CONGRESSIONAL QUARTERLY

Almanac

98th CONGRESS
1st SESSION 1983

VOLUME XXXIX

Congressional Quarterly Inc.

Washington, D.C.

CQ 1983 Almanac

Editor and President
Eugene Patterson

Publisher
Wayne P. Kelley

Deputy Publisher and Executive Editor
Peter A. Harkness

General Manager
Robert C. Hur

Director, Research and Development
Robert E. Cuthriell

EDITORIAL DEPARTMENT

Managing Editor: Kathryn Waters Gest

Assistant Managing Editors: Peg O'Hara, Andy Plattner

Political Editor: Alan Ehrenhalt

News Editors: Martha Angle, Marsha Canfield, Mary Cohn, Michael Glennon, Robin D. Meszoly, Joe Rosenbloom 3rd

Assistant Political Editor: Harrison Donnelly

Reporters: Nadine Cohodas, Rhodes Cook, Joseph A. Davis, Phil Duncan, John Felton, Pamela Fessler, Diane Granat, Rob Gurwitt, Janet Hook, Mary Ann Huser, Brian Nutting, Steven Pressman, Robert Rothman, Dale Tate, Pat Towell, Tom Watson, Elizabeth Wehr, Richard Whittle, Elder Witt

Production Editor: William L. Bonn

Editorial Coordinator: Colleen McGuiness

Proofreaders: Eugene J. Gabler, Tatiana Goodman

Editorial Assistants: Calvin Chin, Lynnemarie Hofman, Dave Kaplan, Leah Fackos Klumph

RESEARCH DEPARTMENT: Michael L. Koempel (Director), Wayne Walker (Assistant Director), Martha Bomgardner (Librarian), Diane Huffman (Indexer), Helen A. Sims (Seminars), Andre D. Adams, Donald F. Baldini, Charles S. Clark, Walter E. Eling, Bena A. Fein, Genevieve Kelley, Joan Levit, Barbara L. Miracle, John Noukas, Mary Anne Rothwell, Teresa L. Sorensen, Pamela Walker, Lenore Webb, Reginald K. Whren

ART DEPARTMENT: Richard A. Pottern (Director), Robert O. Redding (Assistant Director), Belle T. Burkhart

PRODUCTION: I. D. Fuller (Manager), Maceo Mayo (Assistant Manager)

COMPUTER SERVICES: Sydney E. Garriss (Manager)

SALES AND PROMOTION: James V. Bullard (Manager)

BUSINESS MANAGER: Jonathan C. Angier

MARKET RESEARCH: Sandra Stencel (Director)

BOOK DEPARTMENT: David R. Tarr (Director), John L. Moore (Assistant Director), Joanne D. Daniels (Director, CQ Press)

NEWSLETTERS: Kenneth B. Dalecki (Editor)

CONGRESSIONAL MONITOR: Michaela Buhler (Editor), Robert Healy (Managing Editor)

EDITORIAL RESEARCH REPORTS: Hoyt Gimlin (Editor), Martha V. Gottron, Richard L. Worsnop (Associate Editors)

WASHINGTON ALERT SERVICE: Ross Evans (Manager), Steve Newman (Editor), Wayne S. Muhlstein (Marketing Manager)

Chairman of the Board: Nelson Poynter (1903-1978)

Library of Congress No. 47-41081
International Standard Book No. 0-87187-314-1

Copyright 1984 by Congressional Quarterly Inc.
1414 22nd Street, N.W., Washington, D.C. 20037

Congressional Quarterly Inc.

Congressional Quarterly Inc. is an editorial research service and publishing company serving clients in the fields of news, education, business and government. Congressional Quarterly, in its basic publication, the CQ Weekly Report, covers Congress, government and politics. Congressional Quarterly also publishes hardbound reference books and paperback books on public affairs. The service was founded in 1945 by Henrietta and Nelson Poynter.

An affiliated service, Editorial Research Reports, publishes reports each week on a wide range of subjects. Editorial Research Reports also publishes hardbound and paperback books.

Almanac Editor: Mary Cohn
Editorial Coordinator: Renee Amrine
Assistant Editors: Martha Angle, Marsha Canfield, Harrison Donnelly, John Felton, Michael Glennon, Peg O'Hara, Andy Plattner, Elder Witt
Other Contributors: Nadine Cohodas, Rhodes Cook, Richard Cowan, Joseph A. Davis, Leslie Ann DeLong, Phil Duncan, Pamela Fessler, Diane Granat, Rob Gurwitt, Janet Hook, Dupre Jones, Leah Fackos Klumph, Michael R. Meyer, Alan Murray, Brian Nutting, Ann O'Connor, Molly Parrish, Steven Pressman, Robert Rothman, Judy Sarasohn, T. Siafa Sherman Jr., Dale Tate, Pat Towell, Tom Watson, Lenore Webb, Elizabeth Wehr, Richard Whittle, Michael D. Wormser
Appendixes: Colleen McGuiness
Roll-Call Charts: Bena A. Fein; **Vote Studies:** Wayne Walker, Barbara L. Miracle
Editorial Assistants: William L. Bonn, Eugene J. Gabler, Tatiana Goodman
Indexers: Nancy Blanpied, Diane Huffman
Production: I.D. Fuller (manager), Maceo Mayo (assistant manager)

"By providing a link between the local newspaper and Capitol Hill we hope Congressional Quarterly can help to make public opinion the only effective pressure group in the country. Since many citizens other than editors are also interested in Congress, we hope that they too will find Congressional Quarterly an aid to a better understanding of their government.

"Congressional Quarterly presents the facts in as complete, concise and unbiased form as we know how. The editorial comment on the acts and votes of Congress, we leave to our subscribers." Foreword, Congressional Quarterly, Vol. I, 1945.

Henrietta Poynter, 1901-1968
Nelson Poynter, 1903-1978

SUMMARY TABLE OF CONTENTS

CHAPTER 1 — 98th CONGRESS, FIRST SESSION 3
CHAPTER 2 — FOREIGN POLICY 109
CHAPTER 3 — DEFENSE 171
CHAPTER 4 — ECONOMIC POLICY 217
CHAPTER 5 — LAW ENFORCEMENT/JUDICIARY 285
CHAPTER 6 — ENVIRONMENT/ENERGY 325
CHAPTER 7 — AGRICULTURE 373
CHAPTER 8 — HEALTH/EDUCATION/WELFARE 389
CHAPTER 9 — BUDGET AND APPROPRIATIONS 423
CHAPTER 10 — TRANSPORTATION/COMMERCE/CONSUMERS 543
CHAPTER 11 — CONGRESS AND GOVERNMENT 563

APPENDIXES
   SPECIAL REPORTS 1-A
   POLITICAL REPORT 1-B
   VOTING STUDIES 1-C
   LOBBY REGISTRATIONS 1-D
   PRESIDENTIAL MESSAGES 1-E
   PUBLIC LAWS 1-F
   ROLL-CALL CHARTS
      Senate 1-S
      House 1-H
      Roll-Call Index 146-H

INDEX

TABLE OF CONTENTS

Glossary of Congressional Terms xiii
Legislative Process in Brief xxv

Chapter 1 — 98th Congress, First Session

Capitol Hill Map 106
Characteristics of the 98th Congress 29
Committees
   Assignment Index 99
   House 63
Joint 97
Senate 44
Legislative Summary 12
Membership List 10
Organization of the 98th Congress 3

Chapter 2 — Foreign Policy

Introduction 109
Carlucci Commission 153
El Salvador Aid 154
El Salvador Certification Bill Veto 156
El Salvador Reports 164
Foreign Aid Authorizations 140
Grenada Invasion 135
Guatemala Aid, Arms 137
Israel Ties 132
Jordan Military Ties 134
Kissinger Commission 169
Korean Airliner Downing 136
Lebanon Policy 113
National Endowment for Democracy 148
Nicaragua Covert Aid Issue 123
Radio Marti 138
State Department Authorization 145
Stone Confirmation 159
U.S.-Vatican Relations 168

Chapter 3 — Defense

Introduction 171
Adelman Nomination 213
Defense Authorization 175
Joint Chiefs Reorganization 215
Military Construction 193
MX Missile Approval 195
Nuclear Deterrence 202
Nuclear Freeze 205

Chapter 4 — Economic Policy

Introduction 217
Auto Domestic Content 257
Caribbean Trade Plan 252
Credit Card Fraud 267
Credit Card Surcharges 267
Debt Limit Increases 239
Defense Production Act 265
Deficit Reduction Efforts 231
Dislocated Workers Aid 270
Economic Development 229
Export Controls Extension 253
Favored-Nation Trading Status 264
Housing Authorization 277
IMF Funding Increase, Export-Import Bank Extension 241
Industrial Policy 251
Insider Trading Curbs 265
Interest Withholding Repeal 261
Longshore, Corruption Bills 271
Mortgage Aid 267
Mortgage Revenue Bonds 276
Pension 'Equity' Measures 276
Public Service Jobs 268
Public Works Jobs 270
Railroad Retirement 272
Revenue Sharing Extension 226
Social Security Disability 273
Social Security Rescue Plan 219
Tax Cut Cap 249
Trade Adjustment Aid 251
Trade Department 250
Trade Reciprocity, Services 259
Unemployment Benefits Extension 274
Volcker Confirmation 266
Youth Conservation Jobs 230

Chapter 5 — Law Enforcement/Judiciary

Introduction 285
Air Crash Liability Treaty 300
Anti-Abortion Efforts 306
Anti-Crime Grant Program 312
Anti-Crime Package 315
Anti-Tampering Bill 313
Bankruptcy Issues 318
Child Pornography Bill 318
Civil Rights Commission 292
Constitution's Bicentennial 324
Drug Treatment Program 314

Equal Rights Amendment 296
Immigration Bill 287
Insanity Defense Revisions 314
Justice Department Authorization 312
Legal Services Corporation 322
Military Justice Code Revisions 311
New Appeals Court 311
Record Rentals/Copyrights 313
Refugee Program Renewal, 1984 Levels 304
School Prayer Amendments 301
U.S. Judicial Appointments 302

Women's Economic Equity Bills 298

Chapter 6 — Environment/Energy

Introduction 325
Acid Rain Stalemate 340
Alaska Sport Hunting 347
Arizona Wilderness 341
Burford Resignation 332
Clark Profile 330
Clean Air Bill 339
Clean Water Act Rewrite 360
Clinch River Project 362
Coastal Revenue Sharing 359
Dam Safety Repairs 349
Energy Preparedness/IEA 371
Federal Coal Leasing Moratorium 350
Garrison Diversion 356
Hazardous Waste 335
Marine Sanctuaries 359
Matagorda Island Accord 345
Miscellaneous Parks Bill 348

Natural Gas Pricing 366
New Scenic Trails 346
Nuclear Regulatory Commission Authorization 370
Ocean Dumping Legislation 360
Oregon Lands Transfer 344
Park Protection Measure 348
Pribilof Islands 345
RARE II Wilderness Bills 342
Ruckelshaus: EPA Veteran 334
Strategic Petroleum Reserve 372
Temporary Public Land Use 345
Truman Historic Site 348
Utilities Financing 372
Water Projects Bill Authorization 354
Water Resources Research 349
Watt Resignation 327
Wetlands Bill 349
Wild Horses and Burros 346

Chapter 7 — Agriculture

Introduction 373
Dairy Assessments 376
Dairy, Tobacco Programs 375
Drought Aid for Farmers 387
Export Subsidy Program 385
Farm 'Recession Relief' 384
Minor Agriculture Measures 388
Payment-in-Kind (PIK) Plan and Tax Benefits 380

Pesticide Reauthorization 386
Rural Electrification Measure 388
'Sodbuster' Bill 387
Specialty Cotton Program 388
Target Price Freeze 383
Tobacco Price Support 378
U.S.-U.S.S.R. Grain Pact 387
Wheat Program Changes 386

Chapter 8 — Health/Education/Welfare

Introduction 389
Child Food Aid 417
Child Health Plan 419
Child Support Payments 418
Cigarette Labeling 408
Close Up Foundation 405
Desegregation Aid 404
Draft Registration Rules 399
Drug, Alcohol Abuse 402
Education Consolidation Act Amendments 400

Education for Handicapped 402
Educational Summit 400
Endowment Aid 397
Health Emergency Fund 417
Health Planning 420
Hospice Payments 398
Hunger Reports and Food Aid Expansion 412
Jobless Health Insurance 405
Math-Science Education 396
Meals for Elderly 418

Medicare Program Changes 391
National Institutes of Health 409
New GI Bill 418
Saccharin Ban Deferral 401
Sex Discrimination in Education Programs 397
VISTA Authorization 398

Student Loans 400
Tribal Colleges 395
Tuition Tax Credits 395
U.S. Peace Academy 399
Veterans' Health Care Bill 410

Chapter 9 — Budget and Appropriations

Introduction 423
Agriculture 516
Appropriations Chart 422
Budget, Fiscal 1984 425
Budget Resolution 435
Commerce, Justice, State 472
Continuing Resolution, First Fiscal 1984 526
Continuing Resolution, Second Fiscal 1984 528
Defense 479
District of Columbia 494
Energy, Water Projects 500
Water Projects 520

Foreign Aid 521
Housing and Urban Development, Independent Agencies. . . . 495
Interior 462
Labor, Health & Human Services, Education 504
Legislative Branch 539
Military Construction 469
Supplemental, Fiscal 1984/IMF, Housing 536
Supplemental, Fiscal 1983/Jobs, Relief 447
Supplemental, Second, Fiscal 1983 509
Transportation 457
Treasury, Postal Service 531

Chapter 10 — Transportation/Commerce/Consumers

Introduction 543
Amtrak Authorization 561
Boating and Fishing Taxes 562
Broadcast Deregulation 551
Cable TV Deregulation 552
Coal Slurry 549
Consumer Product Safety Commission 557
Daylight-Saving Time 551
Federal Communications Commission 558

Federal Trade Commission 561
Funeral Rule Veto 562
Highway Funding 559
Maritime Antitrust Exemptions 554
Maritime Authorization 549
National Transportation Safety Board 558
Telephone Rate Hike 545
TV Syndication Rights 560
Unisex Insurance 558

Chapter 11 — Congress and Government

Introduction 563
'Abscam' Defendants Enter Prison 585
Boxing Commission 586
Bureau of Standards Funding 587
Censure of Two Members 580
Competitive Bidding 590
Congressional Pay Raises 577
'Debategate' Investigation 594
Drug Investigation 595
Earthquake Hazard Reduction 591
Federal Debt Collection 591
Federal Election Commission 594
Federal Employee Pay 576
Federal Personnel Rules 602
Federal Program Catalog 591
Federal Workers Under Social Security System 573
Franking Privilege 578
Government Ethics Office 584
Hansen, Rep. George, Indictment 592
Historical Publications 595
House Rules Changes 596

Indian Land Claim Veto 586
King Holiday 600
Legislative Veto Invalidation 565
Mail Fraud 604
Minority Businesses 588
NASA/Weather Satellites Authorization 588
National Science Foundation Authorization 604
Paperwork Reduction 590
Procurement Policy Office 589
Relocation Assistance 587
Reorganization Act Renewal 588
Senate Day Care 594
Senate Rules Changes 598
Senate TV Bill 595
Small Business/U.S. Contracts 587
Tax Leasing Plan Veto 603
Terrorist Bomb Explosion at Capitol 592
Transcript Alterations 583
U.S. Pay Change Delay 576
Veterans' Compensation 604
Veterans' Emergency Job Training 599

APPENDIXES

Special Reports

Nominations and Confirmations 23-A
  Federal Regulatory Agencies Membership ... 24-A
Supreme Court Term (1982-83) 3-A
  Legislative Veto Opinions 20-A
  Major Decisions 6-A

Political Report

California, New Jersey Redistricting 5-B
Gubernatorial Elections 3-B
Special House Election 6-B
Special Senate Election 4-B

Voting Studies

Conservative Coalition 37-C
Key Votes 3-C
Party Unity 26-C
Presidential Support 19-C
Voting Participation 32-C

Lobby Registrations

November 1982 - October 1983 .... 3-D
Index 55-D

Presidential Messages

Arms Control Agreement 21-E
Arms Control Policy Letter 32-E
Budget Message 7-E
Central America 28-E
Central America, Democrats' Response 31-E
Civil Rights Commission 38-E
Crime Control Proposal 19-E
Economic Report 12-E
Education Legislation 20-E
Enterprise Zones 14-E
EPA Memorandum of Understanding 16-E
Lebanon Resolution 36-E
MX Commission Report 26-E
Nuclear Arms Control 22-E
Nuclear Arms Talks 33-E
State of the Union Address 3-E
Unemployment 16-E
Vetoes
  Desegregation Funds 35-E
  Farm Announcements 34-E
  Indian Claims Bill 25-E
  Milk Price Support Program 35-E
  Oregon Lands 38-E
  Tax Leasing Plan 34-E

Public Laws 1-F

Roll-Call Charts

House 1-H
Senate 1-S
Roll-Call Index 146-H

Index

ERRATA

1981 Almanac: P. 491, col. 1, last paragraph. The bill authorized $19 million (not $7 million) in each of fiscal years 1982-84 for child abuse prevention and treatment programs.

Glossary of Congressional Terms

Act—The term for legislation once it has passed both houses of Congress and has been signed by the president or passed over his veto, thus becoming law. *(See below.)* Also used in parliamentary terminology for a bill that has been passed by one house and engrossed. *(See Engrossed Bill.)*

Adjournment Sine Die—Adjournment without definitely fixing a day for reconvening; literally "adjournment without a day." Usually used to connote the final adjournment of a session of Congress. A session can continue until noon, Jan. 3, of the following year, when, under the 20th Amendment to the Constitution, it automatically terminates. Both houses must agree to a concurrent resolution for either house to adjourn for more than three days.

Adjournment to a Day Certain—Adjournment under a motion or resolution that fixes the next time of meeting. Under the Constitution, neither house can adjourn for more than three days without the concurrence of the other. A session of Congress is not ended by adjournment to a day certain.

Amendment—A proposal of a member of Congress to alter the language, provisions or stipulations in a bill or in another amendment. An amendment usually is printed, debated and voted upon in the same manner as a bill.

Amendment in the Nature of a Substitute—Usually an amendment that seeks to replace the entire text of a bill. Passage of this type of amendment strikes out everything after the enacting clause and inserts a new version of the bill. An amendment in the nature of a substitute also can refer to an amendment that replaces a large portion of the text of a bill.

Appeal—A member's challenge of a ruling or decision made by the presiding officer of the chamber. In the Senate, the senator appeals to members of the chamber to override the decision. If carried by a majority vote, the appeal nullifies the chair's ruling. In the House, the decision of the Speaker traditionally has been final; seldom are there appeals to the members to reverse the Speaker's stand. To appeal a ruling is considered an attack on the Speaker.

Appropriations Bill—A bill that gives legal authority to spend or obligate money from the Treasury. The Constitution disallows money to be drawn from the Treasury "but in Consequence of Appropriations made by Law."

It usually is the case that an appropriations bill provides the actual monies approved by authorization bills, but not necessarily the full amount permissible under the authorization measures. By congressional custom, an appropriations bill originates in the House, and it is not supposed to be considered by the full House or Senate until the related authorization measure is enacted. Under the 1974 Congressional Budget and Impoundment Control Act, general appropriations bills are supposed to be enacted by the seventh day after Labor Day before the start of the fiscal year to which they apply, but in recent years this deadline rarely has been met.

In addition to general appropriations bills, there are two specialized types. *(See Continuing Resolution, Supplemental Appropriations Bill.)*

Authorization—Basic, substantive legislation that establishes or continues the legal operation of a federal program or agency, either indefinitely or for a specific period of time, or which sanctions a particular type of obligation or expenditure. An authorization normally is a prerequisite for an appropriation or other kind of budget authority. Under the rules of both houses, the appropriation for a program or agency may not be considered until its authorization has been considered. An authorization also may limit the amount of budget authority to be provided or may authorize the appropriation of "such sums as may be necessary." *(See also Backdoor Spending.)*

Backdoor Spending—Budget authority provided in legislation outside the normal appropriations process. The most common forms of backdoor spending are borrowing authority, contract authority and entitlements. *(See below.)* In some cases, such as interest on the public debt, a permanent appropriation is provided that becomes available without further action by Congress. The 1974 budget act places limits on the use of backdoor spending.

Bills—Most legislative proposals before Congress are in the form of bills and are designated by HR in the House of Representatives or S in the Senate, according to the house in which they originate, and by a number assigned in the order in which they are introduced during the two-year period of a congressional term. "Public bills" deal with general questions and become public laws if approved by Congress and signed by the president. "Private bills" deal with individual matters such as claims against the government, immigration and naturalization cases, land titles, etc., and become private laws if approved and signed. *(See also Concurrent Resolution, Joint Resolution, Resolution.)*

Bills Introduced—In both the House and Senate, any number of members may join in introducing a single bill or resolution. The first member listed is the sponsor of the bill, and all members' names following his are the bill's cosponsors.

Many bills are committee bills and are introduced under the name of the chairman of the committee or subcommittee. All appropriations bills fall into this category. A committee frequently holds hearings on a number of related bills and may agree to one of them or to an entirely new bill. *(See also Report, Clean Bill, By Request.)*

Bills Referred— When introduced, a bill is referred to the committee or committees that have jurisdiction over the subject with which the bill is concerned. Under the

standing rules of the House and Senate, bills are referred by the Speaker in the House and by the presiding officer in the Senate. In practice, the House and Senate parliamentarians act for these officials and refer the vast majority of bills.

Borrowing Authority—Statutory authority that permits a federal agency to incur obligations and make payments for specified purposes with borrowed money. The 1974 budget act sets limits on new borrowing authority, except in certain instances, to the extent or amount provided in appropriations acts.

Budget—The document sent to Congress by the president early each year estimating government revenue and expenditures for the ensuing fiscal year.

Budget Authority—Authority to enter into obligations that will result in immediate or future outlays involving federal funds. The basic forms of budget authority are appropriations, contract authority and borrowing authority. Budget authority may be classified by (1) the period of availability (one-year, multiple-year or without a time limitation), (2) the timing of congressional action (current or permanent), or (3) the manner of determining the amount available (definite or indefinite).

Budget Process—The congressional budget process is organized around two concurrent resolutions. The deadline for approval of the first resolution is May 15. The resolution must be passed before the House and Senate consider appropriations, revenue and entitlement legislation. The deadline for the second budget resolution is Sept. 15, two weeks before the Oct. 1 start of the next fiscal year. (Congress has failed to meet these deadlines in recent years.) The purpose of the two budget resolutions is to guide and restrain Congress in its actions on appropriations spending and revenue bills. A concurrent resolution does not have the force of law. Consequently, Congress cannot appropriate money, impose taxes or directly limit federal expenditures by means of a budget resolution. Unless it otherwise stipulates, Congress is not bound by the targets in the first budget resolution when it acts on appropriations and tax legislation. The second resolution sets a ceiling on new budget authority and outlays and a floor on revenues for the coming year. After its adoption a point of order can be raised against any legislation that would cause expenditures to exceed or revenues to drop below budgeted amounts. Congress can revise its budget decisions at any time during the fiscal year by adopting supplementary budget resolutions.

Budget Reconciliation—The 1974 budget act provides for a "reconciliation" procedure for bringing existing tax and spending laws into conformity with the congressional budget resolutions. Under the procedure, Congress instructs designated legislative committees to approve measures adjusting revenues and expenditures by a certain amount. The committees have a deadline by which they must report the legislation, but they have the discretion of deciding what changes are to be made. The recommendations of the various committees are consolidated without change by the Budget committees into an omnibus reconciliation bill, which then must be considered and approved by both houses of Congress.

By Request—A phrase used when a senator or representative introduces a bill at the request of an executive agency or private organization but does not necessarily endorse the legislation.

Calendar—An agenda or list of business awaiting possible action by each chamber. The House uses five legislative calendars. (See Consent, Discharge, House, Private and Union Calendar.)

In the Senate, all legislative matters reported from committee go on one calendar. They are listed there in the order in which committees report them or the Senate places them on the calendar, but may be called up out of order by the majority leader, either by obtaining unanimous consent of the Senate or by a motion to call up a bill. The Senate also uses one non-legislative calendar; this is used for treaties and nominations. (See Executive Calendar.)

Calendar Wednesday—In the House, committees, on Wednesdays, may be called in the order in which they appear in Rule X of the House, for the purpose of bringing up any of their bills from either the House or the Union Calendar, except bills that are privileged. General debate is limited to two hours. Bills called up from the Union Calendar are considered in Committee of the Whole. Calendar Wednesday is not observed during the last two weeks of a session and may be dispensed with at other times by a two-thirds vote. This procedure is rarely used and routinely is dispensed with by unanimous consent.

Call of the Calendar—Senate bills that are not brought up for debate by a motion, unanimous consent or a unanimous consent agreement are brought before the Senate for action when the calendar listing them is "called." Bills must be called in the order listed. Measures considered by this method usually are non-controversial, and debate is limited to a total of five minutes for each senator on the bill and any amendments proposed to it.

Chamber—The meeting place for the membership of either the House or the Senate; also the membership of the House or Senate meeting as such.

Clean Bill—Frequently after a committee has finished a major revision of a bill, one of the committee members, usually the chairman, will assemble the changes and what is left of the original bill into a new measure and introduce it as a "clean bill." The revised measure, which is given a new number, then is referred back to the committee, which reports it to the floor for consideration. This often is a timesaver, as committee-recommended changes in a clean bill do not have to be considered and voted on by the chamber. Reporting a clean bill also protects committee amendments that might be subject to points of order concerning germaneness.

Clerk of the House—Chief administrative officer of the House of Representatives, with duties corresponding to those of the secretary of the Senate. (See also Secretary of the Senate.)

Cloture—The process by which a filibuster can be ended in the Senate other than by unanimous consent. A motion for cloture can apply to any measure before the Senate, including a proposal to change the chamber's rules.

A cloture motion requires the signatures of 16 senators to be introduced, and the cloture motion must obtain the votes of three-fifths of the entire Senate membership (60 if there are no vacancies) to end a filibuster, except that in order to end a filibuster against a proposal to amend the standing rules of the Senate, a two-thirds vote of senators present and voting is required. The cloture request is put to a roll-call vote one hour after the Senate meets on the second day following introduction of the motion. If approved, cloture limits each senator to one hour of debate. The bill or amendment in question comes to a final vote after 100 hours of consideration (including debate time and the time it takes to conduct roll calls, quorum calls and other procedural motions). *(See Filibuster.)*

Committee—A division of the House or Senate that prepares legislation for action by the parent chamber or makes investigations as directed by the parent chamber. There are several types of committees. *(See Standing and Select or Special Committees.)* Most standing committees are divided into subcommittees, which study legislation, hold hearings and report bills, with or without amendments, to the full committee. Only the full committee can report legislation for action by the House or Senate.

Committee of the Whole—The working title of what is formally "The Committee of the Whole House (of Representatives) on the State of the Union." The membership is comprised of all House members sitting as a committee. Any 100 members who are present on the floor of the chamber to consider legislation comprise a quorum of the committee. Any legislation, however, must first have passed through the regular legislative or Appropriations committee and have been placed on the calendar.

Technically, the Committee of the Whole considers only bills directly or indirectly appropriating money, authorizing appropriations or involving taxes or charges on the public. Because the Committee of the Whole need number only 100 representatives, a quorum is more readily attained, and legislative business is expedited. Before 1971, members' positions were not individually recorded on votes taken in Committee of the Whole. *(See Teller Vote.)*

When the full House resolves itself into the Committee of the Whole, it supplants the Speaker with a "chairman." A measure is debated and amendments may be proposed, with votes on amendments as needed. *(See Five-Minute Rule.)* When the committee completes its work on the measure, it dissolves itself by "rising." The Speaker returns, and the chairman of the Committee of the Whole reports to the House that the committee's work has been completed. At this time members may demand a roll-call vote on any amendment *adopted* in the Committee of the Whole. The final vote is on passage of the legislation.

Committee Veto—A requirement added to a few statutes directing that certain policy directives by an executive department or agency be reviewed by certain congressional committees before they are implemented. Under common practice, the government department or agency and the committees involved are expected to reach a consensus before the directives are carried out. *(See also Legislative.)*

Concurrent Resolution—A concurrent resolution, designated H Con Res or S Con Res, must be adopted by both houses, but it is not sent to the president for his signature and therefore does not have the force of law. A concurrent resolution, for example, is used to fix the time for adjournment of a Congress. It also is used as the vehicle for expressing the sense of Congress on various foreign policy and domestic issues, and it serves as the vehicle for coordinated decisions on the federal budget under the 1974 Congressional Budget and Impoundment Control Act. *(See also Bills, Joint Resolution, Resolution.)*

Conference—A meeting between the representatives of the House and the Senate to reconcile differences between the two houses on provisions of a bill passed by both chambers. Members of the conference committee are appointed by the Speaker and the presiding officer of the Senate and are called "managers" for their respective chambers. A majority of the managers for each house must reach agreement on the provisions of the bill (often a compromise between the versions of the two chambers) before it can be considered by either chamber in the form of a "conference report." When the conference report goes to the floor, it cannot be amended, and, if it is not approved by both chambers, the bill may go back to conference under certain situations, or a new conference must be convened. Many rules and informal practices govern the conduct of conference committees.

Bills that are passed by both houses with only minor differences need not be sent to conference. Either chamber may "concur" in the other's amendments, completing action on the legislation. Sometimes leaders of the committees of jurisdiction work out an informal compromise instead of having a formal conference. *(See Custody of the Papers.)*

Confirmations—*(See Nominations.)*

Congressional Record—The daily, printed account of proceedings in both the House and Senate chambers, showing substantially verbatim debate, statements and a record of floor action. Highlights of legislative and committee action are embodied in a Daily Digest section of the Record, and members are entitled to have their extraneous remarks printed in an appendix known as "Extension of Remarks." Members may edit and revise remarks made on the floor during debate, and quotations from debate reported by the press are not always found in the Record.

Beginning on March 1, 1978, the Record incorporated a procedure to distinguish remarks spoken on the floor of the House and Senate from undelivered speeches. Congress directed that all speeches, articles and other matter that members inserted in the Record without actually reading them on the floor were to be set off by large black dots, or bullets. However, a loophole allows a member to avoid the bulleting if he delivers any portion of the speech in person.

Congressional Terms of Office—Terms normally begin on Jan. 3 of the year following a general election and are two years for representatives and six years for senators. Representatives elected in special elections are sworn in for the remainder of a term. A person may be appointed to fill a Senate vacancy and serves until a successor is elected; the successor serves until the end of the term applying to the vacant seat.

Consent Calendar—Members of the House may place on this calendar most bills on the Union or House Calendar that are considered to be non-controversial. Bills

on the Consent Calendar normally are called on the first and third Mondays of each month. On the first occasion that a bill is called in this manner, consideration may be blocked by the objection of any member. The second time, if there are three objections, the bill is stricken from the Consent Calendar. If less than three members object, the bill is given immediate consideration.

A bill on the Consent Calendar may be postponed in another way. A member may ask that the measure be passed over "without prejudice." In that case, no objection is recorded against the bill, and its status on the Consent Calendar remains unchanged. A bill stricken from the Consent Calendar remains on the Union or House Calendar.

Cosponsor—*(See Bills Introduced.)*

Continuing Resolution—A joint resolution drafted by Congress "continuing appropriations" for specific ongoing activities of a government department or departments when a fiscal year begins and Congress has not yet enacted all of the regular appropriations bills for that year. The continuing resolution usually specifies a maximum rate at which the agency may incur obligations. This usually is based on the rate for the previous year, the president's budget request or an appropriation bill for that year passed by either or both houses of Congress, but not cleared.

Contract Authority—Budget authority contained in an authorization bill that permits the federal government to enter into contracts or other obligations for future payments from funds not yet appropriated by Congress. The assumption is that funds will be available for payment in a subsequent appropriation act.

Controllable Budget Items—In federal budgeting this refers to programs, for which the budget authority or outlays during a fiscal year can be controlled without changing existing, substantive law. The concept "relatively uncontrollable under current law" includes outlays for open-ended programs and fixed costs such as interest on the public debt, Social Security benefits, veterans' benefits and outlays to liquidate prior-year obligations.

Correcting Recorded Votes—Rules prohibit members from changing their votes after the result has been announced. But, occasionally, hours, days or months after a vote has been taken, a member may announce that he was "incorrectly recorded." In the Senate, a request to change one's vote almost always receives unanimous consent. In the House, members are prohibited from changing their votes if tallied by the electronic voting system installed in 1973. If taken by roll call, it is permissible if consent is granted.

Current Services Estimates—Estimated budget authority and outlays for federal programs and operations for the forthcoming fiscal year based on continuation of existing levels of service without policy changes. These estimates of budget authority and outlays, accompanied by the underlying economic and policy assumptions upon which they are based, are transmitted by the president to Congress when the budget is submitted.

Custody of the Papers—To reconcile differences between the House and Senate versions of a bill, a conference may be arranged. The chamber with "custody of the papers" — the engrossed bill, engrossed amendments, messages of transmittal — is the only body empowered to request the conference. By custom, the chamber that asks for a conference is the last to act on the conference report once agreement has been reached on the bill by the conferees. Custody of the papers sometimes is manipulated to ensure that a particular chamber acts either first or last on the conference report.

Deferrals of Budget Authority—Any action taken by U.S. government officials that withholds, delays or precludes the obligation or expenditure of budget authority. The 1974 budget act requires a special message from the president to Congress reporting a proposed deferral. Deferrals may not extend beyond the end of the fiscal year in which the message reporting the deferral is transmitted. *(See also Rescission Bill.)*

Dilatory Motion—A motion made for the purpose of killing time and preventing action on a bill or amendment. House rules outlaw dilatory motions, but enforcement is largely within the discretion of the Speaker or chairman of the Committee of the Whole. The Senate does not have a rule banning dilatory motions, except under cloture.

Discharge a Committee—Occasionally, attempts are made to relieve a committee from jurisdiction over a measure before it. This is attempted more often in the House than in the Senate, and the procedure rarely is successful.

In the House, if a committee does not report a bill within 30 days after the measure is referred to it, any member may file a discharge motion. Once offered, the motion is treated as a petition needing the signatures of 218 members (a majority of the House). After the required signatures have been obtained, there is a delay of seven days. Thereafter, on the second and fourth Mondays of each month, except during the last six days of a session, any member who has signed the petition must be recognized, if he so desires, to move that the committee be discharged. Debate on the motion to discharge is limited to 20 minutes, and, if the motion is carried, consideration of the bill becomes a matter of high privilege.

If a resolution to consider a bill is held up in the Rules Committee for more than seven legislative days, any member may enter a motion to discharge the committee. The motion is handled like any other discharge petition in the House.

Occasionally, to expedite non-controversial legislative business, a committee is discharged by unanimous consent of the House, and a petition is not required. *(Senate procedure, see Discharge Resolution.)*

Discharge Calendar—The House calendar to which motions to discharge committees are referred when they have the required number of signatures (218) and are awaiting floor action.

Discharge Petition—*(See Discharge a Committee.)*

Discharge Resolution—In the Senate, a special motion that any senator may introduce to relieve a committee from consideration of a bill before it. The resolution can be called up for Senate approval or disapproval in the same manner as any other Senate business. *(House procedure, see Discharge a Committee.)*

Division of a Question for Voting—A practice that is more common in the Senate, but also is used in the House, whereby a member may demand a division of an amendment or a motion for purposes of voting. Where an amendment or motion can be divided, the individual parts are voted on separately when a member demands a division. This procedure occurs most often during the consideration of conference reports.

Division Vote—*(See Standing Vote.)*

Enacting Clause—Key phrase in bills beginning, "Be it enacted by the Senate and House of Representatives...." A successful motion to strike it from legislation kills the measure.

Engrossed Bill—The final copy of a bill as passed by one chamber, with the text as amended by floor action and certified by the clerk of the House or the secretary of the Senate.

Enrolled Bill—The final copy of a bill that has been passed in identical form by both chambers. It is certified by an officer of the house of origin (clerk of the House or secretary of the Senate) and then sent on for the signatures of the House Speaker, the Senate president pro tempore and the president of the United States. An enrolled bill is printed on parchment.

Entitlement Program—A federal program such as Social Security or unemployment compensation that guarantees a certain level of benefits to persons or other entities who meet the requirements set by law. It thus leaves no discretion with Congress on how much money to appropriate.

Executive Calendar—This is a non-legislative calendar in the Senate on which presidential documents such as treaties and nominations are listed.

Executive Document—A document, usually a treaty, sent to the Senate by the president for consideration or approval. Executive documents are identified for each session of Congress as Executive A, 97th Congress, 1st Session; Executive B, etc. They are referred to committee in the same manner as other measures. Unlike legislative documents, however, treaties do not die at the end of a Congress but remain "live" proposals until acted on by the Senate or withdrawn by the president.

Executive Session—A meeting of a Senate or House committee (or occasionally of either chamber) that only its members may attend. Witnesses regularly appear at committee meetings in executive session — for example, Defense Department officials during presentations of classified defense information. Other members of Congress may be invited, but the public and press are not allowed to attend.

Expenditures—The actual spending of money as distinguished from the appropriation of funds. Expenditures are made by the disbursing officers of the administration; appropriations are made only by Congress. The two are rarely identical in any fiscal year. In addition to some current budget authority, expenditures may represent budget authority made available one, two or more years earlier.

Filibuster—A time-delaying tactic associated with the Senate and used by a minority in an effort to prevent a vote on a bill or amendment that probably would pass if voted upon directly. The most common method is to take advantage of the Senate's rules permitting unlimited debate, but other forms of parliamentary maneuvering may be used. The stricter rules used by the House make filibusters more difficult, but delaying tactics are employed occasionally through various procedural devices allowed by House rules. *(Senate filibusters, see Cloture.)*

Fiscal Year—Financial operations of the government are carried out in a 12-month fiscal year, beginning on Oct. 1 and ending on Sept. 30. The fiscal year carries the date of the calendar year in which it ends. (From fiscal year 1844 to fiscal year 1976, the fiscal year began July 1 and ended the following June 30.)

Five-Minute Rule—A debate-limiting rule of the House that is invoked when the House sits as the Committee of the Whole. Under the rule, a member offering an amendment is allowed to speak five minutes in its favor, and an opponent of the amendment is allowed to speak five minutes in opposition. Debate is then closed. In practice, amendments regularly are debated more than 10 minutes, with members gaining the floor by offering pro forma amendments or obtaining unanimous consent to speak longer than five minutes. *(See Strike Out the Last Word.)*

Floor Manager—A member who has the task of steering legislation through floor debate and the amendment process to a final vote in the House or the Senate. Floor managers are usually chairmen or ranking members of the committee that reported the bill. Managers are responsible for apportioning the debate time granted supporters of the bill. The ranking minority member of the committee normally apportions time for the minority party's participation in the debate.

Frank—A member's facsimile signature, which is used on envelopes in lieu of stamps, for the member's official outgoing mail. The "franking privilege" is the right to send mail postage-free.

Germane—Pertaining to the subject matter of the measure at hand. All House amendments must be germane to the bill being considered. The Senate requires that amendments be germane when they are proposed to general appropriations bills, bills being considered once cloture has been adopted, or, frequently, when proceeding under a unanimous consent agreement placing a time limit on consideration of a bill. The 1974 budget act also requires that amendments to concurrent budget resolutions be germane. In the House, floor debate must be germane, and the first three hours of debate each day in the Senate must be germane to the pending business.

Grandfather Clause—A provision exempting persons or other entities already engaged in an activity from rules or legislation affecting that activity. Grandfather clauses sometimes are added to legislation in order to avoid antagonizing groups with established interests in the activities affected.

Grants-in-Aid—Payments by the federal government to states, local governments or individuals in support

of specified programs, services or activities.

Guaranteed Loans—Loans to third parties for which the federal government in the event of default guarantees, in whole or in part, the repayment of principal or interest to a lender or holder of a security.

Hearings—Committee sessions for taking testimony from witnesses. At hearings on legislation, witnesses usually include specialists, government officials and spokesmen for persons or entities affected by the bill or bills under study. Hearings related to special investigations bring forth a variety of witnesses. Committees sometimes use their subpoena power to summon reluctant witnesses. The public and press may attend open hearings, but are barred from closed, or "executive," hearings. The vast majority of hearings are open to the public. *(See Executive Session.)*

Hold-Harmless Clause—A provision added to legislation to ensure that recipients of federal funds do not receive less in a future year than they did in the current year, if a new formula for allocating funds authorized in the legislation would result in a reduction to the recipients. This clause has been used most frequently to soften the impact of sudden reductions in federal grants.

Hopper—Box on House clerk's desk where members deposit bills and resolutions to introduce them. *(See also Bills Introduced.)*

Hour Rule—A provision in the rules of the House that permits one hour of debate time for each member on amendments debated in the House of Representatives sitting as the House. Therefore, the House normally amends bills while sitting as the Committee of the Whole, where the five-minute rule on amendments operates. *(See Committee of the Whole, Five-Minute Rule.)*

House—The House of Representatives, as distinct from the Senate, although each body is a "house" of Congress.

House as in Committee of the Whole—A procedure that can be used to expedite the consideration of certain measures such as continuing resolutions and, when there is debate, private bills. The procedure, which can be invoked only with the unanimous consent of the House or a rule from the Rules Committee, has procedural elements of both the House sitting as the House of Representatives, such as the Speaker presiding and the previous question motion being in order, and the House sitting as the Committee of the Whole, such as the five-minute rule pertaining.

House Calendar—A listing for action by the House of public bills that do not directly or indirectly appropriate money or raise revenue.

Immunity—The constitutional privilege of members of Congress to make verbal statements on the floor and in committee for which they cannot be sued or arrested for slander or libel. Also, freedom from arrest while traveling to or from sessions of Congress or on official business. Members in this status may be arrested only for treason, felonies or a breach of the peace, as defined by congressional manuals.

Impoundments—Any action taken by the executive branch that delays or precludes the obligation or expenditure of budget authority previously approved by Congress. *(See also Deferrals of Budget Authority, Rescission Bill.)*

Joint Committee—A committee composed of a specified number of members of both the House and Senate. A joint committee may be investigative or research-oriented, an example of the latter being the Joint Economic Committee. Others have housekeeping duties such as the joint committees on Printing and on the Library of Congress.

Joint Resolution—A joint resolution, designated H J Res or S J Res, requires the approval of both houses and the signature of the president, just as a bill does, and has the force of law if approved. There is no practical difference between a bill and a joint resolution. A joint resolution generally is used to deal with a limited matter such as a single appropriation.

Joint resolutions also are used to propose amendments to the Constitution in Congress. They do not require a presidential signature, but become a part of the Constitution when three-fourths of the states have ratified them.

Journal—The official record of the proceedings of the House and Senate. The *Journal* records the actions taken in each chamber, but, unlike the *Congressional Record*, it does not include the substantially verbatim report of speeches, debates, etc.

Law—An act of Congress that has been signed by the president or passed over his veto by Congress. Public bills, when signed, become public laws, and are cited by the letters PL and a hyphenated number. The two digits before the number correspond to the Congress, and the one or more digits after the hyphen refer to the numerical sequence in which the bills were signed by the president during that Congress. Private bills, when signed, become private laws. *(See also Slip Laws, Statutes at Large, U.S. Code.)*

Legislative Day—The "day" extending from the time either house meets after an adjournment until the time it next adjourns. Because the House normally adjourns from day to day, legislative days and calendar days usually coincide. But in the Senate, a legislative day may, and frequently does, extend over several calendar days. *(See Recess.)*

Legislative Veto—A procedure permitting either the House or Senate, or both chambers, to review proposed executive branch regulations or actions and to block or modify those with which they disagree. The specifics of the procedure may vary, but Congress generally provides for a legislative veto by including in a bill a provision that administrative rules or action taken to implement the law are to go into effect at the end of a designated period of time unless blocked by either or both houses of Congress. Another version of the veto provides for congressional reconsideration and rejection of regulations already in effect.

The Supreme Court ruling of June 23, 1983, restricted greatly the form and use of the legislative veto as an

unconstitutional violation of the lawmaking procedure provided in the Constitution.

Lobby—A group seeking to influence the passage or defeat of legislation. Originally the term referred to persons frequenting the lobbies or corridors of legislative chambers in order to speak to lawmakers.

The definition of a lobby and the activity of lobbying is a matter of differing interpretation. By some definitions, lobbying is limited to direct attempts to influence lawmakers through personal interviews and persuasion. Under other definitions, lobbying includes attempts at indirect, or "grass-roots," influence, such as persuading members of a group to write or visit their district's representative and state's senators or attempting to create a climate of opinion favorable to a desired legislative goal.

The right to attempt to influence legislation is based on the First Amendment to the Constitution, which says Congress shall make no law abridging the right of the people "to petition the government for a redress of grievances."

Majority Leader—The majority leader is elected by his party colleagues. In the Senate, in consultation with the minority leader and his colleagues, the majority leader directs the legislative schedule for the chamber. He also is his party's spokesman and chief strategist. In the House, the majority leader is second to the Speaker in the majority party's leadership and serves as his party's legislative strategist.

Majority Whip—In effect, the assistant majority leader, in either the House or Senate. His job is to help marshal majority forces in support of party strategy and legislation.

Manual—The official handbook in each house prescribing in detail its organization, procedures and operations.

Marking Up a Bill—Going through the contents of a piece of legislation in committee or subcommittee, considering its provisions in large and small portions, acting on amendments to provisions and proposed revisions to the language, inserting new sections and phraseology, etc. If the bill is extensively amended, the committee's version may be introduced as a separate bill, with a new number, before being considered by the full House or Senate. (See Clean Bill.)

Minority Leader—Floor leader for the minority party in each chamber. (See also Majority Leader.)

Minority Whip—Performs duties of whip for the minority party. (See also Majority Whip.)

Morning Hour—The time set aside at the beginning of each legislative day for the consideration of regular, routine business. The "hour" is of indefinite duration in the House, where it is rarely used.

In the Senate it is the first two hours of a session following an adjournment, as distinguished from a recess. The morning hour can be terminated earlier if the morning business has been completed. Business includes such matters as messages from the president, communications from the heads of departments, messages from the House, the

presentation of petitions, reports of standing and select committees and the introduction of bills and resolutions. During the first hour of the morning hour in the Senate, no motion to proceed to the consideration of any bill on the calendar is in order except by unanimous consent. During the second hour, motions can be made but must be decided without debate. Senate committees may meet while the Senate conducts morning hour.

Motion—In the House or Senate chamber, a request by a member to institute any one of a wide array of parliamentary actions. He "moves" for a certain procedure, the consideration of a measure, etc. The precedence of motions, and whether they are debatable, is set forth in the House and Senate manuals. (See some specific motions above and below.)

Nominations—Presidential appointments to office subject to Senate confirmation. Although most nominations win quick Senate approval, some are controversial and become the topic of hearings and debate. Sometimes senators object to appointees for patronage reasons — for example, when a nomination to a local federal job is made without consulting the senators of the state concerned. In some situations a senator may object that the nominee is "personally obnoxious" to him. Usually other senators join in blocking such appointments out of courtesy to their colleagues. (See Senatorial Courtesy.)

One-Minute Speeches—Addresses by House members at the beginning of a legislative day. The speeches may cover any subject, but are limited to one minute's duration.

Override a Veto—If the president disapproves a bill and sends it back to Congress with his objections, Congress may try to override his veto and enact the bill into law. Neither house is required to attempt to override a veto. The override of a veto requires a recorded vote with a two-thirds majority in each chamber. The question put to each house is: "Shall the bill pass, the objections of the president to the contrary notwithstanding?" (See also Pocket Veto, Veto.)

Oversight Committee—A congressional committee, or designated subcommittee of a committee, which is charged with general oversight of one or more federal agencies' programs and activities. Usually, the oversight panel for a particular agency also is the authorizing committee for that agency's programs and operations.

Pair—A voluntary arrangement between two lawmakers, usually on opposite sides of an issue. If passage of the measure requires a two-thirds majority vote, a pair would require two members favoring the action to one opposed to it. Pairs can take one of three forms — specific, general and live. The names of lawmakers pairing on a given vote and their stands, if known, are printed in the Congressional Record.

The specific pair applies to one or more votes on the same subject. On special pairs, lawmakers usually specify how they would have voted.

A general pair in the Senate, now rarely used, applies to all votes on which the members pairing are on opposite sides. It usually does not specify the positions of the senators pairing. In a general pair in the House, no agreement is involved. A representative expecting to be absent may

notify the House clerk he wishes to make a "general" pair. His name then is paired arbitrarily with that of another member desiring a pair, and the list is printed in the *Congressional Record*. He may or may not be paired with a member taking the opposite position. General pairs in the House give no indication of how a member would have voted.

A live pair involves two members, one present for the vote, the other absent. The member present casts his vote and then withdraws it and votes "present." He then announces that he has a live pair with a colleague, identifying how each would have voted on the question. A live pair subtracts the vote of the member in attendance from the final vote tabulation.

Petition—A request or plea sent to one or both chambers from an organization or private citizens' group asking support of particular legislation or favorable consideration of a matter not yet receiving congressional attention. Petitions are referred to appropriate committees.

Pocket Veto—The act of the president in withholding his approval of a bill after Congress has adjourned. When Congress is in session, a bill becomes law without the president's signature if he does not act upon it within 10 days, excluding Sundays, from the time he gets it. But if Congress adjourns sine die within that 10-day period, the bill will die even if the president does not formally veto it. *(See also Veto.)*

Point of Order—An objection raised by a member that the chamber is departing from rules governing its conduct of business. The objector cites the rule violated, the chair sustaining his objection if correctly made. Order is restored by the chair's suspending proceedings of the chamber until it conforms to the prescribed "order of business."

President of the Senate—Under the Constitution, the vice president of the United States presides over the Senate. In his absence, the president pro tempore, or a senator designated by the president pro tempore, presides over the chamber.

President Pro Tempore—The chief officer of the Senate in the absence of the vice president; literally, but loosely, the president for a time. The president pro tempore is elected by his fellow senators, and the recent practice has been to elect to the office the senator of the majority party with the longest period of continuous service.

Previous Question—A motion for the previous question, when carried, has the effect of cutting off all debate, preventing the offering of further amendments, and forcing a vote on the pending matter. In the House, the previous question is not permitted in the Committee of the Whole. The motion for the previous question is a debate-limiting device and is not in order in the Senate.

Printed Amendment—A House rule guarantees five minutes of floor debate in support and five minutes in opposition, and no other debate time, on amendments printed in the *Congressional Record* at least one day prior to the amendment's consideration in the Committee of the Whole.

In the Senate, while amendments may be submitted for printing, they have no parliamentary standing or status. An amendment submitted for printing in the Senate, however, may be called up by any senator.

Private Calendar—In the House, private bills dealing with individual matters such as claims against the government, immigration, land titles, etc., are put on this calendar. The private calendar must be called on the first Tuesday of each month, and the Speaker may call it on the third Tuesday of each month as well.

When a private bill is before the chamber, two members may block its consideration, which recommits the bill to committee. Backers of a recommitted private bill have recourse. The measure can be put into an "omnibus claims bill" — several private bills rolled into one. As with any bill, no part of an omnibus claims bill may be deleted without a vote. When the private bill goes back to the House floor in this form, it can be deleted from the omnibus bill only by majority vote.

Privilege—Privilege relates to the rights of members of Congress and to the relative priority of the motions and actions they may make in their respective chambers. The two are distinct. "Privileged questions" deal with legislative business. "Questions of privilege" concern legislators themselves.

Privileged Questions—The order in which bills, motions and other legislative measures are considered by Congress is governed by strict priorities. A motion to table, for instance, is more privileged than a motion to recommit. Thus, a motion to recommit can be superseded by a motion to table, and a vote would be forced on the latter motion only. A motion to adjourn, however, takes precedence over a tabling motion and thus is considered of the "highest privilege." *(See also Questions of Privilege.)*

Pro Forma Amendment—*(See Strike Out the Last Word.)*

Public Laws—*(See Law.)*

Questions of Privilege—These are matters affecting members of Congress individually or collectively. Matters affecting the rights, safety, dignity and integrity of proceedings of the House or Senate as a whole are questions of privilege in both chambers.

Questions involving individual members are called questions of "personal privilege." A member rising to ask a question of personal privilege is given precedence over almost all other proceedings. An annotation in the House rules points out that the privilege rests primarily on the Constitution, which gives him a conditional immunity from arrest and an unconditional freedom to speak in the House. *(See also Privileged Questions.)*

Quorum—The number of members whose presence is necessary for the transaction of business. In the Senate and House, it is a majority of the membership. A quorum is 100 in the Committee of the Whole House. If a point of order is made that a quorum is not present, the only business that is in order is either a motion to adjourn or a motion to direct the sergeant-at-arms to request the attendance of absentees.

Readings of Bills—Traditional parliamentary procedure required bills to be read three times before they were passed. This custom is of little modern significance. Normally a bill is considered to have its first reading when it is introduced and printed, by title, in the *Congressional Record*. In the House, its second reading comes when floor consideration begins. (This is the most likely point at which there is an actual reading of the bill, if there is any.) The second reading in the Senate is supposed to occur on the legislative day after the measure is introduced, but before it is referred to committee. The third reading (again, usually by title) takes place when floor action has been completed on amendments.

Recess—Distinguished from adjournment *(see above)* in that a recess does not end a legislative day and therefore does not interrupt unfinished business. The rules in each house set forth certain matters to be taken up and disposed of at the beginning of each legislative day. The House usually adjourns from day to day. The Senate often recesses, thus meeting on the same legislative day for several calendar days or even weeks at a time.

Recognition—The power of recognition of a member is lodged in the Speaker of the House and the presiding officer of the Senate. The presiding officer names the member who will speak first when two or more members simultaneously request recognition.

Recommit to Committee—A motion, made on the floor after a bill has been debated, to return it to the committee that reported it. If approved, recommittal usually is considered a death blow to the bill. In the House, a motion to recommit can be made only by a member opposed to the bill, and, in recognizing a member to make the motion, the Speaker gives preference to members of the minority party over majority party members.

A motion to recommit may include instructions to the committee to report the bill again with specific amendments or by a certain date. Or, the instructions may direct that a particular study be made, with no definite deadline for further action. If the recommittal motion includes instructions to "report the bill back forthwith" and the motion is adopted, floor action on the bill continues; the committee does not actually reconsider the legislation.

Reconciliation—*(See Budget Reconciliation.)*

Reconsider a Vote—A motion to reconsider the vote by which an action was taken has, until it is disposed of, the effect of putting the action in abeyance. In the Senate, the motion can be made only by a member who voted on the prevailing side of the original question or by a member who did not vote at all. In the House, it can be made only by a member on the prevailing side.

A common practice in the Senate after close votes on an issue is a motion to reconsider, followed by a motion to table the motion to reconsider. On this motion to table, senators vote as they voted on the original question, which allows the motion to table to prevail, assuming there are no switches. The matter then is finally closed and further motions to reconsider are not entertained. In the House, as a routine precaution, a motion to reconsider usually is made every time a measure is passed. Such a motion almost always is tabled immediately, thus shutting off the possibility of future reconsideration, except by unanimous consent.

Motions to reconsider must be entered in the Senate within the next two days of actual session after the original vote has been taken. In the House they must be entered either on the same day or on the next day the House is in session.

Recorded Vote—A vote upon which each member's stand is individually made known. In the Senate, this is accomplished through a roll call of the entire membership, to which each senator on the floor must answer "yea," "nay" or, if he does not wish to vote, "present." Since January 1973, the House has used an electronic voting system for recorded votes, including yea-and-nay votes formerly taken by roll calls.

When not required by the Constitution, a recorded vote can be obtained on questions in the House on the demand of one-fifth (44 members) of a quorum or one-fourth (25) of a quorum in the Committee of the Whole. *(See Yeas and Nays.)*

Report—Both a verb and a noun as a congressional term. A committee that has been examining a bill referred to it by the parent chamber "reports" its findings and recommendations to the chamber when it completes consideration and returns the measure. The process is called "reporting" a bill.

A "report" is the document setting forth the committee's explanation of its action. Senate and House reports are numbered separately and are designated S Rept or H Rept. When a committee report is not unanimous, the dissenting committee members may file a statement of their views, called minority views and referred to as a minority report. Members in disagreement with some provisions of a bill may file additional or supplementary views. Sometimes a bill is reported without a committee recommendation.

Adverse reports occasionally are submitted by legislative committees. However, when a committee is opposed to a bill, it usually fails to report the bill at all. Some laws require that committee reports — favorable or adverse — be made.

Rescission Bill—A bill rescinding or canceling budget authority previously made available by Congress. The president may request a rescission to reduce spending or because the budget authority no longer is needed. Under the 1974 budget act, however, unless Congress approves a rescission bill within 45 days of continuous session after receipt of the proposal, the funds must be made available for obligation. *(See also Deferrals of Budget Authority.)*

Resolution—A "simple" resolution, designated H Res or S Res, deals with matters entirely within the prerogatives of one house or the other. It requires neither passage by the other chamber nor approval by the president, and it does not have the force of law. Most resolutions deal with the rules or procedures of one house. They also are used to express the sentiments of a single house such as condolences to the family of a deceased member or to comment on foreign policy or executive business. A simple resolution is the vehicle for a "rule" from the House Rules Committee. *(See also Concurrent and Joint Resolutions, Rules.)*

Rider—An amendment, usually not germane, which

its sponsor hopes to get through more easily by including it in other legislation. Riders become law if the bills embodying them are enacted. Amendments providing legislative directives in appropriations bills are outstanding examples of riders, though technically, legislation is banned from appropriations bills. The House, unlike the Senate, has a strict germaneness rule; thus, riders usually are Senate devices to get legislation enacted quickly or to bypass lengthy House consideration and, possibly, opposition.

Rules—The term has two specific congressional meanings. A rule may be a standing order governing the conduct of House or Senate business and listed among the permanent rules of either chamber. The rules deal with duties of officers, the order of business, admission to the floor, parliamentary procedures on handling amendments and voting, jurisdictions of committees, etc.

In the House, a rule also may be a resolution reported by its Rules Committee to govern the handling of a particular bill on the floor. The committee may report a "rule," also called a "special order," in the form of a simple resolution. If the resolution is adopted by the House, the temporary rule becomes as valid as any standing rule and lapses only after action has been completed on the measure to which it pertains. A rule sets the time limit on general debate. It also may waive points of order against provisions of the bill in question such as non-germane language or against certain amendments intended to be proposed to the bill from the floor. It may even forbid all amendments or all amendments except those proposed by the legislative committee that handled the bill. In this instance, it is known as a "closed" or "gag" rule as opposed to an "open" rule, which puts no limitation on floor amendments, thus leaving the bill completely open to alteration by the adoption of germane amendments.

Secretary of the Senate—Chief administrative officer of the Senate, responsible for overseeing the duties of Senate employees, educating Senate pages, administering oaths, handling the registration of lobbyists, and handling other tasks necessary for the continuing operation of the Senate. *(See also Clerk of the House.)*

Select or Special Committee—A committee set up for a special purpose and, usually, for a limited time by resolution of either the House or Senate. Most special committees are investigative and lack legislative authority — legislation is not referred to them and they cannot report bills to their parent chamber. *(See also Standing Committees.)*

Senatorial Courtesy—Sometimes referred to as "the courtesy of the Senate," it is a general practice — with no written rule — applied to consideration of executive nominations. Generally, it means that nominations from a state are not to be confirmed unless they have been approved by the senators of the president's party of that state, with other senators following their colleagues' lead in the attitude they take toward consideration of such nominations. *(See Nominations.)*

Sine Die—*(See Adjournment Sine Die.)*

Slip Laws—The first official publication of a bill that has been enacted and signed into law. Each is published separately in unbound single-sheet or pamphlet form. *(See also Law, Statutes at Large, U.S. Code.)*

Speaker—The presiding officer of the House of Representatives, selected by the caucus of the party to which he belongs and formally elected by the whole House.

Special Session—A session held after Congress has adjourned sine die. Special sessions are convened by the president.

Spending Authority—The 1974 budget act defines spending authority as borrowing authority, contract authority and entitlement authority *(see above)*, for which budget authority is not provided in advance by appropriation acts.

Sponsor—*(See Bills Introduced.)*

Standing Committees—Committees permanently established by House and Senate rules. The standing committees of the House were last reorganized by the committee reorganization act of 1974. The last major realignment of Senate committees was in the committee system reorganization of 1977. The standing committees are legislative committees — legislation may be referred to them and they may report bills and resolutions to their parent chambers. *(See also Select or Special Committees.)*

Standing Vote—A non-recorded vote used in both the House and Senate. (A standing vote also is called a division vote.) Members in favor of a proposal stand and are counted by the presiding officer. Then members opposed stand and are counted. There is no record of how individual members voted.

Statutes at Large—A chronological arrangement of the laws enacted in each session of Congress. Though indexed, the laws are not arranged by subject matter, and there is not an indication of how they have altered previously enacted laws. *(See also Law, Slip Laws, U.S. Code.)*

Strike from the Record—Remarks made on the House floor may offend some member, who moves that the offending words be "taken down" for the Speaker's cognizance, and then expunged from the debate as published in the *Congressional Record.*

Strike Out the Last Word—A motion whereby a House member is entitled to speak for five minutes on an amendment then being debated by the chamber. A member gains recognition from the chair by moving to "strike out the last word" of the amendment or section of the bill under consideration. The motion is pro forma, requires no vote and does not change the amendment being debated.

Substitute—A motion, amendment or entire bill introduced in place of the pending legislative business. Passage of a substitute measure kills the original measure by supplanting it. The substitute also may be amended. *(See also Amendment in the Nature of a Substitute.)*

Supplemental Appropriation Bill—Legislation appropriating funds after the regular annual appropriation bill *(see above)* for a federal department or agency has been enacted. A supplemental appropriation provides additional

budget authority beyond original estimates for programs or activities, including new programs authorized after the enactment of the regular appropriation act, for which the need for funds is too urgent to be postponed until enactment of the next year's regular appropriation bill.

Suspend the Rules—Often a time-saving procedure for passing bills in the House. The wording of the motion, which may be made by any member recognized by the Speaker, is: "I move to suspend the rules and pass the bill. . . ." A favorable vote by two-thirds of those present is required for passage. Debate is limited to 40 minutes and no amendments from the floor are permitted. If a two-thirds favorable vote is not attained, the bill may be considered later under regular procedures. The suspension procedure is in order every Monday and Tuesday and is intended to be reserved for non-controversial bills.

Table a Bill—A motion to "lay on the table" is not debatable in either house, and usually it is a method of making a final, adverse disposition of a matter. In the Senate, however, different language sometimes is used. The motion may be worded to let a bill "lie on the table," perhaps for subsequent "picking up." This motion is more flexible, keeping the bill pending for later action, if desired. Tabling motions on amendments are effective debate-ending devices in the Senate.

Teller Vote—This is a largely moribund House procedure in the Committee of the Whole. Members file past tellers and are counted as for, or against, a measure, but they are not recorded individually. In the House, tellers are ordered upon demand of one-fifth of a quorum. This is 44 in the House, 20 in the Committee of the Whole.

The House also has a recorded teller vote, now largely supplanted by the electronic voting procedure, under which the votes of each member are made public just as they would be on a recorded vote. *(See above.)*

Treaties—Executive proposals — in the form of resolutions of ratification — which must be submitted to the Senate for approval by two-thirds of the senators present. Treaties today are normally sent to the Foreign Relations Committee for scrutiny before the Senate takes action. Foreign Relations has jurisdiction over all treaties, regardless of the subject matter. Treaties are read three times and debated on the floor in much the same manner as legislative proposals. After approval by the Senate, treaties are formally ratified by the president.

Trust Funds—Funds collected and used by the federal government for carrying out specific purposes and programs according to terms of a trust agreement or statute such as the Social Security and unemployment compensation trust funds. Such funds are administered by the government in a fiduciary capacity and are not available for the general purposes of the government.

Unanimous Consent—Proceedings of the House or Senate and action on legislation often take place upon the unanimous consent of the chamber, whether or not a rule of the chamber is being violated. Unanimous consent is used to expedite floor action and frequently is used in a routine fashion such as when a senator requests the unanimous consent of the Senate to have specified members of his staff present on the floor during debate on a specific amendment.

Unanimous Consent Agreement—A device used in the Senate to expedite legislation. Much of the Senate's legislative business, dealing with both minor and controversial issues, is conducted through unanimous consent or unanimous consent agreements. On major legislation, such agreements usually are printed and transmitted to all senators in advance of floor debate. Once agreed to, they are binding on all members unless the Senate, by unanimous consent, agrees to modify them. An agreement may list the order in which various bills are to be considered, specify the length of time bills and contested amendments are to be debated and when they are to be voted upon and, frequently, require that all amendments introduced be germane to the bill under consideration. In this regard, unanimous consent agreements are similar to the "rules" issued by the House Rules Committee for bills pending in the House. *(See above.)*

Union Calendar—Bills that directly or indirectly appropriate money or raise revenue are placed on this House calendar according to the date they are reported from committee.

U.S. Code—A consolidation and codification of the general and permanent laws of the United States arranged by subject under 50 titles, the first six dealing with general or political subjects, and the other 44 alphabetically arranged from agriculture to war. The code is revised every six years, and a supplement is published after each session of Congress. *(See also Law, Slip Laws, Statutes at Large.)*

Veto—Disapproval by the president of a bill or joint resolution (other than one proposing an amendment to the Constitution). When Congress is in session, the president must veto a bill within 10 days, excluding Sundays, after he has received it; otherwise, it becomes law without his signature. When the president vetoes a bill, he returns it to the house of origin along with a message stating his objections. *(See also Pocket Veto, Override a Veto.)*

Voice Vote—In either the House or Senate, members answer "aye" or "no" in chorus, and the presiding officer decides the result. The term also is used loosely to indicate action by unanimous consent or without objection.

Whip—*(See Majority and Minority Whip.)*

Without Objection—Used in lieu of a vote on non-controversial motions, amendments or bills that may be passed in either the House or Senate if no member voices an objection.

Yeas and Nays—The Constitution requires that yea-and-nay votes be taken and recorded when requested by one-fifth of the members present. In the House, the Speaker determines whether one-fifth of the members present requested a vote. In the Senate, practice requires only 11 members. The Constitution requires the yeas and nays on a veto override attempt. *(See Recorded Vote.)*

Yielding—When a member has been recognized to speak, no other member may speak unless he obtains permission from the member recognized. This permission is called yielding and usually is requested in the form, "Will the gentleman yield to me?" While this activity occasionally is seen in the Senate, the Senate has no rule or practice to parcel out time.

How a Bill Becomes Law

This graphic shows the most typical way in which proposed legislation is enacted into law. There are more complicated, as well as simpler, routes, and most bills never become law. The process is illustrated with two hypothetical bills, House bill No. 1 (HR 1) and Senate bill No. 2 (S 2). Bills must be passed by both houses in identical form before they can be sent to the president. The path of HR 1 is traced by a solid line, that of S 2 by a broken line. In practice most bills begin as similar proposals in both houses.

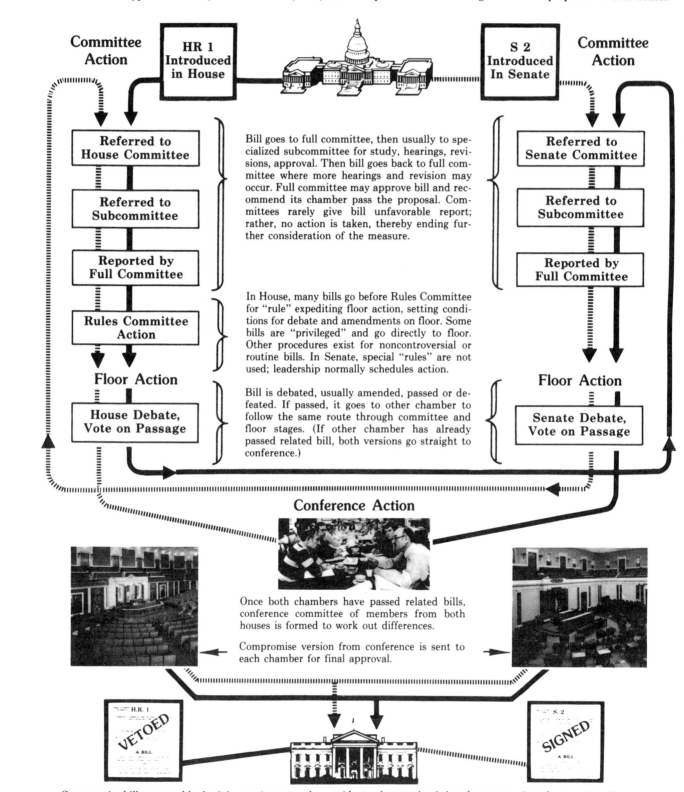

The Legislative Process in Brief

Note: Parliamentary terms used below are defined in the Glossary.

Introduction of Bills

A House member (including the resident commissioner of Puerto Rico and non-voting delegates of the District of Columbia, Guam, the Virgin Islands, and American Samoa) may introduce any one of several types of bills and resolutions by handing it to the clerk of the House or placing it in a box called the hopper. A senator first gains recognition of the presiding officer to announce the introduction of a bill. If objection is offered by any senator the introduction of the bill is postponed until the following day.

As the next step in either the House or Senate, the bill is numbered, referred to the appropriate committee, labeled with the sponsor's name, and sent to the Government Printing Office so that copies can be made for subsequent study and action. Senate bills may be jointly sponsored and carry several senators' names. Until 1978, the House limited the number of members who could co-sponsor any one bill; the ceiling was eliminated at the beginning of the 96th Congress. A bill written in the Executive Branch and proposed as an administration measure usually is introduced by the chairman of the congressional committee which has jurisdiction.

Bills—Prefixed with "HR" in the House, "S" in the Senate, followed by a number. Used as the form for most legislation, whether general or special, public or private.

Joint Resolutions—Designated H J Res or S J Res. Subject to the same procedure as bills, with the exception of a joint resolution proposing an amendment to the Constitution. The latter must be approved by two-thirds of both houses and is thereupon sent directly to the administrator of general services for submission to the states for ratification rather than being presented to the president for his approval.

Concurrent Resolutions—Designated H Con Res or S Con Res. Used for matters affecting the operations of both houses. These resolutions do not become law.

Resolutions—Designated H Res or S Res. Used for a matter concerning the operation of either house alone and adopted only by the chamber in which it originates.

Committee Action

A bill is referred to the appropriate committee by a House parliamentarian n the Speaker's order, or by the Senate president. Sponsors may indicate their preferences for referral, although custom and chamber rule generally govern. An exception is the referral of private bills, which are sent to whatever group is designated by their sponsors. Bills are technically considered "read for the first time" when referred to House committees.

When a bill reaches a committee it is placed upon the group's calendar. At that time it comes under the sharpest congressional focus. Its chances for passage are quickly determined — and the great majority of bills fall by the legislative roadside. Failure of a committee to act on a bill is equivalent to killing it; the measure can be withdrawn from the group's purview only by a discharge petition signed by a majority of the House membership on House bills, or by adoption of a special resolution in the Senate. Discharge attempts rarely succeed.

The first committee action taken on a bill usually is a request for comment on it by interested agencies of the government. The committee chairman may assign the bill to a subcommittee for study and hearings, or it may be considered by the full committee. Hearings may be public, closed (executive session), or both. A subcommittee, after considering a bill, reports to the full committee its recommendations for action and any proposed amendments.

The full committee then votes on its recommendation to the House or Senate. This procedure is called "ordering a bill reported." Occasionally a committee may order a bill reported unfavorably; most of the time a report, submitted by the chairman of the committee to the House or Senate, calls for favorable action on the measure since the committee can effectively "kill" a bill by simply failing to take any action.

When a committee sends a bill to the chamber floor, it explains its reasons in a written statement, called a report, which accompanies the bill. Often committee members opposing a measure issue dissenting minority statements which are included in the report.

Usually, the committee "marks up" or proposes amendments to the bill. If they are substantial and the measure is complicated, the committee may order a "clean bill" introduced, which will embody the proposed amendments. The original bill then is put aside and the "clean bill," with a new number, is reported to the floor.

The chamber must approve, alter, or reject the committee amendments before the bill itself can be put to a vote.

Floor Action

After a bill is reported back to the house where it originated, it is placed on the calendar.

There are five legislative calendars in the House, issued in one cumulative calendar titled *Calendars of the United States House of Representatives and History of Legislation.* The House calendars are:

The Union Calendar to which are referred bills raising revenues, general appropriation bills and any measures directly or indirectly appropriating money or property. It is the Calendar of the Committee of the Whole House on the State of the Union.

The House Calendar to which are referred bills of a public character not raising revenue or appropriating money or property.

The Consent Calendar to which are referred bills of a non-controversial nature that are passed without debate when the Consent Calendar is called on the first and third Mondays of each month.

The Private Calendar to which are referred bills for relief in the nature of claims against the United States or private immigration bills that are passed without debate when the Private Calendar is called the first and third Tuesdays of each month.

The Discharge Calendar to which are referred motions to discharge committees when the necessary signatures are signed to a discharge petition.

There is only one legislative calendar in the Senate and one "executive calendar" for treaties and nominations

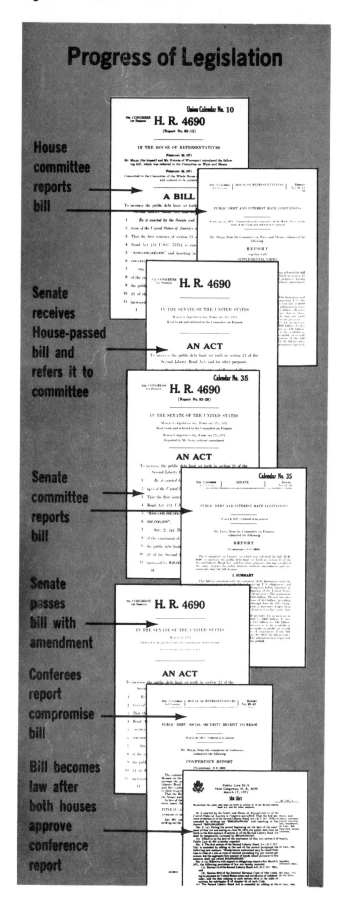

Progress of Legislation

House committee reports bill

Senate receives House-passed bill and refers it to committee

Senate committee reports bill

Senate passes bill with amendment

Conferees report compromise bill

Bill becomes law after both houses approve conference report

submitted to the Senate. When the Senate Calendar is called, each senator is limited to five minutes' debate on each bill.

DEBATE. A bill is brought to debate by varying procedures. If a routine measure, it may await the call of the calendar. If it is urgent or important, it can be taken up in the Senate either by unanimous consent or by a majority vote. The policy committee of the majority party in the Senate schedules the bills that it wants taken up for debate.

In the House, precedence is granted if a special rule is obtained from the Rules Committee. A request for a special rule is usually made by the chairman of the committee that favorably reported the bill, supported by the bill's sponsor and other committee members. The request, considered by the Rules Committee in the same fashion that other committees consider legislative measures, is in the form of a resolution providing for immediate consideration of the bill. The Rules Committee reports the resolution to the House where it is debated and voted upon in the same fashion as regular bills. If the Rules Committee should fail to report a rule requested by a committee, there are several ways to bring the bill to the House floor — under suspension of the rules, on Calendar Wednesday or by a discharge motion.

The resolutions providing special rules are important because they specify how long the bill may be debated and whether it may be amended from the floor. If floor amendments are banned, the bill is considered under a "closed rule," which permits only members of the committee that first reported the measure to the House to alter its language, subject to chamber acceptance.

When a bill is debated under an "open rule," amendments may be offered from the floor. Committee amendments are always taken up first, but may be changed, as may all amendments up to the second degree, i.e., an amendment to an amendment to an amendment is not in order.

Duration of debate in the House depends on whether the bill is under discussion by the House proper or before the House when it is sitting as the Committee of the Whole House on the State of the Union. In the former, the amount of time for debate is determined either by special rule or is allocated with an hour for each member if the measure is under consideration without a rule. In the Committee of the Whole the amount of time agreed on for general debate is equally divided between proponents and opponents. At the end of general discussion, the bill is read section by section for amendment. Debate on an amendment is limited to five minutes for each side.

Senate debate is usually unlimited. It can be halted only by unanimous consent by "cloture," which requires a three-fifths majority of the entire Senate except for proposed changes in the Senate rules. The latter requires a two-thirds vote.

The House sits as the Committee of the Whole when it considers any tax measure or bill dealing with public appropriations. It can also resolve itself into the Committee of the Whole if a member moves to do so and the motion is carried. The Speaker appoints a member to serve as the chairman. The rules of the House permit the Committee of the Whole to meet with any 100 members on the floor, and to amend and act on bills with a quorum of the 100, within the time limitations mentioned previously. When the Committee of the Whole has acted, it "rises," the Speaker returns as the presiding officer of the House and the mem-

ber appointed chairman of the Committee of the Whole reports the action of the committee and its recommendations (amendments adopted).

VOTES. Voting on bills may occur repeatedly before they are finally approved or rejected. The House votes on the rule for the bill and on various amendments to the bill. Voting on amendments often is a more illuminating test of a bill's support than is the final tally. Sometimes members approve final passage of bills after vigorously supporting amendments which, if adopted, would have scuttled the legislation.

The Senate has three different methods of voting: an untabulated voice vote, a standing vote (called a division) and a recorded roll call to which members answer "yea" or "nay" when their names are called. The House also employs voice and standing votes, but since January 1973 yeas and nays have been recorded by an electronic voting device, eliminating the need for time-consuming roll calls.

Another method of voting, used in the House only, is the teller vote. Traditionally, members filed up the center aisle past counters; only vote totals were announced. Since 1971, one-fifth of a quorum can demand that the votes of individual members be recorded, thereby forcing them to take a public position on amendments to key bills. Electronic voting now is commonly used for this purpose.

After amendments to a bill have been voted upon, a vote may be taken on a motion to recommit the bill to committee. If carried, this vote removes the bill from the chamber's calendar. If the motion is unsuccessful, the bill then is "read for the third time." An actual reading usually is dispensed with. Until 1965, an opponent of a bill could delay this move by objecting and asking for a full reading of an engrossed (certified in final form) copy of the bill. After the "third reading," the vote on final passage is taken.

The final vote may be followed by a motion to reconsider, and this motion itself may be followed by a move to lay the motion on the table. Usually, those voting for the bill's passage vote for the tabling motion, thus safeguarding the final passage action. With that, the bill has been formally passed by the chamber. While a motion to reconsider a Senate vote is pending on a bill, the measure cannot be sent to the House.

Action in Second House

After a bill is passed it is sent to the other chamber. This body may then take one of several steps. It may pass the bill as is — accepting the other chamber's language. It may send the bill to committee for scrutiny or alteration, or reject the entire bill, advising the other house of its actions. Or it may simply ignore the bill submitted while it continues work on its own version of the proposed legislation. Frequently, one chamber may approve a version of a bill that is greatly at variance with the version already passed by the other house, and then substitute its amendments for the language of the other, retaining only the latter's bill designation.

A provision of the Legislative Reorganization Act of 1970 permits a separate House vote on any non-germane amendment added by the Senate to a House-passed bill and requires a majority vote to retain the amendment. Previously the House was forced to act on the bill as a whole; the only way to defeat the non-germane amendment was to reject the entire bill.

Often the second chamber makes only minor changes.

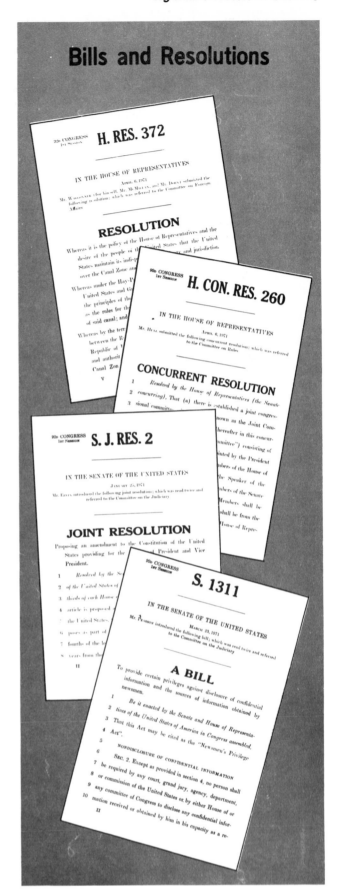

Bills and Resolutions

If these are readily agreed to by the other house, the bill then is routed to the White House for signing. However, if the opposite chamber basically alters the bill submitted to it, the measure usually is "sent to conference." The chamber that has possession of the "papers" (engrossed bill, engrossed amendments, messages of transmittal) requests a conference and the other chamber must agree to it. If the second house does not agree, the bill dies.

Conference, Final Action

CONFERENCE. A conference undertakes to harmonize conflicting House and Senate versions of a legislative bill. The conference is usually staffed by senior members (conferees), appointed by the presiding officers of the two houses, from the committees that managed the bills. Under this arrangement the conferees of one house have the duty of trying to maintain their chamber's position in the face of amending actions by the conferees (also referred to as "managers") of the other house.

The number of conferees from each chamber may vary, the range usually being from three to nine members in each group, depending upon the length or complexity of the bill involved. There may be five representatives and three senators on the conference committee, or the reverse. But a majority vote controls the action of each group so that a larger representation does not give one chamber a voting advantage over the other chamber's conferees.

Theoretically, conferees are not allowed to write new legislation in reconciling the two versions before them, but this curb sometimes is bypassed. Many bills have been put into acceptable compromise form only after new language was provided by the conferees. The 1970 Reorganization Act attempted to tighten restrictions on conferees by forbidding them to introduce any language on a topic that neither chamber sent to conference or to modify any topic beyond the scope of the different House and Senate versions.

Frequently the ironing out of difficulties takes days or even weeks. Conferences on involved appropriation bills sometimes are particularly drawn out.

As a conference proceeds, conferees reconcile differences between the versions, but generally they grant concessions only insofar as they remain sure that the chamber they represent will accept the compromises. Occasionally, uncertainty over how either house will react, or the positive refusal of a chamber to back down on a disputed amendment, results in an impasse, and the bills die in conference even though each was approved by its sponsoring chamber.

Conferees sometimes go back to their respective chambers for further instructions, when they report certain portions in disagreement. Then the chamber concerned can either "recede and concur" in the amendment of the other house, or "insist on its amendment."

When the conferees have reached agreement, they prepare a conference report embodying their recommendations (compromises). The reports, in document form, must be submitted to each house.

The conference report must be approved by each house. Consequently, approval of the report is approval of the compromise bill. In the order of voting on conference reports, the chamber which asked for a conference yields to the other chamber the opportunity to vote first.

FINAL STEPS. After a bill has been passed by both the House and Senate in identical form, all of the original papers are sent to the enrolling clerk of the chamber in which the bill originated. He then prepares an enrolled bill which is printed on parchment paper. When this bill has been certified as correct by the secretary of the Senate or the clerk of the House, depending on which chamber originated the bill, it is signed first (no matter whether it originated in the Senate or House) by the Speaker of the House and then by the president of the Senate. It is next sent to the White House to await action.

If the president approves the bill he signs it, dates it and usually writes the word "approved" on the document. If he does not sign it within 10 days (Sundays excepted) and Congress is in session, the bill becomes law without his signature.

However, should Congress adjourn before the 10 days expire, and the president has failed to sign the measure, it does not become law. This procedure is called the pocket veto.

A president vetoes a bill by refusing to sign it and before the 10-day period expires, returning it to Congress with a message stating his reasons. The message is sent to the chamber which originated the bill. If no action is taken there on the message, the bill dies. Congress, however, can attempt to override the president's veto and enact the bill, "the objections of the president to the contrary notwithstanding." Overriding of a veto requires a two-thirds vote of those present, who must number a quorum and vote by roll call.

Debate can precede this vote, with motions permitted to lay the message on the table, postpone action on it, or refer it to committee. If the president's veto is overridden by a two-thirds vote in both houses, the bill becomes law. Otherwise it is dead.

When bills are passed finally and signed, or passed over a veto, they are given law numbers in numerical order as they become law. There are two series of numbers, one for public and one for private laws, starting at the number "1" for each two-year term of Congress. They are then identified by law number and by Congress — i.e., Private Law 21, 97th Congress; Public Law 250, 97th Congress (or PL 97-250).

98TH CONGRESS, FIRST SESSION

C_Q Organization of Congress

98th Opens With Ceremonies, Partisan Fights

The 98th Congress opened Jan. 3 with the usual festivities and ceremonies but no legislative action.

Newly elected senators, including five freshmen, were sworn in Jan. 3. Then, after meeting for about an hour, the Senate adjourned until Jan. 25, the date of President Reagan's State of the Union address to a joint session of Congress.

Most House members took the oath of office the same day. After Thomas P. O'Neill Jr., D-Mass., was re-elected Speaker, O'Neill and Minority Leader Robert H. Michel, R-Ill., both spoke of the need for bipartisan cooperation.

Immediately thereafter, the House tumbled into partisan bickering. On a party-line vote, Democrats pushed through rules changes they had proposed, which they said would result in a modest streamlining of House procedure. Republicans accused the Democrats of trampling on the rights of the minority.

Representatives remained in town through Jan. 6, when the House approved committee assignments for members. The House then adjourned until Jan. 25, too.

The Senate

The Senate convened Jan. 3 to administer the oath of office to newly elected senators and to formally approve the committee assignments (S Res 8, 9, 10 and 11) both parties had made in December 1982.

SENATE LEADERSHIP

Both parties selected their leaders at party caucuses in December 1982.

The Majority Leadership

The Senate Republican Conference in December 1982 had unanimously re-elected Howard H. Baker Jr., Tenn., as majority leader; Ted Stevens, Alaska, as majority whip; James A. McClure, Idaho, as Republican Conference chairman; and Jake Garn, Utah, as Republican Conference secretary.

Campaign Committee. The only Republican leader not re-elected was Bob Packwood, Ore., who was stripped of his chairmanship of the National Republican Senatorial Committee Dec. 1. Senate Republicans replaced him with Richard G. Lugar, Ind., by a 29-25 secret vote.

The campaign committee raised cash to help elect and re-elect Republican senators. Packwood headed the committee in 1977, 1978, 1981 and 1982 and was generally credited with turning it into a major fund-raising force.

Under Packwood, the committee turned to direct-mail solicitations, and receipts grew from about $2 million in 1975-76 to about $400 million in 1981-82, according to Federal Election Commission records. Committee aide Robert Pipkin said about $10 million was spent on individual Senate campaigns in 1981-82.

But Packwood had had some public differences with President Reagan. In April 1982, after the senator criticized Reagan for ignoring the needs of blacks, women and other minorities, the White House ordered the committee to destroy eight million copies of a fund-raising letter bearing Reagan's signature, at a cost of $2 million.

Lugar portrayed himself as a man who could get along with Reagan. And he was perceived by many senators as Reagan's choice, although both he and Packwood denied White House involvement in the contest. Lugar was nominated by Paul Laxalt, R-Nev., Reagan's close friend, and generally was supported by conservatives. Packwood was nominated by John C. Danforth, R-Mo., and generally was supported by moderates.

After the vote, Baker, Lugar, Packwood and other senators indicated that the contest was not an ideological battle but more of a personality contest. Lugar, who praised Packwood's role in improving the committee, had said he thought the job should be rotated every two years.

Baker Announcement. At a news conference in Knoxville, Jan. 21, Majority Leader Baker said he would not run again for the Senate seat to which he was first elected in 1966. He said he would complete his term but he believed he should not make the Senate a lifetime career and that after three terms he would return to private life in 1985.

Baker had been majority leader since the Republicans took control of the Senate in 1981 and leader of Senate Republicans since 1977.

98th Congress Leadership

SENATE

President Pro Tempore — Strom Thurmond, R-S.C.
Majority Leader — Howard H. Baker Jr., R-Tenn.
Majority Whip — Ted Stevens, R-Alaska
Republican Conference Chairman — James A. McClure, R-Idaho
Republican Conference Secretary — Jake Garn, R-Utah

Minority Leader — Robert C. Byrd, D-W.Va.
Minority Whip — Alan Cranston, D-Calif.
Democratic Conference Secretary — Daniel K. Inouye, D-Hawaii

HOUSE

Speaker — Thomas P. O'Neill Jr., D-Mass.
Majority Leader — Jim Wright, D-Texas
Majority Whip — Thomas S. Foley, D-Wash.

Minority Leader — Robert H. Michel, R-Ill.
Minority Whip — Trent Lott, R-Miss.
Chairman of the Conference — Jack F. Kemp, R-N.Y.
Republican Policy Committee Chairman — Dick Cheney, R-Wyo.

Public Laws

A total of 215 bills cleared by Congress in 1983 became public laws. Following is a list of the number of public laws enacted since 1968:

Year	Public Laws	Year	Public Laws
1983	215	1975	205
1982	328	1974	402
1981	145	1973	247
1980	426	1972	483
1979	187	1971	224
1978	410	1970	505
1977	223	1969	190
1976	383	1968	391

The Minority Leadership

Senate Democrats re-elected their leadership at their party caucus in December 1982. Robert C. Byrd, W.Va., remained minority leader and chairman of the Democratic Conference for the 98th Congress. Alan Cranston, Calif., retained his position as minority whip and Daniel K. Inouye, Hawaii, remained Democratic Conference secretary.

SENATE COMMITTEES

There were no changes in Senate committee chairmen. However, a decision by John C. Stennis, D-Miss., the Senate's senior Democrat, to switch his committee power base set off a chain reaction that scrambled the list of "ranking minority members" on Senate committees.

Although ranking minority members had nowhere near the power of chairmen, they did have some say in the operation of their committees, and they got to hire the minority staff.

Stennis, who had served in the Senate since 1947, was the senior Democrat on both the Armed Services Committee and the Appropriations Committee. He decided in November 1982 to become ranking on Appropriations instead of Armed Services in the 98th Congress. Stennis served as chairman of Armed Services from 1969 to 1981, when he became its ranking minority member.

His shift bumped William Proxmire, Wis., out of his ranking Appropriations slot. Proxmire became ranking Democrat on the Banking, Housing and Urban Affairs Committee, which he chaired form 1975 to 1981, thereby knocking Donald W. Riegle Jr., Mich., out of a ranking job.

Henry M. Jackson, Wash., at that time the ranking Democrat on the Energy and Natural Resources Committee, took Stennis' top slot on Armed Services. J. Bennett Johnston, La., became ranking Democrat on Energy.

Ernest F. Hollings, S.C., who was ranking Democrat on the Budget Committee, chose to become ranking on the Commerce Committee, replacing Howard W. Cannon, Nev., the ranking Democrat who had been defeated for re-election in November 1982.

Lawton Chiles, Fla., the ranking Democrat on the Special Aging Committee, became ranking on Budget. John Glenn, Ohio, took over the ranking minority slot on Aging.

These senators were not giving up seats on any committees; it was only the ranking position that was changing hands.

Stennis felt he could do more for Mississippi as ranking on Appropriations, according to an aide. Hollings, who also had a choice, apparently believed he could do more to help his presidential ambitions on Commerce than on Budget.

Labor Panel Expanded

After weeks of squabbling, Senate Republicans changed the makeup of the Labor and Human Resources Committee. When Republicans made their committee selections in December 1982, Sens. John P. East, N.C., and Paula Hawkins, Fla., left the panel for other committees. But both later wanted to return, although Alfonse M. D'Amato, N.Y., who had joined the committee, did not want to leave it to make room.

On Feb. 3, the Senate agreed to expand the committee by two members, one Republican and one Democrat. D'Amato was removed from the committee and both Hawkins and East went back on. Democratic Sen. Christopher J. Dodd, Conn., also joined the committee. D'Amato took a seat on the Joint Economic Committee, which Hawkins agreed to give up.

The House

After attending to such ceremonial matters as the re-election of its Speaker and the swearing in of new members, the House turned to more partisan matters during the week of Jan. 3.

Democratic and Republican party leadership groups handed out the rewards and punishments of House committee assignments. Resolutions (H Res 26, H Res 27) formalizing the assignments were passed by voice vote Jan. 6.

The House Democratic leadership stripped Rep. Phil Gramm, D-Texas, of his posting to the Budget Committee, punishing Gramm for his two-year collaboration with the White House in supporting the president's budget.

The House Democratic Caucus re-elected all the chairmen of full committees but not before throwing a scare into G. V. "Sonny" Montgomery, D-Miss., chairman of the Veterans' Affairs Committee. Montgomery, like Gramm, had often voted with President Reagan and against the Democratic leadership.

Democrats also forced through a package of changes in House rules over the protests of Republican leaders.

HOUSE LEADERSHIP

House Democrats had re-elected all of their leaders, including Speaker O'Neill and Majority Leader Jim Wright, Texas, during a party caucus in December 1982.

As expected, the House Jan. 3 re-elected O'Neill as Speaker, a post he had held since 1977. O'Neill got 259 votes, all Democratic, compared to 155 votes, all Republican, for Minority Leader Michel. (Vote 1, p. 2-H)

House Republicans had also re-elected their leaders, including Minority Leader Michel and Minority Whip Trent Lott, Miss., during a party caucus in December.

HOUSE COMMITTEES

Democrats increased their voting majority on almost every House committee Jan. 6.

The changes resulted primarily from the 26-seat net gain Democrats made in elections to the 98th Congress in November 1982. The elections gave Democrats a 269-166 majority over Republicans in the House.

The 269-166 lineup worked out to 62 percent Demo-

crats and 38 percent Republicans. But on many panels, Democrats gave themselves a better deal than that ratio would dictate.

For example, the new ratio would have given Democrats a 26:16 edge on the Energy and Commerce Committee, but they took a 27:15 majority. On Foreign Affairs, the new ratio would have given Democrats a 23:14 margin, but they made it 24:13.

Committee Assignments

Significant fights among Democrats came over assignments to four committees: Ways and Means; Energy and Commerce; Budget; and Banking.

Leadership aides and several members discounted published reports that lobbying by outside groups, such as the insurance and auto industries, had much to do with the outcome. They said contests were won because the members worked for the assignments, had key sponsors on Steering and Policy and came from the right area of the country.

Committee Chairmen

With the exception of the Rules Committee, there were no vacancies in chairmanships of standing committees. The Rules Committee chairman was appointed by the Speaker, not named by Steering and Policy, and confirmed, as all chairmen must be, by the Democratic Caucus. Claude Pepper, D-Fla., was named by O'Neill to be Rules chairman and confirmed by the caucus by a 211-5 vote Jan. 4.

The only close vote on nominating chairmen in Steering and Policy came Jan. 3 on Montgomery, who had often voted against the leadership. He was named chairman of Veterans' Affairs on a 16-11 vote. Montgomery said he "was hurting" that night, having expected no more than five votes to be cast against him.

When the full caucus voted on chairmen the next day,

Montgomery was heartened by a 179-53 vote for him. The scare had an impact, though.

"I got the message, loud and clear," Montgomery said, promising he would support the leadership where he could. However, he said on many votes he would have to represent his conservative constituents and vote against the leadership. In the 97th Congress, only six other Democrats voted against the leadership more often than Montgomery.

Montgomery saved his chairmanship by "repenting" late in 1982. He actively campaigned for many Democratic incumbents and after the election asked Democrats for their support for his chairmanship. Montgomery also was helped by his personal popularity with his Democratic colleagues.

The only other chairman to draw much opposition was Melvin Price, D-Ill., who had headed the Armed Services Committee since 1975. Price was nominated by Steering and Policy by a 22-5 vote and confirmed by the caucus 195-36.

Gramm and the Budget Committee

The Democratic Steering and Policy Committee Jan. 3 voted 26-4 to kick Gramm off the Budget Committee. Gramm had worked closely with the White House during the 97th Congress, even supplying presidential aides with Democratic budget strategy. For months, Democratic leaders had been expected to remove him from his slot on Budget, a position they viewed as a reward.

Gramm resigned from the House on Jan. 5 and announced that he would run for his seat as a Republican.

After winning a special election Feb. 12, Gramm returned to Congress Feb. 22 — and to the Budget Committee, but only after Democrats had gone through the embarrassing process of expanding the panel to make room for Gramm's return.

In December 1982, Democrats had promised the GOP

Membership Changes, 98th Congress

SENATE

Party	Member	Died	Resigned	Successor	Party	Appointed	Sworn In
D	Henry M. Jackson, Wash.	9/1/83		Daniel J. Evans	R	9/8/83*	9/12/83

HOUSE

Party	Member	Died	Resigned	Successor	Party	Elected	Sworn In
R	Jack Swigert, Colo.	12/27/82		Daniel L. Schaefer	R	3/29/83	4/7/83
D	Benjamin S. Rosenthal, N.Y.	1/4/83		Gary L. Ackerman	D	3/1/83	3/2/83
D	Phil Gramm, Texas		1/5/83	Phil Gramm	R	2/12/83	2/22/83
D	Phillip Burton, Calif.	4/10/83		Sala Burton	D	6/21/83	6/28/83
D	Harold Washington, Ill.		4/30/83	Charles A. Hayes	D	8/23/83	9/12/83
D	Larry P. McDonald, Ga.	9/1/83		George "Buddy" Darden	D	11/8/83	11/10/83
D	Clement J. Zablocki, Wis.	12/3/83					

Evans was subsequently elected to fill the remaining five years of the term, which expired Jan. 3, 1989.

Vetoes Cast by President Reagan

President Reagan vetoed seven public bills in his third year in office, bringing his total vetoes to 22.

Congress was successful in overriding one of the seven vetoes by the president, the only one on which an override attempt was made. That bill was HR 1062, which authorized the interior secretary to give 3.11 acres of federal land in Lane County, Ore., to persons who had paid for the land after an inaccurate private survey was made when the land was subdivided in 1941. *(Story, p. 344)*

Reagan had two vetoes overridden in 1982.

When Congress is in session, a bill becomes law without the president's signature if he does not act upon it within 10 days, excluding Sundays, from the time he receives it. But if Congress adjourns within that 10-day period, the bill is killed, or pocket vetoed, without the president's signature. One of the seven vetoes in 1983 was a pocket veto. Five of the 13 vetoes in 1982 were pocket vetoes.

Reagan's 22 vetoes exceeded by 12 the number cast by the first six presidents in the 40 years from 1789 to 1829. Seven presidents vetoed no bills. The greatest number of vetoes, 635, was cast by Franklin D. Roosevelt. More recently, Jimmy Carter vetoed 31 bills; Gerald R. Ford vetoed 66; Richard M. Nixon, 43; Lyndon B. Johnson, 30; and John F. Kennedy, 21.

1981

1. H J Res 357 (Continuing Appropriations)
   Vetoed: Nov. 23
   No override attempt
2. HR 4353 (Bankruptcy Fees on Lifetime Communities Inc.)
   Pocket vetoed: Dec. 29

1982

3. S 1503 (Standby Petroleum Allocation)
   Vetoed: March 20
   Senate sustained March 24: 58-36*
4. HR 5118 (Southern Arizona Water Rights Settlement Act)
   Vetoed: June 1
   No override attempt
5. HR 5922 (Urgent Supplemental Appropriations, Fiscal 1982)
   Vetoed: June 24
   House sustained June 24: 253-151*
6. HR 6682 (Urgent Supplemental Appropriations, Fiscal 1982)
   Vetoed: June 25
   House sustained July 13: 242-169*
7. HR 6198 (Manufacturers Copyright Bill)
   Vetoed: July 8
   Veto overridden July 13*
   House: 324-86, July 13
   Senate: 84-9, July 13
8. HR 6863 (Supplemental Appropriations, Fiscal 1982)
   Vetoed: Aug. 28
   Veto overridden Sept. 10*
   House: 301-117, Sept. 9
   Senate: 60-30, Sept. 10
9. HR 1371 (Contract Disputes)
   Vetoed: Oct. 15
   No override attempt
10. S 2577 (Environmental Research and Development)
    Vetoed: Oct. 22
    No override attempt

11. S 2623 (Indian Controlled Community Colleges)
    Pocket vetoed: Jan. 3, 1983
12. HR 5858 (Private Bill for Relief of Certain Silver Dealers)
    Pocket vetoed: Jan. 4, 1983
13. HR 7336 (Education Consolidation and Improvement Act Amendments)
    Pocket vetoed: Jan. 12, 1983
14. HR 9 (Florida Wilderness Act)
    Pocket vetoed: Jan. 14, 1983
15. HR 3963 (Anti-Crime Bill)
    Pocket vetoed: Jan 14, 1983

1983

16. S 366 (Indian Claims Bill)
    Vetoed: April 5, 1983
    No override attempt
17. S 973 (Tax Leasing Plan)
    Vetoed: June 17, 1983
    No override attempt
18. HR 3564 (Feed Grains Bill)
    Vetoed: Aug. 12, 1983
    No override attempt
19. H J Res 338 (Chicago School Desegregation)
    Vetoed: Aug. 13, 1983
    No override attempt
20. S J Res 149 (Dairy Assessment Delay Bill)
    Vetoed: Aug. 23, 1983
    No override attempt
21. HR 1062 (Oregon Land Transfer Bill)
    Vetoed: Oct. 19, 1983
    Veto overridden Oct. 25*
    Senate: 95-0, Oct. 25
    House: 297-125, Oct. 25
22. HR 4042 (El Salvador Certification)
    Pocket vetoed: Nov. 30, 1983

Veto overrides require a two-thirds majority vote of both houses.

---

11 seats on Budget, which was restricted to 30 members by House rules. But in early January, Democrats took 20 Budget seats after kicking Gramm off. Leadership aides said they had intended but forgot to alter the House rules, adopted Jan. 3, to allow 31 members on Budget. Republicans named 10 members to Budget and announced that the 11th seat would be held for Gramm.

With no debate, the House Feb. 7 expanded the Budget Committee to 31 members. The expansion was done in only a few seconds under unanimous consent of the House requested by Gillis W. Long, D-La., chairman of the House Democratic Caucus.

Stump Bumped From Veterans' Affairs

Rep. Bob Stump of Arizona, who switched in 1983 from the Democratic to the Republican Party, wound up

losing his seat on the Veterans' Affairs Committee because the Democrats gave the GOP four fewer seats than in 1982.

Stump, who announced his switch in 1981, had been assured by Republican leaders that he would keep his seniority and stay on his two primary committees, Armed Services and Intelligence, which he did. He also had hoped to be renamed to Veterans' Affairs, but the number of Republicans on the committee was reduced from 15 to 11 and there was no seat for Stump.

Armed Services Squabble

In an unprecedented confrontation, two senior Democrats on the House Armed Services Committee Jan. 26 locked horns over a subcommittee chairmanship. Charles E. Bennett, D-Fla., second-ranking Democrat on the panel, wanted the chairmanship of the procurement subcommittee instead of the Seapower Subcommittee, which he had headed for several years. But Samuel S. Stratton, D-N.Y., right behind Bennett in seniority, did not want to give up his chairmanship of procurement.

Stratton lobbied his colleagues hard. Several defense lobbyists also sought votes for Stratton, as did Sen. Ernest F. Hollings, D-S.C., who asked freshman John M. Spratt Jr., D-S.C., to support Stratton. Amid much tension, Democrats by secret ballot voted 13-16 against Bennett, allowing Stratton to keep the procurement chairmanship. The panel handled the purchase of all weapons systems except ships.

Select Committee on Children

The House Feb. 2 voted 312-69 to establish a 25-member Select Committee on Children, Youth and Families. George Miller, D-Calif., was named chairman. The panel would not have legislative jurisdiction but could hold hearings on issues affecting children. Opponents, mostly Republicans, argued that such select committees tend to grow out of control, and they opposed the panel's estimated $500,000 annual budget.

Rules Committee

The membership of the Rules Committee was reduced from 16 to 13 in the 98th Congress because the House leadership had been unable to persuade any senior members to take vacant seats on the panel. Speaker O'Neill said it soon might be necessary to treat the Rules Committee as a minor panel that members could use as an extra committee assignment.

The transformation of Rules from a committee whose seats were once highly coveted into a body on which few wanted to serve told a great deal about the way the House itself had changed.

A generation earlier, Rules had been filled with legislative specialists of both parties whose interest was the internal workings of the House. Most of them had safe seats in one-party districts, and the "inside game" fascinated them far more than the politics of the places they came from. For every member who found a place on the panel, several were turned away.

In the years since then, however, most members had turned their focus outside the institution and its gamesmanship. The safe House seats for the 1980s were secure because their occupants spent thousands of hours each year planning their local media coverage and collecting the campaign money that could overwhelm a challenger, if it did not scare him away altogether.

For many of these members, strategic placement in the

Senate Cloture Votes, 1983

Following is a list of all cloture votes taken by the Senate during 1983. Cloture motions required a majority of three-fifths of the total Senate (60 members) for adoption, under a rule adopted in 1975. Previously cloture could be invoked by a two-thirds majority vote of those senators present and voting, except between 1949 and 1959, when the rule required a two-thirds majority of the entire Senate.

Since 1979, Senate rules had required, after no more than 100 hours of post-cloture debate, a final vote on a measure on which cloture had been invoked.

The seven cloture votes in 1983 brought to 194 the total number of cloture votes taken since the adoption of Rule 22 first allowed them in 1917. *(Cloture votes, 1919-82, 1982 Almanac p. 5; 1981 Almanac p. 10; 1977 Almanac p. 813)*

Issue	Date	Vote
Emergency Jobs Appropriations/ Interest Withholding	March 16, 1983	50-48
Emergency Jobs Appropriations/ Interest Withholding	March 16, 1983	59-39
International Trade and Investment/Interest Withholding	April 19, 1983	34-53
International Trade and Investment/Interest Withholding	April 19, 1983	39-59
Defense Authorizations, 1984	July 21, 1983	55-41
Radio Broadcasting to Cuba	Aug. 3, 1983	62-33
Natural Gas Policy Act	Nov. 3, 1983	86-7

---

committee system was the first step toward re-election security. And when it came to attracting money and media, the Rules Committee had a hard time competing. The procedural decisions it made were not easy to explain in a press release, and political action committees tended to forget about it except when a crucial piece of legislation was about to come through.

DEMOCRATIC CAUCUS RULES

The House Democratic Caucus made several changes in its own rules during a Dec. 9, 1982, meeting.

It expanded by one member the Democratic Steering and Policy Committee, which made committee assignments for Democrats. Tony Coelho, D-Calif., was added as an ex officio member in his capacity as chairman of the Democratic Congressional Campaign Committee. This brought the committee membership to 30: 10 members of the leadership, 12 elected by region and eight appointed by the Speaker.

The caucus made an exception in its rules to allow Ronald V. Dellums, D-Calif., chairman of the District of Columbia Committee, to keep his chairmanship and take charge of a subcommittee on the Armed Services Committee.

Another change involved the way senior Democrats on committees bid for subcommittee chairmanships. The new rule would allow a senior member who was rejected in a bid for one subcommittee chairmanship to bid on all remaining subcommittee chairmanships. This change could help senior members who had been dumped out of chairmanships in the past.

The caucus prohibited voting by proxy by Democrats in the full caucus or in any caucus of Democrats on a committee or subcommittee.

The caucus also barred members from participating in campaign activities for Republicans seeking federal office. Democrats violating the rule could be thrown out of the caucus. Some Democrats wanted the prohibition to be even stronger.

HOUSE RULES

After dropping the most controversial of several proposed changes in House rules, Democrats forced a package of changes through the House Jan. 3 on a party-line vote.

Democratic leaders claimed the changes were needed to streamline the legislative process, avoiding unnecessary votes and amendments. Republican leaders said the changes trampled on the rights of the minority.

The most contentious of the changes that were approved was one that would make it harder for members to offer "riders" to appropriations bills. Such amendments to limit government actions had become popular in recent years. Riders on school busing and abortion, for example, had been attached to appropriations bills by conservatives. Majority Leader Wright told House members the use of riders had grown from only one being adopted in 1970 to 50 in 1980.

The rules package was approved by voice vote after a key procedural vote was won by Democrats, 249-156. Only two Democrats — Gramm of Texas and Larry P. McDonald of Georgia — voted against the leadership. *(Vote 2, p. 2-H)*

An effort by Republicans to have the change on riders deleted was defeated on a similar party-line vote, 156-250. *(Vote 3, p. 2-H)*

One Change Withdrawn

The rules changes had been agreed to by House Democrats in December 1982, after a task force worked for several months to write the proposals.

As initially approved by the Democratic Caucus, the package also included a change increasing the number of members required to gain House consideration of a constitutional amendment if the Judiciary Committee refused to report it out.

House rules required that to pull a constitutional amendment out of the Judiciary Committee, a majority of the House must sign a discharge petition. The Democrats proposed to increase the number to two-thirds, which is the portion of the House that would have to vote for such an amendment for it to get further consideration in the Senate or the states.

The proposed change drew opposition from a number of Democrats, both liberal and conservative, from Republicans and from a host of interest groups seeking constitutional amendments.

At a brief meeting of the Democratic Caucus Jan. 3, before the full House met, Democrats agreed not to offer the two-thirds requirement. Leadership aides said that while the Democrats probably had the votes to approve the change, the leadership did not want to begin the year with a fight among Democrats over the issue.

The leadership also managed to avoid a split among Democrats over the rules change on appropriations riders. John B. Breaux, D-La., had called the change a "gag rule" after it was approved by the caucus and said he would fight it when the House took it up Jan. 3.

But members of the leadership pressured Breaux to back off, reminding him that he was seeking a coveted slot on the Budget Committee and suggesting that he could have trouble even getting nominated for the position if he fought the rules change.

Breaux spoke against the changes Jan. 3 but voted with the Democratic leadership for the package. Later that day, Budget Committee assignments were handed out; Breaux did not get one.

Rules Changes

The package of rules changes approved Jan. 3 by the House included:

Legislative Riders. Amendments to appropriations bills were prohibited if they were in the form of a general legislative limitation, such as barring the use of funds in the bill for abortions.

Under the new rule, the only way a rider could be offered was for the House to reject a motion to rise out of the Committee of the Whole after all other work on the bill had been completed. If that motion was defeated, one rider could then be offered. The same process would have to occur again before any subsequent riders could be considered.

The Democratic leadership could still get riders it wanted on appropriations bills in one of two additional ways. The Rules Committee, an arm of the Speaker, could allow specific riders to be offered. Or riders could be included in a bill by the Appropriations Committee, which also was usually responsive to the leadership.

'Nuisance' Votes. Two changes were designed to avoid what many members felt were "nuisance" votes on minor procedural issues.

One change allowed the Speaker to resolve the House into the Committee of the Whole without a vote. In the past, members frequently sought a time-consuming, roll-call vote on forming the Committee of the Whole, which was used to debate and amend bills before voting on final passage.

The other change would give the Speaker authority to postpone for up to two legislative days a vote on approval of the previous day's *Journal*, the record of House proceedings. Republicans often forced votes on both procedures to get a quorum of members to the House floor.

Minority Leader Michel criticized the rules changes, saying they would encourage members not to come to the House floor to listen to debate on bills.

"Mr. Speaker," Michel said, "you are converting this body of representatives into robots in a glass-covered dome, who come only when they are called, speak only when they are told and cast their votes only when it is unavoidable."

Resolutions of Inquiry. Another rules change doubled the time granted a committee to consider resolutions of inquiry, which often were investigations of executive branch departments.

Previously, when such a resolution was referred to a committee, the panel had seven legislative days to consider it. Under the new rule, committees would have 14 legislative days for such inquiries.

Secret Hearings. Another change made it easier for three committees — Armed Services, Appropriations and Intelligence — to close hearings to the public.

All House committees were permitted to publicly vote to hold a closed hearing on the day the vote was taken and one additional day. The rules change would allow these

three committees to close meetings for up to five additional days after the vote, for a total of six days of closed hearings.

Tax Jurisdiction. Yet another change tightened the control of the Ways and Means Committee over bills dealing with taxes or tariffs. Although Ways and Means was supposed to have exclusive jurisdiction, other committees occasionally had reported bills dealing with taxes or trade restrictions.

Under the new rule, Ways and Means could use a point of order to block any bill containing a tax or tariff provision from coming to the House floor unless the provision was reported by Ways and Means. The committee also could use a point of order to block House consideration of Senate amendments to a House bill if those amendments contained tax or tariff matters that had not been approved by Ways and Means.

Party Switches. Continued assignment to House committees was made contingent upon members being members of their party caucus. The change was made along with a change in the rules of the Democratic Caucus in December 1982 to throw a member out of the caucus if he or she switched parties.

Office Management. Another change directed the clerk of the House to manage the office of a member who died, resigned or was expelled from the House. There was no provision covering such situations in the existing House rules.

BLACK CAUCUS LEADERS

The Congressional Black Caucus Jan. 4 elected Rep. Julian C. Dixon, D-Calif., as chairman of the 21-member group for the 98th Congress. Dixon replaced Del. Walter E. Fauntroy, D-D.C. The caucus named Reps. Mickey Leland, D-Texas, and William H. Gray III, D-Pa., as vice chairmen. Elected secretary was Rep. Edolphus Towns, D-N.Y. Rep. Harold Washington, D-Ill., was elected treasurer. ∎

Members of the 98th Congress, First Session . . .

As of Jan. 20, 1983

Representatives
D 267; R 165
3 Vacancies*

A

Addabbo, Joseph P., D-N.Y. (6)
Akaka, Daniel K., D-Hawaii (2)
Albosta, Donald J., D-Mich. (10)
Alexander, Bill, D-Ark. (1)
Anderson, Glenn M., D-Calif. (32)
Andrews, Ike, D-N.C. (4)
Andrews, Michael A., D-Texas (25)
Annunzio, Frank, D-Ill. (11)
Anthony, Beryl Jr., D-Ark. (4)
Applegate, Douglas, D-Ohio (18)
Archer, Bill, R-Texas (7)
Aspin, Les, D-Wis. (1)
AuCoin, Les, D-Ore. (1)

B

Badham, Robert E., R-Calif. (40)
Barnard, Doug Jr., D-Ga. (10)
Barnes, Michael D., D-Md. (8)
Bartlett, Steve, R-Texas (3)
Bateman, Herbert H., R-Va. (1)
Bates, Jim, D-Calif. (44)
Bedell, Berkley, D-Iowa (6)
Beilenson, Anthony C., D-Calif. (23)
Bennett, Charles E., D-Fla. (3)
Bereuter, Douglas K., R-Neb. (1)
Berman, Howard L., D-Calif. (26)
Bethune, Ed, R-Ark. (2)
Bevill, Tom, D-Ala. (4)
Biaggi, Mario, D-N.Y. (19)
Bilirakis, Michael, R-Fla. (9)
Bliley, Thomas J. Jr., R-Va. (3)
Boehlert, Sherwood, R-N.Y. (25)
Boggs, Lindy (Mrs. Hale), D-La. (2)
Boland, Edward P., D-Mass. (2)
Boner, Bill, D-Tenn. (5)
Bonior, David E., D-Mich. (12)
Bonker, Don, D-Wash. (3)
Borski, Robert A., D-Pa. (3)
Bosco, Douglas H., D-Calif. (1)
Boucher, Frederick C., D-Va. (9)
Bouquard, Marilyn Lloyd, D-Tenn. (3)
Boxer, Barbara, D-Calif. (6)
Breaux, John B., D-La. (7)
Britt, Robin, D-N.C. (6)
Brooks, Jack, D-Texas (9)
Broomfield, William S., R-Mich. (18)
Brown, George E. Jr., D-Calif. (36)
Brown, Hank, R-Colo. (4)
Broyhill, James T., R-N.C. (10)
Bryant, John, D-Texas (5)
Burton, Dan L., R-Ind. (6)
Burton, Phillip, D-Calif. (5)
Byron, Beverly B., D-Md. (6)

C

Campbell, Carroll A. Jr., R-S.C. (4)
Carney, William, R-N.Y. (1)
Carper, Thomas R., D-Del. (AL)
Carr, Bob, D-Mich. (6)
Chandler, Rod, R-Wash. (8)
Chappell, Bill Jr., D-Fla. (4)
Chappie, Gene, R-Calif. (2)
Cheney, Dick, R-Wyo. (AL)
Clarke, James McClure, D-N.C. (11)
Clay, William, D-Mo. (1)
Clinger, William F. Jr., R-Pa. (23)
Coats, Dan, R-Ind. (4)
Coelho, Tony, D-Calif. (15)
Coleman, E. Thomas, R-Mo. (6)
Coleman, Ron, D-Texas (16)
Collins, Cardiss, D-Ill. (7)
Conable, Barber B. Jr., R-N.Y. (30)
Conte, Silvio O., R-Mass. (1)
Conyers, John Jr., D-Mich. (1)
Cooper, Jim, D-Tenn. (4)
Corcoran, Tom, R-Ill. (14)
Coughlin, Lawrence, R-Pa. (13)

Courter, Jim, R-N.J. (12)
Coyne, William J., D-Pa. (14)
Craig, Larry E., R-Idaho (1)
Crane, Daniel B., R-Ill. (19)
Crane, Philip M., R-Ill. (12)
Crockett, George W. Jr., D-Mich. (13)

D

D'Amours, Norman E., D-N.H. (1)
Daniel, Dan, D-Va. (5)
Dannemeyer, William E., R-Calif. (39)
Daschle, Thomas A., D-S.D. (AL)
Daub, Hal, R-Neb. (2)
Davis, Robert W., R-Mich. (11)
de la Garza, E. "Kika", D-Texas (15)
Dellums, Ronald V., D-Calif. (8)
Derrick, Butler, D-S.C. (3)
DeWine, Michael, R-Ohio (7)
Dickinson, William L., R-Ala. (2)
Dicks, Norman D., D-Wash. (6)
Dingell, John D., D-Mich. (16)
Dixon, Julian C., D-Calif. (28)
Donnelly, Brian J., D-Mass. (11)
Dorgan, Byron L., D-N.D. (AL)
Dowdy, Wayne, D-Miss. (4)
Downey, Thomas J., D-N.Y. (2)
Dreier, David, R-Calif. (33)
Duncan, John J., R-Tenn. (2)
Durbin, Dick, D-Ill. (20)
Dwyer, Bernard J., D-N.J. (6)
Dymally, Mervyn M., D-Calif. (31)
Dyson, Roy, D-Md. (1)

E

Early, Joseph D., D-Mass. (3)
Eckart, Dennis E., D-Ohio (11)
Edgar, Bob, D-Pa. (7)
Edwards, Don, D-Calif. (10)
Edwards, Jack, R-Ala. (1)
Edwards, Mickey, R-Okla. (5)
Emerson, Bill, R-Mo. (8)
English, Glenn, D-Okla. (6)
Erdreich, Ben, D-Ala. (6)
Erlenborn, John N., R-Ill. (13)
Evans, Cooper, R-Iowa (3)
Evans, Lane, D-Ill. (17)

F

Fascell, Dante B., D-Fla. (19)
Fazio, Vic, D-Calif. (4)
Feighan, Edward F., D-Ohio (19)
Ferraro, Geraldine A., D-N.Y. (9)
Fiedler, Bobbi, R-Calif. (21)
Fields, Jack, R-Texas (8)
Fish, Hamilton Jr., R-N.Y. (21)
Flippo, Ronnie G., D-Ala. (5)
Florio, James J., D-N.J. (1)
Foglietta, Thomas M., D-Pa. (1)
Foley, Thomas S., D-Wash. (5)
Ford, Harold E., D-Tenn. (9)
Ford, William D., D-Mich. (15)
Forsythe, Edwin B., R-N.J. (13)
Fowler, Wyche Jr., D-Ga. (5)
Frank, Barney, D-Mass. (4)
Franklin, Webb, R-Miss. (2)
Frenzel, Bill, R-Minn. (3)
Frost, Martin, D-Texas (24)
Fuqua, Don, D-Fla. (2)

G

Garcia, Robert, D-N.Y. (18)
Gaydos, Joseph M., D-Pa. (20)
Gejdenson, Sam, D-Conn. (2)
Gekas, George W., R-Pa. (17)
Gephardt, Richard A., D-Mo. (3)
Gibbons, Sam, D-Fla. (7)
Gilman, Benjamin A., R-N.Y. (22)
Gingrich, Newt, R-Ga. (6)
Glickman, Dan, D-Kan. (4)
Gonzalez, Henry B., D-Texas (20)
Goodling, Bill, R-Pa. (19)
Gore, Albert Jr., D-Tenn. (6)
Gradison, Bill, R-Ohio (2)
Gray, William H. III, D-Pa. (2)
Green, Bill, R-N.Y. (15)
Gregg, Judd, R-N.H. (2)

Guarini, Frank J., D-N.J. (14)
Gunderson, Steve, R-Wis. (3)

H

Hall, Katie, D-Ind. (1)
Hall, Ralph M., D-Texas (4)
Hall, Sam B. Jr., D-Texas (1)
Hall, Tony P., D-Ohio (3)
Hamilton, Lee H., D-Ind. (9)
Hammerschmidt, John Paul, R-Ark. (3)
Hance, Kent, D-Texas (19)
Hansen, George, R-Idaho (2)
Hansen, James V., R-Utah (1)
Harkin, Tom, D-Iowa (5)
Harrison, Frank, D-Pa. (11)
Hartnett, Thomas F., R-S.C. (1)
Hatcher, Charles, D-Ga. (2)
Hawkins, Augustus F., D-Calif. (29)
Hefner, W. G. "Bill", D-N.C. (8)
Heftel, Cecil, D-Hawaii (1)
Hertel, Dennis M., D-Mich. (14)
Hightower, Jack, D-Texas (13)
Hiler, John, R-Ind. (3)
Hillis, Elwood, R-Ind. (5)
Holt, Marjorie S., R-Md. (4)
Hopkins, Larry J., R-Ky. (6)
Horton, Frank, R-N.Y. (29)
Howard, James J., D-N.J. (3)
Hoyer, Steny H., D-Md. (5)
Hubbard, Carroll Jr., D-Ky. (1)
Huckaby, Jerry, D-La. (5)
Hughes, William J., D-N.J. (2)
Hunter, Duncan L., R-Calif. (45)
Hutto, Earl, D-Fla. (1)
Hyde, Henry J., R-Ill. (6)

I, J

Ireland, Andy, D-Fla. (10)
Jacobs, Andrew Jr., D-Ind. (10)
Jeffords, James M., R-Vt. (AL)
Jenkins, Ed, D-Ga. (9)
Johnson, Nancy L., R-Conn. (6)
Jones, Ed, D-Tenn. (8)
Jones, James R., D-Okla. (1)
Jones, Walter B., D-N.C. (1)

K

Kaptur, Marcy, D-Ohio (9)
Kasich, John R., R-Ohio (12)
Kastenmeier, Robert W., D-Wis. (2)
Kazen, Abraham Jr., D-Texas (23)
Kennelly, Barbara B., D-Conn. (1)
Kemp, Jack F., R-N.Y. (31)
Kildee, Dale E., D-Mich. (7)
Kindness, Thomas N., R-Ohio (8)
Kogovsek, Ray, D-Colo. (3)
Kolter, Joe, D-Pa. (4)
Kostmayer, Peter H., D-Pa. (8)
Kramer, Ken, R-Colo. (5)

L

LaFalce, John J., D-N.Y. (32)
Lagomarsino, Robert J., R-Calif. (19)
Lantos, Tom, D-Calif. (11)
Latta, Delbert L., R-Ohio (5)
Leach, Jim, R-Iowa (1)
Leath, Marvin, D-Texas (11)
Lehman, Richard H., D-Calif. (18)
Lehman, William, D-Fla. (17)
Leland, Mickey, D-Texas (18)
Lent, Norman F., R-N.Y. (4)
Levin, Sander M., D-Mich. (17)
Levine, Mel, D-Calif. (27)
Levitas, Elliott H., D-Ga. (4)
Lewis, Jerry, R-Calif. (35)
Lewis, Tom, R-Fla. (12)
Lipinski, William O., D-Ill. (5)
Livingston, Bob, R-La. (1)
Loeffler, Tom, R-Texas (21)
Long, Clarence D., D-Md. (2)
Long, Gillis W., D-La. (8)
Lott, Trent, R-Miss. (5)
Lowery, Bill, R-Calif. (41)
Lowry, Mike, D-Wash. (7)
Lujan, Manuel Jr., R-N.M. (1)
Luken, Thomas A., D-Ohio (1)

Lundine, Stan, D-N.Y. (34)
Lungren, Dan, R-Calif. (42)

M

Mack, Connie, R-Fla. (13)
MacKay, Buddy, D-Fla. (6)
Madigan, Edward R., R-Ill. (15)
Markey, Edward J., D-Mass. (7)
Marlenee, Ron, R-Mont. (2)
Marriott, Dan, R-Utah (2)
Martin, David O'B., R-N.Y. (26)
Martin, James G., R-N.C. (9)
Martin, Lynn, R-Ill. (16)
Martinez, Matthew G., D-Calif. (30)
Matsui, Robert T., D-Calif. (3)
Mavroules, Nicholas, D-Mass. (6)
Mazzoli, Romano L., D-Ky. (3)
McCain, John, R-Ariz. (1)
McCandless, Al, R-Calif. (37)
McCloskey, Frank, D-Ind. (8)
McCollum, Bill, R-Fla. (5)
McCurdy, Dave, D-Okla. (4)
McDade, Joseph M., R-Pa. (10)
McDonald, Larry P., D-Ga. (7)
McEwen, Bob, R-Ohio (6)
McGrath, Raymond J., R-N.Y. (5)
McHugh, Matthew F., D-N.Y. (28)
McKernan, John R. Jr., R-Maine (1)
McKinney, Stewart B., R-Conn. (4)
McNulty, James F. Jr., D-Ariz. (5)
Mica, Daniel A., D-Fla. (14)
Michel, Robert H., R-Ill (18)
Mikulski, Barbara A., D-Md. (3)
Miller, Clarence E., R-Ohio (10)
Miller, George, D-Calif. (7)
Mineta, Norman Y., D-Calif. (13)
Minish, Joseph G., D-N.J. (11)
Mitchell, Parren J., D-Md. (7)
Moakley, Joe, D-Mass. (9)
Molinari, Guy V., R-N.Y. (14)
Mollohan, Alan B., D-W.Va. (1)
Montgomery, G. V. "Sonny", D-Miss. (3)
Moody, Jim, D-Wis. (5)
Moore, Henson, R-La. (6)
Moorhead, Carlos J., R-Calif. (22)
Morrison, Bruce A., D-Conn. (3)
Morrison, Sid, R-Wash. (4)
Mrazek, Robert J., D-N.Y. (3)
Murphy, Austin J., D-Pa. (22)
Murtha, John P., D-Pa. (12)
Myers, John T., R-Ind. (7)

N

Natcher, William H., D-Ky. (2)
Neal, Stephen L., D-N.C. (5)
Nelson, Bill, D-Fla. (11)
Nichols, Bill, D-Ala. (3)
Nielson, Howard C., R-Utah (3)
Nowak, Henry J., D-N.Y. (33)

O

Oakar, Mary Rose, D-Ohio (20)
Oberstar, James L., D-Minn. (8)
Obey, David R., D-Wis. (7)
O'Brien, George M., R-Ill. (4)
Olin, James R., D-Va. (6)
O'Neill, Thomas P. Jr., D-Mass. (8)
Ortiz, Solomon P., D-Texas (27)
Ottinger, Richard L., D-N.Y. (20)
Owens, Major R., D-N.Y. (12)
Oxley, Mike, R-Ohio (4)

P

Packard, Ron, R-Calif. (43)
Panetta, Leon E., D-Calif. (16)
Parris, Stan, R-Va. (8)
Pashayan, Charles Jr., R-Calif. (17)
Patman, Bill, D-Texas (14)
Patterson, Jerry M., D-Calif. (38)
Paul, Ron, R-Texas (22)
Pease, Don J., D-Ohio (13)
Penny, Timothy J., D-Minn. (1)
Pepper, Claude, D-Fla. (18)
Perkins, Carl D., D-Ky. (7)
Petri, Thomas E., R-Wis. (6)
Pickle, J. J., D-Texas (10)
Porter, John Edward, R-Ill. (10)

...Governors, Supreme Court, Cabinet-rank Officers

Price, Melvin, D-Ill. (21)
Pritchard, Joel, R-Wash. (1)
Pursell, Carl D., R-Mich. (2)

Q, R

Quillen, James H., R-Tenn. (1)
Rahall, Nick J. II, D-W.Va. (4)
Rangel, Charles B., D-N.Y. (16)
Ratchford, William R., D-Conn. (5)
Ray, Richard, D-Ga. (3)
Regula, Ralph, R-Ohio (16)
Reid, Harry, D-Nev. (1)
Richardson, Bill, D-N.M. (3)
Ridge, Tom, R-Pa. (21)
Rinaldo, Matthew J., R-N.J. (7)
Ritter, Don, R-Pa. (15)
Roberts, Pat, R-Kan. (1)
Robinson, J. Kenneth, R-Va. (7)
Rodino, Peter W. Jr., D-N.J. (10)
Roe, Robert A., D-N.J. (8)
Roemer, Buddy, D-La. (4)
Rogers, Harold, R-Ky. (5)
Rose, Charlie, D-N.C. (7)
Rostenkowski, Dan, D-Ill. (8)
Roth, Toby, R-Wis. (8)
Roukema, Marge, R-N.J. (5)
Rowland, J. Roy, D-Ga. (8)
Roybal, Edward R., D-Calif. (25)
Rudd, Eldon, R-Ariz. (4)
Russo, Marty, D-Ill. (3)

S

Sabo, Martin Olav, D-Minn. (5)
St Germain, Fernand J., D-R.I. (1)
Savage, Gus, D-Ill. (2)
Sawyer, Harold S., R-Mich. (5)
Scheuer, James H., D-N.Y. (8)
Schneider, Claudine, R-R.I. (2)
Schroeder, Patricia, D-Colo. (1)
Schulze, Richard T., R-Pa. (5)
Schumer, Charles E., D-N.Y. (10)
Seiberling, John F., D-Ohio (14)
Sensenbrenner, F. James Jr., R-Wis. (9)
Shannon, James M., D-Mass. (5)
Sharp, Philip R., D-Ind. (2)
Shaw, E. Clay Jr., R-Fla. (15)
Shelby, Richard C., D-Ala. (7)
Shumway, Norman D., R-Calif. (14)
Shuster, Bud, R-Pa. (9)
Sikorski, Gerry, D-Minn. (6)
Siljander, Mark D., R-Mich. (4)
Simon, Paul, D-Ill. (22)
Sisisky, Norman, D-Va. (4)
Skeen, Joe, R-N.M. (2)
Skelton, Ike, D-Mo. (4)
Slattery, Jim, D-Kan. (2)
Smith, Christopher H., R-N.J. (4)
Smith, Denny, R-Ore. (5)
Smith, Larry, D-Fla. (16)
Smith, Neal, D-Iowa (4)
Smith, Robert F., R-Ore. (2)
Smith, Virginia, R-Neb. (3)
Snowe, Olympia J., R-Maine (2)
Snyder, Gene, R-Ky. (4)
Solarz, Stephen J., D-N.Y. (13)
Solomon, Gerald B. H., R-N.Y. (24)
Spence, Floyd, R-S.C. (2)
Spratt, John M. Jr., D-S.C. (5)
Staggers, Harley O. Jr., D-W.Va. (2)
Stangeland, Arlan, R-Minn. (7)
Stark, Fortney H. "Pete", D-Calif. (9)
Stenholm, Charles W., D-Texas (17)
Stokes, Louis, D-Ohio (21)
Stratton, Samuel S., D-N.Y. (23)
Studds, Gerry E., D-Mass. (10)
Stump, Bob, R-Ariz. (3)
Sundquist, Don, R-Tenn. (7)
Swift, Al, D-Wash. (2)
Synar, Mike, D-Okla. (2)

T

Tallon, Robin, D-S.C. (6)
Tauke, Tom, R-Iowa (2)
Tauzin, W. J. "Billy", D-La. (3)
Taylor, Gene, R-Mo. (7)
Thomas, Lindsay, D-Ga. (1)
Thomas, William M., R-Calif. (20)
Torres, Esteban Edward, D-Calif. (34)

Torricelli, Robert G., D-N.J. (9)
Towns, Edolphus, D-N.Y. (11)
Traxler, Bob, D-Mich. (8)

U, V

Udall, Morris K., D-Ariz. (2)
Valentine, Tim, D-N.C. (2)
Vandergriff, Tom, D-Texas (26)
Vander Jagt, Guy, R-Mich. (9)
Vento, Bruce F., D-Minn. (4)
Volkmer, Harold L., D-Mo. (9)
Vucanovich, Barbara F., R-Nev. (2)

W

Walgren, Doug, D-Pa. (18)
Walker, Robert S., R-Pa. (16)
Washington, Harold, D-Ill. (1)
Watkins, Wes, D-Okla. (3)
Waxman, Henry A., D-Calif. (24)
Weaver, James, D-Ore. (4)
Weber, Vin, R-Minn. (2)
Weiss, Ted, D-N.Y. (17)
Wheat, Alan, D-Mo. (5)
Whitehurst, G. William, R-Va. (2)
Whitley, Charles, D-N.C. (3)
Whittaker, Bob, R-Kan. (5)
Whitten, Jamie L., D-Miss. (1)
Williams, Lyle, R-Ohio (17)
Williams, Pat, D-Mont. (1)
Wilson, Charles, D-Texas (2)
Winn, Larry Jr., R-Kan. (3)
Wirth, Timothy E., D-Colo. (2)
Wise, Bob, D-W.Va. (3)
Wolf, Frank R., R-Va. (10)
Wolpe, Howard, D-Mich. (3)
Wortley, George C., R-N.Y. (27)
Wright, Jim, D-Texas (12)
Wyden, Ron, D-Ore. (3)
Wylie, Chalmers P., R-Ohio (15)

X, Y, Z

Yates, Sidney R., D-Ill. (9)
Yatron, Gus, D-Pa. (6)
Young, C. W. Bill, R-Fla. (8)
Young, Don, R-Alaska (AL)
Young, Robert A., D-Mo. (2)
Zablocki, Clement J., D-Wis. (4)
Zschau, Ed, R-Calif. (12)

Delegates

de Lugo, Ron, D-Virgin Islands
Fauntroy, Walter E., D-D.C.
Sunia, Fofó I. F., D-American Samoa
Won Pat, Antonio Borja, D-Guam

Resident Commissioner

Corrada, Baltasar, New Prog.-Puerto Rico

Senators
R 54, D 46

Abdnor, James, R-S.D.
Andrews, Mark, R-N.D.
Armstrong, William L., R-Colo.
Baker, Howard H. Jr., R-Tenn.
Baucus, Max, D-Mont.
Bentsen, Lloyd, D-Texas
Biden, Joseph R. Jr., D-Del.
Bingaman, Jeff, D-N.M.
Boren, David L., D-Okla.
Boschwitz, Rudy, R-Minn.
Bradley, Bill, D-N.J.
Bumpers, Dale, D-Ark.
Burdick, Quentin N., D-N.D.
Byrd, Robert C., D-W.Va.
Chafee, John H., R-R.I.
Chiles, Lawton, D-Fla.
Cochran, Thad, R-Miss.
Cohen, William S., R-Maine
Cranston, Alan, D-Calif.
D'Amato, Alfonse M., R-N.Y.
Danforth, John C., R-Mo.
DeConcini, Dennis, D-Ariz.

Denton, Jeremiah, R-Ala.
Dixon, Alan J., D-Ill.
Dodd, Christopher J., D-Conn.
Dole, Robert, R-Kan.
Domenici, Pete V., R-N.M.
Durenberger, Dave, R-Minn.
Eagleton, Thomas F., D-Mo.
East, John P., R-N.C.
Exon, J. James, D-Neb.
Ford, Wendell H., D-Ky.
Garn, Jake, R-Utah
Glenn, John, D-Ohio
Goldwater, Barry, R-Ariz.
Gorton, Slade, R-Wash.
Grassley, Charles E., R-Iowa
Hart, Gary, D-Colo.
Hatch, Orrin G., R-Utah
Hatfield, Mark O., R-Ore.
Hawkins, Paula, R-Fla.
Hecht, Chic, R-Nev.
Heflin, Howell, D-Ala.
Heinz, John, R-Pa.
Helms, Jesse, R-N.C.
Hollings, Ernest F., D-S.C.
Huddleston, Walter D., D-Ky.
Humphrey, Gordon J., R-N.H.
Inouye, Daniel K., D-Hawaii
Jackson, Henry M., D-Wash.
Jepsen, Roger W., R-Iowa
Johnston, J. Bennett, D-La.
Kassebaum, Nancy Landon, R-Kan.
Kasten, Bob, R-Wis.
Kennedy, Edward M., D-Mass.
Lautenberg, Frank R., D-N.J.
Laxalt, Paul, R-Nev.
Leahy, Patrick J., D-Vt.
Levin, Carl, D-Mich.
Long, Russell B., D-La.
Lugar, Richard G., R-Ind.
Mathias, Charles McC. Jr., R-Md.
Matsunaga, Spark M., D-Hawaii
Mattingly, Mack, R-Ga.
McClure, James A., R-Idaho
Melcher, John, D-Mont.
Metzenbaum, Howard M., D-Ohio
Mitchell, George J., D-Maine
Moynihan, Daniel Patrick, D-N.Y.
Murkowski, Frank H., R-Alaska
Nickles, Don, R-Okla.
Nunn, Sam, D-Ga.
Packwood, Bob, R-Ore.
Pell, Claiborne, D-R.I.
Percy, Charles H., R-Ill.
Pressler, Larry, R-S.D.
Proxmire, William, D-Wis.
Pryor, David, D-Ark.
Quayle, Dan, R-Ind.
Randolph, Jennings, D-W.Va.
Riegle, Donald W. Jr., D-Mich.
Roth, William V. Jr., R-Del.
Rudman, Warren B., R-N.H.
Sarbanes, Paul S., D-Md.
Sasser, Jim, D-Tenn.
Simpson, Alan K., R-Wyo.
Specter, Arlen, R-Pa.
Stafford, Robert T., R-Vt.
Stennis, John C., D-Miss.
Stevens, Ted, R-Alaska
Symms, Steven D., R-Idaho
Thurmond, Strom, R-S.C.
Tower, John, R-Texas
Trible, Paul S. Jr., R-Va.
Tsongas, Paul E., D-Mass.
Wallop, Malcolm, R-Wyo.
Warner, John W., R-Va.
Weicker, Lowell P. Jr., R-Conn.
Wilson, Pete, R-Calif.
Zorinsky, Edward, D-Neb.

Governors
D 34; R 16

Ala.—George C. Wallace, D
Alaska—Bill Sheffield, D
Ariz.—Bruce Babbitt, D
Ark.—Bill Clinton, D
Calif.—George Deukmejian, R
Colo.—Richard D. Lamm, D
Conn.—William A. O'Neill, D
Del.—Pierre S. "Pete" du Pont IV, R

Fla.—Robert Graham, D
Ga.—Joe Frank Harris, D
Hawaii—George Ariyoshi, D
Idaho—John V. Evans, D
Ill.—James R. Thompson, R
Ind.—Robert D. Orr, R
Iowa—Terry Branstad, R
Kan.—John Carlin, D
Ky.—John Y. Brown, D
La.—David C. Treen, R
Maine—Joseph E. Brennan, D
Md.—Harry R. Hughes, D
Mass.—Michael S. Dukakis, D
Mich.—James J. Blanchard, D
Minn.—Rudy Perpich, D
Miss.—William Winter, D
Mo.—Christopher S. "Kit" Bond, R
Mont.—Ted Schwinden, D
Neb.—Bob Kerrey, D
Nev.—Richard H. Bryan, D
N.H.—John H. Sununu, R
N.J.—Thomas H. Kean, R
N.M.—Toney Anaya, D
N.Y.—Mario M. Cuomo, D
N.C.—James B. Hunt Jr., D
N.D.—Allen I. Olson, R
Ohio—Richard F. Celeste, D
Okla.—George Nigh, D
Ore.—Victor G. Atiyeh, R
Pa.—Richard L. Thornburgh, R
R.I.—J. Joseph Garrahy, D
S.C.—Richard Riley, D
S.D.—William J. Janklow, R
Tenn.—Lamar Alexander, R
Texas—Mark White, D
Utah—Scott M. Matheson, D
Vt.—Richard A. Snelling, R
Va.—Charles S. Robb, D
Wash.—John Spellman, R
W.Va.—John D. "Jay" Rockefeller IV, D
Wis.—Anthony S. Earl, D
Wyo.—Ed Herschler, D

Supreme Court

Burger, Warren E.—Minn., Chief Justice
Blackmun, Harry A.—Minn.
Brennan, William J. Jr.—N.J.
Marshall, Thurgood—N.Y.
O'Connor, Sandra Day—Ariz.
Powell, Lewis F. Jr.—Va.
Rehnquist, William H.—Ariz.
Stevens, John Paul—Ill.
White, Byron R.—Colo.

Cabinet

Baldrige, Malcolm—Commerce
Bell, T. H.—Education
Block, John R.—Agriculture
Dole, Elizabeth Hanford—Transportation †
Donovan, Raymond J.—Labor
Heckler, Margaret M.—HHS ††
Hodel, Donald P.—Energy
Pierce, Samuel R. Jr.—HUD
Regan, Donald T.—Treasury
Shultz, George P.—State
Smith, William French—Attorney General
Watt, James G.—Interior
Weinberger, Caspar W.—Defense

Other Officers With Cabinet Rank

Brock, William E. III—U.S. Trade Representative
Bush, George—Vice President
Casey, William J.—CIA Director
Kirkpatrick, Jeane J.—U.N. Representative
Meese, Edwin III—Counselor to the President
Stockman, David A.—OMB Director

* Colorado 6th District, New York 7th District, Texas 6th District.
† Confirmed Feb. 1, 1983.
†† Confirmed March 3, 1983.

Partisanship Dominated Congressional Year

Congress and President Reagan generally kept to their own turf in 1983 — each branch going about its business with little involvement from the other side.

Unlike the first two years of the Reagan administration, when the president essentially wrote the economic script, Congress conducted its 1983 debate on deficits without Reagan's overt participation.

And while Congress tried to assert itself on foreign policy, Reagan consistently called the global shots.

There were important bipartisan agreements in 1983: on Social Security, jobs legislation, the War Powers Resolution and fiscal 1984 appropriations bills. But these were rare commodities in a year in which political motivations ranked above policy considerations.

The prime example of this dilemma was the way Congress and Reagan reacted to massive federal deficits. No matter how many experts said soaring deficits hurt the economy, few people were willing to take the politically chancy steps needed to cure the problem.

Reagan made a calculated decision to stay out of the deficit debate, thereby ducking any responsibility for the tax increases his advisers viewed as a 1984 election liability.

Anti-deficit rhetoric was a constant refrain in Congress. But Reagan's resistance and their own pre-election jumpiness paralyzed members facing the tax hikes and spending cuts offered in deficit reduction bills.

"The structural deficit is rapidly becoming out of control, and very little was accomplished to reduce deficits," lamented James R. Jones, D-Okla., House Budget Committee chairman.

"The leadership, starting with the president, avoided all the tough problems and basically took the politically safe approach," Jones said.

The reason for the stalemate, according to many members, was the early onset of presidential politics. "I don't remember a presidential election starting so early," said Rep. Bill Gradison, R-Ohio.

1984 Positioning

Reagan was clearly in a re-election mode when he analyzed Congress' deeds in 1983.

"The greatest contribution of the Congress was not what it did for us, but what it didn't do to us," Reagan said in a radio speech Nov. 19, returning to the anti-Washington theme that helped bring him into office.

House Speaker Thomas P. O'Neill Jr., D-Mass., also took a political outlook when he summed up the session Nov. 17.

"If the elections were held tomorrow," O'Neill said, "the polls show that Democrats would [gain] 35 to 50 seats. In the eyes of the American people, we're doing something right."

O'Neill told reporters that 1983 was "very gratifying." One reason had to be the Democrats' new numerical strength. The 1982 elections gave Democrats an extra 26 House seats, allowing O'Neill to wrest control away from the coalition of Republicans and

First Session Summary

Lacking consensus on how to reduce soaring federal deficits, members of Congress called an end to the first session of the 98th Congress Nov. 18 and left Washington for a nine-week vacation before reconvening Jan. 23, 1984. The Senate adjourned *sine die* at 10:04 p.m. The House had adjourned at 7:34 p.m.

Convened at noon on Jan. 3, the session lasted 320 days. It was the shortest non-election-year session since the first session of the 89th Congress in 1965, yet it ranked as the 28th longest in history. The third session of the 76th Congress, from Jan. 3, 1940, to Jan. 3, 1941, was the longest on record. *(CQ Guide to Congress 3rd Edition, p. 410)*

The Senate met for 150 days during the year, the House for 146. There were 8,434 bills and resolutions introduced during the session, as compared to 4,520 in 1982 and 8,719 in 1981, the first session of the 97th Congress.

President Reagan signed into law 215 public bills cleared by Congress, 113 fewer than last year, but 70 more than in 1981. Reagan vetoed seven bills in 1983, one of which was overridden and enacted into law without his signature.

During 1983, the House took 498 recorded votes, 39 more than in 1982. The Senate took 371 recorded votes, 94 fewer than in 1982.

Following are the recorded congressional vote totals between 1971 and 1983:

Year	House	Senate	Total
1983	498	371	869
1982	459	465	924
1981	353	483	836
1980	604	531	1,135
1979	672	497	1,169
1978	834	516	1,350
1977	706	635	1,341
1976	661	688	1,349
1975	612	602	1,214
1974	537	544	1,081
1973	541	594	1,135
1972	329	532	861
1971	320	423	743

conservative "Boll Weevil" Democrats that dominated the 97th Congress.

Reagan and Senate Majority Leader Howard H. Baker Jr., R-Tenn., recognized this new alignment and the need for compromise. With O'Neill, they crafted a plan to revitalize the Social Security system and a $4.6 billion emergency jobs measure.

Bipartisanship also produced unusual progress in the passage of fiscal 1984 appropriations bills.

Congress sent Reagan 10 of the 13 regular 1984 spending bills, its best performance in years. Reagan had threatened to veto any money bills that exceeded his budget targets. But constant give-and-take between Congress and the White House produced bills that Reagan would sign.

On other subjects, though, partisan sniping took over.

O'Neill hammered away all year at the "fairness" issue, charging that Reagan's economic policies had unjustly hurt many Americans. He pushed through the House a cap on the third year of Reagan's tax cut, and a series of bills to aid the unemployed. But the Republican-controlled Senate never approved them.

The Democratic attack on Reaganomics also lost steam as the economy perked up. "As the recovery got started, the attitude was: Let's not rock the boat," Gradison observed.

While partisanship was rampant, party unity did not always flourish.

O'Neill had a 100-vote Democratic margin during most of the year, but he could not always keep his troops in line. In early November, for example, restless freshman Democrats made a symbolic protest against rising deficits and helped kill a spending bill important to their leaders.

In the Senate, Baker no longer could get Republicans to march in lock step, as they often did in the 97th Congress. In May, moderate Republican senators defied GOP leaders when they helped pass a budget calling for increased taxes and domestic spending while slowing the defense buildup.

One major change from Reagan's first two years was that Congress was far more concerned about foreign affairs during 1983.

Throughout the year, Congress focused on trouble spots around the world: El Salvador, Nicaragua, Lebanon and Grenada. Members were jarred by the Soviet Union's downing of a Korean civilian airliner Sept. 1 and the Oct. 23 bombing of the U.S. Marine compound in Beirut.

There were several showdowns over key foreign policy issues. But Congress repeatedly bowed to Reagan's wishes, however reluctantly.

This was partly due to O'Neill's adherence to the adage that "politics should end at the water's edge." Standing behind Reagan, O'Neill in September helped push through a measure allowing Reagan to keep U.S. troops in Lebanon for up to 18 months. And despite grumbling, O'Neill ultimately supported Reagan on the invasion of Grenada.

In backing Reagan on Lebanon, Congress for the first time invoked major parts of the 1973 War Powers Resolution. While he won a free hand this time, Reagan allowed Congress some say in the future commitment of U.S. forces to combat overseas.

Reagan was victorious in most of his defense fights with Congress. He won the go-ahead for production of the MX missile, and he staved off a congressional endorsement of the nuclear freeze proposal. The House passed a freeze resolution, but the Senate rejected a similar measure.

Congress refused, however, to go along with Reagan's plan to resume nerve gas production after a 14-year moratorium. And in the military appropriations bill for fiscal 1984, Congress allowed roughly a 4 percent real-dollar increase in total defense spending, compared to the 10 percent boost that Reagan sought.

The Supreme Court shook Congress June 23 when it decided that the legislative veto device was unconstitutional. The ruling invalidated a tool that Congress had used over the past 50 years to overturn executive branch regulations or orders. The decision — a victory for the executive branch and a potential blow to congressional power — sent lawmakers scrambling for a constitutional replacement.

Congress also was shaken by the sudden deaths in 1983 of two leading Democrats — Sen. Henry M. Jackson, D-Wash., and Rep. Phillip Burton, D-Calif. — as well as the death of Rep. Larry P. McDonald, D-Ga., who died in the Korean airliner incident.

One of the more enduring pieces of legislation approved in 1983 was the creation of a federal holiday in honor of the birthday of slain civil rights leader Dr. Martin Luther King Jr.

Despite a last-minute spurt of activity, Congress left town Nov. 18 with a long list of unfinished business. Among the major pieces of legislation left for 1984 were bills affecting tele-

phone rates, natural gas decontrol, immigration reform, criminal code changes, and revisions in the Clean Air and Clean Water acts.

Following is a summary of major 1983 congressional action:

Agriculture

Dairy/Tobacco/Drought Relief. In one of its last acts of the year, Congress cleared a landmark change in farm policy. The bill (HR 3385 — PL 98-180), meant to curb dairy surpluses, provided for payments to dairy farmers, partly financed by farmers themselves, for producing less milk.

The bill also reduced dairy price supports and included changes in the federal tobacco program, an authorization for egg producers to coordinate marketing, and authorization for livestock producers to buy damaged federal stocks of feed to help them cope with the 1983 summer drought.

Economic and farm officials in the administration objected strongly to the new dairy plan. But a presidential veto would sink the tobacco provisions, which were important to Sen. Jesse Helms, R-N.C., up for re-election in 1984.

PIK Taxes. Congress failed to continue a suspension of federal tax rules that the Reagan administration said was important for its 1984 Payment-in-Kind (PIK) program for wheat farmers. The program gave farmers surplus commodities in return for idling crop land. But Rep. Fortney H. "Pete" Stark, D-Calif., chairman of a key tax subcommittee, said multimillion-dollar payments to individual farmers in the massive 1983 PIK program were illegal.

The Ways and Means Committee Nov. 17 approved a PIK tax extension that could have resulted in caps on the tax break for 1984 PIK payments. But the larger tax legislation (HR 4170), to which the PIK plan was to be added, did not come to the floor.

Farm Credit. Congress adjourned without passing legislation meant to aid debt-ridden farmers, but judicial decisions went part way toward sponsors' goals.

The House May 3 passed a bill (HR 1190) permitting farmers, under certain circumstances, to defer repayments of federal Farmers Home Administration (FmHA) loans. It also re-

quired implementation of an FmHA "economic emergency" loan program the administration had sought to kill.

The Senate did not take up either the House bill or a different version (S 24) reported March 18 by its Agriculture Committee. But Agriculture Secretary John R. Block announced Nov. 4 that, in compliance with a court order, he would reopen the economic emergency program. And on Nov. 15 a federal judge in Bismarck, N.D., ordered a temporary injunction banning FmHA farm foreclosures until he could hear arguments in early January on whether to make the injunction permanent.

Target Prices, Wheat Program. The administration spent much of the year trying, without success, to persuade Congress to block scheduled increases in target prices, a major price support program for wheat and other crops.

The House Agriculture Committee discussed the request in May, but postponed action indefinitely. The Senate Agriculture Committee approved a freeze in target prices and added it as an amendment to a minor House-passed measure (HR 2733). But objections from a few farm-state senators kept that bill off the floor.

Two days before Congress adjourned, the House passed a bill (HR 4072) that trimmed the target price increases. Certain other provisions meant to make the administration's 1984 wheat program financially more attractive to farmers brought administration objections, however, and opposition from prominent Republicans kept the measure from coming to a vote in the Senate.

Pesticide Regulation. Congress passed a one-year authorization of funds for the federal program to regulate pesticides just before adjournment.

Disputes among pesticide makers, environmentalists, labor, farm and health groups kept Congress from overhauling pesticide law in 1982. Environmentalists then drew up an ambitious legislative agenda, but when top Environmental Protection Agency (EPA) officials resigned early in 1983, members decided to postpone action on pesticide policies to give new officials time to settle in at the troubled agency. (EPA administers federal pesticide regulatory programs.) The House passed a one-year reauthorization (HR 2785) in May, and the Sen-

ate cleared the bill Nov. 18 (PL 98-201).

Agricultural Trade. An ambitious bill (S 822) to boost federally backed credits for U.S. farm exports and dump surplus dairy goods abroad failed to reach the floor after the Senate Agriculture Committee reported it in March. There was no comparable House measure.

Rural Telephone, Electric Loans. The House Agriculture Committee Oct. 28 approved a bill (HR 3050) to shore up the federal program that provided financing for rural electrical and telephone systems. The Reagan administration opposed the plan, but sponsors expected to push it in 1984.

"Sodbuster" Conservation Plan. The Senate revised and then passed an important "sodbuster" conservation bill (S 663) Nov. 18. The bill would prohibit federal farm price supports and other benefits for crops produced on highly erodible land.

The Senate Agriculture Committee had reported a broader version Nov. 2, denying benefits to an entire crop if part of it were grown on erodible land. But sponsor William L. Armstrong, R-Colo., persuaded the Senate to amend the committee bill to conform with a narrower version supported by farm groups. A House subcommittee held hearings in September on a more ambitious bill (HR 3457) combining payments to farmers for conservation actions with the "sodbuster" concept.

Appropriations

Appropriations Bills. Congress made unusual progress in sending fiscal 1984 appropriations bills to the president. By the time the fiscal year began Oct. 1, Congress had cleared six of the 13 regular spending bills. When the first session adjourned Nov. 18, it had cleared a total of 10 regular money bills. Those that did not get final action were the agriculture, foreign aid and Treasury-Postal Service funding bills.

Congress approved two stopgap continuing resolutions to fund government offices whose bills had not been enacted. The first (H J Res 368 — PL 98-107) ran from Oct. 1 to Nov. 10. The second (H J Res 413 — PL 98-

151) was to run through Sept. 30, 1984.

Congress cleared two supplemental funding bills for fiscal 1983: a $15.6 billion bill (HR 1718 — PL 98-8) approved March 24, and a $7 billion bill (HR 3069 — PL 98-63) cleared July 29. Congress Nov. 18 cleared a fiscal 1984 supplemental (HR 3959 — PL 98-181) containing a housing authorization, International Monetary Fund contribution and money for veterans and other programs.

Commerce

Telephone Rates. The House Nov. 10 passed a controversial bill (HR 4102) to thwart a Federal Communications Commission (FCC) plan to levy a flat monthly "access charge" on residential and small business phone users for the right to long-distance service. But the Senate decided to wait until 1984 to take up a milder version (S 1660) reported by its Commerce Committee in October.

The FCC proposed a $2-a-month charge on residential users and a $6-a-month per line charge on business users. HR 4102 exempted residential and single-line business phone users from any access charge. S 1660 delayed those charges for two years.

The FCC and the American Telephone & Telegraph Co. (AT&T) said the charges were essential to the Jan. 1, 1984, breakup of AT&T. For years, local phone service had been subsidized by long-distance tolls, but local companies lost that subsidy after separating from AT&T Jan. 1.

The FCC plan would shift the tolls from long-distance to local phone users in the form of long-distance access charges. The FCC wanted to put the charges into effect Jan. 1 but later said it would wait until April 3. The Justice Department joined AT&T in urging the FCC to go ahead with the fees Jan. 1, saying the delay "unnecessarily and inordinately complicates" the breakup of AT&T.

TV Rerun Rights. Just before adjournment, the FCC and the Senate Commerce Committee reached a truce over an FCC plan to let the television networks tap into the lucrative rerun syndication market.

The House had passed a bill (HR 2250) Nov. 8 to bar until June 1, 1984, an FCC plan to modify 1970 rules that prevented the networks — ABC, CBS

and NBC — from controlling or profiting from reruns of shows they had aired. Independent producers, studios and stars objected to the change.

After President Reagan, a former TV and movie actor, said he would support a two-year ban on any changes in the FCC rules, FCC Chairman Mark Fowler Nov. 16 announced that the FCC would put off a final decision until at least May 10. The Senate committee's leadership announced the next day that the committee would take no further action before March 15.

Broadcast Deregulation. The Senate Feb. 17 passed a broadcast deregulation bill (S 55), but the House Energy and Commerce Subcommittee on Telecommunications did not reach a consensus on legislation before adjournment.

S 55 eliminated broadcasting license renewal procedures requiring that a broadcaster's performance be compared to services promised by a new applicant. It essentially required that licenses be renewed automatically unless there had been serious legal violations.

House subcommittee Chairman Timothy E. Wirth, D-Colo., said the Senate bill was too lenient. But he promised to take up legislation by Oct. 15 after broadcasters, charging Wirth with bottling up the legislation, threatened to circumvent his panel. That promise went by the wayside, however, when no consensus emerged from a lengthy series of meetings between the opposing sides on the issue.

Cable TV Deregulation. The House Energy and Commerce Telecommunications Subcommittee Nov. 17 approved a bill (HR 4103) that sharply reduced the power of cities to regulate the cable television business.

Cable operators sought legislation on the grounds that conflicting and overly burdensome local regulations had impeded the development of cable systems. The Senate June 14 passed a bill (S 66) to ease their burden.

But HR 4103 contained restrictions the cable operators opposed, including a requirement that a percentage of channels on large systems be set aside for third-party commercial programmers. It also prohibited cable system owners from owning other media properties, including daily newspapers in their home communities, required landlords to allow cable into their buildings if the cable firm of-

fered compensation under an FCC-approved formula, and allowed cities to require public, educational and government channels on a cable system.

Unisex Insurance. Neither chamber completed action before adjournment on bills (S 372, HR 100) to outlaw sex-based discrimination in all forms of insurance.

The Senate Commerce Committee agreed in June to postpone action until the General Accounting Office studied the effects of S 372; the GAO had not filed its report before Congress adjourned. HR 100 was approved by the House Energy and Commerce Subcommittee on Commerce, Transportation and Tourism, but got no further in the face of insurance industry opposition and the full committee's crowded calendar.

The industry argued that gender was a legitimate factor in determining premiums and benefits. The legislation was pushed by women's and civil rights groups. The Supreme Court ruled July 6 that an employer's retirement plan could not provide smaller benefit payments to women workers than to comparably situated male employees.

Banking Deregulation. As widely predicted, Congress failed to act on a Reagan administration proposal to permit banks to get into insurance, real estate and municipal bond brokerage, or on proposals to impose a moratorium on financial mergers.

There was widespread agreement in Congress and elsewhere that the financial services industry was falling into chaos as banks, insurance firms, securities dealers and others found ways to cross the lines drawn by the 1933 Glass-Steagall Act between banking and other businesses. But there was little incentive for members to act, since any change in the law would damage constituents in every member's state or district.

Senate Banking Committee Chairman Jake Garn, R-Utah, who generally backed administration proposals to deregulate the banking industry, said he would push in 1984 for a bill to expand bank powers. But others, including Sen. John Heinz, R-Pa., a senior Banking Committee member, and key members of the House Banking Committee, backed a financial mergers moratorium.

Congress

Page/Drugs Probe. The House July 20 censured Reps. Daniel B. Crane, R-Ill., and Gerry E. Studds, D-Mass., for having sexual relationships with teenage congressional pages. It was the first time a House member ever had been censured for sexual misconduct. The punishment was stronger than the reprimand recommended by the Committee on Standards of Official Conduct.

The charges stemmed from an investigation of alleged sexual misconduct and Capitol drug use. The ethics panel ended its 16-month probe Nov. 17, concluding there was inadequate evidence to show any current House member used illegal drugs or that a cocaine ring existed at the Capitol.

The panel said insufficient evidence existed to bring charges of illegal drug use by Reps. Ronald V. Dellums, D-Calif., or Charles Wilson, D-Texas. But investigators said three former House members — John L. Burton, D-Calif. (1974-83), Fred Richmond, D-N.Y. (1975-82), and Barry Goldwater Jr., R-Calif. (1969-83) — had used or bought illegal drugs while in office.

Senate TV, Rules Changes. Senate Majority Leader Howard H. Baker Jr., R-Tenn., failed for the third year in his push to broadcast Senate proceedings.

The Senate Rules and Administration Committee approved a resolution (S Res 66) allowing gavel-to-gavel television and radio coverage of the Senate. But the measure was kept off the floor by Senate traditionalists who opposed broadcasting. House floor action was already televised.

Televising major Senate floor debates was one of several recommendations made by former Sens. James B. Pearson, R-Kan. (1962-78), and Abraham Ribicoff, D-Conn. (1963-81), in a study of Senate procedures. The study, which gathered dust on the Rules Committee shelf after it was issued April 5, also called for limits on debate, rules to ensure attendance, election of a permanent presiding officer and elimination of several committees.

Senate Pay Raise. Senators received a 15 percent pay raise, boosting their salaries from $60,662 to $69,800 a year, in a fiscal 1983 supplemental

spending bill (HR 3069 — PL 98-63) cleared by Congress July 29. House members received the same $9,138 pay hike in December 1982.

The legislation also provided that, effective Jan. 1, 1984, the amount of annual income from speeches, articles and appearances that a senator could receive would be capped at 30 percent of his or her congressional salary, or $20,940. House rules included a 30 percent cap on outside earned income for representatives.

Legislative Veto. Congress spent the second half of 1983 sorting through the fallout from the Supreme Court's June 23 decision invalidating the legislative veto, a device used by Congress to block executive branch regulations or orders.

Despite the court's pronouncement that the legislative veto was unconstitutional, Congress continued to include such provisions in a variety of measures enacted after the court's decision. At the same time, members searched for substitutes that could be upheld by the courts. The most popular alternative was to use joint resolutions to overturn executive decisions, instead of concurrent resolutions. A concurrent resolution appeared to be unconstitutional because it did not require the president's signature; a joint resolution needed presidential action.

Defense

Defense Spending. The $250 billion defense appropriations bill (HR 4185 — PL 98-212) cleared Nov. 18 put Congress on a course toward approving a total defense budget for fiscal 1984 that would be about 4 percent larger than the fiscal 1983 budget above the cost of inflation.

President Reagan in his January budget had called for a "real" growth rate of 10 percent in defense funding.

Counting amounts appropriated separately for military construction and for defense nuclear activities conducted by the Energy Department, this amounted to a reduction of nearly $19 billion from the administration's original request. But the reduction was achieved mostly by trimming programs at the edges, rather than by challenging fundamental premises of President Reagan's defense policy. The only major weapons for which Congress denied funds were a new type of lethal nerve gas bombs and

artillery shells called binary munitions.

MX Missile. Production of the 10-warhead MX intercontinental missile was approved by Congress, though by a narrow margin in the House and only after President Reagan adopted a seemingly more flexible stance in strategic arms reduction talks (START) with Moscow.

Although his initial budget request assumed MX would be deployed in a so-called "dense pack" of heavily armored silos, Reagan dropped that approach when he accepted the April 11 recommendation of a bipartisan advisory group chaired by former White House adviser Brent Scowcroft. The Scowcroft panel called for deploying 100 MXs in existing missile silos while developing a new, smaller missile with only one warhead — widely dubbed "Midgetman" — that could be deployed on mobile launchers.

A resolution allowing the start of MX flight testing (S Con Res 26) was approved in late May by large margins in each house. But before funds were approved for the first production-line versions of the missile, a bipartisan group of self-styled moderates in each house demanded that the president further moderate his arms control offer to Moscow.

MX funds were approved by a wide margin in the Senate, in votes on both the defense authorization bill (S 675 — PL 98-94) and the companion appropriations measure (HR 4185 — PL 98-212). But House efforts to delete MX production funds from the budget came close; the funds survived by a 13-vote margin in the authorization bill and by nine votes in the appropriations bill.

Nerve Gas. For the second year in a row, Congress rejected the administration's effort to end a long-time U.S. moratorium on the production of lethal chemical weapons by manufacturing so-called "binary munitions," a new type of nerve gas bombs and artillery shells.

During floor debate on both the defense authorization and appropriations bills, the House voted against the new weapons by a substantial margin. The Senate in each case approved them by a single vote — provided by Vice President George Bush after the Senate tied on the issue.

Conferees on the authorization bill approved nerve gas funding totaling $124.4 million. But the funds were dropped from the appropriations bill

after the House voted 258-166 on Nov. 15 to instruct its conferees to stand fast in opposition to binary weapons.

Nuclear Freeze. The two-year campaign for a U.S.-Soviet nuclear weapons "freeze" scored a tactical victory on Capitol Hill May 4 when the House passed a much amended version of the resolution (H J Res 13) sponsored by the freeze campaign.

The basic freeze resolution would have the president propose to the Soviet Union a mutual and verifiable freeze on the testing, deployment and production of all nuclear weapons. During House debate that sprawled across several weeks, however, various amendments were appended to the resolution, which freeze opponents claimed diluted its significance.

As had been widely expected, the Senate turned aside the freeze resolution by a comfortable margin (58-40) when it was offered Oct. 31 as an amendment to a bill lifting the ceiling on the national debt (H J Res 308).

Though it faced no such direct test of congressional sentiment, a policy calling for a U.S.-Soviet nuclear "build-down" — dropping more existing weapons from the inventory than the number of new ones added — seemed to command broader Senate support.

Adelman Nomination. After a three-month wrangle over administration arms control policy, the Senate April 14 voted 57-42 to approve the nomination of Kenneth L. Adelman to head the Arms Control and Disarmament Agency (ACDA).

Liberal arms control advocates had made Adelman's nomination a symbol of what they insisted was the administration's subordination of arms control efforts to a nuclear build-up.

Economic Affairs

Fiscal 1984 Budget. For the first time since passage of the Congressional Budget Act in 1974, Congress failed to enact deficit reduction measures required by its own budget plan. That measure (H Con Res 91), approved June 23 after months of controversy, called for more federal spending and higher revenues than President Reagan wanted.

The resolution proposed fiscal 1984 spending of $850 billion, rising to

$859 billion if Congress approved 10 anti-recession programs included in a special $8.5 billion reserve fund.

The reserve fund was a way to accommodate the desire of House Democrats to increase spending for social programs, but only two of the 10 reserve fund programs were enacted in 1983: a veterans' job training bill (HR 2355 — PL 98-77), and an extension of supplemental unemployment benefits (HR 3929 — PL 98-135).

With the reserve amounts, the fiscal 1984 deficit was forecast at $179.3 billion; without the reserve fund, $169.9 billion.

To hold the deficit to these levels, the resolution included reconciliation instructions that directed congressional committees to recommend spending cuts of $2.8 billion in fiscal 1984 and $12.3 billion over fiscal 1984-86. The House Ways and Means and Senate Finance committees were directed to raise $12 billion in new taxes in fiscal 1984 and a total of $73 billion in increased revenues over 1984-86.

Despite extended efforts to fashion a deficit reduction package, Congress adjourned without meeting this mandate.

Tax Increases. Neither the House nor the Senate approved any of the tax increases required by the fiscal 1984 budget resolution. And bills reported by the House Ways and Means and Senate Finance committees fell well short of the budget's $73 billion three-year reconciliation goal.

The House Nov. 17 rejected, 204-214, a rule providing for floor consideration of a tax measure (HR 4170) reported by the Ways and Means Committee Oct. 21. The Ways and Means bill would raise approximately $8 billion over three years, mostly by closing loopholes. The main elements of the revenue package dealt with taxation of mortgage revenue bonds, industrial development bonds (IDBs) and fringe benefits; tax simplification; curbs on sale/lease-back schemes by non-profit groups; and the taxation of life insurance companies.

Opponents were unhappy about controversial changes affecting the popular IDBs, as well as the inclusion of provisions that would expand the Medicaid program.

Meanwhile, the Senate never voted on the Finance Committee's $13.4 billion tax increase bill, which was included in an overall three-year budget reconciliation measure (S 2062) brought to the floor Nov. 16.

The Finance bill included provisions to: postpone until 1987 a section of the 1981 tax bill that would exclude from taxes 15 percent of net interest income up to $3,000 ($6,000 for a joint return); curb sale/lease-back schemes by non-profit groups; modify income averaging; reduce the holding period for long-term capital gains; and increase the corporate tax rate for big businesses.

During the final weeks of the session, Finance Committee Chairman Robert Dole, R-Kan., tried in vain to put together a consensus on a $150 billion deficit-reduction plan — equally divided between tax increases and spending cuts. When it became apparent they could not approve the plan before adjournment, Finance members voted Nov. 18 to have the committee staff and Treasury fashion a draft bill along the lines of the Dole plan and report back by Feb. 15, 1984.

Spending Reconciliation. Congress did not approve any of the spending cuts required by the fiscal 1984 budget resolution: $2.8 billion in fiscal 1984 and $12.3 billion over fiscal 1984-86.

On Oct. 25 the House approved a bill (HR 4169) that would cut projected spending by $10.3 billion over three years. The bulk of the savings would come from delaying cost-of-living adjustments for federal retirees' benefits and veterans' compensation, limiting the planned federal civilian pay raise to 4 percent and delaying that pay raise from Oct. 1 to Jan. 1.

The Senate never voted on its $28 billion reconciliation package (S 2062), which contained similar spending cuts plus major savings in the Medicare program and larger tax increases than those included in the House tax bill. After inconclusive debate and the defeat of an amendment offered by Budget Committee Chairman Pete V. Domenici, R-N.M., and ranking Budget Committee Democrat Lawton Chiles, D-Fla., to bring the total deficit reduction to $87.6 billion, the Senate leadership decided to suspend action on the reconciliation bill until 1984.

Interest and Dividend Withholding. Bowing to months of pressure from the banking industry and the public, Congress July 28 cleared legislation (HR 2973 — PL 98-67) to repeal a requirement for 10 percent withholding of taxes on interest and dividend income. The requirement

was one of the tax reforms approved by Congress in 1982.

President Reagan signed the repeal bill Aug. 5. The president initially had threatened to veto a withholding repeal measure, but the addition of special tax incentives for Caribbean nations and stiffer withholding compliance requirements helped ensure his approval. The new compliance provisions required "backup" withholding at a rate of 20 percent for individuals who either did not file a return or under-reported interest and dividend income.

Tax Cap. Democrats lost their bid to limit the last installment of President Reagan's three-year tax-cut plan when the Senate June 29 defeated a bill (HR 1183) to impose a "cap" on the individual tax cut due July 1.

A week earlier the Democratic-controlled House had approved the bill, which would have placed a cap of $720 per family on the scheduled 10 percent cut in individual income taxes.

Democrats tried to portray the tax cap as a way to turn around what they described as the unfair economic policies pursued by Reagan. Although they knew the tax cap plan would fail, they hoped to gain political mileage from the issue. Republicans countered that small businesses, farms and millions of middle-income married couples would be hit by the tax cap.

Senate Democrats had been promised a vote on the issue to win their cooperation in clearing debt limit legislation earlier in the year.

Revenue Sharing. Congress reauthorized the general revenue sharing program of grants to local governments for fiscal 1984-86 after Senate conferees forced the House to back off a desire to increase funding. The bill (HR 2780 — PL 98-185), cleared for the president Nov. 17, mandated the same $4.6 billion-a-year spending level as authorized in fiscal 1980-83.

The House version of HR 2780 would have authorized $5.02 billion a year, or an increase of $450 million annually. The Reagan administration had threatened a veto of any bill authorizing an increase.

Volcker Nomination. With only modest opposition, the Senate July 27 confirmed the nomination of Paul A. Volcker to serve a second four-year term as chairman of the

Federal Reserve Board. Eight Republicans and eight Democrats opposed the nomination on the 84-16 vote.

Ending months of speculation about the Fed chairmanship, President Reagan June 18 announced that he would appoint Volcker for a second term to begin Aug. 6. Volcker was originally appointed by President Carter in 1979.

While Volcker's supporters gave him substantial credit for bringing inflation under control, his critics blamed him and the Fed's tight monetary policy for the longest and deepest recession since the Great Depression.

Debt Limit. Before adjourning for the year, Congress approved a modest $101 billion increase in the public debt limit, an amount sufficient to meet the government's borrowing needs until sometime in April 1984. The bill (H J Res 308 — PL 98-161), cleared Nov. 18, raised the public debt limit to $1.49 trillion, from $1.389 trillion.

The Senate had rejected an earlier version of the bill Oct. 31, 39-56, as many members cast a "no" vote to protest lack of action on reducing the federal deficit.

H J Res 308 was the year's second debt limit increase. An earlier measure (HR 2990 — PL 98-34), cleared May 25, raised the limit to $1.389 trillion from the $1.29 trillion level set in 1982.

Industrial Policy. Industrial policy enjoyed a long run as a congressional buzzword in 1983, but none of the various plans discussed made much legislative progress. Proponents of schemes to develop a national industrial strategy vowed their proposals would receive widespread consideration during the election year.

The House Banking Subcommittee on Economic Stabilization held a hearing on industrial policy legislation (HR 4360) shortly before Congress adjourned, and the Senate Governmental Affairs Committee included an industrial policy component in a bill (S 121), reported Oct. 18, to establish a new Department of International Trade and Industry.

Education

Tuition Tax Credits. One of the top items on President Reagan's education agenda failed a key test Nov. 16 when the Senate by a vote of 59-38 killed a proposal to provide income tax credits for tuition payments to private elementary and secondary schools.

The action came months after the Senate Finance Committee approved a tax credit bill (S 528). Under heavy pressure from the administration to bring the issue to a vote during the waning days of the session, Finance Committee Chairman Robert Dole, R-Kan., introduced the tax credit plan as an amendment to a House-passed tariff bill (H J Res 290).

The amendment provided credits of up to $300 a year for each child attending private school. Its defeat in the Senate was a major setback for tax credit proponents, who had seen no action on comparable legislation in the House.

Math/Science Education. Despite widespread concern about the declining quality of science and mathematics education, Congress failed to finish work on a $425 million bill designed to address the problem.

The House March 2 easily passed HR 1310, which authorized new grants in the Education Department and the National Science Foundation for teacher training and other programs to upgrade instruction in science, mathematics and foreign languages. But a similar bill (S 1285) never made it to the Senate floor after its approval May 11 by the Labor and Human Resources Committee.

That bill was stalled while Labor Committee Chairman Orrin G. Hatch, R-Utah, tried to fend off efforts to use the politically popular measure as a vehicle for extraneous amendments. In particular, Hatch opposed plans by Thomas F. Eagleton, D-Mo., to introduce an amendment authorizing new aid to schools undergoing desegregation.

Education Summit. Responding to a spate of reports calling for major reforms in the public schools, the House passed legislation to finance a national summit conference on education.

The bill (HR 3245) authorized $500,000 for a conference of education leaders who would analyze issues raised by the National Commission on Excellence in Education and other study groups that had drawn attention to weaknesses in the public schools. The conference would draft recommendations for state and federal legis-

lation to boost educational quality. The issue was not considered in the Senate.

Handicapped Education, Vocational Rehabilitation. A bill reauthorizing a number of education programs for the handicapped and the Rehabilitation Act cleared Congress on the last day of the session.

The measures had been tied up in controversy for several months. The logjam was broken Nov. 17 when the House, by a 415-1 vote, passed a bill to reauthorize for three years 11 discretionary handicapped education programs. A portion of the already-passed Rehabilitation Act (HR 3520) was added as an amendment. The Senate approved the bill (S 1341 — PL 98-199) Nov. 18.

The Senate had refused to participate in a conference on the Rehabilitation Act because of objections to House additions increasing authorizations for a number of unrelated education and social programs. Those provisions were discarded by the House Nov. 17.

Energy

Clinch River Breeder Reactor. After hanging on by a thread in 1982, the Clinch River Breeder Reactor project was apparently killed in 1983, as Congress refused on several occasions to provide further federal funds. The last blow came Oct. 26 when the Senate refused to appropriate $1.5 billion requested as part of a new funding scheme for the Oak Ridge, Tenn., nuclear project.

The demise of the demonstration breeder reactor power plant was not unexpected; a series of votes over the previous 10 months had made it clear that Congress was uneasy over the economics of the project.

The government was still liable for an estimated $130 million to $230 million in termination costs.

Strategic Petroleum Reserve. Congress and the president compromised on how fast to fill the Strategic Petroleum Reserve. The fiscal 1984 Interior Department appropriations bill (HR 3363 — PL 98-146) called for a minimum fill rate of 186,000 barrels a day. The administration, citing the need to reduce federal expenditures, had wanted a 145,000-barrel-a-day fill rate, while Congress,

convinced of the need for the reserve in a future oil shortage, wanted the fill rate to remain at the current level of 220,000 barrels per day.

Natural Gas Pricing. Yearlong efforts in both chambers to come up with legislation to change federal controls over the natural gas industry failed, although both the full Senate and the House Energy and Commerce Committee were working on the issue right up to adjournment.

The Reagan administration was pushing a plan (S 615, HR 1760) for decontrol of all gas prices by Jan. 1, 1985. The Senate Energy and Natural Resources Committee, after 30 markup sessions, finally approved a compromise gradual decontrol measure (S 1715) that received administration backing. But in a test vote on the Senate floor Nov. 15, that proposal got only 28 votes. A competing proposal to extend federal controls and roll back some prices to August 1982 levels fared even worse, gaining just 26 votes. As the session ended, senators were working informally on a less comprehensive compromise version.

In the House, John D. Dingell, D-Mich., chairman of the Energy and Commerce Committee, continued to oppose any measure that would result in the decontrol of any "old gas," but Republicans and Democrats representing producing states believed they had convinced a majority of the committee to accept a version that would result in some decontrol. Time ran out before they could push for that version.

Nuclear Regulatory Commission. The Nuclear Regulatory Commission's (NRC) authority to grant temporary operating licenses to nuclear power plants expired Dec. 31, 1983, because Congress was unable to pass an NRC reauthorization bill. Disagreement over emergency planning and whether to continue the commission's temporary licensing authority combined to keep reauthorization bills (S 1291, HR 2510) from reaching the floor in either House or Senate.

The temporary authority was provided in the previous NRC authorization (PL 97-415). Although that authorization expired Sept. 30, 1983, fiscal 1984 NRC funding was provided in the energy and water development appropriations bill (HR 3132 — PL 98-50).

Other measures sought by the administration and the nuclear power in-dustry to streamline the licensing procedure for nuclear power plants were even farther from final consideration.

Oil Company Antitrust Exemption. Oil companies lost their shield from antitrust charges when they participate in joint energy emergency planning activities of the International Energy Agency (IEA). The antitrust exemption expired Dec. 31, 1983, and Congress was unable to clear legislation in the last days of the session to extend that authority through June 30, 1985.

The House passed HR 4194 Nov. 7 and the Senate followed suit Nov. 17. But the Senate version contained an amendment that would end the exemption on June 1, 1984, unless a law giving the president authority to allocate supplies and control prices during an emergency was enacted. On Nov. 18 — the last day of the session — the House refused to accept the Senate's version.

Environment

Watt/Clark. The Senate Nov. 18 confirmed President Reagan's national security adviser, William P. Clark, to replace the contentious James G. Watt as secretary of the interior. Clark was sworn in Nov. 21.

Before the confirmation vote, Senate Democrats tried to push through a non-binding resolution urging changes in the pro-development policies established under Watt. But the Senate Nov. 17 voted 48-42 to table that measure.

Although opposition to Watt's policies had been mounting, it was his penchant for politically damaging remarks that led to his downfall.

Watt resigned Oct. 9, avoiding an almost certain no-confidence vote in the Senate, where his support had eroded steadily in the wake of his Sept. 21 remark characterizing his appointees to a federal coal leasing commission as "a black . . . a woman, two Jews and a cripple."

EPA Dispute. The Senate May 18 unanimously confirmed William D. Ruckelshaus to succeed Anne M. Burford as administrator of the Environmental Protection Agency (EPA). Burford resigned under fire March 9 amid at least six congressional inquiries into charges of unethical conduct, political manipulation and "sweet-heart deals" between EPA and some of the industries it regulates.

The unanimous confirmation of Ruckelshaus, who headed EPA when it was first formed in 1970, reflected Senate confidence in his personal qualifications and integrity.

A constitutional confrontation between Congress and Reagan was eased when the House Aug. 3 effectively dropped its Dec. 16, 1982, contempt of Congress citation against Burford for refusing, on Reagan's orders, to provide materials a House subcommittee sought. The Reagan Justice Department had refused to prosecute Burford on the contempt charge.

Indeed, the only EPA official to be prosecuted as a result of the extensive congressional and Justice Department probes was Rita M. Lavelle, former head of the "superfund" program for cleanup of toxic waste dumps.

Lavelle was acquitted by a federal jury July 22 on a contempt of Congress charge, but she was convicted by another jury Dec. 1 on charges of perjury and obstructing a congressional investigation. On Jan. 9, 1984, she was sentenced to six months in prison and a $10,000 fine.

EPA Funding. Fearful that budget cuts were disabling the EPA, Congress moved to restore some of the funds it had stripped from the agency since Reagan took office. A $3.998 billion overall fiscal 1984 appropriation for EPA was cleared June 29 as part of the funding bill (HR 3133 — PL 98-45) for the Department of Housing and Urban Development and independent agencies.

The agency's operating budget, viewed as a key indicator of its ability to control pollution, was set at $1.11 billion for fiscal 1984. That contrasted with a Reagan request of $948 million and a high-water mark appropriation of $1.35 billion for 1981, the last fiscal year before Reagan's cuts began taking effect.

Hazardous Wastes. Congress made substantial progress during 1983 on bills (HR 2867, S 757) that would tighten and reauthorize for three years the nation's main law for controlling hazardous wastes. House subcommittees earlier in the year heard allegations that EPA had been lax in enforcing the Resource Conservation and Recovery Act of 1976 (PL 94-580), giving efforts to tighten the law a boost.

The House passed HR 2867 by voice vote on Nov. 3. The measure for

the first time would regulate generators of small quantities of hazardous wastes, and it would limit disposal of liquid hazardous wastes in landfills. The Senate Environment and Public Works Committee approved S 757 on July 14.

Interior Appropriation. President Reagan Nov. 4 signed the $7.9 billion fiscal 1984 appropriations bill (HR 3363 — PL 98-146) for the Interior Department and related agencies. Before Congress cleared the bill Oct. 20, it had been the ground for a series of battles over various policies of Interior Secretary James G. Watt. Reagan had requested only $6.7 billion, proposing cutbacks in parkland acquisition, energy conservation, fossil energy research and the Strategic Petroleum Reserve fill rate. Congress ended up giving him more than he wanted on all four.

The bill contained major restrictions on Interior's actions, including a moratorium on leasing of coal on federal lands and offshore oil and gas drilling bans for parts of California, Massachusetts and Florida.

Water Projects. House and Senate committees approved omnibus water project authorizing bills, setting up a potential election-year struggle between Reagan administration budget-cutters and members hoping to bring tangible benefits home to their districts.

The last such omnibus water resources bill was enacted in 1976. Since then, the issue of how much local beneficiaries should share in financing the projects had stymied such legislation. The Reagan administration had urged greater local cost-sharing and lower overall spending, making a presidential veto a possibility even if Congress cleared a bill.

The Public Works and Transportation Committee approved a $12.4 billion House bill (HR 3678) on Aug. 3, but several other committees wanted to act on the bill before it reached the floor. The Senate Environment and Public Works Committee Nov. 8 approved its version (S 1739), authorizing at least $11 billion over more than five years.

Clean Water Act. Conflict over whether to ease or tighten the nation's primary water pollution control law, the Clean Water Act, slowed action on legislation to reauthorize it.

The Senate Environment and

Public Works Committee approved its reauthorization bill (S 431) June 28, leaving some of the law's strictest requirements intact but extending the deadlines for meeting them. That bill, however, left several of the hottest issues to be resolved in a separate bill (S 2006) approved Sept. 21: agricultural runoff, "pre-treatment" of industrial wastes going into municipal sewers, and dredge-and-fill regulations. The House Public Works and Transportation Subcommittee on Water Resources held hearings but did not start marking up a bill.

Clean Air Act. A third year of efforts to overhaul the Clean Air Act came and went in 1983 with little ground gained. Instead, Congress adopted a one-year moratorium on penalties the law would have placed on communities not meeting a 1982 deadline for achieving clean air. That move came in a rider to the appropriations bill (HR 3133 — PL 98-45) funding EPA and other agencies. The Reagan administration had threatened to enforce the penalties rigidly, which many in Congress saw as a move designed to force action on a Clean Air Act rewrite.

Neither the House Energy and Commerce Committee nor the Senate Environment and Public Works Committee approved a clean air reauthorization bill in 1983. But Senate committee Chairman Robert T. Stafford, R-Vt., did reintroduce, as S 768, the comprehensive clean air bill his panel had approved in 1982.

Foreign Policy

Covert Action. U.S. "covert" aid to anti-government guerrillas in Nicaragua was the issue upon which the House Democratic leadership made its stand in opposition to President Reagan's foreign policies.

With Speaker Thomas P. O'Neill Jr., D-Mass., and Intelligence Committee Chairman Edward P. Boland, D-Mass., leading the way, the House voted on July 28 and again on Oct. 20 to force Reagan to stop backing rightist forces that were fighting to overthrow the leftist government of Nicaragua. When the Senate refused to follow suit, the issue was thrown into the lap of two last-minute conference committees that met Nov. 17-18.

Those conferences, on the 1984 defense appropriations bill (HR 4185

— PL 98-212) and the 1984 intelligence agencies authorization bill (HR 2968 — PL 98-215), produced a compromise that limited U.S. aid to the rebels to $24 million — about $11 million less than Reagan had planned to spend. To get more money, Reagan would have to seek the explicit approval of Congress.

El Salvador Aid. Reagan invoked all the persuasive powers of his presidency — including a rare speech to a joint session of Congress on April 27 — to win increased financial backing for El Salvador. He found Congress willing to go along, up to a point.

Under sustained administration pressure, Congress eventually approved $81.3 million in military aid for El Salvador in fiscal 1983. Reagan's various requests for fiscal 1983 had totaled $136.3 million.

For fiscal 1984, a continuing resolution cleared on Nov. 12 (H J Res 413 — PL 98-151) limited El Salvador's military aid to $64.8 million; Reagan had requested $86.3 million. The resolution also contained new restrictions aimed at encouraging progress on land reform and in the trial of those accused of murdering four American churchwomen in December 1980.

Congress approved without debate Reagan's requests for economic and development aid for El Salvador: $170 million in fiscal 1983 and $158 million in 1984. At the very end of the session, Congress also approved a bill (HR 4042) continuing through fiscal 1984 a requirement that the president certify twice each year that El Salvador was making sufficient progress on human rights and other issues to warrant receiving U.S. aid. However, Reagan pocket vetoed the bill.

Foreign Aid. Reagan's rapid expansion of U.S. military aid to friendly countries again made headway in 1983. Congress passed two measures that included significant increases in foreign military aid: a fiscal 1983 supplemental appropriation (HR 3069 — PL 98-63), and the second fiscal 1984 continuing appropriations resolution (H J Res 413 — PL 98-151).

The 1983 supplemental gave Reagan an extra $693 million in military and military-related aid, bringing the year's total for those programs to $8.6 billion — a 16 percent increase over the previous year.

Congress failed to pass regular authorization and appropriations bills for foreign aid in fiscal 1984 and in-

stead approved those programs in the continuing resolution, which included funds for all foreign economic, development and military aid programs. Military and related programs fared best, with $9.4 billion.

Lebanon. With diminishing enthusiasm, Congress at several stages approved the deepening U.S. involvement in the tangled affairs of Lebanon.

There was little debate or objection early in the year when Reagan asked Congress for $150 million in economic aid and $101 million in military aid for Lebanon. That money was authorized in S 639 (PL 98-43), cleared June 15, and appropriated in a fiscal 1983 supplemental bill (HR 3069 — PL 98-63), cleared July 29.

The authorization bill demonstrated congressional hesitation about the presence of more than 1,200 U.S. Marines in Lebanon as part of a four-nation peacekeeping force. The bill required the president to seek congressional authorization for any substantial expansion in the number of Marines or their role.

In late August, the first Marines were killed by hostile fire in Lebanon, and Congress reasserted its authority on the issue. After lengthy negotiations between the administration and House Democratic leaders, Congress on Sept. 29 cleared S J Res 159 (PL 98-119), invoking the 1973 War Powers Resolution (PL 93-148) for the first time and authorizing the Marines to stay in Lebanon for up to 18 months. Reagan signed the bill on Oct. 12, but expressed reservations about its constitutionality. The 18-month period was to expire in mid-April, 1985.

On Oct. 23, 239 U.S. Marines, sailors and soldiers, and 58 French paratroopers, were killed by a terrorist truck bomb in Beirut. Subsequent efforts to revise or revoke PL 98-119 failed in both houses.

Grenada. Reagan won widespread approval in both houses of Congress for the Oct. 25 invasion of Grenada. Reagan said the invasion, which he called a "rescue mission," was necessary to protect some 1,000 Americans from civil strife that erupted following the overthrow and eventual murder of Marxist Prime Minister Maurice Bishop.

While Congress passed no legislation directly concerning the invasion, it did approve $15 million in economic aid for Grenada in a fiscal 1984 continuing appropriations resolution (H J Res 413 — PL 98-151).

Korean Airline Resolution. Congressional action on a resolution (H J Res 353 — PL 98-98) condemning the Soviet Union's destruction of a Korean Air Lines passenger plane demonstrated the extent of conservative unhappiness with the Reagan administration. Rep. Larry P. McDonald, D-Ga., was among the 269 passengers killed on Sept. 1, when the airliner was downed over Soviet territory.

While the resolution condemned the Soviet action in strong terms, it did not go far enough for conservatives who saw the incident as an opportunity to strengthen anti-Soviet attitudes in the United States and the rest of the world. But when the resolution came to the Senate floor Sept. 15, the administration opposed efforts by Jesse Helms, R-N.C., and others to add amendments raising an array of issues in U.S.-Soviet relations.

State Department Authorization. Disputes over secondary issues delayed an authorization bill for the State Department and related agencies. Congress finally cleared the measure (HR 2915 — PL 98-164) on Nov. 18. It authorized $3.2 billion in fiscal 1984 and $3.5 billion in 1985.

One of the major provisions authorized establishment of a new National Endowment for Democracy, which would make grants to private agencies that promote democratic values overseas. But the bill did not allow the Republican and Democratic parties to be among the agencies getting grants, as Reagan proposed.

Radio Marti. Congress approved President Reagan's request for a new U.S. government radio station to broadcast news and opinion to Cuba, but not in the form he wanted.

S 602 (PL 98-111), cleared by Congress on Sept. 29, authorized establishment of the station under the jurisdiction of the Voice of America. Reagan had wanted the station to have more independence, similar to Radio Free Europe and Radio Liberty.

The station was to be called Radio Marti, after Cuban patriot José Marti. Congress in November appropriated $10 million for the station in the fiscal 1984 Commerce, Justice and State departments funding bill (HR 3222 — PL 98-166).

IMF Funding, Export-Import Bank. The legislative battle over funding for the International Monetary Fund (IMF) continued into the final days of the session. The measure to increase by $8.4 billion the U.S. contribution to the fund ran into trouble from conservatives, who termed it a "big bank bailout," and from House Democrats, who refused to act on it until they were guaranteed action on a bill providing housing for the poor.

The final form assumed by the IMF bill was one of the session's most awkward legislative constructions. Negotiations among the chairman of the House Banking Committee, Fernand J. St Germain, D-R.I., his Senate counterpart, Jake Garn, R-Utah, and White House officials resulted in a compromise that joined the IMF and housing bills as a single amendment to a supplemental appropriations measure (HR 3959 — PL 98-181), cleared by Congress Nov. 18.

Besides making extra money available to the IMF, the amendment extended the authorization of the Export-Import Bank for three years, to Sept. 30, 1986. Also reauthorized by HR 3959 were multilateral development banks, including $5.2 billion for the Inter-American Development Bank and $1.3 billion for the Asian Development Bank. The bill also extended the Defense Production Act until March 30, 1984.

General Government

Martin Luther King Holiday. Putting aside his earlier opposition, President Reagan Nov. 2 signed into law a bill (HR 3706 — PL 98-144) declaring the third Monday in January, beginning in 1986, a legal public holiday honoring the late civil rights leader, the Rev. Dr. Martin Luther King Jr.

Enactment of the legislation marked a major victory for civil rights groups, which had pushed for a holiday honoring King since his assassination in 1968. It also marked a major defeat for Sen. Jesse Helms, R-N.C., who led the sometimes virulent opposition to the measure in the Senate.

The Senate passed the bill Oct. 19 by a vote of 78-22. The House had passed it Aug. 2 by a vote of 338-90; there, the principal objection raised to the bill was the cost of an additional public holiday.

Personnel Regulations. Congress voted repeatedly in 1983 to bar the Reagan administration from putting into effect controversial regulations linking federal employees' pay and job security more directly with performance.

But even after the session ended, the battle continued. After Congress adjourned, the Office of Personnel Management (OPM) announced that in its opinion, government agencies could begin implementing the new rules starting Nov. 25. Federal employee unions immediately sought and on Dec. 30 won a court order barring the implementation. OPM said it planned to appeal the ruling.

Congress had inserted provisions in five different bills during the year barring OPM from instituting the new rules. The latest action was an amendment offered by Rep. Steny H. Hoyer, D-Md., to the second fiscal 1984 continuing appropriations resolution (H J Res 413).

Federal Pay Raise. Senate inaction on a budget reconciliation measure reduced a proposed pay increase for white collar federal employees from 4 percent to 3.5 percent, the level proposed by President Reagan. The pay hike took effect Jan. 1, 1984.

By failing to pass the budget-cutting measure (S 2062), the Senate also blocked a proposed delay in cost-of-living increases for federal retirees. However, the delay, expected to save $2.18 billion, was expected to be reintroduced in 1984.

Weather Satellites. In the face of overwhelming opposition from both houses of Congress, the administration dropped its plan to sell weather satellites to the private sector.

The Senate voted three times to bar the sales; the House once. In addition, both chambers passed non-binding resolutions expressing opposition to the proposed sales.

Legislation reauthorizing the National Aeronautics and Space Administration (HR 2065 — PL 98-52) barred the administration from selling the satellites without congressional approval, and an amendment to the Commerce Department's fiscal 1984 funding bill (HR 3222) barred the department from using funds to sell the satellites.

Mail Fraud. Congress Nov. 16 cleared a bill (S 450 — PL 98-186) giving the Postal Service new authority to deal with mail fraud. Under the bill, the Postal Service could issue orders, after a hearing before an administrative law judge, requiring a person to cease and desist from engaging in false representation schemes. The bill also gave the Postal Service investigative and consumer protection authority, and defined penalties for false representation.

Small Business. For the first time since 1980, farmers became entitled to Small Business Administration (SBA) disaster loans, since Congress failed to pass legislation extending the ban on their participation in the program. The ban expired Sept. 30. The legislation was part of the budget reconciliation act (S 2062), which stalled on the Senate floor.

Congress also maintained the SBA direct loan program, which the Reagan administration wanted to eliminate. The Senate voted to abolish the program but the bill (S 1323) was not enacted. A House bill (HR 3020), which would have preserved the program after making several changes, never made it to the floor in 1983.

Legislation designed to set aside a portion of federal procurement funds for small business remained stalled on the House floor. The House Small Business Committee reported a bill (HR 2133), opposed by the Reagan administration and contractors, Nov. 12 by a 37-1 vote.

Federal Procurement Policy. Congress Nov. 17 cleared legislation (HR 2293 — PL 98-191) extending the Office of Federal Procurement Policy for four years and giving the office regulatory authority over procurement policy for the entire executive branch.

Among other things, the bill clarified the office's authority over the Defense Department's procurement policies and required it to make a special study of defense procurement in the last week of each fiscal year.

The Senate also passed a bill (S 338) designed to increase competition in federal contracting by imposing new restrictions on the use of noncompetitive contracts.

Freedom of Information. Congress for the third year in a row failed to endorse the Reagan administration's plan to restrict the Freedom of Information Act.

The Senate Judiciary Committee June 16 approved a bill (S 774) making it easier for the government to close certain files to public view. But the full Senate failed to consider the measure, and Glenn English, D-Okla., chairman of the House Government Operations Subcommittee on Government Information, said he would not consider a bill until the Senate acted.

Meanwhile, the Senate Nov. 17 passed a bill (S 1324) allowing the director of the Central Intelligence Agency to exempt certain operational files containing classified information from search and review under the Freedom of Information Act.

Government Ethics Office. Congress extended for another five years the Office of Government Ethics, closing some loopholes in federal conflict-of-interest laws. The bill (S 461 — PL 98-150) cleared Oct. 27.

It required presidential appointees to update financial disclosure forms the day of their first confirmation hearings and required individuals to report when they had taken actions to comply with agreements made under the law to divest themselves of conflicting interests or to place those interests in a blind trust.

Health

Child Health. Congress in its budget resolution (H Con Res 91) allotted $200 million in fiscal 1984 and extra funds in future years to open Medicaid to more impoverished women during pregnancy, and to young children. The House Energy and Commerce Committee and the Senate Finance Committee both approved such proposals, but neither came to the floor because of problems with the reconciliation measures that were to be used as vehicles for the bills.

Cigarette Warnings. Foes of smoking made some headway when the Senate Labor and Human Resources Committee in July reported a bill (S 772) mandating a tough new health warning label for cigarette packages. The House Energy and Commerce Subcommittee on Health in September endorsed a different version (HR 1824) requiring a series of stiff new warnings, to be rotated on cigarette packages and advertisements so as to catch smokers' attention. But the legislation went no further.

Health Insurance for Job-

less. Despite early support from prominent Republicans and Democrats in both houses, legislation creating new publicly financed health insurance programs for unemployed Americans did not become law.

The House in August approved a two-year, $4 billion plan (HR 3021), and the Senate Finance and Labor and Human Resources Committees each reported more limited versions (S 951, S 242). But the legislation did not come to the Senate floor because conservative Republicans objected strongly to a Finance Committee decision, after its original bill was reported, to include a controversial change in federal income averaging rules for taxes. Revenues from the tax plan were intended to pay for the insurance program.

Administration officials had said they would accept the new health insurance program only if Congress also explicitly provided a way to pay for it.

Health Research. The House passed a compromise three-year reauthorization (HR 2350) for biomedical research programs, including authority for new institutes devoted to arthritis and related diseases, and nursing. Opponents in a bitter fight over setting research priorities had resolved their differences and crafted the compromise that the House approved Nov. 17.

A four-year Senate bill (S 773) with lower authorization levels was reported by the Labor and Human Resources Committee in April but did not come to the Senate floor.

Medicare. Congress enacted a fundamental change in Medicare as part of the Social Security bill (HR 1900 — PL 98-21) cleared in March.

The law authorized a largely untested new method of calculating Medicare payments to hospitals. When Congress acted, the program was paying, within certain limits, what each hospital said it cost to treat Medicare patients. The new method instead fixed payment rates for treatment of each of more than 400 medical conditions. Advocates said this change, put forward by the Reagan administration, could help stem inflation of health-care costs by forcing hospitals to carefully budget the use of their resources.

To meet budget reconciliation requirements, House and Senate committees also readied a series of relatively modest money-saving changes

in Medicare — including a temporary freeze on physician fees with controversial restrictions to keep doctors from passing on more costs to patients. But the reconciliation bills bearing the changes did not come to the floor.

Housing/Development

Housing Authorization. On the eve of adjournment, Congress broke a months-long logjam and cleared a $15.6 billion compromise authorization for housing and community development programs. The measure was attached to a supplemental appropriations bill (HR 3959 — PL 98-181) and linked with a quota increase for the International Monetary Fund (IMF).

The House had passed its bill July 13 (HR 1) after cutting one-third of the funding. The Senate briefly considered its bill (S 1338) June 21, but the threat of an extended debate forced the leadership to pull it from the floor. After the Labor Day recess, key members negotiated with Budget Director David A. Stockman and Treasury Secretary Donald T. Regan to produce the supplemental-IMF compromise.

The administration opposed several provisions in the legislation, but the administration wanted the IMF legislation. The president signed the bill Nov. 30.

A new production and rehabilitation program for rental housing was included, despite administration objections. The program was authorized at $615 million over two years, a level much lower than the $900 million program approved by the House. The bill also included a pilot program of the administration proposal to provide vouchers to be used toward rent by low-income tenants.

Enterprise Zones. An administration proposal to provide tax and regulatory relief to promote the development of inner cities was not enacted.

The Senate Finance Committee May 17 approved a bill (S 863) designating 75 zones over a three-year period, one-third of which would be in rural areas. The Senate attached the measure to a bill (HR 2973) repealing withholding on interest and dividend income, but the provision was dropped in conference with the House.

The House Ways and Means Committee held a hearing on a similar measure (HR 1955) Nov. 17. Chairman Dan Rostenkowski, D-Ill., was skeptical of the proposal, but 231 House members, including a majority on Ways and Means, were cosponsors.

Secondary Mortgage Market. Congress explored several proposals to increase the flow of mortgage money in the secondary market to aid the homebuilding industry.

The Senate Nov. 16 passed legislation (S 2040) removing regulatory impediments limiting the amount of private sector involvement in the buying and selling of mortgage-backed securities. A companion bill (S 1822), affecting tax laws to allow the creation of trusts for investment in mortgages (TIMs), received a hearing in the Senate Finance Committee but was attacked by the industry. Critics objected to the administration's plan to exclude the federally chartered Federal Home Loan Mortgage Corporation and Federal National Mortgage Association from TIMs.

Just before adjournment, Sen. Bob Packwood, R-Ore., and Reps. Ron Wyden, D-Ore., and Richard A. Gephardt, D-Mo., introduced legislation allowing pension funds to invest in mortgage-backed securities. Their bill was supported by the National Association of Home Builders and the AFL-CIO's Building and Construction Trades Department.

Mortgage Aid. Congress failed to enact legislation providing emergency mortgage assistance for the unemployed.

The House acted twice to provide mortgage relief. On May 11, it narrowly approved a program (HR 1983) providing $760 million in direct loans, over the strong objections of the Reagan administration. The House also added funds for a veterans' mortgage aid program to its appropriations bill for the Department of Housing and Urban Development (HUD), but the program was dropped in conference.

The Senate Banking Committee included a loan guarantee program in its housing authorization bill (S 1338). However, when S 1338 reached the Senate floor, Housing Subcommittee Chairman John Tower, R-Texas, deleted the provision. When Congress reached its compromise on the housing authorization, mortgage assistance also was omitted.

Labor/Social Security

Emergency Jobs. Alarmed at recession-spawned unemployment that had hit 10.8 percent in December 1982, Congress March 24 overwhelmingly approved and President Reagan signed into law a $4.6 billion jobs and humanitarian relief package as part of a $15.6 billion fiscal 1983 supplemental appropriations bill (HR 1718 — PL 98-8).

The jobs portion of the bill represented a House-Senate compromise fashioned to fall within a $5 billion limit the president had set. In February, under congressional pressure, Reagan had dropped his opposition to jobs legislation and proposed his own $4.3 billion plan for recession relief. Two-thirds of the final jobs package was allotted to public works, general construction and water projects. The remaining funds were allocated to social services, health and humanitarian aid.

Jobs II. The House Sept. 21 passed by a party-line vote of 246-178 a $3.5 billion jobs bill that got no further in Congress but which Democrats said they would use as a 1984 elections campaign issue. The measure (HR 1036) would have provided federal funds to create jobs for the long-term unemployed through projects to repair and renovate community facilities and public schools in areas of high unemployment.

The jobs plan, sponsored by Rep. Augustus F. Hawkins, D-Calif., had been launched with great momentum in January, when unemployment had only begun to decline from its December 1982 high of 10.8 percent. But it was opposed by President Reagan, who rejected the philosophy behind such public service jobs plans, and it quickly became clear that the Senate would refuse to accept the measure.

When HR 1036 came before the House, Republicans complained that the Democratic leadership was merely playing politics with the issue, since the legislation was doomed. Hawkins and other Democrats responded that jobs were a legitimate political issue and that it was legitimate for them to try to get the other party on record regarding jobs creation.

Social Security. Facing the prospect of funding shortfalls in July and acting on the recommendation of a bipartisan presidential commission, Congress in March approved one of the biggest overhauls of Social Security since the program began in 1937.

The compromise rescue plan (HR 1900 — PL 98-21), pushed through both chambers in just over a month, raised the retirement age from 65 to 67 by the year 2027, delayed for six months annual cost-of-living increases for the system's 36 million recipients and increased payroll taxes for employees and employers.

Intended to raise $165 billion over seven years, the measure also taxed, for the first time, benefits of high-income recipients, authorized transfers from the general Treasury to aid the system's trust funds and brought new federal employees, members of Congress, the president, the vice president and federal judges under Social Security.

Passage of the bill followed a two-year partisan fight over the future of the Social Security program that was provoked in 1981 by Reagan administration proposals to cut benefits to keep the retirement system from insolvency. *(1981 Almanac p. 117)*

Also attached to the legislation were extraneous but major provisions that altered the government's method of reimbursing hospitals for Medicare; extended for six months — through Sept. 30, 1983 — an emergency unemployment benefits program, and increased benefits for the blind, aged and disabled.

Railroad Retirement. After months of deliberation and delay, Congress Aug. 1-2 rapidly cleared a complex bill (HR 1646 — PL 98-76) to keep the federal railroad retirement and unemployment compensation programs solvent. The rescue plan, a compromise backed by rail labor and management, was a combination of benefit reductions, increased taxes and a federal contribution of $1.7 billion. The House passed it Aug. 1 and the Senate cleared it the next day.

The railroad retirement system, the only private pension plan run by the federal government, faced a deficit of $6 billion through fiscal 1988 and $13 billion by 1992 without remedial legislation. But Congress acted under a more pressing deadline: The Railroad Retirement Board had said that starting Sept. 1, 1983, it would send notices to one million retirees warning them that their benefits would have to be trimmed as of the end of fiscal 1983 on Sept. 30 unless Congress restored the system to financial health.

Federal Supplemental Unemployment Compensation. Congress Oct. 21 cleared legislation (HR 3929 — PL 98-135) extending federal supplemental unemployment compensation benefits through March 31, 1985. The bill, cleared after a tangled partisan battle over the program's cost, provided a minimum eight weeks and a maximum 14 weeks of federal supplemental benefits to persons who had used up all other state and federal jobless aid.

It also provided an additional five "reach-back" weeks of benefits to persons who became eligible for supplemental benefits between April 1, 1983, and the week of Oct. 23, 1983, and had exhausted all their benefits, including supplemental benefits, as of Oct. 16, 1983.

Social Security Disability Reviews. House refusal to consider a major tax bill (HR 4170) prevented action on provisions to modify the Social Security disability program and to extend a law permitting Social Security disability aid recipients ruled ineligible to continue to receive benefits while appealing to an administrative law judge.

Disability reform advocates in the Senate failed to attach similar legislation to a supplemental appropriations bill (HR 3959) late in the session. The Senate did pass an extension of the existing review procedures (HR 3391) by 80-0 on the last day of the session, but the House failed to act on that measure.

Congress previously had extended the disability review provisions from Sept. 30 to Dec. 7, trying to provide time to handle a more complex disability bill. Despite the Dec. 7 expiration date, a provision in the law allowed recipients to receive benefits for at least two more months, giving Congress a chance to revise or extend it before it expired early in 1984.

Pension Equity. The Senate Nov. 18 passed a bill (HR 2769) making broad changes in pension law, two days after similar pension "equity" legislation was approved by the House Education and Labor Committee (HR 4280) and the Senate Labor and Human Resources Committee (HR 2110). The House Ways and Means Committee, which shared pension jurisdiction with the Education and Labor panel, was still considering a pension mea-

sure when Congress adjourned.

The Senate and House bills would liberalize pension coverage by strengthening the rights of spouses to pensions if a worker died before retirement age and by permitting workers to leave and subsequently return to a job without losing benefits for which they already had qualified.

Law Enforcement/ Judiciary

Civil Rights. After a six-month battle with President Reagan, Congress Nov. 16 cleared a bill (HR 2230 — PL 98-183) reconstituting the U.S. Civil Rights Commission and extending it for six years. HR 2230 replaced the current six-member presidentially appointed commission with an eight-member panel. The president and Congress each appointed four members, who could be removed only for cause.

Over the last two years, the civil rights panel had issued a number of reports criticizing administration policies. Reagan May 26 announced he was replacing three sitting commissioners with his own nominees. (He already had appointed the chairman and vice chairman of the commission.)

Civil rights activists charged that Reagan's move undermined the commission's independence, and they set out to block the nominations. After months of maneuvering, during which the commission's reauthorization and fiscal 1984 funding became entangled with the confirmation proceedings, the civil rights groups won enough congressional backing to force the White House into accepting a compromise embodied in HR 2230. Reagan, however, had the last word. He joined with congressional Republicans to win control of the commission.

Equal Rights Amendment. The House Nov. 15 failed to revive the Equal Rights Amendment (ERA) when a 278-147 vote on the measure (H J Res 1) fell six short of the two-thirds majority needed for passage of a proposed amendment to the Constitution. House Democratic leaders brought the amendment to the floor under suspension of the rules, a procedure that allows only 40 minutes' debate and no amendments, and generally is reserved for non-controversial matters.

Sponsors tried the parliamentary fast track to avoid amendments making the ERA inapplicable to such areas as abortion, the military draft and military combat regulations. Adoption of such exceptions would have made the ERA unacceptable to many of its supporters.

The suspension tactic angered many House members, and 14 ERA cosponsors voted against the amendment. Democrats supported the proposal 225-38; Republicans voted against it 53-109.

Democrats hoped their votes for the ERA would score points with women's groups who had made the ERA a priority issue, and that Republicans would pay politically for their "nay" votes.

Immigration Reform. House Speaker Thomas P. O'Neill Jr., D-Mass., exercised his power over the calendar Oct. 8 and blocked a wide-ranging immigration reform bill (HR 1510) from reaching the House floor in 1983. The bill was opposed bitterly by Hispanics, who claimed that provisions penalizing employers who knowingly hire illegal aliens would result in discrimination against Hispanics.

O'Neill said there was "no constituency" to counterbalance the concerns of the Hispanics, and that he feared President Reagan might veto any bill that cleared Congress to garner election support within the Hispanic community.

O'Neill's action marked the second year in a row that immigration reform was blocked by the House. The Senate passed bills in 1982 and 1983 that were similar in overall goals to the House bill but differed in some details.

HR 1510 was pending in the House Rules Committee and was likely to be resurrected in 1984.

Abortion. Efforts to pass an anti-abortion constitutional amendment died June 28 when the Senate rejected a proposed amendment giving states and the federal government the right to restrict abortion. It was the first time such an amendment had come to a vote in either chamber since the 1973 Supreme Court decision legalizing abortion.

The vote on the proposal (S J Res 3) was 49-50, with Jesse Helms, R-N.C., voting present. The "yeas" fell 18 votes short of the two-thirds margin required to approve a constitutional amendment.

Although the constitutional amendment drive failed, Helms had said he might try to move an anti-abortion bill in the Senate. A bill would require only a majority vote to pass.

Bankruptcy Courts. The House failed to move on legislation (HR 3) to restructure the nation's bankruptcy courts, although the Senate passed a court reform bill (S 1013) that also included provisions making it harder for consumers to declare bankruptcy and start their financial lives over.

The House bill remained in the Rules Committee, stalled over a proposal to add consumer bankruptcy provisions similar to the Senate measure. House Judiciary Committee Chairman Peter W. Rodino Jr., D-N.J., chief sponsor of HR 3, adamantly opposed adding such provisions to the court bill, but the consumer proposal had enough support of its own to prevent the Rules panel from yielding to Rodino.

The bankruptcy court problem arose from a June 28, 1982, Supreme Court decision invalidating the bankruptcy court system created in 1978.

HR 3 would create a new court of 227 judges with lifetime appointments to handle all bankruptcy and related proceedings.

The Senate bill was modeled on an interim rule for bankruptcy court operations issued by the U.S. Judicial Conference, the policy-making arm of the federal courts. Generally, it would allow existing bankruptcy judges to handle issues that clearly involved bankruptcy law. When parties in a bankruptcy proceeding were involved in other legal disputes, their cases would be handled by district court judges.

Crime. Although the Senate Judiciary Committee approved a consensus anti-crime package (S 1762), the measure was not considered by the full Senate. Key members were unable to work out a time agreement for consideration of separate proposals on controversial issues such as the death penalty.

The bill was expected to be considered in 1984. It included provisions to revise bail and sentencing laws, toughen penalties for drug traffickers and revise the insanity defense.

The House Judiciary Committee, never fond of packaging legislation, preferred instead to work on bills that

dealt with specific subjects. The committee approved a bill (HR 3336) overhauling the insanity defense and was working on selected other subjects covered in S 1762.

Trade

Domestic Content. For the second year in a row, the House gave the United Auto Workers a victory by approving a "domestic content" measure that would require fixed levels of U.S. labor and parts in foreign cars sold in this country. And for the second year in a row, the Reagan administration opposed the bill and the Senate made no effort to consider it.

House consideration of the domestic content bill (HR 1234) in 1983 differed in one respect, however. In 1982 the House by a one-vote margin accepted a weakening amendment that would have prevented domestic content requirements from being enforced if they were found to violate U.S. trade obligations under the General Agreement on Tariffs and Trade (GATT). In 1983 the House handily defeated a similar amendment to the bill, and proponents predicted it would be difficult to ignore domestic content legislation in the upcoming election year.

Export Controls. Despite claims that the flow of sophisticated goods with potential military applications from the United States to Eastern bloc nations amounted to a "hemorrhage," relaxed controls on U.S. exports were approved by the House Oct. 27. The major change in controls made by the legislation (HR 3231), which reauthorized the Export Administration Act for two years, allowed exporters to forgo licensing for shipments to Japan and U.S. allies in Western Europe.

Legislation (S 979) to retain strict controls on exports was reported by the Senate Banking Committee May 23 but failed to gain floor consideration. Because no legislation was enacted, Congress twice extended the president's existing authority to control exports, which expired Sept. 30. The second measure (HR 4476 — PL 98-207), cleared in the last hours before adjournment, continued export controls to Feb. 29, 1984.

Trade Reciprocity. The Senate April 21 passed a so-called reciprocity bill expanding the president's authority to retaliate against unfair trading practices by other countries and requiring the administration to seek new international agreements on trade in services and high technology.

But the bill (S 144) became a legislative vehicle for a controversial measure repealing the withholding of taxes on interest and dividend income. Withholding overshadowed reciprocity, and, in the conference on the withholding-reciprocity measure, the trade provisions were dropped. House leaders promised, however, to consider a reciprocity measure.

The Ways and Means Committee Sept. 27 reported a reciprocity bill (HR 1571) that would put retaliatory power within the Trade Act of 1974, which fell under Ways and Means jurisdiction. The committee reported unfavorably a second measure (HR 2848) that provided separate authority in the Commerce Department, which fell under the jurisdiction of the Energy and Commerce Committee. Neither bill made it to the House floor before adjournment.

Caribbean Basin Plan. A whittled-down version of the Reagan administration's Caribbean Basin Initiative (CBI) won congressional approval July 28 (HR 2973 — PL 98-67). The measure was designed to promote economic development in the region by providing duty-free entry into the United States for certain Caribbean exports and by allowing U.S. businessmen to take tax deductions for the expense of attending conventions in the region.

The administration had envisioned a broader program of trade and tax benefits. But Congress, concerned about domestic unemployment, dropped parts of the legislation until only a modest package of incentives remained.

As passed by Congress, the CBI was made part of a controversial bill repealing a requirement for 10 percent withholding of taxes on interest and dividend income. Though the president opposed the withholding repeal, the addition of the CBI package helped to overcome his opposition to the bill.

Trade Department. A plan (S 121) to establish a new Department of International Trade and Industry was reported by the Senate Governmental Affairs Committee Oct. 18 but went no further. The new department, a combination of the Office of the U.S. Trade Representative and the Commerce Department, would include an "industrial policy" component — an Office of Competitive Analysis and temporary industry "competitiveness councils."

The Senate plan's treatment of industrial policy was inserted by committee Democrats. A stronger industrial policy approach was included in a trade reorganization plan offered by Don Bonker, D-Wash., chairman of the House Foreign Affairs Subcommittee on International Economic Policy and Trade. The Bonker plan would also create competitiveness councils but would replace the U.S. trade representative with the post of assistant to the president for international trade.

Trade Adjustment Assistance. Congress Sept. 30 cleared a two-year extension of the trade adjustment assistance program, hours before it was to expire. The program provided benefits to workers who had been laid off from industries harmed by import competition. A small portion of the benefits also went to small and medium-size firms suffering from imports.

The Reagan administration had sought the termination of trade adjustment assistance. However, high levels of unemployment convinced a majority in both houses that the benefits should be continued. The House had wanted to expand the program but went along with the Senate's simple two-year extension attached to a bill (HR 3813 — PL 98-120) continuing the International Coffee Agreement for three years.

Transportation

Coal Slurry Pipelines. The latest effort of coal slurry pipeline operators to obtain federal eminent domain rights to assist in construction met the same fate as previous efforts: faced with heavy lobbying in opposition by railroads, a bill (HR 1010) was decisively defeated 182-235 by the House Sept. 27.

A similar Senate bill (S 267) was not brought to the floor in light of the defeat in the House.

Railroads fought slurry — pulverized coal mixed with an equal amount of water — as a challenge to their virtual monopoly over coal transporta-

tion in many areas. Supporters attempted to assure Westerners that the legislation contained adequate safeguards to protect precious water rights.

Highway Funds. Congressional inaction jeopardized new Interstate highway construction projects and left a number of emergency highway repair projects without funds.

The House and Senate were unable to agree on a bill (HR 3103) to provide an additional $150 million for emergency highway repair, mostly in California, Utah and Arizona. The bill also permitted the allocation of $4 billion in Interstate construction funds from the Highway Trust Fund. At adjournment, 30 states had less than $9 million each and could not easily award major Interstate construction contracts without the new allocations.

Although both chambers passed HR 3103, House provisions adding $140 million for what critics termed "pork barrel" projects dragged the legislation down. The House also added a controversial trucking antitrust exemption that prompted angry senators to block a conference.

Maritime Administration. Differences over repayment of federal construction subsidies kept the Maritime Administration authorization bill from clearing before adjournment. However, fiscal 1984 funding was provided in the Commerce/Justice/State appropriations bill (HR 3222 — PL 98-166).

The Senate passed S 1037 April 28; the House passed its version Nov. 4. The House drastically curtailed a proposed Transportation Department regulation that would allow vessels built with the aid of federal subsidies to enter domestic trade if the subsidy were repaid. The Senate bill did not address the issue. No action to resolve the difference was taken.

Amtrak. Legislation authorizing a fiscal 1984 operating subsidy for Amtrak (HR 3648, S 1117) was not enacted, but $716.4 million was provided in the Transportation Department appropriations bill (HR 3329 — PL 98-78). The House bill authorized $730 million; the Senate bill, $750 million.

A major concern was the scheduled default of Amtrak on Oct. 1 on about $1 billion in federal loan guarantees. Administrative steps were taken to deal with that problem.

Shipping Antitrust. Both chambers passed legislation to clarify existing antitrust exemptions for the ocean-liner industry. But substantial differences between the versions of S 47 passed by the Senate March 1 and by the House Oct. 17 had not been worked out before adjournment.

The industry sought extended antitrust immunity and an expedited regulatory process. Neither bill went as far as the industry had wanted.

Veterans

Health Care. Congress extended for four additional years, until Sept. 30, 1988, readjustment counseling centers for Vietnam veterans.

The extension was a part of a wide-ranging veterans' health care measure (HR 2920 — PL 98-160), cleared Nov. 3. The bill also required a study of the effects of post-traumatic stress syndrome, a condition affecting Vietnam veterans, and contained provisions aimed at reducing the long-term costs of veterans' health care.

In addition, the Senate Nov. 18 passed a bill (S 1388) increasing the compensation for service-connected disabilities for veterans and dependents. Another measure (S 1651), providing compensation for veterans exposed to Agent Orange and radiation, was expected to be considered by the full Senate early in 1984. A similar measure (HR 1961) was approved by the House Veterans' Affairs Committee.

Job Training. Over administration objections, Congress enacted an emergency job training measure (HR 2355 — PL 98-77) for Korean War and Vietnam-era veterans facing long-term unemployment. The bill, cleared Aug. 3, authorized a two-year, $300 million program to assist the veterans, whose unemployment rate stood at 12.3 percent in July.

A supplemental appropriations bill cleared by Congress just before the end of the session (HR 3959 — PL 98-181) provided $75 million for the program. Another $75 million was provided in the continuing resolution (H J Res 413 — PL 98-151).

Mortgage Aid. Financial assistance for veterans facing foreclosure on home mortgages guaranteed by the Veterans Administration was approved by the House, but was not con-

sidered in the Senate.

The House May 24 approved a bill (HR 2948) providing aid to any veteran or surviving spouse who was unemployed or who suffered a substantial reduction in income.

The House also included $150 million for mortgage assistance for unemployed veterans in a fiscal 1984 appropriations bill (HR 3133 — PL 98-45), but the provision was dropped in conference with the Senate.

Welfare

Food Assistance. Throughout the year, congressional committees held hearings on reports that needy Americans were going hungry because of the recession and budget cuts in federal food programs.

Early in the session, Congress told the Agriculture Department to step up giveaways of surplus federally owned food and, in the same legislation — an emergency jobs bill (HR 1718 — PL 98-8) — provided funds for distribution costs. An August unemployment compensation bill (HR 3409 — PL 98-92) continued the mandate and the funding for two years.

The Reagan administration insisted the hunger reports were exaggerated, but in August, when the nation's poverty rate was reported at a 15-year high, the president ordered a study of the reports.

The House in October voted to restore some funding cut from school lunch and other child nutrition programs and to make this aid available to more children of the "working poor." But that bill (HR 4091) was not acted on by the Senate.

Nor did Congress go ahead with the modest increases in food stamps that the fiscal 1984 budget resolution permitted. Advocates of expanded food aid feared that any move to liberalize food stamps would provoke strong counterattacks from members who thought the program should be cut further.

At the end of the session, Congress cleared a bill (HR 4252 — PL 98-204) postponing a deadline for termination of Puerto Rico's cash nutrition assistance program and giving states more flexibility in coping with new food stamp reporting requirements.

ACTION Authorization. The

House and Senate did not agree on reauthorizing a number of volunteer and anti-poverty programs, and as a result, fiscal 1984 funding for the programs was set lower than envisioned by either chamber.

The Senate Sept. 14 passed S 1129, reauthorizing ACTION for three years. The fiscal 1984 authorization of $147.6 million included $15 million for Volunteers in Service to America (VISTA), which the administration wanted to abolish. The House Oct. 28 passed its version, authorizing about $178.1 million for ACTION, including $25 million for VISTA.

No conference to reconcile the differences was held, and fiscal 1984 ACTION funding was provided through the continuing resolution at 1983 levels: $129.3 million, with $11.8 million for VISTA.

Child Support Enforcement. The House Nov. 16 overwhelmingly approved a measure (HR 4325) designed to encourage payment of child support, but the Senate did not act before adjournment.

The key feature of the bill was the mandatory withholding of payments from the paychecks of those in arrears in court-ordered child support. The bill required states to have such a program in place by 1985 to aid anyone who requested assistance in collecting back child support. It also provided financial incentives to the states to make the collections. ∎

Characteristics of Congress

Characteristics of the 98th Congress

Nearly 50 percent of the members of the 98th Congress were lawyers, the largest single profession represented.

Congressional Quarterly, which has kept occupational statistics since 1948, found that 261 members of the new Congress held law degrees — eight more than in the 97th. The increase marked the reversal of a trend that saw lawyers' numbers drop from 291 in the 95th Congress to 270 in the 96th Congress to 253 in the 97th Congress.

In the Senate, 61 members were lawyers, a slight increase from the 59 lawyers in the 97th. In the 96th and 95th Congresses, lawyers numbered 65 and 68, respectively.

In the House there were 200 lawyers, compared to 223 in the 95th Congress, 205 in the 96th Congress and 194 in the 97th Congress.

Senate—Birth Dates, Past Occupations, Religions, Seniority

(Seniority rank is within the member's party.)

ALABAMA
Heflin (D)—June 19, 1921. Occupation: lawyer, judge. Religion: Methodist. Seniority: 39.
Denton (R)—July 15, 1924. Occupation: naval officer, educator, broadcasting executive. Religion: Roman Catholic. Seniority: 42.

ALASKA
Murkowski (R)—March 28, 1933. Occupation: banker. Religion: Roman Catholic. Seniority: 42.
Stevens (R)—Nov. 18, 1923. Occupation: lawyer. Religion: Episcopalian. Seniority: 6.

ARIZONA
DeConcini (D)—May 8, 1937. Occupation: lawyer. Religion: Roman Catholic. Seniority: 31.
Goldwater (R)—Jan. 1, 1909. Occupation: author, department store executive. Religion: Episcopalian. Seniority: 7.

ARKANSAS
Bumpers (D)—Aug. 12, 1925. Occupation: farmer, hardware company executive, lawyer, governor. Religion: Methodist. Seniority: 22.
Pryor (D)—Aug. 29, 1934. Occupation: newspaper publisher, lawyer, governor. Religion: Presbyterian. Seniority: 35.

CALIFORNIA
Cranston (D)—June 19, 1914. Occupation: author, journalist, real estate executive. Religion: Protestant. Seniority: 13.
Wilson (R)—Aug. 23, 1933. Occupation: lawyer. Religion: Protestant. Seniority: 53.

COLORADO
Hart (D)—Nov. 28, 1937. Occupation: author, educator, lawyer. Religion: Presbyterian. Seniority: 23.
Armstrong (R)—March 16, 1937. Occupation: broadcasting executive. Religion: Lutheran. Seniority: 31.

CONNECTICUT
Dodd (D)—May 27, 1944. Occupation: lawyer. Religion: Roman Catholic. Seniority: 43.
Weicker (R)—May 16, 1931. Occupation: lawyer. Religion: Episcopalian. Seniority: 12.

DELAWARE
Biden (D)—Nov. 20, 1942. Occupation: lawyer. Religion: Roman Catholic. Seniority: 18.
Roth (R)—July 22, 1921. Occupation: lawyer. Religion: Episcopalian. Seniority: 11.

FLORIDA
Chiles (D)—April 3, 1930. Occupation: lawyer. Religion: Presbyterian. Seniority: 15.
Hawkins (R)—June 24, 1927. Occupation: vitamin retailer, public official. Religion: Mormon. Seniority: 42.

GEORGIA
Nunn (D)—Sept. 8, 1938. Occupation: farmer, lawyer. Religion: Methodist. Seniority: 16.
Mattingly (R)—Jan. 7, 1931. Occupation: corporate executive. Religion: Methodist. Seniority: 42.

HAWAII
Inouye (D)—Sept. 7, 1924. Occupation: lawyer. Religion: Methodist. Seniority: 10.
Matsunaga (D)—Oct. 8, 1916. Occupation: lawyer. Religion: Episcopalian. Seniority: 28.

IDAHO
McClure (R)—Dec. 27, 1924. Occupation: lawyer. Religion: Methodist. Seniority: 14.
Symms (R)—April 23, 1938. Occupation: fruit grower, fitness club owner. Religion: Methodist. Seniority: 37.

ILLINOIS
Dixon (D)—July 7, 1927. Occupation: lawyer. Religion: Presbyterian. Seniority: 44.
Percy (R)—Sept. 27, 1919. Occupation: banker, corporate executive. Religion: Christian Scientist. Seniority: 3.

INDIANA
Lugar (R)—April 4, 1932. Occupation: farmer, educator, tool company executive. Religion: Methodist. Seniority: 22.
Quayle (R)—Feb. 4, 1947. Occupation: lawyer, newspaper publisher. Religion: Presbyterian. Seniority: 40.

IOWA
Grassley (R)—Sept. 17, 1933. Occupation: farmer, educator. Religion: Baptist. Seniority: 39.
Jepsen (R)—Dec. 23, 1928. Occupation: insurance salesman, marketing executive. Religion: Lutheran. Seniority: 34.

KANSAS
Dole (R)—July 22, 1923. Occupation: lawyer. Religion: Methodist. Seniority: 8.
Kassebaum (R)—July 29, 1932. Occupation: broadcasting executive. Religion: Episcopalian. Seniority: 26.

KENTUCKY
Ford (D)—Sept. 8, 1924. Occupation: insurance executive, governor. Religion: Baptist. Seniority: 21.
Huddleston (D)—April 15, 1926. Occupation: broadcasting executive. Religion: Methodist. Seniority: 18.

LOUISIANA
Johnston (D)—June 10, 1932. Occupation: lawyer. Religion: Baptist. Seniority: 17.
Long (D)—Nov. 3, 1918. Occupation: lawyer. Religion: Methodist. Seniority: 2.

MAINE

Mitchell (D)—Aug. 20, 1933. Occupation: lawyer, judge. Religion: Roman Catholic. Seniority: 42.

Cohen (R)—Aug. 28, 1940. Occupation: author, educator, lawyer. Religion: Unitarian. Seniority: 31.

MARYLAND

Sarbanes (D)—Feb. 3, 1933. Occupation: lawyer. Religion: Greek Orthodox. Seniority: 30.

Mathias (R)—July 24, 1922. Occupation: lawyer. Religion: Episcopalian. Seniority: 8.

MASSACHUSETTS

Kennedy (D)—Feb. 22, 1932. Occupation: author, lawyer. Religion: Roman Catholic. Seniority: 9.

Tsongas (D)—Feb. 14, 1941. Occupation: author, lawyer. Religion: Greek Orthodox. Seniority: 36.

MICHIGAN

Levin (D)—June 28, 1934. Occupation: lawyer. Religion: Jewish. Seniority: 39.

Riegle (D)—Feb. 4, 1938. Occupation: pricing analyst, professor. Religion: Methodist. Seniority: 27.

MINNESOTA

Boschwitz (R)—Nov. 7, 1930. Occupation: plywood company owner, lawyer. Religion: Jewish. Seniority: 28.

Durenberger (R)—Aug. 19, 1934. Occupation: adhesive manufacturing company executive, lawyer. Religion: Roman Catholic. Seniority: 25.

MISSISSIPPI

Stennis (D)—Aug. 3, 1901. Occupation: lawyer, judge. Religion: Presbyterian. Seniority: 1.

Cochran (R)—Dec. 7, 1937. Occupation: lawyer. Religion: Baptist. Seniority: 27.

MISSOURI

Eagleton (D)—Sept. 4, 1929. Occupation: lawyer. Religion: Roman Catholic. Seniority: 12.

Danforth (R)—Sept. 5, 1936. Occupation: lawyer, clergyman. Religion: Episcopalian. Seniority: 19.

MONTANA

Baucus (D)—Dec. 11, 1941. Occupation: lawyer. Religion: United Church of Christ. Seniority: 34.

Melcher (D)—Sept. 6, 1924. Occupation: veterinarian, cattle feedlot operator. Religion: Roman Catholic. Seniority: 29.

NEBRASKA

Exon (D)—Aug. 9, 1921. Occupation: office equipment retailer, governor. Religion: Episcopalian. Seniority: 37.

Zorinsky (D)—Nov. 11, 1928. Occupation: tobacco and candy wholesaler. Religion: Jewish. Seniority: 25.

NEVADA

Hecht (R)—Nov. 30, 1928. Occupation: clothing store owner. Religion: Jewish. Seniority: 53.

Laxalt (R)—Aug. 2, 1922. Occupation: hotel casino owner, lawyer, governor. Religion: Roman Catholic. Seniority: 17.

NEW HAMPSHIRE

Humphrey (R)—Oct. 9, 1940. Occupation: airline co-pilot. Religion: Baptist. Seniority: 34.

Rudman (R)—May 13, 1930. Occupation: lawyer. Religion: Jewish. Seniority: 42.

NEW JERSEY

Bradley (D)—July 28, 1943. Occupation: author, professional basketball player. Religion: Protestant. Seniority: 39.

Lautenberg (D)—Jan. 23, 1924. Occupation: computer firm executive. Religion: Jewish. Seniority: 45.

NEW MEXICO

Bingaman (D)—Oct. 3, 1943. Occupation: lawyer. Religion: Methodist. Seniority: 46.

Domenici (R)—May 7, 1932. Occupation: lawyer. Religion: Roman Catholic. Seniority: 15.

NEW YORK

Moynihan (D)—March 16, 1927. Occupation: government professor, writer. Religion: Roman Catholic. Seniority: 31.

D'Amato (R)—Aug. 1, 1937. Occupation: lawyer, public official. Religion: Roman Catholic. Seniority: 42.

NORTH CAROLINA

East (R)—May 5, 1931. Occupation: author, college professor. Religion: Methodist. Seniority: 42.

Helms (R)—Oct. 18, 1921. Occupation: journalist, banking association director, broadcasting executive. Religion: Baptist. Seniority: 15.

NORTH DAKOTA

Burdick (D)—June 19, 1908. Occupation: lawyer. Religion: United Church of Christ. Seniority: 7.

Andrews (R)—May 9, 1926. Occupation: farmer. Religion: Episcopalian. Seniority: 36.

OHIO

Glenn (D)—July 18, 1921. Occupation: astronaut, soft drink company executive. Religion: Presbyterian. Seniority: 20.

Metzenbaum (D)—June 4, 1917. Occupation: newspaper publisher, parking lot executive, lawyer. Religion: Jewish. Seniority: 26.

OKLAHOMA

Boren (D)—April 21, 1941. Occupation: lawyer, professor, governor. Religion: Methodist. Seniority: 37.

Nickles (R)—Dec. 6, 1948. Occupation: machine company executive. Religion: Roman Catholic. Seniority: 42.

OREGON

Hatfield (R)—July 12, 1922. Occupation: associate professor, author, governor. Religion: Baptist. Seniority: 5.

Packwood (R)—Sept. 11, 1932. Occupation: lawyer. Religion: Unitarian. Seniority: 10.

PENNSYLVANIA

Heinz (R)—Oct. 23, 1938. Occupation: management consultant, lecturer. Religion: Episcopalian. Seniority: 21.

Specter (R)—Feb. 12, 1930. Occupation: lawyer. Religion: Jewish. Seniority: 42.

RHODE ISLAND

Pell (D)—Nov. 22, 1918. Occupation: investment executive. Religion: Episcopalian. Seniority: 8.

Chafee (R)—Oct. 22, 1922. Occupation: lawyer, governor. Religion: Episcopalian. Seniority: 20.

SOUTH CAROLINA

Hollings (D)—Jan. 1, 1922. Occupation: lawyer, governor. Religion: Lutheran. Seniority: 11.

Thurmond (R)—Dec. 5, 1902. Occupation: lawyer, judge, governor. Religion: Baptist. Seniority: 1.

SOUTH DAKOTA

Abdnor (R)—Feb. 23, 1923. Occupation: rancher. Religion: Methodist. Seniority: 37.

Pressler (R)—March 29, 1942. Occupation: lawyer. Religion: Roman Catholic. Seniority: 33.

TENNESSEE

Sasser (D)—Sept. 30, 1936. Occupation: lawyer. Religion: Methodist. Seniority: 31.

Baker (R)—Nov. 15, 1925. Occupation: lawyer. Religion: Presbyterian. Seniority: 3.

TEXAS

Bentsen (D)—Feb. 11, 1921. Occupation: finance holding institution executive, lawyer, judge. Religion: Presbyterian. Seniority: 14.

Tower (R)—Sept. 29, 1925. Occupation: political science professor. Religion: Methodist. Seniority: 2.

UTAH

Garn (R)—Oct. 12, 1932. Occupation: insurance executive. Religion: Mormon. Seniority: 18.

Hatch (R)—March 22, 1934. Occupation: lawyer. Religion: Mormon. Seniority: 22.

VERMONT

Leahy (D)—March 31, 1940. Occupation: lawyer. Religion: Roman Catholic. Seniority: 23.

Stafford (R)—Aug. 8, 1913. Occupation: lawyer, governor. Religion: Congregation-

alist. Seniority: 13.

VIRGINIA
Trible (R)—Dec. 29, 1946. Occupation: lawyer. Religion: Episcopalian. Seniority: 52.

Warner (R)—Feb. 18, 1927. Occupation: lawyer, farmer. Religion: Episcopalian. Seniority: 30.

WASHINGTON
Jackson (D)—May 31, 1912. Occupation: lawyer. Religion: Presbyterian. Seniority: 3.

Gorton (R)—Jan. 8, 1928. Occupation: lawyer. Religion: Episcopalian. Seniority: 42.

WEST VIRGINIA
Byrd (D)—Nov. 20, 1917. Occupation: lawyer. Religion: Baptist. Seniority: 6.

Randolph (D)—March 8, 1902. Occupation: journalist, professor, airline executive. Religion: Seventh Day Baptist. Seniority: 5.

WISCONSIN
Proxmire (D)—Nov. 11, 1915. Occupa-

tion: author, journalist, printing company executive. Religion: Episcopalian. Seniority: 4.

Kasten (R)—June 19, 1942. Occupation: shoe manufacturing company executive. Religion: Episcopalian. Seniority: 40.

WYOMING
Simpson (R)—Sept. 2, 1931. Occupation: lawyer. Religion: Episcopalian. Seniority: 29.

Wallop (R)—Feb. 27, 1933. Occupation: rancher, meatpacking plant executive. Religion: Episcopalian. Seniority: 22.

House—Birth Dates, Past Occupations, Religions, Seniority

(Seniority rank is within the member's party.)

ALABAMA
1 **Edwards (R)**—Sept. 20, 1928. Occupation: lawyer. Religion: Presbyterian. Seniority: 9.

2 **Dickinson (R)**—June 5, 1925. Occupation: railroad executive, lawyer, judge. Religion: Methodist. Seniority: 9.

3 **Nichols (D)**—Oct. 16, 1918. Occupation: cotton gin company president, fertilizer manufacturing company executive. Religion: Methodist. Seniority: 41.

4 **Bevill (D)**—March 27, 1921. Occupation: lawyer. Religion: Baptist. Seniority: 41.

5 **Flippo (D)**—Aug. 15, 1937. Occupation: accountant. Religion: Church of Christ. Seniority: 120.

6 **Erdreich (D)**—Dec. 9, 1938. Occupation: lawyer. Religion: Jewish. Seniority: 214.

7 **Shelby (D)**—May 6, 1934. Occupation: lawyer. Religion: Presbyterian. Seniority: 151.

ALASKA
AL **Young (R)**—June 9, 1933. Occupation: elementary school teacher, river boat captain. Religion: Episcopalian. Seniority: 48.

ARIZONA
1 **McCain (R)**—Aug. 29, 1936. Occupation: naval officer, beer distributor. Religion: Episcopalian. Seniority: 143.

2 **Udall (D)**—June 15, 1922. Occupation: author, professional basketball player, lawyer. Religion: Mormon. Seniority: 20.

3 **Stump (R)**—April 4, 1927. Occupation: farmer. Religion: Seventh-day Adventist. Seniority: 142.

4 **Rudd (R)**—July 15, 1920. Occupation: lawyer, FBI agent. Religion: Roman Catholic. Seniority: 60.

5 **McNulty (D)**—Oct. 18, 1925. Occupation: Lawyer. Religion: Roman Catholic. Seniority: 214.

ARKANSAS
1 **Alexander (D)**—Jan. 16, 1934. Occupation: lawyer. Religion: Episcopalian. Seniority: 46.

2 **Bethune (R)**—Dec. 19, 1935. Occupation: FBI agent, lawyer. Religion: Methodist. Seniority: 74.

3 **Hammerschmidt (R)**—May 4, 1922. Occupation: lumber company executive. Religion: Presbyterian. Seniority: 16.

4 **Anthony (D)**—Feb. 21, 1938. Occupation: lawyer. Religion: Episcopalian. Seniority: 151.

CALIFORNIA
1 **Bosco (D)**—July 28, 1946. Occupation: lawyer. Religion: Episcopalian. Seniority: 214.

2 **Chappie (R)**—March 28, 1920. Occupation: rancher. Religion: Roman Catholic. Seniority: 104.

3 **Matsui (D)**—Sept. 17, 1941. Occupation: lawyer. Religion: Methodist. Seniority: 151.

4 **Fazio (D)**—Oct. 11, 1942. Occupation: journalist, public official. Religion: Episcopalian. Seniority: 151.

5 **Burton (D)**—June 1, 1926. Occupation: lawyer. Religion: Unitarian. Seniority: 31.

6 **Boxer (D)**—Nov. 11, 1940. Occupation: stockbroker, journalist. Religion: Jewish. Seniority: 214.

7 **Miller (D)**—May 17, 1945. Occupation: lawyer. Religion: Roman Catholic. Seniority: 82.

8 **Dellums (D)**—Nov. 24, 1935. Occupation: social worker, consultant. Religion: Protestant. Seniority: 57.

9 **Stark (D)**—Nov. 11, 1931. Occupation: banker. Religion: Unitarian. Seniority: 66.

10 **Edwards (D)**—Jan. 6, 1915. Occupation: title company executive, lawyer, FBI agent. Religion: Unitarian. Seniority: 22.

11 **Lantos (D)**—Feb. 1, 1928. Occupation: professor, economist. Religion: Jewish. Seniority: 187.

12 **Zschau (R)**—Jan. 6, 1940. Occupation: microcomputer executive, business professor. Religion: Congregationalist. Seniority: 143.

13 **Mineta (D)**—Nov. 12, 1931. Occupation: insurance executive. Religion: Methodist. Seniority: 82.

14 **Shumway (R)**—July 28, 1934. Occupation: lawyer. Religion: Mormon. Seniority: 74.

15 **Coelho (D)**—June 15, 1942. Occupation: congressional aide. Religion: Roman Catholic. Seniority: 151.

16 **Panetta (D)**—June 28, 1938. Occupation: lawyer. Religion: Roman Catholic. Seniority: 120.

17 **Pashayan (R)**—March 27, 1941. Occupation: lawyer, tire retailer. Religion: Protestant. Seniority: 74.

18 **Lehman (D)**—July 20, 1948. Occupation: legislative aide. Religion: Lutheran. Seniority: 214.

19 **Lagomarsino (R)**—Sept. 4, 1926. Occupation: lawyer. Religion: Roman Catholic. Seniority: 49.

20 **Thomas (R)**—Dec. 6, 1941. Occupation: political science professor. Religion: Baptist. Seniority: 74.

21 **Fiedler (R)**—April 22, 1937. Occupation: author, interior decorator, drug store owner. Religion: Jewish. Seniority: 104.

22 **Moorhead (R)**—May 6, 1922. Occupation: lawyer. Religion: Presbyterian. Seniority: 36.

23 **Beilenson (D)**—Oct. 26, 1932. Occupa-

tion: lawyer. Religion: Jewish. Seniority: 120.

24 Waxman (D)—Sept. 12, 1939. Occupation: lawyer. Religion: Jewish. Seniority: 82.

25 Roybal (D)—Feb. 10, 1916. Occupation: social worker, public health teacher. Religion: Roman Catholic. Seniority: 22.

26 Berman (D)—April 15, 1941. Occupation: lawyer. Religion: Jewish. Seniority: 214.

27 Levine (D)—June 7, 1943. Occupation: lawyer. Religion: Jewish. Seniority: 214.

28 Dixon (D)—Aug. 8, 1934. Occupation: legislative aide, lawyer. Religion: Episcopalian. Seniority: 151.

29 Hawkins (D)—Aug. 31, 1907. Occupation: real estate salesman. Religion: Methodist. Seniority: 22.

30 Martinez (D)—Feb. 14, 1929. Occupation: public official. Religion: Roman Catholic. Seniority: 210.

31 Dymally (D)—May 12, 1926. Occupation: author, special education teacher, data processing executive. Religion: Episcopalian. Seniority: 187.

32 Anderson (D)—Feb. 21, 1913. Occupation: savings and loan executive. Religion: Episcopalian. Seniority: 46.

33 Dreier (R)—July 5, 1952. Occupation: public relations executive. Religion: Christian Scientist. Seniority: 104.

34 Torres (D)—Jan. 27, 1930. Occupation: international trade executive. Religion: Roman Catholic. Seniority: 214.

35 Lewis (R)—Oct. 21, 1934. Occupation: public official, insurance executive. Religion: Presbyterian. Seniority: 74.

36 Brown (D)—March 6, 1920. Occupation: management consultant. Religion: Methodist. Seniority: 64.

37 McCandless (R)—July 23, 1927. Occupation: automobile dealer. Religion: Protestant. Seniority: 143.

38 Patterson (D)—Oct. 25, 1934. Occupation: lawyer. Religion: Congregationalist. Seniority: 82.

39 Dannemeyer (R)—Sept. 22, 1929. Occupation: lawyer. Religion: Lutheran. Seniority: 74.

40 Badham (R)—June 9, 1929. Occupation: hardware company executive. Religion: Lutheran. Seniority: 60.

41 Lowery (R)—May 2, 1947. Occupation: public relations executive. Religion: Roman Catholic. Seniority: 104.

42 Lungren (R)—Sept. 22, 1946. Occupation: lawyer. Religion: Roman Catholic. Seniority: 74.

43 Packard (R)—Jan. 19, 1931. Occupation: dentist. Religion: Mormon. Seniority: 143.

44 Bates (D)—July 21, 1941. Occupation: marketing analyst. Religion: Protestant. Seniority: 214.

45 Hunter (R)—May 31, 1948. Occupation: lawyer. Religion: Baptist. Seniority: 104.

COLORADO

1 Schroeder (D)—July 30, 1940. Occupation: lawyer, law instructor. Religion: Congregationalist. Seniority: 66.

2 Wirth (D)—Sept. 22, 1939. Occupation: corporate executive. Religion: Episcopalian. Seniority: 82.

3 Kogovsek (D)—Aug. 19, 1941. Occupation: public official. Religion: Roman Catholic. Seniority: 151.

4 Brown (R)—Feb. 12, 1940. Occupation: meatpacking company executive, lawyer. Religion: United Church of Christ. Seniority: 104.

5 Kramer (R)—Feb. 19, 1942. Occupation: lawyer. Religion: Jewish. Seniority: 74.

6 Vacant. Rep.-elect Jack Swigert, R, died Dec. 27, 1982.

CONNECTICUT

1 Kennelly (D)—July 10, 1936. Occupation: public official. Religion: Roman Catholic. Seniority: 209.

2 Gejdenson (D)—May 20, 1948. Occupation: dairy farmer. Religion: Jewish. Seniority: 187.

3 Morrison (D)—Oct. 8, 1944. Occupation: lawyer. Religion: Lutheran. Seniority: 214.

4 McKinney (R)—Jan. 30, 1931. Occupation: tire retailer. Religion: Episcopalian. Seniority: 27.

5 Ratchford (D)—May 24, 1934. Occupation: lawyer. Religion: Unitarian. Seniority: 151.

6 Johnson (R)—Jan. 5, 1935. Occupation: civic volunteer. Religion: Unitarian. Seniority: 143.

DELAWARE

AL Carper (D)—Jan. 23, 1947. Occupation: public official. Religion: Presbyterian. Seniority: 214.

FLORIDA

1 Hutto (D)—May 12, 1926. Occupation: advertising executive. Religion: Baptist. Seniority: 151.

2 Fuqua (D)—Aug. 20, 1933. Occupation: farmer. Religion: Presbyterian. Seniority: 22.

3 Bennett (D)—Dec. 2, 1910. Occupation: author, lawyer. Religion: Disciples of Christ. Seniority: 3.

4 Chappell (D)—Feb. 3, 1922. Occupation: lawyer. Religion: Methodist. Seniority: 46.

5 McCollum (R)—July 12, 1944. Occupation: lawyer. Religion: Episcopalian. Seniority: 104.

6 MacKay (D)—March 22, 1933. Occupation: lawyer, citrus grower. Religion: Presbyterian. Seniority: 214.

7 Gibbons (D)—Jan. 20, 1920. Occupation: lawyer. Religion: Presbyterian. Seniority: 22.

8 Young (R)—Dec. 16, 1930. Occupation: insurance executive. Religion: Methodist. Seniority: 27.

9 Bilirakis (R)—July 16, 1930. Occupation: lawyer, businessman. Religion: Greek Orthodox. Seniority: 143.

10 Ireland (D)—Aug. 23, 1930. Occupation: banker. Religion: Episcopalian. Seniority: 120.

11 Nelson (D)—Sept. 29, 1942. Occupation: lawyer. Religion: Episcopalian. Seniority: 151.

12 Lewis (R)—Oct. 26, 1924. Occupation: real estate broker, aircraft testing specialist. Religion: Methodist. Seniority: 143.

13 Mack (R)—Oct. 29, 1940. Occupation: banker. Religion: Roman Catholic. Seniority: 143.

14 Mica (D)—Feb. 4, 1944. Occupation: junior high school teacher, congressional aide. Religion: Roman Catholic. Seniority: 151.

15 Shaw (R)—April 19, 1939. Occupation: nurseryman, lawyer, judge. Religion: Roman Catholic. Seniority: 104.

16 Smith (D)—April 25, 1941. Occupation: lawyer. Religion: Jewish. Seniority: 214.

17 Lehman (D)—Oct. 5, 1913. Occupation: high school English teacher, automobile dealer. Religion: Jewish. Seniority: 66.

18 Pepper (D)—Sept. 8, 1900. Occupation: lawyer. Religion: Baptist. Seniority: 22.

19 Fascell (D)—March 9, 1917. Occupation: lawyer. Religion: Protestant. Seniority: 11.

GEORGIA

1 Thomas (D)—Nov. 20, 1943. Occupation: farmer, investment banker. Religion: Methodist. Seniority: 214.

2 Hatcher (D)—July 1, 1939. Occupation: lawyer. Religion: Episcopalian. Seniority: 187.

3 Ray (D)—Feb. 2, 1927. Occupation: exterminator, legislative aide. Religion: Methodist. Seniority: 214.

4 Levitas (D)—Dec. 26, 1930. Occupation: lawyer. Religion: Jewish. Seniority: 82.

5 Fowler (D)—Oct. 6, 1940. Occupation: lawyer. Religion: Presbyterian. Seniority: 149.

6 Gingrich (R)—June 17, 1943. Occupation: history professor. Religion: Baptist. Seniority: 74.

7 McDonald (D)—April 1, 1935. Occupation: physician. Religion: Independent

Methodist. Seniority: 82.

8 Rowland (D)—Feb. 3, 1926. Occupation: physician. Religion: Methodist. Seniority: 214.

9 Jenkins (D)—Jan. 4, 1933. Occupation: lawyer. Religion: Baptist. Seniority: 120.

10 Barnard (D)—March 20, 1922. Occupation: banker. Religion: Baptist. Seniority: 120.

HAWAII

1 Heftel (D)—Sept. 30, 1924. Occupation: broadcast executive. Religion: Mormon. Seniority: 120.

2 Akaka (D)—Sept. 11, 1924. Occupation: elementary school teacher, public official. Religion: Congregationalist. Seniority: 120.

IDAHO

1 Craig (R)—July 20, 1945. Occupation: real estate salesman, cattle and grain farmer. Religion: Methodist. Seniority: 104.

2 Hansen (R)—Sept. 14, 1930. Occupation: science teacher, printer, insurance salesman. Religion: Mormon. Seniority: 50.

ILLINOIS

1 Washington (D)—April 15, 1922. Occupation: lawyer. Religion: African Methodist Episcopal Zion. Seniority: 187.

2 Savage (D)—Oct. 30, 1925. Occupation: journalist, newspaper publisher. Religion: Protestant. Seniority: 187.

3 Russo (D)—Jan. 23, 1944. Occupation: lawyer. Religion: Roman Catholic. Seniority: 82.

4 O'Brien (R)—June 17, 1917. Occupation: lawyer. Religion: Roman Catholic. Seniority: 27.

5 Lipinski (D)—Dec. 22, 1937. Occupation: public official. Religion: Roman Catholic. Seniority: 214.

6 Hyde (R)—April 18, 1924. Occupation: lawyer. Religion: Roman Catholic. Seniority: 51.

7 Collins (D)—Sept. 24, 1931. Occupation: auditor, accountant. Religion: Baptist. Seniority: 76.

8 Rostenkowski (D)—Jan. 2, 1928. Occupation: insurance executive. Religion: Roman Catholic. Seniority: 15.

9 Yates (D)—Aug. 27, 1909. Occupation: lawyer. Religion: Jewish. Seniority: 32.

10 Porter (R)—June 1, 1935. Occupation: lawyer. Religion: Presbyterian. Seniority: 102.

11 Annunzio (D)—Jan. 12, 1915. Occupation: high school industrial arts teacher, labor union executive. Religion: Roman

Catholic. Seniority: 33.

12 Crane, Philip M. (R)—Nov. 3, 1930. Occupation: American history professor, author. Religion: Methodist. Seniority: 25.

13 Erlenborn (R)—Feb. 8, 1927. Occupation: lawyer. Religion: Roman Catholic. Seniority: 9.

14 Corcoran (R)—May 23, 1939. Occupation: railroad executive, public official. Religion: Roman Catholic. Seniority: 60.

15 Madigan (R)—Jan. 13, 1936. Occupation: automobile leasing company executive. Religion: Roman Catholic. Seniority: 36.

16 Martin (R)—Dec. 26, 1939. Occupation: English teacher. Religion: Roman Catholic. Seniority: 104.

17 Evans (D)—Aug. 4, 1951. Occupation: lawyer. Religion: Roman Catholic. Seniority: 214.

18 Michel (R)—March 2, 1923. Occupation: congressional aide. Religion: Apostolic Christian. Seniority: 1.

19 Crane, Daniel B. (R)—Jan. 10, 1936. Occupation: dentist. Religion: Methodist. Seniority: 74.

20 Durbin (D)—Nov. 21, 1944. Occupation: lawyer. Religion: Roman Catholic. Seniority: 214.

21 Price (D)—Jan. 1, 1905. Occupation: journalist. Religion: Roman Catholic. Seniority: 2.

22 Simon (D)—Nov. 29, 1928. Occupation: author, newspaper editor and publisher. Religion: Lutheran. Seniority: 82.

INDIANA

1 Hall (D)—April 3, 1938. Occupation: social studies teacher. Religion: Baptist. Seniority: 211.

2 Sharp (D)—July 15, 1942. Occupation: political science professor, congressional aide. Religion: Methodist. Seniority: 82.

3 Hiler (R)—April 24, 1953. Occupation: foundry executive. Religion: Roman Catholic. Seniority: 104.

4 Coats (R)—May 16, 1943. Occupation: lawyer. Religion: Protestant. Seniority: 104.

5 Hillis (R)—March 6, 1926. Occupation: lawyer. Religion: Presbyterian. Seniority: 27.

6 Burton (R)—June 21, 1938. Occupation: insurance and real estate agent. Religion: Protestant. Seniority: 143.

7 Myers (R)—Feb. 8, 1927. Occupation: banker, farmer. Religion: Episcopalian. Seniority: 16.

8 McCloskey (D)—June 12, 1939. Occupation: lawyer, journalist. Religion: Roman Catholic. Seniority: 214.

9 Hamilton (D)—April 20, 1931. Occupation: lawyer. Religion: Methodist. Seniority: 33.

10 Jacobs (D)—Feb. 24, 1932. Occupation: lawyer. Religion: Roman Catholic. Seniority: 79.

IOWA

1 Leach (R)—Oct. 15, 1942. Occupation: propane gas marketer. Religion: Episcopalian. Seniority: 60.

2 Tauke (R)—Oct. 11, 1950. Occupation: lawyer. Religion: Roman Catholic. Seniority: 74.

3 Evans (R)—May 26, 1924. Occupation: farmer, engineer. Religion: Methodist. Seniority: 104.

4 Smith (D)—March 23, 1920. Occupation: farmer, lawyer. Religion: Methodist. Seniority: 15.

5 Harkin (D)—Nov. 19, 1939. Occupation: lawyer. Religion: Roman Catholic. Seniority: 82.

6 Bedell (D)—March 5, 1921. Occupation: fishing tackle manufacturer. Religion: Methodist. Seniority: 82.

KANSAS

1 Roberts (R)—April 20, 1936. Occupation: congressional aide. Religion: Methodist. Seniority: 104.

2 Slattery (D)—Aug. 4, 1948. Occupation: lawyer, real estate agent. Religion: Roman Catholic. Seniority: 214.

3 Winn (R)—Aug. 22, 1919. Occupation: home builder, real estate developer. Religion: Christian Church. Seniority: 16.

4 Glickman (D)—Nov. 24, 1944. Occupation: lawyer. Religion: Jewish. Seniority: 120.

5 Whittaker (R)—Sept. 18, 1939. Occupation: optometrist. Religion: Christian Church. Seniority: 74.

KENTUCKY

1 Hubbard (D)—July 7, 1937. Occupation: lawyer. Religion: Baptist. Seniority: 82.

2 Natcher (D)—Sept. 11, 1909. Occupation: lawyer. Religion: Baptist. Seniority: 10.

3 Mazzoli (D)—Nov. 2, 1932. Occupation: lawyer. Religion: Roman Catholic. Seniority: 57.

4 Snyder (R)—Jan. 26, 1928. Occupation: farmer, real estate salesman, lawyer. Religion: Lutheran. Seniority: 15.

5 Rogers (R)—Dec. 31, 1937. Occupation: lawyer. Religion: Baptist. Seniority: 104.

6 Hopkins (R)—Oct. 25, 1933. Occupation: stockbroker. Religion: Methodist. Seniority: 74.

7 Perkins (D)—Oct. 15, 1912. Occupation: lawyer. Religion: Baptist. Seniority: 3.

LOUISIANA

1 Livingston (R)—April 30, 1943. Occupation: lawyer. Religion: Episcopalian. Seniority: 71.

2 Boggs (D)—March 13, 1916. Occupation: high school teacher. Religion: Roman Catholic. Seniority: 75.

3 Tauzin (D)—June 14, 1943. Occupation: lawyer. Religion: Roman Catholic. Seniority: 185.

4 Roemer (D)—Oct. 4, 1943. Occupation: farmer, banker, data processing executive. Religion: Methodist. Seniority: 187.

5 Huckaby (D)—July 19, 1941. Occupation: farmer, engineer, corporate executive. Religion: Methodist. Seniority: 120.

6 Moore (R)—Oct. 4, 1939. Occupation: lawyer. Religion: Episcopalian. Seniority: 58.

7 Breaux (D)—March 1, 1944. Occupation: lawyer. Religion: Roman Catholic. Seniority: 63.

8 Long (D)—May 4, 1923. Occupation: lawyer, farmer, investment broker. Religion: Baptist. Seniority: 65.

MAINE

1 McKernan (R)—May 20, 1948. Occupation: lawyer. Religion: Protestant. Seniority: 143.

2 Snowe (R)—Feb. 21, 1947. Occupation: public official. Religion: Greek Orthodox. Seniority: 74.

MARYLAND

1 Dyson (D)—Nov. 15, 1948. Occupation: lumber company executive. Religion: Roman Catholic. Seniority: 187.

2 Long (D)—Dec. 11, 1908. Occupation: economics professor, author. Religion: Presbyterian. Seniority: 22.

3 Mikulski (D)—July 20, 1936. Occupation: social work professor, social worker. Religion: Roman Catholic. Seniority: 120.

4 Holt (R)—Sept. 17, 1920. Occupation: lawyer. Religion: Presbyterian. Seniority: 36.

5 Hoyer (D)—June 14, 1939. Occupation: lawyer. Religion: Baptist. Seniority: 207.

6 Byron (D)—July 27, 1932. Occupation: civic volunteer. Religion: Episcopalian. Seniority: 151.

7 Mitchell (D)—April 29, 1922. Occupation: sociology professor. Religion: Episcopalian. Seniority: 57.

8 Barnes (D)—Sept. 3, 1943. Occupation: lawyer. Religion: Protestant. Seniority: 151.

MASSACHUSETTS

1 Conte (R)—Nov. 9, 1921. Occupation: lawyer. Religion: Roman Catholic. Seniority: 3.

2 Boland (D)—Oct. 1, 1911. Occupation: public official. Religion: Roman Catholic. Seniority: 7.

3 Early (D)—Jan. 31, 1933. Occupation: teacher, basketball coach. Religion: Roman Catholic. Seniority: 82.

4 Frank (D)—March 31, 1940. Occupation: public official. Religion: Jewish. Seniority: 187.

5 Shannon (D)—April 4, 1952. Occupation: lawyer. Religion: Roman Catholic. Seniority: 151.

6 Mavroules (D)—Nov. 1, 1929. Occupation: personnel supervisor. Religion: Greek Orthodox. Seniority: 151.

7 Markey (D)—July 11, 1946. Occupation: lawyer. Religion: Roman Catholic. Seniority: 118.

8 O'Neill (D)—Dec. 9, 1912. Occupation: insurance broker. Religion: Roman Catholic. Seniority: 7.

9 Moakley (D)—April 27, 1927. Occupation: lawyer. Religion: Roman Catholic. Seniority: 66.

10 Studds (D)—May 12, 1937. Occupation: high school teacher. Religion: Episcopalian. Seniority: 66.

11 Donnelly (D)—March 2, 1947. Occupation: high school teacher. Religion: Roman Catholic. Seniority: 151.

MICHIGAN

1 Conyers (D)—May 16, 1929. Occupation: lawyer. Religion: Baptist. Seniority: 33.

2 Pursell (R)—Dec. 19, 1932. Occupation: publisher, high school teacher, real estate salesman, office equipment retailer. Religion: Baptist. Seniority: 60.

3 Wolpe (D)—Nov. 2, 1939. Occupation: author, political science professor, congressional aide. Religion: Jewish. Seniority: 151.

4 Siljander (R)—June 11, 1951. Occupation: restaurant executive. Religion: unspecified Christian. Seniority: 140.

5 Sawyer (R)—March 21, 1920. Occupation: lawyer. Religion: Episcopalian. Seniority: 60.

6 Carr (D)—March 27, 1943. Occupation: lawyer. Religion: Baptist. Seniority: 212.

7 Kildee (D)—Sept. 16, 1929. Occupation: Latin teacher. Religion: Roman Catholic. Seniority: 120.

8 Traxler (D)—July 21, 1931. Occupation: lawyer. Religion: Episcopalian. Seniority: 78.

9 Vander Jagt (R)—Aug. 26, 1931. Occupation: lawyer. Religion: Presbyterian. Seniority: 14.

10 Albosta (D)—Dec. 5, 1925. Occupation: farmer. Religion: Roman Catholic. Seniority: 151.

11 Davis (R)—July 31, 1932. Occupation: funeral director. Religion: Episcopalian. Seniority: 74.

12 Bonior (D)—June 6, 1945. Occupation: public official. Religion: Roman Catholic. Seniority: 120.

13 Crockett (D)—Aug. 10, 1909. Occupation: lawyer, judge. Religion: Baptist. Seniority: 186.

14 Hertel (D)—Dec. 7, 1948. Occupation: lawyer. Religion: Roman Catholic. Seniority: 187.

15 Ford (D)—Aug. 6, 1927. Occupation: lawyer. Religion: United Church of Christ. Seniority: 33.

16 Dingell (D)—July 8, 1926. Occupation: lawyer. Religion: Roman Catholic. Seniority: 13.

17 Levin (D)—Sept. 6, 1931. Occupation: lawyer. Religion: Jewish. Seniority: 214.

18 Broomfield (R)—April 28, 1922. Occupation: insurance salesman. Religion: Presbyterian. Seniority: 1.

MINNESOTA

1 Penny (D)—Nov. 19, 1951. Occupation: sales representative. Religion: Lutheran. Seniority: 214.

2 Weber (R)—July 24, 1952. Occupation: newspaper publisher. Religion: Roman Catholic. Seniority: 104.

3 Frenzel (R)—July 31, 1928. Occupation: warehouse company executive. Religion: unspecified. Seniority: 27.

4 Vento (D)—Oct. 7, 1940. Occupation: science teacher. Religion: Roman Catholic. Seniority: 120.

5 Sabo (D)—Feb. 28, 1938. Occupation: public official. Religion: Lutheran. Seniority: 151.

6 Sikorski (D)—April 26, 1948. Occupation: lawyer. Religion: Roman Catholic. Seniority: 214.

7 Stangeland (R)—Feb. 8, 1930. Occupation: farmer. Religion: Lutheran. Seniority: 70.

8 Oberstar (D)—Sept. 10, 1934. Occupation: congressional aide. Religion: Roman Catholic. Seniority: 82.

MISSISSIPPI

1 Whitten (D)—April 18, 1910. Occupation: author, lawyer, grammar school teacher and principal. Religion: Presbyterian. Seniority: 1.

2 Franklin (R)—Dec. 13, 1941. Occupation: lawyer. Religion: Episcopalian. Seniority: 143.

3 Montgomery (D)—Aug. 5, 1920. Occupation: insurance executive. Religion: Episcopalian. Seniority: 41.

4 **Dowdy (D)**—July 27, 1943. Occupation: broadcasting executive, lawyer. Religion: Methodist. Seniority: 208.

5 **Lott (R)**—Oct. 9, 1941. Occupation: lawyer. Religion: Baptist. Seniority: 36.

MISSOURI

1 **Clay (D)**—April 30, 1931. Occupation: real estate broker, insurance company executive. Religion: Roman Catholic. Seniority: 46.

2 **Young (D)**—Nov. 27, 1923. Occupation: pipe fitter. Religion: Roman Catholic. Seniority: 120.

3 **Gephardt (D)**—Jan. 31, 1941. Occupation: lawyer. Religion: Baptist. Seniority: 120.

4 **Skelton (D)**—Dec. 20, 1931. Occupation: lawyer. Religion: Christian Church. Seniority: 120.

5 **Wheat (D)**—Oct. 16, 1951. Occupation: public official. Religion: Church of Christ. Seniority: 214.

6 **Coleman (R)**—May 29, 1943. Occupation: lawyer. Religion: Protestant. Seniority: 59.

7 **Taylor (R)**—Feb. 10, 1928. Occupation: automobile dealer. Religion: Methodist. Seniority: 36.

8 **Emerson (R)**—Jan. 1, 1938. Occupation: corporate executive. Religion: Presbyterian. Seniority: 104.

9 **Volkmer (D)**—April 4, 1931. Occupation: lawyer. Religion: Roman Catholic. Seniority: 120.

MONTANA

1 **Williams (D)**—Oct. 30, 1937. Occupation: elementary and secondary school teacher. Religion: Roman Catholic. Seniority: 151.

2 **Marlenee (R)**—Aug. 8, 1935. Occupation: rancher. Religion: Lutheran. Seniority: 60.

NEBRASKA

1 **Bereuter (R)**—Oct. 6, 1939. Occupation: residential and commercial development consultant, automobile and hardware dealer. Religion: Lutheran. Seniority: 74.

2 **Daub (R)**—April 23, 1941. Occupation: lawyer, feed company executive. Religion: Presbyterian. Seniority: 104.

3 **Smith (R)**—June 30, 1911. Occupation: farmer. Religion: Methodist. Seniority: 51.

NEVADA

1 **Reid (D)**—Dec. 2, 1939. Occupation: lawyer. Religion: Mormon. Seniority: 214.

2 **Vucanovich (R)**—June 22, 1921. Occu-

pation: congressional aide. Religion: Roman Catholic. Seniority: 143.

NEW HAMPSHIRE

1 **D'Amours (D)**—Oct. 14, 1937. Occupation: lawyer. Religion: Roman Catholic. Seniority: 82.

2 **Gregg (R)**—Feb. 14, 1947. Occupation: lawyer. Religion: Protestant. Seniority: 104.

NEW JERSEY

1 **Florio (D)**—Aug. 29, 1937. Occupation: lawyer. Religion: Roman Catholic. Seniority: 82.

2 **Hughes (D)**—Oct. 17, 1932. Occupation: lawyer. Religion: Episcopalian. Seniority: 82.

3 **Howard (D)**—July 24, 1927. Occupation: elementary school teacher. Religion: Roman Catholic. Seniority: 33.

4 **Smith (R)**—March 4, 1953. Occupation: sporting goods wholesaler. Religion: Roman Catholic. Seniority: 104.

5 **Roukema (R)**—Sept. 19, 1929. Occupation: high school history and government teacher. Religion: Protestant. Seniority: 104.

6 **Dwyer (D)**—Jan. 24, 1921. Occupation: insurance salesman. Religion: Roman Catholic. Seniority: 187.

7 **Rinaldo (R)**—Sept. 1, 1931. Occupation: industrial relations consultant. Religion: Roman Catholic. Seniority: 36.

8 **Roe (D)**—Feb. 28, 1924. Occupation: corporate executive. Religion: Roman Catholic. Seniority: 56.

9 **Torricelli (D)**—Aug. 26, 1951. Occupation: lawyer. Religion: Methodist. Seniority: 214.

10 **Rodino (D)**—June 7, 1909. Occupation: lawyer. Religion: Roman Catholic. Seniority: 3.

11 **Minish (D)**—Sept. 1, 1916. Occupation: labor union executive. Religion: Roman Catholic. Seniority: 22.

12 **Courter (R)**—Oct. 14, 1941. Occupation: lawyer. Religion: Methodist. Seniority: 74.

13 **Forsythe (R)**—Jan. 17, 1916. Occupation: dairy farm manager, association executive. Religion: Society of Friends. Seniority: 26.

14 **Guarini (D)**—Aug. 20, 1924. Occupation: lawyer. Religion: Roman Catholic. Seniority: 151.

NEW MEXICO

1 **Lujan (R)**—May 12, 1928. Occupation: insurance broker. Religion: Roman Catholic. Seniority: 21.

2 **Skeen (R)**—June 30, 1927. Occupation: rancher. Religion: Roman Catholic. Seniority: 104.

3 **Richardson (D)**—Nov. 15, 1947. Occupation: business consultant. Religion: Roman Catholic. Seniority: 214.

NEW YORK

1 **Carney (R)**—July 1, 1942. Occupation: heavy equipment sales representative. Religion: Roman Catholic. Seniority: 74.

2 **Downey (D)**—Jan. 28, 1949. Occupation: public official. Religion: Methodist. Seniority: 82.

3 **Mrazek (D)**—Nov. 5, 1945. Occupation: public official. Religion: Methodist. Seniority: 214.

4 **Lent (R)**—March 23, 1931. Occupation: lawyer. Religion: Methodist. Seniority: 27.

5 **McGrath (R)**—March 27, 1942. Occupation: public official. Religion: Roman Catholic. Seniority: 104.

6 **Addabbo (D)**—March 17, 1925. Occupation: lawyer. Religion: Roman Catholic. Seniority: 18.

7 **Vacant.** Rep. Benjamin S. Rosenthal, D (1962-83), died Jan. 4, 1983.

8 **Scheuer (D)**—Feb. 6, 1920. Occupation: lawyer. Religion: Jewish. Seniority: 79.

9 **Ferraro (D)**—Aug. 26, 1935. Occupation: lawyer. Religion: Roman Catholic. Seniority: 151.

10 **Schumer (D)**—Nov. 23, 1950. Occupation: lawyer. Religion: Jewish. Seniority: 187.

11 **Towns (D)**—July 21, 1934. Occupation: social worker. Religion: Presbyterian. Seniority: 214.

12 **Owens (D)**—June 28, 1936. Occupation: librarian. Religion: Baptist. Seniority: 214.

13 **Solarz (D)**—Sept. 12, 1940. Occupation: public official. Religion: Jewish. Seniority: 82.

14 **Molinari (R)**—Nov. 23, 1928. Occupation: lawyer. Religion: Roman Catholic. Seniority: 104.

15 **Green (R)**—Oct. 16, 1929. Occupation: lawyer. Religion: Jewish. Seniority: 72.

16 **Rangel (D)**—June 11, 1930. Occupation: lawyer. Religion: Roman Catholic. Seniority: 57.

17 **Weiss (D)**—Sept. 17, 1927. Occupation: lawyer. Religion: Jewish. Seniority: 120.

18 **Garcia (D)**—Jan. 9, 1933. Occupation: computer engineer. Religion: Protestant. Seniority: 150.

19 **Biaggi (D)**—Oct. 26, 1917. Occupation: lawyer, police detective. Religion: Roman Catholic. Seniority: 46.

20 **Ottinger (D)**—Jan. 27, 1929. Occupation: lawyer. Religion: Jewish. Seniority: 81.

21 **Fish (R)**—June 3, 1926. Occupation: lawyer. Religion: Episcopalian. Seniority: 21.

22 Gilman (R)—Dec. 6, 1922. Occupation: lawyer. Religion: Jewish. Seniority: 36.

23 Stratton (D)—Sept. 27, 1916. Occupation: public official, radio and television announcer and newscaster. Religion: Presbyterian. Seniority: 15.

24 Solomon (R)—Aug. 14, 1930. Occupation: investment and insurance broker. Religion: Presbyterian. Seniority: 74.

25 Boehlert (R)—Sept. 28, 1936. Occupation: congressional aide. Religion: Roman Catholic. Seniority: 143.

26 Martin (R)—April 26, 1944. Occupation: lawyer. Religion: Roman Catholic. Seniority: 104.

27 Wortley (R)—Dec. 8, 1926. Occupation: newspaper publisher. Religion: Roman Catholic. Seniority: 104.

28 McHugh (D)—Dec. 6, 1938. Occupation: lawyer. Religion: Roman Catholic. Seniority: 82.

29 Horton (R)—Dec. 12, 1919. Occupation: lawyer. Religion: Presbyterian. Seniority: 5.

30 Conable (R)—Nov. 2, 1922. Occupation: lawyer. Religion: Methodist. Seniority: 9.

31 Kemp (R)—July 13, 1935. Occupation: professional football player, radio and television commentator. Religion: Presbyterian. Seniority: 27.

32 LaFalce (D)—Oct. 6, 1939. Occupation: lawyer. Religion: Roman Catholic. Seniority: 82.

33 Nowak (D)—Feb. 21, 1935. Occupation: lawyer. Religion: Roman Catholic. Seniority: 82.

34 Lundine (D)—Feb. 4, 1939. Occupation: lawyer. Religion: Protestant. Seniority: 116.

NORTH CAROLINA

1 Jones (D)—Aug. 19, 1913. Occupation: office supply company executive. Religion: Baptist. Seniority: 40.

2 Valentine (D)—March 15, 1926. Occupation: lawyer. Religion: Baptist. Seniority: 214.

3 Whitley (D)—Jan. 3, 1927. Occupation: congressional aide. Religion: Baptist. Seniority: 120.

4 Andrews (D)—Sept. 2, 1925. Occupation: lawyer. Religion: Baptist. Seniority: 66.

5 Neal (D)—Nov. 7, 1934. Occupation: newspaper publisher, mortgage banker. Religion: Episcopalian. Seniority: 82.

6 Britt (D)—June 29, 1942. Occupation: lawyer. Religion: Methodist. Seniority: 214.

7 Rose (D)—Aug. 10, 1939. Occupation: lawyer. Religion: Presbyterian. Seniority: 66.

8 Hefner (D)—April 11, 1930. Occupation: broadcasting executive. Religion: Baptist. Seniority: 82.

9 Martin (D)—Dec. 11, 1935. Occupation: chemistry professor. Religion: Presbyterian. Seniority: 36.

10 Broyhill (R)—Aug. 19, 1927. Occupation: furniture manufacturing executive. Religion: Baptist. Seniority: 5.

11 Clarke (D)—June 12, 1917. Occupation: farmer, foundation secretary. Religion: Presbyterian. Seniority: 214.

NORTH DAKOTA

AL Dorgan (D)—May 14, 1942. Occupation: public official. Religion: Lutheran. Seniority: 187.

OHIO

1 Luken (D)—July 9, 1925. Occupation: lawyer. Religion: Roman Catholic. Seniority: 119.

2 Gradison (R)—Dec. 28, 1928. Occupation: investment broker. Religion: Jewish. Seniority: 51.

3 Hall (D)—Jan. 16, 1942. Occupation: real estate broker. Religion: Presbyterian. Seniority: 151.

4 Oxley (R)—Feb. 11, 1944. Occupation: FBI agent, lawyer. Religion: Lutheran. Seniority: 141.

5 Latta (R)—March 5, 1920. Occupation: lawyer. Religion: Church of Christ. Seniority: 3.

6 McEwen (R)—Jan. 12, 1950. Occupation: real estate developer. Religion: Protestant. Seniority: 104.

7 DeWine (R)—Jan. 5, 1947. Occupation: lawyer. Religion: Roman Catholic. Seniority: 143.

8 Kindness (R)—Aug. 26, 1929. Occupation: lawyer. Religion: Presbyterian. Seniority: 51.

9 Kaptur (D)—June 17, 1946. Occupation: urban planner. Religion: Roman Catholic. Seniority: 214.

10 Miller (R)—Nov. 1, 1917. Occupation: electrical engineer. Religion: Methodist. Seniority: 16.

11 Eckart (D)—April 6, 1950. Occupation: lawyer. Religion: Roman Catholic. Seniority: 187.

12 Kasich (R)—May 13, 1952. Occupation: legislative aide. Religion: Roman Catholic. Seniority: 143.

13 Pease (D)—Sept. 26, 1931. Occupation: editor. Religion: Protestant. Seniority: 120.

14 Seiberling (D)—Sept. 8, 1918. Occupation: lawyer. Religion: Presbyterian. Seniority: 57.

15 Wylie (R)—Nov. 23, 1920. Occupation: lawyer. Religion: Methodist. Seniority: 16.

16 Regula (R)—Dec. 3, 1924. Occupation: lawyer. Religion: Episcopalian. Seniority: 36.

17 Williams (R)—Aug. 23, 1942. Occupation: barber. Religion: Church of Christ. Seniority: 74.

18 Applegate (D)—March 27, 1928. Occupation: salesman, real estate broker. Religion: Presbyterian. Seniority: 120.

19 Feighan (D)—Oct. 22, 1947. Occupation: lawyer. Religion: Roman Catholic. Seniority: 214.

20 Oakar (D)—March 5, 1940. Occupation: high school English and drama teacher. Religion: Roman Catholic. Seniority: 120.

21 Stokes (D)—Feb. 23, 1925. Occupation: lawyer. Religion: African Methodist Episcopal Zion. Seniority: 46.

OKLAHOMA

1 Jones (D)—May 5, 1939. Occupation: lawyer. Religion: Roman Catholic. Seniority: 66.

2 Synar (D)—Oct. 17, 1950. Occupation: lawyer, rancher, real estate broker. Religion: Episcopalian. Seniority: 151.

3 Watkins (D)—Dec. 15, 1938. Occupation: real estate broker, home builder. Religion: Presbyterian. Seniority: 120.

4 McCurdy (D)—March 30, 1950. Occupation: lawyer. Religion: Lutheran. Seniority: 187.

5 Edwards (R)—July 12, 1937. Occupation: author, journalist, lawyer. Religion: Episcopalian. Seniority: 60.

6 English (D)—Nov. 30, 1940. Occupation: petroleum landman. Religion: Methodist. Seniority: 82.

OREGON

1 AuCoin (D)—Oct. 21, 1942. Occupation: journalist, public relations officer, architectural firm administrator. Religion: Protestant. Seniority 82.

2 Smith, Bob (R)—June 16, 1931. Occupation: cattle rancher. Religion: Presbyterian. Seniority: 143.

3 Wyden (D)—May 3, 1949. Occupation: lawyer. Religion: Jewish. Seniority: 187.

4 Weaver (D)—Aug. 8, 1927. Occupation: home builder. Religion: Protestant. Seniority: 82.

5 Smith, Denny (R)—Jan. 19, 1938. Occupation: newspaper publisher, airline pilot. Religion: Protestant. Seniority: 104.

PENNSYLVANIA

1 Foglietta (D)—Dec. 3, 1928. Occupation: lawyer. Religion: Roman Catholic. Seniority: 187.

2 Gray (D)—Aug. 20, 1941. Occupation: clergyman. Religion: Baptist. Seniority: 151.

3 Borski (D)—Oct. 20, 1948. Occupation: stockbroker. Religion: Roman Catholic. Seniority: 214.

4 Kolter (D)—Sept. 3, 1926. Occupation: accountant. Religion: Roman Catholic. Seniority: 214.

5 Schulze (R)—Aug. 7, 1929. Occupation: household appliance retailer, public official. Religion: Presbyterian. Seniority: 51.

6 Yatron (D)—Oct. 16, 1927. Occupation: professional boxer, ice cream manufacturer. Religion: Greek Orthodox. Seniority: 46.

7 Edgar (D)—May 29, 1943. Occupation: clergyman. Religion: Methodist. Seniority: 82.

8 Kostmayer (D)—Sept. 27, 1946. Occupation: public relations consultant. Religion: Episcopalian. Seniority: 213.

9 Shuster (R)—Jan. 23, 1932. Occupation: corporate executive. Religion: United Church of Christ. Seniority: 36.

10 McDade (R)—Sept. 29, 1931. Occupation: lawyer. Religion: Roman Catholic. Seniority: 5.

11 Harrison (D)—Feb. 2, 1940. Occupation: lawyer, college professor. Religion: Roman Catholic. Seniority: 214.

12 Murtha (D)—June 17, 1932. Occupation: car wash operator. Religion: Roman Catholic. Seniority: 77.

13 Coughlin (R)—April 11, 1929. Occupation: lawyer. Religion: Episcopalian. Seniority: 21.

14 Coyne (D)—Aug. 24, 1936. Occupation: accountant. Religion: Roman Catholic. Seniority: 187.

15 Ritter (R)—Oct. 21, 1940. Occupation: engineering consultant and professor. Religion: Unitarian. Seniority: 74.

16 Walker (R)—Dec. 23, 1942. Occupation: high school teacher, congressional aide. Religion: Presbyterian. Seniority: 60.

17 Gekas (R)—April 14, 1930. Occupation: lawyer. Religion: Greek Orthodox. Seniority: 143.

18 Walgren (D)—Dec. 28, 1940. Occupation: lawyer. Religion: Roman Catholic. Seniority: 120.

19 Goodling (R)—Dec. 5, 1927. Occupation: public school superintendent. Religion: Methodist. Seniority: 51.

20 Gaydos (D)—July 3, 1926. Occupation: lawyer. Religion: Roman Catholic. Seniority: 45.

21 Ridge (R)—Aug. 26, 1945. Occupation: lawyer. Religion: Roman Catholic. Seniority: 143.

22 Murphy (D)—June 17, 1927. Occupation: lawyer. Religion: Roman Catholic. Seniority: 120.

23 Clinger (R)—April 4, 1929. Occupation: lawyer. Religion: Presbyterian. Seniority: 74.

RHODE ISLAND

1 St Germain (D)—Jan. 9, 1928. Occupation: lawyer. Religion: Roman Catholic. Seniority: 18.

2 Schneider (R)—March 25, 1947. Occupation: television producer and moderator. Religion: Roman Catholic. Seniority: 104.

SOUTH CAROLINA

1 Hartnett (R)—Aug. 7, 1941. Occupation: businessman. Religion: Roman Catholic. Seniority: 104.

2 Spence (R)—April 9, 1928. Occupation: lawyer. Religion: Lutheran. Seniority: 27.

3 Derrick (D)—Sept. 30, 1936. Occupation: lawyer. Religion: Episcopalian. Seniority: 82.

4 Campbell (R)—July 24, 1940. Occupation: farmer, real estate broker, parking lot president, restaurant executive. Religion: Episcopalian. Seniority: 74.

5 Spratt (D)—Nov. 1, 1942. Occupation: lawyer. Religion: Presbyterian. Seniority: 214.

6 Tallon (D)—Aug. 8, 1946. Occupation: clothing store executive. Religion: Methodist. Seniority: 214.

SOUTH DAKOTA

AL Daschle (D)—Dec. 9, 1947. Occupation: congressional aide. Religion: Roman Catholic. Seniority: 151.

TENNESSEE

1 Quillen (R)—Jan. 11, 1916. Occupation: newspaper publisher, real estate and insurance salesman. Religion: Methodist. Seniority: 5.

2 Duncan (R)—March 24, 1919. Occupation: lawyer. Religion: Presbyterian. Seniority: 9.

3 Bouquard (D)—Jan. 3, 1929. Occupation: radio station manager. Religion: Church of Christ. Seniority: 82.

4 Cooper (D)—June 19, 1954. Occupation: lawyer. Religion: Presbyterian. Seniority: 214.

5 Boner (D)—Feb. 14, 1945. Occupation: high school and college teacher and coach, banker, lawyer. Religion: Methodist. Seniority: 151.

6 Gore (D)—March 31, 1948. Occupation: journalist, home builder. Religion: Baptist. Seniority: 120.

7 Sundquist (R)—March 15, 1936. Occupation: marketing and printing company owner. Religion: Lutheran. Seniority: 143.

8 Jones (D)—April 20, 1912. Occupation: agricultural representative. Religion: Presbyterian. Seniority: 54.

9 Ford (D)—May 20, 1945. Occupation: mortician. Religion: Baptist. Seniority: 82.

TEXAS

1 Hall, Sam B. Jr. (D)—Jan. 11, 1924. Occupation: lawyer. Religion: Church of Christ. Seniority: 117.

2 Wilson (D)—June 1, 1933. Occupation: lumberyard executive. Religion: Methodist. Seniority: 66.

3 Bartlett (R)—Sept. 19, 1947. Occupation: tool and plastics company owner. Religion: Presbyterian. Seniority: 143.

4 Hall, Ralph M. (D)—May 3, 1923. Occupation: feed company executive, banker, lawyer, judge. Religion: Methodist. Seniority: 187.

5 Bryant (D)—Feb. 22, 1947. Occupation: lawyer. Religion: Methodist. Seniority: 214.

6 Vacant. Rep. Phil Gramm, D (1979-83), resigned Jan. 5, 1983.

7 Archer (R)—March 22, 1928. Occupation: lawyer, feed company executive. Religion: Roman Catholic. Seniority: 27.

8 Fields (R)—Feb. 3, 1952. Occupation: lawyer, cemetery executive. Religion: Baptist. Seniority: 104.

9 Brooks (D)—Dec. 18, 1922. Occupation: lawyer. Religion: Methodist. Seniority: 7.

10 Pickle (D)—Oct. 11, 1913. Occupation: public relations and advertising executive. Religion: Methodist. Seniority: 30.

11 Leath (D)—May 6, 1931. Occupation: banker. Religion: Presbyterian. Seniority: 151.

12 Wright (D)—Dec. 22, 1922. Occupation: advertising executive. Religion: Presbyterian. Seniority: 11.

13 Hightower (D)—Sept. 6, 1926. Occupation: lawyer. Religion: Baptist. Seniority: 82.

14 Patman (D)—March 26, 1927. Occupation: lawyer, rancher. Religion: Methodist. Seniority: 187.

15 de la Garza (D)—Sept. 22, 1927. Occupation: lawyer. Religion: Roman Catholic. Seniority: 33.

16 Coleman (D)—Nov. 29, 1941. Occupation: lawyer. Religion: Presbyterian. Seniority: 214.

17 Stenholm (D)—Oct. 26, 1938. Occupation: cotton grower. Religion: Lutheran. Seniority: 151.

18 Leland (D)—Nov. 27, 1944. Occupation: pharmacist. Religion: Roman Catholic. Seniority: 151.

19 Hance (D)—Nov. 14, 1942. Occupation: lawyer. Religion: Baptist. Seniority: 151.

20 Gonzalez (D)—May 3, 1916. Occupation: lawyer, public official. Religion: Roman Catholic. Seniority: 21.

21 Loeffler (R)—Aug. 1, 1946. Occupation:

rancher, lawyer. Religion: Lutheran. Seniority: 74.

22 Paul (R)—Aug. 20, 1935. Occupation: physician. Religion: Episcopalian. Seniority: 73.

23 Kazen (D)—Jan. 17, 1919. Occupation: lawyer. Religion: Roman Catholic. Seniority: 41.

24 Frost (D)—Jan. 1, 1942. Occupation: lawyer. Religion: Jewish. Seniority: 151.

25 Andrews (D)—Feb. 7, 1944. Occupation: lawyer. Religion: Methodist. Seniority: 214.

26 Vandergriff (D)—Jan. 29, 1926. Occupation: automobile and insurance agent. Religion: Methodist. Seniority: 214.

27 Ortiz (D)—June 3, 1937. Occupation: law enforcement official. Religion: Methodist. Seniority: 214.

UTAH

1 Hansen (R)—Aug. 14, 1932. Occupation: insurance executive, land developer. Religion: Mormon. Seniority: 104.

2 Marriott (R)—Nov. 2, 1939. Occupation: pension consultant, insurance underwriter. Religion: Mormon. Seniority: 60.

3 Nielson (R)—Sept. 12, 1924. Occupation: statistics professor. Religion: Mormon. Seniority: 143.

VERMONT

AL Jeffords (R)—May 11, 1934. Occupation: lawyer. Religion: Congregationalist. Seniority: 51.

VIRGINIA

1 Bateman (R)—Aug. 7, 1928. Occupation: lawyer. Religion: Protestant. Seniority: 143.

2 Whitehurst (R)—March 12, 1925. Occupation: history professor, broadcast journalist. Religion: Methodist. Seniority: 21.

3 Bliley (R)—Jan. 28, 1932. Occupation: funeral director. Religion: Roman Catholic. Seniority: 104.

4 Sisisky (D)—June 9, 1927. Occupation: beer and soft drink distributor. Religion: Jewish. Seniority: 214.

5 Daniel (D)—May 12, 1914. Occupation: textile company executive. Religion: Baptist. Seniority: 46.

6 Olin (D)—Feb. 28, 1920. Occupation: corporate executive. Religion: Unitarian. Seniority: 214.

7 Robinson (R)—May 14, 1916. Occupation: farmer, orchardist, businessman. Religion: Society of Friends. Seniority: 27.

8 Parris (R)—Sept. 9, 1929. Occupation: automobile dealer, commercial pilot,

banker. Religion: Episcopalian. Seniority: 103.

9 Boucher (D)—Aug. 1, 1946. Occupation: lawyer. Religion: Methodist. Seniority: 214.

10 Wolf (R)—Jan. 30, 1939. Occupation: lawyer. Religion: Presbyterian. Seniority: 104.

WASHINGTON

1 Pritchard (R)—May 5, 1925. Occupation: envelope manufacturer. Religion: Presbyterian. Seniority: 36.

2 Swift (D)—Sept. 12, 1935. Occupation: broadcaster. Religion: Unitarian. Seniority: 151.

3 Bonker (D)—March 7, 1937. Occupation: auditor. Religion: Presbyterian. Seniority: 82.

4 Morrison (R)—May 13, 1933. Occupation: fruit grower, nurseryman. Religion: Methodist. Seniority: 104.

5 Foley (D)—March 6, 1929. Occupation: lawyer. Religion: Roman Catholic. Seniority: 33.

6 Dicks (D)—Dec. 14, 1940. Occupation: lawyer, congressional aide. Religion: Lutheran. Seniority: 120.

7 Lowry (D)—March 8, 1939. Occupation: public official. Religion: Baptist. Seniority: 151.

8 Chandler (R)—July 13, 1942. Occupation: public relations consultant, television newsman. Religion: Protestant. Seniority: 143.

WEST VIRGINIA

1 Mollohan (D)—May 14, 1943. Occupation: lawyer. Religion: Baptist. Seniority: 214.

2 Staggers (D)—Feb. 22, 1951. Occupation: lawyer. Religion: Roman Catholic.

Seniority: 214.

3 Wise (D)—Jan. 6, 1948. Occupation: lawyer. Religion: Episcopalian. Seniority: 214.

4 Rahall (D)—May 20, 1949. Occupation: broadcasting executive, travel agent. Religion: Presbyterian. Seniority: 120.

WISCONSIN

1 Aspin (D)—July 21, 1938. Occupation: economics professor. Religion: Episcopalian. Seniority: 57.

2 Kastenmeier (D)—Jan. 24, 1924. Occupation: lawyer. Religion: unspecified. Seniority: 14.

3 Gunderson (R)—May 10, 1951. Occupation: public official. Religion: Lutheran. Seniority: 104.

4 Zablocki (D)—Nov. 18, 1912. Occupation: teacher, musician. Religion: Roman Catholic. Seniority: 3.

5 Moody (D)—Sept. 2, 1935. Occupation: economist. Religion: Protestant. Seniority: 214.

6 Petri (R)—May 28, 1940. Occupation: lawyer. Religion: Lutheran. Seniority: 101.

7 Obey (D)—Oct. 3, 1938. Occupation: real estate broker. Religion: Roman Catholic. Seniority: 55.

8 Roth (R)—Oct. 10, 1938. Occupation: real estate broker. Religion: Roman Catholic. Seniority: 74.

9 Sensenbrenner (R)—June 14, 1943. Occupation: lawyer. Religion: Episcopalian. Seniority: 74.

WYOMING

AL Cheney (R)—Jan. 30, 1941. Occupation: financial consultant. Religion: Methodist. Seniority: 74.

Seniority in the 98th Congress

Senate Seniority

Senate rank generally is determined according to the official date of the beginning of a member's service, which is Jan. 3, except in the case of new members sworn in at times other than the beginning of a Congress. For those appointed or elected to fill unexpired terms, the date of the appointment, certification or swearing-in determines the senator's rank.

When members are sworn in on the same day, custom decrees that those with prior political experience take precedence. Counted as political experience, in order of importance, is senatorial, House and gubernatorial service. Information on prior experience is given where applicable. The

dates following senators' names refer to the beginning of their present service.

REPUBLICANS

1. Thurmond—Nov. 7, 1956[1]
2. Tower—June 15, 1961
3. Baker—Jan. 3, 1967
   Percy—Jan. 3, 1967
5. Hatfield—Jan. 10, 1967
6. Stevens—Dec. 24, 1968
7. Goldwater (ex-senator)—Jan. 3, 1969
8. Dole (ex-representative, four House terms)—Jan. 3, 1969
   Mathias (ex-representative, four House terms)—Jan. 3, 1969
10. Packwood—Jan. 3, 1969
11. Roth—Jan. 1, 1971
12. Weicker—Jan. 3, 1971
13. Stafford—Sept. 16, 1971

14. McClure (ex-representative)—Jan. 3, 1973
15. Helms—Jan. 3, 1973
    Domenici—Jan. 3, 1973
17. Laxalt—Dec. 18, 1974
18. Garn—Dec. 21, 1974
19. Danforth—Dec. 27, 1976
20. Chafee—Dec. 29, 1976
21. Heinz (ex-representative)—Jan. 3, 1977
22. Hatch—Jan. 3, 1977
    Lugar—Jan. 3, 1977
    Wallop—Jan. 3, 1977
25. Durenberger—Nov. 8, 1978
26. Kassebaum—Dec. 23, 1978
27. Cochran—Dec. 27, 1978
28. Boschwitz—Dec. 30, 1978
29. Simpson—Jan. 1, 1979
30. Warner—Jan. 2, 1979
31. Armstrong (ex-representative, three House terms)—Jan. 3, 1979
    Cohen (ex-representative, three House terms)—Jan. 3, 1979
33. Pressler (ex-representative, two House terms)—Jan. 3, 1979
34. Jepsen—Jan. 3, 1979
    Humphrey—Jan. 3, 1979
36. Andrews (ex-representative, eight and one-half House terms)—Jan. 3, 1981
37. Abdnor (ex-representative, four House terms)—Jan. 3, 1981
    Symms (ex-representative, four House terms)—Jan. 3, 1981
39. Grassley (ex-representative, three House terms)—Jan. 3, 1981
40. Kasten (ex-representative, two House terms)—Jan. 3, 1981
    Quayle (ex-representative, two House terms)—Jan. 3, 1981
42. D'Amato—Jan. 3, 1981
    Denton—Jan. 3, 1981
    East—Jan. 3, 1981
    Gorton—Jan. 3, 1981
    Hawkins—Jan. 3, 1981
    Mattingly—Jan. 3, 1981
    Murkowski—Jan. 3, 1981
    Nickles—Jan. 3, 1981
    Rudman—Jan. 3, 1981
    Specter—Jan. 3, 1981
52. Trible (ex-representative, three House terms)—Jan. 3, 1983
53. Hecht—Jan. 3, 1983
    Wilson—Jan. 3, 1983

DEMOCRATS

1. Stennis—Nov. 5, 1947
2. Long—Dec. 31, 1948
3. Jackson—Jan. 3, 1953
4. Proxmire—Aug. 28, 1957
5. Randolph—Nov. 5, 1958
6. Byrd—Jan. 3, 1959
7. Burdick—Aug. 8, 1960
8. Pell—Jan. 3, 1961
9. Kennedy—Nov. 7, 1962
10. Inouye—Jan. 3, 1963

11. Hollings—Nov. 9, 1966
12. Eagleton—Dec. 28, 1968
13. Cranston—Jan. 3, 1969
14. Bentsen (ex-representative)—Jan. 3, 1971
15. Chiles—Jan. 3, 1971
16. Nunn—Nov. 8, 1972
17. Johnston—Nov. 14, 1972
18. Biden—Jan. 3, 1973
    Huddleston—Jan. 3, 1973
20. Glenn—Dec. 24, 1974
21. Ford—Dec. 28, 1974
22. Bumpers (ex-governor)—Jan. 3, 1975
23. Hart—Jan. 3, 1975
    Leahy—Jan. 3, 1975
25. Zorinsky—Dec. 28, 1976
26. Metzenbaum—Dec. 29, 1976
27. Riegle—Dec. 30, 1976
28. Matsunaga (ex-representative, seven House terms)—Jan. 3, 1977
29. Melcher (ex-representative, three and one-half House terms)—Jan. 3, 1977
30. Sarbanes (ex-representative, three House terms)—Jan. 3, 1977
31. DeConcini—Jan. 3, 1977
    Moynihan—Jan. 3, 1977
    Sasser—Jan. 3, 1977
34. Baucus—Dec. 15, 1978
35. Pryor (ex-representative, three and one-half House terms; ex-governor)—Jan. 3, 1979
36. Tsongas (ex-representative, two House terms)—Jan. 3, 1979
37. Boren (ex-governor)—Jan. 3, 1979
    Exon (ex-governor)—Jan. 3, 1979
39. Bradley—Jan. 3, 1979
    Heflin—Jan. 3, 1979
    Levin—Jan. 3, 1979
42. Mitchell—May 8, 1980
43. Dodd (ex-representative)—Jan. 3, 1981
44. Dixon—Jan. 3, 1981
45. Lautenberg—Dec. 27, 1982
46. Bingaman—Jan. 3, 1983

1. Thurmond began his current Senate service Nov. 7, 1956, as a Democrat. He became a Republican Sept. 16, 1964. The Republican Conference allowed his seniority to count from his 1956 election to the Senate.

House Seniority

House rank generally is determined according to the official date of the beginning of a member's service, which is Jan. 3, except in the case of members elected to fill vacancies, in which instance the date of election determines rank.

When members enter the House on the same day, those with prior House experience take precedence, starting with those with the longest consecutive service. Experience as a senator or governor is disregarded. In-

formation on prior experience is given where applicable. The dates following members' names refer to the beginning of their present service.

DEMOCRATS

1. Whitten (Miss.)—Nov. 4, 1941
2. Price (Ill.)—Jan. 3, 1945
3. Bennett (Fla.)—Jan. 3, 1949
   Perkins (Ky.)—Jan. 3, 1949
   Rodino (N.J.)—Jan. 3, 1949
   Zablocki (Wis.)—Jan. 3, 1949
7. Boland (Mass.)—Jan. 3, 1953
   Brooks (Texas)—Jan. 3, 1953
   O'Neill (Mass.)—Jan. 3, 1953
10. Natcher (Ky.)—Aug. 1, 1953
11. Fascell (Fla.)—Jan. 3, 1955
    Wright (Texas)—Jan. 3, 1955
13. Dingell (Mich.)—Dec. 13, 1955
14. Kastenmeier (Wis.)—Dec. 13, 1959
15. Rostenkowski (Ill.)—Jan. 3, 1959
    Smith (Iowa)—Jan. 3, 1959
    Stratton (N.Y.)—Jan. 3, 1959
18. Addabbo (N.Y.)—Jan. 3, 1961
    St Germain (R.I.)—Jan. 3, 1961
20. Udall (Ariz.)—May 2, 1961
21. Gonzalez (Texas)—Nov. 4, 1961
22. Edwards (Calif.)—Jan. 3, 1963
    Fuqua (Fla.)—Jan. 3, 1963
    Gibbons (Fla.)—Jan. 3, 1963
    Hawkins (Calif.)—Jan. 3, 1963
    Long (Md.)—Jan. 3, 1963
    Minish (N.J.)—Jan. 3, 1963
    Pepper (Fla.)—Jan. 3, 1963
    Roybal (Calif.)—Jan. 3, 1963
30. Pickle (Texas)—Dec. 21, 1963
31. Burton (Calif.)—Feb. 18, 1964
32. Yates (Ill.) (seven terms previously)—Jan. 3, 1965
33. Annunzio (Ill.)—Jan. 3, 1965
    Conyers (Mich.)—Jan. 3, 1965
    de la Garza (Texas)—Jan. 3, 1965
    Foley (Wash.)—Jan. 3, 1965
    Ford (Mich.)—Jan. 3, 1965
    Hamilton (Ind.)—Jan. 3, 1965
    Howard (N.J.)—Jan. 3, 1965
40. Jones (N.C.)—Feb. 5, 1966
41. Bevill (Ala.)—Jan. 3, 1967
    Kazen (Texas)—Jan. 3, 1967
    Montgomery (Miss.)—Jan. 3, 1967
    Nichols (Ala.)—Jan. 3, 1967
45. Gaydos (Pa.)—Nov. 5, 1968
46. Alexander (Ark.)—Jan. 3, 1969
    Anderson (Calif.)—Jan. 3, 1969
    Biaggi (N.Y.)—Jan. 3, 1969
    Chappell (Fla.)—Jan. 3, 1969
    Clay (Mo.)—Jan. 3, 1969
    Daniel (Va.)—Jan. 3, 1969
    Stokes (Ohio)—Jan. 3, 1969
    Yatron (Pa.)—Jan. 3, 1969
54. Jones (Tenn.)—March 25, 1969
55. Obey (Wis.)—April 1, 1969
56. Roe (N.J.)—Nov. 4, 1969

57. Aspin (Wis.)—Jan. 3, 1971
    Dellums (Calif.)—Jan. 3, 1971
    Mazzoli (Ky.)—Jan. 3, 1971
    Mitchell (Md.)—Jan. 3, 1971
    Rangel (N.Y.)—Jan. 3, 1971
    Seiberling (Ohio)—Jan. 3, 1971
63. Breaux (La.)—Sept. 30, 1972
64. Brown (Calif.) (four terms previously)—Jan. 3, 1973
65. Long (La.) (one term previously)—Jan. 3, 1973
66. Andrews (N.C.)—Jan. 3, 1973
    Jones (Okla.)—Jan. 3, 1973
    Lehman (Fla.)—Jan. 3, 1973
    Moakley (Mass.)—Jan. 3, 1973
    Rose (N.C.)—Jan. 3, 1973
    Schroeder (Colo.)—Jan. 3, 1973
    Stark (Calif.)—Jan. 3, 1973
    Studds (Mass.)—Jan. 3, 1973
    Wilson (Texas)—Jan. 3, 1973
75. Boggs (La.)—March 20, 1973
76. Collins (Ill.)—June 5, 1973
77. Murtha (Pa.)—Feb. 5, 1974
78. Traxler (Mich.)—April 16, 1974
79. Jacobs (Ind.) (four terms previously)—Jan. 3, 1975
    Scheuer (N.Y.) (four terms previously)—Jan. 3, 1975
81. Ottinger (N.Y.) (three terms previously)—Jan. 3, 1975
82. AuCoin (Ore.)—Jan. 3, 1975
    Bedell (Iowa)—Jan. 3, 1975
    Bonker (Wash.)—Jan. 3, 1975
    Bouquard (Tenn.)—Jan. 3, 1975
    D'Amours (N.H.)—Jan. 3, 1975
    Derrick (S.C.)—Jan. 3, 1975
    Downey (N.Y.)—Jan. 3, 1975
    Early (Mass.)—Jan. 3, 1975
    Edgar (Pa.)—Jan. 3, 1975
    English (Okla.)—Jan. 3, 1975
    Florio (N.J.)—Jan. 3, 1975
    Ford (Tenn.)—Jan. 3, 1975
    Harkin (Iowa)—Jan. 3, 1975
    Hefner (N.C.)—Jan. 3, 1975
    Hightower (Texas)—Jan. 3, 1975
    Hubbard (Ky.)—Jan. 3, 1975
    Hughes (N.J.)—Jan. 3, 1975
    LaFalce (N.Y.)—Jan. 3, 1975
    Levitas (Ga.)—Jan. 3, 1975
    McDonald (Ga.)—Jan. 3, 1975
    McHugh (N.Y.)—Jan. 3, 1975
    Miller (Calif.)—Jan. 3, 1975
    Mineta (Calif.)—Jan. 3, 1975
    Neal (N.C.)—Jan. 3, 1975
    Nowak (N.Y.)—Jan. 3, 1975
    Oberstar (Minn.)—Jan. 3, 1975
    Patterson (Calif.)—Jan. 3, 1975
    Russo (Ill.)—Jan. 3, 1975
    Sharp (Ind.)—Jan. 3, 1975
    Simon (Ill.)—Jan. 3, 1975
    Solarz (N.Y.)—Jan. 3, 1975
    Waxman (Calif.)—Jan. 3, 1975
    Weaver (Ore.)—Jan. 3, 1975
    Wirth (Colo.)—Jan. 3, 1975
116. Lundine (N.Y.)—March 8, 1976
117. Hall, Sam B. Jr. (Texas)—June 19, 1976
118. Markey (Mass.)—Nov. 2, 1976
119. Luken (Ohio) (one term previously)—Jan. 3, 1977
120. Akaka (Hawaii)—Jan. 3, 1977
    Applegate (Ohio)—Jan. 3, 1977
    Barnard (Ga.)—Jan. 3, 1977
    Beilenson (Calif.)—Jan. 3, 1977
    Bonior (Mich.)—Jan. 3, 1977
    Dicks (Wash.)—Jan. 3, 1977
    Flippo (Ala.)—Jan. 3, 1977
    Gephardt (Mo.)—Jan. 3, 1977
    Glickman (Kan.)—Jan. 3, 1977
    Gore (Tenn.)—Jan. 3, 1977
    Heftel (Hawaii)—Jan. 3, 1977
    Huckaby (La.)—Jan. 3, 1977
    Ireland (Fla.)—Jan. 3, 1977
    Jenkins (Ga.)—Jan. 3, 1977
    Kildee (Mich.)—Jan. 3, 1977
    Mikulski (Md.)—Jan. 3, 1977
    Murphy (Pa.)—Jan. 3, 1977
    Oakar (Ohio)—Jan. 3, 1977
    Panetta (Calif.)—Jan. 3, 1977
    Pease (Ohio)—Jan. 3, 1977
    Rahall (W.Va.)—Jan. 3, 1977
    Skelton (Mo.)—Jan. 3, 1977
    Vento (Minn.)—Jan. 3, 1977
    Volkmer (Mo.)—Jan. 3, 1977
    Walgren (Pa.)—Jan. 3, 1977
    Watkins (Okla.)—Jan. 3, 1977
    Weiss (N.Y.)—Jan. 3, 1977
    Whitley (N.C.)—Jan. 3, 1977
    Young (Mo.)—Jan. 3, 1977
149. Fowler (Ga.)—April 5, 1977
150. Garcia (N.Y.)—Feb. 14, 1978
151. Albosta (Mich.)—Jan. 3, 1979
    Anthony (Ark.)—Jan. 3, 1979
    Barnes (Md.)—Jan. 3, 1979
    Boner (Tenn.)—Jan. 3, 1979
    Byron (Md.)—Jan. 3, 1979
    Coelho (Calif.)—Jan. 3, 1979
    Daschle (S.D.)—Jan. 3, 1979
    Dixon (Calif.)—Jan. 3, 1979
    Donnelly (Mass.)—Jan. 3, 1979
    Fazio (Calif.)—Jan. 3, 1979
    Ferraro (N.Y.)—Jan. 3, 1979
    Frost (Texas)—Jan. 3, 1979
    Gray (Pa.)—Jan. 3, 1979
    Guarini (N.J.)—Jan. 3, 1979
    Hall (Ohio)—Jan. 3, 1979
    Hance (Texas)—Jan. 3, 1979
    Hutto (Fla.)—Jan. 3, 1979
    Kogovsek (Colo.)—Jan. 3, 1979
    Leath (Texas)—Jan. 3, 1979
    Leland (Texas)—Jan. 3, 1979
    Lowry (Wash.)—Jan. 3, 1979
    Matsui (Calif.)—Jan. 3, 1979
    Mavroules (Mass.)—Jan. 3, 1979
    Mica (Fla.)—Jan. 3, 1979
    Nelson (Fla.)—Jan. 3, 1979
    Ratchford (Conn.)—Jan. 3, 1979
    Sabo (Minn.)—Jan. 3, 1979
    Shannon (Mass.)—Jan. 3, 1979
    Shelby (Ala.)—Jan. 3, 1979
    Stenholm (Texas)—Jan. 3, 1979
    Swift (Wash.)—Jan. 3, 1979
    Synar (Okla.)—Jan. 3, 1979
    Williams (Mont.)—Jan. 3, 1979
    Wolpe (Mich.)—Jan. 3, 1979
185. Tauzin (La.)—May 17, 1980
186. Crockett (Mich.)—Nov. 4, 1980
187. Coyne (Pa.)—Jan. 3, 1981
    Dorgan (N.D.)—Jan. 3, 1981
    Dwyer (N.J.)—Jan. 3, 1981
    Dymally (Calif.)—Jan. 3, 1981
    Dyson (Md.)—Jan. 3, 1981
    Eckart (Ohio)—Jan. 3, 1981
    Foglietta (Pa.)—Jan. 3, 1981
    Frank (Mass.)—Jan. 3, 1981
    Gejdenson (Conn.)—Jan. 3, 1981
    Hall, Ralph M. (Texas)—Jan. 3, 1981
    Hatcher (Ga.)—Jan. 3, 1981
    Hertel (Mich.)—Jan. 3, 1981
    Lantos (Calif.)—Jan. 3, 1981
    McCurdy (Okla.)—Jan. 3, 1981
    Patman (Texas)—Jan. 3, 1981
    Roemer (La.)—Jan. 3, 1981
    Savage (Ill.)—Jan. 3, 1981
    Schumer (N.Y.)—Jan. 3, 1981
    Washington (Ill.)—Jan. 3, 1981
    Wyden (Ore.)—Jan. 3, 1981
207. Hoyer (Md.)—May 19, 1981
208. Dowdy (Miss.)—July 7, 1981
209. Kennelly (Conn.)—Jan. 25, 1982
210. Martinez (Calif.)—July 15, 1982
211. Hall (Ind.)—Nov. 29, 1982
212. Carr (Mich.) (three terms previously)—Jan. 3, 1983
213. Kostmayer (Pa.) (two terms previously)—Jan. 3, 1983
214. Andrews (Texas)—Jan. 3, 1983
    Bates (Calif.)—Jan. 3, 1983
    Berman (Calif.)—Jan. 3, 1983
    Borski (Pa.)—Jan. 3, 1983
    Bosco (Calif.)—Jan. 3, 1983
    Boucher (Va.)—Jan. 3, 1983
    Boxer (Calif.)—Jan. 3, 1983
    Britt (N.C.)—Jan. 3, 1983
    Bryant (Texas)—Jan. 3, 1983
    Carper (Del.)—Jan. 3, 1983
    Clarke (N.C.)—Jan. 3, 1983
    Coleman (Texas)—Jan. 3, 1983
    Cooper (Tenn.)—Jan. 3, 1983
    Durbin (Ill.)—Jan. 3, 1983
    Erdreich (Ala.)—Jan. 3, 1983
    Evans (Ill.)—Jan. 3, 1983
    Feighan (Ohio)—Jan. 3, 1983
    Harrison (Pa.)—Jan. 3, 1983
    Kaptur (Ohio)—Jan. 3, 1983
    Kolter (Pa.)—Jan. 3, 1983
    Lehman (Calif.)—Jan. 3, 1983
    Levin (Mich.)—Jan. 3, 1983
    Levine (Calif.)—Jan. 3, 1983
    Lipinski (Ill.)—Jan. 3, 1983
    MacKay (Fla.)—Jan. 3, 1983
    McCloskey (Ind.)—Jan. 3, 1983
    McNulty (Ariz.)—Jan. 3, 1983
    Mollohan (W.Va.)—Jan. 3, 1983
    Moody (Wis.)—Jan. 3, 1983
    Morrison (Conn.)—Jan. 3, 1983
    Mrazek (N.Y.)—Jan. 3, 1983
    Olin (Va.)—Jan. 3, 1983

Ortiz (Texas)—Jan. 3, 1983
Owens (N.Y.)—Jan. 3, 1983
Penny (Minn.)—Jan. 3, 1983
Ray (Ga.)—Jan. 3, 1983
Reid (Nev.)—Jan. 3, 1983
Richardson (N.M.)—Jan. 3, 1983
Rowland (Ga.)—Jan. 3, 1983
Sikorski (Minn.)—Jan. 3, 1983
Sisisky (Va.)—Jan. 3, 1983
Slattery (Kan.)—Jan. 3, 1983
Smith (Fla.)—Jan. 3, 1983
Spratt (S.C.)—Jan. 3, 1983
Staggers (W.Va.)—Jan. 3, 1983
Tallon (S.C.)—Jan. 3, 1983
Thomas (Ga.)—Jan. 3, 1983
Torres (Calif.)—Jan. 3, 1983
Torricelli (N.J.)—Jan. 3, 1983
Towns (N.Y.)—Jan. 3, 1983
Valentine (N.C.)—Jan. 3, 1983
Vandergriff (Texas)—Jan. 3, 1983
Wheat (Mo.)—Jan. 3, 1983
Wise (W.Va.)—Jan. 3, 1983

REPUBLICANS

1. Broomfield (Mich.)—Jan. 3, 1957
Michel (Ill.)—Jan. 3, 1957
3. Conte (Mass.)—Jan. 3, 1959
Latta (Ohio)—Jan. 3, 1959
5. Broyhill (N.C.)—Jan. 3, 1963
Horton (N.Y.)—Jan. 3, 1963
McDade (Pa.)—Jan. 3, 1963
Quillen (Tenn.)—Jan. 3, 1963
9. Conable (N.Y.)—Jan. 3, 1965
Dickinson (Ala.)—Jan. 3, 1965
Duncan (Tenn.)—Jan. 3, 1965
Edwards (Ala.)—Jan. 3, 1965
Erlenborn (Ill.)—Jan. 3, 1965
14. Vander Jagt (Mich.)—Nov. 8, 1966
15. Snyder (Ky.) (one term previously)—
Jan. 3, 1967
16. Hammerschmidt (Ark.)—Jan. 3, 1967
Miller (Ohio)—Jan. 3, 1967
Myers (Ind.)—Jan. 3, 1967
Winn (Kan.)—Jan. 3, 1967
Wylie (Ohio)—Jan. 3, 1967
21. Coughlin (Pa.)—Jan. 3, 1969
Fish (N.Y.)—Jan. 3, 1969
Lujan (N.M.)—Jan. 3, 1969
Whitehurst (Va.)—Jan. 3, 1969
25. Crane, Philip M. (Ill.)—Nov. 25, 1969
26. Forsythe (N.J.)—Nov. 3, 1970
27. Archer (Texas)—Jan. 3, 1971
Frenzel (Minn.)—Jan. 3, 1971
Hillis (Ind.)—Jan. 3, 1971
Kemp (N.Y.)—Jan. 3, 1971
Lent (N.Y.)—Jan. 3, 1971
McKinney (Conn.)—Jan. 3, 1971
Robinson (Va.)—Jan. 3, 1971
Spence (S.C.)—Jan. 3, 1971
Young (Fla.)—Jan. 3, 1971
36. Gilman (N.Y.)—Jan. 3, 1973
Holt (Md.)—Jan. 3, 1973
Lott (Miss.)—Jan. 3, 1973
Madigan (Ill.)—Jan. 3, 1973
Martin (N.C.)—Jan. 3, 1973

Moorhead (Calif.)—Jan. 3, 1973
O'Brien (Ill.)—Jan. 3, 1973
Pritchard (Wash.)—Jan. 3, 1973
Regula (Ohio)—Jan. 3, 1973
Rinaldo (N.J.)—Jan. 3, 1973
Shuster (Pa.)—Jan. 3, 1973
Taylor (Mo.)—Jan. 3, 1973
48. Young (Alaska)—March 20, 1973
49. Lagomarsino (Calif.)—March 5, 1974
50. Hansen (Idaho) (two terms previously)—Jan. 3, 1975
51. Goodling (Pa.)—Jan. 3, 1975
Gradison (Ohio)—Jan. 3, 1975
Hyde (Ill.)—Jan. 3, 1975
Jeffords (Vt.)—Jan. 3, 1975
Kindness (Ohio)—Jan. 3, 1975
Schulze (Pa.)—Jan. 3, 1975
Smith (Neb.)—Jan. 3, 1975
58. Moore (La.)—Jan. 7, 1975
59. Coleman (Mo.)—Nov. 2, 1976
60. Badham (Calif.)—Jan. 3, 1977
Corcoran (Ill.)—Jan. 3, 1977
Edwards (Okla.)—Jan. 3, 1977
Leach (Iowa)—Jan. 3, 1977
Marlenee (Mont.)—Jan. 3, 1977
Marriott (Utah)—Jan. 3, 1977
Pursell (Mich.)—Jan. 3, 1977
Rudd (Ariz.)—Jan. 3, 1977
Sawyer (Mich.)—Jan. 3, 1977
Walker (Pa.)—Jan. 3, 1977
70. Stangeland (Minn.)—Feb. 22, 1977
71. Livingston (La.)—Aug. 27, 1977
72. Green (N.Y.)—Feb. 14, 1978
73. Paul (Texas) (one-half of one term previously)—Jan. 3, 1979
74. Bereuter (Neb.)—Jan. 3, 1979
Bethune (Ark.)—Jan. 3, 1979
Campbell (S.C.)—Jan. 3, 1979
Carney (N.Y.)—Jan. 3, 1979
Cheney (Wyo.)—Jan. 3, 1979
Clinger (Pa.)—Jan. 3, 1979
Courter (N.J.)—Jan. 3, 1979
Crane, Daniel B. (Ill.)—Jan. 3, 1979
Dannemeyer (Calif.)—Jan. 3, 1979
Davis (Mich.)—Jan. 3, 1979
Gingrich (Ga.)—Jan. 3, 1979
Hopkins (Ky.)—Jan. 3, 1979
Kramer (Colo.)—Jan. 3, 1979
Lewis (Calif.)—Jan. 3, 1979
Loeffler (Texas)—Jan. 3, 1979
Lungren (Calif.)—Jan. 3, 1979
Pashayan (Calif.)—Jan. 3, 1979
Ritter (Pa.)—Jan. 3, 1979
Roth (Wis.)—Jan. 3, 1979
Sensenbrenner (Wis.)—Jan. 3, 1979
Shumway (Calif.)—Jan. 3, 1979
Snowe (Maine)—Jan. 3, 1979
Solomon (N.Y.)—Jan. 3, 1979
Tauke (Iowa)—Jan. 3, 1979
Thomas (Calif.)—Jan. 3, 1979
Whittaker (Kan.)—Jan. 3, 1979
Williams (Ohio)—Jan. 3, 1979
101. Petri (Wis.)—April 3, 1979
102. Porter (Ill.)—Jan. 22, 1980
103. Parris (Va.) (one term previously)—Jan. 3, 1981

104. Bliley (Va.)—Jan. 3, 1981
Brown (Colo.)—Jan. 3, 1981
Chappie (Calif.)—Jan. 3, 1981
Coats (Ind.)—Jan. 3, 1981
Craig (Idaho)—Jan. 3, 1981
Daub (Neb.)—Jan. 3, 1981
Dreier (Calif.)—Jan. 3, 1981
Emerson (Mo.)—Jan. 3, 1981
Evans (Iowa)—Jan. 3, 1981
Fiedler (Calif.)—Jan. 3, 1981
Fields (Texas)—Jan. 3, 1981
Gregg (N.H.)—Jan. 3, 1981
Gunderson (Wis.)—Jan. 3, 1981
Hansen (Utah)—Jan. 3, 1981
Hartnett (S.C.)—Jan. 3, 1981
Hiler (Ind.)—Jan. 3, 1981
Hunter (Calif.)—Jan. 3, 1981
Lowery (Calif.)—Jan. 3, 1981
Martin (N.Y.)—Jan. 3, 1981
Martin (Ill.)—Jan. 3, 1981
McCollum (Fla.)—Jan. 3, 1981
McEwen (Ohio)—Jan. 3, 1981
McGrath (N.Y.)—Jan. 3, 1981
Molinari (N.Y.)—Jan. 3, 1981
Morrison (Wash.)—Jan. 3, 1981
Roberts (Kan.)—Jan. 3, 1981
Rogers (Ky.)—Jan. 3, 1981
Roukema (N.J.)—Jan. 3, 1981
Schneider (R.I.)—Jan. 3, 1981
Shaw (Fla.)—Jan. 3, 1981
Skeen (N.M.)—Jan. 3, 1981
Smith (N.J.)—Jan. 3, 1981
Smith, Denny (Ore.)—Jan. 3, 1981
Weber (Minn.)—Jan. 3, 1981
Wolf (Va.)—Jan. 3, 1981
Wortley (N.Y.)—Jan. 3, 1981
140. Siljander (Mich.)—April 21, 1981
141. Oxley (Ohio)—June 25, 1981
142. Stump (Ariz.)—Jan. 3, 1983[1]
143. Bartlett (Texas)—Jan. 3, 1983
Bateman (Va.)—Jan. 3, 1983
Bilirakis (Fla.)—Jan. 3, 1983
Boehlert (N.Y.)—Jan. 3, 1983
Burton (Ind.)—Jan. 3, 1983
Chandler (Wash.)—Jan. 3, 1983
DeWine (Ohio)—Jan. 3, 1983
Franklin (Miss.)—Jan. 3, 1983
Gekas (Pa.)—Jan. 3, 1983
Johnson (Conn.)—Jan. 3, 1983
Kasich (Ohio)—Jan. 3, 1983
Lewis (Fla.)—Jan. 3, 1983
Mack (Fla.)—Jan. 3, 1983
McCain (Ariz.)—Jan. 3, 1983
McCandless (Calif.)—Jan. 3, 1983
McKernan (Maine)—Jan. 3, 1983
Nielson (Utah)—Jan. 3, 1983
Packard (Calif.)—Jan. 3, 1983
Ridge (Pa.)—Jan. 3, 1983
Smith, Bob (Ore.)—Jan. 3, 1983
Sundquist (Tenn.)—Jan. 3, 1983
Vucanovich (Nev.)—Jan. 3, 1983
Zschau (Calif.)—Jan. 3, 1983 ∎

1. Stump began his House service Jan. 3, 1977, as a Democrat. He was elected as a Republican to the 98th Congress on Nov. 2, 1982.

CQ Committee Assignments

Committee Posts Important to Members

The bulk of congressional work is done in committees, not on the floor of the House or Senate.

Legislation is written by committees; hearings are held by committees; oversight investigations are conducted by committees.

Particularly in the House, a member's influence often is closely related to the committee or committees on which he or she serves. Assignment to a powerful committee is a virtual guarantee of bountiful campaign contributions.

While many members seek a particular committee because they have an interest in issues within that committee's jurisdiction, others' committee preferences are based on political need.

Members from large agricultural districts gravitate toward the Agriculture committees. Those from districts with major military installations often seek out the Armed Services panels.

Popularity of Committees

In each chamber, a few committees are considered glamorous and powerful and are usually quite difficult to get on. But a number of committees are quite the opposite; congressional leaders often have to go looking for "volunteers" to serve on these lesser committees.

Traditionally, the premier committees sought by representatives have been Appropriations, Ways and Means and Rules, although Rules has lost some of its luster in recent years.

In the Senate, the Appropriations and Finance committees are popular.

In recent years, the Budget committees in both chambers have been the choice of many members. This year, House members fought over a handful of openings on the Budget Committee while there were no Senate Budget Committee openings.

The most sought-after committee assignments this year for freshmen representatives were Energy and Commerce and Banking, Finance and Urban Affairs.

Generally, members assigned to

As published April 2, 1983.

committees stay on those panels throughout their congressional careers, although in every Congress a few veterans switch panels. Only on rare occasions does a party ever remove a member from a committee.

Such a rarity occurred this year when House Democrats booted Texan Phil Gramm off the Budget Commit-

tee. Gramm subsequently resigned and was re-elected as a Republican. The Republicans then gave Gramm a seat on Budget.

The Selection Process

Both House and Senate have major and minor committees; the designation generally is based on the historic importance of the committee.

For example, in the House, Energy and Commerce is a major committee while Post Office and Civil Service is a minor committee.

In the Senate, there are 12 major

committees and 10 minor committees.

Although both the House and Senate have numerous rules governing committee assignments, exceptions are often made, particularly in the Senate.

For example, although Senate rules limit senators to service on only two major committees, the rules have routinely been waived and many senators sit on more than two of these committees.

Most senators serve on four committees, while representatives usually serve on no more than two, and many serve on only one committee.

In both chambers, seniority on committees is determined by the date a member joins the committee, not the date service began in the House or Senate. This results sometimes in junior members being ahead of more senior members on committees.

Committee seniority usually determines the chairman or ranking minority member. In the Senate, the senior majority senator on a committee is always the chairman unless he or she holds a chairmanship of another committee. In the House, controlled by the Democrats, the chairman of each committee is usually the senior Democrat, although chairmanships must be approved by the Democratic Caucus, which has rejected some senior members in the past.

Actual assignments to committees are made by the political parties in each chamber. Those assignments are then routinely ratified by the full House or Senate.

The specific process varies by chamber and party.

Senate. Although the number of members on each committee is set out in the Senate rules, the ratio of Republicans to Democrats is determined by the majority party, currently the Republicans.

Republicans fill committee vacancies strictly by seniority, with senior members picking first. Republican senators are limited to two major committees until all Republicans have at least two. After all Republicans have two, the remaining vacancies are filled as senior Republicans bid for the

openings.

Democratic senators are assigned to committee openings by the Democratic Steering Committee, chaired by Minority Leader Robert C. Byrd of West Virginia. The Steering Committee generally bases its assignments on members' desires and seniority, although it is not bound by it.

House. Democrats are assigned to committee vacancies by the 30-member Democratic Steering and Policy Committee, chaired by Speaker Thomas P. O'Neill Jr., D-Mass. Twelve of that committee's members are elected by geographic region, eight are appointed by O'Neill and 10 serve as a result of other leadership offices they hold.

A member seeking a particular committee assignment must be nominated for it by a member of Steering and Policy. Having a patron on the inside helps a great deal. In 1983, Steering and Policy members were heavily lobbied by representatives seeking assignments.

For example, freshman Jim Slattery, D-Kan., began working for a seat on Energy and Commerce the day after he was elected in November 1982. Slattery personally lobbied each member of Steering and Policy, stressing the importance of geographic and philosophic balance on Energy and Commerce as well as his experience in the Kansas Legislature. He won an Energy and Commerce assignment.

More-senior Democrats fought over assignments to two key committees: the tax-writing Ways and Means Committee and the Budget Committee, which members may serve on without giving up other major committee assignments.

O'Neill and the Steering and Policy Committee tended to reward the members who had supported the Democratic leadership on key votes during the 97th Congress. For example, the committee gave Budget Committee seats to several Democrats who had supported the leadership, but denied a seat there to John B. Breaux of Louisiana, who supported the leadership only slightly more than he opposed it in 1981-82.

In some cases, rewards to freshmen were based on whom they replaced in Congress. For example, Robert J. Mrazek, D-N.Y., was the only freshman to win a seat on Appropriations. Mrazek had O'Neill's vigorous support for the job. Mrazek defeated John LeBoutillier, R-N.Y. (1981-83), who spent much time in Congress calling O'Neill derogatory names.

In addition to making committee assignments, Steering and Policy also determines the chairmen of all the House committees, except for Rules, to which the chairman and all Democrats are named by O'Neill. Steering and Policy also sets the size and party ratios of each committee.

These decisions are then ratified by the House Democratic Caucus and packaged into a resolution for later approval by the House.

House Republicans are assigned to committees by the executive committee of the Republican Committee on Committees, chaired by Minority Leader Robert H. Michel, R-Ill.

There are 19 voting members of this executive committee, elected by state or region to represent fellow Republicans. The number of votes each member has varies according to the number of Republicans he represents. For example, Jerry Lewis, R-Calif., represents California on the panel and has 17 votes, the number of California Republicans.

Michel has considerably less control over the executive committee's selections than O'Neill does over Steering and Policy, where each member only gets one vote and many of the members are chosen by O'Neill.

The executive committee also chooses the ranking Republican member of each House committee. These choices are then submitted to the House Republican Conference — the equivalent of the Democratic Caucus — for ratification, although the conference does not vote on committee assignments. The selections are packaged into a resolution for approval by the House.

Both parties' committee assignment resolutions are generally approved without debate. ∎

Key to Listings, Abbreviations

ORDER OF LISTS — In the Senate Committee section, Republicans are listed on the left in Roman type. Democrats are on the right in italics. In the House, Democrats are listed on the left in Roman type and Republicans are on the right in italics.

Members of legislative committees and subcommittees are listed in order of their seniority on those panels. Members of party committees are listed alphabetically. An index of members' committee assignments begins on p. 99.

ROOM AND TELEPHONE NUMBERS — Phone and room numbers are listed in the body of the book for each committee and subcommittee.

To reach the U.S. Capitol switchboard, call (202) 224-3121.

BUILDINGS, ADDRESSES, ZIP CODES — The following abbreviations are used for congressional office buildings: SD, Dirksen Senate Office Building; SH, Hart Senate Office Building; SR, Russell Senate Office Building; CHOB, Cannon House Office Building; LHOB, Longworth House Office Building; RHOB, Rayburn House Office Building.

A map of Capitol Hill showing the location of each building appears on p. 106.

The ZIP Code for all mail addressed to offices of the Senate is 20510; for the House 20515.

Senate Committee Assignments, 98th Congress

As of April 2, 1983

Agriculture, Nutrition and Forestry

Phone: 224-2035   *Room: SR-328A*

R 10 - D 8

Agriculture in general; animal industry and diseases; crop insurance and soil conservation; farm credit and farm security; food from fresh waters; food stamp programs; forestry in general; home economics; human nutrition; inspection of livestock, meat and agricultural products; pests and pesticides; plant industry, soils and agricultural engineering; rural development, rural electrification and watersheds; school nutrition programs; matters relating to food, nutrition, hunger and rural affairs.

Jesse Helms,
R-N.C.,
chairman*

Robert Dole, Kan.
Richard G. Lugar, Ind.
Thad Cochran, Miss.
Rudy Boschwitz, Minn.
Roger W. Jepsen, Iowa
Paula Hawkins, Fla.
Mark Andrews, N.D.
Pete Wilson, Calif.
Orrin G. Hatch, Utah

Walter D. Huddleston, Ky.
Patrick J. Leahy, Vt.
Edward Zorinsky, Neb.
John Melcher, Mont.
David Pryor, Ark.
David L. Boren, Okla.
Alan J. Dixon, Ill.
Howell Heflin, Ala.

Subcommittees

Agricultural Credit and Rural Electrification

Phone: 224-2035   *Room: SR-328A*

Hawkins - chairman

Jepsen	*Zorinsky*
Andrews	*Heflin*
	Boren

Agricultural Production, Marketing and Stabilization of Prices

Phone: 224-2035   *Room: SR-328A*

Cochran - chairman

Dole	*Leahy*
Boschwitz	*Huddleston*
Andrews	*Zorinsky*
Helms	*Melcher*
	Dixon

Agricultural Research and General Legislation

Phone: 224-2035   *Room: SR-328A*

Lugar - chairman

Hatch	*Boren*
Wilson	*Heflin*
Helms	*Huddleston*
	Pryor

Foreign Agricultural Policy

Phone: 224-2035   *Room: SR-328A*

Boschwitz - chairman

Wilson	*Dixon*
Lugar	*Zorinsky*
Cochran	*Boren*
Jepsen	*Huddleston*
Dole	
Hawkins	

Nutrition

Phone: 224-2035   *Room: SR-328A*

Dole - chairman

Hawkins	*Pryor*
Lugar	*Melcher*
Boschwitz	*Leahy*
Hatch	*Dixon*

Rural Development, Oversight and Investigations

Phone: 224-2035   *Room: SR-328A*

Andrews - chairman

Helms	*Pryor*
	Leahy

Soil and Water Conservation, Forestry and Environment

Phone: 224-2035   *Room: SR-328A*

Jepsen - chairman

Hatch   *Melcher*
Wilson   *Heflin*
Cochran

* Chairman and ranking minority member are members ex officio of all subcommittees of which they are not regular members.

Appropriations

Phone: 224-3471   *Room: S128 Capitol*

R 15 - D 14

Appropriation of revenue for support of the government; rescission of appropriations; new spending authority under the Congressional Budget Act.

Mark O. Hatfield,
R-Ore.,
chairman*

Ted Stevens, Alaska   *John C. Stennis, Miss.**
Lowell P. Weicker Jr., Conn. *Robert C. Byrd, W. Va.*
James A. McClure, Idaho   *William Proxmire, Wis.*
Paul Laxalt, Nev.   *Daniel K. Inouye, Hawaii*
Jake Garn, Utah   *Ernest F. Hollings, S.C.*
Thad Cochran, Miss.   *Thomas F. Eagleton, Mo.*
Mark Andrews, N.D.   *Lawton Chiles, Fla.*
James Abdnor, S.D.   *J. Bennett Johnston, La.*
Bob Kasten, Wis.   *Walter D. Huddleston, Ky.*
Alfonse M. D'Amato, N.Y.   *Quentin N. Burdick, N.D.*
Mack Mattingly, Ga.   *Patrick J. Leahy, Vt.*
Warren B. Rudman, N.H.   *Jim Sasser, Tenn.*
Arlen Specter, Pa.   *Dennis DeConcini, Ariz.*
Pete V. Domenici, N.M.   *Dale Bumpers, Ark.*

Subcommittees

Agriculture, Rural Development and Related Agencies

Phone: 224-7240   *Room: SD-140*

Cochran - chairman

McClure   *Eagleton*
Andrews   *Stennis*
Abdnor   *Byrd*
Kasten   *Chiles*
Mattingly   *Burdick*
Specter   *Sasser*

Commerce, Justice, State and Judiciary and Related Agencies

Phone: 224-7244   *Room: S146A Capitol*

Laxalt - chairman

Stevens   *Hollings*
Weicker   *Inouye*
Rudman   *DeConcini*
Hatfield   *Bumpers*
Specter   *Eagleton*

Defense

Phone: 224-7255   *Room: SD-122*

Stevens - chairman

Weicker   *Stennis*
Garn   *Proxmire*
McClure   *Inouye*
Andrews   *Hollings*
Kasten   *Eagleton*
D'Amato   *Chiles*
Rudman   *Johnston*
Cochran   *Huddleston*

District of Columbia

Phone: 224-2731   *Room: SR-150*

Specter - chairman

Mattingly   *Leahy*
Domenici   *Bumpers*

Energy and Water Development

Phone: 224-7260   *Room: SD-142*

Hatfield - chairman

McClure	*Johnston*
Garn	*Stennis*
Cochran	*Byrd*
Abdnor	*Hollings*
Kasten	*Huddleston*
Mattingly	*Burdick*
Domenici	*Sasser*

Foreign Operations

Phone: 224-7274   *Room: S125 Capitol*

Kasten - chairman

Hatfield	*Inouye*
D'Amato	*Johnston*
Rudman	*Leahy*
Specter	*DeConcini*

HUD-Independent Agencies

Phone: 224-7253   *Room: SD-123*

Garn - chairman

Weicker	*Huddleston*
Laxalt	*Stennis*
D'Amato	*Proxmire*
Abdnor	*Leahy*
Domenici	*Sasser*

Interior and Related Agencies

Phone: 224-7262   *Room: SD-114*

McClure - chairman

Stevens	*Byrd*
Laxalt	*Johnston*
Garn	*Huddleston*
Cochran	*Leahy*
Andrews	*DeConcini*
Rudman	*Burdick*
Weicker	*Bumpers*

Labor, Health and Human Services, Education and Related Agencies

Phone: 224-7283   *Room: SD-186*

Weicker - chairman

Hatfield	*Proxmire*
Stevens	*Byrd*

Andrews	*Hollings*
Rudman	*Eagleton*
Specter	*Chiles*
McClure	*Burdick*
Domenici	*Inouye*

Legislative Branch

Phone: 224-7280   *Room: S128 Capitol*

D'Amato - chairman

Hatfield	*Bumpers*
Stevens	*Hollings*

Military Construction

Phone: 224-7271   *Room: SD-196*

Mattingly - chairman

Laxalt	*Sasser*
Garn	*Inouye*

Transportation and Related Agencies

Phone: 224-0330   *Room: SD-156*

Andrews - chairman

Cochran	*Chiles*
Abdnor	*Stennis*
Kasten	*Byrd*
D'Amato	*Eagleton*

Treasury, Postal Service, General Government

Phone: 224-2726   *Room: SR-150*

Abdnor - chairman

Laxalt	*DeConcini*
Mattingly	*Proxmire*

* Chairman and ranking minority member are members ex officio of all subcommittees of which they are not regular members.

Armed Services

Phone: 224-3871   *Room: SR-222*

R 10 - D 8

Defense and defense policy generally; aeronautical and space activities peculiar to or primarily associated with the development of weapons systems or military operations; maintenance and operation of the Panama Canal, including the Canal Zone; military research and development; national security aspects of nuclear energy; naval petroleum reserves (except Alaska); armed forces generally; Selective Service System; strategic and critical materials.

John Tower,
R-Texas,
chairman

Strom Thurmond, S.C.	Henry M. Jackson, Wash.
Barry Goldwater, Ariz.	John C. Stennis, Miss.
John W. Warner, Va.	Sam Nunn, Ga.
Gordon J. Humphrey, N.H.	Gary Hart, Colo.
William S. Cohen, Maine	J. James Exon, Neb.
Roger W. Jepsen, Iowa	Carl Levin, Mich.
Dan Quayle, Ind.	Edward M. Kennedy, Mass.
John P. East, N.C.	Jeff Bingaman, N.M.
Pete Wilson, Calif.	

Subcommittees

Manpower and Personnel

Phone: 224-9348   *Room: SR-232A*

Jepsen - chairman

Thurmond	Exon
Humphrey	Nunn
Cohen	Kennedy
East	Bingaman

Military Construction

Phone: 224-9354   *Room: SR-222*

Thurmond - chairman

Warner	Hart
Humphrey	Jackson
Quayle	Stennis
East	Exon

Preparedness

Phone: 224-8639   *Room: SR-222*

Humphrey - chairman

Goldwater	Levin
Jepsen	Jackson
Wilson	Kennedy

Sea Power and Force Projection

Phone: 224-8630   *Room: SR-222*

Cohen - chairman

Tower	Nunn
Quayle	Stennis
East	Hart
Wilson	Levin

Strategic and Theater Nuclear Forces

Phone: 224-9349   *Room: SR-222*

Warner - chairman

Tower	Jackson
Thurmond	Stennis
Goldwater	Nunn
Cohen	Hart
Quayle	Exon

Tactical Warfare

Phone: 224-8636   *Room: SR-222*

Goldwater - chairman

Tower	Kennedy
Warner	Levin
Jepsen	Bingaman
Wilson	Vacancy

Banking, Housing and Urban Affairs

Phone: 224-7391   Room: SD-534

R 10 - D 8

Banks, banking and financial institutions; price controls; deposit insurance; economic stabilization and growth; defense production; export and foreign trade promotion; export controls; federal monetary policy, including Federal Reserve System; financial aid to commerce and industry; issuance and redemption of notes; money and credit, including currency and coinage; nursing home construction; public and private housing, including veterans' housing; renegotiation of government contracts; urban development and mass transit; international economic policy.

Jake Garn,
R-Utah,
chairman*

John Tower, Texas	*William Proxmire, Wis.**
John Heinz, Pa.	*Alan Cranston, Calif.*
William L. Armstrong, Colo.	*Donald W. Riegle Jr., Mich.*
Alfonse M. D'Amato, N.Y.	*Paul S. Sarbanes, Md.*
Slade Gorton, Wash.	*Christopher J. Dodd, Conn.*
Paula Hawkins, Fla.	*Alan J. Dixon, Ill.*
Mack Mattingly, Ga.	*Jim Sasser, Tenn.*
Chic Hecht, Nev.	*Frank R. Lautenberg, N.J.*
Paul S. Trible Jr., Va.	

Subcommittees

Consumer Affairs

Phone: 224-7391   Room: SD-534

Hawkins - chairman

D'Amato	*Dodd*
Gorton	*Dixon*

Economic Policy

Phone: 224-7391   Room: SD-534

Gorton - chairman

Hecht	*Dodd*
Armstrong	*Cranston*

Federal Credit Programs

Phone: 224-7391   Room: SD-534

Trible - chairman

Armstrong	*Sasser*
Hecht	*Lautenberg*

Financial Institutions

Phone: 224-7391   Room: SD-534

Armstrong - chairman

Garn	*Cranston*
Tower	*Dixon*
Heinz	*Proxmire*
D'Amato	*Riegle*
Hecht	

Housing and Urban Affairs

Phone: 224-5404   Room: SD-534

Tower - chairman

Garn	*Riegle*
Heinz	*Sasser*
D'Amato	*Lautenberg*
Gorton	*Proxmire*
Hawkins	*Cranston*
Trible	*Sarbanes*

Insurance

Phone: 224-7391   Room: SD-534

Hecht - chairman

Hawkins	*Sarbanes*

International Finance and Monetary Policy

Phone: 224-0891   Room: SD-534

Heinz - chairman

Garn	*Proxmire*
Armstrong	*Dixon*
Mattingly	*Sasser*
Gorton	*Lautenberg*

Rural Housing and Development

Phone: 224-7391   *Room: SD-534*

Mattingly - chairman

Tower   *Cranston*

Securities

Phone: 224-7391   *Room: SD-534*

D'Amato - chairman

Hawkins   *Sarbanes*
Mattingly   *Riegle*
Trible   *Dodd*

* Chairman and ranking minority member are members ex officio *of all subcommittees of which they are not regular members.*

Budget

Phone: 224-0642   *Room: 203 Carroll Arms*

R 12 - D 10

Federal budget generally; concurrent budget resolutions; Congressional Budget Office.

Pete V. Domenici,
R-N.M.,
chairman

William L. Armstrong, Colo.
Nancy Landon Kassebaum, Kan.
Rudy Boschwitz, Minn.
Orrin G. Hatch, Utah
John Tower, Texas
Mark Andrews, N.D.
Steven D. Symms, Idaho
Charles E. Grassley, Iowa
Bob Kasten, Wis.
Dan Quayle, Ind.
Slade Gorton, Wash.

Lawton Chiles, Fla.
Ernest F. Hollings, S.C.
Joseph R. Biden Jr., Del.
J. Bennett Johnston, La.
Jim Sasser, Tenn.
Gary Hart, Colo.
Howard M. Metzenbaum, Ohio
Donald W. Riegle Jr., Mich.
Daniel Patrick Moynihan, N.Y.
J. James Exon, Neb.

(No standing subcommittees.)

Commerce, Science and Transportation

Phone: 224-5115   *Room: SD-508*

R 9 - D 8

Interstate commerce and transportation generally; Coast Guard; coastal zone management; communications; highway safety; inland waterways, except construction; marine fisheries; Merchant Marine and navigation; nonmilitary aeronautical and space sciences; oceans, weather and atmospheric activities; interoceanic canals generally; regulation of consumer products and services; science, engineering and technology research, development and policy; sports; standards and measurement; transportation and commerce aspects of Outer Continental Shelf lands.

Bob Packwood,
R-Ore.,
chairman*

Barry Goldwater, Ariz.
John C. Danforth, Mo.
Nancy Landon Kassebaum, Kan.
Larry Pressler, S.D.
Slade Gorton, Wash.
Ted Stevens, Alaska
Bob Kasten, Wis.
Paul S. Trible Jr., Va.

Ernest F. Hollings, S.C.*
Russell B. Long, La.
Daniel K. Inouye, Hawaii
Wendell H. Ford, Ky.
Donald W. Riegle Jr., Mich.
J. James Exon, Neb.
Howell Heflin, Ala.
Frank R. Lautenberg, N.J.

Subcommittees

Aviation

Phone: 224-4852   *Room: A709 Immigration*

Kassebaum - chairman

Goldwater   *Exon*
Danforth   *Inouye*
Stevens   *Ford*
Trible   *Lautenberg*

Business, Trade and Tourism

Phone: 224-8170   Room: SR-251

Pressler - chairman

Packwood   *Riegle*

Communications

Phone: 224-8144   Room: SR-146

Goldwater - chairman

Pressler	*Hollings*
Stevens	*Inouye*
Gorton	*Ford*

Consumer

Phone: 224-4768   Room: SR-138

Kasten - chairman

Danforth   *Ford*

Merchant Marine

Phone: 224-4766   Room: SR-138

Stevens - chairman

Gorton	*Inouye*
Kasten	*Long*
Trible	*Heflin*

National Ocean Policy Study

Phone: 224-8170   Room: SR-251

Packwood - chairman

Stevens	*Hollings*
Gorton	*Long*
Kasten	*Inouye*
Trible	*Lautenberg*

Science, Technology and Space

Phone: 224-8172   Room: SR-251

Gorton - chairman

Goldwater	*Heflin*
Kassebaum	*Riegle*
Trible	*Lautenberg*

Surface Transportation

Phone: 224-4852   Room: A709 Immigration

Danforth - chairman

Pressler	*Long*
Kassebaum	*Riegle*
Kasten	*Exon*

* Chairman and ranking minority member are members ex officio of all subcommittees of which they are not regular members.

Energy and Natural Resources

Phone: 224-4971   Room: SD-360

R 11 - D 9

Energy policy, regulation, conservation, research and development; coal; energy related aspects of deepwater ports; hydroelectric power, irrigation and reclamation; mines, mining and minerals generally; national parks, recreation areas, wilderness areas, wild and scenic rivers, historic sites, military parks and battlefields; naval petroleum reserves in Alaska; nonmilitary development of nuclear energy; oil and gas production and distribution; public lands and forests; solar energy systems; territorial possessions of the United States.

James A. McClure,
R-Idaho,
chairman*

Mark O. Hatfield, Ore.	*J. Bennett Johnston, La.**
Lowell P. Weicker Jr., Conn.	*Henry M. Jackson, Wash.*
Pete V. Domenici, N.M.	*Dale Bumpers, Ark.*
Malcolm Wallop, Wyo.	*Wendell H. Ford, Ky.*
John W. Warner, Va.	*Howard M. Metzenbaum,*
Frank H. Murkowski, Alaska	*Ohio*
Don Nickles, Okla.	*Spark M. Matsunaga, Hawaii*
Chic Hecht, Nev.	*John Melcher, Mont.*
John H. Chafee, R.I.	*Paul E. Tsongas, Mass.*
John Heinz, Pa.	*Bill Bradley, N.J.*

Subcommittees

Energy and Mineral Resources

Phone: 224-5205   Room: SD-306

Warner - chairman

Heinz	*Melcher*
Wallop	*Bumpers*
Murkowski	*Matsunaga*
Hecht	*Bradley*

Energy Conservation and Supply

Phone: 224-0613   Room: SD-308

Weicker - chairman

Hatfield	*Matsunaga*
Chafee	*Metzenbaum*
Warner	*Tsongas*
Heinz	*Bradley*

Energy Regulation

Phone: 224-5205   Room: SD-306

Murkowski - chairman

Weicker	*Metzenbaum*
Nickles	*Ford*
Domenici	*Melcher*
Chafee	*Bradley*

Energy Research and Development

Phone: 224-4431   Room: S402 Capitol

Domenici - chairman

Warner	*Ford*
Heinz	*Jackson*
Weicker	*Bumpers*
Nickles	*Tsongas*

Public Lands and Reserved Water

Phone: 224-5161   Room: SD-308

Wallop - chairman

Hatfield	*Bumpers*
Hecht	*Jackson*
Chafee	*Matsunaga*
Domenici	*Melcher*

Water and Power

Phone: 224-2366   Room: A420 Immigration

Nickles - chairman

Hatfield	*Tsongas*
Wallop	*Jackson*
Murkowski	*Ford*
Hecht	*Metzenbaum*

* Chairman and ranking minority member are members ex officio of all subcommittees.

Environment and Public Works

Phone: 224-6176   Room: SD-410

R 9 - D 7

Environmental policy, research and development; air, water and noise pollution; construction and maintenance of highways; environmental aspects of Outer Continental Shelf lands; environmental effects of toxic substances, other than pesticides; fisheries and wildlife; flood control and improvements of rivers and harbors; nonmilitary environmental regulation and control of nuclear energy; ocean dumping; public buildings and grounds; public works, bridges and dams; regional economic development; solid waste disposal and recycling; water resources.

Robert T. Stafford,
R-Vt.,
chairman*

Howard H. Baker Jr., Tenn.	*Jennings Randolph, W.Va.**
John H. Chafee, R.I.	*Lloyd Bentsen, Texas*
Alan K. Simpson, Wyo.	*Quentin N. Burdick, N.D.*
James Abdnor, S.D.	*Gary Hart, Colo.*
Steven D. Symms, Idaho	*Daniel Patrick Moynihan,*
Pete V. Domenici, N.M.	*N.Y.*
Dave Durenberger, Minn.	*George J. Mitchell, Maine*
Gordon J. Humphrey, N.H.	*Max Baucus, Mont.*

Subcommittees

Environmental Pollution

Phone: 224-6691   Room: SD-410

Chafee - chairman

Simpson	*Mitchell*
Symms	*Hart*
Durenberger	*Moynihan*

Nuclear Regulation

Phone: 224-2991   Room: SD-625

Simpson - chairman

Baker	*Hart*
Domenici	*Mitchell*
Symms	*Baucus*

Regional and Community Development

Phone: 224-6176   Room: SD-410

Humphrey - chairman

Baker	*Burdick*
Domenici	*Bentsen*
Chafee	*Mitchell*

Toxic Substances and Environmental Oversight

Phone: 224-8215   Room: SD-410

Durenberger - chairman

Simpson	*Baucus*
Abdnor	*Burdick*
Humphrey	*Hart*

Transportation

Phone: 224-7863   Room: SD-625

Symms - chairman

Stafford	*Bentsen*
Baker	*Randolph*
Chafee	*Burdick*
Abdnor	*Moynihan*

Water Resources

Phone: 224-7866   Room: SD-625

Abdnor - chairman

Domenici	*Moynihan*
Durenberger	*Bentsen*
Humphrey	*Baucus*

* Chairman and ranking minority member are members ex officio of all subcommittees of which they are not regular members.

Finance

Phone: 224-4515   Room: SD-221

R 11 - D 9

Revenue measures generally; taxes; tariffs and import quotas; foreign trade agreements; customs; revenue sharing; federal debt limit; Social Security; health programs financed by taxes or trust funds.

Robert Dole,
R-Kan.,
chairman*

Bob Packwood, Ore.	*Russell B. Long, La.**
William V. Roth Jr., Del.	*Lloyd Bentsen, Texas*
John C. Danforth, Mo.	*Spark M. Matsunaga, Hawaii*
John H. Chafee, R.I.	*Daniel Patrick Moynihan,*
John Heinz, Pa.	*N.Y.*
Malcolm Wallop, Wyo.	*Max Baucus, Mont.*
Dave Durenberger, Minn.	*David L. Boren, Okla.*
William L. Armstrong, Colo.	*Bill Bradley, N.J.*
Steven D. Symms, Idaho	*George J. Mitchell, Maine*
Charles E. Grassley, Iowa	*David Pryor, Ark.*

Subcommittees

Economic Growth, Employment and Revenue Sharing

Phone: 224-5487   Room: SD-221

Heinz - chairman

| Roth | *Mitchell* |
| | *Moynihan* |

Energy and Agricultural Taxation

Phone: 224-4515   *Room: SD-221*

Wallop - chairman

Symms	*Bradley*
Durenberger	*Pryor*
	Bentsen

Estate and Gift Taxation

Phone: 224-5487   *Room: SD-221*

Symms - chairman

Grassley	*Boren*

Health

Phone: 224-5471   *Room: SD-221*

Durenberger - chairman

Dole	*Baucus*
Packwood	*Bradley*
Heinz	*Mitchell*

International Trade

Phone: 224-4515   *Room: SD-221*

Danforth - chairman

Roth	*Bentsen*
Chafee	*Matsunaga*
Heinz	*Boren*
Wallop	*Bradley*
Armstrong	*Mitchell*
Grassley	*Moynihan*
Symms	*Baucus*

Oversight of the Internal Revenue Service

Phone: 224-5487   *Room: SD-221*

Grassley - chairman

Dole	*Long*

Savings, Pensions and Investment Policy

Phone: 224-5487   *Room: SD-221*

Chafee - chairman

Packwood	*Pryor*
Roth	*Matsunaga*

Social Security and Income Maintenance Programs

Phone: 224-5470   *Room: SD-221*

Armstrong - chairman

Durenberger	*Moynihan*
Danforth	*Boren*
Dole	*Pryor*
	Long

Taxation and Debt Management

Phone: 224-5487   *Room: SD-221*

Packwood - chairman

Danforth	*Matsunaga*
Chafee	*Bentsen*
Wallop	*Baucus*
Armstrong	*Long*

* Chairman and ranking minority member are members ex officio of all subcommittees of which they are not regular members.

Foreign Relations

Phone: 224-4651   *Room: SD-427*

R 9 - D 8

Relations of the United States with foreign nations generally; treaties; foreign economic, military, technical and humanitarian assistance; foreign loans; diplomatic service; International Red Cross; international aspects of nuclear energy; International Monetary Fund; intervention abroad and declarations of war; foreign trade; national security; oceans and international environmental and scientific affairs; protection of U.S. citizens abroad; United Nations; World Bank and other development assistance organizations.

Charles H. Percy, R-Ill., chairman*

Howard H. Baker Jr., Tenn.	*Claiborne Pell, R.I.**
Jesse Helms, N.C.	*Joseph R. Biden Jr., Del.*
Richard G. Lugar, Ind.	*John Glenn, Ohio*

Charles McC. Mathias Jr., Md.
Nancy Landon Kassebaum, Kan.
Rudy Boschwitz, Minn.
Larry Pressler, S.D.
Frank H. Murkowski, Alaska

Paul S. Sarbanes, Md.
Edward Zorinsky, Neb.
Paul E. Tsongas, Mass.
Alan Cranston, Calif.
Christopher J. Dodd, Conn.

Subcommittees

African Affairs

Phone: 224-5481   *Room: SD-446*

Kassebaum - chairman

Mathias   *Tsongas*
Percy   *Dodd*

Arms Control, Oceans and International Operations and Environment

Phone: 224-4651   *Room: SD-427*

Pressler - chairman

Helms   *Cranston*
Kassebaum   *Zorinsky*

East Asian and Pacific Affairs

Phone: 224-5481   *Room: SD-446*

Murkowski - chairman

Baker   *Glenn*
Helms   *Cranston*

European Affairs

Phone: 224-5481   *Room: SD-446*

Lugar - chairman

Mathias   *Biden*
Boschwitz   *Glenn*
Baker   *Sarbanes*
Percy   *Zorinsky*

International Economic Policy

Phone: 224-4194   *Room: 202 Senate Courts*

Mathias - chairman

Lugar   *Dodd*
Boschwitz   *Biden*
Murkowski   *Sarbanes*

Near Eastern and South Asian Affairs

Phone: 224-5481   *Room: SD-446*

Boschwitz - chairman

Baker   *Sarbanes*
Percy   *Glenn*
Pressler   *Tsongas*

Western Hemisphere Affairs

Phone: 224-3866   *Room: 209 Senate Courts*

Helms - chairman

Lugar   *Zorinsky*
Kassebaum   *Tsongas*
Pressler   *Cranston*
Murkowski   *Dodd*

* Chairman and ranking minority member are members ex officio *of all subcommittees of which they are not regular members.*

Governmental Affairs

Phone: 224-4751   *Room: SD-346*

R 10 - D 8

Budget and accounting measures; census and statistics; federal civil service; congressional organization; intergovernmental relations; government information; District of Columbia; organization and management of nuclear export policy; executive branch reorganization; Postal Service; efficiency, economy and effectiveness of government.

William V. Roth Jr.,
R-Del.,
chairman*

Charles H. Percy, Ill.
Ted Stevens, Alaska
Charles McC. Mathias Jr., Md.
William S. Cohen, Maine
Dave Durenberger, Minn.
Warren B. Rudman, N.H.
John C. Danforth, Mo.
Thad Cochran, Miss.
William L. Armstrong, Colo.

Thomas F. Eagleton, Mo.*
Henry M. Jackson, Wash.
Lawton Chiles, Fla.
Sam Nunn, Ga.
John Glenn, Ohio
Jim Sasser, Tenn.
Carl Levin, Mich.
Jeff Bingaman, N.M.

Subcommittees

Civil Service, Post Office and General Services

Phone: 224-2254   *Room: 57 Capitol Hill Apts.*

Stevens - chairman

Mathias	*Bingaman*
Armstrong	*Sasser*

Energy, Nuclear Proliferation and Government Processes

Phone: 224-9515   *Room: 103 Senate Courts*

Percy - chairman

Durenberger	*Glenn*
Cohen	*Jackson*
Danforth	*Levin*

Governmental Efficiency and the District of Columbia

Phone: 224-4161   *Room: SD-624*

Mathias - chairman

Rudman	*Eagleton*
Cochran	*Chiles*

Information Management and Regulatory Affairs

Phone: 224-0211   *Room: 44 Capitol Hill Apts.*

Danforth - chairman

Percy	*Chiles*
Durenberger	*Jackson*

Intergovernmental Relations

Phone: 224-4718   *Room: 507 Carroll Arms*

Durenberger - chairman

Stevens	*Sasser*
Cochran	*Nunn*
Armstrong	*Levin*

Oversight of Government Management

Phone: 224-5538   *Room: 506 Carroll Arms*

Cohen - chairman

Rudman	*Levin*
Danforth	*Bingaman*

Permanent Subcommittee on Investigations

Phone: 224-3721   *Room: SR-100*

Roth - chairman
Rudman - vice chairman

Percy	*Nunn*
Mathias	*Jackson*
Cohen	*Chiles*
Armstrong	*Glenn*
Cochran	*Sasser*
	Bingaman

* Chairman and ranking minority member are members ex officio of all subcommittees of which they are not regular members.

Judiciary

Phone: 224-5225   *Room: SD-224*

R 10 - D 8

Civil and criminal judicial proceedings generally; penitentiaries; bankruptcy, mutiny, espionage and counterfeiting; civil liberties; constitutional amendments; apportionment of representatives; government information; immigration and naturalization; interstate compacts generally; claims against the United States; patents, copyrights and trademarks; monopolies and unlawful restraints of trade; holidays and celebrations.

Strom Thurmond,
R-S.C.,
chairman

Charles McC. Mathias Jr., Md.	*Joseph R. Biden Jr., Del.*
Paul Laxalt, Nev.	*Edward M. Kennedy, Mass.*

Orrin G. Hatch, Utah
Robert Dole, Kan.
Alan K. Simpson, Wyo.
John P. East, N.C.
Charles E. Grassley, Iowa
Jeremiah Denton, Ala.
Arlen Specter, Pa.

Robert C. Byrd, W.Va.
Howard M. Metzenbaum,
* Ohio*
Dennis DeConcini, Ariz.
Patrick J. Leahy, Vt.
Max Baucus, Mont.
Howell Heflin, Ala.

Subcommittees

Administrative Practice and Procedure

Phone: 224-7703   Room: SR-B10

Grassley - chairman

Laxalt   *Heflin*
Specter   *Baucus*

Constitution

Phone: 224-8191   Room: SR-114

Hatch - chairman

Thurmond   *DeConcini*
Grassley   *Leahy*

Courts

Phone: 224-1674   Room: SD-212

Dole - chairman

Thurmond   *Heflin*
Simpson   *Baucus*
East   *DeConcini*

Criminal Law

Phone: 224-3980   Room: SR-108

Laxalt - chairman

Thurmond   *Biden*
Specter   *Baucus*
Dole

Immigration and Refugee Policy

Phone: 224-7878   Room: A509 Immigration

Simpson - chairman

Grassley   *Kennedy*
Mathias   *Heflin*

Juvenile Justice

Phone: 224-8178   Room: A523 Immigration

Specter - chairman

Denton   *Metzenbaum*
Mathias   *Kennedy*

Patents, Copyrights and Trademarks

Phone: 224-5617   Room: SR-198

Mathias - chairman

Laxalt   *Metzenbaum*
Hatch   *Leahy*
Dole   *DeConcini*

Security and Terrorism

Phone: 224-6136   Room: A521 Immigration

Denton - chairman

Hatch   *Leahy*
East   *Metzenbaum*

Separation of Powers

Phone: 224-6791   Room: SR-B16

East - chairman

Denton   *Baucus*
Simpson   *Metzenbaum*

Labor and Human Resources

Phone: 224-5375   Room: SD-428

R 10 - D 8

Education, labor, health and public welfare generally; aging; arts and humanities; biomedical research and development; child labor; convict labor; American National Red Cross; equal employment opportunity; handicapped individuals; labor standards and statistics; mediation and arbitration of labor disputes; occupational safety and health; private pension plans; public health; railway labor and retirement; regulation of foreign laborers; student loans; wages and hours.

Orrin G. Hatch,
R-Utah,
chairman*

Robert T. Stafford, Vt.
Dan Quayle, Ind.
Don Nickles, Okla.
Gordon J. Humphrey, N.H.
Jeremiah Denton, Ala.
Lowell P. Weicker Jr., Conn.
Charles E. Grassley, Iowa
John P. East, N.C.
Paula Hawkins, Fla.

Edward M. Kennedy, Mass.*
Jennings Randolph, W. Va.
Claiborne Pell, R.I.
Thomas F. Eagleton, Mo.
Donald W. Riegle Jr., Mich.
Howard M. Metzenbaum,
 Ohio
Spark M. Matsunaga, Hawaii
Christopher J. Dodd, Conn.

Subcommittees

Aging

Phone: 224-5375   Room: SD-428

Grassley - chairman

Hawkins	*Eagleton*
Humphrey	*Pell*
Denton	*Metzenbaum*

Alcoholism and Drug Abuse

Phone: 224-5630   Room: 310B Senate Courts

Humphrey - chairman

Quayle	*Matsunaga*
East	*Riegle*

Education, Arts and the Humanities

Phone: 224-2962   Room: 309D Senate Courts

Stafford - chairman

Hatch	*Pell*
Quayle	*Kennedy*
Denton	*Randolph*
Weicker	*Eagleton*
East	*Dodd*

Employment and Productivity

Phone: 224-6306   Room: A613 Immigration

Quayle - chairman

Hawkins	*Metzenbaum*
Hatch	*Pell*
Nickles	*Riegle*
Grassley	*Kennedy*

Family and Human Services

Phone: 224-3491   Room: A624 Immigration

Denton - chairman

Humphrey	*Dodd*
Nickles	*Eagleton*
Weicker	*Metzenbaum*
Grassley	

Handicapped

Phone: 224-6265   Room: SH-113

Weicker - chairman

Stafford	*Randolph*
Hawkins	*Eagleton*
Nickles	*Matsunaga*

Labor

Phone: 224-5546   Room: A609 Immigration

Nickles - chairman

East	*Riegle*
Grassley	*Kennedy*
Hatch	*Randolph*
Stafford	*Matsunaga*
Denton	

* Chairman and ranking minority member are members ex officio of all subcommittees of which they are not regular members.

Rules and Administration

Phone: 224-6352   Room: SR-309

R 7 - D 5

Senate administration generally; corrupt practices; qualifications of senators; contested elections; federal elections generally; Government Printing Office; *Congressional Record;* meetings of Congress and attendance of members; presidential succession; the Capitol, congressional office buildings, the Library of Congress, the Smithsonian Institution and the Botanic Gardens.

Charles McC.
Mathias Jr.,
R-Md.,
chairman

Mark O. Hatfield, Ore.
Howard H. Baker Jr., Tenn.
James A. McClure, Idaho
Jesse Helms, N.C.
John W. Warner, Va.
Robert Dole, Kan.

Wendell H. Ford, Ky.
Claiborne Pell, R.I.
Robert C. Byrd, W.Va.
Daniel K. Inouye, Hawaii
Dennis DeConcini, Ariz.

(No standing subcommittees.)

Select Ethics

Phone: 224-2981   Room: 113 Carroll Arms

R 3 - D 3

Studies and investigates standards and conduct of Senate members and employees and may recommend remedial action.

Ted Stevens,
R-Alaska,
chairman

Howell Heflin,
D-Ala.,
vice chairman

Jesse Helms, N.C.
Dave Durenberger, Minn.

David Pryor, Ark.
Thomas F. Eagleton, Mo.

(No standing subcommittees.)

Select Indian Affairs

Phone: 224-2251   Room: SD-640

R 4 - D 3

Problems and opportunities of Indians including Indian land management and trust responsibilities, education, health, special services, loan programs and Indian claims against the United States.

Mark Andrews,
R-N.D.,
chairman

Barry Goldwater, Ariz.
Slade Gorton, Wash.
Frank H. Murkowski, Alaska

John Melcher, Mont.
Daniel K. Inouye, Hawaii
Dennis DeConcini, Ariz.

(No standing subcommittees.)

Select Intelligence

Phone: 224-1700   Room: SD-G50

R 8 - D 7

Legislative and budgetary authority over the Central Intelligence Agency, the Defense Intelligence Agency, the National Security Agency and intelligence activities of the Federal Bureau of Investigation and other components of the federal intelligence community.

Barry Goldwater,
R-Ariz.,
chairman*

Daniel Patrick
Moynihan,
D-N.Y.,
vice chairman*

Jake Garn, Utah
John H. Chafee, R.I.
Richard G. Lugar, Ind.
Malcolm Wallop, Wyo.
Dave Durenberger, Minn.
William V. Roth Jr., Del.
William S. Cohen, Maine

Walter D. Huddleston, Ky.
Joseph R. Biden Jr., Del.
Daniel K. Inouye, Hawaii
Henry M. Jackson, Wash.
Patrick J. Leahy, Vt.
Lloyd Bentsen, Texas

Subcommittees

Analysis and Production

Phone: 224-1700   *Room: SD-G50*

Lugar - chairman
Jackson - vice chairman

Wallop   *Bentsen*
Roth

Budget

Phone: 224-1700   *Room: SD-G50*

Wallop - chairman
Inouye - vice chairman

Garn   *Jackson*
Durenberger   *Leahy*
Roth   *Bentsen*
Cohen

Collection and Foreign Operations

Phone: 224-1700   *Room: SD-G50*

Chafee - chairman
Huddleston - vice chairman

Garn   *Biden*
Lugar   *Inouye*
Cohen   *Jackson*

Legislation and the Rights of Americans

Phone: 224-1700   *Room: SD-G50*

Durenberger - chairman
Leahy - vice chairman

Garn   *Huddleston*
Chafee   *Biden*
Cohen

* Chairman and ranking minority member are members ex officio of all subcommittees. Majority Leader Howard H. Baker Jr., Tenn., and Minority Leader Robert C. Byrd, W.Va., are members ex officio of the full committee.

Small Business

Phone: 224-5175   *Room: SR-428A*

R 10 - D 9

Problems of small business; Small Business Administration.

Lowell P. Weicker Jr.,
R-Conn.,
chairman*

Bob Packwood, Ore.
Orrin G. Hatch, Utah
Rudy Boschwitz, Minn.
Slade Gorton, Wash.
Don Nickles, Okla.
Warren B. Rudman, N.H.
Alfonse M. D'Amato, N.Y.
Bob Kasten, Wis.
Larry Pressler, S.D.

Sam Nunn, Ga.*
Walter D. Huddleston, Ky.
Dale Bumpers, Ark.
Jim Sasser, Tenn.
Max Baucus, Mont.
Carl Levin, Mich.
Paul E. Tsongas, Mass.
Alan J. Dixon, Ill.
David L. Boren, Okla.

Capital Formation and Retention

Phone: 224-5175   *Room: SR-428A*

Packwood - chairman

Hatch   *Bumpers*
Boschwitz   *Sasser*

Entrepreneurship and Special Problems Facing Small Business

Phone: 224-5175   *Room: SR-428A*

Kasten - chairman

Weicker   *Boren*

Export Promotion and Market Development

Phone: 224-5175   *Room: SR-428A*

Boschwitz - chairman

Gorton   *Huddleston*

Government Procurement

Phone: 224-5175   Room: SR-428A

Nickles - chairman

Rudman   *Levin*
Kasten   *Bumpers*

Government Regulation and Paperwork

Phone: 224-5175   Room: SR-428A

Hatch - chairman

Pressler   *Huddleston*

Innovation and Technology

Phone: 224-5175   Room: SR-428A

Rudman - chairman

Packwood   *Baucus*

Productivity and Competition

Phone: 224-5175   Room: SR-428A

Gorton - chairman

Nickles   *Tsongas*

Small Business: Family Farm

Phone: 224-5175   Room: SR-428A

Pressler - chairman

D'Amato   *Nunn*

Urban and Rural Economic Development

Phone: 224-5175   Room: SR-428A

D'Amato - chairman

Weicker   *Dixon*

* Chairman and ranking minority member are members ex officio of all subcommittees of which they are not regular members.

Special Aging

Phone: 224-5364   Room: SD-G37

R 8 - D 7

Problems and opportunities of older people including health, income, employment, housing and care and assistance. Reports findings and makes recommendations to the Senate, but cannot report legislation.

John Heinz,
R-Pa.,
chairman

Pete V. Domenici, N.M.   *John Glenn, Ohio*
Charles H. Percy, Ill.   *Lawton Chiles, Fla.*
Nancy Landon Kassebaum,   *John Melcher, Mont.*
  Kan.   *David Pryor, Ark.*
William S. Cohen, Maine   *Bill Bradley, N.J.*
Larry Pressler, S.D.   *Quentin N. Burdick, N.D.*
Charles E. Grassley, Iowa   *Christopher J. Dodd,*
Pete Wilson, Calif.   *Conn.*

(No standing subcommittees.)

Veterans' Affairs

Phone: 224-9126   Room: SR-414

R 7 - D 5

Veterans' measures generally; compensation; armed forces life insurance; national cemeteries; pensions; readjustment benefits; veterans' hospitals, medical care and treatment; vocational rehabilitation and education.

Alan K. Simpson,
R-Wyo.,
chairman

Strom Thurmond, S.C.   *Alan Cranston, Calif.*
Robert T. Stafford, Vt.   *Jennings Randolph, W.Va.*
Frank H. Murkowski, Alaska   *Spark M. Matsunaga, Hawaii*
Arlen Specter, Pa.   *Dennis DeConcini, Ariz.*
Jeremiah Denton, Ala.   *George J. Mitchell, Maine*
Rudy Boschwitz, Minn.

(No standing subcommittees.)

Senate Party Committees, 98th Congress

Republican Leaders

Chairman of the Conference — James A. McClure, Idaho. 224-2764
Secretary of the Conference — Jake Garn, Utah 224-1326
Majority Leader — Howard H. Baker Jr., Tenn. 224-3135
Majority Whip — Ted Stevens, Alaska 224-2708

Policy Committee

Phone: 224-2946   *Room: SR-347*

Scheduling of legislation.

John Tower, Texas, chairman

Howard H. Baker Jr., Tenn.† | James A. McClure, Idaho
William S. Cohen, Maine | Bob Packwood, Ore.
Robert Dole, Kan. | Charles H. Percy, Ill.
Pete V. Domenici, N.M. | William V. Roth Jr., Del.
Jake Garn, Utah | Alan K. Simpson, Wyo.
Barry Goldwater, Ariz. | Robert T. Stafford, Vt.
Orrin G. Hatch, Utah | Ted Stevens, Alaska
Mark O. Hatfield, Ore. | Strom Thurmond, S.C.
John Heinz, Pa. | Lowell P. Weicker Jr., Conn.
Jesse Helms, N.C. | Pete Wilson, Calif.
Charles McC. Mathias Jr., Md.

† Member ex officio from the leadership.

Committee on Committees

Phone: 224-4774   *Room: SR-302*

Makes Republican committee assignments.

Nancy Landon Kassebaum, Kan., chairman

James Abdnor, S.D. | William L. Armstrong, Colo.
Mark Andrews, N.D. |

Howard H. Baker Jr., Tenn.† | Chic Hecht, Nev.
Rudy Boschwitz, Minn. | Gordon J. Humphrey, N.H.
John H. Chafee, R.I. | Roger W. Jepsen, Iowa
Thad Cochran, Miss. | Larry Pressler, S.D.
Dave Durenberger, Minn. | Dan Quayle, Ind.
Paula Hawkins, Fla. | Arlen Specter, Pa.
 | Malcolm Wallop, Wyo.
 | John W. Warner, Va.

† Member ex officio from the leadership.

National Republican Senatorial Committee

Phone: 224-2351   *404 C St. N.E. 20002*

Campaign support committee for Republican senatorial candidates.

Richard G. Lugar, Ind., chairman

Howard H. Baker Jr., Tenn.† | Orrin G. Hatch, Utah
Alfonse M. D'Amato, N.Y. | Bob Kasten, Wis.
 | Paul Laxalt, Nev.
John C. Danforth, Mo. | Mack Mattingly, Ga.
Jeremiah Denton, Ala. | Frank H. Murkowski, Alaska
John P. East, N.C. | Don Nickles, Okla.
Slade Gorton, Wash. | Warren B. Rudman, N.H.
Charles E. Grassley, Iowa | Steven D. Symms, Idaho
 | Paul S. Trible Jr., Va.

† Member ex officio from the leadership.

Democratic Leaders

Chairman of the Conference — *Robert C. Byrd, W.Va.* 224-5551
Secretary of the Conference — *Daniel K. Inouye, Hawaii* 224-5551
Minority Leader — *Byrd* 224-5556
Minority Whip — *Alan Cranston, Calif.* 224-2158
Chief Deputy Whip — *Spark M. Matsunaga, Hawaii*
Deputy Whips — *Max Baucus, Mont.; Alan J. Dixon, Ill.; Christopher J. Dodd, Conn.; J. James Exon, Neb.; Wendell H. Ford, Ky.; John Glenn, Ohio; Walter D. Huddleston, Ky.; Patrick J. Leahy, Vt.; David Pryor, Ark.; Donald W. Riegle Jr., Mich.; Paul S. Sarbanes, Md.*

Policy Committee

Phone: 224-5551　　　　　Room: S118 Capitol

Scheduling of legislation.

Robert C. Byrd, W.Va., chairman

Quentin N. Burdick, N.D.	Walter D. Huddleston, Ky.
Alan Cranston	Daniel K. Inouye, Hawaii†
John Glenn, Ohio	
Ernest F. Hollings, S.C.	Claiborne Pell, R.I.

† Members ex officio *from the leadership.*

Legislative Review

Phone: 224-3735　　　　　Room: S208 Capitol

Reviews legislative proposals, provides recommendations.

Dale Bumpers, Ark., chairman

Lloyd Bentsen, Texas	Daniel Patrick Moynihan, N.Y.
J. James Exon, Neb.	
Gary Hart, Colo.	William Proxmire, Wis.
John Melcher, Mont.	Paul S. Sarbanes, Md.

Steering Committee

Phone: 224-3735　　　　　Room: S208 Capitol

Makes Democratic committee assignments.

Robert C. Byrd, W.Va., chairman

Joseph R. Biden Jr., Del.	Patrick J. Leahy, Vt.
David L. Boren, Okla.	Russell B. Long, La.
Lawton Chiles, Fla.	Howard M. Metzenbaum, Ohio
Alan Cranston, Calif.	
Dennis DeConcini, Ariz.	George J. Mitchell, Maine
Christopher J. Dodd, Conn.	
	Sam Nunn, Ga.
Thomas F. Eagleton, Mo.	David Pryor, Ark.
	Donald W. Riegle Jr., Mich.
Wendell H. Ford, Ky.	
Daniel K. Inouye, Hawaii†	Jim Sasser, Tenn.
	John C. Stennis, Miss.
Henry M. Jackson, Wash.	Edward Zorinsky, Neb.
Edward M. Kennedy, Mass.	

† Member ex officio *from the leadership.*

Senatorial Campaign Committee

Phone: 224-2447　　　400 North Capitol St. N.W. 20001

Campaign support committee for Democratic senatorial candidates.

Lloyd Bentsen, Texas, chairman
Alan Cranston, Calif., vice chairman

Robert C. Byrd, W.Va.†	Edward M. Kennedy, Mass.
Christopher J. Dodd, Conn.	Frank R. Lautenberg, N. .
Thomas F. Eagleton, Mo.	Russell B. Long, La.
Wendell H. Ford, Ky.	George J. Mitchell, Maine
Daniel K. Inouye, Hawaii†	Paul S. Sarbanes, Md.
Henry M. Jackson, Wash.	Jim Sasser, Tenn.

† Member ex officio *from the leadership.*

House Committee Assignments, 98th Congress

As of April 2, 1983

Agriculture

Phone 225-2171   *Room: 1301 LHOB*

D 26 - R 15

Agriculture generally; production, marketing and stabilization of agricultural prices; animal industry and diseases of animals; crop insurance and soil conservation; dairy industry; farm credit and security; forestry in general; human nutrition; home economics; inspection of livestock and meat products; plant industry, soils and agricultural engineering; rural electrification; commodities exchanges; rural development.

E. "Kika"
de la Garza,
D-Texas,
chairman*

Thomas S. Foley, Wash.,
  vice chairman
Walter B. Jones, N.C.
Ed Jones, Tenn.
George E. Brown Jr., Calif.
Charlie Rose, N.C.
James Weaver, Ore.
Tom Harkin, Iowa
Berkley Bedell, Iowa
Glenn English, Okla.
Leon E. Panetta, Calif.
Jerry Huckaby, La.
Dan Glickman, Kan.
Charles Whitley, N.C.
Tony Coelho, Calif.
Thomas A. Daschle, S.D.
Charles W. Stenholm,
  Texas
Harold L. Volkmer, Mo.
Charles Hatcher, Ga.
Robin Tallon, S.C.
Harley O. Staggers Jr.,
  W.Va.
Dick Durbin, Ill.

*Edward R. Madigan, Ill.**
James M. Jeffords, Vt.
E. Thomas Coleman, Mo.
Ron Marlenee, Mont.
Larry J. Hopkins, Ky.
George Hansen, Idaho
Arlan Stangeland, Minn.
Pat Roberts, Kan.
Bill Emerson, Mo.
Joe Skeen, N.M.
Sid Morrison, Wash.
Steve Gunderson, Wis.
Cooper Evans, Iowa
Gene Chappie, Calif.
Webb Franklin, Miss.

Lane Evans, Ill.
Lindsay Thomas, Ga.
James R. Olin, Va.
Timothy J. Penny, Minn.

Subcommittees

Conservation, Credit and Rural Development

Phone: 225-1867   *Room: 1336 LHOB*

Jones, Tenn. - chairman

Weaver	*Coleman*
Bedell	*Jeffords*
English	*Skeen*
Glickman	*Morrison*
Daschle	*Gunderson*
Stenholm	
Tallon	
Durbin	
Evans, Ill.	

Cotton, Rice and Sugar

Phone: 225-1867   *Room: 1336 LHOB*

Huckaby - chairman

Coelho	*Stangeland*
Jones, Tenn.	*Emerson*
Rose	*Chappie*
English	*Franklin*
Whitley	
Stenholm	
Hatcher	

Department Operations, Research and Foreign Agriculture

Phone: 225-8408   *Room: 1430 LHOB*

Brown - chairman

Staggers	*Roberts*
Penny	*Gunderson*
Panetta	*Evans, Iowa*
Foley	*Franklin*
Coelho	
Volkmer	
Olin	

Domestic Marketing, Consumer Relations and Nutrition

Phone: 225-8406   *Room: 1430 LHOB*

Panetta - chairman

Olin	*Emerson*
Huckaby	*Coleman*
Glickman	*Hansen*
Staggers	
Foley	

Forests, Family Farms and Energy

Phone: 225-0301   *Room: 1301 LHOB*

Whitley - chairman

Foley	*Hansen*
Brown	*Marlenee*
Weaver	*Morrison*
Huckaby	*Chappie*
Staggers	
Bedell	
Panetta	

Livestock, Dairy and Poultry

Phone: 225-1867   *Room: 1336 LHOB*

Harkin - chairman

Volkmer	*Jeffords*
Olin	*Hopkins*
Jones, Tenn.	*Hansen*
Rose	*Skeen*
Coelho	*Gunderson*
Stenholm	
Hatcher	
Penny	
Daschle	

Tobacco and Peanuts

Phone: 225-8906   *Room: 1430 LHOB*

Rose - chairman

Jones, N.C.	*Hopkins*
Hatcher	*Roberts*
Thomas	*Skeen*
Whitley	*Franklin*
Tallon	
English	
Stenholm	

Wheat, Soybeans and Feed Grains

Phone: 225-1867   *Room: 1336 LHOB*

Foley - chairman

Harkin	*Marlenee*
Bedell	*Stangeland*
English	*Roberts*
Glickman	*Emerson*
Daschle	*Evans, Iowa*
Volkmer	
Durbin	
Evans, Ill.	
Thomas	

* Chairman and ranking minority member are members ex officio of all subcommittees.

Appropriations

Phone: 225-2771   *Room: H218 Capitol*

D 36 - R 21

Appropriation of revenue for support of the federal government; rescissions of appropriations; transfers of unexpended balances; new spending authority under the Congressional Budget Act.

Jamie L. Whitten, D-Miss., chairman*

Edward P. Boland, Mass.	*Silvio O. Conte, Mass.**
William H. Natcher, Ky.	*Joseph M. McDade, Pa.*
Neal Smith, Iowa	*Jack Edwards, Ala.*
Joseph P. Addabbo, N.Y.	*John T. Myers, Ind.*
Clarence D. Long, Md.	*J. Kenneth Robinson, Va.*
Sidney R. Yates, Ill.	*Clarence E. Miller, Ohio*
David R. Obey, Wis.	*Lawrence Coughlin, Pa.*
Edward R. Roybal, Calif.	*C.W. Bill Young, Fla.*
Louis Stokes, Ohio	*Jack F. Kemp, N.Y.*
Tom Bevill, Ala.	*Ralph Regula, Ohio*
Bill Chappell Jr., Fla.	*George M. O'Brien, Ill.*
Bill Alexander, Ark.	*Virginia Smith, Neb.*
John P. Murtha, Pa.	*Eldon Rudd, Ariz.*
Bob Traxler, Mich.	*Carl D. Pursell, Mich.*

Joseph D. Early, Mass.
Charles Wilson, Texas
Lindy (Mrs. Hale) Boggs, La.
Norman D. Dicks, Wash.
Matthew F. McHugh, N.Y.
William Lehman, Fla.
Jack Hightower, Texas
Martin Olav Sabo, Minn.
Julian C. Dixon, Calif.
Vic Fazio, Calif.
W. G. "Bill" Hefner, N.C.
Les AuCoin, Ore.
Daniel K. Akaka, Hawaii
Wes Watkins, Okla.
William H. Gray III, Pa.
Bernard J. Dwyer, N.J.
William R. Ratchford, Conn.
Bill Boner, Tenn.
Steny H. Hoyer, Md.
Bob Carr, Mich.
Robert J. Mrazek, N.Y.

Mickey Edwards, Okla.
Bob Livingston, La.
Bill Green, N.Y.
Tom Loeffler, Texas
Jerry Lewis, Calif.
John Edward Porter, Ill.
Harold Rogers, Ky.

Subcommittees

Agriculture, Rural Development and Related Agencies

Phone: 225-2638   *Room: 2362 RHOB*

Whitten - chairman

Traxler	*Smith, Neb.*
McHugh	*Robinson*
Natcher	*Myers*
Akaka	*Rogers*
Watkins	
Hightower	
Smith, Iowa	
Alexander	

Commerce, Justice, State and Judiciary

Phone: 225-3351   *Room: H309 Capitol*

Smith, Iowa - chairman

Alexander	*O'Brien*
Early	*Miller*
Dwyer	*Porter*
Mrazek	
Carr	

Defense

Phone: 225-2847   *Room: H144 Capitol*

Addabbo - chairman

Chappell	*Edwards, Ala.*
Murtha	*Robinson*
Dicks	*McDade*
Wilson	*Young*
Hefner	
Hightower	
AuCoin	

District of Columbia

Phone: 225-5338   *Room: H301 Capitol*

Dixon - chairman

Natcher	*Coughlin*
Stokes	*Green*
Wilson	*Rogers*
Lehman	
Sabo	

Energy and Water Development

Phone: 225-3421   *Room: 2362 RHOB*

Bevill - chairman

Boggs	*Myers*
Chappell	*Smith, Neb.*
Fazio	*Rudd*
Watkins	
Boner	

Foreign Operations

Phone: 225-2041   *Room: H307 Capitol*

Long - chairman

Obey	*Kemp*
Yates	*Edwards, Okla.*
McHugh	*Livingston*
Lehman	*Lewis*
Wilson	
Dixon	
Gray	

HUD - Independent Agencies

Phone: 225-3241   *Room: H143 Capitol*

Boland - chairman

Traxler	*Green*
Stokes	*Coughlin*
Boggs	*Lewis*
Sabo	
Boner	

Interior

Phone: 225-3081   *Room: B308 RHOB*

Yates - chairman

Murtha	*McDade*
Dicks	*Regula*
Ratchford	*Loeffler*
Boland	
AuCoin	

Labor - Health and Human Services - Education

Phone: 225-3508   *Room: 2358 RHOB*

Natcher - chairman

Smith, Iowa	*Conte*
Obey	*O'Brien*
Roybal	*Pursell*
Stokes	*Porter*
Early	*Young*
Dwyer	
Hoyer	

Legislative

Phone: 225-5338   *Room: H301 Capitol*

Fazio - chairman

Obey	*Lewis*
Murtha	*Conte*
Traxler	*Myers*
Boggs	*Porter* *
Hightower	

Military Construction

Phone: 225-3047   *Room: B300 RHOB*

Hefner - chairman

Bevill	*Regula*
Long	*Edwards, Okla.*
Alexander	*Loeffler*
Addabbo	*Livingston*
Chappell	
Dicks	
Fazio	

Transportation

Phone: 225-2141   *Room: 2358 RHOB*

Lehman - chairman

Sabo	*Coughlin*
Gray	*Conte*
Ratchford	*Edwards, Ala.*
Carr	*Pursell*
Mrazek	

Treasury - Postal Service - General Government

Phone: 225-5834   *Room: H164 Capitol*

Roybal - chairman

Addabbo	*Miller*
Akaka	*Rudd*
Hoyer	*Rogers*
Boland	
Long	

* Chairman and ranking minority member are members ex officio *of all subcommittees of which they are not regular members.*

Armed Services

Phone: 225-4151   *Room: 2120 RHOB*

D 28 - R 16

Common defense generally; Department of Defense; ammunition depots; forts; arsenals; Army, Navy and Air Force reservations and establishments; naval petroleum and oil shale reserves; scientific research and development in support of the armed services; Selective Service System; strategic and critical materials; military applications of nuclear energy; soldiers' and sailors' homes.

Melvin Price, D-Ill., chairman

Charles E. Bennett, Fla.	*William L. Dickinson, Ala.*
Samuel S. Stratton, N.Y.	*G. William Whitehurst, Va.*
Bill Nichols, Ala.	*Floyd Spence, S.C.*
Dan Daniel, Va.	*Marjorie S. Holt, Md.*
G. V. "Sonny" Montgomery, Miss.	*Elwood Hillis, Ind.*
Les Aspin, Wis.	*Robert E. Badham, Calif.*
Ronald V. Dellums, Calif.	*Bob Stump, Ariz.*
Patricia Schroeder, Colo.	*Jim Courter, N.J.*
Abraham Kazen Jr., Texas	*Larry J. Hopkins, Ky.*
Antonio Borja Won Pat, Guam[1]	*Robert W. Davis, Mich.*
Larry P. McDonald, Ga.	*Ken Kramer, Colo.*
Beverly B. Byron, Md.	*Duncan L. Hunter, Calif.*
Nicholas Mavroules, Mass.	*Thomas F. Hartnett, S.C.*
Earl Hutto, Fla.	*Daniel B. Crane, Ill.*
	David O'B. Martin, N.Y.
	John R. Kasich, Ohio

Ike Skelton, Mo.
Marvin Leath, Texas
Dave McCurdy, Okla.
Thomas M. Foglietta, Pa.
Roy Dyson, Md.
Dennis M. Hertel, Mich.
Marilyn Lloyd Bouquard, Tenn.
Norman Sisisky, Va.
Richard Ray, Ga.
John M. Spratt Jr., S.C.
Frank McCloskey, Ind.
Robin Britt, N.C.
Solomon P. Ortiz, Texas
Ron Coleman, Texas

Subcommittees

Investigations

Phone: 225-4221   *Room: 2339 RHOB*

Nichols - chairman

Kazen	*Hopkins*
Mavroules	*Stump*
Leath	*Crane*
Ray	*Martin*
Britt	*Kasich*
Stratton	
Daniel	
Aspin	

Military Installations and Facilities

Phone: 225-1240   *Room: 2343 RHOB*

Dellums - chairman

Montgomery	*Kramer*
Kazen	*Whitehurst*
Won Pat	*Dickinson*
Hutto	*Hartnett*
Foglietta	*Martin*
Hertel	
Sisisky	
Spratt	

Military Personnel and Compensation

Phone: 225-7560   *Room: 2343 RHOB*

Aspin - chairman

Montgomery	*Hillis*
Schroeder	*Holt*
Byron	*Hunter*
Skelton	*Hartnett*
Spratt	*Dickinson*
McCloskey	
Ortiz	
Coleman	

Procurement and Military Nuclear Systems

Phone: 225-7160   *Room: 2120 RHOB*

Stratton - chairman

Byron	*Holt*
Mavroules	*Badham*
Skelton	*Courter*
Leath	*Kramer*
McCurdy	*Davis*
Dyson	
Bouquard	
Ray	

Readiness

Phone: 225-7991   *Room: 420 CHOB*

Daniel - chairman

McDonald	*Whitehurst*
Hutto	*Spence*
Leath	*Crane*
McCurdy	*Kasich*
Foglietta	
Hertel	
Nichols	

Research and Development

Phone: 225-3168   *Room: 2120 RHOB*

Price - chairman

Schroeder	*Dickinson*
Won Pat	*Courter*
McDonald	*Badham*
Hutto	*Davis*
Hertel	*Stump*
McCloskey	*Hopkins*
Coleman	
Bennett	
Dellums	

Seapower and Strategic and Critical Materials

Phone: 225-6704   *Room: 2343 RHOB*

Bennett - chairman

Foglietta	*Spence*
Dyson	*Hartnett*
Bouquard	*Hillis*
Sisisky	*Hunter*
Britt	
Ortiz	
Price	

¹ Delegate from Guam not counted in party ratios.

Banking, Finance and Urban Affairs

Phone: 225-4247   Room: 2129 RHOB

D 29 - R 17

Banks and banking including deposit insurance and federal monetary policy; money and credit; currency; issuance and redemption of notes; gold and silver; coinage; valuation and revaluation of the dollar; urban development; private and public housing; economic stabilization; defense production; renegotiation; price controls; international finance; financial aid to commerce and industry.

Fernand J. St Germain, D-R.I., chairman

Henry B. Gonzalez, Texas	*Chalmers P. Wylie, Ohio*
Joseph G. Minish, N.J.	*Stewart B. McKinney, Conn.*
Frank Annunzio, Ill.	*George Hansen, Idaho*
Parren J. Mitchell, Md.	*Jim Leach, Iowa*
Walter E. Fauntroy, D.C.[1]	*Ron Paul, Texas*
Stephen L. Neal, N.C.	*Ed Bethune, Ark.*
Jerry M. Patterson, Calif.	*Norman D. Shumway, Calif.*
Carroll Hubbard Jr., Ky.	*Stan Parris, Va.*
John J. LaFalce, N.Y.	*Bill McCollum, Fla.*
Norman E. D'Amours, N.H.	*George C. Wortley, N.Y.*
Stan Lundine, N.Y.	*Marge Roukema, N.J.*
Mary Rose Oakar, Ohio	*Bill Lowery, Calif.*
Bruce F. Vento, Minn.	*Douglas K. Bereuter, Neb.*
Doug Barnard Jr., Ga.	*David Dreier, Calif.*
Robert Garcia, N.Y.	*John Hiler, Ind.*
Mike Lowry, Wash.	*Tom Ridge, Pa.*
Charles E. Schumer, N.Y.	*Steve Bartlett, Texas*
Barney Frank, Mass.	
Bill Patman, Texas	
William J. Coyne, Pa.	
Buddy Roemer, La.	
Richard H. Lehman, Calif.	
Bruce A. Morrison, Conn.	
Jim Cooper, Tenn.	
Marcy Kaptur, Ohio	
Ben Erdreich, Ala.	
Sander M. Levin, Mich.	
Thomas R. Carper, Del.	
Esteban Edward Torres, Calif.	

Subcommittees

Consumer Affairs and Coinage

Phone: 226-3280   Room: 212 Annex 1

Annunzio - chairman

St Germain	*Paul*
Gonzalez	*Wylie*
Minish	*Hiler*
Patman	*Ridge*
Vento	
Lowry	

Domestic Monetary Policy

Phone: 226-7315   Room: 109 Annex 2

Fauntroy - chairman

Neal	*Hansen*
Barnard	*Paul*
Hubbard	*McCollum*
Patman	*Lowery*
Roemer	*Hiler*
Morrison	
Cooper	
Carper	

Economic Stabilization

Phone: 225-7145   Room: 2220 RHOB

LaFalce - chairman

Lundine	*Shumway*
Vento	*McKinney*
D'Amours	*Paul*
Oakar	*Bethune*
Minish	*Parris*
Fauntroy	*Wortley*
Schumer	*Roukema*
Coyne	*Bereuter*
Roemer	*Ridge*
Morrison	
Cooper	
Kaptur	
Erdreich	
Levin	
Torres	

Financial Institutions Supervision, Regulation and Insurance

Phone: 225-2924   Room: B303 RHOB

St Germain - chairman

Annunzio	*Wylie*
Hubbard	*Hansen*

D'Amours   *Leach*
Barnard   *Bethune*
LaFalce   *McKinney*
Oakar   *Shumway*
Vento   *McCollum*
Garcia   *Lowery*
Schumer   *Wortley*
Patman   *Dreier*
Neal
Frank
Lehman
Cooper
Erdreich
Carper

General Oversight and Renegotiation

Phone: 225-2828   Room: B304 RHOB

Minish - chairman

Gonzalez   *Parris*
Annunzio   *Wortley*
Mitchell   *Bereuter*
Barnard   *Dreier*
Fauntroy   *Hiler*
Oakar   *Bartlett*
St Germain
Garcia
Roemer

Housing and Community Development

Phone: 225-7054   Room: 2129 RHOB

Gonzalez - chairman

St Germain   *McKinney*
Fauntroy   *Wylie*
Patterson   *Leach*
Lundine   *Bethune*
Oakar   *Roukema*
Vento   *Wortley*
Garcia   *McCollum*
Lowry   *Lowery*
Mitchell   *Bereuter*
Hubbard   *Dreier*
D'Amours   *Hiler*
Schumer   *Ridge*
Frank   *Bartlett*
Coyne
Lehman
Morrison
Cooper
Kaptur
Erdreich
Levin
Carper
Torres

International Development Institutions and Finance

Phone: 226-7511   Room: 604 Annex 1

Patterson - chairman

LaFalce   *Bereuter*
Oakar   *Roukema*
Lowry   *Ridge*
Garcia   *Bartlett*
Levin
Torres

International Trade, Investment and Monetary Policy

Phone: 225-1271   Room: 139 Annex 2

Neal - chairman

Lundine   *Leach*
Barnard   *Hansen*
Patterson   *Shumway*
LaFalce   *Parris*
Lowry   *Dreier*
Patman   *McCollum*
Coyne   *Roukema*
Roemer
Lehman
Kaptur
Cooper
Levin

¹ *Delegate from District of Columbia not counted in party ratios.*

Budget

Phone: 226-7200   Room: 214 Annex 1

D 20 - R 11

Federal budget generally; concurrent budget resolutions; Congressional Budget Office.

James R. Jones,
D-Okla.,
chairman

Jim Wright, Texas   *Delbert L. Latta, Ohio**
Stephen J. Solarz, N.Y.   *Bud Shuster, Pa.*

Timothy E. Wirth, Colo.
Leon E. Panetta, Calif.
Richard A. Gephardt, Mo.
Bill Nelson, Fla.
Les Aspin, Wis.
W. G. "Bill" Hefner, N.C.
Thomas J. Downey, N.Y.
Brian J. Donnelly, Mass.
Mike Lowry, Wash.
Butler Derrick, S.C.
George Miller, Calif.
William H. Gray III, Pa.
Pat Williams, Mont.
Geraldine A. Ferraro, N.Y.
Howard Wolpe, Mich.
Martin Frost, Texas
Vic Fazio, Calif.

Bill Frenzel, Minn.
Jack F. Kemp, N.Y.
Ed Bethune, Ark.
Phil Gramm, Texas
Lynn Martin, Ill.
Bobbi Fiedler, Calif.
Bill Gradison, Ohio
Tom Loeffler, Texas
Connie Mack, Fla.

(No standing subcommittees.)

Task Forces

Budget Process

Phone: 226-7200　　　　Room: 214 Annex 1

Panetta - chairman

Jones	*Shuster*
Wright	*Frenzel*
Gephardt	*Bethune*
Aspin	*Gramm*
Hefner	*Loeffler*
Donnelly	
Derrick	
Miller	

Capital Resources and Development

Phone: 226-7200　　　　Room: 214 Annex 1

Solarz - chairman

Jones	*Fiedler*
Wright	*Martin*
Aspin	
Ferraro	
Wolpe	

Economic Policy and Growth

Phone: 226-7200　　　　Room: 214 Annex 1

Aspin - chairman

Jones	*Bethune*
Wright	*Kemp*
Solarz	*Gramm*
Gray	
Williams	
Ferraro	

Education and Employment

Phone: 226-7200　　　　Room: 214 Annex 1

Gephardt - chairman

Jones	*Martin*
Wright	*Shuster*
Wirth	*Kemp*
Panetta	*Mack*
Hefner	
Downey	
Lowry	
Miller	
Gray	
Williams	
Wolpe	
Frost	

Energy and Technology

Phone: 226-7200　　　　Room: 214 Annex 1

Wirth - chairman

Jones	*Loeffler*
Wright	*Mack*
Nelson	
Derrick	
Frost	
Fazio	

Entitlements, Uncontrollables and Indexing

Phone: 226-7200　　　　Room: 214 Annex 1

Donnelly - chairman

Jones	*Gramm*
Wright	*Gradison*
Hefner	*Mack*
Williams	
Ferraro	
Fazio	

Federalism/State-Local Relations

Phone: 226-7200　　　　Room: 214 Annex 1

Nelson - chairman

Jones	*Frenzel*
Wright	*Gradison*
Downey	
Lowry	
Wolpe	

International Finance and Trade

Phone: 226-7200   *Room: 214 Annex 1*

Lowry - chairman

Jones	*Frenzel*
Wright	*Kemp*
Solarz	*Fiedler*
Wirth	
Gray	
Fazio	

Tax Policy

Phone: 226-7200   *Room: 214 Annex 1*

Downey - chairman

Jones	*Kemp*
Wright	*Frenzel*
Solarz	*Martin*
Aspin	*Fiedler*
Donnelly	*Gradison*
Derrick	
Miller	
Frost	

* Ranking minority member is a member ex officio *of all task forces.*

District of Columbia

Phone: 225-4457   *Room: 1310 LHOB*

D 7 - R 4

Municipal affairs of the District of Columbia.

Ronald V. Dellums,
D-Calif.,
chairman

Walter E. Fauntroy, D.C.[1]
Romano L. Mazzoli, Ky.
Fortney H. "Pete" Stark, Calif.
Mickey Leland, Texas
William H. Gray III, Pa.
Michael D. Barnes, Md.
Mervyn M. Dymally, Calif.

Stewart B. McKinney,
Conn.
Stan Parris, Va.
Thomas J. Bliley Jr., Va.
Marjorie S. Holt, Md.

Subcommittees

Fiscal Affairs and Health

Phone: 226-7556   *Room: 507 Annex 1*

Fauntroy - chairman

Dellums	*Holt*
Stark	*Parris*
Leland	*Bliley*
Gray	

Government Operations and Metropolitan Affairs

Phone: 225-1612   *Room: 441 CHOB*

Gray - chairman

Stark	*Parris*
Barnes	*McKinney*
Fauntroy	*Vacancy*
Vacancy	

Judiciary and Education

Phone: 225-1612   *Room: 441 CHOB*

Dymally - chairman

Mazzoli	*Bliley*
Barnes	*Holt*
Vacancy	*Vacancy*
Vacancy	

[1] Delegate from District of Columbia not counted in party ratios.

Education and Labor

Phone: 225-4527   *Room: 2181 RHOB*

D 20 - R 11

Education and labor generally; child labor; convict labor; labor standards and statistics; mediation and arbitration of labor disputes; regulation of foreign laborers; school food programs; vocational rehabilitation; wages and hours; welfare of miners; work incentive programs; Indian education; juvenile delinquency; human services programs; Gallaudet College; Howard University.

Carl D. Perkins,
D-Ky.,
chairman*

Augustus F. Hawkins, Calif.
William D. Ford, Mich.
Phillip Burton, Calif.
Joseph M. Gaydos, Pa.
William Clay, Mo.
Mario Biaggi, N.Y.
Ike Andrews, N.C.
Paul Simon, Ill.
George Miller, Calif.
Austin J. Murphy, Pa.
Baltasar Corrada, P.R.[1]
Dale E. Kildee, Mich.
Pat Williams, Mont.
Ray Kogovsek, Colo.
Harold Washington, Ill.
Matthew G. Martinez, Calif.
Major R. Owens, N.Y.
Frank Harrison, Pa.
Frederick C. Boucher, Va.
Gary Ackerman, N.Y.[2]

John N. Erlenborn, Ill.*
James M. Jeffords, Vt.
Bill Goodling, Pa.
E. Thomas Coleman, Mo.
Thomas E. Petri, Wis.
Marge Roukema, N.J.
Steve Gunderson, Wis.
Steve Bartlett, Texas
Ron Packard, Calif.
Vacancy
Vacancy

Subcommittees

Elementary, Secondary and Vocational Education

Phone: 225-4368   *Room: B346C RHOB*

Perkins - chairman

Ford	*Goodling*
Andrews	*Packard*
Miller	*Roukema*
Corrada	*Gunderson*
Kildee	*Bartlett*
Williams	*Vacancy*
Hawkins	
Biaggi	
Washington	
Boucher	
Martinez	

Employment Opportunities

Phone: 225-1927   *Room: B346A RHOB*

Hawkins - chairman

Clay	*Jeffords*
Corrada	*Gunderson*
Simon	*Goodling*
Washington	*Coleman*
Martinez	*Petri*
Biaggi	*Bartlett*
Williams	*Vacancy*
Kogovsek	
Owens	
Harrison	
Vacancy	

Health and Safety

Phone: 225-6876   *Room: B245A RHOB*

Gaydos - chairman

Murphy	*Gunderson*
Ford	*Vacancy*
Harrison	

Human Resources

Phone: 225-1850   *Room: 2178 RHOB*

Andrews - chairman

Corrada	*Petri*
Williams	*Coleman*
Owens	*Roukema*
Boucher	
Miller	

Labor-Management Relations

Phone: 225-5768   *Room: 2451 RHOB*

Burton - chairman

Clay	*Roukema*
Ford	*Bartlett*
Kildee	*Jeffords*
Murphy	
Martinez	

Labor Standards

Phone: 226-7594   *Room: 518 Annex 1*

Miller - chairman

Burton	*Petri*
Kildee	*Roukema*
Clay	*Packard*
Martinez	
Owens	
Harrison	

Postsecondary Education

Phone: 225-8881   *Room: 320 CHOB*

Simon - chairman

Ford	*Coleman*
Andrews	*Gunderson*
Kogovsek	*Jeffords*
Harrison	*Goodling*
Boucher	*Petri*
Owens	
Vacancy	

Select Education

Phone: 226-7532   *Room: 617 Annex 1*

Murphy - chairman

Miller	*Bartlett*
Biaggi	*Goodling*
Simon	*Coleman*
Gaydos	
Williams	
Corrada	

* *Chairman and ranking minority member are members* ex officio *of all subcommittees of which they are not regular members. However, Packard replaces Erlenborn as ex-officio member of the Subcommittee on Postsecondary Education.*
¹ *Resident commissioner from Puerto Rico not counted in party ratios.*
² *Subcommittee assignments not available.*

Energy and Commerce

Phone: 225-2927   *Room: 2125 RHOB*

D 27 - R 15

Interstate and foreign commerce generally; national energy policy generally; exploration, production, storage, supply, marketing, pricing and regulation of energy resources; nuclear energy; solar energy; energy conservation; generation and marketing of power; inland waterways; railroads and railway labor and retirement; communications generally; securities and exchanges; consumer affairs; travel and tourism; public health and quarantine; health care facilities; biomedical research and development.

John D. Dingell,
D-Mich.,
chairman*

James H. Scheuer, N.Y.	*James T. Broyhill, N.C.**
Richard L. Ottinger, N.Y.	*Norman F. Lent, N.Y.*
Henry A. Waxman, Calif.	*Edward R. Madigan, Ill.*
Timothy E. Wirth, Colo.	*Carlos J. Moorhead,*
Philip R. Sharp, Ind.	*Calif.*
James J. Florio, N.J.	*Matthew J. Rinaldo, N.J.*
Edward J. Markey, Mass.	*Tom Corcoran, Ill.*
Thomas A. Luken, Ohio	*William E. Dannemeyer,*
Doug Walgren, Pa.	*Calif.*
Albert Gore Jr., Tenn.	*Bob Whittaker, Kan.*
Barbara A. Mikulski, Md.	*Tom Tauke, Iowa*
Al Swift, Wash.	*Don Ritter, Pa.*

Mickey Leland, Texas	*Dan Coats, Ind.*
Richard C. Shelby, Ala.	*Thomas J. Bliley Jr., Va.*
Cardiss Collins, Ill.	*Jack Fields, Texas*
Mike Synar, Okla.	*Mike Oxley, Ohio*
W. J. "Billy" Tauzin, La.	*Howard C. Nielson,*
Ron Wyden, Ore.	*Utah*
Ralph M. Hall, Texas	
Dennis E. Eckart, Ohio	
Wayne Dowdy, Miss.	
Bill Richardson, N.M.	
Jim Slattery, Kan.	
Gerry Sikorski, Minn.	
John Bryant, Texas	
Jim Bates, Calif.	

Subcommittees

Commerce, Transportation and Tourism

Phone: 226-3160   *Room: 151 Annex 2*

Florio - chairman

Mikulski	*Lent*
Tauzin	*Ritter*
Eckart	
Dowdy	
Richardson	

Energy Conservation and Power

Phone: 226-2424   *Room: 316 Annex 2*

Ottinger - chairman

Swift	*Moorhead*
Synar	*Ritter*
Wyden	*Coats*
Hall	
Bryant	
Luken	
Gore	

Fossil and Synthetic Fuels

Phone: 226-2500   *Room: 331 Annex 2*

Sharp - chairman

Synar	*Corcoran*
Tauzin	*Dannemeyer*
Hall	*Tauke*
Dowdy	*Coats*
Richardson	*Fields*
Slattery	
Markey	
Luken	
Walgren	
Shelby	
Collins	

Health and the Environment

Phone: 225-4952   *Room: 2415 RHOB*

Waxman - chairman

Scheuer	*Madigan*
Luken	*Dannemeyer*
Walgren	*Whittaker*
Mikulski	*Bliley*
Shelby	*Nielson*
Wyden	
Eckart	
Sikorski	
Ottinger	
Wirth	
Leland	

Oversight and Investigations

Phone: 225-4441   *Room: 2323 RHOB*

Dingell - chairman

Gore	*Broyhill*
Slattery	*Whittaker*
Sikorski	*Bliley*
Bates	*Oxley*
Scheuer	
Florio	
Markey	
Walgren	

Telecommunications, Consumer Protection and Finance

Phone: 225-9304   *Room: B331 RHOB*

Wirth - chairman

Markey	*Rinaldo*
Swift	*Moorhead*
Collins	*Tauke*
Gore	*Oxley*
Leland	
Bryant	
Bates	
Scheuer	
Waxman	

* Chairman and ranking minority member are members ex officio of all subcommittees of which they are not regular members.

Foreign Affairs

Phone: 225-5021   *Room: 2170 RHOB*

D 24 - R 13

Relations of the United States with foreign nations generally; foreign loans; international conferences and congresses; intervention abroad and declarations of war; diplomatic service; foreign trade; neutrality; protection of Americans abroad; Red Cross; United Nations; international economic policy; export controls including nonproliferation of nuclear technology and hardware; international commodity agreements; trading with the enemy; international financial and monetary organizations.

Clement J. Zablocki,
D-Wis.,
chairman*

Dante B. Fascell, Fla.	*William S. Broomfield, Mich.**
Lee H. Hamilton, Ind.	*Larry Winn Jr., Kan.*
Gus Yatron, Pa.	*Benjamin A. Gilman, N.Y.*
Stephen J. Solarz, N.Y.	*Robert J. Lagomarsino, Calif.*
Don Bonker, Wash.	*Joel Pritchard, Wash.*
Gerry E. Studds, Mass.	*Jim Leach, Iowa*
Andy Ireland, Fla.	*Toby Roth, Wis.*
Daniel A. Mica, Fla.	*Olympia J. Snowe, Maine*
Michael D. Barnes, Md.	*Henry J. Hyde, Ill.*
Howard Wolpe, Mich.	*Gerald B.H. Solomon, N.Y.*
George W. Crockett Jr., Mich.	*Douglas K. Bereuter, Neb.*
Sam Gejdenson, Conn.	*Mark D. Siljander, Mich.*
Mervyn M. Dymally, Calif.	*Ed Zschau, Calif.*
Tom Lantos, Calif.	
Peter H. Kostmayer, Pa.	
Robert G. Torricelli, N.J.	
Larry Smith, Fla.	
Howard L. Berman, Calif.	
Harry Reid, Nev.	
Mel Levine, Calif.	
Edward F. Feighan, Ohio	
Ted Weiss, N.Y.	
Robert Garcia, N.Y.	

Subcommittees

Africa

Phone: 226-7807   Room: 705 Annex 1

Wolpe - chairman

Crockett	*Solomon*
Berman	*Roth*
Reid	*Zschau*
Feighan	
Weiss	

Asian and Pacific Affairs

Phone: 226-7801   Room: 707 Annex 1

Solarz - chairman

Ireland	*Pritchard*
Dymally	*Solomon*
Lantos	*Gilman*
Torricelli	
Levine	

Europe and the Middle East

Phone: 225-3345   Room: B359 RHOB

Hamilton - chairman

Lantos	*Winn*
Ireland	*Siljander*
Dymally	*Zschau*
Torricelli	
Smith	
Levine	

Human Rights and International Organizations

Phone: 226-7825   Room: 703 Annex 1

Yatron - chairman

Bonker	*Leach*
Levine	*Zschau*
Weiss	*Solomon*
Lantos	
Kostmayer	

International Economic Policy and Trade

Phone: 226-7820   Room: 702 Annex 1

Bonker - chairman

Mica	*Roth*
Berman	*Snowe*
Feighan	*Bereuter*
Barnes	
Wolpe	
Gejdenson	

International Operations

Phone: 225-3424   Room: B358 RHOB

Fascell - chairman

Crockett	*Gilman*
Yatron	*Siljander*
Kostmayer	*Pritchard*
Smith	
Solarz	

International Security and Scientific Affairs

Phone: 225-8926   Room: 2103 RHOB

Zablocki - chairman

Fascell	*Broomfield*
Hamilton	*Hyde*
Studds	
Mica	

Western Hemisphere Affairs

Phone: 226-7812   Room: 709 Annex 1

Barnes - chairman

Studds	*Lagomarsino*
Gejdenson	*Hyde*
Kostmayer	*Bereuter*
Reid	
Garcia	
Solarz	

* Chairman and ranking minority member are members ex officio of all subcommittees of which they are not regular members.

Government Operations

Phone: 225-5051   *Room: 2157 RHOB*

D 25 - R 14

Budget and accounting measures; overall economy and efficiency in government including federal procurement; executive branch reorganization; general revenue sharing; intergovernmental relations; National Archives.

Jack Brooks,
D-Texas,
chairman*

Dante B. Fascell, Fla.
Don Fuqua, Fla.
John Conyers Jr., Mich.
Cardiss Collins, Ill.
Glenn English, Okla.
Elliott H. Levitas, Ga.
Henry A. Waxman, Calif.
Ted Weiss, N.Y.
Mike Synar, Okla.
Stephen L. Neal, N.C.
Doug Barnard Jr., Ga.
Barney Frank, Mass.
Tom Lantos, Calif.
Ron Coleman, Texas
Bob Wise, W.Va.
Barbara Boxer, Calif.
Sander M. Levin, Mich.
Buddy MacKay, Fla.
Mel Levine, Calif.
Major R. Owens, N.Y.
Edolphus Towns, N.Y.
John M. Spratt Jr., S.C.
Joe Kolter, Pa.
Ben Erdreich, Ala.

Frank Horton, N.Y.*
John N. Erlenborn, Ill.
*Thomas N. Kindness,
 Ohio*
Robert S. Walker, Pa.
Lyle Williams, Ohio
William F. Clinger Jr., Pa.
Raymond J. McGrath, N.Y.
Judd Gregg, N.H.
Dan L. Burton, Ind.
*John R. McKernan Jr.,
 Maine*
Tom Lewis, Fla.
Al McCandless, Calif.
Larry E. Craig, Idaho
Vacancy

Subcommittees

Commerce, Consumer and Monetary Affairs

Phone: 225-4407   *Room: B377 RHOB*

Barnard - chairman

Coleman   *Gregg*

Spratt   *Clinger*
Conyers   *Lewis*
Levitas
Waxman

Environment, Energy and Natural Resources

Phone: 225-6427   *Room: B371B RHOB*

Synar - chairman

Wise   *Williams*
Boxer   *Clinger*
Levine   *Kindness*
Kolter   *Craig*
Lantos

Government Activities and Transportation

Phone: 225-7920   *Room: B350A RHOB*

Collins - chairman

Owens   *McGrath*
Boxer   *McCandless*
Lantos   *Walker*
Coleman
Wise

Government Information, Justice and Agriculture

Phone: 225-3741   *Room: B349C RHOB*

English - chairman

Neal   *Kindness*
Coleman   *Lewis*
Wise   *Burton*
MacKay
Towns

Intergovernmental Relations and Human Resources

Phone: 225-2548   *Room: B372 RHOB*

Weiss - chairman

Conyers   *Walker*
Levin   *McCandless*
MacKay   *McGrath*
Towns   *Craig*
Erdreich

Legislation and National Security

Phone: 225-5147   Room: B373 RHOB

Brooks - chairman

Fascell	*Horton*
Fuqua	*Erlenborn*
Levitas	*Clinger*
Waxman	*Burton*
Neal	
Lantos	

Manpower and Housing

Phone: 225-6751   Room: B349A RHOB

Frank - chairman

Levine	*McKernan*
Owens	*Burton*
Spratt	*Erlenborn*
Kolter	
Erdreich	

* Chairman and ranking minority member are members ex officio *of all subcommittees of which they are not regular members.*

House Administration

Phone: 225-2061   Room: H326 Capitol

D 12 - R 7

House administration generally; contested elections; federal elections generally; corrupt practices; qualifications of members of the House; *Congressional Record;* the Capitol; Library of Congress; Smithsonian Institution; Botanic Gardens.

Augustus F. Hawkins,
D-Calif.,
chairman*

Frank Annunzio, Ill.
Joseph M. Gaydos, Pa.
Ed Jones, Tenn.
Joseph G. Minish, N.J.

Bill Frenzel, Minn.*
William L. Dickinson, Ala.
Robert E. Badham, Calif.
Newt Gingrich, Ga.

Charlie Rose, N.C.
Al Swift, Wash.
William J. Coyne, Pa.
Thomas S. Foley, Wash.
Mary Rose Oakar, Ohio
Tony Coelho, Calif.
Jim Bates, Calif.

*William M. Thomas,
Calif.
Lynn Martin, Ill.
Rod Chandler, Wash.*

Subcommittees

Accounts

Phone: 226-7540   Room: 611 Annex 1

Annunzio - chairman

Swift	*Badham*
Coyne	*Thomas*
Foley	*Martin*
Oakar	*Frenzel*
Coelho	
Bates	
Gaydos	

Contracts and Printing

Phone: 226-7310   Room: 720 Annex 1

Gaydos - chairman

Jones	*Gingrich*
Oakar	*Martin*
Coyne	

Office Systems

Phone: 225-1608   Room: 722 Annex 1

Rose - chairman

Foley	*Thomas*
Bates	*Dickinson*
Swift	

Personnel and Police

Phone: 226-2307   Room: 612 Annex 1

Minish - chairman

Annunzio	*Chandler*
Rose	*Gingrich*
Coelho	

Services

Phone: 225-4568   Room: 105 CHOB

Jones - chairman

Minish	*Dickinson*
Swift	*Chandler*
Coyne	

Task Forces

Elections

Phone: 226-7616   *Room: 802 Annex 1*

Swift - chairman

Coyne	*Thomas*
Oakar	*Martin*
Coelho	*Frenzel*
Bates	

Telephone Configuration

Phone: 226-7600   *Room: 722 Annex 1*

Rose - chairman

Foley	*Badham*

* Chairman and ranking minority member are members ex officio of all subcommittees and task forces of which they are not regular members.

Interior and Insular Affairs

Phone: 225-2761   *Room: 1324 LHOB*

D 25 - R 14

Public lands, parks and natural resources generally; Geological Survey; interstate water compacts; irrigation and reclamation; Indian affairs; minerals, mines and mining; petroleum conservation on public lands; regulation of domestic nuclear energy industry including waste disposal; territorial affairs of the United States.

Morris K. Udall, D-Ariz., chairman*

Phillip Burton, Calif.	*Manuel Lujan Jr., N.M.**
Abraham Kazen Jr., Texas	*Don Young, Alaska*
John F. Seiberling, Ohio	*Robert J. Lagomarsino, Calif.*

Antonio Borja Won Pat, Guam[1]
James Weaver, Ore.
James J. Florio, N.J.
Philip R. Sharp, Ind.
Edward J. Markey, Mass.
Baltasar Corrada, P.R.[1]
Austin J. Murphy, Pa.
Nick J. Rahall II, W.Va.
Bruce F. Vento, Minn.
Jerry Huckaby, La.
Jerry M. Patterson, Calif.
Ray Kogovsek, Colo.
Dale E. Kildee, Mich.
Tony Coelho, Calif.
Beverly B. Byron, Md.
Ron de Lugo, V.I.[1]
Sam Gejdenson, Conn.
Bill Patman, Texas
Peter H. Kostmayer, Pa.
Jim Moody, Wis.
Alan B. Mollohan, W.Va.
James McClure Clarke, N.C.
James F. McNulty Jr., Ariz.
Richard H. Lehman, Calif.

Dan Marriott, Utah
Ron Marlenee, Mont.
Dick Cheney, Wyo.
Charles Pashayan Jr., Calif.
Larry E. Craig, Idaho
Hank Brown, Colo.
Denny Smith, Ore.
James V. Hansen, Utah
Bill Emerson, Mo.
John McCain, Ariz.
Barbara F. Vucanovich, Nev.

Subcommittees

Energy and the Environment

Phone: 225-8331   *Room: 1327 LHOB*

Udall - chairman

Seiberling	*Lujan*
Florio	*Smith*
Sharp	*Marriott*
Markey	*McCain*
Murphy	*Vucanovich*
Rahall	*Brown*
Vento	*Craig*
Huckaby	*Pashayan*
Patterson	
Gejdenson	
Patman	
Kostmayer	
Moody	
Mollohan	
Clarke	

Insular Affairs

Phone: 225-9297   *Room: 1413A LHOB*

Won Pat - chairman

Burton	*Lagomarsino*
Corrada	*Smith*

Murphy	*Hansen*
Kildee	*Brown*
de Lugo	
Clarke	

Mining, Forest Management and Bonneville Power Administration

Phone: 225-1661   *Room: 1626 LHOB*

Weaver - chairman

Udall	*Marriott*
Kazen	*Vucanovich*
Seiberling	*Young*
Murphy	*Craig*
Rahall	*Emerson*
Huckaby	*McCain*
Kogovsek	
Byron	
Moody	
Mollohan	
McNulty	

Oversight and Investigations

Phone: 226-7610   *Room: 818 Annex 1*

Markey - chairman

Florio	*Marlenee*
Sharp	*Hansen*
Gejdenson	*Vucanovich*

Public Lands and National Parks

Phone: 226-7734   *Room: 812 Annex 1*

Seiberling - chairman

Burton	*Young*
Won Pat	*Marlenee*
Weaver	*Craig*
Vento	*Hansen*
Patterson	*Emerson*
Kogovsek	*Lagomarsino*
Kildee	*Cheney*
Coelho	*Pashayan*
Byron	
de Lugo	
Gejdenson	
Kostmayer	
Moody	
Clarke	
Lehman	

Water and Power

Phone: 225-6042   *Room: 1522 LHOB*

Kazen - chairman

Udall	*Cheney*
Weaver	*Pashayan*
Kogovsek	*Brown*
Coelho	*McCain*
Patman	
McNulty	
Lehman	

*Chairman and ranking minority member are members ex officio *of all subcommittees of which they are not regular members.*
   ¹ Delegates from Guam and Virgin Islands and resident commissioner from Puerto Rico not counted in party ratios.

Judiciary

Phone: 225-3951   *Room: 2137 RHOB*

D 20 - R 11

Civil and criminal judicial proceedings generally; federal courts and judges; bankruptcy, mutiny, espionage and counterfeiting; civil liberties; constitutional amendments; immigration and naturalization; interstate compacts; claims against the United States; apportionment of representatives; meetings of Congress and attendance of members; penitentiaries; patents, copyrights and trademarks; presidential succession; monopolies and unlawful restraints of trade; internal security.

Peter W. Rodino Jr., D-N.J., chairman

Jack Brooks, Texas	*Hamilton Fish Jr., N.Y.*
Robert W. Kastenmeier, Wis.	*Carlos J. Moorhead, Calif.*
Don Edwards, Calif.	*Henry J. Hyde, Ill.*
John Conyers Jr., Mich.	*Thomas N. Kindness, Ohio*
John F. Seiberling, Ohio	*Harold S. Sawyer, Mich.*
Romano L. Mazzoli, Ky.	*Dan Lungren, Calif.*
William J. Hughes, N.J.	*F. James Sensenbrenner Jr.,*
Sam B. Hall Jr., Texas	*Wis.*
Mike Synar, Okla.	*Bill McCollum, Fla.*
Patricia Schroeder, Colo.	*E. Clay Shaw Jr., Fla.*

Dan Glickman, Kan.
Harold Washington, Ill.
Barney Frank, Mass.
George W. Crockett Jr.,
 Mich.
Charles E. Schumer, N.Y.
Bruce A. Morrison, Conn.
Edward F. Feighan, Ohio
Larry Smith, Fla.
Howard L. Berman, Calif.

George W. Gekas, Pa.
Michael DeWine, Ohio

Crime

Phone: 225-1695 *Room: 207 CHOB*

Hughes - chairman

Schumer	*Sawyer*
Morrison	*Shaw*
Feighan	*Sensenbrenner*
Smith	

Subcommittees

Administrative Law and Governmental Relations

Phone: 225-5741 *Room: B351A RHOB*

Hall - chairman

Mazzoli	*Kindness*
Frank	*McCollum*
Schumer	*Shaw*
Berman	

Civil and Constitutional Rights

Phone: 226-7680 *Room: 806 Annex 1*

Edwards - chairman

Kastenmeier	*Sensenbrenner*
Conyers	*Gekas*
Schroeder	*DeWine*
Washington	

Courts, Civil Liberties and Administration of Justice

Phone: 225-3926 *Room: 2137B RHOB*

Kastenmeier - chairman

Brooks	*Moorhead*
Mazzoli	*Hyde*
Synar	*DeWine*
Schroeder	*Kindness*
Glickman	*Sawyer*
Frank	
Morrison	
Berman	

Criminal Justice

Phone: 226-2406 *Room: 362 Annex 2*

Conyers - chairman

Edwards	*Gekas*
Seiberling	*McCollum*
Washington	*DeWine*
Berman	

Immigration, Refugees and International Law

Phone: 225-5727 *Room: 2137 RHOB*

Mazzoli - chairman

Hall	*Lungren*
Frank	*McCollum*
Crockett	*Fish*
Smith	

Monopolies and Commercial Law

Phone: 225-2825 *Room: B353 RHOB*

Rodino - chairman

Brooks	*Fish*
Edwards	*Moorhead*
Seiberling	*Hyde*
Hughes	*Sawyer*
Synar	*Lungren*
Crockett	
Schumer	
Feighan	

Barbara Boxer, Calif.
Solomon P. Ortiz, Texas
Brian J. Donnelly, Mass.[2]

Merchant Marine and Fisheries

Phone: 225-4047   *Room: 1334 LHOB*

D 25 - R 14

Merchant marine generally; oceanography and marine affairs including coastal zone management; Coast Guard; fisheries and wildlife; regulation of common carriers by water and inspection of merchant marine vessels, lights and signals, lifesaving equipment and fire protection; navigation; Panama Canal, Canal Zone and interoceanic canals generally; registration and licensing of vessels; rules and international arrangements to prevent collisions at sea; international fishing agreements; Coast Guard and Merchant Marine academies and state maritime academies.

Walter B. Jones,
D-N.C.,
chairman*

Mario Biaggi, N.Y.,
  vice chairman
Glenn M. Anderson, Calif.
John B. Breaux, La.
Gerry E. Studds, Mass.
Carroll Hubbard Jr., Ky.
Don Bonker, Wash.
Norman E. D'Amours, N.H.
James L. Oberstar, Minn.
William J. Hughes, N.J.
Barbara A. Mikulski, Md.
Earl Hutto, Fla.
W. J. "Billy" Tauzin, La.
Thomas M. Foglietta, Pa.
Fofõ I. F. Sunia,
  American Samoa[1]
Dennis M. Hertel, Mich.
Roy Dyson, Md.
William O. Lipinski, Ill.
Robert A. Borski, Pa.
Thomas R. Carper, Del.
Douglas H. Bosco, Calif.
Robin Tallon, S.C.
Lindsay Thomas, Ga.

*Edwin B. Forsythe, N.J.**
Gene Snyder, Ky.
Joel Pritchard, Wash.
Don Young, Alaska
Norman F. Lent, N.Y.
Robert W. Davis, Mich.
William Carney, N.Y.
Norman D. Shumway,
  Calif.
Jack Fields, Texas
Claudine Schneider, R.I.
Harold S. Sawyer, Mich.
Herbert H. Bateman, Va.
John R. McKernan Jr.,
  Maine
Webb Franklin, Miss.

Subcommittees

Coast Guard and Navigation

Phone: 225-5211   *Room: 217 CHOB*

Studds - chairman

Hughes	*Young*
Tauzin	*Snyder*
Biaggi	*Pritchard*
Oberstar	*Lent*
Mikulski	*Davis*
Hutto	*Sawyer*
Foglietta	*Franklin*
Borski	
Carper	
Thomas	
Hubbard	
Boxer	

Fisheries and Wildlife Conservation and the Environment

Phone: 226-3522   *Room: 2544 Annex 2*

Breaux - chairman

Bonker	*Forsythe*
Oberstar	*Pritchard*
Hutto	*Young*
Dyson	*Carney*
Carper	*Shumway*
Bosco	*Schneider*
Thomas	*Sawyer*
Ortiz	*Bateman*
Anderson	*McKernan*
Studds	*Franklin*
D'Amours	
Hughes	
Tauzin	
Sunia	
Hertel	
Donnelly	
Tallon	

Merchant Marine

Phone: 226-3500   Room: 531 Annex 2

Biaggi - chairman

Anderson	*Snyder*
Mikulski	*Young*
Foglietta	*Davis*
Hertel	*Carney*
Lipinski	*Shumway*
Borski	*Fields*
Tallon	*Sawyer*
Boxer	*Bateman*
Donnelly	*McKernan*
Hubbard	
Bonker	
Dyson	
Ortiz	
Breaux	
Thomas	

Oceanography

Phone: 226-3513   Room: 541 Annex 2

D'Amours - chairman

Sunia	*Pritchard*
Tallon	*Shumway*
Boxer	*Schneider*
Studds	*Bateman*
Hughes	
Mikulski	
Tauzin	
Lipinski	

Panama Canal and Outer Continental Shelf

Phone: 226-3508   Room: 542 Annex 2

Hubbard - chairman

Breaux	*Carney*
Bosco	*Young*
Anderson	*Lent*
Tauzin	*Davis*
Foglietta	*Fields*
Sunia	
Hertel	
Borski	
Ortiz	
Mikulski	

* Chairman and ranking minority member are members ex officio *of all subcommittees of which they are not regular members.*
¹ Delegate from American Samoa not counted in party ratios.
² Member for the first session only.

Post Office and Civil Service

Phone: 225-4054   Room: 309 CHOB

D 15 - R 9

Postal and federal civil services; census and the collection of statistics generally; Hatch Act; holidays and celebrations.

William D. Ford, D-Mich., chairman*

Morris K. Udall, Ariz.	*Gene Taylor, Mo.**
William Clay, Mo.	*Benjamin A. Gilman, N.Y.*
Patricia Schroeder, Colo.	*Tom Corcoran, Ill.*
Robert Garcia, N.Y.	*Jim Courter, N.J.*
Mickey Leland, Texas	*Charles Pashayan Jr., Calif.*
Donald J. Albosta, Mich.	*William E. Dannemeyer,*
Gus Yatron, Pa.	*Calif.*
Mary Rose Oakar, Ohio	*Daniel B. Crane, Ill.*
Katie Hall, Ind.	*Frank R. Wolf, Va.*
Gerry Sikorski, Minn.	*Connie Mack, Fla.*
Thomas A. Daschle, S.D.	
Ron de Lugo, V.I.¹	
Charles E. Schumer, N.Y.	
Douglas H. Bosco, Calif.	
Vacancy	

Subcommittees

Census and Population

Phone: 226-7523   Room: 406 CHOB

Garcia - chairman

Leland	*Courter*
Oakar	*Dannemeyer*
Schumer	

Civil Service

Phone: 225-4025   Room: 209 CHOB

Schroeder - chairman

Udall   Pashayan
Hall   Wolf
Sikorski

Compensation and Employee Benefits

Phone: 226-7546   Room: 608 Annex 1

Oakar - chairman

Bosco   Dannemeyer
Leland   Mack
Garcia

Human Resources

Phone: 225-2821   Room: 601 Annex 1

Albosta - chairman

Daschle   Crane
Yatron   Gilman
Bosco

Investigations

Phone: 225-6295   Room: 122 CHOB

Ford - chairman

Udall   Taylor
Schumer   Gilman
Yatron

Postal Operations and Services

Phone: 225-9124   Room: 219 CHOB

Clay - chairman

Hall   Corcoran
Sikorski   Pashayan
Daschle   Mack
de Lugo

Postal Personnel and Modernization

Phone: 226-7520   Room: 603 Annex 1

Leland - chairman

Clay   Wolf
Albosta   Crane
Daschle

* *Chairman and ranking minority member are members ex officio of all subcommittees of which they are not regular members.*
[1] *Delegate from Virgin Islands not counted in party ratios.*

Public Works and Transportation

Phone: 225-4472   Room: 2165 RHOB

D 30 - R 18

Flood control and improvement of rivers and harbors; construction and maintenance of roads; oil and other pollution of navigable waters; public buildings and grounds; public works for the benefit of navigation including bridges and dams; water power; transportation, except railroads; Botanic Gardens; Library of Congress; Smithsonian Institution.

James J. Howard,
D-N.J.,
chairman*

Glenn M. Anderson, Calif.
Robert A. Roe, N.J.
John B. Breaux, La.
Norman Y. Mineta, Calif.
Elliott H. Levitas, Ga.
James L. Oberstar, Minn.
Henry J. Nowak, N.Y.
Bob Edgar, Pa.
Robert A. Young, Mo.
Nick J. Rahall II, W.Va.
Douglas Applegate, Ohio
Geraldine A. Ferraro, N.Y.
Brian J. Donnelly, Mass.
Donald J. Albosta, Mich.
Ron de Lugo, V.I.[1]
Gus Savage, Ill.
Fofō I. F. Sunia,
  American Samoa[1]
Katie Hall, Ind.
Douglas H. Bosco, Calif.
James F. McNulty Jr., Ariz.
Jim Moody, Wis.
Robert A. Borski, Pa.
Joe Kolter, Pa.
Tim Valentine, N.C.
Edolphus Towns, N.Y.
William O. Lipinski, Ill.
Michael A. Andrews, Texas
Tom Vandergriff, Texas,
J. Roy Rowland, Ga.
James McClure Clarke, N.C.
Bob Wise, W.Va.

Gene Snyder, Ky.*
John Paul Hammerschmidt,
  Ark.
Bud Shuster, Pa.
Arlan Stangeland, Minn.
Newt Gingrich, Ga.
William F. Clinger Jr., Pa.
Guy V. Molinari, N.Y.
E. Clay Shaw Jr., Fla.
Bob McEwen, Ohio
Frank R. Wolf, Va.
Thomas E. Petri, Wis.
Hal Daub, Neb.
Lynn Martin, Ill.
Vin Weber, Minn.
Robert F. Smith, Ore.
Don Sundquist, Tenn.
Nancy L. Johnson, Conn.
Ron Packard, Calif.

Subcommittees

Aviation

Phone: 225-9161   *Room: 2251 RHOB*

Mineta - chairman

Levitas	*Hammerschmidt*
de Lugo	*Shuster*
Hall	*Stangeland*
Valentine	*Gingrich*
Towns	*McEwen*
Lipinski	*Wolf*
Vandergriff	*Petri*
Anderson	*Weber*
Oberstar	*Packard*
Edgar	
Young	
Rahall	
Applegate	
Donnelly	
Bosco	
Ferraro	

Economic Development

Phone: 225-6151   *Room: B370A RHOB*

Oberstar - chairman

Nowak	*Clinger*
Applegate	*Shuster*
Ferraro	*McEwen*
Hall	*Petri*
Bosco	*Sundquist*
Borski	*Johnson*
Kolter	*Martin*
Valentine	
Towns	
Clarke	
Wise	
Sunia	
Roe	

Investigations and Oversight

Phone: 225-3274   *Room: B376 RHOB*

Levitas - chairman

Roe	*Molinari*
Andrews	*Gingrich*
Rowland	*Clinger*
Wise	*Shaw*
Breaux	*Sundquist*
Nowak	*Johnson*
Ferraro	
Albosta	
Borski	
Lipinski	

Public Buildings and Grounds

Phone: 225-9161   *Room: 2251 RHOB*

Young - chairman

Clarke	*Shaw*
Levitas	*Stangeland*
Savage	*Molinari*
Hall	
Andrews	
Rowland	

Surface Transportation

Phone: 225-4472   *Room: 2165 RHOB*

Anderson - chairman

Edgar	*Shuster*
Rahall	*Hammerschmidt*
Donnelly	*Gingrich*
Savage	*Clinger*
Sunia	*Shaw*
McNulty	*Wolf*
Moody	*Daub*
Lipinski	*Smith*
Andrews	*Martin*
Vandergriff	
Breaux	
Mineta	
Applegate	
Albosta	
Bosco	
Borski	
Kolter	
de Lugo	

Water Resources

Phone: 225-0060   *Room: B376 RHOB*

Roe - chairman

Breaux	*Stangeland*
Albosta	*Hammerschmidt*
de Lugo	*Molinari*
Rowland	*McEwen*
Anderson	*Daub*
Oberstar	*Weber*
Nowak	*Smith*
Edgar	*Packard*
Young	
Rahall	
Ferraro	
Donnelly	
Savage	
Sunia	
McNulty	
Moody	

* *Chairman and ranking minority member are members* ex officio *of all subcommittees.*
  [1] *Delegates from Virgin Islands and American Samoa not counted in party ratios.*

Rules

Phone: 225-9486   Room: H312 Capitol

D 9 - R 4

Rules and order of business of the House; emergency waivers under the Congressional Budget Act of required reporting date for bills and resolutions authorizing new budget authority; recesses and final adjournments of Congress.

Claude Pepper,
D-Fla.,
chairman

Gillis W. Long, La.
Joe Moakley, Mass.
Butler Derrick, S.C.
Anthony C. Beilenson, Calif.
Martin Frost, Texas
David E. Bonior, Mich.
Tony P. Hall, Ohio
Alan Wheat, Mo.

James H. Quillen, Tenn.
Delbert L. Latta, Ohio
Trent Lott, Miss.
Gene Taylor, Mo.

Subcommittees

Legislative Process

Phone: 225-1037   Room: 1629 LHOB

Long - chairman

Derrick   Lott
Frost   Taylor
Wheat

Rules of the House

Phone: 225-9091   Room: H152 Capitol

Moakley - chairman

Beilenson   Taylor
Bonior   Lott
Hall

Science and Technology

Phone: 225-6371   Room: 2321 RHOB

D 26 - R 15

Scientific and astronautical research and development including resources, personnel, equipment and facilities; Bureau of Standards, standardization of weights and measures and the metric system; National Aeronautics and Space Administration; National Aeronautics and Space Council; National Science Foundation; outer space including exploration and control; science scholarships; federally owned or operated non-military energy laboratories; civil aviation research and development; energy research, development and demonstration (except nuclear research and development); National Weather Service.

Don Fuqua,
D-Fla.,
chairman*

Robert A. Roe, N.J.
George E. Brown Jr., Calif.
James H. Scheuer, N.Y.
Richard L. Ottinger, N.Y.
Tom Harkin, Iowa
Marilyn Lloyd Bouquard, Tenn.
Doug Walgren, Pa.
Dan Glickman, Kan.
Albert Gore Jr., Tenn.
Robert A. Young, Mo.
Harold L. Volkmer, Mo.
Bill Nelson, Fla.
Stan Lundine, N.Y.
Ralph M. Hall, Texas
Dave McCurdy, Okla.
Mervyn M. Dymally, Calif.
Paul Simon, Ill.

Larry Winn Jr., Kan. *
Manuel Lujan Jr., N.M.
Robert S. Walker, Pa.
William Carney, N.Y.
F. James Sensenbrenner Jr., Wis.
Judd Gregg, N.H.
Raymond J. McGrath, N.Y.
Joe Skeen, N.M.
Claudine Schneider, R.I.
Bill Lowery, Calif.
Rod Chandler, Wash.
Herbert H. Bateman, Va.
Sherwood Boehlert, N.Y.
Al McCandless, Calif.
Tom Lewis, Fla.

Norman Y. Mineta, Calif.
Dick Durbin, Ill.
Michael A. Andrews, Texas
Buddy MacKay, Fla.
Tim Valentine, N.C.
Harry Reid, Nev.
Robert G. Torricelli, N.J.
Frederick C. Boucher, Va.

Subcommittees

Energy Development and Applications

Phone: 225-4494   Room: B374 RHOB

Fuqua - chairman

Ottinger	*Sensenbrenner*
Harkin	*Schneider*
Hall	*Lowery*
Simon	*Bateman*
Durbin	*Lewis*
Boucher	*Carney*
Roe	*Gregg*
Scheuer	
Bouquard	
Young	
Nelson	
McCurdy	
Mineta	

Energy Research and Production

Phone: 225-8056   Room: B374 RHOB

Bouquard - chairman

Roe	*Walker*
Young	*Chandler*
Lundine	*Lujan*
Ottinger	*Lowery*
Hall	
Valentine	

Investigations and Oversight

Phone: 226-3636   Room: 2323 RHOB

Gore - chairman

Reid	*Skeen*
Volkmer	*McCandless*
Roe	*Schneider*
Durbin	
Scheuer	

Natural Resources, Agriculture Research and Environment

Phone: 225-1064   Room: 820 Annex 1

Scheuer - chairman

Valentine	*McGrath*
Harkin	*Schneider*
Andrews	*Chandler*
MacKay	*Lewis*
Torricelli	
Brown	

Science, Research and Technology

Phone: 225-8844   Room: 2319 RHOB

Walgren - chairman

Brown	*Gregg*
McCurdy	*Boehlert*
Dymally	*Sensenbrenner*
Mineta	*McGrath*
MacKay	*Skeen*
Torricelli	*Bateman*
Lundine	*Vacancy*
Simon	
Durbin	
Valentine	
Reid	
Boucher	

Space Science and Applications

Phone: 225-7858   Room: 2324 RHOB

Volkmer - chairman

Nelson	*Lujan*
Andrews	*Lowery*
Brown	*Chandler*
Hall	*Bateman*
Dymally	*Walker*
Mineta	
MacKay	
Torricelli	

Transportation, Aviation and Materials

Phone: 225-9662   Room: 2321 RHOB

Glickman - chairman

Gore	*Carney*
Dymally	*Boehlert*
Ottinger	*McCandless*
Harkin	
Andrews	

Chairman and ranking minority member are members ex officio *of all subcommittees of which they are not regular members.*

Select Aging

Phone: 226-3375   Room: 712 Annex 1

D 38 - R 22

Problems of older Americans including income, housing, health, welfare, employment, education, recreation and participation in family and community life. Studies and reports findings to House, but cannot report legislation.

Edward R. Roybal,
D-Calif.,
chairman

Claude Pepper, Fla.
Mario Biaggi, N.Y.
Ike Andrews, N.C.
Don Bonker, Wash.
Thomas J. Downey, N.Y.
James J. Florio, N.J.
Harold E. Ford, Tenn.
William J. Hughes, N.J.
Marilyn Lloyd Bouquard,
  Tenn.
Stan Lundine, N.Y.
Mary Rose Oakar, Ohio
Thomas A. Luken, Ohio
Geraldine A. Ferraro, N.Y.
Beverly B. Byron, Md.
William R. Ratchford,
  Conn.
Daniel A. Mica, Fla.
Henry A. Waxman, Calif.
Mike Synar, Okla.
Butler Derrick, S.C.
Bruce F. Vento, Minn.
Barney Frank, Mass.
Tom Lantos, Calif.
Ron Wyden, Ore.
Donald J. Albosta, Mich.
George W. Crockett Jr.,
  Mich.
Bill Boner, Tenn.
Ike Skelton, Mo.
Dennis M. Hertel, Mich.
Robert A. Borski, Pa.

Matthew J. Rinaldo, N.J.
John Paul Hammerschmidt,
  Ark.
Ralph Regula, Ohio
Norman D. Shumway, Calif.
Olympia J. Snowe, Maine
James M. Jeffords, Vt.
Tom Tauke, Iowa
Judd Gregg, N.H.
George C. Wortley, N.Y.
Hal Daub, Neb.
Larry E. Craig, Idaho
Pat Roberts, Kan.
Cooper Evans, Iowa
Jim Courter, N.J.
Lyle Williams, Ohio
Claudine Schneider, R.I.
Tom Ridge, Pa.
John McCain, Ariz.
Michael Bilirakis, Fla.
George W. Gekas, Pa.
Mark D. Siljander, Mich.
Christopher H. Smith, N.J.

Frederick C. Boucher, Va.
Ben Erdreich, Ala.
Buddy MacKay, Fla.
Harry Reid, Nev.
Norman Sisisky, Va.
Tom Vandergriff, Texas
Bob Wise, W.Va.
Bill Richardson, N.M.

Subcommittees

Health and Long-Term Care

Phone: 226-3381   Room: 715 Annex 1

Pepper - chairman

Andrews	*Regula*
Florio	*Tauke*
Ford	*Wortley*
Bouquard	*Daub*
Oakar	*Craig*
Luken	*Roberts*
Ratchford	*Courter*
Derrick	*Ridge*
Wyden	*McCain*
Ferraro	*Bilirakis*
Waxman	
Vento	
Skelton	
Hertel	
Borski	

Housing and Consumer Interests

Phone: 226-3375   Room: 712 Annex 1

Bonker - chairman

Lundine	*Hammerschmidt*
Byron	*Wortley*
Crockett	*Ridge*
Boner	*Gekas*
Reid	*Siljander*
Wise	
Synar	
Wyden	

Human Services

Phone: 226-3348   Room: 716 Annex 1

Biaggi - chairman

Hughes	*Snowe*
Albosta	*Rinaldo*

Lantos
Erdreich
MacKay
Richardson
Downey
Florio

Schneider
Bilirakis
Smith

Barbara Boxer, Calif.
Sander M. Levin, Mich.
Bruce A. Morrison, Conn.
J. Roy Rowland, Ga.
Gerry Sikorski, Minn.
Alan Wheat, Mo.

Barbara F. Vucanovich, Nev.

Retirement, Income and Employment

Phone: 226-3335   *Room: 714 Annex 1*

Roybal - chairman

Downey
Synar
Frank
Mica
Boucher
Sisisky
Vandergriff
Oakar

Shumway
Jeffords
Gregg
Evans
Williams

(Subcommittee assignments were not available.)

Select Intelligence

Phone: 225-4121   *Room: H405 Capitol*

D 9 - R 5

Legislative and budgetary authority over the Central Intelligence Agency, the Defense Intelligence Agency, the National Security Agency, intelligence activities of the Federal Bureau of Investigation and other components of the federal intelligence community.

Edward P. Boland, D-Mass., chairman*

Select Children, Youth and Families

Phone: 225-2095   *Room: 2422 RHOB*

D 16 - R 9

Problems of children, youth and families including income maintenance, health, nutrition, education, welfare, employment and recreation. Studies and reports findings to House, but cannot report legislation.

George Miller, D-Calif., chairman

William Lehman, Fla.
Patricia Schroeder, Colo.
Lindy (Mrs. Hale) Boggs, La.
Matthew F. McHugh, N.Y.
Jerry M. Patterson, Calif.
Barbara A. Mikulski, Md.
Ted Weiss, N.Y.
Beryl Anthony Jr., Ark.
Mickey Leland, Texas

Dan Marriott, Utah
Hamilton Fish Jr., N.Y.
Dan Coats, Ind.
Thomas J. Bliley Jr., Va.
Frank R. Wolf, Va.
Dan L. Burton, Ind.
Nancy L. Johnson, Conn.
John R. McKernan Jr., Maine

Clement J. Zablocki, Wis.
Romano L. Mazzoli, Ky.
Norman Y. Mineta, Calif.
Wyche Fowler Jr., Ga.
Lee H. Hamilton, Ind.
Albert Gore Jr., Tenn.
Louis Stokes, Ohio
Dave McCurdy, Okla.

J. Kenneth Robinson, Va.
G. William Whitehurst, Va.
C. W. Bill Young, Fla.
Bob Stump, Ariz.
Bill Goodling, Pa.

Subcommittees

Legislation

Phone: 225-7310   *Room: H405 Capitol*

Mazzoli - chairman

Fowler
Stokes

Whitehurst
Goodling

Oversight and Evaluation

Phone: 225-5657   Room: H405 Capitol

Fowler - chairman

Hamilton	*Young*
Gore	*Goodling*

Program and Budget Authorization

Phone: 225-7690   Room: H405 Capitol

Boland - chairman

Zablocki	*Robinson*
Mineta	*Young*
McCurdy	*Stump*

*Chairman of full committee is a voting member of all subcommittees. House Majority Leader Jim Wright, D-Texas, and Minority Leader Robert H. Michel, R-Ill., are members ex officio of the full committee.

Select Narcotics Abuse and Control

Phone: 226-3040   Room: 234 Annex 2

D 16 - R 9

Problems of narcotics, drug and polydrug abuse and control including opium and its derivatives, other narcotic drugs, psychotropics and other controlled substances; trafficking, manufacturing and distribution; treatment, prevention and rehabilitation; narcotics-related violations of tax laws; international treaties and agreements relating to narcotics and drug abuse; role of organized crime in narcotics and drug abuse; abuse and control in the armed forces and in industry; criminal justice system and narcotics and drug law violations and crimes related to drug abuse. Studies and reports findings to House, but cannot report legislation.

Charles B. Rangel, D-N.Y., chairman

Peter W. Rodino Jr., N.J.   *Benjamin A. Gilman, N.Y.*

Fortney H. "Pete" Stark, Calif.
James H. Scheuer, N.Y.
Cardiss Collins, Ill.
Daniel K. Akaka, Hawaii
Frank J. Guarini, N.J.
Robert T. Matsui, Calif.
Dante B. Fascell, Fla.
Walter E. Fauntroy, D.C.
William J. Hughes, N.J.
Sam B. Hall Jr., Texas
Mel Levine, Calif.
Solomon P. Ortiz, Texas
Larry Smith, Fla.
Edolphus Towns, N.Y.

Lawrence Coughlin, Pa.
E. Clay Shaw Jr., Fla.
Mike Oxley, Ohio
Joel Pritchard, Wash.
Stan Parris, Va.
Gene Chappie, Calif.
Duncan L. Hunter, Calif.
Tom Lewis, Fla.

(No standing subcommittees.)

Small Business

Phone: 225-5821   Room: 2361 RHOB

D 26 - R 15

Assistance to and protection of small business including financial aid; participation of small business enterprises in federal procurement and government contracts.

Parren J. Mitchell, D-Md., chairman*

Neal Smith, Iowa
Joseph P. Addabbo, N.Y.
Henry B. Gonzalez, Texas
John J. LaFalce, N.Y.
Berkley Bedell, Iowa
Henry J. Nowak, N.Y.
Thomas A. Luken, Ohio
Andy Ireland, Fla.
Ike Skelton, Mo.
Charles W. Stenholm, Texas
Romano L. Mazzoli, Ky.
Nicholas Mavroules, Mass.
Charles Hatcher, Ga.

Joseph M. McDade, Pa.*
Silvio O. Conte, Mass.
William S. Broomfield, Mich.
Lyle Williams, Ohio
John Hiler, Ind.
Vin Weber, Minn.
Hal Daub, Neb.
Christopher H. Smith, N.J.
David Dreier, Calif.
Guy V. Molinari, N.Y.
Toby Roth, Wis.
Gene Chappie, Calif.
Sherwood Boehlert, N.Y.

Ron Wyden, Ore.
Dennis E. Eckart, Ohio
Gus Savage, Ill.
Buddy Roemer, La.
Norman Sisisky, Va.
Frank McCloskey, Ind.
Esteban Edward Torres,
  Calif.
Tom Vandergriff, Texas
Jim Cooper, Tenn.
James R. Olin, Va.
Robin Britt, N.C.
Richard Ray, Ga.

Michael Bilirakis, Fla.
Vacancy

General Oversight and the Economy

Phone: 225-8944　　　*Room: B363 RHOB*

Bedell - chairman

Sisisky	*Conte*
Cooper	*Dreier*
Olin	*Boehlert*
Ray	*Bilirakis*
Addabbo	
Gonzalez	
Britt	

Subcommittees

Antitrust and Restraint of Trade Activities Affecting Small Business

Phone: 225-6026　　　*Room: B363 RHOB*

Luken - chairman

Gonzalez	*Weber*
Mazzoli	*Chappie*
McCloskey	

Energy, Environment and Safety Issues Affecting Small Business

Phone: 225-3171　　　*Room: 569 Annex 2*

Skelton - chairman

Mavroules	*Hiler*
Hatcher	*Smith*
Torres	*Roth*
Bedell	

Export Opportunities and Special Small Business Problems

Phone: 225-9368　　　*Room: B363 RHOB*

Ireland - chairman

Stenholm	*Broomfield*
Wyden	*Roth*
Savage	*Chappie*
Sisisky	*Bilirakis*
Torres	
Vandergriff	

SBA and SBIC Authority, Minority Enterprise and General Small Business Problems

Phone: 225-5821　　　*Room: 2361 RHOB*

Mitchell - chairman

Smith	*McDade*
Addabbo	*Daub*
LaFalce	*Molinari*
Wyden	*Boehlert*
Eckart	
Savage	
Luken	

Tax, Access to Equity Capital and Business Opportunities

Phone: 225-7797　　　*Room: B363 RHOB*

Nowak - chairman

Roemer	*Williams*
Vandergriff	*Smith*
Britt	*Dreier*
Eckart	
Olin	

*Chairman and ranking minority member are members ex officio *of all subcommittees of which they are not regular members.*

Standards of Official Conduct

Phone: 225-7103　　　*Room: 2360 RHOB*

D 6 - R 6

Measures relating to the Code of Official Conduct; conduct of House members and employees; Ethics in Government Act.

Louis Stokes,
D-Ohio,
chairman

Nick J. Rahall II, W.Va.
Ed Jenkins, Ga.
Julian C. Dixon, Calif.
Vic Fazio, Calif.
William J. Coyne, Pa.

Floyd Spence, S.C.
Barber B. Conable Jr., N.Y.
John T. Myers, Ind.
Edwin B. Forsythe, N.J.
Hank Brown, Colo.
James V. Hansen, Utah

(No standing subcommittees.)

Thomas A. Daschle, S.D.
Wayne Dowdy, Miss.
Matthew G. Martinez,
  Calif.
Lane Evans, Ill.
Marcy Kaptur, Ohio
Frank Harrison, Pa.
Alan B. Mollohan, W.Va.
Timothy J. Penny, Minn.
Harley O. Staggers Jr.,
  W.Va.
J. Roy Rowland, Ga.
Jim Slattery, Kan.
John Bryant, Texas
Bill Richardson, N.M.

Christopher H. Smith, N.J.
Denny Smith, Ore.
Phil Gramm, Texas[1]
Dan L. Burton, Ind.
Don Sundquist, Tenn.
Michael Bilirakis, Fla.
Nancy L. Johnson, Conn.

Veterans' Affairs

Phone: 225-3527   Room: 335 CHOB

D 21 - R 12

Veterans' measures generally; compensation, vocational rehabilitation and education of veterans; armed forces life insurance; pensions; readjustment benefits; veterans' hospitals, medical care and treatment.

G. V. "Sonny"
Montgomery,
D-Miss.,
chairman*

Don Edwards, Calif.
Bob Edgar, Pa.
Sam B. Hall Jr., Texas
Douglas Applegate, Ohio
Marvin Leath, Texas
Richard C. Shelby, Ala.
Daniel A. Mica, Fla.

John Paul Hammerschmidt,
  *Ark.**
Chalmers P. Wylie, Ohio
Elwood Hillis, Ind.
Gerald B. H. Solomon,
  N.Y.
Bob McEwen, Ohio

Subcommittees

Compensation, Pension and Insurance

Phone: 225-3569   Room: 337 CHOB

Applegate - chairman

Hall	McEwen
Daschle	Wylie
Martinez	Smith, Ore.
Leath	Burton
Shelby	
Mica	
Dowdy	

Education, Training and Employment

Phone: 225-9166   Room: 335 CHOB

Leath - chairman

Edgar	Solomon
Evans	Wylie
Kaptur	Smith, Ore.
Slattery	
Bryant	
Richardson	

Hospitals and Health Care

Phone: 225-9154   Room: 338 CHOB

Edgar - chairman

Mica	Hillis
Dowdy	Solomon

Evans
Kaptur
Harrison
Mollohan
Penny
Staggers
Rowland
Slattery
Bryant
Richardson
Daschle

McEwen
Smith, N.J.
Bilirakis
Johnson

Housing and Memorial Affairs

Phone: 225-9164   Room: 335 CHOB

Shelby - chairman

Applegate
Mollohan
Mica
Bryant
Richardson

Smith, N.J.
Sundquist
Bilirakis

Oversight and Investigations

Phone: 225-3541   Room: 335 CHOB

Montgomery - chairman

Edwards
Hall
Penny
Staggers
Rowland
Evans

Hillis
Solomon
Burton
Sundquist
Johnson

*Chairman and ranking minority member are voting members of all subcommittees.
¹Rep. Gramm's subcommittee assignments were not available.

public moneys; transportation of dutiable goods; tax exempt foundations and charitable trusts; Social Security.

Dan Rostenkowski,
D-Ill.,
chairman*

Sam Gibbons, Fla.
J. J. Pickle, Texas
Charles B. Rangel, N.Y.
Fortney H. "Pete" Stark, Calif.
James R. Jones, Okla.
Andrew Jacobs Jr., Ind.
Harold E. Ford, Tenn.
Ed Jenkins, Ga.
Richard A. Gephardt, Mo.
Thomas J. Downey, N.Y.
Cecil Heftel, Hawaii
Wyche Fowler Jr., Ga.
Frank J. Guarini, N.J.
James M. Shannon, Mass.
Marty Russo, Ill.
Don J. Pease, Ohio
Kent Hance, Texas
Robert T. Matsui, Calif.
Beryl Anthony Jr., Ark.
Ronnie G. Flippo, Ala.
Byron L. Dorgan, N.D.
Barbara B. Kennelly, Conn.

Barber B. Conable Jr., N.Y.*
John J. Duncan, Tenn.
Bill Archer, Texas
Guy Vander Jagt, Mich.
Philip M. Crane, Ill.
Bill Frenzel, Minn.
James G. Martin, N.C.
Richard T. Schulze, Pa.
Bill Gradison, Ohio
Henson Moore, La.
Carroll A. Campbell Jr., S.C.
William M. Thomas, Calif.

Ways and Means

Phone: 225-3625   Room: 1102 LHOB

D 23 - R 12

Revenue measures generally; reciprocal trade agreements; customs, collection districts and ports of entry and delivery; bonded debt of the United States; deposit of

Subcommittees

Health

Phone: 225-7785   Room: 1115 LHOB

Jacobs - chairman

Rangel
Ford
Shannon
Russo

Moore
Duncan
Martin

Oversight

Phone: 225-5522   *Room: 1101 LHOB*

Rangel - chairman

Gibbons	*Martin*
Pickle	*Duncan*
Guarini	*Campbell*
Anthony	*Thomas*
Flippo	
Dorgan	

Public Assistance and Unemployment Compensation

Phone: 225-1025   *Room: B317 RHOB*

Ford - chairman

Stark	*Campbell*
Pease	*Moore*
Hance	*Frenzel*
Matsui	*Thomas*
Fowler	
Kennelly	

Select Revenue Measures

Phone: 225-9710   *Room: 1136 LHOB*

Stark - chairman

| Heftel | *Duncan* |
| Guarini | *Schulze* |

Flippo	*Vander Jagt*
Dorgan	*Moore*
Kennelly	
Jenkins	

Social Security

Phone: 225-9263   *Room: 1105 LHOB*

Pickle - chairman

Jacobs	*Archer*
Gephardt	*Gradison*
Shannon	*Crane*
Fowler	*Thomas*
Matsui	
Anthony	

Trade

Phone: 225-3943   *Room: 1111 LHOB*

Gibbons - chairman

Rostenkowski	*Vander Jagt*
Jones	*Archer*
Jenkins	*Frenzel*
Downey	*Schulze*
Pease	*Crane*
Hance	
Heftel	
Russo	

Chairman and ranking minority member are members ex officio of all subcommittees of which they are not regular members.

House Party Committees, 98th Congress
Democratic Leaders

Chairman of the Caucus — Gillis W. Long, La. 226-3210
Secretary of the Caucus — Geraldine A. Ferraro, N.Y. 226-3210
Majority Leader — Jim Wright, Texas 225-8040
Majority Whip — Thomas S. Foley, Wash. 225-5604
    Chief Deputy Whip — Bill Alexander, Ark. 225-0080
    Deputy Whips — Richard A. Gephardt, Mo.; Norman Y. Mineta, Calif.; Joe Moakley, Mass.; Charles B. Rangel, N.Y.
    At-Large Whips — Tom Bevill, Ala; David E. Bonior, Mich.; Tony Coelho, Calif.; Ron Coleman, Texas; Thomas A. Daschle, S.D.; Byron L. Dorgan, N.D.; Dennis E. Eckart, Ohio; Vic Fazio, Calif.; William D. Ford, Mich.; Martin Frost, Texas; William H. Gray III, Pa.; Carroll Hubbard Jr., Ky.; Ray Kogovsek, Colo.; Parren J. Mitchell, Md.; John P. Murtha, Pa.; Mary Rose Oakar, Ohio; Dan Rostenkowski, Ill.; Patricia Schroeder, Colo.; Philip R. Sharp, Ind.; Gerry Sikorski, Minn.; Pat Williams, Mont.

Assistant Whips, by zone numbers:

1. Bruce A. Morrison, Conn. — Connecticut, Massachusetts, New Hampshire, Rhode Island.
2. Charles E. Schumer, N.Y., and Henry J. Nowak, N.Y. — New York.
3. Austin J. Murphy, Pa. — Pennsylvania.
4. Michael D. Barnes, Md. — Delaware, Maryland, New Jersey.
5. Charles Whitley, N.C. — North Carolina, Virginia.
6. Elliott H. Levitas, Ga. — Georgia, South Carolina.
7. Dale E. Kildee, Mich. — Michigan.
8. David R. Obey, Wis. — Minnesota, Wisconsin.
9. Lee H. Hamilton, Ind. — Indiana, Kentucky.
10. Don J. Pease, Ohio — Ohio, West Virginia.
11. Albert Gore Jr., Tenn. — Louisiana, Mississippi, Tennessee.
12. Daniel A. Mica, Fla. — Alabama, Florida.
13. Ike Skelton, Mo. — Iowa, Missouri.
14. Sidney R. Yates, Ill. — Illinois.
15. J. J. Pickle, Texas, and Henry B. Gonzalez, Texas — Texas.
16. Mike Synar, Okla. — Arkansas, Kansas, Oklahoma.
17. Harry Reid, Nev., and James F. McNulty Jr., Ariz. — Arizona, Colorado, Montana, Nevada, New Mexico, North Dakota, South Dakota.
18. Norman D. Dicks, Wash. — Hawaii, Oregon, Washington.
19. Anthony C. Beilenson, Calif., and Leon E. Panetta, Calif. — California.

(The seven states not covered — Alaska, Idaho, Maine, Nebraska, Utah, Vermont, Wyoming — have no Democratic representatives.)

Steering and Policy Committee

Phone: 226-3260   *Room: 114 Annex 1*

Scheduling of legislation and Democratic committee assignments.

Thomas P. O'Neill Jr., Mass., chairman
Jim Wright, Texas, vice chairman
Gillis W. Long, La., 2nd vice chairman

Charles E. Bennett, Fla.	William Clay, Mo.
Howard L. Berman, Calif.	Tony Coelho, Calif.†
Tom Bevill, Ala.	Thomas A. Daschle, S.D.
Phillip Burton, Calif.	Geraldine A. Ferraro, N.Y.†

Thomas S. Foley, Wash.†	Claude Pepper, Fla.†
Wyche Fowler Jr., Ga.	William R. Ratchford, Conn.
Robert Garcia, N.Y.	
William J. Hughes, N.J.	Dan Rostenkowski, Ill.†
Ed Jenkins, Ga.	Martin Olav Sabo, Minn.
James R. Jones, Okla.†	Patricia Schroeder, Colo.
Thomas A. Luken, Ohio	Wes Watkins, Okla.
Romano L. Mazzoli, Ky.	Jamie L. Whitten, Miss.†
Norman Y. Mineta, Calif.	Charles Wilson, Texas
Joe Moakley, Mass.	Timothy E. Wirth, Colo.

† *Members* ex officio *from the leadership.*

Personnel Committee

Phone: 225-4068   *Room: B343 RHOB*

Selects, appoints and supervises Democratic patronage positions.

Joe Moakley, Mass., chairman

Joseph P. Addabbo, N.Y.	Thomas P. O'Neill Jr., Mass.
Augustus F. Hawkins, Calif.	

Democratic Congressional Campaign Committee

Phone: 789-2920   *400 North Capitol St. 20001*

Campaign support committee for Democratic House candidates.

(Membership had not been determined·)

Republican Leaders

Chairman of the Conference — *Jack F. Kemp, N.Y.* 225-5107
Vice Chairman of the Conference — *Jack Edwards, Ala.* 225-5107
Secretary of the Conference — *Robert J. Lagomarsino, Calif.* 225-5107
Minority Leader — *Robert H. Michel, Ill.* 225-0600
Minority Whip — *Trent Lott, Miss.* 225-0197
Chief Deputy Whip — *Tom Loeffler, Texas* 225-4236
Deputy Whip — *Olympia J. Snowe, Maine* 225-6306

The assistant minority whips are divided into four divisions each with an overall regional whip and assistant whips in charge of specific members as follows:

New England and Middle Atlantic Region — *Jim Courter, N.J. (9 states, 37 members)*:
Judd Gregg, N.H. (8 members)   *Richard T. Schulze, Pa. (10 members)*
David O'B. Martin, N.Y. (10 members)   *Gerald B. H. Solomon, N.Y. (9 members)*

Midwest Region — *Arlan Stangeland, Minn. (7 states, 42 members)*:
Lynn Martin, Ill. (10 members)   *Vin Weber, Minn. (10 members)*
Carl D. Pursell, Mich. (11 members)   *Chalmers P. Wylie, Ohio (11 members)*

Western and Plains Region — *Mickey Edwards, Okla. (15 states, 45 members)*:
Hank Brown, Colo. (9 members)   *Manuel Lujan Jr., N.M. (12 members)*
Duncan L. Hunter, Calif. (14 members)   *Sid Morrison, Wash. (10 members)*

Southern and Border Region — *Bob Livingston, La. (14 states, 42 members)*:
Thomas J. Bliley Jr., Va. (10 members)   *E. Thomas Coleman, Mo. (13 members)*
Carroll A. Campbell Jr., S.C. (8 members)   *William L. Dickinson, Ala. (11 members)*

(The five states not covered — Delaware, Hawaii, North Dakota, South Dakota, West Virginia — have no Republican representatives.)

Committee on Committees

Phone: 225-0600   Room: H230 Capitol

Makes Republican committee assignments.

Robert H. Michel, Ill., chairman

Bill Archer, Texas
William S. Broomfield, Mich.
Hank Brown, Colo.
James T. Broyhill, N.C.
Dick Cheney, Wyo.
E. Thomas Coleman, Mo.
Silvio O. Conte, Mass.
William L. Dickinson, Ala.
John J. Duncan, Tenn.
Mickey Edwards, Okla.
Cooper Evans, Iowa
Edwin B. Forsythe, N.J.
Bill Frenzel, Minn.
Newt Gingrich, Ga.
Judd Gregg, N.H.
John Paul Hammerschmidt, Ark.
George Hansen, Idaho
James V. Hansen, Utah
Marjorie S. Holt, Md.
Frank Horton, N.Y.
James M. Jeffords, Vt.
John R. Kasich, Ohio
Delbert L. Latta, Ohio
Jerry Lewis, Calif.
Trent Lott, Miss.
Ron Marlenee, Mont.
Joseph M. McDade, Pa.
Stewart B. McKinney, Conn.
Henson Moore, La.
John T. Myers, Ind.
Thomas E. Petri, Wis.
Joel Pritchard, Wash.
Harold Rogers, Ky.
Claudine Schneider, R.I.
Joe Skeen, N.M.
Robert F. Smith, Ore.
Virginia Smith, Neb.
Olympia J. Snowe, Maine
Floyd Spence, S.C.
Bob Stump, Ariz.
Barbara F. Vucanovich, Nev.
G. William Whitehurst, Va.
Larry Winn Jr., Kan.
C. W. Bill Young, Fla.
Don Young, Alaska
Ed Zschau, Calif.

Personnel Committee

Phone: 225-0833   Room: 1620 LHOB

Selects, appoints and supervises Republican patronage positions.

John T. Myers, Ind., chairman

Bill Emerson, Mo.
Bill Frenzel, Minn.
Pat Roberts, Kan.
Barbara F. Vucanovich, Nev.

Policy Committee

Phone: 225-6168   Room: 1620 LHOB

Advises on party action and policy.

Dick Cheney, Wyo., chairman

Robert E. Badham, Calif.
Herbert H. Bateman, Va.
Douglas K. Bereuter, Neb.
Rod Chandler, Wash.
Barber B. Conable Jr., N.Y.
Silvio O. Conte, Mass.
William E. Dannemeyer, Calif.
Jack Edwards, Ala.
Edwin B. Forsythe, N.J.

Bill Goodling, Pa.
Judd Gregg, N.H.
Steve Gunderson, Wis.
Nancy L. Johnson, Conn.
Jack F. Kemp, N.Y.
Robert J. Lagomarsino, Calif.
Delbert L. Latta, Ohio
Trent Lott, Miss.
James G. Martin, N.C.
Lynn Martin, Ill.

Bill McCollum, Fla.
Robert H. Michel, Ill.
Henson Moore, La.
Howard C. Nielson, Utah
James H. Quillen, Tenn.
Ralph Regula, Ohio
Floyd Spence, S.C.
Tom Tauke, Iowa
Guy Vander Jagt, Mich.
Vin Weber, Minn.
Vacancy

National Republican Congressional Committee

Phone: 479-7020   320 First St. S.E. 20003

Campaign support committee for Republican House candidates.

Guy Vander Jagt, Mich., chairman

Robert E. Badham, Calif.
Ed Bethune, Ark.
Sherwood Boehlert, N.Y.
Carroll A. Campbell Jr., S.C.
Dick Cheney, Wyo. †
Silvio O. Conte, Mass.
Tom Corcoran, Ill.
Lawrence Coughlin, Pa.
Larry E. Craig, Idaho
Hal Daub, Neb.
William L. Dickinson, Ala.
Jack Edwards, Ala. †
Mickey Edwards, Okla.
Webb Franklin, Miss.
Newt Gingrich, Ga.
Judd Gregg, N.H.
John Hiler, Ind.
Elwood Hillis, Ind.
Marjorie S. Holt, Md.
Larry J. Hopkins, Ky.
James M. Jeffords, Vt.
Nancy L. Johnson, Conn.
Jack F. Kemp, N.Y. †
Ken Kramer, Colo.
Robert J. Lagomarsino, Calif. †
Norman F. Lent, N.Y.

Bob Livingston, La.
Trent Lott, Miss. †
Manuel Lujan Jr., N.M.
Connie Mack, Fla.
Ron Marlenee, Mont.
James G. Martin, N.C. †
Bill McCollum, Fla.
John R. McKernan Jr., Maine
Robert H. Michel, Ill. †
Clarence E. Miller, Ohio
Sid Morrison, Wash.
Howard C. Nielson, Utah
Stan Parris, Va.
Ron Paul, Texas
Matthew J. Rinaldo, N.J.
Pat Roberts, Kan.
Eldon Rudd, Ariz.
Claudine Schneider, R.I.
F. James Sensenbrenner Jr., Wis.
Denny Smith, Ore.
Don Sundquist, Tenn.
Tom Tauke, Iowa
Gene Taylor, Mo.
Barbara F. Vucanovich, Nev.
Vin Weber, Minn.
Frank R. Wolf, Va.
Don Young, Alaska

† *Members* ex officio *from the leadership.*

Research Committee

Phone: 225-0871   Room: 1616 LHOB

At leadership's request, provides information and recommendations on specific policy issues likely to come before Congress.

James G. Martin, N.C., chairman

Steve Bartlett, Texas
Dick Cheney, Wyo. †
E. Thomas Coleman, Mo.
Jack Edwards, Ala. †
Mickey Edwards, Okla.
Newt Gingrich, Ga.
Jack F. Kemp, N.Y. †
Robert J. Lagomarsino, Calif.†
Jerry Lewis, Calif.
Trent Lott, Miss. †

Dan Lungren, Calif.
Raymond J. McGrath, N.Y.
Robert H. Michel, Ill. †
Howard C. Nielson, Utah
Stan Parris, Va.
Marge Roukema, N.J.
Robert F. Smith, Ore.
Gerald B. H. Solomon, N.Y.
Don Sundquist, Tenn.
Guy Vander Jagt, Mich. †
Ed Zschau, Calif.

† *Members* ex officio *from the leadership.*

Task Forces[1]

(and chairmen)

Agriculture — *Smith*

Congressional and Regulatory Reform — *Lewis*

Crime — *Lungren*

Economic Policy — *Parris*

Energy and Natural Resources — *Nielson*

Foreign Policy — *Coleman*

Health and Environment — *McGrath*

High Technology — *Zschau*

Income Maintenance — *Edwards, Okla.*

National Defense Policy — *Solomon*

[1] *Task force memberships had not been determined.*

Joint Committee Assignments, 98th Congress

As of April 2, 1983

Joint Committees are set up to examine specific questions and are established by public law. Membership is drawn from both chambers and both parties. When a senator serves as chairman, the vice chairman is usually a representative, and vice versa. The chairmanship usually rotates from one chamber to the other at the beginning of each Congress.

Democrats are listed on the left in Roman type; Republicans are listed on the right in italics.

Economic

Phone: 224-5171   *Room: SD-G01*

Studies and investigates all recommendations included in the president's annual Economic Report to Congress and reports findings and recommendations to the House and Senate.

Sen. Roger W. Jepsen, R-Iowa, chairman
Rep. Lee H. Hamilton, D-Ind., vice chairman

Senate Members

Lloyd Bentsen, Texas	*William V. Roth Jr., Del.*
William Proxmire, Wis.	*James Abdnor, S.D.*
Edward M. Kennedy, Mass.	*Steven D. Symms, Idaho*
	Mack Mattingly, Ga.
Paul S. Sarbanes, Md.	*Alfonse M. D'Amato, N.Y.*

House Members

Gillis W. Long, La.	*Chalmers P. Wylie, Ohio*
Parren J. Mitchell, Md.	*Marjorie S. Holt, Md.*
Augustus F. Hawkins, Calif.	*Dan Lungren, Calif.*
David R. Obey, Wis.	*Olympia J. Snowe, Maine*
James H. Scheuer, N.Y.	

Subcommittees

Agriculture and Transportation

Phone: 224-5171   *Room: SD-G01*

Sen. Abdnor - chairman
Rep. Snowe - vice chairman

Senate Members

Bentsen	*Roth*

House Members

Long

Economic Goals and Intergovernmental Policy

Phone: 224-5171   *Room: SD-G01*

Rep. Hamilton - chairman
Sen. Bentsen - vice chairman

Senate Members

Jepsen
D'Amato

House Members

Hawkins	*Snowe*

International Trade, Finance and Security Economics

Phone: 224-5171   *Room: SD-G01*

Rep. Long - chairman
Sen. Proxmire - vice chairman

Senate Members

Jepsen
Symms
Mattingly

House Members

Hawkins	*Wylie*
Scheuer	

Investment, Jobs and Prices

Phone: 224-5171   *Room: SD-G01*

Rep. Mitchell - chairman
Sen. Kennedy - vice chairman

Senate Members

Sarbanes	*D'Amato*

House Members

Obey	*Holt*
	Lungren

Monetary and Fiscal Policy

Phone: 224-5171   Room: SD-G01

Sen. Symms - chairman
Rep. Wylie - vice chairman

Senate Members

Kennedy   *Mattingly*
Sarbanes

House Members

Hamilton   *Holt*
Obey

Trade, Productivity and Economic Growth

Phone: 224-5171   Room: SD-G01

Sen. Roth - chairman
Rep. Lungren - vice chairman

Senate Members

Proxmire   *Abdnor*

House Members

Mitchell
Scheuer

Library

Phone: 224-0299   Room: SR-309

Management and expansion of the Library of Congress; receipt of gifts for the benefit of the Library; development and maintenance of the Botanic Gardens; placement of statues and other works of art in the Capitol.

Sen. Charles McC. Mathias Jr., R-Md., chairman
Rep. Augustus F. Hawkins, D-Calif., vice chairman

Senate Members

Daniel K. Inouye, Hawaii   *Mark O. Hatfield, Ore.*
Dennis DeConcini, Ariz.   *John W. Warner, Va.*

House Members

Al Swift, Wash.   *Newt Gingrich, Ga.*
William J. Coyne, Pa.   *Rod Chandler, Wash.*

(No standing subcommittees.)

Printing

Phone: 224-5241   Room: S151 Capitol

Inefficiencies and waste in the public printing, binding and distribution of government publications; federal paper procurement; executive branch department and agency printing plants; purchase of printing and binding equipment; Federal Printing Procurement Program; Depository Library Program; Government Printing Office; congressional publications, including the *Congressional Record.*

Rep. Augustus F. Hawkins, D-Calif., chairman
Sen. Charles McC. Mathias Jr., R-Md., vice chairman

Senate Members

Wendell H. Ford, Ky.   *Mark O. Hatfield, Ore.*
Claiborne Pell, R.I.   *Howard H. Baker Jr., Tenn.*

House Members

Joseph M. Gaydos, Pa.   *Lynn Martin, Ill.*
Ed Jones, Tenn.   *Rod Chandler, Wash.*

(No standing subcommittees.)

Taxation

Phone: 225-3621   Room: 1015 LHOB

Operation, effects and administration of the federal system of internal revenue taxes; measures and methods for simplification of taxes.

Rep. Dan Rostenkowski, D-Ill., chairman
Sen. Robert Dole, R-Kan., vice chairman

Senate Members

Russell B. Long, La.   *Bob Packwood, Ore.*
Lloyd Bentsen, Texas   *William V. Roth Jr., Del.*

House Members

Sam Gibbons, Fla.   *Barber B. Conable Jr., N.Y.*
J. J. Pickle, Texas   *John J. Duncan, Tenn.*

(No standing subcommittees.)

Index of Senators' Committee Assignments

Abdnor: Appropriations; Environment and Public Works; Joint Economic.

Andrews: Agriculture, Nutrition and Forestry; Appropriations; Budget; Select Indian Affairs, chairman.

Armstrong: Banking, Housing and Urban Affairs; Budget; Finance; Governmental Affairs.

Baker: Majority leader; Environment and Public Works; Foreign Relations; Rules and Administration; Joint Printing.

Baucus: Environment and Public Works; Finance; Judiciary; Small Business.

Bentsen: Environment and Public Works; Finance; Select Intelligence; Joint Economic; Joint Taxation.

Biden: Budget; Foreign Relations; Judiciary; Select Intelligence.

Bingaman: Armed Services; Governmental Affairs.

Boren: Agriculture, Nutrition and Forestry; Finance; Small Business.

Boschwitz: Agriculture, Nutrition and Forestry; Budget; Foreign Relations; Small Business; Veterans' Affairs.

Bradley: Energy and Natural Resources; Finance; Special Aging.

Bumpers: Appropriations; Energy and Natural Resources; Small Business.

Burdick: Appropriations; Environment and Public Works; Special Aging.

Byrd: Minority leader; Appropriations; Judiciary; Rules and Administration.

Chafee: Energy and Natural Resources; Environment and Public Works; Finance; Select Intelligence.

Chiles: Appropriations; Budget; Governmental Affairs; Special Aging.

Cochran: Agriculture, Nutrition and Forestry; Appropriations; Governmental Affairs.

Cohen: Armed Services; Governmental Affairs; Select Intelligence; Special Aging.

Cranston: Minority Whip; Banking, Housing and Urban Affairs; Foreign Relations; Veterans' Affairs.

D'Amato: Appropriations; Banking, Housing and Urban Affairs; Small Business; Joint Economic.

Danforth: Commerce, Science and Transportation; Finance; Governmental Affairs.

DeConcini: Appropriations; Judiciary; Rules and Administration; Select Indian Affairs; Veterans' Affairs; Joint Library.

Denton: Judiciary; Labor and Human Resources; Veterans' Affairs.

Dixon: Agriculture, Nutrition and Forestry; Banking, Housing and Urban Affairs; Small Business.

Dodd: Banking, Housing and Urban Affairs; Foreign Relations; Labor and Human Resources; Special Aging.

Dole: Agriculture, Nutrition and Forestry; Finance, chairman; Judiciary; Rules and Administration; Joint Taxation.

Domenici: Appropriations; Budget, chairman; Energy and Natural Resources; Environment and Public Works; Special Aging.

Durenberger: Environment and Public Works; Finance; Governmental Affairs; Select Ethics; Select Intelligence.

Eagleton: Appropriations; Governmental Affairs; Labor and Human Resources; Select Ethics.

East: Armed Services; Judiciary; Labor and Human Resources.

Exon: Armed Services; Budget; Commerce, Science and Transportation.

Ford: Commerce, Science and Transportation; Energy and Natural Resources; Rules and Administration; Joint Printing.

Garn: Appropriations; Banking, Housing and Urban Affairs, chairman; Select Intelligence.

Glenn: Foreign Relations; Governmental Affairs; Special Aging.

Goldwater: Armed Services; Commerce, Science and Transportation; Select Indian Affairs; Select Intelligence, chairman.

Gorton: Banking, Housing and Urban Affairs; Budget; Commerce, Science and Transportation; Select Indian Affairs; Small Business.

Grassley: Budget; Finance; Judiciary; Labor and Human Resources; Special Aging.

Hart: Armed Services; Budget; Environment and Public Works.

Hatch : Agriculture, Nutrition and Forestry; Budget; Judiciary; Labor and Human Resources, chairman; Small Business.

Hatfield: Appropriations, chairman; Energy and Natural Resources; Rules and Administration; Joint Library; Joint Printing.

Hawkins: Agriculture, Nutrition and Forestry; Banking, Housing and Urban Affairs; Labor and Human Resources.

Hecht: Banking, Housing and Urban Affairs; Energy and Natural Resources.

Heflin: Agriculture, Nutrition and Forestry; Commerce, Science and Transportation; Judiciary; Select Ethics.

Heinz: Banking, Housing and Urban Affairs; Energy and Natural Resources; Finance; Special Aging, chairman.

Helms: Agriculture, Nutrition and Forestry, chairman; Foreign Relations; Rules and Administration; Select Ethics.

Hollings: Appropriations; Budget; Commerce, Science and Transportation.

Huddleston: Agriculture, Nutrition and Forestry; Appropriations; Select Intelligence; Small Business.

Humphrey: Armed Services; Environment and Public Works; Labor and Human Resources.

Inouye: Appropriations; Commerce, Science and Transportation; Rules and Administration; Select Indian Affairs; Select Intelligence; Joint Library.

Jackson: Armed Services; Energy and Natural Resources; Governmental Affairs; Select Intelligence.

Jepsen: Agriculture, Nutrition and Forestry; Armed Services; Joint Economic, chairman.

Johnston: Appropriations; Budget; Energy and Natural Resources.

Kassebaum: Budget; Commerce, Science and Transportation; Foreign Relations; Special Aging.

Kasten: Appropriations; Budget; Commerce, Science and Transportation; Small Business.

Kennedy: Armed Services; Judiciary; Labor and Human Resources; Joint Economic.

Lautenberg: Banking, Housing and Urban Affairs; Commerce, Science and Transportation.

Laxalt: Appropriations; Judiciary.

Leahy: Agriculture, Nutrition and Forestry; Appropriations; Judiciary; Select Intelligence.

Levin: Armed Services; Governmental Affairs; Small Business.

Long: Commerce, Science and Transportation; Finance; Joint Taxation.

Lugar: Agriculture, Nutrition and Forestry; Foreign Relations; Select Intelligence.

Mathias: Foreign Relations; Governmental Affairs; Judiciary; Rules and Administration, chairman; Joint Library, chairman; Joint Printing.

Matsunaga: Energy and Natural Resources; Finance; Labor and Human Resources; Veterans' Affairs.

Mattingly: Appropriations; Banking, Housing and Urban Affairs; Joint Economic.

McClure: Appropriations; Energy and Natural Resources, chairman; Rules and Administration.

Melcher: Agriculture, Nutrition and Forestry; Energy and Natural Resources; Select Indian Affairs; Special Aging.

Metzenbaum: Budget; Energy and Natural Resources; Judiciary; Labor and Human Resources.

Mitchell: Environment and Public Works; Finance; Veterans' Affairs.

Moynihan: Budget; Environment and Public Works; Finance; Select Intelligence.

Murkowski: Energy and Natural Resources; Foreign Relations; Select Indian Affairs; Veterans' Affairs.

Nickles: Energy and Natural Resources; Labor and Human Resources; Small Business.

Nunn: Armed Services; Governmental Affairs; Small Business.

Packwood: Commerce, Science and Transportation, chairman; Finance; Small Business; Joint Taxation.

Pell: Foreign Relations; Labor and Human Resources; Rules and Administration; Joint Printing.

Percy: Foreign Relations, chairman; Governmental Affairs; Special Aging.

Pressler: Commerce, Science and Transportation; Foreign Relations; Small Business; Special Aging.

Proxmire: Appropriations; Banking, Housing and Urban Affairs; Joint Economic.

Pryor: Agriculture, Nutrition and Forestry; Finance; Select Ethics; Special Aging.

Quayle: Armed Services; Budget; Labor and Human Resources.

Randolph: Environment and Public Works; Labor and Human Resources; Veterans' Affairs.

Riegle: Banking, Housing and Urban Affairs; Budget; Commerce, Science and Transportation; Labor and Human Resources.

Roth: Finance; Governmental Affairs, chairman; Select Intelligence; Joint Economic; Joint Taxation.

Rudman: Appropriations; Governmental Affairs; Small Business.

Sarbanes: Banking, Housing and Urban Affairs; Foreign Relations; Joint Economic.

Sasser: Appropriations; Banking, Housing and Urban Affairs; Budget; Governmental Affairs; Small Business.

Simpson: Environment and Public Works; Judiciary; Veterans' Affairs, chairman.

Specter: Appropriations; Judiciary; Veterans' Affairs.

Stafford: Environment and Public Works, chairman; Labor and Human Resources; Veterans' Affairs.

Stennis: Appropriations; Armed Services.

Stevens: Majority Whip; Appropriations; Commerce, Science and Transportation; Governmental Affairs; Select Ethics, chairman.

Symms: Budget; Environment and Public Works; Finance; Joint Economic.

Thurmond: Armed Services; Judiciary, chairman; Veterans' Affairs.

Tower: Armed Services, chairman; Banking, Housing and Urban Affairs; Budget.

Trible: Banking, Housing and Urban Affairs; Commerce, Science and Transportation.

Tsongas: Energy and Natural Resources; Foreign Relations; Small Business.

Wallop: Energy and Natural Resources; Finance; Select Intelligence.

Warner: Armed Services; Energy and Natural Resources; Rules and Administration; Joint Library.

Weicker: Appropriations; Energy and Natural Resources; Labor and Human Resources; Small Business, chairman.

Wilson: Agriculture, Nutrition and Forestry; Armed Services; Special Aging.

Zorinsky: Agriculture, Nutrition and Forestry; Foreign Relations.

Index of Representatives' Committee Assignments

Ackerman: Education and Labor.

Addabbo: Appropriations; Small Business.

Akaka: Appropriations; Select Narcotics Abuse and Control.

Albosta: Post Office and Civil Service; Public Works and Transportation; Select Aging.

Alexander: Appropriations.

Anderson: Merchant Marine and Fisheries; Public Works and Transportation.

Andrews (N.C.): Education and Labor; Select Aging.

Andrews (Texas): Public Works and Transportation; Science and Technology.

Annunzio: Banking, Finance and Urban Affairs; House Administration.

Anthony: Select Children, Youth and Families; Ways and Means.

Applegate: Public Works and Transportation; Veterans' Affairs.

Archer: Ways and Means.

Aspin: Armed Services; Budget.

AuCoin: Appropriations.

Badham: Armed Services; House Administration.

Barnard: Banking, Finance and Urban Affairs; Government Operations.

Barnes: District of Columbia; Foreign Affairs.

Bartlett: Banking, Finance and Urban Affairs; Education and Labor.

Bateman: Merchant Marine and Fisheries; Science and Technology.

Bates: Energy and Commerce; House Administration.

Bedell: Agriculture; Small Business.

Beilenson: Rules.

Bennett: Armed Services.

Bereuter: Banking, Finance and Urban Affairs; Foreign Affairs.

Berman: Foreign Affairs; Judiciary.

Bethune: Banking, Finance and Urban Affairs; Budget.

Bevill: Appropriations.

Biaggi: Education and Labor; Merchant Marine and Fisheries; Select Aging.

Bilirakis: Select Aging; Small Business; Veterans' Affairs.

Bliley: District of Columbia; Energy and Commerce; Select Children, Youth and Families.

Boehlert: Science and Technology; Small Business.

Boggs: Appropriations; Select Children, Youth and Families.

Boland: Appropriations; Select Intelligence, chairman.

Boner: Appropriations; Select Aging.

Bonior: Rules.

Bonker: Foreign Affairs; Merchant Marine and Fisheries; Select Aging.

Borski: Merchant Marine and Fisheries; Public Works and Transportation; Select Aging.

Bosco: Merchant Marine and Fisheries; Post Office and Civil Service; Public Works and Transportation.

Boucher: Education and Labor; Science and Technology; Select Aging.

Bouquard: Armed Services; Science and Technology; Select Aging.

Boxer: Government Operations; Merchant Marine and Fisheries; Select Children, Youth and Families.

Breaux: Merchant Marine and Fisheries; Public Works and Transportation.

Britt: Armed Services; Small Business.

Brooks: Government Operations, chairman; Judiciary.

Broomfield: Foreign Affairs; Small Business.

Brown (Calif.): Agriculture; Science and Technology.

Brown (Colo.): Interior and Insular Affairs; Standards of Official Conduct.

Broyhill: Energy and Commerce.

Bryant: Energy and Commerce; Veterans' Affairs.

Burton (Calif.): Education and Labor; Interior and Insular Affairs.

Burton (Ind.): Government Operations; Select Children, Youth and Families; Veterans' Affairs.

Byron: Armed Services; Interior and Insular Affairs; Select Aging.

Campbell: Ways and Means.

Carney: Merchant Marine and Fisheries; Science and Technology.

Carper: Banking, Finance and Urban Affairs; Merchant Marine and Fisheries.

Carr: Appropriations.

Chandler: House Administration; Science and Technology; Joint Library; Joint Printing.

Chappell: Appropriations.

Chappie: Agriculture; Select Narcotics Abuse and Control; Small Business.

Cheney: Interior and Insular Affairs.

Clarke: Interior and Insular Affairs; Public Works and Transportation.

Clay: Education and Labor; Post Office and Civil Service.

Clinger: Government Operations; Public Works and Transportation.

Coats: Energy and Commerce; Select Children, Youth and Families.

Coelho: Agriculture; House Administration; Interior and Insular Affairs.

Coleman (Mo.): Agriculture; Education and Labor.

Coleman (Texas): Armed Services; Government Operations.

Collins: Energy and Commerce; Government Operations; Select Narcotics Abuse and Control.

Conable: Standards of Official Conduct; Ways and Means; Joint Taxation.

Conte: Appropriations; Small Business.

Conyers: Government Operations; Judiciary.

Cooper: Banking, Finance and Urban Affairs; Small Business.

Corcoran: Energy and Commerce; Post Office and Civil Service.

Corrada: Education and Labor; Interior and Insular Affairs.

Coughlin: Appropriations; Select Narcotics Abuse and Control.

Courter: Armed Services; Post Office and Civil Service; Select Aging.

Coyne: Banking, Finance and Urban Affairs; House Administration; Standards of Official Conduct; Joint Library.

Craig: Government Operations; Interior and Insular Affairs; Select Aging.

Crane, Daniel (Ill.): Armed Services; Post Office and Civil Service.

Crane, Philip (Ill.): Ways and Means.

Crockett: Foreign Affairs; Judiciary; Select Aging.

D'Amours: Banking, Finance and Urban Affairs; Merchant

Marine and Fisheries.

Daniel: Armed Services.

Dannemeyer: Energy and Commerce; Post Office and Civil Service.

Daschle: Agriculture; Post Office and Civil Service; Veterans' Affairs.

Daub: Public Works and Transportation; Select Aging; Small Business.

Davis: Armed Services; Merchant Marine and Fisheries.

de la Garza: Agriculture, chairman.

Dellums: Armed Services; District of Columbia, chairman.

de Lugo: Interior and Insular Affairs; Post Office and Civil Service; Public Works and Transportation.

Derrick: Budget; Rules; Select Aging.

DeWine: Judiciary.

Dickinson: Armed Services; House Administration.

Dicks: Appropriations.

Dingell: Energy and Commerce, chairman.

Dixon: Appropriations; Standards of Official Conduct.

Donnelly: Budget; Merchant Marine and Fisheries; Public Works and Transportation.

Dorgan: Ways and Means.

Dowdy: Energy and Commerce; Veterans' Affairs.

Downey: Budget; Select Aging; Ways and Means.

Dreier: Banking, Finance and Urban Affairs; Small Business.

Duncan: Ways and Means; Joint Taxation.

Durbin: Agriculture; Science and Technology.

Dwyer: Appropriations.

Dymally: District of Columbia; Foreign Affairs; Science and Technology.

Dyson: Armed Services; Merchant Marine and Fisheries.

Early: Appropriations.

Eckart: Energy and Commerce; Small Business.

Edgar: Public Works and Transportation; Veterans' Affairs.

Edwards (Ala.): Appropriations.

Edwards (Calif.): Judiciary; Veterans' Affairs.

Edwards (Okla.): Appropriations.

Emerson: Agriculture; Interior and Insular Affairs.

English: Agriculture; Government Operations.

Erdreich: Banking, Finance and Urban Affairs; Government Operations; Select Aging.

Erlenborn: Education and Labor; Government Operations.

Evans (Ill.): Agriculture; Veterans' Affairs.

Evans (Iowa): Agriculture; Select Aging.

Fascell: Foreign Affairs; Government Operations; Select Narcotics Abuse and Control.

Fauntroy: Banking, Finance and Urban Affairs; District of Columbia; Select Narcotics Abuse and Control.

Fazio: Appropriations; Budget; Standards of Official Conduct.

Feighan: Foreign Affairs; Judiciary.

Ferraro: Budget; Public Works and Transportation; Select Aging.

Fiedler: Budget.

Fields: Energy and Commerce; Merchant Marine and Fisheries.

Fish: Judiciary; Select Children, Youth and Families.

Flippo: Ways and Means.

Florio: Energy and Commerce; Interior and Insular Affairs; Select Aging.

Foglietta: Armed Services; Merchant Marine and Fisheries.

Foley: Majority Whip; Agriculture; House Administration.

Ford (Mich.): Education and Labor; Post Office and Civil

Service, chairman.

Ford (Tenn.): Select Aging; Ways and Means.

Forsythe: Merchant Marine and Fisheries; Standards of Official Conduct.

Fowler: Select Intelligence; Ways and Means.

Frank: Banking, Finance and Urban Affairs; Government Operations; Judiciary; Select Aging.

Franklin: Agriculture; Merchant Marine and Fisheries.

Frenzel: Budget; House Administration; Ways and Means.

Frost: Budget; Rules.

Fuqua: Government Operations; Science and Technology, chairman.

Garcia: Banking, Finance and Urban Affairs; Foreign Affairs; Post Office and Civil Service.

Gaydos: Education and Labor; House Administration; Joint Printing.

Gejdenson: Foreign Affairs; Interior and Insular Affairs.

Gekas: Judiciary; Select Aging.

Gephardt: Budget; Ways and Means.

Gibbons: Ways and Means; Joint Taxation.

Gilman: Foreign Affairs; Post Office and Civil Service; Select Narcotics Abuse and Control.

Gingrich: House Administration; Public Works and Transportation; Joint Library.

Glickman: Agriculture; Judiciary; Science and Technology.

Gonzalez: Banking, Finance and Urban Affairs; Small Business.

Goodling: Education and Labor; Select Intelligence.

Gore: Energy and Commerce; Science and Technology; Select Intelligence.

Gradison: Budget; Ways and Means.

Gramm: Budget; Veterans' Affairs.

Gray: Appropriations; Budget; District of Columbia.

Green: Appropriations.

Gregg: Government Operations; Science and Technology; Select Aging.

Guarini: Select Narcotics Abuse and Control; Ways and Means.

Gunderson: Agriculture; Education and Labor.

Hall, Katie (Ind.): Post Office and Civil Service; Public Works and Transportation.

Hall, Ralph (Texas): Energy and Commerce; Science and Technology.

Hall, Sam (Texas): Judiciary; Select Narcotics Abuse and Control; Veterans' Affairs.

Hall, Tony (Ohio): Rules.

Hamilton: Foreign Affairs; Select Intelligence; Joint Economic.

Hammerschmidt: Public Works and Transportation; Select Aging; Veterans' Affairs.

Hance: Ways and Means.

Hansen (Idaho): Agriculture; Banking, Finance and Urban Affairs.

Hansen (Utah): Interior and Insular Affairs; Standards of Official Conduct.

Harkin: Agriculture; Science and Technology.

Harrison: Education and Labor; Veterans' Affairs.

Hartnett: Armed Services.

Hatcher: Agriculture; Small Business.

Hawkins: Education and Labor; House Administration, chairman; Joint Economic; Joint Library; Joint Printing, chairman.

Hefner: Appropriations; Budget.

Heftel: Ways and Means.

Hertel: Armed Services; Merchant Marine and Fisheries;

Select Aging.

Hightower: Appropriations.

Hiler: Banking, Finance and Urban Affairs; Small Business.

Hillis: Armed Services; Veterans' Affairs.

Holt: Armed Services; District of Columbia; Joint Economic.

Hopkins: Agriculture; Armed Services.

Horton: Government Operations.

Howard: Public Works and Transportation, chairman.

Hoyer: Appropriations.

Hubbard: Banking, Finance and Urban Affairs; Merchant Marine and Fisheries.

Huckaby: Agriculture; Interior and Insular Affairs.

Hughes: Judiciary; Merchant Marine and Fisheries; Select Aging; Select Narcotics Abuse and Control.

Hunter: Armed Services; Select Narcotics Abuse and Control.

Hutto: Armed Services; Merchant Marine and Fisheries.

Hyde: Foreign Affairs; Judiciary.

Ireland: Foreign Affairs; Small Business.

Jacobs: Ways and Means.

Jeffords: Agriculture; Education and Labor; Select Aging.

Jenkins: Standards of Official Conduct; Ways and Means.

Johnson: Public Works and Transportation; Select Children, Youth and Families; Veterans' Affairs.

Jones (N.C.): Agriculture; Merchant Marine and Fisheries, chairman.

Jones (Okla.): Budget, chairman; Ways and Means.

Jones (Tenn.): Agriculture; House Administration; Joint Printing.

Kaptur: Banking, Finance and Urban Affairs; Veterans' Affairs.

Kasich: Armed Services.

Kastenmeier: Judiciary.

Kazen: Armed Services; Interior and Insular Affairs.

Kennelly: Ways and Means.

Kemp: Appropriations; Budget.

Kildee: Education and Labor; Interior and Insular Affairs.

Kindness: Government Operations; Judiciary.

Kogovsek: Education and Labor; Interior and Insular Affairs.

Kolter: Government Operations; Public Works and Transportation.

Kostmayer: Foreign Affairs; Interior and Insular Affairs.

Kramer: Armed Services.

LaFalce: Banking, Finance and Urban Affairs; Small Business.

Lagomarsino: Foreign Affairs; Interior and Insular Affairs.

Lantos: Foreign Affairs; Government Operations; Select Aging.

Latta: Budget; Rules.

Leach: Banking, Finance and Urban Affairs; Foreign Affairs.

Leath: Armed Services; Veterans' Affairs.

Lehman (Calif.): Banking, Finance and Urban Affairs; Interior and Insular Affairs.

Lehman (Fla.): Appropriations; Select Children, Youth and Families.

Leland: District of Columbia; Energy and Commerce; Post Office and Civil Service; Select Children, Youth and Families.

Lent: Energy and Commerce; Merchant Marine and Fisheries.

Levin: Banking, Finance and Urban Affairs; Government Operations; Select Children, Youth and Families.

Levine: Foreign Affairs; Government Operations; Select Narcotics Abuse and Control.

Levitas: Government Operations; Public Works and Transportation.

Lewis (Calif.): Appropriations.

Lewis (Fla.): Government Operations; Science and Technology; Select Narcotics Abuse and Control.

Lipinski: Merchant Marine and Fisheries; Public Works and Transportation.

Livingston: Appropriations.

Loeffler: Appropriations; Budget.

Long (La.): Rules; Joint Economic.

Long (Md.): Appropriations.

Lott: Minority Whip; Rules.

Lowery: Banking, Finance and Urban Affairs; Science and Technology.

Lowry: Banking, Finance and Urban Affairs; Budget.

Lujan: Interior and Insular Affairs; Science and Technology.

Luken: Energy and Commerce; Select Aging; Small Business.

Lundine: Banking, Finance and Urban Affairs; Science and Technology; Select Aging.

Lungren: Judiciary; Joint Economic.

Mack: Budget; Post Office and Civil Service.

MacKay: Government Operations; Science and Technology; Select Aging.

Madigan: Agriculture; Energy and Commerce.

Markey: Energy and Commerce; Interior and Insular Affairs.

Marlenee: Agriculture; Interior and Insular Affairs.

Marriott: Interior and Insular Affairs; Select Children, Youth and Families.

Martin (Ill.): Budget; House Administration; Public Works and Transportation; Joint Printing.

Martin (N.Y.): Armed Services.

Martin (N.C.): Ways and Means.

Martinez: Education and Labor; Veterans' Affairs.

Matsui: Select Narcotics Abuse and Control; Ways and Means.

Mavroules: Armed Services; Small Business.

Mazzoli: District of Columbia; Judiciary; Select Intelligence; Small Business.

McCain: Interior and Insular Affairs; Select Aging.

McCandless: Government Operations; Science and Technology.

McCloskey: Armed Services; Small Business.

McCollum: Banking, Finance and Urban Affairs; Judiciary.

McCurdy: Armed Services; Science and Technology; Select Intelligence.

McDade: Appropriations; Small Business.

McDonald: Armed Services.

McEwen: Public Works and Transportation; Veterans' Affairs.

McGrath: Government Operations; Science and Technology.

McHugh: Appropriations; Select Children, Youth and Families.

McKernan: Government Operations; Merchant Marine and Fisheries; Select Children, Youth and Families.

McKinney: Banking, Finance and Urban Affairs; District of Columbia.

McNulty: Interior and Insular Affairs; Public Works and Transportation.

Mica: Foreign Affairs; Select Aging; Veterans' Affairs.

Michel: Minority Leader.

Mikulski: Energy and Commerce; Merchant Marine and

Fisheries; Children, Youth and Families.

Miller (Calif.): Budget; Education and Labor; Select Children, Youth and Families, chairman.

Miller (Ohio): Appropriations.

Mineta: Public Works and Transportation; Science and Technology; Select Intelligence.

Minish: Banking, Finance and Urban Affairs; House Administration.

Mitchell: Banking, Finance and Urban Affairs; Small Business, chairman; Joint Economic.

Moakley: Rules.

Molinari: Public Works and Transportation; Small Business.

Mollohan: Interior and Insular Affairs; Veterans' Affairs.

Montgomery: Armed Services; Veterans' Affairs, chairman.

Moody: Interior and Insular Affairs; Public Works and Transportation.

Moore: Ways and Means.

Moorhead: Energy and Commerce; Judiciary.

Morrison (Conn.): Banking, Finance and Urban Affairs; Judiciary; Select Children, Youth and Families.

Morrison (Wash.): Agriculture.

Mrazek: Appropriations

Murphy: Education and Labor; Interior and Insular Affairs.

Murtha: Appropriations.

Myers: Appropriations; Standards of Official Conduct.

Natcher: Appropriations.

Neal: Banking, Finance and Urban Affairs; Government Operations.

Nelson: Budget; Science and Technology.

Nichols: Armed Services.

Nielson: Energy and Commerce.

Nowak: Public Works and Transportation; Small Business.

Oakar: Banking, Finance and Urban Affairs; House Administration; Post Office and Civil Service; Select Aging.

Oberstar: Merchant Marine and Fisheries; Public Works and Transportation.

Obey: Appropriations; Joint Economic.

O'Brien: Appropriations.

Olin: Agriculture; Small Business.

O'Neill: Speaker of the House.

Ortiz: Armed Services; Merchant Marine and Fisheries; Select Narcotics Abuse and Control.

Ottinger: Energy and Commerce; Science and Technology.

Owens: Education and Labor; Government Operations.

Oxley: Energy and Commerce; Select Narcotics Abuse and Control.

Packard: Education and Labor; Public Works and Transportation.

Panetta: Agriculture; Budget.

Parris: Banking, Finance and Urban Affairs; District of Columbia; Select Narcotics Abuse and Control.

Pashayan: Interior and Insular Affairs; Post Office and Civil Service.

Patman: Banking, Finance and Urban Affairs; Interior and Insular Affairs.

Patterson: Banking, Finance and Urban Affairs; Interior and Insular Affairs; Select Children, Youth and Families.

Paul: Banking, Finance and Urban Affairs.

Pease: Ways and Means.

Penny: Agriculture; Veterans' Affairs.

Pepper: Rules, chairman; Select Aging.

Perkins: Education and Labor, chairman.

Petri: Education and Labor; Public Works and Transportation.

Pickle: Ways and Means; Joint Taxation.

Porter: Appropriations.

Price: Armed Services, chairman.

Pritchard: Foreign Affairs; Merchant Marine and Fisheries; Select Narcotics Abuse and Control.

Pursell: Appropriations.

Quillen: Rules.

Rahall: Interior and Insular Affairs; Public Works and Transportation; Standards of Official Conduct.

Rangel: Select Narcotics Abuse and Control, chairman; Ways and Means.

Ratchford: Appropriations; Select Aging.

Ray: Armed Services; Small Business.

Regula: Appropriations; Select Aging.

Reid: Foreign Affairs; Science and Technology; Select Aging.

Richardson: Energy and Commerce; Select Aging; Veterans' Affairs.

Ridge: Banking, Finance and Urban Affairs; Select Aging.

Rinaldo: Energy and Commerce; Select Aging.

Ritter: Energy and Commerce.

Roberts: Agriculture; Select Aging.

Robinson: Appropriations; Select Intelligence.

Rodino: Judiciary, chairman; Select Narcotics Abuse and Control.

Roe: Public Works and Transportation; Science and Technology.

Roemer: Banking, Finance and Urban Affairs; Small Business.

Rogers: Appropriations.

Rose: Agriculture; House Administration.

Rostenkowski: Ways and Means, chairman; Joint Taxation, chairman.

Roth: Foreign Affairs; Small Business.

Roukema: Banking, Finance and Urban Affairs; Education and Labor.

Rowland: Public Works and Transportation; Select Children, Youth and Families; Veterans' Affairs.

Roybal: Appropriations; Select Aging, chairman.

Rudd: Appropriations.

Russo: Ways and Means.

Sabo: Appropriations.

St Germain: Banking, Finance and Urban Affairs, chairman.

Savage: Public Works and Transportation; Small Business.

Sawyer: Judiciary; Merchant Marine and Fisheries.

Scheuer: Energy and Commerce; Science and Technology; Select Narcotics Abuse and Control; Joint Economic.

Schneider: Merchant Marine and Fisheries; Science and Technology; Select Aging.

Schroeder: Armed Services; Judiciary; Post Office and Civil Service; Select Children, Youth and Families.

Schulze: Ways and Means.

Schumer: Banking, Finance and Urban Affairs; Judiciary; Post Office and Civil Service.

Seiberling: Interior and Insular Affairs; Judiciary.

Sensenbrenner: Judiciary; Science and Technology.

Shannon: Ways and Means.

Sharp: Energy and Commerce; Interior and Insular Affairs.

Shaw: Judiciary; Public Works and Transportation; Select Narcotics Abuse and Control.

Shelby: Energy and Commerce; Veterans' Affairs.

Shumway: Banking, Finance and Urban Affairs; Merchant Marine and Fisheries; Select Aging.

Shuster: Budget; Public Works and Transportation.

Sikorski: Energy and Commerce; Post Office and Civil Service; Select Children, Youth and Families.

Siljander: Foreign Affairs; Select Aging.

Simon: Education and Labor; Science and Technology.

Sisisky: Armed Services; Select Aging; Small Business.

Skeen: Agriculture; Science and Technology.

Skelton: Armed Services; Select Aging; Small Business.

Slattery: Energy and Commerce; Veterans' Affairs.

Smith, Christopher (N.J.): Select Aging; Small Business; Veterans' Affairs.

Smith, Denny (Ore.): Interior and Insular Affairs; Veterans' Affairs.

Smith, Larry (Fla.): Foreign Affairs; Judiciary; Select Narcotics Abuse and Control.

Smith, Neal (Iowa): Appropriations; Small Business.

Smith, Robert (Ore.): Public Works and Transportation.

Smith, Virginia (Neb.): Appropriations.

Snowe: Foreign Affairs; Select Aging; Joint Economic.

Snyder: Merchant Marine and Fisheries; Public Works and Transportation.

Solarz: Budget; Foreign Affairs.

Solomon: Foreign Affairs; Veterans' Affairs.

Spence: Armed Services; Standards of Official Conduct.

Spratt: Armed Services; Government Operations.

Staggers: Agriculture; Veterans' Affairs.

Stangeland: Agriculture; Public Works and Transportation.

Stark: District of Columbia; Select Narcotics Abuse and Control; Ways and Means.

Stenholm: Agriculture; Small Business.

Stokes: Appropriations; Select Intelligence; Standards of Official Conduct, chairman.

Stratton: Armed Services.

Studds: Foreign Affairs; Merchant Marine and Fisheries.

Stump: Armed Services; Select Intelligence.

Sundquist: Public Works and Transportation; Veterans' Affairs.

Sunia: Merchant Marine and Fisheries; Public Works and Transportation.

Swift: Energy and Commerce; House Administration; Joint Library.

Synar: Energy and Commerce; Government Operations; Judiciary; Select Aging.

Tallon: Agriculture; Merchant Marine and Fisheries.

Tauke: Energy and Commerce; Select Aging.

Tauzin: Energy and Commerce; Merchant Marine and Fisheries.

Taylor: Post Office and Civil Service; Rules.

Thomas (Calif.): House Administration; Ways and Means.

Thomas (Ga.): Agriculture; Merchant Marine and Fisheries.

Torres: Banking, Finance and Urban Affairs; Small Business.

Torricelli: Foreign Affairs; Science and Technology.

Towns: Government Operations; Public Works and Transportation; Select Narcotics Abuse and Control.

Traxler: Appropriations.

Udall: Interior and Insular Affairs, chairman; Post Office and Civil Service.

Valentine: Public Works and Transportation; Science and Technology.

Vandergriff: Public Works and Transportation; Select Aging; Small Business.

Vander Jagt: Ways and Means.

Vento: Banking, Finance and Urban Affairs; Interior and Insular Affairs; Select Aging.

Volkmer: Agriculture; Science and Technology.

Vucanovich: Interior and Insular Affairs; Select Children, Youth and Families.

Walgren: Energy and Commerce; Science and Technology.

Walker: Government Operations; Science and Technology.

Washington: Education and Labor; Judiciary.

Watkins: Appropriations.

Waxman: Energy and Commerce; Government Operations; Select Aging.

Weaver: Agriculture; Interior and Insular Affairs.

Weber: Public Works and Transportation; Small Business.

Weiss: Foreign Affairs; Government Operations; Select Children, Youth and Families.

Wheat: Rules; Select Children, Youth and Families.

Whitehurst: Armed Services; Select Intelligence.

Whitley: Agriculture.

Whittaker: Energy and Commerce.

Whitten: Appropriations, chairman.

Williams (Mont.): Budget; Education and Labor.

Williams (Ohio): Government Operations; Select Aging; Small Business.

Wilson: Appropriations.

Winn: Foreign Affairs; Science and Technology.

Wirth: Budget; Energy and Commerce.

Wise: Government Operations; Public Works and Transportation; Select Aging.

Wolf: Post Office and Civil Service; Public Works and Transportation; Select Children, Youth and Families.

Wolpe: Budget; Foreign Affairs.

Won Pat: Armed Services; Interior and Insular Affairs.

Wortley: Banking, Finance and Urban Affairs; Select Aging.

Wright: Majority Leader; Budget.

Wyden: Energy and Commerce; Select Aging; Small Business.

Wylie: Banking, Finance and Urban Affairs; Veterans' Affairs; Joint Economic.

Yates: Appropriations.

Yatron: Foreign Affairs; Post Office and Civil Service.

Young (Alaska): Interior and Insular Affairs; Merchant Marine and Fisheries.

Young (Fla.): Appropriations; Select Intelligence.

Young (Mo.): Public Works and Transportation; Science and Technology.

Zablocki: Foreign Affairs, chairman; Select Intelligence.

Zschau: Foreign Affairs.

Map of Capitol Hill

(Dotted line indicates the city's quadrants, which are noted in the corners of the map)

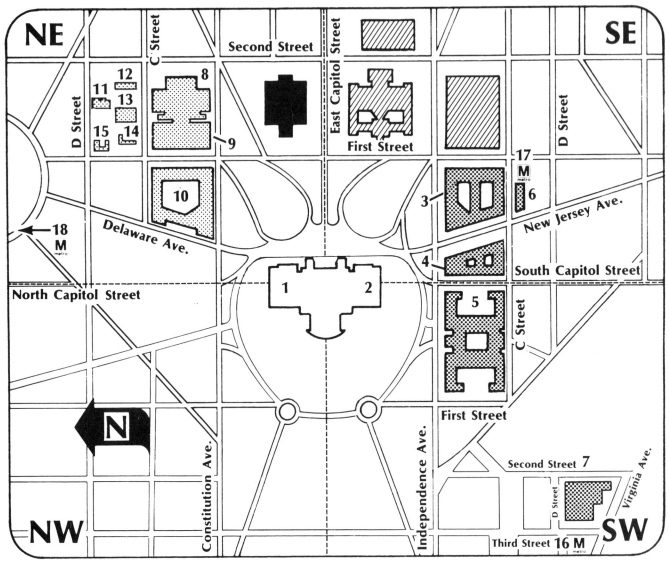

□ U.S. Capitol,
Washington, D.C. 20510 20515*

    1 Senate Wing
    2 House Wing

▨ House Office Buildings,
Washington, D.C. 20515

    3 Cannon
    4 Longworth
    5 Rayburn
    6 House Annex No. 1
    7 House Annex No. 2

▥ Senate Office Buildings,
Washington, D.C. 20510

    8 Hart
    9 Dirksen
    10 Russell
    11 Immigration Building
    12 Capitol Hill Apartments
    13 Senate Courts
    14 Carroll Arms Hotel
    15 Plaza Hotel

■ Supreme Court
Washington, D.C. 20543

▨ Library of Congress,
Washington, D.C. 20540

M Subway System

    16 Federal Center SW Station
    17 Capitol South Station
    18 Union Station Station

* Mail sent to the U.S. Capitol should bear the ZIP code of the chamber to which it is addressed.

MAJOR CONGRESSIONAL ACTION

Foreign Policy

After two years of light sparring, Congress and the Reagan administration slugged it out on foreign policy issues in 1983.

Throughout the year, the two branches of government were at odds on the direction of U.S. policy in Central America. And, as the year progressed, Congress was increasingly unwilling to accept President Reagan's explanations for keeping U.S. Marines in Lebanon; congressional concern becme particularly acute in October after a truck bombing killed 241 U.S. servicemen in Beirut.

The root of nearly every dispute between Congress and Reagan was the use of military muscle to address foreign policy questions. Whether the issue was military aid, arms sales or the introduction of U.S. troops into hostilities, Congress was quick to attack Reagan actions that seemed to emphasize a military approach.

In 1983, Reagan flexed military muscle more than any president since the Vietnam War. During the year, U.S. military forces were fighting in fractured Lebanon and the tiny Caribbean island of Grenada, and were sent to Central America as a signal to Nicaragua, Cuba and the Soviet Union of U.S. resolve to prevent the spread of communism.

The administration contended that it used the military as a last resort and only in response to provocation from U.S. foes. But critics in Congress contended that Reagan was opting for military force before all diplomatic approaches had been tried; by imitating the Soviet Union's military aggressiveness, the critics said, the United States was surrendering its right to be called a peacemaker.

Nevertheless, anxiety about the use of military force was neither unanimous nor consistent in Congress. Most conservatives applauded Reagan's emphasis on security concerns in Central America, and a majority of Democrats supported the Oct. 25 invasion of Grenada once polls showed it was clear that the American public was cheered by the success of the operation.

For the most part, Congress supported Reagan's foreign policy initiatives that did not have a military aspect. Reagan had to fight for every dollar of military aid to El Salvador, for example, but Congress raised few questions or objections to his requests for comparable increases in economic aid to Central America.

Congress was able to insert itself into policy-making on issues such as Central America and Lebanon in spite of a June 23 Supreme Court decision that seemed to threaten the congressional role in such issues.

By overturning the so-called "legislative veto," the court was widely interpreted as eliminating some tools that Congress had available to influence foreign policy. The most important of these were a congressional veto power over major foreign arms sales and the power to force the withdrawal of U.S. troops from foreign combat. Congress had never used either power, but it had won concessions from successive presidents by threatening to wield them.

In its disputes with Reagan during the last half of 1983, Congress found that its political leverage and its ultimate power over spending were sufficient to exact limited concessions from the president.

While the balance of power between the two branches remained essentially the same, the balance of power within Congress shifted during the year.

Early in 1983, the Senate Foreign Relations Committee made a significant claim to power by asserting its right to review and veto the administration's "reprogramming" of funds from one account to another. Previously, only the two Appropriations committees had demanded a right to block such transfers of funds. When Reagan sought to switch $60 million to El Salvador, the Foreign Relations Committee insisted it had the same right to block the money as did the Appropriations committees — and the administration agreed.

But the Foreign Relations Committee and its House counterpart — the Foreign Affairs Committee — later lost a significant chunk of political power when they failed to secure floor action on their foreign aid authorization bills. The Appropriations committees stepped into the breach and made most foreign aid decisions in continuing appropriations resolutions.

The Dec. 3 death of Foreign Affairs Committee Chairman Clement J. Zablocki, D-Wis., seemed likely to signal a new committee approach to legislating. Under the easygoing Zablocki, liberals had been the driving force on the committee. His successor, Dante B. Fascell, D-Fla., who stood to the right of many of his colleagues, was expected to rein in the liberals and prevent the committee from taking stands that the more circumspect House could not accept.

The Middle East

For the first time in a generation, the political consensus in the United States about the Middle East came under challenge in 1983.

The essential elements of the political consensus remained in place: an absolute commitment to Israel's security, encouragement for so-called "moderate" Arab leaders, and a determination to keep the Persian Gulf oil fields free of Soviet control.

But the consequences of Reagan's escalation of U.S. military presence in the region threatened to undermine a general agreement about how the United States should pursue those goals. Perhaps inevitably, the result was an historic confrontation between the president and Congress on the use of U.S. armed forces overseas.

The focus of U.S. policy was Lebanon, the war-torn nation that embodied the hatreds and tension of the Middle East. In 1982, after Israel invaded Lebanon, forcing the eviction of several thousand Palestinian guerrillas from Beirut, the Reagan administration set out to bring stability

to Lebanon, which had suffered nearly 10 years of civil war and occupation by Syrian and Palestinian troops.

Congress at first went along with the experiment, offering no resistance to stationing 1,200 Marines in a peace-keeping force in Beirut, along with soldiers from France, Italy and Great Britain. Early in 1983, Congress approved with no dissent Reagan's request for $251 million in aid to help rebuild the Lebanese economy and arm that country's long-inept army. In September, 1983, after the first Americans were killed in combat in Lebanon, Congress gave its reluctant approval to keeping the Marines there for another 18 months.

But on Oct. 23, a truck carrying more than 10,000 pounds of explosives rammed into a building at Beirut airport, killing 241 U.S. servicemen who were sleeping inside; it was the biggest daily casualty of U.S. Military forces since the Vietnam War. That incident, followed in early December by the first direct military clash between U.S. and Syrian military forces in Lebanon, apparently convinced many Americans and their representatives in Congress the problems of the Middle East were too intractable to be resolved by U.S. armed might.

By the end of the year, Reagan was coming under pressure from Congress and the American public to withdraw from the Lebanon peace keeping force, which had then grown to include 1,600 Marines. Administration officials were increasingly receptive to that pressure, predicting the Marines probably would be withdrawn some time in 1984 regardless of whether there had been much progress toward unity and peace in Lebanon.

Although it quickly unraveled, September's congressional-executive agreement to keep the Marines in Lebanon was an historic, precedent-setting step. By passing a resolution (S J Res 159 — PL 98-119) authorizing the Marines to remain for up to 18 additional months, Congress for the first time invoked key provisions of the 1973 War Powers Resolution (PL 93-148). The 1973 law required the president to obtain congressional approval to keep U.S. troops in combat for more than 60-90 days.

No president had ever acknowledged the constitutionality of the War Powers Resolution, and Reagan held to that tradition. While signing the bill invoking the War Powers act, Reagan questioned its constitutionality and said he would not be bound by its terms.

But in signing it on Lebanon, Reagan gave the War Powers Resolution more political validity than it had acquired during its first 10 years of existence. The political struggle also demonstrated to Congress and the executive branch that it was possible to reach agreement on the War Powers issue without provoking a constitutional crisis.

In concentrating on Lebanon, the administration gave little attention during the year to broader issues of the Middle East — especially the Arab-Israeli peace process begun at Camp David in 1978.

Reagan had sought in September, 1982, to revitalize the Camp David process with a plan that called for Israel to hand over the West Bank of the Jordan River to an "association" of Jordan and local Palestinians. But Israel rejected that plan, and by April Jordan's King Hussein had failed to secure permission from the Palestine Liberation Organization to negotiate on behalf of West Bank Palestinians.

Stymied both in Lebanon and in the broader Middle East peace process, Reagan sought in 1983 to shore up ties to both Jordan and Israel.

Reagan turned first to Jordan, proposing to Hussein that the United States provide financial aid, equipment and training for a Jordanian "rapid deployment force" that could respond to military crises in the region. The prospect of a beefed-up Jordanian army alarmed Israel, whose supporters on the House and Senate Appropriations committees killed some $200 million in funding for the plan.

In November, two months after Israeli Prime Minister Menachem Begin resigned for health reasons, Reagan moved to restore frayed ties between the United States and Israel. During a visit to Washington by Begin's successor, Yitzhak Shamir, Reagan proposed closer military relationships between the two countries and offered major economic advantages, including expanded military aid and a two-way free-trade zone. Reagan did not demand, and did not get, concessions in return from Israel. But he ended the year on much better terms with America's closest ally in the Middle East.

Central America

In 1983, congressional Democrats — occasionally joined by a handful of Republicans — continued their guerrilla warfare against Reagan's Central America policies. The critics were successful in restricting Reagan's flexibility and in forcing the president to make conciliatory gestures but were unable to force any major policy changes.

At the end of the year — as at the beginning — the United States was bolstering the government of El Salvador and undermining the government of Nicaragua. To the chagrin of his critics, Reagan escalated direct U.S. military involvement in the region by sending naval task forces and thousands of armed troops to take part in training exercises, particularly in Honduras.

Reagan took several steps to deflect criticism that he was seeking a purely military solution to the woes of Central America. In April, he appointed former Sen. Richard Stone, D-Fla. (1975-71), as special ambassador to promote negotiations in the region. In July, Reagan named a commission, headed by former Secretary of State Henry A. Kissinger, to propose long-range solutions to the region's woes. And at the end of the year Reagan made his first public effort to convince the Salvadoran government to crack down on right-wing "death squads" that allegedly were responsible for killing thousands of civilians.

But in the midst of those conciliatory gestures, Reagan raised new congressional fears by escalating U.S. military presence in the region. Starting in July, the United States conducted a series of military maneuvers and training exercises in Honduras and off the coast of Central America. Called "Big Pine II," the maneuvers involved 18 ships and more than 4,000 U.S. troops at various times. Coupled with suggestions that the United States might establish permanent bases in Honduras, the maneuvers led to speculation that Reagan was planning an expanded, long-term U.S. military presence in the region.

In his boldest gamble to silence critics, Reagan on April 27 addressed a joint session of Congress and appealed for support of his policies. While the speech raised the visibility of the issues involved in Central America, it failed to create a groundswell of support for the president's actions.

Of all the troubled nations in Central America, El Salvador presented the broadest difficulties for the United States. Each year the United States was giving El Salvador more than $250 million in economic and military aid, yet the economy continued to deteriorate and the guerrillas scored substantial military gains against the government.

Congress responded with caution and skepticism to

the appeals for increased aid. While it provided all the economic and development aid that Reagan requested in 1983, Congress cut his requests for military aid by 40 percent in fiscal 1983 and by 25 percent in fiscal 1984.

Congress also continued to insist that the Salvadoran government could get the military aid only if it made progress on human rights, land reform and other issues. The administration professed agreement with the need for progress on those issues but rejected the linkage between them and the aid.

Reagan made his stand explicit in December, vetoing a bill (HR 4042) that would have extended a 1981 requirement for semi-annual certifications to Congress that El Salvador was making enough progress to warrant the aid. Reagan's critics were outraged by the veto, saying it demonstrated that the president did not really care about human rights in El Salvador. Secretary of State George P. Shultz later gave a more practical explanation, telling reporters that he would not have been able to sign such a certification, given the situation in El Salvador at the end of 1983.

However, Congress kept the human rights issue alive in another fashion: The continuing appropriations resolution for fiscal 1984 made 30 percent of El Salvador's military aid conditional on progress in the trial of five former Salvadoran national guardsmen who were accused of murdering four U.S. churchwomen in December, 1980. The repeated delays in that case had come to symbolize El Salvador's failure to protect human rights. Ten per cent of the military aid also was held up pending a presidential certification that the Salvadoran land reform program was still on track.

A more direct conflict between Congress and the administration centered on the administration's military and political campaigns against the government of Nicaragua. Reagan had been in office for only a few months in 1981 when he suspended a Carter administration program of U.S. economic aid to Nicaragua. Reagan charged that the leftist Sandinistas who had come to power in 1979 were seeking to establish a Marxist state under the influence of Cuba and the Soviet Union. Later in 1981 he authorized U.S. support, through the Central Intelligence Agency, for Nicaraguan exiles in Honduras who had taken up arms against the Sandinistas.

In late 1982 and early 1983, news reports revealed the extent of U.S. backing for the Nicaraguan rebels. The reports showed that an operation that had started as small-scale harassment eventually mushroomed into a full-scale war with some 10,000 rebels battling the 25,000-man Nicaraguan army. By the summer of 1983, guerrilla units were launching air and naval attacks that damaged major Nicaraguan oil storage installations.

Few members of Congress openly sympathized with the Sandinista leadership, which had taken on many of the repressive characteristics of communist regimes. But Democrats in the House, especially the members of the Intelligence Committee, became increasingly alarmed that the administration was expanding the scope of the Nicaragua operation beyond the boundaries of U.S. and international law, with the aim of ousting the sitting government of a foreign country.

In May, the Democratic majority of the House Intelligence Committee broke with Reagan, approving a bill (HR 2760) to prohibit further U.S. aid to the Nicaraguan rebels after a certain date, which remained classified. After Democrats and the administration failed in an attempt to nego-

tiate a compromise on the issue, the House on July 28 passed HR 2760 on a 228-195 vote.

The House action represented a stunning symbolic rejection of one aspect of Reagan's policies toward Central America. But the political and legislative impact of the vote was undermined by the reluctance of key Senate Democrats to press for similar action in their chamber.

The House initiative also lost steam in the wake of the Sept. 1 downing by the Soviet Union of a Korean Air Lines passenger plane carrying 269 persons, including U.S. Rep. Larry McDonald, D-Ga. That incident heightened anti-Soviet sentiment in the United States. It also placed political obstacles in the way of any action that could be seen as a favor to the Soviet Union or its allies, such as Nicaragua.

The issue was decided on Nov. 17, as Congress was rushing to finish its business before adjournment. House-Senate conferees on the defense appropriations bill (HR 4185 — PL 98-212), adopted a compromise that prohibited the CIA and other intelligence agencies from spending more than $24 million in fiscal 1984 to support the Nicaraguan rebels. Although the compromise placed an absolute limit on spending for the Nicaraguan operation, it represented a victory for the administration because it allowed the aid to the rebels to continue.

With no controversy, Congress used its control of the purse to influence U.S. policy in the largest nation in Central America — Guatemala. Under the Carter administration, the United States had blocked military aid and arms sales to Guatemala because of alleged human rights abuses by the military government. When the Reagan administration moved in late 1982 and early 1983 to restore U.S. military ties to Guatemala, liberals in Congress protested that human rights violations had not ceased and the United States should not give its stamp of approval to such a repressive government.

Provisions attached without fanfare to appropriations bills for fiscal 1983 and 1984 banned all U.S. aid to Guatemala except for humanitarian assistance provided through private voluntary organizations. Congressional opposition also helped persuade the administration to shelve a sale to Guatemala of helicopter spare parts and other equipment that had both military and civilian uses.

Critics of Reagan's actions in Central America focused on such narrow issues as foreign aid and arms sales because Congress had more control over such tools of foreign policy than over the basic policies themselves.

Congress always had found it difficult to force a president to abandon or alter a broad policy — such as Reagan's pattern of military involvement in Central America. But over the years, members of Congress had been able to nibble at the edges of policy by attacking presidential requests for specific elements, such as foreign aid, that required congressional approval.

The one aspect of Central American policy that congressional critics found most difficult to address was Reagan's reluctance to press for unconditional negotiations on all the region's political and military problems. The administration insisted that the Nicaraguan government negotiate with its internal opposition as a step toward fulfilling its 1979 promises of democracy, but Reagan officials refused to demand similar negotiations between the government of El Salvador and its opponents.

Responding to congressional pressure, Reagan in April named former Sen. Stone as his special ambassador-at-large for Central America. Stone's mandate was to promote negotiations in the region, but by year's end it was unclear

whether he had moved any of the region's leaders or guerrilla representatives near to the negotiating table.

Some limited progress came from the efforts of the "Contadora group," composed of Mexico, Panama, Colombia and Venezuela. The group took its name from the Panamanian island where leaders of the four nations first met in January, 1983.

The Contadora group sought to get the five countries of Central America (Costa Rica, El Salvador, Guatemala, Honduras and Nicaragua) to agree to a set of principles that would reduce conflict in the region. By September, the four Contadora countries and the five Central American countries had agreed to discuss 21 principles, including such controversial items as phasing out foreign arms shipments and foreign military advisers. Recasting those principles into formal treaties proved more difficult, however. By January, 1984, the nine countries settled for a watered-down agreement that offered no specific promises for reduced conflict.

The proper role of the United States in the Contadora process was the subject of some dispute. The Reagan administration said it endorsed the activities of the Contadora countries, but was keeping its distance from negotiations because U.S. participation might jeopardize any chances for success. But the Contadora negotiations were highly popular in Congress, and some members argued that the United States should support and encourage them more actively.

Foreign Aid

Congress' regular system for handling foreign aid legislation collapsed in 1983. Congress and the administration found it more convenient, from political and parliamentary standpoints, to deal with foreign aid on a stopgap basis.

For the first time in a decade, Congress failed in 1983 to pass a regular bill making statutory authorizations for foreign aid programs. And for the fourth time in five years, Congress failed to pass a regular bill making appropriations for those programs.

Instead, foreign aid funding for fiscal 1984 was included in a continuing appropriations resolution (H J Res 413 — PL 98-151). For Congress, that procedure had the advantage of avoiding lengthy and divisive debates over foreign aid in two separate bills. That stopgap procedure also meant that most foreign aid issues were decided by the two Appropriations committees, which had been remarkably receptive to the administration's foreign aid requests.

The losers were the Senate Foreign Relations and House Foreign Affairs panels, which traditionally had considerable influence on foreign policy decision-making based on their stewardship of the foreign aid legislation.

In 1983 the committees were unable to secure floor action on bills (S 1347, HR 2992) that had taken them months to write. Senate committee Chairman Charles H. Percy, R-Ill., and House committee Chairman Zablocki both attempted repeatedly to move their bills to the floor but were rebuffed by party leaders who were inclined to avoid foreign aid debates whenever possible.

The Democrat-led House committee in particular was sidestepped on important decisions during the year. In practice, the administration disregarded the committee's bill and decided not to press for floor action on it; that meant, for example, that the committee played little direct role in deciding the level of aid to El Salvador, the most controversial foreign aid issue of the year.

The administration's strategy of directing its lobbying efforts toward the Appropriations committees paid off. The continuing resolution cemented into place the administration's shift in foreign aid priorities.

Responding to what it perceived as the urgency of Soviet-inspired military challenges to U.S. allies, such as El Salvador and Turkey, the administration proposed to increase substantially the level of military support. At the same time it held the line on aid for economic advances in developing countries.

Many liberals objected to the administration's emphasis on military aid, but Congress accepted most of the aid proposals nevertheless. The 1984 continuing resolution boosted total military aid by 15 percent over the previous year while cutting economic and development aid spending by nearly 6 percent.

In an effort to devise a new political strategy for getting foreign aid legislation through Congress, Secretary of State Shultz appointed a commission to study aid programs. The commission was chaired by Frank Carlucci, former deputy defense secretary.

The commission report, issued Nov. 21, argued that all types of foreign aid programs were worthwhile, even though it was not possible to document that every foreign aid dollar had been spent wisely. The commission called on the administration and congressional leaders to issue a joint statement endorsing foreign aid as an "essential and integral part of the foreign policy of the United States." As of the end of the year, no such statement had been issued.

Grenada

In the early morning hours of Oct. 25, some 4,600 U.S. Marines, Army rangers and paratroopers landed on the tiny Caribbean island of Grenada. Within a few days, all leaders of the Marxist-led Grenadan government had been arrested and 700 Cuban construction workers who put up an unexpectedly fierce resistance had been overwhelmed.

Reagan said he had ordered the U.S. troops on a "rescue mission" to safeguard nearly 1,000 Americans who were studying at a U.S.-run medical college on the island. The medical students were threatened, Reagan said, by radicals within the Grenadan government who had overthrown Prime Minister Maurice Bishop on Oct. 12 and later killed him. The U.S. troops were requested by Grenada's neighboring nations that belonged to the Organization of Eastern Caribbean States.

The invasion of Grenada brought an immediate chorus of approval from most Republicans in Congress but prompted widespread soul-searching among Democrats.

The reaction of House Speaker Thomas P. O'Neill Jr., D-Mass., was typical. At first, O'Neill declined comment on the invasion, but once the fighting stopped he complained that Reagan had engaged in "gunboat diplomacy." Two weeks after the invasion, however, most members of a House delegation returned from an inspection trip to Grenada saying the invasion was justified, and O'Neill agreed with their assessment. Most Democrats agreed with O'Neill, although with some reluctance.

The impact of the invasion was perhaps greater on the American public than on Congress. Public opinion polls registered immediate approval of the operation, apparently demonstrating that Americans were hungering for a military victory after the embarrassments of the Vietnam War and the Iranian hostage crisis.

—By John Felton

A Reluctant Congress Adopts Lebanon Policy

President Reagan's dispatch of a contingent of Marines to Lebanon in 1982 to take part in a four-nation peacekeeping force evolved during 1983 into a far larger commitment — and a foreign policy dilemma of the first order.

By year's end, the effort to help revive the tiny Mideast country's national life had cost 257 U.S. servicemen their lives. And a Congress that in September had declared itself a partner in Reagan's policy was beginning to move toward rewriting the contract in 1984.

Congress had entered into its bargain with Reagan on Sept. 29, when it passed a resolution (S J Res 159 — PL 98-119) authorizing him to keep U.S. forces in Lebanon for as long as 18 months, or until April 1985. *(Text, p. 37-E)*

But the deal quickly soured as a terrorist bomb killed 241 U.S. servicemen and U.S. naval and air forces clashed with Syrian forces in eastern Lebanon, inflicting more U.S. casualties and provoking fears of a war with Soviet-backed Syria that would risk a superpower confrontation.

Public and congressional concern over Reagan's policy mounted throughout the fall, building pressure on Reagan to withdraw U.S. forces from Lebanon or show why they should stay. The demands for a change gained even more momentum in December, when both a House subcommittee and a Pentagon-appointed panel of military experts issued reports faulting both the military and political conduct of U.S. policy.

Following those reports, House Speaker Thomas P. O'Neill Jr., D-Mass., who had been indispensable to the effort to get S J Res 159 passed, formally asked a Lebanon Oversight Committee he had established to reassess the authorization.

Starting in early December, when U.S. Navy air and Syrian anti-aircraft forces clashed in eastern Lebanon, O'Neill openly expressed his growing uneasiness about the policy he had helped preserve by pushing S J Res 159 in September.

But the opening he chose to signal an open break with the policy came only on Jan. 3, 1984, when the Rev. Jesse Jackson, a black civil rights leader and Democratic presidential candidate, achieved a dramatic political triumph by getting Syria to release a Navy airman, Lt. Robert O. Goodman, whom Syria had captured on Dec. 4.

Critics of the Reagan administration, which had declined to negotiate for Goodman's release, said the grant of Goodman's freedom was a gesture of goodwill that Reagan should seize upon to try to open negotiations with Syria to settle U.S.-Syrian differences over Lebanon.

As the news of Goodman's release broke, O'Neill emerged from a meeting with his Lebanon committee to say that unless the administration soon demonstrated the utility of keeping the Marines in Beirut, he would join those calling on Reagan to pull the Marines out.

"I am saying to the president, 'Those of us who supported the policy must see some action because we can no longer go with the status quo,'" O'Neill said. "Unless measurable progress is achieved in the very near future, I will join with many others in Congress in reconsidering congressional authorization of Marine presence in Lebanon."

Final Provisions

As signed into law (PL 98-119) on Oct. 12, S J Res 159:

● Stated that the removal of all foreign forces from Lebanon was "an essential United States foreign policy objective in the Middle East."

● Stated that the United States was participating in the multinational peacekeeping force in Lebanon "in order to restore full control by the government of Lebanon over its own territory."

● Stated that U.S. armed forces participating in the multinational force were "now in hostilities requiring authorization of their continued presence under the War Powers Resolution [PL 93-148]."

● Stated that Congress "determines" that the requirements of section 4(a)(1) of the War Powers Resolution came into effect on Aug. 29, 1983, when two Marines were killed in Lebanon.

● Authorized the president, "for the purposes of" section 5(b) of the War Powers Resolution, to continue participation by U.S. armed forces in the multinational force in Lebanon, subject to the limitations contained in Sept. 25, 1982, letters between the Lebanese and U.S. governments. The letters stated that 1,200 U.S. armed personnel were to serve in the Beirut area only for peacekeeping and were not to engage in combat.

● Authorized U.S. forces to engage in "such protective measures as may be necessary to ensure the safety of the multinational force...."

● Authorized U.S. forces to remain part of the multinational force in Lebanon "until the end of the 18-month period" beginning on the date of enactment of the joint resolution, which was Oct. 12, 1983. The authorization was to expire before the end of that 18 month period if all foreign forces were withdrawn from Lebanon, unless the president certified to Congress that troops should remain, or if the United Nations or the Lebanese government assumed the duties of the multinational force, or if other "effective security arrangements" had been implemented, or if all other countries had withdrawn from participation in the multinational peacekeeping force.

● Required the president to report to Congress at least every three months on the status of U.S. forces in Lebanon. (Reagan agreed informally to submit such reports every 60 days). The reports were to include statements on: the activities being performed by the multinational force; the composition, responsibilities and areas of deployment of the force; the results of efforts to reduce and eventually eliminate the force; how continued U.S. participation in the force was advancing U.S. foreign policy interests in the Middle East; and what progress had occurred toward political reconciliation among all groups in Lebanon.

● Stated that Congress believed it should be U.S. policy to continue to promote discussions with Israel, Syria and Lebanon on the removal of all foreign forces from Lebanon.

● Stated the sense of Congress that not later than one year after enactment of the resolution, and at least annually thereafter, the United States should discuss with other members of the U.N. Security Council the establishment of a U.N. force to assume the responsibilities of the multinational force in Lebanon.

● Stated that nothing in the resolution precluded the president from withdrawing U.S. forces from Lebanon if circumstances warranted, and nothing precluded Congress by joint resolution from directing such a withdrawal.

● Stated that the resolution did not modify or supersede the War Powers Resolution or the Lebanese Emergency Assistance Act of 1983 (PL 98-43), which required congressional authorization for "any substantial expansion in the number or role of United States Armed Forces in Lebanon."

● Established priority procedures in both houses of Congress for the consideration of any joint resolution or bill to amend or repeal the resolution. *(Text p. 36-E)*

Background

U.S. Marines had participated in a four-nation peacekeeping force in Lebanon that included 2,000 French Legionnaires and paratroopers, 2,100 Italian infantry and Marines and a 100-man British reconnaissance squadron since August 1982. *(1982 Almanac p. 167)*

Initially, the presence of the U.S. Marines, whose number had risen from 1,200 to 1,800 by the fall of 1983, was challenged by only a handful of members of Congress.

But the volume of congressional complaints began to rise in January and early February of 1983 after a series of confrontations between U.S. Marines and Israeli troops.

American and Israeli forces confronted each other several times in January. Then on Feb. 2, a Marine captain waving a loaded pistol stopped three Israeli tanks from advancing into territory held by the peacekeeping force. The incident prompted a heated diplomatic exchange.

The incidents also prompted scattered complaints from members of Congress that the Marines were in greater danger than Reagan had acknowledged. On Feb. 3, Sen. J. James Exon, D-Neb., confronted Defense Secretary Caspar W. Weinberger on the issue in a Senate Budget Committee hearing on the defense budget.

Weinberger told Exon: "It is the judgment of the administration, of the president, that the condition under which the Marines are in Lebanon is not one in which hostilities are imminent."

Exon charged that the administration was "stonewalling" on the issue. He nevertheless admitted that "probably a majority of my colleagues disagree with me."

At the time, a major factor in congressional reticence on the issue was fear of disrupting talks that later led to a May 17 agreement between Israel and Lebanon providing for Israeli troops to withdraw.

The Senate Foreign Relations Committee nevertheless asked Reagan to seek congressional approval before sending more Marines. A Dec. 15, 1982, letter to Reagan signed by 14 of the panel's 17 members said they wanted a chance to consider "the full implications of any extended commitment of U.S. forces" in Lebanon.

The war powers issue festered early in 1983 as the administration was forced to extend its estimates of just how long the Marines would be needed in Beirut.

After an April 18 terrorist bombing at the U.S. Embassy in Beirut killed more than 50 persons, Congress took its first step toward limiting Reagan's use of the Marines by demanding a voice in any decision to reinforce them. The action was taken as part of a bill (PL 98-43) authorizing military and economic aid to Lebanon. *(Box, p. 116)*

But the war powers issue came to a head only after two U.S. Marines were killed in Lebanon on Aug. 29 by artillery fire from Druse Moslem forces fighting the U.S.-backed minority Christian government of Lebanon.

2nd Lt. Donald George Losey, of Winston-Salem, N.C., and Staff Sgt. Alexander M. Ortega, of Rochester, N.Y.,

were killed in the heavy rocket, mortar and small-arms fire. They were the first Marines in the peacekeeping force to die from hostile fire.

In the wake of that incident, pressure in Congress to force the president to invoke the War Powers act quickly mounted.

War Powers Bargain

As it emerged in September, the Lebanon compromise was founded on a desire among members both to limit Reagan's use of U.S. armed forces and to assert Congress' right to do so under the 1973 War Powers Resolution (PL 93-148).

The War Powers Resolution proscribed the deployment of U.S. forces in hostile situations for more than 90 days without congressional authorization for a longer stay. But like presidents before him, Reagan had refused to concede the law's constitutionality and had sidestepped it.

On Aug. 30, Reagan formally notified Congress that two Marines had been killed and 14 others wounded in Beirut on Aug. 29. But in his letter, Reagan refused to cite the section of the 1973 War Powers Resolution that would have enabled Congress to force a withdrawal.

Under Section 4(a)(1) of the act, Congress could, by passing a concurrent resolution, force the president to withdraw U.S. troops from overseas if he had reported that they were sent "into hostilities or into situations where imminent involvement in hostilities is clearly indicated by the circumstances." While acknowledging that the Marines were engaged in "sporadic fighting," Reagan refused to say they were actually involved in "hostilities."

U.S. officials, including Secretary of State George P. Shultz, said they believed the Moslem attacks were directed at the Lebanese Army, not at the Marines.

Reagan wrote to Congress that using U.S. forces in Lebanon was "essential to the objective of helping to restore the territorial integrity, sovereignty and political independence of Lebanon." He said it was "not possible to predict the duration of the presence of these forces in Lebanon. We will continue to assess this question in the light of progress toward this objective."

Congressional Response

Several congressional leaders publicly urged Reagan to invoke Section 4(a)(1) of the War Powers Resolution and were upset when he refused.

House Foreign Affairs Chairman Clement J. Zablocki, D-Wis., who was to succumb to a heart attack Dec. 3, said in the days following the Marine deaths that Reagan was "unnecessarily risking a confrontation with Congress" by "persisting in trying to exclude the Congress from fulfilling its constitutional responsibilities."

Zablocki's Senate counterpart, Charles H. Percy, R-Ill., chairman of the Foreign Relations Committee, agreed that Congress should be involved in the decision-making under terms of the War Powers Resolution.

"We have people up in helicopters, we're shooting rockets and artillery — if that isn't imminent hostilities, I don't know what is," Percy said.

Senate Minority Leader Robert C. Byrd, D-W.Va., wrote Reagan Aug. 31 saying: "American forces are clearly involved in hostilities within the meaning of Section 4(a)(1) of the War Powers Resolution." Byrd said Reagan should invoke Section 4(a)(1) to "assure the fullest possible cooperation" between Congress and the executive.

None of those leaders suggested that Congress would

or should attempt to force withdrawal of the Marines. But members who had been critical of Reagan's decision to send the Marines to Beirut in the first place advocated a withdrawal.

Among them were pro-military conservatives such as Barry Goldwater, R-Ariz., chairman of the Senate Intelligence Committee, and House Armed Services Committee members G. V. "Sonny" Montgomery, D-Miss., and Ike Skelton, D-Mo.

Hill-White House Tensions

The first Marine deaths came at a time when leaders in Congress were still angry at the administration for its failure less than a month before to advise them in advance of plans for extensive military maneuvers in Central America. The administration had calmed that anger only by promising more extensive consultations in the future.

The War Powers controversy also arose at a touchy time for the administration because Congress was to take various important votes in September on tough foreign and defense policy issues, including U.S. policy in Central America and funding for the MX missile.

At an Aug. 31 press conference, Shultz defended Reagan on the War Powers issue. Refusing to characterize the Marines as engaged in hostilities, he said Reagan had complied with the law's requirements.

Shultz also expressed hope that the Lebanese Army, which had received equipment and training from the United States and had moved on Moslem strongholds the same day, would be able to staunch the outbreak of violence.

On Sept. 1, the Pentagon announced that about 2,000 Marines were being sent to join a U.S. naval task force stationed in the eastern Mediterranean off the Lebanese coast. That move was widely seen as a warning that the United States would retaliate for further attacks on the Marines.

Congress earlier in the year had demanded a voice in any decision to increase the number of Marines in Beirut, and Reagan had accepted that demand by signing a bill (PL 98-43) authorizing military and economic aid to Lebanon.

But Reagan refused to submit to Congress the decision to station the additional Marines aboard ships, arguing that they were not part of the peacekeeping force, and therefore not covered by the terms of PL 98-43.

According to Speaker O'Neill, Reagan argued to leaders of Congress on Sept. 4 that invoking the War Powers Resolution would only worsen the situation for the Marines by raising the possibility that they could be withdrawn abruptly. But as the fighting in Lebanon intensified, it became ever more difficult for the administration to sustain the notion that the Marines were not engaged in hostilities.

On Sept. 5, two more Marines were killed, this time by rocket fire, and French members of the peacekeeping force suffered even heavier casualties. On Sept. 8, a U.S. warship fired for the first time on Moslem artillery positions believed responsible for attacking the Marines.

With a confrontation on the issue clearly building, the administration and key congressional leaders soon decided to seek ways to head off a constitutional clash between the executive and legislative branches.

Meanwhile, congressional critics of administration policy began to put their complaints into legislative form.

In the Senate, a plan emerged for Congress to pass a

resolution approving the Marines' deployment but to set limits on the number who could be present in Lebanon and how long they could stay.

But on the day the U.S. warship fired for the first time, Rep. Clarence D. Long, D-Md., chairman of the House Foreign Operations Appropriations Subcommittee, announced that he would offer an amendment to the fiscal 1984 continuing appropriations resolution that would cut off funds for the peacekeeping force in Lebanon after 30 days unless Reagan submitted a Section 4(a)(1) War Powers report to Congress.

Long said the Marines were "sitting duck targets in an undeclared war," and he charged that any resolution that simply approved their posting would be a "Lebanese Gulf of Tonkin resolution, another blank check."

Negotiations Take Shape

In the week of Sept. 12, leaders in Congress and members of the administration began negotiating in earnest, and the edges of the eventual compromise began to appear.

Leaders in both parties on Capitol Hill set as one demand that the president acknowledge the right of Congress to share in setting the terms of the Marines' deployment.

Underlying that demand was a sense that, with Marines under fire, a failure to assert the validity of the War Powers act would cut the law's already shaky legs out from under it for good. Sen. Lloyd Bentsen, D-Texas, said: "I can only suggest that if the War Powers act is not invoked [in such a case] it is worthless. It is a scrap of paper and we ought to throw it away and forget it."

Reagan insisted that, as commander-in-chief of the armed forces, he ultimately was responsible for deciding where and for how long to deploy U.S. military forces. Through aides, Reagan said he wanted Congress to endorse his deployment of the Marines but place no conditions on it.

Providing a foundation for compromise was the fact that, as of September, an apparent majority in Congress agreed that the Marines should stay put for the time being.

On Sept. 12, Reagan decided that Marine commanders could call in air strikes from U.S. ships in the Mediterranean to defend themselves. Yet most leaders of the move to invoke the War Powers act still said they would vote to back the president when given a chance.

The issue thus boiled down to two questions: 1) In what way acceptable to both Congress and the president could the War Powers act be invoked? 2) Should Congress place a formal limit on how long the Marines could remain in Lebanon?

Legislative action was preceded by maneuvering that illustrated the traditional difficulty Congress faced in coming to terms with the president on foreign policy issues. Beyond the customary reluctance of many members to challenge the president on foreign policy, there was the practical question of how Congress could act.

Congress could force the president to abide by the War Powers act only by overriding his certain veto of any bill invoking it. That would be unwieldy at best and impossible politically. Congress never had taken such a step in foreign policy since enacting the War Powers Resolution over President Nixon's veto in 1973. *(1973 Almanac p. 905)*

Moreover, congressional leaders were divided on just what to put in a bill invoking the War Powers act in Lebanon. Even Democrats who had something to gain politically from a congressional rebuke of Reagan had trouble

Congress Approves Aid for Lebanon . . .

The Senate on June 15 cleared legislation (S 639, PL 98-43) authorizing $251 million in economic and military aid to Lebanon in fiscal 1983. The House had passed the bill on June 2 on a 276-76 vote. *(Vote 145, p. 46-H)*

The Senate had first passed its version of the bill, by voice vote, on May 20.

The aid included $150 million in Economic Support Fund loans and grants, $100 million in Foreign Military Sales loans and $1 million in military training aid. The administration had requested the aid in the wake of Israel's June 1982 invasion of Lebanon.

When the House Foreign Affairs Committee and Senate Foreign Relations Committee reported the bill on April 19 and April 20, respectively, they backed off attempts to require the president to obtain permission from Congress before sending more Marines into Lebanon. The committee actions followed a bombing of the U.S. Embassy in Beirut April 18 that resulted in the deaths of an estimated 50 people.

But the bill did require the president to seek congressional authorization for any "substantial expansion" of the number of U.S. troops stationed in Lebanon as part of a multinational peacekeeping force. That provision would apply only to stationing U.S. troops in Lebanon in conjunction with agreements providing for withdrawal of all foreign occupying forces in Lebanon. The United States had more than 1,200 Marines stationed in Lebanon.

The language dealing with the issue stated:

"The president shall obtain statutory authorization from the Congress with respect to any substantial expansion in the number or role in Lebanon of United States Armed Forces, including any introduction of United States Armed Forces into Lebanon in conjunction with agreements providing for the withdrawal of all foreign troops from Lebanon and for the creation of a new multinational peacekeeping force in Lebanon.

"Nothing in this section is intended to modify, limit, or suspend any of the standards and procedures prescribed by the War Powers Resolution of 1973."

Committee Action

At the outset, it was clear that the House and Senate committees would approve amendments dealing with congressional authorization for the troops in Lebanon. It also was clear that the committees and the administration approached the issue from opposite perspectives: most committee members wanted as much congressional involvement as possible and the administration wanted to retain as much flexibility as possible.

The House Foreign Affairs Committee was the first to act. On April 19, it adopted, with little debate, an amendment to HR 2532 requiring the president to get approval from Congress "with respect to the introduction of United States Armed Forces into Lebanon in conjunction with agreements providing for the withdrawal of all foreign troops from Lebanon and for the creation of a new, more permanent multinational peacekeeping force in Lebanon."

That amendment was a watered-down version of a measure approved on April 12 by the panel's Middle East subcommittee that would have required prior approval before more troops could be sent to Lebanon.

Subcommittee Chairman Lee H. Hamilton, D-Ind., said the amendment was weakened because of administration opposition. He said it would not preclude Reagan

agreeing on how long the Marines should be permitted to stay in Beirut.

House Democrats, led by Speaker O'Neill and Chairman Zablocki of the Foreign Affairs Committee, proposed that Congress pass a joint resolution invoking the War Powers Resolution but authorizing Reagan to keep the Marines in Lebanon for at least another 18 months.

This approach was resisted by Senate Democrats, led by Minority Leader Robert C. Byrd, D-W.Va. They wanted legislation to require Reagan to specify how long the Marines would be needed in Lebanon and what their mission was to be, and they objected to an 18-month authorization.

Senate Majority Leader Howard H. Baker Jr., R-Tenn., proposed a variation. He suggested that Reagan write a letter asking Congress "under its constitutional authority and within the scope of the war powers act" to pass a resolution authorizing the Marines to stay in Lebanon for a limited period.

The administration responded to these congressional plans by declining to retreat on either the War Powers or the timing issues. On Sept. 15, White House Chief of Staff James A. Baker III gave congressional leaders a counterproposal: A draft of a letter in which Reagan would accept congressional involvement merely "in the context of the War Powers Resolution."

Leaders in both chambers rejected that plan, saying it would not directly invoke the War Powers act, but White House aide Baker said the president would go no further.

Senate Democrats Act

But Senate Democrats forced Reagan's hand. They caucused on Sept. 15 and voted 29-0 to introduce a resolution (S J Res 163) that simply would have triggered the War Powers act, giving Congress legal control over how long the Marines stayed.

Byrd and other backers of S J Res 163 — a bill requiring the president's signature — maintained that with the Marines in Lebanon suffering casualties, "any blind man" could see that they were engaged in hostilities and that the War Powers Resolution's provisions had been triggered.

"We want to cooperate with the administration," Byrd told reporters. "This is not a partisan matter. But this is the law. The law cannot be winked at."

The Democrats' resolution declared that the Marines had been engaged in hostilities "within the meaning" of the War Powers Resolution since Aug. 28, when Marine positions south of Beirut first came under heavy fire.

S J Res 163 was referred to the Senate Foreign Relations Committee, which also had under consideration a similar measure (S J Res 159) offered Sept. 12 by Charles McC. Mathias Jr., R-Md. As originally introduced, Mathias' bill would have invoked the War Powers Resolution and authorized the Marines to remain in Lebanon only another six months.

. . . But Demands Role in Troop Decision

from increasing the U.S. force of Marines already there.

The Senate Foreign Relations Committee debated the issue during three sessions on April 19 and 20 before settling on somewhat tighter language than the House bill contained.

Sen. Claiborne Pell, D-R.I., wanted to put the Marines under a provision of the 1973 War Powers Resolution (PL 93-148) that would declare them to be facing "imminent hostilities." The War Powers Resolution gave Congress the right, under certain circumstances, to withdraw U.S. troops from overseas combat. Paul S. Sarbanes, D-Md., also proposed requiring congressional approval before additional Marines could be sent to Lebanon. *(War Powers Resolution, 1973 Almanac p. 905)*

The administration strongly objected to those proposals. On April 20 Deputy Secretary of State Kenneth W. Dam sent the committee a letter saying it would be "highly premature and unwise, and potentially damaging to the integrity of the [War Powers] Resolution" to declare the Marines would face "imminent hostilities."

In the face of that opposition, the committee drafted an amendment saying the president must obtain congressional approval for "any substantial expansion in the number or role of United States Armed Forces in Lebanon or for the creation of a new, expanded or extended multinational peace-keeping force in Lebanon."

Lebanon's Army: How Strong?

Congress received conflicting assessments about the effectiveness of the Lebanese army.

In March, the Congressional Research Service of the Library of Congress reported that the army "is in very poor condition" as a result of the 1975-76 civil war and "exists mostly on paper at the present time." The army listed 20,000 members on its rolls, but as few as 11,000 were actually on active duty, the report said.

The report cited estimates that two years would be required to train and equip five brigades, "which would be the minimum size force that could effectively police the country."

But, the report added, "it will be more difficult to restore morale and raise the army's credibility among the Lebanese people who have never trusted, nor demonstrably wanted to strengthen, the central military." Lebanon's religious minorities traditionally had relied on their own militias — several of which were stronger and all of which were better equipped than the regular army, the report said.

Rebutting that report, the State Department on April 26 painted a much more optimistic picture of the Lebanese army. The rebuttal was made in a letter to Rep. Hamilton from Powell A. Moore, assistant secretary of state for congressional relations.

Moore admitted that "only several months ago there was little more than the outward trappings of a Lebanese army. . . ." But the army had gained control throughout the capital city of Beirut and "is now capable of performing basic security missions in the areas to be vacated by the withdrawal of external forces," Moore said.

Moore said there was "growing popular support for the army," adding that a "growing Lebanese national consensus exists to support the government."

Moore did not say how the Lebanese army would assert its authority over the religious militias.

Lengthy Negotiations

The negotiations that led to the eventual compromise were initiated by House Foreign Affairs Chairman Zablocki with firm backing by Speaker O'Neill. Zablocki's aim was to preserve the War Powers Resolution — of which he had been a primary author — and at the same time head off legislative attempts to force an immediate withdrawal of the Marines.

Administration negotiators at first rejected a Zablocki resolution that supported U.S. policy in Lebanon and invoked the War Powers act. The administration wanted the support for the policy but rejected any limit on how long the Marines could remain in Lebanon.

But after Senate Democrats introduced S J Res 163, raising the prospect of a direct vote on the War Powers issue, Reagan's aides resumed their talks with Baker and the House Democrats. A compromise setting an 18-month limit on deployment of the Marines was reached Sept. 19 and ratified by both sets of negotiators the next day. Senate Democrats were left out of the final negotiations — ensuring their opposition to the compromise agreement.

Compromise Resolution

In essence, the compromise required Reagan to sign a joint resolution invoking the War Powers Resolution and imposing an 18-month limit on troop deployment. In turn, the president could declare in writing that he did not recognize the War Powers act's constitutionality and that he retained his constitutional authority as commander-in-chief to deploy U.S. forces.

Zablocki insisted that the compromise was a victory for Congress. "This will be the first administration that has acknowledged the War Powers act," he said.

Yet both sides said the value of the compromise was its avoidance of a confrontation over whether Congress had the power to force the president to withdraw U.S. troops from hostilities overseas.

In more than six hours of hearings before the House Foreign Affairs and Senate Foreign Relations committees on Sept. 21, Secretary of State Shultz repeatedly insisted that enactment of the compromise Lebanon resolution would not impair the president's authority to deploy U.S. forces overseas as he thought necessary.

The key question asked by members of the two committees was: What would happen if the Marines were still in Lebanon at the end of the 18-month period and Congress had not authorized them to remain?

While not answering directly, Shultz made it clear that the president was insisting that his constitutional powers overrode any single piece of legislation.

Shultz told the Senate committee: "The president has no intention of turning over to Congress his constitutional responsibilities as commander in chief." He said the ad-

ministration viewed the compromise as "an effort to put that [constitutional] issue aside for the time being."

Thus for some members, a major motive for passing a resolution on Lebanon was, as Rep. Stephen J. Solarz, D-N.Y., said, to "rescue the War Powers act from what would otherwise be a political and parliamentary grave."

Committee Action

Resolutions (H J Res 364, S J Res 159, as amended) to make the compromise law were approved by the House Foreign Affairs Committee on Sept. 22 (H Rept 98-385) and by the Senate Foreign Relations Committee the next day (S Rept 98-242).

The House panel approved the compromise 30-6, though many members expressed serious misgivings. The measure squeezed through the Senate committee on a party-line vote of 9-7 — and only because Mathias, who said the 18-month time limit was too long, agreed to go along so that a resolution could be reported to the Senate.

Before the compromise could be considered by the full House and Senate, it was challenged in the House Appropriations Committee. While considering a stopgap fiscal 1984 funding measure (H J Res 367) on Sept. 21, that panel adopted an amendment to cut off all funds for the Marines in Lebanon in 60 days unless the president submitted a report to Congress invoking the War Powers act.

The Appropriations action, taken by a 20-16 show of hands, angered Speaker O'Neill. He said it would sabotage the compromise with the White House if allowed to stand, and he ordered H J Res 367 referred to the Foreign Affairs Committee, where the measure died. Appropriations Chairman Jamie L. Whitten, D-Miss., introduced a "clean" fiscal 1984 funding bill (H J Res 368) on Sept. 22 that included no Lebanon amendment.

David R. Obey, D-Wis., and several other Appropriations members said they voted for the amendment as a message that they wanted the Rules Committee to permit the full House to vote on amendments to the Lebanon resolution, which it did.

Foreign Affairs Action

In the Sept. 22 House Foreign Affairs Committee debate on H J Res 364, Zablocki pleaded with his colleagues to approve the compromise without major changes. He said the measure was "a delicate balance of congressional control and executive flexibility." If that balance were upset, he argued, "the Congress will lose, the president will lose and United States foreign policy will greatly suffer."

Several members argued that the compromise was a mistake and that the Marines should be withdrawn from Lebanon right away. Among them was Toby Roth, R-Wis., who said before the final vote: "If we keep the Marines in Lebanon, we're just waiting for a tragedy to happen."

But Rep. Lee H. Hamilton, D-Ind., chairman of the panel's Middle East subcommittee, said that by withdrawing U.S. forces, "we wouldn't be just pulling out 1,200 Marines. We would be sending all the region and all the world a signal that the United States is giving up on its long term commitment to bring stability and unity to Lebanon."

The committee brushed aside two fundamental challenges to H J Res 364 in the form of amendments by liberal Democrats.

One amendment, offered by Ted Weiss, D-N.Y., and rejected by voice vote, would have automatically cut off all funds for the Marines in Lebanon after the 18-month limit. Weiss argued that cutting off funds was the only way Congress could really force the president to withdraw the Marines when the time limit expired.

The second amendment, offered by Peter H. Kostmayer, D-Pa., would have changed the 18-month limit to nine months. The panel rejected that amendment on a 9-25 roll call vote.

Kostmayer said he offered his amendment merely to force Congress to review the Marine deployment before the 1984 elections. "I think to wait past an election, to attempt to insulate ourselves from the voters' sentiments, is not the proper course to pursue," he said.

But Zablocki said Reagan had wanted an "open-ended commitment," so 18 months represented "real compromise." Zablocki added that he wanted to avoid what Kostmayer wanted: a time limit that would raise the Lebanon issue in the midst of the 1984 elections.

Foreign Affairs approved one amendment, by Solarz, requiring withdrawal of the Marines if all other countries withdrew their troops from the multinational force.

The dissenters on the committee's 30-6 vote approving the resolution were Roth, Douglas K. Bereuter, R-Neb., George W. Crockett Jr., D-Mich., Mervyn M. Dymally, D-Calif., Kostmayer, and Gerry E. Studds, D-Mass.

Senate Foreign Relations Action

The next day, Sept. 23, the compromise came before the Senate panel, where it squeezed through thanks to pressure from Senate Majority Leader Baker, a committee member, after a divisive debate and three roll call votes.

At one point, the committee adopted by 9-8 a substitute by Claiborne Pell, D-R.I., that would have limited the deployment of the Marines to six months. That was the key provision of S J Res 159 as introduced by Mathias. The Pell substitute was adopted when Mathias joined the panel's eight Democrats in voting for a six-month limit.

But under pressure from Baker, Mathias later switched and voted with his fellow Republicans to reconsider the vote by which the Pell substitute had been adopted. The committee then adopted the original compromise by 9-7, with Mathias voting "aye." For parliamentary reasons, the committee attached it to S J Res 159.

The Democrats attacked virtually every aspect of the compromise. Paul S. Sarbanes, D-Md., and Alan Cranston, D-Calif., said the resolution had little meaning because the administration had said it would not necessarily be bound by its terms. Cranston offered an amendment to simply invoke the War Powers act, but that was rejected by 9-7.

Committee Republicans said they also had concerns about U.S. policy in Lebanon, and about giving Reagan's policy a stamp of approval. Admitted Chairman Percy: "I don't think any of us knows where this is leading."

But Percy insisted that the compromise was necessary to avoid a constitutional confrontation and to give the president time to seek a diplomatic settlement in Lebanon.

Floor Action

The House passed H J Res 364 on Sept. 28 by 270-161, with all but 27 Republicans voting "aye" and Democrats voting 130-134 against it. *(Vote 342, p. 102-H)*

The Senate adopted S J Res 159 on Sept. 29 by a partisan vote of 54-46. Only two Democrats — George J. Mitchell, Maine, and Edward Zorinsky, Neb. — favored it; three Republicans — Mark O. Hatfield, Ore., William V.

Roth Jr., Del., and Lowell P. Weicker Jr., Conn. — opposed it. Several Republicans voted for the resolution only after last-minute arm-twisting by Majority Leader Baker. *(Vote 264, p. 43-S)*

By a 253-156 vote four hours after the Senate acted, the House accepted minor differences in the Senate version and cleared S J Res 159 for the president. *(Vote 350, p. 104-H)*

The House originally had voted to require presidential reports on the Marines every 60 days and had declared that Congress opposed any partition of Lebanon. The Senate had demanded reports every three months, which the House agreed to after Reagan promised to make such reports each 60 days anyway. The provision opposing partition was dropped.

Reagan praised the "bipartisan spirit" of Congress, but it was clear that his policy lacked genuinely bipartisan support.

A majority of Democrats in both houses voted against the resolution, many charging that it would give Reagan a "blank check" amounting to another Tonkin Gulf Resolution, which Presidents Johnson and Nixon had used to claim congressional backing for the war in Vietnam.

Both houses rejected Democrat-sponsored alternatives that would have forced Reagan to withdraw the Marines before the end of 1983 unless he submitted specific war powers act reports to Congress.

Even some who voted for the resolution asked whether the administration had a clear plan for attaining its goals — strengthening the Lebanese government and getting Syrian, Palestine Liberation Organization and Israeli forces out.

Baker said he had opposed Reagan's decision to send the Marines to Lebanon and still had "grave doubts" about using U.S. military force in the Middle East.

But Baker said he had been obliged to support S J Res 159 because the Marines were "under fire, and I think it would be a mistake of tragic proportions if this Congress were to withdraw them. . . ."

House Action

The House's relatively speedy work on H J Res 364 was eased by the rule governing floor action, which prevented a legislative free-for-all by giving Zablocki great control in managing the measure on the floor.

The Rules Committee approved the rule under pressure from O'Neill, and like his earlier move to torpedo the Lebanon amendment adopted by the Appropriations Committee, the move marked an unusually blunt display of the speaker's power.

H J Res 364 also was boosted by the fact that its foes had no consensus alternative, and members of both parties came under intense pressure to support the resolution.

Wavering Republicans were called to the White House the morning of the House vote. Because of O'Neill's key role in reaching the compromise, the House Democratic leadership made it a test of party loyalty.

Even so, Democratic leaders were edgy about the outcome and briefly considered offering an amendment to shorten the time limit for the deployment of the Marines to nine or 12 months. As debate proceeded, however, it became obvious the resolution would pass by a comfortable margin.

Despite the touchy nature of the issue, the House debate was restrained and generally free of emotional or partisan rhetoric. The major challenge to the resolution came on an amendment by Long and Obey that would have forced the president to pull the Marines out of Lebanon before the end of 1983 unless he submitted specific war powers reports to Congress.

For House members, the Long-Obey amendment constituted the closest thing they had to an opportunity to vote to cut the length of the authorization. The House rejected the amendment by 158-272. *(Vote 341, p. 102-H)*

One apparent flaw in the amendment was that it would have set in motion a complicated process that many members said they had difficulty grasping. But under the rule for floor action fashioned at O'Neill's behest, the complex Long-Obey proposal was the only non-committee amendment permitted.

The essence of the amendment was that 90 days after Aug. 29, when the first Marines had been killed, all funds for stationing the Marines in Lebanon would be suspended unless the president had submitted a section 4(a)(1) War Powers report to Congress concerning hostilities in Lebanon or had certified to Congress that a cease-fire was in effect and "significant progress" was being made in negotiations to broaden the base of the Lebanese government and achieve a political resolution in that country. If the president made a cease-fire certification to Congress, he would have to submit another every 30 days to keep the Marines deployed.

Speaking to a hushed House chamber just before the final vote on the resolution, O'Neill defended the compromise as an affirmation of the validity of the War Powers act.

The War Powers act "is doing what it was intended to do," O'Neill said. By invoking it the Lebanon resolution "clearly limits the scope and role of the U.S. forces in Lebanon so that the danger of a Vietnam-type escalation is avoided," he told the House. "This resolution, believe me, is not a blank check, as some have asserted."

Describing a meeting with Reagan on Sept. 4, O'Neill said the president had wanted an "open-ended" expression of congressional support for his Lebanon policy. O'Neill said he had told Reagan: " 'No way are you or anybody else ever going to have another Tonkin Gulf' " resolution.

"I believe the president of the United States when he says to me head-to-head he has no plans to change the peacekeeping role of the Marines," O'Neill said. He added: ". . . if at any time I have reason to believe that the spirit and the letter of his resolution is not being lived up to, I will do . . . whatever is necessary concerning Lebanon to get our men back."

The House spent relatively little time debating U.S. policy in Lebanon, but several members questioned whether Reagan had clear goals in Lebanon and whether the Marines could — or should — play a role in reaching for them.

Toby Roth, normally a staunch Reagan supporter, launched a vivid attack on administration policy. Facing thousands of Syrian and Palestinian troops and various Lebanese militia, "the Marines can no more keep the peace than you can bring back the dead," Roth said. If the Marines stayed in Lebanon 18 months, he added, "there will be many Americans killed, it's a cinch."

Said Sam Gibbons, D-Fla.: "If we are there to keep the peace, then we are far too few. If we are there to fight, then we are far too few. If we are there to die, then we are far too many."

Middle East Subcommittee Chairman Hamilton said the resolution would allow the Marines to remain in Leba-

non "to give diplomacy a chance to work." A Sept. 25 cease-fire negotiated with the help of U.S. and Saudi Arabian diplomats "shows that the [diplomatic] process in Lebanon is working," Hamilton said, but "it needs more time."

Henry J. Hyde, R-Ill., argued that the Lebanese fighting was "not a religious war but is a struggle for the precious assets of the Middle East." He said an effort by Syria's ally, the Soviet Union, to gain control of Middle East oil was "at the bottom of this terrible conflict."

By voice vote, the House adopted an amendment by Zablocki that made two changes in the resolution:

● The first was a requirement that the president report to Congress every 60 days, rather than every six months. At the suggestion of the House Armed Services Committee, the Zablocki amendment required those reports to include such information as the cost of maintaining the Marines and the military rules under which they were operating.

● A second part of the amendment, suggested by Mary Rose Oakar, D-Ohio, put Congress on record as opposing any partition of Lebanon, parts of which Syria claimed.

Senate Floor Action

In the Senate, only a handful of Republicans took the floor to support the resolution, leaving Foreign Relations Committee Chairman Percy as its chief defender. And Percy sympathized with those who said they were uneasy about the course of U.S. policy in Lebanon.

The major test for S J Res 159 — and a test of Republican party discipline that Majority Leader Baker passed — came on an amendment by Minority Leader Byrd that sought to force the president to withdraw the Marines before the end of 1983 unless he gave Congress specific war powers reports. The Byrd amendment was tabled, and thus killed, on a straight party-line vote of 55-45. *(Vote 259, p. 43-S)*

Senate Democrats, who dominated a debate that spanned four days, from Sept. 26-29, were angered that they had been left out of the talks between the administration and the House Democratic leadership that led to the compromise.

The claim that the compromise was bipartisan, said Lloyd Bentsen, "may be accurate in [the House], but it sure does not apply in the Senate."

The Democrats used the debate to question U.S. goals in Lebanon and the use of Marines to promote them. Led by Joseph R. Biden Jr., D-Del., Sam Nunn, D-Ga., and Sarbanes, Democrats argued that S J Res 159 appeared to commit the United States to goals beyond reach — the removal of all foreign forces, Lebanese government control over its territory and progress toward "national reconciliation" among Lebanon's religious factions.

Percy argued that there was a "distinction" between the administration's broad policy goals and the mission of the Marines. He said the resolution authorized the Marines to remain in Lebanon for the limited purpose of keeping peace.

The resolution itself, Percy asserted, stated that the Marines would perform only the functions outlined in a Sept. 25, 1982, exchange of letters between the U.S. and Lebanese governments: the Marines were not to engage in combat and were to be merely an "interposition force" between warring factions.

At the request of Arlen Specter, R-Pa., Percy read to the Senate an administration-approved statement that S J Res 159 "simply authorizes the president to continue the current role and mission" of the Marines and did not authorize the functions that concerned the Democrats.

Specter told the Senate he had been convinced by top administration officials that Reagan accepted a "limited mission" for the Marines.

However, Democrats noted that the resolution also permitted U.S. forces to take "such protective measures as may be necessary to ensure the safety" of the peacekeeping force. While saying they wanted the Marines to be able to defend themselves, the Democrats called that a "loophole" that might enable Reagan to escalate the fighting.

The Democrats insisted that Reagan should have reported to Congress under section 4(a)(1) of the War Powers act after the first Marines had been killed on Aug. 29, thus giving Congress the right to decide how long the Marines could stay in Lebanon. They cited Reagan's refusal to do so as evidence that S J Res 159 had little meaning.

Percy responded that the resolution expressly invoked the War Powers act and required the president to ask Congress to approve any plan to keep the Marines in Lebanon past the 18 months.

In an effort to quash the Democrats' complaints, Reagan wrote Congress Sept. 27 saying "it would be my intention" to seek congressional authorization for any decision to expand the Marine force. But he was less specific about the 18-month limit. If the Marines had to remain longer, Reagan said, "it would be my intention to work together with the Congress with a view toward taking action on mutually acceptable terms." *(Text, p. 36-E)*

A handful of Republicans disputed the underlying premise of both the Lebanon resolution and the War Powers act — that Congress had a right to help conduct foreign policy.

"We are not capable of formulating and implementing foreign policy in this body, and we are proving it in this very debate," said John Tower, R-Texas, chairman of the Armed Services Committee and a longtime foe of the War Powers act. "If we fool around with this resolution and start putting in conditions, timetables, we run the very grave risk of making the United States irrelevant to the peacemaking process in the Middle East."

After the Senate acted, Barry Goldwater, R-Ariz., defended his vote for the resolution even though he wanted the Marines withdrawn from Lebanon. The president, not Congress, should decide such issues, he said.

"The president is the commander in chief," Goldwater said. "When the commander in chief gives an order, you do it."

The Senate rejected three amendments offered by Democrats in hopes of tightening the language in the resolution:

● By Paul E. Tsongas, D-Mass., to state that one U.S. goal was merely to help the Lebanese government "maintain a secure area" from which it could gain territorial control. The resolution said the Marines were in Lebanon "in order to restore full control" by the government. The Tsongas amendment was tabled, and thus killed, by 56-42. *(Vote 261, p. 43-S)*

● By Carl Levin, D-Mich., to declare that U.S. forces had been involved in hostilities in Lebanon since Aug. 29, 1983. Tabled, 54-45. *(Vote 262, p. 43-S)*

● By Thomas F. Eagleton, D-Mo., saying the Marines could take necessary "defensive" actions. The resolution said the Marines could take "protective" actions, a term Eagleton said was too broad. Tabled, 66-34. *(Vote 263, p. 43-S)*

Support Shattered

Events in Lebanon rapidly conspired to shatter any sense of accomplishment that Speaker O'Neill and others in Congress who supported S J Res 159 might have taken from its enactment.

On Oct. 23, only 11 days after Reagan signed S J Res 159 into law (PL 98-119), a terrorist driving a truck packed with thousands of pounds of explosives plowed into Marine headquarters at Beirut's airport and set off an explosion that killed 241 Americans. About the same time, a car laden with explosives rammed into a Beirut building occupied by French members, killing 58 French soldiers.

Rescue workers struggled for days to free the survivors and recover the dead from the rubble of the U.S. Marine barracks in Beirut. Meanwhile, the shock waves the tragedy sent through Congress were magnified on Oct. 25, when U.S. military forces launched a surprise invasion of the Caribbean island nation of Grenada.

The bombing of the Marine compound in Beirut clearly eroded support for U.S. military involvement in Lebanon, but confusion and mixed emotions over Lebanon and Grenada obstructed the consensus Congress would have needed to act.

In a week fraught with a sense of crisis, members appeared more frustrated by their inability to affect foreign events jeopardizing American lives than they had been since the Iranian hostage crisis in 1979-80. Congress was left to nibble at the edges of policy and insist on its right to play a role.

Moves were begun in both houses to apply the War Powers act to the deployment of U.S. troops in Grenada. But in the case of Lebanon, the earlier passage of S J Res 159 made it difficult for members who had backed the Lebanon compromise to point the finger at Reagan.

Still, the slaughter of the Marines in Beirut clearly haunted members, and it appeared to erase whatever support had existed for a long-term commitment of U.S. troops in Lebanon. Most members who publicly continued to support the use of the Marines in Beirut said they did so only because to withdraw them after the bombing would be to give in to the terrorists who had conceived the act.

A previously unknown group calling itself the Islamic Revolutionary Movement claimed responsibility for the bomb. Reagan said the United States had "strong circumstantial evidence" that the attack "was directed by terrorists who used the same methods" to destroy the U.S. Embassy in Beirut on April 18. In that incident, a van loaded with explosives raced into the embassy driveway and exploded, killing 51 people, including 17 Americans.

Among those who said the United States had to hold its ground in the face of the Oct. 23 massacre was the man perhaps most responsible for enactment of the Lebanon resolution — O'Neill. On Oct. 25, he said withdrawing the Marines "would say to the fanatics and terrorists of the world that they have achieved what they set out to do."

O'Neill maintained that position the next day, when the House Democratic Caucus held a closed session requested by junior Democrats upset by his backing of Reagan on Lebanon and his initial refusal to oppose the invasion of Grenada.

In a speech other members described as perhaps his most emotional and eloquent in years, O'Neill lectured his fellow Democrats on the need for national unity in a time of crisis. He closed, according to members present, with a table-pounding, microphone-rattling declaration that he was standing by the president because "I am a patriot!"

On Oct. 27, in an obvious effort to quell rising concern on Capitol Hill and in the nation at large, Reagan made a nationally-televised address from the White House in which he explained his policies and actions.

Strongly defending his decisions to send U.S. forces into Lebanon and Grenada, the president said: "We are not somewhere else in the world protecting someone else's interests. We are there protecting our own."

Reagan placed the situations in both Lebanon and Grenada within the East-West conflict. "Not only has Moscow assisted and encouraged the violence in both countries, but it provides direct support through a network of surrogates and terrorists," he said.

The president laid much of the responsibility for Lebanon's woes on Soviet-backed Syria, which he said had reneged on promises to withdraw its troops from Lebanon and had "become a home for 7,000 Soviet advisers and technicians who man a massive amount of Soviet weaponry, including SS-21 ground-to-ground missiles capable of reaching vital areas of Israel." Reagan suggested that a U.S. abandonment of Lebanon might lead to a Middle East "incorporated into the Soviet bloc."

On Capitol Hill, Reagan's speech evoked support for his actions in Grenada but not those in Lebanon. Some members said Reagan appeared to be shifting his reasons for U.S. involvement in Lebanon. That view was expressed by Sen. Patrick J. Leahy, D-Vt., who said the U.S. role originally "was a peacekeeping mission" but, as explained by Reagan, had become an effort "to stop the spread of communism."

Bombing Aftermath

In the days following the bombing against the Marines, members of Congress focused on two broad sets of questions — the short-term and the long-term.

Among the immediate questions was why there had not been better protection for the Marines against such an attack. Members proved skeptical of military assurances that everything possible had been done to protect the Marines.

After hearing Defense Secretary Caspar W. Weinberger and top military officials in a closed hearing Oct. 25, Senate Armed Services Committee Chairman Tower said: "The consensus of the committee is that security was not adequate, although it is difficult to defend against a terrorist act of that kind ... a suicide mission."

Tower's assertion was contradicted by Marine Commandant Gen. Paul X. Kelley, who visited the scene of the bombing Oct. 25. "We had very adequate security measures," he said.

The long-range questions disturbing Congress involved the mission of the Marines and U.S. goals in general. Nunn, ranking Democrat on the Senate Armed Services Committee, was a leading congressional critic of the mission given the Marines. He said they were in an "untenable military position" because they had been assigned the "mission impossible" of bringing peace to all of Lebanon while confined to bunkers at the airport.

On Oct. 27, Reagan defined the mission of the Marines in far narrower terms. He said it was "to secure a piece of Beirut, to keep order in their sector and to prevent the area from becoming a battlefield."

Democrats also questioned whether the United States, through its firm support of the government of President Amin Gemayel, had become a participant in the Lebanese

civil war rather than a neutral peacekeeper.

On Oct. 26, Senate Democrats introduced a resolution (S Res 253) calling on the president to try to transfer the peacekeeping mission in Lebanon to the United Nations or to a force composed of troops from "neutral countries."

Kelley Testimony

A week after the bombing, Gen. Kelley faced three days of extraordinary questioning before the House and Senate Armed Services committees.

Kelley had not been in the operational chain of command and had no direct supervision over the Marines in Lebanon but was asked to testify because Reagan had sent him to Beirut after the bombing to investigate security measures there.

In his testimony Oct. 31-Nov. 2, Kelley was blunt and direct, but he failed to satisfy most members of the committees, and the resulting tension led to some sharp exchanges.

Near the end of the third day, when Rep. John R. Kasich, R-Ohio, demanded to know why the Marines had not searched every vehicle entering the Beirut airport, Kelley snapped: "Let's use good judgment about this, Mr. Kasich, and not get emotional for the TV cameras."

Kelley came under pressure to explain published remarks that he had been "totally satisfied" with the measures taken to protect the Marines. Security, Kelly said, "was adequate to meet what any reasonable and prudent commander could have expected" prior to the Oct. 23 attack.

He said the local commander had no reason to suspect such a "massive and unprecedented" terrorist attack, but members questioned that statement in light of the April 18 bombing of the U.S. embassy in Beirut.

Both Kelley and Gen. Bernard Rogers, commander of U.S. forces in Europe, expressed concern about the broad mission of the Marines in Lebanon.

In testimony to the Senate Armed Services Committee, Rogers said flatly that military officials were unhappy with both the mission of the Marines and their exposed position on low ground at the airport.

"There has been continued concern expressed by those of us who wear the uniform about the mission and the location," Rogers said. "We don't like it."

Legislative Action

The Senate Oct. 28 engaged in an intense 4½-hour debate over Reagan's policies in Lebanon and Grenada. The verbal battle was touched off when Majority Leader Baker offered an amendment to a debt ceiling bill (H J Res 308) praising the U.S. military and Reagan for the Grenada operation.

Lowell Weicker, R-Conn., vehemently protested Baker's proposal, saying he was willing to praise the military for its conduct of the invasion but not the commander-in-chief who ordered it. Democrats seized on the occasion to voice concern about Lebanon, seeking to attach a rider to H J Res 308 calling on the president to "vigorously pursue" by "every possible avenue" the replacement of the Marines by United Nations or other "neutral" forces. After a raging debate, however, both amendments were withdrawn.

More ambitious attempts to alter Reagan's policy in Lebanon were launched beginning the next week.

On Nov. 2, the House rejected by 153-274 an amendment to the fiscal 1984 Defense Department appropriations bill (HR 4185) that would have cut off funding for the

Marines after March 1, 1984. *(Vote 411, p. 122-H)*

Proponents of the amendment, offered by Long of Maryland and Samuel Stratton, D-N.Y., said Congress should act to prevent more Marines from dying in a hopeless cause. Foes of the amendment said to withdraw the Marines at that point would be to capitulate to terrorism.

Despite its wide margin, the House vote was far from a strong endorsement of Reagan's policy. Even some members who voted against the amendment said they hoped the United States could find a gracious way out of Lebanon soon.

Also, as in September on the original Lebanon resolution, Reagan's critics were handicapped Nov. 2 by manipulation of House rules and procedures by O'Neill and other leaders who opposed an immediate pullout.

The Democratic leadership upheld a Republican parliamentary objection to the original amendment proposed by Long and Stratton, which would have cut off funds after March 1, 1984, only if Reagan had failed to redefine U.S. policy goals in Lebanon. With that less rigid proposal ruled out of order, Long and Stratton could offer only the less appealing alternative of a flat cutoff.

The amendment was strongly opposed by Middle East Subcommittee Chairman Hamilton, who warned his colleagues they could not act without affecting events elsewhere.

"Both our friends and adversaries see the Lebanon issue as a test of American credibility and resolve in the region," Hamilton said. "Our friends will be disheartened by a signal of withdrawal now. Our adversaries will be heartened by a signal of withdrawal."

Hamilton also argued that a vote to withdraw the Marines would undermine a Lebanese "national reconciliation" conference that had begun Oct. 31 in Geneva, Switzerland. The conference had been promoted by U.S. officials, who hoped it would lead to a new governmental alignment in Lebanon that might end eight years of civil war.

Senate Efforts

In the Senate, Democrats were unable to force a vote on their Oct. 26 proposal, S Res 253, to replace the Marines with a United Nations or other "neutral" force.

Majority Leader Baker himself had made such a proposal in a letter to President Reagan in September. But he said that in the wake of the terrorist bombing, Congress should not abrogate its 18-month agreement with the president. •

Failing to get a floor vote, Democrats led by Alan J. Dixon of Illinois, Thomas F. Eagleton of Missouri and Edward M. Kennedy of Massachusetts proposed Oct. 28 that Congress limit the Marines to three more months in Beirut but give itself the right to vote three-month extensions.

The proposal (S J Res 190), which set the first three-month authorization to expire in mid-January 1984, was referred to the Senate Foreign Relations Committee.

Under the Lebanon resolution (PL 98-119), the Foreign Relations Committee had to consider any legislation to modify the terms of the compromise within 15 days of the amending legislation's introduction. Any such measure reported by the panel would become the Senate's pending business and have to be voted upon within three days. Nov. 12 was the deadline for committee action on S J Res 190.

There, Chairman Percy and other Republicans first blocked committee action on Nov. 10, then stalled a Nov.

15 markup of S J Res 190 long enough to put the issue over until the 1984 session of Congress.

A key player in the last minute maneuvering over S J Res 190 was Mathias, who had voted for the Lebanon compromise in September despite misgivings about the 18-month limit and who often had been a "swing vote" on issues before the committee.

Mathias told the Democrats he would vote for S J Res 190 if it were changed to reflect his September proposal for a limit of six months on the Marines' deployment, beginning Aug. 29, when the first two Marines were killed by hostile fire, and expiring in March 1984. The Democrats said they were willing to compromise on the date.

Deteriorating Support

Growing congressional discontent followed the deaths of more U.S. servicemen in Lebanon in early December and the publication of reports on the Oct. 23 bombing by a House Armed Services subcommittee and a panel of military experts suggesting the tragedy could have been avoided. Members of Congress also were hearing demands by the constituents that the Marines be withdrawn.

Eight Marines and a Navy pilot were killed Dec. 4 after a squadron of Navy fighter-bombers struck Syrian anti-aircraft gun and missile emplacements in eastern Lebanon that had fired on U.S. reconnaissance planes Dec. 3.

A Navy pilot died and his bombardier was captured when their A-6E Intruder fighter-bomber — one of 28 carrier-based U.S. planes participating in the attack — was shot down by Syrian fire. Eight Marines were killed later when Syrian-backed Druse militia fired on their airport post.

On Dec. 9, Rep. Bill Alexander, D-Ark., chairman of a Lebanon Oversight Committee appointed by Speaker O'Neill, said that, given the lack of progress toward U.S. goals and the continued U.S. casualties, the Lebanon compromise had lost majority support in Congress.

On Dec. 13 and 14, U.S. reconnaissance planes were fired upon again and U.S. warships responded by bombarding Syrian positions with long-range guns.

With that, Reps. Hamilton and Les Aspin, D-Wis., both of whom had supported Reagan's use of the Marines, illustrated congressional restiveness by writing Reagan a letter urging him to reduce his use of military force in Lebanon. They said the administration was failing to press strongly enough for a diplomatic settlement in Lebanon.

The same day, Reagan acknowledged public uneasiness about his policy, assuring reporters that the U.S. commitment in Lebanon was not open-ended. He also asserted, without being specific, that there had been "more progress than appears on the surface" toward the U.S. goals of getting foreign forces out of Lebanon and helping stabilize the nation.

Pressure for a withdrawal of the Marines mounted with the release of the House Armed Services and Pentagon-sponsored reports on the Oct. 23 bombing of the Marines.

After an independent investigation, the subcommittee's report produced a report highly critical of the security provided the Marines. The subcommittee also criticized Gen. Kelley personally for his testimony.

More dramatic were the findings of the Pentagon-selected commission, headed by retired Adm. Robert L. J. Long. The report found fault not only with the military's chain-of-command and the way various commanders handled the deployment of the Marines but also with the administration's use of the Marines in a diplomatic rather than purely military role.

Reagan sought to blunt the blow of the Long commission's report. First he forced a delay in its release to give his administration time to formulate a response in advance. He then declared on Dec. 27 that he would forbid any courts-martial of military officers for their handling of Marine security in Beirut. He said he alone was "responsible." ∎

Nicaragua Covert Aid Issue Compromised

Congress and the Reagan administration fought through to a compromise in 1983 that resolved — but only temporarily — the issue of "covert" U.S. aid to anti-government rebels in Nicaragua.

Cleared by Congress on Nov. 18 after months of debate, the Nicaragua compromise gave neither side all it wanted. President Reagan got $24 million to continue aiding some 10,000 rebels seeking to overthrow the leftist government of Nicaragua; congressional opponents got assurances that they would get a better chance to block the program in mid-1984.

Rep. C. W. Bill Young, R-Fla., and other supporters of the president praised the compromise for continuing the formerly "covert" aid to the Nicaraguan rebels for another nine months. Democrats, who led the House in voting twice in 1983 to stop the aid, said they were disappointed for the same reason.

As with many compromises, the Nicaragua agreement postponed a final decision on the issue.

The fiscal 1984 defense appropriations bill (HR 4185 — PL 98-212) and intelligence agencies authorization bill (HR 2968 — PL 98-215) both set a $24 million limit on the formerly covert aid to the Nicaraguan rebels. Both bills

were cleared for the president Nov. 18 and signed Dec. 8 and Dec. 9, respectively.

Reagan apparently had planned to spend $35 million-$50 million to aid the rebels. Congressional leaders said the $24 million would enable the CIA to continue providing arms and other aid to the Nicaraguan rebels through June 1984 — if the 1983 rate of spending were kept up. Once the money ran out, Reagan would have to seek more from Congress or terminate the aid.

House Intelligence Committee Chairman Edward P. Boland, D-Mass., who led opposition to the covert aid, appeared defensive on Nov. 18 as he explained to the House that the compromise was the best deal he could negotiate with the Senate. The only alternative, he said, was to rely on stopgap funding measures that "would mean no limitation on this program," he said.

During the year, Boland and his Democratic colleagues in the House stood almost alone in opposition to the program.

The Republican leadership in both chambers was solidly behind Reagan's Nicaragua policies. And most Senate Democrats, many of them skeptical of the covert aid, chose not to challenge it head-on. In contrast to the House, where

the covert action was a major topic of debate for months, only a handful of senators took to the floor to discuss the issue.

Instead, senators of both parties demanded that Reagan narrow the scope of the aid. Twice, on May 6 and Sept. 21, the Senate Intelligence Committee voted 13-2 to allow the aid to continue, with changes.

Senate committee Vice Chairman Daniel Patrick Moynihan, D-N.Y., on Nov. 18 credited his panel with forcing the administration to "more clearly articulate its goals in Nicaragua."

Final Compromise

As cleared in the 1984 defense and intelligence bills, the Nicaragua compromise stated:

"During fiscal year 1984, not more than $24,000,000 of the funds available to the Central Intelligence Agency, the Department of Defense, or any other agency or entity of the United States involved in intelligence activities may be obligated or expended for the purpose or which would have the effect of supporting, directly or indirectly, military or paramilitary operations in Nicaragua by any nation, group, organization, movement or individual."

The final compromise of the 1983 session brushed aside the first congressional statute on the Nicaragua issue: the so-called "Boland amendment" of 1982. It prohibited the United States from providing aid to any groups in Nicaragua "for the purpose of" overthrowing the Nicaraguan government. *(1982 Almanac p. 246)*

That provision expired on Sept. 30, the end of fiscal 1983, and was not renewed. Boland did not seek to have his amendment renewed, an aide said, because the Senate would not have accepted it. A Senate Intelligence Committee aide said the amendment was made unnecessary by the wording of Reagan's "finding" that governed the covert aid for fiscal 1984. The finding was classified, however.

House and Senate negotiators reached the compromise after starting from directly opposite positions.

House Position

The House would have ended the covert aid early in 1984 and substituted for it $50 million in "overt" aid to help friendly countries in the region combat cross-border arms shipments. The House took that position in two bills: the intelligence authorization bill (HR 2968) and a separate bill (HR 2760) that was explicitly aimed at stopping the covert aid.

Boland had said the House bills included $19 million to continue the covert aid only until April 1, 1984.

Reagan had requested $19 million for fiscal 1984, but said he also would fund the program by using the CIA contingency account and $10 million unspent in fiscal 1983. Congressional sources said the CIA had been running the covert program at a rate of about $35 million a year and reportedly could have spent up to $50 million.

Going into conference, Boland insisted that at a minimum the House be given a chance at some point in fiscal 1984 to veto further funding.

This was accomplished in conference by setting what Boland called "an absolute cap" on the aid that the CIA could provide in fiscal 1984. The administration could "get no more money anywhere else," he told the House, unless it sought a supplemental appropriation that would have to be approved by both houses. Boland called that requirement "a giant step in the right direction."

Senate Position

The Senate had approved $29 million for the covert aid in fiscal 1984. That included $19 million specifically authorized for fiscal 1984 and $10 million to be carried over from unspent funds from fiscal 1983. Once the $29 million ran out, the Senate bill would have allowed the CIA director to dip into his contingency fund to continue the aid unless both Intelligence committees objected — possibly putting total spending as high as $50 million.

The Senate, and through it the administration, flatly opposed the House demand for a legal date for terminating the covert action. The compromise included no such date.

The compromise also gave Reagan three options for the covert aid, rather than the single cutoff option the House had voted.

He could continue the aid at the 1983 rate and allow it to expire when the funds run out; he could continue the program at the 1983 rate and return to Congress for more money in mid-1984; or he could reduce the size of the program to make the $24 million last throughout fiscal 1984, which ended on Sept. 30, 1984.

Wright Amendment

PL 98-215, the 1984 intelligence bill, included a House-passed amendment directing the president to seek intervention by the Organization of American States (OAS) to resolve conflicts in Central America. That amendment had been drafted on July 28 by House Majority Leader Jim Wright, D-Texas, in an apparently successful effort to win votes for HR 2760, the bill originally passed by the House to cut off covert aid.

The major provisions of the Wright amendment:

• Stated that Nicaragua had failed to keep the promises it made to the Organization of American States (OAS) in July 1979. Among the promises were respect for human and political rights and the holding of early elections.

• Stated that Nicaragua, by aiding guerrillas in El Salvador and elsewhere in Central America, had violated the OAS charter, which said that no nation had the right to intervene in the affairs of another nation.

• Asked the president to seek an OAS meeting to evaluate Nicaragua's compliance with its promises and with the OAS charter. It also urged the president to seek "a full range of effective measures" by the OAS to ensure Nicaragua's compliance.

• Asked the president to use "all diplomatic means at his disposal" to get the OAS to settle regional conflicts. It also said the United States should support actions by the OAS and the so-called "Contadora group" to end terrorism, subversion and other activities aimed at the violent overthrow of governments in the region. The Contadora group included Panama, Colombia, Venezuela and Mexico; it took its name from the Panamanian island where representatives of those countries met early in 1983.

• Directed the president to report to Congress by March 15, 1984, on the results of his efforts to achieve peace in Central America, along with his recommendations for further action.

Background

Detailed press reports in 1983 promoted intense congressional scrutiny of the CIA support for Honduras-based rebels who in 1982 invaded Nicaragua with the declared aim of overthrowing the government.

U.S. officials refused publicly to confirm or deny re-

ports of U.S. covert operations in Central America. But CIA Director William J. Casey and other officials were quoted as saying the United States was trying to "harass" the Nicaraguan regime, not to overthrow it.

President Reagan and his top aides called Nicaragua a Marxist state and accused it of supplying Soviet and Cuban arms to leftist guerrillas in neighboring El Salvador. Reagan cut off economic aid to Nicaragua in 1981 and provided millions of dollars in military aid to El Salvador and Honduras.

The Boland Amendment

The first congressional attempt to control the aid to the rebels came from the House Intelligence Committee. In December, 1981, Committee Chairman Boland wrote a letter to Casey expressing concerns about "the number and tactics of the insurgents to be supported, whether these insurgents would be under U.S. control and the possibility of military clashes between Nicaragua and Honduras."

But the committee later said its concerns were ignored.

Under a 1980 law (PL 96-450), which loosened earlier restrictions on covert operations, the president was required to report to the House and Senate Intelligence committees before undertaking covert actions, except when the president declared an emergency. The committees had no formal power to veto plans for covert actions, although there had been cases in which proposed activities were delayed or changed because of objections by the committees. Aside from a requirement that a covert action be "important to national security," there was no legal definition of what constituted a covert action. *(1980 Almanac p. 66)*

In the Nicaragua case, the administration had proceeded with a covert action even though members of both Intelligence committees raised questions about it. The committees could stop the covert action only by passing legislation that would cut off funds for it.

Congress gave itself a bigger handle on the Nicaragua issue in 1982, when it enacted the so-called "Boland amendment." It prohibited U.S. covert actions "for the purpose of" overthrowing the Sandinista regime in Nicaragua or provoking a military exchange between Nicaragua and Honduras.

The Boland amendment was attached secretly to the fiscal 1983 intelligence authorization bill (PL 97-269) and then publicly to the defense portion of the fiscal 1983 continuing resolution (PL 97-377).

The first public congressional debate on the issue came on Dec. 8, 1982, when the House was debating the fiscal 1983 defense appropriations bill (HR 7355). Rep. Tom Harkin, D-Iowa, proposed an amendment to prohibit U.S. aid to any non-governmental group carrying out military activities "in or against Nicaragua."

Boland, with the administration's backing, offered a provision that the two Intelligence committees had included in the classified part of their conference report on the fiscal 1983 authorization bill for U.S. intelligence agencies (PL 97-269). That provision said: "None of the funds provided in this act may be used by the Central Intelligence Agency or any agency of the Department of Defense to furnish military equipment, military training or advice, or other support for military activities, to any group or individual, not part of a country's armed forces, for the purpose of overthrowing the government of Nicaragua or provoking a military exchange between Nicaragua and Honduras."

Boland's provision gave the administration leeway to argue that it was not intending to overthow the Nicaraguan government or to provoke a war between Nicaragua and Honduras.

The House adopted the Boland provision 411-0.

When the Senate took up the fiscal 1983 continuing appropriations resolution (H J Res 631) on Dec. 18, 1982, Christopher J. Dodd, D-Conn., offered an even broader amendment that would have prohibited U.S. support for "irregular or paramilitary groups operating in the Central America region." After a brief debate, the Dodd amendment was tabled on a 56-38 vote. *(Vote 441, 1982 Almanac p. 74-S)*

The Boland amendment was included in the Defense Department portion of H J Res 631, which was cleared by Congress on Dec. 20 and signed into law (PL 97-377) on Dec. 21, 1982. *(1982 Almanac p. 238)*

While Congress was debating the Boland amendment, CIA Director Casey reportedly assured the Intelligence committees that the United States was trying to stop the flow of arms to leftists in El Salvador and was not trying to overthrow the Nicaraguan government.

Reagan's critics accepted the Boland amendment as the maximum step that Congress would take at the time. But they made it clear that they did not expect it to stop U.S. support for the anti-Sandinista rebels. On Dec. 21, Dodd took to the Senate floor to complain that it was "the legislative equivalent of 'blue smoke and mirrors' and we should not have any illusions about it."

New Disclosures

In 1983, renewed press reports about the CIA-managed covert operation in Nicaragua raised controversy in Congress for two reasons. First, many members were opposed to any U.S. effort to undermine the government of another country. Also, there was widespread unease in Congress that the United States appeared to be siding with forces associated with the late Nicaraguan dictator Anastasio Somoza.

Somoza was ousted in July 1979 in a broadly based revolution led by leftist Sandinistas. The Sandinistas later took full control of the government and cracked down on businessmen and other moderates.

Anti-Sandinista rebels, originally numbered at several thousand, organized in Honduras under the banner of the Nicaraguan Democratic Force. According to press reports, some of the key military leaders were members of Somoza's national guard, which was widely charged with human rights abuses.

Although the existence of U.S. support for Nicaraguan rebels had become public knowledge in early 1982, many details of that support remained secret. The CIA and other agencies gave equipment and training to thousands of troops belonging to the Nicaraguan Democratic Force. There were conflicting reports about whether the CIA provided any aid to a rival group based in Costa Rica, the Democratic Revolutionary Alliance.

Press reports in late March and early April 1983 provided the first solid evidence that the Reagan administration was aiding the Nicaraguan rebels.

In its April 4 edition, *Time* magazine reported that the United States and the rebels had established a three-part command structure to disguise U.S. participation in the fighting; on April 3, *The New York Times* reported that the United States had supplied extensive intelligence information, training and plane loads of weapons to the

rebels; and on April 3-5, *The Washington Post* ran articles by a reporter who had accompanied the rebels, reporting that the rebel forces were armed and advised by the United States and were hoping to receive additional U.S. support.

The anti-Sandinista forces, who had been operating in southern Honduras during 1982, reportedly infiltrated about 1,500 troops into Nicaragua early in March. By the end of the year, most accounts put actual rebel force levels at 10,000 to 12,000.

Nicaragua repeatedly protested U.S. support for the rebels, saying it amounted to "undeclared war." Nicaragua took its complaints to the United Nations Security Council in late March. The council debated the issue for a week but took no action.

Renewed Action in Congress

Signs of congressional concern began to blossom in several key committees the week of April 11, 1983.

On April 13, the House Intelligence Committee agreed to demand that the Reagan administration explain what it was doing in Nicaragua. Committee Chairman Boland said he believed the administration was violating the Boland amendment.

The Senate Intelligence panel also met April 12, with Casey. Chairman Barry Goldwater, R-Ariz., stated afterwards that he had concluded that U.S. operations in Nicaragua did not violate the Boland amendment.

The Senate Foreign Relations Committee discussed the Nicaragua issue April 12 and decided only to seek further information from the Senate Intelligence Committee, which along with its House counterpart, had direct jurisdiction over intelligence agencies.

Also on April 12 the Western Hemisphere Affairs Subcommittee of House Foreign Affairs voted along party lines to ban any U.S. support for anti-government rebels in Nicaragua unless Congress expressly approved such aid. The panel added that amendment to its portion of the fiscal 1983-85 foreign aid authorization legislation (HR 2992); the amendment later was deleted from the bill, and the bill itself never reached the House floor. *(Foreign aid bill, p. 140)*

In his first major statement on the issue, Reagan on April 14 said he was "complying with the law" because "we are not doing anything to try and overthrow the Nicaraguan government." Although refusing to discuss details of U.S. covert operations in Central America, Reagan confirmed reports that the United States was attempting to stem the flow of Soviet and Cuban arms through Nicaragua to leftist guerrillas in El Salvador. "Anything that we're doing in that area is simply trying to interdict the supply lines" of those arms, he told reporters.

Thomas O. Enders, assistant secretary of state for inter-American affairs, had seemed to offer a variation of those explanations to the Foreign Relations Committee on April 12. Enders implied that even though the rebels wanted to oust the Nicaraguan government, U.S. aid to the rebels would not violate the Boland amendment because the United States itself was not seeking to overthrow the government.

Faced with mounting congressional challenges not only on his Nicaragua policy, but on other aspects of his Central America policy as well, Reagan on April 27 addressed a joint session of Congress. *(Text, p. 28-E)*

Reagan defended his approach of bolstering El Salvador and other friendly countries in the region against leftist guerrillas supported by Cuba and Nicaragua. The main threat to the region was communist "adventurism," promoted by the Soviet Union, Cuba and Nicaragua, Reagan said.

The president devoted much of his speech to a harsh attack on the leftist government of Nicaragua, saying it "has treated us as an enemy."

In his only direct reference to U.S. activities against Nicaragua, Reagan said the United States was merely trying to prevent the flow of Soviet- and Cuban-supplied arms through Nicaragua to the guerrillas in El Salvador.

"We do not seek [the government's] overthrow," he said. "Our interest is to ensure that it does not infect its neighbors through the export of subversion and violence." *(Speech text, p. 28-E; Democrat response, p. 31-E)*

The day before the speech, liberal Senate Democrats demanded and got an unusual secret meeting of the full Senate to discuss the Nicaragua issue. Their purpose was to press the Intelligence Committee to discuss legislation restricting covert aid in Nicaragua. But the effect was directly opposite. Several moderate and conservative Democrats, notably Lloyd Bentsen of Texas, gave speeches supporting the thrust of Reagan's policy, thus making it clear that it would be difficult for the liberals to assemble a majority to pass any legislation restricting the president's flexibility.

On April 28, Reagan appointed former Sen. Richard "Dick" Stone, D-Fla. (1975-81) as an ambassador-at-large to promote negotiations in Central America. Stone had been a State Department consultant on Central American affairs, primarily lobbying Congress in favor of Reagan's policies. *(Box, p. 159)*

Boland-Zablocki Bill

Just hours before Reagan traveled to Capitol Hill, Boland and fellow committee member Clement J. Zablocki, D-Wis., introduced HR 2760, to end all U.S. support for military groups in Nicaragua. Zablocki also chaired the House Foreign Affairs Committee.

The bill had the support of the Intelligence Committee Democrats and the House Democratic leadership.

As introduced, the bill prohibited any funds being spent by the CIA or any other government agency "for the purpose or which would have the effect of supporting, directly or indirectly, military or paramilitary operations in or against Nicaragua by any nation, group, organization, movement or individual."

The prohibition would have been effective 45 days after the bill was signed into law.

To aid Reagan's effort to stem the flow of arms from Nicaragua to leftist guerrillas in other countries, HR 2760 would have authorized $30 million in fiscal 1983 and $50 million in 1984 for "overt" aid to any Central American country to prevent the use of its territory for the transfer of arms from or through Cuba or Nicaragua.

Five Intelligence committee members — three Republicans and two Democrats — traveled to Central America April 24-26 to investigate U.S. covert actions. Upon their return, the Republicans said they found no evidence that the administration was violating the Boland amendment, and the Democrats said they found just the opposite evidence.

HR 2760: House Intelligence Markup

On May 3, the House Intelligence Committee approved HR 2760, with all Democrats supporting it and all

five Republicans opposing it.

After a closed session, Boland told reporters his panel had done "what the majority of members on the committee believed had to be done, and that was to cut off covert operations in Nicaragua." The committee acted "in the best interests of our government," Boland said. "I think that what we were doing in that area was counterproductive."

The next day, Reagan told several reporters the committee action was "irresponsible" and had "an element in it that looked at partisanship."

Boland had expressed the hope that Reagan would get the "message" of the committee's vote and would voluntarily suspend the covert action.

But Reagan made it clear that he had no such intention. Acknowledging U.S. support for the Nicaraguan rebels, whom he called "freedom fighters," Reagan said he wanted to continue that aid even if it had to be done publicly. "I just don't want the restrictions put on it that they [the House Intelligence Committee] might put on," he said.

The committee's approval of the cut-off legislation came after four weeks of intense debate in private committee sessions. Some parts of the debate spilled into the public domain, as committee members — especially Democrats — became increasingly willing to discuss issues that previously had been highly classified.

In the weeks prior to the committee vote, several Democrats openly accused the administration of misleading them on several issues, but they were prevented by secrecy rules from discussing any details. On the opposite side, several Republicans said they felt hampered by their inability to defend publicly what Reagan was doing.

At its two-part climactic session on May 3, the panel met in the morning for more than three hours with Casey and assistant secretary Enders, then recessed for lunch, and returned in the afternoon for its final vote on adoption of the bill.

In the morning session, the committee rejected, on a 9-5 party-line vote, a proposal by Young to end the U.S. covert action 45 days after the Nicaraguan government signed a "verifiable" agreement to end all its support for the leftist guerrillas in El Salvador. That proposal could have allowed the U.S. covert action to continue indefinitely, since committee members considered Nicaragua unlikely to agree.

To meet objections by the administration and some of its members, the committee did make two changes in the part of its bill dealing with the covert action.

The most important change was to wrap secrecy around the date when the covert action would have to be suspended. The original version of HR 2760 would have suspended the covert action 45 days after the bill was enacted into law. As approved by the committee, the effective date was put into a "classified annex" of the bill.

Committee member Wyche Fowler Jr., D-Ga., said the effective date was made secret to satisfy administration concerns that a publicly stated cutoff date would endanger the U.S.-supported forces inside Nicaragua. The committee wanted to enable those forces to make an "orderly disengagement," Fowler said.

The committee also changed language that prohibited U.S. support for military and paramilitary operations "in or against" Nicaragua. The committee deleted "or against," Fowler said, because its main concern was about operations inside Nicaragua and because any U.S. program to inter-

dict arms supplies running through Nicaragua could be seen as being an action "against" Nicaragua.

As approved by the committee (H Rept 98-122, Pt. 1), the key portion of HR 2760 stated: "None of the funds appropriated for fiscal year 1983 or 1984 for the Central Intelligence Agency or any other department, agency or entity of the United States involved in intelligence activities may be obligated or expended for the purpose or which would have the effect of supporting, directly or indirectly, military or paramilitary operations in Nicaragua by any nation, group, organization or individual."

The bill also authorized $30 million in fiscal 1983 and $50 million in fiscal 1984 to help "friendly" countries in Central America (primarily El Salvador and Honduras) monitor and prevent the use of their territory for the transport of Cuban- or Nicaraguan-supplied military equipment. This part of the bill had to be considered by the Foreign Affairs Committee, because it had responsibility for foreign aid.

Foreign Affairs Action

The House Foreign Affairs Committee broke into partisan bickering before approving HR 2760 on June 7, by a near party-line vote of 20-14.

The Democratic majority on the committee had been divided on a major provision of the bill. They were also divided on the question of how to confront the administration.

Some, including Gerry E. Studds, Mass., argued that the House should state its clear opposition to the covert action to show that Reagan did not have the full support of Congress. But Lee H. Hamilton, Ind., and other Democrats had been negotiating for more than a week with the Republican members and the administration in an attempt to find a middle ground that would show congressional unhappiness with the covert action while preserving some flexibility of action for the president.

Hamilton admitted that HR 2760 was "not going to become law" in the form approved by the Foreign Affairs Committee, since the Republican-controlled Senate was unlikely to approve it and Reagan would certainly veto it in any event.

The committee's action occurred as U.S.-Nicaragua relations deteriorated in the wake of Nicaragua's June 6 expulsion of three American diplomats, and the Reagan administration's retaliation by expelling 21 Nicaraguan diplomats the next day. Each side claimed the ousted diplomats of the other side were guilty of spying.

Partisan emotions on the issue had been building in the Foreign Affairs panel for several weeks. The committee had postponed three meetings it had scheduled earlier on the bill: on May 17, May 25 and June 2.

Republicans used parliamentary tactics to block two of the meetings, and the third was postponed because Hamilton and other senior Democrats were attempting to negotiate a compromise with the administration.

Unusually harsh bickering between Republicans and Democrats exploded just minutes after the committee began the part of the June 6 session that was open to the public.

Noting that he had been a member of Congress for 35 years, Chairman Zablocki said, "I haven't witnessed such partisanship as in the last year, the last 18 months." The blame "lies on both sides of the aisle," he said, "and we can start with the president."

The committee debated the Nicaragua bill in closed

session for nearly two hours on June 6 before opening its doors to the public and press for votes on amendments.

While the committee's doors were closed, three top political officials of the two main rebel groups that were fighting the Nicaraguan government held impromptu press conferences in the hallway. They were Adolfo Calero and Lucia Salazar of the Nicaraguan Democratic Force, which had openly acknowledged receiving CIA assistance, and Alfonso Robelo Callejas of the Democratic Revolutionary Alliance.

The three rebel leaders had met earlier in the day with committee Democrats in a futile, last-minute plea against HR 2760.

All three said they were not demanding the overthrow of the Nicaraguan government and were merely attempting to pressure the government into keeping its 1979 promises of free elections and democratic reforms.

The committee rejected three Republican-sponsored amendments that would have allowed the president to continue the covert action in Nicaragua at least through the remainder of fiscal 1983.

First, on a 12-21 vote, the committee rejected an amendment by William S. Broomfield, R-Mich., that would have allowed the covert action to continue if the president certified to Congress that the United States had attempted and was willing to engage in "good faith efforts to negotiate a peaceful resolution to the conflict in Nicaragua and El Salvador." The amendment would have cut off the covert action only if the president also certified that Nicaragua had ended its support for guerrillas in other countries in the region.

Andy Ireland, Fla., was the only Democrat present to support the Broomfield amendment, and Jim Leach, Iowa, was the only Republican to oppose it.

Next, on a 13-18 vote, the committee rejected an amendment by Toby Roth, R-Wis., that would have required the president to submit to Congress reports on the Nicaraguan government's progress in implementing several reforms — such as improving respect for human rights — similar to reforms Congress had demanded from the government of El Salvador. Under Roth's amendment, the president could not continue covert action in Nicaragua unless he certified that the Nicaraguan government was making those reforms.

Three Florida Democrats — Ireland, Dante B. Fascell and Mica — supported Roth's amendment. Leach and Ed Zschau, Calif., were the only Republicans to oppose it.

Finally, on a 13-22 vote on June 7, the committee rejected an amendment by Zschau that would have allowed the president to continue covert action through the end of fiscal 1983; required the president to submit to Congress a new plan "for the interdiction of arms being shipped from or through Nicaragua" to the guerrillas in El Salvador, taking into account the potential for regional negotiations in Central America; and allowed Congress to veto the new covert action plan by passing a concurrent resolution.

Along with Leach, Zschau was the only committee Republican who openly criticized Reagan's covert action program.

Craig Johnstone, director of the State Department's Central America desk, called Zschau's amendment a "positive step" but refused to endorse it explicitly because of the provision for a congressional veto by concurrent resolution. Johnstone said the administration had a "strong preference" for a veto by joint resolution — which the president himself could veto.

Ireland was the only Democrat to support the Zschau amendment and Leach was the only Republican to oppose it.

One potentially significant amendment, sponsored by Zablocki and adopted by voice vote, limited the $80 million in "overt" aid authorized by the bill to use only for "interdicting the transfer of military equipment to any country in Central America." Another, sponsored by Leach and adopted 24-12, would have allowed Central American countries to use the overt aid to block cross-border arms shipments "to the extent permitted by international law." Leach said his amendment would prevent the aid from being used to establish naval blockades on the high seas.

Aside from the Zablocki amendment, the committee made no major change to the section of the bill that authorized $30 million in fiscal 1983 and $50 million in fiscal 1984 to help "friendly" nations in Central America stop the cross-border shipment of arms to guerrillas in the region.

Several committee Democrats criticized that proposal as backdoor military aid for El Salvador, but no Democrat spoke against it during the committee sessions on June 6-7.

Several Republicans vigorously attacked the proposal, however. Zschau, for example, said it would "expand the conflict" in Central America and require the stationing of U.S. military personnel in the region to carry it out. Most important, he said, the proposal "simply won't work" because the money proposed for it was not adequate.

The provision was included in the bill "as a security blanket" for members who wanted to cut off the covert action, Zschau said.

On the 20-14 committee vote to report HR 2760 (H Rept 98-122, Pt. 2), Leach joined 19 Democrats in supporting the bill and Fascell and Ireland joined 12 Republicans in opposing it. Two Democrats, George W. Crockett Jr. of Michigan and Mervyn M. Dymally of California, passed. Tom Lantos, D-Calif., was the only committee member not present and voting.

House Floor Action

Following the first full debate in either chamber of Congress on Reagan's policies in Central America, the House on July 28 voted against the U.S. covert action in Nicaragua, a key element of those policies.

The 228-195 vote to pass HR 2760 was largely along party lines: Only 18 Republicans joined all but 50 Democrats in supporting HR 2760 on final passage. *(Vote 270, p. 82-H)*

House debate on the issue was intensely partisan and often emotional, with Republicans repeatedly accusing Democrats of abandoning U.S. friends in Central America.

Boland said the House's action sent "a very clear message to the administration" that the Nicaraguan operation should be stopped. He said the vote also would give his committee "more leverage" in bargaining with the Senate on the issue.

"This is not an anti-administration demonstration at all," said Majority Leader Wright, who led the legislative maneuvering that enabled the Democrats to win passage of the bill. Wright noted that he personally supported the other major element of Reagan's policies in Central America: backing for the El Salvador government in its battle against leftist guerrillas.

But Wright acknowledged that passage of HR 2760 was the first time either house of Congress had clearly opposed any aspect of Reagan's policy in Central America. Since

Reagan began escalating support for El Salvador and other pro-U.S. regimes in the region in 1981, Congress had supported the thrust of his actions while paring requests for foreign aid to back those actions.

Noting that the House action came on legislation that probably would never become law, some Republicans disputed its symbolic significance. "It was a free vote," said Trent Lott, Miss., the Republican whip.

Stepped-up Military Role

The House debate took place just as Reagan appeared to be increasing U.S. military involvement in Central America — while denying that he was doing so.

Reagan moved to beef up the U.S. presence in the region in two ways: by sending naval task forces of unprecedented size to patrol both the Pacific and Caribbean coasts of Central America and by boosting the size and duration of planned joint military exercises with Honduras. The exercises were part of "Big Pine II," a follow-up to U.S.-Honduran maneuvers held in February 1982.

In addition, there were press reports that the White House had drafted a plan for expanding the covert operations in Nicaragua that the House was debating.

Reagan tried to downplay the significance of the military moves, saying at a July 26 press conference that the United States "regularly" conducted such military maneuvers and had "no military plans for intervention" in the region.

Several Democrats charged that the maneuvers amounted to "gunboat diplomacy. In a letter to Reagan July 28, House Speaker Thomas P. O'Neill Jr., D-Mass., and Senate Minority Leader Robert C. Byrd, D-W.Va., expressed concern "that officials of your administration did not foresee the need to consult with the Congress prior to initiating such serious action."

Secretary of State George P. Shultz met with senators on July 27 but reportedly could not answer specific questions about the maneuvers.

Both sides said the military escalation jeopardized Reagan's political position on the Nicaragua bill. After the vote, Daniel A. Mica, D-Fla., the chief Democratic proponent of a major pro-administration amendment, said: "I wish the president hadn't sent his boats down there just two days before the vote."

One member who admitted switching sides on the Nicaragua bill because of the military maneuvers was Olympia J. Snowe, R-Maine. She had opposed the bill when it was considered by the Foreign Affairs Committee, on which she sat.

Secret Session

The House debated HR 2760 in an extraordinary four-hour closed session on July 19, then put off further activity until the week of July 25 so that both sides could count votes and try to gain support for the close votes they expected. (*Background of secret sessions, 1980 Almanac p. 334, 1979 Almanac p. 149, Guide to Congress 3rd edition, p. 110*)

According to members who were present, the four-hour secret session was highlighted by presentations by senior members of the Intelligence Committee.

Boland and Fowler justified the committee's unprecedented decision to draft legislation restricting an ongoing covert activity by U.S. intelligence agencies. Both members reportedly said the committee in 1981 and 1982 had insisted that covert activity be limited to blocking the flow of

arms to leftist guerrillas in the region. But, they said, the administration expanded the activity into full-scale support for thousands of anti-government guerrillas in Nicaragua.

Republicans, however, reportedly told the House that the committee had approved covert action in Nicaragua — including aid to the anti-government guerrillas. The Republicans implied that the Democratic majority of the committee withdrew their support for the covert action once it became public.

Rep. Young later told reporters that he had given the House transcripts of private meetings in 1982 during which the committee considered the covert action. The transcripts, he said, "established that the committee had authorized this action to go [foward]" and had placed certain prohibitions on it.

Open Session

House public debate began on July 27, but because about two dozen members — many of them Southern Democrats — remained undecided, all votes were put off until the next day.

Under a rule (H Res 261) providing for action on the bill, two hours was set aside for general debate in public session and 12 hours was set aside for debate on all possible amendments.

Republicans filed more than a dozen amendments to the bill, most of which had the effect of allowing the covert activity to continue indefinitely.

"There are many people in that chamber who are looking for an honorable compromise," said Young, a senior member of the House Intelligence Committee.

Debate on HR 2760 centered around three questions about the covert operation: whether it was legal under U.S. law, whether it had accomplished its objectives, and whether it was hindering or promoting the cause of peace in Central America.

Boland and other Democrats insisted that the covert operation was illegal under the Boland amendment of 1982. Boland told the House that "one with any sense, any legal sense, would have to come to the conclusion that the operation is illegal, that the purpose and the mission of the operation was to overthrow the government in Nicaragua."

Henry J. Hyde, R-Ill., said the Boland amendment was not being violated because the "few little people" the United States was backing in Nicaragua "in no way can overthrow" the Nicaraguan government.

Hamilton said the covert operation had not accomplished its goals of stopping the flow of arms through Nicaragua to guerrillas in El Salvador and forcing the Nicaraguan government to change its policies. "In most cases, things have worsened because of the covert action," he said.

But Robert J. Lagomarsino, R-Calif., said the covert operation had caused "disruptions in the flow of arms" from Nicaragua to the guerrillas in El Salvador and had applied "external pressure" on Nicaragua to accept regional peace negotiations.

Another focus of the debate was on the issue of how to resist communism and promote peace in Central America.

Republicans repeatedly said the Democratic sponsors of HR 2760 were undermining the U.S. efforts to block the spread of communism.

Some of the most direct comments came from Democrat-turned-Republican Phil Gramm of Texas: "I think we are seeing rank partisanship here which does disservice to

the American people, which threatens us in Central America and which some day may bring the rifle shots to our doorstep." Later, he said HR 2760 "is a policy of retreat, it is a policy of abrogation of our responsibility, and it is a policy of surrender."

Gramm's fellow Texan, Jim Wright, said Democrats believed in solving the conflicts of Central America through negotiations involving the countries of the region.

"The question is this," Wright asked. "Do we go it alone? Do we postulate ourselves as a sort of hemispheric Lone Ranger riding throughout the hemisphere shooting silver bullets at people who misbehave from our point of view, or do we call on that organization [the OAS] which has been created for that express purpose ... I believe we should do the latter."

Throughout the action, the key political question was whether the House would accept the original HR 2760, or something similar to it, that would have the effect of ending covert aid at a certain date, or whether the House would support a much milder approach that would enable the administration to continue its covert operation for the foreseeable future.

In an attempt to avert a cut-off, the administration and its supporters developed the concept of "symmetry" — the United States would stop supporting the anti-government rebels in Nicaragua if the Nicaraguan government would stop supporting leftist guerrillas elsewhere in Central America, especially El Salvador.

Floor Votes. The first test vote on the bill, on July 28, was decided at the last second, when Republican Whip Lott pushed forward freshman Sherwood Boehlert, R-N.Y., to change his vote from "yes" to "no," thus scuttling, 213-214, an amendment sponsored by Democrats.

That vote seemed to give the advantage to supporters of the administration, because it killed an amendment by Michael D. Barnes, D-Md., that sought to weaken a key Republican amendment sponsored by Young. *(Vote 264, p. 80-H)*

An hour later, the House reversed itself — and set the pattern for the rest of its action on HR 2760 — by approving, 221-205, a complicated amendment sponsored by Boland and Stephen J. Solarz, D-N.Y., to cut off the covert operation and to require congressional approval for any new proposal by the president to resume it. *(Vote 265, p. 80-H)*

Twelve Democrats and four Republicans who voted against the Barnes amendment switched to support of the Boland-Solarz amendment.

That trend was confirmed five hours later, when the House rejected 203-223, the major Democratic-sponsored amendment that would have permitted Reagan to continue the covert action. *(Vote 266, p. 80-H)*

Written by Mica, and offered by William S. Broomfield, R-Mich., the amendment reflected the symmetry argument.

That vote sealed the outcome of the legislation, since the Mica amendment was widely seen as the administration's best chance for averting a definite House vote to cut off the covert operation. The House then rejected three more Republican attempts to water down or kill the bill by similar margins — 194-229, 196-228 and 189-234 — before passing it, 228-195. *(Votes 267- 270, pp. 80-H — 82-H)*

By voice vote, the House adopted a sweeping substitute sponsored by Wright that wound up as the final version of the bill. It restated the original text of HR 2760 and added a long section calling on the administration to work

through the Organization of American States (OAS) to air U.S. grievances against Nicaragua.

Provisions. The major provisions of the Wright amendment, and the final bill, were:

● A prohibition against direct or indirect support by U.S. intelligence agencies for military or paramilitary operations in Nicaragua, effective at a secret date specified by the House Intelligence Committee.

● A finding by the Congress that a U.S. attempt to oust a government in Central America violated international treaties, including the charters of the United Nations and the OAS.

● A finding that Nicaraguan actions threatened El Salvador and threatened to destabilize Central America.

● Authorization of $30 million in fiscal 1983 and $50 million in fiscal 1984 to help "friendly" governments in Central America prevent use of their territory for the transfer of weapons from Cuba, Nicaragua or other countries to guerrillas.

● A direction to the president to seek a meeting of the OAS to evaluate Nicaragua's compliance with its 1979 promises and with the OAS charter. The OAS also would have been asked to take "effective measures" to force Nicaragua to comply with its 1979 promises and to halt its support for guerrillas elsewhere in Central America.

● A requirement that the president report to Congress by March 15, 1984, on the results of his efforts in Central America and on any need for further funds to carry out the purposes of the bill.

Intelligence Bill

With HR 2760 bottled up in the Senate Intelligence Committee after the House passed it, the focus of Capitol Hill debate on the covert action shifted to other legislation — including the annual authorization bill for U.S. intelligence agencies. In most years, that bill was a routine "must" bill that attracted little attention; most of its provisions were secret.

Both the House and Senate Intelligence committees put provisions in their respective 1984 authorization bills (HR 2968, S 1230) that affected the Nicaragua operation.

Senate Committee Action

The Senate Intelligence Committee, on a 13-2 vote in a closed session on May 6, adopted a compromise provision in its bill (S 1230 — S Rept 98-77) that enabled the CIA to continue its activities in Nicaragua for the remaining five months of fiscal year 1983. But the committee voted to require the president to provide a new plan for those covert actions during fiscal year 1984. A majority of the committee's members could have effectively vetoed the fiscal 1984 plan by refusing to release money for it from the CIA's contingency reserve fund.

The Senate panel's veto plan applied only to itself, but aides said the power almost certainly would be extended to the House Intelligence Committee as well during conference action on the intelligence bill.

Committee Chairman Barry Goldwater said members wanted the president to explain in his plan "just a little more clearly just what it is he wants to do" with covert actions in Central America.

The provision was a compromise between those who would have given Reagan free rein to continue the covert action and those who would have voted to end it quickly. The two members who opposed the compromise reportedly

were John H. Chafee, R-R.I., and Malcolm Wallop, R-Wyo.

The Senate committee provision of May 6 would have changed the existing procedure for approving covert actions in two respects, at least for the Nicaragua action. For the first time, money for a covert action would have been earmarked in the CIA's reserve fund by the intelligence committees, rather than by the administration. Secondly, the administration would have to get explicit approval from one or both intelligence committees before that money could be spent.

Goldwater told reporters that he had discussed the compromise provision with Reagan on May 5 and the president "found no quarrel with it." However, Goldwater said, the president "would have been happier if we had just let the whole thing alone."

The administration presented its plan in September, and the committee approved it Sept. 22 by a 13-2 vote. The dissenters were Joseph R. Biden Jr., D-Del., and Patrick J. Leahy, D-Vt. That plan included a $19 million authorization for the first six months of fiscal 1984, plus $10 million in leftover fiscal 1983 funds, plus an unspecified amount from the CIA contingency fund that could bring the total to as much as $50 million.

As outlined by CIA Director Casey, the plan dropped the contention that the United States was aiding the Nicaraguan rebels in an effort to interdict arms shipments to leftist guerrillas in El Salvador. Instead, Casey reportedly told the committee that the covert aid would force the Nicaraguan government to "turn inward" and thus drop its support for the Salvadoran guerrillas.

House Committee Action

Writing its intelligence authorization bill (HR 2968 — H Rept 98-189, Pt. 1)) on May 11, the House panel included in it the key part of HR 2760, suspending the covert action at a secret date during the remainder of fiscal year 1983. Although the bill contained no specific dollar amounts, it effectively authorized the administration's $19 million request; however, it would not have allowed the CIA to spend used funds or contingency funds on the covert aid.

House Floor Action

Setting up a confrontation with the Senate and the Reagan administration, the House on Oct. 20 reaffirmed its opposition to U.S. backing for rebels fighting against the Nicaraguan government.

By a 227-194 vote, largely along party lines, the House approved for the second time a provision that prohibited U.S. covert aid for the rebels in Nicaragua. The provision was part of the fiscal 1984 intelligence authorization bill (HR 2968). *(Vote 377, p. 112-H)*

In place of that aid, the measure provided $50 million for an "overt" program in Central America during fiscal 1984.

The key vote on the issue was virtually identical to the 228-195 vote by which the House on July 28 adopted the same language in a separate bill (HR 2760). As in July, only 18 Republicans voted for the Oct. 20 measure.

The main Republican effort to sidetrack the Boland-Zablocki provision was a motion by J. Kenneth Robinson, R-Va., ranking Republican on the Intelligence Committee, to return the bill to the committee with instructions to draft a new provision. Robinson's proposal would have enabled the covert operation to continue until the Nicaraguan government stopped supporting leftist guerrillas else-

where in the region and lived up to its 1979 promises to hold elections. Republicans called that approach "symmetry."

The symmetry amendment had great appeal in the House, even among some Democrats. Zablocki, for one, said the idea might provide an "incentive" to the Sandinistas to drop their support for Salvadoran guerrillas.

But symmetry failed, 193-223. Some saw it as permitting the covert action to continue indefinitely and others were not sure how it could be implemented. The House went on to pass the intelligence bill 243-171. *(Votes 378-379, p. 112-H)*

The House debate and votes on Oct. 20 had little of the drama of July 28, when the House first voted to cut off covert aid. Speaker O'Neill and Majority Leader Wright expressed confidence early Oct. 20 that they had the votes to pass the covert aid provision.

For the most part, the House debate on Oct. 20 saw the same members making the same arguments they had made three months earlier — with less passion. The House considered the bill under a rule (H Res 329) that strictly limited debate and permitted only two substantive amendments.

Ironically, Republicans were pinning their hopes for a positive outcome on Wright, whose legislative maneuvering and fiery eloquence had carried the day for HR 2760 in July.

After returning from a trip to Central America during the week of Oct. 9, Wright said he had found that the Sandinistas were imposing a "police state" on Nicaragua. That statement led some Republicans to hope that Wright would soften his support for the Boland-Zablocki provision. Wright dashed those hopes when he took the floor just before the key vote and said he still supported Boland-Zablocki.

The administration made two public appeals to the House prior to the vote, but otherwise spent little energy in trying to persuade members to oppose the Nicaragua amendment.

On Oct. 18, Secretary of State George P. Shultz wrote a letter to O'Neill arguing that cutting off aid for the rebels "would virtually destroy the prospect that Nicaragua may agree to reciprocal and verifiable agreements to end assistance to all guerrilla forces operating in the region."

In an Oct. 19 news conference, Reagan himself staunchly defended the use of covert action. "I think covert actions have been a part of government and a part of government's responsibilities for as long as there's been a government," he said.

An outside appeal came from four members of the Nicaraguan Democratic Force "directorate," who lobbied House members but apparently were unable to change any minds.

Senate Floor Action

The Senate took a stance directly opposite to that of the House Nov. 3 when it approved continued U.S. support for anti-government Nicaraguan rebels as part of the intelligence agencies authorization bill. The Senate passed the bill, HR 2968, by voice vote.

Although the Senate did not vote directly on the Nicaragua issue, there was general agreement that passage of the bill amounted to an endorsement of Reagan's program of aiding the rebels in Nicaragua. As drafted by the Senate Intelligence Committee and approved by the Senate, the bill authorized a fiscal 1984 program of at least $29 million

and as much as $50 million.

Senate Democrats who opposed the covert action chose not to contest it on the floor. Leahy said the covert action probably would have been approved by the Republican-controlled Senate on a direct vote, thus giving its Senate proponents a stronger hand in conference with the House.

"I hold no brief for the Sandinista regime [in Nicaragua]," Leahy said, "but whatever one thinks about it, it is the internationally recognized government of a sovereign nation. It should not be the function of the United States to overthrow regimes because it does not like their ideological character."

Goldwater said the covert action program was "working very well" because the Nicaraguan rebels had attracted "a good deal of popular support." Goldwater said support for the rebels also had forced the government to "focus inward" and thus reduce its backing for guerrillas elsewhere in the region.

While avoiding comment on the merits of the issue, committee Vice Chairman Moynihan lent some support to Goldwater's contentions. The purpose of the covert program, he said, "should be nothing more, nor nothing less, than bringing the government of Nicaragua into conformity with accepted norms of international behavior."

During Senate debate, Goldwater released a Sept. 21 letter from Defense Secretary Caspar W. Weinberger objecting to the overt arms interdiction program included in the House bill. Weinberger said such a program could cost "upwards of $300 million" in the first year and "at least" $100 million for each subsequent year.

Defense Appropriation

Even as the full House was acting on the intelligence bill Oct. 20, the House Appropriations Committee was moving to strike funding for the Nicaraguan rebels. By a 22-24 recorded vote and later by voice vote, the committee rejected attempts to dump a provision of the 1984 defense appropriations bill (HR 4185) that cut out all funds for covert operations in Nicaragua. That provision took effect upon the enactment of an intelligence bill, or on April 1, 1984, if no intelligence bill was enacted.

Appropriations for the intelligence agencies were hidden in the defense bill.

The defense bill also contained a sweeping provision that could have changed the basic method by which all U.S. covert activities were funded. For the first time, the bill required the administration to notify the two Intelligence committees and the two Appropriations committees before spending any money in the "contingency" funds of the CIA and other intelligence agencies. The committees would then have had a chance to block such expenditures.

Many covert activities, including the one in Nicaragua, had received their initial money through the CIA contingency fund. Under existing procedures, the congressional committees were unable to block the use of that fund until after a covert operation was under way.

Rep. Young, a member of both the House Intelligence and Appropriations committees, said the new provision was unacceptable to the administration. "You can't have a secret intelligence-type organization with that kind of requirement," he said. "We're seeing a step-by-step attempt to give Congress a prior veto over covert activities."

The appropriation bill was reported by the House committee Oct. 20 (H Rept 98-427) and passed by the House Nov. 1. The Senate passed the bill with amendments Nov. 8. *(Defense bill, p. 479)*

Conference/Final Action

On Nov. 17, the next-to-the-last day of the 1983 session, conferees on the defense bill hammered out the compromise on the Nicaragua issue. It allocated a maximum of $24 million for the covert aid, and required the president to return to Congress for more funds if he wanted to continue aiding the Nicaraguan rebels.

The next day, conferees on the intelligence authorization bill (HR 2968) adopted the compromise. Both bills (H Repts 98-567, 569) were cleared on Nov. 18.

The advantage in the compromise appeared to be Reagan's. He successfully avoided legislation setting a firm date to cut off the covert operation. And by the time Congress was to reconsider the issue in mid-1984, Reagan would have provided aid to the Nicaraguan rebels for more than two years with little congressional hindrance.

Defending the compromise before the House, Boland said it "will force either a significant phase-down of the covert action or a situation where the administration will have to come back and request additional funds if the covert action is to continue."

Joseph P. Addabbo, D-N.Y., chairman of the House Defense Appropriations Subcommittee, said the compromise set a precedent by requiring approval by both houses for more money for the covert action.

In the past, the covert operation had been funded through CIA contingency funds and the secret parts of intelligence and defense funding bills.

As a result of the fiscal 1984 compromnise legislation, Reagan would have more trouble getting funding through the public legislative procecy, Addabbo said: "We will tear away the sheet of secrecy" that the administration has sought to place over the Nicaragua program.

A State Department spokesman on Nov. 18 expressed satisfaction with the compromise. And Rep. Young, a covert action supporter, said the $24 million was sufficient "to continue the present effort to keep the Sandinistas busy, so they'll stay out of their neighbors' business."

Defense bill conferees eliminated another provision that would have established a new procedure giving the Appropriations and Intelligence committees veto power over all new covert operations by the CIA. ∎

Israel Ties Boosted

A year of bickering between Congress and the administration over aid to Israel came to an amiable conclusion on Nov. 12 as Congress approved one of the biggest single aid increase in years.

The second continuing resolution for fiscal 1984 (H J Res 413, PL 98-151) provided $1.7 billion in military aid for Israel in 1984 — the same amount as in fiscal 1983. But fully half of that amount was designated a forgiven loan (the same as a grant), a $100 million increase over the 1983 amount. The remainder was a regular Foreign Military Sales (FMS) loan, to be repaid at market interest rates. *(Continuing resolution, p. 521)*

Reagan had initially sought $550 million in FMS grants, provoking a storm of protest from pro-Israeli members of Congress who objected to the cut from the 1983

level of $750 million.

The bill also gave Israel $910 million in grants under the Economic Support Fund, an increase of $125 million over 1983. That aid was a subsidy of the Israeli economy. Reagan had requested $785 million.

The administration did not oppose the increases as it had done in late 1982. *(1982 Almanac p. 242)*

The bill also provided $1.365 billion in military aid for Egypt, Israel's partner in the 1979 Middle East peace treaty. Of that amount, $465 million was in forgiven loans and $900 million was in loans to be repaid. Egypt also was given $750 million in ESF grants.

U.S.-Israeli Accord

At the end of 1983, members of Congress were expressing approval of new agreements providing significant U.S. economic and political concessions for Israel.

U.S.-Israeli relations, which had been cool following Israel's invasion of Lebanon in 1982, took a turn for the better during a three-day visit to Washington by Israeli Prime Minister Yitzhak Shamir in November.

Both Reagan and Shamir said the United States and Israel decided to draw closer together as a result of the continuing turmoil in Lebanon and the Soviet Union's staunch backing for Syria.

Items either agreed to or discussed during Shamir's visit were:

● Establishment of a joint U.S.-Israeli committee on political and military affairs.

● Establishment of a free-trade zone, under which the United States and Israel would waive duties on each other's exports.

● A further increase in the grant portion of U.S. military aid to Israel, making $1.4 billion of Israel's 1985 military aid an outright grant.

● The loosening of restrictions on Israel's use of its foreign military aid.

● The lifting of a ban on the sale to Israel of so-called "cluster bombs," which spewed hundreds of small bombs upon impact.

● The storage in Israel of medical supplies and possibly military equipment for use in an emergency.

● Joint training exercises between U.S. and Israeli armed forces.

Some aspects of the agreement mirrored a formal memorandum of understanding that was signed by the United States and Israel on Nov. 30, 1981. The United States suspended that agreement three weeks later, however, when Israel formally annexed the Golan Heights, which technically belonged to Syria.

A senior State Department official involved in the talks said little attempt was made to extract Israeli cooperation on issues of primary interest to the United States. The official admitted that the United States made "no progress" in changing Israeli attitudes or actions on Reagan's Sept. 1, 1982, Middle East "peace initiative" to halt its expansion of Jewish settlements on the West Bank of the Jordan River or on its opposition to U.S. arms sales to Jordan and other "moderate" Arab states. But the administration was satisfied that the visit produced an "institutionalization of discussions" between the United States and Israel on political and military issues, the official said.

Aid Background

Reagan's proposal for a $200 million cut in grant military aid to Israel ran into problems in Congress as soon as it was submitted in January. The proposed cut was attacked in both the House Foreign Affairs and Senate Foreign Relations committees.

Events in the Middle East in March added substantial political weight to the side of Israel's friends in Congress. The installation in Syria of advanced Soviet SA-5 surface-to-air missiles, manned by several hundred Soviet soldiers; Jordan King Hussein's delay in joining the Middle East peace process; the prospect of a controversial arms sale to Jordan; and Israel's continuing economic difficulties all were cited as reasons for increasing, rather than decreasing, aid to Israel.

Administration officials made only tame efforts to defend the Israel aid proposal, saying it was not a cut in the total amount of U.S. aid Israel would get.

Overall, the administration proposed giving Israel the same amount of aid in fiscal 1984 as in 1983: $1.7 billion in military aid under the FMS program and $785 million under the Economic Support Fund.

But, as it had the previous year, the administration proposed reducing the portion provided as a FMS grant to $550 million in fiscal 1984 from the $750 million mandated by Congress for fiscal 1983. The rest of the FMS aid was to be provided as a 30-year loan at market interest rates. Congress mandated the $750 million figure for fiscal 1983, over the administration's adamant opposition.

Nicholas A. Veliotes, assistant secretary of state for Near Eastern and South Asian affairs, repeatedly told the House Middle East subcommittee that the aid proposal was based on budgetary considerations. He said it was not part of a policy of punishing Israel for its actions, such as the invasion of Lebanon and the gradual annexation of the West Bank, which were condemned by the United States.

Veliotes noted that a grant aid increase voted by Congress in 1982 "had to come out of the hide of a lot of other countries."

Notwithstanding the administration's protestations, the Middle East subcommittee voted April 12 to give Israel more aid than the president requested. With little discussion, the subcommittee approved Reagan's request for $1.7 billion in military aid for Israel but boosted the portion of that aid to be given as a grant to $850 million. The subcommittee also voted to boost economic aid for Israel to $850.

The full House Foreign Affairs Committee ratified that decision on May 17 when it reported HR 2992 (H Rept 98-192), its fiscal 1984-85 foreign aid authorization bill.

The Senate Foreign Relations Committee also gave approval to the aid increases when it reported its version of the authorization bill (S 1347 — S Rept 98-146) on May 23. It made one change to the House committee recommendations, by voting $910 million in economic aid.

Floor action did not occur on either bill, and the recommended aid levels were folded into the second continuing resolution (H J Res 413, PL 98-151).

F-16 Jets

The beginnings of a thaw in the U.S. coolness toward Israel occurred on May 20 when Reagan lifted a year-old embargo on U.S. sales of advanced warplanes to Israel, notifying Congress that Israel would be allowed to buy 75 F-16 jets. The embargo was lifted in response to Israel's signing of an agreement to withdraw its troops from Lebanon; the agreement was not carried out in 1983.

Including spare parts and related equipment, the sales price was $2.7 billion, with delivery of the F-16s expected to begin in 1985. Congress had 30 days in which to veto the

sale but declined to object.

When Israel invaded southern Lebanon in June 1982, Reagan suspended the jet sale, informally proposed in May 1982, as one sign of his displeasure. Administration officials explained that the sale would violate the spirit of a 1952 agreement, enforced by U.S. foreign aid laws, that allowed Israel to use weapons bought from the United States only for internal security or self-defense.

In July 1982 and again in September 1982, the State Department notified Congress that a violation of that agreement "may have occurred" when Israel invaded Lebanon using U.S.-supplied weapons and equipment.

The 75 F-16 planes were the second half of Israel's 1977 request for 150 F-16s. President Carter agreed to sell the first 75 F16s in 1978 as part of a package of jet sales to Middle East countries. Reagan in 1981 delayed sending 14 of Israel's first 75 F-16s to protest the bombing of a nuclear reactor in Iraq. *(1981 Almanac p. 131)*

Lavi Fighters

PL 98-151, the fiscal 1984 continuing resolution, also settled a long-simmering dispute: whether the United States should finance Israeli development of a new fighter bomber called the "Lavi."

Of the military aid set aside for Israel, nearly a third, $550 million, was designated to help Israel develop the Lavi (Hebrew for "lion"). Of that amount, $300 million had to be spent in the United States and $250 million could be spent in Israel.

Israel had long sought U.S. support for its rapidly expanding defense industry, but the United States was reluctant to provide it. As part of an effort to thaw the chill in U.S.-Israeli relations, Reagan in late October decided to allow Israel to use foreign military aid on the Lavi project — as long as the money was spent in the United States.

The move to boost funding for the Lavi to $550 million was promoted by Rep. Charles Wilson, D-Texas, who was not widely seen as one of Israel's strongest supporters in Congress. He said he hoped that the Lavi funding might convince Israel to drop its opposition to the training and equiping of two brigades of the Jordanian army as a "rapid deployment task force" in the Middle East. Israel viewed the Jordan proposal as a potential military threat, and its opposition helped convince Congress to kill the plan in 1983.

Favoring the Lavi plan were Grumman Corp., which had a contract to supply wings and tail assemblies for the Lavi, and the Pratt & Whitney Aircraft division of United Technologies Corp., which was to supply engines for the plane.

The main opponent was Northrop Corp., which feared that the Lavi, planned for export in the 1990s, would steal sales from its new F-20 fighter plane. Noting that Northrop had spent more than $600 million of its own money developing the F-20, a company spokesman said it was "unfair" for the U.S. government to subsidize potential competition in Israel. ∎

Military Ties to Jordan

The Reagan administration's hopes for closer military cooperation with Jordan suffered a major setback when Congress rejected a plan to arm and support two brigades of the Jordanian army as a rapid deployment "strike force" in the Middle East.

Congressional opposition also prevented the administration from even proposing to sell Jordan advanced fighter planes and anti-aircraft systems.

The administration sought improved ties with Jordan as a counterweight to Syria and other radical Arab states in the Middle East and as a means of advancing President Reagan's September 1982 Middle East "peace initiative." The peace plan called on Israel to give up control of the West Bank of the Jordan River to an "association" of Jordan and the Palestinians who lived there. *(1982 Almanac p. 170)*

The strike force plan called for U.S. training of Jordanian units in rapid-reaction tactics, such as responding to a military threat to oil facilities in the Persian Gulf. The units were to be equipped with C-130 transport planes, anti-aircraft and anti-tank missiles, tanks, communications equipment and other supplies.

Reagan submitted the plan to Congress in secret. Administration officials asked Congress not to reveal the proposal, saying that Jordan's King Hussein feared that publicity would undermine his standing in the Arab world.

With few members knowing about it, Congress secretly authorized $220 million for the plan when it cleared the fiscal 1984 defense authorization bill (S 675 — PL 98-94) in mid-September.

But in mid-October, press reports about the plan (originating in Israel), created an uproar in Congress, leading the two Appropriations committees to reject funds for the plan while writing legislation (S 2039, HR 4185) that appropriated money for the Defense Department in fiscal 1984. *(Defense authorization, p. 175; appropriation, p. 479)*

Rejection of the plan by the Republican-controlled Senate committee killed it for the current year. At a closed meeting Nov. 1, the committee deleted the Jordan funds. Opposition was led by Defense Appropriations Subcommittee members Alfonse M. D'Amato, R-N.Y., and Daniel K. Inouye, D-Hawaii. Both were strong supporters of Israel, which reportedly had objected to the plan as a military threat.

HR 4185, passed by the House on Nov. 2, also did not include the Jordan funds.

The only public action by Congress on the issue came on Oct. 29, when the Senate by voice vote adopted an amendment to a debt limit bill (H J Res 308 — PL 98-161) prohibiting any funding for the Jordan force unless Congress had expressly approved it "in an unclassified manner." That provision was later dropped when it became clear the Defense Appropriations bill would not include money for the strike force.

The sale of advanced weapons to Jordan was handled in an even more ambiguous manner.

Defense Secretary Caspar W. Weinberger and other administration officials reportedly wanted to sell Jordan F-16 warplanes and mobile Hawk anti-aircraft missile systems. However, the administration did not propose such a sale in 1983, largely because Israel and its allies in Congress vigorously opposed it as a potential threat to Israel's security.

One indication of congressional opposition came in April when the House Foreign Affairs Committee voted to deprive Jordan of advanced U.S. weapons and Foreign Military Sales (FMS) aid until it recognized Israel and agreed to negotiate directly with Israel under the terms of United Nations Security Council resolutions on the Middle East and the 1978 Camp David accords.

The committee acted shortly after Jordan's King Hussein said he was giving up his six-month-long effort to secure the consent of other Arab nations and the Palestine Liberation Organization (PLO) to his entering Middle East peace talks. Committee members complained that Hussein had given the PLO a veto over his participation in peace talks.

The committee attached its conditions to a fiscal 1984-85 foreign aid authorization bill (HR 2992). Although that bill died without reaching the House floor, the committee's action demonstrated that the administration would face strong opposition in Congress to any sale of advanced weapons to Jordan. *(HR 2992, p. 140)* ∎

Invasion of Grenada

President Reagan ordered an invasion of the Caribbean island of Grenada on Oct. 25 and received support from a Congress already in turmoil over the bombing deaths two days before of more than 230 Marines stationed in Lebanon.

However, most members made it clear that their approval was founded on the explanation — and independent evidence for it — that the invasion was necessary to save some 1,000 Americans on the island.

Reagan had declared Grenada a sore spot in March, when he said its anti-American, Marxist regime was permitting Cuba to build military airfields there.

Justification for the invasion, which left 18 U.S. soldiers killed and 115 wounded, also was given because of a request for American help from neighboring island nations in the Organization of Eastern Caribbean States (OECS).

The chairman of the OECS, Prime Minister Eugenia Charles of Dominica, announced the invasion with Reagan on Oct. 25. The OECS nations, lacking military forces, contributed 300 constables to the force.

The island was thrown into turmoil beginning Oct. 12, when an even harder-line Marxist group executed a coup d'etat, killed the previous regime's leaders and imposed a 24-hour "shoot-on-sight" curfew.

Reagan said he ordered U.S. forces to invade after the four other OECS nations (Antigua, Dominica, St. Lucia and St. Vincent), joined by Jamaica and Barbados, urgently requested U.S. help in restoring order and democracy in Grenada. He said he acted because Americans on the island, mostly medical students, were in grave danger.

There were an estimated 30 Soviets on Granada, whom the United States pledged to protect. Cuban Premier Fidel Castro had said there were 700 Cuban "construction workers" on the island. But U.S. forces had captured more than 600 Cubans as of Oct. 28; and, by that date, Defense Department officials said that U.S. troops were fighting several hundred Cuban soldiers.

At the height of the invasion, some 7,300 U.S. Marines, Army Rangers and paratroopers were on Grenada. By Dec. 12 all "combat" troops were withdrawn, leaving some 300 U.S. military "support" personnel on the island.

The War Powers Issue

Some members of Congress sought to emphasize the need for an early withdrawal, and at the same time assert a right to have a hand in decisions to use military force, by trying to invoke the War Powers Resolution (PL 93-148).

The House Foreign Affairs Committee Oct. 27 ap-proved, 32-2 a bill (H J Res 402) to declare under a provision of the 1973 resolution that the U.S. forces must be withdrawn within 90 days unless extended by Congress. On Nov. 1, the full House passed the resolution 403-23. *(Vote 407, p. 122-H)*

The full Senate adopted the same language on Oct. 28, voting 64-20 to attach it to an unrelated debt ceiling bill (H J Res 308). That amendment later died, and Majority Leader Howard H. Baker Jr., R-Tenn., blocked Senate debate on H J Res 402. *(Vote 311, p. 52-S)*

Among those who approved of the operation, Democrats in particular had misgivings about its legality under international and U.S. law. Some complained that Reagan had used the Americans as a pretext to oust Grenada's pro-Cuban regime.

Such criticisms were raised while the invasion was still in progress Oct. 25, but they were all but drowned out the second day, when students from St. George's School of Medicine near the capital, St. George's, who accounted for about 600 of the Americans on the island, were seen on television returning to the United States.

Some kissed the ground. Others said they had feared for their lives before the U.S. troops arrived in Grenada. One told reporters: "God bless America, God bless Reagan, God bless our military."

Such statements helped dash skepticism on Capitol Hill. So did the fierce resistance put up by Cuban as well as Grenadian forces, which U.S. officials admitted was far stronger than anticipated, as did reports that the U.S. forces found large stockpiles of Soviet-made arms and other military equipment once they secured the island Oct. 25.

The most prominent member to switch on the issue was House Speaker Thomas P. O'Neill Jr., D-Mass. Several days after the invasion, O'Neill criticized it as "gunboat diplomacy." But he sent a delegation of House members to the island, and on Nov. 8, after hearing them describe the potential danger to some 1,000 Americans on Grenada prior to the invasion, O'Neill issued a statement in support of the invasion.

Still, an apparent handful remained critical of the invasion. Seven House members, led by Rep. Ted Weiss, D-N.Y., on Nov. 10 offered a resolution to impeach Reagan on grounds that he violated sections of the Constitution in ordering the attack. By Nov. 11, the resolution had no additional cosponsors.

Three congressional delegations visited Grenada during the Nov. 4-8 period: a 14-member delegation (nine Democrats and five Republicans) appointed by O'Neill; a delegation of four Republicans, whose trip was sponsored by the National Defense Council, a conservative lobbying organization; and Senate Armed Services Committee Chairman John Tower, R-Texas.

The official House delegation was headed by Majority Whip Thomas S. Foley, D-Wash., and Minority Leader Robert H. Michel, R-Ill.

The four Republicans on the independent trip were Dan L. Burton, Ind.; Robert W. Davis, Mich.; Don Ritter, Pa.; and Mark D. Siljander, Mich.

For the most part, Democrats in Congress said the invasion was justified only on the narrow grounds of protecting American citizens from being attacked or taken hostage by the revolutionary forces in Grenada.

Foley and others said they were told that chaos reigned in Grenada between Oct. 12, when Bishop was deposed, and Oct. 25, when the United States invaded.

Michael D. Barnes, D-Md., a delegation member, said "there was a sense of terror on the island, not only among foreign nationals, such as American citizens, but among the Grenadians themselves."

Barnes, chairman of the House Foreign Affairs Subcommittee on Western Hemisphere Affairs, was a leading critic of Reagan's political and military policies toward Central America and the Caribbean.

The Democrats insisted that their approval of the invasion did not constitute endorsement for U.S. military action against other countries that were at odds with the United States.

Two dissenters, Louis Stokes, D-Ohio, and Ronald V. Dellums, D-Calif., disputed the administration view that U.S. citizens on Grenada were in real danger.

Some Republicans drew a much broader lesson from the invasion and its aftermath: that it came just in time to prevent the Soviet Union and Cuba from spreading communism to the rest of the Caribbean, if not the entire Western Hemisphere.

Davis, for one, said evidence of Soviet and Cuban military involvement on Grenada "shows me that there is definitely a move in that part of the world to undermine the United States." And Burton said that several tons of military equipment stockpiled in Grenada "was to be used to export terrorism throughout the region."

U.S. Aid

There appeared to be widespread support in Congress for a rapid and relatively large economic aid program for Grenada.

The United States had not provided direct aid to Grenada since the 1979 revolution in which Bishop seized power.

The second continuing appropriations resolution for fiscal 1984 (H J Res 413, PL 98-151), cleared by Congress on Nov. 14, included $15 million for military assistance for peacekeeping forces in the Caribbean. The administration also planned to spend $18.4 million in economic aid to Grenada.

In spite of the controversy it generated in the past, there was backing in Congress for helping the Grenadian government complete its new international airport at Point Salines. The Reagan administration had claimed that the new airport, financed in large part by Cuba and featuring a 9,000-foot runway, was intended for military purposes.

Siljander and other Republicans said the United States should now help complete the airport because it is needed to boost tourism to Grenada.

Barnes put the airport in a larger political context. If the airport was allowed to sit unfinished for a year or two, he said, "it's going to be a symbol of American intervention." ∎

Downing of Korean Airliner

Congress spoke with one voice in condemning the Soviet Union's destruction of a Korean passenger jet and the 269 people aboard it, calling it a "cold-blooded barbarous attack ... [and] one of the most infamous and reprehensible acts in history."

However, some members had sought more than tough words and the resolution (H J Res 353 — PL 98-98), drafted by the White House and congressional leaders, had

the effect of further alienating some hard-line Republicans from President Reagan.

U.S. Rep. Larry P. McDonald (D-Ga.) and some 50 other Americans were among the passengers killed when flight KAL 007 was downed in the Sea of Japan Sept. 1.

The House Sept. 14 voted 416-0 to condemn the "criminal destruction" of the Korean plane; the Senate Sept. 15 voted 95-0. *(House vote 320, p. 96-H; Senate vote 243, p. 41-S)*

In an effort to head off amendments, Senate leaders insisted that the measure had to be passed on Sept. 15 so it could be put before the president without delay. However, Reagan did not sign the resolution into law until Sept. 28.

Despite the unanimity of the votes, many members were unhappy about passing a resolution that urged no specific action to punish the Soviets. Leading conservatives, especially in the Senate, were angered that Reagan had not seized the incident as the opening for an anti-Soviet crusade.

The White House actively opposed all efforts to strengthen the resolution with amendments calling for direct retaliation against the Soviets.

On Sept. 12, the Soviet Union vetoed a resolution in the United Nations Security Council, which deplored the shooting down of flight 007. On Sept. 13, the Soviet Union refused to accept a U.S. demand that it compensate Korean Air Lines and the families of those who died.

The immediate result of the incident was a flurry of harsh accusations from Washington and Moscow.

President Reagan on Sept. 2 cut short a vacation in California to return to Washington for meetings of his National Security Council. Reagan said the Soviets had committed a "barbaric act" that had caused him "anger, disbelief and profound sadness."

Reagan said "the brutality of this act should not be compounded through silence or the cynical distortion of the evidence now at hand."

However, Reagan later decided not to impose specific sanctions on the Soviet Union, such as a grain embargo.

Soviet officials later said they did not know that the plane was a civilian airliner when it was shot down, and they insisted that the plane was spying on sensitive military installations on Sakhalin Island.

While rejecting the latter charge, U.S. officials later admitted that there was no proof that the Soviet Union knew that the plane was a civilian, rather than a military, one.

Provisions

As cleared by Congress, H J Res 353:
- Extended the sympathies of the Congress to the families of the victims and supported their right to obtain reparations from the Soviet Union.
- Called for a "full and frank explanation by the Soviet Union for this brutal massacre."
- Called for an investigation of the incident by the International Civil Aviation Organization. That organization Sept. 16 approved a U.S.-backed proposal for such an investigation.
- Declared the U.S. intention to work with other countries to demand that the Soviet Union change its air defense procedures to assure the safe passage of commercial airliners.
- Stated that the incident, and the Soviet refusal to acknowledge responsibility for it, "will make it more difficult for the United States and other nations to accept the

Soviet Union as a responsible member of the international community."

● Urged the United States and other countries to demand that the Soviet Union apologize for its action, fully compensate the families of the victims and agree to abide by internationally accepted procedures that were designed to prevent such incidents.

House Action

The House debated the resolution for little more than two hours on Sept. 14. Although some conservatives complained about the lack of specific sanctions, none made any move to amend it.

House members had plenty of ideas about how the Soviet Union could be punished. Among them: Eldon Rudd, R-Ariz., proposed boosting economic and military aid to El Salvador; Austin J. Murphy, D-Pa., suggested cutting U.S. contributions to the United Nations and imposing special import duties on Soviet vodka, caviar and sable pelts; and Mary Rose Oakar, D-Ohio, and Clarence E. Miller, R-Ohio, proposed banning imports of Soviet-produced ferroalloy metals, which competed with Ohio-made products.

A warning of another sort was issued by Morris K. Udall, D-Ariz., who said: "The men who made the decision to shoot down flight 007 are the same men who would be making the choices should there be a nuclear confrontation. With anti-Soviet rhetoric at an all-time high, we may be closer to a nuclear holocaust than ever."

Senate Action

The Senate spent nearly eight hours on Sept. 15 debating and voting on the matter before reaching its unanimous vote.

Jesse Helms, R-N.C, and Steven D. Symms, R-Idaho, on Sept. 12 proposed a sweeping set of sanctions, including: expelling most Soviet diplomats from the United States; demanding the withdrawal of all Soviet military personnel and equipment from the Western Hemisphere; temporarily suspending arms control talks with the Soviets; banning all loans to the Soviet Union and its satellites, and banning all high technology sales to the Soviet Union.

Helms and other conservatives for months had been urging Reagan to take some of those actions, and had become increasingly frustrated as he refused to do so.

In an effort to attract support before the vote, Helms and Symms twice softened their proposal, calling for much milder sanctions on the same issues.

Helms dominated Senate debate on the resolution, arguing that Congress should "put some teeth" in any resolution condemning the Soviet Union. "The resolution does not do anything," he said.

Helms, who took a KAL flight that left a refueling stop in Anchorage, Alaska, just minutes after flight 007, recalled for the Senate his meeting at the Anchorage airport with an American family that was traveling on flight 007. Helms said he had told jokes and stories to the two small girls in the family as they waited in the airport, and had watched as they waved and blew kisses to him on their way to board the plane.

"In the name of those two little girls, let us take action which will meet the Soviets on their own ground," Helms pleaded.

Charles H. Percy, R-Ill., expressed sympathy with many of Helms' proposals but argued for rapid approval of a resolution that could command unanimous support of the

Senate and be put on the president's desk without delay. "It is more important to speak with one voice to the Soviet Union than to argue among ourselves about shades of difference," Percy said.

And Daniel Patrick Moynihan, D-N.Y., pointed out that the resolution referred to the Soviet action as a "crime." Saying that the United States had never before formally charged the Soviet Union with committing a crime, Moynihan argued: "This is not a small event. The charge of an international crime is a solemn one."

Helms divided his sweeping amendment into seven parts, and on motions by Majority Leader Howard H. Baker Jr., R-Tenn., the Senate tabled each one on roll-call votes. The widest margin was an 82-14 vote to table a demand that the president formally link the "possible success" of current nuclear arms negotiations in Geneva with "the willingness of the Soviet Union to abide by international law as a responsible member of the community of nations." *(Votes 235-241, p. 40-S)*

The closest margin on a Helms amendment was a 50-45 vote asking the president to report to Congress on the Soviet record of complying with past arms control agreements. *(Vote 237, p. 40-S)*

By an even narrower margin of 49-45, the Senate tabled another amendment, backed by a coalition of members, that would have forced the Soviet Union to "substantially" reduce its diplomatic corps in the United States, to conform to the number of U.S. diplomats stationed in the Soviet Union. Walter D. Huddleston, D-Ky., the amendment's sponsor, said there were about 1,000 Soviet diplomats in the United States, and some 300 U.S. diplomats in the Soviet Union. *(Vote 242, p. 41-S)* ∎

Aid, Arms to Guatemala

Acting sometimes in concert and sometimes at odds, Congress and the Reagan administration in 1983 bluntly warned the Guatemalan government to improve its performance on human rights issues.

With little fanfare, Congress blocked all U.S. aid to the Guatemalan government and the administration halted a long-pending sale of helicopter spare parts and other equipment for that country's army.

The Reagan administration, which had promoted the parts sale and other military aid, went along with its critics after a hard-line general overthrew one who appeared to be easing repression.

The warnings produced no immediate results. The United States had been complaining about human rights abuses by right-wing governments in Guatemala since 1977, with little noticeable effect.

Background

Guatemala had been ruled by military and authoritarian governments since 1954, when a CIA-financed coup overthrew a left-leaning government that irritated the Eisenhower administration.

Rep. Michael D. Barnes, D-Md., chairman of the Foreign Affairs Subcommittee on Western Hemisphere Affairs, cited reports by human rights groups that past Guatemalan governments used U.S.-supplied equipment in an alleged campaign of "systematically massacring the Indian population." Barnes said in 1983 "the jury is still out" on the question of whether the massacres had ended.

The latest change of governments came in August, when Defense Minister Oscar Mejia Victores, a hard-line anti-communist army general, overthrew Gen. Efrain Rios Montt. Rios Montt himself came to power after a March 1982 coup, but alienated powerful groups in the Roman Catholic country with his constant advocacy of fundamentalist Protestantism.

Since the Carter administration, the United States had tried using both the carrot and the stick to persuade Guatemalan governments to ease repression, especially against rural Indians who made up nearly half of the country's population of 7.7 million.

Congress and President Carter applied the stick in 1977, cutting off all arms sales and military aid to Guatemala.

In January 1983, the Reagan administration offered a major political carrot to the Rios Montt government, agreeing to sell the Guatemalan army $6.4 million worth of helicopter parts and other items that could be used for military purposes. The State Department said the sale was justified because Guatemala under Rios Montt had taken "significant steps" to improve respect for human rights.

Under Rios Montt, the department said, "political violence in the cities has declined dramatically; recently there are indications that the level of violence in the countryside has declined as well; villagers have been provided food and medical supplies along with the means to defend themselves; plans are under way for the election of a constituent assembly; the Indian population is increasingly participating in the country's political process; and President Rios Montt has been attacking corruption within the government."

Barnes said he, too, had been encouraged by Rios Montt's promises to hold elections and to respect the rights of Indians.

The administration's January 1983 offer to sell helicopter parts to the Rios Montt government was protested by human rights groups and congressional critics such as Rep. Tom Harkin, D-Iowa, who said there was not enough evidence that Rios Montt had made the improvements the administration claimed.

But the sale never was consummated. Guatemala said it could not afford to pay cash for the equipment, and Congress did not approve the use of U.S. aid to help finance the sale.

The new government of Mejia Victores, according to administration officials, was ready to buy just spare parts and repair work for its three UH-1H helicopters, valued at more than $2 million.

Word of plans for that smaller sale brought new protests from Capitol Hill. On Nov. 9, 51 House members, most of them liberal Democrats, wrote Reagan asking him not to sell Guatemala any equipment "which may be used for offensive military purposes."

Led by Gerry E. Studds, D-Mass., and Barnes, the 51 said there was "no evidence" that the Mejia Victores government "constitutes an improvement over its predecessors." The United States should not "isolate itself from the people or government of Guatemala," they said. "But we also do not believe that offensive military equipment should be made available by the United States to any armed force which is unwilling to respect the fundamental rights of its own citizens."

The administration did not formally respond to that letter, but State Department officials said Nov. 28 the sale was being held in abeyance because of an upsurge in political violence in Guatemala.

After Mejia Victores took power, one linguist working for a U.S.-sponsored educational program was killed and another was kidnapped — allegedly by right-wing death squads with ties to the Guatemalan army or government.

Reagan administration officials first raised the prospect of the sale in autumn of 1981, but delayed any action when Barnes and other liberals introduced legislation to block it. That was when Barnes and Thomas O. Enders, assistant secretary of state for inter-American affairs, reached an agreement on how to handle the issue. Barnes later said the agreement gave the Foreign Affairs Committee an informal veto over the sale; Enders said the agreement merely called for consultations on the issue.

Congress had no automatic power to veto the Guatemala military equipment sale, which fell well below the $50 million threshold for congressional review of overseas arms sale packages.

U.S. Aid

In a related development, Congress in November flatly banned all U.S. military, economic and development aid that would directly benefit the Guatemalan government.

The second continuing appropriations resolution (H J Res 413 — PL 98-151), cleared Nov. 12, barred aid to Guatemala "except for economic development projects through private voluntary organizations."

That provision generated no controversy in Congress and was not actively opposed by the administration. Reagan signed the continuing resolution Nov. 14 without commenting on the Guatemala provision.

Written by the House Appropriations Subcommittee on Foreign Operations, the Guatemala provision was similar to one that had been inserted by the House Foreign Affairs Committee in the fiscal 1984 foreign aid authorization bill (HR 2992). The foreign aid bill never reached the House floor. *(Story, p. 140)*

In his January budget, Reagan had requested $10 million in military loans, $40 million in economic aid and $26.6 million in other aid for Guatemala in fiscal 1984.

The United States had provided small amounts of development and food aid to Guatemala, but after 1977 had given no military or economic aid that might imply active U.S. support for the government. *(1982 Almanac pp. 156, 220)* ∎

Radio Marti

The House Sept. 29 cleared for the president legislation (S 602) authorizing creation of a Voice of America service to broadcast news and information to Cuba. Final approval of "Radio Marti," or "Cuba Service," came on a 302-109 vote. *(Vote 346, p. 104-H)*

The compromise measure had passed the Senate Sept. 13 by voice vote. The Reagan administration and other proponents wanted Radio Marti to be separate from the Voice of America, but opponents had blocked that plan for more than a year.

President Reagan signed S 602 Oct. 4 (PL 98-111).

Advocates had sought a Latin version of Radio Free Europe; opponents feared the project would do more harm than good. Some opponents argued that the station would be used by exiles to irritate Cuban Premier Fidel Castro. Others feared that U.S. commercial radio stations would suffer if Castro jammed Radio Marti broadcasts; Midwest

broadcasters warned that Cuban interference could be costly for domestic broadcasters.

Passage came almost two years after the Reagan administration proposed Radio Marti as a way to counter Cuban influence in Central America and the Caribbean. Authorizing legislation had been passed by the House on Aug. 10, 1982, but was killed by a Senate filibuster in the December 1982 lame-duck session. *(Background, 1982 Almanac p. 147)*

Introduced by Sen. Paula Hawkins, R-Fla., the new proposal was aimed at avoiding Cuban jamming that would interfere with domestic broadcasts in the United States. The administration's original proposal was for Radio Marti to broadcast on 1040 AM, which was used by WHO in Des Moines, Iowa. S 602 offered the option of using the Voice of America Frequency (1180 AM) and facilities in Marathon, Fla.

A key opponent of the 1982 bill, Sen. Roger W. Jepsen, R-Iowa, supported S 602.

The 1180 AM frequency was used by three stations: WHAM in Rochester, N.Y., WLDS in Jacksonville, Ill., and KOFI in Kalispell, Mont.

William F. Rust Jr., owner of WHAM, said he would not oppose putting Radio Marti on 1180 because using the Voice of America facilities "is the logical thing to do." Rust said WHAM had been plagued by Cuban interference for 20 years, "and we gave up fighting it maybe 15 years ago."

Before establishing the broadcast service, Congress agreed to a series of compromises.

Provisions

In final form, the Radio Broadcasting to Cuba Act established the service within the United States Information Agency (USIA), as part of the Voice of America (VOA) — incorporating VOA standards. VOA was already broadcasting to Cuba, but its programs were not prepared specifically for Cuban consumption.

The bill authorized $14 million in fiscal 1984 and $11 million in fiscal 1985 for the station's operations. Also authorized was an additional $54.8 million in each year for modernization of VOA facilities. The figures represented concessions by Radio Marti opponents, who accepted higher amounts in return for putting the Cuba service under VOA auspices.

The bill also provided that:

● U.S. policy supported the right of the Cuban people to "seek, receive and impart information and ideas through any media," regardless of frontiers; and that broadcasts to Cuba could be effective in furthering that goal.

● Transmissions be part of Voice of America broadcasts to Cuba, in accordance with VOA standards; namely, "programs which are objective, accurate, balanced and which present a variety of views."

● The authorized Cuban service use facilities at Marathon, Fla., and the 1180 AM frequency used by the VOA. Other non-commercial AM frequencies also could be used, although they had to be frequencies used for other VOA broadcasts to Cuba.

● Non-governmental shortwave radio stations carry the Cuban service if at least 30 percent of the remaining programs were regular VOA broadcasts.

● If Radio Marti broadcasts on the 1180 AM frequency were jammed 25 percent or more than VOA broadcasts were jammed in the year preceding Sept. 1, 1983, USIA could lease time on commercial or non-commercial AM-band radio stations.

● The director of USIA establish a separately administered Cuba service, with a separate staff.

● An advisory board be established, with nine members appointed by the president with Senate approval. No more than five members could be of one political party. Also authorized was $130,000 to cover the board's incidental expenses.

● The secretary of state should seek settlement of U.S. claims against the Cuban government if Cuba interfered with domestic broadcasts.

● USIA compensate U.S. radio stations for technical expenses incurred as a result of Cuban interference. Procedures for such claims would be established by the Federal Communications Commission. The bill authorized $5 million for USIA, effective Oct. 1, 1984, to pay for such compensation.

● USIA arrange an independent evaluation of Radio Marti programming, with the first report due 18 months after enactment of the bill, then annually for three years. Reports were to be sent to Congress, with any recommendations for legislative action.

● The programs be designated "Voice of America: Cuba Service," or "Voice of America: Radio Marti Program." A previously enacted law (PL 97-241) stipulated that any U.S. broadcast to Cuba be called Radio Marti, after the Cuban patriot José Marti.

Committee Action

President Reagan's revised plan for Radio Marti survived two challenges in the Senate Foreign Relations and House Foreign Affairs committees on June 8-9.

The committees rejected proposals to put Radio Marti under the Voice of America. The vote was 8-9 in the Senate committee and 10-14 in the House panel. Sponsors of those proposals said the move would prevent Radio Marti from being used for propaganda purposes, since the Voice of America was mandated by law to be an "objective" news source.

Both committees went on to approve legislation authorizing the establishment of Radio Marti as an independent station under the supervision of the Board for International Broadcasting, which ran Radio Free Europe and Radio Liberty. The Foreign Relations Committee approved its bill (S 602 — S Rept 98-156) by a 13-4 vote on June 8, and the Foreign Affairs Committee approved its bill (HR 2453 — H Rept 98-284, Pt. I) by a 19-8 vote the next day.

The bills approved by the committees allowed Radio Marti to use the transmitter and 1180 AM frequency of an existing Voice of America station in Marathon, Fla., or to lease time from U.S. radio stations.

Both bills authorized $5 million to compensate U.S. stations for their costs in overcoming any Cuban interference directed at Radio Marti.

Sen. Edward Zorinsky, D-Neb., who killed the Radio Marti proposal in December 1982 by filibustering against it, said on June 8 he had given up trying to block the bill because a filibuster would not be effective without the time pressure of an adjournment deadline.

House Energy Committee. The House Energy and Commerce Committee July 26 approved a Radio Marti bill (HR 2453 — H Rept 98-284, Pt. II) containing strictures the White House opposed.

The committee adopted, 26-16, a major amendment that sought to meet the objections of critics who opposed its proposed propaganda function and of radio station own-

ers who feared Cuban interference with their broadcasts.

Sponsored by Rep. Tom Tauke, R-Iowa, the amendment tightened restrictions in HR 2453 banning Radio Marti from commercial AM and FM frequencies. The station could operate only on shortwave frequencies, or on the 1180 AM frequency used by the Voice of America for limited broadcasts to Cuba. The amendment also gave the Federal Communications Commission (FCC) the responsibility of assigning a frequency to Radio Marti.

Tauke argued that Radio Marti as proposed by the Reagan administration "won't have any impact" because Cuba would jam its broadcasts. But the station "has a chance to succeed" as an arm of the Voice of America, which by U.S. law was required to practice objective journalism, he said.

Matthew J. Rinaldo, R-N.J., argued that Tauke and other Radio Marti critics were attempting to kill "a major foreign policy proposal because of threats by Fidel Castro."

In its major concession to the administration, the committee killed a sweeping amendment by Al Swift, D-Wash., that probably would have prevented Radio Marti from ever reaching the airwaves.

The amendment would have required the U.S. government to reimburse U.S. radio stations for most of the damages caused by Cuban jamming, and prohibited Radio Marti from operating unless all claims filed by U.S. stations and certified by the FCC, had been fully paid.

A broadcaster himself, Swift said his amendment would protect broadcasters in case other provisions, such as Tauke's amendment, were later dropped. But the committee deleted it by voice vote, on a motion by Rinaldo.

The committee also:

● Placed a five-year "sunset" provision on Radio Marti, requiring new authorization for it after that.

● Retained, by a 23-19 vote, a subcommittee amendment offered by Edward J. Markey, D-Mass., banning operation of Radio Marti until after the General Accounting Office had reported to Congress on the potential damages to U.S. broadcasters.

● Retained, by a 22-20 vote, a subcommittee amendment offered by Mickey Leland, D-Texas, banning operation of Radio Marti until after the U.S. government had made "all efforts," through negotiations with Cuba, to reduce Cuban interference with U.S. broadcasts.

Floor Action

Radio Marti cleared a formidable hurdle on Sept. 13 when the Senate, by voice vote, passed a compromise measure (S 602) to establish the station in fiscal 1984.

In its final form, the bill was less than the administration sought, but it won the support of a coalition that had blocked the legislation for more than a year.

The Senate bill, placing Radio Marti under the Voice of America, was the result of negotiations among Hawkins, who had championed the station, and several opponents, including Zorinsky, Lowell P. Weicker Jr., R-Conn., and Charles E. Grassley, R-Iowa.

Hawkins said the compromise was politically necessary and "offers a practical and reasonable way out of this impasse." Weicker said he was satisfied with the compromise because it reduced the chance that the station could be used in a propaganda war with Cuba. "We are not creating a propaganda station, but an accurate, objective and balanced source of news," he told the Senate.

VOA already was broadcasting about five and one-half

hours a day to Latin America, including Cuba. Sponsors of the compromise said the new station should send 14½ hours daily to Cuba.

Virtually every aspect of the Radio Marti issue was compromised in a sweeping amendment incorporated in S 602 — in some cases leaving specific matters unresolved.

Even the name designated for the Cuban broadcasts suggested the give-and-take that preceded the vote: The bill required that they be labeled "Voice of America: Cuba Service" or "Voice of America: Radio Marti." It did not specify which, or who would decide, although an existing law (PL 97-241), enacted in 1982, directed that any U.S. government broadcasts to Cuba be called Radio Marti, after the Cuban patriot José Marti.

In another compromise, the bill authorized $14 million in fiscal 1984 and $11 million in fiscal 1985 for the station's operations and provided an additional $54.8 million in each year for modernization of VOA facilities. The figures represented concessions by Radio Marti opponents, especially Zorinsky. They accepted higher amounts in return for Hawkins' agreement to put the station under the VOA.

The bill also required Radio Marti to use VOA facilities at Marathon, Fla., and the 1180 AM frequency that the VOA had used for 20 years for broadcasts to Cuba. It permitted Radio Marti to use other non-commercial frequencies now used by the VOA.

Proponents of putting Radio Marti under the VOA had argued that Cuba would not jam the station's broadcasts if they met the VOA's standards of objectivity.

Hawkins acknowledged that Radio Marti broadcasts under the VOA banner might be more widely accepted in Cuba than broadcasts by an independent organization. Building on the reputation of VOA programs would "decrease dramatically the problems that would have faced Radio Marti if it had to begin building its reputation on its own," she said.

The House passed S 602 Sept. 29, 302-109, completing congressional action. ∎

Foreign Aid Authorizations

Congress failed in 1983 to complete work on regular legislation authorizing foreign aid programs in fiscal years 1984-85. Leaders in both the House and the Senate turned a deaf ear to committee chairmen and failed to bring either chamber's bill (HR 2992 or S 1347) to the floor.

In the end, most foreign aid issues were resolved by the Appropriations committees during action on a fiscal 1984 continuing resolution (H J Res 413 — PL 98-151). *(p. 521)*

House Foreign Affairs Chairman Clement J. Zablocki, D-Wis, pointed out three obstacles to the foreign aid bill. He said the House bill contained controversial provisions the administration opposed; the administration never pressured for floor action on the aid bills; and leaders of both parties showed no enthusiasm for devoting days of floor time to the politically difficult issues posed by foreign aid.

Congress had not failed to pass a regular aid authorization bill since 1973, when controversy over the Vietnam war blocked passage of an authorization for military aid programs.

Committee Action

The House Foreign Affairs and Senate Foreign Relations committees approved their aid authorization bills in

May following months of agonizing debate on El Salvador. Both panels cut Reagan's request for military aid for El Salvador and imposed conditions on what they did approve. *(El Salvador, p. 154)*

The bills authorized supplemental foreign aid funds for fiscal 1983 — $337.7 million in the House's bill and $346 million in the Senate's. They also provided regular authorizations for fiscal 1984 — $7.7 billion in the House bill and $7.2 billion in the Senate bill. In addition, the House bill authorized $8.3 billion for fiscal 1985; in most cases, the 1985 figures were 4.7 percent higher than those for fiscal 1984.

Those figures did not include authorizations for Foreign Military Sales (FMS) guaranteed loans, which were "off-budget" and were not counted as budget authority. The House committee approved $4.3 billion in FMS loans in 1984 and $4.5 billion in fiscal 1985, and the Senate committee approved $4.5 billion in 1984.

Although members of the Senate committee made public vows of adhering to strict spending limits, they also found themselves adding nearly $200 million to Reagan's overall aid request. But the committee managed to claim a cut from the request because the administration informally boosted the request by $215 million to accommodate the committee's increases in aid for Israel.

The House committee reported its aid bill (H Rept 98-192) on May 17. The Senate panel filed its report (S Rept 98-146) May 23.

MILITARY AID

Both bills continued the rapid expansion of U.S. military aid programs under Reagan. In fiscal 1982, the total authorization for the four major military aid programs was $4.1 billion; for fiscal 1984, both committees approved $6.3 billion, an increase of more than 50 percent. Reagan had wanted even more — $6.45 billion.

The four major military aid programs were FMS guaranteed loans (which carried market interest rates and had to be repaid), FMS forgiven loans (similar to grants), Military Assistance Program (MAP) grants and International Military Education and Training (IMET) loans and grants.

Economic Support Fund (ESF) loans and grants also were included under the administration's "security assistance" budget but were not used directly for military purposes.

Democrats on the Senate committee raised the issue of Reagan's emphasis on military aid, saying it had come at the expense of economic and development aid. At the suggestion of Paul S. Sarbanes (D-Md.), the Senate committee made a small shift of funds from military and military-related aid into development aid. But even though both committees made several cuts in military aid programs, they provided large enough increases for Israel to produce an overall increase in military aid.

In keeping with past practice, both committees made recommendations in their reports for military aid levels for individual countries. However, the committees "earmarked," or mandated in the text of their bills, specific levels for only a few countries, such as Israel and Egypt.

Both committees increased military aid for Israel by a substantial amount above Reagan's request, and the Senate committee voted a much smaller increase for Egypt. *(Story, p. 132)*

Greece, Turkey

The two committees adhered to the traditional con-

gressional practice of protecting aid for Greece while cutting and imposing conditions on military aid for Turkey.

The actions of the committees had the effect of retaining a traditional aid "balance" under which Greece received $7 in U.S. military aid for every $10 that Turkey received. The Reagan administration refused to acknowledge the ratio, which Congress had imposed each year since 1980.

Reagan in February had irritated pro-Greek members of both committees by proposing to increase military aid for Turkey to $755 million from the $465 million he requested for fiscal 1983. The $755 million request included $525 million in FMS loans and $230 million in MAP grants.

Reagan also proposed holding FMS loans to Greece in fiscal 1984 at $280 million — the amount provided annually in fiscal years 1982 and 1983. Faced with protests from pro-Greek members and the certainty that Congress would change his requests, Reagan in March proposed giving Greece "up to" $500 million, if Greece signed an agreement for continued U.S. access to four military bases on Greek soil.

The House committee cut Reagan's military aid request for Turkey by $40 million, to $715 million, including $485 million in FMS loans and $230 million in MAP grants. The committee approved the full $500 million in FMS loans for Greece.

The Senate committee also approved military aid totals of $715 million for Turkey and $500 million for Greece. But that panel sharply pared the MAP grant portion of Turkey's aid to $110 million, with another $605 million to be provided in FMS loans.

Both committees approved Reagan's request of $175 million in ESF loans and grants for Turkey in fiscal 1984. Greece did not receive ESF aid.

The House panel rejected a $55 million ESF supplemental request for Turkey in fiscal 1983. The Senate committee approved additional ESF aid but did not specify an amount.

The Senate committee on May 5 defeated, 8-9, an administration-backed move to provide $160 million in MAP aid for Turkey. All Republicans except Rudy Boschwitz, Minn., and Larry Pressler, S.D., supported the motion, and all Democrats except Edward Zorinsky, Neb., opposed it.

Both committees also approved $15 million in fiscal 1984 ESF aid for refugees on Cyprus, primarily Greek-Cypriots. Reagan had requested $3 million. For years, Congress had voted substantial amounts of aid for Cypriot refugees, over the opposition of successive administrations.

Turkey invaded Cyprus in 1974 and continued to occupy the northern third of the island.

The House committee on May 10 approved a tough amendment aimed at forcing Turkey to remove its 20,000-plus troops from Cyprus, but retreated a day later and adopted a weaker substitute that essentially restated the U.S. policy favoring the removal of Turkish troops from Cyprus.

The first amendment, sponsored by Gus Yatron, D-Pa., was in three parts: a freeze on military aid to either Greece or Turkey so long as either country had more troops on Cyprus than were permitted under a 1959 treaty between the two countries; an embargo on U.S. aid to either country beginning in fiscal 1987 if it was not adhering to the 1959 treaty; and a prohibition on Turkey's use of U.S.-supplied weapons on Cyprus so long as Turkey had more troops than were permitted by the 1959 treaty, which al-

Committees Move to Assert Policy Role

The foreign aid authorization bills reported in May (HR 2992, S 1347) bore the marks of continued strain between Congress' foreign policy committees and the White House.

In acting on foreign aid legislation, the House Foreign Affairs and Senate Foreign Relations committees took several steps to ensure that the Reagan administration lived up to its agreements with Congress. The committees implied that the administration had abused its powers, especially by providing "emergency" aid to El Salvador without congressional approval.

The process by which the two committees made foreign aid authorizations and the administration carried them out was a delicate one that in many cases relied heavily on the equivalent of gentlemen's agreements. With some exceptions, the committees traditionally had "earmarked," or mandated in the law, only portions of the aid budget; otherwise, the executive branch had flexibility to change foreign aid allocations during the course of each fiscal year. In return, the committees expected to be consulted when money was "reprogrammed," or switched from one country or program to another.

Over objections by both committees, the Reagan administration relied heavily on reprogramming and other emergency powers, especially to give aid to El Salvador without Congress' explicit approval.

Some members suggested that Congress should restrict the president's flexibility to change the aid allocations. While leaders of both committees headed off the most extreme of those suggestions — such as earmarking the entire aid budget — the committees did adopt some restrictions and refused the president's requests for more flexibility.

Over White House opposition, both panels continued the longstanding practice of earmarking portions of the aid budget by requiring that specified amounts be spent on certain programs or given to certain countries.

The Senate committee took earmarking a step further than either panel had done in the past when it earmarked all economic support aid.

In another sign of their unhappiness with the administration, both committees flatly rejected an administration effort to limit the sanctity of congressional earmarks.

In the past, Congress had earmarked substantial amounts of aid for a limited number of countries, especially Israel and Egypt, often at levels higher than the administration wanted. At the same time, Congress usually had cut the overall aid budget, thus putting an especially tight squeeze on programs and countries that were not earmarked for specific amounts.

In 1983, President Reagan asked Congress for permission to reduce all countries and programs — even earmarked ones — by an equal percentage if Congress cut the foreign aid budget. For example, if Congress were to reduce the overall military aid budget by 10 percent, all recipients of U.S. military aid would be cut by that percentage.

The Foreign Affairs Committee rejected that request on May 10 by voice vote, on an amendment sponsored by Larry Smith, D-Fla.

Senate Foreign Relations rejected the proposal with little discussion and without a vote. Chairman Charles H. Percy, R-Ill., said it "would permit cuts in programs that we clearly have no intention of [cutting]."

The Senate committee also voted to give itself the same power to veto reprogrammings that the Appropriations Committee had. For years, the Appropriations panels — but not the two authorizing committees — were considered to have the right to veto reprogrammings. Foreign Relations informally declared in 1981 that it should too, and the panel exercised the power in 1983 by reviewing a proposed $60 million military aid reprogramming for El Salvador.

In S 1347, Foreign Relations moved to firm up its jurisdiction over reprogrammings by stating that the committee should receive reprogramming notifications "to the same degree and with the same conditions" as applied to the Senate Appropriations Committee.

---

lowed 950 Greek and 650 Turkish troops on Cyprus.

Yatron's amendment was approved May 10 on a 14-13 vote, over administration opposition.

A day later, the committee approved, by voice vote, a substitute offered by Lee H. Hamilton, D-Ind., allowing the president to waive the restrictions imposed by the Yatron amendment if he determined that the aid was essential to enable either Greece or Turkey to meet its NATO commitments.

The Hamilton amendment also allowed the president to provide increased aid to Greece or Turkey in fiscal 1984 only if he certified to Congress that the aid was necessary for each country to fulfill its NATO responsibilities and would not upset the military balance in the eastern Mediterranean; that each country was taking steps to achieve a settlement of the situation on Cyprus and was publicly committed to moving its troops from the island; that Turkey was implementing a program "for the prompt return to democratic rule" and for observing internationally recog-

nized human rights; and that there were "mutually acceptable arrangements" for U.S. access to military bases in Greece.

The Senate committee adopted a less sweeping provision on Greece and Turkey that avoided the Cyprus issue. It said aid to those countries would be available "only in accordance" with a statement in the committee report. That statement addressed two issues: the 7-10 aid ratio and the status of the negotiations concerning the bases in Greece.

The Senate committee said "the current military balance between Greece and Turkey should be retained" through the 7-10 ratio and "similar steps should be taken to maintain the qualitative military balance between the two countries."

On the bases issue, Foreign Relations said it was approving aid "on the expectation" that both Greece and Turkey would give the United States access to military bases.

Administration officials expressed mild dissatisfaction with the Senate committee actions, saying they preferred not to have any official reference to the 7-10 ratio and wanted a more direct tie between a base agreement and increased aid for Greece.

Latin America

In addition to the strings it attached to aid for El Salvador, the House committee imposed conditions on aid to or U.S. military involvement in six other countries in Latin America: Guatemala, Honduras, Argentina, Chile, Paraguay and Uruguay. However, the committee watered down several restrictions that had been proposed by its Western Hemisphere Affairs Subcommittee.

The Senate committee changed the request for Honduras but did not impose conditions on aid for any of the countries.

Guatemala. The House panel voted a ban on U.S. military aid to Guatemala in fiscal 1984-85, except for $10 million a year to help the Guatemalan military build schools, roads, markets, mobile medical facilities and other civilian projects.

Reagan had requested $10 million annually in FMS loans to help Guatemala buy military equipment. The Senate committee approved the $10 million without comment.

U.S. military aid to Guatemala had been suspended since 1977 because of human rights abuses by the government.

Honduras. The House committee approved Reagan's requests for military aid to Honduras — $37 million in fiscal 1983 and $41 million in 1984 — but expressed concern about the "large number" of U.S. military personnel there. At the time the committee acted, the United States had about 60 military advisers in Honduras; in early June, the Pentagon sent another 120 advisers to Honduras to train troops from El Salvador.

The panel said it wanted to be notified 30 days before new advisers or trainers were stationed in Honduras.

In approving Reagan's full aid requests, the committee overturned a recommendation by its Western Hemisphere Affairs Subcommittee that Honduras be limited to $21 million in military aid annually.

The Senate committee cut the fiscal 1984 request for Honduras, approving only $24.5 million of the $40 million request.

Argentina, Chile. The House committee voted to prohibit military aid to either Argentina or Chile unless an elected civilian government was in power. The military governments of both countries were prohibited from receiving U.S. military aid unless they met several conditions, including compliance with internationally recognized human rights principles. *(1981 Almanac p. 162)*

The committee said its new provision was directed specifically at Argentina, which had scheduled elections for October 1983. The elections were held, and on Dec. 10 Reagan certified to Congress that Argentina qualified for military aid and arms sales.

The committee said it also wanted to encourage the government of Chile to hold elections.

Paraguay, Uruguay. The House committee also established conditions on U.S. military training aid to two South American military dictatorships, Paraguay and Uruguay. Reagan had requested $50,000 in fiscal 1984 training aid for Paraguay and $60,000 for Uruguay.

Paraguay could not receive the aid unless the president certified to Congress that a civilian government was in power following free elections, that the current state of siege had been lifted, political parties were permitted, freedom of the press was observed, and political exiles were allowed to return.

The restrictions on aid to Uruguay were the same, except that they applied only to fiscal 1985 and there was no requirement for the lifting of a state of siege or the return of political exiles. Douglas K. Bereuter, R-Neb., tried unsuccessfully to get the committee to drop the restrictions, saying Uruguay was about to return to democratic government.

Other Military Aid Issues

Zaire. The House committee voted sharp cuts in military aid to Zaire, where the authoritarian government of President Mobuto Sese Seko had been accused of corruption and misuse of U.S. aid.

Reagan requested $10 million in MAP grants and $2 million in FMS loans for Zaire in fiscal 1983 and $10 million in MAP grants in fiscal 1984. The House committee approved $4 million for each year, with 1983 aid to be split between grants and loans and all fiscal 1984 amounts to be grants.

The Senate committee approved $2 million in MAP grants and $5 million in FMS loans for fiscal 1984.

Morocco. The House committee also pared military aid for Morocco in both fiscal 1983 and 1984.

Reagan had requested $100 million for Morocco in fiscal 1983: $75 million in FMS loans and $25 million in MAP grants. The committee approved only $50 million, to be split between the two forms of aid.

For fiscal 1984, Reagan requested $60 million in FMS loans and $30 million in MAP grants. The committee approved $33 million in FMS loans and $17 million in MAP grants.

The Senate committee approved $90 million for Morocco in fiscal 1984, but shifted $5 million from MAP grants to FMS loans.

The House committee repeated its calls of previous years for a negotiated solution to the conflict in the Western Sahara, where Morocco was battling a guerrilla force backed by Algeria and the Soviet Union.

Tunisia. The House panel limited military aid to Tunisia to $95 million in fiscal 1983, including $81 million in FMS loans and $14 million in MAP grants. Reagan had requested $135 million. The committee made a smaller cut for fiscal 1984, approving $115 million (including $43 million in MAP grants) of the $140 million request (which included $50 million in MAP grants).

The Senate committee approved the $140 million total, but with $25 million as MAP grants and $115 million as FMS loans.

Pakistan. The House committee approved the full fiscal 1984 installment of aid for Pakistan: $300 million in FMS loans and $225 million in ESF aid. The Senate committee cut FMS loans to $280 million and ESF aid to $175 million. Fiscal 1984 was the second year of a six-year program of aid for Pakistan approved by Congress in 1981. *(1981 Almanac p. 172)*

Anti-Terrorism. Both committees approved a new program for helping foreign governments combat terrorism, but they imposed restrictions on how the money could be used.

Reagan wanted the money to provide training and equipment to deter bombings, assassinations, hijackings and other terrorist activities. Some liberals in Congress had

expressed concern that repressive governments could use the aid to crack down on political dissidents rather than real terrorists.

The committees voted: to require the president to give them 30 days' advance notice of how the aid would be spent; to prohibit involvement in the program by U.S. intelligence agencies; to require that all training be conducted in the United States; and to limit the program to three fiscal years.

The House committee approved the full $5 million request for the program in fiscal 1984, with another $2.5 million to be transferred from other accounts in fiscal 1983. The Senate committee approved $4 million for fiscal 1984 and the 1983 fund transfer.

Pentagon Repayment. Both committees rejected Reagan's request for $50 million in fiscal 1984 to reimburse the Pentagon for the cost of providing emergency military aid to El Salvador in January 1982.

Reagan provided the aid under section 506(a) of the foreign aid laws, which allowed the president to provide arms, equipment or training from the Defense Department in an emergency.

Guaranty Reserve. Both committees moved to bolster the Guaranty Reserve Fund, which was used to protect the FMS loan program against defaults and reschedulings of debt payments by recipient nations.

The fund was established in 1980, when Congress stopped making annual appropriations to guarantee FMS loans. By law, the fund was supposed to have at least $750 million. There were estimates that the fund would fall below that amount some time in fiscal 1985 because Liberia, Peru, Turkey and other countries had fallen behind on their payments.

To replenish the fund, the House committee added $313 million to its military aid accounts in fiscal 1985, and the Senate committee authorized "up to" $100 million each year beginning in fiscal 1985.

Percy had proposed putting the entire FMS loan program "on budget," thus forcing Congress to authorize and appropriate the full amount of the program. But he dropped that proposal when the administration promised to study the issue.

Glenn Amendment. At the insistence of John Glenn, D-Ohio, the Senate committee included an amendment restricting the administration's ability to add "sensitive technology" items to a foreign arms sale after Congress has approved the original sale. Under the amendment, if the administration wanted to add such items to a sale, Congress must be given an opportunity to veto them.

Glenn pressed his amendment because he became angry late in 1982 when the Reagan administration agreed to include advanced radar gear on F-16 jets that were sold to Pakistan. Congress had approved the sale of F-16s in 1981, but at that time was not told of any plans to include the advanced radar equipment.

Buy American. The Senate committee included a requirement that military aid be used only to buy equipment made in the United States unless the president told Congress that it was in the U.S. "national interest" to make purchases elsewhere.

Military Personnel. Both committees agreed to expand the list of countries where the Pentagon could station more than six military personnel to manage U.S. foreign aid and arms sales programs. The personnel under that limit were administrators; they were not trainers or advisers, such as the 55 trainers in El Salvador.

More than six personnel already were allowed in each of 12 countries. Both committees agreed to add Pakistan, North Yemen, Tunisia, El Salvador, Honduras and Venezuela to that list; the Senate committee also added Liberia, the Sudan and Zaire.

ECONOMIC AID

The Senate committee on May 5 took a small step toward reversing the priorities of the Reagan administration, which had emphasized military over economic aid.

By a 10-7 vote, the committee approved an amendment by Sarbanes to shift $76 million from the MAP and ESF accounts into several economic development aid programs. But the committee later had second thoughts about cutting the ESF aid, so it restored most of the money it had cut.

Although he proposed shifting only 1 percent of the aid budget, Sarbanes said it was "important for the committee to establish the proposition that we ought to be moving in this direction" — toward development aid and away from military aid.

The development aid programs that he proposed to increase were "all winners, all successes," Sarbanes said. He openly admitted that one of his goals was to boost U.S. funding for the United Nations Development Program, partly to ensure that former Rep. F. Bradford Morse, R-Mass. (1961-72), was re-elected as director of the program.

The committee found itself in a quandary on the Sarbanes amendment. Although several members seemed to favor the idea, they realized that any cuts would have a greater impact on small recipients — such as countries in Africa — than on Israel, Egypt and other countries whose allocations were politically untouchable.

But the committee approved the Sarbanes amendment, with the eight Democrats and Republicans Mathias and Pressler casting the "yes" votes.

The panel later restored $30 million for ESF aid to African countries, at the urging of Africa Subcommittee Chairman Nancy Landon Kassebaum, R-Kan.

Earmarks. In a departure from past practice, the Senate committee earmarked the entire ESF account; in some cases it set aside minimum amounts for specific countries, and in other cases for entire regions. In previous years, the committee earmarked amounts for only a few countries.

The committee's ESF earmarks were: Israel, $910 million; Egypt, $750 million; Pakistan, $175 million; Tunisia, $5 million; Morocco, $7 million; Middle East and South Asia region, $50 million; East Asia region, $55 million; Portugal, $40 million; Cyprus, $15 million; Europe region, $187 million; Costa Rica, $70 million; Latin America region, $290 million; and Africa region, $392 million.

House committee earmarks were: Israel, $850 million; Egypt, $750 million; Peru, $50 million; Bolivia, $20 million; Ecuador, $20 million; Panama, $10 million; and southern African countries and regional programs, $225 million.

Zimbabwe. Both committees approved Reagan's request for $75 million in ESF aid to Zimbabwe, despite concerns expressed by Republicans about reports in March and April that government security forces had slaughtered hundreds of civilians in a campaign against "dissidents."

Emergency Fund. Both committees approved $75 million annually for an ESF fund the president could use when the U.S. national interests "urgently require economic support to promote economic or political stability" in foreign nations.

DEVELOPMENT AID

Both committees voted substantial increases over Reagan's requests for population and health programs administered by the U.S. Agency for International Development (AID).

Reagan requested $212.3 million for population programs in fiscal 1984; the House committee voted $275 million, on an amendment by Peter H. Kostmayer, D-Pa., and the Senate committee voted $232 million.

For AID health programs, Reagan had requested $100.7 million; both committees approved $133.4 million.

The House committee also voted a special boost of development aid annually in fiscal 1984 and 1985 of $56.3 million for Latin American countries and $32 million for African countries. The committee took that money out of military aid programs.

Both committees approved the administration's request for authority to establish a revolving fund that would finance AID's programs to encourage investments in developing countries by private businesses. The administration requested a $20 million authorization for the fund in each of the 1984-86 fiscal years. The fund would be limited to $100 million, including reimbursements from loans.

In approving the fund, both committees demanded detailed reports on how the money was being used.

The House committee on April 27 defeated, by a 7-19 vote, a move by several Democrats to kill the revolving fund. The committee also rejected, 9-17, an amendment to limit the fund to $60 million.

OTHER PROVISIONS

China. Both committees dropped an administration-requested provision removing China from the list of communist countries banned from getting U.S. development assistance. Instead, they voted to allow the president to remove any country from the proscribed list if he determined and reported to Congress that such action "is important to the security of the United States."

The committees had taken similar action in 1982, when Reagan first asked that China be made eligible for aid. *(1982 Almanac p. 160)*

The Senate committee rejected 1-10 an amendment by Jesse Helms, R-N.C., that would have allowed the president to remove China from the list of proscribed nations only if he certified to Congress that the Chinese government was making a number of reforms, including improved respect for human rights and adoption of democratic principles. Those restrictions were similar to those that had been imposed on U.S. aid to El Salvador.

Peace Corps. Reagan requested $108.5 million for operations of the Peace Corps in fiscal 1984, $3.5 million more than had been authorized in fiscal years 1982 and 1983.

The House committee approved $118.5 million for 1984 and $124 million for 1985, and the Senate committee approved $113.5 million for 1984.

On an amendment by Jim Leach, R-Iowa, the House committee decided to establish a goal of 10,000 Peace Corps volunteers by the end of fiscal 1986 and require the president to report to Congress on his plans for meeting that goal. The Peace Corps had about 5,000 volunteers, down from a high of about 15,000 in the mid-1960s. Leach's amendment was opposed by the administration.

Narcotics. Both committees adopted provisions requiring the president to suspend assistance to any country that failed to take "adequate steps" to stop traffic to the United States of narcotics and other controlled drugs that were produced, processed or transferred within its borders. The provisions were modified from a proposal by several members that would have forced an automatic cutoff of U.S. aid to Pakistan, Thailand and other countries that were major sources of opium and cocaine.

Similar provisions eventually were included in the fiscal 1984-85 State Department authorization bill (HR 2915 — PL 98-164). *(State Department bill, below)* ∎

State Department Bill

Normally routine legislation making authorizations for the State Department and related agencies was the focus for extended debates in 1982 on broad foreign policy issues.

Congress usually handled such issues in its annual authorizations for foreign aid programs. But the foreign aid legislation for fiscal years 1984-85 died in both chambers.

Members of Congress, especially in the Senate, turned to the State Department bill (HR 2915 — PL 98-164) for a foreign policy vehicle. The Senate adopted 65 amendments to its version of the bill (S 1342), many of which were later deleted by House-Senate conferees. *(Foreign aid, above)*

U.S. participation in the United Nations, diplomatic relations with the Vatican, the War Powers Resolution and Rep. Dante B. Fascell's, D-Fla., chairmanship of the Commission on Security and Cooperation in Europe were among the issues that tied up consideration of the bill.

The House passed HR 2915 by voice vote on June 9. The Senate debated S 1342 on Sept. 22-23; Oct. 5, 19-20. The bill was passed, by voice vote, on Oct. 20.

The legislation cleared Congress Nov. 18, and Reagan signed it into law (PL 98-164) on Nov. 22.

The bill authorized $3.2 billion in fiscal 1984 and $3.5 billion in fiscal 1985 for the State Department, the United States Information Agency (USIA), the Board for International Broadcasting and other programs. *(Chart, p. 146)*

Committee Reports

The House Foreign Affairs Committee filed its report (H Rept 98-130) on HR 2915 May 16, and the Senate Foreign Relations Committee filed its report (S Rept 98-143) on S 1342 May 23.

In drafting their respective bills (HR 2915, S 1342), the House Foreign Affairs and Senate Foreign Relations committees devoted much of their attention to President Reagan's proposal for a "Project Democracy" to promote democratic values around the world.

Rather than put such a program under government auspices, as Reagan had proposed, the committees voted to finance it through four private foundations run by the Democratic and Republican parties, the AFL-CIO and the U.S. Chamber of Commerce. That approach had been recommended in April by a private commission, called the Democracy Program, composed of representatives of those organizations. *(Project Democracy, box, p. 148)*

The House bill made a supplemental authorization of $41.8 million for fiscal 1983, and total authorizations of $3.3 billion in fiscal 1984 and $3.6 billion in fiscal 1985. The Senate bill included a fiscal 1983 supplemental of $13.3 million and total authorizations of $3.2 billion each in fiscal years 1984 and 1985.

State Department Authorization, Fiscal 1984-85

HR 2915 (PL 98-164) made the following authorizations in fiscal years
1984-85 for the State Department and related agencies:

(in thousands of dollars)

Agency	Fiscal 1984 Request	Fiscal 1984 Authorization	Fiscal 1985 Request	Fiscal 1985 Authorization
State Department	$1,479,713	$1,490,213	$1,580,820	$1,580,820
International Organizations	602,343	602,843	645,978	602,343
International Commissions	23,207	23,207	27,503	25,355
Bilateral science/technology agreements	1,700	1,700	1,700	1,700
Asia Foundation	(10,000)[1]	10,000	(10,000)[1]	10,000
Migration/refugee assistance	344,500	344,500	326,400	326,400
United States Information Agency	711,427	648,848	871,039	808,739
Board for International Broadcasting	115,702	106,055	121,268	111,251
Inter-American Foundation	10,705	16,000	[2]	16,000
TOTAL	**$3,289,297**	**$3,243,366**	**$3,574,708**	**$3,482,608**

[1] *For each fiscal year, the administration request for the Asia Foundation was included within the request for the United States Information Agency.*

[2] *For fiscal 1985, the administration requested "such sums as may be necessary" for the Inter-American Foundation.*

State Department

The two committees made only minor changes in Reagan's requests for $2.45 billion in fiscal 1984 and $2.58 billion in fiscal 1985 for operation of the State Department, mandatory donations to United Nations and other international organizations, and U.S. contributions to international refugee programs.

The House committee expressed concern about the impact on the State Department of previous budget cuts, noting that the department lost 1,157 positions between 1967 and 1980 while most other Cabinet agencies were gaining thousands of employees.

USIA

Reagan requested $711.4 million for USIA in fiscal 1984 and $871 million in fiscal 1985, including $65 million each year for Project Democracy. Congress had authorized $559 million for USIA in fiscal 1983 under PL 97-241, and Reagan requested another $20 million for Project Democracy.

The House committee approved a $20 million supplemental, but earmarked $10 million for expansion of cultural and educational exchange programs administered by USIA and $5 million for the Asia Foundation. The Senate committee rejected the $20 million request.

The House committee approved $701.4 million for USIA in fiscal 1984 and $861 million in fiscal 1985. The Senate committee made much sharper reductions, approving $636 million for each year. The committee made the reduction on a 10-5 vote, after rejecting, 7-8, a motion by Nancy Landon Kassebaum, R-Kan., to chop the fiscal 1984 USIA budget to $572 million.

Both committees included in their reports blistering attacks on the USIA operations during the first two years of the Reagan administration.

The House panel said USIA had "arguably violated the letter and spirit of its charter" by using its grantmaking

and personnel policies for partisan political purposes. Without giving specifics, the committee accused the agency of "attempting, unsuccessfully, virtually to eliminate" its educational and cultural affairs programs, "which have stood the test of time and proved their worth."

It also charged USIA with "reflecting partisan ideology in its choice of USIA grantees, ... providing funds to friends of USIA officials without regard to the USIA charter, or proper grant guidelines and procedures, ... attempting to influence the activities and comments of USIA grantees so that they reflected executive branch policy positions," and "withholding or delaying the granting of USIA funds to grantees due to partisan political considerations."

Further, the report charged, USIA was guilty of "placing in career Foreign Service and civil service positions political appointees who reflected partisan political views or who were friends and relations of current government political appointees, without regard to the requirements of specific positions or the effect on the career services." This practice "displaces skilled career employees with people who have little experience in the highly sophisticated war of ideas."

The Senate committee raised similar complaints, saying the USIA "is an agency financially out of control."

That committee specifically complained about the hiring "of friends and relatives of high administration officials without apparent regard for qualifications." This was an apparent reference to the USIA's practice of giving jobs to children of several officials, including Caspar Weinberger Jr., son of Defense Secretary Caspar W. Weinberger, as assistant cultural affairs officer in Bonn; Monica Clark, daughter of national security adviser William P. Clark, to a similar position in Bonn; and Barbara Haig, daughter of former Secretary of State Alexander M. Haig Jr., as assistant to the counselor of USIA.

The House committee said USIA Director Charles Z.

Wick "took immediate steps" to deal with the complaints when they were brought to his attention. On May 4, 1983, Wick sent to the two committees new guidelines for the awarding of grants by the Educational and Cultural Affairs Bureau that prohibited the use of USIA grants and positions for partisan purposes.

The committees also put some bite into their barked complaints, voting to require USIA to notify Congress 15 days before making proposed grants. The House committee said it "intends to scrutinize" USIA grants to prevent their use for "partisan, political" reasons.

The Senate committee also approved a revised charter for USIA's Educational and Cultural Affairs Bureau that, according to the report, would protect "the scholarly integrity, the excellence and the non-political character" of programs such as the Fulbright-Hays scholarships.

House Floor Action

The House debated the bill for only a few hours on June 9, then passed it by voice vote.

In its only major action, the House gutted the proposed National Endowment for Democracy by deleting grants of $5 million each to the institutes established by the Republican and Democratic parties.

The House took two key votes on the endowment. First, by a 194-215 vote, it rejected an amendment by Hank Brown, R-Colo., that would have killed the entire endowment. *(Vote 174, p. 54-H)*

Then, on a 267-136 vote, the House accepted a Brown amendment striking all references in the endowment section of the bill to "the two major political parties." *(Vote 175, p. 54-H)*

Later, by voice vote, the House adopted another Brown amendment actually killing the funds for the two institutes.

The House later rejected an amendment by Dan L. Burton, R-Ind., deleting endowment grants for the AFL-CIO and Chamber of Commerce institutes.

Brown said he supported the idea of promoting democracy abroad but objected to "taking tax money and using it to subsidize the Republican and Democratic parties."

Fascell, prime sponsor of the endowment proposal, said the bill included "sufficient safeguards" to prevent the abuse of the money by the party institutes.

Foreign Affairs Chairman Clement J. Zablocki, D-Wis., said the money would aid "countries that are developing democracies" and told his colleagues that by voting to strike the money, they "will be supporting totalitarian, undemocratic, non-democratic governments." That statement recalled claims by some Republicans that Democrats were aiding communism in Central America by opposing Reagan's policies in the region.

Brown's amendment on the party institutes was adopted with the support of an unusual collection of conservatives and liberals. Fascell later attributed the vote to "an ad hoc coalition that developed on the House floor. That happens sometimes, when people get all worked up."

Senate Action

After debating topics ranging from relations with the Soviet Union to Interior Secretary James G. Watt, the Senate Oct. 20 passed S 1342, the State Department authorization bill.

Because a foreign aid authorization bill was considered dead, the Senate added numerous amendments on a wide range of foreign policy topics. In the past, State Department authorization bills had sailed through the Senate with little debate.

The Senate worked on the bill for five days: Sept. 22-23; Oct. 5, 19-20.

United Nations

The first indication that the bill would become bogged down in foreign policy issues debate came with action on an amendment slashing funding for the United Nations.

The Senate adopted the amendment on Sept. 22, by a 66-23 vote. The measure cut about $500 million from the U.S. contributions to the United Nations and related agencies over the next four years. *(Vote 256, 42-S)*

The amendment limited total U.S. mandatory contributions to U.N. agencies in 1984 to the total of 1980 calendar year contributions to the organizations. Contributions for calendar years 1985-87 were limited to 90 percent, 80 percent and 70 percent, respectively.

Mandatory contributions were ones that the United States was obligated to make under various treaties. The freeze did not apply to "voluntary" contributions to U.N. agencies; those contributions were considered to be foreign aid.

The sponsor, Nancy Landon Kassebaum, R-Kan., insisted the amendment was not intended to signal a withdrawal from the United Nations. "I have been, and remain, a firm believer in the value of the United Nations as a forum for international communication," she said. "I believe, however, that this communication can take place at a significantly lower cost."

She offered her amendment shortly after Charles M. Lichenstein, U.S. alternate delegate to the United Nations, suggested that the organization could leave the United States.

U.N. critics, spurred by Lichenstein's suggestion, were quick to embrace Kassebaum's proposal. Steven D. Symms, R-Idaho, said, "it would send a message that could perhaps show that the United States is going to exert itself and that we are not going to be the doormat for every Third World country and every communist country that wants to come in here and scuff our floor."

War Powers

The Senate addressed a constitutional question relating to the War Powers Resolution (PL 93-148).

In the wake of the Supreme Court's June 23 decision declaring the legislative veto unconstitutional, questions had been raised regarding the constitutionality of the War Powers act, which allowed Congress, by passing a concurrent resolution, to force the withdrawal of U.S. troops engaged in hostilities overseas without specific congressional authorization. *(Court decision, p. 20-A)*

By an 86-11 vote Oct. 20, the Senate approved an amendment offered by Minority Leader Robert C. Byrd, D-W.Va., enabling Congress to force the withdrawal of troops by passing a joint resolution. Such a resolution would require a presidential signature to take effect. Byrd's proposal also called for expedited consideration of a veto message. *(Vote 295, p. 49-S)*

Byrd's amendment was insufficient to satisfy some critics who contended that the War Powers Resolution was unconstitutional. Said Barry Goldwater, R-Ariz.: "Congress does not have the authority to dictate the removal of troops, whether it be by a bill or a joint resolution or a

Program to Promote Democracy Passed . . .

In passing the State Department authorization (HR 2915), Congress granted President Reagan's request for the establishment of a new program to promote democracy overseas. However, the administration request was substantially altered by the House Foreign Affairs and Senate Foreign Relations committees, which opted for private operation of the program, instead of placing it totally under government auspices.

By fall, conferees approved $31.3 million for USIA grants each year to the National Endowment for Democracy, the new agency that was to funnel the money to organizations to carry out the program. The endowment was the result of separate proposals by the administration for a "Project Democracy" and by a bipartisan study group called the "Democracy Program."

Background

In his fiscal 1984 budget, Reagan proposed creating Project Democracy as part of USIA, which ran the Voice of America and such cultural and educational exchange programs as the Fulbright-Hays scholarships.

With a budget of $20 million in fiscal 1983 and $65 million each in fiscal years 1984 and 1985, the project was intended to support a variety of government and private programs that promoted democratic principles and institutions in foreign countries.

USIA submitted to Congress a list of 44 programs that Project Democracy could support, ranging from $1 million for "legislator training" to $13.8 million for a "worldwide initiative to support free labor movements."

The proposal ran into immediate trouble on Capitol Hill. One Republican member of the Senate Foreign Relations Committee privately derided it as a "Buy Democracy" equivalent to the "Buy America" campaigns of U.S. labor unions. Some members expressed concern that the administration might use the money to fund conservative political causes. Members of the House Foreign Affairs Committee also warned Secretary of State George P. Shultz of the difficulty of promoting democracy in the Philippines, South Korea, Taiwan and other countries with authoritarian regimes that were friendly to the United States.

While that debate was under way in Congress, a committee called the Democracy Program was finishing its report on how the United States could promote democracy overseas. In a report issued April 18, the committee said that goal could best be served by U.S. government financing of a private National Endowment for Democracy. The endowment in turn would make grants to foundations created by the Republican and Democratic parties, the AFL-CIO and the Chamber of Commerce — all of which had representatives on the Democracy Program board.

The Democracy Program had no trouble getting its message across to the Reagan administration and Congress. Its chairman was William E. Brock III, Reagan's trade representative, and one member was Rep. Dante B. Fascell, D-Fla., chairman of the House Foreign Affairs International Operations Subcommittee, which had jurisdiction over the issue.

On April 25, Fascell's subcommittee included the Democracy Program's recommendations in legislation authorizing funds for the State Department and related agencies in fiscal years 1983-85. Only one subcommittee member, George W. Crockett Jr., D-Mich., objected, saying he was concerned that the endowment would be exempt from U.S. "affirmative action" requirements and that the endowment board would be self-perpetuating.

The Senate Foreign Relations Committee approved the Democracy Program recommendations on April 28, and the House Foreign Affairs Committee followed suit on May 3.

The administration supported creation of the endowment.

In comparison to Reagan's $65 million request for each of fiscal years 1984 and 1985, the committees approved only $31.3 million for the National Endowment for Democracy and $10 million for the Asia Foundation.

The bills mandated minimum funding for the four institutes in each of fiscal years 1984 and 1985: $13.8 million for the AFL-CIO's Free Trade Union Institute, $5 million each for the National Democratic and National Republican Institutes for International Affairs and $2.5 million for the U.S. Chamber of Commerce's National

concurrent resolution."

National Security Directive

Another skirmish erupted over the administration's proposed regulations requiring all former federal employees who had access to national security information to submit their writings for pre-publication review.

The regulations, known as National Security Decision Directive 84, also permitted the government to control contact between officials and the press and to use polygraphs to investigate unauthorized disclosures.

Charles McC. Mathias Jr., R-Md., and Thomas F. Eagleton, D-Mo., said Congress had not had a chance to assess the implications of the directive. "We must have an opportunity to satisfy ourselves that such a drastic step is warranted," Mathias said.

Although the directive was issued in March, details did not become available until Aug. 25. The Governmental Affairs Committee held a hearing on Sept. 13, and "what the Governmental Affairs Committee learned," said Mathias, "was disturbing." He and Eagleton proposed instead to delay implementation until April 15, 1984, to give the panel a chance to hold more hearings.

Goldwater argued that the directive, particularly the section on pre-publication review, was not sinister. Responding to Mathias' claim that 100,000 Defense Department employees would be affected, Goldwater said, "I cannot possibly conceive of 100,000 people working at the Pentagon ever sitting down and writing anything except a check once in a while."

Eagleton called the directive "an imposition which amounts to a flagrant and indefensible violation of the First Amendment." The amendment was adopted, 56-34, on Oct. 20. *(Vote 296, p. 49-S)*

... After Deleting Funds for Two Parties

Chamber Foundation.

The remaining $5 million of the endowment's $31.3 million annual funding was to support operating expenses and grants to other private agencies.

The two party institutes and the Chamber foundation were created specifically to receive grants from the endowment. The AFL-CIO institute was created in 1978.

The committee's provisions were passed intact by both chambers, with the exception of the House's rejection of earmarked funds for the two political party institutes. Conferees accepted the House provision that deleted language earmarking $5 million each for endowment grants to the party institutes. The House deleted those grants, on a 267-136 vote, after several members said the U.S. government should not be subsidizing overseas activities by the political parties. *(Vote 175, p. 54-H)*

Conference Provisions

As drafted by House-Senate conferees, the State Department bill earmarked annual grants of $13.8 million to the Free Trade Union Institute, an arm of the AFL-CIO, and $2.5 million to the National Chamber Foundation, an arm of the U.S. Chamber of Commerce. Among the programs under consideration were training seminars and trips to the United States for foreign politicians, labor leaders and businessmen.

Conferees deleted the earmarking of funds for the Republican and Democratic party institutes. Fascell noted that conferees merely deleted the earmarking and did not prevent the endowment from making grants to them. The national chairmen of the two parties sat on the endowment's board of directors, and Fascell said the endowment probably would make grants to the party institutes. But the grants "certainly will not go above" the $5 million that had been earmarked before the House action, he said.

In related provisions, the bill directed that the endowment could make grants only to private groups and could not itself carry out programs, prohibited U.S. government employees from being paid by the endowment, required the endowment to submit an annual report to the president for transmittal to Congress and required

officers of the endowment to testify before congressional committees when asked.

Conferees dropped a Senate provision, sponsored by William Proxmire, D-Wis., that would have prohibited the endowment from employing anyone who had been engaged in intelligence activities since 1963. Proxmire had said such a prohibition was needed to ensure that the endowment would not be used as a "cover" for intelligence agents to work abroad.

In exchange for Proxmire's agreement to drop the amendment, CIA Director William J. Casey wrote the senator promising that no intelligence agents would be assigned to the endowment unless Proxmire had approved.

The bill also listed list six broad purposes for the endowment and the institutes:

● Encouraging "free and democratic institutions throughout the world through private sector initiatives, including activities which promote the individual rights and freedoms, including internationally recognized human rights and fundamental freedoms, which are essential to the functioning of democratic institutions";

● Promoting exchanges between U.S. private groups and democratic groups overseas;

● Promoting U.S. non-governmental participation in democratic training programs and "democratic institution-building abroad";

● Strengthening democratic electoral processes abroad "through timely measures in cooperation with indigenous democratic forces";

● Supporting the participation of the Republican and Democratic parties, labor, business and other private groups "in fostering cooperation with those abroad dedicated to the cultural values, institutions and organizations of democratic pluralism"; and

● Encouraging "the establishment and growth of democratic development in a manner consistent both with the broad concerns of United States national interest and with the specific requirements of the democratic groups in other countries which are aided by programs funded by the endowment."

The bill did not define specific activities for the institutes.

Endowment for Democracy

The Senate was more receptive than the House to the proposed National Endowment for Democracy.

The Senate rejected two attempts on Sept. 22 to cut funding for the institute. One, offered by Jesse Helms, R-N.C., would have transferred the $31.3 million for the endowment, as well as $21.6 million the Foreign Relations Committee added to the president's request for Fulbright exchanges, to the Voice of America, to enhance radio transmitters. The Senate rejected Helms' amendment, 26-68. *(Vote 254, p. 42-S)*

Later that day, the Senate rejected, by a 42-49 vote, an attempt by Edward Zorinsky, D-Neb., to eliminate all funding for the endowment. *(Vote 255, p. 42-S)*

The Senate did, however, adopt an amendment by William Proxmire, D-Wis., barring from employment with the endowment anyone who engaged in intelligence activi-

ties since 1963. Proxmire said he wanted to remove any hint that the endowment would be a front for the CIA.

Foreign Aid

Because it was unclear whether the regular foreign aid authorization (S 1347) would be enacted for fiscal 1984, the Senate added several provisions to HR 2915 dealing with foreign aid issues.

On Oct. 20, the Senate approved an amendment offered by Foreign Relations Chairman Charles H. Percy, R-Ill., requiring that fiscal 1984 foreign assistance programs, except for aid to Israel and Egypt, be authorized at the same level as those in the first continuing resolution (PL 98-107), unless Congress specifically authorized funds.

Aid to Israel and Egypt was to be authorized at the level in S 1347, which was higher than that in the continuing resolution.

Percy said he offered the amendment "to prevent the current trend toward [enacting] foreign aid by continuing resolution."

The Senate also adopted a Proxmire amendment barring all U.S. military assistance to the Khmer Rouge faction in Kampuchea, which he said had "pursued the most reprehensible persecution and destruction of a cultural group since the Nazi Holocaust."

The Senate also agreed to de-obligate all funds appropriated in fiscal 1983 to Syria and to earmark $25 million in refugee assistance funds to Lebanon and $10 million in refugee assistance funds to El Salvador.

Nuclear Proliferation

One of the lengthiest debates occurred on a proposal by Rudy Boschwitz, R-Minn., expressing the sense of Congress that three recent administration-approved transfers of nuclear materials and technology should be suspended or revoked.

The three were the transfer to India of spare parts for its Tarapur reactor, the retransfer of U.S.-origin heavy water to Argentina, and the request that U.S. firms be allowed to enter into long-range maintenance contracts for South Africa's Koeberg twin nuclear reactors.

Percy proposed weakening the amendment by adding language permitting transfers "in exceptional cases, when such equipment, material or technology is necessary to protect the health and safety of operations in existing civilian nuclear facilities under international safeguards."

Boschwitz argued that Percy's language would gut the original amendment, and the Senate agreed Oct. 20, rejecting Percy's amendment by a 28-59 vote. The Senate then adopted Boschwitz's amendment by a 70-16 vote. *(Votes 299, 300, p. 49-S)*

Watt Resignation

Although it was never debated, Watt's future as secretary of the interior hung over the Senate's consideration of the State Department bill for weeks. The Senate began debating the bill the day after Watt provoked ire by characterizing his appointees to a coal leasing commission as "a black . . . a woman, two Jews and a cripple."

On Sept. 23, Minority Leader Byrd, calling those and other Watt remarks "totally unbefitting a senior cabinet member of the United States government," offered an amendment declaring the sense of the Senate that the president should ask Watt to resign.

Majority Leader Howard H. Baker Jr., R-Tenn., pulled the measure, partly because the Senate was scheduled to debate the issue of U.S. Marines in Lebanon and the renewal of funds about to expire at the end of the fiscal year. But Byrd reintroduced his amendment Oct. 5 after a Republican caucus indicated that it might pass.

Baker pulled the bill again, promising the Senate would consider it after its October recess. But on Oct. 9, Watt spared the Senate a vote by resigning.

Other Amendments

Soviet-U.S. relations came into play on several amendments. On Oct. 20, Malcolm Wallop, R-Wyo., offered a proposal authorizing the president to deny to the Soviet Union the ownership or possession or use of its Mount Alto embassy site in Washington, D.C.

Wallop noted that the embassy site was on the highest point in the city. "If the Soviets occupy the new embassy site," Wallop said, "their electronic equipment will be in

direct line of sight to every transmitter and relay station in this metropolitan area."

But Baker replied that "the White House and the State Department feel that the adoption of this amendment would cause us grievous damage in our relations with the Soviet Union." The Senate tabled Wallop's amendment by a 46-42 vote. *(Vote 297, p. 49-S)*

In addition, the Senate Oct. 19 approved an amendment by Richard G. Lugar, R-Ind., establishing a Soviet-East European Advisory Board within the State Department. "The gaps in our knowledge of the Soviet Union are enormous," Lugar said.

Earlier, the Senate took a harder anti-Soviet line. On Sept. 22, it adopted by voice vote an amendment by Walter D. Huddleston, D-Ky., declaring the sense of Congress that there should be "substantial equivalence" between the number of Soviet diplomats in the United States and the number of U.S. diplomats in the Soviet Union.

In addition, the Senate, by a 93-0 vote, agreed Sept. 22 to an amendment by James A. McClure, R-Idaho, providing that the president submit to Congress a report on Soviet compliance or non-compliance with existing arms control agreements. *(Vote 253, p. 42-S)*

Conference Report

After an extended series of meetings, House-Senate conferees filed their report on HR 2915 (H Rept 98-563) on Nov. 17.

United Nations

One of the thorniest issues was the Kassebaum amendment which limited U.S. contributions to the United Nations and related agencies.

The House had no comparable provision, and House conferees vigorously opposed any major cutback in contributions to the United Nations. Several Senate conferees had for years fought similar efforts to reduce U.N. funding and were clearly uncomfortable in defending their chamber's position.

A compromise was offered by Sen. Lugar, who said that a failure by conferees to reduce U.N. funds would jeopardize the bill's chances of passage in the Senate.

His compromise, adopted by the conference on Nov. 3, froze total U.S. contributions for 1984 at the 1983 level. It placed no similar restriction on 1985 contributions.

The conference agreement came under immediate attack from some conservatives, who said it abandoned the approach of the Senate amendment. Sen. Helms, for one, claimed that Kassebaum's amendment would have saved $533 million over fiscal years 1984-87, but Lugar's substitute would save only $65 million.

Conferees adopted another Senate amendment calling for a thorough review of U.S. participation in the United Nations.

Among the items to be included in the review were U.S. financial contributions, how the United Nations helped fulfill U.S. policy objectives, and the benefits derived by the United States from its participation in the United Nations. The president was asked, but not required, to report his recommendations on those matters to Congress by June 30, 1984.

In other U.N.-related matters, the legislation:

● Prohibited U.S. assessed contributions that would provide any benefits to the Palestine Liberation Organization or the South-West Africa People's Organization. The secre-

tary of state was directed to conduct an annual study to determine whether any U.S. contributions were being used to benefit those organizations.

● Required the secretary of state to report to Congress by Jan. 31 of each year on the foreign policies of each nation belonging to international organizations of which the United States was a member. Among the subjects to be included in the report were the votes of each nation on issues of concern to the United States.

● Required the United States to suspend participation in the United Nations or any U.N. agency that had expelled Israel or in any way had denied Israel its right to participate. The provision reflected longstanding administration and congressional policy.

Narcotics Control

The bill included a sweeping new provision designed to encourage Pakistan, Thailand and other countries to crack down on the production and export of illicit narcotics, especially opium and cocaine. While not naming any of those countries, the provision threatened suspension of U.S. aid to any nation that failed to take adequate steps on the issue.

Pakistan was the world's second-largest producer of opium (after Iran) and also received one of the biggest doses of U.S. aid: $586 million in military, economic and development aid in fiscal 1984. Thailand also was a major producer of opium and was scheduled to receive $140 million in U.S. aid in fiscal 1984.

The two major producers of cocaine, Colombia and Bolivia, were scheduled to receive $22 million and $30 million in U.S. aid, respectively.

Iran, Burma and other major narcotics-producing countries received little or no U.S. aid.

While acting on the State Department bill, the Senate Oct. 19 adopted, 96-0, an amendment by Paula Hawkins, R-Fla., suspending aid to countries that failed to meet projected reductions in narcotics production. The House bill had no similar provision. *(Vote 294, p. 48-S)*

A compromise worked out by conferees on the State Department bill resembled the Senate provision in most respects. Its major provisions were:

● A requirement that the president submit an annual report to Congress on narcotics production and trafficking in each country that was a major source of narcotics in the United States. The report was to describe each country's plans for eliminating narcotics production, the "maximum achievable reductions" that could be expected for the following fiscal year and the actual reductions that had been made in the previous fiscal year.

● A requirement that the president suspend U.S. direct aid to any narcotics-producing country that had failed to take adequate steps to prevent narcotics from entering the United States. U.S. representatives to international financial institutions, such as the World Bank, also were to vote against loans for such countries.

● A requirement that, once suspended, aid could not be resumed until the president reported to Congress that the affected country had submitted a plan to curtail narcotics production and exports, and had taken legal measures to enforce that plan.

Conferees gave the administration permission to brush aside the narcotics control provision in 1984, noting that it might not be possible to gather all the information to enforce the provision in time for the January 1984 budget submissions to Congress covering fiscal 1985. But they said

they expected full compliance for all future budget requests.

Helsinki Commission

Unable to reach agreement, conferees dropped a Senate provision that would have established a rotating chairmanship between House and Senate members of the Commission on Security and Cooperation in Europe, the so-called Helsinki commission.

Sen. Robert Dole, R-Kan., the commission's vice chairman, had wanted Rep. Fascell, the commission chairman, to agree to a rotating chairmanship, starting in 1984. Fascell had chaired the commission since its founding in 1976 to monitor the Helsinki agreement on human rights issues.

Fascell offered to step aside when his term expired in 1985, but the two men could not agree. In an attempt to force Fascell to give up his post, Dole had offered an amendment in the Senate providing that the commission chairmanship would go to a House member in odd-numbered years and to a Senator in even-numbered years. The Senate adopted the amendment by voice vote on Oct. 20.

When the issue threatened to block a conference agreement on the State Department bill, Dole withdrew his amendment. In its place, the Senate established its own Special Committee on Security and Cooperation in Europe, to begin operations in January, 1984. The Senate created the committee by passing S Res 286 on Nov. 18 by voice vote.

Other Provisions

Other issues addressed in the bill included:

War Powers. Because of the adamant opposition of House Foreign Affairs Committee Chairman Clement J. Zablocki, D-Wis., conferees dropped a Senate amendment that was intended to bolster the constitutionality of the War Powers Resolution.

However, the bill did contain a new provision limiting Senate debate to 20 hours on any bill or joint resolution to force the withdrawal of U.S. forces from overseas combat.

Acid Rain. Conferees retained a Senate provision stating the sense of Congress that the president should take several steps to deal with the problem of "acid rain." Environmentalists charged that acid rain resulted from industrial air pollution and damaged lakes and streams in the Northeast United States and Canada.

Among other things, the president was asked to: "respond constructively" to a Canadian offer to reduce its emissions of sulfur dioxide into the air by 50 percent before 1990 if the United States did the same; negotiate "as expeditiously as possible" an agreement with Canada for significant reductions in transboundary air pollution while keeping economic dislocations in both countries to a minimum; consider initiation of programs to develop new technologies for reduction of air pollution; and instruct the secretary of state to report to Congress by Dec. 1, 1983, on progress toward achieving an acid rain reduction agreement with Canada.

Danger Pay. Both the Senate and House bills had included provisions allowing the State Department to give special pay supplements to diplomats in areas of potential danger even if members of their families were stationed with them. Previously, the State Department had refused to give danger pay to diplomats who were accompanied by their families to such strife-torn areas as El Salvador and Lebanon.

Reprogramming. The bill put into law informal ar-

rangements under which the State Department and the USIA notified Congress before reprogramming, or transferring, money from one account to another. Under the bill, the agencies were required to notify the Foreign Affairs and Foreign Relations committees 15 days before spending any money that had been reprogrammed.

U.S. Embassies. The bill required that American firms be awarded contracts to build U.S. embassies and other State Department facilities valued at $5 million or more. The secretary of state could waive the requirement on a case-by-base basis in the interest of U.S. relations with a host country.

Vatican. Conferees retained a Senate amendment, sponsored by Lugar, repealing an 1867 law that had prohibited the establishment of a U.S. diplomatic mission at the Vatican. There had been recent calls in both chambers for the establishment of diplomatic ties between the United States and the Vatican. In January 1984, Reagan formally established diplomatic relations with the Vatican and named William A. Wilson as ambassador to the Vatican. Wilson was serving as a personal representative of the president. *(Story, p. 168)*

Pre-publication Review. Conferees retained a Senate amendment that delayed until April 15, 1984, the implementation of new rules requiring all former U.S. government employees to submit any writings to the government for review prior to publication. The amendment's sponsor, Sen. Mathias, had wanted the delay to encourage the administration to drop or modify the proposed new rules.

Salvadoran Immigrants. The bill expressed the sense of Congress that several hundred thousand citizens of El Salvador who arrived in the United States before Jan. 1, 1983, should be granted "extended voluntary departure status." That status enabled aliens to remain in the United States after their visas expired if they could show that their lives would be in jeopardy if they returned home.

Endangered Species. The bill declared that the protection of endangered animal and plant species was an important U.S. policy objective and authorized the president to provide aid to help foreign countries establish wildlife sanctuaries and other programs to protect them.

Soviet Studies. Conferees accepted a Senate provision earmarking up to $5 million in fiscal 1984 and $5 million in 1985 for research and training in Soviet and Eastern European studies. Grants for fellowships and research programs would be awarded by the State Department on the advice of a new Soviet-Eastern European Studies Advisory Board, composed of government officials and representatives of various academic groups.

South Africa. The bill earmarked $500,000 in fiscal 1984 and $1 million in fiscal 1985, from State Department funds, for grants to private agencies and international organizations to promote human rights in South Africa.

Syrian Aid. The bill repealed about $80 million in previously approved foreign aid to Syria, except for the training of Syrian students who began their studies before the bill was enacted. A similar provision was included in the second continuing appropriations resolution (H J Res 413 — PL 98-151) for fiscal 1984.

Refugee Aid. For fiscal 1984, the bill earmarked $10 million under the migration and refugee account for relief of displaced persons in El Salvador. At least $5 million, and up to $25 million, also was set aside for refugee relief in Lebanon.

CoCom. The bill authorized $2 million under the international organizations account to modernize the facili-

ties and procedures of the Coordinating Committee on Export Controls (CoCom), a U.S.-European agency that attempted to control exports of sensitive technology to the Soviet Union and its allies. *(Export controls, p. 253)*

Inter-parliamentary Groups. On an issue of direct interest to members of Congress, the bill authorized funds for congressional participation in international parliamentary groups: $50,000 annually for the United States-European Community Inter-parliamentary Group and $450,000 for the U.S. expenses in hosting the annual meeting of the North Atlantic Assembly.

Exchange Programs. Conferees retained a Senate provision establishing a charter for the Bureau of Educational and Cultural Affairs within the USIA. The bureau administered such exchange programs as the Fulbright-Hays scholarships. The charter required the president to ensure that all exchange programs would be non-political and would represent "the diversity of American political, social and cultural life."

In addition, the bill earmarked funds to double the size of the exchange programs between fiscal years 1982-86. Amounts earmarked for fiscal 1984 included $100.5 million for the Fulbright-Hays and International Visitor programs, $3.7 million for the Humphrey Fellowship Program and up to $7.1 million for the Private Sector Program.

Environmental Exchanges. Conferees adopted a Senate provision establishing a new program of exchanges between American and foreign scientists and experts on environmental issues. The program would be funded with 5 percent of the increase earmarked in the bill for all exchange programs run by USIA.

Lobbying. The bill prohibited agencies that received USIA grants from using those funds to lobby or conduct propaganda to influence decisions by federal, state or local governments in the United States.

Foreign Service. The bill maintained a Senate provision merging the USIA's Foreign Service Information Corps with the State Department's Foreign Service. The merger allowed USIA officers to compete with Foreign Service officers for embassy chief of mission and other high-level assignments.

Radio Free Europe. The bill placed new limits on the salary and benefits that could be paid the president of Radio Free Europe and Radio Liberty — starting with the next president. The salary was set at the executive IV level for the federal government (currently $67,200), plus the "normal" allowances and benefits provided employees of that agency under State Department guidelines. The new limits, contained in a House amendment, were in reaction to reports that Radio Free Europe/Radio Liberty president, former Sen. James L. Buckley, C/R-N.Y. (1971-77), was accorded salary and benefits worth about $200,000.

Non-proliferation. The bill included a Senate-passed provision opposing all exports of nuclear supplies and equipment to Argentina, India and South Africa until those countries forswore any attempt to build nuclear weapons and accept international controls (called "safeguards") on all their nuclear facilities. The provision stated the sense of Congress on the issue; it did not directly ban any sales to those countries.

Conferees added a further escape clause saying the president could authorize exports of equipment for India's Tarpur reactor, near Bombay, if he determined that the equipment was necessary for humanitarian reasons and was not available from another supplier.

India Fund. The bill authorized the president to

negotiate with India to establish a United States-India Fund for Cultural, Educational and Scientific Cooperation. The fund would finance exchange programs and joint scholarly studies. It would be established with $200 million remaining from sales in India under the PL 480 Food for Peace Program.

U.S.-Soviet Diplomats. Conferees dropped a Senate provision that would have requested the president to seek "substantial equivalence" between the number of and restrictions on U.S. diplomats permitted in the Soviet Union and Soviet diplomats permitted in the United States.

Baltic States. The bill required that Radio Liberty broadcasts to Estonia, Latvia and Lithuania be organized under a separate division. The broadcasts also were to be given a name that reflected the U.S. policy of not recognizing the incorporation of those Baltic countries into the Soviet Union.

Khmer Rouge. Direct or indirect U.S. aid to the Khmer Rouge faction in Cambodia (Kampuchea) was prohibited by the bill. However, conferees said the prohibition was not intended to stop humanitarian assistance to Cambodian people, even if that aid might fall into the hands of the Khmer Rouge.

Gulf of Thailand. The bill earmarked $5 million in each fiscal year for programs to combat piracy in the Gulf of Thailand. Pirates reportedly had been attacking refugees fleeing from Vietnam. ∎

Carlucci Commission

A commission appointed by Secretary of State George P. Shultz took Congress to task for engaging in "unproductive" debates that endangered foreign aid legislation.

Headed by Frank C. Carlucci, former deputy secretary of defense, the foreign aid commission called on the president and congressional leaders to issue a joint statement endorsing foreign aid as an "essential and integral part of the foreign policy of the United States." As of the end of 1983, no statement had been issued.

The commission released its report Nov. 21, following six months of hearings and studies. Nine of its 24 members were members of Congress.

Among the commission's recommendations, the most controversial were suggestions that the United States provide more of its overseas military aid as grants (and less as loans) and that foreign aid agencies be reorganized into a Mutual Development and Security Administration.

In calling for increased military grants, the commission noted that several countries, including Turkey, Egypt and the Sudan, had built up large debts in U.S. military loans at the same time that the United States was providing them economic aid.

"Thus, the one program is adding to the debt problems of these countries, while the other is seeking to alleviate them through favorable financial terms and economic improvements," the report stated.

An increase in military grants was opposed by several commission members, including Rep. Matthew F. McHugh, D-N.Y., on the grounds that developing countries needed economic aid grants more than military aid grants. They noted that the administration was in the process of reducing U.S. contributions to such agencies as the International Development Association, which made interest-free loans to the world's poorest countries.

The commission said a new agency was needed to direct all U.S. foreign aid programs because the present system was "procedurally and organizationally fragmented." The State, Treasury, Agriculture and Defense departments, along with the Agency for International Development (AID), all ran parts of the foreign aid program, and no single official was responsible for coordinating all of them.

The new agency would be headed by a director, with the rank of a deputy secretary, who would report to the secretary of state. The agency would control the budgets of all foreign aid programs and operate the programs currently conducted by AID.

In a minority report, several unidentified commission members said the reorganization was unnecessary.

The commission concluded that both sides were at fault in the long-running debate about the "balance" of economic vs. military aid to foreign countries. For several years, overseas development groups and their liberal allies in Congress had argued that the United States should boost funding of economic aid; on the opposite side, conservative groups and their congressional allies had advocated increased military aid.

The report said "unproductive debate," coupled with declining public support for foreign aid in general, had allowed "vocal, single-interest constituent groups to influence disproportionately" the aid program.

In addition, the commission said foreign aid bills in Congress "may become hostage to the political pressures." The report noted that Congress had passed both regular foreign aid authorization and appropriations bills only once (1981) in the preceding five years; in other years, foreign aid was included in stopgap funding bills.

"The inability to build a congressional coalition [favoring foreign aid] poses immediate and long-range problems of resource allocation and foreign policy formulation," the report said. "The cumulative effect over the longer run is to diminish confidence in the reliability of U.S. commitments and result in perhaps even more costly challenges to U.S. interests."

The commission itself demonstrated the difficulty of resolving the debate. Commission members could not agree on whether the $3 billion-a-year Economic Support Fund — which aided the economies of U.S. allies such as Israel — should be considered economic or military aid, or whether market-rate military loans should be considered military aid.

The commission said it was difficult to judge the effectiveness of aid programs as a whole and admitted that the issue "will remain a controversial subject." But it said: "While some efforts have not been very successful" in the post-World War II era, "most recipient countries have benefited substantially" from U.S. foreign aid. It added that "both military and economic assistance have been mutually supportive and effective in pursuing U.S. interests."

The report noted that while the United States spent about 50 percent more on foreign aid in the late 1970s and early 1980s than it did a decade earlier, the actual level of aid declined by about 18 percent, after inflation was taken into account. The U.S. share of foreign aid throughout the world also declined during that period, the report said. The United States provided 37 percent of all economic aid to developing nations in 1970; that portion had declined to 22 percent by 1982. ∎

El Salvador Aid Approved — With Strings

For the third year in a row, Congress and the president in 1983 battled to a draw over both the details and the broad outline of U.S. policy toward El Salvador.

As it had done in previous years, Congress used its control over the foreign aid budget to moderate the administration's requests for military aid to the Salvadoran government, which had been battling leftist guerrillas since 1980. Nevertheless, Reagan could take satisfaction from the fact that Congress refused to cut off the aid, thus generally allowing his activist, anti-communist policies in Central America to continue.

The essential political reality in Congress was that there were not enough votes either to give Reagan full backing on El Salvador or to force an immediate withdrawal of U.S. aid from that country. The compromise position was to provide limited aid, but to attach conditions that addressed congressional concerns about human man rights and other issues in El Salvador.

In an attempt to win congressional support, Reagan in the spring of 1983 for the first time took the lead in explaining his policies to Congress and the American public — with modest success. Congress eventually approved little more than half of the president's request for military aid to El Salvador for fiscal 1983. It gave him most of his aid request for fiscal 1984 but attached new conditions that threatened to withhold 30 percent of the money.

Although most Democrats were skeptical of Reagan's policies toward Central America, there was an agreement among some that it was not wise politically to block all of the president's moves. One Democrat who supported the president, Daniel A. Mica of Florida, said his colleagues "do not want to be labeled the party that lost El Salvador, or the group that walked away."

As the year ended, the administration itself was sending mixed signals to El Salvador on human rights issues, long the sticking point in relations between the two countries.

On the one hand, Reagan on Nov. 30 vetoed a bill (HR 4042) that would have continued through fiscal 1984 a ban on military aid to El Salvador unless he certified to Congress every six months that the government there was making progress on human rights and other issues. And a few days later, Reagan voiced the suspicion that so-called "death squads" in El Salvador could be the work of leftist guerrillas as much as right-wing zealots aligned with the security forces.

Human rights groups had said the death squads and government security forces were responsible for many of the 30,000-40,000 civilian deaths in El Salvador since the civil war broke out in 1980.

On the other hand, several administration officials, including Vice President George Bush, publicly and privately admonished the Salvadoran government to halt the work of the death squads. Visiting El Salvador briefly on Dec. 11, Bush warned that Congress "certainly" would cut off further aid if the death squads were not halted. In response to Bush's demands for action, the Salvadoran government demoted or reassigned several military and security officers who were alleged to have ties to the death squads.

Congress had enacted the certification requirement in 1981; it prohibited military aid to El Salvador unless the president certified twice each year that the Salvadoran government was making progress in several areas, including respect for human rights and land reform. Reagan made four certifications: two in 1982 and two in 1983.

The administration originally opposed the certification requirement, but some officials eventually said it gave the United States leverage to press for reforms in El Salvador. Meanwhile, some Reagan critics became disillusioned with the process, saying Reagan was using it to whitewash the situation in El Salvador.

By late summer, Congress seemed ready to allow the certification process to lapse. But in September, leaders in the Foreign Relations and Foreign Affairs committees became concerned that such a change in course would be viewed in El Salvador as a lack of U.S. interest in the reforms, and so they pushed forward with HR 4042 — apparently not knowing that Reagan would veto it.

Aid Highlights

Reagan requested a total of $136.3 million in military aid for El Salvador in fiscal 1983: $76.5 million in Foreign Military Sales (FMS) loan guarantees, $58.5 million in Military Assistance Program (MAP) grants and $1.3 million in International Military Education and Training (IMET) aid. Of the total request, $110 million was sought on March 10 as part of an emergency package of economic and military aid for Central American nations.

Congress approved $81.3 million for fiscal 1983: $26.3 million in loans and grants under the fiscal 1983 emergency funding measure (PL 97-377) approved late in 1982; $30 million in FMS loans that were "reprogrammed," or transferred, from other countries with the approval in April 1983 of the House and Senate Appropriations committees and the Senate Foreign Relations Committee; and $25 million in MAP grants approved in HR 3069 (PL 98-63), an omnibus fiscal 1983 supplemental appropriations bill. *(Previous aid, 1982 Almanac p. 242)*

Congress approved Reagan's full requests of $140 million in Economic Support Fund (ESF) aid and $87.1 million in development and food aid programs for fisal 1983.

For fiscal 1984, Reagan requested $86.3 million in military aid for El Salvador: $30 million in FMS loans, $55 million in MAP grants and $1.3 million in IMET aid. Reagan also requested $120 million in economic aid and $38 million in development aid.

In the second continuing resolution for fiscal 1984 (PL 98-151), Congress set a $64.8 million limit on the military aid, but approved the full economic and development aid requests.

1983 Requests

Faced with a deteriorating military situation in El Salvador, the administration went to Congress in late February with an appeal for emergency military aid to help prop up the embattled Salvadoran government. Its case was hurt, however, by conflicting reports about how much aid would be requested and how desperately it was needed.

Reagan's request came amid indications that members of Congress were torn on what to do about El Salvador. Many were frustrated by the continued human rights violations of the government security forces and by the adminis-

tration's refusal to press for a political reconciliation between the Salvadoran government and its leftist opponents.

On the other hand, several congressional critics of Reagan's policies had returned from visits to El Salvador impressed by pleas for support from the country's moderate politicians. Others apparently feared the political consequences in the United States if the Salvadoran government fell.

Reagan asked Congress for advice on how the aid should be provided, but the administration made clear that it was determined to boost aid to El Salvador — with congressional approval if possible but without it if necessary.

Reagan's move in early 1983 was unusual for two reasons: 1) it was the first time the president personally had entered the controversial El Salvador debate in a highly visible way, and 2) it was the first time his administration publicly involved Congress in formulating a major foreign policy decision.

Three Options

The administration had three ways to provide additional aid, each of which had a serious drawback:

● The quickest way to provide the aid was by invoking the president's power to send Pentagon supplies directly to a foreign government, without seeking congressional authorization. Two-thirds of the military aid given El Salvador in fiscal years 1981 and 1982 was provided under that power. But congressional leaders warned Reagan not to use his emergency power again for El Salvador. Sen. Claiborne Pell, D-R.I., senior Democrat on the Foreign Relations Committee, said it would be "outrageous for the administration to try to go it alone without congressional approval."

● The next quickest way to provide the aid was for the president to transfer, or "reprogram," funds to El Salvador from other foreign aid accounts. By law the president had to notify the House and Senate Appropriations committees 15 days before reprogramming any funds. By tradition, the two committees asserted the right to object to reprogrammings, and various administrations in recent years had honored such objections.

● The most difficult route for Reagan was to get Congress to approve a special supplemental funding measure for El Salvador. Such a request faced numerous legislative hurdles, especially since foreign aid generally was so unpopular in Congress.

Administration Lobbying

In trying to get Congress to approve additional aid, the administration seemed to take several steps backward for each step forward.

The first backward step occurred on Feb. 22 when Defense Secretary Caspar W. Weinberger told the House Foreign Affairs Committee the administration was planning to use the president's "emergency" authority to obtain about $60 million. That statement angered leaders in both houses, who said the administration was attempting to evade Congress' role in authorizing and appropriating funds.

Weinberger said the government of El Salvador was facing "a number of problems" in its military campaign against leftist guerrillas. Ammunition, spare parts and repairs on existing military equipment "are needed and needed quite quickly," he said.

Rep. Michael D. Barnes, D-Md., chairman of the Foreign Affairs Subcommittee on Western Hemisphere Affairs, told Weinberger he was "disheartened" by the administration's repeated requests for additional military aid.

In an interview the following day, Barnes raised complaints about the use of the emergency aid procedure. "This is not the way it ought to be done," he said. "It's an end run around the legislative process."

Administration officials also announced the number of U.S. military advisers in El Salvador would be boosted to a previously established limit of 55, from about 37 at the beginning of the year.

The campaign for the additional aid to El Salvador was opened Feb. 28 at a White House meeting of Reagan, other administration officials and 22 congressional leaders.

Top administration officials attempted to smooth ruffled congressional feathers, giving the leaders the impression they were being consulted before a final decision had been made. But later the White House undermined its campaign with a series of statements that again upset many members.

First, an official traveling with Reagan to California said consideration was being given to expanding the role of U.S. military advisers in El Salvador, whose role had been limited to training Salvadoran troops. That statement later was retracted, but not before members had become alarmed about the prospect of U.S. troops fighting guerrillas in El Salvador.

The same day, Secretary of State George P. Shultz seemed to disparage Catholic Church leaders as "churchmen who want to see Soviet influence in El Salvador improved." Much of the opposition in the United States to military aid for El Salvador had been generated by church groups — largely as a result of the November, 1980, killing of four U.S. churchwomen in that country, allegedly by national guardsmen.

'Domino Theory' Revived

On March 1 and 2, Shultz and other administration officials revived the Vietnam-era "domino theory" as a reason for supporting the Salvadoran government. If El Salvador fell under Marxist influence, they said, other nations in Central America inevitably would follow suit. Mexico then would be threatened, they said, and millions of refugees would pour into the United States.

With a remarkable degree of unanimity, congressional leaders seemed skeptical about the sudden demand for emergency military aid for El Salvador but willing to consider Reagan's arguments. Most leaders said they wanted to see a precise proposal before committing themselves.

A few members flatly opposed any further military aid. Among them, Rep. Gerry E. Studds, D-Mass., likened U.S. policies in Central America to the conduct of the Vietnam War: "Our policy seems to be, if something doesn't work, do more of it."

Perhaps the most positive sign from the administration's viewpoint was the willingness of Rep. Clarence D. Long, D-Md., Foreign Operations Appropriations Subcommittee chairman, to consider Reagan's request.

Long had been a staunch opponent of U.S. military involvement in El Salvador. But he said a trip to the region in mid-February 1983 left him "genuinely undecided" about what should be done in the future. He said he found the economic and military situation in El Salvador to be "really bad," while there had been a "vast improvement" in the government.

Reagan Vetoes El Salvador Certification Bill

President Reagan on Nov. 30, 1983, pocket-vetoed legislation (HR 4042) that would have reinstated during fiscal 1984 a requirement that he certify to Congress every 180 days that El Salvador was making sufficient progress on human rights and other issues to deserve continued U.S. assistance.

The bill was passed by the House Sept. 30 and by the Senate without amendment Nov. 17, completing congressional action. Committee reports were not issued in either house.

Originally enacted in 1981 in PL 97-113, the certification requirement was in effect for fiscal years 1982 and 1983, and expired on Sept. 30, 1983. By not signing HR 4042 by Nov. 30, after Congress had adjourned, Reagan allowed the bill to die.

The veto infuriated Democrats in Congress, many of whom had used the semiannual certification reports to challenge the Reagan administration's support of the Salvadoran government.

Rep. Michael D. Barnes, D-Md., chairman of the Foreign Affairs Subcommittee on Western Hemisphere Affairs, said it was "just unbelievable" that Reagan would veto a bill that had no active opposition in Congress. Both the House and Senate had passed the bill by voice votes.

Critics said the veto conflicted with U.S. diplomatic efforts to get the Salvadoran regime to control an upsurge in human rights abuses by right-wing "death squads" that were thought to have ties to government security forces.

Foreign Relations Chairman Charles H. Percy, R-Ill., expressed concern that the veto "sends a confusing signal to El Salvador just at a time when we are trying to send a strong, clear signal that political violence must cease."

And Christopher J. Dodd, D-Conn., a member of the Foreign Relations Committee, said the veto "is going to be perceived as a green light by those involved in the death squads."

White House spokesman Larry Speakes rejected that interpretation, insisting that the veto "in no way reflects a lessening of our interest in these critical areas" in El Salvador. He said the State Department would continue to report to Congress on El Salvador. The first report subsequent to the president's veto was issued Jan. 16, 1984.

Ironically, the veto pumped new political life into the certification process. House Speaker Thomas P. O'Neill Jr., D-Mass., said renewing the law would have top priority in the second session of the 98th Congress.

As certification reports became routine in 1983, congressional interest waned. The report released in July 1983 drew little attention. Reagan's critics had belittled the certification process and seemed in little hurry to renew it.

But after the veto, Dodd called the process "extremely important."

Administration Dilemma

Reagan's decision to veto the recertification bill came after an apparently vigorous debate within the administration. Some State Department officials had given qualified endorsements of the certification requirement, and they reportedly argued that Reagan should sign HR 4042. But others in the administration prevailed, arguing that the certification law placed undue restraints on the president.

Speakes said the certification requirements "distort our efforts to improve human rights, democracy and recovery in El Salvador." He did not explain why that was so.

One State Department official said the certification law had forced the administration to make an "unacceptable choice." Failure to certify progress would force a withdrawal of U.S. aid and would be seen as "walking away" from El Salvador, he claimed. But he said Secretary of State George P. Shultz was forced to be a "liar" because he was signing reports that exaggerated the progress in El Salvador.

Shultz on Dec. 1, 1983, told reporters that "it would be very difficult" to sign another certification in January 1984 under existing circumstances.

Long said he could support additional aid if the administration put pressure on Salvadoran government officials to take several actions including: a more vigorous waging of the war against the guerrillas; "broadening the base of the government" by seeking the involvement of leftist politicians who had fled the country; and improving respect for human rights, especially by punishing members of the armed forces who killed civilians.

Outright public support for Reagan's request came only from a handful of conservative Republicans. One, Rep. Robert J. Lagomarsino of California, said members of Congress faced a "bottom line" of "Do we wash our hands of the situation and walk away?" If the United States did that, he said, "I think there would be tragic results for all of the things that I think we are all concerned about."

Reagan March 10 Request

After nearly two weeks of consultations with Congress that were intended to smooth the way for approval of the additional aid, Reagan on March 10 staked out a position that jeopardized that effort.

In his first nationwide speech on El Salvador, before the National Association of Manufacturers, Reagan stuck to his positions that for two years had aroused widespread opposition in Congress. He stressed that the United States needed to continue its military support of the Salvadoran government and not be pressured into negotiating with the leftist guerrillas.

At the same time, Reagan dramatically raised the political profile of his policy by proposing a substantial increase in military aid. When he began consulting with Congress on El Salvador in February, Reagan cited an "emergency" need for $60 million. But within a week the amount sought had risen, at the Pentagon's urging, to $110 million in fiscal 1983.

Reagan unveiled an emergency package of aid for Cen-

tral America, totaling $298 million for fiscal 1983. The original intent of the aid package was to bolster the Salvadoran military. But to give the request broader political appeal in Congress the administration added economic aid for El Salvador and three other nations in Central America.

Reagan did not follow through on Weinberger's threat to provide aid to El Salvador through the Defense Department's drawdown authority. But his aides refused to rule out future use of the drawdown authority if Congress decided to block most or all of the administration's request.

For El Salvador, Reagan's March 10 request included $110 million in military aid, including $60 million in FMS loans to be reprogrammed from funds originally intended for other countries and $50 million for MAP grants to be included in a fiscal 1983 supplemental. Congressional approval of the entire package would bring total military aid for El Salvador in fiscal 1983 to $136.3 million.

Reagan's request also included $67.1 million in economic aid, including $35 million to be reprogrammed under the Economic Support Fund (ESF), $23.1 million in development assistance, also reprogrammed, and $9 million reprogrammed under PL 480 Food for Peace assistance. (Approval of the entire request would bring economic aid for El Salvador in fiscal 1983 to $227.1 million.)

The administration's special aid package for Central America also included military and/or economic aid for Honduras, Costa Rica, Belize and Panama.

No U.S. Troops. In his speech to the NAM, Reagan said the military situation there "is not good" but added that the United States would not send in American soldiers or advisers. Reagan called "nonsense" an accusation made by many members that he was interested only in a military solution to the Salvadoran conflict.

Reagan was less explicit about congressional demands that the United States encourage direct negotiations between the Salvadoran government and the guerrillas. The president said he was interested only in negotiations "aimed at expanding participation in democratic institutions." The administration had tried to deflect the negotiations issue by proposing talks on how to assure leftist politicians that they could safely participate in presidential elections.

Reagan also set out his most extensive statement to that point on why El Salvador was important to the United States. Reagan described the essence of the "domino theory" without using the term. If the guerrillas were to win, he said, "El Salvador will join Cuba and Nicaragua as a base for spreading fresh violence to Guatemala, Honduras, even Costa Rica, probably the most democratic country in the world today. The killing will increase, and so will the threat to Panama, the canal, and ultimately Mexico."

The immediate congressional reaction was mostly negative. One critic, Rep. Matthew F. McHugh, D-N.Y., said Reagan's speech "does not convey the impression to the country at large that there is a shift in policy emphasis, which is what it's going to take to convince Americans that it's worth pursuing that policy."

April 27 Address

Reagan addressed a joint session of Congress April 27 to further push his aid policies. He defended his approach of bolstering the Salvadoran government and those of other friendly countries in the region against the leftist guerrillas being supported by Cuba and Nicaragua. Reagan's speech was only the 13th appearance of a president at a joint session of Congress — other than for a State of the Union

address — in the past 20 years. *(Joint session speeches, Guide to Congress, 3rd edition, p. 787)*

The president made no effort to compromise with members critical of his emphasis on military solutions to the economic and political problems of Central America. But by taking his case directly to Congress and the American public Reagan focused new attention on the region and gave encouragement to members who wanted to build a "bipartisan" foreign policy toward Central America. *(Speech text, p. 28-E)*

Reagan broke no new policy ground in his speech. In content, the speech reflected previous administration statements on Central America; it covered the same issues Reagan hit upon on March 10.

Reagan said the problems of Central America should be of immediate concern to the United States because they "directly affect the security and well being of our own people." He noted that two-thirds of all U.S. foreign trade and oil shipments passed through the Panama Canal and the Caribbean Sea.

The main threat to the region was communist "adventurism," promoted by the Soviet Union, Cuba and Nicaragua, Reagan charged.

The president devoted much of his speech to a harsh attack on the leftist government of Nicaragua, saying it "has treated us as an enemy." In his only direct reference to U.S. activities against the Nicaraguan government, Reagan said the United States was merely trying to prevent the flow of Soviet- and Cuban-supplied arms through Nicaragua to the guerrillas in El Salvador.

"We do not seek [the government's] overthrow," he said. "Our interest is to ensure that it does not infect its neighbors through the export of subversion and violence."

Four Goals. Reagan offered "four basic goals of U.S. policy in the region":

● The first, and broadest, goal was support for "democracy, reform and human freedom." He said that entailed U.S. aid, persuasion and leverage "to bolster humane democratic regimes where they already exist" and to help other countries develop democracy. In his only reference to human rights issues, Reagan said: "We will work at human rights problems, not walk away from them."

● The second goal was support for economic development in the region. Reagan asked for passage of the remaining parts of his Caribbean Basin Initiative (CBI), providing trade benefits for countries in the region and tax incentives for businesses that invested there. *(CBI, 1982 Almanac p. 151; 1983 action, p. 252)*

● The third goal was military support for threatened nations in the region. "We do not view security assistance as an end in itself, but as a shield for democratization, economic development and diplomacy," he said.

● Fourth, Reagan said the United States would support "dialogue and negotiations — both among the countries of the region and within each country." He pledged U.S. support for "verifiable and reciprocal" agreements among Central American countries for the withdrawal of all foreign military advisers and troops and for the renunciation of support for insurgents.

The president asked for "prompt" approval by Congress of his pending requests for military and economic aid to the region. He gave only one figure: $600 million for all of Central America in fiscal 1984, which he said was "less than one-tenth of what Americans will spend this year on coin-operated video games." The president did not note that nearly half of the $600 million was for El Salvador.

Helms Leads Conservative Attack on Reagan Policies

In 1982 and 1983 liberals in Congress won widespread public attention for their unrelenting attacks on the Reagan administration's policies in El Salvador.

Less attention was given to criticism from the other side of the political spectrum — by some conservatives in and out of Congress. The most vocal of those critics, Sen. Jesse Helms, R-N.C., argued that the Carter and Reagan administrations had repeated the long history of the United States dictating to Latin American countries. But according to Helms, instead of intervening on behalf of rightist military regimes — as it often did in the past — the United States instead was pushing countries such as El Salvador toward the left.

Helms outlined his view in a lecture to fellow members of the Senate Foreign Relations Committee March 24, as they debated President Reagan's supplemental military aid requests. Helms supported the aid proposal, but almost nothing else Reagan had done involving El Salvador.

Helms described the recent history of U.S. involvement in El Salvador from the opposite perspective of both the Reagan administration and many of its liberal critics. For starters, Helms charged that the Carter administration "organized" the October 1979 coup that overthrew Gen. Carlos Humberto Romero, and later "installed" José Napoleon Duarte as president. The U.S. ambassador at that time, Robert White, had acted, ac-

cording to Helms, as a "proconsul" and ordered the junta to implement a series of "reforms," such as land reform and nationalization of the banks and the export system.

The reforms, Helms said, "disrupted not only the economic system, but the political system as well. They instilled fear, uncertainty, greed, and hatred." Overall, he said: "There is no doubt that everything the United States did in this respect made matters worse, not better."

In March 1982, 80 percent of Salvadorans went to the polls to elect a Constituent Assembly. Helms approved of the election, especially since it resulted in Duarte's departure from office. But Helms said the United States put "tremendous pressure" on the government "to install another president who did not reflect the mandate of the voters [Alvaro Magaña]."

An administration official denied Helms' contentions that the United States "installed" either Duarte or Magaña, or that the U.S.-backed reforms had made matters worse in El Salvador. She noted that the administration repeatedly had indicated that most of the reforms were working well.

Rep. Philip M. Crane, R-Ill., who also was critical of the Reagan administration from a conservative perspective, said it had not pushed hard enough for a military defeat of the leftist guerrillas in El Salvador.

Reagan directly responded to one of the primary concerns among members of Congress: That U.S. troops eventually might be needed to bolster the regimes in El Salvador and other countries in the region. "There is no thought of sending American combat troops to Central America," he said. "They are not needed — indeed, they have not been requested there."

Sen. Christopher J. Dodd, D-Conn., delivered a formal, televised response sanctioned by most of the Democratic leadership. In it he said Reagan ignored the basic cause of unrest in Central America: That "a very few live in isolated splendor while the very many suffer in shantytown squalor. In country after country, dictatorship or military dominance has stifled democracy and destroyed human rights."

Administration policy, he said, was based on "ever increasing military assistance, endless military training, even hiring our own paramilitary guerrillas. This is a formula for failure."

Democrats "are fully prepared to be involved in Central America," Dodd said, but under an alternative policy "that can work." Dodd advanced few specifics, but he called for cease-fires in the conflicts in El Salvador and Nicaragua and for "negotiated political settlements" throughout Central America.

Dodd's speech was repudiated by several Democrats, including House Majority Leader Jim Wright, D-Texas, who said it was too harsh.

REPROGRAMMING REQUEST

Reagan's March 10 request for a $60 million reprogramming of foreign military loans produced extended battles in three committees: the Foreign Operations subcommittees of the Senate and House Appropriations com-

mittees, and the Senate Foreign Relations Committee.

By tradition, the committees were to give the administration an answer to its reprogramming request within 15 days — which would have been March 24. All three committees held rushed hearings and meetings to beat the deadline; the House Foreign Operations Subcommittee was unable to reach a decision by the deadline and demanded more time.

The first to conclude action was the Senate Foreign Operations Subcommittee.

Dominated by Republicans, that panel on March 23 sent Secretary of State George P. Shultz a letter approving the full $60 million, but imposing several conditions on its use. Chairman Bob Kasten, R-Wis., called his panel's action a "modified victory" for the president.

The subcommittee said the extra aid for El Salvador was given "with the understanding that the administration will agree in writing to the following terms and conditions. . . :

● "A reaffirmation by the president of the assurances given to the committee in 1981 that the number of United States military advisers and trainers will not exceed 55 persons;

● "Given the inadequate functioning of the Salvadoran judicial system, the administration will begin a new and immediate effort aimed at addressing the structural defects in this system, with special attention to the effective prosecution of those accused in the murders of United States citizens;

● "The administration will begin a new and immediate diplomatic initiative aimed at securing from the Salvadoran military their guarantee of the physical security and integrity of the participants in the justice system, including

justices, prosecutors, defense attorneys and witnesses;

● "The administration will take the initiative in cooperation with countries in the region, the OAS [Organiation of
American States] and/or other international organizations,
as appropriate, to bring about unconditional discussions
between the government of El Salvador and its adversaries
on the holding of free, fair and safe elections, and any other
subject of concern between the parties."

The letter was signed by seven of the subcommittee's
nine members: Kasten; Alfonse M. D'Amato, R-N.Y.; Warren B. Rudman, R-N.H.; Arlen Specter, R-Pa.; Daniel K.
Inouye, D-Hawaii, J. Bennett Johnston, D-La.; and Dennis
DeConcini, D-Ariz. Inouye signed "with reservations."
Mark O. Hatfield, R-Ore., and Patrick J. Leahy, D-Vt., did
not sign the letter.

The next day — March 24 — the Foreign Relations
Committee approved $30 million of the $60 million requested, without any explicit conditions.

In a letter to Shultz drafted during a testy session, 12
committee members requested, but did not demand,
progress on several El Salvador issues. Chairman Charles
H. Percy, R-Ill., who supported Reagan's request, said the
administration could "get along with the $30 million for
now."

The committee's letter reflected a compromise among
Percy and two other members: Sens. Dodd and Nancy
Landon Kassebaum, R-Kan. Dodd and Kassebaum (along
with Inouye, of the Foreign Operations Subcommittee) had
wanted to impose a limit of $50 million on U.S. military aid
for El Salvador in fiscal 1983 and to insist that the United
States seek an unconditional "dialogue" among all the
Salvadoran parties.

Unlike the Appropriations panel, which had allowed
Reagan also to increase economic, development and food
aid to El Salvador, the Foreign Relations panel objected to
boosting Economic Support Fund (ESF) aid for El Salvador to $140 million from the existing level of $115 million.

The committee accompanied its approval of the aid
with a statement of beliefs. The panel said it "believes that
the United States should use its good offices to encourage
an unconditional dialogue among all parties to the conflict
in El Salvador in the hope of achieving a political resolution.

"The committee also believes that the number of
United States military trainers and advisers in El Salvador
should be limited to no more than 55, and that those
personnel should be subject to current operational restrictions and rules of engagement. Moreover, the committee
believes that any additional training to be provided by
these or other funds for the Salvadoran military in fiscal
year 1983 should be limited strictly to training at facilities
in the United States or in facilities in Panama.

"In addition, the committee firmly believes that an
essential element of continued United States support for
the government of El Salvador must be prompt and far-
reaching reforms of the judiciary in El Salvador, which will
serve to remove corruption, political interference and
intimidation from the judicial process. Moreover, the Salvadoran government must give the highest priority to the
prosecution of those responsible for the murders of the
eight Americans assassinated in El Salvador since December 1980."

House Committees

With the two Senate panels disagreeing on the amount
of aid, pressure was on the House Foreign Operations

Stone Confirmed As Envoy

The Senate by voice vote on May 25, 1983, confirmed former Sen. Richard B. Stone, D-Fla. (1975-80),
as President Reagan's ambassador-at-large for Central
America.

Reagan appointed Stone largely in response to a
demand by Rep. Clarence D. Long, D-Md., for a U.S.
"special negotiator" to settle the civil war in El Salvador. Long, chairman of the House Appropriations
Committee's Foreign Operations Subcommittee, made
the appointment of such a negotiator a condition for
his approval of additional military aid to the Salvadoran government.

Appearing before the Senate Foreign Relations
Committee on May 20, Stone repeatedly said he was
not going to be a "negotiator." Stone described his
special envoy role in much more limited terms than
Long had conceived it, saying it was to be "one of
inducement, invitation and support, rather than co-
optation or domination." He said he would address the
problems of the entire Central American region rather
than just El Salvador.

During the year, Stone traveled repeatedly
throughout the region and successfully arranged meetings between Salvadoran government officials and political representatives of its leftist opposition. However, Stone's efforts were overshadowed by the
workings of the "Contadora group," composed of Mexico, Panama, Venezuela and Colombia. In October,
that group published a list of 21 points for a regional
agreement; in January 1984, the Contadora countries
and the five nations of Central America signed a limited agreement calling for a peaceful settlement of the
region's conflicts.

Appropriations Subcommittee to resolve the issue.

For a six-week period Long's 12-member subcommittee remained sharply divided on the issue. Six of the eight
Democrats favored no additional aid, at least until the
administration made sweeping changes in its policies toward Central America. All four Republicans and Democrat
Charles Wilson of Texas favored the full $60 million re-
quest. Chairman Long occupied the middle ground, saying
all along that he was inclined to approve $30 million, and
that amount only if the administration met several conditions.

Long's conditions were: the appointment of a special
U.S. envoy to arrange negotiations in Central America; the
freeing of political prisoners in El Salvador; the opening of
Salvadoran prisons and detention centers to inspections by
the International Red Cross; and an arrangement for the
families of four American churchwomen murdered in El
Salvador in December 1980 to be allowed to review FBI
evidence in the case.

To assure himself that the Salvadoran government
would accept his proposals, Long had traveled to El Salvador April 23-25. He said President Alvaro Magaña was
"receptive." Upon his return, Long said congressional rejection of any further aid would invite a "military coup" by
the extreme right in El Salvador. "Some of their military
leaders told me they've had a very hard time preventing

that from happening so far," he said.

The panel held its climactic meeting on April 26, the day before Reagan's speech to the joint session of Congress.

The subcommittee met under the most intense pressure it had felt on any issue in several years. The panel faced a phalanx of 12 television cameras and more than 50 reporters. Seated in the front row of the audience during the session was El Salvador's ambassador to the United States, Ernesto Rivas-Gallant.

Republicans on the panel contended that El Salvador needed the full $60 million to fight off leftist guerrillas, who, they said, were getting support from Cuba, Nicaragua and the Soviet Union. "This is international politics, and we're playing for high stakes," said Bob Livingston, R-La.

The panel took three votes:

● Wilson and the four Republicans voted for the full $60 million, but the seven remaining Democrats rejected it.

● The subcommittee split 6-6 and thus rejected a motion by McHugh to delay a decision by as much as another 90 days. Long, Wilson and the four Republicans voted against that motion, while the remaining Democrats supported it.

● Finally, the subcommittee split along the same 6-6 lines on Long's motion to approve only $30 million. But McHugh, noting that the subcommittee's failure to approve any alternative to Reagan's full request would amount to approval of the full $60 million, then switched his vote enabling Long's motion to pass 7-5.

McHugh said he voted for the Long motion only to prevent the approval of the full $60 million by default.

Since the Senate Appropriations and Foreign Relations committees had approved the reprogramming in March, the vote by the House subcommittee completed congressional action on Reagan's reprogramming request.

The House Foreign Affairs Committee did not assert jurisdiction over the $60 million reprogramming request. But at the behest of its Western Hemisphere Affairs Subcommittee, committee Chairman Clement J. Zablocki, D-Wis., agreed to send Shultz a letter saying the committee wanted to review future reprogrammings. "If they want our cooperation, they better bring us into the tent," Zablocki said.

Shultz Letter

Immediately after the committee voted, a State Department official provided the committee with a package containing an undated letter from Shultz responding to Long's conditions on the additional aid.

In his letter, Shultz said the Salvadoran government was making progress on two of Chairman Long's conditions — the freeing of political prisoners in El Salvador and the opening of Salvadoran prisons and detention centers to inspections by the International Red Cross. Shultz noted that President Magaña was reviewing the cases of political prisoners and so far had released 60. Shultz also said Magaña had directed that the Red Cross be allowed "unrestricted and unannounced" visits to prisons and detention centers.

In the case of the murdered churchwomen, Shultz said he had ordered an "independent and high level review" of the evidence and would give useful information to the Salvadoran judiciary.

But several members of Long's subcommittee were skeptical, particularly of the special envoy idea. McHugh said he was concerned that such an appointment could give the president a lever to demand congressional approval of further aid to El Salvador. If it appeared that Congress had

insisted on such an envoy, McHugh said, "the president can argue that Congress should not cut the legs out from under the special negotiator."

Reagan on April 28 appointed former Sen. Richard "Dick" Stone, D-Fla. (1975-81), as an ambassador-at-large. Stone had been a State Department consultant on Central American affairs, primarily lobbying Congress in favor of Reagan's policies. He was confirmed by the Senate May 25. *(Story, see box, p. 159)*

Long and his aides touted the agreement on a special ambassador as a major shift in administration policy. One aide noted that administration officials had vigorously opposed such a step on the grounds that it was unnecessary and could lead to inflated expectations for the outcome of negotiations.

Salvadoran Ambassador Rivas-Gallant said his government would accept the special envoy. But he added it should be limited to helping the government "bring the political parties of the left into the electoral process."

Long dropped several other conditions that he had proposed early in negotiations with the administration. For example, he wanted the United States to demand that the Salvadoran government disband two of its police forces — the treasury police and the civil defense units — which had been widely accused of human rights violations. Long also had said he wanted an "immediate" trial of the five former Salvadoran national guardsmen accused of murdering the four churchwomen.

Administration officials said the Salvadoran government could not be expected to disband its only internal police forces. And while expressing frustration with the slow pace of action in several of the murder cases, Shultz and other officials said they did not want the United States to be seen as interfering in the Salvadoran courts.

SUPPLEMENTAL AID

Besides approving additional aid for El Salvador through the reprogramming process, Congress had to consider Reagan's request for supplemental military aid to El Salvador and other countries in the region for fiscal 1983. In 1983, Congress also considered Reagan's aid requests for fiscal 1984, which began Oct. 1, 1983.

Aid requests for both years were combined in a single authorization measure (S 1347, HR 2992). Although an authorization bill was approved by the House Foreign Affairs and Senate Foreign Relations committees, neither chamber took up the bill in 1983.

Congress approved supplemental appropriations for fiscal 1983 in a bill (HR 3069 — PL 98-63) cleared on July 30. *(1982 action on authorizations, 1982 Almanac p. 156)*

Authorization Bills

El Salvador was the main focus of committee action in both houses on the foreign military and economic aid authorization.

In writing fiscal 1983-84 foreign aid authorization legislation in May, the Foreign Relations and Foreign Affairs committees approved compromise proposals on El Salvador that avoided a complete break with Reagan and allowed him to continue providing substantial U.S. support to the Salvadoran government for the foreseeable future.

In part, the committees were responding to Reagan's April 27 appeal for "bipartisan" support of his policies in Central America. But the committees also were stymied by the inability of either the administration or its opponents to round up enough votes for a complete victory.

Some Democrats wanted to give Reagan enough support to undercut any possibility that he could blame them if that country eventually fell to the guerrillas. Other members, of both parties, were concerned that communist advances in Central America could cause a wave of refugees into the United States. Sen. Edward Zorinsky, D-Neb., spoke to that concern: "Lots of folks in Nebraska want fences, barbed wires and machine guns" if necessary to protect U.S. borders.

The committees approved their compromise aid measures by overwhelming votes, demonstrating that the compromises met the minimum requirements of both the administration and its critics.

But indications of the deep political divisions in the committees came on their key votes. By a 6-11 margin, the Senate committee on May 10 rejected a motion to approve Reagan's full aid request for El Salvador; all six "yes" votes were cast by Republicans, while eight Democrats and three Republicans opposed full funding. On May 11 the House committee adopted, 13-10, a proposal to add $8.7 million in military aid for fiscal 1983 to the $56.3 million that it already had approved. Republicans and a handful of Democrats supported that proposal, while the committee's staunch administration critics opposed it.

In public statements, administration spokesmen protested the restrictions and aid cutbacks. Privately, they expressed satisfaction that the committees had taken much more moderate actions than they had feared.

The committees gave Reagan about half the military aid he wanted for fiscal year 1983. Of the requested $136.3 million, the Senate committee approved $76.3 million and the House committee $65 million. This was better than had appeared likely at one point. On April 19 the House Foreign Affairs Committee had voted narrowly against any additional aid for El Salvador for fiscal 1983. And on March 24 the Senate committee had proposed a $56.3 million limit for fiscal 1983 aid.

The committees approved the same amounts for fiscal 1984. Reagan had requested $86.3 million for that year.

Restrictions

The two committees took drastically different approaches to the issue of what conditions should be placed on U.S. aid to El Salvador.

The House committee voted for a complicated and detailed procedure guaranteeing continued congressional oversight of El Salvador for at least another year and a half. It was drafted by an *ad hoc* group of Democrats, led by Dante B. Fascell of Florida.

The Senate committee gave Reagan more room to maneuver. A compromise sponsored by Nancy Landon Kassebaum, R-Kan., stated that it was U.S. policy to encourage an unconditional dialogue among the parties in El Salvador. Both the Reagan administration and the Salvadoran government opposed unconditional talks. Instead, they advocated negotiations only on procedural issues relating to presidential elections in El Salvador.

Foreign Relations Action

The Senate Foreign Relations Committee reported S 1347 (S Rept 98-146), the fiscal 1983-84 foreign aid authorization bill, on May 23.

In an original compromise drafted in March, committee members Kassebaum and Dodd had proposed to limit military aid for El Salvador in each of fiscal years 1983 and 1984 to $50 million.

When it became obvious that there was enough support in the committee for Reagan to get slightly more money, the two senators changed their proposal to $56.3 million for each year, and they held firm at that figure for several weeks.

But Kassebaum was pressured by Foreign Relations Committee Chairman Charles H. Percy, R-Ill., and the administration to modify the proposal. She eventually agreed to another $20 million, with the stipulation that all of the increase had to be used for military training of Salvadoran forces in the United States.

Kassebaum's last-minute acceptance of the $20 million reportedly caught Dodd off guard, and he accepted the change reluctantly.

When the committee met May 10 to consider the bill, Richard G. Lugar, R-Ind., and Jesse Helms, R-N.C., demanded a committee vote on Reagan's original aid requests.

Lugar said Reagan's April 27 speech had begun to swing American public opinion away from outright opposition to U.S. involvement in El Salvador. And Helms made it clear that he wanted a public record of which senators had supported and opposed the president. For himself, Helms said he wanted to show that "I didn't try to cut down on the fire hydrant when the barn is burning" in El Salvador.

The two senators got the vote, but Reagan's full request was rejected, 6-11. Supporting the president were Percy, Helms, Lugar, Howard H. Baker Jr., R-Tenn., Rudy Boschwitz, R-Minn., and Frank H. Murkowski, R-Alaska.

The committee then approved the revised Kassebaum compromise 17-0.

The Kassebaum proposal:

● Set a limit on U.S. military aid to El Salvador of $76.3 million for each of fiscal years 1983 and 1984, with $20 million of that amount to be used each year only for military training of Salvadoran forces in the United States.

● Approved the president's full requests for economic aid to El Salvador: $140 million in fiscal 1983 and $120 million in fiscal 1984.

● Set a limit of 55 on the total number of U.S. military advisers in El Salvador at any time.

● Prohibited the president from using his emergency powers to provide further aid to El Salvador, without congressional approval.

● Stated that in pursuing peace and democracy in El Salvador, the United States "should use its good offices to encourage an unconditional dialogue among all parties...."

● Stated that the war in El Salvador "cannot be divorced from regional influences;" thus the United States should promote regional talks to reduce tension and instability.

The committee also approved an amendment by John Glenn, D-Ohio, requiring the president to report to Congress on the Salvadoran government's plans for controlling its armed forces, disarming private armies, stopping terrorist activities by "death squads," establishing an "effective" judicial system and bringing to trial those responsible for the murders of the eight Americans. But his amendment, unlike the 1981 certification requirement in PL 97-113, did not include an automatic cutoff of U.S. aid should El Salvador fail to take those steps.

On May 12 the committee voted to continue the PL 97-113 requirement that the president certify to Congress twice each year that El Salvador was making progress on several issues, including respect for human rights.

The committee added a new clause requiring the presi-

Military and Economic Aid to El Salvador

Following are the amounts of direct U.S. aid to El Salvador for fiscal years 1981-84. The figures for 1981-83 are actual amounts that were spent. The fiscal 1984 amounts were approved in a continuing appropriations resolution (PL 98-151); the administration was expected to seek additional funds for that year.

Not included in the chart are housing and agricultural commodity loan guarantee programs.

(in millions of dollars)

	1981	1982	1983	1984
Military Aid				
Foreign Military Sales guaranteed loans	$ 10.0	$ 16.5	$ 46.5	$ 18.5[1]
Military Assistance Program grants	0	8.5	33.5	45.0[1]
Defense Department Drawdown[2]	25.0	55.0	0	
International Military Education/Training	.5	2.0	1.3	1.3[1]
Total, Military aid	$ 35.5	$ 82.0	$ 81.3	$ 64.8
Non-Military Aid				
Economic Support Fund	44.9	115.0	140.0	120.0[3]
Development Assistance	32.8	36.2	60.8	38.0[3]
Food for Peace	26.3	34.4	39.0	32.0[3]
Disaster Assistance	2.6	6.9	0	0[3]
Total, Non-Military Aid	$ 106.6	$ 192.5	$ 239.8	$ 190.0

[1] *For fiscal 1984, PL 98-151 placed a $64.8 million limit on military aid and gave the president discretion to determine under which category that aid would be given.*

[2] *Emergency aid, provided as a grant from Defense Department sup-*

plies and services.

[3] *Fiscal 1984 non-military aid figures as proposed by Reagan in January 1983. Revised figures will be submitted to Congress early in 1984.*

---

dent to certify that El Salvador had taken "concrete steps" to strengthen and ensure the independence and integrity of its judicial system.

In proposing extension of the certification process, Chairman Percy said it "has not lived up to all of the expectations and it has been subject to criticisms, but I think it would send a wrong signal at this particular time" for Congress not to renew it.

The committee also approved an amendment by Helms requiring the president to report to Congress on the "violence, intimidation and lawlessness of the terrorist guerrillas" in El Salvador.

House Committee Bill

The House Foreign Affairs Committee reported its version of the foreign aid authorization bill (HR 2992 — H Rept 98-192) on May 17.

The El Salvador compromise included in HR 2992 was the outgrowth of intense negotiations among the Foreign Affairs panel's Democrats and Republicans over several weeks. The negotiations took on an urgent note after Reagan's April El Salvador speech. By then, some Democrats were inclined to support Reagan, while others remained steadfastly opposed to U.S. policies in El Salvador.

Fascell's own approach essentially was to allow the president to continue providing military aid to El Salvador so long as he could make a credible case that the Salvadoran government was making progress on issues of concern in Congress, such as improving respect for human rights.

The position taken by the committee's Western Hemisphere Affairs Subcommittee, on the other hand, would

have made it virtually impossible for U.S. aid to continue unless the president could convince Congress that El Salvador already had accomplished a wide range of reforms, such as completely stopping the killing of civilians by the military forces. That proposal was written by subcommittee member Stephen J. Solarz, D-N.Y.

Fascell began negotiations with the backing of several fellow Southern Democrats. As the negotiations proceeded, he picked up support from influential moderates and liberals, including subcommittee Chairman Michael D. Barnes, D-Md., and Lee H. Hamilton, D-Ind.

Although a consistent critic of Reagan's policies in Central America, Barnes expressed concern about forcing the president to "certify the uncertifiable" to Congress in order to continue aiding El Salvador.

On May 10 the Democrats narrowed their differences, and Fascell said he had achieved "a policy that has a broad consensus."

When the full committee took up Fascell's proposal on May 11, most members said they were not satisfied with it, but praised it as a masterpiece of political compromise.

One administration supporter, Henry J. Hyde, R-Ill., complained of the restraints in the proposal: "We have taken the president, put him in a straitjacket, locked him in a trunk and dropped him in the river."

But Hyde said Fascell's proposal was "a work of political legerdemain" that enabled members to vote for it in spite of their misgivings about some of the specifics. He added: "If you can't get dinner, get a sandwich."

Committee liberals were able to vote for the compromise because it required the Salvadoran government to engage in an unconditional dialogue with its opponents and

it established a one-house veto over further aid after Oct. 1, 1984.

The Fascell compromise was approved 36-1, with George W. Crockett Jr., D-Mich., casting the "no" vote.

Fascell Compromise. Fascell's proposal required several steps before U.S. military aid could be granted to El Salvador, starting with a requirement that within 60 days of enactment of the bill the president had to submit to Congress a report describing and commenting on the Salvadoran government's plans for addressing nine "objectives." Those were:

● Engagement by the government, within 90 days after enactment of the bill, in a "dialogue, in good faith and without preconditions, with all major parties to the conflict in El Salvador for the purpose of achieving an equitable political solution to the conflict." Two specified "elements" were "free and fair elections" and arrangements for the safety of all participants in the election.

● Establishment of "effective control" by the government over all armed forces in the country, including paramilitary groups, to end involvement by those forces in "indiscriminate violence" and secret detention, abduction, torture and murder.

● Establishment by the government of an "effective judicial system."

● Establishment of "political and social processes" that contribute to strong democratic institutions and a peaceful resolution of conflict in the country.

● Protection of human rights and "ensuring the alleviation of suffering resulting from devastation of the war through the provision of medical services and the basic necessities of life."

● Bringing to trial and disciplining the members of the security forces responsible for human rights violations.

● Bringing to trial and disciplining those "directly or indirectly responsible" for the murders of eight Americans in El Salvador since December 1980.

● Completion of a "successful" land reform program.

● Involvement of the Organization of American States (OAS) or other international organizations in an unconditional dialogue to end the war.

Half of the military aid budgeted for El Salvador for fiscal 1984 was to be made available on Oct. 1, 1983. The remaining 50 percent could not be spent until 30 days after March 30, 1984.

Within 90 days of enactment of the bill, the president had to suspend military aid unless he determined that the government was "actively engaged" in the unconditional dialogue with its opposition or had been unable to enter into such a dialogue because the major opposition groups had refused to participate.

On March 30, 1984, and again on Aug. 31, 1984, the president was required to report to Congress on the Salvadoran government's progress in meeting the nine objectives. If the president did not submit the reports, he would have to suspend all military aid and sales to El Salvador and withdraw all U.S. military advisers.

Congress could reject the March 30 progress report — and thus prevent spending of the remaining half of El Salvador's military aid — by passing a concurrent resolution within 30 days.

The president could not provide military aid to El Salvador in fiscal 1985 unless Congress passed a joint resolution accepting his report of Aug. 31, 1984. This provision effectively created a one-house veto over El Salvador's military aid since approval by both chambers of Congress

was necessary for the aid to continue in fiscal 1985.

The amendment also prohibited the president from using his power to draw from Defense Department stocks to provide military aid to El Salvador without congressional approval. And it required him to obtain approval by Congress for his use of another power, contained in section 614(a) of PL 96-533, allowing him to waive all legal restrictions on providing foreign aid if he said it was in the "national security interest" to do so.

Land Reform. The House committee imposed a similar set of conditions on U.S. Economic Support Fund (ESF) aid to encourage completion of El Salvador's land reform program. The committee proposed to require the president to report to Congress three times in fiscal 1984-85 on progress in the land reform program, with the first report due at the end of March 1984. The committee also froze half of El Salvador's $120 million in ESF aid for fiscal 1984 until Congress had been given 15 days to review the first report. Congress could block fiscal 1985 aid to El Salvador by passing a concurrent resolution.

The House panel also voted to allow ESF aid to be used to implement the land reform program. But on an amendment by Studds, it voted to ban use of the money to compensate Salvadoran landowners for the expropriation of their property.

Aid Amounts. The committee also compromised on amounts of military aid. By a 21-7 vote, the panel adopted an amendment by Mica, to provide $65 million in military aid for El Salvador in each of fiscal years 1984 and 1985. All seven "no" votes were cast by liberal Democrats. Of the total, $10 million was set aside each year for training of Salvadoran forces outside El Salvador and $5 million was for medical supplies and equipment to El Salvador.

The committee subsequently approved, 13-10, an amendment by Barnes authorizing the same amount of aid for fiscal 1983.

Advisers. The committee set a limit of 55 on the number of U.S. military advisers or trainers that could be stationed in El Salvador. But at the administration's request, the committee exempted from the limit any U.S. military personnel "who are in El Salvador solely for the purpose of performing medical training or services."

Supplemental Appropriations

The House Appropriations Committee on May 18, 1983, deferred "without prejudice" consideration of any additional military aid for El Salvador when it considered the fiscal 1983 supplemental bill (HR 3069).

Reagan had requested $50 million in additional Military Assistance Program grants for El Salvador, as part of his March request that would have put total military aid at $136.3 million.

The House then approved HR 3069 on May 25 without allowing any of the additional funds Reagan requested.

Eight days later, on May 26, the Senate Appropriations Committee approved Reagan's $50 million request in adopting its version of HR 3069. The Senate retained the $50 million when it passed HR 3069 on June 16.

House-Senate conferees on the bill agreed July 20 to a $25 million addition in military grants, bringing total U.S. military aid for El Salvador in fiscal 1983 to $81.3 million. HR 3069 was cleared by Congress July 29 and signed the next day by the president (PL 98-63).

Added to the $30 million in arms loans that Reagan had reprogrammed to El Salvador in April, the $25 million raised to $55 million the amount of supplemental military

aid for El Salvador in fiscal 1983 — exactly half of Reagan's $110 million request.

A State Department official said the extra $25 million was "clearly inadequate to meet the needs," but added that the administration "can live with" that amount.

An aide to a senior House member said none of the conferees on the supplemental bill — not even the staunchest opponents of military aid to El Salvador — moved to fight the $25 million.

"There wasn't much of an inclination to fight this, either for it or against it," the aide said. "People seem to be very tired of this [El Salvador] issue."

1984 Appropriations

Neither house in the first session of the 98th Congress acted on a regular foreign aid appropriations bill for fiscal 1984. Although the Foreign Operations subcommittees of the House and Senate Appropriations committees considered fiscal 1984 funding, only the Senate panel formally reported a regular foreign aid bill.

Instead, the panels' recommendations were incorporated in the fiscal 1984 omnibus continuing appropriations resolution (H J Res 413) covering departments and agencies whose regular funding bills were never cleared by Congress.

Because Congress also failed to enact a fiscal 1984 foreign aid authorization bill, the resolution in effect served as the vehicle for the statutory authorization as well as appropriations for foreign aid.

Legislative Action

The 30 percent withholding in the churchwomen's murder case had been proposed Sept. 27 by Sen. Arlen Specter, R-Pa., during action on the foreign aid bill (S 1892) by the the Senate Foreign Operations Subcommittee. The subcommittee approved Reagan's full $86.3 million request for military aid.

The full Senate Appropriations Committee adopted the subcommittee recommendations and reported its foreign aid spending bill Sept. 27 (S Rept 98-245). That bill never reached the Senate floor.

The House Foreign Operations Appropriations Subcommittee, in its Oct. 5 action on foreign aid, cut back Reagan's request for Salvadoran military aid to $51.3 million, including $30 million in FMS loans, $20 million in MAP grants and $1.3 million for military training.

The panel also cut economic assistance, from the $120 million requested to $100 million.

The subcommittee also adopted Sen. Specter's proposal for conditioning the military aid, and added a demand for completion of the investigation into the murders of two AFL-CIO workers in January 1981.

The House panel also voted to condition all aid on a presidential certification that the Salvadoran land reform program was still in effect.

It rejected, however, an appeal by Rep. Barnes that the panel add the sweeping restrictions on aid to El Salvador that had been adopted earlier in the year by the House Foreign Affairs Committee.

The full House Appropriations Committee never considered a regular foreign aid bill. Instead, it folded aid provisions into the continuing resolution on Nov. 2. *(Story, p. 521)*

Neither House voted directly on El Salvador aid issues during their consideration of the continuing resolution.

House-Senate conferees reached agreement on the continuing resolution on Nov. 11. Aid to El Salvador was one of the most contested issues in a meeting of members of the two Foreign Operations Appropriations subcommittees.

For El Salvador, the continuing resolution (H J Res 413 — PL 98-151) limited military aid to $64.8 million, and gave the administration the discretion to determine how much would be in grants and how much would be in the form of loans. The $64.8 million was a limit on all military aid to El Salvador under the bill; to exceed that amount, Reagan would have been required to request a supplemental appropriation or to use his emergency authorities to provide aid.

Reagan had requested $86.3 million for El Salvador.

Of the total amount approved by Congress, 30 percent was withheld until Salvadoran authorities substantially concluded their investigation into the cases of the former national guardsmen accused of murdering four American churchwomen in December 1980, brought the accused to trial and obtained a verdict.

The continuing resolution also withheld 10 percent of the total amount until the president certified to Congress that the Salvadoran regime had not taken any actions that would "modify, alter, suspend, or terminate" the two major portions of the land reform program in a manner that would be detrimental to the rights of those who intended to benefit from the program. The president also was required to certify that the Salvadoran government "continues to make documented progress" in the land reform program.

However, the two withholdings combined were not to exceed 30 percent of the aid.

The continuing resolution allowed the administration to provide economic aid for El Salvador at the requested levels: $120 million in economic aid and $38 million in development assistance.

The bill earmarked $3 million of the economic aid for helping the Salvadoran government improve its judicial system. ∎

Reports on El Salvador

The State Department in 1983 sent Congress two reports on El Salvador's progress in human rights, land reform and other areas. The reports were required by a 1981 law (PL 98-113) that banned military aid to El Salvador unless the president certified to Congress that the Salvadoran government was making progress in those areas.

The 1983 reports were the third and fourth reports issued under PL 97-113; the first two reports were issued in 1982. *(1982 Almanac p. 137)*

January Report

In its third report, issued on Jan. 21, 1983, the administration certified to Congress that the embattled government of El Salvador was "making progress" in several areas, including respect for human rights. "The situation is not perfect and the progress was not as great as desired, but it is progress nonetheless," the State Department said.

That report was roundly criticized by some on Capitol Hill and outside government. Sen. Christopher J. Dodd, D-Conn., a chief author of the certification law, said the administration's "blanket, total approval of conditions" in

El Salvador "is unwarranted" and showed that it "is going to certify regardless of the circumstances."

The American Civil Liberties Union (ACLU) and Americas Watch said the rights situation there was "worse than ever."

The 67-page report backing up the Jan. 21 certification was far tougher than its two predecessors in its criticisms of the Salvadoran government. It made blunt comments about the Salvadoran government's shortcomings, emphasizing failures of the criminal justice and military discipline systems. The report complained of the "systematic ineffectiveness" of the criminal justice system, "particularly in cases originating in political violence." U.S. officials had said the major obstacle to certification was El Salvador's failure to bring to justice those responsible for political murders, especially the murders of eight Americans in 1980 and 1981.

Thomas O. Enders, assistant secretary of state for inter-American affairs, said only a "very few" members of the armed forces charged with abusing human rights actually were brought to justice.

Human Rights

The first criterion in the certification law was that the Salvadoran government had to make "a concerted and significant effort to comply with internationally recognized human rights."

While conceding that "human rights abuses continue," the State Department said the criterion had been met because "political violence" was diminishing and the government was moving to protect its citizens' rights.

The department's main standard for judging compliance on the human rights issue was the number of civilian deaths attributed to political causes, such as murders by right-wing paramilitary "death squads."

The report said such deaths had "declined significantly" and, according to Salvadoran press reports, did not exceed 200 per month in the last half of 1982, compared to a monthly average of nearly 500 in 1981. Press accounts indicated civilian deaths declined from 5,331 in 1981 to 2,630 in 1982. Salvadoran human rights groups reported similar proportionate declines, but their figures were two to three times higher for both years.

The administration's report also listed death totals reported by human rights groups, but it discussed only those in press accounts. The report admitted these accounts were incomplete and possibly unreliable, but it said their use in monitoring deaths "has the benefit of consistency," and thus they were valid for showing trends.

The report said hundreds of persons disappeared in 1982 "and there is compelling information that elements of the security forces are responsible in many cases."

Human rights groups in the United States quickly challenged the facts and assumptions behind the State Department's report. One of the most extensive critiques was issued by the ACLU and Americas Watch. They cited reports by two Catholic Church-related legal aid offices in El Salvador that more than 5,000 civilians were killed in 1982. In 1981 one of these agencies had counted 13,353 civilian deaths.

The ACLU and Americas Watch rejected the State Department's contention that the reduced number of civilian deaths was a sign of progress entitling El Salvador to continued U.S. aid. "The murder of 500 people a month by groups formally or informally connected to the government cannot be seen as acceptable by any standards," their

report said.

The State Department also cited as progress the installation in December of a government human rights commission. But U.S. human rights groups complained that one of the commission members was Col. Reynaldo Lopez Nuila, head of the National Police, which had been accused of numerous human rights abuses.

Controlling the Armed Forces

The second certification standard required evidence that the government was "achieving substantial control over all elements of its own armed forces, so as to bring to an end the indiscriminate torture and murder of Salvadoran citizens by these forces."

The State Department said the Salvadoran government was giving "increased attention" to the need to control human rights abuses by the military, but it said progress was slow.

The report said there had been no recent substantiated reports of "widespread abuses" by the military. But it said "incidents of smaller-scale abuse continue," such as the murder of seven peasants by uniformed men Nov. 20, 1982, in Santa Ana province.

As of January 1983, 141 military personnel were being held "for abuses of authority," the report said.

The report did not address complaints by some human rights groups that previous certification reports overstated the disciplinary actions taken by the military in human rights cases.

Economic Reforms

The third certification standard required El Salvador to make "continued progress in implementing essential economic and political reforms, including the land reform program."

In the United States, most attention centered on the three-part land reform program. The State Department cited some success in the two functioning parts: Phase I, which converted 328 large estates into cooperatives, and Phase III, which allowed sharecroppers and tenant farmers to apply for ownership of the land they farmed. Phase II, designed to convert medium-sized estates into cooperatives, had been shelved.

Both functioning phases encountered difficulties. The civil war forced abandonment of 27 cooperatives and severe problems at 20 others, according to the report. The government also did not have enough money to compensate owners whose land had been taken; thus many of the cooperatives and small farmers had not received official titles.

Of 39,000 farmers who applied for titles to land under Phase III, nearly 5,000 were evicted from their farms in 1982 after the Constituent Assembly voted to suspend some aspects of the program. About half of them later were allowed to return. The Assembly's action was largely responsible for Congress' decision to cut back aid to El Salvador.

Political Reform

The fourth standard for certification said the government had to be "committed to the holding of free elections at an early date and to that end had demonstrated its good-faith efforts to begin discussions with all major political factions in El Salvador which had declared their willingness to find and implement an equitable political solution to the conflict, with such solution to involve a commitment to: (a) a renouncement of further military or paramilitary

activity and (b) the electoral process with internationally recognized observers."

Of all the certification standards, the State Department report cited the greatest progress in the movement toward free elections. A Constituent Assembly was elected in March 1982, and presidential and municipal elections were scheduled for March 1984.

Many members of Congress expressed concern that the Constituent Assembly would be dominated by its new president, Roberto d'Aubuisson, leader of the far-right ARENA party. But the report said d'Aubuisson and the "far-rightist elements" in the Assembly "have not achieved a clear majority." Instead, it said, issues were resolved through bargaining and compromise and "centrist forces have dominated on significant occasions."

The State Department report labeled as a "setback" the October 1982 kidnappings of 17 opposition leaders, including labor union officials and several leaders of the Democratic Revolutionary Front (FDR in Spanish), the political arm of the guerrilla movement. The government acknowledged holding eight of the 17, and six others were reported to be missing. Enders, however, expressed little sympathy for the FDR leaders, who he said "are members of an organization that is allied with and supports an armed insurrection."

Murdered Americans

The State Department reported delays and setbacks in El Salvador's handling of the murders of the eight U.S. citizens in 1980 and 1981. Congress called for a report on the murder investigations in January 1982, and the administration voluntarily had made follow-up reports.

The Salvadoran government's failure to bring to justice those responsible for the murders continued to be embarrassing and frustrating for the Reagan administration. The murder cases helped sustain criticism of administration policy in El Salvador, with some critics charging that the Salvadoran regime's failure to resolve the cases symbolized its inability to protect the lives of civilians.

The trial of five former national guardsmen charged with killing four U.S. churchwomen in December 1980, was delayed several times.

The case of two land reform consultants murdered in January 1981 was more complicated and potentially more explosive. They worked for an arm of the AFL-CIO, which in 1983 opposed certification for the first time. Two national guardsmen confessed to the murders and were ordered to stand trial. They implicated two guard officers, but charges were dropped against one, Lt. Lopez Sibrian, who allegedly had close ties to right-wing politicians. He returned to duty in the national guard.

July Report

The State Department's fourth report, sent to Congress July 20, was by far the most negative one yet given Congress.

The report was signed by Secretary of State George P. Shultz, who made clear his reluctance to state that El Salvador was making substantial progress. Shultz said El Salvador had met the standards of the 1981 law but added: "It is evident that the record falls far short of the broad and sustained progress which both the Congress and the administration believe is necessary for the evolution of a just and democratic society in El Salvador."

Both the State Department and Americas Watch re-

ported that more civilians were killed in El Salvador during the first six months of 1983 than during the last six months of 1982. Citing reports of the pro-government press in El Salvador, the State Department put civilian deaths so far in 1983 at 1,054, compared to 961 in the last half of 1982. Citing figures compiled by human rights groups in El Salvador, Americas Watch said Salvadoran military, police and paramilitary forces had killed 2,527 civilians in the same period, compared to 2,340 in 1982.

As with three previous reports, administration critics rejected the report's facts and conclusions. Rep. Michael D. Barnes, D-Md., said the report showed that "the certification process has become more and more of a joke. There is no way on the facts that anybody can certify with a straight face that progress has been made" on such issues as human rights.

As with the previous certifications, the State Department's report was challenged by several of the groups that monitored human rights conditions in foreign countries. The most comprehensive rebuttal was issued jointly on July 19 by the Americas Watch Committee and the ACLU.

The contrast between the two points of view was predictably sharp.

In his letter accompanying the report to Congress, Shultz admitted that while "progress in some key areas has been disturbingly slow ... our disappointment over the pace of change should not obscure the fact that change is occurring. The people of El Salvador deserve our support in their effort to achieve a truly democratic society, which will provide the best and most lasting safeguard of human rights."

Americas Watch and ACLU insisted, however, that El Salvador had not made the progress required by the 1981 law. Those groups said the Reagan administration "has defeated the main purpose of the certification law by letting it be known that certification is a sure thing. Thereby, it has deprived itself of the capacity to influence the central human rights problem in El Salvador: the routine practice of political murder by the Salvadoran security forces."

Both reports again painted a picture of El Salvador as a country where murder, abduction and torture for political reasons were common.

The Americas Watch/ACLU report was the more graphic, describing in detail several cases of human rights violations, including a mass murder of peasants, the murders of Christian Democratic Party mayors, and aerial bombings of civilians from U.S.-supplied planes.

Different methods were used in counting political victims, and neither side claimed complete accuracy for its figures. A senior administration official said "nobody's statistics are reliable" about the number of El Salvador political murders. The Americas Watch/ACLU report said the real number "is almost certainly considerably higher" than the figure it reported.

The Americas Watch/ACLU report said anything other than a decline in the number of killings and disappearances means "the human rights situation is steadily worsening."

Claiming that some 36,000 civilians had been killed by security forces since 1979, Arieh Neier, an Americas Watch spokesman, said he found it "astonishing that the government of El Salvador can continue to find so many suspect persons to kill."

The State Department declined to lay most of the blame for political atrocities on either the right or the left. Instead, the report said "armed rightist terrorists, includ-

ing members of the government's security forces, bear responsibility for many deaths" and added that leftist guerrillas "also bear responsibility for many violations. . . ."

The Americas Watch/ACLU report betrayed no such hesitation to lay the blame. Their report said rightist groups and government security forces were responsible for all of the 2,527 murders reported by Tutela Legal, the legal aid office of the Roman Catholic Archdiocese in San Salvador.

Still, leftist guerrillas "are themselves responsible for an increasing number of human rights violations," the two groups said. Tutela Legal had found 43 political murders attributed to the guerrillas during the first six months of 1983 — twice the number found during the last half of 1982.

The Americas Watch/ACLU report condemned the guerrillas for the forced recruitment of young men and for its summary executions of soldiers.

At a July 20 briefing, State Department officials acknowledged that the level of political violence was higher in El Salvador than in any other Central American country, but pointed to a new amnesty law and a new human rights commission as signs of progress in the field of human rights.

Americas Watch/ACLU, however, said the commission served only "a marginally useful function," and numbered among its members Col. Lopez Nuila, commander of the National Police, which the groups said "is implicated in many murders, disappearances and cases of torture."

Control of Armed Forces

The State Department reported that leaders of the Salvadoran armed forces had attempted to promote respect for human rights. But it acknowledged that military personnel continued to be involved in "right wing paramilitary activity." It cited as "the most serious incident" the Feb. 22 killing of at least 18 members of a farm cooperative at Las Hojes by government soldiers.

The bluntest comments in the State Department report concerned the El Salvador government's failure to prosecute those responsible for human rights abuses.

It cited 17 cases in which military and security personnel had been charged with serious offenses since late 1982. Eight of the defendants had been convicted as of May, but the report admitted that none of the cases involved crimes that were committed "for apparent political motives."

The Americas Watch/ACLU report said "no one is yet able to cite to us a single case of criminal punishment of a member of the Salvadoran armed forces for a human rights violation." The two groups also said the State Department "engaged in a flim-flam" by promising to monitor the cases of military personnel accused of human rights violations, but then failing to do so.

Judicial System

Both reports said the Salvadoran legal system was incapable of punishing persons responsible for ordinary crimes, let alone those responsible for human rights violations.

As it indicated in past reports, the State Department said the judicature "is in a state of virtual collapse. Convictions in serious criminal cases, in particular those with political overtones of any kind, are virtually unobtainable because of intimidation (usually only implicit) and corruption of judges, lawyers, witnesses and jurors."

The Salvadoran government "has begun reform of its judicial system." But although the United States was providing technical and financial support for that effort, the report said, the reform effort would take time because of "years of neglect and disrespect for the legal system in El Salvador, aggravated by the cruelty of the present conflict."

The Americas Watch/ACLU report agreed but accused the State Department of using the failures of the judicial system as an excuse "for the Salvadoran government's failure to end the political killings."

Murdered Americans

The State Department report offered hope, but little in the way of concrete evidence, that there ever would be a final resolution of the cases of those responsible for the murders of eight Americans in El Salvador since December 1980.

In the case of the four murdered churchwomen, the report said the State Department was "hopeful" that a trial would begin "in the next few weeks," but it noted that "further delays cannot be ruled out."

As if to fulfill the department's expectation, the Associated Press on July 23 quoted the judge handling the case as saying it might be delayed another six months because he had received new evidence implicating six policemen in the case.

The State Department report cited several obstacles to the prosecution of those responsible for the murder of the two land reform workers in January 1981. It noted that only action by the Salvadoran Supreme Court could lead to reinstatement of charges against three persons in the case.

The State Department report could point to no progress in locating the killers of John Sullivan, a freelance journalist who was killed in December 1980. Three soldiers had been detained, and a civilian judge was conducting an investigation, in the case of Michael Kline, an American traveler killed in October 1982.

The State Department also could offer no hope for a resolution of the case of Patricia Cuellar, a U.S. citizen who had worked for a Salvadoran human rights group and who disappeared in July 1982, along with her father and a maid.

The State Department report accepted a claim by leftist guerrilla groups that they were responsible for the May 1983 murder of Navy Lt. Commander Albert A. Schaufelberger.

Schaufelberger was the only American serviceman killed as of the end of 1983 in the Salvadoran civil war.

Political Reform

The State Department report said El Salvador in the first half of 1983 had "made clear progress in strengthening democratic institutions." As evidence of "political reform," the State Department cited these developments:

● The Constituent Assembly, whose members were elected in March 1982, was functioning as "El Salvador's primary organ for political decision and debate." Debate in the Assembly "is often divisive, but the parties have shown themselves capable of reaching compromises."

● Presidential elections were scheduled for 1984, and the government-run Peace Commission attempted to convince leftist opposition groups — including those backing the guerrillas — to participate.

● A draft constitution, debated by the Constituent Assembly, included new rights and protections for individuals.

The Americas Watch/ACLU report did not directly

address the question of political reform in El Salvador. But it charged that "the great number of murders and abductions by the security forces make a mockery" of the State Department's contention that El Salvador was undergoing democratic development.

The two groups noted particularly the "continuing victimization" of the Christian Democratic Party, apparently El Salvador's largest single party. The report said some 35 Christian Democratic mayors had been murdered in recent years, including nine in 1982.

Land Reform

The State Department said El Salvador's land reform program "remains on track and is moving forward." Most U.S. observers said the political and social unrest in El Salvador had been caused in large part by the concentration of agricultural land in the hands of a few families. The State Department report echoed that sentiment, noting that in 1980 "40 percent of all farmland was held by only 0.2 percent of the population."

The legal decree under which the land reform program operated was renewed in December 1983.

House Subcommittee Hearing

At a July 26 hearing, only a handful of the 18 members of the House Foreign Affairs Western Hemisphere Affairs and Human Rights subcommittees showed up to hear one supporter and several critics of the administration discuss the report.

Western Hemisphere Affairs Subcommittee Chairman Barnes issued the harshest attack on the report, saying the administration had found it necessary to "use its imagination to justify the certification," even though "the human rights performance of the government [of El Salvador] continues to be dismal."

A staunch defense of the Salvadoran government came from Rep. Thomas F. Hartnett, R-S.C., who visited El Salvador from July 16-19. Hartnett argued that "violence and killing" had been customary among Salvadorans "for hundreds of years, and now we're trying to hold them to our standards."

"I'm proud of the government of El Salvador and what they're trying to do, and I think they're getting a bum rap from some members of Congress," he said.

U.S.-Vatican Relations

Over the objections of a number of religious groups, Congress in November quietly agreed to repeal an 1867 law that prohibited the use of federal funds to maintain a diplomatic mission to the Vatican.

The action came on an amendment that was added by the Senate to legislation (HR 2915 — PL 98-164) authorizing funds in fiscal 1984 and 1985 for the State Department and related agencies.

President Reagan signed the measure into law Nov. 22. *(State Department authorization, p. 145)*

The Reagan administration announced Jan. 10, 1984, that it would establish full diplomatic ties with the Vatican. A day later, Reagan nominated William A. Wilson, who had been serving as his personal envoy to the Vatican, to become U.S. ambassador to the Vatican.

Because the nomination required Senate confirmation, a variety of religious groups opposed to diplomatic recognition of the Vatican planned to use Senate hearings to lobby against formal ties to the Holy See. One group, Americans United for Separation of Church and State, said it would go to court to block U.S.-Vatican diplomatic relations as a violation of church-state separation if the Senate confirmed an ambassador.

Administration officials contended there were no legal barriers to the move because the U.S. government was recognizing the Vatican as an independent state and was not conferring any special status on the Roman Catholic religion.

Objections Raised

"We feel it is inappropriate for the U.S. government to appoint an ambassador to the [Roman Catholic] Church, to *any* church," said the Rev. Dean M. Kelly, director for religious and civil liberty at the National Council of Churches, soon after Congress had acted.

The council, an umbrella group of Protestant denominations, was joined by other religious groups in opposing U.S. diplomatic ties to the Vatican. All of them argued that such a move would run afoul of the constitutional principle of separation of church and state.

"With respect to the Vatican, we believe the Holy See is principally a religious entity. It is the headquarters of the Roman Catholic Church," said Dr. Gary M. Ross, congressional liaison for the General Conference of Seventh-day Adventists.

Extending diplomatic relations to the Vatican placed the government in a position of giving preferential treatment to a particular religion, in violation of the First Amendment, Ross contended.

Other religious groups and officials opposing U.S.-Vatican ties included the National Association of Evangelicals, the Baptist Joint Committee on Public Affairs, the American Jewish Congress and the Rev. Jerry Falwell, head of the Moral Majority.

Henry Siegman, executive director of the American Jewish Congress, said it was a mistake for the U.S. government to "relate to any particular religious body in any preferential way." Siegman said the existence of the Vatican as a separate geographical entity was simply the result of a historical "fluke" between the Roman Catholic Church and the nation of Italy.

Catholic officials in the United States said they were neutral on the sensitive Vatican issue.

The U.S. Catholic Conference "just doesn't care to get involved with the question," said Russell B. Shaw, a spokesman for the organization, which represented Catholic bishops in the United States on civil and secular issues. "It's something between the U.S. government and the Vatican."

Vatican as Political Force

Reagan, like several other presidents stretching back to Franklin D. Roosevelt, designated a personal representative to the Vatican. But that individual did not enjoy diplomatic status. Reagan's part-time envoy was Wilson, a Southern California rancher and land developer.

Members of Congress who supported U.S.-Vatican relations said such a move was justified because of Pope John Paul II's emergence as a political as well as a religious leader.

Sen. Richard G. Lugar, R-Ind., said John Paul deserved credit for transforming the Vatican into a "significant political force for decency in the world."

Lugar sponsored the amendment to repeal the 1867 law barring U.S.-Vatican diplomatic relations. The amendment was added to HR 2915 by voice vote in the Senate on Sept. 22. There was no dissent during the brief floor debate.

House Foreign Affairs Committee Chairman Clement J. Zablocki, D-Wis., who died Dec. 3, also had introduced legislation (H J Res 316) in the House in June to authorize U.S.-Vatican diplomatic relations.

Lugar argued that by formalizing relations with the Vatican, the United States would be recognizing the pope not as the head of the Catholic Church but rather as leader of a sovereign state that was playing an increasingly important role in world affairs.

The Vatican currently maintained diplomatic relations with 107 nations, including Great Britain, which established such ties in 1980 after a 448-year lapse.

The Vatican also was represented in all major United Nations organizations and sent a permanent observer to the Common Market in Europe and the Organization of American States.

Although the Vatican had no formal diplomatic presence in Washington, an apostolic delegate to the American church, Archibishop Pio Laghi, served in an unofficial diplomatic capacity through occasional meetings with government officials. Laghi was based in Washington.

History of U.S.-Vatican Ties

The United States maintained consular relations with the Vatican from 1797 to 1848, after which it entered into full diplomatic relations for 20 years.

But in 1867, Congress barred the use of federal funds to continue those relations in response to a move in Italy to reunite the independent Papal States with the rest of the country. Since 1870, the Vatican had consisted only of the 108 acres that serve as the headquarters of the Roman Catholic Church.

As a city-state, Vatican City in 1983 had fewer than 1,000 citizens; it nonetheless issued its own license plates and postage stamps.

In the 1950s, President Harry S Truman considered naming an ambassador to the Vatican, but backed down after various non-Catholic religious groups vigorously fought such a move.

Franklin D. Roosevelt, Truman's predecessor, was the first president to send a personal representative to the Vatican. Besides Reagan, Presidents Richard M. Nixon, Gerald R. Ford and Jimmy Carter also sent envoys to the Vatican; Dwight D. Eisenhower, John F. Kennedy and Lyndon B. Johnson did not.

Kennedy, the nation's first Catholic president, might have been reluctant to name a Vatican envoy because of anti-Catholic sentiments during his 1960 campaign. Some critics expressed fears that his election would increase the power of the Roman Catholic Church in U.S. affairs.

In 1977, the Senate voted to repeal the 1867 law barring U.S.-Vatican diplomatic relations, but the provision was dropped in a House-Senate conference. In 1983, however, Lugar's amendment sailed through Congress with only a few dissenting voices.

One who did express concern was Rep. George W. Crockett Jr., D-Mich., who said during a conference committee meeting on the State Department bill that sending an ambassador to the Vatican might run counter to the First Amendment, which guaranteed religious freedom in the United States.

Lugar originally introduced his amendment as a sepa-

rate bill (S 1757) after a spring trip to Europe that included meetings with U.S. staff members who worked for Vatican envoy Wilson in Italy. Lugar later described existing U.S. ties with the Vatican as an "awkward charade" because of their non-diplomatic status.

While in Italy, Lugar, a Methodist, met with Pope John Paul II, but did not discuss the diplomatic issue, according to an aide.   ∎

Kissinger Commission

Besieged by political challenges to his policies toward Central America, President Reagan turned for advice to a 12-member "bipartisan commission" headed by former Secretary of State Henry A. Kissinger.

After five months of closed hearings, meetings and travels to the region, the commission issued its report on Jan. 11, 1984. In general, the report endorsed the thrust of Reagan's policies, saying there was a "crisis" in Central America that was "real and acute" and the United States "must act to meet it, and act boldly."

The commission called for more than $8 billion in economic aid to the region through 1989 and for firm U.S. resistance to the expansion of Soviet and Cuban influence.

The report endorsed a "substantial" increase in military aid for El Salvador and backed indirectly Reagan's program of "covert" aid to anti-government rebels in Nicaragua. It also called on Reagan and Central American leaders to meet to decide on a plan for long-range economic development in the region.

In its most controversial recommendation, the commission backed congressional demands that military aid to El Salvador be conditioned on progress on such human rights concerns as curbing the activities of so-called "death squads."

The commission did not recommend using U.S. military forces to fight in Central America. But it did say the United States should consider force against the leftist Nicaraguan government as a "last resort" if it refused to agree to stop supporting guerrilla movements in other countries.

Commission Established

Reagan announced the establishment of the commission in a July 18 speech to the International Longshoremen's Association convention in Hollywood, Fla. He predicted the panel would "lay the foundation for a long-term unified national approach to the freedom and independence of the countries of Central America."

The idea of a commisssion was proposed in June by Sen. Henry M. Jackson, D-Wash.; Sen. Charles McC. Mathias, Jr., D-Md.; and Reps. Michael D. Barnes, D-Md.; and Jack F. Kemp, R-N.Y.. They introduced legislation (S Res 158, H Res 240) calling on the president to appoint such a body.

Jackson originally had suggested the commission.

The naming of Kissinger produced intense controversy on Capitol Hill. Reagan called Kissinger "virtually a legend" in the field of diplomacy, but several liberals and conservatives in Congress attacked that legend.

Sen. Jesse Helms, R-N.C., and other conservatives had complained for years about Kissinger's promotion of détente between the United States and the Soviet Union in the early 1970s. Several liberals said Kissinger's credibility would be hampered by his actions as secretary of state

under Presidents Nixon and Ford — espcially his reported involvement in the 1973 coup in Chile.

Other commission members appointed by Reagan were: William P. Clements Jr., former Republican governor of Texas; AFL-CIO President Lane Kirkland; former Supreme Court Justice Potter Stewart; Robert S. Strauss, a Washington lawyer and Democratic Party operative; Nicholas Brady, a New Jersey businessman who served as an interim GOP senator for eight months in 1982; San Antonio Mayor Henry G. Cisneros; Carlos F. Diaz-Alejandro, professor of economics at Yale University; Wilson S. Johnson, president of the National Federation of Independent Business; Richard M. Scammon, a Washington political consultant; John Silber, president of Boston University; and William B. Walsh, president of Project Hope.

Eight members of Congress were appointed by congressional leaders to serve as "senior counselors" to the commission: Sens. Jackson; Mathias; Lloyd Bentsen, D-Texas; Pete V. Domenici, R-N.M.; and Reps. Jim Wright, D-Texas; Barnes; Kemp; and William S. Broomfield, R-Mich.

When Jackson died on Sept. 1, he was replaced by Sen. Daniel K. Inouye, D-Hawaii.

Also named as senior counselors by Kissinger on Aug. 10 were William D. Rogers, a former assistant secretary of state for inter-American affairs, and Winston Lord, president of the Council on Foreign Relations. Both worked for Kissinger at the State Department.

Jeane J. Kirkpatrick, U.S. ambassador to the United Nations, was named Reagan's representative to the commission. Harry W. Shlaudeman, then U. S. ambassador to Argentina, was named executive secretary.

The eleven senior counselors — Kirkpatrick, Lord, Rogers and the eight members of Congress — were not official members of the commission and did not possess voting powers, but they attended meetings and participated in the commission's deliberations.

Under its charter, the commission reported to the president "on the elements of a long-term United States policy that will best respond to the challenges of social, economic and democratic development in the region, and to internal and external threats to its security and stability." Reagan also asked the commission to give advice "on means of building a national consensus on a comprehensive United States policy for the region."

Even before the 12 commission members had been sworn in, Cisneros blasted Reagan's current policies in Central America and laid much of the blame for the region's troubles on previous U.S. actions such as "toppling governments and rigging elections."

The commission's only other Hispanic member, Diaz-Alejandro, also was the subject of intense criticism from some conservative leaders and Cuban exile groups, who charged that he was too lenient toward Cuban Premier Fidel Castro. Diaz-Alejandro, who was born in Cuba, became a U.S. citizen in 1974.

The commission racked up more than twenty-five days of hearings and deliberations between its formal organization in early August and the end of the year, hearing testimony on social, humanitarian, religious, economic, security and political considerations. Members undertook two fact-finding missions to Central America: visiting Panama, Costa Rica, El Salvador, Guatemala, Honduras and Nicaragua during a trip Oct. 9 - 16, and Mexico and Venezuela Dec. 12 - 15.

In all, the commission heard from more than four hundred witnesses, including former leaders in the U.S. government; American Church and civil-rights organizations; and representatives of the governments, opposition groups, churches and businesses in Central America. ∎

Defense

Two broad themes dominated the 1983 congressional debate on defense policy: the general pace and scope of Ronald Reagan's planned military buildup and the administration's nuclear weapons policy.

By year's end, hard-line, conservative purists lamented that Reagan had yielded on crucial points in battles over both issues. However, the major outlines of Reagan's original policies seemed intact:

• The president's request for a fiscal 1984 defense budget 10 percent larger than the fiscal 1983 amount in "real" terms — that is, in addition to the cost of inflation — was trimmed by the congressional budget process to allow only a 5 percent real increase. By the time it finished action on the fiscal 1984 appropriations bills, Congress actually had provided a real increase of about 4 percent — a reduction from the January budget request by about $18 billion.

However, that truncated increase still outstripped the rate at which Jimmy Carter had been willing to raise defense spending in all but his last full year in office (1980), when he sought, with evident reluctance, a real increase of 5 percent.

Moreover, the congressional reductions were achieved by cheese-paring across the length and breadth of Reagan's proposal rather than by re-shaping it through substantial cuts in a few major programs.

• Under intense pressure at home and from European allies — and specifically, in response to congressional threats to kill off production of the MX intercontinental ballistic missile (ICBM) — Reagan recast his major arms control offers to Moscow so they would require less sweeping reductions in existing Soviet forces.

But overall, the president gained more than he lost on nuclear issues during the year. Most elements of his nuclear buildup — the B-1 bomber, the Pershing missile and several versions of the cruise missile — handily won congressional approval. Congress also endorsed the initial production of the controversial MX, despite a close shave in the House. The administration's only major defeat — and it was more symbol than substance — came when the House adopted a resolution calling for a freeze on nuclear weapons.

Perhaps as significant as the considerable changes in its negotiating posture was a clear shift in the administration's rhetoric on nuclear arms issues. The hard-nosed willingness to talk of "protracted" nuclear wars in which the United States would try to "prevail" was replaced by the more customary discussion of nuclear war only as something to be deterred at all cost.

The change in rhetoric was accompanied by a search for political allies on nuclear arms issues in the political center and in Washington's bipartisan defense establishment, which the administration had come to office condemning for having presided over a decline of U.S. power.

In contrast to the budget struggle, which was resolved, for all practical purposes, by early summer, the confrontation over nuclear arms continued through the last week of the session. The administration's MX campaign probably benefited from the surge of anti-Soviet sentiment following the destruction of a Korean airliner by Russian warplanes on Sept. 1.

Budget Battle

In the context of burgeoning pressure to reduce federal deficits (that were projected to reach the $200-billion range) without additional deep reductions in domestic spending, congressional support for the rate at which Reagan planned to boost defense budgets clearly had shriveled during 1982.

In fact, the scope of the budget debate was relatively narrow, compared with the heated congressional battles over defense spending of only a few years earlier. Few members disputed the assumption that increases were needed and that they should be measured in terms of "real growth" — only those increases that exceeded the cost of inflation would be considered.

Nevertheless, by the end of 1982 Congress had trimmed a total of some $19 billion from Reagan's $258 billion fiscal 1983 defense request by slowing the administration's buildup plan rather than by substantially altering its shape.

Against that background, pressure was growing within the administration to trim the January 1983 defense request (for fiscal 1984) below the previously planned level of more than $290 billion. It was argued that so large a request in the face of congressional demands for a slower buildup would simply erode the administration's credibility and lead to larger congressional reductions than might otherwise be made.

Fiscal 1984 Request. The January 1983 request for $273.4 billion in new appropriations for the Pentagon was $11.3 billion below the amount the administration originally planned to request. It was $8 billion lower in outlays, the money that actually would be disbursed in fiscal 1984.

But that reduction had little impact on the congressional clamor for additional restraint in Reagan's defense plan. For one thing, nearly half of Reagan's reduction — $4.9 billion — was due to a freeze on military and federal civilian pay, a policy Congress clearly would not abide.

Moreover, the reduction had no dramatic impact on any of the major weapons programs that were the most visible aspect of the buildup. This fed a festering suspicion that the Reagan team was shortchanging the combat-readiness of forces in the field by underfunding maintenance, training costs, spare parts and the like to commit the Pentagon to long-term procurement contracts.

By mid-February, only a few weeks after the president's fiscal 1984 budget reached Capitol Hill, it was evident that the requested real increase of more than 10 percent in defense appropriations enjoyed scant congressional support. A wide range of members from both parties had endorsed as an alternative a real growth rate of 5 percent.

In appearances before several congressional panels, Defense Secretary Caspar W. Weinberger tried to slacken congressional pressure for defense cuts by arguing that it would be nearly impossible to make reductions that would significantly shrink the projected budget deficits. Because of the lag between appropriations and when the money for major weapons is actually spent, a significant, immediate cut in defense outlays would require either a draconian reduction in weapons procurement or a hefty slash in other accounts that would directly reduce the combat readiness of existing forces, Weinberger insisted.

But that argument appeared to have little impact on the congressional debate. Many members insisted that visible reductions in the defense increase — regardless of whether or not they would immediately reduce the deficit — were politically essential to allow further cuts in domestic programs, which would directly affect the deficit.

Procurement Targeted. Moreover, much of the demand for cuts focused specifically on major weapons procurement, long a prime target of liberal Pentagon critics that in 1983 began to draw fire from a much broader span of the political spectrum.

In part, this reflected congressional concern with projected deficits in fiscal 1985 and beyond. Unlike appropriations for pay and operating costs that were spent in a single fiscal year, procurement funds were paid out over the term of long-running weapons contracts. Trimming the procurement budget would serve to reduce future deficits.

The procurement part of the budget also was highlighted by a spate of widely publicized studies of Pentagon cost-overruns that concluded the military systematically underestimated the cost of weapons purchases and, as a consequence, tried to buy too many different kinds of weapons at once.

Budget Committees. On March 17, the House Budget Committee adopted a Democratic-inspired budget resolution generally acknowledged to be a political ploy intended to underscore Reagan's responsibility for the size of the deficit. According to the House panel leadership, the budget resolution would have allowed a real defense increase of 4 percent, though an analysis by the Congressional Budget Office suggested that it would actually provide real growth of less than 3 percent.

The Senate Budget panel clearly was headed for endorsement of a 5 percent defense increase when, on March 15, it acceded to Reagan's last-minute plea to defer action on the issue for three weeks. Budget Committee Chairman Pete V. Domenici, R-N.M., told his colleagues that the president wanted the time to seek "accommodation" with the panel.

But during the grace period, there was little evidence that the White House actually considered any very significant reduction in its request.

At the last moment, the administration offered to trim its request by some $5 billion in budget authority and $4 billion in outlays because of lower-than-predicted inflation rates and fuel costs and a shift to a cheaper basing method for the controversial MX missile. But the gesture was both too late and too small to appease the Senate panel, which voted for a 5 percent real defense increase, the amount eventually approved by the Senate.

Authorization Action. For the fiscal 1984 defense authorization bill (S 675 — PL 98-94), covering about 70 percent of the total Pentagon request, Congress gave $187.5 billion, $10.5 billion less than Reagan had requested for programs covered by the bill.

The two Armed Services committees estimated that this would allow a real defense increase of 5 percent, as allowed by the budget resolution.

The most dramatic skirmish over the overall funding level in the authorization bill came in the Senate. There several members challenged lower-than-budgeted inflation assumptions that had been proposed by the Office of Management and Budget (OMB) and accepted by the Armed Services Committee. In effect, the changed assumptions had allowed the committee to include in its measure $2.1 billion for programs that otherwise would have exceeded the budget ceiling.

A broad coalition of Democrats, ranging from liberal Howard M. Metzenbaum, Ohio, to relatively conservative Lawton Chiles, Fla., the senior Democrat on the Senate Budget Committee, joined with liberal Republicans to charge the Armed Services panel and OMB with creative accounting to skirt the budget ceiling. But an amendment that would have removed the new, more optimistic assumptions from the bill was rejected 53-41.

Appropriations Action. The final version of the fiscal 1984 defense appropriations bill (HR 4185 — PL 98-212), cleared for the president Nov. 18, trimmed $11.1 billion from Reagan's $261 billion appropriations request.

According to congressional supporters of the administration buildup, this bill, when added to the separate legislation funding military construction and defense-related projects of the Energy Department, would allow a real increase above the fiscal 1983 defense budget of less than 4 percent.

In mid-December, the president announced he would seek a $1.8 billion supplemental defense appropriation to cover a 4 percent pay raise for military personnel and Pentagon civilians. But cost-of-living pay hikes for federal employees usually were regarded as a special type of inflation cost that did not add to "real growth" in the defense budget's purchasing power.

During the appropriations battle, as during the authorization fight, the Senate provided the most visible political skirmishes over the scope of the administration's defense program. These centered on the efforts of Defense Appropriations Subcommittee Chairman Ted Stevens, R-Alaska, to head off production rate increases for the Army's M-1 tank and the Navy's *Los Angeles*-class nuclear submarine.

Stevens warned his colleagues that the administration's plans for weapons procurement — and its projected production increases in future years — simply would not be covered by the size of the annual defense spending hikes Congress had shown itself willing to vote. The result, he predicted, would be either further damage to readiness forces as readiness-related funds were used to pay for the procurement buildup or an inefficient cutback in some of the procurement rates once they had been increased.

But Stevens was rebuffed in both efforts.

Tighter Controls. Much of the congressional unhappiness over defense spending was channeled during the year into attempts to change the Pentagon's procurement process. These moves, intended to make the Pentagon a more canny purchaser in the defense marketplace, included:

● establishment of an independent office to test new weapons before they were approved for full-scale production. Critics had charged that expensive weapons routinely were not subjected to realistic tests, partly because the contractors and military personnel with a vested interest in

their production played too large a role in testing. The Pentagon vigorously opposed the testing office but its creation was mandated in an amendment to the defense authorization bill.

● a requirement that manufacturers issue warranties to cover major items bought by the Pentagon against material defects or performance shortfalls, another move the Defense Department had resisted. As enacted in the defense appropriations bill, the warranty provision allowed the defense secretary to waive the warranty requirement on grounds of national security or cost-effectiveness. A waiver would have to be justified to the congressional defense committees.

● various changes in procedures for buying spare parts. Some of the year's most celebrated allegations of Pentagon mismanagement involved very small parts — many of them commercially available for a few dollars or less — for which defense contractors were charging hundreds or thousands of dollars.

Nuclear Arms Politics

The year began with Reagan clearly on the defensive on nuclear arms issues, with two of his fundamental policies reeling under political blows. The administration's premise that the Soviets enjoyed intolerable advantages they would surrender only if faced with the prospect of a matching U.S. buildup was damaged by the success of the grass-roots campaign for a nuclear weapons freeze. By nearly winning in the House in 1982 and prevailing in several state-wide referendums that November, the freeze movement appeared to have won considerable public support for its contention that U.S. and Soviet nuclear arsenals were essentially equivalent and that further modernization of U.S. weaponry would only provoke a corresponding Soviet buildup.

Congress's December 1982 refusal to appropriate funds to buy components for the first production-line MX missiles amounted to an at least momentary rejection of a second administration premise: that it was particularly important to deny Moscow evident superiority in land-based ballistic missiles such as MX (and similar Soviet ICBMs of which more than 600 already were deployed).

In the administration's view, the speed and accuracy with which such weapons could hit their targets gave them military uses and symbolic clout that could not be equaled by bombers or submarine-launched missiles, two types of nuclear arms in which the United States was widely conceded to enjoy superiority over the Soviet Union. This assumption of the primacy of ICBMs justified MX even though the deployment method envisaged at the time — the so-called "dense pack" of heavily armored, closely spaced silos — was regarded by many specialists as vulnerable to Soviet attack.

Shift to the Center. By mid-1982 the White House had begun to try to modify its earlier image as an administration bent on radically breaking with the nuclear arms policy of its predecessors.

Defense Secretary Weinberger's annual report to Congress, released with the January 1983 budget request, continued this shift. A special appendix to the report traced the roots of Reagan's strategic arms doctrine in the annual reports of Weinberger's predecessors as far back as Robert S. McNamara in the 1960s.

At the forceful urging of congressional defense specialists, Reagan tried to salvage MX by seeking an alliance with the same bipartisan national security establishment

his administration had arrived in Washington denouncing. In early January he announced the formation of a blue-ribbon commission chaired by retired Lt. Gen. Brent Scowcroft, President Ford's national security adviser, to recommend a basing method for the MX.

The Scowcroft commission and its group of senior advisers were heavy with veterans of the Nixon, Ford, and Carter administrations, including Carter's defense secretary, Harold Brown, Brown's deputy, William Perry, and Carter's White House counselor, Lloyd N. Cutler.

At the same time, the White House began discussions with a group of congressional defense specialists that threatened to oppose MX unless the administration's negotiating position in the two major U.S.-Soviet arms control parleys became more "flexible." According to these members, the administration's current offers held little promise of agreement either in the Strategic Arms Reduction Talks (START) dealing with intercontinental weapons or in the Intermediate-range Nuclear Force (INF) talks on nuclear weapons in Europe, since the U.S. offers would require far larger reductions of Soviet forces than U.S. forces.

Diversions. In the first few months of 1983, as the administration was groping toward the political middle, it had three major confrontations with liberal critics of its arms control policy. The first occurred in mid-January, when the president suddenly fired Eugene V. Rostow as director of the Arms Control and Disarmament Agency (ACDA) and replaced him with Kenneth L. Adelman, a 36-year-old conservative foreign policy expert who had been a critic of the SALT II treaty negotiated by Jimmy Carter in 1979 and who had been serving as deputy to U.N. ambassador Jeanne Kirkpatrick.

It was widely believed that Rostow had been sacked because he favored too much "flexibility" in the arms control nominations. When Adelman gave non-committal answers to several questions on the first day of his confirmation hearing before the Senate Foreign Relations Committee, committee Democrats had a field day. They charged that Reagan had shown his indifference toward arms control by naming an ACDA director with neither experience in nor enthusiasm for arms control and without the political stature to be an effective advocate for arms control policies within the administration even if he were so inclined.

Adelman's nomination was not confirmed until April, three months after he was named by Reagan.

Liberals again attacked the president after a March 23 televised address in which Reagan called for a new emphasis on developing anti-missile defenses, possibly including satellites armed with laser weapons, that could fend off a Soviet missile attack on the United States.

The suggestion, quickly dubbed the president's "Star Wars" scheme by the press, drew harsh attacks from traditional arms control advocates, who warned that it would undermine the deterrent balance between the superpowers that had prevailed for decades. The deterrent theory held that each country's awareness that an attack on its opponent would bring a devastating retaliation prevented a nuclear exchange.

Administration officials moved quickly to tone down the rhetorical wrapping of Reagan's proposal, emphasizing that decades would pass before such weapons would be available and stressing the importance of accelerating existing research and development programs in the area if only to keep abreast of Soviet activity.

And the administration and its critics squared off on the nuclear freeze. The White House was determined to fight to the end in what was widely understood to be a doomed battle against the nuclear freeze resolution in the House.

Some administration officials bitterly resisted even using the politically potent word "freeze" in drafting an alternative resolution for which administration backers could vote while making a gesture to constituent demands to do "something" about arms control. The House adopted the resolution by a hefty margin, but not before an energetic band of House Republicans and conservative Democrats succeeded in larding the freeze resolution with innumerable amendments they claimed meliorated its impact on administration policy.

The resolution's rejection by the Senate long had been anticipated.

A Limited, Tentative Deal. Meanwhile, in the center ring, the tug-of-war over arms control policy between the administration and self-styled congressional moderates lurched toward a compromise.

In April, Reagan embraced the Scowcroft panel's proposals to:

● abandon the search for an MX basing method that would be invulnerable against Soviet missile attacks and simply deploy 100 MXs in existing Minuteman silos to deprive Moscow of its current monopoly on such large, accurate ICBMs.

● develop a complementary ICBM small enough to be carried in a truly mobile launcher that would make the weapon less vulnerable than the bulky MX. The missiles would carry only a single warhead. Weapons armed with just one warhead were presumed to create a more "stable" strategic balance than multi-warhead missiles, each of which could destroy several enemy missiles in a first strike.

● seek in its arms control policy to induce Moscow to join in the movement toward a more stable nuclear balance via de-emphasis on large, multi-warhead missiles.

Having accepted the Scowcroft prescription, Reagan subsequently tempered his earlier emphasis on seeking radical reductions in U.S. and Soviet missile forces in his arms control offers. However, the Scowcroft group's view was entirely consistent with the administration's fundamental argument that the current Soviet advantage in large, mutli-warhead ICBMs was unacceptable.

By year's end, Reagan had yielded to the congressional moderates' demand for a more "flexible" arms control stance in both of the major U.S.-Soviet negotiations.

In the START discussions, which focused on long-range U.S. and Soviet weapons aimed at each other's homelands, Reagan abandoned his demand for ceilings on ICBMs so low as to require a substantial cut in the Soviets' large, multi-warhead missiles. Moscow's ICBM fleet was the centerpiece of the Soviet nuclear force. He also made explicit offers to limit the number of bomber-launched cruise missiles — a part of the U.S. nuclear arsenal that was due for a very sharp increase under administration plans.

In the INF talks on U.S. missiles based in Western Europe and Soviet missiles aimed at Europe, Reagan gave up his insistence that Moscow abandon its entire force of some 350 existing triple warhead missiles (called SS-20s). He offered to consider any Soviet proposal for a limit that would be equal for both U.S. and Soviet INF warheads.

Reagan's modified posture on nuclear policy secured enough support on Capitol Hill to limit damage to his request to begin production of MX missiles. The number of missiles slated for the assembly line was only slightly reduced (from 27 missiles to 21) during congressional consideration of the weapons system.

After winning an MX go-ahead by an unexpectedly large margin in a preliminary vote in May, the margin of Reagan's success on the issue narrowed dramatically in subsequent House votes in July and November, largely because liberal Democrats pressured their leaders to make MX an issue distinguishing their party from the Reagan-led GOP.

But that dynamic was offset by the strong surge of anti-Soviet feeling that followed the Korean airliner incident Sept. 1.

A Shaky Victory. Reagan seemed to have regained the political initiative on the arms control issue by the end of 1983. But the continued political potency of the issue, and the fragility of Reagan's advantage, was evident in four other fights in which critics beat the administration — or came surprisingly close to it:

● With none of the massive grass-roots pressure that was behind the nuclear freeze resolution, House liberals gained 177 votes for an amendment to the defense authorization bill that would have blocked initial moves toward production of an anti-satellite missile which, they argued, would mark the first step into an arms race in space.

● In a similarly extemporaneous effort on the same bill, Sen. Charles McC. Mathias Jr., R-Md., came within seven votes of blocking continued production of nuclear-armed, ship-launched Tomahawk cruise missiles, which he argued would greatly complicate future arms control agreements because their very small size would make numerical limits hard to enforce.

● Also during the debate on the fiscal 1984 authorization bill, the Senate voted by better than 2-1 to kill a new version of the so-called "neutron bomb" artillery shell intended to destroy Soviet tank columns with lethal radiation. Instead, the funds were shifted to accelerate the development of non-nuclear weapons that could be used against tank forces.

● An administration request to end a 14-year moratorium on the production of lethal chemical weapons was rejected by the House twice, by large margins, and approved in the Senate each time only by grace of Vice President George Bush's tie-breaking vote. The second time around (during debate on the defense appropriations bill) the House dug in and the project was killed for the year.

—By Pat Towell

$187.5 Billion Set for Defense Buildup

Even before powerful anti-Soviet sentiments were aroused by the Soviet destruction of a South Korean passenger jet on Sept. 1, Congress was firmly on the road toward approving a fiscal 1984 defense authorization bill (S 675 — PL 98-94) that made no substantial changes in the overall shape of President Reagan's military buildup. The $187.5 billion conference version of the bill, which had been drafted at the very start of the August recess, was approved in mid-September by hefty margins. The figure approved was $10.5 billion less than Reagan had requested.

The Senate, after scant debate, adopted the conference report on the bill (S Rept 98-213) Sept. 13 by an 83-8 vote. House concurrence came Sept. 15 by a vote of 266-152, despite last-ditch efforts to scuttle the conference report because it approved production of chemical weapons. *(House vote 322, p. 96-H; Senate vote 234, p. 40-S)*

The final measure included hotly disputed authorizations for the MX missile and for a new type of lethal chemical weapons. The $187.5 billion bill authorized funding for virtually all Pentagon programs except military construction, military pay and pensions. *(MX, p. 195)*

Congress Nov. 18 approved a bill (HR 4185) that appropriated $249.8 billion for defense programs in fiscal 1984. That was roughly a 4 percent increase over fiscal 1983, after adjustment for inflation. President Reagan had sought a 10 percent increase. *(Defense funding bill, authorization and appropriation levels compared, p. 488)*

House Committee Action

The $188 billion fiscal 1984 defense authorization bill reported by the House Armed Services Committee May 11 (HR 2969 — H Rept 98-107) incorporated $4.54 billion to begin procurement of MX missiles and $250 million to start work on a much smaller, single-warhead ICBM that could be deployed in the 1990s. The committee thus jumped on the bandwagon of a White House advisory commission, chaired by former presidential adviser Brent Scowcroft.

The Scowcroft panel linked MX deployment to a long-term arms control policy aimed at a more stable nuclear balance through abolition of large, multi-warhead missiles, like MX and current Soviet ICBMs. *(Commissioner recommendations, p. 195)*

Overall, HR 2969 trimmed President Reagan's authorization request by $10.2 billion. The committee said this would provide an increase after inflation of 6 percent, instead of Reagan's proposed 10.2 percent increase.

The House panel praised the Scowcroft commission's linkage of "modernization of our ICBM force and arms control. In a democracy, such linkage is a critical ingredient to developing and maintaining a public consensus in support of such efforts."

The Armed Services panel underscored its insistence that the administration pursue the entire Scowcroft package — not just the MX deployment — by barring the use of any funds authorized for MX until the Pentagon submitted a detailed schedule for development and deployment of the proposed small missile.

Other Nuclear Weapons

The $6.18 billion procurement request for the B-1

bomber program was approved by the committee without change. This covered the purchase of 10 planes with spare parts and components that would be used in 37 planes scheduled for purchase in fiscal 1985.

The bill also included a secret amount for development of the "stealth" bomber, to be designed to evade detection by Soviet radars.

Reflecting a change in Pentagon plans, the committee approved $464 million for 240 air-launched cruise missiles (called ALCM-Bs), designed to be fired from B-1s and existing B-52 bombers, along with spare parts for the missiles.

In January, the Pentagon had planned no further production of the ALCM-B, partly because of its potential vulnerability to a new Soviet anti-aircraft missile, called the SA-10.

A second-generation cruise missile that would incorporate some stealth characteristics — thus being harder for Soviet defenses to attack — and would have one-third again the ALCM-B's 1,500-mile range, was planned.

But in April, the Pentagon decided to continue ALCM-B production for at least one more year, as a hedge against possible problems in developing the new cruise missile. It recommended — and the committee approved — unspecified reductions in other Air Force programs to fund the additional ALCM procurement.

Citing budgetary limits, the panel halved the request for $876 million to put new engines on existing tanker planes, which refuel bombers in midair. The Air Force had requested funds to convert 31 planes in fiscal 1984 and to sign a multi-year contract for future conversions. The committee approved 24 conversions and denied the multi-year contract, for a reduction of $441 million.

Missile Submarines. For the eleventh in a class of submarines designed to fire Trident missiles, the committee approved $1.45 billion, $73 million less than was originally requested. The reduction was in keeping with a later Navy price estimate.

Components that would be used in two future missile subs were approved as requested ($306 million).

Also approved without change were the requests to purchase the final increment of Trident I missiles ($587 million for 52 missiles), and to continue development of the larger Trident II missile ($1.5 billion). The Trident II, which would be able either to carry more warheads than Trident I or to fire the same number of warheads a greater distance, also would be accurate enough to destroy armored, underground targets such as missile silos and command posts. Current submarine missiles lacked that accuracy.

Also approved was a request for $436 million to redesign the Trident sub funded in fiscal 1981 to carry the Trident II missile.

Intermediate-Range Missiles. More than $1 billion was approved without change for Pershing II and ground-launched cruise missiles (GLCMs) designed to reach Soviet territory from launchers in Western Europe. This included $433 million for 95 Pershing IIs and their spare parts and $617 million for 120 GLCMs, 30 of the four-missile GLCM launchers and various other components.

NATO agreed in December 1979 to deploy 108 Per-

Defense Authorizations for Fiscal 1984

S 675 authorized the following amounts for
Defense Department programs in fiscal 1984 *(in millions of dollars):*

	Administration Request	House Passed	Senate Passed	Final Authorization
Procurement	$ 94,087.7	$ 88,449.8	$ 86,900.4	$ 88,259.9
Research and Development	29,625.3	26,837.9	27,250.6	27,303.0
Operations and Maintenance	74,001.6	71,839.8	71,599.6	71,758.8
Civil Defense	253.5	200.0	161.5	169.0
Miscellaneous Adjustments	——	——	75.0	——
Total	$197,968.1	$187,327.5	$185,897.1	$187,490.7

shing IIs and 464 GLGMs beginning in December 1983, unless Moscow agreed in the interim to dismantle its extant force of missiles aimed at Western Europe. Late in the year, Moscow suspended U.S.-Soviet negotiations on these intermediate-range nuclear forces (INF) to protest deployment of the Pershing IIs.

Strategic Defense

The committee approved only $238 million of the $538.4 million requested to develop a "conventional" anti-ballistic missile (ABM) system — one using anti-missile missiles instead of more exotic technologies like laser beams. The panel complained that the program, as requested, was too narrowly focused on defending the so-called Dense Pack version of the MX missile which the administration proposed in 1982 but had since dropped.

A separate $171 million request to develop other kinds of ABM technologies was approved without change.

'Star Wars.' The committee approved essentially the amount requested to develop various kinds of lasers and other "directed-energy" weapons that might be used for the kind of countrywide ABM defense Reagan called for in a March 23 televised address.

But, as it had done in the fiscal 1983 authorization bill, the panel substantially revised the directed-energy research program, insisting that the Pentagon was emphasizing the wrong technical approach. The two approaches could be tested "side-by-side" in 1988, the panel said.

From a total of $462 million requested for various research programs which had some relationship to anti-missile lasers, the committee cut $163 million and added $125 million for its own projects.

Anti-Bomber Defenses. In one of its more sweeping rejections of an aspect of Pentagon planning, the committee attacked Air Force plans to spend $7.5 billion over the next five years to bolster anti-bomber defenses in the United States.

"In view of the accuracy and quantity of Soviet land-based ballistic missiles, it is difficult to justify investing billions of dollars to defend against manned bombers," the committee declared. Instead, it argued, the Air Force should place more emphasis on defending its European bases against Soviet air attack.

That position accounted, in part, for the committee's

approval of only 30 F-15 fighters and components for 30 more in fiscal 1985 ($1.25 billion) instead of the request for 48 F-15s and components for 72 planes in fiscal 1985 ($1.96 billion).

It also was the committee's justification for denying $76 million for components for three AWACS airborne radar planes scheduled for procurement in fiscal 1985. Those three and nine other AWACS planes were intended for anti-bomber defense of the U.S. mainland.

Ground Combat

The committee authorized funds to buy 840 M-1 tanks instead of the 720 tanks requested. Because the panel transferred to this account $112 million authorized but not spent in fiscal 1983, the larger purchase would require authorization of just $1.35 billion — $10 million less than had been requested for the smaller buy.

It also approved $293 million for components of M-1s to be purchased in fiscal 1985, an increase of $42 million above the request.

The Pentagon's planned slowdown in production — 855 M-1s had been authorized in fiscal 1983 — would drive up the cost, the committee complained. And it barred a plan to begin purchasing gas turbine engines for some tanks from a second manufacturer. By the time a second contractor was ready to produce, the panel contended, so few of the planned 7,058 M-1s would remain to be produced that competition between engine manufacturers would produce few savings.

To buy 600 Bradley armored troop carriers, equipped with TOW anti-tank missiles and spare parts, the committee recommended $891 million, $33 million more than the request. The addition was to incorporate into the vehicles the larger TOW II version of the anti-tank missile.

Anti-Tank Weapons. For 112 AH-64 anti-tank helicopters and associated spares and components, the panel approved $1.26 billion, a reduction of $33 million. For 5,351 Hellfire anti-tank missiles, carried by the AH-64, the $239 million request was approved without change.

The panel doubled to $150 million the request for Copperhead artillery shells, enough to buy 3,600 shells. Copperheads were designed to be fired from conventional artillery and to home in on tanks with laser guidance.

The Army had decided in 1982 to end production of

the shell because of cost and performance problems. But the program had been resuscitated for the fiscal 1984 budget. According to the committee, costs were coming down and reliability was improving in test shots. Two Copperheads should be enough to destroy a moving target at distances up to 17 kilometers, it said.

Light Forces. As in previous years, the committee was skeptical of plans to buy 15-ton armored cars to substitute for 60-ton tanks in Army and Marine Corps units intended to be flown quickly to distant trouble spots. The panel complained that the two services could not agree on the versions of the vehicle to be purchased, that they were proving far too expensive and that it was not clear that the versions intended to destroy tanks could do so.

The committee denied the $132 million requested for 176 light armored vehicles (LAVs) for the Army, and approved $52 million of the $78 million requested for the vehicles for the Marines, a reduction to 70 vehicles from a requested 113.

On the other hand, the committee approved $12.6 million requested to develop a new lightweight tank and $7.6 million to develop powerful, lightweight cannons to equip it.

'Deep Strike.' The panel charged that Army-Air Force rivalry was delaying the development of new weapons intended to "thin out" Soviet reinforcements far behind their own lines, before they could join the attack.

The new approach, which had been under development since the mid-1970s, would use an airborne radar to detect Soviet tank columns and steer toward them missiles carrying dozens of separate warheads designed to home in on tanks.

Development of such equipment had been retarded, the committee charged, because of the military services' "not-invented-here syndrome" — an aversion to technology developed outside of the service and to joint programs involving other services.

The committee approved $73 million of $164 million requested to develop the radar — called JSTARS — rejecting an Air Force plan to devise its own radar system. It approved the $50.2 million requested to select the companion missile — called JTACMS — but ordered the two services to select one of two existing missiles, either the Patriot anti-aircraft missile or the Lance artillery rocket, instead of developing a new missile. The panel added $20 million to begin purchasing components of whichever missile was selected.

Anti-Aircraft Defense. The request for 525 Patriot long-range anti-aircraft missiles was trimmed from $992 million to $936 million, disallowing a contingency reserve requested by the Army.

Approved as requested were funds for two short-range anti-aircraft weapons: $178 million for 2,214 Stinger missiles, fired by one man from a bazookalike tube, and $671 million for 130 Divad anti-aircraft tanks and associated spares and components.

Chemical Weapons. The administration had requested $158 million to begin production of lethal nerve gas weapons called binary munitions. This included $18 million for binary artillery shells, $43.2 million for aerial bombs and $96.5 million to equip binary production facilities.

The Pentagon later decided to defer production of the aerial bomb, citing test problems.

The House had voted against binary production in 1982, but the committee approved the $114.6 million still

wanted by the administration. However, it added a provision requiring the administration to dismantle one existing chemical bomb or shell for each new binary weapon deployed.

Air Combat

The committee approved without major change the number of Navy and Marine combat planes requested while making minor reductions in the funds authorized for those purposes. The panel recommended the following amounts for the planes with associated spare parts and components for use in future aircraft of that type:

● 24 F-14 fighters for $1.15 billion, a reduction of $25 million.

● 84 F/A-18 fighters for $2.7 billion, a $102 million reduction reflecting the committee's recommendation to buy only 84 planes in fiscal 1985, rather than the 92 planes budgeted. That permitted a reduction in the purchase in 1984 of components for use in the fiscal 1985 planes.

● 6 A-6E carrier-based bombers for $232 million, the amount requested.

● 6 EA-6B radar-jamming planes for $442 million, a reduction of $57 million reflecting the committee's rejection of a proposal for a multi-year contract.

● 32 Harrier vertical-takeoff small bombers for the Marine Corps, for $1.05 billion as requested.

High-Low Mix. In addition to sharply reducing the request for F-15 Air Force fighters, the committee increased the authorization for smaller F-16s to $2.3 billion for 144 planes, an addition of $407 million and 24 planes to the request.

Apart from the panel's skepticism about the anti-bomber mission for which many of the F-15s were earmarked, the changes also reflected its willingness to buy a larger number of cheaper planes for a slight loss of combat ability. Citing Air Force projections that it needed to buy 270 fighters a year just to keep pace with the retirement of old planes, the committee concluded that the Air Force's future fighter purchases would have to include a larger proportion of the cheaper F-16s.

Current F-16s could not carry the heavy, long-range radar-guided missiles carried by the F-15 to attack other planes. But the committee noted that a new, lighter long-range missile just entering production, called AMRAAM, would give the two planes more nearly equal combat ability.

Future Fighters. The committee's inclinations toward austerity also were evident in its reduction of $149 million — to a total of $350 million — imposed on a group of Air Force programs aimed at developing a version of the F-15 or F-16 that would be used to attack ground targets deep behind enemy lines.

The panel also rejected a $90 million request to continue development of the LANTIRN infrared television, intended to let attack planes fly safely close to the ground and find targets at night or in bad weather. The device simply had become too expensive, the committee said.

To accelerate development of a version of the Tomahawk cruise missile that would be launched from fighters to attack enemy airfields, the committee tripled to $123 million the amount requested.

Airfield Defense. Echoing its criticism of interservice rivalry as an obstacle to deploying new weapons to stop Soviet tank attacks, the panel blamed the same process for the paucity of anti-aircraft defenses around U.S. air bases in Europe. "The deficiency resulted from overlap-

ping service (Army and Air Force) responsibilities and jurisdictional sensitivities together with the relatively low priority the services attached to ... defense of U.S. air bases," the panel charged.

To buy 28 Patriot missile units to be manned by West German troops in defense of U.S. air bases in Germany, the committee added $100 million to the bill.

Another $100 million was added to buy shorter-range anti-aircraft missiles to be manned at U.S. bases outside of Germany by troops of the host nation.

Naval Warfare

The panel approved 22 of the 23 ships requested for the Navy, recommending a total shipbuilding authorization of $12.15 billion, a reduction of $549 million.

The vast bulk of that reduction came from denying $376 million requested to cover increases due to inflation in the cost of ships already on order. Those increases would not occur, the panel argued, because inflation was slowing so rapidly.

Approved as requested were funds for components to be used to refurbish the 25-year-old aircraft carrier *Independence* ($96 million) and to modernize the mothballed battleship *Missouri* and equip it with cruise missiles. Most of the several hundred million dollars each of those two programs would cost was scheduled for inclusion in the fiscal 1985 budget.

Anti-Aircraft Defense. To defend U.S. fleets against Moscow's large arsenal of air- and sea-launched cruise missiles, the committee approved the $3.4 billion request for three cruisers equipped with the Aegis computer-guided anti-aircraft missile.

To continue development and begin buying components for the first of a planned class of more than 50 missile-armed destroyers (the *Arleigh Burke*) equipped with a smaller version of Aegis, the committee approved $190 million, $20.5 million less than the request. The Navy hoped to keep the cost of the *Burke*-class ships to about three-fourths that of the Aegis cruisers. Funds to build the *Burke* were to be included in the fiscal 1985 budget.

Anti-Submarine Warfare. For three nuclear submarines designed principally to hunt other submarines, $2 billion was approved as requested.

For the LAMPS III sub-hunting helicopter, which would be carried by most modern surface warships, the panel recommended $596 million for 21 aircraft and their spare parts. But it denied the $123 million requested for 12 of the smaller LAMPS I helicopters, which were carried by some older small warships. The committee approved only $30 million to close down that production line. The Navy had planned to buy only 18 more LAMPS Is.

Airlift and Sealift

Several programs intended to speed the movement of U.S. combat units abroad were approved by the committee without significant change.

These included the second installment of multi-year contracts for 50 C-5 transports ($1.4 billion) and for 44 KC-10 midair refueling versions of the DC-10 commercial jetliner ($813 million).

Also approved was $144.3 million for the so-called CRAF program, which reimbursed civilian airlines for the cost of equipping their passenger planes for rapid conversion to carry military cargo.

To convert four high-speed cargo container ships (called SL-7s) to carry tanks and other combat vehicles, the

committee recommended the amount requested, $246 million. Also, $31 million was approved to purchase merchant ships to be held in mothballs for activation in case of mobilization.

Amphibious Assault. The committee approved without change the administration's program to expand the size of the Navy's amphibious assault fleet, which was designed to let Marine units fight their way ashore against enemy fire.

Major items included:

● $1.3 billion for the first of a new class of helicopter carriers (LHDs) able to carry 1,800 Marines and upwards of two dozen helicopters to carry them ashore.

● $509 million for another ship (called an LSD) designed to carry combat vehicles and landing barges to carry them ashore. This included funds for components to be used in future LSDs.

● $13.8 million for components to be used to refurbish another class of amphibious ships (LPHs) designed to carry troops and helicopters.

● $191 million for air-cushion landing barges designed to carry tanks and other vehicles from ship to shore at up to 50 mph.

Combat Readiness

The committee argued that reductions could safely be made in two areas frequently cited as indexes of the "combat-readiness" of U.S. forces.

Aircraft Spare Parts. The Army's $390 million request for aircraft spares was nearly $100 million above the fiscal 1983 budget and nearly quadruple the fiscal 1982 budget. And yet, the committee complained, the Army, unlike the Navy and Air Force, provided no statistical basis for its estimate of spare parts use. The committee cut $75 million from the request.

But at the same time, the panel said that it could not verify the Air Force's calculation of its requirement for $3.78 billion worth of aircraft spares. Calling this 46 percent increase over the fiscal 1983 appropriations "excessive," the committee reduced it by $500 million.

Overhauls. The panel also trimmed the Navy's request for ship and aircraft overhauls citing various efficiencies recommended by the General Accounting Office (GAO). It cut $104 million from the $2.2 billion request for aircraft overhauls and $50 million from the $5.9 billion requested for ship repair and overhaul.

House Floor Action

The House, by a 305-114 vote, passed its $187.4 billion version of the defense authorization bill early on July 27. Passage of HR 2969 came on the eighth day of a debate that sprawled over two months, largely because of delays occasioned by the politics of the MX missile and by strong objections to chemical warfare funding. *(Vote 261, p. 80-H)*

Nerve Gas

For the second year in a row, the House initially rejected a Reagan administration effort to begin production of a new type of lethal chemical weapons called binary munitions. During debate June 15 it approved, 256-161, an amendment deleting $114.6 million to prepare for production of 155mm artillery shells that would spew out lethal nerve gas. *(Vote 187, p. 58-H)*

But on the key vote of the battle, binary opponents won by a much narrower margin: A proposal that would

have retained the binary funds in the bill, as requested and as recommended by the Armed Services Committee, was rejected 202-216. *(Vote 186, p. 58-H)*

This 14-vote difference was less than half the margin by which the House blocked binary production in 1982. Binary funds were dropped from the fiscal 1983 defense authorization bill by a vote of 251-159. But, as in 1983, the key test in 1982 came on an earlier vote in which the House rejected by a vote of 192-225 a committee-backed proposal that would have gutted the anti-binary amendment. *(1982 Almanac p. 97)*

The attack on the binary munitions authorization was led by Foreign Affairs Committee Chairman Clement J. Zablocki, D-Wis., and Ed Bethune, R-Ark., who introduced slightly different versions of an amendment to delete binary funds from the bill.

The administration's fundamental case for beginning production of the new weapons — thus lifting a moratorium on the production of lethal chemical weapons that dated from 1969 — was that Moscow's use of its large stockpile of chemical weapons could be deterred only by a similar U.S. capability to use chemical weapons against Soviet forces.

Zablocki and Bethune did not challenge that argument, but cited Pentagon testimony that the current stock of 155mm nerve gas artillery shells could serve as such a deterrent. Replacements for those shells would not be needed until the end of the decade, Bethune maintained.

Moreover, opponents warned, binary production would hand the Soviet Union a propaganda coup. "If we go into production after a 14-year moratorium," Zablocki warned, "they would say, 'The United States intends to use chemical weapons.'"

That kind of image could damage U.S. relations with its NATO allies, Bethune said: "Let us not start a new age of chemical weapons which is going to frighten the bejeebers out of our allies all across Western Europe."

He insisted that there was optimism among delegates to the multilateral Committee on Disarmament in Geneva that a chemical weapons treaty could be negotiated fairly soon.

The budget originally included funds to begin manufacturing an air-dropped binary bomb, called Bigeye, but the Pentagon had withdrawn that request because of technical problems with the weapon's design.

Marvin Leath, D-Texas, insisted that current chemical weapons had to be replaced if deterrence of a Soviet chemical attack was to be maintained. Lacking an adequate chemical response, he argued, the only threat with which NATO could deter a Soviet chemical attack was an early use of nuclear weapons.

He also said that continued U.S. abstention from chemical weapons production would not persuade Moscow to be any more forthcoming in negotiations for a chemical weapons treaty.

He proposed an amendment to the Zablocki amendment that would have retained in the bill the $114.6 million for binary procurement, but would have barred final assembly of any artillery shells until Oct. 1, 1985.

That was about the time they would be assembled under current Pentagon plans. But Leath and his allies emphasized that it would provide enough time for five more rounds of negotiations in Geneva to seek a chemical weapons treaty.

After the Leath amendment was rejected 202-216, the House adopted 256-161 Bethune's slightly different version

of the anti-binary amendment as a substitute for the Zablocki language; it then adopted that version of Zablocki's amendment by voice vote.

After the vote, Bethune — whose district was 30 miles from Pine Bluff, Ark., where the nerve gas was to be produced — credited vigorous White House lobbying for the relatively close vote on the Leath amendment.

B-1 Bomber

As it had done each year since Reagan revived the B-1B bomber in 1981, the House June 15 backed procurement of the plane by a hefty margin. This time it rejected 164-255 an amendment by Ronald V. Dellums, D-Calif., that would have deleted the $6.2 billion earmarked for procurement of 10 B-1Bs with their spare parts and components for additional planes to be bought in future years. *(Vote 185, p. 58-H)*

In July 1982, a similar Dellums amendment to the fiscal 1983 defense authorization bill was rejected 142-257. *(1982 Almanac p. 99)*

Dellums, who long had warned that any nuclear war would quickly escalate into a cataclysmic exchange of the superpowers' nuclear missile forces, dismissed bombers as irrelevant to the nuclear balance.

"If we ever had a nuclear war, the safest place to be would be in the B-1B," he declared, "because by the time you got there, the war would be over."

Supporters of the B-1B insisted that it was needed to replace the current fleet of B-52 bombers built in the late 1950s and early 1960s.

The House also rejected, 171-252, an amendment by Frank McCloskey, D-Ind., that would have barred negotiation of a multi-year contract covering several years of the scheduled B-1 production run. *(Vote 181, p. 56-H)*

McCloskey argued that the B-1B was ineligible for multi-year contracting by Congress' own criteria: The design could not be regarded as stable, he maintained, since it was only 80 percent the same as the earlier B-1 version canceled in 1977 by Jimmy Carter, and the first of the new "B" versions was not to be flight-tested until 1984.

McCloskey insisted that the amendment was not an anti-B-1 move. But that assurance was dismissed by some of his opponents, who noted that the administration's commitment to produce the planned fleet of 100 B-1Bs for $20.5 billion (in fiscal 1981 dollars) depended in part on projected savings of some $600 million due to multi-year procurement.

"[B-1 foes] hope that they can get the multi-year procurement canceled," said Ike Skelton, D-Mo., "and the price of the B-1B will go up and they will say, 'Aha, I told you so.'"

Anti-Satellite Weapons

The House June 14 also rejected 177-243 an amendment by George E. Brown Jr., D-Calif., that would have denied $19.4 million to begin procurement of parts for a missile (ASAT) designed to be launched from F-15 fighter planes to destroy low-flying Soviet space satellites. *(Vote 180, p. 56-H)*

Opponents cited a General Accounting Office (GAO) report which criticized the cost and effectiveness of the ASAT. But most of them emphasized the weapon's threat to prospects for a U.S.-Soviet treaty barring anti-satellite weapons.

ASAT would be "an irreversible step toward a space weapons race," warned Joe Moakley, D-Mass., because

once the 18-foot-long missile was tested, Soviet reconnaissance satellites could not tell whether or not the United States was continuing to deploy it. By contrast, he argued, U.S. intelligence agencies could easily verify Soviet compliance with a ban on Soviet ASATs, which were launched from huge intercontinental missiles.

But senior Armed Services Committee members argued that a U.S. counterpart to the Soviet weapon was needed to encourage Moscow to negotiate an ASAT treaty. Chairman Melvin Price, D-Ill., charged that supporters of the amendment believed that "almost anything the United States does in reaction to Soviet deployments is provocative but that somehow Soviet actions themselves are not provocative."

Pershing II. Also rejected, 73-319, was a Dellums amendment to delete all funds ($432.8 million) for procurement of Pershing II missiles. *(Vote 192, p. 58-H)*

Bradley Vehicles, Divad Guns

Two of the Army's major new weapons easily survived challenges by freshman Democrats who charged that they had not adequately been tested before entering production.

Rejected 124-283 on June 14 was an amendment by Mel Levine, D-Calif., to bar use of any funds for M-2 infantry fighting vehicles ("Bradleys") until production-line versions of the vehicle were tested to prove Army claims for their effectiveness. The tests — spelled out in considerable detail in the nine-page-long amendment — focused on the effectiveness of the M-2's armor against various Soviet weapons. *(Vote 182, p. 56-H)*

HR 2969, which covered the fifth annual increment of M-2 production, included $799 million for 600 M-2s.

Also rejected, 134-283, on June 15 was an amendment by Larry Smith, D-Fla., to delete $671 million for procurement of 130 Divads — radar-guided, 40mm anti-aircraft guns mounted on tank chassis. *(Vote 184, p. 56-H)*

Citing reports by the Congressional Budget Office (CBO), GAO and some Pentagon analysts, Smith maintained that Divad could not meet various performance specifications and that it would have a shorter range than the missile-armed Russian helicopters it was designed to fend off from U.S. tank columns.

But senior committee members questioned the expertise of the GAO and CBO and cited Army Chief of Staff Gen. Edward C. Meyer's plea for the gun. They also claimed it could outrange Soviet helicopters.

Minesweepers. By a standing vote of 6-19, the House rejected an amendment by Thomas F. Hartnett, R-S.C., that would have added to the bill $80 million for a Navy minesweeper.

The committee had trimmed one ship from the Navy's request for four vessels, called MCMs.

MX Missile

MX opponents lobbied to turn around some of the members of the 53-vote majority by which the House had approved flight tests for Reagan's current MX plan on May 24 (H Con Res 113). *(Vote 123, p. 42-H)*

At a caucus of House Democrats June 14, MX opponents expressed unhappiness that senior members of the House Democratic leadership — especially Majority Leader Jim Wright, D-Texas, and Majority Whip Thomas S. Foley, D-Wash. — had voted for MX then.

Some members of the leadership who had voted for the nuclear freeze resolution in early May backed the missile partly in return for White House assurances that Reagan would show new flexibility in seeking an arms control agreement with Moscow. Several also voiced concern that Reagan could blame Democrats for the failure of arms control negotiations if the House rejected the MX, which he insisted was needed for bargaining leverage with the Russians.

Heavily lobbied by both sides, the House July 20 narrowly approved production of the missile. But the close vote was a portent of opposition the missile would face throughout the fiscal 1984 funding process.

The House authorized the missile production funds with only 13 votes to spare. The key vote came on an amendment by Charles E. Bennett, D-Fla., and Nicholas Mavroules, D-Mass., that would have deleted $2.6 billion earmarked for procurement of the first 27 production-line models of the MX. It failed 207-220. *(Vote 248, p. 74-H)*

House Democrats led by Wright accounted for 19 of the 20 members who supported the flight test but opposed the procurement funds. Many Democrats who voted for the missile in May were lobbied intensely by arms control groups, who long had opposed MX.

But Wright and other members of the Democratic leadership came under especially heavy pressure from other House Democrats who opposed the missile and feared that pro-MX Democrats were giving political aid and comfort to Reagan in his campaign to get the missile built and deployed.

Relatively senior members who either held leadership posts or were widely believed to aspire to them accounted for more than a third of the Democrats who voted "pro" MX in May and "against" MX in July.

"We've got more guys running for Speaker than we have running for president," quipped MX advocate Les Aspin, D-Wis., the afternoon after the vote. Aspin was a leader among the dozen or so Democratic moderates who had agreed to support MX procurement after prolonged negotiations with the White House.

These were intended to ensure that the White House was backing MX in the context of a package of nuclear arms policies recommended in April by a blue-ribbon advisory panel — the so-called Scowcroft commission, chaired by former White House national security adviser Brent Scowcroft. The panel recommended deployment of 100 MXs in existing missile silos, abandoning, for the moment, the search for an MX basing mode that would be impervious to Soviet attack. But it also called for developing small, single-warhead missiles that could be made mobile and thus impervious to attack.

It argued that the nuclear balance would be far more stable if single-warhead missiles replaced large, multi-warhead missiles like MX and its 600-plus Soviet counterparts.

The White House made a full-bore effort to convince its more reluctant House allies from the May vote that it was indeed making a strenuous effort to reach an arms control agreement. Wavering members were phoned by Reagan, Scowcroft commission members — several of them prominent Democrats — and senior administration officials.

START (Strategic Arms Reduction Talks) negotiator Edward L. Rowny was called away from consultations with allies to phone eight House members and argue that he needed MX to induce the Russians to negotiate seriously.

In the main, Aspin's Democratic allies and the moderate Republicans who backed MX in May stayed with the president on July 20. Reagan seemed to be living up to his end of the bargain by showing a new flexibility toward the

START talks, they argued.

"The president has operated in good faith," Norman D. Dicks, D-Wash., one of Aspin's key allies, said later, "and ... there has been movement [in START]."

But the House also adopted by voice vote two amendments intended to ensure that the administration would live up to the rest of its deal. These were:

● By Price and Aspin, requiring that future MX procurement and deployment not be allowed to outrun the development of a small, single-warhead missile.

● By Albert Gore Jr., D-Tenn., and Dicks reducing the number of MXs authorized from 27 to 21, a reduction of $358 million.

Credibility. Some members who switched told a reporter later they thought that a production decision was premature and would be too hard to reverse, once made. "Once procured, always procured," warned Dan Glickman, D-Kan.

But a prominent theme in several members' explanations of their anti-MX vote this time was suspicion that too many powerful administration officials were hostile to the kind of negotiating flexibility the members wanted.

And some members who stayed with the administration on this vote warned that its credibility on arms control still was very weak.

"It's not up to us to hold it [a pro-MX majority in the appropriations bill]," Gore told a reporter. "The administration has to come through with more movement on arms control. They've got to deal effectively with the anti-arms control elements within the administration."

Other House Provisions

In the hectic final hours of debate on the bill, late in the evening of July 26, the House adopted an amendment that would add $350 million to the total fiscal 1984 defense budget. By a standing vote of 112-90, it moved forward by three months (to Jan. 1, 1984) the effective date of the 4 percent pay raise for military personnel mandated by the bill. (Since the military payroll was not covered by the authorization bill, this did not increase the amount authorized by the bill.)

Supporters insisted that the amendment by Dennis M. Hertel, D-Mich., was consistent with the first budget resolution.

Another amendment, by G. William Whitehurst, R-Va., that would have similarly extended from six months to nine months the 4 percent pay hike for civilian Pentagon employees, was rejected by voice vote.

Retired Pay. The House shouted down an amendment by Stan Parris, R-Va., that would have repealed:

● the six-month delay on the effective date of the next cost-of-living increase for military retirees, and

● the cap on future cost-of-living increases for military retirees less than 62 years of age.

Parris represented a suburban Washington district that included a large military retired population.

Apart from the MX issue, the House took the following actions during July 21, 22 and 26:

Pershing II. An amendment by Dellums to delay until Dec. 31, 1984, any deployment of Pershing II missiles in Europe was rejected 101-320. *(Vote 259, p. 78-H)*

Deployment in West Germany of the first nine Pershing IIs was scheduled for December 1983, despite strong German opposition. They were the first of a planned U.S. force of 108 Pershings and 464 ground-launched cruise missiles (GLCMs), all of which would be able to hit Soviet

territory from launchers in Western Europe. NATO agreed in December 1979 to deploy the U.S. missiles to counter Moscow's force of some 300 triple-warhead SS-20 ballistic missiles, which was able to strike any target in Europe.

Dellums' central argument against Pershing II echoed a major argument against MX: that the missile was so accurate, and could strike its target in so little time, that it would arouse Soviet fears of a NATO first strike. Under those circumstances, he warned, Soviet weapons would be put on a "hair-trigger" status, and world peace would depend on the reliability of Soviet computers.

But Dellums was deserted on the issue by some members who seemed to share his concern about the destabilizing aspect of MX. Glickman, for example, concurred with Dellums that the Pershing posed a very serious threat to Soviet targets. But that very fact made the missile a useful prod in the Geneva negotiations to limit such weapons, Glickman said.

Anti-satellite Testing. By nearly a 2-1 vote (142-275) the House also rejected an amendment by John F. Seiberling, D-Ohio, that would have barred flight tests of an anti-satellite missile (ASAT) unless authorized in separate legislation. *(Vote 250, p. 76-H)*

During earlier House action on HR 2969, an amendment was rejected that would have deleted funds to purchase components to begin building the ASAT.

Liberal arms control advocates had warned that once ASAT was tested, it would be very difficult to negotiate a U.S.-Soviet ban on anti-satellite weapons. That was because the U.S. weapon — an 18-foot-long missile fired in midair from an F-15 fighter plane — was so small that, once it was tested, Soviet reconnaissance satellites could not verify that it had not been deployed.

According to the Pentagon, Moscow had a crude anti-satellite weapon already deployed on large ballistic missiles. But proponents of an ASAT ban insisted that dismantling of so bulky a weapon could be verified by U.S. intelligence methods.

The basic argument against the test ban was that the Soviet Union would not agree to negotiate an ASAT ban unless confronted with a threat to its own space satellites.

Procurement Reforms

Evidently unwilling to make very substantial cuts in Reagan's weapons procurement request, the House added to the bill two amendments intended to attack widely publicized instances of mismanagement in Pentagon weapons procurement.

Test Oversight. By voice vote, and with the consent of Armed Services Committee leaders, the House agreed to an amendment by Jim Courter, R-N.J., establishing an independent Pentagon office to supervise the so-called operational tests of new weapons.

Operational tests were intended to establish whether new weapons could meet their design specificiations in realistic combatlike conditions when operated by military personnel rather than laboratory technicians.

Allegations had abounded that the operational tests of several major weapons — including the Maverick air-launched anti-tank missile and the Divad anti-aircraft tank — had been designed to show the equipment in a good light, rather than realistically to test its suitability for combat.

Pentagon officials contended that creation of a new test oversight office would simply add to the already impacted layers of bureaucracy that prolong the gestation

period of new U.S. military equipment. But that contention carried little weight against more widespread fears that inadequate testing might endanger U.S. troops by equipping them with unworkable weapons.

Supporters of Reagan's defense buildup — Courter among them — cited an additional reason for trying to tighten up the testing process: a fear that public perceptions of Pentagon incompetence would undermine support for further defense spending increases.

Courter's amendment would have created the position of director of operational testing, to be filled by a civilian presidential appointee. No major weapon could be put into full production until the director reported directly to the secretary of defense and to the congressional Armed Services and Appropriations committees on the weapon's performance in its operational tests and on the adequacy of the test program.

Spare Parts. The House also agreed by voice vote to an amendment by Bill Nichols, D-Ala., requiring the Pentagon to report by June 1, 1984, on the status of various proposed reforms in the procurement of spare parts.

Troops in Europe

An amendment adopted by voice vote expressed the sense of Congress that Japan, Canada and the European NATO members should shoulder a heavier share of the burden of alliance defense, lest they "endanger the vitality, effectiveness and cohesiveness" of their alliances with the United States. The extent to which some allies contributed to mutual defense was "not commensurate with their economic resources," according to the provision.

By a 329-82 vote that language, proposed by Skelton, was substituted for language by Patricia Schroeder, D-Colo., that would have required a 29,000-person reduction in the number of U.S. troops stationed abroad. *(Vote 255, p. 78-H)*

Targeting Unemployment

Members from districts with high unemployment — mostly from Northeastern and Midwestern states — this time won an annual battle over whether to increase the total value of defense contracts that could be earmarked for areas of high unemployment, a policy widely believed to benefit the Frost Belt.

At issue was the yearly effort to enact a limited waiver of the so-called Maybank amendment, which forbade the award of defense contracts to other than the lowest bidder to relieve "economic dislocation."

1983's Maybank waiver amendment, offered by Hertel, was agreed to 218-201. It would allow targeting to high-unemployment areas of contracts for the purchase of routine supplies with a total value of up to $7 billion. *(Vote 260, p. 80-H)*

Senate Committee Action

The bill reported by the Senate Armed Services Committee July 5 (S 675 — S Rept 98-174) authorized $199,958,950,000 for procurement, research and development, operations, maintenance and construction activities of the Defense Department, for nuclear weapons programs of the Energy Department and for nuclear civil defense.

That was $13.4 billion less than the administration requested for those programs. The committee estimated that manpower reductions and other changes in the administration program that did not show up in the authorization

total would reduce eventual defense appropriations in fiscal 1984 by another $200 million or so.

In all, the bill authorized funds for just over 75 percent of the fiscal 1984 defense budget.

The committee's recommendation allowed a real defense spending increase — above the cost of inflation — of 5 percent, the growth allowed for defense in the fiscal 1984 budget resolution (H Con Res 91).

Strategic Warfare

The $4.6 billion recommended by the panel for the MX missile was $1.7 billion less than the sum requested in January. But it was the amount sought by the administration after the president agreed in April to the Scowcroft commission's recommendation to deploy 100 MXs in existing missile silos while developing a new, small, single-warhead missile for future deployment.

The funds approved would buy 27 MXs and continue development of the missile. The committee also agreed to a request of $604 million to begin research on improvements in the ICBM force, including $279 million to begin work on a small missile, $75 million to develop a heavily armored mobile launcher to carry it and $210 million to study ways to "super-harden" missile silos against nuclear attack.

Provisions were added by the committee requiring the Air Force to complete an environmental impact statement on the proposed MX deployment near Cheyenne, Wyo., by Jan. 31, 1984, and to begin deployment of the missiles by Dec. 31, 1986.

The panel also adopted a provision by Sam Nunn, D-Ga., specifying that no more than 21 of the 27 missiles to be purchased in fiscal 1984 would be deployed in operational missile launchers, as the Air Force currently planned. The remaining missiles were to be used instead for training launches and for other purposes.

The provision required the president to identify the number of operational missiles included in each future year's MX procurement and to report to Congress on the impact that the additional increment of operational missiles was expected to have on the stability of the nuclear balance and the prospects for negotiated arms reductions.

According to a Nunn aide, the provision was intended to give Congress a device for enforcing the link between MX deployment and arms control, which was a key component of Congress' endorsement of MX in May. The provision also may have been aimed at forestalling congressional misgivings about the plan to purchase a total of more than 200 MXs, of which only 100 were planned for deployment.

Bomber Weapons. To purchase 240 long-range air-launched cruise missiles (called ALCMs) to be carried by bombers, the committee added $340 million. It also added $23 million to test improvements in the ALCM engine. Most of that money was taken from requested funds to develop an improved cruise missile (ACM).

The Pentagon originally planned to purchase no ALCMs in fiscal 1984, preparatory to beginning production of the ACMs. But in April, the administration decided to continue ALCM procurement, partly because of concerns that the improved missile might be too expensive.

The panel dropped a $254 million request to begin a multi-year contract to equip with new engines the KC-135 tankers assigned to refuel U.S. bombers in midair; it approved the $700 million requested to modify 27 planes. The committee argued that prospective tight budgets would make it impossible for the Air Force to modify the tankers as fast as it planned.

Following the position taken by Congress for the past few years, the committee also added funds ($148 million) to modernize the engines on some other tankers assigned to Air National Guard units. These planes were to be fitted with engines stripped off obsolete airliners.

Sea-Based Missiles. For the 11th submarine of a class designed to carry 24 long-range Trident nuclear missiles, the panel approved $1.77 billion. That was $73 million less than the request, due to a revised Navy cost estimate. The panel denied $197 million requested to pay for cost increases in Trident submarines funded in earlier years.

The entire request to continue development and begin purchasing components for a larger, more accurate Trident II submarine missile ($1.5 billion) was approved. The panel added $10 million to study equipping the new missile with warheads that could fly evasive maneuvers to avoid anti-missile defenses.

Citing cost increases and technical problems in Tomahawk long-range, sea-launched cruise missiles, the committee cut back on the fiscal 1984 production request and warned that "serious consideration should be given to termination of the ... program," if improvements were not forthcoming.

Some of the Tomahawks would be armed with nuclear warheads to attack targets ashore (called TLAM-Ns), and some with conventional warheads to attack ships or shore targets.

The committee complained that the Navy was placing too strong an emphasis on equipping surface ships — particularly refurbished battleships — with nuclear versions at the expense of anti-ship versions. TLAM-Ns aboard submarines would be a sort of ultimate reserve force in case of a nuclear war, the committee said. But it questioned the point of deploying such missiles on large surface ships. Congressional approval of the battleship reactivation was based "primarily [on] their ability to attack and destroy enemy ships with missiles," the committee insisted.

It denied authorization for the 56 TLAM-Ns earmarked for surface ships, and ordered the Navy to report on how it planned to use such weapons before any more were requested. It also increased from 12 to 32 the number of anti-ship Tomahawks in fiscal 1984 and approved as requested the 56 submarine-deployed TLAM-Ns.

In all, $106 million was cut from the $493 million requested for the Tomahawks.

Nuclear Defense. The committee sharply trimmed a request for a large increase in research funds for anti-ICBM defenses. The reduction of $147 million in the $709 million request meant that funds for the program were increased above the fiscal 1983 level by just enough to keep pace with inflation.

For development of more exotic anti-missile defenses, including satellite-borne lasers and other "directed energy" weapons, the committee recommended $269.5 million, $50 million more than the request and almost $80 million more than the corresponding amount in the fiscal 1983 budget.

But in a clear warning to congressional conservatives, some of whom insisted that effective anti-missile defenses could be deployed within a few years, the committee said it "cannot recommend at this time the addition of substantial funds to the development programs falling within this area."

Citing the tight budgetary situation, the committee also sharply reduced the proposed increase in funds for civil defense, as it had done previously. It approved $162

million of the $254 million request — enough, it said, to provide a real increase of 5 percent over the fiscal 1983 program.

Euro-Missiles

The committee strongly endorsed plans to deploy long-range Pershing II and ground-launched cruise missiles able to strike Soviet targets from launchers in Western Europe, unless Moscow abandoned its force of long-range missiles aimed at Western Europe. Though the planned U.S. deployment was backed by the principal NATO governments, it evoked powerful domestic opposition in some European countries.

Deployment of the first U.S. missiles began as scheduled in December.

The committee approved without change the $463 million requested for 95 Pershing IIs and for continued development of the missile.

To procure 120 cruise missiles and to continue development of that weapon, the committee recommended $655 million, all but $17.7 million of the request.

Ground Combat

Citing current and prospective budget limits, the committee ordered the Army to hold down its planned production rates for several of its most important new weapons.

The panel trimmed $227 million (120 tanks) from the request for M-1 tanks. It approved $1.1 billion for 600 tanks and approved Army plans to seek a second manufacturer for the tank's 1,500-horsepower gas turbine engine, made by Avco Corp. in Connecticut. That company was battling hard — successfully in the House, so far — to block competition for future engine production.

The request for 600 Bradley armored infantry carriers was approved with little change ($796 million). But the committee ordered production held at that level in the future, opposing Army plans to seek 720 Bradleys in fiscal 1985.

Also because of the congressional ceiling on defense appropriations, the committee trimmed 16 planes ($121 million) from the $1.3 billion request for 112 Apache anti-tank helicopters. For the same reason, the $219 million request for laser-guided Hellfire anti-tank missiles that were to arm the Apache was cut by $20 million.

Future Tank Hunters. The committee recommended $131 million of the $151 million requested to develop a system of airborne radars (called JSTARS) and missiles (called JTACMS) to disrupt enemy reinforcement units tens of miles behind the front echelon of an enemy attack. After being guided to the target area by the radars, the missiles would dispense dozens of anti-tank warheads to home in on individual vehicles.

Citing Air Force-Army disagreements over the design of both components, the committee barred use of any fiscal 1984 funds for the projects until it received an acceptable plan for the system. It approved without change the $90.5 million requested for the radar, but trimmed $20 million from the $60 million requested for the missile. The panel conceded that the Army and Air Force might in the end need two different missiles for the job because a rocket with a long enough range when fired from the ground might be too bulky to carry on a plane.

Split Decision. The committee recommended an end to the Copperhead laser-guided anti-tank artillery shell, which long had been a favorite target of Pentagon critics because of cost increases and testing problems. The panel

deleted the $100 million Copperhead request.

But the panel stood by another controversial anti-tank weapon: a version of the Maverick air-launched missile that was supposed to home in on heat from tanks and other targets at night or in bad weather but failed to do so in some tests. Critics had long cited the missile as evidence that the services could not be trusted to kill off weapons programs that failed tests.

The Armed Services Committee, however, backed Maverick as the only weapon planes could use against tanks at night. It approved $317 million for 2,300 Mavericks, trimming $30 million to meet the budget ceiling.

Anti-Aircraft Weapons. A favorite target of Pentagon critics, the Divad anti-aircraft tank, also was authorized by the committee at the level requested — $671 million for 130 vehicles and associated spare parts.

The panel acknowledged concern over the weapon's test performance but emphasized its importance against missile-armed Soviet anti-tank helicopters.

Congress' ceiling on the fiscal 1984 budget accounted for the committee's large reduction in another anti-aircraft program: The Patriot missile was cut from $992 million (525 missiles) to $812 million (287 missiles), the same number approved for fiscal 1983.

Tactical Air Combat

As it had done with major Army weapons programs, the panel adjusted the planned procurement rates of several Navy and Air Force combat planes because of current and projected budget limitations.

The Navy took the brunt of the panel's explicit criticism, because of the variety of planes it bought. In part, this reflected the Navy's belief that the limited space aboard an aircraft carrier required a number of very specialized planes, none of which was purchased in very large numbers from year to year.

The committee noted that it had complained about the Navy's large number of small production lines in the fiscal 1983 defense authorization bill: "At that time there were 13 [Navy production] lines. In the fiscal year 1984 request, there are 16 ... and for fiscal year 1985 the Navy projects the number will grow to 20," the committee said.

As a result, the committee insisted, Navy planes had high unit costs which were driving out of the budget projects needed for long-term modernization, including development of a new carrier-based fighter for the mid-1990s and a new engine for the existing F-14 fighter.

In hopes of reversing that trend, the panel ordered a five-year pause in production of the Navy's largest carrier-borne bomber, the A-6E, of which six were planned in fiscal 1984. Meanwhile, it boosted from six to eight the fiscal 1984 production of EA-6Bs, a version of the same plane equipped to jam enemy radars. That increase would cut the unit cost of the EA-6Bs by $10 million, the committee said.

This amounted to a reduction of $111 million in the A-6E account and an increase of $59 million for EA-6Bs.

Citing the congressionally mandated ceiling on the fiscal 1984 defense budget, the committee also slowed down the production rates for two other planes, recommending:

• 27 AV-8B small, vertical-takeoff bombers used by the Marine Corps, for $715 million, a reduction of five planes and $95 million from the request;

• 21 F-14s instead of 24, for a reduction of $94 million to $792 million.

The panel approved the request for 84 F/A-18s, designed to serve as either fighters or bombers, but it denied

$102 million requested for a multi-year contract on the plane's engines. For those planes and for components to be used in 84 F/A-18s planned for purchase in fiscal 1985 (compared with Navy plans for 92) the bill included $2.4 billion.

Air Force Planes. Although the committee did not say so, the effect of its change in Air Force fighter programs was to emphasize procurement of cheaper F-16s at the expense of more expensive — and more technically sophisticated — F-15s.

The request for 48 F-15s ($1.5 billion) in fiscal 1984 and components in preparation for an order of 72 planes in fiscal 1985 ($432 million) was trimmed to 36 planes in fiscal 1984 ($1.3 billion) and advance components for 39 in fiscal 1985 ($144 million). The proposal for a multi-year procurement contract for the plane was rejected.

But the committee boosted the fiscal 1984 F-16 buy to 144 planes ($2 billion), an increase of 24 ($378 million). And it approved $396 million for components for 150 F-16s in fiscal 1985, compared to the request for $344 million to support a purchase of 120 planes the following year.

Future Weapons. The request for $132 million to develop an improved version of the engine used in the F-15 and F-16 was approved without change. The committee emphasized that the choice between an improved version of the current Pratt & Whitney engine and a new General Electric (GE) engine was to be based on their reliability and ease of upkeep, and not on their power.

The Air Force would select either of the two contenders or a mix of both. The Pentagon had insisted for years that it was not looking for additional power in a new engine, but in the superheated competition for contracts to build several thousand engines, the power issue would not go away.

(According to the Air Force, the GE engine was slightly more powerful, but weighed more than the Pratt & Whitney.)

Also approved without change was $94 million requested for development of LANTIRN, a combined infrared television and radar to let fighters seek ground targets at night. But, standing by the position it took in 1982, the committee ordered the Air Force to test some cheaper alternatives to the system.

The panel denied the $41.4 million requested for a medium-range version of the Tomahawk cruise missile (called MRASM), intended to be launched by planes against ships and airfields. The Navy and Air Force, which had been ordered to build a common missile, were not enthusiastic about MRASM, and other weapons could do the job instead, according to the panel.

Naval Warfare

The shipbuilding budget fared better at the hands of the committee than the requests for either airplanes or major Army weapons.

From a $12.7 billion request that included 17 new ships, five conversions of cargo ships and purchase of one supply ship from Britain, the committee cut $1.3 billion, but that deleted only two relatively minor ships. Nearly two-thirds of the reduction amounted to administrative changes that the committee insisted would not slow the Navy program.

Those cuts included $680 million for unanticipated inflation and cost increases in ships funded in prior years. The savings from the administration's revised inflation estimate amounted to $113 million, and an additional $75

million was disallowed from a contingency reserve requested for Aegis anti-missile cruisers.

The committee echoed the Navy's optimism about getting lower-than-anticipated bids on its fiscal 1983 ship contracts. If such savings occurred, the panel said, the Navy would be allowed to use up to $650 million to add another escort frigate or two to the fiscal 1984 budget.

So sanguine had the Navy been about getting lower-than-anticipated bids on its ships in fiscal 1983 that the committee transferred $650 million from that year's ship-building appropriation to the fiscal 1984 budget and told the Navy to build two unbudgeted escort frigates with the windfall.

More than 40 of these anti-aircraft missile-armed ships had been built since the mid-1970s, but the Navy requested none in fiscal 1984. The two added ships would have meant contracts for a Long Beach, Calif., firm (Todd Shipyards) that had built several of the frigates. Most combat ships had been built on the Atlantic or Gulf coasts, but the committee argued it was important to keep several shipyards on all coasts working on combat ship construction.

Battle Groups. Approved as requested was $57.7 million for components to be used in the modernization of the battleship *Missouri*, due for inclusion in the fiscal 1985 budget. It would be the third of four World War II battleships to be equipped with cruise missiles and returned to service.

Also approved was $3.36 billion for three Aegis cruisers, designed to protect U.S. fleets against enemy anti-ship missiles.

The panel recommended $79 million of the $100 million requested to purchase components for the first of a new class of destroyers, the *Arleigh Burke*, due for inclusion in the fiscal 1985 budget. These ships would be scaled-down versions of the Aegis cruiser, designed to replace a few dozen destroyers built in the late 1950s and due for retirement about 1990.

Anti-Submarine Warfare. Approved without change was a request for three *Los Angeles*-class nuclear submarines designed to hunt enemy submarines ($1.7 billion) and components for four of the ships to be requested in fiscal 1986 ($336 million).

The panel boosted to 24 (from 21) the fiscal 1984 purchase of LAMPS III anti-submarine helicopters, which equip most surface combat ships — a $38 million increase. It also halved (to six) the number of smaller LAMPS I helicopters (used on some older ships), citing congressional budget restrictions and the fact that the LAMPS I production line was winding down anyway. The panel approved $44.7 million of $89.4 million sought for LAMPS I.

Mobility

The administration's program to modernize the Navy's amphibious fleet, from which Marine Corps units could fight their way ashore against hostile forces, was supported by the committee but with budget-imposed trimming around the edges.

Approved essentially as requested were funds for a large helicopter carrier, called an LHD, that could house nearly 2,000 Marines ($1.4 billion) and a smaller ship of the LSD-41 class designed to carry tanks and trucks and the small landing barges to haul them to a beach ($337 million).

The panel added $18.3 million to the Navy's budget to continue operating three older ships (LSD-28s) that had been earmarked for retirement in 1982 but which Congress

decided not to retire in December 1982, after the fiscal 1984 budget had been drawn up.

But a request for multi-year procurement of future LSD-41s was rejected ($102 million) as was $14 million that had been earmarked for major overhauls of a similar class of ships (called LPD-4s). The LPD-4 overhauls had been deferred, according to the committee.

The committee also approved without change the requests for two projects to boost the Navy's ability to deliver troops and supplies to distant ports. These were modification of four high-speed container ships (SL-7s) to carry the tanks and other vehicles of an Army division ($246 million) and the purchase of nine commercial freighters for storage in the Navy's reserve fleet ($31 million).

Airlift. The request for eight midair refueling tanker versions of the DC-10 jetliners ($334 million) and for components to be used in future installments on this multi-year contract ($425 million) was approved without change.

For four large C-5 transport planes and components for future purchases, $1.3 billion was approved, a reduction of $18 million.

The committee denied $144 million for a long-troubled program called CRAF under which airlines were reimbursed for equipping their wide-body passenger jets so they could be quickly converted to haul bulky military cargo.

The program had foundered on congressional opposition and airline unhappiness with the funding arrangements. According to the committee, the Air Force planned no continued funding of it in fiscal 1985, which would make the fiscal 1984 conversions prohibitively expensive.

The panel nearly halved (to $14 million) the request to develop a long-range, wide-body cargo plane called the C-17. It warned that the Air Force's development plan for the plane was too rapid in light of the budgets likely to be available. And it barred use of any of the fiscal 1984 funds until the Pentagon reported to Congress on certain issues in the plane's design.

Personnel Issues

The annual authorization bill did not directly address funding levels for military personnel, but it controlled personnel spending indirectly by setting ceilings on Pentagon manpower levels.

The Senate panel set the ceiling on active uniformed personnel at the end of fiscal 1984 at 2,142,674 — an increase of 15,274 over the fiscal 1983 ceiling but 22,026 fewer than the administration requested.

Pay Hike. Rejecting the administration's call for a freeze on all federal pay, the committee proposed a pay hike averaging 4 percent for all military and civilian Pentagon workers. The raise was to come on April 1 or earlier if a similar hike took effect for federal workers not employed by the Pentagon.

Recruits with only a few months of service would receive no raise and mid-level sergeants would receive raises of 5-6 percent.

If the raise took effect on April 1, the military component of it would cost about $750 million, while the civilian raise would cost $433 million. Only the latter amount was included in the authorization total of S 675.

Reliance on Reserves. Like its House counterpart, the Senate panel ordered the Pentagon to rely more heavily on Reserve units than an expanded active duty force for any new missions. That idea appeared to have acquired widespread congressional support on the assumption that Reserve forces, who are paid only for the few days each

month they are in uniform, cost much less to operate than active duty units.

That feeling was a factor in reducing the Pentagon's requested increase in active duty personnel. By contrast, the committee added 9,000 positions to the 37,000 by which the administration wanted to expand the selected Reserve forces — reservists who are organized into units and meet regularly for drill sessions.

The selected Reserve strength set by S 675 was 1,035,000.

In a further effort to prod the Pentagon on the Reserve issue, the panel ordered it to submit a study of the feasibility and prospective savings of strengthening the Reserve role in several ways, including:

● Increasing the number of ground combat units that rely on Reserve forces for some of their components (for instance, one Reserve brigade of three brigades in a division). Four Army divisions were currently relying on such National Guard "round-out" brigades.

● Relying more on Reserve fighter squadrons to defend U.S. airspace against bomber attacks or to reinforce NATO in case of war. There was less debate about the combat readiness of Reserve air units than ground units because Reserve flyers routinely had performed on a par with active duty units in combat exercises.

● Assigning more of the Navy's anti-submarine frigates and large, land-based anti-submarine planes to the Naval Reserve. The Navy planned to assign partly Reserve crews to 24 relatively modern frigates, and it already relied on reservists for a third of its land-based patrol planes.

As had long been routine on defense funding bills, the committee added several hundred million dollars to improve the equipment of Reserve units. Major additions included $125 million for various kinds of electronic and supply equipment, $36 million for 50 additional 155mm cannon, $29 million to modernize existing anti-aircraft guns for Reserve use, and $89 million to modernize various combat planes flown by Reserve units.

The committee earmarked for the Reserves the 24 F-16 fighters it added to the bill. But it took a more tight-fisted approach on other Reserve modernization issues. It opposed a Navy plan to assign new F-18 fighters to Reserve units, telling the service to issue the planes to active duty units first. And it told the Army to equip Reserve units by modernizing existing Cobra anti-tank helicopters until after most active duty units had received the newer Apache helicopter.

Senate Floor Action

After rejecting a move to delete funds for the MX, the Senate approved its $199 billion fiscal 1984 defense authorization bill, S 675, by an 83-15 vote on July 26. *(Vote 217, p. 37-S)*

The Senate bill authorized about $186 billion for weapons procurement, military research and operating costs. The House bill authorized $187.4 billion for the same programs.

MX Retained

President Reagan's plan for the MX missile retained its numerically comfortable but politically tenuous Senate majority when a move to delete MX procurement funds was rejected 41-58.

The move was led by Gary Hart, D-Colo., and Mark O. Hatfield, R-Ore.

Senators lined up essentially as they did May 25, 59-39, when the Senate approved the start of MX flight tests. The pro-MX majority consisted of most Republicans and a dozen Democrats who typically took a hard line on defense issues.

The only change in the July 26 tally compared with the earlier vote was Bob Packwood, R-Ore., who had voted for flight testing but opposed the fiscal 1984 authorization. *(Vote 214, p. 37-S; May 25 tally, vote 114, p. 23-S)*

The Senate then rejected 42-57 an amendment by Daniel Patrick Moynihan, D-N.Y., that would have barred deployment of MX. Lawton Chiles, D-Fla., joined the anti-MX side of that vote. *(Vote 215, p. 37-S)*

But Hart, the leader of a group of about 15 MX opponents that had filibustered the bill for nearly two weeks, claimed a victory far more significant than the gain of one vote.

"A case [against the missile] has been made and not refuted," he told reporters after the vote.

The case Hart and his allies emphasized was that MX would make the U.S.-Soviet nuclear balance more dangerous because of the decision to deploy it in existing missile silos, which were vulnerable to Soviet missile attack. The deployment would force the United States to adopt a policy of "launch-on-warning," the critics said, placing the U.S. nuclear force on a hair trigger to be pulled at the first sign of enemy attack.

During the nearly two weeks that Hart and his allies tried to draw the pro-MX faction into debate, they attacked the new missile for its impact on arms control and on the state of the U.S.-Soviet nuclear balance.

All parties to the battle seemed to endorse the view that the long-term goal of U.S. nuclear arms policy should be abolition of large, accurate multiple-warhead (MIRV) missiles such as the MX, the 600-plus Soviet SS-18s and SS-19s already deployed and the new Soviet SS-24, then undergoing flight tests.

The argument was that if both nuclear superpowers deployed roughly the same number of MIRV missiles, the balance of nuclear terror would be unstable because whichever side attacked first could, theoretically, destroy its opponents' missiles while retaining a large part of its own force for subsequent attacks.

That threat would be obviated if MIRVs were replaced with small, single-warhead missiles, it was argued, since either power then could destroy its opponent's missiles only by using up its own. An amendment by Carl Levin, D-Mich., endorsing that proposition was approved 92-6. *(Vote 216, p. 37-S)*

Earlier the Senate tabled, 60-34, an amendment by Levin that would have added $2.7 billion to various non-nuclear weapons and training programs in the bill — projects Levin charged had been underfunded to pay for MX. *(Vote 190, p. 33-S)*

Chemical Weapons

In the first five days of debate on S 675 July 11-15, the administration's closest shave on a major weapons issue came on an amendment by David Pryor, D-Ark., to delete $131 million earmarked for production of a new generation of chemical weapons called "binary munitions" — artillery shells and air-dropped bombs that produce lethal nerve gas.

A motion to table (and thus kill) the Pryor amendment was agreed to 50-49, with Vice President George Bush — exercising his constitutional role as president of the Senate

— casting the tie-breaking vote after the senators present tied 49-49. *(Vote 180, p. 32-S)*

It was the first time since 1977 that a vice president had cast a Senate vote. Bush was to do so again on Nov. 8 — once more breaking a tie to save nerve gas — during Senate action on defense appropriations. *(p. 479)*

Pryor argued that existing U.S. chemical weapons were adequate to deter Soviet chemical attack and that binary production would surrender "the high ground as far as world opinion is concerned," by ending a self-imposed 14-year moratorium on U.S. chemical weapons production.

Armed Services Chairman John Tower, R-Texas, countered that the existing chemical weapons were "old and deteriorating and dangerous to their handlers." By the end of the decade, he said, the chemicals would have lost their potency, rendering them useless.

He also argued that the new chemical arms were needed to give Moscow an incentive to negotiate a treaty reducing chemical weapons stockpiles.

B-1 Bomber

The B-1 bomber easily survived its opposition when the Senate on July 13 rejected, 68-30, an Edward M. Kennedy, D-Mass., amendment to delete the $6.9 billion earmarked for procurement of 10 bombers and further development of the plane. *(Vote 181, p. 32-S)*

Kennedy called the B-1 "unnecessary and ... virtually obsolete the moment it becomes operational." The air-launched cruise missile had given the B-52 (the current U.S. bomber) a "new lease on life," he said. The missiles launched from B-52s could continue to penetrate Soviet air defenses even after the planes themselves no longer could, he argued, while the B-1 would be only slightly better able than the B-52 to survive Soviet defenses.

A real improvement in the U.S. bomber force, Kennedy argued, would be the so-called "stealth" bomber, designed to evade detection by enemy radar. The plane was planned to enter service about 1991, several years after the B-1. But, Kennedy argued, that timetable could be accelerated, and he warned that production of the planned fleet of 100 B-1s might be so costly that development of the newer plane would be delayed.

Tower countered that the B-1 was "a bird in the hand." Development of the stealth plane might ultimately be delayed, he warned, if Congress tried to accelerate the program unduly.

Multi-Year Contract. By a narrower but still comfortable margin of 56-41, the Senate July 14 rejected an amendment by Nunn that would have barred a multi-year contract to cover the 10 B-1s authorized in fiscal 1984, the 34 planned for fiscal 1985 and the 48 planned for fiscal 1986. *(Vote 186, p. 33-S)*

The amendment would have reduced the B-1 account by $888.7 million slated to be authorized under that production plan. It would have reallocated the money among 47 conventional weapons and operations and maintenance projects that had been trimmed by the Senate Armed Services Committee to remain under the congressional budget ceiling.

Nunn warned that if the B-1 production rate were built up to 48 planes in fiscal 1986, with 60,000 employees engaged in the project, it would be politically impossible to terminate B-1 production abruptly at that point and the B-1 would stay in production at the expense of the stealth bomber.

Budget Battle

The Senate tabled, 53-41, a Slade Gorton, R-Wash., motion to recommit S 675 to the Armed Services Committee with instructions, in effect, to cut some $1.3 billion from the total authorized by the bill. *(Vote 185, p. 33-S)*

The motion would have ordered the panel to report a revised bill with a total authorization below the amount implied by the fiscal 1984 budget resolution but disregarding the administration's June 27 letter to the committee reducing its estimated inflation rate for military purchases.

The effect of the inflation re-estimate was to reduce by $2.1 billion the total cost of programs included in the bill. The committee used $1.3 billion of that amount to add to the bill programs that would not otherwise have been possible under the ceiling set by the budget resolution. This included the $888.7 million for multi-year funding of the B-1 bomber.

On July 11, when the Senate was scheduled to begin debate on S 675, Kennedy and Howard M. Metzenbaum, D-Ohio, used procedural tactics to block action for most of the day, to protest the inflation revision.

Gorton dismissed the new estimates as too optimistic, "without basis in either fact or history." He pointed out that Office of Management and Budget Director David A. Stockman "has not found comparable new room for domestic spending programs."

But Tower and Budget Committee Chairman Pete V. Domenici, R-N.M., insisted that the bill already incorporated all the reductions from the president's request that were called for by the budget resolution.

Chiles, the Budget panel's senior Democrat, agreed that was so, but warned that unrealistically low inflation estimates would wreak havoc on the Pentagon program when weapons prices turned out to be higher than assumed.

Alluding to the Armed Services report on the bill, Chiles warned, "You will not be able to buy what the report says that you expect to be able to buy. So we are adding the $2 billion to the deficit or we are going to take it out of operations and maintenance or we are going to reduce our buy.... You cannot work this with mirrors."

Future Tank Hunters

The Armed Services panel's first defeat of the year on a weapons issue came July 13 with the adoption of an amendment that boosted new conventional weapons as an alternative to new nuclear artillery shells as a way of dealing with the large number of tanks in the Soviet army.

The amendment by Nunn and J. Bennett Johnston, D-La., prohibited the use of $50 million earmarked to begin producing a new 155mm nuclear artillery shell. The shell would have a so-called neutron bomb-type warhead — that is, it would be designed to kill tank crews by releasing a large amount of lethal radiation from a small explosion.

The amendment would use the money instead to accelerate the development of several new non-nuclear weapons designed to destroy opposing tank formations far behind an enemy's front lines. These included air-borne radars designed to locate such targets miles behind the front lines, and missiles equipped with dozens of conventional warheads designed to home in on individual tanks.

Nunn said the Armed Services Committee had cut a total of $413 million from the request for research on these programs.

Nunn warned of "a great overreliance on the early use of nuclear weapons as a key to NATO deterrence" of a

Soviet attack. Technical breakthroughs made a successful non-nuclear defense possible, he insisted, and growing public fear of nuclear weapons in Europe would make it politically necessary, sooner or later, if the Western alliance was to survive.

But according to Nunn, the Pentagon was dragging its feet on developing the new conventional weapons because of "bureaucratic squabbling, service parochialism and opposition from many who see these technologies as a threat to existing programs."

The amendment was adopted by voice vote after a motion to table was rejected 30-67. *(Vote 184, p. 32-S)*

Sea-Launched Cruise Missiles

By a vote of 47-40, the Senate tabled (killed) Charles McC. Mathias', R-Md., amendment declaring the sense of Congress that the president should seek abolition of nuclear-armed, sea-launched cruise missiles in the current START talks. The amendment also asked that the president propose a bilateral moratorium on deployment of such weapons during the negotiations. *(Vote 199, p. 34-S)*

A long-range, nuclear-armed version of the 20-foot Tomahawk missile was due for deployment on U.S. submarines and surface ships beginning in June 1984. Current Soviet cruise missiles were much bulkier and had shorter ranges. But Mathias warned that deployment of the nuclear Tomahawks (called TLAM-Ns) would drive Moscow to develop equally small, long-range weapons.

But Henry M. Jackson, D-Wash., objected that a cruise missile freeze would leave the Soviet Union with hundreds of missiles already deployed.

Space Lasers

In what had become an annual skirmish, Malcolm Wallop's, R-Wyo., effort to accelerate the development of laser-armed space satellites to destroy enemy ballistic missiles was tabled (killed) 65-27. *(Vote 206, p. 35-S)*

Wallop led of a corps of senators, most of them Mountain-states' conservatives, that insisted that recent breakthroughs in lasers and other technologies made it feasible to defend the United States against attack by shooting down approaching missiles. That would mark a radical break from the longstanding policy of seeking to deter an attack by the threat of retaliation against an aggressor.

Since 1980, Wallop had sought to accelerate U.S. laser research and, in particular, to concentrate it on specific kinds of weapons that he and his technical advisers insisted could be tested by 1987. He and other laser advocates warned that a Soviet space laser was likely to be deployed by then.

Most of Wallop's previous efforts were defeated or co-opted by the Senate Armed Services Committee, which seemed to share the Pentagon's skepticism that laser development could prudently be accelerated at the rate Wallop proposed.

In 1983, Wallop might have drawn political momentum from Reagan's embrace of the general concept of missile defense as expressed in a March 23 television address.

But Tower and other committee members warned that the amendment would prejudice the recommendations of a blue-ribbon technical advisory panel established to follow through on Reagan's address.

Anti-Satellite Weapons

By 91-0, the Senate agreed to a compromise amendment negotiated between Armed Services leaders and proponents of a moratorium on space weapons tests. *(Vote 203, p. 35-S)*

The amendment by Paul E. Tsongas, D-Mass., would have barred any tests of anti-satellite (ASAT) weapon warheads against targets in space unless the president certified:

● That the United States was "endeavoring to negotiate in good faith with the Soviet Union a mutual and verifiable ban on anti-satellite weapons," and

● That the tests were necessary to avert "clear and irrevocable harm" to U.S. security interests.

In a colloquy with Armed Services strategic arms subcommittee Chairman John W. Warner, R-Va., Tsongas conceded that the requirement that the United States was endeavoring "to negotiate in good faith" would be met if the U.S. government were merely "actively assessing the possibility of negotiating" on ASAT issues.

Tsongas' immediate target was the planned first test of the 18-foot-long U.S. anti-satellite missile, which was designed to be launched in midair from an F-15 fighter plane. The missile was especially designed to destroy two kinds of Soviet satellites that could be used to locate U.S. warships and provide guidance information to Soviet anti-ship missiles.

In addition to the missile's putative military utility, the administration wanted the ASAT as an incentive to prod Moscow to negotiate a bilateral ASAT ban that would eliminate existing Soviet anti-satellite weapons.

Preliminary U.S.-Soviet ASAT negotiations were conducted in 1978-79 but were suspended when the Soviet Union invaded Afghanistan at the end of 1979.

Tsongas and his allies feared that because the U.S. ASAT was so small, once it was tested an ASAT ban might be impossible to negotiate because Soviet reconnaissance satellites could not tell whether or not the United States was still deploying it. By contrast, they argued, the Soviet ASAT, launched from huge intercontinental ballistic missiles, was so bulky that U.S. intelligence agencies easily could verify Soviet compliance with an ASAT ban.

The House had rejected an amendment to HR 2969 that would have deleted funds to begin purchase of components for the U.S. ASAT.

Foreign Relations Action. On July 19, the day after the Senate adopted the Tsongas amendment, the Foreign Relations Committee approved a resolution (S J Res 129) calling on the president to declare "an immediate, mutual and verifiable moratorium of limited duration" on ASAT tests in space.

The resolution, which also called on the president to "immediately resume negotiations" on an ASAT ban, was sponsored by Larry Pressler, R-S.D., chairman of the panel's Arms Control Subcommittee.

Weapons Testing

Despite Pentagon objections, the Senate adopted, 91-5, an amendment by Pryor establishing within the Pentagon an agency to supervise the tests of new weapons. The agency, to be headed by a civilian requiring Senate confirmation, would report directly to the secretary of defense and to Congress on the effectiveness of new arms. *(Vote 187, p. 33-S)*

The amendment's overwhelming support apparently reflected growing congressional suspicion that much Pentagon weapons testing did not realistically simulate the combat conditions under which the weapon would be used. Moreover, critics complained, even when weapons per-

formed poorly in current tests, they were too often approved for production anyway.

Pentagon research chief Richard D. DeLauer warned repeatedly that the new test agency would simply add to the impacted layers of bureaucracy that contributed to the prolonged gestation period of U.S. weapons. .

But Tower, who had appeared unenthusiastic about other testing proposals, accepted the amendment after its effective date was delayed until November.

Dependents' Schools

Over the Armed Services Committee's objections, the Senate reaffirmed its support for transferring from the Pentagon to the Department of Education control of the elementary and secondary schools operated abroad for the dependents of military personnel. But it provided a loophole that would allow the president to block the transfer.

As reported, the bill repealed the provision of current law that required the transfer by May 4, 1984. The transfer would be administratively chaotic, the committee warned, because the Education Department would have to assume responsibility for various services currently supplied gratis to the schools by U.S. base commanders. And the panel warned that the morale of troops overseas would suffer if the longstanding administrative arrangements for the dependents' schools were disrupted.

Opposing Armed Services' position, Robert T. Stafford, R-Vt., chairman of the Labor and Human Resources Education Subcommittee, argued that the dependents' schools — with the 11th largest student enrollment among U.S. school systems — should be administered by an education agency rather than a military one.

Stafford offered an amendment to delete the committee provision and require the transfer to the Education Department "not later than May 4, 1986." A motion to table Stafford's amendment was rejected 42-50. *(Vote 204, p. 35-S)*

The Senate then agreed, 47-46, to a Dan Quayle, R-Ind., substitute for the Stafford amendment providing that the transfer take place "not earlier than May 4, 1986," and that either the president or Congress could block the move in the interests of military morale or the quality of education in the schools. *(Vote 205, p. 35-S)*

The amended Stafford amendment then was adopted by voice vote.

Draft Registration

The Senate adopted 56-40 a Moynihan amendment delaying until Oct. 1, 1983, the effective date of the current law requiring that college students receiving federal aid certify that they registered with the Selective Service System, as required by law. *(Vote 212, p. 36-S)*

But earlier, the Senate had rejected three efforts to more substantially alter that law.

By a vote of 71-23, it tabled an amendment by Dave Durenberger, R-Minn., that would have repealed the requirement outright. *(Vote 189, p. 33-S)*

Earlier, a Stafford substitute for the Durenberger proposal was tabled 66-29. *(Vote 188, p. 33-S)*

By a vote of 64-19, the Senate later rejected a Bill Bradley, D-N.J., amendment that would have deleted a requirement that students certify their compliance with the registration law. The amendment would instead have required colleges to submit to the Education Department lists of enrolled students receiving federal student aid so that the department could check for student compliance

with the registration law. *(Vote 201, p. 35-S)*

Other Amendments

The Senate also adopted two other amendments:

● By George J. Mitchell, D-Maine, to extend through fiscal 1986 the current ban on "contracting-out" to private firms responsibility for security and firefighting on military bases. Agreed to by voice vote after rejection, 44-53, of a motion to table. *(Vote 182, p. 32-S)*

● By Roger W. Jepsen, R-Iowa, creating the position of assistant secretary of defense for reserve affairs, 91-0. *(Vote 194, p. 34-S)*

Two other amendments were killed:

● By Pressler to add $24.4 million for operating costs of the Army National Guard and Air National Guard. Tabled 47-35. *(Vote 200, p. 35-S)*

● By John Melcher, D-Mont., to provide recruits with the same 4 percent pay hike the bill would grant to other military personnel. Tabled 63-14. *(Vote 202, p. 35-S)*

Conference Action

Conferees on S 675 approved $10.5 billion less than President Reagan's $198 billion request but left it up to the Pentagon to allocate nearly 15 percent of that reduction.

The conference report on the bill, filed in the Senate Aug. 15 (S Rept 98-213), authorized $187.5 billion to cover virtually all Pentagon programs except military construction, military pay and pensions. This was $1.5 billion more than the Senate had approved on July 26, and $163 million more than was included in HR 2969, the companion House bill passed the same day.

The $10.5 billion reduction included $1.3 billion in anticipation of lower-than-budgeted fuel costs. The conferees agreed to half of a controversial $2.1 billion reduction the Senate had made in anticipation of lower-than-budgeted inflation.

But the conferees simply allocated additional unspecified reductions — totaling nearly $1.7 billion — to several major budget accounts. These included cuts of $425 million in spare parts for Air Force planes, $400.2 million in communication and electronic gear for the Army and Navy and $322 million for "miscellaneous" reductions in the Air Force missile account.

In the fiscal 1983 authorization bill (S 2248), such unspecified reductions totaled about $160 million, one-tenth the amount in the current bill.

Binary Munitions Still Opposed

House opposition to the conference report was led by Zablocki and Bethune.

Their target was one part of the report: $114.6 million to produce a new 155mm "binary" artillery shell that could produce lethal nerve gas. The funds had been requested by the president and approved by the Senate, but the House had voted against the new weapons June 15.

Conferees on S 675 tried to mollify House opponents by barring final assembly of the nerve gas shells before Oct. 1, 1985 — allowing U.S. and Soviet negotiators two years to seek a ban on the weapons. The conferees also included a provision requiring that one existing chemical shell be scrapped for each new one produced.

But opponents were not appeased and announced before Congress recessed in August that they would try to beat the conference report in the House.

They conceded that it would be difficult for some

members to vote against the entire defense bill because of a single issue, but hoped that Zablocki's moderate reputation and Bethune's staunchly conservative record would make a "nay" vote easier.

Binary critics also hoped that some members might be further emboldened to challenge the conference report because of their opposition to the MX missile, which had survived a House challenge in July by only 13 votes.

In the last days before the showdown, some longtime arms control lobbyists who opposed nerve gas production nevertheless complained — though not for attribution — that Zablocki's effort simply would give Reagan an easy political victory.

When the House took up the conference report Sept. 15, supporters of the measure insisted that a strong "yea" vote would reinforce the resolution adopted the day before which condemned the Soviet downing of the Korean airliner.

"Will the Kremlin pay more attention to the [condemnatory] resolution ... than it will to the overwhelming passage of this conference report?" asked William L. Dickinson, R-Ala.

Bethune spoke for nerve gas opponents, protesting that the House was being coerced by "the emotions of the moment" into abandoning its earlier opposition to binary weapons.

"Just because the Soviet Union engaged in an immoral act in the shooting down of a jetliner does not mean that this Congress should approve funding for an immoral weapon," such as nerve gas, argued Les AuCoin, D-Ore.

On the other hand, Leath argued that the airliner incident undermined the contention that abstention from producing the new weapons would provide diplomatic leverage against Moscow. "That argument went up in smoke when [flight] 007 went down," Leath declared.

"While we stand on the high ground with our backs turned and our heads bowed, the Soviet butchers are gassing hundreds of thousands of innocent people," in Afghanistan and Southeast Asia, Leath said.

Nerve gas opponents also objected to authorization of a weapon that had been voted down by the House and approved by the Senate only when the vice president broke a tie vote. On those grounds, Zablocki insisted, the conference report was "an affront to the House and to the legislative process."

Retorted Samuel S. Stratton, D-N.Y., "If you'll take out your copies of the Constitution, you'll find that the vice president does have a role."

Compared to the test vote in June, when binary supporters lost by 14 votes, in the 266-152 vote on the conference report Democratic support for the pro-binary position increased by 48 votes, compared with an increase of 16 votes on the Republican side. *(Vote 322, p. 96-H)*

Easy Senate Passage

Nerve gas opponents made no effort to beat the conference report on S 675 in the Senate, although Pryor, one of the most energetic opponents of binary weapons, said he hoped that "the production of chemical weapons will not become our monument to the 269 dead people of the Korean Air Lines tragedy."

The brief Senate debate on the measure Sept. 13 marked the formal debut of Nunn as senior Democrat on the Senate Armed Services Committee, succeeding Jackson, who died Sept. 1.

All senators who voted against the measure on Sept. 13

were Democrats; seven were liberals who frequently opposed selected Pentagon programs.

Nuclear Attack

The two bills were in basic agreement on the MX missile; both houses had voted to start production, though the House vote was a near thing.

The conferees agreed to fund 21 of the missiles ($2.1 billion) rather than the 27 ($2.4 billion) requested and approved by the Senate. During House debate, Gore had insisted on the reduction as the first step in eventually trimming — from the 100 planned by the administration — the total number of MXs to be deployed.

Gore was a leader among House moderates who supported deployment of the 10-warhead MX only on condition that it be linked to development of a smaller, single-warhead ICBM. The conference report also tied the MX deployment schedule to the achievement of certain mileposts in the development of the small missile. That limit originally was sponsored by Aspin, one of Gore's key allies among pro-MX House Democrats.

To begin development of the new small missile and various technologies that might be used in its basing method, the conferees approved the $604 million approved by the Senate. The House had authorized $270 million.

Bomber Modernization. Both bills had authorized the $6.2 billion requested for procurement of 10 B-1 bombers and related equipment.

The conferees also approved a Senate provision ordering the secretary of defense to update the Pentagon's estimate of the total cost of the B-1 program. On Feb. 18, 1982, the president certified to Congress that the planned fleet of 100 B-1s could be bought for $20.5 billion (in fiscal 1981 dollars). The cost issue was politically charged: Some critics warned that the B-1's cost likely would balloon and thus starve out development of its planned successor — the so-called "stealth" bomber, which was being designed to evade detection by enemy radar.

The amount authorized to continue development of the stealth bomber was secret. But conferees included a Senate provision — also added to defense money bills in 1981 and 1982 — barring the Pentagon from diverting any of the secret fund to other projects.

The conferees reduced from $876 million to $578 million the amount earmarked to replace the antiquated jet engines on KC-135 tanker planes — versions of the Boeing 707 jetliner that could refuel strategic bombers and other planes in midair. The budget request would have given new engines to 31 tankers. The conferees directed that 24 planes be given the new engines and that an additional 32 tankers, which were operated by the Air National Guard, be given used engines stripped from scrapped airliners.

Submarine-Launched Missiles. Both houses had approved requests for one Trident-launching submarine ($1.4 billion) and 52 Trident I missiles ($587.2 million).

To continue development of the Trident II submarine-launched missile — a larger and more accurate successor to Trident I — the conferees approved $1.5 billion, $10 million more than requested. The additional funds, a Senate initiative, were intended to preserve the option of equipping the Trident II with a maneuverable re-entry vehicle (MaRV), that might be designed to evade Soviet anti-missile defenses.

Intermediate-Range Missiles. Both houses had approved the request for long-range, ground-launched, nuclear-armed missiles designed to reach Soviet targets from

bases in Western Europe: $407 million for 95 Pershing II ballistic missiles and $563.8 million for 120 ground-launched cruise missiles (GLCMs).

In line with the House position, the conferees deleted $17.7 million requested for financing the GLCM production line.

Senate conferees appeared to relax their evident skepticism toward seaborne versions of the GLCM (called the Tomahawk) based on surface ships. The conference report essentially approved the request for 124 missiles, including nuclear-armed versions to be carried by surface ships.

The Senate had denied funds for nuclear-armed Tomahawks for surface ships, approving 88 missiles, with some nuclear versions earmarked for submarines and non-nuclear models planned for surface ship deployment.

Strategic Defense

The conferees' fundamental premise in dealing with anti-missile defense programs was that no new steps should be taken before a White House commission reported to Reagan on ways to implement his March 23 call for a new look at the feasibility of defending the country against nuclear attack. That report was due in October.

Both houses had substantially cut the $538 million requested to develop a "conventional" kind of anti-missile system — one that would try to shoot down incoming missile warheads with other missiles. The conferees approved $338 million for the project (roughly the midpoint between the amounts authorized by the two bills) and also left the Pentagon room to add up to $40 million currently earmarked for other projects.

Reagan's call for strategic defenses had emphasized more technically exotic weapons that would destroy incoming warheads with beams of energy: lasers, which "aim" streams of concentrated light, or subatomic particles. Such weapons had a small but dedicated band of advocates, mostly among political conservatives.

Reiterating their insistence that no radical new steps be taken before the president commented on the advisory report, the conferees canceled some laser programs not directly related to the strategic defense mission. They also added funds to beef up research on certain types of laser technology.

Anti-Satellite Tests. The conferees also accepted a Senate floor amendment that would bar any tests in space of the U.S. anti-satellite missile unless the president certified that he was attempting to negotiate a ban with the Soviet Union on such weapons, which the Russians had deployed in small numbers.

Civil Defense. Both houses had cut significantly the $253.5 million request for civil defense. The $169 million approved by the conferees was much closer to the lower Senate authorization.

Ground Combat

Programs tailored to confront the tank-heavy forces of the Warsaw Pact fared quite well in the conference.

Following the House's lead, the conferees raised to 840 the number of M-1 tanks authorized, an increase of 120 tanks at about $100 million over the request. The Senate Armed Services Committee had trimmed the M-1 production rate to 600 per year, warning that future Army budgets would not sustain a higher rate.

The Senate had been similarly wary of Army plans to increase in fiscal 1985 the production rate of Bradley armored infantry carriers, which carried TOW anti-tank mis-

siles. But the conferees also disregarded the Senate position that the Bradley's future production rate should be held to 600 per year, the number requested for fiscal 1984 and approved by both houses.

For the 600 Bradleys in fiscal 1984, $699 million was approved, $33 million more than the request, in order to equip the vehicle with a new, larger version of the TOW.

The House also prevailed in its opposition to letting a second contractor bid on the gas turbine engines that powered the M-1. The Army wanted a second source for M-1 engines because of production delays and quality problems with engines made by Avco Corp., the current supplier.

But opponents of the move insisted that the currrent contractor was now performing well, after having made a considerable investment in the M-1 engine production line. The House had voted strongly in favor of the ban after a heated debate dominated by members whose constituents had a direct stake in Avco or one of its potential competitors.

Tank-Hunters. Conferees chose the higher funding alternative for two helicopters armed with laser-guided Hellfire anti-tank missiles:

● $1.2 billion for 112 AH-64 Apaches; the Senate-passed authorization was lower by 16 helicopters ($75.2 million).

● $17.8 million for components to be used in Cobra helicopters to be requested in fiscal 1985 for the Marine Corps. The planned request had been dropped from the administration's January request but added to the Senate bill.

Also approved was $75 million to purchase Copperhead laser-guided artillery shells for the Army. The $25 million requested for Marine Corps Copperheads was denied. The Senate had denied all funds for the program, its committee citing the Pentagon's on-and-off attitude toward the shell because of its cost.

Both houses had approved the request for $177 million to begin equipping small scout helicopters with lasers to "illuminate" enemy tanks for Hellfires and Copperheads. The conferees exempted that program (called AHIP) from the across-the-board reductions they had ordered.

'Deep Strike.' The conferees backed new, non-nuclear weapons designed to destroy opposing tank formations far behind an enemy's front lines. This included $122.5 million to develop an airborne radar (called JSTARS) to locate the tanks and $80.1 million to develop missiles (called JTACMS) equipped with dozens of warheads designed to home in on individual tanks.

Senate Armed Services had sharply trimmed funds for these programs while professing interest in their potential. But by a ratio of more than 2-to-1, the Senate voted to increase funding for the new weapons. The amendment barred production of a new type of nuclear artillery shell, which also was designed to break up tank attacks, and transferred $50 million previously appropriated for that project to the non-nuclear weapons.

Nunn, a leading sponsor of the Senate amendment, argued that the new conventional weapons, designed to reach tens of miles behind enemy lines, would be more militarily effective and politically acceptable than the shorter-range nuclear artillery shell.

The conferees endorsed Nunn's position, declaring "that the utility of short-range nuclear battlefield weapons as a deterrent to war in the NATO area is diminishing and that conventional defensive systems should receive additional emphasis."

Development of the nuclear shell was authorized in a separate measure covering defense projects carried out by the Energy Department, but the conferees agreed that it would be dropped from that bill.

Anti-Aircraft Defense. Following a House initiative, conferees added $200 million for anti-aircraft missiles to protect U.S. air bases in Europe. The missiles, including Patriots, would be operated by troops of the host government. An agreement with West Germany on such an arrangement was to be signed by Sept. 30.

Conferees clearly hoped that in addition to their military significance, such arrangements would defuse congressional arguments that U.S. allies did not pay a fair share of the cost of NATO's defense: "The conferees ... expect increased allied cooperation involving NATO's more prosperous countries to lead to equitable defense burden sharing arrangements."

Lightweight Vehicles. Because of House Armed Services' opposition, the conferees trimmed procurement of novel types of vehicles designed to make it easier to transport U.S. combat units to distant sites or to let them maneuver with greater speed.

Approved amounts included:

● $132.5 million (of $210.5 million requested) for armored cars for Marine and Army units. The conferees told the Army to turn over to the Marines all its so-called "light armored vehicles" and to consider whether it really needed some of its own.

● $2 million for "fast attack vehicles" — dune buggies armed with TOW missile launchers or machine guns to harass an enemy's flanks. The request had been for $4.7 million.

● $1 million (of $9.9 million requested) for cross-country motorcycles for couriers.

Naval Warfare

The report reflected both bills' support for the administration's shipbuilding request, providing:

● Three nuclear-powered, submarine-hunting subs ($1.7 billion).

● Components to modernize a third battleship and equip it with cruise missiles ($57.7 million).

● Three guided-missile cruisers equipped with the Aegis radar, designed to protect U.S. fleets against anti-ship cruise missiles. The conference report trimmed $37.6 million from the cruisers' $3.4 billion price tag, cutting back on a contingency fund and funds earmarked to start production of the ships in a second shipyard. The cost of starting a second production line could not yet be estimated, the report said.

Anti-Submarine Planes. The bill included $447 million for 21 LAMPS III sub-hunting helicopters, which were carried by newer surface combat ships, instead of the 24 aircraft authorized by the Senate. But the conferees told the Pentagon to maintain the 24-per-year rate thereafter.

Funds were authorized for six of the 12 smaller LAMPS I requested, a reduction of $65.1 million (to $44.1 million). This smaller anti-sub helicopter was carried by some older warships. The House had denied authorization for the LAMPS I.

Air Warfare

The Air Force's purchase of fighter planes was shifted slightly toward more emphasis on the F-16 at the expense of the more sophisticated — and more costly — F-15, but not to the extent mandated by the House.

The conference report authorized 36 F-15s ($1.3 billion) rather than the 48 requested ($1.5 billion), and 144 F-16s ($2.3 billion) rather than the 120 asked for ($1.9 billion). The House had authorized only 30 F-15s.

The conferees also told the Air Force to plan on buying 36 F-15s and 150 F-16s in fiscal 1985, rather than the 72 F-15s and 120 F-16s planned.

Navy, Marine Corps. Both bills had approved the request for 84 F-18 fighters for the Navy ($2.3 billion). The conferees agreed to 24 of the larger F-14 fighters, as requested, but trimmed the amount authorized from $886 million to $792 million. This was the amount the Senate had approved to buy 21 F-14s.

Complaining that the Navy was buying too many different kinds of planes at too low a rate, Senate Armed Services had canceled production of the A-6E, the largest carrier-based bomber, and had increased production of the EA-6B, a version of the same plane modified to jam enemy radars.

The conferees restored the six A-6Es requested and approved by the House ($205 million) but also incorporated into the bill the Senate's increase of the electronic warfare planes from six to eight ($435 million).

Another Senate reduction accepted by the conferees cut from 32 to 27 the number of AV-8B Harriers, small, vertical-takeoff jet bombers used by the Marines. This cut $95 million from the $872 million requested.

Airlift and Sealift

Both bills had approved requests for the fiscal 1984 installment of multi-year agreements to buy 50 huge C-5 transport planes ($1.3 billion) and 44 KC-10 midair refueling tankers, the latter a version of the commercial DC-10 jetliner ($759 million).

The conferees approved the $27 million request to continue development of the C-17 transport, designed to carry large combat equipment into primitive airstrips. The Senate had halved that request.

Of $144 million requested, $100 million was approved to modify commercial airliners for rapid conversion to haul military cargo in wartime. Senate Armed Services had denied this request, complaining that the Air Force did not plan to fund this so-called CRAF program in fiscal 1985.

Marine Assault Landings. Approved without controversy was a $1.5 billion request for a large helicopter carrier (an LHD) that could haul 2,000 Marines and $327 million for a smaller ship called an LSD-41 designed to carry the Marines' tanks and combat vehicles and the landing barges to haul them ashore. These had been included in both the Senate and House versions of the bill.

The conferees also approved the request for a multi-year contract to cover future LSD-41s ($182 million) and to continue operating three similar older ships (LSD-28s) the Navy had planned to retire. The Senate had added the LSD-28 funds, but had disapproved the multi-year contracting request for the newer ships.

Pay Raise

A 4 percent pay hike was approved for all Pentagon civilian workers and military personnel except recruits in their first four months of service. The two committees had planned this raise to take effect on April 1 but to occur earlier if other federal employees got a raise.

Citing indications that Congress might grant a civilian federal pay hike Jan. 1, the conferees added to the bill $244 million to cover the additional three months for Pentagon

civilians. (Funds for military pay were not covered by the annual authorization bill.)

Management Reforms

A compromise provision establishing an independent weapons testing office was hammered out of the slightly different versions approved by each house. The new office would have authority to approve or disapprove any plan for operational testing of a new weapon — that is, testing the performance of equipment in the hands of regular combat personnel, rather than by contractors or test specialists.

The office director would be independent of any Pentagon official below the secretary of defense, and congressional defense committees would receive his reports "in precisely the same form and with precisely the same content" as they had when submitted to the secretary.

The conferees also endorsed a Senate provision requiring the secretary of defense to consider an independent estimate of the cost of any weapons system before approving full-scale development, production or deployment of that weapon.

Spare Parts Costs. Both bills had included requirements for Pentagon reports on the purchase of spare parts, a process that had come under close scrutiny in the wake of recent exposés of relatively mundane parts purchased at extremely high cost.

The compromise provision required the Pentagon to give Congress an analysis of the extent of parts overcharges and parts shortages. ∎

Military Construction

Congress completed action Sept. 27 on a bill (HR 2972 — PL 98-115) authorizing $7.35 billion for military construction by the Defense Department in fiscal 1984.

The final authorization was smaller than either the House- or Senate-passed amounts, reflecting conferees' desire to keep defense funding bills within limits set by the fiscal 1984 budget resolution. The authorization was $1.2 billion less than President Reagan's January budget request. *(Chart, p. 194)*

Conferees authorized only $79.2 million of the $207.6 million requested for facilities in Europe from which ground-launched cruise missiles (GLCMs) could strike Soviet territory with nuclear warheads.

And while lawmakers approved the administration's revised request of $72.9 million for MX missile facilities, they required the Pentagon to get $23.3 million of that amount from previous-year authorizations that had not been spent. The administration originally had sought $449 million for the MX program but scaled back its funding request to reflect a new basing plan announced in April.

Congress appropriated $7.1 billion for military construction projects in separate legislation (HR 3263). *(Story, p. 469)*

House Action

Committee

As reported by the House Armed Services Committee May 16 (H Rept 98-166), HR 2972 authorized $7,970,085,000 for military construction projects in fiscal 1984.

The committee made overall reductions of $978 million in the $8.5 billion request; these were partly offset by additions of some $400 million.

Of the reductions, $400 million came from the request for the MX missile program. The $48.7 million approved by the committee was the amount needed to carry out the new basing plan, announced by the president April 18, under which 100 MX missiles would be deployed in existing Minuteman missile silos in Wyoming and Nevada. *(Story, p. 195)*

The original MX request of $449 million was based on a plan to build a "Dense Pack" of 100 newly constructed, super-hard silos. Reagan dropped that plan in April at the suggestion of a White House advisory committee.

Other large elements in the committee's reduction included nearly half the $207.6 million sought for bases in Europe from which ground-launched cruise missiles could reach Soviet territory, and $105.6 million for projects in countries with which U.S. basing agreements were under negotiation.

MX Missile Facilities. In addition to the $48.7 million newly authorized for MX facilities, the panel noted that $23.3 million in authorizations from earlier years also could be used for MX construction.

The bulk of the new funds was earmarked for servicing facilities at Warren Air Force Base ($27.5 million).

GLCM Missile Bases. The committee tried to straddle the two horses of military preparedness and budgetary restraint in handling the $207 million request for construction at five bases in Europe for the GLCM.

On one hand, it voiced support for NATO's declared policy, which was to deploy the 464 missiles (and 108 Pershing II missiles) in Europe unless U.S.-Soviet arms control talks agreed to ban those weapons and similar Soviet missiles, called SS-20s, which targeted Western Europe from Soviet bases.

But the committee noted that if U.S.-Soviet arms talks succeeded, the GLCM bases would become unnecessary. So it deferred authorization totaling $67.2 million for various facilities — such as schools and family housing — to serve the dependents of U.S. personnel assigned to the bases.

Also deferred was $34 million to begin construction at one of the five bases — identity classified — for which a bilateral agreement had not yet been negotiated.

Access Rights. Also because of unsettled negotiations over U.S. base rights, the committee deferred $46.1 million for air and naval facilities in the Philippines, $20.5 million for renovation of the DEW line radar network in Greenland and $4.9 million for a communications station in Greece.

Allied Burden-Sharing. The committee approved $15.5 million to build fuel and ammunition dumps at European-owned air bases to be used by U.S. planes flown to the continent as reinforcements in case of war.

These facilities were eligible for funding by the NATO Infrastructure — the alliance's common fund for facilities of benefit to all members. But the Pentagon wanted to begin work on the projects, recouping the costs when NATO funds became available.

Noting the delay in recouping funds from NATO for this so-called "pre-financing" of NATO-eligible projects, the committee approved the $15.5 million reluctantly.

But it refused to pre-finance the NATO share of a large refueling pier for the air base at Keflavik, Iceland, approving just $30 million for U.S.-only parts. It also approved $31.6 million to expand the Japanese air base at

Military Construction Authorization, Fiscal 1984

Following are the amounts requested by the president and authorized by HR 2972 for military construction projects in fiscal 1984. *(Dollar amounts are in thousands.)*

	Reagan Request	House- Passed	Senate- Passed	Final Authorization
Army	$2,615,879	$2,645,029	$2,426,173	$2,450,959
Navy	1,929,577	1,930,060	1,741,483	1,763,520
Air Force	3,179,086	2,594,268	2,428,908	2,375,071
Defense Agencies	418,144	332,586	341,836	306,386
NATO Infrastructure	150,000	168,000	150,000	150,000
Guard and Reserve	254,900	300,141	260,919	299,591
Total	**$8,587,586**	**$7,970,084**	**$7,349,319**	**$7,345,527**

Misawa, where U.S. F-16 fighter planes would be based, but barred use of that money until Japan provided its agreed-upon share of funds.

Rapid Deployment Force. Approved as requested were two projects intended to speed deployment of troops of the U.S. Central Command — formerly the Rapid Deployment Force — to the Middle East. These were air and naval facilities on Diego Garcia in the Indian Ocean ($90 million) and Air Force refueling facilities in Morocco ($28 million).

Floor

The House June 21 passed HR 2972 by voice vote.

During debate on the authorization bill, the House adopted by voice vote, and with no debate, two amendments by Ronald V. Dellums, D-Calif.

One provided that the $48.7 million authorized for MX-related projects could not be spent until Congress authorized procurement of the missile. Initial procurement funds were included in the fiscal 1984 defense authorization bill.

The other Dellums amendment dropped from the bill provisions that would have extended through fiscal 1984 prior-year authorization of $206.4 million for construction at Ras Banas in Egypt. Plans to construct a large base there for U.S. air and ground forces intervening in the Persian Gulf region had been canceled.

Senate Action

Committee

Following the usual procedure, the Senate Armed Services Committee approved $7.3 billion for military construction as Title II of the omnibus defense authorization bill for fiscal 1984. The committee reported that bill July 5 (S 675 — S Rept 98-174). *(Story, p. 175)*

The committee approved the administration's $74 million revised request for MX-related construction, but told the Air Force to get $23.3 million of it from funds left over from the fiscal 1983 construction program.

According to the committee, the services were reaping the benefits of an "extremely tight construction market" in carrying out their fiscal 1983 construction programs: "The services are getting an unusually high number of bidders

for every job and low bids are averaging 12-15 percent less than the authorized amounts."

Congress added to the fiscal 1983 construction funding bills several projects that were approved as long as the services could fund them out of savings from other projects.

In its report on S 675, the committee said that even after all those contingent projects had been funded, additional windfall savings of $530 million were possible. The panel added to the bill projects with a total estimated cost of $536 million, and it said these could be built if the necessary savings materialized.

Allied Burden-Sharing. In what had become a routine congressional stance in recent years, the committee condemned U.S. allies for not paying more of the cost of keeping U.S. forces in Europe and other overseas sites — deployments that contributed to the defense of those allies.

The panel threatened to begin requiring the use of U.S. material and labor in construction projects for U.S. forces in Europe, as a way to reduce the dollar outflow caused by U.S.-funded overseas defense construction.

Members' Projects. The committee approved several projects located in the districts of Armed Services panel members. Some of these add-ons later were dropped by the House Appropriations Committee during consideration of the military construction appropriations bill.

Floor

The Senate approved the construction authorization by voice vote July 26, after substituting the text of its own provisions — Title II of S 675 — for the text of HR 2972, the authorization bill passed by the House June 21.

Conference

The conference report on HR 2972 was filed Sept. 19 (H Rept 98-359). The House adopted the report Sept. 22 and the Senate followed suit Sept. 27.

As part of an overall effort to keep the defense funding bills under the budget ceiling agreed to in the fiscal 1984 budget resolution, the conferees agreed to reduce the construction authorization to $7.35 billion.

They also listed additional projects, which had not been requested by the president but which the conferees

agreed could be paid for out of surplus funds from earlier years. For many projects, contract bids were running 15-20 percent lower than budgeted amounts; conferees estimated that the difference between budgets and actual bids might be as much as $600 million.

Senate and House versions of the authorization bill approved the administration's revised request of $72 million for MX-related construction. But both required the Pentagon to get $23.3 million of that amount from funds that had been authorized but not spent in earlier years.

Alliance Burden-Sharing. Conferees repeatedly underscored congressional complaints that U.S. allies were not paying a fair share of the cost of a common defense.

They approved a request for $66 million to upgrade two Turkish airfields, to be used by U.S. planes in case of war, though they provided only $18 million in new authorization and directed that the rest be provided out of prior-year savings.

The Turkish projects were eligible for funding by the NATO Infrastructure, the alliance's fund for constructing facilities shared by several members. But because NATO funding would not be available for years, the Pentagon asked for U.S. appropriations, which later would be repaid by the alliance.

This practice — which the Pentagon called "pre-financing" — had drawn fire from congressional critics who complained that the Pentagon was not energetic enough in pursuing recoupment of the funds owed Washington. According to the General Accounting Office, of $832.6 million in NATO projects pre-financed with U.S. appropriations since 1959, only $270 million had been repaid and another $250 million was considered unrecoverable.

The conferees on HR 2972 added a provision barring expenditure of the funds authorized for the Turkish air bases or for any other pre-financed project until the secretary of defense gave Congress a projection of the schedule on which NATO would repay the funds.

Also approved was $17 million (of $19.9 million requested) for the U.S. share of improvements at a Japanese airfield due to house a wing of U.S. Air Force F-16 fighters. But the conferees stipulated that the funds could not be spent until the Japanese government had contributed its agreed-upon share.

Cruise Missiles in Europe. The conference committee cut more deeply than did either house into the $207.6 million requested for facilities in Europe associated with the deployment of ground-launched cruise missiles. The conference report authorized $79.2 million for GLCM projects, compared with $145.9 million approved by the Senate and $106 million by the House.

GLCM deployment was planned for West Germany, Italy, Great Britain, Belgium and the Netherlands.

The conferees' reduction included the entire $34 million earmarked to begin construction in the Netherlands, the only one of the five countries that had not formally approved a specific basing plan for the missiles.

Conferees also reiterated the position taken in 1982 that family housing, dependents' schools and other facilities for the families of U.S. personnel at the GLCM bases should be delayed while there was any chance that a treaty banning the missiles could be negotiated. They cut $67.2 million for dependents' facilities and told the Pentagon to ask for the funds in fiscal 1985 if no such treaty were in prospect. ∎

MX Pulls Through Turbulent Year in Congress

Congress, with three opportunities to vote on testing, production and funding of the MX intercontinental missile in 1983, gave the go-ahead to the controversial weapon, though its popularity in the House waned as the year progressed.

Critical to the congressional endorsement of the MX were the recommendations of a presidential commission on arms control policy and an agreement hammered out between the Reagan administration and a group of congressional moderates. The moderates supported MX in return for President Reagan's pledge to adopt a more flexible approach to arms control negotiations with the Soviet Union.

Reagan's original budget had envisioned deploying the 10-warhead MX in a "dense pack" of fortified silos. The skepticism that greeted dense pack led the president to appoint a bipartisan commission of defense experts to develop a basing plan for MX that would meet with congressional approval. The commission's plan was approved by Congress in May.

Congress had two subsequent opportunities to vote on MX — the fiscal 1984 defense authorization bill and the fiscal 1984 defense appropriations measure. Money for the missile was approved by hefty margins in the Senate. In the House, the vote was tighter: the MX funds in the authorization bill won by 13 votes; in the appropriations measure, the money survived by nine votes.

Scowcroft Commission

President Reagan turned over the question of the future of the U.S. missile force to a blue-ribbon commission Jan. 3 after Congress turned down dense pack in December 1982. The panel had a Feb. 18 deadline for recommending to Reagan whether the MX was needed and, if it were, how it should be based. The deadline was extended, and the panel's report was released April 11.

The commission recommended that the administration deploy 100 MX missiles in existing missile silos while the Pentagon developed a new, smaller missile that could become the keystone of a radical new approach to stabilizing the nuclear balance between U.S. and Soviet nuclear forces. Under the fiscal 1983 continuing resolution, Congress had to approve or reject an MX basing method within 45 days after the president made a recommendation.

The commission said its plan would cost $19.9 billion through fiscal 1988 compared with an estimated $22.9 billion for dense pack. (Amounts were in fiscal 1982 dollars.)

Chaired by Brent Scowcroft, former national security adviser to Presidents Nixon and Ford, the panel was made up of 10 members and seven "senior consultants" who together amounted to a who's who of the national security establishment, including four former secretaries of defense and two former secretaries of state. Efforts were made to devise a politically acceptable plan.

Report Highlights

The presidential commission acknowledged that silo-based MXs would be as vulnerable to Soviet missiles as the Minuteman missiles housed in silos. So after nearly a decade in which the public debate over MX had been dominated by the search for a basing method invulnerable to Soviet attack, Reagan's advisory commission abandoned the argument for MX as being a more "survivable" successor to Minuteman.

Instead, it justified MX on grounds of its military potency and political symbolism — as a counterweight to several hundred existing Soviet missiles, some with even more destructive power than MX.

With 10 warheads, more accurate and potentially more powerful than the three warheads on the existing Minuteman III missile, MX was designed to destroy armored underground targets, such as silos housing intercontinental ballistic missiles (ICBMs) and command centers.

By most estimates, some 600 Soviet ICBMs, carrying 6-10 warheads each, possessed such so-called "hard-target kill capability."

The proposed small, single-warhead missile — dubbed "Midgetman" — would deal with the survivability problem over the long-run, the commission argued. Because the new missile would be designed to weigh about 30,000 pounds — compared to 192,000 pounds for MX — its launchers could be made to be much more mobile than MX launchers, thus thwarting a Soviet attack.

As a third component of its package, linked to the new small missile, the panel held out the hope of inducing Moscow to join the United States in gradually shifting land-based missile forces to single-warhead weapons. The commission said this would restore a degree of stability to the nuclear balance that had been lost with the advent of missiles that could carry accurate MIRVs — multiple warheads.

It was widely agreed that accurate MIRVs made the strategic balance "unstable" because, while both superpowers owned roughly similar numbers of missiles, MIRVs conferred at least a theoretical advantage to whichever side fired its missiles first. Because each attacking multiple-warhead missile could destroy several of the opponent's not yet launched missiles, an aggressor could obliterate his opponent's missile force while retaining most of his own missiles.

Hill Reaction

Early congressional reaction to the commission proposal came largely from liberals who long had opposed MX in any form. Traditional arms control proponents warned that because MX would threaten existing Soviet missiles, it likely would set off a new round in the nuclear arms race as Moscow developed new weapons to counter MX.

And a few moderate members, including Sens. J. James Exon, D-Neb., and Mark Andrews, R-N.D., rejected out of hand support for any deployment of MX that did not promise invulnerability against Soviet attack.

But by divorcing MX from the quest for ICBM survivability, the commission forced out of the closet what long had been a key issue among defense and arms control specialists: whether the United States needed missiles that were militarily and symbolically equivalent to the Soviets'.

Rather than bog down in discussions of basing methods, the commission argued for MX using the public position taken by administrations since at least 1974: Deter-

rence of Soviet aggression depended on the technical plausibility of a U.S. attack that would disrupt Soviet military power without causing so many civilian casualties that retaliation against U.S. cities would be inevitable. "Even before the Soviet leaders, in a grave crisis, consider using the first tank regiment or the first SS-20 missile against NATO, they must be required to face what war would mean to them," the commission said.

"A credible capability for controlled, prompt, limited attack on hard targets ourselves [would cast] a shadow over the calculus of Soviet risk-taking."

MX was the only weapon that could meet those criteria in the near future, according to the commission.

The Scowcroft panel argued, in addition, that the nation had come too far with MX to have the option of abandoning it now: "Canceling the MX when it is ready for flight testing, when over $5 billion have already been spent on it, and when its importance has been stressed by our last four presidents, does not communicate to the Soviets that we have the will essential to deterrence," the panel warned. "Quite the contrary."

In the closing paragraphs of its 26-page report, the commission frankly presented its package as a compromise between proponents of the MX and supporters of small, single-warhead missiles: "For the last decade, each successive administration has made proposals for arms control of strategic offensive systems that have become embroiled in political controversy . . ." As a result, neither an arms control treaty nor a modernization of the U.S. missile force had been possible, the panel said.

Symmetry. With the fate of MX shorn of the battle over basing method survivability, a debate on the commission's program had the potential to force the first clear showdown on the issue of whether deterrence required a rough symmetry in the U.S. and Soviet ICBM forces, apart from the other facets of the nuclear balance.

Both sides carried political albatrosses going into such a debate:

On the one hand, selling the MX basing plan was hindered by the apparent unconcern with which many non-specialists in defense viewed the details of nuclear strategy, such as the differences among nuclear weapons. In addition, too strong an emphasis on the details of nuclear warfighting could have revived the alarm aroused in 1981 when some administration officials' comments appeared to take too casual a view of nuclear war.

On the other hand, MX opponents could have appeared to be calling for unilateral U.S. abstention from deploying the same kinds of weapons that Moscow thought worth the expenditure of tens of billions of dollars.

At first glance, widespread public support for a "freeze" on U.S. and Soviet nuclear weapons, which assumed that current differences in the two nations' arsenals mattered little, implied an advantage for the MX opponents. But it was unlikely much of that support would go to any policy smacking of unilateral U.S. restraint.

The insistence of the freeze resolution (H J Res 13) debated in the House on a "mutual" halt was critical to its congressional support. And most strategists of the freeze campaign went to great lengths to deflect charges that a freeze would have unilaterally encumbered U.S. arms programs in effect, if not as a matter of law. *(Freeze, p. 205)*

Political Mix

Political acceptability to moderate Democrats appeared to loom as large as technical feasibility in the com-

mission's deliberations.

The White House included on the panel and among the senior consultants four officials of the Carter administration who enjoyed formidable reputations for defense expertise, political persuasiveness or both: Defense Secretary Harold Brown, presidential counsel Lloyd N. Cutler, Brown's research and engineering director William J. Perry and Navy Under Secretary R. James Woolsey.

Commission members, in turn, made numerous pilgrimages to Capitol Hill in search of a package that would command substantial Democratic support. This effort included widely reported discussions by commission members with some prominent Democrats, including Reps. Les Aspin, Wis., and Albert Gore Jr., Tenn.

Aspin, widely regarded as a particularly thoughtful, liberal critic of the Pentagon, also had the reputation of being an astute analyst of House politics. Gore, a member of the House Select Intelligence Committee, energetically promoted, since mid-1982, a move to small, single-warhead missiles as a step toward nuclear stability.

First MX Test

Under the terms of the fiscal 1983 continuing resolution passed in December 1982 (PL 97-377), none of the $560 million appropriated by that resolution for development of an MX basing method could be spent unless Congress approved Reagan's basing plan by concurrent resolution within about seven weeks. (An additional $1.95 billion appropriated for development of the MX missile itself in fiscal 1983 was unencumbered.) *(1982 Almanac p. 238)*

Such resolutions were introduced in each house April 20 — S Con Res 26 by Sen. Mark O. Hatfield, R-Ore., and H Con Res 113 by Rep. Jack Edwards, R-Ala. Both were considered under special procedures established by the fiscal 1983 continuing appropriations resolution.

White House Commitment

After the release of the Scowcroft commission report, prospects for the administration's proposal to deploy MX missiles hinged, in large part, on the president's personal assurances to skeptical members of Congress that he viewed the weapon as only the first step toward a radical new nuclear balance.

In two letters to the White House, a dozen key members of the Senate and House warned they would oppose MX deployment unless they were reassured of Reagan's commitment to the entire package of arms and arms control policies recommended April 11 by the Scowcroft panel.

Specifically, the two congressional letters agreed, the administration's embrace of the commission's MX deployment plan had not been matched by enthusiasm for the Scowcroft panel's two other recommendations — development of the Midgetman single-warhead missile that could be deployed in mobile launchers and an arms control policy that sought to move both the U.S. and Soviet ICBM forces away from multiple-warhead missiles toward smaller, single-warhead missiles.

The members' common concern was stated more pointedly in the House members' letter: "Statements in the press — attributed to 'high ranking officials' in the Department of Defense and others — have already raised a suspicion that there are some in the administration who embrace the Scowcroft report, not in its entirety, but only as a means to the end of securing Congress' approval for the deployment of the MX."

In congressional hearings and White House meetings during the week of May 2, Reagan and his aides tried to reassure dubious members of Congress from both political parties that their endorsement of the entire Scowcroft plan was sincere.

Reagan's commitment to arms control was "absolute and complete," Defense Secretary Caspar W. Weinberger told the House Defense Appropriations Subcommittee May 4. "One of the things that concerns the president most is the feeling he is not fully committed."

But the congressional skeptics insisted that Reagan would have to formalize that commitment in various ways before they could support further development of MX.

Who's Who

Three senators signed one letter, dated April 29, and nine House members signed a similar letter May 2.

Among the House members were:

● Gore, who was widely credited as the person most responsible for bringing to public notice the case for seeking a more stable nuclear balance based on single-warhead missiles.

● Aspin, who, with Gore, was closely consulted, before the commission made its recommendation, by members of the Scowcroft panel in search of a package that stood a chance of House approval.

● Norman D. Dicks, D-Wash., the only one of the three liberal Democrats on the House Defense Appropriations Subcommittee who leaned toward approval of the Scowcroft proposal.

The three senators who signed the similar letter to Reagan were no less important to the politics of saving the MX package:

● William S. Cohen, R-Maine, who established solid defense credentials in his four years on the Senate Armed Services Committee, and who might have had special credibility with moderates and conservatives on the MX issue: He took a hard line against the SALT II arms control treaty in 1979, and he had not been a prominent advocate of arms control as a solution to U.S. defense problems.

● Sam Nunn, D-Ga., who in a decade of Senate service, won widespread respect as one of the most thoughtful defense specialists in or out of Congress.

● Foreign Relations Committee Chairman Charles H. Percy, R-Ill., a longtime arms control supporter, who carried considerable weight among the dozen or so other Republican senators who tended to be strong proponents of arms control.

The opposition of any one of the three senators would be a serious blow to the Scowcroft plan. Opposition of all three likely would have been fatal.

START Revision

The two letters agreed that the president should revise his then current proposal in the Strategic Arms Reduction Talks (START) to be compatible with the Scowcroft commission's package.

Reagan's proposed limits of 5,000 ballistic missile warheads and 850 ballistic missiles would promote continued reliance on multiple-warhead missiles, several critics had argued. Moreover, when the Reagan proposal was outlined in May 1982, Gore and several other skeptics warned that it would increase the number of nuclear warheads each country could shoot at each missile launcher in the other country (since the number of missile launchers would be sharply reduced).

Small Missile

Both letters also called for assurances that Reagan would personally promote prompt development of the proposed Midgetman.

The Senate letter asked Reagan for assurance that the program "will retain a high priority despite probable constraints in the overall defense budget."

This reflected a suspicion that elements in the Air Force were not too enthusiastic about the small missile concept and that the project's projected cost could make it a prime candidate for future budgetary restraint.

On May 3 the Pentagon announced the creation of a major program office to manage development of the small missile for which about $500 million would be earmarked in the fiscal 1984 budget. But Gore said he still wanted Reagan's personal declaration that he sponsored the program.

Senate 'Build-Down'

The three senators also asked Reagan to propose to the Soviet Union a "guaranteed mutual build-down" of nuclear forces. In general, a build-down agreement would have required that the deployment of any new strategic weapons be accompanied by the retirement of some larger number of existing weapons, so that the two nuclear arsenals would be reduced as they were modernized. Percy and 42 other senators cosponsored a resolution introduced by Cohen and Nunn that endorsed such a proposal.

The senators recommended continued research on improvements in existing Minuteman missiles, in case deployment of MX seemed either unnecessary — because of arms control progress — or unwise — because of an arms control stalemate.

Administration officials argued that build-down could place the United States at a disadvantage because, compared to the Soviet nuclear force, a much larger proportion of the U.S. arsenal was relatively old and in need of replacement.

Committee Action

In response to the concerns of the moderates, Reagan pledged, in writing, his personal commitment to the entire package of weapons development and arms control initiatives recommended by the Scowcroft panel — of which deployment of 100 MXs was only one element. *(Text of Reagan letter, p. 32-E)*

Soon after, the administration won important early skirmishes in the fight for the MX.

The House Appropriations Committee May 17 approved H Con Res 113 to release some fiscal 1983 appropriations to implement a new MX basing plan and renew flight testing by a 30-26 vote. A companion resolution — S Con Res 26 — was approved by the Senate Appropriations Committee May 12 by a vote of 17-11.

In addition to endorsing the Scowcroft panel's goal of strategic stability, Reagan agreed to the following points in his letters to the members of Congress:

● Revision of his proposal for reducing U.S. and Soviet strategic missiles, to ensure that the U.S. position would encourage evolution of the two nuclear arsenals toward small, single-warhead ICBMs.

● Tying the number of MXs ultimately deployed to the outcome of arms control efforts, and stating that the United States did not seek the ability to launch a surprise attack that would wipe out the Soviet force.

● Development of a small, single-warhead ICBM as a

complement to MX, as a matter of "high priority."

Arms Build-Down. In addition, Reagan's letter to the senators endorsed in general the idea of a strategic arms build-down as an approach to arms reductions. Though the details were left vague, the intent of the approach was to require each country to reduce the overall size of its nuclear arsenal as it deployed new weapons.

Senate Committee

During the Senate committee's debate on the MX resolution, MX opponents, like Dale Bumpers, D-Ark., dismissed the missile's persuasive value, because it would be deployed in existing silos vulnerable to Soviet attack. "The Soviet Union won't even have to retarget their missiles," he said.

But Warren B. Rudman, R-N.H., said that MX approval would be a powerful lever on Moscow: "They don't really know whether this is the first 100 [MXs] or the last 100," he said.

Senate Committee Vote. In addition to Rudman, Appropriations Committee Republicans supporting S Con Res 26 were James Abdnor, S.D.; Thad Cochran, Miss.; Alfonse M. D'Amato, N.Y.; Pete V. Domenici, N.M.; Jake Garn, Utah; Bob Kasten, Wis.; Paul Laxalt, Nev.; Mack Mattingly, Ga.; James A. McClure, Idaho; Arlen Specter, Pa.; and Ted Stevens, Alaska.

Also voting "aye" were Democrats Robert C. Byrd, W.Va.; Lawton Chiles, Fla.; Dennis DeConcini, Ariz.; J. Bennett Johnston, La.; and John C. Stennis, Miss.

Republicans voting against the resolution: Mark Andrews, N.D.; Committee Chairman Mark O. Hatfield, Ore.; and Lowell P. Weicker Jr., Conn.

Democrats voting "nay" were Bumpers; Quentin N. Burdick, N.D.; Thomas F. Eagleton, Mo.; Ernest F. Hollings, S.C.; Daniel K. Inouye, Hawaii; Patrick J. Leahy, Vt.; William Proxmire, Wis.; and Jim Sasser, Tenn.

Walter D. Huddleston, Ky., voted "present."

House Committee

When the House Appropriations panel took up the MX resolution May 17, Edwards, the sponsor of H Con Res 113, urged members to accept the president's claim of a good faith commitment to the entire Scowcroft approach to strategic weapons and arms control. "The president has in fact modified his position in negotiations [with Moscow]," Edwards said.

Edwards also stressed the limited scope of his resolution, pointing out that no procurement funds for the missile would be released by it.

But Defense Subcommittee Chairman Joseph P. Addabbo, D-N.Y., a perennial MX foe, warned that Edwards' resolution would be "a foot in the door" for MX procurement. And he complained that the proposed MX deployment — 100 missiles in existing Minuteman missile silos — would be vulnerable to Soviet attack.

Addabbo offered a substitute resolution that would have endorsed the Scowcroft commission's recommendations, except for the MX proposal. It was rejected 26-29.

Les AuCoin, D-Ore., a leading House supporter of a freeze on nuclear weaponry, discounted the idea that Congress could negotiate a deal with Reagan to pursue arms control in return for MX funds: "An administration that is committed to arms control does not need to be bargained into that position by members of Congress," he said.

Dicks, a leader of the House group that negotiated with the White House to elicit Reagan's letters, insisted

that MX was needed as a negotiating tool, to make Moscow willing to consider reductions in its ICBM force: "When this country has shown resolve and commitment ... then all of a sudden the Soviets are willing to negotiate," Dicks said.

But Dicks also contended that Reagan's acceptance of the entire Scowcroft package, including MX, could set the stage for a bipartisan nuclear arms policy. And he maintained that Congress would have several later opportunities to kill MX, if it decided Reagan was not living up to his broader commitments.

Committee Vote. The vote spotlighted the coalition on which Reagan counted for House approval of MX — a nearly solid bloc of Republicans and conservative Democrats joined by the group of liberal Democrats for whom — as for some GOP moderates — the Scowcroft package was a lever to shift the administration's nuclear arms policy.

Of 21 committee Republicans, 18 supported the president, including four moderates who had voted against MX on the House floor in July 1982: Lawrence Coughlin, Pa., George M. O'Brien and John Edward Porter of Illinois and Carl D. Pursell, Mich. MX had survived the July 1982 vote by a margin of only three votes — 212-209. *(Vote 188, 1982 Almanac p. 56-H)*

"Nay" votes were cast by the panel's two most liberal Republicans — Silvio O. Conte, Mass., and Bill Green, N.Y. — and by Virginia Smith, R-Neb., in whose district 31 of the planned 100 MXs would be deployed. Democrats voted against the resolution 12-23, splitting largely along liberal-conservative lines. Conservatives — mostly Southerners — accounted for most of the "aye" votes.

Dicks was joined by only two other liberal Democrats in supporting the Edwards resolution: Vic Fazio, Calif., and Steny H. Hoyer, Md.

Resolutions' Effect

Apart from the resolutions' symbolic link to the letters exchanged between the White House and Capitol Hill, the technical effect of the two resolutions was difficult to translate precisely into dollars-and-cents terms.

The administration had asked for $560 million in fiscal 1983 to develop the so-called dense pack basing method. Since dense pack had been supplanted by the Scowcroft panel's proposal simply to install MX in existing Minuteman missile silos, an Air Force spokesman said that much less than $560 million would be used in fiscal 1983 for basing development.

The balance of the money could be used on research on the Midgetman missile and on techniques to harden against nuclear blasts missile silos that would be used either for MX or the small missile, he said.

But in addition to formally "fencing" the basing method funds — prohibiting their use without congressional approval — the continuing resolution fenced other MX money, in effect, by barring the missile's initial flight test until Congress agreed to free up the basing money.

Although the initial MX test flight long had been scheduled for January 1983, that date had slipped back to March or April 1983 by the time Congress adopted the continuing resolution. The first test flight took place in June 1983.

Floor Action

President Reagan won a clear victory when the flight testing and basing resolutions reached the Senate and

House floors.

The House resolution was approved 239-186 on May 24; the identical Senate bill passed 59-39 May 25. The House then passed the Senate version May 26, 223-167. *(House votes 123, 133, pp. 42-H, 44-H; Senate vote 114, p. 23-S)*

The pattern established in committee continued when the resolutions received floor consideration: Reagan won with the help of several dozen liberals and moderates who often had questioned the depth of his commitment to arms control policies. The cost of their support was a firm commitment by the president to pursue the Scowcroft commission recommendations.

During the MX debate in each chamber, several members warned the White House that their continued support for MX, in each of the several defense funding bills that would have to be passed before the missile was deployed in early 1987, would depend on the administration's evident good faith in pursuing the Scowcroft goals.

"If they do not perform according to the Scowcroft commission, which I think they will, I believe the votes are here to stop this funding," said Joel Pritchard, R-Wash. "And I am one of them." Pritchard was a participant in the congressional negotiations with the White House.

But longtime MX opponents in each house warned their colleagues that approval of the missile would create momentum that could be very difficult to reverse, regardless of the administration's future performance in the arms control arena.

"No strategic weapons system that has ever passed this stage of funding ... [has] been permanently canceled," AuCoin warned just before the House vote. "This, my friends, is the moment in which the genie leaves the bottle unless we decide to exercise our good judgment and keep it inside."

Vote Analysis

The strings on Reagan's victory were particularly evident in the House.

The administration's 53-vote margin of victory was larger than either observers or participants expected. But a crucial component of that majority was the group of moderates and liberals led by Democrats Aspin, Dicks and Gore.

Compared with the July 21, 1982, vote, in which a move to deny production funds for MX was rejected by a margin of only three votes, 44 members who had opposed MX procurement funds then, voted in May to permit flight testing and development of a basing method.

Among them were 24 Democrats, including such senior liberal stalwarts as Majority Whip Thomas S. Foley, Wash., Lee H. Hamilton, Ind., and Clement J. Zablocki, Wis.

Also supporting the test authorization, after having opposed the procurement funds in 1982, were 20 Republicans, most of them considered relatively liberal, including Carl D. Pursell, Mich., Marge Roukema, N.J., and Olympia J. Snowe, Maine.

Senate Vote. On the other hand, the 59-39 Senate vote in favor of S Con Res 26 — the counterpart resolution — was very similar to the December 1982 Senate vote in favor of Reagan's previous MX plan. *(Vote 420, 1982 Almanac p. 71-S)*

The impact of moderates in the Senate was not as significant as it had been in the House. Despite his stature in the Washington defense community, Nunn failed to win

over any of his liberal co-partisans to the deal: In contrast to the House, none of the Northern Democrats who typically voted "liberal" on arms control issues voted "aye" on the MX resolution. Most of the 12 Democrats who supported S Con Res 26 consistently took a hard line on defense issues.

Only six Republicans — all but one of them (Gordon J. Humphrey, N.H.) moderates — defected from the White House line to oppose the resolution. But the pressure on Reagan for a more flexible arms control approach still was present in the "aye" votes of 10 GOP senators, who, like Percy, typically were regarded as relatively liberal on nuclear arms issues.

House Debate

During the House debate on H Con Res 113 May 23-24, the fundamental attack on MX from most liberal arms control backers was based on the "destabilizing" theory — the weapon was accurate enough to destroy Soviet missiles in their silos, but itself vulnerable to Soviet attack while sitting in existing Minuteman silos.

"The only way MX can be kept safe is if it is used first, before it is struck by an enemy strike," insisted AuCoin. "That is a very destabilizing thing."

The critics charged that Weinberger and various other supporters of the current plan had abandoned their oft-expressed position that MX should only be deployed in some basing method that could survive a Soviet attack — a criterion that existing missile silos would not meet.

But John Edward Porter, R-Ill., spoke for many members who complained that any concern about the "destabilizing" effect of large MIRVed missiles should be directed at the Soviet Union, whose force of SS-18 and SS-19 missiles created the current dilemma by putting U.S. missile silos at risk: "The Soviets already have in place hundreds of SS-18s and are deploying three more of these 10-warhead missiles a month," he said. "That is what is destabilizing."

Bargaining Leverage. The MX opponents also rejected the Scowcroft panel's contention that deployment of the big missile would encourage Moscow to abandon its own large ICBMs.

"A bargaining chip is what this country is capable of deploying, not what we actually deploy," warned Edward J. Markey, D-Mass. "History has shown that the weapons we have deployed have driven the Soviets to the production line, not to the bargaining table."

But Aspin contended that Moscow had not previously been faced with a potential large-scale threat to the land-based missiles, which were by far the most important part of its nuclear arsenal: "We have tried with a number of carrots . . . to get the Soviet Union to abandon the SS-18s and SS-19s . . . which we found so threatening. We were totally unsuccessful," he said. "We cannot seem to get their attention unless we start to do the similar thing to them."

Dealing With Reagan. Some of the most heated exchanges in the House debate focused on Reagan's professed commitment to a new deal in arms control policy, which the MX critics ridiculed.

Thomas J. Downey, D-N.Y., and Markey recited the litany of Reagan's opposition to earlier arms control agreements and warned that his administration was riddled with ideological opponents of arms control: "They believe," charged Downey, "that real men don't control weapons; real men build them."

Gore swung back, arguing essentially that the Scow-

croft package, including MX, was the only game in town for arms controllers: "Do we want to give up on the chance that this administration for the next two years, or possibly the next six years, can achieve an arms control agreement with the Soviet Union?" he demanded. "Do we want to throw away the chance to build a bipartisan approach that might make some sense and might achieve an arms control agreement?"

Senate Debate

The Senate debate on S Con Res 26 on May 20 and May 23-25 struck the same themes as the House battle on the issue.

Rudman was among the members who agreed with the Scowcroft panel's principal argument for deploying MX to secure Soviet concessions: "I for one do not find it reasonable to assume that the Soviet Union will willingly make concessions on its most threatening land-based systems if we fail to proceed with near-term deployment of an improved missile," Rudman declared. "Strong rhetoric unsupported by decisive action will surely be perceived as empty posturing."

On the other hand, Bumpers, after quipping that Reagan "does not like to spend money on anything that does not explode," warned that Moscow would rise to the challenge of an arms race. "Anybody who doubts their resolve to stay in the arms race just does not understand the Soviet mentality," Bumpers said.

Political Calculus. As in the House, much of the battle turned on Reagan's written commitment to accept the whole Scowcroft program.

Huddleston dismissed Reagan's assurances to Cohen, Nunn and Percy as "ambiguous and generalized statements of interest," sentiments echoed by several other MX opponents.

Many senators who endorsed the MX resolution as part of this package underscored their reluctance to buy the missile and their continued wariness of the administration's underlying commitment to arms control.

"What we are discussing here today is not a consensus but a bargain," Cohen warned. "I will begin to deliver on my part of the bargain by voting for release of fiscal 1983 funds [for MX testing]. I will be watching carefully to see if the administration begins similarly to make good on its part of the bargain."

New START Proposals

After Congress gave its approval for MX flight testing and basing, President Reagan announced changes in his negotiating position in the START negotiations with Moscow. The modified negotiating tactic won initial approval from some of the congressional critics who held MX hostage to a more flexible U.S. negotiating posture.

Reagan announced June 8 that he would retain a proposed limit of 5,000 strategic missile warheads on both sides, no more than half of which could be carried on land-based missiles. But he increased the proposed limit on the missiles from 850 to some unspecified higher figure — widely reported to be in the range of 1,100-1,200 — so that the U.S. proposal would require a less radical cut in the existing Soviet missile force. (*Text of Reagan statement, p. 33-E*)

By reducing the ratio of warheads to missiles allowed under the proposal, Reagan brought the new offer more closely in line with the Scowcroft commission's recommen-

dation that U.S. policy encourage a gradual shift of both the U.S. and Soviet arsenals away from their current reliance on large, multi-warhead missiles.

Throw-Weight Issue. Reagan rejected a call by Pentagon officials to propose a limit on missile "throwweight" — the aggregate weight of the warheads and decoys that could be launched by the U.S. and Soviet missile forces. Congressional moderates feared that such a limit would reduce the prospects of an agreement, since it would have far more heavily affected the Soviet force, which had a throw-weight advantage of 3-1.

On the other hand, Pentagon officials long had argued that a large Soviet advantage in ICBM throw-weight was intolerable, in part because it would allow Moscow to "break out" of an arms control agreement by using it to launch a much larger number of smaller warheads.

Even without a direct throw-weight limit, the new Reagan proposal still would have required a substantial reduction in the Soviet force of large ICBMs. A limit of 2,500 ICBM warheads would have at least cut in half the Soviet ICBM warhead arsenal. And a substantial reduction in Soviet throw-weight would have been required by other limits on the largest kinds of Soviet ICBMs. Under the overall limit of some 1,200 missiles — and unchanged from the original U.S. proposal — were sublimits allowing no more than 110 SS-18 missiles and 100 smaller SS-17s and SS-19s — the latter about the size of the MX.

At the time, Moscow had more than 300 SS-18s, each with a throw-weight of nearly 17,000 pounds, and about 450 SS-17s and SS-19s, each with a throw-weight of 6,000-7,500 pounds.

Flexibility

As important politically as the substance of the new position was Reagan's emphasis on "stability" as the goal of his arms control policy and "flexibility" in his negotiating tactics.

"There may be more than one way to achieve our objective of greater stability at reduced levels of arms," Reagan said. Accordingly, he continued, START negotiator Edward L. Rowny had been given the "flexibility to explore all appropriate avenues for meeting our goals."

An administration official briefing reporters on the administration shift underscored the theme of flexibility: "Everything is on the table. We are prepared to negotiate everything." The administration's emphasis on its willingness to talk apparently was meant to satisfy the moderates who had conditioned their continued support for MX on Reagan's commitment to the new arms control approach called for by the Scowcroft panel and to greater flexibility in seeking a START treaty.

Authorization Votes

On June 7, the day before Reagan made his new START position public, several House and Senate members who had insisted on Reagan's renewed arms control commitment as a price for backing MX, accepted the specific changes in the U.S. position — and the administration's emphasis on its "flexibility" in pursuing a START agreement — as evidence that Reagan was living up to his end of the MX bargain, so far.

But despite congressional moderates' general approval of Reagan's new negotiating stance, the fiscal 1984 budget request for $2.6 billion to procure the first 27 of a projected 100 deployed MXs was far from being out of the woods.

More Delay. Another hurdle facing MX was the decision of House Speaker Thomas P. O'Neill Jr., D-Mass., under strong pressure from anti-MX Democrats, to defer action on the MX section of the defense authorization bill until July. After the House vote in favor of the current MX plan in May, anti-MX lobbying groups had sought time to mobilize grass-roots MX opponents in hopes of reversing that outcome.

'Build-Down' Battle

Even if Reagan's position prevailed on the authorization bill, the MX faced a potentially serious problem in the GOP-controlled Senate when the companion defense appropriations bill was considered in early fall. At issue was the Cohen-Percy-Nunn proposal urging Reagan to incorporate into his START negotiating proposal an interim agreement to build down the U.S. and Soviet nuclear forces.

Under Study. In his June 8 announcement, Reagan said that "high-priority work" was continuing within the administration on applying the build-down concept to his negotiating proposal. A White House spokesman speculated that it could take between six weeks and "a few months" for the administration to come up with a detailed application of the general build-down concept that would not be disadvantageous to the United States.

But later that day, Cohen complained to a reporter that officials in the Pentagon and the National Security Council were taking a nit-picking approach to build-down rather than considering ways it might be made to work.

He insisted that a good faith administration effort to produce a workable build-down proposal was extremely important to nearly a score of Republican senators who voted for the MX plan May 25.

Fine Print. One component of Cohen's battle with the defense bureaucracy was the problem of ensuring that a build-down scheme would not work to Moscow's advantage. A basic reason for Pentagon concern was that the most lethal Soviet strategic missiles were relatively new, while all three facets of the U.S. strategic arsenal — bombers, ICBMs and missile submarines — were relatively old by weapons standards.

Accordingly, Moscow could afford to defer new deployments while the United States replaced its older weapons at the cost of reducing the size of its force.

Cohen acknowledged the problem, but insisted it could be handled by fine-tuning the basic build-down idea. For instance, he suggested the proposal could require that if a nation deployed a particularly threatening kind of weapon, such as a large, multi-warhead, land-based missile, it would have to dismantle many more of its existing weapons than it would have to give up if it deployed a small, single-warhead missile.

House, Senate Votes

When the House and Senate took up the fiscal 1984 defense authorization bill in July, the debate on MX closely resembled the discussions preceding the MX votes in May. *(Defense authorization, p. 175)*

The House passed, 305-144, its version of the defense authorization July 26. The lengthy debate on HR 2969 — eight days over a two-month period — was taken up primarily with discussions of the MX and chemical warfare. *(Vote 261, p. 80-H)*

The key MX vote during House debate came on July 20, when the chamber rejected by 13 votes an amendment

What Makes Nuclear Deterrence Work . . .

In terms of overall national security policy, the central issue of the decade-long MX debate had been: What made nuclear deterrence work?

The summary version of the view that prevailed in the Reagan, Carter, Ford and Nixon administrations held that Soviet use of nuclear weapons — or threats to use them — would be forestalled only if U.S. forces could respond in a way that clearly would leave the Russians worse off than if the threats had not been carried out.

But the threatened U.S. reprisal had to be plausible if it were to deter. Specifically, it had to disrupt Soviet military power without causing so many Soviet civilian casualties that Moscow could be expected to reply by devastating U.S. cities. Otherwise, Moscow might threaten a first strike in the expectation that a U.S. second strike would be deterred by the prospect of a Soviet third strike.

By this line of reasoning, it was not enough for U.S. nuclear forces to be able to level Soviet cities. They had to be able to carry out a wide range of "limited" nuclear strikes — for instance, destroying a few Soviet missile launchers to demonstrate U.S. resolve in an international crisis.

In other words, to deter nuclear war, U.S. forces had to be equipped to actually fight one.

However fanciful these scenarios of limited nuclear war might have appeared, Reagan administration officials, like most of their predecessors, insisted that they created perceptions of relative U.S. or Soviet advantage that deeply influenced the diplomatic arena.

From that premise flowed an insistence on what the Carter administration called "essential equivalence" between U.S. and Soviet nuclear forces. That meant rough arms parity had to be maintained lest Soviet strategic forces be perceived as more powerful than their U.S. counterparts.

The Case for ICBMs. The most controversial aspect of the general principle of equivalence was its application to intercontinental ballistic missiles (ICBMs), such as the MX. All four administrations assigned special importance to Moscow's force of large, very accurate, multi-warhead ICBMs and their theoretical ability to destroy

U.S. ICBMs, while the U.S. missiles posed no equivalent threat.

Three factors figured in the significance this school of thought attached to ICBMs:

● They contributed to the diversity of the U.S. strategic force — the "triad" of ICBMs, bombers and submarine-launched missiles, each leg of which was capable of heavily damaging an enemy. This diversity was supposed to provide a hedge against Soviet technical breakthroughs that might nullify any one of the forces.

● In the context of the "war-fighting" notion of how deterrence works, ICBMs had uniquely valuable qualities. Alone of the strategic triad, they combined the speed and accuracy needed to destroy armored Soviet military targets, such as underground missile silos and command posts, on very short notice.

● ICBMs appeared to be the kind of strategic weapon that most impressed Soviet decision-makers — "the coin of the realm," in the words of Brent Scowcroft, who headed the administration's bipartisan panel on the MX. Whatever the arguments of Western strategic analysts, the Soviet Union appeared to think this particular type of weapon worth decades of effort and hundreds of billions of dollars.

The Other View

The core of the opposition to MX over the last decade had been liberal arms control advocates who rejected the strategic policy establishment's fundamental view of how deterrence worked.

They saw mutual U.S.-Soviet nuclear deterrence as an inescapable result of the nuclear balance of terror, regardless of its details.

Each superpower was deterred, they argued, by the sheer destructive potential of even a fraction of the other's nuclear arsenal and not from any detailed calculations of which side would be left less devastated by a particular scenario.

Challenge to ICBMs. From this perspective, the highly touted Soviet ICBM force paled in significance, given the thousands of U.S. warheads on bombers and missile-submarines that would be likely to survive a So-

to delete the $2.6 billion in the bill earmarked for procurement of the first 27 production-line models of MX. *(Vote 248, p. 74-H)*

But the House adopted two amendments designed to maintain pressure on the White House. The first, offered by Aspin and Melvin Price, D-Ill., mandated that MX procurement and development could not outpace the development of the single-warhead Midgetman. The second, offered by Gore and Dicks, reduced from 27 to 21 the number of MXs procured in fiscal 1984.

Gore's long-range goal was to reduce the planned MX production rate so that fewer than 100 of the missiles eventually would be deployed. Gore warned that 100 of the very accurate, 10-warhead missiles, if deployed in conjunction with the almost equally accurate Trident II submarine-launched missiles due to enter service in 1989, theoretically could be capable of wiping out most of the Soviet

ICBM force in a surprise attack, thus destabilizing the nuclear balance.

Senate. In the Senate, MX supporters, backed up by the Scowcroft panel and the administration, insisted that deploying 100 MXs in existing silos would boost the chances of negotiating the eventual abolition of MIRVs by posing the same kind of threat against the Soviet missiles that they currently posed against the U.S. missile force.

"The Soviets do not enter into arms control out of some benevolent desire for peace," said Sen. John Tower, R-Texas, chairman of the Armed Services Committee, but rather when "there is a compelling military rationale for doing so." In this view, the 1972 treaty limiting anti-ballistic missiles (ABM) was the model of how to cut an arms control deal with Moscow: Only after Congress had agreed to build a U.S. ABM system did the Russians agree to a treaty limiting their own similar weapons.

. . . Was Focus Of Decade-long MX Debate

viet attack on U.S. ICBMs.

U.S. efforts to duplicate the Soviet missile force were seen, at best, as a bellicose extravagance.

The utility of ICBMs for "limited" nuclear strikes was seen as downright dangerous since it assumed that any nuclear war was likely to escalate into a global cataclysm. Missiles designed for "limited" war might foster an illusion of strength that could encourage nuclear confrontations and thus increase the risk of war, according to this view.

Regardless of the reasons for Moscow's emphasis on ICBMs rather than bombers or submarines, Soviet leaders could not ignore the brute reality of U.S. strategic power, it was argued.

Enter the MX

Although the philosophical core of the MX battle had been whether the United States needed missiles that were militarily and symbolically equivalent to the Soviets', another question represented the most prominent political and technical issue surrounding MX:

Could a new U.S. missile be based in some way that protected it against increasingly accurate Soviet missile warheads?

The theoretical ability of Soviet missiles to destroy existing Minuteman missiles in their underground silos was the most widely discussed rationale for developing the MX.

Though more than 30 basing techniques had been mentioned before the Scowcroft panel made its report, the Air Force's favorite approach for years had been to move the missiles at random among a large number of potential launch areas, with the total number of sites so large that the Soviet missile fleet would be exhausted in an effort to destroy the MX force.

The Ford administration accepted the shell-game approach. President Carter endorsed it with evident reluctance, apparently reflecting the views of some officials who inclined toward the views of the liberal critics of official deterrence theory.

But by 1979, MX had begun to attract attention — most of it unfavorable — outside the community of nu-clear arms specialists, largely because of the multiple launch-site basing method. In addition to the cost of building thousands of launch sites and the social and environmental impact of their construction in sparsely populated areas of Utah and Nevada, the proposal ran into trouble because of the complicated theory of how it would operate.

Candidate Reagan ridiculed the Carter basing plan during the 1980 presidential campaign, and in October 1981 he decided essentially to build MX but to defer selection of a survivable basing method until 1984. The first few dozen missiles would be installed in existing silos bolstered by additional concrete and steel armor. *(1981 Almanac p. 195)*

That plan eventually was stifled because belief that the new missile should be "survivable" had become widespread in Congress and because the Senate and House Armed Services committees strongly supported the multiple launch-site approach.

President Reagan's second MX plan — dense pack, offered in November 1982 — marked an entirely new approach, based on the assumption that if heavily armored MX silos were close enough together, attacking Soviet warheads would destroy each other while many MXs would survive.

The House swamped this proposal during the post-election session in December 1982, partly because of its exotic technical rationale but also because of two other terms that had entered the MX political equation. *(1982 Almanac pp. 120, 238)*

These were the arguments — especially widespread among Democrats newly heartened by the November 1982 elections in which they gained 26 House seats — that, first, the Reagan administration was spending too much on defense and, second, that it was dangerously inclined to eschew arms control efforts in favor of trying to spend the Russians dry in a nuclear arms race. *(1982 Almanac p. 277)*

Against that background, Reagan in January 1983 formed the Scowcroft commission in hopes of finding a technically and politically acceptable basing method for the MX.

But MX opponents led by Gary Hart, D-Colo., underscored a different bit of arms control history — the deployment in the early 1970s of the very missiles equipped with multiple warheads that had become in the early 1980s the source of strategic instability. Their deployment began as a U.S. effort to gain a military edge over Soviet forces but resulted simply in the Russians matching the U.S. weapon, they argued.

"I defy any senator to cite one weapon system we have built that has brought the Soviets closer to the bargaining table," Hart said. "There are not any."

Moreover, the critics argued, it was unrealistic to expect the Soviet Union to abandon the large land-based MIRVs that made up the vast bulk of its nuclear force, and for the administration to insist that it do so was a sign Washington was not seriously seeking an arms control agreement.

Appropriations Showdown

The last test faced by the MX in 1983 was during consideration of the defense appropriations bill. As the end of the session approached, congressional moderates — the so-called "gang of six" made up of Sens. Cohen, Nunn and Percy and Reps. Aspin, Gore and Dicks — intensified their efforts to secure changes in the administration's arms control policies in return for their support of MX.

Leaders of the group asked the Scowcroft commission to propose specific changes in the U.S. negotiating posture in the START negotiations with Moscow. Scowcroft Sept. 1 agreed to the request. The group began a series of meetings Sept. 13 to hammer out a common position for their dealings with the administration.

Several of them — and other members who followed their lead — threatened to oppose MX procurement if

changes in the administration's START stance were not evident by the time Congress voted on the fiscal 1984 defense appropriations bill.

Bringing in Scowcroft

The maneuvering went public Aug. 30, when Aspin in a letter to Scowcroft urged the advisory commission to "move into high gear for the specific purpose of helping to frame an arms control position."

The commission's participation in the formulation of a new negotiating proposal was politically essential to give the U.S. position a bipartisan flavor, Aspin argued in a press release. "It is in the administration's interest to see that people with arms control credentials have a major hand in framing our arms control position," he said. "Without that, the administration will lose its MX."

Aspin's Suggestions

In his letter to Scowcroft, Aspin suggested three goals he said should be reflected in a new U.S. START offer:

● Gradual movement toward rough equality in the total throw-weight of U.S. and Soviet ballistic missiles.

● Reductions in the total destructive power of both missiles and bombers, but by a formula that took account of bombers' much lower speed (which made them less useful in a surprise attack) and their vulnerability to anti-aircraft defenses (which missiles then did not share).

● Incentives for each country to abandon large, multiple-warhead ICBMs in the course of its normal missile modernization process.

A central premise of Aspin's suggestion was that the administration's insistence on substantial reductions in large Soviet ICBMs would have to be realized gradually.

Senators' Letter

On Sept. 9, Cohen, Nunn and Percy sent a letter to Scowcroft that closely paralleled many of Aspin's arguments from 10 days earlier.

The senators' letter declared it was vitally important that Congress and the president forged a common position on strategic arms policy before early October, when the START negotiations would resume and Congress would begin consideration of the defense appropriations bill. Acknowledging the role of the Scowcroft panel and the House members in putting together such a consensus, the senators offered their own list of principles for Scowcroft's new effort. Many of their suggested goals overlapped Aspin's:

● An immediate ceiling on the number of ballistic missile warheads and a proposal to build down the number of those warheads.

● An immediate ceiling on the total nuclear destructive power of both sides, including missile throw-weight and bomber payload, and a build-down in that overall measure of destructive power.

● Incentives in the proposed build-down formula to discourage new, large multi-warhead ICBMs and to encourage small, single-warhead missiles — Midgetmen.

And the senators insisted that the build-down agreement should be proposed immediately, to serve as a "precursor" to a more comprehensive START agreement.

New Proposal

President Reagan, pressured by the "gang of six," offered new arms control proposals Oct. 4 — including a bilateral nuclear arms build-down — that bolstered his shaky standing with Congress on nuclear arms policy.

But the new formula, which represented the successful outcome of months of negotiations between the White House and Capitol Hill, met with a negative response from Moscow.

In addition to the build-down, Reagan also announced changes in his existing START proposal. And he added to the START negotiating team R. James Woolsey, a member of the Scowcroft commission who was closely allied to key House Democrats.

All three elements of the new Reagan posture — the build-down, the START modification and the Woolsey appointment — were worked out between the White House and the congressional defense moderates.

MX and Beyond

For the short run, Reagan's changes ensured that the congressional "gang of six" would support initial production of the MX missile when Congress took up the defense appropriations bills. The six almost surely could have swung the balance against the missile on the appropriations bill, and had vowed to do so if Reagan did not alter his negotiating posture in ways they thought would improve prospects for an agreement.

Reagan's initial proposals would have required much heftier cuts in Soviet weapons than in U.S. forces, which led to widespread suspicion — not only among liberals, but also in the center of the political spectrum — that the offers were intended only to mollify U.S. public opinion, while continuing a nuclear buildup, rather than to foster an agreement with Moscow.

Charges that Reagan was "inflexible" were less likely to stick after the Oct. 4 announcement. It marked the fourth time since March that Reagan publicly altered a major arms control proposal in a direction deemed more palatable to Moscow.

The earlier public shift in the START position came in June, when Reagan lifted a proposed limit on the number of ICBMs from 850 to some higher number — not publicly specified, but believed to be in the range of 1,100 to 1,200 — thus imposing less of a reduction on Moscow's ICBM fleet, which was much larger than Washington's. *(See above)*

Reagan's two other public shifts were made in the parallel U.S.-Soviet negotiations — also in Geneva — to reduce the number of intermediate-range nuclear forces (INF) in Europe.

As the year ended, the various arms control negotiations with the Soviets were in limbo. The Soviet delegation Nov. 23 walked out of the INF talks to protest the deployment of Pershing II missiles in NATO countries. The START negotiations were adjourned Dec. 8; no date for resuming negotiations was set. *(European missiles, box, p. 206)*

Appropriations Votes

The administration's majority for MX held when the fiscal 1984 defense appropriations bill reached the floor of the House and Senate, though its margin of victory dropped in the House. HR 4185, which cleared Congress Nov. 18, included $2.1 billion for the production of the first 21 MX missiles and $2 billion for continued development work on the weapon. *(Story, p. 479)*

The House Appropriations Committee Oct. 20 approved its version of the bill (H Rept 98-427); the Senate Appropriations Committee reported its measure (S 2039 —

S Rept 98-292) Nov. 1. Despite the controversy the missile had provoked on Capitol Hill earlier in the year, opposition to MX had weakened by the time HR 4185 was moving through committee. The explanation was twofold. A revived get-tough attitude toward Moscow was sparked by the Soviet's Sept. 1 destruction of a Korean airliner. And Reagan's milder approach to arms control — arising out of negotiations with the "gang of six" — apparently paid dividends among members. *(Korean airliner, p. 136)*

The closest opponents came to blocking MX was on a Nov. 1 House vote to bar production of the missile. The amendment was rejected 208-217. *(Vote 409, p. 122-H)*

The nine-vote margin of victory was the smallest of the three key House votes on MX in 1983. The May 24 approval of basing and flight testing won by 53; the July 20 vote turning back a move to halt production won by 13.

On Nov. 7, by a 37-56 vote, the Senate rejected an amendment by Bumpers to delete from the bill the $2.1 billion earmarked for the first 21 production-line versions of the missile. *(Vote 327, p. 54-S))*

The margin was much tighter on a Nancy Landon Kassebaum, R-Kan., amendment to express the sense of the Senate that the administration should propose a mutual moratorium on flight tests of MIRVed ICBMs during the START negotiations. The Kassebaum amendment was rejected 42-50. *(Vote 329, p. 54-S)* ∎

House OKs, Senate Rejects Nuclear Freeze

The House May 4 adopted a much-amended resolution calling for an immediate freeze on U.S. and Soviet nuclear weapons. Five months later, the Senate voted down a similarly worded measure.

Final approval of the House resolution (H J Res 13) came after 42 hours of debate and over the vigorous objections of the Reagan administration. It was approved by a 278-149 vote only after adoption of an amendment that would void a freeze agreement unless it led to mutual arms reductions within a specified period of time. Acceptance of this amendment allowed both sides in the long debate to claim victory. *(Text of House resolution, box, p. 210)*

The Senate Oct. 31 rejected, by a 58-40 vote, an amendment to a debt ceiling bill (H J Res 308) that urged an immediate nuclear weapons freeze. Earlier the Senate Foreign Relations Committee had rejected a freeze proposal (S J Res 2), as well as a proposal for a weapons "build-down" agreement that would have required the United States and the Soviet Union to retire an average of two nuclear weapons for each new one deployed.

The vote in the Senate came as no surprise. Freeze proponents had discounted any prospect of winning in the GOP-controlled Senate. Their goal, they had said, was simply to force all senators to take a public stand on the freeze before the the 1984 elections. The chief sponsors of S J Res 2 were Mark O. Hatfield, R-Ore., and Edward M. Kennedy, D-Mass.

Nationwide Freeze Campaign

Vigorous, grass-roots lobbying was the nuclear freeze campaign's hallmark.

Beginning in 1981, the grass-roots campaign mushroomed, partly in response to remarks by President Reagan and other officials referring to the possibility of "limited" or "protracted" nuclear wars.

Despite energetic lobbying by a network of pro-freeze groups in hundreds of congressional districts, the House narrowly rejected a freeze resolution in 1982 after the administration mounted an all-out assault on the measure. The freeze campaign then concentrated its efforts on November referendums in states and smaller jurisdictions calling, in generally similar terms, for a bilateral nuclear weapons freeze. The freeze proposals were approved in eight of nine states and most of the smaller jurisdictions. *(1982 Almanac p. 113)*

The freeze campaign's fundamental premise was that existing U.S. weapons were an adequate counterweight to the Soviet arsenal. Most freeze backers strongly opposed

new, accurate U.S. weapons such as the Pershing II missile because, they warned, Moscow would inevitably respond with new weapons, thus escalating the nuclear arms race.

In the administration's view, new, more powerful U.S. nuclear weapons were needed to offset intolerable advantages that Moscow enjoyed in certain kinds of nuclear weapons, notably in land-based intercontinental ballistic missiles (ICBMs). Either Moscow had to reduce its armaments to U.S. levels or U.S. forces had to be increased to match the Soviet arsenal, according to the Reagan policy.

Freeze Strategy. In a strategy conference in St. Louis in February 1983, the nuclear freeze campaign reaffirmed its call for congressional approval of a bilateral freeze resolution.

But the freeze conference also set the stage for additional battles in 1983 against specific U.S. weapons programs. Freeze forces decided to work for "interim restraints" on certain U.S. weapons, on the grounds that prospects for a bilateral freeze would be undermined by their deployment.

"Until the U.S. government proposes such a bilateral freeze to the Soviet Union, the National Freeze Campaign will urge the U.S. Congress to suspend funding for testing, production and deployment of U.S. nuclear weapons and to call upon the Soviet Union to exercise corresponding restraint with regard to the testing, production and deployment of Soviet missiles," the freeze conference declared.

House Committee Action

H J Res 13 was approved by the House Foreign Affairs Committee March 3 by a 27-9 vote. The resolution was reported March 14 (H Rept 98-31).

The House freeze resolution was sponsored by Foreign Affairs Chairman Clement J. Zablocki, D-Wis. It expressed the sense of Congress that the U.S.-Soviet nuclear arms talks should include among their objectives "deciding when and how to achieve a mutual and verifiable freeze on testing, production and deployment" of nuclear weapons.

H J Res 13 was similar to a resolution that the House came within a whisker of passing in 1982. The earlier measure, rejected 202-204, went down only because of massive lobbying efforts by the White House.

A joint resolution had the force of law. But since H J Res 13 merely expressed the sense of Congress that a freeze should be an "objective" of U.S.-Soviet negotiations, it would not have compelled the administration to take any

Arms Control Advocates Unsuccessful . . .

Arms control advocates made no headway in 1983 in efforts to delay the European deployment of Pershing II and cruise missiles, despite the Soviet Union's claim that it would break off arms reduction talks if the missiles were put in place.

On Nov. 23, Moscow made good on its threat, walking out of the Intermediate-range Nuclear Forces (INF) talks in Geneva after the West German Parliament reaffirmed — by a clear but not overwhelming margin — its willingness to accept the U.S. missiles.

The first of these missiles, nine Pershing IIs, became operational in December.

In December 1979, NATO agreed to deploy 108 Pershing IIs in Germany and 464 ground-launched cruise missiles (GLCMs) there and in four other Western European countries to offset Moscow's deployment of triple-warhead SS-20 ballistic missiles that could strike any target in Europe. The deployment plan could be waived, the alliance agreed, if U.S.-Soviet negotiations removed the Soviet missile threat.

A total of 32 GLCMs also were due for deployment at the same time as the first nine Pershings — 16 each at Greenham Common in England and Cosimo, Sicily. But construction delays at the Sicilian site delayed deployment of the GLCMs briefly.

The SS-20 force in 1983 numbered more than 350 missiles on mobile launchers, about two-thirds of them within range of Western Europe.

Soviet Offers

As the scheduled NATO deployment date neared, Soviet negotiators offered progressively larger reductions in their INF force, but the talks remained deadlocked over the fundamental issue of land-based ballistic missiles — such as the Pershing II and the SS-20.

Moscow was willing to reduce its force to the number of British and French nuclear missiles — most of which were submarine-launched. But it adamantly rejectd any new U.S. deployments, particularly of the Pershing IIs, citing their great accuracy and their ability to hit targets in the western Soviet Union within a very short time — 10-12 minutes, according to U.S. sources. They were accurate enough to destroy armored underground command posts.

The Reagan administration insisted that as long as NATO was confronted by Soviet SS-20s, it must have the right to confront Moscow with Pershing IIs. In part, this reflected the administration's apparent conviction that land-based ballistic missiles were especially potent diplomatic symbols of military might.

That issue aside, however, there appeared to be a consensus among the major NATO governments that the alliance should not appear to abandon its 1979 decision under Soviet pressure.

Pershing Opposition

Many U.S. arms control activists, insisting the SS-20s had no significant impact on the overall U.S.-Soviet nuclear balance resting on tens of thousands of nuclear weapons, had been critical of the 1979 NATO decision from the outset.

They were particularly opposed to deployment of the Pershing IIs, warning that their potential for a surprise attack would lead Moscow to put its own nuclear missiles on a hair trigger, ready for launch at the first — possibly erroneous — indication of a U.S. attack.

---

particular actions, even if enacted over Reagan's veto.

Committee Views, Votes

Chairman Zablocki opened the Foreign Affairs Committee meeting March 8 by challenging the administration argument that congressional approval of a freeze would undermine U.S. arms negotiators. The resolution "is not an exercise in congressional boat-rocking," he insisted. Because Congress eventually would have to approve the results of any arms control negotiation, he argued, it had an obligation to signal to the president its desires.

Dante B. Fascell, D-Fla., summed up the freeze proponents' belief that each superpower had enough nuclear weapons to devastate the other and that, accordingly, additional refinements in weaponry were irrelevant.

Freshman Robert G. Torricelli, D-N.J., took more specific aim at the credibility of Reagan's arms control position in his endorsement of the freeze: "I want Ronald Reagan to hear a desperate voice from the American people," he said. "No more phony arms control negotiations; no more talk of limited [nuclear] war or winnable [nuclear] war."

William S. Broomfield, R-Mich., the panel's senior Republican, defended Reagan's commitment to arms control, declaring, "I don't think there is an issue on which the president places a higher priority."

Broomfield and Henry J. Hyde, R-Ill., underscored the administration argument that a freeze resolution would destroy any hope of persuading the Soviet Union to substantially reduce its forces. "The freeze is a disincentive to reductions," Hyde said. "Five minutes before we put our Pershing IIs in Europe, the Soviets will get very serious about reductions."

How Immediate? The panel adopted an amendment by Stephen J. Solarz, D-N.Y., stating that the primacy assigned by the resolution to a freeze did not preclude other "concurrent and complementary arms control proposals" that might emerge.

Zablocki objected to Solarz' initial wording, which referred to the "overriding objective of an immediate freeze." Zablocki's resolution referred only to a "mutual and verifiable freeze," and he warned that use of the word "immediate" might be construed as a call for a unilateral U.S. freeze.

As adopted by voice vote, with Zablocki's approval, Solarz' amendment referred to the "overriding objective of negotiating an immediate mutual and verifiable freeze."

How Equal? Also adopted by voice vote was an amendment by Peter H. Kostmayer, D-Pa., declaring that the negotiation of a freeze would be a U.S. objective "con-

. . . In Delaying Pershing II Deployment

The national, grass-roots nuclear freeze campaign, at a strategy conference in St. Louis in February, called for a one-year delay in deploying the Pershing IIs and the GLCMs. Those attending the meeting agreed to a statement which said that such a pause would allow more time for the INF negotiations in Geneva. *(Nuclear freeze, p. 205)*

Amendment to Delay. But despite the freeze movement's political potency, the House July 26 rejected 101-320 Ronald V. Dellums', D-Calif., amendment, to the defense authorization bill (HR 2969), that would have delayed the European deployment of the Pershing IIs and GLCMs until after Dec. 31, 1984. *(Defense authorization, p. 175)*

When the House Appropriations Committee marked up the fiscal 1984 defense appropriations bill (HR 4185) Oct. 20, it rejected two amendments aimed at deferring until July 1, 1984, the planned Pershing deployments:

● By Martin Olav Sabo, D-Minn., delaying both Pershing and GLCM deployment unless the president certified after March 1 that no substantial progress was being made in INF talks; rejected 14-24.

● By David R. Obey, D-Wis., delaying only the Pershings, unless the president certified by March 1, 1984, that Moscow had made no significant reductions in its INF missile force; rejected 17-22.

The committee also rejected 15-29 an effort by defense subcommittee Chairman Joseph P. Addabbo, D-N.Y., to delete from the bill the entire $407.7 million requested for 95 more Pershing IIs.

Over the years, the House had rejected all but one effort to cut Pershing II funds. The sole exception came in 1982, when Addabbo managed to keep Pershing procurement funds out of the fiscal 1983 defense appropria-

tions measure because of dramatic failures in the missile's early test flights. *(1982 Almanac p. 277)*

Gestures. A bipartisan House-Senate coalition of more than 30 members of Congress wrote President Reagan Nov. 17 urging a six-month delay in the European deployment if the Soviet Union agreed to an immediate, verifiable 20 percent reduction in the 243 SS-20s currently deployed within range of Western Europe.

Some of those members also were among the 114 House members — all but two of them Democrats — who signed a second letter the same day calling on Reagan to defer the Pershing deployment for "a reasonable period."

Soviet Deployments

A Nov. 24 statement by Soviet President Yuri Andropov, echoing earlier threats by Soviet spokesmen, declared that new Soviet deployments of land- and sea-based missiles would be made to compensate for the new U.S. weapons.

U.S. officials expected the Soviet steps to include continued deployment in Europe of new, shorter-range missiles — 80-mile-range SS-21s, 600-mile-range SS-22s and 300-mile-range SS-23s. Deployment of these weapons to replace older Soviet missiles had been under way for some years.

The sea-based component of Andropov's threat might consist of new, long-range cruise missiles carried aboard submarines.

On Nov. 26, Assistant Secretary of Defense Richard N. Perle warned that such missiles might threaten a surprise attack on U.S. bombers. The new Soviet missile would be similar to a version of the GLCM being carried aboard U.S. submarines.

---

sistent with the maintenance of essential equivalence in overall nuclear capabilities."

The administration position was that essential nuclear equivalence required deployment of several new weapons, including the MX and Trident II missiles, which the freeze campaign vehemently opposed.

But Kostmayer said the wording of his amendment made it clear that the resolution was affirming, contrary to the administration view, that essential equivalence already existed.

Administration Reaction

Reagan rose to the challenge within a few hours of the committee action, warning a conference of evangelical Christians that the freeze proposal was "a very dangerous fraud . . . merely the illusion of peace."

"A freeze at current levels of weapons would remove any incentive for the Soviets to negotiate seriously and virtually end our chances to achieve the major arms reductions which we have proposed," he said.

House Floor Action

The House passed H J Res 13 on May 4 by a 278-149 vote after rejecting 175-247 a motion to recommit (and

thus kill) the measure. *(Votes 83, 82, p. 30-H)*

Passage came after more than 40 hours of debate spread over six days: March 16, April 13, April 20-21, April 28 and May 4. H J Res 13 called on the United States and the Soviet Union to negotiate an immediate, mutual and verifiable freeze on nuclear weapons. It was approved only after adoption of an amendment by Elliott H. Levitas, D-Ga., that required suspension of a freeze agreement if it were not followed by mutual arms reductions within a specified period of time.

As a result, both freeze supporters and opponents could claim to have come out on top.

"The freeze comes first [before reductions]," Speaker Thomas P. O'Neill Jr., D-Mass., declared immediately before the final vote. "The priorities have not been altered."

This sequence — a freeze first, followed by reductions — was at the heart of the resolution's implicit criticism of the president's policy. The administration maintained that Moscow held important military advantages and would agree to reductions only when faced with the imminent prospect of a U.S. nuclear buildup to offset the Soviet edge.

On the other hand, Minority Leader Robert H. Michel, R-Ill., boasted that three key votes on the Levitas amendment had been won by "those who favor arms reductions now," thus partly vindicating Reagan's position that the

freeze would undermine its proposals for deep reductions in U.S. and Soviet nuclear arsenals.

Symbolic Gesture. Throughout the debate, it seemed clear that many members supported the freeze resolution to nudge the administration toward more rapid arms control progress, rather than to endorse it as a specific arms control proposal. But it was widely believed that the nationwide freeze campaign had been a powerful influence, forcing the administration to moderate its rhetoric on nuclear strategy and to show a more visible enthusiasm for arms control agreements than was evident during its first several months.

On the other hand, the House debate on H J Res 13 forced freeze backers to espouse a circumscribed view of the resolution's effect. Repeatedly they emphasized that any freeze would have to be negotiated and that adoption of the resolution would create no bar to U.S. weapons programs, pending ratification of whatever agreement might be negotiated.

Core of Resolution. Administration supporters sought to reinforce the resolution's limits and to further restrict its effect with dozens of amendments. About 30 amendments were adopted, some as proposed by the critics, others as further amended by freeze backers to protect what they felt was the resolution's symbolic core — the insistence on a freeze first, followed by reductions, and the ban on any provision of a negotiated freeze agreement for "modernization" that would replace current weapons with more lethal arms.

With more than 60 amendments to the resolution still pending after five days of debate, the Democratic leadership, in an unusual move, sought a new rule governing further debate. The new rule, which would have provided for as much as 14 additional hours of debate, was adopted by the House May 4, 270-149. *(Vote 76, p. 28-H)*

After the House adopted the Levitas amendment later that day, allowing the freeze critics to claim some success, leaders on each side of the debate agreed to move promptly to a final vote on the resolution.

Levitas Amendment

As modified by Levitas' amendment, the resolution directed U.S. arms control representatives to negotiate an immediate mutual and verifiable freeze to be followed by reductions, "with such reductions to be achieved within a reasonable, specified period of time."

Despite the amendment's convoluted syntax, Levitas and his opponents agreed on its import: If a U.S.-Soviet freeze agreement contained a time limit on the achievement of post-freeze reductions and that deadline were not met, the freeze would lapse.

Norman D. Dicks, D-Wash., and Les AuCoin, D-Ore., each referred to it as a "sunset provision" on the freeze.

Repeatedly, Levitas emphasized that his amendment would not change the freeze first, reductions second sequence deemed sacrosanct by freeze supporters. But he hammered away at the easy assurances of many freeze advocates that arms reductions would, in some unspecified way, follow from a freeze.

With the choice focused on the linkage — freeze leading directly to reductions — rather than on the sequence — freeze followed by reductions — the freeze leaders dug in: "I would rather have an agreement to freeze than no agreement on anything at all," Solarz, a leading pro-freeze tactician, told the House.

Parliamentary Maneuvers. Solarz offered an amendment to Levitas' amendment that would have left a freeze agreement to stand on its own, "with reductions to be achieved as soon as possible after achievement of a . . . freeze."

Solarz' maneuver followed what had become the freeze leaders' standard — and hitherto successful — tactic for deflecting hostile but politically attractive amendments: It retained the politically seductive aspect of the anti-freeze amendment — in this case, the notion of arms "reductions" — but in a form that preserved the symbolic primacy of the freeze.

Freeze backers feared that the only alternative to this tactic would have been to ask members to vote "against" an amendment that was "for" arms reductions.

Leaders on both sides of the debate had assumed all along that whichever side formulated the final version of any amendment could craft a package sufficiently attractive to prevail. Throughout the debate, freeze backers held the upper hand in this procedural minuet. In general, the rules of the House allowed an amendment to be amended once; but that "second-order" amendment could not itself be amended. This gave the backers of the freeze the final opportunity for amendments in each instance.

But the Solarz amendment was rejected 210-214. *(Vote 78, p. 28-H)*

The procedural advantage thus passed to the anti-freeze side for the first time in the debate. Dicks quickly offered another pro-freeze variation on Levitas' theme, this one specifying that, after negotiating a freeze, negotiators would proceed "immediately to pursuing reductions."

But Dicks offered his amendment as a substitute for the Levitas amendment. House rules allowed one amendment to such substitutes, and Henry J. Hyde, R-Ill., promptly offered it. He proposed a return to the original Levitas language as an amendment to Dicks' substitute.

Levitas' language, as embodied in Hyde's amendment to Dicks' substitute, was approved in two back-to-back votes: 221-203 and 225-191. *(Vote 79, p. 28-H; vote 80, p. 30-H)*

'Sequence,' Modernization Amendments

Throughout the House debate proponents of the freeze turned back other attempts to undermine the resolution's insistence on freeze first, reduce later.

Hank Brown, R-Colo., proposed an amendment that would have given equal priority to a freeze and to Reagan's goal of nuclear arms reductions as the twin goals of arms negotiations. By a vote of 219-195, the House April 13 adopted an amendment to Brown's measure by Jim Leach, R-Iowa, that restored the primacy of the freeze. *(Vote 50 p. 20-H)*

Similarly, freeze backers April 28 eviscerated with an amendment of their own an amendment to the resolution by Mark D. Siljander, R-Mich., that would have set a freeze and reductions as co-equal goals of U.S. arms control negotiators. "All we're trying to make clear is that we're not talking about a freeze with no hope of reductions," Siljander said.

But Leach proposed an amendment to Siljander's amendment to require the sequence of freeze first, followed by reductions. Leach insisted his amendment, which was accepted by a 215-194 vote, was essential to retain the resolution's basic character: a vote of no confidence in the administration's arms control policy. *(Vote 67, p. 26-H)*

Advocates of the freeze also deflected assaults on the other symbolic cornerstone of the resolution: prohibition

within any negotiated freeze of nuclear arms "modernization," in the sense of replacing existing weapons with more deadly ones.

By a vote of 226-195, the House March 16 approved a Zablocki amendment stipulating that the resolution should not be construed to ban "measures necessary for the maintenance of and credibility of the United States' nuclear deterrent." But the Zablocki provision required that such measures be "consistent with the overriding objective" of negotiating a freeze. *(Vote 28, p. 12-H)*

This language was substituted for an amendment by Samuel S. Stratton, D-N.Y., that would have declared the resolution placed no ban on such "modernization" as might be needed to maintain the U.S. deterrent.

Using large charts, Stratton warned that an immediate freeze would doom the United States to disarmament by attrition. A high proportion of existing U.S. missiles, bombers and submarines were approaching obsolescence, he argued, while the bulk of Soviet strategic weapons was less than 10 years old. "Within a mere three or four years, our nuclear deterrent would be washed out as totally unuseful and unserviceable," Stratton said.

Leach countered that U.S. weapons would be quite adequate to deter a Soviet attack, despite their age.

After substituting Zablocki's language for Stratton's, the House adopted the amendment by a standing vote of 112-109.

Freeze backers turned back two "modernization" amendments April 20-21:

● By James G. Martin, R-N.C., stipulating that freeze negotiations take account of the relative age and obsolescence of nuclear weapons. The amendment was rejected 204-211. *(Vote 52, p. 22-H)*

● By William Carney, R-N.Y., stipulating that nothing in the resolution would prevent the United States from deploying new long-range missiles in Europe as agreed to by NATO in 1979. By a vote of 221-195, the House adopted instead a substitute amendment by Zablocki providing that the 1979 agreement could be superseded by a freeze agreement with Moscow. *(Vote 55, p. 22-H)*

Martin Amendment. Faced with another amendment by Martin that could have been construed as an indirect mandate for "modernization" under a freeze, backers of H J Res 13 took another tack April 28.

The amendment provided that a freeze be negotiated with due regard for preserving the essential equivalence of the U.S. and Soviet nuclear forces "at present and in the future." Martin said this was intended to take account of the fact that most U.S. nuclear weapons were older than the Soviets' and would require replacement within the scope of any freeze.

But AuCoin minimized the amendment's significance, arguing that even if U.S. weapons were older, their "technology is so infinitely superior that they are in no way inferior." Then freeze backers deprived Martin's amendment of symbolic value as an "anti-freeze" vote by voting for it unanimously themselves. The amendment was approved 397-0. *(Vote 68, p. 26-H)*

On the last day of debate, the House took up an amendment by Duncan L. Hunter, R-Calif., providing that the resolution would not bar replacement of B-52 bombers with new B-1s. Hunter warned that age was making the existing planes unsafe to fly.

By a vote of 227-189, the House adopted a Solarz amendment to the Hunter amendment providing that the resolution would allow "safety-related improvements" to

existing bombers. The language then was adopted by voice vote. *(Vote 81, p. 30-H)*

Policy or Symbol?

Foreign Affairs Chairman Zablocki had opened the debate on H J Res 13 on March 16 by reminding his colleagues that freeze resolutions had been approved in eight state referendums and by 11 state legislatures and hundreds of other government bodies in 1982. "The people have spoken," he said. "We have an obligation to bring about some kind of action and extend every effort to see that a nuclear holocaust will not come upon us."

Rep. Edward J. Markey, D-Mass., one of the most energetic proponents of the freeze, insisted that it was no mere slogan, but a specific policy to which people were firmly committed.

"People from all walks of life by the millions have reawakened to the danger of nuclear war," Markey declared. "They have begun to analyze strategic doctrines that will bring us peace or megadeaths. And they have begun to ask questions ... that heretofore have been the property of that elite group of nuclear theologians who have controlled the fate of this earth."

Siljander Amendment. But whether members' support for the resolution was an endorsement of the freeze as a concrete policy or whether they intended for the resolution to stand as a symbolic gesture against the threat of nuclear war seemed to be called into question by the close vote on an amendment by Siljander on the first day of debate on H J Res 13.

The amendment, rejected 209-215, would have sanctioned the Reagan administration's insistence on reductions of U.S. and Soviet nuclear arsenals to equal, lower levels, rather than trying to negotiate an immediate freeze. *(Vote 26, p. 12-H)*

It would have made the objective of the resolution the negotiation of "an immediate, mutual and verifiable freeze and/or reduction of" nuclear weapons.

Freeze backers argued the administration position was merely a ruse to permit Reagan's large-scale nuclear arms buildup, since Moscow was unlikely to abandon its existing numerical advantage in ICBMs.

All but 11 voting Republicans supported the Siljander amendment as did 57 Democrats — most of them Southerners or hard-liners on defense issues.

Opponents' Views. In the main, freeze opponents acknowledged the sincerity of grass-roots freeze supporters. But Hyde, one of the more combative freeze opponents, argued that public support for the freeze marked "an expression that the people want to end the arms race," rather than a detailed assessment of the U.S.-Soviet nuclear balance.

Broomfield opened the case against the resolution with the argument that congressional approval of a freeze would undermine administration efforts to negotiate reductions in the most dangerous kinds of weapons — land-based ballistic missiles.

The House vote on the measure "will either show support for the [U.S.] negotiators in Geneva or it will reverse the administration's presently successful efforts," Broomfield said. Broomfield was the sponsor of the principal anti-freeze amendment (H J Res 4), which would have expressly endorsed Reagan's call for "freezing" the U.S. and Soviet strategic arsenals "at equal and substantially reduced levels."

If the president were required to offer Moscow a

Text of House Resolution . . .

Following is the text of H J Res 13 as adopted by the House May 4.

Whereas the greatest challenge facing the Earth is to prevent the occurrence of nuclear war by accident or design;

Whereas the United States and the Soviet Union have signed the Joint Statement of Agreed Principles for Disarmament Negotiations, known as the McCloy-Zorin Agreement, enumerating general principles for future negotiations for international peace and security;

Whereas the increasing stockpiles of nuclear weapons and nuclear delivery systems by both the United States and the Soviet Union have not strengthened international peace and security but in fact enhance the prospect for mutual destruction;

Whereas adequate verification of compliance has always been an indispensable part of any international arms control agreement; and

Whereas a mutual and verifiable freeze and reductions in nuclear weapons and nuclear delivery systems would greatly reduce the risk of nuclear war: Now, therefore, be it

Resolved by the Senate and House of Representatives of the United States of America in Congress assembled, That consistent with the maintenance of essential equivalence in overall nuclear capabilities at present and in the future, the Strategic Arms Reduction Talks (START) between the United States and the Soviet Union should have the following objectives:

(1) Pursuing the objective of negotiating an immediate, mutual, and verifiable freeze, then pursuing the objective of negotiating immediate, mutual, and verifiable reductions in nuclear weapons.

(2) Deciding when and how to achieve a mutual verifiable freeze on testing, production, and further deployment of nuclear warheads, missiles, and other delivery systems and systems which would threaten the viability of sea-based nuclear deterrent forces, and to include all air defense systems designed to stop nuclear bombers. Submarines are not delivery systems as used herein.

(3) Consistent with pursuing the objective of negotiating an immediate, mutual, and verifiable freeze, giving special attention to destabilizing weapons, especially those which give either nation capabilities which confer upon it even the hypothetical advantages of a first strike.

(4) Providing for cooperative measures of verification, including provisions for onsite inspection, as appropriate, to complement National Technical Means of Verification and to ensure compliance.

(5) Proceeding from this mutual and verifiable freeze, pursuing substantial, equitable, and verifiable reductions through numerical ceilings, annual percentages, or any other equally effective and verifiable means of strengthening strategic stability, with such reductions to be achieved within a reasonable, specified period of time as determined by the negotiations.

(6) Preserving present limitations and controls on nuclear weapons and nuclear delivery systems.

(7) Incorporating ongoing negotiations in Geneva on intermediate-range nuclear systems into the START negotiations. Discussing the impact of developing comprehensive defensive systems consistent with all provisions of the Treaty on the Limitation of Anti-Ballistic Missile Systems.

(8) Nothing in this resolution shall be construed by United States negotiators to mandate any agreement that would jeopardize our ability to preserve freedom.

In those negotiations, the United States shall make every effort to reach a common position with our North Atlantic Treaty Organization allies on any element of an agreement which would be inconsistent with existing United States commitments to those allies.

Sec. 2. In the absence of a bilateral agreement embodying the objectives set forth in this joint resolution, nothing in this resolution is intended to prevent the United States from carrying out its responsibilities under the December 1979 North Atlantic Treaty Organization decision regarding intermediate range nuclear forces.

Sec. 3. (a) Consistent with pursuing the overriding objective of negotiating an immediate, mutual, and verifiable freeze, nothing in this resolution shall be construed to prevent the United States from taking advantage of concurrent and complementary arms control proposals.

(b) Nothing in this resolution shall be construed to supersede the treatymaking powers of the President under the Constitution.

---

freeze, opponents maintained, he would lose the flexibility that any negotiator would need to reach an even more far-reaching agreement. Specifically, some warned, he would be unable to threaten the deployment of new U.S. weapons — "bargaining chips" — to provide an incentive for Soviet reductions.

But Markey dismissed that argument: "It is the feeling of the nuclear freeze movement that there are enough bargaining chips."

During the first day of debate, the House rejected or watered down several amendments intended to dilute the freeze resolution's criticism of Reagan policy.

It also rejected 172-249 a motion to kill the measure outright. *(House vote 29, p. 12-H)*

Defining the Freeze

When debate resumed April 13, Zablocki read a statement hammered out among freeze supporters that defined the resolution's effect.

This was intended to forestall a repetition of the debate March 16 when freeze supporters, under questioning by administration allies, appeared to disagree sharply about the measure's intent.

The core of Zablocki's argument was that H J Res 13 would have absolutely no effect on U.S. weapons programs by itself — the resolution was merely a call for negotiations in search of a nuclear freeze.

"Nothing will be frozen until the freeze is signed, approved and ratified," Zablocki said. "The purpose of this

...Calling for Nuclear ''Freeze''

Sec. 4. This resolution does not endorse any type of unilateral disarmament on the part of the United States.

Sec. 5. Consistent with pursuing the overriding objective of negotiating an immediate, mutual, and verifiable freeze, nothing in this resolution should be construed to prevent measures necessary for the maintenance of and credibility of the United States nuclear deterrent.

Sec. 6. Until such time as the final instrument embodying the objectives set forth in section 1 has been fully ratified by both the Soviet Union and the United States, nothing in this joint resolution shall be construed to prevent whatever modernization and deployment of United States weapons may be required to maintain the credibility of the United States nuclear deterrent.

Sec. 7. The Congress proposes that the House Committee on Foreign Affairs and the Senate Committee on Foreign Relations study measures relating to reductions pursuant to the first section, and relating to concurrent and complementary arms control proposals pursuant to section 2, especially those aimed at progressive reductions in the number of destabilizing weapons through a mutual "build-down" or other verifiable processes.

Sec. 8. Any freeze agreement negotiated pursuant to this resolution should not prevent the United States from taking such measures with respect to our strategic systems as are necessary to protect the lives of the United States personnel operating those systems.

Sec. 9. For purposes of this resolution, a nuclear delivery vehicle is a device whose primary or exclusive mission requires it to carry a nuclear weapon into territory of or occupied by hostile forces.

Sec. 10. A freeze agreement in accordance with this resolution will not preclude the one-for-one replacement of nuclear weapons and nuclear delivery vehicles in order to preserve the credibility of the United States nuclear deterrence, provided the new weapon or delivery vehicle is the same type as the old.

Sec. 11. Nothing in this joint resolution shall be construed —

   (1) to prevent, during any negotiations pursuant to this resolution, or
   (2) to require that, in any negotiations pursuant to this resolution, the United States agree to a

provision which would prevent, such modernization and deployment of United States new or improved dual capable delivery systems as the United States may determine is required to maintain the capability of the United States defense posture.

Sec. 12. Consistent with Public Law 88-186, as amended, no action shall be taken under this Act that will obligate the United States to disarm or to reduce or to limit the Armed Forces or armaments of the United States, except pursuant to the treatymaking power of the President under the Constitution or unless authorized by further affirmative legislation by the Congress of the United States.

Sec. 13. Consistent with the provisions of Public Law 92-448, as amended, negotiations undertaken pursuant to this Act shall provide for the maintenance of a vigorous research, development, and safety-related improvements program to assure that the United States would not be limited to levels of nuclear deterrent forces inferior to the force levels of the Soviet Union. Further, such negotiations should recognize the difficulty of maintaining essential equivalence and a stable balance in nuclear deterrent capabilities in a period of rapidly developing technology, and that any future arms control agreements should promote a stable international balance and enhance the survivability of United States nuclear deterrent forces.

Sec. 14. In all negotiations pursuant to this resolution, the United States shall make every effort to ensure that any agreement reached shall provide for full compliance by all parties with preexisting international treaties, obligations, and commitments.

Sec. 15. Any item both sides do not agree to freeze would not be frozen.

Sec. 16. The President shall take all necessary steps to ensure that any agreement embodying the objectives set forth in this joint resolution can be adequately verified, including pursuing the objective of providing for cooperative measures of verification (including provisions for onsite inspection as appropriate) to complement National Technical Means of Verification and to ensure compliance.

Sec. 17. Nothing in this joint resolution shall be construed to prevent safety-related improvements in strategic bombers.

resolution is not unilateral restraint. It is to guide, direct and expedite the process of protecting the nuclear deterrent of the United States through a negotiated, mutual and verifiable freeze."

Zablocki also said those criteria would limit the scope of any freeze agreement: "Any item both sides do not agree to freeze, is not frozen. Any item that cannot be verified, is not frozen," he said.

As envisioned by sponsors of H J Res 13, a freeze would allow maintenance of existing weapons and their replacement by new weapons of the same type, Zablocki declared. For example, a B-1 bomber could be replaced by another B-1, a B-52 bomber by a new B-52, he said. B-52s had not been built since 1962.

Build-Down Rejected

By a vote of 190-229, the House April 13 rejected an amendment by Levitas that would have substituted for the freeze as a U.S. arms control objective a "guaranteed build-down" of nuclear weapons.

This required each superpower to retire two already deployed nuclear warheads for each new warhead deployed. *(Vote 49, p. 20-H)*

The proposal had more than 40 Senate sponsors. *(See Senate action, below)*

Though not endorsed by the administration, the proposal would have allowed deployment of some new weapons, such as the Pershing II and MX missiles, which were strongly opposed by most leading freeze backers.

Levitas and other supporters of build-down insisted it could be compatible with a freeze. But Markey denounced the amendment as "just a public relations cover for the arms buildup the administration wants."

How Binding?

On the final day of House debate, supporters of the freeze easily turned back an amendment by Dan Lungren, R-Calif., that would have specified that the resolution was not "binding on the president or his negotiators in the formulation of strategy, instructions or positions in the conduct of the Strategic Arms Reduction Talks (START)." Lungren and his allies charged that various freeze backers had made contradictory claims as to whether the resolution was binding on the administration or merely symbolic.

The resolution itself was worded in advisory rather than mandatory terms, the freeze critics conceded — it said the president "should" seek a freeze rather than that he "shall" seek a freeze. But they complained that the Foreign Affairs Committee's report on the resolution said it would "mandate" specific guidelines for the president's conduct of foreign policy. This was an unconstitutional intrusion into the president's power to negotiate treaties, Lungren argued.

Freeze leader AuCoin objected that Lungren's amendment would reduce the freeze to the status of "a simple Mother's Day declaration."

"I do not believe there needs to be the spelling out of whether it is binding or mandated," declared Zablocki. "We have every right to give some guidelines and some input into the formulation of foreign policy."

"They want it to be semi-binding," retorted freeze critic Hyde. "They know they cannot tie the president's hands, because then it would be unconstitutional; but they really do not want to say that."

Zablocki offered an amendment to the Lungren measure, which provided simply that nothing in the resolution would supersede the president's constitutional power to make treaties, skirting the question of how "binding" the resolution would be. When freeze critic Jim Courter, R-N.J., restated the Lungren proposal as a substitute amendment, Zablocki offered the same amendment to Courter's amendment.

The Zablocki language prevailed over the Courter substitute, 234-183, and then was adopted as an amendment to the resolution by voice vote. *(Vote 77, p. 28-H)*

Other Amendments

Among the other amendments considered by the House were proposals by:

● Norman F. Lent, R-N.Y., to require that a freeze be verified by on-site inspection. Adopted 426-0, March 16, after the House agreed by voice vote to a Zablocki amendment making this requirement apply only as necessary. *(Vote 25, p. 12-H)*

● By Stratton, providing that the resolution by itself would have no effect on new U.S. weapons deployments, which would be allowed until a freeze agreement was ratified by the U.S. and Soviet governments. Adopted 407-3, April 20. *(Vote 53, p. 22-H)*

● By Newt Gingrich, R-Ga., exempting missile-launching submarines — though not their nuclear missiles — from a freeze. Adopted by voice vote, April 20.

● By Courter, exempting from the freeze planes designed chiefly to carry conventional weapons. Adopted by voice, April 20.

Senate Committee Action

The Senate Foreign Relations Committee Sept. 20 rejected proposals for a nuclear weapons freeze and for a weapons build-down. Both measures were reported to the Senate unfavorably Oct. 24 (S Rept 98-276).

The freeze resolution (S J Res 2), calling on the U.S. and Soviet governments to decide "when and how to begin an immediate mutual and verifiable freeze," failed by a 7-10 vote. The only member to depart from a straight party lineup was Edward Zorinsky, D-Neb., who joined the panel's nine Republicans to vote "nay."

The build-down resolution would have endorsed a U.S.-Soviet agreement that each country retire a larger number of existing nuclear warheads than the number of new ones it deployed. That resolution was rejected by a vote of 8-8, with Charles McC. Mathias Jr., R-Md., joining seven Democrats to vote "nay" and Zorinsky voting "present."

Administration backing for a U.S.-Soviet nuclear arms build-down was a key demand of a group of Senate moderates led by Foreign Relations Chairman Charles H. Percy, R-Ill., William S. Cohen, R-Maine, and Sam Nunn, D-Ga. The three, claiming support from many Senate Republicans, had sought a bargain of sorts: They would support procurement of the MX missile if the administration altered its negotiating position at the START talks in ways the senators thought would improve prospects for an agreement.

The tie vote on build-down was hailed as a tactical victory by freeze proponents. A build-down, while reducing arms levels, would allow some modernization of U.S. forces — including deployment of MX missiles.

Though Percy and other build-down backers insisted there was no conflict between their proposal and the freeze, an aide to committee member Alan Cranston, D-Calif., reflected the view of many freeze backers that the build-down was a political threat — a false but "cosmetically attractive alternative," he said. *(MX and build-down, p. 195)*

Committee Markup

When the committee took up the arms control resolutions Sept. 20, Cranston cited "the inexcusable Soviet trigger-happiness" in the destruction of a Korean airliner on Sept. 1 as a reminder of why the freeze was needed: "The fate of our planet could indeed rest in the hands of a single Soviet [or U.S.] pilot or radar screen or computer," he said. *(Korean airliner story, p. 136)*

Claiborne Pell, D-R.I., another freeze advocate, argued that the administration had failed to meet a commitment to present a specific build-down offer to the committee by mid-September. "As a result," Pell said, "the committee will be put in the untenable position of being asked to endorse a proposal without any clear idea of what its final form may be."

But Pell suggested that his doubts were more fundamental than the timing of a specific proposal. The build-down might "set the stage for deployments of other destabilizing weapons beyond our MX and the Soviet SS-24 [a new Soviet multi-warhead missile similar to MX]," Pell said. "If so, build-down will only be code for build up."

No detailed brief for the build-down was offered during the meeting, but Percy insisted that the specifics of his proposal were much more thoroughly worked out than the details of a freeze.

Under the "freeze first" strategy, Percy argued, any reductions in nuclear armament would have to await negotiation of the freeze's scope and verification procedures.

Joseph R. Biden Jr., D-Del., reiterated his position, taken during the committee's freeze deliberations in 1982, that the freeze should be viewed as a symbol. The freeze movement, he said, is "a reflection of the fact that we lack confidence in this administration's . . . desire and ability to reach an arms control agreement."

Under the agenda established by Percy, the panel's first vote was on a motion to approve or reject the freeze resolution without amendment. The timing, according to one source, forestalled the possibility that freeze backers could score a psychologicial victory by offering an initial motion simply to report the freeze to the Senate floor, without recommendation. In this view, such a motion might have succeeded, after which the panel's meeting might have ended, leaving Percy's build-down resolution stranded.

Senate Floor Action

The Senate turned aside the call for a nuclear freeze Oct. 31 by a 58-40 vote in the first test of Senate sentiment on the measure. *(Vote 317, p. 52-S)*

The Senate vote to table (kill) the measure came on an amendment by Edward M. Kennedy, D-Mass., to the debt ceiling bill (H J Res 308). The result mainly followed party lines: 46 Republicans and 12 Democrats voted to table; 33 Democrats and seven Republicans voted "nay."

The Senate then rejected (13-84) a motion to table a build-down proposal offered by Cohen. *(Vote 318, p. 53-S)*

Having provided an occasion for senators who had voted against the freeze to cast a vote for his alternative arms control approach, Cohen then withdrew the amendment, so there was no direct test of Senate support for the build-down.

Still, the large vote against tabling Cohen's amendment evidently reflected sizable Senate support: By the time it reached the Senate floor, it had been endorsed by 45 senators, including some who also had endorsed the freeze.

But Kennedy and several other build-down opponents also voted against the motion to table — on its face a pro-build-down vote — so that build-down proponents would not be able to cite the vote as an accurate measure of their political strength.

Modernization at Stake

During the Oct. 31 debate, Cohen lauded the freeze movement for having "served to focus our attention and our concentration very much on the subject matter" of arms control.

But floor debate demonstrated the most fundamental issue dividing senators who aligned themselves with the freeze on the one side and build-down on the other: "whether there is a rough [nuclear] balance between the United States and the Soviet Union and whether . . . substantial strategic modernization is needed for American security," in the words of freeze backer Patrick J. Leahy, D-Vt.

Kennedy insisted that the U.S. and Soviet nuclear forces were "in a situation of essential equivalence," with U.S. advantages in bombers and submarine-launched missiles offsetting Soviet advantages in the number and power of ICBMs. A U.S. effort to alter the current weapons balance would be futile, Kennedy said, because the Soviets would match any increases in the U.S. arsenal.

But the freeze backers' objection to Reagan policy was not simply that he favored new arms, but arms that they deemed destabilizing — pre-eminently, the multiple-warhead MX missile, which, launched on a surprise attack, was sufficiently accurate to destroy Soviet missiles in their underground silos.

Cohen argued that the freeze resolution failed to take into account the need to modernize the U.S. strategic force. Existing U.S. B-52 bombers and missile-launching submarines needed replacement as they neared the end of their operational life while existing Minuteman ICBMs were becoming more vulnerable to accurate Soviet missile warheads, he argued.

The merit of the build-down approach, Cohen said, was that it would harness the incentive for modernization. As a result, he asserted, modernization would reduce the number of weapons and encourage a shift of both U.S. and Soviet arsenals away from large, multi-warhead ICBMs like the MX, of which Moscow had more than 600. ∎

Adelman Nomination

After a three-month debate, Kenneth L. Adelman was confirmed April 14 as director of the Arms Control and Disarmament Agency (ACDA).

The vote on Adelman became, in effect, a vote of confidence on the administration's approach to arms control negotiations with the Soviet Union. The Senate approved the nomination, 57-42, following a last-minute lobbying blitz by President Reagan, Vice President George Bush, Secretary of State George P. Shultz and national security adviser William P. Clark, among others. *(Vote 55, p. 13-S)*

A majority of the members of the Senate Foreign Relations Committee Feb. 24 had recommended against confirmation of the nomination, charging that Adelman had neither the strong personal commitment to arms control nor the political stature required to make him an effective arms control advocate within the administration.

Adelman, 36, had been named Jan. 12 to succeed Eugene V. Rostow as ACDA director. Rostow had been fired following months of turmoil in which foreign policy hardliners in the Pentagon and on Capitol Hill had charged that Rostow too eagerly compromised U.S. bargaining positions in arms control talks with Moscow. *(Arms control, p. 205)*

Committee Action

Adelman came under challenge Jan. 27 from Senate Foreign Relations Committee members of both political parties skeptical about his willingness and ability to battle within the administration for arms control.

The question, said committee Chairman Charles H. Percy, R-Ill., was whether Adelman was determined "to aggressively represent the cause of arms control at the highest levels of decision-making."

Several members clearly doubted that Adelman would be a match for the conservative critics of past arms control efforts who had stonewalled Rostow both within the administration and on Capitol Hill.

Adelman's critics on the panel charged that he lacked both a technical background in arms control issues and a history of personal commitment to arms control.

Arms Reductions

In his opening statement to the committee, Adelman tried to demonstrate his support of arms control by lauding as "positive" a long list of arms control agreements "which have contributed to our national security and to world stability and peace." Among the agreements he named were the 1963 Limited Test Ban Treaty and the so-called SALT I agreements — the anti-ballistic missile (ABM) treaty and the interim agreement limiting strategic offensive arms — reached in 1972.

He conceded that he had opposed the SALT II treaty signed by President Carter in 1979, but insisted that it was not a good arms control treaty. "My problems with SALT II were that it was largely irrelevant to the subject of arms control," he told Percy. "It did not reduce nuclear weapons," he said, but rather ratified a continued buildup in both the U.S. and Soviet nuclear arsenals.

He conceded that he had not been very passionate about SALT II. But he insisted, "I could get passionate, damn passionate, about real reductions." Such reductions were Reagan's goal, Adelman maintained.

Evasive Answers

During the Jan. 27 hearing, Adelman antagonized several members by professing to have no views on several politically explosive issues, such as the feasibility of a "limited" nuclear war. And by the end of the meeting enough panel members were dissatisfied with Adelman's performance that a second hearing was scheduled for Feb. 3.

At the second hearing, Adelman apologized to the panel for having been "too cautious" in his earlier appearance, and gave short, crisp answers to the questions he earlier had evaded. Moreover, he gave some answers most committee members wanted to hear, dismissing, for instance, any thought of a "limited" nuclear conflict or the notion that anyone could "win" a nuclear war.

Action Deferred

On Feb. 16, the Foreign Relations Committee voted to defer action on the Adelman nomination. The explicit hope of many panel members was that Reagan would withdraw the nomination.

But at a televised press conference that same evening, Reagan reiterated his support for the nomination. "I'll try to make committee members see the light. If that doesn't work, I'll try to make them feel the heat," Reagan said.

Controversial Column

Adelman made a third appearance before the Foreign Relations panel Feb. 24 at a hearing that had the flavor of a courtroom drama.

During an extraordinary four-hour session, the committee heard sworn testimony first from *New York Daily News* columnist Ken Auletta and then from Adelman. Auletta had written a May 24, 1981, column quoting Adelman's views on arms talks. "My policy would be to do it for political reasons. I think it's a sham," Auletta had quoted Adelman as saying in a May 20 telephone interview.

Opponents of the nomination, had seized on the word "sham" as evidence of Adelman's coolness toward arms control.

Auletta appeared before the committee voluntarily. He presented his notes and a copy of his telephone bill to show that he had interviewed Adelman and that Adelman had made the statements attributed to him.

Several Republican senators challenged Auletta's credibility. Percy, for example, noted that Auletta had originally written "shame" in his notebook and had later changed it to "sham." Auletta insisted the "sham" note was correct. "I distinctly heard Mr. Adelman say sham," he told Percy.

After Auletta testified, Adelman said he had "no recollection of ever granting Mr. Auletta an interview." Adelman insisted he had never held the views Auletta attributed to him.

The hearing prompted Richard G. Lugar, R-Ind., to complain of a "carnival atmosphere." Paul E. Tsongas, D-Mass., said committee members already had made up their minds and were merely "trying to focus on that information that pleases us."

Committee Vote

Following the Feb. 24 hearing the committee rejected, 8-9, a motion to report Adelman's nomination to the full Senate with a favorable recommendation. Republicans Charles McC. Mathias Jr. of Maryland and Larry Pressler of South Dakota joined all committee Democrats except Edward Zorinsky, of Nebraska, in rejecting that motion.

The committee then voted 14-3 to report Adelman's nomination to the Senate with an unfavorable recommendation.

Although it was a clear rebuff to Adelman and Reagan, the committee action did represent a backhanded victory for both men.

Opponents of the nomination had wanted to lock it up in committee, thus forcing Adelman supporters to go through the cumbersome process of getting the full Senate to force the committee to discharge it. In a private meeting before the votes, Senate Majority Leader Howard H. Baker Jr., R-Tenn., had convinced most of his fellow committee members to compromise by reporting the nomination to the full Senate with a negative review.

Floor Action

Vigorous lobbying by top administration officials, including the president, bore fruit April 14 when the Senate confirmed Adelman's nomination by a vote of 57-42. All but four voting Republicans supported the nomination. The four voting against were Mathias, Pressler, Slade Gorton, Wash., and Mark Andrews, N.D. (Bob Packwood, R-Ore., was out of town and did not vote.)

Eight Democrats also voted for the nomination, with 38 Democrats voting "nay."

A common theme among several members who voted for Adelman was that the president had a right to the advisers of his choice and that rejection of Adelman would only create further delay in the search for agreements to control nuclear weapons. Others stressed the heavy burden on the administration to prove its commitment to achieving significant arms control agreements if it hoped to hold on to moderate GOP support of its arms control policy. Members also mentioned another factor that made it easier for them to support the nomination — administration assurances that Secretary of State Shultz, who would be Adelman's immediate superior, would take a much firmer hand in shaping arms control policy. Though he had no track record on the issue, it was widely assumed that Shultz would be a moderating influence on administration policy. ∎

Joint Chiefs Reorganization

The House Oct. 17 passed by voice vote a measure that would give the Joint Chiefs of Staff (JCS) more stature as an independent military counsel to the president. The Senate did not act on the bill (HR 3718).

A similar bill was approved by the House in 1982, but the Senate failed to act on it. *(1982 Almanac p. 110)*

The JCS — a five-member committee consisting of a chairman, and the senior officer of each of the four military services — were, by law, the senior presidential military advisers. But critics charged that JCS effectiveness was diluted by its inability to trespass on the interests of the services.

The House Armed Services Committee — which usually backed the military in battles to boost defense programs — drafted the bill partly in hopes of giving military advice more impact on national decision making.

Currently, though, clear-cut, realistic, feasible and prudent professional military advice was often not available to civilian leaders, the panel complained in its report on the bill (H Rept 98-382), filed Sept. 27.

The administration opposed significant features of the bill; William H. Taft IV, general counsel to the Department of Defense, argued that "current institutional arrangements . . . have served the nation well over an extended period." He also warned that some provisions might undermine "the fundamental principle of civilian control over the military."

Calls for Change

Immediate impetus for the bill came in 1982 from Gen. David C. Jones, chief of staff of the Air Force from 1974 to 1978 and JCS chairman from 1978 until his retirement in 1982.

Jones' thesis was that the JCS organization too often made policy by accommodating the bureaucratic interests of the individual services. He proposed several steps to strengthen the hand of the JCS chairman — the only member of the group not simultaneously responsible for heading one of the military branches.

Jones' approach drew furious opposition from some active and retired military personnel — particularly those with Navy backgrounds — during House Armed Services hearings in 1982. But the committee seemed impressed with Jones' argument, though unwilling to go as far as he recommended by way of weakening the power of the separate services. It reported, and the House passed, HR 6954 on Aug. 16, 1982, incorporating some steps to upgrade the power of the JCS chairman.

In 1983, while House Armed Services was modifying its earlier bill, the Senate Armed Services Committee began to look at decision making in the Defense Department, an investigation much broader in scope than the House committee's inquiry into JCS reform. Senate action on any organizational reform proposals awaited completion of those hearings in 1984.

Strengthening the Chairman

HR 3718 would expressly authorize the Joint Chiefs' chairman to offer military advice to the president in his own right, as well as serving as the JCS' corporate spokesman. It also would make the chairman a member of the National Security Council (NSC) to ensure that professional military advice — both the chairman's view and the JCS position, if different — received a hearing.

The bill also would make the chairman the supervisor and spokesman for the nine senior commanders who actually controlled U.S. combat units in the field. Six of the nine were in charge of "unified" commands — the European Command, for instance — which drew units from more than one military service.

Under the bill, the Army, Navy, Air Force and Marine Corps chiefs would continue to assert their service viewpoints as members of the JCS. But the chairman could more forcefully defend the interests of the nine major commands — which sometimes conflicted with one or more services.

The Defense Department objected to the provision making the chairman supervisor of the major commands. It warned that this smacked too much of creating a supreme military commander, thus undermining the principle of civilian control. It also opposed NSC membership for the chairman, but the JCS broke with its civilian leadership to support that provision.

To free the JCS from what it said was too great a dependence on the staffs of the four services, the bill would repeal current law limiting to 400 officers the size of the Joint Staff — the staff of officers assigned to assist the JCS.

It also would specifically charter the Joint Staff to assist the JCS in forcing the services to meet the needs of the nine major commands. The committee argued that this would "provide unmistakable authority for the chairman to revise the current [Joint Staff] procedures" so that there would be less interference by the separate staffs of the four services.

However, to ensure that all points of view were considered, the bill would allow the chief of any service or any of the nine major commanders to comment on a Joint Staff paper before it was submitted to the Joint Chiefs.

To provide the Joint Staff with more continuity, the bill would extend from three years to four the tenure of any officer on the Joint Staff and would reduce from three years to two the interval between two consecutive Joint Staff assignments. ∎

Economic Policy

The debate over federal deficits dominated economic policy making during 1983 as both Republicans and Democrats jockeyed for political advantage in the 1984 election campaigns.

Despite an unexpectedly strong rebound from the 1981-1982 recession, the deficit for the fiscal year ending Sept. 30, 1983, hit a record $195.4 billion. Most projections indicated that the deficit would hover around the $200 billion mark in fiscal 1984 and subsequent years, barring dramatic action by Congress and the president.

The willingness to take those actions was clearly absent during 1983.

Congress' fiscal 1984 budget resolution, which called on Senate and House committees to reduce spending and raise substantial new revenues, provided the framework for the deficit debate.

But the controversy over how to reduce deficits spilled over into consideration of every major appropriations bill; a Social Security reform measure; jobs, housing and other anti-recession, fiscal stimulus bills; and legislation raising the federal debt ceiling so the government could continue borrowing money to pay its bills.

International relations were affected by the U.S. deficit, as well. At the May 28-30 economic summit conference in Williamsburg, Va., leaders from six nations repeatedly stressed that it was crucial to worldwide economic prosperity for the United States to slash its deficits and bring down interest rates.

Despite pressure from domestic and foreign sources, President Reagan refused to enter the deficit-cutting fray. His posture was a critical factor in Congress' inability to come to terms with deficits.

According to Reagan, there was only one way to stem the flow of red ink: reduce non-defense spending. Throughout 1983, the president repeatedly voiced his adamant opposition to increasing taxes to reduce the deficit.

Without his support, House Democratic leaders were reluctant to expose their membership to charges of "tax and tax, spend and spend" by strongly backing tax increase legislation. They rejected out of hand Reagan's contention that domestic spending was the deficit culprit.

House Speaker Thomas P. O'Neill Jr., D-Mass., said after the House refused to consider a modest tax reform bill, "Today's vote once again proves that we cannot reduce the deficit with the president sitting on the sidelines."

Meanwhile, Senate Republicans were divided into two camps. Some, siding with Reagan, urged that the president be given additional powers to withhold federal spending. Others, including Budget Committee Chairman Pete V. Domenici, R-N.M., and Finance Committee Chairman Robert Dole, R-Kan., tried in vain to push the Senate toward adoption of a spending cut/tax increase package that would reduce deficits by perhaps as much as $150 billion over three years.

The chairman of the president's own Council of Economic Advisers, Martin S. Feldstein, rankled a number of administration officials when he publicly called for tax increases as a necessary element in what he considered the pressing task of reducing the federal deficit. Otherwise, he warned, federal borrowing to finance the deficit would "crowd out" private borrowing, causing interest rates to rise. And the deficit would mushroom as federal borrowing costs increased.

Budget and Taxes

Congress rejected Reagan's fiscal 1984 budget — with its $188.8 billion projected deficit — almost as soon as it appeared. Democrats and Republicans alike looked askance at the administration's priorities — a 10 percent real growth rate for defense spending coupled with a freeze on domestic spending. A White House proposal for a standby tax, to take effect in fiscal 1986 if the deficit were too large, was dead on arrival on Capitol Hill.

Democrats pressed their campaign to portray Reagan's policies as unfair, claiming the budget neglected the needs of the poor and those particularly hard-hit by the recession.

The widespread antipathy toward the administration budget provided House Democrats with the first opportunity since Reagan had taken office to produce a Democratic-inspired fiscal blueprint. In contrast to 1981 and 1982, GOP House members were relegated to the budget sidelines.

The plight of Republicans in the Senate, where it took repeated attempts to find a budget plan that could muster enough votes to pass, was for more tortured.

In the end, fear that the congressional budget process would collapse moved GOP leaders to provide the necessary votes for Senate approval of a spending plan that they themselves did not support. Congress finally approved a compromise fiscal 1984 budget resolution June 23, but the plan proved impossible to implement.

The spending reductions mandated by the fiscal 1984 budget — mostly adjustments in cost-of-living increases for federal retirement programs — were approved with relative ease by House and Senate committees. And the House passed a three-year, $10.3 billion spending cut package by voice vote.

Finding $73 billion in new taxes over fiscal 1984-86 proved considerably more difficult, however. The House Ways and Means Committee and the Senate Finance Committee drafted tax increase legislation that raised only a fraction of the new revenues required by the budget. But neither house ever voted on the tax increase bills.

Monetary Policy

Aside from deficits, members of Congress expressed deep concern over interest rates and the conduct of monetary policy. Many feared that the Federal Reserve would tighten its grip on the money supply in an effort to avert a

new round of inflation, thereby driving up interest rates and choking off the economic recovery.

The debate over monetary policy was fueled by months of speculation preceding the president's June 18 announcement that he would nominate Paul A. Volcker to a second four-year term as chairman of the Federal Reserve Board. The Senate confirmed Volcker July 27.

Volcker's supporters gave him substantial credit for reducing inflation, as measured by the Consumer Price Index, from 13.3 percent during 1979 to less than 4 percent during 1983. But his critics blamed him and the Fed's tight monetary policy for forcing up interest rates, thus triggering the longest and deepest recession since the Great Depression.

During his confirmation hearings, Volcker told the Senate Banking Committee that Congress had to assume a large share of the responsibility for interest rates and continued economic growth. He said the "interest rate outlook depends a great deal" on what Congress did about the deficit. Prospective $200 billion deficits in the next few years posed "looming threats" to the recovery, he warned.

The Economy

Many economists, including the administration's own, were far off the mark in predicting the shape of the economy in 1983. But for the first time in years the economy performed significantly better than economists had anticipated.

Inflation continued to moderate, rising only 3.8 percent during the 12-month period. Civilian unemployment dropped from a high of 10.7 percent (after final year-end adjustments) in December 1982 to 8.2 percent in December 1983 — far below the administration's and most private economists' estimates.

The prime interest rate, or the rate generally offered to a bank's best customers, dropped to 10.5 percent early in the year but edged back up to 11 percent in the latter half of 1983. The prime rate had peaked at 21.5 percent in December 1980.

The "real" gross national product (GNP) — the nation's total output of goods and services, adjusted for inflation — grew 2.6 percent during the first quarter of 1983, as the economy emerged from the 1981-82 recession. It then advanced 9.7 percent in the second quarter and 7.6 percent in the third, before slowing in the final quarter to 4.9 percent.

Early in the year, Congress and the administration responded to record postwar unemployment levels by approving a $4.6 billion jobs and recession relief package. But the unexpectedly robust recovery dashed Democratic plans to capitalize on the ills of the economy by pushing further anti-recession measures.

Congress did extend emergency supplemental unemployment benefits for those who had exhausted their regular unemployment benefits, but other parts of the Democrats' anti-recession program — including bills to provide mortgage foreclosure relief and temporary health insurance for the unemployed — were sidetracked as lawmakers became embroiled in the debate over deficit control.

International Trade

While almost all segments of the economy — from housing, to autos, to retail sales — staged strong rebounds during 1983, the nation's international trade position remained bleak.

Chiefly because of high U.S. interest rates, the value of the dollar reached unprecedented levels, while foreign currencies sagged, weakening the market for U.S. goods abroad. Imports rose 5.9 percent and exports declined 5.5 percent from 1982 levels. The U.S. merchandise trade deficit hit a record $69.4 billion in 1983, and was expected to exceed $100 billion in 1984. Industries and workers hurt by import competition intensified their calls for protectionist trade legislation on Capitol Hill.

—By Dale Tate

Social Security Rescue Plan Swiftly Approved

Setting partisan differences aside, Congress acted with unusual speed at the start of the session to overhaul the Social Security system and to rescue it from possible insolvency. The quick legislative action marked the end of almost two years of bitter political debate and inaction that had allowed the system to fall deeper and deeper into financial trouble.

The package adopted (HR 1900 — PL 98-21) was expected to raise approximately $165 billion over the next seven years, guaranteeing that retirement checks would continue to go out to some 36 million recipients. If Congress had taken no action, the system's largest trust fund — Old-Age and Survivors Insurance (OASI) — would have run short of funds in July and faced serious financial trouble throughout the decade.

If economic projections proved correct, the bill also would keep Social Security solvent after the turn of the century when retirement of the so-called "baby boom" generation was expected to put an even greater strain on the system.

Based primarily on recommendations made earlier in the year by the president's bipartisan National Commission on Social Security Reform, the package raised the retirement age from 65 to 67 by the year 2027, delayed retirees' annual cost-of-living adjustment (COLA) six months and increased payroll taxes for both employers and employees.

Congress also agreed to make fundamental changes in the program by taxing for the first time benefits of high-income recipients and by using transfers from the general Treasury to help bolster the system's trust funds. It also voted to bring new federal employees, members of Congress, the president, the vice president and federal judges under the Social Security system.

Also attached to the bill were extraneous, but major, provisions revamping the way the federal government reimbursed hospitals for Medicare, extending an emergency jobless benefits program six months to help over two million unemployed workers and increasing benefits for the blind, aged and disabled poor.

The legislation left unresolved the possible bankruptcy later in the decade of Medicare's Hospital Insurance (HI) trust fund — also part of the Social Security system.

Passage of the bill followed a lengthy, and often touchy, partisan fight over the future of Social Security, set off in 1981 by Reagan administration proposals to cut benefits to keep the retirement fund from going broke. Democrats charged the administration with trying to balance the budget at the expense of the elderly, and called instead for higher payroll taxes to finance the system. *(1981 Almanac p. 117)*

But with the prospects of a bankrupt Social Security system becoming increasingly real, a truce was called at the end of 1981 with the appointment of the national commission. After some intense political negotiations between the White House and commission members, the commission was able early in 1983 to reach a fragile compromise on saving the system.

Despite some last-minute hitches in the Senate and during conference, legislation based on the commission's recommendations moved rapidly through Congress, largely because of congressional fears that any delay might cause the hard-won political consensus to unravel.

The House adopted the conference report (H Rept 98-47) on the compromise rescue plan on March 24, by a 243-102 vote. *(Vote 43, p. 18-H)*

By a 58-14 vote, the Senate gave its final approval in the early morning hours of March 25. *(Vote 54, p. 12-S)*

President Reagan signed the bill at a large White House ceremony April 20, noting that the legislation would "allow Social Security to age as gracefully as all of us hope to do ourselves, without becoming an overwhelming burden on generations to come."

Final Provisions

As signed into law (PL 98-21), the Social Security Act Amendments of 1983 (effective Jan. 1, 1984, unless otherwise noted):

Social Security

● Required Social Security coverage of all new federal employees, current and future members of Congress, the president, the vice president, sitting federal judges, top political appointees and civil servants and legislative branch workers who did not choose to go under the Civil Service Retirement System by Dec. 31, 1983.

The bill included language assuring current and retired federal workers that their Civil Service retirement benefits would not be reduced because of the bill.

● Required all employees of non-profit organizations to join Social Security as of Jan. 1, 1984, and prohibited any non-profit organization from withdrawing from the system on or after March 31, 1983.

● Prohibited state and local governments from withdrawing from Social Security coverage, as of the date of enactment. The bill allowed those state and local governments that previously had withdrawn from the system to return voluntarily.

● Taxed as regular income the Social Security benefits of individuals whose adjusted gross income (including tax-exempt interest income), combined with half of their Social Security benefits, exceeded $25,000. Benefits above a similar $32,000 threshold for a married couple filing a joint return were also to be taxed.

● Increased payroll taxes for self-employed individuals by 33 percent to equal the combined tax paid by employers and employees. To offset this increase, a tax credit was allowed of 2.7 percentage points in 1984, 2.3 percentage points in 1985 and 2.0 percentage points in 1986-89.

● Increased employer and employee payroll taxes from 6.7 percent to 7 percent of wages in 1984 and from 7.15 percent to 7.51 percent in 1988 and 1989.

● Delayed the annual July cost-of-living adjustment six months, until January, beginning with the July 1983 payment.

The COLA was to be provided in January 1984 even if the increase in the Consumer Price Index (CPI), on which the COLA was based, fell below 3 percent. Afterwards, as under prior law, the COLA would be forgone when the CPI fell that low.

● Allowed employees a .3 percentage point tax credit to offset the 1984 payroll tax increase. In effect, workers were required to pay only 6.7 percent in 1984, with the Treasury

reimbursing the Social Security trust funds for the remaining .3 percentage point.

● Adjusted the annual COLA when reserves in the OASI and Disability Insurance (DI) trust funds were less than 15 percent of what would be needed for the year, for 1985 through 1988. In such cases, the COLA would be based on the lower of the increase in the CPI or the increase in average wages.

After 1988, the lower of the two indexes was to be used whenever the trust funds contained less than 20 percent of what would be needed for the year. Whenever reserves reached 32 percent or more in later years, a "catch-up" benefit was to be paid to those who lost benefits when reserves were low.

● Required the Treasury to credit the Social Security trust funds at the beginning of each month with all of the payroll taxes that were expected to be received during that month. Interest was to be paid by Social Security on any excess funds transferred. Previously, payroll taxes were credited to the funds on a daily basis.

● Required the Social Security board of trustees to inform Congress in its annual report if the system was in danger of falling short of funds.

● Allowed the three Social Security trust funds — OASI, DI and HI — to borrow from each other through 1987. However, OASI and DI would be unable to borrow from the ailing HI trust fund if its reserves fell below a certain level.

● Gradually increased the retirement age from 65 to 67 by the year 2027. The change was to be made in two steps. The age would be raised gradually to 66 over a six-year period ending in the year 2009. The second increase — from 66 to 67 — was to be made over another six-year period ending in the year 2027.

Early retirement still would be allowed at age 62, but benefits would be cut from 80 percent of full retirement benefits to 75 percent by the year 2009 and 70 percent by the year 2027.

● Required the secretary of health and human services (HHS) to study the effects of the retirement age change on those forced to retire early because of physically demanding work. The study, which also was to include recommendations on what if anything should be done to help such workers, was due by Jan. 1, 1986.

● Liberalized an existing penalty on retirees with outside earnings. Under prior law, those under age 70 had their benefits reduced $1 for each $2 they earned above $6,600. The bill provided for a $1 reduction in benefits for each $3 earned, beginning in 1990.

● Increased the bonus individuals received for delaying retirement past the age of 65 from 3 percent of benefits a year to 8 percent a year. The bonus was to be phased in between 1990 and 2008, and was made available for those up to age 70.

● Removed the Social Security system from the "unified" federal budget, in which receipts and outlays from federal funds and trust funds are consolidated, beginning in fiscal year 1992. Until then, Social Security was to be shown as a separate function within the federal budget.

● Reduced the so-called "windfall benefit" some retirees — most often former government employees — received when they worked for only a short time under the Social Security system. The bill cut the base retirement benefit of such workers.

● Permanently reallocated payroll taxes from the healthier DI trust fund to the OASI trust fund.

● Liberalized benefits designed especially to help wid-

owed, divorced and disabled women. These included an increase in benefits for disabled widows and widowers aged 50-59.

● Changed the investment procedures of Social Security trust funds to address criticisms that past investments had yielded low returns.

● Credited the Social Security trust funds with certain military benefits and uncashed Social Security checks. Previously, uncashed checks were credited to Treasury's general revenue fund.

● Included certain elective fringe benefits in the wage base subject to Social Security payroll taxes.

● Eliminated a credit previously allowed certain individuals under age 65, who collected government pensions, to compensate them for the fact that their pension income did not include tax-free Social Security benefits. It also liberalized a similar credit for certain individuals over age 65 who received few, if any, Social Security or Railroad Retirement benefits.

● Allowed the secretary of health and human services to contract with states for death certificate information to help prevent the payment of benefits to deceased individuals.

● Made several miscellaneous and technical changes, including elimination of a number of sex distinctions in the law.

● Required a study by April 1, 1984, on how to turn the Social Security Administration (SSA) into an independent agency. SSA was part of the Department of Health and Human Services.

● Added two public members to the Social Security board of trustees, which had been composed of the secretaries of Treasury, labor and HHS.

● Required the SSA to issue counterfeit-proof Social Security cards.

● Restricted benefits for convicted felons and for survivors and dependents of non-resident aliens.

● Required state and local governments to turn withheld payroll taxes over to the Treasury more rapidly. Previously, such employers could hold onto the funds for about 30 days.

Supplemental Security Income

● Increased the monthly Supplemental Security Income (SSI) benefit $20 for individuals and $30 for couples, effective July 1, 1983.

● Delayed the July 1983 SSI cost-of-living increase for six months, until January 1984, and provided for payment of the annual COLA every January thereafter.

● Allowed payment of SSI benefits for the aged, blind and disabled poor who were housed for up to three months in public shelters. Previously, SSI benefits were allowed for those housed in private, but not public, shelters.

● Waived until Sept. 30, 1984, an existing rule that certain assistance from private non-profit groups be considered as income when determining SSI eligibility.

Unemployment Compensation

● Extended for six months an emergency supplemental jobless benefit program, which had been set to expire March 31. *(Subsequent extension, p. 274)*

The program allowed those who had exhausted up to 39 weeks of regular and extended benefits to qualify for a maximum of from eight to 14 additional weeks of payments, depending on their state's unemployment rate.

Individuals who exhausted emergency benefits under

the existing program on or before April 1 were made eligible for up to 6-10 additional weeks of slightly lower payments under the new law.

Those receiving emergency benefits, but who would not have exhausted them until after April 1, were also made eligible for extra payments. In addition, those who had not exhausted their benefits by Sept. 30, 1983, when the program expired, were allowed to receive up to 50 percent of their remaining payments.

● Allowed states to deduct money from an individual's jobless benefits to pay for health insurance, if the individual elected such coverage.

● Allowed states in debt to the federal unemployment trust fund more time to pay interest on such loans, if the states took certain steps to shore up their own unemployment programs.

● Required states to deny unemployment benefits to non-professional employees of educational institutions between academic years or terms if they had a "reasonable assurance" of returning to work. Such benefits had been denied only for professional employees.

Medicare Changes

Congress attached to the Social Security measure unrelated provisions that fundamentally changed the way Medicare paid for hospital care for elderly and disabled Americans. *(Details, Medicare story, p. 391)*

Background

A delicate, last-minute compromise approved by the National Commission on Social Security Reform Jan. 15 paved the way for quick congressional action to keep the retirement system afloat.

The agreement, reached after hectic negotiations only hours before the commission's midnight deadline, was expected to raise $168 billion for calendar years 1983-89. The commission's members had agreed the previous November that the system's deficit would reach $150 billion-$200 billion over that period if nothing was done. Reagan established the commission in December 1981. Its original Dec. 31, 1982, deadline was extended for 15 days. *(1982 Almanac p. 53)*

The plan, approved by a 12-3 vote, called for both benefit cuts for retirees and tax hikes for employers and employees. The balance between the two measures had proven to be the main sticking point among the commission's 15 members. Rep. Bill Archer, R-Texas, Sen. William L. Armstrong, R-Colo., and former Rep. Joe D. Waggonner Jr., D-La. (1961-79), voted against the plan.

Of the amount to be raised, about $40 billion was to come from a proposed six-month delay in the July 1983 cost-of-living adjustment and a January payment date for all future COLAs. Another $40 billion was to be raised by increasing scheduled payroll tax hikes by 1990. The payroll tax rate would be increased .3 percentage point in 1984 to 7 percent and another .36 percentage point in 1988 to 7.51 percent. A one-time tax credit in 1984 was called for to offset the additional payments.

Self-employed individuals were to be required to pay 33 percent more in payroll taxes to equal the total combined tax paid by employees and employers. A tax deduction was allowed for half of their total payroll tax payment.

The commission also recommended that, for the first time, the Social Security benefits of high-income individuals be taxed. Under the plan, retirees with $20,000 a year

or more in adjusted gross income other than Social Security benefits would have half of their benefits taxed. The threshold was to be $25,000 for those filing joint returns.

Also proposed was mandatory Social Security coverage for all new federal employees, including new members of Congress, and all workers of non-profit organizations. Current members of Congress would not be required to join the system. The commission plan prohibited state and local employers from withdrawing from Social Security.

Additional revenues were to be raised by crediting the Social Security trust funds with certain military service credits and uncashed Social Security checks.

'Baby-Boom' Protection

The commission "agreed to disagree" on how to solve a projected Social Security shortfall in the 21st century when the post-World War II baby-boom generation would begin to retire and there would be insufficient workers paying into the fund.

The commission decided the previous November that the system faced a shortfall equal to about 1.8 percent of expected payroll over 75 years. However, the compromise package raised only approximately two-thirds of that amount.

In a separate opinion, eight of the panel's members — all Republican appointees — called for a gradual increase in the retirement age to address the system's remaining long-term financial problems. They proposed that after the turn of the century the age be raised one month a year from 65 to 66 by the year 2015.

A ninth member, Armstrong, added in his minority views that he also supported this plan.

But five Democratic appointees to the commission called instead for an additional .46 of a percentage point increase in the payroll tax in the year 2010, with a refundable income tax credit for employees. Commission member Claude Pepper, D-Fla., chairman of the strategically important House Rules Committee, made it clear he would not accept any delay in the retirement age.

Last-Ditch Negotiations

The commission's report was the result of days of difficult negotiating between the White House and key members of the panel. Until only a few days before the commission was to dissolve, it appeared the divided membership was unlikely to reach a compromise after almost a year of meetings.

But Republican economist Alan Greenspan, chairman of the commission, said members set aside differences in the end, with the knowledge that not reaching a compromise could endanger the system. "All of us swallowed very hard and accepted individual notions that we personally could not actually support," he said.

The compromise brought together such diverse panel members as AFL-CIO President Lane Kirkland, National Association of Manufacturers President Alexander Trowbridge, Pepper and Senate Finance Committee Chairman Robert Dole, R-Kan.

But the key to a final compromise was the acceptance of the package by both President Reagan and House Speaker Thomas P. O'Neill Jr., D-Mass. It had been the inability of those two to reach an agreement on the volatile Social Security issue that led to appointment of the commission in December 1981. Reagan, O'Neill and Senate Majority Leader Howard H. Baker Jr., R-Tenn., each appointed five members to the panel.

The White House had been reluctant to get too involved in the commission's politically sensitive negotiations. But faced with a difficult budget battle during 1981 and stronger Democratic control of the House, it joined forces with panel members in the final days to avert a possibly embarrassing floor fight on Social Security if no agreement was reached.

The widespread endorsement of the commission's package gave members of Congress — queasy about making any unpopular changes in Social Security — a relatively painless way to take the necessary, but politically difficult steps to keep the system from going broke.

Early Opposition

Groups directly affected by provisions in the compromise package were quick to give notice that they would not be handed a share of the burden without a fight.

The National Council of Senior Citizens said it was "adamantly opposed" to the proposed six-month COLA delay. Removing the provision's protection against inflation — "even for a limited period — is to take a step backward and to abdicate federal responsibility to the aged," the group said.

The 14-million member American Association of Retired Persons was one of several groups, including the National Federation of Independent Business and the National Taxpayers Union, that vowed to wage an all-out grass-roots campaign against the commission plan. Besides the COLA delay, the groups objected to the payroll tax increase and taxation of Social Security benefits.

In addition, federal employee unions joined forces to defeat congressional approval of the proposed requirement that new federal employees join the system. The unions charged that the change would have only minimal long-term advantages for the Social Security system, but would seriously damage the Civil Service Retirement Fund, which paid federal employee pensions.

Archer, Armstrong and other congressional conservatives also attacked the plan for its dependence on tax hikes to fund the system and for its reliance on what they called optimistic economic assumptions.

"The agreement reached continues to leave in doubt, in my opinion, the future stability of the Social Security system," Archer said in his minority views.

Armstrong argued that higher payroll taxes would place a drag on the economy, worsening the prospects for economic growth and he criticized the plan for relying on large sums of scarce general revenues for solving the system's shortfall.

According to preliminary estimates, approximately one-third of the plan's $168 billion target would come from the Treasury, either through tax credits and deductions or direct infusions into the trust funds. Previously, the retirement system had been funded solely through the payroll tax.

Armstrong also charged that another "fundamental principle" violated by the plan was the traditional parity between employer and employee contributors to the system. The proposed 1984 payroll tax credit would be available only to employees.

House Committee Action

Setting the stage for a major House floor fight over raising the retirement age or increasing payroll taxes to keep Social Security solvent, the Ways and Means Committee agreed March 2 to ask the Rules Committee to allow floor votes on both issues.

Ways and Means members agreed to the rule request after adopting by a 32-3 vote a Social Security rescue plan, reported March 4 (HR 1900 — H Rept 98-25), that for the most part followed the recommendations of the National Commission on Social Security Reform.

It included provisions to cover all new federal employees under Social Security, to raise payroll taxes, to delay the July COLA for six months and to tax Social Security benefits for high-income individuals. The package was expected to raise approximately $165.3 billion for 1983-1989, meeting the system's immediate financial problems.

Voting against the measure were Republicans Archer and Reps. Richard T. Schulze, Pa., and Philip M. Crane, Ill. Commission member Archer said the package did not make enough "substantive" changes in the system.

The committee effectively finessed the controversial issue of how to keep the system afloat in the next century when there were expected to be many more retirees and too few workers to support them.

In an effort to block a potentially divisive committee vote on raising the retirement age, Chairman Dan Rostenkowski, D-Ill., told members that the proposed rule allowing two separate floor votes on the issue had been agreed to informally by the House leadership, including Rules Committee Chairman Pepper, a staunch defender of benefits for the elderly.

The proposed rule was expected to pit Pepper, who favored an increase in payroll taxes in the next century, against Social Security Subcommittee Chairman J. J. Pickle, D-Texas, and a large number of Republicans, who preferred an increase in the retirement age after the year 2000.

The Ways and Means Committee took the middle road by including the recommendations of its Social Security Subcommittee to combine both benefit cuts and payroll tax increases. The subcommittee had voted to reduce initial benefits approximately 5 percent for new beneficiaries beginning in the year 2000 and to raise the payroll tax on employers and employees from 7.65 percent to 7.89 percent in 2015.

Under the committee's proposed rule, that provision would be included in the final package if the other two amendments failed on the floor.

Committee Changes

During its speedy two-day markup, the Ways and Means Committee made few changes in the package agreed to by its Social Security Subcommittee Feb. 23.

The committee did, however, agree to revise a controversial provision that would have allowed the Social Security system to borrow from the Treasury in emergency cases.

The change was adopted for the most part to win bipartisan support for the entire package. Republicans had charged that even limited general-revenue borrowing could set a precedent for raiding the Treasury to keep Social Security afloat.

The committee agreed instead to an amendment by Bill Gradison, R-Ohio, that the Social Security trustees would be required to report to Congress if it appeared that any of the system's three trust funds were in danger. Congress could then approve an emergency plan — involving anything from temporary benefit cuts or tax hikes to borrowing from the Treasury — to rebuild trust fund reserves.

The committee also adopted a Kent Hance, D-Texas, amendment to replace a proposed deduction for increased payroll taxes for the self-employed with a new tax credit. The change was made largely to benefit low- and moderate-income taxpayers.

Under the provision, self-employed individuals would be allowed a 2.1 percent credit in 1984 to help offset a 33 percent increase in their payroll taxes called for in the rescue plan. A 1.8 percent credit would be allowed in 1985-87 and a 1.9 percent credit would be allowed each year after 1987.

The committee also agreed to several subcommittee provisions to protect the system from unexpected fluctuations in the economy. These included a measure requiring the annual COLA to reflect the lower of wage or price increases if trust fund reserves fell below a certain level, beginning in 1988. Existing law based the COLA on increases in the price level.

Unemployment Benefits

In another move to win Republican support for the Social Security package, the committee agreed to a proposal by Bill Frenzel, R-Minn., limiting an extension of jobless benefits proposed Feb. 24 by its Subcommittee on Public Assistance and Unemployment Compensation.

The full committee agreed to a six-month extension of the federal emergency jobless benefit program, but cut from 16 to 14 the maximum number of weeks benefits could be paid. The benefits were to be provided in addition to up to 39 weeks of regular state and extended benefits, bringing to 63 the maximum number of weeks a jobless worker could receive payments.

However, the committee agreed to allow up to 65 weeks of benefits for some 1.2 million individuals who were expected to exhaust all existing payments as of April 1. The existing emergency jobless program was to expire March 31.

Frenzel said his plan would cut the cost of the subcommittee's six-month extension by about $200 million. Republicans had complained that the cost of the subcommittee's proposed extension — estimated at $2.6 billion by the Congressional Budget Office and $3.3 billion by the Department of Labor — was too high.

Other Action

The committee also:

● Accepted a $20 increase in monthly SSI benefits for the aged, blind and disabled poor and a six-month delay in the SSI COLA, as recommended by the Subcommittee on Public Assistance and Unemployment Compensation.

● Reversed a Social Security Subcommittee recommendation that the system be kept in the unified budget. The committee agreed instead with the president's commission that the Social Security system's trust funds should be taken out of the federal budget.

● Agreed to cover some 4,000 top political appointees and elected officials, including all sitting federal judges, under Social Security.

● Agreed to round up to $25,000 (for individuals) and $32,000 (for a married couple filing a joint return) the income threshold above which a portion of Social Security benefits would be taxed. The subcommittee had set the threshold at $24,500 and $31,500, respectively.

● Agreed that the income of federal judges under age 70 would be covered by earning restrictions applied to all other Social Security recipients.

● Agreed that interest would have to be paid by the Social Security trust funds on funds advanced to it from the general Treasury at the beginning of each month.

The advances, which were to be made in anticipation of payroll tax revenues to be collected during the month, were recommended by the subcommittee. But Republicans had complained that without the interest requirement, the advances would be little more than interest-free loans from the Treasury.

House Floor Action

The House March 9, by a 282-148 vote, passed a Social Security rescue plan that generally followed the guidelines of the National Commission. But the House also dealt decisively with the system's long-range financial problems — an issue on which the commission could not reach a consensus — by providing for an increase in the retirement age from 65 to 67 by the year 2027. *(Vote 23, p. 10-H)*

Final House passage of HR 1900 did not come without an emotional floor debate over the best way to solve the system's projected financial difficulties in the next century.

Besides an amendment raising the retirement age — offered by Social Security Subcommittee Chairman Pickle — Rules Committee Chairman Pepper proposed a .53 percentage point increase in payroll taxes in the year 2010 to prevent a cut in benefits.

But House members showed during the debate that while they were willing to give Pepper their admiration for his long defense of the elderly, most would not give him their votes. Pepper's measure, despite the backing of House Speaker O'Neill, was rejected by a vote of 132-296. *(Vote 21, p. 10-H)*

"History is being written on this floor. We are changing the tradition of this country," O'Neill said when it became apparent that Pepper's attempts to prevent a retirement age increase would fail. "In America, each generation has always paid for the generation that has gone before them."

Pepper's impassioned plea to his colleagues not to cut benefits won him a standing ovation, but it was not enough to convince most members that the "structural" change of a higher retirement age was the best way to restore the confidence of current workers in the retirement system.

The Pickle amendment was approved by a 228-202 vote, with the backing of 152 Republicans and 76 Democrats, including Ways and Means Chairman Rostenkowski and a majority of committee members. *(Vote 20, p. 10-H)*

The House agreed to raise the retirement age in two stages. The first would be a gradual increase from 65 to 66 over a six-year period ending in the year 2009. The second increase would be from 66 to 67 over another six-year period ending in the year 2027.

While individuals still would be able to take early retirement at age 62, their benefits would be reduced from the current 80 percent of full benefits to 70 percent in 2027.

Opponents seized on this last change and charged it would penalize millions of workers forced to retire early because of poor health or mandatory retirement.

But Pickle defended the age increase as necessary to keep up with changing demographics. He pointed out that life expectancy had increased more than 10 years since the 65-year retirement age was set in place over 40 years earlier.

Raising the retirement age was "not harsh," he said. "That is just in keeping with the times."

Pickle's amendment also required the Department of Health and Human Services to make recommendations by Jan. 1, 1986, on how Congress should deal with individuals who could not retire later because of physically demanding jobs.

Those voting against passage of the bill included both liberals opposed to the higher retirement age and coverage of federal employees and conservatives opposed to additional taxes.

Senate Committee Action

The Senate Finance Committee approved a similar measure the following day by a vote of 18-1, after including long-range funding provisions that dampened much of the conservative opposition to the commission's plan.

The Senate package, reported March 11 (S 1 — S Rept 98-23), included a one-year increase in the retirement age by the year 2015, but it also cut initial retirement benefits 5 percent after the turn of the century.

Committee member Armstrong, one of the most vocal opponents of the commission plan, praised the Finance Committee bill. He observed that quick action in both houses and adoption of the retirement-age increase had proven "the cynics are wrong. There are occasions when Congress will rally to the task and do what is politically hard."

Armstrong and other conservatives had criticized the commission's rescue package because of its reliance on large tax increases, instead of benefit cuts, to keep the system afloat. One critic, Steven D. Symms, R-Idaho, cast the sole dissenting vote in the Finance Committee.

The long-term financing proposal, offered by John Heinz, R-Pa., and adopted 13-4, called for a gradual increase in the retirement age from 65 to 66 over a 15-year period beginning in the year 2000.

It also would have reduced initial benefits by 5 percent beginning the same year. Workers had been receiving an initial Social Security payment equal to about 42 percent of their last paycheck. The package would have reduced this "replacement rate" to 40 percent.

In addition, Heinz' amendment called for elimination — over a five-year period — of a penalty imposed on beneficiaries who worked after they reached retirement age. Benefits were reduced $1 for every $2 retirees up to age 70 earned over $6,600 a year.

The package also would have increased benefits for those leaving the work force to care for their children at home under age six. Under existing law, a worker's five lowest-earning, or non-earning, years were not counted when determining his or her initial Social Security benefit. The committee bill would have allowed two additional "drop-out" years for child care.

The committee rejected 15-2 a proposal by Daniel Patrick Moynihan, D-N.Y., to raise payroll taxes in the year 2010, in place of benefit cuts.

Other Social Security Action

The committee also rejected 6-11 a motion by Russell B. Long, D-La., to delay the effective date of a provision calling for Social Security coverage of new federal employees until a supplemental Civil Service retirement plan could be established.

Members gave assurances that such a supplemental plan would be set up, but federal workers continued to fear that their retirement benefits would be cut if no new work-ers were available to pay into the existing Civil Service Retirement System.

But Finance Committee Chairman Dole charged that a delay in the Jan. 1, 1984, effective date would only give lobbyists a longer time to fight for repeal.

Besides agreeing to the package of long-term provisions, the committee made several other changes in the House-passed package. One of the major ones was a provision to cut beneficiaries' cost-of-living checks, as a last resort, if reserves in the Social Security trust funds fell below a certain level because of unexpectedly bad economic conditions.

The provision was to go into effect in 1985, but was to be used only after all other emergency measures allowed in the bill — including borrowing between the system's three trust funds — had been exhausted.

The bill also would have required the managers of the trust funds to give six-months' notice that such a benefit cut might be necessary so that Congress would have the option to make other adjustments to the system before the COLA cuts went into effect.

The committee also agreed to:

● Include tax-exempt interest when computing a beneficiary's income to determine if his or her Social Security benefits should be taxed.

● Provide a more generous tax credit to offset a proposed 33 percent payroll tax increase for the self-employed. The Finance Committee bill called for a credit against self-employment taxes of 2.9 percent in 1984, 2.5 percent in 1985, 2.2 percent in 1986, 2.1 percent in 1987-89 and 2.3 percent after 1989.

The House bill called for a credit of 2.1 percent in 1984, 1.8 percent in 1985-87 and 1.9 percent after 1987.

● Eliminate Social Security benefits for non-resident aliens, their dependents and survivors, except for payments equal to the amount the alien worker had paid into the system, plus interest.

● Expand Social Security coverage to include all new federal employees, members of Congress, the president and vice president, but not the top political appointees, certain elected officials and sitting federal judges, covered under the House bill.

● Exempt from Social Security coverage members of the Amish religious sect working for Amish employers.

● Allow the three Social Security trust funds to borrow from each other through 1987, as long as no funds were borrowed from the HI trust fund, which financed Medicare, when its reserves were low.

● Eliminate Social Security benefits for imprisoned felons.

Jobless Benefits/SSI

The Finance Committee also agreed to a slightly less generous six-month extension of federal emergency jobless benefits than that adopted by the House.

The Senate measure — expected to cost over $2 billion — provided for up to eight additional weeks of benefits to individuals who exhausted up to 55 weeks of federal and state benefits before April 1. The House bill allowed up to 10 more weeks.

In addition, individuals who did not qualify for the federal emergency benefits until after April 1 were to receive up to 14 weeks of additional benefits depending on their state's jobless rate, under the Finance bill.

Those who did not exhaust their emergency benefits when the extension expired Sept. 30 were to receive up to

50 percent of their remaining payments after the expiration date.

The Senate bill also included a provision to give certain hard-hit states some leeway in repaying interest owed on outstanding loans from the federal unemployment trust fund. States owed about $12 billion to the fund, and many of them saw little chance of being able to repay the loans, or make large interest payments, soon.

Under the plan, states were allowed to spread their interest payments over a five-year period if they could show that they were taking steps to improve the solvency of their state unemployment compensation programs.

The committee also agreed to accept provisions in the House bill to increase monthly SSI benefits $20 and to delay a scheduled SSI COLA six months until January 1985.

Senate Floor Action

The Senate approved the Social Security package March 23, by a vote of 88-9, after brushing aside several attempts to unravel the compromise rescue plan that had sailed through Congress so far. *(Vote 53, p. 11-S)*

"The strength of this package may be the weakness of its parts," Finance Committee Chairman Robert Dole, R-Kan., warned at the start of floor debate March 16. "If during the course of debate one of these should fall by the wayside . . . we probably [would] end up without a compromise and without a Social Security package this year."

Despite the warnings, passage was temporarily threatened March 21 when John Melcher, D-Mont., offered an interest and dividend withholding amendment similar to one that had held up an emergency jobs bill just the week before. *(Withholding, p. 261)*

It took the Senate leadership almost two days to rid the bill of the troublesome amendment — and then only after some muscle flexing by President Reagan.

Melcher's amendment called for a six-month delay in the July 1 effective date of a new law requiring that banks and other financial institutions withhold 10 percent of interest and dividend income for tax purposes.

He said the delay was needed for a "thorough understanding" of the new withholding law, which had provoked a massive letter-writing and repeal campaign.

But a clearly frustrated Dole condemned the Melcher move and threatened to filibuster if the amendment was not withdrawn. Dole reminded members that an agreement had been reached previously to take up the withholding issue on a trade reciprocity measure April 15. He charged the banking lobby with reaching a "new low," adding, "They almost beat the homeless and the jobless and now they're after the senior citizens."

Dole's sharp words and filibuster threats appeared initially to have little impact on his colleagues. A motion by Majority Leader Baker March 21 to table the Melcher amendment lost 37-58. *(Vote 36, p. 9-S)*

The following day, the leadership, along with the White House, took a more forceful stance to get the threatened Social Security package back on track.

After a morning meeting with Republican leaders, Reagan accused the banking lobby of being a "selfish special interest group" and of using "obstructionist tactics."

Baker later stepped up the pressure on the Senate floor by charging in an emotional, and somewhat frustrated, voice that the Melcher amendment would "blow this package apart."

With Vice President Bush presiding in the chair to cast the deciding vote if necessary, the Senate tabled 54-43 a Melcher motion to permit consideration of his amendment even though it violated revenue requirements of the fiscal 1983 budget resolution. Melcher's amendment was then ruled out of order and laid to rest. *(Vote 38, p. 9-S)*

Other Senate Action

But shortly after, another challenge arose to the Social Security plan.

Long, the ranking Democrat on the Finance Committee, proposed an amendment to delay coverage of federal employees under Social Security until a supplemental Civil Service retirement system could be established to provide them with an additional pension, comparable to those offered in private business.

Long's amendment was approved by voice vote, but only after several blocking attempts by the leadership.

Ted Stevens, R-Alaska, charged that the Long amendment would only give federal employees a chance to escape coverage altogether. That loss would cut the value of the rescue plan by $9.3 billion over the next decade, said Dole, who hinted strongly that he would fight the provision in conference if it were passed. The provision was later dropped in conference.

But Long argued it was unfair to expect federal employees to accept the new plan before they knew what supplemental benefits they would receive.

An alternative proposal by Stevens to cover new federal hires under Social Security, but not make them pay into the Civil Service Retirement System until a supplemental plan could be established, Oct. 1, 1985, was rejected 45-50. *(Vote 48, p. 11-S)*

The Senate also:

● Adopted, 96-0, an Armstrong amendment to ease certain payroll tax withholding deposit requirements for small businesses. The change was expected to cost the Social Security trust funds about $1 billion in 1983-89. *(Vote 28, p. 8-S)*

● Accelerated a proposed increase in the bonus benefit that individuals received if they delayed retirement past the age of 65. The bill already had included a provision increasing the existing 3 percent annual delayed retirement credit to 8 percent by the year 2010. The amendment phased in the higher credit by 1995 and removed an existing age limit for receiving the credit, to encourage the elderly to remain in the work force.

● Agreed to a Don Nickles, R-Okla., amendment to deny all Social Security benefits to aliens who worked illegally in the United States. The provision was to apply to those who became eligible for benefits after 1983.

● Agreed to ease interest payment requirements for certain states that owed funds to the federal unemployment trust fund.

● Eliminated all Social Security benefits for the criminally insane.

● Required notices on all Social Security checks that cashing of checks issued to deceased persons would be a felony.

● Allowed the Health and Human Services Department to contract with states for death certificate information to prevent the issuance of checks after a beneficiary's death.

● Allowed clergy members to be considered employees, instead of self-employed, for payroll tax purposes.

● Rejected an Armstrong amendment to delete provisions in the bill calling for higher payroll taxes over the

next decade, by a vote of 27-67. *(Vote 41, p. 10-S)*

● Killed, by a vote of 12-84, an amendment by Steven D. Symms, R-Idaho, that would have increased the retirement age from 65 to 68 over a 36-year period, beginning in 1984. *(Vote 29, p. 8-S)*

Conference Action

House and Senate conferees agreed to the final shape of the bill (H Rept 98-47) during a 12-hour session March 24, as colleagues waited impatiently to leave for the Easter recess.

The primary stumbling block was a difference between the House and Senate on how to solve the system's long-range financial problems. The House measure called for a two-year increase in the retirement age while the Senate bill would have increased the age to 66, cut initial benefit payments 5 percent and eliminated a penalty for retirees earning outside income.

Another major difference was a provision in the Senate bill delaying coverage of new federal employees until a supplemental Civil Service retirement plan could be developed. House conferees charged that if the change were made, the entire Social Security bailout plan could be jeopardized by giving federal workers a chance to escape coverage altogether.

After hours of bargaining, mostly behind closed doors, conferees agreed to the House retirement age change, fearful that any tampering with the sensitive long-term provisions might doom the entire legislative package.

Senate conferees then agreed to recede on federal employee coverage by a vote of 4-3. ∎

Revenue Sharing Extended for Three Years

Congress Nov. 17 gave final approval to a three-year extension of the federal revenue sharing program of aid to local governments.

The measure (HR 2780 — PL 98-185) entitled local governments to $4.6 billion in revenue sharing grants annually in fiscal 1984, 1985 and 1986. The bill was cleared after House conferees yielded to Senate insistence that funding be maintained at the level authorized for fiscal 1980-83. The House had sought a $450 million increase, to $5.02 billion. The Reagan administration had threatened a veto of any bill authorizing an increase.

Revenue sharing was first enacted in 1972 as part of President Nixon's "new federalism." The idea was to transfer money — and thus power — to state and local governments to spend as they pleased. Congress extended the program in 1976 and again in 1980. It lapsed Sept. 30, while Congress was considering a further extension. *(1980 Almanac p. 286)*

Revenue sharing had strong bipartisan support in Congress because it was the only federal aid program that gave localities money they could spend as they saw fit. Since it began, the program had distributed over $60 billion in federal funds to states and localities. States had not participated in the program since 1980.

Local governments used revenue sharing money to pay police and fire personnel, provide health care to residents, buy library books, build and repair highways, support education and for dozens of other purposes.

Final Provisions

As cleared by Congress, HR 2780:

● Extended general revenue sharing grants to local governments for three years, from Oct. 1, 1983, through Sept. 30, 1986.

● Set mandatory, or entitlement, funding for the program at $4.57 billion a year.

● Eliminated the previous authorization allowing state governments to receive revenue sharing funds on a case-by-case basis if specifically appropriated by Congress.

● Permanently extended authority for each state to develop, subject to certain constraints, its own formula for allocating revenue sharing funds to local governments within its borders.

● Provided that a local government whose tax base fell by 20 percent or more due to a plant closing or other economic hardship would not have its revenue sharing allocation cut for at least a year.

● Eliminated the requirement that recipients hold a public hearing on "possible uses" of their revenue sharing funds before holding a hearing on "proposed uses."

● Increased the amount of time a recipient could take to respond to a formal Treasury Department charge that it had used its revenue sharing funds in a discriminatory manner.

● Required governments receiving $100,000 or more a year in revenue sharing to obtain annual independent audits of their use of the funds, or biennial audits in the case of jurisdictions with biennial budgets; required governments receiving from $25,000 to $100,000 a year to obtain an audit once every three years, covering only one of the three years.

● Required the secretary of the Treasury to study various aspects of the revenue sharing program and the formula used to allocate its funding and report to the president and to Congress by June 30, 1985.

● Authorized local governments in Massachusetts to count as taxes collected in 1982 certain taxes actually collected in 1983 to take into account a Massachusetts court ruling that changed the method for valuing property for tax purposes.

House Committee Action

The House Government Operations Committee reported HR 2780 May 16 (H Rept 98-179). As approved by the committee on a 37-2 vote May 11, the bill extended revenue sharing assistance to local governments through fiscal 1988 and increased funding by more than $730 million a year to $5.3 billion.

The House bill also extended a provision in the existing law that was expected to continue excluding states from the program.

By its action, the committee rejected the Reagan administration's request for a three-year reauthorization at the fiscal 1983 level of $4.6 billion.

Committee Democrats joined a number of Republicans in defeating more than a dozen amendments — several

backed by the administration — leaving virtually intact the bill approved April 20 by the committee's Subcommittee on Intergovernmental Relations. The full panel met May 10-11.

Subcommittee Chairman Ted Weiss, D-N.Y., argued that the "modest" funding increase was needed to make up for inflationary erosion of the federal aid program since it began in 1972. The budget resolution passed by the House March 23 allowed for $5.35 billion for the program in fiscal 1984.

Weiss added that the five-year authorization would provide needed stability for local government planners. "This is a very modest, very responsible piece of legislation," he said.

But ranking Republican Frank Horton, N.Y., warned that the five-year authorization could cause trouble for the legislation when it was sent to the president's desk.

The administration earlier in the year opposed any multi-year extension of revenue sharing unless it was consolidated into a new block grant program proposed as part of the administration's New Federalism initiative.

But Treasury Secretary Donald T. Regan admitted in a May 7 letter to Horton that "immediate congressional action on the initiative is not likely," and said a simple, three-year extension would be acceptable.

Not included in the bill was a plan by Weiss to allow state and local governments an additional $1.25 billion a year in so-called "countercyclical" aid.

The subcommittee chairman originally had planned to offer the anti-recession measure — which would target aid to areas hardest hit by the economic downturn — as an amendment to the revenue sharing bill but said he did not want to "endanger" its passage.

No Speedup. Several attempts to liberalize the existing program were defeated by the committee.

A proposal by Barney Frank, D-Mass., to move up the quarterly payments made to local governments from the end of the quarter to the beginning, was defeated by a 19-19 tie vote. Frank argued that the accelerated payments — amounting to a one-time boost of $1.15 billion in fiscal 1983 — were needed to help local governments recover from the recession.

But a number of Republicans, backed by Committee Chairman Jack Brooks, D-Texas, a longtime foe of revenue sharing, argued that the speedup would only add to the federal deficit. "There is no revenue to share," said Brooks, who contended that local governments had become "hooked" on the no-strings aid, draining federal coffers.

A similar speedup provision had been attached to a Senate-passed jobs bill (HR 1718) in March but was dropped in conference because of veto threats from President Reagan. *(Jobs supplemental, p. 447)*

Also defeated by the committee was a proposal by Lyle Williams, R-Ohio, to allocate $350 million of the annual revenue sharing increase to counties with an unemployment rate of 15 percent or more.

Horton argued that the targeting provision would "do violence" to the revenue sharing program, which under existing law allocated payments to local governments according to size, per capita income and tax-raising effort.

Several attempts to revamp the funding formula also were defeated. Instead, the committee agreed to a Weiss amendment to require a Treasury Department study on improving the complex formula.

State Participation. Although the committee agreed to allow an additional $2.3 billion a year through fiscal 1988 for state revenue sharing grants, it retained an existing requirement that the grants be appropriated, making prospects for such funding slim.

Prior to 1980, states automatically received revenue sharing funds as localities continued to do. But since Congress began to require appropriations for state funding in 1980, no appropriations had been made.

However, the committee did eliminate one restriction to state involvement. It agreed with the subcommittee's recommendation to remove a requirement that, if such appropriations were made, states selecting revenue sharing money accept a dollar-for-dollar cut in other federal aid.

A move by Elliott H. Levitas, D-Ga., the original author of the provision, to retain the trade-off requirement was rejected by a vote of 14-22.

Weiss argued that without the Levitas provision, states would at least have "a chance to persuade" the Appropriations Committees to provide additional funds.

The committee also defeated:

● A Horton amendment to limit the reauthorization to three years, by a vote of 16-21.

● An amendment by Al McCandless, R-Calif., to keep funding at its current level, by a vote of 12-27.

● A move by Robert S. Walker, R-Pa., to make the $731 million in new funding contingent on a 5 percent or more annual increase in the gross national product, also 12-27.

● A Horton amendment to allow Puerto Rico and other U.S. territories to participate in the program along with some 39,000 local governments, by a vote of 14-21. The measure was originally adopted 19-18, but the vote was then reconsidered.

Senate Committee Action

The Senate Finance Committee reported a three-year revenue sharing extension July 20 (S 1426 — S Rept 98-189). The panel approved the bill by a 17-0 vote June 29.

In an unusual formulation adopted by unusual procedures, the committee approved changes in the formula for allocating revenue sharing monies, but said they would take effect only if House members in a conference on the measure insisted on increasing the size of the program. The Finance bill provided for a simple three-year reauthorization of the existing revenue sharing program if funding was not increased.

Chairman Robert Dole, R-Kan., permitted absent members to vote on the formula reform amendment after the committee had ordered the bill reported — and let those votes count. Committees customarily let members register late votes in such cases but provided that they could not change the outcome.

The reform plan, sponsored by Dave Durenberger, R-Minn., originally had failed by an 8-10 vote during the panel's markup of S 1426 on the afternoon of June 29. The reversal of that vote was announced the next morning.

Durenberger Plan. The formula reform plan consisted of four provisions contained in a broader measure (S 700) that Durenberger had introduced earlier in the year.

To make his proposal more palatable, Durenberger dropped provisions in S 700 that would establish a revenue sharing trust fund consisting of 4 percent of annual federal income tax receipts and would limit the deductibility on federal income tax returns of state and local taxes.

The proposals adopted by the Finance Committee basically would give certain local governments an increase in their revenue sharing funds by removing what Durenberger

called inequities in the existing formula.

As approved by the committee, S 1426 also contained a "hold harmless" provision assuring that no government receiving federal revenue sharing funds would have its allocation reduced if the formula were changed.

House Floor Action

The House passed HR 2780 Aug. 2 by a 381-35 vote. *(Vote 296, p. 88-H)*

As passed by the House, the bill reauthorized general revenue sharing for only three years, rather than the five the Government Operations Committee proposed. And to comply with the fiscal 1984 budget resolution, the House cut funding to $5.02 billion a year from the $5.3 billion approved by the committee. The House-approved figure was still $1.35 billion above the level acceptable to President Reagan.

In a departure from past practice, the House also voted to drop state governments from the program entirely, a move to make official the actual fact since 1980.

Funding. The House readily adopted, 381-43, an amendment by Frank Horton (R-N.Y.) to cut the funding to the $5.02 billion per year level permissible under the budget resolution. *(Vote 292, p. 88-H)*

In its debate on HR 2780, the House was warned several times that, as Horton, the ranking Republican on the Government Operations Committee, put it, "too much money is in this bill, and we are courting a presidential veto."

But members balked when McCandless proposed cutting the funding to Reagan's proposed $4.6 billion. The House rejected that amendment by a vote of 176-248. *(Vote 291, p. 86-H)*

Three Years. More reluctantly than it accepted the amendment to make the bill's funding comply with the budget resolution, the House also adopted, 226-202, a Horton amendment to hold the reauthorization to three years. *(Vote 290, p. 86-H)*

Weiss argued for retaining the five-year authorization, saying it would "institutionalize" the program and help local governments plan more efficiently.

Walker took Weiss' side — but for a very different motive. He said the virtue of a five-year authorization was that it would keep Congress from adding funds to the program for that much longer.

States Dropped. The closest vote of the day came on an amendment by McCandless to eliminate a $2.3 billion per year authorization for state governments in HR 2780. The amendment was adopted by a vote of 218-193. *(Vote 294, p. 88-H)*

"Frankly, I see no reason to continue the charade," McCandless said. "Revenue sharing funds for the states have not been appropriated since 1980, and I honestly doubt that our budget will allow appropriation in the next three years. Let us be honest with the governors and state legislators and tell them there will be no state share by entitlement or through the appropriations process."

Weiss argued that no state had requested an appropriation for revenue sharing since 1980 because of the stricture requiring it to pay back other funds if it did. And he noted that while many states had budget surpluses in 1980, many were suffering deficits in 1983.

"All we [the Government Operations Committee] are saying is that there should be an authorization so that if the Appropriations Committee at the appropriate time decides that there are good and valid reasons to provide funding, in fact it would be permissible to do so," Weiss said.

Formula. The House spurned attempts to change the formula for allocating revenue sharing, which currently gave more money to areas with large populations, low per capita incomes and high levels of tax effort.

First the House rejected, 154-259, an amendment by Lyle Williams, R-Ohio, to divide the increase over the existing $4.6 billion authorization among localities in counties where unemployment equaled or exceeded the national rate in the prior year. *(Vote 293, p. 88-H)*

Later the House rejected by a much closer 192-220 vote two amendments by Sander M. Levin, D-Mich., that would have changed the allocation formula by replacing personal income as the standard used to gauge a state's capacity to raise taxes and its "tax effort" with the "Representative Tax System" measure, which considered all potential revenues. *(Vote 295, p. 88-H)*

The Levin amendments — considered *en bloc*, or as one — would have put a 10 percent cap on the increase in funds given to localities in any given state as a result of the proposed change in the formula.

But Brooks said the proposal needed further study, Bill Richardson, D-N.M., complained that it would reduce funding under the program for 11 of 13 Western states, and Weiss said he feared the change would disrupt the political coalition that supported revenue sharing.

Other Amendments. The House adopted by voice vote an amendment by Brooks to retain a special authorization for sheriffs in Louisiana to receive revenue sharing funds even though they did not meet the eligibility requirement as a general purpose local government.

In previous revenue sharing reauthorizations, Louisiana sheriffs had been granted a special authorization at the behest of Sen. Russell B. Long, D-La., who chaired the Senate Finance Committee until 1981 and thus exercised profound influence in House-Senate conferences on the issue.

The House previously had deleted the authorization from the bills but, as Weiss said during the debate, with Long leading Senate conferees on the issue, "the basis for the adoption of revenue sharing was the inclusion of Louisiana sheriffs."

Noting that history, Brooks said the House "ought to spare ourselves the futile exercise of deleting Louisiana sheriffs." Weiss argued that the House should reject the amendment on principle.

Members rejected by voice vote an amendment by Walker to permit revenue sharing recipients to apply for a waiver of the Davis-Bacon Act, which required that the prevailing local wage be paid on federally funded projects.

Senate Floor Action

The Senate passed HR 2780 Sept. 21, after substituting its $4.6 billion-a-year reauthorization for fiscal 1984-86 and rejecting moves to increase funding for the program. The vote on the bill was 87-6. *(Vote 252, p. 42-S)*

In a mild-mannered debate lasting a mere two hours, the Senate also dropped an unusual Finance Committee provision designed to force a House-Senate conference to hold the spending line.

The provision would have required changes in the formula for allocating revenue sharing funds among local governments if House conferees insisted on an increase.

Funding. The Senate signaled it would comply with Reagan's spending limit when it rejected, 30-64, the amendment by Daniel Patrick Moynihan, D-N.Y., to increase funding to the $5 billion House level. *(Vote 250, p. 42-S)*

Moynihan argued, as he had in the Finance Committee, that an increase was fair inasmuch as the real (inflation-adjusted) value of revenue sharing funds had declined 40 percent since 1976. Recipients, he said, had lost far more spending power than his $450 million-a-year increase would grant.

The Senate proved only slightly more sympathetic when Bill Bradley, D-N.J., proposed to boost the program by $225 million a year. His amendment failed, 36-58. *(Vote 251, p. 42-S)*

Formula. The provision to change the allocation formula if the House insisted on putting more money into the program was deleted at the behest of Long, the Finance Committee's ranking minority member.

Noting that the House had voted a 10 percent increase in funding and that conferees generally split the difference between disparate funding levels, Long warned that the formula change was likely to be triggered by the conference on HR 2780.

If that happened, he said, most counties and cities would get no increase, while larger cities — he cited New Orleans in his state — would get most of the extra money.

Durenberger, who had sponsored the formula change plan in committee, said he did not object to dropping the plan. Long's amendment was adopted by voice vote.

Davis-Bacon Act. The only tension in the debate came when Gordon J. Humphrey, R-N.H., offered an amendment to exempt revenue sharing projects from the Davis-Bacon Act, which required that the prevailing local wage be paid on federal construction projects.

After asking for a roll-call vote, Humphrey withdrew the amendment at Dole's request when Democrats hinted they might filibuster.

Other Amendments. The Senate also adopted by voice vote the following amendments:

• By John Heinz, R-Pa., to provide that a local government whose tax base was reduced by 20 percent or more due to a plant closing or other economic hardship would not have its revenue sharing cut for at least a year.

• By Durenberger, to authorize a series of studies of federal-state relations by a group including the secretaries of Treasury and commerce, the comptroller general, the Advisory Commission on Intergovernmental Relations and state officials.

Conference, Final Action

Told Nov. 9 that they could take or leave a Senate offer of $4.6 billion a year for revenue sharing in fiscal 1984-86 but would get no part of a House-passed $450 million-a-year increase, House conferees decided Nov. 11 to take it.

In refusing to negotiate a boost in the funding level, Senate conferees, all members of the Finance Committee, had warned that Senate pressure to cut the federal budget deficit was so severe that they could accept no more than the $4.6 billion acceptable to President Reagan.

Minutes after the conference broke up, House conferees seeking the increase had caucused and decided to hold their ground. Brooks, leader of the House conferees, said they ceded their turf two days later.

Brooks said he gave his House colleagues the ensuing Nov. 12-13 weekend to "be sure" that was what they wanted to do — giving representatives of cities and counties a chance to pressure the House conferees to give in.

Brooks said he understood that the other House conferees had indeed "heard from" revenue sharing recipients over the weekend.

On Monday, Nov. 14, he said, all conferees signed the conference report providing $4.6 billion a year. The report was filed the following day (H Rept 98-550).

The House Nov. 17 adopted the conference report on the bill by voice vote. The Senate adopted the report later that day, also by voice vote, clearing the measure for the president's signature. ∎

Economic Development

For the second year in a row, legislation to reauthorize the Economic Development Administration (EDA) bogged down in Congress. EDA operated programs to encourage economic growth in many areas of the country.

The House July 12 voted to extend EDA through fiscal 1986, as part of a broader bill (HR 10) that also extended the Appalachian Regional Commission (ARC), which fostered anti-poverty programs and highways in 13 states.

But in the Senate, a substantially different economic development measure (S 724) reported by the Environment and Public Works Committee did not reach the floor before adjournment. The Senate bill also authorized funding for youth jobs programs, including a proposed American Conservation Corps (ACC) that was patterned after the Depression-era Civilian Conservation Corps (CCC). The House approved the ACC proposal in separate legislation (HR 999). *(Youth conservation jobs, box, next page)*

All of the bills remained alive for further action in the second session of the 98th Congress in 1984.

EDA Under Fire

The Reagan administration had tried since taking office to abolish EDA, which it claimed funded wasteful "pork barrel" projects. Legal authority for the agency had expired Sept. 30, 1982, but Congress nonetheless provided funds to keep it operating. The fiscal 1984 Commerce Department appropriations bill (HR 3222 — PL 98-166), cleared Nov. 16, included $240 million for programs operated by EDA. *(Story, p. 472)*

Critics complained that EDA programs no longer focused on poor communities that needed help priming their economies because Congress had expanded eligibility to encompass most of the country.

House Democrats tried to reform the program in 1982, but their bill died in the face of Senate opposition. The measure would have restricted eligibility for economic development grants to areas with high unemployment or low incomes. *(Background, 1982 Almanac p. 62)*

House Action

Brushing aside Reagan administration and conservative Republican opposition, the House passed HR 10, the National Development Investment Act, by a 306-113 vote July 12. *(Vote 228, p. 70-H)*

HR 10 had been reported April 12 by a 50-0 vote of the Public Works and Transportation Committee (H Rept 98-

Youth Conservation Jobs

The House March 1 passed a bill (HR 999) to establish an American Conservation Corps (ACC) to provide jobs for unemployed and disadvantaged young people on public and Indian lands. The vote was 301-87. *(Vote 8, p. 8-H)*

The Reagan administration opposed the ACC program, which was patterned on the Depression-era Civilian Conservation Corps. The House had passed a similar measure in 1982. *(1982 Almanac p. 505)*

The bill was reported by the Interior Committee Feb. 17 and the Education and Labor Committee March 1 (H Rept 98-7, Parts I and II).

As passed by the House, HR 999 authorized $50 million in fiscal 1983 and $250 million annually in fiscal 1984-89 for the federal program, plus an additional $10 million in 1983 and $50 million annually in 1984-89 for state programs. Funding would come partly from fees for federal permits and leases.

The Senate Energy Committee reported a scaled-down version of HR 999 May 20 (S Rept 98-140), cutting the authorization to $50 million in fiscal 1984, $75 million in fiscal 1985 and $100 million in fiscal 1986. Meanwhile, the Senate Environment and Public Works Committee included a more ambitious youth jobs program in broad economic development legislation reported May 16. Neither bill reached the Senate floor in 1983. *(Economic development, p. 229)*

52, Part 1) and May 16 by voice vote of the Banking, Finance and Urban Affairs Committee (H Rept 98-52, Part 2).

In addition to extending EDA and the Appalachian commission, HR 10 substantially increased funding for both programs: up some $300 million per year for the EDA and, for the ARC, up $100 million in fiscal 1984 from fiscal 1983.

EDA. The bill authorized $500 million annually in fiscal years 1984-86 for EDA grants to governments and other local entities to foster economic development by improving infrastructure — roads, bridges, ports and the like — and by making loans to salvage or start small businesses.

In an attempt to satisfy critics, the bill tightened EDA eligibility standards and required public and private sources on the local level to match the EDA's grants dollar for dollar.

As passed by the House, HR 10 provided for grants of up to $2 million per applicant to distressed communities — those with either an unemployment rate one percentage point above the national average for two successive years or per capita income 80 percent or less of the national average. Areas threatened by the closing of a major plant or some other extensive job loss also would be eligible.

ARC. HR 10 gave the 17-year-old ARC eight more years to finish programs designed to encourage development in economically backward, mountain regions of 13 states. It authorized ARC non-highway programs, which the Reagan administration wanted to drop, at levels of $83 million in fiscal 1984 and 1985, $79 million in 1986 and 1987 and $75 million in 1988. For ARC highway construction, the bill authorized $215 million in fiscal 1984 and $2 billion more stretched over fiscal 1985-91.

Amendments

Before passing HR 10 July 12, the House rejected two amendments offered by Robert S. Walker, R-Pa.

Walker first attempted to amend the bill to implicitly require the secretary of commerce to study whether the Davis-Bacon Act, which required that the local "prevailing wage" be paid on most federal projects, reduced job opportunities. That amendment was rejected 170-245. *(Vote 226, p. 70-H)*

The second Walker amendment, rejected 148-270, would have allowed the secretary of commerce, on application from an EDA grant recipient, to exempt contractors on EDA projects from the requirements of the Davis-Bacon Act if the exemption would increase employment in the area. *(Vote 227, p. 70-H)*

The House adopted by voice vote amendments by the Banking Committee to:

● Bar EDA aid for projects that would relocate industrial or commercial plants, unless such moves would not harm the local economy.

● Authorize $2 million for a study to assess the need for repairs to non-federal infrastructure items — roads, bridges, waterways — essential to economic development.

● Define Indian tribes eligible for aid to include those recognized by states but not by the U.S. Interior Department.

Senate Committee Action

The Senate Environment and Public Works Committee reported S 724 May 16 (S Rept 98-94). The committee authorized $225 million a year for economic development programs as part of a five-year, $4.2 billion bill that also authorized funds for youth jobs programs and historic preservation.

The bill approved by the committee was sharply reduced from the original version of S 724 sponsored by Chairman Robert T. Stafford, R-Vt., and Jennings Randolph, D-W.Va. Even so, S 724 was opposed by most Republicans on the panel.

The vote to report the bill was 9-5. Stafford and Dave Durenberger, Minn., were the only Republicans voting for it.

Economic Development

The Environment Committee had repeatedly voted against EDA funding during the 97th Congress. Stafford and Randolph were able to win committee approval for a successor to EDA in 1983, however, by changing the program and making it smaller.

The new program set up by S 724 would have the same basic goals and methods as the EDA programs, funding a variety of projects aimed at encouraging economic growth. But assistance under the bill would be available only to rural areas and towns with populations of less than 50,000. The new program would be placed under the Army Corps of Engineers instead of under the Commerce Department, which was EDA's overseer. But staff to run the program would be transferred from EDA.

In minority views to the committee report, Alan K. Simpson, R-Wyo., said S 724 marked a return to "those old, worn and tattered ways of legislating and spending — throwing those federal bucks at a problem."

Youth Jobs, Preservation

The Youth Community Conservation and Improve-

ment Program set up by S 724 would concentrate on urban areas. Run by the Department of Health and Human Services, the program would provide grants to non-profit community organizations, which would undertake projects such as rat control, park restoration and removal of architectural barriers.

The other program, the American Conservation Corps (ACC), was designed to replace the Youth Conservation Corps and Young Adult Conservation Corps, which were effectively dismantled by the 1981 budget reconciliation law. *(1981 Almanac p. 108)*

The ACC, to be run by the Interior Department, would provide residential camps in which young people could work on conservation projects on public lands and forests.

S 724 authorized an annual total of $600 million to be divided between the two programs.

The bill also authorized a total of $85 million for historic preservation projects.   ∎

Congress Evades Deficit Reduction Mandate

The 1983 congressional debate over the federal deficit ended with a whimper.

After months of decrying the evils of threatened $200 billion deficits "as far as the eye can see," lawmakers Nov. 18 raised the public debt limit to provide a $101 billion increase in government borrowing authority and then adjourned for the year without meeting their own mandate to approve $85.3 billion in deficit reduction measures over fiscal 1984-86. *(Debt limit, p. 239)*

Defeated, or left in limbo, was every major deficit reduction designed to put Congress in compliance with its own fiscal 1984 budget resolution, adopted in June. It was the first time since passage of the 1974 Congressional Budget Act (PL 93-344) that Congress failed to enact any of the deficit reduction measures required by reconciliation instructions incorporated in its budget resolutions. By adjourning without having met its reconciliation obligations, Congress disregarded one of the key budget control provisions of the 1974 act. *(1974 Almanac p. 145)*

Highlights of action in the closing days of the session:

● The House defeated, 204-214, the rule for floor debate on an $8 billion tax increase bill (HR 4170) drafted by the Ways and Means Committee. Ways and Means Chairman Dan Rostenkowski, D-Ill., said "private interests" had defeated the bill.

"As we leave Washington, word of our impotence will precede us . . .," he said. "We have confessed to an already doubting nation that we are ruled by political fear rather than economic courage."

● The Senate suspended action on a $28 billion reconciliation package (S 2062), containing $14.6 billion in spending cuts and $13.4 billion in tax increases, after the House refused even to consider the Ways and Means tax bill. The House had approved a $10.3 billion spending cut package (HR 4169) in October.

● The Senate turned aside an attempt by Budget Committee Chairman Pete V. Domenici, R-N.M., and ranking Budget Committee Democrat Lawton Chiles, Fla., to increase the reconciliation bill's deficit reductions to $87.6 billion.

● The Senate also rebuffed an effort by William L. Armstrong, R-Colo., and Russell B. Long, D-La., to give the president sweeping authority to impound — refuse to spend — federal funds if Congress did not live up to its own budget guidelines. The amendment was tabled 49-46.

Armstrong argued that the enhanced presidential powers would "get us somewhere back on the track on controlling expenditures." *(Expenditure control, box, p. 238)*

● A $150 billion tax increase/spending cut deficit reduction plan put together by Finance Committee Chairman Robert Dole, R-Kan., remained dead in the water after several weeks of negotiations and repeated rejections from the White House. Dole held three days of hearings on deficit reduction after Congress adjourned, but he put off further committee markups until 1984.

Members cited a long list of scapegoats for their deficit-cutting failures. Republicans blamed Democrats. Democrats blamed Republicans. House Speaker Thomas P. O'Neill Jr., D-Mass., and President Reagan were repeatedly faulted for not leading the assault on the deficit.

The president and his chief economic spokesman, Treasury Secretary Donald T. Regan, downplayed the significance of the deficits and their impact on the recovery throughout the year.

A few members joined Rostenkowski in laying the blame on Congress itself. "We are in a catatonic state. . . . We are immobile. . . . We are unable to act," said Republican Sen. John C. Danforth, Mo.

"The basic problem is one of political decision making," Armstrong said. "There is a lot of lip service paid to the deficit, but not much action."

Still others, chief among them Dole, remained optimistic that Congress would face up to the deficit crisis in 1984. "We haven't succeeded," Dole said. "But we haven't failed." *(Deficits, box, p. 232)*

Background

The fiscal 1984 budget resolution (H Con Res 91), cleared June 23, projected deficits of up to $208.5 billion in fiscal 1983, $179.3 billion in fiscal 1984, $161.1 billion in fiscal 1985 and $130.8 billion in fiscal 1986. To hold the deficits to these levels, the resolution included reconciliation instructions calling for a total of $85.3 billion in spending cuts and tax increases over fiscal 1984-86. *(Budget resolution, p. 435)*

The reconciliation instructions directed four Senate committees and seven House committees to cut existing programs to achieve outlay savings of $2.8 billion in fiscal 1984 and $12.3 billion in fiscal 1984-86. In addition, the Ways and Means and Finance committees were directed to come up with $73 billion in new revenues over the three-year period.

Legislation fulfilling these reconciliation requirements was to be reported back to the House and Senate Budget committees by July 22. That deadline subsequently was extended several times.

House committees required to fulfill reconciliation savings were Armed Services, Energy and Commerce, Foreign Affairs, Post Office and Civil Service, Small Business, Veterans' Affairs and Ways and Means.

Senate committees affected by reconciliation were Fi-

60 Years of Budgets: The Road to $200 Billion Deficits

(in millions of dollars)

Fiscal year*	Budget receipts	Budget outlays	Surplus or deficit (−)	Fiscal year	Budget receipts	Budget outlays	Surplus or deficit (−)
1924	3,871	2,908	+963	1954	69,719	70,890	−1,170
1925	3,641	2,924	+717	1955	65,469	68,509	−3,041
1926	3,795	2,930	+865	1956	74,547	70,460	+4,087
1927	4,013	2,857	+1,155	1957	79,990	76,741	+3,249
1928	3,900	2,961	+939	1958	79,636	82,575	−2,939
1929	3,862	3,127	+734	1959	79,249	92,104	−12,855
1930	4,058	3,320	+738	1960	92,492	92,223	+269
1931	3,116	3,577	−462	1961	94,389	97,795	−3,406
1932	1,924	4,659	−2,735	1962	99,676	106,813	−7,137
1933	1,997	4,598	−2,602	1963	106,560	111,311	−4,751
1934	3,015	6,645	−3,630	1964	112,662	118,584	−5,922
1935	3,706	6,497	−2,791	1965	116,833	118,430	−1,596
1936	3,997	8,442	−4,425	1966	130,856	134,652	−3,796
1937	4,956	7,733	−2,777	1967	148,906	157,608	−8,702
1938	5,588	6,765	−1,177	1968	152,973	178,134	−25,161
1939	4,979	8,841	−3,862	1969	186,882	183,645	+3,236
1940	6,361	9,456	−3,095	1970	192,807	195,652	−2,845
1941	8,621	13,634	−5,013	1971	187,139	210,172	−23,033
1942	14,350	35,114	−20,764	1972	207,309	230,681	−23,373
1943	23,649	78,533	−54,884	1973	230,799	245,647	−14,849
1944	44,276	91,280	−47,004	1974	263,224	267,912	−4,688
1945	45,216	92,690	−47,474	1975	279,090	324,245	−45,154
1946	39,327	55,183	−15,856	1976	298,060	364,473	−66,413
1947	38,394	34,532	+3,862	1977	355,559	400,506	−44,948
1948	41,774	29,773	+12,001	1978	399,561	448,368	−48,807
1949	39,437	38,834	+603	1979	463,302	490,997	−27,694
1950	39,485	42,597	−3,112	1980	517,112	576,675	−59,563
1951	51,646	45,546	+6,100	1981	599,272	657,204	−57,932
1952	66,204	67,721	−1,517	1982	617,766	728,375	−110,609
1953†	69,574	76,107	−6,533	1983	600,562	795,969	−195,407†

*Data prior to 1940 are for the administrative budget.   † Final figures are from fiscal 1985 budget.

SOURCE: Fiscal 1984 Budget

nance, Governmental Affairs, Small Business and Veterans' Affairs.

A provisional instruction was set out for the House and Senate Agriculture committees that would require savings in dairy price supports if the courts found existing milk production charges were unconstitutional. The production charges subsequently were upheld in court.

Energy and Commerce, Ways and Means and Finance were required to find savings in the Medicare program. The Small Business committees were called on to make reductions in disaster loans. Savings from the remaining committees were assumed to come from a six-month delay in cost-of-living adjustments for the full range of federal retirement programs and a three-month delay in an assumed 4 percent pay raise for federal employees.

Committees were to forward their recommendations to the Senate and House Budget committees for incorporation in omnibus reconciliation measures.

While most reconciliation cuts easily won committee approval, the Medicare savings proved controversial. And the Finance and Ways and Means committees showed no

stomach for approving $73 billion in three-year revenue increases in the face of President Reagan's vow to veto any tax increase measure.

Deficit Fever

Deficit reduction efforts remained on the back burner for several months following adoption of the budget resolution, as Congress' preoccupation with foreign affairs overshadowed its concern for domestic issues.

Meanwhile, the economy's recovery from the 1981-82 recession exceeded earlier forecasts, causing short-term deficit projections to decline. Many economists nonetheless warned that tax increases and spending cuts were necessary to keep the recovery going. The Congressional Budget Office said Aug. 20 that failure to enact the reconciliation measures required by the budget resolution would result in budget deficits "on the order of $200 billion for years to come."

By autumn, pressure began building for meaningful action to cut the fiscal 1984-86 deficits. "We must stick with the budget, or we will see the economic recovery go

down the drain," the ranking Democrat on the Senate Budget Committee, Lawton Chiles, D-Fla., warned Sept. 20.

Republicans in both chambers spoke of giving the president new powers to control spending if Congress failed to meet its deficit reduction goals.

House Democrats, pressured by their freshman members, caucused Sept. 22 and agreed that deficit reduction was imperative, although there was no consensus on how to proceed. Democratic leaders feared the political consequences of getting out front on the tax issue. Ways and Means Chairman Rostenkowski insisted it was futile to try to raise taxes without the cooperation and support of the White House.

However, Rostenkowski, along with ranking Ways and Means Republican Barber B. Conable Jr., N.Y., agreed there were a number of tax reform issues with minor revenue impact — such as codifying tax-free fringe benefits and setting new tax rules for the life insurance industry — that should be addressed in 1983. A tax package that included these changes later became the vehicle for what some Democrats hoped would be more ambitious tax increases.

Rostenkowski's restrained approach was, in part, a reaction to the president's oft-repeated remarks that he would not lend his support to any deficit reduction effort that involved tax increases.

"Let them [members of Congress] keep their hands off the recovery and start doing what they were elected to do — get spending under control once and for all," Reagan said in a speech to former campaign workers Nov. 3. "We do not face large deficits because Americans aren't taxed enough. We face those deficits because Congress still spends too much."

House Spending Cuts Passed

As the stalemate over tax increases dragged on, the House Oct. 25 took one step toward deficit reduction when it gave voice vote approval to a reconciliation bill (HR 4169 — H Rept 98-425) that would reduce spending $10.3 billion over fiscal 1984-86.

The bill was reported Oct. 20 by the Budget Committee, which had packaged the spending cuts of various authorizing committees in a single piece of legislation. It did not include Medicare savings that the Ways and Means Committee was considering in conjunction with tax increase measures.

The bulk of the savings in HR 4169 would come from delaying cost-of-living adjustments (COLAs) for federal retirees' benefits and veterans' compensation, limiting the planned federal civilian pay raise to 4 percent and delaying that pay raise from Oct. 1, 1983, until Jan. 1, 1984.

The reconciliation measure also contained a provision, drafted by Budget Committee Chairman James R. Jones, D-Okla., directing the president to convene an "economic summit" meeting to devise a comprehensive plan for reducing federal deficits. Participants would include the president, the House Speaker, the Senate president pro tempore, the majority and minority leaders of the House and Senate, and others from Congress and the executive branch.

Program Savings

Following are the major provisions of the House-passed reconciliation bill. All savings are three-year totals.

Federal Pay Raise (Savings: $6.2 billion). The bill would set the planned federal civilian pay raise at 4 percent and delay its payment until Jan. 1, 1984. The 4 percent cap would save $4.4 billion over fiscal 1984-86; the three-month delay, $1.8 billion. *(Federal pay, p. 576)*

The Post Office and Civil Service Committee had refused to comply with reconciliation instructions to postpone the raise, thus falling $1.8 billion short of its three-year savings requirement. The full House approved a Budget Committee amendment to impose the delay on a 245-176 vote. *(Vote 390, p. 116-H)*

Federal COLAs ($2.18 billion). Starting in 1985, the bill would delay all civil service retirement and disability COLAs until January. COLA increases currently were scattered throughout the year. The COLA change would also affect military, foreign service, Coast Guard and public health retirement systems, which were linked to civil service retirement under existing law.

Veterans' Compensation ($660 million). The bill would delay for six months, until April 1, 1984, the payment of veterans' compensation COLAs.

Small Business Disaster Loans ($1.24 billion). The bill would extend for three years, until Sept. 30, 1986, a requirement that farmers seek disaster loans from the Farmers Home Administration before they could seek more favorable loans from the Small Business Administration.

Farm-related small businesses could take part in the disaster loan program if they were damaged by the Payment-in-Kind (PIK) farm acreage reduction program. *(PIK, p. 380)*

'Puny' Package

Republicans and disenchanted Democrats labeled the spending reduction package "anemic," "puny," "feeble," "a token effort" and a "small drop in the bucket."

Leon E. Panetta, D-Calif., agreed that the package was "not enough," but "this is the only game in town. It is here and now. This is a package that can reduce deficits, it can take them below those of the president. . . ."

The bill was brought to the floor under a rule that permitted only the Budget Committee amendment to delay the federal pay raise. The House adopted the rule on a 224-198 vote, thus barring George Miller, D-Calif., from offering his "pay-as-you-go" budget plan as an amendment to the bill. *(Vote 389, p. 116-H)*

Miller's budget plan would have frozen discretionary spending at fiscal 1984 levels. Any increases in spending thereafter would have to be offset by increasing revenues or cutting spending elsewhere.

Miller was backed by many of the freshman Democrats, who had adamantly urged the House to cut federal deficits.

House Tax Increases Reported

Despite Democratic reluctance to take the lead on taxes, the Ways and Means Committee approved over a period of months several bills dealing with expiring legislation and other urgent items. These measures — plus controversial Medicare savings and changes in the Social Security disability program — were reported as a package Oct. 21 (HR 4170 — H Rept 98-432). Their total revenue yield was estimated at about $8 billion over fiscal 1984-86, far below the $73 billion reconciliation requirement.

The package incorporated the following measures:

Leasing

The Ways and Means Committee approved a bill (HR 3110) July 27 to limit the use of leasing plans by tax-exempt organizations and governments that transferred tax breaks they could not use to private investors.

Chief sponsor J. J. Pickle, D-Texas, said the legislation would "stop one of the most unusual, ingenious and costly tax shelters that we've seen in years."

Although these so-called "sale/lease-backs" had been available to non-profit organizations for many years, their use had escalated since approval of the 1981 tax-cut law (PL 97-34), with its more generous depreciation and investment tax credit provisions. Conservative estimates showed that the federal government could lose $15 billion in revenues over the next five years from use of the device. *(PL 97-34, 1981 Almanac p. 91)*

Interest in the bill was so great that Ways and Means voted unanimously to meet in private, executive session to draft the legislation rather than tackle the politically difficult job in view of hundreds of lobbyists.

The bill that emerged was developed with the advice and approval of the Treasury Department. Staff estimates showed these reforms yielding $3.4 billion in additional revenues over fiscal 1984-86.

The Lease-Back Caper. Since they paid no taxes, non-profit organizations and governments were not entitled to tax benefits such as accelerated depreciation allowances and the investment tax credit.

Accelerated depreciation allowed an investor who was writing off the cost of equipment or real estate, for tax purposes, to receive larger deductions in the early years and smaller deductions later on. The investment credit provided a 10 percent tax credit for investments in certain machinery and equipment.

By using the lease-back arrangement, a tax-exempt entity could sell or lease its assets, most often buildings, to private investors and then lease the assets back for its own use.

The tax benefits — depreciation allowances and investment tax credits that could not be used by the non-profit organization — were passed on to the private investor. Some portion of those benefits was returned to the tax-exempt organization or government in the form of reduced rents.

Bennington College in Vermont, for instance, received considerable publicity after announcing it would sell its entire college campus to a group of alumni investors and then lease back the facilities.

The city of Atlanta used a lease-back plan to rehabilitate its City Hall, and Oakland, Calif., was able to acquire a museum and auditorium through the use of sale/lease-backs.

The federal government was also involved in lease-back schemes. The Navy was planning to lease up to 13 cargo ships for the Rapid Deployment Force from private firms. And the Air Force was considering a leasing arrangement for executive jet aircraft and transport planes.

New Restrictions. The bill approved by the Ways and Means Committee placed restrictions on tax benefits from leasing arrangements by: tax-exempt entities other than farmers' cooperatives; U.S., state and local governmental units; and U.S. possessions.

In general, the measure denied the investment tax credit and slowed down the rate of accelerated depreciation allowances for personal property, such as most business machines. The bill also required the use of the straight-line depreciation method, which meant investors could not choose to take larger depreciation allowances in the earlier years and smaller ones later on, but must spread the allowances out at an equal percentage each year.

Not affected by the bill's restrictions were computers, high-tech hospital equipment and short-lived telecommunications equipment.

Leasing arrangements for real property, such as buildings, owned by tax-exempt entities would be affected by the bill if they met any of the following conditions:

● Financing of the property was achieved through tax-exempt bonds.

● The lease contained a fixed purchase price or sale option.

● The lease term exceeded 80 percent of the property's useful life.

● The tax-exempt entity used the property under a lease, or sale, and lease-back arrangement.

Investors would have to use the straight-line depreciation method for such properties and the current 15-year depreciation period would expand to 40 years or 125 percent of the lease term, whichever was greater.

Rehabilitation, Other Issues. The special tax credit for rehabilitating old buildings would not be allowed if the leasing arrangement was with a non-profit organization or government that used tax-exempt industrial development bonds to finance the rehabilitation.

This would prevent what the staff referred to as "double-dipping" or even "triple-dipping" at the taxpayer's expense.

Property used by foreign entities would be treated the same as property used by a domestic tax-exempt organization if 50 percent or less of the income from the property was subject to U.S. taxes.

The bill also attempted to clarify distinctions between lease arrangements and service contracts. Generally, a private investor had to bear the business risk for it to be exempt from the bill. A special exemption was included for solid waste facilities if they met certain requirements.

Short-term leases — those of less than one year or those using a three-year accelerated depreciation allowance — would not be denied either the investment tax credit or the regular accelerated depreciation allowance.

Fringe Benefits

The committee approved a bill (HR 3525) Oct. 5 that would give statutory authority to most existing tax-free fringe benefits. A congressional moratorium on Treasury regulations governing taxation of fringe benefits was scheduled to expire Dec. 31. *(Moratorium, 1981 Almanac p. 95; 1979 Almanac p. 325)*

The types of fringe benefits that would be excluded from taxation by HR 3525 included:

● Benefits that imposed no additional cost on the employer, such as permitting airline employees to fly free on a space-available basis.

● An employee discount on a product or service. Discounts for employees would be tax-exempt to the extent that the discount did not exceed the amount of profit the employer would make from selling the service or merchandise.

● A working-condition fringe benefit. To qualify for exemption, the property or services must be used primarily for aiding the employee's performance, such as free parking

or an auto salesman's use of a car in the dealer's sales area.

● A "de minimus" fringe — one of such small value that accounting for it would be unreasonable.

● Recreational facilities. A tax exclusion would be allowed for the value of on-premises athletic facilities provided by the employer.

● Tuition reduction. A reduction in tuition to an employee of an educational institution would be excluded from taxes, as would reciprocal arrangements allowing tuition reductions at other institutions.

These provisions would have no revenue impact.

Life Insurance Taxation

Another bill (HR 4065) ordered reported Oct. 5 would restructure the taxation of life insurance companies, dividing the tax burden on the industry so that mutual insurance companies would pay 55 percent and stock insurance companies 45 percent. The three-year revenue yield was estimated at $2.5 billion.

The bill, worked out by the insurance industry and the committee, would allow mutual companies to reduce their tax burden by forming subsidiary firms that would essentially be stock life insurance companies. But these mutual companies would still have to consider the assets of their stock subsidiaries when calculating their taxes.

Life insurance companies would be taxed at the regular corporate rate. However, both mutuals and stock life insurance companies would be allowed a deduction equal to 25 percent of their taxable income coming strictly from their insurance business. Income from investment activities would not receive this deduction.

In addition, the bill included a special "small company deduction" for firms with assets of $500 million or less. These companies would be allowed to deduct 60 percent of the first $3 million of otherwise taxable income. The deduction would be phased down to zero as the company's income increased from $3 million to $15 million.

The insurance industry, according to the staff, would pay an additional $1 billion in 1984 if the bill were enacted.

Individual Retirement Accounts (IRAs)

The committee attached an unrelated provision to the life insurance bill that dealt with Individual Retirement Accounts (IRAs). Under existing law, a person could deposit up to $2,000 of earnings each year into a tax-deferred IRA. If there was a non-working spouse, the contribution could total $2,250.

The committee amendment would permit IRA holders to add an extra $1,750 to their accounts. This extra money would be taxed as earnings, but the interest on the additional money would not be subject to taxes until it was withdrawn. Although the initial revenue loss from the provision would be slight, by 1988 it would cost the Treasury $245 million annually.

Tax Simplification

The committee Oct. 4 approved a tax simplification bill (HR 3475) that would net the Treasury approximately $1.5 billion over the next three years. It tried to conform various income tax credits and apply them more consistently. Under the bill, an individual could take personal tax credits, such as for child-care deductions. But then all business tax credits would be limited to the taxpayer's first $25,000 of tax liability plus 85 percent of his or her remaining liability. The bill also would change the rules for estimated taxes by requiring individuals to make estimated

payments against anticipated minimum tax liabilities.

Miscellaneous Bills

The committee also approved eight additional bills including measures to: provide a special tax exemption for Pennsylvania State University (HR 2504); change the tax rules for offshore commodity funds (HR 3096); and extend federal casualty rules concerning natural disasters to a residence located in a federally declared disaster area (HR 2831).

Private Foundations

On Oct. 6, Ways and Means approved proposals to clarify the taxation of private foundations. Tax-exempt private foundations had hoped Congress would grant them immunity from the requirement that foundations divest themselves of gifts of large business holdings.

Ways and Means refused, but gave the private foundations more time to sell off substantial gifts received after 1969, when the requirement was enacted. The revenue impact was minimal.

Mortgage Subsidy Bonds

The Ways and Means Committee approved the two final elements of its tax package Oct. 19, and HR 4170, the proposed Tax Reform Act of 1983, was ordered reported the following day.

The committee agreed to extend for five years the existing tax exemption for mortgage subsidy bonds, which state and local governments issued to raise money to lend to home buyers at below-market interest rates. The mortgage-bond tax exemption was due to expire at the end of 1983. *(Details, p. 276; background, 1980 Almanac p. 299)*

The committee bill also offered states and localities the option of issuing tax credit certificates instead of bonds. These "mortgage credit certificates" would allow a homeowner to receive a federal tax credit worth up to 50 percent of the mortgage interest on qualified personal residences. The credits, which would be issued directly to the homeowner, would be subject to the existing eligibility requirements for qualified mortgage bonds.

According to committee estimates, the revenue loss from extending the mortgage bonds would be offset by tax increases from changes in industrial development bonds (IDBs), also approved Oct. 19.

Industrial Development Bonds

To curb the use of IDBs, tax-exempt bonds issued by state and local governments to finance private business projects, the committee agreed to impose a $150 per capita limit on the amount of bonds that could be issued within a state annually.

Each state's allocation of bond authority would be divided equally between the state and local issuers, unless the state legislature approved an alternative allocation. The cap would be phased in over two years and would not apply to bonds issued for traditional public purposes, such as schools and roads.

Ways and Means agreed to limit tax write-offs for the following kinds of property funded by IDBs: sewage and solid waste disposal facilities; air and water pollution control facilities; and projects eligible for Urban Development Action Grants (UDAGs).

Under the bill, IDBs could not be used for the purchase of land or existing facilities unless the purchaser was using the proceeds for substantial rehabilitation; or unless

the proceeds were used by a first-time purchaser of a farm or ranch, where there was no more than $250,000 in IDB financing.

House Tax Bill Blocked

The day before Congress' scheduled Nov. 18 adjournment, the House rejected the rule for floor consideration of the Ways and Means package by a 204-214 vote. *(Vote 490, p. 142-H)*

Nearly a month elapsed between the time the Ways and Means Committee reported HR 4170 and the Nov. 17 House action. In the interim, House leaders struggled to defuse opposition to the measure.

From the moment the bill was reported, provisions limiting the use of popular industrial development bonds had run into a wall of opposition from governors, mayors and local officials. They lobbied members of the House Rules Committee to allow a floor vote on an amendment to eliminate the most onerous IDB provision — one that placed a $150 per capita limit on the amount of bonds that could be issued within a state annually.

Under the Ways and Means bill, each state's allocation of bond authority would be divided equally between the state and local issuers, unless the state legislature approved an alternative allocation. The cap would be phased in over two years and would not apply to bonds issued for traditional public purposes, such as schools and roads.

After weeks of impasse, Speaker O'Neill and Rostenkowski came up with an IDB compromise that persuaded enough members on the Rules Committee to move the bill to the floor.

The IDB changes provided that bonds used to finance multifamily housing would be exempted from the cap. IDBs used to finance multifamily housing were also exempted from stricter arbitrage rules, regulations designed to prevent the proceeds of tax-exempt bonds from being used to purchase higher-yielding taxable bonds.

The Ways and Means bill also prohibited the use of IDBs to purchase land or existing facilities, unless they were substantially rehabilitated. The IDB compromise modified this prohibition so that 25 percent of bond proceeds could be used to purchase land, and IDBs could be used to purchase existing structures if rehabilitation expenses constituted at least 15 percent of the cost of the project.

Another element of the compromise stripped the bill of $359 million in controversial Medicare savings. Ways and Means had included a provision extending existing temporary rules for setting Medicare part B premiums — or out-of-pocket expenses for Medicare beneficiaries. Rules Committee Chairman Claude Pepper, D-Fla., was particularly concerned about the Medicare savings, and the elimination of this provision ensured his support.

But when the tax bill finally reached the Rules Committee, additional pressures surfaced. Henry A. Waxman, D-Calif., chairman of the Energy and Commerce Subcommittee on Health and the Environment — which shared jurisdiction with Ways and Means over Medicare and Medicaid — persuaded the Rules Committee to allow a vote on an amendment providing financial incentives to states to extend Medicaid coverage for more needy pregnant women and young children.

In addition to the IDB changes and the Waxman amendment, the Rules Committee agreed to allow separate votes on two additional Ways and Means amendments.

One contained technical tax corrections; the other was a grab bag of tax bills, including postponement of provisions relating to the carry-over of corporate net operating losses and extension of favorable tax treatment for the Payment-in-Kind (PIK) program for farmers.

The Rules Committee further allowed votes on three amendments designed to boost the bill's revenue yield:

● A Rostenkowski proposal to increase revenues $11.5 billion over three years by freezing a number of expiring tax cuts.

● A Democratic Study Group plan to raise an additional $32 billion in revenues over three years through a variety of tax reforms.

● An amendment pushed by Democratic freshmen to impose a $720 cap on the third installment of Reagan's 1981 tax cut. *(Tax cap efforts, p. 249)*

During House debate Nov. 17, Henson Moore, R-La., said, "It's a lousy rule, but a good bill," and urged that the rule be adopted.

But only 13 Republicans voted to approve the rule on the 204-214 House tally. *(Vote 490, p. 142-H)*

Senate Tax-Spending Bill Stalled

In the wake of the House vote, Senate leaders decided to suspend consideration of a $28 billion reconciliation bill (S 2062) on which the Senate had begun debate Nov. 16.

The bill, reported without recommendation by the Budget Committee Nov. 4 (S Rept 98-300), incorporated spending cuts and revenue increases recommended by Senate authorizing committees. Under terms of the 1974 Budget Act, the Budget Committee was not permitted to make any substantive changes in the authorizing committees' proposals.

Three-year spending savings amounted to $14.61 billion, compared to the budget's mandate to shave $12.3 billion.

As in the House, the revenue increases in the reconciliation bill fell well below the budget's $73 billion goal, however. The Finance Committee reported revenue increases of only $13.4 billion, bringing the deficit reduction total to $28 billion over fiscal 1984-86. Eleventh-hour efforts to boost the Finance package proved unsuccessful.

Spending Reductions

Except for the Finance Committee cuts, the savings achieved by Senate committees and incorporated in S 2062 tracked those approved by the House Oct. 25.

The bulk of the spending reductions — $9.6 billion — would come from changes approved by the Governmental Affairs Committee. These savings were achieved primarily by delaying COLAs for federal civilian and military retirees and delaying federal civilian pay raises from October until January.

The Small Business Committee met its directive to save $1.2 billion by extending for three years the requirement that farmers seeking disaster loans must first apply to the Farmers Home Administration before seeking more favorable loans from the Small Business Administration.

The Veterans' Affairs Committee capped the COLA for veterans' compensation at 3.5 percent and delayed payment of the COLA for six months, saving $500 million.

The Finance Committee doubled its mandated savings of $1.7 billion by cutting $3.4 billion in the Medicare, Medicaid, Aid to Families with Dependent Children, Supplemental Security Income, and child support enforcement

programs.

The largest portion of the committee's savings would come from a six-month freeze on Medicare physician fees, without the controversial "assignment" provisions that certain Ways and Means Committee members thought were needed to protect beneficiaries from higher physician charges.

The committee also increased Medicare patients' out-of-pocket costs for non-hospital services, by increasing the "deductible" that patients must pay before Medicare began paying for services, and by making permanent a requirement that patients' premiums be set at rates to recover 25 percent of program costs. Other provisions would set fee schedules for clinical laboratory services, and make several changes in Medicaid.

The bill also would require child support enforcement agencies to seek medical insurance coverage as a part of child support orders.

As part of the reconciliation package, the Finance Committee agreed to reauthorize the maternal and child health block grant program.

Tax Increases

The Finance Committee agreed to increase revenues $1.7 billion in fiscal 1984 and $13.4 billion over fiscal 1984-86. The biggest revenue gainers, and the most important tax changes, in the reconciliation package would:

● Postpone until 1987 a provision of the 1981 tax bill that would allow taxpayers to exclude from taxation 15 percent of net interest income up to $3,000 ($6,000 on a joint return). The provision was due to take effect in 1985. The delay would increase revenues by $3.88 billion over three years. *(Tax bill, 1981 Almanac p. 91)*

● Restrict the use of leasing provisions by tax-exempt entities. As in the measure approved by the Ways and Means Committee, the bill generally would deny non-profit entities the investment tax credit and slow the rate of accelerated depreciation allowances for property. The bill would also restrict the use of leasing arrangements in which equipment, such as planes, was used abroad. Most provisions would apply to arrangements entered into after May 23, 1983. These restrictions would net $3.3 billion over three years.

● Modify provisions of the existing tax law that allowed income averaging. Under existing law, a taxpayer could average income over a five-year period if his current-year taxable income exceeded 120 percent of his average taxable income over the prior four years. Finance increased the threshold to 140 percent. This change would increase revenues $2.9 billion over three years.

● Reduce the long-term capital gains holding period from one year to six months for assets acquired after Nov. 1, 1983. To offset the revenue loss from shortening the holding period, the Finance Committee reduced from $3,000 to $1,000 the amount of capital losses that could be deducted from income.

The holding period change had almost cleared Congress before, but Rostenkowski blocked the measure in conference in 1981 and 1982. *(1982 Almanac p. 52)*

● Increase the corporate tax rate for businesses with income between $1 million and $1.4 million from 46 percent to 51 percent. This was designed to limit a provision of existing law meant to help small business. The change would increase revenues $466 million over three years.

Among other tax changes approved by the Finance Committee were provisions that would: tighten tax compli-ance; apply stricter rules to tax reduction schemes involving commodity straddles; restrict the use of "collapsible corporations" that were used to convert income into capital gains; and require taxpayers subject to the alternative minimum tax, which was designed to ensure that all individuals pay at least some taxes, to make estimated tax payments. *(Tax straddles, 1981 Almanac p. 94; minimum tax, 1982 Almanac p. 31)*

Domenici-Chiles Package

As S 2062 came to the floor Nov. 16, it provided only $14.6 billion in three-year budget savings and $13.4 billion in tax increases recommended by Senate authorizing committees. To try to bring the package into compliance with the congressional fiscal blueprint, Budget Committee Chairman Domenici and ranking Budget Democrat Chiles offered an $87.6 billion deficit reduction package.

In addition to the deficit reduction measures in the bill as reported, the Domenici-Chiles plan sought to reduce discretionary defense and non-defense domestic spending by 2.5 percent over fiscal 1984-86, for savings of $15.7 billion.

The plan aimed to pick up an additional $43.9 billion in taxes by: reducing the indexing of tax rates for inflation to a level 2.5 percent less than the increase in the Consumer Price Index (CPI); imposing a minimum corporate tax and an individual and corporate surtax; and a variety of changes in business tax breaks.

Both expressed their reluctance to offer their savings amendment. But Domenici said, "After months of discussion, nothing has come forth. . . . I think we ought to give the Senate a chance to vote on the tax and expenditure side."

And Chiles insisted, "We do not want to be usurpers, taking the jurisdiction from the Finance Committee."

Both Dole and Long said it was not the prerogative of the Budget Committee to draft major tax legislation. "I don't want to criticize this package," Dole said. "I just don't want to see it adopted."

Armstrong raised a point of order against the amendment, noting that it did not meet germaneness requirements of the 1974 Budget Act. The Senate declined to waive the germaneness rule on a 33-65 vote, and the amendment fell without a vote on its merits. The Senate took no further action on the bill. *(Vote 358, p. 58-S)*

Dole's Deficit Odyssey

Finance Chairman Dole was at the forefront of the Senate drive to fashion a major deficit reduction package in 1983. Before forwarding the Finance proposals to the Budget Committee Oct. 31, Dole told his colleagues he hoped Finance could come up with a much larger savings plan that could be added to the reconciliation measure on the floor.

And until the last day of the session, he tried unsuccessfully to gain committee approval of an expanded deficit reduction plan. On Nov. 18, however, the committee agreed to put off further consideration of deficit reductions until 1984.

Initially, the Dole package would have reduced the deficit by $150 billion over fiscal 1984-86. But after weeks of closed-door negotiations with his committee and other senators, and strong opposition from Democrats to proposed Social Security benefit changes, Dole modified the controversial plan so that the $150 billion in savings would be stretched out over four years — from fiscal 1984-87.

New Spending Control Measures Proposed

Congress' failure to deliver the deficit reduction measures promised in its fiscal 1984 budget resolution (H Con Res 91) intensified dissatisfaction with the budget procedures lawmakers had established in 1974 and brought new demands for additional presidential authority to control federal spending.

The administration indicated President Reagan might ask Congress for expanded authority to impound — refuse to spend — funds appropriated by Congress, as well as authority to veto individual items in appropriations bills. Such action is known as a line-item veto.

"If Congress is unable or unwilling to cut spending, they should give the president expanded authority to do the job," said Treasury Secretary Donald T. Regan.

Congress' existing budget control procedures, established in the 1974 Congressional Budget and Impoundment Control Act (PL 93-344), had been designed to help the legislative branch gain control over the burgeoning federal budget. The law had its genesis in protracted disputes with President Nixon over Nixon's use of executive powers to hold down federal spending and to revise congressionally mandated spending priorities.

Existing Mechanisms

The 1974 act set up two procedures the president could follow if he wished to delay or cancel spending. Both were subject to congressional review.

If the president believed money should not be spent at all, he could propose that Congress enact legislation to rescind the appropriation making the funds available. Unless both houses acted within 45 days, the president had to release the funds.

The law also permitted the president to defer spending temporarily unless either the House or the Senate adopted a resolution directing that the money be spent. *(1974 Almanac p. 145)*

The Supreme Court's June 23 decision that the legislative veto was unconstitutional cast doubt upon the legitimacy of the Budget Act's spending deferral provision. *(Legislative veto, p. 565)*

Presidential Powers

In the wake of the Supreme Court decision, several members of Congress began pushing for a constitutional amendment that would specifically allow the president to veto line items in appropriations bills.

The 1983 stalemate over taxes and spending also prompted other proposals for budget control.

The Senate Nov. 16 killed a plan, offered by William L. Armstrong, R-Colo., and Russell B. Long, D-La., that would have increased the president's powers to rescind or defer spending of appropriated funds.

The Senate tabled the amendment, which was offered to a minor tariff bill (H J Res 290), on a 49-46 vote. *(Vote 357, p. 58-S)*

"For several years I have been thinking that we made a mistake when we tied the hands of the president in limiting his ability to manage the nation's business," Armstrong said. "Literally limited unduly, I think, his ability to not spend amounts that would otherwise need to be spent if conditions change or if our financial resources were not materializing as expected."

Under the Armstrong-Long plan, monthly and quarterly limits on the public debt would be established, in accordance with the most recently adopted congressional budget resolution.

If the president found the debt ceiling for any quarter would have to be exceeded, he would be required to defer or rescind spending to stay within the ceiling. The only limits on the president would be that he could not reduce any program or project by more than 20 percent, and he could not reduce the current level of benefits paid to individuals.

Budget Committee Chairman Pete V. Domenici, R-N.M., opposed the proposal. "This amendment is in theory, perhaps, good. But it just won't work in practice."

Appropriations Committee Chairman Mark O. Hatfield, R-Ore., called the plan "preposterous." Hatfield said it would require an "abdication of our responsibility."

Congressional Procedures

On the issue of spending control, members of Congress disputed not only with the president, but with themselves.

The House Rules Committee held hearings but took no action on several proposals to modify the existing budget process, including measures to reduce the power of the Budget Committee under the 1974 act. One plan was offered by eight chairmen of House authorizing committees, led by Energy and Commerce Chairman John D. Dingell, D-Mich. The Rules Committee task force on budget reform proposed a less ambitious reform package, but failed to complete work on final budget reform recommendations.

In the Senate, a study group led by former Sens. Abraham A. Ribicoff, D-Conn. (1963-81), and James B. Pearson, R-Kan. (1962-68), recommended that the Budget Committee be abolished and its duties taken over by the Appropriations and Finance committees jointly. The Senate took no action on the study group recommendations. *(Story, p. 598)*

Balanced Budget Amendment

A proposal for a constitutional amendment to require balanced budgets remained dormant in Congress in 1983. The Senate had adopted a balanced budget amendment in 1982, but the House defeated a similar measure. *(1982 Almanac p. 391)*

Meanwhile, the drive to force a constitutional convention to draft a balanced budget amendment was two states short of success. Under the Constitution, Congress is required to call a constitutional convention if two-thirds of the states (34) request one. The convention approach has never been tried.

The $150 billion was to be divided evenly between tax increases and spending reductions. Only $39 billion of the spending cuts, however, would come from Finance programs.

"The Finance Committee will look to the other committees of the Senate to make an equal amount of the spending cuts — for example, out of restraint on farm program spending, defense and discretionary expenditures," a committee press release said. ∎

Debt Limit Increases

Congress enacted two increases in the public debt limit in 1983, ultimately boosting the ceiling to $1.49 trillion, an amount expected to meet the Treasury's borrowing needs until April 1984.

The initial increase (HR 2990 — PL 98-34), cleared May 25, raised the debt ceiling to $1.389 trillion from the $1.29 trillion level set in 1982. *(1982 Almanac p. 44)*

The debt ceiling hike provided by HR 2990 bore no expiration date because the bill eliminated an existing distinction between "temporary" and "permanent" ceilings. Previously, the debt ceiling dropped to a permanent level of $400 billion barring periodic action by Congress. Any increases above that level were considered temporary. But since the government would be unable to function at such a low level, the ceiling always had to be raised.

The second increase (H J Res 308 — PL 98-161) became embroiled in Senate maneuvering over deficit reduction measures and cleared only hours before Congress adjourned Nov. 18. The House had passed its version as part of the fiscal 1984 budget resolution under an arrangement adopted in 1979. The procedure was designed to insulate the debt ceiling increases from political pressures that often had caused them to fail in the House. *(1979 Almanac p. 305)*

First Increase: $1.389 Trillion

The first debt-limit increase (HR 2990 — PL 98-34) was cleared May 25 when the Senate passed by a 51-41 vote the $1.389 trillion measure approved by the House May 18. President Reagan signed the bill the following day. *(Senate vote 115, p. 23-S)*

The debt-limit increase, usually a target for politically sensitive amendments and debate because of its urgency, slid through the House May 18 on a surprise voice vote. But House leaders said that if the measure were changed in any way by the Senate and returned to the House for another vote, passage was highly unlikely the second time around.

The Treasury Department had warned that if the ceiling were not raised by May 31, the federal government would be unable to borrow enough funds to continue operating. The new ceiling was expected to meet federal borrowing needs through Sept. 30, the end of the fiscal year.

However, the $1.389 trillion ceiling had no statutory cut-off date, because HR 2990 eliminated the existing distinction between the "temporary" and "permanent" debt ceiling.

The bill also raised from $110 billion to $150 billion the amount of long-term bonds the Treasury was allowed to issue at variable interest rates. Any amount over that

ceiling had to be offered at a prohibitively low 4.25 percent rate.

House Action

The bill was reported by the House Ways and Means Committee May 13 (H Rept 98-121) and passed by the House by voice vote May 18.

Past debate on debt limit increases often had become so politicized that the House had been unable to pass such a bill on the first try, and House leaders had assumed that HR 2990 faced likely defeat.

But as debate ended with only a handful of members on the floor, Speaker Thomas P. O'Neill Jr., D-Mass., took the chair and, with no requests for a recorded vote, gaveled the legislation through to final passage.

"We looked around and saw [the chamber] was empty," said a clearly pleased Barber B. Conable Jr., R-N.Y., co-manager of the bill with Ways and Means Committee Chairman Dan Rostenkowski, D-Ill. "It was not the result of conspiracy, but of great good fortune," he said.

House floor debate on the debt bill began in the usual partisan fashion, with Democrats criticizing the administration's economic policies and Republicans calling for "responsible" congressional action.

In the past, conservative Republicans had used debt limit legislation as a vehicle for attacking "fiscal irresponsibility." But Democrats had delighted in turning the tables once President Reagan took office, putting the onus for passage of the administration's debt ceiling requests on their Republican colleagues.

Budget Committee Chairman James R. Jones, D-Okla., pointed out during floor debate that the Reagan administration had increased the public debt 39 percent in only two years. "It seems to me the first responsibility for passing [the bill] rests on those who ordered supply-side economics from the fiscal menu in the last Congress," he said.

But members on both sides of the aisle nevertheless called for passage of the debt ceiling increase to keep the government in operation.

"We have all danced and now it is time to pay the piper," said Bill Frenzel, R-Minn. "To vote against a debt ceiling after we have voted for spending is a sham."

An effort by Minority Whip Trent Lott, R-Miss., to attach a provision requiring a $7.6 billion cut in fiscal 1983 spending was blocked on a procedural vote of 249-171. *(Vote 120, p. 40-H)*

Lott said he wanted to tie the spending reduction to the debt ceiling hike to make it more "palatable" to conservative members. But Democrats were unwilling to help make the debt ceiling vote easier for their Republican colleagues, and all but nine voted against Lott's plan.

However, when it came time for final passage of the bill no member emerged to request a recorded vote.

Republican leaders were clearly pleased with the result. It had been expected that if such a vote were taken, the bill would fail and a new, 30-day debt limit increase would be brought to the floor. The shorter bill would have had a better chance of passage but also would have meant another debt limit vote in June.

Republicans feared that some Democrats would use a June debt limit bill as a vehicle for tax-increase measures opposed by Reagan.

Debt limit politics had been so volatile in the past that the House approved a measure in 1979 allowing it to approve debt limit increases as part of the congressional

budget resolution. But the fiscal 1984 budget resolution had been bogged down in the Senate for several weeks and House action on a separate debt limit bill was considered necessary to meet the May 31 deadline. *(Budget resolution, p. 435)*

Senate Action

The Finance Committee approved HR 2990 without amendment by an 11-5 vote May 24, and the Senate passed the bill the following day.

Committee approval came only after Chairman Dole promised members another vehicle for a number of pet tax measures — including repeal of a new interest and dividend withholding requirement, extension of tax-exempt mortgage revenue bonds and a so-called "reciprocity" bill aimed at unfair trading practices by foreign countries.

Early debate May 25 was clouded by Democratic threats to bog down the urgent legislation with amendments unless the Senate agreed to a shorter, 20-day increase in the debt ceiling. Minority Leader Robert C. Byrd, D-W.Va., said the shorter bill would allow members to debate a number of tax issues — including a cap on the third installment of President Reagan's 1981 tax cut plan — in June when another debt-limit hike would be needed.

But Majority Leader Howard H. Baker Jr., R-Tenn., warned Democrats that any change in the House-passed measure would mean the "government will stop dead in its tracks" or, more likely, cause a delay or cancellation of the congressional Memorial Day recess.

Senate Republicans had agreed earlier in the day that they would not try to attach controversial abortion and school-prayer amendments to the debt-limit bill, but only if Democrats also refrained from tampering with the measure.

"We're playing a very dangerous game," warned a frustrated Baker, who had been through a grueling floor battle over the federal budget only the week before. "If we add this [20-day increase] amendment, it is my judgment that we will not get this bill."

But after several party caucuses and a commitment from House leaders to send a tax measure to the Senate in June — to which a tax cap could be attached — Democrats agreed to back off. Baker also gave his assurances that he would not block a Senate vote on a tax cap and other tax issues after the recess.

President Reagan strongly opposed any tampering with his tax program and Republican leaders wanted to avoid a vote on the issue, if possible.

Democrats also said they were concerned over a provision in HR 2990 that made the new $1.389 trillion debt ceiling "permanent."

Some charged that the change could give the president power to withhold — or "impound" — funding from selective programs if the ceiling was reached before Congress had a chance to raise it again. They argued that Reagan could use it to prevent funding of certain social programs to which he was opposed.

Finance Chairman Dole assured Democrats, however, that the change would give the president no additional powers, and he was backed up by experts from the Joint Committee on Taxation.

Experts argued that making the higher level permanent would give the government some slight borrowing flexibility because the Treasury could continue to refinance existing debt above the $400 billion mark, as long as it remained below the higher ceiling.

Second Increase: $1.49 Trillion

The second 1983 debt limit increase became entangled in eleventh-hour deficit reduction efforts and did not clear Congress until Nov. 18. *(Deficit reduction, p. 231)*

The bill (H J Res 308 — PL 98-161) provided a $101 billion increase in government borrowing authority, to $1.49 trillion. It was enacted after the Senate first trimmed and then rejected a $1.6 trillion House-passed version to which it had attached various non-germane amendments.

Initial Defeat

Senators anxious to press their case for further deficit-cutting measures succeeded Oct. 31 in defeating a $225.6 billion increase in the public debt limit sought by the administration.

The moving force behind the debt bill's demise was William L. Armstrong, R-Colo. "I think this is the time not to go for business as usual, but to take a stand" to force Congress and the president to agree to hold the line on spending, Armstrong said.

The initial defeat of H J Res 308 came on a 39-56 vote Oct. 31, after four days of debate that ranged from the U.S. invasion of Grenada to Japanese barriers to the importation of beef. *(Vote 320, p. 53-S)*

Several non-germane amendments were adopted, including one to invoke the War Powers act to limit U.S. military involvement in Grenada. *(Vote 311, p. 52-S)*

In its first vote on the issue, the Senate effectively defeated a nuclear freeze proposal. In another vote, members showed broad support for the so-called "build-down" arms control measure. *(Votes 317, 318, pp. 52-S, 53-S)*

When the Senate did discuss the debt ceiling, it was apparent there was little support for the $1.615 trillion limit reported by the Finance Committee Oct. 25 (S Rept 98-279). The House had approved that figure as part of the fiscal 1984 budget resolution, and the Treasury said it would suffice through fiscal 1984.

In initial action Oct. 27, the Senate adopted an amendment by Armstrong, cutting the increase to $1.45 trillion. Armstrong hoped the lower figure would provide "bargaining power" to force action on deficit reduction. The vote was 70-15. *(Vote 309, p. 51-S)*

Before the final vote Oct. 31, Baker moved to recommit the bill to the Finance Committee with instructions to remove all amendments, but that effort failed, 27-68. *(Vote 319, p. 53-S)*

Senate leaders had fought any change in the measure, which would require returning it to the House for further action.

"I think what we did tonight was akin to lighting a match to look in the gas tank," Baker warned following the bill's defeat. "I do not think any of us know what will happen next." But it was clear that the majority in the Senate did not share his sense of crisis.

Although rejection of the debt bill disrupted Treasury borrowing plans, the government faced no immediate shortage of funds. The pressure for swift Senate action was eased further by the knowledge that the existing ceiling of $1.389 trillion would not lapse while Congress debated an increase.

"The Treasury has a lot of money in the till. They can spend all that they have on hand," said the ranking Democrat on the Finance Committee, Russell B. Long, La. "And as the money comes in, they can spend that, too. Nothing

expires."

Long's message — and the message that Armstrong tried to deliver — was simple. "Make no mistake about it," Long said. "When you vote for this [recommittal] motion, you are voting to continue the biggest deficits in the history of this country as far as anybody can see."

Amendments. Amendments adopted by the Senate included proposals by:

● Long, to express the sense of the Senate that the debt limit and budget reconciliation bills should not be used for amendments that would worsen the deficit. Adopted 66-11 Oct. 29. *(Vote 313, p. 52-S)*

● Max Baucus, D-Mont., to express the sense of the Senate that the United States should insist that Japan dismantle all non-tariff trade barriers to the importation of beef. Adopted 92-6 Oct. 31. *(Vote 315, p. 52-S)*

● Charles E. Grassley, R-Iowa, to require the comptroller general to send Congress a report comparing the amounts spent to carry out each federal program in each of the 15 most recent fiscal years ending prior to Oct. 1, 1983. Adopted by voice vote Oct. 31.

● Donald W. Riegle Jr., D-Mich., to limit restrictions on press coverage of the war in Grenada. Adopted 53-18 Oct. 29, modified by voice vote Oct. 31. *(Vote 314, p. 52-S)*

● Daniel Patrick Moynihan, D-N.Y., to deny funds to Jordan for military equipment unless specifically authorized by Congress. Adopted by voice vote Oct. 29.

● Lawton Chiles, D-Fla., to express the sense of Congress that Cuba should be required to take back all Cuban illegal aliens in the United States as a condition for repatriation of Cuban nationals captured by U.S. forces in Grenada. Adopted by voice vote Oct. 28.

The Senate rejected several amendments dealing with budget issues, including those by:

● Chiles, to make the debt limit increase contingent upon enactment of the deficit reduction measures mandated by Congress in the budget resolution. Rejected 31-53 Oct. 28. *(Vote 310, p. 52-S)*

● Alan J. Dixon, D-Ill., to express the sense of the Senate in support of a constitutional amendment authorizing the president to veto individual items in appropriations bills. Tabled 53-25 Oct. 29. *(Vote 312, p. 52-S)*

● Bob Kasten, R-Wis., to express the sense of the Senate in opposition to further tax increases until substantial spending cuts were made. Rejected 42-55 Oct. 31. *(Vote 316, p. 52-S)*

Senate Passage, Final Action

Many senators voted against the debt limit increase to protest congressional inaction on deficit control. They hoped withholding the increase would pressure the president and Congress into approving some form of deficit restraint.

While that pressure did not work, the pressure to adjourn did. Late Nov. 16, the Senate voted 67-31 to reconsider the measure and then passed it 58-40. *(Votes 359, 360, p. 58-S)*

Because the Senate resolution did not agree with the $1.6 trillion House version, a conference was necessary to draft a compromise. Senate-House conferees quickly agreed to strip the bill of all Senate amendments and provide a $1.49 trillion debt ceiling designed to meet government borrowing needs until April 1984.

The Senate approved the conference report on the measure (H Rept 98-566) by voice vote Nov. 17. The House approved the report by a 214-186 vote Nov. 18, thus clearing the bill. *(Vote 498, p. 144-H)* ∎

IMF Funds Increased, Ex-Im Bank Extended

Before adjourning Nov. 18, Congress cleared legislation (HR 3959 — PL 98-181) increasing the U.S. contribution to the International Monetary Fund (IMF) by $8.4 billion, a shot in the arm the fund's proponents said it desperately needed to maintain world economic stability.

Opponents claimed that the increase in the U.S. fund quota represented a "big-bank bailout," a rescue operation for banking institutions that had imprudently lent billions to countries burdened with debt. But with the Reagan administration supporting the IMF, opponents had little chance of blocking the increase.

IMF backers viewed the bill as a necessary, if not particularly palatable, measure. The fund had played a key role in keeping afloat debt-ridden nations, but it threatened to run out of money as early as January 1984, increasing the danger of a worldwide economic crisis.

The IMF was established in 1944 to help member nations meet temporary balance of payments deficits. Nations borrowing from the fund were usually required to adopt adjustment programs, designed to increase export earnings and decrease spending on imports in order to reduce the deficits. The United States provided roughly 20 percent of the IMF's funds.

The IMF was used by both developing and developed nations, but recently had concentrated on newly industrialized countries like Mexico and Brazil that borrowed

heavily from private banks in the 1970s. Hit by a combination of low world commodity prices and high interest rates, these nations were unable to meet their obligations.

The 146 IMF member nations agreed early in 1983 to increase their fund contributions by 47 percent, or nearly $32 billion, thus boosting total IMF resources to about $94.5 billion. All member nations increased their contributions, called quotas, by approximately the same percentage.

The $8.4 billion U.S. contribution to the IMF was not a direct government expenditure. The federal government traded its dollars for Special Drawing Rights (SDRs), an international currency used in transactions between nations. The United States collected interest on the dollars it contributed.

Legislative Hybrid

The yearlong struggle to enact IMF legislation resulted in a legislative hybrid, a housing-IMF bill that was attached to the conference report on a supplemental appropriations bill. *(Supplemental, p. 536; housing, p. 277)*

The IMF measure also included a three-year extension of the Export-Import Bank and authorized funding for the Inter-American Development Bank, the Asian Development Bank and the African Development Fund. In addition, it provided a stopgap six-month extension of the Defense Production Act.

Major Provisions

As cleared by Congress, the IMF section of HR 3959 contained these IMF and related provisions:

IMF Increase

The bill increased the United States' quota in the IMF by approximately $5.8 billion and provided a $2.6 billion increase in the U.S. contribution to the General Arrangements to Borrow (GAB), a contingency fund established by 11 industrialized nations for use when the international financial system was threatened. The dollar figures were not exact because the authority was denominated in Special Drawing Rights, whose dollar value fluctuated daily. The bill also appropriated the $8.4 billion required by increased fund participation.

The measure further required the Treasury secretary to consult with Congress 30 days in advance of any additional increases in the U.S. quota.

The bill also:

● Required the U.S. representative to the IMF to oppose loans to any country that practiced apartheid or was ruled by a communist dictatorship. Loans to such nations were permitted if the Treasury secretary notified Congress 30 days before the IMF vote on the loans and ensured that the loan was in the best interests of a majority of the citizens of the recipient nation.

● Instructed the U.S. representative to the IMF to promote exchange rate stability and avoid manipulation of exchange rates. Directed the representative to back changes in IMF policy to convert the liabilities of debtor nations from short-term, high-interest loans to long-term loans at lower rates of interest.

● Provided that U.S. banking agencies require banks to maintain adequate amounts of capital.

● Mandated that the federal banking agencies require banks to set aside reserves for international loans when, over a period of time, debtor nations failed to abide by the terms of IMF loans or when it appeared unlikely that repayment would proceed in a timely fashion. Also, directed federal banking agencies to require banks to disclose publicly at least four times a year the amount of loans to foreign nations.

Export-Import Bank

The bill extended the Export-Import Bank for three years, through Sept. 30, 1986. It also mandated that, while the bank should consider the cost of money in setting interest rates on loans, all Ex-Im programs should be competitive with the export promotion programs of other nations. *(Background, box, p. 245)*

In addition, the bill:

● Established a "tied aid" credit program for U.S. exports that would permit foreign nations to receive a combination of Ex-Im Bank credits and foreign aid, resulting in very generous credit terms.

● Specified that the bank could provide financing for the export of services, such as insurance, as it did for exports of manufactured products, equipment and other capital goods.

● Mandated special treatment for small business by setting aside percentages of total IMF loans, insurance and guarantees for small businesses — rising from 6 percent in 1984 to 10 percent in 1986.

● Required the Ex-Im board of directors to include at least one small-business representative. The bill changed the terms for board members by providing for staggered terms of fours years except for two directors first appointed on or after Jan. 21, 1985, who were to serve for two years.

● Set up a 12-member advisory committee that was to include representatives from production, commerce, finance, agriculture, labor, services and state government. At least three members were to represent small businesses.

Other Provisions

The IMF measure:

● Authorized $5.2 billion for the Inter-American Development Bank; $1.3 billion for the Asian Development Bank and $150 million for the African Development Fund. *(Foreign aid appropriations, p. 521; background, 1982 Almanac pp. 144, 147)*

● Extended the Defense Production Act for six months, until March 30, 1984. *(Defense Production Act, p. 265)*

Background

The quadrupling of oil prices in 1973-74, followed by another tripling in 1979-81, led to a huge transfer of wealth from oil consumers to the nations of the Organization of Petroleum Exporting Countries (OPEC).

Nations such as Saudi Arabia and Kuwait, with small populations relative to their new riches, could not absorb their billions of petrodollars, and deposited them instead in various international banks.

Flush with deposits, those banks became "desperate to lend," wrote Anthony Sampson in his book *The Money Lenders*. Credit-worthy developing countries, faced with huge oil bills, were equally anxious to borrow. Heated competition among bankers, combined with rising inflation, resulted in very low, and at times negative, "real" interest rates (actual rate minus inflation). Bankers were virtually giving loans away.

"Selling loans," says Sampson, "was like offering crates of whisky to an alcoholic." Bankers felt safe in lending to sovereign nations because, they believed, the chances of default were slim.

The total foreign debt of developing countries grew from $100 billion in 1973 to more than $500 billion, and most of the lending was concentrated in a small group of countries.

The binge ended in 1981, when the U.S. Federal Reserve tightened monetary policy by restricting credit, which pushed up interest rates and reduced inflation.

That caused "real" rates to soar from a level of 1 percent or less, to between 5 and 10 percent. Many of the loans to developing countries had variable interest rates, so the cost of the debt skyrocketed.

At the same time, commodity prices dropped, cutting severely the export incomes of the most heavily indebted nations such as Brazil, Mexico, Argentina and Venezuela. As the cost of their debt rose, the ability to pay that debt plummeted. In mid-1982, debt service (required payments of interest and principal) reached as much as 179 percent of Argentina's total export earnings, 129 percent of Mexico's export earnings, and 122 percent of Brazil's export earnings.

When banks finally recognized the magnitude of the problem, it was too late. They had to extend old loans and provide new ones just to keep indebted nations from defaulting.

That was when the IMF stepped in. It offered new funds to the troubled countries and pressured private

banks to keep lending. In return, the indebted countries agreed to accept IMF austerity programs, designed to increase exports and reduce imports.

Working with the IMF, the banks managed to muddle through the worst of the crisis in 1982, and keep their balance sheets intact. Countries unable to meet their debt payments were provided new loans, and the banks collected hefty "rescheduling" fees up front that made Third World lending continue, on their books, to look profitable.

That process prevented outright default, which could cause a chain reaction in U.S. credit markets. But it did little to relieve the burden of debt on heavy borrowers.

"IMF conditions . . . essentially impose a recession on the economies," said Sen. Bill Bradley, D-N.J. "Apart from the political dangers of these austerity measures, which are substantial, such conditions require the country to take steps that make it virtually impossible for the country to grow again in the short run. How then will these countries generate the foreign exchange earnings needed to repay their loans from international banks?"

Senate Committee Action

The Senate version of the IMF increase (S 695) was reported by the Foreign Relations Committee March 24 (S Rept 98-35) and the Banking Committee May 16 (S Rept 98-122).

The Foreign Relations panel approved the bill March 15, with Jesse Helms, R-N.C., casting the sole dissenting vote. The committee made only minor changes in the bill proposed by the Reagan administration.

The Banking Committee approved the legislation by voice vote April 28.

At the request of John Heinz, R-Pa., the committee required increased public disclosure of banks' lending exposure in foreign countries, and it established new supervisory rules for accounting for fees collected during rescheduling of debt.

The bill required banks to establish loan loss reserves only for loans to those countries that were unable to make payments on the debt, such as Poland and Zaire. For loans to debt-ridden but solvent nations such as Brazil and Argentina, the Heinz bill directed regulators simply to require banks to maintain adequate levels of capital.

Senate Floor Action

The Senate passed S 695 by a 55-34 vote June 8, after defeating attempts by conservative Republicans to restrict the fund's activities. *(Vote 126, p. 25-S)*

Helms said the bill was designed to "bail out the international banks that have made bad loans and now want the taxpayers to back them up."

And Gordon J. Humphrey, R-N.H., heaped heavy criticism on the IMF itself, saying it "has all the trappings of socialism and central planning."

The bill was strongly supported by President Reagan, who sent a letter to the Senate June 6 saying that "passage of this legislation is of the utmost importance to the world economy, to the strength of the recovery and to the U.S. position of leadership in world affairs."

In spite of the president's plea, however, 24 members of his own party refused to support the measure.

Senate Amendments

Helms and Humphrey made numerous attempts dur-

ing consideration of S 695 to tie the hands of the IMF, but virtually all of their amendments were defeated by the Senate.

A Humphrey amendment to deny the increase in funds unless all IMF staff salaries were reduced to no more than $67,000 was killed by a vote of 55-26. *(Vote 118, p. 24-S)*

Humphrey said the IMF compensated its employees "as if there is no end to the money that will flow from member nations."

But Banking Committee Chairman Jake Garn, R-Utah, said that for the United States to mandate salaries for the 146-nation organization would be "a very difficult process, in fact impossible." And Heinz, chairman of the Banking Subcommittee on International Finance and Monetary Policy, said the amendment was actually designed "to kill the bill by a backdoor method."

Another Humphrey amendment would have denied the increase unless all communist nations were expelled from the IMF. Membership of the organization included nations such as Romania, Hungary, Yugoslavia and the People's Republic of China. The Senate killed the amendment, 60-32. *(Vote 119, p. 24-S)*

Two other Humphrey amendments also were rejected. A measure to discourage loans to certain member nations until they held free elections and permitted unrestricted emigration was knocked down by a vote of 63-30. *(Vote 121, p. 24-S)*

Another, to reduce the funding increase by 20 percent and instruct the IMF to sell some of its gold reserves instead, was killed by a vote of 62-30. *(Vote 123, p. 24-S)*

Helms offered an amendment encouraging the IMF to establish a new policy to deny loans to any nation that refused to eliminate direct or indirect "predatory export subsidies" for agricultural goods. The amendment also sought to define a "predatory subsidy" as any subsidy that lowered a nation's export price to a level "below the comparable price for a like product produced in the United States."

The Helms amendment would have suspended U.S. participation in the IMF if the subsidy policy was not fully implemented by Jan. 1, 1985.

The amendment was heavily criticized by the sponsors of the bill, who said the IMF already discouraged export subsidies and the Helms measure went too far.

Recognizing that his amendment was going to fail, Helms offered a substitute that removed the clause suspending U.S. participation in the IMF if the subsidy policy was not implemented. That largely gutted the amendment, since other member nations were unlikely to agree to the proposal. The substitute was adopted by a vote of 81-13. *(Vote 120, p. 24-S)*

Two other Helms proposals also were defeated. A provision to authorize the additional IMF funding only through fiscal 1984 failed 33-57. And a provision requiring congressional approval of any new issues of Special Drawing Rights failed 19-71. *(Votes 125, 124, p. 25-S)*

The Senate narrowly rejected an amendment by William L. Armstrong, R-Colo., expressing the sense of the Senate that an international monetary conference should be called to help restore stability to the world monetary system, and that the IMF should make use of its gold reserves to meet the debt crisis. The amendment also called upon the IMF to revise the conditions that accompanied its loans "to encourage economic growth," and said that any additional resources made available during the debt crisis "should be on a temporary basis, preferably through bilat-

eral arrangements." A move by Heinz to table that amendment was agreed to 47-46. *(Vote 122, p. 24-S)*

Amendments adopted by the Senate by voice vote included those by:

• Mack Mattingly, R-Ga., encouraging the IMF to eliminate practices in member nations inconsistent with the General Agreement on Tariffs and Trade (GATT), and directing the Treasury secretary to study the feasibility of using the IMF gold reserves to raise funds.

• John Melcher, D-Mont., and Pete V. Domenici, R-N.M., to encourage the IMF to deny loans that would increase production of a commodity already in surplus in the world. That provision was sought by the copper industries based in Melcher's and Domenici's home states.

A separate amendment, offered by Garn and also adopted by voice vote, required U.S. banks extending loans for foreign mining, metal or mineral operations to conduct an "economic feasibility evaluation" taking into account the effect of the project on U.S. industry and employment.

• John W. Warner, R-Va., requiring the secretary of the Treasury to study the effect of IMF loans on world oil prices.

• Bill Bradley, D-N.J., requiring the Treasury to prepare a written report on the role of debt restructuring in world recovery.

• Melcher, requiring the secretary of the Treasury to notify Congress if funds in the General Arrangements to Borrow were loaned to nations other than those participating in the GAB.

Major Provisions

In addition to providing new funds for the IMF, S 695 encouraged greater information activities by the fund, and strengthened the government regulation of international lending by U.S. banks. Major provisions would:

• Require bank regulators to ensure that banks heavily involved in overseas lending maintain adequate capital to protect themselves from possible defaults.

• Require banks to establish loan loss reserves for loans to countries such as Poland and Zaire that had been unable to meet the rescheduled payment plans on their debts.

• Require banks to spread the earnings from rescheduling fees over the effective life of the rescheduled loan.

• Require more frequent reporting by banks of their foreign lending.

• Encourage the IMF to examine more closely and report on the external indebtedness of borrowing nations.

• Urge consideration of U.S. membership in the Swiss-based Bank for International Settlements.

House Committee Action

The House Banking Committee reported a package May 16 (HR 2957 — H Rept 98-175), that combined measures to authorize the IMF funding increase (HR 2930 — H Rept 98-177), reauthorize the Export-Import Bank (HR 2842 — H Rept 98-176) and provide additional funding to the multilateral development banks (HR 2832 — H Rept 98-178). The package was approved by a 27-14 vote.

As reported, the IMF measure required banks to establish special reserves to offset loans to nations that had been unable to repay according to the original terms of those loans. That stricture would apply to loans to most of the Third-World borrowers, which had been forced to renegotiate or "reschedule" their foreign debt payments because depressed world commodity markets had severely decreased their export earnings.

Doug Barnard Jr., D-Ga., and Stewart B. McKinney, R-Conn., criticized the reserve provision, saying it would discourage banks from continuing their lending to developing nations at a time when those nations desperately needed new loans to keep afloat. The two members favored more moderate language, like that adopted April 28 by the Senate Banking Committee, which would require reserves only on loans to nations that had repeatedly failed to meet the terms of rescheduling agreements or IMF lending agreements. This would include the most troubled debtors, such as Poland and Zaire, but not fundamentally healthy economies, such as Argentina, Brazil or Mexico.

But Committee Chairman Fernand J. St Germain, D-R.I., argued the stricter language was necessary to ensure that banks did not repeat the mistakes of the past decade, during which "sound, prudent banking ... was too often ignored in pursuit of the quick, high-interest buck in the developing nations."

The effort by Barnard and McKinney to amend the reserve provision was defeated by a vote of 20-23.

Leadership Squabble

The committee rejected a proposal that would pressure the IMF to "stretch out" Third-World debt, requiring banks of all nations to accept longer repayment periods and lower interest rates on outstanding loans.

That proposal had been championed by Charles E. Schumer, D-N.Y., and was added to the IMF bill by St Germain. Schumer believed a stretch-out was necessary to allow for renewed economic growth in the developing countries and in the world.

The controversial proposal, however, was never considered by the International Trade Subcommittee, which had jurisdiction over IMF legislation. That fact caused considerable dissension among the committee's Democrats.

"Apparently when it came to this issue it was deemed that the work of the subcommittee should not be considered relevant," John J. LaFalce, D-N.Y., complained to St Germain.

"Don't give me your theatrics, John," snapped back an angry St Germain, who said, "The chair exercised its prerogative" to incorporate changes in the IMF funding measure.

Stephen L. Neal, D-N.C., chairman of the trade subcommittee, said the stretch-out proposal was "unworkable" and "heavy-handed." Because it would require the U.S. representative to the fund to vote against IMF loans not incorporating a stretch-out of private loans, the measure would tie the hands of the United States in the fund, Neal said.

Neal's amendment to remove the restriction on the U.S. vote was adopted 28-18.

The committee also retained a controversial provision directing the U.S. representative to the fund to oppose IMF loans to South Africa.

An amendment by Ron Paul, R-Texas, requiring the IMF to raise money by selling its gold reserves was defeated 5-31.

The committee adopted two amendments by voice vote. One, sponsored by Mary Rose Oakar, D-Ohio, required that large loans for foreign industrial projects be accompanied by economic feasibility evaluations. Another, sponsored by Jim Leach, R-Iowa, directed bank regulators to establish adequate levels of capital for all U.S. banking institutions, and to work with foreign bank regulators to

strengthen capital bases of all banks involved in international lending.

Other Provisions

Other provisions of the IMF bill would:
- Direct U.S. bank regulators to require that fees charged by banks for rescheduling loans be amortized over the life of the loans.
- Require banks to disclose their foreign country debt exposure.
- Encourage greater credit data gathering and dissemination by the IMF.
- Require congressional approval of any plan to allocate new Special Drawing Rights.
- Require the U.S. representative to the IMF to work toward the elimination of barriers to international trade.

House Floor Action

The House took up HR 2957 July 25 and passed the measure Aug. 3 by a 217-211 vote. *(Vote 304, p. 90-H)*

Opponents of the bill were able to force the sponsors to accept several major amendments.

Led by a coalition of conservative Republicans and populist Democrats, the opposition tagged the bill as a big-bank bailout and a foreign aid giveaway. Armed with more than 60 amendments, they threatened to prolong floor proceedings indefinitely if some of them were not accepted.

The most significant addition was an excess-profits tax on big banks, authored by Ed Bethune, R-Ark. The amendment, adopted by voice vote, would force banks whose loans to Third World countries were made more secure by the IMF to pay the Treasury any interest they collected in excess of the rate charged triple-A-rated corporate borrowers in the United States.

"These are terrible amendments we are accepting," Stephen L. Neal, D-N.C., told reporters after the Bethune amendment had been agreed to. "That's an absolutely insane idea; it would socialize the banks."

Another amendment aimed at the big banks, sponsored by Byron L. Dorgan, D-N.D., prohibited banks from charging fees for restructuring a developing country's debt that exceeded actual administrative costs of restructuring.

Bureaucrats and Communists

Big banks were not alone in taking heat from the House during the IMF debate. The fund itself was saddled with restrictions.

An amendment successfully sponsored by Andrew Jacobs Jr., D-Ind., blocked the increase in the U.S. contribution to the fund unless a salary cap of $67,000 was put on all IMF employees, and unless low-rate mortgages for fund employees were prohibited. According to Jacobs, one-third of the fund's 1,500 employees in Washington earned in excess of the cap. His amendment passed by a voice vote.

A measure forcing the United States to vote against IMF loans to "communist dictatorships," offered by Phil Gramm, R-Texas, was adopted 242-185 Aug. 3. That measure was the conservatives' answer to a provision adopted in the Banking Committee prohibiting loans to countries that practiced apartheid. *(Vote 301, p. 90-H)*

Because the fund was not intended to be a political institution, liberal sponsors of the apartheid provision had defended their action on economic grounds. They argued that apartheid in South Africa was an "impediment to labor mobility."

Export-Import Bank's Role

The Export-Import Bank, a government institution providing low-interest loans for the purchase of U.S. goods by foreign nations and companies, was last extended in 1978. *(1978 Almanac p. 397)*

Ex-Im concentrated its efforts on big-ticket items — airplanes and power plants, for example — and did far less for smaller capital goods exports that could get adequate financing, although at higher rates, from commercial banks.

The bank, a federally chartered independent corporation, did not get appropriated funds from Congress. Rather, it borrowed money from the Federal Financing Bank (FFB), which in turn borrowed from the Treasury; the Treasury raised its funds by the sale of government securities. Because the interest the Treasury had to pay on the securities it sold was generally lower than commercial loan rates, Ex-Im could make loans somewhat below market rates.

The agency had long been subject to complaints that the vast majority of its subsidized loans benefited only a handful of huge U. S. corporations. But by early 1983, with the nation's unemployment rate exceeding 10 percent, subsidized export credit no longer was seen simply as bounty for big business. It was viewed as a way to keep and create jobs.

Many traditional economists — including the three members of President Reagan's Council of Economic Advisers — argued that export subsidies could not create new jobs. Nonetheless, there was growing sentiment that foreign export subsidies had cost the United States jobs, and similar subsidies here might win those jobs back.

Reagan, who attempted to cut the Export-Import Bank's operations in his first two annual budgets, supported a modest expansion of its lending authority in 1983. *(1981 Almanac p. 123)*

"If apartheid represents an impediment to labor mobility," Gramm said, "surely that same logic applies to a system that limits both capital and labor mobility."

An amendment by Philip M. Crane, R-Ill., also directed the U.S. representative to the fund to work toward a policy forcing each member nation to pay for its IMF participation, or "quota," in either dollars, German marks, French francs or Japanese yen, rather than its own currency.

"It is very easy for other countries to urge for quota increases when they pay in toilet paper money," Crane said. The amendment was accepted by voice vote.

Gold Bugs

Paul and William E. Dannemeyer, R-Calif., offered a series of amendments in an attempt to force the IMF to either sell its gold, return the gold to fund members, or reestablish a gold standard. All the gold amendments were defeated without difficulty.

Paul noted that the IMF had 103 million ounces of gold, valued at $40 billion — more than the total increase in IMF quotas. "It is the largest hoard of gold in the world," Paul said. "Giving the IMF a loan is like giving the

richest kid on the block a loan."

Treasury officials argued, however, that any attempt by the IMF to sell its gold reserves would weaken the fund and drive down the price of gold.

Compromise Amendment

In earlier action, supporters of the measure July 29 easily defeated two separate attempts to eliminate the IMF increase, by votes of 181-226 and 178-226. *(Votes 276, 277, p. 84-H)*

The votes in favor of the IMF proposal came after a compromise amendment designed to meet the concerns of some of the bill's opponents was adopted, 332-76. That compromise was engineered July 28 by the House Democratic and Republican leadership, working closely with the Treasury Department. *(Vote 275, p. 82-H)*

The compromise gave some new instructions to the U.S. executive director to the fund and also called for increased regulation of international lending by the major U.S. banks. But it did not substantially alter the heart of the IMF bill.

Bethune criticized the compromise amendment as a "fig leaf," consisting only of cosmetic measures designed to win the support of those who wanted to shield themselves from constituent criticisms that they were bailing out big banks or giving away foreign aid.

Bethune also objected to the successful effort by House Democratic leaders to limit all debate on the amendment to less than two hours.

"When you have a fig leaf," Bethune said, "it is important to get it on the floor, get it voted on and get it out of here quickly. Because if you don't, pretty soon people start to see through your fig leaf."

House Democratic and Republican leaders, as well as the Reagan administration, had been scrambling for two weeks to garner sufficient support in the House for the IMF bill.

Opponents had criticized the measure on three grounds. Some complained that it was a bailout of big banks that had made imprudent loans to developing countries. Others argued that it was a massive, $8.4 billion foreign-aid giveaway at a time when money could better be used within the United States. And others made the more technical criticism that conditions the IMF imposed on debt-burdened nations were too stringent, and tended to restrict growth and decrease U.S. exports to those nations.

The compromise amendment, cosponsored by Banking Chairman St Germain and the committee's ranking Republican, Chalmers P. Wylie, Ohio, attempted to address those criticisms.

Most of the changes probably would have little impact on the operations of the IMF. For example, one provision instructed the U.S. director to the fund to oppose any IMF loan that would be principally for bailing out banks. It also instructed the director to work for fund policies that encouraged growth, low tax rates and free operation of markets.

Another provision would permit use of the $2.6 billion for the General Arrangements to Borrow only if other means of funding had been fully explored.

The amendment also would put new regulations on big bank lending overseas, but only if a bank's loans to a country exceeded that bank's primary capital. Treasury officials said it was not clear whether any banks currently exceeded that relatively loose standard.

The compromise also would require the U.S. director

to the IMF to vote against debt restructuring plans unless they forced private banks to stretch out the maturities and lower the interest rates on their loans.

That provision was similar to an amendment offered July 26 by Charles E. Schumer, D-N.Y., and defeated, 157-268. *(Vote 254, p. 78-H)*

Schumer's earlier amendment, however, would have capped interest and restructuring fees at no more than one-half a percentage point above the international interbank interest rate. The compromise did not include a specific interest cap.

The compromise also required Treasury to consult with Congress before negotiating further increases in U.S. participation in the fund.

Ex-Im Amendment

Amendments to the Export-Import Bank authorization were considered July 26, and the House agreed by voice vote to strike a provision creating a Competitive Tied-Aid Fund.

That provision, sponsored by Neal, would have created a $1 billion "war chest" the bank could have used to subsidize loans for U.S. exporters facing overseas competition from foreign companies receiving subsidized export credit.

House Provisions

The bill passed by the House contained five separate titles, which extended authority for the Export-Import Bank and provided new funds for multilateral development banks as well as providing for increased IMF participation.

The bill also included a section (Title II) attributing many global economic problems to high U.S. interest rates and directing the president to encourage industrialized nations to cooperate in adopting fiscal and monetary policies aimed at sustainable, non-inflationary economic growth.

Ex-Im Bank

Title I of the bill extended authority for the Export-Import Bank until Sept. 30, 1985.

The major proposed change to the Ex-Im law would strengthen the bank's mandate to make loans at rates that were competitive with those offered by foreign governments. Traditionally, the bank had had to balance its mandate to provide competitive credit against its desire not to lose money. The bill directed the bank to continue to pay attention to its balance sheet, but to give competitiveness a higher priority.

If this new policy caused the bank to deplete more than 50 percent of its capital, the bill directed the bank to notify Congress, which then should take "appropriate action."

Small Business. The bill required Ex-Im for the first time to set aside 6 percent of its direct loans and loan guarantees for small businesses in 1984, and 10 percent in 1985. It also directed the president to select at least one of his five appointees to the board from the small business community.

And it provided a congressional mandate for the medium-term financing facility, recently created by the bank, which was expected to boost assistance for small and medium-sized companies. Traditionally, most Ex-Im credit had gone to large companies for big-ticket items such as airplanes and nuclear power plants.

Other Provisions. The bill also would:

● Require the bank to ensure that U.S. insurance companies were given equal opportunity to bid for insurance on sales financed by the bank.

● Establish a 12-person advisory committee to meet quarterly and advise the bank on its programs, and report to Congress.

Senate Bill. The Senate Sept. 23 approved a two-year extension of the Ex-Im Bank in separate legislation (S 869) reported by the Banking Committee May 16 (S Rept 98-111) and the Foreign Relations Committee June 10 (S Rept 98-183). The bill created a new "mixed credit" program allowing the bank to combine its loans with development loans from the Agency for International Development in order to provide credit at lower interest rates. Mixed credit would be given for U.S. exports facing competition from foreign products financed with subsidized credit.

International Monetary Fund

Title III of the House bill increased the U.S. quota in the IMF by approximately $5.8 billion and the contribution to the GAB by about $2.6 billion. The dollar figures were not exact because the authority was denominated in Special Drawing Rights, whose dollar value fluctuated daily.

The increased funds represented a commitment of dollars that the IMF could draw on as they were needed. Interest was paid on the money used by the fund, and SDRs were provided in return for the money in use.

Salary Cap. The Treasury was prohibited from transferring new funds to the IMF until a salary cap of $67,000 was put on all IMF employees and the practice of providing low-rate mortgages for employees was halted.

Stretch-Out. The bill included a modified version of a measure proposed by Schumer, encouraging the IMF to force banks to lower the interest rates and extend the maturities of private bank loans in IMF restructuring programs for debt-ridden nations.

The U.S. representative to the fund was instructed to vote against any restructuring that did not contain such a stretch-out, unless he first determined that an emergency existed in the nation involved, that the debt problem would last for no more than one year, or that other extraordinary circumstances existed.

Congressional Consultation. Congress must be consulted throughout negotiations by the Treasury for any future increase in IMF quotas, under the bill's provisions. The Treasury was prohibited from approving any new allocation of Special Drawing Rights without congressional approval.

Bank Regulation. The bill required federal bank regulators to restrict foreign lending by banks whose foreign loans were "excessive" — defined as banks whose loans in one foreign country exceeded that bank's primary capital.

Restricting the U.S. Vote. The bill also instructed the U.S. representative to the IMF to:

● Propose policies to improve collection and public dissemination of information on a quarterly basis concerning foreign loans made by banks.

● Oppose any use of IMF credit by any country that practiced apartheid or by communist dictatorships.

● Propose policies to the fund to ensure that countries using fund resources take steps to eliminate import restrictions and export subsidies.

● Work for policies to eliminate agricultural export subsidies.

● Work for policies to promote non-inflationary growth, low-rate tax systems, sound monetary and fiscal policy, less government regulation, and contract sanctity in countries that borrowed.

● Work for adoption of policies by the IMF that would contribute to exchange-rate stability.

● Work for the adoption of policies requiring all IMF members to pay for their quota increases in dollars, marks, francs or yen.

● Oppose any loan by the fund drawn principally to repay loans made imprudently by banks.

● Consider whether a country had detonated a nuclear device and signed the nuclear non-proliferation treaty and the nuclear weapons test treaty before voting a loan to that country.

International Banking

Increased regulation of U.S. banks that participated in international lending was called for under Title IV.

A bank would be required to establish special reserves whenever there was a substantial likelihood that it could not repay its loans in accordance with the original terms — a requirement that might affect most of the loans to major Latin American borrowers, such as Brazil and Argentina.

Bank regulators were also directed to use higher standards in determining whether a bank had an adequate level of capital to support a heavy foreign loan portfolio.

Other Provisions. Other banking provisions in the bill would:

● Prohibit banks from charging debt restructuring fees that exceeded the cost of restructuring, and require banks to amortize the fees they charged for restructuring a loan over the life of that loan.

● Require the bank examination council to collect quarterly data on each bank's exposure in foreign countries.

● Require any bank making a loan in excess of $1 million involving a mining or manufacturing project outside the United States to prepare a feasibility evaluation of the project, including a study of its impact on world markets.

Development Banks

Inter-American Bank. The bill authorized a $380 million contribution to the bank's Fund for Special Operations, which made heavily subsidized loans to the poorest Latin American nations. It called for a four-year, $5.2 billion increase in the U.S. subscription to the bank's capital, of which $232 million was to be paid in.

Asian Development Bank. The bill allowed a $520 million increase to the Asian Development Fund, the bank's subsidized loan window. The U.S. subscription to the bank's capital would increase by $1.3 billion, of which $66 million was to be paid in.

The bill also expressed the sense of Congress that support to the Asian Bank should be terminated if the Republic of China (Taiwan) was denied full membership to make room for the People's Republic of China. That provision was added on the House floor Aug. 3 by Jerry M. Patterson, D-Calif.

African Development Fund. HR 2957 allowed a $150 million contribution to the fund, which made concessional loans to poor African nations.

House Stalemate

The IMF legislation remained stalled for three months following House passage. A Republican political propa-

ganda campaign led some House Democrats to consider withdrawing their support for the administration bill, and Banking Chairman St Germain threatened to hold the measure hostage until an unrelated housing bill was passed.

GOP Press Releases

A series of press releases sent out by the Republican congressional campaign committee angered IMF supporters of both parties. The releases were sent to the districts of some 20 Democrats who voted against the Gramm amendment requiring the United States to oppose IMF loans to communist dictatorships.

The Gramm amendment, approved 242-185, was opposed by many of the IMF bill's principal supporters, including President Reagan, House Republican leader Robert H. Michel, Ill., and Wylie, the ranking GOP member of the Banking Committee. Those members argued that the IMF, whose purpose was to preserve the stability of the international monetary system, should not be turned into a political institution.

In spite of that opposition by top Republican leaders, the Republican congressional campaign committee — headed by Rep. Guy Vander Jagt, R-Mich. — decided to send out press releases attacking Democrats who had opposed the amendment.

House Democratic leaders were angry that they had to provide most of the support for the president on the IMF bill, while a majority of members from the president's own party voted against the legislation. The bill was politically unpopular, and many Democrats feared that votes for it would be used against them by the GOP in the 1984 election campaigns.

In a letter to the president, seven House Democrats who were targets of the releases demanded that the charges be rebutted by the White House. "At the very least, those of us who have been targeted with this demagogic attack deserve assurances from you that our support for administration positions will not be distorted for political purposes," they wrote.

The letter was signed by Jerry M. Patterson, Calif.; Howard Wolpe, Mich.; Jim Moody, Wis.; Dante B. Fascell, Fla.; Robert A. Young, Mo.; Katie Hall, Ind.; and Thomas R. Carper, Del.

Housing Bill

Banking Committee Chairman St Germain had repeatedly tied passage of the IMF bill to passage of a housing authorization bill (HR 1, S 1338), and he renewed his threat in a letter to President Reagan Aug. 16.

"I am convinced a housing authorization bill needs to be enacted into law this year," St Germain wrote. "I am also convinced — given the margin of the vote on HR 2957 [the IMF bill], and having talked with a number of members in the House who voted favorably for this legislation — that unless a housing bill is enacted into law this year, they will be constrained to vote against any conference report on IMF legislation."

St Germain said he would hold up the conference on the IMF bill until the Senate acted. "I am seriously constrained from continuing with the legislative process on HR 2957 until the housing authorization bill is completed."

Conference, Final Action

In the final week of the session, the housing authorization sought by House Democrats was mated to the IMF increase sought by the administration. The unusual combination was then attached to the conference report on HR 3959, a non-controversial supplemental appropriations bill, and presented to members in a take-it-or-leave-it package. They took it.

The deal was put together over several weeks of delicate negotiations by key members of the Senate and House along with White House Budget Director David A. Stockman and Treasury Secretary Donald T. Regan. Although the Reagan administration opposed several key provisions of the housing measure, it agreed to swallow them to get the IMF money, which it wanted badly. The administration also won reauthorization of U.S. participation in several international development banks.

As it came out of conference committee Nov. 15, the supplemental looked like a sure bet to clear easily. Controversial amendments had been stripped from the measure.

The House agreed to the conference report (H Rept 98-551) Nov. 16 by a 372-51 vote. *(Vote 475, p. 138-H)*

But when the Senate took up the conference report Nov. 17, Garn offered the housing-IMF package as an amendment. The Senate approved the conference agreement by voice vote and then adopted the package 67-30 after rejecting several amendments that Garn said would destroy the delicate compromise. *(Vote 364, p. 59-S)*

The Senate tabled three such amendments to the Garn package. One, by Gordon J. Humphrey, R-N.H., to reduce the IMF contribution by $584 million, was tabled 52-45. *(Vote 363, p. 59-S)*

Late on the evening of Nov. 17, the House Rules Committee drafted an unusual closed rule (H Res 379), called a "self-executing rule," providing for floor consideration of the Senate changes on Nov. 18. A vote for the rule was a vote for the Senate changes. No amendments were allowed and debate time was limited to one hour and controlled by the Rules Committee.

Many House members objected to the limited debate provided by the rule. "This gives a new meaning to logrolling," said Dennis E. Eckart, D-Ohio. Clarence D. Long, D-Md., called it "a gag rule of the first order."

But Minority Leader Michel took the floor to urge his Republican colleagues to support the Reagan administration and vote for the rule. "*Our* president is on the line here today," Michel told GOP House members.

The House voted 226-186 for the rule Nov. 18, clearing the bill. *(Vote 497, p. 144-H)*

The compromise IMF provisions in HR 3959 featured a toned-down version of the House bill's most controversial provision, a prohibition against U.S. approval of loans to communist dictatorships and countries that practiced apartheid. In its final form, U.S. approval was denied unless the Treasury secretary certified to Congress that the loan was in the best interests of a majority of the recipient nation's citizens.

In the Senate Nov. 17, IMF opponents called the bill a "bailout" for large banks that had engaged in imprudent lending practices, or a foreign aid giveaway. Armstrong argued the funding in the bill was a "bail in" that would encourage the banks to continue their liberal lending policies.

Supporters of the IMF, backed by the Reagan administration, argued the fund's programs helped to keep U.S. export markets healthy and to maintain economic stability.

Rep. Bill Frenzel, R-Minn., Nov. 18 said there was "no more important bill [for U.S. exports] that this House will vote on this year." ∎

Cap on Reagan Tax Cut Fails

Democrats tried unsuccessfully during the fight over fiscal 1984 spending to score some political points by limiting the third installment of President Reagan's three-year tax-cut plan.

The House June 23 passed legislation (HR 1183) placing a $720 per family "cap" on the 10 percent cut in individual income taxes scheduled to take effect July 1, but the measure was squashed easily in the Senate six days later. President Reagan had vowed to veto the bill.

While the defeat of HR 1183 was no surprise, Democratic leaders in both houses used the legislation to brand the proposal as benefiting those in the high-income brackets. It was a theme the party would use repeatedly during the year, in an attempt to discredit Reagan's economic policies. Even the tax cap maneuver would be resurrected later on as the House prepared to deal with a package to raise taxes. *(Deficit reduction story, p. 231)*

In a speech before the American Stock Exchange June 6, House Speaker Thomas P. O'Neill Jr., D-Mass., charged that the scheduled income tax cut would substantially lower taxes for the rich, while having little impact on most other taxpayers. At the same time, he noted, the administration was demanding that Congress reduce a projected $200 billion budget deficit by approving spending cuts that would largely affect those with lower incomes.

"It is time that the rich started to accept their fair share of the burden," he told reporters before the speech.

The July 1 tax cut was the final portion of a three-stage, across-the-board cut in individual income taxes that was a key element of Reagan's 1981 economic program. *(1981 Almanac p. 91)*

House Action

Democrats were not united on the tax-cap issue. While House Democrats caucused June 7 and generally supported O'Neill's call for setting an upper limit on the July 1 tax cut, serious reservations were voiced.

Some members argued that the cap effort could backfire by giving the administration more ammunition in its efforts to label Democrats as big taxers and big spenders. Ways and Means Committee Chairman Dan Rostenkowski, D-Ill., reportedly was concerned that by politicizing the tax-cut issue, the House would have a more difficult time enacting tax-increase legislation needed later in the year to comply with the fiscal 1984 budget resolution.

Two days letter, 79 House Democrats signed a letter to O'Neill calling the tax cap, without an accompanying limit on spending, "flawed policy." "If we're going to be sending signals to the public, let's send one that has meaning," said Dave McCurdy, D-Okla., author of the letter.

But armed with a survey of caucus members showing a majority supported the cap, the House leadership decided to push ahead with the bill. The leadership was prodded on by House freshmen, many of whom had been elected because of their criticism of the Reagan tax-cut program.

Committee Action

The Ways and Means Committee reluctantly approved a bill (HR 1183) June 16 limiting the scheduled July 1 income tax cut to a maximum of $720 per family.

Some Democrats noted that while the bill would likely pass in the House, it had little chance of clearing the

Senate or surviving a presidential veto.

"I think [the cap] is bound to fail. I'm not going to participate in what I think is a futile gesture," said Sam Gibbons, D-Fla., who joined Ways and Means Democrats Thomas J. Downey, N.Y., Wyche Fowler Jr., Ga., and Marty Russo, Ill., and 11 committee Republicans in voting against the bill. The committee adopted the measure by a vote of 18-15.

As reported by Ways and Means June 21 (H Rept 98-252), HR 1183 would have limited the tax cut to $720 for families of four and to $637 for single taxpayers.

According to the Joint Committee on Taxation, the cap would affect about 10 percent of all taxpayers, including almost all those earning over $50,000 a year and a portion of those earning between $30,000 and $50,000.

Because existing law called for a 10 percent across-the-board cut in taxes, those with higher incomes would have the most to lose from the Democrats' plan. For example, a family of four with an adjusted gross income of $100,000 was scheduled to receive a $2,368 tax cut. This would be limited to $720, a reduction of $1,648, under HR 1183. But families with incomes of $50,000 would receive only $108 less than under the existing law.

The committee turned back a number of Republican attempts to link the tax cap to spending cuts, but approved a "preamble" to the bill stating the committee's intention that any revenues raised from the cap should be used to reduce the deficit. HR 1183 was expected to raise $6.2 billion in fiscal 1984 and almost $38 billion through 1989.

At a June 15 hearing on the tax-cap plan, Treasury Secretary Donald T. Regan argued that raising any taxes during the year could jeopardize the emerging economic recovery. He said he expected President Reagan to veto the bill if it reached his desk.

Floor Action

Overcoming opposition within the party, House Democrats scored a symbolic victory against President Reagan June 23 by voting to limit the final installment of his three-year tax cut.

By a largely party-line vote of 229-191, the House agreed to place a cap of $720 per family on the 10 percent cut in individual income taxes scheduled for July 1. *(Vote 207, p. 62-H)*

No Republicans voted for the bill, and 29 Democrats voted against it, despite the strong urgings of the party leadership.

More Democratic defections had appeared likely earlier in the week. But the Rules Committee agreed June 22 to request a rule allowing a watered-down amendment by Rep. McCurdy calling for a $6 billion reduction in fiscal 1984 spending to accompany the $6 billion in revenues expected to come from the cap.

McCurdy had originally requested that Rules allow a floor vote on a more stringent measure that would have repealed the tax cap Jan. 1, 1984, if dollar-for-dollar spending cuts were not made.

Republicans were quick to point out on the floor that the revised amendment included no enforcement mechanism and was little more than a "fig leaf" for Democrats to hide behind. But it was a fig leaf Democrats could live with and the rule was adopted by a vote of 253-166; McCurdy's amendment passed 267-155. *(Votes 203, 205, p. 62-H)*

Democrats defended the cap as the most equitable way to cut the deficit, noting that the cap would largely affect those in the high-income brackets who had benefited most

from the first two years of Reagan's tax-cut program.

But Republicans countered that Democrats were engaged in little more than a futile political exercise aimed at the voters back home. They charged that the tax cap would not only affect wealthy taxpayers but would permanently raise taxes for millions of middle-income families.

Other Republicans accused the Democrats of trying to stifle the emerging economic recovery by raising taxes. "This is the worst possible economic medicine at the worst possible time," said Guy Vander Jagt, R-Mich.

Senate Action

As predicted, the tax-cap issue was laid to rest by the Republican-controlled Senate, which defeated HR 1183 June 29 on a near party-line vote of 45-55.

Only three Republicans — William S. Cohen, Maine; John Heinz, Pa.; and Arlen Specter, Pa. — broke ranks with their party and voted for the Democratic proposal. Four Democrats voted against the tax-cap bill: David L. Boren, Okla.; Howell Heflin, Ala.; J. Bennett Johnston, La.; and Edward Zorinsky, Neb. *(Vote 170, p. 31-S)*

Although the Democrats knew the cap would fail, they hoped to gain political mileage from the issue. Senate leaders had promised Democrats a vote on the tax cap to win vital Democratic support earlier in the year on a debt limit bill. *(Debt limit, p. 239)*

During a June 28 press conference, President Reagan warned that the tax cap "must not and will not become law." He tried to deflect the fairness issue by claiming that 2.4 million small businesses, 350,000 family farms and millions of middle-income married couples would be affected by the cap.

But in a battle of statistics, Senate Democrats argued on the floor that 90 percent of all taxpayers would still receive the full tax cut. "Since when have the top 10 percent of the population been defined as the middle class?" asked Sen. Bill Bradley, D-N.J.

Like their House counterparts, Senate Democrats claimed that the cap would help reduce the federal deficit, while turning around what they described as the unfair economic policies pursued by Reagan.

But the Republicans countered that the deficit would not be reduced by the tax-cap measure. ". . . . Raising taxes will probably do now what it has in the past — that is, raising taxes will only result in more government spending," said Orrin G. Hatch, R-Utah. ∎

Trade Department

A bill that would establish a new Department of International Trade and Industry was reported by the Senate Governmental Affairs Committee Oct. 18, after committee Democrats tacked on a watered-down "industrial policy" proposal. *(Industrial policy, box, next page)*

Approval of the measure (S 121) marked a major victory for Committee Chairman William V. Roth Jr., R-Del., who had been promoting trade reorganization for several years. The full Senate did not act on the bill before adjournment.

Supporters of reorganization argued that the role of foreign trade in the U.S. economy had expanded dramatically, demanding a more coordinated government approach to trade policy. Not only were trade policy matters split

between the Commerce Department and the Office of the U.S. Trade Representative, but several other agencies, such as the Agriculture Department, also held trade responsibilities.

Critics of Roth's proposal said the increased importance of trade issues was the very reason reorganization should not be debated. Many other trade issues should be addressed, they argued, and a reorganization fight could cause confusion in American trade policy for some time.

The Roth bill would combine the trade representative's office and the Commerce Department in a single department, whose secretary would be the president's principal adviser on international trade policy and would assume most of the responsibilities currently held by the secretary of commerce and the U.S. trade representative. The secretary also would chair the interagency trade organization that coordinated trade policy among the executive branch departments and agencies.

The Census Bureau and the National Oceanic and Atmospheric Administration would be moved out of the department and established as independent agencies. The Minority Business Development Agency would be moved to the Small Business Administration, and the Economic Development Administration would become part of the Department of Agriculture.

The Reagan administration endorsed plans for a new "lean and mean" trade department, which had been pushed by Commerce Secretary Malcolm Baldrige. Trade Representative William E. Brock III had defended the existing system, arguing that his office acted as an "honest broker" for the other departments and agencies with an interest in trade. Under any system, he argued, a mechanism was needed for coordinating the views of all the government offices with a legitimate interest in trade.

The House took no action on trade department legislation in 1983. Rep. Don Bonker, D-Wash., chairman of the Foreign Affairs Subcommittee on Trade, attempted to draft a trade reorganization bill that would win Democratic support in the House, but never completed the effort. Bonker admitted it was "certainly not the most urgent step that needs to be taken to improve U.S. international competitiveness."

Industrial Policy Amendment

The Senate Governmental Affairs Committee approved S 121 Oct. 3 on a 13-3 vote.

Although Roth had sufficient support among the committee's Republicans to report the bill, he courted the Democrats in order to improve the legislation's chances of success on the Senate floor, and in the Democratic-controlled House. He delayed final markup for several days to allow Thomas F. Eagleton, D-Mo., and Carl Levin, D-Mich., to offer a compromise industrial policy proposal.

Without some changes to emphasize the need for industrial adjustment and development programs, Eagleton said, he would be hard pressed to support the bill. Roth voted against the industrial policy amendment. But he allowed Eagleton, the committee's ranking minority member, to offer it at a time when the Democrats were a majority of those present at the markup, thus ensuring its success.

"This bill is dead as a doornail in the House of Representatives without an industrial component," Eagleton told Roth before the vote on his amendment.

The "industrial policy" proposal sponsored by Eagleton and Levin came in two parts. The first amendment,

Industrial Policy

Industrial policy enjoyed a long run as a congressional buzzword in 1983. While none of the various plans to develop a national industrial strategy made much legislative progress, many Democrats promoted industrial policy as a potent weapon against the Republicans in the 1984 election campaigns.

In the Senate, the Governmental Affairs Committee included an industrial policy component in legislation to establish a new Department of International Trade and Industry. But the full Senate never acted on that measure (S 121), reported Oct. 18.

In the House, a hearing on an industrial policy plan pushed by Rep. John J. LaFalce, D-N.Y., was held — just two days before Congress adjourned — by the Banking Subcommittee on Economic Stabilization, which LaFalce chaired. The House hearing focused on a bill (HR 4360) that covered two components of La Falce's plan: a Bank for Industrial Competitiveness to provide development money for new and existing industries and a Council on Industrial Competitiveness to map out industrial strategy. Money lent out would have strings attached — borrowers from smokestack industries, for example, would have to agree to modernize and improve competitiveness as a condition for receiving a loan. The Economic Stabilization Subcommittee proposal would also create an Advanced Technology Foundation to support research.

A similar plan was proposed by a task force of the Senate Democratic Policy Committee. In addition to a Council on Economic Competitiveness and Cooperation, the Senate plan would offer tax breaks to promote innovation in industry, upgrade science and math instruction and create programs to help industries and communities adapt to changing technologies.

agreed to by the committee by voice vote with no apparent opposition, would create an Office of Competitive Analysis within the new department. That office would be charged with collecting data on the competitive positions of particular industries in international markets, and providing thorough analysis of the data.

The second, more controversial, amendment charged the Office of Competitive Analysis with preparing a report each March, describing actual and foreseeable economic and technological developments that could affect the competitive positions of particular industries.

The secretary of the new department would then be required to convene temporary industry "competitiveness councils" for those established U.S. industries likely to face "a competitive challenge," "substantial dislocation" or "a significant risk" of being "unable to compete successfully in significant future markets."

Councils also would be convened for industries that were faced with "significant opportunities . . . to compete in new geographical markets or product markets, or to expand their position in established markets."

The councils would consist of representatives of business, labor, government and other groups involved in the industry. And discussions held by the council would be exempted from federal and state antitrust law.

The amendment was adopted by an 8-2 vote.

Other Amendments

During a Sept. 27 markup, the committee accepted by voice vote an amendment by Dave Durenberger, R-Minn., to make the Census Bureau an independent agency.

The Roth bill had placed the bureau in the Treasury Department. Durenberger complained, however, that people responding to census surveys might falsify their answers for fear the information would be shared with the Internal Revenue Service, an arm of the Treasury Department.

The committee also adopted an amendment by Charles H. Percy, R-Ill., which would establish an Administration for Productivity and Technology in the new department. That administration would include the activities of the National Bureau of Standards and the National Technical Information Service, as well as the Office of Patents and Trademarks, the National Telecommunications and Information Administration and the assistant secretary for productivity, technology and innovation.

An amendment by William S. Cohen, R-Maine, to create a Small Business Trade Assistance Office was also adopted Sept. 27.

At a continuation of the markup on Sept. 29, the committee adopted an amendment by Charles McC. Mathias Jr., R-Md., establishing a White House council to coordinate trade policy. Mathias was concerned that by transferring the trade representative to the new department, the Roth bill undermined the president's role as coordinator of trade policy. His council would hold a status similar to that of the National Security Council, and advise the president on trade matters. The plan was adopted 5-2.

The committee also adopted two more amendments by Cohen. One put the Economic Development Administration, which Roth's bill gave to the Department of Housing and Urban Development, into the Department of Agriculture. The other created an under secretary for agricultural trade in the new department. ∎

Trade Adjustment Aid

A two-year extension of the trade adjustment assistance program (HR 3813 — PL 98-120) cleared Congress Sept. 30, just hours before the program was set to expire.

Trade adjustment benefits went to workers who had been laid off from industries harmed by import competition. A small portion of the benefits also went to small and medium-sized firms suffering from imports.

The program was started in 1962 and expanded under the Trade Act of 1974. In the 1981 budget reconciliation act, Congress extended the program through Sept. 30, 1983, but drastically curtailed eligibility for benefits. Some of the more liberal eligibility requirements were restored in 1982. *(1982 Almanac p. 51; 1981 Almanac p. 107)*

The Reagan administration sought the termination of trade adjustment assistance. High levels of unemployment, however, convinced a majority in both houses of Congress that the benefits should be continued.

Legislative History

The House passed a bill (HR 3391) Sept. 15 that would have greatly expanded the program from its fiscal 1983 level. Workers laid off from firms supplying component parts or services to an industry affected by imports would have been eligible for benefits for the first time. And the

government would have been required to approve training assistance under certain circumstances, regardless of whether funds were available. According to Congressional Budget Office estimates, the House bill would have cost $217 million in fiscal 1984. Four attempts by Bill Frenzel, R-Minn., to cut back the program failed by substantial margins. *(Votes 318, 319, p. 94-H; votes 323, 324, p. 96-H)*

The Senate Finance Committee, however, rejected the House changes and approved instead a simple two-year extension of the existing program, expected to cost $95 million in fiscal 1984. The only change made by the Senate was to give preference to firms that adopted employee stock ownership plans when granting trade adjustment assistance to companies.

The Senate Sept. 30 attached its trade adjustment assistance proposal to HR 3813, a House-passed measure extending the International Coffee Agreement for three years. The bill was then approved by voice vote.

Later in the same day, the House gave its approval to the Senate's modest version of the bill, also by voice vote.

"OMB [Office of Management and Budget] has made clear during Senate consideration this week that it would recommend a veto if reauthorization of the trade adjustment assistance programs includes expanded coverage," said Rep. Don J. Pease, D-Ohio, principal sponsor of the House version of the bill, Sept. 30. "Under these circumstances, and because the programs expire today, I recommend the House concur with the Senate." ∎

Caribbean Trade Plan

Congress July 28 handily endorsed the Reagan administration's proposal to provide special tax incentives to aid troubled Central American and Caribbean nations.

The measure (HR 2973 — PL 98-67) was designed to promote economic development in the region by providing duty-free entry into the United States for certain Caribbean exports, and by allowing U.S. businessmen to take tax deductions for the expense of attending conventions in the region.

Passage of the "Caribbean Basin Initiative" fulfilled a promise that President Reagan made to the nations of Central America and the Caribbean in February 1982.

The House that December passed legislation nearly identical to the 1983 Caribbean bill, but it died at the end of the session when the Senate failed to act. *(1982 Almanac p. 54)*

The Reagan administration had envisioned a broader program of trade and tax benefits. But Congress, concerned about heavy unemployment in the United States, whittled away at the bill until only a modest package of incentives remained. Less than 10 percent of the region's exports were to receive new duty-free treatment under the bill.

The administration campaigned energetically for the bill to prove to the politically unstable nations of the Caribbean region that the United States was a reliable friend.

The Caribbean Basin Initiative was contained in tax withholding legislation that otherwise had been opposed by President Reagan, who nevertheless signed the bill Aug. 5. The Senate had added the Caribbean Basin Initiative to the tax bill after the House approved a separate version. *(Withholding provisions, p. 261)*

The House approved the conference report on the bill

(H Rept 98-325) by a 392-18 vote July 28. The Senate vote July 28 was 90-7. *(House vote 263, p. 80-H; Senate vote 224, p. 38-S)*

Final Provisions

As cleared, the Caribbean Basin legislation:

Eligibility. Stipulated that the bill's provisions were applicable to the 27 nations in Central America and the Caribbean as well as Guyana and Surinam, but not Cuba. A nation would be eligible for benefits if it:

● Was not a communist country.

● Had not nationalized, expropriated or otherwise seized ownership of U.S. property, and had not repudiated contracts, patents or trademarks of U.S. citizens.

● Had not failed to act in good faith on the results of binding arbitration in favor of U.S. citizens.

● Did not provide preferential trade treatment to the products of countries other than the United States, to the detriment of U.S. commerce.

● Had not broadcast U.S. copyrighted material without the consent of the owners.

● Cooperated with the United States to prevent drug traffic.

● Had signed an extradition agreement with the United States.

Beneficiary nations wishing to export beef and sugar to the United States must also implement "stable food production plans" to ensure that land needed to provide food for the nation's citizens was not diverted to export crops.

Beneficiary nations were to be designated by the president after notification to Congress. A decision to terminate beneficiary status required 60 days' notice to Congress.

Benefits. Provided duty-free entry into the U.S. market for 12 years for Caribbean products except: textiles and apparel, petroleum products, footwear, handbags, luggage, flat goods (wallets, eyeglass cases, etc.), work gloves, leather wearing apparel, tuna, and watches or watch parts. Sugar would be duty free, but subject to quotas.

● Stipulated that products eligible for duty-free status must be imported directly from a beneficiary country. At least 35 percent of the products' value must consist of Caribbean parts and labor, but U.S. parts and labor could account for up to 15 percent of that 35 percent. Items that were not the product of a beneficiary country and were simply combined, packaged or diluted in the Caribbean would not be eligible for duty-free status.

Duty-free status for any Caribbean export could be suspended through existing import relief procedures. An emergency relief procedure was provided for "perishable" agricultural products. *(Procedures, 1974 Almanac p. 553)*

● Allowed U.S. citizens to take the same tax deduction for conventions held in eligible Caribbean nations as allowed for U.S. conventions, provided the nation had entered into a tax treaty with the United States. That provision was expected to cost the government about $5 million in lost tax revenues per year.

Puerto Rico, Virgin Islands. Included provisions to compensate Puerto Rico and the Virgin Islands for the increased competition they would face in the U.S. market from Caribbean competition. Those provisions:

● Provided that all excise taxes collected on foreign rum brought into the United States, estimated at about $10 million a year, would be transferred to the U.S. islands.

● Included an exemption from U.S. water pollution control laws for a Virgin Islands rum plant.

● Raised the level of permissible foreign content in Vir-

gin Islands exports to the United States from 50 to 70 percent, except for those items exempted from the Caribbean Basin Initiative.

● Permitted travelers entering the United States to carry up to five liters of distilled spirits duty free, provided at least one liter was purchased in Puerto Rico or the Virgin Islands.

Reports. Required the U.S. International Trade Commission to prepare periodic reports on the impact of the Caribbean Basin Initiative on U.S. industries and consumers, and required the Labor Department to undertake a continuing review of the bill's impact on U.S. employment.

● Required the secretary of the Treasury to report on the use of Caribbean nations as tax havens to avoid U.S. taxes, and directed the secretary of state to study establishing a Caribbean Trade Institute in the Harlem section of New York City.

Legislative History

House Action

In spite of heavy labor opposition, the House July 14 voted 289-129 for the initial bill (HR 2769) eliminating duties on certain Caribbean imports. *(Vote 237, p. 72-H)*

The 160-vote margin was 42 votes higher than in 1982, indicating that labor-backed protectionist sentiment in the House might be easing as concern over Central America grew.

Opponents complained the bill would add to U.S. unemployment. "Jobs will be lost in the American workplace," said James L. Oberstar, D-Minn. "They will be replaced by jobs in the Caribbean, but those will be subsistence-type jobs. The workers will have no health benefit plan, no retirement plan, no vacation pay, no overtime, nothing."

Supporters countered that the bill would create jobs in both the Caribbean and the United States. U.S. exports to Caribbean nations totaled more than $6 billion in 1982, they said, and an improvement in the economies of those nations would push exports even higher.

Many members also argued the economic package would contribute to political stability in the troubled region. "We have made many promises to the people of the Caribbean," said Dan Rostenkowski, D-Ill. "If we turn them away, they are likely to seek assistance from others who will promise them easy answers and offer political stability from the barrel of a gun."

No amendments were allowed to the bill under a rule recommended by the Rules Committee and adopted by the House July 13. Oberstar and Richard A. Gephardt, D-Mo., attempted to defeat the rule so they could offer a package of labor-backed amendments. Their effort failed by a narrow vote, however, and the rule passed 212-204. *(Vote 236, p. 72-H)*

Committee Approval. The Ways and Means Committee had approved HR 2769 (H Rept 98-266) on June 21 by voice vote.

During the markup, Ed Jenkins, D-Ga., offered on behalf of the Virgin Islands an amendment that would have restricted Caribbean rum imports, but the measure was defeated 13-21. The Virgin Islands feared the bill might cut into its lucrative bulk rum trade with the United States.

Gephardt offered three labor-backed amendments, which also were defeated. One of them, defeated 10-24, would have dropped Taiwan, South Korea and Hong Kong from the General System of Preferences program.

Senate Action

The Senate Finance Committee May 12 approved, 15-3, a Caribbean Basin bill (S 544), and the full Senate June 16 added its version to HR 2973, the tax withholding bill. *(Votes 156, 157, p. 29-S)*

The major difference between the House and Senate versions had to do with rum. The Senate bill included a provision — similar to the deleted Jenkins amendment — to protect the U.S. Virgin Islands bulk rum industry from Caribbean competition.

The final version contained provisions protecting the Virgin Islands rum trade.   ∎

Export Controls Extension

The Senate and House did not complete action in 1983 on legislation to reauthorize the Export Administration Act, which expired Sept. 30. Instead, Congress temporarily extended the president's authority to control exports under the expiring law and put off final action on its replacement until 1984.

The House Oct. 27 approved a two-year extension of the act (HR 3231) that encouraged increased export trade by lessening the president's authority to impose controls for national security and foreign policy reasons. The major change in controls made by the legislation allowed exporters to forgo licensing for shipments to Japan and U.S. allies in Western Europe.

A six-year export control bill approved by the Senate Banking Committee May 25 did not receive floor consideration in 1983. The Senate bill (S 979) retained tight national security controls and was more to the liking of the Reagan administration, which wanted no relaxation of controls.

The Senate measure, however, contained a "contract sanctity" provision that pleased pro-export forces. It prohibited the president from imposing foreign policy controls that would force exporters to break contracts. The House bill's contract sanctity provision allowed the president to disregard contracts upon Congress' approval or in reaction to terrorism, human rights violations, nuclear weapons tests or imminent acts of aggression.

When it became clear that the Senate and House would not complete action on reauthorizing legislation before the existing act expired Sept. 30, Congress provided a temporary extension of the president's authority to control exports until Oct. 14 (HR 3962 — PL 98-108). Upon expiration of that measure, President Reagan invoked emergency powers to prevent controls from lapsing. A second bill (HR 4476 — PL 98-207), cleared in the last hours before adjournment Nov. 18, extended the president's export control authority until Feb. 29, 1984.

Background

The United States had restricted exports for national security or foreign policy reasons since the 1940s. The Export Administration Act dated from 1969 and had last been extended in 1979 (PL 96-72). *(1979 Almanac p. 300)*

Under the act, exports could be controlled for three purposes: to protect national security, to achieve foreign policy goals, or to prevent the depletion of goods in short supply.

The act was administered by the Office of Export Administration in the Department of Commerce. That of-

fice maintained the Commodity Control List, and items on that list could not be exported without a license.

Most of the goods on the control list were there for national security reasons and required a validated export license regardless of their destination. If the goods were to be exported to a communist country, the secretary of defense could ask to review the license application.

The United States coordinated export controls with its allies through a Coordinating Committee (COCOM) which included the NATO nations (minus Iceland and Spain) and Japan. But the U.S. government was a more ardent controller of exports than its allies, and it restricted many products not on the COCOM list.

Foreign policy controls had been imposed by the Reagan administration and previous administrations for a variety of reasons. Certain products, for instance, were controlled to countries such as Vietnam, Cuba, Cambodia, Libya and South Africa. Foreign policy controls also had been used against the Soviet Union in response to the invasion of Afghanistan and the crisis in Poland.

Short supply controls affected petroleum and certain agricultural products. Under the 1979 export control act, the export of Alaskan crude oil was also prohibited.

Senate, House Committee Action

The president's authority to control exports for foreign policy purposes was greatly restricted by bills approved by the Senate Banking Committee May 25 and the House Foreign Affairs Committee May 26.

The Senate bill, reported June 29 (S 979 — S Rept 98-170), extended the Export Administration Act for six years. The House bill, reported June 22 (HR 3231 — H Rept 98-257, Part 1), extended the act for two years.

The two measures represented a significant victory for U.S. exporting companies, whose businesses were hurt in 1982 by President Reagan's prohibition on shipments of oil and gas pipeline equipment to the Soviet Union to protest Soviet involvement in Poland. U.S. exporters said they not only lost sales to the Soviets, but also gained an international reputation as "unreliable suppliers" due to the controls.

Although the two bills took similar tacks on foreign policy controls — temporary measures intended to punish a specific nation — they diverged drastically on the more sensitive issue of national security controls.

The Senate bill generally followed the recommendations of President Reagan and of defense hard-liners in Congress, maintaining and in some cases tightening national security controls — permanent sanctions designed to prevent the leakage to the communist bloc countries of U.S. technology with possible military applications. The House bill, on the other hand, eased or eliminated national security controls on high-tech products in many cases.

Both bills also extended existing short-supply prohibitions against the export of Alaskan oil.

Foreign Policy Controls

Much to their surprise, exporters won more restrictions on foreign policy controls from the Senate Banking Committee than from House Foreign Affairs.

The Senate bill contained a sweeping "contract sanctity" provision, prohibiting export controls that would force U.S. companies to violate existing contracts. The House bill also had a contract sanctity provision but provided exemptions if Congress gave its approval or if the

president determined breaking contracts was necessary to retaliate for terrorism, human rights violations, nuclear weapons testing or imminent acts of aggression.

The Senate committee was headed by Jake Garn, R-Utah, one of the most fervent advocates of controls, and the panel was believed to be more sympathetic to the administration, which wanted to maintain most of its authority to control exports.

But Garn was more concerned about maintaining national security controls than foreign policy controls. And he also had to contend with John Heinz, R-Pa., who headed the Banking Subcommittee on International Finance and Monetary Policy with jurisdiction over the bill. Heinz sympathized with exporters' complaints against controls, and had promoted measures to limit the president's foreign policy control authority.

The bill marked up by the Banking Committee May 25 was the result of a compromise worked out by Garn and Heinz in advance of the meeting. Garn gave Heinz — and exporters — many restrictions they wanted on foreign policy controls, and got in return many provisions he wanted to tighten national security controls.

During the committee's markup, Garn and Heinz united in opposing attempts to unravel their agreement. Alan J. Dixon, D-Ill., offered an amendment that would have allowed foreign policy controls only on products that were manufactured uniquely by the United States, or were being controlled multilaterally. That amendment was sought by the Caterpillar Tractor Co., which was based in Dixon's home state of Illinois and had suffered heavily from the pipeline sanctions.

But Heinz attacked the amendment, saying it would come close to repealing all foreign policy control authority. And Garn complained that business had already gotten enough from the Garn-Heinz compromise. "I am disappointed after the concessions made on my part that the business community continues to fight," he said.

Dixon finally withdrew his amendment but said he might offer a version of it on the Senate floor.

An amendment by Christopher J. Dodd, D-Conn., which would have weakened the contract sanctity provision but given Congress the power to veto foreign policy controls, also was defeated, 7-10.

In the House, Don Bonker, D-Wash., had geared up for an effort by the Republican right to weaken the tough contract sanctity provision approved by his Subcommittee on International Economic Policy and Trade. But instead the attack came from his Democratic left.

Howard L. Berman, D-Calif., offered an amendment giving the president authority to break contracts if he determined it was necessary to combat terrorism, human rights violations, nuclear weapons testing or imminent acts of aggression.

It was Berman's intent not to allow the president to break contracts as in the 1982 pipeline sanctions, but to permit violation of contracts for sanctions against nations such as Iraq or South Africa.

But Bonker said the amendment would "gut" the contract sanctity provision, providing a loophole the president could use whenever he wished.

In spite of Bonker's protest, Democratic liberals were joined by Republicans to adopt the amendment 13-9.

National Security Controls

The Senate measure did not go as far as Garn would have liked in strengthening national security controls. Garn

wanted to establish an independent Office of Strategic Trade because he felt existing controls, administered by the Commerce Department, were weakened by that department's traditional commitment to export promotion. Instead of establishing an independent office, the Garn-Heinz compromise created a new commerce under secretary for export administration.

The bill gave new authority to the Defense Department to review exports to U.S. allies, in addition to its existing authority to review exports to Soviet bloc countries. The measure also transferred enforcement of the act to the U.S. Customs Service.

The House bill, on the other hand, eliminated controls on exports to U.S. allies who maintained controls cooperatively with the United States. It also provided for the automatic expiration of controls on products that were not controlled by U.S. allies and were readily available overseas. And it automatically ended unilateral controls on products that had been consistently approved for export during a one-year period.

Import Controls

The House Foreign Affairs Committee eliminated a controversial provision that would allow the president to bar imports from foreign companies that violated controls.

That provision had been added in the subcommittee by Olympia J. Snowe, R-Maine. But an amendment by Lee H. Hamilton, D-Ind., to strike it was approved by a vote of 14-8.

Hamilton said the measure would cause dissent between the United States and its allies, who resented U.S. attempts to impose its laws beyond its borders, and said it would "in all likelihood violate the General Agreement on Tariffs and Trade (GATT)," the multilateral treaty that established rules for international trade.

An even tougher import control provision, however, was left in the Senate bill. Snowe's amendment would have applied only to controls maintained in cooperation with U.S. allies, but the Senate provision applied as well to controls maintained unilaterally by the United States.

Both the Snowe amendment and the Senate provision applied only to foreign companies that fell under U.S. jurisdiction, either because they were subsidiaries or affiliates of U.S. firms or had licenses for U.S. technology.

Senate Bill

The Senate Banking Committee approved its version of the bill without objection May 25. The measure included amendments by:

● Mack Mattingly, R-Ga., to require the president to consult with any affected U.S. industry before imposing foreign policy controls.

● Dixon, to exempt small charitable donations of food and other items intended to meet human needs from foreign policy controls.

The bill also:

● Created a multiple export license for exports to U.S. allies who maintained cooperative controls unless the exported item was on the "militarily critical technologies list."

● Controlled sales of goods or technologies to embassies or their affiliates.

● Directed the president to attempt to raise to treaty status COCOM, the international Coordinating Committee that monitored multilateral controls.

● Authorized the president to impose import controls

along with foreign policy export controls.

● Required a review of foreign policy controls every six months.

● Decreased time limits for licensing decisions by one-third.

● Required the president to submit a plan for an Office of Strategic Trade by March 15, 1984.

House Bill

The House Foreign Affairs Committee approved its bill by voice vote May 26. The committee retained most of the basic provisions of the measure drafted by the International Economic Policy and Trade Subcommittee May 4.

Subcommittee Bill. The subcommittee bill eliminated the need for licenses to export high-technology goods to U.S. allies that participated in COCOM. It also removed restrictions on goods that were controlled by the United States but not by COCOM, and which had been routinely granted licenses.

The bill included the broad contract sanctity restriction on foreign policy controls that had been sought by companies hurt when President Reagan limited exports for the Soviet Union's Yamal oil and gas pipeline late in 1981. Under the bill, the president could not impose controls on goods already under contract for exportation.

The bill also eliminated the president's authority to impose controls on companies outside U.S. territory without the specific authorization of Congress.

The subcommittee agreed to the controversial Snowe amendment to enable the president to restrict U.S. imports from companies in foreign countries if those companies violated the U.S. national security controls that were maintained cooperatively with other COCOM countries.

The subcommittee also agreed to an amendment by Toby Roth, R-Wis., that would require the Defense Department to integrate its "militarily critical technologies" list with the Commerce Department's commodity control list by April 1, 1984.

In addition, the panel approved an amendment by Howard Wolpe, D-Mich., to prevent the export of Alaskan oil before Sept. 30, 1987, and an amendment by Douglas K. Bereuter, R-Neb., to prohibit foreign policy export controls on food, medicine, medical supplies or other exports that "help meet basic human needs."

Other provisions of the bill:

● Gave more favorable treatment to exports to the People's Republic of China.

● Increased the Department of Commerce's authority and funding for the enforcement of violations of export controls.

● Allowed a "comprehensive operations license" authorizing multiple shipments of goods and technology from a U.S. company to its subsidiaries and affiliates, eliminating the need to apply for separate licenses on each shipment.

● Decontrolled goods that contained microprocessors, but that would not make a significant contribution to the military capability of the Soviet Union.

● Decontrolled goods that were restricted unilaterally by the United States but were readily available overseas, unless negotiations with allies to eliminate foreign availability were completed within six months.

● Required the president to consult with other countries before imposing foreign policy controls.

● Provided that evidence of foreign availability presented by exporters be considered correct unless contra-

dicted by reliable information.

Committee Amendments. Amendments to the bill adopted by the full committee included those by:

● Hamilton, to prohibit restrictions on the scholarly exchange of scientific information.

● Ed Zschau, R-Calif., to allow the Commerce Department to restrict exports to a company in a country that participated in COCOM if the company had a record of being unreliable in complying with COCOM controls.

● Roth, to strike a provision creating a special, looser standard for exports to China, pending the change in the administration's China policy expected to result from a recent visit to China by Commerce Secretary Malcolm Baldrige.

● Zschau, to prohibit control of a product merely because it included a microprocessor, the most basic component of a computer, if that microprocessor could not be used for any other purpose than that for which it was intended.

● Roth, to encourage the strengthening of COCOM.

● Gerald B. H. Solomon, R-N.Y., to allow Commerce to bar sales to embassies and affiliates.

Subsequent Referrals. After HR 3231 was reported by the Foreign Affairs Committee, a narrow part of the measure was referred to the Armed Services Committee, which filed its views July 22 (H Rept 98-257, Part 2).

In addition, the bill was referred to the Rules Committee for review of its legislative veto provisions in the wake of a June 23 Supreme Court decision that struck down the veto device. Under directions from the Rules panel July 26 (H Rept 98-257, Part 3), Foreign Affairs revised the legislative veto provisions to require passage of a joint resolution, instead of an apparently unconstitutional concurrent resolution, to overrule decisions by the executive. A joint resolution must be sent to the president for his signature or veto. *(Legislative veto, p. 565)*

House Floor Action

The House passed HR 3231 by voice vote Oct. 27, but only after reversing itself on a key provision of the complex measure.

During consideration of the bill Oct. 18, members had approved by a 239-171 vote a Roth amendment deleting a restriction on the president's power to control exports of high-technology products to U.S. allies. Before final passage of the bill Oct. 27, however, the House took a separate vote on the amendment and rejected it, 188-223. Forty-nine House members changed their vote from a "yes" to a "no," thus restoring Foreign Affairs Committee language relaxing curbs on export controls. *(Vote 370, p. 110-H; vote 397, p. 118-H)*

The reversal marked a significant victory for Bonker and his pro-export allies. In earlier floor action, members concerned about the undetected shipment of Western technology to Eastern bloc countries had succeeded in removing some of the bill's other provisions relaxing controls.

The House bill differed in large part from the measure originally approved by Foreign Affairs May 26. Pro-control members added an amendment on the House floor to strike a provision calling for automatic decontrol of any product that was controlled only by the United States and that had been consistently approved for export over a one-year period.

An amendment offered by William H. Gray III, D-Pa., barred all new investments by U.S. individuals and firms in South Africa to censure the government for its practice of apartheid, the policy of segregating the races. As reported, the bill blocked U.S. banks from making loans to the South African government.

The bill also required U.S. firms operating in South Africa to institute fair employment practices. And it prohibited the importation of krugerrands and other gold coins from South Africa.

Roth Amendment

As initially approved by the House Oct. 18, following adoption of amendments by Bonker and Earl Hutto, D-Fla., the Roth amendment allowed the president to continue to require licenses for shipments to COCOM nations if the product was likely to be diverted to a Soviet bloc country.

"What we have done here," complained Zschau, "is to remove from the Export Administration Act amendments the basic reforms that the Committee on Foreign Affairs had crafted over the last several months."

The original Bonker bill also called for automatic decontrol of any product controlled unilaterally by the United States, and not by its allies, which had been consistently approved for export during a one-year period.

But an amendment to strike that provision sponsored by Robert J. Lagomarsino, R-Calif., was adopted by voice vote.

Bonker's bill also called for automatic decontrol of any product readily available from foreign sources, if the administration were unable to convince other countries to control the product within a six-month period.

But an amendment by Jim Courter, R-N.J., which was further amended by Gerald B. H. Solomon, R-N.Y., allowed the president to extend controls for another year even if he had not succeeded in eliminating foreign availability. That amendment was approved by voice vote.

Non-Proliferation

By a 196-189 vote, the House Sept. 30 adopted an amendment prohibiting the export of nuclear technology and nuclear components to countries that did not comply with International Atomic Energy Agency safeguards.

Offered by Howard Wolpe, D-Mich., the amendment was designed to close a loophole in U.S. nuclear non-proliferation laws, which currently banned shipments of fuel and of nuclear facilities, but not technology or component parts, to countries that did not maintain safeguards.

Wolpe said that loophole "is currently being exploited to allow nuclear exports to India, to Argentina and to South Africa." *(Vote 353, p. 106-H)*

Other Amendments

The House Sept. 30 also adopted by voice vote an amendment by Robert H. Michel, R-Ill., requiring the president to lift foreign policy controls after six months if the goods controlled were still readily available from foreign sources and efforts to eliminate foreign availability had been unsuccessful.

And on Oct. 18 it adopted by voice vote an amendment, sponsored by Douglas K. Bereuter, R-Neb., exempting food from all export policy controls. "As the leader of the free world and one of the world's richest nations," Bereuter said, "we should not deny food to our less fortunate neighbors."

Other amendments adopted included those offered by:

● J. J. Pickle, D-Texas, to direct the administration to

seek an agreement among COCOM allies providing for export sanctions against the Soviet Union or any other country if it committed violent acts against unarmed civilians of another country; adopted by voice vote Sept. 29.

● Bonker, to ensure that exports to the People's Republic of China were subject to no greater restrictions than those to any other friendly, nonaligned nation; voice vote, Oct. 19.

Amendments defeated by the House included those by:

● Hutto, to give more authority to the Customs Service in enforcing export controls; standing vote, 8-14, Sept. 29.

● William J. Hughes, D-N.J., to strike the section of the bill giving Commerce Department export control enforcement officials the right to make searches, seizures and arrests; recorded vote, 160-243, Sept. 29. *(Vote 349, 104-H)*

● Larry Smith, D-Fla., to deny licenses for all exports to the Soviet Union until the Soviet Union officially apologized for shooting down Korean Air Lines flight 007 Sept. 1 and compensated the survivors of the victims; standing vote, 9-26, Sept. 30.

● Bill Frenzel, R-Minn., to prohibit the president from imposing foreign policy controls that broke existing export contracts; rejected 172-237, Oct. 19. *(Vote 372, p. 110-H)*

● Courter, to direct the president to attempt to raise COCOM to treaty status; voice vote, Oct. 19.

● John N. Erlenborn, R-Ill., to strike the provision prohibiting the application of foreign policy controls to companies outside the United States; recorded vote, 199-215, Oct. 19. *(Vote 374, p. 112-H)*

A Snowe amendment to allow the president to restrict imports into the United States of goods from companies that violated U.S. national security controls maintained cooperatively with COCOM, was ruled out of order Sept. 29.

Major Provisions of House Bill

As passed by the House, HR 3231 extended for two years, through Sept. 30, 1985, the Export Administration Act of 1979 and authorized $24,600,000 each for fiscal 1984 and fiscal 1985. In addition, it authorized $100,458,000 in each year for Department of Commerce export promotion programs.

The bill also:

● Eliminated licensing requirements for exports to COCOM countries. However, the secretary of commerce could require licenses for exports to specific end-users suspected of diverting goods or technology to controlled countries.

● Required the president to drop national security controls on a product that was readily available from other countries if, after 18 months, he had failed to persuade other nations to control the product. The bill also established an Office of Foreign Availability to gather information on product availability.

● Prohibited the application of foreign policy controls to companies outside the United States, including overseas subsidiaries of U.S. firms.

● Prohibited the export of nuclear technology and nuclear components to nations that failed to comply with the safeguards established by the International Atomic Energy Agency.

● Urged the president to seek the counsel of other foreign countries and Congress before imposing foreign policy controls, and required the president to report to Congress

before foreign policy controls went into effect.

● Barred the president from enacting foreign policy controls that broke existing export contracts unless the controls were in retaliation for actual or imminent acts of aggression, terrorism, human rights violations or nuclear weapons tests, or unless Congress approved.

● Required the president to lift foreign policy controls after six months if the products were readily available from other nations and attempts to eliminate the foreign availability proved unsuccessful.

South Africa

The bill set out several restrictions on U.S. businesses in South Africa and limited commercial transactions between the United States and South Africa. HR 3231:

● Barred all new investment by U.S. firms and individuals in South Africa.

● Banned U.S. banks from lending money to the South African government. Loans to educational, housing and health facilities open to members of all groups were exempted.

● Required all U.S. enterprises in South Africa that employed more than 20 people to establish fair employment practices. These were: desegregated work places; equal employment for all; equal pay for equal work; a minimum wage scale based on a cost-of-living index; increased participation by blacks and other non-whites in managerial, supervisory, administrative, clerical and technical jobs; improvements in wage earners' conditions outside the work place, including housing, schooling and transportation; recognition of labor unions and fair labor practices.

● Prohibited imports of krugerrands and other gold coins minted by the South African government.

● Permitted the president to waive the fair employment provisions of the bill if compliance would harm U.S. national interests. A waiver could be overridden by enactment of a joint resolution disapproving the action.

● Permitted the ban on all new investment in South Africa to lapse if the president determined — and Congress passed a joint resolution supporting the presidential findings — that the South African government "has made substantial progress toward the full participation of all the people of South Africa in the social, political and economic life in that country and toward an end to discrimination based on race or ethnic origin."

Other Provisions

Other provisions of the bill:

● Extended to Sept. 30, 1987, restrictions on the export of Alaskan oil.

● Barred the importation into the United States of gold coins minted in the Soviet Union.

● Reimposed foreign policy controls on Iraq and South Africa that had been lifted in 1982 and 1983.

● Exempted from foreign policy controls food exports and exports of goods donated for humanitarian purposes.

● Prohibited limits on exports to the People's Republic of China stricter than those applied to any other friendly, non-aligned nation. ∎

Auto Domestic Content

For the second year in a row, the House Nov. 3 approved a "domestic content" measure that would require fixed levels of U.S. labor and parts in foreign cars sold in the United States.

The bill (HR 1234) was approved 219-199 with the strong backing of industrial-state Democrats and a sprinkling of Republicans who claimed that foreign-car imports, primarily from Japan, were taking jobs away from U.S. autoworkers and employees in such related industries as rubber and steel. Domestic content had become an important symbolic issue for labor-backed Democrats in Congress, who were anxious to demonstrate their concern about imports and continuing high unemployment in the auto industry and related industries. The Reagan administration actively opposed the measure, which President Reagan described as a "cruel hoax." *(Vote 417, p. 124-H)*

The controversial bill was a creation of the United Auto Workers union (UAW), which thought it would help restore the more than one million jobs lost by workers in automobile and related industries since 1978.

Opposing the legislation was a large coalition of interest groups, including agricultural associations and exporting companies who feared retaliation by other nations in response to domestic content legislation, as well as automobile dealers, longshoremen and other port-related workers who would suffer from a decline in imports. General Motors and the Ford Motor Co. also opposed the bill.

Opponents of the measure claimed that it would lead to a trade war with other countries and result in job losses among U.S. export industries. They also said the bill would add to the sticker price of cars sold in the United States in order to protect members of the UAW.

"This bill is an exercise in greed," Bill Frenzel, R-Minn., said Nov. 2. "It seeks to protect the jobs of a few, to hurt the jobs of the many and to lay the additional costs of job protection on unwilling American consumers."

Supporters hoped to bring the legislation before the Senate in 1984, where they said election-year pressures could help secure passage. "Some people who find it easy to say no to this today just might find it harder to say that in an election year," said UAW President Owen F. Bieber after the House passed HR 1234.

In 1982, the House voted 215-188 for a similar domestic content bill, but the Senate did not act on the measure. *(1982 Almanac p. 55)*

The 1983 bill sparked a power struggle between the Energy and Commerce Committee, which had jurisdiction over interstate commerce, and the Ways and Means Committee, which had jurisdiction over trade. The Energy and Commerce Committee favorably reported the bill June 30 (H Rept 98-287, Part 1), but the Ways and Means Committee reported the bill unfavorably Sept. 21 (H Rept 98-287, Part 2).

Requirement's Impact

The House-passed bill would cover foreign auto manufacturers that sold more than 100,000 cars a year in the United States, beginning in 1985.

Depending upon the number of cars sold, the domestic content requirement would range from 3.3 percent to 30 percent during the first year the law was in effect. The content level would rise to a maximum of 90 percent on companies selling more than 900,000 autos in the United States in 1987 and beyond.

By comparison, five Japanese car companies in 1982 had a domestic content level of 5 percent each for the cars they sold in the United States.

House approval of the domestic content bill came despite a Nov. 1 announcement that Japan would restrict U.S. exports to 1.85 million cars for the year beginnning in April 1984. While that figure was up from the limit of 1.68 million cars in effect for the past three years, U.S. and Japanese trade negotiators had hoped the announcement would reduce protectionist sentiments in Washington.

Energy and Commerce Action

The Energy and Commerce Committee approved the bill by a 25-17 vote June 21.

HR 1234 would require automobile manufacturers to meet certain "domestic content" requirements beginning in 1985. Those requirements would grow tighter each year until 1987, when manufacturers would have to use up to 90 percent U.S. parts and labor in the cars they sold in the United States.

The domestic content requirements of a company would depend on its volume of sales in the United States. Toyota, for example, would have to use 70 percent U.S. labor and parts if its sales stayed at the current level of about 700,000 a year. Honda, with U.S. sales of roughly 350,000 cars each year, would have to use 35 percent domestic labor and parts.

Any company failing to meet the domestic content requirements would have its imports restricted by the secretary of transportation.

During the markup June 21, the committee accepted an amendment by James J. Florio, D-N.J., that would create a U.S. Automobile Advisory Council to formulate a "strategy . . . to increase the domestic production of automotive products." The council would include five labor members, four management members and one representative of a parts manufacturer. An amendment by Richard L. Ottinger, D-N.Y., also added three consumer representatives to the council.

To help avert opposition to the bill on the House floor, the committee also accepted an amendment by Don Ritter, R-Pa., to study the measure's impact on car dealers, and an amendment by Dennis E. Eckart, D-Ohio, to study its impact on prices, the balance of trade, employment at ports, foreign investment and exports of agriculture and other goods.

Ways and Means Action

The Ways and Means Committee, a bulwark of free trade in the House, voted Sept. 20 to disapprove the domestic content bill.

At the same time, the committee approved a moderate trade "reciprocity" bill that would strengthen the president's power to retaliate against foreign unfair trading practices. The reciprocity bill was a more modest response to congressional trade concerns. *(Reciprocity, p. 259)*

In an attempt to save the bill from the committee's censure, Byron L. Dorgan, D-N.D., moved to report the domestic content bill without recommendation. That motion was defeated 13-19. The bill was then ordered reported unfavorably by voice vote.

House Floor Action

Heavily lobbied by the UAW, 187 Democrats joined with 32 Republicans on the 219-199 vote to pass the bill Nov. 3. Voting against the measure were 131 Republicans and 68 Democrats. One member, William Lehman, D-Fla., voted present.

Moments after the vote, Ottinger, his hands held high in victory, was greeted by jubilant UAW lobbyists who lined a corridor leading onto the House floor. Ottinger was floor manager of the bill.

House opponents of HR 1234 had planned to offer a series of amendments during floor consideration Nov. 2. But the House moved surprisingly quickly to final passage Nov. 3 after decisively rejecting a pivotal amendment that would have seriously weakened the bill.

That amendment, offered by Dan Coats, R-Ind., would have prevented domestic content requirements from being enforced if they were found to violate U.S. trade obligations under the General Agreement on Tariffs and Trade (GATT).

Coats said his amendment was designed to protect U.S. exports from Japanese retaliation caused by the domestic content requirements applied to car imports.

"When you pick a fight, someone will retaliate. And the results of that retaliation will be widespread," said Charles W. Stenholm, D-Texas, who backed the Coats amendment.

But others said the Coats amendment would disrupt current procedures for dealing with trade disputes arising under GATT by giving U.S. courts the power to decide if domestic content rules would lead to GATT violations. Currently, such disputes were settled by tribunals operating within the GATT structure.

When the House debated the domestic content bill in 1982, an amendment similar to the one offered by Coats took the bill's sponsors by surprise and was approved 195-194.

In 1983, the sponsors were ready. As the House neared a vote on Coats' amendment early on the evening of Nov. 2, Ottinger quickly moved to end the debate for the day.

That gave the bill's supporters time to round up the votes to defeat the GATT amendment, 178-232, when debate resumed on the bill the next day. *(Vote 415, p. 124-H)*

Twenty-five members — 21 Democrats and four Republicans — who voted for the weakening amendment in 1982 voted against it in 1983. But only 14 members — eight Democrats and six Republicans — switched from no to yes votes.

During consideration of HR 1234, the House adopted, 214-196, an amendment by Don J. Pease, D-Ohio, to place a six-year sunset — termination — provision on the bill, but only if the transportation secretary determined the U.S. auto industry no longer was threatened by car imports. *(Vote 416, p. 124-H)* ▮

Trade Reciprocity, Services

The Senate April 21 passed "reciprocity" trade legislation (S 144) that would expand the president's authority to retaliate against unfair trading practices by other countries and require the administration to seek new international agreements on trade in services and high technology.

But the House never acted on the Senate bill, which became a legislative vehicle for a controversial measure to repeal a requirement for tax withholding on interest and dividend income. Instead, the House May 17 passed a separate withholding measure (HR 2973), which subsequently was enacted into law. And it returned S 144 to the Senate, protesting that the bill violated the constitutional prerogative of the House to originate all revenue legislation. *(Withholding, p. 261)*

Making good on a promise by House leaders to consider reciprocity legislation, however, the Ways and Means Committee Sept. 27 reported a bill (HR 1571) that would

put retaliatory power against unfair trading practices within the Trade Act of 1974, which fell under Ways and Means jurisdiction. The committee reported unfavorably a second measure (HR 2848) that provided separate authority in the Commerce Department, which fell under the jurisdiction of the Energy and Commerce Committee. Neither bill made it to the House floor before adjournment.

Reciprocity legislation had generated considerable controversy in the 97th Congress but never came to a vote in the Senate. Originally sponsored by Sen. John C. Danforth, R-Mo., the measure came under attack in 1982 as "protectionist" legislation. After changes were made under pressure from the Reagan administration, however, the bill came to be viewed as moderate. *(1982 Almanac p. 56)*

Unlike other trade proposals, such as the domestic content bill passed by the House Nov. 3, the reciprocity bill did not mandate trade sanctions. Rather, it left the authority and the initiative for imposing sanctions in the president's hands. The administration supported the modified bill. *(Domestic content, p. 257)*

Senate Action

The Senate passed S 144 by voice vote April 21, after attaching an amendment to delay the withholding of taxes on interest and dividend income. The reciprocity bill had been reported unanimously by the Finance Committee March 14 (S Rept 98-24).

In action on the trade provisions of S 144, the Senate tabled by a 57-32 vote an amendment offered by Arlen Specter, R-Pa., that would have permitted federal courts to issue injunctions against foreign imports if they were being "dumped" (sold at a price below the cost of production) on the U.S. market. It also would have allowed the courts to award damages to U.S. companies injured by foreign dumping. *(Vote 63, p. 15-S)*

The amendment was based on a bill (S 418) cosponsored by Specter and Howell Heflin, D-Ala. Its primary aim was to help the steel industry, which had been dissatisfied with the protection from imports afforded by the International Trade Commission, a U.S. panel that handled dumping and countervailing duty cases.

"The really effective remedy for dumping . . . is injunctive relief, where a federal court would order no further imports of the subsidized goods," Specter said.

Danforth heaped heavy criticism on the Specter amendment, saying it would violate international trade agreements and cause "massive and immediate" disruption in international trade.

"I think it is really terrible policy," Danforth said.

"When I introduced this [reciprocity] bill two years ago . . . I took the position at the time that if it became a Christmas tree for really bad trade policy, I would do everything that I could to abort my own bill," Danforth said. "That is my position on this kind of amendment."

Danforth also read from a letter written by U.S. Trade Representative William E. Brock III, which said the antidumping provisions would "invite retaliation abroad" and have "a strong negative impact on U.S. exporters and workers in our most export-active industries, such as chemicals, paper and wood products."

An amendment offered by Russell B. Long, D-La., and adopted by the Senate April 21 would require administration information and statistics to distinguish between income from foreign investments and that from trade in services. The two were currently lumped together. The

distinction was important, Long said, because "investment abroad provides jobs abroad, whereas providing services from the United States provides jobs here."

The Senate also adopted an amendment offered by Larry Pressler, R-S.D., calling for an investigation by the International Trade Commission of the effects of honey imports on the U.S. bee-keeping industry.

Provisions

In addition to allowing the president to retaliate against barriers to U.S. investment abroad and strengthening his ability to retaliate against trade barriers, the trade provisions of S 144 would:

● Require annual national trade estimates on significant barriers to the export of U.S. goods and services, and on curbs on U.S. foreign investment.

● Direct the president to seek new international agreements removing barriers to trade in services and high-technology products, as well as restrictions on foreign direct investment by U.S. companies.

● Establish a procedure for the administration to receive trade negotiating advice from private business.

● Allow the U.S. trade representative to begin investigations of potential unfair trading practices under Section 301 of the Trade Act of 1974 on his own initiative.

● Provide an exemption from the Freedom of Information Act for information received from private business during investigations of Section 301 trade cases.

● Create a "fast track" legislative process for requests from the president for new authority to retaliate against unfair trading practices.

● Define "unreasonable," "unjustifiable" and "discriminatory" trade acts.

House Committee Action

The House Ways and Means Committee Sept. 20 approved a moderate reciprocity bill that was similar to the Senate-passed measure. The bill, sponsored by James R. Jones, D-Okla., was reported Sept. 27 (HR 1571 — H Rept 98-383, Part 1).

Ways and Means leaders initially were reluctant to move the reciprocity measure, fearing it would attract protectionist amendments on the House floor. Although they finally decided to back the bill, Democratic support for the measure, which generally was viewed as a Republican initiative, remained uncertain.

Trade Subcommittee Chairman Sam Gibbons, D-Fla., was working on a separate trade bill to strengthen the anti-dumping and countervailing duty laws, which was likely to become the Ways and Means Committee's principal trade initiative.

Presidential Authority. As approved by the committee, the reciprocity bill clarified the president's authority to deny licenses to, or otherwise restrict, foreign service companies from nations that had barriers to U.S. services exports.

The bill also allowed the president to retaliate against nations that blocked trade-related foreign investment, or refused to protect U.S. intellectual property rights, such as patents, copyrights and trademarks. And it allowed the U.S. trade representative to initiate investigations into potential unfair foreign trading practices on its own.

The bill mandated that a review of retaliatory measures taken under section 301 of the Trade Act of 1974 be made every two years, and that those measures be rescinded if the offending foreign act had been eliminated or if continuation of the action was not in the national interest.

Negotiating Objectives. The bill required the president to seek international negotiations to eliminate barriers to trade in services and high-technology products, as well as barriers to foreign direct investment.

The existing international trade structure, known as the General Agreement on Tariffs and Trade, dealt primarily with trade in manufactured goods.

Services Program. The measure would establish a Services Industries Development Program in the Department of Commerce to improve the collection of information concerning services industries, and to promote competitiveness and international trade in those industries.

Reports. The U.S. trade representative would be required to submit an annual report to the Ways and Means Committee and the Senate Finance Committee detailing barriers to U.S. exports.

That report would include an inventory of barriers to U.S. goods, services or trade-related investment; and assessment of the effects of those barriers on U.S. trade, and actions taken to eliminate the barriers.

The bill also required the trade representative to report to Congress on factors affecting the competitiveness of U.S. high-technology industries in world markets.

Services Exports

In separate action Sept. 20, the Ways and Means Committee ordered reported unfavorably another bill (HR 2848 — H Rept 98-203, Part 2) to promote service industry exports.

That bill had been reported by the Energy and Commerce Committee May 16 (H Rept 98-203, Part 1), and was similar to provisions contained in the reciprocity bill approved by Ways and Means.

The vote against the services measure did not result from objections to the bill's intent. Rather, it reflected the continuing battle between Energy and Commerce leaders and Ways and Means leaders over jurisdiction on trade issues.

Both the services bill and the reciprocity bill gave the president expanded authority to retaliate against foreign nations that blocked U.S. services exports. Services exports — involving such industries as banking, insurance, telecommunications and engineering and design — had become increasingly important to the United States, amounting to more than $60 billion each year. Members of both panels agreed that action was needed to reduce barriers to services trade.

But the reciprocity bill put the new retaliatory authority within the Trade Act of 1974, which fell under the jurisdiction of the Ways and Means Committee. The services bill, on the other hand, provided separate authority within the Commerce Department, which fell under Energy and Commerce Committee jurisdiction.

By totally rejecting the Energy and Commerce bill, the Ways and Means Committee clouded the outlook for Energy and Commerce action on the reciprocity bill. That measure was jointly referred to Energy and Commerce and Foreign Affairs as well as Ways and Means, and neither of the other two committees had acted. ■

Interest Withholding Requirement Repealed

Bowing to months of intense public pressure, Congress July 28 cleared legislation (HR 2973 — PL 98-67) repealing a new law requiring 10 percent withholding of taxes on interest and dividend income.

Enacted in 1982 as part of the Tax Equity and Fiscal Reponsibility Act (PL 97-248), the withholding requirements came under fire almost as soon as they became law. By the start of 1983, members of Congress began to feel the pressure of one of the most massive mail-in campaigns in Capitol Hill history. *(Tax bill background, 1982 Almanac p. 29)*

Leading the fight were banks and other financial institutions, which were required to withhold interest and dividend taxes starting July 1. The banks charged that the new law would be both an administrative and financial nightmare for them and their customers, as well as an invasion of customer privacy.

They challenged administration claims that withholding was needed to catch tax cheats and to raise much-needed revenues for the federal government.

While many members of Congress were willing to capitulate to the growing public demand for repeal, the administration and leadership in both houses remained firm, decrying the sometimes heavy-handed tactics of the banking lobby.

President Reagan vowed repeatedly to veto any repeal legislation.

Congressional leaders, including House Speaker Thomas P. O'Neill Jr., D-Mass., and Senate Finance Committee Chairman Robert Dole, R-Kan., used their legislative powers to block repeated attempts to bring the issue up for floor votes.

They feared not only that repeal of withholding might unravel further moves to raise revenues through improved tax compliance, but that capitulating to the powerful banking lobby might set a bad legislative precedent.

Lobby Pressure

But the pressure became too much, with literally millions of letters demanding repeal pouring into congressional offices.

Withholding opponents in the Senate brought the issue up on bill after bill, threatening to bog down much of the year's legislative activity. House opponents, using the one legislative tool at their disposal, garnered enough signatures on a "discharge" petition to force a repeal bill to the floor.

Faced with such odds, the leadership agreed to a compromise bill that repealed withholding, but also beefed up compliance and reporting measures. These compliance provisions, as well as attachment of the administration's Caribbean Basin Initiative to the bill, ensured President Reagan's approval. The legislation was signed Aug. 5. *(Caribbean Basin Initiative, p. 252)*

The new compliance requirements were expected to yield $2.4 billion for fiscal 1983-88, assuming $300 million in offsetting appropriations for the Internal Revenue Service (IRS) to beef up its compliance capabilities.

The original withholding law had been expected to raise about $13.4 billion in uncollected tax revenues through 1988.

Final Provisions

As signed into law Aug. 5, HR 2973 (PL 98-67):

Withholding

● Repealed provisions of the 1982 tax-increase law that required banks and other financial institutions to withhold for income taxes 10 percent of all interest and dividend payments as of July 1, 1983.

● Waived penalties for taxpayers who underpaid estimated taxes in the first two quarters of 1983, if the estimated tax payment was reduced to reflect amounts expected to be withheld by banks or financial institutions.

● **Compliance.** Required backup withholding at a rate of 20 percent on interest and dividend payments for all taxpayers who either had interest and dividend income and failed to file a return, or under-reported interest and dividend income by a certain threshold amount. Backup withholding was to take effect Jan. 1, 1984.

● Required IRS to set a secret threshold amount of under-reported income that would trigger backup withholding. Once the threshold was determined, IRS would identify those individuals under-reporting or failing to report and notify institutions to begin the backup withholding process.

The threshold would not be known to the taxpayer or the financial institution.

IRS would base the threshold on the amount of funding available to implement backup withholding. The more money appropriated to the IRS for compliance activities, the lower the threshold IRS would set.

● Required that four notices be sent to an individual asking for an explanation of his under-reporting or failure to report. If the taxpayer did not comply within 120 days, backup withholding would start.

● Continued backup withholding, once it began, until the end of the year. Exemptions were provided for special hardship cases.

IRS Payments. Stated the sense of Congress that $300 million should be appropriated each year for the IRS to implement backup withholding. However, the conferees said in their report that they would prefer a $600 million annual appropriation.

The money would be used to hire new personnel to complete matching and analysis of returns prior to contacting taxpayers, and for increased computer capacity.

Penalties. Made banks and financial institutions subject to civil liability for misuse of backup withholding information.

● Established a $500 penalty for any intentional failure by a retail broker to provide an individual with a tax identification number (TIN) or backup withholding status report.

● Provided that civil and criminal penalties for false backup withholding or TIN certificates would be the same as those for false wage withholding certificates.

● Made taxpayers who under-reported interest and dividend income subject to stricter negligence penalties than

under current law.

Taxpayers would not be required to attach to their tax returns duplicate 1099 forms they received from financial institutions that reported their interest and dividend income. However, banks and financial institutions would be required to send a 1099 form to the taxpayer with a note warning that interest and dividend income was taxable.

Initial Senate Action (S 144)

Amid mounting public concern over the new law, the Senate voted 91-5 on April 21 to delay interest and dividend withholding at least until 1987, and probably forever.

The Senate leadership agreed earlier to allow the repeal vote on an unrelated trade "reciprocity" bill (S 144) in an effort to derail attempts to bog down important jobs (HR 1718) and Social Security (HR 1900) legislation with the controversial withholding issue. *(Social Security, p. 219; jobs, p. 447)*

The face-saving delay — designed to avoid outright repeal of the new law — was attached to S 144 with the leadership's blessings after it became apparent that the leadership did not have sufficient votes to prevent repeal. The trade measure was passed later by voice vote. *(Vote 62, p. 15-S; trade bill details, p. 259)*

Opponents of withholding were clearly pleased with the so-called "compromise." Besides almost guaranteeing repeal of withholding, it called for new interest and dividend reporting requirements, and greater penalties for non-compliance.

Although few expected the House to consider the legislation directly — S 144 was a revenue bill originating in the Senate in violation of the Constitution — repeal proponents felt the vote would send a strong message to the House leadership to allow a similar vote in the House.

To keep the issue from tying up the jobs bill, Senate leaders agreed in March that repeal proponent Bob Kasten, R-Wis., would be allowed to offer an amendment to repeal withholding when S 144 reached the floor.

Senate Finance Committee Chairman Robert Dole, R-Kan., a strong supporter of withholding, planned to filibuster Kasten's amendment but agreed to accept the compromise plan April 19 after discovering he had only 28 votes — not enough to prevent cloture on the amendment or to uphold an expected presidential veto.

Although almost a majority of members had been against withholding for some time, leadership aides said the votes for repeal mounted after members heard from angry constituents during the Easter congressional recess.

"It seemed to me that we had two ways to go: to go ahead and make the fight, and lose . . . or to try to work out some compromise where we could preserve most of the revenue," Dole told colleagues on the Senate floor.

The Senate compromise was expected to raise between $6.3 billion and $8.2 billion for fiscal years 1983-88, depending on whether or not withholding went into effect in 1987. The withholding law was expected to raise about $13.4 billion over that same period, according to Treasury Department estimates.

But another factor in the agreement was Republican concern that the intra-party fight would hurt the majority's chances for unity on critical upcoming votes on both defense and the budget.

Kasten added that the Senate action also gave President Reagan some "wiggle room" so he would not have to face an embarrassing veto override.

Senate Compromise

The Senate measure would delay withholding until July 1, 1987, and implement it then only if the General Accounting Office (GAO) found that interest and dividend tax-cheating had not been cut down substantially and if both houses of Congress affirmed the GAO findings.

To help beef up compliance, the Senate measure would require individuals to submit with their annual tax returns the 1099 forms they received from financial institutions reporting their interest and dividend income. Under existing law, individuals were not required to submit such forms, although institutions were required to send the information to the Internal Revenue Service.

In addition, the compromise called for higher penalties for tax cheating and non-compliance, and "backup" withholding at a rate of 20 percent on those who failed to file a proper tax return or who under-reported interest and dividend income by more than $50.

Institutions also would be required to submit interest and dividend income information to the IRS on computer tape to help the service track down cheaters by matching up the taped information with individual returns.

Withholding would not go into effect in 1987, under the plan, if the GAO found that these new measures boosted taxpayer compliance on interest and dividends to at least 95 percent by 1985.

However, even if the GAO found that compliance was lower than 95 percent, it still would take affirmative votes by both houses of Congress to implement withholding — a requirement that virtually guaranteed that withholding would never go into effect.

Floor Debate

Dole — with the help of liberal Democrats Edward M. Kennedy, Mass., and Howard M. Metzenbaum, Ohio — began a hearty defense of the withholding law April 18, criticizing the banks and financial institutions for waging what he called a deceptive lobbying campaign.

But it was quickly apparent that defenders of the law would not be able to fight back the repeal effort.

With a cloture vote pending on Kasten's amendment, the Senate leadership attempted to adjourn early April 19 to avoid defeat. But the adjournment motion, made by Majority Whip Ted Stevens, R-Alaska, failed by a vote of 31-63 and forced both sides into a lengthy closed-door negotiating session. *(Vote 56, p. 14-S)*

Hours later, with a tentative agreement in hand, Kasten asked his backers to vote against cloture, allowing him to offer the "Kasten-Dole" compromise plan. Two subsequent cloture votes failed, 34-53 and 39-59. *(Votes 57, 58, p. 14-S)*

But while key players on the Republican side had agreed to the compromise plan, Democrats were not eager to help the majority party wiggle out of its intra-party dispute.

Russell B. Long, D-La., made Republican leaders nervous by calling for a straight up-or-down vote on withholding repeal after the compromise had been reached by Dole and Kasten. But Long's amendment was tabled by a vote of 55-40. *(Vote 61, p. 15-S)*

The only Republican to vote against the final compromise, John C. Danforth, Mo., also made an unsuccessful attempt to block the withholding change, criticizing his colleagues for "crumbling" under the pressure of a well-financed lobbying campaign.

Danforth raised a point of order against the bill, claim-

ing that it violated the revenue-raising requirements of the fiscal 1983 budget resolution. However, a subsequent motion by Majority Leader Howard H. Baker Jr., R-Tenn., to waive the Budget Act for the bill was passed by a vote of 94-3. *(Vote 60, p. 14-S)*

Cleared of obstacles, the compromise plan was then approved. Besides Danforth, Democrats Kennedy, Metzenbaum, Alan Cranston, Calif., and Frank R. Lautenberg, N.J., voted against the measure.

House Action

Buoyed by Senate repeal of withholding, House opponents of the law won a key victory May 4 when a majority of House members signed a discharge petition forcing a repeal bill (HR 500) out of the Ways and Means Committee and onto the floor.

Success of the discharge petition, a rarely used device to circumvent the will of the leadership or a strong committee chairman, was a major blow to the House leadership which had kept the bill bottled up in committee for almost four months.

Speaker O'Neill, a supporter of the withholding law, conceded defeat shortly after the necessary 218 signatures were received on the petition. "There's no question there's a clear desire out there to have action on the bill," he said.

Along with the administration and the Senate leadership, he had defended withholding as a law necessary to clamp down on tax cheats. But bombarded with anti-withholding mail, rank-and-file members not only refused to follow the party line, but actively called for repeal.

With a majority of House members signing the petition, the Ways and Means Committee had seven legislative days to report out a repeal bill or face a floor vote "discharging" the committee from its responsibilities on HR 500. The petition was filed in the House in March by Rep. Norman E. D'Amours, D.N.H., sponsor of HR 500.

D'Amours said shortly after the 218th signature was placed on the petition that he would try to substitute the Senate-passed compromise on withholding for his repeal bill to facilitate final passage of the measure through both houses.

The rapid success of D'Amours' petition was unusual. Since they were first allowed in 1910, discharge petitions had been used to force bills to the floor only 26 times. Other petitions were signed by a majority of members, but were invalidated by committee action before the petition could be considered on the floor.

While D'Amours' petition had gathered signatures fairly steadily since it was filed on March 17, the effort appeared to pick up steam after an announcement by Ways and Means Committee Chairman Dan Rostenkowski, D-Ill., April 28 that he would not hold hearings on withholding until June 2.

Some proponents of repeal, including the American Bankers Association, charged that the June 2 date was too late to prevent many financial institutions from investing in the large start-up costs for implementing the new law by July 1. They claimed the Ways and Means scheduling was an effort to diffuse opposition to the law.

Committee Action

The Ways and Means Committee reluctantly cleared the way May 12 for a House vote on repeal of withholding by reporting its own repeal measure (HR 2973 — H Rept 98-120).

While the committee agreed to report the bill, it did so "without recommendation" to indicate its reluctance to comply with the discharge petition's mandate.

Democrats on the panel blasted the banking groups that had lobbied extensively to repeal the law. Thomas J. Downey, D-N.Y., said the committee's capitulation to the banking interests would relay a message that members of Congress were "patsies for every well organized group of lobbyists in America."

In addition, Committee Chairman Rostenkowski warned that new tax revenues would have to be found to make up for the estimated $13.4 billion cost, through 1988, of repealing the withholding tax compliance measure.

Committee Democrats refused to consider a compromise plan by Republicans and the Treasury Department to repeal withholding but beef up certain tax enforcement measures. That plan, similar to one adopted by the Senate, would have raised an estimated $4.9 billion over the next five years.

Rostenkowski argued that any effort by the committee to report out a bill other than straight repeal could be seen as a sign that the Democratic leadership was trying to thwart the will of the House.

But Democrats also hoped privately that passage of a straight repeal bill would mean an embarrassing confrontation between congressional Republicans and President Reagan, who had pledged to veto such a measure.

Floor Action

As predicted by backers of HR 2973, the House voted overwhelmingly May 17 to repeal the controversial interest and dividend withholding law. The measure was approved 382-41.

The vote left it up to the Senate to decide whether it would accept outright repeal or try to work out some compromise that would avoid an embarrassing veto confrontation with President Reagan.

Reagan indicated at a May 17 press conference that he might be willing to consider something short of outright repeal.

The House refused to consider a compromise plan approved earlier by the Senate and attached to an unrelated trade measure, S 144. It voted instead to return that bill untouched to the Senate on grounds that the Constitution required such revenue measures to originate in the House.

In floor debate May 17, Rostenkowski defended withholding as "the most effective means of collecting" taxes and argued that without it new tax revenues would have to be found.

Others charged that the banking industry had deceived the American public by portraying withholding as a new tax.

But opponents of withholding insisted that the repeal effort was a grass-roots reaction against unneeded government interference. D'Amours, sponsor of the discharge petition, said the millions of individuals who had sent mail to Congress calling for repeal were "not the mindless robots that they have been painted to be...."

Voting for repeal were 157 Republicans and 225 Democrats. Nine Republicans and 32 Democrats voted against repeal. *(Vote 115, p. 40-H)*

The measure was brought to the floor under suspension of the rules, which required a two-thirds vote for passage and prohibited any amendments. The step was taken by the House leadership in part to ensure that the

bill would be passed with enough votes to show that a presidential veto could easily be overridden. Such action required a two-thirds majority in both houses.

Senate Action on HR 2973

The Senate Finance Committee agreed May 25 to a compromise plan — similar to one approved by the full Senate April 21 — to prevent interest and dividend tax withholding from going into effect July 1.

But it loaded down the package with a number of unrelated amendments, some of which were intended to make the bill more palatable to the administration.

The committee voted 11-8 along straight party lines to repeal the withholding law, but also agreed to new tax reporting and compliance measures that would raise about $4.9 billion of the $13.4 billion withholding was expected to raise over the following six years.

In addition, the committee voted to attach to the measure several controversial bills, including the administration's Caribbean Basin and "enterprise" zone initiatives, a trade bill and extension of tax-exempt mortgage revenue bonds.

Ranking committee Democrat Russell B. Long, La. — a strong proponent of repeal — complained that the additions would turn the repeal measure into a "Christmas Tree" tax bill that would die before it reached a House-Senate conference.

He vowed to push instead for Senate approval of the House-passed measure, calling for simple repeal of withholding. Long already had prevented HR 2973 from being referred to the Finance Committee when it came over from the House, so that the measure would go directly to the Senate floor.

The package approved by the Finance Committee was to be offered as an amendment to HR 2973 when it was brought up for consideration, according to Committee Chairman Dole.

The committee amendment would repeal the new law, but also would provide for so-called "back-up withholding" of 20 percent for individuals who under-reported interest and dividend income by more than $50 or who failed to file a tax return.

The package also would increase fines for financial institutions that did not provide accurate interest and dividend income information to the Internal Revenue Service and for taxpayers who attempted to avoid paying taxes on such income.

Unrelated — and potentially troublesome — additions to the committee withholding plan included:

● A portion of the administration's Caribbean Basin Initiative.

● The trade "reciprocity" measure (S 144) that was sent back from the House unconsidered.

● The administration's enterprise zone plan (S 863), approved by the Finance Committee May 17. *(Reagan message, p. 14-E; background, 1982 Almanac p. 68)*

● A controversial measure to make permanent an existing law allowing for tax-exempt mortgate revenue bonds, set to expire at the end of the year. *(Story, p. 276)*

Floor Action

The Senate June 16 approved the Finance Committee's withholding repeal package, which was offered on the floor as a committee substitute to the House-passed bill. After adopting the amendment, 48-41, the Senate went on

to pass HR 2973 by an overwhelming 86-4 vote. *(Votes 156, 157, p. 29-S)*

To help smooth approval of the Senate measure, Treasury Secretary Donald T. Regan announced before the final passage vote that the administration would delay implementation of the new law 30 days if the Senate approved more than straight repeal.

The biggest challenge to the Senate withholding package came from ranking Finance Democrat Long, who argued that the extraneous provisions, many of which were opposed in the House, could drag down the entire bill in conference. But Republicans, in a face-saving gesture to the president, blocked Long's motion to table the committee amendment on an almost straight party-line vote of 46-51. *(Vote 154, p. 28-S)*

An amendment by David Pryor, D-Ark., to strip everything except the withholding provisions from the committee amendment was tabled, 50-40. *(Vote 155, p. 28-S)*

Conference

A House-Senate conference agreement (H Rept 98-325) was reached July 27 when a deadlock was broken over an extraneous Senate provision dealing with mortgage revenue bonds.

The House July 28 approved the conference report on the bill by a vote of 392-18. The Senate adopted the report the same day by a vote fo 90-7. *(Vote 263, p. 80-H; vote 224, p. 38-S)*

The way toward final passage was opened when hold-out conferee Sen. Lloyd Bentsen, D-Texas, agreed to drop Senate language that would have made permanent a tax exemption for mortgage revenue bonds. Conferees had been deadlocked over the issue for almost a week.

Fearful that the haggling over the revenue bond provision would delay passage of withholding repeal, Treasury Secretary Regan granted a further extension of the effective date for the new law until Aug. 5 so financial institutions would be spared unecessary start-up costs.

Conferees accepted compliance provisions, less stringent than those passed by the Senate, as well as the tax incentives for Caribbean nations. But they dropped other extraneous Senate provisions, including those involving enterprise zones and trade reciprocity.

Conferees worked under the assumption that President Reagan, who had earlier vowed to veto withholding repeal, would sign the legislation if it included the tougher compliance provisions and his Caribbean Basin Initiative.

The compliance provisions finally adopted were somewhat different from those adopted by the Senate. Conferees agreed to a compliance compromise offered by Rep. Barber B. Conable Jr., R-N.Y., after House members insisted they would not accept the stiff fines in the Senate provisions.

The conferees dropped the trade reciprocity provisions after House Ways and Means leaders agreed to take them up later in the year. ∎

Favored Nation Trade

As in previous years, Congress in 1983 sidetracked legislation to deny most-favored-nation trading status to China, Hungary and Romania.

The House Aug. 1 postponed indefinitely — effectively killing — resolutions to block President Reagan's renewal

of the favorable trading status for the three communist countries. The House postponed a resolution (H Res 256) rejecting the trade status for Romania by a 279-126 vote and postponed resolutions on China and Hungary (H Res 257, 258) by voice votes. The Ways and Means Committee had recommended their rejection (H Repts 98-315, 98-316, 98-317). *(Vote 283, p. 84-H)*

The Senate Finance Committee rejected a related resolution on Romania (S Res 171) July 29.

The resolutions were offered under the Jackson-Vanik amendment to the 1974 Trade Act (PL 93-618), which allowed either house of Congress to deny most-favored-nation status to communist countries by adopting a simple resolution. That "one-house veto" provision probably was invalidated by the Supreme Court's June 23 ruling on legislative vetoes. *(Legislative veto, p. 565; Jackson-Vanik, 1974 Almanac p. 553)*

While discussing the Romania issue on Aug. 1, Sam Gibbons, D-Fla., suggested that the congressional veto portion of the Jackson-Vanik amendment would be allowed to die. "This is probably the last Jackson-Vanik act we will have to put on up here," Gibbons told the House.

A Finance Committee aide said that panel chose not to act on the issue on the assumption that the Jackson-Vanik veto provision was no longer valid.

Background

Reagan on June 3 waived the Jackson-Vanik amendment to allow China, Hungary and Romania access to most-favored-nation benefits. That designation was routinely given to all U.S. trading partners, except communist nations, allowing them to export goods to the United States at reduced rates.

The purpose of Jackson-Vanik was to withhold most-favored-nation status from communist countries that did not permit their citizens to emigrate freely. The president could waive the prohibition on an annual basis for any country if he determined that doing so would promote freedom to emigrate. Jackson-Vanik was directed principally at the Soviet Union's restrictive emigration policies toward Jews and political dissidents; its principal result had been to block a general trade agreement between the United States and the Soviet Union.

For several years, Sen. Jesse Helms, R-N.C., Rep. Larry P. McDonald, D-Ga., and other conservatives in Congress had objected to granting the trading status to Romania. They argued that Romania had placed restrictions on emigration and had persecuted religious and ethnic minorities, especially persons of Hungarian extraction. *(1982 Almanac p. 142)*

Reagan threatened March 4 that he would not renew Romania's most-favored-nation status unless its government revoked an "education repayment tax" on persons wishing to emigrate. Helms said the tax would have amounted to $3,700 for persons with high school educations and $4,000 for each year of college education.

In a June 3 message to Congress, Reagan said he had received assurances from Romanian President Nicolae Ceausescu that the education tax would not be levied and that the Romanian government "will not create economic or procedural barriers to emigration."

Reagan's decision was denounced by sponsors of the legislation to deny the trade status for Romania. Richard T. Schulze, R-Pa., for one, told the House he was "appalled that we are so gullible as to believe that this government in Romania will keep its promises when in the past they have

responded with only short-term improvements in their policies on emigration."

Gibbons, chairman of the Ways and Means Trade Subcommittee, responded that 1,500 Romanians were waiting for U.S. approval to emigrate to the United States. The Romanian authorities, he said, "are not holding people over there. They are turning them loose. They are turning them loose faster than we will accept them or absorb them." ∎

Insider Trading Curbs

The House Sept. 19 passed by voice vote a bill (HR 559) to beef up the Securities and Exchange Commission's power to prosecute a war on insider trading — the use of non-public information to profit in the securities markets.

The Energy and Commerce Committee had reported HR 559 Sept. 15 (H Rept 98-355).

Under the measure, the SEC could ask a federal judge to impose a civil penalty of up to three times the profit gained or loss avoided on an insider trade. Existing law permitted the SEC merely to seek a court-ordered repayment of the gain and to refer such cases to the Justice Department for possible criminal action.

HR 559 also would boost the maximum fine for violations of the Securities Exchange Act to $100,000 from the $10,000 maximum established in 1934. In addition, HR 559 would give the SEC new power to force companies to correct false or misleading statements in proxy materials. The Senate took no action on the bill before adjournment.

The SEC had asked for the new powers as part of a campaign to crack down on insider trading, which had become widespread in recent years as corporate mergers and acquisitions and trading in stock options increased in frequency.

"Insider trading" referred to the illegal practice of exploiting non-public information to buy or sell a security on the expectation that its price would move dramatically up or down once the information became public. ∎

Defense Production Act

In one of its last acts before adjourning Nov. 18, Congress approved a six-month extension of the Defense Production Act, a 1950 law giving the president various powers to ensure the economic health of defense-related industries.

The stopgap extension, until March 30, 1984, was included in a complex supplemental appropriations bill (HR 3959 — PL 98-181) to which a variety of unrelated provisions were attached. *(Supplemental, p. 536)*

The temporary extension of the Defense Production Act became necessary when the Senate and House failed to reach agreement on a longer-term measure (S 1852). The act had expired Sept. 30, when a previous six-month extension (HR 2112 — PL 98-12) ran out.

Senate-House Split

As passed by the Senate Sept. 30, S 1852 extended the Defense Production Act for five years. It also restricted the president's authority to grant loans and loan guarantees for industry and gave Congress broad oversight of loan decisions.

S 1852 initially came to the House floor Oct. 4 under suspension of the rules, a procedure that barred floor amendments. Rep. John J. LaFalce, D-N.Y., chairman of the Banking Subcommittee on Economic Stabilization, attempted to substitute a simple two-year extension of the 1950 law. But the House rejected the bill on a 233-168 vote, 35 short of the two-thirds majority required for passage under the suspension procedure. *(Vote 359, p. 108-H)*

LaFalce returned to the floor Oct. 6 and offered to accept most of the amendments in the Senate-passed bill, but reducing the extension to two years and permitting the administration to give loans and loan guarantees without congressional approval provided the aggregate amount of loans did not exceed certain "threshold" levels. The measure passed by voice vote.

On Oct. 7, however, the Senate refused to accept the House changes and sent the bill back to the House. There was no further action on S 1852.

Defense Stimulus Bill Reported

Earlier in the year, the House Banking Committee included a three-year extension of the Defense Production Act in a defense-related economic stimulus bill reported May 12 (HR 2782 — H Rept 98-110, Part 1). The bill, a scaled-down version of a measure that had run into trouble in 1982, did not receive floor consideration in 1983.

Approved by voice vote, the $2.9 billion bill provided loans and other forms of aid to small- and medium-sized businesses whose products were potentially important to the national defense. The measure also authorized a new vocational education program to train people for certain occupations, such as machinists and tool and die makers, in which skilled workers were expected to be in short supply.

Sponsors of the bill argued that small businesses needed help to modernize their equipment, so that they could survive economic downturns and foreign competition and be ready to produce in the event of war. The bill also sought to encourage domestic production of minerals with strategic importance, to protect against cutoffs of foreign supplies.

The committee had reported a $6.75 billion version of the legislation in 1982, but that bill did not pass. Sponsors pulled it from the floor after the House adopted what the sponsors considered to be a "killer" amendment. *(1982 Almanac p. 63)*

The 1983 version of the bill provided a three-year authorization for the new programs, instead of the five-year authorization contained in the 1982 measure. In addition, annual funding levels for the new business aid program in HR 2782 were substantially lower than those in the earlier bill.

Even so, the 1983 measure faced increased opposition from Republicans, who argued that it was little more than a new subsidy for business largely unrelated to national defense. While a majority of panel Republicans supported the bill in 1982, more than half signed minority views in the committee report opposing HR 2782.

Loan Guarantees. Much of the Republican opposition to HR 2782 was due to the provisions allowing use of funds for loans and loan guarantees to businesses. The bill authorized $400 million in fiscal 1984, $600 million in fiscal 1985 and $800 million in fiscal 1986 for loans and other forms of assistance.

Critics of the bill argued that the loan provisions would lead to further federal interference in the credit markets and result in higher interest rates. They predicted

that, through the use of guarantees, the program could provide a total loan volume up to 10 times as great as the dollar authorization.

The committee rejected, 17-28, an amendment by Tom Ridge, R-Pa., to strike the section of the bill providing business aid.

Vocational Education. Considerably less controversial was a provision authorizing assistance for vocational education. The bill allowed spending of up to $350 million a year for skill training programs.

The measure would provide aid in two forms. The bulk would be in the form of grants to states for vocational education programs. States would have to supplement the programs with an amount of their own funds equal to 10 percent of their federal allocations.

The bill also authorized funds to be distributed to higher education institutions for purchase of equipment to train personnel for key industries.

The Education and Labor Committee, which also had jurisdiction over the bill, reported HR 2782 May 16 (H Rept 98-110, Part 2). Its version of the education proposal was similar to that approved by the Banking Committee.

HR 2782 included a provision, added on the floor in 1982 by an amendment by Education and Labor Committee Chairman Carl D. Perkins, D-Ky., stipulating that any spending authorized by the bill for either business or education aid would not come out of the budget allocation for education and labor programs.   ■

Volcker Confirmation

The Senate July 27 confirmed the nomination of Paul A. Volcker to a second four-year term as chairman of the Federal Reserve Board. Eight Republicans and 8 Democrats opposed the nomination on the 84-16 vote. *(Vote 218, p. 37-S)*

Volcker began his second term Aug. 6. As chairman of the autonomous Federal Reserve, he had primary responsibility for guiding the nation's monetary policy.

President Reagan ended months of speculation June 18 when he announced his intention to renominate Volcker to the Fed chairmanship. Volcker originally was appointed by Democratic President Carter in 1979. *(1979 Almanac pp. 284, 49-A)*

Banking Committee Chairman Jake Garn, R-Utah, praised Volcker's performance during Senate debate July 27. The Banking panel had approved the nomination by a 16-2 vote July 21. "I doubt any chairman has served during a more difficult time," Garn said.

"It is not fair to try and lump all of the problems of this economy on the Federal Reserve Board and not place the emphasis where it really belongs, on those who control the spending," he added.

Volcker's supporters gave him substantial credit for bringing inflation under control. But critics, such as Dennis DeConcini, D-Ariz., charged that the Fed chairman had "almost single-handedly caused one of the worst economic crises" in U.S. history by causing interest rates to skyrocket.

"We should be telling Mr. Volcker that in a democracy, we do not combat inflation by placing 12 million citizens on the rolls of the unemployed," DeConcini said.

Volcker's appointment was considered under provisions of a 1977 law (PL 95-188) that required confirmation

of persons designated as chairman and vice chairman of the Federal Reserve Board. This change was the only tangible result of efforts by several House Democrats to make sweeping reforms in the Federal Reserve Board. *(1977 Almanac p. 152; 1982 action, 1982 Almanac p. 64)*

The law, which took effect on Jan. 1, 1979, guaranteed every Fed chairman and vice chairman a four-year term. If a chairman or vice chairman resigned or died during his term, his successor was to be appointed for a full four years — not merely the remainder of the old term.

Congress created the Federal Reserve Board in 1913. The board consisted of seven members, who were appointed for terms of 14 years. Terms were arranged so that one expired every two years. A member could not be reappointed after serving a full term. *(Board membership, p. 24-A)* ∎

Credit Card Fraud

The House Nov. 16 passed by a 422-0 vote a bill (HR 3622) to beef up laws protecting consumers against fraudulent use of their credit cards. *(Vote 480, p. 140-H)*

The Senate took no action on the measure, which had been reported (H Rept 98-426) by the House Banking Committee Oct. 20.

HR 3622 would make it a federal crime to possess more than five counterfeit credit cards or other payment devices. It also would:

● Broaden existing credit card law by barring fraudulent use not only of the cards themselves but also of credit card numbers, electronic banking cards and other non-check payment devices.

● Prohibit the disclosure of credit card numbers and customer account access codes, except within a corporation or between the corporation and its subsidiaries for legitimate purposes.

● Permit a consumer to sue a consumer reporting agency that illegally disclosed the consumer's credit card or payment device number.

● Close a loophole in existing law that limited federal jurisdiction in cases involving the use of a single credit card to steal more than $1,000 in a single year. HR 3622 would make it a federal crime to steal more than $1,000 in a single year through credit card fraud regardless of how many cards were used. ∎

Credit Card Surcharges

The House Nov. 16 passed — by a 349-73 vote and over Reagan administration objections — a bill (HR 4278) to extend until July 31, 1984, a 1981 ban on surcharges for purchases by credit card or under open-end credit plans. *(Vote 481, p. 140-H)*

The Senate took no action on the bill before adjournment. The existing surcharge ban was scheduled to expire Feb. 27, 1984. *(Background, 1981 Almanac p. 105)*

The sponsor of the bill, Frank Annunzio, D-Ill., chairman of the House Banking Subcommittee on Consumer Affairs and Coinage, said it was needed to allow time for hearings on a Federal Reserve Board study of surcharges that was submitted to Congress July 27, as required by the 1981 law.

The administration viewed the ban on credit card purchase surcharges as unwarranted government intervention in the private sector. It said a credit card surcharge was the same as a discount for paying cash, a practice permitted under federal law. ∎

Mortgage Aid Fails

The widespread belief that the recession was ending helped to block renewed efforts in 1983 to provide emergency mortgage assistance for the unemployed.

House Democrats, whose 1982 drive had been thwarted, tried several times in the new year to establish a mortgage relief program. *(1982 Almanac pp. 205, 71)*

On May 11, the House narrowly approved HR 1983 authorizing $760 million in direct loans in fiscal 1983, over the strong objections of the Reagan administration. The bill called for a revolving loan fund to aid some 100,000 homeowners threatened with foreclosure. A key part of the Democrats' anti-recession program, the bill was approved by a 216-196 vote after eligibility requirements were tightened to meet objections of members. *(Vote 98, p. 34-H)*

But the Senate did not consider that measure, and a plan pushed by some members to provide up to $750 million in loan guarantees was left out of a Housing and Urban Development Department (HUD) authorization and appropriation June 21. *(Appropriations, p. 495; authorization, p. 277)*

The mortgage loan guarantees were dropped first from the authorization (S 1338 — S Rept 98-142) by a floor amendment sponsored by Banking Committee Chairman Jake Garn, R-Utah, and Housing Subcommittee Chairman John Tower, R-Texas, to assuage critics who threatened the bill's passage.

Later that day, during consideration of the HUD appropriation bill (HR 3133 — S Rept 98-152), the Senate tabled an amendment by the sponsors of the mortgage guarantee plan, John Heinz, R-Pa., and Donald W. Riegle Jr., D-Mich., to add the program to the funding bill. They had revised their proposal, cutting the total loans to be guaranteed to $500 million and reducing the length of the program from two years to one year.

Veterans' Aid. The House also included funds in two bills to help unemployed veterans avoid losing their homes. HR 2948 (H Rept 98-118) passed by a vote of 394-23 on May 24 allowed the Veterans Administration (VA) to use up to $150 million from its revolving fund for mortgage aid. *(Vote 124 p. 42-H)*

The Senate did not consider the measure, and the House added language to the HUD appropriation bill (HR 3133) to carry out the program. The provision was dropped in conference.

Mortgage Relief

House Committee. Caught up in a wave of sympathy for victims of the recession, the House Banking, Finance and Urban Affairs Committee March 10 approved a $760 million mortgage aid program. The proposal was similar to one included in the committee's 1982 housing authorization bill, which did not reach the floor. *(1982 Almanac p. 68)*

The 1983 bill (HR 1983 — H Rept 98-32) was ordered reported by a 27-19 vote, with GOP committee members uniformly siding with the Reagan administration in oppos-

ing the bill.

Under the program, which would be triggered by high default rates, HUD would make mortgage payments for needy homeowners for up to three years. Borrowers must contribute 38 percent of their income toward their housing costs during that period, and they must repay the HUD loans. The program would be available only for mortgages below $67,500 in most areas, or a maximum of $90,000 in high-cost regions.

The administration, federal bank supervisors and GOP members argued that the bill was not needed because of the upward swing of the economy and that it would discourage lenders from developing their own programs of forbearance on delinquent loans.

Floor Action. The critics forced Democrats to tighten the eligibility requirements before a final vote was taken. Consideration began April 19, but the measure repeatedly was pulled from the floor because Democrats lacked sufficient votes to pass it. One problem was a widespread belief that the recession was ending and special relief was no longer warranted. Also, critics said HR 1983 was too loosely drawn, and some members were unwilling to support a bill that could add to the federal deficit.

The key vote during House debate May 11 occurred on an amendment by Buddy Roemer, D-La., to gut the bill. It was defeated by a vote of 197-220. *(Vote 94, p. 34-H)*

The House also rejected amendments by:

● Robert S. Walker, R-Pa., to bar spending that violated balanced budget requirements, 157-254. *(Vote 95, p. 34-H)*

● George C. Wortley, R-N.Y., to cut the $760 million plan in half, to $380 million, by voice.

● Steve Bartlett, R-Texas, to require that applicants for mortgage relief first file a wage-earner's plan under the Chapter 13 bankruptcy code, 154-254. *(Vote 96, p. 34-H)*

● Ed Bethune, R-Ark., to ban the mortgage aid program in any area where federal regulators decided it would hinder lender forbearance, 175-234. *(Votes 97, p. 34-H)*

After defeating those amendments, the House by voice vote approved a substitute offered by Housing Subcommittee Chairman Henry B. Gonzalez, D-Texas, to add an assets test to ensure that well-off families with vacation homes or other valuable holdings could not receive mortgage aid.

The test limited assistance to unemployed homeowners whose average income over three years did not exceed $20,000 for a family of four. The family's assets (excluding its residence, car, $5,000 in household goods and job-related equipment) could not exceed $10,000.

Other changes included prohibiting aid to individuals whose unemployment was voluntary or the result of their own misconduct, and excluding from housing expenses used to calculate a borrower's mortgage assistance the cost of upkeep for a golf course, riding stables, swimming pool, tennis court, hot tub or other recreational facilities.

Veterans' Aid

The Veterans' Affairs Committee reported HR 2948 May 13 (H Rept 98-118). Floor consideration began May 23 and the House May 24 passed the bill. The measure made aid available to any veteran or surviving spouse who was unemployed or had suffered a substantial reduction in household income and had fallen at least six months behind in mortgage payments.

It allowed the VA to pay the veteran's mortgage payments for 12 months, including six months of back pay-

ments. The aid could be extended another 12 months. However, the total borrowed from the VA could not exceed $8,400, and the veteran must repay the entire loan within four years at current interest rates or the original loan rate, whichever was less. The aid would be funded out of revolving funds used by the VA to pay claims from lenders. ∎

Democratic Phase II Jobs Bill

By a party-line vote of 246-178, the House Sept. 21 passed a $3.5 billion public service jobs bill (HR 1036), part of a "Phase II" Democratic program aimed at aiding the long-term unemployed. Although the bill went no further in Congress, the Democrats hoped it would come back to haunt its Republican foes in the 1984 election campaign. *(Vote 333, p. 100-H)*

The measure would offer federal funds to create jobs for the long-term unemployed through projects to repair and renovate community facilities and public schools in areas of high unemployment.

The momentum behind HR 1036 — introduced in January, when unemployment had reached its highest point since the Depression — had declined steadily as the unemployment rate dropped from a high of 10.8 percent in December 1982 to 9.5 percent in July and August 1983. *(Anti-recession jobs plans, 1982 Almanac p. 59)*

With bipartisan support, Congress in March enacted a $4.6 billion "Phase I" jobs and humanitarian relief package as part of a fiscal 1983 supplemental appropriations bill (HR 1718 — PL 98-8). *(Story, p. 447)*

But President Reagan, who rejected public service jobs plans, opposed the Phase II legislation, and it quickly became clear that the Republican-controlled Senate would refuse to accept the measure. *(Reagan proposals on structural unemployment, p. 16-E)*

The House never acted on a second Phase II bill, a $3.2 billion public works jobs plan (HR 2544) reported by the Public Works and Transportation Committee May 17. *(Story, p. 270)*

House Committee Action

The House Education and Labor Committee reported HR 1036 May 16 (H Rept 98-199). As reported, the bill authorized $5 billion for the public service jobs program in fiscal 1983. It would create jobs directly, by giving local governments money to hire people for a variety of projects ranging from public school renovation to public safety functions.

The committee finally approved HR 1036 on May 5, after a three-week fight over protections for state and local government workers.

The bill brought to the full committee by Employment Opportunities Subcommittee Chairman Augustus F. Hawkins, D-Calif., the bill's sponsor, had run into opposition from the American Federation of State, County and Municipal Employees (AFSCME), which feared that it would result in displacement of regular employees by federally funded public service workers.

Union ally William Clay, D-Mo., offered an amendment, unacceptable to Hawkins, to penalize local governments that substituted subsidized workers for permanent staff.

The penalties proposed by Clay and AFSCME to prevent potential substitution quickly became the focus of

hard lobbying by other interest groups — principally the AFL-CIO, the U.S. Conference of Mayors and the National League of Cities.

"It was a classic employer-employee negotiation over one key issue — job security," said Nanine Meicklejohn of AFSCME.

The compromise eventually worked out contained "the strongest and most enforceable anti-substitution provisions," according to the committee.

It set up an elaborate reporting and complaint procedure to protect regular employees from being replaced by subsidized workers. But it still allowed financially strapped governments to lay off some workers without being totally excluded from the new program.

Community Renewal Projects

As reported, HR 1036 authorized funds for grants to state and local governments with populations of 50,000 or more. After the $5 billion authorized for fiscal 1983, annual authorization levels would be determined by multiplying 20 percent of the number of long-term unemployed by $10,000.

Of the funds appropriated under the bill, 80 percent would be reserved for community improvement projects such as road and sewer projects, land and water reclamation and various health and social service activities. The remaining 20 percent of the money would go for repair of public school facilities.

Funds would be distributed on the basis of unemployment, with the money concentrated on areas with unemployment rates above the national average. No more than 25 percent of the money provided to each local government could be spent on administration, supervision and supplies. The remainder of the funds would go for wages, which could not exceed $230 a week per person.

Most participants in the program would have to have been unemployed at least 15 of the preceding 20 weeks, with priority given to those who had exhausted their unemployment benefits.

However, local governments would have some discretion in hiring others who did not meet the unemployment criteria. Local governments could use their own funds to supplement the wages of subsidized workers but could not employ any individual for more than 52 weeks in any two-year period.

House Floor Action

With Democrats acknowledging that part of their purpose in forcing House action was to create a 1984 campaign issue, the floor debate Sept. 20-21 was characterized by traditional partisan arguments over whether public service jobs plans work and by a preview of probable 1984 campaign rhetoric.

Majority Leader Jim Wright, D-Texas, for one, launched into a long indictment of the "Reagan deficit" when George W. Gekas, R-Pa., offered an amendment to bar the use of funds in the bill unless the Treasury secretary certified that the spending would not increase the deficit.

"What irony," Wright said. "It must be a terrible disappointment to President Reagan, who promised when he came into his office that he would have a balanced budget by 1984, to see the deficit for 1984 looming larger than it ever has been in the history of the nation."

Gekas replied later: "I ask the majority leader to put aside the history of deficit spending for once in his career and say to the American people, 'I am willing to start with this little bill to show the American public that I want to pay as you go.'"

After two hours of debate on that issue alone, the House rejected the Gekas amendment by a party-line 166-258 vote. *(Vote 330, p. 98-H)*

Other Amendments

On an amendment by Hawkins, the bill's $5 billion fiscal 1983 authorization was dropped and a cap of $3.5 billion for fiscal 1984 was substituted for it, to comply with the fiscal 1984 budget resolution. The Hawkins amendment was adopted 414-0. *(Vote 328, p. 98-H)*

The House also adopted the following amendments by:
● Dick Durbin, D-Ill., providing that not less than 75 percent of the funds in the bill be paid to participants in the program, not more than 15 percent go for administration costs and not more than 10 percent for supplies and equipment. Voice vote.
● Hawkins, to limit salaries for administrators of the program to levels no higher than those a local government paid employees performing comparable functions, or no more than the salary of a federal employee at the GS-10 level, currently $29,000 a year. Voice vote.

The Hawkins amendment was a substitute for a Durbin amendment that would have limited such salaries to the GS-10 level without exception.
● James M. Jeffords, R-Vt., providing that the program's authorization would automatically expire if the national unemployment rate fell below 6 percent, and funding levels would be reduced on a sliding scale for each percentage point drop in unemployment down to 6 percent. Voice vote.

Before adopting the Jeffords amendment, the House rejected, 208-210, a Hawkins substitute to end the authorization if unemployment fell to 4 percent and to target funding to the highest unemployment areas if unemployment was between 4 percent and 6.5 percent. *(Vote 329, p. 98-H)*
● Harold L. Volkmer, D-Mo., to require states to divide funding for rural areas in the same way a formula in the bill would allocate funds to urban areas, targeting areas of high unemployment. Voice vote.
● Gerald B. H. Solomon, R-N.Y., to require that men subject to the draft must register to be eligible for the jobs program. Voice vote.
● Austin J. Murphy, D-Pa., to apply the fraud-and-abuse provisions of the Comprehensive Employment and Training Act to the program authorized by HR 1036. Voice vote.

Amendments Rejected. The House rejected amendments by:
● Robert S. Walker, R-Pa., to require that 100 percent of the jobs created under the program be filled by persons who had been unemployed at least six weeks prior to enactment. Rejected 142-279. *(Vote 331, p. 98-H)*
● Walker, to permit the secretary of labor in effect to waive provisions of the Davis-Bacon Act, which required that the prevailing local wage be paid on federal construction projects, if doing so would substantially increase employment in the area in question. Voice vote.
● Walker, to permit the secretary of labor in effect to waive provisions of the Davis-Bacon Act if doing so would substantially increase employment for minority youth in the area in question. Rejected 92-327. *(Vote 332, p. 98-H)*

● Walker, to require that 100 percent of the jobs created go to persons unemployed at least 15 weeks prior to applying for a job under the program. Rejected by a 23-73 standing vote.

● John N. Erlenborn, R-Ill., to recommit the bill to the Education and Labor Committee. Voice vote.   ▮

Public Works Jobs Plan

The House did not act on a $3.2 billion public works jobs proposal reported by the Public Works and Transportation Committee May 17 (HR 2544 — H Rept 98-202). The measure sought to provide jobs by funding local road and public building projects, chiefly in areas with high unemployment.

HR 2544 was one element in a "Phase II" jobs program pressed by House Democrats in 1983. The House Sept. 21 passed another Phase II bill, a $3.5 billion public service jobs measure (HR 1036). *(Story, p. 268)*

Earlier in the year, Congress enacted a bipartisan $4.6 billion jobs and humanitarian relief package as part of a fiscal 1983 supplemental appropriations bill. *(Story, p. 447)*

That "Phase I" measure had President Reagan's support, but the president opposed further jobs spending. Democrats hoped to gain political mileage from the jobs issue in the 1984 election campaign, but their Phase II plan lost momentum as unemployment dropped more rapidly than expected in 1983.

Committee Action

HR 2544 was approved by the Public Works Committee after a sharp partisan fight. Efforts at compromise fell through, and the bill was ordered reported by a 31-19 party-line vote May 12.

The original version of HR 2544, introduced by Economic Development Subcommittee Chairman James L. Oberstar, D-Minn., provided a $4 billion authorization. It would have established a new program based on the Local Public Works (LPW) program of the mid-1970s, which was operated through the Commerce Department. The LPW program was the target of considerable criticism because it was unable to begin providing jobs before the end of the recession it was intended to combat. *(Background, 1982 Almanac p. 61)*

William F. Clinger Jr., R-Pa., who had helped run the LPW program as a Commerce Department official in the Ford administration, was sharply critical of Oberstar's original approach. He helped develop a Republican alternative, which was rejected 18-32.

Republican Plan. The Republican substitute called for total funding of $2.9 billion. Of that amount, $2.3 billion would be available for new public works projects, distributed basically through the existing revenue sharing program. The remainder would go for increased spending for sewer construction programs.

One-third of the new public works money in the Republican plan would be given to local governments, according to the revenue sharing formula. The revenue sharing formula took into account factors such as population and per capita income, rather than unemployment. The rest of the money would be given to states, which would have discretion to parcel out their share to any local area with unemployment in excess of 8 percent.

The effect of the Republican formula would be to make more money available to small communities and areas with relatively less severe unemployment problems.

Democratic Plan. Unable to reach a compromise with the Republicans, committee Democrats came up with their own new plan that scaled down the original provisions of HR 2544. The scaled-down plan was approved by the panel over Republican opposition.

The second Democratic proposal reduced funding to $3.2 billion from the $4 billion in the original version of HR 2544. In addition, it contained some of the ideas put forward in the Republican plan.

As approved by the committee, HR 2544 would channel funds through the revenue sharing program. But the bulk of the funds, $2.4 billion, would be distributed on the basis of state and local unemployment rates; compared with the Republican plan, the bill required relatively greater focus on areas with the highest levels of unemployment. The remaining $800 million, however, would be distributed on the basis of the revenue sharing formula.

The bill contained other provisions aimed at concentrating aid on high-unemployment areas. Communities with relatively less severe unemployment would have to match their federal allocation with some of their own money; hard-hit areas would not. To prevent funds from going to minuscule projects with minimal job-creation effects, the bill excluded small communities if their formula allocation came to less than $50,000 each.

The bill also included requirements aimed at preventing some of the problems that frequently arose under the LPW program. Local communities would have to ensure that their projects provided work for the long-term unemployed, youth and minorities. They could not use the money to buy real estate, or to construct recreational or cultural facilities. New construction projects could be undertaken only if they could be completed within a year. In addition, the bill urged communities to start projects, such as repair and renovation of public facilities, that provided large numbers of jobs relative to their cost.   ▮

Aid for Dislocated Workers

A bill (S 242) to broaden federal aid to dislocated workers was reported (S Rept 98-181) by the Senate Labor and Human Resources Committee July 14. It failed to receive any further consideration.

S 242, the Employment Opportunities Act of 1983, won committee approval June 22 on a 12-4 vote after the panel accepted five amendments.

S 242 focused on "dislocated workers" — those whose jobs were abolished due to changed economic conditions that made it unlikely they would be re-employed to perform the work for which they were trained.

Among the items approved by the committee was a major amendment by Dan Quayle, R-Ind., primary sponsor of S 242, that attached to the bill the text of another measure (S 1264) to provide health insurance to the unemployed. *(Health insurance for the unemployed, p. 405)*

By a vote of 13-2, the committee also attached to S 242 an amendment by Chairman Orrin G. Hatch, R-Utah, to give block grants to the states to coordinate and fund services to help the elderly and disabled avoid institutionalization.

Two of the other three amendments offered by com-

mittee members also dealt with Quayle's health insurance legislation.

The remaining amendment, offered by Howard M. Metzenbaum, D-Ohio, struck an entire title that would have established a pilot project of "re-employment vouchers" for dislocated workers. The voucher proposal was a variation on one included in President Reagan's fiscal 1984 budget and was opposed by labor unions. *(Story, p. 425)*

Provisions

The fundamental provisions of S 242 were intended to complement the 1982 Job Training Partnership Act (PL 97-300), an aid and training program designed to get the unemployed into private-sector jobs. *(1982 Almanac p. 39)*

The measure was designed to help the out of work receive training for new careers and to provide financial aid to them during the transition from their old jobs to their new positions. Major provisions:

• Allowed a dislocated worker to withdraw funds from an Individual Retirement Account (IRA) without incurring the tax penalty normally imposed on early IRA withdrawals.

• Eased financial eligibility requirements under the federal Pell Grants program, which provided education aid grants to low-income families, and under the federal Guaranteed Student Loans program.

• Authorized $30 million in fiscal 1984 for distribution to the states by the secretary of labor to pay for regional efforts to publicize existing job training programs. ∎

Longshore, Corruption Bills

Two labor reform measures that died in the House in 1982 bogged down there again in 1983. The pair of bills — one to revamp federal workers' compensation for longshoremen, the other to curb union corruption — easily cleared the Senate for a second year in a row but failed to receive House consideration.

The Longshoremen's and Harbor Workers' Compensation Act Amendments of 1983 (S 38) passed the Senate by voice vote June 16. The bill was reported by the Senate Labor and Human Resources Committee May 10 (S Rept 98-81).

The Senate passed the Labor Management Racketeering Act (S 336) 75-0 on June 20. It was reported by the Labor Committee May 11 (S Rept 98-83). *(Vote 158, p. 29-S)*

The Senate in 1982 passed a bill closely resembling S 38, which would exempt some businesses and workers from the expensive longshoremen's compensation program. S 336, which would increase penalties for union officials convicted of bribery or other corrupt practices, was passed by the Senate in identical form in 1982. *(1982 Almanac p. 65)*

But the 1982 measures faced union opposition and failed in the House because the late Phillip Burton, D-Calif. (1964-83), chairman of the House Education and Labor Subcommittee on Labor-Management Relations, declined to act on them.

A subcommittee aide contended that the lack of action in 1983 was simply a matter of the panel having a new chairman, union ally William Clay, D-Mo., who became chairman on Burton's death, and did not signal renewed trouble for the legislation.

Anti-racketeering

One difference in 1983 was that the new general president of the Teamsters union, Jackie Presser, endorsed the anti-racketeering bill in principle. The Teamsters opposed it in 1982, arguing that it was weighted against labor.

Presser's predecessor, Roy Lee Williams, was convicted of bribery and conspiracy in late 1982 and might have been subject to provisions in the bill that would have barred a union official from union office for 10 years following a criminal conviction. Williams agreed to give up all ties to the union so that he could stay out of prison during his appeal.

The bill grew out of an investigation into waterfront corruption that was conducted in 1981 by the Senate Governmental Affairs Permanent Subcommittee on Investigations.

The Senate Labor Committee's report on S 336 noted that in the Investigations Subcommittee's hearings, witnesses "testified that the large network of U.S. ports are [*sic*] controlled by organized crime and charged that payoffs occur with such regularity that they have become a part of normal business operating costs."

Reform Provisions

Major provisions of S 336:

• Increased to five years' imprisonment and a $15,000 fine (from one year and $10,000) the maximum penalty for violations by labor or management officials of three core labor laws: the Labor-Management Relations Act of 1947, known as the Taft-Hartley Act (PL 80-101); the Employee Retirement Income Security Act of 1974, known as ERISA (PL 93-406); and the Labor-Management Reporting and Disclosure Act of 1959, known as the Landrum-Griffin Act (PL 86-257). *(Background, Taft-Hartley, Landrum-Griffin, Congress and the Nation Vol. I, p. 567; ERISA, Vol. IV, p. 690)*

• Expanded the list of offenses for which a convicted person could be disqualified from serving in a union or employee benefit plan office.

• Expanded the list of union or benefit plan offices from which convicted persons would be barred. The committee said in its report that existing law had allowed union officials barred from top jobs to circumvent the penalty by taking clerical or other positions not prohibited to them and exercising authority from there.

• Increased the maximum period of disqualification from union or benefit plan offices to 10 years from five.

• Required that persons convicted of certain labor-related offenses be excluded from union or benefit plan offices immediately upon conviction, rather than upon conclusion of the appeals process, as permitted under existing law.

• Emphasized the Labor Department's responsibility to refer to the Justice Department evidence that could lead to prosecutions under labor and pension statutes.

Longshoremen

The longshore bill was opposed by the East Coast dockworkers' union, the International Longshoremen's Association (ILA). The International Longshoremen's and Warehousemen's Union (ILWU), whose members work in Western ports, did not take a formal position on the issue in 1983.

In 1972 Congress expanded the jurisdiction of the 1927 Longshoremen's and Harbor Workers' Compensation Act, which covered only persons actually working over water, to

include others in maritime jobs.

The Reagan administration advocated a return to more restricted coverage, as called for under S 38. The ILA and ILWU argued in 1982 that the decade-old legislation (PL 92-576) was the product of a labor-industry compromise that should stand. *(1972 Almanac p. 134)*

The bill would have limited benefit increases under the program for disabled longshoremen to 5 percent per year. It would also have scaled back the program's coverage, exempting certain firms, such as builders of small vessels, and certain jobs, such as shipping firm clerks.

Further, the bill would have enacted penalties to combat what another probe by the Governmental Affairs Permanent Subcommittee on Investigations found was a "fraudulent claims racket which flourished under the statutory loopholes in the current act." The anti-fraud provisions stemmed from findings that organized crime had manipulated the program. ∎

Railroad Retirement

Congress moved with rare dispatch to keep the federal railroad retirement and unemployment compensation programs solvent through a combination of benefit reductions, increased taxes and a federal contribution of $1.7 billion.

The House passed the bill (HR 1646) Aug. 1 by a vote of 398-5. The Senate approved it the next day, 95-2, and President Reagan signed it into law Aug. 12 (PL 98-76). *(House vote 282, p. 84-H; Senate vote 230, p. 39-S)*

The railroad retirement system — the only private pension plan run by the federal government — faced a deficit of $6 billion through fiscal 1988 and $13 billion by 1992 if remedial legislation had not been passed.

The urgency surrounding the measure was easily explained: The Railroad Retirement Board, which administered the rail retirement and unemployment compensation programs, said that if Congress failed to act before the start of its summer recess on Aug. 5, the board would notify one million retirees Sept. 1 that a major portion of their benefits would be cut 40 percent as of Oct. 1, when fiscal 1984 began.

The announcement was required under provisions of the fiscal 1982 budget reconciliation act (PL 97-35). *(1981 Almanac p. 106)*

Under PL 97-35, the Railroad Retirement Board was required to report to Congress each April 1 if it estimated a funding shortfall for the next fiscal year. In its report, the board must outline plans to absorb the shortfall by publishing figures on how much so-called Tier II benefits — the portion of railroad retirement equivalent to a private pension plan — were to be cut across-the-board. (Tier I benefits approximated Social Security.)

HR 1646 contained benefits reductions for workers retiring before age 62 and deferred cost-of-living increases for all retirees. But those cuts were far less drastic than the 40 percent cut in fiscal 1984 and a further 40 percent reduction the next year that were scheduled in the absence of legislation.

The Congressional Budget Office (CBO) estimated the changes in benefits would save $256 million in fiscal 1984, $439 million in fiscal 1985 and $512 million in fiscal 1986.

To help cover the deficit created by declines in railroad jobs that had deprived the retirement program of contributions, the legislation increased employer-worker taxes for fiscal 1984-86.

CBO estimated that those changes would bring in $140 million in fiscal 1984, $636 million in fiscal 1985 and more than $1 billion in fiscal 1986.

The bill also authorized federal payments of $1.7 billion for special benefits due retirees covered by both railroad retirement and Social Security pension provisions.

In addition, the bill bolstered the Railroad Unemployment Compensation fund (RRUC) through a 50 percent increase in the wage base on which railroad employers pay unemployment taxes, effective Jan. 1, 1984.

The sharp drop in railroad employment in recent years — there were an estimated 700,000 railroad workers in 1980 but only 400,000 in 1983 — had drained the RRUC, forcing it to borrow from the railroad retirement fund, thus exacerbating the retirement fund's problems.

House Action

The bill as passed was an amalgam of measures approved by the House Energy and Commerce (H Rept 98-30, Part 1) and Ways and Means committees (H Rept 98-30, Part 2). Energy and Commerce reported the bill March 9; Ways and Means, July 1.

HR 1646 retained a Ways and Means amendment that deleted an Energy and Commerce provision permitting RRUC to borrow from the Federal Unemployment Trust Fund with no obligation to repay the loans. Instead, RRUC could continue to borrow from the Railroad Retirement Account until Sept. 30, 1985. After that, rather than permit RRUC to borrow more, the Ways and Means amendment imposed on railroad employers a temporary tax to be collected from July 1, 1986, through Sept. 30, 1990. The RRUC was to use those tax payments to pay back the Railroad Retirement Account.

The Reagan administration opposed the measure as written by the Energy and Commerce Committee but supported it as reported by the Ways and Means Committee and passed by the House and Senate.

Amendments adopted in the House by voice:

● By J. J. Pickle, D-Texas, to advance from July 1, 1984, to Jan. 1, 1984, the effective date of increases in employer and employee payroll taxes needed to finance Tier II benefits.

Under the bill as amended, Tier II taxes for employers would increase from 11.75 percent to 12.75 percent as of Jan. 1, 1984; to 13.75 percent as of Jan. 1, 1985; and to 14.75 percent as of Jan. 1, 1986. Tier II taxes for employees would rise from 2 percent of wages to 2.75 percent on Jan. 1, 1984; to 3.5 percent on Jan. 1, 1985; and to 4.25 percent on Jan. 1, 1986.

The Pickle amendment also required railroad employers to deposit payroll taxes more quickly beginning Jan. 1, 1984 — a change from July 1, 1986, under the bill as reported — to conform with deposit schedules for Social Security taxes.

● By James J. Florio, D-N.J., as an amendment to the Pickle amendment, to phase in — rather than impose at once — benefit cuts affecting railroad employees with 30 years of service who retire before the age of 62.

● By Patricia Schroeder, D-Colo., to instruct the Railroad Retirement Board to honor court orders treating railroad retirement benefits other than Tier I benefits as property that could be divided in divorce proceedings.

Senate Action

The Senate took up HR 1646 only hours after the

Senate Finance Committee held its first hearings on the measure.

At the hearings, Director David A. Stockman of the Office of Management and Budget urged rapid action, saying: "The wolf is at the rail pensioner's door." Representatives of railroad labor and management who had negotiated the terms of the bailout plan in HR 1646 also endorsed the bill as passed by the House.

Final Provisions

As signed by the president, HR 1646:

Taxes. Increased Tier II taxes for employers from 11.75 percent of a given employee's wages to 12.75 percent effective Jan. 1, 1984; to 13.75 percent effective Jan. 1, 1985; and to 14.75 percent effective Jan. 1, 1986.

• Increased Tier II taxes for employees from 2 percent of an employee's wages up to 2.75 percent effective Jan. 1, 1984; to 3.5 percent effective Jan. 1, 1985; and to 4.25 percent effective Jan. 1, 1986.

• Provided that, for the first time, Tier II benefits would be taxed as income, with revenue from the tax to be deposited in the Railroad Retirement Account until the end of fiscal year 1988 or until it totaled $877 million, whichever occurred earlier, and given to the Treasury afterward.

• Imposed on railroad employers a temporary tax, from July 1, 1986, to Sept. 30, 1990, equal to 2 percent of the first $7,000 in wages paid each employee. The tax would rise 0.3 percent each Jan. 1 until it reached 5 percent. The funds would be used to repay loans from the Railroad Retirement Account to the Railroad Unemployment Compensation fund.

• Increased Railroad Retirement Unemployment Compensation taxes 50 percent by raising the monthly wage base from $400 to $600, on which rail employers paid a tax of 8 percent.

• Provided for taxes on the so-called "windfall" benefits some retirees received by virtue of having worked under both the railroad retirement and Social Security pension plans.

• Changed the wage base upon which railroad retirement taxes were paid from a monthly to an annual basis as of Jan. 1, 1985, to conform with the wage base used by the Social Security system.

• Required railroad employers to deposit payroll taxes more quickly beginning Jan. 1, 1984, to conform with deposit schedules other employers must follow for Social Security taxes.

• Provided that sick pay received under railroad unemployment insurance would become subject to income tax beginning Jan. 1, 1984.

Cost of Living. Deferred a scheduled cost-of-living allowance on Tier II benefits from July 1, 1984, to Jan. 1, 1985.

• Provided that future cost-of-living increases in Tier I benefits would be offset by reducing cost-of-living increases on Tier II benefits, up to a cumulative total of 5 percent.

Retirement. Provided that, until July 1, 1984, rail employees with 30 years of service could retire with full benefits at age 60 but that after July 1, 1984, individuals with 30 years of service who retired before they turned 62 would have their benefits permanently cut.

From July 1, 1984, until Dec. 31, 1985, employees with 30 years of service retiring between ages 60 and 62 would receive only 90 percent of Tier I benefits.

After Jan. 1, 1986, the reduction in Tier I benefits for

such early retirees would be 20 percent.

Reports. Required the Railroad Retirement Board to report to Congress each July 1, beginning in 1985, on the financial condition of the railroad retirement system.

• Established a five-member Railroad Unemployment Compensation Committee to report to Congress by April 1, 1984, on benefit and tax changes needed to enable the Railroad Unemployment Compensation fund to repay all its loans from the railroad retirement fund by the year 2000.

The committee also was charged with examining proposals to combine the Railroad Unemployment Compensation program with the federal-state unemployment compensation system.

Others. Authorized the Railroad Unemployment Compensation fund to continue borrowing from the Railroad Retirement Account until Sept. 30, 1985.

• Instructed the Railroad Retirement Board to honor court orders treating railroad retirement benefits other than Tier I benefits as property that could be divided in divorce proceedings.

• Increased from seven to 14 days the waiting period for unemployment benefits during strikes. ∎

Social Security Disability

Congress was unable to reach agreement on changes in the troubled Social Security disability insurance program, despite more than a year of negotiations between legislators and special interest groups.

Instead, certain provisions of existing law were extended, giving Congress until early 1984 to come up with a plan to revise the process used for reviewing the disability rolls.

That process had been the subject of considerable controversy since it was first imposed in 1981 by the Reagan administration, at the direction of Congress. Critics charged that, in an effort to weed the rolls of ineligible recipients, the administration also took away the benefits of thousands of still disabled individuals.

Congress approved stopgap legislation in 1982 to allow those thrown off the rolls to continue collecting benefits while their cases were under appeal, but more comprehensive legislation was postponed. *(Background, 1982 Almanac p. 52)*

The legislation (HR 3755) before Congress in 1983 would revamp the review process, making it more difficult for individuals to be disqualified for benefits.

But despite strong support for some change in the disability program, Republicans challenged the high cost of the proposed legislation and charged that some provisions could allow the kind of program abuses that had led to the 1981 crackdown.

House Action

The Ways and Means Committee agreed Sept. 27 to a bill (HR 3755) to set new rules for dropping from the disability rolls persons judged able to work. However, the legislation was later attached by the committee to a larger tax package (HR 4170 — H Rept 98-432). Reported Oct. 21, HR 4170 never reached the House floor. *(Tax bill, p. 231)*

The committee adopted minor amendments to HR 3755 but left the bill essentially the same as approved Aug.

3 by its Social Security Subcommittee.

The legislation would permit recipients disqualified by the Social Security Administration (SSA) to continue receiving benefits while appealing to an administrative law judge. It also required states to give recipients a hearing at the first stage of a disability review.

The bill further would make it more difficult for SSA to declare a beneficiary sufficiently improved to disqualify him, and it called for a temporary halt of reviews of the mentally disabled until SSA devised new rules for such cases.

As approved by the subcommittee, HR 3755 provided that SSA could halt a person's benefits if it found that:

● New evidence showed he had been helped enough by advances in medical or vocational therapy or technology that he was able to perform "substantial gainful activity."

● New evidence or "new diagnostic techniques" unavailable when he was certified showed he was less impaired than originally thought.

● The original determination that he was eligible for benefits was erroneously made or fraudulently obtained.

In addition, the panel agreed to an amendment by Andrew Jacobs Jr., D-Ind., providing that SSA also could terminate benefits to someone who "is a beneficiary of any additional vocational therapy which results in ability to engage in substantial gainful activity."

The bill was expected to add $2.4 billion to the $18 billion annual cost of the program over fiscal 1984-89.

Stopgap Extension

The Senate Finance Committee Sept. 22 deferred similar legislation but approved, 9-8, a six-month extension of provisions in the 1982 law that let persons ruled ineligible to continue to receive benefits while they appealed. Those provisions had been set to expire Sept. 30.

However, on Sept. 30, the full Senate agreed to extend the law only 60 days as part of an unrelated bill extending federal supplemental unemployment benefits (S 1187). *(Unemployment benefits, below)*

The House approved similar legislation (HR 3929) Sept. 29 that called for a 45-day extension of the disability provisions.

But because conferees did not act quickly on the legislation, Congress Oct. 6 cleared a different bill (HR 4101 — PL 98-118) extending the 1982 disability law until Dec. 7. Despite the Dec. 7 expiration date, however, another provision of the law allowed beneficiaries dropped from the rolls in December to continue receiving benefits through March 1984.

Disability reform advocates in the Senate Nov. 17 attempted to attach legislation similar to the measure approved by the Ways and Means Committee to a supplemental appropriations bill conference report (HR 3959). But the plan, offered by Carl Levin, D-Mich., was tabled (killed) 49-46. *(Vote 365, p. 60-S)*

To allow more time to develop comprehensive disability legislation, the Senate Nov. 18 voted 80-0 for a six-month extension of the existing review procedures, but the House failed to act on the measure (HR 3391). *(Vote 371, p. 60-S)*   ∎

Federal Jobless Aid Extension

Amidst continued high unemployment, Congress voted twice to extend the federal supplemental unemployment

benefits program, which had gone into effect in 1982. *(Background, 1982 Almanac p. 43)*

The first extension was approved in March as part of a larger package (HR 1900 — PL 98-21) to rescue the Social Security system from insolvency. That extension, effective through Sept. 30, allowed from eight to 14 weeks of supplemental benefits for those who had exhausted up to 39 weeks of other benefits. *(Social Security, p. 219)*

In October, the program was again extended — this time through March 1985.

In addition, Congress approved a separate bill (HR 3409 — PL 98-92) in August to clarify some disputed provisions in the first extension dealing with the maximum number of weeks of supplemental benefits states could offer.

No action was taken during the year on the administration's budget proposal to revamp the federal unemployment program by allowing recipients to accept job vouchers in place of weekly unemployment benefits.

Under the plan, the vouchers could be used, in effect, to help a jobless worker buy a job. Once hired, the worker would turn the vouchers over to the employer who would use them to receive tax credits.

Labor groups strongly opposed the plan, charging that the voucher system would encourage employers to get rid of current employees and replace them with those on the unemployment rolls. *(Budget, p. 425)*

Second Extension

President Reagan Oct. 24 signed legislation (HR 3929 — PL 98-135) extending for 18 months federal supplemental unemployment payments to individuals who had exhausted all other unemployment benefits. The program had been scheduled to expire Sept. 30.

The bill provided for a minimum eight weeks and a maximum 14 weeks of supplemental benefits. It also allowed an additional five "reachback" weeks to persons who became eligible for supplemental benefits between April 1 and the week of Oct. 23 and exhausted all their benefits, including supplemental benefits, as of Oct. 16.

The House first passed HR 3929 (H Rept 98-377) Sept. 29 by a 327-92 vote. The measure won Senate approval the next day, 89-0. The conference report (H Rept 98-428) was adopted Oct. 21 — in the House by a vote of 300-5 and in the Senate by voice vote. *(Vote 345, p. 104-H; vote 268, p. 44-S; vote 383, p. 114-H)*

Because conferees failed to quickly agree on the bill, Congress Oct. 6 enacted an emergency measure (HR 4101 — PL 98-118) to extend the unemployment program through Oct. 18.

As originally passed by both houses, HR 3929 also included provisions that extended until Dec. 7 a program permitting persons thrown off the Social Security disability rolls to continue to receive benefits while appealing the decision. But that extension, included in HR 4101, was omitted from the final version of HR 3929. *(Disability, p. 273)*

House, Senate Variants

The House, in HR 3929, agreed to continue the federal benefits for 45 days and to authorize a maximum benefit period of 16 weeks. But the Senate stripped the House language from HR 3929 and substituted its own measure (S 1887 — S Rept 98-240) calling for an 18-month extension, the period endorsed by the Reagan administration. The 18-month extension was approved by the Finance Committee

Sept. 22.

The Senate version also limited the maximum number of weeks an individual could collect benefits to 12, with the exception of a 14-week limit for West Virginia, whose July jobless rate of 17.4 percent was the worst in the nation. The administration had proposed a maximum benefits period of 10 weeks.

The House bill further provided eight extra weeks of federal supplemental benefits to out-of-work individuals who had used up all of their federal benefits. The Senate Sept. 30 rejected by a 37-54 vote an amendment by Minority Leader Robert C. Byrd, D-W.Va., to add a similar reachback provision to S 1887. The White House was opposed to the reachback. *(Vote 266, p. 44-S)*

The Ways and Means Committee approved the 45-day extension Sept. 20 after its subcommittee on unemployment compensation had recommended a nine-month extension. The committee's shorter extension was seen as a maneuver by Chairman Dan Rostenkowski, D-Ill., to make the popular program a vehicle Congress might use to carry a tax increase later in the year. However, the attachment was never made.

Existing law based eligibility for up to 14 weeks of federal unemployment benefits on a state's insured unemployment rate (IUR), which measured the number of individuals collecting unemployment benefits. Long-term unemployed who had run through all their unemployment benefits were not counted in the IUR.

The House bill authorized states to choose between using the IUR and the total unemployment rate for determining how long a state could offer federal supplemental benefits. The Senate stuck with the IUR.

Major Provisions

As signed by the president, HR 3929:

● Extended, from the week of Oct. 23, 1983, through the week of March 31, 1985, federal supplemental unemployment payments providing additional benefits to persons who had exhausted all other state and federal unemployment benefits.

● Provided that the maximum benefit weeks payable in a state would be no fewer than eight and no more than 14, determined by a formula based on a state's IUR.

● Provided reachback benefits payments of up to five extra weeks for the unemployed who exhausted their federal supplemental benefits between April 1 and the week of Oct. 23, 1983.

● Provided "transitional" benefits for up to four weeks to persons eligible for federal supplemental benefits the week of Oct. 16, 1983, but whose eligibility overlapped with the new law.

● Limited, beginning with the week of Oct. 23, 1983, the maximum number of weeks of benefits a state could gain or lose at any time under the program to two weeks, and provided that no state's maximum weeks of benefits could be adjusted up or down more often than each 13 weeks.

● Guaranteed individuals the same number of weeks of benefits they qualified for as of the time they became eligible for supplemental unemployment benefits, irrespective of adjustments to the maximum weeks payable in their state of residence.

● Provided that payments by employers to survivors or to the estates of deceased persons would be exempt from the Federal Unemployment Tax after the end of the calendar year in which the deceased died.

● Extended for two years, from Jan. 1, 1984, to Jan. 1, 1986, a law excluding wages paid to certain alien farm workers from the Federal Unemployment Tax.

● Increased, from $2.5 billion to $2.7 billion, in fiscal 1984 and subsequent fiscal years, the funds available for social services block grants to states authorized by Title XX of the Social Security Act.

● Simplified federal bookkeeping by authorizing direct repayment to the Treasury of funds lent to a state from the unemployment trust fund. Under existing law, such loans had to be paid back to the trust fund and could only be repaid to the general Treasury if the relevant accounts in the trust fund exceeded their statutory limit at the end of the fiscal year.

Unemployment Modification

As one of its last acts before recessing Aug. 4, Congress cleared an intricate piece of legislation that, in essence, was meant to keep promises Congress never meant to make to the nation's long-term unemployed.

The legislation — part of HR 3409 (PL 98- 92), which also extended an emergency food distribution program for two years — arose from the Labor Department's initial misinterpretation and later reinterpretation of a provision in the unemployment compensation law (HR 1900 — PL 98-21) passed in March as part of the Social Security legislation.

As signed into law Sept. 2, HR 3409 prevented any state from having the number of weeks of federal supplemental unemployment compensation benefits it offered reduced beyond what it was able to offer as of July 24.

It also permitted four states — Arizona, Kansas, Massachusetts and North Carolina — to pay benefits to some recipients longer than they would have been able to pay them under a June 10 Labor Department ruling that was meant to correct an initial misinterpretation of the law.

The Labor Department estimated that freezing the benefit period at the July 24 level would mean more weeks of unemployment compensation for 60,000 recipients. The special provision for Arizona, Kansas, Massachusetts and North Carolina, the department estimated, would preserve at least two weeks of benefits for up to 27,000 persons.

To cut the cost of the supplemental unemployment benefit program, HR 1900 reduced the maximum number of weeks of supplemental benefits a state could offer, generally cutting two weeks off the maximum for states with the highest unemployment rates.

HR 1900 also raised the minimum rate of insured unemployment a state had to be suffering to be able to offer its eligible residents at least 10 more weeks of unemployment compensation.

But those working on the legislation discovered that, because of a drop in its IUR, the new standards would cut Delaware's maximum number of weeks of supplemental benefits after March 27, the last week of the original program, from 14 weeks to eight weeks — which was considered too dramatic to be humane.

Consequently, it was provided in HR 1900 that any state whose new maximum would be immediately reduced under the new formula by more than four weeks would suffer a benefits reduction of no greater than four weeks as compared with its maximum as of March 27.

Labor Rulings. But, as explained by the House Ways and Means Committee in its report (H Rept 98-328) on HR 3409, "The Department of Labor misinterpreted the language of the Act. It instructed states that in *no case* could the number of weeks payable in any state throughout

the [six months'] extension be more than 4 weeks less than the number payable in the state for the week of March 27, 1983."

The effect, according to congressional aides, was to make the program more generous than Congress had intended, for the benefits were designed to diminish as a state's insured unemployment rate declined.

But on June 10, the Labor Department issued a new ruling that interpreted the law as originally intended by Congress but had the effect of barring the four states from paying as many weeks of benefits as they had been promising. Also, after the June 10 ruling took effect, the maximum benefit period in 21 states fell by more than four weeks below the maximum under the old program because their IURs dropped.

The difficulty the states faced led members to argue that the original Labor Department interpretation of HR 1900 should stand. The House passed HR 3409 on Aug. 2 by a vote of 338-84 in a form that did just that: provided that, as under the original Labor Department ruling, no state's maximum weeks of supplemental benefits under the extended program would be more than four weeks less than that state could offer under the original program. *(Vote 285, p. 86-H)*

Senate Action. But Senate Finance Committee Chairman Robert Dole, R-Kan., brought the measure to the Senate floor Aug. 4 in a modified form that he said would cost only $56 million, compared to the $208 million it would require to finance the four-week lid.

Rather than capping at four any state's loss of benefits weeks, Dole's amendment provided that a state whose maximum benefit period as of July 24 was four or more weeks less than the maximum that state had been able to offer under the old supplemental unemployment compensation program would have its maximum frozen for the rest of the program.

The amendment also provided that any recipient enrolled for the supplemental benefits as of June 5 would receive a maximum number of weeks of benefits no more than four weeks less than the maximum payable under the old program. A recipient could only receive those benefits if he were still unemployed after Aug. 4.

The Senate passed HR 3409, with Dole's amendment, by voice vote. The House accepted the Senate amendment by voice vote, and cleared the bill for the president the same day. ∎

Pension 'Equity' Measures

A bill (HR 2769) making broad changes in pension law was passed by the Senate Nov. 18. Similiar pension "equity" legislation was approved Nov. 16 by the House Education and Labor Committee (HR 4280) and by the Senate Labor and Human Resources Committee (HR 2110). The House Ways and Means Committee, which shared pension jurisdiction with House Education and Labor, was still considering a pension measure when Congress adjourned.

The Senate Labor and Human Resources Committee gave its approval to HR 2110 after inserting the text of S 1978, a pension bill introduced by Finance Chairman Robert Dole, R-Kan. The Finance Committee had reported the Dole plan in HR 2769 Oct. 29 (S Rept 98-285).

As approved in the Senate by voice vote, HR 2769 liberalized pension coverage by broadening spouses' rights

to a pension if a worker died before retirement age and by permitting employees to leave for as long as five years and then return to a job without suffering a break in service counted for enrollment or vesting (entitlement to receive benefits) in a pension plan.

Under the Employee Retirement Income Security Act (ERISA), employers could exclude any employee under 25 from the plan and could wait until an employee is 22 before counting service for vesting credit. HR 2110 lowered the age for enrollment to 21 and the minimum age for vesting to 18. *(ERISA, 1974 Almanac p. 244)*

House, Senate Differences

The House and Senate pension bills both called for basically similar changes in pension law, though there were some significant differences between the measures. The House bill lowered the enrollment age to 21 for most pension plans, but gave an employer with a defined-benefit plan — which provided a fixed level of benefits at retirement — the option to continue using the 25-year-old enrollment age. Once an employee reached 25, the employer would have to give the worker credit for the previous four years. This provision was designed to avoid paperwork and administrative expenses incurred by processing young employees who leave a company after a brief stay.

Unlike the Senate bill, which entitled a spouse to a pension if an employee had worked at the same firm for 10 years and died after reaching age 45, the House bill provided pension coverage to spouses of employees with 10 years of service regardless of the employee's age at the time of death. ∎

Mortgage Revenue Bonds

A popular program allowing states to increase the supply of mortgage money by issuing tax-exempt bonds expired Dec. 31 after Congress failed to extend the program.

The reauthorization was included in a tax measure (HR 4170 — H Rept 98-432) reported by the Ways and Means Committee Oct. 21. The House Nov. 17 rejected the rule providing for floor consideration of the bill. *(Story, p. 231)*

Under the program, state and local housing finance agencies sold bonds to an investor, who accepted a lower interest rate because he got the advantage of federal tax exemption on the interest income.

Proceeds from the sale were funneled into mortgage funds, and because the state paid a lower interest rate to the bondholder, it could charge the homebuyer a lower interest rate, usually two or three percentage points lower, depending on the bond market.

Controversy Over Tax Loss

Despite the popularity of the program, which states began using in 1970 and cities in 1978, there was controversy over extending tax-exempt mortgage revenue bonds.

State and local governments and housing industry officials strongly backed the program as a way of making low-cost mortgage money available.

But the Reagan administration opposed an extension of the tax exemption because of its concern about the loss of revenue to the federal Treasury.

Use of revenue bonds had increased sharply as interest rates peaked. State and local governments issued a total of

$7.8 billion in bonds for residential property in 1979, up from $3.3 million in 1978. Since $1 billion funded roughly 20,000 homes, about 1.56 million homes were financed through mortgage revenue bonds in 1979.

Congress tried to stem the revenue loss by adding restrictions to the program in the 1980 budget reconciliation act. For example, it limited the use of the bond proceeds to providing funds for single-family residences and to first-time homebuyers, and placed a cap on the volume of bonds a state and all the localities within the state could issue for single-family units. *(1980 Almanac p. 298)*

But the Treasury losses continued. In 1981 and 1982, tax-exempt mortgage revenue bonds cost the federal government a total of more than $2.6 billion in lost revenue, according to the General Accounting Office (GAO).

Critics also charged that the program did not benefit those who needed it most. GAO reported that almost three-fourths of the people who took advantage of the program in 1982 could have afforded homes without it.

Compromise

Because of the popularity of the program, some mem- bers of Congress endorsed a permanent extension. Sen. William V. Roth Jr., R-Del., introduced such a bill (S 147) and more than three-fourths of the Senate signed on as cosponsors.

The Senate Finance Committee, by a 14-3 vote in May, agreed to tack S 147 onto a bill repealing the witholding on interest and dividend income, but the provision was dropped in conference.

The Ways and Means Committee proposal extended the current tax exemption for five years.

Its bill also offered a compromise endorsed by the administration: giving states and localities the option of issuing tax credit certificates instead of bonds.

The "mortgage credit certificates" allowed a homeowner to receive a federal tax credit worth up to 50 percent of the mortgage interest on qualified personal residences. The credits, issued directly to the homeowner, were subject to the existing eligibility requirements for qualified mortgage bonds.

According to committee estimates, the revenue from extending the mortgage bonds would be offset by tax increases from changes in industrial development bonds. ∎

Compromise Reached on Housing Revisions

Congress and the White House put aside some of the sharp divisions that for two years had stymied an overhaul of housing programs and agreed in November on a compromise $15.6 billion housing reauthorization.

Although President Reagan objected to several provisions, he signed the bill Nov. 30 (HR 3959 — PL 98-181) because it was attached to legislation that he wanted badly — an $8.4 billion increase in the U.S. contribution to the International Monetary Fund (IMF). Both were added to a fiscal 1984 funding bill. *(Stories, pp. 241, 536)*

The maneuver of linking the housing and IMF provisions in a "take it or leave it" package was engineered by Fernand J. St Germain, D-R.I., chairman of the House Banking, Finance and Urban Affairs Committee. St Germain wanted to force enactment of a fiscal 1984 authorization for programs run by the Department of Housing and Urban Development (HUD). The last time an authorization reported by congressional committees had cleared Congress was in 1980; in 1981 an authorization was included in the Gramm-Latta II budget reconciliation bill. *(1981 Almanac p. 110; 1982 Almanac p. 68)*

The tactic broke a months-long logjam. The House had passed its $15.6 billion bill (HR 1 — H Rept 98-123) July 13 after cutting one-third of the funding and making other changes.

But the Senate bill ran into serious trouble. The Senate briefly considered a $17.6 billion measure (S 1338 — S Rept 98-142) June 21, but the bill was amended heavily and pulled from the floor because of the threat of extended acrimonious debate.

St Germain's adamant threat to hold up the IMF bill led to negotiations between key members of Congress and the administration, resulting in the compromise cleared by Congress Nov. 18.

The bill put the federal government back in the business of building new rental housing for the first time since Reagan took office. It created a new program of grants for the rehabilitation and construction of rental housing, de- spite administration objections to new construction programs.

The $615 million authorized for the new program over two years was expected to provide 31,000 new units and 30,000 rehabilitated units. The House had authorized a $900 million program, and the Senate proposal provided $300 million.

While some administration proposals were rebuffed, the legislation included a Reagan initiative to replace the current system of subsidies with housing vouchers that low-income persons would apply toward rental housing, although at a reduced level. The vouchers, which tenants could use like cash, were authorized for a demonstration project of 15,000 units, instead of the 80,000 requested by Reagan.

The legislation reflected the drive by House Democrats to reverse policies set by the 1981 budget reconciliation bill. They included reinstating some application requirements for Community Development Block Grants that provided funds for a variety of development programs, and a provision effectively reducing tenant rent.

In other key provisions, the bill:

● Authorized $9.9 billion for subsidized housing programs in fical 1984, which was expected to support 100,000 units. Reagan originally requested $515 million in fiscal 1984 new budget authority, after the rescission or deferral of previously obligated funds. Later revisions to reflect Congress' refusal to defer $3.1 billion in fiscal 1983 funds brought the request to $3.6 billion.

● Authorized $3.5 billion in each of fiscal 1984, 1985 and 1986 for community development grants as requested. But the bill also required recipients to spend at least 51 percent of the aid to benefit low- and moderate-income persons.

● Authorized $440 million in each of fiscal 1984, 1985 and 1986 for Urban Development Action Grants, which were used to foster private investment in deteriorating areas.

● Authorized $1.3 billion in fiscal 1984 for public hous-

ing, including 7,500 new units of public housing and 2,500 units of Indian housing. The administration requested no funds for new construction. Also, the bill authorized $1.6 billion for public housing modernization.

• Authorized $666.4 million to subsidize 14,000 units of housing for the elderly and handicapped.

• Authorized $3.2 billion for rural housing, including $100 million in each of fiscal 1984 and 1985 for a new program of grants to communities for rehabilitation of single-family or rental housing owned or occupied by low- and very-low income persons or families. Reagan originally proposed $1.2 billion for the program run by the Farmers Home Administration (FmHA), a cut from the $3.5 billion 1983 level.

• Permitted the rates for mortgage loans insured by the Federal Housing Administration (FHA) for the first time to match market rates, instead of being set by law.

Provisions

As signed into law, the housing provisions of HR 3959:

Community Development

• **Community Development Block Grants.** Authorized $3.468 billion in each of fiscal 1984, 1985 and 1986 for Community Development Block Grants, and required that each year, at most $68.2 million be set aside for the secretary's discretionary fund.

• Required cities and communities to spend at least 51 percent of their aid to benefit low- and moderate- income persons.

• Required grant recipients to submit to the HUD secretary a statement certifying an estimate of funds to be used to benefit low- and moderate-income families, plans for minimizing displacement, provisions for public review and comment on plans, certification that a plan identified objectives, and a guarantee not to assess low-income individuals for activities assisted by community development funds unless the total community development funds were insufficient to cover those activities.

• Raised the percentage of public service activities eligible for funding from 10 percent to 15 percent.

• Allowed entitlement cities and urban counties that would be ineligible because of lost population to continue to receive entitlement grants through fiscal 1985.

• Required that, after fiscal 1984, a decision by a state to administer the grant program for small cities would be permanent and final, allowing HUD to administer the program if states elected not to, and required that the governor of each state administering the program certify that each unit of local government be required to identify its community and housing needs, including the needs of low- and moderate-income persons.

• Restricted loan guarantees to certain grant recipients who could not complete the financing of an activity on time without the loan, and limited the total amount of guaranteed loans to $225 million in fiscal 1984.

• **Urban Development Action Grants.** Authorized $440 million in each of fiscal 1984, 1985 and 1986 for Urban Development Action Grants, including up to $2.5 million in each year for technical assistance to small cities.

• Clarified that cities of 50,000 or more that were eligible for assistance in fiscal 1983 would continue to be eligible until the secretary revised the standards for eligibility.

• Required that a neighborhood impact analysis be made available to project area residents or organizations.

• Permitted cities of less than 50,000 that are near one another to apply for assistance as consortia.

• Prohibited the secretary from discriminating among programs on the basis of the type of activity involved, whether such activity was primarily a neighborhood, industrial or commercial activity.

• **Urban Homesteading.** Authorized $12 million in fiscal 1984 and $8 million in fiscal 1985 to transfer property to local governments with homesteading programs.

• Extended the required occupancy of a homesteaded property from three to five years prior to the homesteader's receipt of fee simple title, and extended time limits for completion of required repair work.

• Established a demonstration multifamily homesteading program, and required at least 75 percent of the occupants of multifamily homestead properties to be lower-income families.

• Earmarked $1 million for a demonstration project providing assistance to state and local governments for the purchase of real property.

• **Neighborhood Development.** Authorized $2 million in each of fiscal 1984 and 1985 for a demonstration neighborhood development program to create jobs, expand businesses, develop housing or deliver necessary services. The grants would match funds neighborhood development organizations raised privately. Individual grants were limited to $50,000 per year.

• Required that grants be issued on the basis of the extent of neighborhood distress, benefit to low- and moderate-income persons, local participation and voluntary contributions.

• **Section 312 Rehabilitation Loans.** Extended the rehabilitation loan program through fiscal 1984 with no additional authorization.

• Prohibited the secretary from restricting portions of the loans to certain types of property.

• **Neighborhood Investment Corporation.** Authorized $16.5 million in fiscal 1984 and such sums as necessary in fiscal 1985 for the independent corporation to stimulate private sector neighborhood revitalization.

Housing Aid

• Authorized $9.9 billion in budget authority in fiscal 1984 for housing assistance programs. That was expected to support 100,000 units.

• Granted priority for assisted housing to persons and families paying more than 50 percent of income for rent.

• Authorized HUD to issue regulations establishing lease and grievance procedures for public housing tenants in those areas where the secretary found that local eviction procedures did not require a judicial proceeding.

• Retained the requirement that tenants in assisted housing pay 30 percent of their income in rent, but established statutory deductions from income that would substantially reduce rents, including $480 per child, $400 for any elderly or handicapped family, medical expenses above 3 percent of income for elderly and handicapped, and child care expenses.

• **Housing Vouchers.** Authorized $242 million for a demonstration housing voucher program, providing certificates to low-income families to be used toward rent. This was expected to support 15,000 units.

• Set a contract term with public housing agencies for an initial period of five years, and permitted up to two rent adjustments.

• **Public Housing.** Authorized $1.29 billion for fiscal

1984 for public housing, of which $390 million was available for Indian housing. This was expected to support 7,500 units of public housing and 2,500 units of Indian housing.

● Repealed the Section 8 rental assistance new construction program.

● Increased the limitation on single-person occupancy in public housing to 30 percent, if units were not expected to be occupied by families.

● Authorized the use of rental assistance funds for people living in single-room occupancy housing.

● Established demolition and disposition standards for public housing.

● Authorized a demonstration child care program using Community Development Block Grant funds.

● **Elderly, Handicapped.** Authorized $666.4 million in fiscal 1984 for Section 202 units for the elderly and handicapped, expected to fund 14,000 units.

● Authorized funds from existing housing and moderate rehabilitation programs to be used to assist elderly families who elected to live in shared housing arrangements.

● Set the interest rate for Section 202 loans for the elderly and handicapped at 9.25 percent.

● Eliminated the requirement for competitive bidding in construction contracts when the project development cost was less than $2 million, if the project rents would be less than 110 percent of the fair market rents for elderly and handicapped, or if the sponsor was a labor organization.

● Limited the number of efficiency units in a project to 25 percent, unless more was requested by the sponsor.

● Barred owners or managers of federally assisted rental housing from prohibiting elderly or handicapped tenants from owning common pets.

● **Joint HUD/HHS Program.** Authorized $10 million in fiscal 1984 and $15 million in fiscal 1985 to provide a workable linkage between HUD housing assistance and Health and Human Services housing and welfare aid.

● **Section 235 Homeownership Assistance.** Authorized payments to subsidize mortgage payments for a 10-year period but authorized no new budget authority.

● **Homeless Assistance.** Authorized $60 million in fiscal 1984 for grants to states, local governments, Indian tribes and non-profit groups to shelter the homeless.

● **Congregate Services.** Authorized $4 million in fiscal 1984 for the Congregate Housing Services Program and required a report on changes in the administration of the program by March 15, 1984.

New Rental Program

● Authorized $615 million in fiscal 1984 and 1985, including $150 million in fiscal 1984 for rehabilitation and $200 million for new construction, and $150 million in fiscal 1985 for rehabilitation and $115 million for new construction.

● Required rehabilitation grants to be based on a formula, and required construction grants to be available only to communities with a severe rental housing shortage.

● Required 100 percent of grants to benefit lower-income families. .This requirement could be reduced to 70 percent if the recipient certified the reduction was necessary, and could be reduced to not less than 50 percent based on the secretary's determination.

● Allowed a structure to be assisted only if rehabilitation or development would not cause involuntary displacement of very-low-income families by families who were not very-low-income.

● Limited grant assistance to 50 percent of the total

costs associated with rehabilitation and development.

● Prohibited the conversion to condominiums or cooperative ownership for 10 years in the case of rehabilitation grants and 20 years in the case of development grants.

● **Rehabilitation.** Restricted grants to neighborhoods where the median income did not exceed 80 percent of the area median income.

● Required the secretary to assure an equitable distribution of funds for families, including large families with children, and required priority for projects containing units in substandard conditions occupied by very-low-income families.

● **Development.** Required at least 20 percent of the units, during a 20-year period, to be occupied by persons whose income did not exceed 80 percent of the area median income.

● Established criteria for selection, including the severity of rental shortages, non-federal public and private funds, maximum utilization of units for the least cost and the extent to which housing for lower-income persons and families was being met.

● Required the secretary to give priority for selection to those projects that exceeded the minimum requirement of at least 20 percent occupancy by persons whose income did not exceed 80 percent of the area median, projects in areas with long waiting lists for rental housing, and where there were fewer housing units available under other assisted housing programs.

● Limited rents for lower-income families to 30 percent of the adjusted income for families whose income equaled 50 percent of the area median income.

● Permitted states to administer funds for cities of less than 50,000, and permitted a state to administer its own rehabilitation or development program or distribute grants to units of local government.

● Exempted Davis-Bacon prevailing wage requirements for structures containing fewer than 12 units.

● Barred assistance to structures if the state or local government enacted a rent control statute after enactment.

Rural Housing

● **Farmers Home Administration (FmHA).** Required that not less than 40 percent of the units financed by Section 502 loans be available for very-low-income families or persons, and that 30 percent of the units in each state financed by Section 502 be available for very-low-income occupants.

● Permitted Section 502 loans to finance manufactured homes, providing that the home met requirements for any other home.

● Permitted loans under Section 504 to very-low-income families to improve or modernize rural homes.

● Directed FmHA to target rental aid to very-low-income families, by limiting the number of low-income families who were not very-low-income who could receive assistance.

● Limited to 10 percent the amount of farm labor housing grants that could be used for grants to non-profit organizations for farm-worker housing outreach.

● Permitted areas of between 10,000 and 20,000 people no longer classified as rural after the 1980 census to continue to be classified as rural during fiscal 1984.

● Permitted elderly and handicapped persons to receive rental assistance if they elected to live in shared housing, if the shared arrangement was in a single-family dwelling.

● Raised tenant rent contribution for Section 515 rental

assistance to 30 percent of income, and the definition of income was changed to conform to HUD programs.

● **Rural Housing Preservation Grants.** Authorized $100 million in each of fiscal 1984 and 1985 for a new program of grants to communities for rehabilitation of single-family or rental housing owned or occupied by low- and very-low-income persons or families.

● Required the secretary, in making grants, to give priority to families whose income did not exceed 50 percent of the area median income, to areas with populations below 10,000, and to repair and rehabilitation activities that would produce the greatest improvement at the least cost.

Miscellaneous

● **Federal Housing Administration (FHA) Mortgage Insurance.** Limited insured loans to $50.9 million in each of fiscal 1984 and fiscal 1985 and required the secretary to use the authority if qualified applicants were available.

● Eliminated the requirement that FHA interest rates be set by law, allowing the rate to be negotiated.

● Required energy performance standards for newly constructed homes to meet requirements incorporated in minimum property standards in effect on Sept. 30, 1982, and required FHA-insured conventional homes to meet either a nationally recognized building code or a local code the secretary deemed comparable.

● Increased the loan limit for manufactured homes and lots, and allowed refinancing under certain circumstances.

● Authorized a demonstration mortgage reinsurance program allowing contracts with private mortgage insurers.

● Extended FHA insurance to American Samoa, Hawaiian homelands and Indian reservations.

● Permitted the secretary to regulate rents on multifamily structures insured by FHA.

● Reduced down payments for buyers of houses valued at $50,000 or less.

● Authorized a demonstration FHA insurance program for alternative mortgage instruments not to exceed 10 percent of insurance activities of the prior calendar year.

● Required a report within one year on the advisability of establishing a federal program to insure home equity mortgages for the elderly.

● **Flood and Property Insurance.** Authorized the flood insurance program for two years and barred premium rate increases through fiscal 1984.

● Authorized the crime insurance program for one year, terminated the riot insurance program on Nov. 30, 1983, and authorized $1 million to study a sinkhole program.

● **Real Estate Settlement.** Permitted controlled business arrangements in real estate settlement, providing there was written disclosure.

● **Solar Bank.** Authorized $35 million for the Solar Energy and Energy Conservation Bank.

● Authorized $190 million for the Department of Energy's low-income weatherization program.

● **Government National Mortgage Association.** Set commitments at $68.25 billion in each of fiscal 1984 and 1985 for mortgages purchased by GNMA.

Reagan Proposals

Reagan's fiscal 1984 budget recycled many of his earlier housing proposals, once again calling for a sharp cut in subsidized housing funds and a program of cash vouchers to provide housing for the poor.

The administration proposed cutting new budget authority for subsidized housing programs run by the Department of Housing and Urban Development (HUD) and the Agriculture Department from an estimated level of $5.7 billion in 1983, to approximately $400 million in 1984, after the rescission of previously obligated funds. Despite the steep decline, outlays for housing assistance were to rise from $9.6 billion in 1983 to $10.8 billion in 1984 because of commitments made in earlier years.

The cornerstone of the administration's HUD budget was the replacement of most low-income housing construction with a less costly voucher plan. Under the $1.36 billion program, 80,000 families and individuals would receive cash-value certificates to apply toward the rent in existing housing they would find themselves. Each voucher would be worth about $2,000 a year.

All new subsidized households for 1984, except for 10,000 units for the elderly and handicapped, would come under the administration's proposed voucher program. Families would be expected to pay up to 30 percent of their income for rent. The federal subsidy would be the difference between the tenant contribution and a "reasonable rent level," which would be based on local market prices.

The 1984 budget also proposed a $150 million rental rehabilitation program to provide grants to states and cities for the renovation of private rental properties. The program would be used in conjunction with vouchers, and it would help remodel about 30,000 units.

For community development, the budget called for reauthorizing Community Development Block Grants at their existing level. Although $440 million was requested for the popular Urban Development Action Grants, by deferring 1983 spending into 1984, new funds would be cut by more than half.

Low-Income Housing

HUD's 1984 subsidized housing program would require $7.965 billion in budget authority, according to Albert Kliman, director of HUD's budget office. Only $515 million in new budget authority would be required, with the remainder consisting of $4.346 billion "recaptured" from earlier years by canceling previously approved housing units; $3.081 billion that would be deferred from 1983; and $24 million in permanent budget authority.

The proposed budget would allow subsidies for 90,000 new households in 1984. But it would cancel previously scheduled subsidies for approximately 27,000 households. Therefore, the net number of additional households, or units, proposed by the 1984 budget would be about 63,000, a HUD spokesman said.

Although all traditional HUD new construction programs would be ended, the budget would continue to fund Section 202 loans for newly constructed and substantially renovated housing for the elderly and handicapped. The proposed $436 million in new budget authority would cover 10,000 units for the elderly and handicapped.

Cushing N. Dolbeare, president of the National Low Income Housing Coalition, noted that new budget authority for major low-income housing programs had slipped from $30.2 billion in 1981 to approximately $8.65 billion, before rescissions, in 1983, and to a proposed level of $515 million in 1984.

HUD Secretary Samuel Pierce deflected criticisms of the cuts by arguing that the administration's programs would be more efficient. "You don't just have to have a lot of money," he said. "You need to spend it better."

Senate Committee Action

The Republican-controlled Senate Banking, Housing and Urban Affairs Committee April 13 approved a housing authorization bill that defied Reagan's plans to severely trim federal housing programs. Its report (S Rept 98-142) was filed May 23.

The panel unanimously approved a $17.6 billion measure that reauthorized community block grants for three years, created a modified new rental rehabilitation program and provided $7.65 billion in low-income housing subsidies in fiscal 1984, about $7 billion more than Reagan wanted.

By an 11-7 vote, the committee also agreed to an amendment creating a federal loan guarantee program to help unemployed homeowners avoid foreclosure.

The panel's $17.6 billion in budget authority exceeded the administration's fiscal 1984 budget request for HUD. Reagan proposed total new budget authority of $4.1 billion for all HUD activities.

The bill also discarded several policy changes requested by the administration, including a proposal to count food stamps as income when calculating the amount tenants paid for government-assisted housing and a recommendation to convert rural housing programs into a new block grant.

The committee agreed to try the administration's voucher and authorized $800 million for vouchers.

Foreclosure Amendment

The anti-foreclosure amendment was a compromise between a $760 million direct loan program favored by House Democrats and a no-cost system the administration said would encourage lenders to be more lenient with delinquent borrowers. *(Mortgage aid, p. 267)*

John Heinz, R-Pa., and Donald W. Riegle Jr., D-Mich., sponsored the plan to provide federal guarantees on loans that private lenders would offer to help unemployed homeowners meet their monthly mortgage payments. The federal government would guarantee up to 90 percent of a loan, which would prevent the delinquent mortgage from showing up as a decline in a lender's financial status. A $750 million cap on loan guarantees would be authorized, but the program would have no net cost to the government unless owners defaulted.

Funding Levels

The bill's fiscal 1984 programs included:

• A new $850 million rental rehabilitation program that provided grants and loans to cities and states to help construct or refurbish low-cost rental properties. Funding included $300 million for construction and rehabilitation, and $550 million for vouchers to be used by tenants to rent the units.

• Nearly $4 billion anually for community development programs, which were renewed through fiscal 1986. That included approximately $3.5 billion for Community Development Block Grants, $440 million for Urban Development Action Grants and $17 million for the transfer of vacant HUD properties to cities through an urban homesteading program. The block grants had to "principally benefit" persons of low income.

• A variety of low-income housing subsidies totaling $7.65 billion. Those included vouchers, Section 8 and Section 236 rent subsidies, rent supplements, Section 202 housing for the elderly and public housing modernization.

• $1.5 billion in public housing operating subsidies.

• $3.62 billion in rural housing loans and grants.

The bill dropped HUD's crime and riot insurance program, as of Sept. 30, 1983. An amendment by Alfonse M. D'Amato, R-N.Y., to reauthorize the program for three years failed on a 9-9 vote.

By a 9-8 vote, the committee agreed to an amendment by Paula Hawkins, R-Fla., to extend the Section 235 program that helped low-income families purchase homes. No new funding was provided, however. The administration wanted to eliminate the program.

The panel postponed action on changes in the Federal National Mortgage Association, known as Fannie Mae, and the Federal Home Loan Mortgage Corp., or Freddie Mac. It also delayed work on Indian housing.

Senate Floor Action

The Senate substantially revised the bill June 21 in an effort to assuage critics but final action was postponed by the threat of prolonged debate. After nearly two hours of consideration, Majority Leader Howard H. Baker Jr., R-Tenn., pulled the bill from the floor in order to take up a fiscal 1984 appropriations bill (HR 3133) for the Department of Housing and Urban Development and 17 independent agencies. *(Appropriations, p. 495)*

The debate focused on an amendment offered by Banking Committee Chairman Jake Garn, R-UTah, and Housing Subcommittee Chairman John Tower, R-Texas. The amendment, adopted by voice vote, added some $351 million to the bill, bringing the total close to $17.9 billion. It also eliminated the mortgage loan guarantee program.

Other changes it made included authorizing an extra 5,000 public housing units, adding a new Indian housing program and revising the $850 million rental housing rehabilitation proposal.

The amendment was necessary, Tower said, "to attract sufficient support to get this bill on the floor." Since being ordered reported April 13, the bill had drawn criticism from several members.

One of the strongest critics, William L. Armstrong, R-Colo., called the measure "a budget-busting subsidy bill which in my view should not even be on the floor." He was prepared to offer at least 65 amendments to slow its progress, a staff aide said.

Tower, however, wanted to approve the authorization before taking up the fiscal 1984 housing appropriations bill scheduled later that afternoon. He warned that once the funding bill had passed, "... it would be much more difficult for us to return to an authorization bill, especially if our agenda is crowded."

He argued that passage of the authorization was essential because "... the absence of legislative enactment is a relinquishment by Congress of its right and duty to set policy regarding housing for poor Americans and the physical environment of our cities."

Garn-Tower Amendment

The Garn-Tower amendment:

Rental Rehabilitation. Altered the $850 million rental rehabilitation program.

• Targeted all the assistance to benefit low-income families. Under the committee bill, a smaller portion of the funds was required to go to low-income families.

• Required that any housing unit occupied by a very-low-income family, rehabilitated under the program, must

be subsequently occupied by a very-low-income family.

● Limited rehabilitation of units to repairs necessary to correct substandard conditions, make essential improvements and repair major systems in danger of failure.

● Limited the federal grant for rehabilitation to no more than $5,000 per unit, except under certain high cost circumstances. No specific limitation was included in the original bill.

● Required HUD to provide Congress with an evaluation of the program.

Indian Housing. Added a new housing block grant to tribal governments for housing construction, rehabilitation or assistance to individuals.

Public Housing. Authorized $650 million for 5,000 additional units of public housing and required that new construction be permitted only when a city demonstrated that construction was cheaper than acquiring and rehabilitating existing units. The committee bill contained no new funds for additional public housing units.

● Reduced the authorization for public housing modernization by $400 million to $1.6 billion.

● Eliminated the bill's proposed system of public housing agency accreditation and instead created a public housing performance standards advisory commission to develop standards by which housing agencies would be evaluated.

● Required that housing vouchers that were not earmarked for specific programs be used to assist very-low income persons or families displaced by other HUD programs or activities.

House Committee Action

The House Banking, Housing and Urban Affairs Subcommittee on Housing April 26 approved a bill that was considerably more expensive than the legislation reported by the Senate panel and proposed by the president.

In the 22-13 vote to send a fiscal 1984 authorization bill to the full committee, subcommittee Democrats unanimously supported the bill, while GOP members uniformly opposed it.

The bill provided an estimated $24.6 billion in new budget authority.

HR 1 ignored the administration's plea to disband low-income housing construction programs. Instead, it included a new $1.3 billion multifamily housing production program, aimed at areas with critical rental housing shortages.

The annual allocation for Community Development Block Grants jumped from the current level of $3.5 billion to $4.5 billion. Urban Development Action Grants continued to receive $440 million per year. Both programs expired Sept. 30. The panel stipulated that 50 percent of the funds go to low- and moderate-income persons.

The bill reversed several cost-cutting actions Congress took in 1981. It cut the amount tenants paid for rent from 30 percent of their monthly income to 25 percent and reinstated some community development grant application procedures. *(1981 Almanac p. 110)*

In addition, the bill included:

● $12.9 billion for assisted housing, including Section 8 certificates for tenants to apply toward rent in existing buildings, Section 202 housing for the elderly and handicapped, public housing modernization and other housing subsidies.

● $4.2 billion for rural housing, rejecting the administration proposal to cut the FmHA programs by about two-

thirds and to replace them with an $850 million block grant.

● A ceiling of $46 billion for Federal Housing Administration (FHA) mortgage insurance and $68.3 billion for Government National Mortgage Association (GNMA) mortgage-backed securities.

Subcommittee Action

During five days of markup, the subcommittee considered more than 50 amendments. Some highlights:

● Stewart B. McKinney, R-Conn., sponsored an administration-backed amendment to allow communities to use community development grants to build low- and moderate-income housing. The panel rejected the amendment 12-19. Currently, funds could be used to renovate homes but not to build new ones.

● McKinney also proposed a "voucher demonstration" project based on Reagan's proposal, but it was defeated by voice vote.

● The subcommittee by voice approved an amendment by Mike Lowry, D-Wash., to prevent housing aid from being counted as income when considering eligibility for other federal assistance, such as Aid to Families with Dependent Children. The bill already excluded the value of food stamps when determining a family's rent.

Full Committee

The full Banking, Finance and Urban Affairs Committee approved the bill May 10 by voice vote. Its report was filed in two parts May 13 and June 7. Although the Banking panel attached more than 20 amendments, it essentially ratified the bill as approved by the subcommittee.

The full committee swept through HR 1 in about three hours May 9 and 10.

The panel by voice vote agreed to an amendment by Charles E. Schumer, D-N.Y., to target the new rental production program to low-income families. Under the new program, states and local governments would use federal funds to provide loans, grants or other assistance to developers who agreed to reserve 20 percent of the units in a new or rehabilitated rental project for low-income families. The Schumer amendment also stated that developers who set aside more units for poor tenants would be given priority in the selection process.

The committee, by a 23-22 vote, approved an amendment by Barney Frank, D-Mass., allowing developers of federally backed projects to follow local and state building codes instead of HUD "minimum property standards," if the local rules were based on nationally recognized codes.

In a 21-22 vote, the committee rejected an amendment by McKinney to allow community development grants to be spent on new home construction if connected with a neighborhood revival effort. Henry B. Gonzalez, D-Texas, chairman of the housing subcommittee, opposed the amendment on the grounds that community development money already was spread too thin.

House Floor Action

The House July 13 slashed the $24.3 billion funding by about one-third, to $15.6 billion, and passed the bill by a vote of 263-158. The new figure brought the bill in line with the first fiscal 1984 budget resolution and an appropriations measure (PL 98-45). *(Vote 325, p. 72-H; appropriations, p. 495)*

The administration opposed the bill but initially did

not take a position on a possible veto. It objected to the total funding, as well as to a new $900 million program to develop 75,000 subsidized rental housing units.

House consideration of the authorization continued over three days, July 11-13, as members debated more than 20 far-ranging amendments. Republicans made several attempts to dramatically alter the bill, focusing their complaints on its cost, the new programs initiated and the reconciliation policy changes.

Gonzalez said at a press conference July 12 that he agreed to sponsor the substitute amendment cutting the authorizations to "regenerate the bipartisan consensus on national housing issues."

He said he was willing to compromise "to show our good faith, although personally, it does violence to what I perceive as the crying need of the country.

"We don't want to subject this to the accusation that it is a budget buster," said Gonzalez. "At least we'll have a survival authorization. This will keep us alive in the basic housing programs. We've got housing on life support right now."

He added that administration officials agreed to temper their opposition to the housing authorization bill in the Democratic-controlled House only after Committee Chairman St Germain threatened to hold up the administration-backed IMF.

"If IMF weren't a priority on the president's list, we would not be considering HR 1," said Gonzalez.

The Gonzalez amendment cutting the authorizations was adopted July 12 by voice vote over the objections of Chalmers P. Wylie, R-Ohio, the ranking minority member of the Banking Committee. Wylie objected to the new $900 million cost of the multifamily rental housing construction program. Because low-income tenants were assured of getting only 20 percent of the units, he said, the program was "designed more to benefit developers and syndicators than the families in need of decent, safe and sanitary housing."

The reduced funding would support approximately 75,000 units of multifamily housing in areas with a severe rental shortage. Grants would be made on a competitive basis to state or local governments, planning agencies or Indian tribes. Recipients would determine how the grants would be spent for such goals as reducing interest, buying land or making loans.

As amended, HR 1 provided $9.9 billion in new budget authority for assisted housing, supporting approximately 208,817 units, including 5,000 public housing units and 2,500 Indian units.

The amendment also provided $100 million in emergency assistance for the homeless. The funds also were included in HR 1983, a mortgage foreclosure aid bill that passed the House.

It set authorization levels for an urban homesteading program at $24 million and provided $16 million for a new neighborhood reinvestment program designed to help neighborhood development groups create jobs, expand new businesses, develop housing or otherwise improve the neighborhood.

It also reduced public housing operating subsidies for fiscal 1984 to $1.45 billion, $100 million less than the original Banking Committee recommendation.

The community development block grants were authorized at $3.5 billion in each of fiscal years 1984, 1985 and 1986. The urban development grants remained at $440 million for the same periods, including funds for technical assistance to small cities.

Amendments

An amendment offered July 13 by Steve Bartlett, R-Texas, to eliminate the new multifamily program and Section 235 homeownership program for low- and moderate-income families was rejected by a vote of 120-300. He wanted to transfer the $1.06 billion earmarked for those programs to the Section 8 program that helped lower-income families rent existing housing. *(Vote 232, p. 70-H)*

Another amendment offered July 12 by Wylie to prevent funds from the new rehabilitation program from going to areas that established rent control laws after enactment was defeated 206-208. *(Vote 229, p. 70-H)*

A day later, Wylie made a second attempt to add the rent control restriction. But his motion to recommit the bill to committee was defeated 205-217. *(Vote 234, p. 72-H)*

Another amendment offered July 13 by Bartlett to let lenders and borrowers negotiate the interest rate on FHA insured loans was adopted 228-194. *(Vote 233, p. 70-H)*

Other amendments adopted by voice vote July 12 were by:

● Dick Durbin, D-Ill., to allow small cities and towns that would otherwise not be eligible for urban development grants as of August 31, 1983, to remain eligible until HUD revised the selection standards and included the extent of unemployment as a standard of distress.

● Mario Biaggi, D-N.Y., to allow elderly and disabled tenants in federally subsidized housing to have pets.

● George C. Wortley, R-N.Y., to prohibit HUD from selling Section 202 mortgages on housing for low-income and handicapped people.

● Bruce A. Morrison, D-Conn., to allow funds for Section 235 to be used for rehabilitation of existing two- and three-family units and new two-family structures.

● Sander M. Levin, D-Mich., to require that the relative extent of unemployment be given principal consideration in selecting sites for HUD demonstration projects.

● Daniel K. Akaka, D-Hawaii, to extend FHA mortgages to native Hawaiians for property located on Hawaiian Home Lands. Currently, individuals living on these lands were unable to secure FHA insured mortgages.

Final Action

Although negotiations continued in an effort to bring the Senate bill back to the floor, by late summer supporters despaired that it might never again see the light of day. Garn said in a Sept. 28 speech that the bill was "almost impossible to pass."

Meanwhile, St Germain continued to insist that the Senate move on the housing bill as a condition for support for the IMF bill. That legislation was pending before a conference committee, which St Germain would chair.

"If the Senate doesn't act on a housing bill," St Germain said, "then the Senate will have killed the IMF."

By late September, the administration recognized that St. Germain was adamant about tying the IMF with housing. Key members of the administration, principally budget director David A. Stockman and Treasury Secretary Donald T. Regan, sat down with St Germain and Garn to produce a compromise housing bill linked with the IMF. The weeks of intense negotiations produced the package which Garn offered as a floor amendment Nov. 17 to the conference report on the fiscal 1984 supplemental appropriations bill. The Senate adopted the amendment, and the House cleared the measure Nov. 18. ∎

Law Enforcement/Judiciary

Partisan politics heavily influenced Judiciary Committee issues in 1983, producing more rhetoric than action.

In the House, a major immigration reform package was scuttled for the year because Speaker Thomas P. O'Neill Jr., D-Mass., said he feared that President Reagan would try to win Hispanic support by vetoing any bill that passed.

O'Neill's surprise decision to bring the Equal Rights Amendment (ERA) to the House floor under a procedural shortcut angered Republicans, who voted overwhelmingly against the measure, leading to its defeat.

And while a compromise bill renewing and reconstituting the U.S. Civil Rights Commission was enacted Nov. 30, Democrats and civil rights leaders accused the Reagan administration of violating an agreement on the makeup of the panel. The year ended with strained relations between civil rights leaders and key moderate Republican senators, who in the past had been important civil rights allies.

It was a tough year for those pushing anti-abortion legislation. The Senate decisively rejected a proposed constitutional amendment that would have opened the way for new anti-abortion laws. The amendment failed to win even a simple majority, let alone the required two-thirds majority. The proposal was defeated just 13 days after the Supreme Court reaffirmed a woman's constitutional right to have an abortion as it struck down a variety of state and local abortion restrictions.

Although there was considerable talk about anti-crime legislation, Congress made only modest progress on this front. A bill to strengthen the law against tampering with consumer products was the only crime legislation to clear. It was prompted by the deaths in October 1982 of seven people in the Chicago area who ingested extra-strength Tylenol that had been laced with cyanide.

The Senate Judiciary Committee approved a consensus anti-crime package that included, among other things, tougher bail laws, new federal sentencing procedures, harsher penalties for drug offenders and a revised insanity defense. Although sponsors pushed for Senate action in 1983, they were unable to work out a time agreement over related but more controversial crime legislation.

The House Judiciary Committee, which had never liked legislative packages, worked on some of the same bills, but as separate pieces of legislation. A state crime assistance bill and legislation to reauthorize a drug screening program passed the House. The committee approved a bill to create a new, centralized drug enforcement office and revisions in the insanity and international extradition laws.

Eighteen months after the Supreme Court invalidated the bankruptcy court system created in 1978 reform legislation, Congress was still unable to agree on a solution to the court problem.

The Senate passed legislation to restructure the courts but added provisions making it harder for consumers to declare bankruptcy. The House Judiciary Committee passed its own, markedly different bankruptcy court bill that stalled in the House Rules Committee.

Immigration

For the second year in a row, O'Neill was the spoiler on the immigration bill. He announced Oct. 4 that the measure would not come to the floor in 1983 because Hispanics opposed the bill, there was "no constituency" in favor of it, and he had been told that Reagan would veto any measure to win Hispanic political support.

A month later, O'Neill said the bill would come to the floor in 1984 and that he had assurances that Sen. Alan K. Simpson, R-Wyo., chief sponsor of the Senate bill, would work with the White House to make sure Reagan would sign an immigration bill if one cleared Congress.

In 1982, O'Neill reluctantly had allowed a similar immigration measure to come to the floor. But he scheduled it in the waning days of the lame-duck session, when there was no chance to pass the measure.

The Senate had passed immigration reform bills in 1982 and 1983 that were similar in basic thrust to the House bills, but differing in some important details.

Briefly, both measures were designed to curb the flow of illegal aliens into the United States through a system of penalties against employers who knowingly hired illegal aliens. In addition, the measures granted legal status to many of the millions of illegal aliens already in the United States. They also included new, streamlined procedures to handle asylum, deportation and exclusion cases and an expanded program for the agriculture industry to bring in temporary foreign workers for harvesting.

The Senate bill also included a strict new cap on the number of persons allowed to enter the country each year through normal immigration procedures. There was no similar provision in the House bill.

Chief sponsors Simpson and Rep. Romano L. Mazzoli, D-Ky., were particularly disappointed by O'Neill's October decision. They believed they could get a bill through Congress in 1983. In the House, an enormous amount of work had gone into the legislation. Because of its sweep, it had been worked over by four committees — drafted by Judiciary, then amended and revised by the Agriculture, Education and Labor, and Energy and Commerce committees.

At year's end, all four versions were pending at the Rules Committee, where staffers despaired of drafting a rule to take care of all the competing interests involved.

Equal Rights Amendment

The ERA, which died June 30, 1982, three states short of the 38 needed to ratify it, was reintroduced at the start of the 98th Congress.

In November, just six days after the House Judiciary Committee approved the ERA, the amendment was considered on the House floor. O'Neill took the unusual step of bringing it up for consideration under suspension of the

House rules. This procedure, generally reserved for non-controversial matters, provided for only 40 minutes' debate and no amendments.

O'Neill and chief sponsors Don Edwards, D-Calif., and Patricia Schroeder, D-Colo., feared that they could not defeat amendments to limit the ERA's applicability to laws concerning abortion and the military, among others. If any amendment passed, the ERA would be unacceptable to many of its sponsors, so O'Neill decided to use a procedure that barred amendments.

The move outraged Republicans, who claimed the Speaker was playing politics with the ERA and doing violence to House procedures. But ERA proponents pointed out that the constitutional amendment barring the poll tax was approved under suspension of the rules.

In the end, the proposal fell six votes short of the two-thirds majority needed. Democrats voted overwhelmingly in favor of the ERA and hoped this would earn them support from women's groups in the 1984 elections. Republicans voted against the ERA by a 2-1 margin, and women's rights advocates were quick to blame them for dooming the amendment.

Civil Rights Commission

The fight over the Civil Rights Commission was the most bitter and protracted of the year. It started May 26, when Reagan announced he was replacing three commissioners who had frequently criticized administration rights policies. The president nominated three people who had civil rights experience but who also shared his opposition to school busing for integration and hiring quotas.

Meanwhile, Congress was facing a Sept. 30 deadline for action on a commission reauthorization bill. Without such legislation, the six-member, presidentially appointed panel created in 1957 was set to expire.

While urging reauthorization of the commission, civil rights leaders set out to block the president's nominees, not on grounds that they were unqualified but because the rights groups contended Reagan was undermining the commission's traditional independence.

For nearly five months, the Senate Judiciary Committee was in a stalemate. Negotiations among the White House, committee members and the civil rights groups failed to result in a compromise acceptable to all sides. Finally, in mid-October, a compromise appeared to command a majority of the committee. But before the panel could act, Reagan abruptly fired the three commissioners he had been trying to replace.

Members immediately introduced new proposals calling for a commission in the legislative branch appointed solely by Congress. Negotiations with the White House continued, and late Nov. 10, key senators said they had reached agreement with the White House on a compromise.

That proposal, which was cleared by Congress and signed by Reagan, enlarged the commission to eight members, with four to be appointed by the president and four by Congress.

Democratic senators, Senate staffers from both parties and civil rights lobbyists believed the agreement with the White House had included the retention on the commission of two prominent incumbent Republican members, both women, who had joined others on the panel in criticizing administration policies.

But the White House later said there was no such agreement, and the two GOP women were scuttled in favor of Reagan's selections — both Democrats.

Bankruptcy

After working out a compromise on new consumer bankruptcy provisions, the Senate had little trouble passing legislation to restructure the nation's bankruptcy courts. The Senate bill granted overall authority for bankruptcy cases to federal district judges, who would have the discretion to refer clear-cut bankruptcy work to 229 bankruptcy judges authorized in the bill. These judges, adjuncts of the district courts, would have the same status as under the current law. They would be appointed by the president under Article I of the Constitution for 14-year terms.

This scheme was generally the same as an interim rule promulgated in December 1982 by the U.S. Judicial Conference, the policy-making arm of the federal judiciary, to provide for the handling of bankruptcy cases until Congress acted.

In June 1982, the Supreme Court invalidated the bankruptcy court system created in 1978 legislation, ruling that the judges were given too much authority over legal matters and too little independence.

The Senate bill also included provisions to make it more difficult for individuals to declare bankruptcy. Such legislation had been pushed by the consumer credit industry, which claimed that the 1978 law had permitted too many consumers to declare bankruptcy and cancel their debts when they actually could pay off many of them.

The House Judiciary Committee bankruptcy bill was markedly different from the Senate's. The House measure created a new bankruptcy court with 227 judges who would have lifetime appointments and irreducible salaries. These judges would handle all matters in dispute between the parties in a bankruptcy case, even those, such as a contract dispute, that did not involve bankruptcy issues. The Judicial Conference strongly opposed the measure, arguing that a separate court with lifetime judges was not necessary to handle the lion's share of bankruptcy matters.

The House committee bill did not have universal support among members, either. A bipartisan group in June introduced an alternative to the committee proposal that was similar to the Senate bill. Through the rest of the year, sponsors worked to get support for the measure, but at year's end, this measure, like the Rodino proposal, remained stymied.

Judgeships

In 1983, Reagan appointed 34 judges — 29 to the district courts; one to the Court of International Trade, which was equivalent in constitutional status to a district court; and four to the appeals courts.

Reagan appointed seven women to judgeships in 1983 — six to the district courts and one to the international trade court. No blacks were appointed to any judicial posts, while two Hispanics were given district court positions.

Overall in his first three years, Reagan made 123 judicial appointments, including the selection of Sandra Day O'Connor as the first woman to serve on the Supreme Court.

He appointed a total of 11 women, five Hispanics and one black — a man he elevated from his district court seat to a judgeship on a federal appeals court.

By comparison, President Carter in his first three years appointed 166 judges, including 29 women, 26 blacks and nine Hispanics.

—By Nadine Cohodas

O'Neill Blocks Immigration Bill in House

For the second year in a row, the Senate passed wide-ranging immigration reform legislation while the House failed to take final action on a similar bill.

Exercising his authority over the House calendar, Speaker Thomas P. O'Neill Jr., D-Mass., declared Oct. 4 that a House immigration bill (HR 1510 — H Rept 98-115, Parts I-IV) would not come to the floor in 1983.

O'Neill listed three main reasons for his decision: members of the Congressional Hispanic Caucus had told him they bitterly opposed the bill; he could find "no constituency" in favor of it, and he was concerned that President Reagan would veto any bill that cleared Congress to win election support within the Hispanic community.

While Hispanics applauded O'Neill's decision, it was greeted with anger in many quarters, prompting critical floor speeches in the House and Senate and editorials in leading newspapers around the country chastising O'Neill for his unilateral action.

O'Neill's decision was a particularly bitter blow for chief sponsor Romano L. Mazzoli, D-Ky., who saw his hopes for enacting the legislation dashed for the second time in less than a year.

In the 97th Congress, Mazzoli's bill was given a rule for floor action in early December 1982 but was not brought up until the very last days of the lame-duck session, when there was no chance to pass it. *(1982 Almanac p. 405)*

A month after O'Neill declared immigration reform dead for 1983, the Speaker announced that the House would consider the legislation early in 1984. His announcement followed a meeting with the chief Senate sponsor, Alan K. Simpson, R-Wyo., who assured O'Neill he would work with him and the White House to make sure that any bill cleared by Congress in 1984 would not be vetoed.

HR 1510 was pending in the House Rules Committee when Congress adjourned for 1983. Panel members had been unsuccessful in working out a rule for the legislation, which came to Rules with four versions. Because of its broad sweep, the bill, which was drafted by the Judiciary Committee, had been referred to and amended by the Agriculture, Energy and Commerce, and Education and Labor committees.

The Senate passed an immigration reform bill (S 529 — S Rept 98-62) May 18 that was substantially the same as the Senate-passed bill of 1982.

Hispanic, civil rights and lawyers' groups opposing the immigration reform bill continued to press their efforts late in 1983 for an immigration proposal that would phase in reform over a period of years rather than in one comprehensive package.

Background

Believing they had educated many of their colleagues in 1982 about the need for immigration reform, Simpson and Mazzoli plunged ahead early in the 98th Congress with their legislation. Similar in basic thrust but differing in details, HR 1510 and S 529 remained ambitious in their efforts to deal with a number of immigration problems.

To neutralize the magnet — jobs — that was bringing millions of illegal aliens into the country, the bills provided a system of penalties against employers who knowingly hired illegal aliens, or "undocumented workers." The House version was less stringent than the Senate's in its record-keeping requirements.

To improve conditions for the millions of illegals already in the United States, both bills provided an amnesty program granting many of them legal status. The provisions in the House bill were far more generous than the Senate's, granting permanent resident status to those who were in the country by Jan. 1, 1982. The Senate bill created a two-tiered system, with permanent resident status available to those aliens in the United States by Jan. 1, 1977, and temporary resident status available to those in the United States by Jan. 1, 1980.

To bring order to the chaotic system for seeking political asylum in this country, new streamlined procedures were proposed for handling such requests.

In recognition of agriculture's dependence on illegal aliens, an existing temporary worker program was greatly expanded to provide a steady flow of foreign labor for harvesting. This issue proved to be one of the more difficult, and as a result of referrals to Agriculture and Education and Labor, the House bill ended up with three different temporary worker provisions.

The Agriculture Committee provisions gave growers the greatest leeway to recruit foreign workers. The Education and Labor provisions were the most restrictive, while the Judiciary Committee version, similar to S 529, was somewhere in between.

Finally, reflecting concern about the number of legal immigrants coming into the country each year, the Senate bill placed a strict cap of 425,000 on the number of people who would be allowed to enter the United States each year under normal immigration procedures. The House bill did not include this provision.

The current law set an annual immigration cap of 270,000, but the limit was not rigidly enforced because spouses, parents and children of U.S. citizens could be admitted to the country without being charged against the cap.

House Subcommittee Action

The House and Senate bills began their journey through Congress the week of April 4 when the Immigration subcommittees of the House and Senate Judiciary committees approved legislation. The House Immigration, Refugees and International Law panel finished its work April 6, while the Senate Immigration and Refugee Policy Subcommittee completed its markup April 7.

In contrast to the Senate subcommittee markup, which lasted only 30 minutes, the House subcommittee met for more than six hours over two days and processed 36 amendments.

The legislative maneuvering prompted Rep. Dan Lungren, R-Calif., the ranking Republican on the Immigration Subcommittee, to label the bill a good piece of compromise legislation. "It's not the Sistine Chapel," he said, "but it's not a bad paint job."

Several important changes were made during the markup sessions.

Legalization Program

HR 1510 as introduced included a two-tiered legaliza-

tion program identical to that in the Senate bill. Persons who could show they were in the country before Jan. 1, 1977, would be eligible for permanent resident status, but they would be barred from most forms of public assistance, except for certain emergency aid.

Temporary resident status would be available for aliens who had been in the United States before Jan. 1, 1980. They would have to wait three years before seeking to adjust to permanent resident status and would be denied all forms of federal assistance for a total of six years.

On a 5-3 party-line vote, the subcommittee adopted a Mazzoli amendment that would grant permanent resident status to all aliens in the United States before Jan. 1, 1981. They would be ineligible for most forms of welfare, except emergency aid, for four years.

Mazzoli said his amendment "makes sense" and "is more easily implemented" than the two-tiered system of the original bill.

Lungren countered that the amendment made the legalization proposal too much like a blanket amnesty program that would give legal status to any alien, regardless of how long he had been in the United States and what kind of "contribution" he had made to the country.

Larry Smith, D-Fla., retorted that the original proposal was less attractive to aliens and would encourage far fewer of them to come forward than the Mazzoli proposal. "We don't want a *sub rosa* economy," Smith said. "It costs a great deal of money to keep that shadow society going."

As he did in the 97th Congress, Bill McCollum, R-Fla., offered an amendment to strike the entire legalization section. It was rejected 2-5, with Sam B. Hall Jr., D-Texas, joining McCollum.

Temporary-Worker Program

At Lungren's urging, the subcommittee made two changes in the temporary-worker program, known as the "H-2" program.

The first set up a transitional program for phasing out the use of illegal aliens in seasonal agricultural jobs and replacing them with foreign workers entering the country legally but temporarily.

Under the amendment, which was adopted 5-3, growers in the first year after enactment would register with the attorney general the number of illegal aliens they needed at peak season. The attorney general would then issue work permits for that number of aliens.

Over the next three years, the number of permits available for such workers would be decreased by one-third, and by the fourth year after enactment, growers would have to obtain workers through the more stringent H-2 program set out in the legislation.

The other Lungren amendment, adopted by voice vote, permitted growers to give their temporary workers a housing allowance instead of building them housing. The allowance procedure could be used only if rental housing was available in the area.

By voice vote, the panel adopted a Mazzoli amendment to increase the authorization for the Immigration and Naturalization Service to carry out the new law.

Judicial Review

The last amendment adopted by the subcommittee was offered by McCollum to streamline the judicial review process for any legal issues raised under the legislation. McCollum's amendment required all appeals to be heard in the U.S. Court of Appeals for the Federal Circuit, rather than in the various federal appeals courts around the country.

The court, established in 1982, primarily heard patent, trademark and government claims cases. *(Court background, 1982 Almanac p. 396)*

Senate Subcommittee

The Senate markup of S 529 was attended only by Simpson, Sen. Edward M. Kennedy, D-Mass., and Sen. Strom Thurmond, R-S.C., chairman of the full committee, who sat in even though he was not a subcommittee member.

Simpson offered a package of 33 amendments, which he described as "largely technical and minor substantive." They were adopted by voice vote, and the bill was then sent to the full committee.

Several of the Simpson amendments concerned legalization. One redefined "continous residence," which was important to any alien who wanted to meet the terms of the legalization program. The new provision barred an applicant for legalization from leaving the United States for more than 30 days each year during the time he was counting for his legalization.

Senate Committee Action

The Senate Judiciary Committee approved S 529 April 19 by a vote of 13-4. It was formally reported April 21 (S Rept 98-62).

Voting against the bill were Kennedy, John P. East, R-N.C., Howell Heflin, D-Ala., and Dennis DeConcini, D-Ariz.

Amendments Adopted

Sanctions Review. The panel made two changes in S 529 at Kennedy's urging. One amendment authorized the General Accounting Office to conduct an annual review of employer sanctions for five years, with congressional hearings required on the findings.

Fifth Preference. The other gave unmarried brothers and sisters of U.S. citizens the fifth preference for obtaining visas to immigrate. Current law made this preference available to all brothers and sisters of citizens, regardless of marital status, but S 529 as approved by the Immigration Subcommittee had eliminated the preference altogether.

Amendments Rejected

The committee by 5-10 rejected an amendment by Dennis DeConcini, D-Ariz., to make the employer sanction provisions expire after eight years unless Congress reauthorized them. It also rejected, by the following margins, amendments by Kennedy that would have:

● Required the president to certify after five years that employer sanctions had been implemented "satisfactorily," 5-11.

● Increased the yearly immigration cap to 465,000 to accommodate an additional 40,000 visas provided in the bill for Canada and Mexico, 3-12. The subcommittee version of S 529 set the yearly cap at 425,000 persons.

● Required periodic review of the immigration ceiling and authorized the president to set it higher or lower, subject to a motion of disapproval by one chamber, 1-14.

● Moved the cutoff date for eligibility for temporary resident status to Dec. 31, 1981, rejected 3-12. This would

have replaced the two-tiered system, which provided temporary resident status for any illegal alien in the United States by Jan. 1, 1980, and permanent resident status for those in the United States by Jan. 1, 1977.

● Revised the provisions for handling asylum cases to include more judicial review, 7-10.

Senate Floor Action

The Senate passed S 529 on May 18 by a 76-18 vote after making important concessions to the agriculture industry and civil rights groups. *(Vote 101, p. 21-S)*

Although more than 20 amendments were offered during four days of debate on the bill, only a handful were adopted.

Following the final vote, chief sponsor Simpson repeated his favorite description of the legislation: "It's not nativist, not racist, not mean," he said. "I'm proud of it."

Kennedy Opposed

But Kennedy, who led opponents of the bill, said he could not vote for it, despite changes he was able to win.

"In too many areas, what started out as the promise of reform has become the reality of restrictions that are unnecessary and unwise in any fair immigration policy," he said.

A smattering of members from both ends of the political spectrum, along with moderates from Western states, joined Kennedy in voting against the bill.

They included such avowed liberals as Alan Cranston, D-Calif., and Donald W. Riegle Jr., D-Mich., who believed some provisions would exacerbate discrimination; conservatives East and Jesse Helms, R-N.C., who contended it was too lax in its treatment of illegal aliens already here; and Westerners such as Pete V. Domenici, R-N.M., and Pete Wilson, R-Calif., who believed the bill would not accomplish its goals and would cause disruption in their states.

The Senate had started to work on the immigration bill on April 28, but after some critics complained about moving to the floor so quickly after the April 19 committee markup, the Senate worked out an agreement to process some amendments on the 28th and then postpone further action until mid-May.

On April 28, Kennedy offered two amendments he said would improve the bill, but both were rejected, as they were by the Judiciary Committee. One proposal to terminate the employer sanction provisions after five years if they proved discriminatory was rejected 40-51. *(Vote 64, p. 16-S)*

Another amendment to move the eligibility date for temporary resident status from Jan. 1, 1980, to Dec. 31, 1981, was turned down 20-70. *(Vote 65, p. 16-S)*

Concessions to Growers

The Senate resumed consideration of S 529 on May 17.

By voice vote, the Senate approved a compromise amendment giving agricultural employers three years to phase out their use of undocumented workers. In the fourth year after enactment, growers would either have to use American workers or get permission to use foreign employees through a revised temporary-worker program.

For all other industries, the use of illegal aliens was a violation six months after the bill was enacted.

An amendment by Wilson to extend the transition period for growers two more years was rejected 20-72.

(Vote 94, p. 20-S)

Growers conceded that large numbers of their seasonal workers were illegal aliens. But their lobbyists argued that without those workers, or in the absence of some type of broad government program to guarantee an adequate labor supply, crops would perish and consumers would see resulting higher produce prices.

The phase-out amendment was designed to respond to this concern.

The growers won another victory May 18 when the Senate voted 62-33 to accept an amendment by James A. McClure, R-Idaho, requiring federal law enforcement officers to obtain a warrant before searching open fields for illegal aliens. *(Vote 99, p. 21-S)*

Two cases testing whether such warrants were necessary as a matter of constitutional law were argued before the U.S. Supreme Court in November, but the justices had not ruled by year's end. *(Maine v. Thornton, Oliver v. United States)*

Asylum Review

In another important compromise that took two days to negotiate, the Senate by voice vote May 18 adopted a Kennedy-Simpson amendment expanding the right of judicial review for those who were denied political asylum in the United States.

In return for this provision, civil liberties lobbyists, principally the American Civil Liberties Union, had agreed not to lobby in the House or in a conference against another section in the Senate bill that set up new, streamlined procedures within the Justice Department for handling asylum, deportation and exclusion cases.

Sanctions

The sanction provisions, aimed at employers who knowingly hired illegal aliens, required employers of at least four workers to check documents of prospective workers, such as a driver's license and Social Security card, and keep records of those they hire. The bill provided for a fine of $1,000 per alien for the first violation and $2,000 per alien for the second. Criminal penalties were provided in S 529 if the attorney general found a "pattern or practice" of violations.

Hispanic groups were unrelenting in their opposition to the sanctions. They argued that the enforcement scheme would only exacerbate existing discrimination against Hispanics because employers, anxious to avoid penalties, would be increasingly reluctant to hire anyone who looked foreign for fear that the person was in the country illegally.

An amendment offered by Sens. Gary Hart, D-Colo., Carl Levin, D-Mich., Jeff Bingaman, D-N.M., and Kennedy to provide remedies for any discrimination resulting from the sanctions was rejected May 17 by a vote of 29-59. *(Vote 95, p. 21-S)*

Legalization Costs

To help pay for the costs associated with the two-tiered legalization program, S 529 authorized a four-year block grant program of about $1.1 billion to $1.4 billion to help states. The funds were designed to cover such things as educational and health services for the newly legalized population. Allocations would be based on the number of aliens in each state.

The Senate May 18 rejected 37-57 an amendment by Bill Bradley, D-N.J., to adopt a 100 percent reimbursement scheme. *(Vote 96, p. 21-S)*

By a 21-76 vote May 17, the Senate also rejected an amendment by Helms to strike the legalization section. *(Vote 90, p. 20-S)*

Other Amendments

Among the amendments adopted were the following:
- By Paula Hawkins, R-Fla., to create a $35 million revolving fund for immigration emergencies, by voice vote May 17. A similar provision was in HR 1510.
- By John C. Danforth, R-Mo., and Daniel Patrick Moynihan, D-N.Y., to make it easier for foreign students with special skills to remain in the United States, by voice vote May 17.
- By Dale Bumpers, D-Ark., deleting the visa allotment for immigrants who invested at least $250,000 in an enterprise that would employ at least four persons not members of the immigrant's family, by 51-46, May 17. *(Vote 89, p. 20-S)*

Under current regulations, an immigrant who would invest $40,000 and employ at least one person outside his family would be eligible for a visa under this "investor" allotment.

House Judiciary Committee

The House Judiciary Committee approved HR 1510 May 5, following eight hours of markup that stretched over three days. During that time, the committee slogged through more than 35 amendments.

The vote to report the measure to the full House was 20-9, and even though a sizable majority voted to approve it, the often contentious debate reflected the deep concerns many members had about aspects of the bill.

The bill did not go directly from Judiciary to the Rules Committee. Instead, because of its broad sweep, HR 1510 was referred to the Education and Labor, Agriculture, Energy and Commerce, and Ways and Means committees for review. All except Ways and Means acted on the measure.

Legalization Debate

As in 1982, the proposed legalization program was the most controversial subject in the Judiciary markup.

The subcommittee version of HR 1510 granted permanent resident status to any illegal alien who could prove he was in the United States by Jan. 1, 1981, and who met certain conditions. He would be ineligible for most forms of public assistance — except emergency aid — for four years.

On May 5, the full committee by a 15-14 vote adopted an amendment by Barney Frank, D-Mass., to move the eligibility date to Jan. 1, 1982. Frank said this would encourage more illegal aliens to come forward.

"I just don't think it is healthy for us to have a large number of people rattling around in illegal status," Frank said.

Lungren, who opposed the amendment, repeated the argument he had made in the subcommittee against Mazzoli's Jan. 1, 1981, date — that the proposal looked too much like a complete amnesty program for illegal aliens.

Lungren won approval of an amendment to make newly legalized aliens ineligible for federal benefits for five years, instead of four, as the subcommittee bill provided.

The committee rejected, 10-19, a McCollum amendment to strike the legalization program entirely. Two similar proposals at the 1982 markup failed 12-16 and 11-17.

A Lungren amendment incorporating the Senate's two-tiered legalization plan was rejected 10-20.

An amendment by E. Clay Shaw Jr., R-Fla., to move the legalization eligibility date back to Jan. 1, 1980, was rejected 13-17.

Employer Sanctions

The sanctions section proved almost as controversial as legalization, with the strongest opposition coming from Hispanics. In 1982, Hispanics were joined in their objections by the Chamber of Commerce of the United States. But in 1983, the Chamber changed its position and decided instead to press for changes in the sanctions rather than trying to eliminate them.

The Chamber effort paid off May 3, the first day of the markup, when the committee adopted 18-10 an amendment offered by Thomas N. Kindness, R-Ohio, that in essence targeted the use of the sanctions.

Under the Kindness amendment — which was not included in the Senate bill — the panoply of penalties would not come into play unless the Immigration and Naturalization Service (INS) investigated an employer and found an undocumented worker on the payroll.

Once such a finding was made, the employer thereafter would be required to keep records of everyone he hired, and to attest to the fact that he checked documents, such as a Social Security card or driver's license, to verify each person's eligibility to work in the United States.

If INS made a second visit and found any undocumented workers, the employer would be subject to a fine for knowingly hiring such workers, and a fine for not keeping the proper paperwork, if such was the case.

The subcommittee version of the bill had made the screening and record-keeping requirements applicable upon enactment to any employer of more than three workers.

Lungren and Frank, who opposed the amendment, said they believed it would dilute enforcement because employers would still hire undocumented workers and take a chance that INS officials would not get around to inspecting their operations.

Mazzoli and Rodino, who supported the amendment, contended that it did not weaken the sanction provisions but in fact made it easier to call the enforcement scheme into play. Aides to both members pointed out that the original version of the bill required a finding that an employer "knowingly" hired an illegal alien before the sanctions were applicable.

These aides said the Kindness amendment triggered the sanction provisions as soon as INS found an undocumented worker on the payroll, whether he was hired "knowingly" or not.

Other Amendments Adopted

Court Jurisdiction. Under the subcommittee version of HR 1510, court appeals of legal issues raised under the legislation were heard by the year-old Court of Appeals for the Federal Circuit, rather than federal district and appeals courts around the country.

By a vote of 19-11, the committee adopted an amendment by Robert W. Kastenmeier, D-Wis., to delete this provision. The effect of the amendment was to retain current law and have immigration issues heard in the district courts or federal circuit appeals courts.

Asylum Suits. A second Kastenmeier amendment adopted by voice vote would specifically allow "class action" lawsuits for cases involving a pattern or practice of violations of the Constitution in asylum adjudications.

Such suits were brought on behalf of many persons who were similarly situated.

Kastenmeier said the class actions envisioned by his amendment would be authorized only when the litigants could show that other procedural or administrative remedies were inappropriate.

Open Field Searches. By a vote of 20-8 the committee adopted a Lungren amendment — urged by the agriculture industry — requiring immigration officers to obtain a search warrant before coming into "open fields" to look for undocumented workers. S 529 as passed by the Senate included this provision.

Funding for Emergencies. By voice vote, the committee adopted an amendment by Larry Smith, D-Fla., to establish a $35 million trust fund within the Justice Department to be used for immigration emergencies.

Amendments Rejected

A number of amendments that could have changed the bill substantially were rejected.

● By 5-24, the committee rejected an amendment by F. James Sensenbrenner Jr., R-Wis., to set a "flexible" yearly cap on legal immigration of from 300,000 to 420,000 persons. The cap included refugees, defined as those persons who fled their homeland because of a well-founded fear of persecution. (The Senate cap of 425,000 persons did not include refugees.)

● By 11-19, the committee rejected an amendment by Carlos J. Moorhead, R-Calif., to set a yearly cap of 450,000 on legal immigration. This cap did not include refugees.

● By voice vote, the panel rejected a Sensenbrenner amendment to restrict the fifth visa preference to unmarried brothers and sisters of U.S. citizens. This provision was in the Senate bill.

The fifth preference was available to any brother or sister of a U.S. citizen under current law.

Other Committees

The week of June 20, six weeks after the Judiciary Committee approved HR 1510, three other House Committees took up the legislation and made significant modifications.

The three committees — Agriculture, Education and Labor, and Energy and Commerce — changed sections of HR 1510 concerning temporary workers, sanctions and the legalization provisions.

Even though the three panels reported HR 1510, many committee members on these panels expressed opposition to the measure. They emphasized that they were supporting amendments only to improve what they considered to be bad legislation.

Agriculture Amendments

Guest Worker Program. The most significant change was made by the Agriculture Committee, which voted 12-9 June 21 to establish a flexible foreign "guest worker" program for the producers of perishable commodities. This was designed to benefit growers in the Western states.

The amendment, sponsored by California Democrat Leon E. Panetta, was roundly criticized by organized labor — which sent six lobbyists to the committee room — and by Hispanics. Opponents labeled the proposal another "bracero" program, a reference to a controversial program that brought nearly five million Mexican laborers into the

United States from 1942 to 1964, primarily to do agricultural work.

Panetta, whose district had a large agricultural sector, called such charges "ludicrous" and "out to lunch." He said his proposal included certain guarantees that would guard against the kind of abuse in wages and working conditions reported during the bracero program.

The Panetta proposal was in addition to the revised and expanded "H-2" program that already was part of the Judiciary bill.

Panetta said even the revised H-2 program was inadequate. His proposal allowed growers to apply for foreign workers just 72 hours in advance of the anticipated need. Under the Judiciary H-2 program, such a request would have to be made 50 days in advance.

The attorney general was given authority to allow these workers to stay for up to 11 months. The workers were not restricted to just one employer, but could move from employer to employer within a specified "agricultural region" defined by the attorney general. The Judiciary bill restricted the worker to the employer who requested him.

Prior to getting foreign workers, the employer was required to make a "good faith effort" to recruit "willing and qualified" domestic agricultural workers in the area of intended employment. The Judiciary bill required the labor secretary to certify that willing and qualified domestic workers were not available.

Fines for Violations. Sid Morrison, a Washington Republican whose district was heavily agricultural, sponsored an amendment that altered the levels of fines for employers found to have knowingly hired illegal aliens.

Dan Glickman, D-Kan., who was also a member of the Judiciary Committee, objected, contending that Agriculture had no jurisdiction to change the sanction provisions. However, Chairman E. "Kika" de la Garza, D-Texas, overruled Glickman and allowed Morrison to proceed.

The Judiciary bill provided a fine of $1,000 per alien for the first violation and $2,000 for the second. Morrison said he wanted to establish those limits as a maximum, giving a judge flexiblity to impose a lesser amount. Harold L. Volkmer, D-Mo., argued that some minimum was necessary.

By voice vote, the committee accepted a Volkmer substitute that provided a fine of at least $100 but not more than $1,000 for the first offense, at least $500 but not more than $2,000 for the second offense.

Education/Labor Amendments

Organized labor and Hispanic lobbyists had better luck in the Education and Labor Committee, which considered HR 1510 June 23.

H-2 Regulations. During this markup, the committee adopted an amendment by George Miller, D-Calif., that changed several of the H-2 provisions in the Judiciary Committee bill to restore current law. For example, the 50-day application period for requesting foreign workers went back to 80 days. The labor secretary remained in sole control of the certification process for getting the foreign workers, whereas the Judiciary bill gave Agriculture a role.

Miller's amendment also created an 11-member commission that was given 15 months to report to Congress on improving the H-2 program. A Miller aide said the commission was designed to look at two major items — how to "maximize the use of domestic workers," particularly in agriculture, and the type of regulations needed to administer the program. This was intended to include such things

as the length of time required for recruiting domestic workers before foreign workers would be allowed into the country, the length of any worker's stay, and protection of domestic wage rates. The amendment had the strong support of organized labor.

Employer Sanctions. The committee also adopted a package of amendments by Augustus F. Hawkins, D-Calif., that substantially restructured the employer sanctions provisions approved by the Judiciary Committee.

Among the more important Hawkins provisions was one that eliminated criminal penalties for knowingly hiring an illegal alien. Hawkins, however, imposed stiffer fines than Judiciary recommended.

Another Hawkins provision created a "special counsel" within the U.S. Immigration Board, which was created in the Judiciary bill to hear appeals on immigration matters from administrative law judges. The special counsel's office was designed to investigate all allegations against employers concerning the hiring of illegal aliens. No special counsel was in the Judiciary bill.

In addition, the Hawkins amendment made it an unfair "immigration-related employment practice" to discriminate on the basis of national origin or "alienage." Any person who believed he was discriminated against for either reason could file a complaint with the special counsel, and an administrative law judge was authorized to impose penalties, including fines and cease and desist orders.

Energy/Commerce Amendments

Legalization Benefits. The Energy and Commerce Committee, which had jurisdiction over aspects of the legalization program, June 23 expanded the types of federal benefits available to newly legalized aliens.

The Judiciary bill barred benefits to newly legalized aliens for five years, except when required for "public health reasons" or for serious illness or injury. Energy and Commerce, on the recommendation of Henry A. Waxman, D-Calif., chairman of the Health and Environment Subcommittee, changed the exception to "emergency services"

as defined under current Medicaid law.

The panel also provided Medicaid benefits for any newly legalized alien who became pregnant and would otherwise be eligible for Medicaid. The coverage included prenatal and postnatal care, and benefits for the child up to the age of 18.

However, no Medicaid benefits were available for abortions for legalized alien women except to save the woman's life or in a case of incest or rape. The Medicaid ban in effect in 1983 allowed funding only for abortions to save the life of the pregnant woman.

Rules Committee Impasse

When the committees finished their work, all three versions, along with the Judiciary bill, were sent to the Rules Committee.

Rules Chairman Claude Pepper, D-Fla., told the chairmen of the four panels that he wanted them to try to work out a compromise version while Congress was on its August recess. But efforts to come to an agreement were unavailing.

Meanwhile, Hispanic interest groups and members of the Congressional Hispanic Caucus kept up a drumbeat of opposition to the House bill. When Congress returned in late September, the Hispanic members asserted that Reagan was trying to play politics with the Hispanic vote by eventually vetoing any immigration bill to appease Hispanics.

They pointed to a July 27 letter Attorney General William French Smith sent to Judiciary Chairman Peter W. Rodino Jr., D-N.J., outlining the Justice Department's concerns with the Judiciary version of HR 1510.

Administration officials bluntly rejected the veto assertions. And the day after O'Neill announced that HR 1510 was dead for the year, Smith held a news conference to say he was "dismayed" by the Speaker's actions and found O'Neill's explanation "grievously wrong."

A month after he killed HR 1510 for 1983, O'Neill announced that the House would take it up early in 1984. ∎

Civil Rights Commission Reconstituted

A compromise bill reconstituting the U.S. Civil Rights Commission and extending it for six years was signed into law Nov. 30 (HR 2230 — PL 98-183).

Within days, however, an intricately negotiated agreement that had led to congressional approval of the bill unraveled into a bitter dispute involving the White House, moderate Republican senators and civil rights activists.

The disagreement concerned appointments to the commission, which under HR 2230 was changed from a six-member presidentially appointed body to an eight-member panel. The president was to make four appointments and the House and Senate two each.

Power Struggle

For much of the year, President Reagan — disturbed by commission criticism of his civil rights policies — had sought to dismiss three commissioners and replace them with nominees who shared his opposition to busing and affirmative action quotas.

Civil rights lobbyists were concerned that such a move would give Reagan total operational control of the commis-

sion, since he had previously appointed its chairman and vice chairman.

Insisting that the commission, which was established in 1957, was supposed to be independent of the White House, the lobbyists persuaded a majority of the Senate Judiciary Committee to hold up action on Reagan's three nominees.

A long stalemate was broken Nov. 10-11 after marathon negotiations involving the civil rights lobbyists, key members of the Senate Judiciary Committee, Senate Majority Leader Howard H. Baker Jr., and White House staffers in Washington and in Tokyo, Japan, where Reagan was making a state visit.

At the conclusion of the bargaining, civil rights advocates, Democratic senators and a number of staffers from both parties believed they had worked out a deal that would assure reappointment of four members of the old panel who had been critical of administration rights policies — Blandina Cardenas Ramirez, a Democrat; Mary Frances Berry, an independent; and Republicans Mary Louise Smith and Jill Ruckelshaus.

But in early December, less than three weeks after Congress had adjourned for the year, the White House began to say there was no deal on the reappointment of Smith and Ruckelshaus. Both were prominent Republicans — Smith, an Iowa GOP leader, was a former chairman of the Republican National Committee, while Ruckelshaus was the wife of William D. Ruckelshaus, head of the Environmental Protection Agency.

Double Cross Claimed

Civil rights groups claimed a double cross. They contended that the White House reneged on its agreement because administration officials feared they could not control the panel if Smith and Ruckelshaus were reappointed. At an angry news conference Dec. 8, civil rights leaders vowed that the commission flap would become an issue in the 1984 elections.

The White House claimed there was no deal on the appointments; Sen. Robert Dole, R-Kan., and Majority Leader Baker, who mediated between the civil rights groups and the White House during the negotiations, declined to confirm any agreement, although neither had disputed publicly reported details of the purported pact.

When the dust settled, Reagan had appointed to the new commission incumbent Chairman Clarence M. Pendleton Jr., a Republican; Democrat Morris Abram, a well-known civil rights lawyer and former president of Brandeis University; John Bunzel of the Hoover Institution, another Democrat; and Esther Gonzalez-Arroyo Buckley, a Republican high school teacher from Laredo, Tex.

The congressional appointees were incumbents Berry, a Howard University law professor, and Ramirez, a San Antonio educator; Democrat Robert Destro, a law professor at Catholic University; and Francis F. Guess, a black Republican who was serving as Tennessee's labor commissioner.

Provisions

As cleared by Congress, HR 2230 included these major provisions:

● Reconstituted the commission from a six-member, presidentially appointed panel to an eight-member panel. The president had four appointments. The Senate and House had two each.

● Authorized the commission for six years.

● Gave the congressional appointment power to the president pro tempore of the Senate and the Speaker of the House. They were to act upon the recommendations of the minority and majority leaders of both chambers.

● Specified that not more than four commission members could belong to the same political party.

● Set six-year staggered terms for the commissioners.

● Allowed the president to remove commissioners only for "neglect of duty or malfeasance in office."

● Provided $12.18 million for fiscal 1984.

● Allowed the president to name the chairman, vice chairman and staff director of the commission, subject to the approval of a majority of the commissioners.

● Transferred personnel from the old commission to the new commission and guaranteed all existing benefits.

● Gave the new commission the same powers as the old panel to investigate allegations of civil rights violations, collect information, write reports and make recommendations on the need for new laws or other governmental action.

Background

Congressional action on the commission was necessary in 1983 because the panel's existing authorization expired Sept. 30, with a wind-down period of 60 days permitted.

In his State of the Union message Jan. 25, Reagan called the commission "an important part of the ongoing struggle for justice in America" and said the administration would support its reauthorization. *(Address, p. 3-E)*

History of Independence

For most of its 26 years, the Civil Rights Commission, which was created in 1957, had been a little-noticed agency. It was set up as an independent entity charged with surveying the status of civil rights in the country. It had no enforcement authority; its only tools were reports and recommendations for legislation or other governmental responses to civil rights problems. *(Background, 1978 Almanac p. 789)*

Except for President Dwight D. Eisenhower, who appointed the first panel, no president had ever appointed a majority nor summarily dismissed a commissioner.

In 1974, President Richard M. Nixon asked Father Theodore M. Hesburgh to resign as chairman, which Hesburgh did. Nixon appointed Arthur S. Flemming as chairman. Other than that, commissioners had been replaced only as they left voluntarily or died while serving. The law governing the commission was silent on the method of removing its members.

Battle Lines Drawn

Throughout its history, the commission had often criticized whatever administration was in power, but none responded as angrily as the Reagan administration.

On May 26, Reagan announced that he was replacing Berry, Ramirez and Rabbi Murray Saltzman of Baltimore. Their designated replacements were Abram, Bunzel and Destro.

Saltzman, Ramirez and Berry were expected to serve until their successors were confirmed by the Senate.

Civil rights groups vowed to fight the nominations, not because they considered the three men unqualified but because they believed Reagan was undermining the commission's independence by replacing those who were critical of him.

House Committee Action

Although the House Judiciary Civil and Constitutional Rights Subcommittee held hearings on the commission's reauthorization, the panel did not mark up a bill. Instead the full committee acted, approving HR 2230 by voice vote May 12.

As approved by the committee, the measure extended the existing presidentially appointed commission for 15 years and set its fiscal 1984 authorization at $13 million.

An amendment by F. James Sensenbrenner Jr., R-Wis., to extend the commission for 20 years but require fixed staggered terms for its six members was rejected by a vote of 9-19.

The Sensenbrenner proposal was almost identical to a bill (S 1189) Reagan supported that was sent to the Senate Judiciary Constitution Subcommittee, where it remained for the entire year.

HR 2230 was reported officially May 17 (H Rept 98-197).

House Floor Action

The House approved HR 2230 Aug. 4 by voice vote after amendments by chief sponsor Don Edwards, D-Calif., were adopted overwhelmingly.

One amendment, adopted 400-24, scaled back the authorization from 15 years to five years, the length of two previous reauthorizations. *(Vote 306, p. 92-H)*

A second Edwards amendment provided that commissioners could be removed only for "neglect of duty or malfeasance in office." It was adopted 286-128. The existing law was silent on the method of removal. *(Vote 307, p. 92-H)*

Edwards told the House that his amendment was intended to ratify what had been the practice for 25 years. He said commissioners always had served "open-ended" terms, and that, in practice, most commissioners resigned on their own after six or seven years.

Sensenbrenner opposed the amendment, charging that Edwards was making a "not too subtle attempt" to block Reagan's replacement of the three current commissioners. He called that "an infringement" on executive authority.

The Wisconsin Republican offered his committee amendment to extend the commission for 20 years and provide six-year staggered terms for its members, who could be removed only for cause. He said the amendment would terminate the terms of all existing commissioners and give the president six new appointments.

The amendment, opposed by Edwards, was rejected by voice vote.

Senate Committee Action

For the Republican-controlled Senate Judiciary Committee, the main order of business was the confirmation process for Reagan's three nominees, Abram, Bunzel and Destro.

Supporters of the president, led by Orrin G. Hatch, R-Utah, chairman of the Constitution Subcommittee, wanted to move the nominations before voting on a bill to reauthorize the commission.

The committee held a hearing on the nominees July 16, but much of the testimony focused on the independence of the commission.

Sen. Joseph R. Biden Jr., D-Del., ranking panel Democrat, told the nominees, "You are not the issue." Instead, he said the issue was the "perception" that Reagan was eroding the panel's independence. "The question hanging over your head is, if and when you disagree with the president, will you be summarily fired?" Biden said.

The Lobbying Effort

Civil rights lobbyists pressed the committee to put off action on the nominations until the commission was reauthorized.

When the committee met in late July to vote on Abram, Bunzel and Destro, Republican members knew they did not have the votes to confirm all three. Chairman Strom Thurmond, R-S.C., agreed to put off a vote until September. At the request of Democrats, Hatch held a second subcommittee hearing on the nominees Sept. 13.

During the August recess and all through September, lobbyists led by Ralph G. Neas, executive director of the Leadership Conference on Civil Rights, an umbrella organization for 165 groups, kept up a drumbeat of opposition to the appointments. They contended repeatedly that re-

gardless of the nominees' qualifications, Reagan would seriously damage the commission if he replaced three sitting members.

The White House also remained adamant in its position, and extensive negotiations among Senate Judiciary Committee members and staff, the civil rights community and the administration revealed that neither the president nor the civil rights groups had the votes for a clear victory.

Reagan lacked support for his three nominees as outright replacements for Berry, Ramirez and Saltzman. But the civil rights groups could not be sure of the votes for blocking all three nominations and extending the commission in its present six-member form.

Search for Middle Ground

One compromise that emerged would have made the commission a permanent agency, expanding its membership to eight and setting eight-year staggered terms that probably would begin to run in 1985. Under this proposal, drafted by Biden, Dole and Arlen Specter, R-Pa., Reagan would immediately have won two of his three appointments, but the current commissioners also would have remained in office.

Saltzman, who was appointed by President Ford in 1975, was slated under this plan to move off the commission in 1985 because he was the most senior member.

Although this proposal commanded a majority of votes on the committee, the White House still was resisting it, and Republican committee members were unwilling to press ahead without White House support. White House lobbyists were still convinced they could round up enough votes to give Reagan all three of his selections immediately.

While this maneuvering was going on, the commission technically expired Sept. 30. However, the statute creating the panel provided a 60-day wind-down period.

The impasse continued into October. Finally, the Judiciary Committee decided that on Oct. 25, the panel would vote on the compromise plan, which was expected to win approval.

The Reagan Firings

Just hours before the panel was to meet Oct. 25, Reagan abruptly fired Berry, Ramirez and Saltzman. The committee meeting was canceled.

A White House lobbyist conceded Reagan fired the three commissioners because he knew he could not win Senate committee approval for all three of his nominees. "We didn't have the votes. It was either that [the firings] or accept two commissioners," the lobbyist said.

He added that Reagan was determined to change commissioners so he could get a "philosophical balance" on the panel. "The president is upset himself," the lobbyist said. "He feels there's a vendetta against him."

Court Suit Filed

A day after the president's move, Berry and Ramirez went into U.S. District Court in Washington, D.C., seeking to block their firings. Although Judge Norma Holloway Johnson refused to grant a temporary restraining order blocking the president's action, she granted an injunction Nov. 14 against the firings.

"It is not clear that the president has the power to remove commissioners at his discretion and that he should be given the widest latitude to exercise this authority," Judge Johnson said.

The administration appealed the ruling, but the ap-

peal was dismissed after Reagan signed the new commission bill.

Legislative Branch Unit Proposed

The president's firings angered many in Congress and prompted introduction of concurrent resolutions (S Con Res 78, H Con Res 200) to create a new, independent civil rights commission within the legislative branch whose members would be appointed by the House and Senate. Such a resolution would not require a presidential signature to go into effect.

Majority Leader Baker, who opposed the proposal for a legislative branch commission, promised senators that the Senate would consider some type of commission legislation before Congress adjourned.

Senate Floor Action

On Nov. 9, the Senate began debating HR 2230, which extended the existing Civil Rights Commission for five years and permitted removal of commissioners only for cause.

Biden and Specter planned to offer their legislative commission compromise as an amendment in the form of a substitute for the House-passed bill. By Nov. 9 they had rounded up 55 cosponsors, but Baker and Dole asked them to wait, seeking more time to work out a plan acceptable to Reagan.

Funding Eliminated

Meanwhile, $11.89 million in fiscal 1984 funding for the Civil Rights Commission was included in a fiscal 1984 Commerce, Justice, State appropriations bill (HR 3222) sent to conference Oct. 31. *(Story, p. 472)*

Civil rights supporters feared that if Congress cleared the appropriations bill with the commission's funding in it, the action could be taken as a de facto authorization of the panel. That in turn could allow Reagan to give recess appointments to his three nominees after Congress adjourned for the year, bypassing Senate confirmation.

After intense lobbying, the House Nov. 9 voted to strike the commission funding from the bill. The action came as members voted, 170-235, against a motion to accept the Senate's funding level of $11.89 million for the commission. *(Vote 447, p. 132-H)*

This put new pressure on the Senate to work out an agreement on the authorization bill or see the commission go out of business.

Compromise Reached

At midday Nov. 10, negotiations began in earnest among Biden, Specter, Dole, civil rights leaders and White House aides.

When these parties reached agreement, White House lobbyist Pam Turner called presidential counselor Edwin Meese III, who was traveling with Reagan in Tokyo.

Initial offers from the Senate were rejected, largely because of disagreements over removal of commissioners and control of the staff director, Biden said. These issues were finally resolved with another international phone call near midnight, and a deal was struck providing for the eight-member commission, with four presidential and four congressional appointments.

The compromise plan was quickly brought to the Senate Nov. 10 as a Specter amendment, which was adopted 79-5. Opposed to the compromise were Sens. John P. East,

R-N.C.; Jake Garn, R-Utah; Jesse Helms, R-N.C.; Gordon J. Humphrey, R-N.H.; and Steven D. Symms, R-Idaho. *(Vote 345, p. 57-S)*

Immediately after the vote, Biden and Specter spoke to about 25 reporters, congressional staffers and civil rights lobbyists, explaining the details of the agreement. Biden, with Specter looking on, said that an agreement had been reached among all parties over who would be named to the new commission.

The congressional appointees, he said, would be incumbents Berry, Ramirez, Ruckelshaus and another Republican — probably either Lorraine Gutierrez, a New Mexico businesswoman, or George Haley, a Washington lawyer and the brother of author Alex Haley.

At least one of the White House appointments would be incumbent Smith, Biden said. The other three were expected to be chosen from among Abram, Bunzel, Destro and Pendleton.

Senate Passage

HR 2230 as amended was passed by the Senate Nov. 14. The final vote was 78-3, with East, Helms and Symms voting against it. *(Vote 350, p. 57-S)*

Sen. Roger Jepsen, R-Iowa, briefly delayed passage of the bill when he tried to amend it by adding anti-abortion language. But his amendment was tabled (killed) 42-34 on a motion offered by Judiciary Chairman Thurmond, who was a cosponsor of the compromise version of HR 2230. *(Vote 349, p. 57-S)*

Final Action

The bill reconstituting the commission cleared Congress Nov. 16 when the House accepted the Senate amendments incorporating the compromise.

Fiscal 1984 funding for the Civil Rights Commission was quickly restored to the Commerce, Justice, State appropriations bill (HR 3222), which also was cleared Nov. 16.

Reagan did not sign the authorization bill until Nov. 30, when he designated Pendleton as the commission chairman.

At one point, White House aides said the president might not sign the bill, but other officials said Reagan was holding off until the last possible moment to see if a federal appeals court in Washington would rule on Judge Johnson's decision barring him from firing members of the old commission.

Deal Unravels

Early in December, the White House began to say for the first time that there was no agreement to reappoint Smith. Civil rights lobbyists and some Senate staffers said the White House was concerned that if Smith were reappointed by Reagan, and Ruckelshaus were appointed by Congress, there would not be the votes to keep Pendleton as chairman.

On Dec. 6 Reagan made his decision final. He announced that he was naming Abram, Bunzel and Buckley to the commission in addition to Pendleton.

On Dec. 7, House GOP Leader Robert H. Michel, R-Ill., disclosed that he had recommended Destro, a Democrat. House Majority Leader Wright already had recommended Berry.

On Dec. 12, Baker announced the Guess appointment, providing the eighth and final member of the new panel. ■

New Equal Rights Amendment Fails in House

A late-session effort to revive the proposed Equal Rights Amendment to the Constitution failed in the House Nov. 15.

House Democratic leaders tried a parliamentary power play to pass the proposal (H J Res 1), but the 278-147 roll call left it six votes short of the needed two-thirds majority of those present and voting. *(Vote 469, p. 138-H)*

Speaker Thomas P. O'Neill Jr., D-Mass., took the unusual step of bringing the ERA to the floor under suspension of the rules. This procedure, which allowed only 40 minutes debate and no amendments, generally was reserved for non-controversial legislation.

O'Neill's decision angered most Republicans and some Democrats, and prompted 14 ERA cosponsors to vote against the proposal. But O'Neill and chief sponsor Don Edwards, D-Calif., feared that if the ERA went to the floor under normal procedures, amendments relating to abortion and military service would have been adopted, making the ERA unacceptable to many of its own supporters.

Although the ERA was defeated, the showdown created a record of who voted for it and who did not that supporters hoped would haunt the opponents during the 1984 elections.

Background

H J Res 1 and its Senate counterpart, S J Res 10, were identical to the ERA that died June 30, 1982, three states short of the 38 needed to ratify it: "Equality of rights under the law shall not be denied or abridged by the United States or by any state on account of sex."

When the previous ERA came to a House vote in 1971, it was passed by an overwhelming 354-24. Only 12 Republicans and 12 Democrats voted against it. But since 1971, circumstances surrounding the amendment had changed considerably. *(1971 Almanac p. 656)*

The most important new element was the Supreme Court's 1973 decision making abortion legal, and the decade-long controversy that ruling produced.

Anti-abortion groups claimed that unless it was amended, the ERA would lead courts to strike down laws banning federal funding of abortions, because denial of such funding would affect only women and thus amount to sex discrimination.

The 10-year ratification fight over the original ERA also fleshed out old arguments that the ERA could subject women to the military draft and put them in combat, and that it would undermine existing veterans' preferences, which primarily benefited men.

The long-running ERA controversy prompted Sen. Orrin G. Hatch, R-Utah, an ERA critic, and one of his top aides, Stephen J. Markman, to write a book discussing how they thought the ERA would affect various existing laws.

Hatch, chairman of the Judiciary Committee's Constitution Subcommittee, kept the ERA in his panel during 1983. The subcommittee held three hearings on the amendment but took no action on the proposal.

House Committee Action

The House Judiciary Committee debated and battled over H J Res 1 Nov. 9 before approving it by a 21-10 vote.

The Civil and Constitutional Rights Subcommittee had approved the amendment Nov. 7 after a brief meeting.

The tenor of the full committee debate Nov. 9 was at times legalistic, even arcane, and sarcastic. With Phyllis S. Schlafly, a leading ERA opponent, looking on, Republican members grilled Democratic sponsors about the effect of the proposal on various existing laws.

Rep. Patricia Schroeder, D-Colo., the only woman on the 31-member panel, answered most of the questions, getting occasional help from Edwards and Democrats Larry Smith, Fla., and Howard L. Berman, Calif.

The ERA had been approved by the Judiciary Committee 12 years earlier by a 32-3 margin.

Observers present at both that session and the 1983 one said the markups bore only slight resemblance to one another. The first, they said, dealt primarily with large themes such as the role of women in society. The 1983 markup focused mostly on the impact of the ERA on abortion policy, women in the military, veterans' benefits, and public and parochial education.

All of these subjects had become issues in state legislatures that voted on ratifying the amendment.

Nine amendments that attempted to narrow the scope of the ERA were rejected by the House committee. Proponents of those amendments said they were trying to cure some of the problems that plagued the ERA during the ratification fight.

But Smith contended the changes would undercut the basic premise of a constitutional amendment, which is to set broad policy. Smith said the courts would decide how to apply the ERA, just as they had interpreted the rest of the Constitution.

Rep. Henry J. Hyde, R-Ill., charged that Smith was espousing a "trust-me" approach that would send "some warm-sounding words" to the courts for interpretation. He contended this amounted to an abdication of legislative responsibility.

Military Debate

The most emotional committee debate came over proposed amendments that sought to exempt women from military combat duty and the draft.

By 11-20, the panel rejected an amendment by Rep. E. Clay Shaw Jr., R-Fla., that would have made the ERA inapplicable to the military's use of personnel. Currently, women were barred from most combat duties, and Shaw and his supporters claimed the ERA would force the military to put women into combat roles.

Carlos J. Moorhead, R-Calif., said he feared that the ERA could force "the mother of two and three children" into combat. "I support women going into every field they want to. I don't want to force women into combat if they don't desire it, if they want to raise their families," he said.

Schroeder replied that women already served in dangerous military jobs, even though they might not be classified as combat, and said the claim that they were "protected" by the armed forces was "just not the truth."

She cited nurses who served in combat areas, women who flew long-distance supply planes vulnerable to enemy fire and women who served on submarine support boats. She labeled the Shaw proposal a "scare tactic."

By 13-18, the panel rejected an amendment by Sam B. Hall Jr., D-Texas, that would have made the ERA inapplicable to the military draft.

An amendment by Harold S. Sawyer, R-Mich., to

make the ERA inapplicable to congressional powers to raise an army was rejected 13-17.

Abortion, Education Amendments

The committee also rejected, 12-19, an amendment by F. James Sensenbrenner Jr., R-Wis., that would have made the ERA inapplicable to abortion policy. Sensenbrenner and his supporters contended the ERA would require overturning laws banning federal funds for abortion because the laws in effect discriminate by sex.

Schroeder and Edwards, who opposed the amendment, contended that abortion rights decisions by the courts had been based on an implied constitutional right of privacy, and that there was no reason to think the courts would change the legal ground of such decisions if the ERA were passed.

They noted that government funding of abortions had not been required in states with their own ERAs.

By 12-19, the committee rejected an amendment by Dan Lungren, R-Calif., that would have made the ERA inapplicable to private or parochial education.

Voting against the ERA, when all amendments had been disposed of, were Hall, Hyde, Shaw, Moorhead, Sawyer, Sensenbrenner, Lungren, Thomas N. Kindness, R-Ohio; Bill McCollum, R-Fla., and Michael DeWine, R-Ohio.

House Floor Action

Just six days after the Judiciary Committee acted, the full House considered the ERA. Democratic leaders knew they were taking a chance by bringing the proposal up under suspension of the rules, but they decided that the risk was worth it.

Regardless of how it was brought to the floor, the ERA — as a proposed constitutional amendment — would need a two-thirds majority to pass. And under a suspension of the rules, no amendments could be offered. Women's groups and others pushing the ERA wanted it passed in its original form, without exceptions or limitations.

Partisan Split

The ERA was priority item for women's groups such as the National Organization for Women (NOW) and the National Women's Political Caucus. Democrats were hoping their votes for it would score points with women in the 1984 elections and that Republicans would pay politically for "nay" votes.

Democrats voted for the measure 225-38, a margin of 6-1. Republicans voted against it by a 2-1 margin, 53-109.

Shortly after the roll call, Judy Goldsmith, the president of NOW, claimed that Republicans "who orchestrated the loss of the ERA in the House will face the wrath of their constituents at the polls next year. Under the leadership of President Reagan, the Republican members of Congress have consistently opposed equality for women."

Only two of the chamber's 22 women voted against the ERA — Marilyn Lloyd, D-Tenn., and Barbara F. Vucanovich, R-Nev. The latter protested "this blatant abuse of parliamentary procedures," while Lloyd said the ERA should be amended in at least a half-dozen ways.

Backlash on Procedure

The procedural route chosen by Democratic leaders produced one clear backlash: a total of 14 ERA cosponsors, seven from each party, voted "nay."

Republican cosponsors voting against the ERA were William S. Broomfield, Mich.; Robert W. Davis, Mich.; Hamilton Fish Jr.; N.Y., Edwin B. Forsythe, N.J.; Bill Lowery, Calif.; Tom Tauke, Iowa; and Guy Vander Jagt, Mich.

Democratic cosponsors voting "nay" were Berkley Bedell, Iowa; Thomas A. Luken, Ohio; Romano L. Mazzoli, Ky.; Henry J. Nowak, N.Y.; Marty Russo, Ill.; Tom Vandergriff, D-Texas; and Gus Yatron, Pa.

Fish's opposition was of particular importance. A moderate Republican who was the ranking minority member of the House Judiciary Committee, he had stood with Edwards on many controversial committee issues, often against the majority of his party.

He told colleagues that O'Neill's strategy "diminishes the role of each and every member of this House. . . . It is an affront to the deliberative consideration that should be accorded the constitutional amendment process."

Barbara Boxer, D-Calif., put the Democrats' response most succinctly. "If you are for ERA, then vote for it," she said. "If you are against ERA, then vote against it. And explain it any way you want. But do not blame the process, because the people of America will see right through it."

O'Neill chided those who complained about the suspension procedure, charging they were trying to hide their opposition to the ERA. "You are not fooling anybody," he said. "You were looking for the escape. If you think this was the escape, vote 'no.' If you truly believe in a constitutional amendment for women's rights, now is the time to vote 'yes.' "

Mary Rose Oakar, D-Ohio, an ERA cosponsor, said of those who claimed they were upset at the process: "It's a cop-out. Everybody knows it."

But Republicans made much of the leadership's tactic. George W. Gekas, R-Pa., called the process "legislative robbery . . . in broad daylight." Newt Gingrich, R-Ga., accused the Democrats of "bankrupt symbolism," Thomas N. Kindness, R-Ohio, labeled the procedure "legislative martial law," and Minority Leader Robert H. Michel, R-Ill., said O'Neill's tactics "would bring a blush to the cheeks of the most absolute despot of antiquity."

Even some who voted for the ERA denounced the procedure under which it was brought to the floor. Bobbi Fiedler, R-Calif., called O'Neill's strategy "a blueprint for failure." The Democrats, she said, "wanted to beat Republicans who vote 'no' on it over the head between now and the election."

Fiedler said that Democrats were to blame for the defeat of the previous ERA, noting that it was states with Democratic-controlled legislatures that refused to ratify it.

Republicans did not wait until Nov. 15 to express their irritation. When they learned Nov. 14 that the ERA might come up under suspension of the rules, some of them sought to delay House proceedings to express their displeasure. Twice they offered motions to adjourn the House, both of which were defeated on roll-call votes. They further slowed House business by insisting that roll-call votes be taken on eight non-controversial matters. *(Votes 457-466, p. 134-H, 135-H)*

The Amendment Argument

During speeches Nov. 15, many members decried the lack of opportunity to amend the ERA. They said they were for equal rights for women, but that they wanted to make sure that one or another area of law, such as abortion or military combat regulations, was not covered.

At a news conference after the vote, Schroeder contended that their suggestions would amount to writing "an 800-page amendment."

She noted that the First Amendment simply provided that Congress shall make no law abridging freedom of speech, and did not include provisions spelling out a list of exceptions, such as yelling "fire" in a crowded theater or distributing pornographic materials.

The federal courts, she said, would determine how to apply the ERA as specific cases arose — just as they had interpreted the Bill of Rights.

Peter W. Rodino Jr., D-N.J., chairman of the Judiciary Committee, reminded members that in 1962, the House passed a constitutional amendment abolishing the poll tax via suspension of the rules. It became the 24th Amendment two years later, after winning ratification by the required 38 states. *(Congress and the Nation Vol. I, p. 1631)*

Senate Subcommittee

Although Hatch was no fan of the ERA, his Senate Judiciary Constitution Subcommittee began work on the amendment prior to the more friendly House Civil and Constitutional Rights Subcommittee.

The panel held its first ERA hearing on May 26, but the proposal got off to a rocky start.

Hatch made clear his intent was to bore into the possible effects of the amendment, and he contended that "the more the ERA has been exposed to the light of serious legislative discussion and debate, the less successful it has been."

During the hearing, Hatch grilled Sen. Paul E. Tsongas, D-Mass., about the impact of the amendment in a number of areas of the law.

Not expecting such lengthy and detailed questioning, Tsongas told Hatch repeatedly that the courts would decide specific issues. At one point, Tsongas angrily told Hatch, "You knew damn well that these are specific issues that no one coming here unprepared could answer. I will answer them in writing."

Most of the May 26 hearing focused on the relationship between the ERA and federal abortion laws. Rep. Henry J. Hyde, R-Ill., a leading abortion opponent, testified that if the ERA "is ratified without an explicit provision against its use as a pro-abortion device," [it] will be used to sweep away the minimal protection of unborn children that the courts currently allow, and also to mandate tax funding for abortions."

Hatch held two more hearings, one in September devoted to the ERA and its effect on public and private education, and one in November focusing on the ERA and the military.

But the subcommittee did not vote on the ERA in 1983. ∎

Women's Economic Equity Bills Begin Moving

Women's issues took on new prominence in Congress in 1983 as targeted legislation dealing with jobs, child care, individual retirement accounts, pension and insurance reform began moving through the House and Senate.

None of the priority "economic equity" legislation was enacted, and the centerpiece of the women's effort, the Equal Rights Amendment (ERA), was rejected by the House. *(ERA, p. 296)*

But important parts of the legislative package — improvements in pension and child support enforcement laws — had been passed by one chamber, and other bills were advancing in House and Senate committees. *(Pension reform, p. 276; child support, p. 418)*

"I'm very pleased," said Patricia Schroeder, D-Colo., who had served 10 years in Congress, longer than any other woman then in the House except Marjorie S. Holt, R-Md. "We really have seen a willingness by committee chairmen to move issues front and center.... All the movement in both the House and Senate has made people much more aware. Maybe it starts to trickle out that we're more than a token force," Schroeder added, noting there were only 24 women in Congress.

Republican Claudine Schneider, R.I., part of a group of GOP women that worked to gain White House support for some of the economic initiatives, described the year as "more productive than I had anticipated."

Olympia J. Snowe, R-Maine, who chaired the Congressional Caucus for Women's Issues with Schroeder, said there had been a slow but significant shift among male members of Congress. "More than anything I think there were some glaring omissions in our statutes that affected women uniquely and adversely. This was recognized by our male colleagues," she said.

Background

Concerned about the economic plight of women across the country, bolstered by a sophisticated cadre of interest groups, and anxious to milk the so-called "gender gap" for all its political worth, women were taking legislative matters into their own hands in 1983.

While the contentious issues of abortion and ERA remained on the congressional agenda, women for the most part turned their attention to concrete economic issues — jobs, pension and insurance reform, individual retirement accounts for homemakers, tax code revisions to make dependent care more available.

"Women's issues are no longer ERA and reproduction choice," said Geraldine A. Ferraro, D-N.Y. "The economy is becoming a women's issue, which my people, my housewives, my senior citizens can relate to."

Women members drafted proposals on their bread-and-butter concerns that were introduced separately and also packaged into comprehensive legislation (HR 2090, S 888) called the "Economic Equity Act."

A similar comprehensive bill was introduced in the 97th Congress, and portions were enacted that dealt with pensions for former spouses of military personnel, estate taxes and tax code changes concerning day care. *(Military former spouses, 1982 Almanac p. 82; child care, estate taxes, 1981 Almanac p. 92)*

Jobs Legislation

Early in the 98th Congress, women enjoyed a measure of success in the emergency jobs bill signed by President Reagan March 24 (HR 1718 — PL 98-8). While the bill did not include everything women lobbied for, the final mea-

sure provided about $1 billion for jobs and services of benefit to women — significantly more than the original legislation had contained. *(Jobs bill, p. 447)*

"We put ourselves on the map," said Geri Palast, a lobbyist with the Service Employees International Union. "A point was made. . . . Basically what we're talking about in all of this is a reorganization of priorities. If we've been excluded from the pie, they [members of Congress] may have to shift things around if they can't spend more money."

Women and Poverty

According to the Bureau of Labor Statistics (BLS), women in 1982 headed 15.5 percent of all households with children. The unemployment rate for these women was 11.7 percent, compared with a 9.4 percent unemployment rate for all women. The average unemployment rate for men was 9.9 percent, according to the BLS.

The U.S. Civil Rights Commission April 11 released a report, "A Growing Crisis: Disadvantaged Women and Their Children," showing that a "disproportionate number of America's poor in the early 1980s are women." The report found that between 1960 and 1981, the number of persons in poor families headed by women rose 54 percent, while the number in poor families headed by white men dropped by 50 percent.

The report found that the median income in 1981 for husband-wife families was $25,065, compared with $10,960 for female-headed families.

Women and Politics: The Gender Gap

A crucial political tool for women was the so-called "gender gap" revealed by polling data showing women were more likely than men to vote for Democrats over Republicans.

Exit polls in the November 1982 elections by NBC-TV and ABC-TV showed that by 5 percentage points, women were more likely than men to vote for Democrats.

The differential was even more striking when questions were asked about President Reagan's performance. For example, a March Gallup Poll showed that 54 percent of men polled, but only 45 percent of the women surveyed, approved of Reagan's performance as president. This spread was three times as great as the differential for any president since Eisenhower, according to the poll.

Women's groups hoped such studies would make politicians take notice, especially when coupled with data showing that women were voting in greater numbers and mounting drives to increase their registration for the 1984 elections.

Republican women in Congress were paying attention to the current voting trends. In February, six of them held a news conference to express their concerns about the economy's effect on women and to ask for a meeting with Reagan on women's issues. It took six weeks, but after some prodding, particularly by Rep. Schneider, the group met with Reagan and his top aides.

"We became very frustrated that this was going on and on," Schneider said. "He could go to talk to evangelical groups, make speeches for something or other, and we felt frustrated he couldn't take the time to see us earlier."

Participants said Reagan expressed interest in women's issues but made no commitment on legislation.

Rep. Snowe, co-chairman of the women's caucus, noted the Democrats, who controlled Congress for most of the last 30 years, could have done more for women than they

had. but she conceded that "the Republican Party has an image problem. . . . I think we have to take a leadership role [on women's issues]. We need to be up front."

A similar message came from Sen. Nancy Landon Kassebaum, R-Kan. Although she said she distrusted polls, the senator acknowledged that women "seemed to be aligning more closely" with the Democratic Party.

The Women's Network

To rally friends and bypass enemies, sponsors of the equity act relied on a well-organized network in and out of Congress.

At the heart of the legislative operation was the six-year-old women's caucus, which provided information to members and interest groups on a variety of matters affecting women. The caucus began as an organization for women members only, but in 1981 it opened its membership to men. Boasting 125 members by 1983, it was one of the larger groups on Capitol Hill.

Outside Congress, lobbying strategy was being developed under the auspices of the Leadership Conference on Civil Rights, a coalition of 165 national organizations. Executive Director Ralph G. Neas, who directed a highly successful effort in the last Congress to renew the 1965 Voting Rights Act, coordinated dozens of groups working on the equity act, the ERA and jobs legislation.

"You can only translate the gender gap into congressional action if you can demonstrate widespread interest in every congressional district," Neas said. "It is not enough for 35 national organizations to support it. [Members] have got to hear from people these organizations represent."

That message was clear to the membership groups working on the equity act, such as the League of Women Voters, Women's Equity Action League (WEAL), the American Association of University Women (AAUW), the National Federation of Business and Professional Women's Clubs Inc., and the National Organization for Women.

These organizations all had active Washington offices churning out newsletters and memoranda to keep their constituents informed. But the Washington offices were bolstered by energetic local members, many of whom cut their political teeth in the fight for ratification of the ERA. In battling their state legislatures, they learned the value of phone banks, letters, neighborhood meetings and visits with elected officials.

Equity Legislation

Pension Reform

On Nov. 18, the Senate passed a bill (HR 2769) changing the pension laws to give spouses a right to the pensions of workers who died before retirement age but had worked at least 10 years and reached the age of 45. The bill also lowered the age for enrolling a person in a pension plan from 25 to 21, and it permitted workers to leave and return to a job within five years without losing benefits for which they already had qualified. *(Story, p. 276)*

A similar bill (HR 4280) was approved by the House Education and Labor Committee Nov. 16 and referred to the Ways and Means Committee.

There were a few important differences between the two bills. The House committee measure lowered the enrollment age to 21 for most pension plans, but gave an employer with a defined-benefit plan — which provided a fixed level of benefits at retirement — the option to con-

tinue using the 25-year-old enrollment age. Once an employee reaches 25, the employer would have to give the worker credit for the previous four years. This provision was designed to avoid paperwork and administrative expenses for young employees who leave a company after a short stay.

The House bill entitled a spouse to a pension if an employee had worked 10 years, even if he or she died before reaching age 45; the Senate bill required reaching the age of 45.

Child Support Enforcement

The House Nov. 16 unanimously passed a bill (HR 4325) designed to encourage payment of child support. Its major feature was a requirement that states administer child-support withholding by employers from paychecks of parents in arrears in court-ordered support payments.

The bill made state assistance available to all parents who requested help in collecting child support payments. Current law provided such aid only to recipients of Aid to Families with Dependent Children (AFDC), the nation's principal welfare program.

The Senate Finance Committee planned hearings in early 1984 on a child support enforcement bill (S 1691) introduced by the committee's 11 Republican members.

S 1691, a Reagan administration proposal, was similar to the House-passed bill with a few important exceptions. One was a provision in S 1691, rejected by the House, that would reduce the basic federal funding match to cover state administrative costs.

Rep. Barbara B. Kennelly, D-Conn., a chief sponsor of the House bill, said House members feared the provision would deter states that lacked a strong commitment to the current enforcement program.

"We couldn't ask them to do more with less," she explained.

Insurance

In the face of heavy insurance industry opposition, legislation (S 372, HR 100) to outlaw sex-based discrimination in all forms of insurance remained at the committee level when Congress adjourned. *(Insurance discrimination, p. 558)*

The Senate Commerce Committee had been ready to begin markups in late spring, but in June, the panel agreed to postpone action until the General Accounting Office studied the effects the bill would have.

The House Energy and Commerce Committee was poised to consider HR 100 late in the session, but Chairman John D. Dingell, D-Mich., put off action when he determined that he lacked votes for a compromise proposal.

The insurance industry argued that gender was a legitimate factor in determining premiums and benefits. But women's groups and some civil rights groups pushing the legislation disagreed.

They were bolstered somewhat by a July 6 Supreme Court decision holding that an employer's retirement plan could not provide smaller benefit payments to women workers than to comparably situated male employees. *(Court ruling, p. 10-A)*

And the insurance industry itself was not entirely opposed to the anti-discrimination legislation. Early in December, Fireman's Fund Insurance, a subsidiary of American Express Corp., withdrew from the industry lobbying effort against the bills.

Education

While it had only symbolic value, a resolution was passed by the House Nov. 16 opposing any effort to narrow the interpretation of Title IX of the 1972 Education Amendment. That title barred discrimination based on sex in education programs receiving federal funds. *(1972 Almanac p. 390)*

In a case *(Grove City College v. Bell)* before the Supreme Court in its 1983-84 term, the administration and the college argued that the ban applied only to the specific programs in a school that received federal aid, not to all programs at a recipient institution.

Tax Legislation

Several proposals involving tax code changes remained in the Senate Finance and House Ways and Means committees at year's end.

Hearings had been held on the issues, and the administration Oct. 24 released its "Tax Equity for Women" proposals covering some of what Congress was considering.

There appeared to be agreement between the administration and Congress on changing Individual Retirement Accounts (IRAs) to increase the yearly amount a nonworking spouse could contribute.

Another proposal supported by the administration allowed non-profit dependent care organizations for children or the elderly to be treated as tax-exempt organizations, even though they might not have been set up as charitable organizations.

A third area for possible action involved increasing dependent-care tax credits. The Senate and House committees had a day of hearings on this issue, and the administration was supporting legislation to increase the tax credit by 10 percent for taxpayers with an annual adjusted gross income of $10,000 or less. ∎

Air Crash Liability Treaty

Under intense lobbying from trial lawyers, the Senate March 8 rejected a treaty that would have set new limits on passenger damage awards in international air crashes.

The vote on the treaty, known as Montreal Protocols 3 and 4 (S Rept 98-1), was 50-42. This was 12 short of the two-thirds needed (62 in this case) for ratification. There was one vote of "present," by Gordon J. Humphrey, R-N.H., a former airline pilot. *(Vote 9, p. 5-S)*

Leading the opposition to the treaty was Sen. Ernest F. Hollings, D-S.C., who successfully blocked consideration of the pact in the 97th Congress.

Hollings called the treaty unfair, an "outrageous assault on public safety and a sweetheart deal" for foreign governments that own airlines.

Proponents led by Sen. Nancy Landon Kassebaum, R-Kan., countered that for most air crash victims, the treaty would lead to higher, swifter settlements than current law permitted.

Background

The agreement, negotiated by the Ford administration in 1975, had the support of the Carter and Reagan administrations. But it had been ratified by only a handful of countries; most were waiting for the United States to act on the pact.

The March 8 vote marked the first time in more than 20 years that the Senate had rejected a treaty. In 1960,

members refused to ratify an international law of the sea treaty. *(1960 Almanac p. 220)*

On June 23, 1978, the Senate rejected a tax treaty with Great Britain, but four days later it reversed itself and ratified the agreement after adding a restriction. *(1978 Almanac p. 80)*

In theory, there remained a possibility that the treaty could be voted on once more in the 98th Congress, although sponsors said they doubted it would surface again. Just as the vote was ending, Majority Leader Howard H. Baker Jr., R-Tenn., who said he supported the treaty, voted against it. By casting a negative vote, Baker was on the prevailing side and thus eligible to enter a motion to reconsider the vote at a later date.

Limited Liability

Controversy over the Montreal Protocols centered on the treaty's limited liability provision, which would have applied to U.S. citizens on virtually all international flights, not just those to and from the United States.

If a plane on an international flight went down for any reason, all passengers could have recovered up to about $120,000 in "provable economic damages" — the loss of future income suffered by the victim or the victim's family as a result of the crash.

Passengers would not have had to prove that the accident resulted from someone's negligence. They or their survivors would have had to establish only the amount of economic damage suffered.

U.S. citizens flying on any airline could have recovered up to another $200,000 from a fund to be created by a $2 surcharge on their tickets. This fund also would have covered any hospital or medical expenses related to the accident for the rest of the passenger's life.

Existing Law and 'Willful Misconduct'

Under an existing treaty in force since 1934 — which remained unchanged by the March 8 vote — a passenger traveling on a ticket written in the United States could recover up to $75,000 from the airline for economic damages resulting from a crash on any leg of the trip.

Recoveries were limited to $10,000 or $20,000 for crashes involving trips on tickets not written in the United States. The amount varied, depending on which of two international agreements was applicable to the flight in question.

An exception to those existing limits existed if the passenger had his case tried in the United States and proved the airline engaged in "willful misconduct." This exception, which sometimes produced awards well above those allowed by the treaty, would have been eliminated by the pact.

For and Against

The air carriers, represented by the Air Transport Association, the Reagan administration and the American Bar Association contended that the treaty provided fair and swift compensation. They argued that its benefits outweighed the loss of "willful misconduct" suits.

The trial lawyers, represented by the Association of Trial Lawyers of America, who saw the issue from a different vantage point, lobbied furiously against the treaty. They asserted that the treaty impinged upon a passenger's right to full compensation, noting that a liability limit totaling $320,000 did not come close to compensating for the future income loss of many American air passengers. ∎

School Prayer Amendments

The Senate Judiciary Committee decided July 14 to let the full Senate wrestle with alternative constitutional amendments to allow some form of public school prayer.

However, the Senate took no action on the options offered by the committee and there was no substantive House action in 1983 on the school prayer issue.

Rather than choose between competing measures, the Judiciary Committee voted 14-3 to send two resolutions to the Senate without recommendation.

Both proposals were designed to respond to Supreme Court decisions that barred prayer recitations, Bible readings and religious instruction in the public schools. *(CQ Guide to the U.S. Supreme Court, p. 461)*

The Alternatives

One measure (S J Res 73) was strongly supported by President Reagan and conservative religious groups but opposed by a number of mainline religious organizations and the American Civil Liberties Union (ACLU). It allowed organized, recited prayer in public schools. Judiciary Chairman Strom Thurmond, R-S.C., amended the proposal July 14 by adding a sentence barring the United States or any state from composing the words to any school prayer.

The other measure, sponsored by Orrin G. Hatch, R-Utah, permitted silent prayer or meditation in the public schools and barred the federal government and any state government from "encouraging any particular form" of prayer. A second section said that nothing in the Constitution should be interpreted "to prohibit equal access to the use of public school facilities by all voluntary student groups." This was designed to allow student religious groups to use public school buildings for group meetings during non-class hours.

On Sept. 15, the Judiciary Committee approved a separate bill (S 1059) on school access introduced by Sens. Mark O. Hatfield, R-Ore., and Jeremiah Denton, R-Ala.

Hatch said his prayer amendment was intended to meet the concerns of those who believed that any organized, recited prayer would not be truly voluntary and that young students, in particular, would feel pressure to conform with their peers who prayed out loud.

Hatch's proposal, however, was strongly opposed by those who favored S J Res 73. For example, Dick Dingman, legislative director of the Moral Majority, said that the Hatch proposal was too narrow because it dealt only with the "classroom environment" and did not allow such things as Christmas carols and invocations at school ceremonies.

"School prayer goes beyond that moment [of silence]," Dingman said.

Hatch's resolution also found no support from religious and civil liberties groups opposed to any kind of organized prayer in the schools. They suggested that despite the ban on forced participation, anything led by a teacher or sanctioned by a school would in fact carry an unspoken requirement to join in, particularly for elementary school children.

"Children may opt out, but only at the cost of asserting and maintaining their difference from their peers," said Michael J. Malbin, a political scientist at the American Enterprise Institute, in testimony before the Constitution Subcommittee. "This can be a high price to ask of children, one that is not entirely free...."

Reagan Position

The two options were approved June 9 by the Constitution Subcommittee, which was headed by Hatch, after a direct appeal from Reagan.

The action broke a month-long deadlock between subcommittee Republicans and the administration. Hatch, Thurmond and Charles E. Grassley, R-Iowa, had been trying to reconcile their own political judgments with the political wishes of the White House, which had strong backing on S J Res 73 from such conservative religious groups as the Moral Majority and the Christian Broadcasting Network.

Those groups opposed the Hatch measure, contending that it did not go far enough. Hatch had delayed action on the resolution twice in the previous month to accommodate the White House.

Hatch said that Reagan telephoned him shortly before the June 9 markup session and asked that S J Res 73 be sent to the full committee. Hatch said presidential counselor Edwin Meese III had conveyed a similar request the night before.

In addition, Reagan wrote a letter to Thurmond June 6 urging him to block the Hatch proposal and to approve S J Res 73.

Access for Religious Groups (S 1059)

In his letter to Thurmond, Reagan said the issue of religious-group access to public school buildings should be dealt with through legislation rather than as part of a constitutional amendment.

The Judiciary Committee therefore approved S 1059 on Sept. 15. The bill authorized student religious groups in elementary and secondary schools to meet in public school buildings during non-class hours.

Sen. Joseph R. Biden Jr., D-Del., offered an amendment to strike elementary schools from coverage of the bill, but his proposal was rejected 5-10.

The bill allowed religious groups to meet in a school building if the school had a general policy of allowing other student groups to use school facilities. S 1059 specified that any faculty member present at the religous-group meeting could serve only a custodial function to make sure sessions were run in an orderly manner. No faculty member could participate in the meeting.

Court Rulings on Access

Interest in the access issue was roused by a Dec. 8, 1981, Supreme Court decision in the case of *Widmar v. Vincent*, which involved the University of Missouri's refusal to allow a student religious group to meet in school facilities on the same terms as non-religious groups. *(1982 Almanac p. 10-A)*

The court, in an 8-1 decision, ruled that because the university had "an open forum" policy allowing a variety of student groups to use its facilities, implementation of that policy had to be neutral, even if it was a religious group seeking to use the buildings.

The majority said that when an actual "open forum" policy existed, any benefit a religious group extracted from that policy would be merely "incidental."

The justices added that an open forum in the context of a university did not confer the imprimatur of state approval on religious practices or religious sects. "University students are, of course, young adults. They are less impressionable than younger students and should be able to appreciate that the university's policy is one of neutrality towards religion," the court said.

Less than a week after the *Widmar* decision, the Supreme Court took a different stand on a case involving secondary school pupils, rather than university-level students.

The justices refused to review a lower court ruling that barred a group of students from conducting prayer meetings before the start of classes at an Albany, N.Y., high school.

The court also refused to review another case involving religious groups who were denied access to public secondary schools. On Jan. 17, 1983, the court refused to look at a decision of the 5th U.S. Circuit Court of Appeals, which determined that use of school facilities by religious groups in Lubbock, Texas, was not constitutionally permissible.

S 1059 sought to apply the *Widmar* decision to all public schools and colleges. ∎

U.S. Judicial Appointments Go to White Males

After three years, President Reagan's record of federal judicial appointments offered few surprises.

Conservatives, upset at President Carter for appointing what they considered to be liberal, "activist" judges, predicted Reagan would seek judicial candidates with more conservative philosophies. By and large they were right.

Groups representing blacks, Hispanics and women — beneficiaries of Carter's appointment process — expected few gains under Reagan. They, too, generally were right.

By the end of 1983, Reagan had made 123 lifetime, federal judicial appointments. All but 17 of those went to white males.

Reagan named 11 women to the federal bench, including Sandra Day O'Connor, whose 1981 appointment to the Supreme Court made her the first woman justice. *(Story, 1981 Almanac p. 409)*

Nine women were appointed to district court seats, while a 10th was given a seat on the Court of International Trade, which provided lifetime tenure and the same salary as a district court judge.

Reagan appointed only one black to a lifetime federal judgeship. Lawrence W. Pierce was elevated from a district court seat in New York to a seat on the 2nd U.S. Circuit Court of Appeals.

Another black, John Hargrove of Maryland, had been nominated for a district court seat but was not confirmed by the Senate before Congress adjourned.

Five Hispanics were appointed to district court seats. Three of those judgeships were in Puerto Rico, the traditional spot for Hispanic judges. One was in Texas, and the other in Florida.

In his third year, Reagan appointed 34 judges, 29 to the district courts, one to the international trade court and four to the appeals courts. Seven of the appointees at the district court level were women and two were Hispanic. The rest were white men.

Carter-Reagan Comparison

In his first three years in office, Carter appointed 166 judges, 133 to the district courts and 33 to the appellate courts. Of the 133 district court appointees, 19 were women, 18 were black and seven were Hispanic. Of the 33 appeals court appointees, 10 were women, eight were black and two were Hispanic.

With the 1978 Omnibus Judgeship Act (PL 95-486) that gave him 152 new federal judgeships to fill, Carter ended his presidency having appointed 262 federal judges — including 40 women, 38 blacks and 16 Hispanics, more than any other president. *(Judgeship Act, 1978 Almanac p. 173; comparative chart, below)*

Legislation to create an additional 85 federal judgeships was passed by the Senate in 1983 as part of a bill (S 1013) to overhaul the bankruptcy court system. A House bill (HR 3257) to add 76 new district and appeals court judges had not moved, however. *(Story, p. 318)*

Reactions to Reagan Record

The Reagan record followed a "predictable course," said Sheldon Goldman, a political science professor at the University of Massachusetts who had written extensively on federal judicial selection. The record "suggests that administration officials don't feel they have any special obligation to use affirmative action to expand the net, to make a special effort to get qualified women and minorities. They feel they can get away with it politically," Goldman added.

While Reagan's judicial selection policy, by itself, was not likely to be an election issue, women's and minority groups planned to make it part of an overall campaign against the president and Republicans.

"I think the Reagan administration underestimates the black community in terms of a commitment toward getting their fair share," said Althea T. L. Simmons, head of the NAACP's Washington office. "They have written us off, and I think it is dangerous to underestimate 12 percent or 13 percent of the population."

Hispanic leader Arnoldo Torres of the League of United Latin American Citizens said many Hispanics were beyond anger toward the president for his record. "Is it worth getting upset with something you expected to happen? No." Torres said.

"Where the anger comes is when the administration claims they've done something. Our intelligence is insulted."

Susan Ness, a consultant on judicial selection and a member of the board of the National Conference of Women's Bar Associations, was most concerned about Reagan's record on the appeals courts — selections made by the administration with little influence by senators, who exercised considerable power over district court nominations.

"That part of the record is absolutely deplorable," she asserted, pointing out that none of the 23 appeals court appointees was a woman and only one was black.

Ness noted that Deputy Attorney General Edward C. Schmults, in remarks published Nov. 11 in a judiciary newsletter, stated that senators had not come up with many women or minority candidates for district court judgeships. "The administration continually blames senators for failing to come up with women's names," Ness said. "But Reagan's record on the circuit courts basically makes clear what the commitment is."

Jonathan C. Rose, head of the Justice Department's Office of Legal Policy, not surprisingly disagreed with

Ness' assessment. The president "has attempted to make sure that all elements of the population have their fair chance to be represented on the bench," Rose said.

"I suppose for some people there will never be an adequate commitment. But I think Sandra Day O'Connor stands out as the most major example of the president's commitment to appoint qualified women to the highest courts in the country.

"I think the president has continued to appoint a group of outstanding judges to the bench," Rose added. "He has attempted to maintain his position that they should share his philosophy with regard to judicial restraint and his general point of view toward respect for the law, and I think his appointees fully meet those criteria."

Dan Popeo, head of the Washington Legal Foundation, a business-oriented law and research organization, said he was "very pleased" with Reagan's appointments.

Popeo had little patience with women and minority group representatives critical of the president. "They're looking for a drum to beat," Popeo contended, adding that the president could never satisfy these groups "because they are politically motivated.... I don't agree that we need a quota [on the judiciary]," Popeo added. "I'm Italian-American. How many Italian-Americans does he have on the bench?"

The ABA Ratings

Reagan administration officials and Reagan supporters claimed that the president's judicial appointees were better qualified than Carter's. But objective assessments were difficult, in part because the appointees of both presidents had been on the bench such a short time.

The only constant was the ratings of the American Bar Association (ABA), which had been passing on the qualifications of judicial nominees for 35 years.

A comparison of the two administrations showed little difference in ABA ratings. Of all Carter appointees, 6.1 percent were given the highest rating, exceptionally well

Judicial Appointments

U.S. Court of Appeals

	Women	Blacks	Hispanics
Johnson	2.5%	5.0%	Not available
Nixon	0	0	Not available
Ford	0	0	Not available
Carter	19.6	16.1	3.6
Reagan	0	4.3	0

U.S. District Court

	Women	Blacks	Hispanics
Johnson	1.6%	3.3%	2.5%
Nixon	0.6	2.8	1.1
Ford	1.9	5.8	1.9
Carter	14.1	14.1	6.8
Reagan	9.3	0	5.1

Source: The Johnson, Nixon and Ford statistics are from a study by Sheldon Goldman of the University of Massachusetts at Amherst. The Carter and Reagan percentages were compiled by Congressional Quarterly based on figures from the Justice Department.

qualified, while 9.7 percent of Reagan's selections received this rating.

The ABA's "well qualified" rating was given to 49.6 percent of Carter's appointees and 40.6 percent of Reagan's appointees. A "qualified" rating was given to 43.1 percent of Carter's appointees and 49.6 percent of Reagan's selections.

An "unqualified" rating was given to 1.1 percent of Carter's appointees but to none of Reagan's appointees. (The percentages do not total 100 because of rounding.)

Carter Appointees Assessed

One political scientist had attempted to discern what effect Carter's appointments had on the federal judiciary. Jon Gottschall, a political science professor at the State University of New York at Plattsburgh and a former Goldman student, published a study in the October 1983 issue of *Judicature* that looked at selected cases decided by Carter appeals court appointees from July 1, 1979, to June 30, 1981. The study focused on criminal cases and those involving sex and race discrimination.

Gottschall found that in criminal and prisoner rights cases, Carter appointees cast 58 percent of their votes in favor of the criminally accused or prisoners, compared to 52 percent for judges appointed by President Lyndon B. Johnson, 51 percent appointed by President John F. Kennedy, and only 30 percent and 31 percent respectively for Presidents Richard M. Nixon and Gerald R. Ford.

In sex discrimination cases, Gottschall found that Carter appointees cast 59 percent of their votes in favor of the

claimant of sexual discrimination, close to the 63 percent of the Johnson and Kennedy appointees combined. By contrast, Nixon and Ford appointees supported the female claimant of sex discrimination in only 39 and 40 percent of the cases respectively.

In race discrimination cases, Gottschall determined that Carter and Johnson appointees cast 60 percent of their votes in support of the minority claimants of discrimination, while Nixon and Ford appointees voted 43 percent and 45 percent respectively for minority claimants.

"Carter's 56 [appeals court] appointments do appear to have offset an apparent attitudinal conservatism among the 57 Nixon and Ford appointees who preceded them to the courts of appeals," Gottschall concluded.

Based on a survey of the black and women judges among the Carter appointments, Gottschall concluded further that "the apparently greater liberalism of Carter appointees in criminal cases is directly attributable to his appointments of women and blacks, for Carter's white male appointees are virtually indistinguishable in their voting behavior from Johnson and Kennedy appointees."

'A Little Early'

William James Weller, legislative affairs officer for the Administrative Office of the U.S. Courts, said the Gottschall study might be premature, given that the judges were on the bench for such a short time. "It's a little early to be doing this," Weller said, "because the federal judicial experience in the last two decades is that new judges don't really hit full stride for a period of five years." ∎

Refugee Program Renewal, 1984 Levels

The House Nov. 14 approved legislation extending refugee resettlement programs for two years.

The action came slightly more than a month after President Reagan officially authorized the admission of 72,000 refugees in fiscal 1984, down 18,000 from the fiscal 1983 authorized level. It was the third year in a row that the administration had proposed lower admission levels. *(See chart, below)*

The House Nov. 14 passed the refugee program reauthorization bill (HR 3729 — H Rept 98-404) under suspension of the rules by a 300-99 vote. A two-thirds majority was required. *(Vote 460, p. 134-H)*

The measure did not set an overall funding level, but it did earmark $100 million annually for social services for refugees, $14 million to screen refugees for health problems and $50 million for "targeted assistance" to areas with heavy refugee populations.

HR 3729 was sent to the Senate, which did not act on it before adjournment.

Welfare, Medicaid

One of the most controversial aspects of the refugee resettlement program was the high rate of welfare dependency among refugees. Some members of the House Judiciary Committee wanted to bar refugees from receiving welfare for the first 90 days they were in the country. However, the committee refused to adopt such a ban.

The bill did include a section that would make all refugees presumptively eligible for Medicaid, the federal-state medical program for the poor, for the first year they were in the country. This was intended to encourage refugees to take jobs that did not provide health benefits

instead of trying to qualify for welfare programs that entitled them to Medicaid.

Rep. Romano L. Mazzoli, D-Ky., chairman of the Immigration, Refugees and International Law Subcommittee, told the House the welfare dependency rate had dropped from about 70 to 80 percent three years earlier to about 50 percent.

Other Provisions

The bill included these other major provisions:

● Moved the Office of Refugee Resettlement (ORR) from the Social Security Administration to the Office of the Secretary of Health and Human Services.

● Barred refugees from receiving cash assistance if they refused to take a job or go to a job interview arranged by a voluntary agency or local employment service. The first refusal would carry a three-month ban; the second a six-month ban.

● Required the ORR to develop and evaluate alternatives to the present welfare system for refugees. The experimental projects were intended to help Congress decide if resettlement programs could operate without using existing welfare systems.

HR 3729 reauthorized programs established in 1980 legislation that reformed the process for admitting refugees. Part of the law required the administration to consult with Congress each year on the number of refugees to be allowed into the country. *(1980 Almanac p. 378)*

Refugee Admission Levels

President Reagan Oct. 7 formally authorized the admission of 72,000 refugees in fiscal 1984, down 18,000 from

the authorized fiscal 1983 level. (Under the law, refugees were defined as people fleeing persecution in their own countries.)

In addition, the president authorized adjustments to permanent resident status for up to 5,000 aliens who had been granted asylum in the United States.

Reagan set the new levels after completing formal consultations with the House and Senate Judiciary committees as required under the Refugee Act of 1980 (PL 96-212).

It was the third year in a row that the president, with the approval of Congress, reduced the number of refugees authorized to enter the United States. Actual refugee admissions in fiscal 1983 reached only 61,681, which was 28,319 below the authorized level of 90,000. *(1982 Almanac p. 410)*

Both Judiciary committees notified the president in late September that they had no objections to either the overall ceiling or the admissions allocations by region that Reagan had proposed.

The allocations then became official.

Concerns About Central America

However, Sen. Edward M. Kennedy, D-Mass., ranking minority member of the Senate Judiciary Subcommittee on Immigration and Refugee Policy, said in an Oct. 7 letter to Reagan that he harbored "serious reservations" about the authorized limit of 1,000 for refugees from Latin America and the Caribbean, given the turmoil that had been occurring in that region.

Kennedy said State Department reports and materials presented to the Senate Judiciary Committee during the consultation process indicated "there may be as many as 3,500 political refugees seeking asylum next year from El Salvador alone."

He urged the president to make available to refugees from that nation and others in Latin America any unused slots from other regions.

Mazzoli likewise urged Reagan to remain flexible on the number of slots available to refugees from Central America.

And Rep. Hamilton Fish Jr., R-N.Y., ranking House Judiciary Republican, said he preferred an overall ceiling of 83,000 refugees for fiscal 1984.

Committee Action

The House Judiciary Committee approved HR 3729 on Sept. 27.

The bill as approved Aug. 1 by the Subcommittee on Immigration, Refugees and International Law included a provision barring refugees from receiving welfare assistance for the first 90 days they were in the country. However, the full committee Sept. 20 adopted an amendment by Don Edwards, D-Calif., deleting this section. The vote was 16-12.

The bill included a provision that would make all refugees presumptively eligible for Medicaid for the first year they were in the country. Sponsors believed that this provision would encourage refugees to take jobs that did not provide health benefits instead of trying to qualify for welfare programs that then entitled them to Medicaid.

Refugees and Welfare

The most contentious issue during the two House Judiciary markup sessions on HR 3729 dealt with welfare payments to refugees.

It was the second year in a row that members had grappled with the welfare issue. *(1982 Almanac p. 413)*

Under current law, refugees who did not qualify for government assistance under the Aid to Families with Dependent Children program (AFDC) or the Supplemental Security Income (SSI) program for the blind, aged and disabled nonetheless could receive federal cash assistance for the first 18 months they were in the country. They first had to show they had no other source of income.

Mazzoli, chairman of the Immigration Subcommittee, noted that about 55 percent of all refugees who had been in the United States less than three years were getting some form of welfare at either the federal, state or local level. He contended this was much too high a rate, and that Congress needed to change the resettlement system.

He and Dan Lungren, R-Calif., said a 90-day bar to welfare would help voluntary resettlement agencies, such as the U.S. Catholic Conference, get refugees into jobs as soon as they came into the country. Lungren contended that word of the U.S. welfare system circulated through refugee camps overseas, and that too many refugees came to this country expecting to go on welfare.

Edwards, however, argued that barring federal cash

U.S. Refugee Admissions for Fiscal 1984

	Actual Admissions fiscal 1981	Actual Admissions fiscal 1982	Actual Admissions fiscal 1983	Proposed Admissions fiscal 1984
Asia	131,139	73,522	39,408	50,000
Soviet Union/Eastern Europe	20,148	13,536	13,492	12,000
Near East	3,829	6,304	5,465	6,000
Africa	2,119	3,356	2,648	3,000
Latin America/Caribbean	2,017	579	668	1,000
TOTAL	159,252	97,297	61,681	72,000

SOURCE: State Department

assistance to refugees would merely shift refugee costs to the states. The committee agreed Sept. 20 to delete the 90-day ban.

On Sept. 27, the panel by voice vote adopted an amendment by Hamilton Fish Jr., R-N.Y., requiring the secretary of health and human services to develop a pilot program testing alternative income support systems for refugees.

By voice vote Sept. 27, the committee also adopted an amendment of Bill McCollum, R-Fla., providing reimbursement to states that had incurred costs associated with the incarceration of Cubans who came to the United States during the so-called Mariel "boat lift" in 1980. *(1980 Almanac p. 429)*

Court, Senate Rebuff Anti-Abortion Efforts

The anti-abortion movement suffered a double setback in 1983 as the Supreme Court vigorously reaffirmed its landmark 1973 decision legalizing abortion and the Senate defeated a constitutional amendment designed to overturn that decade-old ruling.

The court's 6-3 ruling June 15 came on separate cases from Missouri, Virginia and Akron, Ohio, testing the validity of state and local government efforts to regulate abortion.

Even though no federal law was at issue, the Reagan administration had urged the court to bow out of the abortion controversy and leave "further refinements" of the law to the wisdom of legislative bodies.

Instead, the court told legislatures to stop trying to influence a woman's choice on whether to terminate a pregnancy. Her right to make that decision herself, in consultation only with a physician, was guaranteed by the Constitution along lines spelled out by the 1973 *Roe v. Wade* decision, the court said.

Although anti-abortion groups vowed to redouble their drive to win a constitutional amendment outlawing abortion, the Senate less than two weeks later rejected an amendment designed to overturn *Roe v. Wade.*

It was the first time either chamber of Congress had voted on such an amendment.

The measure (S J Res 3) went down to defeat 49-50, with Jesse Helms, R-N.C., voting present. This was 18 votes short of the two-thirds majority needed for a constitutional amendment. *(Vote 169, p. 31-S)*

The vote was a blow to President Reagan, a foe of abortion who had lobbied senators on the issue.

Background

Prior to *Roe v. Wade,* there was no uniform law governing abortion. Each state had its own approach, and laws varied widely from state to state.

Number of Abortions. In 1972, the year before the Supreme Court decision made abortion legal nationwide, there were 600,000 legal abortions. Thirty-three states allowed abortions to save the life of a pregnant woman; 13 states permitted them if the life of the pregnant woman or her physical or mental health were endangered; four permitted a woman to have an abortion upon consultation with her physician.

In 1980, the most recent year for which figures were available, there were 1,553,900 legal abortions.

Abortion/Childbirth Mortality Rates. In 1972, according to the federal Center for Disease Control, there were 4.1 deaths of women per 100,000 abortions. In 1973, the number dropped to 3.4 per 100,000. In 1978, the most recent year for which figures were available, there were 0.5 deaths per 100,000 abortions.

In 1972, there were 15.2 deaths of women per 100,000

births. In 1973, the number dropped to 12.6 per 100,000, and in 1978, the last year for which figures were available, there were eight deaths per 100,000 births.

Status of Federal Law. The most important existing law was the 1973 *Roe v. Wade* Supreme Court decision, which established the right of a woman to have an abortion based on an implied right of privacy in the Constitution. In the first trimester, the decision to have an abortion was solely between the woman and her doctor. The state was given increasing power to regulate abortion in the second and third trimesters.

Current federal law barred use of federal Medicaid funds for all abortions except those necessary to save the life of the pregnant woman.

The second fiscal 1984 continuing appropriations resolution (H J Res 413 — PL 98-151) cleared by Congress Nov. 12 barred use of federal employee health benefits to pay for abortions except when the mother's life was imperiled. *(H J Res 413, p. 528)*

Since 1973, Congress had cleared a number of other laws containing abortion restrictions. *(Box, p. 310)*

State-Financed Abortions. Although the Supreme Court earlier upheld the validity of state laws banning use of state Medicaid funds for abortions, in 1983 the District of Columbia and the following 15 states still provided abortion funding: Alaska, California, Colorado, Connecticut, Hawaii, Maryland, Massachusetts, Michigan, New Jersey, New York, North Carolina, Oregon, Pennsylvania, Washington and West Virginia. *(Supreme Court case, 1980 Almanac p. 7-A)*

Court Ruling

The Cases: State and Local Regulations

The court's crucial 1983 decision came as the justices by a 6-3 margin held unconstitutional provisions of a 1978 Akron, Ohio, ordinance that was considered a national model for anti-abortion regulation. The decision in the case of *Akron v. Akron Center for Reproductive Health, Akron Center for Reproductive Health v. Akron* struck down the following legal requirements:

● That all abortions after the first three months (trimester) of pregnancy be performed in a hospital.

● That physicians obtain the consent of a parent or legal guardian before performing an abortion on a minor under age 15.

● That physicians recite to women seeking abortions a litany of information about the stages of fetal development, possible abortion complications and birth-giving alternatives.

● That the attending physician, and no one else, inform a patient of the particular risks associated with her own pregnancy or abortion.

● That a waiting period of at least 24 hours be observed between the time a woman signs an "informed consent" form authorizing an abortion and the time one is performed.

● That fetal remains be given some sort of "humane" disposal.

In a companion case, however, the court divided 5-4 to uphold several provisions of a challenged Missouri law. Most significant was one that required "unemancipated" minors to obtain parental or judicial consent for an abortion. Justice Lewis F. Powell Jr. and Chief Justice Warren E. Burger joined the *Akron* dissenters to uphold this requirement in the case of *Planned Parenthood Association of Kansas City, Mo. v. Ashcroft, Ashcroft v. Planned Parenthood Association of Kansas City, Mo.*

Also upheld were Missouri's requirements that abortion tissue, like that from all other surgical procedures, be submitted to a pathologist for examination, and that a second physician be present at abortions late in pregnancy.

In a third case, *Simopoulos v. Virginia,* the court by 8-1 upheld a Virginia law requiring second-trimester abortions to be performed in licensed hospitals. It did so because that law, unlike the invalidated Akron ordinance, permitted outpatient surgical clinics to be licensed as "hospitals." Justice John Paul Stevens dissented.

The Rationale

Respect for settled precedent required the majority to reaffirm *Roe v. Wade,* wrote Powell for the majority in the *Akron* case. Noting that "arguments continue to be made . . . that we erred in interpreting the Constitution" in *Roe v. Wade,* Powell declared that "the doctrine of *stare decisis* . . . demands respect in a society governed by the rule of law."

In a lengthy footnote, Powell said there were "especially compelling reasons" for adhering to precedent in applying the principles of *Roe v. Wade.*

"That case was considered with special care," Powell said, and in the decade since, the court "repeatedly and consistently has accepted and applied the basic principle that a woman has a fundamental right to make the highly personal choice whether or not to terminate her pregnancy."

In his footnote, Powell warned that the three dissenting justices rejected the basic premise of *Roe.* Although they did not argue outright that *Roe* should be overruled, Powell said, they adopted "reasoning that, for all practical purposes, would accomplish precisely that result."

The Dissenters

Justice Sandra Day O'Connor, Reagan's only appointee on the court, led the dissent from the *Akron* ruling. She made clear that she felt *Roe v. Wade* should be drastically modified, if not reversed altogether.

O'Connor was criticized by anti-abortion groups during her September 1981 confirmation hearings for refusing to condemn abortion or to criticize *Roe v. Wade;* the June 15 dissent was the first time since she joined the court that she had spoken officially on that issue. *(O'Connor appointment, 1981 Almanac p. 409)*

The three dissenters — O'Connor, Byron R. White and William H. Rehnquist — were among the youngest justices on the court. The possibility that Reagan, should he serve a second term, would have an opportunity to appoint more justices led some to speculate that the court itself could yet overrule *Roe v. Wade.*

O'Connor, writing for the dissenters, criticized the trimester approach the court adopted in *Roe* for testing state regulation of abortion.

Under that framework, the state could not interfere in a woman's decision to have an abortion in the first trimester of pregnancy beyond requiring that all abortions be performed by licensed physicians. In the second trimester, the state could regulate abortion only to protect maternal health. At the point in pregnancy where the fetus became viable, or able to survive outside the womb, the state could regulate or even ban abortion except to save the life or health of the mother.

The *Roe* rationale, O'Connor warned, was "on a collision course with itself." Under *Roe,* states could regulate second-trimester abortions in the interest of protecting maternal health. Yet the court in the *Akron* case struck down a requirement that all abortions after the first trimester be performed in hospitals, citing new medical evidence that abortions early in the second trimester could safely be performed in an outpatient clinic.

"As the medical risks of various abortion procedures decrease, the point at which the state may regulate for reasons of maternal health is moved forward" to actual childbirth, O'Connor wrote. But at the same time, she continued, "as medical science becomes better able to provide for the separate existence of the fetus, the point of viability [at which, under *Roe,* the state may ban abortion unless necessary to save the life or health of the mother] is moved further back toward conception."

O'Connor, White and Rehnquist indicated they would adopt an approach suggested by the Reagan administration, upholding restrictions on abortion at any stage of pregnancy so long as the particular regulation did not unduly burden a woman's right to choose to have an abortion and was rationally related to some legitimate state purpose.

Under *Roe v. Wade,* the only sufficiently compelling state interest to justify second-trimester regulation was the interest in protecting the mother's health. In the third trimester, that interest was joined by the interest in protecting potentially viable human life, the fetus.

Hospitalization

In the *Akron* case, the court's six-man majority — Powell, Burger, Stevens, William J. Brennan Jr., Thurgood Marshall and Harry A. Blackmun — held that cities and states could not require that all abortions after the first trimester be performed in acute-care, full-service hospitals. Such a requirement made abortions considerably more expensive, Powell noted, and medical evidence showed that most abortions could be safely performed on an outpatient basis in a clinic or other "appropriate non-hospital facilities."

Thus, wrote Powell, a hospitalization requirement like Akron's unreasonably infringed upon a woman's constitutional right to obtain an abortion.

Since 1975, about 75 percent of all abortions nationwide had been performed either in a clinic or at a physician's office. The remaining 25 percent were performed in hospitals, according to the Alan Guttmacher Institute, a special affiliate of Planned Parenthood Federation of America Inc.

Parental Consent

Akron's ordinance required an unmarried minor under 15 years of age to obtain the written consent of one of her

parents or an order approving an abortion from a court "having jurisdiction over her."

Missouri's law, a revised version of one the court struck down in 1976, required parental or judicial consent to an abortion for all unemancipated minors under 18. This law spelled out in some detail, however, the procedure through which a court might decide that a minor was mature enough to make this decision for herself.

The critical difference between the two parental consent requirements was the fact that Missouri spelled out an alternative means of obtaining the necessary consent for a minor who could not or would not obtain that consent from her parents. Although the Akron ordinance mentioned such an alternative, the justices found that it provided an insufficient opportunity for a court, on a case-by-case basis, to decide whether or not a pregnant minor was in fact mature enough to make her own decision.

The question of parental consent had been one of continuing difficulty for the court. In 1976 the court held, 5-4, that states could not require all unmarried minors to obtain parental consent for an early-term abortion.

Three years later, the court by 8-1 struck down a Massachusetts parental consent requirement. Although that law permitted a pregnant minor to obtain judicial, rather than parental, consent, the court struck it down because it let a judge veto a minor's decision to have an abortion even after he had ruled she was mature enough to decide for herself. The majority also found fault with the law for requiring parental notification under all circumstances.

In 1981, the court upheld a Utah law requiring a doctor to notify the parents of a minor before an abortion was performed. The court specifically upheld the notification requirement only as it applied to an immature minor still dependent on her parents.

Other States. According to the Alan Guttmacher Institute, the following six states had laws similar to Missouri's requiring parental or judicial consent before abortions for "unemancipated" minors: Louisiana, Massachusetts, North Dakota and Rhode Island, under laws currently in effect; and Kentucky and Pennsylvania, under laws that were facing federal court challenge but were expected to be upheld in light of the new decision.

The following states required parental notification before abortions on minors: Arizona, Idaho, Indiana, Maryland, Minnesota, Montana, Utah, under laws currently in effect; and Illinois, Maine and Nebraska, under laws facing federal court challenge.

Amendment Background

Disappointed by the failure of the 97th Congress to enact abortion law restrictions, one faction of the anti-abortion movement developed a new strategy for the 98th Congress.

During a Senate subcommittee hearing Feb. 28, Sen. Thomas F. Eagleton, D-Mo., unveiled a proposed constitutional amendment designed to leave regulation of abortion to the 50 states. Eagleton's proposal simply overturned *Roe v. Wade*, returning abortion law to its pre-1973 status, when each state had its own statutes governing abortion.

The Eagleton proposal was only 10 words: "A right to abortion is not secured by this Constitution."

It was actually the first sentence of a proposed constitutional amendment (S J Res 3) introduced by Orrin G. Hatch, R-Utah, chairman of the Senate Judiciary Constitu-

tion Subcommittee. The Feb. 28 hearing was held by that panel.

Hatch's amendment, as introduced, went further, giving states and Congress joint authority to restrict abortion. If both Congress and a state acted, the more restrictive legislation would govern.

In 1982, the Judiciary Committee approved the Hatch proposal, but it never was considered by the full Senate. The amendment became snarled in a dispute over legislation sponsored by Helms that sought to bar abortion through a simple statute rather than a constitutional amendment.

The Helms bill fell victim to a protracted filibuster and eventually was killed on a procedural vote. *(1982 Almanac p. 403)*

"It is my belief, based on numerous conversations with my Senate colleagues, that a constitutional amendment which would return the law to where it was before 1973 . . . would muster the greatest number of votes in the Senate," Eagleton said.

Eagleton did not introduce his proposal as a separate bill. Instead, the Constitution Subcommittee March 24 altered the Hatch amendment, with the Utah senator's blessing, to make it the same as the Eagleton proposal.

Anti-Abortion Movement Split

The strongest opposition S J Res 3 came from those wanting an all-out ban on abortion.

Many of those groups backed a bill (S 467) introduced Feb. 3 by Roger W. Jepsen, R-Iowa.

The Jepsen bill contained congressional findings concerning the protection of a fetus, encouraged states to pass new anti-abortion laws, made permanent the temporary ban on federal funding for abortion and created a federal policy to prevent withholding food or medical treatment from deformed infants.

President Reagan endorsed this proposal Jan. 31, after Rep. Henry J. Hyde, R-Ill., introduced an identical bill in the House (HR 618).

The Hyde bill was referred to seven subcommittees, which took no action on it in 1983. Nor did S 467 advance during the year.

Nellie Gray, head of the Washington-based March For Life, was one of the more emphatic spokesmen for those unhappy with the Eagleton approach. "Government has the responsibility for protecting each and every life, from fertilization through the continuum of life. This is not an option for the United States Congress or the states," she said in an interview.

Asked whether she could support the Eagleton proposal as a first step toward more restrictive abortion law, Gray indicated she could not.

"The real problem with this is that the first step will be the last step. You are putting in the Constitution that it is it all right to kill babies until somebody tells you to stop," she said.

Asked if division within the anti-abortion movement could hurt revision efforts, Gray replied: "I really don't know and I really don't care. My responsibility is to March For Life. All of this effort [to compromise] has brought us nothing but confusion."

The Eagleton approach brought a qualified endorsement from the National Conference of Catholic Bishops. Father Edward Bryce, director of the Bishop's Committee for Pro-Life Activities, said he considered the Eagleton amendment a positive step.

Senate Committee Action

The Constitution Subcommittee of the Senate Judiciary Committee approved the modified S J Res 3 on March 24. The action came on a voice vote, with no dissent. Only the panel's three Republican members were present.

Full Committee Deadlock

On April 19, the Senate Judiciary Committee, deadlocked 9-9 on the proposed constitutional amendment but decided to send it to the floor anyway without a recommendation.

Groups favoring legalized abortion were pleased with the April 19 vote because it represented a turnaround from 1982, when the committee voted 10-7 to send the two-pronged Hatch amendment to the Senate floor. In 1982, Sens. Joseph R. Biden, D-Del., and Alan K. Simpson, R-Wyo., voted for the Hatch proposal. In 1983, they voted against S J Res 3. Howell Heflin, D-Ala., who did not vote in 1982, supported S J Res 3.

Senate Floor Action

Reaction to the Vote

The margin of the June 28 Senate vote defeating S J Res 3 came as something of a surprise. Nineteen Republicans joined 31 Democrats in opposing the amendment.

Hatch said he was "disappointed." But he contended that it was important nonetheless to have had a vote on abortion. He said the vote on his amendment was a "benchmark" that would put senators squarely on record about the nation's abortion policy.

"My job is over," he said. "I've done the best I could to bring this to the Senate floor."

Bob Packwood, R-Ore., who led opponents of S J Res 3, said he believed the vote was a signal from senators that "they want to be done with this issue. The bigger the vote against this, the stronger the message," he said. "The right-to-life forces have crested and are on the decline."

Although the issue of abortion had arisen frequently in the Senate since 1973, it was previously either in the context of preventing the use of federal funds for abortion, or it was enmeshed in a debate over the independence of the federal judiciary. Procedural maneuvering also had prevented clear votes on the merits of abortion. *(Federal funding issue, 1980 Almanac p. 467; federal judiciary debate, 1982 Almanac p. 403)*

The Helms Position

Helms' refusal to vote for the amendment reflected a split within the anti-abortion movement that had persisted for more than two years. On one side were Helms and a handful of anti-abortion groups that favored a statute to define the fetus as a "person" with the same constitutionally guaranteed right to life as any other person. A statute, unlike a constitutional amendment, would require only a majority vote to pass.

On the other side were Hatch and a number of other anti-abortion groups. They believed that a constitutional amendment was required to overturn the *Roe* decision and that any outright ban on abortion — regardless of its form — would never clear Congress.

In a brief speech before the vote, Helms said he could not support S J Res 3 because it "does not advance the principle that human life is inviolable. Instead, it surrenders forever this principle in exchange for the illusory hope that some lives may be saved. . . . It merely rebuts the concept of a right to abortion."

Passage of the amendment, Helms said, would at best be "a Pyrrhic victory for the unborn."

Helms added that he was "convinced a tactical error has been made in bringing up a constitutional amendment without having the necessary votes or being within striking distance."

Asked about Helms' charge, Hatch replied that his North Carolina colleague was entitled to his opinion.

Helms said he intended to push a bill (S 26) similar to Jepsen's and Hyde's (HR 618). A similar Helms proposal was rejected by the Senate in 1982 after a six-week filibuster. *(1982 Almanac p. 403)*

Against Abortion

The Senate's consideration of S J Res 3 was not so much a debate as a series of speeches — some of them emotional — by 32 senators, one after another. Only rarely was there an exchange between those supporting the amendment and those against it.

During the 10 hours of debate, which began June 27, several five-foot-high charts prepared by Hatch's staff lined the back of the chamber. Some provided illustrations of polling data on abortion. One contained pictures of a fetus in its middle and final stages of development, and another related the total number of abortions since 1973 — 15 million, Hatch said — to the number of Americans killed in six wars — 1,160,581.

"The war on the unborn," Hatch said, "has cost 10 times the human lives of all our wars put together."

Jeremiah Denton, R-Ala., contended that the nation's abortion policy "begins the slipperly slope to infanticide." He charged that "we are emulating the Chinese in deciding that girl babies are undesirable. They are not wanted. We will destroy them.

"We are joining the chicken sexers down in Alabama who determine that if the sex of the chicken is male, we're going to destroy them because we don't need that many males."

Mark O. Hatfield, R-Ore., who spoke eloquently on the issue, said that to him, "abortion is a form of violence. It is condoned by a society that has become callous and indifferent to the climate that elevates selfish personal convenience to a supreme status in human decision-making.

"Let us recognize that often, abortion is submitted to by women who have been dehumanized by relationships lacking either commitment or responsibility. These same abortions are ignored — or even encouraged — by the men who caused the pregnancy, since the convenience of abortion eliminates the necessity to view that woman, the relationship, as an integral part of his life. . . ."

Hatfield said more efforts should be made to prevent unwanted pregnancies. "We must promote an uncompromising commitment to sex education and family planning services," he said.

Defending Choice

The opponents of S J Res 3, led by Packwood, consistently portrayed their argument as one of choice for women.

"A woman's right to make a child-bearing decision is part of her right of bodily integrity," Packwood said.

"No other Supreme Court decision has meant more to the health, well-being, freedom and dignity of women than

Federal Abortion Funding Restrictions

Following is a list of federal laws containing abortion restrictions, based on information compiled by the Alan Guttmacher Institute, a research affiliate of the Planned Parenthood Federation of America:

Family Planning Services and Population Research Act of 1970 (PL 91-572). Barred the use of funds for programs in which abortion is a method of family planning.

Health Programs Extension Act of 1973 (PL 93-45). Barred judges or public officials from ordering recipients of federal funds to perform abortions or sterilization procedures or to make facilities available for such procedures if doing so was contrary to a recipient's religious beliefs or moral convictions. Also barred discrimination against personnel for participation or lack of participation in abortions or sterilization procedures.

Legal Services Corporation Act of 1974 (PL 93-355). Barred lawyers in federally funded legal aid programs from providing legal assistance for procuring a "non-therapeutic abortion." Also barred legal aid in proceedings to compel an individual or institution to perform an abortion, assist in an abortion or provide facilities for an abortion.

Public Health Service Act, 1977 Amendments (PL 95-215). Required the secretary of Health, Education and Welfare to conduct a study to determine whether medical, nursing or osteopathic schools denied admission or otherwise discriminated against any applicant because of the applicant's reluctance or willingness to counsel, suggest, recommend, assist or in any way participate in the performance of abortions or sterilizations contrary to the applicant's religious beliefs or moral convictions.

Pregnancy Disability Amendment to Title VII of 1964 Civil Rights Act (PL 95-555). Provided that employers were not required to pay for health insurance benefits for abortion except to save the mother's life, but did not preclude employers from providing abortion benefits.

Public Health Service Act, 1979 Amendments (PL 96-76). Barred recipients of federal funds from denying admission or otherwise discriminating against any applicant for training or study because of the applicant's reluctance or willingness to counsel, suggest, recommend, assist or participate in performing abortions or sterilizations contrary to or consistent with the applicant's religious beliefs or moral convictions.

Budget Reconciliation Act of 1981, Title IX (Health Services and Facilities) (PL 97-35). Allowed grants or payments only to programs or projects that do not provide abortions, abortion counseling or referral, or subcontract with or make payments to any person providing such services, except counseling for a pregnant adolescent if the adolescent and her parents or guardians request such referral.

Appropriations Bills. Since Oct. 1, 1976, appropriations bills for the Department of Health, Education and Welfare (later Health and Human Services) have contained provisions barring the use of Medicaid funds for most abortions. The 1976 amendment barred funding for abortions except to save a mother's life. In subsequent years, funding also was allowed for abortions in cases of rape or incest or when two doctors determined that the woman would suffer serious, long-term physical problems if the pregnancy were carried to term. In June 1981, the ban was tightened again, to cover funding only for abortions to save a mother's life; that restriction has been carried forward to the present.

Other appropriations bills containing abortion restrictions:

Foreign Assistance and Related Programs, fiscal years 1979 and 1982 (PL 95-148, PL 97-121). Barred the use of funds appropriated under the bill for abortions or for lobbying for abortion.

District of Columbia, fiscal 1981 and 1983 (PL 96-530, PL 97-378). Barred federal funding for abortions except to save the mother's life or in cases of rape or incest promptly reported to law enforcement or public health officials.

Department of Defense, fiscal 1982 (PL 97-114). Barred the use of funds in the bill for abortions except to save the mother's life.

Second Continuing Appropriations Resolution, fiscal 1984 (PL 98-151). Prohibited use of federal employee health benefits to pay for abortions except when the mother's life was imperiled.

Roe v. Wade," Packwood said.

Packwood said that S J Res 3 would not solve the abortion dilemma but would "absolutely divide this country for a generation. It is not a plague that should be visited upon this nation."

He added that S J Res 3 would not prevent abortion, but simply drive it underground, where it was before the *Roe* decision. "History proves that women will do anything to rid their bodies of unwanted pregnancies," Packwood said, "and all S J Res 3 will do is restore illegal, unsanitary and lethal backstreet abortions resulting in thousands of deaths to the women, to no benefit of society."

Bill Bradley, D-N.J., said he felt "uneasy as a man determining for women whether they will have the right to a legal abortion, since it is a decision I will never be asked to make."

As if to underscore that point, four women members of the House came to watch the vote: Reps. Geraldine A. Ferraro, D-N.Y., Barbara A. Mikulski, D-Md., Patricia Schroeder, D-Colo., and Olympia J. Snowe, R-Maine.

Sen. Nancy Landon Kassebaum, R-Kan., said she believed abortion "is seldom, if ever, the right moral choice, but it should nevertheless be a choice.

"Many suggest that those who support choice are somehow endorsing abortion as a preferred option," she continued. "This is ridiculous. Abortion is a tragedy which no one is actively promoting."

Edward M. Kennedy, D-Mass., charged that propo-

nents of S J Res 3 often talked of taking "government off people's backs." The amendment, he contended, would "put government into people's bedrooms."

Kennedy also asserted that many proponents of S J Res 3 "have voted consistently against the help and support that can mean fewer abortions. . . . In the name of less government, they turn their backs on proven alternatives to abortion, and then seek to resolve the problem by the most intrusive kind of government of all." ∎

Military Justice Code Revised

A bill revising and streamlining elements of the Uniform Code of Military Justice, the 33-year-old body of law governing the military, was cleared by Congress Nov. 18.

President Reagan signed the measure into law Dec. 6 (S 974 — PL 98-209).

Final action came when the Senate accepted the House version of the bill (S 974). The House had approved the legislation Nov. 16 by voice vote under suspension of the rules.

The Senate Armed Services Committee reported its bill April 5 (S Rept 98-53), while the House Armed Services panel reported the House version Nov. 15 (H Rept 98-549).

Among other things, the bill for the first time gave the Supreme Court direct authority to review certain cases handled by military courts and outlawed, as a matter of military law, various drug offenses already prohibited in civilian life.

Drug Offenses

S 974 prohibited wrongful use, possession, manufacture, distribution, importing or exporting of all drugs illegal in civilian life, including heroin, cocaine and marijuana.

The existing code included no language specifically aimed at drug offenses, an omission which led to litigation over the propriety of using other charges, such as conduct "unbecoming an officer and a gentleman" or action "prejudicial to good order," to reach drug offenses.

Background

The military code was enacted in 1950 (PL 81-506) and amended several times since then, largely to handle procedural problems that arose as the code was being implemented.

The most substantive changes were made when Congress enacted the Military Justice Act of 1968 (PL 90-632). (*Congress and the Nation Vol. I, p. 260; 1968 Almanac p. 639*)

Among other things, the 1968 law created an independent military judiciary, outside the pressure and control of base commanders, that was designed to parallel the civilian judiciary. The 1968 law also required legal counsel and judges in cases where they were not required in the past, and allowed a defendant to be freed pending an appeal of a court martial decision.

Supreme Court Review

The most important provisions of S 974 allowed the Supreme Court to review certain military court decisions. Either party in a case could seek review of a military appeals court ruling, and the high court would have the discretion to accept or reject the case — just as it did with most appeals from civilian courts.

Currently, there was no authority for the court to review decisions by the Court of Military Appeals, the highest court in the military justice system, which was made up of three civilian judges. An accused military person could attempt to get Supreme Court review in a collateral proceeding, a costly and difficult endeavor, but the government had no avenue of appeal from the military appeals court.

The Senate report on S 974 noted that "there is no other major federal judicial body whose decisions are similarly insulated from direct Supreme Court review."

Both the House and Senate reports noted, however, that the military appeals court regularly issued decisions interpreting federal statutes, executive orders and departmental regulations, as well as determining the applicability of constitutional provisions to members of the armed forces.

The Senate committee acknowledged that several justices had expressed concern in the recent past about the Supreme Court's workload. But members said S 974 had been drafted so that only a limited number of cases would qualify for Supreme Court consideration.

For example, cases the Court of Military Appeals declined to review would be ineligible for Supreme Court consideration, and the justices could refuse to review any military case.

Other Provisions

S 974 contained other provisions designed to improve the military justice operations, including those that:

● Formalized the procedure by which staff judge advocates — military lawyers — made detailed written legal determinations concerning charges brought against a military person. The base commander involved in the legal proceeding would still have the authority to determine whether a case should be referred to a general court martial for trial.

● Allowed the "convening authority" for a court martial, normally the base commander, to review a case, but made clear the commander's role primarily involved a determination about whether the sentence imposed by the court should be reduced rather than a formal appellate review. The accused could submit materials to the convening authority and seek to rebut the sentencing recommendation of the judge advocate.

● Permitted the government to appeal rulings by a military judge dismissing charges or excluding important evidence. Currently, no government appeal was available in these matters.

● Provided a procedure for the accused to waive or withdraw an appeal in most cases, except those involving the death penalty. Previously, all cases involving a punitive discharge or confinement for at least one year automatically went to the Courts of Military Review for appellate proceedings. ∎

New Appeals Court

Chief Justice Warren E. Burger early in the year called on Congress to create a temporary new appeals court to help ease the Supreme Court's steadily growing caseload. However, lawmakers took no action on his request in 1983.

In a Feb. 6 speech to an American Bar Association convention in New Orleans, Burger said Congress should create a new court to resolve disputes between federal

appeals courts in the existing 13 circuits — 11 regional circuits, the appeals court for the District of Columbia and the year-old appeals court for the Federal Circuit, which was established primarily to hear patent and trademark disputes.

The chief justice said he envisioned the new court operating for six months to a year while a study commission sought long-range solutions to the Supreme Court's overload. The court would consist of seven or nine judges, to be drawn from a pool of 26 judges, two from each circuit.

"I call on Congress to promptly authorize this panel," Burger said. He told the lawyers: "It will no longer do to say glibly, as some have, that we do not need 'another tier of courts,' or another court, or a change in the structure of appellate procedure at the highest level simply because we have functioned since 1891 with the present structure."

Burger said the high court's load had grown from 1,463 cases and 65 signed opinions in 1953 to 5,311 cases and 141 signed opinions in the 1981-1982 term. In the 1982-83 term, one of the longest and busiest in the court's history, the justices decided 183 cases with 151 written opinions.

Burger noted that a majority of the justices agreed something had to be done to ease the court's workload.

A bill (S 645) incorporating Burger's suggestion was approved June 29 by the Senate Judiciary Courts Subcommittee, but it went no further. ∎

Justice Authorization

The Senate by voice vote Aug. 4 approved a fiscal 1984 authorization bill (S 1192) for the Department of Justice, but the House failed to act on the measure in 1983.

Despite the lack of an authorization bill, funds and operating authority for the department were provided in a fiscal 1984 appropriations measure (HR 3222 — PL 98-166) for the Commerce, Justice and State departments cleared by Congress Nov. 16. *(HR 3222, p. 472)*

As passed by the Senate, S 1192 authorized $3.44 billion for the Justice Department, about $15 million more than President Reagan's request and a shade more than a $3.43 billion House authorization bill (HR 2912) that was reported May 16 by the House Judiciary Committee (H Rept 98-181).

Permanent Authorization

In addition to its annual funding authorization, the Justice Department asked Congress for a permanent authorization for certain activities it said had been hampered by Congress' failure to pass yearly authorization bills. Fiscal 1984 was the fourth consecutive fiscal year that Justice was forced to operate under an appropriations measure, with no formal authorization of its programs.

The fiscal 1983 Justice authorization, for example, passed the Senate, but with a restrictive anti-busing amendment that meant legislative death in the House Judiciary Committee. *(1982 Almanac p. 385)*

The Senate bill provided some of the permanent authority Justice requested, although the House bill did not.

The permanent authority provided in the Senate bill covered such activities as expenses for witnesses, purchase of firearms for some agencies, support for U.S. prisoners housed in non-federal institutions, FBI protection for the president and attorney general, certain Drug Enforcement Administration contracts, and activities of Federal Prison

Industries and the National Institute of Corrections.

House Committee Action

The House bill (HR 2912), as approved May 11 by the Judiciary Committee, included a provision to suspend use of new guidelines that made it easier for the FBI to investigate groups advocating violence for political or social change. The guidelines were implemented in March by Attorney General William French Smith.

Civil liberties groups contended the new guidelines were too broad and could abridge citizens' civil liberties.

The suspension of the guidelines was to begin upon enactment of HR 2912 and last until Jan. 1, 1984. During that time, the committee was to negotiate with Smith and FBI Director William H. Webster on revisions. During the suspension, more restrictive guidelines promulgated in 1976 by Attorney General Edward H. Levi — which were in use prior to the Smith guidelines — were to go back into effect. *(1976 Almanac p. 415)*

Judiciary Chairman Peter W. Rodino Jr., D-N.J., and Don Edwards, D-Calif., chairman of the Civil and Constitutional Rights Subcommittee, had wanted to suspend the Smith guidelines for a year, but they revised that proposal when it appeared they lacked the votes to approve it.

The Senate bill (S 1192), approved May 10, did not include any provisions concerning the Smith guidelines.

The original House bill also included a provision barring the U.S. Secret Service from using the National Crime Information Center computer to track down persons on a Secret Service list — currently 125 names — considered to pose a threat to the president and others entitled to Secret Service protection.

But by voice vote, the committee adopted an amendment by F. James Sensenbrenner Jr., R-Wis., to delete the provision.

Edwards argued that such use of the computer could lead to widespread and unwarranted surveillance of U.S. citizens. But proponents claimed it would help prevent assassination attempts. ∎

Anti-Crime Grant Program

The House May 10 approved legislation creating a new grant program to help states combat crime. Although a similar bill was approved by the Senate Judiciary Committee June 16, there was no further action on the legislation in 1983.

The vote on the House measure (HR 2175 — H Rept 98-68) was 399-16. *(Vote 91, p. 32-H)*

The bill, which authorized funding of $170 million annually for fiscal 1983-86, was essentially the same as one cleared by Congress in 1982 as part of an anti-crime package that was vetoed by President Reagan for unrelated reasons. *(1982 Almanac p. 419)*

Successor to LEAA

The program created by HR 2175 would succeed the old Law Enforcement Assistance Administration (LEAA), an anti-crime grant program created in 1968 that grew into a multibillion-dollar program. By the time it was phased out in 1982, the LEAA had attracted far more congressional enemies than friends. Critics contended that it was wasteful, providing local police forces with Dick Tracy gadgetry instead of helping localities fight crime. *(1982 Almanac p. 378)*

Calling HR 2175 a "modest" initiative, chief sponsor William J. Hughes, D-N.J., told the House the proposed grant program was "a lean and scaled-down operation that would not impose excessive requirements on state and local recipients."

Under the bill, some 80 percent of the total grant money — about $135 million — would be used for block grants distributed to states on the basis of population and crime rate. States would have to provide 50 percent matching funds.

The grants could be used for programs with "a proven record of effectiveness," Hughes said, including community-police anti-crime programs, undercover "sting" operations to recover stolen property, arson and white-collar crime programs.

The House adopted, 401-5, an amendment by Robert S. Walker, R-Pa., adding to the list of eligible programs those aimed at fighting crimes against the elderly. *(Vote 90, p. 32-H)*

To administer the block grants, the bill would establish a new Office of Justice Assistance.

In addition to the block grant program, about $35 million would be available for discretionary grants for multistate and demonstration programs in the area of criminal justice.

The bill also authorized $20 million annually for emergency grants to states and local governments with crime "crisis conditions," such as the 1980-81 investigations into the murders of black children in Atlanta.

Finally, it authorized $25 million annually for the National Institute of Justice and the same amount for the Bureau of Justice Statistics.

Senate Committee Action

The Senate Judiciary Committee approved its own version of the anti-crime grant program (S 53) by voice vote June 16, and the measure was formally reported Sept. 12 (S Rept 98-220).

Like its House counterpart, the measure would create a program of block grants to states, which would have to provide 50 percent matching funds. Federal funds would be distributed essentially on the basis of population and crime rates.   ∎

Record Rentals/Copyrights

The Senate June 28 passed a bill (S 32) aimed at giving record companies and songwriters a greater share of the profits earned by retail stores that rent record albums to their customers. But the measure went no further in 1983.

The bill amended the 1976 Copyright Act (PL 94-553) by prohibiting retail stores from renting record albums without the permission of owners of record copyrights — generally the record company — and of the underlying work — generally music publishers.

The bill was designed to change the "first sale doctrine" in the copyright law under which someone buying copyrighted material had the right to sell or rent it to others. Revising the first sale doctrine would permit record companies to enter into agreements with retail stores for a share of the profits earned from rentals as a condition for permitting the practice to continue.

The bill was sponsored by Sen. Charles McC. Mathias Jr., R-Md., chairman of the Subcommittee on Patents, Copyrights and Trademarks. That subcommittee approved

S 32 on May 26, after adopting an amendment by Sen. Orrin G. Hatch, R-Utah, that required permission of songwriters as well as record companies.

The full committee reported the measure June 23 (S Rept 98-162).

Although a similar bill (HR 1027) was introduced in the House by Rep. Don Edwards, D-Calif., the House Judiciary Committee took no action on it.   ∎

Anti-Tampering Bill Clears

Congress Sept. 30 cleared and sent to President Reagan a bill (S 216 — PL 98-127) making it a federal felony to tamper with consumer products such as drugs, food and cosmetics.

Final action came when the Senate by voice vote adopted a compromise version worked out by the House and Senate Judiciary committees. The House had approved the compromise by voice vote Sept. 29.

The two chambers had approved separate bills May 9 that differed in some of their details.

Tylenol Tragedy

Congress acted one year after seven people in the Chicago area died from taking Extra-Strength Tylenol capsules that had been laced with cyanide. That tragedy, and a rash of copycat incidents elsewhere with less severe consequences, not only prompted the current legislation but also led drug companies and manufacturers of other consumer products to develop tamper-resistant containers.

A bill similar to S 216 cleared Congress in 1982, but it was part of a larger anti-crime package vetoed by President Reagan for unrelated reasons. *(1982 Almanac p. 419)*

Product tampering was a crime under existing federal food and drug laws, but those laws did not cover as wide a range of activities as S 216.

Under current law, it was a misdemeanor to adulterate a food, drug or cosmetic. It was a felony, punishable by a three-year prison term, a $10,000 fine or both, only if there was an intent to defraud.

S 216 also included an unrelated provision extending the patent protection for an anesthetic called "Forane." A wide-ranging patent extension bill that would have covered the drug died in the last Congress. *(1982 Almanac p. 400)*

Provisions

As cleared by Congress, S 216 included the following provisions:

● Made it a felony to tamper with a "consumer product that affects interstate or foreign commerce," or any label or container of such a product, with "reckless disregard" of the risk of injuring a person.

● Made it a felony to attempt to tamper with a consumer product, label or container of such product with reckless disregard of the risk of injuring a person.

● Provided for a fine of up to $100,000, any term of years in prison or life, or both when death resulted from tampering.

● Provided for a fine of up to $100,000, a prison term of up to 20 years or both when serious bodily injury resulted from tampering.

● Provided for a fine of up to $25,000, prison for up to 10 years or both for an attempt to tamper.

● Made it a felony to taint any consumer product or make the label of the product false or misleading with an

intent to damage the reputation of the business involved. (This provision was not in the original House bill.)

• Provided for a fine of up to $10,000, a prison term of up to three years or both for the crime involving damage to a business reputation.

• Made it a felony to "knowingly" falsely claim that a consumer product had been tainted.

• Provided for a fine of up to $25,000 and a prison term of up to five years or both for the false-claim offense.

• Extended patent protection for an anesthetic called "Forane" to cover the time the drug was under review by federal regulatory agencies and not marketable.

House, Senate Committee Action

The Senate Judiciary Committee approved S 216 by voice vote April 12 and formally reported it May 2 (S Rept 98-69).

A similar but not identical measure (HR 2174) was approved by the House Judiciary Committee by voice vote April 26. That bill was reported May 9 (H Rept 98-93).

Both measures made it a felony for anyone to tamper with drugs, food, cosmetics or other consumer products.

House, Senate Floor Action

The House and Senate May 9 approved their respective anti-tampering bills.

Although the bills had the same basic thrust, they differed in certain details.

The House measure (HR 2174) was approved under suspension of the rules by 292-0. *(Vote 86, p. 32-H)*

The Senate bill (S 216 — S Rept 98-69) was approved by voice vote.

Both bills made it a federal crime to tamper with drugs, food and cosmetics as defined by the federal Food, Drug and Cosmetic Act. If death resulted from such tampering, both bills provided for a $100,000 fine, any term of years in prison or life, or both. When serious bodily injury resulted, the Senate bill provided for 20 years in prison, a $50,000 fine or both, while the House bill called for a $100,000 fine, a prison term of 20 years or both.

The House bill required that the offender "knowingly" tamper with a covered product. The Senate bill stated that any person "with intent" to kill, injure or endanger another could be found in violation of law. But S 216 defined intent to include instances when the person knows or "has reason to know" that his conduct could kill or injure a person.

House staffers contended that this amounted to a negligence standard, which they believed was not appropriate for the crimes covered under the bill.

The Senate bill specifically provided for a crime of tampering with the intent to damage a business entity, while the House bill did not include such language.

The Senate measure also included an unrelated amendment by Judiciary Chairman Strom Thurmond, R-S.C., extending patent protection for the anesthetic "Forane" to cover time the drug was under review by federal regulatory agencies and not marketable. ∎

Drug Treatment Program

The House May 9 passed a bill (HR 2173 — H Rept 98-87) to reauthorize for three years a program of drug abuse treatment and monitoring for convicted federal offenders released on parole or probation.

However, the measure went no further in 1983.

The House vote, which came under suspension of the rules, was 275-8. *(Vote 85, p. 32-H)*

The drug program was first authorized by Congress in 1966 (PL 89-793) and had been extended periodically since then. *(Background, 1978 Almanac p. 210)*

Program participants regularly were tested and monitored, largely through urinalysis, to determine if they were using drugs.

A measure similar to HR 2173 was included in an anti-crime package that cleared Congress in 1982 but was vetoed by the president for unrelated reasons. *(1982 Almanac p. 419)*

As passed by the House, HR 2173 authorized $5 million for fiscal 1984, $5.5 million for fiscal 1985 and $6 million for fiscal 1986. ∎

Insanity Defense Revisions

A bill overhauling the federal insanity defense was approved by voice vote Nov. 1 by the House Judiciary Committee, but did not reach the House floor in 1983.

The measure, reported Nov. 21 (HR 3336 — S Rept 98-577), was similar but not identical to insanity-defense provisions in an omnibus anti-crime bill reported Aug. 4 by the Senate Judiciary Committee. *(S 1762, p. 315)*

As approved by the House committee, HR 3336 required a defendant seeking acquittal on grounds of insanity to prove "by a preponderance of the evidence" that he met the legal test for insanity. Under current law, a prosecutor had to prove "beyond a reasonable doubt" that the defendant was sane when he committed a crime.

The bill also changed the federal legal test for insanity. Supporters claimed the new definition was more precise than the current one, while opponents contended it would wreak havoc on the legal system by casting doubt on case law developed under the existing test.

Background

Although members of Congress and many in the legal profession had urged changes in the law for years, there was little movement until a federal court jury's June 21, 1982, acquittal of John W. Hinckley Jr., who was found not guilty by reason of insanity in the March 30, 1981, shooting of President Reagan and three other men. *(1982 Almanac p. 418)*

That verdict provoked a public uproar and brought numerous calls for change in the insanity defense.

On Jan. 19, 1983, the American Psychiatric Association (APA) urged tightening of the defense to protect the public against premature release of potentially dangerous individuals. The APA, which represented about 28,000 psychiatrists, suggested that psychiatric testimony be restricted to an evaluation of a defendant's mental condition, stopping short of conclusions about whether the person was sane according to legal standards, could tell right from wrong, or could control his actions.

On Jan. 27, two committees of the American Bar Association (ABA) jointly recommended restricting the defense. The full ABA later supported in principle HR 3336 and the Senate provisions.

Changing the Test

A key part of HR 3336 was a change in the legal test for insanity. Current law provided that a person could be

considered insane if he suffered from a "mental disease or defect" and as a result was unable to conform his conduct to the law or to appreciate the wrongfulness of his act.

HR 3336 defined insanity as "a severely abnormal mental condition that grossly and demonstrably impaired the defendant's perception and understanding of reality." The defendant would have to prove that, as a result of such a mental condition, he was unable to appreciate the wrongfulness of his act.

According to chief sponsor John Conyers Jr., D-Mich., chairman of the Criminal Justice Subcommittee, the new language was recommended by the American Psychiatric Association. "In other words," Conyers said, "the shrinks are for it."

George W. Gekas, R-Pa., led the opposition to the new test, arguing that it was too broad. "It is an adventurous foray into the unknown," he said.

E. Clay Shaw Jr., R-Fla., echoing Gekas' concerns, said he worried that a person "filled with great hate" who killed someone and thought he was doing the country a favor could use the new definition to win an acquittal.

Shaw, Gekas and several other members argued that the new language would render meaningless court decisions interpreting existing law, creating problems in the legal system.

Chairman Peter W. Rodino Jr., D-N.J., retorted that if such reasoning prevailed, "Congress would never make a change in the law" because to do so might require new court decisions.

Gekas sought to return to the current "mental disease or defect" test, but his amendment lost 10-19.

The Senate bill kept the "mental disease or defect"

language of current law, as well as the provision concerning a defendant's ability to appreciate the wrongfulness of his conduct. However, it eliminated the part of the current test concerning a defendant's ability to conform his conduct to the law.

Bill McCollum, R-Fla., offered an amendment to strike the insanity defense from federal law and instead add provisions allowing a court to determine whether the defendant had the mental state — such as an intent to kill — required as an element of the crime. If the defendant were found not guilty, McCollum said, he could be committed to an institution. The amendment was rejected 12-19.

Other Provisions

HR 3336 provided a new verdict in cases in which insanity was proved — "not responsible only by reason of insanity."

The bill also set forth new procedures for committing to an institution persons found not responsible only by reason of insanity or incompetent to stand trial and not likely to recover.

While all states had commitment procedures, there was no federal commitment law covering those acquitted by reason of insanity.

HR 3336 included a provision to allow psychiatrists to testify about medical issues in a case but prevent them from offering opinions on whether the defendant appreciated the wrongfulness of his conduct, possessed the mental state required as an element of the crime, or should be committed if found not responsible.

An amendment by Harold S. Sawyer, R-Mich., to strike this provision was rejected by voice vote. ∎

Anti-Crime Package Stalls in Senate Again

The Senate Judiciary Committee July 21 approved an anti-crime package designed to deal with problems ranging from sentencing disparities to labor racketeering.

The measure (S 1762), the fifth omnibus anticrime bill approved by the panel in a decade, was ordered reported by a 15-1 vote. Charles McC. Mathias Jr., R-Md., cast the single "no" vote.

The measure was reported Aug. 4 by the Judiciary Committee (S Rept 98-225) and Sept. 20 by the Foreign Relations Committee (S Rept 98-241), which made technical amendments to one title of the measure dealing with extradition of persons sought by other countries.

Although S 1762 was a slimmed-down version of past anti-crime proposals and included only relatively uncontroversial provisions, the legislation did not reach the Senate floor in 1983. Its supporters were unable to obtain a time agreement for its consideration because some senators wanted assurances they would have a chance to debate more controversial crime bills, particularly legislation to restore the death penalty for certain federal crimes.

The House Judiciary Committee, traditionally leery of omnibus crime bills, took no action on HR 2151, a measure similar to S 1762.

Search for Consensus

During Senate committee deliberations, Sen. Joseph R. Biden Jr., D-Del., one of the cosponsors of S 1762, explained the rationale for the consensus package.

"We've learned that the only way to get action is to

agree on what we agree on and move on it, and fight over what is left," Biden said.

He added that he and the other cosponsors, Chairman Strom Thurmond, R-S.C., Paul Laxalt, R-Nev., and Edward M. Kennedy, D-Mass., would resist amendments on the Senate floor that they thought would damage the compromise worked out by the panel.

On July 26, the panel approved four more controversial measures as separate bills. These dealt with drug enforcement (S 1787), the death penalty (S 1765), *habeas corpus* petitions (S 1763) and the "exclusionary rule" barring use in criminal trials of illegally obtained evidence (S 1764).

Background

Congress cleared an omnibus anti-crime bill in 1982 that overlapped in some respects with S 1762, but it was vetoed by President Reagan largely because of administration opposition to creation of a central drug enforcement office dubbed the "drug czar." *(1982 Almanac p. 419)*

In 1983, the drug czar provision was one of the four controversial measures approved separately.

Reagan March 16 sent Congress his own wide-ranging anti-crime package that included a number of controversial proposals such as restoration of the death penalty, easing of the "exclusionary rule" barring use at trial of illegally obtained evidence, and reform of *habeas corpus*, a procedural tool used by prisoners to win release.

The administration proposals also covered a number of

areas addressed in S 1762, including bail and sentencing reform.

Major Provisions: S 1762

As approved by the Judiciary Committee, S 1762 contained 12 separate titles including the following:

Bail Reform

This section permitted a judge to detain before trial a defendant deemed to pose a danger to the community. Under current law, a judge could jail a defendant before trial only after determining there was a real likelihood the person would flee.

A separate bail reform bill (S 215) with the same pretrial detention provision was approved by the committee May 10 and reported May 25 (S Rept 98-147).

But it, too, went no further in 1983.

Sentencing Reform

This title created a commission to write sentencing guidelines for federal judges to use in imposing sentences.

The guidelines were intended to eliminate the widespread disparity that currently existed in sentencing for similar crimes. Under the bill, judges were required to explain in writing any departure from the sentencing guidelines. A defendant could appeal any sentence harsher than the guidelines, while the government could appeal any sentence that was more lenient.

Three Mathias amendments designed to give judges greater flexibility in writing and imposing the guidelines were rejected by votes of 2-15, 3-14 and 3-13. A fourth Mathias amendment that would have added a sentence stating that the new sentencing scheme was not intended to lengthen existing sentences nor dramatically increase the prison population was rejected 1-15.

Under an agreement worked out among Judiciary members, the sentencing provisions of the omnibus bill also were approved as a separate measure (S 668) that was reported Aug. 4 (S Rept 98-223).

Forfeiture of Crime Proceeds

Title III of the bill expanded the federal government's authority to require forfeiture of profits and proceeds from organized crime enterprises and narcotics trafficking. One provision allowed forfeiture of substitute assets where the precise assets sought had been removed from the reach of the government.

Like the sentencing provisions, this foreiture section also was approved as a separate bill (S 948 — S Rept 98-224) and reported Aug. 4.

Insanity Defense

This title limited the insanity defense to those defendants who could prove, by clear and convincing evidence, that they were unable to appreciate the wrongfulness of their acts.

Under current law, once a defendant pleaded not guilty by reason of insanity, the prosecutor bore the burden of proving beyond a reasonable doubt that the defendant did not meet the existing legal test of insanity.

S 1762 shifted the burden of proof from the prosecutor to the defendant, who would have to prove his insanity by clear and convincing evidence.

The section also barred psychiatric experts from testifying on whether the defendant had a particular mental

disease or defect. Howell Heflin, D-Ala., sought to strike this provision, but his motion was rejected 2-12.

The House Judiciary Subcommittee on Criminal Justice approved an insanity bill (HR 3336) June 16 that included a definition of insanity almost identical to the Senate's, but it required the defendant to prove his insanity claim only by a preponderance of the evidence — a lesser test than the "clear and convincing" evidence standard in S 1762. *(Insanity defense, p. 314)*

Efforts to rewrite the insanity defense law were prompted by a federal court jury's June 21, 1982, acquittal of John W. Hinckley Jr., who was found not guilty by reason of insanity in the 1981 shooting of President Reagan and three other men. *(1982 Almanac p. 418)*

Justice Assistance

This section created a program of financial assistance for state and local law enforcement agencies to help finance programs that had proved effective. It amounted to a vastly scaled-down version of the now-defunct Law Enforcement Assistance Administration.

The House passed a similar bill (HR 2175) May 10, 399-16. *(Vote 91, p. 32-H; Anti-crime grants, p. 312)*

Labor Racketeering

This title raised from five to 10 years the period of time a union official convicted of corruption could be barred from union or trust fund positions. The bar was to take effect on the date of conviction rather than the date all appeals were exhausted.

Violent Crime Amendments

This section included 13 separate changes in various federal laws. Among them were provisions that:

Solicitation. Created the crime of "solicitation" to commit a crime of violence, which covered a person who tried to persuade another to commit a crime of violence.

Mandatory Minimum Sentences and Firearms. Provided mandatory minimum sentences for using a firearm in the commission of federal crimes.

Kidnapping Federal Officials. Provided new penalties for kidnapping specified federal officials and for crimes directed at the family members of specified federal officials.

Extradition. Revised the procedures for extraditing foreign criminals found in the United States.

Similar legislation was passed by the Senate and approved by two House committees in the 97th Congress, but it stalled short of the House floor when a coalition of religious and civil liberties groups mounted a lobbying campaign against it. *(1982 Almanac p. 411)*

Sen. Arlen Specter, R-Pa., offered an amendment to require that a federal magistrate find "probable cause" that the person to be extradited had committed a crime in his home country. This was standard procedure for domestic criminal cases, but Thurmond said the Justice Department strongly opposed the amendment, and he persuaded Specter to withdraw it for the time being.

Specter said he would try to work out new language with the department but promised to offer the amendment on the Senate floor if no agreement was worked out.

Specter also wanted to clarify the circumstances under which bail could be granted to persons arrested awaiting extradition. But he agreed to withdraw this amendment to discuss the matter with Justice.

An extradition bill (HR 3347) similar to the provisions

in S 1762 was approved Oct. 4 by the House Judiciary Committee.

The House bill sought to meet most of the concerns of the groups that opposed the 1982 measure, although both the State and Justice departments were unhappy with the language.

The major controversy over the 1982 bill involved protection of persons who claimed they were being sought by their own countries for "political offenses," and therefore should not be extradited.

Under the new House bill, a political offense was defined to exclude any serious offense involving an attack against "internationally protected persons," an offense covered by a treaty that obligated the United States to extradite a person accused of such offense, specified narcotics violations, forcible sexual assault, and "intentional, direct participation in a wanton or indiscriminate act of violence with extreme indifference to the risk of causing death or serious bodily injury" to persons not taking part in armed hostilities.

By a vote of 16-15, the committee adopted an amendment of Robert W. Kastenmeier, D-Wis., that allowed persons about to be extradited to seek judicial review in a federal court. The person would have to allege that he would be subjected to political, racial, nationality-based, sexual or religious persecution if returned to the country seeking his extradition.

Under current law, federal courts had not rejected extradition requests because of human rights concerns. Judges had said in opinions that there could be circumstances in a case that so shocked a court that extradition would be denied, but no such case had yet appeared.

Kastenmeier noted this country had extradition treaties with about 100 other nations, some of which "lack fundamentally fair legal procedures in some instances. . . . I do not quarrel with the law enforcement needs that motivate agreements with these countries," he said. "On the other hand, I am concerned about the potential abuse of our legal system that would be caused if we honored political requests by a repressive regime."

Other Bills

Four other controversial bills, on which there was no consensus, were approved by the Senate panel July 26:

Drug Czar

Although the Justice Department opposed creating a central office for drug enforcement, the committee Aug. 4 voted 12-5 to report this bill (S 1787 — S Rept 98-278). Thurmond, who voted against the measure, told his colleagues they were "spinning their wheels," because the administration would never accept the bill.

But Specter, who supported the measure, said he believed it was worth pursuing the proposal because Attorney General William French Smith, the center of the opposition, might be won over.

Dennis DeConcini, D-Ariz., offered an amendment to S 1762 July 21 to create a select commission on drug enforcement to study how enforcement efforts could be coordinated better. The cosponsors asked DeConcini to withdraw the amendment because they feared it could lead to an eventual veto if it was part of S 1762. DeConcini refused and the amendment failed, 6-8.

The House Judiciary Committee approved a separate drug czar bill (HR 4028) by voice vote Oct. 4.

Although HR 4028 had the support of some Republicans on the Judiciary Committee, Hamilton Fish Jr., R-N.Y., told his colleagues he believed they were making a futile effort. He said he was convinced that even if the House and Senate agreed on another "drug czar" bill, the president "is sure to veto it."

The House bill did not create any new office but rather increased the power of the existing director of the Office of Drug Abuse Policy, which was created when the Drug Abuse Prevention, Treatment and Rehabilitation Act was enacted in 1972. *(1972 Almanac p. 162)*

The bill made the director of the drug office a Cabinet-level position. The president could appoint the vice president to head the office or he could select another person, who would have to be confirmed by the Senate.

The new director would establish federal policies and priorities for combating drug abuse and would have authority to review the annual budgets of the agencies, such as the Drug Enforcement Administration and the U.S. Coast Guard, that were involved in drug control activities. The director could make recommendations to the president on the budgets for such agencies before they were submitted to Congress.

The Senate bill created a brand new anti-drug office and did not give the head of the office the kind of budgetary control the House bill envisioned.

Death Penalty

This measure (S 1765 — S Rept 98-251), ordered reported 13-4, would establish constitutional procedures as mandated by the Supreme Court for imposing the death penalty in certain homicide, treason and espionage cases and in cases involving attempts to assassinate the president.

The bill was virtually identical to a measure approved by the committee in 1981. *(1981 Almanac p. 419)*

Those voting against the bill were Biden, Kennedy, Mathias and Patrick J. Leahy, D-Vt.

Habeas Corpus

This bill (S 1763 — S Rept 98-226), approved 12-5, set out more restrictive federal procedures for looking at state prisoners' claims that they had been imprisoned in violation of their constitutional rights. A time limit was established for filing state appeals in the federal courts.

Max Baucus, D-Mont., offered an amendment to make the new proposal less stringent and allow more federal court review, but his proposal was rejected 7-10.

Exclusionary Rule

Approved 10-6, this bill (S 1764) created an exception to the "exclusionary rule," a longstanding Supreme Court rule that barred the introduction at trial of evidence that was obtained illegally. The exception allowed use of evidence obtained by officers acting with a reasonable, good-faith belief that their conduct was legal.

The Supreme Court in 1983 was expected to endorse or reject the "good faith" modification, but the court sidestepped the issue and resolved the case before it on other grounds. *(Illinois v. Gates, p. 6-A)*

It did agree, however, to consider the exclusionary rule anew in its 1983-84 term. The justices heard arguments in January 1984 on four exclusionary rule cases — two involving search-and-seizure issues and two concerning the use of evidence obtained as a result of improper questioning of suspects. ∎

Child Pornography Bill

Both the House and Senate passed bills to toughen federal child pornography laws, but they failed to resolve differences between the two measures before Congress adjourned for the year.

A bill (HR 3635) to toughen the federal law against the production and distribution of pornographic materials involving children was passed by the House Nov. 14 under suspension of the rules.

The vote was 400-1, with Ted Weiss, D-N.Y., casting the lone "nay." He said he thought the bill was too broad. *(Vote 459, p. 134-H)*

HR 3635 had been approved Oct. 4 by the House Judiciary Committee and was formally reported Nov. 10 (H Rept 98-536).

The Senate passed its own child pornography bill (S 1469) by voice vote July 16.

That measure was reported June 29 by the Senate Judiciary Committee (S Rept 98-169).

House, Senate Bills Compared

Like the Senate bill, the House measure raised from 16 to 18 the maximum age of children protected, removed an existing requirement that sexually explicit materials depicting children be "obscene" before they were banned,

and prohibited the production of child pornography regardless of whether it was commercially disseminated.

The House bill raised the fine for a first offense from $10,000 to a maximum of $100,000, while the Senate bill's maximum was $75,000. For a second offense, the House raised the maximum from $15,000 to $200,000, while the Senate's maximum was $150,000.

The House bill prohibited reproduction of child pornography for distribution through the mails or in commerce. And it authorized the Justice Department to seek court-ordered wiretaps in child pornography cases.

The House bill was limited to visual materials and did not cover written matter. A 1982 Supreme Court decision held that visual material depicting children did not have to meet the legal definition of "obscenity" to be banned, while print material did. *(1982 Almanac p. 10-A)*

HR 3635 also excluded from coverage simulations of sexual activity if there was "no possibility of harm to the minor, taking into account the nature and circumstances of the simulation, and there is redeeming social, literary, educational scientific or artistic value."

S 1469 fined organizations up to $250,000. Neither existing law nor the House bill included this provision. Unlike the House bill and current law, the Senate bill required anyone convicted of sexually exploiting children to forfeit the assets used in producing the pornographic material and the profits accumulated from it. ∎

Bills on Bankruptcy Issues, Courts Stalled

Congress failed to pass legislation in 1983 to reform the nation's bankruptcy court system or to make substantive changes in bankruptcy law, despite action on a variety of proposals.

The Senate April 27 passed a bill (S 1013) designed to put the bankruptcy courts on a sound constitutional footing, but the measure was never considered by the House.

Included in S 1013 and also approved as separate legislation (S 445) was a proposal to make it harder for individuals to declare bankruptcy and start their financial lives anew.

Both Senate measures also contained provisions involving shopping center bankruptcies and grain elevator bankruptcies.

A House bill (HR 3) that took a markedly different approach to the bankruptcy court problem was approved by the House Judiciary Committee but lodged in the Rules Committee, where it got tied up with a House version (HR 1800) of the consumer bankruptcy legislation.

Also caught in the impasse were proposals in both chambers to increase the number of U.S. district court and appeals court judges in the other branches of government.

Background

Congress had struggled with the bankruptcy court issue ever since the Supreme Court on June 28, 1982, declared unconstitutional the court system created under a wide-ranging 1978 bankruptcy reform law. *(1982 Almanac pp. 389, 12-A)*

In that law, Congress authorized bankruptcy judges to hear not only straightforward bankruptcy matters but also a myriad of other civil issues that a bankrupt party might raise. *(1978 Almanac p. 179)*

The court held that Congress had given bankruptcy judges too much power and too little independence from other branches of government. Unlike district and appeals court judges, who were appointed for life at irreducible salaries under Article III of the Constitution, the bankruptcy judges were Article I judges appointed by the president for 14-year terms at salaries that in theory could be reduced by Congress.

The court gave Congress until Dec. 23, 1982, to resolve the court problem. When the 97th Congress failed to act, the U.S. Judicial Conference, the policy-making arm of the federal judiciary, issued an interim rule for handling bankruptcy cases that remained in effect throughout 1983.

Interim Rule Adopted

Essentially, the rule allowed bankruptcy judges to continue to handle all matters that clearly involved bankruptcy issues. Any other legal disputes between the parties involved in a bankruptcy case would be handled by federal district court judges.

Some bankruptcy practitioners were unhappy with the interim rule and challenged it in the federal courts. At year's end, according to the Administrative Office of the U.S. Courts, 16 district courts and five appeals courts had upheld the rule. Three district court judges found some parts of the rule invalid and a fourth judge invalidated the entire rule. Those cases were appealed.

House Committee Action

Subcommittee Action

On Feb. 10, the House Judiciary Committee's Monopolies and Commercial Law Subcommittee approved HR 3.

The measure created a new bankruptcy court network with 227 judges appointed for lifetime terms.

The new judges would be phased in over a two-year period, with no more than 75 appointed by the president and confirmed by the Senate in the first year.

The bankruptcy judges would be on the same constitutional footing as federal district court judges. However, their pay under the subcommittee bill would be $69,500; district court judges earned $73,100.

House Judiciary Chairman Peter W. Rodino Jr., D-N.J., the sponsor of HR 3, had long been an advocate of a separate bankruptcy court whose judges would have lifetime appointments. Rodino favored that approach in 1978, but did not have enough support to push the proposal through Congress.

Rodino was at odds with the Judicial Conference and with Chief Justice Warren E. Burger, who wanted bankruptcy matters heard by regular district court judges. The conference proposed legislation creating bankruptcy administrators in each of the 94 federal judicial districts to handle uncontested cases. Federal district judges would hear contested matters.

In the Judiciary subcommittee, where Democrats held a 9-5 edge, Rodino had no trouble Feb. 10 winning approval of HR 3 and fending off two amendments he did not like.

However, Rodino did compromise with Harold S. Sawyer, R-Mich., on the pay issue. The bill as introduced set the judges' annual salary at $65,000. Sawyer sought to give bankruptcy judges $73,100, the same pay as district court judges, on the ground that they would have similar constitutional standing. After some debate, Rodino proposed a compromise at $69,500, and the panel agreed by voice vote.

As approved, HR 3 did not allow bankruptcy judges to be transferred into the district courts to hear other kinds of cases.

Rep. Henry J. Hyde, R-Ill., offered an amendment that would have allowed bankruptcy judges to be reassigned to other cases if the chief judge of the bankruptcy court certified that the loss of the judge would not result in delays in bankruptcy cases.

Rodino and Sawyer successfully opposed the amendment, saying it was important to send a signal that bankruptcy judges were going to be appointed just to hear bankruptcy cases.

Hyde argued that his proposal would put judicial manpower where it was needed in the federal system. Adopting the HR 3 approach, he contended, was like sitting in a crowded restaurant and being told by a passing waitress, "Sorry, that's not my table."

By 6-8, the subcommittee rejected an amendment by Hamilton Fish Jr., R-N.Y., that would have allowed immediate appointment of all 227 judges. Fish said that if bankruptcy dockets were crowded, there was no reason to delay the appointments.

Full Committee Action

The full Judiciary Committee approved HR 3 Feb. 15 by a 24-6 vote that came after a contentious three-hour meeting. The measure was reported Feb. 24 (H Rept 98-9, Part I).

Because it involved a salary increase for bankruptcy judges, the bill was referred to the House Appropriations Committee. That panel was discharged from consideration March 18 because it failed to act on HR 3 within the required deadline.

During the markup, Reps. Robert W. Kastenmeier, D-Wis., and Thomas N. Kindness, R-Ohio, offered amendments that would have created only 94 new tenured judges for bankruptcy matters. Their proposals were rejected by voice vote.

Kastenmeier said that 94 new judges — one for each judicial district — would be sufficient to handle bankruptcy matters. He said that most bankruptcy cases were uncontested and could be handled by administrative personnel.

But Rodino and Don Edwards, D-Calif., opposed Kastenmeier's proposal. Edwards said it would bifurcate the bankruptcy system, which was exactly what the 1978 reform legislation sought to avoid. That law permitted all matters relating to bankrupt parties to be heard in one proceeding, even if some of the claims involving the parties did not directly concern the actual bankruptcy.

As he had in subcommittee, Fish offered an amendment to appoint all 227 judges at once. Fish said that if the judges were appointed in the piecemeal fashion contemplated in the bill, the Supreme Court could once again invalidate the system because some current non-tenured judges would continue to serve for up to two years.

The Fish proposal was rejected 12-19. William J. Hughes, D-N.J., and 11 Republicans voted "aye."

Sawyer then offered an amendment he said was designed to encourage the president to appoint existing bankruptcy judges to the new Article III positions.

The amendment, which was rejected 13-18, would not have counted in the quota of 75 bankruptcy appointments per year any existing judge who was reappointed under the bill.

Hyde reoffered his subcommittee amendment to allow a bankruptcy judge to shift to other federal courts upon certification by the district court that the judge was needed and a separate certification from the bankruptcy court that the transfer would not delay bankruptcy business.

The amendment was rejected by voice vote.

Entangled With Consumer Bankruptcy Bill

After the Appropriations Committee was discharged from considering HR 3, the measure went to the House Rules Committee, where it remained for the rest of 1983.

While the bill did not move, it nonetheless generated considerable activity. A group of some 200 House members tried for months to make sure that a consumer bankruptcy bill (HR 1800) could be attached as an amendment to HR 3 if the bill ever came to the floor.

Rodino was adamant in his opposition to HR 1800, which made it more difficult for consumers to declare bankruptcy and start fresh financially. But one congressional staffer said that if the Rules panel had drafted a rule precluding consideration of HR 1800, there was "no way in hell" such a rule could win adoption, given the backing for the consumer bill.

HR 1800 allowed a bankruptcy judge to dismiss or suspend a consumer bankruptcy case if the judge decided it would be a "substantial abuse" of the bankruptcy system to allow the bankruptcy to go forward.

The bill was designed to require consumers who were able to pay off their debts to work out a court-approved plan to do so instead of simply canceling them and starting over.

HR 3 had one other serious problem in addition to the consumer bankruptcy issue: the House Democratic leadership was not eager to give President Reagan an opportunity to appoint so many new judges.

Judicial Conference Opposition

Quietly, but consistently, the Judicial Conference opposed HR 3. At one point, the conference, through its legislative affairs office, put together an inch-thick "battle book" — as one congressional staffer called it — to document its position.

The conference asserted that the separate court approach of HR 3 was expensive and unneccessary, arguing that the bulk of bankruptcy work was routine and did not require a judge.

The argument was bolstered by 1983 statistics on bankruptcy cases compiled by the Administrative Office of the U.S. Courts. Those figures showed that less than 2 percent of contested bankruptcy proceedings required the attention of a district court judge.

In 98 percent of the cases, the attorneys involved determined that there were no ancillary legal issues that warranted the use of a district court judge.

New Alternative

On June 8, a bipartisan group of House members introduced a new proposal to reform the bankruptcy courts, hoping to break the impasse over HR 3.

The new bill (HR 3257) was introduced by four Republicans, including Minority Whip Trent Lott, Miss., and two Democrats. It generally followed the Judicial Conference rule and was similar to the Senate's bankruptcy court bill.

HR 3257 gave overall authority for bankruptcy matters to the district court judges. They could refer bankruptcy matters to bankruptcy judges and keep for themselves the cases that included legal issues in addition to bankruptcy. The bankruptcy judges would be appointed by the 12 regional federal appeals courts rather than by the president, as was the case under current law and under the Senate bill.

In an effort to ease overloaded dockets, HR 3257 also created 52 new district court judgeships and 24 appeals court positions. (The Senate bill called for 51 new district judges and 24 appeals court positions.)

In addition to Lott, the other sponsors were Kindness, F. James Sensenbrenner Jr., R-Wis., Bill McCollum, R-Fla., Kastenmeier, and Sam B. Hall Jr., D-Texas.

The sponsors of HR 3257 never expected the bill to be considered by the Judiciary Committee. Instead, they simply wanted the Rules Committee to make it in order as a substitute for HR 3 once that bill was sent to the full House.

But they found themselves in the same boat as backers of HR 1800, the consumer bankruptcy bill — stuck at Rules, which showed no eagerness to act.

Individual Bankruptcies

The consumer-bankruptcy issue was fleshed out somewhat by a General Accounting Office (GAO) report studying the impact of the 1978 law on the number of bankruptcies. The report was released July 25.

Both Rodino and Mike Synar, D-Okla., chief sponsor of HR 1800, found support for their positions in the report.

Rodino asserted July 25 that the study, requested by him on June 10, 1981, showed the bankruptcy law changes "cannot be blamed for a two-year rise in personal bankruptcies. . . . The GAO report found that increased personal bankruptcies were the result of the general downturn in the nation's economy, high inflation and unemployment, recession and overextension of consumer credit."

But Synar in a "Dear Colleague" letter July 26 said the report's conclusions "again demonstrate the need for bankruptcy reform." He specifically cited a finding that "one out of five debtors seeking to discharge all of their debts had incomes in excess of $20,000 per year, and 83 percent were gainfully employed."

Senate Committee Action

The Senate Judiciary Committee March 22 approved compromise legislation (S 1013) to restructure bankruptcy courts. The measure was formally reported April 7 (S Rept 98-55).

New District, Appeals Court Judges

As approved by the committee, the measure also created 51 new U.S. District Court judgeships and 24 new U.S. Circuit Court of Appeals judgeships to relieve overloading in the federal courts. This section was recommended by the Judicial Conference.

HR 3257, the late-starting compromise bill in the House, created 52 new district court judgeships and 24 appeals court positions.

The Senate committee voted 14-1 to report the bill. Sen. John P. East, R-N.C., was the lone dissenter. He said he had no objections to the bankruptcy reforms but opposed the creation of additional district and appeals court judgeships.

East contended that the federal courts were overloaded only because judges had been "too activist" and Congress "has failed to put any restraint on their insatiable and unlimited appetite for involving themselves in areas they ought not be involved in."

Bankruptcy Courts

In contrast to HR 3, the Senate committee decided to keep the bankruptcy judges in their present status, appointed under Article I of the Constitution by the president for 14-year terms. In theory, their salaries could be reduced by Congress.

The bill called for 229 bankruptcy judges who would be adjuncts of the U.S. district courts. District court judges could recall at will any bankruptcy case from the bankruptcy court. A district court judge would be required to take back any part of a case involving ancillary legal issues, as opposed to clear-cut bankruptcy matters, whenever one of the litigants requested the transfer.

In addition, any non-bankruptcy issue that was solely a matter of state law could be referred to a state court for resolution upon request of one of the parties or at the direction of the district judge.

Proponents of the Senate version said their scheme was workable, contending that it was possible to separate bankruptcy matters from other legal issues in a case, such as a contract dispute or antitrust claim. Proponents also contended that relatively few bankruptcy cases involved non-bankruptcy matters that would require the attention of a district court judge.

The Senate bill was a compromise worked out by Chairman Strom Thurmond, R-S.C., and Sen. Howell Heflin, D-Ala., and was similar to legislation the Judicial Conference had proposed in the fall of 1982.

The compromise managed to attract a majority of senators unhappy with both the Rodino approach and with a more recent Judicial Conference proposal (S 443) spon-

sored by Sen. Robert Dole, R-Kan., chairman of the Courts Subcommittee.

The Dole bill would have created 115 new district court judges to handle contested bankruptcy cases. The judges could handle all other types of federal cases as well. Bankruptcy administrators would be created in each judicial district to handle uncontested bankruptcy cases.

The Dole proposal drew enemies from two sides. Some Republicans — particularly East, who had been critical of federal courts since coming to Congress — did not want to create so many new Article III judges. Democrats did not want to give Reagan so many judgeships and were even more concerned that a group of conservative, business-oriented judges would be appointed for bankruptcy matters but still could hear other types of cases, such as civil rights issues.

Consumer Bankruptcy

On April 19, the Senate Judiciary Committee approved compromise legislation on the consumer bankruptcy issue.

The bill (S 445) also included provisions covering grain elevator and shopping center bankruptcies.

The measure was approved by voice vote and with no discussion. Details of the compromise, which was put together by Sens. Dole and Howard M. Metzenbaum, D-Ohio, had been circulated to committee members the previous week.

The credit industry had been lobbying for more than a year for legislation to tighten the consumer bankruptcy law, which was enacted as part of 1978 reform legislation.

Industry spokesmen said the 1978 law permitted consumers to declare bankruptcy when they actually could pay off many of their debts.

The industry originally was pushing legislation to exact payment for debts from a person's future income after he filed for bankruptcy. A bill including this provision was reported by the Judiciary Committee in the 97th Congress, but it was never considered by the Senate because Metzenbaum threatened a filibuster. *(1982 Almanac p. 391)*

The "future income" provisions were opposed vigorously by consumer groups and some bankruptcy specialists, who said they undermined the very purpose of the bankruptcy law.

Dole was pushing the "future income" provision again in the 98th Congress, but to avoid a prolonged fight, he yielded to Metzenbaum and worked out a compromise.

The compromise had two parts. First, when a person filed for bankruptcy under Chapter 7 of the code, a "trustee" would be appointed by the court to administer the estate. The trustee would be required to tell the debtor what options were available under the bankruptcy code. However, the trustee was not supposed to pressure the debtor into taking one avenue or another.

The second part of the compromise allowed a bankruptcy judge, on his own motion, to dismiss a Chapter 7 bankruptcy case when he determined that allowing a debtor to cancel his debts would amount to "a substantial abuse" of the bankruptcy code.

Fran Smith, a spokesman for the National Coalition for Bankruptcy Reform, a group of creditors, said the coalition was satisfied with the compromise, although creditors preferred the tougher original bill. Smith said the provisions in S 445 at least would allow consumers to make more informed decisions about how to restructure their financial lives and would let a judge deny straight bankruptcy if he believed such action were unwarranted.

Shopping Center Bankruptcies

The shopping center provisions in S 445, which were pushed by Orrin G. Hatch, R-Utah, were designed to protect the financial interest of shopping center owners and tenants when a tenant went bankrupt.

Similar legislation was passed by the Senate in 1982 but died in the House. *(1982 Almanac p. 390)*

The key provision required the administrator of a bankrupt tenant's estate to decide within 60 days whether to keep the lease in question, assign it, or let it revert to the shopping center owner, who could then find a new tenant. The 60-day limit could be extended for good cause.

The bill also was reported May 4 as a separate measure (S 549 — S Rept 98-70), but that version did not pass the Senate in 1983.

Grain Elevator Bankruptcies

Dole was the prime mover behind the grain elevator bankruptcy provisions, which expedited procedures for handling bankruptcies involving grain elevators.

The bill was intended to help farmers recoup their investment if a grain elevator operation holding their grain became insolvent.

The Senate passed a similar bill in 1982, but the measure was blocked in the House by Judiciary Chairman Rodino. *(1982 Almanac p. 395)*

Drunken Driving, Time-Share Units

Another provision of S 445, requested by John C. Danforth, R-Mo., barred a person from discharging through bankruptcy proceedings debts incurred as a result of a drunken driving incident.

A fourth section of the bill was designed to protect those who bought time-shared units in developments that subsequently went bankrupt.

Senate Floor Action

By voice vote April 27, the Senate approved the bankruptcy court and consumer bills.

Sen. Jesse Helms, R-N.C., had threatened to tie up the court bill with 11 amendments designed to bar or restrict the federal courts from hearing a variety of legal matters such as busing, school prayer and prisoner appeals. But he withdrew his amendments because he said Reagan had given him assurances that his administration planned its own initiatives for cutting back federal court jurisdiction.

Floor Amendments

Only four changes were made from the Judiciary Committee versions of the bills:

● The consumer bill (S 445) was included by voice vote as an amendment to the court bill (S 1013).

● By voice vote, a Thurmond amendment was adopted providing an additional 10 district court judges, bringing the total number to 61.

● By voice vote another Thurmond amendment was adopted that kept bankruptcy judges' salaries at their current level of $63,600. Salaries could not be increased without specific approval from Congress.

● By voice vote an amendment by Ted Stevens, R-Alaska, was adopted to provide expedited bankruptcy procedures for fishermen who sold their fish to processors whose operations went bankrupt.

Legal Services Corporation Survives Again

The embattled Legal Services Corporation (LSC) survived once again in 1983, despite the continued efforts of the Reagan administration to abolish the agency.

Funding for the corporation was included in the Commerce, Justice, State appropriations bill (HR 3222 — PL 98-166) cleared by Congress on Nov. 16. *(HR 3222, p. 472)*

Although the LSC survived, its operations had to be reduced signficantly because its funding had been slashed 14 percent since fiscal 1981.

The corporation's fiscal 1984 appropriation was set at $275 million, $34 million above the fiscal 1983 level of $241 million. But in fiscal 1981, the last year of President Carter's administration, the agency had received $321 million. *(Background, 1982 Almanac p. 412)*

LSC Board Members

In addition, leadership of the agency in 1983 was in the hands of people who wanted tight controls on the activities of LSC lawyers. At year's end only four of the 11 slots for the LSC board of directors were filled. This was a sufficient number to conduct business, however.

All four board members were appointed by President Reagan during congressional recesses in 1983 and were not confirmed by the Senate. They were Robert E. McCarthy, a San Francisco lawyer, chairman; Milton Masson, a businessman; Donald E. Santarelli, a lawyer who served in the Nixon administration Justice department; and Ronald B. Frankum, a telecommunications consultant. As recess appointees, they could serve through the 1984 session.

Although Reagan nominated 11 members for the board in the fall, none was confirmed by the Senate during 1983 and the nominations died at the end of the session.

Background

The LSC survived since 1979 because of the appropriations process. Its authorization — congressional approval of basic agency programs — ran out in 1979, and no new one was enacted in the succeeding four years despite efforts in both chambers.

The LSC, which distributed grants to local legal aid programs, had been controversial since its inception, with proponents arguing that the poor had a right to the full panoply of legal services available to those who could pay for their own lawyers. Opponents contended over the years that legal services lawyers were more interested in social change than in helping the poor with their legal problems. *(Background, 1977 Almanac p. 587; 1974 Almanac p. 489)*

Opponents were particularly irritated by class action suits brought against government entities on behalf of groups of poor people. They also resented what they believed to be illegal lobbying activities by LSC lawyers.

Both of these issues were debated extensively as legislation involving the LSC was considered during 1983.

Provisions

As cleared by Congress, HR 3222 included not only funding for the LSC but a number of provisions relating to the agency's operations. The most significant of these:

● Barred virtually all lobbying activities by lawyers except on behalf of an eligible client and with specific approval of the director of the LSC-backed program involved. Any lobbying activity, such as writing a letter or making a phone call, would have to be within guidelines established by the particular program.

Under current law, LSC lawyers were permitted to respond to requests for information from legislators or government officials and to lobby on behalf of the corporation's authorization or appropriation.

● Retained current law provisions spelling out the classes of aliens who were entitled to legal representation through the corporation.

The original House bill and a Senate authorization proposal backed by Sens. Thomas F. Eagleton, D-Mo., and Edward M. Kennedy, D-Mass., had expanded the types of aliens who would be entitled to legal aid.

● Barred the use of LSC funds for conducting training programs that dealt with political advocacy. Training programs designed to teach legal skills, such as those needed by paralegals, would still be permitted.

● Retained a provision in current law barring any shifting of money among LSC programs by a governing board whose members had not received Senate confirmation.

● Altered the funding formula for the 326 legal services programs across the country so that each program received at least a 5 percent hike over its fiscal 1983 level.

● Retained language from the first fiscal 1984 continuing appropriations resolution (H J Res 368 — PL 98-107) providing that compensation for LSC board members could not exceed the highest daily rate for a GS-15 federal employee, plus travel expenses in accord with government regulations. The bill also barred reimbursement of LSC board members and employees for membership dues in private clubs. *(PL 98-107, p. 526)*

House Judiciary Committee Action

Subcommittee Approval

Rep. Robert W. Kastenmeier, D-Wis., the agency's chief proponent in the House, began 1983 with the intention of moving an LSC authorization bill.

On May 2, his House Judiciary Subcommittee on Courts, Civil Liberties and Administration of Justice unanimously approved a bill (HR 2909) to reauthorize the LSC for three years.

The measure provided $296 million in fiscal 1984 and such sums as might be necessary for fiscal 1985 and 1986.

Republicans led by Carlos J. Moorhead, Calif., sought to tighten restrictions on lobbying activities by lawyers in LSC-funded programs. The subcommittee could not agree on any new provision, but Kastenmeier deleted temporarily a provision in the bill that allowed lawyers in specified circumstances to communicate with local, state or federal legislators on legislative matters.

Full Committee

The House Judiciary Committee approved HR 2909 May 12 after reversing a vote to cut the agency's budget from the level sought by sponsors.

The bill was approved 23-6, but the sizable margin reflected members' support for the concept of the legal services program rather than their support for the bill's

specific provisions. Extended debate during five hours of markup revealed sharp differences on several issues.

The bill was reported (H Rept 98-201) May 17.

As approved by the committee, HR 2909 provided $296 million for fiscal 1984 and "such sums as necessary" for fiscal 1985 and 1986 — the subcommittee levels.

The fiscal 1984 recommendation also was the amount in the first House concurrent budget resolution (H Con Res 91) approved March 23, and the amount in a Senate LSC reauthorization bill (S 1133) that was pending in the Senate Labor and Human Resources Committee.

The agency, which by law submitted its budget request directly to Congress without review by the Office of Management and Budget, had asked for $257 million in fiscal 1984.

During House committee debate May 11, Dan Glickman, D-Kan., said $296 million was too much for the LSC. Proponents of the higher funding level said the money was necessary to provide legal services adequately.

By a 16-14 vote, the committee adopted Glickman's amendment to authorize $268 million in fiscal 1984, $281 million in fiscal 1985 and $295 million in fiscal 1986.

Four other Democrats — William J. Hughes, N.J., Sam B. Hall Jr., Texas, Romano L. Mazzoli, Ky., and Jack Brooks, Texas — joined Glickman and the committee's 11 Republicans in supporting the amendment.

The vote left chief sponsor Kastenmeier and Chairman Peter W. Rodino Jr., D-N.J., disappointed. After the markup, Rodino asked Hughes to reconsider his vote.

When the committee reconvened May 12, Hughes asked the panel to reconsider the funding issue, and by voice vote, members agreed to restore the subcommittee authorization level of $296 million.

Hughes said Rodino told him he wanted the Judiciary Committee to be consistent with the Appropriations subcommittee and with the budget resolution. Hughes said he agreed to accommodate his fellow New Jersey Democrat but would support a House floor effort to cut the funding.

Lobbying Restrictions

Democrats, who held a 19-11 majority on the committee, overrode Republicans on the issue of lobbying by lawyers in LSC-funded programs.

By a 12-18 vote, the committee rejected a proposal by Moorhead to prevent LSC lawyers from talking to legislators except in response to requests for information. A similar restriction was contained in the second continuing funding resolution for fiscal 1983 (PL 97-377), which provided the agency's funding through Sept. 30. *(1982 Almanac p. 238)*

Hall, a longtime LSC critic, was the only Democrat to vote with the Republicans.

After rejecting the Moorhead proposal, the committee adopted by voice vote a Kastenmeier amendment to broaden existing law. It allowed lawyers to contact state, local or federal legislators concerning authorizations, appropriations or oversight of LSC programs. It also permitted "direct legislative representation" for an eligible client if the LSC-funded program had a policy concerning lobbying, kept records on the amount of time spent lobbying and for what reason, and if the project director approved of the lobbying.

In a bipartisan 18-11 vote, the committee also accepted a Kastenmeier amendment on representation of aliens that broadened existing law. One of its main provisions permitted legal services for illegal aliens asking the government

for asylum. The legal aid provided would cover only the work involved in the application process.

The Kastenmeier proposal was a substitute for a more restrictive Mazzoli proposal.

HR 2909 went to the House Rules Committee following the Judiciary markup, and it remained there for the rest of 1983.

Senate Action

No LSC authorization bill emerged from the Senate Labor and Human Resources Committee, even though several proposals were under discussion by the panel.

The members were split over the LSC, with most of the Democrats and Republican Lowell P. Weicker Jr., Conn., supportive of the agency, while other Republicans, led by Orrin G. Hatch, Utah, looked for ways to curtail lawyers' activities.

Lobbying Probe Requested

The committee held hearings July 12 and 15 focusing on allegations that LSC employees in 1980-82 had misused LSC funds to lobby Congress on behalf of the corporation.

On July 19, Hatch and Jeremiah Denton, R-Ala., both critics of the LSC, asked the Justice Department to investigate the alleged illegal lobbying and other possible improprieties.

On the same day, LSC President Donald P. Bogard sent corporation officials to its nine regional offices with orders to secure documents relating to LSC activities from 1980-82. LSC spokesman Sherrie Miller Bass said some of the records would be brought to Washington. Bass said that in light of the Hatch-Denton request for an investigation, Bogard "decided the files needed to be in a central location for that investigation."

During the July 12 hearing, former LSC President Dan Bradley, now in private practice in Miami, called the allegations of misuse of funds "a bunch of regurgitated crap."

Kastenmeier also contended Hatch and Denton were reviving old charges. "We had that testimony ourselves," Kastenmeier said, referring to hearings his subcommittee held in 1981 and 1983. "It is not new. It is unworthy of all this publicity."

But Hatch insisted his committee's investigation had turned up new evidence of improper use of funds. "We have documents coming out of the woodwork on a daily basis in this area," he contended. "There is more to it than Bradley was indicating."

During the Labor sessions, which drew few Democratic members or staffers, Hatch and Denton sought to document allegations that Legal Services money was improperly used for a range of lobbying activities, particularly after Reagan announced his desire to abolish the agency.

Hatch and Denton said their inquiries were based on documents compiled by committee investigators that showed a coordinated lobbying effort by LSC workers and outside organizations, such as the National Client Counsel and the National Legal Aid and Defender Association.

Bradley said that while some of the documents the committee referred to should not have been written, they were being taken out of context.

"The question is very simple," Bradley added in the interview.

"Were employees permitted to lobby members of the U.S. Congress in support of our authorization and appropriation? I think the answer is unquestionably 'yes.'"

Reagan Nominees

On Oct. 7, Reagan nominated a slate of 11 people for the LSC board. Three of them drew almost immediate criticism from supporters of the corporation: Michael B. Wallace, 31, a Mississippi lawyer who was a clerk for Supreme Court Justice William H. Rehnquist and then an aide to House Minority Whip Trent Lott, R-Miss.; Robert A. Valois, 45, a labor lawyer from Raleigh, N.C., who practiced in the same law firm as Thomas F. Ellis, a close friend and political consultant for Sen. Jesse Helms, R-N.C.; and LeaAnne Bernstein, 33, a Baltimore lawyer who was an aide to LSC President Bogard.

Shortly after Reagan announced his nominees, one of them — Henry Y. Chavira, an El Paso businessman — asked that his name be withdrawn from consideration because of personal legal problems.

Confirmation Hearings

The Senate Labor Committee Nov. 2 held a five-hour hearing on six of the nominees — Wallace, Valois, Bernstein, and Robert F. Kane, 57, a Redwood City, Calif., lawyer who was a former judge; William C. Durant III, 32, a Detroit lawyer, and Claude G. Swofford, a lawyer from Pittsburg, Tenn., who was active in Republican Party politics.

Most of the questioning focused on Wallace, Valois, Bernstein and Kane.

Under existing law, board members were required to disqualify themselves from making decisions involving persons with whom they had a business interest in the previous two years. Questioned about this by committee Democrats, Bernstein said legal opinions from the Justice Department and the LSC stated that her appointment would not violate that provision.

Sen. Howard M. Metzenbaum, D-Ohio, said he would ask the research arm of the Library of Congress to render a separate opinion.

Kane drew questions because he was on the board of trustees of the Pacific Legal Foundation, a conservative public interest legal organization similar to the Mountain States Legal Foundation, which Interior Secretary James G. Watt once headed.

Kane said he had no plans to step down from the legal foundation if confirmed for the LSC board and told senators he saw no conflict of interest in serving both organizations.

Democrats sharply questioned Wallace and Valois about their past legal work, trying to learn how it would affect their LSC stewardship.

Both nominees said they believed in legal services for the poor and that their political philosophies would not interfere with their board work.

When he worked for Lott, Wallace took an active role in opposing elements of a bill to extend and strengthen enforcement sections of the 1965 Voting Rights Act. Congressional sources also contended that Wallace and Lott encouraged the administration to change the Internal Revenue Service (IRS) policy of denying tax exemptions to private schools that practice racial discrimination.

Wallace would not say whether he wrote a letter to administration officials concerning the tax exemption policy, but he said he believed administration officials were right in arguing that without specific congressional authority, the IRS could not deny tax exemptions to schools solely because of their discriminatory policies. The Supreme Court, however, ruled to the contrary May 24. *(p. 10-A)*

Congressional sources contended further that Wallace helped Lott intervene in 1981 to stop a Justice Department investigation into Mississippi jails.

At the hearing, Sen. Thomas F. Eagleton, D-Mo., produced a photocopy of an unsigned letter to the Justice Department on Lott's stationery with Wallace's initials on it. The senator asked Wallace if he wrote the letter. During a heated exchange with Eagleton and Metzenbaum, Wallace refused to say whether he wrote the letter, claiming that to do so would violate his confidential relationship with Lott.

Valois was questioned extensively about his labor work, particularly his representation of a group of employees of J. P. Stevens Co., the textile giant, who were opposed to efforts to unionize Stevens' workers. Valois denied that he was engaged in "union-busting" and contended it would be a "distortion" to say that his practice focused on helping businesses keep unions out of their shops.

The four remaining nominees were Annie Marie Gordon, 50, a mother of 19 children (15 of them living) who operated a community center in Flatonia, Texas; Pepe J. Mendez, 38, a Denver lawyer who worked for President Reagan's election; Paul Eaglin, 35, a Fayetteville, N.C., lawyer, and Bernard Bloom, 57, a judge of the Surrogate Court of Kings County, N.Y.

No hearing was held on their nominations. ∎

Constitution's Bicentennial

Congress Sept. 14 cleared for President Reagan a bill (S 118 — PL 98-101) creating a 23-member commission to plan and conduct a national celebration marking the 200th anniversary of the drafting and ratification of the U.S. Constitution and Bill of Rights.

The presidentially appointed commission, which was to include members recommended by all three branches of government, was given two years to submit to the president, Congress and the Judicial Conference of the United States a report containing specific recommendations for commemorating the 1987 bicentennial of the approval in convention of the Constitution, the nation's basic governing document.

As cleared, S 118 authorized expenditures of $300,000 in fiscal 1983 and "such sums as may be necessary" in subsequent fiscal years.

The commission was to be terminated effective Dec. 31, 1989.

S 118 was reported April 28 by the Senate Judiciary Committee (S Rept 98-68), and passed by voice vote July 18.

The House passed the bill Aug. 4 after adopting several relatively minor amendments, and the Senate cleared it for Reagan's signature Sept. 14. It was signed Sept. 29. ∎

Environment/Energy

In a year when President Reagan's two top environmental appointees, Anne M. Burford and James G. Watt, resigned under withering congressional fire, the environment emerged as a major bone of contention between Congress and the White House.

Day after day, in hearing rooms crowded with TV cameras, House members aired charges that Environmental Protection Agency (EPA) officials led by Burford had been lax in enforcing hazardous waste laws, made "sweetheart deals" with polluters, stood to profit from conflicts of interest, manipulated toxic cleanup grants to influence elections, shredded papers subpoenaed by Congress, and used political "hit lists" to terminate science advisers and civil service employees who disagreed with the Reagan philosophy of rapid deregulation.

None of those charges was prosecuted by the Reagan Justice Department, so no legal test of their validity was available. The only EPA official to be charged in the scandal was Rita M. Lavelle, former head of the "superfund" hazardous waste cleanup program, who was found guilty by a federal jury Dec. 1 of lying under oath before three congressional subcommittees about conflict of interest. She was sentenced to six months in prison and fined $10,000. Lawyers for Lavelle said she had been made a "scapegoat." Chairmen of some of the congressional panels called the Justice Department report on its decision not to prosecute others a "whitewash."

EPA Administrator Burford became the center of the firestorm Dec. 16, 1982, when the House cited her for contempt of Congress. She had refused, on written orders from Reagan and legal advice from the Justice Department, to turn over documents subpoenaed by a House subcommittee.

The administration began to cut Burford adrift in early March 1983, when the Justice Department said it would not defend her against the contempt charge. With anonymous White House sources describing her as a political liability and key congressional Republicans calling for her replacement, she resigned March 9.

Reagan quickly named EPA's first administrator, William D. Ruckelshaus, to succeed her. Ruckelshaus, highly regarded for both policy judgment and personal integrity, was unanimously confirmed by the Senate May 17.

Watt's Downfall

Interior Secretary Watt also met his downfall in 1983. There was growing criticism of his policies, with charges that Watt was engaged in a massive "giveaway" of public resources to private interests. Coal leases, offshore drilling rights, grazing rights, water rights, mineral rights, timber contracts and even title to public lands themselves were under Watt's stewardship.

But Watt's abrasive personality proved a greater liability than his policies. Bitter and personal feuding between Watt and key members of the House Interior Committee had broken out as early as 1981. That year, Watt said: "I never use the words Democrats and Republicans. It's liberals and Americans."

In 1983, Watt continued his string of public relations disasters — for example, banning the popular Beach Boys singing group from the capital's 1983 Fourth of July celebration, saying they attracted "the wrong element." Among their staunchest fans was first lady Nancy Reagan.

And on Sept. 21, 1983, Watt offended four major voting groups in as many seconds by calling members of a coal leasing advisory commission "a black ... a woman, two Jews and a cripple." It proved to be the last gaffe.

Republican senators, worried that Watt might prove to be a millstone around their own necks as well as Reagan's in 1984, deserted him in droves. Facing a Senate "no confidence" vote, Watt finally resigned Oct. 9.

To replace him, Reagan named his trusted national security adviser, William P. Clark, who was confirmed by the Senate on Nov. 18, the final day of the session.

Energy Policy: Reconsidering Past Moves

In the sphere of energy policy, Congress spent most of 1983 reconsidering old decisions rather than undertaking new initiatives.

The year's major development was a decision to halt the Clinch River breeder reactor project, once hailed as the solution to the nation's energy problems. With only one dissenting vote, the House repealed language authorizing the Oak Ridge, Tenn., project. The Senate later voted to refuse additional funding to the breeder reactor, apparently dooming it.

The Clinch River project was intended to demonstrate that "fast breeder" reactors that produced nuclear fuel even while they consumed it to make electricity were a feasible means of generating power for commercial use. Over the years, however, the project fell victim to long delays, sharply rising costs and a flattening of the nation's demands for electric power.

Clinch River in recent years had survived congressional tests by ever-narrowing margins. By 1983, those margins vanished and Congress pulled the plug on the project.

The other important energy issue before Congress was a proposed overhaul of the 1978 Natural Gas Policy Act. Despite months of hearings and committee markup sessions in both chambers, no definitive action was taken.

A natural gas bill did reach the Senate floor late in the session, but members soundly rejected competing proposals to phase out all remaining federal price controls on natural gas or, alternatively, retain existing controls and roll back prices to August 1982 levels.

The legislation remained in limbo at year's end, with no break in sight to the impasse.

Environment Policy: A Power Struggle

The administration for three years had taken Reagan's 1980 election as a mandate to ease or undo scores of pollu-

tion control regulations that industry had complained were excessive, costly and burdensome. At the same time, the Interior Department under Watt swept aside protests from conservationists and pushed forward energy and mineral development on public lands, hoping to reduce the nation's strategic vulnerability to foreign sources.

But many of the same voters who applauded Reagan's promise to get regulatory agencies "off the backs" of the people apparently still wanted government to play an activist role when it came to protecting public health. Legislators felt strong pressure from voters to keep or strengthen environmental controls, especially on toxic substances.

With oil and coal supplies generally exceeding demand during 1983, there was also growing concern that the Treasury would not get a fair return for the resources by selling so many leases on a "soft" market.

The Reagan administration tried several times to test the basic legal and constitutional powers used by Congress to influence environmental policy. And Congress flexed its muscles too, demonstrating the power of the purse, of the contempt of Congress statute, of advice and consent on executive appointments, and of overseeing agency actions.

Even after the smoke had begun to clear, however, there was little certain evidence of change in policies or institutions; only the people had changed for sure.

Some environmentalists conceded that under Ruckelshaus, EPA had begun enforcing environmental laws with more vigor than it had under Burford. But it was not clear whether Ruckelshaus had the leeway to pursue his course over the objections of the Office of Management and Budget, which had final say over many important EPA actions.

If abuses were shown in the EPA hearings, Congress did not write laws correcting them in 1983. Congress fought most of the year's environmental battle not with its legislative power but with its oversight power — the power to investigate how its laws were being enforced, to subpoena witnesses, hold hearings and generate publicity.

Strategically, that made sense for the Democrats and environmentalists; without a veto-proof two-thirds majority in both chambers, Democrats could not work their will.

But if Democrats chose to fight on the front pages and nightly news, Republicans might have checked them there. At least, Republicans partly succeeded in defining the issue in terms of personalities rather than policies, in terms of criminal wrongdoing rather than doing the right thing, in terms of management style rather than management goals. Simply by removing the faces and names that were becoming too painfully familiar on the nightly news, the Reagan administration by year's end pushed the environment issue out of the limelight.

Little New Legislation

While Congress played an unusually active role in overseeing executive branch actions on the environment, it enacted no major new authorizing legislation in 1983. In the most ambitious undertaking, the House passed a bill to tighten and reauthorize the law controlling disposal of hazardous wastes, but the Senate did not act before adjourning.

Most of the half-dozen major environmental laws were due, or even overdue, for overhaul and reauthorization. Congress continued to appropriate money to carry out the laws on a year-to-year basis. The pollution control requirements of those laws stayed in effect.

The inaction was seen by many environmentalists as a victory of sorts. The Reagan administration came into office vowing to ease many of the strict requirements of existing laws. That drive was forestalled, at least in Congress, after three years that might have offered industry its best opportunity to change laws to its liking.

Reagan did, however, achieve much of what he wanted by concentrating on the administrative arena, where his powers were far less fettered, and the issues were usually too technical to invite much public attention.

Perhaps the most fundamental charge made during the EPA scandal of 1983 was that the Reagan administration was failing to carry out the nation's environmental laws. But Reagan's critics found it far easier to identify violations of the spirit of the law than of its letter. In many of the environmental bills Congress moved forward in 1983, it narrowed the leeway and discretion given to the executive branch in carrying out existing law.

Congress Asserts Powers

The biggest environmental decisions Congress made in 1983 were wrapped inside the appropriations bills for EPA and the Interior Department. The fiscal 1984 appropriation for EPA reversed a steady Reagan-era decline in the agency's budget but left it well short of where it had been at the end of the Carter administration.

Congress gave Reagan more money than he wanted for Interior Department conservation programs, and less than he wanted for energy development. And by the time the Interior appropriation cleared, it had blocked some of Watt's major policy initiatives — on coal leasing, offshore drilling, public land sales, wilderness development and other questions.

The Senate in 1983 also played a more active role in reviewing Reagan's environmental appointees than it had in 1981, when it confirmed Burford and Watt.

The Senate got what it wanted in Ruckelshaus, a man with a reputation for saying "no" to presidents, but even so, members of the Environment Committee questioned him carefully at confirmation hearings.

William P. Clark got a more rigorous going-over than Ruckelshaus, partly because his nomination came as a complete surprise to key Senate Republicans. Unable to get any policy commitments from Clark during confirmation hearings, Senate Democrats tried to bring up a sense of the Senate resolution denouncing Watt's Interior policies before allowing the Clark confirmation vote. The effort was killed, 48-42, but a sizable contingent, almost all Democrats, had volunteered some "advice" to go along with their "consent."

As a test of Congress' constitutional powers, the 1983 contempt confrontation was inconclusive. Burford was the highest executive branch official ever cited for contempt by Congress, although Watt had come close to winning that distinction for himself in 1981 and 1982.

But the Justice Department refused to prosecute Burford. The issue of whether such prosecutions were mandatory under law was never settled, and neither was the conflict between Congress' investigative power and the president's "executive privilege" to withhold information. A compromise between the White House and key House Democrats simply finessed such questions.

—By Joseph A. Davis

Clark Replaces Watt at Interior Department

Interior Secretary James G. Watt on Oct. 9 became the second top-level Reagan administration environmental official to resign under fire in 1983.

Although his pro-development natural resource policies long had angered environmental groups and their supporters in Congress, it was Watt's penchant for politically damaging remarks that finally led to his downfall.

The president, in a surprise move, named his national security adviser, William P. Clark, to succeed Watt. The choice was announced Oct. 13, and the Senate confirmed Clark's nomination Nov. 18 by a vote of 71-18. (Vote 369, p. 60-S; Clark profile, p. 330)

Watt resigned his Cabinet post rather than face an almost certain no-confidence vote in the Republican-controlled Senate, where his support had ebbed steadily over the two and a half weeks preceding his Oct. 9 announcement.

His resignation came nine months to the day after Anne M. Burford was forced to quit as administrator of the Environmental Protection Agency. (Story, p. 332)

Watt Resignation

When Watt was named secretary of the interior in 1981, he told Reagan that he would have to "back me and back me and back me, and when he could no longer back me, he'd have to fire me...."

In his resignation letter to the president Oct. 9, Watt began, "The time has come."

"It is my view that my usefulness to you in this administration has come to an end," Watt told Reagan.

Watt's resignation was forced by a political furor that erupted following an off-the-cuff remark he made in a Sept. 21 speech to a Chamber of Commerce audience in Washington, D.C.

In that speech, Watt characterized his appointees to a special commission on federal coal leasing policies as "a black ... a woman, two Jews and a cripple."

It was by no means the first of Watt's casual remarks to kick up a storm, but this one, which managed to offend four key voting blocs within as many seconds, proved to be the last.

Negative reaction mounted steadily despite Watt's apology to his appointees and to the president. Only with difficulty did Senate GOP leaders stave off a Senate vote on a resolution urging Reagan to fire Watt.

Senate Republicans had begun to desert Watt even before the Sept. 21 remark. On Sept. 20 Watt lost a key vote on a coal leasing moratorium, 63-33, although the Senate had backed him narrowly in two previous votes on the same question. (Vote 244, p. 41-S; background, p. 350)

What stampeded Senate Republicans was concern that with an election year nearing, Watt was damaging not only the president but their own political prospects as well.

"There are other Republicans in this country who deserve to be protected," said Sen. Robert Dole, R-Kan. "We want to retain the Senate majority [in 1984].... We just can't stand, every two or three months, Mr. Watt making some comment to offend another 20 or 30 or 40 million people."

As one GOP senator after another denounced Watt, the White House publicly stood behind him. The president made clear he had no intention of firing his embattled appointee, and when Watt finally quit, Reagan accepted his resignation "reluctantly."

Watt's Role: Lightning Rod

Watt understood from the beginning the role he was cast to play as point man for the Reagan administration's environmental policies and a lightning rod to divert the thunderbolts of wrath those policies provoked from environmentalists.

"He's of a combative nature," said Rep. Manuel Lujan Jr., R-N.M., the ranking minority member of the House Interior Committee, who had been viewed as a leading contender to succeed Watt.

"He enjoys a good fight. I could see it in committee all the time," Lujan said. "When you got the real opposition to him that were calling him names and really getting tough on him, you could just see him raise himself up on the chair, ready to do battle."

Watt's resignation quenched the flames of controversy that swirled around his speaking style and political personality, but it appeared unlikely to reverse the course of administration natural resource policies.

"I leave behind people and programs," Watt wrote to Reagan in his resignation letter, "a legacy that will aid America in the decades ahead."

Watt had uprooted the legacy of the Carter administration at his department. Scores of officials, both political appointees and civil service, were fired or transferred and replaced with what he called "good people," those who shared his mission. Virtually every major Interior Department program was reorganized or reoriented. The buffalo on the departmental seal was even shifted to face right instead of left.

Watt sought to tilt the balance in federal resource policy away from environmental protection, which Reagan felt had received too much emphasis in the previous decade, and toward resource development, which the president felt was being slowed to a dangerous degree by federal regulation.

As head of the Interior Department, Watt controlled more than a fifth of the nation's land — and with it vast reserves of oil, gas, coal, minerals, metals, water, timber, grazing lands, fish and wildlife breeding and feeding grounds, recreation areas, historic sites and just plain natural wonders.

The Watt-Reagan goal of "unlocking" some of those resources so that oil and mining companies, cattlemen, loggers and other developers could make use of them won early cheers in the West, where the economy was based on those resources and where the federal government's role as the dominant landlord had conflicted with traditions of personal freedom.

Watt also won plaudits from conservatives, who liked his commitment to free-market economic theory, his opposition to government regulation, and the zeal with which he lambasted liberals and environmentalists.

Both of these constituencies were important elements in the voting coalition that brought Reagan victory in 1980. The White House encouraged Watt to take time for political fence-mending and fund-raising missions out West, but polls showed that even Watt's Western support was slipping.

Relations With Congress

Although his appointment was controversial, Watt was confirmed 83-12 by the Senate on Jan. 22, 1981. *(1981 Almanac p. 17-A)*

In the Senate, Watt faced committees predisposed to cooperate with his agenda. Both the Energy Committee and the Appropriations Subcommittee on Interior were dominated by members from Western or energy-producing states and chaired by James A. McClure, R-Idaho, who shared many of the administration's policy goals.

Watt faced the opposite situation in the Democratic-controlled House, where Interior Committee Chairman Morris K. Udall, D-Ariz., and Rep. Sidney R. Yates, D-Ill., chairman of the Appropriations Subcommittee on Interior, usually leaned as far toward resource conservation as Watt did toward resource development.

Predictably, his relations with House panels were as bitter as his Senate relations were cordial.

Watt did have a few successes on Capitol Hill. A bill he proposed to tighten collection of federal oil and gas revenues sailed through Congress in 1982 with bipartisan support. And he joined environmentalists in supporting a 1982 barrier islands protection measure, partly because a withdrawal of federal subsidies for those areas could save the Treasury hundreds of millions of dollars. *(1982 Almanac p. 436, 446)*

But for most Watt legislative initiatives, especially those central to the administration's policy thrusts, congressional response was lukewarm.

Congress did not directly block his aggressive five-year offshore oil and gas leasing plan, but various appropriations bills were riddled with riders exempting specific coastal areas from leasing.

The Senate twice narrowly upheld his coal leasing program, only to halt it on the third go-round.

Congress went along with Watt's budget proposals for abolishing the Heritage Conservation and Recreation Service, but not those calling for a halt to federal park land acquisition and elimination of the urban parks program and historic preservation funding.

Water Projects

Reagan and Watt also drew congressional fire, just as President Carter had, over the issue of water projects. That fight was not just over whether to build dams, but over who decided to build them — Congress or the executive.

Congress went along with Watt's proposal to abolish the Water Resources Council, the key executive branch water policy center under Carter, and to establish his own Office of Water Policy within Interior.

But Watt's near-promises of more water projects to Westerners raised expectations that he could not fulfill. Budget-cutters in the Reagan administration insisted new projects could be funded only if local and state beneficiaries financed a larger share of construction costs. That drew an April 27, 1983, protest letter from 15 Western Republican senators saying Reagan could harm his 1984 election chances by appearing "anti-West" and "anti-water."

Congress, in the fiscal 1984 energy and water appropriations bill (HR 3132 — PL 98-50), rejected all of the Reagan-proposed new starts, again asserting its own prerogative to decide water spending priorities. To drive home the point, the House Oct. 6 passed a supplemental appropriations bill (HR 3958) funding 43 water projects of members' own choosing. That measure was still pending in the Senate at year's end. *(Water appropriations, p. 520; authorization, p. 354)*

Wilderness Leasing

Early in his tenure, Watt also tramped on congressional toes over the issue of oil and gas leasing in national wilderness areas. Under a 1964 law, these undeveloped, roadless lands were formally designated by Congress to be set aside forever in their undeveloped state as an ecological reserve.

Environmentalists raised an outcry when they intercepted an internal May 7, 1981, memo from Watt to his top aides listing as one of his key goals to "open wilderness areas."

Conservationists wanted to protect, among others, three already designated wildernesses in Montana, including the Bob Marshall, where oil and mineral companies had 343 lease applications pending.

The House Interior Committee fired a warning shot on May 21, 1981, when it approved, largely along party lines, a resolution invoking little-used "emergency" powers under federal law to withdraw the Montana lands temporarily from leasing.

That confrontation was only the opener in a complicated power struggle over wilderness leasing.

The battle soon shifted to the question of a moratorium on leasing in all wilderness areas. The House backed such a ban strongly in a series of legislative actions, but the Senate balked until the leasing ban was finally attached to the fiscal 1983 Interior appropriations bill, which Reagan signed Dec. 30, 1982. *(1982 Almanac p. 461)*

On that same day, Watt finally agreed not to allow oil and gas drilling in wilderness study areas.

Trust and Power Issues

The battle over wilderness leasing revealed much about the basic issues of trust and power that underlay Watt's troubled relations with Congress.

Despite assurances from Watt at various times that he would hold off until Congress had worked its will on the wilderness leasing issue, House Democrats did not fully trust him to refrain from ramming leases through at the last minute before a permanent leasing ban took effect under existing law on Jan. 1, 1984. As the battle dragged on and the "window of opportunity" for such action grew smaller, the quarrel took on proportions far larger than the actual stakes.

That mistrust had been fueled when Watt announced Feb. 21, 1982, that he was proposing legislation to close the wilderness areas to oil and mineral development for the next 18 years. Environmentalists first hailed Watt's proposal, then turned around and denounced it a few days later as a "hoax" after they read the legislative fine print. They said it contained loopholes, including provisions that gave Congress only until Jan. 1, 1985, to act on the existing wilderness recommendations or see the lands "released" for logging, drilling, or mining.

"I have learned to look for 'fishhooks' in Mr. Watt's glittering proposals," said Rep. John F. Seiberling, D-Ohio, chairman of the House Interior Subcommittee on Public Lands.

The issue of power was raised in several ways. At the time of House Interior's 1981 emergency withdrawal of the Bob Marshall wilderness, it was Watt's old alma mater, the Mountain States Legal Foundation, which challenged the action in court on grounds that it was an unconstitutional

"legislative veto." Attorney General William French Smith notified the House that the Justice Department would side with the foundation instead of with Congress. House and Senate lawyers eventually won their case in a federal appeals court, and the Supreme Court ruled the legislative veto unconstitutional in an unrelated case.

But both sides were ready for further constitutional confrontation when House Interior in 1983 invoked the same law to stop a controversial sale of coal leases in the Fort Union area of North Dakota and Montana.

Watt's apparent insistence on testing the limits of congressional authority contributed to his Sept. 20 defeat on the issue of a moratorium on further federal coal leasing.

Watt's challenge to Congress on the coal leasing issue was not an isolated one. With Reagan's backing, he had claimed executive privilege in 1981 in refusing to turn over to a House Energy subcommittee some papers it subpoenaed on how Canadian energy policy affected U.S. companies. The committee voted Feb. 25, 1982, to hold Watt in contempt of Congress, and for a while a showdown seemed likely over where Congress' investigatory power ended and executive privilege began. After lengthy negotiations, however, Watt turned over the documents March 18, 1982. *(1982 Almanac p. 454)*

Clark Selection

The selection of Clark, who had served Reagan as both deputy secretary of state and national security adviser, stunned most of official Washington.

Speculation about a successor to Watt had centered on several present and former members of Congress.

But Reagan said he had "decided once again to turn to someone who has been a trouble-shooter and a result-oriented professional."

He called Clark a "God-fearing Westerner, a fourth-generation rancher, a person I trust."

Sen. Paul Laxalt, R-Nev., one of Reagan's closest Senate allies, said Clark was a "superb" choice, someone who was "totally devoted to the president. Bill will perform the difficult duties of the position in his usual low-key and highly efficient manner."

However, House Minority Leader Robert H. Michel, R-Ill., called the choice "incredible and baffling."

And Sen. Howard M. Metzenbaum, D-Ohio, a member of the Senate Energy and Natural Resources Committee, said Clark "is eminently unqualified to be the secretary of the interior. The appointment demonstrates this administration's insensitivity to environmental concerns."

Clark Hearings

The Senate Energy and Natural Resources Committee completed confirmation hearings on Clark the week of Oct. 31. Clark took few definite policy positions during nearly nine hours of testimony before the committee Nov. 1 and Nov. 2, despite efforts by several senators to pin him down.

Even Clark's sharpest challengers, such as Metzenbaum, acknowledged that his cautiousness under questioning contrasted sharply with the impulsiveness of remarks that repeatedly got Watt into political trouble and ultimately led to his resignation under fire.

"Bill Clark doesn't shout; he listens," said Sen. Pete Wilson, R-Calif., who, as the senator from Clark's home state, presented him to the committee.

Wilson praised the former California judge's "judicial temperament." But Sen. Paul E. Tsongas, D-Mass., asked whether Clark was just "a James Watt who took a Dale Carnegie course in civil behavior."

Leaders of environmental groups opposing the nomination viewed Clark's refusal to take policy positions somewhat skeptically.

"Mr. Clark declines to repudiate specifically a single one of the environmental positions taken by Secretary Watt," said former Sen. Gaylord Nelson, D-Wis. (1963-81), currently chairman of the Wilderness Society.

Democrats Frustrated

Democrats asked Clark how he expected them to exercise their power to advise and consent on presidential appointments if he would not tell them what he thought Interior Department policies should be.

"I'm concerned," said Metzenbaum, "that we're asked to consider a nominee for confirmation who is really dancing the light fantastic around this question of where he stands on some of these issues."

"I can't really help you in indicating which way I lean because I think we have to take it issue-by-issue and case-by-case," Clark replied, invoking the need to protect "the integrity of the decision-making process."

Sen. Dale Bumpers, D-Ark., repeatedly invited Clark to name a single policy of Watt's that he disagreed with. Clark refused. "I don't think it's fair for me to sit here and judge the job of Secretary Watt or any of his predecessor secretaries," Clark said. "All I can assure you of today is an in-depth review from an independent standpoint...."

He spoke often of the "necessity of listening to" environmental groups, who he said "represent some nine million Americans." Watt would not even meet with some of those groups.

Clark also stressed the need to consult with state and local governments and congressional committees. He held several meetings with leaders of environmental groups, and had met with most members of Senate Energy, before the confirmation hearings.

Environmentalists Testify

That apparent openness drew a mixed reaction from environmentalists. While five groups opposed Clark's nomination, two of the largest — the National Wildlife Federation and the National Audubon Society — withheld judgment. They said Clark had taken no positions on which they could base an assessment, and they urged the Senate to get policy commitments before confirming him.

While Clark's judicial background was a major selling point emphasized by his supporters, who claimed he would deliver fair judgments, environmentalists viewed Clark's record on the bench as lopsided.

The National Wildlife Federation (NWF) said its analysis showed that during 1973 to 1981, when Clark sat on California's Supreme Court, it handed down decisions on 18 cases involving environmental issues, in 16 of which the court favored the "pro-conservation" view. Clark, NWF said, took the "anti-conservation" side on 17 of those cases, and the "pro-conservation" side only once.

National Security Concerns

Clark several times indicated that he viewed the nation's dependence on foreign sources of energy and strategic minerals as a "grave concern" from a national security standpoint.

The answer to that problem for Watt, and the Reagan

'Judge' Clark: The President Calls Again

The selection of William P. Clark as interior secretary marked the third time in Ronald Reagan's presidential tenure that he had turned to the 51-year-old California attorney to fill a politically sensitive position.

As with Clark's previous appointments as deputy secretary of state in early 1981 and White House national security adviser a year later, he lacked compelling credentials for the Interior slot, save two: He seemed to share Reagan's attitudes toward national policy and he enjoyed the president's full confidence.

Clark had been chief of staff during Reagan's first term as governor of California, by most accounts bringing managerial order to the administration.

In 1969, Reagan appointed Clark to the first of several state judicial posts, culminating in a 1973 appointment to the state Supreme Court. Opponents to each judicial nomination often cited Clark's undistinguished academic career; he had no undergraduate degree and passed the state bar examination on his second try.

Clark's assignment as deputy secretary of state apparently was intended to let him keep an eye on Reagan's first secretary of state, Alexander M. Haig Jr. The nomination was regarded as a gesture to conservatives who were uneasy about Haig's identification with the Nixon and Ford administrations, in which he had served.

An Embarrassing Debut

Clark's confirmation hearings before the Senate Foreign Relations Committee were an embarrassment. The nominee appeared not to know, among other things, who headed the governments of Zimbabwe and South Africa. One European newspaper headline characterized Clark as a "nitwit," and committee Democrats had a field day.

The Republican-dominated panel nevertheless reported the nomination favorably, and the Senate approved the nomination 70-24. *(1981 Almanac p. 20-A)*

Within a few months, Clark was winning high marks from some skeptics. He worked hard at the State Department job and, in particular, appeared able to smooth out relations between the White House and his mercurial boss, Haig.

Within a year, he was once more on a mission to help Reagan with a personnel problem: He was asked to replace Richard V. Allen as the president's national security adviser.

Under Allen, the National Security Council (NSC) staff — for nearly two decades a powerhouse of foreign policy initiatives — was widely regarded as a backwater, unable to impose coherence on foreign and defense policy. Matters came to a head when Allen became enmeshed in controversy involving the acceptance of cash and gifts from a Japanese firm; he resigned on Jan. 4, 1982. *(1981 Almanac p. 186)*

Clark's appointment met with a mixed reaction: His foreign policy inexperience contrasted sharply with recent national security advisers such as Henry A. Kissinger and Zbigniew Brzezinski, but his reputation as a manager and mediator and his intimacy with Reagan were deemed pluses.

Within weeks of taking charge at NSC, Clark was personally conducting Reagan's morning national security briefing — Allen's briefings had been submitted on paper. He dismissed several of Allen's NSC staff appointments and quickly carved out a larger role for the staff in advising the president on policy options.

To compensate for his lack of personal expertise on security issues, Clark named as his deputy Robert C. McFarlane, a retired Marine Corps officer highly regarded for his foreign policy experience.

Within months after Clark left the State Department, the power struggle between Haig and the White House intensified. Clark was widely seen to be the victor after his former chief, Haig, was pushed out on June 25, 1982. *(1982 Almanac p. 127)*

The Judicial Approach

Clark's preference for the courtesy title "Judge" reflected not only his tenure on the California bench, but his avowed approach to formulating foreign policy. He had described that process using courtroom analogies — hearing out the experts and rendering a judgment.

But the apparent conflict between Clark's hard-line approach to foreign policy and the more conciliatory approach of George P. Shultz — Haig's successor — reinforced the seemingly inevitable struggle between a secretary of state and a national security adviser.

The struggle sometimes went public. Clark, for instance, favored tough bars on Western trade with Moscow in the wake of the martial law crackdown in Poland, and was willing to muscle reluctant Western European governments to go along. Shultz thought that such a policy was ineffective and that the pressure on allies was likely to be self-defeating.

But despite Clark's hard-line views on foreign policy, he seemed not to have lost his gift for mediation — for a non-abrasive kind of advocacy so foreign to outgoing Interior Secretary James G. Watt.

Most recently, that talent was key to the administration's successful negotiations with a bipartisan congressional group that demanded changes in the tone and substance of Reagan's arms control policy in return for its continued support of the MX missile. *(Story, p. 195)*

administration to date, had been a concerted drive to step up dramatically domestic energy and mineral production — especially from public lands over which the interior secretary has control.

While Clark said he believed in "maximum protection of the environment," he also pointed out, "The first mandate of any government is, of course, security and survival."

Some Policy Hints

Although he made virtually no hard commitments, Clark did give a few hints of specific policy stands:

● He said there "may well be" an increase in the administration's budget request for acquisition of land for national parks, on which Watt had tried to impose a moratorium.

● He clearly opposed an increase in the share of costs paid by states and local beneficiaries for federal water projects — thus agreeing with Watt's position and opposing that of Assistant Army Secretary William R. Giannelli, who had oversight over the Corps of Engineers' civil works program.

● He emphasized the importance of using the expertise of career staff within the department and on advisory bodies — many of whom Watt fired, transferred, downgraded or subordinated to political appointees.

● He hinted that during the partial moratorium imposed by Congress on offshore oil and gas leasing under Watt's ambitious five-year plan, "we might be able to come together" on a compromise approach.

● He said "in principle the administration agrees with" an aggressive wetlands protection effort embodied in a bill (S 1329) sponsored by Energy Committee member John H. Chafee, R-R.I. He said he viewed it as "a matter of duty to move out on this." *(Wetlands, p. 349)*

● He acknowledged that the idea of sharing federal revenues from offshore oil and gas leasing with coastal states was "a concept that will not go away," although "the administration, at least for now, recommends against it." *(Coastal revenue sharing, p. 359)*

● He hinted the "answer" to his stand on drilling in federal wildlife refuges "lies in recent history," during which there were few new leases issued for that purpose. Watt sought to increase leasing on these lands.

Clark Confirmation

Committee Vote

The Senate Energy and Natural Resources Committee approved Clark's nomination by a 16-4 vote Nov. 9.

Only Democrats opposed Clark's confirmation. Voting against him were Sens. Wendell H. Ford, Ky.; Paul E. Tsongas, Mass.; Dale Bumpers, Ark.; and Howard M. Metzenbaum, Ohio.

As the nomination was going forward, Watt's resignation took effect on Nov. 8.

Senate Vote

The full Senate confirmed Clark on Nov. 18 after Republicans overcame a challenge to Reagan administration natural resource policies that threatened to snag the nomination.

The vote to confirm Clark was 71-18. All of the "nay" votes were cast by Democrats.

Clark's confirmation was never really in doubt. Many Democrats who forced a delay in the vote until the final hours before Congress adjourned for the year said their concern was not so much Clark's qualifications as administration policies under Watt.

Policy Debate

A group of 37 Democrats and four Republicans tried to switch the spotlight from the nominee to the policies by introducing a resolution Nov. 15 calling for policy changes.

"This policy of dig-dig, chop-chop, dump-dump must stop," declared Sen. Bob Packwood, R-Ore., one of the resolution's cosponsors, in floor remarks Nov. 17.

The administration critics demanded a vote on their resolution before they would allow the Clark nomination to come to a vote. But in an effort to avoid political embarrassment to the White House, Majority Leader Howard H. Baker Jr., R-Tenn., refused to schedule the resolution for floor consideration.

Its sponsors managed to bring it up anyway, by offering it as an amendment to an amendment to the fiscal 1984 supplemental appropriations bill (HR 3959) the evening of Nov. 18. *(HR 3959 story, p. 536)*

However, the Senate agreed, 48-42, to a motion by Appropriations Committee Chairman Mark O. Hatfield, R-Ore., to table the policy statement, which had been introduced by J. Bennett Johnston, D-La. The effect was to kill the amendment. *(Vote 366, p. 60-S)*

Three Republicans, all of them cosponsors of the resolution, joined 39 Democrats in voting against the motion to table: Rudy Boschwitz, Minn.; Gordon J. Humphrey, N.H.; and Packwood.

Dave Durenberger, R-Minn., one of the original cosponsors of the resolution, ended up voting to kill it.

Robert T. Stafford, R-Vt., chairman of the Senate Environment Committee, switched from "nay" to "yea" after it became evident the vote was breaking almost entirely along party lines. And Republicans John H. Chafee, R.I., and Lowell P. Weicker Jr., Conn., who often split with the administration on resource policy, buttonholed colleagues seeking "yea" votes.

Partisan Maneuvering

Republicans expressed confidence all along that they had the votes to confirm Clark. Indeed, even Johnston — chief sponsor of the resolution criticizing administration policies — said from the start he planned to vote in favor of Clark's confirmation.

But the Democrats decided to take advantage of the adjournment pressure to force a public debate on Reagan's natural resource policies.

The White House held a vital trump card in the maneuvering. Baker hinted Nov. 15 that if the Democrats tried to block action on the nomination, he would lay it aside and allow Reagan to put Clark into office with a recess appointment after Congress adjourned for the year.

Such an appointment would have remained in force until at least 40 days after the start of the 1984 session, and possibly until its end.

Policy Resolution

The resolution offered by Johnston was a non-binding "sense of the Senate" resolution expressing "advice" to accompany the Senate's "consent" to the Clark nomination.

The resolution declared that Watt's policies had changed established programs enjoying bipartisan public and congressional support, bringing controversy and litigation.

It advised Reagan and Clark to ensure that Interior Department programs henceforth "conform with the expressed will of Congress."

Specifically, it urged them to halt energy leasing in wilderness study areas, prohibit incompatible commercial development in wildlife refuges, reject plans to sell off large amounts of federal land, resume purchases of park and recreation lands, and lease mineral resources under careful environmental safeguards. ∎

Burford Resigns From EPA Post Under Fire

After months of controversy and a bitter constitutional clash with Congress, Anne M. Burford, administrator of the Environmental Protection Agency (EPA), resigned from her post March 9.

More than a dozen of her top aides either resigned or were fired as well, as EPA went through its worst turmoil since the agency was created in 1970.

The departure of Burford (Anne M. Gorsuch, before her Feb. 20 marriage) came slightly less than three months after the House on Dec. 16, 1982, cited her for contempt of Congress for refusing — on orders from President Reagan — to turn over documents sought by a House subcommittee regarding EPA's management of the nation's hazardous waste cleanup program. *(Contempt, 1982 Almanac p. 451)*

The subcommittee was one of six congressional panels probing allegations of political manipulation, "sweetheart" deals, conflicts of interest, perjury and destruction of documents in connection with the $1.6 billion "superfund" program created under the 1980 Comprehensive Environmental Response, Compensation and Liability Act (PL 96-510). *(Superfund, 1980 Almanac p. 584)*

The congressional investigations and the scandal at EPA spurred action on a major overhaul of the nation's basic hazardous waste law, the 1976 Resource Conservation and Recovery Act (RCRA). By year's end, a three-year reauthorization bill (HR 2867) that significantly tightened existing law had been passed by the House. A similar measure (S 757) was approved by the Senate Environment and Natural Resources Committee. *(Story, p. 335)*

The fracas also focused congressional attention on the deep EPA budget cuts that had taken place since President Reagan took office. It contributed to congressional approval of a sharply increased fiscal 1984 appropriation for the agency.

Ruckelshaus Named

The White House, anxious to start repairing the massive political damage it suffered during the EPA battle, agreed the day Burford resigned to give House subcommittees investigating the agency all the documents they had been seeking.

And on March 21, Reagan named William D. Ruckelshaus, a senior vice president of the Weyerhaeuser Company, to succeed her. The selection of Ruckelshaus, who was EPA's first administrator (1970-73), was almost universally praised. The Senate confirmed his nomination 97-0 on May 17, and he was sworn in a day later. *(Vote 87, p. 20-S; Ruckelshaus biography, p. 334)*

During confirmation proceedings, senators made clear that they had confidence in Ruckelshaus' competence and integrity and trusted him to carry out the environmental laws Congress had enacted, regardless of his own feelings about those laws.

Sen. Robert T. Stafford, R-Vt., chairman of the Senate Environment and Public Works Committee, called Ruckelshaus "one of the few people in this country who could have been confirmed" as head of the battered agency.

"Every step he takes will be watched by a thousand eyes. Levels of distrust and suspicion now run so high that the mere possibility of a wrongful act can and will explode onto the front pages and the evening news," Stafford said.

As predicted, Ruckelshaus came under intensive scru-

tiny at first, but he handled the pressure with aplomb, dealing openly and amiably with the news media and Congress and rapidly restoring morale at his beleaguered agency.

Within weeks, the attention of environmentalists and other administration critics had shifted from EPA to the Interior Department, where Secretary James G. Watt had created nearly as much controversy as Burford, although for different reasons. Seven months to the day after Burford quit, Watt, too, was forced to resign. *(Watt resignation, p. 327)*

While scarcely a half-dozen of EPA's managers were actually accused of wrongdoing, some 20 major officials ultimately resigned in the management change.

By the end of the first session of the 98th Congress, the Senate had confirmed all 12 members of a new management team picked by Ruckelshaus and nominated by Reagan. The final four confirmations on Nov. 18 brought the corps of top EPA officials up to full strength for the first time since Reagan took office.

Background of Investigations

The investigations and hearings into EPA actions grew out of earlier, more routine congressional oversight on how hazardous waste laws were being carried out by the executive branch.

The House Energy and Commerce Subcommittee on Oversight and Investigations, chaired by John D. Dingell, D-Mich., who also chaired the full committee, had begun looking into implementation of the 1980 "superfund" hazardous waste cleanup law as early as September 1980.

Concerned about "the deliberate illegal dumping of hazardous substances and the involvement of organized crime in segments of the toxic waste industry," the subcommittee in a Dec. 16, 1982, report urged "a strong, effective federal deterrent" to illegal disposal.

What the subcommittee found, however, was a "dramatic decline" in hazardous waste enforcement litigation by EPA and the Justice Department since 1981, when the Reagan administration came into office. That was partly due to a Reagan administration policy stressing voluntary compliance by industry.

As other subcommittees joined in with their own investigations, the scope of inquiry widened to include additional charges:

● Possible conflict of interest, as in the case of superfund director Rita M. Lavelle, who eventually legally removed herself from a California dumping case that involved her former employer, Aerojet-General Corp.

● Alleged political manipulation of superfund cleanup grants. Lavelle and Burford, for example, were accused of withholding a grant for the Stringfellow Acid Pits in California to avoid boosting the re-election campaign of Gov. Edmund G. Brown Jr., a Democrat.

● Possible destruction of evidence and obstruction of the congressional inquiry. One concern was raised by the installation of paper shredders at EPA's hazardous waste office after Burford refused to turn over subpoenaed documents.

● Alleged use of political "hit lists" to mark for termination EPA science advisers and civil service employees, as well as political appointees, who disagreed with the Reagan

philosophy of rapid deregulation.

Justice Department Probe

Reagan announced at a Feb. 16 press conference that the Justice Department would probe all allegations of wrongdoing in hazardous waste programs at EPA.

Reagan also said, "I can no longer insist on executive privilege if there's a suspicion in the minds of the people that maybe it is being used to cover some wrongdoing....That we will never stand for."

An initial compromise on the documents was reached two days later, but it was not until March 9 that an agreement was finally reached assuring all House panels the access they sought to EPA documents.

On Aug. 11, six months after Reagan ordered the EPA probe, the Justice Department said its investigation had produced insufficient evidence to warrant criminal prosecution of Burford and five of her top aides.

Besides Burford, the former EPA officials were Robert M. Perry, general counsel; James Sanderson, consultant; John P. Horton and John A. Todhunter, assistant administrators; and Louis J. Cordia, special assistant.

The report said the department's investigation found insufficient evidence of criminal wrongdoing to justify prosecution on some charges. On other charges, the report said criminal intent could not be proved and the department "declined" to prosecute.

Most of the charges under investigation involved conflict of interest, destruction of subpoenaed documents and false testimony. Specific charges varied for each individual.

A statement issued by Attorney General William French Smith said the cases had been "closed without prosecution," but added they were "subject to being reopened in the event new evidence is developed."

Elliott H. Levitas, D-Ga, chairman of one of the House subcommittees probing EPA, used the term "whitewash" to describe the Justice Department report.

Lavelle Only Official Charged

By year's end, former Assistant Administrator Lavelle was the only EPA official who had faced criminal charges. Lavelle headed hazardous waste programs until she was fired by Reagan on Feb. 7.

Lavelle was actually prosecuted twice: once for contempt of Congress and once on charges of perjury and obstructing a congressional investigation.

The House voted 413-0 on May 18 to cite Lavelle for contempt for failing to appear in response to a subpoena from the Dingell subcommittee that was investigating charges of conflict of interest at EPA. *(Vote 119, p. 40-H)*

Lavelle was indicted on the charge May 27, but a federal jury in Washington, D.C., acquitted her on July 22.

On Aug. 4, Lavelle was indicted again — this time on charges of perjury and obstructing a congressional probe.

Lavelle had recused (legally removed) herself from decisions on the Stringfellow Acid Pits dumpsite in California on June 18, 1982, because her former employer, Aerojet-General Corp., was listed as a dumper at the site. She had testified under oath before three congressional hearings that she learned of Aerojet's involvement only on June 17, the day before her recusal. Several witnesses at her trial, however, testified that she had been told of Aerojet's involvement and the need to recuse herself as early as May 28, 1982.

The indictment charged that Lavelle had lied under oath about when she first knew of Aerojet's involvement.

It also charged that she lied when she testified that superfund cleanup grants had not been used for political purposes.

On Dec. 1, a federal jury in Washington, D.C., found Lavelle guilty of four of the five counts on which she had been indicted. On Jan. 9, 1984, she was sentenced to six months in prison and fined $10,000.

Burford Contempt Case

Access by congressional investigators to EPA documents was the issue that escalated the EPA matter from just another policy dispute to a constitutional confrontation. In the end, congressional committees saw almost all the EPA documents they wanted to, but the question of whether Congress had the right to see them remained largely unresolved.

The House had cited Burford for contempt of Congress Dec. 16, 1982, after she followed Reagan's written orders and refused to comply with a congressional subpoena for agency documents. On advice from the Justice Department, Reagan claimed executive privilege, saying that the documents were sensitive because they contained legal enforcement strategy for particular pending dumping cases.

The Justice Department refused to prosecute Burford on the contempt charge. While House attorneys argued that the law made such prosecution mandatory, the Justice Department claimed it was optional.

The department filed suit in U.S. District Court in Washington, D.C., on Dec. 16, 1982, the day of the House vote, seeking to block action on the contempt citation.

The department claimed that the Constitution implied a privilege of the executive to ensure the confidentiality of law enforcement files and of the policy deliberation process.

Leaders of House panels investigating EPA, such as James J. Florio, D-N.J., claimed that the Justice Department had "an inherent conflict" in the Burford contempt matter, since it had advised her not to comply with the subpoena and originally said it would defend her against the contempt charge. Florio and others called for appointment of an independent special prosecutor.

The House Dec. 30 filed a motion seeking dismissal of the Justice Department's suit, and on Feb. 3, 1983, that House motion was granted. U.S. District Court Judge John Lewis Smith Jr. said the department's claims of executive privilege could be raised as part of the defense case in criminal proceedings on the contempt charge.

At the same time, Smith urged a compromise. "The difficulties apparent in prosecuting [Burford] for contempt of Congress should encourage the two branches to settle their differences without further judicial involvement," he wrote. "Compromise and cooperation, rather than confrontation, should be the aim of the parties."

The Compromise

After dismissal of the Justice Department suit, White House officials contacted Rep. Elliott H. Levitas, D-Ga., chairman of the House Public Works Subcommittee on Investigations and Oversight, which had originally subpoenaed the EPA documents, to seek a compromise.

On Feb. 18, an agreement was reached permitting panel members and staff to see the disputed documents under conditions designed to ensure that they were kept confidential.

In return, Levitas promised to try to persuade the House to cancel its Dec. 16 contempt of Congress citation against Gorsuch, who two days later married Robert F. Burford, director of the Interior Department's Bureau of Land Management.

The agreement with Levitas did not end the dispute over access to EPA documents, however. It was not until March 9 that the White House finally met the demands of four other House subcommittees.

Contempt Charge Dropped

In keeping with the deal that resolved the documents dispute, Levitas' subcommittee June 7 approved a resolution (H Res 180) to help cancel the contempt citation against Burford.

The resolution asserted the House's position that executive branch officers must comply with congressional subpoenas, and that federal prosecutors have a duty to proceed against anyone formally cited for contempt for defying such a subpoena. (Smith, in dismissing the Justice Department's suit, had not ruled on this issue).

The resolution said that dropping the contempt citation against Burford "does not constitute a precedent or concession" on that point.

The resolution was approved June 23 (H Rept 98-323) by the full House Public Works and Transportation Committee after Chairman James G. Howard, D-N.J., announced he would introduce a separate bill (HR 3456) to require the U.S. attorney for the District of Columbia to present to a grand jury within 60 days any future contempt action certified by Congress.

The House adopted the resolution Aug. 3 by voice vote.

Howard's bill was one of several proposed to prevent a similar situation from developing in the future.

HR 2684, introduced by Barney Frank, D-Mass., would require appointment of a special prosecutor when Congress cites a member of the executive branch for contempt. HR 3698, introduced by John N. Erlenborn, R-Ill., set up civil procedures under the Freedom of Information Act whereby Congress could challenge in court any president's claim to executive privilege.

Although the House Judiciary Subcommittee on Administrative Law and Governmental Relations held hearings on all of these bills Nov. 15, no further action occurred on them in 1983.

Legislative Legacy

Hazardous Wastes

RCRA. Congress made substantial progress during 1983 on bills (HR 2867, S 757) that would tighten and reauthorize for three years the nation's main law for controlling hazardous wastes. House subcommittees earlier in the year heard allegations that EPA had been lax in enforcing RCRA, giving efforts to tighten the law a boost. *(RCRA background, 1976 Almanac p. 199)*

The House passed HR 2867 by voice vote on Nov. 3 — after easing provisions that for the first time would regulate generators of small quantities of hazardous wastes.

The Senate Environment and Public Works Committee approved S 757 on July 28 and reported it Oct. 28 (S Rept 98-284).

One apparent legislative effect of the charges against EPA was that authors of the new hazardous waste legisla-

Ruckelshaus: EPA Veteran

William D. Ruckelshaus, President Reagan's choice to succeed Anne M. Burford as administrator of the Environmental Protection Agency (EPA), was one of a handful of people who could claim to have on-the-job experience.

Ruckelshaus served as the first administrator of the agency from its formation in 1970 until 1973, taking a bipartisan approach to environmental issues that many members of Congress praised.

But his greatest asset, a reputation for integrity and independence, was earned after he left EPA for the Justice Department.

In October 1973, when Ruckelshaus was deputy attorney general, he refused to carry out President Nixon's order to fire Watergate special prosecutor Archibald Cox, who was seeking tapes of Nixon's White House conversations. Nixon had already fired Attorney General Elliot L. Richardson for balking at his order, and Ruckelshaus, too, was dismissed in that "Saturday night massacre." *(1973 Almanac p. 1009)*

Ruckelshaus then entered private law practice (with the Washington, D.C., firm of Ruckelshaus, Beveridge, Fairbanks, and Diamond). In 1975, he joined the Weyerhaeuser Company, headquartered in Tacoma, Wash., as a senior vice president.

His ties with private industry drew some pointed questions at his Senate confirmation hearing. The appointment of EPA officials with backgrounds in EPA-regulated industries — and the failure of some to divorce themselves completely from those old ties — was one target of House probes into the Reagan EPA.

A major timber products company, Weyerhaeuser needed EPA permits for many parts of its operations. Ruckelshaus also served as a director on the boards of several other corporations that could be affected by EPA decisions.

Ruckelshaus had experience salvaging agencies with damaged integrity. He served for 80 days as acting director of the FBI, beginning April 30, 1973, after it was learned that Nixon's nominee, L. Patrick Gray, had destroyed certain documents. Before taking the job, Ruckelshaus got Nixon to promise him a free hand in pursuing Watergate culprits.

Coming from a well-known family of Indiana Republicans, Ruckelshaus was graduated from Princeton University in 1957 and Harvard Law School in 1960. He served as Indiana's deputy attorney general from 1960 to 1965 and was elected to the Indiana House of Representatives in 1966. There, he was the first freshman ever picked as majority leader.

After an unsuccessful 1968 attempt to unseat Sen. Birch Bayh (D-Ind., 1963-81), he went to the Justice Department as an assistant attorney general, heading the civil division in 1969-70.

During his previous tenure at EPA, Ruckelshaus earned a reputation as an aggressive protector of the environment. But in more recent years, he had advocated changes in environmental laws to reduce excessive cost and paperwork burdens on industry.

tion spelled out requirements in extensive detail, including provisions that would take effect automatically if EPA failed to implement them by the rulemaking process.

Critics charged the bill's authors were trying to make regulations instead of law — going into areas where members of Congress did not have technical competence.

Superfund. There was no legislative action during 1983 on the "superfund" hazardous waste cleanup law (PL 96-510) that was the focus of far more attention during the probes. While RCRA was aimed at preventing unsafe dumping in the future, the $1.6 billion superfund, largely financed by a tax on raw petroleum derivatives used in manufacturing chemicals, was intended for cleanup of existing dumps, often long-abandoned by those responsible for them.

EPA estimated that there could be as many as 14,000 hazardous waste sites nationwide, and that the $1.6 billion would clean up only about 170 of them unless EPA recovered the costs from dumpers. Nonetheless, Burford had signaled that the Reagan administration would not ask for renewal of the superfund law when it expired in 1985.

EPA Funding

In the aftermath of charges that Reagan-proposed budget cuts were disabling the EPA, Congress moved to restore some of the funds it had stripped from the agency since 1981. A $3.998 billion overall fiscal 1984 appropriation for EPA was cleared June 29 as part of the funding bill (HR 3133 — PL 98-45) for the Department of Housing and Urban Development (HUD) and independent agencies. *(HUD appropriations bill, p. 495)*

EPA's operating budget, viewed as a key indicator of its ability to control pollution, was set at $1.11 billion for fiscal 1984. That contrasted with an original 1984 Reagan request of $948 million and a high-water mark appropriation of $1.35 billion for 1981, the last fiscal year before Reagan budget cuts began taking effect. The House June 2 had approved an EPA operating budget of $1.3 billion in a 200-167 vote. *(Vote 139, p. 46-H)*

The Senate waited for Ruckelshaus to make a revised request for the administration, and gave him almost to the dollar what he asked for. It was this sum that ultimately was cleared by Congress.

Pesticide Programs

The Senate Nov. 18 cleared a simple one-year reauthorization (HR 2785 — PL 98-201) of spending for pesticide programs, postponing until next year a more comprehensive rewrite of the law itself. One reason for the postponement was to give EPA time to recover from the shake-up and develop a new legislative position.

EPA Independence

Concern over the Reagan administration's direction of EPA prompted members in both House and Senate to introduce legislation that would reorganize EPA as an independent regulatory commission similar to the Securities and Exchange Commission.

HR 1582, introduced by James H. Scheuer, D-N.Y., drew 42 cosponsors. Neither Scheuer's bill nor a similar one (S 547) introduced by Sens. Daniel Patrick Moynihan, D-N.Y., and George J. Mitchell, D-Maine, emerged from committee in 1983.

Continuing Probes

None of the panels probing EPA — five House subcommittees and a Senate committee — had issued any report on their findings as of the end of the 1983 session.

Some of the panels became less active after the resignation of Burford and confirmation of Ruckelshaus, but none officially closed its investigation.

At least three of the House panels — the House Energy and Commerce Subcommittee on Oversight and Investigations, the House Public Works and Transportation Subcommittee on Investigations and Oversight, and the House Government Operations Subcommittee on Environment, Energy and Natural Resources — continued to hold hearings into the fall, although at a more deliberate pace.

That fact left open the possibility that the EPA issue could be brought up again, through subcommittee hearings and reports, during the 1984 election year.   ∎

House Votes to Tighten Hazardous Waste Law

The House Nov. 3 by voice vote passed a bill (HR 2867) to tighten and reauthorize for three years the chief federal law for controlling the disposal of hazardous wastes.

Similar legislation (S 757) was approved July 28 and reported Oct. 28 (S Rept 98-284) by the Senate Environment and Public Works Committee. It did not reach the Senate floor in 1983, however.

The bill involved a dramatic tightening of the Resource Conservation and Recovery Act (RCRA) of 1976, a law the Environmental Protection Agency (EPA) had been having trouble enforcing. *(RCRA, 1976 Almanac p. 199)*

The House action represented the strongest legislative reaction in 1983 to the hazardous waste enforcement controversy that led to the March 1983 resignation of EPA Administrator Anne M. Burford. *(Burford, EPA controversy, p. 332)*

RCRA Background

The RCRA established more stringent standards for the transport, storage, treatment and disposal of hazardous wastes than for ordinary household and municipal waste. EPA defined hazardous wastes generally as those that were toxic, flammable, corrosive or explosive.

The states administered the hazardous waste program under regulations issued by EPA. The law also authorized federal grants to help states to carry out the program.

Although the law was passed in 1976, EPA did not finish issuing the main regulations for the hazardous waste program until 1982. Environmentalists criticized the Carter administration for foot-dragging in writing the complex regulations needed to actually control landfills and other hazardous waste facilities.

Although it claimed credit for ending the delay, the Reagan administration faced congressional charges that the rules it issued were too lax. Some of those rules proved to be false starts, and EPA reconsidered them.

Facilities handling hazardous waste had to have federal permits, or state permits issued under a federally

approved program, showing that they met safety standards. Bringing existing facilities up to the standards and issuing all the final permits was expected to take years; in the meantime, existing facilities could get "interim status," largely just by applying for a permit.

RCRA also established a system for "cradle-to-grave" tracking of hazardous wastes. A standard EPA manifest form had to accompany such wastes on each stage of shipment, storage, treatment, recycling or final disposal, leaving a paper trail that enforcement officials could use in fixing responsibility for illegal disposal.

RCRA was meant to prevent dumping of toxic materials rather than to clean up hazardous dumps that already existed — a chore left to the "superfund" program created in 1980. *(Superfund, 1980 Almanac p. 584)*

A 1982 RCRA reauthorization bill failed because various controversies could not be resolved before the clock ran out on the 97th Congress. *(1982 Almanac p. 456)*

Closing Loopholes

The 1983 RCRA legislation was designed to close loopholes that allowed roughly half of the nation's hazardous wastes to escape rules requiring their safe disposal, according to chief House sponsor James J. Florio, D-N.J., chairman of the House Energy and Commerce Subcommittee on Commerce, Transportation and Tourism.

In introducing HR 2867, Florio cited the contamination of Times Beach, Mo., by dioxins as an example of the sort of problem Congress needed to address. EPA in February decided to spend some $33 million buying out homeowners in the small community.

Florio noted that neither the toxic chemical wastes — dioxins — nor the practice that put them in Times Beach — the spraying of chemical-laced oil — were regulated under existing law.

Also addressed in the 1983 House and Senate bills was the regulation of small-quantity waste generators. Current EPA regulations exempted generators of less than 1,000 kilograms (kg) per month of hazardous waste — or 2,200 pounds. At least 20 states already regulated small-quantity generators more stringently than the federal government.

However, trade associations for dry cleaners, auto repair shops and other small businesses objected to proposals for bringing small-quantity generators under the regulatory umbrella. To do so would mean unjustified costs and paperwork for their members, they said.

House, Senate Provisions Compared

HR 2867 was unanimously approved April 27 by Florio's Commerce, Transportation and Tourism Subcommittee and reported May 17 by the full House Energy and Commerce Committee (H Rept 98-198, Part I), with a supplemental report filed June 9 (Part II).

The bill was then referred to the House Judiciary Committee, which approved it with amendments June 14 and reported it June 17 (Part III).

The Senate bill (S 757) was approved July 28 by the Senate Environment and Public Works Committee, which formally reported the measure Oct. 28 (S Rept 98-284).

In addition to imposing new requirements on businesses and institutions that generated small quantities of hazardous wastes, both the House and Senate bills strengthened EPA enforcement powers and the right of citizens to sue violators of the law.

They placed tighter restrictions on "land disposal" of

hazardous wastes — that is, disposal in landfills or ponds — than did the current law. And both set ambitious new timetables for EPA to finish regulatory tasks that had dragged on for years.

HR 2867 and S 757 included the following major provisions:

Authorization

● The House bill authorized $163 million for fiscal 1984, $171 million for fiscal 1985 and $176 million for fiscal 1986 to carry out programs under the law.

● The Senate bill authorized $88.6 million for fiscal 1983, $92 million for fiscal 1984, $97 million for fiscal 1985 and $99.5 million for each of fiscal years 1986 and 1987.

Small-Quantity Generators

● The House bill required EPA to issue regulations covering hazardous waste from generators of between 100 and 1,000 kg per month within 18 months of enactment.

● The Senate bill required EPA to study hazardous wastes from generators of less than 1,000 kg per month and to issue regulations covering them by March 31, 1986.

● Both bills required the regulations for sources that generated small quantities to be sufficient to protect human health and the environment but allowed them to be less stringent than those for larger-quantity generators.

● The House bill, over a three-step phase-in period, required generators of between 25 and 1,000 kg per month to report the type and amount of the waste to the transporter on a standard EPA manifest form. Generators of more than 250 kg would have to comply in 270 days from enactment, generators of more than 100 kg in 540 days and generators of more than 25 kg in 810 days.

● The Senate bill, beginning 270 days after enactment, required generators of between 100 and 1,000 kg per month to report the type, amount and destination of the waste to the transporter on a standard EPA manifest form.

● If EPA failed to issue the small-quantity regulations by 30 months from enactment, the House bill required small-quantity generators to report the name of the transporter and destination of the waste; to treat, store or dispose of the waste in a facility with interim status; and to meet other reporting and record-keeping requirements.

● If EPA failed to issue the small-quantity regulations by March 31, 1986, the Senate bill required small-quantity generators to treat, store or dispose of the waste in a facility with a final permit for handling hazardous waste and to meet other reporting and record-keeping requirements.

● Beginning 270 days after enactment, the Senate bill required generators of between 100 kg per month and 1,000 kg of ignitable, corrosive or reactive wastes to ship them only in labeled "suitable, sound, non-leaking containers" that met Transportation Department specifications, were equivalent to the original container or were acceptable to both the generator and transporter. The House bill had no packaging requirement for small-quantity generators.

● The Senate bill, beginning 270 days from enactment, and until the small-generator regulations took effect, required hazardous waste of less than 1,000 kg per month that was not handled in a facility with a final hazardous waste permit to be disposed of only in a state-licensed municipal or industrial solid waste facility.

● Both the House and Senate bills allowed the generator, under the eventual regulations for small-quantity generators, to store up to 1,000 kg per month of hazardous waste on-site for up to 180 days.

The Senate bill added an exemption when wastes had to be shipped more than 200 miles, in which case they could be stored 270 days.

Land Disposal

● Both House and Senate bills required EPA to issue regulations within six months of enactment that minimized to the extent technologically feasible the disposal of containerized liquid hazardous wastes in landfills, and that prohibited the disposal in landfills of bulk or non-containerized liquid hazardous wastes.

● The House bill authorized EPA to issue regulations prohibiting one or more methods of land disposal of hazardous wastes, to be specified by EPA, when it found that those methods might not protect human health and the environment for as long as the waste remained hazardous.

● The Senate bill required EPA to issue regulations prohibiting the disposal of hazardous wastes on land, except for disposal methods for one or more wastes that EPA found would protect human health and the environment. The bill prohibited EPA from determining that a method protected health and environment if a specific waste was highly toxic or mobile, unless an interested party showed that it would not migrate for as long as it remained hazardous.

● The House bill prohibited land disposal, after one year from enactment, of liquid wastes containing certain forms and concentrations of substances listed in the bill, unless EPA found the prohibition was not required to protect health and environment. The substances were cyanides, arsenic, cadmium, chromium, lead, mercury, nickel, selenium, thallium, strong acids, polychlorinated biphenyls (PCBs) and halogenated organic compounds.

The Senate bill required EPA to issue land disposal regulations, within 32 months of enactment, for largely the same forms and concentrations of the same substances.

● The House bill required EPA to determine whether to prohibit land disposal of other wastes already listed as hazardous in EPA regulations according to a published schedule. EPA would have to make determinations on 25 percent of the listed wastes by 24 months after enactment, 50 percent by 34 months, 75 percent by 44 months and 100 percent by 54 months.

The Senate bill required EPA to make the same determinations according to a slightly different schedule: one-third by 32 months after enactment, two-thirds by 42 months and all by 52 months.

● The House bill prohibited land disposal of any waste for which EPA failed to meet the deadline in the schedule. The Senate bill, if deadlines were not met, prohibited land disposal except in facilities with two liners and two leachate collection systems (or technology demonstrated by the landfill owner or operator to be equivalent), as well as groundwater monitoring.

Burning and Blending

● Both House and Senate bills required the owner or operator of any facility that produced, burned, distributed or marketed any fuel made from a listed hazardous waste, used oil or blends of those, to notify EPA and the state, within 12 months of enactment, of the facility's location and the substances and activities involved. Exact information requirements would be set by EPA.

Under the House bill, EPA could exempt residential boilers and other facilities if it determined that notification was not necessary. The Senate bill mandated an exemption

for single-family and two-family residences.

● Both House and Senate bills required EPA to issue regulations within two years of enactment setting such standards as might be needed to protect public health and the environment for facilities that produced, burned, distributed or marketed fuels containing listed hazardous wastes. The Senate bill allowed EPA to exempt facilities that burned "de minimis," or small, amounts of hazardous wastes at the same facility where they were generated, if burned in a device found by EPA to be safe.

● Both bills prohibited distribution or marketing of fuel containing a listed hazardous waste unless the invoice or bill of sale bore a conspicuous warning that the fuel contained hazardous wastes and listed those wastes.

● Both bills required EPA to issue regulations within two years of enactment setting such standards as might be needed to protect public health and the environment for transporters of fuels containing listed hazardous wastes.

● The Senate bill required EPA to issue regulations within 12 months of enactment requiring persons subject to the notice requirement for hazardous waste-derived fuels to keep such records as might be necessary to protect human health and the environment. The House bill had no comparable requirement.

Enforcement

● Both House and Senate bills clarified and broadened the present authority of EPA to sue waste handlers when they present an imminent hazard to health or environment, and to include both past and present actions by any person, including waste generators, contributing to the problem.

● The House bill gave citizens a right to sue waste handlers to abate an imminent hazard if EPA, after being notified of a citizen's intent to sue, failed to file suit itself. The Senate bill narrowed the right of citizens to intervene in ongoing EPA or state legal actions, by giving the right to sue only to citizens who were harmed or had other legally defined interests in the lawsuit.

● The House bill preserved the right of any person or class of persons to sue under common law or statutes other than RCRA for legal relief related to solid or hazardous waste.

The Senate bill contained no comparable provision.

● The House bill allowed the EPA administrator to bring any civil action authorized under RCRA when the attorney general, who normally brought such actions, failed to file it within 150 days after EPA sent him the case.

The Senate bill contained no comparable provision.

● The House bill authorized EPA officers conducting criminal investigations under RCRA to carry firearms; issue warrants, summonses and subpoenas; make arrests without warrants for federal felonies if committed in their presence or if they have reason to believe were committed by the person arrested; and take sworn statements.

The Senate bill contained no comparable provision.

● Both House and Senate bills doubled most criminal penalties for knowing violations of the law, permit requirements or certain regulations, up to a maximum of a $50,000 fine for each day of violation and five years' imprisonment for the gravest offenses. The maximum fine and imprisonment would be doubled for persons previously convicted of a violation.

● Both bills added extra penalties for criminal offenses when the violator knew he was placing another person in imminent danger of death or serious bodily injury. Maximum penalties would be a $250,000 fine ($1 million for

organizations) and 15 years' imprisonment.

Permits and Interim Status

● The House bill restricted the life of permits for hazardous waste facilities to no more than 10 years, subject to renewal under the same requirements as for new permits.

● The Senate bill likewise limited permit life to 10 years but mandated a review of land disposal facility permits every five years to assure compliance with currently applicable requirements.

The Senate bill allowed EPA to review any permit more frequently in light of new technology, regulations and requirements for protection of health and environment.

● The House bill prohibited expansion by more than 10 percent of a hazardous waste treatment, storage or disposal facility operating under interim status unless the facility obtains a final permit before construction begins.

● The Senate bill required operators who expanded, replaced or added units to landfills or surface impoundments operating under interim status to meet many of the same technological requirements that new facilities were required to meet.

● The House bill set deadlines for EPA or the state to take final action on pending permit applications for hazardous waste facilities: four years from enactment for land disposal facilities, with highest priority for existing facilities contaminating groundwater; five years for incinerators; and eight years for any other facility. By these deadlines, EPA or the state was to either issue or deny the permit and interim status would end. The Senate bill contained no comparable provisions.

House Floor Action

The House began work on HR 2867 on Aug. 4, but did not finish it until nearly three months later.

Although consideration of the bill was intermittent, the complex measure sparked intensive debate at times and the House adopted a number of floor amendments.

Amendments Adopted

State Grants. On Aug. 4, members adopted an amendment by David E. Bonior, D-Mich., raising from $2 million to $10 million the authorization for grants to states for carrying out solid waste management plans.

Notice Requirements. Also adopted was an amendment by Richard C. Shelby, D-Ala., and Norman F. Lent, R-N.Y., that was intended to ease requirements that small-quantity generators notify transporters that their wastes were hazardous. As approved by the Energy and Commerce Committee, those requirements applied to businesses generating 25 kg per month or more of hazardous waste. The amendment raised the threshold to 100 kg/mo.

However, this amendment was soon modified by several second-degree amendments. The most important, adopted by 236-180, reinstated the 25 kg/mo. notice requirement. *(Vote 308, p. 92-H)*

Another change lengthened the phase-in period for requirements on the smallest generators to about 27 months. It was approved 218-192. *(Vote 309, p. 92-H)*

Land Disposal. The House Oct. 6 by voice vote adopted an amendment easing the schedule for EPA to decide which hazardous wastes should be banned from land disposal.

Liquid Wastes. Another amendment adopted Oct. 6 banned most disposal of liquid hazardous wastes in salt

domes or underground injection wells without specific approval by EPA or Congress.

Export of Wastes. Still another Oct. 6 amendment allowed EPA to prohibit export of hazardous wastes unless the receiving country certified that it was aware of what it was getting and willing to accept it.

Enforcement Powers. When the House returned to the RCRA bill Nov. 3, it debated two Judiciary Committee amendments to strike provisions in the Energy Committee's bill beefing up EPA's enforcement powers.

The first provision gave the EPA administrator authority to press in court any civil action authorized by RCRA if the attorney general, who normally brought such actions, failed to file it within 150 days after EPA sent him the case.

Proponents of the Judiciary amendment striking this provision were led by William J. Hughes, D-N.J. They argued that the government needed a "centralized and coordinated" litigative authority under the Department of Justice. They said the 150-day time limit was arbitrary and unworkable, and that it indicated Congress believed the Justice Department had been "dilatory and lackadaisical" in enforcing hazardous waste laws.

Albert Gore Jr., D-Tenn., retorted that Justice had indeed failed to take cases to court "in a timely fashion." Allegations of lax enforcement by the department of the "superfund" waste cleanup law were a key focus of congressional investigations into EPA matters.

Gore said at least three other environmental laws gave EPA such litigative power, and Energy Chairman John D. Dingell, D-Mich., said at least four other federal agencies had such power.

Despite these arguments, the House Oct. 31 adopted the Judiciary Committee amendment, 215-165. *(Vote 404, p. 120-H)*

Hughes then pressed the second Judiciary amendment, striking provisions giving EPA criminal investigators certain police powers. He said the FBI had assigned "high priority" to the kinds of illegal waste-dumping cases EPA was concerned about, and that law enforcement authority should be centered as much as possible in the Justice Department.

Dingell, whose committee had probed the involvement of organized crime in illegal hazardous waste-dumping operations, said Justice "has done nothing, nothing...."

"We know the Department of Justice does not have adequate resources," Dingell said, "but we also know they have not done the job."

The House by 292-125 agreed to a compromise amendment directing the attorney general to deputize qualified EPA employees as special deputy U.S. marshals when asked to do so by the EPA administrator, and upon "a showing of need." *(Vote 418, p. 124-H)*

Legislative Veto Rejected

The closest vote Nov. 3 came on an amendment offered by Elliott H. Levitas, D-Ga., that attempted to get around the June 23 Supreme Court decision striking down the legislative veto as unconstitutional. *(Legislative veto, p. 565)*

Levitas sought to prevent EPA from enforcing certain rules to carry out RCRA until those rules had been approved by Congress through a joint resolution passed by both chambers and signed by the president.

That mechanism — not a veto, but a reservation of the rulemaking power Congress commonly delegated to the

executive branch — would have applied only to rules affecting generators of small quantities of wastes and having an annual economic impact of $100 million or more.

Florio opposed the Levitas amendment, saying it would undo much of what the House had accomplished up until then by keeping the law itself from taking effect for an indeterminate length of time.

Such a delay, he said, could trigger a "hammer" provision in the law. This provision, meant to be a penalty for tardy rulemaking by EPA, would impose some requirements now placed on large-scale generators of hazardous wastes on small-scale generators if EPA did not issue special rules for the latter by a certain time.

In cliffhanger votes, Levitas' amendment was first adopted, then rejected. The first vote, held while the House was sitting in the Committee of the Whole, was so close that vote switches changed the outcome several times. The final count was 198-195. *(Vote 419, p. 124-H)*

Florio, the bill's floor manager, asked for a separate vote on the amendment once the bill was reported back to the full House. He won that vote, 189-204. *(Vote 420, p. 124-H)* ∎

No Action on Clean Air Bill

In a move that eased pressure on Congress for any 1983 rewrite of the Clean Air Act, the House voted June 2 to bar the Environmental Protection Agency (EPA) from imposing economic penalties on communities that failed to meet a 1982 deadline for achieving clean air.

The House adopted the one-year sanctions moratorium as an amendment to the fiscal 1984 appropriations bill (HR 3133 — PL 98-45) for the Department of Housing and Urban Development (HUD) and various independent agencies, including EPA. *(HUD funding bill, p. 495)*

The vote was 227-136. *(Vote 141, p. 46-H)*

David O'B. Martin, R-N.Y., said adoption of the amendment meant "you can forget about having clean air legislation" even reported out of committee "during this Congress."

For the first session, at least, his prediction proved accurate.

Clean Air Background

The Clean Air Act, the nation's most complex and far-reaching environmental protection law, was enacted in 1970 (PL 91-604) and amended (PL 95-95) in 1977. *(Background, Congress and the Nation Vol. III, p. 757; 1977 Almanac p. 627)*

Although the law's spending authorization expired in 1981, clean air regulations remained on the books and funding to enforce the act was provided in the fiscal 1983 and fiscal 1984 appropriations bills for HUD and several independent agencies, including the EPA.

In the 97th Congress, committees in both the House and Senate wrestled with clean air legislation throughout 1981-82.

Although the Senate Environment and Public Works Committee reported a massive reauthorization bill, the measure never reached the Senate floor.

In the House, a deadlock on the Energy and Commerce Committee led to a breakoff of markups in August 1982. *(1982 Almanac p. 425)*

Sanctions Threat

As amended in 1977, the Clean Air Act set a Dec. 31, 1982, deadline for meeting EPA's "national ambient air quality standards" — goals for the quality of air in general circulation, rather than for the gas coming out of smokestacks. In certain areas with severe auto-related pollution, an extension to 1987 was allowed.

On Feb. 3, 1983, EPA put approximately 218 communities around the nation — including a number of big cities — on notice that they faced the threat of sanctions as a result of various air act violations.

EPA Administrator Anne M. Burford had put the sanctions machinery into motion in January, claiming existing law gave her no choice. She said communities that missed the Dec. 31, 1982, deadline would face bans on new construction and a cutoff of federal grants for highways and clean air programs.

Environmentalists charged that the administration was using the threat of sanctions as a way of pressuring Congress to act quickly on a clean air reauthorization bill. The Reagan administration, like automobile manufacturers and many other industries, had been seeking a relaxation of the existing law.

Regardless of administration intent, many members unquestionably felt the need to take some action before sanctions actually were imposed.

The Sanctions Moratorium

The amendment adopted by the House prohibited sanctions from being imposed simply because an area failed to meet national air quality standards. That effectively took 75 to 111 communities off the list of 218.

The remaining communities were cited for failure to have an EPA-approved cleanup plan or failure to implement such a plan — and those areas still faced possible sanctions.

The amendment prohibited EPA from spending money provided by the bill to impose the sanctions during the fiscal year running from Oct. 1, 1983, through Sept. 30, 1984.

The Senate Appropriations Committee, in reporting HR 3133 (S Rept 98-152), joined the House in adopting the one-year moratorium, and the provision was not an issue during a House-Senate conference on the bill.

Legislative Maneuvering

Most parties to the clean air battle supported extension of the deadlines in existing law. But few, if any, were willing at first to enact a simple deadline extension without adding some other provisions they considered "musts," and those add-ons inevitably drew opposition from other factions. A deadline extension had become a bargaining chip that no party was willing to give up for free.

The moratorium amendment came up on the floor as a wild card that fractured most traditional coalitions on clean air issues, cutting across parties, regions and philosophies. It was offered by William E. Dannemeyer, R-Calif. — an advocate of the environmental policies of the Reagan administration during the Burford era — who was aligned with conservative and industry positions. But quick to rise in support of the amendment was Henry A. Waxman, D-Calif., a leading environmentalist and a liberal who saw such issues in terms of public health. Both came from Southern California districts facing possible sanctions.

One of the few members whose stand could have been predicted was John D. Dingell, D-Mich., chairman of the

Energy and Commerce Committee responsible for clean air legislation, who opposed the amendment.

Dingell, anxious to act on a clean air bill that would ease auto pollution controls, had been urging the administration to impose the sanctions.

"The law is the law," Dingell told the House. "If you do not like the sanctions, change them."

"Those legislative questions should be reviewed by the legislative committees, not written into this kind of curious amendment under these . . . strange circumstances," Dingell maintained.

The scope of the original Dannemeyer amendment was narrowed in the Speaker's Lobby just off the House floor, only minutes before it was offered, to win the support of Waxman and James T. Broyhill, R-N.C., the ranking minority member on House Energy. Broyhill's support was apparently enough to win the blessing of Minority Leader Robert H. Michel, R-Ill.

The House vote bucked the wishes of the two chairmen whose panels were most directly involved with the measure: Dingell and Edward P. Boland, D-Mass., who headed the Appropriations Subcommittee on HUD and Independent Agencies. But the amendment was supported by both Minority Leader Michel and Majority Leader Jim Wright, D-Texas.

In order to bring up his amendment, Dannemeyer had to use a new rule adopted by House Democrats Jan. 3 that made it more difficult to attach riders to appropriations measures. It was the first time the rule had been tested. *(Rider rule, p. 596)*

No Other Clean Air Action

Sen. Robert T. Stafford, R-Vt., chairman of the Senate Environment and Public Works Committee, early in the year introduced a clean air bill (S 768) identical to the version his panel approved in 1982.

The measure kept most provisions of the existing law, adding new controls for acid rain. It was opposed by many industry groups, and found no favor with the administration.

Although the Environment Committee held a few hearings on the legislation, the panel took no action on it in 1983.

In the House, the Energy and Commerce Committee made no attempt to resume work on the clean air issue in 1983. Dingell and Waxman had clashed repeatedly in 1982, with Dingell pushing an industry-backed bill to relax the existing law and Waxman pressing a package of changes supported by environmental groups. The Energy Committee was often closely divided on crucial issues, with Waxman mustering enough votes to stop or slow Dingell on several fronts, but not enough to carry his own bill through committee.

Following the 1982 elections, seven new Democrats, most of them expected to side with Waxman, were named to the Energy Committee Jan. 6 by the House Democratic Caucus. The caucus passed over several other applicants who had been supported by Dingell. The committee's Democratic majority was raised from 24-18 to 27-15.

The new Democratic appointees were Wayne Dowdy, Miss.; Bill Richardson, N.M.; Jim Bates, Calif.; Dennis E. Eckart, Ohio; Jim Slattery, Kan.; Gerry Sikorski, Minn.; and John Bryant, Texas. The League of Conservation Voters, an environmentalist organization, had worked for the election of Richardson, Bates, Eckart, and Bryant, and said Sikorski had an "extremely good" environmental record. ∎

Acid Rain Stalemate Persists

Despite strong pressure from Canada for action, the Reagan administration remained sharply split over how to combat the problem of acid rain, and Congress took no action on the subject in 1983.

William D. Ruckelshaus, who took over in May as administrator of the Environmental Protection Agency (EPA), struggled in vain to build a consensus on the issue within the administration. But at year's end, a Reagan legislative initiative on acid rain, originally expected to reach Congress by early fall, was nowhere in sight.

Congress was making little headway of its own. Although a wide range of acid rain proposals were introduced in 1983, and hearings on the subject were held in both the House and Senate, there was no action in either body.

The failure to come to grips with acid rain legislation was one factor blocking a resumption of House and Senate committee deliberations on a more comprehensive rewrite of the Clean Air Act. *(Clean air, p. 339)*

Cabinet Clash

President Reagan listed acid rain as a top priority for quick action in a speech at Ruckelshaus' May 18 swearing-in ceremony, telling Ruckelshaus: "I would like you to work with others in our administration, with the Congress, and with state and local officials to meet this issue head-on." *(Ruckelshaus appointment, p. 332)*

Ruckelshaus moved quickly to review proposals for dealing with acid rain, saying at first that he expected "to make our action recommendation to the Cabinet council and the president before the end of summer."

That timetable soon slipped, however. In mid-September Ruckelshaus participated in a flurry of meetings on acid rain attended by Interior Secretary James G. Watt, Energy Secretary Donald P. Hodel, other Cabinet members, White House officials, utility groups, environmentalists, scientists and members of Congress.

President Reagan attended one standing-room-only informational briefing of the Cabinet Council on Natural Resources and Environment on Sept. 15, where a panel of five top scientists answered questions from the president and Cabinet members on acid rain for more than an hour.

Ruckelshaus outlined a range of acid rain options to the council, and recommended a plan that called for a very modest reduction of the coal-fired power plant emissions thought to be a major contributor to acid rain.

But even though his proposal was far more limited than most acid rain bills before Congress, it met strong objections at a Sept. 21 Cabinet council meeting. Leading the opposition were Office of Management and Budget (OMB) Director David A. Stockman and Energy Secretary Hodel, who argued the proposal would be too costly to electric power companies and their ratepayers.

"Ruckelshaus was pretty much on his own within the Cabinet council," said one EPA official. Reportedly, only Secretary of State George P. Shultz backed Ruckelshaus.

Stockman was bolstered by a Sept. 20 letter from Reps. James T. Broyhill, R-N.C., and Edward R. Madigan, R-Ill., that was distributed to all 19 members of the Cabinet council. It urged the administration to hold off on endorsing any acid rain legislation. Broyhill was ranking Republican on the House Energy and Commerce Committee, which has jurisdiction on clean air legislation.

"From a political, scientific and economic standpoint,

we do not believe the timing is ripe for a bill endorsed by the administration," Broyhill and Madigan stated. "Our hope is that the politics of the moment will not lead the administration to rush to judgment. . . ."

Canadian Impatience

The issue came up — as it always did — during routine Cabinet-level meetings Oct. 16 between the United States and its downwind neighbor, Canada. But Ruckelshaus and Shultz could give the Canadians no timetable for an American decision.

Ruckelshaus said he was "not surprised" the decision was taking longer than expected, because acid rain was "a very big, a very controversial issue" that divided the nation along regional lines.

But Canadian Environment Minister Charles L. Caccia expressed impatience, saying: "We are ready to move, we are anxious to move, we have a plan." Caccia said he had urged Ruckelshaus "to take to Washington the impressions he has gotten today of the growing and intense desire to come to grips with the acid rain issue and solve it once and for all."

The Canadians were not the only ones growing impatient. Senate Environment Committee Chairman Robert T. Stafford, R-Vt., said his panel would wait no longer for an administration bill. The committee held acid rain hearings Nov. 2, 8 and 10.

Background

Acid rain is a weak solution of sulfuric or nitric acid caused mainly by sulfur dioxide emitted from coal-burning electric power plants or nitrogen oxide emitted by automobiles. Once aloft, these pollutants can travel hundreds of miles downwind before falling to the ground.

Total man-made sulfur dioxide emissions in the United States amount to about 24.1 million metric tons per year, according to the Interagency Task Force on Acid Precipitation. Although acid rain is a potential problem in many parts of the country, the Northeast and eastern Canada bear the brunt of its effects.

The region emitting the most sulfur dioxide is the Ohio River Valley, where states like Ohio, Indiana, Illinois and Kentucky burn large amounts of high-sulfur coal.

American environmentalists and the Canadian government wanted U.S. emissions cut in half — by about 12 million metric tons per year.

For its first two years, the Reagan administration insisted scientists still knew too little to justify the multibillion-dollar costs of cleanup.

Three major scientific panels issued reports in mid-1983 stating that scientists already knew quite a bit about acid rain. They included the National Research Council, an arm of the National Academy of Sciences; the National Acid Precipitation Task Force, made up of Reagan administration officials from 12 federal agencies; and a nine-person team appointed by the White House Office of Science and Technology Policy.

Political Mine Field

Choosing a strategy for controlling acid rain involved thorny political problems. Some approaches placed the burden of cleanup costs on the utilities emitting the most pollution — and ultimately on their ratepayers. Others spread the cost by charging utility customers nationwide, raising protests in Western areas, where utilities said they were not causing problems.

Utility industry groups said control costs would be huge, and they warned that electric bills in some places could rise by 50 percent. But environmentalists said government studies put costs far lower, involving rate increases of 2.5 percent to 10 percent.

One of the cheaper ways to reduce emissions of sulfur dioxide would be to burn low-sulfur Western coal. But states such as West Virginia, Ohio, Indiana and Illinois feared this would cost miners' jobs and hurt their economies. Consequently, many bills required use of one of the most expensive control technologies: scrubbers that remove sulfur dioxide from smokestack gas.

Competing Bills

In 1982, the Senate Environment and Public Works Committee approved clean air legislation that contained provisions aimed at cutting annual emissions by eight million tons in a 31-state region by 1995. *(1982 Almanac p. 425)*

Chairman Stafford wanted an even greater reduction. In 1983, he introduced S 769, mandating a 12 million-ton reduction, while Sen. George J. Mitchell, D-Maine, introduced S 145, mandating a 10 million-ton reduction.

Stafford saw an eight million-ton reduction as a "barely acceptable minimum effort." In a Sept. 22 speech he said: "I know that Bill Ruckelshaus understands that any proposal to make a token reduction of two or three or four million tons of sulfur dioxide is unacceptable to those of us who want realistic controls on acid rain, and further that such a proposal by the administration would touch off a bitter battle in the Congress."

His remarks did not augur well for the proposals Ruckelshaus advocated a day earlier before the Cabinet council: a narrowly targeted experimental reduction of three million or 4.4 million tons in a handful of Ohio Valley states. What Stockman had rejected as too much, Stafford was rejecting as too little.

In the House, a proposal (HR 3400) by Reps. Henry A. Waxman, D-Calif., and Gerry Sikorski, D-Minn., had more than 80 cosponsors. It would cut emissions by 12 million tons.

The Waxman-Sikorski bill was designed to ease the potential cost burden on Midwestern utility customers by funding capital costs of pollution control equipment through a nationwide charge or fee of one mill on each kilowatt-hour of electricity used.

Arizona Wilderness

The Senate Sept. 13 passed by voice vote a bill (S 626) designating as wilderness 6,670 acres of the Aravaipa Canyon and adjoining lands in southern Arizona.

Sen. Barry Goldwater, R-Ariz., told the Senate the legislation was the first to extend federal wilderness protection to public lands under the jurisdiction of the Interior Department's Bureau of Land Management. Most wilderness areas had been carved from lands under the Agriculture Department's U.S. Forest Service.

S 626 was reported Aug. 4 by the Senate Energy and Natural Resources Committee (S Rept 98-209).

The canyon protected by the measure was often called a miniature version of the Grand Canyon. It was home to more than 158 species of birds and animals.

After passage by the Senate, the bill was referred to the House Interior and Insular Affairs Committee, which took no action on it in 1983.

RARE II Bills Sail Through House, Stall in Senate

The House cranked out wilderness preservation bills at a rapid clip in 1983 in an effort to avert a Reagan administration plan to throw out Carter-era wilderness recommendations and start over.

Only one of the bills was enacted into law, however — a measure (S 96 — PL 98-140) creating a 259,000-acre wilderness area in Montana.

While the House passed wilderness legislation for 10 states, the Senate passed bills for only three states.

Wilderness status under the 1964 Wilderness Act (PL 88-577) and other laws protected federally owned lands that were still largely untouched by man from commercial development, petroleum and mineral leasing, logging and roadbuilding. Off-road vehicle recreation was prohibited, while other activities such as fishing or backpacking were allowed. *(Wilderness Act, Congress and the Nation Vol. I, p. 1061)*

Background: RARE II

Since 1979 Congress had been sorting through recommendations made after the Second Roadless Area Review and Evaluation (RARE II), which was begun in 1977 under President Carter. RARE II was a complete inventory of undeveloped national forest lands meant to sort out which ones should be preserved as wilderness.

The RARE II study looked at 46.1 million acres of forest lands in the lower 48 states. On May 2, 1979, President Carter recommended to Congress that 9.9 million acres in 36 states be designated as wilderness, 28.5 million acres as non-wilderness and 7.7 million acres as further planning areas.

The RARE II study simply made recommendations; only Congress could designate an area as wilderness. Congress was slowly working its way through the recommendations, state by state.

The 96th Congress set aside 4.2 million acres as wilderness in seven states. The 97th Congress set aside 132,011 acres in six states, but President Reagan vetoed the 49,150-acre Florida bill. *(96th Congress, 1980 Almanac p. 617; 97th Congress, 1982 Almanac p. 464)*

RARE II Re-evaluation

On Feb. 1, the Reagan administration decided to throw out the Carter RARE II wilderness recommendations and start over.

The administration's scrapping of RARE II came in response to an October 1982 decision by the 9th U.S. Circuit Court of Appeals that found inadequate the legally required environmental impact statement (EIS) on which the RARE II recommendations were based.

In June 1979, the state of California, joined by environmental groups, sued to block the Agriculture Department from allowing development on 46 roadless areas in the state that had not been recommended for wilderness. They claimed the RARE II study had not adequately assessed environmental effects of such a recommendation. A U.S. district court, and later the appeals court, agreed.

The decision prompted efforts by some in Congress to pass legislation declaring the "sufficiency" of the RARE II EIS nationwide.

Environmentalists and their allies, however, preferred to add a "sufficiency" clause to each state RARE II bill as

it was worked out — waiving the right to sue only after an agreement on wilderness designations had been reached that satisfied all parties.

Although the appeals court's decision applied only to the sufficiency of the EIS on areas recommended for non-wilderness uses, the administration argued that the impact statement for wilderness areas was subject to challenge on the same grounds.

In redoing the whole RARE II study, the administration could drastically cut the areas recommended as wilderness. But Congress could ignore any new recommendations if it chose, continuing to make its own wilderness determinations.

State-by-State List

Alabama

The House June 6 suspended the rules and passed by voice vote a bill (HR 2477 — H Rept 98-98, Pts. I and II) adding approximately 27,865 acres to the existing Sipsey Wilderness in the Bankhead National Forest in Alabama.

The Reagan administration had urged Congress to delay action, citing the potential for oil, gas and logging development in part of the area.

But Rep. Ronnie G. Flippo, D-Ala., whose district included much of the proposed addition, supported the bill. He said the lands made up a tiny fraction (less than two-tenths of 1 percent) of the total 21,333,000 acres of forest land in the state, and that state geological surveys showed their oil and gas value was "minimal."

The measure was referred June 15 to the Senate Agriculture Committee, where it remained at year's end.

California

The House April 12 passed HR 1437 (H Rept 98-40), designating 2.33 million acres of national forest land in California as wilderness. The 297-96 vote may not have reflected the depth of the controversy over the bill, coming as it did two days after the death of Rep. Phillip Burton, D-Calif., who personally crafted the bill. *(Vote 47, p. 20-H)*

The Reagan administration recommended wilderness status for only 1.2 million acres in California.

A Senate Energy subcommittee held hearings on the House bill and other California bills (S 5, S 1515) on July 28 but did not act on any of them.

The House had passed similar California wilderness legislation in 1980 and 1981, only to see those bills — like HR 1437 — languish in the Senate committee. *(1980 Almanac p. 617; 1981 Almanac p. 524)*

As passed by the House, HR 1437 added 58 national forest areas totalling about 2,332,000 acres to the wilderness system.

California already had some 2.1 million acres of national forest wilderness.

The legislation also designated 1,418,230 acres of national park lands as park wilderness — a less controversial move, since the land already had considerable protection. And it added 16,938 acres of national forest and other lands to the park system.

Some 72,000 acres were marked for further evaluation as possible wilderness.

The bill released 4.3 million acres of forest land for development.

Floor Amendments. By voice vote, the House accepted one important amendment by John F. Seiberling, D-Ohio, adding a package of "soft release" provisions sought by conservationists.

"Hard release" language would have prohibited executive branch agencies from ever again considering released lands for possible wilderness designation and from managing those lands to protect that suitability. "Soft release" prohibited renewed wilderness study only through the next U.S. Forest Service planning cycle in 1992-94.

The House rejected, 121-272, an amendment offered by Robert S. Walker, R-Pa., allowing the secretary of agriculture to waive provisions of the bill he found to cause unemployment. *(Vote 45, p. 20-H)*

Also rejected, 136-257, was an amendment offered by Norman D. Shumway, R-Calif., protecting only the 1.2 million acres recommended for wilderness by the Reagan administration. *(Vote 46, p. 20-H)*

Four other amendments, all relating to specific tracts, were rejected by voice or division votes, and a fifth was withdrawn.

Florida

The House June 6 suspended the rules and passed by voice vote HR 9 (H Rept 98-102, Pts. I and II), which added 49,150 acres of national forest land to the federal wilderness system. The bill also banned phosphate leasing and mining in the Osceola National Forest.

HR 9 was similar to a bill vetoed Jan. 14 by President Reagan, who objected to provisions for compensating holders of phosphate mining claims. This time around, those provisions were removed from the bill by the House Interior and Insular Affairs Committee.

Four companies had pending applications to mine phosphates in the forest area covered by the bill. They claimed property rights would be taken from them by the ban on mining accompanying wilderness status.

But the administration said it had rejected the lease applications and ended any legal claim the companies might have against the government. R. Max Peterson, chief of the U.S. Forest Service, told a House Interior subcommittee that a team of Agriculture and Interior technical experts had concluded the forest lands could not be reclaimed at any cost under current technology — which would effectively render the phosphate claims worthless, at least for purposes of compensation.

This represented a reversal of position since 1981, when the Reagan administration supported granting the leases and mining the phosphates. On Oct. 22, 1981, Assistant Agriculture Secretary John B. Crowell had testified that the lands probably could be reclaimed.

After passage by the House, HR 9 was referred June 15 to the Senate Energy and Natural Resources Committee, which took no action on it in 1983.

Missouri

The House Aug. 2 suspended the rules and by 406-18 passed a bill (S 64) designating as the Irish Wilderness approximately 15,500 acres in the Mark Twain National Forest in Missouri. *(Vote 288, p. 86-H)*

The House-passed bill (H Rept 98-337) deleted about 2,000 acres from the 17,562-acre version (S Rept 98-45) passed by the Senate April 13. The area was deleted because the St. Joe Lead Company had applied for mineral prospecting permits in part of the area.

A similar bill passed the Senate in 1982 but was narrowly defeated in the House after objections by Rep. Bill Emerson, R-Mo., in whose district the area lies. Emerson called the 1983 version "a fair and reasonable compromise."

The Irish Wilderness was the largest relatively undisturbed area remaining in Missouri. The name came from the Irish immigrants who settled the area in 1858. The area was currently used for camping, hunting, hiking and other recreational activities.

The Senate did not act on the amended bill before adjournment.

Montana

President Reagan Oct. 31 signed into law a bill (S 96 — PL 98-140) creating a 259,000-acre wilderness area named after the late Sen. Lee Metcalf, D-Mont. (1961-1978), in Montana's Beaverhead and Gallatin National Forests.

The Senate had passed a 244,000-acre version (S Rept 98-16) April 13. The bill released other Montana national forest lands from further wilderness consideration until at least 1995.

The House added acreage to the proposal before approving it Oct. 6 (H Rept 98-405), and the Senate by voice vote Oct. 19 agreed to the House amendments.

New Hampshire

The House Nov. 15 suspended the rules and passed by voice vote HR 3921 (H Rept 98-545), designating as wilderness 77,000 acres in the White Mountain National Forest. The measure covered the Pemigewasset Wilderness Area, the Sandwich Range Wilderness, and the Presidential Dry River Wilderness additions.

The bill was referred to the Senate Agriculture Committee, where the Soil and Water Conservation Subcommittee held hearings on a companion measure (S 1851) Nov. 8.

North Carolina

The House Nov. 16 suspended the rules and passed by a 398-21 vote HR 3960, designating as wilderness 69,000 acres in 11 national forest areas. *(Vote 482, p. 140-H)*

The measure required the secretary of agriculture to review five other national forest areas for wilderness suitability, with the president to make recommendations to Congress on those areas within three years of enactment.

HR 3960 was reported Nov. 10 by the House Interior Committee (H Rept 98-532).

Oregon

The House March 21 passed HR 1149 (H Rept 98-13), which designated as wilderness approximately 1.13 million acres in 30 Oregon national forest areas.

The 252-93 final passage came despite bitter division within the Oregon House delegation. Oregon Republicans Denny Smith and Robert F. Smith opposed the bill and challenged it in a series of House votes, saying it would cost forest industry jobs in their districts. *(Vote 35, 14-H)*

The National Forest Service also opposed the bill on behalf of the Reagan administration.

Proponents, including Oregon Democrats James Weaver, Les AuCoin and Ron Wyden, countered that Oregon's timber industry had a large surplus that it could not cut or sell because of a slump in the housing industry. AuCoin said the bill would make available more board feet

of timber — by releasing wilderness-candidate areas presently off-limits to lumbering — than it preserved in designated wilderness areas.

Wyden said the bill also would protect some 8,900 commercial and Indian fishing jobs by preserving upstream and coastal watersheds on which salmon depended.

Floor Challenges. The first challenge to the bill came on the rule (H Res 141) for its consideration, which was adopted 234-84. *(Vote 31, p. 14-H)*

Denny Smith offered a substitute amendment that would have named no wilderness areas and released all wilderness candidate areas from further consideration or protective management until the year 2000. That amendment was rejected 58-292. *(Vote 32, p. 14-H)*

A substitute offered by Don Young, R-Alaska, would have excluded from wilderness designation any lands in the districts of Robert F. Smith and Denny Smith. It was rejected 91-249. *(Vote 33, p. 14-H)*

Finally, the House rejected 96-240 an amendment by Robert S. Walker, R-Pa., allowing the secretary of agriculture to waive any provision of the bill shown to cause greater unemployment. *(Vote 34, p. 14-H)*

The Senate Energy Subcommittee on Public Lands held hearings on the measure July 21, Aug. 25 and Oct. 20.

Vermont

The House Nov. 15 suspended the rules and passed by voice vote HR 4198 (H Rept 98-533), designating approximately 41,260 acres in the Green Mountain National Forest as wilderness. The areas included the Breadloaf Wilderness, the Big Branch Wilderness, the Peru Peak Wilderness, the George D. Aiken Wilderness and the Lye Brook Wilderness additions.

The bill also created the 36,400-acre White Rock National Recreation Area, which included two of the wilderness areas. Labeled a compromise by sponsors, it included less acreage than was sought by conservationists.

It was referred to the Senate Agriculture Committee, which did not act on it in 1983.

Wisconsin

The House Nov. 16 suspended the rules and by 402-17 passed HR 3578 (H Rept 98-531), which would designate as wilderness 24,339 acres of national forest land. *(Vote 483, p. 140-H)*

The measure covered the 4,235-acre Porcupine Lake Wilderness in the Chequamegon National Forest, the 7,527-acre Kimball Creek wilderness area, 8,872-acre Headwater of the Pine wilderness area, and the 3,705-acre Shelp Lake wilderness area — all in the Nicolet National Forest.

The Senate Agriculture Subcommittee on Soil and Water Conservation held hearings on a companion bill (S 1610) on Nov. 16.

Wyoming

The Senate April 13 passed by voice vote a bill (S 543 — S Rept 98-54) designating approximately 635,729 acres in seven national forest areas as wilderness.

The areas covered were the 157,900-acre Cloud Peak Wilderness in the Bighorn National Forest, the 101,991-acre Popo Agie Wilderness in the Shoshone National Forest, the 228,550-acre Gros Ventre Wilderness in the Bridger-Teton National Forest, the 101,535-acre Jedediah Smith Wilderness in the Targhee National Forest, the 11,100-acre DuNoir addition to the Washakie Wilderness in the Bridger-Teton National Forest, the 28,156-acre Corridor addition to the Teton Wilderness in the Bridger-Teton National Forest, and the 6,497-acre Glacier addition to the Fitzpatrick Wilderness in the Shoshone National Forest.

The total was less than the RARE II recommendation for 713,900 acres of wilderness plus 414,900 acres for further planning.

Conservationists wanted 2.4 million acres of wilderness. As amended by the Senate Energy and Natural Resources Committee, the bill released all non-wilderness forest lands in the state for other uses until the year 2000 and established the legal sufficiency of the RARE II environmental statement for the state.

It also exempted Wyoming from a rider to the fiscal 1983 Interior appropriations bill (PL 97-394), substituting a provision that withdrew all Wyoming wilderness from oil, gas, and mineral leasing and hard rock mining. That exemption left open the possiblity of seismic exploration in the wilderness.

The House Interior Subcommittee on Public Lands held hearings on the bill June 28 and July 21, but did not act on it.

Awaiting Committee Action

Other wilderness bills introduced in 1983 but still awaiting committee action included proposals for Arizona (HR 3562), Arkansas (HR 2452, HR 2917), Texas (HR 2669, HR 3788) and Washington (S 837). ∎

Oregon Lands Transfer

Congress Oct. 25 overrode President Reagan's veto and enacted into law a bill (HR 1062 — PL 98-137) giving 3.11 acres to a handful of Oregon residents, most of them elderly couples who paid for the land years ago only to discover later that it actually belonged to the federal government.

It was the only time in 1983 that Congress overrode a presidential veto. *(Vetoes, p. 4)*

The House vote to override was 297-125, or 15 more than the two-thirds needed. *(Vote 386, p. 114-H)*

The Senate vote, which came scarcely two hours later, was 95-0, or 31 more than the margin needed. *(Vote 304, p. 50-S)*

Background

Reagan's Oct. 19 veto of HR 1062 came as a surprise. The bill had cleared Congress with no objections in either chamber. It was approved on the consent calendar in the House on Oct. 3 and by unanimous consent in the Senate Oct. 6.

The bill authorized the interior secretary to give 3.11 acres of federal land in Lane County, Ore., to individuals who paid for it years ago after an inaccurate private survey was made when the land was subdivided in 1941.

The error was discovered in a 1959 survey by the Interior Department's Bureau of Land Management (BLM), but BLM never formally filed its claim to the land with the Lane County government. The Oregon families continued paying property taxes — more than $20,000 on the federally owned land alone — while beseeching the government to straighten out the title confusion.

At stake were nine small tracts owned by six couples and two corporations, Pacific Northwest Bell and the Pacific and Eastern Railroad Company. Land in the area was

subdivided into lots and sold by a private developer beginning in 1941. But the lots adjoined land owned by the United States and managed by the BLM. An error by a surveyor hired by the developer in 1941 included a 3.11-acre strip of federal land in the lots sold to individual landowners.

Staffers for Rep. James Weaver, D-Ore., the sponsor of HR 1062 who represented the district where the disputed tracts were located, said the BLM land was not being used for any public purpose. The Interior Department had found the land "uneconomical to manage as part of the public lands."

The landowners had been seeking title to the land since the early 1960s, but the BLM under this and previous administrations said it had no legal authority to give them the land.

The administration claimed that there were procedures under the Federal Land Policy and Management Act of 1976 for adjusting claims of this type. The provision it cited turned out to be the one used for sales of surplus land. BLM estimated the fair market value of the land in question at about $45,000 as of July 1982, and said the landowners could buy it at fair market value.

The landowners sought help from Weaver, who introduced the private bill to allow, but not require, the interior secretary to convey the disputed acreage to the landowners without charge.

The Reagan Veto

In his veto message, Reagan contended that the wrong done to the landowners was no fault of the federal government, and that the government should therefore receive fair market value for conveying the lands. "The title defects affecting the beneficiaries of this legislation were caused by the reliance of the developers and subsequent purchasers of this tract on an inaccurate private survey — not by any act of the United States," Reagan said. *(Veto message, p. 38-E)*

But members of both parties denounced the veto as an act of insensitivity and pettiness.

"This bill represents such a small act of generosity and such a large dose of simple justice that it is beyond me what the administration thinks it gains by vetoing it," said Rep. Morris K. Udall, D-Ariz., chairman of the House Interior and Insular Affairs Committee.

The situation, said Rep. Denny Smith, R-Ore., "is a black mark on the Department of Interior or the White House staff or the Office of Management and Budget."

The Reagan administration outlined its objections to the bill in a June 15, 1983, letter from Assistant Interior Secretary Garrey E. Carruthers to Sen. James A. McClure, R-Idaho, chairman of the Senate Energy and Natural Resources Committee. Carruthers' arguments were essentially those used in the Reagan Oct. 19 veto message.

Besides saying that the federal government was not responsible for the survey error, the administration said the bill would create a harmful precedent encouraging other individuals to encroach on federal land.

Rep. Manuel Lujan Jr., R-N.M., ranking minority member on the House Interior Committee, defended the veto.

He called the bill a "sham," saying the original seller or surveyor should pay the damages.

Before the House voted to override, it agreed, 273-144, to a Udall motion to table a Lujan motion to refer the bill back to committee. *(Vote 385, p. 114-H)*   ∎

Matagorda Island Accord

The Senate July 22 cleared for President Reagan a bill (HR 1935) ratifying a state-federal agreement for the management of Matagorda Island, Texas, which provided habitat for the endangered whooping crane and brown pelican.

Reagan signed the measure into law (PL 98-66) on Aug. 4.

Matagorda Island, a 50,500-acre Gulf Coast island, was split between state and federal ownership. Under the agreement ratified by HR 1935, Texas was to make its lands part of the Aransas National Wildlife Refuge. Texas was to manage the wildlife refuge on the island, but under strict and enforceable federal guidelines.

The agreement appeared to resolve a controversy that arose from a 1981 Reagan administration proposal to remove the federal part of the island from the national wildlife refuge system and turn it over to the state.

HR 1935 was reported April 18 by the Merchant Marine and Fisheries Committee (H Rept 98-67). It was passed by voice vote under suspension of the House rules on April 19.

In the Senate, the measure was reported July 11 by the Environment and Public Works Committee (S Rept 98-176).   ∎

Pribilof Islands

The Senate Sept. 28 cleared for President Reagan a bill (HR 2840 — PL 98-129) overhauling the Fur Seal Act of 1966, which governed fur seal management and other federal activities on the Pribilof Islands off Alaska.

As cleared, the measure authorized transfer of federal property on the islands to native and state government entities and provided for a one-time appropriation of $20 million to a Pribilof Island trust fund to help in the transition from an economy dependent on sealing and federal income support to one that was self-sustaining.

In fiscal 1983, $6.3 million was appropriated to carry out federal responsibilities on the islands, with 95 percent going to social welfare programs. The new trust fund was intended to assume the major share of those programs.   ∎

Temporary Public Land Use

The Senate April 5 by voice vote passed a bill (S 612) authorizing temporary use by the military and other federal agencies of public lands controlled by the Interior Department's Bureau of Land Management (BLM). Permits for such temporary use could be issued for a three-year period, with one renewal allowed.

In its Feb. 28 report on the bill (S Rept 98-11), the Senate Energy and Natural Resources Committee noted that on several occasions, existing law had barred BLM from permitting temporary use of lands it controlled.

Once, for example, "BLM was unable to permit the use of a site on public lands by the Environmental Protection Agency for the purpose of monitoring the effects of hazardous waste disposal areas on private lands adjacent to those public lands," the report said.

Another time, the agency had to bar the Federal Aviation Administration from using public lands for its vector analysis program, which required short-term use of moun-

tain tops.

In the House, the bill was referred to the Interior and Insular Affairs Committee, which took no action on it in 1983. ∎

New Scenic Trails Voted

Congress March 15 cleared for the president legislation (S 271 — PL 98-11) establishing three new national scenic trails and authorizing studies of six additional routes.

Final action came when the House by voice vote suspended the rules and passed the bill without amendment. The House Interior and Insular Affairs Committee had reported it March 9 (H Rept 98-28).

The Senate Energy and Natural Resources Committee had reported S 271 (S Rept 98-1) on Jan. 31, and the full Senate passed it Feb. 3.

The measure was generally similar to one passed in 1982 by the House but not the Senate. Unlike that bill, however, S 271 contained no language aimed at blocking imposition of entrance fees at national recreation areas, scenic trails or rivers. The House had supported such language, while the Republican-controlled Senate opposed it. *(1982 Almanac p. 445)*

A more ambitious, and more expensive, national trails bill was also passed by the House in the 96th Congress, only to die in the Senate. *(1980 Almanac p. 617)*

The national trails system was created by Congress in 1968 (PL 90-543), beginning with the Appalachian and Pacific Crest trails. *(1968 Almanac p. 477)*

Provisions

As cleared, S 271 established three new national trails: Potomac Heritage National Scenic Trail, extending along the Potomac River for about 700 miles through Virginia, Maryland, the District of Columbia and Pennsylvania; Florida National Scenic Trail, extending about 1,300 miles in the state of Florida; Natchez Trace National Scenic Trail, extending 694 miles from Nashville, Tenn., to Natchez, Miss.

Studies. The legislation also authorized studies of six additional routes for possible inclusion in the national trail system: Juan Bautista de Anza Trail, following the route of his travels from Mexico to San Francisco; Trail of Tears, the route of the Cherokee Indians' resettlement march from North Carolina to Oklahoma; Illinois Trail, from the Lewis and Clark Trail at Wood River, Ill., to the Chicago Portage National Historic Site; Jedediah Smith Trail, along the route of his exploration from Idaho to California; General Crook Trail, from Prescott, Ariz., to Fort Apache; and Beale Wagon Road Trail, in two national forests in Arizona.

Authorization. The bill authorized expenditures of up to $2.5 million for acquisition and development of the Natchez Trace Trail.

No funds were authorized for the other two new trails, which would be carved out of existing national forests and parks.

Volunteers. The legislation included provisions designed to encourage volunteer groups to plan and manage existing or potential national trails, and to permit use in the trail system of railroad rights-of-way until and unless they were needed for railroad purposes.

Trails Renamed. And finally, S 271 named an existing trail in northern California after former Rep. Harold T.

Johnson, D-Calif. (1959-81), and a portion of the Nantahala National Forest in North Carolina after former Rep. Roy A. Taylor, D-N.C. (1960-77). ∎

Wild Horses and Burros

The Senate Energy and Natural Resources Committee Oct. 28 approved a bill (S 457) to revamp management of fast-breeding herds of wild horses and burros on Western range lands, allowing sale of excess animals to slaughterhouses or other buyers as a last resort.

The committee vote to order the bill reported was 10-9. Before approving S 457, the panel rejected, 8-10, an amendment by Wendell H. Ford, D-Ky., that would have eliminated the option of sale and destruction of excess animals.

The legislation did not reach the Senate floor in 1983.

Background

S 457 amended the Wild Free Roaming Horse and Burro Act of 1971 (PL 92-195), which set up a system for managing and protecting the thousands of "mustangs" running loose on federal lands. *(Congress and the Nation Vol. III, p. 789)*

Before 1971, herds had been decimated by entrepreneurs who rounded them up and sold them — often to rendering plants. The 1971 law made it illegal for private citizens to round up or kill the animals, but it allowed the government to destroy old, sick or lame wild horses it removed from the range.

It also allowed the government to destroy other excess horses when this was the only practical method of disposing of them. That was an option the Bureau of Land Management (BLM) generally avoided exercising; a moratorium on destruction of healthy horses and burros had been in effect since January 1982. The law forbade sale of the destroyed horses' remains.

In 1982, the government estimated there were 44,930 horses and 10,150 burros on its land. It set 25,000 animals as a desirable target population for horses and burros combined.

Sale of Excess Horses

S 457 allowed the government the option of selling unadoptable horses at auction. Proponents claimed the sale would give the horses one more chance to live. But they generally conceded the most likely buyer for many animals would be the packinghouse or rendering plant.

The controversial provision allowing sale of excess animals to slaughterhouses or other buyers drew a large crowd to the committee's hearings, with ranchers and animal lovers alike jamming the room April 11.

Ranchers' View. Ranchers testified that the animals were breeding too fast, overgrazing range land and ruining waterholes needed by cattle and sheep. They said the federal "Adopt-a-Horse" program set up by the 1971 law had not been able to find homes for all the excess horses.

In 1982, the Interior Department estimated the wild horse and burro population at 44,930 horses and 10,150 burros on federal land, and set 25,000 animals as a desirable target population for horses and burros combined. S 457 would have allowed the interior secretary to sell or destroy excess animals that would not be adopted — up to 3,500 per year — subject to state and federal humane laws.

Protectionists' View. But protectionists and the National Academy of Sciences (NAS), while conceding overcrowding existed in certain locations, asserted the evidence was inadequate to show a problem all over the West. Protectionists and a 1980 NAS study challenged BLM claims of a 20 percent growth rate on some ranges, saying 1971 estimates were simply too low. They noted that the range lands supported millions of domestic livestock and game animals.

Protectionists recalled the "atrocities" of the 1950s and 1960s, when the wild horses were indiscriminately rounded up for slaughter by profiteers.

But ranchers told their own stories, also decades old, of starving wild horses eating each others' manes and tails, or dying of thirst during droughts — all because there were too many animals on too little range. ■

Alaska Sport Hunting Bill

The Senate Energy and Natural Resources Committee Aug. 4 ordered reported without recommendation a bill (S 49) reopening to sport hunting approximately five million acres of national park land in Alaska.

The 11-8 committee vote was an indication of the controversy stirred by the legislation, which was formally reported Oct. 26 (S Rept 98-281) but did not reach the Senate floor in 1983.

In the House, Rep. Don Young, R-Alaska, introduced a companion bill (HR 1493), whose cosponsors included 21 of the 42 members of the House Interior Committee, which had jurisdiction over the bill.

However, Rep. John F. Seiberling, D-Ohio, chairman of Interior's Parks Subcommittee, opposed the bill and indicated he would not take it up until and unless the Senate passed it.

The Reagan administration supported the concept of S 49 but urged changes in the boundaries of lands covered. The administration wanted to open about 10.5 million acres to sport hunting.

Background

The sport hunting issue was an emotional one for Alaskans, hunters and conservationists. Advocates of the bill said the hunting ban under current law was a "lock-up" of resources; opponents called the bill a "a raid on the national parks unparalleled in our history."

S 49 was the first legislation dealing with major Alaskan acreage since the Alaska National Interest Lands Conservation Act (ANILCA — PL 96-487) signed by President Carter Dec. 2, 1980. That law marked a cease-fire, if not exactly a peace treaty, in a long and bitterly fought struggle between Alaskans and industries wanting to develop the state's resources on the one hand, and environmentalists and the Carter administration on the other. *(1980 Almanac p. 575)*

The new hunting bill, both sides said, threatened to reopen old wounds suffered by both sides in the struggle. Conservationists had wanted more acres protected in ANILCA, and developers wanted more acres open to development. Some on both sides said they would reopen the whole compromise if they did not get what they wanted on the hunting issue.

The 1980 lands act, nine years in the making, was formally proposed by Carter in 1977. It disposed of hun-

dreds of millions of acres, dividing them among Native Alaskans (44 million acres), the state of Alaska (105 million acres) and the federal government (124 million acres). The state contains a total of 374 million acres.

ANILCA set aside 43.6 million acres of new national parks, 53.8 million acres of new wildlife refuges and 56.7 million acres of wilderness, some of which was already in federal hands.

By Alaskan standards, the five to 12 million acres of national park land under debate in S 49 did not amount to a great deal of land. And even conservation groups did not argue that hunting on those lands was likely to endanger the perpetuation of wildlife populations.

About 19 million of the 43.6 million new national park acres in ANILCA were named national park preserves, a rarely used category differing from park status only in that it allowed hunting. That left about 24 million new park acres closed to hunting, bringing the statewide total to 32 million acres once old parks were added in. That was more than the 30 million acres of federal land in all the lower 48 states where hunting was banned.

In most national park areas created under ANILCA, subsistence hunting, fishing and gathering was still allowed for local residents who had hunted there before 1980. The areas were closed, however, to sport hunting by people from outside the area, as well as to mining, logging, and oil and gas drilling.

S 49 sought to redesignate five million acres of national park as national park preserve.

Symbolic Struggle

The sport hunting bill became a symbol for much larger concerns.

"Only a misbegotten conception that sport hunting is morally wrong can account for any opposition to this bill," said J. Warren Cassidy, head lobbyist for the National Rifle Association (NRA), at an April 15 Senate Energy Committee hearing.

But critics said S 49 would set a precedent for legislation, sought by hunters in the 97th Congress, to open all national parks to hunting. Paul C. Pritchard, president of the National Parks and Conservation Association (NPCA), called it "a double-barrelled shotgun aimed at the national parks in the lower 48 states."

S 49 raised the "right-to-hunt" issue for groups such as the NRA, the Alaska Sportsmen Council, the Alaska Professional Hunters Association, the Foundation for North American Wild Sheep, the American Fur Resources Institute, the Safari Club International and the Wildlife Legislative Fund of America.

Some environmental and conservation groups opposed S 49: NPCA, Defenders of Wildlife, National Audubon Society, the Wilderness Society, and Friends of Animals.

However, the National Wildlife Federation and Izaak Walton League endorsed the bill in concept.

Fun vs. Food

Some Alaskan sport hunters said the issue was one of fairness — that ANILCA created two classes of hunters and gave one (subsistence hunters) superior rights.

But opponents of S 49 argued it would mainly benefit wealthy out-of-state hunters who could afford airplanes and guides to take them to the remote areas in question.

Former Sen. Gaylord Nelson, D-Wis. (1963-81), chairman of the Wilderness Society, said the bear, moose, caribou and Dall sheep likely to be sought in the park areas

appealed mainly to "just a handful of wealthy sportsmen" interested in trophies. Alaska issued 8,270 licenses to out-of-state hunters in 1982.

Proponents of the bill seethed when conservationists asserted that 92 percent of the state's land already could legally be hunted. They noted that land included many areas, such as ice fields and high mountains, that sustained no game animals. Moreover, they said, some of the best hunting was in the park areas closed by the 1980 law, areas they traditionally hunted during the 1970s.

Sen. Ted Stevens, R-Alaska, said many of Alaska's 76,000 licensed hunters supplemented their diets with meat from hunting.

Committee Amendments

As introduced Jan. 25 by Sens. Stevens and Frank H. Murkowski, both Alaska Republicans, the bill would have allowed sport hunting on about 11.8 million acres of Alaska national park lands.

Four amendments approved Aug. 4 by the Energy Committee reduced to about five million acres the amount of land opened to hunting, according to the Interior Department.

Eight parks were affected by the bill as introduced: Katmai, Lake Clark, Denali, Gates of the Arctic, Aniakchak, Kenai Fjords and Glacier Bay, as well as the Noatak Preserve.

The panel approved, 13-6, an amendment offered by Paul E. Tsongas, D-Mass., to delete all of Katmai National Park, about one million acres. By 11-8, it approved another Tsongas amendment deleting about five million acres of Gates of the Arctic National Park, considered the flagship of Alaskan parks.

The committee approved by voice vote two amendments by Murkowski, deleting the 567,000-acre Kenai Fjords National Park and the 523,000-acre Glacier Bay National Park. ∎

Park Protection Measure

After heated debate, the House Oct. 4 passed a bill (HR 2379) meant to protect the national parks from threats posed by federal actions both inside and outside their boundaries.

The 321-82 vote on final passage was comparable to the margin by which the House passed a similar bill in September 1982. That measure died in the Senate Energy Committee, where HR 2379 was referred. The Senate panel took no action on the legislation in 1983. *(Vote 358, p. 106-H; 1982 Almanac p. 445)*

The Reagan administration opposed HR 2379, as it did the earlier version.

The legislation was developed by Rep. John F. Seiberling, D-Ohio, chairman of the House Interior Subcommittee on Public Lands and National Parks, in response to a May 1980 National Park Service report detailing more than 4,000 threats to park resources. Those threats included internal ones, such as too many visitors, and external ones, such as mining on lands next to a park.

The bill required the interior secretary to submit a "State of the Parks Report" to Congress every two years, and it laid out a detailed planning and notification procedure to identify and counter possible threats to the parks.

It applied restrictions not only to Interior Department actions, such as mineral leasing, but also to actions by other federal agencies. The Interior Department and other agencies would have to wait 30 days after notifying Congress of certain proposed actions before carrying them out — giving Congress a chance to second-guess the executive.

The legislation also directed the secretary to maintain an adequate professional staff within the Park Service.

House opposition to HR 2379, led by Western Republicans, centered on a provision requiring the interior secretary to review actions planned by other federal agencies on lands "adjacent to" park boundaries. Opponents argued that the provision, which did not define "adjacent," could stymie needed development in areas far from the parks themselves.

Committee Action

HR 2379 was approved by voice vote May 10 and reported May 16 (H Rept 98-170) by the House Interior and Insular Affairs Committee.

The bill approved April 26 by the Public Lands and National Parks Subcommittee survived the full committee markup virtually unchanged.

The key challenge to HR 2379, an amendment offered by James V. Hansen, R-Utah, was rejected 18-20. It would have authorized state legislatures to define lands "adjacent to" national parks, limiting the scope of the veto power the bill gave to Congress and the National Park Service.

Critics such as Hansen feared the bill would give the federal government veto power over some decisions made by local governments near national parks.

House Floor Action

Hansen tried again on the House floor. Contending that the bill "could lock up most of our Western states," he offered an amendment to delete the provision requiring the interior secretary to review actions planned by other federal agencies on lands adjacent to parks. It was rejected 160-245 after Seiberling said it would effectively gut the bill. *(Vote 357, p. 106-H)* ∎

Harry S Truman Historic Site

The House May 10 cleared for President Reagan a bill (S 287 — PL 98-32) to establish the Harry S Truman National Historic Site at the Independence, Mo., home of the nation's 33rd president.

The Senate had passed the bill May 6 by voice vote.

The bill authorized the interior secretary to acquire and maintain the 2½-story white frame home where Truman and his wife, Bess, lived from the time of their marriage until their deaths. Truman died Dec. 16, 1972; his wife died in October 1982.

Under the measure, the site was to become a unit of the national park system. ∎

Miscellaneous Parks Bill

The House Oct. 20 cleared for President Reagan a noncontroversial "housekeeping" bill (HR 1213 — PL 98-141) related to federal lands and national parks.

The bill authorized a boundary land exchange at the Effigy Mounds National Monument; land acquisition for

four National Park System units; an increase in the budget for development of Perry's Victory and International Peace Memorial in Ohio; funds for the Pennsylvania Avenue Development Corporation; and boundary adjustments for two national forests in Colorado, among other provisions.

The House passed the bill (H Rept 98-15) March 8, while the Senate passed it (S Rept 98-141) with amendments on Oct. 6.

The House-passed bill authorized establishment of the Harry S Truman National Historic Site at the Independence, Mo., home of the 33rd president. But the Senate authorized that site in separate legislation (S 287) May 6. The House cleared S 287 on May 10, and President Reagan signed it into law (PL 98-32) on May 23. *(Story, p. 348)*

The House-passed language on the Truman site was removed from HR 1213 before it cleared. ∎

Water Resources Research

The Senate Nov. 18 approved by voice vote a compromise version of a water resources research authorization bill (S 684) that was only a step away from final clearance when Congress adjourned for the year.

As amended by the Senate Nov. 18, the bill authorized appropriations of $36 million for each of the fiscal years 1985 through 1989. That annual spending figure lay between the $60 million called for by the House and $21.1 million recommended by the Senate in earlier rounds of the legislation.

The administration had requested no funds for the project.

The Senate originally passed the bill (S Rept 98-91) on May 25. The House passed its version Oct. 31 after substituting the provisions of its own bill (HR 2911 — H Rept 98-416).

The Senate Nov. 18 replaced the bill received from the House with a compromise version worked out by House and Senate managers. It provided for $10 million in grants each year to state water research institutes, $20 million each year in matching research grants, and $6 million each year for technology development programs.

In 1982, the Senate passed a $21.1 million water research bill, but the House failed to act on the measure. *(1982 Almanac p. 466)* ∎

Dam Safety Repairs

House and Senate committees reported out companion bills (HR 1652, S 672) to authorize an additional $650 million for safety improvements on some 53 Bureau of Reclamation dams, but neither measure received floor consideration during 1983.

House Bill

The House Interior and Insular Affairs Committee May 10 approved HR 1652 by voice vote. The measure was similar to one that was passed in 1982 by the House but died in the Senate. *(1982 Almanac p. 449)*

The bill amended the Reclamation Safety of Dams Act of 1978 (PL 95-578), which authorized $100 million for dam safety repairs, bringing the total amount authorized to

$750 million. The House bill in 1982 added only $550 million for a $650 million total. *(PL 95-578, 1978 Almanac p. 723)*

As approved by the House panel, HR 1652 was a simple, one-page authorization measure that required no added reimbursement of federal costs by local beneficiaries of the water projects. The 1982 House-passed bill was amended on the floor to include new cost-sharing language, and a similar effort was expected on the floor for HR 1652.

The full House Interior panel accepted the bill as it had been amended and approved April 26 by the Water and Power Resources Subcommittee. The bill was reported May 16 (H Rept 98-168) and placed on the calendar.

Senate Bill

The Senate Energy and Natural Resources Committee approved a similar bill, S 672, on Sept. 21, by a 13-5 vote. It was reported Sept. 29 (S Rept 98-258) and placed on the calendar.

The Senate bill, too, authorized an additional $650 million in safety-related work beyond the 1978 authorization levels. Like the House bill, it allocated no new costs to local beneficiaries.

The Reagan administration supported an increase in the authorization, although only by $550 million. Speaking for the administration, Assistant Interior Secretary Garrey E. Carruthers said local beneficiaries should contribute to the projects when they were able to pay.

Two of the Senators opposing the bill, Howard M. Metzenbaum, D-Ohio, and Bill Bradley, D-N.J., filed minority views in the report saying their opposition was based on the cost-sharing issue. They joined the administration in calling for local cost-sharing. ∎

House Clears Wetlands Bill

The House Nov. 17 cleared a bill (HR 2395 — PL 98-200) extending for one year the Wetlands Loan Act of 1961, through which hunters help pay for federal purchase of waterfowl habitat.

The House had originally passed a 10-year extension of the act on Oct. 31. The Senate passed the same bill Nov. 17, after amending it to reduce the extension to one year. The House by voice vote later on Nov. 17 concurred with the Senate amendment, clearing the bill.

Background

The 1961 law, last renewed in 1976, authorized a total of $200 million in appropriations as a "loan" from the Treasury to speed acquisition of the wetlands that are the habitat of migratory waterfowl. As of Sept. 30, some $147 million of that amount had been appropriated. *(Background, Congress and the Nation Vol. I, p. 1067)*

The money was to be repaid to the Treasury eventually with revenue from the federal "duck stamps," which waterfowl hunters were required to purchase.

Without extension of the act, which expired Sept. 30, 1983, 75 percent of duck stamp revenues would have started going into the Treasury, rather than to purchase wetlands, as they had been doing previously. Those revenues were estimated at $16 million annually.

Both House and Senate were considering more comprehensive bills (HR 3082, S 1329) to beef up wetlands

acquisition. Those measures forgave the wetlands loans altogether.

The House Merchant Marine and Insular Affairs Committee Oct. 25 reported HR 3082 (H Rept 98-440, Part 1), after approving it by voice vote on Sept. 22. The Senate Environment and Public Works Committee approved S 1329 on Sept. 28.

But neither measure reached the floor in 1983.

Legislative History

The House Merchant Marine Committee had intended to combine HR 2395 with the more ambitious HR 3082, but decided to go forward with it alone when the larger bill was referred to two additional committees, the Interior and Insular Affairs Committee and the Public Works and Transportation Committee. Those panels had until March 1, 1984, to report HR 3082.

The House approved HR 2395 by voice vote Oct. 31. As passed, it provided a 10-year extension of the wetlands loan law.

The Senate amended the measure Nov. 17, cutting the extension to one year, and the House accepted that amendment the same day, clearing the bill for President Reagan's signature. ∎

Federal Coal Leasing Moratorium Adopted

Congress froze the leasing of coal on federal lands in 1983 after it became a major bone of contention between Interior Secretary James G. Watt and his congressional critics.

The temporary leasing ban was part of the fiscal 1984 Interior appropriations bill (HR 3363 — PL 98-146) that was cleared Oct. 20 and signed Nov. 4 by President Reagan. *(Interior appropriations bill, p. 462)*

Adoption of the ban by the Senate Sept. 20 marked a sharp reversal for that body, which had narrowly backed Watt's coal leasing program in two previous votes, one in December 1982 and the other in June 1983.

The Sept. 20 Senate vote came after Watt signaled he might defy an emergency ban by the House Interior and Insular Affairs Committee on the next scheduled sale in his coal leasing program.

But a U.S. District Court in Washington, D.C., upheld the House committee for the moment on Sept. 28, barring the next sale until at least the spring of 1984.

Leasing Ban Provisions

As adopted, the ban suspended coal leasing until 90 days after Congress received a report from a blue-ribbon commission appointed by Watt to study the issue. That commission, headed by David F. Linowes, had six months to come up with its report.

The coal leasing ban was contained in an amendment, offered by Sen. Dale Bumpers, D-Ark., that prohibited spending any funds in the fiscal 1984 Interior appropriations for the sale or lease of coal on public lands, except for emergency leasing, lease modifications or lease exchanges.

Exempted from the moratorium were several specific tracts in Montana and Colorado, where individual coal companies claimed they needed coal leased to avert economic hardship to existing mining operations.

The coal leasing prohibition was to stay in effect until the Linowes commission submitted its report and Congress had 90 days to consider it. The 90-day period, Bumpers said, was intended to give Congress a chance to enact any legislation it deemed necessary in response to the commission's recommendations.

The six-month clock for the commission's report actually started running before the leasing ban was enacted.

The commission had been established earlier under the fiscal 1983 supplemental appropriations bill (HR 3069 — PL 98-63) cleared July 29 and signed by the president July 30. That measure gave the interior secretary 30 days from enactment to appoint the commission and gave the commission six months from enactment to report to Congress. *(HR 3069, p. 509)*

Watt Aug. 4 appointed Linowes, a professor at the University of Illinois, to head the Commission on Fair Market Policy for Federal Coal Leasing.

Linowes previously chaired a separate commission appointed by Watt to study the government's oil and gas royalty program. That panel's report served as the basis for a law enacted in 1982 tightening the system for collecting royalties from oil and gas production on federal and Indian lands. *(1982 Almanac p. 446)*

Background

The Leasing System

Under the Federal Coal Leasing Amendments Act of 1976 (PL 94-377) and the Mineral Leasing Act of 1920, the government was authorized to lease certain public lands to companies or individuals for the purpose of mining coal. *(Congress and the Nation Vol. I, p. 1000; Vol. IV, p. 275)*

Under the 1976 law, the interior secretary had to award the leases by competitive bidding, but could accept no bid that he determined to be less than the fair market value of the lease. Leaseholders paid in a number of ways for the privilege of mining publicly owned coal and putting the proceeds in their own pockets.

First, they paid "bonus bids," one-time, up-front payments to the government, to win award of the lease. This was the main area where competition worked to maximize revenue for the federal Treasury.

Second, they paid rents each year the lease was in effect, usually a nominal amount of a few dollars per acre.

Third, they paid royalties, an amount set by the interior secretary at 12½ percent of the value of surface-mined coal (8 percent for underground coal) at the mine.

Fourth, like other corporations, they paid taxes to the state and federal governments. Coal mining firms paid "severance taxes" to states, often amounting to an even higher percentage of the value of coal extracted than that paid for royalties.

Fifth, they paid certain mandatory expenses, such as that for reclamation of strip-mined land, that were required by federal law.

All these items were on top of the basic costs of doing business, such as mining and transporting the coal itself. The ultimate cost of coal delivered to the customer's door was thus likely to be many times its value in the ground.

The Powder River Sale

Watt's yearlong confrontation with Congress over coal leasing was really triggered by an event that happened in April 1982 — the sale of coal leases on federal lands in the Powder River Basin in Wyoming and Montana.

The largest single coal lease sale in the nation's history, it came after a decade when there had been virtually no leasing as a result of various legal and administrative moratoriums.

A May 11 report issued by the General Accounting Office (GAO), a watchdog arm of Congress, found that the government received far less than fair market value for the Powder River leases, and it recommended that Congress change the law to prevent such undercharging.

The GAO report only underscored findings of an April 20 report by the investigations staff of the House Appropriations Committee.

"Such large-scale leasing under poor economic conditions distorts the market by flooding it with leased coal," the Appropriations report stated. "It temporarily reduces fair market value and allows the industry to acquire coal at 'fire sale' prices."

Most of the 146 billion tons of recoverable coal in the Powder River Basin was federally owned. Of that, 1.6 billion tons ended up actually being offered.

Charges of mismanagement and even possible impropriety in the sale centered around a last-minute change in the system for making bonus bids.

Until a few weeks before the Powder River sale, the system called for Interior officials to calculate "minimum acceptable bids" representing "fair market value" before the sale.

But shortly after field officials sent their calculations to Washington, D.C., top headquarters officials decided to change the bidding system.

The new system replaced minimum acceptable bids with what were called "entry-level bids." These were intended to be the point, well below fair market value, at which bidding could open, with an assumption that auction-like competition would bid up the price. Interior officials were to evaluate whether the bids reflected fair market value after the sale. The previously calculated minimum acceptable bids, meant to reflect fair market value, were still supposed to be confidential.

Allegations of a Leak

Critics charged that the minimum acceptable bids for the Powder River sale leaked into the hands of coal companies before the sale was announced. Investigations by the GAO and the inspector general for the Interior Department were unable to substantiate the charge, but their findings pointed in opposite directions.

GAO reported: "There is some evidence that a disclosure occurred, but we were unable to verify details related to it, or to confirm that the disclosure — if it occurred — had an impact on preparations for the April sale."

"The possibility exists that during this time the minimum acceptable bids found their way into industry hands and that industry subsequently pressured Interior into changing bidding systems as a means of lowering coal selling prices," GAO division Director J. Dexter Peach testified May 16 before the House Interior Oversight and Investigations Subcommittee headed by Edward J. Markey, D-Mass.

But Richard Mulberry, Interior's inspector general, said the only allegation he could substantiate turned out to be based on a misunderstanding. An employee who discovered that a company was in possession of bid information was unaware that Interior had already published it.

The question of why Interior changed the bidding system so close to the sale date remained unanswered, in the eyes of Markey and GAO. "Interior had no records documenting and could provide no written quantitative basis supporting the need to change the system," the GAO report stated.

When Markey at a May 16 hearing repeatedly asked for the economic justification for the change, Garrey E. Carruthers, assistant interior secretary, shot back: "It is my view that the public trust was served by that [change] and that is sufficient economic justification for me."

Saying legal documentation was included with the notice of sale, Carruthers added, "It is not necessary to have an economic analysis to change the system."

Sale Results

For the 11 tracts leased in the April 1982 sale, Interior's original minimum acceptable bid values totaled $94.7 million. Interior cut these to entry-level bid values totaling $52.4 million, and received actual bids totaling $54.7 million.

GAO, however, estimated the fair market value of the same 11 tracts at $165.3 million, using Interior's pricing formula but GAO's own judgment in weighting various parts of that equation.

Watt, at a May 12 hearing before the House Appropriations subcommittee, insisted that the bids were within the limits of what he called "fair market value."

The auction effect expected under the new bidding system did not occur, with actual bids only slightly exceeding the entry-level bids. The post-sale evaluation that was meant to backstop those entry levels with real market values did not work as Interior had said it would, either. Interior rejected the high bid for only one of the 11 tracts bid on in April 1982, accepting the others.

The auction effect depends on competition among multiple bidders to drive up the price. Eight of the 11 tracts bid on in April 1982 received only one bid, and the rest received two each. Two more were offered that received no bids.

Eight of the 13 leases offered were so-called "maintenance tracts." These were tracts adjacent to an existing strip mine, often tailored by Interior specifically for the purpose of expanding an existing mine, and usually of economic interest only to the owners of such a mine. Most such tracts got only one bid at the Powder River sale.

"Continuing to sell production maintenance tracts at regional coal sales only creates the pretense of competition and offers little assurance that the government will receive a reasonable return for its coal," GAO's Peach told Markey's panel. "In our view, this problem of 'maintenance leasing' deserves congressional attention."

"Put simply, the procedures unrealistically anticipated genuine bidding competition," Peach testified.

Those procedures had later been changed by Interior, but critics were still not satisfied.

Philosophical Dispute

Watt and Carruthers readily conceded they did not squeeze the last penny out of the coal sale. But they contended their actions were a legitimate exercise of the philosophy of the Reagan administration, not a dereliction of duty.

"I did not seek to maximize the dollar return at the expense of future consumers," Watt told the House Appropriations Interior Subcommittee May 12.

Much of the debate centered on the question of who should set the "price" (meaning minimum bonus bid) of federal coal — the federal government or private industry.

Watt's position, and that of the Reagan administration generally, was based on a belief that free market competition set prices best. GAO said there was no competition with only a single bidder.

Critics such as the House Appropriations staff emphasized the lower immediate dollar return to the federal government that resulted from Watt's policy and leasing practices. The Appropriations report was laden with such terms as "profiteering leaseholders," "fire sale" and "giveaway" — language that Interior officials attacked as unprofessional.

But Carruthers called such criticism shortsighted, questioning its focus on the bonus bid alone: "The bonus is a very small part of the financial reward to the taxpayers of America from leasing coal. The royalty and the tax returns from coal development are much greater than the bonus."

Yet bonuses were the focus of attention because they were the only area where the market could work at all to increase the price the government got for its coal. Royalties and taxes were essentially fixed rates. Sales in which coal leases would be awarded to the company that offered the highest royalty rate were still only a theory.

Earlier Legislative Efforts

Several times before they finally prevailed, Watt's congressional critics had tried — and failed — to slow or block his coal program.

1983 Appropriation

Efforts to thwart the coal program actually began in 1982, with a rider to a fiscal 1983 Interior appropriations bill (PL 97-394). *(1982 Almanac p. 262)*

The House Appropriations Subcommittee on Interior wrote into its version of the bill a funding reduction for the Bureau of Land Management that was designed to slow the coal leasing program. While Reagan had asked for $15.8 million for the program, the committee gave him $13.7 million — a $2.1 million cut.

The panel's report criticized the coal leasing program sharply, and said the cut would delay two sales planned for late fiscal 1983 until early fiscal 1984. Such a "temporary delay," it stated, would allow the economic issues raised by the Powder River sale to be reviewed.

The House passed that measure Dec. 3, 1982, but the Senate Appropriations Subcommittee on Interior restored the funds cut by the House.

During Senate floor consideration of the bill, Bumpers offered an amendment to cut those funds from the bill. His amendment was rejected by a single vote, 47-48, on Dec. 14. *(1982 Almanac, Vote 400, p. 68-S)*

1983 Initiatives

In 1983 several authorizing bills and a resolution were introduced with the similar purpose of slowing or stopping coal leasing.

Rep. Morris K. Udall, D-Ariz., chairman of the House Interior and Insular Affairs Committee, May 12 introduced a bill (HR 3018) to impose a moratorium on coal leasing.

The Udall bill would have barred any coal leasing on

federal lands until certain requirements were satisfied, but in any case for at least one year from the date of enactment. It required the interior secretary to conduct a detailed study of coal leasing economics and come up with new guidelines and procedures for pricing coal, conducting sales and protecting the confidentiality of its pricing information.

Sen. Alan J. Dixon, D-Ill., introduced a bill (S 1142) imposing a one-year leasing moratorium and calling for a broad investigation and report by the General Accounting Office (GAO) of the coal leasing program and possible improvements in it. Dixon also introduced a resolution (S Res 123) calling for a Senate investigation into the matter.

A Senate bill (S 1297) identical to Udall's was introduced May 17 by Bumpers, who in 1982 had offered the appropriations bill amendment to delay leasing.

None of the bills moved in either chamber, however.

Fiscal 1983 Supplemental

The House Appropriations Committee May 18 approved a fiscal 1983 supplemental appropriations bill (HR 3069 — H Rept 98-207) after attaching a rider barring further sale or leasing of coal on public lands through Sept. 30, 1983, the end of the fiscal year. *(Appropriations bill, p. 509)*

The bill also set up the Linowes commission. The House passed it May 25, but the Senate Appropriations Subcommittee on Interior promptly took the moratorium out of the bill, which was already facing serious veto threats from the Reagan administration.

Bumpers sought a second test on the coal leasing issue by offering on the Senate floor an amendment to restore the House-backed moratorium.

After heavy lobbying by the coal industry and the Reagan administration, which opposed any leasing ban, the Senate June 14 rejected the Bumpers amendment by a 48-51 margin. *(Vote 138, p. 26-S)*

Eight senators who had supported Bumpers in 1982 voted against the ban this time, although seven others switched from "nay" to "yea."

Conference/Final. House-Senate conferees, in a report issued July 20, eliminated the House-passed moratorium, but included the provisions that set up the Linowes commission to study the coal issue. Although the study provisions were not in either the House or Senate versions of the supplemental bill, the House had already passed those provisions June 28 as part of the regular fiscal 1984 interior appropriations bill (HR 3363).

Fiscal 1984 Appropriations

House Committee Action

The House Appropriations subcommittee June 7 approved HR 3363 with another coal leasing moratorium attached. The full Appropriations panel reported it June 21 (H Rept 98-253).

Rep. Sidney R. Yates, D-Ill., chairman of the Interior Subcommittee, was the chief architect of the coal leasing ban, which was one of several restrictions on Watt's mineral and energy leasing activities included in the bill.

The moratorium imposed by the House committee in the 1984 funding fill was to stay in effect pending a study by an independent blue-ribbon commission, such as the Linowes panel, which would be appointed by Watt.

The House panel's moratorium started upon enact-

ment. The bill gave the interior secretary 30 days to appoint the commission and gave the commission no more than six months to complete its report.

Under the bill language, the leasing ban was to run until "the secretary and appropriate committees of Congress have agreed on the commission's recommendations to be implemented."

House Floor Action

Before HR 3363 reached the House floor, David A. Stockman, director of the Office of Management and Budget, warned that the leasing restrictions were objectionable to the Reagan administration.

In a June 21 letter to Appropriations Chairman Jamie L. Whitten, D-Miss., Stockman threatened to recommend that Reagan veto the bill, in part because of the coal and oil leasing bans but mainly for budgetary reasons.

Despite Stockman's warning, the House passed the bill, with the leasing bans intact, on June 28.

Senate Committee Action

The Senate Appropriations Subcommittee on Interior, however, stripped the coal leasing ban from the bill before sending it to the full committee on July 18.

The Senate Appropriations Committee reported HR 3363 — without the ban — July 19 (S Rept 98-184).

Fort Union Sale

The Interior Department, in defiance of a House Interior Committee order, went ahead on Sept. 14 with another major coal lease sale in the Fort Union area of North Dakota and a small part of Montana. It was the next in a series of lease sales planned by the department under Watt covering up to 17 billion tons of coal in six Western states over 14 months.

Some congressional critics objected to the sale on environmental grounds, but it took on symbolic significance as a test of whether the Watt leasing program would continue unchecked.

By a party-line 27-14 vote, the House Interior and Insular Affairs Committee on Aug. 3 had approved a resolution directing Watt to withdraw from coal leasing the lands in the Fort Union area.

The committee invoked a little-used provision of the 1976 Federal Land Policy and Management Act (FLPMA — PL 94-579) that required the secretary to withdraw public lands from development temporarily if the appropriate committee of either the House or Senate notified him that emergency measures had to be taken "to preserve values that would otherwise be lost." *(Congress and the Nation Vol. IV, p. 314)*

Watt, in an Aug. 2 letter to Rep. Morris K. Udall, D-Ariz., chairman of the Interior Committee, offered to delay award of the leases until Sept. 30, but no further. Udall, however, wanted to wait until after that date.

The date was critical because fiscal 1984 began on Oct. 1, and the House version of HR 3363 contained the leasing ban rider. Thus, if Watt did not award the leases by Sept. 30, he could have found himself foreclosed from doing so for months to come.

After studying the legal implications of the committee action, the Interior Department Aug. 8 printed notice in the *Federal Register* that the sale would go ahead as scheduled.

The department's action came four days after Congress adjourned for its August recess. But Watt's apparent decision to defy the Interior Committee's resolution guaranteed that the leasing controversy would flare up again when Congress returned Sept. 12.

Legislative Veto? The department considered the committee resolution vulnerable to challenge as a legislative veto — a mechanism ruled unconstitutional June 23 by the U.S. Supreme Court. The panel's action, strictly speaking, was not a veto of executive action, but a directive that the department withdraw the Fort Union lands and report to the committee on its action.

House lawyers said this could be construed as an exercise of Congress' power under Article IV, Section 3, of the Constitution to dispose of public lands. In addition, Stanley Brand, general counsel to the clerk of the House, argued that the provision used by the committee was a "report-and-wait" provision of the type cited as constitutional in a footnote to the Supreme Court decision. Such laws required an executive agency to report to Congress on a proposed action and wait for a specified period before finally carrying it out — giving Congress a chance to avert it with new legislation.

The U.S. District Court for Montana in 1981 upheld the validity of the FLPMA provision in the face of an Interior Department challenge in *Pacific Legal Foundation v. Watt*, saying it was a report-and-wait provision. Although that finding had little value as precedent, the Interior Department did not appeal.

Little Bidding Interest. The Interior Department on Sept. 14 opened bids for eight coal tracts in the Fort Union region, announcing the high bidders. Despite the fuss in Congress, the sale drew comparatively little interest from coal companies. Of the eight tracts offered, totaling 540 million tons of coal, bids totaling $911,800 were made on five tracts with about 115 million tons. Each tract drew only one bid.

The $911,800 worth of bids made on the tracts, Bumpers noted, was only slightly more than the federal government's administrative costs in asking for bids.

Although the bids were opened, the leases were not expected to be awarded until later.

Committee Chairman Morris K. Udall, D-Ariz., said his panel would intervene in a lawsuit filed Sept. 8 by environmental groups seeking to stop final award of the leases. Louis F. Oberdorfer, a U.S. district court judge in Washington, D.C., Sept. 9 denied for the moment a request for a temporary restraining order by the National Wildlife Federation and the Wilderness Society, scheduling further arguments for Oct. 21.

On Sept. 15, however, Interior Department lawyers notified the environmental groups that the department might award the leases within 15 days — before the court had decided the case.

Lawyers for the House and the environmental groups feared that award of the leases could establish a property right in the leases on the part of the coal companies — making it hard to reverse the sale without compensation.

The Court Ruling. On Sept. 16, Oberdorfer issued an order temporarily blocking Watt from making the sale final. "I'm not going to turn my back again," said Judge Oberdorfer.

On Sept. 28, Oberdorfer issued another order barring the Interior Department from issuing the leases in defiance of the committee's withdrawal resolution.

The ruling was not a final decision on the basic constitutional issues in the case, but the judge found enough merit in the House committee's claim to justify postponing

the sale until at least the spring of 1984 while the case was settled in the courts. The Justice Department said it would appeal Oberdorfer's ruling.

"The issue in this case is a constitutional one rather than a challenge to the coal leasing program. Its resolution through the courts could benefit all parties," the Interior Department said in a statement after Oberdorfer's ruling.

Senate Floor Action

The Interior appropriation was stalled on the Senate floor over other issues prior to the August recess, and the Senate did not take it up again until September.

The coal leasing issue came up on Sept. 20, when Bumpers again offered a moratorium amendment. This time around, with the Fort Union flap fresh in the minds of his colleagues, he won by 63-33. *(Vote 244, p. 41-S)*

Vote Switches. Sixteen senators who voted against the Bumpers amendment on coal leasing in June switched and voted for the amendment Sept. 20. They were Howell Heflin, D-Ala.; Paula Hawkins, R-Fla.; Mack Mattingly, R-Ga.; Dan Quayle, R-Ind.; Richard G. Lugar, R-Ind.; Charles E. Grassley, R-Iowa; Roger W. Jepsen, R-Iowa; J. James Exon, D-Neb.; Edward Zorinsky, D-Neb.; Warren B. Rudman, R-N.H.; Alfonse M. D'Amato, R-N.Y.; Mark O. Hatfield, R-Ore.; Arlen Specter, R-Pa.; John H. Chafee, R-R.I.; Slade Gorton, R-Wash.; and Bob Kasten, R-Wis.

One senator, Dave Durenberger, R-Minn., voted for the amendment June 14 but against it on Sept. 20.

Bumpers said the leasing moratorium was needed to keep Watt from "trying to give away our national heritage to whoever happens to show up."

Watt Response and Resignation

Watt responded to the Senate's coal leasing action by accusing Congress of ignoring U.S. energy needs that he said were threatened by ongoing conflicts in Central America and the Middle East.

"The world [is] ready to ignite, and your secretary of the interior has to deal with 535 members of Congress that don't seem to be concerned about the future supply of energy in America," Watt told business lobbyists Sept. 21 at a Chamber of Commerce breakfast speech.

In that same speech, Watt touched off a new round of criticism on Capitol Hill and elsewhere with a remark about the composition of the Linowes commission. "We have every kind of mix you can have. I have a black, I have a woman, two Jews and a cripple. And we have talent," said Watt. He later described his comments as "unfortunate" and apologized for them, but the political furor continued. On Oct. 9, Watt resigned. *(Watt resignation, p. 327)*

Final Action

Bumpers' amendment barred spending for new coal leasing, with certain exceptions, until 90 days after the Linowes commission reported to Congress on the Interior Department's coal leasing policies. The commission was expected to issue its findings in January 1984.

While the House-passed moratorium set no deadline for Congress to act after the Linowes report, the Bumpers amendment was formulated as a report-and-wait provision — a mechanism the Supreme Court indicated was constitutional.

Bumpers' version was adopted by House-Senate conferees, who approved HR 3363 on Sept. 29 (H Rept 98-399).

The conferees called on the Office of Technology Assessment, an arm of Congress, to look separately at the environmental issues involved in coal leasing.

"I'm not sure, since Secretary Watt picked the [coal] commission, that it would be sensitive to environmental problems," Bumpers explained.

When the conference report was called up in the Senate Oct. 20, members by voice vote adopted an amendment, offered by John Melcher, D-Mont., and William L. Armstrong, D-Colo., exempting by name several specific tracts in Montana and Colorado, where individual coal companies claimed they needed coal leased to avert economic hardship to existing mining operations.

The House accepted the Senate amendment the same day, clearing the bill.   ◼

Omnibus Water Projects Bill Starts Moving

Committees in both the House and Senate approved the first major omnibus authorization bill for water projects in seven years, but the legislation did not reach the floor of either chamber in 1983.

The House Public Works and Transportation Committee Aug. 3 unanimously approved a bill (HR 3678) authorizing water projects worth more than $12.4 million.

The Senate Environment and Public Works Committee approved its own, more modest $11 billion version (S 1739) on Nov. 8.

Both bills increased cost-sharing demands on local beneficiaries of federally funded water projects, although the House version did not go as far as the Senate measure. President Reagan had urged significantly greater cost-sharing than either committee proved willing to recommend.

Background

Since the early 1970s, funding for new projects had slowed to a fraction of what it was in the 1950s and 1960s, and Congress had not approved an omnibus water projects authorization bill since 1976. President Ford signed that law authorizing $742 million worth of planning, design and construction in 36 states only weeks before the 1976 election. *(1976 Almanac p. 202)*

Even without new projects, however, the backlog of unfinished water projects, plus those authorized but not yet funded, approached $50 billion in value.

Federal funds for water projects had not totally dried up. Appropriations for the three main water development agencies — the Army Corps of Engineers, the Interior Department's Bureau of Reclamation, and the Agriculture Department's Soil Conservation Service — actually rose in nominal dollars over the last decade, from $2.6 billion or less in 1973-1975 to a peak of $4.1 billion in 1980-1981, before falling back to about $3.7 billion in 1983.

But budget pressures, inflation and high interest rates had reduced what was once a torrent of federal money to a comparative trickle. One result: Most available federal dollars were going to finish projects already started (some took

more than a decade to complete) and to operate and maintain projects that were already built. New authorizations and "new starts" (appropriations to begin construction on projects already authorized) were growing rare.

The corps, the reclamation bureau, and the Soil Conservation Service built or maintained water projects in nearly every congressional district. Those projects provided tangible benefits: municipal and industrial water supply, hydro-electric power, ports and waterways for shipping, irrigation water for farmers, recreational lakes, flood protection — and, in some cases, fish and wildlife habitat.

No less tangible were the political benefits available to members of Congress who could deliver such projects to their districts.

With the 1984 elections approaching, many in Congress were anxious to bring federal water dollars home to their constituents, whether the dollars were for new dams or for replacing antiquated municipal water systems.

But the Reagan administration, to the dismay of many of its most avid supporters, was slow to develop a clear policy for new projects. The administration appeared determined to force state and local beneficiaries of water projects to assume a far greater share of their costs than in the past, but it was worried about the political fallout in the water-dependent West, the president's 1980 electoral stronghold.

The political tensions were heightened by regional rivalries; members from the East and Midwest wanted help for their crumbling infrastructure, while those from the South and West were looking to build new projects.

Appropriations Bill: Jumping the Gun

While the authorizing committees struggled to put together an omnibus bill that contained something for everyone, water subcommittees of the House and Senate Appropriations committees were chafing at the bit.

Without waiting for the authorization bill to clear, both the House and Senate Appropriations committees reported legislation (HR 3958) to finance new and continuing water projects. The House passed a $119 million money bill Oct. 6, but the Senate did not act on its $78 million version before adjournment. *(Story, p. 520)*

Administration Policy

President Carter in 1977 suffered lasting political damage when he put together a "hit list" of water projects he considered wasteful or unnecessary, only to see Congress balk at killing them. *(1977 Almanac p. 650)*

By 1983 President Reagan appeared to be wading into political trouble of his own over the key issue of cost sharing for water projects.

After a year of indecision, the administration in June finally put its stamp of approval on a comprehensive cost-sharing policy that was proposed to the White House a year earlier by the Cabinet Council on Natural Resources and Environment headed by Interior Secretary James G. Watt. The policy would drastically decrease the proportion of federal funding and increase state or local funding requirements.

The idea that beneficiaries and users should pay for certain federal services rested squarely on a belief that the free market made the wisest decisions. That idea was often embraced by Watt and conservative theoreticians — not to mention Office of Management and Budget pragmatists interested in deficit reduction.

An April 27, 1983, letter from Sen. Paul Laxalt, R-

Nev., and 14 other Western Senate Republicans to Reagan had warned the cost-sharing proposal would appear "anti-West" and "anti-water" and be "harmful" to Reagan's Western political support.

Those 14 were Pete V. Domenici, N.M., Malcolm Wallop, Wyo., Orrin G. Hatch, Utah, Barry Goldwater, Ariz., James A. McClure, Idaho, Pete Wilson, Calif., Steven D. Symms, Idaho, Chic Hecht, Nev., Slade Gorton, Wash., Mark Andrews, N.D., Ted Stevens, Alaska, Jake Garn, Utah, Frank H. Murkowski, Alaska, and Larry Pressler, S.D.

"As Republican senators representing Western states," the letter stated, "we are deeply concerned that your administration is going to be painted as 'anti-water' in the 1984 election campaign. The perception exists, fueled by Democratic Western governors, that the Reagan administration has been long on talk and short on substance when it comes to water development. We have yet to initiate construction on any new Western projects in the past two years, and we are now contemplating an up-front financing scheme even more Draconian than that proposed by Jimmy Carter.

"The bottom line here is that we have nothing to gain politically or fiscally from moving on the issue of cost-sharing at this time. We urge you to carefully reconsider these thoughts before putting forth a policy that will be harmful to your administration and your base of support in the West."

Despite this warning, on June 15, exactly one year after the original Cabinet Council proposal, William R. Gianelli, assistant Army secretary for civil works, told the Senate Environment Water Resources Subcommittee that the policy had been "affirmed at the highest levels within the administration." Gianelli oversaw the civil works programs of the Corps of Engineers, one of the principal agencies involved in water projects.

But two days after Gianelli said the cost-sharing policy had been adopted, Watt appeared to contradict him in a letter to subcommittee Chairman James Abdnor, R-S.D., saying the policy was still "under study."

The policy at issue called for a 100 percent non-federal share in financing of hydropower and both municipal and industrial water supply, a 50 percent non-federal share for recreation, and a 35 percent non-federal share for flood control and irrigation. This would impose a degree of uniformity totally lacking under laws in effect during 1983. Under those laws, cost-sharing rates differed from project to project and agency to agency.

The new policy was meant to use market forces to test the merit of proposed projects. It would do this by requiring beneficiaries to pay a major share of project costs — and pay "up front," while projects were being built. Up-front local payment cut out the hefty hidden subsidy that resulted from the artificially low interest rates the federal government used to calculate local paybacks.

The administration in May 1982 proposed nine new water project starts in its fiscal 1983 budget (later increased to 14 for 1984). In all those projects, local and state sponsors had volunteered to pay a greater share of project costs than had historically been the case.

Gianelli said that initiative was meant as a "short-term demonstration of the workability of increased non-federal cost sharing." But its workability in Congress remained unproven. Perhaps because the projects were seen as a stalking horse for the cost-sharing proposal, the Appropriations committees refused to fund them.

The Garrison Diversion in North Dakota . . .

The story of the Garrison Diversion in North Dakota illustrates why Congress is uneasy about water projects. It is a story of the pressures, sometimes undeniable, that pound members from all sides in water resource decisions.

House members voted twice in seven months on this $1.1 billion project to irrigate 250,000 acres of farm land. Both votes were on moves by Silvio O. Conte, R-Mass., that had the practical effect of cutting all appropriations for the project. On Dec. 14, 1982, the House voted against Garrison by a 100-vote margin. On June 23, 1983, members voted for it by a 65-vote margin.

What changed all those minds?

Rep. Byron L. Dorgan, D-N.D., changed many of them himself. As North Dakota's only House member, he bore the entire burden of defending the project in that chamber. Before the June 1983 vote, he appealed personally to "virtually everybody" to support the project.

Water is important to North Dakota, a fairly dry state where agriculture is a major industry. Rainfall averages 18 inches a year statewide, dropping to 14 inches in the arid southwestern part of the state. Agriculture provides at least 40 percent of the jobs in the state, and much of the industry is related to agriculture.

North Dakota finds it hard to ignore water for another big reason: Lake Sakakawea, the reservoir behind Garrison Dam, stretching nearly across the western half of the state, and the Oahe Reservoir, stretching further down into South Dakota, holding back the headwaters of the Missouri River. Dorgan called the reservoirs a "500,000-acre permanent flood."

North Dakota gave up those half-million acres, much of it good farm land, largely to prevent flooding from the Missouri and Mississippi rivers in downstream states. Both reservoirs were built as part of the grander Pick-Sloan Plan, a water project authorized by the Flood Control Act of 1944 that touches at least 10 Missouri Basin states. *(Congress and the Nation Vol. I, p. 801)*

North Dakotans considered the 1944 law a virtual contract: In return for their loss of land and agricultural revenues, they were promised that the massive Garrison reservoir would be used to irrigate approximately one million acres of farm land.

Sen. Quentin N. Burdick, D-N.D., said downstream states had received $1.49 billion in flood protection benefits so far, but North Dakota had yet to receive its part of the bargain. It ranked last among the 17 Western states in acres irrigated by the Bureau of Reclamation, about 33,000 acres so far.

"The motivator here," said Dorgan, "is basically a sense of Western justice. We're last at the table when the tray comes around, and Congressman Conte wants to take the food off. The food we were promised. . . .

"We've played host to the costs, and now Congressman Conte in his Eastern generosity wants to say, 'Well now, you've been saddled with all the costs, now we're going to take the benefits away.' "

The Opposition

The planned diversion of water from the Garrison reservoir for irrigation had come in for heavy criticism from enviromentalists, taxpayers' groups, Canadians and even some farmers in North Dakota.

Environmentalists focused on the effects of building canals and reservoirs to move the water from Garrison to where it can be used, charging the project would destroy or degrade some 73,000 acres of wetlands that provided a breeding habitat for ducks and geese. One of the millions of Americans who liked to hunt ducks was Silvio Conte.

But proponents of the project noted that the U.S. Fish and Wildlife Service had protective control, through ownership or easements, of 5.27 million acres of wetlands and associated wildlife habitat in North Dakota, more than any other central flyway state.

"This is not going to destroy the breeding grounds," says Dorgan. "If Conte wants North Dakota to become a 53-county duck farm, in effect, let him provide loan rates and target prices for raising ducks. If he wants a private game reserve in the Midwest, let him buy it."

The National Taxpayers Union and Sen. William Proxmire, D-Wis., said the project was too expensive, returning only 58 cents in benefits for every dollar of cost at today's interest rates. Proxmire said the project would amount to a subsidy of $3,753 per irrigated acre, or $800,000 for the average farm in the area. These critics said it made no sense to subsidize the creation of new farm land at a time when the government was paying farmers to take land out of production. North Dakota had the highest participation in the Payment-in-Kind program of any state. *(PIK program, p. 380)*

Canadians objected because most of the irrigated land would be in the drainage basin of the Souris River, which runs north across the border and eventually empties into Hudson Bay. They feared that the introduction of fish and aquatic life-forms "foreign" to the ecosystem of the Hudson Bay basin might harm the valuable sport and commercial fishing in Manitoba.

Government plans for mitigating losses of wetland and wildlife habitat caused by the Garrison project called for acquiring or protecting 198,000 other acres of habitat in the state. That would mainly be farm land, and critics said project sponsors had not found farmers who wanted to give up that much land. Some of those critics were

---

"In years past the Congress has pretty well blamed the administration for any deadlock with respect to water development," Gianelli said, "and now it is interesting that Congress is actually holding up approval of at least 14 new starts that have been proposed by the administration. The message here as far as I'm concerned is that this administration wants to move ahead with new water projects. It

doesn't have a hit list. It's not against them — but it feels they have got to move ahead under new guidelines."

House Committee Action

The House Public Works and Transportation Committee unanimously approved HR 3678 on Aug. 3.

... A Case Study in Water Project Politics

farmers themselves, who felt the project would simply transfer productive acreage from one set of farmers to another.

Stop and Go: Fancy Political Footwork

Because more than two decades had gone by since the 1944 Flood Control Act, the Garrison project had to be reauthorized in 1965. Congress appropriated money for the project quite regularly between 1967 and 1978, with spending ranging from $10 million to $20 million yearly during most of that period. Engineering work was completed and actual construction begun; in 1983 it was about 15 percent done. But funding was stalled by a lawsuit in 1979, and sputtered erratically since then as environmentalists lobbied against it. *(Authorization, 1965 Almanac p. 740)*

Project opponents thought they could deliver the coup de grâce in 1982 as the second fiscal 1983 continuing appropriations resolution faced a House vote. Conte offered an amendment Dec. 14, 1982, to bar use of funds in the bill for Garrison, calling it a "boondoggle."

Conte's amendment was adopted 252-152. It was not a party-line vote; Republicans split 126-50 and Democrats 126-102, a fact Conte and the environmentalists later pointed to as a sign that the "pork barrel" era in water politics was waning. As ever in water politics, regional rivalries played a stronger role, with Easterners, who get very few water projects, voting 91-14 to kill the project, and Southerners, who get a lot of them, voting the other way, 44-71. The Midwest, which includes many of the Pick-Sloan states, voted 84-32, and the West, where reclamation projects are important, voted 33-35. *(1982 Almanac p. 240)*

The House defeat for Garrison did not actually kill the appropriation, because the Senate approved funding for the project and the conference committee went along with the Senate. Nonetheless, back in North Dakota, they felt the jolt. Key Republicans publicly criticized Democrat Dorgan for failing in his defense of the project. Dorgan, a potential contender for the state's next Senate vacancy, was hurting.

Although politically wounded, Dorgan did not give up. He seemed to be lying low when the fiscal 1984 energy and water appropriation (HR 3132) passed the House without a dime for Garrison in it. He did not push for a vote on its inclusion. He had a plan.

The Senate Appropriations Subcommittee on Energy and Water Development, of which Burdick was a member, put $22.3 million for Garrison into the House-passed bill. Backers of the project fought off an assault on the Senate floor by Gordon J. Humphrey, R-N.H., tabling his

amendment to kill Garrison by a 62-35 vote. *(Vote 163, p. 29-S)*

This put the issue on the House-Senate conference table once more. Conte, who said the House "got rolled" in last year's conference, sought to "give the House conferees some backbone" this time. He offered a motion on June 23 to instruct the House conferees to insist on zero funding for Garrison.

Dorgan had seen this move coming and he was ready for it — readier, in fact, than Conte. Face to face or by telephone, Dorgan had spent day and night lobbying Republicans and Democrats alike, telling them: "It's important to me and it's important to North Dakota."

Bob Edgar, D-Pa., who opposed Garrison, said Dorgan apppealed to him for support on the grounds that his seat was at stake, although Dorgan denied that.

Stated or unstated, the belief that a Democratic seat was at stake may have played a role in the help Dorgan got from the House Democratic leadership — highly unusual in a non-partisan controversy over a single-district public works project. Majority Leader Jim Wright, D-Texas, spoke against the Conte motion and could be seen "working the door" as members arrived to vote.

Dorgan's strategy also depended on the fact that the challenge came on a "procedural" vote. This allowed Conte's opponents to say they were voting against the instruction procedure rather than casting a substantive vote for the project or against the environment. They could argue that it was a mistake to tie the conferees' hands as a general practice on any single issue, since it could reduce their ability to negotiate successfully on a whole range of House-Senate differences.

"Do not let anyone kid you; this is not a procedural vote," Conte argued before the vote. "This will be counted as one of the most important environmental votes that will be cast in the House this year."

Conte lost, 150-215, a dramatic reversal of the December 1982 vote. *(Vote 208, p. 64-H)*

"We were battered," Conte said, conceding that Dorgan had worked hard and attributing much of the shift to new members unfamiliar with the issue. But analysis shows the voting change in House seats that changed hands was no more drastic than the voting change in the House as a whole. Departing members voted 44-17 with Conte in December, while newly arrived members voted 32-35 against him in June.

Whatever else it demonstrated, the vote showed members still had a big say about projects in their own districts, and that House leaders could still produce votes. Of the 70 members who switched from anti-Garrison to pro-Garrison between the two votes, 54 were Democrats.

The measure, sponsored by Water Resources Subcommittee Chairman Robert A. Roe, D-N.J., caused some qualms in the Reagan administration. Not only did it authorize new spending not contained in the president's budget, but it also required state and local governments to pay a far smaller share of project costs than the administration had sought.

Furthermore, it stripped from the executive branch power to approve many specific projects and established a semi-independent water policy board of a type the administration had opposed.

The Public Works panel approved the bill by a 49-0 vote. The measure, which ran close to 300 pages, had sailed through the Water Resources Subcommittee by voice vote

July 29, two days after it was introduced.

Projects Covered

The Roe measure authorized more than 280 specific projects, at least 60 of which were modifications of existing projects. But the actual number of projects authorized could be far greater, because many provisions simply authorized the Army Corps of Engineers to go ahead with certain types of projects — for example, restoration of unsafe dams, straightening river bends for navigation, river ice control, and changes in completed projects to improve environmental quality.

The bill deauthorized 330 projects that were never funded; these would cost some $11.1 billion to complete.

Because of the open-ended authorizations, it was difficult to assign a precise price tag. But the bill put a cap on annual appropriations for construction by the corps — $1.5 billion for fiscal 1984 and 1985, and $1.6 billion for fiscal 1986, 1987 and 1988. Those amounts compared with $894.1 million actually appropriated for fiscal 1984 for projects already under way.

The Roe bill also contained a sunset provision automatically deauthorizing its projects after five years unless they had received appropriations for planning or construction.

The bill authorized projects for six deep-water ports, 27 general cargo ports, seven major inland waterway lock and dam projects, 79 local flood control projects, 17 shoreline protection projects, and 14 water supply projects, plus various multipurpose and miscellaneous projects.

Cost Sharing

Roe's bill handled the controversial cost-sharing question by charging ports for only 50 percent of the costs of deepening them beyond 45 feet. To recover those costs, ports could collect fees from their users, but only fees already authorized by law. And ports could collect only from ships needing a channel depth greater than 45 feet.

No new user fees for inland waterways were authorized in the Roe bill either. Two-thirds of the construction costs for such projects authorized in the bill would be paid from the general fund of the Treasury, and the remaining third from the Inland Waterway Trust Fund set up under a 1978 law (PL 95-502) establishing a tax on barge fuel. *(1978 Almanac p. 513)*

For flood control, Roe's bill set the non-federal share at 25 percent, most of which was likely to be paid "in kind," in the form of land, easements and rights of way. If the lands needed were worth less than 25 percent of total costs, the remainder of the local share had to be repaid to the Treasury over 15 years. Before projects could be built, local sponsors had to agree to take part in federal flood plain management and flood insurance programs.

Water Board

The bill set up a seven-member National Board on Water Resources Policy, made up of the interior, agriculture and Army secretaries; the administrator of the Environmental Protection Agency; two members nominated by the House or Senate, appointed by the president and confirmed by the Senate; and a chairman appointed by the president and confirmed by the Senate.

This proposal was similar to one that died in the 97th Congress before reaching the House floor. An earlier federal coordinating body, the Water Resources Council, was abolished in the fiscal 1981 and 1982 budgets proposed by

Reagan and approved by Congress. *(1981 Almanac p. 526)*

Environmental Impact

Throughout the Roe bill were provisions that prohibited project construction until the House Public Works and Senate Environment committees saw a final corps report and environmental impact statement, and voted approval of the project. The bill also created a $35 million emergency fund for mitigating any harmful environmental effects from water projects. It reinstated environmental quality as an objective to be used by the government in selecting projects (it had been removed by the Reagan administration).

Senate Committee Action

The Senate Environment and Public Works Committee Nov. 8 approved an $11 billion omnibus water projects authorization bill (S 1739) by a 14-2 vote.

The Senate bill was approved by the Water Resources Subcommittee Sept. 20.

As approved, it hewed more closely than the House measure to a formula sought by the Reagan administration for getting local beneficiaries to share in financing the costs of the projects.

But it ducked one of the hardest cost-recovery issues — whether to impose new fees on vessels using inland waterways and on ocean ports. The Senate bill imposed no such fees. Rather it set caps on spending for those purposes roughly at recent levels, and then created two new study panels to make recommendations on fees to finance additional spending.

And it eased the administration's proposal for the entire cash portion of local contributions to other projects to be paid "up front," or during construction. The Senate bill asked for only 5 percent in cash during construction of flood control, water supply, recreation, and erosion control projects. Commercial navigation and hydroelectric power projects could pay the local share over 30 to 50 years.

Touching Many Bases

Most of the spending authorized in S 1739 was for projects under the Army Corps of Engineers or the Soil Conservation Service. The bill left out entirely Western projects under the jurisdiction of the Bureau of Reclamation.

Still, the bill touched nearly every corner of the country. It authorized the corps to deliver more water to the Everglades National Park, as part of a state program to restore the natural water balance there. It set up a $305 million program of research and demonstration grants aimed at stemming the irreversible "mining" of water from the Ogallala aquifer in the high-plains states. It authorized a breakwater to keep Tangier Island, Va., historic home of watermen who took shellfish from Chesapeake Bay, from eroding away. It authorized $40 million to protect and restore the Acequia, or irrigation ditch, systems set up hundreds of years ago by Spanish land-grant communities in New Mexico. It authorized major work on the Mississippi and Ohio River navigation systems, and port development in the Great Lakes, the Texas Gulf Coast, the Pacific Northwest and other areas.

The exact amount of spending in the Senate bill was difficult to determine, because many authorizations were open-ended. It set an overall cap of $7.9 billion on spending over a five-year period, starting with $1.5 billion for fiscal

1984 and climbing to $1.7 billion for fiscal 1988. But specific authorizations in the bill totaled well over $11 billion over a longer period.

The Senate bill set a cap of $646 million (roughly current levels) on annual spending for inland waterway construction, operation, maintenance and renovation. Some of that, $40 million to $80 million, would come from an existing tax on barge fuel, but most would come from general tax revenues.

It also set up a 21-member Waterway Users Board to determine whether more spending would be needed and how to finance it. If the board recommended new user charges, the bill authorized the Army secretary to impose them.

Port Projects

For ocean ports, the bill proposed a compromise formula that did not fully satisfy any of the wrangling economic and regional interests.

A key question was whether the federal government would finance deepening of major ports to 55 feet or more to allow the largest oceangoing cargo vessels to use them. Eastern coal states with high unemployment, such as West Virginia, wanted deepening of ports like that at Norfolk, Va., to allow more coal to be sold on the export market.

The Senate bill left aspiring superports to finance such deepening (beyond 45-foot depths) on their own, authorizing them to impose their own user fees to pay back the cost of the work.

But, in a new move, the committee authorized federal guarantees for up to 70 percent of the amount of loans made to those ports to finance such work, with an overall cap of $1.5 billion on the amount the federal government would guarantee.

Historically, the federal government had paid almost all costs for port construction, operation, maintenance and improvement, except for land-based commercial loading and transport facilities. The Reagan administration sought to shift 100 percent of those costs to local ports and their beneficiaries through user fees.

The Senate bill left intact the authorization for the corps to do dredging and other harbor maintenance, but put a $350 million annual cap on spending for that purpose. It also set up a Cabinet-level National Commission on Harbor Maintenance and a Shipping Advisory Board made up of representatives from ports, shippers and carriers to make recommendations on cost-sharing and user fees. ■

Marine Sanctuaries

The House June 14 passed a bill (HR 2062) authorizing funding for three years for the national marine sanctuaries program.

The vote was 379-38. *(Vote 179, p. 56-H)*

A companion Senate bill, S 1102, was reported Oct. 26 by the Commerce, Science and Transportation Committee (S Rept 98-280). The full Senate did not act on it in 1983, however.

As passed by the House, HR 2062 authorized $2.264 million in fiscal 1984, $2.5 million in fiscal 1985 and $2.75 million in fiscal 1986.

The marine sanctuaries program, created under Title III of the 1972 Marine Protection, Research and Sanctuaries Act (PL 92-532), permitted the secretary of commerce to designate marine sanctuaries in coastal waters and control activities in them to protect the environment.

Congress, however, could veto the designation if both houses disapproved of it.

As of 1983, six marine areas had been designated as sanctuaries.

Committee Action

The House Merchant Marine and Fisheries Committee approved HR 2062 by voice vote on April 27 after adopting a substitute amendment adding two new provisions to the version approved April 12 in subcommittee.

One set out a 45-day period for committee action on executive branch proposals for new marine sanctuaries before the executive finally designated them. The other provision gave the Regional Fishery Management Council appropriate to a proposed sanctuary the opportunity to draft fishing regulations for the area. The regional councils were interstate planning bodies set up under federal law to recommend appropriate fishing levels to the commerce secretary. ■

Coastal Revenue Sharing

The House Sept. 14 passed a bill (HR 5) to give coastal and Great Lakes states up to $300 million a year in revenue from new offshore oil and gas drilling.

The vote was 301-93. *(Vote 317, p. 94-H)*

The House Merchant Marine and Fisheries Committee, dominated by members from coastal states, had approved the bill April 27 and formally reported it May 16 (H Rept 98-206).

Under the bill, 31 states and five territories would get money for their own ocean and coastal resource programs — including some the Reagan administration wanted to kill. The administration opposed HR 5 on grounds that it diverted funds that otherwise would go to the deficit-ridden general Treasury.

The bill was similar to one that was passed by the House in 1982 but died in the Senate. *(1982 Almanac p. 448)*

Senate Version

In 1983, the Senate Commerce Committee approved its own version of the legislation (S 800) on April 21 and reported it May 16 (S Rept 98-112), but the full Senate took no action on the measure.

The Senate bill required at least 30 percent of the funds going to each state to be passed through to local governments as an entitlement, compared to 35 percent in the House bill.

The Senate measure also set aside 1.5 percent of the funds for a National Coastal Resources Research and Development Institute in Newport, Ore., the home state of Commerce Committee Chairman Bob Packwood, a Republican.

The Senate bill was expected to yield more money to a total of 35 coastal and Great Lakes states than HR 5, which had a $300 million annual cap.

Background

A major source of federal revenue, offshore oil and gas leasing, exploration and production brought about $6.25 billion into the Treasury in fiscal 1982.

That amount was likely to increase in the future if the Interior Department was able to lease tracts as fast as it hoped to under President Reagan.

Although states got half of the revenue produced as a result of energy and mineral leasing on federal lands within their borders, they currently received nothing from leasing off their shores — a discrepancy that coastal states considered unfair.

Provisions

HR 5 required the Treasury to set aside in a special fund each year either $300 million or 10 percent of new offshore leasing revenue — whichever was less. The 10 percent would be calculated only on the increase in revenues above the 1982 level. The money could be spent only after Congress appropriated it.

Of each year's appropriation, 10 to 20 percent would come off the top for the National Sea Grant College Program — a research and technical aid program for ocean-related industries such as fishing.

The rest would be distributed among the states as block grants according to a formula based on each state's coastal energy activity, shoreline mileage and coastal population.

States would have leeway on how to spend the funds, as long as they were used for "enhancement and management of renewable ocean and coastal resources and for the amelioration of any adverse impacts that result from coastal energy activity...."

At least 25 percent of each state's funds, however, would have to be spent on programs authorized under the Coastal Zone Management Act of 1972, which Reagan also wanted to phase out.

House Floor Action

The main opponent to the bill on the House floor was Jack Fields, R-Texas, who wanted a distribution formula based on actual leasing and production off a state's coast.

More than 96 percent of the nation's offshore oil and gas production came from Gulf of Mexico tracts off the coast of Texas and Louisiana, he said. Fields argued that Great Lakes states such as Michigan, with no offshore drilling at all, could get more under the bill than some states with drilling.

Fields offered two blocks of amendments. The first, limiting eligibility to states with offshore energy development and excluding Great Lakes states, was rejected by a standing vote.

The second, striking language that gave a larger share to states taking part in the Coastal Zone Management (CZM) program, was rejected by voice vote. Texas had no CZM program. ∎

Ocean Dumping Legislation

The House Oct. 31 suspended the rules and passed a bill (HR 1761) tightening the nation's main law regulating the ocean dumping of wastes. The Senate, however, took no action on the measure in 1983.

Title I of the Marine Protection, Research and Sanctuaries Act of 1972 (PL 92-532), known as the Ocean Dumping Act, authorized the Environmental Protection Agency (EPA) to issue permits for the dumping of waste materials in the ocean, if such dumping would not harm the ocean environment or endanger public health. *(Congress and the Nation Vol. III, p. 798)*

HR 1761 was designed to speed up the study and designation of dump sites by EPA, beef up standards for choosing and monitoring sites, allow EPA to impose new permit conditions, authorize some permit processing fees, improve the quality of scientific information on which permits were based, and impose criminal penalties for falsifying information and other knowing permit violations.

It authorized $4.2 million in appropriations for fiscal 1984.

The bill was reported May 16 by the House Merchant Marine Committee and Aug. 1 by the Public Works Committee (H Rept 98-200, Parts I and II).

The House passed a similar measure in 1982, but the Senate took no action before the 97th Congress ended. *(1982 Almanac p. 459)*

One part of that bill, limiting ocean dumping of radioactive wastes, was added to the big highway-gas tax bill (PL 97-424) cleared Dec. 23, 1982, just before the 97th Congress adjourned. *(1982 Almanac p. 322)* ∎

Clean Water Act Rewrite

Congress made only slow progress during 1983 on a rewrite of the Clean Water Act, the nation's water pollution control law, with no legislation reaching the floor in either House or Senate.

The Senate Environment and Public Works Committee June 28 unanimously approved a clean water reauthorization bill (S 431 — S Rept 98-233), but it left several of the hardest issues to be settled on the Senate floor.

Later, on Sept. 21, the Senate committee approved a bill (S 2006 — S Rept 98-282) addressing one of those unsettled issues: "non-point source" pollution, which came not from the end of a single pipe, but from water running off agricultural land, logging areas, construction and mining sites, and even city streets.

The committee announced it would offer both those bills as a single substitute to S 1288 (S Rept 98-115), a "shell bill" reported May 16 to meet budget deadlines, when that bill reached the Senate floor. It was not brought up in 1983.

The House Public Works and Transportation Subcommittee on Water Resources held hearings on the Clean Water Act renewal, but did not proceed to mark up a bill.

Background

The Clean Water Act required the Environmental Protection Agency (EPA) and the states to control discharges of pollutants into lakes and streams from industries, public sewers and other sources. The law evolved from the Water Pollution Control Act of 1947 (PL 80-845), with Congress renewing funding authorizations and considering major amendments every five years or so. *(Congress and the Nation Vol. I, p. 1132)*

The most dramatic transformation of the law came in 1972 when Congress enacted a sweeping set of amendments (PL 92-500) establishing a federal permit system to regulate pollution discharges and expanding previous programs of federal grants for construction of municipal sewage systems. *(Congress and the Nation Vol. III, p. 792)*

Congress passed the last comprehensive set of amendments (PL 95-217) in 1977. *(1977 Almanac p. 697)*

Then in 1980, it passed PL 96-483, which reauthorized spending under most sections of the law for fiscal 1981 and 1982. *(1980 Almanac p. 607)*

In 1981, Congress enacted PL 97-117, which overhauled Title II, the section dealing with municipal sewage system construction grants, largely along lines proposed by the Reagan administration. *(1981 Almanac, p. 515)*

Congress was due to act again in 1982, when panels in both the House and Senate held hearings on possible amendments, including a Reagan administration proposal that would have relaxed a number of existing pollution controls. But neither committee reached the markup stage. *(1982 Almanac p. 459)*

Senate Committee Action

The major markup vehicle used by the Senate committee was S 431, introduced Feb. 3 by John H. Chafee, R-R.I., chairman of the Subcommittee on Environmental Pollution.

Chafee's bill, both as introduced and as reported, made little change in the status quo.

Chafee's subcommittee approved S 431 by voice vote on June 22 — with industries expressing disappointment and environmentalists expressing delight at the outcome.

The bill was short in comparison with the 125-page Clean Water Act itself, a minor tuneup rather than a major overhaul.

The measure reauthorized appropriations for four years, fiscal 1984 through 1987, at levels slightly higher than those in the current law.

Chafee said the 1982 committee hearings produced "a consensus that the act is sound and does not require extensive changes."

Pre-treatment

Chafee proposed a significant new approach to the "pre-treatment" of industrial waste discharges to municipal sewage systems.

The 1972 Clean Water Act required the EPA to set up regulations requiring industries that discharged to municipal systems to pre-treat their discharges to remove pollutants that could harm or pass through the municipal treatment plant.

Under the law, the municipalities were to enforce the regulations.

The job of writing those regulations was still not finished in 1983, more than 10 years later. Small cities, in particular, complained the rules were too hard for them to administer. Large cities carried out their own programs without waiting for EPA.

Chafee proposed allowing municipalities to "opt out" of the federal pre-treatment standards if they showed they could carry out local programs to achieve the same result.

The pre-treatment provisions in the Chafee bill would, in practice, have allowed only 50 to 100 of the biggest municipal systems to opt out of EPA standards, and bigcity sewer agencies were among its main supporters.

But EPA Administrator William D. Ruckelshaus joined environmentalists in opposing the opt-out plan, and in response to such criticism, the subcommittee stripped it from the bill.

Other Provisions

Most major provisions of Chafee's bill were approved by both the subcommittee and the full Environment Com-

mittee. Among those approved were the following:

• Extension of the current July 1, 1984, deadline for industries to comply with new discharge limits for certain pollutants, especially toxic ones.

The bill established new deadlines at three years after EPA set the discharge limits, but in no case later than July 1, 1987.

• Tightening of existing limits on the kinds of effluent that municipal sewage systems could discharge into oceans or estuaries, prohibiting the discharge of raw sewage.

• Restrictions that would counter a Reagan administration proposal to allow downgrading of state-set standards for in-stream water quality, by enacting as law some regulations in effect when Reagan took office.

• Increases in civil penalties for violation of the law from $10,000 to $25,000 as a daily maximum in certain cases.

• Increases in the time for which pollution discharge permits run from five years to 10 years.

Chafee's bill as introduced had sought to keep the five-year permit term in existing law. The Reagan administration and industry groups had sought the increase to 10 years.

As approved, however, the bill gave EPA the right to reopen the permits when conditions changed.

• Reaffirmation of the existing right of an injured citizen to sue polluters under state common law for damages caused by non-compliance with the act.

• A new series of deadlines for EPA to issue rules for disposal of municipal sewage sludge — ultimately requiring municipalities to comply with those new rules three years after enactment of the bill.

EPA had failed to meet a deadline set by the existing law.

Non-Point Sources

The Senate Environment Committee approved S 2006, the bill dealing with control of non-point source pollution, by a 16-0 vote on Sept. 21. That unanimity did not reflect the heated controversy that met an earlier proposal by Sen. Dave Durenberger, R-Minn., during markup of S 431. The Durenberger proposal was withdrawn from that bill before it was approved.

As approved by the committee, the non-point source bill included the following provisions:

• A requirement that each state come up with a non-point source control plan within 18 months of enactment. Most states already had such plans.

• Authority for EPA to run a non-point source control program in any state that failed to submit its own plan.

• Requirement that EPA approve or disapprove within six months the plans submitted by the states, with the plan automatically approved if EPA failed to act by then. EPA must act on plan revisions within three months.

• Authorization of $70 million in fiscal 1985, $100 million in fiscal 1986, and $130 million in fiscal 1987 for a program of EPA-administered grants to the states to help them carry out their programs.

The federal grant would pay up to 75 percent of program costs, while state and local sources would have to pay at least 25 percent.

• Allocation of two-thirds of the federal funds among states and territories according to specific proportions written into the law for each.

• Allocation of the remaining one-third to the states according to the discretion of the EPA administrator for achieving the purposes of the law.   ∎

Clinch River Project Scrapped by Congress

The Clinch River breeder reactor project, once hailed as the solution to the nation's energy problems, appeared doomed by the end of 1983.

The Oak Ridge, Tenn., project was the victim of long delays, sharply rising costs, new concerns about nuclear power and an unexpected flattening of the nation's demand for electric power.

Its end came on decisive votes in both chambers of Congress, despite a Reagan administration effort to stave off its demise with a new plan for sharing the project's costs with private industry.

In May the House voted 388-1 to repeal language authorizing funds for the project. *(Vote 104, p. 36-H)*

In October the Senate voted 56-40 to refuse it more money. *(Vote 306, p. 50-S)*

Congress included no money for the Clinch River project in the fiscal 1984 energy and water development appropriation bill (HR 3132 — PL 98-50). *(Story, p. 500)*

The project's demise did not come as a surprise; it had survived in recent years by ever-narrowing margins in Congress. *(1982 Almanac p. 292)*

Background

Once the nation's No. 1 energy project, the breeder reactor was intended to demonstrate that "fast breeder" nuclear power plants that would produce nuclear fuel even while they consumed it to make electricity were a feasible means of generating power for commercial use.

In building the plant the government also hoped to spur the development of an industrial base for building additional plants.

The technology of the breeder reactor dated back to World War II, when scientists were working to develop the atomic bomb. The first prototype breeder, the Experimental Breeder No. 1, went into operation in 1951 in Arco, Idaho. By 1970, several breeder plants were in operation, but the electric power industry still was not convinced of their commercial viability.

Breeder Technology

The nuclear power plants in operation in the United States in 1983 were light water reactors, which did not breed fuel. The difference between those reactors and breeder reactors had to do with the nature of nuclear reactions.

A nuclear reaction occurs when a "fissionable" element — either uranium-235 or man-made plutonium-239 — is packed in concentrated form. Tiny neutrons, which are thrown off at random by the atoms of these elements, will then strike other atoms. This causes the release of more neutrons, and a chain reaction begins. The reaction generates tremendous heat, which converts water into the steam that powers the turbines of an electrical generator.

In light water plants, water is used both to cool the reactor core and to slow down the free neutrons, making the chain reaction easier to control. In the liquid metal fast breeder reactor, however, the neutrons are allowed to travel at much faster speeds, quickening the chain reaction. The reactor core is surrounded with a "blanket" of non-fissionable uranium-238, which absorbs the stray neutrons from the reaction. After absorption, the uranium becomes a new element, plutonium-239, which can then be removed and used as new fuel.

In uranium ore found in nature, the non-fissionable uranium-238 element is much more plentiful than fissionable uranium-235. Before using it in a reactor, the uranium must be "enriched" to increase the concentration of uranium-235. The byproduct of this enrichment is uranium-238, which is stored in large canisters at DOE installations.

Without a breeder reactor, that uranium-238 is of little value. With a breeder, however, it can be converted to plutonium and can provide an abundant energy source. The nation's current supplies of uranium-238 could, with a breeder reactor, provide 700 times more energy than all the coal used in the United States in a year, and 400 times more energy than all the oil used in a year, the Department of Energy said.

Clinch River's Beginning

The Clinch River project effectively began in 1972, the year that the prestigious Club of Rome, an international organization of social scientists, published its book pronouncing with Malthusian certainty that scarce natural resources put limits on society's growth. It was nurtured during the years when the U.S. economy was being turned on its head by a small group of Middle Eastern countries whose power derived from the fact that they were located on top of enormous underground seas of easily accessible petroleum.

The breeder seemed to offer an escape from all that. Because it could produce more fuel than it burned — hence the name "breeder" — it promised an almost limitless source of electrical power.

"The breeder could extend the life of our natural uranium fuel supply from decades to centuries," President Richard M. Nixon told the nation in 1971.

To be sure, there was always opposition. Environmental groups feared the possibility of a horrendous accident — a meltdown of the reactor core which, if secondary safety measures did not go as planned, could release clouds of lethal radioactive gases into the air. Drifting with the wind, those clouds might kill thousands of people.

Others said the breeder would promote the spread of nuclear weapons. Unlike normal "light water" nuclear reactors, breeder reactors used and bred plutonium, a key ingredient of atomic bombs. According to Bill Adler of the Nuclear Control Institute, a breeder "discharges enough plutonium to fashion at least 400 bombs a year."

But in spite of their efforts, environmental and antinuclear groups were unable to kill the Clinch River project. Even when President Carter adopted the non-proliferation argument and called for cancellation of the breeder, the breeder prevailed. Congress overrode the president repeatedly in votes during 1977, 1978 and 1979, and continued to fund the project. *(1977 Almanac p. 692; 1978 Almanac p. 684; 1979 Almanac p. 703; chronology, p. 363)*

Given the nation's uncertain energy future, Congress during the 1970s clearly wanted a breeder reactor.

By the 1980s, however, the energy picture was changing dramatically, and cost considerations loomed bigger.

Changing Energy Picture

In the past several years, a combination of economic

The Clinch River Project: A Chronology

Following is a chronology of major developments affecting the Clinch River breeder reactor project that occurred since 1970:

1970. Congress authorized the demonstration breeder reactor project, to be administered by the government and the electric power industry (PL 91-273).

The plant was to use a fuel consisting of uranium and plutonium, and it would produce additional plutonium as it operated. It was to cost $700 million, of which the government would pay $450 million and industry $250 million.

1971. President Nixon declared that "our best hope today for meeting the nation's growing demand for economical clean energy lies with the fast breeder reactor."

1973. The Atomic Energy Commission signed a contract with the Tennessee Valley Authority, Commonwealth Edison and the Project Management Corporation, representing the utility industry, to build the demonstration plant on the Clinch River near Oak Ridge, Tenn.

1975. Congress reauthorized the project, now estimated to cost $1.7 billion, and directed the federal government to assume complete responsibility for managing it (PL 94-187). Amendments opposing continued work on the project were rejected by the House, 136-227, and by the Senate, 66-30. *(1975 Almanac p. 281)*

1976. The date by which the plant would go into operation slipped from 1980 to 1983; the cost estimate rose to $1.9 billion.

The House rejected, 173-209, an amendment requiring private industry to bear more of the cost of the project. The Senate, 31-50, rejected a similar amendment. *(1976 Almanac p. 153)*

1977. President Jimmy Carter renounced plans to use plutonium as a nuclear fuel in the United States, primarily because of concerns about increasing the world's supply of that element, a key ingredient of nuclear weapons.

Carter asked Congress to terminate the Clinch River project. This request was rejected by the House, 162-146, and by the Senate, 38-49. Carter cast the first veto of his administration to kill a measure (HR 6796) funding the project. *(1977 Almanac p. 692)*

1978. Carter again asked Congress to terminate the project. The House refused, 142-187 and 157-238; the Senate Energy Committee accepted the Carter proposal, but the full Senate did not vote on it. *(1978 Almanac p. 684)*

1979. The House again refused to terminate the project, 182-237. The Senate Energy Committee agreed to terminate it if the administration studied alternative plans for a breeder project. The full Senate again did not vote on the matter. *(1979 Almanac p. 701)*

1980. The estimated cost of the plant rose to $2.9 billion; its estimated operational date slipped to 1988.

1981. The Reagan administration gave full backing to the project, now expected to cost $3.2 billion.

The House Science and Technology Committee voted to terminate the project. The full House overturned that action, refusing, 186-206, to kill the project and including authorizing language in the budget reconciliation measure for that year (PL 97-35). The Senate, 48-46, continued to support funding for the plant as well. *(1981 Almanac p. 304)*

1982. Site clearing began for the plant, now estimated to cost $3.6 billion. The House for the first time voted, 217-196, to deny funds for the project. The Senate kept the project alive by one vote, 48-49. *(1982 Almanac p. 294)*

1983. Cost estimates for the project rose to $4 billion; the Reagan administration searched for a way to increase the share of that cost borne by private industry.

The House voted, 388-1, to deauthorize the Clinch River project, repealing the 1981 language in PL 97-35. The Senate refused, 56-40, to approve the $1.5 billion necessary to complete work on the reactor.

---

recession and energy conservation drastically reduced the need for both oil and electricity.

Energy predictions of a decade earlier came to sound like the words of Chicken Little. U.S. planners consistently overestimated the future need for electricity, and were forced to reduce their forecasts of the need for nuclear power to one-seventh of their 1972 predictions.

No new nuclear plants had been ordered since 1978, and many of those on order had to be canceled. Excessive power plant construction based on faulty forecasts saddled some parts of the nation with multimillion-dollar facilities they could not use. In the Pacific Northwest, a multibillion-dollar power plant fiasco threatened the entire region with financial chaos.

Even the Tennessee Valley Authority (TVA), which had promised to purchase the power from the Clinch River breeder, had no real need for it. Four years ago the TVA was predicting widespread electrical "brownouts." In 1983, according to General Manager W. F. Willis, it saw no need for additional generating capacity until 1994 at the earliest,

and more likely until the next century.

"In light of this, TVA is in no position to buy some or all of the Clinch River plant's capacity," Willis told a Senate Environment and Public Works subcommittee April 20.

In this new environment, energy independence was no longer the obsession it was during the 1970s. The Clinch River project was now looked at with the cool calculus of economics, and more and more people concluded that the payoff was not there.

If uranium reactor fuel were scarce and its price high, the breeder might look like a bargain. Indeed, when Nixon called for a breeder in 1971, uranium was thought to be scarce. Since then, however, vast reserves of uranium had been located around the world and a uranium glut had developed.

The U.S. uranium industry had such a difficult time selling its product in 1982 that it pleaded with Congress to impose import restraints on foreign uranium. *(1982 Almanac p. 310)*

Soaring Costs

The Clinch River project was initially designed as one in which private industry and the government would share costs. When it was first authorized, it was expected to cost $700 million, and private industry agreed to pay $250 million of that, slightly more than one-third the total.

By 1983 Congress had appropriated $1.5 billion for the project, and its total cost had escalated to $4 billion. Private industry was still committed to pay just $250 million, by this time only about one-sixteenth of the total.

The original completion date for the plant was 1980, but that target slipped by a decade: in 1983, the expected operational date was 1989 or 1990.

Not until September 1982 was any work done on the Clinch River site near Oak Ridge. Then, however, site clearing began and a year later, a 100-foot-deep hole the size of a football field was almost ready for concrete pouring.

Half of the $1.5 billion spent on the project had been used for research, development and design, all complete by 1983. In addition, some $749 million in component parts had been ordered.

It was expected to cost between $150 million and $250 million to terminate the project.

Conservative Shift

Uncertainties about breeder economics led a growing number of fiscal conservatives in Congress to oppose the Clinch River project.

These members supported nuclear power in general and gave little weight to traditional arguments that the breeder was environmentally unsafe or a threat to world peace. Their concern was money. Given the current budget squeeze, they said, funneling $200 million to $300 million a year into a research and development project that would not pay off for decades — or possibly ever — was unconscionable.

Among the most active of these conservative Clinch River opponents were Sen. Gordon J. Humphrey, R-N.H., and Rep. Vin Weber, R-Minn. Both helped lead the campaign against the breeder in Congress. Their opposition swayed other key conservatives who previously supported the breeder, such as Reps. Trent Lott, R-Miss., and Phil Gramm, R-Texas.

Backing the efforts of these members was a group of conservative lobbying groups including the National Taxpayers Union and the Heritage Foundation.

Support for Breeder

Breeder opponents liked to attribute the survival of the Clinch River project up to 1983 to the efforts of one man: Sen. Howard H. Baker Jr., R-Tenn.

Backed by the entire Tennessee congressional delegation, the powerful Senate majority leader fought hard for the project.

He helped convince the Reagan administration to support it over the objections of budget director David A. Stockman. And he undoubtedly persuaded more than one of his fellow senators to vote his way. Had it not been for Baker, many observers believed, the Senate would have joined the House in opposing Clinch River funding in 1982.

Members of the Tennessee congressional delegation spent considerable energy devising new arguments for the Clinch River project. In 1982-83, their favorite was jobs.

Breeder work in 1983 employed more than 3,500 people. Once construction began, those jobs would be concen-

trated at the Oak Ridge, Tenn., plant site, in the district of Democrat Marilyn Lloyd. But currently, employment was spread throughout the country, providing some political incentive for members in 32 states to support Clinch River. In California, home of an Atomics International plant and a General Electric plant working on the project, 800 people were employed by the breeder. In Pennsylvania, home of another key contractor, Westinghouse Electric Corp., another 731 were at work on it.

Supporters also argued that the breeder reactor would be needed in the future, if not immediately.

The United States eventually would need breeders, said Percy Brewington Jr., acting director for the Clinch River project, because "it is the only technology we have that we can see as an inexhaustible source of energy."

If the United States did not continue its program to demonstrate and develop a commercial breeder reactor, said Brewington, when commercial breeders did become economically viable the United States would have to buy from overseas. That could be a serious blow to U.S. international competitiveness and could cost the nation many jobs in the future.

But opponents such as Humphrey were quick to dismiss those arguments. "We are deceiving ourselves if we think there is a major race to build a commercial breeder and that Clinch River is the best way to keep the United States in contention," Humphrey told the Senate in December 1982. He cited reports that the United Kingdom had postponed its plans for constructing a breeder until the 21st century and that the breeder programs of France and West Germany were suffering from a lack of political enthusiasm. "The race abroad," he said, "has slowed to a crawl."

Building Clinch River

Research, development and design of the Clinch River reactor continued throughout the 1970s, incorporating new innovations into the project. Breeder engineers dismissed press reports that Clinch River was technologically obsolete; they said the design of the reactor core was unique and far more efficient than the core design being used overseas.

Licensing procedures for the plant proceeded as planned. The NRC issued a final environmental statement in October 1982, and the major court challenges had been dealt with.

When Congress appropriated funds for Clinch River for fiscal 1983, it restrained DOE from initiating "construction of any permanent facility structures or placement of any additional major equipment orders" during the year. That caused no new delays in the project, since construction was not scheduled until fiscal 1984 and most of the major components already had been procured.

House Committee Action

Cost-Sharing Plan

The Department of Energy (DOE) reported to Congress in March that as much as $1 billion more could be raised from private investors to finance the controversial project.

The report, which did not specify a single means of generating such additional private support, was required by Congress when it passed a continuing appropriations resolution in late 1982 (PL 97-377). *(1982 Almanac p. 238)*

The report pointed out that any attempt to raise addi-

tional private funds for the project would be futile unless the government guaranteed that the plant would be completed.

Calling a Halt

On April 26, the House Science and Technology Committee voted 24-16 to halt all work on the Clinch River project on Sept. 30 unless a new plan for sharing its costs with private industry was approved by that date.

The vote came on an amendment to a bill (HR 2587) authorizing $3.3 billion for civilian research and development programs of the Department of Energy in fiscal 1984. The committee then voted to report the bill by a 26-15 party-line vote (H Rept 98-81).

A coalition of taxpayer, environmental and other groups lobbied hard for the Clinch River amendment, sponsored by George E. Brown Jr., D-Calif., and Claudine Schneider, R-R.I. They contended the multibillion-dollar project was too costly in a time of high deficits and that the power to be produced by the reactor was not needed.

Committee Chairman Don Fuqua, D-Fla., offered a substitute amendment that would have allowed the Tennessee site to be prepared and reactor parts to be purchased but would have barred permanent construction work until DOE developed a financing plan.

But opponents pressed for a specific cutoff date for work on Clinch River. "The longer you continue spending money, the less pressure there is on industry to come up with a financing plan," said Richard L. Ottinger, D-N.Y.

Fuqua's substitute was defeated, 19-21, and the Brown amendment then was adopted, 24-16, with the committee's freshman members providing the margin of victory. Of the 12 freshmen on the panel, eight backed Brown and three supported Fuqua. One did not vote.

The committee had been a prime source of support for Clinch River during the four years of the Carter administration, which wanted the project killed. But when the Reagan administration, which backed Clinch River, came to power in 1981, the panel had a change of heart. It voted 22-18 to kill the project, but its action was overturned in the "Gramm-Latta II" budget reconciliation bill (PL 97-35). *(1981 Almanac p. 447)*

In 1982 the full House voted to kill Clinch River but the Senate upheld the project by one vote. Conferees on the continuing appropriations resolution (PL 97-377) finally provided $181 million to keep work going through Sept. 30, 1983, but they prohibited any permanent construction work at the site and directed DOE to explore alternative sources of financing.

House Floor Action

The House voted 388-1 on May 12 to repeal the 1981 law authorizing funds for the Clinch River breeder reactor. Supporters of the project, realizing that they were far outnumbered, did not mount a vigorous opposition to the deauthorization move.

The vote came on an amendment to the Department of Energy authorization measure (HR 2587), which subsequently passed by a vote of 230-132. *(Vote 108, p. 38-H)*

The amendment, which had been approved by the House Science and Technology Committee, was sponsored by Schneider and Brown. It repealed the authorization that Congress had included in the 1981 budget reconciliation act (PL 97-35) after the committee had refused to fund the project.

HR 2587 was primarily a vehicle for the House to express its disagreement with the Reagan administration's energy policy.

The programs it authorized for 1984 were already authorized by PL 97-35 for three years, through 1984. The Senate did not act on HR 2587 in 1983.

Senate Action

New Financing Plan

The Reagan administration Aug. 1 sent Congress a new plan for financing the Clinch River project. Under the plan a total of $1 billion was to be raised from private sources — $150 million through the sale of stock and the remainder from the sale of bonds in 1990 and from money already committed by utilities and other investors.

The plan was developed by a task force formed by the Breeder Reactor Corp., which was to build the plant.

It was endorsed by Reagan but criticized by opponents of the project, who pointed out that private industry assumed no more risk under this plan than under the existing plan, and that the federal government would be liable for repaying the proposed bonds if the plant did not generate sufficient revenue to repay them.

Senate Floor Vote

The Senate Oct. 26 refused, 56-40, to provide $1.5 billion in funding to complete the controversial Clinch River plant.

The vote came on a motion to table an amendment to a fiscal 1984 supplemental appropriations bill (HR 3959) that would have provided $1.5 billion to complete the Clinch River project. *(Vote 306, p. 50-S)*

The amendment had been approved by the Senate Appropriations Committee Oct. 19. It was sponsored by Energy Committee Chairman James A. McClure, R-Idaho.

The margin of defeat was wider than either side had expected. When the Senate had voted 10 months earlier on a similar proposal, the project's supporters had prevailed by a single vote.

Vote Switches

Seven Republicans and one Democrat who voted on Dec. 16, 1982, to continue funding for the Clinch River breeder reactor project switched to oppose it Oct. 26, 1983. They were David L. Boren, D-Okla.; Paula Hawkins, R-Fla.; Roger W. Jepsen, R-Iowa; Mack Mattingly, R-Ga.; Larry Pressler, R-S.D.; Warren B. Rudman, R-N.H.; Alan K. Simpson, R-Wyo., and John W. Warner, R-Va.

Switching from an anti-Clinch River position to a vote for continued funding were Robert C. Byrd, D-W.Va., and Jennings Randolph, D-W.Va.

The project's supporters, led by Majority Leader Howard H. Baker Jr., R-Tenn., and McClure, saw this vote as the last real chance for funding the project.

Although they did not concede defeat outright, McClure acknowledged that the chance for even interim financing was now no more than a bare possibility.

Baker, who in the past had shepherded the project through a series of increasingly close votes, had indicated that the vote would be close, and supporters said it would have been if the majority leader had not released several Republicans to vote "aye" when the votes to table the funding amendment reached 52. Twenty-three GOP senators voted to table the amendment. ∎

Congress Split Over Natural Gas Pricing

Congress in 1983 learned anew the difficulty of legislating natural gas prices.

After three months of work, the Senate Energy and Natural Resources Committee reported a gas bill (S 1715) late in July. But in November, just before the session ended, the Senate soundly rejected both S 1715 and the major alternative (S 996) offered by its critics.

The House Energy and Commerce Subcommittee on Fossil and Synthetic Fuels approved a quite different bill (HR 4227) late in July, but the full Energy Committee had just begun to mark up the measure as the 1983 session ended.

Background

Current Pricing System

Under the 1978 Natural Gas Policy Act (PL 95-621), which ended decades of comprehensive federal control of natural gas prices, gas supplies were divided in various categories and priced accordingly. *(1978 Almanac p. 641)*

"Old" gas, that flowing before April 20, 1977, was kept under price controls at the lowest price, about $1.25 per thousand cubic feet (mcf) in February 1983.

"New" gas could be sold at a higher price, about $3.00 per thousand cubic feet. "Deep" gas, extracted from wells below 15,000 feet or produced under other difficult conditions, could be sold at whatever price purchasers would pay, entirely free of controls. The early 1983 price for that gas was $7.25 per mcf.

This stepladder of prices was intended to encourage the discovery of new gas supplies, and indeed, substantial new reserves of gas were found between 1978 and 1983.

But those advocating an end to all controls on gas criticized the tiered pricing system, saying it distorted the market by encouraging producers to look for expensive gas and discouraging them from producing low-cost gas from existing reservoirs.

Price Surge

Consumer outrage at rapidly rising gas prices spurred Congress to reconsider the issue of natural gas pricing five years after it had passed the landmark 1978 law.

The rapid increases in natural gas prices in 1981 and 1982 were particularly galling because they came at a time of abundant gas supplies. In a properly functioning market, surpluses of a product forced its price lower. Yet the nation's average residential gas price rose from $4.90 per mcf in September 1981 to $5.82 per mcf in September 1982.

One cause of the price jumps was the long-term contracts signed between producers and pipeline companies in the late 1970s.

After the gas shortages during the winter of 1976-77, which forced many schools and industrial plants to shut down and left hundreds of thousands of workers temporarily without jobs, gas pipelines scrambled to get supplies wherever, and at whatever cost, they could. Since federal regulators allowed pipelines to earn a fixed return on their costs, the pipelines had no incentive to keep down those costs. They simply passed price hikes on to consumers.

In many cases, the pipelines agreed to pay the highest price allowed by the 1978 Natural Gas Policy Act. They also agreed to "take or pay" contract provisions requiring them to pay for as much as 90 or 95 percent of the gas they contracted for even if they did not need it when the time came to accept delivery.

Administration Proposal

Much of the gas industry had long sought an end to all federal price controls on natural gas, and in his first two years in office President Reagan had echoed that call.

By 1983, however, the White House realized that there was insufficient support in Congress for immediate decontrol. In February 1983, Reagan sent Congress a natural gas proposal providing for eventual, not immediate, decontrol.

Reagan proposed to deregulate the price of gas for which a new contract was signed or an old contract renegotiated. That gas could be sold at whatever price the purchaser was willing to pay. The price of gas sold under existing contracts would remain controlled. On Jan. 1, 1985, any contract that had not been renegotiated could be broken by producer or pipeline.

Under this plan the price of old gas would presumably rise to the market level, while the price of new gas would fall. But such predictions were difficult to make because of the impossibility of predicting the "mix" of old and new gas pipelines would carry and sell. Advocates of the plan predicted prices lower or at least no higher than current prices; critics predicted that decontrol would result in still another consumer price increase.

To protect consumers from steep rises in gas prices, Reagan proposed to deny pipelines the power to pass through to consumers the cost of the gas they purchased if the increase in gas cost was greater than the rate of inflation.

And to ease financial strains on pipeline companies, the administration proposed to allow them to break contracts with gas producers that contained so-called "take or pay" provisions.

Industry Split

Not all gas producers were enthusiastic about decontrolling old gas prices. Those with large supplies of such gas vigorously supported decontrol, but producers specializing in more expensive new gas or deep gas feared declining revenues as the price of their gas fell to a new, overall market level.

The same split existed among pipeline companies. Those carrying large amounts of old gas would have to pay more for their supplies under deregulation, as would their customers. The opposite was true for interstate and intrastate pipelines delivering new gas.

The contract abrogation provisions of Reagan's plan set up a confrontation between gas producers opposed to contract cancellation and some pipelines that stood to benefit from abrogation.

Consumer Pressure

Mail and other pressure from constituents hard hit by rising gas prices converted a number of Republican senators and representatives usually philosophically opposed to price controls to advocate some such measure to ease the pressure on consumers.

The Citizen/Labor Energy Coalition (CLEC), an amal-

gam of consumer groups and labor unions, was particularly effective in generating grass-roots pressure on Congress to ease the nation's gas bills.

CLEC sent volunteers out to knock on doors in the districts of key members of Congress to urge residents to demand action aimed at easing gas bills.

Also aiding the consumers in this fight were local utility companies, who were more accustomed to battling consumer organizations on issues such as rate hikes. But utilities feared decontrol of old gas prices would mean higher gas prices for them and their customers.

Consumer Alternative

Early in March, a group of House members, mostly Democrats, proposed an alternative to the administration's plan.

The alternative measure would maintain controls on old gas indefinitely, and would impose stricter controls on new gas until 1987. Like the administration plan, however, it would permit pipelines to break their "take or pay" contracts. In addition, it would set strict standards for pipelines to meet in passing through cost increases to consumers, requiring pipelines to demonstrate that they were using the least costly gas available.

This measure (HR 2154) was drafted under the leadership of the CLEC, a five-year-old organization comprised of about 300 organizations including labor unions, farm groups, senior citizens' organizations and other citizen groups. Among the major sponsors of this bill were Democrats Richard A. Gephardt, Mo.; Dan Glickman, Kan.; James L. Oberstar, Minn.; Tom Harkin, Iowa; Norman Y. Mineta, Calif.; Albert Gore Jr., Tenn., and Ike Skelton, Mo.

In the Senate, the CLEC alternative, in slightly different form, was introduced by Nancy Landon Kassebaum, R-Kan.

Senate Committee Action

The Senate Energy Committee began marking up a natural gas measure April 19, using President Reagan's proposal (S 615) as the basis for the markup. This proposal could be amended by a majority vote; in the case of a tie on an amendment, the amendment failed.

But on the most controversial issue, Reagan's proposal to decontrol the price of old gas, Chairman James A. McClure, R-Idaho, said that a majority vote would be required to retain that provision in the bill.

Test Vote: Decontrol

On April 21, the committee by a two-vote margin rejected an attempt to strip from the working draft the provision decontrolling prices of old gas.

But the 8-10 vote was inconclusive, because it came on a non-binding resolution designed only to indicate the "sense of the committee."

Two members — John Melcher, D-Mont., and Spark M. Matsunaga, D-Hawaii — abstained, and several others said their positions were subject to change.

Contract Carriage

Most of the debate in the Energy Committee April 19-21 concerned proposals to encourage pipeline companies to become "contract" gas carriers.

Those proposals had been overshadowed by the controversy over price decontrol. But they could have profound effects on the gas industry.

The purpose of the provisions was to encourage competition in the gas industry by letting utilities and industrial gas users negotiate directly with gas producers.

Under the existing system, pipeline companies were middlemen between producers and consumers. Since many utilities and producers had access to only one pipeline, pipelines often acted as monopolies.

Under the new provisions, utilities and industrial users could buy their gas directly from producers, and simply pay a transportation fee to the pipeline. That would enable them to shop for the best prices, making the gas market operate more efficiently.

McClure put the contract carriage issue at the top of the agenda because he felt it was relatively non-controversial. Both the administration bill and the Kassebaum alternative had provisions encouraging contract carriage.

While committee members seemed to agree that contract carriage provisions were needed, they disagreed on how to fashion those provisions.

Bill Bradley, D-N.J., offered a proposal that became the center of the committee's discussions. His amendment would put more pressure on pipelines to become contract carriers than either the administration or the Kassebaum bill.

Bradley's plan was embodied in a bill (S 1017) he introduced April 12.

Under the Bradley bill — as well as the administration bill — an interstate pipeline would be required to transport gas for a producer, distribution company or industrial user if it had available capacity in its pipeline. But, unlike the administration proposal, the Bradley bill created a presumption that a pipeline did have available capacity unless it could prove otherwise to the Federal Energy Regulatory Commission (FERC), which regulated pipelines.

The purpose of the provision was to encourage competition in the gas industry by allowing gas users — either utilities or industrial users — to buy gas directly from gas producers, and simply pay the pipeline companies a transportation fee. Under the current system, pipelines actually bought gas from producers and sold it to users. They therefore often had a monopoly in the markets they served.

The committee discussed the Bradley amendment for the better part of a month before finally modifying it at the urging of Bradley himself.

As discussion of his plan progressed, Bradley became concerned that industrial gas users would desert the utility companies that served them and buy directly from producers. That would force household gas consumers, who had no choice but to buy from the utilities, to pay a larger proportion of the utilities' fixed costs.

His modifying amendment restricted the ability of industrial gas users who historically had been served by a utility company to desert that company and buy directly from a producer.

After accepting Bradley's amendment by voice vote, the committee adopted the contract carriage proposal, 17-1. The dissenting vote came from Dale Bumpers, D-Ark., who said the amendment gave too much new power to the Federal Energy Regulatory Commission to regulate contract carriage.

Tie Vote on Decontrol

A clever compromise by opponents of natural gas decontrol on the Senate committee brought them closer to victory May 11, but not close enough.

An amendment to S 615, offered by Wendell H. Ford,

D-Ky., and supported by decontrol opponents, was defeated on a 10-10 tie vote.

In the earlier test vote, decontrol advocates had won 8-10, with two members abstaining.

Ford originally intended to offer an amendment eliminating the provision in S 615 lifting controls on old gas. But realizing that such an amendment would not pass, he withdrew it and offered instead an amendment eliminating a key portion of the bill that allowed either gas producers or gas pipeline companies to abrogate or "market out" of their long-term contracts in 1985.

The market-out provision in the administration bill was a sword that cut two ways. It allowed pipeline companies that had contracts forcing them to buy high-priced "new" and "deep" gas to break those contracts and purchase cheaper gas elsewhere. But it also allowed producers who sold large amounts of regulated, low-priced "old" gas to break their contracts and sell the gas at higher prices.

Many decontrol opponents wanted to see the market-out power given to pipelines only, forcing high deep-gas prices down but preventing old gas prices from rising.

In 1983, however, many pipelines that were obligated to buy high-priced gas had found ways to break their obligations without Congress' help.

Given that fact, Ford and other decontrol opponents apparently decided they were willing to give up the new authority for pipelines to break out of unfavorable contracts, provided that producers also forfeited their authority to break out of low-priced old gas contracts.

Without the market-out provisions, Ford believed deregulation of old gas would have much less of an effect on gas prices, since pipelines would not have to agree to price increases on previously contracted gas. The only prices decontrolled would be on new or renegotiated contracts.

By taking this tack, Ford managed to win the support of one member from a gas-producing state — Don Nickles, R-Okla. Nickles supported old gas decontrol but he also represented some independent gas producers who primarily sold high-cost gas and who would have been hurt severely by President Reagan's decontrol proposal. The Ford amendment would have helped protect those independent producers.

Nickles said he also was philosophically opposed to the idea of Congress abrogating private contracts.

Winning Nickles' support, however, did not give Ford a majority, and his amendment lost 10-10.

Stop and Go: Bill Reported

The committee worked on the natural gas issue for three months; in mid-June it put aside S 615 and began using a staff-drafted bill as the vehicle for its discussions. Two weeks later, it put aside that second proposal and began work on a third measure, also drafted by the committee staff.

On July 26, the committee, by a vote of 11-9, finally decided to send to the Senate a bill (S 1715 — S Rept 98-205) that would decontrol all natural gas within 44 months, by Jan. 1, 1986.

However, the committee was forced to report the bill without a recommendation in order to obtain the necessary majority vote to report it.

Lowell P. Weicker Jr., R-Conn., said he would vote against reporting the bill if it was reported favorably, with the recommendation that the Senate pass it. Had he voted against the bill, making the tally 10-10, it would not have been reported.

Just before the final vote July 26, Howard M. Metzenbaum, D-Ohio, a staunch foe of decontrol, was narrowly rebuffed on a move that would have had the effect of keeping price controls on old gas.

Through a parliamentary maneuver, he created a showdown that required the votes of 11 committee members to retain in the bill the provision decontrolling old gas prices.

"I don't think you have 11 votes for decontrol," Metzenbaum told McClure.

But he was wrong. When the roll was called, the vote was 11-8, with John Melcher, D-Mont., voting "present."

Senate Floor Action

Cloture Invoked

After more than three months on the back burner, the issue of natural gas prices moved to the Senate floor Nov. 1.

On Nov. 3, the Senate began consideration of S 1715 after voting 86-7 to shut off a filibuster on a motion to consider the measure, a complex bill that narrowly made it out of the Energy and Natural Resources Committee. *(Vote 321, p. 53-S)*

The bill was subsequently set aside to permit consideration of other business, but not before an interesting parliamentary skirmish took place.

Metzenbaum Maneuver

As soon as the Senate formally began consideration of the bill, Energy Chairman McClure offered a minor amendment. J. Bennett Johnston, La., ranking Energy Committee Democrat, rose to offer a closely related second-degree amendment, which would preclude further amendments at that time and effectively give the bill's proponents control of the initial debate.

But before Johnston could offer his amendment, Metzenbaum, who had been told by McClure and Johnston of their intentions, caught the attention of the presiding officer, John C. Danforth, R-Mo. He then offered his own hastily drafted second-degree amendment — one that prohibited decontrol of gas prices.

The effect of the maneuver was to make Metzenbaum's amendment the pending business when the Senate again took up the bill.

A furious Johnston complained that he should have been recognized before Metzenbaum. And McClure observed that next time, they would "play our cards closer to our vests."

Tables Turned

The Senate briefly resumed debate on natural gas decontrol legislation during the week of Nov. 7, but only long enough to rearrange the procedural pecking order governing consideration of the bill.

On Nov. 9, McClure countered Metzenbaum's move by withdrawing his original amendment, thus removing Metzenbaum's second-degree amendment as well.

Slade Gorton, R-Wash., presiding over the Senate, then recognized in succession McClure and his chief ally, Johnston, who offered two new amendments to the bill, precluding any further modifications until the Senate acted on their proposals.

With that accomplished, the Senate put aside the natural gas legislation and turned to consideration of other business.

Stalemate

After two weeks of desultory off-and-on debate on natural gas prices, the Senate Nov. 15 made clear that it was not ready to approve either of the natural gas pricing proposals before it.

By virtually identical margins it overwhelmingly rejected two diametrically opposed plans to change natural gas price controls.

By a vote of 26-71, the Senate rejected the consumer-backed alternative (S 996) offered by Kassebaum as an amendment to S 1715, the measure reported by the Senate Energy Committee.

S 996 would have retained controls on the price of old gas and rolled back prices on other gas to August 1982 levels. *(Vote 353, p. 58-S)*

Within minutes, the Senate voted 28-67 to reject the committee bill, which would have removed all remaining controls on the price of natural gas over a 44-month period. *(Senate vote 354, p. 58-S)*

Senate Energy Committee Chairman McClure met Nov. 16, 17 and 18 with about a dozen senators representing both sides in the debate in an effort to reach agreement on a new approach.

However, as the Senate pushed to adjourn Nov. 18, he announced that while they had come close to agreeing on a compromise measure, they had not succeeded.

House Committee Action

Subcommittee Markups

The House Energy and Commerce Committee's Subcommittee on Fossil and Synthetic Fuels began markup May 25. As its vehicle, the subcommittee used a plan proposed by Subcommittee Chairman Philip R. Sharp, D-Ind., which retained current price controls on old gas.

On July 29, three days after the Senate committee acted, the subcommittee by a 10-9 vote approved a natural gas bill (HR 4227) that made only modest changes in existing law.

The subcommittee bill retained federal price controls on most old gas, although it lifted price controls on additional volumes of gas produced from old gas wells and fields through the use of "enhanced" recovery techniques.

The bill also permitted pipeline companies to break their "take or pay" contracts as the administration had proposed.

The authors of this bill were Tom Corcoran, Ill., the ranking Republican member of the subcommittee, and Richard C. Shelby, D-Ala.

Chairman Sharp voted against reporting the bill to the full committee, warning that it would permit decontrol of a large amount of old gas. Sharp also cast a proxy vote for full Committee Chairman John D. Dingell, D-Mich., against reporting the bill. Dingell had said that deregulation of old natural gas would take place "over my dead body."

Full Committee

In October, before full committee markup began, Sharp and Dingell unveiled a new consumer-oriented measure that would not only retain price controls on old gas, but would roll back prices on most other gas to September 1982 levels. Only gas brought to market after Jan. 1, 1985, would be deregulated.

The House Energy Committee began marking up the

legislation Nov. 15 and 17, but took no major actions before the end of the first session of the 98th Congress.

Major Issues: A Summary

Price Controls/Old Gas

Under the Natural Gas Policy Act of 1978, the price of old gas was forever controlled.

The Reagan administration proposed eliminating these controls gradually as contracts covering old gas were terminated or renegotiated. By Jan. 1, 1985, all contracts that had not been renegotiated could be broken by either the pipeline or the producer. By Jan. 1, 1986, all gas prices would be decontrolled.

The consumer-oriented bill sponsored by Kassebaum (S 996) retained price controls on old gas.

The Senate Energy Committee bill (S 1715) decontrolled old gas over a 44-month period. The committee adopted this provision by a vote of 11-8.

The House Energy Subcommittee bill (HR 4227) retained federal price controls on old gas, except for gas obtained through special techniques designed to increase the production of an existing well.

The Dingell-Sharp alternative retained price controls on old gas.

Price Controls/New Gas

Under the Natural Gas Policy Act, price controls on new gas expired Jan. 1, 1985.

The Senate Energy Committee bill (S 1715) immediately decontrolled all new gas sold under new or renegotiated contracts. It provided a complex mechanism permitting contracts now covering new gas to be broken or adjusted.

The Kassebaum alternative (S 996) rolled the price of new gas back to August 1982 levels, and delayed decontrol of this gas until 1987.

The House Energy Subcommittee bill did not affect the price of most new gas.

The Dingell-Sharp alternative rolled back the price of new gas to September 1982 levels and permitted deregulation only of gas brought to market after Jan. 1, 1984.

Contract Adjustments: Take or Pay

The Reagan administration proposed permitting pipeline companies to break contracts under which they were forced to take the contracted amount of gas or pay for as much of 90 percent of it even if they did not need it. Under the Reagan proposal, companies could immediately reduce their obligation and pay for only 70 percent of the gas.

The Kassebaum alternative (S 996) allowed the companies to reduce their obligation and pay for only 50 percent of the contracted amount.

The Senate Energy Committee bill (S 1715) reduced take-or-pay requirements to 50 percent during the first year under the new law, 60 percent the second year and 70 percent in the third and final year.

The House subcommittee bill reduced the take-or-pay requirement to 50 percent.

Consumer Prices

The Reagan proposal denied interstate pipelines the power to automatically pass through price increases from the producers to consumers if these increases exceeded the rate of inflation. Larger increases could take effect only

with the approval of the Federal Energy Regulatory Commission (FERC).

The Senate Energy Committee bill permitted pipelines to pass on to consumers only those price increases shown to be prudent. If the price increase were larger, it would have to be reviewed by FERC. Any savings realized by contract adjustments had to be passed on to the consumer.

Contract Carriage

The Senate committee approved provisions to encourage competition in the gas industry by letting utilities and industrial gas users negotiate directly with gas producers, eliminating the middleman role usually played by pipeline companies. Pipelines with available capacity would be required to transport this gas for a fee.

The House Energy Subcommittee bill required pipelines with available capacity to transport gas they did not own; under current law pipelines were not obligated to carry such gas. ∎

NRC Authorization Stalls

Nuclear Regulatory Commission (NRC) authority to grant temporary operating licenses to nuclear power plants ended Dec. 31, 1983, because Congress failed to act on legislation extending it.

As of Jan. 1, 1984, the NRC could no longer grant temporary licenses permitting a nuclear power plant to operate, under certain restrictions, before the lengthy regular licensing process had been completed. The NRC and the nuclear industry sought extension of this interim licensing power as part of an NRC reauthorization for fiscal 1984 and 1985 (HR 2510, S 1291).

HR 2510 was reported May 11 by the House Interior and Insular Affairs Committee and June 24 by the Energy and Commerce Committee (H Rept 98-103, Pts I and II). Only the Energy Committee approved the licensing extension.

The Senate Environment and Public Works Committee Nov. 9 voted 8-7 to delete the extension from S 1291, but the panel did not complete its markup of the bill.

The fiscal 1984 energy and water development appropriations bill (HR 3132 — PL 98-50) cleared by Congress June 29 contained $465.8 million for the NRC. That was the amount the House version of the bill had provided; the Senate-passed bill called for $466.8 million, the amount that had been requested by the Reagan administration. *(Appropriation bill, p. 500)*

Background

The controversial "interim" licensing authority — sought by the nuclear industry as a way to allow plants to begin operating before lengthy licensing hearings were completed — was included in an NRC authorization bill passed in 1982 (PL 97-415). At the time, the NRC warned that 13 plants would not be able to begin operations in a timely fashion without it. *(1982 Almanac p. 310)*

No applications were received for temporary licenses, but the NRC in 1983 again warned that a number of plants — this time five — could face delays unless the temporary licensing authority was extended.

Environmental groups opposed accelerated licensing on grounds public safety could be endangered.

Members of both House committees had hoped to keep HR 2510 non-controversial and had agreed not to deal with such issues as expedited licensing procedures. Those topics were the subject of ongoing hearings.

House Committee Action

Interior Committee. In its markup of HR 2510, the Interior Committee approved a provision stipulating that funds in the bill for work related to the Clinch River Breeder Reactor ($8.2 million in fiscal 1984 and $7.8 million in 1985) should be reallocated to "safety technology activities" in the event the controversial Clinch River project was terminated, as indeed it was later in the year. *(Clinch River, p. 326)*

The committee also included a provision allowing the NRC to issue a license to a nuclear plant "only if it determines that there exists a state, local or utility plan which provides reasonable assurance that public health and safety is not endangered by operation of the facility." And, the committee said, the NRC should not license a plant "when lack of participation in emergency planning by state, county or local governments means it is unlikely that a utility plan could successfully be carried out."

Just such emergency planning problems almost led to the shutdown June 9 of the already-operating Indian Point nuclear plant in New York.

The committee report also said, "The committee believes that the growth of nuclear technology will not continue in the United States in the absence of substantially increased confidence in those responsible for managing it. The committee . . . has found good reason for public apprehension. The NRC's procedures do not provide high assurance that significant safety defects will be found and corrected before reactor operation accidents occur. . . ."

Energy Committee. The amendment to continue the NRC's temporary licensing authority was added to HR 2510 during markup June 15 in the Energy and Commerce Subcommittee on Energy Conservation and Power. On June 21, the full committee defeated efforts by Mike Synar, D-Okla., Edward J. Markey, D-Mass., and subcommittee Chairman Richard L. Ottinger, D-N.Y., to delete that extension of authority.

Synar argued against extending the authority, saying it had yet to be used and that the nuclear industry had failed to make a convincing case that it was needed.

Al Swift, D-Wash., called the authority a "simple safety valve," giving the industry a way to start operations at a plant that had been completed but not licensed. Markey suggested that was "another word for loophole." But Swift and the majority of the committee were not swayed, and voted to retain the temporary authority.

Also on June 21, Albert Gore Jr., D-Tenn., succeeded in including language in the committee report calling on the NRC to make a study of "occupational jet lag" among nuclear plant workers whose changing work shifts might lead to fatigue. He suggested such a problem might have contributed to the 1979 accident at the Three Mile Island nuclear plant in Pennsylvania.

Senate Committee Action

The Senate Environment and Public Works Committee reported a "shell bill" (S 1291 — S Rept 98-118) May 16. But that version was never intended for floor consideration.

The committee later that month began hearings on a number of nuclear policy issues, including licensing reform and emergency preparedness.

On Nov. 9, members voted 8-7 to delete the interim licensing authority extension from S 1291.

Alan K. Simpson, R-Wyo., argued that each day of delay in putting a nuclear power plant in service cost about $1 million. But George J. Mitchell, D-Maine, who moved to delete the interim licensing authority extension, called it a "truly extraordinary circumvention" of normal procedures that was not used in the past and was not needed in the future.

Simpson noted that work had begun in both the Senate and House on bills (S 893, S 894, HR 2511, HR 2512) to overhaul the entire licensing process, and said temporary licensing authority would not be needed if this legislation, aimed at reducing "unnecessary delays," were passed. ∎

Energy Preparedness/IEA

A simple, one-paragraph bill extending an antitrust exemption for oil company participation in international energy planning failed to clear Congress when it became a not-so-simple two-paragraph bill that could lead to a revival of presidential authority to allocate supplies and control prices in an energy emergency.

The effect of the Dec. 31, 1983, expiration of the exemption was likely to be negligible, according to the State Department, as long as the exemption was restored without too much delay after Congress returned in 1984.

"It's like the fire department closing down for a while — if there's no fire, it's not a problem," said a State Department official.

The legislation (HR 4194) began as a simple extension to June 30, 1985, of the exemption from antitrust laws granted to U.S. oil companies when they participated in joint planning activities of the 21-nation International Energy Agency (IEA).

HR 4194 was passed by the House in that form on Nov. 7.

But the Senate Energy and Natural Resources Committee on Nov. 9 adopted an amendment offered by Howard M. Metzenbaum, D-Ohio, adding language that would end the exemption on June 1, 1984, unless a law had been enacted to give the president the authority to allocate supplies and control prices during a severe petroleum shortage.

The Senate passed HR 4194 — with Metzenbaum's amendment attached — on Nov. 17. The House refused to accept the new version, and Metzenbaum would not let the Senate reconsider its position late Nov. 18, the last day of the session.

Background

The IEA, located in Paris, coordinated a 21-nation energy program aimed at reducing international oil demand, increasing stockpiles and sharing available supplies in an emergency.

Because they would be essential to the success of any oil-sharing plan, major oil companies were included in the IEA programs. Their participation required the limited antitrust exemption contained in HR 4194.

The antitrust exemption was extended four times in 1982. Then, as in 1983, the issue of extending the exemption became entangled in the larger question of U.S. readiness for a new energy crisis. *(1982 Almanac p. 300)*

A 1973 law enacted during an Arab embargo on oil shipments to the United States required the president to control allocation and prices during such emergencies. But that law expired Sept. 30, 1981, and President Reagan in 1982 vetoed a measure that would have replaced the mandatory control powers with standby allocation and price control authority.

Reagan argued that the marketplace, not the government, should allocate oil supplies in an emergency. His veto was narrowly upheld as a Senate move to override it fell five votes short of the two-thirds margin needed. *(1982 Almanac p. 301)*

Many members of Congress, however, remained convinced that government plans for an energy emergency needed to be improved.

More Preparation Sought

For example, Sen. James A. McClure, R-Idaho, chairman of the Energy and Natural Resources Committee, introduced S 1678, which was designed to upgrade the United States' preparedness for an energy emergency and included guidelines for the completion and use of the Strategic Petroleum Reserve (SPR).

The IEA antitrust exemption was contained in S 1678, but it was broken out in a separate bill when it became apparent the more extensive package could not clear before the exemption expired Dec. 31, 1983.

McClure, who had long pushed for better emergency planning, sought administration backing for his legislation in exchange for a pledge to support the administration's plan to slow the purchase of oil to fill the SPR, which in 1983 contained more than 365 million of a planned 750 million barrels.

Congress agreed, in the fiscal 1984 Interior appropriations bill (HR 3363 — PL 98-146), to reduce the SPR fill rate from 220,000 barrels per day to 186,000. *(Interior appropriations, p. 462)*

House Action

HR 4194 was reported Nov. 2 by the House Energy and Commerce Committee (H Rept 98-472).

The bill was passed Nov. 7 by voice vote under suspension of the rules.

Senate Action

A similar bill (S 1982) was approved Nov. 9 by an 18-1 vote of the Senate Energy and Natural Resources Committee. There was no written report.

Indicating its continued interest in more comprehensive legislation, the Energy Committee approved, by voice vote, an amendment to S 1982 offered by Metzenbaum.

The amendment called for the termination of the IEA antitrust exemption on June 1, 1984, unless Reagan had signed into law a bill giving him authority to allocate supplies and control prices during a severe petroleum shortage.

Metzenbaum, who opposed the antitrust exemption, argued that if the Reagan administration felt strongly enough about joint emergency planning to provide oil companies antitrust exemption, "then it should support some type of standby allocation program to protect the American public."

After the Senate amended HR 4194 to conform to the language of committee-approved S 1982, the bill was passed Nov. 17.

The House a day later refused to agree to the Senate amendment, and Congress adjourned with the dispute still smoldering. ∎

CWIP Legislation

The House Energy and Commerce Committee July 19 by voice vote approved a bill (HR 555) that restricted the ability of electric utilities to charge their customers for some of the costs of new facilities under construction but not yet completed.

The measure was formally reported (H Rept 98-350) on Aug. 9, but it went no further in 1983.

According to Rep. Richard L. Ottinger, D-N.Y., the bill was drafted in response to an "overly permissive" May 16 ruling by the Federal Energy Regulatory Commission that allowed commission-regulated utilities to recover up to 50 percent of the financing costs of construction work in progress (CWIP).

HR 555 allowed utilities to bill customers for CWIP only "where an obvious cash flow problem exists," subject to consumer protections, which included requirements that the project be the least costly alternative for meeting the need for additional power supplies. ∎

Strategic Petroleum Reserve

Congress and the White House compromised in 1983 on the rate at which the nation should fill the Strategic Petroleum Reserve (SPR), its storehouse of fuel for an emergency.

Congress approved a reduction from 220,000 barrels per day to 186,000 barrels per day in the minimum rate at which the reserve was to be filled. The administration had wanted to slow the fill rate to 145,000 barrels a day.

The compromise reduction came in a provision of the fiscal 1984 Interior Department appropriations bill (HR 3363 — PL 98-146). *(Interior appropriations, p. 462)*

Congress in 1982 (PL 97-229) required the president to fill the reserve at a rate of 300,000 barrels per day unless he certified that to do so was not in the national interest. An absolute minimum rate of 220,000 barrels per day was set. *(1982 Almanac p. 299)*

The administration provoked considerable congressional ire by recommending in its 1984 energy budget proposal a slowdown to 145,000 barrels per day, primarily as a money-saving move. Administration officials argued that because oil imports had decreased and the possibility of an oil embargo was less likely, it was no longer imperative that the nation move quickly to build its reserve.

The Senate Energy Committee March 1 rejected all of Reagan's proposed energy budget cuts and approved the use of $2.5 billion in fiscal 1984 off-budget funds to fill the reserve at the required minimum rate of 220,000 barrels per day.

Funds for purchasing oil for the reserve were not considered part of the budget and thus did not figure into calculations of deficits.

The Interior appropriations bill (HR 3363 — PL 98-146) that contained the reduction in the minimum fill rate also provided $650 million to buy oil for the reserve, permitting purchase of about 15 million barrels for fiscal 1985.

The administration had requested $583.1 million for the reserve; the House provided $1.7 billion and the Senate $1.3 billion. Those large sums had prompted an administration threat to veto the bill, a threat which resulted in the final reduction to one-half the Senate amount.

Facilities Construction

On a related point, the House March 10 rejected Reagan's request to slow the construction of oil storage facilities for the reserve.

The administration wanted to defer spending $57.4 million of the $242.1 million appropriated for the reserve in the fiscal 1983 continuing resolution (PL 97-276). This would delay construction of two storage facilities in Texas and Louisiana, designed to contain 150 million barrels of oil.

The House by voice vote adopted H Res 80 (H Rept 98-23) disapproving the administration request. In debate, members said they hoped their action would put the administration on notice that it should move as quickly as possible to fill the reserve to the mandated level of 750 million barrels. Late in 1983 the reserve contained more than 365 million barrels. ∎

Agriculture

For American agriculture, 1983 was a year of extremes: record drought, grandiose farm programs and startlingly high spending to prop up the farm economy.

Federal expenditures for price supports and other farm subsidy programs reached an extraordinary high — variously estimated at between $19 billion to $22 billion. Those estimates did not include the value of the surplus commodities — about $9.7 billion — used to pay farmers in the administration's ambitious "Payment-in-Kind" (PIK) program.

By contrast, the 1981 price tag for federal aid to farmers was $4 billion, close to the 20-year annual average cost of the programs.

The federal outlays nearly matched net farm income. Preliminary estimates at the end of the year put the net income total at about $29 billion to $34 billion.

Office of Management and Budget Director David A. Stockman, adding in programs not usually considered direct supports for farm income, claimed in May that the federal government would pour close to $38 billion into rural America in 1983.

The high program costs were blamed on the large surpluses of major crops that existed at the beginning of the year and depressed market prices — as in the previous three years. Like food stamps and welfare, farm programs cost more during times of economic stress, when more people depended more heavily upon them.

The surpluses signaled the continuing mismatch between high farm productivity and export markets too weak to siphon off much of the U.S. surplus. Farm exports slid downward in 1983, totaling $34.5 billion in value. The decline continued the downward trend from the 1981 high of $43.8 billion.

In an attempt to prop up exports, the Reagan administration offered subsidized credit and bonuses of commodities to promote foreign sales of U.S. commodities. It also signed a new, long-term grain trade pact with the Soviet Union.

On July 28, Agriculture Secretary John R. Block and U.S. Trade Representative William E. Brock III announced that under the terms of the five-year grain sales agreement, the United States would sell, and the Russians would buy, at least nine million metric tons and as much as 12 million tons of wheat and corn each year. The deal also made special arrangements for soybean sales. The expiring U.S.-U.S.S.R. pact called for annual sales of six million to eight million metric tons, without provision for soybeans.

Politics of Program Costs

Privately and publicly, Stockman attacked the high costs of the farm programs. At a May congressional hearing, he complained that "We are spending more for farm subsidies than we are for welfare for the entire poverty population of this country."

Agriculture Department (USDA) officials turned on the programs they administered, publicly adding to Stockman's complaints. They said that farm programs were in political trouble that could only get worse. They repeatedly reminded audiences, in Congress and elsewhere, that the hefty infusions of federal farm money were going to a relatively small number of people.

According to the most recent Census Bureau figures, the farm population dropped to 5.6 million people in 1982, just 2.4 percent of the total population. Within that number, a still smaller group actually produced the bulk of the nation's food. USDA estimated that about 12 percent of the nation's farms marketed about two-thirds of all farm products.

Because of the way farm programs operated, the larger the size of a farm, the larger the federal farm benefits it could collect. The benefits came in many forms, among them loans on favorable terms, cash payments for price supports, and subsidies for storage facilities and crop insurance.

Paying Not to Grow

The Reagan administration in 1983 swallowed its aversion to meddling in the farm economy and ran the largest crop reduction program in the history of federal farm programs. The president also managed to ignore his free-market philosophy long enough to sign legislation authorizing first-time-ever payments to dairy farmers for not making milk. These two developments seemed clear evidence of the enduring political power of farmers, despite their shrinking numbers.

The PIK program paid farmers for idling part of their crop land; the payments were in the form of wheat or other stocks, not cash. The assumption was that federally owned surpluses would "finance" the program.

As it turned out, the government did not own enough surplus crops to meet its PIK commitments. So to make many of these payments, the government simply forgave price support loans. In effect, the government gave back to farmers full title to crops they owned, but had obligated to the government for loans. (In the price support loan programs, farmers borrowed from the federal government, using crops as collateral.)

Some payments were quite convoluted. Certain participants were required to produce a crop to be put under a price support loan, which was then forgiven. In effect, these farmers grew the crops with which they were paid for not growing more.

These problems did not escape attention, and the program was the butt of jokes and criticism by humorist Art Buchwald and numerous editorial writers and cartoonists.

In one of his nationally syndicated columns, Buchwald quoted a fictional farmer who said that, to pass the time away, he made daily checks to make sure no one had planted anything on his land. "Then I go down to the coffee shop and sit around with the other boys, talking about what great crops we didn't raise this year."

One dire prediction, that farmers would dump their PIK commodities on markets at the same time and ruin prices, failed to come true. At the end of the year, farmers

appeared to be treating the PIK commodities as they would crops they had harvested — watching markets and spacing out sales.

Participation figures suggested that the PIK program was popular in the farm community. About a third of the nation's eligible cropland was idled — more than 80 million acres.

Yet when a devastating drought wiped out crops late in the summer, the PIK program was blamed in some regions for amplifying inequities among farmers. Those in the program were comfortably cushioned because they had stocks to sell while non-participants who lost their crops had also forfeited their claims to federal disaster aid and other assistance. (PIK payments were only part of a broad acreage reduction strategy; farmers were also paid in cash and in farm program eligibility for participating.)

Producers of livestock and dairy animals also grumbled at the combined impact of PIK and the drought because their feed prices soared.

Some participating farms reaped PIK payments worth a million dollars or more. Because compensation for idling crop land was made in the form of surplus crops, the Agriculture Department had decided that these "payments" were exempt from a $50,000 statutory limit on cash program payments to farmers. But this interpretation, and the very large PIK payments it permitted, were sharply criticized in Congress.

The PIK program appeared to put the United States at a disadvantage in world markets. In October, Agriculture Secretary Block told a congressional committee that the large production cuts at home had stimulated extra production by nations that compete with the United States in agriculture.

"While U.S. grain production for 1983/84 is expected to be down by 129 million tons, foreign production is expected to rise by 43 million tons to a new record," Block said.

Nevertheless, Block and other administration officials generally declared the PIK program to be a one-shot success that had headed off yet another surplus and put some badly needed money in farmers' pockets.

Drought Impact

Another exceptional event for agriculture was an unusually broad and long-lasting spell of hot, rainless weather that devastated corn, soybeans and other major crops. The drought, the worst in 50 years, began in July and affected production in at least 28 states across the Southeast, Midwest and Southwest. Drought damage was estimated at about $7 billion.

This natural "production cut" greatly magnified the impact of the PIK program. Corn production was cut in half; carryover stocks — those left over at the end of the year — were reduced by about four-fifths, compared to the previous year. The short supplies produced substantial increases in market prices. In mid-September, according to USDA, the farm price of corn was up more than 50 percent, compared to September 1982; soybeans were up more than 60 percent; cotton prices were up about 15 percent.

Wheat prices, however, did not show the same strong recovery. Wheat producers brought in their winter wheat before the drought hit, harvesting the second largest crop in the nation's history. The PIK program had cut the acreage planted in wheat — from 79 million acres to 60 million acres between 1982 and 1983. Yet because yields rose markedly, the 1983 wheat harvest declined only 14 percent, to 2.4 billion bushels, from the 2.8 billion all-time high of 1982.

—By Elizabeth Wehr

Congress Revises Dairy, Tobacco Programs

President Reagan Nov. 29 signed into law landmark changes in federal dairy policy despite his strong objections to the new program.

The legislation (HR 3385 — PL 98-180) authorized payments to dairymen, partly financed by dairy farmers themselves, for producing less milk.

The bill, which also lowered federal dairy price supports, was meant to reduce surplus dairy production, which had been running about 10 percent more than demand. The federal dairy program had to buy surplus dairy goods at the established support price, and federal expenditures on the program were nearing $3 billion annually.

Since the Depression, American farmers had been paid for idling crop land to head off erosion and to reduce surplus production. But there had never been payments to dairy producers, on a national scale, for producing less milk.

The legislation also included major revisions in the tobacco program, authorization for egg producers to coordinate marketing, and authorization for livestock producers to buy damaged federal stocks of feed to help them cope with the 1983 summer drought.

Administration Role

For much of the year, Agriculture Secretary John R. Block had supported the so-called "paid diversion" dairy plan as part of a larger, unsuccessful strategy to win congressional approval of a freeze on target prices for wheat and other crops. Block, however, had withdrawn his support in the final weeks of the session. *(Target price freeze, p. 383)*

Reagan protested to some members of Congress that paying farmers for not producing violated his free-market philosophy. The president's economic advisers had strongly opposed the bill, but Agriculture Department officials advised him to sign it, arguing that existing law was worse.

Moreover, a veto would have dealt a serious blow to one of Reagan's early Southern supporters, Sen. Jesse Helms, R-N.C. The tobacco provisions were critically important to Helms, who was up for re-election in 1984.

The bill temporarily froze tobacco price supports, ended double payments by growers to special tobacco support funds and phased out the renting of tobacco quotas to land away from the farms to which they were assigned. (Most tobacco could not be sold without a federal quota.)

The tobacco sections, in fact, had been viewed by dairy lobbyists and their congressional allies as solid-gold "insurance" of enactment.

Final Provisions

As signed into law Nov. 29, HR 3385:

Dairy

● Reduced to $12.60 per hundred pounds, from $13.10 per hundred pounds, the federal dairy price support. Authorized two further reductions of 50 cents each on April 1, 1985, and July 1, 1985, if federal purchases of milk in 1985 were estimated to exceed six billion pounds (as of April 1) or five billion pounds (as of July 1). However, the bill would authorize an increase of at least 50 cents on July 1, 1985, if federal purchases were estimated at below five

billion pounds and more milk was needed.

● Authorized a 15-month paid diversion program, from Jan. 1, 1984, until March 31, 1985. Producers who participated would cut production by 5 percent to 30 percent from their previous yields and would be paid at a rate of $10 per hundred pounds.

● Retained an existing 50-cents-per-hundred-pounds assessment paid by dairy producers and earmarked it to help finance the paid diversion program, but repealed a second 50-cent assessment. *(Box, next page)*

● Directed the secretary of agriculture to take all feasible steps to minimize the impact on meat markets from the slaughter of dairy cows.

● Required each dairyman in the paid diversion program to submit a plan showing how much of his production cut would be achieved by selling cows for slaughter, and authorized revisions in diversion contracts to avoid a sudden dumping of dairy cows on the beef market. Directed the secretary to increase federal purchases of meat for food assistance programs.

Drought Relief

● Directed the agriculture secretary to let farmers and ranchers in drought areas buy, at 75 percent of the current price support loan rate (about $2 per bushel), federally owned surplus feed corn that was in poor condition. *(Drought relief, p. 387)*

Tobacco

● Froze the 1984 price support level for flue-cured tobacco at the 1982 level. Retained the customary differential between the flue-cured level and that of burley, effectively permitting the secretary to freeze the burley level for the year. For the 1985 crop, continued the freeze for flue-cured only, but the price support could be raised to reflect a large increase in production costs, if such an increase occurred. (The federal price support established minimum market prices for tobacco. Flue-cured tobacco was grown largely in the Carolinas and Georgia; burley was concentrated in Kentucky and Tennessee.)

● Authorized the secretary to reduce the support price for certain grades of flue-cured tobacco if the reductions were needed to improve the marketability of poor-quality grades. Set certain restrictions on the reductions that could be made and specified that the reductions should not be counted in computing future price support levels.

● Ended the leasing of quotas for flue-cured tobacco for use on other farms after the 1986 crop. For the 1985 and 1986 crops, required that such leasing agreements could not require payment for the lease until after the crop had been sold. For such "off-farm" leasing of burley quotas, reduced by half the total that could be leased and ended the fall leasing of burley quotas.

(Federal quotas determined how many pounds of tobacco a grower could market; they were assigned to specific farms but existing law permitted them to be leased for use on other farms.)

● Ended so-called "double" assessment payments to "no net cost" funds by eliminating a requirement that lessees make the payments.

The assessment-financed funds were established to pay for financial losses in the tobacco price support pro-

Dairy Assessments

HR 3385 (PL 98-180) repealed the second of two controversial assessments that Congress had approved in 1982 (PL 97-253) in an attempt to discourage overproduction in the dairy industry, while offsetting costs of the federal dairy program. The 1982 law had provided for two 50-cent assessments on every hundred pounds of milk equivalent (as measured in butter, cheese and dry milk) produced by dairy farmers above certain levels.

The fee enraged dairymen and generated several lawsuits, one of which blocked the Agriculture Department in December 1982 from collecting the assessment. The department began collecting the first assessment in April 1983 and announced its intentions to collect the second 50-cent assessment if Congress provided no acceptable alternative.

When the legislation overhauling the federal dairy program and replacing the two assessments with a single assessment became entangled in disputes over other farm issues, Congress Aug. 4 abruptly passed a measure (S J Res 149) postponing the second assessment from Sept. 1 to Oct. 1.

President Reagan vetoed S J Res 149 on Aug. 23. His veto message said the $60 million the assessment would yield during September would help offset the $2.4 billion it was estimated the federal dairy program would cost in 1983. *(Veto message, p. 35-E)*

gram, such as interest or losses in sales of surplus tobacco. Some growers renting quotas said they had been paying "twice" — once for themselves, and again because quota owners raised lease prices to cover their assessment payments.

● Postponed for one year, to Dec. 1, 1984, the deadline by which non-farmer owners of flue-cured and burley tobacco quotas had to sell those quotas. Also exempted from the mandatory sale partnerships, estates or family farm corporations if the proceeds from leasing went to individuals, and educational institutions that used their allotments for instruction or demonstration.

Egg Promotion

● Authorized egg producers, subject to approval of the secretary, to adopt marketing orders placing certain limits on the marketing of eggs and providing for disposal of surplus eggs. Also authorized a marketing order for research and promotion of eggs.

Committee Action

The House Agriculture Committee June 9 reported its bill to cut dairy production (HR 1875 — H Rept 98-237). And on June 29 the panel approved legislation making extensive changes in the tobacco program (HR 1440).

The Senate Agriculture Committee June 23 reported a combined dairy-tobacco bill (S 1529 — S Rept 98-163).

House Dairy Bill

The House Agriculture Committee approved HR 1875 on May 24 after weeks of behind-the-scenes negotiations.

At that time, the Reagan administration, in a major departure from its philosophy of a free market for agriculture unhampered by federal programs, reluctantly supported HR 1875.

"We hate it. But we've got to do it, temporarily [to reduce the surplus]," said one high-ranking department official who asked not to be quoted by name. (The administration withdrew its support late in the year.)

The dairy price support program guaranteed that the government would buy dairy products at a set price — at $13.10 per 100 pounds of milk equivalent in mid-1983 — if producers could not sell them elsewhere. The government was buying about 10 percent of the milk produced in the United States, at a cost of nearly $3 billion a year. If no changes were made in the dairy program, the government would buy and store about 16 billion pounds worth of milk, in the form of butter, cheese and non-fat powdered milk.

Under the bill, the price support payments could drop by as much as $1.50 over two years, unless production fell below certain limits. However, dairymen who contracted to reduce production would be paid $10 for each 100 pounds they did not produce, up to certain limits. The new payments would last through part of fiscal 1985.

The bill continued a controversial assessment paid by dairy producers, which partially financed the new payment program.

Industry Split. Major regional dairy cooperatives split over how to cope with the swelling dairy surplus.

On one side were those who wanted strict production limits for individual dairy farms to reduce the surplus. They included the National Milk Producers Federation, an umbrella organization for all co-ops, and the Associated Milk Producers, Inc. (AMPI), a major Midwestern cooperative.

AMPI spokesman Jim Eskin said that about 80 percent of the industry supported production limits, "and we think that's a pretty good showing of unity."

But other elements of the industry, led by the Southeastern cooperatives of Dairymen Inc. and joined by consumer and industrial user groups, objected to production controls. They wanted hefty across-the-board cuts in federal price support levels instead.

The industry divisions delayed action on a subcommittee-approved bill (HR 2822) backed by the federation that provided for production quotas on individual dairy farms, enforced by a sliding scale of price supports.

Compromise. The administration had proposed the new plan to combine temporary production controls with the overall price support cuts in an effort to resolve industry divisions.

But then the administration told members that its support was contingent on Congress simultaneously approving a freeze on target prices, a major type of price support for wheat, corn, cotton and rice. *(Target price freeze, p. 383)*

Rep. James M. Jeffords, R-Vt., generally credited with spearheading the compromise efforts, said he refused to be part of such a tradeoff.

Committee Chairman E. "Kika" de la Garza, D-Texas, said he had promised no more than a fair forum in which the administration could make its case for the crop support freeze.

On May 25, the panel held a day-long session on a hastily introduced freeze bill (HR 3102) but postponed action. Jeffords said any delay on the dairy program was unfortunate because the production-cut program would

have only a relatively short time to work.

J. Dawson Ahalt, the Agriculture Department's deputy assistant secretary for economics, said the target price freeze was needed to offset the cost of the new dairy plan, estimated initially at about $300 million to $400 million a year more than the existing program. Savings from the target price freeze would amount to $370 million in fiscal 1984, Ahalt said.

However, Rep. Edward R. Madigan, R-Ill., ranking minority member of the Agriculture Committee, said that it was not a question of other commodities paying for the dairy program. All of agriculture, Madigan said, must agree to changes that would make U.S. commodities more competitively priced in world markets.

At its May 24 meeting, the committee ignored HR 2822 and instead voted to substitute the compromise for another dairy measure (HR 1875).

The legislation was still opposed by several major segments of the industry, according to a committee aide. But Jeffords said the parties had been convinced that "the other options are so terrible, [and] the pressures building against the program are so incredible" that the compromise was likely to move without serious opposition from within the industry.

Conable Alternative. In mid-June, prominent House Republicans, including Minority Leader Robert H. Michel, R-Ill., unexpectedly objected to the administration-backed dairy bill. Democrats Barney Frank, Mass., John M. Spratt Jr., S.C., and Gillis W. Long, La., joined in opposing HR 1875.

Sponsors of the bill dropped their plan to bring it to the House floor on the June 20 suspension calendar when Barber B. Conable Jr., R-N.Y., Michel and Minority Whip Trent Lott, R-Miss., and the three Democrats publicized their objections in a June 16 "dear colleague" letter. The suspension calendar expedited action by barring amendments and permitting legislation to be considered without going through the House Rules Committee.

Conable introduced an alternative dairy bill (HR 3292), backed by the conservative American Farm Bureau Federation, that omitted a central feature of HR 1875 — payments to dairymen for cutting production.

Senate Dairy-Tobacco Bill

The Senate Agriculture Committee June 16 approved major changes in the federal dairy and tobacco programs (S 1529).

The dairy changes, which basically followed HR 1875 with minor amendments, were approved by a 15-3 vote. The changes would have reduced price supports, retained one of two controversial assessments on dairy payments and used funds from the assessment to pay farmers who cut dairy production.

The committee also voted 17-1 for a multi-year freeze of tobacco price supports and changes in the complex system of allotments and quotas.

Tobacco advocates such as Helms, chairman of the Agriculture Committee, hoped to protect their controversial program by packaging changes with dairy and price support legislation, and thus gain support of other farm groups and the administration. *(Tobacco program, box p. 379)*

Administration strategy to combine the dairy legislation with a freeze on target prices for wheat and other crops was thwarted at the June 16 meeting. Opponents of the freeze blocked attempts to force votes on it. When the dairy bill finally came to the Senate floor, it was under an agreement that barred amendments related to target prices.

House Tobacco Bill

The House Agriculture Committee June 29 approved HR 1440, a measure that called for a two-year freeze on price supports and intricate changes in the tobacco allotment and quota system. The panel also approved legislation (HR 3392) to freeze 1983 tobacco price supports at the 1982 level for one year. *(Tobacco price freeze, box p. 378)*

House, Senate Differences. HR 1440 generally resembled the tobacco provisions in S 1529, except in two respects. First, it mandated that imported tobacco would be subject to the same requirements as domestic tobacco, banning residues of pesticides and other agricultural chemicals that might harm human health.

The House bill also required that individuals who owned federal tobacco allotments and quotas but rented them to tobacco growers had to change over to sharecropping arrangements. The allotments and quotas were the core of the regulatory system, and they limited the number of acres planted and the number of pounds sold. Farmers without an allotment and quota could not sell tobacco.

Instead of cash rent for the allotments and quotas, paid at the beginning of the growing season, the nongrowing owners would share planting costs with the growers and then receive a portion of the profits when the crop was sold, a change meant to defuse criticism of the rental arrangements.

Both bills would, in effect, continue the general system of allotments and quotas, but each would make major changes affecting rental of these allotments and quotas by individuals who did not themselves grow tobacco.

Senate Floor Action

Ignoring objections that it was creating a "socialistic" new farm program that was doomed to failure, the Senate passed landmark dairy legislation Oct. 7. The bill also included important revisions in the federal tobacco program as well as amendments on drought relief and egg marketing, passed by voice vote after the provisions of S 1529 were inserted into HR 3385, a House-passed cotton bill.

Dairy Debate

Advocates said that paying dairymen for reducing their burgeoning herds was the only way to throttle surplus milk production.

But critics of the dairy bill, such as Sen. Daniel Patrick Moynihan, D-N.Y., said that the paid diversion scheme was unfair to producers who did not contribute to the surplus. Once started, opponents warned, the program would be impossible to end. Moreover, Moynihan said, "It seems to me there is something sinful about being paid not to produce food."

Amendment Attempts. Moynihan and his allies insisted that a simple reduction in the dairy price support level would reduce surplus production, as it had in the past. But repeated attempts to substitute a price support cut for the diversion program, or to exempt certain groups of dairy farmers, failed.

The closest the bill's opponents came to success was a 44-40 vote on Oct. 6 to kill an amendment by Sen. Warren B. Rudman, R-N.H., that would have exempted dairymen

who processed and sold the milk they produced. Rudman said these farmers were "not interested in some socialistic form of farming." They were, he added, "just asking to be left alone." *(Vote 276, p. 45-S)*

Sponsors of the legislation insisted that the paid diversion program was the only politically viable solution to industry problems. Senate Agriculture Chairman Helms repeatedly reminded senators that the dairy legislation was supported by a "fragile coalition" that would crack if any changes were made.

Tobacco

The assaults on the bill's dairy provisions contrasted markedly with relatively routine action on the tobacco sections. The Senate accepted several uncontroversial amendments by tobacco state senators and on Oct. 6 killed 57-33 an amendment by Sens. Howard M. Metzenbaum, D-Ohio, and Jake Garn, R-Utah, to repeal the federal tobacco price support program. *(Vote 275, p. 45-S)*

The measure froze price support increases in an attempt to price tobacco more competitively and reduce surpluses. It mandated an end to renting allotments and quotas for use on farms other than those to which they were assigned.

Drought Aid

In other action, the Senate adopted an amendment by Lloyd Bentsen, D-Texas, to provide drought aid to livestock producers. Bentsen's amendment directed the Agriculture Department to sell to drought-stricken livestock farmers surplus grain owned by the federal government that was spoiling in storage.

House Floor Action

Dairy industry lobbyists, with a little help from top House Democrats, won emphatic House approval of the plan to pay dairy farmers, for the first time, not to produce milk.

By a 325-91 vote, the House passed the plan (HR 4196) on Nov. 9 after rejecting, 174-250, an alternative plan offered by Conable. (HR 4196 was the same as HR 1875, the dairy bill reported in June by House Agriculture, but with different effective dates.) *(Votes 443, 441, p. 130-H)*

During the floor debate, the House added two amendments to soften objections from livestock producers and dairymen in states with dairy promotion programs similar to a new national program authorized by the bill.

After approving the bill, the House substituted its language for that of HR 3385, a nearly identical Senate-passed version.

HR 4196, however, did not include provisions to revise the tobacco program, as did the Senate-passed bill. The House Agriculture Committee had approved a separate tobacco bill (HR 1440), but the bill was never reported out of committee. As a result, the House dairy bill alone went to conference with the Senate's combined dairy-tobacco bill.

Reagan Administration Switch

The House votes were a major defeat for the American Farm Bureau Federation and a hastily assembled coalition of consumer and livestock groups that backed Conable. The Reagan administration abruptly had switched its support to Conable's plan, having backed the industry bill through the Oct. 7 Senate vote.

In an Oct. 28 letter to House Minority Leader Michel, Agriculture Secretary Block said his support for the dairy payment program had been contingent on enactment of a freeze on target prices. Because the freeze was not imposed, Block wrote, he switched his support to Conable's plan.

Conable Plan

The plan sponsored by Conable would simply have reduced the federal dairy price support by $1.50 and eliminated the unpopular federal assessment collected from dairy producers.

The Office of Management and Budget (OMB) had declared the industry plan to be the most thrifty but then produced new estimates showing that Conable's plan would save a billion dollars more than HR 4196. "People gave no credence to those estimates," Conable said dryly.

House Agriculture Committee Chairman de la Garza said HR 4196 would save $2.63 billion over four years, compared with existing law.

Backers of the industry plan insisted that its budget savings were greater than those of the Conable plan and

---

Tobacco Price Support Lid

Facing a late July deadline for the opening of tobacco markets, Congress July 14 approved a one-year freeze on tobacco price supports (HR 3392 — PL 98-59).

A major component of the federal tobacco program, price support loans determined the prices at which the crop was sold. Advocates hoped that holding the price support loans at 1982 levels instead of letting them rise in 1983 as scheduled would promote more sales — and less surplus.

The House passed HR 3392 (H Rept 98-288) July 11 by voice vote under suspension of the rules. Sponsor Charlie Rose, D-N.C., held off attacks by an anti-smoking coalition of health groups only by promising floor votes later in 1983 on HR 1440, a more extensive revision of the tobacco program. (HR 1440, however, never was reported out of committee and decisions on major changes in the tobacco program were reached in conference on HR 3385, the Senate's combined dairy-tobacco bill.)

The Senate approved HR 3392 July 13 after accepting an amendment allowing the agriculture secretary to lower the annual burley tobacco marketing quota by 15 percent and requiring a study of imported burley tobacco to determine whether an import quota on the commodity was warranted to protect U.S. producers. Under existing law, the secretary could reduce quotas by 5 percent when it appeared that supply would exceed demand. A lowered quota would cut into farmers' profits because it meant they could sell less tobacco.

The House July 13 dropped the amendment, but the Senate insisted on retaining it and proposed a conference. The House later reconsidered, however, and agreed without conference to a compromise amendment authorizing the secretary to decrease quotas by 10 percent. The Senate passed that version July 14, clearing the bill.

Quota Costs, Tobacco Levies Growing

There's more to growing tobacco than scratching up the dirt and throwing in a few seeds.

Unless a farmer had had what amounted to a federal "license" to sell all but three of the nearly 20 types of tobacco grown in America, he had been subject to heavy financial penalties if he tried to sell tobacco.

And because of legislation passed in 1982, he currently had to help pay the storage and other costs for any excess tobacco left unsold at the end of the season. *(1982 Almanac p. 357)*

But record surpluses had distorted the federal tobacco program, making per-farmer costs rise to uncomfortably high levels for many growers. It was those increases and the certainty that they would continue that were behind the drive for legislation to change the government tobacco program in 1983.

Licensing System

The "licensing" system consisted of federal allotments that specified the number of acres that could be planted in tobacco, together with quotas that limited the number of pounds a farmer could sell. A farmer selling tobacco at auction had to show a card obtained from a county Agricultural Stabilization and Conservation Service office listing his quota.

There was a fixed number of allotments, originally assigned to the land on which farmers were growing tobacco decades ago. Active growers without such land had been able to rent the use of the allotments and quotas from their owners. However, with the passage of PL 98-180, "off-farm" leasing of quotas would end after 1986 for flue-cured tobacco and was greatly reduced for burley tobacco.

For the two major types of American tobacco — flue-cured and burley — the number of allotment owners dramatically outnumbered the number of growers. Burley was grown largely in Kentucky and Tennessee, while flue-cured tobacco was grown primarily in the Carolinas.

The Agriculture Department (USDA) estimated in 1983 there were 40,000 to 50,000 actual producers of flue-cured tobacco and approximately 200,000 owners of allotments and quotas. For burley, the proportion of active farmers who owned their allotments and quotas was higher — approximately 150,000 active growers to 300,000 owners.

The system was subject to referendums every three years in which owners and growers could vote whether to continue it.

Farmers within the system were eligible for federal price support loans set by law at a specific per-pound rate, which increased automatically every year unless Congress legislated otherwise, which it did in 1983. Whatever tobacco they could not sell on the market for a price that equaled or exceeded the loan rate, they could use as collateral for loans from the government. In 1982 the loan rates were $1.70 per pound for flue-cured tobacco and $1.75 per pound for burley.

A number of cooperative growers' groups administered the loan program and held the surplus tobacco put up as collateral for later sale. Once farmers consigned their surplus to a cooperative, they could keep the loan money, and the cooperative was responsible for reselling the crop and repaying the government loan.

The assessment against tobacco farmers approved by Congress in 1982 was meant to pay for any losses that occurred if the cooperative sold the surplus for less than the loan rate, and for interest and other costs.

Until 1982, such losses were borne by the federal government.

To cover anticipated losses from the 1982 crop, the government collected $29.5 million from flue-cured growers and quota-owners, and $7.7 million from burley growers and quota-owners.

That did not prove to be enough, so in 1984, to cover "catch-up" 1982 costs and anticipated losses from the 1983 crop, the department expected to collect at least $32.5 million from burley growers and $85 million from flue-cured growers.

Increasing Costs

According to USDA economists, a grower of burley tobacco in 1982 paid, on an average, 53 cents per pound for combined quota and land, $1.35 per pound for such variable costs as seed and fertilizer, and a 1-cent-per-pound assessment for the new surplus-financing program.

The $1.35 figure included a non-cash allowance of 49 cents for the estimated value of labor and management contributed by a farmer and his family.

The cash and non-cash outlays added up to $1.89 per pound — 8 cents more than the average price of $1.81 for which burley sold in 1982.

For flue-cured tobacco, the 1982 costs were 46 cents per pound for land and quota, $1.10 for variable and other costs and 3 cents for the assessment, for a total of $1.59. The average market prices were about $1.78 per pound in 1982.

For flue-cured tobacco farmers, the non-cash allowance for labor and management was much smaller because there was more mechanization.

Assessments Going Up

There were several program-related factors driving up the cost of growing tobacco. One was that the assessments would jump for the 1983 crop to 7 cents per pound for flue-cured and to as much as 5 cents or 7 cents per pound for burley.

Prior to enactment of HR 3385, many producers who rented their allotments and quotas had been forced to pay the assessments twice: The law had required payments from both farmers and non-growing quota-owners, who often simply increased the rental rate of their quotas by the amount of the assessment. HR 3385 did away with this practice.

Because the allotments and quotas were being reduced administratively by the government in an effort to cut the surplus, fierce competition for renting them had driven up their costs. Rental fees ranged from a low of 25 cents per pound to a high of 80 cents per pound.

that paying farmers to reduce their herds was the most effective way to curb the mountainous federal dairy surplus, while keeping small family dairy farms in business.

Veto Threat

Conable warned that "the director of OMB currently is saying that the president will veto anything but the Conable amendment."

But Charlie Rose, D-N.C., said a veto seemed unlikely because the bill would arrive at the White House with the tobacco program changes that the Senate had included in its dairy measure. Tobacco growers badly wanted the changes.

With Sen. Helms running for re-election next year, Rose said, "They would be out of their minds to veto it." Tobacco was a major North Carolina crop.

De la Garza Maneuver

The strong House votes Nov. 9 for the industry plan surprised observers because House debate Oct. 18 had showed bitter animosity to the plan, and the House had rejected, 188-208, a motion by de la Garza to forgo debate and amendments and proceed directly to a conference with the Senate on HR 3385. *(Vote 371, p. 110-H)*

Opponents attacked both the substance of the legislation and the procedure under which it came to the floor.

De la Garza explained that he wanted to go directly to conference on the Senate measure "to facilitate for the membership some very, very complicated issues." He said that he had been accused of trying to manipulate the House, and that those accusations were "traumatic."

The ranking minority member of de la Garza's committee, Edward R. Madigan, R-Ill., said that the committee was inviting retaliation by bringing agriculture bills to the floor under procedures that blocked amendments. "You will pay a terrible price," he warned.

Farm Groups, Leadership Support

Rose credited the strong showing of the dairy industry to "a lot of hard work" and aid from tobacco, sugar and other segments of agriculture that used federal price support programs, and from Democratic leaders.

Majority Whip Thomas S. Foley, D-Wash., Democratic Campaign Committee Chairman Tony Coelho, D-Calif., and other prominent Democrats were working the House floor on behalf of the dairy industry plan. Said an aide to a member of the leadership, "It was not an official leadership position — but close to it."

Conference Action

Conferees completed work on HR 3385 (H Rept 98-556) on Nov. 15. The Senate passed it just before midnight on Nov. 17 and the House passed it Nov. 18, the last day of the session, clearing it for the president.

During the conference, Agriculture Secretary Block had urged conferees to cap total payments to individual dairymen under the diversion program, lower the rate at which payments were calculated and make other major changes.

House conferees said they could not accept the cap or the lower rate because the changes would require clearance by the House Rules Committee and there was no time.

Still, Rep. James M. Jeffords, R-Vt., urged members to consider a payment cap. Without it, he said, the diversion program would be criticized for "very, very substantial" payments to certain large farms — as much as $4.5 million in one instance.

The House Agriculture Committee scheduled a Nov. 16 session to decide whether to report a separate payment cap bill but then canceled because the dairy industry was divided on the issue.

Some Requests Honored

Other conference actions honored Block's requests — at least in part:

● Conferees eliminated a Senate amendment that would have required tobacco importers to certify that tobacco brought into the United States had not been grown with pesticides banned here.

They retained, in weakened form, a direction that imported tobacco met the same grade standards as American tobacco. Conferees from the Ways and Means Committee agreed with administration objections that the import provisions would invite trade retaliation.

● Conferees weakened a House provision meant to mitigate the impact of dumping slaughtered dairy cows on the beef market. They retained a general instruction that the secretary of agriculture take all feasible steps to avoid the problem but dropped a "trigger" requiring action if beef prices declined a specified amount.

● Conferees tightened the base for calculating dairymen's production cuts although not as much as the administration had wanted. They also kept Senate-passed provisions ordering the secretary to let drought-stricken farmers buy poor condition surplus feed corn owned by the federal government.   ∎

PIK Plan for Farmers Sweetened by Tax Break

Without benefit of a congressional blessing, President Reagan announced Jan. 11 that the federal government would pay farmers in surplus wheat, corn, cotton and rice to not plant those crops in 1983.

Although congressional approval was not required for establishment of the Payment-in-Kind (PIK) program, Congress did enact special tax legislation when it appeared PIK participants could lose tax benefits normally enjoyed by farmers.

Dubbed a "crop swap" by Reagan, PIK was in addition to previously announced production cut programs offering cash payments and eligibility for federal price supports and

other benefits to participating farmers. With federal support, a farmer could retire up to half his normal acreage or, in some cases, whole farms.

The PIK program was based on existing statutory authority, and Agriculture Secretary John R. Block said that no congressional action was needed on the surplus giveaway plan. That suited farm-state members, who feared that PIK action could expose basic farm programs, with their ballooning costs, to hostile budget-cutters. Also, skeptics wanted to make sure that if PIK failed, the blame would fall fully on the administration.

In late 1982, the administration had asked Congress to

exempt the proposal from two statutory limits that could invite lawsuits. Congress failed to act, but Agriculture Department lawyers said they had resolved the legal problems by the start of 1983. *(1982 Almanac p. 361)*

One limit specified that total federal price support payments to individual farmers could not exceed $50,000 a year; the second set a minimum price at which federally owned surplus commodities could be sold. Agriculture Department attorneys believed they neutralized the limits by ensuring that farmers received only commodities, not cash, for PIK transactions.

A General Accounting Office (GAO) report criticizing the multimillion dollar PIK payments to individual farmers — and the congressional reaction it provoked — prompted the Agriculture Department to announce Dec. 21, however, that it would impose a $50,000 limit on payments to individuals participating in the 1984 program. Only wheat farmers could qualify for PIK payments on 1984 crops.

PIK Terms

Under the program, wheat, corn, grain sorghum, cotton and rice farmers who joined previously announced acreage reduction programs could also receive PIK payments for retiring an additional 10 to 30 percent of their land. Sign-up for the program began Jan. 24.

Payment rates were 95 percent of yield per acre in wheat and 80 percent of yield per acre for other crops. PIK payments would be made with crops that farmers had used as collateral for federal price support and farmer-held reserve loans, or from stocks that had become federal property because of default by farmers on the loans. In many cases, farmers could simply reassume full ownership of crops on which they had borrowed.

PIK payments were made at harvest times; to avert dumping the crops on the market, the federal government paid storage costs for 5 months or, for reserve crops, 12 months.

Individual farmers could bid to take entire farms out of production in return for PIK payments; whole-farm bids were accepted if participation in the basic PIK program lagged. In no county could more than half the acreage base in eligible crops be retired.

Farm Policy Shift

Reagan's attempt to induce major cutbacks in farm production marked an extraordinary change in his farm policy, which had stressed all-out production and little government intervention.

But depressed export markets and two bumper-crop years had left the United States with massive surpluses in all major commodities. The excess drove market prices well below farmers' costs and greatly increased their use of federal price support programs, which cost the Treasury an unprecedented $12 billion in fiscal 1982. The administration hoped PIK would shrink existing surpluses while heading off still more overproduction in 1983.

After the president's announcement of the program, Block told reporters that PIK would not greatly raise commodity prices in the next 12 months. Agriculture Department analysts expected PIK to save $3 billion in projected farm-program outlays in fiscal 1983 and 1984, although they did not expect it to drive 1983 outlays below the 1982 high.

Tax Changes

Despite the administration's belief that the PIK program required no legislative action, it soon became clear that program could expose participants to a potentially serious tax burden.

Questions arose concerning whether farmers had to pay taxes on the commodities in the year in which they received them, or could defer tax payments until the commodities were sold. Farmers were not taxed on their crops until they sold them, even if that occurred several years after the harvest.

However, the Internal Revenue Service viewed the PIK commodities as the equivalent of income, liable to taxes in the year in which the commodities were received. Without the change, farmers could have faced tax payments on two crops in the same year — crops they raised and sold and PIK commodities. They would also be shoved into higher tax brackets.

It also was unclear whether land idled in return for commodity payments would still be eligible for special treatment under federal estate tax law.

Fearing the tax liability would make farmers shy away from PIK, the administration pressed for changes in tax law for program participants. Though some members were skeptical, the tax changes received swift congressional approval.

Committee Action

The House Ways and Means Committee March 2 reported a bill (HR 1296 — H Rept 98-14) making one-year alterations in tax law. The bill permitted farmers to defer income tax payments on PIK commodities until they were sold. It also stipulated that land taken out of production could continue to qualify for special treatment accorded farm land by estate tax law.

The Senate Finance Committee also on March 2 reported its version of the bill (S 690) but did not file a report. S 690 made the changes in tax law permanent.

Floor Action

The day before the deadline for farmers to join the (PIK) acreage reduction program, Congress completed legislation clearing the program of federal tax problems.

The Senate on March 10 agreed by voice vote to accept the PIK tax bill that had passed the House by a 401-1 vote on March 8 and was passed again by voice vote, in a revised version, on March 9. *(House vote 19, p. 10-H)*

The president signed the bill March 11 (HR 1296—PL 98-4).

The Senate had passed a different version (S 690) of the legislation by voice vote on March 8.

The final bill exempted farmers in the 1983 program from federal tax law that would have required them to pay income taxes on PIK commodities in the same year that they received them from the federal government.

The second major provision assured that the idled PIK acreage would still qualify for special estate tax treatment.

Rep. Fortney H. "Pete" Stark, D-Calif., chairman of the Ways and Means subcommittee that crafted the bill, told the House that the legislation would cost $323 million in lost receipts in fiscal 1984 and $81 million in fiscal 1985, but would recoup $404 million in fiscal 1986. By then, farmers were expected to have sold the PIK commodities and to have paid the taxes.

PIK Cotton Program Payment Terms

Congress July 29 enacted legislation modifying the terms of cotton farmers' participation in the government's complex Payment-in-Kind (PIK) program after the cotton growers complained they were being treated unfairly.

The PIK provision — reopening cotton bidding on the same terms offered producers of feed grains — was included in the fiscal 1983 supplemental appropriations bill (HR 3069 — PL 98-63). Administration objections to the additional costs generated by the cotton program — estimated at $75 million to $100 million — were not strong enough to threaten enactment of the supplemental. President Reagan signed the measure July 30. *(Supplemental, p. 509)*

The PIK section of HR 3069 was meant to rectify a problem that arose when the administration found it did not own enough surplus cotton, wheat and corn to make promised payments to PIK farmers. Under PIK, producers were paid with surplus crops to take farm land out of production in an effort to reduce the unsold surpluses that were depressing market prices. The Agriculture Department did not own enough of the surplus to meet its commitments to farmers because much of it was being used as collateral for federal price support loans and thus was still owned by individual farmers. *(PIK, p. 380)*

To resolve the problem, the department in May asked farmers what they would accept to supply stocks for PIK needs. But because the department, in an attempt to save money, offered less favorable terms for cotton than for other commodities, it failed to acquire enough cotton.

The Agriculture Department then invoked a clause in the farmers' PIK contracts requiring them to take out price support loans on their 1983 crop. The plan was to foreclose on the loans, so the farmers would keep the loan money and the government would take possession of the cotton.

But changing market conditions made such forced "sales" extremely costly to producers. A large, unexpected Soviet cotton purchase and poor weather had shrunk market supplies and hiked prices well above the "price" farmers would receive from compulsory sales to the government.

Moreover, many farmers had contracted to sell both their PIK cotton and their 1983 crops — crops that would be taken over by the government. They had gone ahead with the contracts after receiving repeated assurances from department officials that the PIK contract clause was not likely to be used.

The cotton language in HR 3069 permitted farmers to again offer to sell their cotton to the government, but on more attractive terms than in the first round of bidding.

The House Agriculture Committee July 12 reported legislation (HR 3385 — H Rept 98-289) making cotton PIK changes; the Senate Agriculture Committee had approved provisions similar to the House's on June 23 in a target price measure (HR 2733 — S Rept 98-164). The cotton-PIK language eventually made its way into several different bills as cotton lobbyists sought to ensure its consideration. It appeared in another farm program bill in the Senate, a dairy-tobacco bill reported June 23 (S 1529 — S Rept 98-163). Cotton provisions also were inserted in the Senate version of the Agriculture Appropriations bill (HR 3223). *(Dairy and tobacco bill, p. 375; target price freeze, p. 383; Agriculture appropriations, p. 516).*

Final Passage

The PIK legislation was not controversial, although Stark and other members of his subcommittee had strong reservations about its impact and forced the Senate to accept just a one-year modification of tax law.

Despite the lack of objections to the substance of the bill, it faced several obstacles. The most difficult was the threat that it would be made a vehicle for the repeal of the controversial law requiring the withholding of taxes from interest and dividend income. *(Withholding, p. 261)*

Senate action on March 8 was delayed for hours while Finance Committee Chairman Robert Dole, R-Kan., persuaded Sen. Bob Kasten, R-Wis., not to force a fight on the withholding issue.

The Senate then passed S 690. In addition to making the tax law changes permanent, it omitted House provisions to discourage speculation, to require a Treasury study of the PIK program and the tax bill, and to confer tax-exempt status on the National Farmers Organization (NFO).

The NFO, which bargained with buyers on behalf of members for the sale of members' commodities, had asked Stark's subcommittee to restore the tax-exempt status that it once held. But the final version of the bill cleared by Congress did not include the exemption.

The version the House passed the second time deleted the NFO section and added some technical changes suggested by the Senate.

Provisions

As signed by the president, HR 1296:

● Permitted participants in the 1983 PIK program to defer income tax payments on the commodities they received in the program until the commodities were sold.

● Permitted crop land idled by 1983 PIK participants to continue to be valued as farm land for estate tax purposes, thereby retaining eligibility for lower tax rates and installment payments of taxes.

● Specified that the income tax and estate tax provisions apply only to the 1983 crop year.

● Restricted eligibility for the tax law changes to owners of farm land as of Feb. 23, 1983, or those who received such land either as an inheritance or a gift from a person who owned it on that date. This provision was meant to discourage speculation.

● Specified that for purposes of self employment tax, income tax credits and Social Security benefits, commodities received in the 1983 PIK program would be treated as if the recipient had grown them.

● Required the Treasury Department, after consulting

with the Agriculture Department, to report to Congress by Sept. 1, 1983, on the impact of the PIK program and its special tax provisions.

Tax Changes: Round Two

The administration faced a not so compliant Congress when it sought to extend the tax changes for a second year to cover a 1984 wheat PIK program the Agriculture Department had unveiled in August. By November, PIK had drawn scathing criticism from several quarters as reports circulated of farmers reaping large payments for not planting crops.

At a Nov. 3 hearing of his Ways and Means Subcommittee on Select Revenue Measures, Stark lashed out at multimillion-dollar PIK payments to individual farmers that had been reported by the GAO. Lawyers from the GAO also declared that the large PIK payments were illegal because they exceeded the $50,000 statutory limit on federal farm program payments to individual farmers.

Agriculture Department officials disputed the GAO interpretation, arguing as they had in January that because the payments were not in cash, they were exempt from the

$50,000 limit. The exemption, they said, was crucial to the success of PIK because without it payments would be too small to get much land out of production.

Stark's subcommittee Nov. 8 approved continuation of the special tax break for PIK farmers. But the subcommittee plan, which was supposed to be attached to the full committee's pending tax bill (HR 4170), included a proviso that could limit the break to the first $50,000-worth of commodities a farmer received in payment for cutting back production, less any cash payment from other federal farm programs.

The subcommittee also instructed GAO to seek a federal district court ruling on the legality of payments above the $50,000 limit; if the court found the limit applied to PIK, the tax treatment of PIK commodities would be limited. Stark also joined in a lawsuit filed Nov. 9 by the California Rural Legal Assistance Association seeking to impose the $50,000 cap on future PIK payments.

The tax break extension was not enacted. HR 4170 failed to make it to the House floor. And Congress failed to pass an unnumbered Ways and Means proposal to continue the tax break, with some limitations. ∎

Congress Refuses to Enact Target Price Freeze

The Reagan administration spent much of 1983 trying, without success, to persuade Congress to block scheduled increases in target prices, a major price support program for wheat and other crops.

The House Agriculture Committee discussed the request in May, but postponed action indefinitely. The Senate Agriculture Committee approved a freeze in target prices and added it as an amendment to a minor House-passed measure (HR 2733), but objections from a few farm-state senators kept that bill off the floor.

On Nov. 16, two days before Congress adjourned, the House, by voice vote, passed a bill (HR 4072) that trimmed the target price increases. Certain other provisions of HR 4072 meant to make the administration's 1984 wheat program financially more attractive to farmers brought White House objections, however, and opposition from prominent Republicans prevented the measure from coming to a vote in the Senate.

Background

The target price program made "deficiency payments" to eligible producers of wheat, corn, cotton and rice whenever the market prices for crops dropped below targets set by law. Secretary of Agriculture John R. Block unsuccessfully sought to end the program in 1981. *(1981 Almanac p. 535)*

The Reagan administration in 1983 wanted Congress to hold target prices at 1983 levels, instead of allowing them to rise automatically over the next two years.

Administration officials said the scheduled increases were expensive and not needed because of low inflation rates. And Block believed that the increases perversely encouraged farmers to overplant at a time of massive surpluses.

Opponents contended that the increases were critical to draw farmers into acreage reduction programs, which were meant to reduce surpluses. To qualify for the payments, farmers had to participate in such programs. *(Pay-*

ment-in-Kind acreage reduction program, p. 380)

Administration Strategy

The administration told members that its support for new dairy legislation was contingent on Congress simultaneously approving the target price freeze. *(Dairy bill, p. 375)*

The administration settled on a strategy of pushing for one bill combining the freeze with the dairy legislation in the hope of buying broad support for the controversial target price list. Severing the issues would have left the freeze more vulnerable to attack, and opponents repeatedly suggested that they would filibuster or otherwise delay further action.

J. Dawson Ahalt, the Agriculture Department's deputy assistant secretary for economics, told the House Agriculture Committee that the freeze was needed to offset the cost of the new dairy plan, which was estimated at about $300 million to $400 million a year more than the existing program. According to Ahalt, the savings from the freeze in fiscal 1984 would amount to $370 million.

House Committee

The Reagan administration tried and failed to prod the House Agriculture Committee into a quick vote to stop increases in target prices.

Appearing before the panel May 25, Agriculture Secretary Block unsuccessfully pressed members to vote on HR 3102, which would have held the target prices for the next two years at 1983 levels.

But after a daylong debate, the committee voted to postpone action.

James M. Jeffords, R-Vt., who led compromise efforts on dairy legislation, said he refused to be part of the administration's proposed tradeoff between White House support for dairy legislation in return for congressional support of the freeze.

Leon E. Panetta, D-Calif., citing budget concerns, was

one of several Democrats who said they were inclined to support the measure. But, Panetta told Block, "We don't slam dunk very much up here in Congress, particularly on a major issue such as this."

Support Disputed. George E. Brown Jr., D-Calif., told Block that the freeze obviously "does help to meet some of the financial problems of the country." But, Brown added, "Would you be able to comment on whether we're signing our political death-knells by supporting this?"

Block replied that major farm groups supported the freeze because they were embarrassed by the enormous cost of farm programs, estimated to reach $21 billion in fiscal 1983. He claimed support from the American Farm Bureau Federation, corn and soybean growers' groups and many rice and cotton producers.

Some supporters, such as the conservative farm bureau, had always been philosophically opposed to target prices, although there were exceptions in the bureau's position for certain crops. Soybean growers tended to think that other commodities could get along with the minimal farm supports that they got.

Ed Jones, D-Tenn., however, disputed Block's claim of farm support. Jones said the bill was opposed by a 17-member coalition, including wheat, peanut and sugar growers, the National Farmers Union and the National Grange. Cotton and rice growers were so divided that their organizations had taken no position, he said.

Senate Committee Action

The Reagan administration had more luck before the Senate Agriculture Committee. The panel reported HR 2733 (H Rept 98-164) June 23, which froze target prices for two years, instead of letting them rise as scheduled. But critics of the freeze endorsed by the Senate committee won a tactical victory when they forced the committee to report it as a separate bill instead of combining it with tobacco and dairy program revisions approved June 16. (The target price language was added by the committee to HR 2733, a House-passed bill promoting development of a domestic rubber plant, guayule.)

Without the protective shield of the tobacco and dairy provisions, the freeze was left open to threats of a filibuster or other delaying tactics. "There is a very strong possibility there would be prolonged debate on the issue," said Sen. David L. Boren, D-Okla.

Grain Belt critics of the freeze said that, contrary to administration claims, the target price payments discouraged excess production, because farmers had to participate in federal acreage reduction programs to qualify for them. Critics also complained that the administration wanted agriculture to give up the increases without having the detailed information about the next year's federal agriculture programs, which farmers needed to make financial decisions. For instance, farmers wanted to know how much they would be paid for idling part of their customary acreage.

"There has to be some kind of assurance to producers as to what kind of deal they're looking at," said Sen. John Melcher, D-Mont.

Still, William G. Lesher, assistant secretary for economics at the Agriculture Department, insisted that the freeze was "imperative" because price supports were making farm goods too costly to compete in world markets.

Provisions. By a 10-7 vote the committee approved the administration plan to let the secretary of agriculture keep target prices at fiscal 1983 levels for fiscal 1984 and 1985.

To gain some support from the affected commodity groups, the committee agreed to include in the bill funds to promote exports of U.S. farm commodities in the next two years.

The bill required that $300 million in Commodity Credit Corporation (CCC) funds be spent in each of the next two fiscal years for export promotion. The CCC manages price support programs.

The bill also extended a revolving export promotion fund and stipulated that it would be funded by repayments of current agricultural export loans.

Administration officials had been cool to the export funding but Agriculture Secretary Block indicated after the committee session that he might not object to it because the target price freeze was such a high priority.

Bill Dropped. Threats of controversial amendments and filibusters prompted Republican leader Howard H. Baker Jr., Tenn., to halt Senate work on HR 2733 July 28. Opponents had begun what they called "a really thorough debate of American agriculture policies" and, after a day and a half of fruitless backstage negotiations to hasten consideration of the administration-supported measure, Baker postponed further action on the bill until Aug. 1. Opponents of HR 2733 prevented formal floor debate during the remainder of the session. ∎

Farm 'Recession Relief'

Despite objections from the Reagan administration, the House May 3 overwhelmingly approved legislation to provide "recession relief" to farmers.

The House bill (HR 1190 — H Rept 98-48), passed by a 378-35 vote, permitted hard-pressed farmers who met certain criteria to delay loan repayments to the Farmers Home Administration (FmHA). It also made it easier for farmers hit by drought or other physical disasters to qualify for FmHA disaster loans, and required the secretary of agriculture to offer "economic emergency" loans. *(Vote 73, p. 26-H)*

The administration claimed these provisions would give a few farmers windfall aid and open the Treasury to enormous expense. Officials said FmHA was already easing terms and deferring payments on a case-by-case basis.

In 1982, an FmHA deferral proposal was included in the fiscal 1983 agriculture appropriations bill (HR 7072 — PL 97-370), but the provision was dropped in conference. The deferral authority also appeared in a separate House-passed FmHA authorization bill, but the Senate failed to act on a companion measure before Congress adjourned. *(1982 Almanac pp. 255, 364)*

A similar FmHA authorization bill (S 24) was pending in the Senate at the end of the session.

Background

A shortfall in a key FmHA lending program strengthened arguments for expanding farm credit. The funding crisis occurred as the House and Senate were preparing to take up the FmHA authorization bills.

During an April 7 session of the Senate Agriculture Appropriations Subcommittee, FmHA officials revealed that strong demand for operating loans, which helped farmers cover the costs of seed, fertilizer and similar expenses, had exhausted funds in 17 states, threatening the year's crops.

Farm-state members were shocked because Agricul-

ture Department (USDA) officials repeatedly had assured them that FmHA had enough money for eligible borrowers. But by April 13, there were $129 million worth of FmHA operating loan applications in the affected state that had received approval but for which there was no money. It was estimated that USDA would need $450 million to cover these loans and those still to come in fiscal 1983.

Under strong congressional pressure to find more money, Secretary of Agriculture John R. Block announced April 15 that he was, in effect, subtracting $400 million from FmHA programs that funded loans for farmland purchases and financed rural water and sewer facility construction, and using it instead for FmHA operating loans.

Congressional aides speculated that the strong demand for FmHA money reflected the reluctance of private lenders to make farm loans in 1983 and the needs of farmers who previously used FmHA "economic emergency" loans that had been discontinued by the administration.

Court Orders. Although Congress had regularly extended the economic emergency loan program since its inception in 1978, the Reagan administration had granted no loans under the program since September 1981. However, in 1983 a federal district court ordered the Agriculture Department to reopen the emergency credit program. From December 1983 to September 1984, a total of up to $600 million in loans was to be available. A provision of HR 1190 would require the secretary of agriculture to make the emergency loans.

And late in 1983, a federal district court judge in Bismarck, N.D., ordered a temporary — until Jan. 9, 1984 — moratorium on foreclosures or the calling of delinquent loans by the FmHA.

House Action

Although House Democrats trimmed and tightened HR 1190 to meet GOP objections before passing it May 3, they failed to satisfy the Reagan administration.

Amendments. When the House began debate April 27, it faced dozens of amendments by Edward R. Madigan, R-Ill., the ranking minority member of the Agriculture Committee. Madigan, who said the administration, bankers and major farm groups all opposed the bill, claimed that the disaster loans alone could cost as much as $4.5 billion.

He said deferral was unfair because most farmers, who borrowed from private lenders, had to keep their repayments up to date. Deferral would also mean less money to be lent in the future, he said. Backers of the deferral said farmers needed it to survive the recession.

The House April 27 adopted an amendment by Berkley Bedell, D-Iowa, 284-121, dropping a committee-passed increase in individual FmHA loans. Bedell said the panel had acted before learning that FmHA had run out of funds in 17 states. *(Vote 62, p. 24-H)*

When debate resumed May 3, a compromise had been worked out calling for Madigan to offer several amendments. The changes, adopted by voice vote:

● Cut the economic emergency loan money in fiscal 1983 to $300 million, from $1.2 billion.

● Placed a greater burden of proof on farmers seeking the loan deferrals or disaster relief for individual farms, and specified that the agriculture secretary's decisions on those matters would be final unless judged in court to be arbitrary and capricious.

Other amendments targeted rural development loans on areas with severe unemployment, authorized grants to retrain the unemployed and earmarked loan money for

Export Subsidy Program

The Senate Agriculture Committee March 16 reported legislation (S 822 — S Rept 98-27) to establish an aggressive export subsidy program for U.S.-produced food and fiber.

The Senate Foreign Relations Committee subsequently considered the bill and reported it (S Rept 98-37) March 24, but the full Senate did not take up S 822. No agricultural trade subsidy legislation made it out of the House Agriculture Committee.

The committee members almost unanimously put a large share of the blame for sagging U.S. farm exports on what they viewed as predatory trade practices by the European Community and a handful of other nations. They contended that American farmers had been unfairly undersold in foreign markets and that U.S. agriculture had to retaliate in kind to regain those markets.

The bill required the secretary of agriculture to sell at least 150,000 metric tons of federally owned surplus dairy stocks abroad annually in fiscal years 1983, 1984 and 1985, at prices not below those established by an international dairy agreement. Those prices were substantially lower than the domestic level set by the federal dairy price support program.

The bill also explicitly authorized export Payment-in-Kind (PIK) arrangements in which bonuses of federally owned surplus commodities could be used to lower prices of exported goods. The measure required the secretary to use half the receipts from the mandated dairy sales and all of the $190 million authorized in the 1982 reconciliation bill (PL 97-253) to subsidize loans and prices of export commodities. *(PL 97-253, 1982 Almanac p. 358)*

It earmarked portions of the reconciliation money for exports of poultry and eggs, raisins and canned fruit — all, according to members, inappropriately subsidized by European nations. Other sections provided for extra PIK bonuses to foreign purchasers who expanded their capacity to take imports by investing in processing and similar facilities.

And it expanded Food for Peace (PL 480) programs of donations and low-cost loans for food purchases by impoverished foreign nations.

small farm service and other businesses adversely affected by the Payment-in-Kind (PIK) program. PIK provided surplus commodities to farmers who agreed to limit production. *(PIK, p. 380)*

Provisions. Major provisions of HR 1190:

● Barred the secretary from foreclosing on FmHA loans and required him to consolidate or reschedule a loan, or defer repayment, at the request of a borrower who could demonstrate to the secretary's satisfaction that he was a good manager, that he could not repay because of circumstances beyond his control and that he had a good chance of repaying after the deferral.

● Continued economic emergency loans until Sept. 30, 1984, and required the secretary to make the loans available. Authorized $300 million annually in fiscal 1983 and 1984.

● Authorized an extra $200 million for farm operating

loans in fiscal 1983, for a total of $1.7 billion, and earmarked the money for new borrowers.

• Earmarked 20 percent of farm ownership and operating loans for low-income, limited-resource borrowers, who qualified for a lower interest rate.

• Extended to 15 years, from seven, the maximum time for repayment of a consolidated or rescheduled FmHA loan and required that interest on such loans be at the original rate or the rate current at the time of rescheduling, whichever was lower.

• Specified that a farmer could qualify for emergency disaster loans on the basis of damage to his farm, though the county in which the farm was located had not been designated a disaster area.

• Conferred eligibility to borrowers for additional disaster-related loans for three or four years after the original emergency loan (depending on the date of the original loan).

• Established selection criteria for community facility and business and industry loans to target areas of high unemployment, and authorized the secretary to make grants, totaling up to $20 million annually, to train unemployed individuals to work in entities assisted by the loans.

• Established an overall $250 million limit on insured or guaranteed loans for business and industrial development. Earmarked 10 percent of fiscal 1984 appropriated loan funds for rural small businesses suffering hardships because of the PIK program, and limited individual loans to $50,000.

• Required the secretary of agriculture to establish a graduated scale for water and waste facility grant rates and take other steps to give priority and favorable terms to very poor rural communities.

• Set annual FmHA authorization ceilings for fiscal years 1984-86: $1 billion for real estate loans; $500 million for insured water and sewer facility loans; $1 billion for industrial development loans; $300 million for insured community facility loans. Also authorized funds as needed for emergency (physical disaster) loans.

Senate Action

The Senate Agriculture Committee March 18 reported S 24 (S Rept 98-28).

The shorter Senate version of the FmHA reauthorization also included deferral, loan repayment extension and increases in farm operating loans. Like the House bill, it continued authority for economic emergency loans but it left the program discretionary, while HR 1190 required that the loans be offered. ∎

Pesticide Reauthorization

A simple one-year authorization (HR 2785 — PL 98-201) of the federal government's controversial pesticide control programs cleared Congress Nov. 18. The president signed the bill Dec. 2.

HR 2785, a reauthorization of the Federal Insecticide, Fungicide and Rodenticide Act (FIFRA), passed the House May 17 by voice vote. It won Senate approval Nov. 18, also by voice. The bill provided $64.2 million in fiscal 1984 for the pesticide regulation program of the Environmental Protection Agency (EPA), about $8 million more than the presidential budget request. HR 2785 also extended through September 1987 the authority for a scientific advisory panel on pesticides.

The bill's sponsors decided to pass a simple funding measure and put aside, for the time being, controversial policy issues surrounding the federal regulation of pesticides. Disputes among pesticide makers, environmentalists, labor, farm and health groups kept Congress from enacting a pesticide bill in 1982. *(1982 Almanac p. 363)*

Environmentalists in 1983 hoped to push for legislative activity in several areas, but the unsettled conditions at the EPA — culminating in the resignation of EPA Administrator Anne M. Burford — convinced members to postpone action until the dust settled at the troubled agency. *(Story, p. 332)*

Pesticide makers and the Reagan administration pushed for a two-year authorization, but environmental groups objected that the longer reauthorization would delay action on issues they considered urgent, including the release of manufacturers' information on the safety of certain chemicals.

The House Agriculture Subcommittee on Department Operations, Research and Foreign Agriculture voted for a two-year bill on April 27. The full House Agriculture Committee, however, reported a one-year authorization (H Rept 98-104) May 11. The Senate, as the session end neared, took the measure from the Senate Agriculture Committee and placed the bill on the Senate calendar Nov. 4, passing it, by voice vote, Nov. 18. ∎

Wheat Program Changes

As predictions of a massive wheat crop in the spring of 1984 began to surface, the House Nov. 16 passed a bill (HR 4072) to make a federal program to cut production more financially attractive to wheat farmers. But objections from prominent Republicans in the Senate blocked consideration there. The House-passed bill was an altered version of the measure approved Nov. 1 by the House Agriculture Committee.

And twice in 1983, Congress approved legislation requiring the Agriculture Department to meet early deadlines for announcing the terms of federal wheat and feed grain programs, such as acreage reduction. President Reagan vetoed the original bill (HR 3564) but signed the second version of the legislation (HR 3914 — PL 98-100). *(Veto message, p. 34-E)*

Acreage Reduction

The administration's program to hobble wheat production in 1984 had so displeased wheat farmers that they threatened to ignore it, increasing the likelihood of another bumper harvest in 1984. The 1983 wheat crop escaped drought damage and, despite the government's Payment-in-Kind (PIK) program to reduce production, was the second largest harvest on record. *(PIK, p. 380)*

In an unsuccessful bid for administration backing, Rep. Thomas S. Foley, D-Wash., the sponsor of HR 4072, had lowered the dollar figures in the bill for wheat target prices, a major type of price support, from those agreed to by the committee.

Provisions. The wheat bill as passed by the House Nov. 16 on a voice vote:

• Set the target price for 1984 and 1985 wheat crops at $4.38 a bushel, instead of $4.45 and $4.65 respectively, as provided by current law. (The target price determined how much farmers received in federal "deficiency payments" when market prices dropped below specified targets.)

● Authorized a 1984 acreage reduction program under which farmers would have to take 20 percent of their customary acreage out of production to qualify for such federal farm program benefits as price supports. If they took out an additional 10 percent, they would be paid at least $3 a bushel on the estimated yield of the idled land — or less under certain circumstances. (The administration had specified a 30 percent acreage reduction to qualify for federal programs, without cash payments.)

● Raised to 85 percent of yield, from 75 percent, the rate of PIK payments to wheat farmers. (The administration offered PIK payments of 75 percent of yield for farmers idling up to 20 percent more acreage, in addition to the basic 30 percent for program eligibility.)

Program Announcements

The president on Aug. 12 vetoed the first version of the measure requiring earlier announcements of wheat programs, arguing that the federal government needed more leeway to cope with unexpected developments, such as drought or early frost.

The bill eventually enacted was identical to the vetoed version except that it also allowed the secretary of agriculture to change a program within 30 days after it was announced if there was a change during that period in the supply of the commodity in question. The bill, approved by voice in the House Sept. 20 and in the Senate Sept. 21, provided that for the 1984 and 1985 feed grain crops, the government's announcement must be made by Sept. 30 (instead of Nov. 15) of the year before that in which the crop was harvested; for the 1985 wheat crop, the deadline was July 1, 1984 (instead of Aug. 15, 1984). ∎

Senate OKs 'Sodbuster' Bill

The Senate quietly passed a notable change in federal land conservation policy on Nov. 18, just hours before adjournment. The House did not act on the measure.

The bill (S 663) made crops grown on easily erodible land ineligible for federal price supports, loans, federally subsidized crop insurance and disaster payments. The Senate passed the bill by voice vote after adopting an amendment by sponsor William L. Armstrong, R-Colo., to narrow the scope of the bill as reported Nov. 2 by the Senate Agriculture Committee (S Rept 98-296).

The committee bill would have barred the farm benefits for an entire crop if any part of it were grown on highly erodible land. Armstrong's amendment restored the bill to the form in which he introduced it.

The bill marked the first time that eligibility for federal farm program benefits would be linked directly to a farmer's conservation practices. Other federal conservation efforts generally relied on financial incentives. Armstrong pointed out that the bill did not dictate land use decisions to farmers, but simply ended federal subsidies for cultivation of fragile land.

The bill was not retroactive. Benefits would be denied only to specified types of land brought into cultivation after enactment. Although some 40 million acres of extremely fragile lands were already cultivated — about 10 percent of the total crop land base — Armstrong claimed another 250 million vulnerable acres could be plowed unless the government made it financially unattractive to do so. ∎

U.S.-U.S.S.R. Grain Pact

Agriculture Secretary John R. Block and U.S. Trade Representative William E. Brock III announced July 28 that the United States and the Soviet Union had concluded a new, five-year grain sales agreement.

The pact, to take effect Oct. 1, committed the United States to sell — and the Soviet Union to buy — at least nine million metric tons and up to 12 million metric tons of wheat and corn each year. It also permitted the Soviet Union to substitute a purchase of 500,000 metric tons of soybeans or soy meal for one million metric tons of wheat or corn; in a year when that occurred, the minimum combined sale of wheat and corn would be eight million tons. The expiring U.S.-U.S.S.R. grain pact called for annual sales of six million to eight million metric tons, with no provision for soybean sales.

Block said the new pact generally followed the terms of the U.S.-U.S.S.R. agreement that expired in 1983. That pact guaranteed delivery of the specified minimums and permitted either side to opt out of its commitment under certain conditions, such as a short supply in the United States. It was the guarantee that continued some grain shipments to the U.S.S.R. during President Carter's grain embargo, imposed after the Soviet invasion of Afghanistan.

President Reagan ended the unpopular Carter embargo in April 1981 but, to protest the establishment of martial law in Poland, refused until 1983 to negotiate a new long-term pact. Instead, the existing agreement was continued on a year-to-year basis. Farm-state critics said that practice encouraged the Soviet Union to find other, apparently more reliable sources of grain. *(Embargo, 1981 Almanac p. 533)*

Drought Aid for Farmers

The spell of hot, rainless weather during the summer of 1983 prompted members from agriculture states to search for ways to provide emergency drought aid to farmers. However, attempts to augment existing federal aid programs with wide-ranging relief were thwarted by the Reagan administration's opposition to additional federal farm aid. Farm supporters, though, met with some success at the end of the session, adding a modest drought-relief measure to the dairy-tobacco bill (HR 3385 — PL 98-180) that cleared Congress Nov. 18. *(Story, p. 375)*

The amendment to HR 3385 directed the agriculture secretary to permit farmers and ranchers in drought areas to buy, at 75 percent of the current price support loan rate (about $2 per bushel), federally owned surplus feed corn that was in poor condition.

The drought was exceptional in its breadth, affecting more than 28 states and devastating corn, soybean and other major crops. In testimony before the House Agriculture Committee on Sept. 21, Agriculture Secretary John R. Block acknowledged that "it probably is the most severe [drought] that we've had in the past 50 years."

But unlike earlier droughts, he said, many farmers could rely in 1983 on hefty payments from the crop insurance and Payment-in-Kind (PIK) programs. The PIK pro-

gram provided payments in the form of surplus commodities to farmers who took crop land out of production in 1983. *(PIK, p. 380)*

House Proposals

The same day that Block testified, the House Appropriations Committee added a drought-aid amendment to the fiscal 1984 continuing resolution (H J Res 367).

The disaster-aid amendment, sponsored by Bill Alexander, D-Ark., and Tom Loeffler, R-Texas, set a 30-day deadline for decisions on farmers' applications for natural disaster-aid loans from the Farmers Home Administration (FmHA) and ordered the federal government either to start an emergency feed program for livestock producers or sell them damaged grain out of storage at reduced rates.

The amendment also specified that farms that had sustained natural disaster damage could qualify for the FmHA disaster loans even if they were in counties that had not been designated disaster areas.

H J Res 367, however, was so top-heavy with controversial non-farm amendments that it was put aside, and Congress enacted a second continuing resolution (H J Res 368 — PL 98-107) that was free of unrelated amendments. *(Continuing resolution, p. 526)*

The House Agriculture Committee Nov. 4 reported a bill (HR 4052 — H Rept 98-488) broadening federal aid to farmers and ranchers harmed by the drought, expanding eligibility for federal disaster relief loans to counties not officially designated disaster areas. The bill also directed the secretary of agriculture to implement two programs already in existing law, permitting eligible producers to either buy grain from government stocks at reduced prices or, if they lived too far away from grain storage facilities to make delivery practical, qualify for cash subsidies to buy feed.

Rural Electrification Measure

Legislation to shore up the federal program that provided financing for rural electrical and telephone systems was approved by the House Agriculture Committee on Oct. 28. The bill did not reach the House floor, and no similar legislation received Senate consideration.

The Rural Electrification Administration (REA) faced financial problems because its congressionally mandated low interest rates on loans were well under the interest payments the government paid in the private market to raise capital for the program. The bill (HR 3050 — H Rept 98-588) raised interest rates on future REA-insured loans to levels high enough to recover what the government paid to borrow the money; however, it also authorized low-interest loans for hardship cases meeting certain criteria.

Another section would, in effect, retain the money repaid by telephone or electrical systems in an REA revolving fund to be lent out again, instead of returning it to the Treasury, as existing law required. The measure was approved Oct. 26 by the House Agriculture Subcommittee on Conservation, Credit and Rural Development.

Minor Agriculture Measures

The House passed by voice vote and sent to the Senate three relatively minor agriculture bills just before adjournment. None was considered there.

One (HR 3867 — H Rept 98-543), passed Nov. 15 by voice vote by the House, was meant to protect sellers of perishable agricultural produce when buyers of their products delayed or did not make payment for produce. In effect, the bill declared that certain assets of the buyers were trusts and that proceeds from those assets could be claimed by sellers, under specified rules, if the buyers reneged on purchasing agreements.

The second (HR 3903 — H Rept 98-538), passed by voice vote Nov. 16, permitted the secretary of agriculture to set up a voluntary water and erosion management program with landowners in the Colorado River basin.

The third (HR 2838 — H Rept 98-255), approved Nov. 16 by voice vote, allowed the federal government to donate tree seedlings for planting on public land when seedlings were not needed for federal forestry programs.

Specialty Cotton Program

A bill to change the terms of federal aid for growers of a special long-fiber cotton ("extra-long staple") was signed by President Reagan Aug. 26. Reported by the House Agriculture Committee (H Rept 98-256) on June 22, the bill (HR 3190 — PL 98-88) passed the House June 27 and the Senate Aug. 4. It was passed by voice vote in both chambers.

HR 3190 was intended to reduce surplus stocks of the cotton by lowering the federal commodity loan rate for it and allowing the agriculture secretary to sell surplus stocks at prices he determined to be appropriate.

The loan rate effectively set minimum market prices; under the new formula authorized in the bill, the 1984 rate would drop to 82.5 cents a pound, instead of 96.25 cents. The bill also made the cotton eligible, for the first time, for "deficiency payments" if market prices dropped below a target price; authorized paid acreage reduction programs for the crop, and permitted the agriculture secretary to require participation in an acreage reduction program as a condition for price support loans and deficiency payments in years when stocks were excessive. Extra-long staple cotton, grown in three Southwestern states, comprised a very small part of total U.S. cotton production.

Health/Education/Welfare

Reports of the declining quality of public education and forecasts that the Medicare hospital fund could be bankrupt within four years concerned Congress throughout 1983. But in neither case did members act directly on the central education and health issues.

A Nation at Risk, the report of the federally appointed National Commission on Excellence in Education, spotlighted high illiteracy rates, falling standardized test scores and poor teacher-training as among the signs that public education was in trouble. Similar conclusions were reached by other national panels. Although the charges prompted public outcry and debate, there was little concrete federal action.

President Reagan, while embracing some of the findings, maintained that more money and an expanded federal role were not the answer. Congress held hearings and laid the groundwork for an examination of the federal role in education. But faced with a soaring deficit, members were hesitant to start costly new programs. A bill to upgrade math and science education was passed by the House but was not acted on by the Senate.

Congress did move quickly to significantly change the way the Medicare program paid for hospital care for elderly and disabled patients. Legislation was enacted establishing a policy of paying "fixed prices" for specific treatments, replacing the current system of generally paying whatever the hospital said patient care cost. The new method was intended to force improved management and more efficient allocation of resources.

However, the change did not address the larger question of the threat of bankruptcy of the Hospital Insurance trust fund. The Congressional Budget Office estimated that the fund, which paid for the hospitalization of Medicare beneficiaries, would run out of money as early as 1987. At the end of the year, Congress had discussed the issue in broad terms but had not developed an answer to the question of how much the nation should pay for the medical care of the elderly and disabled.

Education

Fueled by the array of critical reports, debate about education reform gained new prominence in Congress and state legislatures, on op-ed pages and on the presidential campaign trail.

Most concrete steps took place at the state and local level, largely because key issues such as teachers' salaries, curriculum standards and graduation requirements lay outside the federal purview. And Congress, faced with a threatened $200 billion budget deficit, showed little willingness to move quickly on costly education initiatives.

The April report of the commission on excellence became one of the most celebrated of the education commentaries. Its dire warnings set the tone for the ensuing public debate that some compared to the post-Sputnik reassessment of American education in the late 1950s.

"[T]he educational foundations of our society are presently being eroded by a rising tide of mediocrity that threatens our very future as a nation and a people," said the report presented to President Reagan April 26 by the commission, which had been named by Education Secretary Terrel H. Bell.

"If an unfriendly foreign power had attempted to impose on America the mediocre educational performance that exists today, we might well have viewed it as an act of war," it said.

Among the ills cited by the commission were high illiteracy rates, declining standardized test scores, and increasing need for colleges and businesses to provide remedial education.

The panel's dismal diagnosis was considered by some educators to be overstated. But its basic concerns subsequently were echoed by other organizations, including the Education Commission of the States, the Twentieth Century Fund, the National Science Board and the Carnegie Foundation for the Advancement of Teaching.

The wide publicity given to the excellence commission's report gave new impetus to reform efforts under way in state capitals and local school districts. A survey by the National Conference of State Legislatures found that states had shifted their emphasis in 1983. While reform proposals before 1983 tended to focus on competency testing for students and teachers, the survey found that the changes most frequently sought in 1983 were to improve the curriculum and to provide training for teachers in subjects where there was high demand, such as mathematics or science.

State school plans approved in 1983 included:

● California raised starting teachers' salaries by 30 percent over three years and provided $4,000 bonuses for outstanding teachers; imposed statewide high school graduation requirements; and allowed school districts to extend the school day and year.

● Florida provided new incentives for teachers under a merit pay plan, established a career ladder leading to the status of "master teacher," and offered scholarships and training to reduce the teacher shortage in certain fields.

The idea of rewarding outstanding teachers with higher salaries, rather than paying them strictly on the basis of seniority, became a leading political controversy. Reagan threw his weight behind the idea of merit pay for teachers. He also tossed frequent barbs at the National Education Association (NEA), the largest teachers' union, for its opposition to merit pay.

The NEA and Reagan also were at odds over the federal role in education reform. Saying that financially strapped states and localities needed federal help to foot the bill for improvements, the NEA proposed a $2 billion program of federal aid to local school districts.

Former Vice President Walter F. Mondale, the Democratic presidential candidate endorsed by the NEA, called for $11 billion in new federal spending to promote educa-

MAJOR CONGRESSIONAL ACTION

tional excellence and made a campaign issue out of the administration's efforts to cut the education budget.

Reagan held firm to his view that more money was not the key to improving the schools. But while he continued to advocate a very limited federal role in education, there were signs that he was moderating his stance — even before the surge of public interest in educational excellence.

Scaling back past years' efforts to make deep slashes in the Education Department's budget, the president requested $13.2 billion for the agency for fiscal 1984 — still about $2.1 billion less than was appropriated the previous year but a healthy increase over the $9.95 billion Reagan requested in fiscal 1983.

In his State of the Union message, Reagan also moved to identify himself with a somewhat broader range of education issues than his past agenda of tuition tax credits, school prayer and dismantling the Education Department.

After trying in the past to eliminate science education programs in the National Science Foundation, Reagan called for a new program to improve science and mathematics instruction. To encourage families to save for their children's college educations, Reagan proposed special tax breaks for education savings accounts.

The Education Department seemed to get a new lease on life in 1983, as the administration, for all practical purposes, abandoned its efforts to dismantle the agency.

Health

Although the most significant health issue was the far-reaching change in Medicare payments to hospitals, there were other influential developments.

Leadership of the massive Department of Health and Human Services (HHS) passed from one congressional veteran to another Jan. 12, when former Rep. Margaret M. Heckler was named HHS secretary, succeeding former Sen. Richard S. Schweiker (Senate, 1969-81; House, 1961-1969).

Schweiker's departure unsettled the health community because he had both expertise in the field and adeptness in political fights within the administration.

Heckler, 51, was a moderate Republican who had lost her re-drawn Massachusetts district in 1982 to liberal Barney Frank, D-Mass. Unlike Schweiker, Heckler brought no notable expertise in the programs she would administer, nor was she known as a legislative leader in Congress. During her eight terms in the House, she had served on the Agriculture, Banking, Government Operations, Science and Veterans' Affairs committees but not on panels with jurisdiction over HHS programs.

Reagan nominated Heckler the same day that Schweiker announced his resignation to head a trade and lobbying organization of life insurance companies.

During 1983, Heckler kept a relatively low profile. For instance, when the Senate Finance Committee wanted the administration's opinion of popular legislation providing health insurance for the unemployed, it was budget director David A. Stockman, not Heckler, who testified.

Policies set in motion before her arrival were debated or — in the case of the president's health budget proposals — ignored without much public input from Heckler.

The president's fiscal 1984 budget included a long-promised initiative to stem increases in the cost of health care by promoting more competition. There were no surprises: academic economists had, for years, been recommending the concepts that showed up in the budget.

Reagan's overall goal was to increase the amount that citizens paid out-of-pocket for medical care. Advocates argued that if Americans were more conscious of the high costs of medical care, they more frequently would use organized medical services, which were said to be thrifty in their use of expensive procedures.

The budget's competition initiative proposal included changes in the tax treatment of private employer-based health insurance, to favor plans requiring more cost-sharing by patients; higher out-of-pocket expenditures by Medicare patients, coupled with "catastrophic" coverage for extraordinarily expensive illnesses; and voluntary vouchers for Medicare beneficiaries who wanted to leave the public program and buy private health coverage. None received much attention in Congress, although Finance Committee Chairman Sen. Robert Dole, R-Kan., included the tax changes in a hefty deficit reduction package put together at the end of the year.

On the regulatory front, the administration's conservative agenda suffered several setbacks.

In January, HHS issued regulations requiring birth control clinics that received federal funds to notify parents before prescribing contraceptives for unmarried teenagers. The so-called "squeal" rule was condemned by medical groups. It was struck down in District of Columbia and New York courts on the grounds that HHS had misread congressional intent on parental notification. Current law permitted, but did not require, the notice. The department lost several appeals and, at the end of November, decided that it would not appeal to the Supreme Court.

A second battle concerned the rights of parents to let severely handicapped infants die by withholding nutrition and medical care. The controversy was sparked by a 1982 case in which a family, backed by court decisions, decided to withhold food and medical treatment from a mentally-retarded infant who also could not eat or drink normally because of a defective esophagus. The baby died, at the age of 6 days, in an Indiana hospital.

In March 1983, HHS issued regulations requiring hospitals receiving Medicare or Medicaid funds to place conspicuous notices that "discriminatory failure to feed and care for handicapped infants ... is prohibited by federal law." The notices asked anyone suspecting such behavior to call HHS on a 24-hour hotline.

Medical groups objected that the rule could subject pediatric wards to disruptive federal investigations and impair the treatment of seriously ill children. Privacy issues were also raised. Three medical groups filed suit, and the rule was struck down in April, largely on the grounds that its issuance had violated procedural requirements for federal rulemaking.

The so-called "baby doe" controversy continued for much of the year; at one point the Justice Department went to court in New York, demanding the medical records of a severely handicapped infant with spina bifida. The baby's parents had decided against surgery that would have extended the child's life.

The administration finally rewrote the regulation in consultation with the concerned medical groups, and when the final version was issued in January 1984, there were important changes in tone. Special hospital review committees were given primary responsibility for assuring medical care of handicapped infants. Notices were still required, but with more moderate language and without the requirement for conspicuous posting.

—By Janet Hook and Elizabeth Wehr

Major Changes Made in Medicare Program

Faced with a forecast that the Medicare program could go bankrupt within four years, Congress moved with exceptional speed in 1983 to adopt a radical change in the way the program bought hospital care for elderly and disabled Americans.

To hasten its approval, the new "payment-by-diagnosis" Medicare scheme was attached to major Social Security reform legislation (HR 1900 — PL 98-21) that President Reagan signed into law April 20. *(Story, p. 219)*

The administration first sent the largely untested new Medicare plan to Congress in late December 1982; it was rushed through Congress on a fast track, coupled with the "must" Social Security bill.

The House Ways and Means Health Subcommittee amended and approved the plan Feb. 24, just two days after the administration produced its detailed legislative proposal (HR 1705). The full committee approved the plan March 2 and attached it to HR 1900; the package passed the House March 9. The Senate Finance Committee approved a similar Social Security/Medicare bill (S 1) the next day, and the Senate passed it March 23. The conference version cleared March 25.

The new payment plan replaced the existing system under which Medicare paid hospitals — within certain limits — whatever it cost them to treat Medicare patients. Instead, the bill established the principle of fixed "prices" for treating different types of illnesses. It was meant to force hospitals to budget their resources more effectively, so they would not spend more treating Medicare patients than they could recover from the program.

The Medicare payment reform did not, in itself, end the threat of bankruptcy for Medicare's Hospital Insurance (HI) trust fund. While establishing the new method, Congress still did not speak directly to the central question: how much should the nation pay for medical care of its elderly and disabled citizens, who were the beneficiaries of Medicare? The new payment plan was expected to give hospitals time and incentives to improve their management before Congress overhauled the entire program.

Skeptics warned that the new system could create powerful financial incentives for hospitals to withhold needed medical treatment from patients, or to extract more money from Medicare by deceptive billing or unnecessary hospitalizations.

Advocates maintained that hospital officials would make hard-nosed management improvements and, eventually, influence doctors to use hospital resources more economically. Both sides agreed that the legislation made a fundamental change in Medicare, with broad implications for the structure of American medicine.

President Reagan's fiscal 1984 budget had estimated that Medicare would spend $59.8 billion in 1984 to care for some 30 million beneficiaries. That estimate assumed enactment of a number of money-saving proposals, including the payment reform. But only the payment plan was approved, in somewhat altered form, by Congress.

Three congressional committees approved other Medicare changes to cut anticipated program costs. But these changes were attached to bills that did not come to the floor in either the House or the Senate. *(Details below)*

In late November, the Ways and Means Committee convened a two-day meeting of health policy experts, who described and criticized a wide range of rescue options for Medicare. Members attending the sessions said, however, that given the difficulty of the program's problems and the 1984 election, they did not expect any major revision of Medicare until 1985 at the earliest.

Medicare Provisions

Following are the legislative changes made in Medicare by HR 1900 (PL 98-21). The bill:

● Replaced the existing Medicare hospitalization ("Part A") cost reimbursement system with one in which inpatient hospital operating costs were determined in advance and paid on a per-case basis, according to rates established for specific medical conditions or combinations of conditions (known as "diagnosis related groups," or DRGs).

The rates were to be derived from existing Medicare data, updated to reflect hospital cost increases in fiscal 1983 and updated again in fiscal 1984 and 1985, to reflect cost increases plus 1 percent. The bill specified that for those two years the system would be "budget neutral" — that is, total expenditures under it would be the same as they would have been under the existing reimbursement system with the spending limits enacted as part of the 1982 Tax Equity and Fiscal Responsibility Act. *(1982 Almanac p. 29)*

● Required the secretary of health and human services (HHS), in consultation with an advisory group of experts established by the bill, to decide annually, beginning in fiscal 1986, whether rate adjustments were needed; also required the secretary, with the advice of the group, to readjust the basic DRG classifications in fiscal 1986 and at least every four years thereafter to reflect changing treatment patterns and other factors.

● Generally barred hospitals from billing patients for more than the Medicare DRG payment, except for co-payments required by existing law.

● Authorized the secretary, for the first three years after enactment, to let a hospital continue billing the non-hospitalization Medicare plan ("Part B") for inpatient services, but only if the hospital had used such billing so extensively that immediate compliance with the new law would be disruptive, and if the payments were deducted from the hospital's DRG payments.

● Required DRG adjustments to reflect a hospital's additional costs from being required to join the Social Security system; also, repealed a reduction in Medicare payment rates for a hospital leaving Social Security.

● Excluded from DRG calculations hospital capital costs (for financing construction, major equipment purchases, and similar expenses); also excluded a special Medicare payment for interest ("net return on equity") to investor-owned (for-profit) hospitals.

Both exclusions were to continue until Oct. 1, 1986. Until then, these costs were to be paid under the existing reimbursement system except that the equity payment rate was reduced from 150 percent of the investment return of the Medicare Health Insurance fund to 100 percent of that return. (At the time the bill cleared, this meant a reduction to 12 percent, from 18 percent.)

● Excluded from the DRG a hospital's direct teaching expenses, such as interns' salaries, meaning that these ex-

penses continued to be reimbursed under the existing cost-based system. The bill also provided for DRG payment for indirect educational expenses, at double the rate of the existing system.

● Provided for adjustments in the basic DRG rates to reflect regional differences in labor costs; also provided for separate DRG payment rates for urban and rural hospitals and, for the first three years after enactment, separate DRG rates in each of the nation's nine census divisions.

● Provided for a three-year phase-in of the program, with an increasing portion of hospital costs paid under the new system until DRGs covered 100 percent of hospital costs in the fourth year.

● Required the secretary of HHS to continue the existing hospital cost-reporting system until at least the end of fiscal 1988.

● Required payments in addition to the DRG rate for atypical cases with higher costs because of exceptionally long hospital stays or other reasons.

● Exempted from the DRG system psychiatric, long-term care and children's hospitals and psychiatric and rehabilitation units of acute-care hospitals.

● Required the secretary to provide exceptions or adjustments for: hospitals serving as sole sources of care in a community; public or other hospitals serving a disproportionately large number of low-income or Medicare patients; hospitals serving as regional or national referral centers; hospitals involved in cancer treatment and research, and hospitals in Hawaii and Alaska.

● Required hospitals, as a condition for receiving Medicare payments, to contract by Oct. 1, 1984, with federally designated peer review organizations for reviews of quality of care, appropriateness of admissions, validity of diagnostic information provided by the hospital and other factors. It authorized payment for review activities, as needed, from Medicare Part A funds.

● Authorized certain payment options, if requested, for prepaid health plans such as health maintenance organizations (HMOs).

● Continued authority for Medicare demonstration projects and for different Medicare payments in state hospital cost control programs that met certain criteria; barred the secretary from requiring that the state programs be based on DRGs or that they produce a rate of cost increase lower than national rates; required the secretary to permit state programs to continue as long as they met specified criteria and to make a decision within 60 days on whether to approve new state programs, which would have to meet certain new standards; permitted the secretary to reduce payments to hospitals in a state with a cost control system if the secretary determined that amounts paid for three years for Medicare hospitalizations were higher than they would have been under the national DRG system.

● Continued most existing authority for administrative and judicial review of Medicare payment decisions, but excluded DRG payment rates and classifications from review.

● Required the secretary to study and report to Congress on: inclusion of capital and equity costs in the DRG system; the impact of hospital prospective payment systems on skilled nursing facilities and on other providers, and the feasibility of applying DRGs to nursing facilities; the impact of the DRG system — to be reported each year from 1984 through 1987 — on individual hospitals, classes of hospitals, beneficiaries and other entities, such as private insurers, that paid hospitals; physician fees for inpatient

care and the feasibility of including them in the DRG system; the feasibility of including exempted hospitals in the DRG system; the impact of different state systems, and other matters.

● Barred Medicare payments after three years for new capital projects unless approved by state "1122" review programs.

Background

The Congressional Budget Office (CBO) estimated in February that the HI trust fund, which financed hospitalization of Medicare beneficiaries, would run out of money as early as 1987.

The basic problem, CBO said, was that the cost of hospital care was rising faster than the federal taxes that replenished the fund.

Health experts blamed health care cost increases on a number of factors, including simple price inflation and the aging of the population. But many thought the most important cause of rising health costs was the ever-increasing number and sophistication of treatments — surgical and medical — that ailing Americans, including Medicare beneficiaries, were receiving.

In 1982, the cost of health care rose by 11 percent, nearly three times the 3.9 percent general increase in consumer prices for the year.

Congress had laid the tracks for the Medicare payment change in August 1982 when it passed a major tax bill (PL 97-248) that included two stringent new limits on Medicare payment rates for hospitals. Sponsors assumed that the limits, together with the existing system of calculating Medicare payments to hospitals, would be promptly replaced by a new payment method. The tax bill also ordered the HHS to design and send Congress a new "prospective" payment system for Medicare within five months. *(1982 Almanac p. 471)*

The 1982 limits were intended to save the federal government money, but they had clear political impact as well. Hospital groups said the harsh new limits were insensitive to legitimate differences among hospitals in operating costs. The limits made the payment-by-diagnosis plan appear to be a comparatively attractive alternative.

The new plan thus had the support of major segments of the hospital industry, including the American Hospital Association and the Federation of American Hospitals, as well as of the administration and such key members of Congress as Ways and Means Chairman Dan Rostenkowski, D-Ill., and Finance Committee Chairman Robert Dole, R-Kan. Other groups, such as the American Medical Association and the Blue Cross and Blue Shield Associations, were critical of the plan but did not actively oppose it.

It was opposition from hospital groups that had defeated a major Carter administration hospital cost control bill in 1979. *(1979 Almanac p. 512)*

In ordering a "prospective" reimbursement system, Congress was asking for a method that would let the government determine, in advance, how much the program would pay each year to hospitals for treating Medicare patients.

Critics said the existing system, which paid hospitals for their costs after services were rendered, inflated medical costs because its financial incentives fostered the wasteful overuse of treatments and procedures, instead of discouraging their use. Critics also claimed that Medicare inflation played a major role in driving up the cost of

health care nationally.

Administration Proposal

On Dec. 28, 1982, HHS sent Congress a "prospective" plan that called for standard prices for treating heart attacks, bone fractures and more than 400 other specific medical conditions in Medicare patients.

The HHS report noted that there were wide variations in what different hospitals charged to treat the same condition, although there was "no apparent difference in quality" of care. For instance, hospitals charged anywhere from $1,500 to $9,000 for care of a heart attack victim, while charges for a hip replacement ranged from $2,100 to $8,200, according to the report.

The administration's plan generally would have ended such price differentials in Medicare. It allowed only a few adjustments in the national "prices" to be paid by Medicare: for regional variations in labor costs, for hospitals that were sole sources of care in communities, and for individual medical cases that cost much more than the national average because the patient stayed longer in the hospital. The new payment scheme would not apply to long-term care hospitals, psychiatric hospitals or pediatric hospitals.

The plan barred hospitals from appealing judicially to change Medicare payments, as they could do under existing law. If hospitals found Medicare payments too low under the new system, their options were either to convince HHS to pay more, or to stop treating Medicare patients, the report said.

The report outlined a method of using hospital medical and financial data to assign an average cost, or price, for treating each of 467 "diagnosis related groups" (DRGs). It did not say what the prices would be, but the goal of the plan was to hold overall Medicare expenditures to the same level as that resulting from the 1982 tax law limits.

This tactic also helped allay objections to the plan, because advocates could assure hospitals that in the first two years, the new scheme would gouge no more money out of their government payments than the 1982 limits. When the plan came before the House Ways and Means Committee, members did not debate the wisdom of the plan itself, but instead focused on providing special treatment for different types of hospitals.

The administration plan provided for revisions of the DRGs as needed to reflect changes in medical technology or other factors.

The DRG "prices" were meant to cover all of a hospital's expenses except those for medical teaching programs and "capital" costs such as construction, which would be paid separately. The Medicare DRG payments would be payments in full; hospitals would be barred from trying to collect additional money from individual patients.

If a hospital could treat a case for less money than the DRG provided, it could keep the difference; if it spent more than the DRG allowed on a case, it would have to absorb the loss.

The new system resembled a broader plan being used by the state of New Jersey, which applied the DRG methodology to all payers of hospital bills — Medicare, Medicaid, private health insurance plans and individuals. The HHS report suggested that private insurers could adopt the new Medicare rates as the basis for their hospital payments.

The New Jersey system not only differed markedly from the HHS plan in its scope, but also was too new to have yielded any information on whether it worked.

House Action

The House Ways and Means Committee approved the administration's basic plan on March 2, with changes that gave hospitals more grounds to claim special treatment in the new system, and states more latitude to depart from the DRG methodology.

The administration plan gave the secretary of HHS discretionary authority to broaden the scope of the DRG system substantially, but the committee assumed that Congress would enact such changes. It eliminated discretionary authority for the secretary to expand the system to cover doctors' fees for hospital care and capital costs. Instead, it told HHS to study these and certain other issues and send Congress recommendations for legislation. The committee also provided for a four-year phase-in of the plan.

The committee bill also mandated different DRG schedules for urban and rural hospitals, and for hospitals in different regions of the country. It also permitted states to continue or begin different types of medical cost control programs, including those applying to all payers of hospital bills — private and public.

The administration had wanted as much uniformity as possible, nationally, for Medicare payment methods. It would have allowed the continuation of existing state hospital cost control demonstration projects using different payment methods, but it wanted to end authority for different Medicare payment methods under permanent state cost control programs.

The committee refused to go along with that change and instead required the secretary to grant so-called Medicare "waivers" (authorizing different payment methods) to state cost control programs meeting certain new standards.

The committee also did not go along with the administration's plan to exempt the new payment system from administrative and judicial review; it exempted only DRG payment rates and classifications.

To protect against hospitals skimping or overtreating patients to avoid losses or enhance payments, the committee bill required hospitals to contract with appropriate organizatons for peer review of hospital admissions patterns and other factors.

The committee reported its Medicare plan March 4 (H Rept 98-25) and sent it to the House floor as part of the Social Security rescue legislation, under a rule permitting no amendments to the Medicare section.

The House passed the bill (HR 1900) March 9, 282-148. *(Vote 23, p. 10-H)*

Senate Action

The Senate Finance Committee approved a similar measure (S 1) March 10 by a vote of 18-1, and filed its report March 11 (S Rept 98-23). S 1's Medicare provisions were generally the same as those in the House bill.

Both bills followed the administration's plan of set prices for inpatient treatment of different illnesses, and prohibited charging individual patients more than the set price. Both excluded hospitals' teaching costs and capital expenditures for construction and similar hospital improvements from the system. S 1, however, mandated that capital costs be factored into the new price structure after October 1986.

The two bills substituted a four-year phase-in of the new payment method for the Oct. 1 effective date suggested by the administration. Both required separate rates

for urban and rural hospitals, and for different regions. And both departed from the administration proposal by mandating that hospital admission patterns and other factors be reviewed to guard against costly manipulations of the new system, or poor care for patients. S 1 specified that Professional Review Organizations (PROs) authorized in the 1982 tax bill must do the job, while the House bill permitted the use of other types of organizations. S 1 did not include a House provision authorizing severe penalties for certain violations of the system or compromised quality of care.

Another difference was that the Senate panel decided to let the three Social Security trust funds — including the Medicare HI fund — borrow from each other through 1987. However, the committee stipulated that no funds could be borrowed from the HI fund when its reserves were low.

The Senate passed S 1 March 23 by a vote of 88-9, after adopting an amendment that expanded exceptions from the Medicare payment plan to include certain rural hospitals and large regional and national referral centers. *(Vote 53, p. 11-S)*

Conference, Final Action

House and Senate conferees agreed to the final shape of HR 1900 during a 12-hour session March 24, as colleagues waited impatiently to leave for the Easter recess. The primary points of disagreement were over Social Security issues, not the Medicare plan.

The House adopted the conference report (H Rept 98-47) March 24 by a 243-102 vote. *(Vote 43, p. 18-H)*

By a 58-14 vote, the Senate gave its final approval in the early morning hours of March 25, clearing the bill for the president. *(Vote 54, p. 12-S)*

Other Medicare Proposals

The new payment plan was the only segment of the president's 1984 budget proposals for Medicare to be enacted. Congress' failure to complete work on budget reconciliation legislation left hanging a short list of committee proposals to trim back some projected Medicare costs.

Like the new hospital payment plan, these committee proposals were not expected to make much of a dent in the projected HI budget. But they showed strong sentiment for a clampdown on Medicare payments to doctors.

In his fiscal 1984 budget, Reagan had suggested that:
● Medicare beneficiaries pay substantially more out of their own pockets for short-term hospital stays. This would have been coupled with a plan protecting them from "catastrophic" costs of major illnesses by putting a ceiling on out-of-pocket expenditures for very lengthy hospitalizations.
● Beneficiaries pay higher premiums for non-hospital coverage.
● Doctors accept a one-year freeze on increases in Medicare fees. The administration plan would not have barred physicians from collecting more from patients during the freeze.
● Medicare give vouchers to beneficiaries who chose to leave the public program and buy private health coverage instead.

Much of what the president proposed appeared to be barred by language in the fiscal 1984 congressional budget resolution (H Con Res 91), however.

The resolution directed authorizing committees to

shave $400 million from expected fiscal 1984 Medicare outlays of $60.6 billion, but stipulated that any savings should not raise out-of-pocket costs for beneficiaries or restrict their access to medical services. *(Budget resolution, p. 435)*

Committee debate on Medicare budget savings focused on whether any savings provisions could be constructed that would not violate these restrictions.

Finance Committee Action

On July 13 the Senate Finance Committee included two Medicare savings provisions in a bill (S 951) to set up a new health insurance program for unemployed Americans. *(Story, p. 405)*

One provision would have made permanent a temporary increase in premiums for Part B Medicare coverage (for non-hospital services).

The second would have imposed a nine-month freeze for all physician services on the so-called "prevailing" level of physician charges. Medicare used the level to determine payment rates.

House critics charged that both provisions violated budget resolution language.

The Finance Committee filed its report on the unemployment insurance legislation July 25 (S Rept 98-193), but the bill did not come to the Senate floor in 1983. Its Medicare sections subsequently were transferred to the committee's budget reconciliation plan (S 2062 — S Rept 98-300), which also failed to receive Senate consideration. *(Story, p. 231)*

Ways and Means Action

The Ways and Means Committee Oct. 19 made an unusual decision to send a Medicare physician fee freeze plan to the House floor even though the plan did not have the support of a majority of committt members.

The president's budget had proposed a year-long freeze on fee increases, and there was a general sense in the health community that it was doctors' "turn" to accept some new limitations. Hospitals already faced stringent overall limits on Medicare payments in 1982, and a radical, untested change in the way Medicare payments would be calculated, was adopted early in 1983.

The six-month freeze proposal for doctors' hospital fees had drawn grudging acquiescence from the AMA, but the AMA was vehemently opposed to related "assignment" proposals meant to force doctors to accept Medicare fees as payment in full for their hospital services. These sections were intended to protect beneficiaries from higher costs if doctors decided to elude the freeze by charging patients themselves more.

In a closed session, the committee decided to include other Medicare savings provisions, including limits on payments to laboratories, in its reconciliation tax plan (HR 4170 — H Rept 98-432), and to offer the controversial fee sections as a floor amendment to that plan. Many members feared that including the fee proposal in the bill could lead to the defeat of the entire tax package.

The Medicare provisions were expected to more than meet the budget resolution's mandate to reduce the rate of Medicare spending by $1.7 billion over fiscal 1984-86.

However, the House declined to consider the tax bill, thus foreclosing consideration of the Ways and Means Medicare plan and similar provisions approved Oct. 20 by the Energy and Commerce Committee (HR 4136 — H Rept 98-442, Part I) filed Oct. 26. *(Tax bill, p. 231)*   ∎

Tuition Tax Credits

The Reagan administration was unsuccessful in getting Congress to approve tax breaks for parents who sent their children to private elementary and secondary schools.

The Senate Nov. 16 overwhelmingly rejected the president's tuition tax credit proposal, which was one of the cornerstones of Reagan's education policy. A similar House proposal (HR 1730) introduced by Bill Gradison, R-Ohio, languished in the Ways and Means Committee, whose chairman, Dan Rostenkowski, D-Ill., opposed the idea.

The Senate defeat came on a 59-38 vote to table a tuition tax credit amendment offered by Finance Committee Chairman Robert Dole, R-Kan., to a minor tariff bill (H J Res 290). The margin of defeat cast doubt on the tuition measure's future chances for approval. *(Vote 355, p. 58-S)*

The Dole amendment called for a tax credit — to be subtracted from taxes owed — of 50 percent of the tuition paid to a qualified private school that met standards prohibiting racial discrimination. During the first year, the maximum credit would be $100 per student. The maximum would rise to $200 the second year and $300 in subsequent years. Parents with incomes above $40,000 would receive a smaller credit and, in the case of incomes above $50,000, none at all.

Dole said he brought the measure to the floor to fulfill his pledge to the president, who had included the proposal in his State of the Union message Jan. 25. *(Text, p. 3-E)*

That appeal was not successful, as 24 Republicans, including Majority Leader Howard H. Baker Jr., R-Tenn., voted to table the amendment.

The measure was originally reported June 20 by the Finance Committee, on an 11-7 vote, as S 528 (S Rept 98-154). To avoid the Rostenkowski roadblock, Senate supporters planned all along to attach the tuition tax credit bill as an amendment to another measure, preferably one already passed by the House.

H J Res 290, which passed the House June 28, exempted from duty items brought into the country by foreign participants in the 1984 Summer Olympic Games in Los Angeles.

Threat to Public Schools?

Opponents of the tuition tax credit argued that it would not appreciably help low- and middle-income parents who wished to send their children to private schools, but would be, in the words of David L. Boren, D-Okla., "another major step down the road of destruction of public education in the United States."

They also objected that the administration was proposing an expensive new program at the same time it was invoking the need to reduce budget deficits as a reason not to increase federal aid to public schools. The Congressional Budget Office estimated the tuition tax credit would reduce federal tax revenues by almost $3 billion over five years.

Boren, Robert T. Stafford, R-Vt., and other opponents complained that consideration of such an important proposal should not be attempted during the crush of last-minute activities as the Senate worked toward adjourning for the year.

Court Ruling

Opponents rejected suggestions that the tuition tax credit plan met the requirements of a June 29 Supreme Court 5-4 decision upholding a Minnesota state income tax deduction for public and private school tuition, textbooks and transportation. They argued that the federal proposal was not sufficiently similar to the Minnesota law to pass Supreme Court review.

The Minnesota deduction was available regardless of whether the children attended public or private schools — a fact that was central to the court's decision. In the case of *Mueller v. Allen*, the court held that Minnesota's tax deduction for parents did not amount to state aid to church-related schools in violation of the First Amendment's ban on government "establishment" of religion.

The majority found that the deduction had a secular purpose, did not have the primary effect of advancing religion and did not entangle the state in parochial school affairs. This three-part test for constitutionality had been set out by the justices in a 1971 "parochiaid" case.

The Senate Finance Committee legislation differed from the Minnesota law in several important respects. First, it benefited only parents of private and parochial school students. Second, it provided tax credits rather than deductions. And finally, it covered only tuition outlays, not textbook costs, transportation and similar educational expenditures by parents.

Previous Action

In recent years most activity on tuition tax credit proposals had occurred in the Senate. The Senate Finance Committee approved a tuition tax credit bill in 1982, but there was no further action on the issue and the legislation died when Congress adjourned. *(1982 Almanac p. 489)*

In 1978, both the House and Senate passed bills providing tax credits for college tuition. But the House version also provided credits for elementary and secondary school tuition expenses. When a House-Senate conference committee dropped this provision, the House refused to accept tax credits only for college tuition, and the bill died. *(1978 Almanac p. 248)*

There were a number of tuition tax credit proposals prior to 1978. The Senate passed college tuition tax credit amendments in 1976 and 1977, but they were dropped in conference with the House, which was more interested in credits for elementary and secondary school students. ∎

Tribal Colleges

Congress Nov. 17 cleared a measure authorizing operating, endowment and construction funds for fiscal 1985-87 for 18 colleges controlled by Indian tribes. Both chambers approved the conference report on S 726 (S Rept 98-303, H Rept 98-505) by voice vote Nov. 17.

The president signed the bill Dec. 1 (PL 98-192).

The bill was an altered version of a measure (S 2623) President Reagan had pocket-vetoed in January after objecting to new construction funds and to language referring to the federal government's trust responsibility toward Indians. *(Veto, 1982 Almanac p. 501)*

S 726 did not include the trust responsibility language and authorized "such sums as may be necessary" for new construction or renovation only after the General Services Administration found need for the work. The colleges had to pay 20 percent of the building costs.

The bill authorized for each of the three years $30

million for program grants, $3.2 million for technical assistance and $5 million for a new endowment program.

Legislative History

The House Education and Labor Committee approved HR 2307 unanimously April 13 and reported it April 28 (H Rept 98-77). On May 3, the bill failed in the House, after the Reagan administration expressed opposition to provisions authorizing new endowment and construction expenditures.

It was brought to the floor under suspension of the rules, a procedure that required a two-thirds vote for passage and barred any amendments. It won a majority of votes, 255-148, but fell 14 short of the required two-thirds. *(Vote 69, p. 26-H)*

The Senate Select Committee on Indian Affairs reported S 726 April 26 (S Rept 98-64). The Senate on May 25 passed by voice vote a three-year extension of the federal program.

Mark Andrews, R-N.D., chairman of the Select Indian Affairs Committee, held up action on S 726 to allow the administration time to state its position but no comments were received.

The House on Oct. 20 by voice vote amended the Senate bill to delete the sections that had drawn administration objections.   ▮

Math-Science Education

Despite widespread concern about the deteriorating quality of science and mathematics education, Congress failed to clear legislation designed to address the problem.

The House March 2 overwhelmingly passed a bill (HR 1310 — H Rept 98-6 Parts I and II) that would authorize $425 million in fiscal 1984 to improve math, science and foreign language programs in the nation's schools and colleges. But a companion bill (S 1285 — S Rept 98-151) never made it to the Senate floor after its approval May 11 by the Committee on Labor and Human Resources.

The bills were drafted amid growing concern over the shortage of trained personnel in science and technology and evidence of declining science knowledge among students. Congress was repeatedly warned that those educational inadequacies threatened America's economic and technological position in the world marketplace.

Those fears, already brewing in the 97th Congress, were fueled in 1983 by a spate of highly publicized reports decrying the state of American education — particularly in the areas of math, science and foreign languages.

The Reagan administration, in one of its few proposals to establish a new federal education program, requested $75 million in fiscal 1984 to bolster science education. That request included a new $50 million block grant to states to increase the number of high school math and science teachers.

Both the House and Senate bills far exceeded the President's request, despite complaints from some Republicans in both chambers that it was "irresponsible" to create a new spending program at a time of high budget deficits.

Prompt approval of HR 1310 by the House Education and Labor Committee and the Science and Technology Committee marked a dramatic turnaround from 1982, when a similar science-education bill failed to reach the House floor because the two panels could not agree on how funds would be distributed. *(1982 Almanac p. 499)*

Under HR 1310, $295 million of the new science-education aid would be administered by the Department of Education and $130 million would go to the National Science Foundation.

The science education bill approved by the Senate Committee on Labor and Human Resources also authorized $425 million in fiscal 1984, but allocated $350 million for the Education Department and $75 million for NSF programs.

The Senate bill was stalled for months without reaching the floor, while Labor Committee Chairman Orrin G. Hatch, R-Utah, tried to fend off efforts to use the politically popular measure as a vehicle for extraneous amendments. In particular, Hatch opposed plans by Thomas F. Eagleton, D-Mo., to introduce an amendment authorizing new aid to schools undergoing desegregation.

House Committee Action

Under pressure from Democratic leaders, the Education and Labor Committee and the Science and Technology Committee moved early in the session to resolve the jurisdictional dispute that prevented House action on science education legislation in 1982. The resulting compromise bill, HR 1310, melded provisions of bills introduced earlier by Carl D. Perkins, D-Ky., chairman of the Education Committee, and Don Fuqua, D-Fla., chairman of the Science Committee.

Education and Labor. As approved by the Education and Labor Committee Feb. 8, HR 1310 authorized $400 million in fiscal 1984 to improve math and science courses, alleviate the shortage of teachers in those fields and set a national policy for maintaining an adequate supply of scientific and technical personnel.

The committee approved the bill on a 27-3 vote, after accepting an amendment that allowed some of the money to be used to improve foreign language instruction.

HR 1310 authorized $250 million in fiscal 1984 and "such sums as may be necessary" in fiscal 1985 for grants to states to improve math and science programs in elementary and secondary schools. It also authorized $50 million in assistance to postsecondary institutions.

The state grants, which could be used to benefit private schools as well as public, were provided to finance training projects to improve the skills and knowledge of current math and science teachers and to qualify teachers of other subjects to teach math and science. The money also could be used for the acquisition of instructional materials and equipment, and activities with private businesses, museums, and other agencies.

The $50 million authorized for postsecondary assistance would finance summer institutes and workshops to improve course content and teacher skills, education research, and scholarships for students working toward a teaching degree in math, science, or foreign languages.

HR 1310 also authorized $100 million for the NSF to encourage the training of technical, engineering and scientific personnel, but the Science and Technology Committee was given sole jurisdiction over that section of the bill.

Science and Technology. The Science and Technology Committee Feb. 22 approved HR 1310 after boosting the bill's allocation for postsecondary aid and expanding the NSF's role in administering it.

The science committee increased the authorization for

postsecondary programs from $50 million to $75 million in fiscal 1984. The Science Committee allocated $45 million of the total for Education Department programs and $30 million for the NSF. As approved by the Education Committee, all the postsecondary funds would have been administered by the Department of Education (ED).

The committee earmarked $20 million of ED's share for scholarships for study leading to a teaching degree in math, science or foreign languages that were in great demand in scientific and technical fields. Recipients would have to teach for two years for each year of scholarship assistance received, or repay the aid with interest.

In boosting the postsecondary budget, the committee increased support for summer institutes, education research and postsecondary improvement programs, and added $5-million for the Minority Institutions Science Improvement program.

As approved by the Science Committee, HR 1310 also provided the NSF with $100 million in matching funds each year for five years to encourage the public and private sectors to train adequate numbers of technical, engineering and scientific personnel to meet the nation's needs.

House Floor Action

The House March 2 approved HR 1310 by a vote of 348-54, after rejecting a barrage of amendments from disgruntled Republicans who protested that the bill cost too much and did not adequately address the nation's fundamental short-term need for more math and science teachers. *(Vote 12, p. 8-H)*

The House rejected, 92-323, an amendment by F. James Sensenbrenner Jr., R-Wis., to replace the postsecondary assistance provisions of the bill with $50 million in block grants to states for general program improvements, including salary bonuses and summer employment. *(Vote 10, p. 8-H)*

Another amendment, by E. Thomas Coleman, R-Mo., would have replaced the bill's program of two-year scholarships with one-year scholarships to retrain existing teachers in other fields to be math and science teachers. The amendment was rejected, 138-276. *(Vote 11, p. 8-H)*

John N. Erlenborn, R-Ill., ranking minority member of the Education and Labor Committee, introduced a series of

amendments that would have struck out most parts of the bill, leaving only $75 million for postsecondary assistance programs. The amendments, which were intended to bring the bill more in line with the administration's math and science proposals, were killed by voice vote.

Senate Committee Action

As approved by the Labor and Human Resources Committee by a 16-2 vote May 11, S 1285 authorized $425 million in fiscal 1984 and $540 million in fiscal 1985 to improve instruction for programs designed to increase the supply of trained teachers and to improve instruction in math, science, computer science and "critical" foreign languages.

The publication of a series of reports critical of American schools, including a report April 26 from the National Commission on Excellence in Education appointed by Education Secretary Terrel H. Bell, apparently helped overcome budgetary objections of some fiscal conservatives.

The bill included $350 million in fiscal 1984 and $400 million in 1985 for Education Department grants to states to improve teacher skills and instruction in math, science, computer learning and foreign languages.

The bill required that 70 percent of state funds went for elementary and secondary school programs and 30 percent for higher education programs.

It also authorized $75 million in fiscal 1984 for science education programs in the NSF, including support for teacher institutes, graduate fellowships and merit scholarships to students planning to be math, science or engineering teachers. The bill also provided support for education "partnerships" among schools, businesses, museums, libraries, professional associations and other groups. ∎

Endowment Aid

The House Sept. 26 cleared a compromise bill designed to increase funding to help small developing colleges build their endowment funds.

President Reagan signed the bill (S 1872 — PL 98-95) the same day in a ceremony marking "National Historically Black Colleges Day."

Black colleges were the prime beneficiaries of the extra $4.8 million authorized in fiscal 1984 for challenge grants, which must be matched dollar-for-dollar in non-federal funds. The bill raised the authorization for Title III of the Higher Education Act from the $129.6 million set by the 1981 budget reconciliation law to $134.4 million; challenge grants, originally authorized at $9.6 million, received all the increase. *(1981 Almanac p. 494)*

Between 800 and 1,100 small public and private institutions were eligible for the grants, which in fiscal 1984 would range from $50,000 to $200,000. Twenty percent of the funds were for endowments and 80 percent funded college programs. For fiscal 1985, the grants were authorized at $50 million, all to be used for endowments. The grant ceiling rose to $500,000.

The bill also raised the fiscal 1984 authorization for Howard University in Washington, D.C., by $14.5 million, to $159.7 million.

The legislation was a compromise between HR 2144 reported April 28 by the House Education and Labor Committee (H Rept 98-76) and a proposal sent to the Senate by

Sex Discrimination

While it had only symbolic value, a resolution was passed by the House Nov. 16 opposing any effort to narrow the interpretation of Title IX of the 1972 Education Amendments. That title barred discrimination based on sex in education programs receiving federal funds. *(1972 Almanac p. 390)*

In a case before the Supreme Court, *Grove City College v. Bell*, the administration and the college argued that the ban applied only to the specific programs in a school that received federal aid, not to all programs at a recipient institution.

H Res 190 was agreed to by a vote of 414-8. The resolution had been reported by the Education and Labor Committee Oct. 19 (H Rept 98-418). *(Vote 478, p. 140-H)*

Education Secretary T. H. Bell. S 1872, which tightened federal control over the funds, was passed by the Senate Sept. 22. The House accepted the Senate bill. ∎

VISTA Authorization

Congress failed to clear legislation extending a number of volunteer and anti-poverty programs administered by ACTION, although both chambers passed bills that rebuffed the Reagan administration's effort to eliminate Volunteers in Service to America (VISTA).

Legislation reauthorizing ACTION programs through fiscal 1986 (S 1129) passed the Senate Sept. 14 and the House Oct. 28, but Congress adjourned before a conference committee met to reconcile substantial differences between the two bills.

VISTA, a well-known component of President Johnson's War on Poverty, had been targeted for elimination by the administration for the second year in a row. Only $196,000 was requested for fiscal 1984 — to pay costs associated with the phase-out of the agency.

The administration argued that VISTA had a controversial history of political advocacy and that volunteers ought to be just that, rather than getting paid about $7,000 a year as VISTA volunteers were.

But congressional supporters argued that the program was cost-effective. They maintained that each VISTA volunteer generated about $24,000 in public- and private-sector resources each year.

Rejecting the administration's request to eliminate the program, the Senate authorized $15 million for VISTA in 1984. The House set a $25 million "funding floor" for the program, which meant that the first $25 million appropriated for volunteer anti-poverty programs had to go to VISTA and only then would smaller programs be funded. The floor was among the reasons the bill drew threats of a presidential veto.

Because Congress failed to finish work on the legislation, ACTION's authorization expired Sept. 30. However, the fiscal 1984 continuing resolution contained funding for VISTA. *(Story, p. 526)*

Other ACTION programs under the Domestic Volunteer Service Act of 1973 that would be reauthorized by the House and Senate bills included the Retired Senior Volunteers, Foster Grandparents, Senior Companions, Service Learning and Young Volunteers in Action.

Senate Action

S 1129 was approved by voice vote in the Labor and Human Resources Committee May 25 and the report (S Rept 98-182) was filed July 14. It authorized $147.6 million for all ACTION programs in fiscal 1984, $149.6 million in 1985 and $151.6 million in 1986.

The bill mandated changes in VISTA operating procedures that supporters said would ease doubts about VISTA's activities. For example, the bill made clear that the major focus of VISTA was to alleviate poverty and poverty-related problems. There had been complaints that some VISTA volunteers strayed too far from that goal by engaging in such activities as office work or working as hospital aides.

The Senate Sept. 14 approved the committee bill without change by voice vote, after a floor discussion that was devoted to testimonials on the effectiveness of VISTA and other ACTION programs.

Several senators, including Alan Cranston, D-Calif., and Donald W. Riegle Jr., D-Mich., said they would have preferred more money for VISTA than was provided in the bill. S 1129 authorized $15 million for fiscal 1984 and added $2 million in each of the next two years.

In its heyday, VISTA funding was considerably higher. In 1981, for example, the funding level was $34 million, but by fiscal 1983, it had dropped to $11.8 million.

House Action

The bill reported by the House Education and Labor Committee May 16 (HR 2655 — H Rept 98-161) authorized an estimated $178.1 million for ACTION in fiscal 1984, $188 million in 1985, and $195.6 million in 1986.

The "funding floor" for VISTA increased from $25 million in fiscal 1984 to $28 million in 1985 and $30 million in 1986. The purpose of the floor, the committee said, was to prevent funds from being diverted from VISTA to other programs.

HR 2655 expanded the list of approved volunteer assignments to include such projects as dealing with problems of the hungry, homeless and the illiterate, but required that all VISTA activities be directed toward anti-poverty goals.

The bill also mandated that at least 20 percent of VISTA volunteers be 55 or older. The Senate bill contained no such requirement.

For Older American Volunteers, HR 2655 authorized funds generally to maintain current service levels, with the exception of adding $12 million to the Senior Companions program. Funding for that program was set at $31.4 million, $32.2 million, and $33.1 million respectively for fiscal 1984, 1985 and 1986.

Both Steve Bartlett, R-Texas, and John N. Erlenborn, R-Ill., argued in floor debate Oct. 17 and Oct. 28 that the funding increase for VISTA should be cut considerably.

Bartlett said more than $350 million had been spent on VISTA since 1965. "I do not believe it has made a significant difference in the low-income communities it was designed to serve," he said.

Erlenborn, ranking minority member of the Education and Labor Committee, argued that the expansion of VISTA "jeopardizes the chances of the president signing this legislation."

A Bartlett amendment that would have dropped the specific VISTA authorization and provided "such sums as may be necessary" was defeated Oct. 28 on a party-line vote of 132-215. *(Vote 400, p. 120-H)*

Despite criticism of the bill's VISTA provisions, the House Oct. 28 approved HR 2655 by a 312-30 vote and substituted its text for that of the Senate bill. *(Vote 401, p. 120-H)*. ∎

Hospice Payments

Legislation permitting hospices, which provided home health care and related services for terminally ill patients, to receive up to $6,500 per Medicare patient for such care was signed by the president Aug. 29 (HR 3677 — PL 98-90).

Medicare payments for hospice care had been authorized in 1982 tax legislation, but sponsors said that because of a technical error in that bill, the payments would be capped at a much lower rate — about $4,200 per case — than Congress had intended. The low payment rate would

not cover costs of care and terminally ill Medicare patients were likely to use more expensive hospital or nursing home care instead, they said.

The Ways and Means Committee reported the bill July 28 (H Rept 98-333) and the House passed the bill Aug. 1 by voice vote. The Senate, without committee action, cleared it by voice vote on Aug. 3. ∎

Draft Registration Rules

The Supreme Court agreed Dec. 5 to rule in the 1983-84 term on the constitutionality of a law disqualifying from federal student aid any male college student who failed to register for the military draft.

The law was enacted in 1982 as part of the fiscal 1983 Department of Defense authorization (PL 97-252). *(1982 Almanac p. 485)*

Shortly after its enactment, a lawsuit challenging the law was filed, and in March 1983, a federal district judge in Minnesota declared the law unconstitutional. There also were moves in the House to postpone the law's implementation, but final congressional action was put off pending the Supreme Court decision.

The registration requirement — known as the Solomon amendment for sponsor Rep. Gerald B. H. Solomon, R-N.Y., — went into effect with the 1983-84 school year. It provided that students who failed to register with Selective Service as required by law would be ineligible for any financial aid under Title IV of the Higher Education Act of 1965. The aid programs affected included Pell Grants, Supplemental Educational Opportunity Grants, National Direct Student Loans, State Student Incentive Grants and federally sponsored college work-study progams.

Education Secretary T. H. Bell defended the law as "designed to help us with our emergency preparedness. We all ought to be interested in doing that."

But at hearings Feb. 23-24 before the House Education and Labor Subcommittee on Postsecondary Education, spokesmen for some of the nation's foremost colleges, universities and education organizations testified against the law and the implementing regulations.

House Action

On March 23 the subcommittee approved a bill (HR 2145) to postpone implementation of regulations to enforce the aid law from July 1, 1983, until Feb. 1, 1984. The bill was designed to give schools more time to plan compliance.

The full committee approved the bill April 13 by a vote of 18-8. Its report (H Rept 98-74 Part I) was filed April 28.

Chief sponsor Paul Simon, D-Ill., chairman of the subcommittee, said he had decided on a seven-month delay because the Armed Services Committee agreed to that period. Armed Services shared jurisdiction over the bill but took no action.

The Justice Department subsequently advised the Education Department that until the case was decided or the injunction lifted, the law was "temporarily null and void" and should not be implemented.

On June 29, the Supreme Court lifted the Minnestoa judge's injunction against government enforcement of the law. As of Oct. 1, all college students seeking federal financial aid had to certify that they were in compliance with the draft registration law.

The decision was appealed directly to the Supreme Court under a rule permitting such appeals in cases in which a federal statute was declared unconstitutional. The lower court judge who issued the ruling must certify that the case fell within the class of cases eligible for a direct appeal. The Supreme Court has the discretion to refuse to rule on the case, however. ∎

U.S. Peace Academy

A bill to establish a U.S. Academy of Peace was reported Sept. 27 by the Senate Labor and Human Resources Committee but never reached the floor.

The measure (S 564 — S Rept 98-244) called for a federally sponsored institution to "conduct research . . . into the causes of war . . . and the elements of peace" and to develop "skills in international peace and conflict resolution." It was approved by the committee July 20 on an 11-6 vote.

Sponsored by Spark M. Matsunaga, D-Hawaii, and 52 others, the legislation sought $7.5 million to acquire an academy site, and an additional $16 million for the first two years of operations. After initial federal funding, the academy would establish a private endowment and operate independently. It would offer graduate and postgraduate education — studying the causes of war, teaching techniques for resolving conflicts and giving grants to others to do the same.

Its site and curriculum were to be determined by a 15-member board to be appointed by the president and confirmed by the Senate. The board would include four members of Congress and four ex-officio members — the secretaries of state and defense, the director of the Arms Control and Disarmament Agency and the commandant of the National Defense University.

Committee Action

Matsunaga and his chief ally, Sen. Jennings Randolph, D-W.Va., who had been pushing to get "peace" in the name of a federal entity for decades, tried to deflect Republican opposition during a June 15 markup. Opponents argued that the proposal was idealistic and fraught with danger. While the committee rejected one amendment that would have gutted the bill, Gordon J. Humphrey, R-N.H., raised a point of order that effectively postponed the markup until July 20.

When the committee reconvened, it adopted a number of amendments offered by Chairman Orrin G. Hatch, R-Utah, designed to make the academy "relevant" to "aid U.S. officials in becoming better negotiators against the Soviets and others."

The amendments included adding the four ex-officio members to the board, reducing site acquisition funds from $15 million to $7.5 million and permitting current employees of federal agencies such as the State Department, Defense Department and the intelligence community to be temporarily assigned to the academy staff.

A peace academy bill (HR 1249) introduced by Rep. Dan Glickman, D-Kan., had 148 cosponsors but was never reported by the House Foreign Affairs or Education and Labor committees.

Efforts in 1982 to establish a Peace Academy were unsuccessful. A Senate bill was reported (S 1889 — S Rept 97-499) but did not reach the floor. ∎

Educational Summit

Responding to a spate of reports calling for major reforms in the public schools, the House Oct. 3 passed legislation (HR 3245 — H Rept 98-396) to finance a national summit conference on education.

The bill, which was approved by voice vote by the House Education and Labor Committee Sept. 29, authorized $500,000 for a conference of education leaders to develop recommendations for federal and state legislation to improve the public schools.

The recommendations would address issues raised by the National Commission on Excellence in Education, the Carnegie Foundation for the Advancement of Teaching, the National Science Foundation and other organizations that had issued reports critical of public education.

HR 3245 set a June 15, 1984, deadline for the conference's recommendations to be submitted to the president, Congress and the states.

A 12-member bipartisan executive committee — six members named by the governors and two each appointed by the president, Speaker of the House and Senate majority leader — was authorized to select the summit conferees.

Before sending HR 3245 to the House floor, where it was approved by voice vote, the Education Committee adopted an amendment by Steve Gunderson, R-Wis., to ensure equal representation on the executive committee by requiring that the governors' appointments counterbalance any partisan tilt in the appointments made by the president and the two congressional leaders.

A similar bill (S 1495) was introduced in the Senate, but no action was taken. ∎

ECIA Amendments

Congress Nov. 18 cleared legislation (HR 1035 — PL 98-211) amending the Education Consolidation and Improvement Act (ECIA) of 1981, which included the major programs of federal aid to elementary and secondary schools.

The measure made changes designed to clarify language, resolve questions of legislative intent and eliminate drafting errors in ECIA, which was enacted as part of the 1981 budget reconciliation bill (PL 97-35). *(1981 Almanac pp. 499, 501)*

Provisions

As signed into law by President Reagan Dec. 8, HR 1035:

● Clarified ECIA language that unintentionally excluded preschool children of migratory workers from services covered by the act.

● Blocked Education Department efforts to limit eligibility for the migrant program by changing the definition of a "currently migratory child" and making other regulatory changes.

● Allowed local school districts more flexibility in administering education aid to the disadvantaged.

● Clarified an ambiguity in the 1981 education law by unequivocally extending the bilingual education program through fiscal 1984.

Legislative History

HR 1035 was reported by the House Education and Labor Committee April 7 (H Rept 98-51). The House April 12 passed the bill by voice vote under suspension of the rules, a procedure that required a two-thirds vote for passage and barred any amendments.

As approved by the House, HR 1035 not only clarified and corrected ECIA but also restored "Category B" impact aid payments to school districts around the nation. The payments, which went to districts that educated children whose parents either lived or worked on federal property, were in danger of being cut off because the authorization for them was inadvertently dropped from the hastily drafted 1981 budget reconciliation bill.

The administration had said it "strongly opposed" the impact aid provisions, which subsequently were dropped from the final version. No money was included in the fiscal 1984 budget for the payments, according to the Office of Management and Budget.

Congress had agreed in 1981 to phase out the impact aid program over three years. But due to a drafting error in the reconciliation bill, the payments were eliminated as of the end of fiscal 1983, even though the conference report on the bill stated that the payments should continue through 1984.

HR 1035 corrected that error and authorized "Category B" payments through fiscal 1984.

A similar bill (S 1008 — S Rept 98-166) amending ECIA and extending impact aid was reported by the Senate Labor and Human Resources Committee May 16. Before passing S 1008 by voice vote Aug. 4, the Senate dropped the provision extending "Category B" payments because the authorization had been included in another bill. Conferees on the defense authorization bill (S 675) raised the authorization for impact aid from $455 million to $565 million. *(Story, p. 175)*

On Oct. 7, the Senate by voice vote substituted the text of its bill for HR 1035. The conference report (H Rept 98-574) was approved by both chambers Nov. 18 by voice vote. ∎

Student Loans

Moving to block Reagan administration efforts to rewrite eligibility standards for college student aid, Congress cleared legislation requiring the Department of Education to continue using existing eligibility rules for Pell Grants and Guaranteed Student Loans (HR 3394 — PL 98-79).

However, the principal controversy during debate on HR 3394 involved provisions extending a program that allowed people to consolidate their student loans and take longer to repay them. Faced with administration opposition to a three-year extension of the program, Congress reauthorized loan consolidation only until Nov. 1, 1983.

Efforts were made to revive the program after it died Nov. 1, under a bill (HR 4350) designed to meet the administration's objections to the cost of loan consolidation. But while the House passed HR 4350 Nov. 16 by voice vote, the Senate took no action on the bill before Congress adjourned.

Provisions

As signed into law Aug. 15, HR 3394:

● Wrote into law existing income eligibility requirements for Pell Grants and Guaranteed Student Loans and extended them through the 1985-86 school year. Pell grants

were the principal government aid program for low-income students.

● Increased from $1,100 to $1,600 the living allowance for commuting students who applied for Pell Grants in 1984-85.

● Extended until Nov. 1 the authority of the Student Loan Marketing Association (Sallie Mae) to consolidate student loans. Sallie Mae was the federally chartered corporation that provided capital for student loans.

● Provided protection against discriminatory lending policies for applicants for guaranteed loans and set standard "truth in lending" requirements.

Background

Under past procedures for setting eligibility standards for Pell Grants and Guaranteed Student Loans, the Department of Education published the rules each year in the *Federal Register,* and Congress had the authority to disapprove them. Each year since the Reagan administration took office, Congress had blocked the student aid rules proposed by the Education Department — either through a resolution of disapproval or legislation setting more liberal rules. *(1981 Almanac p. 495; 1982 Almanac p. 483)*

In the wake of a 1983 Supreme Court decision striking down the legislative veto, Congress' authority to disapprove education regulations was thrown into question. *(Story, p. 565)*

The student aid rules for 1984-85 and 1985-86 were set as part of HR 3394, which was needed to extend Sallie Mae's loan consolidation authority past Aug. 1. The program had been established in an effort to reduce student loan defaults by allowing borrowers with large debts (more than $5,000 from more than one lender or more than $7,500 from a single lender) to consolidate their loans and stretch repayments over longer periods of time.

Only Sallie Mae was given the authority to consolidate loans, but Congress was under pressure to allow state loan guarantee agencies and banks to offer similar repayment plans. Private lenders and state agencies argued that if only Sallie Mae had consolidation authority, it could take away their larger loans and leave them with smaller loans that were more costly to administer.

House Commitee Action

As approved July 14 by the House Education and Labor Committee, HR 3394 (H Rept 98-324) mandated the use of existing income eligibility requirements for Pell Grants and Guaranteed Student Loans through the 1985-86 school year.

By extending the standards in place for 1983-84, Congress rejected proposals by the administration that would have involved a major shift in who would be eligible for aid. The House Education and Labor Committee estimated that 100,000 students eligible for Pell Grants would have become ineligible, and they would have been replaced by about 100,000 students who currently did not qualify for the programs.

The committee bill also increased the commuter allowance for Pell Grant applicants from $1,100 to $1,600 for the 1984-85 school year and to $2,100 for 1985-86. The allowance, for students who did not live at home or in approved university housing, was part of a formula used to determine students' cost of attending college.

As approved by the committee, HR 3394 would have extended Sallie Mae's loan consolidation authority to Sept. 30, 1986, and allowed private lenders and state loan guar-

antee agencies to consolidate loans as well.

Before approving the bill, the committee adopted an amendment by James M. Jeffords, R-Vt., allowing states to use tax-exempt bonds to make consolidation loans. The amendment limited total consolidation loans to 15 percent of a state's tax-exempt portfolio.

Floor Action

HR 3394 was passed by the House Aug. 1, after last-minute objections by the Office of Management and Budget (OMB) forced a hasty amendment affecting loan consolidation.

OMB Director David A. Stockman objected to the bill in a telephone call the morning of Aug. 1 to Rep. John N. Erlenborn, Ill., ranking Republican on the Education Committee. Stockman argued that the cost of consolidating the loans was unacceptable. OMB's last-hour intervention drew complaints from Democrats and Republicans in both chambers.

In the face of administration opposition and because existing consolidation authority expired Aug. 1, House committee members amended the bill before floor action to extend Sallie Mae authority only until Nov. 1, 1983. They also dropped provisions allowing state guarantee agencies and private lenders to consolidate loans.

As amended, HR 3394 was passed by the House by voice vote Aug. 1 and approved the next day by the Senate, also by voice vote. A minor Senate amendment — which dropped the provision increasing the Pell Grant commuter allowance to $2,100 in 1985-86 — was accepted by the House Aug. 3, clearing the bill.

Later Action

In an effort to revive the loan consolidation program after it expired Nov. 1, the House Nov. 16 passed a bill (HR 4350) to extend Sallie Mae's authority through fiscal 1986.

HR 4350, passed by voice vote under suspension of the rules, included technical changes designed to meet the administration's earlier objections to the cost of loan consolidation.

The bill gave commercial banks — but not state loan guarantee agencies — authority to consolidate loans. ∎

Saccharin Ban Deferral

President Reagan April 22 signed into law a bill (S 89 — PL 98-22) extending for two years a qualified prohibition on government action against saccharin, the artificial sweetener linked in controversial research to cancer in laboratory animals.

It was the third extension of the prohibition since Congress in 1977 blocked the Food and Drug Administration (FDA) from barring the use of the non-caloric sweetener in the nation's food supply. *(1977 Almanac p. 495)*

The Senate Labor and Human Resources Committee reported S 89 March 23 (S Rept 98-32), and the Senate passed it April 5 by voice vote without debate. The House, without committee action, accepted the Senate bill by voice vote April 13, clearing it for the president.

The bill simply changed the expiration date of the moratorium on FDA action against saccharin, extending it for two years from the date of enactment. The existing law (PL 97-42) was due to expire Aug. 14, 1983.

S 89 left intact requirements that saccharin-sweetened

products, and stores selling them, display health warnings. It also continued authority for studies of the health effects of the substance.

Labor and Human Resources Chairman Orrin G. Hatch, R-Utah, sponsor of the legislation, pointed out that the measure did not bar the FDA from acting "should information become available demonstrating a public health risk from continued use of saccharin." The moratorium applied only to FDA regulations based on old saccharin data, from before 1978, he said.

Hatch noted that new information could be produced from two large-scale animal studies on the safety of saccharin, in progress at the time the bill was passed. "These studies were intended to address numerous questions raised in previous studies, particularly the relevance of past research findings on animals," he said.

Hatch said his support for an extension of the moratorium on FDA action did not mean he had concluded that saccharin was either safe or unsafe for human consumption. But until there are good alternatives or until "saccharin is shown unsafe, we should all be allowed to make personal judgments concerning its use," he said.

Original Ban Proposal

The FDA in 1977 proposed to ban the use of saccharin in processed foods and drinks, while permitting its continued sale to consumers who wanted to add it to food themselves for medical reasons.

The proposal was based on research findings that linked the sweetener to bladder cancer in animals. The "Delaney clause" of federal food law prohibited the use of food additives that had been shown to cause cancer in animals or man.

Soft-drink manufacturers, consumers and others strongly objected to the FDA proposal and ridiculed the research on which it was based. Congress blocked FDA action then, and renewed the moratorium in 1979 and again in 1981. *(1981 Almanac p. 495)*

Each time, sponsors said they would prefer to overhaul the basic federal food safety law so that future exceptions for saccharin would not be needed. But no action was taken on the basic safety law.

Hatch characterized the long-running saccharin controversy as "one illustration of the inflexible and inconsistent nature of our food safety laws." ∎

Drug, Alcohol Abuse

Congress in April approved a two-year authorization of federal research and information programs on alcoholism and drug abuse. The non-controversial measure (S 126 — PL 98-24) passed the Senate April 5 and the House April 13, both by voice vote.

The legislation was similar to a bill that failed to win final approval during the 97th Congress. The 1982 measure (HR 6458) was burdened with a controversial House amendment to extend the health planning system — absent from the 1983 bill. Sponsors with differing views on health planning had worked out a compromise version, but time ran out before 1982 action could be completed. The alcohol and drug abuse programs were funded by the continuing resolution (PL 97-377). *(1982 Almanac p. 238)*

S 126, reported by the Senate Labor and Human Resources Committee March 21 (S Rept 98-29), authorized

$33.5 million in fiscal 1983 and $45.8 million in fiscal 1984 for research and other activities of the National Institute on Alcohol Abuse and Alcoholism, plus $47.4 million in 1983 and $56.2 million in 1984 for activities of the National Institute on Drug Abuse. There was no House committee action on the bill.

The bill also consolidated certain reporting requirements for the two institutes and the White House Office on Drug Abuse Policy; created a top-level position to promote drug and alcohol abuse prevention activities in the two institutes and in the National Institute of Mental Health; and established new procedures for peer review and for dealing with fraud or other scientific misconduct by investigators supported by grants from the institutes. ∎

Education for Handicapped

Legislation reauthorizing major federal programs supporting education and vocational training for the handicapped cleared Congress Nov. 18, after a compromise was reached that ended a two-month-long logjam.

The compromise salvaged the major portions of the billion-dollar Rehabilitation Act, the basic federal aid program for vocational rehabilitation for handicapped persons, which had been stalled by partisan wrangling over House proposals.

As cleared, S 1341 (PL 98-199) reauthorized several discretionary programs that assisted states in providing education for the handicapped, and discretionary and state block grants for vocational rehabilitation of the disabled.

The final bill combined elements of bills that had dealt separately with vocational rehabilitation programs (S 1340, HR 3520) and education for the handicapped (S 1341, HR 3435).

When the Senate passed its two bills, they were relatively straightforward reauthorizations of programs with broad bipartisan support. But problems arose when the House approved a vocational rehabilitation bill (HR 3520) that added $1.6 billion in fiscal 1984 spending authority for 11 unrelated education and social services programs.

The Senate, objecting to the House additions, refused to participate in a conference on the Rehabilitation Act. The logjam was broken when members agreed to postpone until 1984 any attempt to reconcile differences on the non-rehabilitation provisions. A compromise bill cleared Congress after the basic reauthorization of the Rehabilitation Act was attached as an amendment to the bill reauthorizing handicapped education programs (S 1341).

Provisions

As signed into law by President Reagan Dec. 2, S 1341 authorized:

● **Rehabilitation Act.** $1.038 billion for fiscal 1984 and additional amounts for fiscal 1985 and 1986 for the state grant program of the Rehabilitation Act of 1973 (PL 93-112).

● $117.1 million for nine discretionary programs and "such sums as needed" for a 10th program (probably about $1 million) for fiscal 1984.

● **Education of the Handicapped.** $163.8 million for fiscal 1984, $171.6 million for fiscal 1985 and $179.6 million for fiscal 1986 for 11 discretionary programs that supported research and training activities that aided the states in administering the $1 billion state block grant program of

the Education of All Handicapped Children Act (PL 94-142).

● $200,000 for each of fiscal years 1984 through 1986 to re-establish a National Advisory Committee on the Education of Handicapped Children to review programs and laws affecting handicapped children. An earlier committee existed from 1966-1977.

Rehabilitation Act

House Committee Action. Partisan wrangling over HR 3520, ostensibly a five-year reauthorization of the popular vocational rehabilitation program, began long before the bill reached the House floor.

The dispute centered on a Democratic-backed rider to the bill that raised spending limits for a dozen education and social service programs, including grants for education of the poor, impact aid and food programs for low-income children and pregnant women.

Education and Labor Committee Chairman Carl D. Perkins, D-Ky., first proposed the authorization increases moments before the panel completed its April 20 markup of the rehabilitation reauthorization, which was originally introduced as HR 2461. Democrats viewed the increases as necessary to reverse budget cuts required by the 1981 budget reconciliation act, known as Gramm-Latta II (PL 97-35). *(1981 Almanac pp. 399, 488-501)*

The higher authorizations would allow the House to increase appropriations above the Gramm-Latta ceilings, to the targets set by the fiscal 1984 budget resolution (H Con Res. 91). *(Story, p. 435)*

But Republican critics claimed the additions would open the bill to a presidential veto, and they criticized Democratic sponsors for using the popular Rehabilitation Act as a vehicle for increasing authorizations for other, unrelated programs.

Despite those objections, the Perkins amendment was approved on an 18-9 party-line vote, and HR 2461 was ordered reported by voice vote (H Rept 98-137). But the bill failed to receive a rule allowing floor action because the committee's Republicans complained about the "non-germane" increased authorizations.

They charged that Education and Labor staffers, in making technical changes after the committee session, had actually changed the substance of the bill. Although the changes increased the length of the amendment from 67 to 386 words, Perkins insisted they were in order.

After the Rules Committee declined to issue a rule, Perkins introduced a new bill. That measure (HR 3520 — H Rept 98-298) was virtually identical to the original but the section in question became germane by being included in the bill as introduced.

The Education Committee July 14 ordered the new bill reported on a 21-9 party-line vote. In addition to raising the spending ceilings for education and social service programs, HR 3520 extended the Rehabilitation Act for five years. It authorized $1.038 billion for matching grants to states to run vocational rehabilitation programs in fiscal 1984, and additional amounts for subsequent years.

House Floor Action. During floor debate, Democrats described the bill, with its proposed increases for education aid, as a test of members' commitment to improving the schools.

"The entire education community is looking to this vote — and the president's signature of this bill — as an indicator of who is really concerned about education," Perkins said.

The bill was passed Sept. 13 by a vote of 324-79 after a GOP-backed amendment to drop the non-rehabilitation programs failed on a party-line vote of 124-283. *(Votes 316, 313, p. 94-H)*

In action on other floor amendments, the House:

● Defeated, on a standing vote of 17-37, an amendment by Judd Gregg, R-N.H., to deny federal funds authorized by the controversial section of the bill to any district without a procedure for determining functional literacy as a condition for high school graduation.

● Adopted, by voice vote, an amendment by Majority Leader Jim Wright, D-Texas, and E. "Kika" de la Garza, D-Texas, to aid school districts with a large influx of immigrants.

● Adopted, 226-174, an amendment by Carlos J. Moorhead, R-Calif., to alter the formula to allocate low-income energy assistance funds. *(Vote 314, p. 94-H)*

● Approved, by voice vote, an amendment by Pat Williams, D-Mont., to base rehabilitation services authorizations for fiscal 1985-88 on increases in the Consumer Price Index.

● Adopted, by voice vote, an amendment by John J. LaFalce, D-N.Y., to increase the authorization for the National Technical Institute for the Deaf to $28 million, up from $26.5 million.

As passed by the House, the bill included the following fiscal 1984 authorizations for non-rehabilitation programs:

Compensatory Education. $3.83 billion for education of disadvantaged children, up from $3.487 billion set by Gramm-Latta.

Impact Aid. $505 million for school districts educating children of U.S. employees, up from $475 million.

Vocational Education. $825 million, up from $735 million.

Adult Education. $112 million, up from $100 million.

Arts, Humanities. $274 million for the National Endowment for the Arts and National Endowment for the Humanities, up from $233 million.

Museum Services. $10.8 million for the Institute for Museum Services, up from $9.6 million.

Community Services. $398 million for community services block grants, up from $389 million.

Low-Income Energy Aid. $2.25 billion to help low-income people pay energy bills, up from $1.88 billion.

Child Nutrition. $1.36 billion for the supplemental food program for women, infants and children — known as WIC — up from $1.126 billion.

Handicapped Education. $1.5 billion, up from $1.018 billion.

Institute for the Deaf. $28 million, up from $26.3 million.

Senate Action

By contrast with the partisan House squabbling over HR 3520, the Senate passed a simple reauthorization of the rehabilitation programs with little controversy.

The Senate July 26 by voice vote approved a bill (S 1340 — S Rept 98-168) that authorized for fiscal 1984 more than $100 million for discretionary programs and $994 million for state grants for vocational rehabilitation. The authorization levels for fiscal 1985 and 1986 increased about 5.3 percent each year.

Although the rehabilitation authorizations in the House and Senate versions were relatively close, Orrin G. Hatch, R-Utah, chairman of the Labor and Human Resources Committee, objected to the House's addition of the

non-rehabilitation programs and refused to agree to a conference.

The deadlock was broken in the last week of the session. Key House and Senate members agreed to enact the non-controversial aspects of the bills, while postponing bargaining over the other provisions.

The vehicle chosen for enacting the key parts of the rehabilitation bill was pending legislation that extended education programs for the handicapped.

Education of the Handicapped

Senate Action. A measure extending for three years 12 discretionary programs that comprised a portion of the Education of the Handicapped Act was passed by the Senate June 27 by voice vote.

The bill (S 1341 — S Rept 98-191) extended until Sept. 30, 1986, discretionary programs that provided grants to local public and private organizations to conduct research and evaluation programs for improved methods of educating the handicapped. For those programs, S 1341 authorized $186.2 million for fiscal 1984, a $6.1 million increase over fiscal 1983. The 1985 and 1986 authorization figures were increased by about 5 percent over the previous year's total.

S 1341 also increased the authorization level set by the 1981 omnibus reconciliation act for the rest of the programs (Part B) of the Education of the Handicapped Act to $1.071 billion, from $1.017 billion, for fiscal 1984. Part B provided grants to local agencies for educating physically and mentally handicapped students.

House Action. The House Committee on Education and Labor July 26 approved a similar bill (HR 3435 — H Rept 98-410) that extended through fiscal 1987 discretionary programs for education of the handicapped. Although the Senate bill covered fiscal years 1984 through 1986, HR 3435 began with a $186 million authorization in fiscal 1985 and allowed increases of about 5 percent in each of the next two years.

Final Action

The logjam over the Rehabilitation Act was broken when the House brought its version of the handicapped education bill to the floor Nov. 17.

The House accepted an amendment by Steve Bartlett, R-Texas, adding the non-controversial portions of the vocational rehabilitation bill by voice vote.

In addition, the House accepted a committee amendment to its handicapped education bill that brought its authorizations in line with the Senate's.

After passing HR 3435 by a 415-1 vote, the House substituted its language for that of S 1341. The Senate accepted the amendments by voice vote Nov. 18, clearing the measure. *(Vote p. 487, p. 142-H)* ∎

Desegregation Aid

The House June 7 approved legislation that would take a key element of the education block grant set up by the 1981 budget reconciliation act and re-establish it as a separate program.

The bill (HR 2207 — H Rept 98-136) revived a program of aid to school systems experiencing problems as a result of school desegregation. It was one element of a campaign by House Education and Labor Committee Democrats to overturn important parts of the budget reconcilia-

tion law pushed through Congress by the Reagan administration in 1981 (PL 97-35). *(1981 Almanac p. 463)*

In acting on a reauthorization of the 1973 Rehabilitation Act (HR 2461), the House voted to raise fiscal 1984 funding limits imposed by the 1981 law on a number of education and social programs. *(Story, p. 402)*

The drive to enact a new version of the 1972 Emergency School Aid Act (ESAA) had support in the Senate as well as in the House. Republicans and Democrats from states that lost heavily from the abolition of ESAA, such as New York and Missouri, backed a companion to HR 2207 (S 1256).

However, no action was taken on S 1256 after the Senate Labor and Human Resources Subcommittee on Education held a hearing June 27.

Senate supporters had planned to introduce a modified version of S 1256 as an amendment to legislation (S 1285) reported by the Labor and Human Resources Committee to upgrade science and mathematics education, but the bill was not brought to the Senate floor before Congress adjourned. *(Story, p. 396)*

The planned amendment met with strong objections from committee Chairman Orrin G. Hatch, R-Utah, who opposed the resurrection of desegregation aid and wanted to prevent members from using the math-science bill as a vehicle for extraneous amendments.

House Action

As reported by the House Education and Labor Committee May 16, HR 2207 authorized a three-year program of grants at $100 million a year. Funds would be awarded to school districts on a competitive basis.

School systems could use the money for a variety of projects, such as setting up magnet schools or giving special training to teachers, to help them carry out desegregation plans. No funds could be used for busing students.

The House June 7 approved the bill under suspension of the rules, by a 299-120 vote. *(Vote 162, p. 52-H)*

The push for restoration of the emergency school aid program came from big-city school systems that lost substantial amounts of desegregation money after ESAA was folded into the education block grant.

The program originally was keyed to areas experiencing problems with desegregation. Over a decade, some $2.2 billion was distributed, largely to urban school systems with large numbers of minority students. Funding in fiscal 1981 was $149.2 million. *(1972 Almanac p. 389)*

In 1981, however, ESAA was one of the few major education programs to be put into a block grant. Unable to convince Congress to accept a massive education block grant, the Reagan administration settled for a compromise in which ESAA and a number of smaller programs were consolidated. *(1981 Almanac p. 499)*

That caused problems for school districts in two ways. First, the funding level for the block grant was lower than the combined funding for the individual programs. The categorical programs, including ESAA, got a total of $538 million in fiscal 1981; the block grant was funded at $483 million in 1982, according to the House committee report.

In addition, while ESAA funds were focused on racially mixed schools in large urban areas, the formula for distributing block grant funds was based on total student population. Thus, many more districts were eligible for aid under the block grant.

The result of the block grant, supporters of HR 2207 argued, was to take away desegregation funds needed by

urban schools. Schools still were eligible for block grant funds and could use the funds for integration programs, but the amount of money available was less. Buffalo, N.Y., for example, which got $6.6 million in ESAA funds in 1981, had only $1 million available for desegregation programs in 1982.

Sponsors of HR 2207 and S 1256 argued that many school systems needed extra funds, separate from the block grant, to help them implement desegregation.

But even some members sympathetic to the urban schools' plight worried about the implications of the proposed legislation for the block grant, which would be stripped of its major element if HR 2207 became law.

As four Education and Labor Republicans put it in minority views to the committee report on HR 2207: "Is re-establishment of ESAA only a first step in the dismantling of the block grant, as those who did not fare as well under the block grant funding process seek to regain federal dollars?"

The Republicans also argued that the desegregation aid had outlived its usefulness anyway. Instead of providing short-term help for schools undergoing desegregation, they said, the program had become just another form of ongoing aid to schools. ∎

Close Up Foundation

The House Oct. 21 passed a bill extending a program that provided high school students a glimpse of the work-

ings of the federal government, but no action was taken by the Senate.

The bill (HR 3324 — H Rept 98-286), which was passed 233-78, authorized $1.5 million a year in fiscal years 1983-85 for the Allen J. Ellender Fellowship program. The fellowships helped low-income students and their teachers participate in a week-long program in Washington, D.C., conducted by the Close Up Foundation. *(Vote 382, p. 114-H)*

On June 7, a similar bill reauthorizing the fellowship program and another program, the Washington Workshops Foundation, failed to receive the necessary two-thirds vote for passage under suspension of the rules. Opponents of that bill (HR 2943 — H Rept 98-138) objected to linking the two programs, and the bill failed by a vote of 230-190. HR 3324 omitted the Washington Workshops Foundation. *(Vote 165, p. 52-H)*

As passed, the legislation increased fiscal 1984 and 1985 authorizations for the Department of Education's law school clinical program to $2 million each year.

It also removed a law-related education program from the state block grant program, in which a state received a lump sum to spend for a variety of educational needs. The bill shifted the program to the secretary of education's discretionary fund and stipulated that the secretary must spend at least $500,000 a year on it.

An amendment by John N. Erlenborn, R-Ill., to keep the program under the block grants failed 136-173. *(Vote 381, p. 114-H)*

The bill had been reported June 30 by the Education and Labor Committee. ∎

Backing for Jobless Health Insurance Wanes

Legislation to create a temporary health insurance program for out-of-work Americans was passed by the House in August. But although two Senate committees also approved versions of the legislation, neither made it to the Senate floor.

A key part of a Democratic anti-recession program, the House legislation (HR 3021) was passed by a vote of 252-174 Aug. 3. It was intended to help laid-off workers who had lost their job-based health insurance, and who could neither afford private coverage nor qualify for Medicaid, the public program for the poor. *(Vote 300, p. 90-H)*

The House bill authorized $4 billion for block grants for state-administered insurance programs, and for grants for hospitals caring for large numbers of uninsured people. It also included new requirements for private, group-based health insurance to aid the jobless in future recessions.

The Senate Finance and Labor and Human Resources Committees also reported more modest block grant legislation (S 951, S 242). Sponsors encountered substantive objections and tactical problems, however, and the legislation did not come to the Senate floor.

Early in the year, when unemployment stood at double-digit highs, the notion of providing health insurance for the unemployed gained impressive support from both Democrats and prominent Republicans, including Sen. Robert Dole, R-Kan., chairman of the Finance Committee.

By June, Congress had included funds for the new program in its fiscal 1984 budget resolution (H Con Res 91). The resolution assumed spending of $350 million in

fiscal 1983, $2 billion in fiscal 1984 and $1.65 billion in fiscal 1985 for health insurance for the unemployed, with the funding contingent upon enactment of authorizing legislation. *(Story, p. 435)*

Reagan administration officials reluctantly agreed to go along, although they stipulated that Congress must explicitly provide a source of money to pay for the new program.

That stipulation became one of the major stumbling blocks to enactment. By mid-summer, momentum for the bill slowed as sponsors disagreed sharply among themselves about how to finance the new program.

Other conflicts were less visible but equally important in the failure of the bill.

Because of the emotionality of the issue, many members were reluctant publicly to object to the program. But some liberals privately worried about creating a new program at the same time that impoverished Americans were being excluded from Medicaid because of budget reductions. Conservative opponents argued that the deficit did not permit any new programs. And, although the block grant insurance program was meant only to last for two years, critics predicted that it would be difficult or impossible to keep it from continuing indefinitely.

Many of the objections surfaced in the House debate on the bill in August. By fall, the tide had turned against enactment. Unemployment statistics had improved and Congress was struggling unsuccessfully to pass budget-cutting omnibus legislation that some sponsors had hoped

would include the insurance plan. There were strong objections to a tax provision meant to provide funds for the insurance program, and sponsors repeatedly failed to persuade the Senate to include start-up funds for the program in all-purpose appropriations bills.

Background

At the time Congress began considering the legislation, most American workers with health insurance were covered by employment-based group policies, financed partially or entirely by the employer. Such coverage often continued for a short period after a worker left a job, but experts estimated that about 60 percent of group-insured workers lost coverage within 30 days after their jobs ended.

Congressional hearings began in January, when unemployment stood at a 41-year high of 10.8 percent and reached throughout both goods-producing and service industries.

Of the 12 million unemployed, 2.6 million had been out of work for 27 weeks or longer. The Congressional Budget Office (CBO) estimated that by December 1982 approximately 10.7 million Americans had lost employer-based group health coverage because of unemployment. By June, CBO was estimating that in fiscal 1984, 9.6 million persons would be without job-related health benefits. When their dependents were included in the count, some 19.1 million Americans would be uninsured, according to CBO.

Witnesses reported that hospitals and physicians in some regions of the country were turning away uninsured patients or requiring cash deposits before they would treat them. Hospitals, for their part, said they could not afford to keep treating large numbers of people who could not pay their medical bills.

Labor officials, who backed the legislative proposals, said that the unemployed particularly needed health insurance because statistics suggested that they were prone to illness. Stress and skimping on medical care were blamed for upturns in certain types of illness during recessions.

Witnesses representing business and insurance interests cautioned that insuring the unemployed would be an unwelcome new expense for businesses, and/or state and federal governments. CBO Director Alice M. Rivlin estimated that one of the more generous options, Medicare coverage for the jobless, could cost about $6 billion in fiscal 1983.

Budget director David A. Stockman outlined the administration's position at an April 27 hearing of the Senate Finance Committee. Stockman said the problem had been exaggerated and that the federal government could not afford any new programs. However, he indicated that the administration would not stand in the way if Congress were to approve new taxes to pay for additional assistance to the unemployed. "The most important principle is pay-as-you-go financing," Stockman declared.

Stockman wanted a new federal tax on employment-based health insurance plans whose value exceeded certain dollar limits. The new tax, proposed in the president's budget, would have applied only to that part of a plan above the limit. At the time, employees did not pay taxes on these benefits, and employers got a tax break on them too.

Stockman also insisted that the administration would not accept a new entitlement program, but a new block grant program might be permissible. An entitlement program guaranteed benefits to individuals who met certain

criteria. A block grant structure meant stricter control over cost since specific amounts of money would be appropriated each year for a program. Block grants also generally gave states more flexibility to decide who may qualify, and what benefits they may receive.

The last time health insurance for the unemployed came before Congress was in 1975, when unemployment reached 8.5 percent. That year, House and Senate committees approved legislation but became embroiled in disputes over jurisdiction and other matters. Those disputes reflected underlying concerns about setting precedents for national health insurance. *(1975 Almanac p. 627)*

House Action

Energy and Commerce Committee. The legislation cleared its first major hurdle May 24 when the House Energy and Commerce Committee approved an insurance bill (HR 3021 — H Rept 98-236, Part I) sponsored by Henry A. Waxman, D-Calif., chairman of the panel's Health Subcommittee. The vote was 34-8.

The committee approved a state-administered entitlement program, guaranteeing a specified package of medical benefits to all laid-off workers who met eligibility criteria. The program would expire at the end of fiscal 1986.

The measure also included new permanent standards for private employer-based group health insurance plans, requiring them to provide extended coverage for persons losing their jobs. And, it authorized grants for fiscal years 1983-86 to hospitals in areas with high unemployment and many non-paying patients.

The committee by a vote of 15-27 rejected a substitute proposed by Tom Tauke, R-Iowa, which would have substituted block grants for the entitlement program.

Officials in the National Governors' Association (NGA) had objected to a new entitlement program, saying that recession-damaged states could not come up with the matching funds that participation would require. Although the new insurance program was optional for the states, NGA officials said that the political pressures to participate would be "extraordinarily difficult" to ignore.

The bill did not include a funding mechanism. Waxman and other sponsors maintained that preliminary congressional decisions to allot funds for the program in the budget resolution meant that Congress had decided to fund the plan out of general revenues. In addition, the Energy and Commerce Committee lacked jurisdiction to write a revenue-raising section into the bill.

Ways and Means Committee. The second House panel to approve the bill, the Ways and Means Committee, did have authority to include a money-raising device in the bill, but it chose not do so. However, it did agree on a block grant insurance plan, instead of an entitlement.

The version (HR 3021 — H Rept 98-236, Part II) approved June 29 by a 21-11 vote was a compromise that Ways and Means members had worked out with Waxman. At Waxman's insistence, it retained grants to "last resort" hospitals and the new permanent requirments for employment-based group health insurance. The compromise was substituted for the Energy and Commerce text by the committee.

Before agreeing to report the bill, the Ways and Means Committee rejected an amendment by Bill Gradison, R-Ohio, to impose federal taxes on employment-based group health plans with premiums of more than $175 a month for families or $70 a month for individuals. It was the first

formal test of congressional opinion on what was a major Reagan administration tax proposal, with implications for other untaxed "fringe" benefits. Labor and business groups both opposed the new tax.

Gradison argued that the tax would yield more than enough money to pay for the new health insurance program and that it could also help curb inflation in health care costs by indirectly discouraging overuse of medical services.

The panel also rejected three amendments by Republicans that would have required or permitted the use of "means" tests to restrict eligibility for the new insurance program. Labor officials objected to means tests because they wanted laid-off workers to get medical aid without divesting themselves of their houses or other assets.

The committee bill generally limited eligibility for the new program to unemployed workers who received or who had exhausted unemployment compensation benefits.

However, to reach some of the uninsured needy who could not meet this requirement, the bill also earmarked 5 percent of federal funds for covering needy persons meeting different standards, including means tests, as set by states.

Floor Action

It was the Ways and Means version of the bill that came to the House floor Aug. 3 and was essentially passed with one minor change. The final version differed from the Ways and Means Committee bill only in that it authorized both private lawsuits and a temporary tax penalty to enforce the required changes in private group health insurance plans.

The Energy and Commerce panel had authorized the lawsuits, and the Ways and Means panel preferred the tax penalty approach. On the House floor, sponsors offered a substitute with both approaches.

The $4 billion bill, according to House Majority Leader Jim Wright, D-Texas, provided enough money to pay for nine days of hospitalization per person per year, and 10 visits to the doctor annually, for about 12.7 billion people.

Tauke, however, complained that the money would be spread too thinly to do much good.

House Provisions

As passed Aug. 3 by the House, HR 3021:

State Block Grants

● Authorized $350 million in fiscal 1983, $1.869 billion in fiscal 1984 and $1.538 billion in fiscal 1985 for block grants to states wishing to establish health services programs for jobless workers (and immediate dependents), with money allotted among states under a formula based on the number of unemployed persons in a state, the number receiving unemployment compensation (UC) benefits and the number who had exhausted benefits.

● Repealed authority for the block grants on Oct. 1, 1985.

● Required states in fiscal 1984 and 1985, as a condition of receiving federal money, to provide up to 20 percent in matching funds.

● Barred federal matching funds for a state if, after June 1, 1983, it had canceled cash or Medicaid coverage for its welfare families, or if it had dropped Medicaid coverage for children in impoverished two-parent families, or made other significant reductions in Medicaid in order to participate in the jobless insurance program.

● Permitted a state to use money from beneficiary-paid premiums to meet up to half its matching requirement.

● Permitted states, within certain limits, to determine what categories of jobless workers would qualify for health benefits. In general, states would have to design categories to cover individuals receiving unemployment compensation benefits within the previous two years. Also, states would be required to cover workers unemployed for a year or longer before including those out of work for a shorter period. Except for a special program for jobless workers outside the unemployment compensation system, workers unemployed for more than six months were covered.

● Required states to cover all individuals within a specific category and to provide the same benefits for all covered individuals; however, if there was not enough money to cover all individuals within a given category, required coverage of pregnant women and children under the age of five.

● Required states to cover eligible individuals for a year but allowed longer coverage.

● Permitted a state to change categories its program covered to limit costs of the program to available funds.

● Barred income or assets tests for eligibility for benefits except for the program for jobless workers outside the unemployment compensation system.

● Required a state to spend 5 percent of its federal funds to cover jobless workers and dependents who met medical or financial needs standards specified by the state. (This was meant to aid unemployed persons who had worked but for various reasons had not qualified for unemployment compensation.)

● Permitted states to require beneficiaries to pay premiums of no more than 5 percent of an individual's unemployment compensation benefit, or, for individuals not receiving UC benefits, 2 percent of the state's average unemployment compensation payment.

● Required states to require beneficiaries to make some out-of-pocket payments ("copayments") for services.

● Permitted states generally to decide what benefits to provide and, except for pregnancy-related and well-baby care, to limit the amount, scope and duration of services. States would be required at least to provide pregnancy-related and well-baby care, inpatient and ambulatory services.

● Permitted states to pay providers' fees or use alternative arrangements such as contracting for services. Required hospitals and others providing care for beneficiaries to accept program payments as full payment.

Private Health Plans

● Required non-public employers who employed 25 or more workers and who offered group health benefits to provide open enrollment for laid-off spouses (and family members) of covered workers and to provide 90 days of coverage after layoff for their covered workers. Extended coverage would be either the same benefits given employed workers, or 10 physician visits and nine days hospitalization. Employers would have to pay the same proportion of the cost of extended coverage as they did for covered workers.

● Required, by Jan. 1, 1985, that the employment-based plans permit laid-off workers to buy the same coverage they had while working. (This was known as a "conversion option.")

● Authorized a federal tax penalty, effective through 1986, against employers failing to meet new health insur-

ance plan requirements; also authorized private lawsuits against employers failing to comply.

Other Provisions

● Authorized grants for hospitals serving as providers of last resort for unemployed uninsured persons; provided $96 million in fiscal 1984, $77 million in fiscal 1985 and $60 million in fiscal 1986.

Senate Action

Labor and Human Resources Committee. The first panel to act in the Senate was the Labor and Human Resources Committee which, on June 22, agreed to report a jobless health insurance plan as part of a jobs bill (S 242 — S Rept 98-181).

The insurance plan, sponsored by Dan Quayle, R-Ind., provided for a three-year program of block grants to states and required changes in private, group-based health insurance. The committee adopted it without discussion, by voice vote.

The committee bill authorized $200 million in fiscal 1983, $900 million in fiscal 1984 and $700 million in fiscal 1985 for block grants to states for individuals who had been out of work for at least six months. The measure made availability of the money contingent on enactment of a separate revenue-raising bill to fund the program.

The bill generally permitted states to decide what benefits to offer, except that pregnancy care was required.

The panel also included in the jobs measure a new program of block grants for home health care services for elderly and disabled people. The grants were to become available upon the expiration of the jobless insurance program in 1986.

Finance Committee. On July 13, the Finance Committee agreed to report another block grant insurance plan (S 951 — S Rept 98-193) sponsored by Chairman Dole. Finance was the only committee to meet the administration's demand to provide a source of funds for the program. Included in its bill were two money-saving changes in Medicare, the federal medical program for the elderly. Dole said the changes would provide enough savings to offset cost of the $1.8 billion, two-year jobless health insurance program in the bill. *(Medicare, p. 391)*

Dole initially had wanted to finance the insurance plan with new taxes on employment-based group health insurance, as Stockman had advocated. But there was little support in his committee for that plan and it was not formally put to a vote.

Committee Democrats raised strong objections to the tactic of linking the unemployment insurance plan with Medicare cuts. Waxman also called the linkage unacceptable and said that Medicare changes in themselves violated budget resolution language. (The budget resolution had specified that Medicare changes should not increase costs or restrict access to medical care for beneficiaries.)

Reagan administration officials also objected to the tactic of including the Medicare savings provisions in the health insurance bill.

The Medicare sections of the committee bill would have temporarily frozen program payment rates for doctors and given permanent status to a temporary increase in the premiums paid by Medicare beneficiaries.

The Finance Committee bill also included an amendment sponsored by Lloyd Bentsen, D-Texas, that would have required states to provide Medicaid coverage for needy pregnant women during first pregnancies, if they would have qualified once their child was born.

The Senate did not act on either of the two committee bills. Plans to include the legislation in omnibus budget legislation foundered when the larger legislation itself failed to come to the floor.

There were also strong disputes over the funding mechanism, and sponsors worked through the fall, finally agreeing informally to substitute a different revenue-raiser in the insurance bill when it came to the floor. Instead of the Medicare cuts, they agreed to substitute a change in income-averaging rules for federal taxes.

But that plan drew filibuster threats from conservatives. Meanwhile, several attempts to add funds to continuing resolutions for the first year of the program failed in the Senate. ∎

Cigarette Labeling

Facing objections from the tobacco lobby, bills (HR 1824, S 772) to toughen cigarette health warning labels were reported by key committees but did not reach the House or Senate floor in 1983.

The Senate Labor and Human Resources Committee strongly endorsed a stringent new health-warning label for cigarettes June 22, after Chairman Orrin G. Hatch, R-Utah, said that industry efforts to come up with an alternative were "inadequate."

By a 14-1 vote, the panel agreed to report a Hatch-sponsored bill (S Rept 98-177) that required cigarette packages to bear the following statement: "WARNING! Cigarette smoking causes CANCER, EMPHYSEMA, HEART DISEASE; may complicate PREGNANCY; and is ADDICTIVE." The measure was reported July 13.

The language would replace the current warning that "The Surgeon General Has Determined That Cigarette Smoking Is Dangerous to Your Health."

The new label was contained in an amendment offered by Thomas F. Eagleton, D-Mo., and approved by a vote of 15-1. Eagleton's single warning of multiple problems was a substitute for the series of labels that Hatch had originally proposed. Hatch's plan involved rotating warnings of specific diseases so as to attract more attention, but industry officials said the rotation logistics would be difficult.

The bill provided statutory authority for an existing information office on smoking and health in the Department of Health and Human Services (HHS), and it required cigarette makers to disclose to HHS all the additives they used in cigarettes.

The industry, under a voluntary agreement with HHS, was currently disclosing its most-commonly used additives in an arrangement that severely restricted access to the information.

The committee action followed weeks of private meetings between industry representatives and HHS officials, which ended without an agreement on an alternative warning label.

The House Energy and Commerce Subcommittee on Health Sept. 15 approved HR 1824 (no written report) on a 10-6 vote. The legislation, proposed by Chairman Henry A. Waxman, D-Calif., would have required cigarette packaging and advertising to warn smokers that the habit caused or could cause cancer, emphysema, heart disease, miscarriages, premature births, birth weight deficiencies, addic-

tion and death.

That information, plus a statement that quitting smoking "greatly" reduced health risks, would appear in three different labels, to be rotated so as to catch smokers' attention.

The measure also mandated disclosure on packages and advertising of tar, nicotine and carbon monoxide levels of cigarettes; compelled disclosure to the HHS secretary of additives used in cigarettes; and established statutory authority for federal research and education on smoking, including explicit authority for the purchase of radio and television air time to broadcast health and smoking information.

The bill departed from Waxman's original version only in one new section stating that the health warning labels did not relieve cigarette makers of any legal liability for their products. The subcommittee approved the measure by voice vote.

Bills to require stricter health warnings on cigarettes also failed to pass the 97th Congress. *(1982 Almanac p. 499)* ∎

National Institutes of Health

Congress did not complete action on bills to reauthorize funding for the National Institutes of Health (NIH) devoted to research on cancer, heart, lung and blood diseases and to establish a new national research institute on arthritis.

Controversy over the role of Congress in setting research priorities initially blocked a House vote on a reauthorization in July.

But after months of negotiation, the House Nov. 17, by voice vote, passed a compromise bill (HR 2350) authorizing $7.6 billion through fiscal 1986 for the national institutes and other research functions. The measure also created new institutes for research on arthritis and nursing.

The Senate, however, did not take up that bill or a less costly version (S 773 — S Rept 98-110) reported May 16 by the Labor and Human Resources Committee. S 773 contained spending increases for the National Cancer Institute, the National Heart, Lung and Blood Institute, medical libraries and a research awards program. Like HR 2350, the Senate bill would create a new arthritis institute, and called for a study on the care and treatment of laboratory animals used in research.

The 97th Congress failed to take action on a reauthorization for the cancer and heart, lung and blood institutes. *(1982 Almanac p. 494)*

Provisions

As passed by the House, HR 2350:

● Authorized $7.6 billion for fiscal years 1984-86 for national cancer and heart, lung and blood institutes and certain other research activities.

● Required the NIH director to establish regular peer review procedures for all "intramural" research, which was conducted at the institutes; directed the secretary to establish standard procedures for dealing with fraud and other forms of misconduct in NIH-supported research; gave the secretary some flexibility to re-program research funds in response to public health emergencies; and directed the secretary to promote development of research methods

that could be used instead of requiring animal subjects and to conduct a study on the use of live animals in research.

● Required the institutes to focus more attention on prevention of disease, by appointing assistant directors for prevention in each institute and by establishing 25 university-based centers for research and dissemination of information on health promotion and disease prevention.

● Authorized a new National Institute of Arthritis and Musculoskeletal Disease and transferred to it existing activities relating to those diseases, together with research on skin diseases.

● Authorized a new national institute on nursing.

● Authorized grants for research on mental retardation and grants for the support of centers conducting research on Alzheimer's disease and directed institute directors to support research on neurological deficiencies involving genetic engineering and on the role of diet in kidney disease.

● Established new interagency committees on spinal cord injury and on learning disabilities; and established a new coordinating committee on lupus erythematosus.

● Established a national commission on "orphan drugs" — those that often were undeveloped by drug companies because they were for diseases so rare that the drugs did not appear to be profitable.

● Established a presidential commission on human applications of genetic engineering.

● Required recipients of NIH research funds to maintain committees to monitor the care of animals used in research.

● Prohibited NIH from supporting research on living human fetuses or infants intended for abortion or after an abortion, unless the research was directly related to improving the health of the research subject; however, permitted such research if it posed minimal risk to the subject and if the information the research would yield could not be obtained by other means.

House Action

Committee. As reported by the House Energy and Commerce Committee May 16 (HR 2350 — H Rept 98-191), the bill increased spending levels for research on cancer and disease of the heart, lungs and blood by about 15 percent in each of the fiscal years 1984-86. The 1984 authorization was about $2.3 billion, nearly half a billion dollars more than the president's budget request.

For cancer research, the authorization raised spending levels by more than 35 percent in fiscal 1984 compared to fiscal 1983.

The bill, authored by Henry A. Waxman, D-Calif., also recodified authority for the 11 NIH institutes for which there was permanent authorization. Of the 13 institutes, only the two overseeing research on cancer and the diseases of the heart, lung and blood had authorizations that included specific time and dollar limits and thus required periodic reauthorization.

The bill also sought: transfer to the NIH of two national centers for health statistics and for health services research and the National Institute on Occupational Safety and Health; priority status for such things as Alzheimer's disease, spinal cord regeneration and the role of diet therapy in the treatment of end-stage kidney disease; creation of a new arthritis institute; and new university-based research centers on kidney and digestive diseases, disease prevention and bioengineering.

Other sections of the legislation gave statutory status to existing NIH guidelines on the use of human fetuses in

biomedical research and on the care and treatment of laboratory animals. It also established a new presidential commission to study ethical questions raised by genetic engineering.

Floor. House passage of HR 2350 followed a long-running battle over the role of Congress in setting research priorities for the respected institutes.

In floor debate July 25 on the committee bill, opponents charged that the measure inappropriately exposed the institutes' research priorities to political considerations. They said that the bill's numerous directives to set up committees or otherwise highlight research on specific diseases represented pork-barrel politics.

NIH officials, the American Medical Association and the Association of American Medical Colleges all strongly opposed the directive-laden bill. They argued that diseases with high political visibility were not always scientifically "hot" and that rigid directives could squander money on less promising work while underfunding research that was ripe for development.

Backers of the bill included the American Lung Association, the American Cancer Society and the Association of Schools of Public Health. Their congressional allies contended that it was proper for elected members to have some say in how taxpayers' money should be spent on medical research. They said that Congress at times should direct NIH to conduct research on diseases or medical conditions that concerned the public but seemed neglected by the medical establishment.

The final version brought to the floor Nov. 17 still highlighted certain areas for research, but much of what had drawn opposition was omitted. Members on either side in the earlier debate — Waxman and Edward R. Madigan, R-Ill. — agreed that the final bill was acceptable. Waxman

was chairman of the Energy and Commerce Subcommittee on Health, and Madigan was its ranking minority member.

Before passing the bill, the House:

● Agreed to an amendment by William E. Dannemeyer, R-Calif., barring NIH support for research on fetuses intended for abortion or those that had been aborted, unless the research would directly benefit the subject.

● Approved an amendment by Rod Chandler, R-Wash., permitting fetal research if it would produce information that could not be obtained any other way, and if the risk to the fetus were minimal.

● Accepted a Madigan amendment to create a national institute of nursing, and an amendment by Glenn M. Anderson, D-Calif., to establish a coordinating committee on the disease lupus erythematosus.

● Rejected, by a 186-206 vote, an amendment by John D. Dingell, D-Mich., that would have transferred the National Institute for Occupational Safety and Health (NIOSH) to the National Institutes of Health, from the Centers for Disease Control. *(Vote 491, p. 142-H)*

Senate Committee Action

The Senate Labor and Human Resources Committee May 16 reported a four-year reauthorization (S 773 — S Rept 98-110) for the National Cancer Institute and the National Heart, Lung and Blood Institute. For fiscal 1984 the bill proposed funding the two institutes at about 5 percent above the president's request of $1.6 billion.

Like the House version, it also would create a new federal research institute on arthritis and require studies of alternatives to using animals in research. The Senate bill called as well for research on the health effects of nuclear energy.   ▮

Congress Clears Veterans' Health Care Bill

Congress Nov. 3 cleared legislation (HR 2920 — PL 98-160) extending Vietnam veteran readjustment counseling centers for four more years and making other changes in veterans' health care services.

Although the administration opposed several provisions, President Reagan signed the wide-ranging measure into law Nov. 21, citing his "strong commitment to the welfare of America's veterans."

The House passed HR 2920 May 23; the Senate passed its version June 28. A compromise version worked out by the Veterans' Affairs committees was approved by the House Nov. 2 and by the Senate Nov. 3, both by voice vote.

Bob Edgar, D-Pa., chief House sponsor of the bill, called it "the most sweeping veterans' legislation to come before the 98th Congress." And Alan Cranston, Calif., ranking Democrat on the Senate Veterans' Affairs Committee, noted that recent world events showed the need for improved veterans' health care. "Today's battles are creating tomorrow's VA [Veterans Administration] hospital patients," he said.

Besides extending the readjustment centers, the bill required studies on the effects of post-traumatic stress disorder, a condition affecting many Vietnam veterans and one reason for the counseling centers, and on the health effects of radiation testing on veterans who participated in nuclear weapons tests and in the cleanup of Hiroshima and

Nagasaki.

It also contained provisions aimed at reducing the long-term cost of VA health-care services by promoting preventive health care and alternatives to institutionalization, such as adult day care and community health care services.

The bill also established a new advisory committee for women veterans within the VA and expressed the sense of Congress that the VA administrator should have Cabinet-level status.

A Senate-passed provision authorizing VA payments to chiropractors was dropped from the final bill.

Background on Centers

The popular store-front readjustment counseling centers were first authorized in 1979 (PL 96-22) to help Vietnam veterans experiencing war-related emotional problems return to everyday life. *(1979 Almanac p. 522)*

In 1981, Congress extended the program until Sept. 30, 1984 (PL 97-72). *(1981 Almanac p. 481)*

The Reagan administration did not support extension of the centers then, arguing that the veterans could be treated less expensively in VA hospitals. In 1983 it again urged Congress not to pass a new authorization for the program until a task force reported on how readjustment services could best be provided.

The House-passed bill would have extended the centers for three years, the Senate bill for one year. Edgar applauded the decision to extend them for four years. "Keeping this program constantly jumping through authorization hoops impedes rather than improves service for these veterans," he said.

Provisions

As signed into law, HR 2920 (PL 98-160):

● Extended for four years, through Sept. 30, 1988, readjustment counseling centers for Vietnam-era veterans, and gave Vietnam veterans permanent eligibility for readjustment counseling.

● Required a study, with a report to Congress by Oct. 1, 1986, on the incidence, prevalence and effects of posttraumatic stress disorder and other psychological problems of Vietnam-era veterans.

● Increased per diem payments by the VA to state veterans' hospitals to approximately 30 percent of costs. The new rates were: for domiciliary care, $7.30, from $6.35; for nursing care, $17.05, from $12.10; for hospital care, $15.25, from $13.25. Also required a report to Congress every three years on the adequacy of rates; the first report was due June 30, 1986.

● Required the VA to report to Congress by Dec. 1, 1983, on long-range plans to meet the health care needs of veterans in Puerto Rico, the Virgin Islands and other territories.

● Established within the VA an Advisory Committee on Women Veterans to advise the administrator; also required the administrator to take steps to ensure that the VA was able to meet the gender-specific health-care needs of women veterans.

● Required the VA administrator to justify any disposal of real property, and submit any proposal to Congress.

● Authorized, until Sept. 30, 1988, in-house adult day health-care programs for veterans eligible for nursing home care; also clarified the VA's authority to place veterans in private VA-approved community residential care facilities.

● Authorized eligible veterans receiving health care in VA hospitals to receive certain preventive health care services. Also allowed veterans receiving care for service-connected disabilities or veterans rated 50 percent or more disabled to receive at least one preventive health care service as part of their treatment.

● Allowed the VA administrator to set pay rates and qualification standards for three groups of VA health-care personnel: licensed physical therapists, licensed practical or vocational nurses and respiratory therapists. The authority had rested with the Office of Personnel Management.

● Expressed the sense of Congress that the administrator of veterans' affairs should be designated by the president as a member of the Cabinet, and be the president's chief adviser on all matters relating to veterans.

● Required the administrator, unless he deemed it scientifically unfeasible, to provide for the conduct of an epidemiological study on the long-term adverse health effects of exposure of ionizing radiation from detonations of nuclear devices.

● Required the administrator to issue, by Jan. 1, 1984, guidelines on the payment of beneficiary travel.

If regulations were not published by that date, reimbursement would be limited to payment for persons receiving benefits for or in connection with a service-connected disability.

House Action

The House Veterans' Affairs Committee reported HR 2920 on May 13 (H Rept 98-117), and the House passed it May 23 by voice vote under suspension of the rules, a procedure that bars amendments and requires a two-thirds majority for passage.

As passed by the House, the bill reauthorized Vietnam veterans' readjustment counseling centers until Sept. 30, 1987. During the last 12 months of the program, operation of the centers would shift to VA health-care facilities.

Supporters of HR 2920 argued that a three-year extension of the centers was needed because an increasing number of Vietnam-era veterans were experiencing war-related flashbacks, nightmares and psychological trauma. In addition, many former service members and their families were being seen by the veterans' center teams for the first time and could require extended treatment.

During fiscal 1983 the 136 centers in operation had about 80,000 visits from Vietnam-era veterans.

The House bill also required the VA to conduct a comprehensive study of the readjustment of Vietnam veterans to civilian life, and a survey of the health status of Vietnam veterans compared to that of the general population, both due by Dec. 31, 1985.

It also called for the establishment of an Advisory Committee on Women Veterans to advise the VA on how to provide medical care for women veterans, including gender-related care such as gynecological services, which were not available at all VA medical centers.

Although women comprised only about 2.5 percent of all veterans, proponents of the bill noted that the number was growing and women veterans already were making increasing demands on acute, nursing and intermediate care programs.

The House bill also revised procedures for the disposal of excess real property owned by the VA. This provision was designed to prevent the transfer of VA property that might be needed within the next 20 to 25 years to provide for the health care needs of an aging veteran population.

Senate Action

The Senate passed HR 2920 June 28 by voice vote after substituting the text of a bill (S 578) reported by the Veterans' Affairs Committee May 23 (S Rept 98-145).

The Senate bill extended the psychological counseling centers for Vietnam-era veterans until Sept. 30, 1985, and required the VA to evaluate the program and report to Congress by March 1, 1985, on whether it would be needed in the future.

It authorized the VA to pay the bill for women veterans who visited private physicians for gender-related medical care such as gynecological services, if such treatment was not available at VA medical facilities. This provision was included in response to complaints from women veterans that the VA health care program was male-oriented and did not serve their needs.

The Senate bill gave the VA authority to reimburse veterans who sought private adult day care and to set up a pilot project for a similar VA program. The Veterans' Affairs Committee expressed concern about rising VA health care costs as World War II veterans grew older and required additional medical and nursing home care; the day care provisions were designed to provide a less costly alternative to VA hospitalization or nursing homes.

The Senate bill also:

● Clarified provisions of a 1981 law (PL 97-37) to make it easier for prisoners of war suffering from depressive neurosis, a stress-related psychological disorder, to receive disability benefits. *(1981 Almanac p. 472)*

● Limited to $71.2 million the amount the VA could spend in fiscal 1984 to reimburse veterans for travel expenses to receive VA medical care. The committee said the VA should limit travel reimbursement to those who must travel a great distance, were gravely disabled or needed particularly expensive transportation, such as specially outfitted vans, in order to receive VA care. The administration had requested $91.2 million for beneficiary travel.

● Established a VA Advisory Committee on Women Veterans to advise the VA administrator on women veterans' benefits, including health care, pensions and compensation.

● Authorized reimbursement of certain veterans for up to $400 a year for private chiropractic services. The VA already had authority to pay for chiropractic services but rarely did so, primarily because VA physicians seldom recommended the treatment.

● Raised the per diem amount that states charged the VA for housing veterans in state residence homes by 15 percent, effective April 1, 1984. States could raise the daily charge to $7.30, $13.95 or $15, depending on the level of care required for the individual patient.

● Expressed Senate interest in elevating the administrator of the VA to Cabinet-level position.   ∎

Hunger Reports Prompt Food Aid Expansion

Responding to numerous reports of hunger among needy Americans, Congress ordered the secretary of agriculture to donate surplus federally-owned commodities to soup kitchens and other charitable groups feeding the poor.

The legislation ordering the distribution also provided $50 million a year through fiscal 1985 to help pay the costs of distribution and provided additional funds for processing the commodities.

Congress initially passed the commodity distribution legislation as part of a major jobs bill (PL 98-8) that cleared Congress March 24. Then the Senate and House by voice vote passed a two-year extension of the program Aug. 4, as part of an unemployment compensation bill (HR 3409 — PL 98-92). *(Jobs, p. 447; unemployment, p. 274)*

The stories of hunger had come initially from soup kitchens and other emergency feeding centers. As unemployment peaked late in 1982, the centers began reporting massive increases in the number of people turning to them for food, and their reports received wide media coverage.

Local charities and elected officials, and Washington-based anti-poverty groups blamed the increases on the combined impact of the recession and Reagan-era cutbacks in the growth of food stamps and other aid programs for the poor.

Reagan administration officials responded that the federal government was spending more than ever on food aid — $18.6 billion in fiscal 1983. They maintained that the hunger reports were exaggerated. *(Food programs, p. 414)*

The jobs measure that was the original vehicle for the food donations legislation covered only fiscal 1983. As soon as it passed, sponsors focused on similar House and Senate bills (HR 1590, S 17) to continue the donations program through fiscal 1985.

The House June 16 passed the stronger of the two bills (HR 1590), sponsored by Rep. Leon E. Panetta, D-Calif. Panetta was chairman of the House Agriculture Subcommittee on Domestic Marketing, Consumer Relations and Nutrition with jurisdiction over food stamps.

Until early August, however, the Reagan administration objected to extending the donations program past the Sept. 30 expiration date. Senate action on S 17 was delayed by Agriculture Committee Chairman Jesse Helms, R-N.C., who, like the administration, questioned the wisdom of making the food donation program more than a temporary entity.

But the hunger issue continued to receive attention in the media and in Congress. On Aug. 2, when poverty was reported at a 19-year high and when several vivid reports on hunger had been televised nationally, President Reagan ordered a "no holds barred" study of the hunger reports.

Two days later, on Aug. 4, Congress unexpectedly cleared a compromise version of S 17 that closely resembled the language in the jobs bill. The compromise had been negotiated with Helms, Senate sponsor Robert Dole, R-Kan., budget director David A. Stockman, and Panetta. It was included in HR 3409, the unemployment compensation bill.

During the year, Congress also expressed its concern by passing anti-hunger resolutions and by including $450 million for modest food stamp expansions in the fiscal 1984 budget resolution (H Con Res 91). That allotment was in a contingency fund, to be made available if Congress passed legislation authorizing the changes.

However, Congress passed neither the expansions nor any of the $1.1 billion worth of money-saving cuts in food stamps that the president's fiscal 1984 budget had requested. (The budget estimated that the food stamp program would cost $10.9 billion in fiscal 1984, assuming those changes were made.)

Members who wanted more food aid for the needy decided not to press for the food stamp expansions because they did not want to provoke counter-moves by Helms and like-minded members to push the president's budget cuts.

Late in the year, the House passed legislation (HR 4091) that would let more children qualify for federally-subsidized meals, and cut the prices that needy children paid for the food. The bill, which altered eligibility levels and authorized funding for school lunch and other child nutrition programs, restored about a tenth of the $1.5 billion that Congress had cut from the programs in 1981. The Senate did not act on the measure. *(Story, p. 417)*

Provisions

As signed into law Sept. 2, HR 3409 (PL 98-92) included the following provisions relating to commodity distribution:

● Established a two-year program in which the secretary of agriculture was required to make available for distribution commodities acquired by the Commodity Credit Corporation (CCC) that the secretary determined were not

obligated for other programs. Repealed the donations program, except for criminal penalties for misuse, on Sept. 30, 1985.

(The CCC was the Agriculture Department agency that managed farm price support programs and held the commodities acquired through these programs.)

● Specified that eligible recipients, if approved by states and/or the secretary, were: public and non-profit organizations that provided emergency food aid to the poor, including unemployed individuals; school lunch, summer camp and other child nutrition programs providing food service; nutrition projects for the elderly; projects of charitable institutions serving the needy; and disaster relief programs.

● Authorized the CCC to pay for initial processing or packaging of the commodities for institutional or home use before distribution.

● Authorized use in the program of up to 300,000 metric tons of wheat from the international emergency food reserve and required that the reserve be replenished before Oct. 1, 1985. Permitted CCC stocks to be used to replenish the reserve but, if purchases were needed to replenish, required that the purchases be made with appropriated funds.

● Directed the secretary to arrange for private companies to process donated commodities into forms suitable for home or institutional use, with processing expenses to be paid by agencies receiving the commodities.

● Required prompt distribution of commodities by the secretary to designated state agencies or directly to eligible recipient organizations, and prompt redistribution by states; provided that if recipient organizations' requests to a state for a specific commodity exceeded supplies, the state must give priority to organizations providing emergency food aid.

● Required states to determine which individuals were needy enough to qualify for free commodities for household use.

● Directed the secretary to act as needed to assure that organizations receiving the commodities not reduce their other expenditures for food, and to assure that the commodity donations not disrupt commercial sales.

● Prohibited agencies from receiving more commodities than they could use, with use determined by such factors as inventory records and storage capacity.

● Authorized $50 million annually, through fiscal 1985, for distribution to states for storage and distribution costs associated with the commodity donations; earmarked at least 20 percent of that amount each year for redistribution to local soup kitchens and other organizations providing emergency food aid to the needy and unemployed, to help defray their costs.

● Specified that the value of donated commodities and expenditures for processing not be deducted from appropriations made under this authorization.

● Suspended, for the donated commodities, a prohibition against the use of surplus commodities in jurisdictions where food stamps were available.

● Generally prohibited the sale of donated commodities.

● Stipulated that commodities distributed in the program not be counted as income or assets under federal, state or local laws.

● Authorized criminal penalties for fraudulent misuse of program commodities.

● Required publication, by specific deadlines, of the types and quantities of commodities to be made available in the program.

Background

The legislation was meant to respond to problems of emergency "pantries" and other charitable organizations that were providing hot meals (and, often, shelter) or groceries for the needy. A number of volunteer-staffed groups said their budgets were so limited that they could not afford to take the free surplus cheese that the administration had begun handing out late in 1981. They said they lacked money for storage, transportation and similar expenses, and that it was difficult to accept the commodities in bulk, without repackaging or processing into more usable forms.

There also were complaints that the Agriculture Department was rejecting requests for other surplus foods, such as dry milk, honey and wheat.

The stories of hunger surfaced at a time when American farmers had produced massive surpluses of dairy goods and grains, much of which was either owned by or obligated to federal price support programs. (The programs generally provided loans to farmers, who used stocks as collateral. If a farmer defaulted on the loan, the government became the owner of the collateral. In the case of the dairy program, the government bought all surplus dairy products, in the form of cheese, dry milk and butter, that dairymen could not sell at the market price established by the program.)

The federal government had, for decades, donated surplus commodities to schools and other institutions with food services. The administration had initiated the cheese distribution in December 1981, partially to reduce the dairy surplus and partially in response to stories of need.

Stream of Reports

By the beginning of 1983 there was a steady stream of news stories depicting hunger and hard times in cities and suburban neighborhoods. The main sources for the stories were churches and other charitable organizations running food programs for the needy, and mayors and advocacy groups, such as the Food Research and Action Center (FRAC) based in Washington.

They said that emergency food centers were being overwhelmed with growing demands for food and that the food was going not only to the derelicts who had always come to the centers but also, for the first time, to whole families. The families were said to include the "newly poor" — those who had lost their jobs — and those whose food stamps did not last until the end of the month.

Also, some centers said they were feeding more old people because Medicare changes were forcing them to devote more money to medical bills, leaving less for food.

FRAC produced a widely publicized report in January that showed worsening infant mortality rates in seven states and 34 rural and urban areas between 1980 and 1981. Health experts considered poor nutrition during pregnancy to be a contributing factor to infant mortality. The FRAC report, based on a telephone survey by the organization, was criticized by administration officials who said that the data was not statistically reliable.

Congressional Concern

The news stories were followed by congressional hearings, including a series of hearings outside Washington by Panetta's subcommittee, whose members also visited local food centers.

Panetta said he had begun the year with some skepticism about the hunger reports. By the time the House

Federal Food Assistance Programs . . .

	FY83 Budget	Number Served	Benefit	Eligibility
Food Stamps Provides coupons redeemable for foods in grocery stores.	$12 billion*	21.9 million	Average monthly benefit per person is $42.67.	Income cannot be over 130 percent of the poverty line ($12,090 for a family of four).
School Lunch Government-subsidized lunches to children in schools	$3 billion	22.9 million children	3.7 billion school lunches to be served in fiscal 1983. Government gives schools $1.26 for each lunch served free to very needy children; 86 cents for lunches served at a reduced price to needy children (cost to the child cannot exceed 40 cents); 22 cents for lunches served to all other children (approximate cost to the child is 85 cents).	Free lunches served to children from families with income at 130 percent of poverty or below ($12,090 a year for a family of four). Reduced price lunches served to children from families at 185 percent of poverty or below ($17,210 a year for family of four). All other children are eligible for subsidized lunches regardless of income.
School Breakfast Government-subsidized breakfasts to children in schools.	$327 million	3.4 million children	553 million breakfasts to be served in fiscal 1983. Government gives schools 60 cents for each breakfast served free; 30 cents for reduced-price breakfasts (cost to the child cannot exceed 20 cents); 8 cents for breakfasts served to all other children (approximate cost to the child is 40 cents).	Same as for school lunch programs.
Nutrition Education Provides nutrition education for children, teachers and school food service people.	$7 million	3 million children 118,000 teachers 60,000 school food service people	Funds assist in the development of nutrition education curriculum and training.	Funds are allocated to state departments of education based on the number of children in each state.
Summer Food Program Provides a lunch to children in needy areas in summer when school is not in session	$99 million	1.4 million children	Free lunches to all children in the area; 70 million lunches to be served in fiscal 1983.	Program operates in areas in which at least 50 percent of the children served are eligible for free lunches.
Child-Care Food Program Provides federal money for meals served to children in day-care centers.	$334 million	1 million children	Free lunches, snacks, breakfasts and dinners. The amount of cash assistance to the day-care center varies according to the family size and income of children served.	Child-care institutions that are licensed or approved to provide child-care services.

debated HR 1590 in June, he was telling his colleagues, "This country faces a very serious problem with regard to hunger."

Everywhere, he said, the subcommittee "heard the same story. The use of soup kitchens, food pantries and hunger centers is up dramatically in the past two years, in some areas by 400 to 500 percent."

As the House debated the bill, the U.S. Conference of Mayors presented a report on hunger in eight cities to the Senate Agriculture Subcommittee on Rural Development, Oversight and Investigations chaired by Mark Andrews, R-N.D.

That report said, "Although there are several emergency problems of concern to the mayors at this time, hunger is probably the most prevalent and the most insidious."

The number of people, including families with children, "who have little or nothing to eat, have grown tremendously." it said.

City officials agreed, according to the report, that unemployment was the primary cause of increased hunger but contributing factors included cuts in federal funds, high shelter and energy costs, and increased numbers of transients failing to find work.

. . . Serving Millions, Costing Billions

	FY83 Budget	Number Served	Benefit	Eligibility
WIC Provides monthly food packages to pregnant women, infants and young children.	$1.16 billion	2.5 million	Provides vouchers for monthly food packages worth approximately $28. Foods include formula for infants, infant cereal, cheese and milk.	Pregnant and breastfeeding women, children up to four years old. Family's income must be at or below 185 percent of the poverty line ($17,210 for a family of four). There must also be some indication of nutritional need, such as anemia or history of low-birthweight babies.
Commodity Supplemental Food Program Provides monthly food packages to pregnant women and young children. Similar to WIC, but provides the actual food instead of a voucher and distributes a greater variety of food than is available through WIC.	$32 million	135,000	Monthly food package worth approximately $28 per month.	Pregnant and breastfeeding women and children up to five years old. Same income criteria and nutritional criteria as WIC.
Special Milk Program Provides cash assistance to states to reimburse schools, child-care institutions and summer camps for milk served to children.	$20 million	No figure given; 210 million half-pints a day.	Half-pints of milk at a reduced price or free.	Program restricted to institutions that do not use another federal food program.
Food Distribution Provides commodities for programs above, plus these two:				
Commodities on Indian reservations:	$52 million	Approximately 90,000	Food package worth approximately $37.78 a month.	At the request of the tribal organization.
Elderly Feeding Program:	$100 million	184 million meals	Free and reduced-price meals for people in senior-citizen centers or homebound elderly. Cost to recipient depends on the center's ability to supplement the federal reimbursement, which is 54 cents per meal.	

* Includes $1.2 billion supplemental request.   Source: U.S. Department of Agriculture Food and Nutrition Service

Administration Response

Reagan administration officials and their congressional allies maintained throughout the year that the reports of hunger were greatly overstated and that federal food programs were adequate.

In a strongly worded speech in February, budget director Stockman called the FRAC report "absolutely, totally and completely untrue."

The administration's basic argument was that the federal government was spending significantly more on food aid for the needy than ever before and the people excluded from aid programs because of budget cuts were not truly needy.

When queried about the apparent upturn in the use of emergency food centers, administration officials usually suggested that the centers' new clients were taking advantage of giveaways that they did not really need. And they dismissed the stories as insignificant "anecdotes."

In May, concerned by complaints from the cheese industry that the giveaways had cut into commercial sales, the Agriculture Department sharply reduced its cheese distribution.

That decision was later reversed. But in July, Dole chaired a hearing of his Senate Agriculture Subcommittee on Nutrition that focused on the so-called "market displacement" by the free cheese, and other problems in the donations program.

Witnesses told the panel that "greedy" senior citizens were collecting more free cheese than they were supposed to get or than they could eat. Testimony suggested that the dual purpose of the giveaways — to pare down surpluses while helping the hungry — may have led to some initial confusion and laxness in state programs. Witnesses also said that the program had helped the poor.

Wrangling Continues

On Aug. 2, the Census Bureau reported that 15 percent of Americans were living below the poverty level — the highest percentage since 1965 when President Johnson launched his "war on poverty." The poverty level was defined as cash income of less than $9,862 for a family of four.

The same day, Reagan, in a memorandum to presidential Counselor Edwin Meese III, said he was "perplexed" and "deeply concerned" about the hunger reports. The memorandum called for establishment of a study group — subsequently known as the President's Task Force on Food Assistance — to look into the allegations. "If certain aspects of our food assistance programs require more funding, I want to know that too," Reagan wrote.

Meese himself was deluged with criticism in December when he expressed doubts about the extent of reported hunger problems. He said that given the economic upturn and the efforts of federal and state governments and voluntary groups, "if people are going hungry, there must be some problem that's not been addressed, and it isn't the lack of funds."

Meese suggested that some allegations of hunger were "purely political" and that "there may be situations in which there are hungry people," but he had not seen any "authenticated accounts" of hungry people. Meese also observed that "we've had considerable information that people go to soup kitchens because the food is free and that's easier than paying for it."

Task Force Report

The presidential task force Jan. 9, 1984, reported that "allegations of rampant hunger simply cannot be documented." It said that based on testimony it heard, "We cannot doubt that there is hunger in America." However it maintained that there was "no evidence that widespread undernutrition is a major health problem in the United States."

Its major recommendations included allowing states to drop out of the food stamp and other federal food programs and to receive a block grant instead. The proposal drew immediate fire from the National Governors' Association, the U.S. Conference of Mayors, the National Association of Counties and advocates of the poor. They insisted that food aid was a national responsibility and that the proposed grants would be the first step in dumping that responsibility onto state and local governments.

Other recommendations included stiffening the penalties against states that failed to bring their food stamp error rates down to the level mandated by law. It also suggested modest increases in the assets a food stamp recipient could own and in the maximum food stamp allotment, and called for improved collection of nutrition data.

Senate Action

The Senate Agriculture Committee on March 3 approved S 17 (S Rept 98-21). It included the two-year mandate for the secretary to distribute CCC stocks that were found not to be needed for other programs. It differed from the final bill in several respects; most conspicuously, it did not have the $50 million a year authorization for distribution costs. There also were limits on the amount of CCC expenditures devoted to processing and other program costs — $100 million a year, plus an amount equal to the projected costs of commodity storage or spoilage. Those limits did not include the value of the donated commodities, however.

House Action

Two House committees reported similar, stronger versions of the legislation. First, the House Education and Labor Committee, which had jurisdiction over child nutrition programs, reported a bill (HR 1513 — H Rept 98-39) on March 18. That measure ordered the distribution of all unobligated surplus CCC stocks within 60 days of enactment. It also required the federal government to bear the full costs of processing the commodities.

To finance transportation and other administrative costs, the bill required expenditure of so-called "Section 32 funds," which were customs receipts earmarked for agriculture and food programs. State agencies receiving these funds would have been required to pay transportation, storage and other costs of the local agencies distributing the food. In cases where the federal government supplied the commodities directly to the distributing agencies, the federal government would have been required to pay transportation and similar costs.

The bill was referred to the House Agriculture Committee, which then reported a similar version on May 16 (HR 1590 — H Rept 98-148).

Both House bills sought to bypass the appropriations process for the distribution costs — and thereby assure that the money would be available even if the administration opposed the program and refused to request the money later. (Appropriations committees generally resisted appropriating money that had not been explicitly requested in the president's budget.)

The Education and Labor bill specified that the Section 32 funds would be used for that purpose, while the Agriculture Committee bill directed that $50 million a year of CCC funds be used.

Establishing an authorization for this money — thereby requiring an appropriation — was one of the major changes in the final version.

Agriculture Bill Passed

When the Agriculture Committee bill came to the House floor June 16, there was little debate, and it passed by a vote of 389-18. *(Vote 189, p. 58-H)*

The House approved an amendment to assure that a special wheat reserve for international emergencies would be replenished, if it were used for the domestic donations. It also adopted an amendment, sought by the Education and Labor panel, specifying that once money and food needs of emergency feeding centers had been met, the rest of a state's money and food generally could be distributed to other, non-emergency organizations that were eligible, such as schools.

Health Emergency Fund

A new $30 million fund to help federal agencies deal quickly with health emergencies such as the spread of acquired immune deficiency syndrome (AIDS) was signed into law July 13.

The measure (HR 2713 — PL 98-49) established a revolving fund and authorized $30 million for fiscal 1984 and such sums as necessary each year thereafter to bring the fund back to that level.

The money was intended to let such agencies as the Centers for Disease Control and the National Institutes of Health respond to public health emergencies without diverting funds from their other programs. The legislation was a response particularly to the outbreak of AIDS and the 1982 cyanide contamination of Tylenol.

The bill was enacted despite the objections of Health and Human Services Secretary Margaret M. Heckler, who had said that, in the case of AIDS, the extra funds were unneeded. But her predecessor, Richard S. Schweiker, had proposed a $20 million fund.

Legislative History. HR 2713 was approved May 12 by the House Energy and Commerce Committee and reported May 16 (H Rept 98-143). In its original version, the bill called for $40 million in emergency funding, but Health Subcommittee Chairman Henry A. Waxman, D-Calif., agreed to reduce the authorization to $30 million to gain Republican support. It was passed by the House June 13 by voice vote.

The Senate passed HR 2713 June 28, also by voice vote, bypassing committee consideration to expedite the program's implementation. The Senate vote cleared the measure for the president. ∎

Child Food Aid

The House in October voted to let more children qualify for federally subsidized meals and to cut the prices that needy children pay for the food, but the Senate did not act on the legislation before adjournment.

Critics warned that President Reagan would veto the bill (HR 4091), but the House Oct. 25 voted 306-114 to pass it. The bill altered the eligibility levels and authorized funding for school lunch and other child nutrition programs, restoring about one-tenth of the $1.5 billion that Congress had cut from the programs in 1981. *(Vote 387, p. 114-H; 1981 Almanac p. 497)*

The Congressional Budget Office (CBO) estimated that HR 4091 would add $105.5 million to program spending in fiscal 1984 for 10 months, and $160 million in fiscal 1985. The current total program costs under existing law were $3.4 billion annually.

Much of the bill, sponsors said, was meant to restore food aid to children of the "working poor." Many in this category had been dropped because of restrictions enacted in 1981.

A similar bill (S 1913) had been introduced in the Senate. However, the Senate Agriculture Committee did not schedule action on the measure. The chairman of the committee, Jesse Helms, R-N.C., continued to contend that food programs financed by the government should be tightened further.

Administration Objections

The Reagan administration argued that new spending was unwarranted and that the 1981 budget cuts had not hurt impoverished children. Budget director David A. Stockman wrote to House members that the administration had promised "that no needy child would be deprived of nutrition benefits" and "that promise has been kept."

But cosponsor Bill Goodling, R-Pa., in debate Oct. 24 called Stockman's claim "sheer hogwash." Goodling and Carl D. Perkins, D-Ky., chairman of the House Education and Labor Committee, said that many of the nation's most needy children had lost federally subsidized meals as an indirect result of the 1981 cuts.

A major goal of the cuts was sharp reductions in the number of middle-class children in the programs; but a growing number of schools found that without middle-class students making partial payments for the food, they could not afford to run food programs at all. So, Goodling argued, poor children had remained eligible for food programs that often had gone out of existence.

Moreover, of the approximately 3.5 million children disqualified from the school lunch program as a result of the 1981 changes, close to one million were poor, Goodling said.

Incensed by an apparent change in administration policies, Goodling said he had been assured by both the president's counselor (Edwin Meese III) and the White House congressional liaison office that there would be no administration objections to the bill. "I do not appreciate having the rug pulled out from under me," he snapped.

He stressed that the fiscal 1984 budget resolution had allotted money for the child nutrition restorations and disputed arguments that families with incomes slightly above the poverty level did not need subsidized food aid. An annual income of $19,305 — a new eligibility level set by the bill for school lunches — did not mean affluence, once taxes, shelter, health and energy costs were subtracted, he said.

The Education and Labor Committee had approved HR 4091 on Oct. 6. The bill came to the floor without a formal committee report, under suspension of the rules, to avoid a point of order. The budget resolution had made the spending of the additional child nutrition funds contingent upon enactment of legislation to reduce the cost of the federal pension insurance program. However, the panel had not completed that legislation.

Provisions

As passed Oct. 25 by the House, HR 4091:

• Lowered the cost to a student of a reduced-price lunch to 25 cents, from 40 cents, and of a reduced-price breakfast to 15 cents, from 30 cents.

• Raised the income standard determining a student's eligibility for reduced-price meals to 195 percent of the federal poverty level, from 185 percent. The change set the income eligibility standard at $19,305 for a family of four, instead of $18,315.

• Increased by 6 cents the existing per-child, per-meal subsidy for school breakfasts and required new federal regulations to improve the nutritional quality of the meals. The existing subsidy ranged from 9 cents to 75.5 cents, with the higher rates applying to meals for especially needy children.

• Allowed private schools charging annual tuitions of $2,500 or less to participate in the school lunch program.

Existing law limited eligibility to schools charging $1,500 or less.

● Authorized funds for an additional meal and snack per child per day, in the child-care program. That restored the daily total to three meals and two snacks, as before 1981.

● Raised to $7.5 million, from $5 million, the annual authorization for the nutrition education and training program, for fiscal 1984 only.

● Authorized a hardship deduction for unusually high medical expenses in determining eligibility of families for free or reduced-price meals.

● Repealed a requirement that the income eligibility standard for free meals be the same as the standard for food stamps, currently 130 percent of the federal poverty level of $12,870 for a family of four. That meant that future changes in the food stamp eligibility standard would not automatically change the free meal standard.

● Ended a 1981 ban on the use of the special milk program in schools also participating in a federally subsidized meal program, for kindergarten children only. ∎

Child Support Payments

The House Nov. 16 unanimously passed a bill (HR 4325) designed to encourage payment of child support.

The bill was approved 422-0 under suspension of the rules. It had been reported Nov. 10 by the Ways and Means Committee (H Rept 98-527). *(Vote 476, p. 140-H)*

Its major feature was a requirement that states must have in effect by Oct. 1, 1985, a means of mandatory withholding from the paychecks of parents in arrears in court-ordered support payments.

The measure made state assistance available to all those who requested help in collecting child support payments. Current law provided such aid only to recipients of Aid to Families with Dependent Children (AFDC).

A bill (S 1691) introduced by the Senate Finance Committee's 11 Republicans was not acted on by the panel in 1983.

S 1691 was the Reagan administration proposal and was similar to the House-passed bill. There were some differences, however. One of the more important was a provision in S 1691, rejected by the House, that would reduce the basic federal match to cover state administrative costs.

Rep. Barbara B. Kennelly, D-Conn., a chief sponsor of the House bill, said House members feared the provision would deter states that did not have a strong commitment to the current enforcement program. "We couldn't ask them to do more with less," she said. ∎

Meals for Elderly

The House May 24 approved legislation (HR 2807) to provide additional funding for the popular Older Americans meals program.

The bill, reported by the Education and Labor Committee May 16 (H Rept 98-164), passed by a vote of 386-31 under suspension of the rules. There was no Senate action. *(Vote 125, p. 42-H)*

HR 2807 authorized additional spending of $6.8 million in fiscal 1982 and $16 million in 1983 for the program of distribution of cash and commodities to senior nutrition programs. Sponsors said spending limits set by a 1981 reauthorization of the program (PL 97-115) were too low to reimburse states for all the meals they served. *(1981 Almanac p. 496)*

The more controversial part of the bill removed the spending ceiling on the program for fiscal 1984, authorizing "such sums as are necessary." Bill Frenzel, R-Minn., warned that the open-ended funding would restore the program to entitlement status, as it was before 1981. The Reagan administration opposed the bill. ∎

New GI Bill

The House Veterans' Affairs Committee approved a package of education benefits designed to entice qualified young people to join the armed forces and stay in.

The bill, reported May 16 (HR 1400 — H Rept 98-185, Part I), was similar to legislation that stalled in the House during the 97th Congress. It represented a compromise worked out between the Veterans' Affairs Committee and the House Armed Services Committee, which shared jurisdiction. *(1982 action, 1982 Almanac p. 502)*

The measure was never brought to the floor, however. Nor was there any Senate action on a new GI Bill.

The Senate Veterans' Affairs Committee was divided on the issue. Some members agreed with the Reagan administration that the bill was not needed, since none of the branches of the military was having trouble filling its ranks. The administration wanted to delay consideration of any new education benefits until circumstances required such changes.

Senate proponents, however, agreed with House Veterans' Affairs Chairman G. V. "Sonny" Montgomery, D-Miss., that military recruitment and retention problems would surface again as soon as the economy picked up.

Montgomery also was concerned that the declining birthrate that began in the 1960s would adversely affect recruiting during the late 1980s.

The number of males reaching age 18 each year would decline from approximately 2.1 million in 1979 to 1.7 million in 1987, almost a 20 percent drop, Montgomery said at an April 12 hearing. "The armed forces will then have to recruit a larger proportion of the available manpower," he said. "The competition for quality manpower by the end of this decade will be intense."

The Congressional Budget Office estimated that the new education benefits in the bill would cost $2 million in fiscal 1984, $12 million in 1985 and $110 million by 1986.

Provisions

As reported, HR 1400 authorized a basic education benefit for persons who enlisted in the military for three years. The stipend would be $300 per month for up to 36 months. Those who joined the Reserves or National Guard for four years after completing two years of active duty would be eligible for similar benefits.

If needed to attract new recruits for hard-to-fill jobs, the Department of Defense (DOD) could increase the basic benefit by up to $400 a month.

Service members who served five years beyond the initial enlistment period would be entitled to an additional $300 a month in education benefits. DOD could add another $300 to this supplement to encourage those with

critical skills to remain in the service.

The basic benefit would be open to those with a high school diploma or equivalency certificate, or a bachelor's degree. It would not be available to military academy graduates or ROTC scholarship recipients.

To encourage personnel with 10 years or more of active service to remain in the military, the bill would entitle service members to use their benefits while on active duty or transfer the benefits to pay for a spouse's or child's college education. The transferred benefits could be used only while the service member was on active duty or had completed 20 years in the service.

The bill also established a new $140-a-month education benefit, available for 36 months, to members of the National Guard and Reserves who joined, re-enlisted or extended their service for six years. Eligibility for this benefit required no active service, other than basic training. This benefit would be available to high school graduates but not those holding a bachelor's degree or ROTC scholarship students.

The Veterans Administration would pay the basic benefit; the Defense Department would pay for supplemental benefits and those granted to non-active Reserve members.

Left out of the 1983 bill was a "cash-out" provision included in the earlier measure, allowing re-enlisting service members to give up their education benefits in exchange for 25 percent of the benefits' value in cash. The Veterans' Affairs Committee deleted the provision because, it said, the purpose of the legislation was to educate youth, rather than to grant a windfall at the time they completed military service.

Child Health Plan

Children's health advocates took aim at U.S. infant mortality rates which, in 1983, still lagged behind those of other developed nations. But they did not succeed in their drive to expand the availability of free medical care for poor women during pregnancy and for needy youngsters.

Changes in Medicaid that would have opened the federal-state medical program to more poor mothers were approved by the House Energy and Commerce Committee and by the Senate Finance Committee. The House version, the broader of the two plans, included infants and young children as well. But neither measure reached the floor because of tactical problems, substantive objections and the indifference of many members.

Still, the bills signaled a new awareness by some members of the problems plaguing poor women and children. Other signs of that concern were the establishment of three congressional panels focusing on children and families, and the fiscal 1984 budget resolution (H Con Res 91) including $200 million for the children's health initiative, had it been authorized. *(Budget resolution, p. 435)*

The Washington-based Children's Defense Fund led the drive for the so-called Child Health Assurance Program (CHAP) bills. Supporters also included the American Academy of Pediatrics, the American Public Health Association and the United States Catholic Conference.

The focus on problem pregnancies and infancies reflected a pragmatic decision to attack a specific well-documented problem — infant mortality — that would respond to a modest investment. In the Carter administration, the children's fund pushed a more ambitious CHAP bill only to see it fail. *(1979 Almanac p. 499)*

Background

The case for the 1983 measures was based on statistics showing that despite improvements, U.S. infant mortality rates still were worse than those of some other developed nations. Infant mortality rates indicated the number of deaths in the first 12 months of life. The U.S. rate in 1980 was 11.8 deaths per 1,000 live births. Countries with lower rates included Canada, 10.9; Denmark, 8.5; France, 10.0; Japan 7.4; Norway, 8.8; Spain, 11.1; and Sweden, 6.7. Developed nations with rates comparable to or higher than those of the United States included Austria, East Germany, Italy and West Germany.

For black infants, the infant mortality rate was twice that of whites, and comparable to infant death rates in some impoverished, Third-World nations.

Factors associated with infant mortality included absence of or poor medical care during pregnancy, poor nutrition, the youth of the mother, substance abuse and smoking during pregnancy, and poverty.

Supporters of the legislation were particularly concerned with low-birthweight babies — weighing 5.5 pounds or less — who carried a high risk of death within the first year, or lasting illness or disability. The fragile babies were more likely to be born to the poor and to very young mothers. The United States, since 1950, had experienced a 500 percent increase in illegitimate births to teenagers.

Low-weight births in the United States — indicating problem pregnancies — had not declined at the same rate as infant mortality. In 1980, the rate of low birthweights varied from a high of 12.8 percent of births in the District of Columbia to a low of 5 percent in Iowa.

Advocates contended that preventive medical care, beginning before birth, was cheap compared with the long-term costs of untended pregnancies of the poor. For instance, the average cost of comprehensive maternity care was an estimated $2,000, according to the health insurance industry. Per-day costs for intensive hospital care of low-weight, high-risk newborns reached $1,000 or more, for stays averaging 23 days.

Opponents rarely addressed the substance of the child health legislation, instead arguing that the federal government could not afford new spending. Some objected that the House bill unfairly provided richer financial incentives for states that had stinted on Medicaid coverage for pregnancies and young children. States that already had relatively generous eligibility standards would not get comparable treatment under the bill.

Medicaid Selected As Vehicle

Because states generally decided who was poor enough to qualify for Medicaid, a number of people whose incomes fell well below the federal poverty standard were excluded from Medicaid. Rep. Henry A. Waxman, D-Calif., estimated that about six million poor children and 330,000 pregnant women were excluded each year, even though they lived below the federal poverty level of $9,862 for a family of four.

Waxman, chairman of the House Energy and Commerce Subcommittee on Health, sponsored the House CHAP bill. The legislation drew support from both liberals such as Rep. George Miller, D-Calif., and from certain conservatives.

Miller, chairman of the new House Select Committee on Children, Youth and Families, said that his panel's hearings had showed that low-birthweight infants tended to have developmental problems. Those problems could

hamper school performance, and show up in high school dropout rates and teenage pregnancies, and in lifelong dependence on social programs.

"The doctors have said, if we can get to these pregnancies early, we can change the outcome. We can prevent those haunting, long-term costs," Miller said.

Rep. Thomas J. Bliley Jr., R-Va., as conservative as Miller was liberal, linked his support for the bill to his opposition to abortion. "In order to be fair, we are under some obligation to take care of the living," he said. Bliley, who served on both Miller's and Waxman's committees, also said it was "far cheaper in the long run to provide prenatal care to these adolescents."

Committee Action

House Energy and Commerce. The House Energy and Commerce Committee Oct. 20 approved a CHAP bill authorizing full federal funding for states that established new Medicaid coverage for several categories of persons.

The provisions were incorporated in the committee's Medicare budget reconciliation proposals (HR 4136 — H Rept 98-442, Part I) reported Oct. 26. Medicare was the federal medical program for the elderly. *(Story, p. 391)*

Sponsors believed the bill could not come to the floor by itself but needed a larger vehicle. They feared controversial anti-abortion amendments, and objected that the bill promoted new spending in a year of deficits.

Waxman's strategy was to offer the child health plan as a floor amendment to a tax bill (HR 4170), which included the Ways and Means Committee Medicare budget reconciliation proposals. HR 4170 was to be the reconciliation vehicle, and there was no further action on HR 4136.

But the tax bill came to the floor under a rule that provoked resentment because it would have let Waxman offer his amendment, while barring others. That resentment was a major factor in the defeat of the rule on Nov. 17, the day before adjournment. When the tax bill failed to come to the floor, the CHAP amendment was left in limbo. *(Tax bill, p. 231)*

Waxman's proposal authorized full federal funding through Medicaid for comprehensive maternal care for women who were pregnant with a first child, and who would qualify for Medicaid once the child was born. (Eligibility for Medicaid was linked with eligibility for welfare — Aid to Families with Dependent Children. Some states started coverage only after the birth of the first child; some provided Medicaid in the final months of pregnancy; others provided coverage from the time a first pregnancy was diagnosed. Because of problems with federal data collection on the state-administered Medicaid programs, there were differing estimates of how many states fell into each category.)

The bill also provided for full federal funding for coverage of impoverished women and children in intact families, if the principal wage-earner was unemployed. A number of states denied Medicaid coverage to such intact families, regardless of income levels. Another provision allowed states to extend Medicaid to pregnant teenagers, regardless of parents' income.

States already providing the expanded Medicaid coverage could not qualify for the 100 percent federal funding, but they would receive an improved federal matching rate.

The Congressional Budget Office estimated the cost of the plan at $200 million in fiscal 1984, the amount allotted by the fiscal 1984 budget resolution for a children's health initiative.

Senate Finance. The Senate Finance Committee twice approved a modest $10 million-a-year plan sponsored by Lloyd Bentsen, D-Texas, to require state Medicaid programs to cover first-time pregnancies for women who would qualify after birth of the child. The bill authorized the change for two years only and assumed that federal funding for the expanded coverage would continue at existing matching rates.

The provision was added to legislation establishing a new health insurance program for the unemployed. That measure (S 951 — S Rept 98-193) was reported July 25, and again as part of the Senate committee's budget reconciliation bill (S 2062 — S Rept 98-300), reported Nov. 4. Neither came to the Senate floor, however. ■

Health Planning

A multi-year struggle over whether to continue a much-criticized health regulatory system continued in 1983, but with little overt activity and with no resolution.

A bill reauthorizing the federal health planning program, with substantial changes in policy, was reported May 24 by the House Energy and Commerce Committee (HR 2934 — H Rept 98-218). But no further action occurred, and the planning program was simply continued for a year at the existing funding level by the fiscal 1984 continuing appropriations resolution (H J Res 413 — PL 98-151). *(Story, p. 528)*

The task of the health planning program was to promote equitable distribution of health care resources and to combat inflation in health care costs by curbing excessive hospital investments in major medical equipment, new services and construction.

First authorized in 1974, the system consisted of a network of state and local planning agencies supported by federal funds. The agencies surveyed local and state medical resources and decided what additions would be appropriate. The system relied on state "certificate of need" (CON) programs, which federal planning law required states to establish.

The CON programs required hospitals and other health care institutions to receive official approval from state review agencies before embarking on major projects; approval decisions were to be based on data and priorities developed by the planning process.

For years, health planning had been subject to two types of criticism. Liberals worried that it was too weak to have much impact and that hospitals, nursing homes and doctors evaded its strictures. Conservatives complained that its time-consuming procedures hampered the development of a competitive medical marketplace and actually added to the costs of health care.

Since 1981 the Reagan administration — subscribing to the second of the two criticisms — had sought to end health planning altogether. But even conservative supporters of the administration became reluctant to scrap planning without some alternative to control costs, such as competition among medical providers.

In 1981, Congress declined to end health planning. However, as part of the the budget reconciliation legislation (PL 97-35), it substantially reduced its funding to $64.4 million, while extending its authorization for one year. Prior federal spending for the program had been running about $130 million a year. *(1981 Almanac p. 476)*

In 1982, the House twice passed planning reauthorizations, with policy changes, but the Senate did not act. The program was given a second one-year extension by the fiscal 1983 continuing appropriations resolution (PL 97-377). *(1982 Almanac p. 497)*

1983 Proposals

In 1983, critics of the system sought unsuccessfully to convert it to optional block grants to states. But they were unable to persuade the House Energy and Commerce Committee to accept their plan, and on May 24, the panel reported a three-year continuation of the program.

Major provisions of HR 2934 set new higher thresholds for CON reviews: projects costing less than those thresholds would not be required to undergo review. The new

thresholds were $1 million for capital expenditures, up from $600,000; $500,000 for annual operating costs of an institutional health service, up from $250,000; $500,000 for major medical equipment, up from $400,000.

The bill also gave states the power to determine what role — if any — local planning agencies would play in the CON review process. The local agencies frequently had been controversial. The bill continued the authorization for planning through Sept. 30, 1986.

The changes did not satisfy critics of the system, who were strong enough to force further, behind-the-scenes negotiations. The talks were meant to produce a compromise bill for floor action, but the year ended without agreement. There was no action on the issue in the Senate. ∎

Fiscal 1984
Status of Appropriations
98th Congress, First Session

Appropriation Bills	House	Senate	Final	Almanac Page
Agriculture and related agencies (HR 3223)	Passed 6/8	Passed 6/29	Funding included in PL 98-151	516
Defense (HR 4185)	Passed 11/2	Passed 11/8	Signed 12/8 PL 98-212	479
District of Columbia (HR 3415)	Passed 6/29	Passed 7/27	Signed 10/13 PL 98-125	494
Energy and Water Development (HR 3132)	Passed 6/7	Passed 6/22	Signed 7/14 PL 98-50	500
Energy and Water Development Supplemental (HR 3958)	Passed 10/6	Committee reported 10/19		520
Foreign Aid (S 1892)		Committee reported 9/27	Funding included in PL 98-151	521
Housing and Urban Development, Veterans, NASA (HR 3133)	Passed 6/2	Passed 6/21	Signed 7/12 PL 98-45	495
Interior and related agencies (HR 3363)	Passed 6/28	Passed 9/21	Signed 11/4 PL 98-146	462
Labor, Health and Human Services, Education (HR 3913)	Passed 9/22	Passed 10/4	Signed 10/31 PL 98-139	504
Legislative Branch (HR 3135)	Passed 6/3	Passed 6/23	Signed 7/14 PL 98-51	539
Military Construction (HR 3263)	Passed 6/21	Passed 7/27	Signed 10/11 PL 98-116	469
State, Justice, Commerce, Judiciary (HR 3222)	Passed 9/19	Passed 10/21	Signed 11/28 PL 98-166	472
Transportation and related agencies (HR 3329)	Passed 6/22	Passed 7/15	Signed 8/15 PL 98-78	457
Treasury, Postal Service, General Government (HR 4139, S 1646)	Passed 10/27	Committee reported 7/20	Funding included in PL 98-151	531
Continuing Resolution (H J Res 368)	Passed 9/28	Passed 9/29	Signed 10/1 PL 98-107	526
Further Continuing Appropriations (H J Res 413)	Passed 11/10	Passed 11/11	Signed 11/14 PL 98-151	528
Supplemental (HR 3959)	Passed 10/5	Passed 10/27	Signed 11/30 PL 98-181	536

Budget and Appropriations

The nine-year-old congressional budget process endured its most severe test in 1983.

With record-high deficits approaching $200 billion, and no easy solutions for cutting them, Congress abandoned its own budget's mandate to slash the federal deficit by $85 billion over fiscal 1984-86.

Lawmakers did hold the level of appropriations bills at or below the targets set out in their fiscal 1984 budget resolution. But the budget's deficit reduction strategy — to raise $73 billion in additional revenues and cut $12 billion from projected spending over fiscal 1984-86 — remained unfulfilled at year's end.

As in 1982, the budget odyssey began with an administration spending blueprint that found no constituency on Capitol Hill. Members of both parties rejected President Reagan's budget's priorities out of hand. They contended his proposed 10 percent real growth rate for defense spending was too high, his domestic spending freeze was too low and his standby tax plan — to be triggered in 1986 if deficits remained large — was impractical.

"What he sent up was simply not achievable," summed up Senate Budget Committee Chairman Pete V. Domenici, R-N.M. But the budget produced by Congress June 23, after months of rhetoric about closing the deficit gap, did not fare much better.

Budget Resolution

In 1983, the congressional budget process took a sharp turn from the two previous years.

In the House, where Democrats had gained an additional 26 seats in the 1982 elections, the balance of power shifted back to the more traditional, liberal politics of pre-Reagan days.

Splintering of the coalition of Republicans and conservative Southern Democrats that had pushed through budgets in 1981 and 1982 made it easy for the House to adopt a budget that was, in effect, the Democrats' economic manifesto.

The 1982 elections had their impact on the Republican-controlled Senate as well. A number of moderate GOP senators narrowly won re-election, and were able to do so, in part, because they distanced themselves from Reagan's economic policies. These lessons were not lost on their colleagues.

But rather than simplifying the Senate's handling of the budget, the elections and their aftermath helped divide Republican members into two camps — those who were willing to attack future deficits with tax increases, and those who favored only spending cuts. After several abortive attempts, the Senate finally adopted a budget plan that had almost no constituency and was approved almost solely as a means of keeping the budget process alive.

When the House and Senate went to conference, the three critical areas of disagreement were the rate of increase in defense spending, the level of domestic spending and how much to raise taxes.

Conferees split the difference on defense, settling on a 5 percent increase. They finessed problems with House increases in domestic spending by creating an $8.5 billion reserve fund that would kick in only if authorizing legislation for certain programs were enacted into law. The tax hikes included in the House resolution, it was agreed, were unrealistically high. So the conference report included increases very near the Senate level.

For the second year running, the resolution stipulated that if Congress did not complete action on a second budget resolution by the start of the new fiscal year, the targets set in the first resolution would become binding. Congress made no effort to shape a second resolution, and the first measure became binding Oct. 1.

Deficit Reduction

The conference agreement on the budget resolution included "reconciliation" instructions that directed congressional committees to cut program spending by $12.3 billion and increase taxes by $73 billion over fiscal 1984-86.

But at year's end, deficit reduction legislation remained mired in controversy. The House fulfilled most of the reconciliation program reductions when it approved a measure that cut $10.3 billion from projected spending over fiscal 1984-86; missing from the spending cut package were savings contemplated in the Medicare program. Senate committees agreed to parallel spending cuts, but the full Senate never voted on the bill. And neither chamber approved tax increases to meet the budget's revenue reconciliation requirement.

Appropriations

Congress made unusual progress in approving the 13 regular fiscal 1984 appropriations bills. By adjournment of the first session Nov. 18, it had cleared all but three: Agriculture, Foreign Aid and Treasury-Postal Service-General Government. All were scaled to stay within limits acceptable to the president, who had threatened to veto measures that exceeded his budget proposals.

Congress approved two stopgap funding bills, or continuing resolutions, that provided money for government agencies whose regular appropriations had not cleared. The first ran from Oct. 1 to Nov. 10. The second provided funding until Sept. 30, 1984, the end of the fiscal year.

Before adjourning Nov. 18, Congress approved a fiscal 1984 supplemental funding bill that also contained a housing authorization and an increase in the U.S. contribution to the International Monetary Fund (IMF) sought by the administration. The IMF increase had been deleted from a fiscal 1983 supplemental earlier in the year.

Another fiscal 1983 supplemental, cleared March 24, became the vehicle for a bipartisan, $4.6 billion jobs and anti-recession relief package.

—By Dale Tate

Presidents, Congress and the Budget, 1978-84

(in billions of dollars)

	Budget Authority	Outlays	Revenues	Deficit
Fiscal Year 1978				
Ford Budget	480.4	440.0	393.0	−47.0
Carter Revisions	507.3	459.4	401.6	−57.7
First Resolution	503.45	460.95	396.3	−64.65
Second Resolution	500.1	458.25	397.0	−61.25
Actual	500.4	450.8	402.0	−48.8
Fiscal Year 1979				
Carter Budget	568.2	500.2	439.6	−60.6
First Resolution	568.85	498.8	447.9	−50.9
Second Resolution	555.65	487.5	448.7	−38.8
Revised Second Resolution	559.2	494.45	461.0	−33.45
Actual	556.7	493.6	465.9	−27.7
Fiscal Year 1980				
Carter Budget	615.5	531.6	502.6	−29.0
First Resolution	604.4	532.0	509.0	−23.0
Second Resolution	638.0	547.6	517.8	−29.8
Revised Second Resolution	658.9	572.65	525.7	−46.95
Actual	658.8	579.6	520.0	−59.6
Fiscal Year 1981				
Carter Budget	696.1	615.8	600.0	−15.8
Carter Revisions	691.3	611.5	628.0	+16.5
First Resolution	697.2	613.6	613.8	+ 0.2
Second Resolution	694.6	632.4	605.0	−27.4
Revised Second Resolution	717.5	661.35	603.3	−58.05
Actual	718.4	657.2	599.3	−57.9
Fiscal Year 1982				
Carter Budget	809.8	739.3	711.8	−27.5
Reagan Revision	772.4	695.3	650.3	−45.0
First Resolution[1]	770.9	695.45	657.8	−37.65
Revised Second Resolution	777.67	734.10	628.4	−105.7
Actual	779.9	728.4	617.8	−110.6
Fiscal Year 1983				
Reagan Budget	801.9	757.6	666.1	−91.5
First Resolution[2]	822.39	769.82	665.9	−103.92
Revised Resolution	877.2 }*	807.4 }*	604.3	−203.1 }*
	883.36 }	812.85 }		−208.55 }
Actual	866.7	795.97	600.56	−195.4
Fiscal Year 1984				
Reagan Budget	900.1	848.5	659.7	−188.8
First Resolution[2]	919.5 }*	849.5 }*	679.6	−169.9 }*
	928.73 }	858.93 }		−179.33 }

[1] *Second resolution merely reaffirmed figures in first resolution.*
[2] *First resolution became binding at beginning of fiscal year Oct. 1.*
* *Larger figure assumed enactment of 10 programs included in a special $8.5 billion reserve fund.*

Reagan Sees High Deficits Through Fiscal 1988

The $848.5 billion fiscal 1984 budget that President Reagan submitted to Congress Jan. 31 forecast deficits well above $100 billion for the next five years despite a "freeze" on government spending.

The deficit would reach an awesome $188.8 billion in the fiscal year ending Sept. 30, 1984, the budget said, even if the entire $43 billion in budget savings proposed by the administration were adopted.

That shortfall was an improvement over fiscal 1983 when the deficit — dramatically deepened by the longest recession in post-World War II history — was expected to hit $207.7 billion. (In February 1982, the administration had predicted a $91.5 billion deficit for the year.) The fiscal 1985 deficit would climb back up to $194.2 billion, according to the administration's estimates.

Outlays would total $848.5 billion in fiscal 1984 under the Reagan budget. Revenues would be $659.7 billion and budget authority $900.1 billion. *(Budget totals, box, this page; revised estimates, box, p. 429)*

While striking a note for bipartisanship and accommodation, the budget showed that the president remained true to the basic economic policies he set down at the outset of his administration in 1981. Military spending would continue its upward spiral. Discretionary spending for social programs would continue to be whittled away. And the personal and business tax cuts enacted in 1981 would stay firmly in place.

Although the president proposed several initiatives to help the unemployed — including extension of an emergency unemployment benefits program, more money for job training and 718,000 public summer jobs for youth — he remained "adamantly opposed to temporary make-work public jobs."

Most members of Congress were pleased both by the "realism" of the budget and by Reagan's bipartisan rhetoric.

"My administration will now work with the Congress in an effort to accommodate those special concerns

of the legislative branch that have caused unnecessary strains in the past," the president said.

But it was nonetheless clear there would be a heated debate over the details of the final fiscal 1984 spending blueprint. *(Congressional budget resolution, p. 435)*

'Sweeping Changes'

The president's budget message was both upbeat and cautionary.

"The stage is set; a recovery to vigorous, sustainable, non-inflationary economic growth is imminent," Reagan said. "But given the underlying deterioration in the overall budget structure that has occurred over the past two years, only the most sweeping set of fiscal policy changes would help to reverse the trend and set the bud-

get on the path that is consistent with long-term economic recovery." *(Text of message, p. 7-E)*

To achieve this sweeping change, Reagan proposed a four-part plan designed to reduce anticipated spending by $558 billion over the next five fiscal years. *(Savings estimates, box, p. 429)*

● **Federal Spending Freeze.** Taken as a whole, fiscal 1984 budget outlays would increase no more than the rate of inflation under the Reagan plan. But the specifics of the budget showed that spending in some areas — such as defense and interest on the national debt — would increase significantly, while the rate of funding in others would drop.

The freeze would affect aggregate non-defense discretionary programs, medical provider reimbursement and farm price supports. Under the freeze there would be no increase in civilian and military pay and retirement benefits. And a six-month delay would be imposed on cost-of-living adjustments (COLAs) for Social Security and other indexed benefit programs in which payments are automatically adjusted to offset the effects of inflation.

● **Control of 'Uncontrollable' Programs.** A second part of the savings plan focused on long-term structural reforms in entitlement and similar programs under which benefits must be paid to all who qualify.

It included the Social Security plan recommended Jan. 15 by the National Commission on Social Security Reform, which the administration estimated would cut $79 billion from the 1984-88 deficits.

Also included was a cap on Medicare/Medicaid and private health insurance, saving $58 billion from anticipated spending over five years; major reforms of the civil service retirement program, saving $16.2 billion; and better targeting of the means-tested entitlement programs and veterans' benefits, saving $13.6 billion.

● **Defense Adjustments.** The savings plan called for a $55 billion reduction over the next five years in the increases in defense spending the administration proposed in 1982. These savings, which would come from pay, fuel, inflation and program

The Budget Totals

(Fiscal years, in billions of dollars)

	1982 actual	1983 estimate	1984 estimate	1985 estimate	1986 estimate
Budget authority	779.9	847.4	900.1	997.4	1,079.6
Outlays	728.4	805.2	848.5	918.5	989.6
Revenues	617.8	597.5	659.7	724.3	841.9
Deficit	−110.6	−207.7	−188.8	−194.2	−147.7

Budget Terminology

The federal budget is the president's financial plan for the federal government. It accounts for how government funds have been raised and spent, and it proposes financial policies. It covers the **fiscal year**. Fiscal year 1984 begins Oct. 1, 1983, and ends Sept. 30, 1984.

The budget discusses **receipts**, amounts the government expects to raise in taxes; **budget authority**, amounts agencies are allowed to obligate or lend; and **outlays**, amounts actually paid out by the government in cash or checks during the year. Examples of outlays are funds spent to buy equipment or property, to meet the government's liability under a contract or to pay the salaries of employees. Outlays also include net lending — the difference between disbursements and repayments under government lending programs.

The purpose of the budget is to establish priorities, and to chart the government's **fiscal policy**, which is the coordinated use of taxes and expenditures to affect the economy.

Congress adopts its own budget in the form of **budget resolutions**. The **first budget resolution**, due May 15, sets overall goals for taxes and spending, broken down among major budget categories, called **functions**. The **second budget resolution**, due Sept. 15, sets binding budget figures.

An **authorization** is an act of Congress that establishes government programs. It defines the scope of programs and sets a ceiling for how much can be spent on them. Authorizations do not actually provide the money. In the case of authority to enter contractual obligations, though, Congress authorizes the administration to make firm commitments for which funds must later be provided. Congress also occasionally includes mandatory spending requirements in an authorization in order to ensure spending at a certain level.

An **appropriation** provides money for programs, within the limits established in authorizations. An appropriation may be for a single year, a specified period of years, or an indefinite number of years, according to the restrictions Congress wishes to place on spending for particular purposes.

Appropriations generally take the form of **budget authority**. Budget authority often differs from actual outlays. That is because, in practice, funds actually spent or obligated during a year may be drawn partly from the budget authority conferred in the year in question and partly from budget authority conferred in previous years.

---

economies, would "fully protect strategic programs and readiness...," according to the budget.

● **Standby Tax.** The final element of the savings plan was a so-called "deficit insurance policy" that would trigger standby taxes Oct. 1, 1985, but only if three conditions were met: Congress adopted the administration's deficit reduction measures; the forecast for the fiscal 1986 deficit exceeded 2.5 percent of the gross national product (GNP); and on July 1, 1985, the economy was growing.

The taxes would be limited to no more than 1 percent of GNP in fiscal 1986 and would last for three years. They would consist of a $5-per-barrel oil excise tax and a 5 percent surcharge on corporate and individual income tax liability.

Economic Outlook

The administration's own economic and budget estimates indicated the standby tax would be triggered in 1985. The economy would have to perform much better than projected by the White House to prevent the tax from taking effect. *(Economic assumptions, p. 428; administration economic report, p. 12-E)*

The budget forecast that economic recovery would begin during the first half of calendar 1983, "with greater momentum during the year's second half."

The administration estimated that real output as measured by the GNP would rise 3.1 percent from the fourth quarter of 1982 to the fourth quarter of 1983. Output would grow only 4 percent in 1984 — a small in-

crease compared to historic patterns following a recession.

Both inflation and interest rates would continue to moderate, according to administration estimates. The Consumer Price Index (CPI) was expected to rise 5 percent from the fourth quarter of 1982 to the fourth quarter of 1983, and another 4.4 percent in 1984. The average interest rate for three-month Treasury bills, a bench mark for other rates, was estimated at 8 percent in 1983 and 7.9 percent in 1984.

Unemployment, however, would remain at uncomfortably high levels — averaging 10.7 percent in 1983 and 9.9 percent in 1984, the budget said.

Martin S. Feldstein, chairman of the Council of Economic Advisers, described the budget's short-term economic forecast as "cautious, prudent ... designed to reduce the risk of bad surprises in the years ahead."

At a press briefing Jan. 31, Feldstein added that the administration "wanted to make certain when we produced these numbers that they would be credible as a basis for serious legislative discussions with the Congress, and that they also would be regarded by the business and financial community as a clear indication of our intentions to bring down the deficits in a realistic way in the years ahead."

This was a major difference from the two previous years, when the Reagan budget estimates were widely disputed as overly optimistic.

Fiscal Policy

The fiscal policy set out in the 1984 budget adhered to the path set initially by the Reagan administration in 1981 — a downward trend for government spending, with the exception of defense, and a reduced tax burden on individuals and business.

According to the budget, however, "aggregate spending has risen steadily despite the major strides in reducing non-defense spending growth that have been achieved over the past two budget cycles."

Spending would increase $43.3 billion from fiscal 1983 to fiscal 1984, or about 5 percent, matching the expected rate of inflation.

Fiscal 1983 spending would exceed 1981 levels by 21 percent, reflecting "the steady buildup of defense outlays, the explosion of debt service costs, and the continued, largely unchecked rise in basic retirement and medical entitlement programs."

But adoption of the budget plan as proposed, the Office of Management and Budget (OMB) said, would mean that the "overall structural imbalance is substantially reduced, with the 1988 deficit claim on GNP falling by two-thirds compared to the current services baseline."

In addition, the "internal shift in budget priorities toward funding an adequate defense is maintained." Overall spending for non-defense programs would fall 2.9 percent from the 1981 level. And the tax claim on GNP, even if the standby tax were triggered, would remain 2.6 percent lower than would have been the case with pre-1981 tax law.

Structural Deficit

Much of the budget document was an apologia for the Reagan administration's economic program.

Although it attributed the massive deficit problem to the decade of the 1970s and "the inherited budgetary imbalance" bequeathed to the administration, the budget acknowledged that "Reaganomics" had failed to achieve the anticipated goals. And it frankly outlined the deficit problems ahead.

The budget said the "cyclical" element of the deficit — or the portion solely affected by economic conditions — would peak in 1983 at $71 billion, or 2 percent of GNP.

But because of "economic setbacks and divergent policy outcome," the structural deficit would remain in excess of 6 percent of GNP at the end of five years.

"The process of economic adjustment to non-inflationary growth has been far more prolonged, costly and disruptive to financial markets and business activity than originally projected," the budget said. As a result, economic growth was much lower than expected and outlays for debt service were much higher than planned.

The budget also implied that the 1981 tax cuts the president supported had overreached.

The administration had been "more successful in reducing the outyear (1985-88) tax claim on GNP than originally anticipated, and considerably less successful in reducing the non-defense spending claim than initially planned," it said.

The 1984 budget plan, with its deficit reduction initiatives, would begin "steadily eliminating the persisting structural deficit over the next five years," the budget concluded.

1983 Revisions

"The budgetary effects of the large forecasting errors in 1982 turned out to be quite substantial," the budget acknowledged.

Just how substantial the errors were was reflected in the administration's fiscal 1983 budget revisions. The budget said fiscal 1983 revenues would be $55 billion lower than expected and outlays would be $11 billion higher than expected as a result of the net effects of lower inflation, falling interest rates and lower than anticipated growth. Forecasting errors were expected to produce a $66 billion increase in the deficit, or 84 percent of the net change in the fiscal 1983 deficit projection.

The budget revisions projected total fiscal 1983 outlays at $805.2 billion, revenues at $597.5 billion and the deficit at $207.7 billion.

The budget outlined a total of $6.088 billion in budget authority for proposed 1983 supplementals, excluding requests for increased pay costs. The largest request — $5.087 billion

— was for the Labor Department's unemployment benefits programs. The fiscal 1983 pay supplemental request was for $795.96 million.

In addition to the supplemental requests, the administration asked Congress to rescind $5.4 billion in fiscal 1983 appropriations already enacted. Education activities would be the most adversely affected by the rescissions. They would be cut $1.23 billion, including a $900 million rescission in the guaranteed student loan program.

According to OMB figures, the "grand total" of rescissions minus supplementals would cut 1983 budget authority by $1.482 billion. That would bring total 1983 budget authority to $847.4 billion.

Credit Budget

The administration's budget included a credit budget covering all direct loan obligations and loan guarantee commitments of federal agencies.

In fiscal 1982 the credit budget total amounted to $101.3 billion —

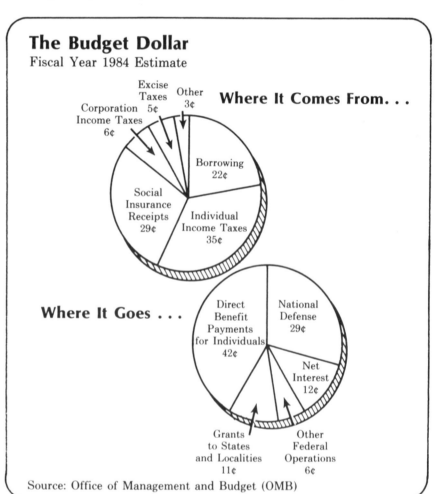

The Budget Dollar
Fiscal Year 1984 Estimate

Where It Comes From . . .

Excise Taxes 5¢
Other 3¢
Corporation Income Taxes 6¢
Borrowing 22¢
Social Insurance Receipts 29¢
Individual Income Taxes 35¢

Where It Goes . . .

Direct Benefit Payments for Individuals 42¢
National Defense 29¢
Net Interest 12¢
Grants to States and Localities 11¢
Other Federal Operations 6¢

Source: Office of Management and Budget (OMB)

Reagan Administration Economic Assumptions

(Calendar years; dollar amounts in billions)

Item	Actual 1981	FORECAST			ASSUMPTIONS			
		1982[1]	1983	1984	1985	1986	1987	1988
Major economic indicators:								
Gross national product, percent change, fourth quarter over fourth quarter:								
Current dollars	9.6	3.3	8.8	9.2	9.0	8.7	8.7	8.6
Constant (1972) dollars	0.7	−1.2	3.1	4.0	4.0	4.0	4.0	4.0
GNP deflator (percent change, fourth quarter over fourth quarter)	8.9	4.6	5.6	5.0	4.8	4.5	4.5	4.4
Consumer Price Index (percent change, fourth quarter over fourth quarter)[2]	9.4	4.4	5.0	4.4	4.7	4.5	4.5	4.4
Unemployment rate (percent, fourth quarter)[3]	8.1	10.5	10.4	9.5	8.5	7.8	7.0	6.2
Annual economic assumptions:								
Gross national product:								
Current dollars:								
Amount	2,938	3,058	3,262	3,566	3,890	4,232	4,599	4,995
Percent change, year over year	11.6	4.1	6.7	9.3	9.1	8.8	8.7	8.6
Constant (1972) dollars:								
Amount	1,503	1,476	1,496	1,555	1,617	1,682	1,749	1,819
Percent change, year over year	1.9	−1.8	1.4	3.9	4.0	4.0	4.0	4.0
Incomes:								
Personal income	2,416	2,570	2,727	2,935	3,142	3,377	3,661	3,956
Wages and salaries	1,494	1,560	1,640	1,780	1,921	2,090	2,281	2,483
Corporate profits	232	175	177	206	246	296	316	329
Price level:								
GNP deflator:								
Level (1972 = 100), annual average	195.5	207.2	218.1	229.4	240.6	251.7	263.0	274.7
Percent change, year over year	9.4	6.0	5.2	5.2	4.9	4.6	4.5	4.4
Consumer Price Index:[2]								
Level (1967 = 100), annual average	272.3	288.6	302.9	316.8	331.4	346.6	362.2	378.3
Percent change, year over year	10.3	6.0	4.9	4.6	4.6	4.6	4.5	4.4
Unemployment rates:								
Total, annual average[3]	7.5	9.5	10.7	9.9	8.9	8.1	7.3	6.5
Insured, annual average[4]	3.5	4.7	5.3	4.7	4.2	3.8	3.5	3.2
Federal pay raise, October (percent)[5]	4.8	4.0	—	6.1	6.0	5.7	5.6	5.5
Interest rate, 91-day Treasury bills (percent)[6]	14.1	10.7	8.0	7.9	7.4	6.8	6.5	6.1
Interest rate, 10-year Treasury notes (percent)	13.9	13.0	10.2	9.8	9.0	8.0	7.4	6.7

[1] *Preliminary actual data.*

[2] *CPI for urban wage earners and clerical workers. Two versions of the CPI are now published. The index shown here is that currently used, as required by law, in calculating automatic cost-of-living increases for indexed federal programs. The figures in this table reflect the actual CPI for December 1982, released January 21, 1983, which was 0.7% lower than had been projected; consequently, the cost-of-living adjustments estimated in the budget are higher than the actual adjustments will be. The manner in which this index measures housing costs will change significantly in 1985.*

[3] *Percent of total labor force, including armed forces stationed in the U.S.*

[4] *This indicator measures unemployment under state regular unemployment insurance as a percentage of covered employment under that program. It does not include recipients of extended benefits under that program.*

[5] *General schedule pay raises become effective in October — the first month of the fiscal year. Thus, the October 1984 pay raise will set new pay scales that will be in effect during fiscal year 1985. The October 1981 pay raise for military personnel was 14.3%.*

[6] *Average rate on new issues within period, on a bank discount basis. These projections assume, by convention, that interest rates decline with the rate of inflation. They do not represent a forecast of interest rates.*

SOURCE: Fiscal 1984 Budget

below the levels for 1981 and 1983. The budget attributed the decline chiefly to the recession and high interest rates on government housing programs, such as Veterans Administration (VA) and Federal Housing Administration loans (FHA).

For fiscal 1984, the administration sought a $14.2 billion decrease in the credit budget, to $137.6 billion.

New direct loan obligations in 1984 would total $38.8 billion; loan guarantee commitments would be $98.7 billion.

The major reductions in the credit budget occurred in direct loans from the Commodity Credit Corporation (CCC) for agriculture price supports and related programs, the Farmers Home Administration and FHA- and CCC-guaranteed loans.

Increases, however, were proposed for the Export-Import Bank, veterans' housing programs and international military aid.

Current Services

The 1974 Congressional Budget Act (PL 93-344) required the president to supply Congress with estimates of outlays and budget authority that would be needed to maintain current government services at the same level as the fiscal year in progress,

---

Reagan Four-Point Savings Plan

(Fiscal years, in billions of dollars)

	1984	1985	1986	1987	1988	Total
1984 Freeze	19	28	33	39	45	164
Defense Savings	8	8	9	10	11	47
Structural Reforms	19	29	41	57	82	228
Standby Revenue Measures	—	—	46	49	51	146
Total Savings*	43	59	123	150	184	558

Table does not add because savings from 1984 freeze include defense savings from military pay and pension freeze.

Source: Office of Management and Budget

---

with no changes in policy. These figures, known as the "Current Services Estimates," could be used as a baseline to measure the budget's proposed program changes and year-to-year growth.

As in 1982, the administration used what it called "current services with adequate defense" for its current services estimates. This level reflected the current services spending for all non-defense programs. But it assumed a level of defense spending that included proposed increases rejected by

Congress in the fiscal 1983 budget. Defense increases were thus obscured in the context of the total budget.

Current services outlays for fiscal 1984 were estimated to be $880.3 billion — 9.2 percent higher than in fiscal 1983. Budget authority was estimated to be $945.8 billion, an increase of 15.3 percent over 1983.

Revenues were expected to increase from $597.5 billion in fiscal 1983 to $648.8 billion in 1984.

The resulting fiscal 1984 current services deficit would be $231.5 billion — $22.9 billion higher than the $208.5 billion deficit for fiscal 1983. In fiscal 1988 the current services deficit was projected to hit $300.4 billion.

CBO Baseline

On Feb. 3, the Congressional Budget Office (CBO) released its baseline budget projections for fiscal years 1984-88.

Like the administration's current services budget, the CBO baseline projected spending based on current policy — the fiscal 1983 appropriations level — with adjustments for inflation.

For 1984-85 defense spending, CBO used the levels specified in the fiscal 1983 budget resolution, and then extrapolated those levels for fiscal 1986-88.

According to CBO, "the principal feature of the baseline budget projections is large and growing deficits." The independent budget office's estimates showed that the fiscal 1983 deficit would hit $194 billion — lower than the administration's own figure. But the deficit would steadily increase — assuming no spending or tax policy changes — to $197 billion in fiscal 1984, $214 billion in fiscal 1985 and to

---

Administration Revises Forecasts

In its mid-session budget review, sent to Congress July 25, the Reagan administration said stronger-than-expected economic growth would cut the fiscal 1984 deficit to $179.7 billion, compared with $188.8 billion forecast in the January budget and $190.2 billion forecast in earlier budget revisions released April 12. Spending was expected to rise to $848.1 billion in fiscal 1984, up from $843.9 billion forecast in April. The revenue forecast was increased from $653.7 billion to $668.4 billion. The administration predicted that the deficit would decline to $82.3 billion by fiscal 1988, from a high of $209.8 billion in 1983.

These projections were based on the assumption that Congress would adopt spending reductions and contingency taxes proposed by the administration that had received little support on Capitol Hill. "Any undisciplined tax or spending increases that exceed those reflected in this review would pose a serious threat to sustained recovery," the report concluded.

The administration's July budget update predicted that the economy would grow at an inflation-adjusted annual rate of 5.5 percent between the fourth quarter of 1982 and the fourth quarter of 1983, up from 4.7 percent forecast in April. The estimate for real economic growth in 1984 was increased from 4 percent to 4.5 percent.

Actual Fiscal 1983 Totals. The federal deficit for the fiscal year that ended Sept. 30, 1983, reached a record $195.4 billion, the government announced Oct. 26. The deficit total was $14.4 billion below the amount estimated by the administration in its July mid-session review, largely due to slower-than-expected spending for agriculture, defense and some other areas. Fiscal 1983 outlays totaled $795.9 billion; receipts, $600.6 billion.

Fiscal 1984 Budget by Function: $848.5 Billion in . . .

(in millions of dollars†)

	BUDGET AUTHORITY‡			OUTLAYS		
	1982	**1983 est.**	**1984 est.**	**1982**	**1983 est.**	**1984 est.**
NATIONAL DEFENSE						
Military Defense	$213,751	$239,407	$273,400	$182,850	$208,932	$238,600
Atomic Energy Defense Activities	4,737	5,700	6,778	4,309	5,471	6,422
Defense-related Activities	219	371	329	263	370	287
Deductions #	−4	−4	−4	−4	−4	−4
TOTAL	$218,704	$245,474	$280,503	$187,418	$214,769	$245,305
INTERNATIONAL AFFAIRS						
International Security Assistance	$ 3,919	$ 4,509	$ 4,692	$ 3,107	$ 4,019	$ 4,598
Foreign Economic and Financial Assistance	4,552	4,755	4,868	3,856	4,335	4,487
Conduct of Foreign Affairs	1,693	1,806	2,042	1,630	1,704	2,001
Foreign Information and Exchange Activities	583	724	832	571	704	828
International Financial Programs	4,612	5,366	4,473	911	1,272	1,430
Deductions #	−92	−94	−94	−92	−94	−94
TOTAL	$ 15,267	$ 17,066	$ 16,813	$ 9,982	$ 11,939	$ 13,250
GENERAL SCIENCE, SPACE AND TECHNOLOGY						
General Science and Basic Research	$ 1,535	$ 1,635	$ 1,943	$ 1,607	$ 1,613	$ 1,865
Space Flight	3,601	4,109	4,049	3,543	4,034	4,028
Space Science, Applications and Technology	1,392	1,568	1,638	1,457	1,517	1,601
Supporting Space Activities	544	610	830	473	604	766
Deductions #	−10	−9	−9	−10	−9	−9
TOTAL	$ 7,063	$ 7,912	$ 8,451	$ 7,070	$ 7,759	$ 8,250
ENERGY						
Energy Supply	$ 2,083	$ 2,391	$ 1,992	$ 3,150	$ 2,752	$ 2,090
Energy Conservation	168	288	74	518	670	343
Emergency Energy Preparedness	191	242	159	191	284	228
Energy Information, Policy and Regulation	889	882	725	886	878	726
Deductions #	−71	−78	−81	−71	−78	−81
TOTAL	$ 3,261	$ 3,725	$ 2,869	$ 4,674	$ 4,506	$ 3,306
NATURAL RESOURCES AND ENVIRONMENT						
Pollution Control and Abatement	$ 3,645	$ 3,653	$ 3,631	$ 5,012	$ 4,330	$ 4,058
Water Resources	3,998	3,957	3,251	4,032	3,955	3,305
Conservation and Land Management	2,565	2,848	2,028	2,746	2,685	2,153
Recreational Resources	1,262	1,405	1,202	1,477	1,677	1,459
Other Natural Resources	1,590	1,503	1,380	1,526	1,572	1,442
Deductions #	−1,860	−2,131	−2,586	−1,860	−2,131	−2,586
TOTAL	$ 11,199	$ 11,234	$ 8,906	$ 12,934	$ 12,087	$ 9,832
AGRICULTURE						
Farm Income Stabilization	$ 17,191	$ 16,460	$ 11,839	$ 13,289	$ 19,360	$ 10,490
Agricultural Research and Services	1,586	1,702	1,647	1,599	1,716	1,662
Deductions #	−14	−2	−2	−14	−2	−2
TOTAL	$ 18,763	$ 18,160	$ 13,484	$ 14,875	$ 21,075	$ 12,150
COMMERCE AND HOUSING CREDIT						
Mortgage Credit and Thrift Insurance	$ 4,055	$ 2,435	$ 5,694	$ 1,216	$ −622	$−1,387
Postal Service	707	789	400	707	789	400
Other Advancement of Commerce	1,660	1,692	1,464	1,943	1,761	1,400
Deductions #	−2	−1	−1	−2	−1	−1
TOTAL	$ 6,419	$ 4,915	$ 7,556	$ 3,865	$ 1,928	$ 413
TRANSPORTATION						
Ground Transportation	$ 14,559	$ 18,869	$ 19,062	$ 14,326	$ 14,562	$ 17,249
Air Transportation	3,785	4,806	5,692	3,564	4,222	4,844
Water Transportation	2,939	2,994	2,995	2,696	3,059	3,019
Other Transportation	88	110	116	90	120	118
Deductions #	−116	−87	−85	−116	−87	−85
TOTAL	$ 21,256	$ 26,692	$ 27,780	$ 20,560	$ 21,876	$ 25,145
COMMUNITY AND REGIONAL DEVELOPMENT						
Community Development	$ 4,291	$ 4,367	$ 4,200	$ 4,583	$ 4,490	$ 4,425
Area and Regional Development	1,984	2,003	1,777	2,735	2,779	2,415
Disaster Relief and Insurance	363	256	128	−119	138	146
Deductions #	−34	−34	−34	−34	−34	−34
TOTAL	$ 6,604	$ 6,592	$ 6,071	$ 7,165	$ 7,373	$ 6,951

... Expenditures, $900.1 Billion in Spending Authority

(in millions of dollars†)

	BUDGET AUTHORITY‡			OUTLAYS		
	1982	1983 est.	1984 est.	1982	1983 est.	1984 est.
EDUCATION, TRAINING, EMPLOYMENT, SOCIAL SERVICES						
Elementary, Secondary and Vocational Education	$ 6,403	$ 6,402	$ 6,030	$ 6,780	$ 6,546	$ 6,437
Higher Education	7,401	6,444	6,202	6,507	6,739	6,084
Research and General Education Aids	999	1,023	867	1,040	1,118	999
Training and Employment	4,386	5,175	5,441	5,464	5,150	4,719
Other Labor Services	600	643	682	589	633	680
Social Services	6,094	6,350	6,475	5,950	6,530	6,394
Deductions #	—29	—42	—57	—29	—42	—57
TOTAL	$ 25,854	$ 25,996	$ 25,640	$ 26,300	$ 26,676	$ 25,256
HEALTH						
Health Care Services	$ 73,469	$ 61,798	$ 85,927	$ 68,350	$ 76,515	$ 84,860
Health Research	3,844	4,228	4,347	3,948	4,204	4,281
Education and Training of Health Care Work Force	494	481	365	670	580	414
Consumer and Occupational Health and Safety	1,037	1,079	1,113	1,034	1,090	1,119
Deductions #	15	—28	—27	15	—28	—27
TOTAL	$ 78,859	$ 67,558	$ 91,725	$ 74,017	$ 82,362	$ 90,647
INCOME SECURITY						
General Retirement and Disability Insurance	$153,316	$189,808	$181,127	$161,805	$176,216	$185,661
Federal Employee Retirement and Disability	32,266	35,440	37,922	19,388	20,856	22,153
Unemployment Compensation	21,177	31,884	29,892	23,756	36,870	28,774
Housing Assistance	13,876	5,660	397	8,043	9,582	10,823
Food and Nutrition Assistance	15,784	17,747	16,302	15,579	17,831	16,322
Other Income Security	17,770	20,789	18,539	19,773	21,117	18,688
TOTAL	$254,188	$301,328	$284,178	$248,343	$282,472	$282,422
VETERANS BENEFITS AND SERVICES						
Income Security	$ 14,510	$ 14,205	$ 14,887	$ 13,710	$ 14,219	$ 14,593
Education, Training and Rehabilitation	1,964	1,666	1,371	1,947	1,624	1,329
Hospital and Medical Care	7,802	8,474	9,188	7,517	8,292	8,900
Housing	—	—82	—90	102	—464	130
Other Benefits and Services	709	742	776	682	744	776
Deductions #	—3	—3	—3	—3	—3	—3
TOTAL	$ 24,982	$ 25,002	$ 26,129	$ 23,955	$ 24,411	$ 25,724
ADMINISTRATION OF JUSTICE						
Federal Law Enforcement Activities	$ 2,658	$ 3,045	$ 3,348	$ 2,529	$ 3,017	$ 3,276
Federal Litigative and Judicial Activities	1,529	1,685	1,592	1,516	1,669	1,592
Federal Correctional Activities	423	404	523	364	424	466
Criminal Justice Assistance	140	137	165	294	189	184
Deductions #	—32	—26	—26	—32	—26	—26
TOTAL	$ 4,718	$ 5,245	$ 5,602	$ 4,671	$ 5,273	$ 5,491
GENERAL GOVERNMENT						
Legislative Functions	$ 1,172	$ 1,260	$ 1,328	$ 1,177	$ 1,253	$ 1,324
Executive Direction and Management	95	103	113	96	104	112
Central Fiscal Operations	2,847	3,293	3,537	2,656	3,275	3,507
General Property and Records Management	386	454	502	334	557	365
Central Personnel Management	141	142	151	136	140	152
Other General Government	507	592	607	504	628	717
Deductions #	—177	—163	—184	—177	—163	—184
TOTAL	$ 4,970	$ 5,682	$ 6,055	$ 4,726	$ 5,794	$ 5,993
GENERAL PURPOSE FISCAL ASSISTANCE						
General Revenue Sharing	$ 4,573	$ 4,574	$ 4,574	$ 4,575	$ 4,573	$ 4,574
Other General Purpose Fiscal Assistance	1,819	1,756	2,394	1,818	1,809	2,394
TOTAL	$ 6,392	$ 6,330	$ 6,969	$ 6,393	$ 6,382	$ 6,968
INTEREST						
Interest on the Public Debt	$117,190	$128,063	$144,500	$117,190	$128,063	$144,500
Interest Received by Trust Funds	—16,067	—16,349	—16,862	—16,067	—16,349	—16,862
Other Interest	—16,427	—22,779	—24,458	—16,427	—22,778	—24,458
TOTAL	$ 84,697	$ 88,935	$103,180	$ 84,697	$ 88,936	$103,180
CIVILIAN AGENCY PAY RAISES	—	—	—	—	—	—
INCREASED EMPLOYING AGENCY RETIREMENT PAYMENTS	—	—	$ 949	—	—	$ 949
CONTINGENCIES	—	—	—	—	—	—
UNDISTRIBUTED OFFSETTING RECEIPTS	$—13,270	$—20,414	$—22,750	$—13,270	$—20,414	$—22,750
GRAND TOTAL	$779,926	$847,433	$900,110	$728,375	$805,202	$848,483

† Figures may not add to totals due to rounding.   ‡ Primarily appropriations.   # For offsetting receipts.

SOURCE: Fiscal 1984 Budget

$267 billion by fiscal 1988.

These deficit projections were based on economic assumptions that showed a modest recovery from the recession — with real growth rates of 2.1 percent in calendar year 1983 and 4.7 percent in 1984. These GNP rates were higher than the administration forecast.

CBO projected that the unemployment rate would average 10.6 percent in 1983 and decline to an average of 9.8 percent in 1984. Inflation was estimated to be less than 5 percent annually during the next two years.

Using these assumptions, CBO estimated fiscal 1984 outlays of $850 billion and revenues of $653 billion.

By 1988, CBO said, spending for national defense, Social Security, Medicare and Medicaid and net interest would account for three-quarters of baseline outlays.

Program Highlights

Taxes. The Reagan budget called for tax increases of $11.7 billion in fiscal 1984, $12.5 billion in fiscal 1985 and $63 billion in fiscal 1986.

These included Social Security payroll tax increases, new taxes on Social Security benefits, a proposal to tax employees on health insurance premiums and higher contributions to civil service retirement. The contin-

gency taxes proposed by the president, which would go into effect in 1986, would make up approximately $46 billion of the $63 billion total.

Tax breaks — totaling $500 million in fiscal 1984, $1.2 billion in fiscal 1985, and $1.9 billion in fiscal 1986 — were proposed for parents who set aside money for their children's education; for tuition tax credits; for tax credits for those who hired the long-term unemployed, and for the Reagan Caribbean Basin Initiative.

National Defense. Reagan continued his quest to build up the defense budget in fiscal 1984. The budget called for an increase in new budget authority for defense from $245.5 billion in fiscal 1983 to $280.5 billion in fiscal 1984. Outlays were estimated to rise from $214.8 billion to $245.3 billion.

The Defense Department accounted for the vast bulk of the defense function. For that agency alone, budget authority would rise from $239.4 billion to $273.4 billion, an increase of 10.15 percent in real purchasing power. Outlays for the Pentagon would increase from $208.9 billion to $238.6 billion, a real increase of 10.26 percent.

Proportionally, the largest increase would come in funds for strategic nuclear forces, up from $20.6 billion in fiscal 1983 to $28.2 billion in

fiscal 1984.

Nearly half of that amount was accounted for by two programs: the MX missile ($2.9 billion for 27 missiles, $3.4 billion for development) and the B-1 bomber ($6.2 billion for 10 planes and $750 million for development).

The administration also planned to propose a $1.6 billion supplemental appropriation for fiscal 1983 that would reverse congressional decisions made in 1982 by including procurement funds for the MX and Pershing II nuclear missiles.

International Affairs. The budget proposed an increase of 19 percent over 1983 in military and military-related foreign aid for fiscal 1984. In dollar terms, the increase was $1.4 billion over the fiscal 1983 base of $7.3 billion.

In addition, the administration requested $201 million in special military and economic aid for Lebanon in fiscal 1983. Military aid for Israel would be reduced in fiscal 1984, but a substantial increase was proposed for Turkey.

Reagan also asked for a fiscal 1983 foreign aid supplemental totaling about $1.25 billion, including nearly $800 million in military-related aid Congress cut in the second fiscal 1983 continuing resolution.

Although the administration took a hold-the-line approach to most economic development aid programs, it did propose increases in U.S. contributions to the international development banks, such as the World Bank.

The amount for guaranteed loans to the Export-Import Bank would go up $2 billion — to $10 billion in fiscal 1984. Direct loan authority for Ex-Im, however, would be reduced from $4.4 billion to $3.8 billion.

Jobs. The Reagan budget's jobs initiatives focused on unemployment benefits. Reagan proposed a six-month extension of emergency supplemental unemployment benefits that were set to expire March 31.

Also, the administration asked for a new job "voucher" plan that would allow those eligible for supplemental benefits to opt instead for vouchers that they could exchange for jobs. The vouchers would be turned over to those who hired the long-term unemployed and could be exchanged by the employer for tax credits.

The administration also proposed a youth subminimum wage of $2.50 per hour. The aim of this program,

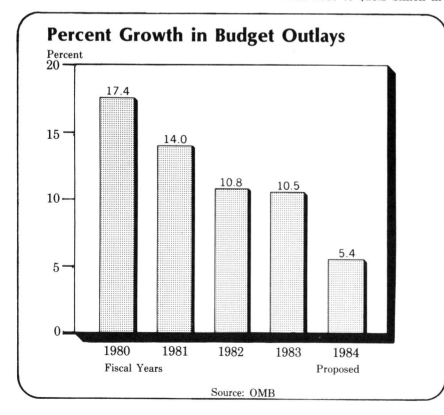

Percent Growth in Budget Outlays

Percent

Fiscal Year	Percent
1980	17.4
1981	14.0
1982	10.8
1983	10.5
1984 Proposed	5.4

Source: OMB

which would run from May to September, was to encourage employers to hire young people.

Funds for basic job training programs would be cut — from $2.2 billion in fiscal 1983 to $1.9 billion in fiscal 1984. Summer youth jobs would also be cut, to $638 million from $725 million, but only if Congress approved the subminimum wage bill.

Reagan wanted to abolish two job-related programs: community service employment for the elderly and the work incentive (WIN) program for welfare recipients.

One program was increased, however — that for dislocated workers who lost their jobs due to long-term changes in the economy. That program would be increased from $25 million in fiscal 1983 to $240 million in fiscal 1984.

Welfare. Coming on top of the reductions of the two previous years, the Reagan administration proposed more cutbacks in programs for the poor. But the fiscal 1984 welfare reductions appeared to hold little that was new, in many cases mimicking cuts from previous years.

The cuts proposed in the budget would fall most heavily on Aid to Families with Dependent Children (AFDC), food stamps, child nutrition programs and energy aid to the poor.

AFDC and child support enforcement funds would be cut $732 million in outlays from the current services level of $8.2 billion.

A mandatory "workfare" proposal, nearly identical to the one that Congress rejected in 1982, also found its way into the budget. Under the plan, states would be required to set up mandatory work programs for AFDC and food stamp recipients, who would have to take jobs in the private or public sector.

Agriculture. Total Agriculture Department outlays were estimated at $35 billion for fiscal 1984, down from a 1983 high of $45 billion. The future reductions in spending would come from improved economic conditions at home and abroad, the administration's "Payment-in-Kind" program to reduce expensive commodity surpluses and a number of controversial legislative changes.

Among the proposed changes for fiscal 1984 were a freeze in a major type of farm price support, known as target prices, and six-month delays in scheduled cost-of-living increases in major food assistance programs. The budget sketched out a $1.1 billion

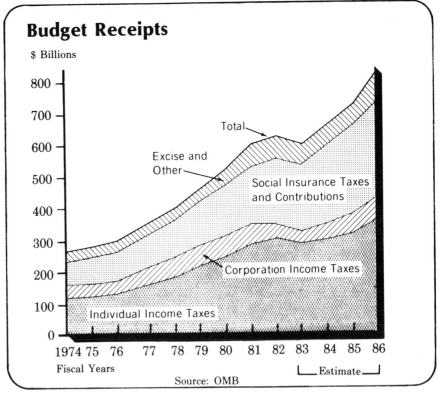

Budget Receipts

$ Billions

Source: OMB

package of money-saving changes for food stamps, including mandatory work programs for able-bodied recipients. And a special feeding and nutrition program for pregnant women and children (WIC) was frozen at the fiscal 1983 level.

The budget included supplementary budget requests for fiscal 1983 totaling nearly $7 billion, and registered a record high outlay figure for major price support programs.

Health. Reagan requested that federal outlays for health total $90.6 billion in fiscal 1984 — nearly a 10 percent increase from fiscal 1983. This increase factored in anticipated savings Congress was asked to make in the Medicare and Medicaid programs.

Proposed budget changes in Medicare and Medicaid would reduce projected outlays by $2.1 billion in fiscal 1984 and $19.3 billion through 1988, according to the Department of Health and Human Services.

Among proposed Medicare changes was a freeze on doctors' fee increases, more out-of-pocket payments for relatively short hospital stays and "catastrophic" coverage for major illnesses.

Medicaid changes included permanent cuts in federal payments to the states and a "nominal" payment of $1 or $2 by beneficiaries for each visit to the doctor.

Energy. The budget proposed drastic cuts in conservation, fossil fuel and solar and other renewable energy programs, while nuclear and defense programs would be strengthened.

Total new budget authority requested by the Energy Department was $11.9 billion, down from $12.8 billion in fiscal 1983.

The biggest chunk of the budget was atomic energy defense activities, which would take $6.77 billion — or 57 percent of all new budget authority.

Funds to state and local governments for assistance in weatherization and other conservation programs, which totaled $262 million in fiscal 1983, would be eliminated.

Natural Resources and Environment. Reagan requested further cuts in natural resources and environmental programs for fiscal 1984, seeking for the second time many cuts Congress refused to make in 1982.

The budget asked for $8.9 billion in budget authority for natural resources and environment programs, compared to $11.23 billion in fiscal 1983.

The proposed reductions came in soil conservation, mining research, environmental research, environmental grants to states and park land acquisition. However, increases were requested for water project construction, toxic dump cleanup and

Budget Authority and Outlays by Agency

(in millions of dollars†)

DEPARTMENT OR OTHER UNIT	BUDGET AUTHORITY			OUTLAYS		
	1982 actual	1983 estimate	1984 estimate	1982 actual	1983 estimate	1984 estimate
Legislative branch	1,410	1,512	1,590	1,362	1,527	1,583
The Judiciary	729	832	925	705	820	907
Executive Office of the President	93	101	111	95	102	109
Funds appropriated to the President	8,550	10,392	9,782	6,073	7,287	7,876
Agriculture	40,591	41,634	39,177	36,213	45,015	34,996
Commerce	1,825	1,576	1,411	2,045	1,969	1,669
Defense — Military[1]	213,751	239,407	273,400	182,850	208,932	238,600
Defense — Civil	2,996	2,987	2,136	2,971	2,929	2,171
Education activities	14,726	13,833	13,138	14,080	14,396	13,496
Energy activities	7,918	8,418	8,945	7,577	8,733	8,832
Health and Human Services	246,153	273,004	285,226	251,267	274,448	288,787
Housing and Urban Development	20,085	10,667	4,145	14,491	14,853	13,737
Interior	3,748	3,789	3,392	3,922	4,047	3,635
Justice	2,595	2,917	3,363	2,584	2,955	3,262
Labor	27,230	38,147	36,300	30,736	42,995	34,268
State	2,586	2,725	2,907	2,185	2,287	2,559
Transportation[2]	20,547	25,945	27,019	19,917	21,157	24,370
Treasury	111,289	118,225	135,074	110,521	118,026	134,997
Environmental Protection Agency	3,673	3,670	3,632	5,080	4,370	4,075
National Aeronautics and Space Administration	6,044	6,831	7,098	6,026	6,713	6,973
Veterans Administration	24,945	24,961	26,083	23,937	24,387	25,696
Other independent agencies	47,781	52,622	53,920	33,074	34,016	34,548
Allowances[3]	—	—	949	—	—	949
Undistributed offsetting receipts:						
Employer share, employee retirement	−7,020	−8,214	−9,853	−7,020	−8,214	−9,853
Interest received by trust funds	−16,067	−16,349	−16,862	−16,067	−16,349	−16,862
Rents and royalties on the Outer Continental Shelf lands	−6,250	−11,793	−11,895	−6,250	−11,793	−11,895
Federal surplus property disposition	—	−408	−1,003	—	−408	−1,003
Total budget authority and outlays	779,926	847,433	900,110	728,375	805,202	848,483

[1] *Includes allowances for civilian and military pay raises for Department of Defense.*
[2] *Includes allowances for military pay raises for the Coast Guard.*
[3] *Includes allowances for civilian agency pay raises and increased employing agency payments for employee retirement.*
† *Figures may not add to totals due to rounding.*

SOURCE: Fiscal 1984 Budget

---

state mine reclamation.

Transportation. The president requested increased highway funding, but not as much as Congress thought would result from the 1982 highway-gas tax increase act (PL 97-424).

A limit of $11.6 billion would be set on obligations from the Highway Trust Fund in fiscal 1983 and $12.6 billion in fiscal 1984.

The budget would eliminate mass transit operating subsidies by the end of fiscal 1984. And Amtrak funds would be reduced from $700 million to $682 million.

Federal aviation programs, however, would increase to more than $5 billion, up from $4.2 billion in 1983.

Housing. The administration renewed efforts to abandon most subsidized housing programs and replace them with cash vouchers that poor families could use to find their own housing.

Law Enforcement. For the third year in a row, no funds for the Legal Services Corporation were requested.

Education. Reagan asked for further cuts, to $13.2 billion from $15 billion in fiscal 1983.

Overall funding levels for three major programs — aid to disadvantaged primary and secondary school students, aid to the handicapped and aid to college and graduate students — would remain virtually unchanged from current levels.

The administration wanted to replace Pell grants and several other college student grant programs with new "self-help" grants, under which students would have to pay 40 percent of their college costs.

Aid to vocational education would be slashed by about $300 million from the current $800 million level. However, the budget asked for new math and science block grants: $50 million in education funds, $25 million for the National Science Foundation. ∎

Budget Resolution Reorders Reagan Priorities

As in 1982, Congress in 1983 bypassed its legal mandate to write a second budget resolution for the fiscal year beginning Oct. 1. Nor did it achieve the deficit reduction measures required by the first resolution (H Con Res 91), cleared June 23.

That measure, designed to set preliminary budget guidelines for fiscal 1984, established higher tax and domestic spending targets and called for lower military funding than President Reagan wanted. In the process, it made substantial reductions in the administration's deficit projections for fiscal 1984-86. Acknowledging the unlikelihood of action on another budget resolution in 1983, H Con Res 91 included a provision that converted its targets into binding budget levels when Congress failed to approve a second resolution by Oct. 1.

Final action on the measure concluded nearly five months of tortuous negotiations during which the future of the congressional budget process often seemed in doubt. Brushing aside the austere budget submitted by Reagan in January, House Democratic leaders won easy passage March 23 of a budget resolution that was essentially a Democratic manifesto. Passage came harder in the Senate, where moderate Republicans and Democrats bent on deficit reduction narrowly won approval May 19 of a budget blueprint that was unacceptable both to Senate GOP leaders and the president. It took another month for Senate-House conferees to patch together the final compromise plan.

The House approved the compromise by a 239-186 vote June 23 — nearly six weeks after the statutory May 15 deadline for final action on the budget. The Senate then went on to clear the resolution, which did not require the president's signature, 51-43. *(House vote 204, p. 62-H; Senate vote 168, p. 30-S)*

"I wish that we could have one [a budget] that met his [Reagan's] every desire," said Senate Budget Committee Chairman Pete V. Domenici, R-N.M. "But what he sent up here was simply not achievable."

Budget Highlights

As cleared, H Con Res 91 called for fiscal 1984 spending of $850 billion, rising to as much as $859 billion if Congress approved 10 anti-recession programs set aside in a special reserve fund. It granted only half of the 10 percent increase in defense funding the president sought. Even so, the congressional spending targets were at least $5.6 billion above the revised budget estimates released by the administration April 12, and revenues were $25.9 billion higher. The fiscal 1984 deficit was forecast at $179.3 billion with the reserve fund amounts; without the reserve fund, $169.9 billion.

The creation of the reserve fund was a way for Senate-House conferees to accommodate the wishes of many House Democrats to provide recession relief money and at the same time appease members intent on controlling the deficit. Congress approved only two of the 10 programs.

The resolution included reconciliation instructions directing congressional committees to approve deficit reduction measures designed to meet the budget's targets. Authorizing committees were required to approve $2.8 billion in program savings in fiscal 1984 and $12.3 billion over fiscal 1984-86. The House Ways and Means and Senate

Finance committees were directed to raise $12 billion in new revenues in fiscal 1984 and a total of $73 billion in new revenues over fiscal 1984-86.

Congress failed to approve any of these savings. *(Reconciliation, p. 231)*

In addition to setting fiscal 1984 budget levels, H Con Res 91 revised the fiscal 1983 levels Congress had set a year earlier. It also set preliminary budget goals for fiscal 1985-86, established "appropriate" levels for the public debt and set non-binding limits on federal credit activity. *(Fiscal 1983-86 budget totals, box, p. 440; details, box, p. 445)*

Process in Peril

The lengthy legislative struggle over H Con Res 91 imposed unprecedented strains on the nine-year-old congressional budget process. *(Budget reform, p. 238)*

In an ironic turnabout, the Reagan administration displayed growing disenchantment with the process, which the president had used as the vehicle for implementing his economic program in 1981 and 1982. *(1982 Almanac p. 186; 1981 Almanac p. 247)*

As lawmakers whittled away at Reagan's proposed military spending increase, Defense Secretary Caspar W. Weinberger suggested to the president that the administration might be better off without a congressional budget. That way, Weinberger reasoned, Reagan might be able to get more money for defense in the appropriations process, and he would be able to veto funding bills for other programs if he thought they were too high.

Weinberger's view was sharply disputed by Office of Management and Budget Director David A. Stockman, who warned the president that without the discipline of a budget resolution there would be $200 billion deficits "as far as the eye could see."

But many Republicans seemed willing to tolerate big deficits in order to maintain both the costly military build-up and Reagan's tax policy, which included the third installment of the 1981 personal tax cut, due July 1, and the indexing of tax rates to offset inflation, scheduled to take effect in 1985. *(Tax law, 1981 Almanac p. 91)*

Reagan, who remained obdurately opposed to any budget resolution that called for 1984 tax increases, blasted congressional deficit reduction efforts in a speech to the National Association of Home Builders May 16. "Yes, the deficit doctors have their scalpels out all right, but they're not poised over the budget," he said. "That's as fat as ever and getting fatter. What they're ready to operate on is your wallet."

Democrats were infuriated by Reagan's comments, which came as Senate Budget Chairman Domenici was making a last-ditch effort to put together a bipartisan budget. Three days later, Domenici and other GOP leaders urged the Senate to adopt a Reagan-opposed budget to stave off collapse of the budget process. The Senate complied by a cliff-hanging one-vote margin.

Reagan Budget

As submitted to Congress Jan. 31, Reagan's budget called for $848.5 billion in outlays and $659.7 billion in revenues in fiscal 1984. The president proposed a 10 percent increase in "real" (adjusted for inflation) defense

spending, within the framework of an overall spending freeze. Although Reagan called for $43 billion in budget savings, he still forecasted a fiscal 1984 deficit of $188.8 billion. The budget included a contingency tax plan to take effect in fiscal 1986 if deficits were still very high. Reagan projected a $147.7 billion budget for that year. *(Story, p. 425)*

Predicting a stronger than expected economic recovery, the administration April 12 lowered its fiscal 1984 spending estimate to $843.9 billion and its revenue estimate to $653.9 billion. That left a deficit of $190.2 billion, a $1.4 billion increase over the January estimate. *(July re-estimates, box, p. 429)*

House Committee Action

The entire Democratic membership of the House took an active role in formulation of the budget resolution reported by the House Budget Committee March 21 (H Con Res 91 — H Rept 98-41).

The Democratic Caucus held several meetings to discuss the budget, and House Democrats were asked to complete a multiple-choice form called "An Exercise in Hard Choices," which laid out the options before members on levels for the deficit, taxes and spending for defense and domestic programs.

When the Budget Committee sat down March 17 and in one whirlwind day approved a fiscal 1984 budget, the outcome was a foregone conclusion. The committee approved the measure on a straight 20-11 party-line vote.

Committee Democrats, who outnumbered the Republicans 20-11, had the input from the Democratic Caucus and the data from the options papers. In closed committee caucuses they arrived at consensus positions on all the major functions in the budget.

The panel called for fiscal 1984 budget authority of $936.55 billion, outlays of $863.55 billion, revenues totaling $689.1 billion and a $174.45 billion deficit.

The committee plan would cut by more than half President Reagan's proposed 10 percent increase in defense spending, raise $30 billion in additional revenues, and restore funding to many domestic programs.

Committee Republicans were rebuffed in every attempt to bring the plan back in line with the president's budget. ". . . This is the most irresponsible budget that has ever been proposed during my four years in Congress," asserted a newly minted Republican, Phil Gramm of Texas, who had served as the Democratic point man for Reagan's budgets in 1981 and 1982.

But Gramm's contention was refuted by Brian J. Donnelly, D-Mass.: "The adoption of this budget was made necessary because Congress made substantial mistakes during the last two years by adopting the budgets of the gentleman from Texas."

What the Republicans called the "Glorious Democratic Economic Recovery Program" did not please all the Democrats, either. In a letter to the Budget Committee outlining revenue recommendations for fiscal 1984, Ways and Means Chairman Dan Rostenkowski, D-Ill., said his panel expected new fiscal 1984 revenues to total $13.2 billion, including $5.2 billion in new Social Security taxes already approved by the House and an additional $8 billion in unspecified revenues. "Increases in revenue beyond this point will be difficult to achieve," the letter said. *(Social Security, p. 219)*

Budget Committee Chairman James R. Jones, D-

Okla., noted that the $30 billion figure — which would probably require elimination of the third installment of the 1981 personal income tax cut — was not necessarily what would come out of conference on the budget resolution.

The Democrats argued that their budget was a "truly Democratic" one that addressed their traditional concerns — education, health and help for the disadvantaged. But there was also a quiet acknowledgment by the Democrats that in many areas — like revenues and defense — the budget was essentially a bargaining tool.

Reflecting the gain of 26 House seats in the 1982 elections, this strategy was markedly different from the one employed by Democrats in 1981 and 1982 when their budgets were only a notch to the left of the Republicans'.

In a March 18 press conference the president lambasted the Democrats' budget as "a giant step backward into an economic quagmire."

Major Policy Shifts

In the introduction to their budget plan, the Democrats stated: "The critical problems of unemployment, business failures and inequitable treatments of the majority of our citizens demand a bold and imaginative Democratic plan to promote economic growth and fairness and equity."

To achieve these goals, which would require the restoration of funds for many social programs as well as money for new programs, the Democrats decided on a path that drastically reduced Reagan's proposed hike in defense spending and called for substantial new revenues.

Committee Republicans did not attempt to change the Democrats' proposal to limit the growth in defense spending to 4 percent after adjustment for inflation, as opposed to Reagan's 10 percent real growth rate. But Tom Loeffler, R-Texas, did offer an amendment that would have required the Democrats to explain how they would achieve that lower growth rate.

Loeffler called the Democrats' proposed $16.4 billion cut in fiscal 1984 defense budget authority and $9.5 billion cut in outlays from the president's request a "plug number." He said it was an "arbitrary political decision not based on what the defense needs of the country are."

But Jones argued that the 4 percent figure was not "totally out of the ballpark" from what people on both sides of the Capitol were considering. Loeffler's amendment was defeated on an 11-20 party-line vote.

The Republicans also failed to convince budget panel Democrats that raising $30 billion in revenues as the nation was emerging from a recession was bad economic policy.

Jack F. Kemp, R-N.Y. — one of the authors of the 1981 personal tax cut plan — offered an amendment that would have eliminated the proposed revenue increase in fiscal 1984. "Don't raise taxes in a recession," Kemp argued. "Don't take $30 billion out of the economy when it is in this fragile situation."

Kemp's amendment failed, as did an amendment to protect the indexing provisions of the 1981 tax law, which were scheduled to take effect in 1985, and an amendment that would have called for the same revenue increase recommended by the Ways and Means Committee.

Domestic Spending

During the debate over revenues, Gramm contended that the Democrats were "raising taxes and cutting defense to pay for domestic programs."

In addition to the $4.9 billion in emergency aid con-

tained in the jobs plan (HR 1718) approved by the House March 3, the Budget Committee agreed to provide money for community renewal, summer feeding and summer youth employment programs, foreclosure assistance for both farmers and homeowners, and health insurance benefits for the unemployed. Much of this money was to be spent in fiscal 1983. *(Jobs bill, p. 447)*

"Long-term growth" programs also were supported by the panel — including $4.25 billion for additional education and employment and training programs; $1.5 billion in added research money; $8.6 billion for physical capital development such as roads, water systems and bridges; $100 million for a National Industrial Development Bank; and $800 million for export assistance.

The fiscal 1984 budget resolution included a revision of the fiscal 1983 spending plan. The new figures estimated that spending in fiscal 1983 would total $886.2 billion in budget authority and $814.7 billion in outlays, with a $208.5 billion deficit.

Over the objections of all Republicans save Kemp, the committee included language stating that monetary policy and economic assumptions in the budget should be consistent. To achieve that goal, the Federal Reserve Board was asked to report to Congress on its objectives with respect to economic growth, inflation and unemployment. If differences existed between the Fed and the administration and Congress, the Fed would be required to explain the discrepancies.

For the fiscal 1984 budget, the committee agreed to use economic assumptions provided by the Congressional Budget Office, which were slightly more optimistic than the administration's.

Rule for Floor Debate

The Budget Committee agreed to ask the Rules Committee for a rule governing floor debate that would allow only one amendment — in the form of a Republican substitute — to be offered.

When Rules met March 21, the Republicans asked to be allowed to offer not a substitute but a series of amendments — perhaps up to 15. In addition to the GOP request, conservative Democrats and William E. Dannemeyer, R-Calif., asked for a rule allowing consideration of their alternative budgets. The Black Caucus decided not to ask for a separate vote on its alternative plan.

The Rules Committee, however, went along with the Budget Committee's request, and the rule provided for votes only on the Budget Committee plan and a GOP substitute.

Despite outcries from the Republicans when the rule came to a vote on the House floor March 22, the rule was approved 230-187. *(Vote 38, p. 14-H)*

House Floor Action

The House passed H Con Res 91 by a 229-196 vote March 23. Since the Republicans offered no substitute, the committee-reported resolution was adopted without change. *(Vote 42, p. 16-H)*

Although it was an unequivocal victory for the Democrats, Republicans maintained that the vote provided them with live political ammunition to fire against the "big-spending" Democrats.

While cutting $14.3 billion from the president's deficit forecast for fiscal 1984, the Democrats' budget would increase domestic spending by approximately $33 billion,

with much of the money earmarked for human needs programs that were significantly cut in the fiscal 1982 and 1983 budgets.

The plan also repudiated Reagan's proposal for further major escalation in defense spending. It called for a 4 percent growth rate after adjustment for inflation, compared to the administration's request for a 10 percent real growth rate.

Finally, in order to arrive at a deficit figure lower than the administration's, the House Democrats proposed that $30 billion in additional revenues be raised in fiscal 1984.

To achieve that goal probably would require elimination of the third installment of the 1981 personal income tax cut. And in 1985, when $40 billion in new revenue would be required under the Democrats' plan, the indexing provision of the 1981 tax bill probably would have to be dropped.

Taken as a whole, the Democratic plan represented a political manifesto. "I think it is very important that we make a statement today that this Congress is not going to turn its back on the millions of people that are unemployed in this nation; that this Congress in the long term wants to deal with the industrial base problems in this nation; that this Congress, albeit without any cooperation from [the Republican] side of the aisle or from this administration, continues to stand on the belief that government has a responsibility to those individuals who realistically and honestly cannot help themselves," said Majority Leader Jim Wright, D-Texas.

Republicans lambasted the Democrats for a return to the old days of "tax and tax, spend and spend."

Minority Leader Robert H. Michel, R-Ill., said the budget resolution should be called the "Revenge on Ronald Reagan Act of 1983." Bill Frenzel, R-Minn., called it "Chairman Jones' letter to Santa Claus."

But after the Democrats' first budget victory in three years, Speaker Thomas P. O'Neill Jr., D-Mass., said: "The people believe that Reagan policies are unfair and have gone too far. This evening, the House voted to restore fairness and balance to our national policies."

Democratic Unity

The difference for the Democrats in 1983 was not merely the 26 House seats they gained in the 1982 elections, although that obviously helped.

The process of putting together the fiscal 1984 budget was what Jones called the "most extraordinary exercise in making hard choices in revenues and spending that has ever occurred in my memory."

"Nearly every Democratic House member helped shape this budget," Wright said on the floor.

Jones made a point of noting that "no one agrees with every single detail in this package." But Wright said the budget "comes as close as we have been able to achieve to a consensus on the Democratic side of the aisle."

The leadership let it be known, especially to the freshmen, that they were expected to stick by the budget when it came to a vote. And stick they did. Fifty-two of the 58 Democratic freshmen voted for the Budget Committee plan. Of the 50 sitting Democrats who voted with Reagan on his first budget in 1981, 23 stuck with their party this time. *(1981 Almanac p. 263)*

Democrats lost a total of 36 votes but picked up four Republicans on the final vote. The GOP defectors were Claudine Schneider, R.I.; Bill Green, N.Y.; James M. Jeffords, Vt.; and Matthew J. Rinaldo, N.J.

The Republicans, on the other hand, could not find an alternative budget around which to coalesce. And because many Republicans did not want to vote for it, the GOP did not want to offer the president's original budget plan.

GOP members berated the Democrats for not allowing them more time to come up with an alternative. But Wright asserted that the lack of a Republican plan was "tellingly revealing of the bankruptcy and abdication of responsibility" of the minority.

The vacuum left by the Republicans' refusal to offer a substitute made it easier for many conservative "Boll Weevil" Democrats to return to the party fold.

The Democrats conceded from the outset that the conference with the Senate was where the real decisions would be made. Majority Whip Thomas S. Foley, D-Wash., told a group of reporters on the day of the House vote, "The final product is the conference report — not the House or the Senate budget."

House Budget Plan

Following is a summary of the budget's major elements:

Revenues. The budget assumed revenue increases totaling $35.2 billion in fiscal 1984, $48.1 billion in fiscal 1985 and $58 billion in fiscal 1986. These totals included $5.2 billion from the tax increase in the Social Security Act amendments (HR 1900). *(Story, p. 219)*

Decisions about how the remaining revenues would be raised were left up to the Ways and Means Committee.

Defense. The resolution called for $263.9 billion in budget authority and $235.4 billion in outlays in fiscal 1984. This was a $16.4 billion decrease in budget authority from the president's request and a $9.3 billion reduction in outlays. However, the resolution made room for a 4 percent increase in military pay, which the administration had proposed to freeze.

Entitlements. The House plan contained no additional reductions in means-tested entitlement programs; instead, it restored funding for some programs cut under previous Reagan budgets and increased funding for others.

● Food stamps would be funded at the current authorized level of $13.14 billion. The budget plan assumed restoration of some of the benefit cuts enacted in the past two years.

● Child nutrition programs would be increased $200 million over current law levels. The special supplemental food program for women, infants and children (WIC) would be increased $300 million.

● Aid to Families with Dependent Children would be increased $100 million over the current law requirement to accommodate repeal of 1981 reconciliation provisions that tended to discourage work.

● The budget rejected the administration's proposals to reduce Medicaid spending below the fiscal 1983 baseline.

Discretionary Domestic Spending. Compared to fiscal 1983, the resolution increased discretionary domestic spending in fiscal 1984 by $22.2 billion in budget authority and $12.45 billion in outlays.

Programs for which funding was increased included compensatory, handicapped, vocational and adult education; job training; social services; community service block grants; child welfare services; mass transportation; low-income housing; and low-income energy weatherization.

Funding was provided for some new domestic programs, including health insurance for the unemployed; foreclosure relief for homeowners and farmers; compensa-

tion for veterans exposed to Agent Orange; and an industrial development bank.

The House budget assumed a 4 percent pay increase for civilian federal employees and a delay in cost-of-living (COLA) increases for federal retirees by six months; the administration had proposed a 12-month delay.

Reconciliation. The resolution directed seven House committees to report reconciliation savings totaling $1.75 billion in budget authority and $2.1 billion in outlays — mostly by delaying COLAs.

Other Provisions. The resolution contained a provision automatically converting it to a binding second resolution if a second resolution were not approved by Oct. 1.

Also included was "sense of Congress" language declaring that the Federal Reserve Board's monetary policy and economic assumptions "shall be consistent" with those of Congress and the administration.

Senate Committee Action

Defying President Reagan, the Republican-controlled Senate Budget Committee April 21 approved a Democratic-inspired budget that called for more than $30 billion in new taxes in fiscal 1984 and provided only half of the increase in defense spending authority the president sought.

Committee Chairman Domenici and three other Republicans joined with nine of the panel's 10 Democrats to report out the budget resolution, 13-4, breaking a deadlock that had prevented the committee from acting the week before. Voting against the resolution were Republicans William L. Armstrong, Colo.; Charles E. Grassley, Iowa; and Dan Quayle, Ind., and Democrat Ernest F. Hollings, S.C., who supported a budget freeze.

As reported April 24, the resolution (S Con Res 27 — S Rept 98-63) called for fiscal 1984 budget authority of $908.6 billion, outlays of $848.8 billion, revenues of $686.7 billion and a $162 billion deficit.

The committee's budget was born more out of frustration than belief. Domenici and others argued that it was more important to keep the budget process moving than to insist on any particular numbers. "The time has come to get a budget resolution," Domenici declared after weeks of fruitless efforts to achieve an accommodation with the White House. The committee had begun its markups March 9.

But both before and after the vote, Domenici vowed he would do his utmost to change the revenue numbers on the Senate floor, as well as fight to increase the resolution's 5 percent real growth rate for defense.

Domenici's decision to push through a resolution — even a Democratic one — came one day after he, Majority Leader Howard H. Baker Jr., R-Tenn., and White House advisers failed to convince all the Republicans on the Budget panel to support a compromise offered by Reagan.

The White House plan — presented to the GOP members by presidential counselor Edwin Meese III, chief of staff James A. Baker III and budget director Stockman — called for 7.5 percent real growth for defense instead of the 10 percent increase proposed by Reagan in January. It also called for $13 billion more in domestic spending than the president had proposed. Reagan had refused to budge on his original revenue plan, which called for minimal tax increases in fiscal 1984 and 1985, but contingency taxes totaling $146 billion from fiscal 1986 to 1988 if the economy did not perform well.

Revenues

Although Domenici and moderate Republicans on the Budget panel agreed to support the Reagan compromise, the committee's fiscal conservatives balked at raising any taxes at all.

The administration tried right up to the vote to convert some of these hard-liners, and Baker called from the White House to ask Domenici if the vote might be postponed. Baker said he thought the administration was only one or two votes shy of victory.

But the White House needed all 12 Republican votes to get its budget plan through, and at least one — Armstrong — refused to relent. Finally, Domenici decided he "couldn't wait any longer" since "there was little chance of getting a solid Republican budget resolution." There was "too much risk in delay," he concluded.

During a luncheon meeting with ranking committee Democrat Lawton Chiles, Fla., Domenici explained what he wanted to do: first — knowing it would fail — vote on the president's revenue figures, and then move to a vote on a Democratic revenue plan proposed by Chiles, which he was certain would carry.

Chiles caucused with committee Democrats and lined up the votes for the revenue package and the budget resolution.

Armstrong, the committee member most adamantly opposed to increasing taxes, said he did not believe a vote against the budget resolution was "a vote against the process." Armstrong said the whole idea behind the budget process was to "raise confrontation.... It wasn't supposed to be painless."

Before the vote on the revenue numbers, Armstrong stated the conservatives' position. "There aren't an unlimited number of possibilities" for raising new revenues, he said. Voting for a standby tax would "trigger a tax increase, and a very sizable one."

But Domenici countered — as he had argued for weeks — that Congress was going to have to raise some revenues in order to help lower the enormous projected deficits. However, Domenici said, "we ought to do it as far away as possible. We ought to do it in the outyears."

Chiles disputed that theory. "We need increased revenues in [fiscal] 1984 and 1985," he said. "The idea that you're going to wait until 1986 to get this additional revenue dooms the recovery."

The revenue proposal Domenici offered was essentially what the president had proposed in his January budget: negligible tax increases in fiscal 1984 and 1985 but sizable revenue hikes between fiscal 1986-88.

The president's plan was defeated on a 6-10 vote. Two Republicans — Armstrong and Grassley — voted against the plan, along with eight Democrats.

The committee then approved, 12-4, the same Chiles tax proposal it had defeated on an 11-11 tie vote a week earlier. It called for $30.2 billion in new revenues in fiscal 1984, $39.1 billion in fiscal 1985, $51.9 billion in fiscal 1986, $68.6 billion in fiscal 1987 and $80 billion in fiscal 1988. These figures closely mirrored the revenue numbers adopted by the House.

Voting for the Chiles revenue figures were four Republicans — Domenici, Slade Gorton, Wash., Mark Andrews, N.D., and Nancy Landon Kassebaum, Kan. — and eight Democrats: Chiles, Joseph R. Biden Jr., Del.; J. Bennett Johnston, La.; Jim Sasser, Tenn.; Howard M. Metzenbaum, Ohio; Donald W. Riegle Jr., Mich.; Daniel Patrick Moyni-

han, N.Y., and J. James Exon, Neb. The four Republicans voting against the Chiles tax plan were: Armstrong, Grassley, Quayle and Rudy Boschwitz, Minn.

Defense

In earlier action, committee Republicans and Democrats joined together April 7, voting 17-4 to cut in half the increase in military spending authority sought by the president for fiscal 1984.

The committee's defense plan would provide a 5 percent real increase in spending authority — to $267 billion — in fiscal 1984, in contrast to Reagan's request for a 10 percent inflation-adjusted growth rate. It voted down Reagan's proposal 19-2.

The Senate panel's action followed House approval of even greater cuts in the administration's defense request. House Democrats maintained their defense figures would provide a 4 percent real growth rate. However, the Congressional Budget Office estimated the House figures would yield a 2.3 to 2.9 percent rate.

Domenici, frustrated and bruised by the president's months-long insistence on his 10 percent figure, laid the blame for the committee's rebuke at the White House steps.

The chairman, who cast his lot with seven other Republicans and nine Democrats for the 5 percent defense growth rate, said the administration was "not responding to its own friends." Then pointing to himself, he added, "at least this one."

Domenici's displeasure flowed from weeks of efforts to convince the president that his defense request would not be approved and that it was time to compromise.

The Budget chairman had acquiesced three weeks earlier to Reagan's plea for additional time to seek "flexibility" on his defense request.

Domenici and the committee's Republican members met with Reagan April 5, and the next day Domenici visited the White House again — this time with Chiles. During those meetings Reagan learned just how little support there was for his continued massive military buildup.

Reagan offered to lower the defense request by perhaps $5 billion in budget authority and $4 billion in outlays because of adjustments in fuel costs, lower inflation and changes in the MX missile program. But he remained unwilling to make any adjustments in major defense programs.

"The president did not basically give any on the 10 percent [growth in military spending]," Chiles said.

Metzenbaum and other Democrats charged that members were "misled" about Reagan's willingness to negotiate. Domenici said he did not believe the "president intentionally misled" him.

But several Republicans were chagrined by the president's intransigence. Grassley, generally a stalwart Reagan supporter, wanted the committee to support a freeze in defense spending over the next several years. Before the final vote, Grassley made what a committee colleague, Armed Services Chairman John Tower, R-Texas, called a "stirring indictment" of the administration.

Grassley cited studies and figures that detailed failures in the Pentagon's procurement procedures. "Why should we dump huge sums of money into the Defense Department," he asked, "when it is rotting with bad management?"

While Tower agreed that Grassley had made some

H Con Res 91: Final Budget Totals Compared

(Fiscal years, in billions of dollars)

	1983	1984	1985	1986
Budget Authority				
Reagan January budget	$847.4	$900.1	$997.4	$1,079.6
Reagan April revisions	867.9	906.4	997.6	1,082.5
House resolution	886.2	936.55	998.65	1,058.4
Senate resolution	875.93	914.7	986.37	1,050.2
Conference agreement, excluding reserve fund items	877.2	919.5	990.5	1,054.6
Conference agreement, including reserve fund items	883.36	928.725	996.75	1,059.3
Outlays				
Reagan January budget	805.2	848.5	918.5	989.6
Reagan April revisions	808.5	843.9	917.0	988.4
House resolution	814.7	863.55	912.6	967.55
Senate resolution	807.33	849.7	910.7	966.0
Conference agreement, excluding reserve fund items	807.4	849.5	906.75	962.95
Conference agreement, including reserve fund items	812.85	858.925	911.6	966.635
Revenues				
Reagan January budget	597.5	659.7	724.3	841.9
Reagan April revisions	598.3	653.7	732.4	843.8
House resolution	606.2	689.1	765.9	831.5
Senate resolution	603.3	671.1	743.1	835.9
Conference agreement	604.3	679.6	750.5	835.8
Deficit				
Reagan January budget	−207.7	−188.8	−194.2	−147.7
Reagan April revisions	−210.2	−190.2	−184.6	−144.6
House resolution	−208.5	−174.45	−146.7	−136.05
Senate resolution	−204.0	−178.6	−167.7	−130.1
Conference agreement, excluding reserve fund items	203.1	169.9	156.25	127.15
Conference agreement, including reserve fund items	208.55	179.325	161.1	130.835

significant points, he argued that "every time Congress tries to second-guess the president on national security and foreign affairs . . . we're wrong." The result, Tower maintained, was that Congress weakened the president's ability to formulate national security and foreign policy.

Tower offered a compromise: a real growth rate in defense spending of 8 percent for the next two fiscal years, with higher growth rates projected for the future. That failed on a 7-14 vote.

Republicans Andrews and Gorton joined Democrats Exon, Johnston, and Moynihan in offering the 5 percent growth course for defense.

Andrews bristled at the argument that the Senate had to opt for a higher growth rate in order to have a bargaining chip with the House. "The committee should come out with a level of spending for programs we think need to be sustained. . . . It's not for trading stock," Andrews argued.

The defense spending path agreed to by the committee would provide fiscal 1984 budget authority of $267 billion and outlays of $241.4 billion.

This would reduce outlays requested by Reagan only $3.3 billion in fiscal 1984. But budget authority — affecting the Department of Defense's ability to plan long-range projects — would be reduced $13.2 billion. Over five years, outlays would be reduced $89 billion from Reagan's request, while budget authority would be about $119 billion lower.

The four Republicans who voted against the 5 percent real growth rate for defense were Tower, Orrin G. Hatch, Utah, Steven D. Symms, Idaho, and Grassley — who said he was voting against it because he did not think the growth rate was low enough.

Budget Details

The budget plan approved by the Senate committee called for about $11.3 billion more in domestic spending than the president proposed, even with the 5 percent growth rate for defense. Highlights of the measure:

Defense. The committee's plan called for $267 billion in fiscal 1984 budget authority and $241.4 billion in out-

lays. While this amounted to a reduction of only $3.3 billion in outlays from the president's defense request, it was $13.2 billion lower in budget authority, affecting the Defense Department's ability to plan long-range projects.

International Affairs. The resolution provided essentially what Reagan requested in this area: $18.2 billion in budget authority and $12.7 billion in outlays. The committee also assumed an $8.5 billion supplemental appropriation for the U.S. contribution to the International Monetary Fund.

Income Security. The committee plan provided $300.9 billion in fiscal 1984 budget authority and $281.2 billion in outlays for welfare and benefit programs included in this category. These numbers reflected spending included in the emergency jobs bill approved in March and took into account the recently approved Social Security bill.

The committee budget would delay for six months cost-of-living adjustments for a number of benefit and retirement programs.

The committee rejected civil service and military reforms proposed by Reagan, and approved additional money for supplemental feeding and child nutrition programs.

Health. The resolution included reforms to the Medicare and Medicaid programs that would save $23.6 billion over five years. This total included $10 billion in savings already enacted as part of the Social Security bill.

The total level of funding for health programs amounted to $93.2 billion in fiscal 1984 budget authority and $92.1 billion in outlays.

Education, Training and Employment. Casting aside Reagan's proposed cuts and reworking of education and training programs, the committee called for $30.8 billion in fiscal 1985 budget authority and $27 billion in outlays. This level provided a 2 percent increase above current levels and added funds for vocational education, math and science education, and compensatory education programs.

Federal Pay Raise. The plan included a six-month delay in the 4 percent pay raise for civilian federal employees.

Reconciliation. The resolution directed four Senate committees and seven House committees to report outlay reductions totaling $3.1 billion in fiscal 1984, $4.8 billion in 1985 and $5.9 billion in 1986. The Finance and Ways and Means committees were directed to achieve revenue increases of $30.2 billion, $39.1 billion and $51.9 billion over that period.

Senate Floor Action

Moderate Senate Republicans and Democrats defied President Reagan and the GOP leadership May 19 by approving a fiscal 1984 budget that increased taxes and domestic spending while slowing the defense buildup.

Unwilling to torpedo the budget process, the Senate approved its budget plan by a 50-49 vote at the end of a grueling session. During the course of the day the Senate twice rejected a leadership plan that had the reluctant endorsement of the president, and initially turned down the budget it ultimately accepted. *(Vote 112, p. 23-S)*

The message of the vote was clear: Big deficits were less tolerable than increased taxes.

And in a striking demonstration of political and philosophical role reversal, a small band of moderate Republicans led the quest for deficit reduction.

As approved by the Senate, S Con Res 27 contained a fiscal 1984 deficit of $178.6 billion, compared to a $193 billion deficit in the leadership plan and $185 billion in the president's own budget.

Perhaps more important, the plan — authored by Gorton — showed declining deficits through fiscal 1988. Projecting the leadership budget to fiscal 1988, the deficit would climb to $220 billion.

The final Senate budget called for fiscal 1984 budget authority of $914.7 billion, outlays of $849.7 billion and revenues totaling $671.1 billion.

In an impassioned speech before the leadership plan went down for the last time, Domenici said: "It's insanity for the U.S. Senate not to vote in a budget resolution.... There's nothing wrong with the budget process. What's wrong is that these are extremely difficult economic times. It's the facts we don't want to vote on, so we blame the budget process."

Domenici opposed the Gorton plan but voted for it to move the budget debate into conference.

Details of Senate floor action:

First Week: Standoff

The Senate debated S Con Res 27 to a standoff the first week in May. Neither the Democrats nor the Republicans had enough votes to push a budget plan to victory.

Several amendments were considered on the floor; a few were adopted. But most of the action took place behind closed doors as both parties worked to develop a strategy and build a majority.

The Republican leadership pinned its hopes on a compromise plan that had the lukewarm endorsement of the president and substantial, but not total, support among Senate Republicans.

As the behind-the-scenes negotiations continued, floor debate inched forward. The Senate solidly rejected four omnibus budget packages that promised lower deficits by the end of the decade.

Conservatives, led by Hatch, backed an overall budget plan that would have preserved the administration's tax cuts, called for higher defense spending than the GOP compromise plan and required drastic reductions in domestic spending.

"We think that, if there is any way of keeping the recovery going, it will not be by increasing taxes. It would be by cutting federal spending or at least by restraining the growth, which is what our budget does," Hatch said. But the Hatch plan, which had the endorsement of the U.S. Chamber of Commerce and a variety of trade groups, failed 23-75. *(Vote 67, p. 16-S)*

A budget freeze proposed by Hollings lost 16-82, a slightly better showing than he achieved on a similar amendment in 1982. The proposal would have allowed a 3 percent after-inflation increase for defense while freezing all domestic discretionary spending for one year. It would have eliminated both the third installment of the personal tax cut and provisions to index taxes to inflation. *(Vote 66, p. 16-S)*

Two other budget packages were also defeated. One, offered by Johnston and other conservative Democrats, would have allowed defense to grow at an inflation-adjusted rate of 5 percent, held all other domestic spending to a 2 percent increase and raised substantial new taxes after fiscal 1985. It was defeated 13-83. *(Vote 69, p. 16-S)*

The other plan, offered by Grassley, would have frozen both domestic and defense spending, but allowed the presi-

dent's tax cuts to remain in place. It was defeated by voice vote.

The Senate tacitly acknowledged that the recession's impact on the unemployed would continue when it voted 90-9 to provide $1.8 billion from fiscal 1983-85 for health insurance for the unemployed. *(Vote 73, p. 17-S)*

The health insurance amendment offered by Finance Chairman Robert Dole, R-Kan., was adopted after the Senate defeated, 36-63, a more generous proposal that mirrored the House-approved budget's $2.7 billion figure. *(Vote 72, p. 17-S)*

Dole stressed, however, that the cost of the program would be offset — either by increasing revenues or finding savings in other programs.

On May 6, the Senate also agreed, 55-32, to a Hollings amendment providing an additional $1 billion in fiscal 1984 for education programs. *(Vote 78, p. 18-S)*

By a 45-50 vote the Senate rejected an amendment by Max Baucus, D-Mont., to restore $440 million for Medicare funding. *(Vote 70, p. 16-S)*

Second Week: Back to Committee

The Senate May 12 tabled, 52-48, a Republican leadership budget and rejected, 46-53, a spending plan introduced by five moderate Republicans and modified by Gorton. *(Votes 85, 86, p. 19-S)*

The resolution then was sent back to the Budget Committee, which was given three days to develop another budget blueprint.

After his first major defeat on an economic issue, Majority Leader Baker said he was "determined, to the extent possible, to get a budget resolution."

The issues that dragged the two Republican budget plans to defeat were the size of the deficits and taxes. Almost every member thought the deficits were too high. Some were willing to bring the deficits down by raising taxes, but others were not — especially if the third installment of the 1981 personal income tax cut were jeopardized in any way.

The GOP leadership plan — known as the Domenici-Baker plan — called for only minimal tax increases in fiscal 1984 and 1985, and as a result showed very high deficits. Moderate Republicans called for higher tax increases in fiscal 1984 and 1985, although not nearly as high as the $30.2 billion included in the Budget Committee's resolution, which was supported by the Democrats.

But the moderates' revenue figure was high enough — $8.9 billion in fiscal 1984 and $13.9 billion in fiscal 1985 — to permit members to interpret a vote for the plan as a vote to cap the personal tax cut. That was how Baker framed the final vote. "I believe that is the real issue before us. . . . Are we going to change the third year of the tax cut or leave it intact?"

There were political as well as substantive reasons for the defeat of the two budget plans. The vote was a test of the Republican leadership's ability to control the budget and its desire to give the White House another, and final, chance to enter serious budget deliberations.

The behind-the-scenes deliberations and deadlock that had characterized the first week of Senate budget debate continued in the days leading up to recommittal of S Con Res 27.

This time, however, the stalemate was not among all Republicans but between the GOP leadership and the "gang of five," who adamantly opposed the Domenici-Baker plan on the grounds that it did not contain enough

new taxes to make a dent in the high deficits projected for the next five years.

The five moderates were: John H. Chafee, R.I.; Mark O. Hatfield, Ore.; Charles McC. Mathias Jr., Md.; Robert T. Stafford, Vt.; and Lowell P. Weicker Jr., Conn.

By midweek the details of the moderates' budget were known. Their plan would have raised $14.3 billion in new taxes in fiscal 1984, $22 billion in fiscal 1985, $34 billion in fiscal 1986, $47 billion in fiscal 1987 and $60 billion in fiscal 1988. While not specifying how the taxes would be raised, these figures would have accommodated a $300 cap on the third installment of the personal tax cut due in July and the repeal of tax indexing, which would adjust tax rates for inflation after 1985.

The Domenici-Baker plan, which was a two-year budget, called for only $2.6 billion in new taxes in fiscal 1984 and $5.7 billion in fiscal 1985.

The moderates' plan would have decreased the defense spending scheme slightly from the GOP leadership's budget. In fiscal 1984, the moderates called for a 6 percent growth rate in defense funding, after adjustment for inflation — as opposed to the Domenici-Baker plan for a 7.5 percent growth rate. In fiscal 1985, both plans called for a 5 percent real growth rate in defense.

On domestic spending, the moderates' plan, like the Domenici-Baker budget, accepted the level of funding included in the Budget Committee's resolution. However, the moderates also included several Senate floor amendments raising fiscal 1984 outlays for domestic spending $12.6 billion above the amount requested by the administration. The GOP leadership plan was $11.3 billion higher than Reagan's.

Amendments included in the moderates' plan called for:

● $900 million in fiscal 1984 for health insurance for the unemployed. *(Vote 73, p. 17-S)*

● $1 billion in fiscal 1984 for education programs. *(Vote 78, p. 18-S)*

● $49 million in fiscal 1984 to increase Medicaid funds for low-income pregnant women and newborn children.

The fiscal 1984 deficit in the moderates' plan was estimated at $181 billion, compared to $192.4 billion in the leadership budget.

Weicker said the five "were willing to negotiate our figures with the leadership and with the White House all week," but the leadership was unwilling to negotiate.

In the end the moderates outlasted the leadership. The five moderates knew, as did the leadership, that without their votes the Domenici-Baker plan would go down to defeat. They wanted the leadership's plan to be voted on first, confident that other moderate Republicans who were committed to the leadership would come over to their side if Domenici-Baker failed. They also expected to pick up considerable Democratic support.

The leadership, meanwhile, hoped that the moderates would be satisfied just to get a vote on their proposal, and thus would be willing to go first. Assuming the moderates' plan would be defeated, the leadership reckoned that they and some Democrats then would vote for Domenici-Baker rather than have no budget resolution at all.

But for the first time in recent years the moderates, not the conservatives, held the balance of power in a major Republican policy battle. It was their chance to make a difference on an issue they all genuinely cared about, and they made it.

When the showdown finally came on May 12, Baker

knew the leadership plan would be defeated, but he also thought that without his backing the moderates' plan would probably go down as well. Then Baker could move to recommit the budget resolution and hope that the committee would come up with something that all Republicans, and perhaps even the White House, could support.

After the Domenici-Baker budget was tabled, Weicker offered the moderates' plan. "In origin, this too is a 'Republican substitute,' but one we sincerely believe addresses serious and widespread bipartisan concerns about correct numbers for defense, deficits and domestic spending," Weicker said.

After speeches by several of its cosponsors, however, the five yielded to Gorton, who outlined his modification of their plan.

Gorton said that "every proposal before us has been an orphan. . . ." He said his plan was an "attempt to bridge the chasm between the president and the Senate" on taxes.

Gorton's plan called for $8.9 billion in new taxes in fiscal 1984, $13.9 billion in fiscal 1985 and $51 billion in fiscal 1986. The fiscal 1984 revenue number, Gorton acknowledged, was the figure that House Ways and Means Chairman Rostenkowski and Senate Finance Chairman Dole had said they could raise.

On defense, Gorton's budget assumed a 6 percent real growth rate in fiscal 1984, 5.5 percent in fiscal 1985 and 5 percent in 1986. These were the same growth rates included in an amendment offered by Sam Nunn, D-Ga., and Henry M. Jackson, D-Wash., that was defeated on a 48-48 tie vote. *(Vote 80, p. 18-S)*

Domestic spending, under Gorton, was the same as in the moderates' plan. And Gorton's projected deficit was $184 billion in fiscal 1984, dropping to $152 billion by fiscal 1988.

But Domenici rose in opposition to Gorton, noting that he had a "lot of doubt" that even the modest revenues contained in the Gorton plan could be raised. Baker also spoke against the plan, while expressing support for maintaining the budget process.

The Senate then defeated Gorton's substitute and recommitted the budget to committee by voice vote.

Committee Tries Again

In a May 18 session, the Budget Committee rejected a Domenici-Chiles plan that would have raised $9 billion in new taxes in fiscal 1984, $15 billion in fiscal 1985 and $51 billion in fiscal 1986.

Their compromise also included real growth rates for defense of 6 percent in fiscal 1984, 5.5 percent in fiscal 1985 and 5 percent in fiscal 1986.

It was the tax increases, however, that made it impossible for Domenici to get a majority of his Republican committee colleagues to support this slight modification of the moderate GOP plan defeated by the Senate a week earlier.

At the outset, Domenici said Baker would not support the plan unless a majority of committee Republicans was willing to vote for it. But only five of the 12 would do so.

A highly charged partisan atmosphere burned any chance for the compromise to be approved, and the plan was defeated 8-12. The committee also rejected, 8-12, the resolution originally reported by the committee.

Domenici then offered a slightly modified version of the Domenici-Baker budget defeated a week earlier by the Senate. With Democratic presidential contenders Hollings and Gary Hart, Colo., absent, the plan was approved 11-9.

Penner Named CBO Head

The Congressional Budget Office (CBO) experienced the first change of command in its eight-year history Sept. 1, when Rudolph G. Penner took over as director of the agency. Penner, a Republican economist, succeeded Democrat Alice M. Rivlin, who had served as CBO's director since its inception in 1975.

Rivlin announced late in 1982 that she would resign to return to the Brookings Institution, a Washington think tank, but she agreed to delay her departure until the fiscal 1984 budget resolution was in place.

CBO was created by the 1974 Congressional Budget and Impoundment Control Act (PL 93-344) to provide Congress with the technical expertise needed to produce and implement a congressional budget. Its directors were to be appointed for four-year terms.

Penner was appointed by House Speaker Thomas P. O'Neill Jr., D-Mass., and Senate President Pro Tempore Strom Thurmond, R-S.C., upon the unanimous recommendation of a congressional search committee. The appointment was made without the controversy that accompanied the selection of Rivlin in 1975. *(1975 Almanac p. 151)*

Penner had held several economic policy positions in the Nixon and Ford administrations, winding up as assistant director for economic policy in the Office of Management and Budget in 1975-76. After the 1976 election, Penner joined the American Enterprise Institute, conservatives' answer to Brookings.

Third Week: Turnabout

Early floor votes May 19 made it clear the GOP leadership could not put together a winning coalition.

After a very brief explanation and debate, the Senate defeated, 43-56, a plan offered by Domenici that had been approved a day earlier in the Budget Committee. *(Vote 102, p. 22-S))*

The Senate had tabled essentially the same budget May 12, 52-48. Domenici altered the budget slightly to lower the real growth rate for defense to 7.1 percent from 7.5 percent in fiscal 1984, although defense outlays were increased $1.2 billion. *(Vote 85, p. 19-S)*

Some of that increase was offset, however, by lower cost estimates for entitlement benefit programs that are affected by cost-of-living adjustments (COLAs). This was due to a downward revision in the fiscal 1984 inflation rate — from 4.1 to 3.5 percent.

Democrats charged that Domenici's plan flew in the face of Republican rhetoric that "deficits are the acid test" of an economic program. "This is the biggest political about-face in the annals of government," charged Metzenbaum.

Gorton and his moderate Republican allies offered their plan, but could not muster enough votes to forge a majority. Their budget was defeated 48-52. *(Vote 103, p. 22-S)*

Domenici tried again, offering his budget with technical changes. "We're going to have chaos in Congress without a budget resolution," he warned.

The Budget chairman said the appropriations process would be in an "absolute muddle." "We will get veto after

veto. . . . I warn you, you'll rue the day."

But with the backing of enough Democrats, the unwavering moderate Republicans were able to defeat Domenici's plan again, 43-57. *(Vote 107, p. 22-S)*

Recognizing that it was Gorton's budget or nothing, Baker offered a motion to reconsider the vote by which Gorton was defeated. "It is essential, in my view," Baker said, "that we pass a budget resolution."

"I did not support the Gorton amendment. I do not support the Gorton amendment. But I am committed to see that the Senate has an opportunity to express its preference and pass a resolution," Baker said. His motion to reconsider was agreed to, 55-45. *(Vote 108, p. 22-S)*

The Senate then went on to adopt the Gorton amendment, 53-47. *(Vote 110, p. 23-S)*

In other action, Jesse Helms, R-N.C., unsuccessfully proposed two budgets. One would have cut spending by 10 percent across-the-board — with the exception of defense, Social Security and interest on the public debt. The second would have required 5 percent cuts. *(Votes 104, 106, p. 22-S)*

In an effort to embarrass the Democrats and make the Republicans' position in conference clear, Dole offered the House budget as a substitute. Dole's proposal was tabled 54-46. *(Vote 109, p. 22-S)*

Finally came the vote on the resolution as amended by Gorton. Until the very end the moderates' budget plan was losing. Domenici originally cast a "no" vote but switched to "aye," and several others switched as well. The Senate's three-week-long budget ordeal ended on a 50-49 vote to approve the Gorton plan. *(Vote 112, p. 23-S)*

Conference Action

Conferees reached agreement on the resolution June 20 (H Rept 98-248). The three touchiest issues dividing the House and Senate were resolved as follows:

● **Taxes.** The House resolution called for $30 billion in fiscal 1984 revenue increases, excluding $5.2 billion in Social Security increases voted earlier in the year; the Senate, $9.9 billion. Conferees finally settled on $12 billion.

● **Defense Spending.** Splitting the difference between the 4 percent increase allowed by the House and the 6 percent increase proposed by the Senate, conferees provided a 5 percent inflation-adjusted growth rate for defense spending.

● **Domestic Spending.** Domestic spending was about $33 billion more than Reagan requested in the House resolution, $12.6 billion more in the Senate version. Chief differences involved money the House provided for new initiatives, such as mortgage foreclosure relief, that the Senate did not include. Conferees agreed to establish a special $8.5 billion reserve fund to accommodate 10 new spending initiatives that might or might not become law.

The conference agreement on H Con Res 91 culminated almost two weeks of confusion, closed-door meetings and uncertainty about the prospects of a budget compromise.

By the time the conferees met for their final session June 20, only a few outstanding issues remained to be resolved: how the so-called contingency, or reserve, fund would work, the level of funding for Medicare and Medicaid, and funding for international affairs.

After approving updated economic assumptions, which had the effect of lowering the deficit forecast by about $14 billion in fiscal 1984, the conferees decided to split the difference on foreign aid funding, providing $12.95 billion in fiscal 1984 outlays. This took care of the House conferees' concern about adequate money for aid to Israel and Egypt.

The last issue confronting conferees was the reconciliation requirement for the Medicare program. While the House agreed to call for savings of $400 million in fiscal 1984, conferees stipulated that the savings could not come from a reduction in services or an increase in costs to beneficiaries.

No House GOP members showed up for the final session, not even Latta, the coauthor of the Reagan-backed Gramm-Latta budgets of 1981-82.

After conferees reached final accord, Domenici said, "I frankly think it's somewhat of a miracle to have reached this agreement."

Reserve Fund

The reserve fund created by the conferees accommodated 10 programs, totaling $8.5 billion in fiscal 1984, $3.45 billion in fiscal 1985 and $1.98 billion in fiscal 1986. The money for each of the programs specified in the resolution would not be included in the congressional budget unless authorizing legislation became law.

If authorizing legislation were enacted, the Appropriations committees would be allowed to increase their spending allocation for that program.

For direct spending or entitlement programs, which do not require appropriations, the committee with jurisdiction would have its budget allocation increased upon enactment of authorizing legislation. Only then would the budget reflect increased spending ceilings and a higher deficit.

The reserve fund programs, with the outlays allowed for fiscal 1984:

● Farmers' mortgage foreclosure relief, $500 million. *(Story, p. 384)*

● Direct loans for farm ownership, operating or economic emergency, $100 million. *(Story, p. 384)*

● Mortgage foreclosure relief for the unemployed, $200 million. *(Story, p. 267)*

● Physical infrastructure program, $75 million. *(Story, p. 270)*

● National Industrial Development Bank, $50 million.

● Jobs for long-term unemployed, $3.5 billion. *(Story, p. 270)*

● Health insurance for the unemployed, $2 billion. *(Story, p. 405)*

● Extension of federal supplemental unemployment compensation benefits, $1.5 billion. Congress extended this program. *(Story, p. 274)*

● Increased benefits and expanded eligibility for food stamps, $450 million. *(Story, p. 412)*

● Veterans' job training program, $150 million. Congress enacted this program. *(Story, p. 599)*

Spending Levels

At the outset the major spending issue facing the conferees was how large the rate of increase in defense spending should be. As expected, the conferees split the difference between the 4 percent inflation-adjusted rate of growth in the House resolution and the 6 percent in the Senate budget. The 5 percent real rate of growth for defense in the conference agreement translated into $268.6 billion in fiscal 1984 budget authority and $240 billion in outlays.

The defense numbers assumed a 4 percent pay raise

Detailed Comparison of Fiscal 1984 Budget Targets

(in billions of dollars, excluding reserved funds)

Category	Reagan Revised April Request	House Target	Senate Target	Conference Agreement
National Defense				
Budget Authority	$280.5	$263.85	$270.65	$268.60
Outlays	245.4	235.40	241.60	240.00
International Affairs				
Budget Authority	16.7	18.85	18.20	18.70
Outlays	13.4	13.20	12.70	12.95
Science, Space & Technology				
Budget Authority	8.5	8.85	8.50	8.70
Outlays	8.2	8.35	8.20	8.30
Energy				
Budget Authority	2.9	4.40	3.90	4.20
Outlays	3.6	4.30	4.10	4.30
Natural Resources & Environment				
Budget Authority	9.0	12.10	12.00	12.05
Outlays	10.3	12.50	12.50	12.50
Agriculture				
Budget Authority	13.5	14.85	11.60	13.00
Outlays	9.7	14.65	11.40	11.50
Commerce & Housing Credit				
Budget Authority	7.6	6.10	5.90	6.00
Outlays	0.9	2.30	1.80	2.25
Transportation				
Budget Authority	27.8	28.30	27.70	28.00
Outlays	25.9	26.15	25.90	26.00
Community & Regional Development				
Budget Authority	6.0	8.25	6.60	6.85
Outlays	7.7	8.55	8.10	8.10
Education, Employment & Social Services				
Budget Authority	25.5	39.15	31.80	33.95
Outlays	25.3	32.70	27.25	28.35
Health				
Budget Authority	94.3	96.25	32.75	32.10
Outlays	90.6	90.60	32.75	32.00
Medical Insurance				
Budget Authority	—	—	61.40	62.50
Outlays	—	—	60.30	60.60
Income Security				
Budget Authority	287.2	310.60	25.90	124.80
Outlays	276.5	284.70	104.00	102.35
Social Security				
Budget Authority	—	—	174.90	176.00
Outlays	—	—	176.40	176.40
Veterans Benefits & Services				
Budget Authority	26.0	26.00	25.70	25.55
Outlays	25.6	25.55	25.60	25.45
Administration of Justice				
Budget Authority	5.5	5.60	6.00	5.85
Outlays	5.5	5.50	6.00	5.85
General Government				
Budget Authority	6.0	5.80	5.70	5.60
Outlays	6.0	6.05	5.70	5.60
General Fiscal Assistance				
Budget Authority	6.8	7.60	7.10	7.25
Outlays	6.8	7.60	7.00	7.15
Net Interest				
Budget Authority	102.3	96.15	95.90	97.10
Outlays	102.3	96.15	95.90	97.10
Allowances				
Budget Authority	0.9	1.20	0.60	.75
Outlays	0.9	1.25	0.60	.80
Offsetting Receipts				
Budget Authority	−20.8	−17.35	−18.10	−18.05
Outlays	−20.8	−17.35	−18.10	−18.05

effective January 1984 for civilian and military defense personnel. Other, non-defense, civilian employees would also receive a 4 percent pay raise.

Non-defense domestic spending, including the reserve fund items, was approximately $21.5 billion higher than Reagan's revised April request, as re-estimated by the Congressional Budget Office.

Domenici maintained that "the House moved 91 percent toward the Senate in domestic spending." However, some House members claimed the domestic spending figures were closer to the House-passed resolution. Part of the difference in perception existed because of the reserve fund.

The funding level was lower than the House resolution in the areas of community and regional development; education, training, employment and social services; and agriculture. Defense spending was almost $5 billion higher than the House provided in both budget authority and outlays.

Revenues

Despite rhetoric by House Democratic conferees about the need to raise revenues in order to reduce the deficit, the revenue reconciliation figures came much closer to the three-year total of $75 billion in the Senate resolution than to the $120 billion called for in the House budget. The final version called for $73 billion in additional revenues in fiscal 1984-86. The reconciliation instruction directed the Finance and Ways and Means committees to raise $12 billion in fiscal 1984, $15 billion in fiscal 1984 and $46 billion in fiscal 1986. However, Domenici noted that the committees could apportion the revenue increases in a different way — backloading the tax hikes so they all would take effect in 1986, for instance.

Economic Assumptions

The conference agreement revised the economic assumptions that had underpinned both the House and Senate resolutions. The forecast for real growth, as measured by the gross national product (GNP), was raised from 2 percent to 2.8 percent in calendar 1983 and from 4.7 percent to 5.1 percent in 1984. The forecast for the annual average unemployment rate was lowered to 10.1 percent from 10.3 percent in 1983 and to 9.3 percent from 9.7 percent in 1984. And the interest rate forecast, as measured by the annual average of 90-day Treasury bills, was increased in 1983 from 6.8 percent to 7.8 percent, but remained at 7.4 percent in 1984 as originally projected.

Reconciliation

The reconciliation instructions included in the conference agreement directed five Senate committees and eight House committees to cut existing programs to achieve outlay savings totaling $2.8 billion in fiscal 1984 and $12.3 billion in fiscal 1984-86. In addition, the Ways and Means and Finance committees were directed to come up with $73 billion in new revenues over the three-year period.

Legislation fulfilling these reconciliation requirements was to be reported back to the House and Senate Budget committees by July 22. That deadline subsequently was extended several times.

House committees required to fulfill reconciliation savings were Armed Services, Energy and Commerce, Foreign Affairs, Post Office and Civil Service, Small Business, Veterans' Affairs and Ways and Means. Senate committees affected by reconciliation were Finance, Governmental Affairs, Small Business and Veterans' Affairs.

A provisional instruction was set out for the House and Senate Agriculture committees that would require savings in dairy price supports, if the courts found existing milk production charges were unconstitutional. The courts upheld the charges.

Energy and Commerce, Ways and Means and Finance were required to find savings in the Medicare program. The Small Business committees were called on to make reductions in disaster loans. Savings from the remaining committees were assumed to come from a six-month delay in cost-of-living adjustments for the full range of federal retirement programs and a three-month delay in federal employee pay increases.

Other Provisions

The conference agreement revised the levels of credit for direct loan obligations and new primary and secondary loan guarantees in fiscal 1983 as well as including nonbinding credit budget targets for fiscal 1984.

Conferees also accepted four Senate "sense of Congress" provisions that called on the president, Congress and the Federal Financing Bank (FFB) to hold loan levels to those set out in the budget resolution.

The conference report urged committees with jurisdiction over the Federal Financing Bank Act of 1973 (PL 93-224) to promptly consider legislation requiring inclusion of budget authority and outlays resulting from FFB transactions in federal agency budgets beginning in fiscal 1985.

The conference agreement stipulated that if Congress had not completed action on a second budget resolution by the Oct. 1 beginning of fiscal 1984, the targets set in the first resolution would become binding budget levels.

In the past, any bill that exceeded the total spending target, even though it was below the amount allocated to the committee of origin, could not be enrolled, or sent to the president, until the adoption of the binding, second resolution. Under H Con Res 91, however, such legislation could be sent to the president.

The conferees modified Senate and House provisions on monetary policy. The new language requested the House and Senate Banking committees to report a resolution expressing the sense of Congress as to the need for coordination of Federal Reserve monetary policy with the fiscal policy set out in the budget resolution. Such a measure was reported in the Senate but did not reach the floor (S Con Res 73 — S Rept 98-263).

The resolution called for a public debt ceiling of $1,389,000,000,000 in fiscal 1983, and $1,614,600,000,000 in fiscal 1984.

Final Action

House Action

The House June 23 adopted the rule for considering the budget compromise, 265-150, and then went on to a predictable partisan debate. *(Vote 201, p. 62-H)*

While House Republicans called the budget agreement a "political document," Democrats countered that without it the economic recovery would be threatened.

"If we don't pass the budget, we're telling the American people that we prefer fiscal anarchy to the discipline of the budget process," said Budget Chairman Jones.

But conferee Frenzel and other Republicans argued that the "process is not worth more than the product." And Delbert L. Latta, Ohio, the Budget Committee's ranking

Republican, described the budget as a "return to the tax and spend policies of the Carter administration."

Another Budget Committee Republican, Lynn Martin, Ill., sarcastically thanked the Democrats for a wonderful campaign issue in 1984. "A tax increase and a ludicrous budget on a platter are being given to my party, not to be used just this year, but next," Martin said.

But Jones accused the Republicans of "standing by and throwing rocks" at the bipartisan compromise, while refusing to offer the president's budget or a House GOP alternative. In the end, Leon E. Panetta, D-Calif., said, it was the "only game in town."

The final 239-186 House vote was remarkably similar to the vote by which the House originally adopted its budget in March. This time only 33 Democrats voted against the budget — 36 did so in March. And 10 Republicans supported the conference agreement, while only four backed the original House budget. *(Vote 204, p. 62-H)*

The House Democratic leadership was able to hold the votes of most liberals, and only one voting member of the Black Caucus — Ronald V. Dellums, D-Calif. — voted against the budget.

Senate

The Senate then went on to clear the resolution by a comfortable 51-43 margin.

Both Domenici and Chiles attributed the budget's success — at least in part — to Majority Leader Baker.

"I think Howard Baker voting with us had a lot to do with it," said Domenici. "Baker helped," Chiles agreed.

Baker, who had voted against Senate adoption of the budget resolution several weeks earlier, was torn between his loyalty to Reagan and his allegiance to both the budget process and one of his hard-working chairmen, Domenici.

By the time the final tally was taken, he had found a way to support all three.

The key to Baker's support was an amendment offered by Dole to the conference resolution that would have reduced the three-year tax increase to $59 billion and extended the Finance Committee's reconciliation reporting date to Sept. 15. "I believe my amendment would satisfy the president," Dole said.

Dole charged that if the Senate adopted the conference agreement without change, it would just be "giving this dead cat to the Finance Committee." Finance would have to come up with 88 percent of the deficit reduction in the budget, he maintained. But only 2 percent of that was in spending reductions, the rest in tax increases. "That's not a very good mix," Dole said.

The ranking Democrat on the Finance Committee, Russell B. Long, La., agreed. "... To try to pass a tax increase of those kind of numbers without the support of the president of the United States is just ridiculous," he said.

But Domenici argued that if "we modify the budget at this late date, we're not going to get one."

Baker supported the Dole amendment, but it was defeated, 41-51. *(Vote 167, p. 30-S)*

The roll call on final adoption of the conference resolution immediately followed, with Baker voting "aye" loud and early.

Among the 32 Democratic senators who voted for the final budget resolution was presidential aspirant Hart. Early in the day, when the outcome was in doubt, Minority Leader Robert C. Byrd, D-W.Va., had asked Hart to hurry back from a campaign appearance in New Jersey. The roll call was extended for almost an hour and a half until Hart made his way back to the Senate chamber. ∎

'83 Supplemental: $4.6 Billion for Jobs, Relief

President Reagan March 24 signed into law (PL 98-8) a $4.6 billion jobs and humanitarian relief package — an amount well within the $5 billion limit House and Senate leaders had said would be acceptable to the president.

The legislation marked the first major effort by the 98th Congress to address the severe economic problems that had left more than 11 million people without jobs.

Congress earlier March 24 overwhelmingly cleared the $4.6 billion compromise program as part of a $15.6 billion supplemental appropriations bill (HR 1718) for the fiscal year ending Sept. 30, 1983.

"This bill will meet neglected urgent needs, result not in make-work but productive jobs, and provide for the indigent and homeless," said House Appropriations Committee Chairman Jamie L. Whitten, D-Miss.

The House March 22 accepted, 329-86, a Senate-House conference agreement on the measure. Senate approval followed several hours later, 82-15. But final passage remained provisional for two days. While there was little debate over specific appropriations, the two chambers became embroiled in a dispute over a complex targeting formula for distributing funds among states and economically distressed areas. As a result, the compromise went from the House to the Senate, only to be bounced back to the House again. *(House vote 39, p. 16-H; Senate vote 44, p. 10-S)*

Conferees had worked under considerable pressure to resolve the targeting dispute quickly. In addition to the jobs package, the bill included $5 billion to fund jobless payments in 27 states and the District of Columbia. The Labor Department said these funds would be depleted by March 23.

The money had been expected to run out earlier, but on three previous occasions the administration at the last moment managed to come up with sufficient funds to continue paying unemployment benefits.

Veto Concerns

The House-Senate compromise was scaled specifically to stay within the limits of what the Reagan administration had signaled it would accept. In February the president abandoned his earlier opposition to a jobs bill when, under pressure from Congress, he proposed his own $4.3 billion recession relief program. The program grew in the House to a $4.9 billion jobs bill passed March 3, and in the Senate to the $5.2 billion package (including $1.1 billion in accelerated revenue sharing payments) approved March 17.

Responding to concern that the size of the Senate bill could trigger a presidential veto, Senate Appropriations Committee Chairman Mark O. Hatfield, R-Ore., said during the conference that he had received "very strong signals

Final Provisions of Jobs Funding Bill . . .

	HOUSE	SENATE	FINAL
Title I — Jobs Program			
Treasury, General Services			
Treasury, corporations study	$ 500,000	$ —	$ —
General Services Administration (GSA) buildings	125,000,000	125,000,000	125,000,000
Transportation			
Highway demonstration project	33,000,000	—	33,000,000
Federal-aid highways (obligation ceiling)	(500,000,000)	(275,000,000)	(275,000,000)
Urban mass transportation	171,000,000	94,300,000	132,650,000
Mass Transit Capital Fund (deferral disapproval)	(229,000,000)	(229,000,000)	(229,000,000)
Amtrak grants	110,000,000	130,000,000	80,000,000
Airport grants (obligation ceiling)	—	(150,000,000)	(150,000,000)
Northeast Corridor improvement	—	25,000,000	—
Housing and Urban Development (HUD), Veterans			
Veterans Administration medical care	75,000,000	75,000,000	75,000,000
HUD expedited mortgage assistance	500,000	—	—
Community Development Block Grants	1,250,000,000	540,000,000	1,000,000,000
(loan guarantee ceiling)	—	(1,000,000,000)	—
Urban Development Action Grants (deferral disapproval)	(244,000,000)	(244,000,000)	(244,000,000)
Assisted housing (deferral disapproval)	(3,081,152,796)	(3,081,152,796)	(3,081,152,796)
Economic Development			
Economic Development Administration	200,000,000	—	100,000,000
Small Business Administration (SBA) loan and investment fund	202,000,000	2,000,000	52,000,000
SBA natural resources development	50,000,000	—	50,000,000
Parks and Recreation, Indians			
National Park Service	100,000,000	100,000,000	130,000,000
Forest Service	45,000,000	115,000,000	85,000,000
Indian health facilities	39,000,000	39,000,000	39,000,000
Fish and Wildlife Service	25,000,000	20,000,000	20,000,000
Bureau of Indian Affairs (BIA) Indian programs	20,000,000	—	20,000,000
BIA construction	—	64,450,000	64,450,000
Indian housing	—	30,000,000	30,000,000
Rural Development, Conservation			
Rural water and waste disposal grants	200,000,000	125,000,000	150,000,000
(loans)	(600,000,000)	(400,000,000)	(450,000,000)
Farmers Home Administration (FmHA) salaries and expenses	6,500,000	6,500,000	6,500,000
Resource conservation and development	15,000,000	—	5,000,000
Watershed and flood prevention	150,000,000	75,000,000	100,000,000
(loans)	(25,000,000)	—	—
Emergency credit measures	10,000,000	—	7,500,000
Agricultural Research Service	—	10,000,000	3,000,000
Food and Drug Administration	—	39,000,000	875,000
Energy and Water Development			
Corps of Engineers	404,000,000	329,000,000	389,000,000
Bureau of Reclamation	101,000,000	116,000,000	116,000,000
Tennessee Valley Authority	40,000,000	40,000,000	40,000,000

. . . Provided $15.6 Billion for Fiscal 1983

	HOUSE	SENATE	FINAL
Miscellaneous Programs			
Prison modernization	$ 90,000,000	$ 70,000,000	$ 80,000,000
(transfer)	(30,000,000)	(10,000,000)	(20,000,000)
Military family housing	243,000,000	100,566,200	179,642,000
Low-income weatherization	150,000,000	100,000,000	100,000,000
Schools and hospitals weatherization	—	75,000,000	50,000,000
GSA motor vehicle purchases	75,000,000	—	—
Employment, Human Services			
Employment and training assistance	207,400,000	257,400,000	217,400,000
Older Americans employment	25,000,000	50,000,000	37,500,000
Job search assistance (trust fund transfer limitation)	—	(50,000,000)	—
Community and migrant health centers	78,000,000	70,000,000	70,000,000
Maternal and child health grants	110,000,000	105,000,000	105,000,000
Centers for Disease Control	—	15,560,000	15,560,000
Public hospitals, emergency rooms	52,000,000	—	—
Alcohol, drug abuse and mental health	30,000,000	30,000,000	30,000,000
Social services block grants	150,000,000	300,000,000	225,000,000
Head Start	30,000,000	—	—
Community services block grant	25,000,000	41,375,000	25,000,000
Impact aid construction	35,000,000	60,000,000	60,000,000
Handicapped education	—	40,000,000	40,000,000
Rehabilitation services and handicapped research	—	5,000,000	5,000,000
Student financial assistance	—	100,000,000	50,000,000
Libraries	—	50,000,000	50,000,000
Food program administration	250,000	—	—
Surplus food distribution	75,000,000	75,000,000	75,000,000
Women, Infants and Children (WIC) food program	100,000,000	100,000,000	100,000,000
Emergency food and shelter program	50,000,000	50,000,000	100,000,000
Railroad unemployment benefits	—	125,750,000	125,750,000
Customs Service, air interdiction	—	3,750,000	3,750,000
Title I, total new budget authority	**$4,898,150,000**	**$3,924,651,200**	**$4,598,577,000**

Title II — Commodities Distribution and Food Assistance

	HOUSE	SENATE	FINAL
Distribution of agricultural commodities	—	100,000,000	50,000,000
Total, Titles I and II	**$4,898,150,000**	**$4,024,651,200**	**$4,648,577,000**

Title III — Supplemental Appropriations

	HOUSE	SENATE	FINAL
Advances to the unemployment trust fund and other funds	5,033,000,000	5,033,000,000	5,033,000,000
Grants to states for unemployment insurance and employment services (limitation on trust fund transfer)	(276,100,000)	(276,100,000)	(276,100,000)
SBA business loan and investment fund	—	434,000,000	200,000,000
Commodity Credit Corporation reimbursement for net realized losses	—	5,707,457,000	5,707,457,000
Total, Title III	**$5,033,000,000**	**$11,174,457,000**	**$10,940,457,000**
Grand total	**$9,931,150,000**	**$15,199,108,200**	**$15,589,034,000**

that this bill is too high for the president to sign."

Hatfield added that the White House was particularly concerned about the controversial Senate provision adding $1.14 billion in accelerated revenue sharing payments to local governments. The bill's chances of gaining Reagan's signature would increase "100 percent" without the revenue sharing measure, Hatfield warned.

The battle over revenue sharing took place almost exclusively within Republican ranks, with Hatfield arguing most strongly against the revenue sharing amendment and Sen. Arlen Specter, R-Pa., supporting it. "We ought to stick with this figure," said Specter, rejecting the notion that the bill might be vetoed.

Senate conferees voted 9-2 to recede to the House and delete the revenue sharing proposal from the conference bill.

Said Sen. Lowell P. Weicker Jr., R-Conn.: "We all want to get this money out on the streets where it will do some good."

Targeting Dispute

The final point of controversy — the targeting issue — was not resolved until March 24, when the House by voice vote approved a compromise engineered by Hatfield and Rep. Bob Edgar, D-Pa., principal authors of the Senate and House targeting formulas.

As framed in the final bill, the targeting mechanism was a hybrid of House and Senate positions. "We took the House version and merged it with the Senate version," said Hatfield. "We have, in effect, two targeting procedures with two sets of programs."

Under the final bill, the House targeting formula covered $1.67 billion in discretionary jobs bill funds appropriated under 17 separate programs, most administered at a municipal rather than state level. The Edgar mechanism reserved 75 percent of these funds for localities or civil jurisdictions having unemployment rates exceeding 8.7 percent.

The Edgar mechanism covered funds for the Economic Development Administration (EDA), federal building repairs, mass transit, rural water and sewer projects, national and urban parks and the Small Business Administration (SBA), among others. The bill specified that the Edgar formula would apply to Army Corps of Engineers projects "to the extent practicable."

The Hatfield targeting mechanism applied to $1.5 billion in non-discretionary funds, appropriated under five programs that were generally administered at the state level. These funds would be distributed in three tiers: one-third would be prorated among states according to their proportionate share of the nation's unemployed; one-sixth would be allotted to 21 "long-term unemployment" states having the highest average unemployment rates; and one-half would be allocated under provisions of existing law.

The Hatfield formula covered all community development, community service and social service block grants, and library and airport construction.

Highlights of Package

Two-thirds of the final jobs package was allotted for public works, general construction and water projects. The remaining funds were allocated for social service, health and humanitarian assistance.

The largest single item in the package — $1 billion for Community Development Block Grants (CDBGs) — was spread fairly evenly between "bricks and mortar" projects

and public service programs. The conferees specified that $500 million of these funds could be used for public service jobs, such as home health and day care. The provision had been sought by women's groups, who noted that few of the construction and public works jobs created by the bill would benefit women. Said Rep. Edward P. Boland, D-Mass.: "This will guarantee a better break for women."

Boland also defended the heavy appropriations for public service programs, which the administration had opposed as "make-work" jobs. "This is one area where you can [get people to work] rapidly," he said.

Backers said the bill would create some 400,000 full-time jobs.

Background

The nucleus of the funding bill was a $4.3 billion jobs package outlined by President Reagan at his Feb. 16 press conference. The administration plan called for:

● $4 billion in accelerated spending for federal construction and repair projects. According to Reagan, "These projects directly and indirectly could provide as many as 470,000 jobs."

● $300 million "in additional humanitarian relief for those in serious distress."

● $2.9 billion for a supplementary unemployment insurance program, not included in the supplemental bill. *(Unemployment insurance, p. 274)*

"Contrary to previous plans, this is consistent with our basic long-term recovery program and my own personal principles," Reagan said. "It funds no make-work jobs." *(Reagan March 11 message on structural unemployment, p. 16-E)*

Democrats called the Reagan initiative a good starting the president "has come a long way toward" the Democratic position on jobs.

"I'm optimistic that we'll be able to conclude legislation the president can sign and [that] has strong bipartisan support in the House and Senate," said Rep. Thomas S. Foley, D-Wash., head of a Democratic task force on jobs.

House Committee Action

The House Appropriations Committee Feb. 25 approved a $4.6 billion emergency employment and recession relief plan that reshuffled and expanded the Reagan administration jobs proposal by about $300 million.

House Democratic leaders the day before agreed to the plan, despite opposition from urban Democrats and Republicans who complained that the public works projects contained in the bill did not go far enough in helping the neediest. Some members also objected that the bill did not address the structural, long-term unemployment problems faced by women, youth and minorities.

"This bill is an important first step in bringing maximum benefits in the quickest possible time to those who need help most," Wright maintained.

Not all members agreed. "This is not a jobs bill, it's a catchall bill," said Silvio O. Conte, R-Mass., the ranking minority member of the Appropriations Committee, in criticizing what he called the public works and "pet project" orientation of the legislation. "It's a rotten bill."

The committee approved the draft bill by voice vote without substantial change.

President Reagan said Feb. 24 that he agreed with three-quarters of the bill but opposed elements that repre-

sented new funding rather than an "acceleration of already budgeted items."

The Democrats tried to put their stamp on the measure without precipitating a presidential veto.

"They're trying to throw the ball back in the president's court," said a Republican aide. "Reagan can either accept the new House bill, or risk being presented with an even fatter jobs plan that he will have to veto."

The largest single component in the House jobs package was $1.25 billion in additional fiscal 1983 funding for Community Development Grants, intended to create 80,000 jobs in the light construction industry. The committee rejected an administration proposal to defer spending $244 million previously appropriated for Urban Development Action Grants.

Other big-ticket items included $200 million for the Economic Development Administration, which the administration hoped to abolish, $202 million for small business loans, and $200 million for rural water and sewer grants.

As reported by the Appropriations Committee March 1 (H Rept 98-11), the bill also contained $5,033,000,000 requested by the administration to continue payment of jobless benefits under existing law.

Departures from Reagan Plan

The committee plan differed from the Reagan proposal in several important respects.

In a major change, the bill increased the ceiling on obligations from the Highway Trust Fund for highway construction from Reagan's proposed $12.2 billion to $12.6 billion.

Funds the White House had slated for mass transit were reduced from $400 million to $100 million, and funds for Veterans Administration (VA) hospital repairs were cut from $200 million to $75 million.

Money freed by these cuts was reallocated to programs advocated by both the House Republican Task Force on Employment Opportunities and the Democratic leadership. These included $100 million for summer youth jobs, $75 million in assistance to displaced workers, $150 million for low-income home weatherization, $150 million for social services block grants, including day care, and $100 million for the Women, Infants and Children (WIC) feeding program.

No funds were allocated to these programs under the administration jobs plan.

The House bill cut $375 million sought by Reagan for deep port dredging and construction, principally because of opposition from the Republican jobs task force. House Republicans had threatened to vote with the Democrats to redirect the funds to summer youth programs and the EDA.

Other major changes increased administration allocations for flood control under the Soil Conservation Service (SCS) and Army Corps of Engineers from $149 million to $564 million.

The House bill also included money for such White House initiatives as repairing federal buildings ($125 million), Amtrak grants ($120 million), military housing ($243 million) and emergency food and shelter ($50 million).

Highlights of Bill

Highlights of jobs funding:

Federal Buildings. The bill provided $125 million to improve and repair public buildings in 47 states and five territories. Funds could be used by the General Services Administration for basic work to correct deterioration, malfunction or obsolescence, fire safety and other protection, aids for the handicapped, and energy and environmental conservation.

A further $75 million was appropriated for Veterans Administration non-recurring maintenance and repair projects. The committee report stipulated that work should be labor-intensive and under way within six months. An estimated 3,000 jobs would be created by the VA projects.

The bill also recommended $35 million for school construction in areas where local revenues and facilities were inadequate to meet educational needs because of federal government activities.

The committee appropriated $90 million to repair and modernize federal prisons.

Highway Construction. The bill included $33 million for a highway demonstration project in Mississippi. It increased the ceiling on obligations from the Highway Trust Fund for highway construction from the administration's proposed $12.2 billion to $12.6 billion.

Mass Transit. To accelerate the construction and modernization of urban transportation systems, the bill appropriated $44 million for projects in Massachusetts, California, Oregon and Minnesota that had been substituted for Interstate highway projects. The bill also included $66 million for urban discretionary grants for seven projects in Florida, Connecticut, Long Island and Michigan.

Amtrak. The bill contained $110 million for the National Railroad Passenger Corporation (Amtrak). Of this, $90 million was reserved for 40 projects in the Northeast Corridor between Boston and Washington, and $10 million was for facility improvements in Massachusetts.

Community Development Block Grants. The bill provided $1.25 billion in additional funding for CDBGs, intended to create 80,000 jobs in the light construction industry. Funds would be distributed under an existing formula allocating 70 percent of the appropriation to metropolitan areas and 30 percent to small cities and rural areas. Of the total, $250 million would be reserved for urban areas with high unemployment.

The committee report specified that these funds were to be used for "brick and mortar" projects such as housing rehabilitation, parks and historic preservation, street repair and public construction that could be started within six months.

The committee removed a 10 percent limitation on the funds allocable to social services such as day care. It also disapproved an administration request to defer spending of $244 million previously appropriated for Urban Development Action Grants.

Economic Development Administration. The committee provided $200 million for EDA public works projects, which it said would create an estimated 33,000 jobs. Funds could be used for a variety of water and sewer, community development and infrastructure projects.

The bill specified that fiscal 1982 recipients of EDA funding would remain eligible for fiscal 1983 programs.

Small Business Administration. Anticipating a rise in loan demand as interest rates fell, the bill appropriated an additional $202 million for SBA loans for plant expansions, working capital and other investments that would clearly create jobs. A further $50 million was provided for small business grants to upgrade state and local parks and recreation facilities.

Parks and Wildlife. The bill appropriated $170 mil-

lion for maintenance of local and national parks and forests, including $50 million for the Urban Park and Recreation Recovery Program, $50 million for the National Park System, $25 million for the National Forest System, $25 million for the Fish and Wildlife Service and $20 million for the Forest Service.

A further $39 million was slated for the construction of sanitary facilities on Indian reservations and in Indian communities in 27 states; $20 million was designated for land improvements and natural resource development on reservations.

Rural Water and Sewer Grants. The Farmers Home Administration (FmHA) provided grants for the construction of water and sewer systems in rural areas and communities having fewer than 10,000 people. HR 1718 appropriated $200 million for grants to small towns under this program, plus $600 million in new loan funds.

By accelerating work on more than 1,000 planned projects, an estimated 44,560 jobs would be created, the committee said. A further $15 million was allocated to the Soil Conservation Service for planning programs with local FmHA sponsors.

Soil Conservation and Flood Control. The bill appropriated $160 million for the Soil Conservation Service to accelerate construction of 453 previously approved watershed and flood control projects in 46 states. A further $545 million was appropriated for irrigation, hydroelectric, flood control, and industrial and municipal water projects, as follows: $101 million for the Bureau of Land Reclamation, Department of Interior; $40 million for the Tennessee Valley Authority; and $404 million for the Army Corps of Engineers.

Military Housing. To create an estimated 10,000 jobs in the construction industry, the bill provided $243 million to repair and improve military housing. To accelerate new construction, the bill rescinded language in earlier legislation (PL 97-321) that would have deferred $200 million in military housing construction until after July 1, 1983.

Home Weatherization. The low-income home weatherization program received $150 million under the bill. The committee said the direct labor involved and the demand generated for weatherization materials would put 10,000 people to work for one year.

Employment and Job Training. The bill included $232.4 million to aid unemployed youths and adults:

● $32.4 million for the Job Corps for in-service training of the unemployed.

● $100 million to create an estimated 100,000 minimum-wage summer jobs for disadvantaged youth.

● $75 million for retraining and relocating displaced workers under the new Job Training Partnership Act. *(1982 Almanac p. 39)*

● $25 million to provide some 4,900 part-time jobs in community service programs for unemployed persons aged 55 or older.

Health and Social Services. More than $535 million was allocated to health and social services for maternal and child health care, Head Start, alcohol and drug abuse services, and home health care. Major items:

● $150 million for Social Service Block Grants directed at maintaining family self-sufficiency and preventing child abuse, neglect and malnutrition. The appropriation was expected to create 4,000 jobs.

The bill earmarked $50 million for child day-care centers, supporting services for some 33,000 children and pro-

viding training and employment for 4,000 new day-care workers.

● $100 million for the WIC program, to provide food to pregnant women, mothers and young children from low-income families. The program was expected to reach 2.2 million people a month in 1983, at an average cost of $40 per person each month.

● $50 million for food and emergency shelter, to be made available through voluntary organizations.

● $75 million for the purchase and distribution of surplus agricultural commodities. Participation in the program would be limited to persons certified by a local government or charitable organization. Federal contributions would have to be matched by a 25 percent non-federal contribution.

House Floor Action

Overriding last-minute opposition, the House March 3 approved HR 1718 by a 324-95 vote. *(Vote 18, p. 10-H)*

The program grew on the floor to $4.9 billion from the $4.6 billion package approved by the Appropriations Committee Feb. 25.

"It's good for the country, it's the best jobs bill we could come up with," said Appropriations Chairman Whitten.

The bill drew sharp and fairly widespread criticism from members of both parties who complained that the measure did not go far enough in helping the needy and that it favored "pork-barrel" projects in the home districts of Appropriations Committee members.

"If you want to vote for pork, this is it," said Delbert L. Latta, R-Ohio. Said Robert S. Walker, R-Pa.: "This bill is a disgrace. It's loaded with political goodies for big-government congressmen."

On passage, the bill was opposed by only 13 Democrats, mostly conservative Southerners, while Republicans split relatively evenly, with 77 supporting the bill and 82 opposing it.

Final passage came just minutes after the House rejected, 158-256, a Republican effort to recommit the bill with instructions to shift some $675 million from public works and water projects to a variety of social programs and "brick and mortar" infrastructure projects that could be started immediately. *(Vote 17, p. 10-H)*

The GOP effort would have cut $31.5 million from the overall plan.

Operating under a rule that limited floor amendments, the House made few changes in the committee bill.

Three amendments were approved in an effort to defuse criticism that funds were not being targeted to people and regions of greatest need.

An amendment by David R. Obey, D-Wis., adopted by voice vote, increased funds for three emergency health care and insurance programs by $200 million. Maternal and child health care block grants received $100 million; community and migrant centers, $48 million; and preventive health services block grants, $52 million.

Also adopted by voice vote was an amendment by James J. Howard, D-N.J., that added $61 million for specific mass transit projects under the Interstate transfer and urban discretionary grant programs. The amendment also disapproved the administration's plan to defer spending of $229 million that would be generated from revenues collected under the new gasoline tax approved in December 1982 (PL 97-424). Funds would be available to any mass

transit project, not merely the 12 specified by the committee.

Edgar offered an amendment requiring that 75 percent of the $2.45 billion in discretionary funding appropriated under the bill — or $1.8 billion — be spent in areas of high unemployment. Cosponsored by Conte and Lawrence Coughlin, R-Pa., the measure was adopted, 335-83. *(Vote 16, p. 10-H)*

Senate Committee Action

As reported by the Senate Appropriations Committee March 7 (S Rept 98-17), the bill contained $3.9 billion in jobs and recession relief, plus the $5 billion approved by the House for advances to the states to continue payment of unemployment benefits under existing law.

The bill also included $5.7 billion to finance losses incurred by the Commodity Credit Corp., the federal agency that administers farm price support programs, and $434 million for the Small Business Administration loan and investment fund. Staff aides said Senate Republicans added these two supplemental funding items, which had not been included in the House bill, to reduce the number of spending bills that might be used for future jobs initiatives.

Comparison with House Bill

Major changes in the House bill:

Federal Buildings. The committee endorsed the House provision appropriating $125 million for public building repairs but cut $20 million from the $90 million House appropriation for prison repairs.

The Senate panel added $263.4 million for VA hospital construction. It concurred with the House in appropriating $75 million for VA maintenance and repair projects.

The Senate bill also increased funds for school construction in areas impacted by federal activities from $35 million to $60 million.

Highway Construction. The committee shaved $225 million from the $12.6 billion obligation ceiling approved by the House for the Highway Trust Fund. It also deleted a $33 million highway demonstration project in Mississippi.

The Senate bill earmarked $775 million in previously appropriated funds for Interstate transfer grants to projects in 16 states.

Mass Transit. The committee proposed $6 million for transit projects in Oregon and Maryland that had been substituted for Interstate highway projects, and $66 million for urban discretionary grants for projects in New York, Florida, Connecticut and Pennsylvania. The House bill appropriated $44 million and $127 million, respectively, for programs in seven states.

Amtrak. The committee increased the House appropriation for Amtrak capital grants from $110 million to $130 million. Rejecting House efforts to earmark these funds, the Senate panel directed Amtrak to give top priority to capital projects that would create the most jobs.

The Senate bill also appropriated $25 million for safety and right-of-way improvements in the Northeast Corridor.

Airports. The committee recommended obligation of an additional $75 million from the Airport Development Trust Fund for airport construction and related projects in seven states. There was no comparable House item.

Community Development Block Grants. The Senate version of the bill cut funding for CDBGs from $1,250,000,000 to $540 million. Of this amount, $250 million would be reserved for urban areas with high unemployment, as provided by the House. These funds would remain available only until Sept. 30, 1984. The House bill allowed the funds to remain available until spent.

To offset the reduction in grants, the Senate provided $1 billion for off-budget loan guarantees under the CDBG program. The House bill contained no similar provision.

The Senate bill restored a 10 percent limitation on the funds allocable to social services such as day care.

Economic Development Administration. Concerned that additional funds could not be spent in fiscal 1983, the Senate committee deleted $200 million appropriated by the House for additional EDA public works projects.

Small Business Administration. Noting that the administration had proposed deferring existing funding for the SBA direct loan program, the committee rejected the additional $200 million appropriation favored by the House. A $50 million appropriation for small business grants to upgrade state and local parks was also deleted.

The panel accepted a House appropriation of $2 million to finance bonds issued by small business development companies.

Parks and Wildlife. The committee added $10 million to the House appropriation for parks and national forests, bringing the total appropriation to $180 million, but shifted some allocations. The Senate bill deleted $50 million for urban parks and doubled the National Park Service appropriation to $100 million: $50 million for land and water conservation, $25 million for historic preservation and $25 million for construction.

The House bill provided $59 million for sanitary and natural resource improvements in Indian communities. The Senate version appropriated $133.5 million for Indian programs, deleting $20 million for the Bureau of Indian Affairs and adding $30 million and $64.5 million for Indian housing and education programs, respectively.

Soil Conservation and Flood Control. The Senate committee cut $75 million from the House bill in appropriating $329 million for water resource projects under the Army Corps of Engineers. Of this total, $123 million was cut from Mississippi River projects and $40 million from new construction funds; $88 million was added for general operations and maintenance.

Allocations for the Bureau of Reclamation ($101 million) and the Tennessee Valley Authority ($40 million) were not altered.

The House bill appropriated $160 million for the Soil Conservation Service (SCS) for accelerated construction of watershed and flood control projects. Believing that an appropriation this large could not be used efficiently in fiscal 1983, the Senate committee cut SCS funding to $75 million. For the same reason the panel deleted $25 million in new loan authority for the Agricultural Credit Insurance Fund.

Rural Water and Sewer Grants. The Senate bill cut $75 million from the $200 million allocated for Farmers Home Administration grants under the House bill. Funds appropriated for new FmHA loans were reduced from $600 million to $400 million, and $15 million allocated to the Soil Conservation Service for FmHA planning programs under the House bill was deleted.

Agricultural Research. The committee recommended $10 million for repair and maintenance work at the

Agricultural Research Service and $39 million to accelerate new Food and Drug Administration construction in Maryland and Arkansas. Neither item was included in the House bill.

Military Housing. The House appropriation for military housing construction was cut from $243 million to $100.6 million, earmarked for use at Air Force, Army and Navy bases in 20 states. The Senate bill endorsed House language accelerating certain projects that would have been deferred until July 1, 1983.

Weatherization. The committee recommended $100 million for low-income home weatherization, estimated to yield energy savings for some 100,000 homes. The House bill proposed $150 million.

The Senate bill appropriated a further $75 million to weatherize some 3,590 schools and 150 hospitals. Funds would be matched by the states.

Unemployment and Job Training. The Senate bill increased aid to unemployed youth and adults from $232.4 million to $282.4 million by adding $50 million to the $75 million House appropriation for retraining and relocating displaced workers. House and Senate appropriations for the Job Corps, summer youth jobs and employment for older persons did not differ.

Health and Social Services. The Senate reallocated and increased funds for health and social services from $510 million to $680.5 million, as follows:

● Three appropriations increased on the House floor under amendments offered by Obey were cut in the Senate bill.

The House appropriation of $78 million for community and migrant health centers was cut to $30 million, $20 million of which was targeted toward some 200,000 people living in underserved areas.

The House provision of $110 million for maternal and child health care was cut to $30 million, and $52 million for preventive health care was deleted from the Senate bill.

● Social service block grants directed at maintaining family health, preventing child abuse and providing day care and adoption services were increased from $150 million to $300 million. Noting that approximately $60 million of these funds would ordinarily flow to day care, the committee deleted House bill language earmarking $50 million for that service.

● Surplus food distribution was increased from $75 million to $175 million.

● The Senate bill appropriated funds for programs not covered by the House, including: $50 million for public library construction; $15.6 million for the Centers for Disease Control; $100 million for college work-study programs designed to help students meet expenses through part-time employment; and $40 million to help colleges make buildings more accessible to handicapped persons.

● Funds for Head Start were cut from the Senate bill. The committee made no changes in House appropriations for the WIC feeding program ($100 million); alcohol, drug abuse and mental health ($30 million) and emergency food and shelter ($50 million).

Customs Service. The committee recommended $3,750,000 in supplemental funding for modification of aircraft to be used in the Customs Service's drug interdiction program. The House bill had contained no appropriation for the program.

Senate Floor Action

The Senate March 17 approved a $5.2 billion emergency jobs and recession relief package, breaking a weeklong deadlock over a controversial amendment to repeal the withholding tax on interest and dividend income.

The jobs program was part of the urgent $16.3 billion fiscal 1983 supplemental appropriations bill (HR 1718) that also included $5 billion needed by March 21 to keep 27 states and the District of Columbia from running out of money to pay unemployment benefits. The Senate passed the bill by an 82-16 vote. *(Vote 30, p. 8-S)*

The White House said existing jobless funds would not last beyond Monday, March 21. "We cannot guarantee payment from the [unemployment trust] fund to the states past Monday," said presidential spokesman Larry M. Speakes. He added that the fund used about $100 million a day and said "our analysis indicates there is $102 million left."

Mindful of the urgency of the compensation issue, Senate leaders worked for days to fashion a compromise that would induce Bob Kasten, R-Wis., and other sponsors of the withholding amendment to abandon their efforts to attach the repealer to the jobs bill. A carefully orchestrated deal was struck only hours before final passage, one day after an obviously frustrated Senate had temporarily dropped the jobs bill to pick up Social Security legislation.

Under the agreement, the divisive withholding tax amendment was removed from the jobs bill and offered to another piece of legislation, a pending trade "reciprocity" bill. Republican leaders assured Kasten that his amendment would be the first item considered when the reciprocity measure came to the Senate floor on April 15, the income tax filing date. *(Withholding repeal, p. 261)*

Withholding Agreement

The break in the Senate stalemate came after a week of sharply divided and frequently acrimonious debate over the Kasten repealer. On March 16, a clearly frustrated Senate temporarily laid aside the jobs bill after failing twice — once by a dramatic one-vote margin — to invoke cloture and break the deadlock.

On one cliff-hanging roll call, Kasten fell one vote short of the 60 votes necessary to shut off a filibuster by Finance Committee Chairman Robert Dole, R-Kan., against the withholding amendment. Under pressure from Dole and Majority Leader Howard H. Baker Jr., R-Tenn., four senators who had lined up with Kasten on a previous vote switched sides and voted against him on the 59-39 tally. *(Vote 27, p. 8-S)*

Dole had already lost his own motion to invoke cloture on the bill, 50-48. *(Vote 26, p. 8-S)*

Triggering Dispute

The Senate bogged down on the withholding issue just moments after tentatively resolving an intense and often acrimonious dispute over a complex "targeting" mechanism designed to channel some $1 billion in jobs funds to 15 states whose unemployment rate exceeded the national average for the past 12 months. Drafted by Republican and Democratic leaders on the Appropriations Committee, the measure ran into opposition from senators representing states not included among the 15.

Senators opposing the targeting plan argued that it discriminated against states with "pockets" of high unemployment. "Unemployed is unemployed whether you live in

Michigan, Ohio or South Dakota," said James Abdnor, R-S.D., whose state was not included under the formula.

Abdnor offered an amendment to dilute the targeting formula by making all states eligible for long-term unemployment aid.

After the Senate rejected, 43-51, his effort to kill the Abdnor amendment, Appropriations Chairman Hatfield offered a perfecting amendment broadening the formula to include six more states. *(Vote 14, p. 5-S)*

The Senate adopted the Hatfield amendment by voice vote after rejecting an Abdnor motion to table 49-50. *(Vote 15, p. 6-S)*

The 21 states that would receive extra funds under the Hatfield long-term unemployment formula were: Alabama, Arkansas, Arizona, California, Illinois, Indiana, Kentucky, Louisiana, Michigan, Mississippi, Nevada, New Mexico, Ohio, Oregon, Pennsylvania, Rhode Island, South Carolina, Tennessee, Washington, West Virginia and Wisconsin.

Democratic Initiative

Further controversy erupted over a Democratic initiative, rejected 34-53, to add $1.7 billion to the committee-drafted $3.7 billion measure. *(Vote 16, p. 7-S)*

Offered by Carl Levin, D-Mich., chairman of the Democratic Task Force on Emergency Human Needs, the amendment proposed an additional $1.3 billion for job creation and human services, including $1 billion for Community Development Block Grants and $390 million for health and humanitarian relief.

Supporters of the measure claimed Levin's proposals would create 280,000 additional jobs. "We're trying to take care of the millions of people whose basic needs have not been met," said Alan J. Dixon, D-Ill.

Other Amendments

Senators spent days slogging through several dozen amendments to the bill — in the process adding $1.3 billion to the $3.9 billion jobs package reported by the Appropriations Committee.

Most of the additional funding came under a proposal by John Heinz, R-Pa., requiring that revenue sharing payments to local governments be made at the beginning of each quarter, effective April 1, 1983, rather than at the end. The proposal, adopted 73-21 on March 14, added $1.1 billion to the bill. *(Vote 19, p. 7-S)*

In other action, the Senate adopted amendments by:

● Bill Bradley, D-N.J., expressing the sense of the Senate in opposition to further cuts in education programs. Adopted March 9, 82-10. *(Vote 13, p. 5-S)*

● Hatfield, striking $263 million for construction work on two Veterans Administration hospitals in Minnesota and Ohio. Adopted March 9 by voice vote.

● Orrin G. Hatch, R-Utah, providing that $5 million of the funds appropriated for health services be reserved for home health care under the Orphan Drug Act, and that another $5 million be used to train home health care aides. Adopted March 9 by voice vote.

● Dan Quayle, R-Ind., requiring that 75 percent of all jobs created by the bill go to people who have been unemployed for 15 of the 26 weeks preceding the date of hire. Adopted March 9 by voice vote.

● Wendell H. Ford, D-Ky., adding $125 million for supplemental unemployment benefits for railroad workers having less than 10 years' service. Supplemental benefits would be paid from the federal Treasury rather than from the Railroad Unemployment Trust Fund. Adopted March

11 by voice vote. *(Railroad retirement, p. 272)*

● Thomas F. Eagleton, D-Mo., adding $115 million for maternal and child care and preventive health services. Adopted March 14, 80-14. *(Vote 20, p. 7-S)*

● Warren B. Rudman, R-N.H., deleting low-income home and school weatherization assistance from programs subject to the Hatfield targeting formula. The proposal was intended to channel funds to Northern states needing such funds the most. Adopted March 15 by voice vote.

● Bradley, adding $20 million in Interstate transfer grants for mass transit projects in New Jersey. Adopted March 15 by voice vote.

● Hatfield, modifying provisions of HR 1718 dealing with the distribution of surplus agricultural commodities to conform with a bill (S 17 — S Rept 98-21) recently approved by the Senate Agriculture Committee. Adopted March 15 by voice vote. *(Story, p. 412)*

● Ted Stevens, R-Alaska, requiring the Agriculture Department to purchase up to $30 million of surplus domestic fish products under Section 32 of the Agricultural Adjustment Act of 1935. Adopted March 15 by voice vote.

● Dennis DeConcini, D-Ariz., adding $15 million for accelerated construction of municipal water and irrigation projects under the Bureau of Land Reclamation. Adopted March 15 by voice vote.

● John Melcher, D-Mont., appropriating an additional $55 million for the National Forest System: $20 million for reforestation and $35 million for timber stand improvements. Adopted March 15 by voice vote.

● Levin, adding $25 million for part-time employment of senior citizens. Adopted March 15 by voice vote.

● Slade Gorton, R-Wash., requiring states to use Federal Emergency Management Agency funds to supplement the activities of such private charitable organizations as United Way and the Salvation Army. Adopted March 15 by voice vote.

● Pete Wilson, R-Calif., accelerating a $2.3 million payment for renovation and maintenance of San Francisco's cable cars. Adopted March 15 by voice vote.

● Daniel Patrick Moynihan, D-N.Y., authorizing the sale of two city-owned theaters in Buffalo, N.Y. Adopted March 15 by voice vote.

Amendments Rejected

Amendments rejected included those by:

● Gordon J. Humphrey, R-N.H., to strike appropriations for all programs other than $5 billion for the unemployment trust fund. Rejected 17-80 on March 14. *(Vote 21, p. 7-S)*

● Mack Mattingly, R-Ga., to strike all jobs bill programs except funds for military construction, shelter for the homeless, distribution of surplus foods, and aid to women, infants and children. Rejected 20-77 on March 14. *(Vote 22, p. 7-S)*

● Mattingly, to reduce appropriations for rural water and sewers by $100 million, Army Corps of Engineers by $100 million, social service block grants by $150 million and college work-study by $50 million. Rejected 16-80 on March 14. *(Vote 23, p. 7-S)*

In proposing the amendment, Mattingly claimed that the Office of Management and Budget (OMB) had identified these programs as causing the president "some problems." Challenging Mattingly, Hatfield said he had "worked directly with [OMB Director David A.] Stockman," who had given the Senate bill his approval.

● Moynihan, to cut $209.7 million from funding for the

Bureau of Reclamation and the Army Corps of Engineers and add $200 million to the Environmental Protection Agency's waste treatment and sewer construction program. Rejected 45-51 on March 15. *(Vote 24, p. 8-S)*

Conference Action

As reported by House-Senate conferees March 21 (H Rept 98-44), the bill contained the $4.6 billion jobs plan, plus $5,033,000,000 requested by the administration for the payment of jobless benefits. Conferees also retained $5.7 billion requested by the administration and appropriated by the Senate to finance losses incurred by the Commodity Credit Corp. Senate language earmarking $500 million of this amount for the Agricultural Export Revolving Fund was deleted.

Conferees also approved $200 million in additional capital for the Small Business Administration loan and investment fund, as opposed to $434 million recommended by the Senate.

The bill denied deferrals sought by the administration for Urban Development Action Grants ($244 million), urban mass transit grants ($229 million) and federal housing assistance ($3,081,152,796). Both houses had rejected the administration's plans to delay spending the previously appropriated funds.

Conferees adopted sense of Congress language calling on the Federal Reserve, in combating inflation, to keep interest rates low enough to stimulate economic growth and reduce unemployment. They also directed the secretaries of the Treasury and commerce to "analyze the current trade crisis with the objective of keeping American exports competitive."

Highlights of conference action:

Federal Buildings. Conferees allotted $125 million to the General Services Administration for repairs and maintenance and $75 million for VA maintenance and repair projects, as recommended by both houses.

Conferees endorsed a Senate increase to $60 million, from $35 million favored by the House, for school construction in areas impacted by federal activities. Splitting the difference between the two chambers, conferees provided $80 million for federal prison repairs and renovation.

Highway Construction. Conferees appropriated $33 million for a highway demonstration project in Mississippi after House Appropriations Chairman Whitten, in whose home state the project lay, insisted that "this project is vital to me."

The fiscal 1983 obligation ceiling on federal-aid highway programs was increased by $275 million, as recommended by the Senate, rather than $500 billion as favored by the House.

Mass Transit. Conferees appropriated $132.7 million for mass transportation. The House had originally proposed $171 million, the Senate $94.3 million. Despite criticism in both houses over "pork barrel" legislation in the mass transit area, conferees allocated the entire amount to specific projects, many in the home states and districts of subcommittee chairmen.

Some $33.8 million went to Dade County, home of William Lehman, D-Fla., chairman of a House transportation subcommittee. Another $20 million went to New Jersey, home of James J. Howard, D, chairman of the House Public Works Committee. Conferees also said they had been lobbied by House Ways and Means Committtee Chairman Dan Rostenkowski, D-Ill., who succeeded in earmarking $10 million for northeastern Illinois.

Amtrak. Capital grants for Amtrak were cut to $80 million, $50 million less than the amount approved by the Senate and $30 million less than the House provided. Spending priority was to be given to labor-intensive capital improvements. Conferees reserved $10 million of this amount for a rail line on Cape Cod, a project favored by Massachusetts Rep. Conte, the ranking minority member of the House Appropriations Committee. Another $2 million was tagged for two station renovations in Michigan.

Conferees rejected a $25 million Senate appropriation for safety and right-of-way improvements in the Northeast Corridor. They appropriated $125.75 million to provide supplemental unemployment benefits for railroad workers having less than 10 years' service.

Airports. The ceiling on obligations for airport grants was raised from $600 million to $750 million, as recommended by the Senate. The list of priority projects was expanded from seven to 16.

Community Development. The Senate originally appropriated $540 million for Community Development Block Grants and provided $1 billion in off-budget loan guarantees under the CDBG program. The House originally recommended $1,250,000,000 in straight grants.

Conferees authorized grants totaling $1 billion, $250 million of which would be reserved for areas of high unemployment, as provided by both House and Senate bills. Funds would remain available until Sept. 30, 1985.

The conferees provided that 50 percent of total community development funds could be used for public service jobs, such as home health and day care. The provision was considered a victory for women's groups, who noted that few of the construction and public works jobs under the jobs program would benefit women.

Economic Development Administration. Conferees appropriated $100 million for the EDA, restoring half the funds appropriated by the House and deleted by the Senate. The administration opposed further EDA funding, but Rep. Neal Smith, D-Iowa, said members "from all over the country" supported the program to provide seed money to communities to attract new industry.

Small Business Administration. The compromise plan appropriated $50 million for the SBA direct loan program and $50 million for small business grants to upgrade state and local parks. The Senate had approved no funds for these programs.

Both houses approved an appropriation of $2 million to finance bonds issued by small business development companies.

Parks and Wildlife. Conferees appropriated $85 million for Forest Service reforestation and timberland improvements, and $130 million for construction, trail maintenance and historic preservation by the National Park Service, including $40 million for urban parks repair — an item not included by the Senate.

The conference bill restored $20 million appropriated by the House for the Bureau of Indian Affairs, bringing the total allocation for Indian programs under the bill to $153.5 million. The final bill followed the Senate plan in other respects.

Soil Conservation and Flood Control. Funding for the Army Corps of Engineers totaled $389 million, as compared to $404 million under the House bill and $329 million under the Senate bill. The increase over the Senate plan came at the insistence of House Appropriations Chairman Whitten, who pushed for a larger allocation for Missis-

sippi River projects. Conferees split the difference between House and Senate recommendations and appropriated $140 million for work along the Mississippi and its tributaries.

The plan also allocated $85 million for Corps of Engineers construction and $164 million for general operations and maintenance.

The conferees appropriated $116 million for the Bureau of Reclamation and $40 million for the Tennessee Valley Authority.

The Soil Conservation Service received $100 million for watershed and flood prevention operations under the joint plan — $25 million more than the Senate proposed but $50 million less than the House recommended. The bill deleted House language appropriating $25 million in new loan authority for the Agricultural Credit Insurance Fund.

Rural Water and Sewers. The conference bill appropriated $150 million for rural water and sewer grants by the Farmers Home Administration. The House had recommended $200 million, the Senate $125 million. Conferees also added $50 million to the Senate bill for new FmHA loans — providing $450 million in new loan authority. The House had proposed $600 million.

The conferees allocated $5 million for resource conservation programs by the SCS, instead of the $15 million proposed by the House. The Senate had deleted these funds.

Agricultural Research. Conferees cut a Senate appropriation for repair and maintenance work at the Agricultural Research Service from $10 million to $3 million.

Food and Drug Administration. A $39 million Senate appropriation for the Food and Drug Administration was reduced to $875,000. The funds were to be used for architectural and engineering design work.

Military Housing. The appropriation for military housing construction and maintenance was set at $179.6 million, compared to $100.6 million in the Senate bill and $243 million in the House bill. The number of states that would receive grants grew from 20 in the House bill to 31 under the final bill.

Weatherization. The conference bill adopted the Senate appropriation of $100 million for low-income home weatherization but cut funds for school and hospital weatherization from $75 million to $50 million.

The House version proposed $150 million for home weatherization. It contained no funding for schools and hospitals.

Unemployment, Job Training. The final bill appropriated $254.9 million in employment and job training assistance. It included $85 million for retraining and relocating displaced workers and waived state matching provisions of the Job Training Partnership Act. The House bill allocated $75 million to the program, the Senate bill $125 million.

The proposed $50 million Senate allocation for the employment of older persons was cut to $37.5 million. The House and Senate appropriations for summer youth employment ($100 million) and the Jobs Corps ($32.4 million) were not changed.

Business, Mortgage Relief. Calling for legislative action by appropriate authorizing committees, the conferees deleted a $500,000 House appropriation that would have allowed the Treasury Department to develop plans for new business and mortgage relief agencies modeled after the Reconstruction Finance Corp. and Home Owners Loan Corp., and a farm credit agency.

Another $500,000 House appropriation for emergency mortgage assistance was also deleted.

Health and Social Services. Conferees followed the Senate in appropriating funds for health and social service programs, including maternal and child health care ($105 million), the Women, Infants and Children feeding program ($100 million), community and migrant health centers ($70 million) and surplus food distribution ($75 million).

A separate title of the bill appropriated $50 million to cover administrative, storage and delivery costs associated with food distribution programs approved by the Senate Agriculture Committee (S 17) and the House Agriculture Committee (HR 1590). The Senate had added the authorizing bill to the jobs measure.

A proposal sponsored by Sen. Ted Stevens required the Agriculture Department to substantially increase purchases of surplus domestic fish products under Section 32 of the Agricultural Adjustment Act of 1935 also was included.

The final bill departed from the Senate plan in four areas:

● Social service block grants directed at maintaining family health, preventing child abuse and providing day care and adoption services were cut from $300 million under the Senate plan to $225 million. The House plan proposed $150 million.

● A Senate college work-study program was cut from $100 million to $50 million.

● The emergency food and shelter program received $100 million. Both House and Senate bills recommended $50 million.

● Community service block grants were reduced from $41,375,000 under the Senate plan to $25 million.

Customs Service. A $3.8 million Senate appropriation for the U.S. Customs Service was retained in conference. Funds were to be used to upgrade aircraft employed in the service's drug interdiction program. ∎

Transportation Funding

Congress Aug. 3 cleared legislation (HR 3329 — PL 98-78) appropriating $10.9 billion for transportation programs in fiscal 1984 after voting to block the administration from implementing controversial federal employee rules.

The conference report for the Transportation Department and related agencies (H Rept 98-318) appropriated only $18.7 million more than Reagan's budget request. The fiscal 1983 spending level was $11.8 billion.

The Senate-passed bill provided slightly less than $10.9 billion while the House version included $11.3 billion. In an effort to avoid a veto confrontation with President Reagan over money, conferees cut $367.7 million from the House level.

The House Aug. 2 adopted the conference report by voice vote. Before adopting the report the next day, the Senate approved, 75-18, an amendment by Charles McC. Mathias Jr., R-Md., to delay until Oct. 15 the implementation of new personnel rules, which would have linked the pay and job security of 1.4 million federal workers to job performance. The rules would have gone into effect Aug. 15. *(Vote 233, p. 39-S; personnel regulations, p. 602)*

Later that day, the House concurred by voice vote in the amendment, thereby clearing the appropriations bill

for the president.

Although the administration had objected strongly to earlier congressional moves to delay the personnel regulations, Reagan signed the bill Aug. 15.

Highlights

HR 3329 included:

● A cap of $800 million on Airport and Airway Trust Fund spending for airport development.

● A ceiling of $12.5 billion on Highway Trust Fund spending for highway programs.

● $716.4 million for Amtrak, the subsidized passenger railroad.

● $2.4 billion for mass transit formula grants, which may be used for operating subsidies and capital projects. Conferees rejected Reagan's efforts to restrict the use of the grants for operating subsidies.

● $1.7 billion for Coast Guard operations.

● $2.5 billion for Federal Aviation Administration operations.

● Provisions that generally blocked implementation of two proposed Transportation Department rules for 60 days — one to reduce a limit on passenger levels at National Airport near Washington, D.C., and the other to allow U.S.-flag tankers in the foreign oil trade to enter the domestic trade. *(Maritime authorization, p. 549)*

● $15 million for rail-highway crossing safety projects.

House Committee Action

As reported June 16 (H Rept 98-246) by the House Appropriations Committee, HR 3329 provided $11.3 billion in new budget authority for the Transportation Department and related agencies, $507.4 million less than appropriated for fiscal 1983. Along with $16.3 billion in obligational authority from various trust funds that do not require annual action, the bill provided a total program level of $27.6 billion. Following are details:

Office of the Secretary. The panel recommended $43.8 million in new budget authority, which was $6.02 million less than requested and $1.1 million less than appropriated in 1983.

Coast Guard. A total of $2.5 billion was provided for the Coast Guard, $27.9 million less than requested but $68.7 million more than 1983 spending. The funding included $1.7 billion for operating expenses, $97.9 million more than in 1983. The bill would have provided 37,645 military and 5,044 civilian positions, an increase over 1983 of 237 and 81 positions respectively. The panel allowed $369 million for acquisition, construction and improvements for vessels, aircraft and facilities, $9.6 million less than requested.

Federal Aviation Administration. The committee provided $2.6 billion for operations, including $310 million from the airport trust fund. It noted that the trust fund contribution amounted to only 12 percent of the operating costs and called the figure a "totally inappropriate cost sharing by the users of the system." However, it said the appropriation followed a "penalty clause" contained in 1982 aviation tax legislation (PL 97-248) that established a formula to reduce trust fund money for operations if facilities and equipment funds were not requested and spent. *(1982 Almanac p. 333)*

The 1982 act authorized $1.39 billion in fiscal 1984 for facilities and equipment, but the administration requested $1 billion and the panel recommended $985.5 million.

The ceiling of $900 million on obligations from the trust fund for airport development and planning grants was necessary to ensure that lagging airport development would not damage the aviation system, the panel said.

The panel recommended $985.5 million from the trust fund for facilities and equipment, which includes airport towers, navigation facilities and other programs. That was $14.5 million below the request and $367.95 million more than 1983 spending.

The new budget authority for the FAA of $3.8 billion was $518.3 million more than current appropriations, primarily because of the FAA's program to upgrade, modernize and consolidate the air traffic control system through 1990. *(1982 Almanac p. 334)*

Federal Highway Administration. The panel provided a program level of $12.7 billion for FHWA, $33.6 million more than requested and $298.5 million less than provided in fiscal 1983. That included the requested $12.6 billion ceiling on obligations from the Highway Trust Fund. The 1982 highway act set a ceiling of $12.75 billion on obligations from the trust fund in fiscal 1984. *(1982 Almanac p. 317)*

National Highway Traffic Safety Administration. A program level of $217.95 million for the agency was recommended, $23 million more than requested. The committee rejected the president's proposal to cut staff levels from 640 to 617, dropping to 586 by the end of the year. It said it doubted the agency could operate at that level without posing additional risks to the public and authorized staffing at 640.

The bill also limited obligations from the Highway Trust Fund for state and community safety grants to $100 million and to $37.95 million for alcohol safety grants.

Federal Railroad Administration. New budget authority was set at $940.5 million, $91.2 million above the amount requested.

The panel provided $35 million not requested for subsistence allowances, moving expenses and other programs to aid employees of the bankrupt Rock Island Railroad. Also, it included $100 million for improvements to the Northeast Corridor, which runs from Boston to Washington, D.C. *(1982 Almanac p. 345)*

Urban Mass Transportation Administration. Recommended total funding was $4.4 billion. Formula grants for mass transit operations and capital aid were set at $2.5 billion, $515.1 million more than requested. The panel rejected the president's plan to restrict operating subsidies, saying it violated the intent of the 1982 transportation act. The president wanted to limit operating aid to $275 million for urban areas and $18.5 million for rural areas.

Discretionary grants for special capital projects would be financed by funds from the new mass transit account established by the 1982 highway act. The panel's cap on obligations of $1.25 billion was $150 million above the budget request.

The bill included $335 million for transit projects substituted by local authorities for planned segments of the Interstate Highway system.

National Transportation Safety Board. The committee included $20.6 million for the agency, which investigates accidents. That was $880,000 above the budget request and provided for 357 positions, 22 more than requested.

Civil Aeronautics Board. The panel approved $69.2 million for the board and special air carrier subsidies.

Fiscal 1984 Transportation Funds

Following is the fiscal 1984 funding for the Department of Transportation and related agencies requested by the president and appropriated by HR 3329 as passed June 22 by the House, July 15 by the Senate and as signed by the president Aug. 15 (PL 98-78).

	Budget Request	House-passed	Senate-passed	Final Appropriation
Department of Transportation				
Office of the Secretary	$ 49,793,000	$ 43,775,000	$ 48,531,000	$ 46,153,000
Coast Guard	2,499,447,456	2,473,030,456	2,451,597,456	2,454,197,456
Federal Aviation Administration	4,037,389,000	3,816,507,000	3,620,159,000	3,619,159,000
Federal Highway Administration	31,620,000	65,220,000	41,590,000	75,590,000
National Highway Traffic Safety Administration	77,998,000	78,000,000	78,000,000	78,000,000
Federal Railroad Administration	849,250,000	940,499,000	949,299,000	949,299,000
Urban Mass Transportation Administration	2,665,166,000	3,182,592,200	2,973,058,200	3,017,922,200
Research and Special Programs Administration	20,287,000	20,200,000	20,200,000	20,200,000
Office of the Inspector General	25,895,000	26,795,000	26,795,000	26,795,000
Subtotal	10,256,845,456	10,646,618,656	10,209,229,656	10,287,385,656
Related Agencies				
Architectural and Transportation Barriers Compliance Board	1,700,000	1,900,000	1,900,000	1,900,000
National Transportation Safety Board	19,735,000	20,615,000	21,062,000	20,858,000
Civil Aeronautics Board	71,690,000	69,200,000	66,900,000	69,200,000
Interstate Commerce Commission	58,038,000	59,000,000	62,000,000	60,000,000
Panama Canal Commission	453,800,000	448,400,000	439,100,000	439,100,000
U.S. Railway Association	0	2,500,000	2,100,000	2,100,000
Washington Metropolitan Area Transit Authority	51,663,569	51,663,569	51,663,569	51,663,569
Subtotal	656,626,569	653,278,569	644,725,569	644,821,569
GRAND TOTAL	$10,913,472,025	$11,299,897,225	$10,853,955,225	$10,932,207,225

Under the 1978 Airline Deregulation Act (PL 95-504), the board was scheduled to go out of existence in 1985. *(1978 Almanac p. 496)*

Interstate Commerce Commission. The panel recommended $59 million, $962,000 above the request and $6.6 million below the 1983 funding. It noted that transportation deregulation legislation had resulted in reducing staff by some 45 percent since 1979.

U.S. Railway Association. Although noting that USRA had largely fulfilled its function of structuring bankrupt railroads into Conrail, the panel recommended $2.9 million, including $400,000 in transfers, to monitor Conrail's performance. Reagan requested no funds.

House Floor Action

The House June 22 approved the committee's $11.3 billion appropriation after defeating an effort to reduce funding by 4 percent.

The appropriations bill was approved 250-156. *(Vote 199, p. 60-H)*

A veto threat hung over the bill largely because it provided $386 million more than Reagan requested and included other provisions objectionable to the administration.

The House, 191-223, rejected a motion by Lawrence Coughlin, R-Pa., ranking minority member of the Appropriations Transportation Subcommittee, to recommit the bill to the full committee with instructions that it be reported back with an amendment to cut discretionary funding by 4 percent. *(Vote 198, p. 60-H)*

Subcommittee Chairman William Lehman, D-Fla., said that 4 percent might seem like "a relatively insignificant sum," but it would mean serious losses for aviation, Coast Guard and railroad programs.

House Provisions

Highlights of the bill included:

● $2.5 billion for mass transit formula grants, used for operating and capital costs.

● A cap of $1.25 billion on spending from the new transit account in the Highway Trust Fund for discretionary tran-

sit grants. The funds, to be used for new rail systems, came from 1 cent of the gas tax. *(1982 Almanac p. 317)*

● A $12.6 billion cap on Highway Trust Fund obligations for Interstate Highway construction and related highway programs.

● A cap of $900 million on spending from the Airport and Airway Trust Fund for airport development. The trust fund is fed by taxes on passenger tickets and aviation fuel. *(1982 Almanac p. 333)*

● $720 million for Amtrak, $58 million more than Reagan proposed.

● $985.5 million to modernize facilities for the nation's air control system. *(1982 Almanac p. 334)*

● A prohibition against using funds to implement a proposed federal rule allowing U.S.-flag tankers involved in foreign trade to enter the domestic oil trade after they repay their federal construction subsidies.

By voice vote, the House approved an amendment by Gerry E. Studds, D-Mass., to add $1.5 million for Coast Guard research and development. Studds said the funds were needed to develop an electronic ocean-dumping surveillance system for enforcing laws regulating disposal of sewage and for other research.

Other amendments included those by:

● Bobbi Fiedler, R-Calif., to delete $127.5 million for a new 18.6-mile subway system in Los Angeles. Rejected 139-280. *(Vote 195, p. 60-H)*

● Christopher H. Smith, R-N.J., to delete statutory language regarding cost-sharing for a high-speed rail link between Philadelphia and Atlantic City. The amendment essentially would have eliminated $30 million for the project. Rejected by a 25-33 division vote.

● Dan Glickman, D-Kan., to eliminate a provision that would bar the use of funds to develop or implement a proposed federal rule to lower the number of passengers below 16 million a year or reducing air carrier slots at National Airport in Washington, D.C. Defeated 170-249. *(Vote 196, p. 60-H)*

The House also rejected an effort to prevent several states from losing their federal highway funds because they had not adopted a motor vehicle inspection and maintenance program to reduce air pollution.

William E. Dannemeyer, R-Calif., said he wanted to offer a rider to the bill to block the sanctions, mandated by the Clean Air Act. But House rules barred the amendment unless a motion for the Committee of the Whole to rise was rejected.

Despite Dannemeyer's urging, the House voted 275-139 for the motion. *(Vote 197, p. 60-H)*

Senate Committee Action

As reported July 14 by the Senate Appropriations Committee (S Rept 98-179), the bill provided $10,856,000,000 in new budget authority for DOT and related agencies.

Office of the Secretary. The panel recommended $48,531,000 in new budget authority, $4.8 million more than the House bill and $1.3 million less than requested.

Coast Guard. The panel included $2.5 billion for the Coast Guard, $21.4 million less than the House and $47.8 million less than requested. It provided $1.6 billion plus another $12.6 million by transfer for operating expenses, $27 million less than the House and $39.6 million less than Reagan requested. The committee also included $370.9 million for the Coast Guard's acquisition, construction and

improvements program. The bill provided for 37,645 military and 5,051 civilian positions.

Federal Aviation Administration. The panel recommended $2.5 billion for operations, $93.3 million less than the House bill and $139.5 million less than requested. It provided that all of the funds for operations come from the general Treasury, while the House included $310 million from the Airport and Airway Trust Fund and Reagan asked for about $1 billion from the trust fund. The trust fund is made up of aviation taxes. The panel said its action was forced by a "penalty clause" in 1982 aviation tax legislation (PL 97-248), which set a formula to cut trust fund money for operations if facilities and equipment funds were not requested and spent. *(1982 Almanac p. 333)*

The bill set a cap of $800 million on spending from the trust fund for airport development, $100 million less than the House and $100 million more than Reagan requested.

The panel eliminated a House recommendation that the FAA consider rehiring some air traffic controllers dismissed for striking, saying that "would be a severe blow to the morale of controllers who stayed on the job."

Federal Highway Administration. The committee provided a total program level of $12.7 billion for FHWA, almost $10 million more than the budget request and $23.6 million less than the House allowance.

Included was a $12.6 billion ceiling on spending from the Highway Trust Fund for Interstate Highway construction and related projects, the same as requested by Reagan and provided by the House.

The committee deleted the House allowance of $35.7 million for railroad-highway crossing projects to resolve safety hazards or traffic impediments.

It also allocated $20 million of available emergency funds to rebuild the Mianus Bridge on I-95 in Connecticut. The bridge collapsed in June. Another $1 million would be provided to Greenwich, Conn., and Port Chester, N.Y., for road repair and police costs caused by the bridge collapse.

National Highway Traffic Safety Administration. The committee recommended a total program level of $219.9 million for NHTSA, $23 million more than requested and $2 million more than the House bill. The total included $78 million for NHTSA operations and research. It also limited spending from the Highway Trust Fund to $100 million for state and community highway safety grants. The panel also capped alcohol safety grants at $37.9 million, the same level requested by the administration and provided by the House.

Federal Railroad Administration. The committee set a total program level of $974.9 million for FRA, $125.6 million more than requested and $2.6 million less than the House provided. The total included $718 million for Amtrak, the federally subsidized passenger railroad. The full Senate cut Amtrak funding to $716.4 million.

The committee met the House level of $35 million for subsistence allowances and other aid to employees of the bankrupt Rock Island Railroad. No funds were requested. The panel met the House and administration level of $100 million for improvements to the Northeast Corridor, which runs from Boston to Washington, D.C. *(1982 Almanac p. 345)*

Urban Mass Transportation Administration. A total program level of $4.2 billion was recommended, $407.9 million more than the budget request and $259.5 million less than the House allowance.

The bill included $2.4 billion for mass transit formula grants, which could be used for operating subsidies and

capital projects. The House bill provided $2.5 billion and Reagan requested $1,974,000,000. Like the House, the Senate panel rejected Reagan's plan to restrict operating subsidies. *(1982 Almanac p. 317)*

The committee recommended a cap of $1.2 billion on spending from the transit account of the Highway Trust Fund for discretionary grants for special capital projects. The House set a ceiling of $1.2 billion and the president sought $1.1 billion. The transit account was funded by revenues from 1 cent of the 9-cents-a-gallon highway gasoline tax. Of the total discretionary funds, the panel recommended $395 million for new rail system starts.

It also included $270 million for transit projects substituted by communities for previously planned Interstate Highway segments, $110 million less than the budget request and $65 million less than the House bill.

National Transportation Safety Board. The panel provided $21.1 million for the agency, which investigated accidents. The total was $447,000 more than the House bill and $1.3 million more than requested. The committee recommended an increase of 22 staff positions over the request, for a total of 357, the same as the House level.

Civil Aeronautics Board. The committee recommended $16.1 million for the CAB through June 30, 1984. The House provided $18.4 million, plus $2.4 million by transfer, for the full fiscal year, and the president requested $20.9 million. Under the 1978 Airline Deregulation Act (PL 95-504), the board was scheduled to disband in 1985. The bill established an Airline Deregulation Study Commission to recommend by April 15, 1984, whether Congress needed to protect travelers from negative effects of deregulation. *(1978 Almanac p. 496)*

Also included in the bill was $50.8 million for special air carrier subsidies, the same level as provided by the House and requested by the president.

Interstate Commerce Commission. The panel provided $62 million for the ICC, $3 million more than the House and almost $4 million more than the budget request.

U.S. Railway Administration. The panel provided $2.5 million, including $400,000 by transfer, for the USRA, which restructured the bankrupt freight railroads of the Northeast into Conrail. The panel said USRA should continue to monitor Conrail at least through a second profitability test in November, which was part of the process of selling the railroad system. The House provided $2.9 million, including $400,000 by transfer, and Reagan requested no funds. *(1981 Almanac p. 561)*

Senate Floor Action

The Senate July 15 approved $10.85 billion in fiscal 1984 appropriations for transportation programs, $60 million under Reagan's budget request.

The bill passed 86-5. The Senate added no money but made a minor cut of $1.6 million in the bill as reported. *(Vote 192, p. 34-S)*

David A. Stockman, director of the Office of Management and Budget, said in a July 14 letter to key senators that any increases to the committee's total of $10.855 billion during floor action or conference "would make it difficult" for him to recommend that Reagan sign the bill.

Mark Andrews, R-N.D., chairman of the Appropriations Transportation Subcommittee, said he was not happy with the total level of spending, but he was told by Stockman and Transportation Secretary Elizabeth Hanford Dole that the level was "signable."

The one cut made by the Senate was contained in an amendment by Malcolm Wallop, R-Wyo., to trim $1.6 million from the committee bill's $718 million for Amtrak, the federally subsidized passenger railroad. Wallop said $1.6 million was the amount Amtrak officials said they would save by rerouting the California Zephyr through Colorado rather than Wyoming.

Senate-House Differences

The bill, as passed by the Senate, included:

● $1.66 billion for Coast Guard operating expenses, $27 million less than the House bill and Reagan's request.

● $2.5 billion for the operation of the air traffic control system by the Federal Aviation Administration (FAA), $139.5 million less than the request and $93.3 million less than the House amount. The bill provided that all of the funds for FAA operations would come from the general Treasury.

● A ceiling of $800 million on trust fund spending for airport development projects, $100 million less than approved by the House but $100 million more than requested by Reagan. *(1982 Almanac p. 333)*

● $716.4 million for Amtrak, $3.6 million less than the House and $54.4 million more than requested.

● $2.39 billion for urban mass transit formula grants, $415.1 million more than the budget request. The grants were for operating subsidies and capital projects. The Senate, like the House, rejected the president's request to allow only $275 million of the formula grant money to be used for urban transit operating subsidies.

Reagan opposed mass transit operating subsidies, contending that they were not a proper use of federal funds. He proposed their elimination in fiscal 1985.

● A ceiling of $1.2 billion on spending from the transit account of the Highway Trust Fund for mass transit capital projects. The House set a $1.25 billion limit, while Reagan requested $1.1 billion. The 1982 Transportation Assistance Act (PL 97-424) established the transit account and financed it with 1 cent of the highway gasoline tax. *(1982 Almanac p. 317)*

● A cap of $12.6 billion on spending from the Highway Trust Fund for Interstate Highway construction and related road projects, the same level approved by the House and proposed by Reagan. The fiscal 1984 ceiling would be $225 million more than the current level (PL 98-8) but $150 million less than authorized by the 1982 transportation act for 1984.

● $20 million from available funds to help repair the Mianus Bridge on I-95 in Connecticut. The bridge collapsed in June. The panel said the disruption of traffic to New England had national consequences.

National Airport. One of the major non-money differences between the Senate and the House bills concerned the use of National Airport in Washington, D.C.

People living near the airport, which is close to downtown Washington, had complained about increasing noise and safety problems. Many members of Congress resisted ordering reduced air traffic because National is convenient to the capital.

DOT had proposed a rule that would limit the number of passengers. One alternative was to cap the number at 14.8 million a year, rather than the current 16 million. The other was to set a ceiling based on future traffic forecasts. The traffic level in 1982 was 13.4 million.

The House bill prohibited the use of funds to develop or implement a rule to reduce the number of passengers below 16 million a year. The Senate eliminated the House language.

The Senate committee report said the proposed DOT rule would not reduce service at National. And the panel said that under the second alternative of the proposed rule, the cap could end up at the 16 million level.

It directed the transportation secretary to work with all interested parties to establish a comprehensive, permanent policy for use of the Washington area airports.

The panel said quick, convenient access to National, Dulles and Baltimore-Washington International (BWI) was more important to travelers than which airport was used. The committee directed the secretary to report to Congress by Feb. 1 on the possibility of a downtown heliport to serve Dulles and BWI. And, the bill included $3.5 million for new buses to improve access to Dulles.

Conference Action

Conferees agreed July 21 on most spending levels for fiscal 1984 transportation programs but found themselves stalemated over a House provision blocking proposed rules reducing the limit on passengers at National Airport and allowing U.S. tankers in foreign trade to enter the domestic oil trade.

On July 26, they agreed to prohibit the enforcement of both rules for 60 days after enactment.

On the airport, the House provision prevented the transportation secretary from implementing a rule to cap the number of passengers at National at 16 million a year. The Senate deleted the provision.

Sen. Andrews proposed holding the rule in abeyance for 90 days, but House conferees rejected the compromise. Rep. Martin Olav Sabo, D-Minn., said the 16-million passenger limit had been approved by former Secretary Drew Lewis two years earlier, and Congress should not continue fighting over the issue.

The other stalemated issue involved a House provision to block the use of funds to implement a proposed Transportation Department rule allowing U.S.-flag tankers operating in foreign trade to enter the domestic oil trade after they repay their federal construction subsidies.

House members argued that the rule would allow vessels that had benefited from cheaper construction costs to compete unfairly with ships in the domestic trade, which were not eligible for the construction subsidies.

Sen. Ted Stevens, R-Alaska, who was not a conferee, told the conference the proposed rule could save $400 million.

Congress Clears 1984 Interior Funding Bill

Congress Oct. 20 cleared for President Reagan a fiscal 1984 appropriations bill (HR 3363 — PL 98-146) for the Interior Department and related agencies that carried riders restricting federal leasing of coal, oil and gas.

Final action came when first the Senate and then the House approved compromise language resolving the last issues in disagreement following their adoption of a conference report (H Rept 98-399) on the bill.

As cleared, the measure provided $7,953,783,000 in new budget authority. President Reagan had requested $6,709,628,000.

The House passed the bill June 28 by a 272-144 vote. *(Vote 213, p. 64-H)*

The Senate followed suit Sept. 21 by a 76-18 vote. *(Vote 249, p. 41-S)*

Coal Leasing Ban

The bill also imposed a moratorium on federal coal leasing until 90 days after a special commission completed a study of the leasing program and made recommendations to Congress. The commission had six months in which to conduct its review. *(Coal leasing, p. 350)*

The moratorium grew out of congressional concern about the coal leasing policies of Interior Secretary James G. Watt, who resigned Oct. 9. *(Watt resignation, p. 327)*

During final consideration of HR 3363, the Senate by voice vote adopted an amendment offered by John Melcher, D-Mont., exempting certain tracts in Montana and Colorado from the coal leasing ban. The House accepted the exemption.

Oil and Gas Leasing

For the third year in a row, Congress banned offshore oil and gas drilling in selected areas. *(1982 Almanac p. 262)*

As cleared, HR 3363 imposed a one-year ban on leasing in a 1.2 million-acre area off the coast of Southern California and a similar ban in the Georges Bank area off New England.

Also, the measure restricted oil and gas leasing off the west coast of Florida in the Gulf of Mexico.

Strategic Petroleum Reserve

HR 3363 set a minimum fill rate of 186,000 barrels per day for the Strategic Petroleum Reserve (SPR) in fiscal 1984. Reagan wanted only 145,000 barrels per day, while the House and Senate had wanted to keep the current rate of 220,000 barrels per day. *(SPR, p. 372)*

The $650 million final appropriation to buy oil for the reserve was expected to allow purchase of about 15 million barrels for fiscal 1985.

The SPR was one of the largest single items in the bill, but it was not counted in budget totals. While Reagan had originally requested $583.1 million for the SPR, the House approved $1.7 billion and the Senate $1.3 billion. Those figures prompted an administration veto threat, hurried negotiations and a reduced figure in the final version.

House Committee Action

The House Appropriations Committee June 21 approved an $8.1 billion version of HR 3363 (H Rept 98-253) with hotly contested riders barring Watt from certain oil and gas leasing off the shores of California and Florida.

Those riders came on top of others, also meant to rein in controversial Interior Department actions, that were put in the bill when it was approved June 7 by the Appropriations Subcommittee on Interior.

The bill exceeded the Reagan budget request by $1.38

Final Provisions of 1984 Interior Funding Bill

Following are the amounts, in budget authority, requested by President Reagan and appropriated by HR 3363 for the Interior Department and related agencies in fiscal 1984 *(in thousands of dollars)*:

	Budget Request*	House Bill	Senate Bill	Final Appropriation
Department of Interior				
Bureau of Land Management	$ 522,449	$ 521,801	$ 538,615	$ 538,828
U.S. Fish and Wildlife Service	266,500	346,422	319,983	353,161
National Park Service	737,080	858,540	822,649	847,201
Geological Survey	356,956	374,951	356,074	367,080
Minerals Management Service	164,218*	155,103	163,803	163,561
Bureau of Mines	117,583	127,865	129,925	136,425
Office of Surface Mining	282,299	316,928	283,829	294,678
Bureau of Indian Affairs	944,840	967,781	963,035	969,122
Territorial & International Affairs	150,139	180,235	198,331	191,371
Secretarial Offices	82,686	79,940	89,470	87,915
Subtotal	3,624,750	3,929,566	3,865,714	3,949,342
Related Agencies				
Forest Service	1,253,924	1,328,404	1,346,988	1,354,006
Department of Energy	666,638	1,296,029	1,479,470	1,191,915
Indian Health	652,706	870,813	766,040	824,003
Indian Education	1,243	71,243	67,248	68,780
Smithsonian	175,894	174,173	164,648	166,803
National Endowment for the Arts	125,000	165,000	143,000	162,000
National Endowment for the Humanities	112,200	150,000	130,000	140,000
Other Agencies	97,273	96,746	91,165	96,934
Subtotal	3,084,878	4,152,408	4,188,559	4,004,441
GRAND TOTAL	$6,709,628	$8,081,974	$8,054,273	$7,953,783

* As amended

billion, but remained $245 million below what Congress appropriated for fiscal 1983.

The total new budget authority recommended in the bill was $8,081,573,000.

The full committee largely accepted the recommendations of the subcommittee, adding only $9.5 million to the total.

Spending Cut Rejected

The committee rejected, 16-27, an amendment offered by Joseph M. McDade, R-Pa., to cut funding 4 percent across-the-board for all programs in the bill. Republicans argued that the bill's total was significantly higher than the committee's report made it seem. They said once off-budget spending, deferrals and supplementals were factored in, the spending total exceeded fiscal 1983 levels.

"This bill is going to get vetoed unless we fix it up here in this room," McDade said, arguing for the cut.

That threat was backed up by David A. Stockman, director of the Office of Management and Budget, in a June 21 letter to Appropriations Chairman Jamie L. Whitten, D-Miss.

In urging approval, however, Interior Subcommittee Chairman Sidney R. Yates, D-Ill., noted that the activities in the bill would bring far more revenue into the Treasury than they took out of it. Some $15,696,982,000 in revenue was anticipated in fiscal 1984, largely from oil, gas, mineral

and timber production.

Permanent appropriations mandated in earlier legislation added $2.38 billion in new budget authority to the amount in the present bill — raising the total new budget authority for fiscal 1984 to $10.46 billion.

Strategic Petroleum Reserve

Off-budget spending, not counted in the totals, was on top of that figure. The biggest such item was funding for the SPR. One of the major disagreements between the committee and the administration was over the rate at which oil was pumped into the reserve — and dollars pumped out of the Treasury. The administration asked $583.1 million for the SPR, while the committee recommended $1.686 billion. Some $2.074 billion was appropriated for fiscal 1983.

Parks, Indian Programs

The committee recommended considerably more spending than the administration wanted in other major areas as well: energy conservation, park land acquisition, fossil energy research and Indian health programs.

Land acquisition for parks and recreation under the Land and Water Conservation Fund had been the subject of continuing dispute between Watt and Congress. The committee voted $242.33 million for land acquisition under the fund in 1984, less than the 1983 appropriation of

$266.89 million but far more than the administration's $64.87 million request. The panel earmarked $75 million of the total for aid to states.

The bill also contained most but not all of the money spent by 12 federal agencies on Indian programs. Governmentwide, appropriations for Indian programs were $2.67 billion in 1983. In this bill, the committee voted $1.92 billion for Indian programs in 1984, more than the administration's $1.62 billion request, but slightly less than the 1983 appropriation of $1.93 billion for comparable programs.

Offshore Drilling Bans

The California and Florida offshore leasing bans proposed by Yates prompted intense committee debate before they were approved, in modified form, by voice vote. The panel softened the bans slightly to allow preparation for lease sales but not the sales themselves.

The California ban applied to waters off Southern California, from the U.S.-Mexico border north through San Diego County and some of Orange County, starting three miles out at the limit of state-controlled waters and reaching to about 20 miles offshore. It also included buffer zones around the Channel Islands and in the Santa Barbara Channel.

The one-year ban was requested in a June 6 letter to Yates signed by 23 of the 45 House members from California. That division within the state delegation, heightened by the pressure to develop a reportedly rich new petroleum find in the area, made the ban hotly controversial.

The bill also renewed less controversial existing leasing bans for most of the northern California coastline and part of the central coastline that were included in the 1983 appropriation.

The Florida rider applied to almost the entire Gulf of Mexico coastline of that state. During the markup, the committee dropped another leasing ban for the southern Atlantic coast, including areas off Florida. The Interior Subcommittee had approved such a ban because of potential conflicts between drilling and military or space agency activities. But Yates said earlier disputes between the Interior Department, the Defense Department and the National Aeronautics and Space Administration had been settled.

The bill also prohibited the sale of leases in the Georges Bank area off the coast of New England. The 30 million acres covered by this sale were scheduled to be offered for lease in February 1984.

Wilderness Study-Area Leasing

Another rider in the appropriations bill barred oil and gas leasing in so-called "wilderness study areas" on lands run by the Bureau of Land Management (BLM). Those areas — lands being studied for possible future inclusion in the federal wilderness system — constituted about 24 million acres of the 397 million acres managed by BLM. Watt had announced Dec. 30, 1982, that he would voluntarily refrain from leasing in the BLM study areas, after Congress banned leasing in national forest wilderness study areas in the fiscal 1983 Interior appropriations bill. (*Wilderness leasing, 1982 Almanac p. 461*)

Wilderness recommendations for BLM lands are handled under a legal and administrative process separate from that for national forest lands — which were the battleground for Watt's fights with Congress over wilderness leasing in 1982.

The Federal Land Policy and Management Act of 1976 (PL 94-579) required Interior to manage BLM study areas so as not to impair their wilderness values, but left the secretary discretion over energy and mineral leasing in those areas. (*Congress and the Nation Vol. IV, p. 314*)

How much acreage in the study areas had been leased already was uncertain. BLM stopped counting in early 1981, when approximately 25 percent nationwide had already been leased. Environmentalists said as much as 80 percent of the study acreage had been leased in some states like Utah and Arizona.

Coal Leasing

The Interior bill also banned sale of coal leases on federal lands until Watt appointed a blue-ribbon study commission to examine the leasing process and Congress reviewed its recommendations. The commission would have six months from the date of enactment to report back to Congress. The leasing ban would run until "the secretary and appropriate committees of Congress have agreed on the commission's recommendations to be implemented."

Interior Department

The committee-approved bill appropriated a total of $3,929,165,000 in fiscal 1984 for the Interior Department — more than Reagan's request of $3,616,050,000 but less than the $4,183,489,000 appropriated for 1983.

One of the biggest additions to Reagan's budget was for the U.S. Fish and Wildlife Service. The panel recommended $346.42 million, up from both the 1983 appropriation of $313.61 million and the administration's request of $266.5 million. Some $42 million of the increase over Reagan's budget was for land acquisition and $23 million for resource management.

Another big boost over Reagan's budget came for the National Park Service, but its funding was still below the fiscal 1983 level of $1.04 billion. Reagan proposed $737.08 million for fiscal 1984, while the committee approved $858.14 million.

Again, the major bone of contention was land acquisition; the committee boosted Reagan's roughly $55 million request to $161 million. The committee also added money for urban parks and historic preservation, programs Reagan wanted to close down, while cutting nearly in half the construction budget request made by the administration.

Agriculture Department

The bill contained $1,328,404,000 for the U.S. Forest Service, a part of the Department of Agriculture. That was more than the administration's 1984 request of $1,253,924,000, but less than the $1,611,283,000 appropriated for fiscal 1983. The largest component of the Forest Service budget was for activities related to the timber sales program — in which private industry pays to harvest timber on U.S. forest land. The rate of sales was important to the forest products industry, which was struggling to come back from a depression.

The committee recommended a sales program of 11.2 billion board feet of new sales in fiscal 1984, funding it at $619.5 million, slightly above the administration's request of $604.2 million. The committee estimated its recommended program would yield $1.39 billion in revenue.

Energy Department

The committee voted budget authority of $1,296,029,000 for the Department of Energy, almost dou-

ble Reagan's request of $666,638,000, and significantly above the 1983 appropriation of $1,202,428,000.

The bulk of the increase was in the area of energy conservation, with the committee voting $528.045 million and the administration requesting only $74.38 million. The bill included $243.5 million for low-income home weatherization and $98 million for conservation in schools and hospitals. The administration wanted no spending on either program.

Another large increase came in fossil energy research and development, which included "synfuels" and other technologies for sqeezing more usable energy from non-nuclear fuels. The committee approved $265.91 million for fossil energy research, well above the 1983 appropriation of $217.51 million, while the administration asked for $94 million.

Other Agencies

Funding for 17 other related agencies and programs was also included in the Interior bill, ranging from Indian health and education programs to cultural and museum programs such as the Smithsonian Institution and the National Endowment for the Arts and Humanities. For these, the committee recommended appropriations totaling $1,527,975,000.

House Floor Action

The House passed HR 3363 on June 28 after rejecting by a razor-thin margin a funding cut Republicans said was needed to avert a presidential veto.

In a classic parliamentary cliffhanger, members first adopted and then rejected an amendment offered by Mc-Dade to cut 4 percent across-the-board from program funding in the bill.

On the initial vote, while the House was sitting as the Committee of the Whole, the amendment was adopted, 211-209. *(Vote 211, p. 64-H)*

Within minutes came an instant replay. The Committee of the Whole rose and reported the bill to the House. Speaker Thomas P. O'Neill Jr., D-Mass., assumed the chair. At this point, the rules allowed a separate vote on one of the amendments reported by the committee.

Although such a second vote is rarely demanded, Sidney R. Yates, D-Ill., chairman of the Appropriations Subcommittee on Interior, asked for one on the McDade amendment. This time, the amendment was rejected, 206-213. *(Vote 212, p. 64-H)*

Six members switched from "yea" on the first McDade amendment vote to "nay" on the second one: Pennsylvania Democrats Joe Kolter, Gus Yatron, Joseph M. Gaydos and Austin J. Murphy; and Carroll Hubbard Jr., D-Ky., and Tony P. Hall, D-Ohio.

Switching from "nay" on the first vote to "yea" on the second were Joe Moakley, D-Mass., and James M. Jeffords, R-Vt.

Frank R. Wolf, R-Va., who voted "yea" on the first vote, did not vote on the second.

Once the McDade amendment was killed, the House passed the bill by 272-144. *(Vote 213, p. 64-H)*

Veto Threat

The veto threat came in a June 21 letter to Appropriations Committee leaders from Office of Management and Budget (OMB) Director David A. Stockman, who called the funding levels in the bill "clearly unacceptable." Stock-

man also said the bill's restrictions on the administration's aggressive program of leasing energy resources on public lands were "seriously objectionable."

Yates said the funding in the bill was $600 million lower than the amount appropriated for fiscal 1983, but Stockman and McDade said it was $300 million more. The administration used 1983 levels as an informal bench-mark in veto decisions. While each side claimed its figures were right, most of the difference seemed to be over how much was appropriated for 1983. That figure was higher if Interior-related funding under the current year's emergency jobs bill (HR 1718) and the main fiscal 1983 supplemental (HR 3069) were added to the department's regular 1983 appropriations bill. *(Jobs bill, p. 447; supplemental, p. 509)*

·The only other recorded vote came over funding for the National Endowment for the Arts and the National Endowment for the Humanities. A set of four amendments offered by John Hiler, R-Ind., to cut their funding by about $40 million, leaving them at fiscal 1983 levels, was rejected, 150-271. *(Vote 210, p. 64-H)*

Senate Committee Action

The Senate Appropriations Committee July 19 approved a $7.6 billion verison of HR 3363 (S Rept 98-184) after modifying it to reduce the threat of a veto.

The Senate committee version of the bill called for appropriations of $7,639,488,000 in new budget authority, well above the administration's $6,700,928,000 request, but $442.5 million less than the $8,081,974,000 approved by the House June 28.

Leasing Bans Removed

At the urging of Sen. James A. McClure, R-Idaho, chairman of the Subcommittee on Interior, the Appropriations Committee stripped from the House bill several provisions banning coal or oil leasing on public lands.

Both the leasing ban riders and the funding levels contained in the House version of the bill figured in administration veto threats conveyed in a July 15 letter to McClure from OMB Director Stockman.

McClure's subcommittee, which marked up the bill one day before the full committee acted, did approve on an 8-7 vote one House provision that would bar oil and gas drilling on some 16 million acres of Bureau of Land Management land and 5.2 million acres of National Forest Service land under consideration for future inclusion in the national wilderness system.

Sen. Lawton Chiles, D-Fla., withdrew a planned amendment to ban oil and gas leasing in some 59 million acres of the Gulf of Mexico off the Florida coast after determining it was likely to be rejected. The amendment was similar to a House-passed provision that would be on the table during a House-Senate conference to resolve differences between the two versions of HR 3363.

The House bill — but not the Senate version — also prohibited leasing in areas offshore from California and in the Georges Bank area, a highly productive commercial fishing region off New England. And it imposed a moratorium of at least six months on coal leasing on federal lands until a blue-ribbon commission studied that issue.

Interior Department

For the Interior Department, the Senate committee bill allotted $3.8 billion, less than the House-passed

amount of $3.9 billion but still above the Reagan request of $3.6 billion.

The biggest cuts the Senate panel made in the House spending levels for Interior came in the Fish and Wildlife Service, down $33 million to $312 million; the National Park Service, down $43 million to $816 million; and the Office of Surface Mining Reclamation and Enforcement, down $33 million to $284 million.

The Senate panel partially offset these and other cuts by increasing above the House level funding for the Bureau of Land Management, up $17 million to $539 million, and for the Office of Territorial Affairs, up $18 million to $198 million.

Agriculture Department

The Senate committee's bill speeded up timber sales from the national forest system. While the House bill aimed at 11.2 billion board feet of new timber sales in fiscal 1984, the Senate version set a target of 11.9 billion board feet. The lands were under control of the Agriculture Department's National Forest Service.

Overall, the Senate panel wanted to spend $1.35 billion for the forest service, compared to the House level of $1.33 billion and the Reagan request of $1.26 billion.

Energy Department

The Senate committee also made cuts in House spending levels for Department of Energy programs funded in this bill, allocating $1.08 billion compared to the House level of $1.30 billion. But that was still far above the Reagan request of $667 million.

A major bone of contention was the weatherization program for energy conservation — popular in the Northeast, where fuel bills were high. McClure's proposal for the program — used mainly for individual low-income homes — was $100 million. The administration had requested no funds for the program, but the House voted $243.5 million.

An amendment offered in subcommittee by Patrick J. Leahy, D-Vt., to raise the Senate level to $245 million was defeated on a 6-9 vote. But a proposal by Warren B. Rudman, R-N.H., to spend $145 million was approved by voice vote.

The single most drastic cut in House-passed spending came for the Strategic Petroleum Reserve, which was not counted in budget totals.

The House voted $1.69 billion to buy oil to fill the reserve against a disruption in foreign oil imports, although the Reagan request was only $583 million. The Senate committee, in a search for budget savings, slashed the funding to $328 million. But McClure threatened during the markup to raise the amount if the administration did not make concessions he thought were needed for emergency preparedness.

On July 20 McClure, who was also chairman of the Energy and Natural Resources Committee, and John W. Warner, R-Va., chairman of that committee's Energy and Mineral Resources Subcommittee, announced that they had received the assurances they sought.

They said Stockman and Energy Secretary Donald P. Hodel had agreed to support legislation and make administrative changes to strengthen energy emergency preparedness programs. In exchange, McClure and Warner said they would not press the administration to increase the reserve's fill rate. The agreement called for a fill rate of 145,000 barrels per day through 1988 and a total reserve of 750 million barrels by 1991.

Other Agencies

The Senate panel also cut into House-passed funding for two cultural programs strongly supported by Yates, chairman of the House Appropriations Subcommittee on Interior. It approved $143 million for the National Endowment for the Arts, $22 million less than the House but $18 million more than Reagan wanted, and $130 million for the National Endowment for the Humanities, $20 million less than the House but $17.8 million more than Reagan sought. These were among more than a dozen small agencies funded in the Interior appropriation.

"Whoops" Rider

Added at the last minute before the Senate committee approved HR 3363 was a rider to help rescue the financially troubled Pacific Northwest power network.

The amendment, offered by McClure, called for creation of a new lending authority to finish construction of as many as three of the five nuclear power plants planned in the 1970s by the Washington Public Power Supply System (WPPSS).

The system, which came to be known as "Whoops," defaulted July 25 on repayment of $2.25 billion in bonds it had issued for construction of the other two nuclear plants. It was the largest municipal bond default in the nation's history — by its largest issuer of municipal bonds — and it left the WPPSS unable to borrow any more.

The Senate committee report said that McClure's amendment would allow creation of a new "entity" under state law to finance completion of the work on plant Nos. 2 and 3, and possibly plant No. 1 as well.

The bonds would be secured by a contract between that entity and the Bonneville Power Administration (BPA), a federally created power distribution network that had been backing the bonds for construction of those three plants.

The new contract would commit BPA to pay the principal and finance costs of the new borrowings directly to the new entity, its obligees or their trustees. In short, BPA would back the new borrowing with revenue from its ratepayers.

The new entity, not burdened by WPPSS's bad credit rating, in theory could borrow money in the same market for the same purpose as WPPSS would have done to complete the plants. The amount would be about $1 billion.

The committee report said the new contracts could be written so as to preclude any attempt by WPPSS's creditors to attach the new funds.

Senate Floor Action

When HR 3363 reached the Senate floor the week of Aug. 1, it was soon stalled by a threatened filibuster over the "Whoops" rider.

McClure said the rider was urgently needed. The key question was "whether or not we are going to force a further collapse in the Northwest power system," he said. But Sen. Howard M. Metzenbaum, D-Ohio, said Aug. 3 that he would filibuster McClure's rider. He was joined by Sen. William Proxmire, D-Wis. The two called the plan a bailout that would be paid for by federal taxpayers.

Metzenbaum announced the filibuster after the Senate by a 40-57 vote Aug. 3 failed to sustain the chair's ruling that McClure's rider was out of order because it added legislation to an appropriations bill. Metzenbaum had raised the point of order. *(Vote 231, p. 39-S)*

McClure introduced his Northwest power system proposal as a separate bill (S 1701) on July 28, and his Energy and Commerce Committee held hearings on it Aug. 3. But he made clear that he wanted to move the measure as a rider to the Interior appropriations bill, largely for parliamentary and political reasons.

An authorizing measure such as S 1701 would inevitably be referred to the House Energy and Commerce Committee after passing the Senate. That panel was chaired by John D. Dingell, D-Mich., one of the most powerful and outspoken of the measure's many opponents in the House.

Impasse Broken

More than six weeks after it first reached the Senate floor, HR 3363 finally passed the Senate Sept. 21 after McClure gave up his effort to win approval of the WPPSS rider.

As passed, the bill provided $8.06 billion for the Interior Department and related agencies, slightly less than the $8.08 billion voted by the House June 28.

The Senate passed the HR 3363 by a 76-18 vote. *(Vote 249, p. 41-S)*

McClure, who managed the bill, warned the Senate the bill could face a veto if cleared at its current spending total.

Coal Leasing Ban

Before approving the spending bill, the Senate adopted an amendment, sponsored by Sen. Dale Bumpers, D-Ark., barring Watt from any new federal coal leasing until 90 days after a special commission, created by the fiscal 1983 supplemental appropriations bill (HR 3069 — PL 98-63), reported on the Interior Department's coal leasing policies.

On June 14, the Senate by 48-51 had defeated a Bumpers amendment to the supplemental appropriations bill that would have imposed a moratorium on coal leasing until Oct. 1. *(Vote 138, p. 26-S)*

But with 16 senators, most of them Republicans, switching to his side, Bumpers' new amendment was adopted 63-33 on Sept. 20. *(Vote 244, p. 41-S)*

Vote Switches. Voting against the leasing ban in June but for it in September were Sens. John H. Chafee, R-R.I.; Alfonse M. D'Amato, R-N.Y.; J. James Exon, D-Neb.; Slade Gorton, R-Wash.; Charles E. Grassley, R-Iowa; Mark O. Hatfield, R-Ore.; Paula Hawkins, R-Fla.; Howell Heflin, D-Ala.; Roger W. Jepsen, R-Iowa; Bob Kasten, R-Wis.; Richard G. Lugar, R-Ind.; Mack Mattingly, R-Ga.; Dan Quayle, R-Ind.; Warren B. Rudman, R-N.H.; Arlen Specter, R-Pa.; and Edward Zorinsky, D-Neb.

Sen. Dave Durenberger, R-Minn., voted for the Bumpers amendment June 14 but against it Sept. 20.

The House-passed Interior bill also included the coal leasing ban. It did not contain the 90-day waiting period, but required Congress to approve the commission's findings before new coal leases could be granted.

Bumpers said the leasing moratorium was needed to keep Watt from "trying to give away our national heritage to whoever happens to show up."

The Fort Union Lease Sale. The Senate's vote came less than a week after Watt's department, in defiance of a House Interior Committee order, on Sept. 14 opened bids for eight coal tracts in the Fort Union region of North Dakota and Montana. Only $911,800 worth of bids were made on five of the tracts — an amount, Bumpers noted, that was nearly exceeded by the federal government's administrative costs in asking for bids.

Although the bids were opened, the leases were not awarded immediately. Two environmental groups went to court seeking to block the sale, and a U.S. District Court judge in Washington, D.C., on Sept. 16 issued an order temporarily blocking Watt from making the sale final. The judge acted after the Interior Department, which days earlier had told him it would not complete the sale for 45 to 60 days, suddenly indicated it would do so by Sept. 30. "I'm not going to turn my back again," said Judge Louis F. Oberdorfer.

Supporters of the Bumpers amendment claimed that Watt had been offering too much federal land for coal mining while the country was in the middle of a coal glut. Citing a recent General Accounting Office (GAO) study, they also charged that Watt had cost the Treasury $100 million by accepting bids at less than market value for coal.

But Sen. Malcolm Wallop, R-Wyo., questioned the GAO finding, saying it was the work of "non-coal fiscal wizards who know nothing about mining and nothing about production of minerals."

Watt responded to the Senate's coal leasing action by accusing Congress of ignoring U.S. energy needs that were threatened by ongoing conflicts in Central America and the Middle East.

"The world [is] ready to ignite, and your secretary of the interior has to deal with 535 members of Congress that don't seem to be concerned about the future supply of energy in America," Watt told business lobbyists Sept. 21 at a Chamber of Commerce breakfast speech.

In that same speech, Watt touched off a new round of criticism on Capitol Hill and elsewhere with a remark about the composition of the special commission studying the coal issue. "We have every kind of mix you can have. I have a black, I have a woman, two Jews and a cripple. And we have talent," said Watt.

Although he later described his comments as "unfortunate" and apologized for them, they proved to be his downfall. *(Watt resignation, p. 327)*

Strategic Petroleum Reserve

The administration suffered another setback in the Senate with the approval of an amendment that would require substantially more oil to be placed in the country's Strategic Petroleum Reserve than thought necessary by the White House.

On a 54-43 vote, the Senate approved an amendment sponsored by Bill Bradley, D-N.J., requiring at least 220,000 barrels per day, the current rate, to be placed in the reserve. The administration, which wanted to cut the daily fill rate to 100,000 barrels next year, had worked out a compromise with McClure to store 145,000 barrels a day. *(Vote 245, p. 41-S)*

The Bradley amendment also would add $370 million to begin construction of a permanent oil reserve storage facility in Big Hill, Texas.

"Our only line of defense against the oil-related threats to our economic and national security is the Strategic Petroleum Reserve," Bradley told the Senate Sept. 20. "We are buying insurance against an economic disaster that could make the Great Depression look tame."

Opponents of Bradley's amendment argued that the worldwide oil picture had brightened in recent years, reducing the need for the United States to place as much oil each year in its petroleum reserve.

To keep the fill rate at 220,000 barrels per day, the

Bradley amendment added $1.3 billion to the bill. The money spent by the government to purchase oil for the reserve was not counted in overall budget amounts. Nonetheless, Senate foes of Bradley's amendment said it would not help in the fight against large budget deficits.

OMB Director Stockman reminded McClure of the administration's "strong opposition" to the higher reserve fill rates in a Sept. 20 letter.

Other Amendments

In other action on the Interior bill, the Senate:

● Adopted by voice vote an amendment to add $27.2 million to energy conservation programs. The amendment was sponsored by Paul E. Tsongas, D-Mass., and John Heinz, R-Pa.

● Adopted 69-25 an amendment by Sen. Pete V. Domenici, R-N.M., to spend up to $450,000 for legal fees for non-Indian defendants in a New Mexico water rights case brought 17 years ago by four Indian pueblos. *(Vote 247, p. 41-S)*

● Rejected 40-53 an amendment by Sen. Don Nickles, R-Okla., that would have deleted $650,000 from the National Park Service budget for the Washington Opera Company. *(Vote 248, p. 41-S)*

Offshore Oil Leasing

The House bill included an oil and gas leasing moratorium for tracts offshore of California, Massachusetts and Florida, but no similar provision was in the Senate version.

Senators from the affected states urged McClure and other Senate conferees to agree to the House-passed moratorium. But only Alan Cranston, D-Calif., voted against the Interior bill because it did not contain an offshore leasing ban.

McClure said there might be some room for compromise on the offshore leasing issue.

Conference

A House-Senate conference committee agreed Sept. 29 on a final verison of HR 3363 appropriating $7,953,783,000. The report was filed Sept. 30 (H Rept 98-399). The total spending was $336,844,000 below fiscal 1983 appropriations. Reagan had sought only $6,709,628,000.

In a slap at Interior Secretary Watt, the measure imposed a moratorium of approximately six months on coal leasing on federal lands, and it banned oil and gas drilling activities off much of the California and New England coasts, and in part of the Gulf of Mexico.

But in a small bow to White House wishes, conferees decided to reduce slightly the amount of oil being placed in the country's Strategic Petroleum Reserve.

Coal Leasing Ban

The coal leasing moratorium barred the Interior Department from making any more federal lands available for coal mining until 90 days after a special commission named by Watt reported on the department's coal leasing policies. While the conferees sided with the Senate position in not requiring specific congressional approval of the commission's report before new coal leasing could occur, they called on an arm of Congress — the Office of Technology Assessment — to look separately at environmental issues involved in coal leasing.

A federal judge in Washington on Sept. 28 barred Watt from issuing five coal leases in the Fort Union region of North Dakota and Montana in defiance of an order by the House Interior and Insular Affairs Committee.

Watt had claimed that the Interior Committee's action amounted to a legislative veto of the type declared unconstitutional by the Supreme Court in its landmark June 23 decision. But U.S. District Judge Louis F. Oberdorfer disagreed.

Interior officials tried to expedite issuance of the Fort Union leases in order to escape the coal leasing moratorium contained in HR 3363. But Oberdorfer ordered Watt not to issue the leases at least until spring of 1984, upholding the House committee's right to withdraw federal lands from coal mining activities.

Offshore Oil Drilling

While the conferees scaled back House-passed provisions banning offshore drilling, they came a long way from the Senate version, which was silent on the issue.

Specifically, the conferees agreed to exclude from oil and gas exploration certain areas in the Georges Bank region off New England. The covered areas include the steep canyons and lobster beds off Massachusetts.

In the Gulf of Mexico, the conferees reduced the number of excluded tracts off the Florida coast covered in the House bill, but still kept a sizable region under the drilling ban.

The conferees adopted somewhat more complex provisions to cover California offshore tracts that stretch southward from Newport Beach to the Mexican border. The compromise extended the state's current three-mile offshore drilling ban to six miles, and set a moratorium until Jan. 1, 1985, on exploration in waters up to 12 miles off the coast. The House moratorium stretched the affected areas to 20 miles offshore.

At the end of the moratorium, various restrictions would be put in place to cover the more distant tracts, including a requirement that both the Interior and Defense departments approve oil and gas leasing and drilling operations. The conference committee also accepted House provisions to bar drilling off the scenic central and northern California coastline.

Strategic Petroleum Reserve

A showdown with the White House over the Interior bill might have been avoided with a conference committee agreement to moderate both the Senate and House stances on filling the Strategic Petroleum Reserve. The conferees agreed to spend $650 million during the 1984 fiscal year to fill the oil reserve at a daily rate of 186,000 barrels.

Both chambers originally had insisted that the current rate of 220,000 barrels per day should be maintained, while the administration wanted to cut back to 145,000 barrels a day. The money used to buy reserve oil was not counted in overall budget amounts, but nonetheless had threatened to make the Interior bill more expensive than the White House would accept.

Conferees also deleted $370 million that was added in the Senate bill to begin construction of a permanent oil storage facility at Big Hill, Texas.

Rep. Tom Loeffler, R-Texas, suggested that less money be spent to buy reserve oil so that construction at Big Hill could begin. But McClure said that would not be acceptable to the administration, which had agreed to begin building the facility in fiscal 1985.

In another action, McClure, acting on behalf of Sen. Domenici, agreed to drop a Senate provision to spend

$450,000 on legal fees for a group of non-Indian defendants involved in a longstanding water rights lawsuit in New Mexico. The money for legal fees was strongly opposed by Rep. Yates, chairman of the House Appropriations Subcommittee on Interior.

Final Approval

Offshore oil and gas leasing was the major bone of contention remaining after the House Oct. 5 approved the conference report by a 296-95 vote. *(Vote 360, p. 108-H)*

The House bill banned leasing for one year on 1.2 million acres off Southern California, while the Senate bill contained no ban. The conference reduced the acreage, but made the ban permanent — a feature not in either original bill and subject to challenge as authorizing legislation on an appropriations bill.

This conference provision was challenged on a point of order by Rep. John B. Breaux, D-La.

As an alternative, the House adopted and sent back to the Senate language insisting on its original Southern California leasing ban.

Another item that threatened to snarl agreement was a House-passed ban on oil and gas leasing off Florida's Gulf Coast. The Senate struck out the House ban, and the conference reduced the acreage subject to an outright leasing ban, requiring only that environmental studies be completed before drilling began in the rest.

The House version had the support of most of the Florida delegation, and Sen. Paula Hawkins, R-Fla., had threatened to stall the conference report.

But her office announced late Oct. 6 that Hawkins had agreed with McClure on an amendment increasing the acreage subject to the ban, but still short of the original House version.

Finally, on Oct. 20, the Senate by voice vote adopted the compromise language sought by Hawkins.

Sen. Pete Wilson, R-Calif., sought to bring up an amendment that would have imposed a permanent California leasing ban similar to that in the conference version, but he was barred on a point of order lodged by Sen. J. Bennett Johnston, D-La. The effect was to leave the House language in the bill. ∎

Military Construction

The Pentagon's fiscal 1984 real property construction budget was trimmed by $1.55 billion — to $7.1 billion — in the military construction appropriations bill (HR 3263 — PL 98-116)) cleared by Congress Sept. 28.

More than $400 million was cut on the assumption that the amount could be made up from a surplus of previously appropriated funds. An additional $417.8 million was cut from President Reagan's January budget request for construction related to the MX missile. But $377 million of that reduction had been requested by the administration when it proposed a new MX basing method after the budget was submitted. *(Appropriations, box, p. 470)*

Slightly smaller reductions were included in the companion construction authorization bill (HR 2972 — PL 98-115), cleared a day before the appropriations bill. The amount authorized by that measure was $7.35 billion, $1.2 billion less than Reagan's January request. *(Authorization, p. 193)*

House Action

Committee

As reported by the House Appropriations Committee June 9 (H Rept 98-238), HR 3263 appropriated $7,052,432,000 for military construction projects in fiscal 1984 — a reduction of $1,602,695,000 from the Pentagon's $8,655,127,000 request.

The reduction included a gross increase of nearly $300 million for some — but not all — of the projects added to the military construction budget by the Armed Services Committee in the authorization bill.

Those congressional add-ons included several projects located in the districts of Armed Services panel members. Among them were a $2.2 million Navy chapel in Pensacola, Fla., in the district of Earl Hutto, D-Fla., and a $23 million trainee barracks at Fort Sill, Okla., in the district of Dave McCurdy, D-Okla.

Nearly a fourth of the Appropriations panel's net reduction in HR 3263 reflected its belief that the Defense Department had overestimated the cost of many facilities.

In anticipation of lower-than-budgeted bids, the committee trimmed the services' requests for new construction projects across-the-board by a total of $361.9 million.

Overseas Construction. The committee reinvoked a long-smoldering congressional concern over continued increases in U.S. military deployments abroad.

It asked rhetorically whether the pattern of expanded commitments abroad reflected a coherent strategy or merely "a series of isolated responses to separate emergent situations." And it warned that unilateral U.S. actions might undermine allied willingness to share more of the burden of the common defense.

The committee approved full funding for overseas projects in HR 3263 only at sites where construction already was under way or where the host government had contributed to funding the project.

"The committee does not intend to continue to fund the unilateral buildup of U.S. forces overseas without actual commitments for similar increases from our allies," the report said.

To strengthen its grip on that process, the panel added to the bill a provision requiring approval by the Senate and House Appropriations committees before construction of any new overseas installation could begin.

NATO Burden-Sharing. Typically, Pentagon plans for construction in Western Europe bore the brunt of the committee's unhappiness with "unilateral" U.S. expansion abroad.

Already, the panel complained, U.S. defense expenditures were growing at an annual rate of 4.6 percent, above the cost of inflation, while the average growth rate above inflation in defense spending for the European members of NATO was less than 2 percent.

Nearly $2 billion was approved for construction funds for Western Europe, with half the amount earmarked for construction, operation and maintenance of military family housing. But, not counting reductions in family housing accounts, the committee cut more than $170 million from requests for military construction in Europe. This was in addition to nearly $250 million dropped for projects that were not authorized in the authorization bill.

Infrastructure. The panel approved $100 million of the $150 million requested for the annual U.S. contribution to the NATO Infrastructure — the alliance's fund for projects of common benefit. It justified the cut partly in

terms of the large balance of unspent funds that had accumulated in the Infrastructure account and partly because the alliance "owed" the United States $256 million.

This was the amount not yet reimbursed to the Pentagon for funds appropriated over several years to "pre-finance" some Infrastructure-eligible projects so that they could be built more quickly than if they awaited their turn for alliance funding.

To encourage the Pentagon to lobby the alliance for more rapid recoupment of the "pre-financing" funds, the committee told the department to use recouped funds to make up for some of the reduction in the Infrastructure appropriation.

Reinforcement Air Bases. The committee approved $18 million of $44.1 million requested to build fuel and ammunition dumps at European-owned air bases that would be used by U.S. air squadrons flown to the continent as reinforcements in case war broke out.

For years, senior military officers had cited these so-called "co-located operating bases" (COBs) as among their highest construction priorities in Europe. But they had fallen victim to congressional insistence that the allies pay a heavier share of their cost.

Of the $44.1 million, $28.6 million had been authorized in fiscal 1983, and the remaining $15.5 million was included in the fiscal 1984 construction authorization bill.

The $18 million included in HR 3263 could not actually be spent, the committee said, until the pending Infrastructure contribution to the COB project was very substantially increased and the Pentagon made "substantial recoupments" of its prior expenditures on pre-financed COB construction.

GLCM Bases. The panel also urged the Pentagon to secure a larger Infrastructure contribution to the construction of ground-launched cruise missile (GLCM) bases, since the United States, in effect, donated to the alliance the personnel, missiles and annual operating cost of the bases. The GLCMs were to be deployed in five European countries, from which they would be able to strike Soviet targets with nuclear warheads.

Concurring with the Armed Services Committee's action on the construction authorization bill, the Appropriations panel trimmed from the request all funds for projects to support the dependents of U.S. personnel assigned to the bases. This was to minimize the amount sunk into facilities that might be abandoned if a U.S.-Soviet arms control agreement were reached banning the GLCMs and corresponding Soviet missiles.

Like the authorizing committee, the Appropriations panel omitted altogether $34 million to begin construction of one of the five GLCM bases for which a bilateral agreement had not yet been negotiated with the host country — which country was secret.

In all, HR 3263 appropriated $78.3 million of the $147.9 million requested for construction of the GLCM facilities and none of the $35.4 million requested for dependents' schools at three of the sites.

Persian Gulf, Caribbean. Defense of oil routes from the Persian Gulf to Europe and Japan was another role the committee complained had been taken on by the Pentagon without commensurate allied contribution. With nearly $1 billion already committed to air and naval bases near the gulf or at critical points on the route thereto, the panel approved most of the request for projects already under construction.

This included $90 million for the Indian Ocean island of Diego Garcia, $28.6 million to improve airfields in Oman and $25 million for aircraft refueling facilities in Morocco.

But the panel told the Pentagon to confine its planning to use of those facilities already in hand or under construction, rather than planning for additional sites.

Egyptian Site Canceled. At the Pentagon's request, the panel dropped from the bill $96.4 million for a large base at Ras Banas on Egypt's Red Sea coast. And it rescinded $91 million appropriated for construction at Ras Banas in fiscal 1983.

According to the committee, plans for the United States to build the facility, which would remain technically under Egyptian control, had "fallen through."

The House committee had fought Pentagon plans for Ras Banas for two years because of the base's projected size, because it would protect oil routes most critical to U.S. allies who bore none of the direct cost, and because the Egyptian government was loath to sign a formal agreement guaranteeing U.S. access to the site. *(1982 Almanac p. 216)*

Honduras Airfield. The committee also denied $8 million requested to improve the runway and servicing facilities at the airfield of La Cieba in Honduras. In 1982,

---

Military Construction Appropriations, Fiscal 1984

Following are the amounts requested by the president and appropriated by HR 3263 for military construction projects in fiscal 1984. *(Dollar amounts are in thousands.)*

	Reagan Request	House-Passed	Senate-Passed	Final Appropriation
Army	$2,615,939	$2,434,416	$2,393,183	$2,419,143
Navy	2,019,444	1,770,146	1,858,900	1,817,010
Air Force	3,196,700	2,172,980	2,344,849	2,306,428
Rescission	0	−91,000	0	−91,000
Defense Agencies	418,144	275,716	331,494	299,643
NATO Infrastructure	150,000	100,000	50,000	50,000
Guard and Reserve	254,900	299,174	261,910	303,013
Total	$8,655,127	$6,961,432	$7,240,336	$7,104,237

the United States agreed to enlarge that field and another one at Comayagua in return for Honduras' agreement that U.S. forces could operate from the fields in case of a regional crisis.

The committee told the Pentagon that Comayagua — for which $13 million had been appropriated in fiscal 1983 — "will provide sufficient access into the region."

MX Missile Facilities. The committee denied the entire request of $449 million for construction associated with the MX missile. That sum had been earmarked for the so-called "dense pack" basing method, which Reagan rejected in April in favor of a plan to put 100 MXs in existing Minuteman missile silos.

At the administration's request, the Armed Services Committee had trimmed the MX construction authorization to $72 million, the amount the Pentagon said was needed to begin work on the new MX plan. But the Appropriations Committee said construction funds would be premature in view of the time needed for environmental impact reviews, site planning and design work.

Although an environmental impact statement (EIS) had not been completed on the new MX plan, the committee did release $30 million for MX site design work that had been appropriated in fiscal 1983 but had been impounded by Congress pending completion of an EIS.

Floor

The House June 21 passed HR 3263 by voice vote without amendment, thus cutting Reagan's $8.6 billion military construction request by nearly $1.7 billion.

The action came a day after Senate-House conferees on the fiscal 1984 budget resolution agreed to trim $11.5 billion from Reagan's overall defense budget request of $280.5 billion. *(Story, p. 435)*

Senate Action

Committee

The Senate Appropriations Committee reported HR 3263 July 14 (S Rept 98-180).

The Senate committee provided $7.2 billion, a $1.4 billion reduction from the request and only $17.7 million more than the fiscal 1983 military construction appropriation. It was $279 million more than the House approved.

MX Missile Projects. Reagan's abandonment of the "dense pack" basing method for the MX missile accounted for the largest single reduction: The administration asked only $72 million for MX-related projects — the amount approved by the Senate — rather than the $390 million originally requested.

Cruise Missile Bases. The Senate cut nearly in half (to $78.3 million) the $147.9 million requested to build bases in Europe for GLCMs.

The panel emphasized its support for NATO's plan to deploy 464 GLCMs (and 108 Pershing II missiles), believed able to hit any target in Western Europe from Soviet launchers. The alliance agreed in 1979 to deploy the new U.S. missiles if Moscow did not agree to dismantle its force of 360 SS-20 missiles, able to reach any target in Western Europe.

Most of the reduction was for facilities to support families of U.S. personnel assigned to GLCM bases. As in 1982, the congressional defense committees agreed to fund only the most essential facilities at the GLCM bases — and to make no provision for dependents, for the time being —

in case U.S.-Soviet arms control talks reached some agreement to reduce the scale of the planned deployment.

Alliance Burden-Sharing. The Senate bill included two dramatic steps that underscored the widespread congressional belief that U.S. allies were bearing too little of the cost of common defense efforts:

● It denied the $44 million requested to build fuel and ammunition dumps at allied air bases in Europe that would be used in wartime by U.S. fighter squadrons flown to the continent as reinforcements. Congress repeatedly had refused to fund these "co-located operating bases" (COBs) in Europe, insisting that they be paid for instead by NATO's fund for projects of common benefit — the so-called Infrastructure.

● It trimmed to $50 million (from $150 million requested) the amount for the annual U.S. contribution to the Infrastructure.

The committee said the cut would demonstrate unhappiness over the Pentagon's repeated ignoring of congressional orders to insist on more rapid payment by the Infrastructure for projects that were eligible for NATO funding but had been paid for by U.S. appropriations. Such "prefinancing" of NATO-eligible projects by the United States had been intended as a temporary measure to allow more rapid construction.

On the other hand, the bill included the $66 million requested to "pre-finance" COB-type facilities at various Turkish air bases. The panel said the strategic importance of these bases justified this exception to its position on pre-finanacing.

Honduran Air Base. The bill included the $8 million requested to improve the Honduran air base at La Cieba, in return for which Honduras had agreed to allow U.S. access to the base. In 1982, Congress approved $13 million for similar improvements at the Honduran base at Comayagua.

Egyptian Base. To build facilities at Ras Banas on Egypt's Red Sea coast, which would be used as a supply base for any U.S. forces moved into the Middle East, the bill approved use in fiscal 1984 of $55 million of the $91 million appropriated for Ras Banas in fiscal 1983.

Plans for U.S. construction of the facility had fallen through because of political objections in Egypt, and the House version of HR 3263 had rescinded the entire $91 million. But the Senate said Egypt might agree to some U.S. construction.

Floor

The Senate passed its version of HR 3263 July 27 by voice vote.

The Senate passed the bill as it was reported by the Appropriations Committee except for two minor amendments:

● By Mack Mattingly, R-Ga., barring the expenditure of 10 percent of the amount appropriated for consultants. (The amendment did not reduce the total appropriation.)

● By Daniel Patrick Moynihan, D-N.Y., requiring an annual report on the allocation of defense expenditures by state and by region.

Conference, Final Action

The conference report on the bill (H Rept 98-378), which was filed Sept. 22, appropriated $7.1 billion of the $8.66 billion requested for fiscal 1984. The House adopted

the report by voice vote Sept. 27, the Senate Sept. 28.

The $1.5 billion reduction included $408 million in anticipation of lower-than-budgeted bids. This was based on intense domestic competition for Pentagon contracts and, overseas, on the strength of the dollar.

The conferees approved $31.2 million for MX-related construction, compared with $69.3 million requested. (One $2.7 million project was dropped by the Pentagon in the interval between action on the authorization bill and action on the appropriations bill.)

NATO Projects. To further drive home the point of congressional sentiment about the alliance burden-sharing issue, the conferees approved only $50 million of the $150 million requested for the annual U.S. contribution to the NATO Infrastructure.

The Senate had made this cut to emphasize its insistence on recoupment of pre-financed funds.

Of $66 million in appropriations requested for improvements at two air bases in Turkey, the conferees approved only $29.3 million.

They barred use of any of the money until the Turkish share of the projects had been funded and they told the Pentagon to seek NATO funding of the rest of the work.

Conferees approved $6.4 million of $44.1 million requested to pre-finance the construction of fuel and ammunition storage dumps at several European air bases to which fighter squadrons would fly from the United States in case of war. These so-called "co-located operating bases" (COBs) long had been a high priority of U.S. commanders in Europe. But the Appropriations committees insisted that they be funded by NATO.

The conferees made an exception to their past policy, approving U.S. pre-financing for COBs in Denmark and Norway. But use of the funds was barred until NATO increased its allocation of Infrastructure funds for COBs.

For GLCM bases in Europe, the conferees approved $74.5 million, slightly less than had been authorized.

Japan Base. For the U.S. F-16 fighter plane base at Misawa, Japan, the conferees approved $17 million on the same terms as the authorization conferees: funds could not be used until Japan allocated its agreed-upon share.

Honduras. As requested, $8 million was approved to improve an air base at La Cieba, Honduras, to which U.S. forces would have access in case of a regional crisis. The funds could not be used until the Appropriations panels reviewed a Pentagon report on all U.S. facilities planned for Central America.

Egypt. Both houses had denied $96.4 million requested in fiscal 1984 for a base at Ras Banas, on Egypt's Red Sea coast, that could be used by U.S. forces en route to intervene in the Persian Gulf region, because of a breakdown in U.S.-Egyptian negotiations over the facility's construction.

The conferees also agreed with the House and rescinded $91 million appropriated for the project in fiscal 1983. But they invited the Pentagon to request a supplemental appropriation for the project if agreement were reached with Cairo.   ∎

Commerce, Justice, State Funding Cleared

Congress Nov. 16 cleared a $10.5 billion fiscal 1984 appropriations bill (HR 3222 — PL 98-166) for the Commerce, Justice and State departments and the federal judiciary.

It was the first time since fiscal 1980 that a regular appropriations bill for these departments and several related agencies had cleared. In the preceding three years, the bill became bogged down in debates over busing and school prayer, and funding for the departments had to be wrapped into continuing appropriations resolutions. *(Background, 1982 Almanac p. 246)*

As cleared, the bill was $473.35 million above Reagan's revised request of $10.03 billion.

It included funding for several agencies Reagan had tried to eliminate.

For example, the bill provided $275 million for the Legal Services Corporation (LSC) and refined several existing restrictions on the activities of LSC lawyers. Reagan had requested no money for the agency since taking office.

Reagan also had sought to abolish the Economic Development Administration (EDA) and to bar funds for juvenile justice programs. But Congress provided $267.5 million for the EDA, and $70 million for juvenile justice.

HR 3222 included a provision barring the Justice Department from using funds in the bill to seek changes in an antitrust prohibition against price-fixing between manufacturers and retailers of their products. The department was urging relaxation of the ban in a case before the Supreme Court.

In signing the bill Nov. 28, Reagan said he had "strong reservations about the constitutional implications" of the antitrust rider.

He also expressed concern about provisions mandating continued funding for current LSC grantees at fiscal 1983 levels unless action to the contrary was taken prior to Jan. 1, 1984, by an LSC board confirmed by the Senate. All LSC board members serving in 1983 had been been given recess appointments; none was confirmed by the Senate. *(LSC, p. 322)*

Reagan said the LSC provision "raises troubling constitutional issues with respect to my recess appointments power. The attorney general has been looking into this matter at my request and will advise me on how to interpret this potentially restrictive condition."

Final Provisions

As cleared by Congress, HR 3222 appropriated the following amounts in budget authority for fiscal 1984 *(in thousands of dollars):*

Agency	Budget Request*	Final Appropriation
Commerce Department		
General administration	$ 33,900	$ 33,561
Bureau of the Census	156,200	155,727
Economic and Statistical Analysis	38,900	38,337
Economic Development Administration	18,100	267,500
International Trade Administration	144,900	167,393
Minority Business Development Agency	54,000	53,342
U.S. Travel and Tourism	5,400	12,000

Agency	Budget Request*	Final Appropriation
National Oceanic and Atmospheric Administration	830,200	1,020,553
Patent and Trademark Administration	82,500	80,444
National Bureau of Standards	98,700	115,718
National Telecommunications and Information Administration	12,200	24,651
Subtotal, Commerce Department	**1,475,000**	**1,969,226**
Related Agencies		
Chrysler Corporation Administrative Expenses	1,005	495
Federal Communications Commission	86,159	86,383
Federal Maritime Commission	11,324	10,756
Federal Trade Commission	59,457	63,500
International Trade Commission	24,335	20,774
Marine Mammal Commission	638	929
Maritime Administration	82,513	84,668
Office of the U.S. Trade Representative	11,897	11,371
Securities and Exchange Commission	91,935	93,000
Small Business Administration	506,200	595,953
Subtotal, Related Agencies	**875,463**	**967,829**
Department of Justice		
General Administration	56,364	63,360
U.S. Parole Commission	7,836	7,248
Legal Activities	708,266	695,416
Interagency Law Enforcement	89,949	89,050
Federal Bureau of Investigation	1,057,690	1,047,000
Drug Enforcement Administration	287,623	286,123
Immigration and Naturalization Service	512,606	501,257
Federal Prison System	483,970	485,995
Office of Justice Assistance, Research and Statistics	152,859	197,352
Subtotal, Justice Department	**3,357,163**	**3,372,801**
Related Agencies		
Civil Rights Commission	12,180	11,887
Equal Employment Opportunity Commission	155,300	151,399
Legal Services Corporation	257,000[1]	275,000
Subtotal, Related Agencies	**424,480**	**438,286**
State Department		
Administration of Foreign Affairs	1,494,001	1,438,997
International Organizations and Conferences	602,343	595,704
International Commissions	23,207	23,625
U.S. Bilateral Science and Technology Agreements	1,700	1,683
The Asia Foundation	--	9,900
Subtotal, State Department	**2,121,251**	**2,069,909**

Agency	Budget Request*	Final Appropriation
Related Agencies		
Arms Control and Disarmament Agency	18,500	18,500
Board for International Broadcasting	106,055	118,182
Commission for Security and Cooperation in Europe	550	544
Japan-United States Friendship Commission	1,700	1,683
Radio Broadcasting to Cuba	8,701	10,000
U.S. Information Agency	711,427	649,665
Subtotal, Related Agencies	**846,933**	**798,574**
The Judiciary		
Supreme Court of the United States	15,649[1]	15,606
U.S. Court of Appeals for the Federal Circuit	6,039[1]	4,680
U.S. Court of International Trade	5,900[1]	5,675
Courts of Appeals, District Courts and other judicial services	861,473[1]	822,559
Administrative Office of the U.S. Courts	27,625[1]	26,075
Federal Judicial Center	9,342[1]	8,445
Subtotal, the Judiciary	**926,028**	**883,040**
Grand Total	**$10,026,318**	**$10,499,665**

[1] Submitted to Congress directly   * As amended

House Committee

The House Appropriations Committee May 25 approved a $10.8 billion version of the Commerce, Justice, State bill and on June 3 formally reported HR 3222 (H Rept 98-232).

Like similar legislation in the past two years, it included money for a number of programs Reagan had tried to abolish.

FTC Provision

In addition, the measure included an unusual provision regarding the troubled Federal Trade Commission (FTC). For the first time, it specified that no money was to be appropriated for the FTC until an authorization bill setting the boundaries for FTC activities was enacted.

In recent years, the FTC had come under attack from industries it had tried to regulate. Currently, the agency was embroiled in a dispute over the scope of its power to regulate doctors and other professionals. *(Story, p. 561)*

Since Sept. 30, 1982, the FTC, like many other agencies and departments, had operated without an authorization. During the 1983 fiscal year, it functioned under provisions of the second fiscal 1983 continuing appropriations resolution (PL 97-377). *(1982 Almanac p. 238)*

This required a waiver of the rule barring appropriations for programs that had not been authorized.

However, in 1980, when a previous FTC authorization bill expired, the Senate and House Appropriations committees refused to continue stopgap funding for the agency. Because there was no authorization, the FTC briefly sus-

pended operations. *(1980 Almanac p. 233)*

The committee report stated that the new provision "should serve as an incentive for the early enactment of authorizing legislation." Without an FTC authorization, the report continued, "there would be no funds available for fiscal year 1984 operations."

Protected Programs

As approved by the Appropriations Committee, HR 3222 provided $937 million more than the administration requested for the departments covered by the bill.

Among the programs protected in the House bill were the following, including their new budget authority:

The Legal Services Corporation, established to provide legal help to the poor, at $296 million; the Economic Development Administration (EDA), designed to spur community development, $315 million; the Sea Grant program, geared to protect marine resources and foster ocean commerce, $35 million; public telecommunications facilities grants, which help finance new public TV and radio facilities, $12 million; and juvenile justice programs, to help states combat juvenile delinquency, $70.15 million. Reagan sought to eliminate all these programs.

Commerce Department

The total recommended for the Commerce Department was $2.05 billion, $608 million more than Reagan requested and $191.63 million above fiscal 1983 appropriations. The bulk of the increase over Reagan's proposal was the $315 million for the EDA.

International Trade Administration (ITA). The committee recommended $183.83 million for programs of the ITA. This was $38.93 million above the Reagan request and $17.4 million above fiscal 1983 appropriations to date. Within this appropriation was $40 million for the Trade Adjustment Assistance program, designed to provide special unemployment benefits to workers who lost their jobs because of foreign competition.

Minority Business Development Agency. HR 3222 recommended $53.88 million, slightly less than Reagan's request, for the Minority Business Development Agency.

National Oceanic and Atmospheric Administration (NOAA). The bill provided $998.47 million in new budget authority for NOAA and an additional $22.51 million in transfers. This was an increase of $198.67 million over the president's request and $105.63 million above fiscal 1983 appropriations to date. The committee said it was not certain that Congress would enact certain mapping and charting user fees contemplated in Reagan's budget request.

U.S. Travel and Tourism Administration. The recommendation for this agency was $10.1 million, up $4.7 million over the Reagan request and $2 million over fiscal 1983 appropriations. The report said that members were impressed with information about increased revenues and job opportunities related to foreign tourism within the United States.

Commerce-Related Agencies

Maritime Administration. The committee provided $85.51 million in new budget authority for the agency. In addition, $401.29 million, the full request, was recommended for payment of operating subsidies to those who run U.S.-flag vessels to help them compete with foreign-operated vessels. This was $52.72 million below the

amount made available in fiscal 1983 for this program.

The bill also included a provision preventing the Maritime Administration from implementing any proposal that would allow owners of vessels built with construction subsidies and restricted to foreign trade from repaying their subsidies and entering "an already overcrowded domestic trade." *(Maritime subsidies, p. 549)*

Chrysler Corporation Loan Guarantee Program. The bill provided $1 million for administrative expenses necessary to carry out the Chrysler loan guarantee program, the full amount requested. *(1979 Almanac p. 285)*

Federal Communications Commission (FCC). The committee recommended $86.98 million for the FCC, $822,000 above the Reagan request and $7.16 million above the fiscal 1983 appropriations to date. The bill provided money for an additional 169 employees.

Federal Trade Commission (FTC). The panel provided $65.12 million for the FTC, $5.66 million more than Reagan's request and $1.59 million above fiscal 1983 appropriations. But the appropriation would not take effect unless the agency's fiscal 1984 authorization bill was enacted.

Small Business Administration (SBA). The SBA recommendation called for $759.24 million, $253 million more than Reagan requested but $99.49 million less than its appropriations to date for fiscal 1983. The largest single increase over Reagan's proposal, offset to some degree by reductions elsewhere, was $261 million extra for SBA's business loan fund, bringing the new capital provided under the bill to $510 million.

Justice Department

The total amount provided for the Justice Department was $3.35 billion, $120.29 million more than the Reagan request and $401.9 million more than fiscal 1983 appropriations enacted to date. A fiscal 1984 Justice authorization bill (HR 2912 — H Rept 98-181) approved by the House Judiciary Committee called for $3.29 billion. *(Justice authorization, p. 312)*

Organized Crime Drug Enforcement. The committee recommended $89.95 million for organized crime drug enforcement, the full budget request. This program initially was funded in the second fiscal 1983 continuing resolution. *(1982 Almanac p. 238)*

The funding supported 12 new regional drug task forces in addition to one in south Florida.

FBI. The bill provided $1.05 billion for the FBI, a reduction of $5.3 million from the administration budget request but an increase of $225.22 million over fiscal 1983 appropriations. The report said the reduction was made solely in requested increases in rent to the General Services Administration (GSA) for space and services.

Immigration and Naturalization Service (INS). The committee recommended $562.97 million for the INS, $23.71 million above the budget request and $78.54 million above fiscal 1983 appropriations. The committee approved all requested program increases, including increased inspections for the 1984 Olympics and a new port of entry scheduled to open in California in 1984.

The report said the committee also recommended $30 million and 750 positions above the budget request to provide enhanced enforcement and additional service to the public.

Related Agencies

Commission on Civil Rights. The committee rec-

ommended $11.88 million for the Civil Rights Commission. The amount reflected the same program level as the administration, but it included a reduction of $293,000 for GSA rental payments.

Without further congressional action, the commission was scheduled to terminate Sept. 30. Reagan said he supported an extension of the commission, but he clashed with some members of Congress on appointments to the board. *(Civil Rights Commission, p. 292)*

Legal Services Corporation (LSC). With an LSC appropriation of $296 million, the committee recommended the agency's first funding boost in two years. The current appropriation was $241 million, the same as in fiscal 1982. The corporation, which submits its request directly to Congress, asked for $257 million.

A bill reauthorizing the LSC for three years (HR 2909 — H Rept 98-201) also set the funding level at $296 million for fiscal 1984 and included revised restrictions on legal aid lawyers' activities. The Appropriations report said funds for the LSC should be used "strictly in accordance" with the authorizing legislation. *(Legal services, p. 322)*

Federal Judiciary

The committee recommended $883.04 million for operations of the federal judiciary, which includes the Supreme Court, the appeals and district courts and several specialized courts. The amount was $42.99 million under the judiciary's request, which is submitted directly to Congress, but $92 million above fiscal 1983 appropriations. The major cut was $26.04 million for space and facilities, the result of a 7-percent cap on increases for rents paid to the GSA.

State Department

The bill provided $2.11 billion for the State Department, $13.15 million less than Reagan's fiscal 1984 request but an increase of $244.96 million over fiscal 1983 appropriations.

The committee cut the most — $19.21 million — from salaries and expenses, but this was offset by additions in other areas.

The largest single addition was $10 million for the Asia Foundation, a 30-year-old private foundation whose current board of trustees included several prominent Washington residents. The report said the $10 million will "fund programs intended to serve broad, long-term American intersts in Asia and the Pacific Ocean . . . with an emphasis on projects which promote the ideals and values of democratic pluralism and respect for the rule of law. . . ."

Related Agencies

Arms Control and Disarmament Agency. The bill provided $18.5 million for the agency, $2.01 million over Reagan's request and $3.36 million above the fiscal 1983 appropriation.

United States Information Agency (USIA). The committee provided $683.31 million for the USIA, $28.12 million less than the administration request but $137.86 million above the fiscal 1983 appropriation. Included was $31.3 million for the "National Endowment for Democracy," which would be established under legislation reported by the Foreign Affairs Committee May 16 (HR 2915 — H Rept 98-130). A similar bill was pending in the Senate (S 1342 — S Rept 98-143). *(Story, p. 145)*

House Floor Action

The House Sept. 19 approved a drastically reduced version of the funding bill (HR 3222) for the Commerce, Justice and State departments and the federal judiciary.

As reported by the Appropriations Committee, the bill had provided $10.69 billion. But by the time the House finished with it, the total had been trimmed to $6.71 billion. The cuts were the result of points of order lodged against funding for programs that had not yet been authorized.

The vote on passage was 228-142. *(Vote 326, p. 98-H)*

Missing from the House-passed version of HR 3222 were, among other things, $2.1 billion for the State Department and funding for two programs Reagan had tried to abolish — the Economic Development Administration, slated to receive $345.14 million, and the Legal Services Corporation, for which the committee had voted $296 million.

Reagan had requested $9.74 billion for Commerce, State and Justice, and a bill reported Aug. 2 by the Senate Appropriations Committee totaled $10.27 billion.

Rep. Neal Smith, D-Iowa, chairman of the Appropriations Subcommittee on Commerce, Justice, State and Judiciary, told colleagues that whatever was stricken on the House floor would be wrapped into a fiscal 1984 continuing appropriations bill that had to be passed to fund government agencies that had not received their regular appropriations by the time the fiscal year began Oct. 1. *(First continuing appropriations resolution, p. 526)*

Procedural Politics

Many programs in HR 3222 were not specifically authorized by Congress, a process by which members set the broad program guidelines for departments and agencies. Under the rules, appropriations were supposed to be withheld for programs that were not formally authorized.

Usually when an appropriations measure contained funds for programs lacking authorizations, the sponsor of the appropriations bill got a special rule from the House Rules Committee to protect those programs.

In this case, however, Smith and the Rules Committee were unable to agree on a rule, and the Iowa Democrat decided to take HR 3222 to the House floor anyway.

In opening remarks to colleagues, Smith acknowledged much of the bill was vulnerable to points of order, but he asked members to refrain from using this procedural tool.

But some Republicans refused to go along. Led by Robert S. Walker, R-Pa., they insisted that the House should abide by its own rules.

"It seems to me that we have got to start holding the Appropriations Committee responsible for the fact that if there is no authorization, there cannot be an appropriation," Walker said. Otherwise, he said, "We will continue to appropriate with no authorization and we will never consider any authorization bills in this Congress."

A variety of unauthorized programs then were stricken from the bill on points of order.

House Provisions

As passed by the House, HR 3222 provided the following funding:

● **Commerce Department.** Several items within Commerce survived, including $33.2 million for general administration; $155.6 million for the Bureau of the Census; $183.8 million for the International Trade Administra-

tion; $888.59 million for the National Oceanic and Atmospheric Administration; $80.4 million for the Patent and Trademark Office; and $759.24 million for the Small Business Administration.

Deleted was funding for the EDA, the Federal Communications Commission, the Federal Trade Commission, the International Trade Commission, and the Securities and Exchange Commission.

● **Justice Department.** Although no Justice Department authorization had cleared Congress, no one lodged a point of order against the department's funding. The House approved $3.35 billion, including $1.05 billion for the FBI; $280.48 million for the Drug Enforcement Administration and $562.97 million for the Immigration and Naturalization Service.

● **Federal Judiciary.** The federal judiciary, which submits its request directly to Congress, received $883 million. The judiciary had requested $926.03 million.

Senate Committee

Without waiting for the House to act, as normal procedure suggested, the Senate Appropriations Committee approved a bill July 28 appropriating $10.3 billion for fiscal 1984 for the State, Justice and Commerce departments and the federal judiciary.

The State, Justice, Commerce Subcommittee had approved the measure July 26.

The Senate bill, formally reported Aug. 2 (S 1721 — S Rept 98-206), was $540 million over the administration request of $9.7 billion and $419 million under the $10.7 billion House measure (HR 3222).

At the time the Senate panel acted, the House bill was in the Rules Committee, where it was snagged in a dispute over funding for Radio Marti, which would broadcast news and information to Cuba. (*Radio Marti, p. 138*)

Like HR 3222, the Senate measure provided funding for several programs President Reagan had tried to abolish, including:

● Legal Services Corporation (LSC), which was given $257 million. The House bill provided $296 million.

● Programs to help states combat juvenile delinquency, at $70 million, roughly the same as the House bill.

● Economic Development Administration (EDA) assistance programs to spur community development, at $198.8 million. EDA also was given $150 million in loan guarantee authority. The House bill provided $315 million.

● Sea Grant program to protect marine resources and foster ocean commerce, at $38 million. The House bill provided $35 million.

The Senate committee provided $59.5 million for the Federal Trade Commission (FTC). The House bill included no money for the FTC because no authorization bill had cleared.

Senate Floor Action

By voice vote, the Senate Oct. 21 passed a $10.2 billion version of HR 3222.

The bill was $539.16 million above Reagan's request and about $3.5 billion above the drastically reduced House version.

The Senate provided $59.5 million for the Federal Trade Commission, but it adopted an amendment by Bob Kasten, R-Wis., to bar the agency from promulgating any final rule until it was reauthorized.

The Senate voted $11.26 million for the U.S. Civil Rights Commission, which technically went out of existence Sept. 30 when Congress failed to extend its life. The House had passed a reauthorization, but similar legislation was snarled in the Senate Judiciary Committee, which balked at Reagan's efforts to replace three sitting commissioners.

Sen. Lloyd Bentsen, D-Texas, offered an amendment to extend the commission until mid-February, but he withdrew it after Judiciary Chairman Strom Thurmond, R-S.C., promised his panel would consider a compromise extension bill endorsed by a majority of the committee but not by the White House.

The Senate bill provided funding for several programs Reagan tried to abolish, including the Legal Services Corporation, $257 million; juvenile justice programs, $70 million; and the Economic Development Administration, $198.8 million and $150 million in loan guarantees.

Legal Services Corporation

In providing $257 million for the LSC, the Senate also clamped down on its operations.

Restrictions on the activities of LSC lawyers had been the subject of continuing dispute between the agency's supporters, who contended such limits would hamper legitimate legal representation, and its detractors, who argued that LSC lawyers were trying to promote social change rather than help poor people with legal problems. By voice vote, the Senate adopted an LSC compromise offered by Orrin G. Hatch, R-Utah, a vocal LSC critic and chairman of the Labor and Human Resources Committee, which had oversight authority for the corporation. The compromise included these provisions:

● Barred virtually all lobbying activities by lawyers except on behalf of an eligible client and with specific approval of the director of the LSC-backed program involved. Any lobbying activity, such as writing a letter or making a phone call, would have to be within guidelines established by the particular program.

Under current law, LSC lawyers were permitted to respond to requests for information from legislators or government officials and to lobby on behalf of the corporation's authorization or appropriation.

● Retained current law provisions spelling out the classes of aliens who were entitled to legal representation through the corporation. The original House bill and a Senate authorization proposal backed by Sens. Thomas F. Eagleton, D-Mo., and Edward M. Kennedy, D-Mass., had expanded the types of aliens who would be entitled to legal aid.

● Barred the use of LSC funds for conducting training programs that dealt with political advocacy. Training programs designed to teach legal skills, such as those needed by paralegals, would still be permitted.

● Revised procedures for taking away funding from a legal services program that violated the law governing the corporation. Under the provision, a program about to lose its money would have to prove why it should retain the funds. Under current law, the corporation had to show why the money should be taken away.

● Retained a provision in current law barring any shifting of money among LSC programs by a governing board whose members had not received Senate confirmation.

Since President Reagan took office, the LSC had been operated by boards whose members were appointed during congressional recesses. These temporary appointments did

Comparing House and Senate Funding

Following are appropriations in budget authority requested by President Reagan and approved by the House and Senate for the Commerce, Justice and State departments; their related agencies; and the federal judiciary for fiscal 1984 *(in thousands of dollars):*

	Administration Request	House-Passed Bill	Senate-Passed Bill
Department of Commerce	$ 1,454,600	$1,523,351[2]	$ 1,915,365
Related Agencies			
Chrysler Corp. Loan Guarantee Administrative Expenses	1,005	500	495
Federal Communications Commission	86,159	Deleted[1]	86,383
Federal Maritime Commission	11,324	10,756	10,648
Federal Trade Commission	59,457	Deleted[1]	59,521
International Trade Commission	24,335	Deleted[1]	20,774
Marine Mammal Commission	638	938	929
Maritime Administration	82,513	Deleted[1]	83,668
Office of the United States Trade Representative	11,897	11,246	11,371
Securities and Exchange Commission	91,935	Deleted[1]	90,592
Small Business Administration	506,200	759,240	529,393
Department of Justice	3,357,163	3,345,979	3,359,624
Related Agencies			
Commission on Civil Rights	12,180	Deleted[1]	11,768
Equal Employment Opportunity Commission	155,300	151,928	151,399
Legal Services Corporation	257,000	Deleted[1]	257,000
Department of State	2,121,251	10,749[2]	2,095,142
Related Agencies			
Arms Control and Disarmament Agency	18,500	18,500	18,315
Board for International Broadcasting	114,756	— —	123,176
Commission on Security and Cooperation in Europe	550	550	544
Japan-United States Friendship Commission	1,700	1,700	1,683
Radio Broadcasting to Cuba	— —	— —	14,130
United States Information Agency	711,427	Deleted[1]	674,932
The Judiciary	926,028[3]	883,040	883,040
TOTAL	$10,005,918	$6,718,477	$10,399,892

[1] *Deleted on the House floor because the agency or program was not authorized.*
[2] *Reduced from the House Appropriation Committee level because the department authorizations had not cleared Congress.*
[3] *Submitted to Congress directly.*

not require Senate confirmation. There currently were only four board members, enough under agency rules to conduct business on a panel that was supposed to have 11 members. None was confirmed by the Senate.

Weather Satellites

By voice vote, the Senate Oct. 21 adopted an amendment by Larry Pressler, R-S.D., to bar the use of Commerce Department funds for the sale or transfer of weather satellites to the private sector.

This was the fourth time the Senate had voted to bar such a sale or transfer. One of the bans was attached to legislation to reauthorize the National Aeronautics and

Space Administration, which was signed into law (PL 98-52). That law barred the sale of any weather satellite without express congressional approval. *(NASA authorization, p. 588)*

Antitrust Changes

Also adopted by voice vote was an amendment by Warren B. Rudman, R-N.H., to bar the Justice Department from using funds in the bill to seek changes in a longstanding antitrust prohibition against price-fixing between manufacturers and retailers of their products.

William F. Baxter, head of the department's antitrust division, had urged Congress to amend antitrust laws

prohibiting manufacturers from setting retail prices for their products, contending that such action was not always anti-competitive.

But the Justice Department also wanted to reverse similar court-ordered prohibitions that dated back more than 70 years. A case pending before the Supreme Court, *Monsanto Co. v. Spray-Rite Service Corp.*, addressed the issue, and rather than waiting for Congress to act, the department submitted a friend-of-the-court brief challenging the existing prohibition.

Rudman's amendment was intended to prevent the department from pressing its arguments before the high court. "It is an outrage that Congress should have to remind the Department of Justice that Congress, not the courts, is the proper body for changing the law, if indeed a change is necessary," said Rudman.

Indian Water Rights Case

The Senate took only two roll-call votes on HR 3222. The first was on an amendment by Pete V. Domenici, R-N.M., adopted 53-16, to provide $450,000 in legal fees for non-Indian defendants in a New Mexico water rights case brought 17 years ago. *(Vote 302, p. 50-S)*

Domenici said the government already had paid almost $3 million in attorneys' fees to lawyers representing the Indian plaintiffs. His amendment originally was added to the Interior Department appropriations bill (HR 3363), but it was dropped from that measure during a conference with the House. *(Interior appropriations, p. 462)*

By 29-52, the Senate rejected a motion by Majority Leader Howard H. Baker Jr., R-Tenn., to table, and thus kill, an amendment by Jesse Helms, R-N.C., to bar the Justice Department from using any money in the bill to bring school busing suits. Although the tabling motion failed, Helms subsequently withdrew his amendment. *(Vote 301, p. 50-S)*

Conference/Final Action

Conferees agreed Oct. 31 to $10.5 billion in fiscal 1984 appropriations for the Commerce, Justice and State departments and the federal judiciary.

The conference went smoothly given the fact that the House came to the session with a pared-down $6.7 billion bill that was missing approximately $4 billion of its original total. A number of items were struck during House floor consideration Sept. 19 because they were not authorized.

The Senate's version totaled $10.4 billion, while President Reagan had requested $10 billion.

Conference Highlights

Legal Services Corporation (LSC). Conferees agreed to an appropriation of $275 million. The Senate bill had provided $257 million — the amount the corporation requested. Reagan recommended no funding. The original House bill had provided $296 million, but that item was deleted on the floor because the agency was not authorized.

Conferees also made a few changes in the language of the Senate bill concerning operation of the corporation. In cases of alleged violation of LSC rules, the Senate had required an LSC program to prove to the corporation why it should not lose its funding. Conferees returned to current law, placing the burden on the corporation to show why the program should lose its money.

Conferees altered the funding formula for the 326 legal services programs across the country so that each program

would receive at least a 5 percent hike over its fiscal 1983 level.

Finally, conferees retained language from the first fiscal 1984 continuing appropriations resolution (PL 98-107) that expired Nov. 10 providing that compensation for LSC board members could not exceed the highest daily rate for a GS-15 federal employee, plus travel expenses in accord with government regulations. Conferees also barred reimbursement for LSC board members and employees for membership dues in private clubs.

Maritime Administration. The House bill had included a provision barring the Maritime Administration from issuing any rule allowing vessels operating in foreign trade to repay their federal shipbuilding subsidies and enter domestic trade.

Senate conferees opposed the provision, and after considerable discussion, conferees agreed to bar the maritime agency from issuing rules only until June 15, 1984. By that time, conferees said they expected an authorization for the Maritime Administration to have cleared Congress that would address the maritime rule. *(Story, p. 549)*

Tennessee Valley Authority (TVA). House Appropriations Committee Chairman Jamie L. Whitten, D-Miss., urged conferees to keep a House provision that barred the Justice Department from using any funds to participate in litigation involving the TVA. Whitten said the TVA was supposed to be an independent agency and that Justice had no authority to assume control of TVA litigation.

The Senate was about to yield to Whitten's position when Deputy Attorney General Edward C. Schmults called the conference room to discuss the provision — which Justice opposed — with Sen. Paul Laxalt, R-Nev., chairman of the Senate Appropriations Subcommittee on Commerce, State, Justice.

A Justice official who was at the conference said the department believed it should have authority to step into a case when issues involving more than one agency were involved.

Conferees accepted Whitten's language after adding a phrase saying that Justice could represent TVA if TVA requested such assistance.

Antitrust Rule. Conferees accepted a Senate amendment barring the Justice Department from using funds in the bill to seek changes in an antitrust prohibition against price-fixing between manufacturers and retailers of their products.

FTC. The House-Senate conference committee adopted compromise language barring use of funds in the bill for the FTC until a reauthorization bill for the agency was cleared or until the end of the first session of the 98th Congress, whichever came first.

Civil Rights Commission

The House Nov. 9 approved the conference report on HR 3222 (H Rept 98-478), but it knocked out money for the embattled U.S. Civil Rights Commission.

The vote to adopt the report was 281-133. *(Vote 444, p. 130-H)*

Meanwhile, the money for the rights commission was put into the second fiscal 1984 continuing resolution (H J Res 413) Nov. 10. *(Second continuing resolution, p. 528)*

The commission technically expired Sept. 30, when Congress failed to pass legislation extending its life. Since then, the six-member watchdog panel, created in 1957, had been in a wind-down period ending Nov. 30.

Early Nov. 11, the Senate reached a compromise, accepted by House leaders and the White House, to reauthorize the panel for six years, reconstitute it and retain two of the three members Reagan had fired.

Rep. Don Edwards, D-Calif., who asked members to vote down the part of the Commerce, Justice, State conference report funding the commission, said that keeping the money in the funding bill amounted to a de facto extension of the commission and would give the president a free hand to replace the three members he had fired.

At Edwards' urging, the House by 170-235 rejected a motion to accept the Senate figure of $11.89 million for the commission. *(Vote 447, p. 132-H)*

Although Edwards and his supporters were initially concerned that the commission's money was restored in H J Res 413, their worries were allayed by the Senate compromise.

FTC Strings

On another roll call, the House rejected a move by

Elliott H. Levitas, D-Ga., to bar use of Federal Trade Commission funds to promulgate final agency rules until Congress cleared a reauthorization for the agency.

By 214-192, members instead accepted language adopted by a House-Senate conference committee that imposed such a bar until a reauthorization was cleared or until the end of the first session of the 98th Congress, whichever came first. *(Vote 446, p. 132-H)*

Final Action

Congress Nov. 16 cleared HR 3222 for the president's signature.

The Senate adopted the conference report on the bill Nov. 15, with the $11.89 million for the rights commission included, and final action came a day later when the House accepted the funding restoration, 417-3. *(Vote 474, p. 138-H)*

An amendment to delete $450,000 for legal fees in a New Mexico water rights case was rejected by the Senate 23-75. *(Vote 352, p. 57-S)*

Funds Voted for Reagan Defense Buildup

Before adjourning Nov. 18, Congress completed action on a fiscal 1984 defense appropriations bill (HR 4185 — PL 98-212) that provided $249.8 billion to continue President Reagan's defense buildup and most of the major weapons involved. *(Funding levels, p. 481; weapons, p. 488)*

While the final appropriation was $11.1 billion below the budget requests, it was $17.3 billion above the fiscal 1983 level. That was roughly a 4 percent increase, after adjustment for inflation.

Reagan's January budget request called for a "real," or inflation-adjusted, growth rate of 10 percent in defense funding. But the fiscal 1984 budget resolution (H Con Res 91), adopted in June, allowed only 5 percent real growth. *(Budget resolution, p. 435)*

The reductions incorporated in HR 4185 were distributed across the Pentagon budget without imposing fundamental changes on Reagan defense policy. The only major weapons program blocked by the bill was a new nerve gas, called binary munitions. It was the second year in a row that Congress had blocked the Reagan administration's effort to resume production of chemical weapons.

Major components of HR 4185 included $2.1 billion for production of the first 21 MX intercontinental missiles, $5.6 billion to buy 10 B-1 bombers and $1.4 billion for the 11th Trident missile-launching submarine, plus $555.3 million for the last 52 Trident I missiles designed to be launched from the subs.

The bill earmarked $407.7 million to procure 95 intermediate-range Pershing II missiles. Under a 1979 NATO decision, the first nine of a planned 108 Pershing IIs were deployed in West Germany in December. Despite vigorous Soviet protests, which cited the missile's short flight time to targets near Moscow, the Bundestag, West Germany's parliament, voted Nov. 22 to proceed with the plan. The Russians thereupon walked out of the Intermediate-range Nuclear Forces (INF) talks in Geneva, which were aimed at curbing the Pershings and their Soviet counterparts, the so-called SS-20s. *(Box, p. 206)*

The House approved the conference report on the bill Nov. 18 by a 311-99 vote. The Senate then approved it 75-

6, thus clearing the measure for the president. *(Vote 496, p. 144-H; vote 370, p. 60-S)*

House Committee Action

The House Appropriations Committee Oct. 20 cut $14 billion out of President Reagan's $261 billion request for the fiscal 1984 defense appropriations bill.

Viewed as defense policy, the cuts were mostly marginal: Major programs were trimmed but not reshaped in the bill (HR 4185 — H Rept 98-427).

The committee voted to restrain two controversial new weapons, despite administration contentions that they were needed to offset similar Soviet arms. Dropped from the bill was $19.4 million to begin production of an anti-satellite missile (called ASAT) and $61.5 million to set up production lines for a new lethal nerve gas weapon.

The panel, though, was unwilling to restrain two major missile programs, both of which stood at the center of the battle over U.S. nuclear arms policy: the multi-warhead, intercontinental-range MX and the intermediate-range Pershing II.

The administration justified these missiles — like the binary weapons and ASATs — by arguing that Moscow would give up a current monopoly in similar weapons only when it faced the unambiguous prospect of a matching U.S. deployment.

For more than a year, political prospects for MX had dimmed steadily on Capitol Hill, partly in reaction to a seeming lack of urgency in the Reagan administration's approach to nuclear arms control negotiations.

But the political threat to MX faded. For one thing, members wanted to take a tougher anti-Soviet stance in the wake of the destruction of a Korean airliner by Soviet forces Sept. 1. Moreover, Reagan struck a more conciliatory arms control tone in 1983, partly as a result of negotiations with a bipartisan congressional group that demanded a more flexible arms negotiating posture as the price for its support of MX. *(MX story, p. 195)*

The committee also approved a provision that would

bar after April 1, 1984, any U.S.-funded covert military operations against the government of Nicaragua, unless a fiscal 1984 intelligence agencies authorization bill became law before that date. An effort by Mickey Edwards, R-Okla., to delete the ban was rejected 22-24. *(Story, p. 140)*

Appropriations Total. As recommended to the Appropriations panel by its Defense Subcommittee, the bill provided new appropriations of $246.24 billion. It added to that amount $709.6 million appropriated for defense programs in earlier years, but not spent. This brought the total funding provided by the bill to $246.95 billion.

On Oct. 20, the full committee adopted several amendments which had the net effect of adding $79.45 million to the bill. This brought new appropriations to $246.31 billion and total funding to $247.03 billion.

Chemical Weapons. The amendment by John Edward Porter, R-Ill., to deny funds for equipment that would be used to produce new chemical weapons was agreed to by a 28-22 vote. This dropped from the bill $61.5 million which the Defense Subcommittee had approved (of $106.3 million requested). The subcommittee had dropped $18.1 million for binary weapons manufacture.

Porter warned that U.S. resumption of nerve gas production after a voluntary moratorium of some 13 years would squander the opportunity to score a major propaganda victory over the Soviet Union.

Continued U.S. abstention from chemical weapons production, in the face of alleged Soviet use of such arms in Afghanistan, would highlight to the world "the difference between our side and theirs," Porter argued.

Ralph Regula, R-Ohio, pointed out that the funds approved by the subcommittee would only equip the production line and that future funding would be required to begin building the binary weapons. But Porter dismissed the distinction: "Once you get the facilities, the next step is production," he said.

Democrats supported Porter 20-9; Republicans opposed him 8-13.

The vote mirrored the opposition to binary production demonstrated in June during floor action on the companion defense authorization bill (HR 2969). Binary production was rejected June 15 by a 256-161 vote. Funds for the new weapons survived a Senate test on the authorization bill only when Vice President Bush cast a tie-breaking vote. House binary opponents were outraged when conferees on the authorization bill approved some funding. *(Authorization story, p. 171)*

Anti-Satellite Weapons. Jack Edwards, R-Ala., proposed deletion of the $19.4 million earmarked to begin production of the ASAT missile, but did so as a maneuver to fend off another amendment by Matthew F. McHugh, D-N.Y.

The McHugh amendment would have left the $19.4 million in the bill but would have barred use of that money and any tests of the ASAT before April 30, 1984. The McHugh amendment also required the president to provide Congress a report by March 31, 1984, on the administration's military plans for space and on the prospects, if any, for arms control negotiations that would avert a U.S.-Soviet race in space weaponry.

Because the ASAT was such a small missile, designed to be fired from an F-15 fighter plane, liberal arms control proponents warned that a mutual U.S.-Soviet ban on anti-satellite weapons would be much harder to police once the U.S. weapon had been tested. The planned date of the first test was secret.

In August, during a meeting with a delegation of eight U.S. senators, Soviet leader Yuri Andropov called for negotiation of an ASAT ban, pledging to dismantle the existing Soviet anti-satellite weapon in that event. "I don't know if [the Russians] are serious or not," McHugh said, "but we have not taken up that expression of interest."

McHugh insisted that the five-month freeze on ASAT tests was needed to make the administration take seriously his amendment's demand for information.

Edwards' proposal was to drop advance procurement funds and require the presidential report. But ASAT testing would go on as scheduled. His amendment was agreed to by voice vote.

Never at issue was the $205.6 million included in Reagan's January request to continue ASAT research and development.

Pershing II. Defense Subcommittee Chairman Joseph P. Addabbo's, D-N.Y., proposal to drop the $407.7 million earmarked to procure 95 Pershing II missiles was rejected 15-29.

The committee subsequently rejected two amendments that would have delayed Pershing II deployment:

● By Martin Olav Sabo, D-Minn., delaying deployment until July 1, 1984, unless the president certified after March 1, 1984, that no substantial progress was being made in INF negotiations. The amendment was rejected 14-24.

● By David R. Obey, D-Wis., delaying deployment until July 1, 1984 unless the president certified by March 1, 1984, that the Soviet Union had not made significant reductions in its INF missile force; rejected 17-22.

MX Missile. An Addabbo amendment to drop the entire $2.1 billion earmarked to purchase the first 21 MX missiles was rejected 23-29.

Addabbo dismissed the administration's argument that unless the United States showed its willingness to deploy the MX, Moscow would not negotiate an arms control treaty cutting back its fleet of more than 600 large multi-warhead missiles.

Others charged that the MX would make the nuclear balance more unstable since the missiles would be accurate enough to threaten a surprise attack on Soviet missile silos while based in U.S. silos that were vulnerable to a Soviet first strike. "That's not deterrence at all," said Les AuCoin, D-Ore. "That's saying to the Soviets, 'Come on; Take 'em out before we use them against you.'"

Committee Report

As reported by the committee Oct. 20, the bill provided $246.3 billion in new appropriations. It added to that amount an additional $709.6 million that had been appropriated in earlier years. According to the committee, these funds were not needed for their various original purposes, and could be used to offset some of the cost of the Defense Department's fiscal 1984 program.

Manpower Savings. The committee cut $281.9 million from the military personnel accounts to reflect the 2,135,900-man ceiling the defense authorization bill had imposed on active-duty military manpower. This would allow 28,800 fewer active-duty personnel than the Reagan administration had requested in its budget.

The committee also argued that a total of $194 million could be saved because re-enlistments were running far higher than had been projected. A planned increase in re-enlistment bonuses thus was excessive, the committee said, allowing a reduction of $155.1 million in the $624 million bonus request.

Fiscal 1984 Department of Defense Appropriations

	Administration Request	House-passed Appropriation	Senate-passed Appropriation	Final Appropriation
Military personnel	$ 47,997,800,000	$ 47,396,850,000	$ 48,607,935,000	$ 47,360,103,000
Retired military personnel	16,772,800,000	16,592,600,000	16,592,600,000	16,592,600,000
Operation and maintenance	74,972,674,000	71,396,066,000	73,800,953,000	72,539,625,000
Procurement	92,594,655,000	84,650,827,000	86,335,012,000	85,617,505,000
(Transfer from other accounts)	——	(454,300,000)	(839,100,000)	(865,100,000)
Research, development, test and evaluation	28,498,840,000	26,465,715,000	26,761,747,000	26,739,269,000
Special foreign currency program	3,050,000	3,050,000	3,050,000	3,050,000
Related agencies	86,300,000	103,383,000	104,740,000	103,623,000
Total, New Appropriations	**260,926,119,000**	**246,608,491,000**	**252,206,037,000**	**248,955,755,000**
(Transfer from other accounts)	——	(454,300,000)	(839,100,000)	(865,100,000)
Total funding available	**$260,926,119,000**	**$247,062,791,000**	**$253,045,137,000**	**$249,820,875,000**

Increased personnel retention also permitted a $143 million cut in the $16.8 billion request for military pensions, a $39.4 million cut in the $1.1 billion budget for recruiting activity including advertising, and $184.7 million in other savings, according to the panel.

But those reductions were partly offset by a projected $327.7 million increase that would be needed in pay and benefits for a force with fewer low-paid recruits in proportion to higher-ranking personnel.

Reserve Buildup. The committee echoed the two Armed Services committees' insistence — which had given rise to the cap on active-duty manpower — that the Pentagon rely more heavily on the reserve components of the four armed services and on the National Guard.

The Appropriations panel ordered the department to plan on transferring to reserve units some of the C-141 cargo jet transports that made up the lion's share of its long-range air cargo fleet. The planes could be taken from active-duty units that would fly the new C-5 transports now entering production, the committee said.

As was typical of the four defense funding committees, the appropriations panel was much more generous to the politically powerful reserve and National Guard forces than were Pentagon budget-writers: It added a total of $1.2 billion to the bill for new equipment or beefed-up programs for the Guard and reserve. The additions included:

● $405 million for 24 additional F-16s, earmarked for the Air National Guard, in addition to the 120 planes budgeted and approved by the panel for active-duty Air Force units.

● $141.9 million to put improved engines on KC-135 midair refueling tankers.

● $158.5 million to modernize various other Guard and reserve combat planes with equipment currently on similar planes assigned to active-duty units.

● $173 million for 10 C-130 transport planes.

Ground Combat. With minor reductions, the committee approved the major weapons intended to protect Western Europe against the tank-heavy forces of the Soviet Union and its Warsaw Pact allies.

It recommended $1.35 billion in new funds and $83.8 million appropriated in fiscal 1983 but not spent to buy 825 M-1 tanks. The authorization bill had allowed for 840 M-1s, assuming that more funds would be available from prior

appropriations. In January, the administration had requested 720 of the tanks ($1.4 billion) but a year earlier, it had projected a January 1983 request for 1,080 M-1s — a plan that fell victim to budgetary constraints.

The committee recommended $759.8 million for 600 Bradley fighting vehicles — armored troop carriers equipped with anti-tank missiles and designed to keep pace with the M-1s better than older, slower troop carriers. The administration had budgeted $766.2 million for 600 Bradleys.

For 96 missile-armed Apache anti-tank helicopters, the committee approved $1.099 billion, a reduction of 16 planes and $120 million from the Pentagon request. The panel objected that a faster production rate budgeted by the Pentagon could be paid for only by dipping into reserve funds it said were needed as a hedge against price increases in the program.

Behind Enemy Lines. Like the two Armed Services panels, House Appropriations appeared to support plans for conventional weapons designed to disrupt attacking forces while they still were far behind an enemy's front lines. But — like the other committees — it was unhappy with signs that the Air Force and Army were not coordinating their development of the new equipment.

The panel approved as requested $60.1 million to develop a missile — called JTACMS — intended to carry several warheads that would home in on attacking tank formations while they still were tens of miles behind enemy lines. But it cut $69 million from the $160 million requested to develop a radar — called JSTARS — intended to locate targets for the missile and guide it toward them.

The committee ordered the Air Force to put the radar in the TR-1, a version of the U-2 spy plane, as favored by the Army, instead of in a Boeing 707 jetliner. One issue behind the disagreement was whether the radar's information should be interpreted in the airplane that carried it — which would be impossible in the one-man TR-1 — or after the information was telemetered to a ground station.

Anti-Aircraft Defense. For long-range Patriot anti-aircraft missiles, the committee recommended $885 million, the $107 million reduction having been mandated by the companion authorization bill.

For the much shorter-range, bazooka-like Stinger mis-

siles carried with combat units, it approved $100.5 million of the $137.8 million requested. To make up the difference, the committee ordered the Army to use $37.3 million appropriated for Stinger but not yet spent in fiscal 1983.

The panel endorsed the $200 million added by the authorization committees to the defense budget to buy anti-aircraft missiles that would be manned by West German troops to defend U.S. air bases in West Germany.

The $541.5 million requested to buy 130 Sergeant York anti-aircraft tanks (formerly called DIVADs) was approved. But the panel denied the $38.7 million requested for components of Sergeant Yorks planned for the fiscal 1985 budget. No more of the weapons would be approved, the panel declared, until the weapon had been tested for military effectiveness and mechanical reliability.

Tactical Air Warfare. The Appropriations Committee concurred in the authorization bill's shift of Air Force fighter production to buy a larger number of less expensive planes: As authorized, it recommended $1.28 billion for 36 F-15s and $2 billion for 144 F-16s, compared with the Pentagon request for 48 F-15s ($1.53 billion) and 120 F-16s ($1.6 billion). The panel also adjusted the funding for components to be used in planes that would be requested in fiscal 1985 to reflect a shift in emphasis to the less expensive F-16. This resulted in an additional reduction of $271.4 million.

In part, the committee based its action on the relatively low priority it said the Air Force placed on anti-bomber defense of U.S. airspace — the mission for which many F-15s were earmarked.

For 24 F-14 fighters for the Navy's aircraft carriers, the panel approved $792.4 million, which was the amount authorized but $94.1 million less than requested. For 84 of the smaller F-18 fighters, the committee recommended $2.07 billion instead of the $2.2 billion requested.

The request for six A-6E carrier-based medium bombers ($205.4 million) was approved and the committee applauded the Navy's desire to develop a so-called A-6F, with improved engines and electronics. This was one of several issues that pitted Navy Secretary John F. Lehman Jr. against Deputy Defense Secretary Paul Thayer: Thayer had ordered the Navy to defer the A-6F project while it studied other options for modernizing its bomber fleet.

New Armament. The $188.6 million requested to continue development of a new air-to-air missile (called AMRAAM) was approved. But the committee said it was premature to appropriate $62.6 million that had been requested to prepare for production of the new missile. AMRAAM would be the first medium-range radar guided missile light enough to be carried by the F-16. Currently, the F-16 carried only short-range heat-seeking Sidewinders that could be used only by day in clear weather.

The $370.8 million requested to equip Navy and Air Force planes with HARM missiles, designed to home in on enemy radars, was approved. But the committee insisted that the two services find a second contractor who would compete with Texas Instruments to produce the missiles. It also added $20 million to the bill to develop a new, cheaper radar homing device for HARM — the current one accounted for nearly half the cost of the missile.

To continue development of the LANTIRN radar and infrared viewing system to allow pilots to attack ground targets at night, the panel approved the $59.9 million authorized, which was $30 million less than the request.

Future Fighters. The $20 million authorized (of $104.7 million requested) to develop a modified version of either the F-15 or F-16 to attack ground targets in bad weather was approved. But the panel denied the $21.4 million earmarked to begin purchasing components for production of either plane.

Also approved was $35 million — the amount authorized of $37.4 million requested — to begin designing a wholly new fighter plane for the late 1990s.

The committee also followed the path of the Armed Services committees through one of the most intensely lobbied defense contract battles in years: the fight between General Electric and United Technology's Pratt & Whitney division for some $10 billion-$14 billion worth of jet engines to be bought in the next decade for current and future fighter planes.

The Appropriations panel approved $48.8 million for two programs focused mainly on improving Pratt & Whitney's F-100 engine, which powered the Air Force's F-15 and F-16 fighters. It also recommended $98.1 million to continue development of GE's F-110 engine, which was put forward as a replacement for the F-100 in future versions of the two planes. And it approved $58.9 million to start buying components of whichever engine won the competition.

Naval Warfare. The $57.7 million requested for components that would be used in fiscal 1985 to take a third battleship out of mothballs and equip it with cruise missiles was approved. But the committee warned that it would not approve the fiscal 1985 funds needed to complete the project until it was informed of the Navy's plans for further modification of the ships.

In their initial modernizations, the Navy planned to give the *Missouri* and *Wisconsin* — like the *New Jersey* and *Iowa* before them — new electronic gear and a few dozen cruise missiles. But Navy officials had held out the promise — without much emphasis on the price — of various options for further modification in the late 1980s, including dozens of additional cruise missiles and a small flight deck for vertical takeoff bombers.

For three cruisers equipped with the Aegis missile system to protect task forces against swarms of anti-ship cruise missiles, the committee recommended $3.2 billion, $234 million less than was recommended.

To continue development of the *Arleigh Burke*-class destroyer, which would carry a smaller version of Aegis, the panel approved $111 million. But it approved only $53 million of $99.5 million requested to begin buying components for the first ship of the new class.

The committee also directed the Pentagon to build an additional ship of a large class of frigates built since the mid-1970s. The panel transferred into the bill $218 million appropriated but not spent for shipbuilding projects in earlier years and told the Pentagon to make up the additional cost of the ship with up to $100 million transferred from other projects in the bill, subject to congressional approval.

These guided-missile armed frigates of the *Perry*-class, the smallest of the Navy's major warship types under construction in the last several years, were designed principally to protect convoys against submarine attack. But the defense funding committees pressed the Navy to equip them with a more versatile radar that could better handle the kind of "saturation" attacks by cruise missiles that the Aegis-equipped ships were built to handle.

Anti-Submarine Warfare. For three attack submarines designed chiefly to hunt other subs, $1.65 billion was approved, $54 million less than the request.

BUDGET AND APPROPRIATIONS

The Navy's two premier aerial sub-hunters were approved with only minor reductions: five P-3C land-based patrol planes, derived from the Electra airliner of the 1950s ($205 million); and 21 LAMPS III helicopters, the principal anti-submarine weapon of most of the Navy's modern cruisers, destroyers and frigates ($398 million).

The number of smaller LAMPS I anti-submarine helicopters bought for use on some older ships was halved to six ($44.7 million), a cut required by the authorization bill.

For anti-submarine homing torpedoes, the committee approved $124.6 million (as requested) for 144 long-range Mark 48s carried by attack submarines and $213 million (a $5 million reduction) for 1,200 smaller Mark 46s carried by surface ships and aircraft.

The committee approved two requests to develop improved torpedoes to deal with faster, deeper diving Soviet subs: $182 million for an improved Mark 48 and $142 million for a lightweight successor to the Mark 46.

Strategic Mobility. The panel approved the request for $228.9 million to charter and operate the flotilla of more than a dozen cargo ships at the Indian Ocean island of Diego Garcia. These so-called "pre-positioning ships" carried the tanks and other heavy equipment of a Marine brigade that could be flown quickly to the region from the United States in case of a crisis.

Also approved was $3 million to begin paying for the charter of ships being extensively rebuilt to replace the current group of floating-arms depots.

To convert four high speed container ships (called SL-7s) to rapidly load and unload the heavy combat vehicles of an Army division, the committee approved $219 million (of $246 million requested).

Also approved was the request for $31 million to buy nine used cargo ships. They would be added to that part of the Navy's mothballed fleet of such ships that was kept ready for service on short notice.

Amphibious Assault. The committee's $1.37 billion recommendation for a new helicopter carrier to haul 2,000 Marines and the transport helicopters to carry them ashore was $14 million less than the request.

Also recommended without significant change was $326 million for a so-called landing ship dock (LSD) to haul Marines and the landing barges to take them ashore. But the panel turned down the request for $102 million to sign a multi-year production contract for LSDs.

To develop a new vertical takeoff cargo plane called JVX that would be used partly to replace aging Marine transport helicopters in the late 1980s, the committee approved $84 million, a $20 million cut.

Airlift. The two largest requests for cargo aircraft were approved without substantial change: $1.08 billion for this installment of a multi-year contract to buy 55 giant C-5Bs; and $311 million for the current installment on a multi-year contract to buy KC-10s — versions of the DC-10 jetliner modified to refuel other planes in midair.

The committee made no change in request for components that would be used in cargo planes bought in fiscal 1985: $240.3 million for C-5 parts and $425 million for KC-10 components.

The $26.8 million requested to continue development of the C-17 — a wide-body cargo plane designed to carry heavy equipment over intercontinental distances to small, ill-equipped airstrips — was approved without change.

The panel cut roughly in half (to $70 million) the $144 million requested to modify passenger planes so they could be converted quickly to haul military cargo in case of an international crisis. It complained that the Air Force had been unenthusiastic about the program.

Strategic Nuclear Weaponry. In addition to approving $4.14 billion for MX, the committee also agreed to administration requests for $279 million to develop a small, mobile ICBM and $75 million for an armored, mobile launcher to carry it.

But the committee rejected two other requests to explore basing methods for small missiles: $210 million to look at ways to further armor missile silos against nuclear blast; and $40 million to design launchers deep underground.

Bomber Weapons. Besides the $6.4 billion earmarked for 10 B-1 bombers and further development, the bill contained a secret amount to continue development of the so-called "stealth" bomber, intended to evade detection by enemy radar.

The committee also recommended $422 million as requested to continue production of long-range, nuclear-armed cruise missiles (or ALCMs) which could be launched from existing B-52 bombers outside the reach of Soviet air defenses. The bill contained a secret amount to develop a new air-launched cruise missile.

The Air Force had requested $996 million to replace the engines on KC-135 tanker planes, which refueled U.S. strategic bombers in midair. Following the lead of the Armed Services panels, House Appropriations approved $636 million of that total in new funds and transferred $62 million from prior years to install reconditioned engines on tanker planes.

The largest part of the reduction ($254 million) came from denial of a multi-year contract to cover future modernizations. The panel also substituted the engines from mothballed airliners — used, but much more powerful than the tanker planes' original engines — for some of the more expensive new engines the Air Force wanted.

Sea-Launched Weapons. For the 11th Trident missile-launching submarine, the committee recommended $1.4 billion — $127 million less than the request, with most of the reduction due to a revised Navy cost estimate. For 52 of the Trident I missiles currently carried by these ships, the panel approved $523 million, $64 million less than the request.

Approved without change was the request for $1.5 billion to continue development of a larger missile — the D-5 or Trident II — intended to be as accurate as the MX.

Rejected Amendments. On Oct. 20, the Appropriations Committee dropped from the bill:

● All funds to prepare for production of a new generation of lethal nerve gas weapons, called binary munitions.

● The $19.4 million requested to buy components to be used in an anti-satellite missile (or ASAT) scheduled to enter production in fiscal 1985. Reportedly, this would delay ASAT production for a year.

The committee stopped short of barring initial ASAT test flights — due to start at some secret, but reportedly early, date. But it demanded that the administration report to Congress by March 31, 1984, on its military plans for space and on the prospects for arms control negotiations to avert a U.S.-Soviet race in space weaponry.

House Floor Action

The House Democratic leadership struck a somewhat leisurely pace when it brought the $247 billion defense appropriations bill to the floor Oct. 25, in part because it

wanted to avert an early vote on an amendment that would cut off funds for U.S. participation in the multinational peacekeeping force in Beirut.

Clarence D. Long, D-Md., and Samuel S. Stratton, D-N.Y., drafted the amendment after a bomb attack in the early hours of Oct. 23 killed more than 220 U.S. Marines. The amendment would have forced the withdrawal of 1,600 Marines from Lebanon after March 1, 1984.

The House rejected the amendment, 153-274, on Nov. 2. It then passed the $247 billion bill by a vote of 328-97. *(Votes 411, 413, p. 122-H)*

During three days of floor debate (Oct. 25-26, Nov. 1), the House approved amendments making a net addition of $292.7 million to the bill as reported by the Appropriations Committee.

As passed Nov. 2, the bill trimmed $14 billion from President Reagan's amended budget request. It contained $5 billion less in new budget authority than the Senate version.

Arms Control Issues

The most significant of the Oct. 26 amendments in terms of national policy was Addabbo's effort to delete all funds earmarked for production of 95 Pershing II missiles. The amendment was rejected by voice vote.

Addabbo emphasized his doubts about the missile's reliability. But most of the opposition was based on controversy over NATO's December 1979 decision to begin deploying 108 of the missiles in West Germany in December unless Moscow agreed to remove similar missiles (called SS-20s) aimed at Western Europe, of which it had deployed some 350 since 1977.

Like the SS-20s, the Pershing IIs were very fast and accurate ballistic missiles — able to reach targets in the Soviet Union from German launch sites within 10 minutes. The nine missiles due for deployment in Germany in December were among 112 funded in fiscal 1982 and 1983.

Under the 1979 agreement, NATO also would deploy 464 ground-launched cruise missiles GLCMs as part of its response to the triple-warhead SS-20s. But the GLCMs — small, drone jet planes, which would take much longer to fly to their targets — had been less controversial than the Pershings.

Money Fights

The House adopted several amendments on Oct. 26 to increase the appropriations provided by HR 4185.

One major increase, adopted 219-193, was an amendment by Armed Services member G. V. "Sonny" Montgomery, D-Miss., to raise the appropriation for Army aircraft by $81.7 million. This included $41.8 million for 16 missile-armed Apache anti-tank helicopters, bringing the number of Apaches funded in the bill to the 112 requested and authorized. *(Vote 391, p. 116-H)*

Also adopted were amendments:

● By David Dreier, R-Calif., adding $37.3 million for Stinger anti-aircraft missiles. The Appropriations Committee had argued that this amount could be provided from prior-year appropriations rather than new funds, but that re-appropriation was killed on a point of order; voice vote.

● By Addabbo, adding $82.7 million to the appropriation for operations and maintenance; voice vote.

● By Addabbo, in which the House agreed, 287-140, that the Navy had to take $218 million out of its own budget to build a guided-missile frigate not included in the president's budget. *(Vote 392, p. 116-H)*

The House rejected, 85-342, an amendment by Charles E. Bennett, D-Fla., chairman of the Armed Services Committee's Seapower Subcommittee, that would have added $355.5 million for various ships, including the frigate, and components for the first of a new destroyer class. *(Vote 393, p. 116-H)*

Close Shave for MX

The MX missile had its closest political shave Nov. 1 when the House rejected, 208-217, an amendment that would have blocked initial production of the controversial ICBM. *(Vote 409, p. 122-H)*

For months, a small bipartisan group of self-styled congressional moderates had negotiated with the Reagan administration over the fate of MX — offering support for the missile in return for Reagan's shift to a more flexible arms control policy.

On May 24, the House had approved the start of MX flight tests by a margin of 53 votes. But by July 20, the moderate group clearly held the balance of power, when the House rejected by only 13 votes an amendment to the defense authorization bill that would have denied the MX production funds.

On Nov. 1, the margin of defeat for MX opponents was only nine votes. A handful of switches and absences that followed no apparent pattern accounted for the difference.

After the vote, Les Aspin, D-Wis., a leader of the congressional moderates, professed to be satisfied that the missile had won by a narrow margin: "Otherwise, there's no heat on the administration" to continue the more flexible arms control approach that Aspin and his allies claimed to have extracted as the price of MX.

In each vote to authorize and appropriate MX funds in future years, Aspin insisted, Congress retained the option of killing the program if Reagan reneged on broader arms control policy: "None of them is *the* [final] vote," he said.

But some MX opponents had warned for months that the fiscal 1984 appropriations bill might offer the last clear shot at blocking MX production. Once procurement contracts actually were signed, they warned, a web of subcontracts — and thus jobs — would give the missile an enlarged network of supporters.

The MX amendment by Addabbo would have deleted the entire $2.2 billion earmarked to purchase the first 21 MXs.

"We have a classic bargaining chip situation out there [in Geneva] now," Aspin told the House. "You are saying to the Soviets: 'We are going ahead with ... 100 MX missiles, and we have an arms control proposal out there for you to sign.... If you do not accept the arms control proposal or something like it, our plan is to build 100 MX missiles.'"

But Thomas J. Downey, D-N.Y., attacked the bargaining chip argument: "Bargaining-chip weapons become weapons. That has been the history of arms control."

And he had a different version of the message that MX deployment would send to Moscow. "We are saying to the Soviets: 'We want you to behave better, and if you don't, we will do something stupid: We will waste a lot of money on a missile that is not survivable.'"

Albert Gore Jr., D-Tenn., and Norman D. Dicks, D-Wash., with Aspin the leading House members of the congressional "moderates" in the MX fight, emphasized another reason for supporting procurement of the missile. They had insisted on — and said they had won — substantial changes in the administration's arms control stance in return for backing MX.

Among other things, this new posture receded from the administration's early insistence on radical reductions in the Soviet ICBM force — a demand the moderates believed would be impossible to negotiate. The administration also offered new reductions in bombers and cruise missiles, which were the U.S. nuclear force's long suit and seemed particularly worrisome to Soviet negotiators.

Gore insisted to his colleagues that the various changes agreed to by the administration "represent not only a change in focus for the [START] negotiations, but — in the aggregate — evidence of serious intent" to pursue arms control agreements.

"The president so far has lived up to his end of this unprecedented agreement," Gore concluded. "We must continue to live up to our end," by funding MX.

B-1 Contracts

The House also turned back (175-247) an Addabbo amendment that would have deleted $438.7 million to begin multi-year procurement of B-1 bombers. *(Vote 408, p. 122-H)*

The amendment would not have affected the $3.8 billion in the bill to buy 10 B-1s in fiscal 1984 nor the $1.4 billion earmarked to buy components that would be used in B-1s bought in fiscal 1985. Addabbo's amendment would, however, have cut funds to buy components for B-1s scheduled for procurement in the fiscal 1986 budget and later.

The savings expected to result from such so-called "multi-year" contracts — which covered items that normally would be purchased on a year-by-year basis — were a key part of the president's guarantee that the planned fleet of 100 B-1s would cost no more than $20.5 billion (in fiscal 1981 dollars).

Addabbo — a longtime critic of the B-1 — insisted that he wanted only to defer commitment to the entire B-1 program until the first planes had come off the assembly line for tests.

If it approved the multi-year contract, Addabbo warned, "Congress will be locked into this procurement and will lose its ability to exercise any future fiscal control over this expensive program."

But Jack Edwards, the senior Republican on the Defense Subcommittee, insisted that the planned multi-year contracts were essential to hold the administration to its $20.5 billion price ceiling.

"If members want to see that lid come off," Edwards warned, "then fail to fund this program in the way it was planned and I guarantee you we will let the Pentagon off the hook."

Other Amendments

The House also agreed by voice vote to amendments:
● By Bill Nichols, D-Ala., adding $110 million for various Army combat vehicles.
● By Melvin Price, D-Ill., as amended by Dicks, to add $30 million to modify civilian airliners so they could be rapidly converted to haul military cargo in an emergency.

Senate Committee Action

Defense Subcommittee

The Senate Appropriations Subcommittee on Defense Oct. 5 recommended a fiscal 1984 defense appropriations bill that trimmed $9.8 billion from Reagan's January request.

But the panel's $251.1 billion bill approved essentially all major weapons programs in the administration budget; basic amounts requested for the MX missile, B-1 bomber and nerve gas weapons were not challenged in the subcommittee.

The only battle over a major weapon involved Chairman Ted Stevens', R-Alaska, unsuccessful effort to delete $57.7 million to begin equipping a World War II-era battleship with cruise missiles, a modernization already funded for two sister ships. The subcommittee approved the battleship funds by a 10-6 vote.

Stevens' version of the bill would provide about $4.9 billion more than the version marked up by the House Defense Appropriations Subcommittee, which would provide about $246.2 billion.

Appropriations Committee

As reported by the full Appropriations Committee Nov. 1 (S 2039 — S Rept 98-292), the bill provided $251.7 billion in new appropriations for military programs in fiscal 1984. This was $5.1 billion more than was provided in the House version of the bill.

The bill also allocated to various fiscal 1984 programs $839.1 million appropriated for the Defense Department in prior years, but not yet spent. Including those funds, the bill provided $8.4 billion less than the $260.9 billion requested by the president.

The Senate panel restored several hundred million dollars in reductions the House Appropriations panel insisted would have no impact on military operations.

For instance, it restored to the bill $680 million deleted by the House to force the Pentagon to buy data processing equipment rather than lease it. Also restored by the Senate panel was $500 million the House committee assumed could be saved by improved management of Pentagon supplies.

The Senate committee's total also included at least two large chunks of money with no counterparts in the House bill:
● $300 million to be transferred to the Coast Guard to improve facilities and buy new equipment.
● $300 million to dispose of hazardous waste and remove debris from abandoned military installations, where required for public safety. The budget request included $59 million for these purposes.

The bill also included $1.87 billion for a 4 percent raise in civilian and military pay, effective Jan. 1, 1984, which the committee expected Congress to enact. The House bill included no funds for a pay increase.

The committee deleted $124 million earmarked for facilities to manufacture the new, nerve gas-dispensing bombs and artillery shells.

Strategic Warfare. In addition to recommending $2.1 billion for the first 21 MX missiles, as authorized, the committee approved the $2 billion requested to continue development of the missile. It also approved $574 million of the $604 million requested to develop a small, single-warhead ICBM as a successor to MX and to explore various methods for protecting it from Soviet attack.

That included $210 million for "super-hardened" silos and $75 million for armored, mobile launchers. The panel's $30 million cut came from the $40 million request to study the feasibility of burying the missiles deep under mountains in launchers designed to burrow to the surface if the missiles were to be fired.

For the 11th in the class of Trident missile-launching submarines, the committee approved $1.4 billion (of the

$1.52 billion requested), with an additional $306 million approved as requested for components to be used for additional Trident ships in future budgets.

Approved without change was the $1.5 billion requested to develop a longer-range, more accurate Trident II (or D-5) missile to be fired from those subs.

For 95 Pershing II ballistic missiles, able to strike Soviet targets from launchers in Western Europe, the committee agreed to the request for $407.7 million.

Bombers, Cruise Missiles. The request for the B-1 bomber program was approved intact: $3.8 billion for 10 planes, $1.9 billion for components that were to be used in planes funded in future budgets and $553 million for spare parts.

The committee also recommended a secret amount to continue development of the so-called "stealth" bomber, intended to evade detection by enemy radars.

For 240 air-launched cruise missiles designed to be launched from bombers flying beyond the reach of Soviet air defenses, the panel approved $392 million, saying that favorable contract negotiations allowed the $30 million reduction from the request.

Airlift, Sealift. The principal requests for long-range air transport planes were supported by the committee:

● $1.1 billion for four C-5 cargo haulers and $240.3 million to buy components for use in future C-5 purchases.

● $334 million for eight KC-10s — DC-10 jetliners modified to haul cargo and refuel other planes in midair — and $425 million for components to be used in KC-10s bought in future budgets.

● $26.8 million to continue development of the C-17 — a wide-body cargo plane intended to land heavy combat gear at primitive airstrips after carrying it transoceanic distances. Defense Subcommittee Chairman Stevens fervently supported the new plane.

The panel approved the request for an additional landing ship dock (LSD) — a large transport carrying Marines, their combat vehicles and landing barges to haul them ashore. But it denied a request for $102.1 million to sign a multi-year contract for several more of the ships. The Pentagon argued that such long-term arrangements frequently reduce weapons costs by allowing contractors to plan on the basis of assured orders. But in this case, the committee maintained, competition among commercial shipyards for future LSD contracts "virtually guarantees savings comparable [to] or better than those available under a multi-year program."

Air Combat. The committee recommended the full amount authorized for Air Force fighter planes: $1.3 billion for 36 F-15s and $2 billion for 144 smaller F-16s. The budget request had placed more emphasis on the larger, more expensive plane: 48 F-15s, 120 F-16s.

Like the House, the committee denied the $21.4 million requested for components that would be used in a modified version of either the F-15 or the F-16, designed to attack ground targets a few hundred miles behind enemy lines in bad weather. The committee agreed with the need for new planes for the mission but said it was unconvinced that the modified planes would be superior to the current F-15 and F-16 models by enough of a margin to warrant the expense of developing the new version.

The committee also denied $10 million requested to develop a ballistic missile called Axe — designed to destroy Soviet air bases with non-nuclear warheads. The panel demanded a firm estimate of the total cost of the program should it be pursued. And it warned that U.S. allies in

Europe might not support the Axe concept, since firing ballistic missiles deep into Warsaw Pact territory at the very start of a conflict might be misread by Soviet generals as a nuclear attack by NATO.

Carrier Planes. The authorized amount was approved by the panel for the two kinds of fighter planes that fly from aircraft carriers: $792.4 million for 24 F-14s and $2.14 billion for 84 F-18s.

But the committee voiced "strong concern" over whether the Navy should proceed with plans to use F-18s as bombers, to attack ships and land targets, as well as fighters — to attack other airplanes. Carrying a bomb load, the F-18 had shorter range than the current A-7 light bomber, which it was scheduled to replace.

The committee told the Navy to explain how it might increase the F-18's bombing range and to identify other planes it might buy in lieu of F-18s for the bombing missions.

New Engines. Overruling its defense panel on yet another issue where billions of dollars in contracts and jobs were at stake, the full Appropriations Committee rejected a subcommittee proposal that would have delayed selection of a new jet fighter engine so Congress could examine the decision.

At issue were tens of billions of dollars for engines in F-15s and F-16s to be bought in the rest of the decade. Plagued by maintenance problems with the engine currently used in the two planes — the F-100 built by United Technologies Corporation's Pratt & Whitney division — the Air Force had sponsored a competition for future engine contracts between an improved F-100 and General Electric's F-110.

The fiscal 1984 budget included $58.9 million to begin purchasing components of new engines.

Stevens' subcommittee recommended that no contract be signed for a new engine until the Armed Services and Appropriations committees had 90 days to review the results of the competition and the Pentagon's final decision.

Critics charged that the delay would, in effect, guarantee that only Pratt & Whitney engines could be used in fighters bought in fiscal 1985, even if they had lost the competition by then.

But Stevens insisted that so major a commitment should be reviewed by Congress before it took effect. And he voiced doubts about the long-term savings the Air Force predicted would result from the choice of a more trouble-free engine, warning that those estimates assumed the annual purchase of far more new fighter planes than now seemed likely.

The committee rejected 8-20 an amendment by Lowell P. Weicker Jr., R-Conn., of Pratt & Whitney's home state, that would have dropped the 90-day delay while retaining other limitations. The panel then dropped all the subcommittee limitations by voice vote.

The committee trimmed $7.7 million from a Navy request for $42.7 million to improve its F-14 fighter, including replacement of the current engine with the winner of the Air Force competition. The panel said it was unconvinced that new engines were needed for the F-14.

New Missile. Procurement funds for components of a new air-to-air missile for U.S. fighter planes (called AMRAAM) were trimmed by $10 million, to $23.8 million. The committee insisted on keeping the new missile's production rate very low until more test flights had been conducted.

For 515 HARM missiles, designed to be fired from U.S.

planes to home in on anti-aircraft radars, the committee recommended $290.9 million in new appropriations. It made up the $80 million reduction from the budget request with a like amount appropriated in fiscal 1983 to initiate a second contractor into production of the missile.

The Defense Subcommittee agreed with the Defense Department — over the objections of the Navy — to abandon the idea of dual-source procurement as a way to cut costs. It agreed instead to look for savings from a cheaper radar homing mechanism for the missile.

The full committee upheld the Defense Subcommittee's view 5-15.

Naval Warfare. The Senate panel approved the $57.7 million requested for components to be used in fiscal 1985 to modernize a third battleship and equip it with long-range cruise missiles. But like its House counterpart, the committee barred use of the funds until the Navy explained its plans for further modification of the ships in the late 1980s.

For three cruisers with the Aegis anti-aircraft system, designed to protect U.S. fleets against swarms of anti-ship missiles, the committee recommended $3.36 billion, $75 million less than requested. This was some $159 million less than the reduction imposed by the House. That difference was not explained by either body, but may have reflected the House panel's long fight to strip these ships of anti-submarine equipment and a backup radar which, it argued, were superfluous to the ship's anti-missile mission.

For components to be used in the first of a new class of destroyers that would carry smaller versions of the Aegis system — the *Arleigh Burke*, due for funding in fiscal 1985 — the committee approved $79 million, the amount authorized.

Submarine Hunting. The request for three attack submarines designed principally to attack other subs was approved ($1.7 billion). But the committee told the Navy to plan on funding only three more of these ships in fiscal 1985 instead of the four planned. It trimmed from $336 million to $168 million the amount provided for components that would be used in attack subs bought in the future.

For a guided missile frigate that was not requested in the budget, the committee added $183.6 million in new appropriations and transferred an additional $116.4 million that had been appropriated but not spent in prior years. But it rejected $37 million the House panel had added to the bill to modify the anti-aircraft radar aboard these ships.

Ground Combat. The committee approved $1.4 billion for 840 M-1 tanks, overriding the Defense Subcommittee, which had approved funds for only 720. The tank was one of several major weapons for which the subcommittee approved lower production rates than were budgeted or authorized, in anticipation of lower-than-planned defense budget increases in future years.

Before the committee increased the M-1 allocation on Oct. 31, subcommittee Chairman Stevens predicted that Congress might approve a real increase in the fiscal 1985 defense budget of as little as 2.5 percent. "If that happens, this is one of the [production] lines that has to come down anyway," he said — to a production rate that might be even lower than the 720 per year approved by his panel.

But Stevens was overridden on a 16-11 vote. Democrats who voted approved the increase 11-1.

After the full committee completed action on the bill — and increased funds for several other programs over

Stevens' objections — he complained to reporters: "The defense bill has become a jobs bill.... We find it impossible to keep reasonable limits on some of the procurements."

The full committee also adopted a provision that would, in effect, nullify a provision of the fiscal 1984 defense authorization bill (PL 98-94) that barred selection of a second manufacturer for the gas turbine engine that powered the M-1. Because of cost and schedule problems with engines produced in Connecticut by Avco Corp., the Army had sought bids from other firms to compete with Avco to build the engines of future M-1s. That was blocked by the authorization bill.

The committee also ordered the Army to report on ways to improve the survivability of the older M-60 tanks, which were to make up half the Army's tank fleet well into the 1990s.

Anti-Tank Weapons. The panel added $33 million (for a total of $799 million) to the subcommittee amount for 600 Bradley armored troop carriers equipped with TOW anti-tank guided missiles. The increase, which the House had adopted by a floor amendment to its version of the bill, was to equip these Bradleys with an improved version of TOW having a larger warhead and aiming devices that could operate at night and in poor visibility.

The committee denied $100 million for the Copperhead laser-guided artillery shell designed to let the Army's large force of 155mm howitzers hit tanks at a range of several miles. The program had a checkered past, in terms of cost, performance and degree of Pentagon support, though the most recent tests had been successful and the Army and Marines restored the shell to their budget plans.

But the Defense Subcommittee remained dubious, and an effort to restore the Copperhead money in the full committee was rejected 4-15.

The panel applauded the Army's decision to give up efforts to perfect the Viper, a portable anti-tank missile which the Senate subcommittee had vigorously opposed because of its cost and its inability to penetrate the front armor of modern Soviet tanks. But it ordered the service to continue evaluating other weapons for the Viper role, including several of European design.

Helicopters. For 112 Apache anti-tank helicopters, the committee approved $1.14 billion, $78 million less than was requested. The House Oct. 26 had adopted a floor amendment increasing from 96 to 112 the number of Apaches funded in its version of the bill.

The panel also told the Army to increase the total number of Apaches it planned to buy so that, starting with the fiscal 1987 budget, it could begin purchasing some of them for National Guard units.

Like the House, the Senate committee added $45.8 million to the request to equip older Cobra attack helicopters with TOW anti-tank missiles.

'Deep Strike.' Like its House counterpart, the Senate panel endorsed the development of a new generation of conventional weapons designed to disrupt attacking ground forces while they still were far behind enemy lines.

It added $20 million not included in the budget to begin buying components for a missile — called JTACMS — designed to carry several warheads that would home in on enemy tank formations.

As required by the companion authorization bill, the committee cut by $49 million (to $42 million) the amount for developing a radar — called JSTARS — intended to locate targets and guide the missiles toward them. But it

Funding for Major Defense Programs, Fiscal 1984

Following is a comparison of the amounts Congress authorized and appropriated
for major defense programs in fiscal 1984 *(in millions of dollars)*:

	Reagan Request		Enacted Authorization (S 675)		Enacted Appropriation (HR 4185)	
	Number	Amount	Number	Amount	Number	Amount
Strategic Weapons						
MX missile	27	$2,770	21	$2,102	21	$2,102
Small ICBM R&D		—		354		354
B-1 bomber	10	3,762	10	3,762	10	3,762
Air-launched cruise missile (ALCM)		—	240	422	240	407
Trident submarine	1	1,526	1	1,452	1	1,398
Trident I missile	52	587	52	587	52	555
Trident II missile R&D		1,496		1,506		1,501
Intermediate-Range Missiles						
Pershing II missile	95	408	95	408	95	408
Ground-launched cruise missile (GLCM)	120	582	120	564	120	564
Ground Combat						
M-1 tank	720	1,361	840	1,463	840	1,463
Bradley troop carrier	600	766	600	799	600	793
Apache anti-tank helicopter	112	1,219	112	1,189	112	1,141
'Deep Strike' weapons (JTACMS and JSTARS)	—	224	—	203	—	183
Sergeant York anti-aircraft tank (Divad)	130	542	130	542	130	542
Patriot anti-aircraft missile	525	992	440	885	440	885
Naval Warfare						
Aegis cruiser	3	3,431	3	3,394	3	3,281
Sub-hunting submarine	3	1,706	3	1,706	3	1,682
LAMPS III anti-submarine helicopter	21	447	21	447	21	398
Parts for a new-design destroyer in 1985	—	100	—	79	—	79
Tactical Air Combat						
F-15 fighter	48	1,529	36	1,282	36	1,282
F-16 fighter	120	1,618	144	1,997	144	1,997
F-14 carrier fighter	24	886	24	792	24	792
F-18 carrier fighter	84	2,151	84	2,136	84	2,100
A-6E carrier bomber	6	205	6	205	6	205
Airlift and Sealift						
LHD helicopter carrier	1	1,380	1	1,380	1	1,366
LSD amphibious ship	1	327	1	327	1	326
Conversion of SL-7 high-speed cargo ship	4	246	4	246	4	230
C-5 transport plane	4	1,076	4	1,076	4	1,076
KC-10 tanker-cargo plane	8	334	8	334	8	317

Note: Amounts for weapons in procurement omit funds for spare parts and for components of items to be bought in future budgets.
They include some funds that are not new appropriations, but money appropriated for the Pentagon but not spent in prior years.

also added $12 million to begin buying components for JSTARS production.

Anti-Aircraft Defense. Like the House, the Senate committee approved the $885 million authorized for Patriot long-range anti-aircraft missiles, designed to protect U.S. installations in Western Europe. This was $107 million less than the request.

But the committee sliced to $10 million the $33 million request to develop a missile — possibly a modified version of the Patriot — to defend European installations against short-range Soviet ballistic missiles.

This so-called "anti-tactical missile" (ATM) was one option the Pentagon thought of using to deal with increasingly accurate short-range Soviet missiles that might be able to destroy U.S. runways, anti-aircraft batteries and command posts with non-nuclear warheads by the late 1980s.

The committee said that the Army's plans for ATM were too indefinite to warrant the funding increase it requested.

The number of Sergeant York anti-aircraft tanks was trimmed from 130 to 113 — a $38.5 million reduction to $503 million — because of the panel's unhappiness over the weapon's increasing cost. It also ordered the Army to test the effectiveness of Yorks — which were just beginning to come off the production line — and to report on alternative weapons.

It trimmed to $23.1 million the $38.7 million requested for components that would be used in Yorks funded in fiscal 1985. The House committee had denied the entire amount for the advance components, but it was restored on the House floor.

The committee complained that the Air Force was dragging its feet in negotiating arrangements for NATO countries that host U.S. airbases to defend those installations with U.S.-bought anti-aircraft missiles. It trimmed $50 million from the $62.9 million requested for the program. The House had not only approved the program but had expanded it by $200 million.

Senate Floor Action

The Senate began debate on the defense bill Nov. 3, first incorporating the committee-approved text of S 2039 in HR 4185, the House-passed bill. It passed HR 4185 five days later by an 86-6 vote. *(Vote 334, p. 55-S)*

Binary Weapons Debate

Prior to passage, the Senate Nov. 8 approved an administration request for $124.4 million related to production of the new chemical arms by the narrowest of margins: 47-46, with Vice President Bush casting the deciding vote. *(Vote 332, p. 55-S)*

Stevens offered the nerve gas amendment, arguing that improvements in the current U.S. chemical weapons stockpile were needed to deter Soviet use of such arms and to persuade Moscow to negotiate a ban on chemical weapons.

Mark O. Hatfield, R-Ore., long a leader among nerve gas opponents, condemned chemical weapons production as "morally and politically indefensible." He also attacked the total cost of the proposed binary program, which he put at $4 billion to $6 billion. "We ought to have every fiscal conservative vote on this," he declared.

David Pryor, D-Ark., another leading binary opponent, challenged the administration's contention that the new

weapons were needed to replace existing U.S. nerve gas systems: Existing gas artillery shells were sufficient for military needs, and the proposed binary air-dropped bomb (called Bigeye) had test problems, he argued.

But Armed Services Chairman John Tower, R-Texas, backed the Pentagon's claim that existing nerve gas weapons were deteriorating chemically — thus losing their potency — and mechanically — thus becoming a danger to U.S. troops.

"Further adherence to a unilateral moratorium on the production of new [chemical] weapons risks unilateral disarmament by obsolescence," Tower said.

Stevens modified his amendment to incorporate an amendment by Rudy Boschwitz, R-Minn., requiring that two existing chemical weapons — or an equivalent amount of lethal chemical agents in bulk storage — be destroyed for each new binary munition deployed.

The Senate then rejected a Hatfield motion to table the Stevens amendment 46-48. During that roll call, the vice president took the presiding officer's chair, poised to break a tie vote, if necessary. *(Vote 331, p. 55-S)*

The Stevens amendment was then agreed to after Bush broke a 46-46 tie.

Since July, when Bush broke a similar tie on the companion defense authorization bill (S 675), three members switched their positions. Majority Leader Robert C. Byrd, D-W.Va., and Jennings Randolph, D-W.Va., abandoned earlier opposition to binary production. Robert T. Stafford, R-Vt., who had been heavily lobbied on the issue by the arms control and environmental communities, switched to opposition.

MX Missile

On Nov. 7, by a 37-56 vote, the Senate rejected an amendment by Bumpers to delete from the bill the $2.1 billion earmarked for the first 21 production-line versions of the missile. *(Vote 327, p. 54-S))*

Bumpers later predicted that his amendment would ultimately be regarded as the Senate's last chance to block MX: No more votes would change until after the 1984 election, he said; and by 1985 the cost of canceling the missile would be prohibitive.

Most senators lined up as they had in the earlier battle on this issue in July, during debate on the defense authorization bill. Only Arlen Specter's, R-Pa., vote against MX represented a change in position.

But the contest was much closer on a Nancy Landon Kassebaum, R-Kan., amendment expressing the sense of the Senate that Reagan should propose to Moscow a mutual moratorium on flight tests of ICBMs with multiple warheads (MIRVs), for the duration of U.S.-Soviet Strategic Arms Reduction (START) Talks.

Such a test ban would block further flight tests on the MX — so far flown twice — as well as a new Soviet missile designated the SS-24 by the Pentagon and improved versions of the already-deployed Soviet SS-18 and SS-19 missiles.

The Kassebaum amendment was rejected 42-50, with eight senators who had voted against the Bumpers measure supporting the test moratorium: Kassebaum, William L. Armstrong, R-Colo., Lloyd Bentsen, D-Texas, Lawton Chiles, D-Fla., Robert Dole, R-Kan., J. Bennett Johnston, D-La., Charles McC. Mathias Jr., R-Md., and Larry Pressler, R-S.D.

The moratorium was opposed by two members of the Armed Services Committee, J. James Exon, D-Neb., and

Gordon J. Humphrey, R-N.H. Both had voted for the Bumpers amendment because they disagreed with the planned deployment of MX in existing missile silos on military grounds rather than because they opposed the missile on arms control grounds. *(Vote 329, p. 54-S)*

Budget Increases

By voice vote, the Senate adopted an amendment by Carl Levin, D-Mich., negotiated with Stevens, that added to the bill $350.6 million for several programs. The largest single addition was $148 million to modernize the industrial equipment in government-owned dockyards and maintenance facilities.

Other elements of the package included $70 million for a Navy electronic warfare plane, $20 million for research on ICBM launchers that would be buried deep underground to escape the blast of attacking nuclear warheads and $10 million to develop a maneuverable re-entry vehicle for the Trident II submarine-launched missile.

Adoption of the Levin amendment followed a 62-31 vote to table (and thus kill) a Tower amendment that would have added $491.2 million for various programs — some of which subsequently were funded by the Levin amendment. But Tower would have offset that increase by reductions of $900 million which had not been authorized. *(Vote 333, p. 55-S)*

Tower's defeat appeared to reflect two factors:

● His 39-page amendment, which revised nearly every major part of the appropriations bill, may have been seen as too sweeping an effort by an authorizing committee to circumscribe the Appropriations Committee's independence of action.

● He would have trimmed from Stevens' bill $300 million earmarked for the Coast Guard. Noting that the Coast Guard came under Navy control in time of war, Stevens and others argued that the funds would also help the current war against drug smugglers, an extremely popular cause.

An amendment by Weicker adding $168 million for components of nuclear submarines, was agreed to 55-36. This restored the account to the level requested, which would buy enough nuclear power plants to allow the production of four submarines each in the fiscal 1985 and 1986 budgets. *(Vote 328, p. 54-S)*

The Appropriations Committee's reduction would have held submarine funding to three ships in each of those years, the number funded in fiscal 1984.

Nuclear Arms Policy

By a vote of 50-29, the Senate tabled (and thus killed) an amendment by Jesse Helms, R-N.C., expressing the sense of the Senate that no U.S. defense program ought to be constrained for the purpose of U.S. compliance with the unratified SALT II nuclear arms treaty, unless the Senate consented to the pact's ratification and the president certified that the Soviet Union was complying with SALT II and several other U.S.-Soviet agreements. *(Vote 325, p. 54-S)*

The amendment was another move in a long campaign by conservatives, including Helms, and Idaho Republicans Steven D. Symms and James A. McClure, among others, to publicize alleged Soviet violations of SALT II and various other agreements, in hopes of dampening public sentiment for further arms control negotiations with Moscow.

"The evidence is overwhelming that the Soviets are violating SALT II, the [1972] SALT I anti-ballistic missile

treaty and the 1962 Kennedy-Khrushchev agreement [governing U.S.-Cuban relations]," Symms charged, citing statements by Reagan and administration officials.

Helms and his allies also denounced the current administration policy as an unconstitutional, de facto ratification of the treaty without Senate consent.

President Carter had shelved his effort to win Senate ratification for the 1979 treaty in January 1980, within days of the Soviet invasion of Afghanistan.

For the most part, Helms' opponents skirted the question of Soviet compliance with SALT II and the other pacts. Defense Subcommittee member Warren B. Rudman, R-N.H., and others argued simply that the administration opposed the amendment and that it might undermine the president's negotiating flexibility in current arms control talks.

The Senate adopted by voice vote two other amendments related to U.S. nuclear arms policy:

● By Paul E. Tsongas, D-Mass., requiring the president to submit by May 15, 1984, a report on the impact on current and prospective arms control agreements of a greater U.S. emphasis on anti-ballistic missile defenses, including the kind of laser-armed space satellites endorsed by Reagan in a March 23 television address.

● By Edward M. Kennedy, D-Mass., barring the use of any funds in the bill to develop a nuclear warhead for the JTACMS missile. The missile had been widely discussed as a non-nuclear alternative to short-range nuclear missiles, designed to dispense multiple conventional warheads that would home in on enemy tanks. But the Army document soliciting contractors' bids to develop JTACMS stipulated that it should be able to carry a nuclear warhead.

Tank Increase

When the Senate began debate on the defense bill Nov. 3, an effort by Stevens to trim $168.7 million from the allowance for M-1 tanks was rejected 45-48. The reduction would have left the number of tanks funded at 720, the number requested in the budget and approved by Stevens' subcommittee, compared to the 840 M-1s authorized and agreed to by the full Senate Appropriations Committee. *(Vote 322, p. 53-S)*

Stevens said his panel had restrained potential production increases for the tank and some other weapons in hopes of averting a funding crisis. He predicted that Congress would allow future defense increases at a much lower rate than budgeted by the Pentagon.

But J. Bennett Johnston, D-La., countered that tanks and other conventional war equipment had been slighted to pay for nuclear weaponry such as the B-1 bomber, which Johnston opposed. "There is a lot bigger chance that these M-1 tanks are going to get into a shooting war than . . . that our strategic weapons are going to be used," he said.

Other Amendments

Several amendments were adopted that put the Senate on record against various reported abuses in Pentagon management:

● By Byrd, requiring the Office of Federal Procurement Policy (OFPP) to report by June 1, 1984, on the Pentagon's spare parts purchasing system. This followed news reports of several instances of commercially available parts being purchased by the Defense Department for vastly more than their list prices. Adopted 66-5. *(Vote 326, p. 54-S)*

● By Byrd, requiring an OFPP study by Feb. 1, 1984, of the Pentagon's award of contracts during the last week of

fiscal 1983, including $4.2 billion worth of contracts awarded on Sept. 30, the last day of the fiscal year. Voice vote.

● By Howard M. Metzenbaum, D-Ohio, adding $10 million to hire an additional 400 auditors for the Defense Department. Voice vote.

● By Mack Mattingly, R-Ga., cutting $100 million from the amount appropriated to hire consultants. In addition to $148 million previously cut from the request by the Appropriations Committee, this left in the bill a total of $1.2 billion for consultants. Voice vote.

● By Metzenbaum, providing that up to $100,000 of the funds appropriated be available to provide transportation to the funeral of any service member who died of a service-connected injury or illness for members of the service member's immediate family. Adopted, 86-0. *(Vote 323, p. 54-S)*

The Senate also rejected an amendment by John Melcher, D-Mont., requiring that recruits in their first four months of service receive the same 4 percent pay raise due to take effect Jan. 1, 1984, for all other military personnel and federal civilian employees. Tabled 69-24. *(Vote 330, p. 54-S)*

Conference Action

The conference report on HR 4185 (H Rept 98-567) was filed Nov. 18, the final day of the session.

The conference featured only two issues that reflected broad national policy differences — and both of them, in simple dollar terms, were marginal to the $250 billion bill.

Only $124 million was at stake in the battle over whether to begin building binary munitions. At the insistence of House conferees, the funds were dropped.

The fight over terms of well-publicized but formally "covert" U.S. aid to Nicaraguan rebels, though central to U.S. policy in Latin America, involved only $24 million of the large, secret amount in the bill for U.S. intelligence agencies. *(Story, p. 123)*

For the most part, funds to continue Reagan's defense buildup — and most of the major weapons involved — simply were not at issue in the Senate-House conference on the bill. Both houses left most weapons at or near budget levels, so conferees had little more to do on those items than reconcile minor differences, many of them amounting to bookkeeping technicalities.

No Basic Challenge

Hundreds of millions of dollars were involved in some issues before the conferees, but these items challenged no basic element of Reagan defense policy. For instance:

● Conferees approved $300 million added by the Senate for modernization of Coast Guard equipment and $150 million (of $300 million) added by the Senate to remove hazardous waste and debris from abandoned military installations.

● They cut $209.3 million (of a $500 million reduction imposed by the House) to enforce tighter management of Pentagon supplies. They also trimmed $148 million (compared with a House-passed $200-million cut) from the $564.5 million requested to modernize industrial equipment in the Pentagon's shipyards and maintenance shops.

● They transferred $150 million from the budget for leased computers to a fund with which they instructed the Pentagon to begin buying out such leases. The House had set up the $150 million purchase fund but cut $680 million from the leasing accounts.

Funding Level

The $249.8 billion approved by defense conferees did not include $1.8 billion included in the Senate bill to fund a 4 percent Pentagon pay hike. Conferees agreed that the money would be included in a later supplemental appropriation.

The pay raise aside, conferees came out slightly closer to the Senate bill ($253 billion) than to the House version ($247 billion). And compared to Reagan's amended request for the bill, conferees trimmed some $11.1 billion.

The reductions were distributed across the Pentagon budget without imposing fundamental changes on Reagan defense policy. Binary munitions were the only major weapons program blocked by the bill.

B-1 bombers ($5.6 billion) and three Aegis cruisers at $1 billion were among the major requests funded essentially without change.

The bill also included funds to begin production of the MX intercontinental missile, although, pursuant to the authorization bill, 21 were funded ($2.1 billion) rather than the 27 requested ($2.4 billion).

Chemical Weapons

A majority of House conferees previously had approved funding for the new nerve gas shells. But the full House voted decisively against the weapons Nov. 15, approving 258-166 a motion to instruct its defense conferees to oppose binary funds. *(Vote 471, p. 138-H)*

The Senate approved nerve gas production in the fiscal 1984 authorization and appropriations measures by a one-vote margin, with Vice President Bush's tie-breaking vote tipping the balance in each case. However, prior to the Senate vote, its Appropriations Committee had stricken chemical weapons funds from the bill by a vote of 14-12.

As the defense conference began Nov. 16, the status of binary munitions seemed much the same as when defense authorization conferees met in late July: the Senate in favor — albeit by the narrowest of margins — and the House opposed, but represented by conferees known to be in favor.

According to several House conferees, the key to preventing a repetition of the authorization conference (which approved binaries) was the Nov. 16 House vote, which insisted on opposition to binary funding.

John Isaacs of the Council for a Livable World, a leading opponent of binary munitions, credited John Edward Porter, R-Ill., with galvanizing nerve gas opponents into action after the Senate voted for binary funding on Nov. 8. "When everyone else was dithering 'what do we do now,' Porter said, 'I'm going to move to instruct,' " according to Isaacs.

When the House took up the question of naming defense appropriations conferees Nov. 15, C. W. Bill Young, R-Fla., a supporter of binary funding, offered a motion that conferees be instructed to insist on the House's more sweeping prohibition on the use of animals for wound experiments.

Under House rules, a so-called "previous question" motion ending debate on the Young motion had to be defeated by Porter and his allies before they could amend the instruction to include nerve gas.

A week had elapsed between the Senate vote on nerve gas and the House vote to instruct defense conferees. Evidently, the time was useful to Porter and his allies, who had to explain a tangled procedural situation to colleagues.

At the end, the votes of most members on the previous

question (rejected 164-256) and on Porter's subsequent amendment to Young's motion (agreed to 258-166) were consistent with their earlier position on binary funding. *(Votes 470, 471, p. 138-H)*

Ground Combat

Conferees agreed to buy 840 M-1 tanks, as approved by the Senate, compared with the budget request for 720 and the House-approved figure of 825. But they provided only $1.31 billion in new budget authority, less than had been approved by either house and less than was budgeted. They added to this amount $149 million appropriated but not spent in earlier years.

They also approved a provision ordering the secretary of defense to report within three months of the bill's enactment on the feasibility of buying the tank's gas turbine engines from more than one contractor and signing a multi-year contract for the engines.

The Army seemed convinced that competition for the engine contracts would save money. An endorsement of that position by the secretary would set the stage for a congressional battle between supporters of Avco Corp., which built the engines in Connecticut, and members who supported competing firms, notably The Garrett Corp.

Tank-Hunters. Both houses had approved the request for 600 Bradley armored infantry carriers. But the conferees provided $792.8 million, much closer to the Senate-passed $799 million than to the $766 million requested and the $759.8 million allowed by the House.

Presumably, the conference amount included the bulk of the $33 million added by the Senate to incorporate into these vehicles an improved version of the TOW anti-tank guided missile. Its anti-tank weaponry accounted for part of the high cost that had made the Bradley controversial. The so-called TOW II had a longer range, a larger warhead and a more accurate guidance system than earlier TOW versions.

The conferees also agreed that the Army should begin buying missile-armed Apache anti-tank helicopters for National Guard units in fiscal 1987, when the current production run for active-duty Army units was due to taper off. Both houses had approved $1.2 billion for 112 Apaches.

Continued production of the Copperhead laser-guided artillery shell, designed to let regular 155mm howitzers kill tanks at a range of 10 miles, was approved ($75 million). However, the conferees complained about the Copperhead's cost per copy and questioned Army claims that earlier testing failures had been overcome. They ordered a report on the reliability tests by Feb. 1, 1984.

They conceded that the planned purchase of some 30,000 Copperheads would not justify involvement of a second contractor — Martin Marietta Corp. currently built the shell in Orlando, Fla. But they told the Army to plan for a competing contractor in case it decided to buy more.

The budget had requested $18 million to develop a 155mm artillery shell that would home in on tanks without needing an observer to shine a laser on the targets, as does Copperhead. Conferees approved $3 million of this amount, compared with $9 million provided by the Senate. The House had denied all funds, insisting that the Pentagon come up with a master plan coordinating the myriad anti-tank weapons being developed.

'Deep Strike' Weapons. The conferees agreed partly with a Senate effort to accelerate deployment of a new family of conventional weapons intended to strike Soviet tank forces long before they could reach the front.

This so-called "deep strike" approach would use a radar called JSTARS to locate attacking ground forces far behind enemy lines. A missile called JTACMS would be guided to those targets by JSTARS and would then spew out several warheads designed to home in on enemy tanks.

Both houses had approved $60.1 million to develop JTACMS, but conferees dropped $20 million the Senate had added to begin buying components for the missiles. They retained a Senate provision barring development of a nuclear warhead for JTACMS.

To develop the radar, they provided $63 million, as approved by the Senate. Both houses had approved $5 million to begin buying JSTARS components, and the conferees added $7 million approved by the Senate to buy ground terminals for the radar.

Mobile Forces. For large armored cars intended to provide mobility and firepower that could be hauled to remote locations more easily than conventional tanks and armored troop carriers, the conferees approved $132.5 million — the amount the Senate provided to buy 172 vehicles.

The request for 289 vehicles ($210.8 million) divided between the Army and Marine Corps had been slashed by the companion authorization bill apparently because the House Armed Services Committee long had been skeptical of the program, particularly the Army's share of it.

Following the Senate's lead, the appropriations conferees shifted the bulk of the funds to the Marine budget, leaving only $8.9 million for the Army to review its need for these so-called light armored vehicles.

Anti-Aircraft Defense. The two houses had agreed to provide $541.5 million as requested for 130 Sergeant York anti-aircraft tanks but agreed to the lower, Senate-passed amount for components to be used in Sergeant Yorks purchased in the fiscal 1985 budget ($23.1 million).

Perhaps reflecting the Army's recent emphasis on protecting front-line troops against the rapidly improving Soviet air force, as well as the longstanding political clout of the National Guard and Reserve forces, the conferees took the Senate position increasing the amount for improving the existing Vulcan anti-aircraft guns from $9.3 million requested to $38.3 million. The Vulcans were due to be assigned to National Guard units as they were displaced from the active-duty forces by new Sergeant Yorks.

To buy anti-aircraft missile batteries that German troops would man to defend U.S. air bases in West Germany, the conferees agreed on $200 million, as provided by the House. But they embargoed use of that money until 45 days after the Pentagon reported to Congress the terms of a U.S.-German agreement on how the costs of such an arrangement would be divided between the two parties.

They split the difference between the House and Senate amounts for developing a missile to intercept short-range Soviet ballistic missiles carrying chemical warheads that might be intended to cripple NATO air bases in the early hours of a European war. The conferees provided $17.5 million for development of this so-called ATM, compared with $25 million approved by the House and $10 million provided by the Senate.

Tactical Air Combat

The conferees faced little significant disagreement on funding for any of the fighter planes requested for the Air Force and Navy. Both houses had approved:
- $1.3 billion for 36 Air Force F-15s;
- $2 billion for 144 smaller Air Force F-16s;

● $792.4 million for 24 Navy F-14s.

The conferees nearly split the difference for 84 smaller Navy F-18s: $2.1 billion, compared with $2.07 billion approved by the House and $2.14 billion allowed by the Senate.

They approved eight EA-6B carrier-based radar jamming planes ($435.1 million) as requested and approved by the House instead of six planes ($382 million) allowed by the Senate.

Improvements. The current generation of fighter planes was likely to be the mainstay of the U.S. combat force well into the 1990s, with the Pentagon relying on modifications rather than brand-new models to keep pace with Soviet modernization.

The most costly single item on the agenda of improvements was selection of a new engine that would be used on future F-15s and F-16s. Competition for an improved engine was sparked by the limited durability of the F-100 engine currently powering the two planes, made by the Pratt & Whitney division of United Technologies Corp. Pratt had developed an improved version of the F-100 while General Electric offered its own fighter engine, the F-110. Up to $14 billion worth of engine sales were at stake in the competition.

The conferees agreed with the Senate provision that would bar the Air Force from signing a contract with the winning firm until it had informed Congress of the competition's outcome. But they insisted their intent was "that Congress extricate itself from the source selection process so this competition can be carried out fairly."

They also approved the full $42.7 million requested to develop an improved version of the Navy's F-14, one that might use the new engine selected by the Air Force.

Anti-Radar Missile. As requested, the conferees approved the $370.9 million for HARM missiles, designed to be fired from U.S. planes against hostile anti-aircraft radars. However, the conferees followed the Senate's lead in requiring that $80 million of that amount be drawn from funds appropriated but not spent on the project in fiscal 1983.

They agreed with the Senate — and with the Pentagon — that the missiles should be purchased only from their current manufacturer, Texas Instruments Inc., of Dallas. The fiscal 1983 defense appropriations bill had supported dual-sourcing for HARM — the $80 million transferred to the 1984 budget by the conferees had been earmarked for that purpose.

But the fiscal 1984 conferees, like the Pentagon hierarchy, decided to rely instead on development of a cheaper radar-homing device to reduce the cost of HARM — the current radar-seeker accounts for about half the cost of the missile. They earmarked $30.2 million of the HARM production funds to accelerate development of the second seeker and added $20 million to the Navy's research budget for the same purpose.

Trainers. The conferees ordered the Navy to buy only versions of the British-designed Hawk jet trainer that had been modified to land on aircraft carriers.

The first of 251 of these so-called "wet" Hawks, to be built in the United States by McDonnell Douglas Corp., were not scheduled for purchase until fiscal 1988. In the interim, the Navy planned to buy 54 "dry" Hawks, made in Britain, without the special landing gear needed to absorb the punishment of carrier landings.

The conferees dropped $4.9 million for components to be used in the first group of "dry" Hawks, scheduled for

purchase in fiscal 1985.

The Hawk deal was based on an agreement that would roughly have split the amount of money spent in Britain and in the United States over the life of the program. Cancellation of the British-made "dry" Hawks likely would reopen those negotiations.

Naval Combat

The major components of the Reagan team's plan to expand the Navy were not in disagreement before the conference. Both houses had approved a $57.7 million down payment on the modernization in fiscal 1985 of a third battleship (due to cost nearly $590 million at that time).

Similarly, both had approved $95.9 million for components that would be used to rebuild the 25-year-old aircraft carrier *Independence*, a project due to cost an additional $800 million in the fiscal 1985 budget.

Anti-Missile Defense. Both houses had approved the request for three cruisers intended to protect U.S. fleets against swarms of anti-ship missiles with the Aegis defense system. The conferees practically split the minor funding difference between the two houses, approving $3.28 billion for the three ships compared with $3.2 billion from the House and $3.36 billion from the Senate.

Conferees also approved the higher Senate-passed amount ($79 million) for equipment that would be used in the first of a fleet of destroyers built to carry smaller versions of the Aegis system. This ship, the *Arleigh Burke* (or DDG-51), was scheduled to receive more than $1.3 billion in the fiscal 1985 budget.

Sub Hunting. The $1.68 billion approved by conferees for three *Los Angeles*-class attack submarines, designed to hunt other subs, incorporated less than half the minor funding reduction the House had imposed.

But the conferees agreed with the House's optimistic projections for the price of 21 LAMPS III anti-sub helicopters, the type scheduled to be stationed on most of the Navy's newer surface warships. The conferees allowed $397.9 million, compared with $427.9 million recommended by the Senate, a reduction the House said was possible because of favorable contract negotiations for the helicopters.

Both houses had approved construction of one additional ship in the large class of guided-missile escort frigates built since the mid-1970s — a vessel not requested by the administration. The conferees agreed with the Senate plan to pay for the ship with $116.4 million in new money added to the budget and an additional $183.3 million transferred to the fiscal 1984 budget from shipbuilding funds appropriated but not spent in earlier years. The House had told the Navy to fund the frigate from within the $11 billion appropriated for shipbuilding in fiscal 1984.

The conferees agreed with the House that the new frigate should be given an improved anti-aircraft missile radar that would be able to deal with more targets at one time. Like the House, the conferees increased by $37 million (to $72.6 million) the funds to develop an improved version of the frigate radar.

Landing the Marines

The modest House reduction in funding for an LSD-41-type amphibious landing ship (to $325.5 million from $326.9 million) was agreed to by the conferees.

They also dropped a Senate provision that would have allowed a multi-year contract for several additional LSD-

41s if it could be shown to cost at least 10 percent less than separate one-ship-per-year contracts for the same ships.

Both houses had agreed to provide $1.4 billion for a larger Marine Corps transport ship and helicopter carrier (called an LHD).

For six air-cushion landing barges (or LCACs) designed to carry tanks from landing ships up onto the beach at nearly 60 mph, four times the speed of conventional landing barges, the conferees approved $127.6 million, accepting the House's $4 million reduction from the request.

However, they also approved $23 million of $29.5 million requested (and denied by the House) for components to be used in LCACs planned for the fiscal 1985 budget.

Following the lead of the Senate, the conferees consolidated in the Navy's research budget the entire $88 million approved (of $104.3 million requested) to develop a combination airplane/helicopter called JVX. Intended initially to replace the aging transport helicopters used by Marines to get some of their troops from assault ships to shore, JVX was expected to have a much higher speed and a much longer range than conventional helicopters.

JVX funds had been divided among the services since all had been expected to use the plane for various missions. But only the Marines (whose research was conducted by the Navy) needed it badly enough to make it a high-priority project, according to the Senate Appropriations Committee.

Nuclear Warfare

The most controversial nuclear weapons funds in the fiscal 1984 budget — $2.1 billion to purchase the first 21 MX missiles and $2 billion to continue development of the missile — had been approved by both houses.

Both also had approved $279 million to develop a small, single-warhead ICBM (commonly called Midgetman) and $75 million to develop an armored mobile launcher for that new missile.

The conferees split the difference between the two houses for research on two other kinds of ICBM basing:

● $110 million to study ways to "super-harden" missile silos against nuclear blast;

● $20 million to study launchers built deep underground.

In each case, the Senate had approved half the conference amount while the House allowed no funds.

Bombers, Cruise Missiles. There was no controversy over the $5.6 billion earmarked to buy 10 B-1 bombers and to begin a multi-year contract on some 80 additional copies of the plane.

The bill also included a secret amount to develop the so-called "stealth" bomber, intended to evade detection by enemy radars.

For 240 of the long-range cruise missiles (or ALCMs) designed to be launched by U.S. bombers from beyond the reach of Soviet air defenses, the conferees approved $407 million (of $422.2 million requested), and they required that $15 million of that amount be made up from funds appropriated for ALCMs in fiscal 1983. This reflected the Senate's position that ALCM prices in fiscal 1983 and 1984 would be lower than budgeted.

Also approved was $7 million (of $8 million added to the budget by the House) for components of ALCMs that might be ordered in fiscal 1985. The Pentagon had budgeted no funds since it was uncertain whether to stop ALCM production in preparation for buying an improved cruise missile.

Submarine Missiles. For the 11th of the huge Trident missile-launching submarines, the conferees agreed on the slightly lower House-passed figure of $1.398 billion.

Approving $55.3 million for the last 52 Trident I missiles designed to be launched from the subs, they split the difference between the Senate ($587.2 million) and House ($523.4 million).

The $1.5 billion approved for development of a larger Trident II missile included half the $10 million added by the Senate to allow the new missile to be equipped with a warhead designed to home in on its target.

Anti-Satellite Missiles. For components of the first production-line versions of a missile (the so-called ASAT) designed to be launched against Soviet space satellites, the conferees approved $19.4 million as requested. ASAT advocates in the House had surrendered the funds to fend off liberal efforts to block initial ASAT tests lest they trigger a new arms race in space.

As a gesture to the House position, conferees blocked use of the ASAT funds until 45 days after the president reported on his plans to seek arms control agreements limiting ASAT weapons; a report was due by March 31, 1984.

Warranties

The conferees also approved a provision requiring that any weapon be covered by a written warranty certifying that it was free from defects and providing that the contractor would bear the cost of bringing the equipment up to its performance specifications.

In contrast to the original Senate-passed provision sponsored by Mark Andrews, R-N.D., the conference provision allowed waiver of this requirement if the secretary of defense found it was not cost-effective. Andrews acknowledged that this was a loophole in the provision but insisted that it was a useful first step, since it also required the secretary to explain to Congress the basis of his waiver decision.

Buy American

The conferees agreed to a Senate-passed provision requiring the use of U.S.-produced coal at U.S. bases in Europe, if available.

Another provision blocked the purchase for U.S. planes of ejection seats made in any country that did not allow U.S.-made ejection seats to compete for use in planes bought by that country. This was an outgrowth of a long wrangle over the use of Martin-Baker ejection seats, made in Britain, for the Navy's F-18 fighter. ∎

D.C. Appropriations

Congress Sept. 29 cleared legislation (HR 3415 — PL 98-125) making fiscal 1984 appropriations for the District of Columbia.

Final action came when the Senate adopted the conference report on the bill (H Rept 98-379) by voice vote. The House approved it earlier in the day by a 231-177 vote. *(Vote 347, p. 104-H)*

As cleared, the bill included $601 million in federal funds, compared to the president's request of $570 million and the fiscal 1983 appropriation of $524 million. The $601 million was $31.2 million over the level contemplated by the fiscal 1984 budget resolution (H Con Res 91), $56.2 million more than the House approved on a 296-124 vote

June 29 (H Rept 98-265) and $5 million more than the Senate approved by voice vote July 27 (S Rept 98-185). *(House vote 219, p. 66-H)*

The bill also appropriated $2.18 billion from the District's own funds, $31.1 million over the budget resolution and $56.1 million over the House-passed version.

The bill included a $386 million federal payment intended to compensate the District for the loss of local tax revenues and to reimburse it for costs associated with its role as the nation's capital. This figure was $25 million over the House-passed version. To make up the difference, House conferees agreed to add $12.2 million for the police, fire and teachers' retirement fund, $4.8 million for St. Elizabeths Hospital for the mentally ill and $8 million for the D.C. General Hospital.

In addition, the House accepted a Senate proposal to add $22.3 million for 422 positions in the Department of Corrections to relieve overcrowding at the D.C. jail. Conferees also approved $2.8 million for 35 positions at the D.C. Superior Court, including seven new judges, but made the funds conditional on congressional enactment of authorizing legislation.

The House agreed to go along with a Senate plan to conduct a study of various alternatives to recognize outstanding teachers through financial or career incentives. The bill included $350,000 for this purpose; the Senate had approved $1.5 million.

Conferees added a new section, appropriating an additional $5.7 million for St. Elizabeths Hospital to eliminate any anticipated deficit. However, the conference report warned that this was the last time the federal government would bail out the hospital; the Reagan administration had wanted to transfer all costs for the hospital to the government of the District. ∎

President Signs $55.8 Billion HUD Measure

President Reagan July 12 signed into law a bill providing $55.8 billion in fiscal 1984 appropriations for the Department of Housing and Urban Development (HUD) and various independent agencies.

The bill (HR 3133 — PL 98-45), the first fiscal 1984 appropriations measure to be signed by the president, exceeded his original budget request of $49.8 billion by about $6 billion. Fiscal 1983 funding was $49.7 billion.

Conference Agreement

House and Senate conferees agreed to drop four provisions and to limit the number of subsidized housing units to be funded, which David A. Stockman, director of the Office of Management and Budget (OMB), said would make the bill acceptable to the administration.

Conferees dropped the following:

● A Senate provision that earmarked $150 million for a new veterans' job training program authorized separately by both the House and Senate (HR 2355). *(Story, p. 599)*

● House language that allowed the use of up to $150 million for mortgage assistance to unemployed veterans.

● A Senate provision prohibiting the HUD secretary from selling Section 202 elderly housing project mortgages without congressional authorization.

● A House level of $4.081 billion for the Environmental Protection Agency (EPA). The Senate figure of $3,998 billion was approved.

Also at the administration's request, conferees approved $9.9 billion for assisted housing that would provide up to 100,000 subsidized housing units. The Senate had provided for 112,000 subsidized housing units, while the House allowed 116,000 units. The administration originally sought funding for 93,000 units.

The $55.8 billion total of the bill was more than $1 billion more than either chamber initially had approved. The Senate June 21 approved $54.25 billion, and the House voted June 2 to spend $54.43 billion.

Conferees reached agreement June 23. The Senate by a vote of 79-17 cleared the conference report (H Rept 98-264) for the president June 29. The House had adopted the report 314-99 earlier in the day. *(Vote 171, 31-S; Vote 215, 64-H)*

Housing Funds

The $9.9 billion in the final bill provided for 61,500 subsidized housing units: 2,500 units of Indian housing, 5,000 units of new public housing, 35,000 units under the regular Section 8 rental housing; 5,000 units of moderately rehabilitated housing; and 14,000 units of new or substantially rehabilitated housing for elderly and handicapped.

However, conferees established a $1.5 billion reserve fund to be available after Jan. 1, 1984, to support 38,500 additional units — up to a total limit of 100,000 units for all housing programs — if new housing programs were authorized. The allocation of the $1.5 billion would be determined by subsequent appropriations legislation.

Conferees omitted Reagan's proposal to provide vouchers that would allow low-income families to seek housing in the private market, pending an authorization. Under the plan, a public housing agency would give vouchers to qualified tenants, who would use them to rent private housing; the landlord would use the voucher to obtain the difference between 30 percent of tenant income and the rent payment standard, to be set by HUD.

The administration sought approval to use vouchers for 50,000 units. Both the House and Senate had approved smaller pilot projects.

Conferees also eliminated a Senate $300 million housing rehabilitation plan that lacked authorization.

The final bill allocated $1.5 billion for public housing modernization and $1.4 billion for operating subsidies.

A limit of $50.9 billion was set on Federal Housing Administration mortgage insurance commitments, the Senate level, instead of $45.9 billion recommended by the House. Commitments for the Government National Mortgage Association's mortgage-backed securities were limited to $68.3 billion, instead of $58.3 billion set by the House bill.

The conferees allocated $3.468 billion to Community Development Block Grants to local and state governments and $440 million to Urban Development Action Grants, which were to be spent in severely distressed areas.

The bill also established a new $2 million demonstration program to provide matching grants to non-profit neighborhood organizations to develop jobs or housing.

In addition, it retained the Section 312 program of

grants to rehabilitate housing and provided funds for the Solar Energy and Energy Conservation Bank, both programs the administration wanted to drop.

The agreement provided $4.6 billion for general revenue sharing in fiscal 1984. The House had deferred funding pending an authorization.

EPA Funds

The $3.998 billion for the embattled Environmental Protection Agency included $295.5 million sought by William D. Ruckelshaus, who was named director of the EPA after Anne M. Burford resigned under fire. Ruckelshaus forwarded a new budget request to Congress, seeking additional funds which were largely for operating expenses. *(Story, p. 332)*

The measure also established a one-year moratorium on the imposition of sanctions by the EPA against those cities that failed to meet Clean Air Act standards. *(Story, p. 339)*

Final Provisions

As signed by the president July 12, HR 3133 (PL 98-45) made the following appropriations for HUD and various independent agencies for fiscal 1984:

	Administration Request	Final Appropriation
Department of Housing and Urban Development		
Housing Programs	$ 2,968,202,896	$ 9,128,870,000
Community Development	3,858,000,000	3,920,000,000
Policy Development and Research	18,000,000	19,000,000
Fair Housing Assistance	4,700,000	4,700,000
Management and Administration	303,107,000	300,950,000
Solar Energy Bank	0	25,000,000
Total, HUD	$ 7,152,009,896	$13,398,520,000
Independent Agencies		
American Battle Monuments Commission	10,837,000	10,462,000
Consumer Product Safety Commission	32,000,000	35,000,000
Cemeterial Expenses, Army	8,203,000	8,203,000
Environmental Protection Agency	3,968,091,000	3,998,100,000
Council on Environmental Quality	913,000	700,000
Office of Science and Technology Policy	2,088,000	1,950,000
Federal Emergency Management Agency	522,407,000	436,594,000
GSA Consumer Information Center	1,449,000	1,349,000
HHS Office of Consumer Affairs	2,011,000	2,011,000
National Aeronautics and Space Administration	7,106,500,000	7,177,500,000
National Science Foundation	1,292,300,000	1,320,300,000
Neighborhood Reinvestment Corporation	15,512,000	15,512,000
Selective Service System	25,499,000	24,500,000
Treasury Department		
General Revenue Sharing	4,566,700,000	4,566,700,000
Salaries and Expenses	7,678,000	7,278,000
Veterans Administration	25,110,661,000*	24,784,661,000
GRAND TOTAL	$49,824,858,896	$55,789,340,000

* This figure includes $263.4 million requested by the administration for two Veterans Administration hospital construction projects in Minneapolis, Minn., and Cleveland, Ohio, that were contained in HR 3069, the fiscal 1983 supplemental appropriations bill.

House Committee Action

The House Appropriations Committee May 24 reported a $54.2 billion fiscal 1984 bill (H Rept 98-223). Some programs were omitted pending enactment of an authorization, such as a rental housing production program and general revenue sharing for local governments.

The committee said its bill provided $9.5 billion more in budget authority than the administration requested and $4.5 billion more than appropriated in fiscal 1983.

Nearly all of the increase over the president's budget — $9.4 billion — was allocated to housing aid.

Reagan originally requested $515 million in new budget authority for housing aid in fiscal 1984 and planned to augment that with $4.37 billion recaptured from canceled housing units and $3.081 billion deferred from 1983.

Edward P. Boland, D-Mass., chairman of the Appropriations Subcommittee on HUD-Independent Agencies, argued that the increase was needed because HUD had miscalculated the money available for recapture and because the subsidized housing programs had been cut disproportionately since 1981. The funds available that year, he said, totaled nearly $25 billion.

Except for adding $15 million for a new National Science Foundation instrumentation program, the full committee adopted the bill as approved May 4 by the HUD subcommittee.

HUD Programs

The committee recommended $16.5 billion for HUD, up $3.4 billion from fiscal 1983. The president requested $7.2 billion.

Major elements of the committee bill included:

● **Assisted Housing.** The bill provided $12.9 billion for 116,000 subsidized housing units. Because no funds had been available for construction in 1982, the committee set aside $1.8 billion for 10,000 units of public housing that it urged be used for large families.

The committee expressed misgivings about the president's housing voucher proposal but recommended $312.5 million to test the plan with 25,000 rental units under the Section 8 program to assist low-income tenants.

The committee matched Reagan's request to rescind up to $93.3 million in annual contract authority, which permits obligations in advance of appropriations, and almost $2.4 billion in budget authority for rent supplements.

The panel also agreed to rescind up to $13.3 million in contract authority and $483.1 million in budget authority in the rental housing assistance program to aid very low-income families living in Section 236 rental units.

● **Housing Payments.** The panel matched Reagan's request for $10.7 billion in contract authority for annual subsidized housing payments for such programs as the Section 8 low-income housing assistance and rent supplement programs, Section 235 homeownership assistance, Section 236 rental housing assistance and low-income public housing and college housing programs.

● **Elderly or Handicapped.** A limit of $666.4 million was set on loans to finance Section 202 housing for the elderly and handicapped, $190.4 million above the request. The funds would provide approximately 14,000 housing units, 4,000 more than requested.

● **Operating Subsidies.** The committee cut $205.5 million from the request for public housing operating subsidies. It approved only $1.4 billion, augmented by $69 million deferred from 1983.

The panel rejected Reagan's plan to base the subsidy on what HUD determined to be the fair market rents in an area. The committee said that public housing could not be equated with private rental housing. It also rejected an administration proposal to shift the basis for allocating funds to modernize low-income housing projects.

● **Government National Mortgage Association.** As requested, the committee approved a $58.6 billion limit on the mortgage-backed securities program of Ginnie Mae.

● **FHA.** It matched the $252.9 million requested by the administration to recover losses through the sale of HUD properties and the liquidation of assigned mortgages. The committee also accepted the president's recommendation to limit to $56.3 million the temporary mortgage assistance payments authorized to be made to homeowners experiencing financial difficulty.

● **Community Development.** The bill trimmed $30 million from the $3.5 billion request for Community Development Block Grants. The panel said the funds had been requested for Indian programs, which were covered elsewhere in the bill. Urban Development Action Grants (UDAG) were funded at $440 million, the 1983 level. The president sought $196 million for UDAG, assuming a 1983 deferral of $244 million. Congress disapproved the deferral in the emergency jobs bill (PL 98-8). *(Story, p. 447)*

● **Solar Energy Bank.** The committee rejected administration attempts to abolish the Solar Energy and Energy Conservation Bank. It provided $25 million, a $5 million increase from fiscal 1983.

● **Rental Rehabilitation.** Some $150 million sought by the administration for grants to rehabilitate housing was rejected on the grounds there was no authorization.

● **Rehabilitation Loans.** The committee rejected the administration efforts to abolish the Section 312 loan program providing low-cost loans for rehabilitation. It ordered the program continued in fiscal 1984 and said an estimated $71.5 million from repayments and other income sources would be available.

Consumer Product Safety Commission

The committee recommended $34.5 million, up $2.5 million over the request. It expressed concern over past budget cuts but while providing funds to maintain the staff at 636, limited the projects CPSC could undertake.

Environmental Protection

Contending that the EPA could not fulfill its mandate on the $3.7 billion requested by the president, the panel recommended $3.9 billion, $142 million more than the 1983 appropriation.

The biggest increase was for abatement, control and compliance, which included water and air quality control, and grants to states to manage hazardous waste. The committee set funding in that category at $370.4 million, adding $76.4 million to the administration's proposal.

For research and development, the panel approved $142 million, $30.3 million more than requested. Of that total, $3 million was earmarked to develop new hazardous waste control technology to decrease the nation's reliance on landfills.

The Hazardous Substance Response Trust Fund, — or "superfund" — was allocated $335 million, $25 million more than requested and $125 million over the 1983 figure. Superfund monies were intended to finance cleanup of emergency hazardous substance spills and of dangerous, uncontrolled and abandoned hazardous waste sites.

The panel provided $567.9 million for EPA salaries and expenses in 1984, up $27.5 million from the president's request and $19.3 million over 1983 funding. It matched the president's $2.4 billion request for wastewater construction grants, a $30 million cut from 1983 spending.

Veterans Administration

The panel recommended $24.8 billion, a $41.5 million cut in the president's budget but a $649.5 million increase over 1983 appropriations.

It matched the request for compensation and pensions of $13.8 billion. The appropriation reflected a savings of $113.3 million due to an anticipated six-month delay in the pension cost-of-living increase, requested by the president. The delay was assumed in the House and Senate-passed budget resolutions. *(Story, p. 435)*

For medical care, the committee added $20 million to the request of $8.07 billion. It provided $350.9 million for major VA construction projects.

National Science Foundation

For the NSF, the panel met the administration's request of $1.3 billion, a $223 million increase over 1983. The bill included $70 million for science education, $31 million more than requested and more than twice the amount appropriated for fiscal 1983.

NASA

The committee recommended $7.2 billion for the National Aeronautics and Space Administration, $70 million over the request. Fiscal 1983 funding was $6.8 billion.

It provided $5.8 billion for research and development which included the space shuttle, a $95 million increase over the president's budget. But the panel slashed $15 million from the request for facilities construction, for a total of $135.5 million. It also cut the request for research and program management by $10 million to $1.2 billion.

The extra NASA money would pay for a fifth space shuttle orbiter and spare parts, a space telescope, advanced turboprop work, technology utilization and research in physics, astronomy and planetary programs.

FEMA

The committee trimmed the president's request for the Federal Emergency Management Agency (FEMA) by $91.6 million and recommended $430.8 million. The 1983 appropriation was $649.9 million.

FEMA carried out a wide range of programs, including civil defense and disaster relief programs. Denied was a $50.5 million increase sought by the administration to assist states and localities with civil defense activities and $43.5 million for other civil defense activities.

Other Programs

Revenue Sharing. The committee deferred consideration of general revenue sharing pending enactment of an authorization, but it included $7.3 million for salaries and operations for the Office of Revenue Sharing. That figure was $300,000 less than requested.

Selective Service System. The committee called for $24 million, a $1.4 million cut in the request but up from the 1983 appropriation of $22.7 million.

House Floor Action

After key amendments affecting the EPA were

adopted, the House June 2 approved a $54.4 billion fiscal 1984 appropriations bill for HUD and the independent agencies by a vote of 216-143. *(Vote 143, p. 46-H)*

Earlier, the House accepted by 227-136 a Republican-backed amendment establishing a one-year moratorium on the imposition of sanctions for violations of the Clean Air Act. The action in effect eased pressures to rewrite the current controversial law. *(Vote 141, p. 46-H; story, p. 339)*

The bill was the first fiscal 1984 appropriations measure to reach the floor, and the clean air rider represented the first test of a new House rule intended to restrict most riders on appropriations bills.

In addition, EPA operating funding was increased on the floor by $219.8 million, bringing the total operating funds to roughly the level that existed before the Reagan administration proposed deep cuts in 1981. The total for EPA covering all activities was $4.086 billion.

The major funding increase was contained in an amendment sponsored by Timothy E. Wirth, D-Colo., and adopted by a vote of 200-167. *(Vote 139, p. 46-H)*

New Rule Used

The clean-air rider, offered by William E. Dannemeyer, R-Calif., barred EPA from using any of its funds to impose sanctions under the Clean Air Act on any area of the country that failed to meet national air quality standards by Dec. 31, 1982, the deadline set by the act.

To bring the issue up, Dannemeyer had to use a new rule adopted by House Democrats Jan. 3 that made it more difficult to attach riders to appropriations measures. The intent was to head off amendments on school busing and abortion, for example.

Under the new rule, the only way a rider could be offered on the floor was for the House to reject a motion to rise out of the Committee of the Whole after all other work on the bill had been completed. If the motion was defeated, one rider could be offered. The same process would have to occur for each individual rider.

The House rejected by a vote of 144-225 Boland's motion that the Committee of the Whole rise, and subsequently adopted Dannemeyer's amendment, 227-136. *(Votes 140, 141, p. 46-H)*

But a second attempt led by Robert S. Walker, R-Pa., to attach another rider to the HUD appropriations bill failed. The House voted 241-120 to rise, thereby precluding Walker from offering his job-related amendment. *(Vote 142, p. 46-H)*

EPA Funding

The EPA funding changes were adopted over the objections of Boland, who warned they might prompt a veto.

Boland, and Bill Green, R-N.Y., ranking minority member on the subcommittee, maintained that Congress should delay increasing funding until the new EPA administrator, Ruckelshaus, reviewed the agency's budget.

Ruckelshaus had written subcommittee leaders that he would consider it a "personal courtesy" for them to wait for his recommendations. "Give him a vote of confidence instead of a slap in the face," Green said.

Morris K. Udall, D-Ariz., a leading House environmentalist, said the agency had been "decimated" by budget cuts over the past two years and the budget increases would strengthen Ruckelshaus' administration.

The budget category of most concern was the EPA's operating budget, which included salaries, research funds and grants to state environmental projects.

Congress in fiscal 1983 had appropriated approximately $1.04 billion for EPA's operating budget, but Reagan requested a cut to about $949 million for fiscal 1984. The Appropriations Committee bill raised that back up to $1.08 billion. Wirth's amendments raised the operating funds to $1.3 billion.

The level set by the Wirth amendment compared to $1.35 billion appropriated by Congress for fiscal 1981, the high-water mark set before Reagan began proposing, and Congress approving, cuts in the agency's budget.

Of the additional money provided in Wirth's amendment, $151.2 million was earmarked for pollution and hazardous waste control, $45 million for salaries and expenses and $23.6 million for research and development.

Another $5 million for EPA's clean lakes program was added to the committee bill by an amendment offered by Robert A. Roe, D-N.J., and accepted by voice vote.

Housing Controversy

Another controversy erupted June 1 on the committee's pilot program testing cash vouchers that low-income families would use to rent private housing. The disagreement was between members of the Appropriations Committee and the authorizing panel, the Banking, Finance and Urban Affairs Committee.

The Appropriations panel had included funds for a modified version of the president's proposed cash-voucher plan, but the HUD authorization reported by the Banking Committee rejected the idea in favor of a new $1.3 billion multifamily housing program.

Boland resolved the issue by agreeing to push for both programs in conference.

Senate Committee Action

The Senate Appropriations Committee June 14 reported a $54.3 billion fiscal 1984 appropriations measure (S Rept 98-152), after adding funds for the EPA to its subcommittee bill.

The committee exceeded the request of EPA administrator Ruckelshaus, who had sought $3.968 billion for the beleaguered agency. The panel boosted that amount another $30 million to provide overall funding of $3.998 billion.

As ordered reported by voice vote, the bill contained $171.7 million less in new budget authority than the House-passed bill.

The Senate panel agreed with the House to grant Reagan's request to rescind up to $93.3 million in annual contract authority and almost $2.4 billion in budget authority for rent supplements. It also met the president's request to rescind up to $13.3 million in contract authority and $483.1 million in budget authority in the Section 236 rental assistance program for very low-income families.

The Senate committee included almost $4.6 billion for general revenue sharing, which the House had deferred pending an authorization.

HUD Funding

The Senate panel set HUD levels at $11.7 billion, including $7.2 billion in budget authority for assisted housing, which would provide 112,000 subsidized housing units. The House bill set overall HUD spending levels at $16.5 billion, with $12.24 billion for assisted housing for 116,000 housing units.

Part of the Senate panel's total was intended for a new experimental housing voucher program that would allow 20,000 low-income families to secure their own housing in the private market. The House-passed bill provided $312.5 million to test the cash voucher system with 25,000 Section 8 rental assistance units.

The House also included $1.8 billion for the construction of 10,000 new units of public housing, while the Senate panel recommended no new funds for public housing construction. But the Senate committee added $1.6 billion for public housing modernization, up $100 million from the House-passed level. Public housing operating subsidies were set at $1.4 billion.

While the House omitted the administration request for $150 million for grants to states and units of local governments for rehabilitation of low- and moderate-income housing, the Senate doubled the figure, to $300 million, which would fund the rehabilitation of 50,000 units.

The Senate panel provided for $10.7 billion to meet contractual payments due in fiscal 1984, the same figure as provided by the House and requested by the administration.

It also matched the House loan limit of $666.4 million for housing for the elderly and handicapped.

Like the House, the Senate committee also provided $25 million for the Solar Energy and Energy Conservation Bank and continued the Section 312 rehabilitation loan program that the administration wanted to phase out.

Community Development

Community development funds were boosted to $4.2 billion, up $293.2 million over the House-passed level. The increase was due largely to including $300 million for the housing rehabilitation program.

The Senate panel funded Community Development Block Grants at $3.46 billion, $6.8 million less than the House. However, the Senate panel earmarked $2.5 million of the secretary's discretionary fund for a new neighborhood demonstration grant program contained in both the House and Senate housing authorizations. The program was designed to stimulate neighborhood revitalization.

The Senate panel matched the House-passed figure of $440 million for the Urban Development Action Grants.

Veterans Administration

The Senate committee also recommended an $111.2 million increase over the House figure of $24.8 billion for the VA, including $150 million for a new emergency veterans' job training program authorized under legislation (HR 2355) passed by the House June 7 and the Senate June 15. (Story, p. 599)

EPA Debate

By a vote of 19-0, the Senate committee June 14 adopted an amendment by Jake Garn, R-Utah, chairman of the Appropriations Subcommittee on HUD-Independent Agencies, setting EPA spending at $3.998 billion. That included a $295.5 million increase over the president's recommendation.

Garn's amendment was a virtual carbon copy of the budget request that Ruckelshaus forwarded to the committee through the Office of Management and Budget.

Ruckelshaus asked for $410 million to spend on superfund hazardous waste cleanup, $100 million more than Reagan sought. His request also included $574.9 million for salaries and expenses, $142.7 million for research

and development, $393.9 million for abatement, control and compliance, and $2.6 million for building and facilities.

The Senate panel agreed to those levels and added $30 million more to the construction grants budget.

A group of senators led by Patrick J. Leahy, D-Vt., sought to provide even more money, arguing that the extra funds were needed to restore the embattled agency's effectiveness. Leahy offered an amendment to give the agency $4.127 billion but it failed, 12-14.

The Senate committee retained the House language establishing a one-year moratorium on imposition of EPA sanctions against cities not meeting certain Clean Air Act standards.

Other funding levels included:

● **National Science Foundation.** The Senate panel trimmed $22.7 million from the National Science Foundation (NSF) budget of $1.3 billion set by the House.

● **Government National Mortgage Association.** The Senate panel set a loan limitation on Ginnie Mae's mortgage-backed securities program at the 1983 level of $68.25 billion, $9.6 billion more than requested.

● **Solar Energy Bank.** The Senate committee accepted an amendment by Dale Bumpers, D-Ark., setting funding for the Solar Energy and Conservation Bank at $25 million, the same level recommended by the House.

● **FEMA.** The committee restored $36.3 million the House trimmed from the president's request of $522.4 million for the Federal Emergency Management Agency. The total funding recommended by the committee was $467.1 million, compared to $430.8 million set by the House.

Senate Floor Action

The Senate June 21 passed the committee bill with little change by a vote of 80-14, after rejecting an attempt by John Heinz, R-Pa., and Donald W. Riegle Jr., D-Mich., to add to the bill a revised mortgage relief program for unemployed homeowners. (Vote 162, p. 29-S)

The amendment, similar to a mortgage aid provision the Senate dropped earlier in the day from a housing authorization bill (S 1338 — S Rept 98-142), was tabled by a vote of 55-39. (Vote 161, p. 29-S)

Under the Heinz-Riegle amendment, the federal government would have guaranteed loans from private lenders to help unemployed homeowners meet their monthly mortgage payments. The government would guarantee up to 90 percent of the loan.

In an effort to head off critics, Heinz and Riegle had cut the total loans that could be guaranteed from $750 million to $500 million and reduced the length of the program from two years to one year. Also, aid would have been targeted to those areas that needed it most.

Other Amendments

Other amendments were by:

● Charles McC. Mathias Jr., R-Md., to earmark $5 million of the EPA budget for the Chesapeake Bay study to improve the quality of the bay. Adopted by voice vote.

● Robert T. Stafford, R-Vt., to transfer $6.415 million from EPA's Hazardous Substance Response Trust Fund to the Department of Health and Human Services to implement its superfund responsibilities. Adopted by voice vote.

● Heinz, to prohibit the secretary of HUD from selling any mortgage held as security for a loan made under Section 202 of the Housing Act of 1959 without prior congressional approval. Adopted by voice vote.

Appropriations Compared

As passed by the House and Senate, HR 3133 appropriated the following amounts for fiscal 1984.

	House-passed Appropriations	Senate-passed Appropriations
Department of Housing and Urban Development		
Housing Programs	$12,242,880,000	$7,167,304,810
Community Development	3,922,000,000	4,215,200,000
Policy Development and Research	15,000,000	21,000,000
Fair Housing Assistance	4,700,000	4,700,000
Management and Administration	300,000,000	300,950,000
Solar Energy Bank	25,000,000	25,000,000
Total, HUD	$16,509,580,000	$11,734,154,810
Independent Agencies		
American Battle Monuments Commission	10,837,000	10,462,000
Consumer Product Safety Commission	34,500,000	35,000,000
Cemeterial Expenses, Army	8,203,000	8,203,000
Environmental Protection Agency	4,081,600,000	3,998,100,000

	House-passed Appropriations	Senate-passed Appropriations
Council on Environmental Quality	700,000	913,000
Office of Science and Technology Policy	1,950,000	1,950,000
Federal Emergency Management Agency	430,758,000	467,087,000
GSA Consumer Information Center	1,449,000	1,349,000
HHS Office of Consumer Affairs	2,011,000	2,011,000
National Aeronautics and Space Administration	7,176,500,000	7,171,500,000
National Credit Union Administration	(600,000,000)	(600,000,000)
National Science Foundation	1,315,300,000	1,292,600,000
Neighborhood Reinvestment Corporation	15,512,000	15,512,000
Selective Service System	24,049,000	24,649,000
Treasury Department:		
General Revenue Sharing	Deferred	4,566,700,000
Salaries and expenses	7,378,000	7,278,000
Veterans Administration	24,805,761,000	24,916,929,000
GRAND TOTAL	$54,426,088,000	$54,254,397,810 ∎

Energy, Water Fiscal 1984 Funding Cleared

Congress cleared the fiscal 1984 energy and water appropriations bill with unusual alacrity, sending the $14.3 billion bill (HR 3132) to the White House June 29. President Reagan signed the bill into law (PL 98-50) July 14.

The measure provided $10 billion for the Department of Energy, of which $6.5 billion was to fund nuclear weapons development and production.

It also provided $3.6 billion for more than 300 ongoing water projects of the Army Corps of Engineers and the Interior Department's Bureau of Reclamation.

In addition, the measure provided funding for six independent agencies, among them the Nuclear Regulatory Commission and the Tennessee Valley Authority.

No Clinch River, Tenn-Tom, Water Starts

Passage of HR 3132 was facilitated by the fact that the bill contained no funds for the controversial Clinch River nuclear breeder reactor, or for any new water projects. Also, no funds were earmarked for the Tennessee-Tombigbee Waterway. In 1982 controversy over the Clinch River and Tenn-Tom projects slowed action on the fiscal 1983 bill to the point that it did not clear. *(1982 Almanac p. 292)*

Work on the Tenn-Tom, which was intended to carry barge traffic from Appalachian coal fields to the Gulf Coast, could continue with $180 million available from fiscal 1983.

The Clinch River project, however, apparently met its demise in 1983 as the Senate in October refused to appropriate any further money for its construction. *(Story, p. 362)*

Funds for new water projects were contained in a supplemental appropriations bill for fiscal 1984 (HR 3958) that passed the House in 1983 but did not reach the Senate floor. *(Story, p. 520)*

PL 98-50 did contain funds for two controversial water projects — the Stonewall Jackson Dam in West Virginia and the Garrison Diversion unit in North Dakota. Neither project was funded by the House when it first passed HR 3132.

The measure also contained $50 million to be used to build production facilities for a new nuclear-tipped artillery shell that the House, but not the Senate, had approved.

Funding Levels

The Energy Department and the other agencies funded by this measure operated during fiscal 1983 with funding provided in the second fiscal 1983 continuing appropriations resolution. *(1982 Almanac p. 292)*

PL 98-50 contained $303.6 million less than the administration requested, and $228.6 million less than the component programs had received in fiscal 1983.

Most of the reduction from the request level was due to the omission of any funds for the Clinch River project, for which the administration had sought $270 million.

House Committee Action

The House Appropriations Committee May 24 reported a $14.2 billion version of HR 3132 (H Rept 98-217). Before reporting the bill, the committee responded to administration pressure by cutting $236.5 million — 3 percent — from the non-defense portion of the bill.

The cut was made after David A. Stockman, director of the Office of Management and Budget (OMB), warned he would recommend a veto unless reductions were made from the version approved May 12 by the Energy and Water Development Subcommittee.

Stockman issued the warning in a May 23 meeting with several committee Republicans and in a letter to

Energy/Water Final Appropriations

Following are the Department of Energy appropriations contained in HR 3132 (PL 98-50). The chart shows the administration request for fiscal 1984, the amounts approved by the House and Senate, and the final amount as cleared by Congress *(amounts in thousands of dollars):*

	Administration Request	House- Passed Amount*	Senate- Passed Amount	Final Amount
Army Corps of Engineers				
Construction	$ 820,700	$ 892,829	$ 885,779	$ 894,104
Operation & maintenance	1,161,300	1,215,032	1,170,620	1,184,492
Flood control, Mississippi River & tributaries	290,000	310,330	297,960	300,480
Other flood control, coastal emergencies	10,000	10,000	10,000	10,000
Other	219,400	267,233	227,435	252,310
Subtotal	2,501,400	2,695,424	2,591,794	2,641,386
Bureau of Reclamation				
Construction	699,388	711,538	683,818	693,818
Operation & maintenance	134,091	134,291	134,291	134,291
Other	127,731	142,151	126,881	133,581
Subtotal	961,210	987,980	944,990	961,690
Department of Energy (DOE)				
Energy Supply, Research and Development	2,099,625	1,964,209	1,943,709	1,951,609
Uranium Enrichment	2,240,000	2,235,000	2,235,000	2,235,000
(Gross Revenues)	(2,240,000)	(2,235,000)	(2,235,000)	(2,235,000)
General Science, Research	645,250	643,250	635,250	638,250
Nuclear Waste Disposal Fund	306,675	306,675	306,675	306,675
Atomic Energy Defense Activities	6,825,575	6,558,375	6,500,875	6,547,875
Administration	351,491	371,056	361,056	366,056
(Miscellaneous revenues)	(209,619)	(209,619)	(209,619)	(34,078)
Power Marketing Administrations				
Alaska Power Administration	3,210	3,410	3,410	3,410
Bonneville Power Administration borrowing authority	203,500	123,400	123,400	123,400
Southeastern Power Administration	20,594	20,594	20,594	20,594
Southwestern Power Administration	36,229	36,229	36,229	36,229
Western Area Power Administration	220,130	185,130	205,130	195,130
Subtotal, Power Marketing Administrations	483,663	368,763	388,763	378,763
Federal Energy Regulatory Commission (FERC)	94,582	89,582	94,582	89,582
(Revenues applied)	(60,000)	(60,000)	(60,000)	(60,000)
Subtotal, FERC	34,582	29,582	34,582	29,582
Geothermal Resources Development Fund	2,100	2,100	2,100	2,100
Subtotal, DOE	10,539,342	10,034,391	9,963,391	10,011,291
Independent Agencies				
Nuclear Regulatory Commission	466,800	465,800	466,800	465,800
Tennessee Valley Authority	61,229	78,679	75,229	78,229
Appalachian Regional Commission, regional development programs	80,000	152,500	127,700	147,700
Delaware River Basin Commission	460	460	460	460
Interstate Commission on the Potomac River Basin	—	68	68	68
Susquehanna River Basin Commission	230	421	421	421
Water Resources Council	—	—	—	—
Subtotal	608,719	697,928	670,678	692,678
General Reduction	—	−235,720	—	—
GRAND TOTAL	**$14,610,671**	**$14,180,003**	**$14,170,853**	**$14,307,045**

* The general reduction in the House-passed total was to be taken from all items except atomic energy and defense activities. Although the administration had some latitude in determining how much each item would be cut, each figure, except the grand total and the atomic energy defense activities line, probably would be about 3 percent lower than indicated in the chart.

Chairman Jamie L. Whitten, D-Miss.

The 3 percent non-defense cut was a compromise offered by John T. Myers, R-Ind., and adopted by voice vote with a handful of dissenting votes. The Myers amendment provided that no line item could be reduced by more than 5 percent. The administration would decide how much to cut from each item and report back to the committee for approval. Myers said the cut was "not a scalpel knife approach, just a shave."

Funding for atomic energy defense activities — $6.6 billion, the largest item in the bill — was exempted from the 3 percent cut. The defense figure already represented a $267.2 million reduction from the administration's budget request.

The committee bill contained no funds for the Clinch River project. Two weeks before the committee vote, the House had voted 388-1 to bar further funding for the project unless Congress approved a new plan for financing it. *(Vote 104, p. 36-H)*

The committee version of HR 3132 also contained no construction funds for the Garrison Diversion project in North Dakota, for which the administration had requested $22.3 million. *(Garrison diversion, p. 356)*

Nor did it contain money for new water project construction. The committee was awaiting action by the House Public Works and Transportation Committee on a water resources authorization bill. *(Water projects, p. 354)*

In addition, there was no money in the bill for the controversial Tenn-Tom project. But Tom Bevill, D-Ala., chairman of the Appropriations Subcommittee on Energy and Water Development, said $180 million in previously appropriated but as yet unspent funding remained available to complete work on the navigation features of the project.

Bevill said the overall committee bill was $330 million less than fiscal 1983 funding provided under PL 97-377, the second continuing appropriations resolution for that year. It was $405 million below Reagan's request and about $1 billion below the target set by the House-passed fiscal 1984 budget resolution. *(Budget resolution, p. 435)*

House Floor Action

With little of the controversy that had surrounded the measure in recent years, the House June 7 passed HR 3132 by a vote of 379-39. *(Vote 160, p. 50-H)*

As passed, the bill appropriated a total of $14,180,003,000 in budget authority.

Stonewall Jackson Dam Deleted

In an unusual episode, freshman Rep. Bob Wise, D-W.Va., succeeded in deleting funds for the proposed Stonewall Jackson Dam in his own district. The House by a vote of 213-161 adopted Wise's amendment deleting $26 million for this dam. Wise's action broke with the tradition that members seek to win such "pork-barrel" projects for their districts rather than to keep such projects out. *(Vote 156, p. 50-H)*

Although every other member of the West Virginia congressional delegation supported the project, Wise successfully argued that there were cheaper methods of flood control that should be considered before the dam, first authorized in 1965, was built. The dam was originally expected to cost $34 million. By 1983, $83 million had been spent and the total cost estimate had risen to $205 million. The $26 million sought for fiscal 1984 was for initial construction work.

Other Water Projects

HR 3132 contained more than $3.5 billion for 206 Corps of Engineers and 95 Bureau of Reclamation ongoing water projects.

With no funding provided for Tenn-Tom, or for new starts, debate on this section of the bill was relatively tame.

Most ongoing water projects were funded at or near the levels proposed by the administration.

Bob Edgar, D-Pa., attempted to cut about $56 million from the Bureau of Reclamation's Dolores and Dallas Creek projects in Colorado, arguing that the bureau had not renegotiated adequate contracts for repayment of construction costs by local users.

But Ray Kogovsek, D-Colo., said the Dallas Creek project was exempt from contract renegotiation requirements. Bevill also opposed Edgar's amendment, which was rejected 140-257. *(Vote 158, p. 50-H)*

MX Missile Warheads

HR 3132 contained $20 million for constructing MX missile warhead production facilities.

The House by voice vote adopted an amendment proposed by Bevill that prohibited expenditure of any of those funds until Congress had authorized MX missile construction and deployment. *(MX story, p. 195)*

Energy Projects

Almost two-thirds of the $10 billion provided to the Department of Energy in the bill was for nuclear weapons programs.

An amendment by F. James Sensenbrenner Jr., R-Wis., to eliminate $10 million earmarked for energy research laboratories at Catholic University in Washington, D.C., and Columbia University in New York City was rejected 105-312. *(Vote 159, p. 50-H)*

Senate Committee Action

The Senate Appropriations Committee approved HR 3132 June 16 by voice vote. As reported (S Rept 98-153), the bill contained $14.2 billion in new budget authority.

Clinch River. Like the House version of the bill, the Senate committee bill contained no funds for the Clinch River breeder reactor project. The panel said it would consider funding for Clinch River if a satisfactory financing plan could be worked out with the private sector.

Water Projects. Again like the House version, the Senate bill contained no money for new water projects, although the committee said it would consider providing such funds at a later date if an authorization bill passed.

The Senate committee did restore the $26 million for the Stonewall Jackson Dam, and it included $22.3 million for the Garrison Diversion unit in North Dakota, which the House declined to fund. But the committee specified that none of the Garrison Diversion funds could be used for parts of the project that would affect Canadian waters. (Canada opposed the project).

MX Missile Warheads. Also approved by the panel was the full $30 million requested by the administration for the construction of MX missile warhead production facilities.

Solar Energy. Although less than 2 percent of the Energy Department's money was devoted to solar energy research, it claimed a significant share of senatorial atten-

tion. The administration proposed to slash funding for the program from a fiscal 1983 level of $202 million to less than $87 million for fiscal 1984.

However, the House voted $180 million and the Senate committee approved $176 million.

The Senate panel made the following argument for continued solar energy research: "The committee agrees that the marketplace must ultimately decide the future role of the solar technologies. The committee does not agree, however, that most solar and renewables research has been developed to the point where the private sector alone can be expected to carry forward with its development."

Senate Floor Action

The Senate approved HR 3132 June 22 by a vote of 91-6. *(Vote 164, p. 30-S)*

As passed, the measure provided $14.17 billion in funding for fiscal 1984.

Garrison Diversion Unit

The only significant floor debate came on an amendment that would have deleted the $22.3 million provided for construction work on the Garrison Diversion unit. It was tabled by a vote of 62-35. *(Vote 163, p. 29-S)*

Gordon J. Humphrey, R-N.H., sponsor of that amendment, argued that the project, designed to take water from the Missouri River in the western part of North Dakota and pump it east for irrigation and municipal water supplies, was not needed and would damage wildlife habitat.

Humphrey said the Garrison unit, with an estimated total cost of $1.1 billion, had a poor cost-benefit ratio and was not needed for irrigation since the United States already had a farm surplus.

In addition, he noted, the project was opposed by the Canadian government, which was concerned about adverse impact from the runoff downstream in the Red River, which flows into Canada.

Humphrey's amendment was opposed by North Dakota Sens. Mark Andrews, a Republican, and Quentin N. Burdick, a Democrat.

Conference/Final Action

Conferees resolved their differences and filed their report (H Rept 98-272) June 28 on a $14.3 billion version of HR 3132.

The final bill appropriated more money than either the House-passed version or the Senate version. The total was $127 million higher than the House amount and $136.2 million above the Senate figure.

But it still was $303.6 million less than the administration requested and $228.6 million less than fiscal 1983 spending.

Even though the bill's total was below the administration request, concerns were voiced throughout its consideration about the possibility of a veto. Administration officials pointed out that most of the reduction came from the elimination of the $270 million sought for Clinch River. That project aside, the bill was close to the administration request.

The bill did not include money for new water project construction. But both Appropriations committees appeared sympathetic to consideration of a supplemental appropriations bill for new projects if they were authorized.

Garrison Unit, Stonewall Jackson Dam

Conferees retained the Senate-approved funding for the Stonewall Jackson Dam and the Garrison Diversion unit.

Rep. Wise, who succeeded in convincing the House to delete funds for the dam — which was in his district — was in the audience as conferees accepted the Senate version. It provided $26 million requested by the administration for work on the project in fiscal 1984.

Sen. Robert C. Byrd, D-W.Va., who said he had called 124 members of the House seeking support for the Senate position, extolled the project's virtues and carried the day. Project opponent Silvio O. Conte, R-Mass., simply said, "I can count the votes."

North Dakota Sens. Burdick and Andrews were on hand to defend the Garrison project, which had received $22.3 million in the Senate bill and nothing in the House.

Conferees restored the money after Burdick and Andrews agreed to accept language stating that none of the funds could be used to build features of the project that affected water flowing north into Canada in any harmful way. Garrison opponents, including the Canadian government, contended the project would result in destruction of wildlife habitat and pollute Canadian waters.

An indication that the House was not adamant in its opposition to funding Garrison came June 23 when a motion by Conte to instruct the conferees to insist on the House position was defeated, 150-215. *(Vote 208, p. 64-H)*

MX Warheads, Nuclear Artillery Shells

The Senate's $30 million appropriation for MX missile production facilities was approved by the conferees, who also retained Senate report language requiring that before the money was spent, approval had to be obtained from the congressional Appropriations and Armed Services committees.

The House had appropriated $20 million.

The House-passed appropriation of $50 million for production facilities for the nuclear artillery shell was approved by conferees after lengthy discussion. But Senate conferees were able to add language that prohibited use of the money unless:

● The president certified to Congress that an old 155mm nuclear shell was being removed from the stockpile for each new one that was added, and,

● Any North Atlantic Treaty Organization member due to have such weapons deployed notified the United States that it approved of deployment of the new weapons.

Savannah River Nuclear Reactor

Conferees also approved language permitting resumption of work to restart the Savannah River L-Reactor in South Carolina. The reactor, which produced material for nuclear weapons, had been shut down since 1968 because its production was not needed. DOE had been trying to restart it since 1980.

Conferees retained Senate language designed to ensure that the plant met state water pollution standards. They called for an expedited environmental impact study, which was due by Jan. 1, 1984.

Final Action

The House adopted the conference report June 29 by a vote of 337-82. *(Vote 218, p. 66-H)*

The Senate cleared the measure the same day by a vote of 82-12. *(Vote 176, p. 31-S)* ∎

Labor-HHS-Education Money Bill Cleared

Congress Oct. 20 cleared a $104.4 billion measure making appropriations for the departments of Labor, Health and Human Services (HHS) and Education and for various smaller agencies.

President Reagan signed the bill (HR 3913 — PL 98-139) Oct. 31.

Enactment of HR 3913 marked the first time in five years that the programs funded in the bill were covered by an appropriations measure fashioned specifically for them. In the recent past, controversies over such subjects as abortion and the busing of school children to achieve desegregation stalled the legislation and required spending for Labor-HHS programs to be included in stopgap continuing appropriations bills. *(Continuing resolution, 1982 Almanac p. 250)*

HR 3913 appropriated $96.5 billion for fiscal 1984 and $7.9 billion for fiscal years 1985-86. For fiscal 1984, it set aside $15.9 billion for the Department of Labor, $64.7 billion for HHS, $15.2 billion for the Education Department and $593.5 million for other agencies, including the Federal Mediation and Conciliation Service, the National Labor Relations Board and the Railroad Retirement Board. *(Further funding, p. 528)*

The bill contained $8.6 billion more in spending than President Reagan had proposed in his budget request.

HR 3913 earmarked $64.5 billion in mandatory spending in fiscal 1984 and $32.1 billion for discretionary expenditures. Mandatory spending is money for federal entitlement programs whose funding is mandated by law. Funding levels for discretionary spending are set annually through appropriations.

The House Appropriations Committee reported HR 3913 Sept. 16 (H Rept 98-357), and the House passed it Sept. 22. The Senate Appropriations Committee reported its version Sept. 28 (S Rept 98-247). The Senate passed the measure Oct. 4.

Conferees met Oct. 18 and had little difficulty settling differences between the House and Senate versions of the bill, emerging with higher spending levels than those set by either chamber. They accepted the Senate bill's figures for many programs because they were based on more recent estimates provided by the Congressional Budget Office.

Final action came when the Senate Oct. 20 adopted the conference report on the bill (H Rept 98-422) by voice vote. The House had approved the conference report earlier in the day by a 323-79 vote. *(Vote 380, p. 112-H)*

Provisions

As signed into law, HR 3913 provided the following specific amounts for the departments of Labor, HHS and Education and related agencies:

	Budget Request	Final Amount
Labor Department		
Employment and Training Administration		
Program administration	$ 86,271,000	$ 82,739,000
Training and employment services	3,593,930,000	6,419,408,000
Community service employment for older Americans	277,100,000	317,300,000
Federal unemployment benefits	7,000,000	12,000,000
Grants to states for unemployment insurance and employment services	25,700,000	72,500,000
Advances to unemployment trust fund	7,109,000,000	7,109,000,000
Labor-Management Services Administration	64,130,000	62,136,000
Employment Standards Administration	1,227,935,000	1,260,527,000
Occupational Safety and Health Administration	210,860,000	212,560,000
Mine Safety and Health Administration	148,032,000	151,397,000
Bureau of Labor Statistics	136,290,000	136,587,000
Departmental Management	133,298,000	132,833,000
Total, Labor Department	13,019,546,000	15,968,987,000
Health and Human Services		
Health resources and services	1,036,816,000	1,304,105,000
Medical facilities guarantee and loan fund	32,000,000	32,000,000
Centers for Disease Control	340,752,000	374,504,000
National Institutes of Health		
Cancer	963,881,000	1,053,442,000
Heart, Lung and Blood	609,248,000	674,674,000
Dental Research	76,944,000	84,312,000
Arthritis, Diabetes, and Digestive and Kidney Diseases	406,505,000	442,543,000
Neurological and Communicative Disorders and Stroke	292,345,000	325,502,000
Allergy and Infectious Diseases	280,809,000	305,678,000
General Medical Sciences	338,255,000	366,844,000
Child Health and Human Development	247,295,000	265,014,000
Eye	138,748,000	150,783,000
Environmental Health Sciences	160,565,000	173,000,000
Aging	97,240,000	112,300,000
Research resources	201,117,000	241,928,000
John E. Fogarty Center	9,189,000	11,336,000
National Library of Medicine	41,963,000	42,113,000
Director	26,720,000	26,720,000

	Budget Request	Final Amount
Buildings and facilities	19,900,000	25,040,000
Alcohol, Drug Abuse and Mental Health Administration	771,152,000	828,869,000
St. Elizabeths Hospital	62,744,000	67,744,000
Assistant secretary for health	201,815,000	187,349,000
Health Care Financing Administration	33,006,016,000	33,340,308,000
(Fiscal 1985 advance)	(5,552,000,000)	(5,552,000,000)
Social Security Administration		
Payments to Social Security trust funds	838,583,000	521,258,000
Black lung payments	1,027,047,000	1,068,000,000
Supplemental Security Income	7,851,518,000	8,223,000,000
Assistance payments	5,376,406,000	6,142,000,000
(Fiscal 1985 advance)	(1,758,454,000)	(2,073,000,000)
Child support enforcement	298,463,000	432,000,000
(Fiscal 1985 advance)	(102,750,000)	(138,000,000)
Low-income energy assistance	1,300,000,000	1,875,000,000
Refugee resettlement	485,328,000	(deferred)
Assistant secretary for human development	4,784,022,000	5,421,313,000
Community services	2,852,000	352,300,000
Departmental management	288,589,000	274,071,000
(Fiscal 1985 advance)	(9,000,000)	(9,000,000)
Total, HHS	61,614,827,000	64,745,050,000
(Fiscal 1985 advance)	(7,422,204,000)	(7,772,000,000)

Education Department

	Budget Request	Final Amount
Compensatory education	3,013,969,000	3,487,500,000
Special programs	478,879,000	527,867,000
Impact aid	455,000,000	585,000,000
Bilingual education	94,534,000	139,365,000
Handicapped education	1,110,252,000	1,214,445,000
Rehabilitation services	1,031,727,000	1,111,400,000
Vocational and adult education	492,839,000	831,314,000
College student assistance	3,517,800,000	3,976,860,000
Guaranteed student loans	2,047,100,000	2,256,500,000
Higher and continuing education	204,716,000	408,366,000
Higher education facilities loans	19,846,000	19,846,000
Education research and statistics	56,978,000	56,978,000
Overseas activities	1,750,000	1,133,000
Libraries	——	86,880,000
Special institutions	228,500,000	228,500,000
Departmental management	293,429,000	292,385,000
Total, Education Department	13,047,319,000	15,224,339,000

Related agencies

	Budget Request	Final Amount
ACTION	109,730,000	(deferred)

	Budget Request	Final Amount
Corporation for Public Broadcasting (Fiscal 1986 advance)	(75,000,000)	(130,000,000)
Federal Mediation and Conciliation Service	21,461,000	23,161,000
Federal Mine Safety and Health Review Commission	3,858,000	3,858,000
National Commission on Libraries and Information Science	553,000	674,000
National Labor Relations Board	134,158,000	133,594,000
National Mediation Board	5,758,000	6,238,000
Occupational Safety and Health Review Commission	6,331,000	5,982,000
Railroad Retirement Board	350,000,000	420,000,000
Total, related agencies	631,849,000	593,507,000
(Fiscal 1986 advance)	(75,000,000)	(130,000,000)
Total, Fiscal 1984	$88,313,541,000	$96,531,883,000
(Fiscal 1985 advance)	(7,422,204,000)	(7,772,000,000)
(Fiscal 1986 advance)	(75,000,000)	(130,000,000)
Grand total	**$95,810,745,000**	**$104,433,883,000**

House Committee Action

As reported by the House Appropriations Committee Sept. 16, the $96.2 billion measure outspent the president's budget requests by $3.5 billion. It did not, however, contain money for several programs that had not been authorized for fiscal 1984 by the time the committee acted. Programs affected included alcohol, drug abuse and mental health research training, the refugee program of the Social Security Administration and impact aid, the program providing funds to school districts that educate large numbers of children of federal employees.

The House bill contained the following amounts for some of the government's largest programs: $13.1 billion for the Labor Department, $62.7 billion for the Department of Health and Human Services — including $38 billion for Medicare and Medicaid — $12.2 billion for the Department of Education and $815.9 million for related agencies.

Labor Department

For the Department of Labor, the House committee approved $13.1 billion, $41.7 million more than the president had requested and $3.9 billion below fiscal 1983 funding. The discrepancies between funding levels for fiscal years 1983 and 1984 were caused by administration plans to phase out some programs — the unemployment provisions of the Trade Act of 1974, for example — and the transfer of programs to other accounts.

Most of the funding — $11.1 billion — was earmarked for the Employment and Training Administration. The fiscal 1984 amount for the agency was $39.2 million above the budget request but nearly $4 billion less than was

provided in fiscal 1983. Part of the money — $6.4 billion — was to fund the Job Training Partnership Act through June 30, 1985. *(1982 Almanac p. 39)*

Other major items included:

Community Service. The panel approved $317.3 million for the community service employment program for older Americans. The politically popular program was funded at $40.2 million over the president's request and at about the same amount the program received in fiscal 1983.

Unemployment, Black Lung. The committee set aside $7.1 billion in advances to the unemployment trust fund, the Employment Security Administration and the black lung disability trust fund. This was the same amount as requested in the budget and $5.3 billion below fiscal 1983 levels.

Occupational Safety. The committee bill provided $212.6 million for the Occupational Safety and Health Administration (OSHA), $1.7 million above the budget and $6 million over the fiscal 1983 amount. The committee, as it did in 1982, rejected an administration proposal to delete language in the appropriations measure limiting OSHA activities, particularly routine inspections of small, relatively safe businesses. The bill also prohibited OSHA inspections of businesses that have been visited by state safety inspectors within the past six months.

Mine Safety. The committee approved $151.4 million for the Mine Safety and Health Administration, an increase of $3.4 million over the administration's budget request and almost $1 million below 1983 levels.

Health and Human Services

The House committee approved $62.7 billion for the Department of Health and Human Services, $1.6 billion above the president's budget figure and $1 billion more than the fiscal 1983 level. Major items included:

Health Resources. $1.3 billion for health resources and services, $215.9 million more than the budget and $1.8 million above the fiscal 1983 amount. The programs covered included maternal and child health block grants, community health centers and the National Health Service Corps.

Disease Control. $373.4 million for the Centers for Disease Control, $32.7 million more than the president's request and $22.1 million above the fiscal 1983 level. The money included $9.3 million to combat Acquired Immune Deficiency Syndrome (AIDS), part of $41 million in AIDS funding in the bill.

National Institutes of Health. $4.3 billion for the National Institutes of Health (NIH). The NIH funding represented an increase of $386.3 million over the budget request and $470.9 million over the fiscal 1983 figures. The House committee awarded each of the 11 NIH institutes an increase above the budget request. As in years past, the National Cancer Institute received the highest level of funding, with $1 billion.

Alcohol, Drug Abuse, Mental Health. $799.2 million for alcohol, drug abuse and mental health programs, $28 million more than the amount requested in the budget and $38.9 million more than was appropriated for fiscal 1983.

Public Health Service Programs. $106.9 million for public health service programs, $15.9 million below the president's budget request and $12.9 million above the fiscal 1983 level.

Medicaid. $20.7 billion for the mandatory federal share of state Medicaid costs. This was the same amount

requested by the budget and $1.4 billion above the amount for fiscal 1983. The committee report noted that, because cost-saving legislation backed by the administration had not been enacted, the grants to the states would fall short and would have to be covered by a supplemental appropriation.

Medicare. $17.3 billion, the amount requested by the administration, for health care trust funds for Medicare benefits. This was $1.9 billion above the 1983 funding amount.

Social Security. $448.6 million for the Social Security trust funds, $390 million below the budget request and $406.6 million less than the 1983 figure. The report explained that because the budget requests were made before enactment of the Social Security Amendments of 1983 (PL 98-21), they did not take into consideration the money transferred to the Social Security System by that law. The Congressional Budget Office had estimated that the changes made by PL 98-21 would reduce fiscal 1984 costs by about $390 million.

Supplemental Security Income. $7.9 billion for the Supplemental Security Income program, the same amount as requested in the budget and $692 million below fiscal 1983. For welfare programs such as Aid to Families with Dependent Children, the committee agreed to the administration's budget requests.

Child Support Enforcement. $298.5 million for the Child Support Enforcement program, an amount equal to the administration's request. In its report, however, the committee claimed the program was chronically underfunded and said it expected the president to submit a supplemental spending request.

Energy Assistance. $1.9 billion for low-income energy assistance, a program that enjoyed wide popularity in Congress. The committee's amount was $575 million more than was included in the budget request and $100 million less than was provided in fiscal 1983.

Human Development. $1.8 billion for human development services, including Head Start and programs for the aging, runaways and Native Americans. The committee's amount was $92.2 million over the budget request and $66.6 million above the fiscal 1983 level.

Family Services. $617.2 million for family social services, including the federal foster care program. This figure was $15.7 million over the budget and $44.6 million above the fiscal 1983 amount.

Work Incentives. $270.8 million — the amount appropriated in fiscal 1983 — in work incentives for individuals who received Aid to Families with Dependent Children. The administration's budget had proposed to eliminate this program.

Community Service Block Grants. $351 million for the grants, an increase of $348 million over the budget request. The administration had proposed shifting community service grants to the Social Services Block Grant program.

Education

The committee approved $12.2 billion for the Department of Education, an amount $684 million above the administration's budget request and $1.4 billion below the levels appropriated in fiscal 1983.

The House committee bill provided:

Compensatory Aid. $3.5 billion for the basic program of federal aid to elementary and secondary education, compensatory education for the disadvantaged. The budget

request was $473.5 million below the committee amount. In fiscal 1983, the program had been funded at $3.2 billion.

Block Grants. $577.3 million for the block grant program authorized by the Education Consolidation and Improvement Act of 1981. This was $98.4 million more than the administration had requested and $42.8 million more than the program received in fiscal 1983.

Bilingual Education. $138 million for bilingual education, the same amount as funded in fiscal 1983 and $43.5 million more than the budget.

Handicapped. $1.2 billion for education programs for the handicapped, $49.5 million above the amount appropriated for fiscal 1983. The administration had requested that funding for this program remain at the 1983 level.

Vocational and Adult Education. $835 million for vocational and adult education, $342.2 million more than the administration request and $18.5 million more than had been approved for fiscal 1983. The committee approved $735 million for vocational education, $100 million for adult education.

College Student Aid. $3.7 billion for college student financial assistance, $179.6 million above the budget figure and $129.6 million over the fiscal 1983 funding level.

Higher Education. $394.3 million for higher education programs, including programs for disadvantaged students, aid to colleges and universities and construction loans. The figure was $194.4 million over the administration's budget amount and $590,000 below the fiscal 1983 amount.

Library Services. $88.8 million to improve library services, $8.5 million above the amount appropriated for fiscal 1983. The budget included no funds for libraries.

House Floor Action

The House Sept. 22 approved HR 3913 by a 310-101 vote. *(Vote 336, p. 100-H)*

As approved by the House, HR 3913 included about $3.8 billion more in discretionary spending than President Reagan's budget request. But it was well below the amounts for discretionary spending established in the fiscal 1984 budget resolution (H Con Res 91) approved by Congress June 23. Comparisons were inexact because HR 3913 did not include money for some programs that were not yet authorized but that were included in the budget resolution. *(Budget resolution, p. 435)*

The measure passed the House easily despite a fight over abortions for poor women and a squabble over education spending between the Democratic leadership and an appropriations subcommittee chairman.

Democrats on Spending

Democratic leaders felt the bill did not contain enough education money. The House adopted an amendment by Majority Leader Jim Wright, D-Texas, to add $300 million for education, and Democrats said more fiscal 1984 education money — at least $450 million more — would be added when the House considered a stopgap, continuing appropriations resolution that had to be enacted before the end of the fiscal year on Sept. 30. However, efforts to add money to the continuing resolution ultimately failed.

As passed by the House, the measure provided $13.2 billion for the Labor Department, $70.1 billion for HHS, $12.4 billion for the Education Department and $593.4 million for several independent agencies.

Abortion Funding

In the House Sept. 23, most of the debate focused on funding for abortion and education.

As approved by the Appropriations Committee, HR 3913 included language that had been a standard feature of the law since 1977, permitting the use of Medicaid money for abortions only when the life of the mother was in danger. Medicaid was the state-federal health care program for the poor.

But Les AuCoin, D-Ore., argued that the language required federal officials to make a determination as to whether a pregnant woman's life was threatened. This, AuCoin said, constituted legislation in an appropriations bill, something that was prohibited by the House rules.

AuCoin's argument was upheld and the prohibition on federal abortion funding was stricken from the bill. However, the House then voted 231-184 for an amendment by the ranking Republican on the Appropriations Committee, Silvio O. Conte, Mass., prohibiting any of the bill's funds from paying for abortions, regardless of the mother's health. *(Vote 334, p. 100-H)*

Education Spending

The fight over funding levels for education programs arose because of the Appropriations Committee's failure to include in the measure programs that were not authorized, including some large items like impact aid. Other programs that had been authorized were provided less money than allowed under the budget resolution.

Some of the authorization problems were taken care of by the House Sept. 13 when it increased by $1.6 billion the authorizations of 12 programs, including grants for the education of the poor and the handicapped. But the Senate did not act on the increased authorizations and, even if it had, the president likely would have vetoed the bill (HR 3520). *(Story, p. 402)*

The amendment to increase education funding by $300 million was the result of a compromise engineered by Wright. It was adopted 302-111. *(Vote 335, p. 100-H)*

As first adopted, Wright's amendment included $400 million, but at Conte's insistence, this was reduced by 25 percent. Wright said the amendment increased spending for six education programs to slightly below their authorized ceilings.

The Wright amendment added $100 million to the Pell grants program, which provided financial aid for needy college students, $100 million for the training programs authorized by the Job Training Partnership Act (PL 97-300), $45 million for handicapped education, $25 million for the Head Start program, $16 million for incentive grants for state scholarships, $10 million for special programs for disadvantaged students, known as the TRIO program, and $4 million for bilingual education.

Senate Committee Action

The Senate Appropriations Committee reported HR 3913 (S Rept 98-357) on Sept. 28.

Responding to the pleas of its leaders, the committee refrained from adding costly, controversial amendments that could have delayed the measure or created White House opposition.

Because the bill had not been enacted by the Oct. 1 start of fiscal 1984, funds for the programs in HR 3913 were included in the stopgap, continuing appropriations resolution (H J Res 368) that cleared Congress Oct. 1. *(First*

1984 continuing resolution, p. 526)

The Senate committee's version of HR 3913 included $4 billion less in total spending than the version approved by the House and $1.2 billion more than Reagan's budget request.

As approved by the Senate panel, HR 3913 included $60.4 billion in mandatory spending and $29.2 billion in discretionary funds.

The House bill contained $67.9 billion in mandatory spending. The discrepancy was caused by the Senate committee's use of updated, lower spending projections provided by the Congressional Budget Office.

Unlike the House, the Senate did not decline to include in its version of the measure programs still awaiting authorization.

Sen. Lowell P. Weicker Jr., R-Conn., chairman of the Appropriations Subcommittee on Labor, Health and Human Services, Education and Related Agencies, was able to fend off most amendments to add money to the bill during markup. The largest increase accepted by the committee was on an amendment offered by Pete V. Domenici, R-N.M., to provide an extra $64.7 million for the TRIO program. The amendment made TRIO funding in the Senate version of the bill equal to the amount approved by the House. Domenici's amendment was adopted by voice.

Busing, Abortion

The committee approved by voice vote three amendments to reinstate language in the bill prohibiting the use of funds for school busing. Offered by Thomas F. Eagleton, D-Mo., the amendments restored bans on the use of money in the bill to bus schoolchildren for purposes of desegregation. The language, which had been removed by Weicker's subcommittee, had been part of the bill in one form or another since 1969, Eagleton said. *(Busing background, 1975 Almanac p. 894; 1969 Almanac p. 545)*

The committee also adopted an Eagleton amendment to restore the bill's prohibition on the use of federal funds to pay for abortions unless the life of the mother was in danger.

Senate Floor Action

The Senate Oct. 4 passed HR 3913 by a 70-23 vote. *(Vote 272, p. 44-S)*

The bill included $91 billion for fiscal 1984 and advance appropriations for fiscal 1985-86 of $7.9 billion.

In fiscal 1984 spending, the Senate version of HR 3913 contained about $500 million less than the $91.5 billion in the House bill. The Senate bill was about $5 billion above the president's budget request in total spending. But in discretionary spending, the Senate bill was more than $600 million above the House measure.

As passed by the Senate, the Labor-HHS bill provided in fiscal 1984 $11.9 billion for the Labor Department, $64.9 billion for HHS, $13.5 billion for the Education Department and $733.7 million for related agencies.

During Senate debate Oct. 4, several attempts were made to add large amounts of money to the bill, but most were frustrated by Weicker.

The most costly amendment — $900 million for health care for the unemployed — was withdrawn after Weicker assured sponsor Edward M. Kennedy, D-Mass., that he would support the program and would oppose "any proposal that calls for the unemployed to pay for their own health premiums." *(Congressional action on health insur-*

ance for the unemployed, p. 405)

An amendment offered by John Heinz, R-Pa., to add $16 million in grants to reward excellence in education was also withdrawn. Weicker told the Senate: "I believe just as strongly as he [Heinz] does in the subject matter he placed before the Senate. Yet I hope that he would back off."

Education Funds

The most acrimonious debate — and Weicker's strongest appeals for restraint — arose during consideration of an amendment offered by Bill Bradley, D-N.J. Bradley's amendment, offered with presidential contender Ernest F. Hollings, D-S.C., would have added $559 million to the bill for education programs.

Weicker said he understood the temptations of adding more than the White House wanted, but added: "My job is to deliver, not to talk about, assistance to the retarded, to the disabled and disadvantaged and the young kids going to college. I have not delivered and our colleagues have not delivered on this matter in this chamber for five years."

The Bradley amendment was defeated on a parliamentary maneuver, with the chair ruling it out of order because it would provide funds above authorized levels. Bradley appealed the ruling, but his appeal was tabled by a 50-45 vote. *(Vote 270, p. 44-S)*

An amendment by Walter D. Huddleston, D-Ky., to add $50 million to help pay for the removal of asbestos from school buildings was similarly killed when the Senate voted 58-35 to table it. *(Vote 269, p. 44-S)*

An amendment offered by Dan Quayle, R-Ind., also was tabled, 50-44. Quayle's amendment would have increased funding for programs covered by the 1982 Job Training Partnership Act by $364 million. *(Vote 271, p. 44-S)*

Amendments Adopted

The Senate adopted several amendments to the bill, all by voice vote. The largest would provide $130 million in fiscal 1984 for ACTION, the volunteer agency. Funding for ACTION was deferred by the House.

The Senate also adopted two amendments dealing with programs named after former senators. One added almost $2 million for a fellowship program to provide financial aid to first-year graduate students. The program was named the Javits National Graduate Fellowships, after Jacob K. Javits, R-N.Y. (1957-81).

The other added $5 million for the Maureen and Mike Mansfield Foundation, which raised money for the planned Mansfield Center for Pacific Affairs and for the University of Montana's Maureen and Mike Mansfield Center. The foundation was named for former Majority Leader Mike Mansfield, D-Mont. (1953-77), and his wife.

Weicker did not oppose a handful of amendments that added substantial amounts to the bill. But he also predicted correctly that most would not survive the conference with the House. The additions included:

● $30 million for public health emergencies such as the crisis involving AIDS. It was offered by Daniel Patrick Moynihan, D-N.Y.

● $29.7 million for trade adjustment assistance, offered by John C. Danforth, R-Mo.

● $38.3 million for buildings at the University of New Mexico and Boston University, money that was sought by Domenici and Kennedy.

● $9 million for a new building at the University of Pennsylvania Dental School. The addition was sponsored

by Pennsylvania Sen. Arlen Specter, R.

Conference

Some of the unauthorized programs the House had not included in HR 3913 had received authorization by the time the conference met, and funding, much of which had been included by the Senate, was kept in the bill. The largest item was $585 million for impact aid, which was included in the defense authorization bill (S 675 — PL 98-94) cleared by Congress Sept. 15, the day HR 3913 was approved by the House Appropriations Committee. *(Defense authorization, p. 175)*

Conferees also agreed to retain $29.7 million for trade adjustment assistance added as an amendment on the Senate floor by John C. Danforth, R-Mo. A two-year extension (HR 3813 — PL 98-120) of the Trade Adjustment Assistance Program cleared Congress Sept. 30. *(Story, p. 251)*

The conference agreed to the House's inclusion of $7.1 billion in advances to the unemployment trust fund. The Senate put in $3.1 billion. The money was in anticipation of an extension (HR 3929 — PL 98-135) of the federal supplemental unemployment compensation program that Congress cleared Oct. 21. *(Federal supplemental unemployment compensation, p. 274)*

The conference dropped the Senate's $130 million for ACTION, the volunteer agency, because an ACTION reauthorization bill had not been enacted. Funding for ACTION was contained in the continuing resolution Congress cleared Sept. 30. *(ACTION, p. 398)*

Education programs that were so strenuously debated during House and Senate consideration of HR 3913 were not a major issue in the conference. Funding for the popular Pell grants program, which provided aid to needy college students, remained at the Senate level of $2.8 billion, $181 million more than the House amount. ∎

Second Fiscal 1983 Supplemental Bill Cleared

The imminent threat of food stamp cutbacks for thousands of poor families prodded Congress to complete work July 29 on the second of two fiscal 1983 supplemental appropriations bills enacted in 1983.

The measure (HR 3069 — PL 98-63) contained $7 billion, including a $1.2 billion infusion for the food stamp program, money that was needed to avoid a reduction in food benefits in August. Progress on the bill was impeded by a drawn-out struggle in the Senate over senators' annual salaries and limits on their outside earnings. In its final form, the measure raised Senate salaries to the same amount earned by House members, $69,800 a year. It also limited the income senators were able to earn for speeches, articles and appearances to 30 percent of their salaries, or $20,940.

In addition to the food stamp money, the bill included $1.3 billion for Social Security, $785.7 million for increased federal pay costs, $615 million for supplement unemployment benefits, $453.6 million for production of Pershing II missiles, funds to rebuild the U.S. Embassy in Beirut, foreign operations funds and money for water projects.

The year's first supplemental (HR 1718 — PL 98-8) had been approved March 24. *(Supplemental, p. 447)*

The House adopted the framework of the conference report on HR 3069 by a 257-133 vote July 28, but it did not finish the technical details until the next day. The Senate then followed suit on July 29, adopting the conference report on a 49-25 vote and clearing the measure for the president. *(House vote 273, p. 82-H; Senate vote 228, p. 39-S)*

President Reagan signed the measure July 30.

To the disappointment of the Reagan administration, the bill did not contain $8.4 billion to increase the U.S. contribution to the International Monetary Fund (IMF). The House did not include the funds when it passed the supplemental in May, but the Senate added the money to HR 3069 in June.

A conference committee was unable to agree on the IMF funding, with House members insisting the money not be added before legislation (HR 2957) authorizing the increased U.S. contribution was approved by the House. The IMF money later was attached to a non-controversial fiscal 1984 supplemental measure (HR 3959 — PL 98-181) Congress cleared Nov. 18. *(IMF, p. 241)*

In addition to the IMF controversy, the bill contained language added by the conferees to help cotton growers avoid huge financial losses that they feared from the administration's Payment-in-Kind (PIK) acreage reduction program. The House narrowly adopted the language by a 204-191 vote. *(Vote 278, p. 84-H; PIK, p. 380)*

Provisions

As cleared, HR 3069 contained the following funding:

	Budget Request	Final Amount
Title I (Program Supplementals)		
Agriculture:		
Agriculture Department	$1,316,156,000	$1,361,799,000
State, Justice, Commerce:		
Commerce Department	20,500,000	51,173,000
U.S. Trade Representative	136,000	130,000
Small Business Administration	152,000,000	152,000,000
Justice Department	16,945,000	16,634,000
State Department	35,399,000	37,799,000
Arms Control & Disarmament Agency	564,000	564,000
Board for International Broadcasting	29,840,000	21,300,000
U.S. Information Agency	42,700,000	23,800,000
Federal Judiciary	9,000,000	5,300,000
Military:		
Defense Department	493,270,000	469,770,000
Energy and Water:		
Corps of Engineers	0	37,000,000
Energy Department	21,288,000	52,288,000
Foreign Operations:		
Multilateral Assistance	8,713,508,776	265,500,000
Bilateral Assistance	360,634,000	307,384,000
Military Assistance	188,000,000	94,325,000
Housing/Independent Agencies:		
Community Development (Urban Renewal)	0	6,000,000
Environmental Protection Agency	0	9,000,000
Veterans Administration	2,280,000	265,680,000

	Budget Request	Final Amount
Natural Resources:		
Interior Department	79,490,000	211,752,000
Agriculture Department		
(National Forest System)	59,000,000	0
Department of Health &		
Human Services		
(Indian Health Services)	0	21,297,000
Labor/Education/Human Services:		
Unemployment Trust Fund	615,000,000	615,000,000
Black Lung Trust Fund	186,000,000	186,000,000
Department of Health &		
Human Services	2,650,000	14,650,000
Social Security	1,300,000,000	1,300,000,000
Education Department	4,816,000	140,486,000
Legislative Branch:		
Death Benefits	0	139,600
Senate Expenses	546,000	546,000
House Expenses/Allowances	11,946,000	7,946,000
Attending Physician	19,000	19,000
Mailing Costs	38,064,000	37,965,000
Office of Technology		
Assessment	245,000	165,000
Capitol Architect	161,245,000	49,525,000
Transportation:		
Federal Aviation		
Administration	45,000,000	44,000,000
Federal Highway		
Administration	0	400,000
Panama Canal Commission	375,000	378,635
General Government:		
Treasury (Customs Service)	2,430	2,430
Office of the President	810,000	810,000
Office of Personnel		
Management		
(Retirement/Disability		
Fund)	342,269,000	342,269,000
Merit Systems Protection	1,000,000	1,600,000
Total, Title I	14,250,698,206	6,152,396,665
Title II (Pay Supplemental)	787,355,602	785,664,602
Title IV (General Provisions)		
Agency for International Development	100,000,0000	100,000,000
TOTAL (HR 3069)	$15,138,053,808	$7,038,061,267

Major provisions of the bill:

● Directed the agriculture secretary to reopen bids for cotton producers to sell their 1983 crop to the federal government for the PIK acreage reduction program. This was the provision that gave cotton growers a chance to avoid the massive financial losses they feared from the PIK program.

The measure also made rented farm lands eligible for the PIK program.

● Included $50 million for guaranteed farm operating loans, $25 million for insured farm ownership loans and $25 million for rural water and waste disposal grants.

● Appropriated $1.2 billion for food stamps to avert an August cutback of 25 percent in the program.

● Provided $16 million for the elderly feeding program and $118 million for child nutrition programs.

● Appropriated $5 million for emergency conservation measures to repair flood damage.

● Appropriated $1 million for a Food and Drug Administration contingency fund to meet unanticipated costs of emergency activities similar to the Tylenol investigation.

Commerce, State, Justice

● Appropriated $48.9 million for the National Oceanic and Atmospheric Administration.

● Provided $152 million for the Small Business Administration to purchase business loan guarantees that were in default.

● Appropriated $3.7 million for federal prisons and for expansion of a program to relieve overcrowding in federal institutions.

● Appropriated $22.3 million to build a new U.S. Embassy in Beirut to replace the building destroyed by the April 1983 terrorist bombing. The bill also included almost $8 million for temporary office space for embassy staff in Beirut, replacement of materials and payment of personal damage costs related to the bombing.

● Appropriated $13 million for the U.S. Information Agency and $10.8 million for acquisition and construction of radio facilities.

Defense

● Appropriated $453.6 million to continue production of 91 Pershing II missiles. *(Pershing missile, p. 175)*

● Allowed the Air Force to purchase B-1B bomber components in sufficient quantities to sustain multi-year procurement if Congress approved subsequent legislation providing multi-year contracting authority for the bomber.

● Restored a pre-1982 exemption of specialty metals and chemical warfare protective clothing from "Buy America" restrictions. The exemption originally had been deleted in an effort to protect the U.S. specialty metal industry. But the restrictions created problems with NATO allies.

● Appropriated $9.7 million for equipment to be used by West German reservists who would assist U.S. combat units in Europe in case of war.

● Included $5 million for training for so-called POMCUS equipment storage depots in Europe. The depots would be used by U.S. Army reinforcements flown to Europe if war appeared imminent.

Energy and Water Development

● Appropriated $37 million for flood control, coastal emergencies and other Army Corps of Engineers expenses.

● Authorized a number of flood control and other water projects.

● Appropriated $30 million for Western Area Power Administration construction near Sidney, Neb.

● Prohibited the use of funds for restarting the L-Reactor at the Savannah River nuclear plant at Aiken, S.C., until the Energy Department completed an environmental impact statement and until a water pollution permit was issued. Under this provision, some preliminary work could be performed. *(Story on energy/water appropriations, p. 500)*

Foreign Operations

● Appropriated $245 million for the International Development Association (IDA), the controversial arm of the World Bank that made low-interest loans to poor countries.

● Appropriated $4.5 million for the International Atomic Energy Agency and $16 million for the International Fund for Agricultural Development.

● Appropriated $301.3 million for foreign economic support, including $150 million in grants for Lebanon.

● Appropriated $93.3 million for the military assistance program, including $25 million for El Salvador.

● Appropriated $293.5 million for foreign military sales credits, including $100 million for Lebanon. *(Security and allocations, chart, p. 514)*

HUD Appropriations

● Provided the housing and urban development secretary with some flexibility to redistribute funds among various housing assistance programs.

● Required the Department of Housing and Urban Development to pay the full cost of increases — incurred by raised rent charges or changes of tenant income — in rent supplement and rental housing assistance programs for state-aided units through fiscal 1983. Beginning Oct. 1, the department would pay 90 percent of the increased amount.

● Deferred $69 million of fiscal 1983 operating subsidies for low-income housing projects and made the funds available for fiscal 1984. Any additional funds in excess of fiscal 1983 requirements also would be available for 1984.

● Increased the ceiling on FHA-insured mortgages for residences built to replace homes destroyed by natural disasters from $14,400 to $67,500; larger amounts could be made available for high-cost areas.

● Provided $263.4 million for Veterans Administration construction in Minneapolis and Cleveland.

Interior

● Appropriated $4 million for construction of a national fish research facility in Gainesville, Fla.

● Appropriated $68.2 million for federal land acquisition.

● Appropriated $51.9 million for the Abandoned Mine Reclamation Fund.

● Appropriated $53.2 million for operation of Indian programs.

● Appropriated $19.4 million for Indian health services.

● Directed the interior secretary to appoint a commission within 30 days of enactment of the bill to review the Interior Department's coal leasing procedures. The commission was directed to make its recommendations for ensuring receipt of fair market value for coal leases on public lands within six months of enactment.

● Stated the sense of Congress that it is not in the national interest to allow the Forest Service to sell large amounts of national forest until the service identified the tracts that were no longer needed by the federal government, evaluated the tracts as to their public benefit and provided for public discussion and completed environmental assessments of such sales.

Labor, Health, Education

● Appropriated $615 million for emergency federal supplemental unemployment benefits required by a law (PL 98-13) enacted in March to extend the program from March 31 to Sept. 30. *(Federal supplemental unemployment compensation, p. 274.*

● Appropriated $186 million for the Black Lung Disability Trust Fund, which paid disability benefits to miners who suffered from black lung disease. The basic financing for the trust fund came from coal excise taxes. The additional appropriation was necessary because of a decline in coal sales and higher than expected benefit payments.

● Appropriated $12 million for research on Acquired Immune Deficiency Syndrome (AIDS).

● Included $1.3 billion for a one-time credit to the Social Security System for the value of Social Security checks issued by the Treasury but never cashed. *(Social Security, p. 219)*

● Appropriated $47.9 million for grants to states for education of handicapped children.

● Appropriated $40 million to moderate losses that some Southern and other states expected in federal grants for compensatory education for low-income children. The funds ensured that the states would receive not less than 95 percent of their fiscal 1982 funding.

The expected loss in funds was a result of the impact of the 1980 census on the allocation formula.

● Provided $42.9 million for construction of academic facilities: $20.4 million for the Biomedical Information Communication Center at the Oregon Health Sciences University in Portland, Ore.; $15 million for the advanced technology center at the University of New Hampshire; and $7.5 million for library construction at Boston College.

Legislative Branch

● Increased senators' salaries by 15 percent to $69,800 a year, the same level of House members. The measure also provided that effective Jan. 1, 1984, the annual income from speeches, articles and appearances that a senator could receive would be capped at 30 percent of salary, or $20,940. House rules included a 30 percent cap on outside earned income for representatives. *(1982 Almanac p. 544)*

● Appropriated $38 million for official mail costs.

● Included $49 million for restoration of the crumbling sandstone West Front wall of the Capitol. The measure also provided for an outside consulting architect to oversee the restoration.

Other Provisions

● Limited obligations for boating safety programs to $7.5 million.

● Appropriated $44 million for the Federal Aviation Administration to settle aircraft purchase loan guarantee defaults.

● Appropriated $342.3 million for the Civil Service Retirement and Disability Fund to cover raised benefit levels, which were based on recently increased pay levels.

● Prohibited the Internal Revenue Service from using funds to enforce a ruling that would tax the value of campus lodgings furnished by colleges and universities for faculty members.

● Rescinded $37.2 million in budget authority for the District of Columbia in governmental support, economic development, education, transportation and other programs.

● Appropriated $15 million for public safety, human support services and other District programs.

Titles II, III, IV

● Appropriated $785.7 million for previously approved federal employee pay increases.

● Provided that payment for damages incurred in the earthquake at Coalinga, Calif., be paid promptly from previously appropriated federal emergency funds.

● Made $100 million in deobligated funds for the Agency for International Development available for use.

● Instructed the U.S. executive director of the IMF to oppose the use of fund loans for production of any commodity that would hurt U.S. producers of the same commodity.

House Committee Action

The House Appropriations Committee reported HR 3069 May 18 by voice vote (H Rept 98-207) after passionate debate over providing health benefits to the unemployed,

restoring the West Front of the Capitol and increasing foreign aid.

The House committee version, which appropriated $4.8 billion for fiscal 1983, contained $359 million less than the amount requested by President Reagan.

An amendment that would have both authorized and appropriated $2.7 billion for emergency health insurance benefits for the jobless was rejected 24-25. The committee also rejected, by voice vote, an amendment to reduce funds in the bill for repairing and extending the West Front. The amendment would have eliminated funding for the controversial extension.

However, the committee accepted an amendment adding $133 million for economic and military aid to eight countries. The approval of this amendment headed off a Republican move in committee to delete $245 million for an arm of the World Bank.

David A. Stockman, director of the Office of Management and Budget, said in a letter to the Appropriations Committee that the administration did not oppose the totals in HR 3069 but did object strongly to some of the provisions the committee added.

Among the items Stockman criticized were the committee's language blocking the administration from implementing new federal personnel rules or from leasing public lands for the mining of coal.

Committee members noted that more than 60 percent of the funds in HR 3069, including $1 billion for food stamps and $615 million for emergency unemployment benefits, were required by existing law. The $615 million in unemployment benefits, for example, was required by a law (PL 98-13) enacted in March to extend the program from March 31 to Sept. 30. *(Federal supplemental benefits, p. 274)*

Another large chunk of the bill, which members said they had little choice but to approve, was $785 million for increased pay costs for federal civilian agencies. This money provided only a portion of the raise costs; the rest was absorbed by the various agencies.

Jobless Health Benefits

Joseph M. McDade, R-Pa., unsuccessfully sought an amendment to provide health insurance benefits for jobless workers no longer covered by employment-based health plans and not eligible for Medicaid. The amendment would have authorized $2.7 billion in federal funds and required the states to pay 20 percent of the program's costs. Unemployed workers participating in the program would contribute $3 to $5 a week.

Committee leaders opposed the McDade amendment, although some said they would support a benefits program for unemployed workers if one were authorized. *(Health insurance for the unemployed, p. 405)*

West Front Fix

The House Committee revived the debate, begun in earnest 20 years ago, over restoration of the deteriorating sandstone West Front wall of the Capitol building.

Bill Boner, D-Tenn., unsuccessfully offered an amendment to reduce the bill's $70.5 million to renovate and extend the West Front to $49 million to simply restore it.

Supporters of extending the wall said it would provide additional office space in the Capitol and improve access to the building for the handicapped. The extension was designed also to buttress the wall.

But opponents of the extension argued that added space in the Capitol was not needed and would diminish the building's historic importance.

"If we do extend, we forget the historic value of the Capitol," said Edward R. Roybal, D-Calif. *(Background, 1977 Almanac p. 244)*

Honoraria Limit

The House committee also adopted an amendment, offered by Silvio O. Conte, R-Mass., ranking minority member, to limit the outside earnings of senators to 30 percent of annual salary. Designed as a direct slap at the Senate, it was approved by voice vote.

House rules already limited outside earnings to 30 percent, or $20,940, for representatives. But there was no limit on the total senators could earn beyond their salary. Representatives in 1982 got a $9,138 pay raise, increasing their pay to $69,800, but senators stayed at the old level of $60,662.50 a year while eliminating limits on outside earnings. *(1982 Almanac p. 544)*

Many members of both chambers long had contended congressional pay was inadequate because of the cost of living and the expense of maintaining homes both in their states and the Washington area. But they had been reluctant to vote for pay hikes, fearing the political backlash that traditionally accompanied such pay raises.

Some representatives resented the criticism they had been subjected to for raising their pay, while many senators earned much more because senators' outside earnings were not subject to any limits.

Senators' honoraria reports for 1982 were made public in May 1983. Senate members, because they generally were better known than representatives, were able to command larger speaking fees. The top earner was Finance Committee Chairman Robert Dole, R-Kan., who received $135,750, contributing $51,500 of that to charity.

Personnel Rules

The committee approved a prohibition on the use of federal funds to implement or enforce controversial regulations proposed by the Office of Personnel Management (OPM) until the Comptroller General completed a review.

The regulations would more closely link to job performance the pay raises and job security of most white-collar federal workers. The administration said the changes would make personnel practices of the federal work force more like those of the private sector. But some members of Congress believed the administration overstepped its bounds in proposing the new regulations. *(Personnel regulations, p. 602)*

House Floor Action

The House May 25 approved its $4.8 billion version of the fiscal 1983 supplemental appropriations bill. The vote on HR 3069 was 309-92. *(Vote 131, p. 44-H)*

On the House floor, the two-decade stalemate over the West Front was settled when the House agreed to a $49 million restoration of the crumbling sandstone West Front wall, instead of an extension as approved by the committee. The Senate had traditionally supported a simple restoration, not extension.

The House decision was made overwhelmingly by a 325-86 vote. *(Vote 130, p. 44-H)*

The West Front dispute dominated the House debate May 25. Heavy lobbying by the American Institute of Architects and the National Trust for Historic Preservation

convinced the House to reject the committee's $70.5 million to extend and repair the West Front and allow only $49 million to be used solely for restoration.

House Rule Controversy

Many representatives were unhappy with the rule (H Res 209) under which the supplemental bill was debated on the House floor. The rule prohibited points of order that could have been made against more than half of the bill. It was necessary because appropriations exceeded the existing 1983 budget ceiling, some funding had not been authorized, and some provisions amounted to authorizing legislation on an appropriations bill, which was against House rules.

The rule was narrowly approved 212-195. *(Vote 129, p. 42-H)*

Opponents of the rule argued that the Appropriations Committee was encroaching on the jurisdiction of the authorizing committees. Critics said the supplemental bill should provide money only for emergency situations, but that the bill included non-emergency "pork." Opponents were particularly critical of waivers for water projects that had not been authorized.

The House Appropriations Committee leadership, however, maintained that the water projects and other items, such as $1 billion for food stamps, $186 million for Black Lung disability benefits and $615 million for unemployment benefits, were emergency needs. Supporters of the rule also said the bill was within the revised 1983 budget ceiling included in the House budget resolution (H Con Res 91).

Appropriations Committee Chairman Jamie L. Whitten, D-Miss., said the "supreme" House rule was that which enables the House to make exceptions to its rules.

Other House Amendments

The House also adopted an amendment, offered by William H. Natcher, D-Ky., to provide $12 million for research and other activities relating to Acquired Immune Deficiency Syndrome (AIDS). The funds were for the Centers for Disease Control and the National Institutes of Health.

The House rejected an amendment, offered by Appropriations Defense Subcommittee Chairman Joseph P. Addabbo, D-N.Y., to reduce by $135.4 million the bill's $453.6 million funds to continue production of the Pershing II missile. The House turned down the amendment by a 9-18 non-record vote.

The House also rejected by voice vote an amendment by Ronald V. Dellums, D-Calif., to eliminate all the Pershing II funds in the bill.

Senate Committee Action

The Senate Appropriations Committee reported its version of HR 3069 May 26 (S Rept 98-148), jacking up the total to $15.6 billion, mostly through the inclusion of $8.4 billion for the International Monetary Fund. The committee also added $1.3 billion for Social Security that was not in the House-passed bill and $370 million for the construction of Strategic Petroleum Reserve (SPR) storage facilities.

The House declined to include the IMF funding because the authorization had not yet been enacted. And the president's Social Security request was not made in time for House action. The House provided the $370 million for

SPR construction, but identified the funds as "off-budget."

The committee rejected the House-passed cap on senators' outside earnings. The cap was restored on the Senate floor, however.

El Salvador

The Senate committee, with little debate, rejected 8-15 an amendment by Daniel K. Inouye, D-Hawaii, to pare supplemental military aid for El Salvador to $20 million, from the $50 million the president had requested. The money — part of an emergency aid package Reagan proposed in March — was in addition to $56.3 million Congress already had approved for El Salvador in fiscal 1983. *(El Salvador aid, p. 154)*

Inouye's amendment would have made the bill conform to a recommendation by the Foreign Relations Committee that military aid for El Salvador in 1983 be limited to $76.3 million.

The House bill deferred the $50 million request pending further progress in El Salvador on issues of concern to Congress, such as human rights improvements in that country.

IMF

The largest single item in the bill was an $8.4 billion boost in the U.S. participation in the IMF, which lends money to countries having trouble paying their foreign debts. The appropriation was made contingent on the enactment of authorizing legislation.

Under pressure from the administration, the panel deleted a provision that would have required the U.S. representative to the IMF to vote against loans to several leftist countries, such as Libya, Vietnam and Nicaragua.

IDA, Foreign Aid

On a related issue, the committee cut to $125 million Reagan's $245 million request for the U.S. contribution to the World Bank's IDA.

Reagan's full request of $251 million in economic and military aid to Lebanon was approved, but the panel made substantial cuts in military aid for Pakistan (to $55 million, from the $75 million requested), Turkey (deleting all of the $65 million request for military aid and approving instead $10 million for economic aid), the Sudan (to $25 million, from the $50 million requested) and Jordan (to $15 million, from the $35 million requested).

By a 12-16 vote, the panel rejected an amendment by J. Bennett Johnston, D-La., to eliminate multi-year contracting authority for production of the B-1B bomber.

OPM Regulations

In addition, the Senate committee eliminated the House language in HR 3069 covering the OPM regulations. Ted Stevens, R-Alaska, chairman of the Civil Service Subcommittee of the Governmental Affairs Committee, said he did not offer an amendment to block the rules after the administration assured him the regulations would not be implemented until his panel had time to consider legislation on the subject.

Senate Floor Action

HR 3069 won Senate approval June 16 but only after senators, in response to public criticism, voted to limit the extra income they may receive for speeches, appearances and articles. The cap — 30 percent of annual salary — took

Foreign Operations: 'Security Aid' Allocations

Following are amounts for major "security assistance" programs for key countries. The fiscal 1983 final figures include amounts appropriated by Congress in the continuing resolution (PL 97-377) and the 1983 supplemental (PL 98-63). The fiscal 1984 amounts were allocated under a continuing resolution, PL 98-151. The chart shows allocations for Foreign Military Sales (FMS) loans, Economic Support Fund (ESF) and Military Assistance Program (MAP). *(Dollar figures are in millions; country figures are in bold type.)*

Country	Fiscal 1983 Request	Fiscal 1983 Final	Fiscal 1984 Preliminary
Egypt	**$2,075**	**$2,075**	**$2,115**
FMS [1]	1,325	1,325	1,365
ESF	750	750	750
Israel	**2,485**	**2,485**	**2,485**
FMS [2]	1,700	1,700	1,700
ESF	785	785	910
Jordan	**95**	**71.5**	**135**
FMS	75	51.5	115
ESF	20	20	20
Lebanon [3]	**250**	**250**	**15**
FMS	100	100	15
ESF	150	150	0
Pakistan	**475**	**460**	**525**
FMS	275	260	300
ESF	200	200	225
Turkey	**765**	**685**	**853.5**
FMS	355	290	585
ESF	300	285	138.5
MAP	110	110	130
Greece [4]	**280**	**280**	**500**
FMS	280	280	500
Cyprus	**15**	**15**	**15**
ESF	15	15	15
Spain	**412**	**412**	**412**
FMS	400	400	400
ESF	12	12	12

Country	Fiscal 1983 Request	Fiscal 1983 Final	Fiscal 1984 Preliminary
Korea	**200**	**185**	**230**
FMS	200	185	230
Philippines	**100**	**100**	**100**
FMS	50	50	50
ESF	50	50	50
Sudan	**170**	**125.25**	**165**
ESF	95	82.25	120
MAP	75	43	45
Zaire	**19**	**11.5**	**15**
FMS	2	2	0
ESF	7	5	8
MAP	10	4.5	7
El Salvador	**275**	**220**	**183.5**
FMS	76.5	46.5	18.5
ESF	140	140	120
MAP	58.5	33.5	45
Guatemala	**16.35**	**0**	**0**
FMS	0	0	0
ESF	16.35	0	0
Honduras	**81.5**	**89.5**	**80**
FMS	9	9	0
ESF	45	53	40
MAP	27.5	27.5	40

[1] *For 1983, includes $425 million in forgiven loans and $900 million in loans to be repaid; for fiscal 1984, includes $465 million in forgiven loans and $900 million in loans to be repaid.*

[2] *For 1983, includes $750 million in forgiven loans and $950 million in loans to be repaid; for 1984, includes $850 million in forgiven loans and $850 million in loans to be repaid.*

[3] *Fiscal 1983 aid to Lebanon included a special $250 million program.*

[4] *Reagan proposed "up to" $500 million for Greece in fiscal 1984, contingent on the United States and Greece reaching an agreement to continue U.S. military bases in Greece.*

effect Jan. 1, 1984. The Senate also gave itself a raise, up to $69,800 a year, the salary paid to representatives, after first voting against a pay hike.

The honoraria issue slowed debate on HR 3069, which extended through five days. The Senate's $16.1 billion supplemental was approved 64-33. *(Vote 153, p. 28-S)*

The supplemental bill included $650 million more than the president had requested and $11.3 billion more than the House version.

The major differences between the Senate and House bills were the Senate's addition of $8.4 billion for the IMF, $1.3 billion for Social Security and $370 million for construction of SPR storage facilities.

Veto Threatened

Throughout consideration of HR 3069, the administration raised the possibility of a presidential veto. David A. Stockman, director of the Office of Management and Budget (OMB), threatened Senate leaders with a veto in a June 8 letter. He warned that Reagan's senior advisers would find it difficult to recommend a presidential signature unless the bill's total was reduced and other objectionable provisions eliminated.

Stockman said the bill provided $780 million in unrequested program funds, including the $370 million for SPR facilities. And he was critical of the addition of $325 million in unrequested increases on loan limits for rural water and farm programs.

The veto threat infuriated some senators, particularly Appropriations Committee Chairman Mark O. Hatfield, R-Ore. Hatfield was upset that Stockman was threatening a veto when the big money items — IMF, Social Security and military funds — had been requested by Reagan.

Despite the threat, the Senate approved amendments adding over $407 million more in spending, including $225 million for health insurance benefits for jobless workers.

Senate Pay, Honoraria

The Senate voted June 16 to raise senators' salaries to $69,800 a year and limit honoraria after Senate leaders met and worked out a final amendment. Henry M. Jackson, D-Wash., one of the leading advocates on the earning limit, offered it on behalf of Baker and Minority Leader Robert C. Byrd, D-W.Va.

The new salary went into effect July 1. The vote on the Jackson amendment raising salaries and capping honoraria

was adopted 49-47. *(Vote 152, p. 28-S)*

A week earlier, on June 9, the Senate had approved an honoraria cap on a vote of 51-41 but declined to raise annual salaries. *(Vote 130, p. 25-S)*

Jackson forced the Senate June 9 to vote on various pay and honoraria options. The Senate rejected his first amendment, 20-67, to raise senators' salary to the House level and place a 30 percent cap on honoraria. *(Vote 127, p. 25-S)*

Jackson's second amendment, rejected 13-78, would have given each senator the choice of the higher salary and the honoraria cap or the existing pay and no cap. *(Vote 128, p. 25-S)*

His third amendment, rejected 3-88, would have increased senators' salaries to $69,800 but not placed any limit on honoraria. Even Jackson voted against this amendment. *(Vote 129, p. 25-S)*

Jake Garn, R-Utah, who led the fight against the amendments, argued it was unfair to limit the ability of anyone to earn outside income. "I resent my colleagues trying to impose on my children what my future income will be," Garn said.

By a vote of 6-89, the Senate June 16 rejected an amendment, offered by Lowell P. Weicker Jr., R-Conn., to raise the salary to $100,000 and prohibit the acceptance of honoraria. *(Vote 150, p. 28-S)*

The Senate also on June 16 voted 9-84 to reject a Jackson amendment raising senators' pay to $80,100 — the level of a Cabinet member — and bar honoraria. *(Vote 151, p. 28-S)*

After disposing of the pay and honoraria issue, the Senate June 16 passed the supplemental funding bill by a 64-33 vote. *(Vote 153, p. 28-S)*

Other Amendments

The Senate June 9 rejected an effort to eliminate multi-year contracting authority for production of the B-1B bomber. It voted 52-38 for a Stevens amendment to provide $185 million for multi-year contracting authority. This authority had been included by the Appropriations Committee but knocked out on a point of order. *(Vote 131, p. 25-S)*

Other amendments to the supplemental appropriations bill considered by the Senate included those by:

● Patrick J. Leahy, D-Vt., to delete $376 million of foreign economic and military assistance funds. Rejected 39-45, June 9. *(Vote 132, p. 26-S)*

● Daniel Patrick Moynihan, D-N.Y., to appropriate $225 million for health insurance benefits for the unemployed. Accepted 75-23, June 15. *(Vote 146, p. 27-S)*

● Bumpers, to prohibit federal coal leasing through fiscal 1983. Rejected 48-51, June 14. *(Vote 138, p. 26-S)*

● Edward M. Kennedy, D-Mass., to appropriate $30 million for summer jobs for youths. Accepted by voice vote, June 15.

● Howard M. Metzenbaum, D-Ohio, to bar the use of federal funds to indemnify companies against the loss of tax breaks involved in government leasing contracts. Adopted by voice vote, June 15.

The amendment was aimed at Navy ship-leasing contracts that contained clauses that could result in the payment of as much as $2.7 billion by the Navy if planned tax breaks for the lessors were disallowed, Metzenbaum said.

A June 14 motion to table, or kill, the amendment failed 49-50. *(Vote 140, p. 27-S)*

Conference

As the threats of a presidential veto mounted and as the deadline for the food stamp program neared, House-Senate conferees accepted reduced spending levels in HR 3069. The conferees agreed to $7 billion in new spending in the bill, which was reported July 20 (H Rept 98-308).

However, the Senate conferees insisted on another $8.5 billion for the IMF, which the House conferees opposed.

The food stamp cutoff encouraged conferees to make deep slashes in budget and loan authority in hopes of making it acceptable to the president. Major cuts included $370 million for SPR facilities and $225 million for emergency health insurance benefits for unemployed workers.

It was difficult to compare the conference report directly to Reagan's request. House and Senate conferees did not recognize the same items as budget requests, and the administration scored appropriations and loan authority programs differently.

According to the conferees, the bill was $100.6 million more than the conference-considered administration requests. Senate aides estimated that cuts of roughly $1 billion were made in the Senate version of the bill.

Senate Pay Hike

The controversial subject of senators' compensation was laid to rest when House conferees agreed to accept the Senate's cap on outside earnings and a $9,137.50 pay raise for senators, bringing their annual salaries to the $69,800 level of House members.

Foreign Aid

House conferees accepted higher foreign military aid spending in exchange for the full House allowance of $245 million for the World Bank's IDA.

The conferees approved $93.3 million in foreign military assistance, a split between the Senate level of $155.7 million and the House level of $31 million. The House bill had no El Salvador monies.

Also included was $293.5 million for foreign military sales credits, instead of $398 million provided by the Senate and $189 million proposed by the House.

Foreign economic aid was set at $301.3 million. The Senate provided $322.5 million and the House allowed $253 million.

Other Provisions

In other action conferees:

● Eliminated $370 million for the Strategic Petroleum Reserve with the understanding that the administration would request SPR construction funds for fiscal 1985. The conferees also reaffirmed congressional commitment to an average daily fill rate of 220,000 barrels.

● Retained a House prohibition on the controversial OPM rules.

● Deleted $225 million in loan authority provided by the Senate for rural water and waste disposal loans.

● Eliminated the Senate provision of multi-year contracting authority for production of the B-1B bomber. The conference agreement allowed the purchase of components in sufficient quantities to sustain multi-year procurement if Congress approved subsequent legislation providing multi-year contracting authority for the bomber.

● Eliminated a House prohibition on the sale or lease of coal on public lands through Sept. 30, 1983. ∎

Agriculture Funding Included in Stopgap Bill

Congress cleared legislation Nov. 12 making fiscal 1984 appropriations for farm and food programs.

Disagreements between congressional committees and the Reagan administration over funding levels for farm and food programs stalled progress on the regular agriculture money bill (HR 3223) and, as a result, agriculture appropriations were incorporated into two stopgap funding bills.

Final action came Nov. 12 as Congress gave approval to a $316 billion emergency spending measure (H J Res 413 — PL 98-151) that included $33.9 billion in funding for agriculture, food and related programs. The agriculture spending levels had been agreed to in the conference on HR 3223 (H Rept 98-450).

The primary purpose of H J Res 413, known as a continuing resolution, was to provide appropriations for the remainder of the 1984 fiscal year for programs covered in the Agriculture, Commerce-State-Justice, Defense, Foreign Operations and Treasury-Postal Service money bills. *(Continuing resolution, p. 528)*

Agriculture funding in the continuing resolution came to a total of $33,984,209,000 in new budget authority and so-called "Section 32" funds, customs receipts earmarked by law for Agriculture Department programs. The House-passed bill had provided $34,029,527,000, and the Senate version had provided $34,117,290,000, compared with a presidential budget request of $34,083,299,000. Budget Director David A. Stockman had objected vehemently that both bills underfunded some programs and added substantial amounts of money, above the requested figures, to others.

The House adopted the conference report on H J Res 413 (H Rept 98-540) by a 173-136 vote, and the Senate approved the measure by voice. President Reagan signed the continuing resolution Nov. 14. *(House vote 455, p. 134-H).*

Congress Sept. 30 had cleared H J Res 368, which provided agriculture and food money — and appropriations for other programs as well — from the Oct. 1 start of the fiscal year through Nov. 10. *(First continuing resolution, p. 526)*

Provisions

As signed into law, H J Res 413 (PL 98-151) provided the following amounts for the Department of Agriculture and related programs:

	Budget Request	Final Amount
Agriculture Programs		
Office of the Secretary	$ 5,045,000	$ 5,045,000
Standard Level User Charges	69,402,000	64,270,000
Advisory Committees	1,398,000	1,398,000
Departmental Administration	17,819,000	17,999,000
Governmental and Public Affairs	7,092,000	7,407,000
Congressional Affairs	477,000	——
Inspector General	29,754,000	29,211,000
General Counsel	14,348,000	14,253,000
Federal Grain Inspection Service	6,861,000	6,861,000
Agricultural Research Service	478,559,000	509,003,000
Cooperative State Research Service	231,715,000	247,655,000
Extension Service	287,082,000	334,340,000
National Agricultural Library	9,873,000	9,873,000
Animal and Plant Health Inspection Service	227,126,000	265,624,000
Food Safety and Inspection Service	333,696,000	333,696,000
Economic Research Service	45,024,000	43,841,000
Statistical Reporting Service	55,778,000	53,903,000
Agricultural Cooperative Service	3,677,000	4,639,000
World Agricultural Outlook Board	1,522,000	1,500,000
Agricultural Marketing Service	31,448,000	34,252,000
Packers and Stockyards Administration	9,013,000	9,013,000
Agricultural Stabilization & Conservation Service	51,986,000	53,786,000
Federal Crop Insurance Corporation	473,870,000	310,000,000
Commodity Credit Corporation	10,173,636,000	9,673,636,000
Subtotal	$12,566,201,000	$12,031,205,000
Rural Development Programs		
Office of Rural Development Policy	2,388,000	2,000,000
Farmers Home Administration	3,356,271,000	3,375,725,000
Rural Electrification Administration	29,960,000	29,960,000
Soil Conservation Service	424,406,000	601,756,000
Agricultural Stabilization & Conservation Service	56,000,000	211,300,000
Subtotal	$ 3,869,025,000	$ 4,220,741,000
Domestic Food Programs		
Child Nutrition Programs	700,919,000	705,919,000
Special Milk Program	11,720,000	11,920,000
Women, Infants & Children (WIC) Program	1,060,000,000	1,060,000,000
Commodity Supplemental Food Program	32,600,000	40,150,000
Food Stamps	10,916,705,000	10,916,705,000
Nutrition Assistance for Puerto Rico	825,000,000	825,000,000
Food Donations Programs	150,061,000	166,936,000
Temporary Emergency Food Assistance	——	50,000,000
Food Program Administration	80,387,000	81,352,000

	Budget Request	Final Amount
Nutrition Information	6,564,000	6,564,000
Subtotal	$13,783,956,000	$13,864,546,000
International Programs		
Foreign Agricultural Service	85,217,000	83,717,000
Food for Peace (PL 480)	1,052,000,000	1,052,000,000
Office of International Cooperation and Development	4,016,000	5,016,000
Subtotal	$ 1,141,233,000	$ 1,140,733,000
Other Agencies		
Food and Drug Administration	385,058,000	387,449,000
Commodity Futures Trading Commission	24,691,000	26,400,000
Subtotal	$ 409,749,000	$ 413,849,000
TOTAL	**$31,770,164,000**	**$31,671,074,000**
Section 32 Transfers	$ 2,313,135,000	$ 2,313,135,000
TOTAL OBLIGATIONAL AUTHORITY:	**$34,083,299,000**	**$33,984,209,000**

Loan Authorization. HR 3223 also provided the following loan authorizations:

● $9,012,000,000 in direct and insured loans (budget request: $5,384,000,000).

● $3,816,000,000 in guaranteed loans (budget request: $3,466,000,000).

House Committee Action

The House Appropriations Committee June 3 approved a $34 billion version of HR 3223, essentially ignoring warnings from the administration that, unless major changes were made in the measure, the president would veto it.

In a letter to the committee, Budget Director Stockman complained that key programs were subjected to bookkeeping "gimmicks." According to Stockman, the bill exceeded the president's budget request for farm and food programs by $652 million. But, according to the Appropriations Committee report (H Rept 98-231), the total appropriation of $34,029,527,000 was $53,772,000 less than the president's budget request and $6,196,669,000 less than fiscal 1983 appropriations.

The committee customarily reported agriculture appropriations bills below presidential budget totals and invariably drew administration complaints that it misrepresented savings and masked over-budget funding decisions.

The $6.2 billion difference between the 1983 and 1984 bills represented lower estimated spending by the Commodity Credit Corporation (CCC), the agency that administered price support and other farm programs. The administration had forecast that its Payment-in-Kind (PIK) program, in which farmers were paid in surplus stocks of grains and cotton for cutting the size of their harvests,

would reduce the demand for CCC funds in 1984. *(PIK, p. 380)*

The committee bill set aside $9.7 billion for reimbursing past CCC losses, $500 million below the budget request. Stockman called this a "scorekeeping gimmick," noting the money would have to be found eventually because it was needed for losses already incurred.

As in previous years, the committee found too optimistic the administration's expectations of the growth of the federal crop insurance program, which provided farmers with protection against crop damage. The bill provided $90 million less than the budget requested for the program.

Partial-Year Funding

As in 1982, the committee bill also provided less than a full year of funding for food stamps and other federal feeding programs. To keep the bill within the House-passed budget resolution totals, the committee used the same numbers as the president's budget and simply cut off funding on the dates when it estimated funds would run out. For instance, money for child nutrition programs, including school lunches, was appropriated for a period ending Aug. 15, 1984, six weeks before the end of the fiscal year. *(1982 Almanac p. 255)*

The fiscal 1984 budget request assumed that Congress would save some money by delaying cost-of-living adjustments, freezing certain spending levels and making other changes in these programs. But the Agriculture Committee failed to make these alterations, so the Appropriations panel funded the food programs at current spending levels.

To make up the shortfall, Appropriations recommended that the administration submit supplemental budget requests.

Agriculture Programs

For basic farm programs, including price supports, research and crop insurance, the House committee bill provided $12.1 billion, about $470 million less than the budget request and $6.6 billion less than appropriated in fiscal 1983, with the CCC funding accounting for the reduction between the two fiscal years.

Research. The committee pointedly rejected the administration's research policies, including a six-year plan for the Agricultural Research Service (ARS) to identify high-priority areas for research for the future. The plan, the report said, was "heavily oriented toward basic research" and suggested an unsatisfactory "retreat from the hard cases" such as research on gypsy moths, boll weevils, fruit flies, beetles and bees.

The panel also restored more than $50 million worth of budget cuts in programs to combat boll weevils, grasshoppers, certain weeds and brucellosis, a cattle disease that can also infect humans.

PIK Administration. The bill included an extra $50 million for the Agricultural Stabilization and Conservation Service for administrative expenses of the PIK program.

In providing less money to reimburse the CCC than requested, the committee noted the administration had revised its estimate of fiscal 1984 CCC outlays down, by $2.5 billion, in an April budget update. That suggested the need for reimbursement was also "overstated."

Rural Development

For loan, grant and other programs that financed individual farming operations, rural housing, water and elec-

trification projects and businesses, the bill provided a total of $4.3 billion, $386 million more than the budget request and $579 million more than fiscal 1983.

The bill continued existing funding levels for rural housing programs, ignoring an administration plan to replace them with a new rural housing block grant, which, "from all indications, . . . will not become law," according to the report. The bill generally retained 1983 funding levels, which meant, in the case of rural rental assistance, an appropriation of $940 million, which was $924 million more than the budget request.

Farmers Home. For the Farmers Home Administration (FmHA), which provided loans to individual farmers, the committee rejected an administration plan to limit lending for physical disaster losses to a total of $1.5 billion, and instead provided funds "as necessary." It included $600 million for economic emergency loans, which the administration opposed, with the money to become available "if authorized by law."

Water, Industrial Development. For rural water and sewer facility loans and grants and industrial development loans, the committee continued funding at 1983 levels, substantially above the fiscal 1984 budget requests.

For watershed and flood prevention operations of the Soil Conservation Service, the bill provided $183 million, $136.6 million more than the budget request.

Rural Electrification. For the Rural Electrification Administration (REA), which financed electrical and telephone systems, the bill provided a total of $1.1 billion in insured loan authorizations, $525 million more than the budget request, and $4.7 billion in guaranteed loan authorizations, $1.4 billion more than the budget request. It also provided $197.9 million for a special fund that paid an interest subsidy on REA loans; the administration had not requested money for this fund.

Food Programs

For domestic food programs, the bill provided $13.8 billion, $29.7 million more than the budget request but $232.5 million less than fiscal 1983.

Child Nutrition. For child nutrition programs, including school lunches, the committee provided $3 billion, through Aug. 15, 1984. It estimated that an additional $312.8 million would be needed to finish the year unless Congress enacted the administration's proposed reductions.

Women and Infants. For the women, infants and children (WIC) program, which provided nutritional supplements to low-income pregnant and nursing women and young children, the committee provided $1 billion through July 10, 1984, enough to support the same caseload as in 1983. It recommended that the administration submit a supplemental budget request, but did not suggest how much more would be needed.

Food Stamps. For food stamps, the committee provided $10.9 billion through Sept. 6, 1984, and estimated at least $766 million more would be needed to get through the year.

Other Programs

Of the $1.1 billion provided for international programs, $1 billion was for the Food for Peace (PL 480) program, which made food available to needy foreign nations through donations and subsidized loans for purchase.

The bill appropriated a total of $386.9 million for the Food and Drug Administration (FDA) and $24.9 million for

the Commodity Futures Trading Commission (CFTC).

House Floor Action

The House easily passed HR 3223 on June 8, despite warnings that members were being deceived about the budget-busting potential of the measure.

It was approved by a 297-115 vote. There were no amendments to the bill on the House floor. *(Vote 167, p. 52-H)*

The administration's criticisms of the measure failed to have much of an effect on the outcome. The bill's total spending figure was sharply disputed by Stockman and administration supporters such as Rep. Bill Frenzel, R-Minn. They said the bill actually exceeded the presidential budget requests by $1.9 billion and obligated the government for many billions of dollars in unwarranted loan program increases.

Stockman's complaints were that the bill exceeded the budget and the bill followed familar practices of earlier years, subtracting money from requests for such key accounts as the CCC and adding money for politically popular programs, such as conservation projects on individual farms.

Senate Committee Action

The Senate Appropriations Committee reported its version of HR 3223 (S Rept 98-160) on June 22, one day after its Agriculture Subcommittee finished work on it.

As reported, the bill appropriated $31,702,780,000 for Agriculture Department programs and the related agencies, and it provided $2,313,135,000 in Section 32 funds.

The total fiscal 1984 funding of $34,015,915,000 was, the panel said, $67.4 million less than the presidential budget request and $13.6 million less than the version passed by the House.

The Senate bill largely followed the House in funding federal food programs for less than a full 12 months, chopping $500 million from the budget request for the CCC, reducing the request for the federal crop insurance program, ignoring proposed cuts in federal credit programs, and restoring research and conservation funds. As with the House version, the bill drew vehement complaints from Budget Director Stockman that it used "gimmicks" to disguise "massive" over-budget excesses.

Agriculture Programs

For price supports, research, crop insurance and other basic farm programs, the bill provided $12.1 billion, $17.6 million less than the House version.

Research. For agricultural research programs, the panel's total of $1.1 billion was $35.5 million more than the House bill. Some $10 million of the extra funding was for postgraduate fellowships to head off what the committee called "predicted shortages in agricultural scientific and professional personnel."

The panel added and subtracted modest amounts from House totals for a handful of the more than 40 Agricultural Research Service (ARS) programs.

The Senate committee said it would closely monitor implementation of a six-year departmental plan to reorder ARS research priorities, which had been flatly repudiated by the House.

For the Cooperative State Research Service, the committee total of $252.8 million was $19.2 million more than

the House total; it included an $11.5 million increase over the House figure for competitive research grants, for the total requested by the administration of $21.5 million.

For the Animal and Plant Health Inspection Service, the committee provided $251.4 million for salaries and expenses, $26 million less than the House bill.

Brucellosis Eradication. The biggest reduction made by the Senate panel was a $21.4 million cut in the House figure for the program to eradicate brucellosis. The committee recommended $60 million. It said that Reagan's budget had under-funded many federal disease-control programs, but, in the case of brucellosis, higher levels of funding in recent years had not lowered the incidence of the disease below .4 percent. There also was evidence that states were spending brucellosis funds for other purposes, it said.

Crop Insurance. For the Federal Crop Insurance program, the committee went even further than the House in cutting the budget request, providing a total of $353.9 million, which was $120 million below the budget estimate and $30 million below the House total.

Participation in the program was much lower than anticipated and rapid program growth was unlikely in 1984, according to the committee, because of the expected continuation of an extensive federal acreage reduction program.

PIK Program. The committee directed the administration to specifically identify funds in its fiscal 1985 budget that would be used to repay the CCC for the cost of the PIK program.

The panel also eliminated a $500 million ceiling on the direct export credits that the CCC could provide.

Rural Development

The committee bill provided a total of $4.3 billion — $10.4 million less than the House bill — for programs financing farming operations, rural housing, water and electrification projects and businesses.

Like the House, the Senate panel did not reduce funds for rural housing and package them into a block grant, as requested by the administration. Also like the House, it increased rural rental assistance loans by $924 million over the budget request.

The committee also provided a total of $73 million, $11 million more than the House, for rent supplements for low-income families. The administration budget had not funded this program.

FmHA. In the Farmers Home Administration programs, the committee followed the House in rejecting an administration request for a $1.5 billion cap on emergency disaster loans for losses from natural disasters, such as drought.

Unlike the House, however, the committee did not fund a $600 million economic emergency loan program that the administration opposed.

Water, Sewers. The panel trimmed back to $270 million the water and sewer facility loan program that the House had funded at $375 million. The budget requested $250 million.

It also cut back funding for rural water and waste disposal grants to the $90 million requested by the budget, instead of the $125 million provided by the House.

Industrial Development. Like the House, the Senate provided $300 million for guaranteed industrial development loans that the budget did not fund, and it added $30 million to the budget request of $100 million for com-

munity facility loans. It also followed the House in expressing concern about the economic troubles of many FmHA borrowers, urging the secretary of agriculture to avoid foreclosures and to use existing legal authority to defer loans and make other concessions to borrowers with repayment problems.

REA. For the REA, the committee went along with the House in providing $525 million more than the budget in insured loan authorizations, for a $1.1 billion total.

But for guaranteed REA loans, the Senate measure provided the budget figure of $3.4 billion, instead of the $4.7 billion provided by the House. Like the House, the committee added $197.9 million for a special fund that paid the interest subsidy on REA loans; the administration had not requested money for the fund.

Food Programs

The bill provided $13.8 billion for domestic food programs, which was $3 million more than the House. As in the House bill, funding for major federal food programs stopped before the end of the fiscal year.

For child nutrition programs the committee provided $3 billion through Aug. 15, 1984.

WIC. For the women, infants and children program, the bill provided $1 billion through July 10, 1984, and it required the department to keep the WIC caseload from falling below 2.8 million persons during that period.

Food Stamps. For the food stamp program, the committee provided $10.9 billion through Sept. 6, 1984, and it prohibited administrative actions to reduce benefit levels without "ample" opportunity for Congress to consider supplemental funding.

Most particularly, the committee barred the secretary from changing procedures used to calculate the amount of food stamps a household received in order to lower the recipient's allotment.

The committee also permitted Puerto Rico to use its food assistance block grant to provide cash assistance as well as non-cash aid, such as food stamps.

Other Programs

The Senate bill provided $1.1 billion for international programs, including $1 billion for the Food for Peace program, the same amount as provided by the House.

For the FDA, the panel provided $392 million, $5.6 million more than the House.

The extra money was largely to establish a contingency fund to enable the agency to respond to major medical emergencies, such as the 1982 recall of infant formula and the contamination of the painkiller Tylenol. The bill provided $4 million for the fund, in addition to the $1 million earmarked by the House.

CFTC. For the Commodity Futures Trading Commission, the bill provided $26.6 million, $1.8 million more than the House bill. The committee noted that the agency's budget request had not included money for a series of studies that had been ordered by Congress in the 1982 CFTC reauthorization (PL 97-444). *(1982 Almanac p. 365)*

Senate Floor Action

The Senate June 29 gave its strong approval to HR 3223 despite repeated warnings of a presidential veto. The vote was 77-18. *(Vote 175, p. 31-S)*

The bill approved by the Senate appropriated $31,804,155,000 for Agriculture Department programs and

several related agencies and $2,313,135,000 in Section 32 funds.

The total fiscal 1984 funding of $34,117,290,000, according to Appropriations Committee calculations, was $33,991,000 more than the presidential budget request. It was also $87,763,000 more than the House-passed bill.

The Senate Appropriations committee bill had been well under the presidential budget, according to committee calculations. Floor amendments added a little more than $100 million to the committee bill.

As with the House bill, however, Stockman argued that the legislation actually mandated "massive" over-budget spending that was disguised by bookkeeping sleights-of-hand.

Floor Amendments

Major changes made in the committee bill on the Senate floor included:

● An amendment by Mark Andrews, R-N.D., accepted by voice vote, to require the Agriculture Department to honor its original obligations under its PIK program. The amendment was meant to address the problems of cotton producers, who were being required in effect to sell their cotton to the government at unfavorable prices. (Cotton PIK legislation, p. 380)

● An amendment by Carl Levin, D-Mich., accepted by voice vote, to add $875,000 to reimburse states for past costs of elderly feeding programs.

● An amendment by Rudy Boschwitz, R-Minn., adopted by a 61-36 vote, to add $96 million for Food for Peace programs. (Vote 174, p. 31-S)

The Senate also agreed, on a 63-33 vote, to table and thus kill an amendment by Edward Zorinsky, D-Neb., that would have raised grain storage payments to farmers. (Vote 172, p. 31-S)

Conference

House and Senate conferees completed work Oct. 27 on HR 3223 (H Rept 98-450), paring its spending levels in an attempt to ward off a Reagan veto.

The final version of the bill provided for a total of $33,984,209,000 in new budget authority and Section 32 funds.

Some of the administration's objections to the bill were resolved in conference. The recovering economy appeared to defuse the partial year funding issue; Sen. Thad Cochran, R-Miss., chairman of the Appropriations Subcommittee on Agriculture, Rural Development and Related Agencies, said that the improved economic outlook meant that the food stamp money — some $10.9 billion — would probably last for the full year. Committee staff estimated that the other food programs would require a supplemental appropriation of about $750 million.

The conferees dropped the House-passed provision calling for a $600 million "economic emergency" loan program for farmers. A court order had directed the department to go ahead with the program, using funds left over from 1982. Conferees also dropped an earmark of CCC funds for export promotion.

But other features objectionable to the administration remained. The final bill retained the $500 million cut in CCC funds and provided substantially less for the Federal Crop Insurance Program than the White House requested. And the bill provided more rural rental aid, conservation and credit programs than the administration wanted.

Administration officials did not press their objections to these features, however, because they were preoccupied with funding levels in the continuing resolution for various social programs. ∎

New Water Project Funds

The House Oct. 6 approved a bill (HR 3958) providing the first money for new water projects in four years, but the Senate did not act on the measure before Congress adjourned.

HR 3958, a fiscal 1984 supplemental appropriations bill, provided almost $119 million for 43 new water projects.

Of the 43 projects funded by the House-passed bill, 23 had been previously authorized by Congress but not funded. The remaining 20 projects were authorized by a bill (HR 3678) that was approved by the House Public Works and Transportation Committee in August but did not pass the House in 1983. (Story, p. 354)

House Committee Action

The House Appropriations Committee approved HR 3958 on Sept. 21 and reported it (H Rept 98-873) the following day.

The bill was opposed by the Reagan administration, which had requested funds for only 16 new projects costing $33.2 million. Thirteen of the projects funded by HR 3958 were Reagan requests.

David A. Stockman, director of the Office of Management and Budget (OMB), informed the committee that without passage of legislation authorizing the 20 projects in the bill that had not yet been approved by Congress, he would have difficulty recommending that the president sign HR 3958.

HR 3958 provided construction and planning funds for 39 Corps of Engineers and four Bureau of Reclamation projects. It included $103.1 million for construction work on 28 Corps of Engineers projects, and planning and development work on 11 others. These projects included deepening inland waterways and upgrading a number of ports, including Baltimore, Mobile, Norfolk, Sacramento, San Francisco and Tampa.

The four Bureau of Reclamation projects funded by the bill were flood control, power and irrigation projects in Arizona, Colorado, New Mexico and Wyoming. The bill contained $15.85 million for these projects.

Environmentalists had criticized two of the projects — the Animas-La Plata project in Colorado and New Mexico, and the Narrows Unit in Colorado. The latter was included in President Carter's famous "hit list" of projects he did not want built. (1977 Almanac p. 650)

House Floor Action

Over the derisive protests of Rep. Silvio O. Conte, R-Mass., the ranking minority member of the Appropriations Committee, the House Oct. 6 passed HR 3958 by voice vote. The funds provided by the bill were unchanged from those recommended by the Appropriations Committee.

Conte wore a pig mask in a press conference held during debate on HR 3958 to dramatize his point that the bill was pork-barrel legislation. "These congressmen have their schnozzle right in the trough ... slurping up the money," he said, referring to the supporters of the bill.

"And when this bill gets over to that greedy other

body, they will not resist the temptation to get into the trough — slup, slup, slup — and slop up more and more," Conte warned the House later.

The House took two test votes on the bill, focusing on the fact that half of the projects it funded were not yet authorized by Congress. By a vote of 270-124, the House adopted the rule for the measure (H Res 331) waiving points of order against the bill on this issue. *(Vote 361, p. 108-H)*

The House also rejected, 133-271, an amendment offered by Bob Edgar, D-Pa., to delete all unauthorized projects from the bill. *(Vote 364, p. 108-H)*

Senate Committee Action

The Senate Appropriations Committee Oct. 19 approved a trimmed-down version of HR 3958 (S Rept 98-274), providing $78 million to start work on 27 new water projects.

The Senate cut 20 projects from the House bill and added four of its own. Its measure included $70 million for 24 Corps of Engineers projects and $8 million for three projects of the Bureau of Reclamation.

The reclamation projects were the Animas-La Plata Project in Colorado and New Mexico, the Headgate Rock Hydroelectric Project in Arizona, and the Buffalo Bill Dam Modification in Wyoming.

Among the major corps projects were inland waterway improvements for the Sacramento River Deepwater Channel, Calif.; Mississippi River Locks and Dam No. 26 at Alton, Ill.; the Mississippi River Ship Channel from the Gulf of Mexico to Baton Rouge, La.; Gallipolis Locks and Dam on the Ohio River, Ohio and W.Va.; and Bonneville Navigation Lock on the Columbia River, Ore. and Wash.

The Senate panel deleted several other key inland navigation projects sought by the House: Lock and Dam No. 7 and Lock No. 8 on the Monongahela River, Pa. and W.Va., and Oliver Lock and Dam on the Black Warrior-Tombigbee Waterway, Ala.

Major ocean port projects approved by the Senate panel included: Mobile Harbor, Ala.; Baltimore Harbor and Channels, Md.; Gulfport Harbor, Miss.; Freeport Harbor, Texas; and Norfolk Harbor, Va.

Among the flood control projects in the Senate panel's bill were Eight Mile Creek, Ark.; Merced County Streams, Calif.; Kahoma Stream, Hawaii; Atchafalaya Basin Floodway System, La.; and Ellicott Creek, N.Y.

Included in the Senate committee bill but not the House version were Jonesport Harbor, Maine; Basset Creek, Minn.; Gulfport Harbor, Miss.; and Little Dell Lake, Utah.

Twelve of the Senate-funded projects lacked authorizing legislation. ∎

Omnibus Bill Includes Foreign Aid Programs

In an unusual step, Congress in 1983 lumped together authorizations and appropriations for $11.5 billion in foreign aid programs in one bill — the second continuing appropriations resolution (H J Res 413 — PL 98-151) for fiscal 1984.

Putting foreign aid appropriations in a continuing resolution was not unusual: Congress had done so for fiscal years 1980, 1981, and 1983. But since 1973, Congress had regularly passed a separate authorizations bill for foreign aid; its failure to do so in 1983 forced congressional leaders to put stop-gap authorization language in the continuing resolution.

In theory, Congress each year would pass two separate bills on foreign aid: an authorization bill to set overall funding limits and establish foreign policy guidelines, and an appropriations bill to determine how much the administration could spend on aid programs.

Because foreign aid was an unpopular subject, especially in election years, Congress had not passed either type of bill since 1981, when it approved an authorization measure covering fiscal years 1982-1983 and an appropriations bill for fiscal 1982. For fiscal 1983, appropriations were covered in a continuing resolution. *(1981 Almanac pp. 161, 339; 1982 Almanac pp. 156, 242)*

Congressional Plans

Early in the fall of 1983, congressional leaders began planning to put foreign aid programs in an omnibus continuing resolution. From their viewpoint, such an action had the virtue of avoiding lengthy floor debates on foreign policy, especially such touchy issues as aid to El Salvador. As part of an omnibus continuing resolution, foreign aid would evoke less controversy than if it were raised in a separate bill.

As H J Res 413 was snaking its way through the legislative process, both Senate Foreign Relations Committee Chairman Charles H. Percy, R-Ill., and House Foreign Affairs Committee Clement J. Zablocki, D-Wis., tried to use it to preserve at least some of their influence over foreign aid.

Percy on Nov. 10 sought to force action on his committee's authorizations bill by placing an amendment in the continuing resolution to prevent foreign aid spending after April 15, 1984, unless it had been authorized. The Senate approved that amendment by voice vote with little debate.

Zablocki simply pared his committee's complex bill down to the minimum necessary to authorize the funds in H J Res 413. The House adopted Zablocki's limited authorizations amendment on Nov. 8.

The final version of H J Res 413 contained the bulk of Zablocki's amendment. *(Foreign aid authorizations, p. 140)*

Both Appropriations committees acted on foreign aid issues, but their actions were made moot by later action on the continuing resolution.

The Senate Appropriations Committee reported a separate aid appropriations bill (S 1892, S Rept 98-245) on Sept. 27.

The House Appropriations Committee brushed aside an unnumbered bill that had been drafted on Oct. 5 by its Foreign Operations Subcommittee. Instead, the committee on Nov. 2 included stop-gap foreign aid funding in the continuing resolution.

Most decisions on foreign aid were made in private caucuses during negotiations on the continuing resolution. The key House position on foreign aid was hammered out during a Nov. 3 meeting of selected members of the House Foreign Operations Appropriations Subcommittee. Even the subcommittee's chairman, Clarence D. Long, D-Md., was excluded from the meeting — although he later ap-

Foreign Aid Appropriations, Fiscal 1984

The following chart shows amounts in new budget authority of President Reagan's request, the House- and Senate-approved amounts, and the final amounts for foreign aid appropriations in fiscal 1984. Foreign aid programs were included in a continuing resolution, PL 98-

151. *(Figures in parentheses show program limitations; except for a portion of the Export-Import Bank loans, the limitations do not count as new budget authority. Figures for individual development banks include only paid-in capital.)*

Program	Request	House-Passed Amount	Senate-Passed Amount	Final Amount
Inter-American Development Bank	$ 171,623,983	$ 127,380,983	$ 138,423,983	$ 118,423,983
International Bank for Reconstruction and Development	109,720,549	79,720,549	109,720,549	79,720,549
International Development Association	1,095,000,000	945,000,000	700,000,000	945,000,000
Asian Development Bank	160,348,846	61,604,261	160,348,846	113,232,676
African Development Fund	50,000,000	50,000,000	50,000,000	50,000,000
African Development Bank	17,986,678	17,986,678	17,986,678	17,986,678
Total callable capital for development banks	(2,889,522,779)	(2,095,022,666)	(2,889,522,779)	(2,095,022,666)
International Organizations and Programs	239,950,000	314,164,000	285,136,000	314,164,000
Subtotal, Multilateral Aid	$ 1,844,630,056	$ 1,595,856,471	$ 1,461,616,056	$ 1,638,527,886
Agriculture aid	725,213,000	725,213,000	705,000,000	715,106,500
Population aid	212,231,000	244,600,000	212,231,000	240,000,000
Health aid	100,656,000	100,656,000	133,405,000	125,000,000
Education, human resources aid	121,477,000	121,477,000	103,550,000	116,477,000
Energy, selected development aid	172,423,000	150,000,000	140,288,000	140,288,000
Science and technology aid	10,000,000	10,000,000	10,000,000	10,000,000
Private sector revolving fund	(20,000,000)	(20,000,000)	(20,000,000)	(20,000,000)
American schools and hospitals abroad	7,500,000	30,000,000	25,000,000	30,000,000
International disaster aid	25,000,000	25,000,000	25,000,000	25,000,000
Sahel development	103,000,000	103,000,000	103,000,000	103,000,000
Foreign Service retirement and disability	39,316,000	36,537,000	39,316,000	36,537,000
Economic Support Fund	2,949,000,000	2,894,500,000	2,912,000,000	2,903,250,000[1]
Peacekeeping	46,200,000	31,100,000	46,200,000	46,200,000
Agency for International Development (AID) operating expenses	378,512,000	353,066,500	370,000,000	361,533,250
Trade and Development program	22,000,000	10,500,000	22,000,000	16,250,000
AID reappropriation	0	0	40,000,000	(40,000,000)
International narcotics control	53,030,000	41,200,000	46,645,000	41,200,000
Inter-American Foundation	10,705,000	14,000,000	12,000,000	13,000,000
African Development Foundation	3,000,000	3,000,000	0	3,000,000
Peace Corps	108,500,000	116,000,000	113,500,000	115,000,000
Migration, refugee aid	344,500,000	323,000,000	339,500,000	323,000,000
Anti-terrorism program	5,000,000	0	5,000,000	2,500,000
Subtotal, Bilateral Aid	$ 5,437,263,000	$ 5,332,849,500	$ 5,403,635,000	$ 5,366,341,750
Military assistance program grants	747,000,000	420,400,000	697,000,000	510,000,000
International military education and training	56,532,000	46,000,000	56,532,000	51,532,000
Foreign military sales: forgiven loans	1,000,000,000	1,315,000,000	1,395,000,000	1,315,000,000[2]
Foreign military sales: guaranteed loans	(4,656,000,000)	(4,446,500,000)	(4,356,000,000)	(4,401,250,000)[3]
Defense acquisition fund limitation	(325,000,000)	(125,000,000)	(325,000,000)	(225,000,000)
Subtotal, Military Aid	$ 1,803,532,000	$ 1,781,400,000	$ 2,148,532,000	$ 1,876,532,000
Housing guaranty program	(150,000,000)	(150,000,000)	(150,000,000)	(150,000,000)
Overseas Private Investment Corporation				
Direct loans	(15,000,000)	(10,000,000)	(15,000,000)	(10,000,000)
Loan guarantees	(150,000,000)	(100,000,000)	(150,000,000)	(100,000,000)
Export-Import Bank total limitation	(13,846,899,000)	(13,381,007,000)	(14,416,899,000)	(13,881,899,000)
Budget authority effect of Ex-Im Bank limitations	2,552,000,000	2,587,000,000	3,111,000,000	2,587,000,000
Direct loans	(3,830,000,000)	(3,865,000,000)	(4,400,000,000)	(3,865,000,000)
Loan guarantees	(10,000,000,000)	(9,500,000,000)	(10,000,000,000)	(10,000,000,000)
Administration	(16,899,000)	(16,007,000)	(16,899,000)	(16,899,000)
Grand Total	$11,637,425,056	$11,297,105,971	$12,124,783,056	$11,468,401,636

[1] Includes $910 million for Israel and $750 million for Egypt.
[2] Includes $850 million for Israel and $465 million for Egypt.
[3] Includes $850 million for Israel and $835 million for Egypt.

proved the decisions reached in it. Subcommittee members acted when it became clear that the continuing resolution provisions adopted by the Appropriations Committee on Nov. 2 would never pass the full House.

Final decisions on foreign aid were made at a private four-hour meeting, on Nov. 11, of several Senate and House conferees on the continuing resolution.

Still, both chambers recorded votes on foreign aid funding.

In a preliminary vote Nov. 7, the House approved, 262-150, an amendment by Long to include in the continuing resolution the compromise proposal that had been worked out at the Nov. 3 meeting of his subcommittee members. That compromise substantially boosted military aid above the amounts that would have been provided by a simple extension of the first continuing resolution (PL 98-107), which expired Nov. 10. *(Vote 426, p. 126-H)*

The Senate's only vote on foreign aid came on Nov. 10, when it tabled, 46-37, an amendment by Charles McC. Mathias Jr., R-Md., to trim a large increase in funds for the Military Assistance Program. That program made grants to help financially strapped countries buy U.S. weapons. *(Vote 344, p. 56-S)*

Totals

The "foreign operations" section of the continuing resolution included $11.468 billion in new budget authority, of which $8.881 billion was for traditional economic, development and military aid programs and $2.587 billion represented the technical budget effect of loans made by the Export-Import Bank. *(Chart, p. 245)*

Another $18.266 billion was authorized for off-budget items, such as foreign military loan guarantees and Ex-Im Bank guaranteed loans.

President Reagan had requested $11.637 billion in new budget authority, including $9.1 billion for foreign aid and $2.5 billion for the Ex-Im Bank. Reagan's budget also included $19.5 billion for off-budget items.

In new budget authority alone, the final bill was $169 million below Reagan's request, $171 million above the House bill and $656 million below the Senate bill.

The bill specified minimum or maximum amounts of military and military-related aid for only a few countries; the State Department on Dec. 19 announced the preliminary allocations of aid. *(Box, p. 514)*

El Salvador

El Salvador was a major issue in foreign aid discussions at the House-Senate conference on the continuing resolution — as it had dominated foreign aid issues during much of the year. *(El Salvador story, p. 154)*

The bill set a $64.8 million limit on military aid for El Salvador, a cut of $21.5 million from Reagan's request. The House had approved the $64.8 million, while the Senate had approved Reagan's full request.

Conferees made a significant concession to Reagan by not stipulating the accounts under which the aid would be provided. That gave Reagan a free hand to dispense much of the military aid on a grant basis.

The State Department announced Dec. 19 that El Salvador would get $18.5 million in Foreign Military Sales (FMS) loans, $45 million in Military Assistance Program (MAP) grants and $1.3 million in International Military Education and Training (IMET) grants.

That breakdown was slightly more generous, in the proportion of aid given as a grant, than Reagan's original

budget request submitted in January. In that request, Reagan had proposed giving El Salvador $55 million in MAP grants, $30 million in FMS loans and $1.3 million in IMET aid.

The $64.8 million limit was the first statutory cap that Congress had imposed on aid to El Salvador.

The continuing resolution mandated the toughest conditions yet imposed by Congress on aid to El Salvador.

One provision withheld expenditure of 30 percent of the military aid until the Salvadoran government completed its investigation into the murders of four U.S. churchwomen in December 1980, brought the accused murderers to trial and obtained a verdict. Five former national guardsmen had been charged, but their trial was delayed repeatedly.

The bill did not state who would determine when those conditions had been met. In the past, critics had accused the administration of overlooking the shortcomings of the Salvadoran government in a rush to certify its eligibility for U.S. aid.

Another major condition withheld 10 percent of El Salvador's military aid until the president certified to Congress that the government had taken no actions that would "modify, alter, suspend or terminate" the two key parts of its land reform program in a manner that would undermine the rights of those who were intended to benefit from the program. The president also would have to certify that the government "continues to make documented progress" in the land reform program.

Although the bill withheld 30 percent in the churchwomen's case and 10 percent for land reform, conferees nevertheless mandated that total aid to be withheld would be limited to 30 percent.

The bill did not limit economic and development aid to El Salvador — an issue that had generated little controversy in Congress. Reagan had requested $120 million in economic aid and $38 million in development aid for El Salvador in 1984.

The bill did earmark $3 million in economic aid for improvements in the Salvadoran judicial system.

Military vs. Development Aid

The continuing resolution represented a substantial victory for the administration's effort to boost military aid to friendly countries.

Counting both on- and off-budget items, the bill increased foreign military aid programs by 15 percent over fiscal 1983 amounts. By contrast, total funding for economic and development aid programs was cut by 5.6 percent from 1983 levels.

The largest single increase in the bill was for military assistance grants. When Reagan entered office in 1981, the MAP program provided $110 million in grants to help economically strapped nations buy U.S. weapons. By fiscal 1983, it had grown to $383 million; the 1984 continuing resolution provided $510 million.

In another category — foreign military loans — the bill had the effect of giving Reagan slightly more than he requested. By shifting $300 million of Israel's military aid from loans to grants, the bill ended up with $3.551 billion for arms loans to other countries, $45 million more than Reagan had requested.

The bill also gave Reagan much more freedom to allocate military aid among countries than any president had in recent years. Traditionally, amounts for most countries were specified in foreign aid bills or in the reports issued by

Reagan Wins in Foreign Aid Supplemental

President Reagan won a significant victory for his foreign aid program in the second supplemental appropriations bill (HR 3069 — PL 98-63) for fiscal 1983.

Although the bill made substantial cuts from President Reagan's requests, it set foreign aid spending at levels that were "more than we ever hoped for," said a State Department official.

The bill provided about two-thirds of the $1 billion-plus that Reagan had requested for "security assistance." Security assistance included military aid, such as loans and grants to help foreign governments buy U.S. arms, and economic aid to U.S. allies.

The bill also included Reagan's $245 million request for the International Development Association (IDA), an arm of the World Bank. That sum was an addition to $700 million previously approved by Congress.

Security Aid

HR 3069 gave Reagan $689 million of the $1.067 billion he had requested for security assistance programs. The major items included in the bill were:

● $301.3 million for the Economic Support Fund (ESF), which bolstered the economies of countries friendly to the United States. Reagan had requested $354 million.

● $293.5 million for Foreign Military Sales (FMS) market-rate loans that helped friendly countries buy U.S. weapons. Reagan had requested $525 million.

● $93.3 million for Military Assistance Program (MAP) grants, which also helped foreign countries buy U.S. arms. Reagan had requested $187 million.

Conferees on the bill gave Reagan virtually complete discretion to allocate the security aid among the more than 30 countries for which money was requested. There were three exceptions to that rule: Lebanon, El Salvador and Somalia. *(Allocations, box, p. 514)*

The bill earmarked $251 million for Lebanon, including $150 million in ESF aid, $100 million in FMS loans and $1 million in military training aid.

In their report, but not in the text of the bill, House-Senate conferees also placed limits of $25 million on military aid to El Salvador and $2 million to Somalia.

The El Salvador money was one of the most controversial issues facing the conferees.

Reagan had requested an additional $50 million in fiscal 1983 for military grants to El Salvador as part of a $110 million boost in military aid announced in March. The House Appropriations Committee had rejected the $50 million request and the Senate committee had ap-proved it. Conferees split the difference at $25 million.

The $25 million limit for El Salvador was not included in the bill itself, and thus was not legally binding, but Reagan accepted it. Combined with $26.3 million previously appropriated and $30 million reprogrammed from other countries, the $25 million put military aid to El Salvador in fiscal 1983 at $81.3 million.

Another informal $2 million limit was placed on FMS loans to Somalia, which was engaged in a border dispute with Ethiopia. Reagan asked for $4 million in loans and $5 million in military grants for Somalia.

A State Department official on July 27 expressed satisfaction that HR 3069 eliminated the need for sharp cutbacks in foreign aid programs.

"It's fair to say that instead of having disasters all around the world, we have reduced it to disappointment in the major cases, and some new programs that we had planned probably won't get started," he said.

Other Provisions

Other major foreign aid provisions of HR 3069 were:

● A flat prohibition on additional FMS loans for Jordan. Reagan had requested $35 million in supplemental loans for Jordan, largely to encourage King Hussein to participate in Middle East peace negotiations. Congress previously had approved $51.5 million. But Hussein had shied away from direct negotiations, prompting moves in Congress to cut Jordan's aid.

● A prohibition on all forms of aid to Guatemala except for development projects conducted by private voluntary organizations. Reagan had requested $6 million in supplemental 1983 funds for economic aid for Guatemala. Although Reagan did not request military aid for Guatemala in fiscal 1983, he had requested $10 million in such aid for fiscal 1984, and the prohibition in HR 3069 was widely viewed as a signal of congressional reluctance to provide military aid to that nation's repressive government.

● A similar requirement that economic aid for Zaire be used only to fund development projects sponsored by private organizations. Reagan had requested $7 million in supplemental ESF aid for Zaire, where the U.S. aid program had faced frequent charges of corruption and misspent money.

● A ban on spending of any of the foreign aid money until Sept. 15, 1983, or until Congress enacted supplemental foreign aid authorization legislation, whichever came first. The authorization legislation (HR 2992, S 1347) later died in Congress. *(Story, p. 140)*

congressional committees.

But the continuing resolution specified amounts for only a few countries and allowed Reagan to shift amounts among countries, as long as he notified Congress in advance and stayed within his original budget requests, submitted in January and February.

Mathias raised the military aid issue in the Senate on Nov. 10 with an amendment that would have pared the increase in the Military Assistance Program. In particular, he questioned aid to Costa Rica, which had no army.

Mathias noted that the $697 million in the Senate bill represented an 81 percent increase over fiscal 1983. Mathias proposed $421 million — a 10 percent increase — which he called "a reasonable amount."

Mathias said that under the Reagan administration military aid had increased by 100 percent, while "humanitarian development assistance" had increased by only 10 percent. "If you want to look at the root of instability and

insecurity, there it is," he said.

Patrick J. Leahy, D-Vt., put the issue in a direct foreign vs. domestic context, saying Reagan had proposed to double or triple the aid to some countries. "I am not sure how I could explain my voting for doubling or tripling of their aid to my farmers back in counties in Vermont, for example, and explain why we are cutting a number of domestic programs that involve them."

Opponents of Mathias' amendment contended that it would have required significant cuts in aid for several key countries, including Turkey, Portugal, Morocco, Somalia and the Sudan.

Bob Kasten, R-Wis., said aid to those countries was "the guts" of the entire U.S. foreign aid program.

And Pete Wilson, R-Calif., argued that countries friendly to the United States could "defend their own freedom" only with help from the United States.

"We are not policemen to the world, but whether we like it or not we are cast in the position of being the leader of the free world and of certainly being the major supplier to those who would defend their freedom [and] who lack the economic means to do so," Wilson said.

Israel, Egypt

Israel, long the most popular item in the foreign aid bill among members of Congress, got one of its biggest single aid increase in years.

The bill provided $1.7 billion in military aid for Israel in 1984 — the same amount as in fiscal 1983. But fully half of that amount was to be a forgiven loan (the same as a grant), a $100 million increase over the 1983 amount. The remainder was to be a regular FMS loan, which must be repaid at market interest rates.

The bill also gave Israel $910 million in grants under the Economic Support Fund, an increase of $125 million over 1983. That aid essentially was a subsidy of the Israeli economy. Reagan had requested $785 million.

The administration did not oppose the increases in 1983, as it had done in late 1982. *(1982 Almanac p. 242)*

The bill also authorized Israel to spend up to $550 million of its military aid for research and development on its new fighter-bomber, the Lavi.

Egypt, in a smaller aid boost, was to receive $1.365 billion in military aid under the bill, of which $465 million was to be a forgiven loan and $900 million was to be a regular FMS loan. Reagan had requested $400 million as a forgiven loan and $900 million as a regular loan. Egypt was to receive another $750 million in economic aid.

International Banks

The bill included $1.3 billion in direct contributions and $2.1 billion in so-called "callable capital" (similar to loan guarantees) for the World Bank and other international development banks. Conferees cut $280.3 million in direct contributions and $794.5 million in callable capital from Reagan's request.

As in previous years, the most controversial item was the U.S. contribution to the International Development Association (IDA), the World Bank agency that made no-interest, long-term loans to the world's poorest countries. Conservatives in Congress for years had criticized IDA's lending policies and had fought U.S. support for the agency.

Reagan requested $1.1 billion in fiscal 1984 for the final payment on the U.S. pledge of $3.24 billion to the sixth replenishment of IDA resources.

The House had approved $945 million — the same as the fiscal 1983 amount — but the Senate approved only $700 million. The final bill provided $945 million.

Conferees also pared Reagan's requests for U.S. contributions to the main arm of the World Bank, the International Bank for Reconstruction and Development. That agency made loans at near-market rates to middle-income developing countries, such as Mexico and Brazil.

Reagan had requested $109.7 million in direct contributions to that agency and $1.4 billion in callable capital. Conferees cut those amounts to $79.7 million and $983.2 million, respectively.

Export-Import Bank

Conferees approved what they called a "symbolic" increase in funding for the Export-Import Bank, a U.S. government agency that made loans and loan guarantees to help American firms sell their products overseas.

The key funding item for the bank was the direct loan program, under which the bank actually lent money to foreign countries and firms that bought American products. Congress approved $4.4 billion for that program in fiscal 1983, but the bank used only $890 million. Reagan requested $3.83 billion for fiscal 1984.

Complaining that the bank had failed to "pursue aggressively policies which would result in greater lending," the conferees approved $3.865 billion for fiscal 1984 and said they would again approve $4.4 billion if there was enough demand.

Greece, Turkey

On its face, the bill appeared to give Reagan a free hand to provide Turkey all of the $755 million in military aid he had proposed. However, the conferees on the bill included a statement in their report that had the effect of cutting that aid by $35 million.

Reagan's request for Turkey was bitterly opposed by pro-Greek members of Congress, and most congressional committees responsible for foreign aid voted to reduce it. Greece and Turkey were traditional rivals. The $755 million request was a substantial increase over the $400 million Congress had approved for fiscal 1983.

While the continuing resolution itself set no limits on aid to either Greece or Turkey, the conferees in their report directed the administration to adhere to a 7-10 ratio in military aid to those countries. For several years, at congressional insistence, Greece had received $7 for every $10 that Turkey received; Turkey got more aid because it had a much bigger army than did Greece.

Under congressional pressure, Reagan in March agreed to increase aid to Greece to $500 million, from the $280 million he originally had proposed, if Greece renewed an agreement providing for several U.S. military bases on Greek soil. Greece and the United States signed a five-year bases agreement in September.

Adhering to the 7-10 ratio, the administration in December allocated $500 million in FMS loans to Greece and $715 million in aid to Turkey (including $585 million in FMS loans and $130 million in MAP grants).

Syria

In a move unusual for its directness, the continuing resolution withdrew some $80 million in past appropriations for economic aid to Syria and shifted $15 million of that money to Grenada and $10 million to Italy.

The aid repeal did not affect money for training stu-

dents whose studies began before enactment of the bill.

The Syrian money was appropriated during the Carter administration but never spent. The Grenada money was to be used for economic development and reconstruction in the wake of the U.S. invasion on Oct. 25, provided that the House and Senate Appropriations committees were notified 15 days before the funds were obligated.

Other members insisted, without much direct evidence, that there was another trade-off — the Syrian money was transferred to Israel.

Other Provisions

In other foreign aid provisions, PL 98-151:

• Appropriated $1.4 billion for development assistance programs of the Agency for International Development.

• Appropriated $10 million in development assistance for Botswana.

• Prohibited all military, economic and development aid to Guatemala, except for economic development projects conducted through private voluntary organizations.

• Authorized the establishment of a revolving fund within the Agency for International Development to finance development activities by the private sector. Up to $20 million could be placed in the fund in fiscal 1984.

• Authorized the establishment of a program to provide assistance to enable foreign countries to combat terrorism. For fiscal 1984, $2.5 million was appropriated.

• Directed the secretaries of state and Treasury to report to Congress by Feb. 1, 1984, on the economic policies of nations receiving foreign aid.

• Directed the president to submit to Congress each January a report on the extent to which nations receiving U.S. foreign aid supported the foreign policy of the United States.

• Prohibited aid for any country certified by the president to have failed to take adequate measures to prevent narcotic drugs from entering the United States.

• Appropriated $1.6 billion in direct payments and $2.1 billion in callable capital (similar to loan guarantees) for international development banks.

• Set aside 10 percent of development aid funds for activities by economically and socially disadvantaged enterprises, black colleges and universities, and private and voluntary organizations controlled by black Americans, Hispanic Americans and other disadvantaged persons, including women. The administrator of the Agency for International Development was permitted to waive this provision. ∎

Congress Clears 1984 Continuing Resolution

Congress acted with rare dispatch Sept. 30 by sending President Reagan a 41-day, stopgap spending bill with hours to spare before the 1984 fiscal year began Oct. 1.

Instead of the typical beat-the-clock chaos that traditionally had accompanied passage of the temporary money bill for most government agencies, Congress cleared the first fiscal 1984 continuing resolution (H J Res 368 — PL 98-107) early in the evening Sept. 30.

Floor and conference action on the continuing resolution was condensed into three days. On Sept. 28, the House passed the massive money bill in 25 minutes, by a 261-160 vote. The Senate, with even more speed, approved the measure by voice vote Sept. 29. *(Vote 343, p. 102-H)*

House and Senate conferees met the morning of Sept. 30 and completed the bill in less than two hours. The House adopted the conference report that afternoon by a vote of 232-136. The Senate followed suit in a voice vote, clearing the bill for the president. Reagan signed the bill Oct. 1. *(Vote 354, p. 106-H)*

Neither the House nor Senate added any extraneous amendments to the bill on the floor, another departure from tradition. Such bills often were laden with ornaments by members hoping to attach controversial legislation to a bill the president must sign to keep the government in business.

The outlook was not as bright, however, when the continuing resolution first began traveling through legislative channels. The House Appropriations Committee Sept. 21 loaded its first version (H J Res 367 — H Rept 98-374) with so many controversial amendments that the entire bill was ditched.

The key to passage of the streamlined bill, which expired Nov. 10, was the promise from House and Senate leaders that lawmakers could attach their amendments to a pending supplemental appropriations bill (HR 3959) for fiscal 1984. Another explanation for the restraint on the

continuing resolution was that legislators were exhausted from the intense debate on stationing U.S. Marines in Lebanon, which preceded action on the money bill, and they were not up to a last-minute fight over government funding.

The continuing resolution provided interim financing, from Oct. 1 to Nov. 10, for programs normally funded under nine regular appropriations bills that had not become law by the beginning of the 1984 fiscal year. Four other appropriations bills had been signed into law. Two of the nine that had not become law were cleared by Congress and awaiting presidential approval. Those two were the bills for the District of Columbia and for military construction programs.

In 1983, Congress completed more regular spending bills by the Oct. 1 start of the fiscal year than it had since 1978, when eight bills were cleared and five were law by Oct. 1.

Before its final adjournment Nov. 18, Congress was forced to approve a further continuing resolution (H J Res 413 — PL 98-151) to maintain funding for agencies covered by the three regular appropriations bills that did not clear before the session ended. *(Story, p. 528)*

Provisions

H J Res 368 provided the following funding levels through Nov. 10:

• For the District of Columbia and for military construction programs, spending was at the conference report level for each bill. Congress cleared the District of Columbia bill (HR 3415) Sept. 29 and the military construction bill (HR 3263) Sept. 28.

• For agriculture, food and related programs, spending was at an annual level of $33.9 billion, about the same level as in both the House- and Senate-passed versions of the agriculture spending bill (HR 3223). The bill assumed cur-

rent levels of spending for food stamps and other major food programs, instead of the lower levels in the Reagan budget.

• For the departments of Commerce, Justice, State and the federal judiciary, the bill put spending at the lower of the House-passed or Senate committee-reported bill (HR 3222). There were a few exceptions, such as for the Legal Services Corporation, which was allocated $275 million, about halfway between the House and Senate versions.

• For Interior, the rate was set at the level agreed to by conferees Sept. 29 on the Interior appropriations bill (HR 3363).

• For the departments of Labor, Health and Human Services and Education, spending was at the lower of the House-passed or Senate committee-reported level in HR 3913. The bill retained the terms and conditions of the fiscal 1983 continuing resolution (PL 97-377) for this category. This provision softened anti-abortion language approved in the House Sept. 22 by restoring the so-called Hyde amendment, which permitted the use of Medicaid money for abortions when the life of the mother is in danger.

• For the Defense Department, funding was set at an annual rate of $247 billion prorated for the 41-day duration of the continuing resolution. This was the level approved by the House Appropriations Subcommittee on Defense Sept. 29. The bill also banned new starts for major new programs.

• For foreign assistance programs, the bill set spending at the fiscal 1983 rate or the president's fiscal 1984 budget request, whichever was lower. There was no disagreement between the House and Senate bills on this issue.

• For programs covered by the Treasury-Postal Service bill (HR 3191), spending was at the rate of the fiscal 1983 continuing resolution (PL 97-377). *(1982 Almanac p. 238)*

House Action

When the House Appropriations Committee took up its first version of the fiscal 1984 continuing resolution Sept. 21, it attached so many controversial amendments that the bill (H J Res 367) was doomed from the start.

One of those amendments was to cut off financing for U.S. Marines in Lebanon on Dec. 1, 1983, if Reagan refused to invoke the War Powers Resolution by then. This provision set off a complicated snarl with House leaders, who had reached a separate agreement with the White House to keep Marines in Lebanon for at least 18 months.

With the war powers clause and other volatile amendments, H J Res 367 was a sure candidate for a presidential veto. In addition to the Lebanon limitation, there were amendments to increase assistance for Israel and Egypt, provide drought aid for American farmers, block a contested Federal Communications Commission regulation affecting television programming and defy Reagan's veto of school desegregation aid for Chicago.

As often happens with omnibus continuing resolutions, members saw it as the only vehicle to which they could attach proposals that had little chance of passing independently. And, recognizing that the Senate usually added dozens of unrelated amendments to such resolutions, some members tried "to get even with the Senate," said Appropriations Committee Chairman Jamie L. Whitten, D-Miss.

Accusing Appropriations members of "meddling with the rights of other committees," Speaker Thomas P. O'Neill Jr., D-Mass., Sept. 22 sent H J Res 367 to the Foreign Affairs Committee to review the war powers sec-

tion. Such referral of an appropriations bill to a legislative committee was without precedent, according to the House parliamentarian's office. The measure never emerged from Foreign Affairs.

After shuttling H J Res 367 to Foreign Affairs, O'Neill had Whitten put together a slimmed-down bill (H J Res 368), which was stripped of the 19 amendments added by Appropriations Sept. 21.

H J Res 368 was handled only by the Rules Committee because Whitten was reluctant to bring the new bill back to his committee, where he said members would "offer the same amendments and we'd get into the same fix." It was possible to bypass the Appropriations panel and go straight to Rules because the Rules Committee could send any bill to the floor, even if it was not reported by a committee.

By skipping over Appropriations, Rules became the forum for frustrated members and lobbyists who wanted to stick their pet projects on the continuing resolution. California Democrat Vic Fazio, for one, asked for permission to offer an amendment delaying a controversial Federal Communications Commission rule concerning television syndication rights. Bill Alexander, D-Ark., and Tom Loeffler, R-Texas, wanted aid for drought-stricken farmers. Others came with special requests, but the Rules Committee denied them all Sept. 27 and, by voice vote, issued a closed rule barring amendments.

H J Res 368 was brought to the floor Sept. 28 and there were only 25 minutes of debate. The measure was approved in a 261-160 vote. *(Vote 343, p. 102-H)*

Senate Action

The tightly controlled situation in the House apparently had a salutary effect on the Senate Appropriations Committee, where members Sept. 28 heeded Chairman Mark O. Hatfield's plea to withhold non-essential amendments. "This is only a simple stopgap measure, not an omnibus vehicle for every stray measure," said Hatfield, R-Ore.

After listening to what Hatfield called his "sermonette," committee members agreed not to offer their amendments. One influence was Hatfield's announcement that Senate Majority Leader Howard H. Baker Jr., R-Tenn., had agreed not to offer his proposal seeking more money for the controversial Clinch River Breeder Reactor in Tennessee.

The only amendment adopted by the committee was one offered by Ted Stevens, R-Alaska, to set defense spending at $253 billion. The House-passed bill called for $228 billion.

Before taking the measure to the floor, Hatfield said he believed the biggest hurdle was cleared when the Appropriations panel stayed in line.

"You have 29 senators, just shy of one-third of the Senate, who all restrained themselves. I think anyone who raises their head in the brush out there [on the floor] will get shot at from 29 different directions," he said.

Hatfield's prediction proved true, when the Senate took up the bill the next day. After Baker won a unanimous agreement from senators not to offer any amendments, the bill was passed in just 17 minutes. It was approved by voice vote.

The Senate-passed version of H J Res 368 substituted the Senate's recommended spending levels for those accepted by the House.

The Senate also changed the bill's expiration date from Nov. 15, as passed by the House, to Nov. 10, to avoid

bumping up against the proposed adjournment date of Nov. 18.

Conference Committee Action

House and Senate conferees met Sept. 30 and completed the bill in less than two hours (H Rept 98-397).

Most differences in the bill were settled amicably. One problem arose when Hatfield offered language, at Baker's request, to make it clear that already appropriated but unobligated money could be spent for the Clinch River reactor, but no new appropriations would be allowed.

Several House conferees balked at the proposal, warning that it would alarm anti-Clinch River members in the House, who might try to hold up the conference report. With that warning, the language was modified to make sure there would be no new spending on the nuclear power plant.

Another minor scuffle occurred over how much money Congress should appropriate to help Los Angeles pay for anti-terrorist security at the 1984 Olympic Games. The House asked for $50 million and the Senate wanted $5 million. The smaller Senate figure was accepted. ∎

Congress Clears 2nd Continuing Resolution

Three days after several government departments ran out of money, President Reagan Nov. 14 signed a stopgap spending bill to fund those agencies through the Sept. 30, 1984, end of the fiscal year. Because of a three-day, Veterans Day holiday weekend and White House assurances that Reagan would sign the bill (H J Res 413 — PL 98-151), there was no disruption in government services.

The second continuing resolution for fiscal 1984 cleared Congress Nov. 12. The House adopted the bill's conference report (H Rept 98-540) by a 173-136 vote that day. The Senate approved the measure by voice vote. *(Vote 455, p. 134-H)*

After defeating its original version Nov. 8, the House passed H J Res 413 Nov. 10 by a 224-189 vote. The Senate approved it by voice vote in the early morning hours Nov. 11. *(Vote 452, p. 132-H)*

A first continuing resolution for fiscal 1984 (H J Res 368 — PL 98-107) provided agencies with funding from Oct. 1 through Nov. 10. *(Story, p. 526)*

Final passage of the continuing resolution came after a week-long confrontation between House Democrats and Reagan over nearly $1 billion in extra domestic spending the House attached to the bill. Reagan's veto threat dissipated, though, when House and Senate conferees Nov. 11 whittled down the extra education and social welfare spending to $98.7 million, one-tenth of the $997.7 million that House Majority Leader Jim Wright, D-Texas, first proposed.

The main purpose of the second continuing resolution was to provide appropriations for the remainder of the 1984 fiscal year for programs whose regular annual funding bills did not clear Congress before adjournment Nov. 18.

The end-of-the-session battle over the stopgap spending bill had different themes in the House and Senate. But in both chambers, the common thread was the desire of lawmakers to attach controversial items to one of the last pieces of legislation they felt certain would clear before the 1983 adjournment Nov. 18.

In the House, the first version of the interim spending bill fell victim to a band of freshman Democrats making a symbolic protest against soaring federal deficits. Teaming up with Republicans and more senior Democrats, the young rebels helped defeat the first resolution (H J Res 403) by a three-vote margin Nov. 8. The defeat was the first time the House had rejected a continuing appropriations resolution since 1967.

The House battle also focused on Wright's controversial plan to add money for education and social programs.

In the Senate, the major sticking point was abortion funding by federal employee health insurance plans. After a filibuster and several close votes, the Senate joined the House in barring the use of federal employee health benefits to pay for abortions except when the mother's life was in danger.

The Senate also engaged in its regular practice of decorating a catchall money bill with extraneous amendments. These ranged from pork-barrel projects for various members to a $100,000 appropriation for a reward for information leading to the arrest and conviction of persons involved in the Nov. 7 bombing of the Capitol's Senate wing.

The irony in the continuing resolution drama was that Congress had made unusual progress in 1983 in passing regular 1984 money bills.

Of the 13 standard appropriations measures, eight had been signed into law by the time H J Res 413 began moving through Congress. The continuing resolution was needed only for programs in the Agriculture, Commerce-State-Justice, Defense, Foreign Aid and Treasury-Postal Service bills.

The Commerce-State-Justice bill (HR 3222 — PL 98-166) was signed into law Nov. 28, superseding part of the continuing resolution.

The Defense bill (HR 4185 — PL 98-212) was signed into law Dec. 8, also superseding a large part of the continuing resolution.

Major Provisions

As enacted, the following were the major provisions of H J Res 413:

● **Foreign Aid.** The bill made both authorizations and appropriations of $11.5 billion in new budget authority for foreign aid and related programs. *(Story, p. 521)*

● **Defense.** Set 1984 spending levels at $247 billion, the level passed by the House in the defense appropriations bill (HR 4185). Allowed work to proceed on new programs and multi-year contracts, for items such as the MX missile and B-1 bomber, if they were contained in both the House- and Senate-passed versions of HR 4185. *(Story, p. 479)*

● **Labor-HHS-Education.** Divided the $98.7 million education-social welfare package among the following programs: education for the handicapped, $25 million; vocational rehabilitation, $10 million; schooling for immigrant children, $30 million; college work-study, $5 million; supplemental educational opportunity grants, $5 million; community health centers, $10 million; National Technical Institute for the Deaf, $1.7 million; Gallaudet College, $2 million; food distribution and emergency shelter for the

needy, $10 million. Congress previously had enacted HR 3913, a $104.4 billion Labor-HHS-Education appropriations bill for fiscal 1984. *(Story, p. 504)*

● **Agriculture.** Provided the $31.7 billion in funding for agriculture, food and related programs that was agreed to in the conference report for HR 3223 (H Rept 98-450). *(Story, p. 516)*

● **Commerce-State-Justice.** Set spending for the departments of Commerce, State, Justice and the federal judiciary at the lower of the House-passed or Senate-reported bill, with some exceptions. *(Story, p. 472)*

● **Treasury-Postal Service.** Provided funding at the level reported by the Senate Appropriations Committee in S 1646, but with the terms and conditions in the House-passed Treasury-Postal Service bill (HR 4139). Also allocated $879 million for the postal revenue forgone subsidy, which prevented a rate increase for preferred mailers, mostly non-profit organizations. A key provision prohibited the use of federal employee health benefits to pay for abortions except when the mother's life was imperiled.

● **HUD-Independent Agencies.** Appropriated $75 million for job training for Vietnam-era veterans. Another $75 million for veterans' job training was included in HR 3959 (PL 98-181), a fiscal 1984 supplemental appropriations bill. *(Story, p. 495)*

House Committee Action

The legislative journey of the second continuing resolution started with a novel approach used by the House Appropriations Committee when it took up the measure Nov. 2.

The committee simply approved a one-paragraph resolution to fund government agencies whose fiscal 1984 money bills had not been enacted. The bill (H J Res 403 — H Rept 98-473) merely extended the first continuing resolution from its expiration date of Nov. 10 to Feb. 29, 1984.

The Appropriations panel then tore off the 13 extraneous amendments it had added to H J Res 403 and packaged them in a new, less urgent supplemental spending bill (HR 4293 — H Rept 98-474).

Despite the panel's restraint on the continuing resolution, the Rules Committee Nov. 4 voted to allow consideration of major amendments dealing with foreign aid, education and housing when the bill reached the House floor, including Wright's amendment adding money for domestic programs.

For Appropriations leaders, the Rules action negated the unusual work they had done Nov. 2 to produce a "clean" stopgap money bill. During the Appropriations meeting, Chairman Jamie L. Whitten, D-Miss., fought against amendments, but members added several. At that point, Whitten pushed through a plan to report a simple extension and a separate supplemental bill with the amendments. Both measures were approved by voice vote.

A key amendment in the supplemental provided extra military aid for foreign countries, which Reagan had requested. Other provisions included $50 million in overt aid to Central America and drought relief for U.S. farmers.

While the continuing resolution made it to the House floor, and ultimately was defeated on the first try, the supplemental never was considered by the House.

David R. Obey, D-Wis., a veteran Appropriations member, said he had never seen the panel split the amendments from a continuing resolution and compile them in a separate measure. Obey said the maneuver, which he supported, represented the failure of the system by which

members and lobbyists tried to attach pet projects to the catchall money bill. "This is what happens when every goddamned interest group in America tries to harass the committee for one more try. It turns the legislative process into a zoo. It's just nuts," he said.

House Floor Action

On Tuesday, Nov. 8, the House began work on H J Res 403 (H Rept 98-473), the one-paragraph continuing resolution reported by the Appropriations Committee Nov. 2. But the Rules Committee decision to allow major amendments opened the door for a complicated fight.

Approving the first amendment, on foreign aid, was relatively painless. The bipartisan amendment was a compromise offered by Clarence D. Long, D-Md., and Jack F. Kemp, R-N.Y., respectively the chairman and the ranking Republican on the Appropriations Subcommittee on Foreign Operations. Their amendment was amended by Foreign Affairs Committee Chairman Clement J. Zablocki, D-Wis., to authorize the spending levels in the Long-Kemp proposal. The House approved the package by a vote of 262-150. *(Vote 426, p. 126-H)*

The amendment's key points provided Israel with $1.7 billion in military aid and $910 million in economic aid, and Egypt with $1.3 billion in military aid and $750 million in economic aid. Also included was $64.8 million in military aid for El Salvador, but with 30 percent to be withheld until a verdict was reached in the murder case involving four U.S. churchwomen three years ago in El Salvador.

Serious problems began when Wright offered the Democratic leadership's proposal to add $997.7 million for education, job training, low-income energy assistance and other social programs.

Democratic supporters of the Wright amendment argued that it would restore some of the domestic spending cuts that Reagan won from Congress in 1981. They also said it would force Congress and Reagan to decide whether to back up their recent cries for improved education. But Silvio O. Conte, R-Mass., the senior Republican on Appropriations, attacked Wright's proposal, claiming that education funding had increased the past few years.

Republicans demanded separate votes on the various components of the Wright amendment. In these votes, the House adopted extra money for vocational education, schooling for immigrant children, community health centers, job training, child nutrition and several other services. But members soundly rejected — 122-286 — the section providing $43 million for science centers at three universities. *(Vote 428, p. 126-H)*

After deleting the money for the science centers, the House then passed the remaining $954.4 million in the Wright amendment as a package. The vote was 254-155. *(Vote 434, p. 128-H)*

While attention on the floor focused on Wright's plea for more domestic money, another important fight was occurring in leadership offices just off the floor. There, Speaker Thomas P. O'Neill Jr., D-Mass., was meeting with rebellious freshman Democrats who were threatening to vote against the entire continuing resolution unless speedy action was taken on legislation to reduce the federal deficit.

Freshmen at the meeting later said they were close to prying a stalled tax increase bill (HR 4170) out of the Rules Committee when the bells rang signaling the final vote on the continuing resolution. Having failed to get a satisfactory answer from leaders, 24 freshman Democrats joined 43 more senior Democrats and 139 Republicans to defeat the

bill, 203-206. *(Vote 436, p. 128-H)*

House leaders were furious with the freshmen, who had clearly been the difference between winning and losing. O'Neill called the freshman tactic "kind of ridiculous." But they began to pick up the pieces and put together a new continuing resolution. And to placate the freshmen, attempts were made to dislodge the tax bill, including additional meetings between Ways and Means Committee Chairman Dan Rostenkowski, D-Ill., and Rules Committee members.

Under a plan hatched Nov. 9 by Democratic leaders, Appropriations Committee Chairman Whitten introduced a new, unamended continuing resolution (H J Res 413) identical to the one-paragraph bill reported by Appropriations Nov. 2.

Bypassing the Appropriations panel, the Rules Committee then met in emergency session to consider the fresh bill. At the request of Democratic leaders, Rules approved a floor procedure by which Wright would offer an amendment to H J Res 413 incorporating all the extras, including the Long-Kemp-Zablocki foreign aid package, that the House had accepted before the bill was defeated Nov. 8. Rules also permitted Steny H. Hoyer, D-Md., to offer an amendment attaching the text of the House-passed Treasury-Postal Service spending bill (HR 4139) to the continuing resolution.

Thursday, Nov. 10 — the day the first continuing resolution expired at midnight — opened with an abbreviated rerun of the House activity two days before.

Angry that Democrats wanted another chance to pass essentially the same measure that had been rejected Nov. 8, Republicans fought to defeat the rule for floor debate. Conte begged the 24 dissident Democratic freshmen from Nov. 8 to again join Republicans and reject the rule. The Democrats prevailed, however, and the rule (H Res 367) was adopted 238-177. *(Vote 450, p. 132-H)*

During debate on the new continuing resolution, H J Res 413, Republicans blasted Democratic leaders for again offering the Wright money for education and social services. In its second incarnation, the amendment contained $954.4 million, compared to the $997.7 million in the first version. Conte repeatedly warned that adding "the Wright stuff" would prompt a White House veto. Liberal Democrats responded by daring Reagan to veto money to help "the poorest of the poor," as one member put it.

Before adopting Wright's amendment, 235-181, the House by voice vote accepted Hoyer's addition to attach the Treasury-Postal Service appropriations bill to H J Res 413. The Treasury bill included the language preventing federal workers from using government health insurance to pay for abortions. *(Vote 451, p. 132-H)*

On final passage of the new continuing resolution, Democrats rounded up the votes they had lost two days earlier. H J Res 413 was approved 224-189. Those voting yes included 14 repentant freshman Democrats who had voted no on final passage Nov. 8. *(Vote 452, p. 132-H)*

Senate Action

With a Nov. 10 deadline looming, pressure to pass the continuing resolution was so intense that the House and Senate worked simultaneously on the measure. Typically, the Senate waited until the House completed its action.

The Senate Appropriations Committee approved its own bill (S J Res 194 — S Rept 98-304) Nov. 8. One major difference was the Senate bill would have run through the end of the fiscal year, to Sept. 30, 1984, instead of the House expiration date of Feb. 29, 1984.

Mark O. Hatfield, R-Ore., chairman of the Senate Appropriations Committee, cautioned that Reagan would veto the bill if the committee agreed to amendments similar to those in the House. Heeding his warning, panel members attached mostly minor amendments to the bill.

After the House's unusual defeat of the spending bill Nov. 8, an impatient Senate started debating its own version Nov. 9.

The Senate made progress on technical amendments but then stumbled over an anti-abortion amendment by Jeremiah Denton, R-Ala. Denton's amendment inserted the so-called Ashbrook language (after the late Rep. John M. Ashbrook, R-Ohio (1961-82)), which barred the use of federal employee health benefits to pay for abortions except where the mother's life was in danger.

In a series of close votes, including one tie, Denton won his point. This prompted a filibuster by Bob Packwood, R-Ore., an advocate of free choice on abortion. Finally, a frustrated Majority Leader Howard H. Baker Jr., R-Tenn., pulled the bill from the floor until the next day.

After the House finished its new bill (H J Res 413) Nov. 10, the Senate set aside its own continuing resolution, S J Res 194, and took up H J Res 413. But Baker warned that Reagan probably would veto the bill, as approved by the House, because of the Wright amendment.

To get a sense of how senators stood on the Wright provisions, Hatfield offered an amendment to delete the $954 million the House had added for domestic spending. The Senate adopted Hatfield's amendment, 53-36. *(Vote 338, p. 56-S)*

The Senate then plunged back into its abortion troubles. Noting that the House-passed bill contained the Ashbrook anti-abortion language, Hatfield offered an amendment to strip that wording from the bill. The Senate rejected Hatfield's proposal, 43-44. After two more close procedural votes, the Senate retained the abortion restrictions, and pro-choice senators abandoned their filibuster. *(Vote 339, p. 56-S)*

A long chain of Senate amendments followed, keeping the Senate in session until 3:40 a.m. Nov. 11. The amendments adopted ranged from a $100,000 reward for information on the Nov. 7 Capitol bombing to $150 million in job training for veterans.

Several controversial amendments were rejected. Those defeated included proposals to severely reduce foreign military assistance, to provide health insurance benefits to the unemployed and to require the president to send a balanced budget to Congress.

After finishing the stack of amendments, the Senate passed the continuing resolution by voice vote.

Conference Action

House and Senate conferees met Nov. 11 to iron out differences between the two bills. The biggest dispute concerned the Wright domestic money, which was in the House version but not in the Senate bill.

By late Nov. 11, hours after their Nov. 10 deadline, House and Senate conferees reached agreement on a common version of H J Res 413 that they could send to Reagan, who was to return to Washington Nov. 14 from a trip to Japan and Korea.

After days of White House warnings that Reagan would veto the bill because of the nearly $1 billion in education and social service spending, conferees finally settled on a compromise that cut the domestic money to

$98.7 million. Democratic leaders, who seemed to savor the week-long confrontation with Reagan over politically popular social programs, settled for only 10 percent of what they had wanted.

As agreed to by the conferees, the bill provided money for education for the handicapped, vocational rehabilitation, immigrant education, college student aid, community health centers, colleges for the deaf and emergency shelters for the homeless. But all of these programs were funded at levels substantially below what the House had approved.

Conferees also set the expiration date for the continuing resolution at the Senate date of Sept. 30, 1984, instead of the House's date of Feb. 29, 1984.

Final Action

The House and Senate met in an unusual Saturday session Nov. 12 to take final action on the bill's conference report. The House adopted the conference report (H Rept 98-540) by a 173-136 vote, and the Senate approved the measure by voice vote, clearing it for the president. Reagan signed it Nov. 14. *(Vote 455, p. 134-H)*

Total spending in the continuing resolution, with all its provisions to run for the remainder of fiscal 1984, amounted to about $316 billion, more than half the total 1984 appropriations Congress had enacted for the government, according to Senate Appropriations Committee staff estimates.

As an urgent measure late in the session, the second continuing resolution was a vehicle for legislators' favorite pork-barrel projects and pet issues.

For example, Senate Majority Leader Baker won $6.4 million to help the Tennessee Valley Authority pay for white-water rafting on the Ocoee River in his home state. Conferees, however, insisted that the cost be reimbursed from user fees.

Rep. James J. Howard, D-N.J., chairman of the Public Works and Transportation Committee, picked up $9 million for a new federal courthouse in Newark, N.J.

During House consideration of the conference report, some Republicans attacked the bill's pork-barrel contents. But Conte, the top Republican on Appropriations, replied: "There are some piglets in here, not pork." ∎

Treasury/Postal Service Bill Fails to Clear

After traveling a rocky legislative road, a funding bill for the Treasury Department, Postal Service, executive offices and several independent agencies failed to clear Congress by the end of the session. Instead, for the fourth year in a row, funds for these agencies were included in a continuing appropriations resolution.

The second fiscal 1984 continuing resolution (H J Res 413 — PL 98-151), cleared by Congress Nov. 12, provided a total of $11,944,900,000 in new budget authority for the agencies in the bill. That was $368.6 million more than President Reagan had requested and $467.9 million more than the fiscal 1983 appropriation. *(Continuing resolution, p. 528; fiscal 1983 bill, 1982 Almanac p. 273)*

Besides the new budget authority, the bill made available funds for agencies under permanent authority that did not require consideration by Congress during the appropriations process. The biggest item in that category was interest on the public debt, expected to reach $144.5 billion in fiscal 1984. Together with the new budget authority, the bill provided a total of $207.9 billion for the Treasury and other agencies covered by the bill.

The bill also contained a number of controversial provisions, including a ban on the use of federal employee health benefits funds to pay for abortions, except to save the life of the mother; language that barred the Office of Personnel Management (OPM) from implementing regulations linking pay raises and job security for 1.4 million white-collar federal employees more closely to job performance, and language barring the Office of Management and Budget (OMB) from reviewing agricultural marketing orders. *(Federal employee regulations, p. 602)*

Legislative History

The House passed its version of the Treasury/Postal Service funding bill (HR 4139) Oct. 27, after rejecting a similar measure (HR 3191) on June 8 — the first time an appropriations bill had been defeated on the House floor since 1979. The defeat was attributed to opposition by two groups: fiscal conservatives who felt the funding in the bill

was too high and liberals angered by the anti-abortion provision.

The Senate Appropriations Committee reported a bill (S 1646 — S Rept 98-186) July 20, but the full Senate did not consider it.

Conferees on the continuing resolution included funding for the agencies at the level in the Senate bill, except for Postal Service subsidies, which were funded at the higher level in the House bill. An amendment on the House floor added the terms and conditions of the House-passed bill, which had the effect of enacting the bans on abortion and on the personnel regulations.

The biggest single increase over the president's budget came in funding for postal subsidies, which made up for revenue forgone from free and reduced-rate mail by nonprofit organizations and newspaper, book and magazine publishers. The president wanted mailers to share a greater proportion of the actual cost of mailing and recommended only $400 million in subsidies, but Congress appropriated $879 million.

In other additions, Congress voted $584.9 million for the Customs Service, $39.7 million more than Reagan had requested. The additional money funded 1,600 positions for drug interdiction — positions the administration had proposed to eliminate.

Congress also voted to restore 986 positions and $25 million for the Internal Revenue Service's (IRS) taxpayer assistance program. The administration had proposed cutting those positions, but Congress, citing in particular the volunteers in programs of tax assistance and tax counseling for the elderly, voted to maintain the fiscal 1983 funding level for taxpayer assistance.

Provisions

As cleared by Congress, H J Res 413 contained the following appropriations in new budget authority for the Treasury Department, Postal Service, executive office of the president and certain independent agencies:

Agency	Budget Request	Final Amount
Treasury Department		
Office of the Secretary	$ 69,949,000	$ 65,743,000
International Affairs	—	—
Federal Law Enforcement Training Center	14,481,000	14,481,000
Bureau of Government Financial Operations	242,995,000	239,995,000
Bureau of Alcohol, Tobacco and Firearms	157,122,000	157,260,000
U.S. Customs Service	574,999,000	615,943,000
Bureau of the Mint	52,628,000	52,070,000
Bureau of the Public Debt	205,605,000	196,427,000
Internal Revenue Service	3,291,551,000	3,264,800,000
Payment where energy credit exceeds liability for tax	200,000	200,000
Secret Service	270,860,000	294,555,000
Subtotal	$ 4,880,390,000	$ 4,901,474,000
U.S. Postal Service		
Payment to the Postal Service Fund	$ 400,000,000	$ 879,000,000
Subtotal	$ 400,000,000	$ 879,000,000
Executive Office of the President		
President's Compensation	$ 250,000	$ 250,000
Office of Administration	14,900,000	14,295,000
The White House Office	23,413,000	22,830,000
Executive Residence	4,550,000	4,550,000
Official Residence of the Vice President	262,000	262,000
Special Assistance to the President	1,593,000	1,593,000
Council of Economic Advisers	2,464,000	2,464,000
Office of Policy Development	2,861,000	2,861,000
National Security Council	4,497,000	4,497,000
Office of Management and Budget	34,246,000	31,603,000
Office of Information and Regulatory Affairs	5,397,000	5,397,000
Office of Federal Procurement Policy	2,714,000	2,556,000
Property Review Board	415,000	415,000
Unanticipated Needs	1,000,000	1,000,000
Subtotal	$ 98,562,000	$ 94,573,000
Independent Agencies		
Administrative Conference of the United States	$ 1,406,000	$ 1,100,000
Advisory Commission on Intergovernmental Relations	2,020,000	2,000,000
Advisory Committee on Federal Pay	215,000	215,000
Committee for Purchase from the Blind and Other Severely Handicapped	687,000	687,000
Federal Election Commission	10,000,000	10,649,000

Agency	Budget Request	Final Amount
General Services Administration	600,036,000	477,486,000
Office of Personnel Management	5,525,375,000	5,521,875,000
Merit Systems Protection Board	24,041,000	23,981,000
Federal Labor Relations Authority	16,695,000	16,695,000
U.S. Tax Court	16,871,000	15,165,000
Subtotal	$ 6,197,346,000	$ 6,069,853,000
Grand Total	$11,576,298,000	$11,944,900,000

Major Legislative Provisions

● Prohibited the use of funds appropriated for federal employee health insurance benefits to pay for abortions, except when the life of the mother would be endangered by continuation of the pregnancy.

● Barred the use of funds in the bill to implement, administer or enforce a series of federal personnel rules changes issued by the Office of Management and Budget.

● Limited pay increases of federal wage-scale (blue-collar) workers in fiscal 1984 to the same percentage increase that federal white-collar workers received; provided that any delays in pay increases be the same for both groups.

● Barred the Office of Management and Budget from reviewing marketing orders under the 1937 Agricultural Marketing Agreement Act.

● Barred the Bureau of Alcohol, Tobacco and Firearms from issuing regulations requiring ingredient labeling on alcoholic beverages until federal courts ruled on the validity of the regulations.

● Barred the General Services Administration from contracting out certain positions held by veterans, including guards, messengers, custodians and elevator operators.

● Limited to 14 percent any fiscal 1984 increase in rental rates GSA charged other federal agencies.

House Committee Action

The House Appropriations Committee reported HR 3191 on June 2 (H Rept 98-229).

As reported, the bill provided $11,987,584,000, an increase of $981,422,000 over fiscal 1983 appropriations for the covered agencies and $331.4 million above President Reagan's $11.6 billion budget request.

Major provisions included:

Treasury Department

A total of $4.9 billion was recommended for the Treasury Department, $45.8 million more than Reagan requested. The bulk of the increase was to restore the IRS's taxpayer assistance program and prevent layoffs at the U.S. Customs Service. The department's fiscal 1983 appropriation was $4.46 billion.

Bureau of Alcohol, Tobacco and Firearms (BATF). The House added $3.1 million to Reagan's $157.1 million request, primarily to continue enforcement of a cigarette-smuggling prevention program the administration wanted to terminate. Fiscal 1983 BATF funding was $145 million.

U.S. Customs Service. The committee balked at Reagan's proposal to eliminate 2,000 Customs Service positions. The bill provided $651.2 million for the Service, an increase of $76.1 million over the administration's proposal of $575 million and $93.7 million over 1983 funding.

IRS. The committee voted $3.2 billion for the IRS, a $296 million increase over fiscal 1983 funding but a $47 million cut from Reagan's request.

Reagan wanted to change the structure of the appropriations accounts for the IRS and eliminate the personnel and salaries category, but the committee refused to go along. Instead, members added $102.3 million for personnel and salaries and slashed by $121.3 million Reagan's $989 million request for processing tax returns.

The committee also trimmed $27.2 million from the administration's proposal to spend $1.3 billion on tax examinations and appeals. It cut $1.3 million from Reagan's request of $1.02 billion for investigations, collections and taxpayer services, but added $25 million to continue the IRS's taxpayer assistance program at its 1983 level.

Secret Service. The committee set fiscal 1984 spending levels for the service at $284.9 million — $14 million more than Reagan requested and $49.9 million above the fiscal 1983 appropriation.

U.S. Postal Service

The $879 million subsidy payment voted by the committee would cover the Postal Service's revenue loss from free and reduced-rate mail, including second-class publications such as rural newspapers and third-class letters from non-profit groups. Reagan had proposed a $400 million subsidy. The 1983 appropriation was $789 million.

White House, Other Agencies

White House and Executive Offices. The committee trimmed $1.4 million from Reagan's $98.6 million request, primarily by refusing to fill 10 positions at the Office of Management and Budget and eliminating the Property Review Board. The bill provided $11.3 million more than fiscal 1983 funding.

Federal Election Commission (FEC). To help the FEC gear up for the 1984 elections, the committee added $400,000 to Reagan's $10 million request. In 1983, Congress provided $9.7 million.

General Services Administration (GSA). The committee chopped $112.5 million from the administration's $600 million request. The $487.5 million funding level was $78.6 million below GSA's 1983 appropriations.

The committee included language limiting to 14 percent any fiscal 1984 increase in the rental rates GSA charges other federal agencies. Reagan wanted a 23 percent rate increase.

OPM. The committee approved language barring the use of funds in the bill to implement, administer or enforce the personnel rules changes proposed by OPM March 30, to link pay raises and job security of 1.4 million federal white-collar workers more closely to job performance.

It rejected an amendment by Eldon Rudd, R-Ariz., to bar the use of funds in the bill to pay for abortions under federal employee health benefit plans, except to save the life of the mother.

House Floor Action

The House defeated HR 3191 June 8 by a vote of 149-259. *(Vote 171, p. 54-H)*

The last time an appropriations measure had been defeated on the House floor was in 1979, when the House by a 186-232 vote rejected the fiscal 1980 legislative appropriations bill because of a controversial provision allowing a 5.5 percent congressional pay raise. *(1979 Almanac p. 271)*

The defeat of the 1984 money bill was attributed to an odd, informal coalition of House conservatives convinced that the bill was too expensive and "pro-choice" liberals angered by the anti-abortion rider added to the bill on the floor. The amendment banned the use of federal health insurance benefits for abortions for federal employees or their families.

"There was a hell of a war going on here," said Silvio O. Conte, R-Mass., ranking minority member of the House Appropriations Committee, after the vote. "If you had had the pro-choice people voting for this, it would have passed."

The Reagan administration opposed the bill, primarily because it exceeded the president's budget request. The administration also objected to several specific items in the bill, including the 14 percent limit on increases in the rent the GSA assessed federal agencies for office space; the deletion of funds for the Property Review Board, which was established in 1982 to expedite the review and disposal of federal properties; and the provisions barring changes in federal personnel rules.

During more than six hours of debate, the House cut $79.9 million from the bill as reported by the Appropriations Committee.

It also adopted an amendment by Mickey Edwards, R-Okla., barring the use of funds in the bill to implement the withholding of taxes on dividends and interest. The House already had voted May 17 to repeal the controversial new law, due to go into effect July 1. *(Story, p. 261)*

Adopted by voice vote, Edwards' amendment would have applied only to funds spent in fiscal 1984, which began Oct. 1, three months after the repeal law was to take effect. But proponents argued it would warn the Treasury Department and IRS not to begin withholding the tax.

Abortion Rider

None of the changes made on the floor provoked more emotional debate than the anti-abortion amendment offered by Christopher H. Smith, R-N.J., and adopted by a 226-182 vote. *(Vote 170, p. 54-H)*

The amendment, similar to a rider passed by the House in previous years, prohibited the use of federal employee health insurance benefits to pay for an abortion except to save the life of the mother. It also banned outlays for administrative expenses of any health insurance plan that allowed abortions.

Opponents of the amendment, including members representing large numbers of federal workers, tried but failed to defeat the House rule (H Res 222) allowing consideration of the anti-abortion amendment. But the rule was adopted, 229-183. *(Vote 168, p. 52-H)*

Amendment foes then tried to block the rider itself. "This [insurance benefits for abortion costs] is compensation to the people who are in the federal government. It is not taxpayer money," said Patricia Schroeder, D-Colo. "It is not a handout."

But the amendment's backers called the test a "key abortion vote." The amendment, they said, would not prevent federal employees from paying for abortions themselves. "The issue today is simply whether or not the taxpayer will continue to fund federal employees' abortions,"

argued Smith.

Ex-Presidents' Staffs

Another controversy erupted over an amendment by Andrew Jacobs Jr., D-Ind., to delete $910,700 for staff and office expenses for former Presidents Jimmy Carter, Richard M. Nixon and Gerald R. Ford. The amendment was adopted 244-169. *(Vote 169, p. 52-H)*

The amendment did not affect the $260,300 provided by the bill for pensions for the former presidents and for the widow of former President Lyndon B. Johnson. Nor did it affect funding for Secret Service protection for the former presidents, which was contained in another section of the bill.

Other Amendments

The House by voice vote adopted an amendment by Bill Frenzel, R-Minn., cutting $23.4 million from funds for the Customs Service's Operation Exodus, a border program aimed at preventing the export of strategic defense items to the Soviet Union. Frenzel said the program did not need as much money as the committee provided.

The entire $52.6 million appropriation for the Bureau of the Mint was also knocked out of the bill on a ruling of the chair at the request of Frank Annunzio, D-Ill., who said the agency's funding had not been authorized.

The House also trimmed $3 million from the $243 million earmarked for the Bureau of Government Financial Operations.

House Democrats, joined by Harold Rogers, R-Ky., beat back an attempt by Judd Gregg, R-N.H., to trim the $879 million postal subsidy in the bill to the $400 million level sought by Reagan.

Proponents of the higher subsidy maintained that Reagan's plan would harm charities and veterans' organizations and double the price of rural, weekly newspaper subscriptions. But Gregg argued that these groups, some of which were charged as little as 3.3 cents per piece of mail, should pay a greater share of postal costs.

The House left untouched the provision barring the use of funds in the bill to implement the personnel rule changes proposed by OPM. Clarence E. Miller, R-Ohio, ranking minority member on the Appropriations Subcommittee on Treasury, Postal Service and General Government, dropped a planned amendment to strike the restrictive language after noting that the intent of the regulations was "widely misunderstood."

Senate Committee Action

The Senate Appropriations Committee reported its version of the Treasury/Postal Service funding bill July 20 (S 1646 — S Rept 98-186).

S 1646 provided a total of $11,864,000,000, about $288 million more than President Reagan requested and $858 million more than the fiscal 1983 appropriation.

The single largest increase over the president's budget was for postal subsidies. The committee provided $802 million.

The Treasury/Postal Service subcommittee originally voted to set the subsidy at $750 million — $39 million below the fiscal 1983 amount. However, Postmaster General William F. Bolger and commercial mailers lobbied members of the subcommittee overnight, and the next day, Dennis DeConcini, D-Ariz., offered an amendment setting the subsidy at $802 million.

A DeConcini aide said Bolger argued that if the postal subsidy were lowered, commercial mailers such as daily newspapers would end up subsidizing non-profit mailers.

Under DeConcini's amendment, postal rates for non-profit mailers such as veterans' organizations would rise between 4 and 12 percent, a subcommittee report said. For example, the classroom mail rate would go from 6.7 cents to 7 cents per piece; third-class rates for non-profit organizations would go from 3.3 cents per piece to 3.7 cents.

In another departure from the president's budget, the committee cut only 400 of the 2,000 U.S. Customs Service positions Reagan wanted to eliminate. "We just couldn't go for this," said James Abdnor, R-S.D., chairman of the Treasury/Postal Service Subcommittee. "We felt this would mean a wholesale foreclosure of customs offices."

The committee adopted an amendment by Abdnor adding $15 million to pay for 390 new positions at the IRS designed to catch those who did not declare income from interest and dividends.

During subcommittee action, an amendment by Mack Mattingly, R-Ga., was added to the bill, providing for a 10 percent across-the-board reduction in the amount of money available to pay consultants who work for agencies funded under the bill.

The Senate bill did not contain the House provisions barring the use of federal funds for abortions under federal employees' health insurance programs or to implement the personnel rule changes proposed by OPM.

The bill contained $157.3 million for BATF, compared to $160.2 million in the House bill. Like the House, the committee refused to go along with the president's proposal to eliminate the interstate cigarette smuggling prevention program, although the panel noted it expected to curtail funding for the program in fiscal 1985.

The committee included $615.9 million for the Customs Service; $3.265 billion for the IRS; $294.5 million for the Secret Service; $94.6 million for the executive office of the president and $10.6 million for the FEC.

The committee slashed the president's $600 million request for the GSA to $473.8 million, well below the House level of $487.5 million. It also went along with House language limiting to 14 percent any increase in rental rates that GSA charged other federal agencies.

Second House Bill

After the defeat of HR 3191, the House Appropriations Committee went back to the drawing board and reported a second Treasury/Postal Service funding bill on Oct. 18.

The $11.9 billion bill (HR 4139 — H Rept 98-417) contained about $100 million less than HR 3191, but was still $301 million over President Reagan's budget request.

It contained the same anti-abortion provision that helped send HR 3191 down to defeat. But, chastened by that defeat, committee members were reluctant during markup of HR 4139 to add any additional provisions that might spark opposition. "We've got enough controversy," said Conte. "We are walking a very, very tight rope with this bill."

One provision added to the bill by the Treasury/Postal Service Subcommittee did arouse controversy in the full committee, however. It banned duty-free imports of agricultural products from Caribbean nations, a key element of the administration's Caribbean Basin Initiative (HR 2973 —PL 98-67), cleared by Congress July 28. *(Story, p. 252)*

By a 17-18 vote, the committee refused to delete the

ban from HR 4139. In its report, the committee said it was "concerned about the possible use of insecticides and pesticides on agricultural products, particularly when the use of such insecticides and pesticides, or the marketing of commodities on which they have been used, has been restricted by" U.S. regulatory agencies.

Provisions

As reported by the House Appropriations Committee, HR 4139 provided $4.85 billion for the Treasury Department — $80 million less than the amount the committee approved in June; $53 million of the reduction came from elimination of the entire appropriation for the Bureau of the Mint, whose funding had not yet been authorized.

That cut and others made during floor action on HR 3191 were incorporated into HR 4139 by the Treasury/Postal Service Subcommittee.

The panel cut $23 million from the Customs Service by eliminating 855 permanent positions. However, the bill retained 1,775 positions for drug interdiction — positions the administration proposed to eliminate.

The committee also shaved $3 million from the BATF, and added $50 million for the IRS to upgrade its computer system (for a total of $75 million). The Treasury Department had requested $100 million.

As in the first bill, the committee approved $879 million for postal subsidies. Edward R. Roybal, D-Calif., chairman of the Treasury/Postal Service Subcommittee, said the $400 million level requested by Reagan would mean a doubling of postal rates for non-profit organizations.

The committee trimmed $3.7 million from the Executive Office of the President, including slight cuts in the White House Office, the Office of Administration and OMB. The total for the Executive Office was $93.5 million, $5.1 million below the administration's request.

The panel included $260,300 for pensions for former Presidents Carter, Ford and Nixon and for the widow of Lyndon Johnson. But it cut $910,700 for their staff and office expenses, reflecting the amendment adopted on the floor during action on HR 3191.

The panel trimmed $4.3 million from funding for the National Archives and Records Service, bringing the total to $89.8 million. Funding for the National Historical Publications and Records Commission and for records preservation were cut in half, to $1.5 million each.

The bill also barred the use of funds to implement the OPM personnel regulations; limited the pay increases of federal wage-scale (blue-collar) workers in fiscal 1984 to the same percentage increase that federal white-collar workers received, and provided that any delays in pay increases be the same for both groups, and barred OMB from reviewing agricultural marketing orders.

Floor Action on HR 4139

The House passed HR 4139 Oct. 27 by voice vote.

As passed, the bill contained $4.9 billion for the Treasury Department, $879 million for the Postal Service, $93.5 million for the Executive Office of the President and $6.1 billion for other independent agencies.

Although the bill contained more money than the president had requested, members voted for it to move the appropriations process along. No amendments affecting the dollar totals of the bill were offered.

Conte admitted the bill contained provisions that members might not like. But, he said, "at least give this a

chance to go over to the Senate, and then we will go to conference, see if we can iron out some of these things."

Roybal also pleaded with his colleagues to pass the bill, and to avoid relying on a continuing resolution to fund the programs in the bill. "It is a bad practice and should be discontinued," he said.

Marketing Orders

In contrast with the House debate in June, abortion and funding levels were barely discussed Oct. 27. Most of the debate centered around the provision barring OMB from reviewing agricultural marketing orders under the 1937 Agricultural Marketing Agreement Act.

An amendment by Barney Frank, D-Mass., to delete the provision failed on a 97-319 vote. *(Vote 395, p. 118-H)*

Frank argued that marketing orders — under which producers, principally California citrus growers, agreed to set production quotas in order to ensure a stable market for their perishable goods — amounted to a "government-sanctioned price fixing scheme."

The orders are subject to approval by the U.S. Department of Agriculture. Under the Reagan administration's regulatory reform policy (Executive Order 12291, issued Feb. 17, 1981), OMB was empowered to review any departmental regulation.

But some farm producers, and their backers in Congress, claimed that OMB Director David A. Stockman opposed marketing orders and had used his regulatory review to stymie them. "The actions taken by OMB are uncalled for, and possibly even illegal," said George E. Brown Jr., D-Calif.

Frank and his allies countered that OMB was the only independent agency reviewing the orders. "The question is not whether OMB is interfering in the regulatory process; the issue is whether the market is controlled to the detriment of the consumer," said Conte.

Leon E. Panetta, D-Calif., chairman of the Agriculture subcommittee with jurisdiction over marketing orders, said the issue should be settled in Congress, not through regulation.

Abortion

Although there was no substantive debate on the issue of abortion, supporters of the bill's anti-abortion provision had to go through a parliamentary maze to keep it in the bill.

Barbara Boxer, D-Calif., tried to strike the section, arguing that the qualifying clause regarding the mother's life violated House rules by placing a legislative provision on a spending bill.

But Christopher H. Smith, who offered the original anti-abortion amendment June 8, then proposed to offer an amendment banning all abortions paid for under federal employee health insurance programs — without any exception covering saving the life of the mother.

Foes of the more restrictive language tried to cut off debate, which would have barred Smith from offering his amendment. That attempt failed, 193-229. *(Vote 396, p. 118-H)*

Smith then offered his amendment, adding the qualifying clause, and it passed by voice vote. Pro-choice members made no attempt to block it. "It would eventually wind up being in there, we knew that," said Boxer.

Other Floor Action

Parliamentary maneuvering deleted a provision

prohibiting duty-free imports of agricultural products from Caribbean nations. Ways and Means Committee Chairman Dan Rostenkowski, D-Ill., invoking for the first time a new House rule adopted at the start of the 98th Congress, argued that the prohibition amounted to a change in tariff schedules, which under the rule the Ways and Means Committee would have to approve. The provision was deleted on a point of order.

Sam Gibbons, D-Fla., also succeeded in eliminating a provision that would have barred the procurement of flatware from foreign sources. Gibbons argued that the provision required a Customs official to make a determination not required by federal law. Gibbons later chastised the Appropriations Committee for inserting provisions that should be approved by other panels, including his own Ways and Means Trade Subcommittee.

The House adopted an amendment by David R. Obey, D-Wis., clarifying that a provision prohibiting BATF from issuing regulations requiring ingredient labeling on alcoholic beverages would last only until federal courts decided finally on the validity of the regulations.

The House also adopted an amendment by Bob Edgar, D-Pa., clarifying a section in the bill that barred the GSA from contracting out certain positions currently held by veterans, including guards, messengers, custodians and elevator operators.

Final Action

Conferees on the continuing resolution agreed to ac-cept the funding levels in the Senate committee version of the bill, one of only three appropriations bills that had not been passed by both chambers.

However, the conferees agreed to accept the House-passed appropriation for Postal Service subsidies, making the bill $77 million higher than the amount reported by the Senate Appropriations Committee.

The House, in considering the continuing resolution, adopted by voice vote an amendment by Hoyer, attaching the "terms and conditions" of the House-passed bill. This had the effect of enacting the bans on abortion funding and personnel regulations, as well as OMB review of agricultural marketing orders.

When the Senate originally considered its version of the continuing resolution (S J Res 194) Nov. 9, Jeremiah Denton, R-Ala., offered an amendment to insert the anti-abortion language. In a series of close votes, including one tie, Denton won his point. *(Votes 335, 336, p. 55-S)*

But Bob Packwood, R-Ore., began a filibuster, causing Majority Leader Howard H. Baker Jr., R-Tenn., to pull the measure from the floor until the next day.

Then, after the House passed its continuing resolution, including the anti-abortion language from HR 4139, the Senate considered that vehicle (H J Res 413). Mark O. Hatfield, R-Ore., offered an amendment to strike the language, but that attempt failed, 43-44. *(Vote 339, p. 56-S)*

After two more close procedural votes, the Senate retained the abortion restrictions. *(Votes 340, 341, p. 56-S)*

Pro-choice senators soon afterward dropped their filibuster, and the abortion restrictions remained in the bill. ∎

Biggest 'Deal' Cleared in 1984 Supplemental

Mixing subsidized housing for some of the nation's poorest citizens with what some members called a "bailout" for the nation's largest banks, Congress made its biggest legislative deal of 1983 just before it adjourned Nov. 18.

Congress mated a $15.6 billion housing authorization measure, sought by House Democrats, to an $8.4 billion U.S. contribution to the International Monetary Fund (IMF), sought by the Reagan administration.

The unusual combination was then attached to the conference report of a non-controversial, $302 million fiscal 1984 supplemental appropriations bill (HR 3959) and presented to members in a take-it-or-leave-it package. They took it.

The deal was put together over several weeks of delicate negotiations by key members of the Senate and House along with White House Budget Director David A. Stockman and Treasury Secretary Donald T. Regan. Although the Reagan administration opposed several key provisions of the housing measure, it agreed to swallow them to get the IMF money, which it wanted badly. The administration also won reauthorization of U.S. participation in several international development banks. President Reagan signed the measure into law (PL 98-181) Nov. 30.

The linkage of the issues had been insisted on for months by House Banking Committee Chairman Fernand J. St Germain, D-R.I., who said many House Democrats would not vote for the IMF increase without a housing bill.

Senate Banking Committee Chairman Jake Garn, R-Utah, said he did not like the combination but finally agreed to it. "It's like mating a turkey and a camel and hoping it would fly," said Garn.

Senate Minority Leader Robert C. Byrd, D-W.Va., objected to the procedure, saying, "This is a reprehensible way to legislate."

Major Provisions

Before the addition of the housing-IMF package, the bill was a relatively minor appropriations measure. The conference agreement on HR 3959 included $75 million for a new Vietnam veterans' job training program and $54 million for a medical study of Vietnam veterans exposed to the defoliant Agent Orange.

The bill originally contained $150 million for veterans' job training, but half of that was included in the fiscal 1984 continuing resolution enacted Nov. 14. *(Story, p. 528)*

Other items included $30 million for emergency food and shelter for the poor; $20 million for construction by the National Aeronautics and Space Administration; and $57 million for nuclear waste disposal. It also contained funds for several public works projects including $9.4 million for Appalachian Regional Commission highway construction in Mississippi and Alabama that had been sought by leaders of the House Appropriations Committee.

The Senate dropped this money, but conferees quietly reinserted it.

The chairman of the House Appropriations Committee was Jamie L. Whitten, D-Miss., and the chairman of the panel's Subcommittee on Energy and Water was Tom Bevill, D-Ala.

The bill also included $69,800 payments to the widows of Larry P. McDonald, D-Ga., who died in the Korean airliner shot down Sept. 1, and Henry M. Jackson, D-Wash., who died Sept. 1 of a heart attack. The amount equaled one year's congressional salary and was the customary compensation for members' survivors.

When the Senate added the housing and IMF provisions after the conference, the bill gained $8.4 billion in IMF appropriations.

Housing. The bill authorized $15.6 billion in housing programs including $3.5 billion for community development funds and $9.9 billion for subsidized housing.

It contained several provisions strongly opposed by the Reagan administration, yet at a scale smaller than many members in both chambers would have liked. Those provisions included new production of rental housing and rent reductions for subsidized housing tenants.

However, it also included, at a reduced level, a Reagan administration initiative to provide housing vouchers for low-income persons to use toward renting private housing. *(Detailed provisions, story p. 277)*

The bill's authorization totals were to be provided by money that had already been included in the fiscal 1984 appropriations bill for the Department of Housing and Urban Development (HR 3133). *(Story, p. 495)*

International Banking. The bill increased the U.S. contribution to the IMF by $8.4 billion — $5.8 billion for the U.S. quota in the fund and $2.6 billion to the General Arrangements to Borrow, a contingency fund established financial system is threatened. The bill both authorized and appropriated the $8.4 billion.

The bill extended the authorization of the Export-Import Bank for three years, to Sept. 30, 1986. It also mandated that the bank offer financing at rates competitive with loans offered by other nations. The Ex-Im Bank provided long-term loans for the purchase of U.S. exports by foreign companies and nations.

Also reauthorized in HR 3959 were multilateral development banks, including $5.2 billion for the Inter-American Development Bank and $1.3 billion for the Asian Development Bank. The bill also extended the Defense Production Act until March 30, 1984. *(Story, p. 265)*

Legislative History

Initial House Action

Only five days into the 1984 fiscal year, the House Oct. 5 passed HR 3959, a supplemental money bill to boost funding for programs that had already received regular 1984 appropriations. It initially had been reported Sept. 22 (H Rept 98-375).

As passed 363-30 by the House, it included $444.7 million for veterans' services, nuclear waste studies, Appalachian highways and other miscellaneous programs. *(Vote 363, p. 108-H)*

Despite expectations that the bill would become a magnet for controversial amendments, the House adopted only minor add-ons.

Whitten said $406 million of the supplemental bill's total was sought by President Reagan. In particular, Reagan wanted $150 million for a veterans' job training program Congress authorized in August.

A letter from David A. Stockman, director of the Office of Management and Budget, indicated the bill's funding levels generally were acceptable to the White House.

But he had reservations about certain sections, including the $9.4 million for the Appalachian Regional Commission, which Reagan had sought, unsuccessfully, to abolish.

Supplemental spending bills normally came up later in the fiscal year. But because several 1984 money bills were signed as early as July, new budget needs arose in the Veterans Administration (VA), Energy Department and other agencies that had already received their 1984 money.

Rules Committee. Although 18 House members trooped before the Rules Committee Oct. 4 seeking permission to offer amendments to the supplemental, the panel, by voice vote, barred unrelated amendments.

Rules member Gillis W. Long, D-La., later said leaders of Rules and Appropriations feared that a loose rule would open "a can of worms" by allowing authorizing legislation on a spending bill.

Among those whose amendments were turned down was Vic Fazio, D-Calif., who had a proposal to block a change in Federal Communications Commission rules on television syndication rights. Fazio said he did not fight the rule on the floor because a battle on a procedural question "would have poisoned the well on a close and contentious issue anyway."

And Bill Alexander, D-Ark., who had wanted an amendment to provide drought relief to farmers, shrugged and said, "I'd like to open it up, but this is not the Senate," referring to the easier amending process in the Senate.

With $444.7 million, HR 3959 was then small by appropriations bill standards. But it still contained morsels of "pork-barrel" spending for Appropriations Committee members.

Whitten and Bevill slipped in money for road projects in their states without clearly identifying where the money would go.

The committee report simply said $9.4 million in the Appalachian Regional Commission highway fund would be spent for construction of "critical portions of corridor X" and to complete "gaps in corridor V."

During floor debate Oct. 5, Silvio O. Conte, R-Mass., demanded to know where those highways were located. Bevill rose and muttered, "They are in Mississippi and Alabama." Conte, the senior Republican on Appropriations, caustically replied, "Well, let us include Massachusetts next time."

Besides the Appalachian highway money, the House also included in HR 3959:

● $150 million for the new job training program for unemployed veterans from the Korean and Vietnam War eras.

● $57.4 million for research on the health risks for veterans exposed to Agent Orange, a herbicide used in Vietnam.

● $66 million for veterans' compensation and pensions, requested by the VA because costs were higher than first estimated.

● $40 million for additional veterans' education and training payments, and an additional $4 million for VA operating costs.

● A $69,800 payment to Kathryn McDonald, widow of Rep. McDonald.

● $57 million for the Energy Department's military atomic energy activities, to fund a nuclear waste burial facility in New Mexico. The bill also provided $12 million for a nuclear waste disposal study.

● $42 million to relocate residents of Centralia and Byrnesville, Pa., who lived over a burning coal mine.

An additional $6.7 million was added to HR 3959 in

floor amendments. This amount included $4 million for health care for Pacific atoll residents affected by U.S. nuclear tests; $1.7 million for a preschool program on Indian reservations; and $1 million for fossil energy research.

Initial Senate Action

Senate Appropriations. The bill gained in controversy when the Senate Appropriations Committee reported it (S Rept 98-275) Oct. 19.

The Clinch River breeder reactor was resuscitated when the committee added $1.5 billion to the bill for the nuclear plant if private industry shared the project's costs.

Appropriations also stepped into another controversy by voting to temporarily block a Federal Communications Commission (FCC) proposal to give television networks financial rights to independently produced programs.

Clinch River, a long-planned demonstration power plant to be located near Oak Ridge, Tenn., had been on its death bed since 1982 when Congress said there had to be a new financing arrangement before it would approve any more money for the reactor. *(Story, p. 362)*

Such an alternative financing plan, dependent on a $1 billion contribution from utility companies and other private firms, was embodied in the amendment Appropriations approved Oct. 19 by an 18-10 vote. The committee traditionally had looked kindly on the project, but it faced potent resistance on the Senate and House floors.

The Reagan administration's opinion on the Clinch River money was unclear. Appropriations Chairman Mark O. Hatfield, R-Ore., said budget director Stockman opposed any additions to the House-passed funding levels for HR 3959.

But James A. McClure, R-Idaho, who sponsored the Clinch River amendment, said Energy Secretary Donald P. Hodel endorsed the new financing plan for the reactor. McClure offered the amendment at the behest of Senate Majority Leader Howard H. Baker Jr., R-Tenn. Baker had been the project's congressional godfather, guarding it against attacks by environmentalists, anti-nuclear groups and others who said the project cost too much, might be hazardous and was unneeded as a power source.

The FCC amendment, sponsored by Ted Stevens, R-Alaska, was adopted 16-13. It would have blocked for six months a proposed FCC rule change that would allow TV networks to acquire a financial interest in programs produced by other companies. Networks also could obtain rerun syndication rights for those shows under the FCC proposal.

The FCC rule was heavily lobbied in Washington, with the three major TV networks on one side and Hollywood producers, writers and actors on the other side. Since 1970, the networks had been barred from obtaining syndication rights for reruns of prime-time programs and the FCC rule would lift this ban.

The committee also made other changes in the House-approved version of HR 3959.

It deleted $66 million for veterans' compensation and pensions and $40 million for veterans' education and training benefits, with aides saying the VA did not need the money in fiscal 1984.

The panel also deleted $9.4 million for Appalachian Regional Commission highways in Mississippi and Alabama, arguing that the commission received $100 million for highways in its fiscal 1984 appropriation Oct. 1 and extra money is unwarranted.

The committee added $20 million for two National Aeronautics and Space Administration projects: a solid rocket booster and warehousing for the space shuttle's supplies, spare parts and ground support equipment.

Another addition was $25 million to acquire land at the Congaree Swamp National Monument in South Carolina.

Also added was a $69,800 payment to Helen Jackson, widow of Sen. Jackson.

The committee also adopted an amendment by Patrick J. Leahy, D-Vt., to force the Interior Department to prepare an environmental impact statement on the effect of oil and gas drilling in the national wildlife refuge system, before processing any applications for drilling leases.

Senate Floor. The FCC and Clinch River amendments were the main focus when the bill was considered on the Senate floor Oct. 26-27.

The Senate passed HR 3959 Oct. 27 by voice vote. The day before, it handed a crushing defeat to Clinch River supporters. It rejected the financing scheme the Appropriations Committee had added to the bill.

After $1.5 billion for the nuclear reactor was scratched, the bill contained $390.8 million for veterans' benefits, nuclear waste disposal and other programs.

The Senate also added an amendment to create a "drug czar" to coordinate federal drug enforcement efforts, an idea President Reagan opposed.

The Appropriations Committee's inclusion of Clinch River money had galvanized the project's opponents, who argued in a lengthy debate Oct. 26 that the project was too expensive and a needless energy source. They also condemned the public-private financing arrangement.

Baker was silent during debate on his home-state project, which he had protected during a decade of attacks. McClure virtually stood alone to defend the funding plan, which Reagan endorsed.

After voting 56-40 against the financing plan, the biggest Senate hurdle was the amendment on the FCC television rule. *(Vote 306, p. 50-S)*

When the issue reached the floor Oct. 27, Commerce Committee Chairman Bob Packwood, R-Ore., raised a point of order, asking that the amendment be dropped because it was not within the Appropriations Committee's jurisdiction. Television issues generally came under Commerce's purview.

Although Packwood's point of order was upheld by the chair, Stevens appealed the ruling. Packwood tried to table the appeal, but lost 32-57. The Senate then approved the FCC delay by voice vote. *(Vote 308, p. 51-S)*

Stevens insisted the six-month moratorium was not based on the issue's merits. "It provides the Senate with breathing time, time within which to hold a hearing to have a more complete study of the impacts of the proposed action of the FCC," he said. Hearings by the Commerce Subcommittee on Communications were held in November.

Another major amendment to HR 3959 was offered by Joseph R. Biden Jr., D-Del., to create a Cabinet-level drug czar to combat international drug trafficking and the use and sale of drugs within the United States. The Senate adopted Biden's amendment by voice, after rejecting, 40-53, a motion by Strom Thurmond, R-S.C., to table it. *(Vote 307, p. 50-S)*

Congress cleared an anti-crime bill in the 97th Congress with a drug czar provision, but Reagan vetoed it on the grounds that the new drug czar would disrupt existing anti-drug programs. *(1982 Almanac p. 419)*

Also on the supplemental appropriations measure, proponents of a new health insurance program for the unemployed briefly attempted to add $900 million for that program to the bill. But they withdrew their proposal after Appropriations Chairman Hatfield promised to consider it on the next stopgap continuing resolution, needed after Nov. 10.

The Senate agreed to aid for the needy, though, when it adopted an amendment providing $40 million for emergency food and shelter.

The Senate adopted more than a dozen other minor amendments. They ranged from $5 million to renovate buildings at two black colleges in Pennsylvania to an amendment renaming Alaska's time zones.

Conference Report

As it came out of the conference committee Nov. 15, the supplemental contained $302 million for an array of government programs.

Conferees dropped the controversial Senate FCC amendment when Stevens said the FCC proposal would be considered in a separate piece of legislation expected on the Senate floor before Congress adjourned.

The conference also dropped another disputed Senate amendment to create a "drug czar" to coordinate federal drug enforcement efforts.

Hatfield said the administration opposed the drug czar language. "It puts the whole supplemental in jeopardy," Hatfield said.

Conte said conferees stripped some, but not all, of the "special interest programs" added by the Senate. "We won some; we lost some."

Legislative Mating — Final Action

As it came out of conference committee, the supplemental looked like a sure bet to clear easily. Controversial amendments had been stripped from the measure.

The House agreed to the conference report (H Rept 98-551) Nov. 16 by a 372-51 vote. *(Vote 475, p. 138-H)*

But when the Senate took up the conference report Nov. 17, Garn offered the housing-IMF package as an amendment. The Senate approved the conference agree-

ment by voice vote and then adopted the package 67-30 after rejecting several amendments that Garn said would destroy the delicate compromise. *(Vote 364, p. 59-S)*

The Senate tabled three such amendments to the Garn package. One, by William L. Armstrong, R-Colo., to target rental rehabilitation housing money to very low-income people, was rejected 74-23. Another Armstrong amendment, to eliminate funds for a voucher program to give poor people cash certificates that could be used in renting private housing, was tabled by a division vote. The third, by Gordon J. Humphrey, R-N.H., to reduce the IMF contribution by $584 million, was rejected 52-45. *(Votes 362, 363, p. 59-S)*

In other action on the supplemental conference report, the Senate also tabled, 49-46, an amendment by Carl Levin, D-Mich., making changes in the Social Security disability insurance program; tabled, 48-42, an amendment by J. Bennett Johnston, D-La., dealing with the policies of the Interior Department; tabled, 51-40, an amendment by Howard M. Metzenbaum, D-Ohio, to block a proposed Securities and Exchange Commission ruling limiting disclosure of corporate benefits by executives; and tabled, 71-20, another Johnston amendment to loosen restrictions in the bill on petroleum drilling off the Florida coast. *(Votes 365-368, p. 60-S)*

Late on the evening of Nov. 17, the House Rules Committee drafted an unusual closed rule (H Res 379), called a "self-executing rule," providing for floor consideration of the Senate changes on Nov. 18. A vote for the rule was a vote for the Senate changes. No amendments were allowed and debate time was limited to one hour and controlled by the Rules Committee.

Many House members objected to the limited debate provided by the rule. "This gives a new meaning to logrolling," said Dennis E. Eckart, D-Ohio. Clarence D. Long, D-Md., called it "a gag rule of the first order."

But Minority Leader Robert H. Michel, R-Ill., took the floor to urge his Republican colleagues to support the Reagan administration and vote for the rule. "*Our* president is on the line here today," Michel said.

The House voted 226-186 for the rule Nov. 18, clearing the bill. *(Vote 497, p. 144-H)* ∎

$1.5 Billion Legislative Appropriations Cleared

For the first time in five years, Congress cleared a separate appropriations measure for itself and its agencies.

House and Senate conferees June 28 agreed on a $1.473 billion fiscal 1984 spending bill (HR 3135 — PL 98-51) for the legislative branch. The House adopted the conference report (H Rept 98-271) by a 241-175 vote June 29. The Senate cleared the bill later that day by voice vote. *(Vote 217, p. 66-H)*

President Reagan signed the bill July 14. The White House by tradition did not interfere with appropriations for congressional operations.

Because of controversies such as congressional pay raises, Congress had not enacted a legislative branch money bill since 1978. Instead, Congress received money through stopgap continuing resolutions.

In 1979 the legislative appropriations bill was defeated in the House, and in 1980 the House passed a bill but the

Senate never acted. *(1979 Almanac p. 271; 1980 Almanac p. 176)*

Neither the House nor the Senate ever brought a legislative spending bill to the floor in 1981 or 1982. *(1981 Almanac p. 286; 1982 Almanac p. 236)*

Vic Fazio, D-Calif., chairman of the House Appropriations Legislative Subcommittee, said it was easier in 1983 because "the problems we're hassling over are in the supplemental."

Fazio referred to HR 3069, a supplemental appropriations bill for fiscal 1983. That bill contained a hotly contested pay raise for senators, a limit on the honoraria income senators could earn and a plan to restore, rather than extend, the decaying West Front of the Capitol.

HR 3069 was eventually cleared by Congress after the legislative funding bill and was signed into law (PL 98-63) by President Reagan July 30. *(Story, p. 509)*

"We're dealing with less controversial things in here," Fazio said about HR 3135. The bill's only effect on congressional pay was to preclude members from getting a very large raise at the time federal white-collar workers were given a raise. However, members did get a 3.5 percent pay raise Jan. 1, 1984, equal to what the federal employees received. *(Story, p. 577)*

The House passed its $1.2 billion version of HR 3135 by a 184-104 vote June 3. *(Vote 153, p. 48-H)*

After adding money for its own operations and a few other areas, the Senate passed a $1.476 billion version by a 78-15 vote June 23. *(Vote 166, p. 30-S)*

The conference agreement provided $138 million more than had been enacted for the legislative branch for fiscal 1983. When funds in the supplemental appropriations bill were considered, the 1984 level in HR 3135 was only about $7 million more than the 1983 total, according to a Senate Appropriations Committee aide.

HR 3135 contained $22 million less than Reagan proposed. Although the president made a legislative branch budget request, Congress wrote the figures and the administration included them in the budget without comment.

Provisions

As cleared, HR 3135 provided $1,473,359,000 for Congress and related agencies.

For congressional operations, the bill provided $981,876,000, which included:
- $384 million for House operations.
- $245 million for Senate operations.
- $117 million for joint operations.
- $14.7 million for the Office of Technology Assessment.
- $16.3 million for the Congressional Budget Office.
- $81.2 million for the Architect of the Capitol.
- $36.7 million for the Congressional Research Service.
- $86.6 million for the Government Printing Office to do congressional printing.

For the operations of related congressional agencies, the bill provided $491,483,000, which included:
- $2 million for the Botanic Garden.
- $177 million for the Library of Congress.
- $6 million for the Architect of the Capitol to run the library's buildings.
- $210,000 for the Copyright Royalty Tribunal.
- $39.1 million for the Government Printing Office for non-congressional printing.
- $267.1 million for the General Accounting Office.

House Appropriations Committee

When the House Appropriations Committee considered HR 3135 May 25, it added a provision blocking members from getting a large pay raise in the fall of 1983. The previous year members of the House had received a controversial 15 percent raise. *(1982 Almanac p. 544)*

The committee-reported (H Rept 98-227) bill would have reset the pay levels for which representatives were eligible in permanent law to $69,800 a year, the level set in December 1982. House members formerly received $60,662.50 a year; senators earned that amount until July 1983 when the supplemental, HR 3069, was enacted.

Before the bill's action on pay, the salary for members in permanent law was $77,300. Members got less than the full amount for which they were eligible because Congress had chosen to limit raises for itself over the past several years.

The committee included $1.211 billion for staff sala-

ries, operating Capitol buildings and for several related agencies, including the Library of Congress, General Accounting Office (GAO) and Government Printing Office (GPO).

Its bill did not include funding for the Senate, which traditionally inserted its own figures. The committee report estimated a $269 million appropriation for Senate activities.

The funding included by the committee in HR 3135 was $125 million more than the amount appropriated for fiscal 1983. Considering additional 1983 money in the supplemental appropriations bill (HR 3069) that passed the House May 25, HR 3135 would actually be $17.8 million below the final 1983 level. *(1982 Almanac p. 236)*

As reported by the Appropriations Committee, HR 3135 included $720 million for congressional operations and $491 million for other legislative agencies.

House Operations. The bill contained $384 million for the House, up from $349 million in fiscal 1983. The largest portion was for staff salaries: $150 million for personal staff members, $35 million for standing committee employees and $45 million for salaries of House supporting officers, such as the doorkeeper, sergeant-at-arms and chaplain.

This included $103 million for members' allowances and expenses, up $21 million from 1983.

The committee included $3 million for House leadership offices, with $721,000 set aside for the Speaker's office. In 1983, $2.7 million went to the leadership.

Money for members' salaries was not included in the bill because it was an automatic, or permanent, appropriation. The committee noted that $34 million was anticipated for members' compensation and related expenses.

For the first time, this amount included a $1.1 million payment to the Social Security program. This was to cover the employer contribution for members of Congress, who were to enter the system Jan. 1, 1984, under the Social Security rescue plan (PL 98-21) enacted in March. Members would have the 7 percent employees' contribution deducted from their salaries. *(Social Security story, p. 219)*

Joint Expenses. The committee provided $117 million for joint House and Senate activities. The 1983 total was $64 million.

This included $107 million for members' official mail costs, almost double the 1983 appropriation of $55 million. With additional funds for franked mail included in the 1983 supplemental bill, however, the increase would be only $14 million. Congressional mailing costs traditionally increase during an election year.

The committee included $29 million for the Capitol police force to cover salaries and expenses for 1,226 officers. It also inserted $295,000 for the education of pages, $775,000 for the Capitol Guide Service, $2.4 million for the Joint Economic Committee and $3.4 million for the Joint Taxation Committee.

Other Accounts. The committee bill also contained:
- $14 million for the Office of Technology Assessment, a congressional advisory body.
- $16 million for the Congressional Budget Office.
- $69 million for the Capitol architect, who runs and maintains the Capitol buildings and grounds.
- $177 million for the Library of Congress. The bill also contained $38 million for the Congressional Research Service, a branch of the library.
- $87 million for GPO printing and document binding

for Congress. Other GPO activities would get $39 million.

● $2 million for the Botanic Garden, which supplies plants to members' offices.

● $267 million for the GAO, an agency that monitors government efficiency and adjudicates federal compensation questions.

House Action

By a 184-104 vote, the House passed HR 3135 June 3, avoiding touchy issues, such as a congressional pay raise. *(Vote 153, p. 48-H)*

Although floor action was smoother than in recent years, the bill still faced a barrage of Republican amendments during debate June 2 and 3.

Orchestrated by Hank Brown, R-Colo., the amendments would have trimmed funds for members' official expenses, committee staffs, franked mail, the Congressional Budget Office and Capitol elevator operators.

All the amendments failed, except for one by Thomas F. Hartnett, R-S.C., to cut $2.3 million from the Congressional Research Service, a branch of the Library of Congress.

The amendments included proposals by:

● Robert S. Walker, R-Pa., to reduce funds for committee staffs by $1.1 million, from $34.7 million to $33.6 million. It was defeated 142-213. *(Vote 144, p. 46-H)*

● Judd Gregg, R-N.H., to cut overall funding for committees by $6 million, from $44 million to $38 million. Rejected 133-189. *(Vote 148, p. 48-H)*

● Steve Bartlett, R-Texas, to slice $6.9 million out of the bill's $67 million for members' expense accounts. Rejected 156-160. *(Vote 149, p. 48-H)*

● Duncan L. Hunter, R-Calif., to cut $9.3 million from official mail costs. Rejected 134-173. *(Vote 150, p. 48-H)*

● John Hiler, R-Ind., to reduce funds for the Congressional Budget Office by $733,850. Rejected 141-164. *(Vote 151, p. 48-H)*

● Brown, of Colorado, to eliminate the jobs of 14 operators for automatic elevators in House office buildings, for a savings of $169,876. Rejected 101-193. *(Vote 152, p. 48-H)*

Republican proponents of the amendments argued that Congress must set an example in austerity by cutting its own funds.

"The question is whether or not we are going to behave responsibly with our own budget," Brown said.

Democrats said they already were holding the line. "This is not a profligate spending bill," protested Vic Fazio, D-Calif., chairman of the Appropriations Legislative Subcommittee.

Fazio argued that the legislative branch budget had grown at an average annual rate of 5.3 percent since 1979, compared to a rate of 11.6 percent for the entire federal budget.

The most vocal debate focused on members' expense accounts and mail franking costs.

Fazio said the bill contained $17 million less than the House Administration Committee had authorized for members' allowances, which were used for travel, telephones, and other business costs. He added that members who did not want the money could return it to the Treasury.

"If we do not need it, we do not need to spend it," Fazio said.

But Republicans said the increase proposed in HR 3135, from $57 million in fiscal 1983 to $67 million in 1984, was too large.

"Do we not owe the working men and women of this country at least this example of holding our increases to reasonable levels?" Brown asked.

Hunter said his amendment to reduce official mail costs "should spark some restraint in the election year use of the franking privilege by members of Congress." He said House members would send out about 422 million pieces of mail in 1983, and about 839 million pieces in 1984, an election year.

But Democrats said members needed more money to respond to the large volume of constituent mail.

Senate Appropriations

The Senate Appropriations Committee reported the bill (S Rept 98-161) June 22 by voice vote.

Alfonse M. D'Amato, R-N.Y., chairman of the Appropriations Legislative Branch Subcommittee, said HR 3135 contained $19 million less than the amount proposed by President Reagan.

The measure provided $9 million more than total fiscal 1983 appropriations for the legislative branch.

The committee included several housekeeping changes in the bill. One abolished the Senate's longevity compensation program, under which employees of the Secretary of the Senate and the sergeant-at-arms could receive salary increases based on length of service.

The committee report said, "There is no longer a justification for rewarding employees solely on the basis of length of service, irrespective of the quality of their performance. Annual cost-of-living raises provide employees pay comparability, and other raises should be based on merit."

The committee also allowed senators to purchase computer equipment or computer services with money from their office expense accounts, if approved by the Rules Committee. Previously, there were restrictions on the use of office funds to buy computer equipment.

Senate Action

The Senate debate over the bill June 23 centered on the compensation of senators. The Senate passed the bill 78-15 after rejecting a proposal to place part of senators' unearned income, such as dividends and interest, in restricted trust funds. *(Vote 166, p. 30-S)*

The proposal, aimed at wealthy senators who received money from investments and inheritance, was defeated 34-58. Majority Leader Howard H. Baker Jr., R-Tenn., joked that "the rich caucus is opposed to it," and many of the Senate's best-known millionaires voted against it. *(Vote 165, p. 30-S)*

Jake Garn, R-Utah, saying he was angry about the $20,940 cap on honoraria earned by senators that was approved by the Senate June 9, offered the plan to place outside unearned income in a special trust.

Garn was one of the Senate's top honoraria earners in 1982, collecting $60,799 for speeches and articles. In an often sarcastic speech, Garn attacked the Senate's "rich boys," who he said adhered to a "self-righteous double standard" by capping honoraria income without limiting the amount they could receive in unearned income.

"We have two classes of senators here," Garn said. Some senators, he said, did not inherit wealth from "a rich father" or did not have "a rich wife."

"Some of us married for love," he said.

Under Garn's amendment, all of a senator's unearned income above 30 percent of his or her annual salary would have been placed in a trust fund. The money would not

have been available during the senator's term in office.

However, if a senator's unearned income in any year was less than 30 percent of his or her annual salary, he or she would be able to withdraw some money from the trust fund.

"We realize that some of the rich boys, with their country club memberships and their several houses on the beach and in Europe and in Mexico might get into a cash flow problem," Garn said. Such senators might complain that "'we may have to sell one of our cathedrals in Europe, or one of our beach houses in the Mediterranean,'" he added.

Though no one spoke against the amendment on the floor, most of the Senate's wealthiest members cast "no" votes.

Afterwards, Garn said, "This vote is exactly what I expected. This is a lousy amendment and it should never become law." But he said he offered it to prove the point that limits also should not be placed on honoraria.

Aside from the Garn amendment, HR 3135 faced no other problems on the Senate floor.

Conference Action

There were few differences between the House and Senate in the brief conference June 28.

The only issue to stir up conferees was whether to provide money for a chauffeur-driven automobile for Capitol Architect George M. White.

White currently had a government-paid car and driver, but the Senate wanted to eliminate the chauffeur. The Senate bill also stated that the car could not be used to transport White between his home and office.

Conferees agreed to provide funding for the car and driver for meetings but not allow funds for trips between White's home and the Capitol.

Several conferees were generally unhappy about chauffeur-driven cars provided to other congressional officers. Silvio O. Conte, R-Mass., said, "I'm sick and tired of seeing these guys with chauffeurs, sitting on their fat asses. They ought to take those chauffeurs out of everybody's cars."

The provision that had been inserted by House Appropriations to prevent members from getting larger raises was included in the final version.

Transportation/Commerce/Consumers

Congress generally found itself in the role of a spectator as the transportation industry struggled to cope with its deregulated environment and the effects of the 1982-83 recession.

Overall, the transportation field was healthier in 1983 than in 1982, but some individual firms within a particular segment of the industry were at risk.

For example, members of the Air Transport Association were expected to reap a cumulative operating profit of several hundred million dollars in 1983, compared to operating losses in 1982 of more than $700 million. But Continental Airlines declared bankruptcy, Eastern Airlines was forced to seek wage concessions from employees and several other airlines were in poor financial health.

The situation was the same in the trucking industry. American Trucking Association's figures showed that the largest dozen or so trucking firms were profitable and increasing their share of business but hundreds of much smaller firms had to curtail or shut down operations.

There was no concentrated push on Capitol Hill for legislation to ease the financial turmoil. It was difficult to separate the effects of the recession from the impact of the deregulation of the airline, railroad, trucking and bus industries, and Congress was reluctant to initiate major legislation.

Supporters of deregulation argued that a painful shakeout had to be expected when long-standing government regulation changed. Deregulation, for example, generally meant ending restrictions on who could enter an industry. While increased competition might damage some firms, the purpose of deregulation was to make the industry more efficient by eliminating marginal companies or business practices, thus benefiting the consumer.

Transportation Secretary Elizabeth Hanford Dole, sworn in Feb. 7 to replace Drew Lewis who resigned, argued that transportation industries "are drawing new energy from competition. Those who would succeed must put aside the old ways of thinking and acting. The consumers will now decide who is efficient and who is not. They are no longer merely along for the ride. They are driving the train."

Dole said she believed that the recession, far more than deregulation, was to blame for economic problems in the transportation industry.

But that view was not universally held, particularly by those who regarded themselves as victims of the new competitive environment — including some transportation employees.

Hard Times Continue

Management of many financially troubled firms sought employee concessions, such as pay cuts, arguing that high labor costs made it impossible for them to compete with a host of new, mostly non-union firms that took advantage of deregulation to enter the industry.

Continental Airlines declared bankruptcy after its workers refused to accept a pay cut and went on strike. A reorganized Continental Airlines returned to business with employees who were paid a fraction of their precedessors' salaries.

Cut-rate fares offered by new entrants in the airline industry had far reaching impact on other segments of the transportation business. Greyhound Bus Lines, the nation's largest intercity bus line, told its employees that it could not compete with the low air fares and remain profitable without lower labor costs. Workers staged a seven-week strike but eventually agreed to a 7.8 percent pay cut.

Even accepting a reduction in pay was not enough to save the jobs of thousands of trucking industry workers. Although the International Brotherhood of Teamsters agreed to a master labor agreement calling for lower wages, dozens of firms closed or greatly reduced operations in the face of competition of thousands of new non-union firms, who offered lower costs to shippers. An estimated 100,000 Teamsters were still out of work at year's end.

Truckers in particular turned to Capitol Hill for help. They complained that the Interstate Commerce Commission (ICC) was going beyond the intent of Congress in administering the 1980 Motor Carrier Act, letting virtually anyone enter the industry and allowing unlawful discriminatory rates.

They also sought relief from the scheduled sixfold increase in heavy-truck user fees mandated by the 1982 Surface Transportation Assistance Act. The 30,000-member Independent Truckers Association staged a violence-marred strike Jan. 31 through Feb. 10, 1983, to protest the higher road-use fees. The strike ended after 35 members of Congress promised to review the fees.

1983 Congressional Action

Among the matters before Congress in 1983 were the following:

Trucking Issues. While there was no major trucking bill, Congress took preliminary steps on issues important to the industry.

A number of bills were introduced to raise the federal tax on diesel fuel from 9 to 14 cents per gallon in exchange for the repeal of the increased user fees on heavy trucks. The user fees were to increase from a $240 maximum to $1,600 July 1, 1984. The issue was a high priority of the trucking lobby.

Another area involved extending antitrust immunity for certain collective ratemaking practices in the trucking industry. The immunity was scheduled to expire July 1, 1984. Trucking labor and management wanted the extension while shippers and the administration favored its end. A House effort to continue the immunity was blocked by Senate opponents.

A bill to deregulate the trucking industry completely and end the trucking functions of the ICC was introduced by Sen. Bob Packwood, R-Ore., chairman of the Commerce Committee. Packwood was unable to win strong White

House backing for his bill. The Teamsters, who opposed deregulation, had endorsed President Reagan in the 1980 presidential election.

Coal Slurry Pipelines. In a big victory for the railroads, the House decisively defeated legislation granting the right of federal eminent domain to coal slurry pipeline companies. The pipeline industry had sought such legislation for years and believed it had won enough support to make the vote close. But railroads, whose virtual monopoly over coal transportation was threatened, conducted a heavy lobbying effort, and the measure, HR 1010, was defeated by 53 votes — 182-235.

After assessing the defeat, sponsors of a similar bill in the Senate declined to bring it to the floor.

Air Bags. The highway death rate continued to drop in 1983; the toll was an estimated 2.63 per 100 million vehicle miles compared to 2.88 in 1982 and 5.70 in 1966. But consumer groups and many members of Congress insisted that more could be done to make the highways safer.

The National Highway Traffic Safety Administration, after dropping in 1981 a requirement that new automobiles be equipped with air bags, was told by the Supreme Court to consider the matter again.

Legislation (S 1108) to require large automobile manufacturers to offer air bags in some models beginning with the 1986 model year was ordered reported by the Senate Commerce, Science and Transportation Committee, but no floor action was taken.

Amtrak. Legislation (HR 3648, S 1117) authorizing fiscal 1984 operating and capital improvement grants for Amtrak, the federally subsidized passenger railroad, did not clear, partly because of controversy over an Amtrak default on more than $1 billion in federal loans.

Maritime Issues. Two major maritime bills were considered in 1983, but action was not completed:

● Bills authorizing fiscal 1984 funds for the Maritime Administration (S 1037, HR 2114) passed. A provision in the House bill that would restrict the Department of Transportation from giving blanket approval for U.S.-flag vessels in foreign trade to enter the domestic market held up final passage. The Senate version left the door open for a DOT proposal to permit the entry of vessels whose federal construction subsidy was repaid.

● Legislation (S 47) sought by shipping lines to broaden antitrust immunity for collective ratemaking also was approved by both chambers but a conference agreement was not reached by year's end.

Highway Construction and Repair Funds. A bill (HR 3103) to provide an additional $150 million in emergency highway repair funds and to permit the distribution

of $4 billion for Interstate highway construction and $700 million for other projects was held up by a House-Senate dispute over other provisions of the bill.

Commerce

Telephone and broadcasting controversies placed heavy demands on Congress, with the House and Senate in several cases unable to agree on legislation.

The Jan. 1, 1984, breakup of the American Telephone & Telegraph Co. (AT&T) raised the specter of rapidly rising telephone rates. The fears were fed by a Federal Communications Commission (FCC) proposal to shift costs that had been paid by long-distance users to local telephone users, in effect increasing local rates.

Both chambers took steps to head off the FCC charges and to establish a safety net for low-income persons who might be unable to afford service if rates should rise. But only the House completed floor action, passing its bill (HR 4102) Nov. 10 banning the charges. The Senate did not complete action on a milder measure (S 1660) that established a two-year moratorium.

House and Senate members were sharply divided over broadcast deregulation. The Senate had approved legislation (S 55) in February ratifying a number of FCC rulings deregulating such aspects of the industry as license renewal. Broadcasters had lobbied hard for the Senate action. But legislation was blocked in House subcommittee by disagreement.

The Senate also met some of the requests of cable television operators who wanted freedom from what they called a bewildering array of local restrictions. The bill (S 66) was opposed by some cities that objected to the loss of local control of the industry. Another measure, approved by the House Energy and Commerce Subcommittee on Telecommunications, brought complaints from the industry and was not acted upon by the full committee.

The FCC was at the center of a controversy that pitted the giant television networks against the equally large Hollywood studios and producers. The FCC proposed to modify long-standing rules and allow the major television networks — ABC, NBC and CBS — to profit from TV reruns. Hollywood producers, studios and others objected to the plan.

In November the House passed legislation (HR 2550) to delay the FCC change for six months, and just as the Senate was poised to do the same, the agency reached a truce and agreed to hold off a final decision until May 1984.

—By Brian Nutting

Congress Moves to Bar FCC Phone Rate Hike

Foes of a Federal Communications Commission (FCC) plan to raise local telephone rates scored a ringing victory Nov. 10 when the House passed by voice vote a bill to reject the FCC proposal.

The bill (HR 4102) prohibited the FCC from imposing a new monthly fee on residential or single-line business phone users but permitted the charge to be levied on multi-line businesses. The action marked a bitter defeat for the FCC and the American Telephone & Telegraph Co. (AT&T), which had spent an estimated $4 million lobbying against the bill.

The Senate, however, did not act on a milder bill reported by its Commerce Committee (S 1660 — S Rept 98-270) that would delay the FCC plan for two years. The leadership announced the legislation would be considered in 1984.

The issue involved an FCC proposal to levy a flat charge on residential and small business phone users for the right of access to long-distance service, whether they used long-distance service or not. The fee, originally set to begin Jan. 1 but later delayed by the FCC until April, would start at $2 per month for residential customers and $6 per month for businesses, rising yearly until 1990.

The fees were designed to eventually recover $6.5 billion that currently was being paid by long-distance users to help maintain wires, poles and other equipment shared by all users. The $6.5 billion amounted to a subsidy that helped keep local rates low.

The FCC and AT&T said that shifting the charges from long-distance to local users was essential to the success of the Jan. 1, 1984, court-ordered breakup of AT&T. Local companies would separate from AT&T on Jan. 1 and would no longer get that subsidy from AT&T. AT&T would become one of several long-distance companies. *(1982 Almanac p. 331)*

However, because AT&T accounted for more than 90 percent of long-distance billings, it had billions of dollars riding on whether long-distance or local customers covered the costs. AT&T and the FCC argued that continuing to make long-distance users pay would drive up long-distance prices and encourage the development of private systems bypassing the local network. They said the FCC plan recognized the new competitive environment of telecommunications and reflected a proper shift to cost-based pricing.

Backers of the legislation said the FCC proposal would mean an increase of $7-to-$8 per month in the average monthly phone bill of American consumers by 1990, undermining a policy dating to 1934 that called for universal telephone service. Telephone service would become too expensive for the poor, they said.

House Bill

Under HR 4102 as passed by the House Nov. 10, residential and single-line business customers would pay no access charge, but businesses with more than one telephone line still would pay the $6 per month envisioned by the FCC. The multi-line businesses would provide $1.3 billion of the $6.5 billion in question.

The bill would require long-distance companies, including AT&T and its competitors, to put up $3.9 billion of the cost of jointly used facilities, with the remaining $1.3 billion recovered through charges on private phone systems

that indirectly interconnected with the local phone system.

Two funds to help keep phone rates affordable for high-cost rural areas and low-income customers were established by the bill. The money would come from a small surcharge added to long-distance calls.

Legislative Summary

The specter of rising telephone rates led to the introduction of legislation in both chambers. A bipartisan group of key House and Senate members July 21 introduced bills (HR 3621, S 1660) to help hold rates down.

Sponsors included John D. Dingell, D-Mich., and Timothy E. Wirth, D-Colo., chairmen of the House Energy and Commerce Committee and its Telecommunications Subcommittee, respectively, and Bob Packwood, R-Ore., and Barry Goldwater, R-Ariz., who chaired the Senate Commerce Committee and its Communications Subcommittee. (Goldwater later withdrew his sponsorship.)

Although differing in details, both bills were aimed at blocking the FCC decision. Joint hearings of the two Commerce Committees were held July 28-29.

On Sept. 20, the Senate panel refused to approve Packwood's bill and tentatively approved a one-year moratorium on imposing the FCC fees. The moratorium was later extended to two years and the bill ordered reported Sept. 27.

On Sept. 28, the House Subcommittee on Telecommunications marked up a clean bill (subsequently introduced as HR 4102) and approved it by a party-line vote of 10-5. The full committee, after sometimes contentious debate spanning seven meetings, ordered the bill reported Oct. 27. The report (H Rept 98-479) was filed Nov. 3.

AT&T had launched its offensive against the legislation Oct. 5 with chairman Charles Brown writing all members of the House and Senate. Brown pleaded with Congress not to "disrupt the final step in the restructuring of the telephone industry." In 1982, a massive lobbying effort by the firm that flooded congressional offices with letters from stockholders helped to kill telephone legislation. *(1982 Almanac p. 331)*

House Provisions

As passed by the House, HR 4102:

● **Access Charges.** Retained the existing system of subsidizing local service from long-distance revenues from Jan. 1, 1984, when the AT&T divestiture was to take effect, until the system of access charges did take effect.

● Prohibited the FCC from imposing its planned flat monthly access charge on residential telephone customers, businesses with only one telephone line or non-profit orphanages.

● **Lifeline Service.** Required state public utility commissions to establish "lifeline" — *i.e.*, discount — telephone service for low-income residential telephone customers.

● Established a Universal Service Fund, overseen by a joint federal-state board, to make payments to local telephone companies to help defray the cost of serving high-cost rural areas to provide state-approved lifeline service for the poor. The fund would be financed by a surcharge on long-distance telephone companies.

To be eligible for payments from the fund, a local phone company's expenses had to exceed the national average and its lifeline service had to offer reduced rates of 33-50 percent below the average local telephone rate. The fund would reimburse the local company for 50 percent of the difference between the reduced rate for lifeline service and the average charge for residential service. The other 50 percent would be recovered from other customers, statewide, in a manner approved by the state public utility commission.

● Established a Universal Service Board, consisting of the five FCC commissioners and four state public utilities commissioners, to oversee the Universal Service Fund and determine how to apportion the costs of jointly used facilities between interstate and intrastate sources within each state.

● Declared the board's decisions administratively final, and thus not subject to FCC review.

● Limited at the 1983 level the share of the costs of jointly used lines, wires or other equipment recovered by local phone companies from interstate long-distance firms.

● **Private Systems.** Imposed a special access charge, paid to the local phone company, on so-called "indirectly interconnected" users — those that established private communication systems that indirectly interconnected with the local system through a PBX (private branch exchange) or other facilities. The charge would help support the local public telephone system.

The bill exempted from the special access charge any private system unable to use the local exchange as a reliable or commercially valuable alternative to its own system. The exemption applied to systems used for radio and television transmission, radio or other mobile services used for public safety purposes, systems on private property used solely for internal communication or facilities necessary to safe, efficient operation of railroads, pipelines and utilities along their rights of way.

● Imposed an "insurance" charge no greater than 10 percent of the special access charge paid by indirectly interconnected systems on so-called "unconnected users" — private systems that could call on the local phone system as a backup or supplement but were not connected to it.

Systems unable to use the public system as a commercially valuable backup or supplement were exempt from the charge.

● Exempted from payments to the Universal Service Fund any private system that was exempt from the special access charge on indirect interconnection.

● Required that the local phone company use any revenues collected from the charges on unconnected users to reduce the rates paid by local phone company customers.

● Imposed a fine of up to $100,000 for an individual and $500,000 for a company that evaded or attempted to evade the special charges through fraud or misrepresentation.

● Permitted local phone companies to ensure that they recovered all of their cost of maintaining jointly used equipment by providing that local firms could charge long-distance firms for any shortfall between the costs of such equipment and the revenue provided by special access charges on indirectly interconnected users, charges on unconnected users or long-distance access charges on businesses.

● Required the FCC to ensure that AT&T and other long-distance companies pass through to their customers "to the maximum extent possible and practicable" reductions in the long-distance share of the cost of jointly used facilities.

● **Long-Distance Access.** Froze until July 1, 1985 — except for increases to cover inflation — the amount of charges levied on long-distance competitors of AT&T for access to local exchanges at the rates in effect as of July 1, 1983; and permitted AT&T's competitors to continue receiving a discount on their local access charges until the FCC determined that the quality of the interconnections they received was equivalent to AT&T's. Before July 1, 1985, the FCC could permit the competitors' local access charges to be raised to the same level as AT&T's if the competitors were provided with interconnections as good as AT&T's.

● **Miscellaneous.** Required, beginning 90 days after enactment, that anyone owning or operating facilities permitting him to originate or terminate communications between phone exchanges, notify the FCC and the "appropriate exchange" of that fact or face a fine of up to $50,000.

● Prohibited any local exchange from imposing a charge on residential subscribers for using computer terminals not leased from the exchange carrier.

● Prohibited any local or long-distance phone company from charging telephone users for the first six calls a month for long-distance directory assistance.

● Overturned a Dec. 22, 1982, FCC decision requiring state regulatory commission rules for depreciation of telephone equipment to match FCC rules, and made recommendations for state commissions to follow in setting depreciation rules.

● Authorized states to require phone companies to lease one dial telephone and the wiring necessary to operate it to anyone requesting to lease such basic equipment rather than purchase it.

● Prohibited telephone companies from using revenues from regulated services to underwrite their unregulated business.

● Protected pension rights and other benefits for current AT&T employees after divestiture.

● Invalidated any tariff, rule or other action that prohibited or restricted the rights of telephone users to share the use of telephone facilities in any way that did not infringe on the rights of other users.

● **Public Participation.** Authorized the FCC to provide financial assistance, including reasonable fees for lawyers and expert witnesses, to persons who could not afford to participate at their own expense in FCC proceedings, who represented interests that otherwise would be inadequately represented and whose exclusion would prevent the proceedings from being fair.

● Authorized the creation of private, non-profit associations of residential telephone users in each state and the District of Columbia to represent consumer interests in FCC or state regulatory commission proceedings or other civil or administrative proceedings affecting the interests of telephone users. Membership would be open to telephone customers over 16 years of age.

● Permitted such consumer associations to include, at the associations' expense, information in customer billings mailed by local telephone firms.

● Created a National Consumer Telephone Resource Center to act as an umbrella organization providing research and other support for the telephone consumer groups established by the bill.

● Prohibited telephone companies from interfering with the activities of the consumer groups.

House Committee Action

The Subcommittee on Telecommunications approved the bill Sept. 28 by a 10-5 party-line vote. Earlier it rejected by 5-10 a Republican alternative that would have kept the FCC's access charge but would have phased it in over a longer period of time.

The subcommittee adopted by a 12-3 vote a plan drafted by Edward J. Markey, D-Mass. Matthew J. Rinaldo, R-N.J., and Tom Tauke, R-Iowa, who had offered the Republican plan, voted with the Democrats.

Besides barring the residential access charge, Markey's amendment assessed a fee on firms that used private lines and bypassed the local phone company. The FCC plan would charge firms that bypassed local lines by using phone company equipment, but it would exempt those using other equipment.

The subcommittee also adopted amendments clarifying the universal service and lifeline funds.

Under one amendment, offered by Al Swift, D-Wash., small telephone companies with fewer than 100,000 lines would receive money from the universal service fund if their costs exceeded the national average, to be determined by a sliding scale. According to subcommittee staff, the fund, financed by long-distance charges, would total between $400 million and $500 million when fully implemented.

In addition, the panel agreed that up to one-half of the cost of telephone service for low-income persons should be subsidized. Under an amendment offered by Mickey Leland, D-Texas, state public service commissions would determine eligibility.

The subcommittee also approved an amendment by Swift to establish non-profit associations of residential telephone consumers in each state. The associations would represent consumers before telephone companies and governmental bodies, and would receive funds through membership dues.

Full Committee

Brushing aside the intensive lobbying effort by AT&T, the Energy and Commerce Committee Oct. 27 approved HR 4102 on a strict party-line vote of 27-15.

The committee had begun its markup Oct. 18 in a charged atmosphere because a 1982 telephone bill (HR 5158) opposed by AT&T died during committee markup in an unusually bitter fight.

HR 5158 would have tightened restrictions on AT&T more than the consent decree, requiring the firm to divest itself of its operating companies. In 1982, panel member Tom Corcoran, R-Ill., urged on by AT&T, suffocated HR 5158 by employing uncommon dilatory tactics that halted committee action. *(1982 Almanac p. 331)*

With the FCC's access charge set to take effect Jan. 1, 1984, and Congress hoping to adjourn for 1983 in November, Corcoran and other opponents of HR 4102 had indicated that delay again would be their chosen weapon.

But as he opened the Oct. 18 markup, Dingell declared that he would use his power as chairman to prevent the delays that had killed HR 5158. When it came Corcoran's turn to make a five-minute opening statement, Dingell showed he meant business.

"I plan to be active and do my part to make sure that this committee has the time to fully discuss this legislation," Corcoran announced. But then, with Corcoran in the middle of another sentence, his five minutes expired.

As it did, Dingell slammed his gavel down with a bang that echoed through the committee room like a rifle shot, startling many spectators and Corcoran as well.

When Corcoran sought recognition to ask for the usual unanimous consent to finish his statement, Dingell ignored his cries of "Mr. Chairman, Mr. Chairman," and recognized someone else instead.

Then Dingell leaned back in his chair, turned to Corcoran and grinned broadly.

Time Agreement

The Oct. 18 session continued its contentious course until Wirth undertook a parliamentary move that gave him and Dingell the leverage they needed to get a time agreement limiting committee debate on the measure.

Wirth offered a slightly different version of the bill in the form of a substitute amendment, which had the effect of restricting the number of amendments permitted and giving Wirth the right to demand a vote on his substitute at any time.

When Republicans on the committee protested, Dingell suspended the markup and took Wirth and ranking minority member James T. Broyhill, R-N.C., behind closed doors to negotiate the time agreement.

As those talks were proceeding, the FCC decided to delay the access charge until April 3.

The FCC decision was announced late on Oct. 18. At noon on Oct. 19, Broyhill announced the time agreement, under which Wirth agreed to withdraw his substitute amendment, thus lifting the limit on amendments.

As debate proceeded, committee members rejected amendments that AT&T supported.

Two crucial amendments, the defeat of which paved the way for final approval of HR 4102, came up Oct. 25.

One, offered by Matthew J. Rinaldo, R-N.J., would have placed a one-year moratorium on the FCC's proposed access charge for business and residential customers. It also would have set an initial $1 maximum monthly charge and permitted a yearly increase of $1 per month up to a maximum of $4 per month.

Rinaldo characterized his amendment as a compromise between the bill's prohibition of any residential access charge and the FCC's plan to begin the access charge at $2 per month next year.

But the bill's sponsors said the amendment would gut the measure.

"The issue is simple," said Dingell. "Do you want to stick it to your residential and small business constituents to benefit long-distance companies, principally AT&T with its 97 percent market share, and big business customers who account for the overwhelming bulk of long-distance calling?"

Rinaldo's amendment was turned down on a 16-26 vote.

The second key amendment, offered by Barbara A. Mikulski, D-Md., involved competition among long-distance companies. Mikulski wanted to delete a section of HR 4102 that would temporarily keep in place significant discounts to AT&T's long-distance competitors on the costs of hooking into local phone networks. The bill maintained those discounts until competing companies such as MCI and Sprint were able to offer the same level and quality of long-distance service as AT&T.

Mikulski said she was concerned that local phone companies would have to underwrite the cost of the discounts and would therefore pass on the costs to customers.

But opponents of her amendment said AT&T, rather than the local companies, would be responsible for absorbing the discounts. The amendment failed 16-26.

The committee also agreed to an amendment that would require the company to pass along to its customers any savings in the form of reduced long-distance rates that resulted from the FCC access charge order and phone legislation. The amendment was offered by Bill Richardson, D-N.M., and passed by voice vote.

Supporters of HR 4102 estimated that AT&T would earn a "windfall" profit of $2.25 billion under the FCC plan. That profit, according to the estimates, was on top of the $1.75 billion in reduced long-distance charges that AT&T had promised if the FCC plan were allowed to go into effect. AT&T officials announced they would reconsider their plans to lower long-distance rates if HR 4102 became law.

Sponsors of the bill, however, contended that AT&T would still have an extra $2.8 billion to pass on to customers in the form of long-distance reductions if the measure was enacted.

AT&T enjoyed one victory when, on a 22-19 vote, the panel Oct. 25 agreed to an amendment by James J. Florio, D-N.J., aimed at discouraging the FCC from nationally averaging long-distance calling costs. Florio said the practice would penalize phone customers in urbanized areas where fixed long-distance costs were lower than in more sparsely populated regions.

Florio's amendment permitted the FCC to average fixed, or "non-traffic-sensitive," long-distance costs but only upon finding that the step was needed to further the overall purposes of the Communications Act of 1934.

Florio said that without his amendment, states in the urbanized Northeast and Midwest would become "exporters" of long-distance subsidies to other parts of the country. But Bob Whittaker, R-Kan., charged that the amendment would be "detrimental and discriminatory" to rural areas.

Government agencies, meanwhile, faced higher phone charges under HR 4102. The Commerce Committee approved an amendment by Wirth that treated local, state and federal agencies the same as large firms. As a result, government offices would pay long-distance access charges or other fees imposed by the bill on those who used private telephone systems.

House Floor Action

House passage of the bill was forecast by a 142-264 party-line vote Nov. 10 rejecting a substitute offered by Tauke that would have phased in the FCC residential access charge beginning in 1985 and limited it to $1 a month at first, rising to $4 a month by 1988. *(Vote 453, 134-H)*

The vote split almost strictly along party lines. Only eight Democrats voted for the Tauke substitute; 245 voted against it. Only 19 Republicans voted against it; 134 voted for it.

Tauke had cast his amendment as a compromise retaining the best of both HR 4102 and the FCC's plan, which Tauke and other Republicans argued was essential to preserve the long-distance telephone system after the breakup of AT&T.

Wirth and other backers of HR 4102 argued that banning the access charge was essential to keep local phone rates from rising too much.

Tauke said his substitute was more generous in subsidies financed by surcharges on long-distance companies. He said it would provide $883 million a year to subsidize low-income users, compared to $679 million in HR 4102, and $1 billion a year to defray the high costs of rural service, compared to $544 million in Wirth's bill.

About five of the seven hours of debate were spent on Tauke's plan, which foes said would gut the bill.

Albert Gore Jr., D-Tenn., derided the Tauke substitute for delaying its access charge until 1985, which he said was a ploy to avoid taking responsibility for it in the 1984 elections.

Wirth and others also complained that Tauke's provisions favoring rural phone users were intended to "Balkanize" the House. Much of the debate centered on whether the Tauke substitute or HR 4102 would better protect rural phone service.

Other Amendments. The only other roll call was a 122-270 defeat of an amendment by Rinaldo that was nearly identical to the Tauke amendment. *(Vote 454, 134-H)*

The House rejected by voice vote an amendment by Corcoran that would have made it easier for AT&T's long-distance competitors to lose discounts they got on charges they paid for connecting with local phone systems. Such firms got a discount because the connections were not as good as those AT&T enjoyed.

Senate Committee Action

A divided Senate Commerce Committee refused at a Sept. 20 meeting to endorse Packwood's bill, which would have banned the FCC fees. After agreeing 9-6 to adopt an amendment by Frank R. Lautenberg, D-N.J., wiping out the provisions of Packwood's bill and substituting the one-year moratorium, the committee voted 10-6 to delay a final vote on the bill until Sept. 27.

Lautenberg, contending that the committee had received revisions to Packwood's bill only the night before the markup, urged delay in acting on the measure.

"We are moving along pell-mell into chaos," he warned, adding that technology and the industry were changing so rapidly that Congress must move cautiously.

Packwood objected to the one-year moratorium, saying the congressional schedule would prohibit considered deliberations and pointing out Congress would be in recess during the two national political conventions and elections.

Packwood urged that the moratorium be extended to two years and include a prohibition of access fees for business customers, and that the FCC be required to submit a plan to Congress of any new fees it planned.

On Sept. 30 the panel agreed 15-2 to a compromise between Lautenberg's one-year moratorium and Packwood's original bill.

Lautenberg had changed his original proposal by exempting small businesses with only one telephone line from the FCC's access fee and agreeing to the two-year moratorium.

In addition, he agreed to add a section from a revised version of Packwood's bill establishing a $200 million universal service fund to subsidize service in high-cost rural areas, and a $200 million so-called "lifeline" fund to assure service for low-income users.

The committee tentatively agreed to the Lautenberg plan Sept. 27 by a 10-2 vote, with Communications Subcommittee Chairman Barry Goldwater, R-Ariz., and Slade

Gorton, R-Wash., opposing.

Goldwater argued that more study was necessary to determine the effect of the FCC's proposal, as well as the telephone industry changes.

Goldwater said that Congress should wait to see what happened after the FCC access charge took effect Jan. 1, 1984. "We can always repeal what the FCC has done," he said. "In fact, we can abolish the FCC."

But Lautenberg insisted that "if we do nothing here and allow the forces at play to take effect, we will be imposing a fairly heavy burden on individual subscribers."

Gorton had proposed that the legislation place a cap on whatever access fee might emerge, to ensure predictability that "a certain policy will take place." Gorton also wanted a larger universal service fund. Packwood had originally proposed a $1.2 billion fund to help local telephone firms cover high costs caused by new equipment. ∎

Maritime Authorization

Congress failed to complete action on a one-year re-authorization of maritime programs administered by the Department of Transportation. One key provision on ship construction subsidies remained to be reconciled when the first session of the 98th Congress ended.

The fiscal 1984 funding authorized by the House and Senate versions of the bill (S 1037) was similar.

The bill (HR 2114) passed by the House by a vote of 281-35 Nov. 4 authorized $486.8 million in fiscal 1984, while the Senate measure, passed by voice vote April 28, provided for $498.1 million. The Senate figure included $11.3 million for the Federal Maritime Commission (FMC). The FMC was authorized for fiscal 1984 in a previous year and was not included in the House bill. The administration had requested $483.8 million for maritime programs. *(Vote 423, p. 126-H)*.

The bills differed substantially, however, on ship construction subsidies. The issue was whether to allow U.S.-flag vessels that had been built with federal construction subsidies to automatically enter the lucrative domestic shipping trade, if the subsidies were repaid.

The subsidies were designed to help equalize the costs of shipbuilding in the United States, which were higher than in foreign yards. The federal government could subsidize up to 50 percent of the cost of the ship.

Recipients of the construction subsidies had not been permitted to engage in domestic trade, although the law permitted the transportation secretary to grant temporary entry if the vessel owner reimbursed the government for some of the subsidy. New construction subsidies were ended by Congress in 1981. *(1981 Almanac p. 570)*

DOT proposed that vessels that had received construction subsidies in the past be allowed permanent entry into domestic trade, if their subsidies were paid back with interest.

Opponents argued that U.S.-flag vessels currently in domestic trade were not eligible for the subsidies and the rule would allow vessels that had benefited from cheaper construction costs to compete unfairly.

Supporters said the DOT plan would enrich the Treasury and lower shipping costs by increasing competition.

The House-passed bill curbed DOT's plan and provided that the department could, on a case-by-case basis,

allow vessels to enter the domestic trade after the subsidy had been repaid, if certain other conditions were met.

The Senate bill did not mention the subsidies, and its version would have permitted the Transportation Department to go ahead with its broader proposal.

DOT was barred from putting the rule into effect until June 15, 1984, by a provision in the appropriations bill for the Commerce, Justice and State departments (PL 98-166). *(Story, p. 472)*

Legislative Action

On April 27, the Senate Commerce, Science and Transportation Committee reported and sent S 1037 to the floor (no written report). It was approved by the Senate by voice vote April 28.

The House Merchant Marine and Fisheries Committee May 10 approved a $401.29 million fiscal 1984 maritime authorization (HR 2114) with an amendment that effectively blocked the DOT proposal.

The amendment by Roy Dyson, D-Md., was accepted by the committee by a vote of 28-7. It allowed the subsidized tankers to enter domestic trade only under very limited conditions. Dyson said the amendment would "veto" the DOT's proposed rule. The bill was reported May 16 (H Rept 98-131).

After approval by the House by voice vote Nov. 4, the text of HR 2114 was substituted for that of the Senate bill (S 1037). Both versions authorized the following amounts:

● $401.29 million for operating subsidies in fiscal 1984.

● $11.5 million for research and development of improved shipboard machinery, ship design, construction methods and operations.

● $35.66 million for maritime education and training, including $20.27 million for the U.S. Merchant Marine Academy at Kings Point, N.Y.; $10.67 million for state maritime academies; and $3 million for state academy training vessel fuel.

● $8.05 million for national security support capabilities, including almost $7 million for reserve fleet expenses.

● $30.31 million for other operating expenses. ∎

Coal Slurry Defeated

The House Sept. 27 decisively defeated a bill that would have granted the right of federal eminent domain to coal slurry pipeline companies.

The margin of defeat — 182-235 — surprised supporters of the measure (HR 1010), who had expected a close vote. But the bill picked up only a few more votes than in 1978, when the last slurry bill to reach the House floor was rejected by 161-246. *(Vote 339, p. 102-H; 1978 Almanac p. 674)*

The vote was a victory for railroads, whose virtual monopoly in coal transportation in many areas would have been threatened by the pipelines. The bill would have made it easier for pipeline companies to obtain railroad and other rights-of-way needed for construction; eminent domain authority permitted them to acquire rights-of-way through the courts.

Another factor in the vote was the concern of some members over the allocation to pipelines of scarce water in arid Western states. Slurry is crushed coal mixed with water shipped by pipe.

The bill was a compromise version of a measure reported by the Interior Committee April 15 and the Public Works and Transportation Committee June 14 (H Rept 98-64, Parts I and II). The chief differences involved which agency would certify pipeline companies as eligible for eminent domain; the compromise gave certification authority to both the Interior Department and the Interstate Commerce Commission.

Water rights would have to be obtained from affected states before eminent domain authority could be exercised.

A similar bill (S 267 — S Rept 98-61) was ordered reported April 14 by the Senate Energy and Natural Resources Committee but never reached the floor.

Background

Several pipelines had been proposed to carry coal from Western states, southern Illinois and the Appalachian Mountains to power plants as much as 1,500 miles away, where the water would be used to cool the plants.

The 273-mile Black Mesa Pipeline, the only line in operation, carried about 4 million tons of coal a year from a mine in northeastern Arizona to a power plant in Nevada.

Slurry proponents said they needed the ability to invoke federal eminent domain to secure the rights of ways needed to build the other pipelines.

For years, railroads and rail-worker unions vigorously fought coal slurry bills on the grounds that pipelines would reduce the amount of coal hauled by trains and lead to a loss of railroad jobs. *(1982 Almanac p. 341)*

They were joined in opposing the legislation by some environmental groups, which feared potential damage caused by pipelines, and an array of agricultural organizations worried about water supplies and higher rail rates.

Pipeline proponents maintained that transporting the coal by pipeline would be cheaper than by railroad. They said it would foster competition and would result in lower electricity costs to consumers.

Backers of the legislation included such groups as the Consumer Federation of America and the American Association of Retired Persons.

House Committee Action

As approved by the Interior Committee by a vote of 27-13 April 6, the bill established that eminent domain authority did not apply to the taking of state water. And, state water permits must have been secured before a company could apply to the interior secretary for certification.

One previous opponent, Dick Cheney, R-Wyo., voted to report HR 1010 after the Interior Committee accepted amendments he offered on states' water and other rights.

One Cheney amendment gave express authority to the states to control whether a pipeline might use their water. Another Cheney amendment accepted by the committee provided that in a court case involving federal eminent domain and slurry pipeline construction, state rules applied to questions about jury trials, compensation and pipeline siting alternatives.

The panel rejected several amendments that supporters of the bill referred to as "killer amendments."

By a vote of 15-24, it rejected an amendment by Nick J. Rahall II, D-W.Va., that would have prohibited certification of a pipeline company unless it promised to pay benefits for up to six years to railroad employees laid off or shifted to lower-paying jobs because of construction of the pipelines. Railroads and rail labor had maintained that the pipelines would result in a loss of 71,000 jobs.

In addition, the committee voted 16-20 against an amendment by Austin J. Murphy, D-Pa., that would have required pipelines to be built only with U.S. steel and other domestic materials, except under limited circumstances.

Public Works. The Public Works and Transportation Committee June 8 ordered its version reported by a vote of 32-10. It was reported June 14.

By narrower margins, the committee rejected attempts by slurry opponents to scuttle the bill.

Bud Shuster, R-Pa.,tried to delay the markup on jurisdictional grounds. The grant of primary jurisdiction to the Interior Committee over HR 1010 left Public Works only 30 days to act on a bill.

Arguing that 11 of the bill's 13 titles were under the purview of Public Works, Shuster asked that action on the bill be postponed until Public Works and Interior were given joint referral. Under joint referral, both panels would receive the bill at the same time, without a time limit for action. Shuster's proposal was defeated on a 20-29 vote, signaling the degree of support for the pipelines.

Slurry opponents then offered several amendments that would have made it more difficult for pipelines to be financed and built. The most sweeping proposal — and the one that generated the most heated debate — was made by John Paul Hammerschmidt, R-Ark. His plan, which lost in the Surface Transportation Subcommittee by one vote, would have required all states that shared a water source, such as an underground aquifer or a natural body of water, to enter into an interstate compact to control its allocation before a state was permitted to divert water for a pipeline.

John B. Breaux, D-La., a leading slurry supporter, claimed the amendment was unnecessary, because the bill did nothing to affect state water rights. Breaux added that the mandate for an interstate agreement would make it more difficult to construct pipelines, since a single state could virtually veto the decision to start a pipeline.

Searching for a compromise, Elliott H. Levitas, D-Ga., proposed striking the requirement that all states in a compact consent to the use of the water for a pipeline, but his attempt failed 23-27. The Hammerschmidt amendment then fell 21-28.

House Floor Action

Potential problems with the bill were forecast Sept. 14 when the Rules Committee approved a rule for the bill with no votes to spare.

Two Democrats — Tony P. Hall of Ohio and Alan Wheat of Missouri — joined three GOP members in voting against the rule, which was approved 7-5. Two other Democrats — David E. Bonior of Michigan and Martin Frost of Texas — said they voted to send the bill to the floor only in response to leadership requests.

Because at least 91 amendments had been prepared for introduction, the quick floor vote killing the bill came as a surprise to many observers, including the supporters of the bill and lobbyists.

After debating the bill Sept. 15 and 19, the House began considering amendments Sept. 27. The first amendment, sponsored by Bruce F. Vento, D-Minn., was defeated, but when no one responded to the chair's call for additional amendments, the bill moved to final passage. Vento's amendment would have prohibited a state from granting a slurry pipeline company rights to water that passed through more than one state, unless all the affected states had entered into an interstate compact agreeing to the use of that water.

Supporters of the bill argued that it effectively would give one state veto authority over another state's use of water. Adoption, they argued, would render the bill useless. The amendment was rejected 162-257. *(Vote 338, p. 102-H)*

Slurry opponents had decided secretly the week before to scrap the 91 amendments and to vote quickly on the bill. They believed they could win and that any amendments might have made the measure more palatable to critics, leading to its enactment.

The text of the compromise, HR 3857, was substituted for the text of HR 1010 before the final vote.

Senate Committee Action

As approved by the Senate Energy and Natural Resources panel April 14 by a 13-7 vote, S 267 established a procedure for allowing slurry pipeline companies to exercise federal eminent domain.

A company first would have to secure state approval for the use of water before applying for eminent domain power. After the firm received the water permits, the energy secretary would determine if construction would be in the national interest.

Once certified by the secretary, a firm could go to court to exercise eminent domain to secure easements.

The panel accepted a package of amendments proposed by Malcolm Wallop, R-Wyo., and Chairman James A. McClure, R-Idaho, to ensure that the bill would not erode state control over water supplies. One amendment, for example, expressly provided that state water law would be enforced even if it prevented the construction of a pipeline.

Wendell H. Ford, D-Ky., offered an amendment that would have prevented the bill from pre-empting state laws that would result in prohibiting building or operating a slurry pipeline, or acquiring easements through eminent domain.

But his amendment was blocked when the panel approved 13-7 a substitute by J. Bennett Johnston, D-La., that provided that the bill would not pre-empt state laws and rules except when they discriminated against slurry pipelines.

Ford argued that the consideration given to Western states worried about water rights should be granted to Eastern states concerned about their laws designed to protect land.

The panel accepted a revised version of a Ford amendment that would make up to 10 percent of a pipeline's capacity available under certain conditions to small coal producers.

The pipeline company would be required to offer that capacity before applying for certification. Coal slurry supporters were concerned that Ford's original amendment would have left the 10 percent capacity offer open too long, making it difficult for a company to secure financing for construction. ∎

Daylight-Saving Time

Reversing action it took in 1981, the House July 14 defeated a bill (HR 1398) to extend daylight-saving time (DST) by two months. The House rejected the bill 199-211, after voting 221-187 for an amendment allowing states to exempt themselves from the additional two months. *(Votes 240, 239, p. 72-H)*

Under the bill, DST would have started the first Sunday in March instead of the last Sunday in April. It would have run to the last Sunday of October, as under existing law.

Supporters said the extra daylight hours would save energy and give people time for more work, errands and recreation. Critics said the change would hurt farmers, who begin work at sunrise, and children in the western portion of time zones who would have to wait for school buses in the early-morning darkness.

In 1981, the House passed similar legislation 243-165, but the Senate took no action. *(1981 Almanac p. 577)* ∎

Broadcast Deregulation

For the second time in two years, the Senate in 1983 saw legislation it had passed to deregulate the broadcasting industry blocked by opposition in the House.

Although the Senate Feb. 17 passed the deregulation bill (S 55), the House Energy and Commerce Subcommittee on Telecommunications did not reach a consensus before adjournment in November.

S 55 eliminated broadcasting license renewal procedures requiring that a broadcaster's performance be compared to services promised by a new applicant. It essentially required that licenses be renewed automatically unless there had been serious legal violations.

House subcommittee Chairman Timothy E. Wirth, D-Colo., said the Senate bill was too lenient. But he promised to take up legislation by Oct. 15 after broadcasters, charging Wirth with bottling up the legislation, threatened to circumvent his panel.

But that promise fell by the wayside when no consensus emerged from a lengthy series of meetings between opposing sides on the issue.

A similar Senate-passed bill died in 1982 when the House failed to act on it, and Senate provisions attached to a 1981 reconciliation bill were dropped at the insistence of House members. *(1982 Almanac p. 341; 1981 Almanac pp. 569, 256)*

Senate Action

The Senate Commerce Committee Feb. 15 reported S 55 (no written report) and it was passed by voice vote with little debate two days later.

Proponents of the bill said regulation originally was justified on the grounds that airwaves were a limited natural resource and that in return for their use, broadcasters had to meet special responsibilities. But there currently were enough radio stations and other sources of information and entertainment competing for the public's attention to ensure that the public interest will be met without government interference, they argued.

The legislation codified radio deregulation efforts by the Federal Communications Commission (FCC), which were being challenged in court. The bill, for example, barred the FCC from requiring radio broadcasters to provide news and public affairs programming, and limiting the number of commercials. The bill did not affect "equal time" rules for political candidates.

In addition, S 55 eliminated the current license renewal requirement that the performance and qualifications of radio and TV stations be compared to the services promised by a new applicant.

The bill also required broadcasters to pay fees to help cover the cost of remaining FCC regulation. Under S 55, there would be annual fees for commercial TV and radio stations and fees for FCC services, such as construction permits. The annual fees for TV stations would range from $900 to $9,000, while radio fees would range from $200 to $1,250, generally based on size.

House Reaction

The legislation ran into renewed opposition in the House.

Wirth objected to eliminating the existing license renewal process, which he said would leave broadcasters with a virtually permanent license.

In addition, he opposed deregulation legislation that did not require broadcasters to provide meaningful compensation for the use of the public airwaves, an aide said.

Wirth proposed that broadcasters compensate the public for use of the airwaves, much as a timber company was required to pay for lumbering rights in national forests. The aide said the bill's proposed cost-of-regulation fees did not constitute the significant compensation for the use of a valuable public resource that Wirth wanted.

In the spring, broadcasters backing the bill charged that Wirth's subcommittee had bottled up the legislation. They sought the support of full committee chairman John D. Dingell, D-Mich., and other panel members to attach language they wanted to another bill before the full committee.

During several weeks of behind-the-scenes maneuvering, Wirth's allies threatened to load the bill — a reauthorization of the Federal Communications Commission (FCC) — with controversial amendments to counteract the broadcasters' efforts. Wirth protested to Dingell about the end-run attempt and a compromise was reached.

As part of the compromise, Wirth began hearings May 24 to develop a deregulation proposal and agreed to submit legislation to the full committee by Oct. 15.

The general proposal under review included the broadcasters' request to eliminate the existing license renewal process. But it also included a controversial mechanism for determining the quantity of special programming that a station must provide to serve the public interest.

In pursuing that "quantification" approach, Wirth dropped his effort to make broadcasters pay spectrum fees for the use of public airwaves.

While broadcasters had grave reservations about quantification, they strongly opposed spectrum fees. ∎

Cable TV Deregulation

Efforts to reduce the power of cities to regulate cable television systems moved forward in 1983, with measures passed by the full Senate and approved by a key House subcommittee.

Cities and other interest groups had succeeded in blocking similar legislation in 1981 and 1982, contending that the bills would intrude into local affairs and would restrict local governments' authority. The coalition, however, split over the legislation proposed in 1983. *(1982 Almanac, p. 341; 1981 Almanac p. 558)*

The bill passed by the Senate by a vote of 87-9 June 14 (S 66 — S Rept 98-67) encompassed a compromise reached by the National League of Cities and the National Televi-

sion Cable Assocation (NCTA). However, the U.S. Conference of Mayors and a group of cities including New York City and Dallas, the American Civil Liberties Union and others continued to oppose the bill. They objected that it allowed automatic rate increases by cable firms and virtually required cities to renew franchises. *(Vote 143, p. 27-S)*

The measure approved Nov. 17 by the House Energy and Commerce Subcommittee on Telecommunications (HR 4103) sharply reduced local power to regulate cable and contained restrictions on the systems that cable operators opposed.

The operators, for example, objected to a requirement that a percentage of channels on large systems be set aside for third-party commercial programmers. They also opposed a provision barring cable system owners from owning other media properties, including daily newspapers, in their home communities; requiring landlords to allow cable into their buildings if the cable firm offered compensation under an FCC-approved formula; and allowing cities to require public educational and governmental channels on a cable system.

Background

A cable system picked up programming signals from antennas, microwave or satellite relays, and sent the signals by cable to subscribers' television sets. Cable re-transmitted over-the-air television signals and provided special programming, such as movies, sports and 24-hour news shows.

There were more than 4,800 cable systems in the United States, serving 31.1 million households, or 37 percent of the households that had television.

The industry began to boom in the 1970s when the Federal Communications Commission (FCC) started relaxing its controls and cable operators were able to offer more than distant over-the-air television programs.

But cable operators contended that as federal regulation decreased, local and state governments stepped up their controls.

The operators argued that burdensome and uncertain local regulation impeded their development. They said local regulatory schemes put them at a competitive disadvantage with other types of telecommunications companies that were not regulated.

The city interests and cable operators fought for two years over proposals by the cable operators to diminish local government control. Negotiations that began in September 1982 and ended in March 1983 resulted in a partial compromise that split the urban interests.

Senate Committee Compromise

The Senate Commerce Committee had begun debate on S 66 March 22 but delayed a vote when Democratic senators protested that they had not received a copy of the bill until the day before.

When the committee reconvened April 21, it agreed to add to the bill the compromise offered by Barry Goldwater, R-Ariz., chairman of the Subcommittee on Communications. The panel approved the bill 15-2.

The agreement had been reached March 4 by representatives of the National League of Cities and the NCTA. The league's board of directors approved it March 6, and the NCTA approved the compromise March 22. League officials said they backed the compromise partly to avoid more restrictive legislation sought by cable firms.

Two of the major areas of compromise involved franchise fees and local regulation of rates.

Franchise Fees. Currently, local governments and cable firms established long-term contracts that provided the terms and conditions of the franchise, including the use of public rights-of-way by the operator. Generally a company was granted a monopoly and agreed to pay the government a portion of its revenues.

Previous bills authorized the FCC to establish a ceiling on franchise fees and provided that the fees could permit only the recovery of the reasonable cost of regulation.

The compromise allowed a city to charge a cable operator a franchise fee of up to 5 percent of the operator's annual gross revenues. No limitation was set on the use of the fees.

Cities had been concerned that the FCC might restrict the level of the fee to below that amount. And, they did not want to be told how to spend the funds.

Rates. The compromise allowed local governments to regulate the subscription rates charged by operators for basic service only when the system was located in an area receiving fewer than four television signals.

Basic service was defined as "the lowest cost tier of service," which included re-transmission of broadcast signals; public, educational and governmental programming; and other programming service offered by the operator.

The agreement permitted current franchise agreements that allowed rate regulation of basic service in an area with four television signals to continue for five years or half the remainder of the franchise term, whichever was longer.

Current law generally prohibited the regulation of rates for "pay-per-channel" service — feature-length programs, data processing or electronic publications — would be continued.

Senate Floor Action

Before the Senate June 14 overwhelmingly approved the bill after two days of debate, the measure became enmeshed in two issues regarding telephone service. One involved rates and the other, the regulation of certain telecommunications services such as data processing.

Rates. Members of Congress had been worried about increases in residential and rural telephone rates that were expected after the divestiture in January 1984 of American Telephone & Telegraph Company's (AT&T) local phone companies from the parent firm and from increased competition from unregulated telecommunications firms. *(Story, p. 545)*

The Senate by a vote of 97-0 adopted an amendment to the cable bill that lent significant support to efforts to hold rates down. The amendment was sponsored by James Abdnor, R-S.D. *(Vote 135, p. 26-S)*

Abdnor and others feared that after divestiture and further entry into telecommunications markets by unregulated companies, some big telephone users might bypass the local telephone networks by using new, less expensive technology. They believed that if the local companies had to increase their rates substantially to make up for the lost business, some rural and residential customers would be unable to afford basic telephone service, undermining the nation's policy of universal service.

The amendment attached to the cable bill said "... it is in the public interest to ensure that all providers of telecommunication services share in the obligation of providing universal service."

Data Processing. The wide margin of victory passing the bill belied a hard-fought battle by AT&T against the measure. The firm said the bill gave cable companies an unfair advantage in selling data services. The bill allowed cable firms to offer the services without regulation. Similar services provided by local telephone companies were regulated by the states.

The turning point came when the Senate June 14 rejected 44-55 another amendment by Abdnor. It would have required cable firms to be subject to the same regulatory restrictions as phone companies when offering telecommunications services that could be provided by the phone companies. *(Vote 136, p. 26-S)*

Abdnor said the bill would lead to increased local telephone rates because it would allow cable firms to skim off the local telephone companies' lucrative telecommunications business.

"Let us not rush into legislation that replaces the ghost on a bad television picture with the ghost of what today is the world's finest telephone service," he said.

But Commerce Committee Chairman Bob Packwood, R-Ore., said the bill would not lead to telephone rate hikes, contending that telephone companies were the dominant providers of data processing services.

Abdnor said, "The telephone companies must serve all customers no matter how big or how small. The cable companies will be free to pick off only the most profitable routes and services."

Packwood contended that Abdnor's proposal would undermine the purpose of the bill by requiring the regulation of a host of potential cable services, such as burglar alarms, electronic banking and shopping, electronic "yellow pages" and electronic publishing.

In an effort to deflect opposition to the bill, the Commerce Committee prior to floor action had modified its original version and provided that a telephone company's data services would be deregulated when the market became competitive. The modification also allowed states to require a cable operator to file an "informational tariff" on rates and conditions of local data processing services.

In other action, the Senate:

● Rejected 19-79 an amendment by Lloyd Bentsen, D-Texas, to grandfather all existing cable contracts with franchising authorities. *(Vote 137, p. 26-S)*

● Agreed 82-16 to a motion by Packwood to kill an amendment by Alan J. Dixon, D-Ill., to place the burden of proof on the cable company seeking franchise renewal to show that it had substantially conformed with applicable law. *(Vote 141, p. 27-S)*

● Rejected 26-72 an amendment by Dixon to eliminate a provision that allowed cable companies to raise regulated rates automatically based on the regional consumer price index. *(Vote 142, p. 27-S)*

Summary of Legislation

As passed by the Senate, S 66 limited the ability of communities to regulate cable systems. It eventually would end local control of viewers' rates in many areas and would limit the fee that cities could charge cable systems to a maximum of 5 percent of annual gross revenues.

Cities would be required to renew an operator's franchise agreement except under limited circumstances.

The bill left in place current law generally barring the regulation of rates for non-basic cable or "pay-per-channel service" — feature-length movies or data processing.

The bill also ensured the cities' rights to grant monopoly franchises, and clarified their rights to negotiate franchises and to require that firms provide channels for gov-

ernment use. It also allowed cities to require cable systems to provide channels for public and educational use.

The committee's modification eliminated a provision that would have prevented a community from considering applications from competitors at the time the existing franchise was being renewed. In addition, it provided that a regulated rate for basic cable service could be automatically increased to a level tied to the regional consumer price index (CPI).

The original committee bill would have provided for a 5 percent annual increase or the regional CPI, whichever was higher.   ∎

Maritime Antitrust Differences Unsettled

Congress adjourned in 1983 before completing action on legislation that would broaden and clarify antitrust exemptions for the nation's ocean-line industry.

The Senate by a vote of 64-33 passed its bill (S 47) March 1 after a leading opponent dropped his filibuster against it. *(Vote 6, p. 4-S)*

Howard M. Metzenbaum, D-Ohio, said he abandoned his filibuster because he believed the public had been alerted to the substance of the bill over five days of debate and nothing would be gained by further delay. Metzenbaum had stalled action on similar legislation in 1982, arguing that it would decrease competition and raise prices. *(1982 Almanac p. 343)*

The House passed a compromise measure Oct. 17 by voice vote (HR 1878 — H Rept 98-53, Parts I and II) under suspension of the rules, a procedure that barred amendments. The compromise was developed by the Merchant Marine and Fisheries Committee, which drafted the bill, and the Judiciary Committee, which had criticized some provisions as not fostering competition.

Both the House and Senate versions of the legislation clarified the antitrust immunity granted to agreements made by cartels or conferences of ocean-liners that fixed prices or took other collective actions to limit competition. A key issue in both chambers was whether to continue to require the Federal Maritime Commission (FMC), which regulated the industry, to approve the agreements before immunity was granted. Both bills continued FMC enforcement but differed in details. Conferees did not meet before adjournment.

The legislation generally was backed by the Reagan administration; the FMC; the U.S. liners; foreign ship companies; maritime labor; and some shippers, the firms that exported and imported products.

Arrayed against the bills were consumer groups, free market advocates and other shippers, especially smaller ones that feared large firms would benefit more than they under the legislation.

Background

Backers of changes in the maritime antitrust law were counting on pent-up support and early timing to win passage in the 98th Congress of legislation that had been blocked in previous years. At issue was how much immunity from prosecution under antitrust laws should be granted to U.S. liners engaged in foreign trade when they set prices or took other steps collectively.

The Senate had passed a bill in 1980 granting broad immunity, but a more complex measure was held up in the House because of various controversies, including Abscam. *(1980 Almanac p. 259)*

In 1982, the House overwhelmingly passed legislation, only to see a similar Senate bill tied up in the lame-duck session by Metzenbaum's objections.

Critics contended that the legislation provided too broad a grant of antitrust immunity for practices that would be illegal in other businesses.

But Sen. Slade Gorton, R-Wash., chief sponsor of S 47, argued that changes were needed because of the special nature of international shipping.

Ship liners — both American and foreign-flag — generally organized into cartels or conferences according to trade routes. The cartels fixed rates, determined levels of service and took other steps to limit competition.

The 1916 Shipping Act granted the cartels some immunity from prosecution under antitrust laws for their collective agreements. But court interpretations of the law and of federal regulations created uncertainty over what was acceptable and what was not. There was confusion, for example, over the guidelines the FMC followed in approving agreements reached by a conference. That delayed implementation of agreements and placed U.S. ships in an untenable competitive position, Gorton said.

In addition, U.S. shipping companies were at a disadvantage because foreign companies generally did not have to answer to a counterpart to the FMC in their own nations and they escaped the restrictions placed on U.S. vessels.

Supporters said the proposed legislation would put the ailing U.S.-flag ship liner industry on an equal footing with foreign liners by clarifying the 1916 law.

The bills ensured that ship liners — both American and foreign-flag — in cartels involved in U.S. trade could fix rates, determine levels of service and take other actions to limit competition free of antitrust laws.

They applied only to liners, which operated on a regular schedule between specified ports between two or more countries and carried packaged goods, such as machinery parts. The bills did not affect bulk carriers, which handled loose commodities such as grain and oil and which were not regulated by the federal government.

Senate Committee Action

Commerce Committee. The Senate Commerce Committee Feb. 15 ordered S 47 reported by a vote of 14-0 after amending it to satisfy the concerns of some shippers. There was no written report.

One of the amendments narrowed the cartels' antitrust immunity. Under current law, cartel agreements, such as those setting rates, must be judged by the FMC to be in the public interest and approved by the FMC before going into effect. The liners must prove that the agreements met the public interest standard, and they did not receive immunity until the FMC had acted. The original S 47 would have granted immunity even to liners operating under agreements not officially in effect.

The amendment provided that immunity would be granted only to agreements officially in effect and only to activities undertaken in the reasonable belief that they were pursuant to an effective agreement.

However, the agreements still would not have to meet the public interest standard, which the bill's supporters said was vague. Instead, the bill prohibited specific acts, such as unfairly discriminating against certain shippers in the setting of rates.

The committee also reported an identical bill (S 504 — S Rept 98-3) and referred it to the Judiciary Committee. The two bills were reported in the hopes that if one were blocked, the other would reach the floor.

Judiciary Committee. The Judiciary Committee reported S 504 Feb. 22 (no written report) with amendments to moderate what members said were anti-competitive effects of the bill.

One of the most controversial amendments eliminated the requirement that tariffs be filed with and enforced by the FMC. Supporters of the amendment, which included the Reagan administration and the Federal Trade Commission, contended that the government should not enforce price-fixing agreements.

Without FMC enforcement, liners could decide to disregard a cartel agreement and negotiate lower rates with a shipper.

Supporters of the filing and enforcement provisions said that they were needed to ensure that the complicated tariffs were accessible to small shippers and ports.

Senate Floor Action

The Senate Feb. 24 ended two days of parliamentary stalemate and began debating the maritime antitrust bill.

Metzenbaum and other opponents accepted a unanimous consent agreement Feb. 24 that allowed debate to begin and provided for a March 1 cloture vote to limit discussion. (Later the cloture vote was vitiated.) The agreement also ensured that the Senate would consider the Judiciary Committee amendments backed by Metzenbaum and others.

Two key issues continued to be how much immunity from antitrust prosecution would be granted to cartels and whether the FMC should enforce the cartels' price-fixing agreements.

Passage of the bill March 1 came shortly after the Senate by a vote of 24-71 rejected a Metzenbaum amendment that would have killed antitrust immunity for the liner cartels altogether. *(Vote 5, p. 4-S)*

Several of the Judiciary Committee amendments were adopted by voice vote. However, the Judicary panel's most important proposal, which would have ended government enforcement of cartel price-fixing, was effectively killed by an amendment offered by Ted Stevens, R-Alaska. The amendment, which maintained FMC enforcement, was adopted 61-31. *(Vote 3, p. 4-S)*

Judiciary Committee amendments adopted by voice vote included the following:

● Barred the FMC from exempting a cartel pact from the law's requirements, if the exemption would significantly lessen competition.

● Allowed permitting a shipper under a loyalty contract to a cartel to use a non-cartel liner for 5 percent of its goods that otherwise would have been subject to the contract. A loyalty contract allowed a shipper to obtain lower rates by committing all or a fixed portion of its cargo to a liner or

conference. Critics said the contracts were a way of tying up cargo and preventing competition.

● Eliminated a provision allowing the establishment of shippers' councils. The councils would receive antitrust immunity to allow them to confer with liner cartels about rates and practices, and to negotiate certain special rates. Critics of the councils said the bill extended the evils of price fixing to another industry, but backers said the councils would help balance cartel power.

The amendment, however, did allow for small shippers to form joint ventures, which would be able to do almost all the councils could, a Commerce Committee staffer said.

Other Amendments

An amendment by Orrin G. Hatch, R-Utah, providing for independent action by a cartel liner, was designed to promote competition for shipments. The amendment, supported by members of the Judiciary and Commerce committees, was adopted by voice vote.

The amendment allowed any cartel member to independently negotiate rates and services with a shipper if the cartel used loyalty contracts or if it served a trade route between the United States and Organization for Economic Cooperation and Development (OECD) nations. The OECD was a coalition of industrial nations, including the United States, European countries, Japan, Canada and Australia.

The Senate rejected another Metzenbaum amendment that would have eliminated antitrust immunity for cartels to fix through rates that included charges for the land portion of a shipment. He said the bill would extend immunity to a truck, for example, that picked up a container of cargo carried to the United States by a liner. The vote was 25-69. *(Vote 4, p. 4-S)*

Gorton said the amendment would prevent the U.S. liner industry from taking advantage of the efficiencies of "intermodal" transportation that led to lower rates. He maintained that S 47 did not change the laws affecting other transportation industries.

House Committee Action

Merchant Marine Committee. The House Merchant Marine and Fisheries Committee showed unflagging enthusiasm for its maritime antitrust bill by ordering it (HR 1878) reported by a 39-0 vote March 23. Its version was similar in many respects to the Senate-passed bill. The committee report (H Rept 98-53 Part I) was filed April 12.

Like S 47, HR 1878 granted broad antitrust immunity to liner cartels to fix prices in U.S. foreign shipping. Supporters said it would help increase competition by putting U.S.-flag liners on an equal regulatory footing with foreign ships in an international industry in which price-fixing and other joint practices were normal.

The committee bill provided that the cartel agreements would not have to meet the public interest standard. A pact generally would go into effect automatically, allowing immediate antitrust immunity for the parties participating in the agreement.

Instead of requiring the public interest standard, the bill prohibited specific acts, such as unfairly discriminating against certain shippers in the setting of rates.

The committee approved two amendments relating to dealings with foreign countries.

HR 1878 and S 47 provided that the FMC could cancel or modify an agreement by liners to pool traffic or revenues

if it determined that the agreement substantially reduced competition, except under certain circumstances. One of the exceptions in S 47 was if the agreement allowed U.S.-flag liners to carry cargo of a foreign country that otherwise restricted the cargo to its own liners.

Transportation Secretary Elizabeth Hanford Dole told the Merchant Marine Subcommittee March 22 that the administration strongly opposed that exception because it would allow U.S.-flag liners "to enter into arrangements to implement the cargo reservation schemes of foreign governments."

She said, "The response of the United States to the restrictive practices of foreign governments must remain the prerogative of the federal government, since the interests of both shippers and carriers, as well as the foreign relations of the United States, may be vitally affected."

HR 1878 did not include that exception. However, the committee approved an amendment that provided that in determining whether the agreement substantially reduced competition, the FMC should consider the effect of any cargo reservation laws of the foreign country on competition. Also, the FMC was directed to "have due regard for the foreign and trade policy interests of the United States."

The amendment was offered by Glenn M. Anderson, D-Calif.

Another Anderson amendment accepted by the committee provided that if the FMC determined that a foreign government had unduly impaired a U.S.-flag vessel's access to trade between foreign ports, the FMC could suspend the tariffs of the foreign government's flag carriers in U.S. trade. Under law, a liner could not operate in U.S. trade without proper tariffs — schedules of rates and practices.

The president could disapprove a suspension order for reasons of national defense or foreign policy.

The Senate bill directed the FMC to suspend the tariffs if it found that the foreign nation unfairly restricted U.S.-flag liner access to trade.

Judiciary Committee. The Judiciary Committee June 15 approved changes in the bill that weakened the power of cartels to take collective actions. Its report (H Rept 98-53 Part II) was filed July 1.

Even though they had been seeking for several years to clarify their antitrust situation, some industry officials said that no bill would be better than the Judiciary Committee version.

"Unless it is changed, I don't think anyone would want to see the bill passed. It would be ruinous," said Albert E. May, executive vice president of the Council of American-Flag Ship Operators.

Major changes approved by the Judiciary panel included:

● **Sunset.** The committee added a provision to terminate antitrust immunity for cartels and marine terminal operators by Dec. 31, 1988, or two years after a presidential study commission made recommendations on deregulation of the industry, whichever was earlier. The study commission would be established by the bill.

Several panel members believed that the provision was necessary to ensure that Congress would review the commission's recommendations on possibly deregulating the industry.

The liner industry, Merchant Marine panel and the Reagan administration opposed the sunset clause. They contended that the uncertainty about continued antitrust immunity would make it impossible for liner operators to raise funds to make necessary improvements in their fleets.

Since 1978, Congress had narrowed or eliminated antitrust immunity for joint activities in the airline, railroad, trucking and intercity bus industries. But "unlike the domestic transportation industries, the need for antitrust immunity in the maritime industry is not in any way transitional," Secretary Dole said in a June 13 letter to Judiciary Committee Chairman Peter W. Rodino Jr., D-N.J. *(1982 Almanac p. 336; 1980 Almanac pp. 248, 242; 1978 Almanac p. 496)*

● **Enforcement.** The Judiciary panel eliminated FMC enforcement of cartel price-fixing agreements.

Judiciary Committee members and administration officials viewed eliminating tariff filing and enforcement as a way of promoting competition. If the government did not enforce the cartel-approved tariffs, then some conference members might try to seek business by offering lower rates.

Liners and some shippers believed that the filing and enforcement requirements were necessary to ensure that liners were not violating the law.

The Senate had rebuffed an effort by its Judiciary Committee to end government enforcement of cartel price-fixing.

● **Public Interest.** The Judiciary panel streamlined procedures for putting an agreeement into effect and included a "public interest" standard for challenged agreements.

It stipulated that if the FMC did not act on a proposed agreement, the agreement would go into effect with antitrust immunity in 45 days. One 45-day extension would be allowed. In order to block an agreement, the FMC would have to prove in court that the agreement was not in the public interest because it was likely to substantially reduce competition in a manner that outweighed benefits to the public.

The Merchant Marine panel had eliminated the original public interest standard and instead listed specifically prohibited acts, such as unfair rate discrimination against certain shippers. The Judiciary bill also included the prohibited acts.

The Merchant Marine version also provided that a pact generally would go into effect automatically in 45 days. The FMC could have up to another 180 days to disapprove it.

● **Independent Action.** The Judiciary panel required conferences to allow a member the right of independent action — to make an individual arrangement with a shipper — upon 10 days' notice. The Merchant Marine Committee allowed independent action if a conference utilized a loyalty contract with shippers.

House Floor Action

The bill passed Oct. 17 by voice vote was a compromise between the Merchant Marine and Fisheries Committee and the Judiciary Committee. After passing HR 1878, the House substituted its language for that of S 47.

The compromise eliminated two Judiciary Committee provisions that were troublesome to the ocean-liner industry.

One provision that was dropped would have eliminated the antitrust exemption for the industry on Dec. 31, 1988. The other would have deleted a section of the law providing for the filing of tariffs with the FMC and relying on the FMC to enforce those tariffs.

The bill, however, created a special 22-member commission to conduct a comprehensive study of the ocean-

liner industry and make recommendations concerning deregulation. The commission would report to Congress one year after its first meeting.

The Senate bill required the General Accounting Office to study and report on the antitrust aspects of the industry.

Other Provisions Compared

The compromise bill included streamlined procedures for filing requests with the FMC to establish new conferences and joint ventures among ocean carriers. The Senate bill also included new procedures, but the House version had stricter time limits designed to provide quicker decisions for the parties involved.

The bill also permitted the FMC to seek a court injunction against any conference agreement whose likely anti-competitive effect outweighed likely benefits. This provision was in the Judiciary Committee version, but in the compromise, the standard for determining the anti-competitive effects of any proposal was made more specific. The Senate bill included a similar provision.

Both the House and Senate bills eliminated the existing law allowing private antitrust suits for treble damages when the alleged violation involved an infraction under the shipping act.

Both allowed a member of a conference independently to alter a rate or service, provided that other members of the conference were notified. The House bill required notice of two working days for a pricing change and 10 working days for a change in service.

The House bill also added a new provision concerning "loyalty contracts." It permitted loyalty contracts only if they otherwise met antitrust rules for exclusive contracts that governed other industries. The Senate included a less restrictive provision on loyalty contracts.

The House bill also included a provision making clear that the FMC had the authority to approve shipping rates that covered land travel on the way to a port as well as travel from one port to another.

The Senate bill included a similar provision. ∎

CPSC Authorization

Legislation reauthorizing funding for the Consumer Product Safety Commission (CPSC) was caught up in the confusion over the validity of legislative vetoes and House-Senate differences were not resolved before adjournment.

The Senate passed its CPSC reauthorization (S 861 — S Rept 98-57) by voice vote June 16, before the Supreme Court ruled that a legislative veto that was not presented to the president was unconstitutional. The Senate in effect extended the current veto, which permitted one chamber to veto a CPSC rule if the other chamber did not object (PL 97-35). *(Story, p. 565; 1981 Almanac p. 572)*

The House version of S 861, passed June 29 after the court decision, included two floor amendments that presented alternatives to the existing legislative veto.

One, offered by Elliott H. Levitas, D-Ga., barred the spending of funds to implement a major rule unless a joint resolution approving it had been passed by Congress and sent to the president. The other, proposed by Henry A. Waxman, D-Calif., provided that a rule would not go into effect for 90 days, allowing time for Congress to enact a resolution of disapproval, which would be sent to the president.

In addition, there were differences over funding. The Senate bill authorized $35 million in fiscal 1984 and 1985, the amounts reported by the Commerce Committee March 22. The House measure authorized $35.7 million in fiscal 1984, $37.5 million in 1985 and $39.4 million in 1986. President Reagan requested $32 million for fiscal 1984.

Funding Reductions

The bill passed by voice vote by the House slashed the funding and reduced the authorization period recommended by its Energy and Commerce Committee. Waxman, chairman of the Subcommittee on Health, said the cuts were due partly to fears that Congress would lose control over regulatory agencies as a result of the court ruling.

The full committee by a vote of 19-5 May 3 had ordered reported a bill (HR 2668) authorizing $47 million in fiscal 1984, rising to $57 million by 1988. It also established a minimum staff level of 650 full-time employees. Its report (H Rept 98-114) was filed May 12.

Many committee members were concerned that CPSC effectiveness might have been damaged by Reagan's budget cuts. The fiscal 1981 appropriation was $42.2 million and the 1982 appropriation was $33.5 million. *(1982 Almanac p. 231)*

The reductions forced the agency to delay or cancel investigations of deaths and injuries associated with many products, Waxman said.

The committee rejected 19-23 an amendment by Richard C. Shelby, D-Ala., that would have eliminated all provisions but the funding authorizations and would cut the funding to $35.7 million in fiscal 1984, rising to $39.36 million in 1986.

Shelby and James T. Broyhill, R-N.C., said the reductions provided more realistic funding and that the original amounts were excessive.

House Floor Action

The House began deliberating the bill June 20 and, before passing the measure by voice vote June 29, adopted the Shelby amendment by a vote of 238-177. *(Vote 220, p. 66-H)*

In addition, the House by voice vote adopted the Waxman and Levitas alternatives to the current legislative veto, in effect allowing Congress to block major CPSC rules through legislative action.

Levitas said his proposal would better ensure that unelected bureaucrats, whose actions had the force of law, followed congressional intent.

Waxman argued that the Levitas method would reduce the agency to a study commission and could result in "interminable delays" in important safety regulations. He said his own plan would allow Congress to deal with the most controversial regulations without becoming bogged down in all of the agency's work.

Levitas disputed contentions that his amendment would overload Congress, saying that the CPSC had issued only 35 regulations over its 10-year existence. And he maintained that Congress had an obligation to review regulations that had the force of law.

After HR 2668 as amended was approved, the House substituted its language for the Senate bill (S 861).

Also on June 29, Congress cleared a bill (HR 3133 — PL 98-45) appropriating $35 million in fiscal 1984 for the CPSC. *(Story, p. 495)* ∎

Safety Board Funding

The president June 6 signed into law a bill authorizing increased funding for the National Transportation Safety Board (NTSB) through fiscal 1986.

The board investigated transportation and pipeline accidents, and made special studies relating to transportation safety.

The legislation (S 967 — PL 98-37) authorized $22.6 million for fiscal 1984, $24.5 million for 1985 and $26.1 million for 1986.

In reporting the bill March 31 (S Rept 98-43), the Senate Commerce Committee noted that the fiscal 1982 appropriation had been cut to $17.1 million, a reduction of more than 10 percent, resulting in a staff reduction of 27 percent.

The fiscal 1983 appropriation was $19.97 million. The Senate approved the bill by voice vote April 7.

Identical authorizations were contained in the bill (HR 1707 — H Rept 98-154 Parts I and II) reported by the House Public Works and Transportation Committee May 16 and by the Energy and Commerce Committee May 17. The House May 24 passed the measure by a vote of 372-43 and then cleared the Senate bill. *(Vote 126, p. 42-H)* ∎

Unisex Insurance

In the face of heavy insurance industry opposition, legislation (S 372, HR 100) to outlaw sex-based discrimination in all forms of insurance remained at the committee level when Congress adjourned.

The Senate Commerce Committee had been ready to begin markups in late spring, but in June, the panel agreed to postpone action until the General Accounting Office studied the effects the bill would have.

The House Energy and Commerce Committee was poised to consider HR 100 late in the session, but Chairman John D. Dingell, D-Mich., put off action when he determined that he lacked votes for a compromise proposal.

The insurance industry argued that gender was a legitimate factor in determining premiums and benefits. It argued that equalizing benefits would cost $2.5 billion a year and that women would face higher rates for some insurance, such as automobile coverage.

But women's groups and some civil rights groups pushing the legislation disagreed. They were bolstered somewhat by a July 6 Supreme Court decision holding that an employer's retirement plan could not provide smaller benefit payments to women workers than to comparably situated male employees.

Dingell and Senate Commerce Committee Chairman Bob Packwood, R-Ore., May 12 publically criticized an insurance industry group that switched position and decided to oppose the legislation. The board of the American Council of Life Insurance had offered a compromise requiring that after a specified date, all employer-sponsored insurance, annuity and pension programs provide equal benefits to men and women. However, after member companies rebelled, the organization May 11 reconsidered the compromise and renewed its support for sex-based pricing for individual insurance contracts.

The Senate panel had reported a unisex insurance bill in 1982 (S 2204 — S Rept 97-161). ∎

FCC Authorization Clears

The public broadcasting system got a boost in its funding in each of fiscal years 1984-86 under a Federal Communications Commission (FCC) authorization Congress cleared just before adjournment Nov. 18.

The bill (HR 2755) was passed by voice vote in both chambers Nov. 18. After a brief debate Nov. 17, the House had rejected by 141-277 an amendment to cut the public broadcasting authorizations in the measure. *(Vote 489, p. 142-H)*

As signed into law Dec. 8 (PL 98-214), the legislation authorized funding for the Corporation for Public Broadcasting (CPB) at $145 million in fiscal 1984, $153 million in 1985 and $162 million in 1986.

The increases recouped a portion of CPB funding cut in 1981, when Congress provided $80 million more than President Reagan requested but still reduced CPB authorizations from $220 million in fiscal 1983 to $130 million a year in 1984-86. *(1981 Almanac p. 567)*

The bill also authorized $91.2 million in each of fiscal 1984 and 1985 for FCC operations, including 200 new staff positions. It further imposed a series of financial controls on National Public Radio (NPR), which was forced to borrow money and negotiate other aid from the CPB during the summer to overcome a financial mismanagement crisis.

HR 2755 was reported by the House Energy and Commerce Committee Sept. 15 (H Rept 98-356). There was no Senate committee consideration.

Focus on NPR

The amendment rejected by the House was offered by Mike Oxley, R-Ohio, who proposed to cut the CPB authorizations in the bill by $11 million in fiscal 1984, $15 million in fiscal 1985 and $20 million in fiscal 1986.

"The issue is whether we are in fact going to increase massively . . . the levels of funding for the Corporation for Public Broadcasting at a time when there are some serious questions that have been raised about the efficacy and the fiscal mismanagement of NPR," Oxley said.

NPR, which provided programming and a satellite link for 280 member public radio stations, sharply curtailed its operations and dismissed more than 140 employees in 1983 after it was revealed that the network faced a $9.1 million deficit.

The financial crisis, resolved only after the CPB agreed to a bailout plan, led to the resignations of NPR President Frank Mankiewicz and other top executives.

Timothy E. Wirth, D-Colo., chairman of the House Energy and Commerce Telecommunications Subcommittee, noted that not all of the $70 million increase for the CPB would go to NPR.

Wirth also argued that a new management team was in place at NPR, that new procedures had been adopted that would prevent future financial mismanagement and that HR 2755 itself provided further safeguards.

The bill barred the CPB from distributing federal subsidies to NPR unless the CPB certified that the radio network had adopted a system of financial controls approved by both a certified public accountant and the General Accounting Office and that it had a balanced budget.

Wirth said he had "reluctantly supported" the 40 percent cut in the public broadcasting authorization in 1981 while hoping funds from other sources would cover the

shortfall. He said such funds had not materialized and warned that revenues were not being generated quickly enough to prevent program curtailment.

Final Provisions

As signed into law, HR 2755:
• Authorized $91.2 million for the Federal Communications Commission in each of fiscal 1984 and 1985.
• Authorized $145 million in fiscal 1984, $153 million in fiscal 1985 and $162 million in fiscal 1986 for CPB.

NPR

• Prohibited the CPB from distributing federal funds to NPR unless NPR had implemented financial procedures recommended by a certified public accountant and deemed prudent by the comptroller general; adopted a balanced budget; and provided the CPB with continuous access to all NPR financial records.
• Required the CPB to report to Congress within 15 days of enactment on steps NPR had taken to meet the conditions in the bill and to repay a CPB loan.
• Provided that the financial supervision and controls on NPR imposed by the bill would be lifted when NPR had covered debts accumulated before Oct. 1, 1983, when fiscal 1984 began.
• Reversed a 1981 law that would have permitted the CPB president to serve as chairman of the board and allowed the board to elect one of its members as chairman.
• Clarified that a broadcast station exempt from the FCC's regional concentration rules by virtue of a "grandfather" clause could make technical changes in its facilities without losing its exemption. The regional concentration rules forbade the same entity from directly or indirectly controlling three stations when any two of the stations were within 100 miles of the third.

Obscene Messages

• Made it a crime to provide obscene telephone messages, such as so-called "dial it" services, whether made directly or by recording and without regard to whether the sender of the message initiated the call, in the District of Columbia or across state lines or U.S. borders that could be received by a person under the age of 18.
• Provided for violators of the ban on obscene messages to be subject to criminal penalties of up to $50,000 in fines and up to six months in prison and a civil fine of up to $50,000 a day for each day during which a violation occurred for commercial purposes.
• Provided that a defendant could escape conviction if he met regulations to be prescribed by the FCC to prevent persons under the age of 18 from receiving the obscene messages.
• Required the FCC to establish a plan to ensure that the needs of state and local police and public safety agencies would be taken into account when the FCC decided frequency assignments or spectrum allocations.
• Authorized persons who voluntarily administered amateur radio license examinations for the FCC to charge examinees up to $4 each.
• Declared it U.S. policy to encourage new communications technologies and services; declared the burden of proof in FCC proceedings on new technologies or services to lie with persons opposed to them; and ordered the FCC to rule within one year on applications to provide new technologies or service. ■

Highway Funding Snarled

The failure of Congress to complete action on a highway bill snarled funding for a number of new Interstate Highway construction projects and left some emergency highway repair projects without funds.

The legislation (HR 3103) would have allowed the Transportation Department to allocate some $4 billion to the states that Congress had earlier authorized for fiscal 1984 for Interstate projects. The funds would have come directly from the Highway Trust Fund and would not have affected projects under way.

In addition, the bill would have increased the existing fiscal 1984 authorization for emergency work from $100 million to $250 million. It exempted Western states hard hit by floods and storms from the current $30 million maximum annual emergency allocation.

Both chambers passed measures that would have freed the Interstate construction funds and provided the additional emergency repair money. But the legislation was dragged down by added baggage, including House amendments earmarking about $140 million for "pork-barrel" highway projects and extending antitrust immunity to trucking firms in certain rate-making actions.

When it became evident that HR 3103 was not likely to pass, at least two other attempts were made to salvage the critical portions of the bill, but those efforts were unsuccessful during the waning days of the session.

A joint resolution (S J Res 195) to approve the Interstate fund allocations was quickly reported by the Senate Environment and Public Works Committee Nov. 8, but it did not reach the floor before adjournment Nov. 18.

And S J Res 199, an unrelated highway measure, was amended by the House by voice vote Nov. 17 to provide the additional $150 million for emergency road repair. But the Senate did not act on the House amendment.

No Agreement

As passed by the House by voice vote June 13, HR 3103 provided an additional $150 million from the Highway Trust Fund for emergency road repairs and made a number of changes in the Surface Transportation Assistance Act of 1982 (PL 97-424). The bill had been reported June 13 by the Public Works and Transportation Committee (H Rept 98-240). *(1982 Almanac p. 317)*

The legislation was reported by the Senate Environment and Public Works Committee June 14 (S Rept 98-253) and by the Banking and Urban Affairs Committee Oct. 6 (no written report).

When the Senate passed the bill Oct. 25 by a vote of 91-2, it added the Interstate fund allocations to the states and made a number of other changes, sending the measure back to the House. *(Vote 305, p. 50-S)*

Under the Interstate Highway program, Congress was to approve by Oct. 1 the state allocations for the next fiscal year, based on cost estimates approved by the Transportation Department. Then, the states were able to obligate the funds set aside for them.

The House took up the bill again Nov. 1 and added amendments extending antitrust exemptions for trucking companies that engaged in certain rate-setting practices and earmarking an additional $140 million for a number of highway projects.

The new projects added by the House included:
• $50 million for design and construction of a highway in

Passaic County, N.J.
- $8 million for two projects in Altoona, Pa.
- $12 million for a highway near Johnstown, Pa.
- $8.5 million to widen a highway and improve traffic signals near Fort Smith, Ark.
- $3 million for a project near Moorhead, Minn.
- $20.5 million for a highway from Dry Ridge, Ky., to Owenton, Ky.
- $38 million to improve access to Ontario, Calif., International Airport.
- Planning and design funds for a center-city Boston highway project that would have otherwise been ineligible for Interstate funds.

Complaints Aroused

The House additions brought quick complaints from senators and administration officials.

Senate Commerce Committee Chairman Bob Packwood, R-Ore., objected to the antitrust exemption, a matter his committee had been working on for months.

Packwood did not want a conference committee to attempt to resolve the differences without assurances from House Public Works and Transportation Committee Chairman James J. Howard, D-N.J., that the antitrust exemption would not be included in the final version. Howard said he was willing to provide such assurances but was never able to contact Packwood.

Packwood had held deregulation hearings but had not planned to introduce a bill without negotiations with the trucking industry, which objected to further deregulation. He was angered by what he regarded as the House's unilateral extension of antitrust immunity, which the industry wanted, without industry concessions in return.

In response to the House action, Packwood Nov. 1 introduced S 2038, the "Trucking Competition Act of 1983," which would deregulate the trucking industry and abolish the trucking regulatory functions of the Interstate Commerce Commission on Jan. 1, 1987. The bill would end certain antitrust immunity for truckers' rate-making on July 1, 1984.

Most of the complaints from senators focused on the antitrust issue, since pork barrel was not an exclusive province of the House.

But the Office of Management and Budget and Transportation Secretary Elizabeth Hanford Dole complained about both issues. Dole, in a letter to Senate Environment and Public Works Committee Chairman Robert T. Stafford, R-Vt., said she would recommend a presidential veto if the House version prevailed. ∎

TV Syndication Rights

A November truce between the Federal Communications Commission (FCC) and a Senate committee stalled a bill that would have barred the FCC temporarily from letting the major television networks profit from TV reruns.

As passed by the House Nov. 8 by voice vote, the bill (HR 2250 — H Rept 98-483) would have delayed until at least June 1, 1984, an FCC plan to modify 1970 rules that had prohibited the networks — ABC, CBS and NBC — from controlling or selling reruns of programs they aired.

Senate action had been expected in 1983. But on Nov. 16, the Senate Commerce Committee suspended its mark-

up of HR 2250 until at least March 15, 1984, after the FCC decided to delay any rules change at least until May 10.

In a letter to Sen. Ted Stevens, R-Alaska, FCC Chairman Mark S. Fowler said the agency would hold off to give the networks and their opponents — Hollywood studios, producers, actors and others — time to negotiate a compromise.

Fowler wrote Stevens after President Reagan, a former movie and television actor, said through his counselor, Edwin Meese III, that he backed a two-year moratorium on any change in the FCC rules.

Before Reagan's support for a two-year moratorium was announced, the Justice and Commerce departments and the Federal Trade Commission had supported the FCC's effort to modify the rules. Afterward, the Justice and Commerce departments said they would back a two-year moratorium.

FCC Proposal

Acting on network petitions, the FCC had issued a tentative decision Aug. 4 proposing to lift almost all aspects of its financial interest and syndication rules on the grounds that they limited competition and were unnecessary to curb network dominance.

At issue were the FCC's:
- Financial interest rule, which barred the networks from sharing in the profits from syndication or distribution of television programs.
- Syndication rule, which barred the networks from controlling the syndication or distribution within the United States of reruns of programs they had aired.
- Prime time access rule, which barred network affiliates from filling more than three hours of the four-hour prime time viewing period with network programming or syndicated programming originally produced by a major network. Prime time included the hours 7-11 p.m. Eastern Standard Time, and 6-10 p.m. in the Central and Mountain time zones.

The FCC plan would have let the networks have a financial interest in reruns of their programs on independent TV stations or cable systems. But it would have required that syndication of programs be controlled by an independent company until 1990.

The networks ardently supported the FCC decision, arguing that it would mean greater diversity and competition. They said they needed to share in the $800 million-a-year syndication and rerun market to contend with emerging competition from cable and satellite networks.

Independent producers argued the opposite. They said independent television stations and program producers had made major gains under the FCC rules and would be at a competitive disadvantage without them. They said the networks would dominate TV if the rules were lifted.

House Action

There were a number of efforts to block the FCC plans. On Sept. 21, the House Appropriations Committee voted 26-25 to add an amendment to a stopgap funding measure (H J Res 367) that would have barred the FCC from changing the syndication rules for one year. But the House leadership insisted on a continuing appropriations resolution (H J Res 368) stripped of all ornaments — including the FCC rider.

On Sept. 22, the House Energy and Commerce Subcommittee on Telecommunications approved by 9-4 an

original version of HR 2250 that would have imposed a five-year ban on the FCC's proposed rules changes.

But on Nov. 1, the full Energy and Commerce Committee unanimously approved an amendment to the bill providing for a six-month moratorium on the proposed rules changes. That action was taken after the Senate adopted a six-month ban in an amendment to a fiscal 1984 supplemental appropriations bill (HR 3959). *(Story, p. 536)*

The Energy and Commerce Committee's report on the bill said a six-month moratorium would give Congress a chance to study the issues and might induce the networks and their foes to compromise.

The non-controversial nature of preserving the status quo for another half-year enabled the House to pass HR 2250 Nov. 8 under suspension of the rules, a procedure that limited debate and prohibited amendments. ∎

FTC Authorization Pending

Legislation to reauthorize the Federal Trade Commission (FTC) was approved by House and Senate committees but neither chamber completed floor action before adjournment Nov. 18.

Legislative veto and the regulation of professionals were major issues in the legislation (S 1714, HR 2970, HR 2974).

The bill reported by the Senate Commerce Committee Sept. 1 (S 1714 — S Rept 98-215) was silent on the legislative veto because of the uncertainty following an earlier decision of the Supreme Court that the vetoes were unconstitutional. However, a veto alternative was expected to be offered on the floor. *(Court, p. 565)*

HR 2970, as reported by the Commerce Committee May 16 (H Rept 98-156, Part I) prior to the court's decision, made permanent the power of Congress to veto FTC rules. The authority was provided by the 1980 FTC act (PL 96-252). *(1980 Almanac p. 233)*

However, both the Rules and Judiciary Committees ordered that bill reported without recommendation (H Rept 98-156, Parts II and III) and May 16 reported another authorization bill, HR 2974 (H Rept 98-157). HR 2974 continued the veto authority only through fiscal 1984, pending a decision by the Supreme Court, and authorized funding for one year.

On the regulation of professionals, the Senate bill included a compromise forged by the American Medical Association (AMA) and FTC staffs. It provided that the agency could not challenge anti-competitive activity by professionals if the activity was required and supervised by the states. The FTC was not allowed to pre-empt state licensing rules establishing training or experience requirements.

HR 2970 contained a similar provision, but it also contained language to allow the FTC to challenge a state law or rule that purported to relate to training and educational requirements but in fact dealt with business practices. The report said such situations as a state board's imposing unreasonable restrictions to limit entry into a profession would be affected by the addition. HR 2974 did not address the regulation of professionals.

The AMA in 1982 backed reauthorizing legislation that exempted professionals from FTC regulation. But

agency supporters let it die Sept. 30 rather than accept the exemption. *(1982 Almanac p. 347)*

The AMA had argued that the FTC did not have jurisdiction over professionals, who were regulated by the states. Spokesmen also said the agency was interfering with issues concerning the quality of care.

FTC supporters countered that federal regulation was needed to prevent professionals and their associations from conducting boycotts, price-fixing and other activities that limited competition, led to higher consumer costs and reduced the choice of services.

Authorizations

The House Commerce Committee bill authorized $70.71 million for the FTC in fiscal 1984; $75.65 million for 1985; and $80.95 million for 1986. President Reagan requested $59.5 million for the FTC in 1984. A stopgap funding measure (PL 97-377) provided an appropriation of about $64 million for fiscal 1983. *(1982 Almanac pp. 246, 238)*

HR 2974 authorized $70.71 million for fiscal 1984.

S 1714 authorized $69.9 million for the FTC in fiscal 1984, $71.1 million for 1985 and $72.4 million for 1986. ∎

Amtrak Authorization

Congress failed to enact a fiscal 1984 authorization for Amtrak, partly because of concerns about government debts owed by the federally subsidized railroad.

About $880 million in principal and $200 million in interest was due Oct. 1 on loans made by the Federal Financing Bank (FFB). Bills were reported by committees in both chambers (HR 3648 — H Rept 98-371, S 1117 — S Rept 98-79), but Congress adjourned before completing floor action.

Although Amtrak was technically in default Oct. 1, the railroad was relieved of having to pay its debt to the FFB under an administrative agreement reached with the Department of Transportation (DOT). The department took title to the FFB notes that it had guaranteed when Amtrak loans were negotiated prior to 1976, and assumed liability for the FFB obligation.

Fiscal 1984 funding of $716.4 million was provided for the railroad in the Transportation Department appropriations bill (PL 98-78). Default did not affect the operations of Amtrak. *(Story, p. 457)*

Background

Amtrak, created by Congress to take over the nation's unprofitable passenger rail business, began service in 1971. *(1971 Almanac p. 835; 1970 Almanac p. 804)*

Prior to 1976, Amtrak received federal loans guaranteed by the Transportation Department (DOT) for capital costs, such as equipment. At the time, it was thought that Amtrak would become profitable and be able to repay the loans.

But it soon became clear that Amtrak would require continued federal aid, and Congress began appropriating direct grants for both operating and capital costs.

In 1981, Congress deferred the interest on the FFB loans until Sept. 30, 1983, to help the railroad hold down fare increases and asked DOT for recommendations for ways of relieving the debt. DOT did not make an overall recommendation but noted some possibilities, such as sim-

ply forgiving the debt and interest. *(1981 Almanac p. 565)*

Senate Action

The Senate Commerce Committee bill reported May 9 allowed Amtrak to issue preferred stock to the FFB to retire the debt. The bill also authorized $750 million in grants for fiscal 1984 for Amtrak operating and capital subsidies, and $800 million for 1985.

A proposed committee amendment, worked out after the Budget and Banking committees criticized its first solution, would make the transportation secretary responsible for repaying the FFB.

However, the legislation, along with the proposed amendment, was held up partly to explore questions raised by members and the Congressional Budget Office about its impact on the budget. A Senate Budget Committee staffer said it was not clear whether repaying the debt would be considered a fiscal 1983 or 1984 expense.

House Action

Committee. The House Energy and Commerce Committee reported a $730 million fiscal 1984 authorization Sept. 21. The bill deferred Amtrak's obligations until Oct. 1, 1984.

Transportation Subcommittee Chairman James J. Florio, D-N.J., said Amtrak was being held hostage to another issue, a dispute over Congress' role in the sale of Conrail.

A 1981 law (PL 97-35) allowed Congress, without presidential review, to veto any DOT plan to sell Conrail. Some members feared that the administration might sell Conrail in such a way that some vital freight service in the Northeast would be lost. *(1981 Almanac p. 561)*

But Supreme Court decisions in June and July effectively invalidated legislative vetoes not presented to the president for his signature. *(Story, p. 565)*

The committee bill required the passage of a law before allowing the sale of Conrail to go through.

In an Aug. 3 letter to Committee Chairman John D. Dingell, D-Mich., Transportation Secretary Elizabeth Hanford Dole said the requirement that a law be passed approving the sale would hamper DOT negotiations with potential buyers. She said the uncertainty would discourage potential purchasers from even expressing interest in the railroad. She said she would rather allow Amtrak to default on the loan than accept the bill.

Floor Action. When the bill was brought to the floor Oct. 6, the House rejected 151-198 an attempt by Florio to discharge Amtrak of its federal debt by allowing the federally subsidized passenger railroad to issue preferred stock to DOT. The transfer of stock would have eliminated the debt. *(Vote 365, p. 108-H)* ∎

Boating and Fishing Taxes

The House July 12 passed a bill (HR 2163) expanding a tax on sport fishermen and redirecting a tax on boaters to set aside more funds in fiscal 1984-88 for boating safety and fish restoration programs such as stream stocking.

The Senate Finance Committee, however, Nov. 15 reported a substitute version (S Rept 98-312) deleting all of the provisions pertaining to boating and fishing taxes. There was no floor action in the Senate.

HR 2163, reported by the Merchant Marine and Fisheries Committee May 16 and by Ways and Means July

1 (H Rept 98-133 Parts I, II), aimed to resolve problems in allocating motorboat fuel tax revenues.

HR 2163 created the Aquatic Resources Trust Fund within the Treasury to receive the revenues. It allocated two-thirds of the money — about $150 million over five years — for state boating safety projects. The other third was for Coast Guard services to recreational boaters.

HR 2163 also expanded the number of articles subject to the existing 10 percent excise tax on sport fishing equipment. Revenues from that tax, plus additional funds from a motorboat fuel levy, were slated for sport fisheries, improved access for recreational boaters and aquatic resource education. ∎

Funeral Rule Veto Failed

An effort to block a Federal Trade Commission (FTC) rule concerning funeral home directors' practices was unsuccessful in 1983.

The House Commerce, Transportation and Tourism Subcommittee May 9 unfavorably reported a resolution of disapproval (H Con Res 70) to the full Energy and Commerce Committee. The full committee did not act on the resolution before the June 23 ruling of the Supreme Court holding legislative vetoes unconstitutional. No similar resolution was introduced in the Senate. *(Court, p. 565)*

Congressional aides said that the pending court decision may have been a factor in the lack of enthusiasm for vetoing the rule.

Another may have been concern about bad publicity surrounding the 1982 congressional veto of an FTC rule requiring disclosure of certain information by used car dealers.

The used-car veto was the first under a 1980 law (PL 96-252) that allowed Congress to overturn an FTC rule without the president's signature if both chambers passed a resolution of disapproval within 90 calendar days of continuous session after the rule had been submitted. *(1980 Almanac p. 233; 1982 Almanac p. 346)*

The funeral rule, in the making since 1975, required funeral directors to disclose the prices of individual services and goods included in a package, and barred a director from making misrepresentations.

The industry opposed the regulation, contending that it imposed an unnecessary and costly burden for the majority of funeral directors, who were honorable. Spokesmen also argued that there was not sufficient evidence showing the need for the rule.

Supporters contended that the rule was necessary so that vulnerable bereaved customers would have full information.

The FTC scheduled part of the funeral home rule to go into effect Jan. 1, 1984, but implementation of another section of the rule was delayed until April 30.

The section becoming effective in January barred funeral homes from making misrepresentations, such as saying that embalming was required by law when that was not the case. The more controversial section of the rule, requiring funeral home directors to disclose detailed price information to customers, was delayed.

The 4th Circuit Court of Appeals in Richmond, Va., in a suit brought by the National Funeral Directors Association, upheld the rule in January, clearing the way for full implementation. ∎

Congress and Government

While Congress itself did little in 1983 to alter the way it conducts business, a Supreme Court decision in June had the potential to fundamentally change the balance of power between Congress and the executive branch.

The high court sent a tremor through the Capitol June 23 when it ruled that the legislative veto was unconstitutional. The veto device, included in some 200 laws over the past 50 years, allowed one or both houses of Congress to overturn an executive branch regulation or order, without requiring the president's approval. The statutes included some major foreign policy tools, such as the War Powers Resolution and the Arms Export Control Act, as well as the Congressional Budget and Impoundment Control Act.

Immediately after the ruling, experts said Congress would have to change the way it wrote legislation delegating authority to the executive branch. But by year's end, Congress did not come up with a sweeping replacement to the legislative veto, choosing instead to repair on an individual basis those statutes containing vetoes. And, in fact, Congress left itself open to further legal challenges when it continued to include veto provisions in laws enacted after the Supreme Court's June 23 decision.

Aside from the commotion created by the legislative veto ruling, Congress in 1983 went through a wide range of internal problems, from the censure of two House members for sexual misconduct to a struggle over a pay raise in the Senate.

The year opened with the organizational rites for the 98th Congress. Benefiting from their 26-seat gain in the 1982 elections, Democrats increased their voting majority on almost every House committee. And in retribution for Texas Democrat Phil Gramm's collaboration with the Republican White House in supporting President Reagan's budget in 1981 and 1982, House Democratic leaders stripped Gramm of his seat on the Budget Committee. After he resigned from Congress and was re-elected in a special election as a Republican, Gramm was reappointed to the Budget panel.

House Democrats also forced through a series of changes in House rules, which they deemed necessary to streamline the legislative process. The key change made it harder for members to offer amendments to appropriations bills, known as riders, that limit spending for specific purposes.

In the Senate, comprehensive rules changes were recommended in a report by former Sens. James B. Pearson, R-Kan., who served from 1962-78, and Abraham Ribicoff, D-Conn., a senator from 1963-81. Their proposals included placing stricter limits on Senate debate, electing a permanent presiding officer, televising floor debate on major issues, overhauling the budget process and eliminating several committees. But the Pearson-Ribicoff report gathered dust on the Senate Rules Committee shelf, where members briefly examined it in the spring but never acted on its suggestions.

Meanwhile, Senate Majority Leader Howard H. Baker Jr., R-Tenn., had more trouble getting the unruly Senate to work on legislation in a timely fashion. The Senate was repeatedly bogged down by filibusters and a lengthy amending process on major bills. Baker also failed for the third year in his push to broadcast Senate proceedings.

Baker was still highly regarded by his colleagues in 1983, but he operated as a lame duck following his January announcement that he would not seek re-election to his Tennessee Senate seat in 1984. His announcement set off subtle jockeying for the majority leader's job among several prominent Republicans.

Pay raises are always a traumatic issue in Congress, where members fear the wrath of voters when they increase their salaries. So it went in the Senate, where senators in June nervously awarded themselves the same 15 percent pay hike that House members accepted in December 1982. The $9,138 pay raise boosted their salaries from $60,662.50 to $69,800 a year. But senators also imposed a limit on the amount of annual income from speeches, articles and appearances that they could accept after Jan. 1, 1984. The cap was set at 30 percent of a senator's congressional salary.

Without taking any legislative action, members of Congress assured themselves of another pay raise Jan. 1, 1984, which was automatically tied to wage hikes for federal employees under the provisions of a 1981 law. The 3.5 percent pay raise was to be offset, though, by the requirement passed in 1983 that lawmakers must begin paying Social Security taxes in 1984.

The House took a sharp look at two of its own in July, when it voted to censure Daniel B. Crane, R-Ill., and Gerry E. Studds, D-Mass., for sexual misconduct with congressional pages, the teenagers who run errands at the Capitol. A report by the Committee on Standards of Official Conduct — the ethics committee — found that Crane had a sexual relationship with a 17-year-old female page, while Studds had a sexual relationship with a 17-year-old male page.

By choosing to censure the two members, the House rejected the ethics committee's recommendation to merely issue a reprimand, a less severe form of punishment. The vote July 20 marked the first time a member ever was censured for sexual misconduct and the first time since 1980 that the House censured one of its members.

The House's action was the result of the ethics committee's yearlong investigation, conducted by special counsel Joseph A. Califano Jr., of published allegations of widespread sexual misconduct and drug use by members and pages in 1981 and 1982. The committee in November ended its probe of Capitol drug use, concluding there was inadequate evidence to show any current House member used illegal drugs or that a drug ring ever operated at the Capitol.

Congress' attention was captured briefly by a controversy that arose in June over the appearance of Carter White House documents in the 1980 Reagan campaign.

Rep. Donald J. Albosta, D-Mich., had his Post Office and Civil Service Subcommittee on Human Resources investigate how Reagan's campaign obtained briefing papers used to prepare President Carter for a televised debate with Reagan. The so-called "Debategate" probe produced no firm results at year's end.

Transcript tampering was the focus of another internal flap in the House. At issue were charges that improper changes were made in transcripts of House committee proceedings. Although a House ethics committee report found no pattern of wrongdoing, it did find improper changes made in the record of a 1982 hearing by four subcommittees on Environmental Protection Agency actions. The staff member who made the changes resigned in September.

The Supreme Court may have dealt a blow to congressional power with its legislative veto ruling, but it did issue a decision protecting one political advantage that incumbents enjoy. On May 2, the high court rejected a challenge to the free mailing rights of members of Congress, ending a longstanding lawsuit against the congressional franking privilege.

The year ended on a tense note for Congress when a bomb exploded Nov. 7 just outside the Senate chamber. A terrorist group claimed responsibility, saying the action was to protest U.S. military "aggression" in Grenada and Lebanon. The bomb blast, which caused no injuries, led to strengthened security measures at the Capitol, including tighter entrance procedures for visitors.

—By Diane Granat

Supreme Court Invalidates Legislative Veto

In a decision that dramatically altered the balance of power between Congress and the executive branch, the Supreme Court June 23 declared the legislative veto unconstitutional.

The 7-2 ruling invalidated a device that had been included in one guise or another in more than 200 laws enacted over the past 50 years, beginning with a 1932 government reorganization act. Some of those laws permitted a single chamber to veto an executive branch regulation or order; others required action by both the House and Senate. Still others gave committees of Congress veto authority.

Among the laws affected by the court's ruling were the 1973 War Powers Resolution and the 1974 Budget and Impoundment Control Act. (Partial listing, p. 566; foreign policy impact, p. 569)

The decision was a major victory for the executive branch. Presidents had long viewed the legislative veto as an incursion upon executive authority to carry out laws.

But the ruling precipitated a flurry of activity in Congress, as committees moved to review existing laws with veto provisions and to seek new ways to assert Congress' control over the manner in which laws were implemented by executive branch and independent agencies.

At least five laws containing legislative veto provisions were enacted subsequent to the June 23 decision. All had been well along in the legislative process before the court ruled: the fiscal 1984 appropriations bill for the Department of Housing and Urban Development and Independent Agencies (PL 98-45); the fiscal 1984 authorization for the National Aeronautics and Space Administration (PL 98-52); fiscal 1983 supplemental appropriations (PL 98-63); the Caribbean Basin Economic Recovery Act (PL 98-67); and fiscal 1984 appropriations for the Department of Transportation (PL 98-78).

It was not clear whether the agencies affected by those provisions would challenge them at some future date.

In addition, Congress at year's end was exploring new ways of reining in executive branch rule-making discretion. Alternatives under consideration ranged from a constitutional amendment to allow legislative vetoes to the use of amendments on appropriations bills to prohibit spending to implement any agency rule that Congress disliked.

"Ultimately, Congress will prevail," predicted Rep. Elliott H. Levitas, D-Ga., the leading congressional advocate of the legislative veto. "But we should do it in a responsible way that's not obtrusive. We're at a critical crossroads in the evolution of our government."

Background

The legislative veto had been a source of controversy ever since Congress wrote into the fiscal 1933 legislative appropriations act a provision enabling either house of Congress to block President Hoover's executive branch reorganization proposal by voting to disapprove it before it could go into effect. The next year, when Hoover issued his reorganization order, the House voted to disapprove it.

Types of Veto

Although many varieties of legislative veto were adopted over the years, they shared one common feature: they permitted all or part of Congress to block an executive action, with or without the president's approval.

One form of legislative veto permitted either house of Congress to block an agency plan or rule by passing a simple resolution of disapproval within a fixed period from the time of the agency's action. A variation permitted a one-house veto only if the second chamber did not overturn the first's action within a specified time.

Another common type of veto required passage of a concurrent resolution of disapproval by both houses.

A third form permitted one or more congressional committees to block an agency action. Yet another type required passage of a resolution approving a proposed rule or plan by one or both houses, or one or more congressional committees, before the plan or rule could be carried out.

Finally, some two-house veto plans required the president's signature, essentially making the congressional action equivalent to the passing of a whole new law.

Pros and Cons

Backers of the veto device contended Congress needed authority to overturn federal rules to keep overzealous regulators in check when they went beyond the intent of Congress in implementing laws.

In recent years, the veto had become a rallying point for members who believed that a burgeoning federal bureaucracy was eroding congressional power.

"The legislative veto will make certain that the people who are elected make the laws — not unelected bureaucrats who are obviously not accountable," Levitas explained in one 1981 interview.

Critics charged that the legislative veto was an unconstitutional encroachment on the authority of the executive branch. They also warned that Congress would be overburdened if it were forced to review an ever-growing range of regulations.

The Reagan View

Although presidents since Hoover had objected to the legislative veto, President Reagan nearly broke the mold. While campaigning for the presidency in 1980, he appeared to endorse some form of the device. In an Oct. 8, 1980, speech in Youngstown, Ohio, Reagan said, "To better control the growth of federal regulations we should ... grant both Congress and the president greater authority to veto regulations approved by executive agencies."

After Reagan took office, though, administration officials repeatedly modified his pro-veto stand.

On March 18, 1981, Attorney General William French Smith said the administration believed the legislative veto was unconstitutional if it "intrudes on the power of the president to manage the executive branch."

James C. Miller III, then an official with the Office of Management and Budget (OMB) and later chairman of the Federal Trade Commission, said the administration opposed legislative vetoes of executive branch rules but would accept them for independent regulatory agency actions.

In November 1981, the administration modified its position further, saying it would back a two-house veto for all agencies provided it required the president's signature.

Finally, in December 1981, Christopher C. DeMuth, OMB director for information and regulatory affairs, said

Court Ruling Negates Veto Provisions . . .

Following is a list of some of the current major laws that included legislative veto provisions. The list was compiled from the dissenting opinion of Justice Byron R. White, who obtained the information from a brief in *INS v. Chadha* filed by the Office of Senate Legal Counsel in 1981.

Foreign Affairs and National Security

● **Act for International Development of 1961 (PL 87-195).** Act's foreign assistance funds may be terminated by a resolution approved by both chambers.

● **War Powers Resolution, 1973 (PL 93-148).** Absent a declaration of war, the president may be directed by a resolution approved by both chambers to remove U.S. armed forces engaged in foreign hostilities.

● **Department of Defense Appropriation Authorization Act, 1974 (PL 93-155).** National defense contracts obligating the United States for any amount in excess of $25 million may be disapproved by a resolution of either chamber.

● **Department of Defense Appropriation Authorization Act, 1975 (PL 93-365).** Applications for export of defense goods, technology or techniques may be disapproved by a resolution approved by both chambers.

● **House Joint Resolution 683, 1975 (PL 94-110).** Assignment of civilian personnel to the Sinai may be disapproved by a resolution approved by both chambers.

● **International Development and Food Assistance Act of 1975 (PL 94-161).** Foreign assistance to countries not meeting human rights standards may be terminated by a resolution approved by both chambers.

● **International Security Assistance and Arms Control Act of 1976 (PL 94-329).** The president's letter of an offer to sell major defense equipment may be disapproved by a resolution approved by both chambers.

● **National Emergencies Act, 1976 (PL 94-412).** Presidentially declared national emergency may be terminated by a resolution approved by both chambers.

● **International Navigational Rules Act of 1977 (PL 95-75).** Presidential proclamation of International Regulations for Preventing Collisions at Sea may be disapproved by a resolution approved by both chambers.

● **International Security Assistance Act of 1977 (PL 95-92).** President's proposed transfer of arms to a third country may be disapproved by a resolution of both chambers.

● **Act of December 8, 1977 (PL 95-223).** A presidentially declared national emergency and exercise of conditional powers may be terminated by a resolution of both chambers.

● **Nuclear Non-Proliferation Act of 1978 (PL 95-242).** Cooperative agreements concerning storage and disposition of spent nuclear fuel, proposed export of nuclear facilities, materials or technology and proposed agreements for international cooperation in nuclear reactor development may be disapproved by a resolution passed by both chambers.

Budget

● **Congressional Budget and Impoundment Control Act of 1974 (PL 93-344).** The president's proposed deferral of budget authority provided for a specific project may be disapproved by a resolution passed by either chamber.

Rulemaking

● **Education Amendments of 1974 (PL 93-380).** Department of Education regulations may be disapproved by a resolution passed by both chambers.

● **Federal Election Campaign Act Amendments of 1979 (PL 96-187).** Proposed rules and regulations of the Federal Election Commission may be disapproved by a resolution of either chamber.

● **Act of January 2, 1975 (PL 93-595).** Proposed amendments to federal evidence rules by Supreme Court may be disapproved by resolution of either chamber.

● **Act of August 9, 1975 (PL 94-88).** Social Security standards proposed by the health and human services secretary may be disapproved by a resolution passed by either chamber.

● **Airline Deregulation Act of 1978 (PL 95-504).** Rules or regulations governing employee protection programs may be disapproved by a resolution of either chamber.

● **Education Amendments of 1978 (PL 95-561).** Rules and regulations proposed under the act may be disapproved by a resolution passed by both chambers.

● **Federal Trade Commission Improvements Act of 1980 (PL 96-252).** Federal Trade Commission rules may be disapproved by a resolution passed by both chambers.

● **Department of Education Organization Act, 1979 (PL 96-88).** Rules and regulations promulgated for various programs transferred by the act may be disapproved by a resolution passed by both chambers.

● **Multiemployer Pension Plan Amendments Act of 1980 (PL 96-364).** Schedules proposed by the Pension Benefit Guaranty Corporation (PBGC) that require an increase in premiums must be approved by a resolution passed by both chambers. Revised premium schedules for voluntary supplemental coverage proposed by the PBGC may be disapproved by a resolution passed by both chambers.

● **Farm Credit Act Amendments of 1980 (PL 96-592).** Certain Farm Credit Administration regulations may be delayed by resolution of either chamber.

● **Comprehensive Environmental Response, Compensation and Liability Act of 1980 (PL 96-510).** Environmental Protection Agency regulations concerning hazardous substances releases, liability and compensation may be disapproved by a resolution approved by both chambers or by the adoption by either chamber of a concurrent resolution that is not disapproved by the other chamber.

● **National Historic Preservation Act Amendments of 1980 (PL 96-515).** Regulation proposed by the secretary of the interior may be disapproved by a resolution approved by both chambers.

Reagan might veto a bill that would allow Congress to overturn executive agency rules without requiring the president's signature.

The Court's Decision

The decision in the case of *Immigration and Naturalization Service v. Chadha* was the court's most important separation-of-powers ruling since the White House tapes case of the Watergate era, when the struggle was between President Nixon and the judicial branch of government. Indeed, the veto ruling is among its most important such decisions in history. *(Nixon case, 1974 Almanac p. 879)*

The court said the framers of the Constitution had decided that "the legislative power of the federal government [should] be exercised in accord with a single, finely wrought and exhaustively considered procedure." That procedure demands that a measure be approved by both houses of Congress and presented to the president for his signature or veto, the court said.

. . . In Wide Range of Laws on the Books

● **Coastal Zone Management Improvement Act of 1980 (PL 96-464).** Rules proposed by the commerce secretary may be disapproved by a resolution of either chamber.

● **Act of December 17, 1980 (PL 96-539).** Rules or regulations promulgated by the administrator of the Environmental Protection Agency under the Federal Insecticide, Fungicide and Rodenticide Act may be disapproved by a resolution passed by both chambers.

● **Omnibus Budget Reconciliation Act of 1981 (PL 97-35).** The education secretary's schedule of expected family contributions for Pell Grant recipients may be disapproved by resolution of either chamber. Specified rules promulgated by the transportation secretary may be disapproved by resolution of either chamber. Amendments to Amtrak's route and service criteria may be disapproved by resolution of either chamber. Consumer Product Safety Commission regulations may be disapproved by a resolution approved by both chambers or by a concurrent resolution of disapproval by either chamber that is not disapproved by the other chamber.

Energy

● **Act of November 16, 1973 (PL 93-153).** Continuation of oil exports being made pursuant to the president's finding that such exports are in the national interest may be disapproved by a resolution approved by both chambers.

● **Federal Nonnuclear Energy Research and Development Act of 1974 (PL 93-577).** Rules or orders proposed by the president about allocation or acquisition of essential materials may be disapproved by resolution of either chamber.

● **Energy Policy and Conservation Act, 1975, (PL 94-163).** Certain presidentially proposed "energy actions" involving fuel economy and pricing may be disapproved by resolution of either chamber.

● **Naval Petroleum Reserves Production Act of 1976 (PL 94-258).** The president's extension of the production period for naval petroleum reserves may be disapproved by resolution of either chamber.

● **Energy Conservation and Production Act, 1976 (PL 94-385).** Proposed sanctions involving federal assistance and the energy conservation performance standards for new buildings must be approved by resolution of both chambers.

● **Department of Energy Act of 1978 (PL 95-238).** International agreements and expenditures by the secretary of energy of appropriations for foreign spent nuclear fuel storage must be approved by a resolution passed by both chambers, if not agreed to by legislation. Plans for such use of appropriated funds may be disapproved by either chamber. Financing in excess of $50 million for demonstration facilities must be approved by resolution in both chambers.

● **Outer Continental Shelf Lands Act Amendments of 1978 (PL 95-372).** Establishment by the secretary of energy of oil and gas lease bidding system may be disapproved by resolution of either chamber. Export of oil and gas may be disapproved by a resolution passed by both chambers.

● **Natural Gas Policy Act of 1978 (PL 95-621).** Presidential reimposition of natural gas price controls may be disapproved by a resolution passed by both chambers. Congress may reimpose natural gas price controls by a resolution passed by both chambers. A federal Energy Regulatory Commission (FERC) amendment to pass through incremental costs of natural gas, and exemptions from this rule, may be disapproved by resolution of either chamber.

● **Export Administration Act of 1979 (PL 96-72).** The president's proposal for domestic production of crude oil must be approved by a resolution passed by both chambers. Action by the commerce secretary to prohibit or curtail export of agricultural commodities may be disapproved by a resolution approved by both chambers.

● **Energy Security Act, 1980 (PL 96-294).** Loan guarantees by the departments of Defense, Energy and Commerce in excess of specified amounts may be disapproved by resolution of either chamber. The president's proposal to provide loans or guarantees in excess of established amounts may be disapproved by resolution of either chamber. A proposed award by the president of individual contracts for purchase of 75,000 barrels per day of crude oil may be disapproved by resolution of either chamber. Certain actions of the Synthetic Fuels Corporation are subject to disapproval by a resolution of one chamber or both, as specified in the act.

International Trade

● **Trade Expansion Act of 1962 (PL 87-794).** Tariff or duties recommended by the Tariff Commission may be imposed by a resolution of approval passed by both chambers.

● **Trade Act of 1974 (PL 93-618).** Proposed presidential actions on import relief and actions concerning certain countries may be disapproved by a resolution passed by both chambers. Various presidential proposals for waiver extensions and for extension of non-discriminatory treatment of products of foreign countries may be disapproved either by a resolution of one chamber or a resolution approved by both chambers.

Miscellaneous

● **Federal Land Policy and Management Act of 1976 (PL 94-579).** Sale of public lands larger than 2,500 acres and withdrawal of public lands totaling at least 5,000 acres may be disapproved by a resolution passed by both chambers.

● **National Aeronautics and Space Act of 1958 (PL 85-568).** President's transfer to NASA of functions of other departments and agencies may be disapproved by a resolution passed by both chambers.

● **Emergency Unemployment Compensation Extension Act of 1977 (PL 95-19).** The president's recommendations regarding rates of salary payment may be disapproved by a resolution of either chamber.

● **Civil Service Reform Act of 1978 (PL 95-454).** Continuation of the Senior Executive Service may be disapproved by a resolution approved by both chambers.

When Congress delegated to the executive branch the authority to issue regulations or make certain kinds of decisions, it "must abide by its delegation of authority until that delegation is legislatively altered or revoked," the court said. *(Excerpts of majority and dissenting opinions, next page; opinion texts, p. 20-A)*

The Court Lineup

Chief Justice Warren E. Burger spoke for six members of the majority in striking down the legislative veto. Joining him were Justices William J. Brennan Jr., Thurgood Marshall, Harry A. Blackmun, John Paul Stevens and Sandra Day O'Connor.

Justice Lewis F. Powell Jr. concurred in the court's judgment in the specific case at hand, but for different reasons.

Justice Byron R. White wrote a stinging dissent, decrying the "destructive scope" of the ruling. "Today's decision," said White, "strikes down in one fell swoop provisions in more laws enacted by Congress than the court has

cumulatively invalidated in its history." (By the end of the 1981-82 term, the court had struck down as unconstitutional all or part of 110 federal laws.)

Justice William H. Rehnquist wrote his own dissent, which dealt only with the case before the court and did not discuss the legislative veto in general.

The Chadha Case

The case decided by the court June 23 began in 1974 when Jagdish Rai Chadha, a Kenyan East Indian who had overstayed his student visa, won a decision from the Immigration and Naturalization Service (INS) suspending his deportation. In December 1975, the House of Representatives, exercising the one-house veto power granted it under a section of the 1952 Immigration and Naturalization Act, vetoed that suspension.

Chadha filed suit challenging the power of the House to overrule the INS. In 1980, the 9th U.S. Circuit Court of Appeals agreed and held the one-house veto of INS action unconstitutional. The Supreme Court agreed in October 1981 to review that ruling.

The justices heard the case argued in February 1982, but on July 2, 1982, the last day of the 1981-82 term, the court ordered a second round of arguments in the case. Those arguments were held Oct. 7, 1982.

Chadha, meanwhile, had married an American citizen, become a father and settled down in this country.

The Majority Opinion

Writing for the court, Chief Justice Burger vigorously endorsed the Constitution's scheme for separating and balancing the powers of the three branches of government — legislative, executive and judicial.

He acknowledged the practical and political difficulties this arrangement sometimes created but said: "Convenience and efficiency are not the primary objectives — or the hallmarks — of democratic government, and our inquiry is sharpened rather than blunted by the fact that congressional veto provisions are appearing with increasing frequency in statutes which delegate authority to executive and independent agencies."

"The hydraulic pressure inherent within each of the separate branches to exceed the outer limits of its power, even to accomplish desirable objectives, must be resisted," Burger said.

The Constitution sets out, in "explicit and unambiguous provisions" the manner in which the legislative power is to be exercised, Burger noted. Article I states that bills shall be approved by both the House and the Senate and shall be presented to the president for his approval.

"It is beyond doubt that lawmaking was a power to be shared by both houses and the president," wrote Burger. The one-house legislative veto runs afoul of these requirements, both of which have a clear purpose.

"The president's participation in the legislative process was to protect the executive branch from Congress and to protect the whole people from improvident laws," Burger said.

"The division of the Congress into two distinctive bodies assures that the legislative power would be exercised only after opportunity for full study and debate in separate settings. . . ."

The majority's view that the legislative veto did not comport with this constitutional prescription was further reinforced, the chief justice explained, by the fact that the framers did set out four specific situations in which one

house should act alone — the House to initiate impeachments, and the Senate to try impeachments, to confirm or reject presidential appointments, and to ratify or reject treaties.

Some of the choices made by those who drafted the Constitution seemed to result in "clumsy, inefficient, even unworkable processes," the chief justice acknowledged.

Nonetheless, he concluded, "with all the obvious flaws of delay, untidiness and potential for abuse, we have not yet found a better way to preserve freedom than by making the exercise of power subject to the carefully crafted restraints spelled out in the Constitution."

The Dissent

In one of the longest dissenting opinions of his judicial career, equaling the majority opinion in length, Justice White declared that the "prominence of the legislative veto mechanism in our contemporary political system and its importance to Congress can hardly be overstated."

By denying Congress the use of that mechanism, he said, the court presented Congress with "a Hobson's choice: either to refrain from delegating the necessary authority, leaving itself with a hopeless task of writing laws with the requisite specificity to cover endless special circumstances across the entire policy landscape, or in the alternative, to abdicate its lawmaking function to the executive branch and independent agencies.

"To choose the former leaves major national problems unresolved; to opt for the latter risks unaccountable policy-making by those not elected to fill that role."

White said the legislative veto was "an important if not indispensable political invention that allows the president and Congress to resolve major constitutional and policy differences, assures the accountability of independent regulatory agencies and preserves Congress' control over lawmaking."

History showed, White wrote, that Congress had not used this veto as a "sword" with which it struck out to "aggrandize itself at the expense of the other branches." Instead, he said, it had used the veto as "a means of defense, a reservation of ultimate authority necessary if Congress is to fulfill its designated role under Article I as the nation's lawmaker."

"In my view, neither Article I of the Constitution nor the doctrine of separation of powers is violated by this mechanism by which our elected representatives preserve their voice in the governance of the nation," White concluded.

He said the power to exercise a legislative veto was not the same as the power to write new law without the approval of both chambers and the president.

The veto must in the first place be authorized by statute, he pointed out, and can only negate a proposal from the executive branch or an independent agency. "On its face," he wrote, "the legislative veto no more allows one house of Congress to make law than does the presidential veto confer such power upon the president."

The Follow-up Rulings

Less than two weeks after its ruling in the *Chadha* case, the court made clear that it intended to invalidate not just one-house legislative vetoes, but most if not all existing forms of the device.

In a brief statement July 6, the court affirmed two lower court decisions holding unconstitutional a one-house legislative veto provision in the 1978 Natural Gas Policy

Congress Loses Major Foreign Policy Tool

By striking down the legislative veto, the Supreme Court stripped from Congress one of the major tools it had used to influence foreign policy in the past decade.

Congress had relied on the legislative veto to curb presidential powers ranging from arms sales to declarations of national emergencies. It enacted the laws containing foreign policy vetoes in the early 1970s in response to President Nixon's conduct of the Vietnam War — and over the bitter objections of Nixon's successor, Gerald R. Ford.

Reflecting on the battles that Congress went through to get its powers, House Foreign Affairs Committee Chairman Clement J. Zablocki, D-Wis., said the court "by the stroke of a pen has negated everything Congress has done in the past 10 years."

Sen. Henry M. Jackson, D-Wash., said the decision "leaves us in a very unrealistic situation, in terms of being able to share responsibility between the Congress and the president" on foreign policy.

There were signs in the aftermath of the court's decision that Congress would not willingly cede the powers it had claimed over foreign policy. But it was apparent that both Congress and the Reagan administration were hoping to avoid confrontations.

"From our point of view, nothing has changed," said one administration lawyer who dealt with foreign policy statutes. "We never conceded the constitutionality of the legislative veto in the first place. But as a practical matter, we would be fools to thumb our noses at Congress now."

A key aide to Senate Majority Leader Howard H. Baker Jr. echoed that sentiment, saying that in the interests of "political accommodation," the administration should act as if the vetoes were still valid.

"Absent an extraordinary emergency," he added, "Congress probably will not rush to pass new laws that would recapture the foreign policy vetoes in another form."

Although Congress had never actually used any of its foreign policy vetoes, its leaders frequently had threatened a veto to force the executive branch to consult more closely and accept compromises.

War Powers

The two most important vetoes were in the War Powers Resolution of 1973 (PL 93-148) and the Arms Export Control Act of 1976 (PL 94-329). Other major laws allowed Congress to veto exports of nuclear materials (the 1978 Nuclear Nonproliferation Act, PL 95-242), and to overturn the granting of most-favored-nation trading status to certain communist countries (the Jackson-Vanik amendment of 1974, PL 93-618). *(Laws, p. 566)*

The War Powers Resolution allowed Congress, by passing a concurrent resolution, to force the withdrawal of U.S. troops engaged in hostilities overseas without specific congressional authorization. That veto provision appeared to be nullified by the court's decision. *(1973 Almanac, p. 905)*

However, another major section of the law could remain intact. It prohibited the president from keeping U.S. forces in hostile situations overseas for more than 90 days unless Congress had declared war, had specifically authorized the president's action or had extended the time period. Although that provision had the effect of a legislative veto, it did not involve the simple or concurrent resolution vetoes that the Supreme Court challenged.

Congress invoked this section of the War Powers act for the first time when it cleared a compromise measure (S J Res 159 — PL 98-119) authorizing U.S. Marines who were in Lebanon as part of a multinational peacekeeping force to remain there for up to 18 months.

Although Reagan signed the bill Oct. 12, he expressed reservations about its constitutionality. *(Lebanon resolution, p. 113)*

Presidents Ford, Carter and Reagan submitted reports to Congress under the War Powers Resolution in sending troops to Southeast Asia and the Middle East, but Congress never tried to use its veto power to force a withdrawal of troops.

Arms Export Law

The arms export law allowed Congress to veto major arms sales by passing a concurrent resolution within 30 days of receiving a presidential notification of a planned sale. As amended in 1981, the veto applied to individual weapons or military equipment worth $14 million or more, and to package sales of $50 million or more. *(1981 Almanac p. 162)*

Congress never had actually vetoed an arms sale, but it forced Presidents Carter and Reagan to make compromises during dramatic battles over sales to the Middle East. The closest fight was in 1981, when the Senate narrowly rejected a veto of the sale of AWACS radar planes to Saudi Arabia. *(1981 Almanac p. 129)*

By coincidence, the court's decision came down just as the two foreign policy committees of Congress were moving to place new restrictions on the president's powers to give aid to foreign countries. The Senate Foreign Relations and House Foreign Affairs committees took those actions in response to President Reagan's repeated use of his emergency powers to provide military aid to El Salvador without congressional approval. *(Foreign aid authorization, p. 140)*

Remaining Tools

Even without a legislative veto, Congress still retained some major foreign policy powers, including its control over foreign aid funds, its right to declare war and the Senate's power to approve treaties and confirm presidential nominees.

A senior aide to the Foreign Relations Committee predicted the decision would give the president more flexibility "in the short term," but that eventually Congress could make life "much more complicated" for the president by passing even more restrictive laws.

Zablocki, echoing that theme, said: "I'm sure there will be some means and methods sought to return the gains, so to speak, of the Congress."

Act and a two-house legislative veto provision in the Federal Trade Commission Improvements Act of 1980.

In both cases, the U.S. Court of Appeals for the District of Columbia had ruled that the vetoes permitted Congress to intrude too far into the powers reserved by the Constitution to the other two branches of the federal government.

Justice Powell did not take part in the court's consideration of the requests for review in these cases. Justices Rehnquist and White, who dissented in *Chadha*, voted to review the cases. White argued that the vetoes involved were different from the one struck down in *Chadha*. He noted that the *Chadha* case involved a congressional veto of an executive branch decision, while in these cases, Congress was overturning decisions of independent regulatory commissions — the Federal Energy Regulatory Commission (FERC) and the Federal Trade Commission (FTC).

"To invalidate the device which allows Congress to maintain some control over the lawmaking process merely guarantees that the independent agencies, once created, for all practical purposes are a fourth branch of the government not subject to the direct control of either Congress or the executive branch. I cannot believe that the Constitution commands such a result," White wrote.

The FERC case involved the House's 1980 veto of the agency's so-called "Phase II" plan for deregulating natural gas prices. *(1980 Almanac p. 492)*

The FTC case grew out of a 1982 congressional veto of a proposed rule requiring used-car dealers to disclose information on auto defects before a sale. *(1982 Almanac p. 346)*

Congress in 1980 included a provision in the Federal Trade Commission authorization (PL 96-252) allowing it to block any regulation of the independent regulatory agency if both houses passed a resolution of disapproval. *(1980 Almanac p. 233)*

The used-car proposal was the only FTC rule vetoed prior to the court's ruling. A 1983 effort to block an FTC rule requiring funeral home directors to disclose detailed price information to customers failed when neither chamber considered a disapproval resolution. *(Story, p. 562)*

Congressional Response

Reaction to Court Ruling

The court's decision drew a mixed reaction in Congress, but most members agreed they would have to re-examine and probably rewrite laws that contained legislative veto provisions. They also said Congress had to find new ways to monitor executive branch actions.

"It will mean some readjustment of a lot of laws," said Senate Majority Leader Howard H. Baker Jr., R-Tenn.

"We're going to be less willing to delegate in the future," said Charles E. Grassley, R-Iowa, a key Senate supporter of the veto.

"The unelected, unaccountable bureaucrats have gained too much power. They have become the fourth branch of government and we need to exert more authority over them," said Sen. Carl Levin, D-Mich., who along with Levitas had been seeking to expand use of the legislative veto by including it in omnibus regulatory reform legislation.

The veto's opponents, however, long had maintained that the device was unconstitutional, and they applauded the decision. "It's been a long time in coming," said Rep.

Peter W. Rodino Jr., D-N.J., chairman of the House Judiciary Committee. "The legislative veto violates the orderly process of government. It's an invasion of the principle of separation of powers," Rodino said.

Sen. Patrick J. Leahy, D-Vt., said Congress would have to be more precise about its intent when it passed laws.

"We pass such fuzzy legislation. Then we pass it on to administrative agencies and say: 'You work it out.' Then members and the president go out and campaign against those 'crazy bureaucrats,' " said Leahy.

Several members said the ruling would dramatically change the relationship between the legislative and executive branches.

"Up to now, Congress and the president have shared power in hundreds of laws," said Levin.

In those statutes, he said, "the Congress has permitted the president certain leeway subject to its saying no. If it is no longer permitted to veto such actions of the president, it is less likely to grant him the authority in the first place.

"The result," Levin said, "is that shared power is out the window and either a more costly legislative process or an imperial presidency will take its place."

Legislative Forays

Consumer Product Safety Commission. The House wasted no time in reacting to the court's ruling. Acting on a bill (HR 2668) to reauthorize the Consumer Product Safety Commission (CPSC), the House June 29 approved two alternative amendments that would restrict the agency's regulatory authority. *(Story, p. 557)*

One amendment, written by Levitas, required proposed CPSC actions to be approved by both the House and Senate as well as the president before going into effect. A narrower option, offered by Rep. Henry A. Waxman, D-Calif., permitted CPSC decisions to go into effect unless disapproved by Congress and the president.

The House approved both amendments, leaving a House-Senate conference committee to choose between them. The Senate, acting before the court's *Chadha* decision, had passed a CPSC bill June 16 (S 861) that contained a more traditional legislative veto provision of the type struck down by the court. The differing versions of the CPSC bill were still awaiting conference action at year's end.

Since Levitas' amendment required the president's signature on a disapproval resolution, its supporters said it would be acceptable under the Supreme Court ruling.

After the House approved his veto plan, Levitas said, "The first one out of the bag is important. This is the first measure since the Supreme Court decision to show where we're headed."

Caribbean Basin Initiative. The House Rules Committee, meeting June 28, wrestled with the veto issue while discussing the Reagan administration's Caribbean Basin Initiative (CBI).

The Caribbean measure (HR 2769) did not contain a veto but portions of the bill could trigger a veto provision in the 1974 Trade Act (PL 93-618) dealing with import decisions made by the International Trade Commission. After a few minutes of uncertain discussion, Rules members chose to avoid the veto issue and agreed to send HR 2769 on to the House floor. *(CBI, p. 252)*

Hearings on Veto Alternatives

Majority Leader Jim Wright, D-Texas, said members of Congress were "groping around" for responses to the

court's decision.

Some members said the court's decision left Congress with little choice but to act swiftly. "There is never a convenient time for this type of sweeping governmental review and reform, but the Supreme Court decision has left us no choice. The time is now," declared Sen. Sam Nunn, D-Ga., in a June 27 speech in Atlanta.

Back in Washington, Rep. Andrew Jacobs Jr., D-Ind., began soliciting sponsors for a constitutional amendment to expressly give either the Senate or House authority to veto administrative rules and regulations.

"When an unelected Supreme Court decides that an unelected bureaucracy has more say than Congress in determining what Congress means when it passes a law, it is time for Congress ... to clear things up on behalf of the people," Jacobs said.

At hearings the week of July 18, a number of options were discussed:

● Repealing all statutes that contained unconstitutional legislative vetoes, and rewriting the laws to limit power delegated to the executive branch.

● Excising the veto from laws that included severability clauses, which would delete the offending passage while preserving the remainder of the statute.

● Requiring that before any agency regulation took effect, it must be approved by the House and Senate in a joint resolution, which then must be signed by the president. This method was included in a Consumer Product Safety Commission bill (HR 2668) passed by the House June 29.

● Requiring a "report and wait" procedure, by which agency regulations would be submitted to Congress, where they would sit for a specific period of time. The rules would go into effect unless disapproved by Congress and the president during that period.

This concept was also embodied in HR 2668, providing that a proposed rule could not take effect for 90 days, giving Congress time to enact a joint resolution of disapproval. Senators Carl Levin, D-Mich., and David L. Boren, D-Okla., introduced a similar plan (S 1650) July 20.

● Using amendments — riders — to appropriations bills to bar spending money to implement an agency regulation that Congress disliked.

● Passing a constitutional amendment overturning the Supreme Court's decision. Such an amendment would have to be ratified by three-fourths of the states.

● Passing legislation that would remove the federal courts' jurisdiction over the legislative veto, or giving members of Congress weight in federal appeals courts if they challenged the validity of rules that were disapproved by concurrent resolution. Rep. Charles Pashayan Jr., R-Calif., offered these ideas.

"Whatever the range of solutions, it is clear that the Supreme Court decision will mean more problems for the executive in carrying out its functions and a much greater workload for Congress," observed Norman J. Ornstein, a Catholic University professor of politics, at a July 20 hearing of the Senate Judiciary Subcommittee on Administrative Practice and Procedure.

The other hearings were held in the House Judiciary Subcommittee on Administrative Law and the House Foreign Affairs Committee.

Other Responses

Besides the House action on the Consumer Product Safety Commission bill, there already had been several other responses to the Supreme Court's ruling.

The House Rules Committee July 12 returned a foreign aid authorization bill (HR 2992) to the Foreign Affairs Committee because the measure contained a legislative veto.

And the Senate Armed Services Committee June 27 decided to restrict the president's control over military pay raises by requiring that any presidential pay proposal that varied from his defense secretary's recommendation be submitted as legislation.

This process replaced a plan the committee was considering before the Supreme Court ruling. That proposal would have subjected the president's alternative pay scheme to a one-house legislative veto.

The most drastic reply to the high court's ruling came from Stanley Brand, general counsel to the House, in testimony July 19 before the Foreign Affairs Committee.

Brand said Congress would be best off to discard all laws that contained legislative vetoes and then rewrite them to restrict the delegation of power to the executive branch.

But Committee Chairman Clement J. Zablocki, D-Wis., said Brand's suggestion was unworkable because it would create an excessive workload for Congress.

"It does not address the practical problems that will arise if Congress is forced to promulgate every executive regulation," Zablocki said.

Levin, in testimony July 20 before the Senate subcommittee, said he believed his proposed joint resolution veto would be constitutional because it needed action by both chambers and the president.

Deputy Attorney General Edward C. Schmults said the Reagan administration would work with Congress in a "spirit of comity" to resolve problems resulting from the decision.

Schmults said only minor adjustments were needed to fix laws that contained vetoes. In place of the veto, he said, "there are many effective and fully constitutional mechanisms whereby Congress can carry out its constitutional oversight function."

He said the administration would continue to honor existing report and wait provisions.

Rules Committee Crackdown

The House Rules Committee July 26 said it would not act on any bill containing a legislative veto if the measure was reported by a committee after the June 23 Supreme Court decision.

Veto-bearing bills reported before the decision would be considered only if the veto provisions were removed, Rules added.

The policy was prompted by two bills with legislative vetoes that Rules sent back to the Foreign Affairs Committee.

The first was a foreign aid authorization bill (HR 2992), which Foreign Affairs July 27 changed to require that a joint resolution would be necessary to suspend military aid to El Salvador, instead of using an apparently unconstitutional concurrent resolution. Foreign Affairs took the same action on the Export Administration Act (HR 3231), which Rules had returned.

A joint resolution must be sent to the president for his signature, unlike a concurrent resolution. One Rules Committee aide said Supreme Court justices "were almost putting up neon lights pointing to the joint resolution as something they would accept."

Business as Usual?

By mid-summer, Louis Fisher, a government specialist with the Congressional Research Service of the Library of Congress, had identified five laws enacted since the court's ruling that contained at least 17 legislative vetoes: the fiscal 1984 appropriations for the Department of Housing and Urban Development and Independent Agencies (PL 98-45); fiscal 1984 National Aeronautics and Space Administration (NASA) authorization (PL 98-52); fiscal 1983 supplemental appropriations (PL 98-63); the Caribbean Basin Economic Recovery Act (PL 98-67); and the fiscal 1984 Transportation Department appropriations (PL 98-78).

One of the new vetoes, for example, stated that construction grants by the Environmental Protection Agency were subject to approval by the House and Senate Appropriations committees.

Another stipulated that up to 5 percent of NASA's 1984 money could be transferred between accounts with the approval of the Appropriations committees.

Steven R. Ross, House legal counsel, said Congress might have accidentally overlooked these and other vetoes when they were enacted. "Each bill isn't gone through with a fine-tooth comb to compare it to what the Supreme Court said in *Chadha*," he said.

Looking the Other Way

Several experts thought the new vetoes were left in the measures as part of an informal understanding between Congress and executive agencies that if a veto device worked well for both sides, it would continue to be used, regardless of its legal status.

This was particularly true with "reprogramming" restrictions included in appropriations bills. Reprogramming, or the transfer of money from one account to another within an agency's budget, often was barred by Congress unless the Appropriations committees gave their prior consent.

Although such a restraint on an agency's money transfer technically was a veto, the agency and Congress were likely to ignore the Supreme Court's invalidation of the procedure, as long as it was not challenged in court, according to congressional analysts.

"The agencies are legally free to ignore the committees and spend the funds . . .," Fisher told the Senate Judiciary Subcommittee on Administrative Practice during the summer. "They defer to the committees because they fear retribution in the form of budget cutbacks . . . and other sanctions."

Theodore B. Olson, the Justice Department legal counsel, said he did not think Congress deliberately defied the court when it passed the new vetoes.

"It was probably not intentional to include legislative veto provisions or expect them to be enforced. The legislation might have been so far in the pipeline that people didn't catch them," he said.

Also, Olson said, the vetoes related to reprogramming were "relatively minor flaws in the legislation."

But a House Appropriations Committee staffer said the presence of the new vetoes in the money bills was not accidental. Many of the reprogramming clauses had been carried in spending bills for years, and until their constitutionality was specifically tested, they would continue to be used, the aide said.

Fisher said the new vetoes signified a move toward casual accommodation between congressional committees and executive agencies.

"Some matters that were open under the legislative veto [before the court's ruling] will start to go underground," Fisher said. "It will be done in a subterranean manner."

Fisher predicted that in future bills, committees might delegate power to an agency with the caveat: " 'Before you do this, notify us.' Notification will be the code word for legislative veto."

Levitas said he believed agencies "are trying to seek accommodation and not seek confrontation" with Congress. If agencies tried to grab power, Congress would respond with tighter restraints on their authority, he said.

Search for Alternatives

Because the legislative veto was so pervasive — it was included in laws ranging from budget control to the War Powers Resolution to District of Columbia self-government — a search was on for an all-encompassing replacement that could survive a legal challenge.

The list of alternatives included:

● Regulatory reform legislation, which would revamp federal rule-making procedures on an across-the-board basis. Several measures had been introduced, but no action was taken on them in 1983.

A bill (HR 2327) offered by Sam B. Hall Jr., D-Texas, chairman of the House Judiciary Subcommittee on Administrative Law, subjected proposed regulations to a joint resolution of disapproval by both houses of Congress. Such a resolution also must be signed by the president.

S 1080, a regulatory reform bill pending in the Senate, included an unconstitutional one-house veto. But sponsor Charles E. Grassley, R-Iowa, was expected to substitute a more acceptable device. At year's end, his bill had bypassed the Senate Judiciary Committee and was pending on the Senate calendar.

House Minority Whip Trent Lott, R-Miss., introduced a regulatory reform measure (HR 3939) that required a joint resolution of approval for major rules proposed by executive agencies, and a joint resolution of disapproval for minor rules. Lott's bill was referred to the House Judiciary and Rules committees.

In the 97th Congress, the Senate passed a broad regulatory reform bill, but a similar bill never emerged from the House. *(1982 Almanac p. 523)*

● A more limited regulatory reform bill (S 1650) was introduced in the Senate by Levin, David L. Boren, D-Okla., and others, providing for a joint resolution of disapproval over agency rules. Their bill was referred to the Governmental Affairs Committee.

The Levin-Boren proposal used a "report and wait" procedure, under which agency rules would be submitted to Congress, where they would sit for a specific period of time. A proposed rule could not take effect for 30 days. During that time, if a committee approved a joint resolution of disapproval, the rule would be delayed 60 more days, during which time both houses could act on the resolution, which would need the president's signature to become law.

● Sen. Daniel Patrick Moynihan, D-N.Y., introduced a bill (S 1591) to create a commission on an alternative to the legislative veto. The bill was referred to Governmental Affairs.

Other substitutes were also floating around, such as using amendments to appropriations bills to prohibit spending money to implement an agency rule that Congress disliked.

A House Republican task force also had proposed

methods to curb presidential and regulatory agency powers in the post-*Chadha* era.

Its alternatives included: setting a strict time limit for the president to act on foreign affairs, national security or economic crises; writing into law an automatic expiration of an agency's major rules; approving agency rules as part of authorizing legislation for the agency; and establishing a special congressional committee on regulation.

"In some cases, no single alternative to the veto may be appropriate, but a hybrid of several approaches may be necessary," said Jerry Lewis, R-Calif., GOP task force chairman.

Constitutional Amendments

Aside from legislative alternatives, several members were pushing for a constitutional amendment to allow legislative vetoes.

An amendment (H J Res 313) proposed by Jacobs provided for one-house vetoes of certain regulations issued by the executive branch. Sen. Dennis DeConcini, D-Ariz., introduced a constitutional amendment (S J Res 135) that said executive powers delegated by Congress could be subject to one-house or two-house approval.

Such amendments, if they emerged from Congress, would have to be ratified by three-fourths of the states. The Jacobs and DeConcini proposals were referred to the respective Judiciary committees.

Actions on Substitutes

In the months after the Supreme Court decision, Congress considered several legislative veto substitutes on an individual basis.

The Senate Oct. 20 voted to alter the War Powers Resolution to bring it in line with the court's ruling. Instead of Congress using a concurrent resolution to withdraw troops from hostilities abroad, the new version required a joint resolution to bring troops home. A concurrent resolution would not require the president's signature; a joint resolution would.

The Senate action came on the fiscal 1984-85 authorization bill for the State Department. The war powers provision was subsequently modified in conference with the House. *(Story, p. 145)*

Another case involved the District of Columbia self-government law (PL 93-198), which allowed either the House or Senate to overturn laws passed by the District government. On Oct. 4, the House passed amendments (HR 3932) to the Home Rule Act to replace the unconstitutional legislative vetoes with disapproval by joint resolution.

The House Energy and Commerce Committee in September deleted one-house vetoes from the Amtrak Improvement Act (HR 3648) and replaced them with a "report and wait" provision, requiring 120 days of continuous session before a route change proposed by Amtrak could take effect. The House debated HR 3648, but no final action was taken. *(Story, p. 561)*

New Litigation

In addition to the legislative action, there were several new lawsuits involving the veto following the Supreme Court's decision.

Two federal employee unions filed suits challenging the way pay raises for federal workers were granted the past few years. The lawsuits were pending in the U.S. District Court for the District of Columbia.

The Pay Comparability Act of 1970 required a group of officials to recommend a wage increase that would make federal white-collar salaries comparable to those in the private sector. But the president could submit an alternative pay plan to Congress, and that plan could be vetoed by either the House or Senate. Because the veto was unconstitutional, the unions argued that the president's right to propose his own pay plan also was invalid.

The president typically recommended a lower pay raise than the one called for by the comparability group, and Congress generally accepted the president's proposal.

Another lawsuit involved the coal leasing policy of Interior Secretary James G. Watt.

The House Interior and Insular Affairs Committee Aug. 3 ordered Watt not to sell government coal leases in the Fort Union area of North Dakota and Montana. But Watt said the committee's action was unconstitutional under *Chadha* and he proceeded with bid openings. *(Story, p. 350)*

In response, the National Wildlife Federation and The Wilderness Society filed suit asking the U.S. District Court for the District of Columbia to block the sale. Judge Louis F. Oberdorfer issued a preliminary injunction Sept. 28 preventing the Fort Union lease sale. ∎

Federal Workers Join Social Security System

Over the vehement protests of federal workers and their unions, Congress decided to require all new federal employees hired after Jan. 1, 1984, to join the Social Security system.

Current federal workers, who had their own retirement plan providing far more generous benefits than Social Security, were not affected by the move. *(Comparison of civil service, Social Security plans, next page)*

The change for new U.S. workers was made in a massive Social Security overhaul (HR 1900 — PL 98-21) that President Reagan signed into law on April 21. *(Social Security, p. 219)*

As cleared by Congress March 25, the bill extended Social Security coverage to new federal employees, current and future members of Congress, the president, the vice president, sitting federal judges, top political appointees and top civil servants. Legislative branch employees who did not choose to go under the Civil Service Retirement System by Dec. 31, 1983, also were covered.

Effective Jan. 1, 1984, all of these U.S. employees were subject to Social Security payroll taxes, which amounted to 7 percent of wages for 1984, rising to 7.51 percent in 1988 and 7.65 percent in 1990.

HR 2077: Retirement Plan, Physician Contracts

Federal employees already were contributing 7 percent of their pay to the Civil Service Retirement System. To avoid forcing new workers to pay 14 percent toward retirement, Congress Nov. 16 cleared a separate bill (HR 2077) that limited their contribution to the civil service plan to 1.3 percent until a new supplemental retirement program was adopted or until January 1986, whichever was earlier.

Reagan signed that measure into law (PL 98-168) on Nov. 29.

The civil service provisions were adopted by the Senate Nov. 4 as an amendment to HR 2077, which was principally designed to extend for four years the authority of the federal government to contract for physicians. HR 2077, which passed the House Sept. 19, also relieved physicians who exceeded the statutory limit on compensation from being required to repay the excess.

House-Senate conferees agreed to keep the civil service retirement language in the bill.

HR 2077 required federal agencies to continue paying their full 7 percent share to the Civil Service Retirement System, with the general Treasury making up the shortfall caused by lowered employee contributions.

Sen. Ted Stevens, R-Alaska, principal sponsor of the adjustment provision, said he would introduce legislation in 1984 to set up a new supplemental retirement plan for federal employees covered by Social Security.

Background

Commission Recommendation

The proposal to bring new federal workers under the system was one recommendation of a sweeping financial rescue plan for Social Security proposed by a bipartisan commission that was appointed by Reagan in late 1981 and issued its recommendations Jan. 15. *(Commission background, 1982 Almanac p. 53)*

The Social Security panel said it believed an independent pension plan should be available to new federal workers to complement their Social Security coverage, which — unlike the current civil service pension plan — was never meant to be the sole source of a worker's retirement income.

But the commission did not say whether the existing plan should be preserved, or a new one developed.

The commission recommended, and Congress subsequently agreed, that Social Security coverage also be extended to employees of all non-profit organizations.

This step, together with coverage of new federal employees, was expected to pump nearly $20 billion into the financially struggling system between 1983 and 1989.

The commission projected that the revenue Social Security would gain from the payroll taxes paid by new participants would exceed the amount it had to pay out to new beneficiaries over the next 75 years.

Besides their interest in the cash infusion from coverage of federal workers, members of the commission based their support for the idea on their belief that the Social Security system should provide universal coverage to all Americans, without excluding one group of workers.

The commission said the proposal would not adversely affect financing of benefits for present federal employees. But in a dissenting view, AFL-CIO President Lane Kirkland, a commission member, said, "The commission cannot know in advance whether the pension rights of present and future employees will be adequately protected if Congress enacts mandatory coverage."

This was not the first time Social Security coverage of federal employees had been seriously considered.

Most recently, Congress in 1977 rejected a plan to bring nearly 7 million government workers and non-profit corporation employees into the system, after federal unions and state and local governments lobbied hard against com-

---

Civil Service/Social Security

Coverage: The Civil Service Retirement System covered more than 2.7 million civilian workers and paid benefits to approximately 1.7 million retirees and survivors in fiscal 1981. About 116 million workers participated in Social Security, and 36 million individuals drew benefits.

Contributions: Federal employees contributed 7 percent of their basic pay through payroll deductions to the civil service retirement fund, compared to a 6.7 percent payroll deduction for Social Security participants. In addition, federal workers as of Jan. 1, 1983, paid 1.3 percent of their basic pay for Medicare coverage, which was included in the 6.7 percent payroll deduction of workers covered by Social Security.

Federal agencies put in a matching amount for each employee, just as private employers matched their workers' Social Security contributions. The U.S. Treasury also contributed to the civil service fund from general revenues to help cover unfunded future liabilities caused by an anticipated gap between contributions received and benefits owed.

Benefits: In early 1983, the average monthly civil service benefit was $1,047, according to the Office of Personnel Management, compared to $406 a month for Social Security. Many Social Security recipients supplemented their retirement income with private pension benefits. Also, civil service benefits were taxable, whereas Social Security payments were tax-free.

Retirement Age: A federal worker could collect a full pension if he retired at age 55 with 30 years of service, age 60 with 20 years, or age 62 with five years in government. Under Social Security, a worker could retire at age 62 with partial benefits and age 65 with full benefits.

---

pulsory participation. *(1977 Almanac p. 161)*

Reaction

Vincent Sombrotto, president of the National Association of Letter Carriers, warned that the existing civil service retirement fund would run out of money in about 20 years if new workers were pulled out.

To cover the fund's existing liability at that point, Sombrotto said, would cost the government at least $185 billion from the general treasury.

"Extending Social Security coverage to new federal and postal employees will bankrupt the present Civil Service Retirement System and cost the taxpayers billions more," he said.

While congressional leaders embraced the broad Social Security reform package, members who represented large pockets of federal workers criticized the portion affecting their constituents.

"It's being very penny-wise and pound-foolish," said Rep. Mary Rose Oakar, D-Ohio, who chaired the House Post Office and Civil Service Subcommittee on Compensation and Employee Benefits. "In the short term, injecting new employees helps the Social Security system. But it hurts the Civil Service Retirement System," Oakar said.

Senate Majority Whip Stevens, chairman of the Governmental Affairs Subcommittee on Civil Service, said he

was inclined to oppose the Social Security commission's proposal unless Congress also addressed the future of the entire federal retirement program.

"I can't see using federal employee contributions to solve the short-term solvency problems of Social Security unless we're willing to look at the long-term problems of the civil service system," Stevens said.

The Lobbying Effort

Federal employee groups mounted a $6 million lobbying effort against the commission's proposal. The Fund for Assuring an Independent Retirement (FAIR), a coalition of 25 organizations representing 6 million active and retired employees, took the lead role.

As the Social Security legislation began moving through Congress, the federal employee groups showered members with letters of protest and brought in workers from all over the nation, who roamed the corridors of Capitol Hill seeking to derail the provisions affecting them.

In opposing universal Social Security coverage, federal employee and retiree groups argued that:

● Removing new workers from the civil service system would deplete its assets, forcing annual appropriations by Congress to keep the system afloat.

● Universal coverage would cost taxpayers more because the government, as the employer of federal workers, would have to contribute to both Social Security and a supplemental pension plan to bring retirement benefits up to their present level.

● A lucrative pension program had long been one of the attractions of federal service, and the government might have trouble recruiting and retaining good workers if the plan was changed.

● Employee morale would be hurt if one set of workers was covered by the traditional civil service pension plan and another was covered by Social Security and a new supplemental program.

House Committee Action

The House Ways and Means Committee opened hearings on the Social Security reform package the week of Jan. 31, and by Feb. 9, when the hearings concluded, members had heard testimony from about 100 witnesses.

Subcommittee Action

The Ways and Means Subcommittee on Social Security Feb. 23 approved by a straight 7-4 party-line vote a package incorporating almost all of the recommendations made by the bipartisan National Commission on Social Security Reform.

The panel agreed to require mandatory Social Security coverage of all new federal employees and employees of non-profit organizations, despite a strong lobbying effort by federal employee unions to block the change. The subcommittee required that as of Jan. 1, 1984, all new federal employees be covered under the Social Security system. Currently, such workers belonged to the more generous Civil Service Retirement System. The bill included language stating congressional intent to develop some supplemental retirement plan for new federal employees so they would not have a reduction in total retirement benefits.

In addition, all members of Congress, the president and vice president were to be covered by Social Security as of Jan. 1, 1984. All new hires of the legislative and judicial branches, including new federal judges, also were to be

covered under the system. Current legislative branch employees who had chosen to participate in the Civil Service Retirement System were not covered.

The bill also prohibited state and local governments from withdrawing from the system. Those employers currently had the option of belonging to Social Security, but in recent years many had chosen to withdraw. The bill gave those state and local governments the option of returning to the Social Security fold.

The measure wiped out so-called "windfall" benefits that some workers, especially federal government retirees, received from Social Security even though they worked only a short period of time under the system. The bill eliminated the benefit by using a different formula for workers who collect pensions from jobs that were not covered by Social Security than was used for other workers. The provision applied to those reaching the age of 60 after Dec. 31, 1983.

Full Committee Action

After a speedy, two-day markup, the full Ways and Means Committee on March 2 approved the Social Security rescue bill (HR 1900) by a 32-3 vote.

The measure was formally reported March 4 (H Rept 98-25).

The committee made few changes in the package agreed to by its Social Security Subcommittee, but it did tinker with the provisions affecting federal workers.

The panel agreed to cover some 4,000 top political appointees and elected officials, including all sitting federal judges, under Social Security. The bill already called for coverage of new federal employees, as well as all members of Congress, the president and the vice president.

A move by Andrew Jacobs Jr., D-Ind., to delete coverage of new federal employees from the bill was defeated by voice vote.

House Floor Action

The House passed HR 1900 on March 9 by a 282-148 vote. *(House vote 23, p. 10-H)*

Those voting against passage of the bill included liberals opposed to the higher retirement age and the coverage of federal employees, and conservatives opposed to additional taxes.

There was no separate vote on the federal employee provisions.

Senate Committee Action

The Senate Finance Committee approved its own version of the Social Security bill (S 1) on March 10 by a vote of 18-1. The measure was formally reported the following day (S Rept 98-23).

Like the House bill, S 1 called for the coverage of all new federal employees and workers in non-profit organizations beginning Jan. 1, 1984, and included all current and new members of Congress under the Social Security system.

But it did not contain the House bill provisions extending coverage to all top political appointees, certain elected officials and sitting federal judges.

The committee rejected 6-11 a motion by Russell B. Long, D-La., to delay the effective date of a provision calling for Social Security coverage of new federal employees until a supplemental Civil Service retirement plan

could be established.

Members had given assurances that such a supplemental plan would be set up, but federal workers feared they faced retirement benefit cuts if no new workers were available to pay into their current system.

Finance Chairman Robert Dole, R-Kan., charged that a delay in the Jan. 1, 1984, effective date would only give lobbyists a longer time to fight for repeal.

Senate Floor Action

The Senate passed the Social Security package March 23 by a vote of 88-9. *(Vote 53, p. 11-S)*

Long proposed on the floor the amendment he had offered unsuccessfully in committee to delay coverage of federal employees under Social Security until a supplemental Civil Service retirement system could be established to provide them with an additional pension, comparable to those offered in private business.

Long's amendment was approved by voice vote, but only after several blocking attempts by the leadership.

Stevens charged that the Long amendment would only give federal employees a chance to escape coverage altogether. That loss would cut the value of the rescue plan $9.3 billion over the next decade, said Dole, who hinted strongly that he would fight the provision in conference if it was passed.

But Long argued it was unfair to expect federal employees to accept the new plan before they knew what supplemental benefits they would receive. "I do not think it's fair to ask these people to buy a pig in a poke," he said.

An alternative proposal by Stevens to cover new federal hires under Social Security, but not make them pay into the Civil Service Retirement System until a supplemental plan could be established, was rejected 45-50. *(Vote 48, p. 11-S)*

Conference/Final

House and Senate conferees agreed to the final shape of the bill during a 12-hour session March 24, as colleagues waited impatiently to leave for the Easter recess.

The primary stumbling block was a difference between the House and Senate bills on how to solve the system's long-range financial problems when the so-called baby-boom generation began to retire after the turn of the century.

But conferees also grappled with the provision in the Senate bill delaying coverage of new federal employees until a supplemental Civil Service retirement plan could be developed. House conferees charged that if the change were made, the entire Social Security bailout plan could be jeopardized by giving federal workers a second chance to persuade Congress that they should escape coverage altogether.

After hours of bargaining, mostly behind closed doors, conferees agreed to the House provision. The Senate conferees agreed to recede on the federal employee provisions by a vote of 4-3.

The House adopted the conference report (H Rept 98-47) on March 24 by a 243-102 vote. *(Vote 43, p. 18-H)*

By a 58-14 vote, the Senate gave final approval to the plan in the early morning hours of March 25, clearing HR 1900 for the president. *(Vote 54, p. 12-S)*

Reagan signed the landmark bill into law (PL 98-21) on April 20. ∎

Federal Employee Pay

Some 1.4 million federal white-collar workers received a 3.5 percent pay increase effective Jan. 1, 1984, after Senate inaction on a fiscal 1984 budget reconciliation measure blocked them from receiving a 4 percent raise.

President Reagan had recommended the 3.5 percent level in an Aug. 31 executive order that also provided for a three-month delay in the annual federal pay raise scheduled for Oct. 1. By law, Reagan's proposal took effect when Congress did not overrule it.

Members of Congress also received a 3.5 percent raise effective Jan. 1. *(Story, next page)*

The Senate reconciliation bill (S 2062) provided for a 4 percent pay raise as of Jan. 1, 1984. It also sought to delay until January 1985 a scheduled May 1984 cost-of-living (COLA) increase for federal retirees. The bill did not reach a Senate vote before adjournment.

The House Oct. 25 passed its own reconciliation bill (HR 4169), which likewise called for a 4 percent increase in white-collar pay and a delay in retiree COLAs. By a 245-176 vote, the House agreed to delay the pay raise from Oct. 1, 1983, until Jan. 1, 1984. The House Post Office and Civil Service Committee had sought an Oct. 1 effective date. The reconciliation bills were designed to achieve deficit reductions required by the fiscal 1984 budget resolution. *(House vote 390, p. 116-H; details of Senate and House action on reconciliation, p. 231)*

Under provisions of the fiscal 1984 Treasury-Postal Service funding bill that were incorporated in the second fiscal 1984 continuing appropriations resolution (PL 98-151), pay raises for blue-collar ("wage scale") federal workers were limited to the same percentage and timetable as those for white-collar workers. *(PL 98-151, p. 528)*

In his fiscal 1984 budget proposal, Reagan called for a one-year freeze on federal wages and fiscal 1984 cost-of-living adjustments (COLAs) for federal retirees.

The proposed pay freeze would have affected about 2.7 million civilian employees and 2.1 million active military personnel. Administration officials said it would save about $6 billion in fiscal 1984.

U.S. Pay Change Delayed

President Reagan Oct. 11 signed into law a bill (HR 3871 — PL 98-117) delaying for three months a bookkeeping change that resulted in a slight pay cut for federal workers.

The measure had been passed by the House Sept. 20 and by the Senate Sept. 27.

It delayed from Oct. 1, 1983, until Jan. 1, 1984, the effective day of a minor change enacted as part of the fiscal 1983 budget reconciliation act (PL 97-253). The modification extended the number of hours used to compute biweekly paychecks for most annual-rate federal employees.

The change was expected to cost workers between $3.20 and $8.80 per pay period.

With enactment of HR 3871, the shift took effect at the same time as a 3.5 percent pay boost for federal white-collar workers.

The COLA freeze would have affected some 1.4 million civil service retirees and 1.3 million military retirees.

Chilly Reception

Federal employee and retiree groups attacked the Reagan proposals angrily.

"They're outrageous. I have never seen such a direct, all-out attack on a group of employees like this," declared Jane McMichael, legislative director for the American Federation of Government Employees, a large federal union.

The House Post Office and Civil Service Committee March 2 rejected the Reagan proposals, recommending that the House Budget Committee ignore them.

The committee voted 4-18 against a proposal by William E. Dannemeyer, R-Calif., that the one-year freeze on pay be approved.

The Senate Governmental Affairs Committee later approved a 4 percent pay boost, effective Jan. 1, 1984.

COLA Delay for Retirees Blocked

The House Post Office Committee voted 3-18 against a 13-month delay in federal retiree COLAs that was offered by Dannemeyer.

"We have treated the civil service retirees exceedingly well, especially in the 1970s," Dannemeyer argued. He said federal outlays for the retirement plan had increased nine times faster than inflation in the past 20 years, and that federal retirees enjoyed benefits far more generous than those of most private sector retirees.

However, the reconciliation bill (HR 4169) passed Oct. 25 by the House did include a delay from May 1984 until January 1985 in COLAs for federal retirees.

The Senate Governmental Affairs Committee also approved a delay in the retiree COLA from May 1984 to January 1985, but the failure of the full Senate to approve a budget reconciliation measure blocked this proposed delay. ∎

Congressional Pay Raises

Six months after the House took a 15 percent pay raise for its members, Congress provided an identical raise to senators, making their salary $69,800 a year effective July 1.

In return for the raise, the Senate limited senators to receiving no more than 30 percent of their salaries in honoraria for speeches, appearances and articles. This limit — $21,660 — went into effect Jan. 1, 1984. Members of the House were already at the 30 percent limit.

In addition, by not acting in 1983, all members of Congress got another raise effective Jan. 1, 1984. This 3.5 percent pay increase brought congressional salaries to $72,200 a year, although members actually faced a net loss in 1984 because they had to start paying Social Security taxes.

Increasing members' pay had traditionally been one of the most difficult political chores for members of Congress. Members generally felt they were worth more than they got in pay but seldom had the political courage to risk the wrath of their constituents by voting for more.

In 1982, Congress broke with nearly two centuries of tradition by agreeing to pay larger salaries to representatives than senators while allowing senators to make unlimited outside earnings. *(1982 Almanac p. 544)*

In 1983, senators caught up in pay and agreed to limit their honoraria earnings to 30 percent of their salaries, the same limit representatives faced on all their outside earned income. The change came as part of a fiscal 1983 supplemental appropriations bill (HR 3069 — PL 98-63) that Congress cleared July 29. *(Supplemental story, p. 509)*

Senate Pay Raise

Ironically, the Senate pay raise evolved from a House slap at senators over their honoraria earnings. The House Appropriations Committee marked up the supplemental May 18, a few days after 1982 honoraria figures were made public. Those revealed that more than half the Senate earned more than 30 percent of their salaries in honoraria, with several earning more than their Senate salaries. This outraged many members of the House, who were generally less in demand as speakers and who also faced a 30 percent limit on outside earned income.

The Appropriations Committee adopted an amendment offered by Silvio O. Conte, R-Mass., ranking minority member, to limit such earnings of senators to 30 percent of their salaries. This was seen as a direct slap at senators. Traditionally, neither chamber had interfered with the internal workings of the other.

The issue was not contested on the floor of the House, which passed the bill May 25.

The Senate spent a week in June trying to negotiate a satisfactory arrangement on pay and honoraria. It initially voted for a cap on honoraria but declined to accept a pay raise. Finally, it approved, 49-47, an amendment by Sen. Henry M. Jackson, D-Wash., limiting honoraria to 30 percent of senators' salaries, which were increased 15 percent to $69,800. Based on that figure, the honoraria cap was to be $20,940 on Jan. 1, 1984, but with the 1984 pay raise, the cap moved up to $21,660. *(Vote 152, p. 28-S)*

The Senate passed the bill June 16. A conference committee agreed to the pay arrangement and the bill was cleared July 29.

1984 Raise

Under the Social Security rescue plan approved in March 1983, representatives and senators were to have approximately $2,500 deducted from their paychecks in 1984 to provide them with Social Security coverage for the first time. *(Social Security story, p. 219)*

But under the provisions of another law, their $69,800-a-year salaries grew by $2,400 — to $72,200 — Jan. 1, 1984, offsetting the Social Security bite.

The only thing that could have stopped the automatic 3.5 percent pay raise for members was passage of a bill barring the salary hike. Such legislation was not passed in 1983 but was expected to be considered in early 1984.

Sen. Jake Garn, R-Utah, who had fought the Senate limit on honoraria, said he would try to rescind the Jan. 1 pay raise. Garn and Sen. Don Nickles, R-Okla., first tried to block the raise in November, as an amendment to the fiscal 1984 Department of Defense appropriations bill (HR 4185). They were forced to withdraw the amendment because of procedural problems, but were assured by Senate leaders that they could offer the proposal in January as an amendment to another bill.

Garn and Nickles argued that the House in 1982 and the Senate in 1983 had awarded themselves a 15 percent pay raise, making another increase unwarranted. While Garn had opposed congressional pay raises, he argued that members should be allowed to earn as much as they wanted

from honoraria, without the constraints currently imposed.

If approved, the Garn-Nickles measure would have rescinded the 3.5 percent raise retroactive to Jan. 1 for members of Congress, but it would not affect other federal workers.

But it was unclear that the repeal would be successful.

"The raise will already be in effect when they get back here, and a repeal of money already in people's pockets would be difficult," said Jonathan W. Delano, administrative assistant to Rep. Doug Walgren, D-Pa., who had opposed backdoor congressional pay raises in the past.

Social Security. The paycheck changes for legislators were the result of laws that put them on an equal footing with other federal employees.

Like other federal civilian workers, members of Congress never were covered by the Social Security system. Instead, they received pension benefits from a separate retirement plan.

But under the legislation approved in March to help keep Social Security afloat (HR 1900 — PL 98-21), new federal employees and all members of Congress had to join the system.

As of Jan. 1, 1984, federal employees and members of Congress had to begin contributing 6.7 percent of their salaries to Social Security. Their employer — the federal government — must also contribute 7 percent for each worker.

There was a $37,800 ceiling on the amount of wages subject to the payroll tax in 1984. That left the remaining $34,443 in lawmakers' earnings untouched by the Social Security tax. In 1984, each member of Congress would pay the maximum Social Security tax of $2,532.60.

Pay Raise. The 3.5 percent pay raise for members was linked to an identical cost-of-living wage hike that went to most federal white-collar workers.

Congressional salaries had been tied to federal employee pay raises since 1975. From 1975 to 1981, members still needed to appropriate money separately for their own raises. But a 1981 law (PL 97-51) provided an automatic appropriation that did not require a politically sensitive vote each year. *(1981 Almanac p. 286)*

Members of Congress typically were reluctant to vote themselves pay raises because of their fear of voter backlash. Yet many complained that with the expense of maintaining homes in their state and in high-cost Washington, D.C., only the wealthy could afford to serve in Congress.

It was during the December 1982 post-election session that House members had the political nerve to vote themselves a 15 percent raise. The Senate at that time passed up the pay raise and opted instead for unlimited outside earnings, including honoraria from speeches and appearances.

Unlike the 1982 House pay raise and the 1983 Senate increase, no legislative action was needed to produce the 3.5 percent annual increase ($2,400) that members began getting in 1984.

When members were similarly poised — before the 1982 elections — to receive an automatic cost-of-living raise along with other federal workers, several House members blocked the increase. In 1983, though, many traditional pay raise critics avoided the issue.

"We're not going to do anything," said an aide to Rep. Patricia Schroeder, D-Colo., who opposed the automatic increase last year. "We've carried the water enough on this issue. It's only gotten us black and blue."

Walgren's assistant, Delano, said the Pennsylvania Democrat also would not attempt to revoke the 3.5 percent

increase later in 1984 after Congress reconvened. "It's very frustrating fighting these issues," Delano said.

Another reason members were reluctant to fight the increase was that, in effect, it was canceled out by the Social Security tax. The difference between the $2,532.60 Social Security deduction and the $2,400 pay raise actually was a $132.60 net loss to members. ∎

Franking Privilege Upheld

The Supreme Court May 2 rejected a challenge to the free mailing privileges of members of Congress.

Putting an end to a decade-old lawsuit, the court voted 6-3 not to consider the case. The result left standing a lower court decision upholding the constitutionality of the congressional franking privilege. *(Background, 1982 Almanac p. 521)*

Members of Congress have enjoyed free mailings since the 1st Congress in 1789. The privilege was intended to make it easy for members to communicate with their constitutents on matters of official business.

In recent years, with the advent of computerized mailing lists, the amount of franked mail emanating from Capitol Hill had mushroomed and the costs had skyrocketed.

In 1983, Congress appropriated $107 million for the cost of the frank in fiscal 1984, an average of $200,000 per voting member.

In 1973, Common Cause, the self-styled citizens' lobby, filed suit, charging that the frank was unconstitutional because it promoted the re-election of incumbents and therefore placed an unfair disadvantage on challengers. *(Background, CQ Guide to Congress 3rd Edition, p. 730)*

On Sept. 7, 1982, a special three-judge panel of the U.S. District Court for the District of Columbia dismissed the Common Cause suit. The panel said the franking privilege "confers a substantial advantage to incumbent congressional candidates over their challengers," but it found no constitutional violation.

Common Cause appealed the outcome to the Supreme Court, which decided May 2 against hearing the appeal in the case of *Common Cause v. William F. Bolger.*

Despite its ultimate rejection, the Common Cause suit had a substantial effect. In the 10 years since the case was first filed, Congress passed two laws (PL 93-191, PL 97-69) governing the use of the frank, and both House and Senate established their own rules on the subject. *(1981 Almanac p. 394)*

Currently, members were restricted from sending franked mass mailings within 60 days before an election. Members were also restricted in their use of the frank for letters that merely expressed a member's condolences or congratulations.

However, the changes still left incumbents with an unfair advantage, Common Cause had argued in its effort to get the Supreme Court to take the case.

Common Cause said Congress either should not allow the frank to be used for mass mailings or should also allow non-incumbent challengers to take advantage of the frank.

In its brief to the court, Common Cause also suggested that franked mail should not be allowed for mailings to groups of people whose selection identified the mailing as political.

New Restrictions

Congress also put additional limits on the use of the

frank in 1983, although the restrictions were delayed and watered down.

At the same time, lax regulation of the privilege drew a growing number of complaints from members. Criticisms included the high costs as well as charges that it had been politically abused.

The issue was a particularly sensitive one for members of Congress, who traditionally had balked at any attempts to regulate what they saw as the rights of their offices.

In 1984, an election year, members of Congress planned to send an estimated 840 million pieces of mail under the frank — 3.6 letters for every man, woman and child in the United States. This was nearly double the 423 million pieces of franked mail Congress sent in 1983.

In place of postage, franked mail — ranging from individual letters to mass-mailed newsletters — carried a reproduction of the signature of the member sending it. Congress then appropriated funds to cover the anticipated bill from the Postal Service for the postage costs.

Each chamber set its own rules on mailings. Most of the regulations were put in place in 1973 (PL 93-191). Additional rules were added in 1977, when changes were made in the House and Senate ethics codes. In 1981, Congress enacted a law (PL 97-69) codifying some of those changes, and added some new regulations. The changes relaxed some standards and tightened others. *(1981 Almanac p. 394)*

Responsibility for regulating the frank in the House rested with the Commission on Congressional Mailing Standards, called the franking commission, established by the 1973 law. In the Senate, the Rules and Administration Committee set standards while the Select Committee on Ethics interpreted them.

While the court affirmed Congress' right to police its own use of the frank, some members questioned its ability. On June 7, the House franking commission watered down stricter regulations it had proposed only two months earlier and issued a set of general, non-binding guidelines. The commission basically left responsibility for regulating the style and content of mailings up to each member. Commission member William D. Ford, D-Mich., called this "the mature approach."

Other members of the six-member panel disagreed, however. "They're as next to nothing as you can get," said Trent Lott, R-Miss., a commission member since 1977, who resigned from the commission June 15 in protest. "I'm not going to be a party to the situation," Lott said.

In the Senate, an attempt to curb a proliferation of newsletters met with resistance from senators. The Rules Committee failed to meet a self-imposed June 27 deadline to develop regulations on "postal patron" mail — mail sent to every mailbox, rather than a specific address. Members of the House had been sending postal patron mail districtwide since 1977. The 1981 franking law extended the postal patron right to senators, pending regulations by the Rules Committee, which had been unable to agree on them.

The committee Nov. 1 approved postal patron mail for senators effective Dec. 1, but only for the announcement of town meetings.

Laws governing the frank allowed it to be used for "official business," such as "the conveying of information to the public, and the requesting of views from the public." The law forbade use of the frank for personal business or friendships, and letters that dealt with partisan politics. Despite these restrictions, some members charged that

other members had stretched the definition of official business.

Since 1981, the franking commission had reviewed every House newsletter before it got in the mail. If the commission found no violation of franking rules, the newsletter was mailed. The commission later heard complaints from anyone who felt there was a violation. Most complaints, almost all of which had been filed during election years, had been dismissed. If the commission did find a violation, it could refer the case to the House Committee on Standards of Official Conduct.

In the Senate, responsibility for reviewing franked mail rested with the Senate Select Ethics Committee. Chairman Ted Stevens, R-Alaska, said interpretations of the law were "very, very sticky," and required a "subjective kind of decision."

Although members of Congress were limited to sending only six newsletters per year, the costs of the franking system had escalated sharply. The fiscal 1984 legislative branch appropriations bill (HR 3135 — PL 98-51), cleared by Congress June 29, provided $107 million for franked mail, a $14 million increase over what Congress expected to spend in 1983. *(Story, p. 539)*

By contrast, the total amount spent in 1981 was $52 million.

House

During House debate on HR 3135, Duncan L. Hunter, R-Calif., offered an amendment to cut proposed funding by $7 million to $98 million, but that was rejected, 134-173. *(Vote 150, p. 48-H)*

In presenting his proposal, Hunter said, "This is one place where we can demonstrate some fiscal discipline." But Vic Fazio, D-Calif., chairman of the Appropriations Legislative Subcommittee, insisted "We are really attempting to reflect reality. We do not want to put a figure in here that will require a supplemental [appropriations bill] in the next fiscal year. We think this is truth in appropriations."

Mary Rose Oakar, D-Ohio, said that what Hunter was trying to do "is to cut off our ability to communicate with our constituents.... People demand a response to their inquiries and to their points of view about issues."

To avoid political use of the frank, the House franking commission in April proposed a new set of rules. Among other things, the commission restricted the use of photos in newsletters, limited the size of the newsletters, limited the colors allowed in newsletters and restricted the size of a member's name in a headline. In addition, the commission proposed that its staff issue advisory opinions on the frankability of all mass mailings of more than 1,000 pieces.

These proposed changes provoked a sharply negative reaction from other members and their staffs.

Many members sent letters of objection to the commission. Some thought the content restrictions smacked of censorship. Others objected to a provision allowing members to send mail only in the capacity of a "federal-level representative," prohibiting them from sending franked mail on purely local matters.

After the combination of the negative feedback from other members, the Supreme Court decision upholding the frank and the House vote against Hunter's amendment, the House franking commission issued a new set of guidelines on June 7.

"The primary responsibility for ensuring proper and cost-efficient use of the franking privilege," the commission wrote, "lies with each individual member of the House

who uses the privilege."

Rather than the strict April limits, the June guidelines encouraged members to hold newsletters to four pages and to limit the size and type of photographs in newsletters. The commission also suggested — but did not require — that members submit mass mailings to the commission for advice.

The commission said it would review the guidelines at the end of the year, but the June changes were enough to cause Lott to resign.

Senate

In the Senate, attempts to control the frank had met with similar resistance. Senate Rules and Administration Committee Chairman Charles McC. Mathias Jr., R-Md., proposed a set of guidelines for newsletters that he wanted adopted before the Senate permitted postal patron mail.

Mathias' major concern was cost. When Rules held its first hearing on the law in 1982, Stevens, who had written the law, argued that postal patron mail would save money, since it could be sent third-class rather than first-class. In addition, Stevens said, Congress could save money because postal patron mail did not have to be returned for incorrect addresses.

But Howard S. Liebengood, Senate sergeant-at-arms, testified that the postal-patron provision would actually add costs, since senators could use postal patron in addition to regular mail.

In 1982, Mathias and the Rules Committee decided to postpone implementation of the postal-patron provision for a year. In February 1983, the Rules panel met again, and Mathias indicated that he wanted to tie implementation to guidelines for newsletters. The committee again postponed a decision.

Mathias' original proposal would permit postal-patron mail to be used only for announcements of upcoming meetings. Other senators on the committee had objected, noting that Mathias' constituents could read all about his congressional activities in *The Washington Post* and *The Baltimore Sun*. They contended that elsewhere in the country, voters could learn about a senator's activities only from a newsletter.

In addition, some senators, particularly those from states with only one House member, wanted to make Senate regulations closer to those of the House. Larry Pressler, R-S.D., said his constituents had asked him what he was doing after seeing a great deal more information from South Dakota's lone representative, Democrat Thomas A. Daschle.

Finally, on Nov. 1, the committee approved rules allowing postal-patron mailings only for announcing town meetings. The regulations, which took effect Dec. 1, also barred all franked mass mailings 60 days before any primary or general election, even if the senator was not up for re-election. ∎

Two Members Censured

The House July 20 censured Daniel B. Crane, R-Ill., and Gerry E. Studds, D-Mass., for sexual misconduct with teenage congressional pages.

The action marked the first time that a member had ever been censured for sexual misconduct and the first time since 1980 the House had censured one of its members. *(Box, next page)*

In voting to censure the two members, the House overturned a recommendation by its ethics committee, the Committee on Standards of Official Conduct, which had recommended a reprimand. A reprimand was the least severe form of punishment the House could impose.

The penalty associated with either a reprimand or censure was public condemnation. A censured member, however, must also appear in the well of the House to hear the charges read against him or her. In addition, under the rules of the House Democratic Caucus, a censured Democrat lost any chairmanship of a committee or subcommittee that he or she held.

The ethics committee July 14 reported that both Crane and Studds had sexual relationships with teenage pages, and had thus committed a "serious breach of the duty owed by the House and its individual members to the young people who serve the House as its pages."

Several members, though, felt a reprimand was too mild. Newt Gingrich, R-Ga., said, "With no malice toward any individual, I cannot see how a reprimand is in any way adequate." Gingrich wanted the two expelled.

The mood on the House floor was somber, and many members expressed appreciation to the ethics committee for performing a function members would rather not do. Minority Leader Robert H. Michel, R-Ill., called the position "the most distasteful job in the House." When ethics Chairman Louis Stokes, D-Ohio, sat down after his final remarks, he received a standing ovation.

Those who felt Studds and Crane deserved only a reprimand insisted that the punishment was indeed severe. "The member must live with this condemnation forever," said Stokes.

Floyd Spence, R-S.C., ranking Republican on ethics, said, "The public disclosure of the facts of these cases has already placed an indelible stain on the reputations of these members."

But Gingrich insisted, "Our focus should not be on what [Crane and Studds] are going through and what has happened to them." Rather, Gingrich said, "Our decisions are made today about the integrity of freedom, about belief in our leaders, about the future of this country, about what we should become."

Before the vote on the ethics committee's recommendations, Michel moved to change the recommendation of reprimand to censure. Michel said he sensed that members wanted a more severe form of punishment.

Michel's motion in Crane's case (H Res 266) was adopted 289-136. The censure resolution was then agreed to by a 421-3 vote. *(Votes 243, 244, p. 74-H)*

In Studds' case (H Res 265), Michel's motion was adopted 338-87, and the House voted to censure Studds by a 420-3 vote. *(Votes 245, 246, p. 74-H)*

Crane voted for his own censure. Studds voted present when the House voted on his censure.

Crane, who admitted to having a sexual relationship with a 17-year-old female page, approached the well of the House, then faced his silent colleagues as Speaker Thomas P. O'Neill Jr., D-Mass., read the resolution of censure to him. Studds, who the ethics committee found had a sexual relationship with a male page, faced the Speaker, hands clasped behind him, as O'Neill read his resolution of censure.

As a result of the censure, Studds lost his chairmanship of the Merchant Marine and Fisheries Coast Guard and Navigation Subcommittee. Walter B. Jones, D-N.C., who chaired the full Merchant Marine Committee, was

Censure Proceedings in the House

Congress	Session	Year	Member	Grounds	Disposition
5th	2nd	1798	Matthew Lyon, Anti-Fed-Vt.	Assault on representative	Not censured
5th	2nd	1798	Roger Griswold, Fed-Conn.	Assault on representative	Not censured
22nd	1st	1832	William Stanbery, D-Ohio	Insult to Speaker	Censured
24th	1st	1836	Sherrod Williams, Whig-Ky.	Insult to Speaker	Not censured
25th	2nd	1838	Henry A. Wise, Tyler Dem.-Va.	Service as second in duel	Not censured
25th	3rd	1839	Alexander Duncan, Whig-Ohio	Offensive publication	Not censured
27th	2nd	1842	John Q. Adams, Whig-Mass.	Treasonable petition	Not censured
27th	2nd	1842	Joshua R. Giddings, Whig-Ohio	Offensive paper	Censured
34th	2nd	1856	Henry A. Edmundson, D-Va.)	Complicity in assault	Not censured
34th	2nd	1856	Laurence M. Keitt, D-S.C.)	on senator	Censured
35th	1st	1858	Orsamus B. Matteson, Whig-N.Y.	Corruption	Censured
36th	1st	1860	George S. Houston, D-Ala.	Insult to representative	Not censured
38th	1st	1864	Alexander Long, D-Ohio	Trasonable utterance	Censured
38th	1st	1864	Benjamin G. Harris, D-Md.	Treasonable utterance	Censured
39th	1st	1866	John W. Chanler, D-N.Y.	Insult to House	Censured
39th	1st	1866	Lovell H. Rousseau, R-Ky.	Assault on representative	Censured
40th	1st	1867	John W. Hunter, Ind-N.Y.	Insult to representative	Censured
40th	2nd	1868	Fernando Wood, D-N.Y.	Offensive utterance	Censured
40th	3rd	1868	E. D. Holbrook, D-Idaho [1]	Offensive utterance	Censured
41st	2nd	1870	Benjamin F. Whittemore, R-S.C.	Corruption	Censured
41st	2nd	1870	Roderick R. Butler, R-Tenn.	Corruption	Censured
41st	2nd	1870	John T. Deweese, D-N.C.	Corruption	Censured
42nd	3rd	1873	Oakes Ames, R-Mass.	Corruption	Censured
42nd	3rd	1873	James Brooks, D-N.Y.	Corruption	Censured
43rd	2nd	1875	John Y. Brown, D-Ky.	Insult to representative	Censured [2]
44th	1st	1876	James G. Blaine, R-Maine	Corruption	Not censured
47th	1st	1882	William D. Kelley, R-Pa.	Offensive utterance	Not censured
47th	1st	1882	John D. White, R-Ky.	Offensive utterance	Not censured
47th	2nd	1883	John Van Voorhis, R-N.Y.	Offensive utterance	Not censured
51st	1st	1890	William D. Bynum, D-Ind.	Offensive utterance	Censured
67th	1st	1921	Thomas L. Blanton, D-Texas	Abuse of leave to print	Censured
96th	1st	1979	Charles C. Diggs Jr., D-Mich.	Misuse of clerk-hire funds	Censured
96th	2nd	1980	Charles H. Wilson, D-Calif.	Financial misconduct	Censured
98th	1st	1983	Daniel B. Crane, R-Ill.	Sexual Misconduct	Censured
98th	1st	1983	Gerry E. Studds, D-Mass.	Sexual Misconduct	Censured

[1] *Holbrook was a territorial delegate, not a representative.*
[2] *The House later rescinded part of the censure resolution against Brown.*

SOURCE: Hinds and Cannon, *Precedents of the House of Representatives of the United States,* 11 vols. (1935-41); Joint Committee on Congressional Operations, *House of Representatives Exclusion, Censure and Expulsion Cases from 1789 to 1973,* committee print, 93rd Cong., 1st sess., 1973.

elected July 29 by committee Democrats to also chair Studds' subcommittee.

The House's action was the result of yearlong investigation by the ethics committee, led by special counsel Joseph A. Califano Jr., who was secretary of health, education and welfare during the Carter administration. *(Story, p. 595)*

Even while the ethics committee investigation was going on, Congress was quietly overhauling the page system, from how pages were appointed to how they were housed and educated. Most of the changes had occurred in the House, which employed about 70 pages during the academic year, compared with about 30 Senate pages. More were hired during the summer.

The House was quicker to act because allegations of misconduct touched its members. During the Califano in-

vestigation, though, the committee heard allegations of drug use involving Senate employees. The committee released its inch-thick report (H Rept 98-297) July 14 along with a separate report (H Rept 98-295) on Studds and one (H Rept 98-296) on Crane.

The ethics committee found that Studds, in 1973, had a sexual relationship with a 17-year-old male page, who might have been 16 at the time the relationship began. In addition, the panel said Studds made sexual advances on two other male pages in 1973. Studds July 14 told his House colleagues that he was gay.

Crane, the panel said, had a sexual relationship with a 17-year-old female page in 1980. Since the legal age of consent in the District of Columbia was 16, the panel accused neither Studds nor Crane of a crime. Nevertheless, the panel felt that any sexual relationship, consensual or

Studds and Crane: A Congressional Contrast

Though caught in the same web of sexual misconduct, Daniel B. Crane, R-Ill., and Gerry E. Studds, D-Mass., were a contrast in political philosophies and legislative styles.

Crane, 47, elected in 1978, had exhibited little of the drive and intensity that led his more famous brother, Philip, who represented Illinois' 12th District, to seek the presidency in 1980. The two shared a conservative ideology but little else.

Flippant and relaxed, Dan Crane ambled into the House chamber from the gym most afternoons, slapping his fellow members on the back and trading stories, but rarely staying to participate in the debate.

Crane had some clear legislative priorities, but they tended to be away from the center of national debate — such as his efforts to repeal the 55-miles-per-hour speed limit, to allow the minting of gold coins to compete with Federal Reserve notes, and to stop the torture of dogs in the Philippines.

Although he was the ranking minority member on the Post Office and Civil Service Subcommittee on Human Resources, which was investigating the Carter briefing book affair at the time of the ethics committee charges against him, he took a back seat to Republican colleagues in the probe. *(Story, next page)*

Crane represented a conservative district, highlighted by corn farms and the University of Illinois. His 1982 Democratic opponent, John Gwinn, held Crane to only 52 percent of the vote. Initial reports from Illinois' 19th District indicated that Crane, the father of six, might be hurt politically by his affair with a teenage page. Crane said he would not resign and held a district tour of town meetings in August.

When the ethics committee report was first released, Crane issued a terse statement: "I'm sorry that I made a mistake. It happened three years ago. I'm hu-man, and in no way did I violate my oath of office. I only hope my wife and children will forgive me."

When the House considered his punishment, a tearful Crane took the floor to apologize to his colleagues.

Unlike Crane, Studds, 46, was not apologetic. He did not speak during debate on his censure but later reiterated his feeling that his conduct did not warrant punishment. Studds had been known as a liberal activist, particularly on the Foreign Affairs Committee, where he had been one of the leading critics of American military ventures, from Vietnam to Central America.

He had been free to pursue his foreign policy interests, largely because of his vigorous defense of New England's fishing interests, and his political shrewdness, as shown by his learning Portuguese to communicate with his New Bedford constituents.

Studds' seaside constituents remembered him best for pushing through a measure in his first term extending U.S. territorial waters to a 200-mile limit, a bill considered vital by his state's fishing interests.

In the 97th Congress, as chairman of the Merchant Marine and Fisheries Committee's Coast Guard Subcommittee, Studds fought against cutbacks in the Coast Guard's budget, warning, "Lives will be lost if the administration budget is enacted." Studds lost his chairmanship as a result of being censured.

Studds was first elected in 1972 on an anti-Vietnam War platform. In recent years, he challenged the Reagan administration's support for the government of El Salvador, and sought to overturn the administration's certifications of human rights progress in that country.

Although Studds had a comfortable 1982 winning margin of 69 percent, it was the lowest since he was first elected narrowly in 1972. The conservatives of his district might object to his homosexuality but there was a large homosexual community in Provincetown.

---

not, between a member and a page constituted improper sexual conduct.

In addition, the panel voted July 14 to initiate disciplinary proceedings against James Howarth, former majority chief page in the House Doorkeeper's Office. According to the report, Howarth had a sexual relationship in 1980 with a female page under his direct supervision, and he gave that page preferential treatment. The report also charged Howarth with purchasing cocaine in the House cloakroom from Robert Yesh, a former House employee. On Nov. 15, the ethics committee issued its final report (H Rept 98-548) on the page scandal. It recommended that Howarth be dismissed. Howarth resigned after the report was issued.

In choosing an appropriate penalty for Crane and Studds, Califano cited as precedents the two most recent cases of censure and expulsion. In 1980, the House censured Charles H. Wilson, D-Calif. (1963-81) for bribery. The same year, the House expelled Michael "Ozzie" Myers, D-Pa. (1976-80), who was convicted on Abscam bribery charges. Califano concluded, "Measured against the precedents, neither expulsion nor censure is warranted." Califano added, though, "The institutional integrity of the

House of Representatives requires that the House itself act." He recommended a reprimand, and the committee agreed by an 11-1 vote. *(1980 Almanac pp. 522, 514)*

But for some members, this was not enough. "I want to change the precedent," Gingrich said. "The precedent is ridiculous." He said if Studds or Crane were teachers or police officers, they would be fired.

Supporting Gingrich, Chalmers P. Wylie, R-Ohio, said July 18 he would support a stiffer penalty unless both members resigned.

Without mentioning Wylie's suggestion, Studds announced July 19 he would stay in the House. "I look forward," he said, "to concentrating all my energies once again on the job my constituents expect me — and elected me — to do."

Page Scandal Background

The ethics probe came after published allegations of widespread sexual misconduct and drug use by members and pages during the period July 1981 to June 1982. In a preliminary report issued in December 1982, Califano found the charges groundless, although he did learn of misconduct before that period, and he continued his inves-

tigation. *(1982 Almanac p. 528)*

Referring to the charges that set off the investigation, Califano said most of the "allegations and rumors of misconduct were the product of teenage exaggeration, gossip, or even out-and-out fabrication that was often repeated mercilessly in a political capital that thrives on rumor."

On June 30 and July 1, 1982, CBS television aired news reports quoting former pages who said that pages had been the victims of sexual misconduct on the part of House members. Later news reports identified the accusers as Leroy Williams, 18, of Arkansas, and Jeffrey Opp, 16, of Colorado. Both later admitted that they had lied.

On July 13, 1982, the House authorized the ethics committee to investigate the charges, which eventually led to the censures. At the same time, the Justice Department began an investigation, only to close it Aug. 31, 1982, when it was unable to corroborate Williams' allegations.

But the House also decided, for the third time in 20 years, to undertake an extensive examination of the page system.

Speaker O'Neill set up a special commission to look at the page system. It recommended that the system be retained, but improved.

The commission rejected proposals to use college students and senior citizens as pages. It said pages should be 11th graders who were at least 16 years old and who would serve for only one semester. To monitor the program, the commission recommended the creation of a Page Board, which was created Nov. 30, 1982.

Also, the House converted two floors of an office building to be used as a page dormitory. House pages were required to live in the residence hall; Senate pages could live there if space was available. The residence hall was staffed by a director and five resident assistants. There was a nightly curfew.

Page School Changes

In addition, Congress had been considering changes in the schooling of pages. Under legislation (HR 3034) passed by the House and reported in the Senate (S Rept 98-201), pages would be named for up to one year, during their junior year in high school.

Apparently for the 1983-84 school year, the House and Senate would operate separate page schools for the first time. In the past, both chambers signed a joint contract with the Washington, D.C., Board of Education. In 1983, the House, based on a decision by its Page Board, elected not to renew its contract, preferring instead to operate its own school. The Senate, however, expected to continue to contract with the District of Columbia for page schooling.

The decision to create a separate school came about because of concerns over the present school. The Speaker's commission on pages reported, "Every witness, including the pages, with whom the commission met, spoke of deficiencies in the page school." The Page Board noted a decline in scholastic aptitude test scores, as well as a high absentee rate.

Page school principal John C. Hoffman, a teacher and administrator for 25 years, challenged that assessment. Hoffman said any problems with the school had come about because of time constraints imposed by congressional duties.

On July 21, the House passed a resolution (H Res 279) limiting attendance at the House page school to pages only. In the past, some high-school age House employees and interns also had attended the school.

Joseph G. Minish, D-N.J., who chaired the Page Board, felt the changes made so far had "alleviated a great deal of the concern" members had about the system. Vic Fazio, D-Calif., a member of the Page Board and the ethics committee, said, "I don't think there is ever any foolproof way" to avoid problems, but added, "We will continue to do what we can to make the program more safe."

The changes were not enough to satisfy Gingrich, who felt that the system remained open to abuse. "If we do not expel Studds," Gingrich said July 19, "I would abolish the page system."

And Bill Frenzel, R-Minn., ranking Republican of the House Administration Committee, won a round of applause during the House debate on the Crane censure resolution by proposing to scrap the page system. "We are not and cannot be real parents," Frenzel said, adding that page duties should be taken over by regular employees.

Frenzel later introduced a resolution (H Res 291) to abolish the system. ∎

Transcript Alterations

The House ethics committee in 1983 investigated charges of improper changes being made in transcripts of committee proceedings.

But in a report (H Rept 98-544) issued Nov. 9, the committee found "absolutely no evidence whatsoever of a pattern of improper alteration" of transcripts, but recommended committees clarify how far they want to go in routine smoothing out of grammar and diction.

The ethics panel, however, did find improper changes made in the record of a bitterly partisan July 1982 joint hearing by four subcommittees on Environmental Protection Agency actions. Those changes, it found, were made by Lester O. Brown, who resigned Sept. 2 from the staff of the House Government Operations Subcommittee on Energy, Environment and Natural Resources.

Government Operations Committee Chairman Jack Brooks, D-Texas, said Brown told him "he personally had made unofficial changes in the record of a hearing conducted last year."

The ethics committee probe began after Republicans charged that their remarks in a hearing transcript entitled "EPA Oversight: One Year Review" had been changed in such a way as to make them look foolish. The hearing was held jointly July 21 and 22, 1982, by five subcommittees, one from Government Operations and two each from Energy and Commerce and from Science and Technology.

When the record was published in May, an aide to Robert S. Walker, R-Pa., noticed one of Walker's comments had been changed from "Many members of the other party know that I am willing to take part in reasonable hearings," to "Many members of the other party know that I am *not* willing to take part in reasonable hearings."

Walker and others first asked the Science Committee and then the full House to conduct an open investigation, but the House voted 409-0 June 30 to authorize an ethics committee investigation, which was done behind closed doors. *(Vote 222, p. 66-H)*

Brown had been hired in May 1980 by former subcommittee Chairman Toby Moffett, D-Conn. (1975-83), who ran unsuccessfully for the Senate in 1982. Brown was regarded as an expert on environmental issues and was co-author of a book published by the Sierra Club entitled "Hazardous Waste in America." ∎

Government Ethics Office

Congress Oct. 27 completed action on a bill (S 461 — PL 98-150) that extended the Office of Government Ethics for five years, through Sept. 30, 1988, and closed some loopholes in federal conflict-of-interest laws.

The ethics office, created by the Ethics in Government Act of 1978 (PL 95-521), was an arm of the Office of Personnel Management (OPM). It was responsible for reviewing financial disclosure forms required of many executive branch officials, including the president and vice president, candidates for those offices, and presidential appointees requiring Senate confirmation.

It also advised officials on how to comply with various provisions of the federal ethics law, including those designed to avoid conflicts of interest. *(Background, 1978 Almanac p. 835)*

S 461 contained several provisions designed to strengthen the independence of the ethics office, including one that provided a five-year term for the ethics director and required a report to Congress if the president decided to remove him before his term expired.

"It is crucial that the director be free from political interference and from the threat of removal by the president," said Sen. William S. Cohen, R-Maine, chief sponsor of the bill.

Under previous law, the director served at the pleasure of the president, and the Reagan administration opposed limitations on the president's removal authority.

Other provisions of the bill tightened financial disclosure rules for top presidential appointees and imposed new reporting rules on individuals who were required to divest themselves of conflicting interests or to place those interests in a blind trust. The bill also made top White House aides subject to the 15 percent limit on outside earned income that applied to other high-level executive branch officials.

Provisions

As signed into law Nov. 11, S 461 (PL 98-150):

Ethics Office. Provided a five-year term for any person appointed or reappointed by the president as director of the Office of Government Ethics, beginning Oct. 1, 1983. If the president removed a director from office before expiration of the five-year period, he was required to inform the appropriate committees of Congress of his reasons for doing so.

The Senate bill originally had permitted premature removal of the director only for "good cause."

● Gave the ethics office authority to issue its own regulations pertaining to financial disclosure, conflicts of interest and ethics in the executive branch. Previously, the office had authority to develop and recommend these rules, but only the OPM had authority to issue them.

● Set the ethics office apart as a separate line item in the OPM budget.

● Gave the ethics office director statutory authority to request the assistance of inspectors general of other agencies in conducting investigations.

● Permitted the director to recommend replacement of the official in each government agency responsible for enforcing the ethics law.

Outside Earned Income. Provided that White House personnel who were compensated at rates equivalent to level II of the Executive Schedule (currently $69,800 or more a year) could not have outside earnings exceeding 15 percent of their annual salary. The provision was applicable to 25 top White House positions, as the Senate had proposed. The House bill would have covered 69.

The limit on outside earnings already applied to political appointees requiring Senate confirmation, such as Cabinet secretaries and other high-ranking administration officials. The Reagan administration had extended the policy to White House aides, even though it was not required to do so by existing law.

Financial Disclosure. Required presidential appointees to positions requiring Senate confirmation to file by the first day of their confirmation hearings updated financial disclosure statements showing income and honoraria as of five days before the hearings.

● Permitted an individual to file a financial disclosure statement with the ethics office before formally being nominated by the president.

● Extended financial disclosure requirements to high-level staff members of federal advisory committees.

Ethics Agreements. Stipulated that if an official agreed to take action to comply with federal ethics or conflict-of-interest laws, he must report steps taken toward compliance to the ethics office, a designated agency ethics officer or the appropriate Senate committee. Such a report was to be made within three months after the date of the agreement.

● Stipulated that an official who agreed to "recuse" himself, or withdraw from consideration of a particular matter, must file a report clarifying the recusal agreement with the agency or committee requesting the agreement.

The new reporting requirements were drawn from the House bill.

Blind Trusts. Permitted any trust to be approved as a "qualified blind trust," provided it met certain requirements set out in the bill. Previously, only trusts established before enactment of the 1978 ethics law could be so designated.

Under the 1978 law, the qualified blind trust was one of two main types of blind trust open to executive branch personnel who wished to avoid an appearance of conflict of interest. Under both types, the individual gave up control of his financial assets. But the qualified blind trust imposed more restrictions on the holder than the "qualified diversified blind trust," which was available only to persons requiring confirmation.

The Senate originally had proposed that all executive branch employees be permitted to place their assets in the less restrictive qualified diversified blind trusts.

Legislative History

The Senate Governmental Affairs Committee reported S 461 March 24 (S Rept 98-59), and the Senate passed the bill April 6 by voice vote without debate.

The House Judiciary Committee reported its version of the bill May 5 (HR 2717 — H Rept 98-89, Part 1), and the Post Office and Civil Service Committee, to which the measure was also referred, reported HR 2717 May 16 (H Rept 98-89, Part 2).

A compromise between the two committees' versions of the bill was passed by the House by voice vote under suspension of the rules Sept. 19.

After being bounced back and forth between the two chambers to reconcile Senate-House differences, S 461 was cleared Oct. 27, when the Senate accepted final House changes in the bill. ∎

Abscam Defendants Enter Prison

After exhausting their legal appeals, four of the seven members of Congress convicted in the FBI's Abscam investigation entered federal prisons in 1983.

A fifth former member went to jail in early 1984 and the two others were expected to begin serving time in 1984.

Abscam rocked the Capitol in February 1980 when the investigation was first revealed. Posing as businessmen and Arab shieks, FBI agents videotaped members of Congress and other politicians accepting money and promising illegal favors in return.

Two years later, all seven members were out of Congress. Three were defeated in the 1980 election, three resigned in the face of disciplinary action and one was expelled by the House. All seven were convicted in federal court.

In three separate instances in 1983, all without comment, the Supreme Court rejected the appeals of six of the members.

On May 31, the Supreme Court rejected the appeals of four former members of the House and three others convicted on Abscam bribery charges.

The four former members of Congress were Michael "Ozzie" Myers, D-Pa., (1976-80), Raymond F. Lederer, D-Pa., (1977-81), John M. Murphy, D-N.Y., (1963-81), and Frank Thompson Jr., D-N.J., (1955-81).

The others were former Mayor Angelo J. Errichetti of Camden, N.J., and Philadelphia lawyers Louis C. Johanson and Howard L. Criden.

By refusing to hear the cases, the Supreme Court let stand a 1982 appeals court decision upholding the seven convictions. In that decision, a three-judge panel of the 2nd U.S. Circuit Court of Appeals found that the "conduct of the investigation, though subject to some criticism, affords no basis for rejecting the convictions." Moreover, the panel said, the "essential characteristic" of the Abscam operation "was the creation of an opportunity for the commission of a crime by those willing to do so."

On Oct. 11, the Supreme Court left standing the conviction of former Rep. Richard Kelly, R-Fla., (1975-81). Kelly was the only congressional Abscam defendant to have won a reversal of his conviction. In May 1982, Kelly's conviction was overturned by a U.S. district court judge in Washington, D.C., who found the government had violated Kelly's rights.

However, the U.S. Circuit Court of Appeals for the District of Columbia reinstated Kelly's conviction May 10, 1983, a move the Supreme Court left intact.

On Dec. 5, the Supreme Court refused to hear the appeal of former Sen. Harrison A. Williams Jr., D-N.J. (1959-82), the only senator nabbed in the Abscam operation.

The only case the Supreme Court had not heard was that of former Rep. John W. Jenrette Jr., D-S.C., (1975-80).

By late January 1984:

● Murphy was serving a three-year sentence at the federal prison camp in Danbury, Conn.

● Thompson was serving a three-year sentence at the federal penitentiary in Lexington, Ky.

● Williams was serving a three-year sentence at the federal prison camp at Allenwood, Pa.

● Lederer was also serving a one-year sentence at Allenwood.

● Myers was also serving a three-year sentence at Allenwood.

● Jenrette was sentenced Dec. 9 to two years in prison but had not yet entered prison and could still appeal.

● Kelly was sentenced Jan. 12, 1984, to a prison term of six to 18 months. Because Kelly's sentencing came after the Supreme Court rejected his initial appeal, it was still possible for Kelly to again appeal to the high court.

Abscam Background

The cases against the members of Congress first came to light in February 1980, when press reports revealed the undercover FBI investigation, where agents disguised themselves as businessmen and Arab sheiks. The FBI eventually charged seven members of Congress in criminal wrongdoing, alleging that the members accepted money from the phony sheiks, promising favors in return. (1980 Almanac p. 513)

An eighth member, John P. Murtha, D-Pa., was named an unindicted co-conspirator. He testified for the government in one trial. Over the objections of the attorney conducting the investigation for the House Committee on Standards of Official Conduct (the ethics committee), the committee decided not to cite Murtha for misconduct. (1981 Almanac p. 388)

The linchpin of the government's case against the defendants was a series of videotapes showing the members actually accepting cash or stock. In one, an agent handed Myers an envelope stuffed with hundred-dollar bills, saying, "Spend it well." Myers responded, "Pleasure."

After witnessing that, the House ethics committee unanimously recommended expelling him. Convinced of his innocence, Myers took his case to the House floor, where he pleaded, "When you push the 'yes' button on the voting machine, it will have the same effect as hitting the button on the electric chair." The House voted 376-30 to expel him. Myers was the first member to be expelled since the Civil War, the first ever to be expelled for misconduct other than treason.

Kelly was seen on a videotape stuffing bills in his pockets and asking if the money made visible bulges in his clothing. He was forced to resign from the House Republican Conference, and later lost in the 1980 Republican primary. Murphy and Thompson lost in the general election.

Jenrette, who said on a tape he had "larceny in my blood," also lost in the 1980 election. The ethics committee recommended expelling him during the lame-duck session that year. He resigned the next day.

Lederer was the only Abscam defendant to win reelection in 1980. When he took his seat in January 1981, House Democrats kicked him off the Ways and Means Committee. In April, the ethics committee recommended his expulsion. He resigned the next day. (1981 Almanac p. 386)

Williams, whose term was scheduled to expire in 1983, became the first senator in 61 years to have been convicted while in office. Although the Senate Select Ethics Committee recommended his expulsion in August 1981, the full Senate did not consider the recommendation until March 1982. Williams resigned on March 11. (1982 Almanac p. 509)

Williams' case was the most complicated of the seven. Unlike the six House members, Williams actually turned down a bribe when undercover agents offered him one. He was convicted for his participation in a complicated business scheme involving a hidden interest in a mining venture owned by several of Williams' friends.

FBI's Role Questioned

From the start, press reports of the Abscam investigation stirred concern about the FBI's role. Much of the strongest criticism was aimed at the premature leaking of allegations to the news media. Although the probe had been conducted secretly for two years, law enforcement authorities learned in January 1980 that news organizations were preparing reports on the investigation.

The authorities decided to abandon the undercover operation, notify the suspects, and begin organizing the evidence.

Many lawmakers also expressed fear that the FBI had "entrapped" members into breaking the law by its undercover techniques. Lederer used that argument unsuccessfully in his defense. Others were concerned about the bureau's use of paid informants.

Allegations about the FBI's conduct reached a head during the Senate's debate on Williams' expulsion in 1982. During that debate, Sen. Alan Cranston, D-Calif., said he believed that abuses occurred in Abscam "on the magnitude of Watergate." He added that "Abscam was an undercover operation totally out of control."

Responding to those charges, the Senate set up a special committee to study the FBI's role. That panel, composed of four Republicans and four Democrats and chaired by Charles McC. Mathias Jr., R-Md., released its final report on Dec. 16, 1982. The report gave Abscam a "mixed review," with the good outweighing the bad. *(1982 Almanac p. 510)*

But the panel warned of the improper use of undercover techniques that "create risks to citizens' property, privacy and civil liberties, and may compromise law enforcement itself." It said "the undercover technique may on occasion create crime where none would otherwise have existed."

In March 1983, the eight members of the panel introduced legislation (S 804) designed to establish permanent authority for undercover operations, but only under specific guidelines. The bill would prohibit such operations in cases when law enforcement officials could show a "reasonable suspicion of criminal conduct." It would also allow defendants to use the defense of entrapment in certain cases, and would authorize compensation for innocent victims of undercover operations. The bill was referred to the Judiciary Committee, where no action was taken.

In May, the House Judiciary Committee added language to the Justice Department authorization bill (HR 2912) strengthening the requirement that the FBI report to Congress on undercover activities. The committee approved the bill May 11 (H Rept 98-181). The bill would require the bureau to submit to Congress detailed information about FBI undercover operations. However, the bill was not passed in 1983. ▮

Boxing Commission

The House July 26 defeated a bill (HR 2498) to establish a Congressional Advisory Commission on Boxing.

The measure was rejected when the House refused, 167-254, to suspend the rules and pass the bill. A two-thirds majority was needed for passage. *(Vote 253, p. 78-H)*

The commission would have looked into the need to establish a federal agency to oversee boxing and set national licensing standards.

The bill, sponsored by Rep. James J. Florio, D-N.J., was prompted by the 1982 death of Korean fighter Duk Koo Kim following a match with Youngstown, Ohio, boxer Ray "Boom Boom" Mancini.

Florio said the existing regulation of boxing was a "non-system," with wide variations state to state. There was no central data source on the fight and injury records of boxers, he noted. "The absence of uniform minimum standards and a central source of data on medical and ring records poses a continuing threat to the health and safety of boxers," Florio said.

Opponents, led by Rep. John N. Erlenborn, R-Ill., said no other sport was subject to such federal regulatory action. "Wherever there have been problems with a professional sport or a collegiate sport, the people engaged in that activity have found a method of policing themselves rather than turning to the federal government," he said. ▮

Indian Land Claim Veto

President Reagan April 5 vetoed a bill (S 366) to settle claims of the Mashantucket Pequot Indian Tribe to 800 acres of land in eastern Connecticut.

Congress made no attempt to override the veto, the 16th of Reagan's presidency and his first of legislation cleared by the 98th Congress. The measure — a compromise agreed to by the state, the Indian tribe and 14 eastern Connecticut landowners — had been passed by voice vote in the Senate Feb. 24 and the House March 22.

In his April 5 veto message, the president objected to a provision of S 366 that established a $900,000 federal claims settlement fund to compensate the Indians for their claims to the disputed land near Ledyard, Conn. The Indians contended that the land, currently in private ownership, was sold by the state in 1855 without the consent of the federal government and in violation of the provisions of the Indian Non-Intercourse Act of 1790.

The president said the state should pay at least half of the settlement costs. *(Veto message, p. 25-E)*

Under the bill, the state would give the Indians 20 acres of land, which the administration contended was worth only about $50,000. During House debate on the measure, Sam Gejdenson, D-Conn., said Connecticut's percentage of participation was higher than that of other states involved in similar claims settlements.

The president also criticized the bill for giving federal recognition to the tribe, thereby bypassing the Department of Interior's administrative procedures for determining whether federal recognition should be extended to Indian groups.

In 1982, the administration had opposed an earlier version of the bill on essentially the same grounds.

Gejdenson, who represented the area, said the presidential veto left a continuing cloud on the title of the land that was depressing land prices there.

Earlier Veto

Reagan's veto of S 366 was his second of legislation aimed at resolving longstanding Indian claims to land or

water. In 1982, he vetoed a bill designed to settle a water rights dispute between the Papago Indian Tribe of Arizona and landowners in the Tucson area. Then, as in 1983, the president complained that the federal government was being asked to bear too great a share of the cost of settling the Indian claims. *(Papago bill, 1982 Almanac p. 441)*

Congress did not attempt to override Reagan's veto of the Papago Indian settlement bill. Instead, the settlement formula was revised and the new provisions were incorporated into major legislation (PL 97-293) overhauling an 80-year-old Western reclamation water law. *(1982 Almanac p. 353)* ∎

Relocation Assistance

The Senate May 20 passed by voice vote a bill (S 531) to revise the Uniform Relocation Act, a 1970 law that required payments to individuals and businesses displaced by federally assisted projects such as highway construction and urban renewal.

The House did not act on the measure, which would provide the first major overhaul of the 1970 relocation law (PL 91-646). *(Background, Congress and the Nation Vol. III, p. 650)*

As passed by the Senate, S 531 significantly broadened the class of individuals and businesses eligible for relocation aid and provided for payments of up to $10,000 to help small businesses and non-profit organizations re-establish at new locations. It also required the administration to develop a uniform set of federal regulations pertaining to the act. Under a floor amendment adopted by voice vote, utility companies displaced by federally funded projects would be allowed to receive relocation assistance under certain circumstances.

The Senate passed a similar measure in 1982, but the House failed to act. *(1982 Almanac p. 535)*

Committee Action

The Senate Governmental Affairs Committee May 5 reported S 531 May 5 (S Rept 98-71).

In recent years, as urban renewal diminished and construction was substantially completed on the Interstate Highway System, there had been a pronounced decline in the number of families and businesses displaced by federally assisted projects. But the committee said the current drive by Congress to improve the nation's infrastructure of highways, bridges and other public facilities "presages a significant reversal of such trends."

Under the bill, persons displaced by private entities with the power of eminent domain — such as public utilities and private development corporations — would become eligible for relocation assistance if their property was acquired under a federally funded program or project.

Also, persons displaced by non-acquisition activities such as rehabilitation, code enforcement or demolition projects would become eligible for benefits. This section was specifically intended to cover persons displaced by activities funded under the community development block grant program, the committee said.

In addition to moving expenses allowed by existing law, the bill would permit payments of up to $10,000 to help small businesses and non-profit organizations get re-established at their new locations. The measure also increased from $10,000 to $20,000 the amount a small busi-

ness or non-profit organization could receive in lieu of itemized moving expenses.

The bill also changed the definition of the replacement dwelling to which a person was entitled to be relocated from a "comparable replacement dwelling" to a "suitable replacement dwelling." The latter was defined as a dwelling that was decent, safe and sanitary.

In the past, according to the committee report, a "comparable" dwelling had been rigorously interpreted to mean "most nearly identical, or better property."

The emphasis on physical comparability rather than comparability in value or utility had made the entitlement expensive and difficult to administer, the committee said.

The bill also required the president to designate a lead federal agency that would be responsible for promulgating a single, uniform set of federal regulations so that state and local governments did not have to bear the administrative costs of following a multiple set of federal regulations. ∎

Bureau of Standards Funding

Congress did not complete action on a fiscal 1984 authorization for the National Bureau of Standards.

The Senate April 7 passed a $114.8 million authorization bill reported by the Commerce, Science and Transportation Committee March 31 (S 821 — S Rept 98-49), but the House did not act on a $130.1 million version reported by its Science and Technology Committee May 9 (HR 2513 — H Rept 98-95). Fiscal 1984 began Oct. 1.

President Reagan had requested $98.7 million for the bureau, a Commerce Department agency responsible for developing standards, measures and technologies in many fields. Both the Senate and House bills rejected Reagan's proposals to eliminate the Center for Fire Research and the Center for Building Technology and to slash funding for the Institute for Computer Sciences and Technology.

Congress appropriated $115.7 million for the Bureau of Standards in the Commerce Department's fiscal 1984 appropriations bill (HR 3222). *(Story, p. 472)* ∎

Small Business/U.S. Contracts

President Reagan Aug. 11 signed into law a bill (S 272 — PL 98-72) designed to increase competition for government procurement contracts and make it easier for small businesses to receive these contracts, primarily by requiring advance notice.

The bill was cleared Aug. 1, when the House approved the conference report (H Rept 98-263) by voice vote. The Senate approved the report June 27.

The bill originally was reported by the Senate Small Business Committee Feb. 2 and passed the Senate the next day. The House passed the bill with amendments March 8. The conference report was filed June 23.

Parren J. Mitchell, D-Md., chairman of the House Small Business Committee, called the measure "a vital tool for small business entrepreneurs who seek a larger share of federal contracts for goods and services."

Provisions

S 272 required federal agencies and departments to publish notice of upcoming federal contracts worth $10,000

or more in the *Commerce Business Daily* at least 15 days prior to soliciting contract bids. In addition, federal agencies had to allow at least 30 days for receipt of bids or proposals.

Exemptions. There were a number of exemptions from these rules, including:

- Purchases that were classified for security reasons.
- Goods or services for which the agency or department had an "unusual and compelling" urgency.
- Transactions in which a foreign government was reimbursing the United States for the cost and only one source was available, or if the terms of an international agreement or treaty authorized or required that the procurement be from specified sources.
- Purchases made from another government department or a mandatory source of supply.
- Utility services if only one source was available.
- Purchases made against an order placed under a "requirements" contract allowing federal departments to purchase goods regularly as needed, such as meat to feed military personnel.
- Research resulting from unsolicited proposals if publication would disclose originality of thought or innovation.
- Purchases on which the Small Business Administration and the department agreed that advance notice was not appropriate or reasonable.

Federal departments also were required to publish notice in the *Commerce Business Daily* of prime contract awards exceeding $25,000 in which subcontracting was likely, unless the procurement was classified because of security reasons.

Sole Source Contracts. The measure also made it more difficult for federal departments to negotiate a sole-source contract with a single company by requiring, in most circumstances, the approval of the head of the procurement division or his deputy.

The sole source provision of the bill applied to procurement contracts valued at $1 million in fiscal year 1984, $500,000 in fiscal 1985 and $300,000 in fiscal 1986 and subsequent years. It took effect Oct. 1, 1983. All other provisions applied to procurement actions initiated 90 days after the date of enactment. ∎

Reorganization Act Renewal

Efforts to revive the president's authority to reorganize executive branch agencies made little headway in 1983.

The House Government Operations Committee reported a bill May 16 (HR 1314 — H Rept 98-128, Part 1) to renew the president's reorganization authority through 1984. But the House Rules Committee, to which the bill was also referred, did not act on the measure.

The Reorganization Act, in effect off and on since 1949, permitted the president to reorganize government agencies without seeking legislation from Congress. The last extension of the act (PL 96-230) expired April 7, 1981. *(Background, 1980 Almanac p. 543)*

Under HR 1314, a presidential reorganization plan could go into effect only if both the Senate and House within 90 days passed a joint resolution approving it and the measure was subsequently signed by the president.

In the past, a presidential reorganization plan became effective automatically unless either the House or Senate

adopted a resolution disapproving the plan. The Supreme Court ruled June 23 that such one-house legislative vetoes were unconstitutional. *(Story, p. 565)* ∎

Minority Businesses

Congress June 30 cleared for President Reagan a bill (S 273 — PL 98-47) reauthorizing two pilot programs of the Small Business Administration (SBA) aimed at assisting minority-owned and other disadvantaged small businesses.

Final action came when the House agreed to a conference report (H Rept 98-262) on the bill that had been approved June 27 by the Senate.

The Senate had originally passed S 273 on Feb. 3. The House passed its own version (HR 861) Feb. 15, then adopted the Senate bill number.

As cleared, S 273 revived two expired pilot programs involving minority businesses. Section 8(a) of the Small Business Act of 1953 gave the SBA authority to enter into procurement contracts with federal agencies and then subcontract the work to socially and economically disadvantaged small businesses.

A 1978 law (PL 95-507) set up a two-year pilot procurement program under which the president designated the Department of the Army as the agency from whom SBA was to take procurement contracts for minority enterprises.

That 1978 law also authorized SBA to waive, under certain circumstances and conditions, the federal bonding requirements that otherwise would be in force for government contracts awarded through the 8(a) program.

Both pilot programs were extended for one year under PL 96-481, but they had expired Sept. 30, 1981.

The House Committee on Small Business noted in reporting HR 861 (H Rept 98-2) that SBA and the Army had engaged in "a considerable amount of bickering" over the program, and that only 14 contracts worth approximately $100 million had been awarded during its three-year existence.

The 1983 legislation (S 273) reopened the pilot programs effective Oct. 1 and required the president, within 60 days, to select a new agency other than the Defense Department or a component thereof to participate in the programs. ∎

NASA/Weather Satellites

Congress cleared a fiscal 1984 authorization for the National Aeronautics and Space Administration (NASA) that included a provision barring the sale of the nation's land and weather satellites to private industry unless Congress passed a law approving any sale. President Reagan had advocated such sales.

Final action on the NASA bill (HR 2065 — PL 98-52), which provided $7.3 billion for the agency, came June 29 when the House by voice vote accepted a compromise version of the bill. The Senate accepted the compromise June 28, also by voice vote.

The House and Senate had passed differing NASA authorizations, with the House providing $620,000 more than the compromise and the Senate bill (S 1096) providing $10.5 million above the final version.

Weather Satellites

There was strong congressional opposition to any sale of the nation's weather satellites almost from the day the administration announced plans to auction them off to the highest bidder.

Reagan March 8 proposed that private firms be allowed to bid on the satellites separately or as a package. The government would then purchase needed weather information from the private owners and distribute some of it free of charge. Other data would be sold.

Congressional concerns centered on how much the sale would end up costing taxpayers, especially for specialized weather services that had been available free through the National Weather Service. Critics feared, too, that such a sale could lead to a monopoly of weather information since only one firm, Communications Satellite Corp. (COMSAT), had proposed to purchase both the land and weather satellite systems.

Members also feared the sale could result in less accurate weather predictions — especially of hazards such as tornadoes and hurricanes — and could be detrimental to national security, since the weather satellites served as a backup to Pentagon satellites.

The prohibition on selling weather satellites applied to the nation's five existing satellites and any future land, meteorological or ocean remote sensing space satellites. The existing satellites, valued at $1.6 billion, were developed and launched by NASA. After orbit, the satellites were operated by a division within the National Oceanic and Atmospheric Administration (NOAA).

As cleared, HR 2065 provided that no satellite could be sold unless the secretary of commerce submitted to Congress a comprehensive statement of recommended policies, procedures, conditions and limitations on the transfer. Congress then would have to pass legislation approving the transfer.

Commerce Appropriation (HR 3222). The Commerce, Justice, State Department appropriations bill for fiscal 1984 (HR 3222) contained a rider barring use of any funds in the bill to transfer or sell the weather satellites. The rider had been added on the floor of the Senate at the urging of Sen. Larry Pressler, R-S.D. *(HR 3222, p. 472)*

NOAA Authorization. Provisions barring the sale of weather satellites also were part of House and Senate authorization bills (S 1097, HR 2900) for NOAA programs.

As approved May 10 and reported May 16 by the House Science and Technology Committee, HR 2900 (H Rept 98-135, Pt. I) barred sale of the land and weather satellites without express consent of Congress.

The Senate Commerce Committee included a similar prohibition in S 1097, which was reported May 16 (S Rept 98-109) and passed by the full Senate June 15.

Neither HR 2900 nor S 1097 cleared before Congress adjourned.

S Con Res 67. Just to drive home its concern about the proposed satellite sale, the Senate Oct. 7 passed a concurrent resolution (S Con Res 67) expressing the sense of Congress in opposition to the transfer of weather satellites to private ownership.

NASA Authorization

HR 2065, with its $7.27 billion authorization, provided $161 million more than President Reagan asked for NASA operations and allowed NASA to spend $82 million more than he requested to initiate procurement of a fifth space shuttle orbiter in fiscal 1984.

Reagan had provided money for space shuttle production and development activities.

This allocation included funds for operation and production activities of the first four shuttles, but no money for a fifth orbiter.

The administration had requested approximately $1.6 billion for space transportation operations. The House provided the administration request while the Senate provided $35 million less. The substitute that cleared provided $1,545,000,000, a decrease of $25 million from the request.

NASA had requested $205 million for planetary exploration activities in fiscal 1984.

The Senate provided $215.4 million in its version of the authorization bill, and the House provided $220.4 million, which was the amount in the final bill. ∎

Procurement Policy Office

Congress Nov. 17 cleared and sent to President Reagan a bill (HR 2293) reauthorizing for four years the Office of Federal Procurement Policy (OFPP), a unit within the Office of Management and Budget (OMB).

The legislation, which Reagan signed into law Dec. 1 (PL 98-191), strengthened the role of the OFPP in developing and guiding government procurement policies.

Among other things, it restored the office's authority — dropped by Congress in 1979 — to issue procurement policies and regulations. *(1979 Almanac p. 202)*

The office was created by Congress in 1974 to improve the federal procurement process and provide overall direction of executive branch procurement ranging from the purchase of canned tuna for the military to pencils for government offices. *(1974 Almanac p. 669)*

HR 2293 was passed by the House June 1 by voice vote, and passed with amendments by the Senate Nov. 15. The House agreed to the Senate amendments Nov. 17, clearing the measure for the president.

Provisions

As cleared, HR 2293 contained the following major provisions:

● Authorized the OFPP administrator to prescribe government-wide policies, regulations, procedures and contract forms to be followed and used by executive agencies for all their procurement activities.

● Authorized the OFPP administrator, with the concurrence of the director of OMB, to veto or rescind any procurement rule adopted by an executive branch agency if the administrator found it inconsistent with established government-wide procurement policies.

● Authorized development and testing of innovative procurement methods and procedures with the consent of the heads of agencies involving in the pilot programs.

● Required executive agency heads to increase use of competition in procurement activities and to establish clear lines of responsibility for procurement within their agencies.

● Required the OFPP, by Feb. 1, 1984, to study and report to Congress on all procurement actions of the Department of Defense within a one-week period ending Sept. 30, 1983, the final week of fiscal 1983.

● Required the OFPP, by June 1, 1984, to study and report to Congress on Defense Department procurement of spare parts for weapons systems.

● Set the OFPP's annual authorization at $4.5 million.

Legislative History

The House Government Operations Committee approved HR 2293 on May 3. That version of the bill continued the office for three years at $4 million per year and restored the office's authority — dropped by Congress in 1979 — to issue procurement policies and regulations.

As amended by Rep. Frank Horton, R-N.Y., HR 2293 also required the administrator of the OFPP to submit a plan to Congress for testing "innovative" procurement methods and procedures in selected agencies.

The bill was reported May 16 (H Rept 98-146) and passed June 1 under suspension of the rules.

The Senate Governmental Affairs Committee reported its own version of the legislation (S 1001) on Aug. 1 (S Rept 98-214).

Among other things, that version called for a five-year reauthorization at $5 million annually.

Staff of the House and Senate committees worked out a compromise between the two versions, and provisions of that compromise were adopted on the Senate floor Nov. 15 as a substitute for the House-passed language of HR 2293.

In urging passage of the measure, Senate floor manager William S. Cohen, R-Maine, said a stronger OFPP was needed "to resolve agency disputes and turf battles if we are ever to implement significant procurement reforms on a government-wide basis." ∎

Competitive Bidding

The Senate Nov. 11 passed legislation (S 338) aimed at promoting competition for government contracts.

The measure, which was referred jointly to the House Government Operations Committee and House Armed Services Committee on Nov. 16, was designed to make it harder for government agencies to purchase goods and services without competitive bids.

According to the Federal Procurement Data Center, $79.2 billion of the $146.9 billion spent on property and services over $10,000 in fiscal 1982 was negotiated non-competitively.

The Senate Governmental Affairs Committee March 17 unanimously approved S 338, which was formally reported March 23 (S Rept 98-50). It was then referred to the Senate Armed Services Committee, which reported it (S Rept 98-297) June 27.

The legislation was designed to save the government money. The Congressional Budget Office estimated that $1.5 billion per year could be saved with more competitive bidding, said Sen. William S. Cohen, R-Maine, sponsor of the bill.

Exceptions Limited

The heart of the bill reduced from 17 to six the circumstances under which civilian and defense contracts could be issued without soliciting competitive bids. Agencies could no longer justify non-competitive purchases on the often cited grounds that soliciting bids was not "practicable."

Under the bill, a government agency could bypass the competitive bidding process only if:

● The property or service was available from only one source.

● The agency's need was so urgent the government would be seriously injured by a delay.

● It was necessary to award a contract to a particular contractor to maintain essential industrial capability or for national industrial mobilization.

● Federal law required procurement through a specific source such as a minority firm.

● National security was jeopardized by competitive bidding.

● A non-competitive purchase was required by international treaty or agreement.

To facilitate oversight by Congress, S 338 required agencies to maintain a record by fiscal year identifying all sole-source procurements.

To ensure that companies were aware of procurement contract opportunities, the measure required agencies to publish a notice of all prospective contracts in excess of $10,000 in *Commerce Business Daily*. A similar provision was contained in a separate bill (S 272) cleared by Congress Aug. 1. *(Story, p. 587)* ∎

Paperwork Reduction

The House Nov. 7 suspended the rules and by voice vote passed a bill (HR 2718) aimed at decreasing the amount of government paperwork while improving the quality and availability of federally generated information.

The measure, a three-year reauthorization of the Paperwork Reduction Act of 1980, was then referred to the Senate Governmental Affairs Committee, where it remained when Congress adjourned for the year.

As passed by the House, the bill authorized $9 million in fiscal 1984 and $9.5 million in fiscal 1985 and 1986 for the Office of Information and Regulatory Affairs, the part of the Office of Management and Budget (OMB) responsible for carrying out the 1980 law.

Other Provisions

As approved, HR 2718 also:

● Required that the paperwork burden imposed on the public through federal collection of information be reduced 10 percent by Oct. 1, 1984, and another 5 percent by Oct. 1, 1985.

● Amended the Federal Property and Administrative Services Act to combine the existing federal telecommunications fund and automatic data processing fund in a new revolving Information Technology Fund, which agencies could use to buy information technology such as computers.

● Created a separate line item in the OMB budget for information management and paperwork reduction.

● Created a chief statistician within OMB's Office of Information and Regulatory Affairs to help develop uniform government statistical policies.

● Transferred from OMB to the General Services Administration (GSA) the authority to audit the approach adopted by each federal agency to collect, process and distribute information.

● Gave GSA authority to develop and issue principles, standards and guidelines for managing federal information. OMB already had this authority. Under the bill, the two agencies were to share this responsibility.

Background

The Paperwork Reduction Act (PL 96-511) was intended to reduce the burden of lengthy and redundant federal reporting requirements and to make government

agencies more productive, primarily by encouraging the use of modern information technology including computers, electronic mail and electronic funds transfer. *(1980 Almanac p. 528)*

The 1980 law required OMB to reduce the amount of information requested by the government by 25 percent over three years.

OMB told the House Government Operations Committee that paperwork burdens to individuals and businesses had been reduced by 27 percent since the act became law.

But in reports released April 25, the General Accounting Office (GAO) found that only limited progress had been made in developing uniform information policies, promoting more effective use of advanced information technology and overseeing the federal statistics system.

GAO said the major cause of these failures was OMB's decision to assign to the Office of Information and Regulatory Affairs, created to implement the paperwork legislation, the primary responsibility for the Reagan administration's regulatory review program.

Committee Action

The House Government Operations Committee approved HR 2718 on May 3 and formally reported it May 16 (H Rept 98-147).

The measure was ordered reported by voice vote amid charges by committee Chairman Jack Brooks, D-Texas, that OMB had failed to take the lead in adapting modern information technology to government programs, as required under the act.

"It is unfortunate that the administration, despite its recent talk about high technology, does not appear to recognize the enormous benefits that could be achieved by just following the law," said Brooks.

Brooks asserted that the Reagan administration had concentrated too heavily on reviewing regulations rather than on computerizing federal offices.

To ensure that funds appropriated for the office were used to improve government information management rather than for regulatory review, HR 2718 created a separate line item in the budget for information management and paperwork reduction.

The administration opposed this provision and had privately threatened to veto the bill, according to both Republican and Democratic staffers.

Rep. Elliott H. Levitas, D-Ga., warned that creating a separate fund as a practical matter would abolish regulatory reform analysis. But Brooks argued that the bill did not preclude such activity.

"The problem is this legislation is not regulatory reform," said Brooks. "They're using the money [for regulatory reform] and they don't have that authority...." ∎

Federal Debt Collection

Congress completed action Nov. 14 on a bill (S 376 — PL 98-167) to make it easier for federal agencies to contract with private debt collection firms for the collection of debts owed to the federal government.

S 376 amended the Federal Debt Collection Act of 1982 (PL 97-365) to permit federal agencies to pay private debt collection services a percentage of the total amount of debt collected without having an advance appropriation. If a collection contract called for a fixed fee, an advance appropriation would still be required. Contingent-fee contracts had been barred under the 1982 act, but the practice was common in private business. *(1982 Almanac p. 520)*

The non-controversial measure was reported by the Senate Governmental Affairs Committee May 5 (S Rept 98-75) and passed by the Senate by voice vote May 20. The House Judiciary Committee reported the bill without change Nov. 4 (H Rept 98-482), and the House passed it by a 397-3 vote Nov. 14, completing congressional action. *(Vote 461, p. 136-H)* ∎

Earthquake Hazard Reduction

The Senate April 7 by voice vote passed a bill (S 820) reauthorizing the Earthquake Hazards Reduction Act for three years.

The bill, which was reported March 31 by the Senate Commerce Committee (S Rept 98-42), authorized $61 million for four federal agencies in fiscal year 1984 to conduct research and set housing construction standards to prevent or ready the nation for future earthquakes. The administration requested $60.5 million for the program in fiscal year 1984.

The multiagency earthquake reduction act involved the Federal Emergency Management Agency, the U.S. Geological Survey (USGS), the National Bureau of Standards and the National Science Foundation.

Meanwhile, the House Science, Research and Technology Subcommittee of the House Science and Technology Committee April 7 marked up similar legislation (HR 2465) that authorized $67 million for the earthquake program in fiscal 1984. The House panel increased the administration's $29.5 million request for the USGS by $6 million.

The full House Interior Committee reported HR 2465 on May 10 (H Rept 98-99, Pt. I), while the Science Committee reported it May 16 (Pt. II). ∎

Federal Program Catalog

President Reagan Nov. 29 signed into law a bill (HR 2592 — PL 98-169) that transferred to the General Services Administration (GSA) responsibility for annual publication of the catalog of federal domestic assistance programs.

The catalog, previously the responsibility of the Office of Management and Budget (OMB), was the only comprehensive list available of federal financial assistance programs. HR 2592 transferred to GSA only the printing and distribution of the catalog, leaving OMB responsible for collecting the data.

The legislation, which was requested by the Reagan administration, was reported May 12 by the House Government Operations Committee (H Rept 98-112) and passed by the House June 1.

The Senate Governmental Affairs Committee Sept. 1 reported a companion bill (S 1267 — S Rept 98-216), which was passed by the Senate Oct. 27. On Oct. 28, the Senate vitiated that action and passed HR 2592 after amending it to conform with the provisions of S 1267. The House agreed to the Senate amendments on Nov. 17, clearing the bill for the president. ∎

George Hansen Indicted

Rep. George Hansen, R-Idaho, was indicted April 7 by a federal grand jury, which charged him with failing to disclose several of his financial transactions as required by law.

Hansen, a 12-year House veteran, issued a statement proclaiming his innocence and saying the charges were "politically motivated."

The indictment was returned in U.S. District Court for the District of Columbia and contained four counts, one for each of Hansen's financial disclosure statements for 1978, 1979, 1980 and 1981. It alleged that Hansen failed to disclose: $135,000 in personal loans made to him in 1981 by three individuals from southern Virginia; a $61,503.42 personal loan made in 1980 to Hansen and his wife, Connie, in her name, by wealthy Texan Nelson Bunker Hunt; an $87,475 profit made by the Hansens on the purchase and sale of silver futures contracts during a two-day period in 1979, and a $50,000 personal loan made in 1978 to the Hansens by a Dallas bank and guaranteed by Hunt.

Ethics Act

The indictment said Hansen was required to disclose the transactions under the 1978 Ethics in Government Act (PL 95-521). The indictment was the first ever returned under the 1978 law, which provided a penalty of up to five years in prison and a $10,000 fine for each count. *(1978 Almanac p. 835)*

In a written statement April 7, Hansen said, "I am convinced both as a matter of law and as a matter of fact that I am innocent of any wrongdoing of any sort or degree in the conduct of my affairs as a member of the House . . . and that I will be vindicated. I am further convinced that this selective and bogus prosecution is either a product of failed supervision of very young attorneys in the Department of Justice or a product of the politically motivated desire of the Department of Justice to silence my strong dissents and my opposition to federal intrusion into all our lives through uncontrolled taxation policies and enforcement procedures."

This was not the first time Hansen had run afoul of federal financial disclosure laws. In 1975 he pleaded guilty to charges of filing false reports concerning his 1974 House primary. He was initially sentenced to prison but the penalty was suspended after his lawyer argued that Hansen had been stupid but not evil, and the judge agreed. *(1975 Almanac p. 698)*

Hansen Appeals

After the April indictment, Hansen was allowed to appeal to the U.S. Circuit Court of Appeals for the District of Columbia. He argued that the filing required by the 1978 law could not result in criminal prosecution because it was a legislative activity protected by the Constitution's speech and debate clause.

In August, the appeals court rejected Hansen's argument. Hansen appealed further to the U.S. Supreme Court, which also turned him down on Jan. 9, 1984. The Supreme Court's action left intact the lower court ruling, clearing the way for Hansen's trial on the charges in the April 1983 indictment. ∎

Terrorist Bomb Explosion Rocks Capitol

Police tightened security throughout the U.S. Capitol following the Nov. 7 explosion of a bomb just outside the Senate chamber.

The blast caused no injuries but brought the fear of terrorism home to those people who worked at the Capitol.

A group called the "Armed Resistance Unit" claimed responsibility, saying the action was a protest against U.S. military "aggression" in Grenada and Lebanon.

By early 1984, no suspects had been apprehended by police in the case.

Not long before the bombing, some members of Congress had warned of the possibility of a terrorist strike against the Capitol because of political violence overseas and at home. Capitol Police, armed with a new Secret Service study of security problems in the Capitol, had begun to implement extra security measures shortly before the explosion occurred. More elaborate and costly anti-terrorist protective steps were taken after Congress adjourned for the year Nov. 18.

Political violence, and the increased security that followed it, were not new to Congress. The last time the Capitol was bombed, in 1971, lawmakers virtually doubled the size of the Capitol police force (the force currently stood at 1,222) and spent over $4 million on new security equipment.

The Bombing

Shortly before 11 p.m. on Monday, Nov. 7, a powerful bomb exploded in an alcove on the second-floor hallway near the office of Minority Leader Robert C. Byrd, D-W.Va., about 30 feet away from the Senate chamber.

Witnesses outside the building said the blast sounded like "a sonic boom" or "a heavy clap of thunder."

The explosion blew out a wall partition and sent a shower of splintered wood, plaster and brick flying across the hall, shattering the windows of the Republican cloakroom. Furniture and walls in the cloakroom were peppered with the glass and rubble.

The doors to Byrd's office were blown off their hinges, nearby windows were blown out and surrounding walls were pockmarked with fist-sized holes. Major damage was done to arches, walls and the glazed-tile floor near the blast, but there was no structural damage to the building.

Several old and valuable works of art were also heavily damaged by the explosion, Capitol officials said. Glass in two ornate chandeliers was shattered, a grandfather clock that had stood outside the Senate chamber since 1859 was torn and stopped by the blast, and at least six paintings were ripped, shredded or damaged.

Repairs, expected to cost about $1 million, began the next morning.

FBI officials, who investigated the incident in conjunction with the Secret Service, Capitol Police and District of Columbia police, said the bomb was set hours earlier, and apparently consisted of several sticks of dynamite with a pocket watch as a timer.

"It was a high-explosive device with delayed timing," said Theodore M. Gardner, FBI special agent in charge of

the Washington Field Office.

A closed-circuit TV system monitored the hall, and police studied videotapes for clues to who might have set the bomb.

By sheer coincidence, no one was around when the bomb went off. The Senate had gone into session at 9 a.m. and was expected to work late into the night on a military appropriations bill (HR 4185).

However, the bill moved much faster than anticipated, and the Senate adjourned at 7:02 p.m. The Mansfield Room, immediately adjacent to where the bomb exploded, had been crowded with a reception just hours before the blast.

"It was indeed fortunate that the Senate was not in session last night, as had been announced," Majority Leader Howard H. Baker Jr., R-Tenn., said the day after the blast. "Had we been in session at 11 o'clock, undoubtedly there would have been grave injury and perhaps loss of life."

Byrd, the next day, said: "I told my staff yesterday something like this was going to happen . . . . I was sort of anticipating something, especially in light of other occurrences that have taken place around the world recently. I'm just glad we were not here when it did happen."

Sen. Ted Stevens, R-Alaska, predicted just two weeks before the latest bombing occurred that terrorist violence would soon come to Washington. Speaking to reporters Oct. 26 in the Mansfield Room, a few feet from where the bomb later exploded, Stevens said: "It's not too long before we have some of this [violence] at home . . . . It's almost impossible to provide the kind of security you need and still accommodate the public. We've looked at this before, and decided to go with public access."

Despite the damage outside its chamber, the Senate convened early the morning after the blast. "The Senate will not be deterred from its business," Baker said. "We'll do that in the rubble. We'll do that in the mess."

The Suspects

Moments before the bomb went off, a tape-recorded message was telephoned to the news desk of *The Washington Post*, saying the action was being taken by the Armed Resistance Unit in support of "all nations' struggle" against U.S. military aggression in Grenada and Lebanon. A second recorded phone call to the Capitol switchboard also warned that a bomb was about to go off, officials said.

The day after the explosion, National Public Radio received a letter titled "Communique from the Armed Resistance Unit," apparently mailed before the bombing. Part of the letter stated: "We attacked the U.S. government to retaliate against imperialist aggression that has sent the Marines, the CIA, and the Army to invade sovereign nations, to trample and lay waste the lives and rights of the peoples of Grenada, Lebanon, El Salvador, and Nicaragua, to carry out imperialism's need to dominate, oppress, and exploit."

The letter also said the group purposely aimed its attack at American institutions, as opposed to individuals. It called for "Victory to the FMLN/FDR" and support for the Palestine Liberation Organization.

According to FBI officials, FMLN was the Spanish acronym for Farabundo Marti Liberation Front, a group of El Salvador-based leftist guerrillas. FDR, or the Democratic Revolutionary Front, was its political arm.

The FBI believed that the Armed Resistance Unit was also responsible for other 1983 bombing incidents in Wash-

ington at Fort McNair April 26, and at the Navy Yard Aug. 18.

The Response

Initial hearings into Capitol security were held after the bombing but full-scale hearings were put off until 1984 because of the Nov. 18 adjournment.

Jurisdiction over the Capitol and the surrounding grounds was held by the Senate Committee on Rules and Administration and the House Committee on House Administration. Funding for any new measures designed to improve security at the Capitol would be handled by the House and Senate Appropriations subcommittees on the legislative branch, which, at the time, were drawing up their budgets for the next fiscal year.

Lawmakers immediately decried the bombing. Byrd called it "an offense against all the people." Sen. Jeremiah Denton, R-Ala., chairman of the Senate Judiciary Subcommittee on Security and Terrorism, said the blast was "an attack that strikes at the heart of our constitutional democracy."

Denton was especially critical of the news media for not adequately covering his subcommittee's earlier hearings and reports.

"It takes incidents such as the attack on our Marines in Lebanon or a bomb going off in the Capitol to obtain the attention that could have and should have been accorded to the problem earlier," Denton said at a news conference.

Other officials described the conflict of security vs. access — keeping governmental buildings open to the people who needed to use them.

"I think a free society such as ours owes a degree of access of the public to the public buildings," said House Majority Leader Jim Wright, D-Texas. "This is not our building. It's the building of the people of the United States."

"God forbid anyone should lose their life visiting the Capitol," said Senate Sergeant-at-Arms Larry E. Smith. But, he added, "it is impossible to make any building entirely secure unless you close it down."

Police said the Capitol complex was difficult to defend, because of the size of the buildings, their numerous entrances and interconnecting underground tunnel system, and the vast number of people who worked in or visited the Capitol every day.

After the bombing, police sealed off the bomb-damaged area and greatly increased the number of guards in the building itself — although security at some other parts of the Capitol complex proved sporadic. A reporter entering the Cannon House Office Building the morning after the blast found a main door completely unguarded by the Capitol Police. She entered without the customary search of visitors' briefcases and purses.

Numerous bomb threats were phoned in to police during the day following the explosion, prompting a brief evacuation of the House restaurant and temporary closing of the nearby Metro subway station. Security was beefed up at federal and local government buildings, courthouses, embassies and police stations.

In the Capitol building itself, several new steps were taken. Visitors were admitted through only four or six of the Capitol's doors (about 10 had been in use), and metal detectors were to screen all visitors who came through (only gallery visitors were screened before).

Lobbyists and tourists no longer were allowed in the hallways just outside the House and Senate chambers. Car

traffic and parking on the East Front lot was restricted, and delivery trucks were searched. Officials planned to require identification badges to be worn by staff, visitors and press in the Capitol in 1984.

Among the security proposals under study were a new generation of screening devices that could pick up non-metallic explosives; segregated entrances for reporters, staff and the public; computerized press and staff passes; and a transparent plastic shield between visitors' galleries and the House and Senate floors. A 1973 study concluded bulletproof glass was impractical, partly because of its weight. Plastic was considerably lighter, but either material would be expensive.

Even before the bombing, concern about Capitol security had been heightened by terrorist bombings overseas and by the Oct. 18 arrest of a tourist in the House visitors' gallery who threatened to blow up the building with a homemade bomb he had concealed under his clothes.

Officials said that device failed to set off metal detectors because it consisted of two plastic soda bottles filled with a black powder and flammable liquid, wrapped in stone, ceramic and small metal fragments.

Capitol police said the man, Israel Rabinowits, a 22-year-old Israeli, tried to explode the device, but its battery-powered detonator was not rigged properly. The visitors' gallery was packed at the time, and lawmakers were crowding onto the House floor for a vote. He was charged with making threats of bodily harm.

After the incident, police readjusted their metal detectors and installed more sensitive bomb-detection gear. ∎

'Debategate' Investigated

A House subcommittee spent the second half of 1983 investigating charges that the 1980 presidential campaign of Ronald Reagan had received pilfered briefing material from the Carter White House before a Carter-Reagan election debate.

The investigation, briefly matched by one at the Justice Department, was quickly dubbed "Debategate."

The House Post Office and Civil Service Subcommittee on Human Resources, a relatively obscure panel with oversight over the 1978 Ethics in Government Act (PL 95-521), interviewed many officials connected with both campaigns.

All that was produced in 1983, however, were charges and allegations. The committee did not issue a report. Public hearings had been scheduled for January 1984, but early that month, Chairman Donald J. Albosta, D-Mich., canceled them, saying he wanted to avoid "partisan bickering and a media extravaganza" in a presidential election year.

The controversy arose in June 1983, triggered by an account by David A. Stockman, director of the Office of Management and Budget, of the use of Carter documents to help prepare Reagan for the debate. Stockman, a Republican member of the House from 1977 to 1981, worked for Reagan's election. The Stockman account appeared as a passage in a book called *Gambling with History*, written by Time Magazine correspondent Laurence I. Barrett.

An Elkhart, Ind., newspaper quoted Stockman as saying on Oct. 28, 1980, the day of the debate, that he had used "a pilfered copy" of a Carter briefing book in preparing Reagan.

Among the revelations about the flap that came to light in 1983 was the contention by James A. Baker III, Reagan's White House chief of staff, that he had received a copy of the Carter briefing book during the campaign from William J. Casey, CIA director who was manager of Reagan's 1980 campaign. Casey adamantly denied the Baker contention, however.

House Republicans opposed the Albosta investigation, concerned that it would expose politically embarrassing internal fights in the Reagan administration. And House Democratic leaders gave Albosta little encouragement, fearing that Reagan might turn to his advantage what could be considered a partisan investigation.

At a June 28 news conference, Reagan denied ever having seen the Carter briefing materials. "I never knew until you people made it public in the press a few days ago that there ever had been such material in possession of any people in our campaign organization," Reagan said. "It seems strange to me that, since I was the debater, no one on our side ever mentioned anything of this kind." ∎

Federal Election Commission

The House passed and a Senate committee reported a $10.8 million fiscal 1984 authorization bill (HR 2621) for the Federal Election Commission (FEC), but the bill went no further in 1983.

The House action came April 26 by voice vote, just four days after the bill was reported by the House Administration Committee (H Rept 98-71).

The Senate Committee on Rules and Administration approved HR 2621 on May 12 and formally reported it May 16 (S Rept 98-102).

Sen. Jesse Helms, R-N.C., a member of the Rules Committee, said he would offer a controversial floor amendment to prohibit unions from using their members' dues for political contributions. But the bill did not reach the Senate floor in 1983.

It was the third year in a row that the House passed an FEC authorization bill only to see the measure stall in the Senate. The commission, a frequent target of congressional attack, had not been officially authorized since fiscal 1981. *(1980 Almanac p. 545)*

Fiscal 1984 funding for the FEC was included in the second continuing appropriations resolution (H J Res 413 — PL 98-151). *(Story, p. 528)* ∎

Senate Day Care Approved

A day-care center for the children of Senate employees was authorized by the Senate Nov. 14, along with $20,000 in start-up costs for the program.

The Senate voted 50-31 to approve a resolution (S Res 269) establishing the child care center. The money came from Senate contingency funds. *(Vote 351, p. 57-S)*

The center, which was scheduled to open in January 1984 in a Senate annex, eventually would be self-supporting. The $20,000 was to be used to pay a director for two months and to purchase equipment and supplies.

Charles McC. Mathias Jr., R-Md., chairman of the Senate Rules and Administration Committee, said, "I believe this modest investment will pay substantial benefits to the Senate in the form of increased employee morale, greater work force efficiency, and in the inestimable value of the Senate's example to other employers."

Mack Mattingly, R-Ga., who voted against the resolution, said the day-care proposal was "purely frivolous."

And Jim Sasser, D-Tenn., another opponent, argued that the proposal "could easily be construed as an unnecessary benefit to a distinguished elite."

Sasser said, "Is it fair that the children of Senate employees, including senators, should be afforded the luxury of day care when, since 1982, 32 states have cut funding for child care? I think not."

The idea of a work-site day-care center came from a group of Senate employees. They surveyed Senate workers and found that parents of more than 130 preschoolers were interested in such a program.

The center was open to all Senate employees, from secretaries, committee lawyers and cafeteria workers to senators. The center initially planned to accept 40 to 60 children, and parents would pay a weekly or monthly fee. The House did not have a day-care program of its own. ▪

Historical Publications

A five-year reauthorization bill (HR 2196 — PL 98-189) for the National Historical Publications and Records Commission was cleared by Congress Nov. 18.

Final action came when the House accepted Senate amendments increasing the annual authorization levels for the commission. As reported May 16 by the House Government Operations Committee (H Rept 98-129) and passed by the House June 1, the measure had authorized $3 million annually for fiscal 1984-88.

As cleared, however, the bill gave the commission, a part of the National Archives, authority to spend $4 million in each of fiscal years 1984 and 1985, and $5 million annually in fiscal years 1986-88.

The commission encouraged government and private institutions to collect, preserve, edit and publish the papers of outstanding American citizens and other historic documents. The papers of George Washington, William Penn, Robert Morris, Thomas Jefferson, and others were among collections supported by the commission.

Since taking office, the Reagan administration had recommended eliminating funds for the program, but Congress refused to go along.

The last authorization for the commission had cleared Congress in 1979, but the commission continued to operate on $2.5 million appropriated in fiscal 1982 and $3 million for fiscal 1983. ▪

Drug Investigation Ended

The House ethics committee ended its 16-month investigation into Capitol drug use with a Nov. 17 report that said there was insufficient evidence to conclude allegations of drug use by two current members of the House were true.

The committee noted allegations against Reps. Ronald V. Dellums, D-Calif., and Charles Wilson, D-Texas, but found the evidence too skimpy to seek House action against them.

The Justice Department had announced July 27 that it had found insufficient evidence to prosecute Dellums, Wilson or former Rep. Barry M. Goldwater Jr., R-Calif. (1969-83), on cocaine charges. (1969-83)

All three men maintained their innocence of the allegations.

The Nov. 17 report (H Rept 98-559) of the ethics committee said the panel had found "substantial evidence" that three former representatives either purchased or used cocaine or marijuana while they served in the House between 1978 and 1982.

However, the committee did not name the three and, citing past House policy, did not pursue an investigation of former members.

Allegations of drug use by members and staff surfaced during the summer of 1982 about the same time as charges of sexual misconduct involving members and teenage pages. The ethics committee investigated both sets of allegations simultaneously. It hired Joseph A. Califano Jr., secretary of health, education and welfare under President Carter, as its chief investigator. *(1982 Almanac p. 528)*

The committee's findings on the page scandal led to the censure of Reps. Gerry E. Studds, D-Mass., and Daniel B. Crane, R-Ill. *(Story, p. 580)*

The investigation also resulted in the resignations of three House employees.

● James C. Howarth, former chief of Democratic House pages, resigned after the committee issued a report in November finding Howarth had a sexual relationship in 1980 with a 17-year-old female page. The committee cleared Howarth of drug charges.

● Robert T. Yesh, former Democratic assistant cloakroom manager, resigned and negotiated a plea bargain with the Justice Department after the committee initiated an inquiry in December 1982. Yesh, the committee found, had shared drugs with pages. He testified that he personally supplied cocaine and marijuana to Dellums and a member of Dellums' staff.

● James M. Beattie, who worked in the House doorkeeper's office, was identified by Yesh as having sold narcotics. Beattie resigned and pleaded guilty to two federal misdemeanor offenses.

The committee found that another employee, who first worked for the doorkeeper and then on a member's personal staff, also had dealt in drugs with Yesh and Beattie and a Capitol tour guide. That employee was identified only as "Employee A" by the committee, which said the member had fired him.

The ethics committee recommended:

● The House leadership should assure that the capacity existed — either within the Capitol Police or another law enforcement agency — to carry out criminal investigations, including drug investigations, at the Capitol.

● The House should establish employee assistance programs to provide counseling and guidance to employees who had drug or alcohol problems.

● The House should establish fair and effective procedures for disciplining and discharging employees accused of misconduct. ▪

Senate TV Bill Fails Again

For the third time in three years, Senate Majority Leader Howard H. Baker Jr.'s plan to televise the Senate remained a glimmer in the Tennessee Republican's eye.

Although the Senate Rules and Administration Committee reported a resolution to authorize television broadcasting of Senate proceedings, the measure faced adamant opposition and the full Senate did not even take the resolution up in 1983.

By a 5-3 vote June 15, the panel ordered reported without recommendation a broadcast measure (S Res 66)

that was substantially identical to one it approved in July 1982. S Res 66 provided continuous, gavel-to-gavel television and radio coverage of Senate proceedings. It required no Senate rules changes, and permitted the camera to be focused only on the senator who was recognized to speak.

In addition, it barred political or commercial use of tapes but provided them free to news organizations. Six cameras would have been installed, and the resolution had authorized $3.5 million to pay for coverage.

Opposition to the concept was strong, however. To ensure that the resolution would be cleared for floor debate, chief backer Baker omitted the word "favorably" in moving to report the measure.

One senator who agreed to send the measure to the full Senate, Mark O. Hatfield, R-Ore., indicated he would vote against it when it reached the floor. Hatfield said full television coverage might "reduce our stature."

One of the leading critics of a televised Senate, Wendell H. Ford, D-Ky., the ranking Democrat on the Rules Committee, did not attend the June 15 markup, and some Democrats asked to delay consideration of the resolution so Ford could offer a substitute. But, citing time pressures, Rules Chairman Charles McC. Mathias Jr., R-Md., went ahead with the markup, adding that Ford could offer his amendment on the floor.

Ford's substitute, similar to ones he offered in 1981 and 1982, would allow only radio, not television, coverage. Ford had argued that radio broadcasting would be considerably less expensive, and would reach more homes than television. His amendment failed on a 5-7 party-line vote in committee in 1981 and 1982.

When Baker became majority leader at the start of the 97th Congress, he made televising the Senate his No. 1 priority. The House began televising its proceedings in 1979, and Baker said he wanted "an extension electronically of the public gallery."

He convinced the Rules Committee to report a television resolution in August 1981, but the measure did not reach the floor until the following year. *(1981 Almanac p. 391)*

During 1982 floor consideration, Russell B. Long, D-La., led the opposition to the resolution. Arguing that televising the Senate would be "a very great mistake and a net minus to the Senate," Long filibustered against the measure. A cloture vote to cut off the filibuster failed 47-51, 13 votes short of the 60 necessary to limit debate.

Before the Senate took a second cloture vote, Baker agreed to a compromise with Senate Democrats that sent the proposal back to the Rules Committee for rewriting.

Subsequently, the Rules Committee agreed to report a second resolution, but that measure was never brought up on the floor. *(1982 Almanac p. 540)*

Reintroducing the proposal at the start of the 98th Congress, Mathias and Baker hoped to bring the issue to the floor relatively quickly. However, Democrats on the Rules panel forced delays.

In April, two former senators endorsed a more-limited televising of the Senate than that sought by Baker. James B. Pearson, R-Kan. (1962-78), and Abraham Ribicoff, D-Conn. (1963-81), suggested limited broadcasting in their report on Senate rules changes. However, their report did little more than gather dust in 1983.

After the television resolution was reported by Rules and Administration in June, Baker said it would be at least Labor Day before the Senate debated it. Throughout the fall, he kept listing it on his agenda of things the Senate would do, although it never came up. ∎

Democrats Make Changes in House Rules

After dropping the most controversial of several proposed changes in House rules, Democrats forced a package of changes through the House Jan. 3 on a party-line vote.

Democratic leaders claimed the changes were needed to streamline the legislative process, avoiding unnecessary votes and amendments.

Republican leaders said the changes trampled on the rights of the minority.

The most contentious of the changes that were approved was one that would make it harder for members to offer "riders" to appropriations bills.

Such amendments to limit government actions had become popular in recent years. Riders on school busing and abortion, for example, had been attached to appropriations bills by conservatives for the past several years.

In addition to restricting appropriations riders, the rules changes gave the Democratic leadership the power to avoid what it viewed as "nuisance" votes on approving the previous day's *Journal* or resolving into the Committee of the Whole House for consideration of a bill.

The rules package was approved by voice vote after a key procedural vote was won by Democrats, 249-156. Only two Democrats — Phil Gramm of Texas and Larry P. McDonald of Georgia — voted against the leadership. *(Vote 2, p. 2-H)*

(Later on Jan. 3, the leadership threw Gramm off the House Budget Committee. Two days later he resigned his seat and announced that he would seek re-election as a Republican, which he did successfully. McDonald, an ultra-conservative, died Sept. 1 in the Soviet downing of a Korean airliner.)

An effort by Republicans to have the change on riders deleted was defeated on a similar party-line vote, 156-250. *(Vote 3, p. 2-H)*

The rules changes had been agreed to by House Democrats in December 1982 after a task force worked for several months to write the proposals.

As approved by the Democratic Caucus in December, the package also included a change increasing the number of members required to gain House consideration of a constitutional amendment if the Judiciary Committee refused to report it out.

House rules required that to pull a constitutional amendment out of the Judiciary Committee, a majority of the House must sign a discharge petition. The Democrats proposed to increase the number to two-thirds, which was the portion of the House that would have to vote for such an amendment for it to get further consideration in the Senate or the states.

The proposed change drew opposition from a number of Democrats, both liberal and conservative, from Republicans and from a host of interest groups seeking constitutional amendments.

At a brief meeting of the Democratic Caucus Jan. 3, before the full House met, Democrats agreed not to offer the two-thirds requirement. Leadership aides said that

while the Democrats probably had the votes to approve the change, the leadership did not want to begin the year with a fight among Democrats over the issue.

The leadership also managed to avoid a split among Democrats over the rules change on appropriations riders. John B. Breaux, D-La., had called the change a "gag rule" after it was approved by the caucus and said he would fight it when the House took it up Jan. 3.

But members of the leadership pressured Breaux to back off, reminding him that he was seeking a coveted slot on the Budget Committee and suggesting that he could have trouble even getting nominated for the position if he fought the rules change.

Breaux spoke against the changes Jan. 3 but voted with the Democratic leadership for the package. Later that day, Budget Committee assignments were handed out; Breaux did not get one.

During the brief floor debate, House Majority Leader Jim Wright, D-Texas, called the package of changes "rather modest."

But Minority Leader Robert H. Michel, R-Ill., said, "This further concentration of power in the hands of the few is a travesty and I doubt that it will stop here. It will continue until all of our rights, all of our responsibilities, all of our prerogatives are gone, wiped away by the hand of authoritarian government."

Minority Whip Trent Lott, R-Miss., was even more emphatic, calling the changes "the paranoidal palpitations of an imperiled party."

Lott said the change restricting riders on appropriations bills would hurt Democrats as well as Republicans. He noted that riders had been used by liberals attempting to end the war in Southeast Asia, to limit foreign aid to various countries and to kill massive public works projects, such as the Clinch River breeder reactor.

Wright argued that the proper place for legislative limitations was on authorization bills, not on appropriations measures. He said the use of riders had grown from only one being adopted in 1970 to 50 in 1980.

Wright said the change would make it more difficult to offer a rider, but not impossible. Indeed, a number of riders were successfully attached to appropriations bills in 1983.

The package of rules changes approved Jan. 3 by the House included:

Legislative Riders. Under the new rule, the only way a rider could be offered to an appropriations bill was for the House to reject a motion to rise out of the Committee of the Whole after all other work on the bill had been completed. If that motion was defeated, one rider could then be offered. The same process would have to occur again before any subsequent riders could be considered.

The Democratic leadership could still get riders it wanted on appropriations bills in one of two additional ways. The Rules Committee, which was an arm of the Speaker, could allow specific riders to be offered. Or riders could be included in a bill by the Appropriations Committee, which also was usually responsive to the leadership.

'Nuisance' Votes. Two changes were designed to avoid what many members felt were "nuisance" votes on minor procedural issues.

One change allowed the Speaker to resolve the House into the Committee of the Whole without a vote.

In the past, members frequently sought a time-consuming, roll-call vote on forming the Committee of the Whole, which was used to debate and amend bills before voting on final passage.

The other change gave the Speaker authority to postpone for up to two legislative days a vote on approval of the previous day's *Journal*, the record of House proceedings.

Previously, Republicans had often forced votes on both procedures to get a quorum of members to the House floor.

Michel criticized the rules changes, saying they would would encourage members not to come to the House floor to listen to debate on bills.

"Mr. Speaker," Michel said, "you are converting this body of representatives into robots in a glass-covered dome, who come only when they are called, speak only when they are told and cast their votes only when it is unavoidable.

"It is more than tradition we are discarding. It is the fabric, character and personality of an institution that for almost 200 years has stood as a symbol of freedom, open deliberation, and true representative democracy worldwide," Michel said.

Resolutions of Inquiry. Another rules change doubled the time a committee had to consider resolutions of inquiry, which often were investigations of executive branch departments.

Previously, when such a resolution was referred to a committee, the panel had seven legislative days to consider it. As a result of the change, committees had 14 legislative days for such inquiries.

Secret Hearings. Another change made it easier for three committees — Armed Services, Appropriations and Intelligence — to close hearings to the public.

All House committees were permitted to publicly vote to hold a closed hearing on the day the vote was taken and one additional day. The rules change allowed these three committees to close meetings for up to five additional days after the vote, for a total of six days of closed hearings.

Tax Jurisdiction. Another change tightened the control of the Ways and Means Committee over bills dealing with taxes or tariffs. Although Ways and Means was supposed to have exclusive jurisdiction, other committees occasionally had reported bills dealing with taxes or trade restrictions.

Under the new rule, Ways and Means could use a point of order to block any bill containing a tax or tariff provision from coming to the House floor unless the provision was reported by Ways and Means. The committee also could use a point of order to block House consideration of Senate amendments to a House bill if those amendments contained tax or tariff matters that had not been approved by Ways and Means.

Party Switches. Continued assignment to House committees was made contingent upon members being members of their party caucus. The change was made along with a change in the rules of the Democratic Caucus in December 1982 to throw a member out of the caucus if he or she switched parties.

Had these new rules been in effect during the 97th Congress, when Eugene V. Atkinson, D-Pa., switched to become a Republican, he would have lost his committee assignments. As it was, Atkinson continued to hold his Democratic committee assignments. He was defeated for re-election in November 1982.

Office Management. Another change directed the clerk of the House to manage the office of a member who died, resigned or was expelled from the House.

There was no provision covering such situations in the existing House rules. ∎

Changes in Senate Rules Recommended

Noting the continuing problems of the Senate in considering legislation, two former members April 5 recommended sweeping changes in the way that chamber conducted its business.

The recommendations included limits on debate, rules to ensure attendance, election of a permanent presiding officer, elimination of several committees and all staffed subcommittees, and changes in the congressional budget process.

The suggestions, however, did little more than gather dust for the remainder of 1983, and the Senate continued to have problems acting on bills.

Former Sens. James B. Pearson, R-Kan. (1962-78), and Abraham Ribicoff, D-Conn. (1963-81), authors of the report, acknowledged that their recommendations could be considered "quite radical." But they said the basic nature of the Senate would not be changed, even though "these recommendations do represent a dramatic change in the daily life of the Senate and in how the Senate and its committee system work."

The Senate Committee on Rules and Administration held brief hearings on the recommendations in May.

The report came at a time when the Senate was floundering in a sea of filibusters and dilatory maneuvering, frustrating its members and leaders. Wendell H. Ford, Ky., ranking Rules Committee Democrat, said it "goes directly to the heart of the problems we now are experiencing and lays out options that justify consideration, if we are serious about improving the operation of the Senate."

Once considered a collegial institution, since mid-1982 the Senate sometimes had dissolved into disarray, with Majority Leader Howard H. Baker Jr., R-Tenn., often unable to prevent small groups of senators from using the intricate Senate rules to block major pieces of legislation.

Filibusters had been used by both conservatives and liberals. In December 1982, a handful of conservatives tied the Senate up for weeks, trying unsuccessfully to block passage of an increase in the federal gasoline tax. Earlier that fall, liberal and moderate senators filibustered successfully to block approval of social policy amendments, including one to ban abortion.

In the spring of 1983, Baker was frustrated when some senators insisted on offering an amendment to repeal a tax withholding law, first to a jobs bill and then to the Social Security bill. *(Story, p. 219)*

Ford said Senate rules designed to guarantee deliberative debate "have been distorted and exploited, putting serious strains on floor procedures." Even the Senate chaplain noted the strain in his prayer opening the April 5 session. The Rev. Richard C. Halverson asked God to "prevent the Senate from being like Humpty Dumpty. Keep it from being so fractured and fragmented that no one will be able to put it together again."

Recommendations

The Senate passed a resolution (S Res 392) in the spring of 1982 calling for a study of its operations. Pearson and Ribicoff were appointed to do the study, assisted by senior Senate staffers.

Most of their report focused on changes in the way floor debate was handled. A smaller portion dealt with changes in the committee system.

Presiding Officer. The report called for election of a senator as the Senate's permanent presiding officer.

Although the Constitution named the vice president as the presiding officer, in practice he rarely attended Senate sessions. The Senate's president pro tem, Strom Thurmond, R-S.C., also rarely presided, leaving the chore to a rotating cadre of junior members, usually inexperienced in Senate procedures. This had not established a presiding officer who was "sufficiently impressive that the membership gives proper deference to the chair's control and direction of the Senate," the report said.

The elected presiding officer should be given extra compensation and the important power to determine on his own whether a quorum was present, and, if not, whether to adjourn or recess the Senate, the report said. Now, the roll was called to determine a quorum, a procedure often used to delay debate.

Set Agenda. The report recommended that at the beginning of each year the Senate set an agenda of subjects to be considered during that session. Only by a two-thirds vote could issues not on this agenda be considered. Senate committees could not report bills that did not fall within the scope of the agenda.

Limit Controversy. The rules should be changed to prohibit Senate consideration of a particular controversial issue more than once a year, the report said. In recent years, some issues, such as abortion, had surfaced again and again, wasting the time of the Senate, it said.

Eliminate "Holds." Senators often blocked debate on bills by registering "holds" on the bills with Senate leaders. Pearson and Ribicoff recommended doing away with the practice by creating a calendar committee for each party to decide which bills could be handled without objection and which would require extensive debate.

Limits on Debate. The report recommended limiting to an hour the debate on a motion for the Senate to consider a bill. In recent years, senators had filibustered these motions and then engaged in another filibuster when the bill was actually debated.

To reduce debating time, the report suggested barring senators from reading speeches. Written speeches would be inserted in the record and senators would be allowed to speak only extemporaneously or from notes.

Cloture Rule. Although filibusters could be stopped by a cloture vote by at least 60 senators, senators frequently had engaged in further delay by proposing numerous amendments after cloture had been invoked. The report recommended that senators be permitted to offer only two amendments once cloture was invoked and that only one vote be allowed on an amendment after cloture, rather than allowing an amendment to be voted on in sections.

Television. Baker had been trying unsuccessfully for more than two years to convince his colleagues to allow the televising of all Senate floor debate. The report recommended that debate on "major issues confronting the country" — but not the daily business of the Senate — be televised. *(Story, p. 595)*

Budget Process. The report suggested an overhaul of the congressional budget process, including eliminating the Budget committees and considering two-year appropriations bills, rather than annual bills.

Committee Changes

The recommendations on Senate committees were even more controversial than the proposed changes in floor procedures.

The report recommended greatly contracting the committee system, and thus shrinking or eliminating the power base of many senators.

"Senators now have too many committee assignments to do their work successfully," the report said. It recommended cutting the number of committees from 20 to 12 or 13 and eliminating all joint committees.

The report suggested scrapping the Intelligence, Budget, Veterans' Affairs, Small Business, Aging, Ethics and Indian Affairs committees. The remaining committees would be divided into three groups. Senators could serve on only three committees, one from each group; they currently served on as many as five committees.

Traditionally, the primary power base for many senators had been the chairmanship of subcommittees and the staff that went with those panels. The report said this had resulted in extreme specialization. To avoid that, it recommended prohibiting all staffed subcommittees. Subcommittees could only hold hearings and compile data but not report legislation. The report said the restriction of subcommittees would cut the Senate's workload and give members more opportunity to study legislative proposals. ∎

Veterans' Emergency Job Training Approved

Congress Aug. 3 cleared an "emergency" veterans' job training bill (HR 2355) authorizing a two-year, $300 million program to pay employers to hire and train long-term unemployed Vietnam-era and Korean War veterans.

Although the administration had strongly opposed the measure, President Reagan signed it into law Aug. 15 (PL 98-77).

The bill was prompted by congressional concern over unemployment rates that remained high among veterans despite a dip in the national jobless rate.

Unemployment among veterans hit its highest level since World War II in February, and although it declined after that, the unemployment rate for veterans between 25 and 29 was still at 12.3 percent in July.

In June, 365,000 Vietnam-era veterans between the ages of 25 and 44 had been unemployed for 15 weeks or longer, Marvin Leath, D-Texas, told the House Aug. 2.

It was that group that HR 2355 originally was designed to serve, although it subsequently was broadened to include Korean War veterans.

The measure was supported by the American Legion, Disabled American Veterans, Amvets, Paralyzed Veterans of America, Vietnam Veterans of America and Veterans of Foreign Wars.

While acknowledging that Vietnam-era veterans faced serious unemployment problems, the administration opposed the legislation throughout its consideration in Congress on grounds that the economy was improving and would yield additional job opportunities for veterans.

Provisions

As signed into law, PL 98-77:

● Established a new emergency veterans' job training program providing subsidies to employers to hire and train eligible unemployed veterans.

● Authorized $150 million in each of fiscal years 1984 and 1985 for the program.

● Limited eligibility for the program to veterans who served in the active military, naval or air service for at least 180 days during the Korean conflict or the Vietnam era or suffered a service-connected disability during those years. To receive the aid, a veteran must be jobless and must have been unemployed for at least 15 of the 20 weeks immediately preceding his application for the program.

● Limited payments to employers who hire and train eligible veterans to 50 percent of the veteran's starting salary, up to a maximum of $10,000. The training could last up to nine months for most veterans. The subsidy for disabled veterans could continue for 15 months.

● Provided that the training program in most cases must last for at least six months for occupations in growth industries, for jobs requiring new technological skills or in fields for which jobs outnumber the labor supply.

● Required employers to certify that after completion of the job training program, the veteran would be hired in a permanent, stable job for which he was trained; also required employers to certify that training would not be offered to a veteran who was already qualified for the job.

● Stipulated that employers could not lay off or fire other workers in order to participate in the new program.

● Allowed employers to contract with an educational institution to provide job training.

● Expanded GI Bill eligibility for Vietnam-era veterans to enable them to pursue associate degree programs that are predominantly vocational; barred veterans from receiving job training benefits under both the new program and other federal programs.

● Authorized the Veterans Administration and the Labor Department to jointly administer the program, but designated the VA as the lead agency.

● Provided that eligible veterans could enroll in the program between Oct. 1, 1983, and Sept. 30, 1985; payments would continue through Sept. 30, 1986.

Legislative History

HR 2355 was reported by the House Veterans' Affairs Committee May 13 (H Rept 98-116) and passed the House June 7, 407-10, under suspension of the rules. The suspension procedure bars floor amendments and requires a two-thirds majority for passage. *(Vote 163, p. 52-H)*

As passed by the House, the bill authorized $325 million for a 27-month program covering only Vietnam-era veterans (those who served between Aug. 5, 1964, and May 7, 1975). It provided two forms of aid: subsidies to employers covering up to half of a veteran's salary during on-the-job training, or payments of up to $500 a month to veterans for tuition and fees for vocational education courses.

The Senate version of the bill was reported by the Veterans' Affairs Committee May 19 (S 1033 — S Rept 98-132) and passed the Senate by voice vote June 15. It made all unemployed wartime veterans, from World War II through the Vietnam conflict, eligible for job training. It authorized a one-year, $150 million program covering on-the-job training only, not vocational education.

The final compromise, worked out informally by the House and Senate Veterans' Affairs committees, authorized $150 million a year for two years for the program. It limited eligibility to Vietnam-era and Korean War veterans who served at least 180 days or had a service-connected disability. The House provision authorizing benefits for vocational education was dropped, but employers were allowed to conduct their job training programs at vocational schools if they wished.

The House passed the final version of the bill Aug. 2, the Senate the following day, both by voice vote.

Alan Cranston, Calif., ranking Democrat on the Senate Veterans' Affairs Committee, warned that "a presidential veto would be futile in light of the overwhelming, bipartisan support for this measure in both houses." ∎

Martin Luther King Holiday

Brushing aside earlier opposition, President Reagan Nov. 2 signed into law a bill (HR 3706 — PL 98-144) declaring the third Monday in January, beginning in 1986, a legal public holiday honoring the late civil rights leader, the Rev. Dr. Martin Luther King Jr.

Enactment of the legislation marked a major victory for civil rights groups, which had pushed for a holiday honoring King since his assassination in 1968.

It also marked a major defeat for Sen. Jesse Helms, R-N.C., who led the sometimes virulent opposition to the measure in the Senate. Helms questioned whether King was worthy of the recognition and objected to the cost of another public holiday.

King's birthday would become the 10th legal holiday for federal employees.

The cost of another holiday was the principal objection raised in the House. The administration also opposed the measure on grounds that King could be remembered more inexpensively without requiring another paid holiday for federal workers. Supporters of the bill, however, cited estimates of the government's cost as only about $18 million in 1986 and insisted that the symbolic value of honoring King was of greater importance.

The House passed the bill Aug. 2 by a vote of 338-90. The Senate passed it Oct. 19 by a 78-22 vote.

On the day of Senate passage, Reagan told a nationally televised press conference: "Since they seem bent on making it a national holiday, I believe the symbolism of that day is important enough that I would — I'll sign that legislation when it reaches my desk."

Background

Bills to honor King's Jan. 15 birthday had been introduced repeatedly since he was assassinated in Memphis, Tenn., on April 4, 1968.

The House came close to passing one of them in November 1979. Members, under a procedure known as suspension of the rules, which bars amendments and requires a two-thirds majority for approval, voted 252-133 for a bill designating Jan. 15 a national holiday. The vote split along party lines and fell four votes short of the necessary two-thirds majority. *(1979 Almanac p. 584)*

Backers brought the bill back to the floor later that year under an open rule. Members then adopted an amendment that called for celebrating King's birthday on the third Monday in January. Hoping to counter arguments that another federal holiday was too expensive, proponents said designating a Monday would be less costly because employers would not have to shut down in the middle of the week and absenteeism was less before and after Monday holidays.

However, the House subsequently adopted an amendment that called for honoring King on the third Sunday in January and barred the government from providing paid leave for the day, the normal procedure when federal holidays fell on weekends. In the end, supporters withdrew the bill.

House Action

Committee. The House Post Office and Civil Service Committee July 26 reported HR 3345 (H Rept 98-314) to designate the third Monday in January as a federal holiday honoring King's memory.

The bill had 16 cosponsors. Because a number of other members wanted to be listed as original sponsors of the legislation, an identical bill, HR 3706, with 109 cosponsors, was introduced July 29.

Floor. The House passed HR 3706 Aug. 2 by a vote of 338-90, under suspension of the rules. *(Vote 289, p. 86-H)*

Democrats voted heavily for the measure; only one Northern and 12 Southern Democrats voted against it. Republicans were sharply divided, voting 89-77 for it.

Among the bill's supporters were 35 members (26 of them Republicans) who had voted against the 1979 bill.

One who changed his position was Jack F. Kemp, R-N.Y. He did so, he said, because "I really think that the American Revolution will not be complete until we commemorate the civil rights revolution and guarantee those basic declarations of human rights for all Americans and remove those barriers that stand in the way of people being what they were meant to be." Kemp said he wanted the Republican Party to stand for an end to social segregation. "If we turn our backs," he said, "we are not going to be the party of human dignity we want as Republicans to be known for."

Floor manager Katie Hall, D-Ind., said after the vote, "Men and women of good will on both sides of the aisle showed this was a human concern, not a political or racial issue." She also credited the strong support of the Democratic leadership in getting the bill through.

Floor Debate

Backers of the bill argued that a paid federal holiday would give deserved recognition to King and the civil rights movement he led. Opponents maintained the nation did not need a 10th federal holiday and that the measure would be too costly.

William E. Dannemeyer, R-Calif., who led the opposition, argued that it would cost taxpayers $225 million a year in lost productivity in the federal work force and three times that much in the private sector.

But Parren J. Mitchell, D-Md., countered angrily: "What do you mean 'cost'? What was the cost of keeping us blacks where we were?"

Supporters cited a Congressional Budget Office estimate that the bill would cost the government only about $18 million in 1986, the first year the holiday would be in effect.

Dannemeyer contended the bill should be considered under regular floor procedures, instead of under suspension

of the rules, which barred amendments, so that he could offer an amendment designating the third Sunday in January as the day to honor King.

In an emotional plea that quieted the noisy chamber before the vote, Speaker Thomas P. O'Neill Jr., D-Mass., invoked the memory of King's famous "I have a dream" speech, delivered at the Lincoln Memorial Aug. 28, 1963.

"Martin Luther King changed America — all of America," O'Neill said in urging passage of the bill. "He changed it not by a force of arms but by moral force. He asked us to become the country that we always claimed to be — a country of equal justice, of equal opportunity, a country where all men — all men — are created equal."

Senate Action

After two days of often acrimonious and occasionally eloquent debate, the Senate passed HR 3706 Oct. 19 by a vote of 78-22. *(Vote 293, p. 48-S)*

There was no Senate committee action on the bill.

Though the debate took up more time than the Senate often takes to consider multibillion-dollar spending bills, the King holiday issue had assumed a symbolic importance transcending its actual effect.

"I have seldom approached a moment in this chamber when I thought the action we are about to take has greater potential for good and a greater symbolism for unity than the vote we are about to take," said Majority Leader Howard H. Baker Jr., R-Tenn.

As a testament to the symbolic importance of the vote, the galleries were full, packed with some of the leading figures in the civil rights movement. Among those present for the final vote were King's widow, Coretta Scott King, his son, Martin Luther King III, NAACP Executive Director Benjamin L. Hooks and Southern Christian Leadership Conference President Rev. Joseph E. Lowery.

Also present were several members of the House Black Caucus, including John Conyers Jr., D-Mich., who was a civil rights lawyer before coming to Congress in 1965. Conyers had introduced a bill in each Congress since King's assassination to make King's birthday a national holiday.

Defeat for Helms

Passage of the measure was a major setback for Jesse Helms, who tried in a variety of ways to scuttle it.

Helms doubted King was worthy of the recognition a public holiday would grant. When the bill first came up Oct. 3, he referred to King's "action-oriented Marxism." Later he alleged that King had links with members of the Communist Party, and objected to King's denunciation of the Vietnam War. Helms also opposed the bill on economic grounds, citing estimates that the holiday would cost the national economy between $4 billion and $12 billion.

Helms not only lost on the Senate floor, he also lost in the courts. His lawyers, along with lawyers from the Conservative Caucus, sought the release of FBI tapes on King, which were sealed until 2027 by a 1977 court order. On Oct. 18, U.S. District Judge John Lewis Smith Jr. refused to break the seal.

Filibuster. Senate leaders had hoped to act Oct. 3 on HR 3706, but when it was brought up, Helms launched a filibuster. He provoked heated debate when he denounced King and his career. "Although there is no record that Dr. King himself ever joined the Communist Party," Helms said, "he kept around him as his principal advisers and associates certain individuals who were taking their orders

and directions from a foreign power."

"Those charges," Edward M. Kennedy, D-Mass., shot back, "were raised first and most vigorously by the archsegregationists bent on retaining the rule of racism. It is their heirs in the last-ditch stand against equal justice who seek to divert us today on this legislation with such matters."

Helms inserted into the *Congressional Record* eight pages of material on the political activities and associations of King. When asked later if he believed King was a Marxist, he replied, "If something has webbed feet and has feathers and so forth, it's a fair bet it's a you-know-what."

Vote Agreement. The leadership of both parties quickly filed a cloture motion to limit debate. If debate had been cut off and the Senate moved to consider the bill Oct. 5, proposed amendments could have tied the Senate up as it was trying to conclude business before the Columbus Day recess.

Instead, under an agreement announced Oct. 5 by Baker, the cloture motion was withdrawn, and the Senate began debate on a tobacco and dairy bill (S 1529) backed by Helms, who chaired the Agriculture Committee. The pact called for the Senate to return to the King bill Oct. 18, with debate on amendments limited and a vote set for no later than 4 p.m. Oct. 19.

Senate Debate

The debate produced inflamed rhetoric that harkened back to the civil rights debates of the 1960s. It also produced genuine eloquence and feeling seldom heard in the Senate of the 1980s.

The fireworks began immediately. Helms launched an attack on King and on the procedures used to move the bill through Congress, and Kennedy responded with a sharp rebuke.

When Kennedy, citing joint House-Senate hearings held in 1979, characterized as "inaccurate and false" Helms' assertion that the Senate had held no hearings on the bill, Helms sought to strike the words from the record as a violation of the Senate rule prohibiting one senator from impugning the motives of another.

Baker intervened, and the Senate agreed to expunge Kennedy's word "false" from the record.

In response to Helms' allegation that King had an "association with far-left elements and elements in the Communist Party U.S.A.," Kennedy quoted the Church committee which investigated intelligence agencies in 1975 and reported that the FBI had stated that "at no time did it have any evidence that Dr. King himself was a Communist or connected with the Communist Party."

Later, Daniel Patrick Moynihan, D-N.Y., holding a file containing FBI documents on King's personal life, said, "The Congress of the United States has never been so sick as it could be today if we were to pay attention to the filth in this brown binder that has been passed around the chamber today." An enraged Moynihan flung the binder to the floor.

The heat continued the next day, when Bill Bradley, D-N.J., said of Helms and Sen. John P. East, R-N.C.: "I want to give the senators of North Carolina the due respect of a colleague, but I must say it is just not possible in this case. They speak for a past that the vast majority of Americans have overcome," Bradley said.

Aside from Helms and East, most senators, even those who opposed the legislation, chose to pay tribute to King. "I believe, and have stated many times," said James Abd-

nor, R-S.D., "that Martin Luther King probably was the most outstanding leader of black citizens in our country and individually contributed most to the advancement of civil rights in our country." But Abdnor opposed the establishment of another public holiday, and voted against the bill because of its cost.

Other senators noted the symbolic value of the issue.

"The vote we are about to cast may not balance the budget," Baker said, "but it is proof positive that the country and the Senate have a soul and that we intend to acknowledge and to celebrate the nobility of all of our citizens in the opportunity which they must have to participate in the fullness of America's future."

Kennedy said, "Long after all of us have left the Senate, long after all our other actions have been forgotten, people will remember that this was the Congress that gave Martin Luther King the highest honor our nation can bestow on any of its citizens."

The symbolism inherent in the issue introduced political considerations into the debate. Republicans who favored the bill were quick to distance themselves from Helms and the other opponents, and instead claimed that they were in the forefront of civil rights.

"I'm very proud of my party today," said Robert Dole, R-Kan., after the vote. "We're in the mainstream."

Even some conservative Republicans, particularly those from states with large black populations, voted for the bill. For example, Jeremiah Denton, R-Ala., after voting with Helms on several amendments, voted for final passage. "I believe that there were some things about Martin Luther King which were not perfect," Denton said, "but I believe they are transcended by the national importance of the deserving character of the man and the significance of what it meant to the whole nation to effect the change that occurred in the South."

Amendment Attempts

Before the vote on final passage, there were a number of attempts to delay or change the bill. All but one were offered by opponents of the legislation.

First, Helms moved to send the bill to the Judiciary Committee for hearings. The motion failed, 12-76, virtually assuring the bill's success. *(Vote 281, p. 47-S)*

The Senate then rejected 12 amendments, four of them by Helms. One would have required the Senate to obtain and examine the sealed documents the district court refused to release before voting on a public holiday in honor of King. It lost, 3-90. *(Vote 286, p. 47-S)*

Another Helms amendment would have expressed the sense of Congress that the president should pardon Marcus Garvey, the Jamaican-born leader of a back-to-Africa movement in the United States in the 1910s. Garvey was convicted of mail fraud in 1923, served time in prison and was deported in 1927. He is a national hero in Jamaica. That amendment was defeated, 5-92. *(Vote 290, p. 48-S)*

A third Helms amendment would have barred a holiday honoring King unless Congress first created one honoring Thomas Jefferson. It lost, 10-82. *(Vote 289, p. 48-S)*

The final Helms amendment would have created a separate legal holiday honoring Hispanic Americans. That also failed, 4-93. *(Vote 291, p. 48-S)*

Two Democrats offered amendments to change the date of the holiday from the third Monday in January to King's actual birthday, Jan. 15. The first, by Jennings Randolph, D-W.Va., failed 23-71. An attempt by J. James Exon, D-Neb., to designate Jan. 15 a commemorative day

rather than a public holiday failed 24-69. Both men voted against the bill. *(Votes 284, 285, p. 47-S)*

An amendment by Gordon J. Humphrey, R-N.H., to change the date of the holiday to the third Sunday in January failed 16-74. *(Vote 287, p. 47-S)*

Four other amendments would have changed the name and date of the holiday. One, by East, would have made March 16 (James Madison's birthday) a non-paid holiday called "National Civil Rights Day." It lost, 18-76. *(Vote 283, p. 47-S)*

Another, by Warren B. Rudman, R-N.H., would have created a national legal holiday called "National Equality Day," to be celebrated on Feb. 12, Abraham Lincoln's birthday. That failed, 22-68. *(Vote 282, p. 47-S)*

The third, by Humphrey, would have declared the second Sunday in February a national holiday honoring Abraham Lincoln. It lost, 11-83. *(Vote 288, p. 47-S)*

The fourth, by Charles E. Grassley, R-Iowa, would have declared the third Sunday in January "National Heroes Day." Each year, an unpaid committee of eight persons would determine which hero would be honored on the holiday. The amendment failed by voice vote.

The final amendment received the most votes, partly because it was offered by senators who favored the bill. Proposed by David L. Boren, D-Okla., and Sam Nunn, D-Ga., the amendment would have declared that all holidays honoring a particular individual — George Washington's Birthday, Columbus Day, and Martin Luther King's birthday — be celebrated on the actual date, rather than a Monday, even if the date occurred on a weekend.

Nunn said the amendment would honor King and at the same time address the issue of the cost of federal holidays. He said that 13 times between 1986 and 2000, one of those three holidays would occur on a weekend. The amendment failed, 45-52. *(Vote 292, p. 48-S)*

After the amendment failed, Boren introduced it as separate legislation (S 1971), and it was placed on the Senate calendar.

Pete Wilson, R-Calif., offered but withdrew an amendment to limit the number of federal holidays to 10. He subsequently offered that as separate legislation (S 1970) too, and the Senate passed it Oct. 20 by a vote of 86-2. *(Vote 298, p. 49-S)* ∎

Federal Personnel Rules

A federal judge Dec. 30 blocked the Reagan administration from implementing regulations designed to link pay raises and job security for federal employees more closely to job performance.

Congress voted repeatedly in 1983 to halt the new rules, but the Office of Personnel Management (OPM) announced Nov. 21 — the Monday after Congress adjourned — that it would put them into effect Nov. 25.

The National Treasury Employees Union, joined by other federal employee unions, filed a lawsuit challenging the action, and U.S. District Court Judge Barrington D. Parker ruled Dec. 30 that the regulations were null and void. OPM said it planned to appeal the ruling.

The rules would have eliminated automatic, within-grade pay raises and established instead a pay-for-performance system for 1.4 million white-collar federal workers.

The new system would have been phased in over three years. Employees would be rated on a five-level scale and

must earn at least a rating of "fully successful," the third level in the scale, to receive a raise.

Under existing rules, federal employees got pay hikes every one, two or three years if they received a "satisfactory" job rating.

More controversial than the new pay system were the proposed rules covering job security. They provided that workers would receive points for performance as well as for seniority. This provision enraged federal employee unions; they argued that a worker with many years' seniority could be laid off before a worker with less seniority but with better performance ratings.

Kenneth T. Blaylock, president of the American Federation of Government Employees, charged the administration with "attempting to replace the civil service system with one of political patronage."

Rules Blocked

The dispute over the rules began in March, when OPM issued its first set of regulations. Congress, backing the unions' claims that the regulations were unfair to workers who had attained seniority and could lead to politicization of the work force, blocked the March rules, and subsequently delayed a revised set of rules published in July.

President Reagan endorsed the merit pay plan Aug. 20 in his weekly radio address.

OPM issued a third set of regulations Oct. 25, and Congress responded by adopting an amendment to the second continuing appropriations resolution (H J Res 413 — PL 98-151) barring the use of funds in the bill to implement, administer or enforce the proposed regulations in fiscal 1984. *(Continuing resolution, p. 528)*

The amendment specifically mentioned only the regulations published March 30 and July 14, not the final version, although the sponsor of the ban, Rep. Steny H. Hoyer, D-Md., said Congress intended to block the Oct. 25 regulations as well.

OPM Director Donald J. Devine maintained that the amendment to the continuing resolution only barred the agency from spending money to implement the rules, "but no funds are necessary for the regulations to become the rules of the civil service."

Congressional Actions

The first set of regulations, issued March 30, caused a furor in Congress.

Rep. Patricia Schroeder, D-Colo., chairman of the House Post Office and Civil Service Subcommittee on Civil Service, introduced a bill (HR 2449) to block them.

On May 11 the full committee voted 17-4 to instruct the House Appropriations Treasury/Postal Service Subcommittee to block the regulations, and the panel agreed, adopting an amendment offered by Hoyer to the first Treasury-Postal Service appropriations bill (HR 3191).

However, HR 3191 was defeated on the House floor, for reasons unrelated to the amendment. *(Story, p. 531)*

The House attached a similar amendment to a supplemental appropriations bill (HR 3069 — PL 98-63) passed in May, and the Senate threatened to follow suit in June. The administration first threatened to veto the bill if the restrictive language remained in it, then announced it would delay implementation of the rules temporarily. *(HR 3069, p. 509)*

OPM proposed a new set of regulations July 14, addressing some concerns about the original proposals. But the regulations did not go far enough to satisfy critics, and

Sen. Charles McC. Mathias Jr., R-Md., successfully offered an amendment to the fiscal 1984 transportation appropriations bill (HR 3329 — PL 98-78), delaying their implementation until Oct. 15. *(Story, p. 457)*

Mathias hoped Congress would address the issue legislatively, but a bill (S 958) to establish a demonstration pay-for-performance project for 150,000 workers, with unions participating in the design of the demonstration, was stalled in the Senate Governmental Affairs Committee. *(See below)*

On Oct. 25, after the transportation bill provision expired, OPM proposed a third set of regulations. Hoyer made sure the provision blocking their implementation stayed in the second Treasury-Postal Service funding bill (HR 4139) passed by the House, but the Senate did not consider HR 4139. Instead, funding for the agencies in that bill were included in the continuing resolution. On the House floor, Hoyer attached the text of HR 4139 to the resolution, which had the effect of including the ban on the implementation of the OPM rules in that legislation.

Pending Legislation

The Senate Governmental Affairs Committee Nov. 15 approved a bill (S 958) making changes in the existing merit pay system for federal managers. It did not include the proposal for a demonstration project affecting 150,000 workers. Civil Service Subcommittee Chairman Ted Stevens, R-Alaska, who had pushed that idea as a compromise, abandoned it after reaching agreement with Devine on the final set of regulations.

Hoyer said he also would introduce legislation early in 1984 addressing some aspects of the disputed pay system. Hoyer said the bill would apply only to managers in GS grades 13-15, who had been under a merit pay system since 1978. *(1978 Almanac p. 818)*

Hoyer also called for a demonstration project to see if the merit pay system should be extended across the federal work force. ∎

Tax Leasing Plan Vetoed

President Reagan June 17 vetoed a bill (S 973) that would have allowed a North Carolina school to "lease" to outside investors tax benefits attributable to a building that had been rehabilitated with federal funds.

The amendment, sponsored by Sen. Jesse Helms, R-N.C., had been added on the Senate floor to a bill making minor and technical amendments to the Indian Self-Determination and Education Assistance Act of 1974 (PL 93-638) and several other laws affecting Indians.

Reagan said he had no objections to those amendments, but he said the tax leasing arrangement was "totally unjustifiable." He noted there had been "a great deal of concern" about the sale of tax benefits by tax-exempt entities through leasing transactions. The Economic Recovery Tax Act of 1981 (PL 97-34) liberalized leasing laws to make it easier to transfer tax benefits from businesses that were not profitable enough to use them to businesses that could use them. *(1981 Almanac p. 91)*

Such leasing transactions "present tremendous potential for abuse and could result in billions of dollars of revenue loss to the federal government," Reagan said. *(Veto text, p. 34-E)*

S 973 was the second public bill vetoed by Reagan

during the 98th Congress. Earlier, he vetoed an Indian land claims measure (S 366). *(Story, p. 586)*

The Helms amendment to S 973 was intended to benefit the North Carolina School of the Arts in Winston-Salem. The school had renovated a building for use as a performing arts center, using a combination of private funds and a federal Economic Development Act (EDA) grant. Helms said the school faced "significant" operating losses on the new theater and sought a lease-back arrangement on the building to get funds to offset those losses. Such an arrangement would be technically illegal, and the school would have to repay the EDA grant immediately, Helms said. His amendment would permit the lease-back arrangement but eliminate the necessity of immediate repayment of the EDA grant.

S 973 was reported by the Senate Select Committee on Indian Affairs May 5 (S Rept 98-73). The Senate passed the bill by voice vote May 25 after adopting the Helms amendment; the House passed it June 1 without debate, clearing it for the president.

The Senate Indian Affairs panel June 28 approved a new version of the bill, (S 1530), without the North Carolina tax-leasing provision. There was no written report. The full Senate passed it by voice vote Sept. 30. However, the House did not act on the measure. ∎

NSF Authorization

The House May 12 passed a bill (HR 2066) authorizing $1.34 billion in fiscal 1984 for programs of the National Science Foundation (NSF).

The Senate Labor and Human Resources Committee reported a similar bill May 16 (S 1087 — S Rept 98-195) but the full Senate did not act on it, so the NSF authorization did not become law.

NSF programs were funded at $1.32 billion in the fiscal 1984 appropriations bill for the Department of Housing and Urban Development and various independent agencies (HR 3133 — PL 98-45). President Reagan had requested $1.29 billion. *(Story, p. 495)*

The NSF supports research in all non-medical fields of science and engineering through grants and contracts with colleges, universities and private research organizations.

HR 2066, passed by a vote of 297-111, restored some funds cut from the NSF budget during the previous two years for social, behavioral and information science programs. *(Vote 103, p. 36-H)*

The bill also included about $230 million for new high-technology instrumentation programs; the money was intended to upgrade equipment at advanced research facilities, develop new laboratories and promote university use of high-technology equipment.

The House rejected, 150-257, an amendment by Larry Winn Jr., R-Kan., to delete $50 million of that amount. It also rejected, 150-255, an amendment by George E. Brown Jr., D-Calif., to add another $49 million for the instrumentation program. *(Votes 101, 100, p. 36-H)*

The House Science and Technology Committee had reported the bill April 26 (H Rept 98-73). ∎

Veterans' Compensation

The Senate passed a bill (S 1388) Nov. 18 to increase by 3.5 percent the rate of compensation to disabled veterans, their dependents and survivors.

However, the House did not act on a bill reported by the Veterans' Affairs Committee June 1 (HR 2937 — H Rept 98-228) authorizing a 4.1 percent cost-of-living (COLA) increase in disability payments and postponing the increase from Oct. 1, 1983, to April 1, 1984, as requested by the administration.

The Senate bill, reported Sept. 28 (S Rept 98-249), also extended VA home loan guarantee authority to manufactured homes, repealed the 1989 termination date of the Vietnam-era GI Bill, expressed the sense of Congress that the compensation increases take effect on Dec. 1 beginning in 1985, expanded the membership of the Board of Veterans Appeals from 50 to 65 and established a pilot project to expedite certain medical facility construction projects.

The House passed bills affecting the home loan guarantee program (HR 2948) and expanding the appeals board (HR 2936), but none of the bills became law.

The Veterans' Affairs committees were directed by the fiscal 1984 budget resolution (H Con Res 91) to trim $226 million from 1984 outlays for veterans' benefits and services. The Senate committee agreed to a 3.5 percent COLA increase and the six-month delay. Although HR 2937 became part of the House-passed budget reconciliation measure (HR 4169), that bill did not clear and the cuts were never made. *(HR 4169, p. 231)*

The administration had proposed a 5.1 percent hike in service-connected disability compensation. In 1982 Congress voted a 7.4 percent raise. *(1982 Almanac p. 488)* ∎

Mail Fraud

Congress Nov. 16 cleared a bill (S 450 — PL 98-186) giving the Postal Service new authority to deal with mail fraud. The bill was reported by the Senate Governmental Affairs Committee March 31 (S Rept 98-51) and passed the Senate Nov. 3. The House passed the measure Nov. 16.

The bill authorized the Postal Service, after a hearing before an administrative law judge, to issue orders requiring a person to cease and desist from engaging in false representation schemes, and provided a civil penalty of up to $10,000 a day for anyone who tried to evade such orders.

It also gave the Postal Service power to tender cash for items advertised through the mail, in order to speed up investigations, and expanded its authority to carry out a consumer education program.

Left out of the bill was a controversial proposal to give the Postal Service authority to issue civil investigative demands, similar to subpoenas, to examine books, records or other material related to a mail fraud investigation. The House dropped that provision after civil liberties groups complained that it could dangerously expand the Postal Service's police powers.

Mail fraud legislation was passed by both the House and Senate in 1982, but Congress adjourned before a conference committee could work out minor differences in the two bills. *(1982 Almanac p. 531)* ∎

SPECIAL REPORTS

Supreme Court......................... 3-A
   Major Decisions 6-A
   Opinions on Legislative Veto 20-A
Nominations and Confirmations......... 23-A

CQ

Supreme Court Rebuffs Reagan on Policies

The Supreme Court is "almost never a really contemporary institution," wrote Attorney General Robert H. Jackson in 1940, the year before he was appointed to that court. "The judiciary is . . . the check of a preceding generation on the present one."

Jackson was writing of the battle between the court and the Roosevelt administration over key New Deal legislation. But 42 years later, President Ronald Reagan learned the truth of Jackson's words.

In the 1982-83 court term that ended July 6, Reagan in a number of cases urged the justices to make dramatic changes in national policy. In all but one or two of those cases, the court rejected or sidestepped such administration requests.

The administration was not without its victories, but it prevailed primarily in cases involving institutional issues or preservation of the status quo, not policy initiatives of the Reagan presidency. The single most important decision of the term — in which the court struck down as unconstitutional the legislative veto, a device Congress had used to block executive branch orders or regulations — was an institutional victory for the chief executive.

More often, despite administration calls for change, a court appointed largely by earlier presidents upheld policies adopted by earlier administrations and laws passed by previous Congresses. In so doing, the justices often invoked Supreme Court decisions of the 1960s and 1970s as the basis for their actions.

Reagan's sole appointee on the court, Sandra Day O'Connor, sided with the president's position on these key cases more often than any justice except William H. Rehnquist, with whom she attended Stanford Law School.

But a majority of the justices, including those named by Republican Presidents Eisenhower, Nixon and Ford, repeatedly rebuffed the administration on major policy questions. And even O'Connor split with Reagan on almost half of the publicized cases in which the administration took a position.

The Rebuffs to Reagan

One of the biggest blows came when the justices voiced strong support for a longstanding Internal Revenue Service (IRS) policy denying tax-exempt status to racially discriminatory private colleges and schools.

The Reagan administration had suffered massive political damage in 1982 when it sought to reverse this policy, claiming that in the absence of explicit authorization from Congress, the IRS lacked the power to deny tax exemptions to discriminatory schools.

In May 1983, the justices by 8-1 rejected the Reagan position with a ringing declaration that "racial discrimination in education is contrary to public policy," and that schools practicing such discrimination thus were not entitled to tax-exempt status. Rehnquist alone dissented.

In its first attempt to influence the court on the issue of school busing for desegregation, the administration sought to persuade the court to use a Nashville case as the

vehicle for reconsidering its support for busing. But the justices refused to do so, leaving intact a lower court decision that required more busing of Nashville pupils.

In another major setback for Reagan, the court by 6-3 reaffirmed a woman's constitutional right to an abortion and made clear that state and local efforts to curtail that right will continue to be strictly scrutinized. The administration had urged the justices to bow out of the abortion controversy, leaving the issue to elected legislators to resolve. O'Connor, Rehnquist and Justice Byron R. White sided with Reagan on this issue.

The court struck down as arbitrary and capricious the administration's effort to rescind a requirement for passive restraints — air bags or automatic seat belts — in automobiles. The court said any move to rescind federal regulations must be backed up by reasons as good as those that supported adoption of the regulations in the first place.

And over administration objections, the court allowed states to block construction of new nuclear power plants until an adequate federal plan for disposing of nuclear waste was developed.

The court temporarily postponed consideration of two other Reagan requests for legal change. After hearing arguments, the court decided it had picked the wrong case for weighing a major change in the controversial "exclusionary rule," which denies prosecutors the use of evidence police have obtained by improper methods.

And the justices avoided a major ruling on affirmative action, holding moot a case in which the administration had argued for limits on the use of that principle.

In both instances, the justices agreed to review other cases in their next term that presented the same issues.

Reagan Victories

The president enjoyed one victory in principle when the court by 5-4 upheld the constitutionality of a Minnesota law granting parents of private and public school students a state income tax deduction for tuition, textbook and transportation expenses. The administration had supported Minnesota in this case, and Reagan had been pressing Congress to approve federal tuition tax credits for parents of private school students.

The court ruling was a mixed blessing for Reagan, however. It effectively required the administration to choose between making its proposed tax credits available to parents of public school children or abandoning the concept altogether. The potential budget cost in lost revenues had been a major stumbling block to the original Reagan proposal, which involved only private school tuition tax credits; an even more costly package was too much for Congress to swallow in a period of high deficits.

The administration could also claim to be on the winning side of the court's decision striking down sex-based discrimination in employer-sponsored retirement plans. While not involved in the case decided by the court, the government had filed a brief on the side of the women in a related case raising the same issue.

Virtually all of the administration's other significant wins before the court came when it argued for preserving the status quo, rather than for shifts in national policy directions. Among its major victories in this category was the court's unanimous verdict in suppport of the 1980 windfall profits tax on oil, a decision of great import for a government battling record budget deficits.

On other issues, the court adopted the executive branch position upholding an existing federal ban on age discrimination as applied to state employees, requiring pre-marketing clearance by the Food and Drug Administration of generic drugs, and reversing lower court decisions that required the Nuclear Regulatory Commission to consider community stress and nuclear waste disposal more closely than it now does in considering a request to grant or amend a license for a nuclear power plant.

The Aging Court

President Reagan, pondering the fate of his policy initiatives before the Supreme Court this term, could take some comfort from history.

The year after Attorney General Jackson wrote of the generation gap between the court and the elected branches of the government, he became the seventh justice appointed by President Franklin D. Roosevelt. And thus transformed, a court that had frustrated Roosevelt and Congress during the 1930s became a court that operated in philosophical harmony with them in the 1940s.

Not until the 1950s did a generation gap again open, with a court notably more liberal than the other branches.

The court in 1983 was an aging court. When the 1983-84 term began on Oct. 3, five justices were 74 or older. William J. Brennan Jr., leader of the court's liberal wing, was the oldest and the most senior justice. Born April 25, 1906, he joined the court in October 1956. The youngest justices were Rehnquist, 59 (born Oct. 1, 1924), and O'Connor, 53 (born March 26, 1930), both conservatives. The average age was 69. With the exception of O'Connor and John Paul Stevens, all the justices had served on the court for well over 10 years.

History, as well as the age of the sitting justices, suggested that changes would occur in the court in the next presidential term. Although the court, on the average, had welcomed a new member every two years, O'Connor's appointment in 1981 was the only change in its membership since 1975. After a similar period of stability in the mid-1930s, Roosevelt named seven justices in four years.

Legislative Veto

Not since the New Deal collisions of the 1930s had Congress felt so keenly the power of the court to curtail its actions. By denying Congress the use of the legislative veto, a tool it has employed since 1932, the Supreme Court abruptly altered the delicate balance of power between the other two branches of government.

Although Congress appeared to be the loser for the short term, it was by no means certain that the presidency was strengthened for the long haul. Indeed, the opposite could be true if Congress henceforth refused to delegate flexible powers to the executive branch.

Observers compared the historic significance of the veto decision in *Immigration and Naturalization Service v. Chadha* with that of the court's 1974 Watergate tapes ruling and with its pivotal 1803 decision in the case of *Marbury v. Madison,* in which the court for the first time exercised its power to hold an act of Congress unconstitu-

tional. But neither comparison was particularly apt.

The veto ruling was far broader in its effect than the Watergate decision, which had a dramatic impact in a single historic situation that was unlikely to be repeated.

And while the court in *Chadha* invalidated more federal laws or parts of laws than it had declared unconstitutional in its entire history, such a move would not even have been possible without its assertion of judicial power under *Marbury v. Madison.*

In *Chadha*, the court majority held the legislative veto a breach of the lines separating the powers of the legislative and executive branches, a violation of the "carefully crafted restraints" that the Constitution imposed on each branch of the federal government.

Only Justice White accepted the argument of Congress that the legislative veto was a useful and necessary modern invention, enabling Congress to delegate authority without abdicating responsibility.

Individual Rights

As in previous terms, the court maintained a generally liberal record on questions of individual rights, while compiling a clearly conservative profile on criminal law issues.

The court reaffirmed the importance of the "one person, one vote" principle for congressional redistricting, invalidating New Jersey's new district map because the state had failed to justify a population difference of less than 1 percent in the districts created after the 1980 census. In the *Bob Jones University* tax-exemption case, the court reaffirmed the nation's commitment to end racial discrimination in education. Its equally vigorous majority opinion in the abortion cases made clear that the court as presently constituted stood firmly behind the 1973 decision granting women a constitutional right of privacy in deciding whether to have an abortion.

Moving against sex discrimination in the work place, the court held that the 1964 Civil Rights Act forbids employers to discriminate between male and female employees in the breadth of medical coverage afforded their spouses. And the court also held it illegal under that law for employers to offer retirement plans that provided women smaller monthly benefits than men on grounds that women as a group live longer than men as a group.

In separate cases the court denied federal military and civilian employees the right to sue their superiors for allegedly infringing on their constitutional rights. Other procedures and remedies were available, the court said.

First Amendment

The elasticity of the First Amendment was demonstrated again this term by the wide variety of cases in which it was cited.

By far the most notable of the First Amendment decisions came in two major church-state cases.

In the first, the court upheld Minnesota's plan for granting parents of both private and public school pupils a tax deduction for tuition and related expenses. And in a Nebraska case, the justices endorsed the practice of opening sessions of Congress and state legislatures with prayers.

Both rulings were departures for this court, which had insisted repeatedly — especially in "parochiaid" cases — on maintaining a high wall between church and state.

The court in the legislative prayer case, however, made clear that it considered the decision in this case an exception to its usual rules for judging state entanglement with religion, primarily because of the "unique history" of the

practice in this country.

Both decisions came by relatively narrow margins — 5-4 in the tax case and 6-3 in the prayer case.

In a different kind of First Amendment case, the court unanimously upheld the decision of Congress to give veterans' groups tax-exempt status, no matter how much lobbying they do, while restricting the lobbying activities of all other tax-exempt organizations.

A Washington organization had claimed this unequal treatment violated the First Amendment's guarantee of freedom of expression by effectively barring lobbying by most tax-exempt groups. The court disagreed, saying Congress had not barred lobbying by anyone, but had simply chosen not to subsidize it except for veterans' groups.

In almost all the remaining First Amendment cases it considered fully, the court struck down the challenged law or practice as a violation of that amendment's guarantee of freedom of the press, speech or association.

Among the statutes that fell was a federal law barring peaceful protests on the sidewalk in front of the court itself, and a second federal law banning the mailing of unsolicited advertisements for contraceptives.

In addition, the court held unconstitutional Minnesota's law taxing the use of ink and paper by the state's large newspapers, and Ohio's laws requiring independent presidential candidates to declare themselves months earlier than major party candidates and compelling minority political parties to disclose the names of their contributors.

But once again, public employees ended up on the short end of this issue. By a 5-4 vote in the Louisiana case of *Connick v. Myers*, the court held the First Amendment does not protect from dismissal public employees who complain about their working conditions or supervisors.

State Powers

The states won several major victories before the court this term, effectively rebutting assertions that their laws were in irreconcilable conflict with federal statutes.

The court unanimously upheld California's law imposing a moratorium on the construction of new nuclear power plants until a federal plan for disposing of nuclear waste was in place. The decision rebuffed the joint argument of the Reagan administration and the nuclear power industry that such a law was pre-empted by the federal Atomic Energy Act.

And in another California case, the court upheld the "worldwide unitary" method for state taxation of U.S.-based multinational corporations, a victory worth billions of dollars to state treasuries.

The court emphasized that despite its strict application of the "one person, one vote" rule to congressional districts, states have more leeway in drawing the districts for their own legislatures. The day that New Jersey saw its congressional redistricting map discarded by the court, Wyoming won — also 5-4 — the right to give its least populous county its own representative in the Legislature, even though that resulted in far greater population variation among state legislative districts than was held impermissible among New Jersey's congressional districts.

In yet another case, the court held that states do not have to provide a free public education to children who live within their bounds just to attend school. The justices upheld a Texas law that allowed school districts to charge such students tuition.

A number of state officials had hoped the court this term would resurrect as a guarantee of states' rights the

10th Amendment, which reserves power to the states and the people. As in the 1981-1982 term, however, the justices by a one-vote margin declined to do so. In the case of *Equal Employment Opportunity Commission v. Wyoming*, the court rejected, 5-4, state arguments that a 1974 federal law barring age discrimination against state employees infringed too far on states' rights.

Criminal Law

In this term, as in the last several, prosecutors and police were generally successful in persuading the court to uphold their challenged actions. Prosecutors won three out of four criminal cases heard by the court this term.

The court resolved nine cases in which a search by law enforcement agents was challenged as unconstitutional. In seven, the court upheld the search or arrest at issue — and in an eighth, it upheld the police practice in general, while holding that in the particular case at hand, law enforcement agents had unconstitutionally infringed upon the suspect's rights.

The most closely watched search case of the term produced an anticlimactic ruling. Putting off for another day the question of major modifications in the much-criticized exclusionary rule, the court in the case of *Illinois v. Gates* made it easier for police to use tips from anonymous informers as the basis for search warrants.

In other cases the court permitted warrantless searches of boats by customs officials, and of autos by police in certain circumstances.

In criminal cases not involving search and seizure issues, the court ruled against drunk drivers who claimed it was unconstitutional for the state to use against them their refusal to take a blood alcohol test when stopped for erratic driving.

In a 5-4 decision, the court overruled a lower court's order barring Los Angeles police from using a controversial "chokehold" on suspects. The justices said the man who brought the case lacked standing to sue the city to stop the practice altogether because he could not show it would ever be used against him again.

By the time the court ruled, however, police officials had prohibited use of one type of chokehold and had imposed a six-month moratorium on use of another such hold.

Finally, the court said a person acquitted of a crime on grounds of insanity may be confined to a mental institution for a period longer than the sentence he would have received if convicted of the offense in question.

Four inmates on Death Row won a full review of their sentences, but all four death penalties were upheld. In one of these rulings, *Barefoot v. Estelle*, the court also backed as "tolerable" the use of expedited procedures by courts of appeals considering both a constitutional challenge to a death sentence and a request for a stay of execution.

In a rare victory for a defendant, the court struck down as unconstitutionally vague a California law that permitted police to arrest anyone stopped on suspicion of a crime who did not provide them with reliable identification. Such a law left too much to police discretion, the court said.

The court also held that it was unconstitutionally cruel and unusual punishment for South Dakota to jail for life, without possibility of parole, a man convicted of seven relatively minor and non-violent crimes. And it granted a prison inmate who was beaten and raped by his cellmates the right to sue the prison guard on duty at the time for damages. Both of these rulings came by 5-4 votes. ∎

—By Elder Witt

Major Decisions, 1982-1983 Term

CRIMINAL LAW

Search and Seizure

United States v. Knotts, decided by a 9-0 vote, March 2, 1983. Rehnquist wrote the opinion.

Minnesota law enforcement officers did not violate the Fourth Amendment guarantee against unreasonable search and seizure when they monitored signals from a beeper placed inside a container sold to a suspected drug manufacturer. The signals enabled police to follow the suspect's car to a cabin where police, armed with a search warrant, found a clandestine drug laboratory.

Monitoring the beeper signal did not violate the suspect's privacy and so was neither a "search" nor a "seizure" within the meaning of the Fourth Amendment.

Florida v. Royer, decided by a 5-4 vote, March 23, 1983. White announced the judgment of the court in an opinion joined by three other justices; Brennan concurred; Rehnquist, Burger, O'Connor and Blackmun dissented.

Florida detectives acted illegally when they detained a man at the Miami International Airport because his appearance and manner fit a "drug courier profile." Therefore, the suspect's consent to a subsequent search of his luggage by the detectives was tainted by the illegality of his detention and was not valid. The profile alone does not constitute probable cause for the suspect's arrest.

Texas v. Brown, decided by a 9-0 vote, April 19, 1983. Rehnquist announced the decision in an opinion joined by three justices; the other justices concurred in separate opinions.

The court upheld the seizure of a party balloon of the type often used to store narcotics. It was taken from the seat of a car stopped by police at a routine driver's license checkpoint. The officer knew from experience of the use of these balloons to store drugs, and from observation of the balloon in plain view here thought that to be the situation.

Illinois v. Gates, decided by a 6-3 vote, June 8, 1983. Rehnquist wrote the opinion; Brennan, Marshall and Stevens dissented.

Making it easier for police to obtain search warrants on the basis of anonymous tips, the court held that a magistrate asked to issue a warrant on this basis should make a common-sense decision based on the totality of the circumstances surrounding the tip and the efforts and success of police in verifying it. Among the factors to be considered are evidence of the veracity of the informant, the reliability of the report and the basis of the tipster's knowledge.

The court heard two rounds of arguments in this case. The second, at the court's request, had focused on the issue of a "good-faith" exception to the controversial exclusionary rule, which bars the use as evidence of illegally obtained items.

The question before the court was whether to permit the use of evidence taken by police who thought they were operating within constitutional bounds. The court finally decided not to resolve that issue in this case.

United States v. Villamonte-Marquez, decided by a 6-3 vote, June 17, 1983. Rehnquist wrote the opinion; Brennan, Marshall and Stevens dissented.

Customs officers are authorized by Congress to board a vessel and inspect its documentation, even without a warrant or any suspicion of unlawful activity. A vessel on a waterway with ready access to the sea is subject to such boarding in order that customs officials may effectively police the waterways.

Florida v. Casal, dismissed by a 9-0 vote, June 17, 1983. Per curiam (unsigned) opinion.

The court dismissed this case after hearing oral arguments, deciding that the lower court ruling under review rested on adequate and independent state grounds. The case involved the suppression of 100 pounds of marijuana discovered on a fishing boat and used to convict two men of importing that drug. The Florida Supreme Court held the evidence could not be used against the men; the Supreme Court found that ruling to rest on sufficient grounds in state law, making federal review unnecessary.

Illinois v. Lafayette, decided by a 9-0 vote, June 20, 1983. Burger wrote the opinion.

The court held reasonable and constitutional a police search and inventory of the possessions of a suspect who has been arrested and taken to the police station to be booked. No search warrant is required for this type of search.

United States v. Place, decided by votes of 9-0 and 6-3, June 20, 1983. O'Connor wrote the opinion; Brennan, Blackmun and Marshall dissented in part.

The court held unanimously that federal narcotics agents acted unreasonably when they detained for 90 minutes the luggage of an airline passenger suspected of carrying drugs in order to have the luggage sniffed by a dog trained to detect drugs. Six members of the court went on to say, however, that this sort of "sniff" test was permissible, despite the Fourth Amendment's guarantee against unreasonable searches, so long as the detention of the luggage was brief.

Illinois v. Andreas, decided by a 6-3 vote, July 5, 1983. Burger wrote the opinion; Brennan, Marshall and Stevens dissented.

Police officers do not need a search warrant to reopen a locked container that has already been lawfully opened by a customs agent who found it to contain narcotics, resealed it, and delivered it to its owner.

Michigan v. Long, decided by a 6-3 vote, July 6, 1983. O'Connor wrote the opinion; Brennan, Marshall and Stevens dissented.

Police may conduct a "protective search" of the interior of a car they have stopped, just as — under the 1968 decision in *Terry v. Ohio* — they may pat down or frisk a suspect they stop on the street.

This sort of warrantless search is reasonable and constitutional so long as it is limited to the areas of the passenger compartment in which a weapon might be hidden and is based upon a reasonable belief that the suspect is dangerous and may be able to seize a weapon from the area around him.

Self-Incrimination

Pillsbury Co. v. Conboy, decided by a 7-2 vote, Jan. 11, 1983. Powell wrote the opinion; Stevens and O'Connor dissented.

Grand jury witnesses who are granted immunity from use of their testimony against them may not be compelled, at a later time in civil proceedings, to verify their prior immunized testimony.

In such a situation, a witness is entitled to claim his Fifth Amendment privilege to remain silent rather than incriminate himself, and he may not be forced to testify over a valid assertion of that privilege.

South Dakota v. Neville, decided by a 7-2 vote, Feb. 22, 1983. O'Connor wrote the opinion; Stevens and Marshall dissented.

An individual's privilege against self-incrimination is not violated when his refusal to submit to a blood-alcohol test is used as evidence against him when he is tried on charges of drunken driving.

United States v. Hasting, decided by votes of 7-2 and 9-0, May 23, 1983. Burger wrote the opinion. Brennan and Marshall dissented.

A court of appeals impermissibly ignored the "harmless error" doctrine when it overturned the convictions of four men for kidnapping and rape, basing its action on the prosecutor's comments to the jury noting that the defendants did not attempt to rebut the government's evidence against them. The court of appeals found this to be a violation of the defendants' right to remain silent rather than be compelled to incriminate themselves.

The Supreme Court found these comments by the prosecutor amounted to harmless error in the face of the overwhelming evidence of guilt presented by the prosecutor and the weak defense mounted by the suspects.

Double Jeopardy

Missouri v. Hunter, decided by a 7-2 vote, Jan. 19, 1983. Burger wrote the opinion; Marshall and Stevens dissented.

If a state legislature decides expressly to authorize multiple sentences for the same criminal action — for example, separate sentences for a person convicted both of first degree robbery and of an "armed criminal action" — imposition of such sentences does not violate the constitutional guarantee against double jeopardy.

Due Process

Marshall v. Lonberger, decided by a 5-4 vote, Feb. 22, 1983. Rehnquist wrote the opinion; Stevens, Brennan, Marshall and Blackmun dissented.

A federal court erred when it threw out a state court murder conviction on grounds that the defendant was denied due process by the admission, at his trial, of the fact that four years before the murder he had pleaded guilty to attempted murder.

This was not admitted as evidence to prove his guilt of the pending charge but to serve as a factor upon which a death sentence could be based. He was sentenced to die. He challenged the use of the prior plea, arguing that it was not voluntarily made. The Supreme Court held that the federal court should not have disturbed the state court holding that the plea was voluntary and its use in this situation appropriate.

Jones v. United States, decided by a 5-4 vote, June 29, 1983. Powell wrote the opinion; Brennan, Marshall, Blackmun and Stevens dissented.

A person found not guilty of a crime by reason of insanity may be confined in a mental institution for a longer period than he would have been imprisoned had he been convicted on the charge. The length of his hypothetical sentence is irrelevant to the purpose for which he was committed, and confinement beyond that term does not deprive him of liberty without due process of law.

Once it is established that a defendant is not guilty by reason of insanity, it is constitutional for the government to confine him until he has regained his mental health or is no longer a danger to himself or society.

Fair Trial

Connecticut v. Johnson, decided by a 5-4 vote, Feb. 23, 1983. Blackmun announced the court's judgment, joined in that opinion by three other justices; Justice Stevens concurred in that judgment; Powell, Burger, Rehnquist and O'Connor dissented.

The court upheld a decision by the Connecticut Supreme Court that a man on trial for attempted murder, kidnapping and sexual assault was denied a fair trial when the judge instructed jurors that "the law presumes that a person intends the ordinary consequences of his voluntary acts."

The state Supreme Court based its holding on a U.S. Supreme Court decision, *Sandstrom v. Montana* (1979), that such an instruction denied a defendant due process of law by giving a juror the idea that whatever criminal action the defendant committed was committed with intent, instead of leaving it to the prosecutor to prove intent in that case.

The court did not resolve the primary question in the Johnson case — whether such an error in jury instructions could be considered harmless enough to permit the ensuing conviction to stand. Four justices felt that such a mistake could never be harmless and would always require reversal of a conviction. Justice Stevens felt the case should simply have been dismissed, but he joined the four other justices to form a majority to dispose of it.

Right to Counsel

Morris v. Slappy, decided by a 9-0 vote, April 20, 1983. Burger wrote the opinion.

A California trial judge did not deny a rape and burglary defendant his constitutional right to the aid of legal counsel when he refused to delay the trial after the defendant's first appointed defense counsel became ill and had to be replaced by another appointed attorney.

Oregon v. Bradshaw, decided by a 5-4 vote, June 23, 1983. Rehnquist wrote the opinion announcing the judgment of the court and joined by three other justices; Powell concurred; Marshall, Brennan, Blackmun and Stevens dissented.

A man arrested for drunken driving and informed of his right to remain silent and have the assistance of an attorney, who first says that he wishes to have his attorney present before any further questioning but later, before the attorney arrives, asks a policeman, "Well, what is going to happen to me now?" is not denied his constitutional rights by police who remind him of his request for counsel and then go on to converse with the suspect.

Jones v. Barnes, decided by a 7-2 vote, July 5, 1983. Burger wrote the opinion; Brennan and Marshall dissented.

Court-appointed defense attorneys are not required to raise on appeal every non-frivolous claim suggested by their clients.

Cruel and Unusual Punishment

Zant v. Stephens, decided by a 7-2 vote, June 22, 1983. Stevens wrote the opinion; Marshall and Brennan dissented.

The court upheld a death sentence imposed upon a man convicted of a murder committed after he had escaped from jail, even though one of the factors upon which the court relied in determining his sentence was later found to be unconstitutional. Because two other valid factors were properly considered by the sentencing jury, the sentence could stand.

Solem v. Helm, decided by a 5-4 vote, June 28, 1983. Powell wrote the opinion; Burger, White, Rehnquist and O'Connor dissented.

South Dakota violated the constitutional guarantee against cruel and unusual punishment when it imposed a life sentence without possibility of parole on a man convicted on seven separate occasions of non-violent felonies.

For the first time, the court applied this constitutional provision to judge the relative severity of a prison sentence. The court said the Constitution prohibits not only barbaric punishments but also sentences that are disproportionate to the crime committed.

Barefoot v. Estelle, decided by a 6-3 vote, July 6, 1983. White wrote the opinion; Brennan, Marshall and Blackmun dissented.

It is permissible, although not preferred procedure, for a federal appeals court to consider and decide simultaneously a death row inmate's request for a stay of execution and the merits of his appeal from a district court's denial of his petition for a writ of *habeas corpus.*

Such expedited procedures may only be used when an inmate is bringing a collateral challenge to his sentence after he has unsuccessfully appealed his state court conviction and sentence. Courts employing these procedures must give full consideration to the inmate's arguments.

On a separate point, the court held that the Constitution does not forbid the state to use at the sentencing proceedings the testimony of psychiatrists as to a defendant's future dangerousness to society, even if they have not interviewed or examined the inmate himself. Federal rules of evidence permit the use of such expert witnesses.

Barclay v. Florida, decided by a 6-3 vote, July 6, 1983. Rehnquist announced the decision in an opinion joined by three justices; Marshall, Brennan and Blackmun dissented.

A death sentence imposed on a man convicted of a racially motivated murder need not be held invalid because the judge, in explaining his decision to impose a death sentence instead of the jury-recommended sentence of life in prison, cited his own Army experiences during World War II when he saw Nazi concentration camps and their victims. A judge in such a situation need not act as if he were in a vacuum, as if he had no experience, the court said. "It is entirely fitting for the moral, factual and legal judgment of judges and juries to play a meaningful role in sentencing."

The sentence need not be overturned just because one of the aggravating factors upon which it was based — the defendant's criminal record — is not a factor spelled out by state law for consideration during sentencing.

California v. Ramos, decided by a 5-4 vote, July 6, 1983. O'Connor wrote the opinion; Brennan, Marshall, Blackmun and Stevens dissented.

Nothing in the Constitution prohibits a state from requiring judges to instruct juries in capital punishment cases that a sentence of life imprisonment without parole may be commuted by the governor to a sentence permitting parole.

Equal Protection

Bearden v. Georgia, decided by a 9-0 vote, May 24, 1983. O'Connor wrote the opinion.

The guarantee of equal protection of the laws prohibits states from automatically revoking the probation of a defendant who fails to pay a fine or make some sort of financial restitution.

Such a revocation may be constitutional if an evaluation of the particular case in question shows the probationer has not made sufficient good faith efforts to pay the fine, and no alternative, such as community service or an extended payment schedule, is adequate to fulfill the state's interest in punishing him and deterring future crimes.

General

Dickerson v. New Banner Institute Inc., decided by a 5-4 vote, Feb. 23, 1983. Blackmun wrote the opinion; Brennan, Rehnquist, Stevens and O'Connnor dissented.

The federal law that makes it illegal for convicted felons to ship, transport or receive any firearm or ammunition in interstate commerce or to engage in the business of importing, manufacturing, or dealing in firearms applies to a man who pleaded guilty to a state crime of carrying a concealed handgun, was placed on probation for that crime, and subsequently had his record expunged of that judgment.

Tuten v. United States, decided by a 9-0 vote, March 30, 1983. Marshall wrote the opinion.

In imposing sentence under a recidivist sentencing law, a trial court may consider the fact that the defendant was earlier placed on probation for two years under the Youth Corrections Act, and that this probationary sentence had not been set aside.

Bell v. United States, decided by an 8-1 vote, June 13, 1983. Powell wrote the opinion; Stevens dissented.

The Federal Bank Robbery Act, which makes it a crime to steal money from a bank, proscribes the crime of obtaining money from a bank under false pretenses as well as the crime of actually robbing a bank.

CIVIL RIGHTS

Damage Suits

Briscoe v. LaHue, decided by a 6-3 vote, March 7, 1983. Stevens wrote the opinion; Brennan, Marshall and Blackmun dissented.

A police officer who allegedly commits perjury during a state criminal trial is immune from a suit for damages by

the defendant against whom he testified. The law that permits damage suits against persons who violate another's rights while acting "under color of law" does not permit such suits based on testimony in judicial proceedings. Nor does it authorize such suits against judges, prosecutors and others who perform official roles in the judicial process.

Kush v. Rutledge, decided by a 9-0 vote, April 4, 1983. Stevens wrote the opinion.

The provision of the Civil Rights Act of 1871 that prohibits conspiracies to interfere with the administration of justice in the federal courts may be invoked as the basis of a federal lawsuit by a white male football player against his former football coaches and the state university athletic director, whether or not his race or sex played any part in the matter under dispute.

Smith v. Wade, decided by a 5-4 vote, April 20, 1983. Brennan wrote the opinion; Rehnquist, O'Connor, Burger and Powell dissented.

A prison inmate who was beaten and raped by his cellmates can recover punitive damages under the Civil Rights Act of 1871 against the guard on duty at the time of the assault if he can show the guard acted with reckless or callous indifference to the prisoner's rights.

Hensley v. Eckerhart, decided by a 5-4 vote, May 16, 1983. Powell wrote the opinion; Brennan, Marshall, Blackmun and Stevens dissented.

The court set out guidelines for federal judges to follow under the Civil Rights Attorneys' Fee Awards Act of 1976 in awarding attorneys' fees to successful plaintiffs in civil rights cases.

The court held that fees for winners may be reduced if they did not prevail on all their claims. The court ordered a federal judge to reconsider an award of $133,000 to attorneys representing inmates of Missouri state prisons and hospitals who won a suit contending that the state was violating the constitutional rights of inmates.

Chappell v. Wallace, decided by a 9-0 vote, June 13, 1983. Burger wrote the opinion.

Military servicemen may not sue for damages superior officers who have allegedly violated their constitutional rights in the course of their military service.

Haring v. Prosise, decided by a 9-0 vote, June 13, 1983. Marshall wrote the opinion.

A defendant who pleads guilty to state drug charges — and does not challenge as illegal the police search uncovering the evidence against him — can still sue police for damages, claiming that their search violated his constitutional rights.

Chardon v. Soto, decided by a 6-3 vote, June 20, 1983. Stevens wrote the opinion; Rehnquist, White and Powell dissented.

Until Congress approves a federal statute of limitations governing civil rights damage suits, federal courts must apply state statutes of limitations where applicable. Thus a federal court was correct in applying Puerto Rico's statute to a suit brought by several education officials who charged they were demoted because of their political views.

United Brotherhood of Carpenters & Joiners of America, Local #610 v. Scott, decided by a 5-4 vote, July 5, 1983.

White wrote the opinion; Blackmun, Brennan, Marshall and O'Connor dissented.

Without some state involvement, victims of a conspiracy by union members to attack non-union workers to deprive them of their First-Amendment right not to join a union may not use the Civil Rights Act of 1871 to sue their attackers.

Use of the provision of the 1871 law that permits federal damage suits by persons deprived of equal protection of the laws or equal privileges and immunities does not apply to conspiracies in which there is no evidence of racial or class-based motive. The law was originally known as the Ku Klux Klan Act and it was designed to protect blacks against mob violence; it does not reach conspiracies motivated by economic concerns.

Job Discrimination

U.S. Postal Service Board of Governors v. Aikens, decided by a 9-0 vote, April 4, 1983. Rehnquist wrote the opinion.

A plaintiff in a job discrimination suit under Title VII of the 1964 Civil Rights Act is not required to produce direct proof of deliberate discrimination; indirect or circumstantial evidence is sufficient to move his case into the next stage, in which the employer must justify his decision to hire or promote someone else rather than the plaintiff.

Boston Firefighters Union, Local 718 v. Boston Chapter, NAACP, Boston Police Patrolmen's Association v. Castro, Beecher v. Boston Chapter, NAACP, decided by an 8-0 vote, May 16, 1983. Per curiam (unsigned) opinion; Marshall did not participate in the ruling.

After hearing oral arguments in this major affirmative action case, the court sent it back to lower courts for consideration of whether the matter was moot.

The Boston police and firemen's unions, backed by the Reagan administration, had argued that the principle of affirmative action had been extended too far by a federal judge. In order to preserve recent court-ordered minority hiring gains, the judge had ordered the city to ignore the usual seniority rule of "last hired, first fired" in making budget-dictated lay-offs.

Subsequently, the Massachusetts Legislature ordered the police and fire departments to reinstate the laid-off workers and to guarantee them that they would not again be laid off for fiscal reasons.

Crown, Cork & Seal Co. v. Parker, decided by a 9-0 vote, June 13, 1983. Blackmun wrote the opinion.

The pendency of a class action job discrimination suit halts the running of the 90-day statute of limitations on individual suits by persons who have been notified by the Equal Employment Opportunity Commission (EEOC) of their right to challenge their discharge as illegal.

Even if the class action case fails to win certification, a discharged worker can file an individual lawsuit against his employer under Title VII of the 1964 Civil Rights Act even though more than 90 days have passed since his receipt of the EEOC notice.

Guardians Association v. Civil Service Commission of City of New York, decided by votes of 7-2 and 5-4, July 1, 1983. White announced the judgment of the court and wrote an opinion joined in part by Rehnquist; Marshall and White dissented in part; Burger, Powell, Rehnquist and

O'Connor dissented in part; Brennan, Stevens and Blackmun dissented in part.

Without proof of intent to discriminate, private plaintiffs who sue their employer, a recipient of federal funds, for discriminating against them on the basis of race and national origin may not win compensatory relief such as back pay or retroactive seniority.

In the absence of a showing of intent, Title VI of the 1964 Civil Rights Act, which bars racial or ethnic discrimination by recipients of federal funds, entitles plaintiffs only to injunctions against such practices or judgments declaring them illegal. The vote on this point was 7-2.

However, five members of the court indicated that government agencies are free to adopt regulations to enforce Title VI by denying federal aid to recipients whose actions are discriminatory in effect, regardless of their intent.

Sex Discrimination

Newport News Shipbuilding & Dry Dock Co. v. Equal Employment Opportunity Commission, decided by a 7-2 vote, June 20, 1983. Stevens wrote the opinion; Rehnquist and Powell dissented.

Employers violate Title VII of the 1964 Civil Rights Act and discriminate among their employees on the basis of sex when their health insurance plans provide less comprehensive pregnancy coverage for the wives of male employees than for the company's female employees. Such discrimination gives male employees a less inclusive package of health benefits for their dependents than female employees receive.

Arizona Governing Committee for Tax Deferred Annuity and Deferred Compensation Plans v. Norris, decided by two 5-4 votes, July 6, 1983. Per curiam (unsigned) opinion; Burger, Blackmun, Powell and Rehnquist dissented; Marshall, White, Brennan and Stevens dissented in part.

An employer's retirement plan may not include an annuity option under which women workers upon retirement receive smaller monthly payments than men who have contributed the same amounts during their working career.

Title VII of the 1964 Civil Rights Act requires that employees be treated by their employers as individuals, not members of groups, in determining pay and other conditions of employment.

The fact that women as a group live longer than men as a group is not a permissible basis for paying them different monthly retirement benefits. Marshall, White, Brennan, Stevens and O'Connor formed the majority on this point.

However, O'Connor, Burger, Blackmun, Powell and Rehnquist formed a majority to hold that this decision would not affect retirement benefits paid to women already retired and no longer contributing to a system, but instead would apply only to retirement benefits derived from contributions made after this decision. Those benefits must be calculated without regard to the sex of the recipient.

Tax Exemptions

Bob Jones University v. United States, Goldsboro Christian Schools v. United States, decided by an 8-1 vote, May 24, 1983. Burger wrote the opinion; Rehnquist dissented.

The Internal Revenue Service (IRS) did not exceed its authority when it denied tax-exempt status to private schools that discriminate against blacks. In light of the clear national policy against racial discrimination in education, the IRS was correct in declaring in 1970 that it would no longer grant tax-exempt status to discriminatory private schools.

Although the two schools in these cases contended their discriminatory policies were based upon sincerely held religious beliefs, the court held that the First Amendment did not preclude IRS denial of tax-favored status. The national interest in eradicating racial discrimination in education "substantially outweighs whatever burden denial of tax benefits places" on the exercise of the First Amendment freedom of religion.

INDIVIDUAL RIGHTS

Abortion

City of Akron v. Akron Center for Reproductive Health Inc., Akron Center for Reproductive Health Inc. v. City of Akron, decided by a 6-3 vote, June 15, 1983. Powell wrote the opinion; White, Rehnquist and O'Connor dissented.

The court held unconstitutional provisions of an Akron, Ohio, ordinance requiring that all abortions after the first trimester of pregnancy be performed in full-service hospitals; that physicians obtain the consent of a parent or legal guardian before performing an abortion on a minor under age 16; that physicians recite to women seeking abortions a litany of information about fetal development, alternatives to abortion and possible abortion complications; that the attending physician and no one else inform a patient of the particular risks associated with her own pregnancy or abortion; that there be a 24-hour waiting period between the time a woman signs a consent form authorizing an abortion and the time it is performed; and that fetal remains be given a "humane" disposal.

The court held all these requirements to be unreasonable infringements upon a woman's right to decide to have an abortion.

Planned Parenthood Association of Kansas City, Mo. v. Ashcroft, Ashcroft v. Planned Parenthood Association of Kansas City, Mo., decided by votes of 5-4 and 6-3, June 15, 1983. Powell wrote the opinion; Blackmun, Brennan, Marshall and Stevens dissented in part; O'Connor, White and Rehnquist dissented in part.

The court upheld provisions of a Missouri law requiring "unemancipated" minors to obtain parental or judicial consent for an abortion. This requirement was permissible, while a similar one in the Akron ordinance (above) was not, because Missouri's requirement spelled out an alternative means of obtaining consent for a minor who could not or would not obtain parental consent. The vote on this issue was 5-4.

The court also upheld requirements that tissue from an abortion be submitted to a pathologist for examination and that a second physician be present at late-pregnancy abortions. These rulings came by a 5-4 vote.

The court struck down, 6-3, a requirement that all abortions after the first trimester be performed in a general-care hospital.

Simopoulos v. Virginia, decided by an 8-1 vote, June

15, 1983. Powell wrote the opinion; Stevens dissented.

The court upheld Virginia's law requiring that second-trimester abortions be performed in licensed hospitals. The court distinguished this hospitalization requirement from those struck down in the Akron and Missouri cases (above) because the Virginia law defined licensed outpatient surgical clinics as hospitals, and thus did not automatically increase the cost of an abortion.

Aliens

Landon v. Plasencia, decided by votes of 9-0 and 8-1, Nov. 15, 1982. O'Connor wrote the opinion; Marshall dissented in part.

A permanent resident alien, charged upon return from temporary absence from the country with smuggling aliens, is not entitled to demand that the issues of 'entry' and possible exclusion be resolved in a deportation hearing instead of the exclusion hearing convened immediately, at the border, by the Immigration and Naturalization Service.

Handicapped Persons

Community Television of Southern California v. Gottfried, Federal Communications Commission (FCC) v. Gottfried, decided by a 7-2 vote, Feb. 22, 1983. Stevens wrote the opinion; Brennan and Marshall dissented.

The Federal Communications Commission (FCC) is not required to use its licensing procedures to enforce the 1973 Rehabilitation Act, which requires recipients of federal grants to make special provisions for the handicapped population. That law is to be enforced by the agencies that administer the grant programs.

Public television stations are under no greater obligation than commercial stations to provide captioned programming or otherwise accommodate the needs of hearing-impaired viewers.

Illegitimate Children

Pickett v. Brown, decided by a 9-0 vote, June 6, 1983. Brennan wrote the opinion.

A Tennessee law requiring all paternity and support actions in behalf of illegitimate children to be filed by the time the child is two years old is unconstitutional. Such a law denies illegitimate children the equal protection of the law because it imposes a time limit on their right to paternal support that is not imposed on legitimate children.

Lehr v. Robertson, decided by a 6-3 vote, June 27, 1983. Stevens wrote the opinion; White Marshall and Blackmun dissented.

An unwed father who has developed no significant relationship with his child and does not seek to establish any legal tie with the child until after the child is two years old has no right to be notified by the state when the child is to be adopted by someone else.

The Constitution's guarantee of equal protection does not prevent a state from dealing differently with a parent who has established a relationship with his illegitimate child than it deals with one who has not.

Taxpayers

United States v. Rodgers, decided by votes of 9-0 and 5-4, May 31, 1983. Brennan wrote the opinion; Blackmun, Rehnquist, Stevens and O'Connor dissented.

The Internal Revenue Service can force the sale of a couple's jointly owned home if one of the owners is delinquent in paying federal taxes. The existence of a state homestead law, which gives both husband and wife full legal interest in the property, does not protect such property from this tax sale.

DUE PROCESS

Inmates

Hewitt v. Helms, decided by a 5-4 vote, Feb. 22, 1983. Rehnquist wrote the opinion; Stevens, Brennan, Marshall and Blackmun dissented.

Prisoners retain only a narrow range of protected liberty interests. A prisoner suspected of a key role in a prison riot was not denied his rights to liberty or due process when he was confined to administrative, non-disciplinary segregation following the riot, while prison officials investigated his role in the disturbance. The prisoner received notice of the charges against him, hearings on the evidence and the opportunity to present a statement to the hearing.

Olim v. Wakinekona, decided by votes of 6-3 and 7-2, April 26, 1983. Blackmun wrote the opinion; Marshall, Brennan and Stevens dissented.

A prisoner is not denied his right to due process when he is transferred from the state of his residence where he was convicted to an out-of-state prison. Once convicted, a person's constitutionally protected liberty is curtailed to the point that the state may confine him in any prison it selects.

Citizens

Kolender v. Lawson, decided by a 7-2 vote, May 2, 1983. O'Connor wrote the opinion; White and Rehnquist dissented.

The court struck down as unconstitutionally vague a California law that permitted police to arrest anyone whom they stopped, suspecting of criminal activity, who failed to provide "credible and reliable" identification. By providing no standard by which police could judge the identification such a person might offer, the law left too much discretion in the hands of police. This encouraged arbitrary enforcement in violation of the constitutional guarantee of due process, the court said.

Customs

United States v. $8,850 in U.S. Currency, decided by an 8-1 vote, May 23, 1983. O'Connor wrote the opinion; Stevens dissented.

An 18-month delay between the seizure of currency for failure to declare it upon entering the country and the filing of a civil forfeiture action in federal court does not, without evidence of prejudice to the person from whom the currency was taken, violate that person's right to due process of law.

Mortgage Holders

Mennonite Board of Missions v. Adams, decided by a 6-3 vote, June 22, 1983. Marshall wrote the opinion; O'Connor, Powell and Rehnquist dissented.

Mortgage holders have a constitutional right to be notified by mail or in person of the pending tax sale of property in which they have an interest. An Indiana law entitling a mortgage holder only to notice by publication was insufficient.

FIRST AMENDMENT

Church and State

Larkin v. Grendel's Den, decided by an 8-1 vote, Dec. 13, 1982. Burger wrote the opinion; Rehnquist dissented.

The First Amendment ban on state action establishing religion is violated by a Massachusetts law that gives schools and churches the power to block issuance of a liquor license to any establishment located within a 500-foot radius of the church or school.

Mueller v. Allen, decided by a 5-4 vote, June 29, 1983. Rehnquist wrote the opinion; Marshall, Brennan, Blackmun and Stevens dissented.

A Minnesota law that gives parents a state income tax deduction for the cost of tuition, textbooks and transportation for their elementary and secondary school children — up to a limit of $700 per older child and $500 per younger — is permissible under the First Amendment.

Because the deduction is available to public school patrons as well as private school patrons, and because any aid to church schools is the result of individual choices, not state design, the court found that it met the test for such aid. The majority found that the deduction had a secular purpose, did not have the primary effect of advancing religion and did not entangle the state in religious affairs.

Marsh v. Chambers, decided by a 6-3 vote, July 5, 1983. Burger wrote the opinion; Brennan, Marshall and Stevens dissented.

The First Amendment ban on establishment of religion is not offended by Nebraska's practice of opening daily sessions of the state Legislature with a prayer by a chaplain paid by the state. This practice has a long and unique history, dating back to the First Congress of the United States, which also adopted the First Amendment. "The practice of opening legislative sessions with prayer has become part of the fabric of our society," wrote the court.

Freedom of Speech

Perry Education Association v. Perry Local Educators' Association, decided by a 5-4 vote, Feb. 23, 1983. White wrote the opinion; Brennan, Marshall, Powell and Stevens dissented.

The First Amendment is not violated by a collective bargaining agreement between a school board and the local teachers' union that grants the union access to the interschool mail system and teacher mailboxes while denying such access to all rival unions.

The state may reserve the use of public property that is a forum for public communication for certain intended purposes, so long as the restriction thus imposed on speech is reasonable and is not an effort to suppress expression of particular views.

Connick v. Myers, decided by a 5-4 vote, April 20, 1983. White wrote the opinion; Brennan, Marshall, Blackmun and Stevens dissented.

The First Amendment does not protect from dismissal public employees who complain about their working conditions or their supervisors. The First Amendment does not require a public employer to tolerate action that he reasonably believes will undermine his authority or the operation of his office.

United States v. Grace, decided by votes of 9-0 and 7-2, April 20, 1983. White wrote the opinion; Marshall and Stevens dissented in part.

The First Amendment protects the freedom of individuals to use leaflets or picket signs to express their views while standing on the public sidewalks adjacent to the Supreme Court building. The court struck down as unconstitutional a federal law barring all demonstrations on those sidewalks.

Regan v. Taxation with Representation of Washington, Taxation with Representation of Washington v. Regan, decided by a 9-0 vote, May 23, 1983. Rehnquist wrote the opinion.

Congress did not infringe upon the freedom of expression guaranteed by the First Amendment when it denied tax-exempt status to non-profit organizations who devote a substantial amount of their efforts to lobbying.

Congress did not violate the Fifth Amendment guarantee of equal protection when it exempted from this restriction all veterans' groups, permitting them to retain tax-exempt status no matter how much lobbying they did. This was a legitimate way of repaying veterans for the time they spent in military service to the country.

Bush v. Lucas, decided by a 9-0 vote, June 13, 1983. Stevens wrote the opinion.

A federal employee demoted for criticizing his agency does not, in view of the statutory remedies for such allegedly unconstitutional action, have the right to bring a damage suit against his employer for violating his First Amendment rights.

Bolger v. Youngs Drug Products Corp., decided by an 8-0 vote, June 24, 1983. Marshall wrote the opinion. Brennan did not take part in the decision.

The court held unconstitutional a federal law prohibiting the mailing of "any unsolicited advertisement of matter which is designed, adapted, or intended for preventing conception. . . ." This unduly infringed upon the freedom of speech protected by the First Amendment, a guarantee which provides some protection for commercial speech.

Freedom of the Press

Minneapolis Star & Tribune Co. v. Minnesota Commissioner of Revenue, decided by votes of 8-1 and 7-2, March 29, 1983. O'Connor wrote the opinion; White and Rehnquist dissented.

Minnesota violated the First Amendment's guarantee of freedom of the press when it taxed the use of paper and ink by newspapers that use those items in large volume.

ELECTION LAW

Apportionment

Karcher v. Daggett, decided by a 5-4 vote, June 22, 1983. Brennan wrote the opinion; White, Burger, Powell and Rehnquist dissented.

The court struck down the New Jersey congressional redistricting plan adopted following the 1980 census, although there was less than a 1% variation between the most populous district and the least populous district. The court reaffirmed that states must adhere as closely as possible to the "one person, one vote" standard of reapportionment. When precise equality is not achieved, the state

must prove that the variations were necessary to achieve some important state goal. New Jersey had not proved that point in this case, the court held.

Brown v. Thomson, decided by a 5-4 vote, June 22, 1983. Powell wrote the opinion; Brennan, White, Marshall and Blackmun dissented.

Wyoming law, which requires that each county have at least one representative in the state House of Representatives, is constitutional even though the population variance between the smallest county and the largest is 89 percent. The law is permissible in light of the state's legitimate interest in assuring each county its own representative, the court held.

Political Association

Brown v. Socialist Workers '74 Campaign Committee (Ohio), decided by a 6-3 vote, Dec. 8, 1982. Marshall wrote the opinion; O'Connor, Rehnquist and Stevens dissented.

The court held unconstitutional, as applied to minor party candidates, an Ohio law requiring candidates for public office to disclose the name and address of each campaign contributor. The justices declared that such disclosure of contributors to minor parties might subject those persons to harassment, violating their First Amendment right to associate freely with persons of similar political views.

Anderson v. Celebrezze, decided by a 5-4 vote, April 19, 1983. Stevens wrote the opinion; Rehnquist, White, Powell and O'Connor dissented.

Ohio law burdened the voting and First Amendment rights of independent candidates and voters by requiring independent candidates for president to file in March of an election year in order to appear on the ballot in November, while major party candidates were not compelled to meet such an early deadline. The issue was raised by John B. Anderson, who ran in 1980 as an independent candidate for president.

Voting Rights

City of Port Arthur, Texas v. United States, decided by a 6-3 vote, Dec. 13, 1982. White wrote the opinion; Powell, Rehnquist, and O'Connor dissented.

A federal district court acted within its powers when it required the city of Port Arthur to elect certain members of its City Council by a plurality, rather than a majority vote, and conditioned its approval of a new plan for electing the City Council upon this change.

Federal approval of a change in the city's electoral system was required under the Voting Rights Act. The district court imposed the plurality requirement because it felt this would enhance the chances that black candidates would be elected to the council. The new electoral plan was adopted following the consolidation of Port Arthur and two nearby cities, a move that reduced the percentage of blacks in the city population from 45 to 40 percent.

City of Lockhart, Texas v. United States, decided by votes of 8-1 and 6-3, Feb. 23, 1983. Powell wrote the opinion; White, Marshall and Blackmun dissented.

The city of Lockhart is entitled to federal approval of changes in the way in which members of its City Council are elected at-large to numbered posts on a staggered basis because although those changes may have some discrimina-

tory effect, they have no retrogressive effect on minority voting strength.

Campaign Finance

Federal Election Commission v. National Right to Work Committee, decided by a 9-0 vote, Dec. 13, 1982. Rehnquist wrote the opinion.

The Supreme Court refused to expand the target population from which certain political action committees (PACs) can solicit funds. Federal election law restricts nonstock corporate PACs, such as the Employee Rights Campaign Committee set up by the National Right to Work Committee, to soliciting funds from their members, executives and administrative staff. The National Right to Work Committee argued that its "members" were all persons who could be identified as sharing its philosophy and supporting its work. The court rejected this broad definition and ruled that because the PAC's charter, adopted under state law, declared that it had no members, it could only solicit funds from its executives and administrative staff.

BUSINESS LAW

Antitrust

Associated General Contractors of California Inc. v. California State Council of Carpenters, decided by an 8-1 vote, Feb. 22, 1983. Stevens wrote the opinion; Marshall dissented.

A union that charges that a contractors' association and its members have conspired to weaken the collective bargaining relationship between the union and the contractors is not a "person" injured by a potential antitrust violation within the meaning of the Clayton Act. It is therefore not eligible to sue for treble damages. Such suits may only be brought by persons who have been injured by the alleged conspiracy; the union did not show such injury.

Jefferson County Pharmaceutical Association Inc. v. Abbott Laboratories, decided by a 5-4 vote, Feb. 23, 1983. Powell wrote the opinion; O'Connor, Brennan, Rehnquist and Stevens dissented.

Sales to state and local government agencies are not exempt from the price discrimination ban of the Robinson-Patman Act when those agencies are competing in the public marketplace with private business.

Falls City Industries Inc. v. Vanco Beverage Inc., decided by a 9-0 vote, March 22, 1983. Blackmun wrote the opinion.

A company charged with violating the Robinson-Patman Act's ban on price discrimination may successfully defend itself against those charges by arguing that it lowered its prices for all customers in a certain area in order to meet the prices of its competitors. This "meeting competition" defense is available even if the lower prices are set on an area-wide, rather than a customer-by-customer, basis.

Illinois v. Abbott & Associates, decided by a 9-0 vote, March 29, 1983. Stevens wrote the opinion.

In approving the Hart-Scott-Rodino Antitrust Improvements Act of 1976, Congress did not give state attorneys general any special right to see grand jury materials unless they can show a particularized need to gain access to such information.

BankAmerica Corp. v. United States, decided by a 5-3 vote, June 8, 1983. Burger wrote the opinion; Powell did not participate in the decision; White, Brennan and Marshall dissented.

The Clayton Act, which prohibits persons from serving simultaneously as the director of two or more competing million-dollar corporations other than banks or common carriers, does not bar such interlocking directorates between a bank and a competing non-bank corporation such as an insurance company.

Banking

First National City Bank v. Banco Para El Comercio Exterior de Cuba, decided by votes of 9-0 and 6-3, June 17, 1983. O'Connor wrote the opinion; Stevens, Brennan, Blackmun dissented.

A U.S. bank whose assets in Cuba were nationalized in 1960 can make counterclaim for those losses against a Cuban bank that serves as an official autonomous credit institution for foreign trade and that sued the U.S. bank to collect a debt owed it by the U.S. bank.

Bankruptcy

United States v. Security Industrial Bank, decided by a 9-0 vote, Nov. 30, 1982. Rehnquist wrote the opinion.

The provisions of the Bankruptcy Reform Act of 1978 (PL 95-598) that exempt certain personal property from liens by creditors do not apply to consumer loans made before the law was enacted. With this holding, the court sidestepped a decision on whether such an exemption, had it applied retroactively, was unconstitutional.

United States v. Whiting Pools Inc., decided by a 9-0 vote, June 8, 1983. Blackmun wrote the opinion.

A bankruptcy court can compel the Internal Revenue Service to return to a company in bankruptcy property which the IRS has seized to satisfy the company's tax bills.

Patents

General Motors Corp. v. Devex Corp., decided by a 9-0 vote, May 24, 1983. Marshall wrote the opinion.

The court upheld an award of $11 million in interest — which had accrued before the judgment in a patent infringement case — to a company that had sued General Motors for infringing on its patent for making car bumpers. The court held that it was appropriate in some cases for courts to award interest dating back to the point at which the infringement began in order to adequately compensate the patent holder for his loss.

Railroads

Burlington Northern Inc. v. United States, decided by a 9-0 vote, Dec. 13, 1982. Burger wrote the opinion.

A federal appeals court, reviewing a contested order from the Interstate Commerce Commission (ICC) concerning rail-freight rates, may order the ICC to reconsider those rates but may not itself decide what rates should be charged in the interim. It is the responsibility of the ICC to set such interim rates.

Regulation

United States v. Generix Drug Corp., decided by a 9-0 vote, March 22, 1983. Stevens wrote the opinion.

Generic prescription drugs must receive pre-marketing approval from the Food and Drug Administration even if they contain exactly the same active ingredients as already approved brand name drugs.

Motor Vehicle Manufacturers Association of the United States v. State Farm Mutual Automobile Insurance Co., Consumer Alert v. State Farm, Department of Transportation v. State Farm, decided by votes of 9-0 and 5-4, June 24, 1983. White wrote the opinion. Rehnquist, Burger, Powell and O'Connor dissented in part.

Federal agencies may not rescind existing regulations without a reasoned justification for the rescission. The National Highway Transportation Safety Administration acted arbitrarily and capriciously in 1981 when it rescinded a requirement that all cars be equipped with passive safety restraints — air bags or automatic seat belts — by September 1983.

Four justices felt that although the rescission was unjustified on the issue of air bags and one type of seat belt, the agency did justify its rescission of the rule as to detachable seat belts.

Securities

Herman & MacLean v. Huddleston, Huddleston v. Herman & MacLean, decided by an 8-0 vote, Jan. 24, 1983. Marshall wrote the opinion; Powell did not participate in the court's consideration of the case.

Making it easier for individual victims of stock fraud to sue those who have defrauded them, the court held that such charges need only be proved by a preponderance of the evidence, rather than the stiffer standard of clear and convincing evidence. Such cases can be brought under both the Securities Exchange Act of 1934 and the Securities Act of 1933.

Dirks v. Securities and Exchange Commission, decided by a 6-3 vote, July 1, 1983. Powell wrote the opinion; Blackmun, Brennan and Marshall dissented.

A securities analyst did not violate federal securities law — which forbids the trading of stocks on the basis of inside information — when he acted on the basis of a tip from a corporate insider and advised several of his clients to sell stock in a company that was about to collapse.

Individuals who receive such inside information are obligated to disclose it to the Securities and Exchange Commission or to abstain from trading on it altogether only if the person who gave them the information breached his duty to his stockholders by doing so and stands to gain personally as a result. No such breach occurred in this case.

Taxation

Hillsboro National Bank v. Commissioner of Internal Revenue, United States v. Bliss Dairy, decided by votes of 6-3 and 7-2, March 7, 1983. O'Connor wrote the opinion; Brennan, Stevens, Marshall and Blackmun dissented.

Physical recovery of funds, as in a tax refund, is not required to trigger the application of the so-called tax benefit rule. Under that rule, a taxpayer who deducts in one year an amount he expects to expend on some deductible item must report that amount as income in a subsequent year if the expected expense does not occur.

United States v. Rylander, decided by an 8-1 vote, April 19, 1983. Rehnquist wrote the opinion; Marshall dissented.

A taxpayer held in civil contempt for refusing to produce certain corporate records sought by the Internal Revenue Service cannot force the IRS to prove that he has those records simply by declaring that he does not and then invoking the Fifth Amendment privilege against compelled self-incrimination to avoid answering any further questions.

Commissioner of Internal Revenue v. Tufts, decided by a 9-0 vote, May 2, 1983. Blackmun wrote the opinion.

The amount of gain realized on sale of a property subject to a non-recourse mortgage which exceeded the fair market value of the property is not limited by the fair market value, but must be considered as the full value of the forgiven debt. (A non-recourse mortgage is one secured only by the value of the mortgaged property; the borrower assumes no personal liability for the loan.)

United States v. Ptasynski, decided by a 9-0 vote, June 6, 1983. Powell wrote the opinion.

The windfall profits tax on domestic oil producers, enacted in 1980, is constitutional despite the fact that Congress exempted from the tax new oil produced on Alaska's North Slope. This exemption, even though framed in geographic terms, does not violate the constitutional requirement that taxes be uniform throughout the United States.

LABOR LAW

Bowen v. United States Postal Service, decided by a vote of 5-4, Jan. 11, 1983. Powell wrote the opinion; Rehnquist, White, Marshall and Blackmun dissented.

Labor unions that fail to provide fair representation to their members in cases of wrongful dismissal may be held jointly liable with the employer for wages the employee lost as a result of their misconduct or failure to act.

Shepard v. National Labor Relations Board (NLRB), decided by an 8-1 vote, Jan. 18, 1983. Rehnquist wrote the opinion; O'Connor dissented.

The NLRB acted within the area of discretion granted it by Congress when it decided not to order a union or contractors, who had illegally agreed not to deal with non-union dump truck drivers, to reimburse a dump truck operator who was compelled by this illegal agreement to join the union for the amount he paid in dues, initiation fees and fringe benefit contributions.

The NLRB issued an order directing the union and the contractors to cease this illegal boycott of independent truck drivers, but it refused to order the reimbursement, holding that it would not in any way carry out the remedial purposes of the National Labor Relations Act. Such a decision is within the authority granted the board by Congress.

Metropolitan Edison Co. v. National Labor Relations Board, decided by a 9-0 vote, April 4, 1983. Powell wrote the opinion.

Union leaders cannot be punished by employers more severely than other workers for participating in illegal strikes, unless the labor contract specifically requires them to prevent such strikes.

This case involved a 1977 strike during construction of the Three Mile Island nuclear plant near Harrisburg, Pa. Metropolitan Edison, operator of the plant, disciplined

leaders of the International Brotherhood of Electrical Workers when members of the union refused to cross a picket line set up by another union.

Jim McNeff Inc. v. Todd, decided by a 9-0 vote, April 27, 1983. Burger wrote the opinion.

A construction union can sue a contractor to enforce a "pre-hire agreement," a contract between the contractor and union before the union had been selected to represent the contractor's employees. The agreement at issue required the contractor to contribute to a union health and pension fund.

Such agreements are generally prohibited under federal labor law but are allowed in the construction industry so that bidding contractors can estimate labor costs.

Bill Johnson's Restaurants Inc. v. National Labor Relations Board, decided by a 9-0 vote, May 31, 1983. White wrote the opinion.

The NLRB may not halt proceedings in a state court lawsuit so long as the suit has a reasonable legal or factual basis, even if the suit is allegedly filed by an employer to retaliate against employees who are attempting to organize a union.

W. R. Grace & Co. v. Local #759, International Union of the United Rubber, Cork, Linoleum and Plastic Workers of America, decided by a 9-0 vote, May 31, 1983. Blackmun wrote the opinion.

A company that furloughed white males in order to preserve the jobs of more recently hired women and black employees cannot escape damage claims by the fired workers because its lay-off decision was the result of an anti-discrimination agreement. A discriminatory employer who signs conflicting labor agreements — one with a union and one with the Equal Employment Opportunity Commission — cannot use the latter as a shield against a suit charging it with violating the former agreement.

DelCostello v. International Brotherhood of Teamsters, United Steelworkers of America v. Flowers, decided by a 7-2 vote, June 8, 1983. Brennan wrote the opinion; Stevens and O'Connor dissented.

Federal labor law, not state laws limiting the period within which arbitration awards can be set aside, governs the right of employees to file suit against employers and unions alleging breach of a collective bargaining agreement and breach of the union's duty of fair representation in handling the resulting grievance or arbitration.

National Labor Relations Board v. Transportation Management Corp., decided by a 9-0 vote, June 15, 1983. White wrote the opinion.

The NLRB properly concluded that an employer violated federal labor law when it was shown, by a preponderance of the evidence, that hostility toward an employee's union organizing activities was a motivating factor in his dismissal — and the employer had not proved by a preponderance of the evidence that the employee would have been discharged anyway for legitimate reasons.

Edward J. DeBartolo Corp. v. National Labor Relations Board, decided by a 9-0 vote, June 24, 1983. Stevens wrote the opinion.

A union handbilling campaign urging a boycott of a shopping mall because the union has a dispute with the

contractor building a store for one mall tenant is a secondary boycott prohibited by the National Labor Relations Act. This campaign is not protected by the "publicity proviso," which permits a union to advise the public that one company sells the product of another company with which the union has a primary dispute.

Belknap Inc. v. Hale, decided by a 6-3 vote, June 30, 1983. White wrote the opinion; Brennan, Marshall and Powell dissented.

Non-union workers, hired during a strike as permanent replacements for striking workers and then fired when the striking workers came back to work, may sue the employer in state courts for misrepresentation and breach of contract. State court jurisdiction over such cases is not pre-empted by the National Labor Relations Act.

Longshoremen and Harbor Workers

Director, Office of Workers' Compensation Programs v. Perini North River Associates, decided by an 8-1 vote, Jan. 11, 1983. O'Connor wrote the opinion; Stevens dissented.

A construction worker injured while building a sewage disposal plant over a navigable waterway is engaged in "maritime employment" for the purposes of compensation under the Longshoremen's and Harbor Workers' Compensation Act.

Pallas Shipping Agency Ltd. v. Duris, decided by a 9-0 vote, May 23, 1983. Marshall wrote the opinion.

Acceptance by an injured longshoreman of compensation voluntarily paid by his employer, but terminated after two years, does not trigger the provision of the Longshoremen's and Harbor Workers' Compensation Act that assigns to his employer after six months his right to sue any third party responsible for his injury.

Morrison-Knudsen Construction Co. v. Director, Office of Workers' Compensation Programs, U.S. Department of Labor, decided by an 8-1 vote, May 24, 1983. Burger wrote the opinion; Marshall dissented.

In calculating the death benefits to be paid under the Longshoremen's and Harbor Workers' Compensation Act, the "wages" upon which those benefits are based do not include employer payments to union trust funds on behalf of the deceased employee.

Jones & Laughlin Steel Corp. v. Pfeifer, decided by a 9-0 vote, June 15, 1983. Stevens wrote the opinion.

A longshoreman injured at work on a barge owned by his employer may sue the vessel owner — his employer — under the Longshoremen's and Harbor Workers' Compensation Act for causing his injury through negligence, even though he has already received compensation from his employer under the law.

ENERGY

Energy Reserves Group Inc. v. Kansas Power & Light Co. Inc., decided by a 9-0 vote, Jan. 24, 1983. Blackmun wrote the opinion.

States retain the power to limit prices for the in-state sale of gas produced in the state even though Congress has moved to deregulate the price of natural gas sold interstate. The court upheld a 1979 Kansas law that permitted the state to continue regulating the intrastate price of gas produced under contracts already in effect when federal deregulation began in 1978.

Metropolitan Edison Co. v. People Against Nuclear Energy (PANE), United States Nuclear Regulatory Commission (NRC) v. PANE, decided by a 9-0 vote, April 19, 1983. Rehnquist wrote the opinion.

The National Environmental Policy Act does not require the NRC to assess the risk of psychological harm to residents of communities near nuclear power plants before it approves a change in the operation of those plants.

Pacific Gas & Electric Co. v. State Energy Resources Conservation and Development Commission, decided by a 9-0 vote, April 20, 1983. White wrote the opinion.

The Atomic Energy Act leaves the states sufficient power to block construction of new nuclear power plants until an adequate federal plan for disposing of nuclear waste has been developed.

The court upheld a California law that imposed a moratorium on the construction of new plants until such a plan was adopted by the federal government. The court found the state law was not based on concern about the safety of nuclear power plants, an area in which state power is pre-empted by federal law, but on concern about the economic viability of nuclear power.

Arkansas Electric Cooperative Corp. v. Arkansas Public Service Commission, decided by a 7-2 vote, May 16, 1983. Brennan wrote the opinion; White and Burger dissented.

Neither the Constitution's grant of power to Congress to regulate interstate commerce, nor its clause stating that federal laws have supremacy over state laws when they conflict, is offended by a state commission's assertion of jurisdiction over the wholesale rates a rural power cooperative within the state charges to its members.

American Paper Institute Inc. v. American Electric Power Service Corp., Federal Energy Regulatory Commission (FERC) v. American Electric Power Service Corp., decided by an 8-0 vote, May 16, 1983. Marshall wrote the opinion; Powell did not participate in the decision.

The FERC acted properly in issuing two key regulations under the Public Utility Regulatory Policies Act of 1978. The first required utilities purchasing electricity from small firms that generate electricity as well as other forms of energy from the same source to pay these "cogenerators" the "full avoided cost" of producing that amount of power themselves or purchasing it elsewhere. The second regulation required these utilities to make the interconnections necessary to receive power from cogenerators.

Baltimore Gas & Electric Co. v. Natural Resources Defense Council Inc., decided by an 8-0 vote, June 6, 1983. O'Connor wrote the opinion; Powell did not participate in the decision.

The Nuclear Regulatory Commission does not have to consider the problem of the permanent storage of nuclear waste each time it licenses a new nuclear power plant. The court upheld an NRC rule that permits its licensing boards to assume, when licensing a new plant, that there will be a means of storing the wastes that plant generates without damaging the environment.

Public Service Commission of New York v. Mid-Louisiana Gas Co., Arizona Electric Power Cooperative v. Mid-Louisiana Gas Co., Michigan v. Mid-Louisiana Gas Co., Federal Energy Regulatory Commission v. Mid-Louisiana Gas Co., decided by a 5-4 vote, June 28, 1983. Stevens wrote the opinion; White, Brennan, Marshall and Blackmun dissented.

Natural gas pipeline companies that produce gas must be allowed to charge the same rates for their gas as independent producers are permitted under the Natural Gas Policy Act of 1978. The Federal Energy Regulatory Commission misinterpreted the 1978 law when it ruled to the contrary.

ENVIRONMENT

North Dakota v. United States, decided by a 7-2 vote, March 7, 1983. Blackmun wrote the opinion; O'Connor and Rehnquist dissented.

States that consent to the federal acquisition of waterfowl breeding and nesting grounds, authorized and funded under the Migratory Bird Hunting and Conservation Stamp Act and the Wetlands Act of 1961, cannot subsequently revoke that consent or impose new restrictions and conditions on those acquisitions.

Block v. North Dakota, decided by an 8-1 vote, May 2, 1983. White wrote the opinion; O'Connor dissented.

The Quiet Title Act of 1972 is the exclusive means by which states, or other adverse claimants, can challenge the U.S. title to real property. That law's 12-year statute of limitations applies to states just as it does to other parties suing under it.

Watt v. Western Nuclear Inc., decided by a 5-4 vote, June 6, 1983. Marshall wrote the opinion; Powell, Rehnquist, Stevens and O'Connor dissented.

Gravel is a mineral within the meaning of the Stock-Raising Homestead Act of 1916, and thus gravel on land settled by homesteaders under that law remains the property of the U.S. government.

Nevada v. United States, Truckee-Carson Irrigation District v. United States, Pyramid Lake Paiute Tribe of Indians v. Truckee-Carson Irrigation District, decided by a 9-0 vote, June 24, 1983. Rehnquist wrote the opinion.

The United States is barred by earlier federal court decisions from reopening water rights cases between Indians and state residents in order to seek additional allocation of water to Indians.

Ruckelshaus v. Sierra Club, decided by a 5-4 vote, July 1, 1983. Rehnquist wrote the opinion; Stevens, Brennan, Marshall and Blackmun dissented.

Clean Air Act provisions that authorize federal judges in emissions-standards review cases to award attorneys' fees when appropriate authorize such fee awards only to parties who have succeeded in some measure on their claims.

STATE POWERS

Federal Funds

Bell v. New Jersey, decided by a 9-0 vote, May 31, 1983. O'Connor wrote the opinion.

States that misspend federal education funds granted under Title I of the Elementary and Secondary Education Act of 1965 can be required to repay those misspent funds to the federal government. This repayment obligation can be enforced even if the funds were misused before 1978, when Congress specifically amended Title I to authorize repayment in such circumstances.

Indians

New Mexico v. Mescalero Apache Tribe, decided by a 9-0 vote, June 13, 1983. Marshall wrote the opinion.

Federal law pre-empts the application of New Mexico hunting and fishing regulations to on-reservation hunting and fishing by non-members of an Indian tribe, once a tribe has with federal assistance set up a comprehensive plan for managing its wildlife resources.

Municipal Liability

City of Revere v. Massachusetts General Hospital, decided by a 9-0 vote, June 27, 1983. Blackmun wrote the opinion.

The constitutional ban on cruel and unusual punishment obligated a city to see that persons injured while being arrested by police receive appropriate medical care, but it does not obligate the city to pay the medical bills which result. It is up to the state to decide who should pay the bill.

Privileges and Immunities

White v. Massachusetts Council of Construction Employers, decided by votes of 9-0 and 7-2, Feb. 28, 1983. Rehnquist wrote the opinion; Blackmun and White dissented in part.

The power of a city to require that at least half the workers on each city-funded construction project be residents of the city is not pre-empted by the federal power to regulate interstate commerce.

Equal Employment Opportunity Commission (EEOC) v. Wyoming, decided by a 5-4 vote, March 2, 1983. Brennan wrote the opinion; Burger, Powell, Rehnquist and O'Connor dissented.

The Age Discrimination in Employment Act, which forbids states to mandate retirement for certain employees at age 55, does not violate the 10th Amendment guarantee of state power and sovereignty.

Martinez v. Bynum, decided by an 8-1 vote, May 2, 1983. Powell wrote the opinion; Marshall dissented.

States do not have to provide a free education to children who reside within their boundaries solely for the purpose of attending school. The court upheld a Texas law that allows school districts to require minors who live apart from their parents or legal guardians and within the district for the primary purpose of attending its schools to pay tuition.

Regulation

Philko Aviation Inc. v. Shacket, decided by a 9-0 vote, June 15, 1983. White wrote the opinion.

Congress pre-empted state law when it approved part of the Federal Aviation Act that required that any transfer of title to an aircraft would not be valid against a third party until it was recorded with the Federal Aviation Administration. This provision of federal law pre-empts state

laws that permit conveyance of title to aircraft by transfer of possession alone, without such FAA recording.

Shaw v. Delta Air Lines Inc., decided by a 9-0 vote, June 24, 1983. Blackmun wrote the opinion.

New York's Human Rights Law, which forbids discrimination in employee benefit plans on the basis of pregnancy, is pre-empted with respect to plans subject to the federal Employee Retirement Income Security Act (ERISA) only insofar as it bars practices that are lawful under federal law. New York's Disability Benefits Law, which requires employers to pay sick leave benefits to employees unable to work because of pregnancy, is not pre-empted by ERISA.

Rice v. Rehner, decided by a 6-3 vote, July 1, 1983. O'Connor wrote the opinion; Blackmun, Brennan and Marshall dissented.

California is not precluded by federal law from requiring a federally licensed Indian storekeeper who operates a store on an Indian reservation to obtain a state license to sell liquor for consumption off the premises.

State Courts

Gillette Co. v. Miner, dismissed Dec. 6, 1982, without dissent.

A month after the court heard oral arguments in the case — which involved state court jurisdiction over a class action suit in which many members of the class had no connection with the state — it dismissed the case, stating simply that there was no final judgment in it for the Supreme Court to review.

Local 926, International Union of Operating Engineers, AFL-CIO v. Jones, decided by a 6-3 vote, April 4, 1983. White wrote the opinion; Rehnquist, Powell and O'Connor dissented.

The National Labor Relations Act pre-empts state court jurisdiction over a case in which a supervisory employee charges that a union had coerced his employer into firing him. This is a matter over which the National Labor Relations Board has exclusive jurisdiction. Although the NLRB official acting on this complaint in the first place dismissed it as based on insufficient evidence, the employee may not take this complaint to state courts, seeking damages from the union and the company.

Arizona v. San Carlos Apache Tribe of Arizona, Montana v. Northern Cheyenne Tribe of the Northern Cheyenne Indian Reservation, decided by a 6-3 vote, July 1, 1983. Brennan wrote the opinion; Marshall, Stevens and Blackmun dissented.

State courts, as well as federal courts, have jurisdiction to hear water rights disputes involving Indian tribes.

Taxation

Xerox Corp. v. County of Harris, Texas, decided by an 8-1 vote, Dec. 13, 1982. Burger wrote the opinion; Powell dissented.

State property taxes on goods held in a customs bonded warehouse after being assembled in a foreign country and prior to shipment to another foreign country conflict with the comprehensive customs system Congress has created, which permits duty-free storage in such warehouses.

Memphis Bank & Trust Co. v. Garner, decided by a 9-0 vote, Jan. 24, 1983. Marshall wrote the opinion.

Tennessee's bank tax, which is imposed on the net earnings of banks doing business in the state, including interest the banks receive on U.S. bonds and on bonds issued by other states, is a discriminatory tax in favor of Tennessee. It violates federal law exempting U.S. bonds from most state and local taxes.

Washington v. United States, decided by a 5-4 vote, March 29, 1983. Rehnquist wrote the opinion; Blackmun, Marshall, Stevens and White dissented.

Federal contractors are not immune from state taxation. Washington state laws imposing a sales tax on contractors who build on federal land, but not on contractors building on non-federal land (because in those cases the tax is imposed on the landowner) is not unconstitutional. A tax is not invalid just because it treats those who deal with the federal government differently from others.

Exxon Corp. v. Eagerton, Exchange Oil and Gas Corp. v. Eagerton, decided by a 9-0 vote, June 8, 1983. Marshall wrote the opinion.

Alabama may impose a severance tax on natural gas produced in-state, but it may not prohibit gas producers from passing on the cost of that gas to interstate customers. It can impose a ban on the pass-through of that cost to in-state customers, but federal law governs with regard to interstate sales.

Container Corporation of America v. Franchise Tax Board, decided by 5-3 vote, June 27, 1983. Brennan wrote the opinion; Stevens did not participate; Powell, Burger and O'Connor dissented.

States may consider the worldwide income of U.S.-based multinational corporations in calculating the corporations' state tax liability. The income of foreign subsidiaries may be considered in the tax base for this assessment. This "worldwide unitary" method of taxation does not violate the due process guarantee or the Constitution's grant of power to the federal government to regulate interstate and foreign commerce.

American Bank & Trust Co. v. Dallas County, decided by a 6-2 vote, July 5, 1983. Blackmun wrote the opinion; O'Connor did not participate; Rehnquist and Stevens dissented.

Texas, which imposes a property tax on the value of the stock of a commercial bank, cannot include the value of the U.S. securities held by the bank in the value of the bank stock. By including this value in the bank share value, Texas violates the federal law that exempts all U.S. obligations from state and local taxes.

INTERSTATE DISPUTES

Colorado v. New Mexico, decided by a 9-0 vote, Dec. 13, 1982. Marshall wrote the opinion.

This case concerned an effort by Colorado to divert water for the use of its residents from the Vermejo River, a non-navigable river that originates in southern Colorado and flows into New Mexico. The river's water is at present used entirely by New Mexicans.

A special master had been appointed by the Supreme Court in 1979 to resolve this water-rights dispute between

Colorado and New Mexico. The special master recommended that Colorado be permitted to divert 4,000-acre-feet of water from the river each year; New Mexico objected, and the Supreme Court sent the matter back to the special master for more specific findings to support his recommendation.

Arizona v. California, decided by votes of 8-0 and 5-3, March 30, 1983. White wrote the opinion; Marshall did not participate in the case; Brennan, Blackmun and Stevens dissented.

The court refused to grant five Indian tribes additional rights to water from the Colorado River. This case, an original one in the Supreme Court (that is, it had not been heard by any other court), was the oldest live case on the court's docket. It had been there since 1952, when Arizona sued California to limit its use of Colorado River water.

The government acknowledged that because of a mistake made in 1964, when water rights were allotted to the tribes and the states, the tribes had received less than they should have. But the court in this case refused to redistribute those rights, emphasizing the need for finality in such matters.

Texas v. New Mexico, exceptions to the report of a special master sustained in part, overruled in part, by a 9-0 vote, June 17, 1983. Brennan wrote the opinion.

The court ordered further hearings in a dispute between Texas and New Mexico over the amount of water each state is entitled to from the Pecos River. The court rejected a plan to permit the U.S. representative on the Pecos River Commission to vote to resolve such disputes.

Idaho v. Oregon and Washington, decided by a 6-3 vote, June 23, 1983. Blackmun wrote the opinion; O'Connor, Brennan and Stevens dissented.

The court dismissed an Idaho action against Oregon and Washington regarding the apportionment of certain fish that migrate between the Pacific Ocean and Idaho. The court found, on the basis of a special master's report, that Idaho had not shown that it had suffered sufficient injury under the present situation to justify a court order to remedy it.

FEDERAL COURTS

Moses H. Cone Memorial Hospital v. Mercury Construction Corp., decided by a 6-3 vote, Feb. 23, 1983. Brennan wrote the opinion; Rehnquist, Burger and O'Connor dissented.

A federal district court abused its discretion in staying, and effectively dismissing, a lawsuit filed by a contractor against a hospital to compel the hospital to submit contract disputes between them to arbitration under federal arbitration law. The federal court cited as the reason for its action parallel state court litigation in the case.

Only in exceptional circumstances should a federal district court decline to exercise its jurisdiction because of parallel state litigation. No such circumstances existed here.

District of Columbia Court of Appeals v. Feldman, decided by an 8-1 vote, March 23, 1983. Brennan wrote the opinion; Stevens dissented.

Denial by the highest local court in the District of Columbia of petitions seeking waiver of a D.C. bar admis-

sion rule is a judicial action not subject to review by any federal court but the Supreme Court.

Federal district courts do have jurisdiction over general challenges to state bar rules, which are usually set out by state courts in non-judicial proceedings.

City of Los Angeles v. Lyons, decided by a 5-4 vote, April 20, 1983. White wrote the opinion; Marshall, Brennan, Blackmun and Stevens dissented.

The court overturned a federal district judge's order barring Los Angeles police officers from using certain choke holds on suspects unless the officers were threatened with death or great bodily harm.

The Supreme Court held that a man subjected to this potentially fatal type of hold after being stopped by police for a traffic violation lacked standing to seek an injunction against its future use because he could not show that the choke hold would ever again be used against him.

Verlinden B.V. v. Central Bank of Nigeria, decided by a 9-0 vote, May 23, 1983. Burger wrote the opinion.

It is within the power of Congress to grant federal courts jurisdiction over cases brought by foreign corporations against foreign countries, even when the dispute is not a federal matter. Congress granted federal courts such jurisdiction in the Foreign Sovereign Immunities Act of 1976.

Franchise Tax Board of California v. Construction Laborers Vacation Trust for Southern California, decided by a 9-0 vote, June 24, 1983. Brennan wrote the opinion.

A federal court lacks jurisdiction to hear a suit by a state to enforce state tax levies against funds held in trust for an employee benefit plan when the only federal issue is the defensive claim that the employee benefit plan is subject to the federal Employee Retirement Income Security Act.

United States v. Sells Engineering Inc., decided by a 5-4 vote, June 30, 1983. Brennan wrote the opinion; Burger, Powell, Rehnquist and O'Connor dissented.

Attorneys in the civil division of the Justice Department are not automatically entitled to access to transcripts or other records of federal grand jury investigations. To gain such access, these lawyers must obtain a federal court order by demonstrating a strong and particular need to see the records.

United States v. Baggot, decided by an 8-1 vote, June 30, 1983. Brennan wrote the opinion; Burger dissented.

The Internal Revenue Service may not seek disclosure of otherwise secret grand jury materials for use in a civil tax audit. Such disclosure is permitted by court order only if the materials will be used to prepare for particular litigation.

POWERS OF CONGRESS

Immigration and Naturalization Service v. Chadha, United States House of Representatives v. Chadha, United States Senate v. Chadha, decided by a 7-2 vote, June 23, 1983. Burger wrote the opinion; White and Rehnquist dissented.

The one-house legislative veto, under which Congress claimed for itself the power to review and veto executive branch decisions implementing laws, is unconstitutional. It violates the separation of powers between the executive

and legislative branches, and it runs counter to the "single, finely wrought and exhaustively considered procedure" the Constitution prescribes for the enactment of legislation — approval by both chambers and presentation to the president for his signature.

With this decision, invalidating a device included in one form or another in more than 200 laws enacted since 1932, the court struck down at one time more provisions in more federal laws than it had invalidated in its entire history. As of mid-1982, the court had struck down all or part of 110 federal laws as unconstitutional. *(Opinion excerpts, below)*

MISCELLANEOUS

Lockheed Aircraft Corp. v. United States, decided by a 7-2 vote, Feb. 23, 1983. Powell wrote the opinion; Rehnquist and Burger dissented.

The Federal Employees' Compensation Act does not bar a suit against the government by an aerospace company seeking contribution or indemnity to the company, which itself was sued for wrongful death by the estate of a government employee who died in the crash of an aircraft being used by the United States.

This case arose after the crash of an Air Force cargo plane during the Vietnam "baby lift" of 1975. One hundred forty-four people were killed. Relatives of some government employees who were killed sued the airplane's manufacturer, Lockheed, for damages. Lockheed, in turn, sought to sue the government, contending the crash was caused by government negligence, which resulted in the failure of a rear loading door to close properly. The Supreme Court's decision permitted Lockheed to pursue its suit against the government.

Block v. Neal, decided by a 9-0 vote, March 7, 1983. Marshall wrote the opinion.

Persons who receive Farmers Home Administration (FmHA) loans to build their homes can sue the federal government if FmHA inspectors fail adequately to inspect the construction of their homes, which are later found to be defective.

United States v. Mitchell, decided by a 6-3 vote, June 27, 1983. Marshall wrote the opinion; Powell, Rehnquist and O'Connor dissented.

The United States can be sued for money damages by Indian tribes charging mismanagement of valuable timber lands on their reservations. The basis for these suits is the Tucker Act, which permits some suits against the government for grievances, and several other laws that give the federal government full responsibility to manage Indian resources for the benefit of Indians.

Bowsher v. Merck & Co., Merck & Co. v. Bowsher, decided by votes of 5-4 and 7-2, April 19, 1983. O'Connor wrote the opinion; White, Marshall, Blackmun and Stevens dissented.

The authority of the comptroller general of the United States to examine the records of a contractor with whom the government has entered into a fixed-price negotiated contract for drugs extends only to the contractor's records of the direct costs of producing those drugs, and not to records concerning indirect costs such as research, marketing and promotion.

Heckler v. Campbell, decided by votes of 9-0 and 8-1, May 16, 1983. Powell wrote the opinion; Marshall dissented.

The Social Security Administration may properly use standard medical-vocational guidelines to determine whether jobs exist that a claimant for disability benefits could perform despite his or her disability.

Federal Trade Commission v. Grolier Inc., decided by a 9-0 vote, June 6, 1983. White wrote the opinion.

A Freedom of Information Act exemption that protects from disclosure under the law "interagency or intraagency memorandums or letters which would not be available by law to a party . . . in litigation with the agency" protects the documents used by government lawyers to prepare for litigation even after the litigation has ended.

National Association of Greeting Card Publishers v. U.S. Postal Service, United Parcel Service of America v. U.S. Postal Service, decided by a 9-0 vote, June 22, 1983. Blackmun wrote the opinion.

The Postal Rate Commission has broad discretion in setting rates for different classes of mail. It is not required by law to maximize its use of the "cost-of-service" principle, under which each class of mail pays the share of costs for the overall postal system directly attributable to it.

The Commission has the discretion to use whatever reliable way it chooses to attribute these costs to the various classes of mail. ∎

Text of Court Opinions on Legislative Veto

The following are excerpts from the Supreme Court's June 23 majority and dissenting opinions in the case of Immigration and Naturalization Service v. Chadha, *which tested the constitutionality of the legislative veto.*

The majority opinion was written by Chief Justice Warren E. Burger on behalf of himself and Justices Harry A. Blackmun, William J. Brennan Jr., Thurgood Marshall, Sandra Day O'Connor and John Paul Ste- *vens. Justice Byron R. White wrote the dissenting opinion quoted below.*

Majority Opinion

We turn now to the question whether action of one House of Congress under § 244(c)(2) violates strictures of the Constitution. We begin, of course, with the presumption that the challenged statute is valid. Its wisdom is not the concern of the courts; if a challenged action does not violate the Constitution, it must be sustained:

"Once the meaning of an enactment is discerned and its constitutionality determined, the judicial process comes to an end. We do not sit as a committee of review, nor are we vested with the power of veto."

By the same token, the fact that a given law or procedure is efficient, convenient, and useful in facilitating functions of government, standing alone, will not save it if it is contrary to the Constitution. Convenience and efficiency are not the primary objectives — or the hallmarks — of democratic government and our inquiry is

sharpened rather than blunted by the fact that Congressional veto provisions are appearing with increasing frequency in statutes which delegate authority to executive and independent agencies.

* * * *

The records of the Constitutional Convention reveal that the requirement that all legislation be presented to the President before becoming law was uniformly accepted by the Framers. Presentment to the President and the Presidential veto were considered so imperative that the draftsmen took special pains to assure that these requirements could not be circumvented....

The decision to provide the President with a limited and qualified power to nullify proposed legislation by veto was based on the profound conviction of the Framers that the powers conferred on Congress were the powers to be most carefully circumscribed. It is beyond doubt that lawmaking was a power to be shared by both Houses and the President....

The President's role in the lawmaking process also reflects the Framers' careful efforts to check whatever propensity a particular Congress might have to enact oppressive, improvident, or ill-considered measures.

* * * *

The bicameral requirement of Art. I, §§ 1, 7 was of scarcely less concern to the Framers than was the Presidential veto and indeed the two concepts are interdependent. By providing that no law could take effect without the concurrence of the prescribed majority of the Members of both Houses, the Framers reemphasized their belief, already remarked upon in connection with the Presentment Clauses, that legislation should not be enacted unless it has been carefully and fully considered by the Nation's elected officials.

* * * *

...The President's participation in the legislative process was to protect the Executive Branch from Congress and to protect the whole people from improvident laws. The division of the Congress into two distinctive bodies assures that the legislative power would be exercised only after opportunity for full study and debate in separate settings. The President's unilateral veto power, in turn, was limited by the power of two thirds of both Houses of Congress to overrule a veto thereby precluding final arbitrary action of one person. It emerges clearly that the prescription for legislative action in Art. I, §§ 1, 7 represents the Framers' decision that the legislative power of the Federal Government be exercised in accord with a single, finely wrought and exhaustively considered, procedure.

* * * *

Finally, we see that when the Framers intended to authorize either House of Congress to act alone and outside of its prescribed bicameral legislative role, they narrowly and precisely defined the procedure for such action. There are but four provisions in the Constitution, explicit and unambiguous, by which one House may act alone with the unreviewable force of law, not subject to the President's veto:

(a) The House of Representatives alone was given the power to initiate impeachments. Art. I, § 2, cl. 6;

(b) The Senate alone was given the power to conduct trials following impeachment on charges initiated by the House and to convict following trial. Art. I, § 3, cl. 5;

(c) The Senate alone was given final unreviewable power to approve or to disapprove presidential appointments. Art. II, § 2, cl. 2;

(d) The Senate alone was given unreviewable power to ratify treaties negotiated by the President. Art. II, § 2, cl. 2.

Clearly, when the Draftsmen sought to confer special powers on one House, independent of the other House, or of the President, they did so in explicit, unambiguous terms. These carefully defined exceptions from presentment and bicameralism underscore the difference between the legislative functions of Congress and other unilateral but important and binding one-House acts provided for in the Constitution. These exceptions are narrow, explicit, and separately justified; none of them authorize the action challenged here. On the contrary, they provide further support for the conclusion that Congressional authority is not to be implied and for the conclusion that the veto provided for in § 244(c)(2) is not authorized by the constitutional design of the powers of the Legislative Branch.

...The bicameral requirement, the Presentment Clauses, the President's veto, and Congress' power to override a veto were intended to erect enduring checks on each Branch and to protect the people from the improvident exercise of power by mandating certain prescribed steps. To preserve those checks, and maintain the separation of powers, the carefully defined limits on the power of each Branch must not be eroded.

* * * *

The veto authorized by § 244(c)(2) doubtless has been in many respects a convenient shortcut; the "sharing" with the Executive by Congress of its authority over aliens in this manner is, on its face, an appealing compromise. In purely practical terms, it is obviously easier for action to be taken by one House without submission to the President; but it is crystal clear from the records of the Convention, contemporaneous writings and debates, that the Framers ranked other values higher than efficiency. The records of the Convention and debates in the States preceding ratification underscore the common desire to define and limit the exercise of the newly created federal powers affecting the states

and the people. There is unmistakable expression of a determination that legislation by the national Congress be a step-by-step, deliberate and deliberative process.

The choices we discern as having been made in the Constitutional Convention impose burdens on governmental processes that often seem clumsy, inefficient, even unworkable, but those hard choices were consciously made by men who had lived under a form of government that permitted arbitrary governmental acts to go unchecked. There is no support in the Constitution or decisions of this Court for the proposition that the cumbersomeness and delays often encountered in complying with explicit Constitutional standards may be avoided, either by the Congress or by the President. With all the obvious flaws of delay, untidiness, and potential for abuse, we have not yet found a better way to preserve freedom than by making the exercise of power subject to the carefully crafted restraints spelled out in the Constitution.

Dissenting Opinion

Today the Court not only invalidates § 244(c)(2) of the Immigration and Nationality Act, but also sounds the death knell for nearly 200 other statutory provisions in which Congress has reserved a "legislative veto." For this reason, the Court's decision is of surpassing importance. And it is for this reason that the Court would have been well-advised to decide the case, if possible, on the narrower grounds of separation of powers, leaving for full consideration the constitutionality of other congressional review statutes operating on such varied matters as war powers and agency rulemaking, some of which concern the independent regulatory agencies.

The prominence of the legislative veto mechanism in our contemporary political system and its importance to Congress can hardly be overstated. It has become a central means by which Congress secures the accountability of executive and independent agencies. Without the legislative veto, Congress is faced with a Hobson's choice: either to refrain from delegating the necessary authority, leaving itself with a hopeless task of writing laws with the requisite specificity to cover endless special circumstances across the entire policy landscape, or in the alternative, to abdicate its lawmaking function to the executive branch and independent agencies. To choose the former leaves major national problems unresolved; to opt for the latter risks unaccountable policymaking by those not elected to fill that role. Accordingly, over the past five decades, the legislative veto has been placed in nearly 200 statutes. The device is known in every field of governmental concern: reorganization, budgets, foreign affairs, war powers, and regulation of trade, safety, energy, the environment and the economy.

* * * *

Even this brief review suffices to demonstrate that the legislative veto is more than "efficient, convenient, and useful." *Ante,* at 23. It is an important if not indispensable political invention that allows the President and Congress to resolve major constitutional and policy differences, assures the accountability of independent regulatory agencies, and preserves Congress' control over lawmaking. Perhaps there are other means of accommodation and accountability, but the increasing reliance of Congress upon the legislative veto suggests that the alternatives to which Congress must now turn are not entirely satisfactory.

The history of the legislative veto also makes clear that it has not been a sword with which Congress has struck out to aggrandize itself at the expense of the other branches — the concerns of Madison and Hamilton. Rather, the veto has been a means of defense, a reservation of ultimate authority necessary if Congress is to fulfill its designated role under Article I as the nation's lawmaker. While the President has often objected to particular legislative vetoes, generally those left in the hands of congressional committees, the Executive has more often agreed to legislative review as the price for a broad delegation of authority. To be sure, the President may have preferred unrestricted power, but that could be precisely why Congress thought it essential to retain a check on the exercise of delegated authority.

For all these reasons, the apparent sweep of the Court's decision today is regrettable. The Court's Article I analysis appears to invalidate all legislative vetoes irrespective of form or subject. Because the legislative veto is commonly found as a check upon rulemaking by administrative agencies and upon broad-based policy decisions of the Executive Branch, it is particularly unfortunate that the Court reaches its decision in a case involving the exercise of a veto over deportation decisions regarding particular individuals. Courts should always be wary of striking statutes as unconstitutional; to strike an entire class of statutes based on consideration of a somewhat atypical and more-readily indictable exemplar of the class is irresponsible.

* * * *

If the legislative veto were as plainly unconstitutional as the Court strives to suggest, its broad ruling today would be more comprehensible. But, the constitutionality of the legislative veto is anything but clearcut. The issue divides scholars, courts, attorneys general, and the two other branches of the National Government. If the veto devices so flagrantly disregarded the requirements of Article I as the Court today suggests, I find it incomprehensible that Congress, whose members are bound by oath to uphold the Constitution, would have placed these mechanisms in nearly 200 separate laws over a period of 50 years.

The reality of the situation is that the constitutional question posed today is one of immense difficulty over which the executive and legislative branches — as well as scholars and judges — have understandably disagreed. That disagreement stems from the silence of the Constitution on the precise question: The Constitution does not directly authorize or prohibit the legislative veto. Thus, our task should be to determine whether the legislative veto is consistent with the purposes of Art. I and the principles of Separation of Powers which are reflected in that Article and throughout the Constitution. We should not find the lack of a specific constitutional authorization for the legislative veto surprising, and I would not infer disapproval of the mechanism from its absence. From the summer of 1787 to the present the government of the United States has become an endeavor far beyond the contemplation of the Framers. Only within the last half century has the complexity and size of the Federal Government's responsibilities grown so greatly that the Congress must rely on the legislative veto as the most effective if not the only means to insure their role as the nation's lawmakers. But the wisdom of the Framers was to anticipate that the nation would grow and new problems of governance would require different solutions. Accordingly, our Federal Government was intentionally chartered with the flexibility to respond to contemporary needs without losing sight of fundamental democratic principles.

* * * *

If Congress may delegate lawmaking power to independent and executive agencies, it is most difficult to understand Article I as forbidding Congress from also reserving a check on legislative power for itself. Absent the veto, the agencies receiving delegations of legislative or quasi-legislative power may issue regulations having the force of law without bicameral approval and without the President's signature. It is thus not apparent why the reservation of a veto over the exercise of that legislative power must be subject to a more exacting test. In both cases, it is enough that the initial statutory authorizations comply with the Article I requirements.

* * * *

I regret that I am in disagreement with my colleagues on the fundamental questions that this case presents. But even more I regret the destructive scope of the Court's holding. It reflects a profoundly different conception of the Constitution than that held by the Courts which sanctioned the modern administrative state. Today's decision strikes down in one fell swoop provisions in more laws enacted by Congress than the Court has cumulatively invalidated in its history. I fear it will now be more difficult "to insure that the fundamental policy decisions in our society will be made not by an appointed official but by the body immediately responsible to the people." I must dissent. ∎

Reagan Cabinet Nominees Include Two Women

President Reagan appointed three new Cabinet secretaries in 1983, including the first two women to head Cabinet departments in his administration.

Early in the year, Reagan appointed and the Senate easily confirmed Elizabeth Hanford Dole as secretary of transportation and Margaret M. Heckler as secretary of health and human services. United Nations Representative Jeane J. Kirkpatrick also held Cabinet rank.

Before adjourning Nov. 18, the Senate confirmed Reagan's third Cabinet nominee, William P. Clark, to be secretary of the interior. Clark, Reagan's national security adviser, succeeded James G. Watt, who resigned under fire Oct. 9.

In other confirmations to major policy-making posts:

● With only modest opposition, the Senate July 27 confirmed Paul A. Volcker to a second four-year term as chairman of the Federal Reserve Board. Volcker thus retained primary responsibility for guiding U.S. monetary policy.

● Kenneth L. Adelman, Reagan's choice to head the Arms Control and Disarmament Agency (ACDA), faced tougher opposition but finally was confirmed April 14.

● William D. Ruckelshaus won unanimous Senate endorsement May 17 to become director of the scandal-ridden Environmental Protection Agency (EPA).

Reagan in 1983 continued to have problems with his nominations to the Legal Services Corporation (LSC) board of directors. And, in attempting to appoint a majority of members to the U.S. Civil Rights Commission, he started a six-month struggle between himself and Congress.

On the sensitive issue of the number of women named to high places, a Congressional Quarterly survey found that in his first two and one-half years in office, Reagan successfully appointed 19 percent fewer women to jobs requiring Senate approval than did President Carter during the comparable period. Between the time he took office in 1977 and the congressional recess in August 1979, the Senate confirmed 166 women nominated by Carter to posts ranging from Cabinet jobs to ambassadorships to advisory commissions. Between the time Reagan moved into the White House in 1981 and the 1983 August recess, the Senate had confirmed 134 women nominated by Reagan. (*Reagan judicial appointments, story, p. 302*)

In all, the president sent 3,454 civilian nominations to the Senate in 1983. The Senate confirmed 2,978 and two were withdrawn.

Cabinet Nominees

Dole. The first woman to head a Cabinet department in the Reagan administration, Elizabeth Hanford Dole, was confirmed as secretary of transportation by the Senate on a 97-0 vote Feb. 1. (*Vote 1, p. 2-S*)

Dole, 46, succeeded Drew Lewis, who resigned to become chief executive officer of Warner Amex Cable Communications Inc. The wife of Sen. Robert Dole, R-Kan., she was serving as Reagan's assistant for public liaison when Reagan announced her appointment to the Cabinet post

Jan. 5. Her past service included a stint as Federal Trade commissioner. Like Lewis, who was widely regarded as one of Reagan's most able Cabinet secretaries, she had little background in the transportation field.

Heckler. President Reagan's second woman Cabinet appointee, former Rep. Margaret M. Heckler, R-Mass. (1967-83), was tapped by Reagan on Jan. 12 to serve as secretary of health and human services. Two months earlier, Heckler had lost an often bitter re-election campaign in a newly redrawn district to Barney Frank, D-Mass.

The Senate confirmed the Heckler nomination March 3 on an 82-3 vote. All three "nay" votes were cast by Republicans: Bob Packwood, R-Ore.; Jesse Helms, R-N.C.; and John P. East, R-N.C. (*Vote 8, p. 4-S*)

Heckler, 51, succeeded Richard S. Schweiker who resigned to become president of the American Council of Life Insurance, a trade and lobbying organization for life insurance companies. She brought to office no notable expertise in the programs she was to administer at HHS — the largest Cabinet agency, with 145,000 employees. During her eight terms in the House, she served on the Agriculture, Banking, Government Operations, Science and Veterans' Affairs committees, but not on the panels with legislative responsibility for HHS programs.

Clark. After Republicans overcame a challenge to Reagan natural resource policies that threatened to snag the nomination, the Senate Nov. 18 voted 71-18 to confirm William P. Clark as secretary of the interior. All of the nay votes were cast by Democrats. (*Vote 369, p. 60-S*)

Clark, 51, had served Reagan as deputy secretary of state and national security adviser. In a surprise move, the president Oct. 19 nominated him to succeed James G. Watt, who resigned Oct. 9, thus avoiding an almost certain no confidence vote in the Senate. Many Democrats who forced a delay in the Clark confirmation vote until the final hours before Congress adjourned for the year said their concern was not so much Clark's qualifications as administration policies under Watt. (*Story, p. 327*)

Federal Reserve

Volcker. Ending months of speculation, Reagan announced June 18 that he would nominate Paul A. Volcker to a second four-year term as chairman of the Federal Reserve Board. Volcker's supporters gave him substantial credit for controlling inflation, which had exceeded 13 percent in 1979. But his critics maintained that the price paid for lowering inflation — the longest and deepest recession since the Great Depression — was too high.

The Senate confirmed Volcker July 27. Eight Republicans and eight Democrats opposed the nomination on the 84-16 vote. (*Vote 218, p. 37-S*)

Volcker began his second term as chairman Aug. 6. He was originally appointed by President Carter in 1979, when he was confirmed by a 98-0 vote. His term as board member ran until Jan. 31, 1992. (*Story, p. 266*)

Membership of Federal Regulatory Agencies, 1983

Civil Aeronautics Board

(Five members appointed for six-year terms; not more than three members from one political party; agency due to expire Jan. 1, 1985.)

Member	Party	Term Expires	Nominated	Confirmed by Senate
Clinton D. McKinnon (C)	R	12/31/84	10/6/81	10/26/81
Gloria Schaffer	D	12/31/84	7/13/78	9/13/78
James R. Smith	I	12/31/84	7/25/80	8/27/80
Diane Kay Morales	R	12/31/84	12/6/82	12/16/82
Barbara E. McConnell	R	12/31/84	8/31/83	9/21/83

Commodity Futures Trading Commission

(Five members appointed for five-year terms; not more than three members from one political party.)

Member	Party	Term Expires	Nominated	Confirmed by Senate
Susan M. Phillips (C)	R	4/13/85	9/10/81	10/27/81
Kalo A. Hineman	R	6/19/86	12/10/81	12/16/81
Fowler C. West	D	4/13/87	9/17/82	10/1/82
William E. Seale	D	4/13/88	11/4/83	11/15/83
Vacancy				

Consumer Product Safety Commission

(Five members appointed for seven-year terms; not more than three members from one political party.)

Member	Party	Term Expires	Nominated	Confirmed by Senate
Nancy Harvey Steorts (C)	R	10/26/84	7/13/81	7/27/81
Samuel D. Zagoria	R	10/26/85	9/29/78	10/10/78
Stuart M. Statler	R	10/26/86	6/14/79	7/26/79
Terrence M. Scanlon	D	10/26/89	1/26/83	3/23/83
Saundra B. Armstrong	D	10/26/90	8/31/83	11/18/83

Federal Communications Commission

(Five members appointed for seven-year terms; not more than three members from one political party.)

Member	Party	Term Expires	Nominated	Confirmed by Senate
Mark S. Fowler (C)	R	6/30/86	4/27/81	5/14/81
James H. Quello	D	6/30/84	7/8/81	7/31/81
Henry M. Rivera	D	6/30/87	7/8/81	7/31/81
Mary Ann Weyforth-Dawson	R	6/30/88	5/12/81	6/4/81
Dennis Patrick	R	6/30/85	10/18/83	*

* Member sitting on commission pending Senate confirmation.

Federal Election Commission

(Six members appointed for six-year terms; not more than three members from one political party.)

Member	Party	Term Expires	Nominated	Confirmed by Senate
Danny Lee McDonald (C)	D	4/30/87	1/26/82	7/1/82
Frank P. Reiche	R	4/30/85	5/1/79	7/25/79
John W. McGarry	D	4/30/89	6/15/83	7/29/83
Joan D. Aikens	R	4/30/89	6/15/83	7/29/83
Thomas E. Harris	D	4/30/85	5/1/79	6/19/79
Lee Ann Elliott	R	4/30/87	1/26/82	7/1/82

Federal Energy Regulatory Commission

(Five members appointed to staggered four-year terms; not more than three members from one political party.)

Member	Party	Term Expires	Nominated	Confirmed by Senate
Raymond J. O'Connor (C)	R	10/20/87	10/3/83	10/28/83
John D. Hughes	D	10/20/83†	6/27/80	8/27/80
Georgianna Sheldon	R	10/20/84	5/14/81	6/4/81
Anthony G. Sousa	R	10/20/84	6/30/81	7/27/81
Oliver G. Richard III	D	10/20/85	7/16/82	8/19/82

† Will sit on commission until successor is appointed.

Federal Reserve System Governors

(Seven members appointed for 14-year terms; no statutory limitation on political party membership.)

Member	Party	Term Expires	Nominated	Confirmed by Senate
Paul A. Volcker (C)	D	1/31/92	7/25/79	8/2/79
Nancy H. Teeters	D	1/31/84	8/28/78	9/15/78
J. Charles Partee	I	1/31/86	12/5/75	12/19/75
Henry C. Wallich	R	1/31/88	1/11/74	2/8/74
Emmett J. Rice	D	1/31/90	4/13/79	6/12/79
Lyle E. Gramley	D	1/31/94	2/2/80	5/15/80
Preston Martin	R	1/31/96	1/11/82	3/30/82

Federal Trade Commission

(Five members appointed for seven-year terms; not more than three members from one political party.)

Member	Party	Term Expires	Nominated	Confirmed by Senate
James C. Miller III (C)	R	9/25/88	7/16/81	9/21/81
Michael J. Pertschuk	D	9/25/84	3/25/77	4/6/77
Patricia P. Bailey	R	9/25/87	6/10/80	6/26/80
George W. Douglas	D	9/25/89	9/20/82	12/16/82
Terry Calvani	R	9/25/90	9/14/83	11/16/83

Interstate Commerce Commission

(Membership is being reduced gradually under a 1982 law, PL 97-253. As of Jan. 1, 1986, the ICC will have five members, not more than three from one political party. Any appointments made after Jan. 1, 1984, are for five years.)

Member	Party	Term Expires	Nominated	Confirmed by Senate
Reese H. Taylor Jr. (C)	R	12/31/83	5/5/81	6/16/81
Frederic N. Andre	R	12/31/87	9/24/81	3/16/82
Malcolm M. B. Sterrett	R	12/31/87	9/24/81	2/9/82
Heather J. Gradison	R	12/31/88	3/22/82	6/16/82
Three Vacancies				

Nuclear Regulatory Commission

(Five members appointed for five-year terms; not more than three members from one political party.)

Member	Party	Term Expires	Nominated	Confirmed by Senate
Nunzio J. Palladino (C)	R	6/30/86	6/11/81	6/19/81
Victor Gilinsky	D	6/30/84	5/15/79	6/27/79
Thomas M. Roberts	R	6/30/85	7/9/81	7/31/81
James K. Asselstine	I	6/30/87	4/26/82	5/13/82
Frederick M. Bernthal	R	6/30/88	7/26/83	8/4/83

Securities and Exchange Commission

(Five members appointed for five-year terms; not more than three members from one political party.)

Member	Party	Term Expires	Nominated	Confirmed by Senate
John S. R. Shad (C)	R	6/5/86	4/1/81	4/8/81
Bevis Longstreth	D	6/5/84	6/23/82	8/20/82
James C. Treadway Jr.	R	6/5/87	7/22/82	8/19/82
Charles C. Cox	R	6/5/88	7/11/83	11/18/83
Vacancy				

Foreign Policy

Adelman. White House lobbying bore fruit April 14 as the Senate confirmed Kenneth L. Adelman to head the Arms Control and Disarmament Agency by a 57-42 vote. *(Vote 55, p. 13-S)*

Adelman, deputy ambassador to the United Nations, was named to replace Eugene V. Rostow Jan. 12.

The three-month debate over the nomination was, in large part, a debate on Reagan's strategy for nuclear arms control. The Senate Foreign Relations Committee reported the nomination unfavorably Feb. 24 on a 14-3 vote. The committee rejected by an 8-9 vote a motion to report the nomination with a favorable recommendation. Opponents said Adelman had neither the strong personal commitment to arms control nor the political stature to fight for it within the administration.

Motley. With unusual speed and no debate, the Senate June 29 confirmed Langhorne A. "Tony" Motley as assistant secretary of state for inter-American affairs, by voice vote. Ambassador to Brazil since 1981, Motley won praise from Brazilian government officials, top political appointees of the Reagan administration and several members of Congress.

Motley's controversial predecessor, Thomas O. Enders was fired on May 27 — ostensibly as part of a routine personnel shuffle, but reportedly because White House aides were dissatisfied with Enders' approach to Central American policy.

Environmental Protective Agency

Ruckelshaus. William D. Ruckelshaus was sworn in as administrator of the troubled Environmental Protection Agency on May 18, one day after his unanimous confirmation by the Senate. Ruckelshaus, who headed EPA from its creation in 1970 until 1973, was confirmed by the Senate by a 97-0 vote. *(Vote 87, p. 20-S)*

He replaced Anne M. Burford, who resigned from the post March 9 amid at least six congressional inquiries into charges of unethical conduct, political manipulation and "sweetheart deals" between EPA and regulated industries.

Sen. Robert T. Stafford, R-Vt., chairman of the Environment and Public Works Committee, which unanimously approved the nomination May 6, called Ruckelshaus "one of the few people in this country who could have been confirmed" as head of EPA. Ruckelshaus was "about to enter a political minefield," Stafford warned. *(Story, p. 332)*

Civil Rights Commission

Civil rights activists protested when Reagan May 26 announced that he was replacing three sitting members of the U.S. Civil Rights Commission with his own appointees. Reagan previously had appointed the chairman and vice chairman of the six-member commission.

Opponents charged that Reagan's move undermined the commission's independence, and they set out to block the nominations. After a six-month battle, Congress and the president agreed on compromise legislation reconstituting the commission and extending it for six years. The six-member presidentially appointed commission was to be replaced by an eight-member panel to be appointed half by the president and half by Congress. *(Story, p. 292)*

Legal Services Corporation

Although the embattled Legal Services Corporation once again survived Reagan's attempts to abolish it, only four of the 11 slots for the LSC's board of directors — the minimum required to do business — were filled at year's end.

All four board members were appointed by Reagan during congressional recesses in 1983 and were not confirmed by the Senate. They were Robert E. McCarthy, a San Francisco lawyer, chairman; Milton Masson, a businessman; Donald E. Santarelli, a lawyer who served in the Justice Department during the Nixon administration; and Ronald B. Frankum, a telecommunications consultant. As recess appointees, they could serve through the 1984 session.

Reagan nominated 11 members for the board in the fall, but none was confirmed by the Senate during 1983, and the nominations died at the end of the session. *(Legal Services, p. 322)*

1983 Confirmations

Listed below are 140 persons appointed by President Reagan to major federal posts and confirmed by the Senate in 1983. Information is given in the following order: name of office, salary (as of confirmation date), appointee, legal residence, last occupation before appointment, selected political or public policy posts held, date of birth, party affiliation (where available) and confirmation date.

EXECUTIVE OFFICE OF THE PRESIDENT

Office of the U.S. Trade Representative

Deputy U.S. trade representative with rank of ambassador, $68,400 — **Robert E. Lighthizer;** Rockville, Md.; chief minority counsel and then chief counsel and staff director, U.S. Senate Finance Committee (1978-83); associate, Covington & Burling (1973-78); Oct. 11, 1947; Republican; April 15.

Deputy U.S. trade representative with rank of ambassador, $68,400 — **Peter O. Murphy;** Washington, D.C.; chief textile negotiator, Office of the U.S. Trade Representative (1981-83); March 23, 1948; May 25.

Council on Environmental Quality

Member, $67,200 — **William L. Mills;** Nashville, Tenn.; associate professor, environmental and water resources engineering, Vanderbilt University (1977-83); associate professor, environmental health sciences and engineering, North Carolina Central University (1973-77); Nov. 20, 1944; Republican; Nov. 18.

CABINET DEPARTMENTS

Department of Agriculture

Assistant secretary for administration, $67,200 — **John J. Franke Jr.;** Merriam, Kan.; deputy assistant secretary for administration, Agriculture Department (1982-83); commissioner, Johnson County, Kan. (1973-81); June 28, 1930; Republican; March 11.

Under secretary for international affairs and commodity programs, $68,400 — **Daniel G. Amstutz;** New York City; general partner in charge of commodity activities, Goldman, Sachs & Co. (1978-83); various positions leading to president and chief executive officer, Cargill Investor Services (1960-1978); Nov. 8, 1932; Republican; May 16.

General counsel, $67,200 — **Daniel Oliver;** Greenwich, Conn.; general counsel, Education Department (1981-83); president, Rincon Communications Corp. (1980-81); member, Alexander & Green (1976-79 and 1971-73); executive editor, *National Review* (1973-76); April 10, 1939; Republican; Nov. 15.

Commodity Credit Corporation

Member while serving as under secretary for international affairs and commodity programs, $68,400 — **Daniel G. Amstutz;** New York City; general partner in charge of commodity activities, Goldman, Sachs & Co. (1978-83); various positions leading to president and chief executive officer, Cargill Investor Services (1960-78); Nov. 8, 1932; Republican; July 29.

Department of Commerce

Assistant secretary for international economic policy, $67,200 — **Alfred Hugh Kingon;** New York City; editor in chief, Macro Communications Inc. (1971-83); May 11, 1931; Republican; April 27.

Assistant secretary for communications and information, $67,200 — **David J. Markey;** Washington, D.C.; legal assistant to the chairman, Federal Communications Commission (1983); chief of staff and legislative director to U.S. Sen. Frank H. Murkowski (1981-83); legislative counsel and then vice president for congressional relations, National Association of Broadcasters (1974-81); administrative assistant to U.S. Sen. J. Glenn Beall Jr. (1969-74); July 25, 1940; Republican; Aug. 1.

Deputy secretary, $69,800 — **Clarence J. Brown;** Urbana, Ohio; U.S. representative, 7th Congressional District, Ohio (1965-83); president and then board chairman, Brown Publishing Co. (1965-83); editor and then publisher, *Urbana* (Ohio) *Daily Citizen* (1957-70); June 18, 1927; Republican; Oct. 7.

Assistant secretary for trade development, $67,200 — **Richard L. McElheny;** Phoenix, Ariz.; director general of the commercial service, International Trade Administration, Commerce Department (1982-83); director general of the foreign commercial service, International Trade Administration, Commerce Department (1981-82); president and chief executive officer, Econo Therm Energy Systems (1979-81); May 24, 1936; Republican; Sept. 30.

Department of Defense

Assistant secretary (comptroller), $67,200 — **Vincent Puritano;** Annandale, Va.; executive assistant to the deputy secretary, Defense Department (1981-83); special assistant to the deputy director, Central Intelligence Agency (1978-80); Jan. 10, 1930; Republican; Feb. 24.

Inspector general, $67,200 — **Joseph H. Sherick;** Annandale, Va.; assistant to the secretary for review and oversight, Defense Department (1981-83); deputy assistant secretary for program/budget, Defense Department (1976-81); deputy comptroller, Department of the Army (1973-76); Oct. 1, 1924; April 28.

Assistant secretary for international security affairs, $67,200 — **Richard Lee Armitage;** Fairfax, Va.; deputy assistant secretary for East Asia and Pacific affairs, Office of the Assistant Secretary for International Security Affairs, Defense Department (1981-83); administrative assistant to U.S. Sen. Robert Dole (1978-79); partner, SEATHAI Ltd. (1976-78); senior management consultant, Defense Department (1975-76); April 26, 1945; Republican; May 25.

Assistant secretary of the Navy for manpower and reserve affairs, $67,200 — **Chapman Beecher Cox;** Arlington, Va.; deputy assistant secretary of the Navy for logistics, Department of the Navy (1981-83); partner, Sherman & Howard (1972-81); July 31, 1940; Republican; May 25.

Assistant secretary for health affairs, $67,200 — **William E. Mayer;** Rockville, Md.; administrator, Alcohol, Drug Abuse and Mental Health Administration, Health and Human Services Department (1981-83); medical director, San Diego County Department of Health Services (1980-81); chief deputy director of health and director, California State Department of Health (1973-75); Sept. 24, 1923; Republican; Nov. 15.

Assistant secretary for public affairs, $67,200 — **Michael I. Burch;** Woodbridge, Va.; deputy chief, operations branch, armed forces news division, and then military assistant to the assistant

secretary of defense for public affairs, Office of the Secretary of Defense, Defense Department (1976-83); public affairs officer, operations branch, and then special assistant to the director of public affairs, Office of the Secretary of the Air Force, Defense Department (1972-76); June 20, 1941; Republican; Nov. 18.

Army

Assistant secretary for manpower and reserve affairs, $67,200 — **Delbert L. Spurlock Jr.;** Reston, Va.; general counsel, Department of the Army (1981-83); partner, Spurlock & Thatch (1977-81); chief, conflicts and interest division, California Fair Political Practices Commission (1975-77); April 3, 1941; July 13.

Department of Education

Assistant secretary for special education and rehabilitative services, $67,200 — **Madeleine C. Will;** member, Governmental Affairs Committee, National Association for Retarded Citizens (1981-82); founding member, Real Rights (1981); chairman, Governmental Affairs Committee, Maryland Association for Retarded Citizens (1981); member, board of directors, Montgomery County, Md., Association for Retarded Citizens (1979); Chevy Chase, Md.; Aug. 9, 1945; June 28.

Department of Energy

General counsel, $67,200 — **Theodore J. Garrish;** Alexandria, Va.; special assistant to the secretary, Energy Department (1982-83); legislative counsel, Office of Congressional and Legislative Affairs, Interior Department (1981-82); partner, Deane, Snowdon, Shutler, Garrish & Gherardi (1978-81); general counsel, Consumer Product Safety Commission (1976-78); Jan. 6, 1943; Republican; May 6.

Under secretary, $68,400 — **William Patrick Collins;** Alexandria, Va.; vice president of political affairs, National Association of Home Builders (1981-83); assistant to the senior adviser, Office of Executive Branch Management, Reagan Presidential Transition (1980-81); director of political affairs, National Association of Home Builders (1979-80); administrative assistant to U.S. Rep. Ron Marlenee (1976-79); legislative assistant to U.S. Rep. Alan Steelman (1973-76); March 16, 1946; Republican; Aug. 4.

Deputy secretary, $69,800 — **Danny J. Boggs;** Bowling Green, Ky.; senior policy adviser and then assistant director and special assistant to the president, Office of Policy Development, Executive Office of the President (1981-83); deputy minority counsel, U.S. Senate Energy and Natural Resources Committee (1977-79); assistant to the chairman, Federal Power Commission (1975-77); assistant to the solicitor general, Justice Department (1973-75); Oct. 23, 1944; Republican; Oct. 28.

Assistant secretary for international affairs, $67,200 — **Helmuth A. Merklein;** Dallas, Texas; professor, petroleum engineering department, Texas A&M University (1982-83); dean, graduate school of management, University of Dallas (1980-82); assistant professor, associate professor and then professor of energy economics, international economics and macroeconomics, University of Dallas and University of Nice, France (1970-80); May 26, 1935; Republican; Nov. 15.

Federal Energy Regulatory Commission

Member for term expiring Oct. 20, 1987; $67,200 — **Raymond J. O'Connor;** Whitestone, N.Y.; senior vice president and manager of the public utility and then executive vice president and director of the energy group, corporate finance department, Prudential-Bache Securities Inc. (1975-81); vice president, energy systems department, Citibank Corp. (1968-75); Sept. 16, 1932; Republican; Oct. 28.

Department of Health and Human Services

Secretary, $80,100 — **Margaret M. Heckler;** Wellesley, Mass.; U.S. representative, 10th Congressional District, Mass.

(1967-83); lawyer, private practice (1956-66); June 21, 1931; Republican; March 3.

Under secretary, $68,400 — **John A. Svahn;** Severna Park, Md.; commissioner, Social Security Administration (1981-83); administrator, Social and Rehabilitation Service, Health, Education and Welfare Department (1975-1976); May 13, 1943; Republican; March 8.

Department of Housing and Urban Development

Assistant secretary for public and Indian housing, $67,200 — **Warren T. Lindquist;** Washington, D.C.; chairman, SCETAM Inc. (1977-81); senior associate to David Rockefeller (1951-77); June 18, 1919; Republican; Aug. 4.

Under secretary, $69,800 — **Philip Abrams;** West Newton, Mass.; assistant secretary for housing and federal housing commissioner, Housing and Urban Development Department (1982-83); general deputy assistant secretary for housing, Housing and Urban Development Department (1981-82); developer, builder, cofounder and treasurer, Abreen Corp. (1966-81); Nov. 13, 1939; Republican; Sept. 27.

Department of the Interior

Under secretary, $68,400 — **J. J. Simmons III;** Washington, D.C.; commissioner, Interstate Commerce Commission (1982-83); vice president, government relations, Amerada Hess Corp. (1970-82); deputy administrator and then administrator, Oil Import Administration, Interior Department (1968-70); March 26, 1925; Feb. 24.

Secretary, $80,100 — **William P. Clark;** Paso Robles, Calif.; assistant to the president for national security affairs, Executive Office of the President (1982-83); deputy secretary, State Department (1981-82); associate justice, California Supreme Court (1973-81); chief of staff for Gov. Ronald Reagan, state of California (1967-69); Oct. 23, 1931; Republican; Nov. 18.

Department of Justice

Assistant attorney general for the Office of Justice Assistance, Research and Statistics, $67,200 — **Lois H. Herrington;** McLean, Va.; acting director, Office of Justice Assistance, Research and Statistics, Justice Department (1983); chairman, President's Task Force on Victims of Crime (1982-83); deputy district attorney, Alameda County, Calif., district attorney's office (1976-81); Dec. 6, 1939; Republican; June 22.

Assistant attorney general for the criminal division, $67,200 — **Stephen S. Trott;** Los Angeles; U.S. attorney, Central District of California (1981-83); chairman, Law Enforcement Coordinating Committee for the Central District of California (1981-83); coordinating U.S. attorney, Central California/Nevada Regional Drug Trafficking Task Force (1981-83); head deputy district attorney, Western District, Office of the District Attorney of Los Angeles County (1979-81); Dec. 12, 1939; Republican; July 18.

Assistant attorney general for land and natural resources, $67,200 — **Frank H. Habicht II;** Washington, D.C.; special assistant to the attorney general and then deputy assistant attorney general for land and natural resources, Justice Department (1981-83); associate, Kirkland & Ellis (1978-81); April 10, 1953; Republican; Nov. 15.

Bureau of Justice Statistics

Director, $67,200 — **Steven Roger Schlesinger;** Silver Spring, Md.; assistant professor, then associate professor and associate chairman, politics department, Catholic University of America (1977-83); March 28, 1944; Republican; April 13.

Drug Enforcement Administration

Administrator, $68,400 — **Francis M. Mullen Jr.;** Vienna, Va.; acting administrator, Drug Enforcement Administration (1981-83); various positions leading to executive assistant director

for investigations, Federal Bureau of Investigation (1962-81); Dec. 14, 1934; Republican; Oct. 7.

Department of Labor

Under secretary, $68,400 — **Ford Barney Ford;** Woodbridge, Va.; assistant secretary for mine safety and health, Labor Department (1981-83); vice president, California Institute for Industrial and Governmental Relations (1978-81); chairman and public member, California Occupational Safety and Health Appeals Board (1973-78); Nov. 19, 1922; Democrat; July 12.

Inspector general, $67,200 — **James Brian Hyland;** Fredericksburg, Va.; deputy inspector general, National Aeronautics and Space Administration (1980-83); assistant inspector general, National Aeronautics and Space Administration (1979-80); director, surveys and investigations staff, U.S. House of Representatives Appropriations Committee (1978-79); May 31, 1938; Independent; Aug. 3.

Assistant secretary for legislative affairs, $67,200 — **John J. O'Donnell;** Washington, D.C.; vice president, Executive Council, AFL-CIO (1979-83); airline captain, Eastern Airlines Inc. (1956-83); president, Air Line Pilots Association (1971-82); Jan. 14, 1925; July 13.

Assistant secretary for mine safety and health, $67,200 — **David A. Zegeer;** Lexington, Ky.; owner and manager of private consulting business (1977-83); manager and division superintendent, Bethlehem Mines Corp. (1956-77); Aug. 27, 1922; Republican; Nov. 18.

Department of State

Assistant secretary for economic and business affairs, $67,200 — **Richard T. McCormack;** Washington, D.C.; assistant secretary for economic and business affairs designate, State Department (1982-83); international economics consultant, State Department (1981-82); legislative assistant to U.S. Sen. Jesse Helms, R-N.C. (1979-81); March 6, 1941; Republican; Feb. 16.

Assistant secretary for European affairs, $67,200 — **Richard R. Burt;** Washington, D.C.; director, Bureau of Politico-Military Affairs, State Department (1981-82); Feb. 3, 1947; Republican; Feb. 16.

Counselor, $67,200 — **Edward J. Derwinski;** Flossmoor, Ill.; counselor designate, State Department (1983); U.S. representative, 4th Congressional District, Ill. (1959-83); Sept. 15, 1926; Republican; March 17.

Assistant secretary for inter-American affairs, $67,200 — **Langhorne A. Motley;** Anchorage, Alaska; U.S. ambassador to Brazil (1981-83); president, Valeria Inc. (1981); executive vice president, Citizens for the Management of Alaska Lands Inc. (1977-80); commissioner of commerce and economic development, state of Alaska (1975-77); June 5, 1938; Republican; June 29.

Ambassadors

Colombia, $68,400 — **Lewis Arthur Tambs;** Mesa, Ariz.; consultant, National Security Council (1982-83); professor, Arizona State University (1975-82); July 7, 1927; March 8.

Switzerland, $67,200 — **John D. Lodge;** Westport, Conn.; speaker and writer (1974-83); U.S. ambassador to Argentina (1969-74); U.S. ambassador to Spain (1955-61); governor, Connecticut (1951-55); U.S. representative, 4th Congressional District, Conn. (1947-51); Oct. 20, 1903; Republican; March 17.

At-large ambassador serving as special representative of the president to Central America, $69,800 — **Richard B. Stone;** Washington, D.C.; special representative of the president for public diplomacy in Central America, State Department (1983); senior resident partner, Proskauer Rose Goetz & Mendelsohn (1981-82); U.S. senator, Florida (1975-80); secretary of state, state of Florida (1970-74); member, Florida Senate (1966-70); Sept. 22, 1928; Democrat; May 25.

Rank of ambassador while serving as U.S. representative to international organizations in Vienna, Austria, $67,200 — **Richard S. Williamson;** McLean, Va.; assistant to the president for

intergovernmental affairs, Executive Office of the President (1981-83); associate and then partner, Winston & Strawn (1977-81); deputy to the chairman, Reagan-Bush campaign (1979-80); Illinois director, Reagan for President campaign (1976); administrative assistant and legislative counsel to U.S. Rep. Philip M. Crane (1974-76); May 9, 1949; Republican; May 16.

Austria, $68,400 — **Helene A. von Damm;** Flanders, N.J.; assistant to the president for presidential personnel, Executive Office of the President (1982-83); special assistant to the president and then director of presidential personnel with the rank of deputy assistant to the president, Executive Office of the President (1981-82); Northeast regional finance director, Reagan-Bush campaign (1979-80); executive assistant to former Gov. Ronald Reagan (1975-79); personal secretary to Gov. Ronald Reagan (1969-75); May 4, 1938; Republican; May 3.

Costa Rica, $67,200 — **Curtin Winsor Jr.;** Washington, D.C.; president, Winsor Pittman Co. (1982-83); president, Winsor Pittman Coal Co. (1980-83); member of the transition team for the State Department and the Agency for International Development (1980); manager for international affairs, Chase Manhattan Bank (1973-79); special assistant to the chairman, Republican National Committee (1971-73); April 28, 1939; Republican; May 25.

Democratic Republic of Madagascar and Federal and Islamic Republic of the Comoros, $63,800 — **Robert B. Keating;** Washington, D.C.; consultant, Office of the General Counsel, Department of the Navy (1982-83); consultant for international security affairs, Office of the Secretary, Defense Department (1981-82); May 7, 1924; June 29.

United Nations, deputy representative, $67,200 — **Jose S. Sorzano;** Arlington, Va.; U.S. representative, Economic and Social Council, United Nations (1981-83); associate professor, Georgetown University (1969-76 and 1979-81); director, Peace Corps in Bogotá, Colombia (1976-79); Nov. 9, 1940; July 26.

NATO, U.S. permanent representative, $69,800 — **David M. Abshire;** Alexandria, Va.; executive director, chairman and then president, Center for Strategic and International Studies, Georgetown University (1962-83); director, national security group, Transition Office of President-Elect Reagan (1980-81); assistant secretary for congressional relations, State Department (1970-73); April 11, 1926; Republican; July 13.

United Nations, rank of ambassador while serving as U.S. representative to the Food and Agriculture Organization, $63,800 — **Millicent Fenwick;** Bernardsville, N.J.; U.S. representative, 5th Congressional District, New Jersey (1975-83); director, Division of Consumer Affairs, state of New Jersey (1973-74); Feb. 25, 1910; Republican; Sept. 22.

Hungary, $67,200 — **Nicolas M. Salgo;** Key Largo, Fla.; founder and owner, Nicolas Salgo and Company (1959-83); chairman, Watergate Companies (1977-83); consultant, United States Information Agency (1982-83); founder and limited partner, Watergate Improvement Associates (1960-77); Aug. 17, 1914; Republican; Oct. 6.

Kenya, $69,800 — **Gerald E. Thomas;** San Diego, Calif.; ambassador, Cooperative Republic of Guyana (1981-83); commander, Training Command of the Pacific Fleet, U.S. Navy (1978-81); regional director, Near East and South Asia, Office of the Assistant Secretary for International Security Affairs, Defense Department (1976-78); June 23, 1929; Oct. 6.

Belgium, $68,400 — **Geoffrey Swaebe;** Los Angeles; rank of ambassador while serving as U.S. representative to the European Office of the United Nations (1981-83); private business and management consultant (1972-81); chairman of the board and president, May Department Stores of California (1962-72); March 23, 1911; Nov. 17.

Department of Transportation

Secretary, $80,100 — **Elizabeth Hanford Dole;** Russell, Kan.; assistant to the president for public liaison, Executive Office of the President (1981-83); chairman, Voters for Reagan-Bush (1980); commissioner, Federal Trade Commission (1973-79); July 29, 1936; Republican; Feb. 1.

General counsel, $67,200 — **James H. Burnley IV;** Falls Church, Va.; associate deputy attorney general, Justice Department (1982-83); director, VISTA (1981-82); partner, Turner, Enochs, Foster, Sparrow & Burnley (1975-81); July 30, 1948; Republican; May 3.

Assistant secretary for policy and international affairs, $67,200 — **Matthew V. Scocozza;** Kingsport, Tenn.; deputy assistant secretary for transportation and telecommunications affairs, State Department (1982-83); senior counsel, U.S. Senate Commerce, Science and Transportation Committee (1977-82); senior attorney, Bureau of Investigations and Enforcement, Interstate Commerce Commission (1976-77); minority counsel, Transportation Subcommittee, U.S. House of Representatives Appropriations Committee (1975-76); Oct. 13, 1948; Republican; Sept. 21.

Deputy secretary, $69,800 — **James H. Burnley IV;** Falls Church, Va.; general counsel, Transportation Department (1983); associate deputy attorney general, Justice Department (1982-83); director, VISTA (1981-82); partner, Turner, Enochs, Foster, Sparrow & Burnley (1975-81); July 30, 1948; Republican; Nov. 18.

Administrator for urban mass transportation, $68,400 — **Ralph L. Stanley;** Alexandria, Va.; special assistant to the secretary and then chief of staff, Transportation Department (1981-83); associate, Bracewell and Patterson (1978-81); Sept. 13, 1951; Republican; Nov. 18.

Assistant secretary for public affairs, $67,200 — **Mari Maseng;** Columbia, S.C.; speechwriter, Executive Office of the President (1981-83); press aide to Nancy Reagan, Office of the President-Elect (1980-81); special assistant to the chairman, Reagan-Bush Committee (1980); March 15, 1954; Republican; Nov. 18.

Federal Railroad Administration

Administrator, $68,400 — **John H. Riley;** Falls Church, Va.; chief counsel to U.S. Sen. Dave Durenberger, R-Minn. (1979-83); member, Meagher, Geer, Markham, Anderson, Adamson, Slaskamp & Brennan (1975-79); Jan. 19, 1947; Republican; Nov. 17.

National Highway Traffic Safety Administration

Administrator, $68,400 — **Diane K. Steed;** Washington, D.C.; deputy administrator, National Highway Traffic Safety Administration, Transportation Department (1981-83); chief, regulatory policy branch, Office of Management and Budget (1978-81); Nov. 29, 1945; Republican; Nov. 3.

St. Lawrence Seaway Development Corporation

Administrator for term expiring Nov. 21, 1990, $67,200 — **James L. Emery;** Geneseo, N.Y.; president, Emery Corp. (1983); member, New York State Assembly (1964-82); July 22, 1931; Republican; Nov. 18.

Department of the Treasury

Assistant secretary for domestic finance, $67,200 — **Thomas J. Healey;** Chatham, N.J.; various management positions, Dean Witter Reynolds Inc. (1975-82); vice president of finance, Instrumentation Engineering Inc. (1971-75); Sept. 14, 1942; Aug. 4.

Treasurer of the United States, $80,100 — **Katherine D. Ortega;** Alamogordo, N.M.; commissioner, Copyright Royalty Tribunal (1982-83); president and director, Santa Ana Bank (1975-77); vice president and cashier, Pan American National Bank (1972-75); July 16, 1934; Republican; Sept. 22.

INDEPENDENT AGENCIES

Agency for International Development

Assistant administrator for Africa, $67,200 — **Frank J. Donatelli;** Alexandria, Va.; member, Patton, Boggs & Blow

(1981-83); regional political director, Reagan for President Committee (1979-80); executive director, Young Americans for Freedom Inc. (1973-77); July 4, 1949; Republican; Nov. 9.

Civil Aeronautics Board

Member for term expiring Dec. 31, 1989, $67,200 — **Barbara E. McConnell;** Washington, D.C.; executive assistant to the chairman, Civil Aeronautics Board (1982-83); assistant secretary and associate general counsel, Southwest Forest Industries Inc. (1980-82); law clerk and then attorney, Greyhound Corp. (1976-80); Dec. 26, 1950; Republican; Sept. 21.

Commodity Futures Trading Commission

Chairman for term expiring April 15, 1985, $68,400 — **Susan M. Phillips;** Iowa City, Iowa; commissioner, Commodity Futures Trading Commission (1981-83); associate professor, finance department, University of Iowa (1978-81); economic fellow, Securities and Exchange Commission (1977-78); Dec. 23, 1944; Republican; Nov. 15.

Commissioner for term expiring April 15, 1988, $67,200 — **William E. Seale;** McLean, Va.; vice president of government relations, Commodity Exchange Inc. (1979-83); legislative assistant to U.S. Sen. Walter D. Huddleston, D-Ky. (1975-79); area farm management specialist and then assistant professor, agricultural economics department, University of Kentucky (1970-75); Feb. 10, 1941; Democrat; Nov. 15.

Consumer Product Safety Commission

Commissioner for term expiring Oct. 26, 1989, $67,200 — **Terrence M. Scanlon;** Washington, D.C.; various positions leading to chief of industry and technology division, Minority Business Development Agency, Commerce Department (1969-83); industry specialist, Small Business Administration (1967-69); May 1, 1939; Democrat; March 23.

Commissioner for term expiring Oct. 26, 1990, $67,200 — **Saundra Brown Armstrong;** Oakland, Calif.; trial attorney, criminal division, Justice Department (1982-83); deputy district attorney, Alameda County, Calif. (1977-78 and 1980-82); senior consultant, committee on criminal justice, California State Assembly (1979-80); March 23, 1947; Democrat; Nov. 18.

Environmental Protection Agency

Administrator, $69,800 — **William D. Ruckelshaus;** Medina, Wash.; senior vice president, Weyerhaeuser Co. (1975-83); partner, Ruckelshaus, Beveridge, Fairbanks and Diamond (1973-75); deputy attorney general, Justice Department (1973); acting director, Federal Bureau of Investigation (1973); administrator, Environmental Protection Agency (1970-73); assistant attorney general, civil division, Justice Department (1969-70); member and majority leader, Indiana House of Representatives (1967-69); July 24, 1932; Republican; May 17.

Assistant administrator for solid waste and emergency response, $67,200 — **Lee M. Thomas;** Woodbridge, Va.; acting assistant administrator for solid waste and emergency response and then acting deputy administrator, Environmental Protection Agency (1983); associate director for state and local programs and support, Federal Emergency Management Agency (1981-83); director, Office of Public Safety, South Carolina Governor's Office (1980-81); private consultant (1978-80); director, Office of Criminal Justice, South Carolina Governor's Office (1972-78); June 13, 1944; June 29.

Assistant administrator for administration, $67,200 — **Howard Messner;** Columbia, Md.; controller, Energy Department (1983); assistant director for management improvement and evaluation, Office of Management and Budget (1977-83); assistant director of management programs, Congressional Budget Office (1975-77); deputy assistant administrator for administration, Environmental Protection Agency (1971-75); June 10, 1937; Aug. 4.

Deputy administrator, $68,400 — **Alvin L. Alm;** Cambridge, Mass.; director, Energy Security Program, Harvard University (1979-83); lecturer, John F. Kennedy School of Government, Harvard University (1979-83); assistant secretary for policy and evaluation, Energy Department (1977-79); Jan. 27, 1937; Democrat; Aug. 4.

Assistant administrator (general counsel), $67,200 — **A. James Barnes;** Washington, D.C.; general counsel, Agriculture Department (1981-83); member and then partner, Beveridge, Fairbanks & Diamond (1975-81); assistant to the administrator, Environmental Protection Agency (1970-73); Aug. 30, 1942; Republican; Oct. 7.

Assistant administrator for congressional and external affairs, $67,200 — **Josephine S. Cooper;** Alexandria, Va.; staff assistant to U.S. Sen. Howard H. Baker Jr. and professional staff member, U.S. Senate Environment and Public Works Committee (1981-83); special assistant to the assistant administrator for research and development, Environmental Protection Agency (1979-81); Aug. 2, 1945; Republican; Oct. 7.

Assistant administrator for air and radiation, $67,200 — **Joseph A. Cannon;** Vienna, Va.; associate administrator for policy and resources management, Environmental Protection Agency (1981-83); associate, Andrews, Kurth, Campbell & Jones (1979-81); associate, Morgan, Lewis & Bockius (1978-79); July 31, 1949; Republican; Nov. 18.

Assistant administrator for enforcement and compliance monitoring, $67,200 — **Courtney M. Price;** Washington, D.C.; acting associate administrator for legal and enforcement counsel and acting general counsel, Environmental Protection Agency (1983); deputy chief counsel and then associate administrator for rulemaking, National Highway Traffic Safety Administration, Transportation Department (1981-83); staff attorney, Office of the General Counsel, Energy Department (1979-81); Sept. 12, 1942; Republican; Oct. 28.

Assistant administrator for policy, planning and evaluation, $67,200 — **Milton Russell;** Washington, D.C.; senior fellow and director, center for energy policy research, Resources for the Future (1976-83); senior staff economist, Council of Economic Advisers, Executive Office of the President (1974-76); assistant professor and then associate professor, economics department, Southern Illinois University (1964-74); Oct. 28, 1933; Nov. 18.

Assistant administrator for research and development, $67,200 — **Bernard D. Goldstein;** Westfield, N.J.; professor and chairman, environmental and community medicine department and professor, medicine department, Rutgers Medical School (1980-83); assistant professor and then associate professor, departments of environmental medicine and medicine, New York University School of Medicine (1970-80); Feb. 28, 1939; Independent; Nov. 18.

Assistant administrator for toxic substances, $67,200 — **John A. Moore;** Raleigh, N.C.; various positions leading to director, toxicology research and testing program, National Institute of Environmental Health Sciences, National Institutes of Health (1973-83); adjunct professor, pathology department, Duke University (1975-82); Feb. 9, 1939; Nov. 18.

Assistant administrator for water programs, $67,200 — **Jack E. Ravan;** Dunwoody, Ga.; vice president, project development, Signal Clean Water Corp. (1982-83); director, Energy Department, state of Alabama (1980-82); regional administrator, Southeastern region, Environmental Protection Agency (1971-77); June 18, 1937; Nov. 3.

Federal Election Commission

Member for term expiring April 30, 1989, $67,200 — **Joan D. Aikens;** Washington, D.C.; member, Federal Election Commission (1975-83); vice president and account executive, Lew Hodges Communications Inc. (1974-75); May 1, 1928; Republican; July 29.

Member for term expiring April 30, 1989, $67,200 — **John W. McGarry;** Washington, D.C.; member, Federal Election Commission (1978-83); special counsel on elections, U.S. House of Representatives House Administration Committee (1974-78); partner, Sheff and McGarry (1964-73); June 11, 1922; Democrat; July 29.

Federal Emergency Management Agency

Associate director, National Preparedness Programs, $67,200 — **Bernard A. Maguire;** Vienna, Va.; president, VPA Corp. (1982-83); project manager, Tera Corp. (1978-82); Sept. 12, 1942; March 17.

Deputy director, $67,200 — **Robert H. Morris;** Bethesda, Md.; assistant director for enterprise development, Minority Business Development Agency, Commerce Department (1981-83); chairman and principal owner, Johnson Bronze Co. (1970-81); March 31, 1919; Republican; Nov. 18.

Federal Home Loan Bank Board

Member for term expiring June 30, 1983, and reappointment for term expiring June 30, 1987, $67,200 — **Edwin J. Gray;** La Jolla, Calif.; senior vice president and director of public affairs, San Diego Federal Savings and Loan Association (1982-83); director of policy information, Executive Office of the President (1982); deputy assistant to the president for policy development, Executive Office of the President (1981-82); associate director of policy coordination for human services, Office of the President-Elect (1980-81); deputy chief of staff and director of policy communications, Reagan-Bush Committee (1980); Aug. 22, 1935; Republican; March 23.

Member for term expiring June 30, 1985, $67,200 — **Donald I. Hovde;** McLean Va.; under secretary, Department of Housing and Urban Development (1981-83); March 6, 1931; June 10.

Federal Maritime Commission

Commissioner for term expiring June 30, 1987, $67,200 — **Robert Setrakian;** San Francisco; president, part-owner and director, Mid-State Horticultural Co. Inc. (1962-83); chairman and chief executive officer, California Growers Winery Inc. (1971-82); Jan. 21, 1924; Democrat; May 20.

Commissioner for term expiring June 30, 1988, $67,200 — **Thomas F. Moakley;** Alexandria, Va.; commissioner, Federal Maritime Commission (1977-83); port director, Massachusetts Port Authority (1970-77); Nov. 3, 1921; Democrat; Nov. 18.

Federal Trade Commission

Commissioner for term expiring Sept. 25, 1990, $67,200 — **Terry Calvani;** Nashville, Tenn.; assistant professor, associate professor and then professor, Vanderbilt University Law School (1974-80); associate, Pillsbury, Madison & Sutro (1973-74); Jan. 29, 1947; Nov. 16.

International Trade Commission

Member for the remainder of the term expiring Dec. 16, 1991, $67,200 — **Seeley G. Lodwick;** Arlington, Va.; under secretary for international affairs and commodity programs and president of the Commodity Credit Corporation, Agriculture Department (1981-82); co-director, farm and food division, Reagan-Bush Committee (1980); Iowa administrator for U.S. Sen. Roger W. Jepsen (1979-80); Oct. 19, 1920; Aug. 4.

Merit Systems Protection Board

Member for term expiring March 1, 1990, $67,200 — **Maria Lucia Johnson;** Anchorage, Alaska; consultant, Equal Employment Opportunity Commission (1982-83); commercial loan officer, Security National Bank (1982); commercial real estate loan officer, National Bank of Alaska (1981-82); associate, Lambert, Griffin & McGovern (1979-81); Jan. 27, 1947; Republican; May 6.

National Labor Relations Board

Member and chairman for term expiring Dec. 16, 1987, $68,400 — **Donald L. Dotson;** Pittsburgh, Pa.; assistant secretary for labor management services, Labor Department (1981-83);

chief labor counsel, Wheeling-Pittsburgh Steel Corp. (1976-81); Oct. 8, 1938; Feb. 17.

Member for term expiring Aug. 27, 1986, $67,200 — **Patricia Diaz Dennis;** Los Angeles; attorney and then assistant attorney general, American Broadcasting Co. (1978-83); attorney, Pacific Lighting Co. (1976-78); Oct. 2, 1946; Democrat; April 15.

National Mediation Board

Member for term expiring July 1, 1986, $67,200 — **Robert O. Harris;** Washington, D.C.; member and chairman (1979-80 and 1982), National Mediation Board (1977-83); staff director and counsel, U.S. Senate District of Columbia Committee (1971-77); Nov. 11, 1929; Democrat; Nov. 4.

Member for term expiring July 1, 1985, $67,200 — **Helen M. Witt;** Pittsburgh, Pa.; private arbitrator (1972-83); assistant to the chairman, Board of Arbitration, U.S. Steel Corp. and United Steel Workers of America (1975-82); partner, Cleland, Hurtt & Witt (1970-74); July 13, 1933; Republican; Nov. 4.

National Science Foundation

Director, $69,800 — **Edward A. Knapp;** Los Alamos, N.M.; assistant director and then director on recess appointment, National Science Foundation (1982-83); division leader, Accelerator Technology Division, University of California, Los Alamos National Laboratory (1978-82); March 7, 1932; April 15.

Nuclear Regulatory Commission

Member for term expiring June 30, 1988, $68,400 — **Frederick M. Bernthal;** Oak Ridge, Tenn.; chief legislative assistant to U.S. Sen. Howard H. Baker Jr. (1980-83); associate professor, Michigan State University (1970-80); Jan. 10, 1943; Republican; Aug. 4.

Railroad Retirement Board

Member and chairman for term expiring Aug. 29, 1987, $68,400 — **Robert A. Gielow;** Glencoe, Ill.; senior vice president, member of the board of directors and member of the executive committee, Alexander & Alexander Services Inc. (1982-83); director, risk analysis and management group, Alexander & Alexander Inc. (1976-82); Aug. 18, 1919; March 1.

Securities and Exchange Commission

Member for term expiring June 5, 1988, $67,200 — **Charles C. Cox;** Washington, D.C.; chief economist, Securities and Exchange Commission (1982-83); assistant professor of management, Texas A&M University (1980-82); private law practice (1978-80); assistant professor, economics department, Ohio State University (1972-80); May 8, 1945; Republican; Nov. 18.

U.S. Arms Control and Disarmament Agency

Director, $69,800 — **Kenneth L. Adelman;** Arlington, Va.; U.S. deputy representative, United Nations (1981-83); senior political scientist, Strategic Studies Center, Stanford University (1977-81); assistant to the secretary, Defense Department (1976-77); congressional liaison officer, Agency for International Development (1975-76); June 9, 1946; Republican; April 14.

Deputy director, $67,200 — **David F. Emery;** Rockland, Maine; U.S. representative, 1st Congressional District, Maine (1975-83); member, Maine House of Representatives (1971-75); Sept. 1, 1948; Republican; June 6.

JUDICIARY

U.S. Circuit Courts

Judge, 7th Circuit, $77,300 — **Joel M. Flaum;** Chicago; judge, U.S. District Court, Northern District of Illinois (1975-83); Nov. 26, 1936; May 4.

Judge, 8th Circuit, $77,300 — **Pasco M. Bowman II;** Kansas City, Mo.; dean and professor of law, University of Missouri at Kansas City School of Law (1979-83); Dec. 20, 1933; Republican; July 18.

Judge, District of Columbia Circuit, $77,300 — **Kenneth W. Starr;** McLean, Va.; counselor to the attorney general, Justice Department (1981-83); member, Gibson, Dunn & Crutcher (1977-80 and 1974-75); law clerk to Chief Justice Warren E. Burger, United States Supreme Court (1975-77); July 21, 1946; Republican; Sept. 20.

Judge, 5th Circuit, $77,300 — **W. Eugene Davis;** New Iberia, La.; judge, U.S. District Court, Western District of Louisiana (1976-83); associate and then partner, Caffery, Duhe & Davis (1964-76); Aug. 18, 1936; Republican; Nov. 15.

U.S. District Courts

Judge, Central District of California, $73,100 — **Pamela A. Rymer;** Los Angeles; partner, Toy and Rymer (1975-83); Jan. 6, 1941; Republican; Feb. 23.

Judge, Southern District of New York, $73,100 — **Shirley W. Kram;** New York City; judge, New York City Family Court (1970-83); Dec. 25, 1922; Republican; March 2.

Judge, Northern District of Texas, $73,100 — **A. Joe Fish;** Dallas; associate justice, Texas Court of Civil Appeals, 5th Supreme Judicial District (1981-83); judge, Texas District Court, 95th District (1980-81); associate, McKenzie and Baer (1968-80); Nov. 12, 1942; Republican; Feb. 23.

Judge, Southern District of Mississippi, $73,100 — **William H. Barbour Jr.;** Yazoo City, Miss.; partner, Henry, Barbour & DeCell (1966-83); Feb. 4, 1941; April 21.

Judge, District of Maine, $73,100 — **Gene Carter;** Portland, Maine; associate justice, Maine Supreme Judicial Court (1980-83); Nov. 1, 1935; June 22.

Judge, District of New Mexico, $73,100 — **Bobby Ray Baldock;** Roswell, N.M.; partner, Sanders, Bruin & Baldock (1965-83); New Mexico co-chairman, Reagan-Bush campaign (1976); Jan. 24, 1936; Republican; June 6.

Judge, Eastern District of New York, $73,100 — **Leonard D. Wexler;** Islip, N.Y.; partner, Meyer & Wexler (1956); Nov. 11, 1924; June 22.

Judge, Western District of Tennessee, $73,100 — **Julia Smith Gibbons;** Memphis, Tenn.; judge, Tennessee Circuit Court, 15th Judicial Circuit (1981-83); deputy counsel and then legal adviser to Gov. Lamar Alexander (1979-81); Dec. 23, 1950; June 6.

Judge, Eastern District of Tennessee, $73,100 — **H. Ted Milburn;** Chattanooga, Tenn.; judge, Tennessee Circuit Court, 6th Judicial Circuit (1973-83); May 26, 1931; Republican; June 6.

Judge, Southern District of Texas, $73,100 — **Ricardo H. Hinojosa;** McAllen, Texas; associate, Ewers, Toothaker, Ewers, Abbott, Talbot, Hamilton & Jarvis (1976-83); Jan. 24, 1950; Republican; May 4.

Judge, District of Connecticut, $73,100 — **Peter C. Dorsey;** New Haven, Conn.; partner, Flanagan, Dorsey, Mulvey & Oliver (1977-83); March 24, 1931; July 18.

Judge, Eastern and Western District of Missouri, $73,100 — **Stephen N. Limbaugh;** Cape Girardeau, Mo.; partner, Limbaugh, Limbaugh, Russell & Syler (1951-83); Nov. 17, 1927; Republican; July 18.

Judge, Eastern District of Pennsylvania, $73,100 — **Marvin Katz;** Philadelphia; partner, Mesirov, Gelman, Jaffe, Cramer & Jamieson (1981-83); special partner, Wolf, Block, Schorr and Solis-Cohen (1981); assistant to the commissioner, Internal Revenue Service (1977-81); Nov. 22, 1930; Aug. 4.

Judge, Eastern District of Pennsylvania, $73,100 — **James McGirr Kelly;** Philadelphia; coordinator system rate counsel and then vice president for regulatory practices, American Water Works Service Co. (1979-83); member and then administrative assistant, Pennsylvania Public Utility Commission (1967-78); March 24, 1928; Aug. 4.

Judge, Eastern District of Pennsylvania, $73,100 — **Thomas**

N. **O'Neill;** Gladwyne, Pa.; partner, Montgomery, McCracken, Walker & Rhoads (1956-83); July 6, 1928; Aug. 4.

Judge, District of Puerto Rico, $73,100 — **Hector M. Laffitte;** San Juan, Puerto Rico; partner, Laffitte, Dominguez & Totti (1970-83); April 13, 1934; Republican; July 26.

Judge, Northern District of California, $73,100 — **John P. Vukasin Jr.;** Oakland, Calif.; judge, Superior Court of California, Alameda County (1974-83); commissioner, California Public Utilities Commission (1969-74); May 25, 1928; Republican; Sept. 20.

Judge, Northern District of Florida, $73,100 — **C. Roger Vinson;** Pensacola, Fla.; attorney, Beggs & Lane (1971-83); Feb. 19, 1940; Republican; Oct. 4.

Judge, Eastern District of Louisiana, $73,100 — **Martin L. C. Feldman;** New Orleans, La.; member and then partner, Bronfin, Heller, Feldman & Steinberg (1959-83); special counsel to governor, state of Louisiana (1980-83); general counsel, Louisiana Republican Party (1965-72); Jan. 28, 1934; Republican; Oct. 4.

Judge, District of New Jersey, $73,100 — **Maryanne T. Barry;** Sparta, N.J.; various positions leading to first assistant U.S. attorney, U.S. Attorney's Office, District of New Jersey (1976-83); April 5, 1937; Republican; Oct. 6.

Judge, Southern District of New York, $73,100 — **John F. Keenan;** Bronx, New York; criminal justice coordinator, City of New York (1982-83); chairman and president, New York City Off-Track Betting Corp. (1979-82); special prosecutor for the investigation into corruption in the criminal justice system, City of New York (1976-79); Nov. 23, 1929; Republican; Sept. 20.

Judge, Middle District of Florida, $73,100 — **G. Kendall Sharp;** Vero Beach, Fla.; judge, Florida Circuit Court, 19th Judicial Circuit (1979-83); private law practice (1977-79); member and then partner, Sharp & Johnston (1963-76); Dec. 30, 1934; Republican; Nov. 15.

Judge, Southern District of Florida, $73,100 — **Lenore C. Nesbitt;** Coral Gables, Fla.; judge, Florida Circuit Court, 11th Judicial Circuit (1975-83); member, Norman Somberg law firm (1975); associate, Petersen, McGowan & Feder (1973-75); associate, John Robert Terry law firm (1969-73); July 19, 1932; Republican; Nov. 15.

Judge, Eastern District of Michigan, $73,100 — **George E. Woods;** Rochester, Mich.; judge, U.S. Bankruptcy Court, Eastern District of Michigan (1981-83); private law practice (1962-81); Oct. 10, 1923; Republican; Nov. 15.

Judge, Eastern District of Tennessee, $73,100 — **Thomas G. Hull;** Greeneville, Tenn.; private law practice (1981-82); legal counsel to the governor, state of Tennessee (1979-81); judge, Tennessee Circuit Court, 20th Judicial Circuit (1972-79); May 20, 1926; Republican; Nov. 9.

Judge, Eastern District of Wisconsin, $73,100 — **Thomas J. Curran;** Mauston, Wis.; partner, Curran, Curran & Hollenbeck (1948-83); April 30, 1924; Republican; Nov. 4.

U.S. Court of International Trade

Judge, $73,100 — **Gregory W. Carman;** Farmingdale, N.Y.; partner, Carman, Callahan, Carman & Sabino (1961-83); U.S. representative, 3rd Congressional District, N.Y. (1981-83); Republican; March 2.

Judge, $73,100 — **Jane A. Restani;** Arlington, Va.; various positions leading to director, commercial litigation branch, civil division, Justice Department (1973-83); Feb. 27, 1948; Nov. 15.

U.S. Tax Court

Judge, $73,100 — **Charles E. Clapp II;** Barrington, R.I.; associate then partner, Edwards & Angell (1955-83); Dec. 25, 1923; Republican; June 22.

Judge, $73,100 — **Stephen J. Swift;** Danville, Calif.; senior tax counsel, Tax Department, Bank of America (1977-83); assistant U.S. attorney, tax division, U.S. Attorney's Office, San Francisco (1970-74); Sept. 7, 1943; July 14.

POLITICAL REPORT

Gubernatorial Elections. 3-B
Special Senate Election. 4-B
California, New Jersey Redistricting. 5-B
Special House Elections 6-B

CQ

Democrats Win Three Gubernatorial Races

The 1983 elections were a dramatic illustration of the continuing weakness of the Republican Party in the South. Despite the popularity of President Reagan in the region, and the party's successes in congressional elections there, the GOP had sunk to its lowest levels — at least as shown by governorships — in years.

At the beginning of 1982, the Republicans held the Statehouse in four Southern states. After losing two of those states, Texas and Arkansas, in 1982, the party also lost Louisiana in 1983, with the defeat of incumbent David C. Treen. By the end of the year, the only Republican governor in the region was Lamar Alexander of Tennessee.

Treen lost to Democrat Edwin W. Edwards, who had served two terms as Louisiana governor, from 1972 to 1980. Two other Democrats, Kentucky Lt. Gov. Martha Layne Collins and Mississippi Attorney General Bill Allain, also were elected governors of their states in the 1983 elections.

The electoral clout of the Democrats in Southern state-level contests was underscored by the somewhat unusual character of the gubernatorial winners, and the size of their victories. All three Democratic candidates were outside the conventional mode — one was the first woman governor of her state, another allegedly was involved in homosexual escapades, and the third was a flamboyant wheeler-dealer dogged by accusations of corruption. Yet each was elected with a large majority.

The GOP's loss of Southern governorships has paralleled its decline in statehouses nationally. Entering the 1982 elections with 23 governors' chairs, the GOP by the end of 1983 had only 15, compared to the Democrats' 35.

Off-year congressional elections did not reveal any similarly clear pattern. There were six special elections to the House and one to the Senate. Only one of the contests — Phil Gramm's successful attempt to regain as a Republican the Texas House seat from which he had resigned as a Democrat — resulted in a change in the partisan breakdown of the House. At the end of 1983, there were 267 Democrats and 167 Republicans in the House, and one vacant seat.

The 1983 elections had a much more significant impact on the Senate. The death of veteran Washington Democratic Sen. Henry M. Jackson (1953-83), led to the appointment by the state's GOP governor of Republican Daniel J. Evans to fill the vacant seat. Evans went on to defeat Democratic Rep. Mike Lowry in the November special election, thus earning the right to serve the five years remaining in Jackson's term.

Evans' appointment and election victory fixed the Senate partisan ratio at 55-45. That one-seat gain in the Republicans' margin of control of the chamber could play a major role in the future, weakening Democratic chances of recapturing the Senate in the 1984 or 1986 elections.

Gubernatorial Results

Louisiana

Long known as brash and colorful, Democrat Edwin W. Edwards proved Oct. 22 that he was also one of the most popular politicians in recent Louisiana history. By easily defeating GOP Gov. David C. Treen, Edwards became the state's first elected three-term governor.

Treen's defeat was not unexpected; polls showed him trailing Edwards throughout the year. But the size of the incumbent's loss was startling. As a little-known New Orleans lawyer in 1972, Treen lost his first gubernatorial race against Edwards by 14 percentage points. As a well-known incumbent, Treen lost by 26 percentage points.

Treen was the state's first GOP governor in this century and it took bitter Democratic infighting for him to win narrowly in 1979.

With Edwards back on the ballot in 1983 — he was forced out of office in 1979 by the state's two-terms-and-out law — Treen needed some breaks to win.

He did not get them. Compared with the brash and fun-loving Edwards, the hard-working Treen was labeled "dull Dave." And the state's oil-and-gas-based economy, which had boomed during the 1970s when Edwards was in office, turned sour during the Treen years.

Treen stressed his personal integrity and the accusations of corruption that had dogged Edwards over the years. But Edwards was able to surmount this liability with disarming displays of candor and a vibrant populism that recalled Huey and Earl Long.

Treen had hoped to win re-election by capturing nearly 60 percent of the white vote and close to 20 percent of the black vote. But while Treen appointed a large number of blacks to his administration, he drew barely 10 percent of the black vote. Whites split their votes almost evenly between the two candidates.

Under Louisiana's unique open election system, all candidates, regardless of party designation, were listed on the Oct. 22 ballot. There was no primary. Since Edwards won a majority of the vote, a November runoff was unnecessary. In spite of bad weather and the opening of squirrel-hunting season, more Louisianans voted for governor in 1983 than for president in 1980.

Official results:

Edwin W. Edwards (D)	1,006,561	62.3%
David C. Treen (R)	588,508	36.4
Seven others	20,836	1.3

In his two previous gubernatorial bids, Treen had carried at least 22 of the state's 64 parishes. In 1983, he won only two affluent parishes in the suburbs of New Orleans — St. Tammany and his home base of Jefferson. Even there, his margins were narrow.

A French-speaking Cajun, Edwards rolled up his biggest majorities in his native Acadiana and the predominantly black parishes along the Mississippi River. He swept rural Louisiana by a margin of more than 2-1.

But that was largely expected. More surprising was Treen's failure to run more strongly in the state's population centers, where Republican statewide victories are usually fashioned. About half the voters in Louisiana live in the nine most populous parishes. In 1972, Treen nearly split the vote there with Edwards. In 1979, population centers like Baton Rouge, Shreveport, Monroe, Lafayette and the suburban New Orleans parishes gave Treen the margin of votes that carried him to victory.

But this time even Republican strongholds rejected him. Treen was swamped in population centers from New Orleans to Shreveport by nearly 15 percentage points.

Kentucky

There was virtually no controversy or suspense in Kentucky's Nov. 8 gubernatorial election. With a significant Democratic registration advantage and the party united behind her, Lt. Gov. Martha Layne Collins essentially ignored her Republican opponent, state Sen. Jim Bunning.

Collins replaced Democratic Gov. John Y. Brown, who was forced to leave office by the state's one-term-and-out law.

Collins, 46, was a seasoned campaigner and officeholder. She became Kentucky's Democratic national committeewoman in 1972, and was elected clerk of the Kentucky Supreme Court in 1975. Four years later, she pushed through a crowded field to win nomination and election as lieutenant governor.

In May 1983, Collins narrowly won a bitterly fought gubernatorial primary against Louisville Mayor Harvey Sloane and Grady Stumbo, who served as human resources secretary under Brown.

Collins sought to soothe voters who might be uncomfortable voting for a female governor by emphasizing her Kentucky roots, traditional family background and experience in the executive branch of state government. She noted that on the frequent occasions Brown was out of the state, she was the acting governor.

Bunning, 51, was a baseball pitcher and manager from 1950-72, working for the Detroit Tigers' and Philadelphia Phillies' organizations. He won election to the Fort Thomas City Council in 1977, and two years later moved up to the state Senate, where he was minority leader.

Bunning agreed to enter the race only because no other Republican of stature was willing to make the effort. He used a "tough man" theme in the campaign, arguing that he would be a more aggressive fighter for jobs and education than his female foe. He also warned that Collins would be a figurehead governor controlled by a few key politicians who supported her, such as state Senate President Pro Tem Joe Prather, Collins' campaign manager.

Official returns:

Martha L. Collins (D)	561,674	54.5%
Jim Bunning (R)	454,650	44.1
Nicholas McCubbin (Ind.)	14,347	1.4

Bunning carried two of seven congressional districts — the northern Kentucky 4th, which included his home base in the Cincinnati suburbs, and the traditionally Republican 5th in the mountainous southeastern corner of the state. But Collins won elsewhere, including populous Jefferson County (Louisville).

Mississippi

As expected, Democratic Attorney General Bill Allain, 55, won Mississippi's Nov. 8 gubernatorial election. But Allain's easy win came after one of the most bizarre and bitter election campaigns in the state's history.

Allain had a difficult time making it to the general election. He had finished second in the Aug. 2 Democratic primary to former Lt. Gov. Evelyn Gandy. But, in the Aug. 23 runoff, he beat Gandy by the margin of 403,743 votes (52.3 percent) to 367,706 votes (47.7 percent).

After winning the Democratic nomination, Allain seemed like a sure bet for the general election. His Republican opponent was wealthy Clarksdale planter Leon Bramlett, 60, who benefited from only a few defections by prominent Democrats. Veteran civil rights candidate

Charles Evers, 61, the former mayor of Fayette, was on the ballot as an independent candidate. But he had much less support from blacks than he had in 1978, when his independent candidacy for the Senate drained away Democratic votes and helped elect Republican Thad Cochran.

Allain ran a populist campaign centered on opposition to utility rate increases. Bramlett emphasized his personal background (an All-America football player at the Naval Academy), his Democratic roots and "nice guy" reputation. Bramlett was Democratic state party chairman from 1968 to 1972, but later left the party, saying it was too liberal.

The specifics of the campaign faded from view, however, once allegations that Allain had engaged in homosexual activities with male prostitutes became public. The accusations, made in late October by prominent Bramlett supporters, dominated the last two weeks of the campaign.

Allain's accusers, mainly wealthy Jackson oilmen, hired a detective agency to investigate rumors about Allain's private life. The detectives found three black transvestites who gave graphic descriptions of encounters with Allain, and several Jackson policemen who claimed they had seen Allain driving in the section of the city where "drag queens" congregated.

Allain denied any impropriety, contending that his opponents had employed "the big lie technique" because their campaign was going nowhere on the issues. He passed a lie detector test arranged by his lawyer, but declined a Republican challenge to submit to a battery of tests conducted by independent sources.

Although he ran a late set of ads critical of Allain's character, Bramlett had distanced himself from the allegations of his supporters. But in his campaign speeches, he emphasized the importance of having a family man as governor.

Official returns:

Bill Allain (D)	409,209	55.1%
Leon Bramlett (R)	288,764	38.9
Charles Evers (Ind.)	30,593	4.1
Billy Taylor (Ind.)	7,869	1.0
Helen M. Williams (Ind.)	6,302	.8

In the end, the allegations against Allain probably did not change many votes. Democratic officials, led by outgoing Gov. William Winter, remained supportive of Allain.

To stand a chance in Mississippi, a Republican must carry virtually all the major population centers. But Bramlett could win only six of the 12 most populous counties. And in many urban centers, he won only by a narrow margin.

In the rest of the state, Bramlett trailed Allain badly. The sex allegations failed to make a significant dent in the rural following Allain had built with his populist rhetoric. Returns showed the Democrat winning all but two of the 50 smaller white-majority counties and all 20 rural counties with a black majority.

But Evers, who carried a dozen counties as an independent Senate candidate in 1978, drew only 5 percent of the vote in 1983 in black-majority counties.

Special Senate Election

Washington

Republican Daniel J. Evans survived a hard-charging campaign by liberal Rep. Mike Lowry to win Washington's

Nov. 8 special Senate election. Evans, appointed to the Senate on an interim basis after the Sept. 1 death of Democratic Sen. Henry M. Jackson, was to serve the five years remaining in Jackson's term.

Lowry, a three-term U.S. House member from Seattle and a fierce critic of President Reagan's foreign and domestic policies, labored mightily to cast the Senate election as a referendum on Reaganism. But there were two reasons why that strategy failed.

First, Lowry found it difficult to persuade Washington state voters to view Evans as a pro-Reagan partisan lackey. The characterization did not ring true to the voters who recalled Evans' tenure as governor from 1965 to 1977. Evans' moderate-to-liberal record during twelve years in that office earned bipartisan support and brought him three consecutive election victories, in 1964, 1968 and 1972.

Evans had never been close to conservative elements in the state GOP. In 1976, when he supported Gerald R. Ford over Ronald Reagan for the party's presidential nomination, pro-Reagan forces then dominant in the state party denied the governor a seat at the national convention. As late as the month before the election, in the special primary that launched the campaign for Jackson's seat, conservatives united behind Seattle businessman Lloyd E. Cooney in an effort to block Evans' nomination. But Evans easily won the Oct. 11 Republican primary, beating Cooney by a wide margin.

Lowry had beaten Seattle Mayor Charles Royer in the Democratic primary.

Many voters apparently agreed with the way Evans characterized Lowry's strategy when the two candidates met in a debate. "Mike," Evans said, "if you want to run against President Reagan, you are a year too early."

The second reason Lowry's "Reagan referendum" approach failed was that voters became less tolerant of the congressman's attacks on the administration after the bombing of U.S. Marine headquarters in Lebanon and the military intervention in Grenada. Those events dominated the closing days of the campaign, and promoted a "rally 'round the flag" mentality that enhanced Reagan's prestige and stalled Lowry, who until then had been gaining ground on Evans.

After the Lebanon bombing, Lowry stopped using an advertisement that criticized Evans for voting to keep Marines in Lebanon for 18 months. But even when it became clear that most voters endorsed Reagan's decision to use force in Grenada, Lowry continued to call it a dangerous precedent that might lead to armed U.S. intervention in nearby Central American countries.

Official returns:

Daniel J. Evans (R)	672,326	55.4%
Mike Lowry (D)	540,981	44.6

Labor unions and liberal groups were intensely loyal to Lowry, but the votes they delivered were not enough to match the broad appeal Evans displayed. The Republican won all but three of the state's 39 counties, and he carried King County (Seattle), the state's most populous and Lowry's political base, with 56 percent.

Lowry's best showings came in areas of the state where high unemployment persisted, such as Jefferson and Wahkiakum counties, whose economies were based on logging and fishing.

An important factor in Evans' victory was his success in conservative eastern Washington.

California, New Jersey Redistricting

In a development with potentially major consequences for partisan control of the House, the California Supreme Court Sept. 15 barred a GOP-sponsored redistricting initiative in the state.

The court decided to remove from the ballot an initiative on congressional and state legislative lines that was to have been voted on in a special election Dec. 13. The plan, pushed by Republican state Assemblyman Don Sebastiani, would have replaced a Democrat-drawn district map for the 1984 elections with districts that Republicans had hoped would lead to the defeat of several congressional Democrats and turn the state Legislature over to the GOP. But in a 6-1 decision, the court held that the initiative violated a constitutional rule allowing only one reapportionment per decade after the federal census.

The Democratic "gerrymander" that Sebastiani tried to replace was the second set of district lines that California had had since the 1980 census. But the court reasoned that the first set, passed by the Legislature in 1981, did not count because it had been voided by a June 1982 ballot referendum. The 1981 plan was ordered into place by the court solely for the 1982 elections and never took effect as the reapportionment plan for the decade.

Another important action relating to congressional redistricting came June 22, when the U.S. Supreme Court struck down New Jersey's congressional district map as redrawn following the 1980 census.

In a 5-4 vote, the court ruled in *Karcher v. Daggett* that states must adhere as closely as possible to the "one man, one vote" standard of reapportionment — and ultimately bear the burden of proving that deviations from precise population equality were made in pursuit of a legitimate goal.

The ruling upheld a three-judge federal panel's decision on March 3, 1982, to overturn the New Jersey map. The lower court found that the 0.69 percent deviation between the state's most and least populous districts was too great, violating the "one man, one vote" principle applied to redistricting in the Supreme Court's 1964 *Wesberry v. Sanders* decision.

Dissenters argued that the decision would leave even the most minuscule population deviance open to constitutional attack.

The majority decision was written by Justice William J. Brennan Jr., the author of the landmark 1962 *Baker v. Carr* decision, which began the involvement of courts in apportionment.

Brennan argued that population differences between districts in the New Jersey map "could have been avoided or significantly reduced with a good-faith effort to achieve population equality." He contended that New Jersey legislators failed to prove that the deviations from population equality were made in pursuit of a non-discriminatory goal.

Justice Byron R. White, writing in dissent, was joined by Chief Justice Warren E. Burger, and Justices Lewis F. Powell Jr. and William H. Rehnquist. Powell also filed a separate dissenting opinion.

White criticized the court for its "unreasonable insistence on an unattainable perfection in the equalizing of congressional districts."

Special House Elections

Texas

Phil Gramm, who quit his 6th District Democratic House seat to run as a Republican, was returned to Washington Feb. 12 by Texas voters who preferred him over 10 other candidates in a special election.

With 55.3 percent of the vote, Gramm was able to escape a runoff election, which would have been required by Texas law had he received under 50 percent of the vote.

Gramm ran an almost textbook-perfect campaign to deliver the traditionally Democratic House seat into the Republican Party column for the first time in Texas history.

Gramm's only threat turned out to be former Democratic State Rep. Dan Kubiak, 44, of Hilltop Lake, who received almost 40 percent of the vote.

Gramm, 40, forced the special election when he resigned his House seat Jan. 5 and switched parties. This all happened after Gramm's fellow House Democrats knocked him off the House Budget Committee for conspiring with the administration to fashion the Republicans' successful 1981 budget proposal.

Throughout the campaign, Gramm succeeded in focusing voters' attention on himself. He said he was being penalized for voting his own conservative convictions and those of his like-minded constituents.

Gramm carried eight of the sprawling 6th District's 14 counties. His real strength remained in three counties: Brazos, his home county, and two suburban GOP counties south of Dallas and north of Houston.

Kubiak lost his home base, Leon County, to Gramm by 71 votes.

Kubiak's strength was in six rural counties — Freestone, Hill, Johnson, Limestone, Navarro and Robertson. He beat Gramm in each but generally by only the barest of margins.

Official results:

Phil Gramm (R)	46,371	55.3%
Dan Kubiak (D)	33,201	39.6
John Henry Faulk (D)	3,070	3.7
Bill Powers (D)	318	.4
Rex L. Carey (D)	268	.3
H. Martin Gibson	223	.3
George M. Chamberlain (D)	153	.2
Louis C. Davis (D)	84	.1
Joe R. English (D)	80	.1
Carl A. Nigliazzo (D)	78	.1
Joseph Agris (D)	59	.1

New York

Democratic New York state Sen. Gary Ackerman won a special election March 1 to replace the late Rep. Benjamin S. Rosenthal, D-N.Y., in the House.

Ackerman, 40, relied heavily on the Queens County Democratic organization to capture the 7th District seat.

The seat had been vacant since Jan. 4, when Rosenthal died of cancer. Rosenthal represented the Democratic area in Congress for 20 years.

Ackerman's closest competitor was Republican Albert Lemishow, a 57-year-old accountant. Douglas Schoen, a 29-year-old pollster who placed third, reportedly spent close to $350,000 of his own and family money on television and radio advertisements.

The founder of four Queens County community newspapers, Ackerman was well-known throughout the district. He won the race primarily on the strength of the Queens County Democratic Party's endorsement, usually considered tantamount to winning the election.

Official results:

Gary L. Ackerman (D, Liberal)	18,388	48.7%
Albert Lemishow (R, Conservative, Queens Independent)	8,331	22.1
Douglas F. Schoen (Neighborhood)	5,997	15.9
Sheldon Leffler (Ind.)	4,318	11.4
Unrecorded	690	1.8

Colorado

Republican state Sen. Daniel L. Schaefer easily defeated his Democratic opponent March 29 to win election to the Colorado 6th District congresssional seat left vacant by the death of former astronaut Jack Swigert.

Schaefer defeated Democrat Steve Hogan, an Aurora city councilman, and independent John Heckman.

Schaefer, 47, was favored to replace fellow Republican Swigert, who died of cancer Dec. 27, a week before he was to be sworn in to represent the new GOP-oriented district.

Schaefer, a public relations consultant who served two years in the Colorado House before moving to the state Senate in 1978, had taken conservative stands against school busing, the Equal Rights Amendment and legalized abortion.

The special election brought Hogan, 34, his second defeat in five months. Hogan had lost to Swigert in the November 1982 election by a 2-to-1 margin.

Schaefer led Hogan by about 2-to-1 in Arapahoe and Jefferson counties, the largest portions of the district.

Official results:

Daniel L. Schaefer (R)	49,816	63.3%
Steve Hogan (D)	27,779	35.3
John Heckman (Ind.)	1,112	1.4

California

San Francisco Democrat Sala Burton swept past 10 opponents June 21 to win the U.S. House seat left vacant in April by the death of her husband, Democratic Rep. Phillip Burton.

Burton took 57 percent of the vote. Her nearest competitor was Republican real estate broker Duncan Howard, who received 23.3 percent.

By winning more than 50 percent of the vote, Burton avoided a runoff election.

Throughout her campaign, Burton worked to convince voters that she was almost as familiar with the Washington scene as her late husband had been. She would be "effective from the start," she told voters.

Burton had been heavily favored to take the seat since she announced shortly after Phillip Burton's funeral that she intended to campaign for it. In heavily Democratic San Francisco, Burton's backing from the U.S. House leadership, the California Democratic congressional delegation, and the state and local Democratic organizations gave her an overwhelming edge over her opponents.

Official results:

Sala Burton (D)	44,790	56.9%
Dunan Howard (R)	18,305	23.3
Richard Doyle (D)	6,582	8.4
Tom Spinosa (R)	2,933	3.7
Gary Arnold (R)	1,596	2.0
Tibor Uskert (D)	1,117	1.4
Bill Dunlap (R)	1,043	1.3
Evelyn Lance (D)	880	1.1
Michael Plunkett (D)	560	0.7
A. Paul Kangas (Peace and Freedom)	448	0.6
Eric Garris (Libertarian)	408	0.5
Write-ins	6	

Illinois

Democratic labor leader Charles A. Hayes easily won an Aug. 23 special election to fill the Illinois congressional seat vacated by Democrat Harold Washington when he took over as mayor of Chicago. Hayes took 93.7 percent of the vote in defeating Republican Diane Preacely, a community newspaper columnist.

Hayes' election in the overwhelmingly Democratic 1st District virtually was guaranteed by his July 26 primary victory, in which he defeated 13 other black Democrats. An international vice president of the United Food and Commercial Workers Union, Hayes had played a prominent fund-raising role in Washington's mayoral campaign, and was the mayor's choice in the primary contest.

Washington's support in the primary was vital to Hayes. Although Hayes' labor ties gave him an advantage in raising funds, he lacked the political base of his chief opponents in the contest. Radio commentator and community activist Lu Palmer and civil rights activist Al Raby, themselves prominent figures in Washington's mayoral campaign, both were better known than Hayes. But Washington's ability to pull South Side political leaders in line behind him gave Hayes access to ward and precinct organizations that his opponents lacked.

Official results:

Charles A. Hayes (D)	39,623	93.7%
Diane Preacely (R)	2,272	5.4
Ed Warren (Ind.)	394	.9
Write-ins	2	—

Georgia

Georgia State Rep. George W. "Buddy" Darden easily defeated Democrat Kathryn McDonald in a Nov. 8 special House election runoff.

Darden replaced Democratic Rep. Larry P. McDonald, Kathryn's husband, who died aboard the Korean Air Lines jet shot down by a Soviet fighter plane Sept. 1. Kathryn McDonald echoed her husband's militant conservatism and his hostility to the national Democratic Party. Darden took a more moderate approach.

Darden was the first candidate in a decade to challenge successfully the coalition of national conservative organizations, local John Birch Society adherents and rural conservatives that sparked Larry McDonald's campaigns. An ally of powerful state House Speaker Tom Murphy, Darden was able to pick up the support of a range of elected Democrats and party officials despite the official neutrality of the party itself.

The face-off between McDonald and Darden was set up Oct. 18, when they finished first and second, respectively, in the first round of the non-partisan special election. McDonald's 30.6% of the vote in the initial round was far less than her supporters had hoped for, and it signaled trouble for her campaign.

McDonald's initial weakness stemmed in part from voters' doubts about her suitability to succeed her husband. Originally from California, she had spent most of her time after their marriage in Washington, D.C., and seemed to have little in common with the voters of northwest Georgia. Moreover, some tradition-minded voters questioned whether a widow with two young children should be in Congress.

Darden campaigned as a "responsible conservative" and labeled McDonald an extremist. The McDonald campaign attacked Darden as a liberal for his support for the Equal Rights Amendment and his financial backing from organized labor.

Although McDonald carried the four northern counties in the district — traditionally her husband's stronghold — Darden picked up most of the vote in those counties that had gone to other candidates on the first round.

Official results:

George W. "Buddy" Darden	56,267	59.1%
Kathryn McDonald	38,949	40.9 ∎

VOTING STUDIES

Key Votes 3-C
Presidential Support 19-C
Party Unity 26-C
Voting Participation. 32-C
Conservative Coalition 37-C

CQ

CQ Key Votes

GOP Senate Plays Gatekeeper Role in 1983

Key House and Senate votes in 1983 demonstrated that the salient feature of the 98th Congress, as with the 97th, was Republican control of the Senate.

With Republican President Reagan and the Democratic House at odds on many major issues, GOP Senate leaders had been acting for the past three years as the nation's legislative gatekeepers.

The Senate leadership generally had been able and willing to close the gate on measures the House had passed against Reagan's wishes. And since 1981 it often had fallen to the Senate leadership to find and open the door to compromise when confrontation between Reagan and the House threatened to disrupt the government's business.

In 1983, as in the preceding two years, many key votes were decided along party lines, and Democratic initiatives passed by the House over Reagan's opposition were killed or compromised in the Senate.

For example, when the House passed an emergency mortgage aid program, only six Republicans voted for the measure and only 41 Democrats — 33 of them conservative Southerners — opposed it. The aid plan died in the Senate.

The House passed a nuclear freeze resolution opposed by Reagan, but the Senate tabled a similar measure.

On the other hand, a compromise $4.6 billion jobs package was crafted to fall within limits Reagan would approve after the Senate rejected, by a party-line vote, a move by Democrats to add $1.7 billion to a $3.7 billion relief measure.

Likewise, the Senate refused to follow suit when the House passed a bill to halt Reagan's use of covert aid to assist anti-government rebels in Nicaragua.

But it did agree to a compromise under which Congress gave Reagan $24 million in additional funding for covert aid on the condition that Congress must approve any further amounts.

Exceptions to Rule

Naturally, there were exceptions to the rule. Perhaps the most conspicuous came in action on the fiscal 1984 budget resolution.

House Democrats rammed through their own budget plan after House Republicans proved unwilling to back Reagan's budget.

But when the Senate GOP leadership sought passage of a compromise Reagan was willing to accept, moderate Senate Republicans joined Democrats in rejecting it — twice.

In the end, Senate leaders such as Pete V. Domenici, R-N.M., the Budget Committee chairman, had to give ground to avoid a stalemate.

Neither did the Senate play its customary broker's role on the issue of Reagan's request for an $8.4 billion increase in the U.S. contribution to the International Monetary Fund.

Many Republicans opposed Reagan, so he had to bargain with House Democrats for support. That proved costly. To taste victory on the IMF bill, the president was

forced to swallow a $15.6 billion housing authorization measure that the House Democrats wanted and he had opposed.

Bipartisan Votes

Partisanship was generally less prominent on the broader issues of national security.

The House approved Reagan's request for funding for the MX missile on the strength of votes from moderate Democrats who hoped to modify the administration's arms control policy. In the Senate, a move to cut funding for the MX failed by a sizable margin, with almost a fourth of Senate Democrats voting in favor of the missile program.

Similarly, House Speaker Thomas P. O'Neill Jr., D-Mass., usually a vigorous Reagan critic, played a major role in getting the House to pass a compromise resolution on Lebanon. The measure authorized Reagan to keep U.S. Marines in Lebanon for another 18 months but asserted that Congress had the right under the 1973 War Powers Resolution to decide the ultimate length of their stay.

The Senate did split along party lines when it voted on the Lebanon resolution, following the failure of separate negotiations between Senate Democrats and Reagan.

Party politics played little role in the Senate's vote to approve Reagan's plan to begin production of nerve gas for the first time since 1969. Vice President Bush twice was forced to cast a tie-breaking vote for the plan, which was ultimately scrapped at the insistence of the House.

But partisanship in its purest form could be seen in some House votes on controversial measures brought up to get Republicans on the record before the 1984 elections.

One such vote came on the Equal Rights Amendment, which the House leadership took to the floor under suspension of the rules, a procedure requiring a two-thirds vote of those present for passage. The bill fell six votes short of the necessary majority. Democrats supported it overwhelmingly; Republicans opposed it by 2-1.

How Votes Were Selected

Congressional Quarterly each year selects a series of key votes on major issues.

Selection of Issues. An issue is judged by the extent it represents one or more of the following:

- A matter of major controversy.
- A test of presidential or political power.
- A decision of potentially great impact on the nation and lives of Americans.

Selection of Votes. For each group of related votes on an issue, one key vote usually is chosen. This is the vote, in the opinion of Congressional Quarterly editors, that was important in determining the outcome.

In the description of the key votes, the designation "ND" denotes Northern Democrats and "SD" denotes Southern Democrats.

Senate Key Votes

1. Anti-Recession Assistance

Double-digit unemployment resulting from the worst recession since World War II stimulated a variety of emergency relief proposals early in the 1983 session. Attempting to capitalize on what they saw as a traditional Democratic issue, Democratic members of Congress tried to beef up a limited job stimulus and humanitarian aid package announced by President Reagan Feb. 16.

During floor debate March 11, Senate Democrats proposed a nearly $1.7 billion increase in a $3.7 billion emergency relief measure (HR 1718) reported by the Senate Appropriations Committee. Offered by Sen. Carl Levin, D-Mich., chairman of the Democratic Task Force on Emergency Human Needs, the amendment would have added $1.3 billion for job creation and human services, including $1 billion for community development block grants, and $390 million for health and humanitarian relief.

Supporters claimed Levin's proposals would create an additional 280,000 jobs. "We're trying to take care of the millions of people whose basic needs have not been met," said Alan J. Dixon, D-Ill.

But the Republican-controlled Senate rejected the plan on a near party-line vote of 34-53: R 2-46; D 32-7 (ND 25-4, SD 7-3).

A $4.6 billion jobs and relief package cleared Congress March 24 as part of a $15.6 billion supplemental appropriations bill for fiscal 1983. The final House-Senate compromise was scaled specifically to stay within limits acceptable to the Reagan administration.

2. Fiscal 1984 Budget

Defying President Reagan and the GOP leadership, moderate Republicans and Democrats won Senate passage May 19 of a fiscal 1984 budget blueprint that increased taxes and domestic spending while slowing the defense buildup sought by the president and cutting $14.5 billion from his revised deficit estimates.

The Senate approved its budget resolution (S Con Res 27) at the end of a grueling session during which members twice rejected a leadership plan that had the reluctant support of the president and initially turned down the budget they ultimately adopted. Final approval came after Budget Committee Chairman Pete V. Domenici, R-N.M., and other opponents of the plan switched their votes to keep the nine-year-old congressional budget process from collapsing. The final tally was 50-49: R 21-32; D 29-17 (ND 24-8, SD 5-9).

The House-passed budget resolution called on Congress to approve much higher tax increases, a lower rate of defense spending, and significantly higher domestic spending than the Senate budget plan. *(House key vote 2)*

3. Senators' Pay Raise

The Senate June 16 voted to give senators a 15 percent pay raise, increasing their annual salaries from $60,662.50 to $69,800. The $9,138 pay hike, which took effect July 1, 1983, put senators at the same salary level as House members. The House raised members' pay in December 1982.

At the same time, the Senate approved a 30 percent cap, effective Jan. 1, 1984, on the honoraria income sena-

tors may receive for speeches, articles and appearances. The $20,940 annual limit already applied to all outside income earned by House members.

The pay raise and honoraria cap were included in an amendment to a fiscal 1983 supplemental appropriations bill (HR 3069 — PL 98-63) that Congress cleared July 29. The Senate agreed to the pay raise by a vote of 49-47: R 29-25; D 20-22 (ND 16-13, SD 4-9).

Although senators did not take a pay raise when House members did in 1982, they had no cap on their honoraria earnings. After honoraria reports for 1982 were made public in May, showing that 19 senators received more than $40,000 each, the House attached an amendment to HR 3069 extending the 30 percent cap to senators. The Senate Appropriations Committee eliminated the honoraria limit, but the full Senate reversed that action June 9, imposing the cap while rejecting amendments to raise senators' pay. Finally, on June 16, Henry M. Jackson, D-Wash., offered the successful amendment that raised salaries and capped honoraria.

Despite frequent complaints that their salaries were insufficient to support homes in their states and in the Washington, D.C., area, members were reluctant to approve pay hikes. Of senators up for re-election in 1984, 24 voted against the pay raise and seven supported it.

4. Abortion

The Senate June 28 rejected a proposed constitutional amendment designed to overturn the Supreme Court's 1973 *Roe v. Wade* decision that made abortion legal.

The vote on the amendment (S J Res 3) was 49-50, with Jesse Helms, R-N.C., voting present. This was 18 votes short of the two-thirds majority needed to pass an amendment. Republicans voted almost 2-1 in favor of the proposal, while Democrats opposed it by almost the same ratio: R 34-19; D 15-31 (ND 7-25, SD 8-6).

The Senate action on S J Res 3 marked the first time either house of Congress had voted on a constitutional amendment aimed at overturning the Supreme Court's abortion ruling.

Sponsored by Orrin G. Hatch, R-Utah, the measure simply stated: "A right to abortion is not secured by this Constitution." By knocking out the constitutional underpinnings for abortion rights, it was designed to authorize Congress and the states to pass new laws to restrict or prohibit abortion.

The anti-abortion movement was split on the strategy behind S J Res 3. Some favored Hatch's approach, while others — led by Helms — thought Congress should pass a statute defining a fetus as a "person" with the same constitutionally guaranteed right to life as any other person. This would require only a simple majority vote in Congress, and no ratification by the states.

Neither the House nor its Judiciary Committee acted on any comparable abortion amendment or bill in 1983.

5. Chemical Weapons

The Senate July 13 approved Reagan administration plans to begin manufacturing lethal chemical weapons for the first time since 1969, but only by the narrowest of margins, with Vice President George Bush casting a tie-breaking vote. It was the first time since 1977 that the vice

president had cast a Senate vote.

At stake were new types of nerve gas bombs and artillery shells, called "binary munitions." The administration insisted that binary production was needed to deter Moscow's use of its large arsenal of chemical weapons and to provide an incentive for Soviet agreement to a ban on chemical weapons. Existing U.S. chemical weapons were inadequate, they said, because they were dangerous for U.S. troops to handle and were losing some of their potency because of chemical deterioration.

Opponents countered that the new weapons were militarily superfluous since there was a large enough supply of usable U.S. chemical weapons to force enemy troops to don clumsy protective suits and masks. Moreover, they argued, production of new chemical weapons would surrender the propaganda advantage the United States had earned from 14 years' abstention from chemical weapons production.

The key Senate vote on the issue came on a motion to table (and thus kill) an amendment to delete binary weapons production funds from the fiscal 1984 defense authorization bill (S 675). The motion was agreed to 50-49: R 35-17; D 14-32 (ND 5-27, SD 9-5), with Vice President Bush casting the deciding "yea" vote to break a 49-49 tie.

The scenario was replayed Nov. 8, when an amendment adding the nerve gas funds to the fiscal 1984 defense appropriations bill (HR 4185) was agreed to 47-46. Again, Bush cast the deciding vote for binary production.

Although the nerve gas provision remained in the authorization bill, it was ultimately deleted — at the insistence of the House — from HR 4185, the defense appropriations measure. *(House key vote 15)*

6. Interest and Dividend Withholding

Months of pressure from the banking industry and the public persuaded Congress to undo a tax reform it had approved only a year earlier: a requirement for 10 percent withholding of taxes on interest and dividend income.

The banking industry stimulated a massive letter-writing campaign against the plan, arguing that the withholding requirement would impose an unfair financial burden on honest taxpayers, as well as banks.

Opponents of repeal countered that the banks were deceiving the American public by portraying withholding as a new tax, rather than as a means of enforcing tax laws already on the books, but the lobbying campaign paid off.

Sealing a major victory for the banks, the Senate July 28 cleared a withholding repeal measure (HR 2973) by a vote of 90-7: R 51-2; D 39-5 (ND 25-5, SD 14-0).

President Reagan, who initially vowed to veto a withholding repealer, yielded when it became clear that such a veto almost certainly would be overridden. The addition of stiffer withholding compliance requirements, plus inclusion of the trade and tax portions of his Caribbean Basin Initiative, helped ensure Reagan's approval of the bill.

7. Coal Leasing

A collapse of Senate support for the coal-leasing policies of Interior Secretary James G. Watt was evident in a Sept. 20 vote to impose a moratorium on federal coal leasing.

The vote came on an amendment offered by Dale Bumpers, D-Ark., to the fiscal 1984 Interior Department appropriations bill (HR 3363 — PL 98-146). That amendment barred the use of funds in the bill for any leasing of coal on federal lands until 90 days after a study commission created to review leasing policies reported its recommendations. It was adopted 63-33: R 23-29, D 40-4 (ND 29-1, SD 11-3).

Bumpers charged that Watt's leasing program was selling too much coal too fast, and bringing less than the fair market value of the coal as a return to the Treasury.

Twice in the preceding year, the Senate had narrowly rejected similar Bumpers amendments. The first vote came Dec. 14, 1982, when a leasing-ban rider to the fiscal 1983 Interior appropriations bill (PL 97-394) was rejected 47-48. On June 14, 1983, the Senate by 48-51 rejected a similar amendment to a fiscal 1983 supplemental appropriations measure (HR 3069 — PL 98-63).

Those two votes split along party lines, with most Republicans backing Watt and most Democrats opposing him. Thirteen of the 16 senators who switched to Bumpers' side between June 14 and Sept. 20 were Republicans.

The House had approved a slightly different version of the coal-leasing ban, but the variances were easily reconciled in conference.

On Sept. 21, the day after the Senate vote, Watt sparked an uproar by characterizing his appointees to the leasing study commission as "a black ... a woman, two Jews and a cripple."

That remark proved to be the last straw for many Republican senators, who feared Watt's penchant for politically damaging remarks was harming their own prospects as well as President Reagan's. With his Senate support eroding rapidly, Watt resigned Oct. 9.

8. Marines in Lebanon

In late August, the first combat casualties among U.S. Marines in Lebanon prompted members of Congress to question U.S. policies and goals in that troubled country. President Reagan had sent more than 1,200 Marines to Lebanon in 1982 to serve in a multinational peacekeeping force.

To calm growing fears on Capitol Hill, Reagan in early September conducted private negotiations with key congressional leaders. The result was an agreement among Reagan, House Speaker Thomas P. O'Neill Jr., D-Mass., and Senate Majority Leader Howard H. Baker Jr., R-Tenn. Reagan agreed to sign legislation specifically invoking for the first time the major provision of the 1973 War Powers Resolution (PL 93-148) that required congressional approval for U.S. troops to be stationed in combat situations for more than 60 to 90 days. In return, O'Neill and Baker agreed to authorize the Marines to stay in Lebanon for an additional 18 months.

The compromise agreement was put into a joint resolution, which the House passed, 270-161, on Sept. 28. *(House key vote 9)*

When the Senate took up the measure (S J Res 159, as amended) the following day, the ultimate outcome was not seriously in doubt, but it was uncertain how many Republican senators would oppose the resolution. Senate Democrats, unable to reach an agreement with Reagan during separate negotiations, had refused to accept the Reagan-O'Neill-Baker compromise.

As it happened, the vote broke almost purely along party lines. After rejecting several amendments offered by Democrats to tighten limits on the mission of the Marines,

the Senate passed the resolution 54-46: R 52-3; D 2-43 (ND 2-29, SD 0-14).

On Oct. 23, just 11 days after Reagan signed the resolution into law (PL 98-119), terrorist bombings in Beirut killed 239 Marines, sailors and soldiers and 58 French paratroopers. Efforts to revise or revoke the Lebanon resolution in the wake of the bombings fell short in both houses.

9. Education Spending

Senators supporting more money for federal education programs came up short Oct. 4 during debate over the fiscal 1984 Labor, Health and Human Services, Education appropriations bill (HR 3913 — PL 98-139). An amendment by Bill Bradley, D-N.J., Ernest F. Hollings, D-S.C., and Robert T. Stafford, R-Vt., that would have added $559 million to the bill's $13.5 billion total for Department of Education programs was killed on a procedural move.

House Democrats succeeded Sept. 22 in adding $300 million in education and job training programs to the House-passed version of HR 3913. But education supporters in the Senate met with less success.

Led by Bradley, the amendment's backers argued that the extra money would bring the bill's total up to spending levels contained in the fiscal 1984 budget approved by the Senate in May. They were beaten back, however, by the Republican manager of the bill, Lowell P. Weicker Jr., Conn., himself a longtime supporter of increased funding for education. Weicker used the threat of a presidential veto to win enough support to kill the Bradley amendment with a parliamentary maneuver.

The Bradley amendment was ruled out of order by the chair because it would have increased funding above authorized levels, a judgment immediately appealed by Bradley. His appeal was tabled (killed) by a 50-45 party-line vote: R 49-5; D 1-40 (ND 1-26, SD 0-14).

10. Martin Luther King Holiday

After a two-day debate that was alternately bitter and eloquent, the Senate Oct. 19 overcame a recalcitrant conservative minority led by Jesse Helms, R-N.C., and voted to declare the third Monday in January, beginning in 1986, a legal public holiday honoring the Rev. Dr. Martin Luther King Jr., the civil rights leader assassinated in 1968.

The bill (HR 3706) passed by a vote of 78-22: R 37-18; D 41-4 (ND 28-3, SD 13-1).

Setting aside earlier opposition to the legislation, President Reagan signed it into law (PL 98-144) at a ceremony in the Rose Garden. The ceremony, attended by leaders of the civil rights establishment, was indicative of the symbolism the measure had taken on. Supporters argued that creation of the holiday honored not only King, but the entire civil rights movement as well. Leaders of the Aug. 27 march on Washington commemorating the 20th anniversary of King's "I have a dream" speech, made creation of the holiday a priority.

The House passed the bill relatively quickly, by a 338-90 vote Aug. 2. The Senate leadership then placed it directly on the calendar, where it could be brought up at any time. Majority Leader Howard H. Baker Jr., R-Tenn., tried to bring it up just before the August recess, but decided not to when Helms indicated he would begin a lengthy debate.

While some opponents argued against the cost of a 10th public holiday, others, especially Helms, suggested

King was not worthy of the singular recognition a legal holiday would confer. When the measure came up after the recess, Helms began a brief filibuster, based on allegations that King had ties with the Communist Party. Along with several conservative groups, Helms sued demanding release of FBI documents on King, sealed until the year 2027 by a court order. However, a federal judge refused to break the seal.

Helms and his allies attempted to send HR 3706 to the Judiciary Committee for hearings and offered numerous amendments to the bill, but all their efforts fell by lopsided margins. However, concern about the cost of additional federal holidays did lead the Senate to pass a separate measure limiting to 10 the number of legal public holidays.

11. Clinch River Breeder Reactor

Congress in 1983 voted not to provide any more funds for the construction of the controversial Clinch River Breeder Reactor project. The apparent death of the demonstration nuclear power plant came after a series of votes over the preceding three years showed steadily dwindling support for the plutonium-powered project near Oak Ridge, Tenn.

Before the decisive vote was cast by the Senate Oct. 26, both the House and Senate Appropriations committees had declined to recommend fiscal 1984 funding, and the House May 12 had voted overwhelmingly against the project.

Thus, when the Senate voted on a proposal to provide $1.5 billion to complete the federal share of payments under a new funding scheme, Clinch River's demise was not completely unexpected.

Opponents were concerned that Majority Leader Howard H. Baker Jr., R-Tenn., the project's godfather, would once more be able to prevail on his colleagues to support the project. But Baker did not argue in its defense during floor debate — leaving that task to Energy and Natural Resources Committee Chairman James A. McClure, R-Idaho.

Unmoved by McClure's arguments, the Senate turned down the Clinch River funding, which was contained in an amendment to a fiscal 1984 supplemental appropriations bill (HR 3959). The vote, on a motion to table the amendment, was 56-40: R 23-30; D 33-10 (ND 26-4, SD 7-6).

Both sides said they believed concern over the ultimate cost of the project, which was authorized by Congress in 1970, was the deciding factor in its defeat. The federal government had already spent $1.6 billion on the project.

12. Nuclear Freeze

In its first vote on the issue, the Senate Oct. 31 turned aside a resolution calling for a mutual and verifiable freeze on the testing, production and deployment of U.S. and Soviet nuclear weapons.

The resolution had earned widespread, grass-roots backing since late 1981. A heavily amended version of it was passed by the House in May. *(House key vote 3)*

Freeze advocates argued that a rough balance currently existed between U.S. and Soviet nuclear forces, with each sufficient to deter an attack by the other. U.S. advantages in bombers and missile-firing submarines offset Soviet advantages in the number and size of land-based ICBMs, they maintained. By this logic, President Reagan's planned nuclear buildup was not only unnecessary but dangerous, because of its emphasis on missiles such as the

MX, accurate enough to threaten a first strike on armored Soviet missile launchers.

Opponents warned that a freeze would block the replacement of older American weapons with modern ones. They also argued a freeze would bar the development of new weapons — such as the small, single-warhead ICBM dubbed Midgetman — that might make the nuclear balance more stable.

The fundamental objection to the freeze by many administration officials and others rested on the belief that ICBMs were unique among nuclear weapons because of the short time within which they could deliver a surprise attack. From that premise, it followed that the Soviet advantages in ICBMs could not be tolerated nor would Moscow agree to reduce its ICBM force unless threatened by similar U.S. weapons — particularly, the MX missile, which a freeze would prevent.

The freeze was offered as an amendment to the bill (H J Res 308) increasing the ceiling on the national debt. A motion to table (and thus kill) the amendment was agreed to 58-40: R 46-7; D 12-33 (ND 3-28, SD 9-5).

13. Debt Limit/Deficit Control

Senators anxious to press their case for deficit control measures succeeded Oct. 31 in defeating an urgent increase in the public debt limit sought by the Reagan administration. The vote was 39-56: R 28-25; D 11-31 (ND 10-19, SD 1-12).

Conservative Republicans led the attack on the legislation (H J Res 308), without which the government could not continue to borrow money to pay its bills. They hoped to force action on bold steps to reduce federal spending — including enhanced presidential authority to impound, or withhold from spending, funds appropriated by Congress.

The GOP conservatives were joined by members of both parties who hoped to pressure Congress in the waning days of the session to agree on a major package of spending cuts and administration-opposed tax increases. That deficit-reduction effort failed, however, and before adjourning for the year the Senate joined the House in approving a $1.49 trillion debt limit measure.

14. MX Missile

The Senate Nov. 7 decisively rejected an effort to bar funding for production of the MX missile, the centerpiece of the Reagan administration's nuclear arms buildup.

The vote came just six days after the House, by a much tighter nine-vote margin, had likewise voted to keep $2.1 billion in MX money in the fiscal 1984 defense appropriations bill (HR 4185). The funds were earmarked to build the first 21 production-line versions of the big ICBM. *(House key vote 10)*

The missile, which was flight-tested for the first time in June, would carry 10 nuclear warheads, each with enough power and accuracy to destroy armored Soviet missile launchers and command posts.

The administration insisted the MX was needed to offset a Soviet force of more than 600 ICBMs of comparable power and accuracy. It argued that such land-based missiles cast a political influence far more powerful than other nuclear weapons and, accordingly, that continued Soviet advantages in the number and power of ICBMs could not be tolerated.

Members who shared this view were joined in supporting MX by others who were more skeptical about the importance of MX, but were willing to support it in return for a shift by the administration to arms control negotiating positions deemed more likely to win Soviet agreement.

MX opponents argued that the missile would destabilize the U.S.-Soviet nuclear balance. They said MX would threaten the ICBMs that comprised the bulk of the Soviet nuclear force while itself being vulnerable to Soviet attack, since it would be deployed in existing U.S. missile silos.

They also rejected claims that ICBMs enjoyed unique diplomatic potency compared with other nuclear weapons, and insisted that superior U.S. bombers and missile submarines offset any Soviet advantage in land-based missiles.

The key Senate vote on the missile came on a motion offered by Sen. Dale Bumpers, D-Ark., to delete from HR 4185 the $2.1 billion earmarked to begin MX production. That amendment was rejected 37-56: R 6-46; D 31-10 (ND 24-3, SD 7-7).

House Key Votes

1. Social Security

Acting on one of the sensitive issues left unresolved by the National Commission on Social Security Reform, the House March 9 voted to raise the normal Social Security retirement age gradually from 65 to 67 between the year 2000 and 2027. It thus rejected a Ways and Means Committee plan to reduce initial benefit levels beginning in 2000 and raise payroll taxes beginning in 2015. The vote was 228-202: R 152-14; D 76-188 (ND 23-152, SD 53-36).

The choice between raising the retirement age and increasing taxes to help maintain long-term solvency of the Social Security system had been one of the main points of controversy surrounding the crisis over Social Security financing. The bipartisan reform commission had been unable to reach agreement on measures to deal with the system's long-range problems.

The Senate ultimately went along with the House in approving a two-year increase in the retirement age. In other respects, the Social Security financing bill (HR 1900) closely paralleled the Jan. 15 recommendations of the bipartisan reform commission.

2. Fiscal 1984 Budget

After two years as mere onlookers, House Democrats scored a major budget victory March 23, when the House approved the first budget resolution for fiscal 1984 (H Con Res 91). The vote was 229-196: R 4-160; D 225-36 (ND 168-6, SD 57-30).

The budget plan adopted by the House was essentially a Democratic political manifesto. Conceived by the entire Democratic membership, it added approximately $33 billion in domestic spending to the president's fiscal 1984 requests. Much of that money was earmarked for human needs programs that were significantly cut in the fiscal 1982 and 1983 budgets.

To pay for these programs, the plan reduced the president's proposed rate of growth in defense spending from 10 percent to 4 percent. And it also called for $30 billion in additional revenues in fiscal 1984. Reagan opposed tax increases.

The Republicans charged that the plan was a return to the old policies of "tax and tax, spend and spend." But

they were unable to contrive a plan of their own and unwilling to bring the president's original budget up for a vote. The vacuum left by the Republicans allowed conservative Democratic "Boll Weevils," who had voted with the Republicans in 1981-82, to return to the fold and vote with their party leadership.

The Republican-controlled Senate also reordered Reagan's budget priorities. *(Senate key vote 2)*

3. Nuclear Freeze

The House May 4 approved a resolution (H J Res 13) calling for negotiation of a mutual and verifiable freeze on the testing, production and deployment of U.S. and Soviet nuclear arms. But the measure passed only after days of debate spread over three months and the adoption of several amendments intended by freeze opponents to mute its impact on Reagan administration nuclear arms policy.

The Senate later rejected a slightly different version of the freeze resolution. *(Senate key vote 12)*

Freeze advocates insisted that U.S. and Soviet nuclear forces currently were in overall balance and that a freeze was the only way to prevent escalation of the race by both sides to deploy new or improved weapons. In addition, they warned that both military establishments planned new weapons, such as the MX missile, that would make the nuclear balance more unstable because they would be sufficiently fast and accurate to threaten a first strike.

The administration opposed a freeze, arguing it would block new U.S. programs that were needed both to replace obsolescent weapons and to give Moscow an incentive to agree to substantial mutual reductions in the U.S. and Soviet nuclear arsenals. To freeze the arsenals at this point merely would cement Soviet advantages, officials said.

Freeze critics succeeded in attaching some amendments, including one specifying that any freeze agreement would expire if it did not lead to substantial reductions in the U.S. and Soviet missile forces.

The amended resolution was passed by a 278-149 vote: R 60-106; D 218-43 (ND 168-4, SD 50-39).

4. Emergency Mortgage Aid

As part of an effort to provide federal anti-recession aid — and to distance itself from the Republican administration — the Democratic leadership in the House pushed for passage of a measure providing $760 million in fiscal 1983 for a temporary loan program to help unemployed homeowners meet mortgage payments. The bill also included $100 million in fiscal 1984 funding for emergency shelter for the homeless.

Debate on the bill (HR 1983) was bitter and partisan. The House considered it May 11, after weeks in which the leadership pulled the measure from the schedule because it lacked the votes needed for passage. Opponents argued the program was too expensive in a time of high deficits and would eventually lead to the creation of a new entitlement program.

To make it more palatable to doubting members, House Democrats agreed to tighten eligibility requirements for the temporary loan program.

The House narrowly rejected an attempt by Buddy Roemer, D-La., to gut the bill by stripping out the loan program and simply asking lenders to practice forbearance. It then voted 216-196 for the program: R 6-155; D 210-41 (ND 158-8, SD 52-33).

However, the mortgage assistance program never became law. The Senate Banking Committee agreed to a loan guarantee program and included it in its housing authorization bill (S 1338). But the final housing authorization, which cleared Congress Nov. 18, omitted mortgage assistance. In addition, an appropriation for mortgage assistance loans, passed by the House, was dropped in conference with the Senate. Shelter for the homeless was authorized, however, at $60 million.

5. Clean Air Act Sanctions

The House defused a political time bomb June 2 when it voted to bar the Environmental Protection Agency (EPA) from imposing penalties on communities that had missed a Dec. 31, 1982, deadline for meeting national clean air standards.

The Reagan administration had threatened to impose the sanctions on some 218 communities around the nation. Environmentalists charged the administration was trying to pressure lawmakers into moving on a long-stalled reauthorization of the Clean Air Act in hopes that a new version would ease a range of existing anti-pollution requirements. Congress had been deadlocked for more than two years on competing proposals to rewrite the law.

Neither side had been willing to allow a simple extension of the air quality deadlines without getting other concessions it wanted. But in a surprise move, the House June 2 voted a one-year moratorium on the penalties, 227-136: R 89-50; D 138-86 (ND 88-58, SD 50-28).

The vote was on an amendment prohibiting use of funds in the fiscal 1984 Housing and Urban Development appropriations bill (HR 3133) to impose the sanctions.

The vote fractured most existing coalitions on clean air issues, cutting across parties, regions and regulatory philosophies. The amendment was offered by William E. Dannemeyer, R-Calif., an advocate of Reagan administration environmental policies who usually was aligned with conservative and industry forces seeking relaxation of the Clean Air Act. But it also won support from a number of House members who favored the existing law.

The moratorium on penalties was included in the version of the bill passed by the Senate and signed into law by President Reagan July 12. Its adoption put an end to efforts to move a Clean Air Act reauthorization in the first session of the 98th Congress.

6. Covert Action in Nicaragua

In their one symbolic challenge to President Reagan's foreign policy, House Democrats twice voted to end "covert" U.S. aid to some 10,000 guerrillas fighting to overthrow the leftist government of Nicaragua. Congress had not publicly questioned a secret CIA operation since 1976, when it forced the Ford administration to drop its support for a pro-Western faction fighting for control of Angola.

The Democrats insisted the covert aid in Nicaragua violated international law, undermined U.S. credibility as a peacemaker in Central America and actually strengthened the Nicaraguan government's support among its own people. Administration officials gave varying reasons for the aid. First, they said it was aimed at interdicting the flow of arms through Nicaragua to leftist guerrillas in El Salvador and elsewhere in Central America. Later, they said the covert aid was forcing the Sandinista government in Nicaragua to "turn inward" and thus reduce its support for the

Salvadoran guerrillas.

The House first took a stand against the covert aid on July 28, when it passed a bill (HR 2760) terminating the aid at a secret date and substituting for it a program to openly help nations in Central America combat cross-border arms shipments. The vote was 228-195: R 18-145; D 210-50 (ND 163-9, SD 47-41).

The GOP-controlled Senate refused to follow suit, and Reagan and Congress ultimately reached a compromise on the issue. Congress provided $24 million to continue the covert aid in fiscal 1984, but Reagan was required to seek congressional approval for additional funds.

7. IMF Participation

President Reagan had to fight with his fellow Republicans and court House Democrats to win approval for an increase in the U.S. contribution to the International Monetary Fund (IMF). The effort nearly backfired, however, after Democrats who had sided with the president on a key amendment were attacked by Republicans. The $8.4 billion U.S. share of a nearly $32 billion IMF increase finally cleared Congress as part of an unrelated measure.

The IMF increase was needed to provide short-term aid to debt-ridden developing countries, and proponents said failure to approve it could cause a drop in world trade and possibly a global financial collapse. Opponents, however, called the increase a "big-bank bailout," a rescue operation for banking institutions that had imprudently made huge loans to countries burdened with debt.

The House originally passed the IMF increase (HR 2957) Aug. 3 on a 217-211 vote: R 72-94; D 145-117 (ND 106-68, SD 39-49).

But some Democrats later threatened to withdraw their support for the bill to protest a Republican press release criticizing their votes against an amendment that was also opposed by the president. Reagan ultimately sent a thank-you letter to every Democrat who supported him on the amendment.

A second obstacle to the IMF increase was the refusal of House Democrats to go to conference on the bill until the Senate agreed to an unrelated housing authorization. A deal was struck late in the session that combined the IMF measure with the housing bill as a single amendment to the conference report on a supplemental fiscal 1984 appropriations bill (HR 3959).

8. Coal Slurry Pipeline

By a surprising margin, the House Sept. 27 rejected a bill (HR 1010) giving the right of federal eminent domain to qualified coal slurry pipeline companies.

It was the first time in five years that such legislation had reached the House floor. In 1978, a similar bill was defeated 161-246. Coal slurry backers believed support for the idea had increased substantially since then.

But the tally of 182-235: R 85-75; D 97-160 (ND 52-120, SD 45-40) showed the continued lobbying muscle of the railroads, which in many areas enjoyed a virtual monopoly on coal transportation. They were joined by a number of farmers' organizations in fighting the bill.

Sen. J. Bennett Johnston, D-La., chief sponsor of a similar Senate bill (S 267), assessed the margin of the House vote and declined to press for Senate consideration of his measure.

Several pipeline companies proposed to carry coal slurry, fine particles of pulverized coal mixed with water, from Western states, southern Illinois and the Appalachian Mountains to power plants as much as 1,500 miles away.

Federal eminent domain rights were viewed as crucial to the development of the slurry industry. Only one slurry line was currently in operation; other efforts to obtain the needed rights of way had been blocked, often by railroads.

Supporters argued that moving coal via pipelines would result in lower electricity costs to consumers. But the railroads contended that coal slurry pipelines would deprive them of much-needed revenue, and farmers' groups were concerned the railroads would recoup by charging higher costs for transporting farm goods.

9. Marines in Lebanon

The backing of Speaker Thomas P. O'Neill Jr., D-Mass., was the key that led to House passage Sept. 28 of a controversial resolution (H J Res 364) allowing President Reagan to keep U.S. Marines in Lebanon until early 1985.

Reagan had sent more than 1,200 Marines to Lebanon in 1982 to serve in a multinational peacekeeping force. Congress accepted that action without question until several Marines were killed by sniper and artillery fire in late August and early September 1983.

With congressional concern on the rise, Reagan in early September conducted private negotiations with O'Neill and Senate Majority Leader Howard H. Baker Jr., R-Tenn. As a result, Reagan agreed to sign legislation specifically invoking for the first time the major provision of the 1973 War Powers Resolution (PL 93-148), which required congressional approval for U.S. troops to be stationed in combat situations for more than 60-90 days. In return, O'Neill and Baker agreed to authorize the Marines to stay in Lebanon for an additional 18 months.

The House passed the compromise agreement Sept. 28 after rejecting an effort by some Democrats to force an earlier withdrawal of the Marines. Nearly half the Democrats in the House went along with O'Neill and supported the agreement. The vote was 270-161: R 140-27; D 130-134 (ND 70-105, SD 60-29).

The Senate passed its version of the resolution (S J Res 159, as amended) the next day, 54-46. The House accepted the Senate's slightly different version later that day, clearing it for the president. *(Senate key vote 8)*

Reagan signed the bill into law (PL 98-119) on Oct. 12. Just 11 days later, terrorist bombings in Beirut killed 239 Marines, sailors and soldiers and 58 French paratroopers. Efforts to revise or revoke the Lebanon resolution in the wake of the bombings fell short in both houses.

10. MX Missile

The House Nov. 1 approved production of the first 21 MX missiles by a margin of only nine votes.

The Senate followed suit by a far wider margin Nov. 7, assuring inclusion of $2.1 billion for MX in the fiscal 1984 defense appropriations bill. *(Senate key vote 14)*

The administration viewed the missile as the most significant element of its nuclear buildup. The planned deployment of 100 MXs, each with 10 very accurate warheads, would pose the same threat to armored Soviet missile silos that the Soviet Union's missile force currently posed to U.S. missiles. Only that kind of threat would give

Moscow an incentive to negotiate substantial mutual reductions in such large, multi-warhead ICBMs, some MX supporters insisted.

They were joined by a small group of moderate Democrats who were less certain that MX was required in its own right, but who were willing to support it in return for a moderation of administration arms control policy.

MX opponents warned that the missile would make the U.S.-Soviet nuclear balance dangerously unstable because of the threat it posed to Soviet ICBMs. They argued the MX threat might tempt Moscow to launch its land-based missiles — which comprise the bulk of its nuclear arsenal — at the first, possibly erroneous sign of a U.S. attack.

If a new U.S. ICBM were needed, some MX foes argued, it should be a small missile that could be made relatively invulnerable to Soviet attack — unlike the large silo-based MXs — by being carried around in a mobile launcher. Such a smaller missile — dubbed Midgetman — would have to carry only a single warhead and thus would remove uncertainty introduced into the current nuclear balance by each ICBM's ability to destroy several enemy missiles, thus conferring a potential advantage to whichever side launched its missiles first.

The key House vote on the missile came on an amendment to delete from the fiscal 1984 defense appropriations bill (HR 4185) $2.1 billion for 21 MX missiles. The amendment was rejected 208-217: R 18-145; D 190-72 (ND 156-18, SD 34-54).

11. Social Programs Spending

Seeking to restore domestic spending cuts made in 1981, House Democratic leaders Nov. 8 produced an amendment to a stopgap spending bill adding $997.7 million for education, job training, low-income energy assistance and other social programs.

The amendment to the second fiscal 1984 continuing resolution (H J Res 403) was offered by Majority Leader Jim Wright, D-Texas. Supporters said the proposal would force Congress and Reagan to decide whether to back up with hard cash their expressed concern over the state of American education. Democratic leaders also wanted to force Reagan to choose between more domestic spending or a veto of politically popular programs.

Reagan adamantly opposed the extra money, and Republicans demanded separate votes on the various components of the Wright amendment. In those votes, the House adopted more money for vocational education, schooling for immigrant children, community health centers, job training, child nutrition and other services, rejecting only a section providing $43 million for science centers at three universities.

After deleting the money for science centers, the House approved the remaining $954.4 million in the Wright amendment as a package. The vote was 254-155: R 22-134; D 232-21 (ND 162-7, SD 70-14).

Although the Wright amendment was adopted, the entire continuing resolution was rejected later that night by a 203-206 vote. The defeat came when impatient freshman Democrats mounted a symbolic protest against the stalemate on deficit reduction legislation and joined Republicans to reject the stopgap money bill.

When the House considered a new continuing resolution (H J Res 413) Nov. 10, the Wright amendment again was accepted. But the Senate voted 53-36 against the extra

domestic money.

With Reagan threatening to veto the continuing resolution because of the Wright money, House and Senate conferees Nov. 11 trimmed the $954.4 million down to $98.7 million. The money was divided among education for the handicapped, vocational rehabilitation, immigrant education, college student aid, community health centers, colleges for the deaf and emergency shelters for the homeless. Reagan signed H J Res 413 (PL 98-151) Nov. 14.

12. Dairy Program

Faced with an expensive, continuously growing dairy surplus, the House Nov. 9 had a clear choice between two alternative methods of dealing with the problem. It endorsed a plan, pushed by the dairy industry, to pay dairy farmers for the first time to cut back production. For years, the federal government had compensated crop farmers for holding down production, but there had been no payments on a national scale to dairymen for producing less milk.

The House rejected an alternative plan to authorize immediate, sharp cuts in federal dairy price supports. The support establishes the price paid by the federal dairy program for surplus milk. Advocates said price support cuts in past years had reduced surplus production and would do so again; they called the 15-month payment program an expensive mistake, and said dairy farmers would figure out ways to collect the payments without permanently reducing productive capacity.

But the House rejected these arguments, and the price support cut, proposed by Barber B. Conable Jr., R-N.Y., lost 174-250: R 97-65; D 77-185 (ND 52-122, SD 25-63).

The House subsequently passed the payment plan (HR 4196). Its supporters noted dairy farmers themselves would be financing part of the program, and they argued that family dairy farms should be protected from unreasonable economic shocks associated with production cuts.

The administration initially backed the payment plan, but Agriculture Secretary John R. Block later announced he preferred Conable's price support cut. The American Farm Bureau Federation, consumer representatives and livestock producers also lined up behind Conable.

The paid diversion plan was controversial enough that the House emphatically refused in mid-October to let sponsors scoot a Senate-passed version (HR 3385) straight through to conference, without amendments. But when the bill came up a second time Nov. 9, dairy lobbyists had mustered enough support from key Democratic leaders — and from commodity groups benefiting from other provisions dealing with tobacco program changes, egg production and drought relief — to soundly defeat Conable's amendment.

13. Universal Telephone Service

A $4 million lobbying campaign by the American Telephone & Telegraph Co. (AT&T) failed Nov. 10 when the House rejected by a party-line vote a Federal Communications Commission (FCC) plan to raise local phone rates.

The FCC had proposed levying a flat charge of $2 per month for residential users and $6 per month per line for small-business users, beginning Jan. 1, 1984, for the right of access to long-distance service. The fees would rise in the future.

The FCC and AT&T argued the access charges were essential to the success of the scheduled Jan. 1, 1984, court-ordered breakup of AT&T.

Under the existing system, local telephone companies received some $6.5 billion a year from interstate long-distance tolls to help cover the costs of wires, poles and other equipment. After Jan. 1, when the local companies separated from AT&T, they no longer would get that subsidy.

The FCC plan would shift the subsidy to local users. AT&T, the FCC and their Republican allies argued that unless long-distance users were relieved of the burden of paying the subsidy, allowing long-distance rates to fall, the large firms that make the bulk of long-distance calls would turn to new technologies to set up their own communications networks. The result, they said, would shrink the rate base, requiring local phone users to pay higher rates in the long run.

The bill under consideration (HR 4102) would prohibit the FCC from imposing the access charge on residential customers and business users that had only one line, and would require long-distance users to continue to pay part of the costs of the wires, poles and other facilities shared with local users.

The bill's sponsor, Timothy E. Wirth, D-Colo., chairman of the House Energy and Commerce Subcommittee on Telecommunications, and his allies argued that the FCC plan was unfair. They said it would shift a cost properly borne by long-distance callers to local users and would charge local users for the right to use long-distance even if they made no such calls. They contended phone service would become so expensive that the poor and some rural citizens could not afford it.

The key vote came when the House rejected by 142-264 a substitute bill offered by Tom Tauke, R-Iowa, that would have let the FCC phase in the access charges at lower levels than the $2 a month the FCC planned. The vote was 142-264: R 134-19; D 8-245 (ND 1-169, SD 7-76).

The House went on to pass the bill by voice vote, but final action on the issue awaited Senate action on a milder bill (S 1660) that would delay the FCC plan for two years.

14. Equal Rights Amendment

The House Democratic leadership tried to revive the Equal Rights Amendment (ERA) Nov. 15 by putting the proposal on a parliamentary fast track, but the tactic angered a number of House members and the ERA failed.

The vote on H J Res 1 was 278-147, six short of the two-thirds majority required to pass it. Democrats voted overwhelmingly for the ERA, while Republicans voted against the measure by a 2-1 margin: R 53-109; D 225-38 (ND 164-13, SD 61-25).

The wording of H J Res 1 was identical to that of an earlier ERA that died June 30, 1982, three states short of the three-fourths (38) needed to ratify it: "Equality of rights under the law shall not be denied or abridged by the United States or by any state on account of sex."

Speaker Thomas P. O'Neill Jr., D-Mass., took the unusual step of bringing the ERA to the floor under suspension of the rules, a procedure that allows only 40 minutes' debate and no amendments. Generally, it is reserved for non-controversial measures.

O'Neill and ERA sponsors feared that if H J Res 1 went to the floor under normal procedures, amendments would be adopted making it inapplicable to abortion policy, the military draft and military combat regulations, among other areas of existing law. Realizing that such amendments would make the ERA unacceptable to many of its supporters, they opted to send the proposal to the floor under a procedure barring amendments entirely.

The ERA was a priority issue for many women's groups, and Democrats hoped the sharp partisan divergence on the amendment would weigh heavily in the 1984 elections.

Although ERA hearings were held in a Senate Judiciary subcommittee, that panel took no action on the proposal in 1983.

15. Nerve Gas Production

For the third time in two years, the House Nov. 15 voted against resuming the production of lethal chemical weapons. It instructed conferees on the fiscal 1984 defense appropriations bill (HR 4185) to oppose adamantly $124.4 million for production of so-called "binary munitions." These are aerial bombs and artillery shells designed to dispense lethal nerve gas.

The administration insisted Moscow's use of its large stocks of chemical weapons could be deterred only if U.S. forces possessed comparable weapons. And officials also contended that only a viable U.S. chemical weapons threat would induce Moscow to negotiate a chemical weapons ban.

Binary weapons opponents insisted that existing U.S. chemical weapons would be adequate in case of a conflict. Critics also argued that, because of the widespread revulsion against chemical weapons, U.S. binary production would surrender a propaganda advantage that Washington reaped from its own 14-year abstention from chemical weapons production, while Soviet forces and allies were widely believed to have used such weapons in Afghanistan, Laos and Cambodia.

The key vote was on an amendment to a motion to instruct the House conferees that had the effect of insisting on the House position of denying production funding for the nerve gas weapons. The amendment was agreed to 258-166: R 60-103; D 198-63 (ND 162-12, SD 36-51).

16. Tax Increases

The House killed any chance for consideration of a limited $8 billion tax increase measure (HR 4170) during the 1983 session when it refused Nov. 17 to approve the rule governing floor consideration of the measure. The vote against the rule was 204-214: R 13-149; D 191-65 (ND 147-23, SD 44-42).

Many House Democrats believed that they could co-opt the deficit-reduction issue by urging increases in taxes. President Reagan, however, was unequivocal in his opposition to tax increases of any size.

House leaders were lukewarm toward the measure. Although they ultimately backed the effort, they saw little to be gained by approving a controversial tax bill that the Senate was unlikely to approve and the president would certainly veto.

The chief controversy over the bill, which was drafted in part to meet deficit-reduction requirements in the fiscal 1984 budget resolution, involved proposed limits on tax-exempt industrial development bonds (IDBs). Other provisions of the bill would extend the mortgage revenue bond program, revamp the taxation of life insurance companies, give statutory tax exemption to most existing fringe benefits, and restrict the use of sale/lease-back schemes by nonprofit entities.

	1	2	3	4	5	6	7
ALABAMA							
Denton	N	N	Y	Y	Y	Y	N
Heflin	N	N	N	Y	Y	Y	Y
ALASKA							
Murkowski	N	N	Y	Y	+	Y	N
Stevens	N	Y	Y	N	Y	Y	N
ARIZONA							
Goldwater	N	?	Y	N	?	Y	N
DeConcini	N	N	Y	Y	N	Y	Y
ARKANSAS							
Bumpers	Y	N	N	N	Y	Y	Y
Pryor	Y	N	N	N	N	Y	Y
CALIFORNIA							
Wilson	N	N	N	N	Y	Y	Y
Cranston	#	N	?	N	N	N	Y
COLORADO							
Armstrong	?	N	N	Y	Y	Y	N
Hart	?	Y	?	N	N	?	Y
CONNECTICUT							
Weicker	?	Y	N	N	N	Y	N
Dodd	Y	Y	N	N	N	N	Y
DELAWARE							
Roth	N	N	Y	N	N	Y	Y
Biden	Y	Y	N	N	N	Y	Y
FLORIDA							
Hawkins	N	N	Y	Y	Y	Y	Y
Chiles	Y	Y	Y	Y	N	Y	Y
GEORGIA							
Mattingly	N	N	N	Y	Y	Y	Y
Nunn	N	N	N	Y	Y	Y	Y
HAWAII							
Inouye	Y	Y	?	N	N	Y	?
Matsunaga	?	Y	Y	N	N	Y	Y
IDAHO							
McClure	N	N	N	Y	Y	Y	N
Symms	?	N	N	Y	Y	Y	N
ILLINOIS							
Percy	N	Y	Y	N	N	Y	Y
Dixon	Y	Y	N	N	Y	N	Y
INDIANA							
Lugar	N	N	Y	Y	Y	Y	Y
Quayle	N	N	Y	Y	Y	Y	Y

	1	2	3	4	5	6	7
IOWA							
Grassley	N	N	N	Y	N	Y	Y
Jepsen	N	N	N	Y	Y	Y	Y
KANSAS							
Dole	?	N	Y	Y	Y	Y	N
Kassebaum	N	Y	Y	N	N	Y	Y
KENTUCKY							
Ford	Y	N	N	Y	Y	Y	Y
Huddleston	Y	Y	N	Y	N	Y	Y
LOUISIANA							
Johnston	?	N	N	Y	Y	Y	N
Long	Y	N	Y	Y	Y	Y	Y
MAINE							
Cohen	N	Y	N	Y	N	Y	Y
Mitchell	Y	Y	N	N	N	Y	Y
MARYLAND							
Mathias	Y	Y	Y	N	N	N	?
Sarbanes	Y	Y	Y	N	N	Y	Y
MASSACHUSETTS							
Kennedy	Y	Y	Y	N	N	N	Y
Tsongas	Y	Y	Y	N	N	N	Y
MICHIGAN							
Levin	Y	Y	N	N	N	Y	Y
Riegle	Y	Y	N	N	N	Y	Y
MINNESOTA							
Boschwitz	N	Y	N	Y	Y	Y	Y
Durenberger	?	N	Y	N	Y	N	Y
MISSISSIPPI							
Cochran	N	Y	N	Y	N	Y	N
Stennis	N	Y	Y	Y	Y	Y	Y
MISSOURI							
Danforth	N	Y	N	Y	N	N	N
Eagleton	Y	Y	Y	N	Y	N	Y
MONTANA							
Baucus	Y	N	N	N	N	Y	Y
Melcher	Y	N	Y	N	Y	N	Y
NEBRASKA							
Exon	N	N	N	Y	Y	Y	Y
Zorinsky	N	N	N	Y	Y	Y	Y
NEVADA							
Hecht	N	N	N	Y	Y	Y	N
Laxalt	N	N	Y	Y	Y	Y	N

	1	2	3	4	5	6	7
NEW HAMPSHIRE							
Humphrey	N	N	N	Y	Y	Y	Y
Rudman	N	Y	Y	N	Y	Y	Y
NEW JERSEY							
Bradley	Y	Y	N	N	N	Y	Y
Lautenberg	Y	Y	Y	N	N	N	Y
NEW MEXICO							
Domenici	N	Y	N	Y	Y	?	N
Bingaman	Y	Y	Y	N	N	Y	Y
NEW YORK							
D'Amato	N	Y	Y	Y	Y	Y	Y
Moynihan	Y	Y	Y	N	N	Y	Y
NORTH CAROLINA							
East	N	N	N	Y	Y	Y	N
Helms	N	N	N	P	Y	Y	N
NORTH DAKOTA							
Andrews	N	Y	Y	Y	N	Y	N
Burdick	Y	Y	Y	N	N	Y	N
OHIO							
Glenn	Y	Y	Y	N	Y	?	Y
Metzenbaum	Y	Y	Y	N	N	N	Y
OKLAHOMA							
Nickles	N	N	N	Y	Y	Y	N
Boren	X	N	N	N	N	Y	N
OREGON							
Hatfield	N	Y	Y	Y	N	Y	Y
Packwood	N	Y	Y	N	N	Y	Y
PENNSYLVANIA							
Heinz	N	Y	N	N	N	Y	Y
Specter	Y	Y	N	N	N	Y	Y
RHODE ISLAND							
Chafee	N	Y	Y	N	Y	Y	Y
Pell	Y	Y	N	N	N	Y	Y
SOUTH CAROLINA							
Thurmond	N	N	Y	Y	Y	Y	-
Hollings	?	N	N	N	Y	Y	Y
SOUTH DAKOTA							
Abdnor	N	N	N	Y	Y	Y	N
Pressler	N	N	N	Y	N	Y	N
TENNESSEE							
Baker	N	N	Y	Y	Y	Y	?
Sasser	Y	Y	-	N	N	Y	N

KEY

Y	Voted for (yea).
#	Paired for.
+	Announced for.
N	Voted against (nay).
X	Paired against.
-	Announced against.
P	Voted "present".
C	Voted "present" to avoid possible conflict of interest.
?	Did not vote or otherwise make a position known.

Democrats   Republicans

	1	2	3	4	5	6	7
TEXAS							
Tower	?	N	Y	N	Y	Y	N
Bentsen	?	Y	Y	N	Y	Y	Y
UTAH							
Garn	N	N	Y	Y	Y	Y	N
Hatch	N	N	Y	Y	Y	Y	N
VERMONT							
Stafford	N	Y	Y	N	Y	Y	Y
Leahy	Y	N	N	N	N	Y	Y
VIRGINIA							
Trible	N	N	Y	Y	Y	Y	N
Warner	N	N	N	Y	Y	Y	Y
WASHINGTON							
Gorton	N	Y	Y	N	Y	Y	Y
Evans [1]							Y
WEST VIRGINIA							
Byrd	Y	Y	Y	N	N	Y	Y
Randolph	Y	Y	Y	N	N	Y	Y
WISCONSIN							
Kasten	N	N	N	Y	N	Y	Y
Proxmire	N	N	N	N	Y	N	Y
WYOMING							
Simpson	N	Y	N	N	Y	Y	Y
Wallop	N	N	Y	N	Y	Y	N

ND - Northern Democrats   SD - Southern Democrats (Southern states - Ala., Ark., Fla., Ga., Ky., La., Miss., N.C., Okla., S.C., Tenn., Texas, Va.)

1. Sen. Daniel J. Evans, R-Wash., sworn in Sept. 12, 1983, to succeed Henry M. Jackson, D, who died Sept. 1, 1983.

1. HR 1718. Emergency Supplemental Appropriations, Fiscal 1983/Jobs. Levin, D-Mich., amendment to add $1.665 billion for job creation, emergency food and shelter assistance and emergency health assistance. Rejected 34-53: R 2-46; D 32-7 (ND 25-4, SD 7-3), March 11, 1983.

2. S Con Res 27. First Budget Resolution, Fiscal 1984. Adoption of the concurrent resolution to set fiscal 1984 budget targets as follows: budget authority, $914.7 billion; outlays, $849.7 billion; revenues, $671.1 billion; and deficit, $178.6 billion. Adopted 50-49: R 21-32; D 29-17 (ND 24-8, SD 5-9), May 19, 1983.

3. HR. 3069. Supplemental Appropriations, Fiscal 1983. Jackson, D-Wash., amendment to raise senators' salaries to $69,800 beginning July 1, 1983, and, beginning Jan. 1, 1984, to limit the acceptance of honoraria to 30 percent of pay. Adopted 49-47: R 29-25; D 20-22 (ND 16-13, SD 4-9), June 16, 1983.

4. S J Res 3. Human Life Federalism Amendment. Passage of the joint resolution to propose an amendment to the Constitution that would overturn the 1973 Supreme Court decision, *Roe v. Wade*, which made abortion legal. Rejected 49-50: R 34-19; D 15-31 (ND 7-25, SD 8-6), June 28, 1983. A two-thirds majority of those present and voting (67 in this case) of both houses is required for passage of a joint resolution proposing an amendment to the Constitution. A "yea" was a vote supporting the president's position.

5. S 675. Omnibus Defense Authorizations. Tower, R-Texas, motion to table (kill) the Pryor, D-Ark., amendment to prohibit the production of lethal binary chemical munitions and related production facilities. Motion agreed to 50-49: R 35-17; D 14-32 (ND 5-27, SD 9-5), July 13, 1983, with Vice President Bush casting a "yea" vote to break the 49-49 tie. A "yea" was a vote supporting the president's position.

6. HR 2973. Interest and Dividend Tax Withholding/Caribbean Basin Initiative. Adoption of the conference report on the bill to repeal interest and dividend withholding requirements due to take effect Aug. 5; to impose new tax compliance requirements and penalties; and to provide trade and tax incentives to certain Caribbean nations. Adopted (thus cleared for the president) 90-7: R 51-2; D 39-5 (ND 25-5, SD 14-0), July 28, 1983.

7. HR 3363. Interior Appropriations, Fiscal 1984. Bumpers, D-Ark., amendment to ban all further coal leasing on federal lands until 90 days after a special commission created to study the Interior Department's coal leasing policies has completed its report. Adopted 63-33: R 23-29; D 40-4 (ND 29-1, SD 11-3), Sept. 20, 1983.

	8	9	10	11	12	13	14
ALABAMA							
Denton	Y	Y	Y	N	Y	N	N
Heflin	N	N	Y	N	Y	N	N
ALASKA							
Murkowski	Y	Y	N	N	Y	N	N
Stevens	Y	Y	Y	N	Y	Y	N
ARIZONA							
Goldwater	Y	Y	N	X	Y	N	N
DeConcini	N	N	N	Y	Y	N	?
ARKANSAS							
Bumpers	N	N	Y	Y	N	N	Y
Pryor	N	N	Y	Y	N	N	Y
CALIFORNIA							
Wilson	Y	Y	Y	Y	Y	N	N
Cranston	N	?	Y	Y	N	?	?
COLORADO							
Armstrong	Y	Y	Y	Y	Y	N	N
Hart	N	N	Y	Y	N	?	?
CONNECTICUT							
Weicker	N	Y	Y	N	N	?	Y
Dodd	N	N	Y	Y	N	Y	Y
DELAWARE							
Roth	N	Y	Y	Y	Y	Y	N
Biden	N	N	Y	Y	N	N	Y
FLORIDA							
Hawkins	Y	Y	Y	Y	Y	N	N
Chiles	N	N	Y	Y	Y	N	N
GEORGIA							
Mattingly	Y	Y	Y	Y	Y	N	N
Nunn	N	N	Y	Y	Y	N	N
HAWAII							
Inouye	N	?	Y	Y	N	N	?
Matsunaga	N	N	Y	Y	N	Y	Y
IDAHO							
McClure	Y	Y	N	N	Y	Y	N
Symms	Y	Y	N	N	Y	N	N
ILLINOIS							
Percy	Y	Y	Y	Y	Y	Y	N
Dixon	N	N	Y	Y	N	N	?
INDIANA							
Lugar	Y	Y	Y	Y	Y	Y	N
Quayle	Y	Y	Y	Y	Y	N	N

	8	9	10	11	12	13	14
IOWA							
Grassley	Y	Y	N	N	Y	N	N
Jepsen	Y	Y	N	Y	Y	N	N
KANSAS							
Dole	Y	Y	Y	N	Y	Y	N
Kassebaum	Y	Y	Y	Y	Y	Y	N
KENTUCKY							
Ford	N	N	Y	Y	Y	N	Y
Huddleston	N	N	Y	N	N	N	Y
LOUISIANA							
Johnston	N	N	Y	N	Y	N	N
Long	N	N	Y	N	Y	N	N
MAINE							
Cohen	Y	N	Y	Y	Y	Y	N
Mitchell	Y	N	Y	Y	N	N	Y
MARYLAND							
Mathias	Y	?	Y	N	N	Y	N
Sarbanes	N	N	Y	N	Y	N	N
MASSACHUSETTS							
Kennedy	N	N	Y	N	Y	N	N
Tsongas	N	N	Y	Y	N	Y	Y
MICHIGAN							
Levin	N	N	Y	N	Y	N	Y
Riegle	N	-	Y	+	N	N	Y
MINNESOTA							
Boschwitz	Y	Y	Y	Y	?	?	N
Durenberger	Y	Y	Y	Y	Y	Y	?
MISSISSIPPI							
Cochran	Y	N	Y	N	Y	N	N
Stennis	N	N	N	N	Y	Y	N
MISSOURI							
Danforth	Y	Y	Y	N	Y	N	N
Eagleton	N	N	Y	Y	N	Y	Y
MONTANA							
Baucus	N	N	Y	Y	N	N	Y
Melcher	N	N	Y	Y	N	N	Y
NEBRASKA							
Exon	N	N	N	Y	Y	N	Y
Zorinsky	Y	N	N	N	Y	N	N
NEVADA							
Hecht	Y	Y	N	N	Y	N	N
Laxalt	Y	Y	Y	N	?	Y	N

	8	9	10	11	12	13	14
NEW HAMPSHIRE							
Humphrey	Y	Y	N	Y	Y	N	Y
Rudman	Y	Y	N	Y	Y	N	N
NEW JERSEY							
Bradley	N	N	Y	Y	N	Y	Y
Lautenberg	N	N	Y	Y	N	N	+
NEW MEXICO							
Domenici	Y	Y	Y	N	Y	N	N
Bingaman	N	N	Y	Y	N	Y	Y
NEW YORK							
D'Amato	Y	Y	Y	N	Y	N	N
Moynihan	N	N	Y	Y	N	Y	Y
NORTH CAROLINA							
East	Y	Y	N	N	Y	N	N
Helms	Y	Y	N	N	Y	N	N
NORTH DAKOTA							
Andrews	Y	Y	Y	N	N	Y	Y
Burdick	N	N	Y	N	N	N	Y
OHIO							
Glenn	N	?	Y	Y	N	Y	N
Metzenbaum	N	N	Y	Y	N	N	N
OKLAHOMA							
Nickles	Y	Y	N	Y	Y	N	N
Boren	N	N	Y	Y	N	Y	N
OREGON							
Hatfield	N	Y	Y	Y	N	Y	Y
Packwood	Y	Y	Y	Y	Y	Y	?
PENNSYLVANIA							
Heinz	Y	Y	Y	N	Y	N	N
Specter	Y	N	Y	N	N	Y	Y
RHODE ISLAND							
Chafee	Y	Y	Y	Y	N	Y	N
Pell	N	N	Y	N	Y	N	Y
SOUTH CAROLINA							
Thurmond	Y	Y	Y	N	Y	N	N
Hollings	N	N	Y	+	N	?	Y
SOUTH DAKOTA							
Abdnor	Y	Y	N	N	Y	N	N
Pressler	Y	N	N	Y	Y	N	N
TENNESSEE							
Baker	Y	Y	Y	N	Y	N	N
Sasser	N	N	Y	N	N	N	Y

KEY

Y Voted for (yea).
\# Paired for.
+ Announced for.
N Voted against (nay).
X Paired against.
- Announced against.
P Voted "present".
C Voted "present" to avoid possible conflict of interest.
? Did not vote or otherwise make a position known.

Democrats   *Republicans*

	8	9	10	11	12	13	14
TEXAS							
Tower	Y	Y	N	N	Y	N	N
Bentsen	N	N	Y	Y	Y	N	N
UTAH							
Garn	Y	Y	N	N	Y	Y	N
Hatch	Y	Y	N	N	Y	N	N
VERMONT							
Stafford	Y	N	Y	#	N	Y	Y
Leahy	N	N	Y	N	Y	N	Y
VIRGINIA							
Trible	Y	Y	Y	Y	Y	N	N
Warner	Y	Y	Y	Y	Y	N	N
WASHINGTON							
Gorton	Y	Y	Y	Y	Y	Y	N
Evans	Y	Y	Y	N	Y	Y	?
WEST VIRGINIA							
Byrd	N	N	Y	N	N	N	N
Randolph	N	N	N	N	N	N	N
WISCONSIN							
Kasten	Y	Y	Y	N	Y	N	N
Proxmire	N	Y	Y	Y	N	N	Y
WYOMING							
Simpson	Y	Y	Y	Y	Y	Y	N
Wallop	Y	Y	N	N	Y	Y	N

ND - Northern Democrats   SD - Southern Democrats (Southern states - Ala., Ark., Fla., Ga., Ky., La., Miss., N.C., Okla., S.C., Tenn., Texas, Va.)

8. S J Res 159. Multinational Force in Lebanon. Passage of the joint resolution to provide statutory authorization under the War Powers Resolution for continued U.S. participation in the multinational peacekeeping force in Lebanon for up to 18 months after the enactment of the resolution. Passed 54-46: R 52-3; D 2-43 (ND 2-29, SD 0-14), Sept. 29, 1983. A "yea" was a vote supporting the president's position.

9. HR 3913. Labor, Health and Human Services, Education Appropriations, Fiscal 1984. Weicker, R-Conn., motion to table (kill) the Bradley, D-N.J., appeal of the chair's ruling that a Bradley amendment to add $559 million for education programs was out of order because it would have increased funding above authorized levels. Motion agreed to 50-45: R 49-5; D 1-40 (ND 1-26, SD 0-14), Oct. 4, 1983. A "yea" was a vote supporting president's position.

10. HR 3706. Martin Luther King Jr. Holiday. Passage of the bill to declare the third Monday in January a legal public holiday honoring Martin Luther King Jr. Passed 78-22: R 37-18; D 41-4 (ND 28-3, SD 13-1), Oct. 19, 1983.

11. HR 3959. Supplemental Appropriations, Fiscal 1984. Humphrey, R-N.H., motion to table (kill) the Senate Appropriations Committee amendment to add $1.5 billion to the bill to complete the Clinch River breeder reactor in Tennessee. Motion agreed to 56-40: R 23-30; D 33-10 (ND 26-4, SD 7-6), Oct. 26, 1983.

12. H J Res 308. Debt Limit Increase. Dole, R-Kan., motion to table (kill) the Kennedy, D-Mass., amendment to call for a mutual and verifiable freeze on and reduction in nuclear weapons. Motion agreed to 58-40: R 46-7; D 12-33 (ND 3-28, SD 9-5), Oct. 31, 1983. A "yea" was a vote supporting the president's position.

13. H J Res 308. Debt Limit Increase. Passage of the bill to increase the public debt limit to $1.45 trillion, from $1.389 trillion. Rejected 39-56: R 28-25; D 11-31 (ND 10-19, SD 1-12), Oct. 31, 1983.

14. HR 4185. Defense Department Appropriations, Fiscal 1984. Bumpers, D-Ark., amendment to delete $2.1 billion for 21 MX missiles. Rejected 37-56: R 6-46; D 31-10 (ND 24-3, SD 7-7), Nov. 7, 1983. A "nay" was a vote supporting the president's position.

1. HR 1900. Social Security Act Amendments. Pickle, D-Texas, amendment to gradually raise the normal Social Security retirement age from 65 to 67 after the year 2000, and to delete provisions of the Ways and Means Committee bill that would reduce initial benefit levels beginning in the year 2000 and raise payroll taxes beginning in the year 2015. Adopted 228-202: R 152-14; D 76-188 (ND 23-152, SD 53-36), March 9, 1983. A "yea" was a vote supporting the president's position.

2. H Con Res 91. First Budget Resolution, Fiscal 1984. Adoption of the first concurrent budget resolution to set spending and revenue targets for the fiscal year ending Sept. 30, 1984, as follows: budget authority, $936.55 billion; outlays, $863.55 billion; revenues, $689.1 billion; and deficit, $174.45 billion. The resolution also set preliminary goals for fiscal 1985-86, revised budget levels for fiscal 1983 and included reconciliation instructions requiring House committees to recommend legislative savings to meet the budget targets. Adopted 229-196: R 4-160; D 225-36 (ND 168-6, SD 57-30), March 23, 1983.

3. H J Res 13. Nuclear Freeze. Passage of the joint resolution calling for a mutual and verifiable freeze on and reduction in nuclear weapons. Passed 278-149: R 60-106; D 218-43 (ND 168-4, SD 50-39), May 4, 1983. A "nay" was a vote supporting the president's position.

4. HR 1983. Emergency Housing Assistance Act. Passage of the bill to authorize $760 million in fiscal 1983 for a temporary loan program to help unemployed homeowners make their mortgage payments, and $100 million in fiscal 1984 for emergency shelter for the homeless. Passed 216-196: R 6-155; D 210-41 (ND 158-8, SD 52-33), May 11, 1983. A "nay" was a vote supporting the president's position.

5. HR 3133. Department of Housing and Urban Development Appropriations, Fiscal 1984. Dannemeyer, R-Calif., amendment to prohibit the Environmental Protection Agency from using any funds provided by the bill to impose sanctions during fiscal 1984 on any area for failing to attain any national ambient air quality standard established under the Clean Air Act. Adopted 227-136: R 89-50; D 138-86 (ND 88-58, SD 50-28), June 2, 1983.

6. HR 2760. Prohibition on Covert Action in Nicaragua. Passage of the bill to prohibit, at a classified date specified by the House Intelligence Committee, support by U.S. intelligence agencies for military or paramilitary operations in Nicaragua and to authorize $30 million in fiscal 1983 and $50 million in fiscal 1984 to help friendly countries in Central America interdict cross-border shipments of arms to anti-government forces in the region. The bill also directed the president to seek action by the Organization of American States to resolve the conflicts in Central America and to seek an agreement by the government of Nicaragua to halt its support for anti-government forces in the region. Passed 228-195: R 18-145; D 210-50 (ND 163-9, SD 47-41), July 28, 1983. A "nay" was a vote supporting the president's position.

7. HR 2957. International Recovery and Financial Stability Act. Passage of the bill to authorize an $8.4 billion increase in U.S. participation in the International Monetary Fund, extend for two years with some changes the authority for the Export-Import Bank, and provide multilateral development aid. Passed 217-211: R 72-94; D 145-117 (ND 106-68, SD 39-49), Aug. 3, 1983. A "yea" was a vote supporting the president's position.

8. HR 1010. Coal Pipeline Act. Passage of the bill to grant federal power of eminent domain to certified coal slurry pipeline companies. Rejected 182-235: R 85-75; D 97-160 (ND 52-120, SD 45-40), Sept. 27, 1983.

1. Rep. Sala Burton, D-Calif., sworn in June 28, 1983, to succeed her husband, Phillip Burton, D, who died April 10, 1983.

2. Rep. Daniel L. Schaefer, R-Colo., sworn in April 7, 1983, to succeed Rep.-elect Jack Swigert, R, who died Dec. 27, 1982.

3. Rep. George W. "Buddy" Darden, D-Ga., sworn in Nov. 10, 1983, to succeed Larry P. McDonald, D, who died Sept. 1, 1983.

4. Rep. Charles A. Hayes, D-Ill., sworn in Sept. 12, 1983, to succeed Harold Washington, D, who resigned April 30, 1983.

5. Rep. Thomas P. O'Neill Jr., D-Mass., as Speaker, votes at his own discretion.

6. Rep. Gary L. Ackerman, D-N.Y., sworn in March 2, 1983, to succeed Benjamin S. Rosenthal, D, who died Jan. 4, 1983.

7. Rep. Phil Gramm, D-Texas, resigned Jan. 5, 1983, and was re-elected Feb. 12 as a Republican and was sworn in Feb. 22, 1983.

KEY

Y Voted for (yea).
\# Paired for.
\+ Announced for.
N Voted against (nay).
X Paired against.
\- Announced against.
P Voted "present".
C Voted "present" to avoid possible conflict of interest.
? Did not vote or otherwise make a position known.

Democrats   *Republicans*

	1	2	3	4	5	6	7	8
ALABAMA								
1 *Edwards*	Y	N	N	N	Y	N	Y	N
2 *Dickinson*	Y	N	N	X	?	Y	N	N
3 Nichols	N	N	N	N	Y	N	Y	N
4 Bevill	N	Y	N	Y	N	Y	N	N
5 Flippo	Y	Y	N	Y	Y	Y	N	N
6 Erdreich	N	N	N	Y	Y	Y	N	N
7 Shelby	Y	N	N	Y	N	N	N	N
ALASKA								
AL *Young*	Y	N	Y	N	?	N	N	Y
ARIZONA								
1 *McCain*	Y	N	N	N	?	N	Y	N
2 Udall	Y	Y	Y	Y	Y	Y	Y	Y
3 *Stump*	N	N	N	N	N	N	N	N
4 *Rudd*	N	N	N	N	N	N	N	N
5 McNulty	Y	Y	Y	N	Y	Y	Y	Y
ARKANSAS								
1 Alexander	Y	Y	Y	Y	?	Y	Y	Y
2 *Bethune*	Y	N	N	N	N	N	N	N
3 *Hammerschmidt*	Y	N	N	N	N	N	N	N
4 Anthony	Y	Y	Y	N	N	Y	N	Y
CALIFORNIA								
1 Bosco	N	Y	Y	Y	N	Y	N	Y
2 *Chappie*	Y	N	N	Y	N	?	N	Y
3 Matsui	Y	Y	Y	Y	Y	Y	Y	Y
4 Fazio	N	Y	Y	Y	Y	Y	Y	N
5 Burton[1]						Y	Y	N
6 Boxer	N	Y	Y	Y	Y	Y	Y	N
7 Miller	N	Y	Y	Y	Y	Y	Y	N
8 Dellums	N	Y	Y	Y	Y	Y	Y	N
9 Stark	Y	Y	Y	Y	Y	Y	Y	N
10 Edwards	N	Y	Y	Y	Y	Y	Y	N
11 Lantos	N	Y	+	#	Y	Y	Y	N
12 *Zschau*	Y	N	Y	Y	Y	Y	Y	N
13 Mineta	N	Y	Y	Y	Y	Y	Y	Y
14 *Shumway*	N	Y	N	N	N	Y	N	N
15 Coelho	N	Y	Y	Y	Y	Y	Y	N
16 Panetta	N	Y	Y	Y	+	Y	Y	Y
17 *Pashayan*	Y	N	N	N	?	N	N	?
18 Lehman	N	Y	Y	Y	Y	Y	Y	N
19 *Lagomarsino*	Y	N	Y	N	Y	Y	Y	N
20 *Thomas*	Y	N	Y	N	Y	N	N	N
21 *Fiedler*	Y	N	Y	N	N	Y	N	N
22 *Moorhead*	N	N	N	N	N	N	Y	N
23 Beilenson	Y	Y	Y	N	Y	Y	Y	Y
24 Waxman	N	Y	?	Y	Y	Y	Y	N
25 Roybal	N	Y	Y	Y	N	Y	N	N
26 Berman	N	Y	Y	Y	?	Y	Y	Y
27 Levine	N	Y	Y	Y	+	Y	Y	Y
28 Dixon	N	Y	Y	#	?	Y	Y	N
29 Hawkins	N	Y	Y	Y	?	Y	Y	Y
30 Martinez	N	Y	Y	?	?	Y	Y	Y
31 Dymally	N	Y	Y	Y	Y	Y	Y	Y
32 Anderson	N	Y	Y	Y	Y	Y	Y	N
33 *Dreier*	Y	N	N	N	Y	N	N	Y
34 Torres	N	Y	Y	Y	+	Y	Y	N
35 *Lewis*	Y	N	N	N	N	Y	N	N
36 Brown	N	Y	Y	Y	Y	Y	N	Y
37 *McCandless*	Y	N	N	N	Y	N	N	Y
38 Patterson	N	Y	Y	Y	Y	Y	Y	N
39 *Dannemeyer*	Y	N	X	N	Y	N	N	N
40 *Badham*	Y	N	N	N	?	N	Y	Y
41 *Lowery*	Y	N	N	N	Y	N	Y	Y
42 *Lungren*	Y	N	N	N	Y	N	N	Y

	1	2	3	4	5	6	7	8
43 *Packard*	Y	N	N	N	Y	N	N	Y
44 Bates	Y	Y	Y	Y	Y	Y	N	Y
45 *Hunter*	Y	N	N	N	Y	N	N	Y
COLORADO								
1 Schroeder	N	Y	Y	N	Y	Y	N	N
2 Wirth	N	Y	Y	Y	Y	Y	Y	N
3 Kogovsek	N	Y	Y	Y	Y	Y	Y	N
4 *Brown*	Y	N	N	N	N	N	N	Y
5 *Kramer*	Y	N	N	N	Y	N	N	N
6 *Schaefer*[2]			N	N	Y	N	N	Y
CONNECTICUT								
1 Kennelly	N	Y	Y	Y	N	Y	Y	N
2 Gejdenson	N	Y	Y	Y	Y	Y	Y	N
3 Morrison	N	Y	Y	Y	Y	Y	Y	N
4 *McKinney*	Y	Y	N	Y	N	Y	N	N
5 Ratchford	N	Y	Y	Y	Y	Y	Y	N
6 *Johnson*	N	N	Y	N	N	N	N	Y
DELAWARE								
AL Carper	Y	Y	Y	N	Y	Y	N	N
FLORIDA								
1 Hutto	Y	N	N	N	Y	N	N	Y
2 Fuqua	Y	Y	Y	N	N	Y	N	Y
3 Bennett	Y	N	N	N	Y	N	N	Y
4 Chappell	Y	Y	Y	N	N	Y	N	Y
5 *McCollum*	Y	N	N	N	Y	N	X	Y
6 MacKay	Y	Y	Y	N	Y	Y	Y	Y
7 Gibbons	Y	Y	Y	N	Y	Y	Y	?
8 *Young*	Y	N	N	N	Y	N	N	N
9 *Bilirakis*	Y	N	N	N	Y	N	N	Y
10 *Ireland*	Y	N	N	N	Y	N	N	Y
11 Nelson	N	Y	Y	N	N	Y	N	Y
12 *Lewis*	N	N	N	N	Y	N	N	Y
13 *Mack*	Y	N	N	N	N	N	N	Y
14 Mica	N	Y	Y	?	N	Y	Y	Y
15 *Shaw*	Y	N	N	N	Y	N	N	Y
16 Smith	Y	Y	Y	?	Y	Y	Y	Y
17 Lehman	N	Y	Y	?	Y	Y	Y	Y
18 Pepper	N	Y	Y	Y	Y	Y	Y	N
19 Fascell	N	Y	Y	N	Y	Y	N	Y
GEORGIA								
1 Thomas	Y	N	N	N	Y	N	N	N
2 Hatcher	Y	N	?	N	Y	N	Y	N
3 Ray	Y	N	N	N	Y	N	N	N
4 Levitas	Y	N	N	N	Y	N	N	N
5 Fowler	N	Y	Y	Y	N	Y	Y	N
6 *Gingrich*	Y	N	N	N	Y	N	N	N
7 Darden[3]								
8 Rowland	Y	N	N	?	N	Y	N	N
9 Jenkins	Y	N	N	N	Y	N	N	N
10 Barnard	Y	N	N	N	N	N	Y	N
HAWAII								
1 Heftel	Y	Y	Y	?	?	?	?	?
2 Akaka	N	Y	Y	Y	N	Y	Y	Y
IDAHO								
1 *Craig*	Y	N	N	?	N	N	N	
2 *Hansen*	Y	N	N	N	Y	N	N	N
ILLINOIS								
1 Hayes[4]								Y
2 Savage	N	Y	Y	Y	Y	Y	Y	N
3 Russo	N	Y	Y	Y	N	Y	N	N
4 *O'Brien*	Y	N	Y	Y	N	Y	Y	N
5 Lipinski	Y	N	Y	Y	N	Y	N	N
6 *Hyde*	Y	N	N	N	Y	N	N	N
7 Collins	N	Y	Y	?	Y	N	N	
8 Rostenkowski	Y	Y	Y	N	Y	Y	N	N
9 Yates	N	Y	Y	Y	Y	Y	Y	N
10 *Porter*	Y	N	Y	Y	N	Y	Y	
11 Annunzio	N	Y	Y	Y	N	Y	N	
12 *Crane, P.*	Y	N	N	N	N	N	N	N
13 *Erlenborn*	Y	N	N	N	Y	N	N	N
14 *Corcoran*	Y	N	N	N	Y	N	N	X
15 *Madigan*	Y	N	N	Y	N	N	N	
16 *Martin*	Y	N	N	N	Y	N	N	N
17 Evans	N	Y	Y	Y	Y	Y	Y	N
18 *Michel*	Y	N	N	X	Y	N	N	Y
19 *Crane, D.*	Y	N	N	N	Y	N	N	Y
20 Durbin	N	Y	Y	Y	Y	Y	Y	N
21 Price	Y	Y	Y	?	Y	N	N	
22 Simon	N	Y	Y	Y	?	Y	N	Y
INDIANA								
1 Hall	N	Y	Y	Y	N	Y	Y	N
2 Sharp	N	Y	Y	Y	Y	Y	Y	N
3 *Hiler*	Y	N	N	N	N	N	N	Y
4 *Coats*	Y	N	N	N	Y	N	N	Y
5 Hillis	Y	N	N	N	Y	N	N	Y

ND - Northern Democrats   SD - Southern Democrats

	1	2	3	4	5	6	7	8
6 ***Burton***	Y	N	N	N	Y	N	N	Y
7 ***Myers***	Y	N	N	N	Y	N	N	?
8 McCloskey	N	Y	Y	Y	N	Y	N	N
9 Hamilton	Y	Y	Y	N	Y	Y	Y	N
10 Jacobs	N	Y	Y	Y	Y	Y	N	N
IOWA								
1 ***Leach***	Y	N	Y	N	?	Y	Y	N
2 ***Tauke***	Y	N	Y	N	N	N	Y	?
3 ***Evans***	Y	N	Y	N	N	Y	Y	N
4 Smith	N	N	Y	Y	N	Y	Y	Y
5 Harkin	N	Y	Y	Y	?	Y	N	N
6 Bedell	Y	Y	Y	Y	N	Y	Y	N
KANSAS								
1 ***Roberts***	Y	N	N	N	N	N	N	N
2 Slattery	Y	Y	Y	N	N	Y	N	N
3 ***Winn***	Y	N	N	N	N	N	N	N
4 Glickman	Y	Y	Y	N	N	Y	Y	N
5 ***Whittaker***	Y	N	Y	N	N	N	N	N
KENTUCKY								
1 Hubbard	N	Y	N	Y	Y	N	Y	N
2 Natcher	N	Y	Y	Y	N	Y	N	N
3 Mazzoli	Y	Y	Y	Y	N	Y	Y	N
4 ***Snyder***	N	N	N	N	Y	N	N	N
5 ***Rogers***	Y	N	N	N	Y	N	N	N
6 ***Hopkins***	Y	N	Y	N	N	N	N	#
7 Perkins	N	Y	Y	Y	N	Y	N	N
LOUISIANA								
1 ***Livingston***	Y	N	N	N	N	N	Y	Y
2 Boggs	N	Y	Y	Y	Y	Y	Y	Y
3 Tauzin	Y	N	N	N	N	N	N	Y
4 Roemer	Y	N	N	N	N	N	N	Y
5 Huckaby	N	N	N	N	N	N	Y	Y
6 ***Moore***	Y	N	N	N	N	N	N	Y
7 Breaux	Y	N	N	N	N	N	N	Y
8 Long	N	Y	Y	Y	Y	Y	Y	Y
MAINE								
1 ***McKernan***	Y	N	Y	N	N	Y	Y	Y
2 ***Snowe***	Y	N	Y	N	N	Y	Y	Y
MARYLAND								
1 Dyson	N	N	N	Y	Y	N	N	N
2 Long	N	Y	Y	Y	?	Y	N	N
3 Mikulski	N	Y	Y	Y	Y	Y	N	N
4 ***Holt***	Y	N	N	N	?	N	N	Y
5 Hoyer	N	Y	Y	Y	N	#	Y	N
6 Byron	Y	N	N	N	Y	N	N	N
7 Mitchell	N	Y	Y	Y	N	Y	N	N
8 Barnes	N	Y	Y	Y	Y	Y	Y	N
MASSACHUSETTS								
1 ***Conte***	N	N	Y	N	?	Y	Y	N
2 Boland	?	Y	Y	Y	N	Y	Y	Y
3 Early	N	Y	Y	?	N	Y	N	Y
4 Frank	N	Y	Y	Y	Y	Y	Y	Y
5 Shannon	N	Y	Y	Y	N	Y	Y	Y
6 Mavroules	N	Y	Y	Y	N	Y	Y	Y
7 Markey	N	Y	Y	Y	Y	Y	Y	N
8 O'Neill [5]								
9 Moakley	N	Y	Y	Y	N	Y	Y	N
10 Studds	Y	Y	Y	Y	N	Y	Y	N
11 Donnelly	N	Y	Y	Y	N	Y	N	Y
MICHIGAN								
1 Conyers	N	Y	Y	Y	?	Y	N	Y
2 ***Pursell***	Y	N	Y	N	?	N	Y	Y
3 Wolpe	N	Y	Y	Y	Y	Y	Y	?
4 ***Siljander***	Y	N	N	N	?	N	N	N
5 ***Sawyer***	Y	N	Y	N	N	N	Y	Y
6 Carr	N	Y	Y	Y	N	Y	N	N
7 Kildee	N	Y	Y	Y	N	Y	N	N
8 Traxler	N	Y	Y	Y	?	Y	N	N
9 ***Vander Jagt***	Y	N	Y	N	N	N	Y	Y
10 Albosta	N	Y	Y	Y	N	Y	N	Y
11 ***Davis***	N	N	Y	Y	N	N	N	Y
12 Bonior	N	Y	Y	Y	N	Y	Y	N
13 Crockett	N	Y	?	Y	?	N	N	N
14 Hertel	N	Y	Y	Y	N	Y	N	N
15 Ford	N	Y	Y	Y	N	Y	N	N
16 Dingell	N	Y	Y	Y	N	Y	Y	Y
17 Levin	N	Y	Y	Y	Y	Y	Y	N
18 ***Broomfield***	Y	N	N	N	N	N	Y	N
MINNESOTA								
1 Penny	Y	Y	Y	Y	Y	Y	N	N
2 ***Weber***	Y	N	N	N	N	N	N	N
3 ***Frenzel***	Y	N	Y	N	?	N	Y	?
4 Vento	N	Y	Y	Y	Y	Y	Y	N
5 Sabo	N	Y	Y	Y	?	Y	Y	N
6 Sikorski	N	Y	Y	Y	Y	Y	Y	N

	1	2	3	4	5	6	7	8
7 ***Stangeland***	Y	N	Y	N	Y	?	Y	N
8 Oberstar	N	Y	Y	Y	Y	Y	N	N
MISSISSIPPI								
1 Whitten	N	Y	Y	Y	N	Y	N	N
2 ***Franklin***	Y	N	N	N	Y	N	N	Y
3 Montgomery	Y	N	N	N	Y	N	N	Y
4 Dowdy	N	Y	Y	Y	Y	?	N	N
5 ***Lott***	Y	N	N	N	Y	N	N	Y
MISSOURI								
1 Clay	N	Y	Y	Y	?	Y	Y	N
2 Young	N	Y	Y	Y	Y	Y	Y	Y
3 Gephardt	N	Y	Y	Y	Y	Y	N	N
4 Skelton	N	N	Y	Y	?	N	N	N
5 Wheat	N	Y	Y	Y	Y	Y	N	N
6 ***Coleman***	Y	N	N	N	N	N	N	N
7 ***Taylor***	Y	N	N	N	Y	N	N	N
8 ***Emerson***	Y	N	N	N	Y	N	N	N
9 Volkmer	N	Y	Y	Y	Y	Y	N	N
MONTANA								
1 Williams	N	Y	Y	Y	Y	Y	Y	N
2 ***Marlenee***	Y	N	N	X	?	N	N	N
NEBRASKA								
1 ***Bereuter***	Y	N	N	N	N	N	Y	N
2 ***Daub***	Y	N	N	N	Y	N	N	N
3 ***Smith***	Y	N	N	N	Y	N	N	N
NEVADA								
1 Reid	N	Y	Y	Y	Y	Y	N	N
2 ***Vucanovich***	Y	N	N	N	+	N	N	Y
NEW HAMPSHIRE								
1 D'Amours	N	Y	Y	Y	N	Y	N	N
2 ***Gregg***	Y	N	Y	N	Y	N	N	Y
NEW JERSEY								
1 Florio	N	Y	Y	Y	+	Y	N	N
2 Hughes	N	Y	Y	Y	N	Y	N	N
3 Howard	N	Y	Y	Y	?	Y	N	Y
4 ***Smith***	Y	N	Y	Y	N	N	Y	N
5 ***Roukema***	Y	N	Y	N	N	Y	Y	Y
6 Dwyer	N	Y	Y	#	N	Y	Y	Y
7 ***Rinaldo***	N	Y	Y	Y	N	N	N	N
8 Roe	N	Y	Y	Y	N	Y	Y	Y
9 Torricelli	N	Y	Y	Y	Y	Y	Y	N
10 Rodino	N	Y	Y	Y	N	Y	Y	Y
11 Minish	N	Y	Y	Y	N	Y	Y	N
12 ***Courter***	Y	N	N	N	N	N	N	Y
13 ***Forsythe***	Y	N	?	N	+	N	Y	Y
14 Guarini	N	Y	Y	Y	N	Y	Y	Y
NEW MEXICO								
1 ***Lujan***	Y	N	Y	N	Y	N	N	Y
2 ***Skeen***	Y	N	N	N	Y	N	Y	N
3 Richardson	N	Y	Y	Y	Y	Y	N	N
NEW YORK								
1 ***Carney***	Y	N	N	N	?	N	N	Y
2 Downey	Y	Y	Y	Y	N	Y	Y	N
3 Mrazek	N	Y	Y	N	N	Y	N	N
4 ***Lent***	Y	N	Y	N	N	N	Y	N
5 ***McGrath***	Y	N	Y	N	N	N	N	Y
6 Addabbo	N	Y	Y	Y	Y	#	N	N
7 Ackerman [6]	N	Y	Y	Y	N	Y	Y	Y
8 Scheuer	N	Y	Y	Y	Y	Y	Y	N
9 Ferraro	N	Y	Y	Y	N	Y	N	Y
10 Schumer	N	Y	Y	Y	Y	Y	Y	Y
11 Towns	N	Y	Y	Y	N	Y	Y	Y
12 Owens	N	Y	Y	?	N	Y	Y	N
13 Solarz	N	Y	Y	Y	Y	+	Y	Y
14 ***Molinari***	N	N	N	N	N	X	Y	N
15 ***Green***	Y	Y	Y	N	N	Y	Y	Y
16 Rangel	N	Y	Y	Y	Y	Y	Y	Y
17 Weiss	N	Y	Y	Y	+	Y	Y	Y
18 Garcia	N	Y	Y	Y	N	Y	Y	N
19 Biaggi	N	Y	Y	Y	Y	Y	N	?
20 Ottinger	N	Y	Y	Y	Y	Y	Y	N
21 ***Fish***	Y	N	Y	N	Y	Y	Y	Y
22 ***Gilman***	N	N	N	N	Y	N	Y	N
23 Stratton	Y	N	N	Y	?	N	Y	N
24 ***Solomon***	Y	N	N	N	N	N	N	N
25 ***Boehlert***	Y	N	Y	N	N	Y	Y	N
26 ***Martin***	Y	N	N	N	N	N	Y	Y
27 ***Wortley***	Y	N	N	N	Y	N	Y	Y
28 McHugh	N	Y	Y	Y	Y	Y	Y	N
29 ***Horton***	Y	N	Y	N	Y	Y	Y	N
30 ***Conable***	Y	N	N	N	Y	N	Y	Y
31 ***Kemp***	Y	N	N	N	Y	N	N	N
32 LaFalce	N	Y	Y	?	N	Y	Y	N
33 Nowak	N	Y	Y	Y	Y	Y	Y	N
34 Lundine	Y	Y	Y	Y	Y	Y	Y	Y

	1	2	3	4	5	6	7	8
NORTH CAROLINA								
1 Jones	Y	Y	Y	Y	N	Y	N	Y
2 Valentine	Y	N	N	N	Y	Y	N	Y
3 Whitley	Y	N	N	Y	Y	Y	N	N
4 Andrews	N	Y	Y	N	Y	Y	Y	Y
5 Neal	?	#	Y	Y	Y	Y	Y	Y
6 Britt	N	Y	Y	Y	N	Y	Y	Y
7 Rose	N	Y	Y	Y	Y	Y	N	Y
8 Hefner	Y	Y	Y	#	Y	Y	N	N
9 ***Martin***	Y	N	Y	N	Y	N	Y	Y
10 ***Broyhill***	Y	N	Y	N	Y	N	N	Y
11 Clarke	N	Y	Y	N	N	Y	Y	Y
NORTH DAKOTA								
AL Dorgan	N	Y	Y	N	Y	Y	N	N
OHIO								
1 Luken	N	Y	Y	Y	N	Y	Y	?
2 ***Gradison***	Y	N	N	N	?	N	Y	Y
3 Hall	N	Y	Y	Y	Y	Y	Y	N
4 ***Oxley***	Y	N	N	N	Y	N	Y	N
5 ***Latta***	Y	N	N	N	Y	N	Y	N
6 ***McEwen***	Y	N	N	N	Y	N	Y	N
7 ***DeWine***	Y	N	N	N	N	N	Y	N
8 ***Kindness***	Y	N	N	N	N	N	Y	N
9 Kaptur	N	Y	Y	Y	N	Y	N	N
10 ***Miller***	N	N	N	N	Y	N	N	N
11 Eckart	N	Y	Y	Y	Y	Y	N	N
12 ***Kasich***	Y	N	N	N	Y	N	N	N
13 Pease	N	Y	Y	Y	Y	Y	Y	N
14 Seiberling	N	Y	Y	Y	Y	Y	Y	Y
15 ***Wylie***	Y	N	Y	N	N	N	Y	N
16 ***Regula***	N	N	Y	N	N	N	Y	N
17 ***Williams***	N	X	Y	Y	N	Y	Y	N
18 Applegate	N	Y	Y	Y	Y	Y	N	N
19 Feighan	N	Y	Y	Y	Y	Y	N	N
20 Oakar	N	Y	Y	Y	Y	Y	Y	N
21 Stokes	N	Y	Y	Y	N	Y	#	N
OKLAHOMA								
1 Jones	Y	Y	Y	N	Y	Y	Y	Y
2 Synar	Y	Y	Y	Y	Y	Y	Y	Y
3 Watkins	Y	Y	Y	Y	Y	Y	N	Y
4 McCurdy	Y	Y	N	N	Y	Y	N	Y
5 ***Edwards***	Y	X	N	N	Y	N	N	Y
6 English	Y	N	N	N	Y	Y	N	Y
OREGON								
1 AuCoin	Y	Y	Y	Y	?	Y	Y	N
2 ***Smith, R.***	Y	N	Y	X	Y	N	N	Y
3 Wyden	N	Y	Y	Y	Y	Y	Y	N
4 Weaver	N	Y	Y	Y	Y	Y	N	N
5 ***Smith, D.***	Y	N	N	N	?	N	N	Y
PENNSYLVANIA								
1 Foglietta	N	Y	Y	Y	?	Y	Y	Y
2 Gray	N	Y	Y	Y	N	Y	Y	Y
3 Borski	N	Y	Y	Y	Y	Y	Y	Y
4 Kolter	N	Y	Y	Y	?	Y	N	N
5 ***Schulze***	Y	N	Y	N	?	N	N	Y
6 Yatron	N	?	Y	Y	Y	Y	N	N
7 Edgar	N	Y	Y	+	N	Y	Y	N
8 Kostmayer	N	Y	Y	Y	?	Y	Y	Y
9 ***Shuster***	Y	N	Y	N	?	N	N	N
10 ***McDade***	N	N	Y	?	N	?	Y	N
11 Harrison	N	Y	Y	Y	Y	Y	N	X
12 Murtha	N	Y	Y	Y	Y	N	Y	N
13 ***Coughlin***	Y	N	Y	N	N	Y	Y	N
14 Coyne	N	Y	Y	Y	N	Y	Y	N
15 ***Ritter***	Y	N	N	N	N	N	N	Y
16 ***Walker***	Y	N	N	N	Y	N	N	N
17 ***Gekas***	Y	N	N	N	Y	N	Y	N
18 Walgren	N	Y	Y	Y	Y	Y	N	Y
19 ***Goodling***	N	N	Y	N	N	Y	Y	N
20 Gaydos	N	?	Y	Y	Y	N	Y	N
21 ***Ridge***	Y	N	Y	Y	Y	Y	Y	N
22 Murphy	N	Y	Y	Y	Y	Y	N	N
23 ***Clinger***	Y	N	Y	N	N	N	Y	Y
RHODE ISLAND								
1 St Germain	N	Y	Y	Y	N	Y	Y	Y
2 ***Schneider***	N	Y	Y	Y	?	Y	Y	N
SOUTH CAROLINA								
1 ***Hartnett***	Y	N	N	N	Y	N	N	X
2 ***Spence***	Y	N	N	N	Y	N	N	N
3 Derrick	N	Y	Y	N	?	Y	Y	N
4 ***Campbell***	Y	N	N	N	Y	N	Y	N
5 Spratt	N	Y	Y	?	Y	Y	Y	N
6 Tallon	N	Y	Y	N	Y	N	N	N
SOUTH DAKOTA								
AL Daschle	Y	Y	Y	Y	Y	Y	N	Y

	1	2	3	4	5	6	7	8
TENNESSEE								
1 ***Quillen***	Y	N	N	N	Y	N	Y	N
2 ***Duncan***	Y	N	N	N	?	N	N	N
3 Lloyd	Y	Y	N	N	?	N	N	N
4 Cooper	Y	Y	N	N	N	Y	Y	N
5 Boner	N	Y	Y	Y	Y	N	Y	N
6 Gore	N	Y	Y	Y	Y	Y	Y	N
7 ***Sundquist***	Y	N	N	N	Y	N	N	Y
8 Jones	N	Y	Y	Y	?	X	N	N
9 Ford	N	Y	Y	#	Y	Y	Y	?
TEXAS								
1 Hall, S.	Y	N	N	Y	Y	N	N	Y
2 Wilson	Y	X	N	?	?	N	?	Y
3 ***Bartlett***	Y	N	N	N	Y	N	Y	Y
4 Hall, R.	Y	N	N	Y	Y	N	?	N
5 Bryant	N	Y	Y	Y	Y	Y	N	N
6 Gramm [7]	Y	N	N	N	Y	N	N	Y
7 ***Archer***	Y	N	N	N	Y	N	N	Y
8 ***Fields***	Y	N	N	N	Y	N	N	Y
9 Brooks	Y	#	Y	Y	Y	Y	N	#
10 Pickle	Y	Y	Y	N	N	Y	N	Y
11 Leath	Y	N	N	?	Y	N	N	Y
12 Wright	Y	Y	Y	Y	Y	Y	Y	Y
13 Hightower	Y	Y	N	Y	N	N	Y	Y
14 Patman	N	Y	N	Y	Y	N	N	Y
15 de la Garza	Y	Y	Y	Y	N	Y	N	Y
16 Coleman	Y	Y	Y	Y	Y	Y	Y	N
17 Stenholm	Y	N	N	N	Y	N	N	Y
18 Leland	N	Y	Y	Y	Y	Y	Y	Y
19 Hance	Y	N	N	Y	Y	N	N	Y
20 Gonzalez	N	Y	Y	Y	Y	Y	N	Y
21 ***Loeffler***	Y	N	N	N	Y	N	N	Y
22 ***Paul***	Y	N	N	N	Y	N	N	N
23 Kazen	Y	N	Y	Y	?	N	N	Y
24 Frost	N	Y	Y	Y	?	Y	Y	N
25 Andrews	Y	Y	N	Y	Y	Y	Y	Y
26 Vandergriff	Y	N	Y	N	Y	N	Y	#
27 Ortiz	Y	Y	N	Y	Y	Y	N	Y
UTAH								
1 ***Hansen***	Y	N	N	N	?	N	N	Y
2 ***Marriott***	Y	N	N	N	Y	N	Y	Y
3 ***Nielson***	Y	N	N	N	+	N	N	Y
VERMONT								
AL ***Jeffords***	Y	Y	Y	N	N	Y	Y	N
VIRGINIA								
1 ***Bateman***	Y	N	N	N	Y	N	Y	N
2 ***Whitehurst***	Y	N	N	N	Y	N	Y	N
3 ***Bliley***	Y	N	N	N	Y	N	N	N
4 Sisisky	N	Y	N	Y	?	N	N	N
5 Daniel	Y	N	N	N	Y	N	N	N
6 Olin	Y	Y	Y	N	N	Y	N	N
7 ***Robinson***	Y	N	N	N	Y	N	N	Y
8 ***Parris***	Y	N	N	N	N	N	N	Y
9 Boucher	N	Y	Y	Y	Y	Y	Y	N
10 ***Wolf***	Y	N	N	N	N	N	N	Y
WASHINGTON								
1 ***Pritchard***	Y	N	Y	N	?	Y	Y	Y
2 Swift	N	Y	Y	Y	Y	Y	Y	N
3 Bonker	N	Y	Y	Y	+	Y	Y	N
4 ***Morrison***	Y	N	Y	N	+	N	Y	N
5 Foley	N	Y	Y	Y	Y	Y	Y	N
6 Dicks	N	Y	Y	Y	Y	Y	Y	N
7 Lowry	N	Y	Y	Y	Y	Y	Y	N
8 ***Chandler***	Y	N	Y	N	Y	N	Y	Y
WEST VIRGINIA								
1 Mollohan	N	Y	Y	Y	Y	Y	N	N
2 Staggers	N	Y	Y	Y	Y	Y	N	N
3 Wise	N	Y	Y	Y	Y	Y	N	N
4 Rahall	N	Y	Y	Y	?	Y	N	N
WISCONSIN								
1 Aspin	N	Y	Y	Y	Y	Y	Y	N
2 Kastenmeier	N	Y	Y	Y	N	Y	Y	N
3 ***Gunderson***	Y	N	Y	N	N	N	N	N
4 Zablocki	N	Y	Y	Y	Y	Y	Y	Y
5 Moody	N	Y	Y	Y	Y	Y	Y	Y
6 ***Petri***	Y	N	Y	N	N	N	N	Y
7 Obey	N	Y	Y	Y	Y	Y	Y	N
8 ***Roth***	Y	N	Y	N	Y	N	N	Y
9 ***Sensenbrenner***	Y	N	Y	N	Y	N	N	N
WYOMING								
AL ***Cheney***	Y	N	N	N	?	N	Y	Y

Southern states - Ala., Ark., Fla., Ga., Ky., La., Miss., N.C., Okla., S.C., Tenn., Texas, Va.

9. H J Res 364. Multinational Force in Lebanon. Passage of the joint resolution to provide statutory authorization under the War Powers Resolution for continued U.S. participation in the multinational peacekeeping force in Lebanon for up to 18 months after the enactment of the resolution. Passed 270-161: R 140-27; D 130-134 (ND 70-105, SD 60-29), Sept. 28, 1983. A "yea" was a vote supporting the president's position.

10. HR 4185. Defense Department Appropriations, Fiscal 1984. Addabbo, D-N.Y., amendment to delete $2.1 billion for procurement of 21 MX missiles. Rejected 208-217: R 18-145; D 190-72 (ND 156-18, SD 34-54), Nov. 1, 1983. A "nay" was a vote supporting the president's position.

11. H J Res 403. Continuing Appropriations, Fiscal 1984. Wright, D-Texas, amendment to increase funding in the bill by approximately $955 million for an assortment of programs, most of them concerning education. Adopted 254-155: R 22-134; D 232-21 (ND 162-7, SD 70-14), Nov. 8, 1983. A "nay" was a vote supporting the president's position.

12. HR 4196. Dairy Production Stabilization. Conable, R-N.Y., substitute to authorize the secretary of agriculture to reduce the existing $13.10 (per hundred pounds) federal dairy support by as much as $1.50, and to repeal two existing dairy assessments, each 50 cents per hundred pounds. Rejected 174-250: R 97-65; D 77-185 (ND 52-122, SD 25-63), Nov. 9, 1983. A "yea" was a vote supporting the president's position.

13. HR 4102. Universal Telephone Service. Tauke, R-Iowa, substitute to phase in, rather than ban, the Federal Communications Commission plan to impose an access charge on residential and small business telephone users for the right to long-distance service, but only as of Jan. 1, 1985, rather than April 3, 1984, and at levels of no more than $1 a month the first year, rather than $2, rising to $4 a month by 1988. Rejected 142-264: R 134-19; D 8-245 (ND 1-169, SD 7-76), Nov. 10, 1983.

14. H J Res 1. Equal Rights Amendment. Rodino, D-N.J., motion to suspend the rules and pass the joint resolution to propose an amendment to the Constitution declaring, "Equality of rights under the law shall not be denied or abridged by the United States or by any state on account of sex." Motion rejected 278-147: R 53-109; D 225-38 (ND 164-13, SD 61-25), Nov. 15, 1983. A two-thirds majority of those present and voting (284 in this case) is required for passage under suspension of the rules. A "nay" was a vote supporting the president's position.

15. HR 4185. Defense Department Appropriations, Fiscal 1984. Porter, R-Ill., amendment, to the Young, R-Fla., motion to instruct House conferees, to insist on the House position, namely opposition to $124.4 million for production facilities for and procurement of chemical munitions. Motion agreed to 258-166: R 60-103; D 198-63 (ND 162-12, SD 36-51), Nov. 15, 1983. A "nay" was a vote supporting the president's position.

16. HR 4170. Tax Reform Act. Adoption of the rule (H Res 376) providing for House floor consideration of the bill to raise $8 billion in revenues over fiscal 1984-86 through a variety of changes in tax law. The main elements of the bill dealt with mortgage revenue bonds, industrial development bonds, fringe benefits, tax simplification, curbs on sale/lease-back schemes by non-profit groups and the taxation of life insurance companies. The bill also made substantial savings in the Medicare program and revised administration of the Social Security Disability Insurance program. Rejected 204-214: R 13-149; D 191-65 (ND 147-23, SD 44-42), Nov. 17, 1983.

---

1. Rep. George W. "Buddy" Darden, D-Ga., sworn in Nov. 10, 1983, to succeed Larry P. McDonald, D, who died Sept. 1, 1983.
2. Rep. Thomas P. O'Neill Jr., D-Mass., as Speaker, votes at his own discretion.

KEY

Y	Voted for (yea).
#	Paired for.
+	Announced for.
N	Voted against (nay).
X	Paired against.
-	Announced against.
P	Voted "present".
C	Voted "present" to avoid possible conflict of interest.
?	Did not vote or otherwise make a position known.

Democrats   **Republicans**

	9	10	11	12	13	14	15	16
ALABAMA								
1 *Edwards*	Y	N	N	N	Y	N	N	N
2 *Dickinson*	Y	N	N	?	N	N	N	N
3 Nichols	N	N	N	N	N	N	N	N
4 Bevill	Y	N	Y	N	Y	N	Y	
5 Flippo	N	N	N	N	Y	N	Y	
6 Erdreich	Y	N	Y	N	N	Y	Y	N
7 Shelby	N	N	Y	N	N	N	N	N
ALASKA								
AL *Young*	Y	N	?	N	Y	Y	N	N
ARIZONA								
1 *McCain*	N	N	N	Y	Y	N	N	N
2 Udall	N	Y	Y	N	Y	Y	Y	
3 *Stump*	Y	N	N	Y	Y	N	N	N
4 *Rudd*	Y	N	N	Y	Y	N	N	N
5 McNulty	N	Y	Y	N	Y	Y	Y	
ARKANSAS								
1 Alexander	Y	N	Y	N	Y	Y	N	Y
2 *Bethune*	Y	N	N	Y	Y	N	Y	N
3 *Hammerschmidt*	Y	N	N	Y	N	N	N	N
4 Anthony	Y	Y	Y	Y	N	+	N	Y
CALIFORNIA								
1 Bosco	N	Y	Y	N	N	Y	Y	Y
2 *Chappie*	Y	N	N	Y	Y	N	N	N
3 Matsui	Y	Y	Y	N	Y	Y	Y	Y
4 Fazio	Y	N	Y	N	Y	Y	?	Y
5 Burton	Y	Y	Y	N	Y	Y	Y	Y
6 Boxer	N	Y	N	N	Y	Y	Y	Y
7 Miller	N	Y	N	N	Y	Y	Y	Y
8 Dellums	N	Y	Y	N	Y	Y	Y	Y
9 Stark	N	Y	Y	X	Y	Y	Y	Y
10 Edwards	N	Y	N	N	Y	Y	Y	Y
11 Lantos	Y	Y	Y	N	Y	Y	Y	Y
12 *Zschau*	Y	N	N	Y	Y	Y	Y	N
13 Mineta	N	Y	N	N	Y	Y	Y	Y
14 *Shumway*	Y	N	N	Y	Y	N	N	N
15 Coelho	?	Y	Y	N	Y	Y	Y	Y
16 Panetta	N	Y	N	N	Y	Y	Y	Y
17 *Pashayan*	Y	N	N	Y	N	N	Y	Y
18 Lehman	Y	?	Y	N	Y	Y	Y	Y
19 *Lagomarsino*	Y	N	N	Y	Y	N	N	N
20 *Thomas*	Y	N	N	Y	Y	N	N	N
21 *Fiedler*	Y	N	N	Y	Y	N	N	N
22 *Moorhead*	Y	N	N	Y	N	N	N	N
23 Beilenson	Y	Y	Y	N	N	Y	Y	Y
24 Waxman	N	Y	Y	N	Y	Y	Y	Y
25 Roybal	N	Y	Y	N	Y	N	?	Y
26 Berman	Y	Y	Y	N	Y	Y	Y	Y
27 Levine	Y	Y	Y	N	Y	Y	Y	Y
28 Dixon	N	Y	Y	N	Y	Y	Y	Y
29 Hawkins	Y	Y	Y	N	Y	Y	Y	#
30 Martinez	N	Y	Y	N	Y	Y	Y	Y
31 Dymally	N	?	Y	Y	Y	Y	Y	#
32 Anderson	Y	N	Y	N	Y	Y	N	Y
33 *Dreier*	Y	N	N	Y	Y	N	N	N
34 Torres	Y	Y	Y	Y	N	Y	Y	Y
35 *Lewis*	Y	N	N	Y	Y	?	?	X
36 Brown	Y	Y	Y	?	Y	Y	Y	Y
37 *McCandless*	Y	N	N	Y	N	N	N	N
38 Patterson	Y	Y	Y	N	Y	Y	Y	Y
39 *Dannemeyer*	N	N	N	Y	Y	N	N	N
40 *Badham*	Y	N	N	Y	N	N	N	N
41 Lowery	Y	N	Y	N	Y	Y	N	N
42 *Lungren*	Y	N	N	Y	Y	N	N	N

	9	10	11	12	13	14	15	16
43 *Packard*	Y	N	N	Y	Y	N	N	N
44 Bates	N	Y	Y	N	N	Y	Y	Y
45 *Hunter*	Y	N	N	Y	N	N	N	N
COLORADO								
1 Schroeder	N	Y	Y	N	Y	N	Y	N
2 Wirth	N	Y	Y	N	N	Y	Y	Y
3 Kogovsek	Y	Y	Y	N	Y	Y	Y	Y
4 *Brown*	N	N	N	Y	Y	Y	Y	N
5 *Kramer*	Y	N	N	N	?	N	N	N
6 *Schaefer*	Y	N	N	N	Y	N	Y	N
CONNECTICUT								
1 Kennelly	N	Y	Y	N	N	Y	Y	Y
2 Gejdenson	Y	Y	Y	N	N	Y	Y	Y
3 Morrison	N	Y	N	N	Y	Y	Y	Y
4 *McKinney*	Y	Y	Y	Y	Y	Y	Y	Y
5 Ratchford	N	Y	N	N	Y	Y	Y	Y
6 *Johnson*	Y	Y	Y	N	Y	Y	Y	Y
DELAWARE								
AL Carper	N	Y	Y	Y	Y	Y	Y	N
FLORIDA								
1 Hutto	Y	N	N	N	N	N	N	N
2 Fuqua	Y	N	Y	N	Y	N	N	N
3 Bennett	N	Y	N	N	N	N	N	Y
4 Chappell	Y	N	Y	N	N	N	Y	N
5 *McCollum*	Y	N	Y	N	Y	N	N	N
6 MacKay	Y	Y	Y	N	Y	N	Y	Y
7 Gibbons	N	Y	Y	N	Y	Y	Y	Y
8 *Young*	N	N	N	N	N	N	N	N
9 *Bilirakis*	Y	N	N	N	N	N	N	Y
10 Ireland	Y	N	Y	N	N	N	N	N
11 Nelson	Y	N	Y	N	Y	N	N	Y
12 *Lewis*	Y	N	Y	N	#	Y	Y	Y
13 *Mack*	Y	N	N	Y	Y	N	N	N
14 Mica	Y	Y	Y	N	X	Y	N	N
15 *Shaw*	Y	N	Y	N	Y	N	N	N
16 Smith	Y	Y	Y	N	Y	Y	Y	Y
17 Lehman	Y	Y	Y	N	Y	Y	Y	Y
18 Pepper	Y	Y	Y	N	Y	Y	Y	Y
19 Fascell	Y	Y	Y	N	Y	Y	Y	Y
GEORGIA								
1 Thomas	Y	N	Y	N	Y	N	Y	N
2 Hatcher	Y	N	Y	N	Y	N	Y	Y
3 Ray	N	N	N	N	Y	N	N	X
4 Levitas	N	N	N	Y	N	Y	N	Y
5 Fowler	Y	Y	Y	N	Y	Y	Y	Y
6 *Gingrich*	Y	N	N	N	Y	N	N	N
7 Darden [1]					N	Y	N	N
8 Rowland	Y	N	N	Y	N	N	N	N
9 Jenkins	Y	N	?	N	?	?	?	?
10 Barnard	Y	?	N	N	Y	N	N	N
HAWAII								
1 Heftel	?	Y	Y	N	N	Y	Y	Y
2 Akaka	Y	Y	Y	N	N	Y	Y	Y
IDAHO								
1 *Craig*	Y	N	N	Y	N	N	N	N
2 *Hansen*	Y	N	N	Y	N	N	N	N
ILLINOIS								
1 Hayes	N	Y	Y	N	N	Y	Y	Y
2 Savage	N	Y	Y	N	N	Y	Y	Y
3 Russo	N	Y	N	Y	N	?	N	Y
4 *O'Brien*	Y	N	?	Y	#	Y	N	N
5 Lipinski	N	N	N	N	N	N	Y	Y
6 *Hyde*	N	N	Y	Y	N	N	N	N
7 Collins	N	Y	Y	N	N	Y	Y	?
8 Rostenkowski	Y	Y	N	N	Y	N	Y	Y
9 Yates	N	Y	N	N	Y	Y	Y	Y
10 *Porter*	Y	N	Y	N	Y	Y	Y	N
11 Annunzio	Y	Y	Y	N	Y	Y	Y	Y
12 *Crane, P.*	N	N	N	Y	N	N	N	N
13 *Erlenborn*	Y	N	N	Y	N	N	N	N
14 *Corcoran*	Y	X	N	Y	N	N	N	N
15 *Madigan*	Y	N	Y	N	Y	N	Y	N
16 *Martin*	Y	N	N	Y	N	N	N	N
17 Evans	N	Y	N	Y	Y	Y	Y	Y
18 *Michel*	Y	N	N	Y	N	N	N	N
19 *Crane, D.*	N	N	N	Y	N	N	N	N
20 Durbin	N	Y	Y	N	N	Y	Y	Y
21 Price	Y	N	Y	N	Y	N	N	Y
22 Simon	Y	#	Y	N	X	Y	Y	?
INDIANA								
1 Hall	N	Y	Y	N	Y	Y	Y	Y
2 Sharp	N	Y	Y	N	Y	Y	Y	Y
3 *Hiler*	Y	N	N	Y	N	N	N	N
4 *Coats*	Y	N	N	Y	N	Y	N	N
5 *Hillis*	N	N	N	Y	N	N	N	N

ND - Northern Democrats   SD - Southern Democrats

	9	10	11	12	13	14	15	16
6 ***Burton***	Y	N	N	N	?	N	N	N
7 ***Myers***	N	N	N	N	Y	N	N	N
8 McCloskey	N	Y	Y	Y	N	Y	Y	Y
9 Hamilton	Y	Y	Y	N	N	Y	Y	Y
10 Jacobs	N	Y	Y	N	N	Y	Y	Y
IOWA								
1 ***Leach***	Y	Y	Y	Y	Y	Y	Y	?
2 ***Tauke***	N	Y	N	N	Y	N	Y	N
3 ***Evans***	Y	#	Y	Y	Y	Y	Y	N
4 Smith	N	Y	N	N	N	Y	Y	N
5 Harkin	N	Y	Y	N	N	Y	Y	N
6 Bedell	N	Y	Y	N	N	N	Y	N
KANSAS								
1 ***Roberts***	Y	N	N	Y	Y	N	Y	N
2 Slattery	Y	Y	N	N	N	Y	Y	Y
3 ***Winn***	Y	N	?	?	#	N	N	N
4 Glickman	Y	Y	N	Y	N	Y	Y	Y
5 ***Whittaker***	Y	N	N	Y	Y	N	Y	N
KENTUCKY								
1 Hubbard	N	N	Y	N	N	N	N	N
2 Natcher	N	Y	N	N	N	Y	Y	N
3 Mazzoli	N	Y	Y	Y	N	N	Y	Y
4 ***Snyder***	N	N	N	N	N	N	N	N
5 ***Rogers***	Y	N	N	N	Y	N	N	N
6 ***Hopkins***	N	N	N	N	Y	Y	Y	N
7 Perkins	N	Y	Y	N	N	Y	Y	N
LOUISIANA								
1 ***Livingston***	Y	N	N	Y	Y	N	N	N
2 Boggs	Y	N	Y	N	N	Y	Y	N
3 Tauzin	Y	N	N	N	N	Y	N	N
4 Roemer	N	N	N	Y	N	N	Y	N
5 Huckaby	Y	N	N	N	Y	Y	Y	N
6 ***Moore***	Y	N	N	Y	Y	N	N	Y
7 Breaux	Y	N	N	N	N	Y	N	N
8 Long	Y	Y	Y	Y	N	Y	Y	Y
MAINE								
1 ***McKernan***	Y	N	Y	N	N	Y	Y	N
2 ***Snowe***	Y	N	Y	N	N	Y	Y	N
MARYLAND								
1 Dyson	Y	Y	N	Y	N	Y	N	N
2 Long	N	Y	Y	N	N	Y	N	Y
3 Mikulski	Y	Y	Y	N	N	Y	Y	N
4 ***Holt***	Y	N	N	Y	Y	Y	N	N
5 Hoyer	Y	N	Y	N	N	Y	Y	Y
6 Byron	N	N	Y	N	N	Y	N	N
7 Mitchell	N	Y	Y	Y	N	Y	Y	Y
8 Barnes	Y	Y	Y	Y	N	Y	Y	Y
MASSACHUSETTS								
1 ***Conte***	N	Y	N	Y	Y	Y	Y	N
2 Boland	Y	Y	Y	Y	N	Y	Y	Y
3 Early	N	Y	?	?	?	Y	Y	N
4 Frank	N	Y	Y	Y	N	Y	Y	Y
5 Shannon	N	Y	Y	Y	N	Y	Y	Y
6 Mavroules	Y	Y	Y	Y	?	Y	Y	Y
7 Markey	Y	Y	Y	Y	N	Y	Y	Y
8 O'Neill [2]						Y		
9 Moakley	Y	Y	Y	Y	N	Y	Y	Y
10 Studds	N	Y	Y	Y	N	Y	Y	Y
11 Donnelly	N	Y	Y	Y	N	Y	N	Y
MICHIGAN								
1 Conyers	N	Y	Y	N	N	Y	Y	Y
2 ***Pursell***	Y	N	N	N	N	Y	Y	N
3 Wolpe	N	Y	Y	N	N	Y	Y	Y
4 ***Siljander***	Y	N	N	N	Y	N	N	N
5 ***Sawyer***	Y	?	N	N	N	?	?	N
6 Carr	Y	Y	Y	N	N	Y	Y	N
7 Kildee	N	Y	Y	N	N	Y	Y	Y
8 Traxler	N	Y	Y	N	N	Y	Y	Y
9 ***Vander Jagt***	Y	X	N	Y	Y	N	Y	Y
10 Albosta	N	Y	Y	N	N	Y	Y	N
11 ***Davis***	Y	N	Y	N	Y	N	N	N
12 Bonior	Y	Y	Y	N	N	Y	Y	Y
13 Crockett	N	Y	Y	N	N	Y	Y	Y
14 Hertel	N	Y	Y	N	N	Y	Y	Y
15 Ford	N	Y	Y	N	N	Y	Y	Y
16 Dingell	N	Y	Y	N	N	Y	Y	Y
17 Levin	Y	Y	Y	N	N	Y	Y	Y
18 ***Broomfield***	Y	N	N	Y	?	N	Y	N
MINNESOTA								
1 Penny	N	Y	Y	N	N	Y	Y	Y
2 ***Weber***	Y	N	N	N	N	N	Y	N
3 ***Frenzel***	Y	N	N	N	Y	Y	Y	Y
4 Vento	N	Y	Y	N	N	Y	Y	Y
5 Sabo	N	Y	Y	N	N	Y	Y	Y
6 Sikorski	N	Y	Y	N	N	Y	Y	Y
7 ***Stangeland***	Y	N	N	N	N	N	N	N
8 Oberstar	N	Y	Y	N	N	Y	Y	N
MISSISSIPPI								
1 Whitten	Y	Y	Y	N	N	Y	Y	N
2 ***Franklin***	Y	N	N	Y	Y	N	N	N
3 Montgomery	Y	N	N	Y	?	N	N	N
4 Dowdy	N	Y	Y	N	N	Y	N	?
5 ***Lott***	Y	N	N	N	Y	N	N	N
MISSOURI								
1 Clay	N	Y	Y	N	N	Y	Y	?
2 Young	N	Y	Y	N	N	N	N	N
3 Gephardt	Y	Y	Y	N	N	Y	Y	Y
4 Skelton	N	N	Y	N	N	N	N	N
5 Wheat	N	Y	Y	N	N	Y	Y	Y
6 ***Coleman***	Y	N	N	N	N	N	N	N
7 ***Taylor***	Y	N	N	N	Y	N	N	N
8 ***Emerson***	Y	N	N	N	Y	N	N	N
9 Volkmer	N	Y	Y	N	N	Y	Y	Y
MONTANA								
1 Williams	Y	Y	Y	N	N	Y	Y	Y
2 ***Marlenee***	Y	N	N	N	N	N	N	N
NEBRASKA								
1 ***Bereuter***	N	Y	N	N	Y	Y	N	N
2 ***Daub***	Y	N	N	N	Y	Y	Y	N
3 ***Smith***	Y	Y	N	Y	#	Y	N	N
NEVADA								
1 Reid	Y	N	Y	N	N	N	Y	Y
2 ***Vucanovich***	Y	N	N	Y	Y	N	N	N
NEW HAMPSHIRE								
1 D'Amours	Y	Y	Y	Y	N	Y	Y	N
2 ***Gregg***	Y	N	N	Y	Y	Y	Y	N
NEW JERSEY								
1 Florio	N	Y	?	N	N	Y	Y	Y
2 Hughes	Y	Y	N	N	N	Y	N	Y
3 Howard	N	Y	?	Y	N	Y	Y	Y
4 ***Smith***	Y	Y	Y	Y	Y	N	Y	N
5 ***Roukema***	Y	Y	Y	Y	Y	Y	Y	Y
6 Dwyer	Y	Y	Y	Y	N	Y	Y	Y
7 ***Rinaldo***	Y	N	Y	N	Y	Y	Y	N
8 Roe	Y	Y	Y	Y	N	Y	Y	Y
9 Torricelli	Y	Y	Y	N	N	Y	Y	Y
10 Rodino	N	Y	Y	N	N	Y	Y	Y
11 Minish	Y	Y	Y	Y	N	Y	Y	Y
12 ***Courter***	Y	N	N	Y	Y	Y	N	N
13 ***Forsythe***	Y	Y	N	N	Y	N	Y	N
14 Guarini	N	Y	Y	N	N	Y	Y	Y
NEW MEXICO								
1 ***Lujan***	Y	N	N	Y	Y	Y	N	N
2 ***Skeen***	Y	N	N	Y	Y	N	N	N
3 Richardson	N	Y	Y	N	N	Y	Y	N
NEW YORK								
1 ***Carney***	Y	N	N	Y	Y	N	Y	N
2 Downey	N	Y	Y	Y	N	Y	Y	Y
3 Mrazek	Y	Y	Y	Y	N	Y	Y	Y
4 ***Lent***	Y	N	N	Y	Y	?	N	N
5 ***McGrath***	Y	N	N	Y	Y	N	Y	N
6 Addabbo	N	Y	Y	N	N	Y	Y	Y
7 Ackerman	Y	Y	Y	Y	N	Y	Y	Y
8 Scheuer	Y	Y	Y	N	N	Y	Y	Y
9 Ferraro	N	Y	Y	N	N	Y	Y	Y
10 Schumer	Y	Y	Y	Y	N	Y	Y	Y
11 Towns	N	Y	Y	N	N	Y	Y	Y
12 Owens	N	Y	Y	N	N	Y	Y	Y
13 Solarz	Y	Y	Y	?	X	Y	Y	?
14 ***Molinari***	Y	N	?	?	?	?	?	N
15 ***Green***	Y	Y	Y	Y	Y	Y	Y	N
16 Rangel	N	Y	Y	Y	N	Y	Y	Y
17 Weiss	N	Y	Y	Y	N	Y	Y	Y
18 Garcia	N	N	?	N	N	#	Y	Y
19 Biaggi	Y	Y	Y	Y	N	Y	Y	N
20 Ottinger	N	Y	Y	Y	N	Y	Y	Y
21 ***Fish***	Y	N	N	N	Y	N	Y	N
22 ***Gilman***	Y	N	Y	N	Y	Y	N	N
23 Stratton	N	N	?	N	N	Y	N	Y
24 ***Solomon***	Y	N	N	N	Y	N	N	N
25 ***Boehlert***	Y	N	Y	N	Y	Y	Y	N
26 ***Martin***	Y	N	N	Y	#	N	N	N
27 ***Wortley***	Y	N	N	Y	Y	Y	Y	N
28 McHugh	N	Y	Y	N	N	Y	Y	Y
29 ***Horton***	N	N	Y	N	Y	Y	Y	N
30 ***Conable***	Y	N	N	Y	Y	Y	N	Y
31 ***Kemp***	Y	N	N	Y	Y	N	N	?
32 LaFalce	N	Y	Y	Y	N	Y	Y	Y
33 Nowak	N	Y	Y	Y	N	N	Y	Y
34 Lundine	N	Y	Y	N	N	Y	Y	N
NORTH CAROLINA								
1 Jones	Y	N	Y	N	N	Y	Y	N
2 Valentine	Y	Y	Y	N	N	N	N	Y
3 Whitley	Y	N	Y	N	N	Y	N	Y
4 Andrews	N	Y	Y	N	N	Y	N	Y
5 Neal	N	N	Y	N	N	Y	Y	Y
6 Britt	Y	N	Y	Y	?	Y	Y	Y
7 Rose	Y	Y	Y	N	N	Y	N	Y
8 Hefner	Y	N	?	N	N	Y	N	Y
9 ***Martin***	Y	N	N	Y	Y	N	Y	N
10 ***Broyhill***	Y	N	N	Y	Y	N	Y	N
11 Clarke	Y	Y	Y	Y	N	Y	N	Y
NORTH DAKOTA								
AL Dorgan	N	Y	Y	N	N	Y	Y	#
OHIO								
1 Luken	N	Y	?	Y	N	N	Y	Y
2 ***Gradison***	N	Y	N	Y	Y	Y	Y	N
3 Hall	Y	Y	Y	Y	N	Y	Y	Y
4 ***Oxley***	Y	N	N	N	Y	N	Y	N
5 ***Latta***	Y	N	N	Y	Y	N	N	N
6 ***McEwen***	Y	N	N	N	Y	N	N	N
7 ***DeWine***	Y	N	?	N	Y	N	N	N
8 ***Kindness***	Y	N	N	N	Y	N	N	N
9 Kaptur	N	Y	Y	N	N	Y	Y	Y
10 ***Miller***	N	N	N	N	Y	N	Y	N
11 Eckart	N	Y	Y	N	N	Y	Y	Y
12 ***Kasich***	N	N	N	N	Y	N	N	N
13 Pease	N	Y	Y	N	N	Y	Y	Y
14 Seiberling	Y	Y	Y	N	N	Y	Y	Y
15 ***Wylie***	Y	N	N	N	Y	N	N	Y
16 ***Regula***	Y	N	N	N	Y	Y	Y	N
17 ***Williams***	Y	N	?	N	N	Y	Y	N
18 Applegate	N	Y	Y	N	N	Y	Y	Y
19 Feighan	Y	Y	Y	N	N	Y	Y	Y
20 Oakar	Y	Y	Y	N	N	Y	Y	Y
21 Stokes	N	Y	Y	Y	N	Y	Y	Y
OKLAHOMA								
1 Jones	N	N	Y	N	N	Y	N	Y
2 Synar	Y	Y	Y	N	N	Y	Y	N
3 Watkins	N	N	Y	Y	N	Y	Y	N
4 McCurdy	N	N	Y	N	N	Y	Y	Y
5 ***Edwards***	Y	N	?	Y	Y	N	Y	N
6 English	N	N	Y	N	N	Y	Y	N
OREGON								
1 AuCoin	N	Y	N	N	N	Y	Y	N
2 ***Smith, R.***	Y	N	N	Y	N	N	Y	N
3 Wyden	N	Y	Y	N	N	Y	Y	N
4 Weaver	N	Y	Y	N	N	Y	Y	N
5 ***Smith, D.***	N	N	N	Y	?	N	N	N
PENNSYLVANIA								
1 Foglietta	Y	Y	Y	Y	N	Y	Y	Y
2 Gray	N	Y	Y	N	N	Y	Y	Y
3 Borski	Y	Y	Y	N	N	Y	Y	Y
4 Kolter	Y	Y	Y	N	N	Y	Y	Y
5 ***Schulze***	N	N	N	N	?	N	N	N
6 Yatron	Y	N	Y	N	N	N	Y	Y
7 Edgar	N	Y	+	N	N	Y	Y	Y
8 Kostmayer	Y	Y	Y	N	N	Y	Y	Y
9 ***Shuster***	Y	N	N	N	Y	N	N	N
10 ***McDade***	Y	N	N	N	N	N	N	N
11 Harrison	Y	Y	Y	N	N	Y	Y	Y
12 Murtha	Y	N	Y	N	N	N	N	Y
13 ***Coughlin***	Y	N	Y	Y	Y	Y	Y	N
14 Coyne	Y	Y	Y	Y	N	Y	Y	Y
15 ***Ritter***	Y	N	N	N	Y	N	N	N
16 ***Walker***	N	N	N	Y	Y	N	Y	N
17 ***Gekas***	Y	N	N	N	Y	Y	Y	N
18 Walgren	N	Y	Y	Y	N	Y	Y	Y
19 ***Goodling***	Y	Y	N	N	Y	Y	Y	N
20 Gaydos	N	N	Y	N	N	N	N	Y
21 ***Ridge***	Y	Y	Y	N	N	Y	N	N
22 Murphy	N	Y	Y	N	N	Y	Y	Y
23 ***Clinger***	Y	N	N	N	Y	Y	Y	N
RHODE ISLAND								
1 St Germain	N	Y	Y	Y	N	N	Y	Y
2 ***Schneider***	Y	Y	Y	Y	Y	Y	Y	N
SOUTH CAROLINA								
1 ***Hartnett***	Y	N	N	Y	Y	N	N	N
2 ***Spence***	Y	N	N	Y	Y	N	N	N
3 Derrick	N	Y	Y	Y	N	Y	Y	Y
4 ***Campbell***	Y	N	N	Y	Y	N	N	N
5 Spratt	Y	Y	Y	Y	N	Y	Y	Y
6 Tallon	Y	Y	Y	N	N	Y	Y	N
SOUTH DAKOTA								
AL Daschle	N	Y	Y	N	N	Y	Y	N
TENNESSEE								
1 ***Quillen***	Y	N	N	N	Y	N	N	Y
2 ***Duncan***	Y	N	N	N	Y	N	Y	Y
3 Lloyd	Y	N	Y	N	N	N	N	N
4 Cooper	Y	N	Y	N	N	N	Y	Y
5 Boner	Y	N	Y	N	N	Y	N	N
6 Gore	Y	N	Y	N	N	Y	Y	N
7 ***Sundquist***	Y	N	N	N	Y	N	N	Y
8 Jones	Y	N	Y	N	N	N	N	N
9 Ford	Y	Y	?	N	N	Y	Y	Y
TEXAS								
1 Hall, S.	N	N	N	N	N	N	N	Y
2 Wilson	Y	N	Y	N	N	Y	N	Y
3 ***Bartlett***	Y	N	N	Y	Y	N	N	N
4 Hall, R.	N	N	Y	Y	N	Y	N	N
5 Bryant	N	Y	Y	N	N	Y	Y	Y
6 ***Gramm***	Y	N	?	?	?	N	N	N
7 ***Archer***	N	N	N	Y	Y	N	N	N
8 ***Fields***	N	N	N	Y	Y	N	N	N
9 Brooks	N	Y	Y	Y	N	Y	N	N
10 Pickle	Y	N	Y	Y	N	Y	Y	Y
11 Leath	Y	N	?	N	N	N	N	N
12 Wright	Y	Y	Y	N	N	Y	N	Y
13 Hightower	Y	N	Y	Y	N	X	N	N
14 Patman	N	N	Y	Y	N	Y	N	N
15 de la Garza	Y	N	Y	N	?	Y	N	Y
16 Coleman	Y	Y	Y	Y	N	Y	N	Y
17 Stenholm	N	N	N	N	?	N	N	N
18 Leland	N	Y	?	N	N	Y	Y	Y
19 Hance	N	N	Y	?	X	#	?	?
20 Gonzalez	N	Y	Y	N	N	Y	Y	N
21 ***Loeffler***	Y	N	N	Y	Y	N	N	N
22 ***Paul***	N	Y	?	?	?	?	?	N
23 Kazen	Y	N	Y	Y	N	N	N	N
24 Frost	Y	N	Y	N	N	Y	Y	N
25 Andrews	Y	N	Y	N	N	Y	N	Y
26 Vandergriff	Y	N	Y	N	N	N	N	N
27 Ortiz	Y	N	Y	Y	N	Y	N	Y
UTAH								
1 ***Hansen***	Y	N	N	Y	Y	N	N	X
2 ***Marriott***	Y	N	N	Y	Y	N	N	N
3 ***Nielson***	Y	N	N	Y	Y	N	N	N
VERMONT								
AL ***Jeffords***	Y	Y	Y	N	N	Y	Y	N
VIRGINIA								
1 ***Bateman***	Y	N	N	Y	Y	N	N	N
2 ***Whitehurst***	Y	N	N	Y	Y	Y	N	N
3 ***Bliley***	Y	N	N	Y	Y	N	N	N
4 Sisisky	Y	Y	Y	N	N	Y	N	Y
5 Daniel	Y	N	N	N	Y	N	N	N
6 Olin	Y	Y	Y	Y	N	Y	Y	Y
7 ***Robinson***	Y	N	N	Y	Y	N	N	N
8 ***Parris***	Y	N	N	Y	Y	Y	Y	N
9 Boucher	Y	Y	Y	N	N	Y	?	N
10 ***Wolf***	Y	N	N	Y	Y	N	N	N
WASHINGTON								
1 ***Pritchard***	Y	N	?	?	Y	Y	Y	?
2 Swift	N	Y	Y	N	N	Y	Y	Y
3 Bonker	Y	Y	Y	N	N	Y	Y	Y
4 ***Morrison***	Y	N	Y	N	Y	Y	N	N
5 Foley	Y	N	Y	N	N	Y	Y	Y
6 Dicks	Y	N	Y	N	N	Y	Y	Y
7 Lowry	N	Y	?	?	N	Y	Y	Y
8 ***Chandler***	Y	N	Y	Y	Y	Y	N	N
WEST VIRGINIA								
1 Mollohan	Y	N	Y	N	N	N	N	Y
2 Staggers	Y	Y	Y	N	N	Y	Y	Y
3 Wise	N	Y	Y	Y	N	Y	Y	Y
4 Rahall	Y	Y	Y	N	N	Y	Y	Y
WISCONSIN								
1 Aspin	Y	N	Y	N	N	Y	Y	Y
2 Kastenmeier	N	Y	Y	N	N	Y	Y	Y
3 ***Gunderson***	N	N	N	N	N	Y	Y	N
4 Zablocki	Y	N	Y	N	N	Y	Y	Y
5 Moody	N	Y	Y	Y	N	Y	?	Y
6 ***Petri***	N	Y	N	N	N	Y	N	Y
7 Obey	N	Y	Y	N	N	Y	Y	Y
8 ***Roth***	N	N	N	N	Y	N	N	N
9 ***Sensenbrenner***	N	N	N	N	Y	N	Y	N
WYOMING								
AL ***Cheney***	Y	N	?	Y	Y	N	N	N

Southern states - Ala., Ark., Fla., Ga., Ky., La., Miss., N.C., Okla., S.C., Tenn., Texas, Va.

Democrats Showed Renewed Strength in '83

A rejuvenated Democratic Party asserted itself on Capitol Hill in 1983, giving President Reagan his lowest level of support in three years and generating the highest level of Democratic unity in three decades.

These and other findings were based on four statistical vote studies conducted by Congressional Quarterly. The studies, provided annually, measured presidential support, party unity, voting participation and the strength of the conservative coalition in Congress.

The new studies statistically confirmed anecdotal evidence that Reagan had more political troubles with Congress in 1983 than he did during the first two years of his administration.

The numerical results also reinforced impressions that Democrats voted together more frequently than they had in years, and that partisanship in the House was exceptionally high in 1983.

In addition, there was a substantial weakening in the coalition of Republicans and Southern Democrats that helped produce Reagan's major victories in 1981 and 1982. Not only did this conservative alliance come together less often in 1983, but when it appeared, it won fewer votes than it had in 1981 or 1982.

Democrats' Enlarged Margin

The chief reason given for the drop in presidential support and the rise in Democratic Party unity was the Democrats' capture of 26 House seats in the 1982 elections. With this additional numerical strength, House Democratic leaders worked hard to establish an agenda different from Reagan's.

"Unlike 1982, we had a clear majority in 1983. There were, therefore, certain priorities we wanted to see achieved," said a House Democratic leadership aide. A major priority was a package of legislation to help recession victims, much of which passed the House but died in the Senate.

Another factor in 1983 was the administration's reluctance to press House Republicans to take politically risky steps as often as it did in Reagan's first two years. This change in tactics was in reaction to the political realities of the year: The GOP stood a greater chance of losing in the House, but the Republican-controlled Senate still could thwart many efforts that were unpalatable to the White House.

"You didn't see the direct intervention [by the White House] that you saw the first two years," said a Republican leadership aide.

"Issues like health insurance for the unemployed, which they would have vetoed, they saw no reason to push on, since it wasn't going anywhere. They tended to play the House against the Senate."

Southern Democrats

An important influence on Democratic Party unity was that many Southern Democrats, who aligned themselves

with Reagan during the previous two years, returned to their party's fold during 1983.

One reason Southern Democrats were more loyal was that some interpreted the Republican losses in the 1982 election as a rebuff of the Reagan administration's program.

This was particularly true of Southerners first elected in 1982, who tended to be more moderate than their recent predecessors.

Also, by tolerating high budget deficits that resulted from his tax cut and military buildup, the president made it easier for Southern Democrats to vote with their party for more social spending, while blaming massive deficits on Reagan's policies.

Voting attendance in 1983 tied the 30-year high established in 1981. Leaders in the House and the Senate made it simpler for members to show up for votes by scheduling the vast majority of roll calls on Tuesdays, Wednesdays or Thursdays, when members were most likely to be in Washington.

Candidates' Voting Scores

Of the four Democratic senators running for their party's 1984 presidential nomination, Gary Hart, D-Colo., disagreed with President Reagan's position on recorded votes most often in 1983.

A Congressional Quarterly vote analysis showed that Hart disagreed with Reagan on 46 percent of the votes on which the president took a stand. Alan Cranston, D-Calif., opposed Reagan on 40 percent of the votes, while John Glenn, D-Ohio, and Ernest F. Hollings, D-S.C., disagreed with his position on 35 percent of the votes.

These numbers were skewed somewhat by the four senators' irregular attendance; failure to vote lowered each member's score on each of the CQ vote studies.

Of the four White House contenders, Hollings showed up for the fewest number of votes. He voted "yea" or "nay" on only half of the 1983 roll calls. Glenn voted 64 percent of the time; Hart, 63 percent; and Cranston, 56 percent. In terms of party unity votes — those votes in which a majority of voting Democrats opposed a majority of voting Republicans — Hart voted in agreement with his party 61 percent of the time. The party unity score for Glenn was 57 percent; Cranston, 55 percent; Hollings, 49 percent. On votes where the conservative coalition of Republicans and Southern Democrats appeared, Hollings agreed with the coalition 23 percent of the time. The conservative coalition support score for Glenn was 20 percent; Hart, 9 percent; Cranston, 7 percent.

Congress' Backing for Reagan Continues to Decline Steadily

President Reagan's support in Congress continued to weaken in 1983, falling to its lowest level since he was elected in 1980, a Congressional Quarterly analysis showed.

After a strong start in 1981, when Congress backed his positions 82.4 percent of the time, Reagan encountered steadily dwindling enthusiasm for his policies on Capitol Hill. Congress supported Reagan 72.4 percent of the time in 1982 and just 67.1 percent in 1983. *(Box, this page)*

The decline was caused primarily by the further erosion of Reagan's support in the House, where Democrats solidified their control with a 26-seat gain in the 1982 elections and thereafter exhibited renewed party unity.

CQ's annual presidential support study measures how often congressional votes matched the president's announced position.

On Senate votes on which he took a stand, Reagan won 85.9 percent of the time, an increase of 2.7 percentage points from the 1982 level. But on House votes on which he established a position, Reagan won 47.6 percent of the time, a drop of 8.2 percentage points from 1982.

Although backing for Reagan's position climbed slightly in the Republican-dominated Senate, it was not enough to offset the large drop in House support. Overall, Reagan suffered a 5.3 percentage point decline in his score from 1982 to 1983.

Such a drop in presidential support is not unusual in the latter years of a president's term. With the exception of President Kennedy, every executive since Eisenhower saw his support score drop from the second to third year of his term.

CQ's study was based on 167 recorded votes on which Reagan declared a position. Eighty-five of the votes were in the Senate; the remaining 82 were in the House.

Reagan's Progress

Although Reagan lost more votes in 1983 on which he staked out a position than he had in 1981 and 1982, he did not ask Congress for as much as he did in his first two years, when he sought major economic policy changes.

Most of Reagan's victories in both chambers were on his proposals to expand military spending. Two other major issues that provided favorable votes for the president were his request to increase the U.S. contribution to the International Monetary Fund and a measure allowing U.S. Marines to stay in Lebanon for an 18-month period.

Many of Reagan's House losses were on votes to increase domestic spending for such items as subsidized housing, education, health insurance for the unemployed or meals for the elderly.

White House officials attributed the overall drop in Reagan's support score to the higher number of Democratic House members in the 98th Congress, compared to the 97th.

The Democratic Edge

With the House Democratic majority having a 100-vote margin over Republicans in 1983, compared to a 50-vote margin at the end of 1982, it was more difficult for the White House to patch together the coalition of Republicans and conservative Democrats that helped pass Reagan's economic program in the 97th Congress.

Also in 1983, Democrats in Congress displayed the highest level of party loyalty they had shown in any year since 1954, when CQ began analyzing party unity. *(Party unity, p. 26-C)*

Recognizing the limits to its power imposed by this big Democratic majority, the White House did not ask House Republicans to back the president on politically difficult votes as often as they did during Reagan's first two years in office, GOP officials said.

Study's Limitations

Although the study showed that Reagan had more political problems on Capitol Hill than he did during the first two years of his administration, it did not gauge how much of his program actually was adopted. And as a measure of an individual lawmaker's loyalty to the president, the study should be used with caution.

First, the study counted only issues that reached a roll-call vote on the House or Senate floor. It did not count portions of the White House program that were scuttled or defeated before they reached the floor, quietly compromised behind the scenes, or passed on a voice vote.

Second, the study considered only votes where the president publicly indicated clear personal support or opposition.

Third, all votes received equal weight. No distinction was made between major votes and minor ones, slim victories and lopsided decisions, administration proposals and congressional initiatives. *(Ground rules, box, p. 21-C)*

Thus, the Senate's razor-thin approval of Reagan's request to renew production of nerve gas, a major defense

---

Success Rate

Following are the annual percentages of presidential victories since 1953 on congressional votes where the presidents took a clear-cut position:

Eisenhower		Nixon	
1953	89.0%	1969	74.0%
1954	82.8	1970	77.0
1955	75.0	1971	75.0
1956	70.0	1972	66.0
1957	68.0	1973	50.6
1958	76.0	1974	59.6
1959	52.0		
1960	65.0	**Ford**	
		1974	58.2%
		1975	61.0
Kennedy		1976	53.8
1961	81.0%		
1962	85.4	**Carter**	
1963	87.1	1977	75.4%
		1978	78.3
		1979	76.8
		1980	75.1
Johnson			
1964	88.0%	**Reagan**	
1965	93.0	1981	82.4%
1966	79.0	1982	72.4
1967	79.0	1983	67.1
1968	75.0		

priority for the president, counted the same as the near-unanimous Senate vote to confirm former House member Margaret M. Heckler, R-Mass. (1967-83), as secretary of health and human services.

Finally, issues that took many roll calls to resolve may have influenced the study more than matters settled by a single vote. The classic recent example was in 1978, when President Carter's Senate support score was dramatically enhanced because the administration came out on top on 55 roll calls — mostly procedural — related to ratification of the Panama Canal treaties.

In 1983 some issues were controversial enough to require several roll calls to resolve. For example, six Senate votes were devoted to the resolution authorizing the stationing of U.S. troops in Lebanon. A Senate decision not to place a cap on the third year of Reagan's tax cut took only one vote.

Although some subjects were important to the president, he never publicly expressed a solid position on the legislation. This was true during Senate consideration of the fiscal 1984 budget resolution. Therefore, the CQ vote study did not reflect Reagan's view on a long string of Senate budget votes.

A reporter or researcher interested in how an individual member of Congress voted on the various parts of the administration's program is advised to look at the specifics of the member's legislative actions, including his or her record on CQ's selection of key votes. *(Key votes, p. 3-C)*

The presidential support score is a rough measure of the relationship between Congress and the president. Over time, the score reflects numerically the rises and dips in relations between the two branches of government, and individual scores show how particular lawmakers fit the trends.

The study was started in 1953 and long was considered an indicator of the president's success on Capitol Hill. A closer reading of the study's ground rules showed its limitations as a measure of executive clout, but not all readers have been discriminating in using the figures.

During the 1980 presidential campaign, President Carter's supporters, citing his 77 percent support score in 1979, claimed that Congress had passed four-fifths of the Carter agenda. A Carter aide later admitted that CQ's statistics had been "mistranslated or misused."

Party, Regional Differences

Not surprisingly, Republicans agreed with Reagan more often than Democrats in 1983, although support among Senate Republicans was down 1 percentage point, from 74 percent of the roll calls counted in 1982 to 73 percent in 1983. In the House, though, Republican loyalty to the president was up 6 percentage points from 1982 to 1983, from 64 to 70 percent.

House Democratic backing for the president fell from 39 percent in 1982 to 28 percent. Reagan's support among Senate Democrats slipped only 1 percentage point, from 43 to 42 percent.

In the Senate, Reagan derived most of his support from Midwestern Republicans, who agreed with him on 77 percent of the roll calls on which he took a position. Western Democrats supplied him with his lowest level of support in the Senate. It was Western Republicans, though, who gave Reagan the most regional support in the House.

House Democrats from every region but the South gave Reagan low support scores, averaging about 21 percent. Southern Democratic representatives voted with him on 42 percent of the affected roll calls.

Top Supporters, Opponents

Reagan's top supporter in the Senate was Richard G. Lugar, R-Ind., who voted with the president on 95 percent of the roll calls on which he expressed a stand.

Majority Whip Ted Stevens, R-Alaska, was the second-ranked supporter, at 92 percent. Majority Leader Howard H. Baker Jr., R-Tenn., slipped from 89 to 81

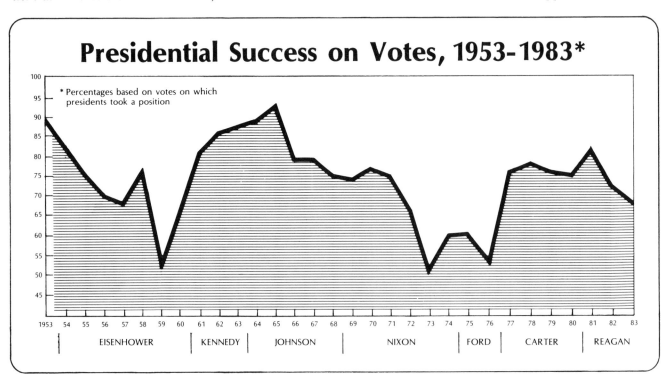

Presidential Success on Votes, 1953-1983*

* Percentages based on votes on which presidents took a position

Ground Rules for CQ Presidential Support-Opposition

Presidential Issues — CQ tries to determine what the president personally, as distinct from other administration officials, does and does not want in the way of legislative action by analyzing his messages to Congress, press conference remarks and other public statements and documents. Members must be aware of the position when the vote is taken.

Borderline Cases — By the time an issue reaches a vote, it may differ from the original form in which the president expressed himself. In such cases, CQ analyzes the measure to determine whether, on balance, the features favored by the president outweigh those he opposed or vice versa. Only then is the vote classified.

Some Votes Excluded — Occasionally, important measures are so extensively amended on the floor that it is impossible to characterize final passage as a victory or defeat for the president.

Procedural Votes — Votes on motions to recommit, to reconsider or to table often are key tests that govern the legislative outcome. Such votes are necessarily included in the presidential support tabulations.

Appropriations — Generally, votes on passage of appropriations bills are not included in the tabulations, since it is rarely possible to determine the president's position on the revisions Congress almost invariably makes in the sums allowed. However, some votes on amendments to cut or increase specific funds requested in the president's budget are included.

Failure to Vote — In tabulating the support or opposition scores of members on the selected presidential-issue votes, CQ counts only "yea" and "nay" votes on the ground that only those affect the outcome. Most failures to vote reflect absences because of illness or official business. Failures to vote lower both support and opposition scores equally.

Weighting — All presidential-issue votes have equal statistical weight in the analysis.

Changed Positions — Presidential support is determined by the position of the president at the time of a vote, even though that position may be different from an earlier position, or may have been reversed after the vote was taken.

---

percent. Baker announced early in 1983 that he would retire when his term ended in 1984.

Robert Dole, R-Kan., and Pete V. Domenici, R-N.M. — two senators with substantial influence over economic matters — were not among Reagan's top 10 Senate supporters, as they had been in 1982. This reflected a growing distance between the president and Dole, the Finance Committee chairman, and Domenici, the Budget Committee chairman, on economic issues. Dole sided with the president 78 percent of the time; Domenici took the president's position 74 percent of the time.

Among Senate Democrats, Sam Nunn, D-Ga., voted most often for Reagan's position in 1983, agreeing with him 64 percent of the time. The Democrat who opposed Reagan's position most frequently was David Pryor, D-Ark., whose opposition score was 71 percent.

Some of the Senate's most conservative Republicans disagreed with Reagan the most, a departure from past years when liberals dominated the Republican opposition list. Gordon J. Humphrey, N.H., had the highest opposition score among GOP senators, followed by Jesse Helms, N.C.

In the House, Dan Daniel, D-Va., was the Democrat who backed Reagan's position most often. Other frequent supporters also were from Southern states.

Among House Republicans, freshman Al McCandless, R-Calif., showed Reagan the most support, voting with him 90 percent of the time.

Another House freshman, Lane Evans, D-Ill., was the Democrat who disagreed with Reagan's position on the most occasions. His opposition score was 90 percent.

Among GOP House members, Claudine Schneider, a moderate from Rhode Island, disagreed with Reagan's position 71 percent of the time. She was followed by other Northeastern moderates. Schneider also had the highest opposition to party score among House Republicans.

Average Scores

Following are composites of Democratic and Republican scores for 1983 and 1982:

	1983		1982	
	Dem.	Rep.	Dem.	Rep.
SUPPORT				
Senate	42%	73%	43%	74%
House	28	70	39	64
OPPOSITION				
Senate	51%	22%	51%	21%
House	66	25	51	27

Regional Averages

SUPPORT

Regional presidential support scores for 1983; scores for 1982 are in parentheses:

	East		West		South		Midwest	
DEMOCRATS								
Senate	42%	(34)	38%	(38)	42%	(55)	45%	(42)
House	22	(34)	20	(34)	42	(50)	21	(34)
REPUBLICANS								
Senate	68	(64)	73	(75)	74	(80)	77	(77)
House	60	(56)	75	(70)	74	(70)	71	(62)

OPPOSITION

Regional presidential opposition scores for 1983; scores for 1982 are in parentheses:

	East		West		South		Midwest	
DEMOCRATS								
Senate	54%	(62)	49%	(54)	49%	(41)	51%	(53)
House	73	(56)	73	(56)	52	(41)	75	(56)
REPUBLICANS								
Senate	27	(31)	20	(18)	23	(17)	20	(19)
House	35	(35)	19	(18)	22	(23)	25	(30)

*(CQ defines regions of the United States as follows: **East:** Conn., Del., Maine, Md., Mass., N.H., N.J., N.Y., Pa., R.I., Vt., W.Va. **West:** Alaska, Ariz., Calif., Colo., Hawaii, Idaho, Mont., Nev., N.M., Ore., Utah, Wash., Wyo. **South:** Ala., Ark., Fla., Ga., Ky., La., Miss., N.C., Okla., S.C., Tenn., Texas, Va. **Midwest:** Ill., Ind., Iowa, Kan., Mich., Minn., Mo., Neb., N.D., Ohio, S.D., Wis.)*

Highest Scorers — Support

Highest individual scorers in presidential support — those who voted most often for Reagan's position in 1983:

SENATE

Democrats [1]		Republicans	
Nunn, Ga.	64%	Lugar, Ind.	95%
Stennis, Miss.	59	Stevens, Alaska	92
Zorinsky, Neb.	56	Hecht, Nev.	91
Johnston, La.	55	Quayle, Ind.	88
Dixon, Ill.	54	Thurmond, S.C.	86
Exon, Neb.	54	Tower, Texas	86
Bentsen, Texas	51	Rudman, N.H.	85
Proxmire, Wis.	51	Gorton, Wash.	85
Randolph, W.Va.	51	Trible, Va.	84
		Warner, Va.	82
		Baker, Tenn.	81
		Denton, Ala.	81

[1] *Sen. Henry M. Jackson, D.-Wash., who died Sept. 1, 1983, scored 72 percent in presidential support.*

HOUSE

Democrats [2]		Republicans	
Daniel, Va.	77%	McCandless, Calif.	90%
Ireland, Fla.	72	Hyde, Ill.	89
Montgomery, Miss.	68	Erlenborn, Ill.	88
Ray, Ga.	66	Bartlett, Texas	87
Stenholm, Texas	63	Bateman, Va.	87
Hutto, Fla.	61	Latta, Ohio	87
Leath, Texas	61	Cheney, Wyo.	87
Chappell, Fla.	60	Bliley, Va.	85
Barnard, Ga.	59	Lagomarsino, Calif.	85
Hightower, Texas	57	Oxley, Ohio	85
Fuqua, Fla.	57	Conable, N.Y.	85
Byron, Md.	57	Whitehurst, Va.	85
Stratton, N.Y.	55	Dreier, Calif.	85
Nelson, Fla.	55	Robinson, Va.	85

[2] *Rep. Larry P. McDonald, D-Ga., who died Sept. 1, 1983, scored 76 percent in presidential support.*

1983 Presidential Position Votes

Following is a list of all Senate and House recorded votes in 1983 on which President Reagan took a position. The votes, listed by CQ vote number, appear in the vote charts beginning on pages 1-S and 1-H.

Senate Votes (85)

Presidential Victories (73) — 1, 2, 6, 7, 8, 10, 11, 54, 55, 61, 63, 87, 88, 90, 91, 92, 94, 96, 97, 101, 113, 114, 115, 126, 154, 155, 159, 160, 170, 178, 180, 181, 183, 185, 186, 199, 206, 214, 215, 218, 219, 235, 236, 237, 238, 239, 240, 241, 242, 250, 251, 252, 254, 255, 258, 259, 260, 261, 262, 263, 264, 270, 317, 325, 327, 328, 329, 331, 332, 338, 364, 366, 369.

Presidential Defeats (12) — 3, 9, 36, 99, 169, 173, 184, 187, 210, 245, 304, 355.

House Votes (82)

Presidential Victories (39) — 19, 20, 21, 22, 23, 43, 69, 123, 133, 145, 165, 170, 174, 180, 181, 182, 184, 185, 192, 237, 248, 250, 256, 258, 259, 264, 276, 277, 290, 303, 304, 341, 342, 408, 409, 411, 469, 497, 498.

Presidential Defeats (43) — 8, 35, 83, 94, 98, 115, 125, 134, 135, 136, 162, 164, 175, 186, 207, 228, 235, 241, 266, 270, 278, 291, 300, 316, 317, 353, 358, 364, 374, 377, 378, 382, 385, 386, 387, 398, 400, 417, 434, 441, 443, 451, 471.

High Scorers — Opposition

Highest individual scorers in presidential opposition — those who voted most often against Reagan's position in 1983:

SENATE

Democrats		Republicans	
Pryor, Ark.	71%	Humphrey, N.H.	42%
Levin, Mich.	66	Helms, N.C.	41
Melcher, Mont.	65	Specter, Pa.	41
Riegle, Mich.	64	East, N.C.	38
Mitchell, Maine	60	Symms, Idaho	35
Metzenbaum, Ohio	60	Armstrong, Colo.	34
Biden, Del.	60	Nickles, Okla.	34
Baucus, Mont.	60	Andrews, N.D.	34
Huddleston, Ky.	59	Kasten, Wis.	32

HOUSE

Democrats		Republicans	
Evans, Ill.	90%	Schneider, R.I.	71%
Kildee, Mich.	89	Conte, Mass.	56
Gonzalez, Texas	88	Horton, N.Y.	56
Traxler, Mich.	88	Leach, Iowa	55
Towns, N.Y.	87	McKinney, Conn.	51
Penny, Minn.	87	Rinaldo, N.J.	51
Wheat, Mo.	87	Jeffords, Vt.	51
Savage, Ill.	87	Smith, N.J.	50
Hayes, Ill.	86 [3]	McKernan, Maine	50
		Snowe, Maine	50
		Green, N.Y.	50

[3] *Not eligible for all presidential-issue votes in 1983.*

	1	2		1	2		1	2
ALABAMA			**IOWA**			**NEW HAMPSHIRE**		
Denton	81	18	*Grassley*	74	26	*Humphrey*	55	42
Heflin	42	52	*Jepsen*	78	21	*Rudman*	85	15
ALASKA			**KANSAS**			**NEW JERSEY**		
Murkowski	69	14	*Dole*	78	21	Bradley	42	58
Stevens	92	5	*Kassebaum*	78	20	Lautenberg	40	56
ARIZONA			**KENTUCKY**			**NEW MEXICO**		
Goldwater	62	6	Ford	40	56	*Domenici*	74	18
DeConcini	32	47	Huddleston	39	59	Bingaman	45	54
ARKANSAS			**LOUISIANA**			**NEW YORK**		
Bumpers	32	56	Johnston	55	44	*D'Amato*	67	28
Pryor	27	71	Long	42	38	Moynihan	46	51
CALIFORNIA			**MAINE**			**NORTH CAROLINA**		
Wilson	78	18	*Cohen*	66	29	*East*	60	38
Cranston	28	40	Mitchell	40	60	*Helms*	56	41
COLORADO			**MARYLAND**			**NORTH DAKOTA**		
Armstrong	60	34	*Mathias*	60	26	*Andrews*	62	34
Hart	31	46	Sarbanes	41	58	Burdick	46	54
CONNECTICUT			**MASSACHUSETTS**			**OHIO**		
Weicker	56	31	Kennedy	36	54	Glenn	39	35
Dodd	41	53	Tsongas	38	56	Metzenbaum	36	60
DELAWARE			**MICHIGAN**			**OKLAHOMA**		
Roth	76	22	Levin	33	66	*Nickles*	66	34
Biden	38	60	Riegle	34	64	Boren	41	56
FLORIDA			**MINNESOTA**			**OREGON**		
Hawkins	61	28	*Boschwitz*	80	15	*Hatfield*	64	29
Chiles	48	49	*Durenberger*	75	19	*Packwood*	66	24
GEORGIA			**MISSISSIPPI**			**PENNSYLVANIA**		
Mattingly	74	26	*Cochran*	71	22	*Heinz*	76	20
Nunn	64	33	Stennis	59	35	*Specter*	59	41
HAWAII			**MISSOURI**			**RHODE ISLAND**		
Inouye	33	42	*Danforth*	80	16	*Chafee*	80	18
Matsunaga	46	53	Eagleton	45	51	Pell	41	48
IDAHO			**MONTANA**			**SOUTH CAROLINA**		
McClure	69	31	Baucus	38	60	*Thurmond*	86	12
Symms	62	35	Melcher	33	65	Hollings	8	35
ILLINOIS			**NEBRASKA**			**SOUTH DAKOTA**		
Percy	80	15	Exon	54	46	*Abdnor*	80	19
Dixon	54	41	Zorinsky	56	42	*Pressler*	59	31
INDIANA			**NEVADA**			**TENNESSEE**		
Lugar	95	5	*Hecht*	91	9	*Baker*	81	9
Quayle	88	7	*Laxalt*	79	13	Sasser	39	58

KEY

† Not eligible for all recorded votes in 1983 (sworn in after Jan. 3, died or resigned during session, or voted "present" to avoid possible conflict of interest).

———

Democrats   *Republicans*

	1	2
TEXAS		
Tower	86	11
Bentsen	51	45
UTAH		
Garn	72	28
Hatch	72	28
VERMONT		
Stafford	66	21
Leahy	41	58
VIRGINIA		
Trible	84	15
Warner	82	16
WASHINGTON		
Evans [1]	74†	6†
Gorton	85	15
WEST VIRGINIA		
Byrd	48	51
Randolph	51	45
WISCONSIN		
Kasten	68	32
Proxmire	51	49
WYOMING		
Simpson	76	20
Wallop	72	22

Presidential Support and Opposition: Senate

1. Reagan Support Score, 1983. Percentage of 85 Reagan-issue recorded votes in 1983 on which senator voted "yea" or "nay" *in agreement* with the president's position. Failures to vote lower both Support and Opposition scores.

2. Reagan Opposition Score, 1983. Percentage of 85 Reagan-issue recorded votes in 1983 on which senator voted "yea" or "nay" *in disagreement* with the president's position. Failures to vote lower both Support and Opposition scores.

1. Sen. Daniel J. Evans, R-Wash., sworn in Sept. 12, 1983, to succeed Henry M. Jackson, D, who died Sept. 1, 1983. Jackson's 1983 presidential support score was 72 percent; opposition was 28 percent.

Presidential Support and Opposition: House

1. Reagan Support Score, 1983. Percentage of 82 Reagan-issue recorded votes in 1983 on which representative voted "yea" or "nay" *in agreement* with the president's position. Failures to vote lower both Support and Opposition scores.

2. Reagan Opposition Score, 1983. Percentage of 82 Reagan-issue recorded votes in 1983 on which representative voted "yea" or "nay" *in disagreement* with the president's position. Failures to vote lower both Support and Opposition scores.

---

1. *Rep. Sala Burton, D-Calif., sworn in June 28, 1983, to succeed her husband, Phillip Burton, D, who died April 10, 1983. Phillip Burton's 1983 presidential support score was 25 percent; opposition was 63 percent.*

2. *Rep. Daniel L. Schaefer, R-Colo., sworn in April 7, 1983, to succeed Rep.-elect Jack Swigert, R, who died Dec. 27, 1982.*

3. *Rep. George W. "Buddy" Darden, D-Ga., sworn in Nov. 10, 1983, to succeed Larry P. McDonald, D, who died Sept. 1, 1983. McDonald's 1983 presidential support score was 76 percent; opposition was 19 percent.*

4. *Rep. Charles A. Hayes, D-Ill., sworn in Sept. 12, 1983, to succeed Harold Washington, D, who resigned April 30, 1983. Washington's 1983 presidential support score was zero; opposition was zero.*

5. *Rep. Thomas P. O'Neill Jr., D-Mass., as Speaker, votes at his own discretion.*

6. *Rep. Gary L. Ackerman, D-N.Y., sworn in March 2, 1983, to succeed Benjamin S. Rosenthal, D, who died Jan. 4, 1983.*

KEY

† Not eligible for all recorded votes in 1983 (sworn in after Jan. 3, died or resigned during session, or voted "present" to avoid possible conflict of interest).

Democrats　*Republicans*

	1	2
43 *Packard*	83†	16†
44 Bates	20	77
45 *Hunter*	74	24
COLORADO		
1 Schroeder	11	84
2 Wirth	18	78
3 Kogovsek	22	78
4 *Brown*	67	33
5 *Kramer*	73	20
6 *Schaefer* [2]	74†	20†
CONNECTICUT		
1 Kennelly	16	80
2 Gejdenson	20	79
3 Morrison	16	83
4 *McKinney*	38	51
5 Ratchford	17	83
6 *Johnson*	51	46
DELAWARE		
AL Carper	33	66
FLORIDA		
1 Hutto	61	37
2 Fuqua	57	37
3 Bennett	41	59
4 Chappell	60	35
5 *McCollum*	78	17
6 MacKay	44	50
7 Gibbons	45	50
8 *Young*	74	23
9 *Bilirakis*	79	20
10 Ireland	72	23
11 Nelson	55	40
12 *Lewis*	67	32
13 *Mack*	77	20
14 Mica	49	48
15 *Shaw*	78	16
16 Smith	23	74
17 Lehman	17†	78†
18 Pepper	34	55
19 Fascell	33	62
GEORGIA		
1 Thomas	49	51
2 Hatcher	51	40
3 Ray	66	33
4 Levitas	41	54
5 Fowler	27	68
6 *Gingrich*	72	24
7 Darden [3]	40†	60†
8 Rowland	44	55
9 Jenkins	49	38
10 Barnard	59	30
HAWAII		
1 Heftel	16	17
2 Akaka	28	66
IDAHO		
1 *Craig*	73	16
2 *Hansen*	74	15
ILLINOIS		
1 Hayes [4]	7†	86†
2 Savage	7	87
3 Russo	16	74
4 *O'Brien*	66	22
5 Lipinski	40	55
6 *Hyde*	89	10
7 Collins	5	80
8 Rostenkowski	41	52
9 Yates	17	77
10 *Porter*	73	22
11 Annunzio	29	62
12 *Crane, P.*	76	16
13 *Erlenborn*	88	2
14 *Corcoran*	70	10
15 *Madigan*	74	20
16 *Martin*	61	35
17 Evans	9	90
18 *Michel*	84	7
19 *Crane, D.*	77	16
20 Durbin	13	85
21 Price	37	61
22 Simon	15	59
INDIANA		
1 Hall	13	80
2 Sharp	22	77
3 *Hiler*	83	17
4 *Coats*	78	21
5 Hillis	80	17

	1	2
ALABAMA		
1 *Edwards*	71	24
2 *Dickinson*	78	16
3 Nichols	49	44
4 Bevill	37	54
5 Flippo	45	46
6 Erdreich	37	63
7 Shelby	54	44
ALASKA		
AL *Young*	52	34
ARIZONA		
1 *McCain*	80	17
2 Udall	24	71
3 *Stump*	77	18
4 *Rudd*	74	20
5 McNulty	28	70
ARKANSAS		
1 Alexander	34	52
2 *Bethune*	61	34
3 *Hammerschmidt*	66	32
4 Anthony	45	51
CALIFORNIA		
1 Bosco	20	76
2 *Chappie*	67	20
3 Matsui	32	67
4 Fazio	28	68
5 Burton [1]	19†	69†
6 Boxer	15	84
7 Miller	11	78
8 Dellums	7	83
9 Stark	21	72
10 Edwards	15	84
11 Lantos	21	73
12 *Zschau*	78	22
13 Mineta	16	84
14 *Shumway*	82	11
15 Coelho	28	62
16 Panetta	20	79
17 *Pashayan*	73	21
18 Lehman	22	76
19 *Lagomarsino*	85	15
20 *Thomas*	74	21
21 *Fiedler*	70	29
22 *Moorhead*	78	16
23 Beilenson	29	66
24 Waxman	22	71
25 Roybal	15	83
26 Berman	24	67
27 Levine	21	77
28 Dixon	13	71
29 Hawkins	12	76
30 Martinez	10	59
31 Dymally	16	77
32 Anderson	29	70
33 *Dreier*	85	15
34 Torres	21	77
35 *Lewis*	70	20
36 Brown	16	77
37 *McCandless*	90	10
38 Patterson	20	77
39 *Dannemeyer*	77	15
40 *Badham*	82	4
41 *Lowery*	79	20
42 *Lungren*	83	15

	1	2
6 Burton	83	16
7 Myers	68	27
8 McCloskey	17	82
9 Hamilton	35	65
10 Jacobs	23	68
IOWA		
1 *Leach*	39	55
2 *Tauke*	59	38
3 *Evans*	62	33
4 Smith	30	68
5 Harkin	7	85
6 Bedell	26	74
KANSAS		
1 *Roberts*	73	27
2 Slattery	39	61
3 *Winn*	76	18
4 Glickman	43	57
5 *Whittaker*	68	30
KENTUCKY		
1 Hubbard	46	35
2 Natcher	32	68
3 Mazzoli	40	59
4 *Snyder*	70	29
5 *Rogers*	70	29
6 *Hopkins*	65	34
7 Perkins	20	79
LOUISIANA		
1 *Livingston*	77	18
2 Boggs	38	60
3 Tauzin	54	45
4 Roemer	54†	44†
5 Huckaby	54	45
6 *Moore*	68	30
7 Breaux	52	40
8 Long	29	68
MAINE		
1 *McKernan*	50	50
2 *Snowe*	50	50
MARYLAND		
1 Dyson	39	60
2 Long	20	78
3 Mikulski	15	84
4 *Holt*	77	9
5 Hoyer	32	67
6 Byron	57	40
7 Mitchell	10	78
8 Barnes	23	76
MASSACHUSETTS		
1 *Conte*	40	56
2 Boland	24	63
3 Early	6	83
4 Frank	17	82
5 Shannon	17	80
6 Mavroules	21	76
7 Markey	21	77
8 O'Neill [5]		
9 Moakley	22	74
10 Studds	18	77
11 Donnelly	17	80
MICHIGAN		
1 Conyers	6	73
2 *Pursell*	63	28
3 Wolpe	16	82
4 *Siljander*	73	23
5 Sawyer	63	23
6 Carr	12	83
7 Kildee	11	89
8 Traxler	6	88
9 *Vander Jagt*	66	22
10 Albosta	16	82
11 *Davis*	52	44
12 Bonior	21	78
13 Crockett	13	71
14 Hertel	20	80
15 Ford	12	78
16 Dingell	23	67
17 Levin	28	72
18 *Broomfield*	77	18
MINNESOTA		
1 Penny	13	87
2 *Weber*	63	35
3 *Frenzel*	68	26
4 Vento	17	82
5 Sabo	18	80
6 Sikorski	16	83

	1	2
7 *Stangeland*	68	28
8 Oberstar	12	84
MISSISSIPPI		
1 Whitten	30	66
2 *Franklin*	76	20
3 Montgomery	68	30
4 Dowdy	27	59
5 *Lott*	73	22
MISSOURI		
1 Clay	9	80
2 Young	33	66
3 Gephardt	26	70
4 Skelton	45	50
5 Wheat	12	87
6 *Coleman*	65	33
7 *Taylor*	70	26
8 *Emerson*	70	27
9 Volkmer	26	74
MONTANA		
1 Williams	18	72
2 *Marlenee*	63	32
NEBRASKA		
1 *Bereuter*	61	37
2 *Daub*	76	23
3 *Smith*	72	28
NEVADA		
1 Reid	29	67
2 *Vucanovich*	78	16
NEW HAMPSHIRE		
1 D'Amours	27	62
2 *Gregg*	78	20
NEW JERSEY		
1 Florio	13	80
2 Hughes	34	66
3 Howard	18	74
4 *Smith*	50	50
5 *Roukema*	61	35
6 Dwyer	22	76
7 *Rinaldo*	46	51
8 Roe	24	72
9 Torricelli	17	78
10 Rodino	16	65
11 Minish	24	73
12 *Courter*	70	23
13 *Forsythe*	57	27
14 *Guarini*	18	76
NEW MEXICO		
1 Lujan	72	26
2 *Skeen*	82	17
3 Richardson	16	82
NEW YORK		
1 *Carney*	67	27
2 Downey	26	71
3 Mrazek	23	73
4 *Lent*	68	24
5 *McGrath*	60	35
6 Addabbo	9	80
7 *Ackerman* [6]	20†	79†
8 Scheuer	21	77
9 Ferraro	15	77
10 Schumer	23	73
11 Towns	12	87
12 Owens	12	77
13 Solarz	24	55
14 *Molinari*	65	24
15 *Green*	48	50
16 Rangel	20	71
17 Weiss	15	78
18 Garcia	16	68
19 Biaggi	23	63
20 Ottinger	18	80
21 *Fish*	54	37
22 Gilman	57	43
23 Stratton	55	43
24 *Solomon*	76	21
25 *Boehlert*	52	43
26 *Martin*	73	23
27 *Wortley*	76	23
28 McHugh	24	76
29 *Horton*	39	56
30 *Conable*	85	12
31 *Kemp*	77	21
32 LaFalce	30	67
33 Nowak	23	74
34 Lundine	22	74

	1	2
NORTH CAROLINA		
1 Jones	38	57
2 Valentine	44	56
3 Whitley	46	54
4 Andrews	35	56
5 Neal	38	50
6 Britt	33	65
7 Rose	26	61
8 Hefner	40	54
9 *Martin*	77	20
10 *Broyhill*	73	22
11 Clarke	41	55
NORTH DAKOTA		
AL Dorgan	18	77
OHIO		
1 Luken	29	68
2 *Gradison*	72	27
3 Hall	21	74
4 *Oxley*	85	12
5 *Latta*	87	10
6 *McEwen*	72	28
7 *DeWine*	84	15
8 *Kindness*	84	15
9 Kaptur	12	85
10 *Miller*	68	29
11 Eckart	18	82
12 *Kasich*	77	23
13 Pease	20	80
14 Seiberling	20	79
15 *Wylie*	79	17
16 *Regula*	66	32
17 *Williams*	40	43
18 Applegate	27	72
19 Feighan	20	78
20 Oakar	26	73
21 Stokes	11	80
OKLAHOMA		
1 Jones	45	52
2 Synar	33	66
3 Watkins	34	63
4 McCurdy	41	51
5 *Edwards*	68	27
6 English	46	51
OREGON		
1 AuCoin	20	76
2 *Smith, B.*	71	21
3 Wyden	13	85
4 Weaver	7	83
5 *Smith D.*	78	16
PENNSYLVANIA		
1 Foglietta	24	68
2 Gray	11	78
3 Borski	21	73
4 Kolter	13	67
5 *Schulze*	72	23
6 Yatron	28	70
7 Edgar	17	73
8 Kostmayer	16	77
9 *Shuster*	71	21
10 McDade	57	30
11 Harrison	20	76
12 Murtha	54	40
13 *Coughlin*	57	41
14 Coyne	26	67
15 *Ritter*	76	22
16 *Walker*	80	20
17 *Gekas*	79	20
18 Walgren	11	83
19 *Goodling*	54	40
20 Gaydos	40	59
21 *Ridge*	51	46
22 Murphy	22	77
23 *Clinger*	61	39
RHODE ISLAND		
1 St Germain	20	71
2 *Schneider*	23	71
SOUTH CAROLINA		
1 *Hartnett*	80	12
2 *Spence*	74	26
3 Derrick	35	57
4 *Campbell*	82	15
5 Spratt	37	61
6 Tallon	32	66
SOUTH DAKOTA		
AL Daschle	16	76

	1	2
TENNESSEE		
1 *Quillen*	79	16
2 *Duncan*	61	34
3 Lloyd	54	41
4 Cooper	32	59
5 Boner	44	51
6 Gore	29	61
7 *Sundquist*	70	29
8 Jones	37	51
9 Ford	20	65
TEXAS		
1 Hall, S.	49	48
2 Wilson	45	37
3 *Bartlett*	87	12
4 Hall, R.	48	49
5 Bryant	24	76
6 *Gramm*	73	16
7 *Archer*	77	22
8 *Fields*	83	17
9 Brooks	32	63
10 Pickle	44	49
11 Leath	61	32
12 Wright	43	55
13 Hightower	57	35
14 Patman	52	48
15 de la Garza	41	50
16 Coleman	37	61
17 Stenholm	63	35
18 Leland	10	83
19 Hance	41	32
20 Gonzalez	11	88
21 *Loeffler*	80	18
22 *Paul*	48	34
23 Kazen	48	50
24 Frost	34	59
25 Andrews	45	54
26 Vandergriff	54	41
27 Ortiz	44	52
UTAH		
1 *Hansen*	77	13
2 *Marriott*	79	11
3 *Nielson*	80	13
VERMONT		
AL *Jeffords*	41	51
VIRGINIA		
1 *Bateman*	87	10
2 *Whitehurst*	85	11
3 *Bliley*	85	12
4 Sisisky	43	56
5 Daniel	77	22
6 Olin	41	57
7 *Robinson*	85	12
8 *Parris*	70	27
9 Boucher	22	74
10 *Wolf*	77	23
WASHINGTON		
1 *Pritchard*	50	28
2 Swift	18	80
3 Bonker	23	71
4 *Morrison*	68	28
5 Foley	29	59
6 Dicks	38	61
7 Lowry	16	79
8 *Chandler*	66	33
WEST VIRGINIA		
1 Mollohan	34	66
2 Staggers	16	84
3 Wise	13	85
4 Rahall	15	78
WISCONSIN		
1 Aspin	30	63
2 Kastenmeier	11	82
3 *Gunderson*	61	39
4 Zablocki	41	55
5 Moody	22	73
6 *Petri*	60	39
7 Obey	22	77
8 *Roth*	71	27
9 *Sensenbrenner*	70	30
WYOMING		
AL *Cheney*	87	6

Party Voting Study:

House Partisanship Increases; Democrats Exhibit New Unity

The House took on a far more partisan flavor in 1983 than it had in 1982 or 1981, reflecting a determined effort by Democratic leaders to separate their party from Republican White House policies.

And Democrats in Congress as a whole stuck together on partisan votes more often in 1983 than in any year since 1954, when Congressional Quarterly began its annual study of party unity.

The CQ vote analysis showed that in 56 percent of recorded House votes in 1983, a majority of Democrats voted against a majority of Republicans. This was a sharp jump from 1982, when only 36 percent of the House votes were along party lines. In 1981, 37 percent were strongly partisan votes.

Partisan voting in 1983 was at the highest level in the House since 1957, according to the CQ study.

Party-line voting in the Senate, in contrast, had been fairly consistent during the three years of the Reagan administration. In 1983 a majority of Democratic senators voted against a majority of Republicans in 44 percent of the recorded votes. The comparable figures for 1982 and 1981 were 43 percent and 48 percent, respectively.

Party unity — the percentage of votes on which a member voted in agreement with a majority of his party — was up among House Democrats, but down slightly among Senate Democrats. The average House Democrat voted with the majority of the party 76 percent of the time in 1983, compared to 72 percent the year before. The party unity score among Senate Democrats dropped from 72 to 71 percent.

But because, in calculating a party score, the House numbers were weighted more heavily than the Senate to take into account the greater number of representatives, the composite Democratic party unity score in 1983 was 76 percent. This was the highest level since CQ began collecting the statistic in 1954. The next highest year was 1959, when Democrats were united on partisan votes 75 percent

---

Definitions

Party Unity Votes. Recorded votes in the Senate and House that split the parties, a majority of voting Democrats opposing a majority of voting Republicans.

Party Unity Scores. Percentage of Party Unity votes on which a member votes "yea" or "nay" *in agreement* with a majority of his party. Failure to vote, even if a member announced his stand, lowers his score.

Opposition-to-Party Scores. Percentage of Party Unity votes on which a member votes "yea" or "nay" *in disagreement* with a majority of his party. A member's Party Unity and Opposition-to-Party scores add up to 100 percent only if he voted on all Party Unity votes.

---

of the time.

Party unity slipped among Senate Republicans as divisions between GOP conservatives and moderates re-emerged. From a high of 81 percent in 1981, party unity among Senate Republicans dropped to 76 percent in 1982, and to 74 percent in 1983. House Republicans, however, displayed party loyalty more often in 1983, raising their score up to 74 percent from 69 percent in 1982. The composite GOP score was 74 percent.

Partisan Voting

The CQ statistical study confirmed anecdotal evidence that the House split along party lines more frequently in 1983 than it did during the first two years of the Reagan administration.

The statistics also reinforced impressions that Democrats were more cohesive on votes that were defined as partisan.

Unlike 1981 and 1982, when the House was dominated by a coalition of Republicans and conservative "Boll Weevil" Democrats, in 1983 the Democratic majority — bolstered by the party's gain of 26 House seats in the 1982 elections — reasserted itself. Democratic leaders interpreted the election results as a mandate to press for anti-recession legislation and other party-backed programs.

Despite early signs of House bipartisanship, such as the vote in March on Social Security changes, many votes later in the year became political statements for the two parties. Some major partisan votes included the Democratic-backed fiscal 1984 budget (H Con Res 91), the nuclear freeze (H J Res 13) and the Equal Rights Amendment (H J Res 1).

In total, 277 of the 498 recorded votes in the House reflected party-line voting in 1983. In 1982, 167 of the 459 recorded House votes were highly partisan.

Other Findings

The CQ vote study also found:

● House Democrats won and Republicans lost 214 of the 277 party-line votes in 1983, or 77 percent. This was up from 1982, when Democrats won 106 of the 167 partisan votes, or 63 percent.

● Senate Democrats also did better than they did in 1982 in winning party-divided votes. In the Senate, Democrats won 57 of the 162 partisan votes, or 35 percent. In 1982, Democrats won and Republicans lost 55 of the 202 partisan votes, or 27 percent.

● Southern Democrats voted with their party more frequently in 1983, in both the House and Senate. In the Senate, the figure went up from 59 percent in 1982 to 65 percent in 1983. On partisan votes, Southern Democrats in the House joined their party on 62 percent of the roll calls, up from 56 percent in 1982.

● A group of moderate Republican senators made up the most frequent voters against the GOP majority. In the House, Southern conservative Democrats had the highest opposition-to-party scores, while Northern liberal Republicans voted against their party position most often. Rep. Larry P. McDonald, D-Ga., who died Sept. 1, scored 93 percent in opposition to his party, the highest in the House.

Individual Scores

Donald W. Riegle Jr., D-Mich., was the Senate Democrat who voted most consistently with his party majority against the majority of Republicans. His party unity score

was 93 percent. Freshman Chic Hecht, R-Nev., was the Senate Republican who voted the GOP party line most often, with a score of 94 percent.

In the House, freshman Alan Wheat, D-Mo., had an almost perfect record of voting with his party majority against a majority of Republicans. His score was 97 percent. David Dreier, R-Calif., held the same 97 percent party unity score, the highest among Republican members of the House.

Three of the four Democrats in the Connecticut House delegation ranked among the highest eight representatives on the party loyalty question, all scoring 95 percent: William R. Ratchford, Barbara B. Kennelly and Sam Gejdenson.

The Senate Democrat to vote most consistently against his party's majority was Edward Zorinsky of Nebraska. He voted in disagreement with a majority of his party on 52 percent of the party unity votes. Zorinsky was once a Republican, and while he switched to the Democratic party to run for the Senate, he had contemplated returning to the GOP.

The other Democratic senators who voted most often against the party were also generally conservative; this group included Nebraska's other senator, J. James Exon.

Arlen Specter, R-Pa., was the Republican senator who voted against his party on partisan votes most often. His opposition-to-party score was 54 percent. He was followed by other GOP senators with moderate leanings.

While many Southern Democratic "Boll Weevils" returned to the party's fold in 1983, they still had the highest opposition-to-party scores in the House. After McDonald, the highest was Dan Daniel, D-Va., who voted in disagreement with the majority of the Democrats on 79 percent of the party-line votes. He was followed by Charles W. Stenholm, D-Texas, who scored 77 percent against his party. Stenholm was coordinator of the Conservative Democratic Forum in the House.

Claudine Schneider, R-R.I., voted against a majority of her party on partisan votes more often than any other House Republican. Her opposition score was 66 percent. The other Republican representatives who disagreed with their party line most often were all from the Northeast, members of the informal group of moderate Republicans known as the "Gypsy Moths."

Party Unity Scoreboard

The following table shows the proportion of Party Unity recorded votes in recent years:

	Total Recorded Votes	Party Unity Recorded Votes	Percent of Total
1983			
Both Chambers	869	439	51
Senate	371	162	44
House	498	277	56
1982			
Both Chambers	924	369	40
Senate	465	202	43
House	459	167	36
1981			
Both Chambers	836	363	43
Senate	483	231	48
House	353	132	37
1980			
Both Chambers	1,135	470	41
Senate	531	243	46
House	604	227	38
1979			
Both Chambers	1,169	550	47
Senate	497	232	47
House	672	318	47
1978			
Both Chambers	1,350	510	38
Senate	516	233	45
House	834	277	33
1977			
Both Chambers	1,341	567	42
Senate	635	269	42
House	706	298	42
1976			
Both Chambers	1,349	493	37
Senate	688	256	37
House	661	237	36
1975			
Both Chambers	1,214	584	48
Senate	602	288	48
House	612	296	48
1974			
Both Chambers	1,081	399	37
Senate	544	241	44
House	537	158	29
1973			
Both Chambers	1,135	463	41
Senate	594	237	40
House	541	226	42
1972			
Both Chambers	861	283	33
Senate	532	194	36
House	329	89	27
1971			
Both Chambers	743	297	40
Senate	423	176	42
House	320	121	38
1970			
Both Chambers	684	219	32
Senate	418	147	35
House	266	72	27
1969			
Both Chambers	422	144	34
Senate	245	89	36
House	177	55	31
1968			
Both Chambers	514	172	33
Senate	281	90	32
House	233	82	35

Victories, Defeats

	Senate	House	Total
Democrats won, Republicans lost	57	214	271
Republicans won, Democrats lost	105	63	168
Democrats voted unanimously	8	2	10
Republicans voted unanimously	12	14	26

Party Scores

Party Unity and Opposition-to-Party scores below are composites of individual scores and show the percentage of time the average Democrat and Republican voted with his party majority in disagreement with the other party's majority. Failures to vote lower both Party Unity and Opposition-to-Party scores. Averages are closer to House figures because the House has more members.

	1983		1982	
	Dem.	**Rep.**	**Dem.**	**Rep.**
Party Unity	76%	74%	72%	71%
Senate	71	74	72	76
House	76	74	72	69
Opposition	17%	20%	20%	21%
Senate	22	20	23	19
House	17	19	19	22

Sectional Support, Opposition

SENATE	Support	Opposition
Northern Democrats	74%	19%
Southern Democrats	65	28
Northern Republicans	72	22
Southern Republicans	81	16

HOUSE	Support	Opposition
Northern Democrats	84%	10%
Southern Democrats	62	31
Northern Republicans	72	21
Southern Republicans	81	13

Party Unity History

Composite Party Unity scores showing the percentage of time the average Democrat and Republican voted with his party majority in partisan votes in recent years:

Year	Democrats	Republicans
1983	76%	74%
1982	72	71
1981	69	76
1980	68	70
1979	69	72
1978	64	67
1977	67	70
1976	65	66
1975	69	70

Individual Scores

Highest Party Unity Scores. Those who in 1983 most consistently voted with their party majority against the majority of the other party:

SENATE

Democrats		Republicans	
Riegle, Mich.	93%	Hecht, Nev.	94%
Leahy, Vt.	89	Lugar, Ind.	92
Sarbanes, Md.	88	Thurmond, S.C.	92
Levin, Mich.	86	Garn, Utah	91
Burdick, N.D.	85	Wilson, Calif.	90
Bumpers, Ark.	85	Hatch, Utah	90
Sasser, Tenn.	85	Abdnor, S.D.	88
		Dole, Kan.	88

HOUSE

Democrats[1]		Republicans	
Wheat, Mo.	97%	Dreier, Calif.	97%
Roybal, Calif.	95	Loeffler, Texas	95
Mineta, Calif.	95	Lungren, Calif.	94
Ratchford, Conn.	95	Hiler, Ind.	94
Kennelly, Conn.	95	Mack, Fla.	94
Yates, Ill.	95	Walker, Pa.	94
Seiberling, Ohio	95	Schaefer, Colo.	93[2]
Gejdenson, Conn.	95		

Highest Opposition-to-Party Scores. Those who in 1983 most consistently voted against their party majority:

SENATE

Democrats		Republicans	
Zorinsky, Neb.	52%	Specter, Pa.	54%
Nunn, Ga.	48	Andrews, N.D.	46
Proxmire, Wis.	43	Weicker, Conn.	45
Exon, Neb.	43	Mathias, Md.	41
Heflin, Ala.	41	Stafford, Vt.	41

HOUSE

Democrats[3]		Republicans	
Daniel, Va.	79%	Schneider, R.I.	66%
Stenholm, Texas	77	Conte, Mass.	65
Roemer, La.	73[2]	Green, N.Y.	64
Montgomery, Miss.	67	Horton, N.Y.	61
Ray, Ga.	62	Rinaldo, N.J.	61
Ireland, Fla.	62	Boehlert, N.Y.	61
Sam B. Hall Jr., Texas	61	Jeffords, Vt.	60
Tauzin, La.	60	McKinney, Conn.	60
Leath, Texas	60		

[1] *Rep. Phillip Burton, D-Calif., who died April 10, 1983, scored 100 percent in party support.*
[2] *Not eligible for all votes in 1983.*
[3] *Rep. Larry P. McDonald, D-Ga., who died Sept. 1, 1983, scored 93 percent in opposition to his party.*

	1	2		1	2		1	2	KEY
ALABAMA			**IOWA**			**NEW HAMPSHIRE**			† Not eligible for all recorded votes in 1983 (sworn in after Jan. 3, died or resigned during session, or voted "present" to avoid possible conflict of interest).
Denton	83	9	*Grassley*	81	19	*Humphrey*	70	25	
Heflin	57	41	*Jepsen*	82	17	*Rudman*	82	17	
ALASKA			**KANSAS**			**NEW JERSEY**			
Murkowski	73	8	*Dole*	88	8	Bradley	82	18	
Stevens	80	17	*Kassebaum*	71	25	Lautenberg	77	20	
ARIZONA			**KENTUCKY**			**NEW MEXICO**			
Goldwater	56	9	Ford	81	17	*Domenici*	72	14	Democrats *Republicans*
DeConcini	55	31	Huddleston	73	22	Bingaman	81	15	
ARKANSAS			**LOUISIANA**			**NEW YORK**			
Bumpers	85	10	Johnston	54	40	*D'Amato*	67	30	
Pryor	78	14	Long	47	40	Moynihan	74	21	
CALIFORNIA			**MAINE**			**NORTH CAROLINA**			
Wilson	90	9	*Cohen*	60	36	*East*	80	19		1	2
Cranston	55	7	Mitchell	84	15	*Helms*	77	20	
COLORADO			**MARYLAND**			**NORTH DAKOTA**			
Armstrong	83	12	*Mathias*	40	41	*Andrews*	50	46	**TEXAS**		
Hart	61	13	Sarbanes	88	9	Burdick	85	14	*Tower*	77	12
CONNECTICUT			**MASSACHUSETTS**			**OHIO**			Bentsen	63	31
Weicker	44	45	Kennedy	70	17	Glenn	57	12	**UTAH**		
Dodd	67	17	Tsongas	80	15	Metzenbaum	80	19	*Garn*	91	6
DELAWARE			**MICHIGAN**			**OKLAHOMA**			*Hatch*	90	9
Roth	80	18	Levin	86	12	*Nickles*	83	16	**VERMONT**		
Biden	82	12	Riegle	93	4	Boren	60	35	*Stafford*	51	41
FLORIDA			**MINNESOTA**			**OREGON**			Leahy	89	10
Hawkins	73	20	*Boschwitz*	62	32	*Hatfield*	56	33	**VIRGINIA**		
Chiles	69	30	*Durenberger*	60	28	*Packwood*	56	35	*Trible*	86	14
GEORGIA			**MISSISSIPPI**			**PENNSYLVANIA**			*Warner*	84	14
Mattingly	86	14	*Cochran*	69	28	*Heinz*	57	38	**WASHINGTON**		
Nunn	49	48	Stennis	54	40	*Specter*	46	54	*Evans* [1]	55†	10†
HAWAII			**MISSOURI**			**RHODE ISLAND**			Gorton	76	23
Inouye	70	9	*Danforth*	72	27	*Chafee*	67	33	**WEST VIRGINIA**		
Matsunaga	82	14	Eagleton	79	15	Pell	81	15	Byrd	81	19
IDAHO			**MONTANA**			**SOUTH CAROLINA**			Randolph	71	28
McClure	80	9	Baucus	77	21	*Thurmond*	92	6	**WISCONSIN**		
Symms	84	12	Melcher	82	16	Hollings	49	8	*Kasten*	78	17
ILLINOIS			**NEBRASKA**			**SOUTH DAKOTA**			Proxmire	57	43
Percy	63	27	Exon	56	43	*Abdnor*	88	12	**WYOMING**		
Dixon	70	26	Zorinsky	45	52	*Pressler*	64	31	*Simpson*	78	13
INDIANA			**NEVADA**			**TENNESSEE**			*Wallop*	83	9
Lugar	92	8	*Hecht*	94	6	*Baker*	79	16	
Quayle	85	11	*Laxalt*	86	4	Sasser	85	11	

Party Unity and Party Opposition: Senate

1. Party Unity, 1983. Percentage of 162 Senate Party Unity votes in 1983, on which senator voted "yea" or "nay" *in agreement* with a majority of his party. (Party Unity roll calls are those on which a majority of voting Democrats opposed a majority of voting Republicans. Failures to vote lower both Party Unity and Party Opposition score.)

2. Party Opposition, 1983. Percentage of 162 Senate Party Unity votes in 1983, on which senator voted "yea" or "nay" *in disagreement* with a majority of his party.

1. Sen. Daniel J. Evans, R-Wash., sworn in Sept. 12, 1983, to succeed Henry M. Jackson, D, who died Sept. 1, 1983. Jackson's 1983 party unity score was 69 percent; opposition was 31 percent.

KEY

† Not eligible for all recorded votes in 1983 (sworn in after Jan. 3, died or resigned during session, or voted "present" to avoid possible conflict of interest).

———————

Democrats   *Republicans*

Party Unity and Party Opposition: House

1. Party Unity, 1983. Percentage of 277 House Party Unity recorded votes in 1983 on which representative voted "yea" or "nay" *in agreement* with a majority of his party. (Party unity roll calls are those on which a majority of voting Democrats opposed a majority of voting Republicans. Failures to vote lower both Party Unity and Party Opposition scores.)

2. Party Opposition, 1983. Percentage of 277 House Party Unity recorded votes in 1983 on which representative voted "yea" or "nay" *in disagreement* with a majority of his party.

	1	2
ALABAMA		
1 *Edwards*	60	32
2 *Dickinson*	75	17
3 Nichols	42	49
4 Bevill	62	31
5 Flippo	57	35
6 Erdreich	56	40
7 Shelby	43	54
ALASKA		
AL *Young*	57	21
ARIZONA		
1 *McCain*	83	9
2 Udall	86	5
3 *Stump*	91	6
4 *Rudd*	83	11
5 McNulty	84	10
ARKANSAS		
1 Alexander	68	10
2 *Bethune*	74	17
3 *Hammerschmidt*	75	21
4 Anthony	69	25
CALIFORNIA		
1 Bosco	78	10
2 *Chappie*	78	6
3 Matsui	93	6
4 Fazio	91	6
5 Burton[1]	88†	3†
6 Boxer	94	3
7 Miller	83	8
8 Dellums	82	7
9 Stark	83	7
10 Edwards	94	3
11 Lantos	91	5
12 Zschau	74	25
13 Mineta	95	4
14 *Shumway*	90	2
15 Coelho	83	4
16 Panetta	85†	10†
17 *Pashayan*	77	9
18 Lehman	91	4
19 *Lagomarsino*	88	12
20 *Thomas*	81†	10†
21 *Fiedler*	82	16
22 *Moorhead*	92	3
23 Beilenson	91	7
24 Waxman	84	3
25 Roybal	95	3
26 Berman	85	5
27 Levine	86	6
28 Dixon	81	1
29 Hawkins	78	3
30 Martinez	65	2
31 Dymally	82	5
32 Anderson	76	21
33 *Dreier*	97	2
34 Torres	88	4
35 *Lewis*	74	17
36 Brown	84	5
37 *McCandless*	86	10
38 Patterson	84	9
39 *Dannemeyer*	91	4
40 *Badham*	79†	4†
41 *Lowery*	83	13
42 *Lungren*	94	3

	1	2
43 *Packard*	92†	5†
44 Bates	86	11
45 *Hunter*	88	10
COLORADO		
1 Schroeder	81	16
2 Wirth	82	7
3 Kogovsek	91	7
4 *Brown*	82	18
5 *Kramer*	87	9
6 *Schaefer*[2]	93†	5†
CONNECTICUT		
1 Kennelly	95	3
2 Gejdenson	95	3
3 Morrison	88	4
4 *McKinney*	32	60
5 Ratchford	95	3
6 *Johnson*	43	49
DELAWARE		
AL Carper	76	23
FLORIDA		
1 Hutto	45	51
2 Fuqua	64	30
3 Bennett	61	39
4 Chappell	53	39
5 *McCollum*	89	6
6 MacKay	62	28
7 Gibbons	68	23
8 *Young*	77	18
9 *Bilirakis*	90	9
10 Ireland	31	62
11 Nelson	52	39
12 *Lewis*	78	18
13 *Mack*	94	4
14 Mica	73	22
15 *Shaw*	87	8
16 Smith	89	6
17 Lehman	85†	5†
18 Pepper	77	9
19 Fascell	86	11
GEORGIA		
1 Thomas	64	36
2 Hatcher	62	29
3 Ray	37	62
4 Levitas	58	38
5 Fowler	83	11
6 *Gingrich*	83	10
7 Darden[3]	48†	48†
8 Rowland	60	38
9 Jenkins	47	39
10 Barnard	41	53
HAWAII		
1 Heftel	30†	7†
2 Akaka	86	9
IDAHO		
1 *Craig*	86	4
2 *Hansen*	85	3
ILLINOIS		
1 Hayes[4]	87†	7†
2 Savage	88	4
3 Russo	76†	13†
4 O'Brien	53	32
5 Lipinski	66	24
6 *Hyde*	83	15
7 Collins	85	3
8 Rostenkowski	77	12
9 Yates	95	4
10 *Porter*	69	29
11 Annunzio	83	12
12 *Crane, P.*	92	4
13 *Erlenborn*	74	11
14 *Corcoran*	74	6
15 *Madigan*	73	22
16 *Martin*	74	22
17 Evans	91	6
18 *Michel*	71†	20†
19 *Crane, D.*	90	3
20 Durbin	77	17
21 Price	79	17
22 Simon	74	4
INDIANA		
1 Hall	89	2
2 Sharp	79	20
3 *Hiler*	94	4
4 *Coats*	88†	12†
5 Hillis	72†	21†

1. Rep. Sala Burton, D-Calif., sworn in June 28, 1983, to succeed her husband, Phillip Burton, D, who died April 10, 1983. Phillip Burton's 1983 party unity score was 100 percent.

2. Rep. Daniel L. Schaefer, R-Colo., sworn in April 7, 1983, to succeed Rep.-elect Jack Swigert, R, who died Dec. 27, 1982.

3. Rep. George W. "Buddy" Darden, D-Ga., sworn in Nov. 10, 1983, to succeed Larry P. McDonald, D, who died Sept. 1, 1983. McDonald's 1983 party unity score was 2 percent; opposition was 93 percent.

4. Rep. Charles A. Hayes, D-Ill., sworn in Sept. 12, 1983, to succeed Harold Washington, D, who resigned April 30, 1983. Washington's 1983 party unity score was 8 percent; opposition was zero.

5. Rep. Thomas P. O'Neill Jr., D-Mass., as Speaker, votes at his own discretion.

6. Rep. Gary L. Ackerman, D-N.Y., sworn in March 2, 1983, to succeed Benjamin S. Rosenthal, D, who died Jan. 4, 1983. Rosenthal did not vote on the one party unity vote for which he was eligible.

7. Rep. Phil Gramm, R-Texas, resigned Jan. 5, 1983. He had been elected as a Democrat and cast his first three votes of 1983 as a member of that party. His party unity score as a Democrat was 33 percent; opposition was 67 percent. Gramm was re-elected Feb. 12, 1983, as a Republican and sworn in Feb. 22. The scores in the chart reflect his votes as a Republican.

	1	2
6 *Burton*	92	4
7 Myers	72	25
8 McCloskey	89	10
9 Hamilton	82	17
10 Jacobs	61	31
IOWA		
1 *Leach*	40	51
2 *Tauke*	65	32
3 Evans	62	35
4 Smith	84	13
5 Harkin	82	10
6 Bedell	81	16
KANSAS		
1 *Roberts*	87	11
2 Slattery	57	38
3 *Winn*	81	9
4 Glickman	73	23
5 *Whittaker*	84	14
KENTUCKY		
1 Hubbard	44	46
2 Natcher	83	17
3 Mazzoli	78	20
4 *Snyder*	77	21
5 *Rogers*	80	19
6 *Hopkins*	84	14
7 Perkins	87	12
LOUISIANA		
1 *Livingston*	76	17
2 Boggs	77	14
3 Tauzin	35	60
4 Roemer	27†	73†
5 Huckaby	44	51
6 *Moore*	80	18
7 Breaux	41	50
8 Long	87	11
MAINE		
1 *McKernan*	48	51
2 *Snowe*	46	53
MARYLAND		
1 Dyson	63	36
2 Long	81	12
3 Mikulski	90	6
4 *Holt*	77	9
5 Hoyer	91	6
6 Byron	43	51
7 Mitchell	88	4
8 Barnes	91	6
MASSACHUSETTS		
1 *Conte*	30	65
2 Boland	84	7
3 Early	74	10
4 Frank	88	8
5 Shannon	90	6
6 Mavroules	87	7
7 Markey	91	6
8 O'Neill [5]		
9 Moakley	89	5
10 Studds	91	5
11 Donnelly	84	12
MICHIGAN		
1 Conyers	73	6
2 *Pursell*	56	33
3 Wolpe	93	4
4 *Siljander*	83	9
5 Sawyer	62	31
6 Carr	86	10
7 Kildee	92	8
8 Traxler	82	8
9 *Vander Jagt*	70	19
10 Albosta	79	15
11 Davis	53	44
12 Bonior	87	6
13 Crockett	77	6
14 Hertel	87	11
15 Ford	87	2
16 Dingell	84	6
17 Levin	94	6
18 *Broomfield*	77	16
MINNESOTA		
1 Penny	84	16
2 *Weber*	79	16
3 *Frenzel*	71	21
4 Vento	94	4
5 Sabo	93	3
6 Sikorski	89	8

	1	2
7 *Stangeland*	75	20
8 Oberstar	90	6
MISSISSIPPI		
1 Whitten	71	22
2 *Franklin*	85	8
3 Montgomery	28	67
4 Dowdy	68	17
5 *Lott*	86	7
MISSOURI		
1 Clay	83	2
2 Young	78	17
3 Gephardt	90	6
4 Skelton	56	37
5 Wheat	97	3
6 *Coleman*	70	27
7 *Taylor*	81	14
8 *Emerson*	85	13
9 Volkmer	71	29
MONTANA		
1 Williams	77	9
2 *Marlenee*	71	17
NEBRASKA		
1 *Bereuter*	69	26
2 *Daub*	89	10
3 *Smith*	74	23
NEVADA		
1 Reid	86	13
2 *Vucanovich*	87	6
NEW HAMPSHIRE		
1 D'Amours	71†	21†
2 *Gregg*	85	10
NEW JERSEY		
1 Florio	81	9
2 Hughes	74	26
3 Howard	87	3
4 *Smith*	44	56
5 *Roukema*	49	47
6 Dwyer	93	4
7 *Rinaldo*	36	61
8 Roe	87	9
9 Torricelli	82	6
10 Rodino	86	2
11 Minish	90	7
12 *Courter*	74	22
13 *Forsythe*	59	22
14 Guarini	90	4
NEW MEXICO		
1 *Lujan*	81	16
2 *Skeen*	89	8
3 Richardson	87	9
NEW YORK		
1 *Carney*	77	15
2 Downey	90	4
3 Mrazek	85	11
4 *Lent*	65	29
5 *McGrath*	69	25
6 Addabbo	84	2
7 Ackerman [6]	91†	4†
8 Scheuer	92	5
9 Ferraro	92	3
10 Schumer	89	5
11 Towns	90	2
12 Owens	79	2
13 Solarz	76	5
14 *Molinari*	57	24
15 *Green*	33	64
16 Rangel	88	4
17 Weiss	87	6
18 Garcia	83	1
19 Biaggi	78	8
20 Ottinger	92†	4†
21 *Fish*	45	47
22 *Gilman*	42	56
23 Stratton	59	34
24 *Solomon*	92	5
25 *Boehlert*	34	61
26 *Martin*	72	18
27 *Wortley*	75	21
28 McHugh	92	5
29 *Horton*	32	61
30 *Conable*	78	18
31 *Kemp*	75	16
32 LaFalce	84	12
33 Nowak	91	6
34 Lundine	86	8

	1	2
NORTH CAROLINA		
1 Jones	70	19
2 Valentine	54	42
3 Whitley	65	31
4 Andrews	73	18
5 Neal	64	20
6 *Britt*	77	19
7 Rose	74	12
8 Hefner	66	21
9 *Martin*	77†	15†
10 *Broyhill*	82	11
11 Clarke	78	18
NORTH DAKOTA		
AL Dorgan	77	18
OHIO		
1 Luken	82	12
2 *Gradison*	72	23
3 Hall	75	17
4 *Oxley*	87	10
5 *Latta*	88	7
6 *McEwen*	82	13
7 *DeWine*	88	9
8 *Kindness*	81	16
9 Kaptur	85	10
10 *Miller*	80	18
11 Eckart	84	14
12 *Kasich*	90	10
13 Pease	91	9
14 Seiberling	95	4
15 *Wylie*	73	20
16 *Regula*	68	31
17 *Williams*	34	49
18 Applegate	69	27
19 Feighan	86	11
20 Oakar	86	13
21 Stokes	86	3
OKLAHOMA		
1 Jones	65	32
2 Synar	85	12
3 Watkins	65	32
4 McCurdy	55	37
5 *Edwards*	79†	14†
6 English	53	46
OREGON		
1 AuCoin	75	16
2 *Smith, B.*	74	8
3 Wyden	91	8
4 Weaver	77	15
5 *Smith D.*	83	3
PENNSYLVANIA		
1 Foglietta	87	4
2 Gray	93	1
3 Borski	91	6
4 Kolter	77	12
5 *Schulze*	75	11
6 Yatron	78	18
7 Edgar	84	6
8 Kostmayer	86	5
9 *Shuster*	85	5
10 *McDade*	44	43
11 Harrison	83	8
12 Murtha	74	22
13 *Coughlin*	56	42
14 Coyne	91	4
15 *Ritter*	81	16
16 *Walker*	94	6
17 *Gekas*	82	17
18 Walgren	82	14
19 *Goodling*	71	26
20 Gaydos	76	17
21 *Ridge*	56	40
22 Murphy	78	18
23 *Clinger*	62†	37†
RHODE ISLAND		
1 St Germain	80	8
2 *Schneider*	27	66
SOUTH CAROLINA		
1 *Hartnett*	90	4
2 *Spence*	87	10
3 Derrick	72	16
4 *Campbell*	84	9
5 Spratt	74	20
6 Tallon	79	20
SOUTH DAKOTA		
AL Daschle	75	12

	1	2
TENNESSEE		
1 *Quillen*	70	21
2 *Duncan*	69	27
3 Lloyd	41	50
4 Cooper	69	24
5 Boner	67	20
6 Gore	77	13
7 *Sundquist*	83	14
8 Jones	61	23
9 Ford	78	3
TEXAS		
1 Hall, S.	38	61
2 Wilson	53	28
3 *Bartlett*	88	9
4 Hall, R.	38	57
5 Bryant	84	10
6 *Gramm* [7]	79†	1†
7 *Archer*	92†	5†
8 *Fields*	91	6
9 Brooks	81	14
10 Pickle	68	25
11 Leath	29	60
12 Wright	81	15
13 Hightower	44	46
14 Patman	44	56
15 de la Garza	70	17
16 Coleman	81	16
17 Stenholm	21	77
18 Leland	86	3
19 Hance	35	32
20 Gonzalez	88	10
21 *Loeffler*	95	4
22 *Paul*	71	9
23 Kazen	55	38
24 Frost	79	13
25 Andrews	61	37
26 Vandergriff	48	49
27 Ortiz	75	21
UTAH		
1 *Hansen*	83	3
2 *Marriott*	74	17
3 *Nielson*	88	5
VERMONT		
AL *Jeffords*	31	60
VIRGINIA		
1 *Bateman*	81	17
2 *Whitehurst*	78	12
3 *Bliley*	87	10
4 Sisisky	61	32
5 Daniel	18	79
6 Olin	64	33
7 *Robinson*	90	8
8 *Parris*	74	19
9 Boucher	88	7
10 *Wolf*	79	19
WASHINGTON		
1 *Pritchard*	38	25
2 Swift	91	4
3 Bonker	84	7
4 Morrison	67	26
5 Foley	83	8
6 Dicks	83	11
7 Lowry	84	6
8 *Chandler*	67	28
WEST VIRGINIA		
1 Mollohan	78	21
2 Staggers	86	12
3 Wise	84	13
4 Rahall	76	16
WISCONSIN		
1 Aspin	84	9
2 Kastenmeier	90	6
3 *Gunderson*	70	30
4 Zablocki	84	12
5 Moody	84	10
6 *Petri*	76	23
7 Obey	94	5
8 *Roth*	84	14
9 *Sensenbrenner*	85	14
WYOMING		
AL *Cheney*	82	5

Voting Participation Record Equaled by Congress in 1983

Members of Congress in 1983 missed, on the average, less than one in every 10 recorded votes taken in the House and Senate.

Congressional Quarterly's study of 1983 voting participation showed that members on average recorded a position on 92 percent of the votes taken, 2 percentage points above the 1982 mark. The figure tied the 1981 score, the highest voting participation percentage in 30 years.

Scores traditionally are lower in election years, when members must campaign for re-election. In 1980 the average for all members was 87 percent.

The chief explanation for the high voting participation average appeared to be the accommodating vote schedules adopted in both chambers. By scheduling most roll calls on Tuesdays, Wednesdays or Thursdays, House and Senate leaders made it easier for members to show up for votes. Many members were absent on Fridays and Mondays, spending long weekends in their districts and states.

In the Senate, for example, more than 80 percent of the recorded votes in 1983 were taken on Tuesdays, Wednesdays and Thursdays, according to a Congressional Quarterly analysis. Similarly, House leaders also scheduled most votes for midweek.

Although 1983 was not an election year, four senators were actively seeking the 1984 Democratic presidential nomination, and their voting participation records were among the lowest in the Senate. Their absences helped bring the Senate Democrats' voting participation rate below the 1982 election-year level.

The voting participation study is the closest approach to an attendance record for Congress, but it is only an approximation. *(Definition, box, p. 33-C)*

In 1983, as in most years, Republicans voted more often than Democrats. Senate Democrats had outscored their Republican counterparts in only four of the past 32 years; House Democrats only twice.

Two senators and three representatives had perfect scores for voting participation. Six senators and four representatives voted less than 70 percent of the time.

Chamber, Party Scores

Total recorded votes in the House and Senate in 1983 numbered 869, 55 fewer than in 1982 and 481 fewer than the record 1,350 votes in 1978. There were 371 Senate votes in 1983, 94 fewer than in 1982 and 317 fewer than the record 688 in 1976.

The House took 498 votes in 1983, 39 more than in 1982, but 336 fewer than the record 834 in 1978.

Senators' and representatives' voting participation scores were the same in 1983: 92 percent. In 1982 senators scored 94 percent, representatives 89 percent.

House Republicans on average voted 93 percent of the time in 1983, compared to 90 percent in 1982 and 92 percent in 1981. Democratic House members scored 92 percent in 1983, 88 percent in 1982 and 90 percent in 1981.

In the Senate, Republicans scored 94 percent, Democrats 91 percent. In 1982 Senate Republicans scored 95 percent, Democrats 94 percent. Senate Republicans had 94

percent in 1981 to the Democrats' 92 percent.

For the two chambers combined, the 1983 scores were 93 percent for Republicans and 92 percent for Democrats. In 1982 Republicans led Democrats 91 percent to 89 percent. The 1981 scores were 93 percent for Republicans, 91 percent for Democrats.

Republican senators from the Midwest and South led members from all regions in both chambers, voting 95 percent of the time. The lowest regional score came from Democratic senators for the West: 85 percent.

Individual Highs and Lows

Two senators, Democrat William Proxmire of Wisconsin and Republican Richard G. Lugar of Indiana, answered every roll call in 1983. Proxmire last missed a vote in 1966 and extended his record of consecutive votes to 8,343. Twelve other senators — 10 Republicans and two Democrats — scored 99 percent.

Three representatives, all Democrats, had perfect scores in 1983: William H. Natcher of Kentucky, Charles E. Bennett of Florida and Dale E. Kildee of Michigan. Natcher had not missed a vote since his election to Congress in 1954 and extended his record to 9,511 consecutive votes.

The lowest scoring senator was Ernest F. Hollings of South Carolina, 50 percent. Hollings, a candidate for the 1984 Democratic presidential nomination, was followed by three of his fellow Democrats also seeking the nomination: Alan Cranston, Calif., 56 percent; Gary Hart, Colo., 63 percent; and John Glenn, Ohio, 64 percent. The lowest scoring Senate Republican was Barry Goldwater of Arizona, 61 percent.

The lowest scoring representative was Democrat Cecil Heftel of Hawaii, 34 percent. Heftel was ill much of the year. Joel Pritchard of Washington had the lowest Republi-

---

Absences

Among members of Congress absent for a day or more in 1983 because they were sick or because of illness or death in their families were:

Senate Democrats: Biden, Del.; Lautenberg, N.J.; Matsunaga, Hawaii; Randolph, W.Va.; Riegle, Mich.; Sasser, Tenn.

Senate Republicans: Baker, Tenn.; Domenici, N.M.; Goldwater, Ariz.; Mathias, Md.; Murkowski, Alaska; Packwood, Ore.

House Democrats: Anthony, Ark; Boland, Mass.; Dyson, Md.; Foley, Wash.; Ford, Mich.; Gaydos, Pa.; Gephardt, Mo.; Hefner, N.C.; Heftel, Hawaii; Jones, Tenn.; Kolter, Pa.; Lehman, Fla.; Lloyd, Tenn.; Mica, Fla.; Mikulski, Md.; Neal, N.C.; Pickle, Texas; Rodino, N.J.; Slattery, Kan.; Waxman, Calif.; Yates, Ill.; Yatron, Pa.

House Republicans: Carney, N.Y.; Courter, N.J.; Forsythe, N.J.; Franklin, Miss.; Lewis, Calif.; Lott, Miss.; McDade, Pa.; McEwen, Ohio; Michel, Ill.; Morrison, Wash.; Porter, Ill.; Winn, Kan.

Failure to vote often is due to conflicting duties. Members frequently have to be away from Washington on official business. Leaves of absence, not listed here, are granted members for these purposes.

can score in the House, 64 percent.

State Delegations

The Senate delegations with the highest voting participation scores in 1983 were Iowa, Utah and West Virginia, all 99 percent; and Georgia, Indiana, Virginia and Wisconsin, all 98 percent.

In the House, the highest scoring delegations with two or more members were Maine, 98 percent; Kentucky, Nebraska and New Mexico, all 97 percent; West Virginia and Wisconsin, both 96 percent.

Party Scores

Composites of Democratic and Republican voting participation scores for 1983 and 1982:

	1983		1982	
	Dem.	Rep.	Dem.	Rep.
Senate	91%	94%	94%	95%
House	92	93	88	90

Regional Scores

Regional voting participation breakdowns for 1983 with 1982 scores in parentheses:

	East	West	South	Midwest
DEMOCRATS				
Senate	94% (94)	85% (90)	90% (95)	93% (95)
House	92 (88)	90 (88)	92 (89)	93 (88)
REPUBLICANS				
Senate	94% (94)	91% (93)	95% (96)	95% (96)
House	93 (89)	91 (87)	94 (91)	94 (91)

*(CQ defines regions of the United States as follows: **East:** Conn., Del., Maine, Md., Mass., N.H., N.J., N.Y., Pa., R.I., Vt., W.Va. **West:** Alaska, Ariz., Calif., Colo., Hawaii, Idaho, Mont., Nev., N.M., Ore., Utah, Wash., Wyo. **South:** Ala., Ark., Fla., Ga., Ky., La., Miss., N.C., Okla., S.C., Tenn., Texas, Va. **Midwest:** Ill., Ind., Iowa, Kan., Mich., Minn., Mo., Neb., N.D., Ohio, S.D., Wis.)*

Highest Scorers

SENATE

Democrats[1]		Republicans	
Proxmire, Wis.	100%	Lugar, Ind.	100%
Byrd, W.Va.	99	Specter, Pa.	99
Mitchell, Maine	99	Mattingly, Ga.	99
Melcher, Mont.	98	Grassley, Iowa	99
Leahy, Vt.	98	Hecht, Nev.	99
Levin, Mich.	98	Rudman, N.H.	99
Ford, Ky.	98	Warner, Va.	99
Burdick, N.D.	98	Hatch, Utah	99
Bingaman, N.M.	98	Gorton, Wash.	99
		Abdnor, S.D.	99
		Jepsen, Iowa	99

Definition

Voting Participation. Percentage of recorded votes on which a member voted "yea" or "nay." Failures to vote "yea" or "nay" lower scores — even if the member votes "present," enters a live pair or announces his stand in the *Congressional Record.* Only votes of "yea" or "nay" directly affect the outcome of a vote. Voting participation is the closest approach to an attendance record, but it is only an approximation. A member may be present and nevertheless decline to vote "yea" or "nay" — usually because he has entered a live pair with an absent member.

HOUSE

Democrats		Republicans	
Natcher, Ky.	100%	Kasich, Ohio	99%
Bennett, Fla.	100	Lagomarsino, Calif.	99
Kildee, Mich.	100	Walker, Pa.	99
Thomas, Ga.	99	Brown, Colo.	99
Hughes, N.J.	99	Gunderson, Wis.	99
Levin, Mich.	99	Zschau, Calif.	99
Patman, Texas	99	Moore, La.	99
Hamilton, Ind.	99	Sensenbrenner, Wis.	99
Roemer, La.	99[2]	Wolf, Va.	99
Penny, Minn.	99	Regula, Ohio	99
Pease, Ohio	99	Smith, N.J.	99
Wheat, Mo.	99	Petri, Wis.	99
Volkmer, Mo.	99	Clinger, Pa.	99[2]

Lowest Scorers

SENATE

Democrats		Republicans	
Hollings, S.C.	50%	Goldwater, Ariz.	61%[3]
Cranston, Calif.	56	Evans, Wash.	67[2]
Hart, Colo.	63	Percy, Ill.	82
Glenn, Ohio	64	Mathias, Md.	83[3]
Dodd, Conn.	81		
Inouye, Hawaii	81		

HOUSE

Democrats[4]		Republicans	
Heftel, Hawaii	34%[2,3]	Pritchard, Wash.	64%
Martinez, Calif.	62	Corcoran, Ill.	77
Hance, Texas	68	Young, Alaska	77
Conyers, Mich.	74	Hansen, Idaho	79
Simon, Ill.	75	Paul, Texas	80
Solarz, N.Y.	77		

[1] *Another Democrat, Henry M. Jackson, Wash., who died Sept. 1, 1983, also scored 100 percent.*
[2] *Not eligible for all votes in 1983.*
[3] *Member absent a day or more in 1983 due to sickness or because of illness or death in family.*
[4] *Benjamin S. Rosenthal, D-N.Y., who died Jan. 4, 1983, scored zero. Harold Washington, D-Ill., who resigned April 30, 1983, scored 4 percent.*

Voting Participation Scores: House

Voting Participation, 1983. Percentage of 498 recorded votes in 1983 on which representative voted "yea" or "nay."

KEY

†   Not eligible for all recorded votes in 1983 (sworn in after Jan. 3, died or resigned during session, or voted "present" to avoid possible conflict of interest).

\#   Member absent a day or more in 1983 due to illness or illness or death in family.

———

Democrats   ***Republicans***

ALABAMA		
1 *Edwards*	88	
2 *Dickinson*	90	
3 Nichols	88	
4 Bevill	93	
5 Flippo	92	
6 Erdreich	96	
7 Shelby	97	
ALASKA		
AL *Young*	77	
ARIZONA		
1 *McCain*	90	
2 Udall	92	
3 *Stump*	96	
4 *Rudd*	92	
5 McNulty	93	
ARKANSAS		
1 Alexander	81	
2 *Bethune*	91	
3 *Hammerschmidt*	96	
4 Anthony	90#	
CALIFORNIA		
1 Bosco	88	
2 *Chappie*	87	
3 Matsui	98	
4 Fazio	96†	
5 Burton [1]	91†	
6 Boxer	95	
7 Miller	89	
8 Dellums	86	
9 Stark	89	
10 Edwards	97†	
11 Lantos	94	
12 *Zschau*	99	
13 Mineta	97	
14 *Shumway*	92	
15 Coelho	87	
16 Panetta	94†	
17 *Pashayan*	85	
18 Lehman	92	
19 *Lagomarsino*	99	
20 *Thomas*	92†	
21 *Fiedler*	97	
22 *Moorhead*	95	
23 Beilenson	97	
24 Waxman	86	
25 Roybal	95	
26 Berman	87	
27 Levine	93	
28 Dixon	82	
29 Hawkins	81	
30 Martinez	62	
31 Dymally	82	
32 Anderson	97	
33 *Dreier*	98	
34 Torres	90	
35 *Lewis*	87#	
36 Brown	88	
37 *McCandless*	96	
38 Patterson	91	
39 *Dannemeyer*	94	
40 *Badham*	82†	
41 *Lowery*	95	
42 *Lungren*	96	
43 *Packard*	97†	
44 Bates	95	
45 *Hunter*	96	
COLORADO		
1 Schroeder	95	
2 Wirth	91	
3 Kogovsek	95	
4 *Brown*	99	
5 *Kramer*	95	
6 *Schaefer* [2]	96†	
CONNECTICUT		
1 Kennelly	98	
2 Gejdenson	98	
3 Morrison	93	
4 *McKinney*	88	
5 Ratchford	98	
6 *Johnson*	91	
DELAWARE		
AL Carper	98	
FLORIDA		
1 Hutto	95	
2 Fuqua	92	
3 Bennett	100	
4 Chappell	86	
5 *McCollum*	95	
6 MacKay	90	
7 Gibbons	92	
8 *Young*	93	
9 *Bilirakis*	97	
10 Ireland	92	
11 Nelson	92	
12 *Lewis*	96	
13 *Mack*	96	
14 Mica	93#	
15 *Shaw*	94	
16 Smith	94	
17 Lehman	90†#	
18 Pepper	84	
19 Fascell	95	
GEORGIA		
1 Thomas	99	
2 Hatcher	90	
3 Ray	98	
4 Levitas	95	
5 Fowler	94	
6 *Gingrich*	91	
7 Darden [3]	98†	
8 Rowland	98	
9 Jenkins	87	
10 Barnard	91	
HAWAII		
1 Heftel	34†#	
2 Akaka	94	
IDAHO		
1 *Craig*	88	
2 *Hansen*	79	
ILLINOIS		
1 Hayes [4]	92†	
2 Savage	88	
3 Russo	92†	
4 O'Brien	85	
5 Lipinski	90	
6 *Hyde*	97	
7 Collins	86	
8 Rostenkowski	88	
9 Yates	96#	
10 *Porter*	96#	
11 Annunzio	94	
12 *Crane, P.*	91†	
13 *Erlenborn*	86	
14 *Corcoran*	77	
15 *Madigan*	91	
16 *Martin*	95	
17 Evans	98	
18 *Michel*	89†#	
19 *Crane, D.*	92†	
20 Durbin	95	
21 Price	96	
22 Simon	75	
INDIANA		
1 Hall	90	
2 Sharp	98	
3 *Hiler*	98	
4 *Coats*	97†	
5 *Hillis*	92†	

1. Rep. Sala Burton, D-Calif., sworn in June 28, 1983, to succeed her husband Phillip Burton, D, who died April 10, 1983. Phillip Burton's 1983 voting participation score was 88 percent.

2. Rep. Daniel L. Schaefer, R-Colo., sworn in April 7, 1983, to succeed Rep.-elect Jack Swigert, R, who died Dec. 27, 1982.

J. Rep. George W. "Buddy" Darden, D-Ga., sworn in Nov. 10, 1983, to succeed Larry P. McDonald, D, who died Sept. 1, 1983. McDonald's 1983 voting participation score was 95 percent.

4. Rep. Charles A. Hayes, D-Ill., sworn in Sept. 12, 1983, to succeed Harold Washington, D, who resigned April 30, 1983. Washington's 1983 voting participation score was 4 percent.

5. Rep. Thomas P. O'Neill Jr., D-Mass., as Speaker, votes at his own discretion.

6. Rep. Gary L. Ackerman, D-N.Y., sworn in March 2, 1983, to succeed Benjamin S. Rosenthal, D, who died Jan. 4, 1983. Rosenthal did not vote on the one roll call for which he was eligible in 1983.

7. Rep. Phil Gramm, D-Texas, resigned Jan. 5, 1983, and was re-elected as a Republican on Feb. 12, 1983. He was sworn in Feb. 22, 1983.

6 Burton 95
7 Myers 97
8 McCloskey 98
9 Hamilton 99
10 Jacobs 88

IOWA
1 Leach 91
2 Tauke 97
3 Evans 97
4 Smith 96
5 Harkin 89
6 Bedell 97

KANSAS
1 Roberts 96
2 Slattery 95#
3 Winn 91#
4 Glickman 96
5 Whittaker 97

KENTUCKY
1 Hubbard 89
2 Natcher 100
3 Mazzoli 97
4 Snyder 97
5 Rogers 98
6 Hopkins 98
7 Perkins 98

LOUISIANA
1 Livingston 91
2 Boggs 90
3 Tauzin 96
4 Roemer 99†
5 Huckaby 93
6 Moore 99
7 Breaux 89
8 Long 97

MAINE
1 McKernan 98
2 Snowe 98

MARYLAND
1 Dyson 98#
2 Long 91
3 Mikulski 94#
4 Holt 86
5 Hoyer 97
6 Byron 90
7 Mitchell 89
8 Barnes 96

MASSACHUSETTS
1 Conte 94
2 Boland 90#
3 Early 85
4 Frank 96
5 Shannon 95
6 Mavroules 91
7 Markey 96
8 O'Neill [5]
9 Moakley 93
10 Studds 95†
11 Donnelly 96

MICHIGAN
1 Conyers 74
2 Pursell 88
3 Wolpe 98
4 Siljander 92
5 Sawyer 90
6 Carr 94
7 Kildee 100
8 Traxler 90
9 Vander Jagt 89
10 Albosta 95
11 Davis 96
12 Bonior 91
13 Crockett 79
14 Hertel 98
15 Ford 81#
16 Dingell 86
17 Levin 99
18 Broomfield 92

MINNESOTA
1 Penny 99
2 Weber 96
3 Frenzel 92
4 Vento 98
5 Sabo 95
6 Sikorski 98

7 Stangeland 93
8 Oberstar 87

MISSISSIPPI
1 Whitten 94
2 Franklin 91#
3 Montgomery 96
4 Dowdy 83
5 Lott 92#

MISSOURI
1 Clay 83
2 Young 93
3 Gephardt 94#
4 Skelton 93
5 Wheat 99
6 Coleman 97
7 Taylor 92
8 Emerson 97
9 Volkmer 99

MONTANA
1 Williams 84
2 Marlenee 85

NEBRASKA
1 Bereuter 96
2 Daub 97
3 Smith 98

NEVADA
1 Reid 98
2 Vucanovich 93

NEW HAMPSHIRE
1 D'Amours 91†
2 Gregg 94

NEW JERSEY
1 Florio 91
2 Hughes 99
3 Howard 88
4 Smith 99
5 Roukema 97
6 Dwyer 96
7 Rinaldo 95
8 Roe 96
9 Torricelli 91
10 Rodino 86#
11 Minish 95
12 Courter 96#
13 Forsythe 83#
14 Guarini 95

NEW MEXICO
1 Lujan 96
2 Skeen 97
3 Richardson 96

NEW YORK
1 Carney 92#
2 Downey 94
3 Mrazek 93
4 Lent 93
5 McGrath 93
6 Addabbo 86
7 Ackerman [6] 94†
8 Scheuer 95
9 Ferraro 93
10 Schumer 94
11 Towns 80
12 Owens 77
13 Solarz 84
14 Molinari 84
15 Green 97
16 Rangel 90
17 Weiss 94
18 Garcia 84
19 Biaggi 85
20 Ottinger 88†
21 Fish 91
22 Gilman 95
23 Stratton 93
24 Solomon 94
25 Boehlert 93
26 Martin 86
27 Wortley 95
28 McHugh 94
29 Horton 94
30 Conable 94
31 Kemp 89
32 LaFalce 94
33 Nowak 96
34 Lundine 88

NORTH CAROLINA
1 Jones 85
2 Valentine 95
3 Whitley 96
4 Andrews 88
5 Neal 83#
6 Britt 95
7 Rose 84
8 Hefner 88#
9 Martin 90†
10 Broyhill 94
11 Clarke 95

NORTH DAKOTA
AL Dorgan 94

OHIO
1 Luken 93
2 Gradison 96
3 Hall 91
4 Oxley 94
5 Latta 94
6 McEwen 97#
7 DeWine 97
8 Kindness 96
9 Kaptur 96
10 Miller 96
11 Eckart 98
12 Kasich 99
13 Pease 99
14 Seiberling 96
15 Wylie 93
16 Regula 99
17 Williams 83
18 Applegate 88
19 Feighan 93
20 Oakar 98
21 Stokes 88

OKLAHOMA
1 Jones 97
2 Synar 97
3 Watkins 95
4 McCurdy 91
5 Edwards 92†
6 English 98

OREGON
1 AuCoin 89
2 Smith, B. 85
3 Wyden 98
4 Weaver 89
5 Smith D. 86

PENNSYLVANIA
1 Foglietta 90
2 Gray 91
3 Borski 98
4 Kolter 85#
5 Schulze 87
6 Yatron 95#
7 Edgar 88
8 Kostmayer 92
9 Shuster 91
10 McDade 86#
11 Harrison 91
12 Murtha 95
13 Coughlin 95
14 Coyne 96
15 Ritter 96
16 Walker 99
17 Gekas 97
18 Walgren 95
19 Goodling 90
20 Gaydos 92#
21 Ridge 94
22 Murphy 94
23 Clinger 99†

RHODE ISLAND
1 St Germain 80
2 Schneider 92

SOUTH CAROLINA
1 Hartnett 89
2 Spence 97
3 Derrick 87
4 Campbell 89
5 Spratt 95
6 Tallon 96

SOUTH DAKOTA
AL Daschle 88

TENNESSEE
1 Quillen 91
2 Duncan 96
3 Lloyd 91#
4 Cooper 93
5 Boner 89
6 Gore 91
7 Sundquist 97
8 Jones 85#
9 Ford 83

TEXAS
1 Hall, S. 97
2 Wilson 78
3 Bartlett 96
4 Hall, R. 95
5 Bryant 93
6 Gramm [7] 81†
7 Archer 97
8 Fields 95
9 Brooks 93
10 Pickle 91#
11 Leath 90
12 Wright 94
13 Hightower 91
14 Patman 99
15 de la Garza 86
16 Coleman 96
17 Stenholm 97
18 Leland 88
19 Hance 68
20 Gonzalez 98
21 Loeffler 98
22 Paul 80
23 Kazen 94
24 Frost 92
25 Andrews 97
26 Vandergriff 96
27 Ortiz 95

UTAH
1 Hansen 85
2 Marriott 91
3 Nielson 93

VERMONT
AL Jeffords 90

VIRGINIA
1 Bateman 95
2 Whitehurst 91
3 Bliley 97
4 Sisisky 95
5 Daniel 96
6 Olin 97
7 Robinson 98
8 Parris 92
9 Boucher 96
10 Wolf 99

WASHINGTON
1 Pritchard 64
2 Swift 95
3 Bonker 90
4 Morrison 93#
5 Foley 89#
6 Dicks 93
7 Lowry 91
8 Chandler 95

WEST VIRGINIA
1 Mollohan 98
2 Staggers 97
3 Wise 97
4 Rahall 91

WISCONSIN
1 Aspin 89
2 Kastenmeier 95
3 Gunderson 99
4 Zablocki 96
5 Moody 94
6 Petri 99
7 Obey 97
8 Roth 97
9 Sensenbrenner 99

WYOMING
AL Cheney 87

State / Senator	Score	State / Senator	Score	State / Senator	Score
ALABAMA		**IOWA**		**NEW HAMPSHIRE**	
Denton	91	*Grassley*	99	*Humphrey*	92
Heflin	94†	*Jepsen*	99	*Rudman*	99
ALASKA		**KANSAS**		**NEW JERSEY**	
Murkowski	85#	*Dole*	96	Bradley	97
Stevens	92	*Kassebaum*	96	Lautenberg	95#
ARIZONA		**KENTUCKY**		**NEW MEXICO**	
Goldwater	61#	Ford	98	*Domenici*	88#
DeConcini	84	Huddleston	94	Bingaman	98
ARKANSAS		**LOUISIANA**		**NEW YORK**	
Bumpers	91	Johnston	92	*D'Amato*	96
Pryor	92	Long	86	Moynihan	92
CALIFORNIA		**MAINE**		**NORTH CAROLINA**	
Wilson	98	*Cohen*	95	*East*	96
Cranston	56	Mitchell	99	*Helms*	97
COLORADO		**MARYLAND**		**NORTH DAKOTA**	
Armstrong	93	*Mathias*	83#	*Andrews*	94
Hart	63	Sarbanes	97	Burdick	98
CONNECTICUT		**MASSACHUSETTS**		**OHIO**	
Weicker	87	Kennedy	87	Glenn	64
Dodd	81	Tsongas	94	Metzenbaum	96
DELAWARE		**MICHIGAN**		**OKLAHOMA**	
Roth	98	Levin	98	*Nickles*	97
Biden	94#	Riegle	96†#	Boren	96
FLORIDA		**MINNESOTA**		**OREGON**	
Hawkins	90	*Boschwitz*	94	*Hatfield*	88
Chiles	96	*Durenberger*	90	*Packwood*	94#
GEORGIA		**MISSISSIPPI**		**PENNSYLVANIA**	
Mattingly	99	*Cochran*	94	*Heinz*	95
Nunn	96†	Stennis	95	*Specter*	99
HAWAII		**MISSOURI**		**RHODE ISLAND**	
Inouye	81	*Danforth*	98	*Chafee*	98
Matsunaga	95#	Eagleton	92	Pell	95
IDAHO		**MONTANA**		**SOUTH CAROLINA**	
McClure	89	Baucus	96	*Thurmond*	97
Symms	94	Melcher	98	Hollings	50
ILLINOIS		**NEBRASKA**		**SOUTH DAKOTA**	
Percy	82	Exon	97	*Abdnor*	99
Dixon	93	Zorinsky	95†	*Pressler*	95
INDIANA		**NEVADA**		**TENNESSEE**	
Lugar	100	*Hecht*	99	*Baker*	94#
Quayle	95	*Laxalt*	91	Sasser	95†#

KEY

† Not eligible for all recorded votes in 1983 (sworn in after Jan. 3, died or resigned during session, or voted "present" to avoid possible conflict of interest).

\# Member absent a day or more in 1983 due to illness or illness or death in family.

———

Democrats *Republicans*

State / Senator	Score
TEXAS	
Tower	89
Bentsen	92
UTAH	
Garn	98
Hatch	99
VERMONT	
Stafford	93
Leahy	98
VIRGINIA	
Trible	98
Warner	99
WASHINGTON	
Evans [1]	67†
Gorton	99
WEST VIRGINIA	
Byrd	99
Randolph	97#
WISCONSIN	
Kasten	96
Proxmire	100
WYOMING	
Simpson	92
Wallop	94

Voting Participation Scores: Senate

Voting Participation, 1983. Percentage of 371 roll calls in 1983 on which senator voted "yea" or "nay."

1. *Sen. Daniel J. Evans, R-Wash., sworn in Sept. 12, 1983, to succeed Henry M. Jackson, D, who died Sept. 1, 1983. Jackson's 1983 voting participation score was 100 percent.*

Coalition Vote Study:

Conservative Strength Falters In Wake of United Democrats

Republicans and Southern Democrats joined forces in Congress less frequently in 1983 than in any year since 1964, according to a Congressional Quarterly vote analysis.

When this conservative coalition did appear, it won fewer votes than it did in 1981 or 1982. But the conservative alliance still won more victories in 1983 than it did in the years before President Reagan took office in 1981.

The decline in the conservative coalition's strength in 1983 was due in large part to the Democrats' gain of 26 House seats in the 1982 elections, renewed unity among House Democrats and a drop in congressional support for Reagan's policies.

The conservative coalition score is based on recorded votes in which a majority of Republicans and Southern Democrats vote together against a majority of Northern Democrats.

In 1983 the alignment appeared in 15 percent of the recorded votes for both houses, the lowest coalition appearance rate since 1964 — the year of major civil rights and anti-poverty victories — when it also was 15 percent.

In 1982 the conservative coalition appeared in 18 percent of the recorded votes, and it was apparent in 21 percent of the 1981 roll calls.

In Congress as a whole, the Republican-Southern Democratic alliance was successful 77 percent of the time it was a factor in 1983 votes, down from an 85 percent success rate in 1982 and 92 percent in 1981. But the conservative coalition's 1983 victory rate was still better than its record in the nine years prior to Reagan's inauguration.

In the House, the coalition's success rate continued to slip from the 1981 high of 88 percent. In 1983 the coalition won 71 percent of the affected votes, down from 78 percent in 1982.

The number of conservative coalition triumphs dipped slightly in the Senate, from 90 percent in 1982 to 89 percent in 1983. In 1981, the year Republicans took control of the Senate, the score was 95 percent.

While CQ's vote study reflected common views held by Southern Democrats and Republicans on certain legislation, it did not involve any sort of organized conservative entity, nor any philosophic definitions of conservatism.

The coalition showed up most frequently in roll calls favoring increased defense spending or the procurement of new weapons.

One explanation for the declining strength of the conservative coalition was that many Southern Democrats returned to the fold in 1983, after two years in which they frequently had teamed up with Republicans.

Southern Democratic senators supported the conservative coalition 62 percent of the time in 1983, compared to 73 percent in 1982. In the House, Democrats from the South agreed with the coalition 65 percent of the time, down from 66 percent in 1982.

While Southern Democrats and Republicans tended to vote with the conservative alliance more than members from other regions, Easterners from both parties usually voted with the coalition least often. The sole exception was among House Democrats, where Western representatives opposed the coalition 75 percent of the time, compared to a

Definitions

Conservative Coalition. As used in this study, the term "conservative coalition" means a voting alliance of Republicans and Southern Democrats against the Northern Democrats in Congress. This meaning, rather than any philosophic definition of the "conservative coalition" position, provides the basis for CQ's selection of coalition votes.

Conservative Coalition Vote. Any vote in the Senate or the House on which a majority of voting Southern Democrats and a majority of voting Republicans opposed the stand taken by a majority of voting Northern Democrats. Votes on which there is an even division within the ranks of voting Northern Democrats, Southern Democrats or Republicans are not included.

Southern States. The Southern states are Alabama, Arkansas, Florida, Georgia, Kentucky, Louisiana, Mississippi, North Carolina, Oklahoma, South Carolina, Tennessee, Texas and Virginia. The other 37 states are grouped as the North in this study.

Conservative Coalition Support Score. Percentage of conservative coalition votes on which member votes "yea" or "nay" *in agreement* with the position of the conservative coalition. Failures to vote, even if a member announces a stand, lower the score.

Conservative Coalition Opposition Score. Percentage of conservative coalition votes on which a member votes "yea" or "nay" *in disagreement* with the position of the conservative coalition.

74 percent opposition rate among Eastern Democrats.

Individual Members' Scores

Among Senate Republicans, Mack Mattingly, R-Ga., and Jake Garn, R-Utah, joined the conservative coalition on every vote on which it was united in 1983. The Southern Democratic senator voting most consistently with the coalition was Sam Nunn, D-Ga. The Northern Democratic senators who registered the highest coalition support scores were Nebraskans Edward Zorinsky and J. James Exon.

Paul E. Tsongas, D-Mass., opposed the coalition 89 percent of the time in 1983, more than any other senator.

Lowell P. Weicker Jr., R-Conn., voted against the conservative coalition more often than any other Republican senator. The Southern Democrat who differed the most with the coalition was Jim Sasser, D-Tenn.

While a 100 percent conservative coalition support score in the House went to George W. "Buddy" Darden, D-Ga., he was present for only a handful of votes because he was not elected until Nov. 8 to take the seat of Larry P. McDonald, D-Ga., who died Sept. 1. The next highest coalition support score among House Southern Democrats went to Earl Hutto, D-Fla.

Among House Republicans, Tom Loeffler, R-Texas, and J. Kenneth Robinson, R-Va., voted with the coalition 98 percent of the time. Two Maryland Democrats, Beverly B. Byron and Roy Dyson, had the highest support scores among Northern Democrats.

The House member who opposed the conservative coalition most often was Bruce F. Vento, D-Minn. He was followed by William H. Gray III, D-Pa., and Barbara

Boxer, D-Calif. Jim Leach, R-Iowa, and Claudine Schneider, R-R.I., voted against the coalition more than any other House Republicans.

Coalition Victories

Many of the conservative coalition's 1983 victories in the House and Senate were on defense spending.

With the coalition's backing, Reagan won endorsement for nearly every major weapons system he sought, including the MX missile. The exception was the production of binary chemical weapons, which Congress refused to fund — a loss for the conservative coalition.

The Senate's conservative alliance faltered during consideration of the fiscal 1984 budget resolution, and Democrats and moderate Republicans joined to pass a budget more to their liking.

In the House, the conservative coalition lost a series of amendments designed to water down the nuclear freeze proposal. The coalition also was defeated when it tried to block passage of an administration-backed $8.4 billion increase in the U.S. contribution to the International Monetary Fund.

The House coalition was successful, however, in stopping an effort to cut off financing for U.S. troops in Lebanon within a certain period. Instead, with the coalition's support, Congress agreed to keep Marines in Lebanon for up to 18 months after the measure's passage.

Coalition Appearances

Following is the percentage of the recorded votes for both houses of Congress on which the coalition appeared:

Year	%	Year	%
1964	15%	1974	24
1965	24	1975	28
1966	25	1976	24
1967	20	1977	26
1968	24	1978	21
1969	27	1979	20
1970	22	1980	18
1971	30	1981	21
1972	27	1982	18
1973	23	1983	15

Coalition Victories

Year	Total	Senate	House
1964	51%	47%	67%
1965	33	39	25
1966	45	51	32
1967	63	54	73
1968	73	80	63
1969	68	67	71
1970	66	64	70
1971	83	86	79
1972	69	63	79
1973	61	54	67
1974	59	54	67
1975	50	48	52
1976	58	58	59
1977	68	74	60
1978	52	46	57
1979	70	65	73
1980	72	75	67
1981	92	95	88
1982	85	90	78
1983	77	89	71

Average Scores

Following are the composite conservative coalition support and opposition scores for 1983 (scores for 1982 are in parentheses):

	Southern Democrats	Republicans	Northern Democrats
Coalition Support			
Senate	62% (73)	75% (76)	28% (28)
House	65 (66)	78 (75)	21 (24)
Coalition Opposition			
Senate	28% (23)	18% (18)	64% (65)
House	30 (25)	18 (18)	74 (68)

Regional Scores

Following are the parties' coalition support and opposition scores by region for 1983 (scores for 1982 are in parentheses):

SUPPORT

	East	West	South	Midwest
DEMOCRATS				
Senate	21% (19)	28% (34)	62% (73)	38% (35)
House	21 (23)	18 (23)	65 (66)	24 (26)
REPUBLICANS				
Senate	58% (53)	77% (83)	88% (91)	75% (77)
House	63 (62)	86 (82)	88 (85)	77 (74)

OPPOSITION

	East	West	South	Midwest
DEMOCRATS				
Senate	74% (74)	57% (57)	28% (23)	56% (59)
House	74 (68)	75 (69)	30 (25)	72 (66)
REPUBLICANS				
Senate	37% (41)	13% (11)	8% (4)	20% (19)
House	33 (31)	9 (9)	9 (9)	19 (19)

*(CQ defines regions of the United States as follows: **East:** Conn., Del., Maine, Md., Mass., N.H., N.J., N.Y., Pa., R.I., Vt., W.Va. **West:** Alaska, Ariz., Calif., Colo., Hawaii, Idaho, Mont., Nev., N.M., Ore., Utah, Wash., Wyo. **South:** Ala., Ark., Fla., Ga., Ky., La., Miss., N.C., Okla, S.C., Tenn., Texas, Va. **Midwest:** Ill., Ind., Iowa, Kan., Mich., Minn., Mo., Neb., N.D., Ohio, S.D., Wis.)*

Individual Scores

SUPPORT

Highest Coalition Support Scores. Those who voted with the conservative coalition most consistently in 1983:

SENATE

Southern Democrats		Republicans	
Nunn, Ga.	84%	Mattingly, Ga.	100%
Long, La.	82	Garn, Utah	100
Johnston, La.	82	East, N.C.	98
Heflin, Ala.	77	Helms, N.C.	95
Boren, Okla.	73	Lugar, Ind.	95

Northern Democrats

Zorinsky, Neb.	79%
Exon, Neb.	70
Randolph, W.Va.	57
Dixon, Ill.	55
DeConcini, Ariz.	52

HOUSE

Southern Democrats[1]		Republicans	
Darden, Ga.	100%[2]	Loeffler, Texas	98%
Hutto, Fla.	96	Robinson, Va.	98
Montgomery, Miss.	94	Spence, S.C.	97
Daniel, Va.	93	Dreier, Calif.	97
Leath, Texas	92	Lott, Miss.	97
Stenholm, Texas	92	Moorhead, Calif.	96
Ray, Ga.	91	Franklin, Miss.	96
Valentine, N.C.	90	Bliley, Va.	96
Tauzin, La.	90	Archer, Texas	96
Lloyd, Tenn.	90		

Northern Democrats

Byron, Md.	87%
Dyson, Md.	75
Skelton, Mo.	74
Stratton, N.Y.	70
Slattery, Kan.	58
Murtha, Pa.	58
Price, Ill.	56
Lipinski, Ill.	55
Mollohan, W.Va.	54

OPPOSITION

Highest Coalition Opposition Scores. Those who voted against the conservative coalition most consistently in 1983:

SENATE

Southern Democrats		Republicans	
Sasser, Tenn.	65%	Weicker, Conn.	61%
Bumpers, Ark.	45	Specter, Pa.	55
Ford, Ky.	43	Mathias, Md.	55
Huddleston, Ky.	39	Chafee, R.I.	50
Pryor, Ark.	34	Hatfield, Ore.	45
Bentsen, Texas	34	Heinz, Pa.	45
Chiles, Fla.	34	Andrews, N.D.	43

Northern Democrats

Tsongas, Mass.	89%
Metzenbaum, Ohio	86
Riegle, Mich.[2]	86

1983 Coalition Votes

Following is a list of all 1983 Senate and House votes on which the conservative coalition appeared. The votes are listed by CQ vote number and may be found in the vote charts beginning on pages 1-S and 1-H.

SENATE VOTES (44)

Coalition Victories (39) — 10, 24, 33, 34, 35, 40, 45, 64, 65, 81, 88, 95, 98, 100, 103, 114, 127, 161, 180, 181, 188, 200, 225, 227, 247, 257, 267, 278, 301, 317, 330, 331, 332, 335, 341, 347, 352, 353, 369.

Coalition Defeats (5) — 104, 110, 112, 169, 297.

HOUSE VOTES (89)

Coalition Victories (63) — 20, 21, 22, 78, 79, 80, 100, 123, 133, 168, 180, 181, 182, 184, 185, 220, 231, 233, 236, 237, 239, 240, 247, 248, 250, 253, 254, 256, 257, 258, 259, 261, 264, 279, 290, 293, 294, 295, 301, 309, 314, 322, 338, 341, 342, 346, 350, 365, 368, 369, 370, 390, 391, 402, 404, 408, 409, 411, 412, 419, 428, 477, 491.

Coalition Defeats (26) — 26, 28, 49, 50, 52, 55, 57, 67, 139, 186, 187, 260, 276, 277, 304, 339, 353, 397, 416, 417, 420, 446, 470, 471, 497, 498.

Sarbanes, Md.	84
Leahy, Vt.	82
Kennedy, Mass.	82
Levin, Mich.	82
Pell, R.I.	82

HOUSE

Southern Democrats		Republicans	
Leland, Texas	84%	Leach, Iowa	71%
Lehman, Fla.	77[2]	Schneider, R.I.	71
Ford, Tenn.	74	Conte, Mass.	67
Smith, Fla.	72	Jeffords, Vt.	67
Fascell, Fla.	66	Green, N.Y.	64
Boucher, Va.	64	McKinney, Conn.	60
Gonzalez, Texas	63	Tauke, Iowa	53
Fowler, Ga.	62	Roukema, N.J.	51
Perkins, Ky.	61	McKernan, Maine	51
Long, La.	61		

Northern Democrats[3]

Vento, Minn.	96%
Gray, Pa.	93
Boxer, Calif.	92
Kildee, Mich.	91
Dellums, Calif.	91
Edgar, Pa.	91
Ottinger, N.Y.	91
Seiberling, Ohio	91
Kastenmeier, Wis.	91

[1] *Rep. Larry P. McDonald, D-Ga., who died Sept. 1, 1983, scored 93 percent support.*
[2] *Not eligible for all conservative coalition votes in 1983.*
[3] *Rep. Phillip Burton, D-Calif., who died April 10, 1983, scored 100 percent opposition.*

Conservative Coalition Support and Opposition: House

1. Conservative Coalition Support, 1983. Percentage of 89 conservative coalition recorded votes in 1983 on which representative voted "yea" or "nay" *in agreement* with the position of the conservative coalition. Failures to vote lower both support and opposition scores.

2. Conservative Coalition Opposition, 1983. Percentage of 89 conservative coalition recorded votes in 1983 on which representative voted "yea" or "nay" *in disagreement* with the position of the conservative coalition. Failures to vote lower both support and opposition scores.

KEY

† Not eligible for all recorded votes in 1983 (sworn in after Jan. 3, died or resigned during session, or voted "present" to avoid possible conflict of interest).

———————

Democrats   *Republicans*

	1	2
ALABAMA		
1 *Edwards*	80	15
2 *Dickinson*	83	10
3 Nichols	82	11
4 Bevill	80	17
5 Flippo	80	13
6 Erdreich	78	21
7 Shelby	76	20
ALASKA		
AL *Young*	78	7
ARIZONA		
1 *McCain*	90	7
2 Udall	22	69
3 *Stump*	92	7
4 *Rudd*	88	6
5 McNulty	33	65
ARKANSAS		
1 Alexander	39	44
2 *Bethune*	75	20
3 *Hammerschmidt*	88	7
4 Anthony	64	36
CALIFORNIA		
1 Bosco	28	61
2 *Chappie*	91	1
3 Matsui	24	76
4 Fazio	24	72
5 Burton [1]	11†	79†
6 Boxer	4	92
7 Miller	13	75
8 Dellums	2	91
9 Stark	12	83
10 Edwards	7	89
11 Lantos	20	76
12 *Zschau*	73	27
13 Mineta	8	88
14 *Shumway*	90	2
15 Coelho	21	64
16 Panetta	21	78
17 *Pashayan*	85	4
18 Lehman	15	79
19 *Lagomarsino*	88	12
20 *Thomas*	84	10
21 *Fiedler*	92	8
22 *Moorhead*	96	2
23 Beilenson	16	84
24 Waxman	6	85
25 Roybal	7	89
26 Berman	10	88
27 Levine	20	76
28 Dixon	8	80
29 Hawkins	11	72
30 Martinez	7	73
31 Dymally	11	78
32 Anderson	45	54
33 *Dreier*	97	2
34 Torres	12	85
35 *Lewis*	74	8
36 Brown	11	82
37 *McCandless*	85	11
38 Patterson	24	74
39 *Dannemeyer*	84	9
40 *Badham*	84	4
41 *Lowery*	83	15
42 Lungren	91	6
43 *Packard*	91	2
44 Bates	18	78
45 *Hunter*	93	7
COLORADO		
1 Schroeder	18	78
2 Wirth	16	81
3 Kogovsek	17	79
4 *Brown*	75	25
5 *Kramer*	88	7
6 *Schaefer* [2]	92†	7†
CONNECTICUT		
1 Kennelly	12	83
2 Gejdenson	9	90
3 Morrison	8	88
4 *McKinney*	30	60
5 Ratchford	11	88
6 *Johnson*	54	46
DELAWARE		
AL Carper	35	65
FLORIDA		
1 Hutto	96	2
2 Fuqua	80	15
3 Bennett	72	28
4 Chappell	88	4
5 *McCollum*	94	3
6 MacKay	56	37
7 Gibbons	38	55
8 *Young*	87	11
9 *Bilirakis*	93	4
10 Ireland	89	7
11 Nelson	84	12
12 *Lewis*	91	8
13 *Mack*	92	6
14 Mica	52	46
15 *Shaw*	93	4
16 Smith	26	72
17 Lehman	18†	77†
18 Pepper	36	57
19 Fascell	31	66
GEORGIA		
1 Thomas	84	16
2 Hatcher	76	12
3 Ray	91	8
4 Levitas	73	25
5 Fowler	35	62
6 *Gingrich*	87	8
7 Darden [3]	100†	0†
8 Rowland	88	12
9 Jenkins	79	12
10 Barnard	78	12
HAWAII		
1 Heftel	17	25
2 Akaka	42	56
IDAHO		
1 *Craig*	93	3
2 *Hansen*	84	1
ILLINOIS		
1 Hayes [4]	9†	85†
2 Savage	4	84
3 Russo	26	72
4 *O'Brien*	74	18
5 Lipinski	55	42
6 *Hyde*	88	12
7 Collins	7	88
8 Rostenkowski	33	64
9 Yates	7	87
10 *Porter*	67	30
11 Annunzio	38	56
12 *Crane, P.*	92	6
13 *Erlenborn*	79	12
14 *Corcoran*	73	6
15 *Madigan*	75	18
16 *Martin*	66	31
17 Evans	13	84
18 *Michel*	81	15
19 *Crane, D.*	87	7
20 Durbin	31	69
21 Price	56	40
22 Simon	17	56
INDIANA		
1 Hall	7	88
2 Sharp	35	64
3 *Hiler*	92	8
4 *Coats*	84	16
5 *Hillis*	79	18

1. Rep. Sala Burton, D-Calif., sworn in June 28, 1983, to succeed her husband, Phillip Burton, D, who died April 10, 1983. Phillip Burton's 1983 conservative coalition support score was zero; opposition was 100 percent.

2. Rep. Daniel L. Schaefer, R-Colo., sworn in April 7, 1983, to succeed Rep.-elect Jack Swigert, R, who died Dec. 27, 1982.

3. Rep. George W. "Buddy" Darden, D-Ga., sworn in Nov. 10, 1983, to succeed Larry P. McDonald, D, who died Sept. 1, 1983. McDonald's 1983 conservative coalition support score was 93 percent; opposition was 5 percent.

4. Rep. Charles A. Hayes, D-Ill., sworn in Sept. 12, 1983, to succeed Harold Washington, D, who resigned April 30, 1983. Washington did not vote on any of the 11 conservative coalition votes for which he was eligible.

5. Rep. Thomas P. O'Neill Jr., D-Mass., as Speaker, votes at his own discretion.

	1	2
6 Burton	93	6
7 Myers	88	8
8 McCloskey	29	69
9 Hamilton	42	58
10 Jacobs	31	64
IOWA		
1 Leach	28	71
2 Tauke	42	53
3 Evans	49	48
4 Smith	29	66
5 Harkin	16	81
6 Bedell	20	78
KANSAS		
1 Roberts	85	13
2 Slattery	58	38
3 Winn	90	6
4 Glickman	46	53
5 Whittaker	92	8
KENTUCKY		
1 Hubbard	70	25
2 Natcher	53	47
3 Mazzoli	51	48
4 Snyder	83	17
5 Rogers	89	10
6 Hopkins	85	12
7 Perkins	37	61
LOUISIANA		
1 Livingston	85	12
2 Boggs	51	44
3 Tauzin	90	10
4 Roemer	79	21
5 Huckaby	85	13
6 Moore	89	11
7 Breaux	85	9
8 Long	37	61
MAINE		
1 McKernan	48	51
2 Snowe	49	49
MARYLAND		
1 Dyson	75	24
2 Long	35	62
3 Mikulski	18	76
4 Holt	87	3
5 Hoyer	29	70
6 Byron	87	10
7 Mitchell	4	82
8 Barnes	17	83
MASSACHUSETTS		
1 Conte	31	67
2 Boland	24	70
3 Early	17	73
4 Frank	9	89
5 Shannon	11	88
6 Mavroules	18	80
7 Markey	8	90
8 O'Neill [5]		
9 Moakley	11	82
10 Studds	6	88
11 Donnelly	22	75
MICHIGAN		
1 Conyers	4	73
2 Pursell	69	26
3 Wolpe	11	88
4 Siljander	90	9
5 Sawyer	73	18
6 Carr	25	72
7 Kildee	9	91
8 Traxler	24	70
9 Vander Jagt	79	13
10 Albosta	49	51
11 Davis	73	24
12 Bonior	13	81
13 Crockett	8	82
14 Hertel	20	78
15 Ford	8	82
16 Dingell	16	78
17 Levin	19	81
18 Broomfield	80	16
MINNESOTA		
1 Penny	29	69
2 Weber	72	25
3 Frenzel	61	34
4 Vento	4	96
5 Sabo	9	90
6 Sikorski	13	87

	1	2
7 Stangeland	75	21
8 Oberstar	9	89
MISSISSIPPI		
1 Whitten	63	31
2 Franklin	96	0
3 Montgomery	94	3
4 Dowdy	49	37
5 Lott	97	1
MISSOURI		
1 Clay	2	85
2 Young	44	51
3 Gephardt	25	69
4 Skelton	74	22
5 Wheat	10	90
6 Coleman	83	13
7 Taylor	91	6
8 Emerson	90	9
9 Volkmer	46	54
MONTANA		
1 Williams	18	74
2 Marlenee	80	9
NEBRASKA		
1 Bereuter	70	29
2 Daub	88	12
3 Smith	80	20
NEVADA		
1 Reid	35	65
2 Vucanovich	90	7
NEW HAMPSHIRE		
1 D'Amours	39	57
2 Gregg	73	20
NEW JERSEY		
1 Florio	26	70
2 Hughes	38	62
3 Howard	12	79
4 Smith	60	39
5 Roukema	47	51
6 Dwyer	17	82
7 Rinaldo	53	44
8 Roe	26	71
9 Torricelli	16	80
10 Rodino	6	79
11 Minish	21	76
12 Courter	74	20
13 Forsythe	44	35
14 Guarini	15	80
NEW MEXICO		
1 Lujan	91	7
2 Skeen	94	4
3 Richardson	29	71
NEW YORK		
1 Carney	84	13
2 Downey	10	84
3 Mrazek	27	73
4 Lent	78	19
5 McGrath	79	20
6 Addabbo	10	81
7 Ackerman	12	87
8 Scheuer	10	90
9 Ferraro	16	80
10 Schumer	13	84
11 Towns	7	89
12 Owens	6	78
13 Solarz	16	72
14 Molinari	70	24
15 Green	35	64
16 Rangel	9	87
17 Weiss	9	87
18 Garcia	9	84
19 Biaggi	19	65
20 Ottinger	7	91
21 Fish	55	40
22 Gilman	61	38
23 Stratton	70	28
24 Solomon	94	4
25 Boehlert	49	47
26 Martin	88	11
27 Wortley	80	19
28 McHugh	12	87
29 Horton	43	47
30 Conable	73	25
31 Kemp	83	10
32 LaFalce	19	75
33 Nowak	12	85
34 Lundine	18	76

	1	2
NORTH CAROLINA		
1 Jones	62	29
2 Valentine	90	8
3 Whitley	88	11
4 Andrews	47	45
5 Neal	55	33
6 Britt	52	46
7 Rose	42	42
8 Hefner	72	22
9 Martin	82	17
10 Broyhill	82	11
11 Clarke	54	44
NORTH DAKOTA		
AL Dorgan	33	60
OHIO		
1 Luken	27	67
2 Gradison	73	26
3 Hall	26	72
4 Oxley	83	16
5 Latta	81	13
6 McEwen	87	9
7 DeWine	89	10
8 Kindness	83	17
9 Kaptur	15	82
10 Miller	73	25
11 Eckart	26	74
12 Kasich	87	13
13 Pease	18	82
14 Seiberling	9	91
15 Wylie	72	20
16 Regula	80	20
17 Williams	56	28
18 Applegate	48	49
19 Feighan	22	75
20 Oakar	22	75
21 Stokes	6	85
OKLAHOMA		
1 Jones	64	34
2 Synar	43	55
3 Watkins	79	21
4 McCurdy	79	13
5 Edwards	90	7
6 English	85	15
OREGON		
1 AuCoin	19	75
2 Smith, B.	90	7
3 Wyden	15	84
4 Weaver	17	74
5 Smith D.	85	6
PENNSYLVANIA		
1 Foglietta	11	85
2 Gray	2	93
3 Borski	16	83
4 Kolter	30	62
5 Schulze	83	8
6 Yatron	42	57
7 Edgar	4	91
8 Kostmayer	8	84
9 Shuster	90	8
10 McDade	60	31
11 Harrison	24	70
12 Murtha	58	38
13 Coughlin	52	45
14 Coyne	12	85
15 Ritter	82	16
16 Walker	81	19
17 Gekas	76	22
18 Walgren	17	80
19 Goodling	61	38
20 Gaydos	35	58
21 Ridge	66	31
22 Murphy	38	57
23 Clinger	66	34
RHODE ISLAND		
1 St Germain	17	69
2 Schneider	24	71
SOUTH CAROLINA		
1 Hartnett	89	3
2 Spence	97	2
3 Derrick	42	49
4 Campbell	93	6
5 Spratt	60	40
6 Tallon	55	43
SOUTH DAKOTA		
AL Daschle	42	51

	1	2
TENNESSEE		
1 Quillen	85	10
2 Duncan	85	10
3 Lloyd	90	7
4 Cooper	56	35
5 Boner	61	31
6 Gore	39	58
7 Sundquist	91	6
8 Jones	65	25
9 Ford	10	74
TEXAS		
1 Hall, S.	89	11
2 Wilson	66	13
3 Bartlett	85	13
4 Hall, R.	83	11
5 Bryant	36	60
6 Gramm	93	0
7 Archer	96	4
8 Fields	92	4
9 Brooks	47	51
10 Pickle	72	21
11 Leath	92	1
12 Wright	56	39
13 Hightower	87	8
14 Patman	82	18
15 de la Garza	61	27
16 Coleman	48	49
17 Stenholm	92	7
18 Leland	4	84
19 Hance	67	6
20 Gonzalez	31	63
21 Loeffler	98	1
22 Paul	48	35
23 Kazen	88	8
24 Frost	48	47
25 Andrews	78	21
26 Vandergriff	85	12
27 Ortiz	66	29
UTAH		
1 Hansen	89	2
2 Marriott	83	10
3 Nielson	92	7
VERMONT		
AL Jeffords	27	67
VIRGINIA		
1 Bateman	85	13
2 Whitehurst	87	10
3 Bliley	96	3
4 Sisisky	75	21
5 Daniel	93	3
6 Olin	65	34
7 Robinson	98	2
8 Parris	79	11
9 Boucher	29	64
10 Wolf	87	13
WASHINGTON		
1 Pritchard	45	29
2 Swift	11	89
3 Bonker	18	80
4 Morrison	79	19
5 Foley	25	55
6 Dicks	34	60
7 Lowry	7	83
8 Chandler	78	22
WEST VIRGINIA		
1 Mollohan	54	46
2 Staggers	30	70
3 Wise	30	67
4 Rahall	29	62
WISCONSIN		
1 Aspin	29	57
2 Kastenmeier	8	91
3 Gunderson	65	35
4 Zablocki	35	64
5 Moody	15	82
6 Petri	72	28
7 Obey	11	88
8 Roth	82	18
9 Sensenbrenner	74	25
WYOMING		
AL Cheney	89	6

Southern states · Ala., Ark., Fla., Ga., Ky., La., Miss., N.C., Okla., S.C., Tenn., Texas, Va.

	1	2		1	2		1	2
ALABAMA			**IOWA**			**NEW HAMPSHIRE**		
Denton	91	7	*Grassley*	77	23	*Humphrey*	82	11
Heflin	77†	16†	*Jepsen*	89	11	*Rudman*	80	20
ALASKA			**KANSAS**			**NEW JERSEY**		
Murkowski	80	0	*Dole*	89	7	Bradley	23	75
Stevens	77	16	*Kassebaum*	59	36	Lautenberg	14	80
ARIZONA			**KENTUCKY**			**NEW MEXICO**		
Goldwater	61	7	Ford	52	43	*Domenici*	75	9
DeConcini	52	32	Huddleston	61	39	Bingaman	25	73
ARKANSAS			**LOUISIANA**			**NEW YORK**		
Bumpers	41	45	Johnston	82	5	*D'Amato*	70	27
Pryor	57	34	Long	82	2	Moynihan	16	80
CALIFORNIA			**MAINE**			**NORTH CAROLINA**		
Wilson	86	7	*Cohen*	73	23	*East*	98	2
Cranston	7	52	Mitchell	30	70	*Helms*	95	2
COLORADO			**MARYLAND**			**NORTH DAKOTA**		
Armstrong	89	5	*Mathias*	32	55	*Andrews*	52	43
Hart	9	52	Sarbanes	11	84	Burdick	36	59
CONNECTICUT			**MASSACHUSETTS**			**OHIO**		
Weicker	36	61	Kennedy	11	82	Glenn	20	52
Dodd	14	64	Tsongas	9	89	Metzenbaum	11	86
DELAWARE			**MICHIGAN**			**OKLAHOMA**		
Roth	77	20	Levin	14	82	*Nickles*	91	5
Biden	23	68	Riegle	14†	86†	Boren	73	25
FLORIDA			**MINNESOTA**			**OREGON**		
Hawkins	80	9	*Boschwitz*	66	30	*Hatfield*	45	45
Chiles	64	34	*Durenberger*	57	36	*Packwood*	50	41
GEORGIA			**MISSISSIPPI**			**PENNSYLVANIA**		
Mattingly	100	0	*Cochran*	77	16	*Heinz*	52	45
Nunn	84	11	Stennis	73	20	*Specter*	45	55
HAWAII			**MISSOURI**			**RHODE ISLAND**		
Inouye	9	66	*Danforth*	64	32	*Chafee*	45	50
Matsunaga	27	70	Eagleton	27	61	Pell	14	82
IDAHO			**MONTANA**			**SOUTH CAROLINA**		
McClure	82	0	Baucus	45	55	*Thurmond*	93	7
Symms	86	9	Melcher	39	61	Hollings	23	20
ILLINOIS			**NEBRASKA**			**SOUTH DAKOTA**		
Percy	57	27	Exon	70	25	*Abdnor*	93	7
Dixon	55	43	Zorinsky	79†	19†	*Pressler*	80	16
INDIANA			**NEVADA**			**TENNESSEE**		
Lugar	95	5	*Hecht*	91	9	*Baker*	84	9
Quayle	86	5	*Laxalt*	82	7	Sasser	35†	65†

KEY

† Not eligible for all recorded votes in 1983 (sworn in after Jan. 3, died or resigned during session, or voted "present" to avoid possible conflict of interest).

———

Democrats *Republicans*

	1	2
TEXAS		
Tower	73	14
Bentsen	64	34
UTAH		
Garn	100	0
Hatch	93	7
VERMONT		
Stafford	48	41
Leahy	18	82
VIRGINIA		
Trible	84	11
Warner	89	11
WASHINGTON		
Evans [1]	44†	0†
Gorton	70	30
WEST VIRGINIA		
Byrd	36	61
Randolph	57	43
WISCONSIN		
Kasten	93	7
Proxmire	50	50
WYOMING		
Simpson	75	18
Wallop	82	9

(Southern states - Ala., Ark., Fla., Ga., Ky., La., Miss., N.C., Okla., S.C., Tenn., Texas, Va.)

Conservative Coalition
Support and Opposition: Senate

1. Conservative Coalition Support, 1983. Percentage of 44 conservative coalition votes in 1983 on which senator voted "yea" or "nay" *in agreement* with the position of the conservative coalition. Failures to vote lower both support and opposition scores.

2. Conservative Coalition Opposition, 1983. Percentage of 44 conservative coalition votes in 1983 on which senator voted "yea" or "nay" *in disagreement* with the position of the conservative coalition. Failures to vote lower both support and opposition scores.

1. Sen. Daniel J. Evans, R-Wash., sworn in Sept. 12, 1983, to succeed Henry M. Jackson, D, who died Sept. 1, 1983. Jackson's 1983 conservative coalition support score was 46 percent; opposition was 54 percent.

LOBBY REGISTRATIONS

CQ

November 1982 Registrations

Citizens' Groups

COALITION FOR ENVIRONMENTAL-ENERGY BALANCE, Columbus, Ohio. Lobbyist — James M. Friedman, 700 Terminal Tower, Cleveland, Ohio 44113. Filed 11/5/82. Legislative interest — "Environmental and energy legislation, generally, and proposed amendments to the Clean Air Act, 42 U.S.C. Section 7401 et seq., specifically."

MOVE DETROIT FORWARD FUND, Detroit, Mich. Lobbyist — Gnau, Carter, Jacobsen & Associates Inc., 1777 F St. N.W., Washington, D.C. 20006. Filed 11/3/82. Legislative interest — "Housing, job training, government business loan guarantees."

NANA REGIONAL CORP. INC., Kotzebue, Alaska. Lobbyist — Baenen, Timme, De Reitzes & Middleton, 1049 30th St. N.W., Washington, D.C. 20007. Filed 11/1/82. Legislative interest — "... including but not limited to all matters relating generally to Alaska, its lands and natural resources, the Alaska Native Claims Settlement Act, matters relating to Indians, Eskimos and Aleuts, generally."

NATIONAL AUDUBON SOCIETY, 950 Third Ave., New York, N.Y. 10022. Filed for self 11/8/82. Legislative interest — "Public land issues, wilderness legislation, Clean Air Act (support), Clean Water Act (support); and related appropriations and budget legislation...." Lobbyist — Brock Evans, 645 Pennsylvania Ave. S.E., Washington, D.C. 20003.

Corporations and Businesses

AMURCON CORP., Southfield, Mich. Lobbyist — Gnau, Carter, Jacobsen & Associates Inc., 1777 F St. N.W., Washington, D.C. 20006. Filed 11/3/82. Legislative interest — "... housing."

BEZTAK CO., Southfield, Mich. Lobbyist — Gnau, Carter, Jacobsen & Associates Inc., 1777 F St. N.W., Washington, D.C. 20006. Filed 11/3/82. Legislative interest — "Housing and taxation laws."

BROWNING-FERRIS INDUSTRIES INC., P.O. Box 3151, Houston, Texas 77253. Filed for self 11/8/82. Legislative interest — Not specified. Lobbyist — John Shuey.

CAC ASSOCIATES, Muskegon, Mich. Lobbyist — Gnau, Carter, Jacobsen & Associates Inc., 1777 F St. N.W., Washington, D.C. 20006. Filed 11/3/82. Legislative interest — "Government loan guarantees to business."

R. J. CHAMBERS, Royal Oak, Mich. Lobbyist — Gnau, Carter, Jacobsen & Associates Inc., 1777 F St. N.W., Washington, D.C. 20006. Filed 11/3/82. Legislative interest — "Housing."

FRONTIER AIRLINES INC., Denver, Colo. Lobbyist — Baker & Hostetler, 818 Connecticut Ave. N.W., Washington, D.C. 20006. Filed 11/4/82. Legislative interest — "... Department of Transportation and related agencies Appropriations Bill of 1983 ... S 2914 ... supporting provision for settlement of claims for compensation under the Federal Aviation Act."

GENERAL TELEPHONE & ELECTRONICS, Washington, D.C. Lobbyist — Preston, Thorgrimson, Ellis & Holman, 1776 G St. N.W., Washington, D.C. 20006. Filed 11/1/82. Legislative interest — "Tax legislation, specifically in suppport of HR 1524, to amend the normalization method under the Internal Revenue Code for treating public utility property."

GRAND TRAVERSE DEVELOPMENT INC., Bloomfield Hills, Mich. Lobbyist — Gnau, Carter, Jacobsen & Associates Inc., 1777 F St. N.W., Washington, D.C. 20006. Filed 11/3/82. Legislative interest — "Farmers home loan guarantees, housing."

POTTER INSTRUMENT CO. INC., Gonic, N.H. Lobbyist — Gnau, Carter, Jacobsen & Associates Inc., 1777 F St. N.W.,

Washington, D.C. 20006. Filed 11/3/82. Legislative interest — "Government business loan guarantees."

SANDERS CORP., Detroit, Mich. Lobbyist — Gnau, Carter, Jacobsen & Associates Inc., 1777 F St. N.W., Washington, D.C. 20006. Filed 11/3/82. Legislative interest — "Government business loan guarantees."

URBAN REVITALIZATION INC., Detroit, Mich. Lobbyist — Gnau, Carter, Jacobsen & Associates Inc., 1777 F St. N.W., Washington, D.C. 20006. Filed 11/3/82. Legislative interest — "Housing, job training legislation."

WESTINGHOUSE ELECTRIC CORP., Washington, D.C. Lobbyist — Powell, Goldstein, Frazer & Murphy, 1110 Vermont Ave. N.W., Washington, D.C. 20005. Filed 11/8/82. Legislative interest — "... authorization of the Clinch River Breeder Reactor."

Trade Associations

AMERICAN LOGISTICS ASSOCIATION, 1133 15th St. N.W., Washington, D.C. 20005. Filed for self 11/8/82. Legislative interest — "... issues related to military commissaries and exchanges ... support measures to strengthen commissaries and exchanges as a valuable service to the armed forces." Lobbyist — A. Kolbet Schrichte.

CONTACT LENS MANUFACTURERS ASSOCIATION, Newark, N.J. Lobbyist — Rogers, Hoge & Hills, 1111 19th St. N.W., Washington, D.C. 20036. Filed 11/8/82. Legislative interest — Not specified.

NATIONAL COUNCIL OF FARMER COOPERATIVES, 1800 Massachusetts Ave. N.W., Washington, D.C. 20036. Filed for self 11/3/82. Legislative interest — Not specified. Lobbyist — Randall M. Russell.

ROCHESTER TAX COUNCIL, Rochester, N.Y. Lobbyist — Ivins, Phillips & Barker, 1700 Pennsylvania Ave. N.W., Washington, D.C. 20006. Filed 11/1/82. Legislative interest — "Generally, all legislation relating to federal income taxation of corporations. Specifically, lobbying for International Sales Corporation Tax Act of 1981 (S 2708)."

Miscellaneous

H. K. ALLEN, 1325½ Wisconsin Ave. N.W., Washington, D.C. 20007. Filed for self 11/8/82. Legislative interest — "Legislation dealing with project of the U.S. Air Force known as European Distribution System Aircraft."

FRANK G. KINGSLEY, New Canaan, Conn. Lobbyist — Max N. Edwards, 1511 K St. N.W., Washington, D.C. 20005. Filed 11/3/82. Legislative interest — "Legislation relating to non-fuel minerals and metals."

EVANS W. NORTH, 1216 16th St. N.W., Washington, D.C. 20036. Filed for self 11/4/82. Legislative interest — "... all legislative matters that relate to the various plans under which dental care is offered throughout the United States...."

December 1982 Registrations

Citizens' Groups

CITIZEN/LABOR ENERGY COALITION, 1300 Connecticut Ave. N.W., Washington, D.C. 20036. Filed for self 12/30/82. Legislative interest — "Energy policy legislation, with special attention to oil and gas, energy conservation and renewable technologies, low-income fuel assistance, leasing policies." Lobbyist — Cathy Hurwit.

COW CREEK BAND OF UMPQUA TRIBE OF INDI-ANS, Canyonville, Ore. Lobbyist — Whittlesey & O'Brien, 1607 New Hampshire Ave. N.W., Washington, D.C. 20009. Filed 12/16/82. Legislative interest — "HR 6588 and S 2819."

COWLITE INDIAN TRIBE, Tacoma, Wash. Lobbyist — Whittlesey & O'Brien, 1607 New Hampshire Ave. N.W., Washington, D.C. 20009. Filed 12/16/82. Legislative interest — "HR 3612 and S 2931."

METLAKATLA INDIAN COMMUNITY, Metlakatla, Alaska. Lobbyist — Hobbs, Straus, Dean & Wilder, 1735 New York Ave. N.W., Washington, D.C. 20006. Filed 12/30/82. Legislative interest — Not specified.

MICCOSUKEE TRIBE OF INDIANS OF FLORIDA, Washington, D.C. Lobbyist — Hobbs, Straus, Dean & Wilder, 1735 New York Ave. N.W., Washington, D.C. 20006. Filed 12/30/82. Legislative interest — "Florida Indian Land Claims Settlement legislation - HR 7155, S 2893 (97th Congress); registrant favors passage."

NATIONAL COUNCIL FOR A WORLD PEACE TAX FUND, 2121 Decatur Place N.W., Washington, D.C. 20008. Filed for self 12/28/82. Legislative interest — "...the World Peace Tax Fund Act HR 4897, S 880." Lobbyist — Marian C. Franz.

PUBLIC VOICE FOR FOOD AND HEALTH POLICY, 1001 Connecticut Ave. N.W., Washington, D.C. 20036. Filed for self 12/22/82. Legislative interest — "...food safety, food prices and agriculture price supports, health policy, and related areas...." Lobbyist — Thomas Blaisdell Smith.

Corporations and Businesses

AMERICAN GLOBAL LINES INC., New York, N.Y. Lobbyist — Whittlesey & O'Brien, 1607 New Hampshire Ave. N.W., Washington, D.C. 20009. Filed 12/16/82. Legislative interest — "HR 3191."

CHAMPLIN PETROLEUM CO., Forth Worth, Texas. Lobbyist — Hogan & Hartson, 815 Connecticut Ave. N.W., Washington, D.C. 20006. Filed 12/21/82. Legislative interest — "Continuing appropriations resolution H J Res 631 - opposing a proposed rider to the resolution."

COMBINED INSURANCE COMPANY OF AMERICA, Northbrook, Ill. Lobbyist — O'Connor & Hannan, 1919 Pennsylvania Ave. N.W., Washington, D.C. 20006. Filed 12/29/82. Legislative interest — "Seek amendment to section 269 of TEFRA."

COMPO INDUSTRIES INC., Lowell, Mass. Lobbyist — Hale and Dorr, 1201 Pennsylvania Ave. N.W., Washington, D.C. 20004. Filed 12/20/82. Legislative interest — "Matters relating to tariff treatment of coated, laminated and filled fabrics including, but not limited to, HR 7118 and S 2859 (for)."

EDWARD HINES LUMBER CO., Chicago, Ill. Lobbyist — Gardner, Carton & Douglas, 1875 I St. N.W., Washington, D.C. 20006. Filed 12/14/82. Legislative interest — "Legislation relating to federal timber contracts."

FEDERAL KEMPER LIFE ASSURANCE CO., Kemper Building, Long Grove, Ill. Filed for self 12/28/82. Legislative interest — "...including but not limited to legislation having an impact on federal regulatory controls of the life insurance industry and federal tax issues." Lobbyist — Michael F. Dineen, 600 Pennsylvania Ave. S.E., Washington, D.C. 20003.

INTERNATIONAL SOFTWARE AND CONSULTING, 7961 S. Webster Way, Littleton, Colo. 80123. Filed for self 12/21/82. Legislative interest — "Computerized Moment Stability System...." Lobbyist — K. Michael Neudeck.

KANE PAPER CORP., Baldwin, N.Y. Lobbyist — O'Connor & Hannan, 1919 Pennsylvania Ave. N.W., Washington, D.C. 20006. Filed 12/14/82. Legislative interest — "Defense appropriations bill (HR 7355 and S 2951)."

KEMPER INVESTORS LIFE INSURANCE CO., 120 S. LaSalle St., Chicago, Ill. 60603. Filed for self 12/28/82. Legislative interest — "...including but not limited to legislation having an impact on federal regulatory controls of the life insurance industry and federal tax issues." Lobbyist — Michael F. Dineen, 600 Pennsylvania Ave. S.E., Washington, D.C. 20003.

LEHMAN BROTHERS KUHN LOEB INC., New York, N.Y. Lobbyist — O'Connor & Hannan, 1919 Pennsylvania Ave. N.W., Washington, D.C. 20006. Filed 12/29/82. Legislative interest — "Seek passage of HR 5699."

LUMBERMENS MUTUAL CASUALTY CO., 600 Pennsylvania Ave. N.W., Washington, D.C. 20003. Filed for self 12/28/82. Legislative interest — "...including but not limited to legislation having an impact on federal regulatory controls of the life insurance industry and federal tax issues." Lobbyist — Michael F. Dineen.

MeOH INC., Burr Ridge, Ill. Lobbyist — Hale and Dorr, 1201 Pennsylvania Ave. N.W., Washington, D.C. 20004. Filed 12/20/82. Legislative interest — "Matters regarding the taxation of alcohol fuels including but not limited to HR 6211."

NELCO PRODUCTS INC., Anaheim, Calif. Lobbyist — Jensen, Sanders & McConnell, 1875 I St. N.W., Washington, D.C. 20006. Filed 12/21/82. Legislative interest — "Unfair trade and competition...."

NORTHEASTERN INTERNATIONAL AIRWAYS INC., Fort Lauderdale, Fla. Lobbyist — Lois D. Cohen Associates, 360 E. 65th St., New York, N.Y. 10021. Filed 12/20/82. Legislative interest — "Aviation, legislation, including authorizing and appropriations measures."

PILOT PETROLEUM CORP., Long Beach, Calif. Lobbyist — Kirkpatrick, Lockhart, Hill, Christopher & Phillips, 1900 M St. N.W., Washington, D.C. 20036. Filed 12/17/82. Legislative interest — "HR 6211."

R. J. REYNOLDS TOBACCO CO., Winston-Salem, N.C. Lobbyist — Camp, Carmouche, Palmer, Barsh & Hunter, 2550 M St. N.W., Washington, D.C. 20037. Filed 12/16/82. Legislative interest — "Matters pertaining to excise taxes on tobacco products."

ST. JOE MINERALS CORP., New York, N.Y. Lobbyist — Patton, Boggs & Blow, 2550 M St. N.W., Washington, D.C. 20037. Filed 12/16/82. Legislative interest — "Supporting legislation that would extend deadline for mineral exploration in the Irish Wilderness area (Mark Twain National Forest in Missouri), S 1964."

SECURITY NEW YORK STATE CORP., Rochester, N.Y. Lobbyist — Brainard E. Prescott, 670 Main St., East Aurora, N.Y. Filed 12/22/82. Legislative interest — "...all aspects of the banking industry."

SHELL OIL CO., Washington, D.C. Lobbyist — Camp, Camouche, Palmer, Barsh & Hunter, 2550 M St. N.W., Washington, D.C. 20037. Filed 12/16/82. Legislative interest — "Matters pertaining to motor fuels tax legislation (HR 6211)."

TURNER BROADCASTING SYSTEM INC., Atlanta, Ga. Lobbyist — Mintz, Levin, Cohn, Ferris, Glovsky & Popeo, 1015 15th St. N.W., Washington, D.C. 20005. Filed 12/16/82. Legislative interest — "Copyright legislation."

WARNER COMMUNICATIONS INC., 75 Rockefeller Plaza, New York, N.Y. 10019. Filed for self 12/15/82. Legislative interest — "Legislation dealing with telecommunications and copyright matters." Lobbyist — Timothy A. Boggs, 2020 K St. N.W., Washington, D.C. 20006.

Labor Groups

NATIONAL FEDERATION OF FEDERAL EMPLOYEES, 1016 16th St. N.W., Washington, D.C. 20036. Filed for self 12/28/82. Legislative interest — "...the working conditions and welfare of federal employees." Lobbyists — Sandy Arnold, Stephen Herm, Frank James, Pat Riley, Marie Winslow.

State and Local Governments

CITY OF AUSTIN, Austin, Texas. Lobbyist — Creamer, Dickson and Basford, 1625 K St. N.W., Washington, D.C. 20006. Filed 12/20/82. Legislative interest — "S 2172, cable television."

CITY OF DALLAS, Dallas, Texas. Lobbyist — Creamer, Dickson and Basford, 1625 K St. N.W., Washington, D.C. 20006. Filed 12/20/82. Legislative interest — "S 2172, cable television."

CITY OF HOUSTON, Houston, Texas. Lobbyist — Creamer, Dickson and Basford, 1625 K St. N.W., Washington, D.C. 20006. Filed 12/20/82. Legislative interest — "S 2172, cable television."

CITY OF SAN ANTONIO, San Antonio, Texas. Lobbyist — Creamer, Dickson and Basford, 1625 K St. N.W., Washington, D.C. 20006. Filed 12/20/82. Legislative interest — "S 2172, cable television."

MAYOR OF KANSAS CITY, Kansas City, Mo. Lobbyist — Creamer, Dickson and Basford, 1625 K St. N.W., Washington, D.C. 20006. Filed 12/20/82. Legislative interest — "Natural gas prices. . . ."

STATE OF DELAWARE, Wilmington, Del. Lobbyist — Dickstein, Shapiro & Morin, 2101 L St. N.W., Washington, D.C. 20037. Filed 12/16/82. Legislative interest — "Distribution to the states by the Department of Energy (DOE) of overcharges recovered from companies which violated DOE Petroleum Price and Allocation Regulations. For S 1439; against HR 4404 and HR 5290. Also any oversight hearings held relating to DOE's plans for distribution of such revenues."

STATE OF IOWA, Des Moines, Iowa. Lobbyist — Dickstein, Shapiro & Morin, 2101 L St. N.W., Washington, D.C. 20037. Filed 12/16/82. Legislative interest — "Distribution to the states by the Department of Energy (DOE) of overcharges recovered from companies which violated DOE Petroleum Price and Allocation Regulations. For S 1439; against HR 4404 and HR 5290. Also any oversight hearings held relating to DOE's plans for distribution of such revenues."

STATE OF LOUISIANA, New Orleans, La. Lobbyist — Dickstein, Shapiro & Morin, 2101 L St. N.W., Washington, D.C. 20037. Filed 12/16/82. Legislative interest — "Distribution to the states by the Department of Energy (DOE) of overcharges recovered from companies which violated DOE Petroleum Price and Allocation Regulations. For S 1439; against HR 4404 and HR 5290. Also any oversight hearings held relating to DOE's plans for distribution of such revenues."

STATE OF NORTH DAKOTA, Bismarck, N.D. Lobbyist — Dickstein, Shapiro & Morin, 2101 L St. N.W., Washington, D.C. 20037. Filed 12/16/82. Legislative interest — "Distribution to the states by the Department of Energy (DOE) of overcharges recovered from companies which violated DOE Petroleum Price and Allocation Regulations. For S 1439; against HR 4404 and HR 5290. Also any oversight hearings held relating to DOE's plans for distribution of such revenues."

STATE OF RHODE ISLAND, Providence, R.I. Lobbyist — Dickstein, Shapiro & Morin, 2101 L St. N.W., Washington, D.C. 20037. Filed 12/16/82. Legislative interest — "Distribution to the states by the Department of Energy (DOE) of overcharges recovered from companies which violated DOE Petroleum Price and Allocation Regulations. For S 1439; against HR 4404 and HR 5290. Also any oversight hearings held relating to DOE's plans for distribution of such revenues."

Trade Associations

CHEMICAL MANUFACTURERS ASSOCIATION, Washington, D.C. Lobbyist — Camp, Carmouche, Palmer, Barsh & Hunter, 2550 M St. N.W., Washington, D.C. 20037. Filed 12/16/82. Legislative interest — "Patent extension legislation (HR 6444)."

FLORIDA ASSOCIATION OF MARINE INDUSTRIES, Miami, Fla. Lobbyist — Alcalde, Henderson & O'Bannon, 1901 N. Fort Myer Drive, Rosslyn, Va. 22209. Filed 12/15/82. Legislative interest — ". . . marine industries, particularly HR 6975 (for) and S 3023 (for)."

FLORIDA CARIBBEAN CRUISE ASSOCIATION, Miami, Fla. Lobbyist — Alcalde, Henderson & O'Bannon, 1901 N. Fort Myer Drive, Rosslyn, Va. 22209. Filed 12/15/82. Legislative

interest — "All legislation affecting the cruise industry, particularly HR 6975 (for) and S 3023 (for)."

FOOD MARKETING INSTITUTE, 1750 K St. N.W., Washington, D.C. 20006. Filed for self 12/21/82. Legislative interest — ". . . the farm bill and other general agricultural legislation." Lobbyist — Nancy Foster.

GROCERY MANUFACTURERS OF AMERICA, Washington, D.C. Lobbyist — Randall, Bangert & Price, 1625 K St. N.W., Washington, D.C. 20006. Filed 12/15/82. Legislative interest — "The Federal Anti-Tampering Act (to amend Title 18)."

MOTION PICTURE ASSOCIATION OF AMERICA, Washington, D.C. Lobbyist — Donovan, Leisure, Newton & Irvine, 1850 K St. N.W., Washington, D.C. 20006. Filed 12/21/82. Legislative interest — "Caribbean Basin Economic Recovery Act, S 2237, HR 5900."

THE NEW ENGLAND COUNCIL INC., 1800 Massachusetts Ave. N.W., Washington, D.C. 20036. Filed for self 12/16/82. Legislative interest — "Legislative matters of interest to the New England economy, business interests, tax and energy legislation, including but not limited to support for HR 3809." Lobbyist — Jeanne Campbell.

Miscellaneous

ASIAN PACIFIC ECONOMIC, EDUCATIONAL, CULTURAL ORGANIZATION INC., P.O. Box 891, Manila, Philippines. Filed for self 12/20/82. Legislative interest — "HR 6514 (Immigration Reform and Control Act of 1982), HR 7397 (Caribbean Basin Economic Recovery Act) and other bills affecting the people of the Philippines and other Asian-Pacific nations." Lobbyist — Angelesio C. Tugado, 2302 Jackson Parkway, Vienna, Va.

INTERNATIONAL LEGAL DEFENSE COUNSEL, 1420 Walnut St., Philadelphia, Pa. 19102. Filed for self 12/14/82. Legislative interest — Not specified. Lobbyist — Leora Kusher.

WASHINGTON WORKSHOPS, Washington, D.C. Lobbyist — Alcalde, Henderson & O'Bannon, 1901 N. Fort Myer Drive, Rosslyn, Va. 22209. Filed 12/15/82. Legislative interest — "General legislation affecting education community, especially HR 7205 (for)."

January 1983 Registrations

Citizens' Groups

ALLIANCE TO SAVE ENERGY, 1925 K St. N.W., Washington, D.C. 20006. Filed for self 1/10/83. Legislative interest — ". . . Authorizations, appropriations, tax credits, depreciation provisions, and other financial incentives promoting energy efficiency (*e.g.*, industrial energy tax credits - S 750); appropriations for Department of Energy energy efficiency programs; legislation involving utility participation in energy efficiency initiatives; vanpooling legislation (*e.g.*, S 239); low income energy assistance legislation, particularly as it authorizes expenditures for weatherizing buildings (*e.g.*, S 1165); and deregulation of natural gas and other energy supplies. . . . favor deregulation and measures promoting energy efficiency." Lobbyist — Wayne Gathers.

AMERICAN LUNG ASSOCIATION, 1740 Broadway, New York, N.Y. 10019. Filed for self 1/19/83. Legislative interest — ". . . TB project grants, reauthorization of Clean Air Act, pending reauthorization of NHLBI, appropriations for federal lung research, deregulation of tobacco support programs, and postal rates for non-profit organizations." Lobbyist — Fran Du Melle, 1101 Vermont Ave. N.W., Washington, D.C. 20005.

AMERICAN RIVERS CONSERVATION COUNCIL, 323 Pennsylvania Ave. S.E., Washington, D.C. 20003. Filed for self

1/4/83. Legislative interest — "... generally in favor of additions to the National Wild and Scenic River System and other proposals which protect rivers; opposed to those water resource projects which unwisely or unnecessarily destroy rivers...." Lobbyist — Christopher N. Brown.

COMMITTEE TO STOP ILLEGAL IMMIGRATION, 314 E. Capitol St., Washington, D.C. 20003. Filed for self 1/10/83. Legislative interest — Not specified. Lobbyists — Edmund J. Gannon, David A. Hennig, Gary M. Sukow.

LEAGUE OF WOMEN VOTERS OF THE UNITED STATES, 1730 M St. N.W., Washington, D.C. 20036. Filed for self 1/13/83. Legislative interest — "... support CETA reauthorization and budgeting; civil rights; day care; education; employment; food stamps; HUD authorizations and appropriations; unemployment compensation; vocational education ... oppose legislation to rescind IRS regulations on private school non-profit status; tuition tax credits; anti-busing legislation ... support international development banks; foreign economic development assistance; free flow in international trade/reduction of trade barriers ... support clean air act; clean water act; energy conservation; sound land use legislation; Surface Mining Control and Reclamation Act; low income energy assistance; environmental protection measures generally ... support D.C. representation; looking into problems of early projections; Voting Rights Act reauthorization ... support urban mass transit; Economic Development Administration; CDBG/UDAG; general revenue sharing." Lobbyist — Stephanie Teff.

NATIONAL ASSOCIATION OF ARAB AMERICANS, 1825 Connecticut Ave. N.W., Washington, D.C. 20009. Filed for self 1/11/83. Legislative interest — "Middle East related legislation, including, but not limited to FY '83 Foreign Assistance Act; FY '83 Foreign Appropriations." Lobbyists — Howard Cook, Christina Hammond.

NATIONAL COMMITTEE FOR POOR PEOPLE, 2178 Atlantic Ave., Brooklyn, N.Y. 11233. Filed for self 1/13/83. Legislative interest — "... human needs of the little tax payers and really poor of U.S.A." Lobbyist — Grady O'Cummings III.

NATIONAL RIGHT TO WORK COMMITTEE, 8001 Braddock Road, Springfield, Va. 22160. Filed for self 1/11/83. Legislative interest — "Legislative proposals related to compulsory unionism in private industry, farm labor, and public sector employees." Lobbyist — Gary Glenn.

Corporations and Businesses

ABBOTT LABORATORIES, Abbott Park, North Chicago, Ill. 60064. Filed for self 1/7/83. Legislative interest — "... legislation affecting the health care industry. Specific legislative interests are health care policy, medical research, energy and environment, and transportation." Lobbyist — Victoria Stewart-Shain, 1730 M St. N.W., Washington, D.C. 20036.

ACACIA MUTUAL LIFE INSURANCE CO., Washington, D.C. Lobbyist — Reasoner, Davis & Vinson, 800 17th St. N.W., Washington, D.C. 20006. Filed 1/18/83. Legislative interest — "Representation in connection with passage of S 3114, 97th Congress, 2nd Session - a bill to amend Acacia's charter. For such bill."

AIRBUS INDUSTRIE, Blagnac, France. Lobbyist — DGA International Inc., 1225 19th St. N.W., Washington, D.C. 20036. (Former U.S. Sen. Charles E. Goodell, R-N.Y., 1968-71, House 1959-68, was listed as agent for this client.) Filed 1/20/83. Legislative interest — "Legislation affecting U.S. trade policy, the U.S. Export Import Bank legislation and any legislation affecting commercial aircraft manufacturing...."

AIR FLORIDA INC., Miami, Fla. Lobbyist — Cook, Purcell, Henderson & Zorack, 1015 18th St. N.W., Washington, D.C. 20036. Filed 1/14/83. Legislative interest — "... HR 5930 - Extension of Airline War Risk Insurance, HR 4961 - Tax Equity and Fiscal Responsibility Act of 1982, Montreal Protocols."

ALASCOM INC., Vancouver, Wash. Lobbyist — Birch, Horton, Bittner and Monroe, 1140 Connecticut Ave. N.W., Washington, D.C. 20036. Filed 1/17/83. Legislative interest — "Telecommunication issues."

ALASKA LUMBER & PULP, Sitka, Alaska. Lobbyist — Heffernan & Moseman, 1875 I St. N.W., Washington, D.C. 20006. Filed 1/9/83. Legislative interest — "... exportation of Alaskan crude oil ... Alaskan timber resources...." Lobbyist — Robertson, Monagle, Eastaugh & Bradley, 200 National Bank of Alaska Building, P.O. Box 1211, Juneau, Alaska 99802. Filed 1/10/83. Legislative interest — "... exportation of Alaskan crude oil ... Alaskan timber resources...."

ALASKA PACIFIC BANCORP., Anchorage, Alaska. Lobbyist — Birch, Horton, Bittner and Monroe, 1140 Connecticut Ave. N.W., Washington, D.C. 20036. Filed 1/17/83. Legislative interest — "General banking issues."

ALASKA PULP & RESOURCES INC., Sitka, Alaska. Lobbyist — Heffernan & Moseman, 1875 I St. N.W., Washington, D.C. 20006. Filed 1/10/83. Legislative interest — "... exportation of Alaska crude oil...." Lobbyist — Robertson, Monagle, Eastaugh & Bradley, 200 National Bank of Alaska Building, Juneau, Alaska 99802. Filed 1/10/83. Legislative interest — "... exportation of Alaskan crude oil...."

AMERICAN PRESIDENT LINES LTD., Oakland, Calif. Lobbyist — Finley, Kumble, Wagner, Heine, Underberg & Casey, 1120 Connecticut Ave. N.W., Washington, D.C. 20036. Filed 1/12/83. Legislative interest — "Tax Equity and Fiscal Responsibility Bill of 1982, HR 4961, opposed."

AVON PRODUCTS INC., 9 W. 57th St., New York, N.Y. 10019. Filed for self 1/11/83. Legislative interest — "... government regulation of the manufacture and distribution of products, the environment and taxation. Specifically, including withholding federal income taxes, and withholding and paying taxes of the Federal Insurance Contributions Act and the Federal Unemployment Tax Act." Lobbyist — P. Richard Biondo.

BACARDI IMPORTS INC., Miami, Fla. Lobbyist — Busby, Rehm and Leonard, 1629 K St. N.W., Washington, D.C. 20006. Filed 1/14/83. Legislative interest — "Legislation to promote exportation of distilled spirits."

BURGER KING CORP., P.O. Box 520783, Miami, Fla. 33152. Filed for self 1/17/83. Legislative interest — "Legislation which may arise from time to time affecting restaurant operations." Lobbyist — Stephen A. Finn.

CAMP, CARMOUCHE, PALMER, BARSH & HUNTER, Washington, D.C. Lobbyist — Heffernan & Moseman, 1875 I St. N.W., Washington, D.C. 20006. Filed 1/10/83. Legislative interest — "Providing advice and counsel on any and all tax-related issues."

CONRAIL, Washington, D.C. Lobbyist — Fred B. Rooney, 1050 Thomas Jefferson St. N.W., Washington, D.C. 20007. (Former U.S. rep., D-Pa., 1963-79.) Filed 1/12/83. Legislative interest — "Legislation affecting Safe Harbor Tax Bill."

CORNING ASSOCIATES, Corning, N.Y. Lobbyist — Powell, Goldstein, Frazer & Murphy, 1110 Vermont Ave. N.W., Washington, D.C. 20005. Filed 1/10/83. Legislative interest — "Gift and estate tax matters."

CROWN LIFE INSURANCE CO., Toronto, Ontario, Canada. Lobbyist — Thompson & Mitchell, One Mercantile Center, St. Louis, Mo. 63101. Filed 1/12/83. Legislative interest — "... the termination accounting rules in section 257 of the Tax Equity and Fiscal Responsibility Act of 1982, HR 4961. In the form originally proposed, Crown Life Insurance Co. opposed this provision."

DOW CHEMICAL U.S.A., 1800 M St. N.W., Washington, D.C. 20036. Filed for self 1/17/83. Legislative interest — "... include but are not limited to Clean Air Act, Clean Water Act, Toxic Substances Control Act, Comprehensive Environmental Response, Compensation and Liability Act, Occupational Safety and Health legislation ... HR 5252, HR 5735, HR 7300, S 3041 ... support responsible and equitable environmental legislation." Lobbyist — James M. Kuszaj.

DREYFUS TAX-EXEMPT BOND FUND, New York, N.Y. Lobbyist — Stroock & Stroock & Lavan, 1150 17th St. N.W., Washington, D.C. 20036. Filed 1/11/83. Legislative interest — "In support of certain technical amendments to HR 6056, the Technical Corrections Act of 1982."

DREYFUS TAX-EXEMPT MONEY MARKET FUND, New York, N.Y. Lobbyist — Stroock & Stroock & Lavan, 1150 17th St. N.W., Washington, D.C. 20036. Filed 1/11/83. Legislative interest — "In support of certain technical amendments to HR 6056, the Technical Corrections Act of 1982."

GENSTAR CONTAINER CORP., San Francisco, Calif. Lobbyist — Finley, Kumble, Wagner, Heine, Underberg & Casey, 1120 Connecticut Ave. N.W., Washington, D.C. 20036. Filed 1/12/83. Legislative interest — "Tax Equity and Fiscal Responsibility Bill of 1982, HR 4961, opposed."

HAMBROS BANK LTD., London, England. Lobbyist — Gray and Co., 3255 Grace St. N.W., Washington, D.C. 20007. Filed 1/13/83. Legislative interest — "For HR 5858."

HARZA ENGINEERS, Washington, D.C. Lobbyist — Birch, Horton, Bittner and Monroe, 1140 Connecticut Ave. N.W., Washington, D.C. 20036. Filed 1/17/83. Legislative interest — "Issues on hydroelectric power in Alaska."

INTERNATIONAL MARITIME ASSOCIATES INC., 1800 K St. N.W., Washington, D.C. 20006. Filed for self 1/14/83. Legislative interest — "Maritime matters, with specific relation to Buy America legislation, Navy shipbuilding funding and shipbuilding industry." Lobbyists — James R. McCaul, James E. Wilson.

KALEIDOSCOPE RESEARCH AND MARKETING GROUP, 5128 Sauer, Houston, Texas 77004. Filed for self 1/5/83. Legislative interest — Not specified. Lobbyists — Steven Bryant, George Dillard.

KEMPER INVESTORS LIFE INSURANCE CO., 120 S. LaSalle St., Chicago, Ill. 60603. Filed for self 1/19/83. Legislative interest — "...including but not limited to legislation dealing with federal tax issues and legislation having an impact on federal regulatory controls of the life insurance industry." Lobbyist — Charles M. Kierscht.

LANGHAM ENERGY CORP., Houston, Texas. Lobbyist — C. H. Mayer Inc., 3421 N. Causeway, Metairie, La. Filed 1/10/83. Legislative interest — "Energy interests including support for repeal of sections of the Crude Oil Windfall Profit Tax Act/sections of the tax bill/deregulation of natural gas."

LANGHAM PETROLEUM EXPLORATION CORP., Houston, Texas. Lobbyist — C. H. Mayer Inc., 3421 N. Causeway, Metairie, La. Filed 1/10/83. Legislative interest — "Energy interests including support for repeal of sections of the Crude Oil Windfall Profits Tax Act/sections of the tax bill/deregulation of natural gas."

LARS KROGH & CO., Oslo, Norway. Lobbyist — Arent, Fox, Kintner, Plotkin & Kahn, 1050 Connecticut Ave. N.W., Washington, D.C. 20036. Filed 1/11/83. Legislative interest — "General legislative interests relate to appropriations, fill rates, and interim and regional storage for the Strategic Petroleum Reserve."

LONE STAR INDUSTRIES INC., Washington, D.C. Lobbyist — Fred B. Rooney, 1050 Thomas Jefferson St. N.W., Washington, D.C. 20007. (Former U.S. rep., D-Pa., 1963-79.) Filed 1/12/83. Legislative interest — "Railway Safety Act of 1982."

MANVILLE CORP., Washington, D.C. Lobbyist — C & B Associates Inc., 1750 New York Ave. N.W., Washington, D.C. 20006. Filed 1/3/83. Legislative interest — "Interest in prospective legislation dealing with compensation for victims of occupational disease and bankruptcy-related legislation."

MERRILL LYNCH & CO. INC., 1828 L St. N.W., Washington, D.C. 20036. Lobbyist — Witkowski, Weiner, McCaffrey & Brodsky, 1575 I St. N.W., Washington, D.C. 20005. Filed 1/13/83. Legislative interest — "General: housing, consumer finance and banking legislation. Specific: Real Estate Settlement Practices Amendments of 1982." Filed for self 1/10/83. Legislative interest — "Financial, banking, securities, taxation, real estate and related legislation." Lobbyist — Lois A. Noack.

NATIONAL RURAL DEVELOPMENT AND FINANCE CORP., Washington, D.C. Lobbyist — Moss, McGee & Bellmon, 1740 N St. N.W., Washington, D.C. 20036. Filed 1/3/83. Legislative interest — "Community Services Block Grant Act, Community Economic Development Act, Labor/HHS Appropriations Act, Budget Act."

OCEAN DRILLING AND EXPLORATION CO., New Orleans, La. Lobbyist — Groom and Nordberg, 1775 Pennsylvania Ave. N.W., Washington, D.C. 20006. Filed 1/10/83. Legislative interest — "Federal legislation affecting Title 26 of U.S.C."

OCCIDENTAL PETROLEUM CORP., Los Angeles, Calif. Lobbyist — Finley, Kumble, Wagner, Heine, Underberg & Casey, 1120 Connecticut Ave. N.W., Washington, D.C. 20036. Filed 1/12/83. Legislative interest — "Tax Equity and Fiscal Responsibility Act of 1982, HR 4961, opposed."

SAMARITAN HEALTH SERVICE, 1410 N. Third St., Phoenix, Ariz. 85002. Filed for self 1/17/83. Legislative interest — "General interest in legislation affecting health care...." Lobbyist — Burton Lewkowitz.

SEARS, ROEBUCK AND CO., Sears Tower, Chicago, Ill. 60684. Filed for self 1/10/83. Legislative interest — "Legislation generally affecting the operation of Sears, Roebuck and Co., as a part of the retail industry, its employees and customers and more specifically those issues that might affect advertising and distribution of consumer products." Lobbyist — Donald Forsyth Craib III, 1211 Connecticut Ave. N.W., Washington, D.C. 20036.

SHARPS, PIXLEY & CO. LTD., London, England. Lobbyist — Gray and Co., 3255 Grace St. N.W., Washington, D.C. 20007. Filed 1/13/83. Legislative interest — "For HR 5858."

SIGNAL COMMUNICATIONS, Metairie, La. Lobbyist — Arthur E. Cameron, 499 S. Capitol St. S.W., Washington, D.C. 20003. Filed 1/11/83. Legislative interest — "Surface Transportation Assistance Act of 1982 ... HR 6211...."

THE SIGNAL COMPANIES INC., 11255 N. Torrey Pines Road, La Jolla, Calif. 92037. Filed for self 1/11/83. Legislative interest — "Of specific interest ... are DOD, DOE, DOT authorizations and appropriations; export policy; clean air and tax legislation...." Lobbyist — Ricardo R. Alvarado, 1575 I St. N.W., Washington, D.C. 20005.

SONAT INC., Birmingham, Ala. Lobbyist — Stephen W. Still, 1100 15th St. N.W., Washington, D.C. 20005. Filed 1/10/83. Legislative interest — "...legislation generally affecting Sonat Inc. and its subsidiaries, including interstate natural gas transmission, offshore drilling, oil and gas exploration and production, forest products and marine transportation."

THE STANDARD OIL CO. (OHIO), Midland Building, Cleveland, Ohio 44115. Filed for self 1/9/83. Legislative interest — "General legislative matters pertaining to the interests of the company respecting petroleum products, refining and distribution, petro-chemicals and coal and metal/non-metal minerals." Lobbyist — Robert J. Araujo, 1001 22nd St. N.W., Washington, D.C. 20036.

STORER COMMUNICATIONS INC., 1220 19th St. N.W., Washington, D.C. 20036. Filed for self 1/6/83. Legislative interest — "... principally broadcasting." Lobbyist — Walter L. Threadgill.

TENNECO INC., P.O. Box 2511, Houston, Texas 77001. Filed for self 1/10/83. Legislative interest — Not specified. Lobbyists — John A. Armbruster, Robert F. Lockhart Jr., 490 L'Enfant Plaza East S.W., Washington, D.C. 20024.

TRANSCANADA PIPELINES LTD., Toronto, Ontario, Canada. Lobbyist — Mayer, Brown & Platt, 888 17th St. N.W., Washington, D.C. 20006. Filed 1/9/83. Legislative interest — "All legislation affecting natural gas imports."

TRANS WORLD AIRLINES INC., New York, N.Y. Lobbyist — Chadbourne, Parke, Whiteside & Wolff, 1101 Vermont Ave. N.W., Washington, D.C. 20005. Filed 1/10/83. Legislative interest — "Ratification of Montreal Protocol."

TURNER BROADCASTING SYSTEM INC., Washington, D.C. Lobbyist — Verner, Liipfert, Bernhard and McPherson, 1660 L St. N.W., Washington, D.C. 20036. Filed 1/14/83. Legislative interest — "Legislation concerning cable TV copyright royalties, particularly with regard to a recent decision by the Copyright Royalty Tribunal."

UNION PACIFIC CORP., 345 Park Ave., New York, N.Y. 10154. Filed for self 1/19/83. Legislative interest — "Pending and prospective legislation affecting the petroleum and natural gas industries." Lobbyist — Jeffery A. Fritzlen, 1120 20th St. N.W., Washington, D.C. 20036.

UNION TEXAS PETROLEUM CORP., P.O. Box 2120, Houston, Texas 77252. Lobbyist — Groom and Nordberg, 1775 Pennsylvania Ave. N.W., Washington, D.C. 20006. Filed 1/10/83. Legislative interest — "Federal legislation affecting Title 26 of U.S.C." Filed for self 1/12/83. Legislative interest — ". . . oil and gas legislation." Lobbyist — Craig Liske.

WESTINGHOUSE CORP., Washington, D.C. Lobbyist — White, Fine & Verville, 1156 15th St. N.W., Washington, D.C. 20005. Filed 1/11/83. Legislative interest — "Any and all nuclear legislative matters concerning nuclear power, nuclear equipment export, the Export-Import Bank of the United States, the Clinch River Breeder Reactor and such other international concerns as may affect the corporation's international interests; certain amendments to the Clean Air Act."

International Relations

REPUBLIC OF GABON, Libreville, Gabon. Lobbyist — Cramer, Hoffman & Haber, 1320 19th St. N.W., Washington, D.C. 20036. (Former U.S. Rep. William C. Cramer, R-Fla., 1955-71, was listed among agents for this client.) Filed 1/14/83. Legislative interest — "Any legislation, including budget authorization or appropriation, which may affect federal funding or federal programs for the Republic of Gabon."

REPUBLIC OF HAITI, Port au Prince, Haiti. Lobbyist — Gray and Co., 3255 Grace St. N.W., Washington, D.C. 20007. Filed 1/10/83. Legislative interest — "To encourage a more positive U.S. attitude toward the Republic of Haiti through dialogue with Members of Congress and U.S. government officials resulting in increased foreign investment, foreign aid and tourism."

State and Local Governments

COMMONWEALTH OF PUERTO RICO, San Juan, Puerto Rico. Lobbyist — Gray and Co., 3255 Grace St. N.W., Washington, D.C. 20007. Legislative interest — Not specified.

STATE OF LOUISIANA, Baton Rouge, La. Lobbyist — Carol R. Emery, P.O. Box 1300, McLean, Va. 22102. Filed 1/13/83. Legislative interest — Not specified.

Trade Associations

AIR FORCE SERGEANTS ASSOCIATION, Suitland, Md. Lobbyist — Rudy I. Clark, 3179 Colchester Brook Lane, Fairfax, Va. 22031. Filed 1/7/83. Legislative interest — ". . . legislation affecting the enlisted men and women of the U.S. Air Force and their dependents, and the national security of the United States."

AMERICAN BUS ASSOCIATION, Washington, D.C. Lobbyist — Birch, Horton, Bittner & Monroe, 1140 Connecticut Ave. N.W., Washington, D.C. 20036. Filed 1/11/83. Legislative interest — "General transportation excise tax bills and the 5-cents-a-gallon tax bill."

AMERICAN COUNCIL OF LIFE INSURANCE, 1850 K St. N.W., Washington, D.C. 20006. Filed for self 1/11/83. Legislative interest — "Proposed legislation which would affect the life insurance industry." Lobbyist — Beverly L. Bennett.

AMERICAN DENTAL ASSOCIATION, 1101 17th St. N.W., Washington, D.C. 20036. Filed for self 1/10/83. Legislative interest — "Appropriations bills; legislation regarding dental disease prevention; nutrition and child health; radiation; Safe Drinking Water Act." Lobbyist — Beverly J. Bailey.

AMERICAN GAS ASSOCIATION, 1515 Wilson Blvd., Arlington, Va. 22209. Filed for self 1/12/83. Legislative interest — "Natural gas pricing, taxation." Lobbyist — Randall Griffin.

AMERICAN IRON AND STEEL INSTITUTE, Washington, D.C. Lobbyist — Gray & Co., 3255 Grace St. N.W., Washington, D.C. 20007. Filed 1/13/83. Legislative interest — "For the Heinz 'Buy American' amendment to the highway gas tax bill, HR 6211."

AMERICAN MARITIME ASSOCIATION, New York, N.Y. Lobbyist — Gray & Co., 3255 Grace St. N.W., Washington, D.C. 20007. Filed 1/13/83. Legislative interest — "For Maritime Authorization Bill."

AMERICAN MEAT INSTITUTE, P.O. Box 3556, Washington, D.C. 20007. Filed for self 1/13/83. Legislative interest — "Legislation affecting the food industry in general and particularly the livestock and meat industry including, but not limited to: livestock production and feeding, animal diseases, meat inspection, food additives, labeling, transportation, environmental protection, safety, trade practices, consumer protection, energy, food safety, regulatory reform." Lobbyist — Gary Jay Kushner.

AMERICAN PETROLEUM INSTITUTE, 2101 L St. N.W., Washington, D.C. 20037. Filed for self 1/11/83. Legislative interest — "Legislation affecting petroleum industry." Lobbyist — Barbara L. Bush.

AMERICAN PUBLIC TRANSIT ASSOCIATION, Washington, D.C. Lobbyist — Fred B. Burke, 1620 I St. N.W., Washington, D.C. 20006. Filed 1/14/83. Legislative interest — "Surface Transportation Act of 1982, HR 6211 and other urban transportation legislation in the future."

AMERICAN ROSE COUNCIL, Washington, D.C. Lobbyist — Joseph B. McGrath, 1320 19th St. N.W., Washington, D.C. 20036. Filed 1/17/83. Legislative interest — "HR 6370 and S 2466, bills to impose tariffs on imported roses."

THE AMERICAN WATERWAYS OPERATORS INC., 1600 Wilson Blvd., Arlington, Va. 22209. Filed for self 1/13/83. Legislative interest — Not specified. Lobbyist — Joseph A. Farrell.

ASSOCIATION OF LOCAL HOUSING FINANCE AGENCIES, Washington, D.C. Lobbyist — Kutak, Rock & Huie, 1101 Connecticut Ave. N.W., Washington, D.C. 20036. Filed 1/9/83. Legislative interest — "Monitoring legislation affecting the housing industry."

AUTOMOBILE IMPORTERS OF AMERICA INC., Arlington, Va. Lobbyist — Busby, Rehm and Leonard, 1629 K St. N.W., Washington, D.C. 20006. Filed 1/14/83. Legislative interest — "Legislation affecting importation, distribution and sale of foreign automobiles." Lobbyist — Robert N. Hampton, 7010 Girard St., McLean, Va. 22101. Filed 1/14/83. Legislative interest — "Legislation affecting importation, distribution, and sale of foreign automobiles, including HR 5133 (against)."

BUILDING SERVICE CONTRACTORS ASSOCIATION INTERNATIONAL, Fairfax, Va. Lobbyist — Arent, Fox, Kintner, Plotkin & Kahn, 1050 Connecticut Ave. N.W., Washington, D.C. 20036. Filed 1/18/83. Legislative interest — "Seeking repeal of 'Edgar Amendment,' section 120 of Public Law 97-377."

BUSINESS EXECUTIVES FOR NATIONAL SECURITY, Washington, D.C. Lobbyist — David Cohen, 2010 Massachusetts Ave. N.W., Washington, D.C. 20036. Filed 1/10/83. Legislative interest — "National security; arms control, particularly limitation or control of nuclear weapons; military spending issues, particularly as they impact on the U.S. economy; and U.S.-Soviet relations." Lobbyist — Stanley A. Weiss, 2126 Connecticut Ave. N.W., Washington, D.C. 20008. Filed 1/14/83. Legislative interest — "National security; arms control, particularly limitation or control of nuclear weapons; military spending issues, particularly as they impact on the U.S. economy; and U.S.-Soviet relations."

CALIFORNIA SAVINGS AND LOAN LEAGUE, Los Angeles, Calif. Lobbyist — McKenna, Conner & Cuneo, 3435 Wilshire Blvd., Los Angeles, Calif. 90010. Filed 1/10/83. Legislative interest — "Amendments to legislation affecting financial institutions."

CHAMBER OF COMMERCE OF THE UNITED STATES, 1615 H St. N.W., Washington, D.C. 20062. Filed for self 1/10/83. Legislative interest — "RCRA, hazardous wastes legislation." Lobbyist — Douglas K. Walker.

COLLEGE OF AMERICAN PATHOLOGISTS, Skokie, Ill. Lobbyist — Gray & Co., 3255 Grace St. N.W., Washington,

D.C. 20007. Filed 1/11/83. Legislative interest — "Including but not limited to health legislation."

COMMITTEE FOR PRUDENT DEREGULATION, New York, N.Y. Lobbyist — Akin, Gump, Strauss, Hauer & Feld, 1333 New Hampshire Ave. N.W., Washington, D.C. 20036. Filed 1/10/83. Legislative interest — "Legislation relating to the syndication of network television programming, HR 7347."

DAIRY-FARMER DISTRIBUTORS OF AMERICA INC., Chittenango, N.Y. 13037. Filed for self 1/10/83. Legislative interest — "Repeal of the Omnibus Budget Reconciliation Act of 1982 at the dairy sub-part, and any similar legislation." Lobbyist — Daniel F. Gates.

FEDERAL NATIONAL MORTGAGE ASSOCIATION, 3900 Wisconsin Ave. N.W., Washington, D.C. 20016. Lobbyist — Dewey, Ballantine, Bushby, Palmer & Wood, 1775 Pennsylvania Ave. N.W., Washington, D.C. 20006. Filed 1/14/83. Legislative interest — Not specified. Filed for self 1/14/83. Legislative interest — "Legislation regarding residential mortgages, housing, and various tax issues. Specifically, HR 1 and HR 3." Lobbyist — Dale P. Riordan.

FOREST FARMERS ASSOCIATION, P.O. Box 95385, Atlanta, Ga. 30347. Filed for self 1/12/83. Legislative interest — "Appropriation bills, including U.S. Forest Service items ... proposals to amend the Fair Labor Standards Act ... legislation affecting forestry and forest landowners ... environmental and land use legislation ... proposals to amend the Internal Revenue Code." Lobbyist — B. Jack Warren.

HEALTH INDUSTRY MANUFACTURERS ASSOCIATION, 1030 15th St. N.W., Washington, D.C. 20005. Filed for self 1/6/83. Legislative interest — "... health and business issues ... any proposal relating to prospective reimbursement of health care costs." Lobbyist — Ronald L. Geigle.

INDEPENDENT INSURANCE AGENTS OF AMERICA INC., New York, N.Y. Lobbyist — Batzell, Nunn & Bode, 1015 15th St. N.W., Washington, D.C. 20005. Filed 1/7/83. Legislative interest — "Legislation that involves sales of property and casualty insurance by bank holding companies; especially S 2879, HR 2255 and HR 6267, bills that would amend the Bank Holding Company Act of 1956. Additionally, legislation contemplating the sale of insurance through other instrumentalities (S 734, HR 6016)."

INVESTMENT COMPANY INSTITUTE, 1775 K St. N.W., Washington, D.C. 20006. Filed for self 1/11/83. Legislative interest — "S 1424, amend the Investment Company Act - oppose; S 1427, State and Local Government Financing Reform Act of 1981 - oppose; S 1541, a bill to amend ERISA - may favor amendment; S 1720, to enhance the competitiveness of depository institutions - oppose; S 1888 to amend the Internal Revenue Code - oppose; S 2536, to amend the Securities Acts of 1933 and 1934 and the Investment Company Act of 1940 - oppose; HR 1916, Financial Industry Equity Act - oppose; HR 2591, Federal Reserve Act Amendments of 1981 - oppose; HR 2916, to amend the Internal Revenue Act - oppose; HR 3058, to amend the Internal Revenue Act - oppose; HR 3097, to amend the Internal Revenue Act - oppose; HR 3230, to amend the Federal Reserve Act - oppose; HR 3456, to amend the Investment Company Act - oppose; HR 2980, to amend the Federal Reserve Act - oppose; HR 4049, to amend the Glass-Steagall Act - oppose; HR 5004, to amend the Internal Revenue Code - oppose; HR 5053, to amend the Internal Revenue Code - support; HR 5699, to amend the Internal Revenue Code - support; HR 6124, to extend the Credit Control Act - oppose; HR 6410, to amend the Internal Revenue Code - oppose; S 3059, to amend the Federal Reserve Act - may favor amendment." Lobbyist — Sandra Cohen Lieberman.

METRO GARAGE BOARD OF TRADE, New York, N.Y. Lobbyist — Stroock & Stroock & Lavan, 1150 17th St. N.W., Washington, D.C. 20036. Filed 1/11/83. Legislative interest — "Drafting of an amendment to HR 6211, the Surface Transportation Act of 1982, concerning the proposed gasoline tax provisions of the bill."

MOTION PICTURE ASSOCIATION OF AMERICA INC., 1600 I St. N.W., Washington, D.C. 20006. Filed for self 1/10/83. Legislative interest — "Legislation dealing with: amendments to Copyright Act of 1976, S 2044 and HR 5949; pay television antipiracy, HR 4727, S 2172; export trade, S 734, HR 1799, HR 2326, HR 2459, HR 2812, HR 6755, S 2237; in-home taping, S 1758; amendment 1333 to S 1758, HR 5705, HR 4794, HR 4783, HR 5250; the Communications Act of 1934, as amended, S 2172; financial interest and syndication rules, HR 7347; cable copyright rates, H J Res 631; antitrust, censorship of motion pictures and audiovisual works, and miscellaneous tax bills affecting films." Lobbyist — Tom Railsback (Former U.S. rep., R.-Ill., 1967-83.).

NATIONAL ASSOCIATION OF BROADCASTERS, 1771 N St. N.W., Washington, D.C. 20036. Filed for self 1/12/83. Legislative interest — "... relating directly or indirectly to the Communications Act of 1934, 47 U.S.C. 151; Copyright Law of 1909, 17 U.S.C. 1; Communications Satellite Act of 1962, 47 U.S.C. 701; regulation of advertising; taxation; appropriations; public broadcasting; newsmen's privilege; and consumer protection." Lobbyist — Timothy X. Moore.

NATIONAL ASSOCIATION OF INDEPENDENT COLLEGES AND UNIVERSITIES, 1717 Massachusetts Ave. N.W., Washington, D.C. 20036. Filed for self 1/13/83. Legislative interest — "All legislative matters affecting independent colleges and universities, including but not limited to reauthorization of the Higher Education Act of 1965, tax, budget, and appropriations legislation." Lobbyist — Kathleen Curry.

NATIONAL ASSOCIATION OF INSURANCE BROKERS, 311 First St. N.W., Washington, D.C. 20001. Filed for self 1/11/83. Legislative interest — "Legislation involving insurance industry and related interests." Lobbyist — David F. Lambert III.

NATIONAL ASSOCIATION OF MANUFACTURERS, 1776 F St. N.W., Washington, D.C. 20006. Filed for self 1/12/83. Legislative interest — "... product liability tort reform including, but not limited to S 2621. All legislation concerning the allocation of product liability risks between the federal government and its contractors and providing, in certain cases, indemnity from those risks, including but not limited to, HR 1504. All legislation affecting workers' compensation systems, including, but not limited to HR 5375, S 1182." Lobbyist — James A. Anderson Jr.

NATIONAL ASSOCIATION OF PUBLIC HOSPITALS, Washington, D.C. Lobbyist — Dewey, Ballantine, Bushby, Palmer & Wood, 1775 Pennsylvania Ave. N.W., Washington, D.C. 20006. Filed 1/14/83. Legislative interest — Not specified.

NATIONAL ASSOCIATION OF REALTORS, 777 14th St. N.W., Washington, D.C. 20005. Filed for self 1/11/83. Legislative interest — "Tax legislation." Lobbyist — Jeff DoBoer.

NATIONAL FROZEN FOOD ASSOCIATION, Hershey, Pa. Lobbyist — Rose Mary Mims, 600 Maryland Ave. S.W., Washington, D.C. 20024. Filed 1/19/83. Legislative interest — "National School Lunch and Child Nutrition Acts ... emergency standby petroleum allocation legislation, highway trust fund authorization, Social Security and immigration legislation."

NATIONAL RIFLE ASSOCIATION OF AMERICA, 1600 Rhode Island Ave. N.W., Washington, D.C. 20036. Filed for self 1/11/83. Legislative interest — "... all aspects of the acquisition, possession, and use of firearms and ammunition as well as legislation relating to hunting and wildlife conservation." Lobbyist — Terri O'Grady.

NATIONAL TIRE DEALERS AND RETREADERS ASSOCIATION INC., 1343 L St. N.W., Washington, D.C. 20005. Filed for self 1/11/83. Legislative interest — "... bills to amend regulations concerning tire identification and record keeping, the Internal Revenue Code provisions dealing with the excise tax on tread rubber, the Motor Vehicle Safety Act, regulations promulgated under the Occupational Safety and Health Act, and the issue of allowing post exchanges to retail and service new tires...." Lobbyist — Michael DeSanto.

PHILIPPINE SUGAR COMMISSION, P.O. Box 2279, Manila, Philippines. Filed for self 1/10/83. Legislative interest — Not specified. Lobbyist — Ralph R. Harding, 2600 Virginia Ave. N.W., Washington, D.C. 20037. (Former U.S. rep., D-Idaho, 1961-65.)

PRIVATE TRUCK COUNCIL OF AMERICA INC., Washington, D.C. Lobbyist — Billig, Sher & Jones, 2033 K St.

N.W., Washington, D.C. 20006. Filed 1/10/83. Legislative interest — "Legislation affecting the operation of truck fleets."

THE RAILROAD RETIREMENT ASSOCIATION, 400 First St. N.W., Washington, D.C. 20001. Filed for self 1/10/83. Legislative interest — "... The Railroad Retirement Act of 1937, as amended ... the Financial Interchange Act between Social Security and the Railroad Retirement Fund ... the Social Security portion of Railroad Retirement benefits ... employment in the railroad industry as it affects tax contributions to the Railroad Retirement Fund on the part of employees and/or employers ... the financing of the phase out of the so called 'dual benefits' under the Railroad Retirement Act ... amount of benefits under said act." Lobbyist — L. L. Duxbury.

RECORDING INDUSTRY ASSOCIATION OF AMERICA INC., New York, N.Y. Lobbyist — DeHart Associates Inc., 1505 22nd St. N.W., Washington, D.C. 20037. Filed 1/17/83. Legislative interest — "Copyright and other legislation of interest to the recording industry...."

SHIPBUILDERS COUNCIL OF AMERICA, 1110 Vermont Ave. N.W., Washington, D.C. 20005. Filed for self 1/13/83. Legislative interest — "Defense authorization and appropriations bills; Maritime Administration authorization." Lobbyist — John J. Stocker.

SWAZILAND SUGAR ASSOCIATION, Mbabane, Swaziland. Lobbyist — Murray and Scheer, 2550 M St. N.W., Washington, D.C. 20037. Filed 1/20/83. Legislative interest — "Legislation affecting the increased U.S. import of sugar."

TRAVEL INDUSTRY ASSOCIATION OF AMERICA, 1899 L St. N.W., Washington, D.C. 20036. Filed for self 1/7/83. Legislative interest — "National Tourism Policy Act; legislation to amend Immigration and Nationality Act." Lobbyist — Thomas N. Shoemaker.

Miscellaneous

GEORGE WASHINGTON UNIVERSITY STUDENT ASSOCIATION, 800 21st St. N.W., Washington, D.C. 20052. Filed for self 1/18/83. Legislative interest — "All legislation which may have an impact on post-secondary education, post-secondary students, and the D.C. metropolitan area." Lobbyist — Matthew G. Dobson.

LEGAL SERVICES CORP., 733 15th St. N.W., Washington, D.C. 20005. Filed for self 1/3/83. Legislative interest — "... annual appropriation and congressional actions directly affecting the activities of the corporation, particularly the appropriations bills of the House and Senate Appropriations Subcommittees on State, Justice, Commerce, the Judiciary and related agencies containing funds for the corporation and bills of the House Judiciary Subcommittee on Courts, Civil Liberties and the Administration of Justice and the Senate Labor and Human Resources Subcommittee on Aging, Family and Human Services regarding reauthorization of the corporation." Lobbyist — Donald P. Bogard.

EDWARD MULROY, Marcellus, N.Y. 13108. Filed for self 1/10/83. Legislative interest — "Repeal of the Omnibus Budget Reconciliation Act of 1982 at the Dairy sub-part, and any similar legislation."

HRH PRINCE TALAL BIN ABDUL AZIZ AL SAUD, Riyadh, Saudi Arabia. Lobbyist — Gray and Co., 3255 Grace St. N.W., Washington, D.C. 20007. Filed 1/17/83. Legislative interest — "For continued UNICEF funding, H J Res 631."

UNITED NATIONS CHILDREN'S FUND, New York, N.Y. Lobbyist — Gray and Co., 3255 Grace St. N.W., Washington, D.C. 20007. Filed 1/10/83. Legislative interest — "For continued UNICEF funding, H J Res 631."

February Registrations
Citizens' Groups

AUDIO RECORDING RIGHTS COALITION, Washington, D.C. Lobbyist — Cornell, Pelcovits & Brenner Economists Inc., 1211 Connecticut Ave. N.W., Washington, D.C. 20036. Filed 2/24/83. Legislative interest — "... pending proposals to amend the copyright laws, Title 17 of the United States Code, to exempt from copyright liability off-air recording by videotape recorders and/or establish a compulsory license fee or make other revisions of the copyright laws relating to such activities.... Supports exemption from copyright liability of off-air recording by videotape and audiotape recorders. Opposes establishment of any taxes or fees on home recording, and any changes in First Sale Doctrine."

THE BIPARTISAN BUDGET APPEAL, P.O. Box 9, New York, N.Y. 10004. Filed for self 2/25/83. Legislative interest — "... certain aspects of the federal budget...." Lobbyist — Peter G. Peterson.

HOME RECORDING RIGHTS COALITION, Washington, D.C. Lobbyist — Cornell, Pelcovits & Brenner Economists Inc., 1211 Connecticut Ave. N.W., Washington, D.C. 20036. Filed 2/24/83. Legislative interest — "... pending proposals to amend the copyright laws, Title 17 of the United States Code, to exempt from copyright liability off-air recording by videotape recorders and/or establish a compulsory license fee or make other revisions of the copyright laws relating to such activities.... Supports exemption from copyright liability of off-air recording by videotape and audiotape recorders. Opposes establishment of any taxes or fees on home recording, and any changes in First Sale Doctrine."

OGLALA SIOUX TRIBE, Pine Ridge, S.D. Lobbyist — Hobbs, Straus, Dean & Wilder, 1735 New York Ave. N.W., Washington, D.C. 20006. Filed 2/28/83. Legislative interest — "Legislation affecting American Indians."

PUBLIC VOICE FOR FOOD & HEALTH POLICY, 1001 Connecticut Ave. N.W., Washington, D.C. 20036. Filed for self 2/2/83. Legislative interest — "General legislative interests include bills expected to be introduced in the 98th Congress addressing areas of food safety, food prices and agriculture price supports, health policy, and related areas." Lobbyist — Ellen Haas.

Corporations and Businesses

ALASKA LUMBER & PULP INC., Sitka, Alaska. Lobbyist — Anderson, Hibey, Nauheim & Blair, 1605 New Hampshire Ave. N.W., Washington, D.C. 20009. Filed 2/22/83. Legislative interest — "Any and all legislation dealing with the exportation of Alaskan crude oil."

AMERICAN SCIENCE AND TECHNOLOGY CORP., 600 Water St. S.W., Washington, D.C. 20024. Filed for self 2/28/83. Legislative interest — "Interested in all bills concerning transfer of ownership of remote sensing satellites from the government to the private sector. Generally, in support of commercializing land remote sensing satellites." Lobbyists — Kathleen Bonner, Diana H. Josephson.

ANEUTRONIX INC., New York, N.Y. Lobbyist — Gray and Co., 3255 Grace St. N.W., Washington, D.C. 20007. Filed 2/28/83. Legislative interest — "Including but not limited to legislation concerning energy issues and appropriations."

ATLANTA LIFE INSURANCE CO., Atlanta, Ga. Lobbyist — Sutherland, Asbill & Brennan, 1666 K St. N.W., Washington, D.C. 20006. Filed 2/28/83. Legislative interest — "General interest in legislation dealing with Section 4943 of the Code."

BELL AEROSPACE TEXTRON, New Orleans, La. Lobbyist — James E. Guirard Jr., 1090 Vermont Ave. N.W., Washington, D.C. 20005. Filed 2/28/83. Legislative interest — "Defense authorization and appropriations bills. Coast Guard authorization and appropriations bills."

BRUNSWICK CORP., One Brunswick Plaza, Skokie, Ill. 60077. Filed for self 2/23/83. Legislative interest — "Taxation, international trade, anti-trust, regulatory reform; issues pertaining to the areas of recreation, transportation, defense and technical." Lobbyist — Veronica M. Floyd, 2001 S. Jefferson Davis Highway, Arlington, Va. 22202.

FREEPORT-McMoRan INC., New York, N.Y. Lobbyist — R. Duffy Wall & Associates Inc., 11 Dupont Circle N.W.,

Washington, D.C. 20036. Filed 2/24/83. Legislative interest — "For legislation to convert DISC to a GATT legal territoriality system; for amendments to the Clean Air Act to exclude fugitive dust from PSD increments; for legislation to correct inequities in the NGPA; for legislation to give Frasch sulphur mines parallel treatment with oil and gas wells under the UIC regulations of the Safe Drinking Water Act; against legislation to reduce percentage depletion for hard rock mining or for independent oil producers; against legislation to violate the sanctity of contracts for the purchase or sale of domestic natural gas from independent producers. . . ."

MARTIN BAKER AIRCRAFT CO. LTD., Middlesex, England. Lobbyist — Gray and Co., 3255 Grace St. N.W., Washington, D.C. 20007. Filed 2/28/83. Legislative interest — "Including but not limited to legislation concerning military appropriations."

NATIONAL BROADCASTING CO., New York, N.Y. Lobbyist — Gray and Co., 3255 Grace St. N.W., Washington, D.C. 20007. Filed 2/28/83. Legislative interest — "Including but not limited to legislation which would codify the financial interest and syndication rules, sponsored by Congressman Waxman."

NEW YORK STATE ELECTRIC & GAS CO., Binghampton, N.Y. Lobbyist — Van Ness, Feldman, Sutcliffe, Curtis & Levenberg, 1050 Thomas Jefferson St. N.W., Washington, D.C. 20007. Filed 2/28/83. Legislative interest — "Amendments to the Clean Air Act with respect to emissions offsets."

PENNSYLVANIA ELECTRIC CO., Washington, D.C. Lobbyist — Van Ness, Feldman, Sutcliffe, Curtis & Levenberg, 1050 Thomas Jefferson St. N.W., Washington, D.C. 20007. Filed 2/28/83. Legislative interest — "Amendments to the Clean Air Act with respect to emissions offsets."

PROVIDENT LIFE AND ACCIDENT INSURANCE CO., Chattanooga, Tenn. Lobbyist — Scribner, Hall & Thompson, 1875 I St. N.W., Washington, D.C. 20006. Filed 2/22/83. Legislative interest — "Proposed legislation with respect to the taxation of life insurance companies."

STEDMAN CORP., P.O. Box 1288, Asheboro, N.C. 27203. Filed for self 2/23/83. Legislative interest — "American Eagle Gold Coin Act, and other matters affecting the Stedman Corporation." Lobbyist — Donald R. Vaughan.

TANO CORP., New Orleans, La. Lobbyist — James E. Guirard Jr., 1090 Vermont Ave. N.W., Washington, D.C. 20005. Filed 2/28/83. Legislative interest — "Defense authorization and appropriations bills. Energy conservation legislation. Legislation affecting small business set-asides. Legislation affecting government R & D programs generally."

TEXAS EASTERN CORP., Washington, D.C. Lobbyist — Bliss, Craft & Richards, 1050 Thomas Jefferson St. N.W., Washington, D.C. 20007. Filed 2/24/83. Legislative interest — "Any legislation dealing with coal slurry pipelines."

UNITED DISTRIBUTION COS., 159 Town Hall Square, Falmouth, Mass. 02540. Filed for self 2/2/83. Legislative interest — "Amendments to the Natural Gas Policy Act; and amendments to the Natural Gas Act." Lobbyist — C. William Cooper.

R. DUFFY WALL & ASSOCIATES INC., 11 Dupont Circle N.W., Washington, D.C. 20036. Filed for self 2/24/83. Legislative interest — "For legislation to convert DISC to a GATT legal territoriality system; for amendments to the Clean Air Act to exclude fugitive dust from PSD increments; for legislation to correct inequities in the NGPA; for legislation to give Frasch sulphur mines parallel treatment with oil and gas wells under the UIC regulations of the Safe Drinking Water Act; against legislation to reduce percentage depletion for hard rock mining or for independent oil and gas producers; against legislation to violate the sanctity of contracts for the purchase or sale of domestic natural gas from independent producers. . . ." Lobbyist — R. D. Folsom.

Trade Associations

THE CONSUMER BANKERS ASSOCIATION, 1300 N. 17th St., Arlington, Va. 22209. Filed for self 2/22/83. Legislative interest — ". . . Usury preemption, HR 2501, S 1406, 12 U.S.C. 1731 *et seq.*; Financial Institution Restructuring and Services Act of 1981, S 1720; Bankruptcy Improvements Act of 1981, S 2000, HR 4786." Lobbyist — Marcia Z. Sullivan.

Miscellaneous

HARVARD SCHOOL OF PUBLIC HEALTH, Boston, Mass. Lobbyist — D.C. Associates Inc., 402 Third St. S.E., Washington, D.C. 20003. Filed 2/24/83. Legislative interest — "All matters affecting health, health-related research activities and programs; prospective hospital payment system measures."

March Registrations

Citizens' Groups

THE AMERICAN LEGION, 700 N. Pennsylvania St., Indianapolis, Ind. Filed for self 3/31/83. Legislative interest — "Americanism . . . children and youth . . . economics . . . foreign relations . . . internal affairs . . . national security . . . veteran affairs and rehabilitation. . . ." Lobbyist — Joseph E. Miller Jr., 1608 K St. N.W., Washington, D.C. 20006.

ASBESTOS LITIGATION GROUP, New York, N.Y. Lobbyist — Carol Tucker Foreman, 11 Dupont Circle N.W., Washington, D.C. 20036. Filed 3/28/83. Legislative interest — "For amendments to the Bankruptcy Code to prevent discharge of future claims in bankruptcy proceedings."

COMMITTEE FOR PRUDENT DEREGULATION, New York, N.Y. Lobbyist — Wexler, Reynolds, Harrison & Schule Inc., 1317 F St. N.W., Washington, D.C. 20004. Filed 3/11/83. Legislative interest — ". . . support of retention of 47 CFR 73.685 (j) and other matters pertaining to FCC Docket No. 82-345."

COMMITTEE FOR SAVERS' INTEREST, 315 Union St., Nashville, Tenn. 37201. Filed for self 3/2/83. Legislative interest — ". . . a portion of Title 3 of the 1982 Tax Equity and Fiscal Responsibility Act. . . ." Lobbyist — Ron Samuels.

ENVIRONMENTAL POLICY INSTITUTE, 317 Pennsylvania Ave. S.E., Washington, D.C. 20003. Filed for self 3/7/83. Legislative interest — "To influence public policy to improve management of the nation's public lands and mineral resources." Lobbyist — J. Stevens Lanich.

FRIENDS OF ANIMALS INC., 1 Pine St., Neptune, N.J. 07753. Filed for self 3/16/83. Legislative interest — "Legislation affecting animals." Lobbyist — Yvonne B. Eider.

FRIENDS OF THE COLUMBIA GORGE, 1306 Main St., Vancouver, Wash. 98660. Filed for self 3/8/83. Legislative interest — "Passage of act to protect the Columbia River Gorge . . . 'Columbia River Gorge Act of 1983'; S 627." Lobbyist — Bowen Blair Jr., 4140 S.W. Greenhills Way, Portland, Ore. 97221.

HOME RECORDING RIGHTS COALITION, Washington, D.C. Lobbyist — Carol Tucker Foreman, 11 Dupont Circle N.W., Washington, D.C. 20036. Filed 3/28/83. Legislative interest — "For HR 175 and S 175. Opposed to HR 1027, HR 1029, HR 1030, S 31, S 32, S 33."

MICCOSUKEE TRIBE OF INDIANS OF FLORIDA, Miami, Fla. Lobbyist — Hobbs, Straus, Dean & Wilder, 1735 New York Ave. N.W., Washington, D.C. 20006. Filed 3/1/83. Legislative interest — "Legislation affecting American Indians."

MONTANA WILDERNESS ASSOCIATION, P.O. Box 635, Helena, Mont. 59624. Filed for self 3/17/83. Legislative interest — Not specified. Lobbyist — Bill Cunningham.

NATIONAL ASSOCIATION OF ARAB AMERICANS, 1825 Connecticut Ave. N.W., Washington, D.C. 20009. Filed for self 3/31/83. Legislative interest — "Middle East related legislation . . . FY '84 Foreign Assistance Act . . . S 637, HR 1850. . . ." Lobbyists — Annette Najjar, Gregory A. Sahd.

NATIONAL CONSUMERS LEAGUE INC., Washington, D.C. Lobbyist — Barbara F. Warden, 3100 Connecticut Ave. N.W., Washington, D.C. 20008. Filed 3/8/83. Legislative interest — "First budget resolution; Consumer Product Safety Commission reauthorization; FTC reauthorization."

NATIONAL PARKS & CONSERVATION ASSOCIATION, Washington, D.C. Lobbyist — Laura Loomis, 419 N. Nelson St., Arlington, Va. 22203. Filed 3/7/83. Legislative interest — "General legislative interest relating to national park system areas, management and development and to natural resource conservation issues generally ... Alaska Hunting bill; S 49, HR 1493; oppose. Mono Lake National Monument bill; HR 1341; support."

SIERRA CLUB, 530 Bush St., San Francisco, Calif. 94108. Filed for self 3/15/83. Legislative interest — "Clean Air Act ... Clean Water Act ... national parks issues ... national wilderness issues." Lobbyist — Spencer Black.

YOUNG AMERICANS FOR FREEDOM INC., Box 1002, Woodland Road, Sterling, Va. 22170. Filed for self 3/22/83. Legislative interest — "Legislation affecting young people." Lobbyist — Michael Boos, 251 S. Reynolds St., Alexandria, Va. 22304.

Corporations and Businesses

AETNA LIFE & CASUALTY, Hartford, Conn. Lobbyist — Robert N. Giaimo, 499 S. Capitol St. S.W., Washington, D.C. 20003. (Former U.S. rep., D-Conn., 1959-81.) Filed 3/14/83. Legislative interest — "Insurance, taxation, banking and pension legislation."

AIWA AMERICA INC., Moonachie, N.J. Lobbyist — Patton, Boggs & Blow, 2550 M St. N.W., Washington, D.C. 20037. Filed 3/29/83. Legislative interest — "Legislation amending the Copyright Act that affects the home recording of television and radio broadcasts and the 'first sale' doctrine such as HR 175, S 175, S 3131, S 3132, S 3133."

AMERICAN PETROFINA INC., Dallas, Texas. Lobbyist — Black, Manafort and Stone Inc., 435 N. Lee St., Alexandria, Va. 22314. Filed 3/15/83. Legislative interest — "46 C.F.R. Part 276 regarding Department of Transportation policy in considering requests for repayment of construction-differential subsidy (CDS). ..."

AMERICAN PRESIDENT LINES, Washington, D.C. Lobbyist — Bliss, Craft & Richards, 1050 Thomas Jefferson St. N.W., Washington, D.C. 20007. Filed 3/10/83. Legislative interest — "S 47, the Ocean Shipping Act of 1983, and related House of Representatives legislation."

ANEUTRONIX INC., New York, N.Y. Lobbyist — Gray and Co., 3255 Grace St. N.W., Washington, D.C. 20007. Filed 3/5/83. Legislative interest — "Including but not limited to legislation concerning energy issues and appropriations."

ASHLAND OIL INC., Houston, Texas. Lobbyist — Sisk, Foley, Hultin & Driver, 2501 M St. N.W., Washington, D.C. 20037. Filed 3/10/83. Legislative interest — "Legislation with impact upon independent gasoline refiner-marketers, including opposition to legislation forcing divorcement or divestiture by independent refiners. Legislation being followed includes: the 'Small Business Motor Fuel Marketers Preservation Act,' HR 1755 and S 40."

BANKAMERICA CORP., San Francisco, Calif. Lobbyist — Fred J. Martin Jr., 1800 K St. N.W., Washington, D.C. 20006. Filed 3/9/83. Legislative interest — Not specified.

BATUS INC., Louisville, Ky. Lobbyist — Gray & Co., 3255 Grace St. N.W., Washington, D.C. 20007. Filed 3/9/83. Legislative interest — "Including but not limited to agricultural and tax issues."

BENDONE-DeROSSI INTERNATIONAL, Vineland, N.J. Lobbyist — Surrey & Morse, 1156 15th St. N.W., Washington, D.C. 20005. Filed 3/25/83. Legislative interest — "Bendone-DeRossi International supplies uniforms to the U.S. Army. The Department of Defense has proposed a reduction in the number of uniforms it procures for each serviceman. Bendone-DeRossi opposes the proposed reduction. ..."

BETHLEHEM STEEL CORP., Bethlehem, Pa. Lobbyist — Charls E. Walker Associates Inc., 1730 Pennsylvania Ave. N.W., Washington, D.C. 20006. Filed 3/11/83. Legislative interest — "... may concern issues relating to the promotion of the economic interests of the basic industries of the nation."

BEVERLY ENTERPRISES, Pasadena, Calif. Lobbyist — Gray and Co., 3255 Grace St. N.W., Washington, D.C. 20007. Filed 3/9/83. Legislative interest — "Including but not limited to health and tax legislation."

BUDD CO., Troy, Mich. Lobbyist — Gray and Co., 3255 Grace St. N.W., Washington, D.C. 20007. Filed 3/9/83. Legislative interest — "Including but not limited to environmental and transportation legislation."

BURNS & ROE INC., Washington, D.C. Lobbyist — Wagner & Baroody Inc., 1100 17th St. N.W., Washington, D.C. 20036. Filed 3/10/83. Legislative interest — "For funding of the Clinch River Breeder Reactor."

CHAMPLIN PETROLEUM CO., Fort Worth, Texas. Lobbyist — Sisk, Foley, Hultin & Driver, 2501 M St. N.W., Washington, D.C. 20037. Filed 3/10/83. Legislative interest — "Legislation with impact upon independent gasoline refiner-marketers, including opposition to legislation forcing divorcement or divestiture by independent refiners. Legislation being followed includes: the 'Small Business Motor Fuel Marketers Preservation Act,' HR 1755 and S 40."

CHEMICAL WASTE MANAGEMENT INC., Oak Brook, Ill. Lobbyist — Richard N. Sharood, 510 Seward Square S.E., Washington, D.C. 20003. Filed 3/5/83. Legislative interest — "HR 5723 and S 2336 - FY 83 Maritime Authorization - against enactment of amendment extending Jones Act to include ocean incineration of toxic waste."

CHICAGO AND NORTHWESTERN RAILROAD, Chicago, Ill. Lobbyist — Wagner & Baroody Inc., 1100 17th St. N.W., Washington, D.C. 20036. Filed 3/10/83. Legislative interest — "Any legislation affecting the railroad industry."

CITIES SERVICE OIL AND GAS CORP., Box 300, Tulsa, Okla. 74102. Lobbyist — Skadden, Arps, Slate, Meagher & Flom, 919 18th St. N.W., Washington, D.C. 20006. Filed 3/1/83. Legislative interest — "Natural gas deregulation legislation." Filed for self 3/15/83. Legislative interest — "Legislation impacting the following industries: petroleum, natural gas, chemicals, synthetic fuels." Lobbyist — Jean L. Mestres, 1747 Pennsylvania Ave. N.W., Washington, D.C. 20006.

COLUMBIA GAS SYSTEM SERVICE CORP., Washington, D.C. Lobbyist — Van Ness, Feldman, Sutcliffe, Curtis & Levenberg, 1050 Thomas Jefferson St. N.W., Washington, D.C. 20007. Filed 3/30/83. Legislative interest — "Opposition to S 615 and HR 1760."

COMBINED HEALTH RESOURCES INC., Phoenix, Ariz. Lobbyist — Perito, Duerk, Carlson & Pinco, 1140 Connecticut Ave. N.W., Washington, D.C. 20036. Filed 3/5/83. Legislative interest — "Legislation affecting ... Medicare prospective payments system; and ... report of the National Commission on Social Security Reform, January 1983."

COMERICA INC., Detroit, Mich. Lobbyist — Miller, Canfield, Paddock and Stone, 2555 M St. N.W., Washington, D.C. 20037. Filed 3/14/83. Legislative interest — "HR 1900 and Senate version - Social Security amendments against provisions to tax cafeteria plans Section 125, and flexible compensation plans Section 401(k)."

DILLINGHAM SHIP REPAIR, Portland, Ore. Lobbyist — Jack Ferguson Associates Inc., 203 Maryland Ave. N.E., Washington, D.C. 20002. Filed 3/23/83. Legislative interest — "Export Administration Act of 1979."

E-SYSTEMS, Arlington, Va. Lobbyist — Wagner & Baroody, 1100 17th St. N.W., Washington, D.C. 20036. Filed 3/10/83. Legislative interest — "Legislation affecting research and development and anything relating to the electronics industry."

FEDERAL NATIONAL MORTGAGE ASSOCIATION, 3900 Wisconsin Ave. N.W., Washington, D.C. 20016. Filed for self 3/22/83. Legislative interest — "Amendments pertaining to the Housing and Urban Rural Recovery Act of 1983 (HR 1) and S 644." Lobbyists — Thomas H. Stanton, Judy Winchester.

FORD AEROSPACE, Arlington, Va. Lobbyist — Van Fleet Associates Inc., 499 S. Capitol St. S.W., Washington, D.C. 20003. Filed 3/10/83. Legislative interest — "Generally to act in Ford Aerospace's behalf regarding the FY 84 DOD authorization and appropriations bills."

FUJI PHOTO FILM U.S.A. INC., New York, N.Y. Lobbyist — Patton, Boggs & Blow, 2550 M St. N.W., Washington, D.C. 20037. Filed 3/29/83. Legislative interest — "Legislation amending the Copyright Act that affects the home recording of television and radio broadcasts and the 'first sale' doctrine such as HR 175, S 175, S 3131, S 3132 and S 3133."

G A TECHNOLOGIES INC., La Jolla, Calif. Lobbyist — Clair W. Burgener, 530 Broadway, San Diego, Calif. 92101. (Former U.S. rep., R-Calif., 1973-83.) Filed 3/14/83. Legislative interest — "Authorization and appropriation levels for such energy programs as fusion and the high temperature gas cooled reactor (HTGR)."

GENERAL ELECTRIC CO., San Jose, Calif. Lobbyist — Fried, Frank, Harris, Shriver & Kampelman, 600 New Hampshire Ave. N.W., Washington, D.C. 20037. Filed 3/17/83. Legislative interest — "Support for nuclear licensing reform legislation."

GREENS CREEK JOINT VENTURE, Denver, Colo. Lobbyist — Jones, Jones, Bell, Close & Brown, 1110 Vermont Ave. N.W., Washington, D.C. 20005. (Former U.S. Rep. James D. Santini, D-Nev., 1975-83, was listed as agent for this client.) Filed 3/30/83. Legislative interest — "Monitoring and reporting on legislative activity dealing with public lands, United States-Canadian relations, and critical and strategic minerals issues."

GRUMMAN AEROSPACE CORP., Arlington, Va. Lobbyist — Leo C. Zeferetti, 9912 Fort Hamilton Parkway, Brooklyn, N.Y. 11209. (Former U.S. rep., D-N.Y., 1975-83.) Filed 3/7/83. Legislative interest — ". . . including but not limited to the E2C aircraft program."

HUNT BUILDING CORP., El Paso, Texas. Lobbyist — Fried, Frank, Harris, Shriver & Kampelman, 600 New Hampshire Ave. N.W., Washington, D.C. 20037. Filed 3/21/83. Legislative interest — ". . . proposed changes in federal housing and urban development laws."

INGRAM TANKSHIPS INC., 4100 One Shell Square, New Orleans, La. 70139. Lobbyist — Hansell & Post, 1915 I St. N.W., Washington, D.C. 20006. Filed 3/2/83. Legislative interest — "Any legislation affecting U.S. flagship shipping." Filed for self 3/2/83. Legislative interest — "Any legislation affecting U.S. flagship shipping." Lobbyist — Cyrus E. Webb.

KENWOOD U.S.A. CORP., Carson, Calif. Lobbyist — Patton, Boggs & Blow, 2550 M St. N.W., Washington, D.C. 20037. Filed 3/29/83. Legislative interest — "Legislation amending the Copyright Act that affects the home recording of television and radio broadcasts and the 'first sale' doctrine such as HR 175, S 175, S 3131, S 3132, and S 3133."

KONISHIROKU AMPEX CO. LTD., Tokyo, Japan. Lobbyist — Patton, Boggs & Blow, 2550 M St. N.W., Washington, D.C. 20037. Filed 3/29/83. Legislative interest — "Legislation amending the Copyright Act that affects the home recording of television and radio broadcasts and the 'first sale' doctrine such as HR 175, S 175, S 3131, S 3132, and S 3133."

LAKE ONTARIO CEMENT LTD., Toronto, Ontario, Canada. Lobbyist — Dow, Lohnes & Albertson, 1225 Connecticut Ave. N.W., Washington, D.C. 20036. Filed 3/15/83. Legislative interest — "Surface Transportation Assistance Act of 1982 and other international trade legislation affecting cement imports from Canada . . . HR 621/Public Law 424 . . . in opposition to any legislation which restricts cement imports from Canada."

LANIHAU CORPS., Honolulu, Hawaii. Lobbyist — Wagner & Baroody, 1100 17th St. N.W., Washington, D.C. 20036. Filed 3/10/83. Legislative interest — "For an equitable land swap with the federal government."

LEGGETTE & CO. INC., Dallas, Texas. Lobbyist — Johnson & Swanson, 4700 InterFirst Two, Dallas, Texas 75270. Filed 3/3/83. Legislative interest — "To represent the interests of certain non-profit hospitals in connection with the report of the National Commission on Social Security Reform."

LONE STAR STEEL, Dallas, Texas. Lobbyist — Akin, Gump, Strauss, Hauer & Feld, 1333 New Hampshire Ave. N.W., Washington, D.C. 20036. Filed 3/3/83. Legislative interest — "Legislation relating to the importation of steel pipe and tube products."

LONG ISLAND TRUST CO., Garden City, N.Y. Lobbyist — Wagner & Baroody Inc., 1100 17th St. N.W., Washington, D.C. 20036. Filed 3/10/83. Legislative interest — "Any legislation affecting the banking industry."

LORIMAR PRODUCTIONS, Culver City, Calif. Lobbyist — Jones, Jones, Bell, Close & Brown, 1110 Vermont Ave. N.W., Washington, D.C. 20005. (Former U.S. Rep. James D. Santini, D-Nev., 1975-83, was listed as agent for this client.) Filed 3/30/83. Legislative interest — "Monitoring legislation, particularly the syndication and financial interest rules; oppose repeal of these rules."

MARRIOTT CORP., Washington, D.C. Lobbyist — Akin, Gump, Strauss, Hauer & Feld, 1333 New Hampshire Ave. N.W., Washington, D.C. 20036. Filed 3/22/83. Legislative interest — "Hearings and any legislation affecting Social Security payroll taxes, particularly so-called 'cafeteria plans,' including S 1 and HR 1900, the 'Social Security Act Amendments of 1983.' "

MAXELL CORPORATION OF AMERICA, Moonachie, N.J. Lobbyist — Patton, Boggs & Blow, 2550 M St. N.W., Washington, D.C. 20037. Filed 3/29/83. Legislative interest — "Legislation amending the Copyright Act that affects the home recording of television and radio broadcasts and the 'first sale' doctrine such as HR 175, S 175, S 3131, S 3132, and S 3133."

McDONNELL DOUGLAS ASTRONAUTICS CORP., Huntington Beach, Calif. Lobbyist — Van Ness, Feldman, Sutcliffe, Curtis & Levenberg, 1050 Thomas Jefferson St. N.W., Washington, D.C. 20007. Filed 3/5/83. Legislative interest — "Monitor and plan opportunities to educate appropriate Congressmen with visits as appropriate, towards drafting, introducing and pursuing passage of measure for affirmative commitment on the energy tax credit . . . sections 46 & 48 of the Internal Revenue Code. . . ."

McGIFFERT, MUELLER, JONES & DARCY, 1701 K St. N.W., Washington, D.C. 20006. Filed for self 3/11/83. Legislative interest — "Foreign relations and non-military, foreign economic aid to the Hashemite Kingdom of Jordan." Lobbyist — Enüd McGiffert.

MONSANTO CO., 800 N. Lindbergh Blvd., St. Louis, Mo. 63167. Filed for self 3/16/83. Legislative interest — Not specified. Lobbyist — Thomas M. Helscher, 1101 17th St. N.W., Washington, D.C. 20036.

NAKAMICHI U.S.A. CORP., Santa Monica, Calif. Lobbyist — Patton, Boggs & Blow, 2550 M St. N.W., Washington, D.C. 20037. Filed 3/29/83. Legislative interest — "Legislation amending the Copyright Act that affects the home recording of television and radio broadcasts and the 'first sale' doctrine such as HR 175, S 175, S 3131, S 3132, S 3133."

NATIONAL SECURITY AND RETIREMENT PROGRAM, West Chester, Pa. Lobbyist — O'Connor & Hannan, 1919 Pennsylvania Ave. N.W., Washington, D.C. 20006. (Former U.S. Rep. Thomas B. Evans Jr., R-Del., 1977-83, was listed as agent for this client.) Filed 3/2/83. Legislative interest — "Possible amendment to Social Security Act."

NORANDA EXPLORATION INC., Denver, Colo. Lobbyist — Jones, Jones, Bell, Close & Brown, 1110 Vermont Ave. N.W., Washington, D.C. 20005. (Former U.S. Rep. James D. Santini, D-Nev., 1975-83, was listed as agent for this client.) Filed 3/30/83. Legislative interest — "Monitoring and reporting on legislative activity dealing with public lands, United States-Canadian relations, and critical and strategic minerals issues."

NORANDA MINING INC., Denver, Colo. Lobbyist — Jones, Jones, Bell, Close & Brown, 1110 Vermont Ave. N.W., Washington, D.C. 20005. (Former U.S. Rep. James D. Santini, D-Nev., 1975-83, was listed as agent for this client.) Filed 3/30/83. Legislative interest — "Monitoring and reporting on legislative activity dealing with public lands, United States-Canadian relations, and critical and strategic minerals issues."

NORTHVILLE INDUSTRIES CORP., Melville, N.Y. Lobbyist — Charls E. Walker Associates Inc., 1730 Pennsylvania

Ave. N.W., Washington, D.C. 20006. Filed 3/18/83. Legislative interest — "... may concern issues relating to the export of goods from the United States."

PACIFIC RESOURCES INC., Honolulu, Hawaii. Lobbyist — Sisk, Foley, Hultin & Driver, 2501 M St. N.W., Washington, D.C. 20037. Filed 3/10/83. Legislative interest — "Legislation with impact upon independent gasoline refiner-marketers, including opposition to legislation forcing divorcement or divestiture by independent refiners. Legislation being followed includes: the 'Small Business Motor Fuel Marketers Preservation Act,' HR 1755 and S 40."

PAN AMERICAN NATIONAL BANK, Dallas, Texas. Lobbyist — Gray and Co., 3255 Grace St. N.W., Washington, D.C. 20007. Filed 3/9/83. Legislative interest — "Including but not limited to small business issues."

PIONEER ELECTRONICS (U.S.A.) INC., Long Beach, Calif. Lobbyist — Patton, Boggs & Blow, 2550 M St. N.W., Washington, D.C. 20037. Filed 3/29/83. Legislative interest — "Legislation amending the Copyright Act that affects the home recording of television and radio broadcasts and the 'first sale' doctrine such as HR 175, S 175, S 3131, S 3132, S 3133."

PIRELLI CABLE CORP., Union, N.J. Lobbyist — Schlossberg-Cassidy and Associates Inc., 955 L'Enfant Plaza S.W., Washington, D.C. 20024. Filed 3/9/83. Legislative interest — "All legislation and appropriations affecting public works, the Department of Energy, the Department of Defense, the Department of Transportation and other government funded construction works."

PPG INDUSTRIES INC., Washington, D.C. Lobbyist — Patton, Boggs & Blow, 2550 M St. N.W., Washington, D.C. 20037. Filed 3/17/83. Legislative interest — "Natural Gas Policy Act of 1978 and amendments thereto - S 615, S 60, S 239, S 291, S 293, S 370, S 689, HR 2012. For the bill with amendments."

RIVIANA FOODS INC., Houston, Texas. Lobbyist — Akin, Gump, Strauss, Hauer & Feld, 1333 New Hampshire Ave. N.W., Washington, D.C. 20036. Filed 3/22/83. Legislative interest — "Hearings and any legislation relating to commodity distribution programs including HR 1590, the 'Emergency Food Assistance and Commodity Distribution Act of 1983' and HR 1718, providing emergency supplemental appropriations for FY 1983."

RLC CORP., Wilmington, Del. Lobbyist — O'Connor & Hannan, 1919 Pennsylvania Ave. N.W., Washington, D.C. 20006. (Former U.S. Rep. Thomas B. Evans Jr., R-Del., 1977-83, was listed as agent for this client.) Filed 3/2/83. Legislative interest — "... including, but not limited to, changes in the gas tax."

ROCKWELL INTERNATIONAL CORP., Arlington, Va. Lobbyist — Hansell & Post, 1915 I St. N.W., Washington, D.C. 20006. Filed 3/9/83. Legislative interest — "Legislative action relating to the authorization of and appropriation for additional shuttle orbiters including long lead items."

SAMARITAN HEALTH SERVICE, Phoenix, Ariz. Lobbyist — Perito, Duerk, Carlson & Pinco, 1140 Connecticut Ave. N.W., Washington, D.C. 20036. Filed 3/14/83. Legislative interest — "... Medicare prospective payment system and ... report of the National Commission on Social Security Reform, January 1983."

SANSUI ELECTRONICS CORP., Lyndhurst, N.J. Lobbyist — Patton, Boggs & Blow, 2550 M St. N.W., Washington, D.C. 20037. Filed 3/29/83. Legislative interest — "Legislation amending the Copyright Act that affects the home recording of television and radio broadcasts and the 'first sale' doctrine such as HR 175, S 175, S 3131, S 3132, and S 3133."

SHELL OIL CO., P.O. Box 2463, Houston, Texas 77001. Filed for self 3/1/83. Legislative interest — "... oil and gas production, chemicals, health, safety and the environment, taxation concerns, and employee/employer relations." Lobbyists — Paul D. Ching, 1025 Connecticut Ave. N.W., Washington, D.C. 20036; Thomas G. Johnson, P.O. Box 2463, Houston, Texas 77001.

THE SHERWIN-WILLIAMS CO., Cincinnati, Ohio. Lobbyist — Taft, Stettinius & Hollister, 1800 Massachusetts Ave. N.W., Washington, D.C. 20036. Filed 3/1/83. Legislative interest — "Advice in regard to legislation to extend moratorium on application of food and drug laws to saccharin. Of particular interest are S 89 and HR 968."

RICHARD L. SINNOTT AND CO., Washington, D.C. Lobbyist — Gray and Co., 3255 Grace St. N.W., Washington, D.C. 20007. Filed 3/8/83. Legislative interest — "Including but not limited to legislation to provide a limited exemption from the antitrust laws for professional football."

SOLAREX CORP., Rockville, Md. Lobbyist — Farnsworth, Martin & Gallagher, 1823 Jefferson Place N.W., Washington, D.C. 20036. Filed 3/17/83. Legislative interest — "Solar tax legislation."

THE SOUTHLAND CORP., P.O. Box 719, Dallas, Texas 75221. Filed for self 3/11/83. Legislative interest — "Legislative interest shall be those determined to have an effect on the retail industry." Lobbyists — W. M. Click, William L. Fisher, Pamela Sederholm.

SUMITOMO 3M LTD., Toyko, Japan. Lobbyist — Patton, Boggs & Blow, 2550 M St. N.W., Washington, D.C. 20037. Filed 3/29/83. Legislative interest — "Legislation amending the Copyright Act that affects the home recording of television and radio broadcasts and the 'first sale' doctrine such as HR 175, S 3131, S 3132, and S 3133."

SUN CO. INC., 100 Matsonford Road, Radnor, Pa. 19087. Filed for self 3/17/83. Legislative interest — "Petroleum, environment, transportation, marine shipping, pipelines, and energy related matters, such as product liability, divorcement, and Caribbean Basin Initiative." Lobbyist — Ralph Zaayenga, 1800 K St. N.W., Washington, D.C. 20006.

TDK U.S.A. CORP., Port Washington, N.Y. Lobbyist — Patton, Boggs & Blow, 2550 M St. N.W., Washington, D.C. 20037. Filed 3/29/83. Legislative interest — "Legislation amending the Copyright Act that affects the home recording of television and radio broadcasts and the 'first sale' doctrine such as HR 175, S 175, S 3131, S 3132, and S 3133."

TEAC CORP., Tokyo, Japan. Lobbyist — Patton, Boggs & Blow, 2550 M St. N.W., Washington, D.C. 20037. Filed 3/29/83. Legislative interest — "Legislation amending the Copyright Act that affects the home recording of television and radio broadcasts and the 'first sale' doctrine such as HR 175, S 175, S 3131, S 3132, and S 3133."

TEKNIKA ELECTRONICS CORP., New York, N.Y. Lobbyist — Patton, Boggs & Blow, 2550 M St. N.W., Washington, D.C. 20037. Filed 3/29/83. Legislative interest — "Legislation amending the Copyright Act that affects the home recording of television and radio broadcasts and the 'first sale' doctrine such as HR 175, S 175, S 3131, S 3132, and S 3133."

TENNECO INC., Houston, Texas. Lobbyist — Sisk, Foley, Hultin & Driver, 2501 M St. N.W., Washington, D.C. 20037. Filed 3/10/83. Legislative interest — "Legislation with impact upon independent gasoline refiner-marketers, including opposition to legislation forcing divorcement or divestiture by independent refiners. Legislation being followed includes: the 'Small Business Motor Fuel Marketers Preservation Act,' HR 1755 and S 40."

TEXAS OIL & GAS CORP., Dallas, Texas. Lobbyist — Beveridge & Diamond, 1333 New Hampshire Ave. N.W., Washington, D.C. 20036. Filed 3/25/83. Legislative interest — "Congressional action affecting natural gas decontrol."

TWENTIETH CENTURY-FOX FILM CORP., Beverly Hills, Calif. Lobbyist — Swidler, Berlin & Strelow, 1000 Thomas Jefferson St. N.W., Washington, D.C. 20007. Filed 3/29/83. Legislative interest — "Copyright and communications legislation: The Consumer Video Sales/Rental Amendment of 1983, HR 1029; The Home Recording Act of 1983, HR 1030; To provide a moratorium on changes in FCC Syndication and Financial Interest Rules, HR 2250."

UNIROYAL INC., Middlebury, Conn. Lobbyist — Barnes, Richardson & Colburn, 1819 H St. N.W., Washington, D.C. 20006. Filed 3/11/83. Legislative interest — "Proposed tariff suspension on imports of dimethylbenzylphenylamine ... 19 U.S.C. section 1202 (Tariff Schedules of the United States)...."

UNION PACIFIC RAILROAD CORP., Washington, D.C. Lobbyist — Wagner & Baroody Inc., 1100 17th St. N.W., Washington, D.C. 20036. Filed 3/10/83. Legislative interest — "Any legislation affecting the railroad industry, especially opposition to coal slurry pipelines."

U.S. BANKNOTE CORP., New York, N.Y. Lobbyist —

Gray & Co., 3255 Grace St. N.W., Washington, D.C. 20007. Filed 3/9/83. Legislative interest — "Including but not limited to immigration and food stamps legislation."

VICTOR MAGNETAPE CO. LTD., Ibaragi, Japan. Lobbyist — Patton, Boggs & Blow, 2550 M St. N.W., Washington, D.C. 20037. Filed 3/29/83. Legislative interest — "Legislation amending the Copyright Act that affects the home recording of television and radio broadcasts and the 'first sale' doctrine such as HR 175, S 175, S 3131, S 3132 and S 3133."

WANG LABORATORIES INC., Lowell, Mass. Lobbyist — Gadsby & Hannah, One Post Office Square, Boston, Mass. 02109. Filed 3/10/83. Legislative interest — "Issues involving telecommunications policy."

WEBSTER, JEPPSON, JONES & AGRAN, Los Angeles, Calif. Lobbyist — Miller & Chevalier, 655 15th St. N.W., Washington, D.C. 20005. Filed 3/18/83. Legislative interest — "Legislation affecting Title 26 of the U.S. Code."

WHEELS INC., Chicago, Ill. Lobbyist — Cohen and Uretz, 1775 K St. N.W., Washington, D.C. 20006. Filed 3/18/83. Legislative interest — "Tax legislation affecting leasing, particularly support of HR 1607, and any similar legislation."

Labor Groups

AMERICAN FOREIGN SERVICE ASSOCIATION, 2101 E St. N.W., Washington, D.C. 20037. Filed for self 3/14/83. Legislative interest — "Any legislation affecting the terms and conditions of appointment to or employment in the Foreign Service of the United States." Lobbyist — Robert M. Beers.

BUILDING AND CONSTRUCTION TRADE DE-PARTMENTS, AFL-CIO, Washington, D.C. Lobbyist — Leo C. Zeferetti, 9912 Fort Hamilton Parkway, Brooklyn, N.Y. 11209. (Former U.S. rep., D-N.Y., 1975-83.) Filed 3/7/83. Legislative interest — ". . . including but limited to the Davis-Bacon Act."

METAL TRADES DEPARTMENT, AFL-CIO, Washington, D.C. Lobbyist — D.C. Associates Inc., 402 Third St. S.E., Washington, D.C. 20003. Filed 3/7/83. Legislative interest — "All legislation affecting Federal and private shipyards; legislation affecting maritime matters, port development, and related issues."

NATIONAL ASSOCIATION OF LETTER CARRI-ERS, Washington, D.C. Lobbyist — Frank J. Brasco, 108 Greenwich St., New York, N.Y. 10006. (Former U.S. rep., D-N.Y., 1967-75.) Filed 3/9/83. Legislative interest — Not specified.

State and Local Governments

KANSAS CORPORATION COMMISSION, Topeka, Kan. Lobbyist — Jerris Leonard & Associates, 900 17th St. N.W., Washington, D.C. 20006. Filed 3/5/83. Legislative interest — ". . . natural gas, telecommunications, etc."

Trade Associations

ASSOCIATED BUILDERS AND CONTRACTORS INC., Washington, D.C. Lobbyist — Wagner & Baroody Inc., 1100 17th St. N.W., Washington, D.C. 20036. Filed 3/10/83. Legislative interest — "For reform of the Davis-Bacon Act."

AMERICAN BUS ASSOCIATION, Washington, D.C. Lobbyist — Wagner & Baroody Inc., 1100 17th N.W., Washington, D.C. 20036. Filed 3/10/83. Legislative interest — "Any legislation affecting the bus industry."

AMERICAN LEAGUE FOR EXPORTS AND SECU-RITY ASSISTANCE INC., 475 L'Enfant Plaza S.W., Washington, D.C. 20024. Filed for self 3/7/83. Legislative interest — "Matters dealing with U.S. export policy, legislation and procedures to include taxes, incentives, Eximbank, DISC, tax policy, licensing procedures and other matters relating to the interests of ALESA." Lobbyists — George C. Axtell, Joel L. Johnson.

AMERICAN MARITIME ASSOCIATION, New York, N.Y. Lobbyist — Gray and Co., 3255 Grace St. N.W., Washington, D.C. 20007. Filed 3/9/83. Legislative interest — "Including but not limited to maritime legislation."

AMERICAN SOYBEAN ASSOCIATION, St. Louis, Mo. Lobbyist — Akin, Gump, Strauss, Hauer & Feld, 1333 New Hampshire Ave. N.W., Washington, D.C. 20036. Filed 3/29/83. Legislative interest — "Hearings and any legislation affecting the FY 1984 budget for the PL 480 program."

COALITION FOR ENVIRONMENTAL DATA, Washington, D.C. Lobbyist — Chwat/Weigend Associates, 226 Massachusetts Ave. N.E., Washington, D.C. 20002. Filed 3/10/83. Legislative interest — "General legislative interests regarding the potential transfer of federal government meteorological and earth resources satellites, monitoring stations and other related facilities to the private sector."

FAIR TRADE SUBCOMMITTEE OF THE INTERNA-TIONAL TRADE COMMITTEE OF THE CAST METALS FEDERATION, Des Plaines, Ill. Lobbyist — Simonelli and Hall, 1420 N St. N.W., Washington, D.C. 20005. Filed 3/25/83. Legislative interest — "All matters pertaining to international trade."

FEDERAL LAW ENFORCEMENT OFFICERS ASSO-CIATION, Carle Place, N.Y. Lobbyist — Nickerson, Ingram & Associates Inc., 1150 17th St. N.W., Washington, D.C. 20036. Filed 3/7/83. Legislative interest — "All legislation concerning the financing, operation and regulation for federal law enforcement agencies. . . ."

FUTURES INDUSTRY ASSOCIATION INC., 1825 I St. N.W., Washington, D.C. 20006. Filed for self 3/14/83. Legislative interest — "The FIA has a general interest in all legislation affecting and involving the trading of futures contracts. The FIA is specifically interested in any legislation to amend the Commodity Exchange Act or other laws governing the regulation of futures markets by the Commodity Futures Trading Commission or other agency." Lobbyists — John W. Clagett, John M. Damgard, Leighton W. Lang.

HEALTH INSURANCE ASSOCIATION OF AMER-ICA, Washington, D.C. Lobbyist — Gray and Co., 3255 Grace St. N.W., Washington, D.C. 20007. Filed 3/14/83. Legislative interest — "Including but not limited to HR 4961."

HIGHWAY USERS FEDERATION FOR SAFETY AND MOBILITY, 1776 Massachusetts Ave. N.W., Washington, D.C. 20036. Filed for self 3/14/83. Legislative interest — "General legislative interest concerns highway development and use; specifically . . . the federal-aid highway and highway safety acts and amendments thereto . . . related federal-aid highway program bills . . . emergency energy contingency planning and environmental legislation pertinent to highway transportation; positions typically favor legislation which provides for safe and efficient highway transportation." Lobbyist — K. H. Kruke.

INVESTMENT COMPANY INSTITUTE, Washington, D.C. Lobbyist — Fried, Frank, Harris, Shriver & Kampelman, 600 New Hampshire Ave. N.W., Washington, D.C. 20037. Filed 3/4/83. Legislative interest — "Legislative representation in support of amendments to the Internal Revenue Code concerning tax-exempt obligations."

JOINT MARITIME CONGRESS, 444 N. Capitol St. N.W., Washington, D.C. 20001. Lobbyist — Gray and Co., 3255 Grace St. N.W., Washington, D.C. 20007. Filed 3/9/83. Legislative interest — "Including but not limited to maritime legislation." Filed for self 3/7/83. Legislative interest — "Transportation and maritime related legislation." Lobbyist — Michael J. Balzano.

NATIONAL ASSOCIATION OF REALTORS, 777 14th St. N.W., Washington, D.C. 20005. Filed for self 3/7/83. Legislative interest — "Any and all legislation affecting the real estate industry including specifically, tax relief; independent contractor; restructuring of financial institutions; enterprise zone legislation; coastal barrier protection; emergency tax proposals to spur housing; and 1983 budget." Lobbyists — John B. Blount, Vickie L. Erickson.

NATIONAL BEER WHOLESALERS ASSOCIATION, 5205 Leesburg Pike, Falls Church, Va. 22041. Lobbyist — Wagner & Baroody Inc., 1100 17th St. N.W., Washington, D.C. 20036. Filed

3/10/83. Legislative interest — "For legislation to codify existing court decisions granting exclusive territories for malt beverages." Filed for self 3/8/83. Legislative interest — ". . . legislation affecting the business interests of small businessmen involved in beer wholesaling. Specific legislative interests include alcohol excise taxes, the Malt Beverage Interbrand Competition Act which would affirm the beer industry's practice of granting exclusive territorial distribution franchises; funding for the Department of Treasury's Bureau of Alcohol, Tobacco and Firearms and any amendment of the Federal Alcohol Administration Act." Lobbyist — Linda S. Rearick.

NATIONAL INHOLDERS ASSOCIATION, Sonoma, Calif. Lobbyist — Douglas Smith, 3219 Magnolia Ave., Falls Church, Va. 22041. Filed 3/14/83. Legislative interest — "Public land legislation affecting inholders. . . ."

NATIONAL MASS RETAILING INSTITUTE, New York, N.Y. Lobbyist — Peabody, Lambert & Meyers, 1150 Connecticut Ave. N.W., Washington, D.C. 20036. Filed 3/23/83. Legislative interest — "Opposing Department of Justice policies on resale price maintenance."

NATIONAL SOYBEAN PROCESSORS ASSOCIA-TION, Washington, D.C. Lobbyist — Akin, Gump, Strauss, Hauer & Feld, 1333 New Hampshire Ave. N.W., Washington, D.C. 20036. Filed 3/29/83. Legislative interest — "Hearings and any legislation affecting the FY 1984 budget for the PL 480 program."

NATIONAL TOOLING AND MACHINE ASSOCIA-TION, Fort Washington, Md. Lobbyist — Ruttenberg, Phelps & Slocum, 5201 Leesburg Pike, Falls Church, Va. 22041. Filed 3/23/83. Legislative interest — "Interested in supporting legislation that increases competition in government procurement by eliminating barriers to small business participation."

NATIONAL TOUR ASSOCIATION, Lexington, Ky. Lobbyist — Jones, Jones, Bell, Close & Brown, 1110 Vermont Ave. N.W., Washington, D.C. 20005. (Former U.S. Rep. James D. Santini, D-Nev., 1975-83, was listed as agent for this client.) Filed 3/30/83. Legislative interest — ". . . travel and tourism issues before the 98th Congress, such as USTTA funding, immigration laws affecting tourism travel, tax issues such as the '3-martini lunch deduction,' energy policy and taxes, bus regulatory reform act oversight, National Park Service legislation."

POTATO CHIP/SNACK FOOD ASSOCIATION, 1735 Jefferson Davis Highway, Arlington, Va. 22202. Filed for self 3/18/83. Legislative interest — "All legislation affecting the snack food industry, including energy, agricultural, and nutrition legislation." Lobbyist — Marjorie Carroll Kicak.

SOUTHEASTERN FISHERIES ASSOCIATION INC., Tallahassee, Fla. Lobbyist — Galloway & Greenberg, 1725 I St. N.W., Washington, D.C. 20006. Filed 3/31/83. Legislative interest — "All legislation affecting commercial fisheries in the Gulf of Mexico and the South Atlantic Ocean, including FY 1984 State/Justice/Commerce appropriations bills, federal Unemployment Tax Act (S 146), fish net tariff reductions, Capital Construction Fund (S 254)."

THE TOBACCO INSTITUTE, Washington, D.C. Lobbyist — William B. Prendergast, 6215 Kellogg Drive, McLean, Va. Filed 3/1/83. Legislative interest — "General legislative interests are equitable tax treatment of tobacco and other legislation affecting tobacco. HR 230 - Favor; HR 698 - Oppose; HR 1473 - Oppose."

TRANSPORTATION INSTITUTE, Washington, D.C. Lobbyist — Leo C. Zeferetti, 9912 Fort Hamilton Parkway, Brooklyn, N.Y. 11209. (Former U.S. rep., D-N.Y., 1975-83.) Filed 3/7/83. Legislative interest — ". . . including but not limited to the Cargo Bulk bill."

UNITED TOBACCO GROWERS ASSOCIATION, Wendell, N.C. Lobbyist — Howard D. Moye Jr., P.O. Box 28, Farmville, N.C. 27828. Filed 3/8/83. Legislative interest — Not specified.

Miscellaneous

OTTO BREMER FOUNDATION, St. Paul, Minn. Lobbyist — Davis, Polk & Wardwell, 1575 I St. N.W., Washington, D.C. 20005. Filed 3/16/83. Legislative interest — "Legislation relating to sections 4942 and 4943 of the Internal Revenue Code affecting charitable foundations." Lobbyist — Winthrop, Weinstine & Sexton, 444 Cedar St., St. Paul, Minn. 55101. Filed 3/22/83. Legislative interest — "Legislation relating to sections 4942 and 4943 of the Internal Revenue Code affecting charitable foundations."

THEODORE S. J. DAVI, 6 Magnolia Ave., Montvale, N.J. 07645. Filed for self 3/11/83. Legislative interest — "General environmental issues. . . ."

WILLIAM C. GIBB, 1140 Connecticut Ave. N.W., Washington, D.C. 20036. Filed for self 3/23/83. Legislative interest — "The general legislative interest is transportation. . . ."

HARRIS METHODIST HEALTH SYSTEM, Fort Worth, Texas. Lobbyist — Johnson & Swanson, 4700 InterFirst Two, Dallas, Texas 75270. Filed 3/3/83. Legislative interest — "To represent the interests of certain non-profit hospitals in connection with the report of the National Commission on Social Security Reform."

HARVARD MEDICAL CENTER, Boston, Mass. Lobbyist — O'Neill and Haase, 1333 New Hampshire Ave. N.W., Washington, D.C. 20036. Filed 3/4/83. Legislative interest — "Health legislation."

JACK C. JORGENSEN, 6534 Spring Valley Drive, Alexandria, Va. 22312. Filed for self 3/28/83. Legislative interest — "Water resources research legislation and appropriations. HR 2031, its companion Senate bill and the appropriations bills for the U.S. Bureau of Reclamation - Public Works; for passage of these bills."

JOHN LASTER, 1133 15th St. N.W., Washington, D.C. 20005. Filed for self 3/29/83. Legislative interest — ". . . issues related to higher education, particularly with regard to providing financial assistance for the children of participants in the Social Security system."

LEGAL SERVICES CORP., 733 15th St. N.W., Washington, D.C. 20005. Filed for self 3/10/83. Legislative interest — ". . . passage of the appropriations bills of the House and Senate Appropriation Subcommittees of State, Justice, Commerce, the Judiciary and related agencies containing funds for the corporation . . . bills of the House Judiciary Subcommittee on Courts, Civil Liberties and the Administration of Justice and the Senate Labor and Human Resources Subcommittee on Aging, Family and Human Services regarding reauthorization of the corporation." Lobbyist — James R. Streeter.

JAMES W. LOGAN, 12416 W. Old Baltimore Road, Boyds, Md. 20841. Filed for self 3/15/83. Legislative interest — Not specified.

MEMORIAL HOSPITAL OF GARLAND, Garland, Texas. Lobbyist — Johnson & Swanson, 4700 InterFirst Two, Dallas, Texas 75270. Filed 3/3/83. Legislative interest — "To represent the interests of certain non-profit hospitals in connection with the report of the National Commission on Social Security Reform."

METHODIST HOSPITALS OF DALLAS, Dallas, Texas. Lobbyist — Johnson & Swanson, 4700 InterFirst Two, Dallas, Texas 75270. Filed 3/3/83. Legislative interest — "To represent the interests of certain non-profit hospitals in connection with the report of the National Commission on Social Security Reform."

OSTEOPATHIC MEDICAL CENTER, Fort Worth, Texas. Lobbyist — Akin, Gump, Strauss, Hauer & Feld, 1333 New Hampshire Ave. N.W., Washington, D.C. 20036. Filed 3/3/83. Legislative interest — "Hearings and any legislation relating to Social Security reform, including S 1, the 'Social Security Act Amendments of 1983,' particularly as related to non-profit hospitals." Lobbyist — Johnson & Swanson, 4700 InterFirst Two, Dallas, Texas 75270. Filed 3/3/83. Legislative interest — "To represent the interests of certain non-profit hospitals in connection with the report of the National Commission on Social Security Reform."

UNIVERSITY OF ALABAMA HEALTH SERVICES FOUNDATION, Birmingham, Ala. Lobbyist — Piper & Marbury, 888 16th St. N.W., Washington, D.C. 20006. Filed 3/18/83. Legislative interest — "To seek amendments to 'Social Security Amendments of 1983' (S 1 and HR 1900)."

April Registrations

Citizens' Groups

AMERICAN AUTOMOBILE ASSOCIATION, 8111 Gatehouse Road, Falls Church, Va. 22047. Filed for self 4/11/83. Legislative interest — "Legislation relating to American motorists and travel generally."

AMERICAN REFUGEES IN AMERICA, P.O. Box 44141, Tucson, Ariz. 85733. Filed for self 4/7/83. Legislative interest — "The poor, homeless and hungry." Lobbyists — Emily Matusow, Job Matusow.

CITIZENS FOR GAULEY RIVER, Cross Lanes, W.Va. Lobbyist — Brown, Roady, Bonvillian & Gold, 1300 19th St. N.W., Washington, D.C. 20036. Filed 4/9/83. Legislative interest — "CFGR is interested in a proposal and report of the U.S. Army Corps of Engineers entitled 'The Summersville Lake Modification Study and Report.' No bills have been introduced. Statutes involved include HR Res of May 10, 1962, 1970 Flood Control Act (PL 91-611), approved 31 December 1970."

FRIENDS OF ANIMALS, 400 First St. N.W., Washington, D.C. 20001. Filed for self 4/11/83. Legislative interest — "All legislation affecting animals and the environment." Lobbyist — Yvonne B. Eider.

INTER-TRIBAL COUNCIL OF MICHIGAN INC., Sault Ste. Marie, Mich. Lobbyist — Gnau, Carter, Jacobsen & Associates Inc., 1777 F St. N.W., Washington, D.C. 20006. Filed 4/20/83. Legislative interest — "Government and agency liaison to provide information on funding sources and legislation affecting their organization."

THE MAJORITY PARTY, P.O. Box 28347, Washington, D.C. 20005. Filed for self 4/7/83. Legislative interest — "Change in structure of Congress...." Lobbyist — Charles Lefkoff.

NATIONAL AUDUBON SOCIETY, Washington, D.C. Lobbyist — Winston & Strawn, 2550 M St. N.W., Washington, D.C. 20037. Filed 4/15/83. Legislative interest — "Lobbying related to statutes affecting fish and wildlife resources and public lands, particularly the Endangered Species Act, the Alaskan National Interest Land Conservation Act, and the National Wildlife Refuge Administration Act."

NATIONAL COALITION FOR LOWER PRICES, 765 Fifth Ave., New York, N.Y. 10001. Filed for self 4/19/83. Legislative interest — "15 U.S.C. 1 - Amend Sherman Act to prohibit restricted distribution...." Lobbyist — Richard B. Kelly.

NATIONAL COMMITTEE AGAINST REPRESSIVE LEGISLATION, 201 Massachusetts Ave. N.E., Washington, D.C. 20002. Filed for self 4/20/83. Legislative interest — "Seek to prevent passage of legislation that conflicts with First Amendment rights of free speech, press & association; specifically, opposed to H Res 48 (re-establishment of House Committee on Internal Security); S 829 and S 830 (reform of federal sentencing procedures)." Lobbyist — Stephanie T. Farrior.

THE NATIONAL PEACE ACADEMY CAMPAIGN, 110 Maryland Ave. N.E., Washington, D.C. 20002. Filed for self 4/4/83. Legislative interest — "The National Peace Academy legislation, HR 1249 and S 564." Lobbyist — Marcia L. Harrington.

NATURAL RESOURCES DEFENSE COUNCIL, 1725 I St. N.W., Washington, D.C. 20006. Filed for self 4/18/83. Legislative interest — "Clinch River Breeder Reactor, for and against various amendments and sections of authorization and appropriation bills." Lobbyist — Martha M. Broad.

PASCUA-YAQUI TRIBE, Tucson, Ariz. Lobbyist — Anne L. Howard and Associates, 888 17th St. N.W., Washington, D.C. 20006. Filed 4/18/83. Legislative interest — "Legislation, policies, programs and other administrative actions affecting the Pascua-Yaqui Tribe to include, but not limited to, tax legislation and other laws, rules or regulations affecting bingo and similar economic development projects. Other legislation would include that which would affect the social and economic well-being of the Pascua-Yaqui Tribe."

SHAKOPEE-MDEUAKANTON SIOUX COMMUNITY, Prior Lake, Minn. Lobbyist — Anne L. Howard and Associates, 888 17th St. N.W., Washington, D.C. 20006. Filed 4/18/83. Legislative interest — "Legislation, policies, programs and other administrative actions affecting the Shakopee-Mdeuakanton Sioux Community to include, but not limited to, tax legislation and other laws, rules or regulations affecting bingo and similar economic development projects. Other legislation would include that which would affect the social and economic well-being of the Shakopee-Mdeuakanton Sioux Community."

UNITED ACTION FOR ANIMALS INC., New York, N.Y. Lobbyist — Joseph F. Meadow, 7100 Baltimore Ave., College Park, Md. 20740. Filed 4/18/83. Legislative interest — "All legislation dealing with animal welfare...."

Corporations and Businesses

AIR PRODUCTS & CHEMICALS INC., Washington, D.C. Lobbyist — Patton, Boggs & Blow, 2550 M St. N.W., Washington, D.C. 20037. Filed 4/5/83. Legislative interest — "In favor of legislation amending the Natural Gas Policy Act of 1978 including S 615, S 60, S 239, S 291, S 293, S 370, S 689, HR 2012, and HR 2154."

ALASKA LUMBER & PULP CO. INC., Sitka, Alaska. Lobbyist — Heffernan & Moseman, 1875 I St. N.W., Washington, D.C. 20006. Filed 4/9/83. Legislative interest — "Any and all legislation dealing with the exportation of Alaskan crude oil." Lobbyist — Sullivan & Worcester, 1025 Connecticut Ave. N.W., Washington, D.C. 20036. Filed 4/12/83. Legislative interest — "Export Administration Act ... 50 U.S.C. app. sec 2406(d)...."

ALLIED TUBE & CONDUIT CORP., Harvey, Ill. Lobbyist — Manatt, Phelps, Rothenberg & Tunney, 1200 New Hampshire Ave. N.W., Washington, D.C. 20036. Filed 4/7/83. Legislative interest — "Legislation relating to authorization and appropriations for Department of Commerce." Lobbyist — David M. Barrett, 2555 M St. N.W., Washington, D.C. 20037. Filed 4/1/83. Legislative interest — "Budget or legislative items affecting fire safety research or building standards; trade legislation, particularly as to steel tariffs, S 414, HR 1319, S 144."

BANGOR & AROOSTOOK RAILROAD, Bangor, Maine. Lobbyist — RBC Associates, 324 Fourth St. N.E., Washington, D.C. 20002. Filed 4/8/83. Legislative interest — "Coal slurry; jobs bill; regulatory reform; railroad retirement ... HR 1010 and S 267; HR 1718; S 48; HR 1646...."

BASF WYANDOTTE CORP., Parsippany, N.J. Lobbyist — James E. Guirard Jr., 1730 Rhode Island Ave. N.W., Washington, D.C. 20036. Filed 4/20/83. Legislative interest — "Enactment of legislation granting temporary suspension of import duties on certain chemicals: HR 908, HR 2335, HR 2336, HR 2258 and similar Senate bills not yet introduced."

GEORGE K. BAUM & CO., Kansas City, Mo. Lobbyist — Camp, Carmouche, Barsh, Hunter, Gray & Hoffman, 2550 M St. N.W., Washington, D.C. 20037. Filed 4/13/83. Legislative interest — "Work in connection with tax proposals affecting industrial revenue bonds, (HR 1635)."

BLYTH EASTMAN PAINE WEBBER INC., New York, N.Y. Lobbyist — Camp, Carmouche, Barsh, Hunter, Gray & Hoffman, 2550 M St. N.W., Washington, D.C. 20037. Filed 4/13/83. Legislative interest — "Work in connection with tax proposals affecting industrial revenue bonds, (HR 1635)."

THE BOEING CO., Seattle, Wash. Lobbyist — Timmons and Co. Inc., 1850 K St. N.W., Washington, D.C. 20006. Filed 4/11/83. Legislative interest — "Interests include revenue and tax matters, trade regulation and control, regulation and control of transportation and authorization and appropriation bills such as FY 84 Department of Defense procurement authorization bill, FY 84 Department of Defense appropriation bill, and FY 84 Department of Transportation appropriation bill."

BOSTON & MAINE RAILROAD, North Billerica, Mass. Lobbyist — RBC Associates, 324 Fourth St. N.E., Washington, D.C. 20002. Filed 4/8/83. Legislative interest — "Coal slurry; jobs

bill; regulatory reform; railroad retirement ... HR 1010 & S 267; HR 1718; S 48; HR 1646...."

CHAPMAN & CUTLER, Chicago, Ill. Lobbyist — Camp, Carmouche, Barsh, Hunter, Gray & Hoffman, 2550 M St. N.W., Washington, D.C. 20037. Filed 4/13/83. Legislative interest — "Work in connection with tax proposals affecting industrial revenue bonds, (HR 1635)."

CHEMICAL WASTE MANAGEMENT INC., Oak Brook, Ill. Lobbyist — Richard N. Sharood, 510 Seward Square, Washington, D.C. 20003. Filed 4/11/83. Legislative interest — "All legislation generally implementing federal policy regarding chemical waste disposal and in particular amendments to Resource Recovery and Reclamation Act and Ocean Dumping Act...."

CHICAGO & NORTH WESTERN TRANSPORTATION CORP., Chicago, Ill. Lobbyist — RBC Associates, 324 Fourth St. N.E., Washington, D.C. 20002. Filed 4/8/83. Legislative interest — "Coal slurry; jobs bill; regulatory reform; railroad retirement ... HR 1010 & S 267; HR 1718; S 48; HR 1646...."

COFFEE SUGAR & COCOA EXCHANGE INC., 4 World Trade Center, New York, N.Y. 10048. Filed for self 4/12/83. Legislative interest — "Legislation which affects commodity futures trading or the commodities related thereto, in particular that which relates to coffee, sugar, cocoa, the Commodity Futures Trading Commission, taxation and bankruptcy." Lobbyist — Anthony R. Macchia.

CROWN ZELLERBACH CORP., 1 Bush St., San Francisco, Calif. 94104. Filed for self 4/19/83. Legislative interest — "Legislation directly affecting pulp, paper, and forest products." Lobbyist — Elizabeth W. Heilig.

CRUM & FORSTER INSURANCE COS., Washington, D.C. Lobbyist — Powell, Goldstein, Frazer & Murphy, 1110 Vermont Ave. N.W., Washington, D.C. 20005. Filed 4/8/83. Legislative interest — "No specific legislation but generally tax matters affecting the property and casualty insurance industry."

CUMBERLAND SECURITIES, Knoxville, Tenn. Lobbyist — Camp, Carmouche, Barsh, Hunter, Gray & Hoffman, 2550 M St. N.W., Washington, D.C. 20037. Filed 4/13/83. Legislative interest — "Work in connection with tax proposals affecting industrial revenue bonds, (HR 1635)."

DAMSON OIL CORP., New York, N.Y. Lobbyist — Breed, Abbott & Morgan, 1875 I St. N.W., Washington, D.C. 20006. Filed 4/9/83. Legislative interest — "Sections 512 and 514 of the Internal Revenue Code; HR 821."

DELAWARE OTSEGO SYSTEM, Cooperstown, N.Y. Lobbyist — RBC Associates, 324 Fourth St. N.E., Washington, D.C. 20002. Filed 4/8/83. Legislative interest — "Coal slurry; regulatory reform; railroad retirement ... HR 1010 & S 267; S 48; HR 1646...."

DILLINGHAM CONSTRUCTION GROUP, San Francisco, Calif. Lobbyist — Jack Ferguson Associates Inc., 203 Maryland Ave. N.E., Washington, D.C. 20002. Filed 4/14/83. Legislative interest — "Military construction appropriation, PL 97-323."

ENERGY CYCLE INC., Lincoln, Neb. Lobbyist — Spriggs, Bode & Hollingsworth, 1015 15th St. N.W., Washington, D.C. 20005. Filed 4/14/83. Legislative interest — "Legislation that involves the inclusion of anaerobic digestion equipment as qualified property under the energy investment tax credit provisions of Section 48(L)(15)(C) of the Internal Revenue Code of 1954, as amended. Our interests include HR 1876 and other draft legislation to be introduced to amend this IRC section."

ENHANCED ENERGY RESOURCES INC., 14141 Southwest Freeway, Sugarland, Texas 77478. Lobbyist — Foreman & Dyess, 1920 N St. N.W., Washington, D.C. 20036. Filed 4/11/83. Legislative interest — "Restrictions on operation of take-or-pay clauses in natural gas contracts and natural gas legislation affecting occluded gas from coal seams." Filed for self 4/11/83. Legislative interest — "Restrictions on operation of take-or-pay clauses in natural gas contracts and natural gas legislation affecting occluded gas from coal seams."

ENVIRITE CORP., Blue Bell, Pa. Lobbyist — Mintz, Levin, Cohn, Ferris, Glovsky & Popeo, 1015 15th St. N.W., Washington, D.C. 20005. Legislative interest — "S 757 and S 431, and other legislation relating to the reauthorization of the Resource Conservation and Recovery Act and the Clean Water Act."

ESSEX, Montgomery, Ala. Lobbyist — Camp, Carmouche, Barsh, Hunter, Gray & Hoffman, 2550 M St. N.W., Washington, D.C. 20037. Filed 4/13/83. Legislative interest — "Work in connection with tax proposals affecting industrial revenue bonds, (HR 1635)."

THE FRAZER LANIER CO., Montgomery, Ala. Lobbyist — Camp, Carmouche, Barsh, Hunter, Gray & Hoffman, 2550 M St. N.W., Washington, D.C. 20037. Filed 4/13/83. Legislative interest — "Work in connection with tax proposals affecting industrial revenue bonds, (HR 1635)."

FIRST PENNSYLVANIA BANK, Philadelphia, Pa. Lobbyist — O'Connor & Hannan, 1919 Pennsylvania Ave. N.W., Washington, D.C. 20006. Filed 4/15/83. (Former U.S. Rep. Thomas B. Evans Jr., R-Del. (1977-83), was listed as agent for this client.) Legislative interest — "Issues of interest to the client including, but not limited to, matters involving the FDIC and the IMF."

FOOTHILLS PIPE LINES (YUKON) LTD., Calgary, Alberta, Canada. Lobbyist — McHenry & Staffier, 1300 19th St. N.W., Washington, D.C. 20036. Filed 4/14/83. Legislative interest — "All natural gas legislation ... HR 2182, H Con Res 88, HR 2054, HR 1759, HR 1701, HR 1685, HR 1422, H Con Res 29, HR 910, HR 873, HR 796, H J Res 58, HR 583, HR 4, HR 131, HR 2154, H J Res 192, HR 2012, HR 1752, HR 1686, HR 1441, HR 1359, H Res 38, HR 909, HR 827, HR 705, HR 619, HR 482, HR 232, H 1760 ... S 823, S 689, S J Res 46, S 512, S 293, S 239, S 3069, S 2771, S 740, S 615, S 370, S 291, S 60, S 2892, S 2770."

GENERAL ELECTRIC CO., 3135 Easton Turnpike, Fairfield, Conn. 06431. Filed for self 4/4/83. Legislative interest — Not specified. Lobbyist — P. S. Peter, 777 14th St. N.W., Washington, D.C. 20005.

GENERAL ELECTRIC CREDIT CO., Stamford, Conn. Lobbyist — Lane and Edson, 1800 M St. N.W., Washington, D.C. 20036. Filed 4/14/83. Legislative interest — "Aspects of housing legislation relating to financial markets, including HR 1."

GENERAL MILLS INC., Washington, D.C. Lobbyist — Barnett & Alagia, 1000 Thomas Jefferson St. N.W., Washington, D.C. 20007. Filed 4/11/83. Legislative interest — "Nutritional guidelines of the WIC program; for."

GENESEE & WYOMING CORP., Greenwich, Conn. Lobbyist — RBC Associates, 324 Fourth St. N.W., Washington, D.C. 20002. Filed 4/8/83. Legislative interest — "Coal slurry; regulatory reform; railroad retirement ... HR 1010 & S 267; S 48; HR 1646...."

GEORGIA PACIFIC CORP., Washington, D.C. Lobbyist — Patton, Boggs & Blow, 2550 M St. N.W., Washington, D.C. 20037. Filed 4/5/83. Legislative interest — "In favor of legislation amending the Natural Gas Policy Act of 1978, including S 615, S 60, S 239, S 291, S 293, S 370, S 689, HR 2012 and HR 2154."

GOLDMAN SACHS & CO., New York, N.Y. Lobbyist — Camp, Carmouche, Barsh, Hunter, Gray & Hoffman, 2550 M St. N.W., Washington, D.C. 20037. Filed 4/13/83. Legislative interest — "Work in connection with tax proposals affecting industrial revenue bonds, (HR 1635)."

BILL HECHT & ASSOCIATES, 499 S. Capitol St., Washington, D.C. 20003. Filed for self 4/15/83. Legislative interest — "General legislative interests, including but not limited to: HR 2041 (opposed); S 772 (opposed); HR 1824 (opposed)." Lobbyist — John J. Connolly.

HUDSON WATERWAYS, New York, N.Y. Lobbyist — Preston, Thorgrimson, Ellis & Holman, 1776 G St. N.W., Washington, D.C. 20006. Filed 4/13/83. Legislative interest — "Support of legislative efforts to extend the restriction on the export of Alaska oil. HR 1197, any companion legislation or any other legislation with the same or similar purpose."

INTERNATIONAL TELEPHONE & TELEGRAPH CORP., 320 Park Ave., New York, N.Y. 10022. Filed for self 4/12/83. Legislative interest — "Clean Air Act amendments - for; Export Trading Company - for; Clean Water Act reauthorizations - for; Regulatory Reform bills - for." Lobbyist — Linda Anzalone Woolley, 1707 L St. N.W., Washington, D.C. 20036.

JAMAICAN BROADCASTING CORP., Kingston, Jamaica. Lobbyist — O'Connor & Hannan, 1919 Pennsylvania Ave.

N.W., Washington, D.C. 20006. Filed 4/18/83. (Former U.S. Rep. Thomas B. Evans, R-Del. (1977-83), was listed as agent for this client.) Legislative interest — "Matters affecting copyright provisions of Caribbean Basin legislation."

KAISER ALUMINUM & CHEMICALS CORP., Washington, D.C. Lobbyist — Patton, Boggs & Blow, 2550 M St. N.W., Washington, D.C. 20037. Filed 4/5/83. Legislative interest — "In favor of legislation amending the Natural Gas Policy Act of 1978 including S 615, S 60, S 239, S 291, S 293, S 370, S 689, HR 2012 and HR 2154."

KIDDER, PEABODY, New York, N.Y. Lobbyist — Camp, Carmouche, Barsh, Hunter, Gray & Hoffman, 2550 M St. N.W., Washington, D.C. 20037. Filed 4/13/83. Legislative interest — "Work in connection with tax proposals affecting industrial revenue bonds, (HR 1635)."

KING & SPALDING, Atlanta, Ga. Lobbyist — Camp, Carmouche, Barsh, Hunter, Gray & Hoffman, 2550 M St. N.W., Washington, D.C. 20037. Filed 4/13/83. Legislative interest — "Work in connection with tax proposals affecting industrial revenue bonds, (HR 1635)."

SAM KANE PACKING, Corpus Christi, Texas. Lobbyist — Sam White, 412 First St. S.E., Washington, D.C. 20003. Filed 4/6/83. Legislative interest — "Legislation affecting agriculture."

LEHMAN BROTHERS, New York, N.Y. Lobbyist — Camp, Carmouche, Barsh, Hunter, Gray & Hoffman, 2550 M St. N.W., Washington, D.C. 20037. Filed 4/13/83. Legislative interest — "Work in connection with tax proposals affecting industrial revenue bonds, (HR 1635)."

LIBERTY MUTUAL INSURANCE CO., Boston, Mass. Lobbyist — Mintz, Levin, Cohn, Ferris, Glovsky and Popeo, 1015 15th St. N.W., Washington, D.C. 20005. Filed 4/3/83. Legislative interest — "S 38, Longshoremen's and Harbor Workers' Compensation Act and other legislation affecting the property and casualty insurance industry."

LITCHSTREET CO., Northport, N.Y. Lobbyist — Schwabe, Williamson, Wyatt, Moore & Roberts, 1000 Potomac St. N.W., Washington, D.C. 20007. Filed 4/8/83. (Former U.S. Rep. Robert Duncan, D-Ore. (1963-67; 1975-81), was listed as agent for this client.) Legislative interest — "Air traffic control - collision avoidance."

LOUISIANA WORLD EXPOSITION INC., New Orleans, La. Lobbyists — Carol R. Emery, John C. McCarthy, John C. Stone, P.O. Box 1300, McLean, Va. 22102. Filed 4/12/83. Legislative interest — "HR 2019, to provide for a commemorative coin to recognize the 1984 Louisiana World Exposition."

M.A.N. TRUCK & BUS CORP., Charlotte, N.C. Lobbyist — Burch, Wilhelm & McDonald, 1320 19th St. N.W., Washington, D.C. 20036. Filed 4/8/83. Legislative interest — Not specified.

McDONALD & CO., Cleveland, Ohio. Lobbyist — Camp, Carmouche, Barsh, Hunter, Gray & Hoffman, 2550 M St. N.W., Washington, D.C. 20037. Filed 4/13/83. Legislative interest — "Work in connection with tax proposals affecting industrial revenue bonds, (HR 1635)."

THE MEAD CORP., Dayton, Ohio. Lobbyist — Howrey & Simon, 1730 Pennsylvania Ave. N.W., Washington, D.C. 20006. Filed 4/11/83. Legislative interest — "Legislation to provide for claim reduction and contribution in antitrust damages cases: S 380, S 904, HR 2244."

MONSANTO CO., 800 N. Lindbergh Blvd., St. Louis, Mo. 63167. Filed for self 4/8/83. Legislative interest — Not specified. Lobbyist — Carl F. St. Cin, 1101 17th St. N.W., Washington, D.C. 20036.

MOUNTAIN STATES ENERGY INC., Butte, Mont. Lobbyist — Schwabe, Williamson, Wyatt, Moore & Roberts, 1000 Potomac St. N.W., Washington, D.C. 20007. Filed 4/8/83. (Former U.S. Rep. Robert Duncan, D-Ore. (1963-67; 1975-81), was listed as agent for this client.) Legislative interest — "Funding for MHD (Magnetohydrodynamics) - low cost, clean electric power derived from coal."

NORTH, HASKELL, SLAUGHTER, YOUNG & LEWIS, Birmingham, Ala. Lobbyist — Camp, Carmouche, Barsh, Hunter, Gray & Hoffman, 2550 M St. N.W., Washington, D.C. 20037. Filed 4/13/83. Legislative interest — "Work in connection

with tax proposals affecting industrial revenue bonds, (HR 1635)."

NORTHERN TIER PIPELINE CO., Washington, D.C. Lobbyist — Cook, Purcell, Henderson & Zorack, 1015 18th St. N.W., Washington, D.C. 20036. Filed 4/13/83. Legislative interest — "General interest - Monitor all legislation affecting the transportation of oil produced in Alaska. Specific interest - All legislation and amendments to facilitate rights-of-way and permits acquisition to construct an oil pipeline for the transportation of Alaskan oil from Seattle to the Northern tier states."

NORTHVILLE INDUSTRIES CORP., Melville, N.Y. Lobbyist — Vinson & Elkins, 1101 Connecticut Ave. N.W., Washington, D.C. 20036. Filed 4/12/83. Legislative interest — "HR 1197 (Wolpe-McKinney bill) (in support thereof)."

NORTHWEST BANCORP., Minneapolis, Minn. Lobbyist — Davis, Polk & Wardwell, 1575 I St. N.W., Washington, D.C. 20005. Filed 4/18/83. Legislative interest — "Matters affecting domestic bank holding companies generally."

OHIO CASUALTY INSURANCE CO., Hamilton, Ohio. Lobbyist — Watt, Tieder, Killian, Toole & Hoffar, 1742 R St. N.W., Washington, D.C. 20009. Filed 4/7/83. Legislative interest — "Our firm is working with the House and Senate Appropriations Subcommittees on Military Construction on a reprogramming request. This request is for funds to pay for a settlement of a contract dispute between our client and the Air Force and Corps of Engineers. There is no specific legislation involved."

OTIS ELEVATOR CO., Denver, Colo. Lobbyist — Schwabe, Williamson, Wyatt, Moore & Roberts, 1000 Potomac St. N.W., Washington, D.C. 20007. Filed 4/8/83. (Former U.S. Rep. Robert Duncan, D-Ore. (1963-67; 1975-81), was listed as agent for this client.) Legislative interest — "Funding for AGRT (Advanced Group Rapid Transit)."

PACIFIC GREEN CORP., Camarillo, Calif. Lobbyist — Latham, Watkins & Hills, 1333 New Hampshire Ave. N.W., Washington, D.C. 20036. Filed 4/8/83. Legislative interest — "Energy and water development, authorization and appropriations bills to be introduced in fiscal 1984."

PAKHOED, Houston, Texas. Lobbyist — Camp, Carmouche, Barsh, Hunter, Gray & Hoffman, 2550 M St. N.W., Washington, D.C. 20037. Filed 4/13/83. Legislative interest — "Matters relating to HR 1700."

PANDROL, Bridgeport, N.J. Lobbyist — RBC Associates, 324 Fourth St. N.E., Washington, D.C. 20002. Filed 4/8/83. Legislative interest — "Jobs bill; tax legislation ... HR 1718...."

PITTSBURG & SHAWMUT RAILROAD, Kittanning, Pa. Lobbyist — RBC Associates, 324 Fourth St. N.E., Washington, D.C. 20002. Filed 4/8/83. Legislative interest — "Coal slurry; jobs bill; regulatory reform; railroad retirement ... HR 1010 & S 267; HR 1718; S 48; HR 1646...."

QUALICARE INC., New Orleans, La. Lobbyists — Carol R. Emery, John C. Stone, P.O. Box 1300, McLean, Va. 22102. Filed 4/12/83. Legislative interest — "Health-related legislation."

RAUSCHER PIERCE REFSNES, Dallas, Texas. Lobbyist — Camp, Carmouche, Barsh, Hunter, Gray & Hoffman, 2550 M St. N.W., Washington, D.C. 20037. Filed 4/13/83. Legislative interest — "Work in connection with tax proposals affecting industrial revenue bonds, (HR 1635)."

SAMARITAN HEALTH SERVICE, Phoenix, Ariz. Lobbyist — Perito, Duerk, Carlson & Pinco, 1140 Connecticut Ave. N.W., Washington, D.C. 20036. Filed 4/13/83. Legislative interest — "Legislation affecting ... Medicare prospective payment system; and ... report of the National Commission on Social Security Reform, January 1983."

SAN FRANCISCO PUBLIC UTILITIES COMMISSION, San Francisco, Calif. Lobbyist — Brown, Roady, Bonvillian & Gold, 1300 19th St. N.W., Washington, D.C. 20036. Filed 4/20/83. Legislative interest — "Retained to advise on governmental public mass transit programs and funding; may include advising on transit authorizing and appropriation legislation; in favor of such legislation."

SANTA FE INTERNATIONAL CORP., Alhambra, Calif. Lobbyist — O'Melveny & Myers, 1800 M St. N.W., Washington, D.C. 20036. Filed 4/6/83. Legislative interest — "Defeat or amendment of proposed legislation to amend the Mineral Lands Leasing

Act of 1920...."

SCHLENAKER DRILLING CO., Richardson, Texas. Lobbyist — Daniel A. Dutko, 412 First St. S.E., Washington, D.C. 20003. Filed 4/8/83. Legislative interest — "Legislation affecting oil and gas matters."

SIX FLAGS CORP., Los Angeles, Calif. Lobbyist — Pierson, Semmes, Crolius and Finley, 1054 31st St. N.W., Washington, D.C. 20007. Filed 4/12/83. Legislative interest — "Legislative interests concern any attempt to amend section 3 of the Consumer Product Safety Act, 15 U.S.C. section 2052(a)(1), to provide the CPSC with jurisdiction over mechanical devices that carry or convey passengers along, around, or over a fixed or restricted route or course or within a defined area for the purpose of giving passengers amusement where such devices are permanently fixed to a site."

SPENO RAIL SERVICES, East Syracuse, N.Y. Lobbyist — RBC Associates, 324 Fourth St. N.E., Washington, D.C. 20002. Filed 4/8/83. Legislative interest — "Tax legislation...."

THE STANDARD OIL CO. (OHIO), Midland Building, Cleveland, Ohio 44115. Filed for self 4/19/83. Legislative interest — "General legislative matters pertaining to the interests of the company respecting petroleum products, refining and distribution, petro-chemicals and coal, and metal/non-metals minerals." Lobbyist — Mark L. Schneider, 1001 22nd St. N.W., Washington, D.C. 20037.

STERN, AGEE & LEACH, Montgomery, Ala. Lobbyist — Camp, Carmouche, Barsh, Hunter, Gray & Hoffman, 2550 M St. N.W., Washington, D.C. 20037. Filed 4/13/83. Legislative interest — "Work in connection with tax proposals affecting industrial revenue bonds, (HR 1635)."

SUMMIT ENTERPRISES INC., Fredericksburg, Va. Lobbyist — Howrey & Simon, 1730 Pennsylvania Ave. N.W., Washington, D.C. 20006. Filed 4/15/83. Legislative interest — "Opposition to antitrust legislation to overrule the decisions of the United States Supreme Court in *Community Communications Co. v. City of Boulder*; and *Lafayette v. Louisiana Power & Light Co.*"

TENNECO INC., P.O. Box 2511, Houston, Texas 77001. Filed for self 4/8/83. Legislative interest — Not specified. Lobbyist — Robert H. Maloney, 480 L'Enfant Plaza East S.W., Washington, D.C. 20024.

TEXACO INC., 2000 Westchester Ave., White Plains, N.Y. 10650. Filed for self 4/11/83. Legislative interest — "Interest, if any, will be in legislation related to production, refining, marketing and transportation of oil, gas, synthetic fuels and other minerals insofar as they affect the business of my employer." Lobbyist — Paul T. Burke, 1050 17th St. N.W., Washington, D.C. 20036.

THORNTON, FARISH & GAUNTT, Montgomery, Ala. Lobbyist — Camp, Carmouche, Barsh, Hunter, Gray & Hoffman, 2550 M St. N.W., Washington, D.C. 20037. Filed 4/13/83. Legislative interest — "Work in connection with tax proposals affecting industrial revenue bonds, (HR 1635)."

ULTRASYSTEMS INC., 10340 Democracy Lane, Fairfax, Va. 22030. Filed for self 4/13/83. Legislative interest — "General legislative interests concerning energy policy issues." Lobbyist — Mark H. R. Lyons, 1882 Columbia Road N.W., Washington, D.C. 20009.

WALD MANUFACTURING CO. INC., Maysville, Ky. Lobbyist — Taft, Stettinius & Hollister, 21 Dupont Circle N.W., Washington, D.C. 20036. Filed 4/11/83. Legislative interest — "Advice on possible amendments to the Foreign Trade Zone Act. Of particular interest is HR 657 and S 722."

WESTINGHOUSE INFORMATION SYSTEMS, Washington, D.C. Lobbyist — RBC Associates, 324 Fourth St. N.E., Washington, D.C. 20002. Filed 4/8/83. Legislative interest — "Surface Transportation Act ... HR 6211...."

WEST TEXAS UTILITIES CO., P.O. Box 841, Abilene, Texas 79604. Filed for self 4/12/83. Legislative interest — "All legislation affecting generation and distribution of electricity ... Coal Slurry Pipeline legislation: S 267, lobbying for and HR 1010, lobbying for ... Clean Air Act amendments: S 768, lobbying on ... legislation to control acid deposition: S 769, lobbying against; S 145, lobbying against; S 766, lobbying on; S 454, lobbying for; HR 1405, lobbying for; HR 132, lobbying against ... Clean Water Act amendments: S 431, lobbying on." Lobbyist — Walter B. Grubbs, 3510 S. 20th St., Abilene, Texas 79605.

WHEAT FIRST SECURITIES, Richmond, Va. Lobbyist — Camp, Carmouche, Barsh, Hunter, Gray & Hoffman, 2550 M St. N.W., Washington, D.C. 20037. Filed 4/13/83. Legislative interest — "Work in connection with tax proposals affecting industrial revenue bonds, (HR 1635)."

International Relations

GOVERNMENT OF BELIZE, Belize City, Belize. Lobbyist — McMurray & Pendergast, 1575 I St. N.W., Washington, D.C. 20005. Filed 4/7/83. Legislative interest — "All legislative matters pertaining to the regulation and importation of sugar."

REPUBLIC OF KENYA, Nairobi, Kenya. Lobbyist — Van Ness, Feldman, Sutcliffe, Curtis & Levenberg, 1050 Thomas Jefferson St. N.W., Washington, D.C. 20007. Filed 4/19/83. Legislative interest — "For a congressional authorization and appropriation for purchases for the U.S. national defense stockpile of strategic and critical materials."

REPUBLIC OF PANAMA, Panama City, Panama. Lobbyist — McMurray & Pendergast, 1575 I St. N.W., Washington, D.C. 20005. Filed 4/7/83. Legislative interest — "All legislative matters pertaining to the regulation and importation of sugar."

Labor Groups

AMERICAN ASSOCIATION OF RETIRED PERSONS, 1909 K St. N.W., Washington, D.C. 20049. Filed for self 4/7/83. Legislative interest — "Support of improved Social Security and Medicare/Medicaid laws ... improved tax treatment of older Americans ... improved nursing home standards ... consumer protection legislation ... employment of older workers ... national health insurance ... transportation for the elderly ... housing for the elderly." Lobbyist — Leon Harper.

COUNCIL ON MULTIEMPLOYER PENSION SECURITY INC., 1000 Potomac St. N.W., Washington, D.C. 20007. Filed for self 4/13/83. Legislative interest — "The Council supports the position that contributors to multiemployer pension plans must not be subject to 'withdrawal liabilities' as stipulated in the Multiemployer Pension Plan Amendments Act of 1980; that contributors to multiemployer plans must be held accountable only for defined contributions as agreed in collective bargaining; and that trustees of multiemployer funds be required to adjust benefits to conform to actual funding levels." Lobbyist — Ben Jarratt Brown.

THE RAILROAD RETIREMENT ASSOCIATION, 236 Massachusetts Ave. N.W., Washington, D.C. 20002. Filed for self 4/8/83. Legislative interest — "All legislation in any way relating to, amending or affecting, directly or indirectly, any of the following: The Railroad Retirement Act of 1937, as amended; The Financial Interchange Act between Social Security and the Railroad Retirement Fund; The Social Security portion of Railroad Retirement benefits; Employment in the railroad industry as it affects tax contributions to the Railroad Retirement Fund on the part of employees and/or employers; the financing of the phase-out of the so-called 'dual benefits' under the Railroad Retirement Act; amount of benefits under said Act." Lobbyist — L. L. Duxbury.

SHEET METAL WORKERS' INTERNATIONAL ASSOCIATION, 1750 New York Ave. N.W., Washington, D.C. 20006. Filed for self 4/13/83. Legislative interest — "All labor legislation, solar legislation, S 336." Lobbyists — Edward J. Carlough, Lawrence J. Cassidy.

State and Local Governments

CAMBRIDGE REDEVELOPMENT AUTHORITY, Cambridge, Mass. Lobbyist — O'Connor & Hannan, 1919 Pennsyl-

vania Ave. N.W., Washington, D.C. 20006. Filed 4/6/83. (Former U.S. Sen. Edward W. Brooke, R-Mass. (1967-79), was listed as agent for this client.) Legislative interest — "Monitor housing and community development legislation."

CITY OF EL PASO, El Paso, Texas. Lobbyist — Vinson & Elkins, 1101 Connecticut Ave. N.W., Washington, D.C. 20036. Filed 4/12/83. Legislative interest — "State water rights issue."

COUNTY OF SUFFOLK, Hawppaugh, N.Y. Lobbyist — Kirkpatrick, Lockhart, Hill, Christopher & Phillips, 1900 M St. N.W., Washington, D.C. 20036. Filed 4/20/83. Legislative interest — "Legislation relative to the licensing of nuclear power plants; support public health and safety requirements."

NORTH CENTRAL NEBRASKA RECLAMATION DISTRICT, O'Neill, Neb. Lobbyist — Jim Casey, 3470 Mildred Drive, Falls Church, Va. 22042. Filed 4/20/83. Legislative interest — "All legislative matters affecting the O'Neill unit, Pick Sloane Missouri Basin Project."

STATE OF OREGON, Portland, Ore. Lobbyist — Schwabe, Williamson, Wyatt, Moore & Roberts, 1000 Potomac St. N.W., Washington, D.C. 20007. Filed 4/8/83. (Former U.S. Rep. Robert Duncan, D-Ore. (1963-67; 1975-81), was listed as agent for this client.) Legislative interest — "Transportation (mass transit); interstate transfer highway funds; safe harbor leasing; tax legislation affecting mass transportation systems."

Trade Associations

AMERICAN BANKERS ASSOCIATION, 1120 Connecticut Ave. N.W., Washington, D.C. 20036. Filed for self 4/4/83. Legislative interest — "Legislation that is of direct interest to the banking industry in general and specifically, HR 1190 and S 24 the Emergency Agricultural Credit Act and HR 500 *et al.*, to repeal the withholding of interest and dividends." Lobbyist — Ann Todd Free.

AMERICAN HELLENIC INSTITUTE PUBLIC AFFAIRS COMMITTEE INC., 1730 K St. N.W., Washington, D.C. 20006. Filed for self 4/6/83. Legislative interest — "All matters affecting trade and commerce between the United States and Greece, between the United States and Cyprus and within the American Hellenic community." Lobbyist — Georgia L. Delyannis.

AMERICAN MEAT INSTITUTE, P.O. Box 3556, Washington, D.C. 20007. Filed for self 4/12/83. Legislative interest — "Legislation affecting the food industry in general and particularly the livestock and meat industry - including, but not limited to: livestock production and feeding, animal diseases, meat inspection, food additives, labeling, transportation, environmental protection, safety, trade practices, consumer protection, energy, food safety, regulatory reform." Lobbyist — Susan Magaw.

AMERICAN MEDICAL RECORDS ASSOCIATION, Chicago, Ill. Lobbyist — Phillip Porte & Associates Inc., 1301 S. Arlington Ridge Road, Arlington, Va. 22202. Filed 4/11/83. Legislative interest — "General legislative matters affecting health and welfare; health legislation affecting medical records; the data necessary for Medicare/Medicaid reimbursement."

AMERICAN NURSES ASSOCIATION, 2420 Pershing Road, Kansas City, Mo. 64108. Filed for self 4/8/83. Legislative interest — "Legislation relating to nurses, nursing and health including, but not limited to Nurse Training Act, Nurse Research, Community Health Grants, Medicare, Medicaid, mental health, block grants, pro-competition proposals, appropriations and budget." Lobbyist — Deborah A. Smith, 1101 14th St. N.W., Washington, D.C. 20005.

AMERICAN PAPER INSTITUTE INC., 260 Madison Ave., New York, N.Y. 10016. Filed for self 4/1/83. Legislative interest — "Legislative interests are those affecting the pulp, paper and paperboard industry, its operation, practices and properties; tax legislation to amend Federal Food Drug and Cosmetic Act." Lobbyist — Red Cavaney Jr., 1619 Massachusetts Ave. N.W., Washington, D.C. 20036.

THE ASSOCIATED GENERAL CONTRACTORS OF

AMERICA, 1957 E St. N.W., Washington, D.C. 20006. Filed for self 4/8/83. Legislative interest — "Longshoremen's and Harbor Workers' Compensation Reform Act - support." Lobbyist — David A. Johnston.

ASSOCIATION OF BUSINESS ADVOCATING TARIFF EQUITY, Detroit, Mich. Lobbyist — Sutherland, Asbill & Brennan, 1666 K St. N.W., Washington, D.C. 20006. Filed 4/12/83. Legislative interest — "Legislation relating to natural gas imports."

THE ASSOCIATION OF PRIVATE PENSION AND WELFARE PLANS INC., Washington, D.C. Lobbyist — Steptoe & Johnson, 1250 Connecticut Ave. N.W., Washington, D.C. 20036. Filed 4/8/83. Legislative interest — "Social Security Amendment; Fair Insurance Practice Act; Pension Equity Acts; Health Insurance for Unemployed Workers . . . HR 1900, HR 100 and S 372; S 10, S 888 and HR 2090; S 307. . . ."

AUTO INTERNACIONAL ASSOCIATION, Whittier, Calif. Lobbyists — John Russell Deane III, Steven T. Miller, 1607 New Hampshire Ave. N.W., Washington, D.C. 20009. Filed 4/14/83. Legislative interest — "To insure free trade between the United States and its foreign partners in trade."

BEER INDUSTRY ALLIANCE, Falls Church, Va. Lobbyist — Webster, Chamberlain & Bean, 1747 Pennsylvania Ave. N.W., Washington, D.C. 20006. Filed 4/18/83. Legislative interest — Not specified.

THE BUSINESS ROUNDTABLE, 1828 L St. N.W., Washington, D.C. 20036. Filed for self 4/15/83. Legislative interest — "Legislative matters, generally, which may affect business and industry operations - including, but not limited to proposals in the fields of labor relations, employment, budget and health. . . ." Lobbyist — Margaret L. Gehres.

CENTRAL & SOUTHERN MOTOR FREIGHT TRAFFIC ASSOCIATION, Louisville, Ky. Lobbyist — Camp, Carmouche, Barsh, Hunter, Gray & Hoffman, 2550 M St. N.W., Washington, D.C. 20037. Filed 4/7/83. Legislative interest — "Motor Carrier Act of 1980."

CENTRAL STATES MOTOR FREIGHT BUREAU, Chicago, Ill. Lobbyist — Camp, Carmouche, Barsh, Hunter, Gray & Hoffman, 2550 M St. N.W., Washington, D.C. 20037. Filed 4/7/83. Legislative interest — "Motor Carrier Act of 1980."

COALITION OF AUTOMOTIVE ASSOCIATIONS, Whittier, Calif. Lobbyist — Steven T. Miller, 1607 New Hampshire Ave. N.W., Washington, D.C. 20009. Filed 4/14/83. Legislative interest — "The Association has general interest in legislation affecting the automobile industry. . . ."

COALITION FOR COMPETITION, Washington, D.C. Lobbyist — Cook, Purcell, Henderson & Zorack, 1015 18th St. N.W., Washington, D.C. 20036. Filed 4/14/83. Legislative interest — "General interest - All legislation affecting the contractual relationships between office equipment suppliers and retailers. Specific interest - Oppose HR 1159 and S 286." Lobbyist — Powell, Goldstein, Frazer & Murphy, 1110 Vermont Ave. N.W., Washington, D.C. 20005. Filed 4/4/83. Legislative interest — "Legislative interests are in defeating the Office Equipment Dealers Act, S 286, HR 1159, on the ground they are non-competitive."

DOMESTIC PETROLEUM COUNCIL INC., Washington, D.C. Lobbyist — Webster & Sheffield, 1200 New Hampshire Ave. N.W., Washington, D.C. 20036. Filed 4/12/83. Legislative interest — "Natural Gas legislation, including S 615."

THE FERTILIZER INSTITUTE, 1015 18th St. N.W., Washington, D.C. 20036. Filed for self 4/11/83. Legislative interest — ". . . legislation relating to the fertilizer industry and agriculture in general." Lobbyists — Diane Bateman, Larry D. Meyers, Gary D. Myers.

INDEPENDENT CATTLEMEN'S ASSOCIATION, Austin, Texas. Lobbyist — Sam White, 412 First St. S.E., Washington, D.C. 20003. Legislative interest — "General farm bill."

MANUFACTURED HOUSING INSTITUTE, 1745 Jefferson Davis Highway, Arlington, Va. 22202. Filed for self 4/6/83. Legislative interest — "General interest in housing legislation, specifically mobile and modular . . . HR 1, Housing and Urban Rural Recovery Act of 1983, partial support . . . S 445, Omnibus Bankruptcy Amendments Act of 1983, partial support . . . HR

1800, Consumer Debtor Bankruptcy Amendments Act of 1983, partial support ... S 644, Emergency Homeowners Relief Act of 1983, partial support."

MIDDLE ATLANTIC CONFERENCE, Riverdale, Md. Lobbyist — Camp, Carmouche, Barsh, Hunter, Gray & Hoffman, 2550 M St. N.W., Washington, D.C. 20037. Filed 4/7/83. Legislative interest — "Motor Carrier Act of 1980."

MIDDLEWEST MOTOR FREIGHT BUREAU, Kansas City, Mo. Lobbyist — Camp, Carmouche, Barsh, Hunter, Gray & Hoffman, 2550 M St. N.W., Washington, D.C. 20037. Filed 4/9/83. Legislative interest — "Motor Carrier Act of 1980."

NATIONAL ASSOCIATION OF BROADCASTERS, 1771 N St. N.W., Washington, D.C. 20036. Filed for self 4/8/83. Legislative interest — "... Those relating directly or indirectly to the radio and television broadcasting industry, especially amendments relating to Communications Act of 1934, 47 U.S.C. 151, Copyright Law of 1909, 17 U.S.C. 1, Communications Satellite Act of 1962, 47 U.S.C. 701, regulation of advertising, taxation, appropriations, public broadcasting, newsmen's privilege and consumer protection."

NATIONAL ASSOCIATION OF BUSINESS DEVELOPMENT CORPS., Lincoln, Neb. Lobbyist — Neece, Cator & Associates Inc., 1050 17th St. N.W., Washington, D.C. 20036. Filed 4/8/83. Legislative interest — "Issues affecting 501 business development company program; Small Business Act."

NATIONAL ASSOCIATION OF CATALOG SHOWROOM MERCHANDISERS, New York, N.Y. Lobbyist — Richard B. Kelly, 770 Lexington Ave., New York, N.Y. 10021. Filed 4/19/83. Legislative interest — "15 U.S.C. 1 - Amend Sherman Act to prohibit restricted distribution - No pending bills."

NATIONAL ASSOCIATION OF INDEPENDENT COLLEGES AND UNIVERSITIES, 1717 Massachusetts Ave. N.W., Washington, D.C. 20036. Filed for self 4/14/83. Legislative interest — "All legislative matters affecting independent colleges and universities, including but not limited to reauthorization of the Higher Education Act of 1965, tax, budget, and appropriations legislation." Lobbyist — Heather Stevens-Kittner.

NATIONAL ASSOCIATION OF MANUFACTURERS, 1776 F St. N.W., Washington, D.C. 20006. Filed 4/13/83. Legislative interest — "... Social Security Reform, FY '84 First Concurrent Budget Resolution, Emergency Supplemental Appropriations - Fiscal Year 1983/Jobs ... HR 1900, H Con Res 91, HR 1718...." Lobbyist — Patricia S. Koziol, 1719 Route 10, Parsippany, N.J. 02054.

NATIONAL ASSOCIATION OF PRIVATE PSYCHIATRIC HOSPITALS, 1319 F St. N.W., Washington, D.C. 20004. Filed for self 4/6/83. Legislative interest — "Issues affecting mental health, hospitals, manpower, and patients." Lobbyist — Katherine Millard.

NATIONAL ASSOCIATION OF REALTORS, 777 14th St. N.W., Washington, D.C. 20005. Filed for self 4/18/83. Legislative interest — "Any legislation that affects the real estate industry, including subsidized housing issues and housing authorization and appropriations legislation. Condominium legislation, public buildings legislation, Farmers Home Administration legislation and enterprise zone legislation." Lobbyist — Esther Liss.

NATIONAL ASSOCIATION OF SMALL BUSINESS INVESTMENT COS., Washington, D.C. Lobbyist — McClure & Trotter, 1100 Connecticut Ave. N.W., Washington, D.C. 20036. Filed 4/14/83. Legislative interest — "Legislation in connection with the amendment of subchapter M of the Internal Revenue Code."

NATIONAL CABLE TELEVISION ASSOCIATION INC., 1724 Massachusetts Ave. N.W., Washington, D.C. 20036. Filed for self 4/8/83. Legislative interest — "Amendments to the Communications Act of 1934 and other legislation affecting cable television generally." Lobbyists — Lois Richerson, Douglas R. Watts.

NATIONAL GROCERS ASSOCIATION, 1825 Samuel Morse Drive, Reston, Va. 22090. Filed for self 4/7/83. Legislative interest — "Issues related to food distribution industry ... Federal Anti-Tampering Act, S 216, support; Heavy Use Vehicle Tax

Adjustment Act of 1983, S 343, support; A bill to repeal interest and dividend withholding, HR 500, support." Lobbyists — Elizabeth C. Nanni, Janet L. Oliver, Richard P. Swigart, Thomas K. Zaucha.

NATIONAL PEANUT GROWERS GROUP, Gorman, Texas. Lobbyist — Sam White, 412 First St. S.E., Washington, D.C. 20003. Filed for self 4/6/83. Legislative interest — "General farm bill."

NATIONAL RURAL ELECTRIC COOPERATIVE ASSOCIATION, 1800 Massachusetts Ave. N.W., Washington, D.C. 20036. Filed for self 4/11/83. Legislative interest — "All legislation affecting the rural electrification program provided for under the REA Act of 1936 as amended." Lobbyist — Rae E. Cronmiller.

NATIONAL SMALL BUSINESS GOVERNMENT CONTRACTORS ASSOCIATION, Nutley, N.J. Lobbyist — Bowman, Conner, Touhey & Thornton, 2828 Pennsylvania Ave. N.W., Washington, D.C. 20007. Filed 4/18/83. Legislative interest — "Legislation relating to government procurement and small business matters generally including S 272 (for) and S 338."

NEW ENGLAND MOTOR RATE BUREAU, Burlington, Mass. Lobbyist — Camp, Carmouche, Barsh, Hunter, Gray & Hoffman, 2550 M St. N.W., Washington, D.C. 20037. Filed 4/7/83. Legislative interest — "Motor Carrier Act of 1980."

NIAGARA FRONTIER TARIFF BUREAU, Buffalo, N.Y. Lobbyist — Camp, Carmouche, Barsh, Hunter, Gray & Hoffman, 2550 M St. N.W., Washington, D.C. 20037. Filed 4/7/83. Legislative interest — "Motor Carrier Act of 1980."

PACIFIC INLAND TARIFF BUREAU, Portland, Ore. Lobbyist — Camp, Carmouche, Barsh, Hunter, Gray & Hoffman, 2550 M St. N.W., Washington, D.C. 20037. Legislative interest — "Motor Carrier Act of 1980."

PACIFIC SEAFOOD PROCESSORS ASSOCIATION, Seattle, Wash. Lobbyist — Bogle & Gates, 1 Thomas Circle, Washington, D.C. 20005. Filed 4/11/83. Legislative interest — Not specified.

PHARMACEUTICAL MANUFACTURERS ASSOCIATION, Washington, D.C. Lobbyist — O'Neill and Haase, 1333 New Hampshire Ave. N.W., Washington, D.C. 20036. Filed 4/8/83. Legislative interest — "Patent Term Restoration Act."

PIPELINE INDUSTRY ADVANCEMENT FUND, Dallas, Texas. Lobbyist — Akin, Gump, Strauss, Hauer & Feld, 1333 New Hampshire Ave. N.W., Washington, D.C. 20036. Filed 4/20/83. Legislative interest — "Hearings and any legislation affecting coal slurry pipelines, including HR 1010, 'Coal Slurry Pipeline Act,' and S 267, 'Coal Distribution and Utilization Act of 1983.'"

ROCKY MOUNTAIN MOTOR TARIFF BUREAU, Denver, Colo. Lobbyist — Camp, Carmouche, Barsh, Hunter, Gray & Hoffman, 2550 M St. N.W., Washington, D.C. 20037. Filed 4/7/83. Legislative interest — "Motor Carrier Act of 1980."

SOUTHERN MOTOR CARRIERS RATE CONFERENCE, Atlanta, Ga. Lobbyist — Camp, Carmouche, Barsh, Hunter, Gray & Hoffman, 2550 M St. N.W., Washington, D.C. 20037. Filed 4/7/83. Legislative interest — "Motor Carrier Act of 1980."

SPECIALTY EQUIPMENT MARKET ASSOCIATION, Whittier, Calif. Lobbyist — Steven T. Miller, 1607 New Hampshire Ave. N.W., Washington, D.C. 20009. Filed 4/14/83. Legislative interest — "We are interested in general activities affecting the automotive market...."

SUGAR ASSOCIATION OF THE CARIBBEAN, Port of Spain, Trinidad. Lobbyist — McMurray and Pendergast, 1575 I St. N.W., Washington, D.C. 20005. Filed 4/7/83. Legislative interest — "All legislative matters pertaining to the regulation and importation of sugar."

Miscellaneous

H. L. ARONSON JR., 1511 34th St. N.W., Washington, D.C. 20007. Filed for self 4/4/83. Legislative interest — "Legislative interests are concerning the Alaskan gas pipeline and legislation

involving natural gas regulation."

BI-COUNTY CONSORTIUM, Gwinn, Mich. Lobbyist — Gnau, Carter, Jacobsen & Associates Inc., 1777 F St. N.W., Washington, D.C. 20006. Filed 4/20/83. Legislative interest — "Government and agency liasion to provide information on funding sources and legislation affecting their organization."

THE CLEVELAND CLINIC FOUNDATION, Cleveland, Ohio. Lobbyist — Hogan & Hartson, 815 Connecticut Ave. N.W., Washington, D.C. 20006. Filed 4/11/83. Legislative interest — "Represent employer's interests with respect to legislation to amend sections of the Social Security Act dealing with the Medicare and Medicaid programs."

INDIANA UNIVERSITY, Bloomington, Ind. Lobbyist — Schlossberg-Cassidy & Associates Inc., 955 L'Enfant Plaza S.W., Washington, D.C. 20024. Filed 4/8/83. Legislative interest — "Legislation relating to federal research, education and development programs."

PETER J. KIERNAN, 2712 N St. N.W., Washington, D.C. 20007. Filed for self 4/15/83. Legislative interest — "All statutes and bills relating to the Export Administration Act and the Export of Alaska North Slope Oil."

THE METHODIST HOSPITAL, Houston, Texas. Lobbyist — Hogan & Hartson, 815 Connecticut Ave. N.W., Washington, D.C. 20006. Filed 4/11/83. Legislative interest — "Represent employer's interests with respect to legislation to amend sections of the Social Security Act not dealing with the Medicare and Medicaid programs." Lobbyist — Vinson & Elkins, 1101 Connecticut Ave. N.W., Washington, D.C. 20036. Filed 4/14/83. Legislative interest — "General legislative interests in connection with Medicare legislation."

PRATT INSTITUTE, Brooklyn, N.Y. Lobbyist — Schlossberg-Cassidy & Associates Inc., 955 L'Enfant Plaza S.W., Washington, D.C. 20024. Filed 4/8/83. Legislative interest — "Legislation relating to federal research, education and development programs."

SCHICK SHADEL HOSPITAL, Fort Worth, Texas. Lobbyist — Bill Newbold and Associates, 1510 N. 12th St., Arlington, Va. 22209. Filed 4/12/83. Legislative interest — "Medical treatment of alcoholism. Medicare reimbursement for medical treatment of alcoholism."

TYRONE STALLWORTH, 220 N. Devillers St., Pensacola, Fla. 32501. Filed for self 4/8/83. Legislative interest — "Military Justice and civil rights and education (elementary through higher education)."

MRS. WINNIE M. TSE, Hoboken, N.J. Lobbyist — Chwat/Weigend Associates, 226 Massachusetts Ave. N.W., Washington, D.C. 20002. Filed 4/4/83. Legislative interest — "Private immigration legislation before the House and Senate Judiciary Committees."

May Registrations

Citizens' Groups

ARMENIAN NATIONAL COMMITTEE, 419-A W. Colorado St., Glendale, Calif. 91204. Filed for self 5/5/83. Legislative interest — "Legislation and congressional actions affecting or of interest to the Armenian-American community." Lobbyist — Michael Mahdesian, 1514 17th St. N.W., Washington, D.C. 20009.

COALITIONS FOR AMERICA, 721 Second St. N.E., Washington, D.C. 20002. Filed for self 5/23/83. Legislative interest — "Working in favor of reintroduction and passage of Tsongas-Ritter resolution calling upon the United States government to support the people of Afghanistan with material assistance in their struggle to be free from foreign domination." Lobbyists — Andrew Eiva, Charles A. Moser.

COMMON CAUSE, 2030 M St. N.W., Washington, D.C. 20036. Filed for self 5/5/83. Legislative interest — "Legislative interests are in such areas as open government, campaign finance reform, Federal Election Commission, lobby disclosure, government ethics, Senate confirmation process, extension of the Clean Air Act, court jurisdiction issues, congressional budget process, congressional reform, freedom of information, energy policy, waste in government, merit selection of federal judges and U.S. attorneys, regulatory reform, public participation in federal agency proceedings, Legal Services Corporation, the Equal Rights Amendment, nuclear arms control and military spending. In the 98th Congress, Common Cause has supported legislation to provide for public financing of Congressional elections, PAC limits and response time for independent expenditures. Common Cause has supported H J Res 13 calling for a mutual and verifiable freeze on nuclear weapons and has opposed production funds for the MX missile. Common Cause has supported retention of the interest and dividend withholding provision adopted last year as part of the Tax Equity and Fiscal Responsibility Act of 1982. In addition, Common Cause has supported the reauthorization of the Office of Government Ethics and has supported the FY 84 budget reported by the House Budget committee and adopted by the House." Lobbyists — Jay Keller, Jennifer Vasiloff.

WASHINGTON COALITION ON REDRESS, 318 Sixth Ave. South, Seattle, Wash. 98104. Filed for self 5/2/83. Legislative interest — "Legislative interest is to pass legislation that will provide individuated payments to Japanese Americans whose civil liberties were violated by the U.S. government during World War II." Lobbyists — Charles T. Kato; Philip Nash, 399 Oak Ave., Maywood, N.J. 07607.

ZERO POPULATION GROWTH INC., 1346 Connecticut Ave. N.W., Washington, D.C. 20036. Filed for self 5/23/83. Legislative interest — "Support legislation to establish a national population policy and foresight capability: 'The Global Resources, Environment and Population Act of 1983,' Senate and House Bills S 1025 and HR 2491. Support legislation to reform U.S. immigration policy: 'Immigration Reform and Control Act of 1983,' HR 1510. In general, seek Congressional consideration of national population planning issues." Lobbyist — Rhea L. Cohen.

Corporations and Businesses

ALASKA LUMBER AND PULP CO., Washington, D.C. Lobbyist — Bliss, Craft & Richards, 1050 Thomas Jefferson St. N.W., Washington, D.C. 20007. Filed 5/26/83. Legislative interest — "Any legislation dealing with lifting the ban on exporting Alaskan oil."

ALPHA DATA INC., Nashville, Tenn. Lobbyist — Paul Tendler Associates Inc., 818 Connecticut Ave. N.W., Washington, D.C. 20006. Filed 5/4/83. Legislative interest — "All legislation or regulations dealing with export licenses and trade matters for high technology to European countries."

AMERICAN GENERAL LIFE INSURANCE CO., Houston, Texas. Lobbyist — Davis & McLeod, 499 South Capitol St. S.W., Washington, D.C. 20003. Filed 5/23/83. Legislative interest — "All tax legislation affecting the life insurance industry."

AMERICAN STOCK EXCHANGE INC., New York, N.Y. Lobbyist — Dewey, Ballantine, Bushby, Palmer & Wood, 1775 Pennsylvania Ave. N.W., Washington, D.C. 20006. Filed 5/2/83. Legislative interest — "Possible changes in section 1092 of the Internal Revenue Code as regards exchange traded stock options."

APACHE CORP., Minneapolis, Minn. Lobbyist — Wilmer, Cutler & Pickering, 1666 K St. N.W., Washington, D.C. 20006. Filed 5/25/83. Legislative interest — "Representing Apache Corp. in connection with any current or future legislation affecting the tax status of income from working interests in oil and gas properties as unrelated taxable business income under the Internal Revenue Code, including HR 821 introduced in the 98th Congress, and similar legislation."

ARMCO INC., Washington, D.C. Lobbyist — Richard C. White, 499 South Capitol St. S.W., Washington, D.C. 20003. Filed 5/24/83. (Former U.S. rep., D-Texas, 1965-83.) Legislative interest — "Export Administration Act."

BANKAMERICA CORP., 555 California St., San Francisco, Calif. 94104. Filed for self 5/25/83. Legislative interest —

"None." Lobbyist — Patrick S. Antrim, 1800 K St. N.W., Washington, D.C. 20006.

BKK CORP., Torrance, Calif. Lobbyist — Manatt, Phelps, Rothenberg & Tunney, 1200 New Hampshire Ave. N.W., Washington, D.C. 20036. Filed 5/31/83. (Former U.S. Rep. James C. Corman, D-Calif., 1961-81, was listed as agent for this client.) Legislative interest — "Legislation dealing with waste disposal."

CECOS CER CO., Cincinnati, Ohio. Lobbyist — William H. Harsha & Associates Inc., P.O. Box 24157, Washington, D.C. 20024. Filed 5/6/83. (Former U.S. Rep. William H. Harsha, R-Ohio, 1961-81, was listed as agent for this client.) Legislative interest — "Harzardous Waste Disposal ... HR 2867, HR 2478."

CERTAINTEED CORP., P.O. Box 860, Valley Forge, Pa. 19482. Filed for self 5/5/83. Legislative interest — Not specified.

CHARTER OIL CO., 2550 M St. N.W., Washington, D.C. 20037. Filed for self 5/19/83. Legislative interest — "... Tax treatment of single premium deferred annuities and other tax legislation affecting insurance industry; Position: retain current law ... Buy America provisions or other requirements on domestic content ... natural gas decontrol; Position: Support S 615 ... petroleum regulatory legislation ... superfund legislation; HR 2503, S 80, S 86."

COMMITTEE FOR FAIR INSURANCE RATES, 600 Pennsylvania Ave. S.E., Washington, D.C. 20003. Filed for self 5/23/83. Legislative interest — "Opposition to legislation which prohibits gender based pricing of insurance ... Fair Insurance Practices Act ... Non-Discrimination in Insurance Act ... HR 100, S 372...." Lobbyist — Nancy Haragan.

COMPUTERIZED SECURITY SYSTEMS INC., Troy, Mich. Lobbyist — Gnau, Carter, Jacobsen & Associates Inc., 1777 F St. N.W., Washington, D.C. 20006. Filed 5/27/83. Legislative interest — "Exploring possible market in Federal government for sale of their product."

CONNECTICUT MUTUAL LIFE INSURANCE CO., Hartford, Conn. Lobbyist — Murray and Scheer, 2550 M St. N.W., Washington, D.C. 20037. Filed 5/24/83. Legislative interest — Not specified.

DAMSON OIL CORP., New York, N.Y. Lobbyist — Dewey, Ballantine, Bushby, Palmer & Wood, 1775 Pennsylvania Ave. N.W., Washington, D.C. 20006. Filed 5/2/83. Legislative interest — "Sections 512 and 514 of the Internal Revenue Code; HR 821."

ECOLOGICAL PROFESSIONAL INDUSTRIES INC., Cincinnati, Ohio. Lobbyist — William H. Harsha & Associates Inc., P.O. Box 24157, Washington, D.C. 20024. Filed 5/6/83. (Former U.S. Rep. William H. Harsha, R-Ohio, 1961-81, was listed as agent for this client.) Legislative interest — "RECRA, superfund."

FORD MOTOR CO., The American Road, Dearborn, Mich. 48121. Filed for self 5/20/83. Legislative interest — "... natural gas, toxic substance victim compensation, motor vehicle theft, product liability, vehicle safety, noise legislation." Lobbyist — Robert M. Howard, 815 Connecticut Ave. N.W., Washington, D.C. 20006.

GLOBAL COMMUNICATIONS INC., Williamston, Mich. Lobbyist — Gnau, Carter, Jacobsen & Associates Inc., 1777 F St. N.W., Washington, D.C. 20006. Filed 5/27/83. Legislative interest — "Working with FmHA, Economic Development Administration, HUD, for federal loan guarantees for economic development."

GOVERNMENT EMPLOYEES INSURANCE CO., Chevy Chase, Md. Lobbyist — Zuckert, Scoutt, Rasenberger & Delaney, 888 17th St. N.W., Washington, D.C. 20006. Filed 5/5/83. Legislative interest — "Legislation relating to property and casualty insurance tax."

INDIANA ASSOCIATES, Landover, Md. Lobbyist — Arent, Fox, Kintner, Plotkin & Kahn, 1050 Connecticut Ave. N.W., Washington, D.C. 20036. Filed 5/27/83. (Former U.S. Sen. John C. Culver, D-Iowa, Senate 1975-81, House 1965-75, was listed as agent for this client.) Legislative interest — "Resolution before House Committee on Public Works for approval of GSA lease for 633 Indiana Ave."

INTELSAT, Washington, D.C. Lobbyist — Arent, Fox,

Kintner, Plotkin & Kahn, 1050 Connecticut Ave. N.W., Washington, D.C. 20036. Filed 5/4/83. (Former U.S. Sen. John C. Culver, D-Iowa, Senate 1975-81, House 1965-75, was listed among agents for this client.) Legislative interest — "Opposition to section 304(a) of S 999."

LINEAR AIR MOTORS INC., Ortonville, Mich. Lobbyist — Gnau, Carter, Jacobsen & Associates Inc., 1777 F St. N.W., Washington, D.C. 20006. Filed 5/20/83. Legislative interest — "Working with DOT and other federal agencies for support in funding Linear Air Motor's cost effective urban transit system."

MASSACHUSETTS MUTUAL LIFE INSURANCE CO., Springfield, Mass. Lobbyist — Murray and Scheer, 2550 M St. N.W., Washington, D.C. 20037. Filed 5/24/83. Legislative interest — Not specified. Lobbyist — Reid & Priest, 1111 19th St. N.W., Washington, D.C. 20036. Filed 5/31/83. Legislative interest — "Revision of Subchapter L of the Internal Revenue Code or extension of and/or modifications of sections 259-263 and 267 of PL 97-248."

MUTUAL BENEFIT LIFE INSURANCE CO., Newark, N.J. Lobbyist — Murray and Scheer, 2550 M St. N.W., Washington, D.C. 20037. Filed 5/24/83. Legislative interest — Not specified.

MUTUAL PROTECTION TRUST, Los Angeles, Calif. Lobbyist — Webster, Chamberlain & Bean, 1747 Pennsylvania Ave. N.W., Washington, D.C. 20006. Filed 5/5/83. (Former U.S. Rep. Charles E. Chamberlain, R-Mich., 1957-74, was listed as agent for this client.) Legislative interest — "In support of HR 2095 and HR 2486, to amend the Internal Revenue Code of 1954 relative to physicians' and surgeons' mutual protection associations."

NEW ENGLAND MUTUAL LIFE INSURANCE CO., 501 Boylston St., Boston, Mass. 02116. Lobbyist — Murray and Scheer, 2550 M St. N.W., Washington, D.C. 20037. Filed 5/24/83. Legislative interest — Not specified. Filed for self 5/2/83. Legislative interest — "HR 100 - Non-Discrimination in Insurance Act. S 372 - Fair Practices in Insurance Act - opposed." Lobbyist — Jeanne Campbell, 1800 Massachusetts Ave. N.W., Washington, D.C. 20036.

NORTHWESTERN MUTUAL LIFE INSURANCE CO., Milwaukee, Wis. Lobbyist — Reid & Priest, 1111 19th St. N.W., Washington, D.C. 20036. Filed 5/31/83. Legislative interest — "Revision of Subchapter L of the Internal Revenue Code for extension of and/or modifications of sections 259, 263 and 267 of PL 97-248."

PANHANDLE EASTERN PIPE LINE CO., Houston, Texas. Lobbyist — Dewey, Ballantine, Bushby, Palmer & Wood, 1775 Pennsylvania Ave. N.W., Washington, D.C. 20006. Filed 5/2/83. Legislative interest — "Energy taxation, any related issues."

THE PENN MUTUAL LIFE INSURANCE CO., Philadelphia, Pa. Lobbyist — Murray and Scheer, 2550 M St. N.W., Washington, D.C. 20037. Filed 5/24/83. Legislative interest — Not specified.

PROVIDENT LIFE & ACCIDENT INSURANCE CO., Chattanooga, Tenn. Lobbyist — Corporate Consulting Services Inc., Key Largo, Fla. Filed 5/20/83. (Former U.S. Rep. L. A. "Skip" Bafalis, R-Fla., 1973-83, was listed as agent for this client.) Legislative interest — "Tax issues relating to the life insurance industry." Lobbyist — Davis & McLeod, 499 South Capitol St. S.W., Washington, D.C. 20003. Filed 5/23/83. Legislative interest — "All tax legislation affecting the life insurance industry."

RIO BLANCO PROPERTIES, Meeker, Colo. Lobbyist — DAR Investment Corp., 600 Water St. S.W., Washington, D.C. 20024. Filed 5/18/83. Legislative interest — "General legislation - Interior appropriations supplemental."

SAFEKEEPER SYSTEMS INC., Troy, Mich. Lobbyist — Gnau, Carter, Jacobsen & Associates Inc., 1777 F St. N.W., Washington, D.C. 20005. Filed 5/27/83. Legislative interest — "Exploring possible market in federal government for sale of the product."

STEPAN CHEMICAL CO., Northfield, Ill. Lobbyist — Mayer, Brown & Platt, 888 17th St. N.W., Washington, D.C. 20006. Filed 5/3/83. Legislative interest — "Registrant's interest is

limited to seeking DOE budget authorizations and appropriations for the cleanup of radiological waste materials, including authorizations in HR 2587."

THOMSON-CSF INC., Bagneux, France. Lobbyist — King & Spalding, 1915 I St. N.W., Washington, D.C. 20006. Filed 5/23/83. (Former U.S. Sen. Charles E. Goodell, R-N.Y., Senate 1968-71, House 1959-68, was listed as agent for this client.) Legislative interest — "Legislation relating to the Short Range Air Defense (SHORAD) System known as SICA."

TRANSCO ENERGY CO., 2800 South Post Oak Road, Houston, Texas 77251. Filed for self 5/31/83. Legislative interest — "Amendments to the Natural Gas Policy Act - all legislation; Coal Slurry Legislation - S 267, HR 1010." Lobbyist — Ross Workman.

TURNER BROADCASTING SYSTEM INC., Atlanta, Ga. Lobbyist — Ginn & Edington Inc., 1006 Cameron St., Alexandria, Va. 22314. Filed 5/20/83. Legislative interest — "Legislation impacting upon and of interest to the broadcasting and communications industries." Lobbyist — Don Wallace Associates Inc., 232 East Capitol St., Washington, D.C. 20003. Filed 5/19/83. (Former U.S. Rep. John L. Napier, R-S.C., 1981-83, was listed as agent for this client.) Legislative interest — "Copyright legislation (S 1270 ... HR 2902 and other legislation); Communications issues (HR 2250, HR 2382 and HR 2755)."

UCI INC., Springfield, Va. Lobbyist — Manatt, Phelps, Rothenberg & Tunney, 1200 New Hampshire Ave. N.W., Washington, D.C. 20036. Filed 5/23/83. (Former U.S. Rep. James C. Corman, D-Calif., 1961-81, was listed as agent for this client.) Legislative interest — "Legislation affecting small businesses."

U.S. MANUFACTURING CO., Fraser, Mich. Lobbyist — Gnau, Carter, Jacobsen & Associates Inc., 1777 F St. N.W., Washington, D.C. 20006. Filed 5/27/83. Legislative interest — "Exploring possible market in federal government for sale of their products. Also looking for possible federal loan guarantees for economic development."

UNITED STATES STEEL CORP., 600 Grant St., Pittsburgh, Pa. 15230. Filed for self 5/27/83. Legislative interest — "Matters pertaining to judiciary or labor, health and social service issues. These include: Employee Retirement Income Security Act; Single Employer Pension Plan Termination; Occupational Health and Safety; Mine Safety and Health Act (S 1173); Insurance Improvements Act. Health Care for the Unemployed (HR 3021); Plant Closings (HR 2847); Taxpayer Antitrust Enforcement Act (S 915); Joint Research and Development Act (S 737)." Lobbyist — Marilyn A. Harris, 818 Connecticut Ave. N.W., Washington, D.C. 20006.

VELO-BIND INC., Sunnyvale, Calif. Lobbyist — Dewey, Ballantine, Bushby, Palmer & Wood, 1775 Pennsylvania Ave. N.W., Washington, D.C. 20006. Filed 5/2/83. Legislative interest — "Resolve certain difficulties in the workings of section 186 of the Internal Revenue Code."

VISA U.S.A. INC., Washington, D.C. Lobbyist — Bingham, Dana & Gould, 1724 Massachusetts Ave. N.W., Washington, D.C. 20036. Filed 5/25/83. Legislative interest — "Support for legislation involving credit and debit card fradulent activities and imposing criminal penalties therefor."

International Relations

EMBASSY OF THE REPUBLIC OF SOUTH AFRICA, Washington, D.C. Lobbyist — Baskin and Sears, 818 Connecticut Ave. N.W., Washington, D.C. 20006. Filed 5/24/83. Legislative interest — "Baskin and Sears P.C. will endeavor to assist in developing and maintaining mutually beneficial relations between the United States and the Republic of South Africa; HR 2957, section 303 (directing President to instruct the U.S. executive director of the IMF to oppose credit drawings by South Africa) oppose; HR 1693 (ban on importation of Krugerrands and other measures) oppose; Senate Foreign Aid Authorization bill (amendment to impose tariff of Krugerrands) oppose."

REPUBLIC OF KOREA, Washington, D.C. Lobbyist — Baron/Canning and Co. Inc., 540 Madison Ave., New York, N.Y.

10022. Filed 5/5/83. Legislative interest — "General matters pertaining to U.S.-Republic of Korea relations."

Labor Groups

FOOD AND BEVERAGE TRADES DEPARTMENT, AFL-CIO, 815 16th St. N.W., Washington, D.C. 20006. Filed for self 5/26/83. Legislative interest — Not specified. Lobbyist — John Vincent Harvey.

State and Local Governments

CITY OF LAKEWOOD, Lakewood, Calif. Lobbyist — Preston, Thorgrimson, Ellis & Holman, 1735 New York Ave. N.W., Washington, D.C. 20006. Filed 5/23/83. Legislative interest — "Legislation affecting municipal interests in cable television including S 66."

CITY OF ST. LOUIS, St. Louis, Mo. Lobbyist — Preston, Thorgrimson, Ellis & Holman, 1735 New York Ave. N.W., Washington, D.C. 20006. Filed 5/23/83. Legislative interest — "Legislation affecting municipal interests in cable television including S 66."

LOS ANGELES RAPID TRANSIT DISTRICT, Los Angeles, Calif. Lobbyist — Manatt, Phelps, Rothenberg & Tunney, 1200 New Hampshire Ave. N.W., Washington, D.C. 20036. Filed 5/25/83. Legislative interest — "Congressional approval of funds for the Los Angeles Metro Rail Project."

PUERTO RICO MARITIME SHIPPING AUTHORITY, San Juan, Puerto Rico. Lobbyist — McAuliffe & Associates, 812 D St. N.E., Washington, D.C. 20002. Filed 5/5/83. Legislative interest — "Insurance industry and maritime shipping authority."

STATE OF ALASKA, Juneau, Alaska. Lobbyist — Preston, Thorgrimson, Ellis & Holman, 1735 New York Ave. N.W., Washington, D.C. 20006. Filed 5/23/83. Legislative interest — "Legislation affecting telephone rates and other telecommunications issues."

Trade Associations

AMERICAN NEWSPAPER PUBLISHERS ASSOCIATION, Washington, D.C. Lobbyist — Blum & Nash, 1015 18th St. N.W., Washington, D.C. 20036. Filed 5/25/83. Legislative interest — "Cable legislation before the House Energy and Commerce Committee, S 66."

AMERICAN PAPER INSTITUTE INC., 260 Madison Ave., New York, N.Y. 10016. Filed for self 5/31/83. Legislative interest — "Legislative interests are those affecting the pulp, paper and paperboard industry, its operation, practices and properties." Lobbyists — James L. Hutchison, Ronald J. Slinn.

ASSOCIATION OF FLORAL IMPORTERS OF FLORIDA, Miami, Fla. Lobbyist — Heron, Burchette, Ruckert & Rothwell, 1200 New Hampshire Ave. N.W., Washington, D.C. 20036. Filed 5/6/83. Legislative interest — "HR 1146; All legislation affecting floral importers."

THE CANNED AND COOKED MEAT IMPORTERS ASSOCIATION, Washington, D.C. Lobbyist — Anderson & Pendleton, 1000 Connecticut Ave. N.W., Washington, D.C. 20036. Filed 5/4/83. Legislative interest — "Tariff rates applicable to canned corned beef. For HR 2502."

THE COMMITTEE ON UNITED STATES BUSINESS OF THE CANADIAN LIFE & HEALTH INSURANCE ASSOCIATION, Toronto, Ontario, Canada. Lobbyist — Cornelius B. Kennedy, 4801 Massachusetts Ave. N.W., Washington, D.C. 20016. Filed 5/2/83. Legislative interest — Not specified.

INSTITUTE OF INTERNATIONAL CONTAINER LESSORS, Box 605, Bedford, N.Y. 10506. Lobbyist — Cadwalader, Wickersham & Taft, 1333 New Hampshire Ave. N.W., Washington, D.C. 20036. Filed 5/24/83. Legislative interest

— "U.S. tax treaties with Australia and New Zealand ... for in part, against in part." Lobbyist — Lund & O'Brien, 1625 I St. N.W., Washington, D.C. 20006. Filed 5/19/83. Legislative interest — "U.S. tax treaties with Australia and New Zealand ... for in part, against in part." Filed for self 5/31/83. Legislative interest — "U.S. tax treaties with Australia and New Zealand ... for in part, against in part." Lobbyist — Edward A. Woolley.

INSURANCE ASSOCIATION OF CONNECTICUT, Hartford, Conn. Lobbyist — O'Connor & Hannan, 1919 Pennsylvania Ave. N.W., Washington, D.C. 20006. Filed 5/3/83. Legislative interest — "Seek amendments to HR 100, 'Nondiscrimination in Insurance Act.'"

INTERNATIONAL ASSOCIATION OF DRILLING CONTRACTORS, 1901 L St. N.W., Washington, D.C. 20036. Filed for self 5/24/83. Legislative interest — "General interest in legislation affecting the drilling industry." Lobbyist — Brian T. Petty.

INTERNATIONAL CHIROPRACTIC ASSOCIATION, Washington, D.C. Lobbyist — Craig Hackler, 421 First St. S.E., Washington, D.C. 20003. Filed 5/19/83. Legislative interest — "HR 3016, to authorize reimbursement for the reasonable charges for chiropractic services provided to certain veterans; for."

INTERSTATE NATURAL GAS ASSOCIATION OF AMERICA, Washington, D.C. Lobbyist — Nossaman, Guthner, Knox & Elliott, 1140 19th St. N.W., Washington, D.C. 20036. Filed 5/3/83. Legislative interest — "Measures relating to natural gas regulation or deregulation."

NATIONAL ASSOCIATION OF BUSINESS DEVELOPMENT CORPS., Lincoln, Neb. Lobbyist — Neece, Cator & Associates Inc., 1050 17th St. N.W., Washington, D.C. 20036. Filed 5/20/83. Legislative interest — "Issues affecting 501 business development company program; Small Business Act."

NATIONAL ASSOCIATION OF INSURANCE COMMISSIONERS, Brookfield, Wis. Lobbyist — McAuliffe & Associates, 812 D St. N.E., Washington, D.C. 20002. Filed 5/5/83. Legislative interest — "Insurance industry and maritime shipping authority."

NATIONAL BEER WHOLESALERS' ASSOCIATION OF AMERICA INC., Falls Church, Va. Lobbyist — Don Wallace Associates Inc., 232 East Capitol St., Washington, D.C. 20003. Filed 5/18/83. Legislative interest — "'Malt Beverage Interbrand Competition Act,' HR 2262."

NATIONAL MACHINE TOOL BUILDERS' ASSOCIATION, McLean, Va. Lobbyist — Richard C. White, 499 South Capitol St. S.W., Washington, D.C. 20003. Filed 5/24/83. (Former U.S. rep., D-Texas, 1965-83). Legislative interest — "Export Administration Act."

NATURAL GAS SUPPLY ASSOCIATION, Washington, D.C. Lobbyist — Dickstein, Shapiro & Morin, 2101 L St. N.W., Washington, D.C. 20037. Filed 5/20/83. Legislative interest — "Natural gas matters affecting industry."

PETROLEUM EQUIPMENT AND SUPPLY ASSOCIATION, Houston, Texas. Lobbyist — Richard C. White, 499 South Capitol St. S.W., Washington, D.C. 20003. Filed 5/24/83. (Former U.S. rep., D-Texas, 1965-83.) Legislative interest — "Export Administration Act."

RISK AND INSURANCE MANAGEMENT SOCIETY INC., New York, N.Y. Filed for self 5/25/83. Legislative interest — "Seeking amendments to sections 461 and 165 of the Internal Revenue Code of 1954 to allow deductions for self-insurance costs; HR 2642 and other legislation favoring tax equality; insurance and related insurance matters."

Miscellaneous

ESTATE OF CHARLES G. BLUHDORN, New York, N.Y. Lobbyist — McClure & Trotter, 1100 Connecticut Ave. N.W., Washington, D.C. 20036. Filed 5/27/83. Legislative interest — "Legislation in connection with Subtitle B, Chapter 11 of the Internal Revenue Code, as amended."

THE MORRIS AND GWENDOLYN CAFRITZ FOUNDATION, Washington, D.C. Lobbyist — Rogers & Wells, 1737 H St. N.W., Washington, D.C. 20006. Filed 5/4/83. Legislative interest — "Tax legislation relating to private foundations; PL 91-172, the Tax Reform Act of 1969."

COMMITTEE FOR SAVERS' INTEREST, 315 Union St., Nashville, Tenn. 37201. Filed for self 5/26/83. Legislative interest — "Specific legislative interest is to support the repeal of a portion of Title III of the 1982 Tax Equity and Fiscal Responsibility Act. Several bills have been introduced to accomplish this. Our Committee supports the repeal in general." Lobbyist — Ronald Samuels.

NICHOLAS JOHNSON, Box 1876, Iowa City, Iowa 52244. Filed for self 5/31/83. Legislative interest — "Telecommunications, communications, broadcasting and cable policy issues (*e.g.*, oppose S 66)."

ALAN W. LONG JR., 500 W. 22nd St., New York, N.Y. 10011. Filed for self 5/25/83. Legislative interest — "HR 2713, HR 2762, HR 2763 ... AIDS research and patient services."

DOUGLAS P. WACHHOLZ, 7002 Bright Ave., McLean, Va. 22101. Filed for self 5/18/83. Legislative interest — "Lobbying in support of S 544 ('Caribbean Basin Economic Recovery Act')."

ROBERT P. WILL, Washington, D.C. Lobbyist — Karl R. Klingelhofer, 5417 Thetford Place, Alexandria, Va. 22310. Filed 5/25/83. Legislative interest — "S 752."

June Registrations

Citizens' Groups

AMERICAN BORDER BROADCASTERS FREE SPEECH COMMITTEE INC., 2000 M St. N.W., Washington, D.C. 20036. Lobbyist — Lionel Van Deerlin, 2945 Fruitland Drive, Vista, Calif. 92083. (Former U.S. rep., D-Calif., 1963-81.) Filed 6/21/83. Legislative interest — "The Committee favors repeal of section 325(b) of the Communications Act of 1934, as amended (47 U.S.C. section 325(b))." Filed for self 6/21/83. Legislative interest — "The Committee favors repeal of section 325(b) of the Communications Act of 1934, as amended (47 U.S.C. section 325(b))." Lobbyist — William J. Potts Jr.

COMMITTEE FOR AD VALOREM EQUITY, Washington, D.C. 20006. Lobbyist — David P. Stang, 1629 K St. N.W., Washington, D.C. 20006. Filed 6/6/83. Legislative interest — "HR 2381, to amend the Tariff Act of 1930."

COOK INLET REGION INC., Anchorage, Alaska. Lobbyist — Nossaman, Guthner, Knox & Elliott, 1140 19th St. N.W., Washington, D.C. 20036. Filed 6/22/83. Legislative interest — "Legislative representation of Cook Inlet Region Inc., an Alaska Native Corporation. Legislative interests include public lands matters affecting Alaska, including the Alaska Native Claims Settlement Act (43 U.S.C. section 1601 *et seq.*), S 1232 and the Alaska National Interests Lands Conservation Act (16 U.S.C. section 3101 *et seq.*)."

MINNESOTANS FOR PEACE IN CENTRAL AMERICA, 920 Nicollet Mall, Minneapolis, Minn. 55402. Filed for self 6/27/83. Legislative interest — "Following all legislation relating to Central America; we oppose increased military aid to El Salvador, Guatemala and Honduras as found in Foreign Aid Authorization and Appropriations Bills." Lobbyist — Doug Nethercut.

NATIONAL CITIZENS' LOBBY INC., 934 First Capitol Drive, St. Charles, Mo. 63301. Filed for self 6/24/83. Legislative interest — Not specified. Lobbyist — Clifford E. Sims, 3021 Flamingo Drive, St. Charles, Mo. 63301.

NATIONAL PEACE ACADEMY CAMPAIGN, 110 Maryland Ave. N.E., Washington, D.C. 20002. Filed for self 6/24/83. Legislative interest — "General legislative interests designed to establish a National Academy of Peace (and Conflict Resolution). Specific legislation: S 564 and HR 1249, the United States Academy of Peace (and Conflict Resolution) Act." Lobbyist — Mark Alan Rilling.

NINTH PRO-LIFE CONGRESSIONAL DISTRICT ACTION COMMITTEE, 1120 Michigan Blvd., Dunedin, Fla. 33528. Filed for self 6/6/83. Legislative interest — "... S J Res 110, S J Res 3 and any other proposed human life amendments." Lobbyist — John Kelley.

TRIBAL COUNCIL OF THE COUSHATTA TRIBE OF LOUISIANA, Elton, La. Lobbyist — Jim D. Bowmer, P.O. Box 844, Temple, Texas 76503. Filed 6/30/83. Legislative interest — "Support passage of HR 2337 and H Res 114."

TRUST FOR PUBLIC LANDS, San Francisco, Calif. Lobbyist — Nossaman, Guthner, Knox & Elliott, 1140 19th St. N.W., Washington, D.C. 20036. Filed 6/22/83. Legislative interest — "Legislative representation of Trust for Public Lands. Legislative interests include appropriations for purchase of park and other conservation system lands and other issues affecting non-profit conservation organizations."

THE WILDERNESS SOCIETY, 1901 Pennsylvania Ave. N.W., Washington, D.C. 20006. Filed for self 6/2/83. Legislative interest — "Wilderness and other public land issues relating to Alaska public lands." Lobbyist — Amy Skilbred.

Corporations and Businesses

ALAMO CEMENT CO., San Antonio, Texas. Lobbyist — Squire, Sanders & Dempsey, 1201 Pennsylvania Ave. N.W., Washington, D.C. 20004. Filed 6/21/83. Legislative interest — "Tariff and trade matters...."

ALUMINUM COMPANY OF AMERICA, Washington, D.C. Lobbyist — Patton, Boggs & Blow, 2550 M St. N.W., Washington, D.C. 20037. Filed 6/27/83. Legislative interest — "In favor of amendments to the foreign tax credit rules of the Internal Revenue Code. HR 3140, the Foreign Tax Credit Conformity Act of 1983...."

AMERICAN CAN CO., Stamford, Conn. Lobbyist — Dewey, Ballantine, Bushby, Palmer & Wood, 1775 Pennsylvania Ave. N.W., Washington, D.C. 20006. Filed 6/22/83. Legislative interest — Not specified.

APACHE CORP., Minneapolis, Minn. Lobbyist — Chambers Associates Inc., 1411 K St. N.W., Washington, D.C. 20005. Filed 6/30/83. Legislative interest — "Bills revising tax code; particularly HR 821 and S 1549. Education issues."

ARMCO INC., Washington, D.C. Lobbyist — Patton, Boggs & Blow, 2550 M St. N.W., Washington, D.C. 20037. Filed 6/27/83. Legislative interest — "In favor of amendments to the foreign tax credit rules of the Internal Revenue Code. HR 3140, the Foreign Tax Credit Conformity Act of 1983...."

BANKAMERICA CORP., San Francisco, Calif. Lobbyist — Patrick S. Antrim, 1800 K St. N.W., Washington, D.C. 20006. Filed 6/24/83. Legislative interest — Not specified.

BARBER BLUE SEA LINE/BARBER WEST AFRICA LINE, New York, N.Y. Lobbyist — Billig, Sher & Jones, 2033 K St. N.W., Washington, D.C. 20006. Filed 6/17/83. Legislative interest — "Interest is in legislation which would impose fees on vessels in connection with calls at U.S. ports, including S 865, S 970, HR 1512 and similar legislation."

BECHTEL POWER CORP., San Francisco, Calif. Lobbyist — Morgan, Lewis & Bockius, 1800 M St. N.W., Washington, D.C. 20036. Filed 6/1/83. Legislative interest — "S 267 and HR 1010."

BLUE CROSS AND BLUE SHIELD ASSOCIATION, 1709 New York Ave. N.W., Washington, D.C. 20006. Filed for self 6/6/83. Legislative interest — "Legislation impacting the financing and delivery of health care in the United States ... legislation impacting Blue Cross and Blue Shield plans as non-profit entities or as employers." Lobbyist — Alan K. Richards. Filed for self 6/6/83. Legislative interest — "Legislation impacting the financing and delivery of health care." Lobbyist — Stephan E. Chertoff.

BOWMAN, CONNER, TOUHEY & THORNTON, 2828 Pennsylvania Ave. N.W., Washington, D.C. 20007. Filed for self 6/24/83. Legislative interest — "Tax legislation affecting shipping ... Tax Equity and Fiscal Responsibility Act of 1982 ... HR 4961 ... title 26, U.S. Code...." Lobbyist — Samuel H. Black.

BROWN & ROOT, Houston, Texas. Lobbyist — David P. Stang, 1629 K St. N.W., Washington, D.C. 20006. Filed 6/6/83. Legislative interest — Not specified.

BROWNING-FERRIS INDUSTRIES INC., Houston, Texas. Lobbyist — Dewey, Ballantine, Bushby, Palmer & Wood, 1775 Pennsylvania Ave. N.W., Washington, D.C. 20006. Filed 6/17/83. Legislative interest — "HR 3110 - leasing bill." Lobbyist — Gray and Co., 3255 Grace St. N.W., Washington, D.C. 20007. Filed 6/24/83. Legislative interest — "Including but not limited to hazardous waste issues, environmental legislation and tax legislation."

CAVALIER CLOTHING CO., Jamaica, N.Y. Lobbyist — Surrey & Morse, 1250 I St. N.W., Washington, D.C. 20005. Filed 6/14/83. Legislative interest — "Cavalier Clothing supplies uniforms to the U.S. Army. The Dept. of Defense has proposed a reduction in the number of uniforms it procures for each serviceman. Cavalier Clothing opposes the proposed reduction. This matter is the subject of the House and Senate Supplemental Appropriation Bill for FY 1983 (HR 3069) and the Dept. of Defense Authorization Bill for FY 1984."

CITIBANK N.A., 399 Park Ave., New York, N.Y. 10043. Filed for self 6/15/83. Legislative interest — "Tax legislation affecting banks and bank holding companies ... bills to amend the Tax Equity and Fiscal Responsibility Act of 1982 ... tax reform bills arising out of budget reconciliation process...:" Lobbyist — Henry C. Ruempler, 1200 New Hampshire Ave. N.W., Washington, D.C. 20036.

CLEVELAND CLIFFS IRON CO., Cleveland, Ohio. Lobbyist — Murray & Scheer, 2550 M St. N.W., Washington, D.C. 20037. Filed 6/17/83. Legislative interest — Not specified.

CONNECTICUT MUTUAL LIFE INSURANCE CO., Hartford, Conn. Lobbyist — Murray & Scheer, 2550 M St. N.W., Washington, D.C. 20037. Filed 6/17/83. Legislative interest — Not specified.

DALE FASHIONS, Vineland, N.J. Lobbyist — Surrey & Morse, 1250 I St. N.W., Washington, D.C. 20005. Filed 6/14/83. Legislative interest — "Dale Fashions supplies uniforms to the U.S. Army. The Dept. of Defense has proposed a reduction in the number of uniforms it procures for each serviceman. Dale Fashions opposes the proposed reduction. This matter is the subject of the House and Senate Supplemental Appropriations Bill for FY 1983 (HR 3069) and the Dept. of Defense Authorization Bill for FY 1984."

DIRECT BROADCAST SATELLITE CORP., Bethesda, Md. Lobbyist — Finley, Kumble, Wagner, Heine, Underberg, Manley & Casey, 1120 Connecticut Ave. N.W., Washington, D.C. 20036. Filed 6/2/83. Legislative interest — "Any [legislation] or legislative action pertaining to direct broadcast satellite services. To date, no legislation on this topic has been introduced, but there have been hearings before the Subcommittee on Telecommunications, Consumer Protection, and Finance of the House Committee on Energy and Commerce."

DOUGHERTY, DAWKINS, STRAND & YOST, Minneapolis, Minn. Lobbyist — O'Connor & Hannan, 1919 Pennsylvania Ave. N.W., Washington, D.C. 20006. Filed 6/20/83. Legislative interest — "HR 3110; modification of transitional rule contained in the bill."

DREYFUS CORP., New York, N.Y. Lobbyist — Stroock & Stroock & Lavan, 1150 17th St. N.W., Washington, D.C. 20036. Filed 6/28/83. Legislative interest — "Generally following HR 3413 and S 1532 concerning depository institutions moratorium."

DRIFTWOOD DAIRY, El Monte, Calif. Lobbyist — Latham, Watkins & Hills, 1333 New Hampshire Ave. N.W., Washington, D.C. 20036. Filed 6/22/83. Legislative interest — "In favor of National Dairy Equity Act of 1983, S 658; HR 1875."

FANUC LTD., Tokyo, Japan. Lobbyist — Global USA Inc., 1825 I St. N.W., Washington, D.C. 20006. Filed 6/24/83. Legislative interest — "The legislative interests of our client relate to the extension of the Export Administration Act (S 979 and HR 2971). Our employers interest is to have Global USA Inc. monitor the legislative progress of these bills...."

FINANCIAL INVESTMENT ASSOCIATES INC., Washington, D.C. Lobbyist — Gray and Co., 3255 Grace St. N.W.,

Washington, D.C. 20007. Filed 6/29/83. Legislative interest — "Including but not limited to amendments to HR 3110."

FREEPORT-McMORAN INC., New York, N.Y. Lobbyist — Murray & Scheer, 2550 M St. N.W., Washington, D.C. 20037. Filed 6/17/83. Legislative interest — Not specified.

GENERAL MILLS CORP., Washington, D.C. Lobbyist — Don Wallace Associates Inc., 232 East Capitol St., Washington, D.C. 20003. Filed 6/23/83. (Former U.S. Rep. John L. Napier, R-S.C., 1981-83, was listed as agent for this client.) Legislative interest — "S 1440."

GENERAL MOTORS CORP., 3044 West Grand Blvd., Detroit, Mich. 48202. Filed for self 6/29/83. Legislative interest — Not specified. Lobbyist — Ronald L. Beeber, 1660 L St. N.W., Washington, D.C. 20036.

GENERAL PORTLAND INC., Dallas, Texas. Lobbyist — Squire, Sanders & Dempsey, 1201 Pennsylvania Ave. N.W., Washington, D.C. 20004. Filed 6/21/83. Legislative interest — "Tariff and trade matters...."

GIFFORD-HILL & CO. INC., Dallas, Texas. Lobbyist — Squire, Sanders & Dempsey, 1201 Pennsylvania Ave. N.W., Washington, D.C. 20004. Filed 6/21/83. Legislative interest — "Tariff and trade matters...."

GLOBAL COMMUNICATIONS, Williamston, Mich. Lobbyist — Gnau, Carter, Jacobsen & Associates Inc., 1777 F St. N.W., Washington, D.C. 20006. Filed 6/2/83. Legislative interest — "Working with FmHA, Economic Development Administration, HUD for federal loan guarantees for economic development."

GROVE, JASKIEWICZ, GILLIAM AND COBERT, 1730 M St. N.W., Washington, D.C. 20036. Filed for self 6/16/83. Legislative interest — "Appropriation of funds under PL 97-468, specifically Title III on amendments to improvements to the Northeast Corridor authorizing $30 million for a highspeed rail line from Philadelphia, Pa., to Atlantic City, N.J., to be considered in the DOT FY 1984 appropriations bill (opposition). HR 2429, amending the Rail Passenger Service Act (45 U.S.C. section 563) (opposition)." Lobbyists — Robert E. Campbell, William H. Shawn, Alan J. Thiemann.

HELLENIC LINES/HESSA LINE, New York, N.Y. Lobbyist — Billig, Sher & Jones, 2033 K St. N.W., Washington, D.C. 20006. Filed 6/17/83. Legislative interest — "Interest is in legislation which would impose fees on vessels in connection with calls at U.S. ports, including S 865, S 970, HR 1512 and similar legislation."

HOME LIFE INSURANCE CO., New York, N.Y. Lobbyist — Manatt, Phelps, Rothenberg & Tunney, 1200 New Hampshire Ave. N.W., Washington, D.C. 20036. Filed 6/15/83. (Former U.S. Rep. James C. Corman, D-Calif., 1961-81, was listed as agent for this client.) Legislative interest — "Tax legislation relating to life insurance companies."

HOME OWNERS WARRANTY CORP., Washington, D.C. Lobbyist — Crowell & Moring, 1100 Connecticut Ave. N.W., Washington, D.C. 20036. Filed 6/23/83. Legislative interest — "Support for S 1046, amending the Risk Retention Act (PL 97-45)."

INTERNATIONAL GOLD CORP. LTD., 645 Fifth Ave., New York, N.Y. Filed for self 6/15/83. Legislative interest — "Generally interested in legislation regarding gold in general and Krugerrands in particular. Specifically interested in HR 1662, HR 1663 and S 42, all of which are entitled 'American Gold Eagle Coin Act of 1983,' HR 1693, a bill which would mandate certain fair employment practices for U.S. companies operating in South Africa, restrict the making of loans to South Africa and ban the importation of Krugerrands and HR 3231, entitled 'Export Administration Amendment Act of 1983.' Positions for and against provisions of these bills." Lobbyists — Kenneth W. Watson, Michael F. Vigil Jr.

KAISER CEMENT CORP., Oakland, Calif. Lobbyist — Squire, Sanders & Dempsey, 1201 Pennsylvania Ave. N.W., Washington, D.C. 20004. Filed 6/21/83. Legislative interest — "Tariff and trade matters...."

LINEAR AIR MOTORS, Ortonville, Mich. Lobbyist — Gnau, Carter, Jacobsen & Associates Inc., 1777 F St. N.W., Washington, D.C. 20006. Filed 6/2/83. Legislative interest —

"Working with DOT and other Federal agencies for support on funding Linear Air Motor's cost effective urban transit system."

LYKES BROTHERS STEAMSHIP CO., New Orleans, La. Lobbyist — Billig, Sher & Jones, 2033 K St. N.W., Washington, D.C. 20006. Filed 6/17/83. Legislative interest — "Interest is in legislation which would impose fees on vessels in connection with calls at U.S. ports, including S 865, S 970, HR 1512 and similar legislation."

M/A-COM DEVELOPMENT CORP., Rockville, Md. Lobbyist — Finley, Kumble, Wagner, Heine, Underberg, Manley & Casey, 1120 Connecticut Ave. N.W., Washington, D.C. 20036. Filed 6/2/83. Legislative interest — "General in the nature of legislative proposals affecting international communications common carriers; S 999."

A. P. MOLLER MAERSK LINE, New York, N.Y. Lobbyist — Billig, Sher & Jones, 2033 K St. N.W., Washington, D.C. 20006. Filed 6/17/83. Legislative interest — "Interest is in legislation which would impose fees on vessels in connection with calls at U.S. ports, including S 865, S 970, HR 1512 and similar legislation."

MAJOR CLOTHING CO., Bridgeton, N.J. Lobbyist — Surrey & Morse, 1250 I St. N.W., Washington, D.C. 20005. Filed 6/14/83. Legislative interest — "Major Clothing Co. supplies uniforms to the U.S. Army. The Dept. of Defense has proposed a reduction in the number of uniforms it procures for each serviceman. Major Clothing Co. opposes the proposed reduction. This matter is the subject of the House and Senate Supplemental Appropriation Bill for FY 1983 (HR 3069) and the Dept. of Defense Authorization Bill for FY 1984."

MASSACHUSETTS MUTUAL LIFE INSURANCE CO., Springfield, Mass. Lobbyist — Murray & Scheer, 2550 M St. N.W., Washington, D.C. 20037. Filed 6/17/83. Legislative interest — Not specified.

MEAD CORP., Washington, D.C. Lobbyist — Patton, Boggs & Blow, 2550 M St. N.W., Washington, D.C. 20037. Filed 6/27/83. Legislative interest — "In favor of amendments to the foreign tax credit rules of the Internal Revenue Code. HR 3140, the Foreign Tax Credit Conformity Act of 1983...."

MILLER & SCHROEDER MUNICIPALS INC., Minneapolis, Minn. Lobbyist — O'Connor & Hannan, 1919 Pennsylvania Ave. N.W., Washington, D.C. 20006. Filed 6/30/83. Legislative interest — "Modification of rehabilitation tax credit provision in section 1(c) of HR 3110."

MONOLITH PORTLAND CEMENT CO., Glendale, Calif. Lobbyist — Squire, Sanders & Dempsey, 1201 Pennsylvania Ave. N.W., Washington, D.C. 20004. Filed 6/21/83. Legislative interest — "Tariff and trade matters...."

MUTUAL BENEFIT LIFE INSURANCE CO., Newark, N.J. Lobbyist — Murray & Scheer, 2550 M St. N.W., Washington, D.C. 20037. Filed 6/17/83. Legislative interest — Not specified.

NATIONAL SHIPPING COMPANY OF SAUDI ARABIA, New York, N.Y. Lobbyist — Billig, Sher & Jones, 2033 K St. N.W., Washington, D.C. 20006. Filed 6/17/83. Legislative interest — "Interest is in legislation which would impose fees on vessels in connection with calls at U.S. ports, including S 865, S 970, HR 1512 and similar legislation."

NEDLLOYD LINES, New York, N.Y. Lobbyist — Billig, Sher & Jones, 2033 K St. N.W., Washington, D.C. 20006. Filed 6/17/83. Legislative interest — "Interest is in legislation which would impose fees on vessels in connection with calls at U.S. ports, including S 865, S 970, HR 1512 and similar legislation."

NETCO, Ann Arbor, Mich. Lobbyist — Gnau, Carter, Jacobsen & Associates Inc., 1777 F St. N.W., Washington, D.C. 20006. Filed 6/29/83. Legislative interest — "Research and development funding and continuing funding from various agencies within the Federal government for energy cost saving programs."

NEW ENGLAND MUTUAL LIFE INSURANCE CO., Boston, Mass. Lobbyist — Murray & Scheer, 2550 M St. N.W., Washington, D.C. 20037. Filed 6/17/83. Legislative interest — Not specified.

OWENS-CORNING FIBERGLAS CORP., Fiberglas Tower, Toledo, Ohio 43659. Filed for self 6/17/83. Legislative interest — "Social Security Reform (HR 1900); First Budget

Resolution (H Con Res 91); Product Liability (S 44; HR 2729); S 654; HR 1837." Lobbyist — Herbert A. Jolovitz, 900 17th St. N.W., Washington, D.C. 20006.

PACIFIC MUTUAL LIFE INSURANCE CO., Newport Beach, Calif. Lobbyist — Manatt, Phelps, Rothenberg & Tunney, 1200 New Hampshire Ave. N.W., Washington, D.C. 20036. Filed 6/15/83. (Former U.S. Rep. James C. Corman, D-Calif., 1961-81, was listed as agent for this client.) Legislative interest — "Tax legislation relating to life insurance companies."

PENN MUTUAL LIFE INSURANCE CO., Philadelphia, Pa. Lobbyist — Murray & Scheer, 2550 M St. N.W., Washington, D.C. 20037. Filed 6/17/83. Legislative interest — Not specified.

PHILLIPS PETROLEUM CO., Phillips Building, Bartlesville, Okla. 74004. Filed for self 6/21/83. Legislative interest — Not specified. Lobbyist — John N. Scott, 1825 K St. N.W., Washington, D.C. 20006.

PORTLAND GENERAL ELECTRIC CO., 121 S.W. Salmon St., Portland, Ore. 97204. Filed for self 6/3/83. Legislative interest — "Legislation regarding the utilities industry; energy programs; tax; natural resources; Department of Energy; Nuclear Regulatory Commission; Federal Energy Regulatory Commission." Lobbyist — Jill W. Eiland, 507 Second St. N.E., Washington, D.C. 20002.

PRIMARK CORP., Washington, D.C. Lobbyist — Gnau, Carter, Jacobsen & Associates Inc., 1777 F St. N.W., Washington, D.C. 20006. Filed 6/29/83. Legislative interest — Not specified.

PROVIDENT MUTUAL LIFE INSURANCE CO., Philadelphia, Pa. Lobbyist — Manatt, Phelps, Rothenberg & Tunney, 1200 New Hampshire Ave. N.W., Washington, D.C. 20036. Filed 6/15/83. (Former U.S. Rep. James C. Corman, D-Calif., 1961-81, was listed as agent for this client.) Legislative interest — "Tax legislation relating to life insurance companies."

PUROLATOR INC., Piscataway, N.J. Lobbyist — Akin, Gump, Strauss, Hauer & Feld, 1333 New Hampshire Ave. N.W., Washington, D.C. 20036. Filed 6/22/83. Legislative interest — "HR 2197, HR 2198 amending section 9(b)(3) of the National Labor Relations Act to redefine the term 'guard.'"

R. J. REYNOLDS TOBACCO CO., Winston-Salem, N.C. Lobbyist — Ragan & Mason, 900 17th St. N.W., Washington, D.C. 20006. Filed 6/21/83. Legislative interest — "All matters affecting manufacturing, labeling, taxing and regulating cigarettes."

SAFEKEEPER SYSTEMS INC., Troy, Mich. Lobbyist — Gnau, Carter, Jacobsen & Associates Inc., 1777 F St. N.W., Washington, D.C. 20006. Filed 6/2/83. Legislative interest — "Exploring possible market in Federal government for sale of the product."

SAFLOK, Troy, Mich. Lobbyist — Gnau, Carter, Jacobsen & Associates Inc., 1777 F St. N.W., Washington, D.C. 20006. Filed 6/2/83. Legislative interest — "Exploring possible market in Federal government for sale of their product."

JOSEPH E. SEAGRAM & SONS INC., New York, N.Y. Lobbyist — Van Ness, Feldman, Sutcliffe, Curtis & Levenberg, 1055 Thomas Jefferson St. N.W., Washington, D.C. 20007. Filed 6/7/83. Legislative interest — "S 544, the Caribbean Basin Initiative, relating to amendments to the Clean Water Act."

SNECMA, Paris, France. Lobbyist — DGA International Inc., 1225 19th St. N.W., Washington, D.C. 20036. Filed for self 6/16/83. (Former U.S. Sen. Charles E. Goodell, R-N.Y., Senate 1968-71; House 1959-68, was listed as agent for this client.) Legislative interest — "Legislation affecting U.S. Department of Defense authorizations and appropriations. In the immediate period the 1983 Defense Authorization bill and the 1983 Defense Appropriation bill are of specific interest. Also any other legislation that would affect U.S. Defense Department procurement decisions related to large military aircraft engines (*i.e.*, engines for tankers, transport, surveillance, or other similar type aircraft). We plan to monitor current legislation of the type described above and plan to take positions that would support legislation that calls for continuing utilization by the U.S. Air Force of military engines produced by our foreign principal."

SOUTH JERSEY CLOTHING, Minotola, N.J. Lobbyist — Surrey & Morse, 1250 I St. N.W., Washington, D.C. 20005. Filed 6/14/83. Legislative interest — "South Jersey Clothing supplies

uniforms to the U.S. Army. The Dept. of Defense has proposed a reduction in the number of uniforms it procures for each serviceman. South Jersey Clothing opposes the proposed reduction. This matter is the subject of the House and Senate Supplemental Appropriation Bill for FY 1983 (HR 3069) and the Dept. of Defense Authorization Bill for FY 1984."

SOUTHERN HOTEL DEVELOPMENT CO., Columbus, Ohio. Lobbyist — Vorys, Sater, Seymour and Pease, 1828 L St. N.W., Washington, D.C. 20036. Filed 6/16/83. Legislative interest — "Advance client's interests with respect to HR 3110, 'To amend the Internal Revenue Code of 1954 to deny tax incentives for property used by governments and other tax-exempt entities.' Client's concerns center on section 1(c) of HR 3110."

SOUTHERN PACIFIC CO., 1 Market Plaza, San Francisco, Calif. 94105. Filed for self 6/27/83. Legislative interest — "Legislation affecting the transportation, taxation, regulatory and other legislative interests of employer named above." Lobbyist — Wiley N. Jones, 1828 L St. N.W., Washington, D.C. 20036.

SOUTHWESTERN PORTLAND CEMENT CO., Los Angeles, Calif. Lobbyist — Squire, Sanders & Dempsey, 1201 Pennsylvania Ave. N.W., Washington, D.C. 20004. Filed 6/21/83. Legislative interest — "Tariff and trade matters...."

STATE MUTUAL LIFE ASSURANCE COMPANY OF AMERICA, Worcester, Mass. Lobbyist — Manatt, Phelps, Rothenberg & Tunney, 1200 New Hampshire Ave. N.W., Washington, D.C. 20036. Filed 6/15/83. (Former U.S. Rep. James C. Corman, D-Calif., 1961-81, was listed as agent for this client.) Legislative interest — "Tax legislation relating to life insurance companies."

STEPHENS INC., Little Rock, Ark. Lobbyist — Patton, Boggs & Blow, 2550 M St. N.W., Washington, D.C. 20037. Filed 6/28/83. Legislative interest — "Natural gas deregulation and other energy related legislation...."

STOCKTON TERMINAL AND EASTERN RAILROAD, Stockton, Calif. Lobbyist — Damrell, Damrell & Nelson, 911 13th St., Modesto, Calif. 95353. Filed 6/17/83. Legislative interest — "Exemption from regulation - box car traffic and hearings relating thereto in the U.S. Senate."

SWAZILAND SUGAR CO., Mbabane, Swaziland. Lobbyist — Murray & Scheer, 2550 M St. N.W., Washington, D.C. 20037. Filed 6/17/83. Legislative interest — Not specified.

TEXAS EASTERN TRANSMISSION CO., Washington, D.C. Lobbyist — Bliss, Craft & Richards, 1050 Thomas Jefferson St. N.W., Washington, D.C. 20007. Filed 6/20/83. Legislative interest — "Any legislation in the House of Representatives or the Senate pertaining to the coal slurry pipeline including S 267 and HR 1010."

TOYOTA MOTOR CORP., Toyota City, Aichi Prefecture, Japan. Lobbyist — Arent, Fox, Kintner, Plotkin & Kahn, 1050 Connecticut Ave. N.W., Washington, D.C. 20036. Filed 6/3/83. Legislative interest — "General interests relate to Congressional activities (*e.g.*, oversight hearings) concerning the proposed Toyota Motor Corporation/General Motors joint venture to manufacture a new line of subcompact automobiles in the U.S."

TRANSCO ENERGY CO., Houston, Texas. Lobbyist — Skadden, Arps, Slate, Meagher & Flom, 919 18th St. N.W., Washington, D.C. 20006. Filed 6/24/83. Legislative interest — "Coal Slurry Pipeline legislation and Natural Gas Deregulation legislation."

TRT TELECOMMUNICATIONS CORP., Washington, D.C. Lobbyist — Finley, Kumble, Wagner, Heine, Underberg, Manley & Casey, 1120 Connecticut Ave. N.W., Washington, D.C. 20036. Filed 6/2/83. Legislative interest — "General in the nature of legislative proposals affecting international communications common carriers; S 999."

TURNER BROADCASTING SYSTEM INC., Atlanta, Ga. Lobbyist — Finley, Kumble, Wagner, Heine, Underberg, Manley & Casey, 1120 Connecticut Ave. N.W., Washington, D.C. 20036. Filed 6/2/83. Legislative interest — "General in the nature of legislative proposals affecting international communications common carriers; S 999."

UNION PACIFIC CORP., 345 Park Ave., New York, N.Y. 10154. Filed for self 6/6/83. Legislative interest — "Pending and

prospective legislation affecting the railroad industry." Lobbyists — Judy C. Durand, John M. Edsall, 1120 20th St. N.W., Washington, D.C. 20036.

UNITED ARAB SHIPPING CO., Cranford, N.J. Lobbyist — Billig, Sher & Jones, 2033 K St. N.W., Washington, D.C. 20006. Filed 6/17/83. Legislative interest — "Interest is in legislation which would impose fees on vessels in connection with calls at U.S. ports, including S 865, S 970, HR 1512 and similar legislation."

U.S. MANUFACTURING CO., Fraser, Mich. Lobbyist — Gnau, Carter, Jacobsen & Associates Inc., 1777 F St. N.W., Washington, D.C. 20006. Filed 6/2/83. Legislative interest — "Exploring possible market in Federal government for sale of their products. Also looking for possible Federal loan guarantees for economic development."

U.S. TELEPHONE INC., Dallas, Texas. Lobbyist — Wiley, Johnson & Rein, 1776 K St. N.W., Washington, D.C. 20006. Filed 6/22/83. Legislative interest — Not specified.

URBAN NEIGHBORHOOD ENTERPRISES INC., 730 N.W. First St., Miami, Fla. 33136. Filed for self 6/28/83. Legislative interest — "Laws governing the utilization of public funds for the development of economic activities in low income communities. . . ." Lobbyist — David A. Rosemond.

WALTON & SON STEVEDORING CO., Houston, Texas. Lobbyist — Robert C. Eckhardt, 1750 Pennsylvania Ave. N.W., Washington, D.C. 20006. Filed 6/22/83. (Former U.S. rep., D-Texas, 1967-81.) Legislative interest — Not specified.

WATERMAN STEAMSHIP CO., New York, N.Y. Lobbyist — Billig, Sher & Jones, 2033 K St. N.W., Washington, D.C. 20006. Filed 6/17/83. Legislative interest — "Interest is in legislation which would impose fees on vessels in connection with calls at U.S. ports, including S 865, S 970, HR 1512 and similar legislation."

International Relations

EMBASSY OF THE REPUBLIC OF SOUTH AFRICA, Washington, D.C. Lobbyist — Kimberley C. Hallamore, 1725 K St. N.W., Washington, D.C. 20006. Filed 6/15/83. Legislative interest — "Legislation pertaining to South Africa, especially HR 1693."

INVESTMENT COUNCIL OF PANAMA, Panama City, Panama. Lobbyist — Manchester Associates Ltd., 1155 15th St. N.W., Washington, D.C. 20005. Filed 6/21/83. Legislative interest — "Caribbean Basin Initiative - S 544 plus possibly other legislation affecting Panama."

REPUBLIC OF TURKEY, Ankara, Turkey. Lobbyist — Gray and Co., 3255 Grace St. N.W., Washington, D.C. 20007. Filed 6/21/83. Legislative interest — "Including but not limited to economic and security assistance issues."

State and Local Governments

CITY OF CINCINNATI, Cincinnati, Ohio. Lobbyist — Preston, Thorgrimson, Ellis & Holman, 1735 New York Ave. N.W., Washington, D.C. 20006. Filed 6/1/83. Legislative interest — "Legislation affecting municipal interests in cable television including S 66."

CITY OF SCOTTSDALE, Scottsdale, Ariz. Lobbyist — Preston, Thorgrimson, Ellis & Holman, 1735 New York Ave. N.W., Washington, D.C. 20006. Filed 6/8/83. Legislative interest — "Legislation affecting municipal interests in cable television including S 66."

COMMONWEALTH OF PUERTO RICO, San Juan, Puerto Rico. Lobbyist — Gray and Co., 3255 Grace St. N.W., Washington, D.C. 20007. Filed 6/27/83. Legislative interest — Not specified.

INTERGOVERNMENTAL CABLE COMMUNICATIONS AUTHORITY OF OAKLAND COUNTY, MICH., Huntington Woods, Mich. Lobbyist — Preston, Thorgrimson, Ellis & Holman, 1735 New York Ave. N.W., Washington, D.C. 20006. Filed 6/1/83. Legislative interest — "Legislation affecting munici-

pal interests in cable television including S 66."

NATIONAL CONFERENCE OF BLACK MAYORS, Washington, D.C. Lobbyist — Wald, Harkrader and Ross, 1300 19th St. N.W., Washington, D.C. 20036. Filed 6/16/83. Legislative interest — "HR 3110 and other bills affecting governmental leasing."

NEW YORK POWER AUTHORITY, New York, N.Y. Lobbyist — Wexler, Reynolds, Harrison & Schule Inc., 1317 F St. N.W., Washington, D.C. 20004. Filed 6/24/83. Legislative interest — "The registrant will represent the employer with regard to energy regulation, water and air pollution control, the tax code, nuclear energy controls and any other subjects that the employer deems necessary."

WESTERN GOVERNORS POLICY OFFICE, Denver, Colo. Lobbyist — Akin, Gump, Strauss, Hauer & Feld, 1333 New Hampshire Ave. N.W., Washington, D.C. 20036. Filed 6/2/83. Legislative interest — "Hearings and any legislation relating to federal formula and block grant programs, including but not limited to general revenue sharing, housing, infrastructure, unemployment and education programs."

Trade Associations

AD HOC COMMITTEE OF FLOOR BROKERS, Washington, D.C. Lobbyist — Cadwalader, Wickersham & Taft, 1333 New Hampshire Ave. N.W., Washington, D.C. 20036. Filed 6/23/83. Legislative interest — "Legislative interests with respect to legislation dealing with the taxation of commodity futures contracts."

AMERICAN BAKERS ASSOCIATION, Washington, D.C. Lobbyist — Billig, Sher & Jones, 2033 K St. N.W., Washington, D.C. 20006. Filed 6/17/83. Legislative interest — "Interest in transportation legislation affecting the baking industry."

AMERICAN INSTITUTE OF MERCHANT SHIPPING, Washington, D.C. Lobbyist — Terrence W. Modglin, 3248 Prospect St. N.W., Washington, D.C. 20007. Filed 6/29/83. Legislative interest — ". . . any possible amendment of sections 1411-1418 of the Panama Canal Act of 1979."

AMERICAN PETROLEUM INSTITUTE, 2101 L St. N.W., Washington, D.C. 20037. Filed for self 6/16/83. Legislative interest — "Any new or proposed legislation affecting the taxation of the petroleum industry." Lobbyists — Carlton Jackson, 111 N. Gadsden St., Tallahassee, Fla. 32301; Andrew Yood.

AMERICAN PROTESTANT HOSPITAL ASSOCIATION, Schaumberg, Ill. Lobbyist — Perito, Duerk, Carlson & Pinco, 1140 Connecticut Ave. N.W., Washington, D.C. 20036. Filed 6/27/83. Legislative interest — "Legislation affecting general health care policy matters, including tax-exempt bond financing for non-profit hospitals."

AMERICAN PULPWOOD ASSOCIATION, 1619 Massachusetts Ave. N.W., Washington, D.C. 20036. Filed for self 6/7/83. Legislative interest — Not specified. Lobbyist — Richard Lewis.

AMUSEMENT AND MUSIC OPERATORS ASSOCIATION, Oak Brook, Ill. Lobbyist — Jenner & Block, 1 IBM Plaza, Chicago, Ill. 60611. Filed 6/6/83. Legislative interest — "Copyright legislation 17 U.S.C. section 101 *et seq.*, particularly section 116."

ASSOCIATION OF AMERICAN RAILROADS, Washington, D.C. Lobbyist — Wexler, Reynolds, Harrison & Schule Inc., 1317 F St. N.W., Washington, D.C. 20004. Filed 6/24/83. Legislative interest — "Registrant seeks to amend or defeat S 267 and HR 1010."

BASIC INDUSTRIES COALITION INC., Washington, D.C. Lobbyist — Patton, Boggs & Blow, 2550 M St. N.W., Washington, D.C. 20037. Filed 6/27/83. Legislative interest — "Enhancement of access by basic industries to the capital investment incentives of the Internal Revenue Code. For enactment of the Work Opportunities and Renewed Competition Act of 1983. . . ."

THE BUSINESS ROUNDTABLE, Washington, D.C. Lobbyist — Hogan & Hartson, 815 Connecticut Ave. N.W.,

Washington, D.C. 20006. Filed 6/3/83. Legislative interest — "Taxpayer Antitrust Enforcement Act of 1983 (S 915), against. Antitrust Fairness Amendments of 1983 (HR 2244), against." Lobbyist — Richard C. White, 499 South Capitol St., Washington, D.C. 20003. Filed 6/22/83. (Former U.S. rep., D-Texas, 1965-83.) Legislative interest — "Export Administration Act."

CENTRAL SAN JOAQUIN RIVER ASSOCIATION, Modesto, Calif. Lobbyist — Damrell, Damrell & Nelson, 911 13th St., Modesto, Calif. 95353. Filed 6/17/83. Legislative interest — "Hearings relating to HR 3132, a bill allocating funds for channel maintenance and flood control."

CHAMBER OF COMMERCE OF THE UNITED STATES, 1615 H St. N.W., Washington, D.C. 20062. Filed for self 6/20/83. Legislative interest — Not specified. Lobbyist — Kathryn Eleanor Young.

CREDIT UNION NATIONAL ASSOCIATION, Washington, D.C. Lobbyist — Dave Evans Associates, 160 North Carolina Ave. S.E., Washington, D.C. 20003. Filed 6/14/83. Legislative interest — Not specified.

EMPLOYEE STOCK OWNERSHIP ASSOCIATION, Washington, D.C. Lobbyist — David P. Stang, 1629 K St. N.W., Washington, D.C. 20006. Filed 6/6/83. Legislative interest — "S 748, pertaining to Employee Stock Option Plans."

FORMALDEHYDE INSTITUTE, Scarsdale, N.Y. Lobbyist — Cleary, Gottlieb, Steen & Hamilton, 1752 N St. N.W., Washington, D.C. 20036. Filed 6/29/83. Legislative interest — "General interest in HR 2668 and S 861, Amendment and Reauthorization of the Consumer Product Safety Act, 15 U.S.C. section 2051."

IRON ORE LESSORS ASSOCIATION, St. Paul, Minn. Lobbyist — Murray & Scheer, 2550 M St. N.W., Washington, D.C. 20037. Filed 6/17/83. Legislative interest — Not specified.

NATIONAL ASSOCIATION OF BEDDING MANUFACTURERS, Arlington, Va. Lobbyist — Rogers & Wells, 1737 H St. N.W., Washington, D.C. 20006. Filed 6/2/83. Legislative interest — "Legislation affecting the rulemaking authority and procedures of the Consumer Product Safety Commission; HR 2668, to amend the Consumer Product Safety Act, and for other purposes."

NATIONAL ASSOCIATION OF PUBLIC TELEVISION STATIONS, Washington, D.C. Lobbyist — Dickstein, Shapiro & Morin, 2101 L St. N.W., Washington, D.C. 20037. Filed 6/6/83. Legislative interest — "Authorization bills and appropriations bill affecting industry."

NATIONAL BUSINESS AIRCRAFT ASSOCIATION, Washington, D.C. Lobbyist — Murray & Scheer, 2550 M St. N.W., Washington, D.C. 20037. Filed 6/17/83. Legislative interest — Not specified.

NATIONAL CABLE TELEVISION ASSOCIATION, Washington, D.C. Lobbyist — Epstein, Becker, Borsody & Green, 1140 19th St. N.W., Washington, D.C. 20036. Filed 6/17/83. Legislative interest — "Our interests are concerned with the Cable Telecommunications Act of 1983 (Senate Commerce Committee Bill S 66)."

NATIONAL CORN GROWERS ASSOCIATION, 1015 15th St. N.W., Washington, D.C. 20005. Filed for self 6/20/83. Legislative interest — "Current and ongoing legislation that affects grain production, storage, marketing and trade." Lobbyist — Michael L. Hall.

NATIONAL COUNCIL OF COAL LESSORS INC., Charleston, W.Va. Lobbyist — Murray & Scheer, 2550 M St. N.W., Washington, D.C. 20037. Filed 6/17/83. Legislative interest — Not specified.

NATIONAL COUNCIL OF FARMER COOPERATIVES, 1800 Massachusetts Ave. N.W., Washington, D.C. 20036. Filed for self 6/15/83. Legislative interest — "None." Lobbyist — Wayne A. Boutwell.

NATIONAL FUTURES ASSOCIATION, 200 W. Madison St., Chicago, Ill. 60606. Filed for self 6/8/83. Legislative interest — "PL 97-444, Futures Trading Act of 1982 contains provisions (*i.e.* section 233 and section 237) that have an impact on the operations of National Futures Association. The law requires NFA to develop certain programs and rules and submit them to

the Commodity Futures Trading Commission for approval. Also, the law requires CFTC [to] submit to Congress a report containing the result of a study of the regulatory experience of NFA during the period between Jan. 1, 1983, to Sept. 30, 1985." Lobbyist — Wayne A. Fletcher, 1415 N. Dearborn Parkway, Chicago, Ill. 60610.

NATIONAL RESTAURANT ASSOCIATION, 311 First St. N.W., Washington, D.C. 20002. Filed for self 6/23/83. Legislative interest — "Any legislation affecting the restaurant and food service industries is of interest to the Association. Generally, this is legislation involving small business, labor laws, wages and hours, taxation, consumer protection, food marketing and economic stabilization." Lobbyists — Ronald A. Sarasin, Laura VanEtten.

TEXAS CATTLE FEEDERS ASSOCIATION, Amarillo, Texas. Lobbyist — David P. Stang, 1629 K St. N.W., Washington, D.C. 20006. Filed 6/23/83. Legislative interest — "Issues relating to estate and gift taxes."

TEXAS & SOUTHWESTERN CATTLE RAISERS ASSOCIATION, Fort Worth, Texas. Lobbyist — David P. Stang, 1629 K St. N.W., Washington, D.C. 20006. Filed 6/23/83. Legislative interest — "Issues relating to estate and gift taxes."

VIDEOTEX INDUSTRY ASSOCIATION, Washington, D.C. Lobbyist — Blum & Nash, 1015 18th St. N.W., Washington, D.C. 20036. Filed 6/2/83. Legislative interest — "Cable legislation before the House Energy and Commerce Committee, S 66."

WEST INDIES RUM AND SPIRITS PRODUCERS ASSOCIATION, Bridgetown, Barbados, West Indies. Lobbyist — Akin, Gump, Strauss, Hauer & Feld, 1333 New Hampshire Ave. N.W., Washington, D.C. 20036. Filed 6/17/83. Legislative interest — "Hearings and any legislation relating to tariffs on the importation of rum and spirits from the West Indies, including but not limited to S 554, the 'Caribbean Basin Economic Recovery Act.' "

Miscellaneous

GEORGE PAUL ALEXA, 5021 Seminary Road, Alexandria, Va. 22311. Filed for self 6/2/83. Legislative interest — "Child Custody and Visitation Reform."

BENNINGTON COLLEGE, Bennington, Vt. Lobbyist — Cohen and Uretz, 1775 K St. N.W., Washington, D.C. 20006. Filed 6/6/83. Legislative interest — "Tax legislation affecting sale and leaseback of property, particularly HR 3110, and any similar legislation."

BUFFALO PHILHARMONIC ORCHESTRA, Buffalo, N.Y. Lobbyist — Donald C. Lubick, 1776 Pennsylvania Ave. N.W., Washington, D.C. 20006. Filed 6/29/83. Legislative interest — "Effective date of HR 3110. . . ."

ESTATE OF GEORGE W. BUNN, Springfield, Ill. Lobbyist — McDermott, Will & Emery, 1850 K St. N.W., Washington, D.C. 20006. Filed 6/22/83. Legislative interest — "Support of S 1180 and HR 2813, bills to amend the Internal Revenue Code to provide transitional rules for estate and gift tax treatment of disclaimer of property interest created by transfers before November 15, 1958."

RICHARD H. SCHECK, 1650 Fitzgerald Lane, Alexandria, Va. 22302. Filed for self 6/7/83. Legislative interest — "All bills favoring space communications and opposing space weaponization."

July Registrations

Citizens' Groups

AD HOC COMMITTEE IN DEFENSE OF LIFE INC., 150 E. 35th St., New York, N.Y. 10016. Filed for self 7/7/83. Legislative interest — "Generally, any legislation which promotes the right to life of all human beings, at any stage of their biological development, and any legislation which opposes so-called 'abortion on demand' and euthanasia. Specifically, any legislation which

seeks to modify by Constitutional amendment or otherwise, the Supreme Court decisions of *Roe v. Wade* and *Doe v. Bolton* of 1/22/73." Lobbyist — Robert Tobin, 605 14th St. N.W., Washington, D.C. 20005.

BOAT OWNERS ASSOCIATION OF THE UNITED STATES, 880 S. Pickett St., Alexandria, Va. 22304. Filed for self 7/9/83. Legislative interest — "Interested in all legislation pertinent to water pollution, recreational boating and other legislation impacting on boating and boat owners, including but not limited to ... amendments to the Federal Safe Boating Act ... PL 96-451 appropriations ... Coast Guard and NOAA budgets."

COALITION FOR LEGAL SERVICES INC., 1625 K St. N.W., Washington, D.C. 20006. Filed for self 7/26/83. Legislative interest — "All legislation concerning the reauthorization of and appropriations to the Legal Services Corporation and all other legislation regarding provision of legal services to the poor, and including confirmation proceedings...." Lobbyist — Robert J. Rhudy.

COMMITTEE FOR EQUITABLE COMPENSATION, 1901 N. Fort Myer Drive, Rosslyn, Va. 22209. Filed for self 7/25/83. Legislative interest — "To improve the system of asbestos disease compensation ... HR 3175, Occupational Disease Compensation Act of 1983...." Lobbyist — Albert D. Bourland.

COMMITTEE TO IMPROVE PUBLIC SCHOOL LIBRARIES, Washington, D.C. Lobbyist — Harold A. Thornton & Associates, 1301 15th St. N.W., Washington, D.C. 20005. Filed 7/15/83. Legislative interest — "Housing, health, education and labor issues."

CONGRESS WATCH, 215 Pennsylvania Ave. S.E., Washington, D.C. 20003. Filed for self 7/11/83. Legislative interest — "Bankruptcy; food safety; dairy and sugar price support legislation." Lobbyist — Louise S. Greenfield.

COOLEY'S ANEMIA FOUNDATION, New York, N.Y. Lobbyist — John T. Grupenhoff, 10000 Falls Road, Potomac, Md. 20854. Filed 7/18/83. Legislative interest — "...Concerned with issues of blood diseases research, especially Cooley's Anemia, in appropriations, authorization and Medicare/Medicaid legislation...."

ENVIRONMENTAL POLICY INSTITUTE, 317 Pennsylvania Ave. N.W., Washington, D.C. 20003. Filed for self 7/27/83. Legislative interest — "Legislation relating to management of the nation's public land and mineral resources." Lobbyist — Andrew Palmer.

LEAGUE OF WOMEN VOTERS OF THE UNITED STATES, 1730 M St. N.W., Washington, D.C. 20036. Filed for self 7/12/83. Legislative interest — "...CETA reauthorization and budgeting, civil rights, day care, education, employment, food stamps, HUD authorizations and appropriations, unemployment compensation, vocational education ... legislation to rescind IRS regulations on private school non-profit status, tuition tax credits, anti-busing legislation ... international development banks, foreign economic development assistance, free flow in international trade/reduction of trade barriers ... Clean Air Act, Clean Water Act, energy conservation, sound land use legislation, Surface Mining Control and Reclamation Act, low income energy assistance, environmental protection measures generally ... D.C. representation, looking into problems of early projections, Voting Rights Act reauthorization ... urban mass transit, Economic Development Administration, CDBG/UDAG, general revenue sharing." Lobbyist — Elizabeth Lawson.

NATIONAL ALLIANCE FOR ANIMAL LEGISLATION, P.O. Box 77012, Washington, D.C. 20013. Filed for self 7/25/83. Legislative interest — "Support all animal protection legislation." Lobbyist — Connie Kagan.

NATIONAL INCORPORATION OF TENANTS, Great Neck, N.Y. Lobbyist — Paul M. Tendler, 1110 Vermont Ave. N.W., Washington, D.C. 20005. Filed 7/11/83. Legislative interest — "Legislation and regulations regarding tenants, housing, tax and urban redevelopment. Legislation and regulations regarding credit unions."

PEACE POLITICAL ACTION COMMITTEE, 100 Maryland Ave. N.E., Washington, D.C. 20002. Filed for self 7/25/83. Legislative interest — "Legislation on arms control and

disarmament, FY 1984 authorization and appropriation bill for Department of Defense, State Department, AEC, ACDA...." Lobbyist — Katherine Magraw.

UNITED STATES DEFENSE COMMITTEE, 3238 Wynford Drive, Fairfax, Va. 22031. Filed for self 7/11/83. Legislative interest — "Legislative proposals related to defense and foreign affairs ... Garn-Heinz bill, Garn alternative to a Nuclear Freeze, Wallop resolution for a space-based defense, Whitehurst resolution for a space-based defense, Boland-Zablocki bill ... S 979, S J Res 74, S Res 100, HR 215, HR 2761...." Lobbyist — William S. Baker.

Corporations and Businesses

ALAMO CEMENT CO., San Antonio, Texas. Lobbyist — Williams & Jensen, 1101 Connecticut Ave. N.W., Washington, D.C. 20036. Filed 7/22/83. Legislative interest — "Trade and tariff matters of interest to the company."

AMERICAN AIRLINES INC., 1101 17th St. N.W., Washington, D.C. 20036. Filed for self 7/5/83. Legislative interest — Not specified. Lobbyist — Gene E. Overbeck.

AMERICAN NATURAL RESOURCES CO., One Woodward Ave., Detroit, Mich. 48226. Filed for self 7/26/83. Legislative interest — "S 1475/HR 2124 - To amend the Internal Revenue Code of 1954, to repeal the highway use tax on heavy trucks and to increase the tax on diesel fuel used in heavy trucks." Lobbyist — Roland Dolly, 1899 L St. N.W., Washington, D.C. 20036.

ANHEUSER-BUSCH COS. INC., St. Louis, Mo. Lobbyist — Charls E. Walker Associates Inc., 1730 Pennsylvania Ave. N.W., Washington, D.C. 20006. Filed 7/11/83. Legislative interest — "Legislative interests may concern issues relating to the federal excise taxes on beer."

ATLANTIC RICHFIELD CO., 515 S. Flower St., Los Angeles, Calif. 90071. Filed for self 7/14/83. Legislative interest — Not specified. Lobbyist — Henry H. Paige, 1333 New Hampshire Ave. N.W., Washington, D.C. 20036.

BERENERGY CORP., Denver, Colo. Lobbyist — Chadbourne, Parke, Whiteside & Wolff, 1101 Vermont Ave. N.W., Washington, D.C. 20005. Filed 7/19/83. Legislative interest — "Oil and gas tax legislation."

BONNEVILLE INTERNATIONAL CORP., Salt Lake City, Utah. Lobbyist — Wilkinson, Barker, Knauer & Quinn, 1735 New York Ave. N.W., Washington, D.C. 20006. Filed 7/22/83. Legislative interest — "Opposing S 880 and HR 2385 insofar as it would impede operation of clear channel radio broadcasters increased operating hours for daytime AM radio stations."

BORDEN INC., Columbus, Ohio. Lobbyist — O'Connor & Hannan, 1919 Pennsylvania Ave. N.W., Washington, D.C. 20006. Filed 7/25/83. Legislative interest — "Natural gas deregulation legislation."

BRISTOL-MYERS CO., New York, N.Y. Lobbyist — Kaye, Scholer, Fierman, Hays & Handler, 1575 I St. N.W., Washington, D.C. 20005. Filed 7/25/83. Legislative interest — "General interest in congressional action relating to policies affecting incentives to conduct research and development."

CALIFORNIA ALMOND GROWERS EXCHANGE, Sacramento, Calif. Lobbyist — Heron, Burchette, Ruckert & Rothwell, 1200 New Hampshire Ave. N.W., Washington, D.C. 20036. Filed 7/5/83. Legislative interest — "FTC authorization bill, DISC legislation, user fee legislation-USDA, regulatory reform legislation ... support legislation to exclude agriculture from the generalized system of preferences."

CASTLE & COOKE INC., San Francisco, Calif. Lobbyist — Van Ness, Feldman, Sutcliffe, Curtis & Levenberg, 1050 Thomas Jefferson St. N.W., Washington, D.C. 20007. Filed 7/11/83. Legislative interest — "Amendments to Shipping Act of 1916 ... 46 U.S.C. section 800 *et seq.*"

CBS INC., New York, N.Y. Lobbyist — Wiley, Johnson & Rein, 1776 K St. N.W., Washington, D.C. 20006. Filed 7/5/83. Legislative interest — "... opposition to HR 2250 (moratorium on

changes to FCC financial interest syndication and prime time access rules)."

CFS CONTINENTAL, Chicago, Ill. Lobbyist — Kent & O'Connor Inc., 1919 Pennsylvania Ave. N.W., Washington, D.C. 20006. Filed 7/9/83. Legislative interest — "Meat grading legislation."

CHRISTIAN BJELLAND & CO. INC., Millburn, N.J. Lobbyist — Chapman, Duff and Paul, 1730 Pennsylvania Ave. N.W., Washington, D.C. 20006. Filed 7/1/83. Legislative interest — "Revision of trade remedy laws."

COLORADO-UTE ELECTRIC ASSOCIATION INC., Montrose, Colo. Lobbyist — Groom and Nordberg, 1775 Pennsylvania Ave. N.W., Washington, D.C. 20006. Filed 7/8/83. Legislative interest — "Federal legislation affecting Title 26 of U.S.C."

COLORTYME INC., Athens, Texas. Lobbyist — Zimmer & Carnavos, 2501 M St. N.W., Washington, D.C. 20037. Filed 7/6/83. Legislative interest — "Legislative interests involve supporting the enactment of reasonable legislation which regulates terminable consumer leases; S 1152 with modifications."

COLT INDUSTRIES INC., Washington, D.C. Lobbyist — McNair, Glenn, Konduros, Corley, Singletary, Porter & Dibble, 1155 15th St. N.W., Washington, D.C. 20005. Filed 7/1/83. Legislative interest — "Antitrust legislation with potential application to industry."

COMMONWEALTH EDISON CO., Chicago, Ill. Lobbyist — Gordon R. Corey, 2511 Park Place, Evanston, Ill. 60201. Filed 7/13/83. Legislative interest — "...Clinch River Breeder Reactor."

CONOCO INC., 1007 Market St., Wilmington, Del. 19898. Filed for self 7/11/83. Legislative interest — "All congressional bills dealing with oil and gas leasing on federally-owned lands, onshore and offshore; emergency preparedness and international economic energy policy legislation; Department of Interior appropriations; Export Administration Act; Energy Emergency Preparedness Act." Lobbyist — Nancie S. Johnson, 1701 Pennsylvania Ave. N.W., Washington, D.C. 20006. Filed for self 7/11/83. Legislative interest — "All congressional bills dealing with health, safety and environmental issues including appropriations and legislation dealing with the transportation of hazardous waste, endangered species and compensation of victims of hazardous substances exposure." Lobbyist — Robert M. Heine, 1701 Pennsylvania Ave. N.W., Washington, D.C. 20006.

CONSOLIDATED EDISON COMPANY OF NEW YORK, New York, N.Y. Lobbyist — John McElroy Atkisson, 1717 K St. N.W., Washington, D.C. 20036. Filed 7/18/83. Legislative interest — "Nuclear Regulatory Commission licensing reform; Federal emergency planning as pertaining to commercial nuclear power plants and reform thereof."

CONTAINER TRANSPORT INTERNATIONAL INC., White Plains, N.Y. Lobbyist — Piper & Marbury, 888 16th St. N.W., Washington, D.C. 20006. Filed 7/22/83. Legislative interest — "For amendment to legislation (S 1564, HR 3110, or later bills of similar effect) to prevent it from denying capital cost recovery tax allowances to U.S. taxpayers for their investments in productive equipment."

CONTINENTAL WINGATE CO., New York, N.Y. Lobbyist — Latham, Watkins & Hills, 1333 New Hampshire Ave. N.W., Washington, D.C. 20036. Filed 7/6/83. Legislative interest — "Opposition to HR 3110 as presently drafted."

CRINCO INVESTMENTS INC., El Paso, Texas. Lobbyist — Chadbourne, Parke, Whiteside & Wolff, 1101 Vermont Ave. N.W., Washington, D.C. 20005. Filed 7/19/83. Legislative interest — "Oil and gas tax legislation."

THE DETROIT EDISON CO., 2000 Second Ave., Detroit, Mich. 48226. Filed for self 7/14/83. Legislative interest — "Regulation affecting the utility industry including energy, the environment and regulatory issues." Lobbyist — Barbara Bauman, 1990 M St. N.W., Washington, D.C. 20036.

DETROIT & MACKINAC RAILWAY CO., Tawas City, Mich. Lobbyist — Gnau, Carter, Jacobsen & Associates Inc., 1777 F St. N.W., Washington, D.C. 20006. Filed 7/29/83. Legislative interest — Not specified.

DETROIT MADISON CO., Detroit, Mich. Lobbyist —

Dickinson, Wright, Moon, Van Dusen & Freeman, 1901 L St. N.W., Washington, D.C. 20036. Filed 7/26/83. Legislative interest — "HR 3110."

DOSIMETER CORPORATION OF NORTH AMERICA, Cincinnati, Ohio. Lobbyist — Taft, Stettinius & Hollister, 21 Dupont Circle N.W., Washington, D.C. 20036. Filed 7/3/83. (Former U.S. Sen. Robert A. Taft Jr., R-Ohio, 1971-76 (House 1963-65, 1967-71), was listed among agents for this client.) Legislative interest — "Attempting to get Congressional direction against production engineering of dosimeters by FEMA."

EAGLE-PICHER INDUSTRIES, Cincinnati, Ohio. Lobbyist — The Hoving Group, 2550 M St. N.W., Washington, D.C. 20037. Filed 7/15/83. Legislative interest — "Occupational Disease Compensation Act of 1983 ... HR 3175."

ELECTRONIC PROCESSING INC., P.O. Box 1340, Kansas City, Kan. Filed for self 7/11/83. Legislative interest — "In support of amendment to supplemental appropriation bill affecting employer." Lobbyist — M. Caldwell Butler, P.O. Box 720, Roanoke, Va. 24004. (Former U.S. rep., R-Va., 1972-83.)

ELKEM METALS CO., New York, N.Y. Lobbyist — Robert N. Pyle, P.O. Box 3731, Washington, D.C. 20007. Filed 7/7/83. Legislative interest — "National defense; strategic metals."

EXPRESS FOODS CO. INC., Louisville, Ky. Lobbyist — Leighton, Conklin, Lemov, Jacobs & Buckley, 2033 M St. N.W., Washington, D.C. 20036. Filed 7/15/83. Legislative interest — "All legislation affecting the marketing of modified whey products."

FEDERATION EMPLOYMENT & GUIDANCE SERVICE, New York, N.Y. Lobbyist — Howard M. Groedel, 1000 Potomac St. N.W., Washington, D.C. 20007. Filed 7/7/83. Legislative interest —"... potential private relief bill on behalf of the Federation Employment & Guidance Service, which is engaged in the training and employment of handicapped workers."

FLEXI-VAN LEASING INC., New York, N.Y. Lobbyist — Piper & Marbury, 888 16th St. N.W., Washington, D.C. 20006. Filed 7/22/83. Legislative interest — "For amendment to legislation (S 1564, HR 3110, or later bills of similar effect) to prevent it from denying capital cost recovery tax allowances to U.S. taxpayers for their investments in productive equipment."

FLOATING POINT SYSTEM, Portland, Ore. Lobbyist — Blum & Nash, 1015 18th St. N.W., Washington, D.C. 20036. Filed 7/8/83. Legislative interest — "Export Administration legislation, S 979."

F M S CORP., Los Angeles, Calif. Lobbyist — Patterson, Belknap, Webb & Tyler, 1730 Pennsylvania Ave. N.W., Washington, D.C. 20006. Filed 7/28/83. Legislative interest — "FY 84 Department of Defense authorization bill, S 675, section 1024, amendments to the Freedom of Information Reform Act, S 775, and amendments to the Export Administration Act, HR 3231."

FORUM COMMUNICATIONS, Seattle, Wash. Lobbyist — RBC Associates, 324 Fourth St. N.E., Washington, D.C. 20002. Filed 7/12/83. Legislative interest — "Department of Transportation FY 84 appropriations...."

CARL M. FREEMAN ASSOCIATES INC., Potomac, Md. Lobbyist — Kendall & Associates, 1750 New York Ave. N.W., Washington, D.C. 20006. Filed 7/11/83. Legislative interest — "Coastal Barrier Island legislation."

SAMUEL GARY OIL PRODUCER INC., Englewood, Colo. Lobbyist — Fulbright & Jaworski, 1150 Connecticut Ave. N.W., Washington, D.C. 20036. Filed 7/20/83. Legislative interest — "Amendment of section 613A of the Internal Revenue Code."

GC SERVICES CORP., Houston, Texas. Lobbyist — Cook, Purcell, Henderson & Zorack, 1015 18th St. N.W., Washington, D.C. 20036. Filed 7/13/83. Legislative interest — "Support of an appropriation for Debt Collection Act of 1982 (PL 97-365). HR 3069, FY 83 supplemental appropriations bill."

GENERAL ELECTRIC CO., 3135 Easton Turnpike, Fairfield, Conn. 06430. Filed for self 7/26/83. Legislative interest — "Involves various matters of business concern to the General Electric Company such as aerospace and defense matters, labor law, regulation of trade, interstate and foreign commerce, government procurement, environmental and customer items, etc." Lobbyist — Mary Ann Freeman, 777 14th St. N.W., Washington, D.C. 20005.

GENERAL MILLS INC., Washington, D.C. Lobbyist — McNair, Glenn, Konduros, Corley, Singletary, Porter & Dibble, 1155 15th St. N.W., Washington, D.C. 20005. Filed 7/1/83. Legislative interest — "Legislation relating to trademark protection."

GENERAL MOTORS CORP., Detroit, Mich. Lobbyist — Sutherland, Asbill & Brennan, 1666 K St. N.W., Washington, D.C. 20006. Filed 7/12/83. Legislative interest — "To seek amendments to HR 3110 and S 1564 relating to leasing by tax-exempt entities."

GENERAL PORTLAND INC., Dallas, Texas. Lobbyist — Williams & Jensen, 1101 Connecticut Ave. N.W., Washington, D.C. 20036. Filed 7/22/83. Legislative interest — "Trade and tariff matters of interest to the company."

GIFFORD-HILL & CO. INC., Dallas, Texas. Lobbyist — Williams & Jensen, 1101 Connecticut Ave. N.W., Washington, D.C. 20036. Filed 7/22/83. Legislative interest — "Trade and tariff matters of interest to the company."

GRUMMAN CORP., Arlington, Va. Lobbyist — Gray and Co., 3255 Grace St. N.W., Washington, D.C. 20007. Filed 7/7/83. Legislative interest — "Including but not limited to defense issues and military appropriations."

HAHN AND MATKOV, Boston, Mass. Lobbyist — Donald W. Whitehead, 1120 Connecticut Ave. N.W., Washington, D.C. 20036. Filed 7/1/83. Legislative interest — "Legislation affecting U.S. Indian tribes, especially Gay Head Indians of Massachusetts."

HALE & DOUGHERTY, 1625 K St. N.W., Washington, D.C. 20006. Filed for self 7/22/83. Legislative interest — Not specified.

JOHN HANCOCK MUTUAL LIFE INSURANCE CO., Boston, Mass. Lobbyist — Milbank, Tweed, Hadley & McCloy, 1825 I St. N.W., Washington, D.C. 20006. Filed 7/1/83. Legislative interest — "Legislation relating to natural gas industry including S 615 and HR 1760 and related bills."

HARRIS CORP., Melbourne, Fla. Lobbyist — McNair, Glenn, Konduros, Corley, Singletary, Porter & Dibble, 1155 15th St. N.W., Washington, D.C. 20005. Filed 7/1/83. Legislative interest — "Antitrust legislation with potential application to industry."

HAWAIIAN ELECTRIC CO. INC., Honolulu, Hawaii. Lobbyist — Cades, Schutte, Fleming & Wright, 1001 22nd St. N.W., Washington, D.C. 20037. Filed 7/8/83. Legislative interest — "Tax legislation affecting tax exempt financial property - HR 1635 and section 103 Internal Revenue Code."

HELLER, EHRMAN, WHITE, AND McAULIFFE, San Francisco, Calif. Lobbyist — Kendall & Associates, 1750 New York Ave. N.W., Washington, D.C. 20006. Filed 7/11/83. Legislative interest — "Interest in pension reform as it applies to ERISA."

HERCULES INC., Salt Lake City, Utah. Lobbyist — Ginn & Edington Inc., 121 S. Columbus St., Alexandria, Va. 22314. Filed 7/13/83. Legislative interest — "Defense-oriented legislation."

HOLCOMB INVESTMENTS INC., Dallas, Texas. Lobbyist — Avenel Associates Inc., P.O. Box 53131, Washington, D.C. 20009. Filed 7/9/83. Legislative interest — "Legislative tracking on natural gas deregulation."

HOSPITAL CORPORATION OF AMERICA, 2000 L St. N.W., Washington, D.C. 20035. Lobbyist — Shea & Gould, 1627 K St. N.W., Washington, D.C. 20006. Filed 7/12/83. Legislative interest — "Tax and health related legislation." Filed for self 7/12/83. Legislative interest — "Tax and health related legislation." Lobbyist — James Smith.

HOUGHTON MIFFLIN CO., Boston, Mass. Lobbyist — Mintz, Levin, Cohn, Ferris, Glovsky & Popeo, 1825 I St. N.W., Washington, D.C. 20006. Filed 7/9/83. Legislative interest — "HR 1310 and S 1285."

INDUSTRIAL SIDERURGICA INC., Bayamon, Puerto Rico. Lobbyist — Chapman, Duff and Paul, 1730 Pennsylvania Ave. N.W., Washington, D.C. 20006. Filed 7/1/83. Legislative interest — "Revisions of trade remedy laws."

INSURANCE SERVICES OFFICE, 160 Water St., New York, N.Y. Filed for self 7/13/83. Legislative interest — "Fair Insurance Practices Act; Non-Discrimination in Insurance Act; Economic Equity Act, Title III ... S 888; S 2204; HR 100; HR 2090...." Lobbyist — Mavis A. Walters, 900 17th St. N.W.,

Washington, D.C. 20006.

KAISER ALUMINUM & CHEMICAL CORP., 900 17th St. N.W., Washington, D.C. 20006. Filed for self 7/18/83. Legislative interest — "... S 615 and HR 1760 - Natural Gas Consumer Regulatory Reform Amendments of 1983...." Lobbyist — Ann R. Wieseneck.

KAISER CEMENT CORP., 300 Lakeside Drive, Oakland, Calif. 94612. Lobbyist — Williams & Jensen, 1101 Connecticut Ave. N.W., Washington, D.C. 20036. Filed 7/22/83. Legislative interest — "Trade and tariff matters of interest to the company." Lobbyist — Squire, Sanders & Dempsey, 21 Dupont Circle N.W., Washington, D.C. 20036. Filed 7/27/83. Legislative interest — "International trade ... health care ... environmental bills ... transportation ... taxes ... product liability." Filed for self 7/27/83. Legislative interest — "International trade ... health care ... environmental bills ... transportation ... taxes ... product liability." Lobbyist — Lauren Cronin.

KIRO INC., Seattle, Wash. Lobbyist — Wilkinson, Barker, Knauer & Quinn, 1735 New York Ave. N.W., Washington, D.C. 20006. Filed 7/22/83. Legislative interest — "Opposing S 880 and HR 2385 insofar as it would impede operation of clear channel radio broadcasters increased operating hours for daytime AM radio stations."

KOMATSU LTD., Tokyo, Japan. Lobbyist — Global USA Inc., 1825 I St. N.W., Washington, D.C. 20006. Filed 7/29/83. Legislative interest — "... extension of the Export Administration Act (S 979 and HR 2971)...."

LONG ISLAND LIGHTING CO., 250 Old Country Road, Mineola, N.Y. 11501. Filed for self 7/8/83. Legislative interest — Not specified.

M/A-COM INC., 1350 Piccard Drive, Rockville, Md. 20850. Filed for self 7/13/83. Legislative interest — "Telecommunications, tax policy, international trade policy, government procurement policy, such as S 999 and S 738." Lobbyist — Jeffrey Krauss.

THE MANUFACTURERS LIFE INSURANCE CO., Toronto, Canada. Lobbyist — Chadbourne, Parke, Whiteside & Wolff, 1101 Vermont Ave. N.W., Washington, D.C. 20005. Filed 7/15/83. Legislative interest — "Trade Act of 1974; Fair Insurance Practice Act ... HR 2973, HR 100, S 372 ... 19 U.S.C. 2411...."

MANVILLE CORP., 1025 Connecticut Ave. N.W., Washington, D.C. 20036. Lobbyist — Kendall & Associates, 1750 New York Ave. N.W., Washington, D.C. 20006. Filed 7/11/83. Legislative interest — "Interest in prospective legislation dealing with compensation for victims of occupational disease and bankruptcy related legislation." Lobbyist — Wilkinson, Barker, Knauer & Quinn, 1735 New York Ave. N.W., Washington, D.C. 20006. Filed 7/28/83. (Former U.S. Rep. Thomas L. Ashley, D-Ohio, 1955-81, was listed as being "of counsel" for this client.) Legislative interest — "Legislation to compensate victims of asbestos-related diseases, in general; HR 3175, the Occupational Disease Compensation Act, and the proposed Asbestos Claimants Compensation Act, in particular." Lobbyist — Chambers Associates Inc., 1411 K St. N.W., Washington, D.C. 20005. Filed 7/18/83. Legislative interest — "HR 3175 and related issues." Filed for self 7/8/83. Legislative interest — "General legislative interests; energy conservation; specifically, HR 1, S 1338." Lobbyist — Joseph L. Lach.

MARION LABORATORIES INC., Kansas City, Mo. Lobbyist — Taggart & Associates, 1015 15th St. N.W., Washington, D.C. 20005. Filed 7/22/83. Legislative interest — "Matters that pertain to health legislation."

MASSACHUSETTS MUTUAL LIFE INSURANCE CO., Springfield, Mass. Lobbyist — Birch, Horton, Bittner, Pestinger and Anderson, 1140 Connecticut Ave. N.W., Washington, D.C. 20036. Filed 7/7/83. Legislative interest — "Tax legislative matters." Lobbyists — Carol R. Emery, Jay Stone, 412 First St. S.E., Washington, D.C. 20003. Filed 7/12/83. Legislative interest — "Tax legislation affecting mutual insurance companies."

MAZAK CORP., Florence, Ky. Lobbyist — Global USA Inc., 1825 I St. N.W., Washington, D.C. 20006. Filed 7/25/83. Legislative interest — "... extension of the Export Administration Act (S 979 and HR 2971)...."

MERRILL LYNCH & CO. INC., 1828 L St. N.W., Washington, D.C. 20036. Filed for self 7/13/83. Legislative interest —

"Financial, banking, securities, taxation, real estate and related legislation." Lobbyist — Charles Maguire, 3315 P St. N.W., Washington, D.C. 20036.

METROPOLITAN INSURANCE COS., Washington, D.C. Lobbyist — Camp, Carmouche, Barsh, Hunter, Gray & Hoffman, 2550 M St. N.W., Washington, D.C. 20037. Filed 7/28/83. Legislative interest — "Legislation affecting the income taxation of life insurance companies." Lobbyist — McNair, Glenn, Konduros, Corley, Singletary, Porter & Dibble, 1155 15th St. N.W., Washington, D.C. 20005. Filed 7/1/83. Legislative interest — Not specified.

MICHIGAN CONSOLIDATED GAS CO., Detroit, Mich. Lobbyist — Plunkett, Cooney, Rutt, Watters, Stanczyk & Pedersen, 900 Marquette Building, Detroit, Mich. 48226. Filed 7/8/83. (Former U.S. Rep. William M. Brodhead, D-Mich., 1975-83, was listed as agent for this client.) Legislative interest — "Amendments to Social Security Act dealing with vendors services to AFDC recipients."

MID-CONTINENT TELEPHONE CORP., 100 Executive Parkway, Hudson, Ohio 44236. Lobbyist — Thompson, Hine and Flory, 1920 N St. N.W., Washington, D.C. 20036. Filed 7/15/83. Legislative interest — "General interest is legislation affecting the telephone and telecommunications industries, especially S 1382, H Res 231 and HR 3440...." Filed for self 7/15/83. Legislative interest — "General interest is legislation affecting the telephone and telecommunications industries, especially S 1382, H Res 231 and HR 3440...." Lobbyist — Jon F. Kelly.

MIDDLE SOUTH SERVICES INC., P.O. Box 61000, New Orleans, La. 70161. Filed for self 7/14/83. Legislative interest — Not specified. Lobbyist — George E. White Jr.

MILLER BREWING CO., Milwaukee, Wis. Lobbyist — Webster, Chamberlain & Bean, 1747 Pennsylvania Ave. N.W., Washington, D.C. 20006. Filed 7/8/83. Legislative interest — Not specified.

MONEGON LTD., Gaithersburg, Md. Lobbyist — Chadbourne, Parke, Whiteside & Wolff, 1101 Vermont Ave. N.W., Washington, D.C. 20005. Filed 7/19/83. Legislative interest — "Solar tax legislation."

MONOLITH PORTLAND CEMENT CO., Glendale, Calif. Lobbyist — Williams & Jensen, 1101 Connecticut Ave. N.W., Washington, D.C. 20036. Filed 7/22/83. Legislative interest — "Trade and tariff matters of interest to the company."

NETCO, Ann Arbor, Mich. Lobbyist — Gnau, Carter, Jacobsen & Associates Inc., 1777 F St. N.W., Washington, D.C. 20006. Filed 7/5/83. Legislative interest — "Research and development funding and continuing funding from various agencies within the Federal government for energy cost saving programs."

NL INDUSTRIES, New York, N.Y. Lobbyist — Daniel J. Piliero II, 1750 Pennsylvania Ave. N.W., Washington, D.C. 20006. Filed 7/18/83. Legislative interest — "The company is interested in legislation pertaining to the Department of Energy remedial action programs and related issues."

PHH GROUP INC., 11333 McCormick Road, Hunt Valley, Md. 21031. Filed for self 7/5/83. Legislative interest — "...HR 1607 and S 1161." Lobbyist — Samuel H. Wright.

PHILADELPHIA FACILITIES MANAGEMENT CORP., Philadelphia, Pa. Lobbyist — Butler & Binion, 1747 Pennsylvania Ave. N.W., Washington, D.C. 20006. Filed 7/15/83. Legislative interest — "HR 3110, Government Leasing Act; HR 6135, Industrial Development Bond Limitation Act."

PILLSBURY CO., Minneapolis, Minn. Lobbyist — Hogan & Hartson, 815 Connecticut Ave. N.W., Washington, D.C. 20006. Filed 7/27/83. Legislative interest — "...Federal income tax proposals relating to DISC - S 28, HR 981 and HR 1673...."

PIPER, JAFFRAY & HOPWOOD, Minneapolis, Minn. Lobbyist — Taft, Stettinius & Hollister, 21 Dupont Circle N.W., Washington, D.C. 20036. Filed 7/3/83. (Former U.S. Sen. Robert A. Taft Jr., R-Ohio, 1971-76 (House 1963-65, 1967-71), was listed as agent for this client.) Legislative interest — "Requesting development of transition language in HR 3110 covering St. Paul, Minn., Civic Center bond issue."

PRIMARK CORP., Washington, D.C. Lobbyist — Gnau, Carter, Jacobsen & Associates Inc., 1777 F St. N.W., Washington,

D.C. 20006. Filed 7/5/83. Legislative interest — Not specified.

PRUDENTIAL INSURANCE COMPANY OF AMERICA, Washington, D.C. Lobbyist — O'Connor & Hannan, 1919 Pennsylvania Ave. N.W., Washington, D.C. 20006. Filed 7/28/83. Legislative interest "... including, but not limited to, opposition of bank entry into the insurance business."

PUEBLO INTERNATIONAL INC., New York, N.Y. Lobbyist — Arent, Fox, Kintner, Plotkin & Kahn, 1050 Connecticut Ave. N.W., Washington, D.C. 20036. Filed 7/25/83. Legislative interest — "Provisions of HR 3223 concerning nutrition assistance to Puerto Rico."

RCA GLOBAL COMMUNICATIONS INC., New York, N.Y. Lobbyist — Taft, Stettinius & Hollister, 21 Dupont Circle N.W., Washington, D.C. 20036. Filed 7/11/83. (Former U.S. Sen. Robert A. Taft Jr., R-Ohio, 1971-76 (House 1963-65, 1967-71), was listed as agent for this client.) Legislative interest — "Advice in connection with international telecommunications decisions in S 999."

ROSES INC., Haslett, Mich. Lobbyist — J. Philip Carlson, 1435 G St. N.W., Washington, D.C. 20005. Filed 7/13/83. Legislative interest — "To amend tariff schedules of the U.S. to align those rates on fresh cut roses to those imposed by the EEC... HR 1146 and S 1296... 19 U.S.C. 1202 item 192.18...."

ST. JOE MINERALS CORP., Washington, D.C. Lobbyist — Craig Hackler, 412 First St. S.E., Washington, D.C. 20003. Filed 7/19/83. Legislative interest — "S 64, HR 2170, wilderness designation, opposed."

SANTA ANITA REALTY ENTERPRISES INC., Los Angeles, Calif. Lobbyist — Fulbright & Jaworski, 1150 Connecticut Ave. N.W., Washington, D.C. 20036. Filed 7/20/83. Legislative interest — Not specified.

SCHOCHET ASSOCIATES, Boston, Mass. Lobbyist — Brownstein, Zeidman and Schomer, 1025 Connecticut Ave. N.W., Washington, D.C. 20036. Filed 7/8/83. Legislative interest — "All legislation affecting real estate development, particularly HR 3110, HR 1 and S 1338."

SHEA PRODUCTS INC., P.O. Box 184, Clawson, Mich. 48017. Filed for self 7/8/83. Legislative interest — "... increase the amount of federal R&D money available to developing such [communications aids for the severely speech impaired] technology; or ... hold down the costs of such aids to those who need them through a direct subsidy and/or tax credits." Lobbyist — Robert R. Williams, 2400 Virginia Ave. N.W., Washington, D.C. 20037.

SINGAPORE AIRLINES LTD., Singapore, Singapore. Lobbyist — Barrett, Smith, Schapiro, Simon & Armstrong, 1201 Pennsylvania Ave. N.W., Washington, D.C. 20004. Filed 7/11/83. Legislative interest — "Interested in legislation that would adversely affect foreign aircraft lease transactions ... HR 3110, to amend the Internal Revenue Code of 1954 to deny certain tax incentives for property used by governments and other tax-exempt entities. S 1564, Governmental Lease Financing Reform Act."

SKYLINK CORP. INC., Boulder, Colo. Lobbyist — Hamel, Park, McCabe & Saunders, 888 16th St. N.W., Washington, D.C. 20006. Filed 7/8/83. Legislative interest — "Communications legislation affecting the interests of Skylink, including possible amendments to the Communications Act of 1934."

SMITH, BARNEY, HARRIS, UPHAM & CO. INC., New York, N.Y. Lobbyist — Kendall & Associates, 1750 New York Ave. N.W., Washington, D.C. 20006. Filed 7/11/83. Legislative interest — "Legislation affecting industrial development bonds."

SOCIETE NATIONALE D'ETUDE ET DE CONSTRUCTION DE MOTEURS D'AVIATION, Paris, France. Lobbyist — DGA International Inc., 1225 19th St. N.W., Washington, D.C. 20036. Filed 7/11/83. Legislative interest — "Legislation affecting U.S. Department of Defense authorization and appropriations. In the immediate period the 1983 Defense authorization bill and the 1983 Defense appropriation bill are of specific interest. Also any other legislation that would affect U.S. Defense Department procurement decisions related to large military aircraft engines (*i.e.*, engines for tankers, transport, surveillance, or other similar type aircraft)...."

SOLAREX CORP., Rockville, Md. Lobbyist — Chadbourne, Parke, Whiteside & Wolff, 1101 Vermont Ave. N.W., Washing-

D.C. 20005. Filed 7/19/83. Legislative interest — "Solar tax legislation."

SOUTHEASTERN EXPORTERS, Nashville, Tenn. Lobbyist — Paul M. Tendler Associates Inc., 1110 Vermont Ave. N.W., Washington, D.C. 20005. Filed 7/11/83. Legislative interest — "Legislative interests regarding matters of trade and securing general distributors license."

SOUTHERN CALIFORNIA EDISON CO., Rosemead, Calif. Lobbyist — Akin, Gump, Strauss, Hauer & Feld, 1333 New Hampshire Ave. N.W., Washington, D.C. 20036. Filed 7/28/83. Legislative interest — "Hearings and any legislation relating to the 1920 Federal Power Act." Lobbyist — Groom and Nordberg, 1775 Pennsylvania Ave. N.W., Washington, D.C. 20006. Filed 7/8/83. Legislative interest — "Federal legislation affecting Title 26 of U.S.C."

SOUTHWESTERN PORTLAND CEMENT CO., Los Angeles, Calif. Lobbyist — Williams & Jensen, 1101 Connecticut Ave. N.W., Washington, D.C. 20036. Filed 7/22/83. Legislative interest — "Trade and tariff matters of interest to the company."

SPANISH INTERNATIONAL COMMUNICATION CORP., New York, N.Y. Lobbyist — Munger, Tolles & Rickershauser, 612 Flower St., Los Angeles, Calif. 90017. Filed 7/6/83. Legislative interest — "Immigration Reform and Control Act of 1983, HR 1510 and S 529. . . ."

SUN CO. INC., Radnor, Pa. Lobbyist — David P. Stang, 1629 K St. N.W., Washington, D.C. 20006. Filed 7/22/83. Legislative interest — "S 1066, concerning supplemental retirement benefits."

SUN-DIAMOND GROWERS OF CALIFORNIA, Stockton, Calif. Lobbyist — Heron, Burchette, Ruckert & Rothwell, 1200 New Hampshire Ave. N.W., Washington, D.C. 20036. Filed 7/5/83. Legislative interest — "Export Equity Act, FTC authorization bill, user fee legislation-USDA, regulatory reform legislation . . . support legislation to exclude agriculture from the generalized system of preferences. HR 2327, HR 2970."

SUNKIST GROWERS INC., Van Nuys, Calif. Lobbyist — Heron, Burchette, Ruckert & Rothwell, 1200 New Hampshire Ave. N.W., Washington, D.C. 20036. Filed 7/5/83. Legislative interest — "FTC authorization bill, fruit frost appropriations, user fee legislation-USDA, regulatory reform legislation, HR 2327, HR 2970. Support legislation to exclude agriculture from the generalized system of preferences."

TAYLOR & MIZELL, 2700 Republic Bank Tower, Dallas, Texas 75210. Filed for self 7/7/83. Legislative interest — "This firm anticipates being retained for the purpose of influencing legislation primarily dealing with Title 26, U.S.C. (the Internal Revenue Code). . . ." Lobbyists — E. Philip Bush, Robert C. Taylor, Robert E. Wilbur.

TEXAS EASTERN TRANSMISSION CORP., Washington, D.C. Lobbyist — Corcoran, Hardesty, Whyte, Hemphill & Ligon, 1575 I St. N.W., Washington, D.C. 20005. Filed 7/25/83. Legislative interest — "Support of Coal Slurry Pipeline legislation . . . Coal Pipeline Act of 1983 . . . HR 1010, S 267."

THERMO ELECTRON CORP., 101 First Ave., Waltham, Mass. 02254. Filed for self 7/22/83. Legislative interest — "Followed the House passage of the Interior and HUD/Independent agencies appropriations bills; interested in specific provisions in each." Lobbyist — Robert L. Pratt, 1 Ivy Road, Wellesley, Mass. 02181.

THOMPSON & CO., 1924 South Utica, Tulsa, Okla. 74104. Filed for self 7/18/83. Legislative interest — "Tax matters, oil and gas matters, and other miscellaneous; specifically now HR 2163." Lobbyist — Robert J. Thompson.

THOMSON-CSF INC., Bagneux, France. Lobbyist — Gil Nettleton, 4101 Cathedral Ave. N.W., Washington, D.C. 20016. Filed 7/25/83. Legislative interest — "Legislation relating to the Short Range Air Defense (SHORAD) System known as SICA."

TITANIUM METALS CORPORATION OF AMERICA (TIMET DIVISION), Pittsburgh, Pa. Lobbyist — Ullman Consultants Inc., 1000 Potomac St. N.W., Washington, D.C. 20007. Filed 7/11/83. (Former U.S. Rep. Al Ullman, D-Ore., 1957-81, was listed as agent for this client.) Legislative interest — "Appropriations affecting the national defense stockpile."

TOYOTA MOTOR SALES USA INC., Torrance, Calif. Lobbyist — Kendall & Associates, 1750 New York Ave. N.W., Washington, D.C. 20006. Filed 7/11/83. Legislative interest — "General interest in trade matters, automobile matters. Specific interest in legislation dealing with Domestic Content."

TRANSAMERICA-ICS INC., New York, N.Y. Lobbyist — Piper & Marbury, 888 16th St. N.W., Washington, D.C. 20006. Filed 7/22/83. Legislative interest — "For amendment to legislation (S 1564, HR 3110, or later bills of similar effect) to prevent it from denying capital cost recovery tax allowances to U.S. taxpayers for their investments in productive equipment."

TRANSCO ENERGY CO., 2800 S. Post Oak Road, Houston, Texas 77251. Filed for self 7/9/83. Legislative interest — "Coal - Coal Pipeline legislation - specifically, HR 1010, The Coal Pipeline Act of 1983 (support) and S 267, The Coal Distribution and Utilization Act of 1983 (support). Natural gas - amendments to the Natural Gas Policy Act - all legislative initiatives." Lobbyist — Curtis E. Whalen, 490 L'Enfant Plaza S.W., Washington, D.C. 20024.

UNITED STATES CRUISES INC., Seattle, Wash. Lobbyist — Whittlesey & O'Brien, 1607 New Hampshire Ave. N.W., Washington, D.C. 20009. Filed 7/9/83. Legislative interest — "HR 2883."

UNITED STATES SURGICAL CORP., Norwalk, Conn. Lobbyist — Cummings & Lockwood, 1090 Vermont Ave. N.W., Washington, D.C. 20005. Filed 7/21/83. Legislative interest — "Use of animals in research . . . Animal Welfare Act . . . S 657 and other animal bills . . . 7 U.S.C. section 2131-2156. . . ."

WARNER AMEX CABLE COMMUNICATIONS INC., 75 Rockefeller Plaza, New York, N.Y. 10019. Filed for self 7/29/83. Legislative interest — "Cable Telecommunications Act of 1983 . . . S 66. . . ." Lobbyist — Richard M. Berman.

WEYERHAEUSER CO., Corporate Headquarters, Tacoma, Wash. 98477. Filed for self 7/12/83. Legislative interest — Not specified. Lobbyist — Frederick S. Benson III, 1625 I St. N.W., Washington, D.C. 20006.

WORLDWIDE INFORMATION RESOURCES INC., Washington, D.C. Lobbyist — Kendall & Associates, 1750 New York Ave. N.W., Washington, D.C. 20006. Filed 7/11/83. Legislative interest — "Opposed to any bill limiting states' coal severance tax."

International Relations

GOVERNMENT OF SUDAN, Washington, D.C. Lobbyist — O'Connor & Hannan, 1919 Pennsylvania Ave. N.W., Washington, D.C. 20006. Filed 7/25/83. (Former U.S. Rep. Thomas B. Evans Jr., R-Del., 1977-83, was listed as agent for this client.) Legislative interest — Not specified.

REPUBLIC OF TURKEY, Washington, D.C. Lobbyist — Gray and Co., 3255 Grace St. N.W., Washington, D.C. 20007. Filed 7/9/83. Legislative interest — "Including but not limited to economic and security assistance issues."

Labor Groups

AMERICAN FEDERATION OF TEACHERS, 11 Dupont Circle N.W., Washington, D.C. 20036. Filed for self 7/22/83. Legislative interest — Not specified. Lobbyist — Mary Granger.

AMERICAN POSTAL WORKERS UNION, Washington, D.C. Lobbyist — Plunkett, Cooney, Rutt, Watters, Stanczyk & Pedersen, 900 Marquette Building, Detroit, Mich. 48226. Filed 7/8/83. (Former U.S. Rep. William M. Brodhead, D-Mich., 1975-83, was listed as agent for this client.) Legislative interest — "Social Security amendments of 1983."

FARM LABOR ALLIANCE, Fresno, Calif. Lobbyist — Heron, Burchette, Ruckert & Rothwell, 1200 New Hampshire Ave. N.W., Washington, D.C. 20036. Filed 7/5/83. Legislative interest — "Immigration legislation, HR 1510."

MAJOR LEAGUE BASEBALL PLAYERS ASSOCIATION, New York, N.Y. Lobbyist — Onek, Klein and Farr, 2550 M St. N.W., Washington, D.C. 20037. Filed 7/15/83. Legislative interest — "Legislation affecting the interests of and the terms and conditions of employment for major league baseball players, including HR 3094, S 1036 and other legislation concerning application of the antitrust laws to professional sports."

OVERSEAS EDUCATION ASSOCIATION, 1201 16th St. N.W., Washington, D.C. 20036. Filed for self 7/29/83. Legislative interest — "Goal is to pass HR 2302 to amend 20 U.S.C. 901 *et seq.* and to stop changes to PL 96-88, the Dept. of Education Organization Act that would place overseas teachers in the Dept. of Defense rather than in the Dept. of Education...." Lobbyist — Ronald R. Austin.

State and Local Governments

CITY OF DETROIT, Detroit, Mich. Lobbyist — Plunkett, Cooney, Rutt, Watters, Stanczyk & Pedersen, 900 Marquette Building, Detroit, Mich. 48226. Filed 7/29/83. (Former U.S. Rep. William M. Brodhead, D-Mich., 1975-83, was listed as agent for this client.) Legislative interest — Not specified.

NEW MEXICO PUBLIC SERVICE COMMISSION, Santa Fe, N.M. Lobbyist — Butler & Binion, 1747 Pennsylvania Ave. N.W., Washington, D.C. 20006. Filed 7/18/83. Legislative interest — "Pending Natural Gas Deregulation legislation including, but not limited to, S 615 and HR 1760."

ORANGE COUNTY TRANSIT DISTRICT, Garden Grove, Calif. Lobbyist — Nickerson, Ingram & Associates Inc., 1150 17th St. N.W., Washington, D.C. 20036. Filed 7/27/83. Legislative interest — "Safe Harbor Leasing ... generally interested in its retention and broadest possible utility for the transit agency."

SAN FRANCISCO PUBLIC UTILITIES COMMISSION, San Francisco, Calif. Lobbyist — Smith Dawson Associates Inc., 1000 Connecticut Ave. N.W., Washington, D.C. 20036. Filed 7/14/83. Legislative interest — "Monitor, evaluate and report on the status of legislation including but not limited to transportation and energy authorizations and appropriations bills."

SOUTHERN CALIFORNIA RAPID TRANSIT DISTRICT, Los Angeles, Calif. Lobbyist — Nickerson, Ingram & Associates Inc., 1150 17th St. N.W., Washington, D.C. 20036. Filed 7/27/83. Legislative interest — "Safe Harbor Leasing ... Generally interested in its retention and broadest possible utility for the transit agency." Lobbyist — Bill Hecht, 499 South Capitol St., Washington, D.C. 20003. Filed 7/21/83. Legislative interest — "General legislative interests, including but not limited to HR 3329." Lobbyist — Heron, Burchette, Ruckert & Rothwell, 1200 New Hampshire Ave. N.W., Washington, D.C. 20036. Filed 7/5/83. Legislative interest — "Mass transit funds. Department of Transportation appropriations."

STATE OF NEVADA, Las Vegas, Nev. Lobbyist — Duncan, Weinberg & Miller, 1775 Pennsylvania Ave. N.W., Washington, D.C. 20006. Filed 7/9/83. Legislative interest — "Matters relating to allocation and marketing of power from Hoover Dam."

Trade Associations

AIR CONDITIONING AND REFRIGERATION INSTITUTE, 1815 N. Fort Myer Drive, Arlington, Va. 22209. Filed for self 7/20/83. Legislative interest — "Legislation affecting the air conditioning industry, including bills related to regulation of chlorofluorocarbons, the Clean Air Act, energy conservation, tax credit for solar energy, and budget measures affecting the Department of Energy and the Federal Trade Commission." Lobbyist — Joseph M. McGuire.

ALASKA BANKERS ASSOCIATION, Juneau, Alaska. Lobbyist — Birch, Horton, Bittner, Pestinger and Anderson, 1140 Connecticut Ave. N.W., Washington, D.C. 20036. Filed 7/7/83. Legislative interest — "General banking issues."

AMERICAN ASSOCIATION OF MEAT PROCESSORS, P.O. Box 269, Elizabethtown, Pa. 17022. Filed for self 7/14/83. Legislative interest — "Meat inspection amendments of 1983 and Federal Meat and Poultry Products Inspection Act of 1983 ... HR 1795 and S 593." Lobbyist — A. Joan Dannelley.

AMERICAN INDEPENDENT REFINERS ASSOCIATION, 114 Third St. S.E., Washington, D.C. 20003. Filed for self 7/3/83. Legislative interest — "All legislative issues affecting small refiners such as refining policy legislation and other measures including but not limited to the President's energy proposal." Lobbyist — Raymond F. Bragg Jr.

AMERICAN IRON AND STEEL INSTITUTE, Washington, D.C. Lobbyist — Gray and Co., 3255 Grace St. N.W., Washington, D.C. 20007. Filed 7/9/83. Legislative interest — "Including but not limited to clean water legislation."

AMERICAN NURSES' ASSOCIATION, 2420 Pershing Road, Kansas City, Mo. 64108. Filed for self 7/6/83. Legislative interest — "Legislation relating to nurses, nursing and health including but not limited to Nurse Training Act, nurse research, community health grants, Medicare, Medicaid, mental health, block grants, pro-competition proposals, appropriations and budget." Lobbyist — Richard G. Miller, 1101 14th St. N.W., Washington, D.C. 20005.

AMERICAN SOCIETY OF COMPOSERS, AUTHORS AND PUBLISHERS, New York, N.Y. Lobbyist — Landis, Cohen, Singman and Rauh, 1019 19th St. N.W., Washington, D.C. 20036. Filed 7/9/83. Legislative interest — "All matters of legislative concern; amendments to Copyright Act, 17 U.S.C., including S 32."

AMERICAN WATERWAYS OPERATORS INC., 1600 Wilson Blvd., Arlington, Va. 22209. Filed for self 7/25/83. Legislative interest — "All legislation of interest to the barge and towing industry." Lobbyist — Marcia Y. Kinter, Jeffrey A. Smith.

ASSOCIATED GENERAL CONTRACTORS OF AMERICA, 1957 E St. N.W., Washington, D.C. 20006. Filed for self 7/7/83. Legislative interest — "Port and inland waterways development." Lobbyist — Jeffrey L. Beard. Filed for self 7/7/83. Legislative interest — "Occupational safety and health issues affecting the construction industry." Lobbyist — Michael I. Fanning. Filed for self 7/7/83. Legislative interest — "Federal tax legislation." Lobbyist — Barbara V. Hess.

ASSOCIATION OF AMERICAN CANCER INSTITUTES, Buffalo, N.Y. Lobbyist — John T. Grupenhoff, 10000 Falls Road, Potomac, Md. 20854. Filed 7/16/83. Legislative interest — "Interest in HR 2350 and S 773, biomedical research legislation and appropriations, Medicare/Medicaid and other legislation affecting cancer research."

ASSOCIATION OF AMERICAN RAILROADS, 1920 L St. N.W., Washington, D.C. 20036. Filed 7/11/83. Legislative interest — Not specified. Lobbyist — John F. Wetzel Jr., 412 First St. S.E., Washington, D.C. 20003.

ASSOCIATION OF TRIAL LAWYERS, 1050 31st St. N.W., Washington, D.C. 20007. Filed for self 7/8/83. Legislative interest — "Legislation relative to admiralty, automobile reparation, aviation, consumer protection, criminal law, the environment, health, the administration of justice, legal services, and worker's compensation." Lobbyist — Daniel L. Cohen.

CHAMBER OF COMMERCE OF THE UNITED STATES, 1615 H St. N.W., Washington, D.C. 20062. Filed for self 7/8/83. Legislative interest — Not specified. Lobbyist — M. Frank Sellers.

CHOCOLATE MANUFACTURERS ASSOCIATION OF THE USA, 7900 Westpark Drive, McLean, Va. 22102. Lobbyist — Richard T. O'Connell & Associates Inc., 3208 Traveler St., Fairfax, Va. 22030. Filed 7/14/83. Legislative interest — "General agricultural legislation with particular interest pertaining to sugar, milk, peanuts and almonds; *i.e.*, S 788. Food safety legislation and other legislation pertaining to the food industry." Filed for self 7/14/83. Legislative interest — "General agricultural legislation with particular interest pertaining to sugar, milk, peanuts and almonds; *i.e.*, S 788. Food safety legislation and other legislation pertaining to the food industry." Lobbyist — Timothy R. Rugh.

CLEAR CHANNEL BROADCASTING SERVICE,

Washington, D.C. Lobbyist — Wiley, Johnson & Rein, 1776 K St. N.W., Washington, D.C. Filed 7/13/83. Legislative interest — "Wiley, Johnson & Rein will represent the Clear Channel Broadcasting Service in opposition to S 880 and HR 2385 (extended hours for daytime stations)."

COMPUTER AND BUSINESS EQUIPMENT MANUFACTURERS ASSOCIATION, Washington, D.C. Lobbyist — Hogan & Hartson, 815 Connecticut Ave. N.W., Washington, D.C. 20006. Filed 7/20/83. Legislative interest — "HR 3110, legislation limiting the tax benefits of lessors of property to tax-exempt institutions and companion legislation in the Senate." Lobbyist — Richard C. White, 499 South Capitol St., Washington, D.C. 20003. Filed 7/25/83. (Former U.S. rep., D-Texas, 1965-83.) Legislative interest — "Export Administration Act."

COMPUTER AND COMMUNICATION INDUSTRY ASSOCIATION, Arlington, Va. Lobbyist — Tendler, Black & Biggins, 1110 Vermont Ave. N.W., Washington, D.C. 20005. Filed 7/29/83. Legislative interest — ". . . international trade legislation. . . ."

COMPUTER DEALERS AND LESSORS ASSOCIATION INC., Washington, D.C. Lobbyist — Patton, Boggs & Blow, 2550 M St. N.W., Washington, D.C. 20037. Filed 7/6/83. Legislative interest — "Tax treatment of computers; the appropriate depreciation period thereof; HR 3110."

EMERGENCY COMMITTEE FOR AMERICAN TRADE, Washington, D.C. Lobbyist — Richard C. White, 499 South Capitol St., Washington, D.C. 20003. Filed 7/8/83. (Former U.S. rep., D-Texas, 1965-83.) Legislative interest — " . . . Export Administration Act."

FREIGHT FORWARDERS INSTITUTE, Washington, D.C. Lobbyist — Williams & Jensen, 1101 Connecticut Ave. N.W., Washington, D.C. 20036. Filed 7/27/83. Legislative interest — "Tax matters of interest to the Institute."

HAZARDOUS WASTE TREATMENT COUNCIL, Washington, D.C. Lobbyist — Richard C. Fortuna, 4201 Massachusetts Ave. N.W., Washington, D.C. 20016. Filed 7/12/83. Legislative interest — "All legislation affecting the control of hazardous wastes and toxic substances. Specifically, the Treatment Council is interested in the passage of legislation to reauthorize the Resource Conservation and Recovery Act (HR 7867, S 757), and legislation to reauthorize the Toxic Substances Control Act (TSCA)."

IMPERIAL VALLEY ASPARAGUS GROWERS ASSOCIATION, El Centro, Calif. Lobbyist — Heron, Burchette, Ruckert & Rothwell, 1200 New Hampshire Ave. N.W., Washington, D.C. 20036. Filed 7/5/83. Legislative interest — "Support legislation to change tariff schedules for asparagus from Mexico."

INTELLECTUAL PROPERTY OWNERS INC., 1800 M St. N.W., Washington, D.C. 20036. Filed 7/11/83. Legislative interest — "Pending or proposed bills affecting patent, trademark and copyright laws, including S 1535, S 1538, HR 2610, S 1306, S 875, HR 2447, HR 2995, S 1440, HR 3320, S 1201, HR 1028, HR 3285 and HR 3296. Favor bills which provide effective protection for patent, trademark and copyright rights."

LONDON CHAMBER OF COMMERCE AND INDUSTRY, 69 Cannon St., London EC4, England. Lobbyist — Surrey & Morse, 1250 I St. N.W., Washington, D.C. 20005. Filed 7/13/83. Legislative interest — "Registrant supports amendments to HR 3231 and S 979, authorization bills to amend the Export Administration Act of 1979, which would deregulate unnecessary unilateral constraints on exports of American products and technology abroad and improve the system of multilateral export controls, to maximize the free flow of trade between the U.S. and Great Britain." Filed for self 7/13/83. Legislative interest — "Registrant supports amendments to HR 3231 and S 979, authorization bills to amend the Export Administration Act of 1979, which would deregulate unnecessary restraints on exports of American products and technology abroad and improve the system of multilateral export controls to maximize the free flow of trade between the U.S. and Great Britain." Lobbyist — W. F. Nicholas.

MOTOR VEHICLE MANUFACTURERS ASSOCIATION OF THE U.S. INC., 300 New Center Building, Detroit, Mich. 48202. Filed for self 7/25/83. Legislative interest — "Legislation affecting the international trade and investment position of the motor vehicle industry." Lobbyist — Neil D. Schuster, 1909 K St. N.W., Washington, D.C. 20006.

NATIONAL ASSOCIATION OF BROADCASTERS, 1771 N St. N.W., Washington, D.C. 20036. Lobbyist — Chadbourne, Parke, Whiteside & Wolff, 1101 Vermont Ave. N.W., Washington, D.C. 20005. Filed 7/8/83. (Former U.S. Sen. Edmund S. Muskie, D-Maine, 1959-80, was listed as agent for this client.) Legislative interest — "Radio Broadcasting to Cuba Act . . . S 602 . . . 22 U.S.C. 2871 *et seq.*" Lobbyist — Wiley, Johnson & Rein, 1776 K St. N.W., Washington, D.C. 20006. Filed 7/12/83. Legislative interest — ". . . opposition to HR 2453, S 602 and S 659 (radio broadcasting to Cuba)." Filed for self 7/25/83. Legislative interest — "Radio Broadcasting to Cuba Act . . . S 602 . . . 22 U.S.C. 2871 *et seq.*" Lobbyist — Steven F. Stockmeyer.

NATIONAL ASSOCIATION OF INSURANCE COMMISSIONERS, Brookfield, Wis. Lobbyist — Heron, Burchette, Ruckert & Rothwell, 1200 New Hampshire Ave. N.W., Washington, D.C. 20036. Filed 7/5/83. Legislative interest — Not specified.

NATIONAL ASSOCIATION OF MANUFACTURERS, Washington, D.C. Lobbyist — Crowell & Moring, 1100 Connecticut Ave. N.W., Washington, D.C. 20036. Filed 7/7/83. Legislative interest — "Legislation relating to contribution and indemnification for government contractors."

NATIONAL ASSOCIATION OF PHARMACEUTICAL MANUFACTURERS, 747 Third Ave., New York, N.Y. 10017. Filed for self 7/19/83. Legislative interest — "The association opposes the enactment of 'Patent Term Restoration' bills as introduced in Senate by Mathias and in House by Synar." Lobbyist — Thomas G. Goodwin, 1401 S. Edgewood St., Arlington, Va. 22204.

NATIONAL ASSOCIATION OF TRUCK STOP OPERATORS, 700 N. Fairfax St., Alexandria, Va. 22314. Filed for self 7/13/83. Legislative interest — "The interests are those that affect the truck stop industry including but not limited to, fuel and energy issues, trucking and highway regulation, agricultural and food service issues, labor issues and regulatory reform." Lobbyists — Richard P. Schweitzer, Thomas N. Willess.

NATIONAL CONFECTIONERS ASSOCIATION OF THE U.S., 7900 Westpark Drive, McLean, Va. 22102. Lobbyist — Richard T. O'Connell & Associates Inc., 3208 Traveler St., Fairfax, Va. 22030. Filed 7/14/83. Legislative interest — "General agricultural legislation with particular interest pertaining to sugar, milk, peanuts, and almonds; *i.e.*, S 788. Food safety legislation and other legislation relative to the food industry." Filed for self 7/14/83. Legislative interest — "General agricultural legislation with particular interest pertaining to sugar, milk, peanuts and almonds; *i.e.*, S 788. Food safety legislation and other legislation relative to the food industry." Lobbyist — Peter J. Pantuso.

NATIONAL HOSPICE ORGANIZATION, Arlington, Va. Lobbyist — Hogan & Hartson, 815 Connecticut Ave. N.W., Washington, D.C. 20006. Filed 7/11/83. Legislative interest — "Represent employer's interests with respect to proposed legislation to amend section 122 of the Tax Equity and Fiscal Responsibility Act of 1982."

NATIONAL NEWSPAPER ASSOCIATION, 1627 K St. N.W., Washington, D.C. 20006. Filed for self 7/31/83. Legislative interest — ". . . Legislation affecting the newspaper business ranging from First Amendment concerns to business interests." Lobbyist — Robert J. Brinkmann.

NATIONAL OFFICE MACHINE DEALERS ASSOCIATION, Wood Dale, Ill. Lobbyist — Williams & Jensen, 1101 Connecticut Ave. N.W., Washington, D.C. 20036. Filed 7/27/83. Legislative interest — "Enact legislation clarifying the rights of office machine dealers with respect to equipment manufacturers. (HR 1159)."

NATIONAL PASSENGER TRAFFIC ASSOCIATION, New York, N.Y. Lobbyist — Francis & McGinnis Associates Inc., 1050 Thomas Jefferson St. N.W., Washington, D.C. 20007. Filed 7/27/83. Legislative interest — Not specified.

NATIONAL PRINTING EQUIPMENT AND SUPPLY ASSOCIATION INC., 6849 Old Dominion Drive, McLean, Va. 22101. Filed for self 7/11/83. Legislative interest — "Model Product Liability . . . HR 2729, S 44."

NATIONAL SOLID WASTES MANAGEMENT ASSOCIATION, Washington, D.C. Lobbyist — Bayh, Tabbert & Capehart, 1575 I St. N.W., Washington, D.C. 20005. Filed 7/29/83. Legislative interest — "S 757 and related issues."

NATURAL GAS SUPPLY ASSOCIATION, Washington, D.C. Lobbyist — Communications Management Inc., 1925 N. Lynn St., Arlington, Va. 22209. Filed 7/8/83. Legislative interest — "Legislative interests are supporting enactment of legislation intended to remove controls on prices charged for all natural gas and opposing legislation intended to preserve such controls." Lobbyist — Pappanastos, Samford, Roberts & Blanchard, One Court Square, Montgomery, Ala. 36102. Filed 7/12/83. Legislative interest — "Natural gas pricing legislation."

PHARMACEUTICAL MANUFACTURERS ASSOCIATION, 1100 15th St. N.W., Washington, D.C. 20005. Filed for self 7/14/83. Legislative interest — "All matters relating to health care and, particularly, prescription medicines." Lobbyist — Alberta L. Henderson.

SOUTHERN ARIZONA WATER RESOURCES ASSOCIATION, Tucson, Ariz. Lobbyist — Bracy Williams & Co., 1000 Connecticut Ave. N.W., Washington, D.C. 20036. Filed 7/7/83. Legislative interest — "Legislation affecting the Central Arizona Project, HR 3132 (for)."

U.S. LEAGUE OF SAVING INSTITUTIONS, Washington, D.C. Lobbyist — Dave Evans Associates, 160 North Carolina Ave. S.E., Washington, D.C. 20003. Filed 7/26/83. Legislative interest — "Housing issues."

U.S. RECREATIONAL SKI ASSOCIATION, 1919 Pennsylvania Ave. N.W., Washington, D.C. 20006. Filed for self 7/8/83. Legislative interest — "Public lands, energy and consumer loans." Lobbyist — Nancy J. Ingalsbee.

VOLUME FOOTWEAR RETAILERS OF AMERICA, 1319 F St. N.W., Washington, D.C. 20004. Filed for self 7/21/83. Legislative interest — "Legislation regarding labor laws, revenue, trade and other legislation." Lobbyist — Peter T. Mangione.

WASHINGTON PSYCHIATRIC SOCIETY, Washington, D.C. Lobbyist — Chadbourne, Parke, Whiteside & Wolff, 1101 Vermont Ave. N.W., Washington, D.C. 20005. Filed 7/15/83. (Former U.S. Sen. Edmund S. Muskie, D-Maine, 1959-80, was listed among agents for this client.) Legislative interest — "... the Federal Health Benefits Plan Amendments of 1983 ... HR 656 and S 1004 ... chapter 89, Title 5 U.S. Code...." Lobbyist — Kendall & Associates, 1750 New York Ave. N.W., Washington, D.C. 20006. Filed 7/11/83. Legislative interest — "... mental health legislation."

WESTERN FUELS ASSOCIATION INC., Washington, D.C. Lobbyist — McCarthy, Sweeney & Harkaway, 1750 Pennsylvania Ave. N.W., Washington, D.C. 20006. Filed 7/11/83. (Former U.S. Rep. Robert C. Eckhardt, D-Texas, 1967-81, was listed as agent for this client.) Legislative interest — "Amendment to Sherman Antitrust Act relating to joint use of trackage and other similar legislative interests."

Miscellaneous

APPALACHIAN COMMUNITY SERVICE NETWORK, Washington, D.C. Lobbyist — Donald W. Whitehead, 1120 Connecticut Ave. N.W., Washington, D.C. 20036. Filed 7/1/83. Legislative interest — "Legislation affecting TV broadcasting, especially cable TV, and particularly S 1285."

J. ARMANDO BERMUDEZ, Santiago, Dominican Republic. Lobbyist — Thomas J. Scanlon, 3248 Prospect St. N.W., Washington, D.C. 20007. Filed 7/18/83. Legislative interest — "Legislative interests are to continue while the Congress is considering the Caribbean Basin Initiative, including S 544, HR 1992, HR 2819, H Res 246, HR 2769, HR 2249, and CBI provisions of HR 2973. Representation will be in behalf of a provision in the CBI legislation that would effect the duty-free entry of Caribbean rum."

BRIGHAM AND WOMEN'S HOSPITAL INC., Boston, Mass. Lobbyist — O'Neill and Haase, 1333 New Hampshire Ave.

N.W., Washington, D.C. 20036. Filed 7/13/83. Legislative interest — "Governmental Lease Financing Reform Act of 1983."

COMMUNITY REDEVELOPMENT AGENCY, Los Angeles, Calif. Lobbyist — Latham, Watkins & Hills, 1333 New Hampshire Ave. N.W., Washington, D.C. 20036. Filed 7/6/83. Legislative interest — "Opposition to HR 3110 as presently drafted."

COUNCIL OF MICHIGAN FOUNDATIONS, Grand Haven, Mich. Lobbyist — Plunkett, Cooney, Rutt, Watters, Stanczyk & Pedersen, 900 Marquette Building, Detroit, Mich. 48226. Filed 7/8/83. (Former U.S. Rep. William M. Brodhead, D-Mich., 1975-83, was listed as agent for this client.) Legislative interest — "HR 3043, Conable-Shannon foundation bill; in support of the bill."

EXECUTIVE COUNCIL ON FOREIGN DIPLOMATS, Washington, D.C. Lobbyist — Gray and Co., 3255 Grace St. N.W., Washington, D.C. 20007. Filed 7/7/83. Legislative interest — "Including but not limited to foreign policy issues."

LEGAL SERVICES CORP., 733 15th St. N.W., Washington, D.C. 20005. Filed for self 7/18/83. Legislative interest — "... appropriations bills of the House and Senate Subcommittee of State, Justice, Commerce, the Judiciary and related agencies containing funds for the Corporation ... bills of the House Judiciary Subcommittee on Courts, Civil Liberties and the Administration of Justice and the Senate Labor and Human Resources Subcommittee on Aging, Family and Human Services regarding reauthorization of the Corporation." Lobbyist — James O. E. Norell.

THE MIAMI CONSERVANCY DISTRICT, Dayton, Ohio. Lobbyist — Taft, Stettinius & Hollister, 21 Dupont Circle N.W., Washington, D.C. 20036. Filed 7/11/83. Legislative interest — "Advice on various legislative matters relating to the Rivers and Harbors Act and the Clean Water Act."

NORTHROP UNIVERSITY, Inglewood, Calif. Lobbyist — Dorsey & Whitney, 1800 M St. N.W., Washington, D.C. 20036. Filed 7/8/83. Legislative interest — "Amendments to Federal Property and Administrative Services Act of 1949, (63 Stat. 377, as amended), 40 U.S.C. section 471, *et seq.*, regarding surplus real property disposal."

August Registrations

Citizens' Groups

ALLIANCE AGAINST HANDGUNS, P.O. Box 75700, Washington, D.C. 20013. Filed 8/9/83. Legislative interest — "Develop national handgun registration requirements. HR 3407, for; HR 3415, con; HR 3714, con; HR 3716, con; HR 3454, for."

AMERICAN VETERANS OF WORLD WAR II, KOREA & VIETNAM (AMVETS), 4647 Forbes Blvd., Lanham, Md. 20706. Filed for self 8/8/83. Legislative interest — "Legislation affecting all veterans, their dependents in relation to employer, hospitalization, rehabilitation, pensions, disability compensation and housing; welfare of servicemen of the Armed Forces and their dependents; matters relating to national security, immigration and naturalization, the combating of subversive activities and the resolutions adopted by the National Convention and National Executive Committee." Lobbyists — David J. Passamaneck, Morgan S. Ruph, Peggy Seipel, Noel C. Woosley.

FEDERATION OF AIDS ORGANIZATIONS, New York, N.Y. Lobbyist — Gerald R. Connor, 6500 Wisconsin Ave., Chevy Chase, Md. 20815. Filed 8/17/83. Legislative interest — "Amendments to the Public Health Service Act; amendments to the Social Security Act; appropriations for the Department of Health and Human Services."

HALT INC., 201 Massachusetts Ave. N.E., Washington, D.C. 20002. Filed for self 8/19/83. Legislative interest — "Fair Tax Act of 1983, S 1421 ... FTC appropriations, HR 2970 ... National Child Support Enforcement Act, HR 3354...." Lobbyist — Thomas Mostowy.

MORAL MAJORITY, 499 S. Capitol St. S.W., Washington, D.C. 20003. Filed for self 8/25/83. Legislative interest — "Legislative interests include pro-family, anti-abortion, school prayer, tuition tax credits, pornography, nuclear freeze, national defense, civil rights and other issues supporting traditional Judeo-Christian values." Lobbyist — Richard B. Dingman.

NATIONAL CONSUMERS LEAGUE INC., 1522 K St. N.W., Washington, D.C. 20005. Filed for self 8/11/83. Legislative interest — "FTC reauthorization, CPSC reauthorization, HR 1034, product liability legislation." Lobbyist — Gus Avrakotos.

NATIONAL COUNCIL OF LA RAZA, 20 F St. N.W., Washington, D.C. 20001. Filed for self 8/16/83. Legislative interest — "Legislative interests include education, employment/training, immigration, housing and community development, civil rights, and other areas of importance to Hispanics. Specific legislative interests include against HR 1510 (Simpson-Mazzoli bill); in favor of HR 1036 (Community Renewal Employment Act); against HR 2682 (Bilingual Education Improvement Act)." Lobbyist — Martha M. Escutia.

NEGATIVE POPULATION GROWTH INC., 16 E. 42nd St., New York, N.Y. 10017. Filed for self 8/15/83. Legislative interest — "Immigration reform. We are in favor of the Simpson-Mazzoli bill, and would also favor a bill to reduce legal immigration." Lobbyist — Donald W. Mann, 60B Franklin St., Tenafly, N.J. 07670.

SIERRA CLUB, 530 Bush St., San Francisco, Calif. 94108. Filed for self 8/29/83. Legislative interest — "California Wilderness legislation, support HR 1437 and S 5, interests in offshore oil drilling legislation." Lobbyist — Bob Hattoy, 2410 Beverly Blvd., Los Angeles, Calif. 90057.

Corporations and Businesses

AETNA LIFE AND CASUALTY CO., Hartford, Conn. Lobbyist — Wexler, Reynolds, Harrison & Schule Inc., 1317 F St. N.W., Washington, D.C. 20004. Filed 8/24/83. Legislative interest — "The registrant seeks to represent the employer with respect to matters pertaining to taxation of insurance."

AIRBUS INDUSTRIE, Blagnac, France. Lobbyist — DGA International Inc., 1225 19th St. N.W., Washington, D.C. 20036. Filed 8/10/83. Legislative interest — "Legislation affecting U.S. trade policy (HR 2971, S 979, HR 2157, S 414, S 121, HR 1234), the U.S. Export-Import Bank legislation (S 869, HR 2842), and any other legislation affecting commercial aircraft manufacturing (HR 3110). . . ."

AMERICAN PETROFINA INC., P.O. Box 2159, Dallas, Texas 75221. Filed for self 8/31/83. Legislative interest — "Ad valorem duties on foreign repairs of U.S. ships . . . HR 2381, to amend the Tariff Act of 1930; HR 3156, Merchant Marine Act of 1983; HR 3330, to amend the Tariff Act of 1930; S 1038, Merchant Marine Act of 1983. . . ." Lobbyist — Gary W. Bruner.

APEX MARINE CORP., Lake Success, N.Y. Lobbyist — Kominers, Fort, Schlefer & Boyer, 1776 F St. N.W., Washington, D.C. 20006. Filed 8/3/83. Legislative interest — "Maritime authorization and appropriations bills, HR 2114, HR 3222 and HR 3329; against CDS amendment."

BABCOCK & BROWN INC., San Francisco, Calif. Lobbyist — Royer & Shacknai, 1747 Pennsylvania Ave. N.W., Washington, D.C. 20006. Filed 8/5/83. Legislative interest — "Governmental Lease Financing Reform Act of 1983 . . . HR 3110, S 1564."

THE BRAE CORP., San Francisco, Calif. Lobbyist — Van Ness, Feldman, Sutcliffe, Curtis & Levenberg, 1050 Thomas Jefferson St. N.W., Washington, D.C. 20007. Filed 8/30/83. Legislative interest — "Enactment of new legislation concerning boxcar compensation. . . ."

CABOT CORP., 125 High St., Boston, Mass. 02110. Filed for self 8/12/83. Legislative interest — "Energy, chemicals, strategic minerals and metals, trade issues including HR 3801 to amend the trade laws, and HR 1441, HR 2508, HR 2154 to amend the Natural Gas Policy Act." Lobbyist — Kenneth R. Adams, 1850 K St. N.W., Washington, D.C. 20006.

CBS INC., New York, N.Y. Lobbyist — McNair, Glenn, Konduros, Corley, Singletary, Porter & Dibble, 1155 15th St. N.W., Washington, D.C. 20005. Filed 8/29/83. Legislative interest — "Legislation with respect to financial interest rules and syndication rules and other communications matters."

CHEVRON U.S.A. INC., 1700 K St. N.W., Washington, D.C. 20006. Filed for self 8/16/83. Legislative interest — Not specified. Lobbyist — Lydia I. Beebe.

CHRISTIAN BJELLAND & CO., Millburn, N.J. Lobbyist — Chapman, Duff and Paul, 1825 I St. N.W., Washington, D.C. 20006. Filed 8/19/83. Legislative interest — "Revisions of trade remedy laws."

CROCKER NATIONAL BANK, San Francisco, Calif. Lobbyist — Morrison & Foerster, 1920 N St. N.W., Washington, D.C. 20036. Filed 8/10/83. Legislative interest — Not specified.

DIRECT MARKETING INSURANCE GROUP, Frazer, Pa. Lobbyist — Sutherland, Asbill & Brennan, 1666 K St. N.W., Washington, D.C. 20006. Filed 8/24/83. Legislative interest — "Interest in legislation which would restrict the dissemination of credit card account numbers and similar payment device numbers. In particular, HR 2885."

EMPLOYERS REINSURANCE CORP., Overland Park, Kan. Lobbyist — Preston, Thorgrimson, Ellis & Holman, 1735 New York Ave. N.W., Washington, D.C. 20006. Filed 8/16/83. Legislative interest — "Support legislative efforts (including S 916) to adjust federal timber sales contracts."

EQUITABLE LIFE ASSURANCE SOCIETY, Washington, D.C. Lobbyist — Cummings & Lockwood, 1090 Vermont Ave. N.W., Washington, D.C. 20005. Filed 8/7/83. Legislative interest — "Interest directed at taxation of life insurance companies."

FOOTHILLS PIPE LINE (YUKON) LTD., Calgary, Alberta, Canada. Lobbyist — Wexler, Reynolds, Harrison & Schule Inc., 1317 F St. N.W., Washington, D.C. 20004. Filed 8/24/83. Legislative interest — "The registrant seeks to represent the employer in matters regarding . . . the monitoring of natural gas legislation."

GENERAL ELECTRIC CO., Washington, D.C. Lobbyist — Richard C. White, 499 S. Capitol St., Washington, D.C. 20003. (Former U.S. rep., D-Texas, 1965-83.) Filed 8/22/83. Legislative interest — "Export Administration Act."

GENERAL MILLS INC., P.O. Box 1113, Minneapolis, Minn. Lobbyist — Swidler, Berlin & Strelow, 1000 Thomas Jefferson St. N.W., Washington, D.C. 20007. Filed 8/23/83. Legislative interest — "S 1440, amendments to the Lanham Act." Filed for self 8/3/83. Legislative interest — ". . . In general, issues relating to taxation, international trade, employee benefits and human resources." Lobbyist — Mark S. Gorman, 1200 New Hampshire Ave. N.W., Washington, D.C. 20036.

GETTY OIL CO., 3810 Wilshire Blvd., Los Angeles, Calif. 90010. Filed for self 8/12/83. Legislative interest — "Registrant has interest in legislation pertaining to public lands and coal issues." Lobbyist — Phillip W. Rivers.

GOVERNMENT EMPLOYEES INSURANCE CO., Washington, D.C. Lobbyist — Quinn, Racusin, Young & Delaney, 1000 Connecticut Ave. N.W., Washington, D.C. 20036. Filed 8/17/83. Legislative interest — "All legislation and statutes pertaining to the taxation of insurance companies. . . ."

HARTFORD FIRE INSURANCE CO., Hartford, Conn. Lobbyist — Theodore L. Jones, 3081 Teddy Drive, P.O. Box 65122, Baton Rouge, La. 70896. Filed 8/22/83. Legislative interest — "Legislation relating to the taxation of life insurance companies."

HBO & CO., Atlanta, Ga. Lobbyist — Charls E. Walker Associates Inc., 1730 Pennsylvania Ave. N.W., Washington, D.C. 20006. Filed 8/11/83. Legislative interest — "Legislative interests may concern issues arising out of the providing of services for hospitals."

HUFFY CORP., Dayton, Ohio. Lobbyist — Collier, Shannon, Rill & Scott, 1055 Thomas Jefferson St. N.W., Washington, D.C. 20007. Filed 8/29/83. Legislative interest — "Trade legislation including but not limited to HR 657."

ICELANDAIR, Reykjavik, Iceland. Lobbyist — Steven A. Martindale, 1000 Potomac St. N.W., Washington, D.C. 20007.

Filed 8/3/83. Legislative interest — "To engage in discussions with Congressmen, Senators and their staffs concerning the disposition of DC-10 airplanes currently held by the Export-Import Bank."

INGRAM CORP., New Orleans, La. Lobbyist — Kominers, Fort, Schlefer & Boyer, 1776 F St. N.W., Washington, D.C. 20006. Filed 8/3/83. Legislative interest — "HR 3110 and S 1564. . . ."

INTERNATIONAL TRADE SERVICES CORP., P.O. Box 2593, Washington, D.C. 20013. Filed for self 8/20/83. Legislative interest — "S 121 and similar bills in the House, involving creation of a U.S. Dept. of International Trade and Industry. . . ." Lobbyist — Harry Ganderson.

INVESTORS MORTGAGE INSURANCE CO., Boston, Mass. Lobbyist — Foley, Lardner, Hollabaugh & Jacobs, 1775 Pennsylvania Ave. N.W., Washington, D.C. 20006. Filed 8/9/83. Legislative interest — "Investors Mortgage Insurance Co. has authorized Foley, Lardner, Hollabaugh & Jacobs to comment with regard to those provisions in S 1609 and related or successor legislation which would allow bank and S&L holding companies to engage in insurance underwriting and brokerage."

LEXITEL CORP., Birmingham, Mich. Lobbyist — Bayh, Tabbert & Capehart, 1575 I St. N.W., Washington, D.C. 20005. Filed 8/3/83. Legislative interest — "HR 3621, S 1660 and other legislation related to universal telephone service."

M/A-COM INC., Rockville, Md. Lobbyist — George R. Moses, 1341 G St. N.W., Washington, D.C. 20005. Filed 8/25/83. Legislative interest — "Legislative and oversight activities affecting high-technology manufacturing and government contracting."

MANVILLE CORP., 1025 Connecticut Ave. N.W., Washington, D.C. 20036. Lobbyist — Wexler, Reynolds, Harrison & Schule Inc., 1317 F St. N.W., Washington, D.C. 20004. Filed 8/23/83. Legislative interest — "The registrant seeks to represent the employer with respect to matters pertaining to victim compensation of the asbestos industry." Lobbyist — Wilkinson, Barker, Knauer & Quinn, 1735 New York Ave. N.W., Washington, D.C. 20006. Filed 8/4/83. Legislative interest — "Legislation to compensate victims of asbestos-related diseases, in general; HR 3175, the Occupational Disease Compensation Act, and the proposed Asbestos Claimants Compensation Act, in particular." Filed for self 8/9/83. Legislative interest — "General legislative interests; energy conservation, specifically: HR 1, S 1338." Lobbyist — Joseph L. Lach.

MARRIOTT CORP., Washington, D.C. Lobbyist — O'Neill and Haase, 1333 New Hampshire Ave. N.W., Washington, D.C. 20036. Filed 8/11/83. Legislative interest — "Legislation affecting the tax code's depreciation period for buildings."

MASTERCARD INTERNATIONAL INC., New York, N.Y. Lobbyist — Morrison & Foerster, 1920 N St. N.W., Washington, D.C. 20036. Filed 8/26/83. Legislative interest — "The legislative interests are related to credit card fraud, and include specifically House of Representatives Bills 2885, 3570, 3181 and 3622. The titles of these bills are, respectively, Credit Card Protection Act, Counterfeit Access Device and Computer Fraud Act of 1983, Credit Card Counterfeiting and Fraud Act of 1983 and Credit Card Protection Act. The employer is in favor of such bills."

MERCHANTS GRAIN AND TRANSPORTATION INC., St. Louis, Mo. Lobbyist — Don Wallace Associates Inc., 232 E. Capitol St., Washington, D.C. 20003. Filed 8/19/83. Legislative interest — "Legislation related to agricultural commodities; user fees; and inland waterway transportation systems."

PETRO-LEWIS CORP., Denver, Colo. Lobbyist — Baker & Botts, 1701 Pennsylvania Ave. N.W., Washington, D.C. 20006. Filed 8/4/83. Legislative interest — "Tax legislation affecting percentage depletion for crude oil and natural gas, including but not limited to S 1661."

PIPER AIRCRAFT CORP., 3806 Maryland St., Alexandria, Va. 22309. Filed for self 8/5/83. Legislative interest — "All legislation pertaining to or affecting the business interest of Piper Aircraft Corp., such as aviation legislation, Defense Authorization Act (HR 2969, S 675), authorization for aircraft procurement and tax measures that may affect our business." Lobbyist — James I. Granger.

PITTSBURGH CORNING CORP., Pittsburgh, Pa. Lobbyist — Collier, Shannon, Rill & Scott, 1055 Thomas Jefferson St.

N.W., Washington, D.C. 20007. Filed 8/19/83. Legislative interest — "Legislation regarding compensation for asbestos-related diseases, including HR 3175."

PUGET SOUND POWER & LIGHT CO., Bellevue, Wash. Lobbyist — O'Neill and Haase, 1333 New Hampshire Ave. N.W., Washington, D.C. 20036. Filed 8/11/83. Legislative interest — "S 1701, a bill providing certain directives to the Bonneville Power Administration."

REDFIELD LAND CO., Reno, Nev. Lobbyist — Jones, Jones, Bell, Close & Brown, 1110 Vermont Ave. N.W., Washington, D.C. 20005. Filed 8/8/83. Legislative interest — "HR 1428, which would authorize the land transfer of Redfield Estate land to the U.S. Forest Service to offset accumulated estate tax liabilities."

ROSENBERG REAL ESTATE EQUITY FUND INC., San Francisco, Calif. Lobbyist — Morrison & Foerster, 1920 N St. N.W., Washington, D.C. 20036. Filed 8/10/83. Legislative interest — "The legislative interests are tax-related, and include specifically Senate Bill 1815. The Employer is in favor of such bill."

SOCIETE NATIONALE D'ETUDE ET DE CONSTRUCTION DE MOTEURS D'AVIATION, Paris, France. Lobbyist — DGA International Inc., 1225 19th St. N.W., Washington, D.C. 20036. Filed 8/10/83. Legislative interest — "Legislation affecting U.S. Department of Defense authorization and appropriations. In the immediate period the 1983 Defense Authorization bill and the 1983 Defense Appropriation bill are of specific interest. Also any other legislation that would affect U.S. Defense Department procurement decisions related to large military aircraft engines (*i.e.*, engines for tankers, transport, surveillance, or other similar type aircraft). We plan to monitor current legislation of the type described above and plan to take positions that would support legislation that calls for continuing utilization by the U.S. Air Force of military engines produced by our foreign principal."

SOFREAVIA, Paris, France. Lobbyist — DGA International Inc., 1225 19th St. N.W., Washington, D.C. 20036. Filed 8/10/83. Legislative interest — "Legislation affecting U.S. trade policy (HR 2971, S 979, HR 2157, S 414, S 121, HR 1234), the U.S. Export Import Bank legislation (S 869, HR 2842) and any other legislation affecting commercial aircraft manufacturing (HR 3110). . . ."

TELEPHONE AND DATA SYSTEMS INC., Chicago, Ill. Lobbyist — Taggart & Associates, 1015 15th St. N.W., Washington, D.C. 20005. Filed 8/19/83. Legislative interest — "Rural telecommunications legislation."

UNION OIL COMPANY OF CALIFORNIA, 461 S. Boylston St., Los Angeles, Calif. 90017. Filed for self 8/12/83. Legislative interest — Not specified. Lobbyist — Milly S. Blumel, 1050 Connecticut Ave. N.W., Washington, D.C. 20036.

UNION PACIFIC CORP., New York, N.Y. Lobbyist — Deloitte, Haskins & Sells, 655 15th St. N.W., Washington, D.C. 20005. Filed 8/10/83. Legislative interest — "Interest is in tax legislation which might have an impact on the business of employer."

U.S. CAPITAL CORP., Columbia, S.C. Lobbyist — Pappanastos, Samford, Roberts & Blanchard, One Court Square, Montgomery, Ala. 36102. Filed 8/18/83. Legislative interest — "Coastal Barrier Resources System legislation."

U.S. WEST INC., Washington, D.C. Lobbyist — Wilkinson, Barker, Knauer & Quinn, 1735 New York Ave. N.W., Washington, D.C. 20036. Filed 8/11/83. Legislative interest — "Following HR 3621 to amend the Communications Act of 1934 to assure universal telephone service within the U.S. and for other purposes; S 1660 relating to preservation of universal telephone service and S 66, the Cable Telecommunications Act of 1983."

VENABLE, BAETJER AND HOWARD, 1800 Mercantile Bank and Trust Building, Baltimore, Md. 21201. Filed for self 8/16/83. Legislative interest — ". . .to defeat HR 3110 and S 1564. . . ." Lobbyist — Jaques T. Schlenger.

VULCAN FOUNDRY INC., Denham Springs, La. Lobbyist — Adduci, Dinan and Mastriani, 1140 Connecticut Ave. N.W., Washington, D.C. 20036. Filed 8/3/83. Legislative interest — "In the House we propose amendment to HR 1986 (to amend the Tariff Act of 1930 regarding Country of marking requirements for certain imported pipe and pipe fitting) to include material relating to marking of construction castings. These matters are covered

generally by 19 U.S.C. section 1304...."

WEST INDIES INVESTMENT CO., Christiansted, U.S. Virgin Islands. Lobbyist — W. J. Chandler Associates, 1717 Massachusetts Ave. N.W., Washington, D.C. 20036. Filed 8/4/83. Legislative interest — "Department of the Interior and related agencies appropriation bill, 1984; HR 3363; for such legislation."

WOODSTREAM CORP., Lititz, Pa. Lobbyist — Sutherland, Asbill & Brennan, 1666 K St. N.W., Washington, D.C. 20006. Filed 8/5/83. Legislative interest — "General legislative interest in HR 2163 with regard to a manufacturer's Excise tax."

International Relations

GOVERNMENT OF THE REPUBLIC OF CHINA, Taipei, Republic of China. Lobbyist — Whitman & Ransom, 1333 New Hampshire Ave. N.W., Washington, D.C. 20036. Filed 8/9/83. Legislative interest — "Support of legislation relating to the continued membership of the Republic of China in the Asian Development Bank, specifically S Res 137 and similar resolutions."

HASHEMITE KINGDOM OF JORDAN, Amman, Jordan. Lobbyist — Neill & Co. Inc., 1100 17th St. N.W., Washington, D.C. 20036. Filed 8/11/83. Legislative interest — "Promoting the passage of the administration's military and economic assistance program insofar as it may relate to the Hashemite Kingdom of Jordan, including the foreign assistance authorization and appropriations bills."

LE DIRECTEUR DES AFFAIRES INTERNATIONALES DE LA DELEGATION GENERALE POUR L'ARMEMENT (FRENCH MINISTRY OF DEFENSE), Paris, France. Lobbyist — DGA International Inc., 1225 19th St. N.W., Washington, D.C. 20036. Filed 8/10/83. Legislative interest — "Department of Defense authorization and appropriations bills for FY 1983...."

Labor Groups

GRAPHIC COMMUNICATIONS INTERNATIONAL UNION, AFL-CIO, 1900 L St. N.W., Washington, D.C. 20036. Filed for self 8/22/83. Legislative interest — "General interest on all tax, pension and health, unemployment, and workers compensation legislation: a) manufacturing clause of the U.S. Copyright Act, S 1880 - HR 3940 for such bill; Federal Contract Debarment Bill, HR 1743, for such bill; Plant Closure Bill, HR 2487, for such bill." Lobbyist — John M. Greer.

State and Local Governments

CITIES FOR RESPONSIBLE CABLE POLICY, Austin, Texas. Lobbyist — Geary, Stahl & Spencer, 2800 One Main Place, Dallas, Texas 75250. Filed 8/29/83. Legislative interest — "Legislation affecting municipal interests in cable television, including S 66."

MARYLAND PEOPLE'S COUNSEL, Baltimore, Md. Lobbyist — Swidler, Berlin & Strelow, 1000 Thomas Jefferson St. N.W., Washington, D.C. 20007. Filed 8/8/83. Legislative interest —"... securing legislative reforms to the Natural Gas Policy Act of 1978, 15 U.S.C. section 3301 *et seq.*, that are fair to residential consumers of natural gas ... Support HR 2154 and oppose all other bills concerning natural gas, including S 615 and S 1715."

SOUTH CAROLINA PUBLIC SERVICE AUTHORITY, Moncks Corner, S.C. Lobbyist — Swidler, Berlin & Strelow, 1000 Thomas Jefferson St. N.W., Washington, D.C. 20007. Filed 8/5/83. Legislative interest — "The South Carolina Public Service Authority supports the enactment of the Santee Cooper Earthquake Protection Amendment to the Supplemental Appropriation Act of 1983, HR 3069, PL 98-63."

Trade Associations

AMERICAN ACADEMY OF PEDIATRICS, Arlington, Va. Lobbyist — Pierson, Ball & Dowd, 1200 18th St. N.W., Washington, D.C. 20036. Filed 8/17/83. Legislative interest — "Legislation of interest to pediatricians, including childhood immunization and legislation affecting seriously ill newborns."

AMERICAN ASSOCIATION OF HOMES FOR THE AGING, 1050 17th St. N.W., Washington, D.C. 20036. Filed for self 8/22/83. Legislative interest — "Federal health and housing programs serving the elderly and other issues of concern to the aging." Lobbyist — Vitina Biondo.

AMERICAN COUNCIL OF LIFE INSURANCE, 1850 K St. N.W., Washington, D.C. 20006. Filed for self 8/19/83. Legislative interest — "Proposed legislation which affects the life insurance industry; specifically HR 100, S 372." Lobbyist — Anthony Valanzano.

AMERICAN INSTITUTE OF MERCHANT SHIPPING, Washington, D.C. Lobbyist — Keller and Heckman, 1150 17th St. N.W., Washington, D.C. 20036. Filed 8/9/83. Legislative interest — "General interests relate to statutory requirements for cargo vessels. Specific interests relate to Title III, part II of the Communications Act of 1934 (47 U.S.C. sections 351-362) which governs certain radio communications requirements."

AMERICAN MINING CONGRESS, 1920 N St. N.W., Washington, D.C. 20036. Filed for self 8/17/83. Legislative interest — "Measures affecting mining such as income taxation, social security, public lands, monetary policy, mine safety, stockpiling, environmental quality control, etc." Lobbyist — Lisa A. Vehmas.

CHAMBER OF COMMERCE OF THE UNITED STATES, 1615 H St. N.W., Washington, D.C. 20062. Filed for self 8/4/83. Legislative interest — Not specified. Lobbyist — Ellen B. Brown.

CONSEJO NACIONAL DE COMMERCIO EXTERIOR DEL NORESTE A.C., Monterrey, Mexico. Lobbyist — Adduci, Dinan & Mastriani, 1140 Connecticut Ave. N.W., Washington, D.C. 20036. Filed 8/5/83. Legislative interest — "Support of extension of Generalized System of Preferences. Submission of testimony to House Ways and Means Trade Subcommittee on proposed 'Generalized System of Preferences Renewal Act of 1983.' "

CONTRACT CARRIAGE COALITION, Washington, D.C. Lobbyist — Sutherland, Asbill & Brennan, 1666 K St. N.W., Washington, D.C. 20006. Filed 8/5/83. Legislative interest — "Legislation relating to natural gas."

DEALER BANK ASSOCIATION, 1800 K St. N.W., Washington, D.C. 20006. Filed for self 8/9/83. Legislative interest — "Legislative interests may concern issues relating to corporate powers of dealer banks as they relate to state and local government financing." Lobbyists — Richard L. DeCair, Richard K. Liggitt.

EDISON ELECTRIC INSTITUTE, Washington, D.C. Lobbyist — LeBoeuf, Lamb, Leiby & MacRae, 1333 New Hampshire Ave. N.W., Washington, D.C. 20036. Filed 8/3/83. Legislative interest — "Support of enabling and funding legislation related to the Clinch River Breeder Reactor."

INSURANCE ASSOCIATION OF CONNECTICUT, Hartford, Conn. Lobbyist — Gibson, Dunn & Crutcher, 1776 G St. N.W., Washington, D.C. 20006. Filed 8/31/83. Legislative interest — "The general purpose is to represent the interests of IAC relating to legislation dealing with women's equity and sex discrimination in employee benefits ... The Fair Insurance Practices Act (S 372/HR 100) ... The Economic Equity Act of 1983 (S 888) ... The Retirement Equity Act of 1983 (S 19)."

INTERNATIONAL AIRFORWARDER AND AGENTS ASSOCIATION, Rockville Center, N.Y. Lobbyist — Robert Henri Binder, 1150 Connecticut Ave. N.W., Washington, D.C. 20036. Filed 8/15/83. Legislative interest — "General interest in legislation which positively or negatively affects international airforwarders and agents."

INTERNATIONAL ANTICOUNTERFEITING COALITION, New York, N.Y. Lobbyist — Swidler, Berlin & Strelow, 1000 Thomas Jefferson St. N.W., Washington, D.C. 20007. Filed 8/23/83. Legislative interest — "S 875 and HR 2447,

the Trademark Counterfeiting Act of 1983."

INTERNATIONAL ASSOCIATION OF ICE CREAM MANUFACTURERS/MILK INDUSTRY FOUNDATION, 888 16th St. N.W., Washington, D.C. 20006. Filed for self 8/11/83. Legislative interest — Not specified. Lobbyist — Constance D. Broadstone. Filed for self 8/8/83. Legislative interest — Not specified. Lobbyist — Dawn M. Brydon.

LAND MOBILE COMMUNICATIONS COUNCIL, Washington, D.C. Lobbyist — Keller & Heckman, 1150 17th St. N.W., Washington, D.C. 20036. Filed 8/17/83. Legislative interest — "Legislation affecting the land mobile communications industry, including bills dealing with allocating spectrum, deployment of new technologies, bypass access charges, and matters relating to the Communications Act of 1934."

THE MARYLAND SAVINGS SHARE INSURANCE CORP., Baltimore, Md. Lobbyist — Quinn, Racusin, Young & Delaney, 1000 Connecticut Ave. N.W., Washington, D.C. 20036. Filed 8/17/83. Legislative interest — ". . . Internal Revenue Code section 501(c). . . ."

NATIONAL ASSOCIATION OF MANUFACTURERS, 1776 F St. N.W., Washington, D.C. 20006. Filed for self 8/8/83. Legislative interest — "Legislation affecting domestic and international tax treatment of American manufacturers, and related fiscal and monetary policy issues." Lobbyist — Robert A. Ragland.

NATIONAL ASSOCIATION OF ROYALTY OWNERS INC., Ada, Okla. Lobbyist — David P. Stang, 1629 K St. N.W., Washington, D.C. 20006. Filed 8/30/83. Legislative interest — "Issues relating to energy and tax legislation."

NATIONAL ASSOCIATION OF STATE UTILITY CONSUMER ADVOCATES, Washington, D.C. Lobbyist — Swidler, Berlin & Strelow, 1000 Thomas Jefferson St. N.W., Washington, D.C. 20007. Filed 8/8/83. Legislative interest — ". . . securing legislative reforms to the Natural Gas Policy Act of 1978, 15 U.S.C. section 3301 *et seq.*, that are fair to residential consumers of natural gas . . . support HR 2154 and oppose all other bills concerning natural gas, including S 615 and S 1715."

NATIONAL CABLE TELEVISION ASSOCIATION, Washington, D.C. Lobbyist — Wexler, Reynolds, Harrison & Schule Inc., 1317 F St. N.W., Washington, D.C. 20004. Filed 8/24/83. Legislative interest — "The registrant seeks to represent the employer with respect to legislation of cable telecommunications including S 66."

NATIONAL COUNCIL OF HEALTH CENTERS, 2600 Virginia Ave. N.W., Washington, D.C. 20037. Filed for self 8/5/83. Legislative interest — "Interest in legislation related to long-term care and the nursing home industry." Lobbyist — Gary C. Hong.

NATIONAL EMPLOYEE BENEFITS INSTITUTE, Washington, D.C. Lobbyist — Reinhart, Boerner, Van Deuren, Norris & Rieselbach, 111 E. Wisconsin Ave., Milwaukee, Wis. 53202. Filed 8/5/83. Legislative interest — "Legislation and regulations affecting deferred compensation and employee fringe benefits generally. Specifically, Retirement Equity Act of 1983 (S 19), Economy Equity Act (S 888) and Economic Equity Act of 1983 (HR 2090)."

NATIONAL MULTIFAMILY HOUSING FINANCE ASSOCIATION, Washington, D.C. Lobbyist — Dunnells, Duvall, Bennett & Porter, 1220 19th St. N.W., Washington, D.C. 20036. Filed 8/26/83. Legislative interest — "Authorization and appropriations for the Department of HUD (HR 1 and Senate Housing and Community Development Act of 1983)."

NATIONAL SHORTHAND REPORTERS ASSOCIATION, Vienna, Va. Lobbyist — Swidler, Berlin & Strelow, 1000 Thomas Jefferson St. N.W., Washington, D.C. 20007. Filed 8/23/83. Legislative interest — "Legislative oversight of court system."

SECURITIES INDUSTRIES ASSOCIATION, Washington, D.C. Lobbyist — Pierson, Ball & Dowd, 1200 18th St. N.W., Washington, D.C. 20036. Filed 8/17/83. Legislative interest — Not specified.

THE SOCIETY OF THE PLASTICS INDUSTRY, 355 Lexington Ave., New York, N.Y. 10017. Filed for self 8/16/83. Legislative interest — "Any legislation affecting the well-being of the plastics industry, including that affecting petrochemical feed-

stocks workplace and product health and safety, international trade, transportation, and the economy." Lobbyist — Marina L. Brockmann, 605 14th St. N.W., Washington, D.C. 20005.

UTILITIES TELECOMMUNICATIONS COUNCIL, Washington, D.C. Lobbyist — Keller & Heckman, 1150 17th St. N.W., Washington, D.C. 20036. Filed for self 8/17/83. Legislative interest — "Legislation affecting telecommunications, including bills dealing with allocating spectrum, deployment of new technologies, bypass, regulating common carriers, access charges, and matters relating to the Communications Act of 1934."

WESTERN FUELS ASSOCIATION INC., 1225 19th St. N.W., Washington, D.C. 20036. Filed 8/15/83. Legislative interest — "Supporting coal slurry legislation (HR 1010, S 267); modifications to the Staggers Act through Rahall Bill (HR 2584) and Ford Bills (S 1081 and S 1082) and limitations on railroad monopoly pricing powers through other potential legislation; Federal coal leasing programs; re-enactment of the Clean Air Act with modifications, including a moderate program of Acid Rain abatement; Clean Water Act." Lobbyist — Orren Beaty Jr.

Miscellaneous

THE ALTMAN FOUNDATION, New York, N.Y. Lobbyist — Ernest Wittenberg Associates Inc., 1616 H St. N.W., Washington, D.C. 20006. Filed 8/9/83. Legislative interest — "Amendment to section 4943 of the Internal Revenue Code of 1954."

AMERICAN RED CROSS RETIREMENT SYSTEM, Alexandria, Va. Lobbyist — Stroock & Stroock & Lavan, 1150 17th St. N.W., Washington, D.C. 20036. Filed 8/12/83. Legislative interest — "Generally following S 1227 concerning premiums paid to the Pension Benefit Guaranty Corp."

THE CHELONIA INSTITUTE, Arlington, Va. Lobbyist — W. J. Chandler Associates, 1717 Massachusetts Ave. N.W., Washington, D.C. 20036. Filed 8/4/83. Legislative interest — "Department of the Interior and related agencies appropriation bill, 1984; HR 3363; for such legislation."

THE DAY TRUST, New Haven, Conn. Lobbyist — Pierson, Ball & Dowd, 1200 18th St. N.W., Washington, D.C. 20036. Filed 8/5/83. Legislative interest — "In support of HR 1649."

FEDERAL NATIONAL MORTGAGE ASSOCIATION, 3900 Wisconsin Ave. N.W., Washington, D.C. 20016. Filed for self 8/22/83. Legislative interest — "Legislation re residential mortgages, housing and various tax legislation. Specifically, HR 1, S 1147, HR 3357, S 1821." Lobbyist — William R. Maloni, William L. Warfield.

GARRISON DIVERSION CONSERVANCY DISTRICT, Garrison, N.D. Lobbyist — Christopher U. Sylvester, 1831 Briar Ridge Court, McLean, Va. 22101. Filed 8/22/83. Legislative interest — "Further the prospects of the Garrison Diversion Irrigation Unit, specifically in the area of the Energy and Water Development Appropriations Bills."

THE GEORGE WASHINGTON UNIVERSITY STUDENT ASSOCIATION, 800 21st St. N.W., Washington, D.C. 20052. Filed for self 8/9/83. Legislative interest — Not specified.

OREGON INLET COMMISSION, Manteo, N.C. Lobbyist — Don Wallace Associates Inc., 232 E. Capitol St., Washington, D.C. 20003. Filed 8/4/83. Legislative interest — "HR 3288 and S 1471."

SEAMEN'S CHURCH INSTITUTE, 15 State St., New York, N.Y. 10004. Filed for self 8/4/83. Legislative interest — "The welfare and rights of foreign seafarers in United States ports." Lobbyist — Earl Kooperhamp, 99 Claremont Ave., New York, N.Y. 10027. Filed for self 8/4/83. Legislative interest — "The welfare and rights of foreign seafarers in United States ports." Lobbyist — Paul K. Chapman.

RONALD G. SILLS, c/o 38832-066, A-1, F.C.I. Box 7000, Texarkana, Texas 75501. Filed for self 8/30/83. Legislative interest — "All legislation dealing with the military and federal criminal justice system, including prisons, parole and criminally punitive statutes."

JON R. WEINSTEIN, 9 Wildwood Gardens, Port Washington, N.Y. 11050. Filed for self 8/3/83. Legislative interest — "...trade, tariffs, plastic safety, defense appropriations... Export Administration Act, Tariff Act, Defense Appropriations Act."

September Registrations

Citizens' Groups

ALEUTIAN/PRIBILOF ISLANDS ASSOCIATION INC., Anchorage, Alaska. Lobbyist — Cook, Purcell, Henderson & Zorack, 1015 18th St. N.W., Washington, D.C. 20036. Filed 9/22/83. Legislative interest — "...all legislation affecting welfare of Aleut people. Specific Interest — legislation to implement recommendations of Commission on Wartime Relocation and Internment of civilians."

AMERICAN AUTOMOBILE ASSOCIATION, POTOMAC DIVISION, 8111 Gatehouse Road, Falls Church, Va. 22047. Filed for self 9/19/83. Legislative interest — Not specified. Lobbyists — Thomas R. Crosby Jr., Norman E. Grimm Jr., Mary Anne Reynolds.

COMMUNITY ART ALLIANCE INC., 1801 Polk St., P.O. Box 1675, Hollywood, Fla. 33022. Filed for self 9/13/83. Legislative interest — "... arts, charitable organizations bills: HR 1285, HR 1315, S 337, S 427, HR 1773, S 825, S 722. Fight against budget cuts for Arts in Education and other arts related items. For all of the above bills." Lobbyist — Wade J. Adams, 4111 Stirling Road, Ft. Lauderdale, Fla. 33314.

JAPANESE AMERICAN CITIZENS LEAGUE, Washington, D.C. Lobbyist — Wise & Wrenn Inc., 2600 Virginia Ave. N.W., Washington, D.C. 20037. Filed 9/22/83. Legislative interest — "... legislation concerning redress for Japanese American citizens and resident aliens interned during World War II...."

MIGRANT LEGAL ACTION PROGRAM INC., 806 15th St. N.W., Washington, D.C. 20005. Filed for self 9/9/83. Legislative interest — "... legislation dealing with the admission of alien laborers for temporary employment in agriculture ... Simpson-Mazzoli Immigration Reform and Control Act, S 529 and HR 1510, particularly section 211 dealing with temporary foreign laborers; opposed to any provisions expanding temporary farm labor program. HR 2909, Legal Services Corporation Amendments of 1983, particularly that section dealing with representation of aliens holding H-2 visas; in favor of representation of H-2 workers by legal services attorneys." Lobbyist — H. Michael Semler.

NATIONAL WOMEN'S POLITICAL CAUCUS, 1411 K St. N.W., Washington, D.C. 20005. Filed for self 9/29/83. Legislative interest — "Abortion: opposed to all bills and amendments to restrict abortion. Education: support Title IX Resolution HR 268, S 478. Budget: oppose block grants and cuts in domestic spending for FY83. Economic Equity: support Economic Equity Act S 888, HR 3117 and related bills HR 100, S 2204. Equal Rights Amendment: support. Civil Rights: support HR 2230. Child Care: support S 1531, HR 1991. Child Support Enforcement: support HR 2374, S 888. Social Security: support HR 2738, HR 2744, HR 2739, S 3...." Lobbyists — Linda D. Anderson, Catherine East.

Corporations and Businesses

AETNA LIFE AND CASUALTY INSURANCE CO., Hartford, Conn. Lobbyist — Robert E. Juliano Associates, 1101 New Hampshire Ave. N.W., Washington, D.C. 20037. Filed 9/30/83. Legislative interest — Not specified.

AIR QUALITY RESEARCH INC., Berkeley, Calif. Lobbyist — D.C. Associates Inc., 402 Third St. S.E., Washington, D.C. 20003. Filed 9/26/83. Legislative interest — "All legislation, appropriation, and budget measures affecting indoor air quality matters, including HR 2533 and HR 3819."

ALASKA LUMBER AND PULP CO., Sitka, Alaska. Lobbyist — C. Deming Cowles, 1050 Thomas Jefferson St. N.W., Washington, D.C. 20007. Filed 9/27/83. Legislative interest — "Monitor clean water legislation for applicability to both mills' water discharges."

ALLIED CORP., P.O. Box 3000-R, Morristown, N.J. 07960. Filed for self 9/28/83. Legislative interest — "Energy, employee relations, taxes, environmental and other matters...." Lobbyist — Ken W. Cole, 1150 Connecticut Ave. N.W., Washington, D.C. 20036.

ALLIS-CHALMERS CORP., Washington, D.C. Lobbyist — O'Connor & Hannan, 1919 Pennsylvania Ave. N.W., Washington, D.C. 20006. Filed 9/30/83. Legislative interest — "Advice and assistance on legislative efforts to amend S 1564, the Governmental Lease Financing Reform Act of 1983."

AMERADA HESS CORP., New York, N.Y. Lobbyist — Akin, Gump, Strauss, Hauer & Feld, 1333 New Hampshire Ave. N.W., Washington, D.C. 20036. Filed 9/21/83. Legislative interest — "Hearings and any legislation relating to national energy policy, including bills providing for the recapture of certain tax losses through the use of foreign tax credits, S 1584 and HR 3140."

AMERICAN BROADCASTING CO., Washington, D.C. Lobbyist — Patton, Boggs & Blow, 2250 M St. N.W., Washington, D.C. 20037. Filed 9/30/83. Legislative interest — "... HR 2250 and S 1707, the Competition in Television Production Act, providing a moratorium on changes to the Federal Communications Commission rules regarding television syndication. Opposed."

AMERICAN EXPRESS CO., American Express Plaza, New York, N.Y. 10004. Filed for self 9/20/83. Legislative interest — Not specified. Lobbyist — Denise G. Ferguson, 1700 K St. N.W., Washington, D.C. 20006.

AMERICAN INCOME LIFE INSURANCE CO., Waco, Texas. Lobbyist — David P. Stang, 1629 K St. N.W., Washington, D.C. 20006. Filed 9/23/83. Legislative interest — "Life Insurance Tax Act of 1983."

AMERICAN PETROFINA INC., Dallas, Texas. Lobbyist — Bowman, Conner, Touhey & Petrillo, 2820 Pennsylvania Ave. N.W., Washington, D.C. 20007. Filed 9/9/83. Legislative interest — "Ad valorem duties on foreign repairs of U.S. ships ... HR 2381, to amend the Tariff Act of 1930; HR 3156, Merchant Marine Act of 1983; HR 3330, to amend the Tariff Act of 1930; S 1038, Merchant Marine Act of 1983 ... 19 U.S.C., section 1466 ... for all such bills...."

ARCO SOLAR INC., Woodland Hills, Calif. Lobbyist — Chadbourne, Parke, Whiteside & Wolff, 1101 Vermont Ave. N.W., Washington, D.C. 20005. Filed 9/10/83. Legislative interest — "Increase in, and extension of, the tax credits for photovoltaics."

BABCOCK & BROWN, San Francisco, Calif. Lobbyist — Royer & Shacknai, 1747 Pennsylvania Ave. N.W., Washington, D.C. 20006. Filed 9/14/83. Legislative interest — "Governmental Lease Financing Reform Act of 1983; HR 3110; S 1654; 26 U.S.C. Section 168; opposing certain provisions of both bills."

BOND AND LAXALT INC., 813 Maryland Ave. N.E., Washington, D.C. 20002. Filed for self 9/29/83. Legislative interest — "Financial Interest and Syndication Rule, Video Copyright on behalf of the Motion Picture Association of America." Lobbyist — Michelle Laxalt.

CARR-GOTTSTEIN PROPERTIES INC., Anchorage, Alaska. Lobbyist — Robertson, Monagle, Eastaugh & Bradley, 210 Ferry Way, Juneau, Alaska 99801. Filed 9/26/83. Legislative interest — "Legislation affecting the status of the Department of Education Housing Loan Program."

CBS INC., New York, N.Y. Lobbyist — John S. Erthein & Associates Inc., 1800 M St. N.W., Washington, D.C. 20036. Filed 9/28/83. Legislative interest — "... opposition to HR 2250 (Moratorium on changes to FCC financial interests, syndication and prime time access rules.)" Lobbyist — Charls E. Walker Associates Inc., 1730 Pennsylvania Ave. N.W., Washington, D.C. 20006. Filed 9/7/83. Legislative interest — "... may concern issues which may arise out of proposed changes in network television financial interest rules."

JERRY CHAMBERS OIL PRODUCER, Chicago, Ill. Lobbyist — Holme, Roberts & Owen, 1700 Broadway, Denver, Colo. 80290. Filed 9/6/83. Legislative interest — "Seeking amendment and passage of S 1661, 98th Cong. 1st Sess., relating to

availability of percentage depletion allowance for oil produced using secondary and tertiary recovery methods...."

COMBINED INSURANCE CO., Northbrook, Ill. Lobbyist — Daley and George, 111 W. Washington St., Chicago, Ill. 60602. Filed 9/30/83. Legislative interest — "Consideration of Federal Income Tax treatment of life insurance companies by Subcommittee of Ways and Means...."

CONTROL DATA CORP., Minneapolis, Minn. Filed for self 9/8/83. Legislative interest — Not specified. Lobbyist — Barbara J. Washburn, 1201 Pennsylvania Ave. N.W., Washington, D.C. 20004.

COOPERATIVE POWER ASSOCIATION, 14615 Lone Oak Road, Eden Prairie, Minn. 55344. Filed for self 9/6/83. Legislative interest — "Rural electric cooperative concerns: Rural Electrification Act; Environmental laws." Lobbyist — Robert P. Ambrose.

DAVIS & McLEOD, Washington, D.C. Lobbyist — Corporate Consulting Services Inc., P.O. Box 2768, Key Largo, Fla. 33037. Filed 9/16/83. (Former U.S. Rep. L. A. "Skip" Bafalis, R-Fla., 1973-83, was listed as agent for this client.) Legislative interest — "Unemployment compensation relating to H-2 workers."

DOW CHEMICAL CO., Midland, Mich. Lobbyist — Akin, Gump, Strauss, Hauer & Feld, 1333 New Hampshire Ave. N.W., Washington, D.C. 20036. Filed 9/22/83. Legislative interest — "Hearings and any legislation relating to the tax treatment of foreign sales corporations including the 'Foreign Sales Corporation Act of 1983,' S 1804 and HR 3810."

FEDERAL HOME LIFE INSURANCE CO., Battle Creek, Mich. Lobbyist — Miller, Canfield, Paddock and Stone, 2555 M St. N.W., Washington, D.C. 20037. Filed 9/29/83. Legislative interest — "Taxation of life insurance companies...."

SAMUEL GARY OIL PRODUCER INC., Englewood, Colo. Lobbyist — Holme, Roberts & Owen, 1700 Broadway, Denver, Colo. 80290. Filed 9/6/83. Legislative interest — "Seeking amendment and passage of S 1661, 98th Cong. 1st Sess., relating to availability of percentage depletion allowance for oil produced using secondary and tertiary recovery methods...."

GOLDMAN SACHS & CO., New York, N.Y. Lobbyist — Akin, Gump, Strauss, Hauer & Feld, 1333 New Hampshire Ave. N.W., Washington, D.C. 20036. Filed 9/22/83. Legislative interest — "Hearings and any legislation relating to federal bankruptcy reform, including HR 3, HR 1800, S 445 and S 1013."

HALLMARK CARDS INC., Kansas City, Mo. Lobbyist — Deloitte, Haskins & Sells, 655 15th St. N.W., Washington, D.C. 20005. Filed 9/28/83. Legislative interest — "Interest is in tax legislation which might have an impact on business of employer."

HANSEN ENGINE CO., Minnetonka, Minn. Lobbyist — Thomas M. Hagedorn, 1201 S. Jefferson Davis Highway, Arlington, Va. 22202. (Former U.S. rep., R-Minn., 1975-83.) Filed 9/8/83. Legislative interest — "To seek funding for innovative valve technology via 1983 Defense Authorizations and Appropriations legislation."

HARTFORD FIRE INSURANCE CO., Hartford Plaza, Hartford, Conn. 06115. Filed for self 9/23/83. Legislative interest — Not specified. Lobbyists — Theodore L. Jones, Stephen I. Martin.

INGERSOLL & BLOCH, Washington, D.C. Lobbyist — Stroock & Stroock & Lavan, 1150 17th St. N.W., Washington, D.C. 20036. Filed 9/23/83. Legislative interest — "In favor of the exclusion of the leasing of postal facilities from HR 3110 and S 1564 which deny certain tax exemptions for property used by governments and other tax exempt entities."

INGERSOLL-RAND CO., Woodcliff Lake, N.J. Lobbyist — Stovall, Spradlin, Armstrong & Israel, 1819 H St. N.W., Washington, D.C. 20006. Filed 9/22/83. Legislative interest — "Legislation concerning amendments of Export Administration Act of 1969, Overseas Private Investment Corporation Act Amendments of 1981, and Export-Import Bank Act of 1945."

INTERNATIONAL GOLD CORP. LTD., New York, N.Y. Lobbyist — Rubenstein, Wolfson & Co. Inc., 220 E. 42nd St., New York, N.Y. 10017. Filed 9/8/83. Legislative interest — "Generally interested in legislation regarding gold in general and

Krugerrands in particular. Specifically interested in HR 1662, HR 1663 and S 42, all of which are entitled 'American Gold Eagle Coin Act of 1983,' HR 1693, a bill which would mandate certain fair employment practices for U.S. companies operating in South Africa, restrict the making of loans to South Africa and ban the importation of Krugerrands and HR 3231, entitled 'Export Administration Amendment Act of 1983'...."

ISFA CORP., Tampa, Fla. Lobbyist — Lud Ashley, 1735 New York Ave. N.W., Washington, D.C. 20006. (Former U.S. rep., D-Ohio, 1955-81.) Filed 9/20/83. Legislative interest — "Financial institution reform legislation."

ITEL CORP., San Francisco, Calif. Lobbyist — O'Connor & Hannan, 1919 Pennsylvania Ave. N.W., Washington, D.C. 20006. (Former U.S. Rep. Thomas B. Evans Jr., R-Del., 1977-83, was listed as agent for this client.) Filed 9/14/83. Legislative interest — "Legislation affecting client including, but not limited to: amendments to the Staggers Rail Act of 1980."

KETCHIKAN PULP CO., Ketchikan, Alaska. Lobbyist — C. Deming Cowles, 1050 Thomas Jefferson St. N.W., Washington, D.C. 20007. Filed 9/27/83. Legislative interest — "Monitor clean water legislation for applicability to both mills' water discharges."

KIAWAH ISLAND CO. LTD., P.O. Box 12910, Charleston, S.C. 29412. Filed for self 9/27/83. Legislative interest — "... proposed legislation relating to federal flood insurance and coastal barriers ... draft legislation that may impact on the availability of tax deductions for resort or second homes, and the proposed Preservation of Wetlands and Duck Resources Act. Registrant supports equitable treatment and responsible development of coastal barriers and favors the maintenance of a federal tax policy that would allow such developments." Lobbyist — C. Leon Murphy.

MANVILLE CORP., Denver, Colo. Lobbyist — Baker & Hostetler, 818 Connecticut Ave N.W., Washington, D.C. 20006. Filed 9/21/83. Legislative interest — "... issues relating to energy conservation and the 1983 Housing Act; (a) Housing and Community Development Act of 1983; Housing and Urban-Rural Recovery Act of 1983; (b) S 1338; HR 1...."

NATIONAL BROADCASTING CO., Lobbyist — Gray and Co., 3255 Grace St. N.W., Washington, D.C. 20007. Filed 9/28/83. Legislative interest — "Including but not limited to legislation which would codify the financial interest and syndication rules, sponsored by Congressman Waxman (HR 2250)."

NATIONWIDE INSURANCE CO., One Nationwide Plaza, Columbus, Ohio 43216. Filed for self 9/6/83. Legislative interest —"In opposition to HR 100/S 372." Lobbyist — William E. Long.

NORANDA MINING INC., Juneau, Alaska. Lobbyist — Robertson, Monagle, Eastaugh & Bradley, 210 Ferry Way, Juneau, Alaska 99801. Filed 9/26/83. Legislative interest — "Legislation affecting mining in the Tongass National Forest, Alaska."

NOVA SCOTIA RESOURCES LTD., Halifax, Nova Scotia. Lobbyist — Corcoran, Hardesty, Whyte, Hemphill & Ligon, 1575 I St. N.W., Washington, D.C. 20005. Filed 9/6/83. Legislative interest — "Natural gas importation under the Natural Gas Act, Natural Gas Policy Act of 1978, and future legislation."

PACIFIC EXPRESS INC., Chico, Calif. Lobbyist — Stroock & Stroock & Lavan, 1150 17th St. N.W., Washington, D.C. 20036. Filed 9/19/83. Legislative interest — "General aviation matters and specific interest in and involvement with the industry computer reservation system controversy."

PEABODY HOLDING CO. INC., St. Louis, Mo. Lobbyist — Christopher G. Farrand, 1120 20th St. N.W., Washington, D.C. 20036. Filed 9/9/83. Legislative interest — "Legislative matters pertaining to the coal industry."

PENNZOIL CO., Pennzoil Place, Box 2967, Houston, Texas 77001. Filed for self 9/21/83. Legislative interest — "Refinery policy; deregulation of natural gas; end use controls; environmental matters; tax matters; international matters; public lands; and related matters." Lobbyist — Frank A. Verrastro, 1155 15th St. N.W., Washington, D.C. 20005.

PITNEY BOWES INC., Walter H. Wheeler Jr. Drive, Stamford, Conn. 06926. Filed for self 9/14/83. Legislative interest — Not specified. Lobbyist — Peter J. Cotch.

PLASTICS MANUFACTURING CO., Dallas, Texas. Lobbyist — Barnett & Alagia, 1000 Thomas Jefferson St. N.W., Washington, D.C. 20007. Filed 9/23/83. Legislative interest — "Oppose S 1542 and HR 2158."

POTTS INDUSTRIES INC., St. Louis, Mo. Lobbyist — David P. Stang, 1629 K St. N.W., Washington, D.C. 20006. Filed 9/16/83. Legislative interest — "Issues related to the taxation of shipping income."

SCHULMAN MANAGEMENT CO., Hollywood, Calif. Lobbyist — R. Duffy Wall & Associates Inc., 11 Dupont Circle N.W., Washington, D.C. 20036. Filed 9/20/83. Legislative interest — "Issues relating to real estate taxation."

SEACO INC., New York, N.Y. Lobbyist — Charls E. Walker Associates Inc., 1730 Pennsylvania Ave. N.W., Washington, D.C. 20006. Filed 9/28/83. Legislative interest — "... may concern proposals which would attempt to treat foreign corporations as though they were domestic corporations."

SECURITY PACIFIC INTERNATIONAL LEASING (EUROPE) INC., London, England. Lobbyist — Morgan, Lewis & Bockius, 1800 M St. N.W., Washington, D.C. 20036. Filed 9/29/83. Legislative interest — "HR 3110 and S 1564."

SOCIETE NATIONALE D'ETUDE ET DE CONSTRUCTION DE MOTEURS D'AVIATION, Paris, France. Lobbyist — DGA International Inc., 1225 19th St. N.W., Washington, D.C. 20036. Filed 9/23/83. Legislative interest — "Legislation affecting U.S. Department of Defense authorization and appropriations. In the immediate period the 1984 Defense Authorization bill and the 1984 Defense Appropriations bill are of specific interest. Also any other legislation that would affect U.S. Defense Department procurement decisions related to large military aircraft engines (*i.e.*, engines for tankers, transport, surveillance, or other similar type aircraft). We plan to monitor current legislation of the type described above and plan to take positions that would support legislation that calls for continuing utilization by the U.S. Air Force of military engines produced by our foreign principal. ..."

TEXAS ELECTRIC SERVICE CO., P.O. Box 970, Fort Worth, Texas 76101. Filed for self 9/27/83. Legislative interest — "Legislation affecting the electric utility industry, including energy, environment and regulatory issues." Lobbyist — Justin W. Johnson.

TRANS AMERICA DEVELOPERS INC., 1600 W. Camelback Road, Phoenix, Ariz. 85015. Filed for self 9/14/83. Legislative interest — "... transportation issues, bills, regulations ... small and minority business issues, bills, regulations." Lobbyist — Wesley A. Plummer.

U.S. TELEPHONE INC., Dallas, Texas. Lobbyist — Daniel A. Dutko, 412 First St. S.E., Washington, D.C. 20003. Filed 9/22/83. Legislative interest — Not specified.

VULCAN MATERIALS CO., Winston-Salem, N.C. Lobbyist — Boothe, Prichard & Dudley, 1199 N. Fairfax St., Alexandria, Va. 22313. Filed 9/12/83. Legislative interest — Not specified.

WASTE MANAGEMENT INC., 3003 Butterfield Road, Oak Brook, Ill. 60521. Filed for self 9/28/83. Legisiative interest — "Legislation relating to the solid waste, hazardous waste industry ... Resource Recovery and Conservation Act amendments, Superfund amendments ... HR 2867, S 757, HR 3200. ..." Lobbyist — Francis B. Moore.

WESTERN UNION TELEGRAPH CO., Washington, D.C. Lobbyist — F/P Research Associates, 1700 K St. N.W., Washington, D.C. 20006. Filed 9/7/83. Legislative interest — "S 1660 and HR 3621."

WESTINGHOUSE ELECTRIC CORP., Washington, D.C. Lobbyist — Benjamin L. Palumbo, 11 Dupont Circle, Washington, D.C. 20036. Filed 9/13/83. Legislative interest — "Clinch River Breeder Reactor."

XTRA CORP., Boston, Mass. Lobbyist — Piper & Marbury, 888 16th St. N.W., Washington, D.C. 20006. Filed 9/27/83. Legislative interest — "For enactment of legislation, such as S 1231 and HR 3003 or other legislation of similar effect, which would exempt certain piggyback trailers and semitrailers from the federal excise tax on the sale of heavy trucks and trailers."

International Relations

COMMISSION ON FUTURE POLITICAL STATUS AND TRANSITION, THE FEDERATED STATES OF MICRONESIA, Kolonia, Ponape, E.C.I. Lobbyist — Stovall, Spradlin, Armstrong & Israel, 1819 H St. N.W., Washington, D.C. 20006. Filed 9/23/83. Legislative interest — "All matters pertaining to the Government of the Federated States of Micronesia, including Omnibus Territories Acts, Territories Appropriation Acts."

EUROPEAN TRAVEL COMMISSION, 630 Fifth Ave., New York, N.Y. 10111. Filed for self 9/19/83. Legislative interest — "Legislation affecting tax treatment of expenses incurred by U.S. citizens attending foreign conventions. HR 1672 and other bills which have been or may be introduced — Against restrictions."

JAPANESE EMBASSY, Washington, D.C. Lobbyist — Manatos & Manatos Inc., 1750 New York Ave. N.W., Washington, D.C. 20006. Filed 9/13/83. Legislative interest — "Pro free trade legislation. ..."

KOREAN TRADERS ASSOCIATION, Seoul, Korea. Lobbyist — International Business & Economic Research Corp., 1819 H St. N.W., Washington, D.C. 20006. Filed 9/20/83. Legislative interest — "Renewal legislation for the Generalized System of Preferences. ..." Lobbyist — Daniels, Houlihan & Palmeter, 1819 H St. N.W., Washington, D.C. 20006. Filed 9/20/83. Legislative interest — "Renewal legislation for the Generalized System of Preferences. ..."

REPUBLIC OF TURKEY, Ankara, Turkey. Lobbyist — Gray and Co., 3255 Grace St. N.W., Washington, D.C. 20007. Filed 9/20/83. Legislative interest — "Including but not limited to economic and security assistance issues."

REPUBLIQUE D'HAITI, Washington, D.C. Lobbyist — Patton, Boggs & Blow, 2550 M St. N.W., Washington, D.C. 20037. Filed 9/30/83. Legislative interest — "Legislation affecting the government of Haiti such as HR 2769 and S 544, the Caribbean Basin Initiative, and HR 1850, the Foreign Aid Authorization bill."

TRADE, INDUSTRY & CUSTOMS DEPARTMENT, GOVERNMENT OF HONG KONG. Lobbyist — International Business & Economic Research Corp., 1819 H St. N.W., Washington, D.C. 20006. Filed 9/20/83. Legislative interest — "Renewal legislation for the Generalized System of Preferences. ..." Lobbyist — Daniels, Houlihan & Palmeter, 1819 H St. N.W., Washington, D.C. 20006. Filed 9/20/83. Legislative interest — "Renewal legislation for the Generalized System of Preferences. ..."

Labor Groups

AMERICAN FEDERATION OF GOVERNMENT EMPLOYEES, LOCAL 2677, Washington, D.C. Lobbyist — Harold A. Thornton & Associates, 1301 15th St. N.W., Washington, D.C. 20005. Filed 9/30/83. Legislative interest — Not specified.

UNITED PLANT GUARD WORKERS ASSOCIATION, Roseville, Mich. Lobbyist — Patton, Boggs & Blow, 2559 M St. N.W., Washington, D.C. 20037. Filed 9/28/83. Legislative interest — "Opposed to amendments to section 9(b)(3) of the National Labor Relations Act such as HR 2198, PL 80-101."

State and Local Governments

CITY OF ANAHEIM, Anaheim, Calif. Lobbyist — Arnold & Porter, 1200 New Hampshire Ave. N.W., Washington, D.C. 20036. Filed 9/29/83. Legislative interest — "To oppose efforts to repeal or amend the public preference provisions of the Federal Power Act."

MUNICIPALITY OF ANCHORAGE, Anchorage, Alaska. Lobbyist — C. Deming Cowles, 1050 Thomas Jefferson St. N.W., Washington, D.C. 20007. Filed 9/26/83. Legislative interest — "Monitor for impact on the municipality various funding legisla-

tion in area of general and OCS revenue sharing, housing, mass transit and highway construction and planning. Generally favor those funding measures which best address municipality's needs."

CITY OF AZUSA, Azusa, Calif. Lobbyist — Arnold & Porter, 1200 New Hampshire Ave. N.W., Washington, D.C. 20036. Filed 9/29/83. Legislative interest — "To oppose efforts to repeal or amend the public preference provisions of the Federal Power Act."

CITY OF BANNING, Banning, Calif. Lobbyist — Arnold & Porter, 1200 New Hampshire Ave. N.W., Washington, D.C. 20036. Filed 9/29/83. Legislative interest — "To oppose efforts to repeal or amend the public preference provisions of the Federal Power Act."

CALIFORNIA STATE LANDS COMMISSION, Sacramento, Calif. Lobbyist — Lobel, Novins & Lamont, 1523 L St. N.W., Washington, D.C. 20005. Filed 9/23/83. Legislative interest — "Legislation affecting state-owned public lands."

CHICAGO BOARD OF EDUCATION, Chicago, Ill. Lobbyist — Jeffrey A. Simering, 5320 Five Fingers Way, Columbia, Md. 21045. Filed 9/27/83. Legislative interest — Not specified.

CITY OF COLTON, Colton, Calif. Lobbyist — Arnold & Porter, 1200 New Hampshire Ave. N.W., Washington, D.C. 20036. Filed 9/29/83. Legislative interest — "To oppose efforts to repeal or amend the public preference provisions of the Federal Power Act."

MASSACHUSETTS PORT AUTHORITY, Boston, Mass. Lobbyist — John D. Cahill, 444 N. Capitol St. N.W., Washington, D.C. 20001. Filed 9/12/83. Legislative interest — "Transportation issues related to aviation and maritime."

NORTHERN CALIFORNIA POWER AGENCY, Citrus Heights, Calif. Lobbyist — Arnold & Porter, 1200 New Hampshire Ave. N.W., Washington, D.C. 20036. Filed 9/29/83. Legislative interest — "To oppose efforts to repeal or amend the public preference provisions of the Federal Power Act."

CITY OF RIVERSIDE, Riverside, Calif. Lobbyist — Arnold & Porter, 1200 New Hampshire Ave. N.W., Washington, D.C. 20036. Filed 9/29/83. Legislative interest — "To oppose efforts to repeal or amend the public preference provisions of the Federal Power Act."

SACRAMENTO PUBLIC UTILITY DISTRICT, Sacramento, Calif. Lobbyist — Arnold & Porter, 1200 New Hampshire Ave. N.W., Washington, D.C. 20036. Filed 9/29/83. Legislative interest — "To oppose efforts to repeal or amend the public preference provisions of the Federal Power Act."

CITY OF ST. PETERSBURG, St. Petersburg, Fla. Lobbyist — Krivit & Krivit, 101 Duddington Place S.E., Washington, D.C. 20003. Filed 9/23/83. Legislative interest — "Amendments to the IRS Code of 1954, to Deny Certain Tax Incentives for Property to be Used by Governments and Other Tax-Exempt Entities ... HR 3110 and S 1564. ..."

CITY OF SANTA CLARA, Santa Clara, Calif. Lobbyist — Arnold & Porter, 1200 New Hampshire Ave. N.W., Washington, D.C. 20036. Filed 9/29/83. Legislative interest — "To oppose efforts to repeal or amend the public preference provisions of the Federal Power Act."

Trade Associations

AMERICAN MEDICAL PEER REVIEW ASSOCIATION, 440 First St. N.W., Washington, D.C. 20001. Filed for self 9/7/83. Legislative interest — "Interest is with PL 92-603 and resulting Professional Standards Review Organizations (PSRO) and will continue for as long as the law exists. Interest is also with PL 97-248, the Tax Equity and Fiscal Responsibility Law and funding for fiscal year 1984." Lobbyist — Andrew H. Webber.

AMERICAN SEED TRADE ASSOCIATION, 1030 15th St. N.W., Washington, D.C. 20005. Filed for self 9/30/83. Legislative interest — "Changes to the Federal Seed Act. Changes to HR 1510 and S 529, the Immigration Reform and Control Act of 1983." Lobbyist — William T. Schapaugh.

AMERICAN SKI FEDERATION, 499 S. Capitol St. S.W., Washington, D.C. 20003. Filed for self 9/2/83. Legislative interest — "Legislation impacting public lands." Lobbyist — Joseph T. Prendergast.

BRICK INSTITUTE OF AMERICA, 1750 Old Meadow Road, McLean, Va. 22102. Filed for self 9/30/83. Legislative interest — "... energy, housing and tax legislation." Lobbyist — Leslie M. Taylor.

COAL SLURRY ASSOCIATION, Washington, D.C. Lobbyist — Thomas M. Hagedorn, 1201 S. Jefferson Davis Highway, Arlington, Va. 22202. (Former U.S. rep., R-Minn., 1975-83.) Filed 9/8/83. Legislative interest — "... S 267 and HR 1010."

FARM CREDIT COUNCIL, 1800 Massachusetts Ave. N.W., Washington, D.C. 20036. Filed for self 9/15/83. Legislative interest — Not specified. Lobbyist — Joseph L. S. Terrell.

FEDERATION OF APPAREL MANUFACTURERS, New York, N.Y. Lobbyist — Gibson, Dunn & Crutcher, 1776 G St. N.W., Washington, D.C. 20006. Filed 9/26/83. Legislative interest — "... to represent the interests of FAM relating to legislation dealing with the Multiemployer Pension Plan Amendments Act of 1980."

JAPAN IRON & STEEL EXPORTERS' ASSOCIATION, Tokyo, Japan. Lobbyist — Wald, Harkrader & Ross, 1300 19th St. N.W., Washington, D.C. 20036. Filed 9/13/83. Legislative interest — "Oppose legislation that would amend the trade laws of the United States in ways that appear to be adverse to the interest of exports of steel from Japan to the United States, specifically, the Trade Act of 1974, and Trade Agreements Act of 1979."

JAPAN TELESCOPES MANUFACTURERS ASSOCIATION, Tokyo, Japan. Lobbyist — Mike M. Masaoka, 900 17th St. N.W., Washington, D.C. 20006. Filed 9/29/83. Legislative interest — "... Relating to the tariff treatment of certain telescopes not designed for use with infrared light ... HR 3174 and S 1642. ..."

LAUNDRY CLEANING COUNCIL, Philadelphia, Pa. Lobbyist — Patton, Boggs & Blow, 2550 M St. N.W., Washington, D.C. 20037. Filed 9/30/83. Legislative interest — "Legislation affecting the laundry and dry cleaning industry such as HR 2867 and S 767, the Resource Conservation and Recovery Act."

MEAT PRICE INVESTIGATORS ASSOCIATION, Des Moines, Iowa. Lobbyist — Alston & Bird, 1800 M St. N.W., Washington, D.C. 20036. Filed 9/23/83. Legislative interest — "Proponent of amendments to the antitrust laws to provide explicitly that indirect sellers may sue for damages for violations of such laws."

MICHIGAN INSURANCE ASSOCIATION, Washington, D.C. Lobbyist — Patton, Boggs & Blow, 2550 M St. N.W., Washington, D.C. 20036. Filed 9/30/83. Legislative interest — "Legislation affecting the insurance industry such as HR 100, Non-discrimination in Insurance Act and S 372, the Fair Insurance Practices Act."

NATIONAL-AMERICAN WHOLESALE GROCERS' ASSOCIATION, 201 Park Washington Court, Falls Church, Va. 22046. Filed for self 9/15/83. Legislative interest — "Matters affecting the U.S. wholesale grocery and food distribution industries including, HR 7233 (Multi-employer pension withdrawal liability); S 44 (Product liability); S 529 (Immigration Reform); HR 4961 (Tax Equity Fiscal Responsibility Act)." Lobbyist — Denis R. Zegar.

NATIONAL ASH ASSOCIATION INC., 1819 H St. N.W., Washington, D.C. 20006. Filed for self 9/22/83. Legislative interest — Not specified. Lobbyist — Tobias Anthony.

NATIONAL POTATO COUNCIL, Denver, Colo. Lobbyist — Heron, Burchette, Ruckert & Rothwell, 1200 New Hampshire Ave. N.W., Washington, D.C. 20036. Filed 9/22/83. Legislative interest — "HR 3193 - tracking. S 50 - tracking. ..."

NATIONAL SCHOOL TRANSPORTATION ASSOCIATION, Springfield, Va. Lobbyist — Palumbo & Cerrell, 11 Dupont Circle N.W., Washington, D.C. 20036. Filed 9/13/83. Legislative interest — "Legislation affecting school bus operations."

NATURAL GAS SUPPLY ASSOCIATION, Washington, D.C. Lobbyist — Lerch & Co. Inc., 1030 15th St. N.W., Washington, D.C. 20005. Filed 9/20/83. Legislative interest —

"... to support the deregulation of natural gas (S 1715)."

NORTH WEST TIMBER ASSOCIATION, Eugene, Ore. Lobbyist — Preston, Thorgrimson, Ellis & Holman, 1735 New York Ave. N.W., Washington, D.C. 20006. (Former U.S. Rep. Lloyd Meeds, D-Wash., 1965-79, was listed as agent for this client.) Filed 9/21/83. Legislative interest — "To promote legislation effecting timber contract relief. S 916 and similiar legislation."

UNITED STATES PHOTOVOLTAICS MANUFACTURERS' AD HOC COMMITTEE, Washington, D.C. Lobbyist — Chadbourne, Parke, Whiteside & Wolff, 1101 Vermont Ave. N.W., Washington, D.C. 20005. Filed 9/10/83. Legislative interest — "Increase and extension of the tax credits for photovoltaics."

WATER AND WASTEWATER EQUIPMENT MANUFACTURERS ASSOCIATION INC., P.O. Box 17402, Dulles International Airport, Washington, D.C. 20041. Filed for self 9/20/83. Legislative interest — "Federal Water Pollution Control Act Amendments (S 431, HR 3282) support with amendments. Omnibus Water Act (S 1739, HR 3678) support with amendments. Safe Drinking Water Act Amendments (HR 3200) support with amendments. Products Liability Act (S 44, HR 2726) support. Sales Representation Contractual Relations Act (HR 3591) oppose. Governmental Leasing Tax Act (HR 3110, S 1564) support with amendments. Appropriations bills for U.S. EPA, Dept. of Agriculture, FmHA, support. Infrastructure measures (S 23, S 532, S 1330) support." Lobbyists — Dawn C. Kristof, John M. Scheer.

WESTERN COTTON GROWERS ASSOCIATION, Fresno, Calif. Lobbyist — Heron, Burchette, Ruckert & Rothwell, 1200 New Hampshire Ave. N.W., Washington, D.C. 20036. Filed 9/22/83. Legislative interest — "PIK Legislation."

WESTERN FOREST INDUSTRIES ASSOCIATION, Portland, Ore. Lobbyist — Preston, Thorgrimson, Ellis & Holman, 1735 New York Ave. N.W., Washington, D.C. 20006. (Former U.S. Rep. Lloyd Meeds, D-Wash., 1965-79, was listed as agent for this client.) Filed 9/21/83. Legislative interest — "To promote legislation effecting timber contract relief. S 916 and similar legislation."

Miscellaneous

AD HOC COMMITTEE FOR EQUITABLE TRANSPORTATION, Washington, D.C. Lobbyist — Sutherland, Asbill & Brennan, 1666 K St. N.W., Washington, D.C. 20006. Filed 9/19/83. Legislative interest — "Legislation relating to natural gas."

AMERICAN DRUZE PUBLIC AFFAIRS COMMITTEE, Hotel Washington, 15th St. and Pennsylvania Ave. N.W., Washington, D.C. 20004. Filed for self 9/22/83. Legislative interest — "... United States policy in regard to the Middle East...."

ASSOCIATION FOR DEVELOPMENT POLICY RESEARCH, 1309 L St. N.W., Washington, D.C. 20005. Filed for self 9/6/83. Legislative interest — Not specified. Lobbyist — John A. Viola.

CITIZENS FOR SENSIBLE CONTROL OF ACID RAIN, 7926 Jones Branch Drive, McLean, Va. 22102. Lobbyist — Communications Management Inc., 1925 North Lynn St., Arlington, Va. 22209. Filed 9/14/83. Legislative interest — "... supporting or opposing enactment of legislation intended to control and reduce acid deposition (*i.e.*, 'acid rain'), including without limitation the following currently pending bills: For — Acidic Deposition Mitigation and Research Act of 1983 (S 454). Against — Clean Air Act Amendments of 1983 (S 768)." Filed for self 9/14/83. Legislative interest — "... supporting or opposing enactment of legislation intended to control and reduce acid deposition (*i.e.*, 'acid rain'), including without limitation the following currently pending bills: For — Acidic Deposition Mitigation and Research Act of 1983 (S 454). Against — Clean Air Act Amendments of 1983 (S 768)." Lobbyist — Christopher G. Farrand.

RICHMOND R. FARRING, Weirsdale, Fla. Lobbyist — C. Deming Cowles, 1050 Thomas Jefferson St. N.W., Washington, D.C. 20007. Filed 9/26/83. Legislative interest — "Monitor trade legislation which may impact on Mr. Farring's citrus and meat businesses, and work on his prospects for appointment to a federal

trade position."

FEDERAL NATIONAL MORTGAGE ASSOCIATION, 3900 Wisconsin Ave. N.W., Washington, D.C. 20016. Filed for self 9/15/83. Legislative interest — "Legislation re residential mortgages, housing and various tax legislation. Specifically, HR 1, S 1146, HR 3357, S 1821." Lobbyist — David W. Roderer.

KNIGHT FOUNDATION, Akron, Ohio. Lobbyist — Baker & Hostetler, 818 Connecticut Ave. N.W., Washington, D.C. 20006. Filed 9/28/83. Legislative interest — "General legislative interest is in tax laws relating to charitable and educational organizations described in section 501(c)(3) of the Internal Revenue Code and possible amendments thereto and IRC Chapter 42 and specifically HR 3427."

MASSACHUSETTS GENERAL HOSPITAL, Boston, Mass. Lobbyist — O'Neill and Haase, 1333 New Hampshire Ave. N.W., Washington, D.C. 20036. Filed 9/16/83. Legislative interest — "Legislation affecting teaching hospitals."

NATIONAL PUBLIC RADIO, 2025 M St. N.W., Washington, D.C. 20036. Filed for self 9/22/83. Legislative interest — "... to pursue legislation which is consistent with the public interest, First Amendment, and full development of public radio ... FY 1985 rescissions for the Corporation for Public Broadcasting; CPB appropriations for FY 1985 and 1986; HR 2755, FCC Authorization; S 880, AM Daytimers Legislation; broadcast deregulation; copyright...."

THE PATHFINDER FUND, Chestnut Hill, Mass. Lobbyist — Surrey & Morse, 1250 I St. N.W., Washington, D.C. 20005. Filed 9/2/83. Legislative interest — "... to seek the withdrawal of an objection filed by Senator Robert Kasten with the Agency for International Development (AID) regarding AID's intent to award a new cooperative agreement to The Pathfinder Fund...."

UNITED HELLENIC AMERICAN CONGRESS AND AMERICAN HELLENIC ALLIANCE INC., Lobbyist — Manatos & Manatos Inc., 1750 New York Ave. N.W., Washington, D.C. 20006. Filed 9/19/83. Legislative interest — "Foreign military aid specifically to Greece and Turkey ... Foreign Assistance Act."

WASHINGTON COORDINATING COUNCIL ON PRODUCTIVITY, Washington, D.C. Lobbyist — Manatos & Manatos Inc., 1750 New York Ave. N.W., Washington, D.C. 20006. Filed 9/20/83. Legislative interest — "Productivity improving pieces of legislation including — tax credits, for investment, antitrust, training. S 121, The Trade Reorganization Act of 1983. HR 1310, Emergency Math & Science Education Act. S 568, Joint Venture for Research and Development."

October Registrations

Citizens' Groups

AMERICAN SOCIAL HEALTH ASSOCIATION, Palo Alto, Calif. Lobbyist — Kaye, Scholer, Fierman, Hays & Handler, 1575 I St. N.W., Washington, D.C. 20005. Filed 10/27/83. Legislative interest — "General interest in government policies regarding certain health and funding issues."

ASSINIBOINE TRIBE, Fort Belknap, Mont. Lobbyist — Fried, Frank, Harris, Shriver & Kampelman, 600 New Hampshire Ave. N.W., Washington, D.C. 20037. Filed 10/19/83. Legislative interest — "... HR 3555. Supported."

CITIZENS FOR AMERICA, Washington, D.C. Lobbyist — Bond and Laxalt, 813 Maryland Ave. N.E., Washington, D.C. 20002. Filed 10/17/83. Legislative interest — "Informing members of Congress of Citizens for America, a 501(c)4, which is a national citizens lobby advocating economic growth policies and a strong national security policy."

CITIZENS FOR A NUCLEAR FREEZE, 324 4th St. N.E., Washington, D.C. 20002. Filed for self 10/26/83. Legislative interest — "S J Res 2 - Favor (Nuclear Freeze Resolution). H J Res 13 - Favor (Conte-Markey Resolution)." Lobbyist — Anne M. Kronenberg, 1004 South Carolina Ave. S.E., Washington, D.C. 20003.

PROJECT CURE INC., 2020 K St. N.W., Washington, D.C. 20006. Filed for self 10/24/83. Legislative interest — ". . . advocating a full scale Congressional investigation of the National Cancer Institute and the medical profession relating to the suppression of alternative cancer treatments . . . and the unnecessary delays in the testing and use of potential cures to cancer. . . . address the issue of advising the public about cancer prevention and/or treatment using dietary controls and techniques." Lobbyist — Robert DeBragga, 26 Flanders Road, Stonington, Conn. 06378.

SANTA CLARA PUEBLO, Espanola, N.M. Lobbyist — Gerard, Byler & Associates, 1100 17th St. N.W., Washington, D.C. 20036. Filed 10/24/83. Legislative interest — "Working toward enactment of legislation to restore land to reservation."

SIERRA CLUB, 530 Bush St., San Francisco, Calif. 94108. Filed for self 10/10/83. Legislative interest — "Reauthorization of Clean Air Act; reauthorization of Clean Water Act; reauthorization of Safe Drinking Water Act; miscellaneous wilderness legislation and other environmental legislation." Lobbyist — James M. Price, P.O. Box 11248, Knoxville, Tenn. 37919.

UNITED STATES DEFENSE COMMITTEE, 3238 Wynford Drive, Fairfax, Va. 22031. Filed for self 10/10/83. Legislative interest — "Legislative proposals related to defense and foreign affairs . . . Garn-Heinz bill, Boland-Zablocki bill, FY 84 [Department of Defense] Appropriations . . . For S 979, against HR 2760, for some parts of [Department of Defense] Appropriations." Lobbyists — M. Louise Tate, Robert G. Mills.

UNITED WAY OF AMERICA, Alexandria, Va. Lobbyist — Wellford, Wegman, Krulwich, Gold & Hoff, 1775 Pennsylvania Ave. N.W., Washington, D.C. 20006. Filed 10/10/83. Legislative interest — ". . . legislation affecting relations between non-profits and federal government."

THE WILDERNESS SOCIETY, 1901 Pennsylvania Ave. N.W., Washington, D.C. 20006. Filed for self 10/13/83. Legislative interest — "Wilderness and other public land issues, particularly those relating to Colorado, Arizona, New Mexico, West Texas and Utah." Lobbyist — Michael Scott.

WOMEN'S LEGAL DEFENSE FUND, 2000 P St. N.W., Washington, D.C. 20036. Filed for self 10/24/83. Legislative interest — ". . . employment discrimination, equal education, domestic relations, and federal appointments." Lobbyist — Claudia A. Withers.

Corporations and Businesses

ACUREX SOLAR CORP., Mountain View, Calif. Lobbyist — Chadbourne, Parke, Whiteside & Wolff, 1101 Vermont Ave. N.W., Washington, D.C. 20005. Filed 10/10/83. Legislative interest — "Energy tax credits."

ALIGNPAC, Portland, Ore. Lobbyist — Morgan, Lewis & Bockius, 1800 M St. N.W., Washington, D.C. 20036. Filed 10/13/83. Legislative interest — "HR 4065 and related measures."

AM INTERNATIONAL, Chicago, Ill. Lobbyist — McDermott, Will & Emery, 1850 K St. N.W., Washington, D.C. 20006. Filed 10/28/83. Legislative interest — "Subchapter C issues, specifically, net operating losses provisions."

AMERICAN EXPRESS CO., American Express Plaza, New York, N.Y. 10004. Filed for self 10/18/83. Legislative interest — "Legislation regarding travel, miscellaneous financial services. . . ." Lobbyist — Howard A. Menell, 1700 K St. N.W., Washington, D.C. 20006.

AMERICAN SECURITY INSURANCE CO., Atlanta, Ga. Lobbyist — Hansell & Post, 1915 I St. N.W., Washington, D.C. 20006. Filed 10/12/83. Legislative interest — "Legislative action relating to the taxation of the U.S. Life Insurance Industry."

AMERICAN TELEPHONE & TELEGRAPH INC., New York, N.Y. Lobbyist — Donovan, Leisure, Newton & Irvine, 30 Rockefeller Plaza, New York, N.Y. 10122. Filed 10/31/83. Legislative interest — "HR 4102, Universal Telephone Service Preservation Act of 1983."

AMYTEX CORP., South Kearny, N.J. Lobbyist — Reid & Priest, 1111 19th St. N.W., Washington, D.C. 20036. Filed 10/26/82. Legislative interest — "Agreement between the United States and Mexico relating to trade in cotton, wool and man-made fiber textiles and textile products, with annexes effected by exchange of notes February 26, 1979, as amended and Category 604 (part) TSUSA 310.5049."

ANDERSON, HIBEY, NAUHEIM AND BLAIR, Washington, D.C. Lobbyist — Kendall & Associates, 1750 New York Ave. N.W., Washington, D.C. 20006. Filed 10/13/83. Legislative interest — "Tax legislation."

ASPEN TECHNOLOGY INC., Cambridge, Mass. Lobbyist — Charles J. Micoleau, One Canal Plaza, Portland, Maine 04112. Filed 10/7/83. Legislative interest — "HR 1236." Lobbyist — J. William W. Harsch, 1825 K St. N.W., Washington, D.C. 20006. Filed 10/7/83. Legislative interest — "HR 1236."

AVIS INC., Garden City, N.Y. Lobbyist — Bregman, Abell & Kay, 1900 L St. N.W., Washington, D.C. 20036. Filed 10/12/83. Legislative interest — ". . . matters of interest to the client concerning telecommunications."

BALLARD, SPAHR, ANDREWS & INGERSOLL, 1850 K St. N.W., Washington, D.C. 20006. Filed for self 10/27/83. Legislative interest — ". . . Industrial development bond financing . . . to preserve the present authority for use of IDB's." Lobbyists — Rebecca L. Halkias, William C. Smith.

BANKAMERICA CORP., San Francisco, Calif. Filed for self 10/20/83. Legislative interest — "None." Lobbyist — Connie M. Downs, 1800 K St. N.W., Washington, D.C. 20006.

BANKERS LIFE CO., Des Moines, Iowa. Lobbyist — Groom and Nordberg, 1775 Pennsylvania Ave. N.W., Washington, D.C. 20006. Filed 10/11/83. Legislative interest — "Federal legislation affecting Title 26 of U.S.C."

THE BARNESS ORGANIZATION, Warrington, Pa. Lobbyist — Bond and Laxalt Inc., 813 Maryland Ave. N.E., Washington, D.C. 20002. Filed 10/24/83. Legislative interest — ". . . issues relating to housing."

C. F. BEAN, New Orleans, La. Lobbyist — Patton, Boggs & Blow, 2550 M St. N.W., Washington, D.C. 20037. Filed 10/27/83. Legislative interest — "Legislation relating to equitable administration of small business set-aside program . . . to amend the Small Business Act; HR 2133; 72 Stat. 395."

BECHTEL POWER CORP., Washington, D.C. Lobbyist — Thomas E. Thomason, 6024 Western Ave., Chevy Chase, Md. 20815. Filed 10/14/83. Legislative interest — Not specified.

BRISTOL-MYERS CO., Washington, D.C. Lobbyist — McNair, Glenn, Konduros, Corley, Singletary, Porter & Dibble, 1155 15th St. N.W., Washington, D.C. 20005. Filed 10/5/83. Legislative interest — ". . . S 1762."

BROADCAST MUSIC INC., New York, N.Y. Lobbyist — Peabody, Lambert & Meyers, 1150 Connecticut Ave. N.W., Washington, D.C. 20036. Filed 10/17/83. Legislative interest — "Opposing S 1734 and HR 3858."

BUDGET RENT-A-CAR CORP., Chicago, Ill. Lobbyist — Bregman, Abell & Kay, 1900 L St. N.W., Washington, D.C. 20036. Filed 10/12/83. Legislative interest — ". . . matters of interest to client concerning telecommunications."

BURLINGTON NORTHERN RAILROAD, 176 E. 5th St., St. Paul, Minn. 55101. Filed for self 10/31/83. Legislative interest — "Legislation affecting railroad transportation." Lobbyist — Ronald H. Reimann.

CBS INC., 51 West 52nd St., New York, N.Y. 10019. Filed for self 10/20/83. Legislative interest — "The Financial Interest and Syndication Rule . . . for repeal of." Lobbyist — Rebecca R. Lambert, 813 Maryland Ave. N.E., Washington, D.C. 20002. Filed for self 10/14/83. Legislative interest — "F.C.C. Financial Interest and Syndication Rules (HR 2250 and S 1707)." Lobbyist — Heidi Ann Hanson, 1608D Belmont St. N.W., Washington, D.C. 20019.

CHICAGO MERCANTILE EXCHANGE, Chicago, Ill. Lobbyist — Heron, Burchette, Ruckert & Rothwell, 1200 New Hampshire Ave. N.W., Washington, D.C. 20035. Filed 10/20/83. Legislative interest — ". . . commodities trade."

CLAYMARK CORP. INC., 30 Rockefeller Plaza, New York, N.Y. 10112. Lobbyist — Milbank, Tweed, Hadley & McCloy, 1 Chase Manhattan Plaza, New York, N.Y. 10005. Filed 10/4/83. Legislative interest — "Seeking amendments to Internal Revenue

Code Section 311. . . ." Filed for self 10/4/83. Legislative interest — "Seeking amendments to Internal Revenue Code Section 311. . . ." Lobbyist — Richard E. Salomon.

THE COASTAL CORP., Houston, Texas. Lobbyist — Birch, Horton, Bittner, Pestinger and Anderson, 1140 Connecticut Ave. N.W., Washington, D.C. 20036. Filed 10/13/83. Legislative interest — "Natural resource development issues including S 750."

CONSOLIDATED EDISON COMPANY OF NEW YORK, New York, N.Y. Lobbyist — Charlie McBride Associates Inc., 1717 K St. N.W., Washington, D.C. 20036. Filed 10/12/83. Legislative interest — "Revisions to Federal laws and regulations in regard to emergency evacuation from areas adjacent to nuclear power plants." Lobbyist — Miller & Chevalier, 655 15th St. N.W., Washington, D.C. 20005. Filed 10/31/83. Legislative interest — "Revisions to Federal laws and regulations in regard to emergency evacuation plans in areas adjacent to nuclear power plants." Lobbyist — Charles L. Fishman, 1717 K St. N.W., Washington, D.C. 20036. Filed 10/31/83. Legislative interest — "Revisions to Federal laws and regulations in regard to emergency evacuation from areas adjacent to nuclear power plants."

CONTRACT STAFFING OF AMERICA INC., Tustin, Calif. Lobbyist — Sidley & Austin, 1722 I St. N.W., Washington, D.C. 20006. Filed 10/21/83. Legislative interest — "Tax legislation concerning pension return and employee leasing . . . Tax Equity and Fiscal Responsibility Act of 1982."

JOHN COOLEY CONSTRUCTION CO., Ferndale, Mich. Lobbyist — Gnau, Carter, Jacobsen & Associates Inc., 1777 F St. N.W., Washington, D.C. 20006. Filed 10/14/83. Legislative interest — "General housing and urban development interests."

COPIAT, Washington, D.C. Lobbyist — Charls E. Walker Associates Inc., 1730 Pennsylvania Ave. N.W., Washington, D.C. 20006. Filed 10/14/83. Legislative interest — ". . . issues relating to the importation of items subject to United States trademarks without the consent of the trademark owners."

CRAWFORD FITTING CO., Solon, Ohio. Lobbyist — Fred B. Rooney, 1050 Thomas Jefferson St. N.W., Washington, D.C. 20007. (Former U.S. rep., D-Pa., 1963-79.) Filed 10/11/83. Legislative interest — "Tax legislation."

DELOITTE, HASKINS & SELLS, 655 15th St. N.W., Washington, D.C. 20005. Filed for self 10/19/83. Legislative interest — "Governmental Leasing Act, HR 3110, S 1564. In opposition to definition of exempt organization." Lobbyist — Randall A. Snowling.

DYCO PETROLEUM CO., Minneapolis, Minn. Lobbyist — Hale and Dorr, 1201 Pennsylvania Ave. N.W., Washington, D.C. 20004. Filed 10/26/83. Legislative interest — "Legislation affecting oil and gas exploration and production including, but not limited to, S 1715 and the natural gas bill reported out of the House Subcommittee on Fossil and Synthetic Fuels (opposed)."

EHA VENTILFABRIK WILHELM FRITZ KG, Mühlheim (Main), West Germany. Lobbyist — Barnes, Richardson & Colburn, 1819 H St. N.W., Washington, D.C. 20006. Filed 10/20/83. Legislative interest — "Miscellaneous Tariff Bills; S 1518. Portion relating to tubeless tire valves; opposed to passage of this legislation."

EQUITABLE LIFE ASSURANCE SOCIETY OF THE UNITED STATES, 1285 Avenue of the Americas, New York, N.Y. 10019. Lobbyist — Cummings & Lockwood, 1090 Vermont Ave N.W., Washington, D.C. 20005. (Former U.S. Rep. John J. Rhodes, R-Ariz., 1953-83, was listed as agent for this client.) Filed 10/4/83. Legislative interest — "Taxation of life insurance companies." Filed for self 10/17/83. Legislative interest — "Life Insurance Taxation." Lobbyist — William C. Mattox, 1775 Pennsylvania Ave. N.W., Washington, D.C. 20006.

FIFTH AVENUE & 59TH CORP., New York, N.Y. Lobbyist — Stroock & Stroock & Lavan, 1150 17th St. N.W., Washington, D.C. 20036. Filed 10/21/83. Legislative interest — "Involved in the drafting of proposed legislation to amend section 216 of the Internal Revenue Code concerning cooperative housing corporations."

GENERAL AMERICAN LIFE INSURANCE CO., St. Louis, Mo. Lobbyist — James C. Corman, 1420 16th St. N.W., Washington, D.C. 20036. (Former U.S. rep., D-Calif., 1961-81.)

Filed 10/21/83. Legislative interest — "To support HR 4065 and similar legislation. To oppose legislation adverse to Mutual Insurance companies."

GREAT LAKES DREDGE & DOCK, Oakbrook, Ill. Lobbyist — Patton, Boggs & Blow, 2550 M St. N.W., Washington, D.C. 20037. Filed 10/27/83. Legislative interest — "Legislation relating to equitable administration of small business set-aside program. . . . To amend the Small Business Act; HR 2133; 72 Stat. 395."

GRINDLAYS BANK LTD., London, England. Lobbyist — Thacher, Proffitt & Wood, 1140 Connecticut Ave. N.W., Washington, D.C. 20036. Filed 10/14/83. Legislative interest — "S 1564, Public Property Leasing and HR 3110, Governmental Leasing Tax Act of 1983."

THE GUARDIAN LIFE INSURANCE COMPANY OF AMERICA, New York, N.Y. Lobbyist — Groom and Nordberg, 1775 Pennsylvania Ave. N.W., Washington, D.C. 20006. Filed 10/11/83. Legislative interest — "Federal legislation affecting Title 26 of U.S.C."

GULF OIL CORP., Washington, D.C. Lobbyist — Bliss, Craft & Richards, 1050 Thomas Jefferson St. N.W., Washington, D.C. 20008. Filed 10/18/83. Legislative interest — "All legislation dealing with the issue of coal leasing."

HAPAG-LLOYD A.G., Hamburg, West Germany. Lobbyist — Billig, Sher & Jones, 2033 K St. N.W., Washington, D.C. 20006. Filed 10/4/83. Legislative interest — "Legislation affecting companies operating vessels in international commerce."

HILATURAS LERMA S.A., Mexico City, Mexico. Lobbyist — Reid & Priest, 1111 19th St. N.W., Washington, D.C. 20036. Filed 10/26/82. Legislative interest — "Agreement between the United States and Mexico relating to trade in cotton, wool and man-made fiber textiles and textile products, with annexes effected by exchange of notes February 26, 1979, as amended and Category 604 (part) TSUSA 310.5049."

HOME LIFE INSURANCE CO., New York, N.Y. Lobbyist — James C. Corman, 1420 16th St. N.W., Washington, D.C. 20036. (Former U.S. rep., D-Calif., 1961-81.) Filed 10/21/83. Legislative interest — "To support HR 4065 and similar legislation. To oppose legislation adverse to Mutual Insurance companies."

INDEPENDENT CEMENT CORP., Albany, N.Y. Lobbyist — Heron, Burchette, Ruckert & Rothwell, 1200 New Hampshire Ave. N.W., Washington, D.C. 20036. Filed 10/10/83. Legislative interest — "HR 3103 - for."

INEXCO OIL CO., Houston, Texas. Lobbyist — Hale and Dorr, 1201 Pennsylvania Ave. N.W., Washington, D.C. 20004. Filed 10/26/83. Legislative interest — "Legislation affecting oil and gas exploration and production including, but not limited to, S 1715 and the natural gas bill reported out of the House Subcommittee on Fossil and Synthetic Fuels (opposed)."

INTERNATIONAL MINERALS & CHEMICAL CORP., 2315 Sanders Road, Northbrook, Ill. 60062. Filed for self 10/14/83. Legislative interest — "Legislation affecting mining, the fertilizer industry and trade regulation, particularly ammonia and ferroalloy import pricing proposals, and the Canadian Tax Treaty." Lobbyist — Joan T. Bier, 1726 M St. N.W., Washington, D.C. 20036.

INTERNATIONAL TECHNICAL EXPERTISE LTD., 7297J Lee Highway, Falls Church, Va. 22042. Filed for self 10/5/83. Legislative interest — "Defense matters and legislation related thereto." Lobbyists — Stephen F. Rohrkemper, Dennis L. Petersen, Phillip A. Hogue, Jesse H. Johnson, Louis F. Finch.

KELLY, APPLEMAN, HART & HALLMAN, Fort Worth, Texas. Lobbyist — Williams & Jensen, 1101 Connecticut Ave. N.W., Washington, D.C. 20036. Filed 10/31/83. Legislative interest — "Legislative developments affecting the taxation of corporations and their shareholders."

KMS FUSION INC., Ann Arbor, Mich. Lobbyist — James E. Guirard Jr., 1780 Rhode Island Ave. N.W., Washington, D.C. 20036. Filed 10/11/83. Legislative interest — "Authorization and appropriations bills (DOE and DOD) affecting the inertial confinement fusion program of the Department of Energy."

LAKE ONTARIO CEMENT LTD., Toronto, Ontario, Canada. Lobbyist — Kirby, Gillick, Schwartz & Tuohey, 600

Maryland Ave. S.W., Washington, D.C. 20024. Filed 10/17/83. Legislative interest — "Support HR 3103 as reported by the Senate Environment and Public Works Committee."

LOCKHEED CORP., P.O. Box 551, Burbank, Calif. 91520. Filed for self 10/21/83. Legislative interest — ". . . international export policy, the Export Administration Act, the Security Assistance Act, the annual DOD and NASA authorization and appropriation legislation, Airport and Airway Development Act and aircraft noise legislation. . . ." Lobbyist — Powell A. Moore, 8637 Winthrop Drive, Alexandria, Va. 22307.

M LIFE INSURANCE CO., Portland, Ore. Lobbyist — Paul, Hastings, Janofsky & Walker, 1050 Thomas Jefferson St. N.W., Washington, D.C. 20007. Filed 10/11/83. Legislative interest — "Legislation affecting life insurance company taxes and life insurance product taxes."

MARRIOTT CORP., Washington, D.C. Lobbyist — Kendall & Associates, 1750 New York Ave. N.W., Washington, D.C. 20006. Legislative interest — "Tax legislation."

MATSUSHITA ELECTRIC INDUSTRIAL CO. LTD., Osaka, Japan. Lobbyist — Wald, Harkrader & Ross, 1300 19th St. N.W., Washington, D.C. 20036. Filed 10/5/83. Legislative interest — ". . . legislation involving international trade. . . ."

MEDTRONIC INC., Minneapolis, Minn. Lobbyist — Hogan & Hartson, 815 Connecticut Ave. N.W., Washington, D.C. 20006. Filed 10/11/83. Legislative interest — ". . . legislation to amend sections of the Social Security Act dealing with the Medicare and Medicaid programs."

MESA PETROLEUM CO., Amarillo, Texas. Lobbyist — Akin, Gump, Strauss, Hauer & Feld, 1333 New Hampshire Ave. N.W., Washington, D.C. 20036. Filed 10/5/83. Legislative interest — "Hearings and any legislation relating to amendments to the Natural Gas Policy Act of 1978."

MICROBAND CORPORATION OF AMERICA, New York, N.Y. Lobbyist — Squire, Sanders & Dempsey, 1201 Pennsylvania Ave. N.W., Washington, D.C. 20004. Filed 10/12/83. Legislative interest — "Revisions to the Communications Act of 1934."

THE MINNESOTA MUTUAL LIFE INSURANCE CO., St. Paul, Minn. Lobbyist — Groom and Nordberg, 1775 Pennsylvania Ave. N.W., Washington, D.C. 20006. Filed 10/11/83. Legislative interest — "Federal legislation affecting title 26 of U.S.C."

MISSISSIPPI CHEMICAL CORP., Yazoo City, Miss. Lobbyist — Sutin, Thayer & Browne, P.O. Box 1945, Albuquerque, N.M. 87103. Filed 10/31/83. Legislative interest — "Senate bill 1715."

MITEX, Boston, Mass. Lobbyist — Wellford, Wegman, Krulwich, Gold & Hoff, 1775 Pennsylvania Ave. N.W., Washington, D.C. 20006. Filed 10/10/83. Legislative interest — ". . . legislation and nominations affecting the regulation of hydropower licensing. . . ."

MUSIC CORPORATION OF AMERICA INC., Universal City, Calif. Lobbyist — James C. Corman, 1420 16th St. N.W., Washington, D.C. 20036. (Former U.S. rep., D-Calif., 1961-81.) Filed 10/21/83. Legislative interest — "To support legislation protecting the copyright of motion picture producers. To oppose legislation diminishing copyright and syndication rights, or tax laws adverse to motion picture producers."

NATIONAL BROADCASTING CO. INC., 1825 K St. N.W., Washington, D.C. 20006. Lobbyist — Gray and Co., 3255 Grace St. N.W., Washington, D.C. 20007. Filed 10/11/83. Legislative interest — "Including but not limited to the financial interest and syndication rules." Filed for self 10/12/83. Legislative interest — "Legislation affecting employer, principally broadcasting, including: S 1707, HR 2250, S 55, HR 2382." Lobbyist — Terence P. Mahony.

NATIONAL CAR RENTAL SYSTEM INC., Minneapolis, Minn. Lobbyist — Bregman, Abell & Kay, 1900 L St. N.W., Washington, D.C. 20036. Filed 10/12/83. Legislative interest — ". . . matters of interest to the client concerning telecommunications."

NATIONAL INVESTMENT DEVELOPMENT CORP., Los Angeles, Calif. Lobbyist — Manatt, Phelps, Rothenberg &

Tunney, 1200 New Hampshire Ave. N.W., Washington, D.C. 20036. Filed 10/31/83. Legislative interest — "Various legislative proposals affecting the real estate industry."

NATIONAL STEEL AND SHIPBUILDING CO., San Diego, Calif. Lobbyist — Wilmer, Cutler & Pickering, 1666 K St. N.W., Washington, D.C. 20006. Filed 10/13/83. Legislative interest — ". . . involve the Department of Defense Appropriations budget for the Navy Shipbuilding Program, Hospital Ships."

NEWMONT MINING CORP., Washington, D.C. Lobbyist — Chadbourne, Parke, Whiteside & Wolff, 1101 Vermont Ave. N.W., Washington, D.C. 20005. Filed 10/27/83. Legislative interest — "To increase the amount authorized to be expended for emergency relief under Title 23, U.S. Code, in fiscal year 1983 from $100,000,000 to $250,000,000; HR 3103; tracking legislation. . . ."

NEW YORK LIFE INSURANCE CO., New York, N.Y. Lobbyist — Groom and Nordberg, 1775 Pennsylvania Ave. N.W., Washington, D.C. 20006. Legislative interest — "Federal legislation affecting Title 26 U.S.C."

NEW YORK TELEPHONE CO., New York, N.Y. Lobbyist — Leo. C. Zeferetti, 9912 Fort Hamilton Parkway, Brooklyn, N.Y. 11209. (Former U.S. rep., D-N.Y., 1975-83.) Filed 10/12/83. Legislative interest — Not specified.

NIU INC., Lobbyist — Gray and Co., 3255 Grace St. N.W., Washington, D.C. 20007. Filed 10/20/83. Legislative interest — ". . . pending telephone restructuring legislation."

NORTHWESTERN BELL (IOWA DIVISION), Des Moines, Iowa. Lobbyist — Davis, Hockenberg, Wine, Brown & Koehn, 2300 Financial Center, Des Moines, Iowa 50309. Filed 10/11/83. Legislative interest — "To implement the FCC order of July 27, 1983, without modification by Congress."

PACIFIC MUTUAL LIFE INSURANCE CO., Newport Beach, Calif. Lobbyist — James C. Corman, 1420 16th St. N.W., Washington, D.C. 20036. (Former U.S. rep., D-Calif., 1961-81.) Filed 10/21/83. Legislative interest — "To support HR 4065 and similar legislation. To oppose legislation adverse to Mutual Insurance companies."

PFIZER INC., 235 E. 42nd St., New York, N.Y. 10017. Filed for self 10/10/83. Legislative interest — Not specified. Lobbyist — David W. Landsidle, 1700 Pennsylvania Ave. N.W., Washington, D.C. 20006.

PINTO VALLEY COPPER CORP., P.O. Box 100, Miami, Ariz. 85539. Filed for self 10/14/83. Legislative interest — "Legislation affecting mineral resources, products and conduct of business in these fields." Lobbyist — Charles T. Brown.

PLAZA 400 OWNERS CORP., New York, N.Y. Lobbyist — Stroock & Stroock & Lavan, 1150 17th St. N.W., Washington, D.C. 20036. Filed 10/21/83. Legislative interest — "Involved in the drafting of proposed legislation to amend Section 216 of the Internal Revenue Code concerning cooperative housing corporations."

PROVIDENCE CAPITOL CORP., New York, N.Y. Lobbyist — McClure & Trotter, 1100 Connecticut Ave. N.W., Washington, D.C. 20036. Filed 10/12/83. Legislative interest — "Legislation in connection with the taxation of life insurance companies and their products, particularly HR 4065, Life Insurance Tax Act of 1983."

PROVIDENT MUTUAL LIFE INSURANCE COMPANY OF PHILADELPHIA, Philadelphia, Pa. Lobbyist — Groom and Nordberg, 1775 Pennsylvania Ave. N.W., Washington, D.C. 20006. Filed 10/11/83. Legislative interest — "Federal legislation affecting Title 26 of U.S.C." Lobbyist — James C. Corman, 1420 16th St. N.W., Washington, D.C. 20036. (Former U.S. rep., D-Calif., 1961-81.) Filed 10/21/83. Legislative interest — "To support HR 4065 and similiar legislation. To oppose legislation adverse to Mutual Insurance companies."

T. RAMIREZ AND CO. INC., Lobbyist — Hill and Knowlton Inc., 1201 Pennsylvania Ave. N.W., Washington, D.C. 20004. Filed 10/11/83. Legislative interest — "Legislation affecting Central American policy. A private bill may be sought to compensate Mr. Ramirez for damages caused to his property by U.S. actions in Honduras."

SALOMON BROTHERS INC., New York, N.Y. Lobbyist — Thacher, Proffitt & Wood, 1140 Connecticut Ave. N.W., Wash-

ington, D.C. 20036. Filed 10/14/83. Legislative interest — "Various housing finance securities and secondary mortgage market activities ... S 1821 for secondary mortgage market enhancement and S 1821 for trusts in mortgage securities (TIMS)."

SANTA ANITA REALTY ENTERPRISES INC., Los Angeles, Calif. Lobbyist — Robert C. McCandless, 1707 H St. N.W., Washington, D.C. 20006. Filed 10/23/83. Legislative interest — "Promotion or furtherance of general legislative programs felt to be in the interests of Santa Anita. Specifically, protecting the interests of Santa Anita with regard to HR 3475 and Staple - REITS."

SANTA FE INDUSTRIES INC., 224 South Michigan Ave., Chicago, Ill. 60604. Filed for self 10/14/83. Legislative interest — "... including but not limited to ... HR 1010, S 267, Coal Distribution & Utilization Act of 1983; HR 1646, Railroad Retirement Solvency Act of 1983; S 48, Transportation Improvement Act of 1983 ... Omnibus tax legislation, Mineral Leasing Act revisions, oil pipeline regulatory reform, public land management, hazardous waste...."

SHAH & ASSOCIATES, Gaithersburg, Md. Lobbyist — James C. Corman, 1460 16th St. N.W., Washington, D.C. 20036. (Former U.S. rep., D-Calif., 1961-81.) Filed 10/21/83. Legislative interest — "To support legislation favorable to small businesses engaged in contracting with the Federal government."

SONY CORPORATION OF AMERICA, New York, N.Y. Lobbyist — Debevoise & Plimpton, 1777 F St. N.W., Washington, D.C. 20006. Filed 10/7/83. Legislative interest — "Pending proposals to amend the copyright laws, Title 17 of the U.S. Code, to exempt from copyright liability off-air recording by video and audio recorders, and/or establish compulsory license fee relating to such activities, and to otherwise modify the copyright laws ... HR 175, 1027, 1029, 1030; S 31, 32, 33, 175...."

STANDARD OIL COMPANY OF INDIANA, Chicago, Ill. Lobbyist — Chadbourne, Parke, Whiteside & Wolff, 1101 Vermont Ave. N.W., Washington, D.C. 20005. Filed 10/10/83. Legislative interest — "Photovoltaic tax credits."

STATE MUTUAL LIFE ASSURANCE COMPANY OF AMERICA, Worchester, Mass. Lobbyist — James C. Corman, 1420 16th St. N.W., Washington, D.C. 20036. (Former U.S. rep., D-Calif., 1961-81.) Filed 10/21/83. Legislative interest — "To support HR 4065 and similiar legislation. To oppose legislation adverse to Mutual Insurance companies."

STONE & WEBSTER ENGINEERING CORP., Boston, Mass. Lobbyist — Charlie McBride Associates Inc., 1717 K St. N.W., Washington, D.C. 20036. Filed 10/12/83. Legislative interest — "Nuclear waste disposal legislation; Clinch River Breeder Reactor legislation; nuclear matters in general."

STROH BREWERY CO., Detroit, Mich. Lobbyist — Gray and Co., 3255 Grace St. N.W., Washington, D.C. 20007. Filed 10/11/83. Legislative interest — "Including but not limited to antitrust and tax issues."

SUN LIFE ASSURANCE COMPANY OF CANADA (U.S.), Wellesley Hills, Mass. Lobbyist — Covington & Burling, 1201 Pennsylvania Ave. N.W., Washington, D.C. 20044. Filed 10/31/83. Legislative interest — "Taxation of annuities; 'Tax Reform Act of 1983,' HR 4170 (section 222), S 1922 (section 222); against."

SYSTEMS AND APPLIED SCIENCES, Riverdale, Md. Lobbyist — James C. Corman, 1420 16th St. N.W., Washington, D.C. 20036. (Former U.S. rep., D-Calif., 1961-81.) Filed 10/21/83. Legislative interest — "To support legislation favorable to small businesses engaged in contracting with the Federal government."

THE TEST MARKETING GROUP INC., 140 S. Dearborn St., Chicago, Ill. 60603. Lobbyist — Pepper & Corazzini, 1776 K St. N.W., Washington, D.C. 20006. Filed 10/27/83. Legislative interest — "S 66 Cable Telecommunications Act of 1983." Filed for self 10/27/83. Legislative interest — "S 66 Cable Telecommunications Act of 1983." Lobbyist — William J. McKenna.

TEXAS AIR CORP., Houston, Texas. Lobbyist — Hughes, Hubbard & Reed, 1201 Pennsylvania Ave. N.W., Washington, D.C. 20004. Filed 10/7/83. Legislative interest — "To bring to the attention of relevant committees, members and staff of the House and Senate positions on regulation of the airline industry after the

Civil Aeronautics Board sunset." Lobbyist — Van Ness, Feldman, Sutcliffe, Curtis & Levenberg, 1050 Thomas Jefferson St. N.W., Washington, D.C. 20007. Filed 10/20/83. Legislative interest — "Opposition to any legislation that would ... reregulate the airline industry ... modify the bankruptcy laws that affect any voluntary reorganization under Chapter 11, that was filed prior to September 25, 1983, or ... modify the present Federal law concerning labor protective provisions." Lobbyist — James C. Corman, 1420 16th St. N.W., Washington, D.C. 20036. (Former U.S. rep., D-Calif., 1961-81.) Filed 10/21/83. Legislative interest — "Opposition to any legislation that would ... reregulate the airline industry ... modify the bankruptcy laws that affect any voluntary reorganization under Chapter 11, that was filed prior to September 25, 1983, or ... modify the present Federal law concerning labor protective provisions."

TIMBER REALIZATION, Jackson, Miss. Lobbyist — McDermott, Will & Emery, 1850 K St. N.W., Washington, D.C. 20006. Filed 10/28/83. Legislative interest — "Subchapter C issues, specifically, publicly traded partnership provisions."

TIPPERARY CORP., Midland, Texas. Lobbyist — Akin, Gump, Strauss, Hauer & Feld, 1333 New Hampshire Ave. N.W., Washington, D.C. 20036. Filed 10/5/83. Legislative interest — "Hearings and any legislation relative to the regulation of disposal of brine including HR 3200, the 'Safe Drinking Water Amendments of 1983.' "

TRADE MAX INC., Dallas, Texas. Lobbyist — Daniel A. Dutko, 412 1st St. S.E., Washington, D.C. 20003. Filed 10/12/83. Legislative interest — "Legislation affecting trademark infringement."

TRANSCO INC., Houston, Texas. Lobbyist — Nancy Whorton George, 499 South Capitol St. S.W., Washington, D.C. 20003. Filed 10/10/83. Legislative interest — "Coal slurry legislation."

TYMNET INC., San Jose, Calif. Lobbyist — Squire, Sanders & Dempsey, 1201 Pennsylvania Ave. N.W., Washington, D.C. 20004. Filed 10/12/83. Legislative interest — "Revisions to the Communications Act of 1934 ... Universal Telephone Service Preservation Act of 1983 ... S 1660 ... HR 3621...."

UCI INC., Springfield, Va. Lobbyist — James C. Corman, 1420 16th St. N.W., Washington, D.C. 20036. (Former U.S. rep., D-Calif., 1961-81.) Filed 10/21/83. Legislative interest — "To support legislation favorable to small businesses engaged in contracting with the Federal government."

WESTINGHOUSE ELECTRIC CORP., Washington, D.C. Lobbyist — Charlie McBride Associates Inc., 1717 K St. N.W., Washington, D.C. 20036. Filed 10/12/83. Legislative interest — "Legislation concerning Clinch River Breeder Reactor, nuclear export, nuclear waste disposal, Export-Import Bank funding."

YUKON PACIFIC CORP., Houston, Texas. Lobbyist — Birch, Horton, Bittner, Pestinger and Anderson, 1140 Connecticut Ave. N.W., Washington, D.C. 20036. Filed 10/13/83. Legislative interest — "Legislation involving North Slope natural gas development."

International Relations

GOVERNMENT OF JAMAICA, Kingston, Jamaica. Lobbyist — O'Connor & Hannan, 1919 Pennsylvania Ave. N.W., Washington, D.C. 20006. (Former U.S. Rep. Thomas B. Evans Jr., R-Del., 1977-83, was listed as agent for this client.) Filed 10/24/83. Legislative interest — "General legislative matters including, but not limited to passage of the Caribbean Basin Initiative...."

KINGDOM OF MOROCCO, Rabat, Morocco. Lobbyist — Neill and Co. Inc., 1100 17th St. N.W., Washington, D.C. 20036. Filed 10/19/83. Legislative interest — "Promoting the passage of the Administration's military and economic assistance programs insofar as it may relate to the Kingdom of Morocco, including the foreign assistance authorization and appropriations bills."

Labor Groups

BROTHERHOOD OF RAILWAY, AIRLINE & STEAMSHIP CLERKS, FREIGHT HANDLERS, EX-

PRESS & STATION EMPLOYEES, 3 Research Place, Rockville, Md. 20850. Filed for self 10/25/83. Legislative interest — "Interested in all legislation affecting labor, especially railroad and airline labor." Lobbyists — John B. Spears, Anthony Padilla, Claude W. Merlo, Elden C. McKeen, Gilbert Mattox, John W. Matthews, Brian M. Kilbury, Daniel W. Kaluza, Thomas J. Dwyer, Thomas F. Donovan, Michael M. Cunniff, Harold L. Crosier, Florian J. Anfang, 815 16th St. N.W., Washington, D.C. 20006.

NATIONAL ASSOCIATION OF RETIRED FEDERAL EMPLOYEES, 1533 New Hampshire Ave. N.W., Washington, D.C. 20036. Filed for self 10/21/83. Legislative interest — "... all proposals affecting Federal Civil Service annuitants. During the 3rd Quarter, 1st Session of the 98th Congress, we supported HR 656 (Oakar)-FEHBP; opposed HR 3798 (Dannemeyer)-Administration voucher plan; on the Budget Reconciliation, opposed any COLA reductions or delays beyond those in budget resolution; supported purpose of HR 3371 (Ford) and S 1522 (Stevens) to provide relief for double retirement coverage of post-83 Federal employees." Lobbyist — Thomas J. Trabucco.

NATIONAL EDUCATION ASSOCIATION, 1201 16th St. N.W., Washington, D.C. 20036. Filed for self 10/17/83. Legislative interest — "Bills pending before Congress relating to public education." Lobbyist — Donna Gold.

NATIONAL FEDERATION OF FEDERAL EMPLOYEES, 1016 16th St. N.W., Washington, D.C. 20036. Filed for self 10/10/83. Legislative interest — "... First and Second Concurrent Budget Resolutions, Agency Appropriations and Authorizations, Budget Reconciliation, Social Security Benefits, Mandatory Social Security coverage, contracting out (OMB circular A-76) Federal Employees Compensation Act, Civil Service Reform Act (U.S.C. Title V), overall compensation and working conditions for Federal employees and retirees ... Proposed Revisions to Office of Management and Budget Circular A-76 (opposed). Fiscal Year 1984 appropriations (support or oppose). HR 3871, delay change in work hours (support). HR 3466, provide Secretary of Army and Air Force authority to establish regulations governing the performance of National Guard civilian technicians (oppose). HR 3511, to eliminate 30-day notice of termination for civilian technicians who cease to be members of the National Guard (oppose). HR 828/829, to restrict the contracting out of certain Veterans' position (support). HR 2969, Department of Defense Authorization Bill. HR 3752, to establish a new supplementary civil service retirement system (oppose). S 1385 - HR 2449, to prohibit implementation of Office of Personnel Management regulations (support). HR 656, to restructure Federal Employees Health Benefit Program. S 958, to establish a demonstration project placing Federal Employees under a new performance appraisal system (support). HR 622, to provide death benefits for Federal Law Enforcement Officers and Firefighters (support)." Lobbyists — Suzanne Kalfus, Clinton Wolcott.

SHEET METAL WORKERS' INTERNATIONAL ASSOCIATION, 1750 New York Ave., N.W., Washington, D.C. 20006. Filed for self 10/21/83. Legislative interest — "All labor legislation, all solar legislation, S 1462." Lobbyist — Cecil D. Clay.

State and Local Governments

CLAVEY-WARDS FERRY PROJECT/TURLOCK IRRIGATION DISTRICT/MODESTO IRRIGATION DISTRICT, Turlock, Calif. Lobbyist — Damrell, Damrell & Nelson, 911 13th St., Modesto, Calif. 95353. Filed 10/11/83. Legislative interest — "Hearings on any related legislation concerning United States environmental and energy policy, including but not limited to legislation affecting the Tuolumne River."

17TH GUAM LEGISLATURE, Agana, Guam. Lobbyist — Hale and Dorr, 1201 Pennsylvania Ave. N.W., Washington, D.C. 20004. Filed 10/26/83. Legislative interest — "... tax legislation and legislation affecting territories generally."

COMMISSIONER OF PUBLIC LANDS FOR STATE OF NEW MEXICO, Santa Fe, N.M. Lobbyist — Eric M. Rubin, 1730 M St. N.W., Washington, D.C. 20036. Filed 10/13/83. Legisla-

tive interest — "Legislation concerning compensation for lands within White Sands Test Range."

CITY OF WHITTIER, Whittier, Alaska. Lobbyist — Birch, Horton, Bittner, Pestinger and Anderson, 1140 Connecticut Ave. N.W., Washington, D.C. 20036. Filed 10/13/83. Legislative interest — "Issues dealing with the transfer of the Alaska railroad."

Trade Associations

AD HOC COMMITTEE ON ALTERNATIVE ENERGY TAX CREDITS, Washington, D.C. Lobbyist — Van Ness, Feldman, Sutcliffe, Curtis & Levenberg, 1050 Thomas Jefferson St. N.W., Washington, D.C. 20007. Filed 10/11/83. Legislative interest — "... extending the duration of existing energy tax credits ... S 1305, S 1396, HR 3072, and HR 3358."

ALASKA RAILROAD LEASEHOLDERS ASSOCIATION, Anchorage, Alaska. Lobbyist — Birch, Horton, Bittner, Pestinger and Anderson, 1140 Connecticut Ave. N.W., Washington, D.C. 20036. Filed 10/13/83. Legislative interest — "Issues dealing with transfer of a railroad."

AMERICAN ASSOCIATION OF HOMES FOR THE AGING, 1050 17th St. N.W., Washington, D.C. 20036. Filed for self 10/4/83. Legislative interest — "Federal health and housing programs serving the elderly and other issues of concern to the aging." Lobbyist — Charles H. Edwards.

AMERICAN CONSULTING ENGINEERS COUNCIL, 1015 15th St. N.W., Washington, D.C. 20005. Filed for self 10/11/83. Legislative interest — "Matters relating to public works; transportation; the environment; pollution control; housing; equal employment opportunity; public health and safety; economy and efficiency in government; and energy legislation. Primary interests are in fields of international policy, trade and finance." Lobbyist — Julian K. Morrison III.

AMERICAN FARM BUREAU FEDERATION, 225 Touhy Ave., Park Ridge, Ill. 60068. Filed for self 10/19/83. Legislative interest — "... natural resources...." Lobbyist — Dennis C. Stolte, 600 Maryland Ave. S.W., Washington, D.C. 20024.

AMERICAN FISHING TACKLE MANUFACTURERS ASSOCIATION, Arlington Heights, Ill. Lobbyist — Gray and Co., 3255 Grace St. N.W., Washington, D.C. 20007. Filed 10/11/83. Legislative interest — "HR 2163."

AMERICAN HARDWARE MANUFACTURERS ASSOCIATION, Schaumburg, Ill. Lobbyist — Sheldon I. London, 1725 DeSales St. N.W., Washington, D.C. 20036. Filed 10/12/83. Legislative interest — "... legislation which relates to tax policy, consumer, product liability, environment, labor...."

AMERICAN MEAT INSTITUTE, Arlington, Va. Lobbyist — Kaye, Scholer, Fierman, Hays & Handler, 1575 I St. N.W., Washington, D.C. 20005. Filed 10/27/83. Legislative interest — "General interest in government policies regarding the red meat industry."

AMERICAN MEDICAL PEER REVIEW ASSOCIATION, 440 1st St. N.W., Washington, D.C. 20001. Filed for self 10/19/83. Legislative interest — "... PL 92-603 and resulting Professional Standards Review Organizations (PSRO) ... PL 97-248, the Tax Equity and Fiscal Responsibility Law and funding for fiscal year 1984." Lobbyist — Andrew H. Webber.

AMERICAN PETROCHEMICAL CONSUMERS, 1815 H St. N.W., Washington, D.C. 20006. Lobbyist — Kenneth L. Holland, P.O. Drawer 940, Gaffney, S.C. 29342. (Former U.S. rep., D-S.C., 1975-83.) Filed 10/20/83. Legislative interest — "Legislation relating to the importation of petrochemicals." Filed for self 10/19/83. Legislative interest — "Legislation relating to the importation of petrochemicals and any amendments to the Trade Act of 1930 (Title 19 U.S.C.)...." Lobbyist — Edwin M. Wheeler.

ASSOCIATION OF BANK HOLDING COS., 730 15th St. N.W., Washington, D.C. 20005. Lobbyist — Moss Associates Inc., 2440 Virginia Ave. N.W., Washington, D.C. 20037. Filed 10/10/83. Legislative interest — "In support of the proposed regional Banking Deregulation Act...." Filed for self 10/12/83.

Legislative interest — "... In support of the proposed Financial Institutions Deregulation Act, S 1609, and the proposed Regional Banking Deregulation Act. In oposition to 'moratorium' legislation, such as S 1532 and HR 3499." Lobbyist — James C. Sivon.

CHAMBER OF COMMERCE OF THE UNITED STATES, 1615 H St. N.W., Washington, D.C. 20062. Filed for self 10/12/83. Legislative interest — Not specified. Lobbyists — Melody J. Blank, Samuel A. Roth.

COALITION OF COMMUNITY BANKS OF FLORIDA, Miami, Fla. Lobbyist — Smathers, Symington & Herlong, 1700 K St. N.W., Washington, D.C. 20008. Filed 10/4/83. Legislative interest — "Legislation that would allow banks to pay interest on demand deposit transactional accounts maintained by commercial depositors, generally; specifically HR 3535, the 'Demand Deposit Equity Act of 1983,' oppose; HR 3895, the 'Demand Deposit Equity Act of 1983,' oppose in part; S 1875, the 'Demand Deposit Deregulation Act,' oppose in part."

COMMITTEE OF CORPORATE TELECOMMUNICATIONS USERS, Washington, D.C. Lobbyist — Peabody, Lambert & Meyers, 1150 Connecticut Ave. N.W., Washington, D.C. 20036. Filed 10/20/83. Legislative interest — "Universal Telephone Service Preservation Act of 1983: S 1660 and HR 4102 - Opposed to Bypass Charge and other provisions thereof."

COMMITTEE FOR PRUDENT DEREGULATION, New York, N.Y. Lobbyist — Williams & Jensen, 1101 Connecticut Ave. N.W., Washington, D.C. 20036. Filed 10/13/83. Legislative interest — "Legislation relating to the syndication of network TV programming, including HR 2250 and S 1707."

CONTACT LENS MANUFACTURERS ASSOCIATION, Newark, N.J. Lobbyist — Thompson & Mitchell, 1120 Vermont Ave. N.W., Washington, D.C. 20005. Filed 10/5/83. Legislative interest — Not specified.

COOPERATIVE OF AMERICAN PHYSICIANS INC., Los Angeles, Calif. Lobbyist — James C. Corman, 1420 16th St. N.W., Washington, D.C. 20036. (Former U.S. rep., D-Calif., 1961-81.) Filed 10/21/83. Legislative interest — "To support HR 2486...."

CORDAGE INSTITUTE, Washington, D.C. Lobbyist — The Keefe Co., 444 N. Capitol St., Washington, D.C. 20001. Filed 10/21/83. Legislative interest — "Support for bills relating to trade, production liability, small business and taxation."

COSMETIC, TOILETRY AND FRAGRANCE ASSOCIATION INC., 1110 Vermont Ave. N.W., Washington, D.C. 20005. Filed for self 10/17/83. Legislative interest — Not specified. Lobbyist — Michael J. Petrina Jr.

DESIGN PROFESSIONALS COALITION, Washington, D.C. Lobbyist — Williams & Jensen, 1101 Connecticut Ave. N.W., Washington, D.C. 20036. Filed 10/31/83. Legislative interest — "Legislative developments affecting federal procurement of architectural-engineering services."

ELECTRONIC INDUSTRIES ASSOCIATION OF JAPAN, Lobbyist — Gray and Co., 3255 Grace St. N.W., Washington, D.C. 20007. Filed 10/7/83. Legislative interest — "Including but not limited to unitary tax issues, anti-dumping cases and general matters affecting the electronic industry."

GREATER PHILADELPHIA CHAMBER OF COMMERCE, 1346 Chestnut St., Philadelphia, Pa. 19107. Filed for self 10/14/83. Legislative interest — "...federal budget, taxation issues, energy and environmental issues and water/port issues affecting Philadelphia and the State of Pennsylvania ... HR 3678, Omnibus Water Resources Bill - GPCC supports. HR 3790, Ways and Means 2% Tax Indexation Bill - GPCC supports. HR 1234, Domestic Content Legislation - GPCC opposes." Lobbyists — Camille Kearns Rudy, Cris Penn, James E. Panyard.

INDEPENDENT RADIO COMMON CARRIERS ASSOCIATION, Austin, Texas. Lobbyist — Schlossberg-Cassidy & Associates, 955 L'Enfant Plaza, Washington, D.C. 20024. Filed 10/25/83. Legislative interest — "All legislative matters affecting radio common carriers."

INTERNATIONAL TAXICAB ASSOCIATION, Rockville, Md. Lobbyist — James C. Corman, 1460 16th St. N.W., Washington, D.C. 20036. (Former U.S. rep., D-Calif., 1961-81.) Filed 10/21/83. Legislative interest — "To support continuation of gasoline franchise tax laws affecting taxicab industry."

JOINT MARITIME CONGRESS, Washington, D.C. Lobbyist — Gray and Co., 3255 Grace St. N.W., Washington, D.C. 20007. Filed 10/3/83. Legislative interest — "Including but not limited to maritime legislation."

NATIONAL ASSOCIATION FOR HOSPITAL DEVELOPMENT, Washington, D.C. Lobbyist — Swidler, Berlin & Strelow, 1000 Thomas Jefferson St. N.W., Washington, D.C. 20007. Filed 10/10/83. Legislative interest — "... all bills pending in the Congress that affect the ability of the donor to freely donate money or assets to not-for-profit hospitals. NAHD's principal interest currently is in HR 501 and HR 850."

NATIONAL ASSOCIATION OF MUTUAL SAVINGS BANKS, 200 Park Ave., New York, N.Y. 10166. Filed for self 10/14/83. Legislative interest — Not specified. Lobbyist — Peter E. Knight, 1709 New York Ave. N.W., Washington, D.C. 20006.

NATIONAL ASSOCIATION OF PRIVATE PSYCHIATRIC HOSPITALS, 1319 F St. N.W., Washington, D.C. 20004. Filed for self 10/11/83. Legislative interest — "Issues affecting mental health, hospitals, manpower and patients." Lobbyist — Charles J. Campisis.

NATIONAL ASSOCIATION OF WHOLESALER-DISTRIBUTORS, 1725 K St. N.W., Washington, D.C. 20006. Filed for self 10/24/83. Legislative interest — "Product liability tort reform ... S 44, HR 2729; budgetary issues ... S J Res 5, H J Res 243; regulatory reform ... S 1080, HR 220, HR 2327; Multiemployer Pension Plan Act; Single Employer Pension Plan Reforms ... S 1227; Sales Representatives Protection Act ... HR 797, HR 3591; Office Machine and Equipment Retail Dealers' Agreement Act ... HR 1159, S 286."

NATIONAL CABLE TELEVISION ASSOCIATION, 1724 Massachusetts Ave. N.W., Washington, D.C. 20036. Lobbyist — Heron, Burchette, Ruckert & Rothwell, 1200 New Hampshire Ave. N.W., Washington, D.C. 20036. Filed 10/18/83. Legislative interest — "Support legislation to pre-empt local regulation of cable TV." Filed for self 10/18/83. Legislative interest — "Amendments to the Communications Act of 1934...." Lobbyist — Edward A. Merlis.

NATIONAL CONFERENCE OF BANKRUPTCY JUDGES, Lexington, Ky. Lobbyist — M. Caldwell Butler, P.O. Box 720, Roanoke, Va. 24004. (Former U.S. rep., R-Va., 1972-83.) Filed 10/18/83. Legislative interest — "Passage of HR 3."

NATIONAL COUNCIL OF COMMUNITY HOSPITALS, Washington, D.C. Lobbyist — Swidler, Berlin & Strelow, 1000 Thomas Jefferson St. N.W., Washington, D.C. 20007. Filed 10/10/83. Legislative interest — "... HR 1900 and S 1."

NATIONAL COUNCIL OF FARMER COOPERATIVES, 1800 Massachusetts Ave. N.W., Washington, D.C. 20036. Filed for self 10/24/83. Legislative interest — "None." Lobbyist — Nancy E. Foster.

NATIONAL SOCIETY OF PUBLIC ACCOUNTANTS, 1010 N. Fairfax St., Alexandria, Va. 22314. Filed for self 10/10/83. Legislative interest — "Legislation affecting public accountants; tax legislation affecting small business; S 1510 'The Uniform Single Financial Audit Act of 1983.' " Lobbyist — Maryalyce Reilly.

NATIONAL TOOLING & MACHINING ASSOCIATION, 9300 Livingston Road, Fort Washington, Md. 20744. Filed for self 10/12/83. Legislative interest — Not specified. Lobbyist — Anna Mary Hoovler.

NEW BEDFORD SEAFOOD COUNCIL INC., 17 Hamilton St., New Bedford, Mass. 02740. Filed for self 10/14/83. Legislative interest — "... Fish Net Tariff Reduction, FCMA, Funding of fisheries and Coast Guard Programs, Oil Drilling on Outer Continental Shelf, Maritime Safety." Lobbyist — Allyn M. Fritts, 5006 N. 34th Road, Arlington, Va. 22207.

OFFSHORE MARINE SERVICE ASSOCIATION, New Orleans, La. Lobbyist — David P. Stang, 1629 K St. N.W., Washington, D.C. 20006. Filed 10/14/83. Legislative interest — "S 1564/HR 3110 'Governmental Lease Financing Reform Act of 1983.' "

PHARMACEUTICAL MANUFACTURERS ASSOCIATION, Washington, D.C. Lobbyist — F/P Research Associates,

1700 K St. N.W., Washington, D.C. 20006. Filed 10/11/83. Legislative interest — "S 44, legislation to regulate interstate commerce by providing for a uniform product liability law."

SHIPBUILDERS COUNCIL OF AMERICA, 1110 Vermont Ave. N.W., Washington, D.C. 20005. Filed for self 10/12/83. Legislative interest — "Maritime legislation, tax law related thereto, naval shipbuilding, government procurement regulations, maritime related labor, health and environmental regulations." Lobbyist — M. Lee Rice.

THE SOCIETY OF THE PLASTICS INDUSTRY INC., New York, N.Y. Lobbyist — James M. Bennett, 642 S. Dakota Trail, Franklin Lakes, N.J. 07417. Filed 10/12/83. Legislative interest — "Product Liability Tort Reform, Natural Gas Deregulation, Food Safety, Energy Taxes, Hazardous Air Pollutants, Hazardous Waste Small Generator Exemption, Toxic Victims Compensation Fund, Export-Import Bank Rechartering, Federal Spending, Social Security, Clean Water Act Effluent Guidelines, Hazardous Materials Transportation Chlorofluorocarbons...."

TELOCATOR NETWORK OF AMERICA, Washington, D.C. Lobbyist — Finley, Kumble, Wagner, Heine, 1120 Connecticut Ave. N.W., Washington, D.C. 20036. Filed 10/18/83. Legislative interest — "Pending legislation on access charges and surcharges as it relates to radio common carriers; to assure universal telephone service, HR 4102 and S 1660; RCC Amendment."

THE TOBACCO INSTITUTE, 1875 I St. N.W., Washington, D.C. 20006. Filed 10/10/83. Legislative interest — Not specified. Lobbyists — Ralph Vinovich, Howard S. Liebengood.

UNITED STATES LEAGUE OF SAVING INSTITUTIONS, 111 E. Wacker Drive, Chicago, Ill. Filed for self 10/10/83. Legislative interest — "...legislation affecting savings and loans, housing, home financing, thrift and financial institutions...." Lobbyists — Roy G. Green, Michael G. Troop, 1709 New York Ave. N.W., Washington, D.C. 20006.

UNITED STATES LIFESAVING MANUFACTURERS ASSOCIATION, Washington, D.C. Lobbyist — Patton, Boggs & Blow, 2550 M St. N.W., Washington, D.C. 20037. Filed 10/13/83. Legislative interest — "Legislation relating maritime safety including equipment requirements on inspected vessels and manufacturing inspection procedures, such as HR 3486 and S 1910."

UTILITY NUCLEAR WASTE MANAGEMENT GROUP, Washington, D.C. Lobbyist — Lowenstein, Newman, Reis & Axelrad, 1025 Connecticut Ave. N.W., Washington, D.C. 20036. Filed 10/11/83. Legislative interest — "Congressional consent legislation for state compacts developed pursuant to the Low-Level Radioactive Waste Policy Act (PL 96-573); in favor of bills consenting to regional compacts (such as S 247 & HR 1012, S 1581 & HR 3022, and S 1749 & HR 3777)...."

Miscellaneous

CORPORATION FOR PUBLIC BROADCASTING, Washington, D.C. Lobbyist — Preston, Thorgrimson, Ellis & Holman, 1735 New York Ave. N.W., Washington, D.C. 20006. Filed 10/11/83. Legislative interest — "HR 2755, HR 3913, S 607 and other bills affecting public broadcasting authorization and appropriations."

RAMZI A. DALLOUL, Washington, D.C. Lobbyist — Gray and Co., 3255 Grace St. N.W., Washington, D.C. 20007. Filed 10/3/83. Legislative interest — "...immigration/visa matters."

THE FARM CREDIT COUNCIL, 1800 Massachusetts Ave. N.W., Washington, D.C. 20036. Filed for self 10/21/83. Legislative interest — "None." Lobbyists — Delmar K. Banner, Joseph L. S. Terrell.

FLOOD CONTROL ADVISORY COMMITTEE, Minneapolis, Minn. Lobbyist — Powell, Goldstein, Frazer & Murphy, 1110 Vermont Ave. N.W., Washington, D.C. 20005. Filed 10/31/83. Legislative interest — "...to obtain Congressional approval of a flood control project in Rochester, Minn."

DYKE JOHNSON JR., P.O. Box 7000 A, Texarkana, Texas 75501. Filed for self 10/10/83. Legislative interest — "Civil rights, criminal justice administration, minority job programs."

ANDREW L. LUI, West Newton, Mass. Lobbyist — Charles J. Micoleau, One Canal Plaza, Portland, Maine 04112. Filed 10/6/83. Legislative interest — "HR 1236." Lobbyist — J. William W. Harsch, 1825 K St. N.W., Washington, D.C. 20006. Filed 10/7/83. Legislative interest — "HR 1236."

JOHN D. AND CATHERINE T. MacARTHUR FOUNDATION, Northbrook, Ill. Lobbyist — Verner, Liipfert, Bernhard and McPherson, 1660 L St. N.W., Washington, D.C. 20036. Filed 10/11/83. Legislative interest — "Legislation seeking relief from 5-year divestment requirement."

NEW ENGLAND EDUCATIONAL LOAN MARKETING CORP., Braintree, Mass. Lobbyist — Larry S. Snowhite, 1825 I St. N.W., Washington, D.C. 20006. Filed 10/14/83. Legislative interest — "Student Loan Consolidation and Financing Corp. Legislation."

ROBERT RICHARD SCHMITT, 11304-047, Unit C, P.O. Box 888, Ashland, Ky. 41101. Filed for self 10/11/83. Legislative interest — "Lobby House and Senate for better prison and jail conditions and fair and equal enforcement of laws."

PHILIP WILLIFORD, #12140 057, U.J., P.O. Box 888, Ashland, Ky. 41101. Filed for self 10/11/83. Legislative interest — "Lobby House and Senate for better prison and jail conditions and fair and equal enforcement of laws." ■

Lobby Registration Index

A

Abbott Laboratories · 6-D
Acacia Mutual Life Insurance Co. · 6-D
Acurex Solar Corp. · 49-D
Ad Hoc Committee for Equitable Transportation · 48-D
Ad Hoc Committee in Defense of Life Inc. · 31-D
Ad Hoc Committee of Floor Brokers · 30-D
Ad Hoc Committee on Alternative Energy Tax Credits · 53-D
Adams, Kenneth R. · 40-D
Adams, Wade J. · 44-D
Adduci, Dinan and Mastriani
  Consejo Nacional de Commercio Exterior del Noreste A.C. · 42-D
  Vulcan Foundry Inc. · 41-D
Aetna Life & Casualty Co. · 12-D

Aetna Life and Casualty Insurance Co. · 40-D, 44-D
Airbus Industrie · 6-D, 40-D
Air Conditioning and Refrigeration Institute · 37-D
Air Florida Inc. · 6-D
Air Force Sergeants Association · 8-D
Air Products & Chemicals Inc. · 17-D
Air Quality Research Inc. · 44-D
AIWA America Inc. · 12-D
Akin, Gump, Strauss, Hauer & Feld
  Amerada Hess Corp. · 44-D
  American Soybean Association · 15-D
  Committee for Prudent Deregulation · 9-D
  Dow Chemical Co. · 45-D
  Goldman Sachs & Co. · 45-D
  Lone Star Steel · 13-D
  Marriott Corp. · 13-D
  Mesa Petroleum Co. · 51-D

  National Soybean Processors Association · 16-D
  Osteopathic Medical Center · 16-D
  Pipeline Industry Advancement Fund · 22-D
  Purolator Inc. · 29-D
  Riviana Foods Inc. · 14-D
  Southern California Edison Co. · 36-D
  Tipperary Corp. · 52-D
  Western Governors Policy Office · 30-D
  West Indies Rum and Spirits Producers Association · 31-D
Alamo Cement Co. · 27-D, 32-D
Alascom Inc. · 6-D
Alaska Bankers Association · 37-D
Alaska Lumber and Pulp Co. Inc. · 6-D, 10-D, 17-D, 23-D, 44-D
Alaska Pacific Bancorp. · 6-D
Alaska Pulp & Resources Inc. · 6-D
Alaska Railroad Leaseholders Association · 53-D

Alaska, State of · 25-D
Alcalde, Henderson & O'Bannon
  Florida Association of Marine Industries · 5-D
  Florida Caribbean Cruise Association · 5-D
  Washington Workshops · 5-D
Aleutian/Pribilof Islands Association Inc. · 44-D
Alexa, George Paul · 31-D
Alignpac · 49-D
Allen, H. K. · 3-D
Alliance Against Handguns · 39-D
Alliance to Save Energy · 5-D
Allied Corp. · 44-D
Allied Tube & Conduit Corp. · 17-D
Allis-Chalmers Corp. · 44-D
Alpha Data Inc. · 23-D
Alston & Bird
  Meat Price Investigators Association · 47-D

Altman Foundation, The - 43-D
Aluminum Company of America - 27-D
Alvarado, Ricardo R. - 7-D
AM International - 49-D
Ambrose, Robert P. - 45-D
Amerada Hess Corp. - 44-D
American Academy of Pediatrics - 42-D
American Airlines Inc. - 32-D
American Association of Homes for the Aging - 42-D, 53-D
American Association of Meat Processors - 37-D
American Association of Retired Persons - 20-D
American Automobile Association - 17-D
American Automobile Association, Potomac Division - 44-D
American Bakers Association - 30-D
American Bankers Association - 21-D
American Border Broadcasters Free Speech Committee Inc. - 26-D
American Broadcasting Co. - 44-D
American Bus Association - 8-D, 15-D
American Can Co. - 27-D
American Consulting Engineers Council - 53-D
American Council of Life Insurance - 8-D, 42-D
American Dental Association - 8-D
American Druze Public Affairs Committee - 48-D
American Express Co. - 44-D, 49-D
American Farm Bureau Federation - 53-D
American Federation of Government Employees, Local 2677 - 46-D
American Federation of Teachers - 36-D
American Fishing Tackle Manufacturers Association - 53-D
American Foreign Service Association - 15-D
American Gas Association - 8-D
American General Life Insurance Co. - 23-D
American Global Lines Inc. - 4-D
American Hardware Manufacturers Association - 53-D
American Hellenic Institute Public Affairs Committee Inc. - 21-D
American Income Life Insurance Co. - 44-D
American Independent Refiners Association - 37-D
American Institute of Merchant Shipping - 30-D, 42-D
American Iron and Steel Institute - 8-D, 37-D
American League for Exports and Security Assistance Inc. - 15-D
American Legion, The - 11-D
American Logistics Association - 3-D
American Lung Association - 5-D
American Maritime Association - 8-D, 15-D
American Meat Institute - 8-D, 21-D, 53-D
American Medical Peer Review Association - 47-D, 53-D
American Medical Records Association - 21-D
American Mining Congress - 42-D
American Natural Resources Co. - 32-D
American Newspaper Publishers Association - 25-D
American Nurses' Association - 21-D, 37-D
American Paper Institute Inc. - 21-D, 25-D
American Petrochemical Consumers - 53-D
American Petrofina Inc. - 12-D, 40-D, 44-D

American Petroleum Institute - 8-D, 30-D
American Postal Workers Union - 36-D
American President Lines Ltd. - 6-D, 12-D
American Protestant Hospital Association - 30-D
American Public Transit Association - 8-D
American Pulpwood Association - 30-D
American Red Cross Retirement System - 43-D
American Refugees in America - 17-D
American Rivers Conservation Council - 5-D
American Rose Council - 8-D
American Science and Technology Corp. - 10-D
American Security Insurance Co. - 49-D
American Seed Trade Association - 47-D
American Ski Federation - 47-D
American Social Health Association - 48-D
American Society of Composers, Authors and Publishers - 37-D
American Soybean Association - 15-D
American Stock Exchange Inc. - 23-D
American Telephone & Telegraph Inc. - 49-D
American Veterans of World War II, Korea & Vietnam (AMVETS) - 39-D
American Waterways Operators Inc. - 8-D, 37-D
Amurcon Corp. - 3-D
Amusement and Music Operators Association - 30-D
Amytex Corp. - 49-D
Anaheim, City of - 46-D
Anchorage, Municipality of - 46-D
Anderson & Pendleton
    Canned and Cooked Meat Importers Association, The - 25-D
Anderson, Hibey, Nauheim & Blair
    Alaska Lumber & Pulp Inc. - 10-D
    Lobby registration - 49-D
Anderson, James A. Jr. - 9-D
Anderson, Linda D. - 44-D
Aneutronix Inc. - 10-D, 12-D
Anfang, Florian J. - 53-D
Anheuser-Busch Cos. Inc. - 32-D
Anthony, Tobias - 47-D
Antrim, Patrick S. - 24-D, 27-D
Apache Corp. - 23-D, 27-D
Apex Marine Corp. - 40-D
Appalachian Community Service Network - 39-D
Araujo, Robert J. - 7-D
Arco Solar Inc. - 44-D
Arent, Fox, Kintner, Plotkin & Kahn
    Building Service Contractors Association International - 8-D
    Indiana Associates - 24-D
    Intelsat - 24-D
    Lars Krough & Co. - 7-D
    Pueblo International Inc. - 35-D
    Toyota Motor Corp. - 29-D
Armbruster, John A. - 7-D
Armco Inc. - 23-D, 27-D
Armenian National Committee - 23-D
Arnold, Sandy - 4-D
Arnold & Porter
    Anaheim, City of - 46-D
    Azusa, City of - 47-D
    Banning, City of - 47-D
    Colton, City of - 47-D
    Northern California Power Agency - 47-D
    Riverside, City of - 47-D
    Sacramento Public Utility District - 47-D
    Santa Clara, City of - 47-D
Aronson, H. L., Jr. - 22-D
Asbestos Litigation Group - 11-D

Ashland Oil Inc. - 12-D
Ashley, Lud - 45-D
Asian Pacific Economic, Educational, Cultural Organization Inc. - 5-D
Aspen Technology Inc. - 49-D
Assiniboine Tribe - 48-D
Associated Builders and Contractors Inc. - 15-D
Associated General Contractors of America - 21-D, 37-D
Association for Development Policy Research - 48-D
Association of American Cancer Institutes - 37-D
Association of American Railroads - 30-D, 37-D
Association of Bank Holding Cos. - 53-D
Association of Business Advocating Tariff Equity - 21-D
Association of Floral Importers of Florida - 25-D
Association of Local Housing Finance Agencies - 8-D
Association of Private Pension and Welfare Plans Inc. - 21-D
Association of Trial Lawyers - 37-D
Atkisson, John McElroy - 33-D
Atlanta Life Insurance Co. - 10-D
Atlantic Richfield Co. - 32-D
Audio Recording Rights Coalition - 10-D
Austin, City of - 4-D
Austin, Ronald R. - 37-D
Auto Internacional Association - 21-D
Automobile Importers of America Inc. - 8-D
Avenel Associates Inc. - 34-D
Avis Inc. - 49-D
Avon Products Inc. - 6-D
Avrakotos, Gus - 40-D
Axtell, George C. - 15-D
Azusa, City of - 47-D

B

Babcock & Brown Inc. - 40-D, 44-D
Bacardi Imports Inc. - 6-D
Baenen, Timme, De Reitzes & Middleton
    Nana Regional Corp. Inc. - 3-D
Bafalis, L. A. "Skip" - 24-D
Bailey, Beverly J. - 8-D
Baker & Botts
    Petro-Lewis Corp. - 41-D
Baker & Hostetler
    Frontier Airlines Inc. - 3-D
    Knight Foundation - 48-D
    Manville Corp. - 45-D
Baker, William S. - 32-D
Ballard, Spahr, Andrews & Ingersoll - 49-D
Balzano, Michael J. - 15-D
Bangor & Aroostook Railroad - 17-D
Bankamerica Corp. - 12-D, 23-D, 27-D, 49-D
Bankers Life Co. - 49-D
Banner, Delmar K. - 55-D
Banning, City of - 47-D
Barber Blue Sea Line/Barber West Africa Line - 27-D
Barnes, Richardson & Colburn
    EHA Ventilfabrik Wilhelm Fritz - 50-D
    Uniroyal Inc. - 14-D
Barness Organization, The - 49-D
Barnett & Alagia
    General Mills Inc. - 18-D
    Plastics Manufacturing Co. - 46-D
Baron/Canning and Co. Inc. - 25-D
Barrett, David M. - 17-D
Barrett, Smith, Schapiro, Simon & Armstrong

    Singapore Airlines Ltd. - 35-D
BASF Wyandotte Corp. - 17-D
Basic Industries Coalition Inc. - 30-D
Baskin and Sears
    South Africa, Embassy of the Republic of - 25-D
Bateman, Diane - 21-D
Batus Inc. - 12-D
Batzell, Nunn & Bode
    Independent Insurance Agents of America Inc. - 9-D
Baum, George K., & Co. - 17-D
Bauman, Barbara - 33-D
Bayh, Tabbert & Capehart
    Lexitel Corp. - 41-D
    National Solid Wastes Management Association - 39-D
Bean, C. F. - 49-D
Beard, Jeffrey L. - 37-D
Beaty, Orren Jr. - 43-D
Bechtel Power Corp. - 27-D, 49-D
Beebe, Lydia I. - 40-D
Beeber, Ronald L. - 28-D
Beer Industry Alliance - 21-D
Beers, Robert M. - 15-D
Belize, Government of - 20-D
Bell Aerospace Textron - 10-D
Bendone-DeRossi International - 12-D
Bennett, Beverly L. - 8-D
Bennett, James M. - 55-D
Bennington College - 31-D
Benson, Frederick S. III - 36-D
Berenergy Corp. - 32-D
Berman, Richard M. - 36-D
Bermudez, J. Armando - 39-D
Bethlehem Steel Corp. - 12-D
Beveridge & Diamond
    Texas Oil and Gas Corp. - 14-D
Beverly Enterprises - 12-D
Beztak Co. - 3-D
Bi-County Consortium - 23-D
Bier, Joan T. - 50-D
Billig, Sher & Jones
    American Bakers Association - 30-D
    A. P. Moller Maersk Line - 28-D
    Barber Blue Sea Line/Barber West Africa Line - 27-D
    Hapag-Lloyd A. G. - 50-D
    Hellenic Lines/Hessa Line - 28-D
    Lykes Brothers Steamship Co. - 28-D
    National Shipping Company of Saudi Arabia - 28-D
    Nedlloyd Lines - 28-D
    Private Truck Council of America Inc. - 9-D
    United Arab Shipping Co. - 30-D
    Waterman Steamship Co. - 30-D
Binder, Robert Henri - 42-D
Bingham, Dana & Gould
    Visa U.S.A. Inc. - 25-D
Biondo, P. Richard - 6-D
Biondo, Vitina - 42-D
Bipartisan Budget Appeal, The - 10-D
Birch, Horton, Bittner and Monroe
    Alascom Inc. - 6-D
    Alaska Pacific Bancorp. - 6-D
    American Bus Association - 8-D
    Harza Engineers - 7-D
    Massachusetts Mutual Life Insurance Co. - 34-D
Birch, Horton, Bittner, Pestinger and Anderson
    Alaska Bankers Association - 37-D
    Alaska Railroad Leaseholders Association - 53-D
    Coastal Corp., The - 50-D
    Whittier, City of - 53-D
    Yukon Pacific Corp. - 52-D
BKK Corp. - 24-D
Black, Manafort and Stone Inc.
    American Petrofina Inc. - 12-D
Black, Samuel H. - 27-D
Black, Spencer - 12-D

Blair, Bowen - 11-D
Blank, Melody J. - 54-D
Bliss, Craft & Richards
    Alaska Lumber and Pulp Co. - 23-D
    American President Lines - 12-D
    Gulf Oil Corp. - 50-D
    Texas Eastern Corp. - 11-D
    Texas Eastern Transmission Co. - 29-D
Blount, John B. - 15-D
Blue Cross and Blue Shield Association - 27-D
Bluhdorn, Charles G., Estate of - 26-D
Blum & Nash
    American Newspaper Publishers Association - 25-D
    Floating Point System - 33-D
    Videotex Industry Association - 31-D
Blumel, Milly S. - 41-D
Blyth Eastman Paine Webber Inc. - 17-D
Boat Owners Association of the United States - 32-D
Boeing Co., The - 17-D
Bogard, Donald P. - 10-D
Boggs, Timothy A. - 4-D
Bogle & Gates
    Pacific Seafood Processors Association - 22-D
Bond and Laxalt Inc.
    Barness Organization, The - 49-D
    Citizens for America - 48-D
    Lobby registration - 44-D
Bonner, Kathleen - 10-D
Bonneville International Corp. - 32-D
Boos, Michael - 12-D
Boothe, Pritchard & Dudley
    Vulcan Materials Co. - 46-D
Borden Inc. - 32-D
Boston & Maine Railroad - 17-D
Bourland, Albert D. - 32-D
Boutwell, Wayne A. - 31-D
Bowman, Conner, Touhey & Petrillo
    American Petrofina Inc. - 44-D
Bowman, Conner, Touhey & Thornton
    Lobby registration - 27-D
    National Small Business Government Contractors Association - 22-D
Bowmer, Jim D. - 27-D
Bracy Williams & Co. - 39-D
Brae Corp., The - 40-D
Bragg, Raymond F. Jr. - 37-D
Brasco, Frank J. - 15-D
Breed, Abbott & Morgan
    Damson Oil Corp. - 18-D
Bregman, Abell & Kay
    Avis Inc. - 49-D
    Budget Rent-A-Car Corp. - 49-D
    National Car Rental System Inc. - 51-D
Brick Institute of America - 47-D
Brigham and Women's Hospital Inc. - 39-D
Brinkmann, Robert J. - 38-D
Bristol-Myers Co. - 32-D, 49-D
Broad, Martha M. - 17-D
Broadcast Music Inc. - 49-D
Broadstone, Constance D. - 43-D
Brockmann, Marina L. - 43-D
Brodhead, Willian M. - 35-D
Brotherhood of Railway, Airline & Steamship Clerks, Freight Handlers, Express & Station Employees - 52-D
Brown & Root - 27-D
Brown, Ben Jarratt - 20-D
Brown, Charles T. - 51-D
Brown, Christopher N. - 6-D
Brown, Ellen B. - 42-D
Brown, Roady, Bonvillian & Gold
    Citizens for Gauley River - 17-D
    San Francisco Public Utilities Commission - 19-D
Browning-Ferris Industries Inc. - 3-D, 27-D
Brownstein, Zeidman and Schomer

Schochet Associates - 35-D
Bruner, Gary W. - 40-D
Brunswick Corp. - 10-D
Bryant, Steven - 7-D
Brydon, Dawn M. - 43-D
Budd Co. - 12-D
Budget Rent-A-Car Corp. - 49-D
Buffalo Philharmonic Orchestra - 31-D
Building and Construction Trade Departments, AFL-CIO - 15-D
Building Service Contractors Association International - 8-D
Bunn, George W., Estate of - 31-D
Burch, Wilhelm & McDonald
    M.A.N. Truck & Bus Corp. - 19-D
Burgener, Clair W. - 13-D
Burger King Corp. - 6-D
Burke, Fred B. - 8-D
Burke, Paul T. - 20-D
Burlington Northern Railroad - 49-D
Burns & Roe Inc. - 12-D
Busby, Rehm and Leonard
    Automobile Importers of America Inc. - 8-D
    Bacardi Imports Inc. - 6-D
Bush, Barbara L. - 8-D
Bush, E. Philip - 36-D
Business Executives for National Secutity - 8-D
Business Roundtable - 21-D, 30-D
Butler & Binion
    New Mexico Public Service Commission - 37-D
    Philadelphia Facilities Management Corp. - 35-D
Butler, M. Caldwell - 33-D, 54-D

C

C & B Associates Inc.
    Manville Corp. - 7-D
Cabot Corp. - 40-D
CAC Associates - 3-D
Cades, Schutte, Fleming & Wright
    Hawaiian Electric Co. Inc. - 34-D
Cadwalader, Wickersham & Taft
    Ad Hoc Committee of Floor Brokers - 30-D
    Institute of International Container Lessors - 25-D
Cafritz, Morris and Gwendolyn, Foundation - 26-D
Cahill, John D. - 47-D
California Almond Growers Exchange - 32-D
California Savings and Loan League - 8-D
California State Lands Commission - 47-D
Cambridge Redevelopment Authority - 20-D
Cameron, Arthur E. - 7-D
Camp, Carmouche, Barsh, Hunter, Gray & Hoffman
    Blyth Eastman Paine Webber Inc. - 17-D
    Central & Southern Motor Freight Traffic Association - 21-D
    Central States Motor Freight Bureau - 21-D
    Chapman & Cutler - 18-D
    Cumberland Securities - 18-D
    Essex - 18-D
    Frazer Lanier Co. - 18-D
    George K. Baum & Co. - 17-D
    Goldman Sachs & Co. - 18-D
    Kidder, Peabody - 19-D
    King & Spaulding - 19-D
    Lehman Brothers - 19-D
    McDonald & Co. - 19-D
    Metropolitan Insurance Cos. - 35-D
    Middle Atlantic Conference - 22-D

Middlewest Motor Freight Bureau - 22-D
New England Motor Rate Bureau - 22-D
Niagara Frontier Tariff Bureau - 22-D
North, Haskell, Slaughter, Young & Lewis - 19-D
Pacific Inland Tariff Bureau - 22-D
Pakhoed - 19-D
Rauscher Pierce Refsnes - 19-D
Rocky Mountain Motor Tariff Bureau - 22-D
Southern Motor Carriers Rate Conference - 22-D
Stern, Agee & Leach - 20-D
Thornton, Parish & Gauntt - 20-D
Wheat First Securities - 20-D
Camp, Carmouche, Palmer, Barsh & Hunter
    Chemical Manufacturers Association - 5-D
    Lobby registration - 6-D
    R. J. Reynolds Tobacco Co. - 4-D
    Shell Oil Co. - 4-D
Campbell, Jeanne - 24-D
Campbell, Robert E. - 28-D
Campisis, Charles J. - 54-D
Canned and Cooked Meat Importers Association - 6-D
Carlough, Edward J. - 20-D
Carlson, J. Philip - 35-D
Carr-Gottstein Properties Inc. - 44-D
Casey, Jim - 21-D
Cassidy, Lawrence J. - 20-D
Castle & Cooke Inc. - 32-D
Cavalier Clothing Co. - 27-D
Cavaney, Red Jr. - 21-D
CBS Inc. - 32-D, 40-D, 44-D, 49-D
Cecos Cer Co. - 24-D
Central & Southern Motor Freight Bureau - 21-D
Central San Joaquin River Association - 31-D
Central States Motor Freight Bureau - 21-D
Certainteed Corp. - 24-D
CFS Continental - 33-D
Chadbourne, Parke, Whiteside & Wolff
    Acurex Solar Corp. - 48-D
    Arco Solar Inc. - 44-D
    Berenergy Corp. - 32-D
    Crinco Investments Inc. - 33-D
    Monegon Ltd. - 35-D
    National Association of Broadcasters - 38-D
    Newmont Mining Corp. - 51-D
    Solarex Corp. - 35-D
    Standard Oil Company (Indiana) - 52-D
    The Manufacturers Life Insurance Co. - 34-D
    Transworld Airlines Inc. - 7-D
    United States Photovoltaics Manufacturers' Ad Hoc Committee - 48-D
    Washington Psychiatric Society - 39-D
Chamber of Commerce of the United States - 8-D, 31-D, 37-D, 42-D, 54-D
Chamberlain, Charles E. - 24-D
Chambers Associates Inc.
    Apache Corp. - 27-D
    Manville Corp. - 34-D
Chambers, Jerry, Oil Producer - 44-D
Chambers, R. J. - 3-D
Champlin Petroleum Co. - 4-D, 12-D
Chandler, W. J., Associates
    Chelonia Institute, The - 43-D
    West Indies Investment Co. - 42-D
Chapman & Cutler - 18-D
Chapman, Duff and Paul
    Christian Bjelland & Co. Inc. - 33-D, 40-D
    Industrial Siderurgica Inc. - 34-D
Chapman, Paul K. - 43-D

Charter Oil Co. - 24-D
Chelonia Institute, The - 43-D
Chemical Manufacturers Association - 5-D
Chemical Waste Management Inc. - 12-D, 18-D
Chertoff, Stephan E. - 27-D
Chevron U.S.A. Inc. - 40-D
Chicago and Northwestern Railroad - 12-D
Chicago & Northwestern Transportation Corp. - 18-D
Chicago Board of Education - 47-D
Chicago Mercantile Exchange - 49-D
Ching, Paul D. - 14-D
Chocolate Manufacturers Association of the USA - 37-D
Christian Bjelland & Co. Inc. - 33-D, 40-D
Chwat/Weigend Associates
    Coalition for Environmental Data - 15-D
    Mrs. Winnie M. Tse - 23-D
Cincinnati, City of - 30-D
Citibank N. A. - 27-D
Cities for Responsible Cable Policy - 42-D
Cities Service Oil and Gas Corp. - 12-D
Citizen/Labor Energy Coalition - 3-D
Citizens for America - 48-D
Citizens for a Nuclear Freeze - 48-D
Citizens for Gauley River - 17-D
Citizens for Sensible Control of Acid Rain - 48-D
Clagett, John W. - 15-D
Clark, Rudy I. - 8-D
Clavey-Wards Ferry Project/Turlock Irrigation District/Modesto Irrigation District - 53-D
Clay, Cecil D. - 53-D
Claymark Corp. Inc. - 49-D
Clear Channel Broadcasting Service - 37-D
Cleary, Gottlieb, Steen & Hamilton
    Formaldehyde Institute - 31-D
Cleveland Cliffs Iron Co. - 27-D
Cleveland Clinic Foundation - 23-D
Click, W.M. - 14-D
Coal Slurry Association - 47-D
Coalition for Competition - 21-D
Coalition for Environmental Data - 15-D
Coalition for Environmental-Energy Balance - 3-D
Coalition for Legal Services Inc. - 32-D
Coalition of Automotive Associations - 21-D
Coalition of Community Banks of Florida - 54-D
Coalitions for America - 23-D
Coastal Corp., The - 50-D
Coffee Sugar & Cocoa Exchange Inc. - 18-D
Cohen and Uretz
    Bennington College - 31-D
    Wheels Inc. - 15-D
Cohen, Daniel L. - 37-D
Cohen, David - 8-D
Cohen, Lois D. Associates - 4-D
Cohen, Rhea - 23-D
Cole, Ken W. - 44-D
College of American Pathologists - 8-D
Collier, Shannon, Rill & Scott
    Huffy Corp. - 40-D
    Pittsburgh Corning Corp. - 41-D
Colorado-Ute Electric Association Inc. - 33-D
Colortyme Inc. - 33-D
Colt Industries Inc. - 33-D
Colton, City of - 47-D
Columbia Gas System Service Corp. - 12-D
Combined Health Resources Inc. - 12-D
Combined Insurance Company of America - 4-D, 45-D

Comerica Inc. - 12-D

Commission on Future Political Status and Transition, The Federated States of Micronesia - 46-D

Committee for Ad Valorem Equity - 26-D

Committee for Equitable Compensation - 32-D

Committee for Fair Insurance Rates - 24-D

Committee for Prudent Deregulation - 9-D, 11-D, 54-D

Committee for Savers' Interest - 11-D, 26-D

Committee of Corporate Telecommunications Users - 54-D

Committee on United States Business of the Canadian Life & Health Insurance Association - 25-D

Committee to Improve Public School Libraries - 32-D

Committee to Stop Illegal Immigration - 6-D

Common Cause - 23-D

Commonwealth Edison Co. - 33-D

Commonwealth of Puerto Rico - 8-D

Communications Management Inc.
  Citizens for Sensible Control of Acid Rain - 48-D
  Natural Gas Supply Association - 39-D

Community Art Alliance Inc. - 44-D

Community Redevelopment Agency - 39-D

Compo Industries Inc. - 4-D

Computer and Business Equipment Manufacturers Association - 38-D

Computer and Communication Industry Association - 38-D

Computer Dealers and Lessors Association Inc. - 38-D

Computerized Security Systems Inc. - 24-D

Congress Watch - 32-D

Connecticut Mutual Life Insurance Co. - 24-D, 27-D

Connolly, John J. - 18-D

Connor, Gerald R. - 39-D

Conoco Inc. - 33-D

Conrail - 6-D

Consejo Nacional de Commercio Exterior del Noreste A. C. - 42-D

Consolidated Edison Company of New York - 33-D, 50-D

Consumer Bankers Association, The - 11-D

Contact Lens Manufacturers Association - 3-D, 54-D

Container Transport International Inc. - 33-D

Continental Wingate Co. - 33-D

Contract Carriage Coalition - 42-D

Contract Staffing of America Inc. - 50-D

Control Data Corp. - 45-D

Cook Inlet Region Inc. - 26-D

Cook, Howard - 6-D

Cook, Purcell, Henderson & Zorack
  Air Florida Inc. - 6-D
  Aleutian/Pribilof Islands Association Inc. - 44-D
  Coalition for Competition - 21-D
  GC Services Corp. - 33-D
  Northern Tier Pipeline Co. - 19-D

Cooley, John, Construction Co. - 50-D

Cooley's Anemia Foundation - 32-D

Cooper, C. William - 11-D

Cooperative of American Physicians Inc. - 54-D

Cooperative Power Association - 45-D

Copiat - 50-D

Corcoran, Hardesty, Whyte, Hemphill & Ligon
  Nova Scotia Resources Ltd. - 45-D

Texas Eastern Transmission Corp. - 36-D

Cordage Institute - 54-D

Corey, Gordon R. - 33-D

Corman, James C.
  BKK Corp. - 24-D
  Cooperative of American Physicians Inc. - 54-D
  General American Life Insurance Co. - 50-D
  Home Life Insurance Co. - 28-D, 50-D
  International Taxicab Association - 54-D
  Music Corporation of America Inc. - 51-D
  Pacific Mutual Life Insurance Co. - 29-D, 50-D
  Provident Mutual Life Insurance Company of Philadelphia - 51-D
  Shah & Associates - 52-D
  State Mutual Life Assurance Company of America - 52-D
  Systems and Applied Sciences - 52-D
  Texas Air Corp. - 52-D
  UCI Inc. - 25-D, 52-D

Cornell, Pelcovits & Brenner Economists Inc.
  Audio Recording Rights Coalition - 10-D
  Home Recording Rights Coalition - 10-D

Corning Associates - 6-D

Corporate Consulting Services Inc.
  Davis & McLeod - 45-D
  Provident Life and Accident Insurance Co. - 24-D

Corporation for Public Broadcasting - 54-D

Cosmetic, Toiletry and Fragrance Association Inc. - 54-D

Cotch, Peter J. - 45-D

Council of Michigan Foundations - 39-D

Council of Multiemployer Pension Security Inc. - 20-D

Covington & Burling
  Sun Life Assurance Company of Canada - 52-D

Cow Creek Band of Umpqua Tribe of Indians - 4-D

Cowles, C. Deming
  Alaska Lumber and Pulp Co. - 44-D
  Ketchikan Pulp Co. - 45-D
  Municipality of Anchorage - 46-D
  Richmond R. Farring - 48-D

Cowlite Indian Tribe - 4-D

Craib, Donald Forsyth III - 7-D

Cramer, Hoffman & Haber
  Republic of Gabon - 8-D

Cramer, William C. - 8-D

Crawford Fitting Co. - 50-D

Creamer, Dickson and Basford
  City of Austin - 4-D
  City of Dallas - 5-D
  City of Houston - 5-D
  City of San Antonio - 5-D
  Mayor of Kansas City - 5-D

Credit Union National Association - 31-D

Crinco Investments Inc. - 33-D

Crocker National Bank - 40-D

Cronin, Lauren - 34-D

Cronmiller, Rae E. - 22-D

Crosby, Thomas R. - 44-D

Crosier, Harold L. - 53-D

Crowell & Moring
  Home Owners Warranty Corp. - 28-D
  National Association of Manufacturers - 38-D

Crown Life Insurance Co. - 6-D

Crown Zellerbach Corp. - 18-D

Crum & Forster Insurance Cos. - 18-D

Culver, John C. - 24-D

Cumberland Securities - 18-D

Cummings & Lockwood
  Equitable Life Assurance Society of the United States - 40-D, 50-D
  United States Surgical Corp. - 36-D

Cunniff, Michael M. - 53-D

Cunningham, Bill - 11-D

Curry, Kathleen - 9-D

D

Dairy-Farmer Distributors of America - 9-D

Dale Fashions - 27-D

Daley and George
  Combined Insurance Co. - 45-D

Dallas, City of - 5-D

Dalloul, Ramzi A. - 55-D

Damgard, John M. - 15-D

Damrell, Damrell & Nelson
  Central San Joaquin River Association - 31-D
  Clavey-Wards Ferry Project/Turlock Irrigation District/Modesto Irrigation District - 53-D
  Stockton Terminal and Eastern Railroad - 29-D

Daniels, Houlihan & Palmeter
  Korean Traders Association - 46-D
  Trade Industry & Customs Department, Government of Hong Kong - 46-D

Dannelley, A. Joan - 37-D

Damson Oil Corp. - 18-D, 24-D

DAR Investment Corp. - 24-D

Davi, Theodore S.J. - 16-D

Davis & McLeod
  American General Life Insurance Co. - 23-D
  Lobby registration - 45-D
  Provident Life & Accident Insurance Co. - 24-D

Davis, Hockenberg, Wine, Brown & Koehn
  Northwestern Bell (Iowa Division) - 51-D

Davis, Polk & Wardwell
  Northwest Bancorp. - 19-D
  Otto Bremer Foundation - 16-D

Day Trust, The - 43-D

D.C. Associates Inc.
  Air Quality Research Inc. - 44-D
  Harvard School of Public Health - 11-D
  Metal Trades Department, AFL-CIO - 15-D

Dealer Bank Association - 42-D

Deane, John Russell III - 21-D

Debevoise & Plimpton
  Sony Corporation of America - 52-D

DeCair, Richard L. - 42-D

DeHart Associates Inc.
  Recording Industry Association of America Inc. - 10-D

DeBragga, Robert - 49-D

Deleware Otsego System - 18-D

Delaware, State of - 5-D

Deloitte, Haskins & Sells
  Hallmark Cards Inc. - 45-D
  Lobby registration - 50-D
  Union Pacific Corp. - 41-D

Delyannis, Georgia L. - 21-D

DeSanto, Michael - 9-D

Design Professionals Coalition - 54-D

Detroit & Mackinac Railway Co. - 33-D

Detroit, City of - 37-D

Detroit Edison Co., The - 33-D

Detroit Madison Co. - 33-D

Dewey, Ballantine, Bushby, Palmer & Wood
  American Can Co. - 27-D
  American Stock Exchange Inc. - 23-D
  Browning-Ferris Industries Inc. - 27-D
  Damson Oil Corp. - 24-D
  Federal National Mortgage Association - 9-D

National Association of Public Hospitals - 9-D

Panhandle Eastern Pipe Line Co. - 24-D

Velo-Bind Inc. - 25-D

DGA International Inc.
  Airbus Industrie - 40-D
  Le Directeur des Affaires Internationales de la Delegation Generale pour L'Armement (French Ministry of Defense) - 42-D
  Snecma - 29-D
  Societe Nationale D'Etude et De Construction De Moteurs D'Aviation - 35-D, 41-D, 46-D
  Sofreavia - 41-D

Dickinson, Wright, Moon, Van Dusen & Freeman
  Detroit Madison Co. - 33-D

Dickstein, Shapiro & Morin
  National Association of Public Television Stations - 31-D
  Natural Gas Supply Association - 26-D
  State of Delaware - 5-D
  State of Iowa - 5-D
  State of Louisiana - 5-D
  State of North Dakota - 5-D
  State of Rhode Island - 5-D

Dillard, George - 7-D

Dillingham Construction Group - 18-D

Dillingham Ship Repair - 12-D

Dineen, Michael F.
  Federal Kemper Life Assurance Co. - 4-D
  Kemper Investors Life Insurance Co. - 4-D
  Lumbermens Mutual Casualty Co. - 4-D

Dingman, Richard B. - 40-D

Direct Broadcast Satellite Corp. - 27-D

Direct Marketing Insurance Group - 40-D

DoBoer, Jeff - 9-D

Dobson, Matthew G. - 10-D

Dolly, Roland - 32-D

Domestic Petroleum Council Inc. - 21-D

Donovan, Leisure, Newton & Irvine
  American Telephone & Telegraph Inc. - 49-D
  Motion Picture Association of America - 5-D

Donovan, Thomas F. - 53-D

Dorsey & Whitney
  Northrop University - 39-D

Dosimeter Corporation of North America - 33-D

Dougherty, Dawkins, Strand & Yost - 27-D

Dow Chemical Co. - 45-D

Dow Chemical U.S.A. - 6-D

Dow, Lohnes & Albertson
  Lake Ontario Cement Ltd. - 13-D

Downs, Connie M. - 49-D

Dreyfus Corp. - 27-D

Dreyfus Tax-Exempt Bond Fund - 6-D

Dreyfus Tax-Exempt Money Market Fund - 7-D

Driftwood Dairy - 27-D

DuMelle, Fran - 5-D

Duncan, Robert - 19-D

Duncan, Weinberg & Miller
  State of Nevada - 37-D

Dunnells, Duvall, Bennett & Porter
  National Multifamily Housing Finance Association - 43-D

Durand, Judy C. - 30-D

Dutko, Daniel A. - 20-D, 46-D, 52-D

Duxbury, L.L. - 10-D, 20-D

Dwyer, Thomas J. - 53-D

Dyco Petroleum Co. - 50-D

E

Eagle-Picher Industries - 33-D

East, Catherine - 44-D

Eckhardt, Robert C. - 30-D
Ecological Professional Industries Inc. - 24-D
Edison Electric Institute - 42-D
Edsall, John M. - 30-D
Edward Hines Lumber Co. - 4-D
Edwards, Charles H. - 53-D
Edwards, Max N. - 3-D
EHA Ventilfabrik Wilhelm Fritz - 50-D
Eider, Yvonne B. - 11-D, 17-D
Eiland, Jill W. - 29-D
Eiva, Andrew - 23-D
El Paso, City of - 21-D
Electronic Industries Association of Japan - 54-D
Electronic Processing Inc. - 33-D
Elkem Metals Co. - 33-D
Embassy of the Republic of South Africa - 25-D, 30-D
Emergency Committee for American Trade - 38-D
Emery, Carol R. - 8-D, 19-D, 34-D
Employee Stock Ownership Association - 31-D
Employers Reinsurance Corp. - 40-D
Energy Cycle Inc. - 18-D
Enhanced Energy Resources Inc. - 18-D
Envirite Corp. - 18-D
Environmental Policy Institute - 11-D, 32-D
Epstein, Becker, Borsody & Green
 National Cable Television Association - 31-D
Equitable Assurance Society of the United States - 40-D, 50-D
Erickson, Vickie L. - 15-D
Erthein, John S., & Associates Inc. - 44-D
Escutia, Martha M. - 40-D
Essex - 18-D
E-Systems - 12-D
European Travel Commission - 46-D
Evans, Brock - 3-D
Evans, Dave, Associates - 31-D, 39-D
Evans, Thomas B. Jr. - 13-D, 14-D, 19-D
Executive Council on Foreign Diplomats - 39-D
Express Foods Co. Inc. - 33-D

F

Fair Trade Subcommittee of the International Trade Committee of the Cast Metals Federation - 15-D
Fanning, Michael I. - 37-D
Fanuc Ltd. - 27-D
Farm Credit Council, The - 47-D, 55-D
Farm Labor Alliance - 36-D
Farnsworth, Martin & Gallagher
 Solarex Corp. - 14-D
Farrand, Christopher G. - 45-D, 48-D
Farrell, Joseph A. - 8-D
Farring, Richmond R. - 48-D
Farrior, Stephanie T. - 17-D
Federal Home Life Insurance Co. - 45-D
Federal Kemper Life Assurance Co. - 4-D
Federal Law Enforcement Officers Association - 15-D
Federal National Mortgage Association - 9-D, 12-D, 43-D, 48-D
Federation of Apparel Manufacturers - 47-D
Federation Employment & Guidance Service - 33-D
Federation of AIDS Organizations - 39-D
Ferguson, Denise G. - 44-D
Ferguson, Jack, Associates Inc.
 Dillingham Construction Group - 18-D
 Dillingham Ship Repair - 12-D

Fertilizer Institute - 21-D
Fifth Avenue & 59th Corp. - 50-D
Financial Investment Associates Inc. - 27-D
Finch, Louis F. - 50-D
Finley, Kumble, Wagner, Heine, Underberg, Manley & Casey
 American President Lines Ltd. - 6-D
 Direct Broadcast Satellite Corp. - 27-D
 Genstar Container Corp. - 7-D
 M/A-Com Development Corp. - 28-D
 Occidental Petroleum Corp. - 7-D
 Telocator Network of America - 55-D
 TRT Telecommunications Corp. - 29-D
 Turner Broadcasting System Inc. - 29-D
Finn, Stephen A. - 6-D
First Pennsylvania Bank - 18-D
Fisher, William L. - 14-D
Fishman, Charles L. - 50-D
Fletcher, Wayne A. - 31-D
Flexi-van Leasing Inc. - 33-D
Floating Point System - 33-D
Flood Control Advisory Committee - 55-D
Florida Association of Marine Industries - 5-D
Florida Caribbean Cruise Association - 5-D
Floyd, Veronica M. - 10-D
F M S Corp. - 33-D
Foley, Lardner, Hollabaugh & Jacobs
 Investors Mortgage Insurance Co. - 41-D
Folsom, R. D. - 11-D
Food and Beverage Trades Department, AFL-CIO - 25-D
Food Marketing Institute - 5-D
Foothills Pipe Lines (Yukon) Ltd. - 18-D, 40-D
Ford Aerospace - 13-D
Ford Motor Co. - 24-D
Foreman & Dyess
 Enhanced Energy Resources Inc. - 18-D
Foreman, Carol Tucker
 Asbestos Litigation Group - 11-D
 Home Recording Rights Coalition - 11-D
Forest Farmers Association - 9-D
Formaldehyde Institute - 31-D
Fortuna, Richard C. - 38-D
Forum Communications - 33-D
Foster, Nancy E. - 5-D, 54-D
F/P Research Associates
 Pharmaceutical Manufacturers Association - 54-D
 Western Union Telegraph Co. - 46-D
Francis & McGinnis Associates Inc. - 38-D
Franz, Marian C. - 4-D
Frazer Lanier Co., The - 18-D
Free, Ann Todd - 21-D
Freeman, Carl M. Associates Inc. - 33-D
Freeman, Mary Ann - 33-D
Freeport-McMoran Inc. - 10-D, 28-D
Freight Forwarders Institute - 38-D
Fried, Frank, Harris, Shriver & Kampelman
 Assiniboine Tribe - 48-D
 General Electric Co. - 13-D
 Hunt Building Corp. - 13-D
 Investment Company Institute - 15-D
Friedman, James M. - 3-D
Friends of Animals - 17-D
Friends of Animals Inc. - 11-D
Friends of the Columbia Gorge - 11-D
Fritts, Allyn M. - 54-D
Fritzlen, Jeffery A. - 7-D
Frontier Airlines Inc. - 3-D
Fulbright & Jaworski
 Samuel Gary Oil Producer Inc. - 33-D
 Santa Anita Realty Enterprises Inc. - 35-D
Fuji Photo Film U.S.A. Inc. - 13-D
Futures Industry Association Inc. - 15-D

G

G A Technologies Inc. - 13-D
G C Services Corp. - 33-D
Gadsby & Hannah
 Wang Laboratories Inc. - 15-D
Galloway & Greenberg
 Southeastern Fisheries Association Inc. - 16-D
Ganderson, Harry - 41-D
Gannon, Edmund J. - 6-D
Gardner, Carton & Douglas
 Edward Hines Lumber Co. - 4-D
Garrison Diversion Conservancy District - 43-D
Gary, Samuel, Oil Producer Inc. - 33-D, 45-D
Gates, Daniel F. - 9-D
Gathers, Wayne - 5-D
Geary, Stahl & Spencer
 Cities for Responsible Cable Policy - 42-D
Gehres, Margaret L. - 21-D
Geigle, Ronald L. - 9-D
General American Life Insurance Co. - 50-D
General Electric Co. - 13-D, 18-D, 33-D, 40-D
General Electric Credit Co. - 18-D
General Mills Inc. - 18-D, 34-D, 40-D
General Mills Corp. - 28-D
General Motors Corp. - 28-D, 34-D
General Portland Inc. - 28-D, 34-D
General Telephone & Electronics - 3-D
Genesee & Wyoming Corp. - 18-D
Genstar Container Corp. - 7-D
George, Nancy Whorton - 52-D
George Washington University Student Association - 10-D, 43-D
Georgia Pacific Corp. - 18-D
Gerard, Byler & Associates
 Santa Clara Pueblo - 49-D
Getty Oil Co. - 40-D
Giaimo, Robert N. - 12-D
Gibb, William C. - 16-D
Gibson, Dunn & Crutcher
 Federation of Apparel Manufacturers - 47-D
 Insurance Association of Connecticut - 42-D
Gifford-Hill & Co. Inc. - 28-D, 34-D
Ginn & Edington Inc.
 Hercules - 34-D
 Turner Broadcasting System Inc. - 25-D
Glenn, Gary - 6-D
Global Communications Inc. - 24-D, 28-D
Global USA Inc.
 Fanuc Ltd. - 27-D
 Komatsu Ltd. - 34-D
 Lobby registration - 1757
 Mazak Corp. - 34-D
Gnau, Carter, Jacobsen & Associates Inc.
 Amurcon Corp. - 3-D
 Beztak Co. - 3-D
 Bi-County Consortium - 23-D
 CAC Associates - 3-D
 Computerized Security Systems Inc. - 24-D
 Detroit & Mackinac Railway Co. - 33-D
 Global Communications Inc. - 24-D, 28-D
 Grand Traverse Development Inc. - 3-D
 Inter-Tribal Council of Michigan Inc. - 17-D
 John Cooley Construction Co. - 50-D
 Linear Air Motors Inc. - 24-D, 28-D
 Move Detroit Forward Fund - 3-D
 Netco - 28-D, 35-D
 Potter Instrument Co. Inc. - 3-D
 Primark Corp. - 29-D, 35-D
 R. J. Chambers - 3-D

Safekeeper Systems Inc. - 24-D, 29-D
Saflok - 29-D
Sanders Corp. - 3-D
Urban Revitalization Inc. - 3-D
U.S. Manufacturing Co. - 25-D, 30-D
Gold, Donna - 53-D
Goldman Sachs & Co. - 18-D, 45-D
Goodell, Charles E. - 6-D, 25-D, 29-D
Goodwin, Thomas G. - 38-D
Gorman, Mark S. - 40-D
Government Employees Insurance Co. - 24-D, 40-D
Government of the Republic of China - 42-D
Grand Traverse Development Inc. - 3-D
Granger, James I. - 41-D
Granger, Mary - 36-D
Graphic Communications International Union, AFL-CIO - 42-D
Gray and Co.
 American Fishing Tackle Manufacturers Association - 53-D
 American Iron and Steel Institute - 8-D, 37-D
 American Maritime Association - 8-D, 15-D
 Aneutronix Inc. - 10-D, 12-D
 Batus Inc. - 12-D
 Beverly Enterprises - 12-D
 Browning-Ferris Industries Inc. - 27-D
 Budd Co. - 12-D
 College of American Pathologists - 8-D
 Commonwealth of Puerto Rico - 8-D, 30-D
 Electronic Industries Association of Japan - 54-D
 Executive Council on Foreign Diplomats - 39-D
 Financial Investment Associates Inc. - 27-D
 Grumman Corp. - 34-D
 Hambros Bank Ltd. - 7-D
 Health Insurance Association of America - 15-D
 HRH Prince Talal Bin Abdul Aziz Al Saud - 10-D
 Joint Maritime Congress - 15-D, 54-D
 Martin Baker Aircraft Co. Ltd. - 11-D
 National Broadcasting Co. - 11-D, 45-D, 51-D
 NIU Inc. - 51-D
 Pan American National Bank - 14-D
 Ramzi A. Dalloul - 55-D
 Republic of Haiti - 8-D
 Republic of Turkey - 30-D, 36-D, 46-D
 Richard L. Sinnott and Co. - 14-D
 Sharps, Pixley & Co. Ltd. - 7-D
 Stroh Brewery Co. - 52-D
 United Nations Children's Fund - 10-D
 U.S. Banknote Corp. - 14-D
Great Lakes Dredge & Dock - 30-D
Greater Philadelphia Chamber of Commerce - 54-D
Green, Roy G. - 55-D
Greenfield, Louise S. - 32-D
Greens Creek Joint Venture - 13-D
Greer, John M. - 42-D
Griffin, Randall - 8-D
Grimm, Norman E. Jr. - 44-D
Grindlays Bank Ltd. - 50-D
Grocery Manufacturers of America - 5-D
Groedel, Howard M. - 33-D
Groom and Nordberg
 Bankers Life Co. - 49-D
 Colorado-Ute Electric Association Inc. - 33-D
 Guardian Life Insurance Company of America, The - 50-D
 Minnesota Mutual Life Insurance Co., The - 51-D
 New York Life Insurance Co. - 51-D
 Ocean Drilling and Exploration Co. - 7-D

Provident Mutual Life Insurance Company of Philadelphia - 51-D
Southern California Edison Co. - 36-D
Union Texas Petroleum Corp. - 8-D
Grove, Jaskiewicz, Gilliam and Cobert - 28-D
Grubbs, Walter B. - 20-D
Grumman Aerospace Corp. - 13-D
Grumman Corp. - 34-D
Grupenhoff, John T. - 32-D, 37-D
Guam Legislature, 17th - 53-D
Guardian Life Insurance Company of America - 50-D
Guirard, James E. Jr.
Base Wyandotte Corp. - 17-D
Bell Aerospace Textron - 10-D
KMS Fusion Inc. - 50-D
Tano Corp. - 11-D
Gulf Oil Corp. - 50-D

H

Haas, Ellen - 10-D
Hackler, Craig - 26-D, 35-D
Hagedorn, Thomas M. - 45-D, 47-D
Hahn and Matkov - 34-D
Hale and Dorr
Compo Industries Inc. - 4-D
Dyco Petroleum Co. - 50-D
Guam Legislature, 17th - 53-D
Inexco Oil Co. - 50-D
MeOH Inc. - 4-D
Hale & Dougherty - 34-D
Halkias, Rebecca L. - 49-D
Hall, Michael L. - 31-D
Hallamore, Kimberley C. - 30-D
Hallmark Cards Inc. - 45-D
Halt Inc. - 39-D
Hambros Bank Ltd. - 7-D
Hamel, Park, McCabe & Saunders
Skylink Corp. Inc. - 35-D
Hammond, Christina - 6-D
Hampton, Robert N. - 8-D
Hancock, John, Mutual Life Insurance Co. - 34-D
Hansell & Post
American Security Insurance Co. - 49-D
Ingram Tankships Inc. - 13-D
Rockwell International Corp. - 14-D
Hansen Engine Co. - 45-D
Hanson, Heidi Ann - 49-D
Hapag-Lloyd A. G. - 50-D
Haragan, Nancy - 24-D
Harding, Ralph R. - 9-D
Harper, Leon - 20-D
Harrington, Marcia L. - 17-D
Harris Corp. - 34-D
Harris, Marilyn A. - 25-D
Harsch, J. William W. - 49-D, 55-D
Harsha, William H., & Associates Inc.
Cecos Cer Co. - 24-D
Ecological Professional Industries Inc. - 24-D
Hartford Fire Insurance Co. - 40-D, 45-D
Harvard Medical Center - 16-D
Harvard School of Public Health - 11-D
Harvey, John Vincent - 25-D
Harza Engineers - 7-D
Hashemite Kingdom of Jordan - 42-D
Hattoy, Bob - 40-D
Hawaiian Electric Co. Inc. - 34-D
Hazardous Waste Treatment Council - 38-D
HBO & Co. - 40-D
Health Insurance Association of America - 15-D
Health Industry Manufacturers Association - 9-D
Hecht, Bill, & Associates - 18-D, 37-D
Heffernan & Moseman
Alaska Lumber & Pulp - 6-D, 17-D

Alaska Pulp & Resources Inc. - 6-D
Camp, Carmouche, Palmer, Barsh & Hunter - 6-D
Heilig, Elizabeth W. - 18-D
Heine, Robert M. - 33-D
Hellenic Lines/Hessa Line - 28-D
Heller, Ehrman, White and McAuliffe - 34-D
Helscher, Thomas M. - 13-D
Henderson, Alberta L. - 39-D
Hennig, David A. - 6-D
Hercules Inc. - 34-D
Herm, Stephen - 4-D
Heron, Burchette, Ruckert & Rothwell
Association of Floral Importers of Florida - 25-D
California Almond Growers Exchange - 32-D
Chicago Mercantile Exchange - 49-D
Farm Labor Alliance - 36-D
Imperial Valley Asparagus Growers Association - 38-D
Independent Cement Corp. - 50-D
National Cable Television Association - 54-D
National Potato Council - 47-D
National Association of Insurance Commissioners - 38-D
Southern California Rapid Transit District - 37-D
Sun-Diamond Growers of California - 36-D
Sunkist Growers Inc. - 36-D
Western Cotton Growers Association - 48-D
Hess, Barbara V. - 37-D
Highway Users Federation for Safety and Mobility - 15-D
Hilaturas Lerma S.A. - 50-D
Hill and Knowlton Inc.
T. Ramirez and Co. Inc. - 51-D
Hines, Edward, Lumber Co. - 4-D
Hobbs, Straus, Dean & Wilder
Metlakatla Indian Community - 4-D
Miccosukee Tribe of Indians of Florida - 4-D, 11-D
Oglala Sioux Tribe - 10-D
Hogan & Hartson
Business Roundtable - 30-D
Champlin Petroleum Co. - 4-D
Cleveland Clinic Foundation - 23-D
Computer and Business Equipment Manufacturers Association - 38-D
Medtronic Inc. - 51-D
National Hospice Organization - 38-D
Pillsbury Co. - 35-D
The Methodist Hospital - 23-D
Hogue, Phillip A. - 50-D
Holcomb Investments Inc. - 34-D
Holland, Kenneth L. - 53-D
Holme, Roberts & Owen
Jerry Chambers Oil Producer - 44-D
Samuel Gary Oil Producer Inc. - 45-D
Home Life Insurance Co. - 28-D, 50-D
Home Owners Warranty Corp. - 28-D
Home Recording Rights Coalition - 11-D
Hong, Gary C. - 43-D
Hoovler, Anna Mary - 54-D
Hospital Corporation of America - 34-D
Houghton Mifflin Co. - 34-D
Houston, City of - 5-D
Hoving Group, The - 33-D
Howard, Anne L. and Associates
Pascua-Yaqui Tribe - 17-D
Shakopee-Mdeuakanton Sioux Community - 17-D
Howard, Robert M. - 24-D
Howrey & Simon
Summit Enterprises Inc. - 20-D
The Mead Corp. - 19-D
HRH Prince Talal Bin Abdul Aziz Al Saud - 10-D

Hudson Waterways - 18-D
Huffy Corp. - 40-D
Hughes, Hubbard & Reed
Texas Air Corp. - 2751
Hunt Building Corp. - 13-D
Hurwit, Cathy - 3-D
Hutchison, James L. - 25-D

I

Icelandair - 40-D
Imperial Valley Asparagus Growers Association - 38-D
Independent Cattlemen's Association - 21-D
Independent Cement Corp. - 50-D
Independent Insurance Agents of America Inc. - 9-D
Independent Radio Common Carriers Association - 54-D
Indiana Associates - 24-D
Indiana University - 23-D
Industrial Siderurgica Inc. - 34-D
Inexco Oil Co. - 50-D
Ingalsbee, Nancy J. - 39-D
Ingersoll & Bloch - 45-D
Ingersoll-Rand Co. - 45-D
Ingram Corp. - 41-D
Ingram Tankerships Inc. - 13-D
Institute of International Container Lessors - 25-D
Insurance Association of Connecticut - 26-D, 42-D
Insurance Services Office - 34-D
Intellectual Property Owners Inc. - 38-D
Intelsat - 24-D
Intergovernmental Cable Communications Authority of Oakland County, Mich. - 30-D
International Airforwarder and Agents Association - 42-D
International Anticounterfeiting Coalition - 42-D
International Association of Drilling Contractors - 26-D
International Association of Ice Cream Manufacturers/Milk Industry Foundation - 43-D
International Business & Economic Research Corp.
Korean Traders Association - 46-D
Trade, Industry & Customs Department, Government of Hong Kong - 46-D
International Chiropractic Association - 26-D
International Gold Corp. Ltd. - 28-D, 45-D
International Legal Defense Counsel - 5-D
International Maritime Associates Inc. - 7-D
International Minerals & Chemical Corp. - 50-D
International Software and Consulting - 4-D
International Taxicab Association - 54-D
International Technical Expertise Ltd. - 50-D
International Telephone & Telegraph Corp. - 18-D
International Trade Services Corp. - 41-D
Interstate Natural Gas Association of America - 26-D
Inter-Tribal Council of Michigan Inc. - 17-D
Investment Company Institute - 9-D, 15-D
Investment Council of Panama - 30-D

Investors Mortgage Insurance Co. - 41-D
Iowa, State of - 5-D
Iron Ore Lessors Association - 31-D
Isfa Corp. - 45-D
Itel Corp. - 45-D
Ivins, Phillips & Barker
Rochester Tax Council - 3-D

J

Jackson, Carlton - 30-D
Jamaica, Government of - 52-D
Jamaican Broadcasting Corp. - 18-D
James, Frank - 4-D
Japan Iron & Steel Exporters' Association - 47-D
Japan Telescopes Manufacturers Association - 47-D
Japanese American Citizens League - 44-D
Japanese Embassy - 46-D
Jenner & Block
Amusement and Music Operators Association - 30-D
Jensen, Sanders & McConnell
Nelco Products Inc. - 4-D
Johnson & Swanson
Harris Methodist Health System - 16-D
Leggette & Co. Inc. - 13-D
Memorial Hospital of Garland - 16-D
Methodist Hospitals of Dallas - 16-D
Osteopathic Medical Center - 16-D
Johnson, Dyke Jr. - 55-D
Johnson, Jesse H. - 50-D
Johnson, Joel L. - 15-D
Johnson, Justin W. - 46-D
Johnson, Nancie S. - 33-D
Johnson, Nicholas - 26-D
Johnson, Thomas G. - 14-D
Johnston David A. - 21-D
Joint Maritime Congress - 15-D, 54-D
Jolovitz, Herbert A. - 29-D
Jones, Jones, Bell, Close & Brown
Greens Creek Joint Venture - 13-D
Lorimar Productions - 13-D
National Tour Association - 16-D
Noranda Exploration Inc. - 13-D
Noranda Mining Inc. - 13-D
Redfield Land Co. - 41-D
Jones, Theodore L. - 40-D, 45-D
Jones, Wiley N. - 29-D
Jorgensen, Jack C. - 16-D
Josephson, Diana H. - 10-D
Juliano, Robert E. Associates - 44-D

K

Kagan, Connie - 32-D
Kaiser Aluminum & Chemical Corp. 19-D, 34-D
Kaiser Cement Corp. - 28-D, 34-D
Kaleidoscope Research and Marketing Group - 7-D
Kalfus, Suzanne - 53-D
Kaluza, Daniel W. - 53-D
Kane Paper Corp. - 4-D
Kane, Sam, Packing - 19-D
Kansas City, Mayor of - 5-D
Kansas Corporation Commission - 15-D
Kato, Charles T. - 23-D
Kaye, Scholer, Fierman, Hays & Handler
American Meat Institute - 53-D
American Social Health Association 48-D
Bristol-Myers Co. - 32-D
Keefe Co., The - 54-D
Keller and Heckman
American Institute of Merchant Shipping - 42-D

Land Mobile Communications Council - 43-D
  Utilities Telecommunications Council - 43-D
Keller, Jay - 23-D
Kelley, John - 27-D
Kelly, Appleman, Hart & Hallman - 50-D
Kelly, Jon F. - 35-D
Kelly, Richard B. - 17-D, 22-D
Kemper Investors Life Insurance Co. - 4-D, 7-D
Kendall & Associates
  Anderson, Hibey, Nauheim and Blair - 49-D
  Carl M. Freeman Associates Inc. - 33-D
  Heller, Ehrman, White and McAuliffe - 34-D
  Manville Corp. - 34-D
  Marriott Corp. - 51-D
  Smith, Barney, Harris, Upham & Co. Inc. - 35-D
  Toyota Motor Sales USA Inc. - 36-D
  Washington Psychiatric Society - 39-D
  Worldwide Information Resources Inc. - 36-D
Kennedy, Cornelius B. - 25-D
Kent & O'Connor
  CFS Continental - 33-D
Kenwood U.S.A. Corp. - 13-D
Kenya, Republic of - 20-D
Ketchikan Pulp Co. - 45-D
Kiawah Island Co. Ltd. - 45-D
Kicak, Marjorie Carroll - 16-D
Kidder, Peabody - 19-D
Kiernan, Peter J. - 23-D
Kierscht, Charles M. - 7-D
Kilbury, Brian M. - 53-D
Kilpatrick, Lockhart, Hill, Christopher & Phillips
  Pilot Petroleum Corp. - 4-D
King & Spaulding
  Lobby registration - 19-D
  Thomson-CSF Inc. - 25-D
Kingsley, Frank G. - 3-D
Kinter, Marcia Y. - 37-D
Kirby, Gillick, Schwartz & Tuohey
  Lake Ontario Cement Ltd. - 50-D
Kirkpatrick, Lockhart, Hill, Christopher & Phillips
  Pilot Petroleum Corp. - 4-D
  County of Suffolk - 21-D
Kiro Inc. - 34-D
Klingelhofer, Karl R. - 26-D
KMS Fusion Inc. - 50-D
Knight Foundation - 48-D
Knight, Peter E. - 54-D
Komatsu Ltd. - 34-D
Kominers, Fort, Schlefer & Boyer
  Apex Marine Corp. - 40-D
  Ingram Corp. - 41-D
Konishiroku Ampex Co. Ltd. - 13-D
Kooperhamp, Earl - 43-D
Korea, Republic of - 25-D
Korean Traders Association - 46-D
Koziol, Patricia S. - 22-D
Krauss, Jeffrey - 34-D
Kristof, Dawn C. - 48-D
Krivit & Krivit
  City of St. Petersburg - 47-D
Kronenberg, Anne M. - 48-D
Kruke, K. H. - 13-D
Kusher, Leora - 5-D
Kushner, Gary Jay - 8-D
Kuszaj, James M. - 6-D
Kutak, Rock & Huie
  Association of Local Housing Finance Agencies - 8-D

L

Lach, Joseph L. - 34-D, 41-D

Lake Ontario Cement Ltd. - 13-D, 50-D
Lakewood, City of - 25-D
Lambert, David F. III - 9-D
Lambert, Rebecca R. - 49-D
Landis, Cohen, Singman and Rauh
  American Society of Composers, Authors and Publishers - 37-D
Land Mobile Communications Council - 43-D
Landsidle, David W. - 51-D
Lane and Edson
  General Electric Credit Co. - 18-D
Lang, Leighton W. - 15-D
Langham Energy Corp. - 7-D
Langham Petroleum Exploration Corp. - 7-D
Lanich, J. Stevens - 11-D
Lanihau Corps - 13-D
Lars Krogh & Co. - 7-D
Laster, John - 16-D
Latham, Watkins & Hills
  Community Redevelopment Agency - 39-D
  Continental Wingate Co. - 33-D
  Driftwood Dairy - 27-D
  Pacific Green Corp. - 19-D
Laundry Cleaning Council - 47-D
Lawson, Elizabeth - 32-D
Laxalt, Michelle - 44-D
League of Women Voters of the United States - 6-D, 32-D
LeBoeuf, Lamb, Leiby & MacRae
  Edison Electric Institute - 42-D
Le Directeur des Affaires Internationales de la Delegation Generale pour L'Armement (French Ministry of Defense) - 42-D
Lefkoff, Charles - 17-D
Legal Services Corp. - 10-D, 16-D, 39-D
Leggette & Co. Inc. - 13-D
Lehman Brothers - 19-D
Lehman Brothers Kuhn Loeb Inc. - 4-D
Leighton, Conklin, Lemov, Jacobs & Buckley
  Express Foods Co. Inc. - 33-D
Leonard, Jerris, & Associates - 15-D
Lerch & Co. Inc.
  Natural Gas Supply Association - 47-D
Lewis, Richard - 30-D
Lewkowitz, Burton - 7-D
Lexitel Corp. - 19-D
Liberty Mutual Insurance Co. - 19-D
Liebengood, Howard S. - 55-D
Lieberman, Sandra Cohen - 9-D
Liggitt, Richard K. - 42-D
Linear Air Motors Inc. - 24-D, 28-D
Liske, Craig - 8-D
Liss, Esther - 22-D
Litchstreet Co. - 19-D
Lobel, Novins & Lamont
  California State Lands Commission - 47-D
Lockhart, Robert F. Jr. - 7-D
Lockheed Corp. - 51-D
Logan, James W. - 16-D
London Chamber of Commerce and Industry - 38-D
London, Sheldon I. - 53-D
Lone Star Industries Inc. - 7-D
Lone Star Steel - 13-D
Long, Alan W. Jr. - 26-D
Long Island Lighting Co. - 34-D
Long Island Trust Co. - 13-D
Long, William E. - 45-D
Loomis, Laura - 12-D
Lorimar Productions - 13-D
Los Angeles Rapid Transit District - 25-D
Louisiana, State of - 5-D, 8-D
Louisiana World Exposition Inc. - 19-D
Lowenstein, Newman, Reis & Axelrad
  Utility Nuclear Waste Management Group - 55-D

Lubick, Donald C. - 31-D
Lui, Andrew L. - 55-D
Lumbermens Mutual Casualty Co. - 4-D
Lund & O'Brien
  Institute of International Container Lessors - 26-D
Lykes Brothers Steamship Co. - 28-D
Lyons, Mark H. R. - 20-D

M

M Life Insurance Co. - 51-D
M/A-Com Development Corp. - 28-D
M/A-Com Inc. - 34-D, 41-D
MacArthur Foundation, John D. and Catherine T. - 55-D
Macchia, Anthony R. - 18-D
Magaw, Susan - 21-D
Magraw, Katherine - 32-D, 35-D
Maguire, Charles - 35-D
Mahdesian, Michael - 23-D
Mahony, Terence P. - 51-D
Major Clothing Co. - 28-D
Major League Baseball Players Association - 37-D
Majority Party, The - 17-D
Maloney, Robert H. - 20-D
Maloni, William R. - 43-D
M.A.N. Truck & Bus Corp. - 19-D
Manatos & Manatos Inc.
  Japanese Embassy - 46-D
  United Hellenic American Congress and American Hellenic Alliance Inc. - 48-D
  Washington Coordinating Council on Productivity - 48-D
Manatt, Phelps, Rothenberg & Tunney
  Allied Tube & Conduit Corp. - 17-D
  BKK Corp. - 24-D
  Home Life Insurance Co. - 28-D
  Los Angeles Rapid Transit District - 25-D
  National Investment Development Corp. - 51-D
  Pacific Mutual Life Insurance Co. - 29-D
  Provident Mutual Life Insurance Co. - 29-D
  State Mutual Life Insurance Company of America - 29-D
  UCI Inc. - 25-D
Manchester Associates Ltd.
  Investment Council of Panama - 30-D
Mangione, Peter T. - 39-D
Mann, Donald W. - 40-D
Manufactured Housing Institute - 21-D
Manufacturers Life Insurance Co. - 34-D
Manville Corp. - 7-D, 34-D, 41-D, 45-D
Marion Laboratories Inc. - 34-D
Marriott Corp. - 13-D, 41-D, 51-D
Martin Baker Aircraft Co. Ltd. - 11-D
Martin, Fred J. - 12-D
Martin, Stephen I. - 45-D
Martindale, Steven A. - 40-D
Maryland People's Counsel - 42-D
Maryland Savings Share Insurance Corp. - 43-D
Masaoka, Mike M. - 47-D
Massachusetts General Hospital - 48-D
Massachusetts Mutual Life Insurance Co. - 24-D, 28-D, 34-D
Massachusetts Port Authority - 47-D
Mastercard International Inc. - 41-D
Matsushita Electric Industrial Co. Ltd. - 51-D
Matthews, John W. - 53-D
Mattox, Gilbert - 53-D
Mattox, William C. - 50-D
Matusow, Emily - 17-D
Matusow, Job - 17-D
Maxell Corporation of America - 13-D

Mayer, Brown & Platt
  Stepan Chemical Co. - 24-D
  Transcanada Pipelines Ltd. - 7-D
Mayer, C.H., Inc. - 7-D
Mazak Corp. - 34-D
McAuliffe & Associates
  National Association of Insurance Commissioners - 26-D
  Puerto Rico Maritime Shipping Authority - 25-D
McBride, Charlie, Associates Inc.
  Consolidated Edison Company of New York - 50-D
  Stone & Webster Engineering Corp. - 52-D
  Westinghouse Electric Corp. - 52-D
McCandless, Robert C. - 52-D
McCarthy, John C. - 19-D
McCarthy, Sweeney & Harkaway
  Western Fuels Association Inc. - 39-D
McCaul, James R. - 7-D
McClure & Trotter
  Estate of Charles G. Bluhdorn - 26-D
  National Association of Small Business Investment Cos. - 22-D
  Providence Capitol Corp. - 51-D
McDermott, Will & Emery
  AM International - 49-D
  Estate of George W. Bunn - 31-D
  Timber Realization - 52-D
McDonald & Co. - 19-D
McDonnell Douglas Astronautics Corp. - 13-D
McGiffert, Enud - 13-D
McGiffert, Mueller, Jones & Darcy - 13-D
McGrath, Joseph B. - 8-D
McGuire, Joseph M. - 37-D
McHenry & Staffier
  Foothills Pipe Lines (Yukon) - 18-D
McKeen, Elden C. - 53-D
McKenna, Conner & Cuneo
  California Savings and Loan League - 8-D
McKenna, William J. - 52-D
McMurray & Pendergast
  Government of Belize - 20-D
  Republic of Panama - 20-D
  Sugar Association of the Caribbean - 22-D
McNair, Glenn, Konduros, Corley, Singletary, Porter & Dibble
  Bristol-Myers Co. - 49-D
  CBS Inc. - 40-D
  Colt Industries Inc. - 33-D
  General Mills Inc. - 34-D
  Harris Corp. - 34-D
  Metropolitan Insurance Cos. - 35-D
Mead Corp., The - 19-D, 28-D
Meadow, Joseph F. - 17-D
Meat Price Investigators Association - 47-D
Medtronic Inc. - 51-D
Memorial Hospital of Garland - 16-D
Menell, Howard A. - 49-D
MeOH Inc. - 4-D
Merchants Grain and Transportation Inc. - 41-D
Merlis, Edward A. - 54-D
Merlo, Claude W. - 53-D
Merrill Lynch & Co. Inc. - 7-D, 34-D
Mesa Petroleum Co. - 51-D
Mestres, Jean L. - 12-D
Metal Trades Department, AFL-CIO - 15-D
Methodist Hospital - 23-D
Methodist Hospitals of Dallas - 16-D
Metlakatla Indian Community - 4-D
Metro Garage Board of Trade - 9-D
Metropolitan Insurance Cos. - 35-D
Meyers, Larry D. - 21-D
Miami Conservancy District, The - 39-D
Miccosukee Tribe of Indians of Florida - 4-D, 11-D

Michigan Consolidated Gas Co. - 35-D
Michigan Insurance Association - 47-D
Micoleau, Charles J. - 49-D, 55-D
Microband Corporation of America - 51-D
Mid-Continent Telephone Corp. - 35-D
Middle Atlantic Conference - 22-D
Middle South Services Inc. - 35-D
Middlewest Motor Freight Bureau - 22-D
Migrant Legal Action Program Inc. - 44-D
Milbank, Tweed, Hadley & McCloy
  Claymark Corp. Inc. - 49-D
  John Hancock Mutual Life Insurance Co. - 34-D
Millard, Katherine - 22-D
Miller & Chevalier
  Consolidated Edison Company of New York - 50-D
  Webster, Jeppson, Jones & Agran - 15-D
Miller & Schroeder Municipals Inc. - 28-D
Miller Brewing Co. - 35-D
Miller, Canfield, Paddock and Stone
  Comerica Inc. - 12-D
  Federal Home Life Insurance Co. - 45-D
Miller, Joseph E. - 11-D
Miller, Richard G. - 37-D
Miller, Steven T. - 21-D, 22-D
Mills, Robert G. - 49-D
Mims, Rose Mary - 9-D
Minnesota Mutual Life Insurance Co. - 51-D
Minnesotans for Peace in Central America - 26-D
Mintz, Levin, Cohn, Ferris, Glovsky & Popeo
  Envirite Corp. - 18-D
  Houghton Mifflin Co. - 34-D
  Liberty Mutual Insurance Co. - 19-D
  Turner Broadcasting System Inc. - 4-D
Mississippi Chemical Corp. - 51-D
Mitex - 51-D
Modglin, Terrence W. - 30-D
Moller Maersk, A. P., Line - 28-D
Monegon Ltd. - 35-D
Monolith Portland Cement Co. - 28-D, 35-D
Monsanto Co. - 13-D, 19-D
Montana Wilderness Association - 11-D
Moore, Francis B. - 46-D
Moore, Powell A. - 51-D
Moore, Timothy X. - 9-D
Moral Majority - 40-D
Morgan, Lewis & Bockius
  Alignpac - 49-D
  Bechtel Power Corp. - 27-D
  Security Pacific International Leasing (Europe) Inc. - 46-D
Morocco, Kingdom of - 52-D
Morrison & Foerster
  Crocker National Bank - 40-D
  Mastercard International Inc. - 41-D
  Rosenberg Real Estate Equity Fund Inc. - 41-D
Morrison, Julian K. III - 53-D
Moser, Charles A. - 23-D
Moses, George R. - 41-D
Moss Associates Inc.
  Association of Bank Holding Cos. - 53-D
Moss, McGee & Bellmon
  National Rural Development and Finance Corp. - 7-D
Mostowy, Thomas - 39-D
Motion Picture Association of America Inc. - 5-D, 9-D
Motor Vehicle Manufacturers Association of the U.S. Inc. - 38-D
Mountain States Energy Inc. - 19-D
Move Detroit Forward Fund - 3-D

Moye, Howard D. Jr. - 16-D
Mulroy, Edward - 10-D
Munger, Tolles & Rickershauser
  Spanish International Communication Corp. - 36-D
Murphy, C. Leon - 45-D
Murray and Scheer
  Cleveland Cliffs Iron Co. - 27-D
  Connecticut Mutual Life Insurance Co. - 24-D, 27-D
  Freeport-McMoran Inc. - 28-D
  Iron Ore Lessors Association - 31-D
  Massachusetts Mutual Life Insurance Co. - 24-D, 28-D
  Mutual Benefit Life Insurance Co. - 24-D, 28-D
  National Business Aircraft Association - 31-D
  National Council of Coal Lessors Inc. - 31-D
  New England Mutual Life Insurance Co. - 24-D, 28-D
  Penn Mutual Life Insurance Co. - 24-D, 29-D
  Swaziland Sugar Association - 10-D
  Swaziland Sugar Co. - 29-D
Music Corporation of America Inc. - 51-D
Mutual Benefit Life Insurance Co. - 24-D, 28-D
Mutual Protection Trust - 24-D
Myers, Gary D. - 21-D

N

Najjar, Annette - 11-D
Nakamichi U.S.A. Corp. - 13-D
Nana Regional Corp. Inc. - 3-D
Nanni, Elizabeth C. - 22-D
Napier, John L. - 25-D, 28-D
Nash, Philip - 23-D
National Alliance for Animal Legislation - 32-D
National-American Wholesale Grocers' Association - 47-D
National Ash Association Inc. - 47-D
National Association for Hospital Development - 54-D
National Association of Arab Americans - 6-D, 11-D
National Association of Bedding Manufacturers - 31-D
National Association of Broadcasters - 9-D, 22-D, 38-D
National Association of Business Development Corps. - 22-D, 26-D
National Association of Catalog Showroom Merchandisers - 22-D
National Association of Independent Colleges and Universities - 9-D, 22-D
National Association of Insurance Brokers - 9-D
National Association of Insurance Commissioners - 26-D, 38-D
National Association of Letter Carriers - 15-D
National Association of Manufacturers - 9-D, 22-D, 38-D, 43-D
National Association of Mutual Savings Banks - 54-D
National Association of Pharmaceutical Manufacturers - 38-D
National Association of Private Psychiatric Hospitals - 22-D, 54-D
National Association of Public Hospitals - 9-D
National Association of Public Television Stations - 31-D
National Association of Realtors - 9-D, 15-D, 22-D
National Association of Retired Federal Employees - 53-D

National Association of Royalty Owners - 43-D
National Association of Small Business Investment Cos. - 22-D
National Association of State Utility Consumer Advocates - 43-D
National Association of Truck Stop Operators - 38-D
National Association of Wholesaler-Distributors - 47-D
National Audubon Society - 3-D, 17-D
National Beer Wholesalers' Association of America Inc. - 15-D, 26-D
National Broadcasting Co. - 11-D, 45-D
National Broadcasting Co. Inc. - 51-D
National Business Aircraft Association - 31-D
National Cable Television Association Inc. - 22-D, 31-D, 43-D, 54-D
National Car Rental System Inc. - 51-D
National Citizens' Lobby Inc. - 26-D
National Coalition for Lower Prices - 17-D
National Committee Against Repressive Legislation - 17-D
National Committee for Poor People - 6-D
National Confectioners Association of the U.S. - 38-D
National Conference of Bankruptcy Judges - 54-D
National Conference of Black Mayors - 30-D
National Consumers League Inc. - 12-D, 40-D
National Corn Growers Association - 31-D
National Council for a World Peace Tax Fund - 4-D
National Council of Black Mayors - 30-D
National Council of Coal Lessors Inc. - 31-D
National Council of Community Hospitals - 54-D
National Council of Farmer Cooperatives - 3-D, 31-D, 54-D
National Council of Health Centers - 43-D
National Council of La Raza - 40-D
National Education Association - 53-D
National Employee Benefits Institute - 43-D
National Federation of Federal Employees - 4-D, 53-D
National Frozen Food Association - 9-D
National Futures Association - 31-D
National Grocers Association - 22-D
National Hospice Organization - 38-D
National Incorporation for Tenants - 32-D
National Inholders Association - 16-D
National Investment Development Corp. - 51-D
National Machine Tool Builders' Association - 26-D
National Mass Retailing Institute - 16-D
National Multifamily Housing Finance Association - 43-D
National Newspaper Association - 38-D
National Office Machine Dealers Association - 38-D
National Parks and Conservation Association - 12-D
National Passenger Traffic Association - 38-D
National Peace Academy Campaign, The - 17-D, 26-D
National Peanut Growers Group - 22-D
National Potato Council - 47-D
National Printing Equipment and Supply Association Inc. - 38-D

National Public Radio - 48-D
National Restaurant Association - 31-D
National Rifle Association of America - 9-D
National Right to Work Committee - 6-D
National Rural Development and Finance Corp. - 7-D
National Rural Electric Cooperative Association - 22-D
National School Transportation Association - 47-D
National Security and Retirement Program - 13-D
National Shipping Company of Saudi Arabia - 28-D
National Shorthand Reporters Association - 43-D
National Small Business Government Contractors Association - 22-D
National Society of Public Accountants - 54-D
National Solid Wastes Management Association - 39-D
National Soybean Processors Association - 16-D
National Steel and Shipbuilding Co. - 51-D
National Tire Dealers and Retreaders Association Inc. - 9-D
National Tooling and Machine Association - 16-D, 54-D
National Tour Association - 16-D
National Women's Political Caucus - 44-D
Nationwide Insurance Co. - 45-D
Natural Gas Supply Association - 26-D, 39-D, 47-D
Natural Resources Defense Council - 17-D
Nedlloyd Lines - 28-D
Neece, Cator & Associates Inc.
  National Association of Business Development Corps. - 22-D, 26-D
Negative Population Growth Inc. - 40-D
Neill & Co. Inc.
  Hashemite Kingdom of Jordan - 42-D
  Morocco, Kingdom of - 52-D
Nelco Products Inc. - 4-D
Netco - 28-D, 35-D
Nethercut, Doug - 26-D
Nettleton, Gil - 36-D
Neudeck, K. Michael - 4-D
New Bedford Seafood Council Inc. - 54-D
New England Council Inc. - 5-D
New England Educational Loan Marketing Corp. - 55-D
New England Motor Rate Bureau - 22-D
New England Mutual Life Insurance Co. - 24-D, 28-D
New Mexico, Commissioner of Public Lands for State of - 53-D
New Mexico Public Service Commission - 37-D
New York Life Insurance Co. - 51-D
New York Power Authority - 30-D
New York State Electric & Gas Co. - 11-D
New York Telephone Co. - 51-D
Newbold, Bill, and Associates
  Schick Shadel Hospital - 23-D
Newmont Mining Corp. - 51-D
Niagara Frontier Tariff Bureau - 22-D
Nicholas, W. F. - 38-D
Nickerson, Ingram & Associates Inc.
  Federal Law Enforcement Officers Association - 15-D
  Orange County Transit District - 37-D
  Southern California Rapid Transit District - 37-D

Ninth Pro-Life Congressional District Action Committee - 27-D
NIU Inc. - 51-D
NL Industries - 35-D
Noranda Exploration Inc. - 13-D
Noranda Mining Inc. - 13-D, 45-D
Norell, James O. E. - 39-D
North Central Nebraska Reclamation District - 21-D
North Dakota, State of - 5-D
North, Evans W. - 3-D
North, Haskell, Slaughter, Young & Lewis - 19-D
Northeastern International Airways Inc. - 4-D
Northern California Power Agency - 47-D
Northern Tier Pipeline Co. - 19-D
Northrop University - 39-D
Northville Industries Corp. - 13-D, 19-D
Northwest Bancorp. - 19-D
North West Timber Association - 48-D
Northwestern Bell (Iowa Division) - 51-D
Northwestern Mutual Life Insurance Co. - 24-D
Nossaman, Guthner, Knox & Elliott
   Cook Inlet Region Inc. - 26-D
   Interstate Natural Gas Association of America - 26-D
   Trust for Public Lands - 27-D
Nova Scotia Resources Ltd. - 45-D

O

Occidental Petroleum Corp. - 7-D
Ocean Drilling and Exploration Co. - 7-D
O'Connell, Richard T., & Associates Inc.
   Chocolate Manufacturers Association of the USA - 37-D
   National Confectioners Association of the U.S. - 38-D
O'Connor & Hannan
   Allis-Chalmers Corp. - 44-D
   Borden Inc. - 32-D
   Cambridge Redevelopment Authority - 20-D
   Combined Insurance Company of America - 4-D
   Dougherty, Dawkins, Strand & Yost - 27-D
   First Pennsylvania Bank - 18-D
   Government of Sudan - 36-D
   Insurance Association of Connecticut - 26-D
   Itel Corp. - 45-D
   Jamaica, Government of - 52-D
   Jamaican Broadcasting Corp. - 18-D
   Kane Paper Corp. - 4-D
   Lehman Brothers Kuhn Loeb Inc. - 4-D
   Miller & Schroeder Municipals Inc. - 28-D
   National Security and Retirement Program - 13-D
   Prudential Insurance Company of America - 35-D
   RLC Corp. - 14-D
O'Cummings, Grady III - 6-D
Offshore Marine Service Association - 54-D
Oglala Sioux Tribe - 10-D
O'Grady, Terri - 9-D
Ohio Casualty Insurance Co. - 19-D
Oliver, Janet L. - 22-D
O'Melveny & Myers
   Santa Fe International Corp. - 19-D
O'Neill and Haase
   Brigham and Women's Hospital Inc. - 39-D
   Harvard Medical Center - 16-D

Marriott Corp. - 41-D
Massachusetts General Hospital - 48-D
Pharmaceutical Manufacturers Association - 22-D
Puget Sound Power & Light Co. - 41-D
Onek, Klein and Farr
   Major League Baseball Players Association - 37-D
Orange County Transit District - 37-D
Oregon Inlet Commission - 43-D
Oregon, State of - 21-D
Osteopathic Medical Center - 16-D
Otis Elevator Co. - 19-D
Otto Bremer Foundation - 16-D
Overbeck, Gene E. - 32-D
Overseas Education Association - 37-D
Owens-Corning Fiberglas Corp. - 28-D

P

Pacific Express Inc. - 45-D
Pacific Green Corp. - 19-D
Pacific Inland Tariff Bureau - 22-D
Pacific Mutual Life Insurance Co. - 29-D, 51-D
Pacific Resources Inc. - 14-D
Pacific Seafood Processors Association - 22-D
Padilla, Anthony - 53-D
Paige, Henry H. - 32-D
Pakhoed - 19-D
Palmer, Andrew - 32-D
Palumbo & Cerrell
   National School Transportation Association - 47-D
Palumbo, Benjamin L. - 46-D
Pan American National Bank - 14-D
Pandrol - 19-D
Panhandle Eastern Pipe Line Co. - 24-D
Pantuso, Peter J. - 38-D
Panyard, James E. - 54-D
Pappanastos, Samford, Roberts & Blanchard
   Natural Gas Supply Association - 39-D
   U.S. Capital Corp. - 41-D
Pascua-Yaqui Tribe - 17-D
Passamaneck, David J. - 39-D
Pathfinder Fund, The - 48-D
Patterson, Belknap, Webb & Tyler
   F M S Corp. - 33-D
Patton, Boggs & Blow
   Air Products & Chemicals Inc. - 17-D
   AIWA America Inc. - 12-D
   Aluminum Company of America - 27-D
   American Broadcasting Co. - 44-D
   Armco Inc. - 27-D
   Basic Industries Coalition Inc. - 30-D
   C. F. Bean - 49-D
   Computer Dealers and Lessors Association Inc. - 38-D
   Fuji Photo Film U.S.A. Inc. - 13-D
   Georgia Pacific Corp. - 18-D
   Great Lakes Dredge & Dock - 50-D
   Kaiser Aluminum & Chemicals Corp. - 19-D
   Kenwood U.S.A. Corp. - 13-D
   Konishiroku Ampex Co. Ltd. - 13-D
   Laundry Cleaning Council - 47-D
   Maxell Corporation of America - 13-D
   Mead Corp. - 28-D
   Michigan Insurance Association - 47-D
   Nakamichi U.S.A. Corp. - 13-D
   Pioneer Electronics (U.S.A.) Inc. - 14-D
   PPG Industries Inc. - 14-D
   Republique D'Haiti - 46-D
   Sansui Electronics Corp. - 14-D
   St. Joe Minerals Corp. - 4-D
   Stephens Inc. - 29-D
   Sumitomo 3M Ltd. - 14-D
   TDK U.S.A. Corp. - 14-D
   TEAC Corp. - 14-D

Teknika Electronics Corp. - 14-D
United Plant Guard Workers Association - 46-D
United States Lifesaving Manufacturers Association - 55-D
   Victor Magnetape Co. Ltd. - 15-D
Paul, Hastings, Janofsky & Walker
   M Life Insurance Co. - 51-D
Peabody Holding Co. Inc. - 45-D
Peabody, Lambert & Meyers
   Broadcast Music Inc. - 49-D
   Committee of Corporate Telecommunications Users - 54-D
   National Mass Retailing Institute - 16-D
Peace Political Action Committee - 32-D
Penn, Cris - 54-D
Penn Mutual Life Insurance Co. - 24-D, 29-D
Pennsylvania Electric Co. - 11-D
Pennzoil Co. - 45-D
Pepper & Corazzini
   Test Marketing Group Inc., The - 52-D
Perito, Duerk, Carlson & Pinco
   American Protestant Hospital Association - 30-D
   Combined Health Resources Inc. - 12-D
   Samaritan Health Service - 14-D, 19-D
Peter, P. S. - 18-D
Petersen, Dennis L. - 50-D
Peterson, Peter G. - 10-D
Petrina, Michael J. Jr. - 54-D
Petro-Lewis Corp. - 41-D
Petroleum Equipment and Supply Association - 26-D
Petty, Brian T. - 26-D
Pfizer Inc. - 51-D
Pharmaceutical Manufacturers Association - 22-D, 39-D, 54-D
PHH Group Inc. - 35-D
Philadelphia Facilities Management Corp. - 35-D
Philippine Sugar Commission - 9-D
Phillips Petroleum Co. - 29-D
Pierson, Ball & Dowd
   American Academy of Pediatrics - 42-D
   Day Trust, The - 43-D
   Securities Industries Association - 43-D
Pierson, Semmes, Crolius and Finley
   Six Flags Corp. - 20-D
Piliero, Daniel J. II - 35-D
Pillsbury Co. - 35-D
Pilot Petroleum Corp. - 4-D
Pinto Valley Copper Corp. - 51-D
Pioneer Electronics (U.S.A.) Inc. - 14-D
Pipeline Industry Advancement Fund - 22-D
Piper Aircraft Corp. - 41-D
Piper, Jaffray & Hopwood - 35-D
Piper & Marbury
   Container Transport International Inc. - 33-D
   Flexi-van Leasing Inc. - 33-D
   Transamerica-ICS Inc. - 36-D
   University of Alabama Health Services Foundation - 16-D
   Xtra Corp. - 46-D
Pirelli Cable Corp. - 14-D
Pitney Bowes Inc. - 45-D
Pittsburg & Shawmut Railroad - 19-D
Pittsburgh Corning Corp. - 41-D
Plastics Manufacturing Co. - 46-D
Plaza 400 Owners Corp. - 51-D
Plummer, Wesley A. - 46-D
Plunkett, Cooney, Rutt, Watters, Stanczyk & Pederson
   American Postal Workers Union - 36-D
   City of Detroit - 37-D
   Council of Michigan Foundations - 39-D
   Michigan Consolidated Gas Co. - 35-D
Porte, Phillip, & Associates Inc.
   American Medical Records Association - 21-D

Portland General Electric Co. - 29-D
Potato Chip/Snack Food Association - 16-D
Potter Instrument Co. Inc. - 3-D
Potts Industries Inc. - 46-D
Potts, William J. Jr. - 26-D
Powell, Goldstein, Frazer & Murphy
   Coalition for Competition - 21-D
   Corning Associates - 6-D
   Crum & Foster Insurance Cos. - 18-D
   Flood Control Advisory Committee - 55-D
   Westinghouse Electric Corp. - 3-D
PPG Industries Inc. - 14-D
Pratt Institute - 23-D
Pratt, Robert L. - 36-D
Prendergast, Joseph T. - 47-D
Prendergast, William B. - 16-D
Prescott, Brainard E. - 4-D
Preston, Thorgrimson, Ellis & Holman
   City of Cincinnati - 30-D
   City of Lakewood - 25-D
   City of Scottsdale - 30-D
   City of St. Louis - 30-D
   Corporation for Public Broadcasting - 55-D
   Employers Reinsurance Corp. - 40-D
   General Telephone & Electronics - 3-D
   Hudson Waterways - 18-D
   Intergovernmental Cable Communications Authority of Oakland County, Mich. - 30-D
   North West Timber Association - 48-D
   State of Alaska - 25-D
   Western Forest Industries Association - 48-D
Price, James M. - 49-D
Primark Corp. - 29-D, 35-D
Private Truck Council of America Inc. - 9-D
Project Cure Inc. - 49-D
Providence Capitol Corp. - 51-D
Provident Life and Accident Insurance Co. - 11-D, 24-D
Provident Mutual Life Insurance Co. - 29-D
Provident Mutual Life Insurance Company of Philadelphia - 51-D
Prudential Insurance Company of America - 35-D
Public Voice for Food and Health Policy - 4-D, 10-D
Pueblo International Inc. - 35-D
Puerto Rico, Commonwealth of - 30-D
Puerto Rico Maritime Shipping Authority - 25-D
Puget Sound Power & Light Co. - 41-D
Purolator Inc. - 29-D
Pyle, Robert N. - 33-D

Q

Qualicare Inc. - 19-D
Quinn, Racusin, Young & Delaney
   Government Employees Insurance Co. - 40-D
   Maryland Savings Share Insurance Corp., The - 43-D

R

Ragan & Mason
   R. J. Reynolds Tobacco Co. - 29-D
Ragland, Robert A. - 43-D
Railroad Retirement Association - 10-D, 20-D
Railsback, Tom - 9-D
Ramirez, T., and Co. Inc. - 51-D
Randall, Bangert & Price
   Grocery Manufacturers of America - 5-D

Rauscher Pierce Refsnes - 19-D
RBC Associates
    Bangor & Aroostook Railroad - 17-D
    Boston and Maine Railroad - 17-D
    Chicago & North Western Transportation Corp. - 18-D
    Delaware Otsego System - 18-D
    Forum Communications - 33-D
    Genesee & Wyoming Corp. - 18-D
    Pandrol - 19-D
    Pittsburg & Shawmut Railroad - 19-D
    Speno Rail Services - 20-D
    Westinghouse Information Systems - 20-D
RCA Global Communications Inc. - 35-D
Rearick, Linda S. - 16-D
Reasoner, Davis & Vinson
    Acacia Mutual Life Insurance Co. - 6-D
Recording Industry Association of America Inc. - 10-D
Redfield Land Co. - 41-D
Reid & Priest
    Amytex Corp. - 49-D
    Hilaturas Lerma S.A. - 50-D
    Massachusetts Mutual Life Insurance - 24-D
    Northwestern Mutual Life Insurance Co. - 24-D
Reilly, Maryalyce - 54-D
Reimann, Ronald H. - 49-D
Reinhart, Boerner, Van Deuren, Norris & Rieselbach
    National Employee Benefits Institute - 43-D
Republic of Gabon - 8-D
Republic of Haiti - 8-D
Republic of Panama - 20-D
Republic of Turkey - 30-D, 46-D
Republique D'Haiti - 46-D
Reynolds, Mary Anne - 44-D
Reynolds, R. J., Tobacco Co. - 4-D, 29-D
Rhode Island, State of - 5-D
Rhodes, John J. - 50-D
Rhudy, Robert J. - 32-D
Rice, M. Lee - 55-D
Richards, Alan K. - 27-D
Richerson, Lois - 22-D
Riley, Pat - 4-D
Rilling, Mark Alan - 26-D
Rio Blanco Properties - 24-D
Riordan, Dale P. - 9-D
Risk and Insurance Management Society Inc. - 26-D
Rivers, Phillip W. - 40-D
Riverside, City of - 47-D
Riviana Foods Inc. - 14-D
RLC - 14-D
Robertson, Monagle, Eastaugh & Bradley
    Alaska Lumber and Pulp - 6-D
    Alaska Pulp & Resources Inc. - 6-D
    Carr-Gottstein Properties Inc. - 44-D
    Noranda Mining Inc. - 45-D
Rochester Tax Council - 3-D
Rockwell International Corp. - 14-D
Rocky Mountain Motor Tariff Bureau - 22-D
Roderer, David W. - 48-D
Rogers & Wells
    National Association of Bedding Manufacturers - 31-D
    The Morris and Gwendolyn Cafritz Foundation - 26-D
Rogers, Hoge & Hills
    Contact Lens Manufacturers Association - 3-D
Rohrkemper, Stephen F. - 50-D
Rooney, Fred B. - 6-D, 7-D, 50-D
Rosemond, David A. - 30-D
Rosenberg Real Estate Equity Fund Inc. - 41-D
Roses Inc. - 35-D

Roth, Samuel A. - 54-D
Royer & Shacknai
    Babcock & Brown Inc. - 40-D, 44-D
Rubenstein, Wolfson & Co.
    International Gold Corp. Ltd. - 45-D
Rubin, Eric M. - 53-D
Rudy, Camille Kearns - 54-D
Ruempler, Henry C. - 27-D
Rugh, Timothy R. - 37-D
Ruph, Morgan S. - 39-D
Russell, Randall M. - 3-D
Ruttenberg, Phelps & Slocum
    National Tooling and Machine Association - 16-D

S

Sacramento Public Utility District - 47-D
Safekeeper Systems Inc. - 24-D, 29-D
Saflok - 29-D
Sahd, Gregory A. - 11-D
Salomon Brothers Inc. - 51-D
Salomon, Richard E. - 50-D
Samaritan Health Service - 7-D, 14-D, 19-D
Samuels, Ron - 11-D, 26-D
San Antonio, City of - 5-D
San Francisco Public Utilities Commission - 19-D, 37-D
Sanders Corp. - 3-D
Sansui Electronics Corp. - 14-D
Santa Anita Realty Enterprises Inc. - 35-D, 52-D
Santa Clara, City of - 46-D
Santa Clara Pueblo - 49-D
Santa Fe Industries Inc. - 52-D
Santa Fe International Corp. - 19-D
Santini, James D. - 13-D
Sarasin, Ronald A. - 31-D
Scanlon, Thomas J. - 39-D
Schapaugh, William T. - 47-D
Scheck, Richard H. - 31-D
Scheer, John M. - 48-D
Schick Shadel Hospital - 23-D
Schlenaker Drilling Co. - 20-D
Schlenger, Jaques T. - 41-D
Schlossberg-Cassidy and Associates Inc.
    Independent Radio Common Carriers Association - 54-D
    Indiana University - 23-D
    Pirelli Cable Corp. - 14-D
    Pratt Institute - 23-D
Schmitt, Robert Richard - 55-D
Schneider, Mark L. - 20-D
Schochet Associates - 35-D
Schrichte, A. Kolbet - 3-D
Schulman Management Co. - 46-D
Schuster, Neil D. - 38-D
Schwabe, Williamson, Wyatt, Moore & Roberts
    Litchstreet Co. - 19-D
    Mountain States Energy Inc. - 19-D
    Otis Elevator Co. - 19-D
    State of Oregon - 21-D
Schweitzer, Richard P. - 38-D
Scott, John N. - 29-D
Scott, Michael - 49-D
Scottsdale, City of - 30-D
Scribner, Hall & Thompson
    Provident Life and Accident Insurance - 11-D
Seaco Inc. - 46-D
Seagram, Joseph E., & Sons Inc. - 29-D
Seamen's Church Institute - 43-D
Sears, Roebuck and Co. - 7-D
Securities Industries Association - 43-D
Security New York State Corp. - 14-D
Security Pacific International Leasing (Europe) Inc. - 46-D
Sederholm, Pamela - 14-D

Seipel, Peggy - 39-D
Sellers, M. Frank - 37-D
Semler, H. Michael - 44-D
Shah & Associates - 52-D
Shakopee-Mdeuakanton Sioux Community - 17-D
Sharood, Richard N. - 12-D, 18-D
Sharps, Pixley & Co. Ltd. - 7-D
Shawn, William H. - 28-D
Shea & Gould
    Hospital Corporation of America - 34-D
Shea Products Inc. - 35-D
Sheet Metal Workers' International Association - 20-D, 53-D
Shell Oil Co. - 4-D, 14-D
Sherwin-Williams Co., The - 14-D
Shipbuilders Council of America - 10-D, 55-D
Shoemaker, Thomas N. - 10-D
Shuey, John - 3-D
Sidley & Austin
    Contract Staffing of America Inc. - 50-D
Sierra Club - 12-D, 40-D, 49-D
Signal Communications - 7-D
Signal Companies Inc., The - 7-D
Sills, Ronald G. - 43-D
Simering, Jeffrey A. - 47-D
Simonelli and Hall
    Fair Trade Subcommittee of the International Trade Committee of the Cast Metals Federation - 15-D
Sims, Clifford E. - 26-D
Singapore Airlines Ltd. - 35-D
Sinnott, Richard L., and Co. - 14-D
Sisk, Foley, Hultin & Driver
    Ashland Oil Inc. - 12-D
    Champlin Petroleum Co. - 12-D
    Pacific Resources Inc. - 14-D
    Tenneco Inc. - 14-D
Sivon, James C. - 54-D
Six Flags Corp. - 20-D
Skadden, Arps, Slate, Meagher & Flom
    Cities Service Oil and Gas Corp. - 12-D
    Transco Energy Co. - 29-D
Skilbred, Amy - 27-D
Skylink Corp. Inc. - 35-D
Slinn, Ronald J. - 25-D
Smathers, Symington & Herlong
    Coalition of Community Banks of Florida - 54-D
Smith, Barney, Harris, Upham & Co. Inc. - 35-D
Smith Dawson Associates Inc. - 37-D
Smith, Deborah A. - 21-D
Smith, Douglas - 16-D
Smith, James - 34-D
Smith, Jeffrey A. - 37-D
Smith, Thomas Blaisdell - 4-D
Smith, William C. - 49-D
Snecma - 29-D
Snowling, Randall A. - 50-D
Snowwhite, Larry S. - 55-D
Societe Nationale D'Etude et De Construction De Moteurs D'Aviation - 35-D, 41-D, 46-D
Society of the Plastics Industry, The - 43-D, 55-D
Sofreavia - 41-D
Solarex Corp. - 14-D, 35-D
Sonat Inc. - 7-D
Sony Corporation of America - 52-D
South Carolina Public Service Authority - 42-D
South Jersey Clothing - 29-D
Southeastern Exporters - 36-D
Southeastern Fisheries Association Inc. - 16-D
Southern Arizona Water Resources Association - 39-D
Southern California Edison Co. - 36-D

Southern California Rapid Transit District - 37-D
Southern Hotel Development Co. - 29-D
Southern Motor Carriers Rate Conference - 22-D
Southern Pacific Co. - 29-D
Southland Corp., The - 14-D
Southwestern Portland Cement Co. - 29-D, 36-D
Spanish International Communication Corp. - 36-D
Spears, John B. - 53-D
Specialty Equipment Market Association - 22-D
Speno Rail Services - 20-D
Spriggs, Bode & Hollingsworth
    Energy Cycle Inc. - 18-D
Squire, Sanders & Dempsey
    Alamo Cement Co. - 27-D
    General Portland Inc. - 28-D
    Gifford-Hill & Co. Inc. - 28-D, 34-D
    Kaiser Cement Corp. - 28-D
    Microband Corporation of America - 51-D
    Monolith Portland Cement Co. - 28-D
    Southwestern Portland Cement Co. - 29-D
    Tymnet Inc. - 52-D
St. Cin, Carl F. - 19-D
St. Joe Minerals Corp. - 4-D, 35-D
St. Louis, City of - 25-D
St. Petersburg, City of - 47-D
Stallworth, Tyrone - 23-D
Standard Oil Company (Indiana) - 52-D
Standard Oil Company (Ohio) - 7-D, 20-D
Stang, David P. - 26-D, 31-D, 36-D, 43-D, 44-D, 46-D, 54-D
Stanton, Thomas H. - 12-D, 27-D
State Mutual Life Assurance Company of America - 29-D, 52-D
State of Nevada - 37-D
Stedman Corp. - 11-D
Stepan Chemical Co. - 24-D
Stephens Inc. - 29-D
Steptoe & Johnson
    Association of Private Pension and Welfare Plans Inc. - 21-D
Stern, Agee & Leach - 20-D
Stevens-Kittner, Heather - 22-D
Stewart-Shain, Victoria - 6-D
Still, Stephen W. - 7-D
Stocker, John J. - 10-D
Stockmeyer, Steven F. - 38-D
Stockton Terminal and Eastern Railroad - 29-D
Stolte, Dennis C. - 53-D
Stone & Webster Engineering Corp. - 52-D
Stone, Jay - 34-D
Stone, John C. - 19-D
Storer Communications Inc. - 7-D
Stovall, Spradlin, Armstrong & Israel
    Commission on Future Political Status and Transition, The Federated States of Micronesia - 46-D
    Ingersoll-Rand Co. - 45-D
Streeter, James R. - 16-D
Stroh Brewery Co. - 52-D
Stroock & Stroock & Lavan
    American Red Cross Retirement System - 43-D
    Dreyfus Corp. - 27-D
    Dreyfus Tax-Exempt Bond Fund - 6-D
    Dreyfus Tax-Exempt Money Market Fund - 7-D
    Fifth Avenue & 59th Corp. - 50-D
    Ingersoll & Bloch - 45-D
    Metro Garage Board of Trade - 9-D
    Pacific Express Inc. - 45-D
    Plaza 400 Owners Corp. - 51-D

Sudan, Government of - 36-D

Suffolk, County of - 21-D

Sugar Association of the Caribbean - 22-D

Sukow, Gary M. - 6-D

Sullivan & Worcester
Alaska Lumber & Pulp Co. Inc. - 17-D

Sullivan, Marcia Z. - 11-D

Sumitomo 3M Ltd. - 14-D

Summit Enterprises Inc. - 20-D

Sun Co. Inc. - 14-D, 36-D

Sun-Diamond Growers of California - 36-D

Sun Life Assurance Company of Canada - 52-D

Sunkist Growers Inc. - 36-D

Surrey & Morse
Bendone-DeRossi International - 12-D
Cavalier Clothing Co. - 27-D
Dale Fashions - 27-D
London Chamber of Commerce and Industry - 38-D
Major Clothing Co. - 28-D
South Jersey Clothing - 29-D
The Pathfinder Fund - 48-D

Sutherland, Asbill & Brennan
Ad Hoc Committee for Equitable Transportation - 48-D
Association of Business Advocating Tariff Equity - 21-D
Atlanta Life Insurance Co. - 10-D
Contract Carriage Coalition - 42-D
Direct Marketing Insurance Group - 40-D
General Motors Corp. - 34-D
Woodstream Corp. - 42-D

Sutin, Thayer & Browne
Mississippi Chemical Corp. - 51-D

Swaziland Sugar Association - 10-D

Swaziland Sugar Co. - 29-D

Swidler, Berlin & Strelow
General Mills Inc. - 40-D
International Anticounterfeiting Coalition - 42-D
Maryland People's Counsel - 42-D
National Association for Hospital Development - 54-D
National Association of State Utility Consumer Advocates - 43-D
National Council of Community Hospitals - 54-D
National Shorthand Reporters Association - 43-D
South Carolina Public Service Authority - 42-D
Twentieth Century-Fox Film Corp. - 14-D

Swigart, Richard P. - 22-D

Sylvester, Christopher U. - 43-D

Systems and Applied Sciences - 52-D

T

Taft, Stettinius & Hollister
Dosimeter Corporation of North America - 33-D
Miami Conservancy District, The - 39-D
Piper, Jaffray & Hopwood - 35-D
RCA Global Communications Inc. - 35-D
Sherwin-Williams Co., The - 14-D
Wald Manufacturing Co. Inc. - 20-D

Taggart & Associates
Marion Laboratories Inc. - 34-D
Telephone and Data Systems Inc. - 41-D

Tano Corp. - 11-D

Tate, M. Louise - 49-D

Taylor & Mizell - 36-D

Taylor, Leslie M. - 47-D

Taylor, Robert C. - 36-D

TDK U.S.A. Corp. - 14-D

TEAC Corp. - 14-D

Teff, Stephanie - 6-D

Teknika Electronics Corp. - 14-D

Telephone and Data Systems Inc. - 41-D

Telocator Network of America - 55-D

Tendler, Black & Biggins
Computer and Communication Industry Association - 38-D

Tendler, Paul, Associates Inc.
Alpha Data Inc. - 23-D
Southeastern Exporters - 36-D

Tendler, Paul M. - 32-D

Tenneco Inc. - 7-D, 14-D, 20-D

Terrell, Joseph L. S. - 47-D

Test Marketing Group Inc., The - 52-D

Texaco Inc. - 20-D

Texas Air Corp. - 52-D

Texas & Southwestern Cattle Raisers Association - 31-D

Texas Cattle Feeders Association - 31-D

Texas Eastern Corp. - 11-D

Texas Eastern Transmission Co. - 29-D, 36-D

Texas Electric Service Co. - 46-D

Texas Oil and Gas Corp. - 14-D

Thatcher, Proffitt & Wood
Grindlays Bank Ltd. - 50-D
Salomon Brothers Inc. - 51-D

Thermo Electron Corp. - 36-D

Thiemann, Alan J. - 28-D

Thomason, Thomas E. - 49-D

Thompson & Co. - 36-D

Thompson & Mitchell
Contact Lens Manufacturers Association - 54-D
Crown Life Insurance Co. - 6-D

Thompson, Hine and Flory
Mid-continent Telephone Corp. - 35-D

Thompson, Robert J. - 36-D

Thomson-CSF Inc. - 25-D, 36-D

Thornton, Farish & Gauntt - 20-D

Thornton, Harold A., & Associates
American Federation of Government Employees, Local 2677 - 46-D
Committee to Improve Public School Libraries - 32-D

Threadgill, Walter L. - 7-D

Timber Realization - 52-D

Timmons and Co. Inc.
The Boeing Co. - 17-D

Tipperary Corp. - 52-D

Titanium Metals Corporation of America (Timet Division) - 36-D

Tobacco Institute, The - 16-D, 55-D

Tobin, Robert - 32-D

Toyota Motor Corp. - 29-D

Toyota Motor Sales USA Inc. - 36-D

Trabucco, Thomas J. - 53-D

Trade Industry & Customs Department, Government of Hong Kong - 46-D

Trade Max Inc. - 52-D

Trans America Developers Inc. - 46-D

Transamerica-ICS Inc. - 36-D

Transcanada Pipelines Ltd. - 7-D

Transco Energy Co. - 25-D, 29-D, 36-D

Transco Inc. - 52-D

Transportation Institute - 16-D

Trans World Airlines Inc. - 7-D

Travel Industry Association of America - 10-D

Tribal Council of the Coushatta Tribe of Louisiana - 27-D

Troop, Michael G. - 55-D

TRT Telecommunications Corp. - 29-D

Trust for Public Lands - 27-D

Tse, Mrs. Winnie M. - 23-D

Tugado, Angelesio C. - 5-D

Turkey, Republic of - 36-D

Turner Broadcasting System Inc. - 4-D, 7-D, 25-D, 29-D

Twentieth Century-Fox Film Corp. - 14-D

Tymnet Inc. - 52-D

U

UCI Inc. - 25-D, 52-D

Ullman Consultants Inc.
Titanium Metals Corporation of America (Timet Division) - 36-D

Ultrasystems Inc. - 20-D

Union Oil Company of California - 41-D

Union Pacific Corp. - 7-D, 29-D, 41-D

Union Pacific Railroad Corp. - 14-D

Union Texas Petroleum Corp. - 8-D

Uniroyal Inc. - 14-D

United Action for Animals Inc. - 17-D

United Arab Shipping Co. - 30-D

United Distribution Cos. - 11-D

United Hellenic American Congress and American Hellenic Alliance Inc. - 48-D

United Nations Children's Fund - 10-D

United Plant Guard Workers Association - 46-D

United States Cruises Inc. - 36-D

United States Defense Committee - 32-D, 49-D

United States League of Saving Institutions - 55-D

United States Lifesaving Manufacturers Association - 55-D

United States Photovoltaics Manufacturers' Ad Hoc Committee - 48-D

United States Steel Corp. - 25-D

United States Surgical Corp. - 36-D

United Tobacco Growers Association - 16-D

United Way of America - 49-D

University of Alabama Health Services Foundation - 16-D

Urban Neighborhood Enterprises Inc. - 30-D

Urban Revitalization Inc. - 3-D

U.S. Banknote Corp. - 14-D

U.S. Capital Corp. - 41-D

U.S. League of Saving Institutions - 39-D

U.S. Manufacturing Co. - 25-D, 30-D

U.S. Recreational Ski Association - 39-D

U.S. Telephone Inc. - 30-D, 46-D

U.S. West Inc. - 41-D

Utilities Telecommunications Council - 43-D

Utility Nuclear Waste Management Group - 55-D

V

Valanzano, Anthony - 42-D

Van Deerlin, Lionel - 26-D

Van Etten, Laura - 31-D

Van Fleet Associates Inc.
Ford Aerospace - 13-D

Van Ness, Feldman, Sutcliffe, Curtis & Levenberg
Ad Hoc Committee on Alternative Energy Tax Credits - 53-D
Brae Corp., The - 40-D
Castle & Cooke Inc. - 32-D
Columbia Gas System Service Corp. - 12-D
Joseph E. Seagram & Sons Inc. - 29-D
McDonnell Douglas Astronautics Corp. - 13-D
New York State Electric & Gas Co. - 11-D
Pennsylvania Electric Co. - 11-D
Republic of Kenya - 20-D
Texas Air Corp. - 52-D

Vasiloff, Jennifer - 23-D

Vaughan, Donald R. - 11-D

Vehmas, Lisa A. - 42-D

Velo-Bind Inc. - 25-D

Venable, Baetjer and Howard - 41-D

Verner, Liipfert, Bernhard and McPherson
John D. and Catherine T. MacArthur Foundation - 55-D
Turner Broadcasting System Inc. - 7-D

Verrastro, Frank A. - 45-D

Victor Magnetape Co. Ltd. - 15-D

Videotex Industry Association - 31-D

Vigil, Michael F. - 28-D

Vinovich, Ralph - 55-D

Vinson & Elkins
City of El Paso - 21-D
Northville Industries Corp. - 19-D
The Methodist Hospital - 23-D

Viola, John A. - 48-D

Visa U.S.A. Inc. - 25-D

Volume Footwear Retailers of America - 39-D

Vorys, Sater, Seymour and Pease
Southern Hotel Development Co. - 29-D

Vulcan Foundry Inc. - 41-D

Vulcan Materials Co. - 46-D

W

Wachholz, Douglas P. - 26-D

Wagner & Baroody
American Bus Association - 15-D
Associated Builders and Contractors Inc. - 15-D
Burns & Roe Inc. - 12-D
Chicago and Northwestern Railroad - 12-D
E-Systems - 12-D
Lanihau Corps. - 13-D
Long Island Trust Co. - 13-D
National Beer Wholesalers Association - 15-D
Union Pacific Railroad Corp. - 14-D

Wald, Harkrader and Ross
Japan Iron & Steel Exporters' Association - 47-D
Matsushita Electric Industrial Co. Ltd. - 51-D
National Conference of Black Mayors - 30-D

Wald Manufacturing Co. Inc. - 20-D

Walker, Charls E., Associates Inc.
Anheuser-Busch Cos. Inc. - 32-D
Bethlehem Steel Corp. - 12-D
CBS Inc. - 44-D
Copiat - 50-D
HBO & Co. - 40-D
Northville Industries Corp. - 13-D
Seaco Inc. - 46-D

Walker, Douglas K. - 8-D

Wall, R. Duffy, & Associates Inc.
Freeport-McMoRan Inc. - 10-D
Lobby registration - 11-D
Schulman Management Co. - 46-D

Wallace, Don, Associates Inc.
General Mills Corp. - 28-D
Merchants Grain and Transportation Inc. - 41-D
National Beer Wholesalers' Association of America Inc. - 26-D
Oregon Inlet Commission - 43-D
Turner Broadcasting System Inc. - 25-D

Walters, Mavis A. - 34-D

Walton & Son Stevedoring Co. - 30-D

Wang Laboratories Inc. - 15-D

Warden, Barbara F. - 12-D

Warfield, Wiliam L. - 43-D

Warner Amex Cable Communications Inc. - 36-D

Warner Communications Inc. - 4-D

Warren, B. Jack - 9-D

Washburn, Barbara J. - 45-D
Washington Coalition of Redress - 23-D
Washington Coordinating Council on Productivity - 48-D
Washington Psychiatric Society - 39-D
Washington Workshops - 5-D
Waste Management Inc. - 46-D
Water and Wastewater Equipment Manufacturers Association Inc. - 48-D
Waterman Steamship Co. - 30-D
Watson, Kenneth W. - 28-D
Watt, Tieder, Killian, Toole & Hoffar
  Ohio Casualty Insurance Co. - 19-D
Watts, Douglas R. - 22-D
Webb, Cyrus E. - 13-D
Webber, Andrew H. - 47-D, 53-D
Webster & Sheffield
  Domestic Petroleum Council Inc. - 21-D
Webster, Chamberlain & Bean
  Beer Industry Alliance - 21-D
  Miller Brewing Co. - 35-D
  Mutual Protection Trust - 24-D
Webster, Jeppson, Jones & Agrann - 15-D
Weinstein, Jon R. - 44-D
Weiss, Stanley A. - 8-D
Wellford, Wegman, Krulwich, Gold & Hoff
  Mitex - 51-D
  United Way of America - 49-D
Western Cotton Growers Association - 48-D
Western Forest Industries Association - 48-D
Western Fuels Association Inc. - 39-D
Western Governors Policy Office - 30-D
Western Union Telegraph Co. - 46-D
Westinghouse Corp. - 8-D
Westinghouse Electric Corp. - 3-D, 46-D, 52-D
Westinghouse Information Systems - 20-D

West Indies Rum and Spirits Producers Association - 31-D
West Indies Investment Co. - 42-D
West Texas Utilities Co. - 20-D
Western Fuels Association Inc. - 43-D
Western Governors Policy Office - 30-D
Wetzel, John F. Jr. - 37-D
Wexler, Reynolds, Harrison & Schule Inc.
  Aetna Life and Casualty Co. - 40-D
  Association of American Railroads - 30-D
  Committee for Prudent Deregulation - 11-D
  Foothills Pipe Line (Yukon) Ltd. - 40-D
  Manville Corp. - 41-D
  National Cable Television Association - 43-D
  New York Power Authority - 30-D
Weyerhaeuser Co. - 36-D
Whalen, Curtis E. - 36-D
Wheat First Securities - 20-D
Wheeler, Edwin M. - 53-D
Wheels Inc. - 15-D
White, Fine & Verville
  Westinghouse Corp. - 8-D
White, George E. Jr. - 35-D
White, Richard C. - 23-D, 26-D, 31-D, 38-D, 40-D
White, Sam - 19-D, 21-D, 22-D
Whitehead, Donald W. - 34-D, 39-D
Whitman & Ransom
  Government of the Republic of China - 42-D
Whittier, City of - 53-D
Whittlesey & O'Brien
  American Global Lines Inc. - 4-D
  Cow Creek Band of Umpqua Tribe of Indians - 4-D
  Cowlite Indian Tribe - 4-D
  United States Cruises Inc. - 36-D
Wieseneck, Ann R. - 34-D

Wilbur, Robert E. - 36-D
Wilderness Society, The - 27-D, 49-D
Wiley, Johnson & Rein
  CBS Inc. - 32-D
  Clear Channel Broadcasting Service - 38-D
  National Association of Broadcasters - 38-D
  U.S. Telephone Inc. - 30-D
Wilkinson, Barker, Knauer & Quinn
  Bonneville International Corp. - 32-D
  Kiro Inc. - 34-D
  Manville Corp. - 34-D, 41-D
  U.S. West Inc. - 41-D
Will, Robert P. - 26-D
Willess, Thomas N. - 38-D
Williams & Jensen
  Alamo Cement Co. - 32-D
  Committee for Prudent Deregulation - 54-D
  Design Professionals Coalition - 54-D
  Freight Forwarders Institute - 38-D
  General Portland Inc. - 34-D
  Gifford-Hill & Co. Inc. - 34-D
  Kaiser Cement Corp. - 34-D
  Kelly, Appleman, Hart & Hallman - 50-D
  Monolith Portland Cement Co. - 35-D
  National Office Machine Dealers Association - 38-D
  Southwestern Portland Cement Co. - 36-D
Williams, Robert R. - 35-D
Williford, Philip - 55-D
Wilmer, Cutler & Pickering
  Apache Corp. - 23-D
  National Steel and Shipbuilding Co. - 51-D
Wilson, James E. - 7-D
Winchester, Judy - 12-D
Winslow, Marie - 4-D
Winston & Strawn
  National Audubon Society - 17-D

Winthrop, Weinstine & Sexton
  Otto Bremer Foundation - 16-D
Wise & Wrenn Inc.
  Japanese American Citizens League - 44-D
Withers, Claudia A. - 49-D
Witkowski, Weiner, McCaffrey & Brodsky
  Merrill Lynch & Co. Inc. - 7-D
Wittenberg, Ernest, Associates Inc.
  Altman Foundation, The - 43-D
Wolcott, Clinton - 53-D
Women's Legal Defense Fund - 49-D
Woodstream Corp. - 42-D
Woolley, Edward A. - 26-D
Woolley, Linda Anzalone - 18-D
Woosley, Noel C. - 39-D
Workman, Ross - 25-D
Worldwide Information Resources Inc. - 36-D
Wright, Samuel H. - 35-D

X, Y, Z

Xtra Corp. - 46-D
Yood, Andrew - 30-D
Young Americans for Freedom Inc. - 12-D
Young, Kathryn Eleanor - 31-D
Yukon Pacific Corp. - 52-D
Zaayenga, Ralph - 14-D
Zaucha, Thomas K. - 22-D
Zeferetti, Leo C. - 13-D, 15-D, 16-D, 51-D
Zegar, Denis R. - 47-D
Zero Population Growth Inc. - 23-D
Zimmer & Carnavos
  Colortyme Inc. - 33-D
Zuckert, Scoutt, Rasenberger & Delaney
  Government Employees Insurance Co. - 24-D

PRESIDENTIAL MESSAGES

CQ

Reagan's State of the Union Address

Following is the Congressional Record *text of President Reagan's State of the Union address to a joint session of Congress Jan. 25.*

The PRESIDENT: Mr. Speaker, Mr. President, distinguished Members of the Congress, honored guests and fellow citizens: This solemn occasion marks the 196th time that a President of the United States has reported on the state of the Union since George Washington first did so in 1790. That is a lot of reports, but there is no shortage of new things to say about the state of the Union. The very key to our success has been our ability, foremost among nations, to preserve our lasting values by making change work for us rather than against us.

I would like to talk with you this evening about what we can do together — not as Republicans and Democrats, but as Americans — to make tomorrow's America happy and prosperous at home, strong and respected abroad, and at peace in the world.

As we gather here tonight, the state of our Union is strong, but our economy is troubled. For too many of our fellow citizens — farmers, steel and auto workers, lumbermen, black teenagers, and working mothers — this is a painful period. We must all do everything in our power to bring their ordeal to an end. It has fallen to us, in our time, to undo damage that was a long time in the making, and to begin the hard but necessary task of building a better future for ourselves and our children.

We have a long way to go, but thanks to the courage, patience, and strength of our people, America is on the mend.

Let me give you just one important reason why I believe this — it involves many Members of this body.

Social Security Reform

Just 10 days ago, after months of debate and deadlock, the bipartisan Commission on Social Security accomplished the seemingly impossible.

Social security, as some of us had warned for so long, faced disaster. I, myself, have been talking about this problem for almost 30 years. As 1983 began, the system stood on the brink of bankruptcy, a double victim of our economic ills. First, a decade of rampant inflation drained its reserves as we tried to protect beneficiaries from the spiraling cost of living. Then the recession and the sudden end of inflation withered the expanding wage base and increasing revenues the system needs to support the 36 million Americans who depend on it.

When the Speaker of the House, the Senate majority leader, and I formed the bipartisan Commission on Social Security, pundits and experts predicted that party divisions and conflicting interests would prevent the Commission from agreeing on a plan to save social security.

Well, sometimes, even here in Washington, the cynics are wrong. Through compromise and cooperation, the members of the Commission overcame their differences and achieved a fair, workable plan. They proved that, when it comes to the national welfare, Americans can still pull together for the common good.

Tonight, I am especially pleased to join with the Speaker and the Senate majority leader in urging the Congress to enact this plan by Easter.

There are elements in it, of course, that none of us prefers, but taken together it forms a package that all of us can support. It asks for some sacrifice by all — the self-employed, beneficiaries, workers, Government employees, and the better-off among the retired — but it imposes an undue burden on none. And, in supporting it, we keep an important pledge to the American people: the integrity of the social security system will be preserved — and no one's payments will be reduced.

The Commission's plan will do the job. Indeed, it must do the job. We owe it to today's older Americans — and today's younger workers.

So, before we go any further, I ask you to join with me in saluting the members of the Commission who are here tonight, and Senate Majority Leader Howard Baker and Speaker Tip O'Neill, for a job well done.

Bipartisan Spirit

I hope and pray the bipartisan spirit that guided you in this endeavor will inspire all of us as we face the challenges of the year ahead.

Nearly half a century ago, in this Chamber, another American President, Franklin Delano Roosevelt, in his second state of the Union message, urged America to look to the future — to meet the challenge of change and the need for leadership that looks forward, not backward.

"Throughout the world," he said, "change is the order of the day. In every nation economic problems long in the making have brought crises of many kinds for which the masters of old practice and theory were unprepared."

He also reminded us that, "the future lies with those wise political leaders who realize that the great public is interested more in Government than in politics."

So, let us, in these next 2 years — men and women of both parties and every political shade — concentrate on the long-range, bipartisan responsibilities of Government, not the short-range or short-term temptations of partisan politics.

Economic Recovery

The problems we inherited were far worse than most inside and out of Government had expected; the recession was deeper than most inside and out of Government had predicted. Curing those problems has taken more time, and a higher toll, than any of us wanted. Unemployment is far too high. Projected Federal spending — if Government refuses to tighten its own belt — will also be far too high and could weaken and shorten the economic recovery now underway.

This recovery will bring with it a revival of economic confidence and spending for consumer items and capital goods — the stimulus we need to restart our stalled economic engines. The American people have already stepped up their rate of saving, assuring that the funds needed to modernize our factories and improve our technology will once again flow to business and industry.

The inflationary expectations that led to a 21½ percent interest prime rate and soaring mortgage rates 2 years ago are now reduced by almost half. Lenders have started to realize that double-digit inflation is no longer a way of life. So interest rates have tumbled, paving the way for recovery in vital industries like housing and autos.

The early evidence of that recovery has started coming in. Housing starts for the fourth quarter of 1982 were up 45 percent from a year ago. And housing permits — a sure indicator of future growth — were up a whopping 60 percent.

We are witnessing an upsurge of productivity and impressive evidence that American industry will once again become competitive in markets at home and abroad — insuring more jobs and better incomes for the Nation's workforce.

But our confidence must also be tempered by realism and patience. Quick fixes and artificial stimulants, repeatedly applied over decades, are what brought us the inflationary disorders that we have now paid such a heavy price to cure.

The permanent recovery in employment, production, and investment we seek will not come in a sharp, short spurt. It will build carefully and steadily in the months and years ahead.

In the meantime, the challenge of Government is to identify the things we can do now to ease this massive economic transition for the American people.

Federal Budget and Deficits

The Federal budget is both a symptom and a cause of our economic problems. Unless we reduce the dangerous growth rate in Government spending, we could face the prospect of sluggish economic growth into the indefinite future. Failure to cope with this problem now could mean as much as a trillion dollars more in national debt in the next 4 years alone. That would average $4,300 in additional debt for every man, woman, and child and baby in our Nation.

To assure a sustained recovery, we

must continue getting runaway spending under control to bring those deficits down. If we do not, the recovery will be too short, unemployment will remain too high, and we will leave an unconscionable burden of national debt for our children. That we must not do.

Let us be clear about where the deficit problem comes from. Contrary to the drumbeat we have been hearing for the last few months, the deficits we face are not rooted in defense spending. Taken as a percentage of the gross national product, our defense spending happens to be only about four-fifths of what it was in 1970. Nor is the deficit, as some would have it, rooted in tax cuts. Even with our tax cuts, taxes as a fraction of gross national product remain about the same as they were in 1970.

The fact is, our deficits come from the uncontrolled growth of the budget for domestic spending. During the 1970s the share of our national income devoted to this domestic spending increased by more than 60 percent — from 10 cents out of every dollar produced by the American people to 16 cents. In spite of all our economies and efficiencies, and without adding any new programs, basic, necessary domestic spending provided for in this year's budget will grow to almost $1 trillion over the next 5 years.

The deficit problem is a clear and present danger to the basic health of our Republic. We need a plan to overcome this danger — a plan based on these principles.

It must be bipartisan. Conquering the deficits and putting the Government's house in order will require the best efforts of all of us.

It must be fair. Just as all will share in the benefits that will come from recovery, all would share fairly in the burden of transition.

It must be prudent. The strength of our national defense must be restored so that we can pursue prosperity in peace and freedom while maintaining our commitment to the truly needy.

And finally, it must be realistic. We cannot rely on hope alone.

Four-Part Plan for Recovery

With these guiding principles in mind, let me outline a four-part plan to increase economic growth and reduce deficits.

First, in my budget message, I will recommend a Federal spending freeze. I know this is strong medicine, but so far we have only cut the rate of increase in Federal spending. The Government has continued to spend more money each year, though not as much more as it did in the past. Taken as a whole, the budget I am proposing for the next fiscal year will increase no more than the rate of inflation — in other words, the Federal Government will hold the line on real spending. Now, that is far less than many American families have had to do in these difficult times.

I will request that the proposed 6-month freeze in cost-of-living adjustments recommended by the bipartisan Social Se-

curity Commission be applied to other Government-related retirement programs. I will also propose a 1-year freeze on a broad range of domestic spending programs, and for Federal civilian and military pay and pension programs.

Let me say right here, I am sorry, with regard to the military, in asking that of them because for so many years they have been so far behind and so low in reward for what the men and women in uniform are doing, but I am sure they will understand that this must be across the board and fair.

Second, I will ask Congress to adopt specific measures to control the growth of the so-called uncontrollable spending programs. These are the automatic spending programs, such as food stamps, that cannot be simply frozen — and that have grown by over 400 percent since 1970. They are the largest, single cause of the built-in or structural deficit problem. Our standard here will be fairness — insuring that the taxpayers' hard-earned dollars go only to the truly needy; that none of them are turned away; but that fraud and waste are stamped out. And, I am sorry to say, there is a lot of it out there. In the food stamp program alone, last year we identified almost $1.1 billion in overpayments. The taxpayers are not the only victims of this kind of abuse; the truly needy suffer as funds intended for them are taken not by the needy but by the greedy. For everyone's sake, we must put an end to such waste and corruption.

Third, I will adjust our program to restore America's defenses by proposing $55 billion in defense savings over the next 5 years. These are savings recommended to me by the Secretary of Defense, who has assured me they can be safely achieved and will not diminish our ability to negotiate arms reductions or endanger America's security. We will not gamble with our national survival.

Fourth, because we must insure reduction and eventual elimination of deficits over the next several years, I will propose a standby tax limited to no more than 1 percent of the gross national product to start in fiscal 1986. It would last no more than 3 years and it would start only if the Congress has first approved our spending freeze and budget control program. And there are several other conditions also that must be met, all of them in order for this program to be triggered. You could say that this is an insurance policy for the future, a remedy that will be at hand if needed, but only resorted to if absolutely necessary.

In the meantime, we will continue to study ways to simplify the Tax Code and make it more fair for all Americans. This is a goal that every American who has ever struggled with a tax form can understand.

At the same time, however, I will oppose any efforts to undo the basic tax reforms that we have already enacted — including the 10-percent tax break coming to taxpayers this July and the tax indexing which will protect all Americans from inflationary bracket creep in the years ahead.

Now, I realize that this four-part plan

is easier to describe than it will be to enact. But the looming deficits that hang over us — and over America's future — must be reduced. The path I have outlined is fair, balanced, and realistic. If enacted, it will insure a steady decline in deficits, aiming toward a balanced budget by the end of the decade. It is the only path that will lead to a strong, sustained recovery.

Let us follow that path together.

Employment

No domestic challenge is more crucial than providing stable, permanent jobs for all Americans who want to work. The recovery program will provide jobs for most, but others will need special help and training for new skills. Shortly, I will submit to the Congress the Employment Act [of] 1983 designed to get at the special problems of the long-term unemployed as well as young people trying to enter the job market. I will propose extending unemployment benefits, including special incentives to employers who hire the long-term unemployed, providing programs for displaced workers, and helping federally funded and State-administered unemployment insurance programs to provide workers with training and relocation assistance. Finally, our proposal will include new incentives for summer youth employment to help young people get a start in the job market.

We must offer both short-term help and long-term help for our unemployed. I hope we can work together on this, as we did last year in enacting the landmark Job Training Partnership Act. Regulatory reform legislation, a responsible Clean Air Act, and passage of Enterprise Zone legislation will also create new incentives for jobs and opportunity.

Trade

One out of every five jobs in our country depends on trade. So, I will propose a broader strategy in the field of international trade — one that increases the openness of our trading system and is fairer to America's farmers and workers in the world marketplace. We must have adequate export financing to sell American products overseas. I will ask for new negotiating authority to remove barriers and get more of our products into foreign markets. We must strengthen the organization of our trade agencies and make changes in our domestic laws and international trade policy to promote free trade and the increased flow of American goods, services, and investments.

Our trade position can also be improved by making our port system more efficient. Better, more active harbors translate into stable jobs in our coalfields, railroads, trucking industry, and ports. After 2 years of debate, it is time for us to get together and enact a port modernization bill.

Education, training, and retraining are fundamental to our success, as are re-

search, development, and productivity. Labor, management, and government at all levels can and must participate in improving these tools of growth. Tax policy, regulatory practices, and Government programs all need constant reevaluation in terms of our competitiveness. Every American has a role, and a stake, in international trade.

Education

We Americans are still the technological leaders in most fields. We must keep that edge, and to do so we need to begin renewing the basics — starting with our educational system. While we grew complacent, others have acted. Japan, with a population only about half the size of ours, graduates from its universities more engineers than we do. If a child does not receive adequate math and science teaching by the age of 16, he or she has lost the chance to be a scientist or an engineer.

We must join together — parents, teachers, grassroots groups, organized labor, and the business community — to revitalize American education by setting a standard of excellence.

In 1983, we seek four major education goals:

A quality education initiative to encourage a substantial upgrading of math and science instruction through block grants to the States.

Establishment of education savings accounts that will give middle and lower income families an incentive to save for their children's college education and, at the same time, encourage a real increase in savings for economic growth.

Passage of tuition tax credits for parents who want to send their children to private or religiously affiliated schools.

A constitutional amendment to permit voluntary school prayer; God should never have been expelled from America's classrooms in the first place.

Discrimination Against Women

Our commitment to fairness means that we must assure legal and economic equity for women, and eliminate, once and for all, all traces of unjust discrimination against women from the United States Code. We will not tolerate wage discrimination based on sex and we intend to strengthen enforcement of child support laws to insure that single parents, most of whom are women, do not suffer unfair financial hardship. We will also take action to remedy inequities in pensions. These initiatives will be joined by others to continue our efforts to promote equity for women.

Civil Rights Commission

Also in the area of fairness and equity, we will ask for extension of the Civil Rights Commission which is due to expire this year. The Commission is an important part of the ongoing struggle for justice in America, and we strongly support its reauthorization. Effective enforcement of our Nation's fair housing laws is also essential to ensuring equal opportunity. In the year ahead, we will work to strengthen enforcement of fair housing laws for all Americans.

Criminal Justice Reform

The time has also come for major reform of our criminal justice statutes and acceleration of the drive against organized crime and drug trafficking. It is high time that we make our cities safe again. This administration hereby declares an all-out war on big-time organized crime and the drug racketeers who are poisoning our young people. We will also implement recommendations of our Task Force on Victims of Crime, which will report to me this week.

Agriculture

American agriculture, the envy of the world, has been the victim of its own successes. With one farmer now producing enough food to feed himself and 77 other people, America is confronted with record surplus crops and commodity prices below the cost of production. We must strive, through innovations like the payment-in-kind "crop swap" approach, and an aggressive export policy, to restore health and vitality to rural America. Meanwhile, I have instructed the Department of Agriculture to work individually with farmers with debt problems to help them through these tough times.

Private Sector Initiatives Task Force

Over the past year, our Task Force on Private Sector Initiatives has successfully forged a working partnership involving leaders of business, labor, education, and government to address the training needs of American workers. Thanks to the task force, private sector initiatives are now underway in all 50 States of the Union and thousands of working people have been helped in making the shift from dead-end jobs and low-demand skills to the growth areas of high technology and the service economy. Additionally, a major effort will be focused on encouraging the expansion of private community child care. The new Advisory Council on Private Sector Initiatives will carry on and extend this vital work of encouraging private initiative in 1983.

Health Care

In the coming year we will also act to improve the quality of life for Americans by curbing the skyrocketing cost of health care that is becoming an unbearable financial burden for so many. And we will submit legislation to provide catastrophic illness insurance coverage for older Americans.

State and Local Governments

I will also shortly submit a comprehensive federalism proposal that will continue our efforts to restore to States and local governments their roles as dynamic laboratories of change in a creative society.

During the next several weeks, I will send to the Congress a series of detailed proposals on these and other topics and look forward to working with you on the development of these initiatives.

Pioneer Spirit

So far, now, I have concentrated mainly on the problems posed by the future. But in almost every home and workplace in America, we are already witnessing reason for great hope — the first flowering of the man-made miracles of high technology, a field pioneered and still led by our country.

To many of us now, computers, silicon chips, data processing, cybernetics, and all the other innovations of the dawning high technology age are as mystifying as the workings of the combustion engine must have been when that first Model T rattled down Main Street U.S.A.

But, as surely as America's pioneer spirit made us the industrial giant of the 20th century, the same pioneer spirit today is opening up another vast frontier of opportunity — the frontier of high technology. In conquering this frontier we cannot write off our traditional industries, but we must develop the skills and industries that will make us a pioneer of tomorrow. This administration is committed to keeping America the technological leader of the world now and into the 21st century.

America as World Leader

But let us turn briefly to the international arena. America's leadership role in the world came to us because of our own strength and because of the values which guide us as a society: Free elections, a free press, freedom of religious choice, free trade unions, and, above all, freedom for the individual and rejection of the arbitrary power of the State. These values are the bedrock of our strength. They unite us in a stewardship of peace and freedom with our allies and friends in NATO, in Asia, in Latin America and elsewhere. There are also the values which in the recent past some among us have begun to doubt and view with a cynical eye.

Fortunately, we and our allies have rediscovered the strength of our common democratic values. And we are applying them as the cornerstone of a comprehensive strategy for peace with freedom. In London last year, I announced the commitment of the United States to developing the infrastructure of democracy throughout the world. We intend to pursue this democratic initiative vigorously. The future belongs not to governments and ideologies which oppress their peoples but to democratic systems of self-government which encourage individual initiative and guarantee personal freedom.

But our strategy for peace with freedom must also be based on strength — economic strength and military strength. A strong American economy is essential to the well-being and security of our friends and allies. The restoration of a strong,

healthy American economy has been and remains one of the central pillars of our foreign policy. The progress I have been able to report to you tonight will, I know, be as warmly welcomed by the rest of the world as it is by the American people.

We must also recognize that our own economic well-being is inextricably linked to the world economy. We export over 20 percent of our industrial production, and 40 percent of our farmland production is for export. We will continue to work closely with the industrialized democracies of Europe and Japan and with the International Monetary Fund to insure it has adequate resources to help bring the world economy back to strong, noninflationary growth. As the leader of the West and as a country that has become great and rich because of economic freedom, America must be an unrelenting advocate of free trade. As some nations are tempted to turn to protectionism, our strategy cannot be to follow them but to lead the way toward freer trade. To this end, in May of this year, America will host an economic summit meeting in Williamsburg, Va.

Defense Program

As we begin our third year, we have put in place a defense program that redeems the neglect of the past decade. We have developed a realistic military strategy to deter threats to peace and to protect freedom if deterrence fails. Our Armed Forces are finally properly paid, after years of neglect, are well trained, and becoming better equipped and supplied — and the American uniform is once again worn with pride. Most of the major systems needed for modernizing our defenses are already underway and we will be addressing one key system — the MX missile — in consultation with the Congress in a few months.

Foreign Policy

America's foreign policy is once again based on bipartisanship — on realism, strength, full partnership and consultation with our allies, and constructive negotiation with potential adversaries. From the Middle East to Southern Africa to Geneva, American diplomats are taking the initiative to make peace and lower arms levels. We should be proud of our role as peacemakers.

In the Middle East last year, the United States played the major role in ending the tragic fighting in Lebanon, and negotiated the withdrawal of the PLO from Beirut.

Last September, I outlined principles to carry on the peace process begun so promisingly at Camp David. All the people of the Middle East should know that, in the year ahead, we will not flag in our efforts to build on that foundation to bring them the blessings of peace.

In Central America and the Caribbean Basin, we are likewise engaged in a partnership for peace, prosperity, and democracy. Final passage of the remaining por-

tions of our Caribbean Basin Initiative, which passed the House last year, is one of this administration's top legislative priorities for 1983.

The security and economic assistance policies of this administration, in Latin America and elsewhere, are based on realism and represent a critical investment in the future of the human race. This undertaking is a joint responsibility of the executive and legislative branches, and I am counting on the cooperation and statesmanship of the Congress to help us meet this essential foreign policy goal.

U.S.-Soviet Relations

At the heart of our strategy for peace is our relationship with the Soviet Union.

The past year saw a change in Soviet leadership. We are prepared for a positive change in Soviet-American relations. But the Soviet Union must show, by deeds as well as words, a sincere commitment to respect the rights and sovereignty of the family of nations. Responsible members of the world community do not threaten or invade their neighbors and they restrain their allies from aggression.

For our part, we are vigorously pursuing arms reduction negotiations with the Soviet Union. Supported by our allies, we put forward draft agreements proposing significant weapons reductions to equal and verifiable lower levels. We insist on an equal balance of forces. And, given the overwhelming evidence of Soviet violations of international treaties concerning chemical and biological weapons, we also insist that any agreement we sign can and will be verifiable.

In the case of intermediate-range nuclear forces, we have proposed the complete elimination of the entire class of land-based missiles. We are also prepared to carefully explore serious Soviet proposals. At the same time, let me emphasize that allied steadfastness remains a key to achieving arms reductions.

With firmness and dedication, we will continue to negotiate. Deep down, the Soviets must know it is in their interests as well as ours to prevent a wasteful arms race. And once they recognize our unshakeable resolve to maintain adequate deterrence, they will have every reason to join us in the search for greater security and major arms reductions. When that moment comes — and I am confident that it will — we will have taken an important step toward a more peaceful future for all the world's people.

America's Noble Vision

A very wise man, Bernard Baruch, once said that America has never forgotten the nobler things that brought her into being and that light her path. Our country is a special place because we Americans have always been sustained, through good times and bad, by a noble vision — a vision not only of what the world around us is today, but what we, as a free people, can make it be tomorrow.

We are realists; we solve our problems instead of ignoring them, no matter how loud the chorus of despair around us.

But we are also idealists, for it was an ideal that brought our ancestors to these shores from every corner of the world.

Right now we need both realism and idealism. Millions of our neighbors are without work. It is up to us to see they are not without hope. This is a task for all of us. And may I say Americans have rallied to this cause, proving once again that we are the most generous people on Earth.

We who are in Government must take the lead in restoring the economy.

[Applause, the Members rising.]

The PRESIDENT. Here all that time I thought you were reading the paper. [Laughter.]

The single thing that can start the wheels of industry turning again is further reduction of interest rates. Just another one or two points can mean tens of thousands of jobs. Right now, with inflation as low as it is, 3.9 percent, there is room for interest rates to come down.

Only fear prevents their reduction. A lender, as we know, must charge an interest rate that recovers the depreciated value of the dollars loaned, and that depreciation is, of course, the amount of inflation. Today, interest rates are based on fear, fear that Government will resort to measures, as it has in the past, that will send inflation zooming again.

We who serve here in this Capital must erase that fear by making it absolutely clear that we will not stop fighting inflation; that, together, we will do only these things that will lead to lasting economic growth.

Yes, the problems confronting us are large and forbidding. And, certainly, no one can or should minimize the plight of millions of our friends and neighbors who are living in the bleak emptiness of unemployment. But we must and can give them good reason to be hopeful.

Back over the years, citizens like ourselves have gathered within these walls when our Nation was threatened; sometimes when its very existence was at stake. Always, with courage and commonsense, they met the crises of their time and lived to see a stronger, better, and more prosperous country.

The present situation is no worse and in fact is not as bad as some of those they faced. Time and again, they proved that there is nothing we Americans cannot achieve as free men and women.

Yes, we still have problems — plenty of them. But it is just plain wrong — unjust to our country and unjust to our people — to let those problems stand in the way of the most important truth of all: America is on the mend.

We owe it to the unfortunate to be aware of their plight and to help them in every way we can. No one can quarrel with that — we must and do have compassion for all the victims of this economic crisis. But the big story about America today is

the way that millions of confident, caring people — those extraordinary "ordinary" Americans who never make the headlines and will never be interviewed — are laying the foundation, not just for recovery from our present problems, but for a better tomorrow for all our people.

From coast to coast, on the job and in classrooms and laboratories, at new construction sites and in churches and in community groups, neighbors are helping neighbors. And they have already begun the building, the research, the work, and the giving that will make our community great again.

I believe this because I believe in them — in the strength of their hearts and minds, in the commitment that each one of them brings to their daily lives, be they high or humble. The challenge for us in Government is to be worthy of them — to make Government a help, not a hinderance to our people in the challenging but promising days ahead.

If we do that, if we care what our children and our children's children will say of us, if we want them one day to be thankful for what we did here in these temples of freedom, we will work together to make America better for our having been here — not just in this year, or in this decade, but in the next century and beyond.

Thank you and God bless you.
[Applause, the Members rising.] ∎

President's Budget Message

Following is the text of President Reagan's budget message sent to Congress Jan. 31.

TO THE CONGRESS OF THE UNITED STATES:

Two years ago, in my first address to the country, I went before the American people to report on the condition of our economy, which had suffered from many years of seriously misguided policies. I made a strong commitment to change the traditional shortsighted view that had previously been taken on economic priorities so that we could achieve our goal of long-term prosperity. I stated that we had a massive job before us.

Government spending was taking a rapidly increasing share of national income, burdensome Government regulation had stunted productivity increases, and excessive tax rates combined with erratic monetary policy resulted in serious disincentives to investment and long-term real economic growth. Inflation was at double-digit levels. Interest rates were at record highs. Real growth and job creation had ceased. New investment, productivity, and personal saving were stagnant. Our economy was in the worst mess in half a century.

To make matters worse, our military strength had been allowed to run down relative to the aggressively expanding military might of the Soviet Union. We were in serious danger of becoming powerless to deter or counter Soviet aggression around the world.

The economic program that I proposed at that time focused on long-range real growth. My tax proposals were designed to provide badly needed private incentives to stimulate saving and productive investment. I supported the Federal Reserve in its pursuit of sound monetary policy. I worked with the Congress to reverse the growth of Government programs that had become too large or outlasted their usefulness. I worked to eliminate or simplify unnecessary or burdensome regulations.

The unprecedented buildup of inflationary forces in the 1970's, however, exacerbated in severity and duration the economic downturn of recent years. One of the key detrimental forces has been the growing Federal budget. Despite our success in reducing the rate of growth of nondefense spending in the last two budgets, spending in 1983 will exceed 1981 levels by 21%, reflecting continued increases in basic entitlement programs, essential increases in defense spending, and rapid growth of interest costs.

Thus, the full effect of the changes we have made is taking time to develop. Over-reactive short-term remedies are not the answer. What is essential now is that we continue to work together to rebuild this country — without losing sight of the four fundamentals of our economic program:

• Limiting tax burdens to the minimum levels necessary to finance essential Government services, thus maintaining incentives for saving, investment, work effort, productivity, and economic growth.

• Reducing the growth of overall Federal spending by eliminating Federal activities that overstep the proper sphere of Federal Government responsibilities and by restraining the growth of spending for other Federal activities.

• Reducing the Federal regulatory burden in areas where the Federal Government intrudes unnecessarily into our private lives or interferes unnecessarily with the efficient conduct of private business or of State or local government.

• Supporting a moderate and steady monetary policy, to bring inflation under control.

Two Years of Accomplishment

Over the past 2 years, dramatic improvements have been made in the way the Government affects our economy. The Congress joined with my administration in a cooperative and politically courageous effort to reverse a decade of runaway growth in spending and tax burdens, proliferation of unnecessary regulations and red tape,

and erosion of our military strength.

Both the Omnibus Reconciliation Acts of 1981 and 1982 effected fundamental reforms in numerous Federal programs, and demonstrated a greatly heightened level of maturity and responsibility of the congressional budget process that has come to fruition with the help and support of this administration. Although I am disappointed that many administration spending-reduction proposals did not pass last year — which has resulted in higher deficits — I believe that the revitalized congressional budget process signifies a refreshing willingness on the part of the Congress to work with my administration to address squarely the many crucial, complex, and politically difficult budgetary dilemmas before us. The results have been impressive:

• Where the growth rate of spending was almost out of control at 17.4% a year in 1980, it is now declining dramatically — to 10.5% this year, and, with this budget, to 5.4% next year — which is no more than the projected rate of inflation; in effect, a comprehensive freeze on total Federal spending.

• Where spending growth totaled $220 billion from 1978 to 1981, a 48% increase, spending will rise by only 27% from 1981 to 1984, despite legislated cost-of-living adjustments and the needed defense buildup.

• For the first time since the Second World War, the Federal tax system has been fundamentally restructured. Income tax rates have been substantially reduced, greatly improving the climate for savings and investment. Excessive taxation of business income resulting from depreciation allowances rendered inadequate by inflation has been eliminated through depreciation reform. Tax loopholes have been closed, making the tax structure more equitable. Emphasis is shifting to financing programs through user fees commensurate with benefits and services provided.

• The excessive rates of growth of entitlement programs were curbed. Overly-broad eligibility criteria were tightened to limit benefit awards more to the truly needy, and eliminate or restrict unnecessary and costly payments of welfare-type benefits to those who are relatively well off and are, or ought to be, self-supporting. Overly-generous and unnecessarily frequent cost-of-living adjustments were pared back. Nonetheless, the growth of these programs has proven difficult to control and continues to be the primary cause of higher deficits.

• Limitation of Federal credit activity and off-budget spending is being achieved.

• The burgeoning growth of Federal regulations and red tape has been capped. The number of proposed new regulations has been reduced by one-third in the past 2 years. Unnecessary costs of Federal regulation to individuals, businesses, and State and local governments have been reduced by $6 billion in annual expenditures and $9 to $11 billion in capital costs. By the end of 1983, the time our citizens spend filling out Federal forms and reports will have been

cut by over 300 million hours annually.

● Improvements in the management of Federal operations, such as better procedures for the collection of debts owed the Government and better cash-management practices, are being carried out. These improvements have helped reduce waste, fraud, and abuse in Government programs.

● And by the end of the 1982 fiscal year, the Federal nondefense workforce has been reduced by 91,300 employees since I took office.

During the past 2 years, we have also taken decisive measures to increase our military strength. At the same time, diplomatic approaches to increase our national security, such as arms reduction talks, have been vigorously pursued.

The improvement in our defense posture includes all of its major elements. Long-overdue modernization of our strategic forces is proceeding with new bomber-, submarine-, and land-based missile programs. Our conventional forces are also being modernized and strengthened, with new ships, tanks, and aircraft. Above all, successful recruiting and retention over the past 18 months have resulted in all of our armed services being more fully manned with capable, high-caliber men and women. The All Volunteer Force is now working well.

By any standards, these are accomplishments to be proud of. And I am proud of them. We have come far in restoring order to the chaos prevailing in our economy and Government affairs just 2 years ago.

This is not to say that we do not still face great problems such as excessive unemployment, slower than desired economic growth, and high deficits. During the past 2 years our Nation has labored to purge itself of the inflationary disease that for nearly two decades had progressively undermined the economy's ability to generate growth, capital formation, worker productivity incentives, and financial stability. Those inflationary fevers have largely subsided in the aftermath of my decision 2 years ago to redirect economic policy toward a more modest size and scope for the Federal Government, a series of tax rate reductions to reward productive investment and work effort, and a restrained monetary policy to sustain the purchasing power of individual savings and income.

Accompanying the marked progress in unwinding the damaging inflation spiral that plagued our Nation for so many years, financial markets in 1982 experienced their first sustained improvement in more than 5 years. Interest rates throughout the maturity spectrum declined substantially, and by yearend we can proudly report that key rates for home mortgages, consumer loans, and business investment were able to sustain their lower levels, indicating new confidence in administration policies and bringing much needed relief to the housing and auto industries, the farm community, and the export sector.

Inflationary pressures of the sort experienced during the past two decades extracted a heavy toll from our economy. We have learned that the problems we inherited were far worse than most inside and out of Government had expected; the recession was deeper and longer than most inside and out of Government had predicted. Curing those problems has taken more time and a higher toll than any of us wanted. Unemployment is far too high.

Fortunately, the long nightmare of runaway inflation is now behind us. Slowly, but steadily and unmistakably, our national economy is completing the transition from recession to recovery. The interaction of lower tax rates, reduced inflation, and falling interest rates has placed the consumer and the producer in a much strengthened position with respect to balance sheets, liquidity, after-tax income, and purchasing power.

There are numerous signs that the battered, sputtering inflation-warped economy that we found 2 years ago is on the mend, and that the dislocation and hardship we have suffered in the interim will prove to be a corrective interlude on the path of sustained recovery. But our confidence must also be tempered by realism and patience. Quick fixes and artificial stimulants, repeatedly applied over decades, are what brought on the inflationary disorders that we have now paid such a heavy price to cure.

In part as a result of the difficult period of disinflation, during the past year and one-half our projections of the Federal deficit have steadily risen. They have now reached very high levels, creating uncertainty in the financial markets and threatening to block the economic recovery ahead of us.

But before we consider what is to be done, we must review how we got here. And the truth is that as in the case of the social security fund, the looming gaps in our national budget are the consequence of both the inflation that got out of hand and the correctives that have been unavoidably applied to cure it.

During the 1970's, the share of our national income devoted to domestic programs and transfer payments soared by more than 50% — from 10 cents to 16 cents on every dollar produced by the American people. For a brief time, it appeared that we could afford all of this generosity because inflation badly misled us.

As inflation reached higher and higher peaks, the Treasury's coffers swelled from its take on inflated incomes and the upward creep of tax rates. For a time, we even financed our trillion dollar national debt on the cheap with interest rates that had not yet caught up with the spiraling inflation.

Meanwhile, defense spending grew at less than 60% of inflation, making room in the budget for extra domestic programs. The real purchasing power available to maintain our readiness, modernize our weapons, and maintain strategic nuclear safety declined by a startling 20%.

But it couldn't last — and it didn't.

Today the Federal budget itself has become a major victim of the economic transition:

● The inflationary revenue windfall has dried up.

● Our staggering national debt until recently was being financed at the highest interest rates in peacetime history.

● The undelayable process of restoring our inflation-eroded military budgets and our decayed military strength has further strained our resources.

● Despite our great strides in reducing the spending growth over the last 2 years, the vast edifice of domestic programs remains significantly in place.

The social security system has also been a victim of our economic ills. First, the rampant inflation drained its reserves as Government tried to keep beneficiaries up with the spiraling cost of living that its own mistaken policies had created in the first place. Now the recessionary adjustments to disinflation have temporarily deprived it of the expanding wage base and growing revenues required to support commitments to the retired and disabled. As a result, for too long the specter of social security insolvency has haunted our Nation's elderly citizens and threatened to rupture the lifeline on which 36 million retired and disabled Americans depend.

But however obvious the threat of insolvency, one thing is certain: social security cannot and will not be allowed to fail the 36 million Americans who depend on it. With this commitment in mind, it is especially pleasing to me to join with the Speaker of the House and the Senate Majority Leader in urging the Congress to enact the bipartisan compromise plan developed by the National Commission on Social Security Reform.

There are elements in it that none of us prefers, but taken together it forms a package all of us can support. It asks for some sacrifice by all — the self-employed, beneficiaries, workers, new government employees, and the better-off among the retired — but it imposes an undue burden on none. And, in supporting it, we keep an important pledge to the American people: the integrity of the social security system will be preserved — and no one's payments will be reduced.

Toward Economic Recovery

To enhance prospects for sustained economic recovery and lower unemployment, I am proposing a sweeping set of fiscal policy changes designed to reduce substantially the mounting Federal deficits that threaten the renewal of economic growth. My plan is based on these principles.

It must be bipartisan. Overcoming the deficits and putting the Government's house in order will require the best efforts of all of us.

It must be fair. Just as all will share in the benefits that will come from recovery, all should share fairly in the burden of transition.

It must be prudent. The strength of our national defense must be restored so that we can pursue prosperity in peace and freedom, while maintaining our commitment to the truly needy.

Finally, it must be realistic. We cannot rely on hope alone.

With these guiding principles in mind, let me outline a four-part plan to increase economic growth and reduce deficits.

First, I am recommending a Federal spending freeze. I know this is strong medicine, but so far we have cut only the rate of increase in Federal spending. The Government has continued to spend more money each year, though not as much more as it did in the past. Taken as a whole, the budget I am proposing for the next fiscal year will increase no more than the rate of inflation — in other words, the Federal Government will hold the line on real spending. That is far less than many American families have had to do in these difficult times.

I will request that the proposed 6-month freeze in cost-of-living adjustments recommended by the bipartisan National Commission on Social Security Reform be applied to other Government benefit programs. I will also propose a 1-year freeze on a broad range of domestic spending programs, and for Federal civilian and military pay and pension programs.

Second, I will ask the Congress to adopt specific measures to control the growth of the so-called "uncontrollable" spending programs. These are the automatic spending programs, such as food stamps, that cannot be simply frozen — and that have grown by over 400% since 1970. They are the largest single cause of the built-in or "structural" deficit problem. Our standard here will be fairness — ensuring that the taxpayers' hard-earned dollars go only to the truly needy; that none of them is turned away; but that fraud and waste are stamped out. And, I am sorry to say, there is a lot of it out there. In the food stamp program alone, last year we identified almost $1.1 billion in overpayments. The taxpayers are not the only victims of this kind of abuse; the truly needy suffer, as funds intended for them are taken by the greedy. For everyone's sake, we must put an end to such waste and corruption.

Third, I will adjust our program to restore America's defenses by proposing $55 billion in defense savings over the next 5 years. These are savings recommended to me by the Secretary of Defense, who has assured me they can be safely achieved and will not diminish our ability to negotiate arms reductions or endanger America's security. We will not gamble with our national survival. As a percent of GNP, the level I am requesting for defense spending in 1984 is less than the United States spent during the decade of the 1960's. As a percent of the total Federal budget it is far less than was allocated for national defense in those years. We are 2 years into the program to re-arm America. Sustaining the momentum of this program is essential if

---

The Budget Totals
(in billions of dollars)

	1982 Actual	1983 Estimate	1984 Estimate	1985 Estimate	1986 Estimate
Budget receipts	617.8	597.5	659.7	724.3	841.9
Budget outlays	728.4	805.2	848.5	918.5	989.6
Surplus or deficit (−)	−110.6	−207.7	−188.8	−194.2	−147.7
Budget authority	779.9	847.4	900.1	997.4	1,079.6

---

we are to avoid slipping back into the inefficient and counterproductive pattern of wildly fluctuating defense spending levels.

Fourth, because we must ensure reduction and eventual elimination of deficits over the next several years, I will propose a stand-by tax limited to no more than 1% of the gross national product to start in fiscal year 1986. It would last no more than 3 years and would start *only* if the Congress has first approved our spending freeze and budget control program. You could say that this is an insurance policy for the future — a remedy that will be at hand if needed, but resorted to only if absolutely necessary.

In the meantime, we will continue to study ways to simplify the tax code and make it more fair for all Americans. This is a goal that every American who has ever struggled with a tax form can understand.

At the same time, however, I will oppose any efforts to undo the basic tax reforms we have already enacted — including the 10% tax break coming to taxpayers this July and the tax indexing that will protect all Americans from inflationary bracket creep in the years ahead.

This plan is urgently needed and is geared toward solving the problems of the growing deficits. But it naturally requires the cooperation of both branches of Government, both Houses, and both parties. Thus, our plan is aimed at bridging the institutional, philosophical, and political differences that separate us — which are not as important as the overriding common objective of economic recovery and sustained prosperity for America.

After 2 years of reducing much of the overspending, we have now reached the bone in many places — programs where we will not propose further reductions. My administration will now work with the Congress in an effort to accommodate those special concerns of the legislative branch that have caused unnecessary strains in the past.

Thus, we will propose $3 billion more for education programs than was proposed last year, and almost $2 billion more for employment and training. Proposals for new rescissions of already-enacted budget authority will be held to an absolute minimum.

This budget process must be a two-way street, for the problem of large deficits is very real. Even when all reasonable measures are applied to the vast detail of the budget, the resulting deficits are large and progress toward reducing them slow. The political risks entailed in these deficit-containment measures are considerable. But the risk of doing nothing at all due to partisanship or legislative stalemate is much greater. I therefore urge the Congress to join with my administration behind this common-sense strategy.

Meeting — and Reshaping — Federal Responsibilities

My administration seeks to limit the size, intrusiveness, and cost of Federal activities as much as possible, and to achieve the needed increase in our defense capabilities in the most cost-effective manner possible. This does not mean that appropriate Federal responsibilities are being abandoned, neglected, or inadequately supported. Instead, ways are being found to streamline Federal activity, to limit it to those areas and responsibilities that are truly Federal in nature; to ensure that these appropriate Federal responsibilities are performed in the most cost-effective and efficient manner; and to aid State and local governments in carrying out their appropriate public responsibilities in a similarly cost-effective manner. The Nation must ask for no more publicly-provided services and benefits than the private sector can reasonably be asked to finance.

Education. One of the high priorities I have set for my administration is the return to a more appropriate role for the Federal Government in the Nation's education systems and policies. We have slowed the alarming rate of growth of Federal spending for education, an area that is rightfully and primarily a family and State and local government responsibility. From 1974 to 1981, Federal spending for education increased by 172%. From 1981 to 1982, however, outlays declined by more than $1 billion. My administration has accomplished a major consolidation of small fragmented education programs into a flexible education block grant to States and localities. We have cut back on unnecessary regulation and Federal intrusion in local affairs.

The 1984 budget seeks to stabilize education spending, requesting $13.1 billion in budget authority for 1984. It reflects several important new initiatives to strengthen American education:

● Passing of tuition tax credits for parents who want to send their children to qualified private or religiously-affiliated schools.

● Establishing education savings accounts to give middle- and lower-income families an incentive to save for their children's college education and, at the same time, to encourage a real increase in savings for economic growth.

● Reorienting student aid programs to ensure that students and families meet their responsibilities for financing higher education, while making funds available across a wider spectrum of schools for the low-income students most in need.

● Allowing States or localities, if they so choose, to use their compensatory education funds to establish voucher programs to broaden family choice of effective schooling methods for educationally disadvantaged children.

● Helping States to train more mathematics and science teachers.

These initiatives represent the administration's continuing commitment to avoid improper Federal involvement in State, local, and family decisions, while preserving proper Federal support for key national policy goals such as supporting compensatory and handicapped education, facilitating access to higher education, and helping States improve science and mathematics education.

Research. My administration recognizes the Federal responsibility to maintain U.S. leadership in scientific research. Although support of basic scientific research represents a small share of the Federal budget, it is a vital investment in the Nation's future. Such research lays the foundation for a strong defense in the years to come, and for new technologies and industries that will help maintain our industrial competitiveness, create new jobs, and improve our quality of life. By carefully establishing budget priorities, my administration has been able to reinvigorate Federal support for basic scientific research. With my 1984 budget proposals, such support across the Government will have increased by more than 20% over the 1982 level.

Health care. A major problem for both individuals and the Federal Government in meeting health care needs is the rapid inflation of health care costs. The rate of increase in health care costs is excessive and undermines people's ability to purchase needed health care. Federal policies have contributed significantly to health care cost increases. The budget contains several major initiatives to reduce cost increases. We must eliminate the tax incentive for high-cost employee health insurance programs. Savings from medicare cost controls will be used to protect the aged from catastrophic hospital costs. Incentives will also be proposed to slow the growth of medicaid costs.

Agriculture. The administration seeks to move agricultural supply toward a better balance with demand by reducing farm production and Government program stocks. The budget proposes a four-part approach to solving the current surplus supply problem:

● establishing a payment-in-kind (PIK) program, under which farmers would receive surplus commodities now held for Federal loans, or owned by the Government, in return for reducing their production;

● freezing farm crop target prices at current levels;

● donating Government-held commodities through international humanitarian organizations for needy people around the world; and

● selling our agricultural produce abroad, both through commercial channels and through government negotiation.

Efforts are also continuing to identify surplus Federal land holdings for sale from those administered by the Departments of Agriculture and of the Interior. Planned sales total $500 million in 1984.

Transportation. In the transportation area, my administration has made major strides in implementing one of the fundamental principles in my program for economic recovery: having users pay for program costs that are clearly allocable to them. During the past year, I signed into law two administration-backed proposals to increase excise taxes on aviation and highway users and thereby provide funding needed to revitalize and modernize these important segments of the Nation's transportation system. The 1984 budget reflects the administration's continued commitment to the "users pay" principle by again proposing user fees for:

● construction and maintenance of deep-draft ports;

● the inland waterway system;

● selected direct Coast Guard services; and

● nautical and aviation maps and charts.

Recognizing the importance of our transportation system in maintaining and contributing to the Nation's economic and social well being, my administration secured passage of legislation designed to rebuild the Nation's highway and public transportation facilities. This legislation substantially increased funds available to the States and local communities to complete and repair the aging interstate highway system, to rehabilitate principal rural and urban highways and bridges, and to improve mass transit systems.

Fully capable ports and channels are essential to make U.S. coal exports competitive in world markets. My administration will work with the Congress to provide for timely and efficient port construction. We propose a system of user fees for existing port maintenance and new port construction. Local governments would be empowered to set up their own financing arrangements for the immediate construction of facilities in their areas.

Reducing the Federal presence in commercial transportation, currently regulated by the Interstate Commerce Commission, the Civil Aeronautics Board, and the Federal Maritime Commission, will improve the efficiency of the industry. To this end, my administration will seek further deregulation of trucking, airlines, and ocean shipping. Experience since the adoption of initial transportation deregulation legislation has shown clearly that both consumers and industry benefit from reduced Federal involvement in these activities.

Energy. The administration has significantly reoriented the country's approach to energy matters in the past 2 years. Reliance on market forces — instead of Government regulation and massive, indiscriminate Federal spending — has resulted in greater energy production, more efficient use of energy, and more favorable energy prices. For example:

● The U.S. economy today is using 18% less energy to produce a dollar's worth of output than it did in 1973 when energy prices first began to rise.

● The price of heating oil and gasoline has actually fallen in real terms by 12% in the past 2 years — confounding past theories that insisted that these prices could only increase.

Federal energy programs and policies have been refocused and made more productive:

● Wasteful spending on large, unprofitable technology demonstrations has been curtailed.

● At the same time, spending has increased in areas where the Government has a key role to play — for example, in supporting long-term energy research.

● The strategic petroleum reserve has more than doubled in size over the past 2 years.

Criminal justice. My administration has also sought to strengthen the Federal criminal justice system by proposing major legislative initiatives, such as bail for sentencing reform, by attacking drug trafficking and organized crime, and by achieving a better balance among law enforcement, prosecutorial, and correctional resources. Twelve regional task forces will focus on bringing to justice organized crime drug traffickers. The administration will strengthen efforts to identify, neutralize, and defeat foreign agents who pose a threat to the Nation.

International affairs. Our foreign policy is oriented toward maintaining peace through military strength and diplomatic negotiation; promoting market-oriented solutions to international economic problems; telling the story abroad of America's democratic, free-enterprise way of life; and increasing free trade in the world while assuring this country's equitable participation in that trade.

● The security assistance portion of the international affairs program has been increased to assist friendly governments facing threats from the Soviet Union, its sur-

Impact of Stronger Economic Growth

● If the recovery of real GNP growth over the next 2 fiscal years is *about 1%* above our cautious projections, the deficit estimates would improve by an average of about $20 billion per year, and would result in lower deficits as follows:

	1984	1985	1986	1987	1988
Deficit (−) ($ billions)	−177	−177	−127	−119	−90

● An average real GNP growth rate *1.33%* higher each year over the next 6 years, compared to the prudent projections made in the 1984 budget, would result in a balanced budget by 1988. This is a "high growth" scenario but within the range of previous historical experience. My administration remains committed to the goal of a balanced budget and will propose additional policy actions, as needed, to achieve it.

rogates, and from other radical regimes.

● Development aid emphasizes encouraging the private sectors of developing nations and increasing U.S. private sector involvement in foreign assistance.

● A major expansion of international broadcasting activities aimed primarily at communist countries is planned, and a new initiative will be undertaken to strengthen the infrastructure of democracy around the world.

● Special attention is being given to assuring adequate financing of U.S. exports while my administration seeks to obtain further reductions in the export subsidies of other governments.

My administration will submit to the Congress a proposal to increase the U.S. quota in the International Monetary Fund and the U.S. obligations under the IMF's General Arrangements to Borrow, as soon as negotiations on these issues are completed. This is necessary to ensure that the IMF has adequate resources to help bring the world economy back to strong, noninflationary growth.

Although now less than 2% of the budget, international programs are critical to American world leadership and to the success of our foreign policy.

Minority-owned businesses. My administration will assist in the establishment or expansion of over 120,000 minority-owned businesses over the next 10 years. The Federal Government will procure an estimated $15 billion in goods and services from minority business during the 3-year period 1983-1985. It will make available approximately $1.5 billion in credit assistance and $300 million in technical assistance to promote minority business development during this period.

Civil service retirement. The 97th Congress made some improvements in the civil service retirement system. However, civil service retirement still has far more generous benefits and is much more costly than retirement programs in the private sector or in State and local governments. Accordingly, this budget proposes fundamental changes in civil service retirement designed to bring benefits into line with

those offered in the private sector and reduce the cost of the system to affordable levels. Retirement benefit changes will be phased in over a period of years in order to avoid upsetting the plans of those at or near retirement.

Unemployment Demands Specific Attention

My administration seeks to provide appropriate assistance to the unemployed. There are three major groups who need help: the largest, those who are unemployed now but will find jobs readily as the economy improves; those whose jobs have permanently disappeared; and youth who have trouble finding their niche in the labor market.

Those in the first group need interim help because, historically, increases in jobs always lag in an economic recovery. Last year we provided a temporary program to give the long-term unemployed up to 16 added weeks of unemployment compensation, in addition to the up to 39 weeks available from our permanent unemployment insurance. This temporary program expires March 31, 1983. I propose to modify and extend the program for 6 more months, and provide an option for recipients to receive assistance in securing work through a system of tax credits to employers. This will give employers a significant incentive to hire the long-term unemployed, while workers will get full wages rather than the lower unemployment benefit.

Those whose jobs have permanently disappeared must be helped to find new long-term occupations. The Job Training Partnership Act, enacted last year, authorizes grants to States to help retrain such workers and assist them in locating and moving to new jobs. The Congress appropriated $25 million to start this new program in 1983. I am requesting $240 million to implement the program fully in 1984. In addition, I propose that the Federal unemployment law be changed to allow States to use a portion of the unemployment taxes they collect to provide such retraining and

job search assistance to their unemployed workers. Regulatory reform and passage of enterprise zone legislation will also create new incentives for jobs and opportunity.

Those youth who have problems finding jobs after they leave school are often condemned to a lifetime of intermittent employment and low earnings. The new Job Training Partnership Act is designed to help disadvantaged youth acquire the basic skills potential employers look for when they hire. I am requesting $1.9 billion for the block grant to States under that Act. The States must use at least 40% of that for youth.

One of the problems hampering youth is inability to get meaningful work experience during school vacations. Such experience is invaluable to demonstrate their qualifications to potential permanent employers. The budget provides for 718,000 public summer job opportunities for disadvantaged youth. But we must also make it possible for youth to experience work in the private sector. The minimum wage law now frequently prevents this. Inexperienced youth cannot produce enough of value to make it worthwhile for employers to pay them the full minimum wage during short periods of employment. I therefore propose that the minimum wage for summer jobs for youth be reduced to $2.50 an hour. Limitation of the reduced minimum wage to the summer months will make it unlikely that employers will substitute youths for older workers.

I remain adamantly opposed to temporary make-work public jobs or public works as an attempted cure for non-youth unemployment. There are several reasons for this. The cost per "job" created is excessive; we cannot afford major new programs, particularly in our current budgetary straits; the actual number of new jobs "created" is minimal; the jobs created tend to be temporary and of a dead-end nature; and most such jobs do not materialize until after recovery is well underway.

Improving the Efficiency of Government

The proposed freeze on program funding levels will compel program managers in every agency of the Government to find more efficient ways of carrying out their programs. For too long, costs of Federal operations have been mounting unchecked.

Good management has not always been a priority of the executive branch. I have been correcting that situation.

My administration has redirected programs to improve their efficiency and to achieve cost savings Government-wide. My administration is committed to improving management and reducing fraud, waste, and abuse. The President's Council on Integrity and Efficiency (PCIE), made up of 18 Inspectors General, reported that almost $17 billion has been saved or put to better use in the past 2 years.

In 1982, I signed into law the Federal Managers' Financial Integrity Act. Under this Act, my Cabinet officers and other

agency heads will report to me and the Congress annually on the status of their efforts to improve management controls that prevent fraud and mismanagement. A number of agencies have already begun to make significant improvements in this important area.

But the Government can go only so far with the seriously outdated and inefficient management/administrative systems that are currently in place. One-third of our large-scale computers, for example, are more than 10 years old. A comprehensive management improvement program was needed, so "Reform '88" was initiated. We intend to upgrade and modernize our administrative systems to make them more effective and efficient in carrying out the Government's business and serving the public.

We are already saving tax dollars by managing our almost $2 trillion yearly cash flow more effectively, collecting the Government's $250 billion of just debts, cutting Government administrative costs, modernizing Federal procurement systems, reducing internal regulations, controlling our office space and equipment more prudently, and streamlining the workforce in many departments and agencies. These cost-reduction efforts will continue.

Continuing Reform of Our Federal System

The overall efficiency of Government in the United States can also be improved by a more rational sorting out of governmental responsibilities among the various levels of government — Federal, State, and local — in our Federal system, and eliminating or limiting overlapping and duplication.

In 1981, the Congress responded to my proposals by consolidating 57 categorical programs into 9 block grants. In 1982, block grants were created for job training in the Jobs Training Partnership Act, and for urban mass transit in the Surface Transportation Act. The initiatives to be proposed this year will expand on these accomplishments.

Four new block grants will be proposed, with assured funding for major functions now addressed through categorical grants:

● A general Federal-State block grant covering approximately 15 categorical programs.

● A Federal-local block grant that would include the entitlement portion of the community development grant program and the general revenue sharing program.

● A transportation block grant.

● A rural housing block grant.

The administration is improving the management of intergovernmental assistance by providing State and local elected officials with greater opportunity to express their views on proposed Federal development and assistance actions before final decisions are made. Under Executive Order 12372, Intergovernmental Review of Federal Programs, which I signed in July 1982, Federal agencies must consult with State and local elected officials early in the assistance decision process and make every effort to accommodate their views. The Order also encourages the simplification of State planning requirements imposed by Federal law, and allows for the substitution of State-developed plans for federally required State plans where statutes and regulations allow.

Through the President's Task Force on Regulatory Relief and the regulatory review process, the administration is eliminating and simplifying regulations affecting State and local governments that are burdensome, unnecessary, and counterproductive. These changes have improved local efficiency and accountability and reduced program costs. Twenty-five reviews were completed during the past 2 years by either the Task Force or by various Federal agencies. Available data indicate that regulatory relief actions will save State and local governments approximately $4 to $6 billion in initial costs, and an estimated $2 billion on an annual basis. My administration is also simplifying selected, generally applicable crosscutting requirements that are imposed on State and local governments as a condition of accepting financial assistance.

Federal Credit Programs: More Selective

The administration continues its strong commitment to control Federal credit assistance, which has serious effects on the Nation's financial markets. To this end, I propose a credit budget that reverses the accelerated rate of growth in direct and guaranteed lending by the Federal Government that occurred during the second half of the 1970's and the first years of the 1980's.

Federal intervention through guarantees and provision of direct lending misdirects investment and preempts capital that could be more efficiently used by unsubsidized, private borrowers. Because federally assisted borrowers are frequently less productive than private borrowers, large Federal credit demands must be reduced in order to improve prospects for economic growth.

Conclusion

The stage is set; a recovery to vigorous, sustainable, noninflationary economic growth is imminent. But given the underlying deterioration in the overall budget structure that has occurred over the past 2 years, only the most sweeping set of fiscal policy changes could help to reverse the trend and set the budget on a path that is consistent with long-term economic recovery.

If the challenge before us is great, so, too, are the opportunities. Let us work together to meet the challenge. If we fail, if we work at cross purposes, posterity will not forgive us for allowing this opportunity to slip away.

RONALD W. REAGAN

January 31, 1983   ∎

Reagan's Economic Report

Following is the text of President Reagan's Economic Report sent to Congress Feb. 2.

TO THE CONGRESS OF
THE UNITED STATES:

Two years ago, I came to Washington with a deep personal commitment to change America's economic future. For more than a decade, the economy had suffered from low productivity growth and a rising rate of inflation. Government spending absorbed an increasing share of national income. A shortsighted view of economic priorities was destroying our prospects for long-term prosperity.

The economic program that I proposed shortly after I took office emphasized economic growth and a return to price stability. My tax proposals were designed to encourage private initiative and to stimulate saving and productive investment. I have supported and encouraged the Federal Reserve Board in its pursuit of price stability through sound monetary policy. My Administration has slowed the growth of Federal regulation, strengthening the forces of competition in a number of economic sectors. And I have worked with the Congress to enact legislation that has reversed or limited the growth of government programs that have become too large or outlasted their usefulness.

Although the full effect of these changes in government policy will take time to develop, some of the benefits have already become apparent. The rate of consumer price inflation between December 1981 and December 1982 was only 3.9 percent, about one-third of the rate in the year before I took office. Interest rates are now lower than when I took office, and have fallen rapidly during the last 6 months.

The Administration will propose many additional measures over the next several years to strenghten economic incentives, reduce burdensome regulations, increase capital formation, and raise our standard of living. It is easy to lose sight of these long-term goals in a year, like 1982, when the economy was in an extended recession. I am deeply troubled by the current level of unemployment in the United States and by the suffering and anxiety that it entails for millions of Americans. The unemployment that many of our citizens are experiencing is a consequence of the disinflation that

must necessarily follow the accelerating inflation of the last decade. Allowing the upward trend of inflation to continue would have risked even greater increases in unemployment in the future. In spite of the present high unemployment rate and the accompanying hardships, it is essential that we maintain the gains against inflation that we have recently achieved at substantial cost. Continuing success in restraining inflation will provide a stronger foundation for economic recovery in 1983 and beyond.

Reducing Unemployment

The Federal Government can play an important role in reducing unemployment. I believe, however, that the government should focus its attention on those groups that will continue to face high unemployment rates even after the recovery has begun. By helping them to develop their job-related skills, we will foster productive careers in the private sector rather than dead-end jobs. This emphasis on training and private sector employment is the focus of the Jobs Training Partnership Act that I supported and signed into law in 1982. I am proposing additional steps this year to strengthen Federal training and retraining programs and to help the structurally unemployed find lasting jobs.

It is understandable that many well-meaning members of the Congress have responded to the current high unemployment rate by proposing various public works and employment programs. However, I am convinced that such programs would only shift unemployment from one industry to another at the cost of increasing the Federal budget deficit.

Although programs to help the structurally unemployed are important, only a balanced and lasting recovery can achieve a substantial reduction in unemployment. There are now over four million more unemployed people than there were at the peak of the last business cycle. Nine million new workers are expected to join the labor force by 1988. Only a healthy and growing economy can provide the more than 13 million jobs needed to achieve a progressively lower level of unemployment over the next 5 years.

The Prospects for Economic Recovery

There are now signs that an economic recovery will begin soon. By December 1982 the index of leading economic indicators had risen in 7 of the last 8 months. Housing starts have risen substantially over the last year, and by December 1982 were 39 percent higher than 12 months earlier. Inventory levels have fallen sharply, so that increased sales should translate quickly into increased production and employment. Both long-term and short-term interest rates have fallen substantially. The Administration's economic forecast predicts that the gross national product will begin to rise in the first quarter of 1983 and will then rise more quickly as the year continues. Most private forecasters also predict a recovery in 1983.

Monetary policy will play a critical role in achieving a sound and sustainable economic recovery. If the monetary aggregates grow too slowly, the economy will lack the level of financial resources needed for continued economic growth. But if these aggregates are allowed to expand too rapidly, an increase in inflation and a short-lived recovery will result. I recognize the difficulties that the Federal Reserve has faced and will continue to face in guiding the growth of the money supply at a time when major regulatory changes have made it difficult to rely on old guidelines. I expect that in 1983 the Federal Reserve will expand the money supply at a moderate rate consistent with both a sustained recovery and continued progress against inflation.

Investment and Economic Growth

An economic recovery beginning in 1983 should bring not only a reduction in unemployment but also an increase in business investment over the next several years. A higher level of investment is an important ingredient in raising productivity and economic growth. The Accelerated Cost Recovery System that I proposed and that the Congress enacted in 1981 was designed to encourage a substantial expansion of business investment above the relatively low levels of the 1970s. Since that time the adverse effects of the recession have outweighed the positive effects of the new tax rules. As the economy turns from recession to recovery, however, incentives to invest will become more powerful. But business investment may not grow rapidly unless measures proposed by the Administration to reduce potentially large Federal budget deficits are enacted.

Federal borrowing competes with private investment for available savings. If the government continues to borrow large amounts to finance its deficit, the real interest rate will remain high and discourage private investment. This process of "crowding out" will tend to depress private investment in the years ahead unless the budget deficit is progressively reduced.

Fiscal Year 1984 Budget Proposals

It is important to distinguish the cyclical part of the budget deficit from the structural part, which would remain even at the peak of the business cycle. Approximately one-half of the 1983 budget deficit is due to the depressed state of the economy. With earnings and profits reduced, tax receipts have significantly decreased, and expenditures have increased. As the economy recovers, the cyclical part of the deficit will shrink. But cyclical recovery alone will not bring the deficit down to an acceptable size.

In the budget I am now submitting to the Congress, I am proposing the dramatic steps needed to reduce Federal budget deficits in future years. My budget proposals

are designed to reduce the deficit by dealing directly with the rapid growth of the domestic spending programs (apart from interest payments) of the Federal Government. In 1970 these programs accounted for 10 percent of the gross national product and 48 percent of Federal spending. By 1980 these programs had grown to 14 percent of gross national product and 63 percent of the budget. I remain committed to the idea that we can reduce budget deficits without increasing the burden on the poor, without weakening our national defense, and without destroying economic incentives by counterproductive tax increases.

Rapid congressional enactment of the budget would provide clear and credible evidence that the Federal Government intends not to place heavy burdens on the capital markets in future years. Such reassurance should hasten the decline in interest rates, especially long-term interest rates on bonds and residential mortgages, and improve prospects for the recovery of the housing, automobile, and capital investment sectors of the economy.

I recognize the special importance of protecting the social security and medicare programs for aged retirees and their dependents. These programs now face very serious financial problems. The bipartisan National Commission on Social Security Reform has recently recommended a series of measures, which I have endorsed, to eliminate the cumulative deficiency of $150 billion to $200 billion projected for the social security system in the years 1983 through 1989. It is critically important at this time to make changes in the social security programs that will protect their solvency and financial viability for the years to come.

The Remaining Burden of Federal Economic Regulation

For many decades, the Federal Government has regulated the price and entry conditions affecting several sectors of the American economy. Much of this regulation is no longer appropriate to the conditions of the contemporary economy. Over time, most of this regulation — by restraining competition and the development of new services and technologies — has not served the interests of either consumers or producers. Since deregulation of some markets began several years ago, the experience has been almost uniformly encouraging. My Administration has supported these step-by-step efforts to reduce these regulations in markets that would otherwise be competitive. It is now time to consider broad measures to eliminate many of these economic regulations especially as they affect the natural gas, transportation, communications, and financial markets.

Interest Rates and the U.S. Trade Deficit

The very high levels of real interest rates over the last several years are a principal cause of the sharp rise in the ex-

change value of the dollar relative to foreign currencies. This rise has reduced the ability of American exporters to compete in foreign markets and increased the competitiveness of imports in the domestic market. Largely as a result, the U.S. merchandise trade balance showed a substantial deficit in 1982.

Our current trade deficit is a reminder of the importance of international trade to the American economy. The export share of U.S. gross national product has more than doubled over the last three decades. American workers, businesses, and farmers suffer when foreign governments prevent American products from entering their markets, thus reducing U.S. export levels. While the United States may be forced to respond to the trade distorting practices of foreign governments through the use of strategic measures, such practices do not warrant indiscriminate protectionist actions, such as domestic content rules for automobiles sold in the United States. Widespread protectionist policies would hurt American consumers by raising prices of the products they buy, and by removing some of the pressures for cost control and quality improvement that result from international competition. Moreover, protectionism at home could hurt the workers, farmers, and firms in the United States that produce goods and services for export, since it would almost inevitably lead to increased protectionism by governments abroad. I am committed to a policy of preventing the enactment of protectionist measures in the United States, and I will continue working to persuade the other nations of the world to eliminate trade distorting practices that threaten the viability of the international trading system upon which world prosperity depends.

Trade in goods and services is only one aspect of our economic relations with the rest of the world. The international flow of capital into the United States and from the United States to other countries is also of great importance. The United States should play a primary role in preserving the vitality of the international capital market. Severe strains on that market developed in 1982 as several nations found it difficult to service their overseas debt obligations. In 1982, the Federal Government worked closely with debtor and creditor nations and the major international lending agencies to prevent a disruption in the functioning of world capital markets. Now, with the cooperation of a wide variety of creditors, countries with especially severe debt-servicing difficulties are establishing economic and financial programs that will permit them to meet their international obligations.

The Years Ahead

We are now at a critical juncture for the American economy. The recession has led to strong pressures from some members of the Congress and from others to abandon our commitment to a policy that is aimed at long-term economic growth, capi-

tal accumulation, and price stability. There are many who urge new government spending programs and forcing the Federal Reserve to raise monetary growth rates to levels that would rekindle inflation.

I am convinced that such policies would prove detrimental to the long-run interests of the American people. Our economy, despite the recession, is extraordinarily resilient and is now on the road to a

healthy recovery. It is essential in the year ahead that the Administration and the Congress work together, take a long-term perspective, and pursue economic policies that lead to sustained economic growth and to greater prosperity for all Americans.

RONALD REAGAN

February 2, 1983 ∎

Message on Enterprise Zones

Following is the Congressional Record *text of President Reagan's March 7 message to Congress on enterprise zones.*

TO THE CONGRESS OF
THE UNITED STATES:

I am transmitting to the Congress today legislation entitled, "The Enterprise Zone Employment and Development Act of 1983." This legislation will provide for the creation of meaningful jobs within the private sector and the long-term revitalization of our Nation's most depressed areas. It is offered as one element of a comprehensive jobs package intended to attack unemployment, including such other elements as supplemental unemployment benefits, tax credits for hiring the long-term unemployed, a summer youth program, and additional funds for job training and relocation assistance.

In my January 25 state of the Union message, I indicated that we would reintroduce Enterprise Zone legislation in the 98th Congress. While this legislation carries forward the tax and regulatory relief measures of our earlier proposal in the 97th Congress, it contains several important additions which reflect the combined wisdom of the growing coalition supporting this idea, including the ideas of the small business community, State and local officials, labor organizations and the many members of Congress who studied and debated our earlier legislation. We are confident that the net result is strong, farsighted legislation designed to unleash the creative energies of our free market economy in our most distressed urban areas. In these difficult days of high unemployment, the legislation is drafted to be of direct primary benefit to disadvantaged workers and the long-term unemployed.

The high level of success experienced by the dozen or so State and local Enterprise Zone programs is very encouraging. Prompt Federal action is warranted to bolster State and local efforts, and it is in that spirit that I urge the early enactment of this legislation.

The Concept of Enterprise Zones

The Enterprise Zone program will improve the private sector's ability to provide new employment opportunities, and in

turn, urban regeneration. It creates a productive free market environment in economically depressed areas by reducing taxes, regulations and other government burdens on economic activity. The removal of these burdens will create and expand economic opportunity within the zone areas, allowing business firms and entrepreneurs to create jobs — particularly for disadvantaged workers — and expand economic activities.

Enterprise Zones are a fresh approach for promoting economic growth in the inner cities. The old approach relied on heavy government subsidies and central planning. A prime example was the Model Cities program of the 1960s, which concentrated government programs, subsidies and regulations in specific, depressed urban areas. The Enterprise Zone approach would remove government barriers, freeing individuals to create, produce and earn their own wages and profits.

Mindful of the need to control public expenditures, Enterprise Zones require no Federal appropriations other than necessary administrative expenses. Of course, states and cities have the option of allocating existing Federal funds for their Enterprise Zones if they desire, or to appropriate additional funds of their own for such zones. Enterprise Zones are more than just a Federal initiative. State and local contributions to these zones will be critically important in these competitive, Federal designation of zones, and probably determine whether individual zones succeed or fail. In keeping with Constitutional requirements of federalism, State and local governments retain broad flexibility to develop the contributions to their zones most suitable to local conditions and preferences.

The Elements of Enterprise Zones

The Enterprise Zone program includes four basic elements:

● Tax reduction at the Federal, State and local levels to lessen the economic impediments to business investment and employment.

● Regulatory relief at the Federal, State and local levels to reduce costly burdens which are unnecessary to legitimate health and safety concerns.

● New efforts to improve local services, including experimentation with private al-

ternatives to provide those services.

• Neighborhood involvement so that local residents participate in the economic success of their zones. For example, resident owned Enterprise Zones businesses might provide local services which were previously monopolized by government.

By combining all these elements we will create the right economic environment for our Nation's depressed areas.

The Structure of the Enterprise Zone Program

Title I of the Act describes the program's structure and how the zones will be established.

The initial designation or establishment of each zone will depend on local leadership and initiative. To obtain the Federal incentives for Enterprise Zones, State and local governments must nominate eligible areas to the Secretary of HUD.

As defined by the Act, eligible areas include all UDAG eligible jurisdictions which have significant unemployment, poverty or population loss. Based on these criteria, currently more than 2,000 cities, rural areas and Indian reservations qualify. The Enterprise Zone program is a potential source of economic assistance to distressed areas of all types, shapes and sizes, all across the country.

The Secretary of HUD will be authorized to designate up to 75 zones over a three-year period. The actual number designated will depend on the number and quality of the applications.

Federal designation of nominated zones is not automatic. The Secretary of HUD will evaluate the various applications on a competitive basis, choosing the best applications for the limited number of Federal designations authorized. The key criterion in this competitive process will be the nature and strength of the State and local efforts to remove government burdens and to revitalize Enterprise Zone areas.

Thus, the Federal evaluation of State and local contributions will be highly flexible and not prescriptive. In this regard, the Secretary of HUD will not insist upon any particular item of tax and regulatory relief. A weakness of State and local incentives in one area, such as tax relief, could be offset by greater strength in another area such as regulatory relief.

Each Enterprise Zone will last for the period chosen by the nominating State and local governments. The Federal incentives will apply to an approved zone for this entire period, up to a maximum of 20 years plus a 4-year, phase-out period.

The Federal Incentives of the Enterprise Zone Program

Title II of the Act describes the Federal Tax incentives applying within Enter-

prise Zones, which include:

• A 5 percent tax credit for capital investments in personal property in an Enterprise Zone;

• A 10 percent tax credit for the construction or rehabilitation of commercial, industrial or rental housing structures within a zone;

• A 10 percent tax credit to employers for payroll paid to qualified zone employees in excess of payroll paid to such employees in the year prior to zone designation, with a maximum credit of $1,700 per worker;

• A special, strengthened tax credit to employers for wages paid to qualified zone employees who were disadvantaged individuals when hired, with the credit equal to 50 percent of wages in each of the first 3 years of employment, and declining by 10 percentage points in each year after that;

• A 5 percent tax credit, up to $525 per worker to qualified zone employees for wages earned in zone employment;

• The elimination of capital gains taxes for qualified property within Enterprise Zones;

• The designation of suitable Enterprise Zones areas as Foreign Trade Zones, providing relief from tariffs and import duties for goods subsequently exported to other countries;

• The continued availability of Industrial Development Bonds to small business in Enterprise Zones, even if the availability of such bonds is terminated elsewhere; and

• The permission for excess Enterprise Zone tax credits to be carried back three years and forward up to the life of the zone.

The Federal tax reductions applying to Enterprise Zones are substantial. They include reductions for employers, employees, entrepreneurs and investors. They include incentives for attracting venture capital, hiring workers, particularly disadvantaged workers, and starting and building up new businesses. They include the reduction, and in some case elimination, of corporate income taxes, individual income taxes and capital gains taxes.

The cost of the Enterprise Zone tax package should be minimal given the small amount of tax revenue presently generated in Enterprise Zones. Moreover, as the Enterprise Zone concept succeeds, the tax revenue attendant to increased economic activity should offset the tax losses in the initial years.

Title III of the Act describes the Federal regulatory relief applying within Enterprise Zones. Under these provisions, State and local governments may request relief for their Enterprise Zones from any Federal regulation, unless it would directly violate a requirement imposed by statute. There is no authority for any Federal regulatory relief within an Enterprise Zone without a request for such relief from both the State and local governments.

This regulatory relief authority expressly does not apply, however, to regulations designed to protect any person against discrimination because of race, color, religion, sex, marital status, national origin, age or handicap. It also does not cover any regulation whose relaxation would likely present a significant risk to the public safety, including environmental pollution. The minimum wage law would not be covered by this authority because it is specifically imposed and spelled out by statute.

The Role of State and Local Governments

While these Federal incentives are substantial, strong State and local contributions to the zones will be necessary for the program to succeed.

These contributions can be from each of the four basic categories noted earlier: tax relief; regulatory relief; improved local services; and increased participation by neighborhood organization. More traditional urban efforts, such as job training, minority business assistance or infrastructure grants, can also be contributed to the zone. Once again, consistent with the Administration's policy of restoring the Constitutional principle of federalism, the Federal government will not dictate to State and local governments what they must contribute to the zones.

The State and local contributions to the zones need not be costly. For example, regulatory relief, service improvements through privatization, and private sector involvement all entail no budgetary cost. Finally, as with the Federal tax relief, the cost of State and local tax relief should be modest because of the little economic activity currently existing in potential Enterprise Zone areas. State and local expenditures would be reduced as individuals who formerly received government aid are employed in the zone.

The legislation I am sending you today is based on the work of many Members from both sides of the aisle. I encourage these innovative individuals to work for early, bipartisan passage of this legislation.

More than government expenditures and subsidies, resident of economically-depressed areas need opportunities. This is the focus of the Enterprise Zone program. The program will identify and remove government barriers to entrepreneurs who can create jobs and economic growth. It will spark the latent talents and abilities already in existence in our Nation's most depressed areas. The success of State Enterprise Zones confirms that the concept deserves to be given a chance to work at the Federal level.

RONALD REAGAN

The White House,
March 7, 1983

∎

EPA Memorandum of Understanding

Following is the text of the March 9 memorandum of understanding between the chairman and ranking minority member of the House Energy and Commerce Subcommittee on Oversight and Investigations, John D. Dingell, D-Mich., and James T. Broyhill, R-N.C., and Counsel to the President Fred F. Fielding concerning subpoenaed Environmental Protection Agency documents.

MEMORANDUM OF UNDERSTANDING

1. The Environmental Protection Agency (EPA) will deliver all documents that are within the subpoena dated February 10, 1983, issued by the Subcommittee on Oversight and Investigations, Committee on Energy and Commerce, on or before 10:00 a.m. of Thursday, March 10, 1983.

2. The EPA shall identify at the time of delivery any document or portion thereof that is "enforcement sensitive." The designation of "enforcement sensitive" shall be used to identify any document or portion thereof the public disclosure of which could jeopardize the ability of the Executive Branch to pursue any enforcement action.

3. The Subcommittee agrees that delivery of the documents described in paragraph 1 of this memorandum shall be in full and complete satisfaction of the subpoenas dated October 14, 1982, and February 10, 1983.

4. The Subcommittee agrees to afford any document or portion thereof designated as "enforcement sensitive" the confidential treatment of executive session materials. If the Subcommittee votes to release or use in public session any document or portion thereof designated as "enforcement sensitive," reasonable advance notice with opportunity for consultation shall be given to the EPA. Every effort should be made to reach agreement as to whether or not the document should be released or used in public session. If agreement cannot be reached, such documents shall not be released or used in public session. If agreement cannot be reached, such documents shall not be released or used in public session without the concurrence of the Chairman or Ranking Minority Member of the Subcommittee. In the event such concurrence cannot be reached, such documents shall be released or used in public session only upon a further vote of the members of the Subcommittee. The documents shall be kept in a locked safe with sign-in procedures for those obtaining access. Staff access shall be limited to those individuals designated jointly by the Chairman and Ranking Minority Member.

5. Nothing in this memorandum shall constitute a waiver of Executive Privilege with regard to any document. The Subcommittee does not acknowledge the applicability of Executive Privilege to any document subpoenaed.

6. Title to "enforcement sensitive" documents shall remain in the EPA and shall not transfer to the Subcommittee. Upon notice by the Subcommittee to the EPA that the documents are no longer needed, the EPA may retrieve them.

Dated: March 9, 1983

John D. Dingell
Chairman, Subcommittee on
Oversight and Investigations

James T. Broyhill, Ranking
Minority Member, Subcommittee on
Oversight and Investigations

Fred F. Fielding
Counsel to the President ∎

Message on Structural Unemployment

Following is the White House text of President Reagan's March 11 message to Congress on programs to relieve structural unemployment.

TO THE CONGRESS OF
THE UNITED STATES:

Two years ago when I took office, the U.S. economy was suffering from back-to-back years of double digit inflation; interest rates exceeded 20 percent. The Economic Recovery Program which we put in place — slowing the rate of growth of Federal spending, reducing the Federal tax burden, eliminating unnecessary regulations, and supporting a stable and moderate growth in the money supply — has cleared the way for recovery and laid the foundation for a period of sustained, non-inflationary economic growth. Unfortunately, every economy which has successfully made this transition has experienced a period of increased unemployment. Because the 1981-82 recession, closely following the 1980 recession, was longer and deeper than anyone in or out of government had predicted, it sent the unemployment rate to painfully high levels.

In January over 11 million American men and women who were seeking work could not find jobs. Nearly 60 percent of the unemployed had lost their previous jobs and were either looking for new ones or waiting for recall by their previous employers. Nearly 2 million of the unemployed were teenagers most of whom were looking for their first job or struggling with the difficult transition from school to work. Unemployment is particularly painful to the long-term unemployed. About 40 percent of those now out of work have been unemployed for more than 14 weeks and nearly one-fourth have been unemployed for 6 months or longer.

Reducing unemployment without re-igniting the fires of inflation is the most significant domestic challenge we face. In designing policies to reduce unemployment, we must first have a clear understanding of its dimensions and its underlying causes.

There are two primary types of unemployment: cyclical unemployment and structural unemployment. Cyclical unemployment results from downturns in business conditions. As the general level of business activity declines, employers reduce their demand for workers, and unemployment increases, as the economy picks up, cyclical unemployment automatically goes down. Structural unemployment, on the other hand, is largely unaffected by swings in business conditions. It can result from the continuous change in a dynamic economy where some industries are declining while others are expanding; from a mismatch of skills needed for available jobs versus the skills in the available work force; from barriers to labor market entry; and from increases in the proportion of the population looking for work. Thus, structural unemployment will remain a problem even after the economy has fully recovered.

Cyclical Unemployment

The present period of economic stagnation began in January 1980 when the economy went into a brief recession. The recovery that followed later that year was anemic, especially in construction and in many of our basic manufacturing industries. By mid-1981, the short upturn in economic activity could not be maintained, and the economy entered the current recession.

In December 1979, before the present period of stagnation, 6.4 million people were unemployed. Today, 11.4 million Americans are out of work. The back-to-back recessions have caused most of the 5 million increase in unemployment since 1979.

A major part of our current unemployment problem is the result of economic stagnation. The single most effective long-term cure for much of our unemployment

problem is to get the economy moving again. There is every reason to believe that we are now on the road to economic recovery. Construction activity, which has significantly contributed to past recoveries, has shown marked improvement in recent months. Industrial production is up for two months in succession. Automobile sales and new orders for manufacturing goods have also increased. Not least, the unemployment rate, normally a lagging indicator, has finally begun to moderate. The economic assumptions in my budget, which many have characterized as very cautious, project an increase of nearly 5 million additional jobs by the end of 1984. I am confident we can accomplish this without re-igniting inflation.

Structural Unemployment

Even after the economy has fully recovered, however, we will still face the challenge of structural unemployment. Government can play an important role in assisting three groups of structurally unemployed workers: the long-term unemployed, displaced workers, and youth.

We can help the long-term unemployed by providing needed financial assistance and offering new incentives to employers to hire and train them.

We can help our displaced workers obtain the training needed to make the transition from declining to growth industries.

And we can help our young people by removing impediments that prevent them from gaining the initial skills they need for a lifetime of productive work.

Only by moving forward on all these fronts can we successfully meet the challenge of structural unemployment. The Employment Act of 1983, which I am sending the Congress today, contains a balanced and comprehensive set of programs to help the long-term unemployed, displaced workers, and youth secure productive jobs in our economy.

Assisting the Long-Term Unemployed

Extending Federal Supplemental Compensation

Many of the long-term unemployed will continue to face economic hardship during the coming months. Last year I signed legislation to assist them during this difficult period. In my State of the Union Address, I said I would propose the extention and modification of the temporary Federal Supplemental Compensation (FSC) program, which is scheduled to terminate March 31, 1983.

The program I am proposing provides additional unemployment compensation until the end of the current fiscal year to aid those individuals who have exhausted their unemployment insurance benefits and who have demonstrated workforce attachment and have lost their jobs through

no fault of their own.

Our proposed extension will also eliminate the unnecessary complexity in the current program while continuing to provide the longest benefit durations in those states with the most severe unemployment problems.

This FSC program should help those who most deserve assistance. Our proposal will ensure this by changing the workforce attachment requirement and excluding voluntary job quitters. This approach is both fair and fiscally responsible.

Inducing More Employment Through Job Vouchers

While unemployment compensation reduces the hardship of being out of work, it does not help the unemployed to find work. We must adopt programs that will help the long-term unemployed secure jobs by providing incentives for businesses to hire them. Therefore, I propose supplementing the extension of FSC with a new job voucher program to help the long-term unemployed obtain productive jobs. Under this new program, a worker eligible for FSC will be allowed to convert his or her unemployment benefits into vouchers that would entitle a new employer who hires the individual to receive a tax credit.

The job voucher program will have much broader coverage than existing employment tax credit programs, such as the targeted jobs tax credit. An employer will be able to use the voucher to offset state or Federal unemployment insurance taxes or Federal income tax liabilities. This new incentive to hire the long-term unemployed will extend to all private sector employers including nonprofit institutions. Of course, individual state unemployment trust funds will be reimbursed from federal general revenues so as not to penalize the states. The employer hiring incentive would last for one year after March 31, 1983, six months beyond the termination date of FSC on October 1, 1983.

Extending FSC and establishing the job voucher program have the advantage that they can be enacted swiftly through Federal legislation. Unlike other elements of the unemployment insurance program, the states would not have to change their legislation. These proposals constitute a cost effective, fair, and efficient program to help those most in need and help them immediately.

Enterprise Zones to Increase Employment in Distressed Inner Cities and Rural Towns

I have also proposed the creation of enterprise zones in inner cities and in rural towns. Through Federal, State, and local tax and regulatory relief, and strong neighborhood and local participation, enterprise zones will offer a significant economic incentive to businesses, large and small, looking for opportunities to expand or revitalize their operations. Several provisions in the proposed legislation provide direct

benefits and incentives to employers to hire, train, and promote disadvantaged workers, and the long-term unemployed. The increase in economic activity in these zones will offer new job opportunities for individuals and stimulate a revival in distressed local economies.

Assisting Displaced Workers

Displaced workers are a second group suffering structural unemployment. Our economy is currently undergoing extensive changes due to international developments, technological advances, and environmental needs. Many of these changes will help increase our productivity and improve our standard of living. But they also mean that many workers must face significant adjustments as some plants close and individual production lines are idled. While we as a nation must revitalize our industrial base to meet the economic challenges of the 1980s and beyond, we must also vigorously pursue labor market policies which ensure that our experienced workforce has the skills to match the needs of our expanding industries. Sustained economic growth and a rising standard of living can only be fully realized if our labor force receives the necessary training and if it is sufficiently mobile geographically and occupationally.

The Congressional Budget Office estimates that about 15 percent of those currently unemployed are displaced workers, defined as people who have lost their jobs from either declining industries or declining occupations. Of those from declining industries, nearly half are from automobiles, fabricated metals, primary metals, and wearing apparel; more than 60 percent reside in the northeast and midwest. Of those displaced from declining occupations, three-quarters are semi-skilled operatives and laborers.

Achieving enhanced employment security for our experienced work force is a shared responsibility. No single level of government or single segment of society has exclusive responsibility. All have significant roles.

Our proposals to the Congress:
- Constitute a meaningful assistance policy for displaced workers;
- Are consistent with the principle of shared responsibility; and
- Utilize existing government institutions and service delivery mechanisms.

The Job Training Partnership Act

On October 13, 1982, I signed into law the Job Training Partnership Act (JTPA). Title III of the Act provides for a state administered training and placement assistance program for displaced workers.

The JTPA establishes a partnership among business, labor, and elected officials at the state and local levels. Through this partnership, the private sector, in cooperation with elected officials, will play a deci-

sive role in planning and implementing programs to assure that training is responsive to the job needs of business and industry.

I am requesting an appropriation for Title III of the JTPA of $240 million for fiscal year 1984. This represents an almost ten-fold increase over fiscal year 1983 funding. When combined with non-Federal matching funds, this appropriation will support much needed training and placement assistance for 100,000 displaced workers.

Using Unemployment Insurance for Reemployment Assistance

Since 1935, our unemployment insurance program has served the nation well in providing temporary financial assistance for unemployed workers. But, while income maintenance helps cushion the financial strain of unemployment, it does not directly assist people in finding jobs. I believe we can modify the Unemployment Insurance (UI) system to improve the occupational and geographic mobility of permanently displaced workers without violating the integrity and insurance nature of the system.

Recognizing the unique Federal-State structure of the system and that many different adjustment assistance policies may prove effective, the bill I am sending to the Congress would amend the Federal Unemployment Tax Act to allow states the flexibility to use up to 2 percent of state unemployment insurance tax revenues to pay for training, job search, and relocation assistance.

These two reemployment assistance programs can help our displaced working men and women acquire the skills they need to adjust to the changes in a dynamic economy.

Assisting Youth

Young people are a third group suffering from structural unemployment. Unemployment among youth constitutes over 30 percent of our overall unemployment. The rate among the 16-21 age group is an unacceptable 23 percent, over twice the national average, and among minority youth, the unemployment rate of 44 percent represents the single most important social labor market problem.

The consequences of youth unemployment are different from those of adult unemployment. Among adults, unemployment is primarily a matter of financial loss and temporary economic hardship. Most of our nation's youth, on the other hand, live in families in which they are the second or third breadwinner. Unemployment among the majority of youth, therefore, does not usually create severe financial hardship. In 1981, the annual income of families with unemployed youth averaged almost $25,000.

Prolonged periods of unemployment among many youths, however, often lead to serious long-term consequences. First, sustained unemployment can tempt some to channel their energies and ambitions into antisocial or criminal activities. Second, long-term unemployment undermines a young person's potential for success. Recent studies show that those who have prolonged unemployment during their formative years also have less stable employment and diminished earning capacity during their adult years.

Prolonged unemployment among youth is partially due to a lack of initial labor market skills. The problem of skill deficiencies is exacerbated by a lack of career-oriented job opportunities. To combat the problem of skill deficiencies, the Administration worked with Congress to enact the landmark Job Training Partnership Act (JTPA) of 1982. Under the Act, in FY 1984, $724 million in resources are targeted at economically disadvantaged youth in need of training. These resources will provide young people with a fresh chance to develop fully their potential for a productive career.

As a second step toward improving the job skills of our nation's youth, the Administration worked with Congress to extend the Targeted Jobs Tax Credit (TJTC) Program. As part of the extension, the program was modified to target resources more tightly on economically disadvantaged youth. The tax credits provided by the program will encourage employers to aid in the process of developing the skills of many of our young people.

Enactment of enterprise zone legislation would be a third step in this process of improving employment opportunities for youth, particularly disadvantaged youth in our inner cities and rural areas. However, the problem of youth unemployment is too large and too severe for the Federal government alone to provide the sole remedy. The private sector must also help open up career-oriented job opportunities.

One of the most important causes of the lack of career-oriented jobs in which young people can start their careers is the minimum wage. When many young people first enter the labor market their job skills are well below those of older, experienced workers. In a free market, unhampered by government restrictions, young people could compensate for their relative lack of experience and skills by offering to work for a lower wage. Then, as they gain experience on the job, their growing skills would make them more valuable to employers and they would progress up the pay scale. The minimum wage destroys this opportunity: young people are prevented from offering their services at less than a government mandated wage. Faced with the prospect of hiring an unskilled youth at a wage in excess of the current value of his labor, many firms not surprisingly turn young people away. Unable to get an initial job, many young workers never learn the job skills that are needed to earn more than the minimum wage.

Evidence of the effects of the minimum wage is abundant. For nearly a century and a half, this nation experienced no significant youth unemployment problem. Then, just after the turn of the century, state legislatures began enacting minimum wage laws. At first, these mandated wages were not far from market wages and there was little impact. In 1938, however, the Federal government imposed a Federal minimum wage applicable to firms engaged in interstate commerce. Initially this meant that the Federal minimum wage was largely confined to manufacturing. The Federal minimum wage contributed to declining youth employment in manufacturing. But other industries such as retail trade and the service sector still provided an outlet for the energies of youth who wished to work.

During the 1960s and 1970s the minimum wage was increased and its coverage was expanded. At the same time, the youth unemployment problem continued to worsen, especially among minorities.

Youth Employment Opportunity Wage

To help those young people who want to work find jobs, I am proposing a youth employment opportunity wage for youngsters under the age of 22. This youth opportunity wage will be $2.50 per hour, 25 percent below the regular minimum wage of $3.35 per hour. Young people will not, of course, be forced to accept the lower wage, and many will receive more than $2.50 an hour. But all will have the opportunity to offer their services at $2.50 if lack of job skills or other factors make this appropriate.

I am not the first to propose a youth differential minimum wage; indeed, the government more than once has come close to implementing such a proposal. Each time it failed, however, due to concerns that adults would be displaced by younger workers. I am unconvinced by such arguments but I appreciate the concern behind them. Therefore, I am proposing that the youth employment opportunity wage only be effective during the summer — specifically from May 1 to September 30. This is the period when the greatest number of youth are in the labor market and, therefore, the period in which this proposal will generate the most employment opportunities. By restricting the youth opportunity wage to the summer months, the jobs of older workers will be protected. An employer will not wish to disrupt his or her work force by attempting to use youth during the summer and adults the rest of the year.

To ensure that existing jobs are protected, the Employment Act of 1983 prohibits displacement of current workers by those hired at the youth employment opportunity wage. It also protects the wages of youth employed at the current minimum wage by prohibiting employers from reducing their rate of pay. Thus it expands youth employment opportunities, but not at the expense of older workers.

Some may try to use this proposed legislation as an opportunity to raise the level of the Federal minimum wage above the current $3.35 per hour. I will vigorously oppose any such attempt. Raising the level of the minimum wage would cause many adult workers to lose their jobs. At a time of 10.4 percent unemployment, it would simply create further job loss and more unemployment.

Summary

The Employment Act of 1983 is a balanced and realistic approach to addressing our economy's structural unemployment problem. It provides appropriate incentives for employers to hire the long-term unemployed. It provides needed financial assistance to men and women suffering from the hardship of prolonged joblessness, and provides Federal funds for a cooperative effort by industry, labor, and local officials in assisting displaced workers. It gives States the flexibility needed to further assist these workers, and supplements the major effort already underway to provide meaningful training to our disadvantaged youth by establishing a youth employment opportunity wage which will give all our youth a chance to get the work experience they need. Our enterprise zone legislation will stimulate new jobs in economically distressed areas. Together these proposals will provide the foundation for expanding job opportunities for our unemployed. I urge the Congress to enact this legislation promptly.

RONALD REAGAN

March 11, 1983

Crime Control Bill Proposal

Following is the White House text of President Reagan's March 16 message to Congress proposing crime control legislation.

TO THE CONGRESS OF
THE UNITED STATES:

I am transmitting to the Congress today a legislative proposal entitled, the "Comprehensive Crime Control Act of 1983."

As you know, my Administration has made major efforts to fight crime in America. Soon after taking office, I directed the Attorney General and other Federal law enforcement officials to improve the efficiency and coordination of Federal law enforcement, with special emphasis on violent and drug-related crime. This has been accomplished largely through the work of the Cabinet Council on Legal Policy, chaired by the Attorney General, as well as through leadership provided by the White House Office on Drug Abuse Policy. As a result of these efforts, Federal law enforcement is better coordinated than ever before.

Of even greater importance, this Administration is attacking crime at its source by providing increased resources to Federal law enforcement agencies for apprehension, conviction, and incarceration. Last October, for example, I announced a national strategy to cripple organized crime and put drug traffickers out of business. We established twelve interagency task forces in key areas of the country — modeled in part on the Task Force that has been operating very successfully in South Florida — to work with State and local law enforcement officials to shut down organized criminal enterprises. We established a National Center for State and Local Law Enforcement Training to assist and train State and local officials in combatting syndicated crime. We also have taken many other actions, including use of the FBI in drug cases, to bring the full resources of the United States Government to bear on the critical problem of crime.

Our efforts are beginning to bear fruit. During 1982, for example, Federal cocaine seizures totalled nearly 12,500 pounds — nearly three times the amount seized in 1981. Heroin seizures almost doubled, and seizures of marijuana increased by 50 percent. I have every reason to believe that these and other administrative actions will continue to increase arrests and convictions of persons who violate Federal law.

But administrative action, however successful, is not enough. If the forces of law are to regain the upper hand over the forces of crime, ensuring that criminals are convicted and put and kept behind bars, basic legislative changes are needed.

During the 97th Congress, the Senate passed S. 2572, the Violent Crime and Drug Enforcement Improvements Act. Among its principal provisions, this legislation would have made major and urgently needed changes in our laws concerning bail, criminal forfeiture, and sentencing. It is unfortunate that S. 2572 was not enacted during the last Congress, but I look forward to working with the 98th Congress to secure, at long last, passage of critically needed substantive criminal law reform.

The legislative proposal that I am transmitting today provides a thorough and comprehensive reform of those aspects of Federal criminal law that have proven to be the largest obstacles in our fight against crime. Many of our proposals were considered by the 97th Congress. Others are new. Each is important in rolling back the tide of criminal activity that threatens our Nation, our families and our way of life.

Our proposal is summarized in some detail in the materials accompanying this message. I do, however, want to highlight six especially critical reforms:

● **Bail.** Our bill would make it much more difficult for a defendant likely to be a threat to his community to be released on bail pending trial.

● **Sentencing.** The bill would change the sentencing system to ensure that sentences would be determinate and consistent throughout the Federal system, with no parole possible.

● **Exclusionary rule.** Under our proposal, evidence in a criminal case that may have been improperly seized, which is now excluded from evidence, would be admissible upon a showing that the officer making the seizure acted in reasonable good faith.

● **Criminal forfeitures.** Our bill would strengthen the ability of Federal prosecutors to confiscate the assets and profits of criminal enterprises.

● **Insanity defense.** The bill would replace the current Federal insanity defense with a narrower defense applicable only to a person who is unable to appreciate the nature or wrongfulness of his acts.

● **Narcotics enforcement.** Our proposal would substantially increase the penalties for trafficking in drugs and would strengthen the regulatory authority of the Drug Enforcement Administration with respect to the diversion of legitimate drugs into illegal channels.

The bill contains many other important provisions, as well, concerning labor racketeering, capital punishment, consumer product tampering, and extradition, to name only a few. These proposals, taken together, will provide Federal law enforcement officials with important new tools with which to combat crime and will help once again to make our streets safe for all our citizens.

We must not allow further delay in protecting the rights, safety, and quality of life of all Americans. We must act now. Accordingly, I urge prompt consideration and passage of these legislative proposals.

RONALD REAGAN

The White House,
March 16, 1983

Education Legislation Proposal

Following is the White House text of President Reagan's March 17 message to Congress proposing three education bills, "The Student Assistance Improvement Amendments," "The Education Savings Account Act" and "The Equal Education Opportunity Act."

TO THE CONGRESS OF
THE UNITED STATES:

I am herewith transmitting to the Congress three bills to improve equity and quality in American education: "The Student Assistance Improvement Amendments," "The Education Savings Account Act" and "The Equal Educational Opportunity Act."

All Americans, and especially today's parents, are deeply concerned about our system of education — and rightly so. For generations we have been justly proud of the quality and openness of our education system from kindergarten to post-graduate levels, both public and private. It has served the nation well, but now it is in need of significant changes in key areas.

The programs and budget requests I recommended to the Congress this year address a wide range of education issues. They reflect my strong conviction that education decisions should be made by parents, students, States and local officials. The national government also has an important, but limited, role to play in the education system. Thus, while I have worked to brake the runaway growth in education spending, my budget calls for over $13 billion for the coming fiscal year. Within this total is over $4 billion for supplemental educational services for the educationally disadvantaged and for the handicapped. I have also included over $5.6 billion for post-secondary student aid.

Despite these huge investments and its own basic strengths, our education system has not been immune to the stresses and strains of a changing society. Its problems are complex and varied. They call for a broad range of creative approaches by concerned parents, by educators, by the private sector, and by government.

Two of these critical problems are the reasons for the bills I am proposing today. These problems are:

Meeting Higher Education Costs. The cost of higher education rose 30% in just three years, from 1978 to 1981, making it more difficult for qualified students from lower and middle-income families to meet the cost of attending many institutions despite very rapidly rising Federal student aid. At the same time, many more affluent families who could contribute more have been paying a smaller share of these costs, relying instead on increasingly generous Federal aid.

Parental Choice. At the elementary and secondary level, parents too often feel excluded from the education of their own children by education bureaucracies. Parents who turn to private schools are burdened with a double payment — they must pay private school tuition in addition to taxes for the public schools. As a practical matter the ability to choose and the opportunity to obtain a private education are made difficult if not impossible for many Americans — particularly those from low- and middle-income families.

Administration Proposals

The three bills I am transmitting to Congress today take on squarely these two important issues.

Meeting Higher Education Costs

The "Student Assistance Improvement Amendments" I am transmitting will:

● Redirect the present student aid system from one in which some students can get Federal grants without contributing any of their own money, to a system which begins with self-help, with parents and students shouldering their fair share of the cost of education before Federal grants are made;

● Increase by almost 60% the funds available for work-study to help students help themselves meet their obligations;

● Increase by two-thirds the maximum Pell grant students can receive under current law; and

● Require all applicants for guaranteed student loans to prove need before receiving the generous interest subsidy.

With these changes, Federal student aid dollars will help more low-income persons meet the burden of education costs and will help restore confidence in the fairness of our system of education.

In addition, I am asking the Congress to enact my Education Savings Account proposal. This bill speaks to another aspect of the education cost problem I have described: the difficulty parents have in saving for college costs.

Everyone has trouble saving for the future, especially when today's demands on our resources are so great. Nevertheless, the importance of saving for higher education has never been so critical. We need a strong, diverse higher education system to which all Americans have access. Moreover, many of the nation's better job opportunities will be limited to those who have a higher education. So I have today proposed an additional special incentive for parents to begin, as early as possible, to set aside money for their children's college education.

Under my proposal many parents will be able to put aside up to $1,000 per year in special accounts whose interest income will be tax free. The full benefit will be available to all those with incomes below $40,000 per year; reduced benefits are included for families with incomes up to $60,000.

Over time, this tax incentive will greatly enhance parents' ability to contribute to the cost of the higher education they want for their children. It cannot, of course, substitute for the student's own work and savings, nor for Federal aid. It will, however, help to restore a better balance in the system and make meeting the family's share of education costs a less burdensome task in future years.

Parental Choice

At the elementary and secondary level, we face different problems. The public education system, as it has evolved over the decades, is the backbone of American education and one of the great strengths of our democracy. However, many parents want to use alternative approaches to meet the educational needs of their children. This option should be theirs in our free society. But there can be meaningful choice only if our system also makes access to alternatives a reality.

Several weeks ago I sent to Congress a bill to make tuition tax credits available to all parents, within eligible income limits, who choose to send their children to nondiscriminatory private schools. Today, I am proposing a bill, the "Equal Educational Opportunity Act," to permit States and localities to offer another kind of choice to parents whose children are selected for participation in our $3 billion compensatory education program, Chapter 1 of the Education Consolidation and Improvement Act.

Chapter 1 helps meet the costs of supplemental educational services, like remedial reading, for millions of educationally disadvantaged children each year. In some cases, we believe that the parents of those children would prefer a greater range of educational choice in their selection of a school. Under this bill, in States or school districts which choose to provide the option, parents would be able to participate in a voucher program to exercise that choice at whatever school they felt provided the greatest educational opportunity for their children.

I firmly believe that in districts where the voucher option is implemented, education will be strengthened for all. The potential for competition for enrollments and resources will raise the quality of both public and private education. Parents will gain a greater measure of control. Children will receive a better education.

Conclusion

These three bills address central issues in American education. They will bring

greater order and balance to Federal, family and student efforts to meet the rising cost of higher education. They will help bring parental choice and the benefits of competition to elementary and secondary education. They, and all my proposals in the education area, make clear the limited role of the Federal government and wherever possible restore more choice and control to the family. Their ultimate goal is more diverse, higher quality education for all Americans. I ask your support for rapid consideration and passage of these proposals.

RONALD REAGAN

The White House,
March 17, 1983

Reagan Statement on Arms Control Agreement

Following is the White House text of President Reagan's March 30 statement as delivered on intermediate-range nuclear forces negotiations.

THE PRESIDENT: Thank you very much. Last week, when I addressed the American people on this administration's defense program, I expressed our determination to reduce our reliance on the terrible power of nuclear weapons to assure the peace.

And today, I want to say a few words about this critical aspect of our security policy — our efforts to drastically reduce the arsenals which burden the lives of our own citizens, of our friends and allies, and, yes, of our adversaries as well.

As you know, over the last year and a half, this administration has undertaken a comprehensive and far-reaching arms control program designed to achieve deep reductions in nuclear arms, to rid the world of chemical weapons, and to cut the size of conventional forces in Europe. I'll be saying more about these initiatives in a speech tomorrow. But this morning, let me focus on one of these negotiations.

I have just met with the Ambassadors of the countries of the North Atlantic Alliance. We invited them here because the citizens of their countries share with Americans a profound hope for success in the Geneva negotiations on intermediate-range nuclear missiles.

Geneva Negotiations

The forces being discussed in the I.N.F. negotiations directly affect the security of our allies. As I told you last week, the Soviet Union has deployed hundreds of powerful, new SS-20 missiles, armed with multiple warheads and capable of striking the cities and defense installations of our allies in Europe, and of our friends and allies in Asia as well. The Soviets have built up these forces even though there's been no comparable threat from NATO. They've deployed them without let-up — there now are more than 350 SS-20 missiles, with more than 1,000 nuclear warheads. NATO will begin deploying a specific deterrent to this threat late this year, unless, as we hope, an agreement to eliminate such weapons would make this deployment unnecessary.

The United States, with the full support of our allies, has been negotiating in Geneva for more than a year to persuade the Soviet Union that it is a far better course for both of us to agree to eliminate totally this entire category of weapons. Such an agreement would be fair and far-reaching. It would enhance the security of the Soviet Union as well as the security of NATO. And it would fulfill the aspiration of people throughout Europe and Asia for an end to the threat posed by these missiles.

So far, the Soviet Union has resisted this proposal and has failed to come up with a serious alternative. They insist on preserving their present monopoly on these weapons. Under their latest proposal, the Soviets would retain almost 500 warheads on their SS-20 missiles in Europe alone and hundreds more in the Far East, while we would continue to have zero. Their proposal would actually leave them with more SS-20 missiles than they had when the talks began in 1981. In addition, the Soviets have launched a propaganda campaign aimed apparently at dividing America from our allies and our allies from each other.

From the opening of these negotiations nearly 18 months ago, I have repeatedly urged the Soviets to respond to our zero-zero proposal with a proposal of their own. I've also repeated our willingness to consider any serious alternative proposal.

Their failure to make such a proposal is a source of deep disappointment to all of us who have wished that these weapons might be eliminated or at least significantly reduced. But I do not intend to let this shadow that has been cast over the Geneva negotiations further darken our search for peace.

When it comes to intermediate nuclear missiles in Europe, it would be better to have none than to have some. But if there must be some, it is better to have few than to have many.

An Interim Agreement

If the Soviets will not now agree to the total elimination of these weapons, I hope that they will at least join us in an interim agreement that would substantially reduce these forces to equal levels on both sides.

To this end, Ambassador Paul Nitze has informed his Soviet counterpart that we are prepared to negotiate an interim agreement in which the United States would substantially reduce its planned deployment of Pershing II and ground-launched cruise missiles, provided the Soviet Union reduce the number of its warheads on longer-range I.N.F. missiles to an equal level on a global basis.

Ambassador Nitze has explained that the United States views this proposal as a serious initial step toward the total elimination of this class of weapons. And he has conveyed my hope that the Soviet Union will join us in this view. Our proposal for the entire elimination of these systems remains on the table.

We've suggested that the negotiations resume several weeks earlier than originally planned. The Soviets have agreed to that and talks will resume on May 17th.

I hope this initiative will lead to an early agreement. We remain ready to explore any serious Soviet suggestions that meet the fundamental concerns which we have expressed.

I invited the NATO Ambassadors here today not only to review these developments, but to express my appreciation for the firm support which the allies have given to our negotiating effort in Geneva. And I can assure them of my personal commitment to the closest possible consultations with them on the I.N.F.

This consultation process has already proven one of the most intensive and productive in the history of the North Atlantic Alliance. It has made the initiative announced today an Alliance initiative in the best sense of that term. And over the past months, we and our allies have consulted intensively on the I.N.F. negotiations.

I have been in frequent and close contact with other Heads-of-Government. Vice President Bush had a very productive discussion with allied leaders on I.N.F. during his trip to Europe. Secretaries Shultz and Weinberger have exchanged views with their counterparts from allied governments. And the NATO Special Consultative Group has met regularly to review the negotiations and consider criteria which should form the basis for the Alliance position in I.N.F.

The very thoughtful views expressed by the allies in these consultations have been of significant help in shaping this new initiative. This process is a model for how an alliance of free and democratic nations can and must work together on critical issues. It is the source of our unity, and gives us a strength that no one can hope to match. And it gives me great confidence in the eventual success of our efforts in Geneva to create a safer — safer world for all the Earth's people.

Thank you very much. (Applause.) ∎

Reagan Address on Nuclear Arms Control

Following is the White House text of President Reagan's March 31 remarks made before the Los Angeles World Affairs Council, in Los Angeles.

THE PRESIDENT: Thank you. Thank you all very much. Thank you, Dr. Singleton, the President, and Presidents past and distinguished guests and you, ladies and gentlemen, thank you all for a very warm welcome.

I can tell you that our eyes turn westward constantly in Washington. The only problem with coming out here is it's so hard to go back. (Laughter.) (Applause.)

Last week, I spoke to the American people about our plans for safeguarding this nation's security and that of our allies. And I announced a long-term effort in scientific research to counter some day the menace of offensive nuclear missiles. What I have proposed is that nations should turn their best energies to moving away from the nuclear nightmare. We must not resign ourselves to a future in which security on both sides depends on threatening the lives of millions of innocent men, women and children.

And today, I would like to discuss another vital aspect of our national security: our efforts to limit and reduce the danger of modern weaponry.

We live in a world in which total war would mean catastrophe. We also live in a world that's torn by a great moral struggle between democracy and its enemies, between the spirit of freedom and those who fear freedom.

In the last 15 years or more, the Soviet Union has engaged in a relentless military buildup, overtaking and surpassing the United States in major categories of military power, acquiring what can only be considered an offensive military capability. All the moral values, which this country cherishes, freedom, democracy, the right of peoples and nations to determine their own destiny, to speak and write, to live and worship as they choose, all these basic rights are fundamentally challenged by a powerful adversary which does not wish these values to survive.

This is our dilemma, and it's a profound one. We must both defend freedom and preserve the peace. We must stand true to our principles and our friends while preventing a holocaust.

The Western commitment to peace through strength has given Europe its longest period of peace in a century. We cannot conduct ourselves as if the special danger of nuclear weapons did not exist. But we must not allow ourselves to be paralyzed by the problem, to abdicate our moral duty. This is the challenge that history has left us.

We of the 20th Century who so pride ourselves on mastering even the forces of nature — except last week when the Queen was here — (laughter) — we are forced to wrestle with one of the most complex moral challenges ever faced by any generation. Now, my views about the Soviet Union are well known. Although, sometimes I don't recognize them when they're played back to me. (Laughter.) And our program for maintaining, strengthening, and modernizing our national defense has been clearly stated.

Today, let me tell you something of what we are doing to reduce the danger of nuclear war. Since the end of World War II, the United States has been the leader in the international effort to negotiate nuclear arms limitations. In 1946, when the United States was the only country in the world possessing these awesome weapons, we did not blackmail others with threats to use them, nor did we use our enormous power to conquer territory, to advance our position, or to seek domination.

Doesn't our record alone refute the charge that we seek superiority, that we represent a threat to peace. We proposed the Baruch Plan for international control of all nuclear weapons and nuclear energy, for everything nuclear to be turned over to an international agency. And this was rejected by the Soviet Union. Several years later, in 1955, President Eisenhower presented his "open skies" proposal that the United States and the Soviet Union would exchange blueprints of military establishments and permit aerial reconnaissance to ensure against the danger of surprise attack. This, too, was rejected by the Soviet Union.

Now, since then, some progress has been made, largely at American initiative. The 1963 Limited Test Ban Treaty prohibited nuclear testing in the atmosphere, in outer space, or under water. The creation of the "Hot Line" in 1963, upgraded in 1971, provides direct communication between Washington and Moscow to avoid miscalculation during a crisis. The Nuclear Non-Proliferation Treaty of 1968 sought to prevent the spread of nuclear weapons. In 1971, we reached an agreement on special communication procedures to safeguard against accidental or unauthorized use of nuclear weapons, and on a seabed arms control treaty, which prohibits the placing of nuclear weapons on the seabed of the ocean floor. The Strategic Arms Limitation Agreements of 1972 imposed limits on anti-ballistic missile systems and on numbers of strategic, offensive missiles. And the 1972 Biological Warfare Convention bans — or was supposed to ban — the development and production and stockpiling of biological and toxin weapons.

But while many agreements have been reached, we've also suffered many disappointments. The American people had hoped, by these measures, to reduce tensions and start to build a constructive relationship with the Soviet Union.

Instead, we have seen Soviet military arsenals continue to grow in virtually every significant category. We have seen the Soviet Union project its power around the globe. We have seen Soviet resistance to significant reductions and measures of effective verification, especially the latter. And, I'm sorry to say, there have been increasingly serious grounds for questioning their compliance with the arms control agreements that have already been signed and that we've both pledged to uphold. I may have more to say on this in the near future.

Coming into office, I made two promises to the American people about peace and security: I promised to restore our neglected defenses, in order to strengthen and preserve the peace, and I promised to pursue reliable agreements to reduce nuclear weapons. Both these promises are being kept.

Today, not only the peace but also the chances for real arms control depend on restoring the military balance. We know that the ideology of the Soviet leaders does not permit them to leave any Western weakness unprobed, any vacuum of power unfilled. It would seem that to them negotiation is only another form of struggle. Yet, I believe the Soviets can be persuaded to reduce their arsenals — but only if they see it's absolutely necessary. Only if they recognize the West's determination to modernize its own military forces will they see an incentive to negotiate a verifiable agreement establishing equal, lower levels. And, very simply, that is one of the main reasons why we must rebuild our defensive strength.

All of our strategic force modernization has been approved by the Congress except for the land-based leg of the TRIAD. We expect to get congressional approval on this final program later this spring. A strategic forces modernization program depends on a national bipartisan consensus. Over the last decade, four successive administrations have made proposals for arms control and modernization that have become embroiled in political controversy. No one gained from this divisiveness; all of us are going to have to take a fresh look at our previous positions. I pledge to you my participation in such a fresh look and my determination to assist in forging a renewed bipartisan consensus.

My other national security priority on assuming office was to thoroughly re-examine the entire arms control agenda. Since then, in coordination with our allies, we've launched the most comprehensive program of arms control initiatives ever undertaken. Never before in history has a nation engaged in so many major simultaneous efforts to limit and reduce the instruments of war. Last month in Geneva, the Vice President committed the United States to nego-

tiate a total and verifiable ban on chemical weapons. Such inhumane weapons, as well as toxin weapons, are being used in violation of international law in Afghanistan, in Laos, and Kampuchea.

Together with our allies, we've offered a comprehensive new proposal for mutual and balanced reduction of conventional forces in Europe.

We have recently proposed to the Soviet Union a series of further measures to reduce the risk of war from accident or miscalculation. And we are considering significant new measures resulting in part from consultations with several distinguished Senators.

We've joined our allies in proposing a Conference on Disarmament in Europe. On the basis of a balanced outcome of the Madrid meeting, such a Conference will discuss new ways to enhance European stability and security.

We have proposed to the Soviet Union improving the verification provisions of two agreements to limit underground nuclear testing, but, so far, the response has been negative. We will continue to try.

And, most importantly, we have made far-reaching proposals, which I will discuss further in a moment, for deep reductions in strategic weapons and for elimination of an entire class of intermediate-range weapons.

I am determined to achieve real arms control — reliable agreements that will stand the test of time, not cosmetic agreements that raise expectations only to have hopes cruelly dashed.

In all these negotiations certain basic principles guide our policy: First, our efforts to control arms should seek reductions on both sides — significant reductions. Second, we insist that arms control agreements be equal and balanced. Third, arms control agreements must be effectively verifiable. We cannot gamble with the safety of our people and the people of the world. Fourth, we recognize that arms control is not an end in itself but a vital part of a broad policy designed to strengthen peace and stability. It's with these firm principles in mind that this administration has approached negotiations on the most powerful weapons in the American and Soviet arsenals — strategic nuclear weapons.

In June of 1982, American and Soviet negotiators convened in Geneva to begin the Strategic Arms Reduction Talks, what we call START. We've sought to work out an agreement reducing the levels of strategic weapons on both sides. I proposed reducing the number of ballistic missiles by one-half and the number of warheads by one-third. No more than half the remaining warheads could be on land-based missiles. This would leave both sides with greater security at equal and lower levels of forces.

Not only would this reduce numbers — it would also put specific limits on precisely those types of nuclear weapons that pose the most danger.

The Soviets have made a counter proposal. We've raised a number of serious concerns about it. But — and this is important — they have accepted the concept of reductions. Now, I expect this is because of the firm resolve that we have demonstrated. In the current round of negotiations, we have presented them with the basic elements of a treaty for comprehensive reductions in strategic arsenals. The United States also has, in START, recently proposed a draft agreement on a number of significant measures to build confidence and reduce the risks of conflict. This negotiation is proceeding under the able leadership of Ambassador Edward Romney on our side — Edward Rowny, I should say, on our side.

We're also negotiating in Geneva to eliminate an entire class of new weapons from the face of the earth. Since the end of the mid-1970s, the Soviet Union has been deploying an intermediate range nuclear missile, the SS-20, at a rate of one a week. There are now 351 of these missiles, each with three highly accurate warheads capable of destroying cities and military bases in Western Europe, Asia and the Middle East.

NATO has no comparable weapon; nor did NATO in any way provoke this new, unprecedented escalation. In fact, while the Soviets were deploying their SS-20s, we were taking a thousand nuclear warheads from shorter range weapons out of Europe.

This major shift in the European military balance, prompted our West European allies themselves to propose that NATO find a means of righting the balance. And in December of '79, they announced a collective two-track decision.

First, to deploy in Western Europe 572 land-based cruise missiles and Pershing II ballistic missiles, capable of reaching the Soviet Union. The purpose, to offset and deter the Soviet SS-20s. The first of these NATO weapons are scheduled for deployment by the end of this year.

Second, to seek negotiations with the Soviet Union for the mutual reduction of these intermediate-range missiles.

In November of 1981, the United States, in concert with our allies, made a sweeping new proposal: NATO would cancel its own deployment if the Soviets eliminated theirs. The Soviet Union refused and set out to intensify public pressures in the West to block the NATO deployment, which has not even started. Meanwhile, the Soviet weapons continue to grow in number.

Our proposal was not made on a take-it-or-leave-it basis. We are willing to consider any Soviet proposal that meets these standards of fairness:

An agreement must establish equal numbers for both Soviet and American intermediate-range nuclear forces.

Other countries' nuclear forces, such as the British and French, are independent and are not part of the bilateral U.S.-Soviet negotiations. They are, in fact, strategic weapons and the Soviet strategic arsenal more than compensates for them.

Next, an agreement must not shift the threat from Europe to Asia. Given the range in mobility of the SS-20s, meaningful limits on these and comparable American systems must be global.

An agreement must be effectively verifiable.

And an agreement must not undermine NATO's ability to defend itself with conventional forces.

We've been consulting closely with our Atlantic allies and they strongly endorse these principles.

Earlier this week, I authorized our negotiator in Geneva, Ambassador Paul Nitze, to inform the Soviet delegation of a new American proposal which has the full support of our allies.

We are prepared to negotiate an interim agreement to reduce our planned deployment if the Soviet Union will reduce their corresponding warheads to an equal level. This would include all U.S. and Soviet weapons of this class, wherever they're located. Our offer of zero on both sides will, of course, remain on the table as our ultimate goal. At the same time, we remain open — as we have been from the very outset — to serious counter-proposals. The Soviet negotiators have now returned to Moscow where we hope our new proposal will receive careful consideration during the recess. Ambassador Nitze has proposed and the Soviets have agreed that negotiations resume in mid-May, several weeks earlier than scheduled.

I am sorry that the Soviet Union, so far, has not been willing to accept the complete elimination of these systems on both sides. The question I now put to the Soviet Government is: If not elimination, to what equal level are you willing to reduce? The new proposal is designed to promote early and genuine progress at Geneva. For arms control to be truly complete and world security strengthened, however, we must also increase our efforts to halt the spread of nuclear arms. Every country that values a peaceful world order must play its part.

Our Allies, as important nuclear exporters, also have a very important responsibility to prevent the spread of nuclear arms. To advance this goal, we should all adopt comprehensive safeguards as a condition for nuclear supply commitments that we make in the future. In the days ahead, I will be talking to other world leaders about the need for urgent movement on this and other measures against nuclear proliferation.

Now, that is the arms control agenda we have been pursuing. Our proposals are fair. They are far-reaching and comprehensive. But we still have a long way to go. We Americans are sometimes an impatient people. I guess it is a symptom of our traditional optimism, energy, and spirit. Often, this is a source of strength. In a negotiation, however, impatience can be a real handicap. Any of you who have been involved in labor-management negotiations or any kind of bargaining know that patience strengthens your bargaining position. If one side seems too eager or desper-

ate, the other side has no reason to offer a compromise and every reason to hold back, expecting that the more eager side will cave in first.

Well, this is a basic fact of life we cannot afford to lose sight of when dealing with the Soviet Union. Generosity in negotiation has never been a trademark of theirs. It runs counter to the basic militancy of Marxist-Leninist ideology. So it is vital that we show patience, determination, and above all, national unity. If we appear to be divided, if the Soviets suspect that domestic, political pressure will undercut our position, they will dig in their heels. And that can only delay an agreement, and may destroy all hope for an agreement.

That is why I have been concerned about the nuclear freeze proposals, one of which is being considered at this time by the House of Representatives. Most of those who support the freeze, I am sure, are well-intentioned, concerned about the arms race and the danger of nuclear war. No one shares their concern more than I do. But however well-intentioned they are, these freeze proposals would do more harm than good. They may seem to offer a simple solution. But there are no simple solutions to complex problems. As H. L. Mencken once wryly remarked, he said, "For every problem, there's one solution which is simple, neat, and wrong." (Laughter.)

The freeze concept is dangerous for many reasons. It would preserve today's high, unequal, and unstable levels of nuclear forces, and, by so doing, reduce Soviet incentives to negotiate for real reductions.

It would pull the rug out from under our negotiations in Geneva, as they have testified. After all, why should the Soviets negotiate if they've already achieved a freeze in a position of advantage to them?

Also, some think a freeze would be easy to agree on, but it raises enormously complicated problems of what is to be frozen, how it is to be achieved and, most of all, verified. Attempting to negotiate these critical details would only divert us from the goal of negotiating reductions for who knows how long.

The freeze proposal would also make a lot more sense if a similar movement against nuclear weapons were putting similar pressures on Soviet leaders in Moscow. As former Secretary of Defense Harold Brown has pointed out — the effect of the freeze "is to put pressure on the United States, but not on the Soviet Union."

Finally, the freeze would reward the Soviets for their 15-year build-up while locking us into our existing equipment, which in many cases is obsolete and badly in need of modernization. Three-quarters of Soviet strategic warheads are on delivery systems five years old or less. Three-quarters of the American strategic warheads are on delivery systems 15 years old or older. The time comes when everything wears out. The trouble is, it comes a lot sooner for us than for them. And, under a freeze, we couldn't do anything about it.

Our B-52 bombers are older than many of the pilots who fly them. If they were automobiles, they'd qualify as antiques. A freeze could lock us into obsolescence. It's asking too much to expect our service men and women to risk their lives in obsolete equipment. The two million patriotic Americans in the armed services deserve the best and most modern equipment to protect them and us.

I'm sure that every President has dreamt of leaving the world a safer place than he found it. I pledge to you, my goal — and I consider it a sacred trust — will be to make progress toward arms reductions in every one of the several negotiations now underway.

I call on all Americans of both parties and all branches of government to join in this effort. We must not let our disagreements or partisan politics keep us from strengthening the peace and reducing armaments.

I pledge to our Allies and friends in Europe and Asia — we will continue to consult with you closely. We're conscious of our responsibility when we negotiate with our adversaries on conditions of — or issues of concern to you and your safety and well being.

To the leaders and people of the Soviet Union, I say, join us in the path to a more peaceful, secure world. Let us — (Applause) — Let us vie in the realm of ideas, on the field of peaceful competition. Let history record that we tested our theories through human experience, not that we destroyed ourselves in the name of vindicating our way of life. And let us practice restraint in our international conduct, so that the present climate of mistrust can some day give way to mutual confidence and a secure peace.

What better time to rededicate ourselves to this undertaking than in the Easter season, when millions of the world's people pay homage to the One who taught us peace on earth, good will toward men?

This is the goal, my fellow Americans, of all the democratic nations — a goal that requires firmness, patience and understanding. If the Soviet Union responds in the same spirit, we're ready. And we can pass on to our posterity the gift of peace — that and freedom are the greatest gifts that one generation can bequeath to another.

Thank you. And God bless you. (Applause.)

MR. HADDAD: Thank you very, very much, Mr. President.

Ladies and gentlemen, President Reagan has graciously agreed to answer a few questions from the audience. We respectfully ask that the questions be short and to the point and no speeches. (Laughter.)

We'll start over here. Yes, sir?

Q: Would the President please give us an update on the nomination of Kenneth Adelman?

P: It will be taken up now by the Senate because it has passed out of committee to the floor, although it passed out with a one margin negative vote against him.

I am optimistic that the Senate will ratify him. He is an excellent choice. He does have the knowledge and experience and ability that we need and he is highly respected in diplomatic circles. And I just think that since the biggest thing that they could ever find out against him in the committee was that somebody wrote him a letter and they didn't like the letter — he didn't write it, he received it. (Laughter.) And I think he should be ratified and I'm looking forward to it.

MR. HADDAD: Thank you, another question. That gentleman right over there. Yes, sir?

Q: Thank you. The gentleman says in view of the delay of an agreement or of the Soviets on arms control, wouldn't it be better for the President to declare his intention to run for office again earlier? (Applause.)

P: I can't give a very specific answer to that. I can only say that, you know, if too early you become a lame duck and then you can't get anything done — if the answer is one way. And if the answer is the other way, then everything you try to do is viewed as being political and part of a campaign.

I have said that I think the people tell you whether you should seek re-election or not and I will remember your response to the question. (Applause.)

MR. HADDAD: The gentleman in the tan suit standing in the back.

Q: The gentleman questions the new guidelines set by the White House and the President on the press. Are we now imitating our adversaries when we set such tough guidelines?

P: No. I don't believe so. What we are trying to control is what seems to be the favorite game of Washington, even more popular than the Redskins. And that is leaks. As a matter of fact, I think sometimes that we ought to just turn to the chandeliers and tell them what it is — (laughter) — that we are trying to do, because they must have ears. (Laughter.)

The trouble is some of the leaks are unfounded. Or they are from people down in the bureaucracy someplace who only know a part of what they are leaking. Sometimes it is misinformation on, maybe, a memorandum of options that has been presented to the Cabinet and to the President. And they are leaked before they have even been seen. And they are leaked as being decisions that have already been made.

But the worst part of it is that, then, the interpretation that is very often put on this incomplete or misinformation is such that it actually can endanger the things that I have been talking about here today. If you are going to negotiate, you cannot be in the position of saying in advance, "Well, what is your back up position? Or what are you going to do, and what is your strategy?" And yet, this comes about in the press. And leads the other side of the table to believe, "Well, they are considering something else."

We have actually had to do something

in the line of explaining and apologizing when leaks that are absolutely fallacious have brought a difference — a kind of confrontation between ourselves and some of our friends and allies in the world. And all we have proposed is methods of intercepting the leaks from the government, itself, to the press. But I do not believe that we are making it difficult at all. As a matter of fact, I have increased the amount of time that I am going to spend with the press. And we started last week on that, so that they will have greater access to me.

And I just think that the press must recognize it, too, has a responsibility for the welfare of the nation. (Applause.)

Q: Mr. President, Ambassador Habib has just returned from the Middle East. I wonder if you could give us an update on your peace initiative, where it stands in the Middle East at this time.

P: Well, it has been a frustrating experience. And there have been gains made. But there are still some points of disagreement.

We believed in the original proposal. And this has been confirmed by many nations in the Middle East, that we cannot proceed with the general subject of overall peace for that troubled area until the forces that are in Lebanon get out. And the Lebanese Government is at last, after all these years, allowed to establish its own sovereignty over its own land. Lebanon has asked for this at the — the Israelis are still in there, the Syrians are still with occupying forces and there are elements of the PLO still there. And what we have sought is a withdrawal of these forces to their own borders. This is one of the reasons for the multinational forces being there, to help Lebanon maintain order while they bring this about, and then proceed at the negotiating table to take up the overall problems.

Very simply, what the whole goal of our plan is, and it's being delayed until we can get this clearing of Lebanon, the goal is to create more Egypts. Egypt and Israel were once at war and they came together with a peace treaty and became friends there in the Middle East. I don't think that it's impossible to believe that among the Arab states there are other potential Israels and that — my dream is that Israel can only know real security if it doesn't have to remain an armed camp far beyond what its size warrants, but could know that the security of having — being surrounded by neighbors that recognize its right to exist as a nation and have signed peace treaties

with them. (Applause.)

Thank you.

Q: This lady compliments the President. She's just returned from a trip in Latin America and says they all support us there or —

P: Thank you very much.

Q: The gentleman wonders with the installation of Soviet SAM-5s in Syria, is the President prepared to release the American planes scheduled for shipment to Israel?

P: You must realize that under the law — the law exists now — those weapons must be for defensive purposes. And this is, again, one of the obstacles presented by the stalemate in Lebanon. While those forces are in the position of occupying another country that now has asked them to leave, we are forbidden by law to release those planes. They're F-16s, the planes that are on order. And it's as simple as the other forces returning to their own countries and letting Lebanon be Lebanon. (Applause.)

Q: This will be the last question. And before — Would all please remain seated until the Presidential party leaves the room.

Would the President support a greater public relations for a closer relationship with the peoples of Europe, inasmuch as they seem to be our first line of defense?

P: Yes. And we have been trying to do more in that regard. I think the relationship that we have with the countries of Western Europe now, between our government and theirs, is probably better and firmer than it's ever been. But it is true that there is a great counter-propaganda effort there trying to divide us from our allies, divide them from us, and at the same time to prevent the deployment, the scheduled deployment of the Pershings and the cruise missiles versus the SS-20s.

And we have, this was part of the reason for Vice President Bush's trip there. We are using other measures, I don't know whether we can actually turn around some of the people that have organized, as they have here, in regard to the nuclear freeze and so forth, I understand they're planning over this weekend sizeable demonstrations there.

But you're right, we have not been in the best, in years past, at matching our adversaries in propaganda. And we've got something to sell and we better start selling it. (Applause.)

Thank you all very much.

Thank you. ∎

Indian Claims Bill Veto

Following is the Congressional Record *text of President Reagan's April 5 message accompanying his veto of S 366, to settle claims of the Mashantucket Pequot Indians. It was Reagan's first veto of a public bill during the 98th Congress.*

TO THE SENATE:

I am returning, without my approval, S. 366, the "Mashantucket Pequot Indian Claims Settlement Act."

This bill would settle claims in the Mashantucket Band of the Western Pequot Indian Tribe to approximately 800

acres of land in the town of Ledyard, Connecticut. In settling the claims, the legislation would generally: (1) extinguish any aboriginal title and any tribal claims for damages or possession of the land and natural resources; (2) establish a $900,000 Federal claims settlement fund to compensate the Indians for extinguishment of the claims; and (3) extend Federal recognition, with all attendant benefits and services, to the Western Pequot Indian Tribe.

The claim that would be settled by this bill is not against the federal Government, but against the State of Connecticut, which sold the Indian land, and against the present owners of the lands concerned. However, the costs of the settlement provided in this bill would be borne almost entirely by the Federal Government.

Given the concerted effort that has already been made to develop a mutually satisfactory settlement for the Western Pequot's land claims, I agree that the most desirable approach to resolution and extinguishment of these claims is through agreements negotiated among the parties concerned and ultimately ratified by the Federal Government. However, this process must recognize certain principles if equity and fairness to all parties are to be achieved. Unfortunately, I find S. 366 violates several of these principles.

First, even if Federal participation in this settlement is warranted, sufficient information does not exist to determine the validity of the claim or the appropriateness of the proposed $900,000 settlement. This settlement is not based on the formula for Eastern Indian land claims settlements supported by my Administration. The Administration formula is based on the difference between land value and compensation received at the time of the land transfer (in this case 1855), plus interest. If the type of valuation for land claims settlements contemplated by this bill were applied across the board to all potential claims of this nature, it could require payment by the taxpayers of billions of dollars.

Second, S. 366 provides for an unacceptably low level of State contribution to the settlement — only 20 acres of State land with an estimated value of about $50,000. The Administration has urged that an affected State should pay for at least one-half of settlement costs in claims such as this, which are not against the Federal Government but against the State and private parties who would be the primary beneficiaries of any settlement.

Finally, the Tribe may not meet the standard requirements for Federal recognition or services that are required of other tribes. The Federal Government has never entered into treaties with this Tribe, and the Bureau of Indian Affairs has never provided services to them or exercised jurisdiction over any Indian lands in Connecticut. The government-to-government relationship between the Western Pequot Tribe and the Federal Government that would be established by this bill is not warranted at this time, pending further

study by Interior. Extending Federal recognition to the Tribe would bypass the Department of the Interior's administrative procedures that apply a consistent set of eligibility standards in determining whether or not Federal recognition should be extended to Indian groups.

I am convinced that a satisfactory resolution of the Western Pequot's land claims can be achieved. However, this will require (1) verification of the claim, including the amount of any monetary settlement based on the formula I have outlined above, (2) completion by Interior of its administrative procedure for determining whether or not Federal recognition of the Tribe is appropriate, and (3) payment by the State of Connecticut of at least one-half of any settlement costs.

I am directing the Secretary of the Interior to enter negotiations with the parties at interest in this case to determine an acceptable settlement, consistent with the Administration's principles, and report his recommendation to me and to the Congress.

RONALD REAGAN

The White House,
April 5, 1983

Report of President's MX Commission

Following are excerpts from the April 11 report of the President's Commission on Strategic Forces.

The Commission has concluded that the preferred approach for modernizing our ICBM force seems to have three components: initiating engineering design of a single-warhead small ICBM, to reduce target value and permit flexibility in basing for better long-term survivability; seeking arms control agreements designed to enhance strategic stability; and deploying MX missiles in existing silos now to satisfy the immediate needs of our ICBM force and to aid that transition.

A more stable structure of ICBM deployments would exist if both sides moved toward more survivable methods of basing than is possible when there is primary dependence on large launchers and missiles. Thus from the point of view of enhancing such stability, the Commission believes that there is considerable merit in moving toward an ICBM force structure in which potential targets are of comparatively low value — missiles containing only one warhead. A single-warhead ICBM, suitably based, inherently denies an attacker the opportunity to destroy more than one warhead with one attacking warhead. The need to have basing flexibility, and particularly the need to keep open the option for different types of mobile basing, also suggests a missile of small size. If force survivability can be additionally increased by arms control agreements which lead both sides toward more survivable modes of basing than is possible with large launchers and missiles, the increase in stability would be further enhanced. In the meantime, however, deployment of MX is essential in order to remove the Soviet advantage in ICBM capability and to help deter the threat of conventional or limited nuclear attacks on the alliance....

The Commission stresses that these two aspects of ICBM modernization and this approach toward arms control are integrally related. They point toward the same objective — permitting the U.S. and encouraging the Soviets to move toward more stable ICBM deployments over time in a way that is consistent with arms control agreements having the objective of reducing the risk of war. The Commission is unanimous that no one part of the proposed program can accomplish this alone.

Small, Single-Warhead ICBM

The commission believes that a single-warhead missile weighing about fifteen tons (rather than the nearly 100 tons of MX) may offer greater flexibility in the long-run effort to obtain an ICBM force that is highly survivable, even when viewed in isolation, and that can consequently serve as a hedge against potential threats to the submarine force.

The Commission thus recommends beginning engineering design of such an ICBM, leading to the initiation of full-scale developments in 1987 and an initial operating capability in the early 1990s. The design of such a missile, hardened against nuclear effects, can be achieved with current technology. It should have sufficient accuracy and yield to put Soviet hardened military targets at risk. During that period an approach toward arms control, consistent with such deployments, should also seek to encourage the Soviets to move toward a more stable ICBM force structure at levels which would obviate the need to deploy very large numbers of such missiles. The development effort for such a missile need not and should not be burdened with the uncertainties accompanying a crash program; thus its timing can be such that competitive development is feasible.

Decisions about such a small missile and its basing will be influenced by several potential developments: the evolution of Soviet strategic programs, the path of arms control negotiations and agreements, general trends in technology, the cost of the program, operational considerations, and the results of our own research on specific basing modes. Although the small missile program should be pursued vigorously, the way these uncertainties are resolved will inevitably influence the size and nature of the program. We should keep in mind, however, that having several different modes of deployment may serve our objective of stability. The objective for the United States should be to have an overall program that will so confound, complicate, and frustrate the efforts of Soviet strategic war planners that, even in moments of stress, they could not believe that they could attack our ICBM forces effectively.

Different ICBM deployment modes by the U.S. would require different types of planned Soviet attacks. Deployment in hardened silos would require the Soviets to plan to use warheads that are large, accurate, or both. Moreover, for those silos or shelters holding a missile with only one warhead, each would present a far less attractive target than would be the case for a silo containing a large missile with many MIRVs. Mobile deployments of U.S. missiles would require the Soviets to try to barrage large areas using a number of warheads for each of our warheads at risk, to develop very sophisticated intelligence systems, or both. In this context, deployment of a small single-warhead ICBM in hardened mobile launchers is of particular interest because it could permit deployment in peacetime in limited areas such as military reservations. Land-mobile deployments without hard launchers could be threatened by a relatively small attack — in the absence of an appropriate arms control agreement — unless our own missiles were distributed widely across the country in peacetime. The key advantages of a small single-warhead missile are that it would reduce the value of each strategic target and that it is also compatible with either fixed or mobile deployments, or with combinations of the two.

As discussed below ... deployment of such small missiles would be compatible with arms control agreements reducing the number of warheads, in which case only a small number of such missiles would probably need to be deployed. If the Soviets proved unwilling to reach such agreements, however, the U.S. could deploy whatever number of small missiles were required — in whatever mix of basing modes — to maintain an adequate overall deterrent.

The MX in Minuteman Silos

There are important needs on several grounds for ICBM modernization that cannot be met by the small, single-warhead ICBM.

First, arms control negotiations — in particular the Soviets' willingness to enter agreements that will enhance stability — are heavily influenced by ongoing programs. The ABM Treaty of 1972, for example, came about only because the United States maintained an ongoing ABM pro-

gram and indeed made a decision to make a limited deployment. It is illusory to believe that we could obtain a satisfactory agreement with the Soviets limiting ICBM deployments if we unilaterally terminated the only new U.S. ICBM program that could lead to deployment in this decade. Such a termination would effectively communicate to the Soviets that we were unable to neutralize their advantage in multiple-warhead ICBMs. Abandoning the MX at this time in search of a substitute would jeopardize, not enhance, the likelihood of reaching a stabilizing and equitable agreement. It would also undermine the incentives to the Soviets to change the nature of their own ICBM force and thus the environment most conducive to the deployment of a small missile.

Second, effective deterrence is in no small measure a question of the Soviets' perception of our national will and cohesion. Cancelling the MX, when it is ready for flight testing, when over $5 billion have already been spent on it, and when its importance has been stressed by the last four Presidents, does not communicate to the Soviets that we have the will essential to effective deterrence. Quite the opposite.

Third, the serious imbalance between the Soviets' massive ability to destroy hardened land-based military targets with their ballistic missile force and our lack of such a capability must be redressed promptly. Our ability to assure our allies that we have the capability and will to stand with them, with whatever forces are necessary, if the alliance is threatened by massive conventional, chemical or biological, or limited nuclear attack, is in question as long as this imbalance exists.... [W]e cannot safely permit a situation to continue wherein the Soviets have the capability promptly to destroy a range of hardened military targets and we do not.

Fourth, our current ICBM force is aging significantly. The Titan II force is being retired for this reason and extensive Minuteman rehabilitation programs are planned to keep those missiles operational. ... As Soviet ABM modernization and modern surface-to-air missile development and deployment proceed — even within the limitations of the ABM treaty — it is important to be able to match any possible Soviet breakout from that treaty with strategic forces that have the throw-weight to carry sufficient numbers of decoys and other penetration aids.... Having in production a missile that could effectively counter such a Soviet step should help deter them from taking it.... These objectives can all be accomplished, at reasonable cost, by deploying MX missiles in current Minuteman silos.

In the judgment of the Commission, the vulnerability of such silos in the near term, viewed in isolation, is not a sufficiently dominant part of the overall problem of ICBM modernization to warrant other immediate steps being taken such as closely-spacing new silos or ABM defense of those silos. This is because of the mutual

survivability shared by the ICBM force and the bomber force in view of the different types of attacks that would need to be launched at each, as explained above.... To deter ... surprise attacks we can reasonably rely both on our other strategic forces and on the range of operational uncertainties that the Soviets would have to consider in planning such aggression — as long as we have underway a program for long-term ICBM survivability such as that for the small, single warhead ICBM to hedge against long-term vulnerability for the rest of our forces....

Arms Control

Over the long run, stability would be fostered by a dual approach toward arms control and ICBM deployments which moves toward encouraging small, single-warhead ICBMs. This requires that arms control limitations and reductions be couched, not in terms of launchers, but in terms of equal levels of warheads of roughly equivalent yield. Such an approach could permit relatively simple agreements, using appropriate counting rules, that exert pressure to reduce the overall number and destructive power of nuclear weapons and at the same time give each side an incentive to move toward more stable and less vulnerable deployments.

Arms control agreements of this sort — simple and flexible enough to permit stabilizing development and modernization programs, while imposing quantitative limits and reductions — can make an important contribution to the stability of the strategic balance. An agreement that permitted modernization of forces and also provided an incentive to reduce while modernizing, in ways that would enhance stability, would be highly desirable. It would have the considerable benefit of capping both sides' strategic forces at levels that would be considerably lower than they would otherwise reach over time. It would also recognize, realistically, that each side will naturally desire to configure its own strategic forces. Simple aggregate limits of this sort are likely to be more practical, stabilizing, and lasting than elaborate, detailed limitations on force structure and modernization whose ultimate consequences cannot be confidently anticipated.

Encouraging stability by giving incentives to move toward less vulnerable deployments is more important than reducing quickly the absolute number of warheads deployed. Reductions in warhead numbers, while desirable for long-term reasons of limiting the cost of strategic systems, should not be undertaken at the expense of influencing the characteristics of strategic deployments. For example, warhead reductions, while desirable, should not be proposed or undertaken at a rate that leads us to limit the number of launching platforms to such low levels that their survivability is made more questionable.

For a variety of historical, technical, and verification reasons, both the SALT II unratified teaty and the current START

proposal contain proposals to limit or reduce the number of ICBM launchers or missiles. Unfortunately this has helped produce the tendency to identify arms control with launcher or missile limits, and to lead some to identify successful arms control with low or reduced launcher or missile limits. This has, in turn, led to an incentive to build launchers and missiles as large as possible and to put as many warheads as possible into each missile. Such an incentive has been augmented by the cost savings involved in putting a given number of warheads on a few large missiles rather than on a number of smaller ones....

We will have for some time strategic forces in which the number of launchers on one side are outnumbered many times over by the number of warheads on the other. Under such circumstances, it is not stabilizing to use arms control to require mutual reductions in the number of launching platforms (e.g. submarines or ICBM launchers) or missiles. Such a requirement further increases the ratio of warheads to targets. It does not promote deterrence and reduce the risk of war for the Soviets to have many more times the number of accurate warheads capable of destroying hard targets than the U.S. has ICBM launchers.

In time we should try to promote an evolution toward forces in which — with an equal number of warheads — each side is encouraged to see to the survivability of its own forces in a way that does not threaten the other. But if the Soviet Union chooses to retain a large force of large missiles, each with many warheads, the U.S. must be free to match this by the sort of deployment it chooses. Any arms control agreement equating SS-18s and small single-warhead ICBMs because each is one missile or because each is on one launcher would be destabilizing in the extreme.

The approach toward arms control suggested by the Commission, moreover, is compatible with the basic objectives and direction of several other current arms control proposals.

... [I]t should be noted that, as a method of restricting ICBM modernization, the negotiated SALT II Treaty, which would have expired in 1985, would have prohibited testing of more than one new ICBM. The two-part ICBM modernization program suggested by the Commission would not violate that negotiated agreement because testing of a small, single-warhead ICBM could not begin before this expiration date. Of more long-term importance, however, the approach toward arms control and force modernization suggested here is fundamentally compatible with the sort of stability that SALT II sought to achieve. SALT II specifically contemplated the negotiation of extension agreements with improved terms, and there is no reason to doubt that future extension agreements would have allowed the testing and deployment of a second new ICBM missile with the stabilizing potential of a small, single-warhead ICBM. Moreover, the Soviets have tested two new ICBMs since Octo-

ber 1982.

The current Administration's START proposal is centered on warhead limitations and reductions, with some attention to throw-weight limitations. These are consistent with the Commission's recommended program. It also contains a proposed limit on launchers that the Commission believes should be reassessed since it is not compatible with a desirable evolution toward small, single-warhead ICBMs.

Some current arms control proposals in Congress concentrate on warhead limitations in which reductions are forced in warhead numbers as a price of modernization; others seek explicitly to encourage movement toward small, single-warhead ICBMs on both sides. These general directions are also consistent with the approach suggested in this report.... ∎

Reagan Speech on Central America

Following is the Congressional Record *text of President Reagan's April 27 address on Central America as delivered before a joint session of Congress.*

THE PRESIDENT. Mr. Speaker, Mr. President, distinguished Members of the Congress, honored guests and my fellow Americans:

A number of times in the past years, Members of Congress and a President have come together in meetings like this to resolve a crisis. I have asked for this meeting in the hope that we can prevent one.

It would be hard to find many Americans who are not aware of our stake in the Middle East, the Persian Gulf, or the NATO line dividing the free world from the Communist bloc, and the same could be said for Asia. But in spite of, or maybe because of, a flurry of stories about places like Nicaragua and El Salvador and, yes, some concerted propaganda, many of us find it hard to believe we have a stake in problems involving those countries. Too many have thought of Central America as just a place way down below Mexico that cannot possibly constitute a threat to our well being.

That is why I have asked for this session. Central America's problems do directly affect the security and the well being of our own people. And Central America is much closer to the United States than many of the world trouble spots that concern us. As we work to restore our own economy, we cannot afford to lose sight of our neighbors to the south.

El Salvador is nearer to Texas than Texas is to Massachusetts. Nicaragua is just as close to Miami, San Antonio, San Diego, and Tucson as those cities are to Washington where we are gathered tonight.

But nearness on the map does not even begin to tell the strategic importance of Central America, bordering as it does on the Caribbean, our lifeline to the outside world. Two-thirds of all our foreign trade and petroleum pass through the Panama Canal and the Caribbean. In a European crisis at least half our supplies for NATO would go through these areas by sea. It is well to remember that in early 1942 a handful of Hitler's submarines sank more tonnage there than in all of the Atlantic Ocean. And they did this without a single naval base anywhere in the area.

Today the situation is different. Cuba is host to a Soviet combat brigade, a submarine base capable of servicing Soviet submarines, and military air bases visited regularly by Soviet military aircraft.

Because of its importance, the Caribbean Basin is a magnet for adventurism. We are all aware of the Libyan cargo planes refueling in Brazil a few days ago on their way to deliver medical supplies to Nicaragua. Brazilian authorities discovered the so-called supplies were actually munitions and prevented their delivery. You may remember that last month, speaking on national television I showed an aerial photo of an airfield being built in the Island of Grenada. Well, if that airfield had been completed those planes could have refueled there and completed their journey.

If the Nazis during World War II and the Soviets today could recognize the Caribbean and Central America as vital to our interests, should not we also?

For several years now, under two Administrations, the United States has been increasing its defense of freedom in the Caribbean Basin. And I can tell you tonight, democracy is beginning to take root in El Salvador, which until a short time ago knew only dictatorship. The new government is now delivering on its promises of democracy, reforms and free elections. It was not easy and there was resistance to many of the attempted reforms, with assassinations of some of the reformers. Guerrilla bands and urban terrorists were portrayed in a worldwide propaganda campaign as freedom fighters representative of the people. Ten days before I came into office, the guerrillas launched what they called a "final offensive" to overthrow the government. And their radio boasted that our new Administration would be too late to prevent their victory. Well, they learned that democracy cannot be so easily defeated.

President Carter did not hesitate. He authorized arms and munitions to El Salvador. The guerrilla offensive failed, but not America's will. Every President since this country assumed global responsibilities has known that those responsibilities could only be met if we pursued a bipartisan foreign policy.

As I said a moment ago, the Government of El Salvador has been keeping its promises, like the land reform program which is making thousands of farm tenants farm owners. In a little over 3 years, 20 percent of the arable land in El Salvador has been redistributed to more than 450,000 people. That is one in ten Salvadorans who have benefited directly from this program.

El Salvador has continued to strive toward an orderly and democratic society. The government promised free elections. On March 28th, little more than a year ago, after months of campaigning by a variety of candidates, the suffering people of El Salvador were offered a chance to vote — to choose the kind of government they wanted. Suddenly the so-called freedom fighters in the hills were exposed for what they really are: a small minority who want power for themselves and their backers, not democracy for the people. The guerrillas threatened death to anyone who voted. They destroyed hundreds of buses and trucks to keep the people from getting to the polling places. Their slogan was brutal: "Vote today, die tonight." But on election day, an unprecedented 80 percent of the electorate braved ambush and gunfire, and trudged for miles, many of them, to vote for freedom. That is truly fighting for freedom. We can never turn our backs on that.

Members of this Congress who went there as observers told me of a woman who was wounded by rifle fire on the way to the polls, who refused to leave the line to have her wound treated until after she had voted. Another woman had been told by the guerrillas that she would be killed when she returned from the polls, and she told the guerrillas, "You can kill me, you can kill my family, you can kill my neighbors; you can't kill us all." The real freedom fighters of El Salvador turned out to be the people of that country — the young, the old, the in-between — more than one million of them out of a population of less than five million. The world should respect this courage and not allow it to be belittled or forgotten. Again, I say in good conscience, we can never turn our backs on that.

The democratic political parties and factions in El Salvador are coming together around the common goal of seeking a political solution to their country's problems. New national elections will be held this year and they will be open to all political parties. The government has invited the guerrillas to participate in the election and is preparing an amnesty law. The people of El Salvador are earning their freedom and they deserve our moral and material support to protect it.

Yes, there are still major problems regarding human rights, the criminal justice system and violence against non-combatants and, like the rest of Central America, El Salvador also faces severe economic problems. But in addition to recession — depressed prices for major agricultural exports, El Salvador's economy is being deliberately sabotaged.

Tonight in El Salvador — because of ruthless guerrilla attacks — much of the fertile land cannot be cultivated, less than half the rolling stock of the railways remains operational, bridges, water facilities, telephone and electrical systems have been destroyed and damaged. In one 22-month period there were 5,000 disruptions of electrical power. One region was without electricity for a third of a year.

I think Secretary of State Shultz put it very well the other day: "Unable to win the free loyalty of El Salvador's people, the guerrillas," he said, "are deliberately and systematically depriving them of food, water, transportation, light, sanitation, and jobs. And these are the people who claim they want to help the common people."

They do not want elections because they know they would be defeated. But as the previous election showed the Salvadoran people's desire for democracy will not be defeated.

The guerrillas are not embattled peasants armed with muskets. They are professionals, sometimes with better training and weaponry than the government soldiers. The Salvadoran battalions that have received United States training have been conducting themselves well in the battlefield and with the civilian population. But so far we have only provided enough money to train 1 Salvadoran soldier out of 10, fewer than the number of guerrillas that are trained by Nicaragua and Cuba.

And let me set the record straight on Nicaragua, a country next to El Salvador. In 1979 when the new government took over in Nicaragua, after a revolution which overthrew the authoritarian rule of Somoza, everyone hoped for the growth of democracy. We in the United States did too. By January of 1981, our emergency relief and recovery aid to Nicaragua totaled $118 million — more than provided by any other developed country. In fact, in the first 2 years of Sandinista rule, the United States directly or indirectly sent five times more aid to Nicaragua than it had in the 2 years prior to the revolution. Can anyone doubt the generosity and the good faith of the American people?

These were hardly the actions of a nation implacably hostile to Nicaragua. Yet the government of Nicaragua has treated us as an enemy. It has rejected our repeated peace efforts, it has broken its promises to us, to the Organization of American States and, most important of all, to the people of Nicaragua.

No sooner was victory achieved than a small clique ousted others who had been part of the revolution from having any voice in the government. Humberto Ortega,

the Minister of Defense, declared Marxism-Leninism would be their guide, and so it is.

The government of Nicaragua has imposed a new dictatorship, it has refused to hold the elections it promised, it has seized control of most media and subjects all media to heavy prior censorship. It denied the bishops and priests of the Roman Catholic Church the right to say mass on radio during Holy Week, it insulted and mocked the Pope, it has driven the Miskito Indians from their homelands — burning their villages, destroying their crops, and forcing them into involuntary internment camps far from home; it has moved against the private sector and free labor unions; it condoned mob action against Nicaragua's independent human rights commission and drove the director of that commission into exile.

In short, after all of these acts of repression by the government, is it any wonder that oppositoin has formed? Contrary to propaganda, the opponents of the Sandinistas are not die-hard supporters of the previous Somoza regime. In fact, many are anti-Somoza heroes who fought beside the Sandinistas to bring down the Somoza government. Now they have been denied any part of a new government because they truly want a democracy for Nicaragua, and they still do. Others are Miskito Indians fighting for their homes, their lands and their lives.

The Sandinista revolution in Nicaragua turned out to be just an exchange of one set of autocratic rulers for another, and the people still had no freedom, no democratic rights, and more poverty. Even worse than its predecessor, it is helping Cuba and the Soviets to destabilize our hemisphere.

Meanwhile, the Government of El Salvador, making every effort to guarantee democracy, free labor unions, freedom of religion, and a free press, is under attack by guerrillas dedicated to the same philosophy that prevails in Nicaragua, Cuba and, yes, the Soviet Union.

Violence has been Nicaragua's most important export to the world. It is the ultimate in hypocrisy for the unelected Nicaraguan Government to charge that we seek their overthrow when they are doing everything they can to bring down the elected Government of El Salvador. The guerrilla attacks are directed from a headquarters in Managua, the capital of Nicaragua.

But let us be clear as the American attitude toward the Government of Nicaragua. We do not seek its overthrow. Our interest is to insure that it does not infect its neighbors through the export of subversion and violence. Our purpose, in conformity with American and international law, is to prevent the flow of arms to El Salvador, Honduras, Guatemala, and Costa Rica. We have attempted to have a dialogue with the Government of Nicaragua, but it persists in its efforts to spread violence.

We should not — and we will not — protect the Nicaraguan Government from

the anger of its own people. But we should, through diplomacy, offer an alternative. And, as Nicaragua ponders its options, we can and will — with all the resources of diplomacy — protect each country of Central America from the danger of war.

Even Costa Rica, Central America's oldest and strongest democracy, a government so peaceful it does not even have an army, is the object of bullying and threats from Nicaragua's dictators.

Nicaragua's neighbors know that Sandinista promises of peace, non-alliance, and non-intervention have not been kept. Some 36 new military bases have been built — there were only 13 during the Somoza years.

Nicaragua's new army numbers 25,000 men supported by a militia of 50,000. It is the largest army in Central America supplemented by 2,000 Cuban military and security advisers. It is equipped with the most modern weapons, dozens of Soviet-made tanks, 800 Soviet-bloc trucks, Soviet 152-MM howitzers, 100 anti-aircraft guns, plus planes and helicopters. There are additional thousands of civilian advisers from Cuba, the Soviet Union, East Germany, Libya, and the PLO. And we are attacked because we have 55 military trainers in El Salvador.

The goal of the professional guerrilla movements in Central America is as simple as it is sinister — to destabilize the entire region from the Panama Canal to Mexico. And if you doubt me on this point, just consider what Cayetano Carpio, the now-deceased Salvadoran guerrilla leader, said earlier this month. Carpio said that after El Salvador falls, El Salvador and Nicaragua would be "arm-in-arm and struggling for the total liberation of Central America."

Nicaragua's dictatorial junta, who themselves made war and won power operating from bases in Honduras and Costa Rica, like to pretend that they are today being attacked by forces based in Honduras. The fact is, it is Nicaragua's government that threatens Honduras, not the reverse.

It is Nicaragua who has moved heavy tanks close to the border, and Nicaragua who speaks of war. It was Nicaraguan radio that announced on April 8th the creation of a new, unified revolutionary coordinating board to push forward the Marxist struggle in Honduras.

Nicaragua, supported by weapons and military resources provided by the Communist bloc, represses its own people, refuses to make peace, and sponsors a guerrilla war against El Salvador.

President Truman's words are as apt today as they were in 1947, when he, too, spoke before a Joint Session of Congress:

At the present moment in world history nearly every nation must choose between alternative ways of life. The choice is not too often a free one.

One way of life is based upon the will of the majority, and is distin-

guished by free institutions, representative government, free elections, guarantees of individual liberty, freedom of speech and religion, and freedom from political oppression.

The second way of life is based upon the will of a minority forcibly imposed upon the majority. It relies upon terror and oppression, a controlled press and radio, fixed elections, and the suppression of personal freedoms.

I believe that it must be the policy of the United States to support free peoples who are resisting attempted subjugation by armed minorities or by outside pressures.

I believe that we must assist free peoples to work out their own destinies in their own way.

I believe that our help should be primarily through economic and financial aid which is essential to economic stability and orderly political processes.

... Collapse of free institutions and loss of independence would be disastrous not only for them but for the world. Discouragement and possibly failure would quickly be the lot of neighboring peoples striving to maintain their freedom and independence.

The countries of Central America are smaller than the nations that prompted President Truman's message. But the political and strategic stakes are the same. Will our response — economic, social, military — be as appropriate and successful as Mr. Truman's bold solutions to the problems of postwar Europe?

Some people have forgotten the successes of those years — and the decades of peace, prosperity, and freedom they secured.

Some people talk as though the United States were incapable of acting effectively in international affairs without risking war or damaging those we seek to help.

Are democracies required to remain passive while threats to their security and prosperity accumulate?

Must we just accept the destabilization of an entire region from the Panama Canal to Mexico on our southern border?

Must we sit by while independent nations of this hemisphere are integrated into the most aggressive empire the modern world has seen?

Must we wait while Central Americans are driven from their homes, like the more than four million who have sought refuge out of Afghanistan or the 1½ million who have fled Indochina or the more than one million Cubans who have fled Castro's Caribbean utopia? Must we, by default, leave the people of El Salvador no choice but to flee their homes, creating another tragic human exodus?

I do not believe there is a majority in the Congress or the country that counsels passivity, resignation, defeatism, in the face of this challenge to freedom and security in our own hemisphere.

I do not believe that a majority of the Congress or the country is prepared to stand by passively while the people of Central America are delivered to totalitarianism and we ourselves are left vulnerable to new dangers.

Only last week an official of the Soviet Union reiterated Brezhnev's threat to station nuclear missiles in this hemisphere — five minutes from the United States. Like an echo, Nicaragua's Commandate, Daniel Ortega, confirmed that, if asked, his country would consider accepting those missiles. I understand that today they may be having second thoughts.

Now, before I go any further, let me say to those who invoke the memory of Vietnam: There is no thought of sending American combat troops to Central America; they are not needed and, indeed, they have not been requested there. [Applause.]

All our neighbors ask of us is assistance in training and arms to protect themselves while they build a better, freer life.

We must continue to encourage peace among the nations of Central America. We must support the regional efforts now underway to promote solutions to regional problems.

We cannot be certain that the Marxist-Leninist bands who believe war is an instrument of politics will be readily discouraged. It is crucial that we not become discouraged before they do. Otherwise, the region's freedom will be lost and our security damaged in ways that can hardly be calculated.

If Central America were to fall, what would the consequences be for our position in Asia, Europe, and for alliances such as NATO? If the United States cannot respond to a threat near our own borders, why should Europeans or Asians believe that we are seriously concerned about threats to them? If the Soviets can assume that nothing short of an actual attack on the United States will provoke an American response, which ally, which friend, will trust us then?

The Congress shares both the power and the responsibility for our foreign policy.

Tonight, I ask you, the Congress, to join me in a bold, generous approach to the problems of peace and poverty, democracy and dictatorship in the region. Join me in a program that prevents Communists victory in the short run but goes beyond to produce for the deprived people of the area the reality of present progress and the promise of more to come.

Let us lay the foundation for a bipartisan approach to sustain the independence and freedom of the countries of Central America. We in the Administration reach out to you in this spirit. We will pursue four basic goals in Central America:

First: in response to decades of inequity and indifference, we will support democracy, reform and human freedom. This means using our assistance, our powers of persuasion and our legitimate "leverage" to bolster humane democratic systems where they already exist and to help countries on their way to that goal complete the process as quickly as human institutions can be changed. Elections — in El Salvador and also in Nicaragua — must be open to all, fair and safe. The international community must help. We will work at human rights problems, not walk away from them.

Second: In response to the challenge of world recession and, in the case of El Salvador, to the unrelenting campaign of economic sabotage by the guerrillas, we will support economic development. By a margin of two to one, our aid is economic now, not military. Seventy-seven cents out of every dollar we will spend in the area this year goes for food, fertilizers, and other essentials for economic growth and development. And our economic program goes beyond traditional aid: The Caribbean Basin Initiative introduced in the House earlier today will provide powerful trade and investment incentives to help these countries achieve self-sustaining economic growth without exporting United States jobs. Our goal must be to focus our immense and growing technology, to enhance health care, agriculture, industry, and to insure that we who inhabit this interdependent region come to know and understand each other better, retaining our diverse identities, respecting our diverse traditions and institutions.

Third: In response to the military challenge from Cuba and Nicaragua, to their deliberate use of force to spread tyranny, we will support the security of the region's threatened nations. We do not view security assistance as an end in itself, but as a shield for democratization, economic development and diplomacy. No amount of reform will bring peace so long as guerrillas believe they will win by force.

No amount of economic help will suffice if guerrilla units can destroy roads and bridges and power stations and crops again and again with impunity. But with better training and material help our neighbors can hold off the guerrillas and give democratic reform time to take root.

Fourth: We will support dialogue and negotiations both among the countries of the region and within each country. The terms and conditions of participation in elections are negotiable. Costa Rica is a shining example of democracy. Honduras has made the move from military rule to democratic government. Guatemala is pledged to the same course. The United States will work toward a political solution in Central America which will serve the interests of the democratic process.

To support these diplomatic goals I offer these assurances:

The United States will support any agreement among Central American countries for the withdrawal — under fully verifiable and reciprocal conditions — of all foreign military and security advisors and troops.

We want to help opposition groups join the political process in all countries

and compete by ballots instead of bullets.

We will support any verifiable reciprocal agreement among Central American countries on the renunciation of support for insurgencies on neighbors' territory.

And, finally, we desire to help Central America end its costly arms race, and will support any verifiable, reciprocal agreements on the non-importation of offensive weapons.

To move us toward these goals more rapidly I am tonight announcing my intention to name an Ambassador-at-Large as my special envoy to Central America. He or she will report to me through the Secretary of State. The Ambassador's responsibilities will be to lend United States support to the efforts of regional governments to bring peace to this troubled area and to work closely with the Congress to assure the fullest possible bipartisan coordination of our policies toward the region.

What I am asking for is prompt Congressional approval for the full reprogramming of funds for key current economic and security programs so that the people of Central America can hold the line against externally supported aggression.

In addition, I am asking for prompt action on the supplemental request in these same areas to carry us through the current fiscal year and for early and favorable Congressional action on my request for fiscal year 1984. And, finally, I am asking that the bipartisan consensus which last year acted on the trade and tax provisions of the Caribbean Basin Initiatives in

the House again take the lead to move this vital proposal to the floor of both chambers. And, as I said before, the greatest share of these requests is targeted toward economic and humanitarian aid, not military.

What the administration is asking for on behalf of freedom in Central America is so small, so minimal, considering what is at stake. The total amount requested for aid to all of Central America in 1984 is about $600 million; that is less than one-tenth of what Americans will spend this year on coin-operated video games.

In summation, I say to you that tonight there can be no question: The national security of all the Americas is at stake in Central America. If we cannot defend ourselves there, we cannot expect to prevail elsewhere. Our credibility would collapse, our alliances would crumble, and the safety of our homeland would be put in jeopardy.

We have a vital interest, a moral duty, and a solemn responsibility.

This is not a partisan issue. It is a question of our meeting our moral responsibility to ourselves, our friends, and our posterity.

It is a duty that falls on all of us — the President, the Congress, and the people. We must perform it together. Who among us would wish to bear responsibility for failing to meet our shared obligation?

Thank you. God bless you and good night.

[Applause, the Members rising.] ∎

gion. Let me share some facts with you about Central America.

Most of the people there are appallingly poor. They can't afford to feed their families when they're hungry. They can't find a doctor for them when they're sick. They live in rural shacks with dirt floors or city slums without plumbing or clean water. The majority can't read or write, many of them don't even know how to count.

It takes all five Spanish-speaking countries of Central America more than a year to produce what this nation does in less than three days. Virtually none of even that meager amount ever reaches the bulk of the people. In short, a very few live in isolated splendor while the very many suffer in shantytown squalor. In country after country, dictatorship or military dominance has stifled democracy and destroyed human rights.

If Central America were not racked with poverty, there would be no revolution. If Central America were not racked with hunger, there would be no revolution. If Central America were not racked with injustices, there would be no revolution. In short, there would be nothing for the Soviets to exploit. But unless those oppressive conditions change, that region will continue to seethe with revolution — with or without the Soviets.

Instead of trying to do something about the factors which breed revolution, this Administration has turned to massive military buildups at a cost of hundreds of millions of dollars. Its policy is ever increasing military assistance, endless military training, even hiring our own paramilitary guerrillas. This is a formula for failure. And it is a proven prescription for picking a loser. The American people know that we have been down this road before — and that it only leads to a dark tunnel of endless intervention.

Tonight the President himself told us that things were not going well in Central America. But for this the President cannot blame Congress. We have given him what he has asked. $700 million in economic and military assistance has been delivered or is on its way to El Salvador since Ronald Reagan came to office . . . all at his request and all with Congressional approval. One of every five Salvadoran soldiers fighting for its government was trained right here in the United States. American soldiers are there now training Salvadoran army units which are employing modern weapons built in American factories.

Now the President asks for an even greater commitment. His requests for El Salvador alone will bring the total aid to that country during his term to more than $1 billion.

One billion dollars to counter a rebel army that, according to all reports, does not exceed 7,000 guerrillas.

That means you are paying $140,000 in heard-earned tax dollars for each one of those guerrillas we are trying to defeat.

While your tax dollars have been pouring into El Salvador, the money skimmed

Democrats Respond to Speech By Reagan on Central America

Following is the text of the Democratic response as prepared for delivery by Sen. Christopher J. Dodd, D-Conn., to President Reagan's April 27 speech on U.S. policy toward Central America.

Good evening. Tonight the President may have brought people to their feet, but I do not think he brought them to their senses. In the months and years that follow this evening, after the applause has faded and the ringing phrases are forgotten, Americans will have to live with the choices we make in this fateful time of decision.

In the past, we as a nation have learned painfully that the truth is never as simple as some would paint it. Charts and statistics can be used or misused to prove any side of a case. And speeches can sound very good without being very right.

So first of all, let me state clearly that on some very important things, all Americans stand in agreement.

We will oppose the establishment of Marxist states in Central America.

We will not accept the creation of Soviet military bases in Central America.

And, we will not tolerate the placement of Soviet offensive missiles in Central America — or anywhere in this hemisphere.

Finally, we are fully prepared to defend our security and the security of the Americas, if necessary, by military means.

All patriotic Americans share these goals. But many of us in Congress, Democrats and Republicans alike, disagree with the President because we believe the means he has chosen will not fulfill them.

Those of us who oppose the President's policy believe that he is mistaken in critical ways. To begin with, we believe the Administration fundamentally misunderstands the causes of the conflict in Central America. We cannot afford to found so important a policy on ignorance — and the painful truth is that many of our highest officials seem to know as little about Central America in 1983 as we knew about Indochina in 1963.

I've lived with the people in this re-

off by that nation's rich is leaving the country. For every dollar we've sent in, more than a dollar has gone out — to numbered accounts in Zurich or to buy stocks on Wall Street. It raises the question of why we should invest in the future of El Salvador when the wealthiest citizens of that country are investing in Swiss banks.

What return have we achieved for all we have spent? The army in El Salvador has been reluctant to fight — and it is led by an Officer Corps working a nine to five shift with weekends off. Land reform has been abandoned. At least 30,000 civilians have been killed and the majority of them have been victims of the government's own security forces. American nuns and labor advisors have been murdered — and the judicial system is so intimidated that it cannot even bring accused murderers to trial.

For those 30,000 murders, confirmed by our own Embassy, there have been fewer than 200 convictions.

American dollars alone cannot buy military victory — that is the lesson of the painful past and of this newest conflict in Central America. If we continue down that road, if we continue to ally ourselves with repression, we will not only deny our own most basic values, we will also find ourselves once again on the losing side. It is folly, pure and simple, to pursue a course which is wrong in principle — in order to wage a conflict which cannot be won.

After 30,000 deaths, after hundreds of millions of dollars, with the ante going up, with no end in sight, with no hope for any real change, the time has come for a different approach. Yes, we are fully prepared to be involved in Central America. But the question is the nature and quality of our involvement. We must offer an alternative policy that can work.

First, we should use the power and influence of the United States to achieve an immediate cessation of hostilities in both El Salvador and Nicaragua. Already in both those countries too many people have died. It is time for the killing to stop.

Second, the United States should use all its power and influence to work for negotiated political settlements in Central America.

In El Salvador, the rebels have offered to negotiate unconditionally. Let us test their sincerity. We certainly have the leverage to move the government to the bargaining table. On his recent trip to that very Catholic region, the Pope lent the moral force of his office to such a step. It is practical and realistic to expect, that if we support it, these talks can get underway. And every major ally of ours in the region — Mexico, Panama, Venezuela, and Colombia — is anxious for such a step to be taken and has offered to make the arrangements.

Those same nations have volunteered to bring Nicaragua into negotiations — and Nicaragua has agreed to talk. Instead, as we know from press accounts, this Administration is conducting a not so secret war inside that country.

No one in this Congress or this country is under the delusion that the Sandinista government is a model democracy or a force for stability. But the insurgents we have supported are the remnants of the old Somoza regime — a regime whose corruption, graft, torture, and despotism made it universally despised in Nicaragua. The Sandinistas may not be winners, but right now we are backing sure losers. We are doing for the Sandinista Marxists what they could not do for themselves. We are weakening the very groups inside Nicaragua which believe in a free and democratic society. And that is the sad irony of the Administration's policy.

Third, we must restore America's role as a source of hope and a force for progress in Central America. We must help governments only if they will help their own people. We must hear the cry for bread, schools, work, and opportunity that comes from campesinos everywhere in this hemisphere. We must make violent revolution preventable by making peaceful revolution possible.

Most important, this approach would permit the United States to move with the tide of history rather than stand against it.

For us, the stakes are diplomatic, political, and strategic. But for the people of El Salvador, life itself is on the line.

I have been to that country and I know about the morticians who travel the streets each morning to collect the bodies of those summarily dispatched the night before by Salvadoran security forces — gangland-style — the victim on bended knee, thumbs wired behind the back, a bullet through the brain.

We recoil at such an image for our association with criminals such as these is not America's tradition. In other, brighter days we have stood for the aspirations of all the people who are part of the Americas. Two centuries ago, our nation raised the light of liberty before the world — and all of this hemisphere looked to us as an example and an inspiration. In this Capitol building, from which I speak tonight, men like Daniel Webster, Henry Clay, and Abraham Lincoln once spoke of an America leading the way to human progress and human rights — and people everywhere listened with hope.

There is no greater or larger ideal than the one which was forged here in the early days of this Republic. That ideal of liberty is our greatest strength as a nation; it is a powerful and peaceful weapon against tyranny of any kind anywhere in this hemisphere. We can take the road of military escalation. But we really don't know what the next step will be, where it will lead or how much it will cost.

This much, however, we do know. It will mean greater violence. It will mean greater bloodshed. It will mean greater hostilities. And, inevitably, the day will come when it will mean a regional conflict in Central America.

When that day comes — when the "dogs of war" are loose in Central America, when the cheering has stopped — we will know where the President's appeal for more American money and a deeper American commitment has taken us. ∎

Reagan Letter on Arms Control Policy

Following is the text of a letter on arms control policy sent by President Reagan to Rep. Norman D. Dicks, D-Wash., on May 11.

May 11, 1983

Dear Norm:

Thank you for your recent letter on our strategic modernization program and its relationship to our arms control proposals. Your letter represents the bipartisan spirit which I believe will help achieve our common goals of ensuring effective deterrent forces and equitable and verifiable arms reductions.

The fundamental U.S. goal in negotiations concerning arms reduction, and especially in our approach to the START negotiations, is to seek agreements that would enhance security and stability by reducing overall force levels while permitting modernization of U.S. forces necessary for a credible deterrent. As you know, the Scowcroft Commission noted that elements of our START proposal are consistent with and supportive of the Commission's findings. I agree wholeheartedly with the essential theme of the Scowcroft Commission's approach to arms control: the attainment of stability at the lowest possible level of forces.

The Scowcroft Commission's recommendations on modernization and arms control are integrally related. Our action with respect to these recommendations must be equally comprehensive. That is why I am now conducting a review of our START proposal with the intention of developing such modifications as are necessary to reflect the Commission's approach, which I share. To cite just one example, the Commission report recommended that the proposed limit on deployed ballistic missiles currently contained in the U.S. START position be reassessed since it is not compatible with a desirable evolution toward small, single-warhead ICBMs. There are a number of alternative approaches available to integrate this and the

other Commission recommendations into our approach to arms reductions. As modifications are made to our START proposal, I will continue to seek stability at the lowest possible level of forces.

The planned deployment of the Peacekeeper missile as proposed by my Administration is compatible with the long-term objective of the Scowcroft Commission Report. The Peacekeeper missile, deployed in a mix with small single-warhead ICBMs, would permit us to maintain the effectiveness of our deterrent and enhance stability while serving as a hedge against Soviet temptation to exploit their present advantage.

At the same time, let me emphasize that we do not seek a first strike capability. To this end, we have constrained the number of Peacekeeper missiles that we plan to deploy to the minimum number needed to assure the effectiveness of our deterrent and no more. Our task, of course, would be much easier if the Soviets would agree to work with us to reduce the ratio of accurate warheads to missile silos. Clearly, consistent with our national security requirements, the overall level of Peacekeeper deployment will be influenced by Soviet strategic programs and arms reductions agreements.

In addition, I fully recognize the central role that the small, single-warhead ICBM plays in the overall modernization program recommended by the Scowcroft Commission Report. We will promptly undertake a major effort to bring the proposal of a small, single-warhead ICBM to fru-

ition on a high priority basis.

In considering the implementation of the essential ICBM modernization program, the Scowcroft Commission also recognized that a series of decisions involving both the Executive Branch and the Congress would be necessary in the months ahead in order to determine the future shape of our ICBM force. Further, it noted that not all of these decisions can or should be made in 1983. The deliberate approach to decision making proposed by a number of members of Congress is fully in keeping with the intent of the Scowcroft Commission Report. I fully recognize that a lasting consensus on such an important issue must be built up carefully and I intend to take the time necessary to forge that lasting consensus.

I urge all concerned, however, to keep in mind that if we draw out critical elements of the decision-making process unnecessarily, we encourage the Soviets to delay in negotiations while continuing apace in their own weapons modernization programs. To avoid this, I am seeking a clear show of support from Congress to signal U.S. resolve. A case in point is the clear necessity of approving funds promptly to procure Peacekeeper missiles. Working together, this should be achievable while simultaneously meeting our mutual desire to deal with deployment issues, whenever possible, in a careful, deliberate manner.

Finally, I want to stress the extraordinary contribution made by the Scowcroft Commission. It provided an opportunity

for nonpartisan analysis of an exceptionally difficult issue as a prelude to obtaining necessary bipartisan support for critically needed modernization of our strategic forces. While not prescribing the details or the timing, the Commission report suggested certain directions that the continued evolution of our complementary strategy for arms reduction could take. Over the short term, follow-on arrangements involving members of the Commission, as well as close coordination with the Congress, will be extremely helpful both technically and politically in thinking through this evolution. However, we are giving careful consideration to determining which follow-on arrangements best meet our common objectives.

In this regard, I do see merit in a panel with bipartisan composition and with staggered terms of membership to provide advice and continuity in this area. I will work with the Congress, building upon the experience of the Scowcroft Commission, to strengthen and supplement our consultative and advisory processes to assure a lasting, national, bipartisan consensus concerning arms control initiatives — a consensus which will deserve to be sustained from one Administration to the next.

Sincerely,
RONALD REAGAN

The Honorable Norman D. Dicks
House of Representatives
Washington, D.C. 20515 ∎

Reagan Statement on Nuclear Arms Talks

Following are excerpts from the White House prepared text of President Reagan's June 8 statement on the Strategic Arms Reductions Talks and the recommendations of the Scowcroft commission.

. . . Before discussing [specific negotiating changes], I would like to comment on what I see as very positive developments taking place both here and abroad. I am happy to say that today there is a growing sense that we are making progress. I just met in Williamsburg with the leaders of the major industrialized nations, and I was struck there not only by the facts and figures pointing toward economic recovery, but also by a spirit of optimism and cooperation which was remarkable. This same spirit is visible in our discussions of security issues. In NATO, as in our other alliances, there is a new feeling of partnership. The Atlantic Alliance is alive and well, and its close consultations are a source of strength and participation for each of its members.

At least as important, and very gratify-

ing to me, is the new spirit of bipartisanship on national security issues which is increasingly evident in both Houses of Congress. When I established the Scowcroft Commission I could not then foresee the impact that this outstanding panel would have. Clearly, the Commission's work, which went beyond MX to address critical issues of deterrence and arms control, has become a major stimulus to the rethinking of national policy. The Commission's report challenged some favorite assumptions, and called for changes in our strategic planning. At the same time, it expressed support for my Administration's most heartfelt objectives in arms control: deep reductions, modernization for stability's sake, and the elimination of the first-strike threat.

I have pledged to Congress my full support for the Scowcroft Commission recommendations and my intention to incorporate them in our START proposal. So that we can continue to benefit from the wisdom of its counsel, I intend to ask the Commission to continue to serve. Its bipartisan membership will thus be able to provide timely advice to me both with respect to the adoption of its proposals into our

defense program and our arms control policies. . . .

. . . Three full rounds of negotiations on START are now behind us. It is my judgment that these rounds have been useful and have permitted us to cover necessary ground. However, due largely to Soviet intransigence, we have not yet made meaningful progress on the central issues.

I remain firmly committed to take whatever steps are necessary to increase the likelihood of real, substantive progress towards an agreement involving significant reductions in U.S. and Soviet strategic nuclear arsenals — and in the national security interests of both sides. Above all, our goal is to maintain a stable nuclear balance in order to reduce the risk of war. Our efforts in the START negotiations must be guided by that objective.

The report of the Scowcroft Commission offers us a new opportunity for progress. It has provided a consistent and coherent framework to guide our thinking about the fundamental elements of our national security policy — deterrence, defense and arms control. But, more than that, it has provided the basis for renewed, bipartisan support for that policy.

To capitalize on this critical opportunity and on the basis of the widest possible range of advice, I have directed new steps toward progress in achieving real arms reductions at the START negotiations. The purpose of this guidance, provided to Ambassador Ed Rowny, our Chief START Negotiator, is to adjust the U.S. START position to bring it into line with the Scowcroft Commission's recommendations and to provide additional flexibility to our negotiators in pursuing our basic goals.

Although we have put forth a comprehensive proposal on limiting strategic ballistic missiles and bombers, our primary aim in the START negotiations has been, and continues to be, to reduce the threat posed by the most destabilizing systems, namely ballistic missiles. To achieve that aim, measures that constrain the number and destructive capability and potential of ballistic missile warheads are essential. Our proposed limit of 5,000 total ballistic missile warheads — a reduction by one-third of the current level — remains the central element of the U.S. START position.

The U.S. START position tabled in previous negotiating rounds includes another constraint. It would have limited each side to no more than 850 deployed ballistic missiles. This measure was never viewed as being as useful or important a constraint as the limit on total ballistic missile warheads. The Scowcroft Commission report specifically suggested that it should be reassessed since it could constrain the evolution we seek toward small, single-warhead ICBM's.

Acting upon the Scowcroft Commission's recommendation, I have now directed our negotiators to adjust our position on deployed ballistic missiles by relaxing our current proposal for an 850 deployed ballistic missile limit.

At the same time, the U.S. remains firm on the point that the destructive capability and potential of ballistic missiles must be addressed in START. Our current position includes a network of constraints designed to lead to a more stable strategic balance at reduced force levels — while addressing the destructive potential of missiles. The Soviets and others have complained that these constraints are designed to dictate Soviet force structure according to U.S. standards. This is not the case. We believe, as does the Scowcroft Commission, that stability can be increased by limitations on the destructive capability and potential of ballistic missiles. As a consequence, we will continue to propose such constraints which indirectly get to the throw weight problem while making clear to the Soviets our readiness to deal directly with the corresponding destructive capability if they prefer.

There may be more than one way to achieve our objective of greater stability at reduced levels of arms. So I have instructed Ambassador Rowny to make clear to the Soviet delegation our commitment to our fundamental objectives, but I have also given him the flexibility to explore all ap-

propriate avenues for meeting our goals. I sincerely hope that the Soviet Union will respond with corresponding flexibility.

Finally, high-priority work is continuing on how the mutual and guaranteed build-down concept proposed by several United States Senators can be applied in our quest for significant and stabilizing strategic arms reductions.

These actions reflect a bipartisan consensus on arms control, and new flexibility in the negotiations — steps to be viewed seriously by the Soviets and all others who have a stake in world peace. To the leaders of the Soviet Union, I urge that this new opportunity not be lost. To America's friends and allies around the world, I say that your steadfast support for the goals of both deterrence and arms control is essential in the future. To Congress and to the American people, I say let us continue to work together in a bipartisan spirit so that these days will be spoken of in the future as the time when America turned a corner.

Let us put our differences behind us. Let us demonstrate measured flexibility in our approach, while remaining strong in our determination to reach our objectives of arms reductions, stability, and security. Let us be leaders in the cause of peace. ∎

Tax Leasing Plan Veto Message

Following is White House text of President Reagan's June 17 message accompanying his veto of S 973, to make technical amendments to the Indian Self-Determination and Education Assistance Act and other acts and to allow a school to transfer to taxable investors tax benefits attributable to a building that it refurbished with federal funds. It was Reagan's second veto of a public bill during the 98th Congress.

TO THE SENATE OF
THE UNITED STATES:

I am returning, without my approval, S. 973, "an Act to make technical amendments to the Indian Self-Determination and Education Assistance Act and other Acts." I have no objections to these technical amendments.

However, section 5 of the bill, added by an amendment on the Senate floor, would allow a particular school to transfer to taxable investors tax benefits attributable to a building that it refurbished with Federal funds. Without this legislation, the proposed transaction would result in the school being required to repay the Federal funds used to refurbish the building.

Recently there has been a great deal of concern about the sale of tax benefits by tax-exempt entities through leasing transactions. Leasing transactions similar to the one contemplated by this legislation present tremendous potential for abuse and could result in billions of dollars of revenue loss to the Federal Government. The transaction that this legislation would condone would permit a school that has already received tax deductible contributions and Federal grant money to sell certain tax benefits to outside investors. This case is particularly offensive in that the tax benefits being sold are attributable to property that was paid for with Federal grant money. In addition to receiving money for selling tax benefits, the school, as a tax-exempt entity, would be able to invest the proceeds of the sale and receive the income from such investment tax-free.

The propriety of leasing transactions involving the sale by tax-exempt organizations of tax benefits needs to be scrutinized very carefully. Where the tax benefits being sold are attributable to expenditures of Federal funds, the transaction becomes totally unjustifiable. We cannot condone the sale by a tax-exempt entity of tax benefits produced through the use of Federal funds.

As I have noted, the Indian-related amendments contained in this bill are not objectionable. Accordingly, I urge the Congress to reenact sections 1-4 of S. 973 without delay.

RONALD REAGAN

The White House,
June 17, 1983   ∎

Farm Announcements Veto

Following is the White House text of President Reagan's Aug. 12 message accompanying his veto of HR 3564, to require earlier announcements of the terms of federal farm programs. It was Reagan's third veto of a public bill during the 98th Congress.

TO THE HOUSE OF
REPRESENTATIVES:

I am returning herewith without my approval H.R. 3564, "To require the Secretary of Agriculture to make an earlier announcement of the 1984 crop feed grain program and of the 1985 crop wheat and feed grain programs."

H.R. 3564 directs the Secretary of Ag-

riculture to announce the 1984 and 1985 feed grain programs no later than September 30 of the preceding year and to announce the 1985 wheat program no later than July 1, 1984. Current law sets November 15 as the announcement date for feed grains; the wheat program announcement date in current law is August 15. Thus, in each case the announcements would have to be made approximately six weeks earlier than the current law now requires.

The main purpose of acreage adjustment programs is to assist producers in adjusting supplies to meet demand. When projecting the supply/demand situation for the next crop year, it is essential to have the best possible information about the current crop year, while giving due consideration to producers' planning needs. Sound estimates of production as well as timely announcements are a vital component for designing successful programs. Good program design ultimately serves the best interests of producers, consumers, and taxpayers.

The Administration is sympathetic to the need for making acreage adjustment program announcements as early as possible. When conditions warrant, the Secretary of Agriculture will continue the ongoing practice of announcing commodity programs before the statutory deadlines. However, when the appropriate program decision is not obvious, it is essential that the Secretary retain the discretion to announce wheat as late as August 15 and feed grains as late as November 15.

This flexibility will enable the Secretary to respond quickly to unforeseen circumstances, such as drought or early frost. Without this flexibility, the mandate in H.R. 3564 could either exacerbate a surplus supply situation and needlessly increase budget outlays by substantial amounts or unnecessarily create a grain shortage and cause food prices to increase sharply.

RONALD REAGAN

The White House,
August 12, 1983 ∎

Under these circumstances, I must reluctantly veto this bill.

RONALD REAGAN

The White House,
August 13, 1983 ∎

Milk Price Support Program Veto Message

Following is the White House text of President Reagan's Aug. 23 message accompanying his veto of S J Res 149, to temporarily suspend the authority of the secretary of agriculture to impose a second 50 cents per hundredweight deduction from the proceeds of sale of all milk marketed commercially in the United States. It was President Reagan's fifth veto of a public bill during the 98th Congress.

TO THE SENATE OF
THE UNITED STATES:

I am returning herewith without my approval S.J. Res. 149, "To temporarily suspend the authority of the Secretary of Agriculture, under the milk price support program, to impose a second 50 cents per hundredweight deduction from the proceeds of sale of all milk marketed commercially in the United States."

Current law allows the Secretary to deduct 50 cents per hundredweight from the proceeds of sale of all milk marketed, if the Commodity Credit Corporation (CCC) purchases of surplus milk are expected to exceed 5 billion pounds. This deduction program became effective April 16, 1983. Current law also authorizes the Secretary to deduct another 50 cents per hundredweight if CCC purchases of surplus milk are expected to exceed 7.5 billion pounds. Dairy farmers who reduce their milk production according to Department of Agriculture guidelines will be entitled to refunds of this second 50 cents.

This second deduction and the refund program are scheduled to go into effect on September 1 and are expected to produce net receipts by CCC of about $60 million during September. Even with both deductions in effect, the Department of Agriculture projects that CCC purchases of milk will still exceed 16 billion pounds for the current marketing year at a net cost to taxpayers of $2.4 billion.

I cannot support S.J. Res. 149, as it would reduce by $60 million the amount of funds available to be used to defray the cost of the milk price support program and would reduce the desired downward effect upon milk production. Without the added downward pressure of the second 50-cent deduction there will be less incentive to decrease milk production.

Desegregation Funds Veto

Following is the White House text of President Reagan's Aug. 13 message accompanying his veto of H J Res 338, to provide funds to assist the Chicago school system in complying with a desegregation consent decree. It was Reagan's fourth veto of a public bill during the 98th Congress.

TO THE HOUSE OF
REPRESENTATIVES:

I am returning herewith without my approval H.J. Res. 338. This bill was originally included in the 1983 Supplemental Appropriation bill, which I recently signed (P.L. 98-63), but was separately passed because it was inadvertently omitted from the enrolled version of that bill. Normally such bills passed as a result of enrollment errors are signed as a matter of course. I am taking this unusual action because of the extraordinarily important constitutional principles raised by this particular measure.

H.J. Res. 338 appropriates $20 million for the purpose of providing a source of funds from which the Secretary of Education could comply with the June 30, 1983 order issued in *United States v. Board of Education of the City of Chicago*, No. 80C5124 (N.D. Ill.), if the order is upheld on appeal. The case was brought by the United States to desegregate the Chicago school system. The court ordered the United States to provide a minimum of $14.6 million and froze more than $250 million appropriated by Congress for other educational programs in order to meet expenses incurred by the Chicago Board of Education in carrying out its constitutional responsibilities to desegregate its school

system. The court enjoined the Department of Education from providing grants to hundreds of other worthy grantees under several programs of national significance, including grants intended to facilitate local desegregation efforts and others intended to follow up on the report of the National Commission on Excellence in Education.

I well understand the reasons motivating the Congress to pass this legislation. Under the order of the court in Chicago, other education programs throughout the country were denied the funding they rightfully expected to receive. The Chicago court's ostensible purpose in issuing this order was to provide a source of funds for the implementation of its decree. Congress hoped by the passage of this legislation to induce the court to release the funds that were impounded by the court. But I believe that the better course is to seek swift reversal of the district court's order.

This veto is not premised on a desire to protect the Federal budget. It is based upon my conviction that the Constitution and its process of separated powers and checks and balances does not permit the judiciary to determine spending priorities or to reallocate funds appropriated by Congress. Those are exclusively the functions of the Legislative and Executive branches, and the use of judicial decrees to assume such powers raises problems of profound constitutional significance.

If finally ordered to pay additional funds to the Board of Education of the City of Chicago, the Federal government will of course do so. It is inappropriate, however, for a court to withhold millions of dollars worth of unrelated and necessary education programs to enforce its orders.

In addition, if I signed S.J. Res. 149, there would be even greater confusion on the part of milk producers. The first deduction has been the subject of extensive litigation. Since Secretary Block has announced that the second deduction and the refund program will begin on September 1, a delay of one month would only add to the confusion and make planning by producers even more difficult.

Implementation of the deduction has already been delayed considerably. As a result, the cost savings contemplated when this provision was enacted have not materialized, further worsening the Federal deficit.

The annual cost of the dairy price support program is now over $2 billion and will continue to grow unless something is done. We cannot continue to absorb these enormous costs. The Administration's position last year, which the Congress failed to accept, called for increased flexibility to set support levels that would facilitate a more favorable supply and demand balance and reduce Federal outlays. We remain committed to an economically sound dairy industry with adequate supplies of milk and dairy products for consumers, and we will continue to work with the Congress to achieve that end. However, until Congress can act on a mutually acceptable dairy program that accomplishes the objectives stated above, we must continue to exercise without further delay what authority we have to deal with our dairy problem.

RONALD REAGAN

The White House,
August 23, 1983

Reagan Signs Lebanon Resolution Into Law

Following is the White House text of remarks made Oct. 12 by President Reagan on the signing into law of H J Res 159 (PL 98-119), to authorize the president to keep U.S. Marines in Lebanon for up to 18 months as part of a multinational peacekeeping force.

I am pleased to sign into law today S.J. Res. 159, the Multinational Force in Lebanon Resolution. This Resolution provides important support for the United States presence and policies in Lebanon, and facilitates the pursuit of United States interests in that region on the bipartisan basis that has been the traditional hallmark of American foreign policy. In my view, the participation and support of the Congress are exceedingly important on matters of such fundamental importance to our national security interests, particularly where United States Armed Forces have been deployed in support of our policy objectives abroad. I am grateful to those of both political parties who joined in the expression of resolve reflected by the enactment of this Resolution, and especially to the bipartisan leadership of Senate Majority Leader Baker, House Speaker O'Neill, House Foreign Affairs Committee Chairman Zablocki and Senate Foreign Relations Committee Chairman Percy.

The text of this Resolution states a number of congressional findings, determinations, and assertions on certain matters. It is, of course, entirely appropriate for Congress to express its views on these subjects in this manner. However, I do not necessarily join in or agree with some of these expressions. For example, with regard to the congressional determination that the requirements of section 4(a)(1) of the War Powers Resolution became operative on August 29, 1983, I would note that the initiation of isolated or infrequent acts of violence against United States Armed Forces does not necessarily constitute actual or imminent involvement in hostilities, even if casualties to those forces result. I think it reasonable to recognize the inherent risk and imprudence of setting any precise formula for making such determinations.

However, complete accord on such debatable issues is less important than the process that has taken place and the bipartisan policy goals that have been articulated. We must not let disagreements on interpretation or issues of institutional powers prevent us from expressing our mutual goals to the citizens of our Nation and the world. I therefore sign this Resolution in full support of its policies, but with reservations about some of the specific congressional expressions.

There have been historic differences between the Legislative and Executive Branches of government with respect to the wisdom and constitutionality of section 5(b) of the War Powers Resolution. That section purports to require termination of the use of United States Armed Forces in actual hostilities or situations in which imminent involvement in hostilities is clearly indicated by the circumstances unless Congress, within sixty days, enacts a specific authorization for that use or otherwise extends the sixty-day period. In light of these historic differences, I would like to emphasize my view that the imposition of such arbitrary and inflexible deadlines creates unwise limitations on presidential authority to deploy United States Forces in the interests of United States national security. For example, such deadlines can undermine foreign policy judgments, adversely affect our ability to deploy United States Armed Forces in support of these judgments, and encourage hostile elements to maximize United States casualties in connection with such deployments.

I believe it is, therefore, important for me to state, in signing this Resolution, that I do not and cannot cede any of the authority vested in me under the Constitution as President and as Commander-in-Chief of the United States Armed Forces. Nor should my signing be viewed as any acknowledgment that the President's constitutional authority can be impermissibly infringed by statute, that congressional authorization would be required if and when the period specified in section 5(b) of the War Powers Resolution might be deemed to have been triggered and the period had expired, or that section 6 of the Multinational Force in Lebanon Resolution may be interpreted to revise the President's constitutional authority to deploy United States Armed Forces. Let me underscore, however, that any differences we may have over institutional prerogatives will in no way diminish my intention to proceed in the manner outlined in my letter of September 27, 1983, to achieve the important bipartisan goals reflected in this Resolution.

Indeed, I am convinced that congressional support for the continued participation of United States Forces alongside those of France, Italy, and the United Kingdom helped bring about the recent cease-fire and the start of the reconciliation process in Lebanon. The security and the stability of the Beirut area and the successful process of national reconciliation are essential to the achievement of United States policy objectives in Lebanon, as stated in the Resolution. It is my fervent hope and belief that this reaffirmation of the support of the Executive and Legislative Branches for the Government of Lebanon and for our partners in the Multinational Force will promote a lasting peace and hasten the return home of our Armed Forces.

Reagan Letter

Following is the White House text of President Reagan's Sept. 27 letter to House Speaker Thomas P. O'Neill Jr., D-Mass.

Dear Mr. Speaker:

I know you were as gratified as I with Sunday's announcement of a cease fire in Lebanon. While there were many things that contributed to the cease fire, it is my belief that your agreement to advance the compromise resolution on war powers — and the favorable action by the Foreign

Affairs and Foreign Relations Committees — were particularly important. At a crucial point, your agreement and the supporting committee actions expressed a commitment to bipartisanship in U.S. foreign policy. Please accept my thanks.

Let me also take this opportunity to clarify an issue with respect to the interpretation of the compromise resolution. The compromise resolution refers to the requirements of section 4(a) of the Lebanon Emergency Assistance Act; I gather that a question has arisen as to the Executive Branch's understanding and intention in this regard. My understanding and intent remain exactly as they were when I signed the Lebanon Emergency Assistance Act: It would be my intention to seek Congressional authorization — as contemplated by the Act — if circumstances require any substantial expansion in the number or role of U.S. armed forces in Lebanon.

In addition, regarding the Administration's intentions with respect to the 18-month time period, I can assure you that if our forces are needed in Lebanon beyond the 18-month period, it would be my intention to work together with the Congress with a view toward taking action on mutually acceptable terms.

Again let me thank you for your support for the compromise agreement. I believe its prompt enactment will only further improve the chances for the stable peace we seek in Lebanon.

Sincerely,

/s/ Ron ∎

Resolution Text

Following is the Congressional Record *text of S J Res 159, as cleared by Congress Sept. 29.*

Resolved by the Senate and House of Representatives of the United States of America in Congress assembled,

SHORT TITLE

SECTION 1. This joint resolution may be cited as the "Multinational Force in Lebanon Resolution."

FINDINGS AND PURPOSE

Sec. 2. (a) The Congress finds that

(1) the removal of all foreign forces from Lebanon is an essential United States foreign policy objective in the Middle East;

(2) in order to restore full control by the Government of Lebanon over its own territory, the United States is currently participating in the multinational peacekeeping force (hereafter in this resolution referred to as the "Multinational Force in Lebanon") which was established in accordance with the exchange of letters between the Governments of the United States and Lebanon dated September 25, 1982;

(3) the Multinational Force in Lebanon better enables the Government of Lebanon to establish its unity, independence, and territorial integrity;

(4) progress toward national political reconciliation in Lebanon is necessary; and

(5) United States Armed Forces participating in the Multinational Force in Lebanon are now in hostilities requiring authorization of their continued presence under the War Powers Resolution.

(b) The Congress determines that the requirements of section 4(a)(1) of the War Powers Resolution became operative on August 29, 1963. Consistent with section 5(b) of the War Powers Resolution, the purpose of this joint resolution is to authorize the continued participation of United States Armed Forces in the Multinational Force in Lebanon.

(c) The Congress intends this joint resolution to constitute the necessary specific statutory authorization under the War Powers Resolution for continued participation by United States Armed Forces in the Multinational Force in Lebanon.

AUTHORIZATION FOR CONTINUED PARTICIPATION OF UNITED STATES ARMED FORCES IN THE MULTI-NATIONAL FORCE IN LEBANON

SEC. 3. The President is authorized, for purposes of section 5(b) of the War Powers Resolution, to continue participation by United States Armed Forces in the Multinational Force in Lebanon, subject to the provisions of section 6 of this joint resolution. Such participation shall be limited to performance of the functions, and shall be subject to the limitations, specified in the agreement establishing the Multinational Force in Lebanon as set forth in the exchange of letters between the Governments of the United States and Lebanon dated September 25, 1982, except that this shall not preclude such protective measures as may be necessary to ensure the safety of the Multinational Force in Lebanon.

REPORTS TO THE CONGRESS

SEC. 4. As required by section 4(c) of the War Powers Resolution, the President shall report periodically to the Congress with respect to the situation in Lebanon, but in no event shall he report less often than once every three months. In addition to providing the information required by that section on the status, scope, and duration of hostilities involving United States Armed Forces, such reports shall describe in detail —

(1) the activities being performed by the Multinational Force in Lebanon;

(2) the present composition of the Multinational Force in Lebanon, including a description of the responsibilities and deployment of the armed forces of each participating country;

(3) the results of efforts to reduce and eventually eliminate the Multinational Force in Lebanon;

(4) how continued United States participation in the Multinational Force in Lebanon is advancing United States foreign policy interests in the Middle East; and

(5) what progress has occurred toward national political reconciliation among all Lebanese groups.

STATEMENTS OF POLICY

SEC. 5. (a) The Congress declares that the participation of the armed forces of other countries in the Multinational Force in Lebanon is essential to maintain the international character of the peacekeeping function in Lebanon.

(b) The Congress believes that it should continue to be the policy of the United States to promote continuing discussions with Israel, Syria, and Lebanon with the objective of bringing about the withdrawal of all foreign troops from Lebanon and establishing an environment which will permit the Lebanese Armed Forces to carry out their responsibilities in the Beirut area.

(c) It is the sense of the Congress that, not later than one year after the date of enactment of this joint resolution and at least once a year thereafter, the United States should discuss with the other members of the Security Council of the United Nations the establishment of a United Nations peacekeeping force to assume the responsibilities of the Multinational Force in Lebanon. An analysis of the implications of the response to such discussions for the continuation of the Multinational Force in Lebanon shall be included in the reports required under paragraph (3) of section 4 of this resolution.

DURATION OF AUTHORIZATION FOR UNITED STATES PARTICIPATION IN THE MULTINATIONAL FORCE IN LEBANON

SEC. 6. The participation of United States Armed Forces in the Multinational Force in Lebanon shall be authorized for purposes of the War Powers Resolution until the end of the eighteen-month period beginning on the date of enactment of this resolution unless the Congress extends such authorization, except that such authorization shall terminate sooner upon the occurrence of any one of the following:

(1) the withdrawal of all foreign forces from Lebanon, unless the President determines and certifies to the Congress that continued United States Armed Forces participation in the Multinational Force in Lebanon is required after such withdrawal in order to accomplish the purposes specified in the September 25, 1982, exchange of letters providing for the establishment of the Multinational Force in Lebanon; or

(2) the assumption by the United Nations or the Government of Lebanon of the responsibilities of the Multinational Force in Lebanon;

(3) the implementation of other effective security arrangements in the area; or

(4) the withdrawal of all other countries from participation in the Multinational Force in Lebanon.

INTERPRETATION OF
THIS RESOLUTION

SEC. 7. (a) Nothing in this joint resolution shall preclude the President from withdrawing United States Armed Forces participation in the Multinational Force in Lebanon if circumstances warrant, and nothing in this joint resolution shall preclude the Congress by joint resolution from directing such a withdrawal.

(b) Nothing in this joint resolution modifies, limits, or supersedes any provision of the War Powers Resolution or the requirement of section 4(a) of the Lebanon Emergency Assistance Act of 1983, relating to congressional authorization for any substantial expansion in the number or role of United States Armed Forces in Lebanon.

CONGRESSIONAL
PRIORITY PROCEDURES
FOR AMENDMENTS

SEC. 8. (a) Any joint resolution or bill introduced to amend or repeal this Act shall be referred to the Committee on Foreign Affairs of the House of Representatives or the Committee on Foreign Relations of the Senate, as the case may be. Such joint resolution or bill shall be considered by such committee within fifteen calendar days and may be reported out, together with its recommendations, unless such House shall otherwise determine pursuant to its rules.

(b) Any joint resolution or bill so reported shall become the pending business of the House in question (in the case of the Senate the time for debate shall be equally divided between the proponents and the opponents) and shall be voted on within three calendar days thereafter, unless such House shall otherwise determine by the yeas and nays.

(c) Such a joint resolution or bill passed by one House shall be referred to the committee of the other House named in subsection (1) and shall be reported out by such committee together with its recommendations within fifteen calendar days and shall thereupon become the pending business of such House and shall be voted upon within three calendar days, unless such House shall otherwise determine by the yeas and nays.

(d) In the case of any disagreement between the two Houses of Congress with respect to a joint resolution or bill passed by both Houses, conferees shall be promptly appointed and the committee of conference shall make and file a report with respect to such joint resolution within six calendar days after the legislation is referred to the committee of conference. Notwithstanding any rule in either House concerning the printing of conference reports in the *Record* or concerning any delay in the consideration of such reports, such report shall be acted on by both Houses not later than six calendar days after the conference report is filed. In the event the conferees are unable to agree within forty-eight hours, they shall report back to their respective Houses in disagreement. ∎

Oregon Lands Bill Veto

Following is the Congressional Record text of President Reagan's Oct. 19 message accompanying his veto of HR 1062, to authorize the secretary of the interior to convey certain land in Lane County, Oregon. It was President Reagan's sixth veto of a public bill during the 98th Congress.

TO THE HOUSE OF
REPRESENTATIVES:

I am returning herewith, without my approval, H.R. 1062, a bill "To authorize the Secretary of the Interior to convey, without consideration, certain lands in Lane County, Oregon."

H.R. 1062 would authorize the Secretary of the Interior to convey to any person, without consideration, the real property they claim to have been deprived of in Lane County, Oregon, as a result of a particular Bureau of Land Management (BLM) resurvey. All right, title, and interest of the United States to such property could be conveyed if an application, accompanied by such proof of title, description of land, and other information as the Secretary of the Interior may require, is received by the Secretary within five years after enactment of the bill.

The title defects affecting the beneficiaries of this legislation were caused by the reliance of the developers and subsequent purchasers of this tract on an inaccurate private survey — not by any act of the United States. To authorize the United States to convey public lands to persons who rely on erroneous private surveys is not in the pubic interest. Moreover, enactment of this legislation would create a clearly undesirable precedent, encouraging other persons who do not verify the validity of their title to assert claims for conveyance, at no charge, of the Federal lands on which they are encroaching. Without doubt, these claims would hinder effective public land management.

Moreover, administrative procedures exist under conditions set out in section 203 of the Federal Land Policy and Management Act whereby the purposes of this legislation could be accomplished through a conveyance of the property at fair market value.

H.R. 1062 is clearly inconsistent with this policy of requiring fair market value for conveyance of Federal lands. There was no error in the survey by the United States. Instead, the problem arose because of an improper private survey. There is, therefore, no justification for legislating a conveyance of this tract without payment of fair market value or for bypassing administrative procedures that already exist for the conveyance of public lands in appropriate cases.

For these reasons, I have withheld my approval of H.R. 1062.

RONALD REAGAN

The White House,
October 19, 1983 ∎

Reagan Signs Bill Creating New Civil Rights Commission

Following is the White House text of statements by President Reagan and the Department of Justice issued Nov. 30 on the signing into law of HR 2230, reconstituting the Commission on Civil Rights and extending it for six years. The president and Congress each will appoint four members, who can be removed only for cause.

I have signed today H.R. 2230, establishing a new Commission on Civil Rights. I believe that the birth of this Commission can serve as another milestone in our long struggle as a nation to assure that individuals are judged on the basis of their abilities, irrespective of race, sex, color, national origin or handicap.

I take this opportunity to reaffirm this Administration's commitment to these ideals, which the civil rights laws of the United States were designed to implement and which it will be the central mission of this Commission to articulate and defend.

The bill I have signed today is, of course, a product of negotiation and compromise. While, as noted, I am pleased that the Commission has been recreated so that it may continue the missions assigned to it, the Department of Justice has raised concerns as to the constitutional implications of certain provisions of this legislation. I have appended a recitation of these reservations.

During the preceding six months there has been considerable debate on the past and the future of the Commission on Civil Rights. But all seem to agree that the Commission's best and most productive years were its earlier ones. I believe that it is no coincidence that those years were characterized by open debate and a devotion to the principle of equal treatment under the law. With the bill I have signed today, and

the quality of appointments that can be made to the Commission, there is cause for confidence that the Commission's best years are yet to come.

Justice Department Statement

Under the terms of H.R. 2230, four members of the Commission will be appointed by the President, two members by the President pro tempore of the Senate, and two members by the Speaker of the House of Representatives. The Commission itself is not placed clearly within any of the three branches of government created by the United States Constitution, and restrictions have been placed upon the power of the President to remove members of the Commission.

Agencies which are inconsistent with the tripartite system of government established by the Framers of our Constitution should not be created. Equally unacceptable are proposals which impermissibly dilute the powers of the President to appoint and remove Officers of the United States. The Civil Rights Commission is, however, unique in form and function and should therefore not become a precedent for the creation of similar agencies in the future.

The new appointment procedure created by the Congress has effectively imposed constitutional limitations on the duties that the Commission may perform. The basic purpose of the old Commission on Civil Rights — to investigate, study, appraise and report on discrimination — would be maintained, and most of its current authorities would remain intact. However, because half of the members of the Commission will be appointed by the Congress, the Constitution does not permit the Commission to exercise responsibilities that may be performed only by "Officers of the United States" who are appointed in accordance with the Appointments Clause of the United States Constitution (Article II, Section 2, clause 2). Therefore, it should be clear that although the Commission will continue to perform investigative and informative functions, it may not exercise enforcement, regulatory, or other Executive responsibilities that may be performed only by Officers of the United States. ∎

PUBLIC LAWS

Public Laws, 98th Congress, 1st Session

PL 98-1 (S 61) Designate the "Nancy Hanks Center" in Washington, D.C., to commemorate the accomplishments of Nancy Hanks in the fields of government and culture. Introduced by STAFFORD, R-Vt., Jan. 26, 1983. Senate Environment and Public Works reported Jan. 26. Senate passed Jan. 27. House passed Feb. 2. President signed Feb. 5, 1983.

PL 98-2 (H J Res 60) Designate Feb. 16, 1983, as "Lithuanian Independence Day." Introduced by RUSSO, D-Ill., Jan. 6, 1983. House Post Office and Civil Service discharged. House passed Feb. 2. Senate passed Feb. 3. President signed Feb. 16, 1983.

PL 98-3 (S J Res 37) Provide that the week containing March 8, 1983, 1984 and 1985, shall be designated as "Women's History Week." Introduced by HATCH, R-Utah, Feb. 17, 1983. Senate Judiciary reported Feb. 28. Senate passed March 2. House Post Office and Civil Service discharged. House passed March 3. President signed March 8, 1983.

PL 98-4 (HR 1296) Amend the Internal Revenue Code of 1954 relating to the treatment for income and estate tax purposes of commodities received under 1983 payment-in-kind programs. Introduced by HARKIN, D-Iowa, Feb. 7, 1983. House Ways and Means reported March 2 (H Rept 98-14). House passed, under suspension of the rules, March 8. Senate passed, amended, March 8. House agreed to Senate amendment with an amendment March 9. Senate agreed to House amendment March 10. President signed March 11, 1983.

PL 98-5 (S J Res 15) Designate the month of March 1983 as "National Eye Donor Month." Introduced by MOYNIHAN, D-N.Y., Jan. 26, 1983. Senate Judiciary reported Feb. 22. Senate passed Feb. 24. House Post Office and Civil Service discharged. House passed March 3. President signed March 11, 1983.

PL 98-6 (HR 1572) Repeal section 311 of the Federal Transportation Act of 1982. Introduced by LEVITAS, D-Ga., Feb. 22, 1983. House Public Works and Transportation discharged. House passed Feb. 24. Senate passed March 2. President signed March 16, 1983.

PL 98-7 (S J Res 21) Designate the month of April 1983 as "National Child Abuse Prevention Month." Introduced by DeCONCINI, D-Ariz., Jan. 26, 1983. Senate Judiciary reported Feb. 22. Senate passed Feb. 24. House Post Office and Civil Service discharged. House passed March 3. President signed March 16, 1983.

PL 98-8 (HR 1718) Appropriate funds to provide for emergency expenditures to meet neglected needs and to provide supplemental funds for advances to the unemployment trust fund for fiscal year 1983. Introduced by WHITTEN, D-Miss., March 1, 1983. House Appropriations reported March 1 (H Rept 98-11). House passed March 3. Senate Appropriations reported March 7 (S Rept 98-17). Senate passed, amended, March 17. House agreed to conference report March 22 (H Rept 98-44). Senate agreed to conference report March 22. House agreed to further Senate amendment March 24. President signed March 24, 1983.

PL 98-9 (S J Res 35) Designate the week beginning March 20, 1983, as "National Mental Health Counselors Week." Introduced by HUDDLESTON, D-Ky., Feb. 16, 1983. Senate Judiciary reported March 17. Senate passed March 18. House passed March 21. President signed March 24, 1983.

PL 98-10 (S J Res 65) Designate March 21, 1983, as "Afghanistan Day." Introduced by PELL, D-R.I., March 18, 1983. Senate passed March 18. House passed March 21. President signed March 24, 1983.

PL 98-11 (S 271) Designate additional national scenic and historic trails. Introduced by McCLURE, R-Idaho, Jan. 27, 1983. Senate Energy and Natural Resources reported Jan. 31 (S Rept 98-1). Senate passed Feb. 3. House Interior and Insular Affairs reported March 9 (H Rept 98-28). House passed, under suspension of the rules, March 15. President signed March 28, 1983.

PL 98-12 (HR 2112) Extend the expiration date of the Defense Production Act of 1950. Introduced by LaFALCE, D-N.Y., March 16, 1983. House passed, under suspension of the rules, March 22. Senate passed, amended, March 23. House disagreed to Senate amendments March 24. Senate receded from its amendments March 24. President signed March 29, 1983.

PL 98-13 (HR 2369) Prevent the temporary termination of the Federal Supplemental Compensation Act of 1982. Introduced by FORD, D-Tenn., March 24, 1983. House Ways and Means discharged. House passed March 24. Senate passed March 25. President signed March 29, 1983.

PL 98-14 (HR 1936) Amend title 37, U.S. Code, to extend certain expiring enlistment and re-enlistment bonuses for the armed forces. Introduced by ASPIN, D-Wis., March 7, 1983. House Armed Services reported March 9 (H Rept 98-27). House passed, under suspension of the rules, March 15. Senate passed March 21. President signed March 30, 1983.

PL 98-15 (S J Res 64) Commemorate the 200th anniversary of the signing of the Treaty of Amity and Commerce between Sweden and the United States. Introduced by BOSCHWITZ, R-Minn., March 17, 1983. Senate passed March 18. House Post Office and Civil Service discharged. House passed March 24. President signed April 4, 1983.

PL 98-16 (H J Res 175) Authorize and request the president to proclaim May 1983 as "National Amateur Baseball Month." Introduced by GARCIA, D-N.Y., March 3, 1983. House Post Office and Civil Service discharged. House passed March 21. Senate Judiciary discharged. Senate passed March 24. President signed April 4, 1983.

PL 98-17 (S 926) Establish uniform national standards for the continued regulation by the several states of commercial motor vehicle width on interstate highways. Introduced by PACKWOOD, R-Ore., March 24, 1983. Senate passed March 24. House passed March 24. President signed April 5, 1983.

PL 98-18 (S J Res 32) Provide for the designation of May 1983 as "National Arthritis Month." Introduced by SYMMS, R-Idaho, Feb. 3, 1983. Senate Judiciary reported March 17. Senate passed March 18. House Post Office and Civil Service discharged. House passed March 24. President signed April 5, 1983.

PL 98-19 (S J Res 52) Authorize and request the president to designate the week of April 10-16, 1983, as "National Mental Health Week." Introduced by QUAYLE, R-Ind., March 3, 1983. Senate Judiciary reported March 17. Senate passed March 18. House Post Office and Civil Service discharged. House passed April 12. President signed April 15, 1983.

PL 98-20 (H J Res 80) Authorize and request the president to issue a proclamation designating April 17-24, 1983, as "Jewish Heritage Week." Introduced by ADDABBO, D-N.Y., Jan. 25, 1983. House Post Office and Civil Service discharged. House passed April 12. Senate passed April 15. President signed April 19, 1983.

PL 98-21 (HR 1900) Implement the consensus recommendations of the National Commission on Social Security Reform. Introduced by ROSTENKOWSKI, D-Ill., March 3, 1983. House Ways and Means reported March 4 (H Rept 98-25, Part I). House passed March 9. Senate passed, amended, March 23. House agreed to conference report March 24 (H Rept 98-47). Senate agreed to conference report March 25. President signed April 20, 1983.

PL 98-22 (S 89) Amend the Saccharin Study and Labeling Act to extend the period during which the secretary of health and human services may not take certain actions to restrict the continued use of saccharin or of any food, drug or cosmetic containing saccharin. Introduced by HATCH, R-Utah, Jan. 26, 1983. Senate Labor and Human Resources reported March 23 (S Rept 98-32). Senate passed April 5. House passed April 13. President signed April 22, 1983.

PL 98-23 (S J Res 53) Authorize and request the president to designate the month of May 1983 as "National Physical Fitness and Sports Month." Introduced by THURMOND, R-S.C., March 8, 1983. Senate Judiciary reported March 17. Senate passed March 18. House Post Office and Civil Service discharged. House passed April 12. President signed April 26, 1983.

PL 98-24 (S 126) Establish in the Alcohol, Drug Abuse, and Mental Health Administration an associate administrator for prevention to promote and coordinate prevention research programs of the National Institutes of Mental Health, Drug Abuse and Alcoholism, authorize funds for 1983 and 1984 for alcohol and drug abuse research, transfer specified alcohol and drug abuse statutory authority to the Public Health Service Act, and consolidate various reporting requirements. Introduced by HUMPHREY, R-N.H., Jan. 26, 1983. Senate Labor and Human Resources reported March 21 (S Rept 98-29). Senate passed April 5. House passed April 13. President signed April 26, 1983.

PL 98-25 (S 304) Hold a parcel of land in trust for the Burns Paiute Trust. Introduced by HATFIELD, R-Ore., Jan. 31, 1983. Senate Indian Affairs reported Feb. 23. Senate passed Feb. 24. House Interior and Insular Affairs discharged. House passed April 19. President signed May 2, 1983.

PL 98-26 (H J Res 245) Provide for corrections of errors in the enrollment of HR 1718, Emergency Jobs Appropriations, 1983. Introduced by WHITTEN, D-Miss., April 21, 1983. House passed April 21. Senate passed April 21. President signed May 4, 1983.

PL 98-27 (S J Res 62) Provide for the designation of the week beginning May 15, 1983, as "National Parkinson's Disease Week." Introduced by MATHIAS, R-Md., March 17, 1983. Senate Judiciary reported April 12. Senate passed April 13. House Post Office and Civil Service discharged. House passed April 26. President signed May 4, 1983.

PL 98-28 (HR 2600) Dedicate the Golden Gate National Recreation Area to Congressman Phillip Burton. Introduced by MILLER, D-Calif., April 19, 1983. House Interior and Insular Affairs reported April 25 (H Rept 98-72). House passed, under suspension of the rules, April 26.

Senate passed April 28. President signed May 10, 1983.

PL 98-29 (S 1011) Amend the Federal Deposit Insurance Act to provide for the issuance of income capital certificates. Introduced by HAT-FIELD, R-Ore., April 7, 1983. Senate passed April 15. House passed, under suspension of the rules, May 3. President signed May 16, 1983.

PL 98-30 (S J Res 51) Designate May 21, 1983, as "Andrei Sakharov Day." Introduced by DOLE, R-Kan., March 3, 1983. Senate Judiciary reported April 12. Senate passed April 13. House Post Office and Civil Service discharged. House passed May 17. President signed May 18, 1983.

PL 98-31 (H J Res 219) Declare the support of the United States government for efforts of the U.S. Soccer Federation to bring the World Cup to the U.S. in 1986; designate the secretary of commerce as the official representative of the U.S. government to the Federation Internationale de Football Association. Introduced by FLORIO, D-N.J., March 24, 1983. House passed, under suspension of the rules, May 3. Senate passed May 6. President signed May 20, 1983.

PL 98-32 (S 287) Establish the Harry S Truman National Historic Site in the state of Missouri. Introduced by EAGLETON, D-Mo., Jan. 31, 1983. Senate Energy and Natural Resources discharged. Senate passed May 6. House Interior and Insular Affairs discharged. House passed May 10. President signed May 23, 1983.

PL 98-33 (S 957) Provide for an increase in the number of members of the Congressional Award Board. Introduced by BYRD, D-W.Va., March 24, 1983. Senate passed March 24. House Education and Labor discharged. House passed, amended, May 9. Senate agreed to House amendment May 12. President signed May 25, 1983.

PL 98-34 (HR 2990) Increase the permanent public debt limit. Introduced by ROSTENKOWSKI, D-Ill., May 12, 1983. House Ways and Means reported May 13 (H Rept 98-121). House passed May 18. Senate Finance reported May 24. Senate passed May 25. President signed May 26, 1983.

PL 98-35 (H J Res 265) Provide for the temporary extension of certain insurance programs relating to housing and community development. Introduced by GONZALEZ, D-Texas, May 10, 1983. House passed, under suspension of the rules, May 17. Senate passed, amended, May 20. House agreed to Senate amendment with an amendment May 24. Senate agreed to House amendment to Senate amendment May 24. President signed May 26, 1983.

PL 98-36 (S 653) Amend Chapter 104, title 10, United States Code, to establish the Foundation for the Advancement of Military Medicine. Introduced by JACKSON, D-Wash., and TOWER, R-Texas, March 2, 1983. Senate Armed Services reported March 22 (S Rept 98-39). Senate passed March 23. House passed, amended, under suspension of the rules, May 9. Senate agreed to House amendments May 12. President signed May 27, 1983.

PL 98-37 (S 967) Amend the Independent Safety Board Act of 1974 and authorize funds for fiscal years 1984, 1985 and 1986. Introduced by PACKWOOD, R-Ore., March 31, 1983. Senate Commerce, Science and Transportation reported March 31 (S Rept 98-43). Senate passed April 7. House passed May 24. President signed June 6, 1983.

PL 98-38 (HR 2681) Make certain amendments to sections 4, 13, 15 and 15B of the Securities Exchange Act of 1934. Introduced by DINGELL, D-Mich., April 21, 1983. House Energy and Commerce reported May 11 (H Rept 98-106). House passed, under suspension of the rules, May 17. Senate passed May 25. President signed June 6, 1983.

PL 98-39 (H J Res 201) Designate June 14, 1983, as "Baltic Freedom Day." Introduced by DONNELLY, D-Mass., March 16, 1983. House Foreign Affairs and House Post Office and Civil Service discharged. House passed June 9. Senate passed June 10. President signed June 13, 1983.

PL 98-40 (S J Res 75) Provide for the designation of June 12-18, 1983, as "National Scleroderma Week." Introduced by SYMMS, R-Idaho, April 6, 1983. Senate Judiciary reported May 26. Senate passed June 6. House Post Office and Civil Service discharged. House passed June 9. President signed June 14, 1983.

PL 98-41 (H J Res 234) Designate the week beginning June 19, 1983, as "National Children's Liver Disease Awareness Week." Introduced by MOLINARI, R-N.Y., and COURTER, R-N.J., April 12, 1983. House Post Office and Civil Service discharged. House passed May 12. Senate Judiciary discharged. Senate passed June 15. President signed June 20, 1983.

PL 98-42 (S J Res 42) Designate Jan. 3, 1984, as "Alaska Statehood Day." Introduced by MURKOWSKI, R-Alaska, Feb. 24, 1983. Senate Judiciary reported May 19. Senate passed May 20. House Post Office and Civil Service discharged. House passed June 9. President signed June 22, 1983.

PL 98-43 (S 639) Authorize supplemental assistance to aid Lebanon in rebuilding its economy and armed forces. Introduced by PERCY, R-Ill., March 1, 1983. Senate Foreign Relations reported May 5 (S Rept 98-72). Senate passed May 20. House passed, amended, under suspension of the rules, June 2. Senate agreed to House amendment June 15.

President signed June 27, 1983.

PL 98-44 (S 925) Make certain technical corrections in the Atlantic Salmon Convention Act of 1982. Introduced by PACKWOOD, R-Ore., March 24, 1983. Senate Commerce, Science and Transportation reported May 9 (S Rept 98-78). Senate passed June 29. House passed June 29. President signed July 12, 1983.

PL 98-45 (HR 3133) Appropriate funds for fiscal year 1984 for programs of the Department of Housing and Urban Development, and certain independent agencies. Introduced by BOLAND, D-Mass., May 24, 1983. House Appropriations reported May 24 (H Rept 98-223). House passed June 2. Senate Appropriations reported June 14 (S Rept 98-152). Senate passed, amended, June 21. House agreed to conference report June 29 (H Rept 98-264). Senate agreed to conference report June 29. President signed July 12, 1983.

PL 98-46 (S 680) Designate the Baltimore-Washington Parkway in Maryland as the Gladys Noon Spellman Parkway. Introduced by SARBANES, D-Md., March 3, 1983. Senate Energy and Natural Resources reported May 20 (S Rept 98-135). Senate passed June 15. House passed June 29. President signed July 12, 1983.

PL 98-47 (S 273) Extend the authority of the Small Business Administration section 8(a)(1) pilot procurement program. Introduced by WEICKER, R-Conn., Jan. 27, 1983. Senate Small Business reported Feb. 2. Senate passed Feb. 3. House passed, amended, Feb. 15. Senate agreed to conference report June 27 (H Rept 98-262). House agreed to conference report June 30. President signed July 13, 1983.

PL 98-48 (HR 1746) Authorize funds through Sept. 30, 1983, and for fiscal year 1984 for the Navajo and Hopi Indian Relocation Commission. Introduced by UDALL, D-Ariz., March 1, 1983. House Interior and Insular Affairs reported May 16 (H Rept 98-173). House passed, under suspension of the rules, June 1. Senate Indian Affairs discharged. Senate passed June 29. President signed July 13, 1983.

PL 98-49 (HR 2713) Amend the Public Health Service Act to authorize funds to be made available to the secretary of health and human services for research on the cause, treatment and prevention of public health emergencies. Introduced by WAXMAN, D-Calif., April 21, 1983. House Energy and Commerce reported May 16 (H Rept 98-143). House passed, under suspension of the rules, June 13. Senate passed June 28. President signed July 13, 1983.

PL 98-50 (HR 3132) Appropriate funds for fiscal year 1984 for energy and water development programs. Introduced by BEVILL, D-Ala., May 24, 1983. House Appropriations reported May 24 (H Rept 98-217). House passed June 7. Senate Appropriations reported June 16 (S Rept 98-153). Senate passed, amended, June 22. House agreed to conference report June 29 (H Rept 98-272). Senate agreed to conference report June 29. President signed July 14, 1983.

PL 98-51 (HR 3135) Appropriate funds for fiscal year 1984 for the legislative branch of the federal government. Introduced by FAZIO, D-Calif., May 25, 1983. House Appropriations reported May 25 (H Rept 98-227). House passed June 3. Senate Appropriations reported June 23 (S Rept 98-161). Senate passed, amended, June 23. House agreed to conference report June 29 (H Rept 98-271). Senate agreed to conference report June 29. President signed July 14, 1983.

PL 98-52 (HR 2065) Authorize funds for fiscal year 1984 for programs administered by the National Aeronautics and Space Administration. Introduced by FUQUA, D-Fla., March 11, 1983. House Science and Technology reported April 15 (H Rept 98-65). House passed April 26. Senate Commerce, Science and Transportation reported June 27. Senate passed, amended, June 28. House agreed to Senate amendment June 29. President signed July 15, 1983.

PL 98-53 (HR 1271) Regards presidential certifications on conditions in El Salvador. Introduced by STUDDS, D-Mass., Feb. 3, 1983. House passed, under suspension of the rules, June 7. Senate Foreign Relations reported June 28. Senate passed June 29. President signed July 15, 1983.

PL 98-54 (S J Res 68) Authorize and request the president to designate July 16, 1983, as "National Atomic Veterans' Day." Introduced by SPECTER, R-Pa., March 22, 1983. Senate Judiciary reported May 3. Senate passed May 4. House Post Office and Civil Service discharged. House passed June 30. President signed July 15, 1983.

PL 98-55 (S J Res 18) Designate Sept. 22, 1983, as "American Business Women's Day." Introduced by JEPSEN, R-Iowa, Jan. 26, 1983. Senate Judiciary reported March 1. Senate passed March 2. House Post Office and Civil Service discharged. House passed June 30. President signed July 19, 1983.

PL 98-56 (S J Res 34) Designate Nov. 7-13, 1983, as "National Reye's Syndrome Week." Introduced by RIEGLE, D-Mich., Feb. 15, 1983. Senate Judiciary reported June 20. Senate passed June 23. House Post Office and Civil Service discharged. House passed June 30. President signed July 19, 1983.

PL 98-57 (S 929) Amend the act of July 2, 1940, as amended, pertaining to appropriations for the Canal Zone Biological Area. Introduced by GOLDWATER, R-Ariz., March 24, 1983. Senate Rules and Adminis-

tration reported May 16 (S Rept 98-96). Senate passed May 25. House Merchant Marine and Fisheries reported June 29 (H Rept 98-283). House passed, under suspension of the rules, July 12. President signed July 22, 1983.

PL 98-58 (S J Res 96) Designate Aug. 1, 1983, as "Helsinki Human Rights Day." Introduced by DeCONCINI, D-Ariz., May 5, 1983. Senate Judiciary reported May 19. Senate passed May 20. House Foreign Affairs and House Post Office and Civil Service discharged. House passed June 22. President signed July 25, 1983.

PL 98-59 (HR 3392) Provide that for the 1983 crop of any kind of tobacco for which marketing quotas are in effect or for which marketing quotas are not disapproved by producers, the support level in cents per pound shall be the support level in cents per pound at which the respective 1982 crop was supported. Introduced by ROSE, D-N.C., June 22, 1983. House Agriculture reported July 1 (H Rept 98-288). House passed, under suspension of the rules, July 11. Senate passed, amended, July 13. House agreed to Senate amendment with an amendment July 13. Senate disagreed to House amendment July 14. House receded from its amendment and agreed to Senate amendment with an amendment July 14. Senate agreed to House amendment to Senate amendment July 14. President signed July 25, 1983.

PL 98-60 (S J Res 77) Designate the week of July 24-31, 1983, as "National Animal Agriculture Week." Introduced by DOLE, R-Kan., April 6, 1983. Senate Judiciary reported July 14. Senate passed July 16. House Post Office and Civil Service discharged. House passed July 25. President signed July 27, 1983.

PL 98-61 (S 459) Authorize and direct the secretary of the interior to convey by quitclaim deed all right, title and interest of the United States in and to certain lands that were withdrawn or acquired for the purpose of relocating a portion of the City of American Falls, Idaho, out of the area flooded by the American Falls Reservoir. Introduced by McCLURE, R-Idaho, Feb. 3, 1983. Senate Energy and Natural Resources reported Feb. 23 (S Rept 98-5). Senate passed March 2. House Interior and Insular Affairs reported June 28 (H Rept 98-270). House passed July 18. President signed July 28, 1983.

PL 98-62 (H J Res 258) Designate Aug. 3, 1983, as "National Paralyzed Veterans Recognition Day." Introduced by MOAKLEY, D-Mass., May 3, 1983. House Post Office and Civil Service discharged. House passed June 9. Senate Judiciary reported July 14. Senate passed July 16. President signed July 29, 1983.

PL 98-63 (HR 3069) Appropriate supplemental funds for the fiscal year ending Sept. 30, 1983, for the federal government. Introduced by WHITTEN, D-Miss., May 18, 1983. House Appropriations reported May 18 (H Rept 98-207). House passed May 25. Senate Appropriations reported May 26 (S Rept 98-148). Senate passed, amended, June 16. House agreed to conference report July 28 (H Rept 98-308). Senate agreed to conference report July 29. President signed July 30, 1983.

PL 98-64 (S 419) Provide that per capita payments to Indians may be made by tribal governments. Introduced by HATFIELD, R-Ore., Feb. 3, 1983. Senate Indian Affairs reported Feb. 23. Senate passed Feb. 24. House Interior and Insular Affairs reported June 3 (H Rept 98-230). House passed, amended, June 20. Senate agreed to House amendment July 20. President signed Aug. 2, 1983.

PL 98-65 (HR 2637) Amend the District of Columbia Self-Government and Governmental Reorganization Act, increasing the amount authorized to be appropriated as the annual federal payment to the District of Columbia. Introduced by FAUNTROY, D-D.C., April 20, 1983. House District of Columbia reported May 11 (H Rept 98-100). House passed June 27. Senate passed July 20. President signed Aug. 2, 1983.

PL 98-66 (HR 1935) Ratify an exchange agreement concerning National Wildlife Refuge System lands located on Matagorda Island, Texas. Introduced by PATMAN, D-Texas, March 7, 1983. House Merchant Marine and Fisheries reported April 18 (H Rept 98-67). House passed, under suspension of the rules, April 19. Senate Environment and Public Works reported July 11 (S Rept 98-176). Senate passed July 22. President signed Aug. 4, 1983.

PL 98-67 (HR 2973) Repeal the withholding of tax from interest and dividends. Introduced by JACOBS, D-Ind., May 11, 1983. House Ways and Means reported May 13 (H Rept 98-120). House passed, under suspension of the rules, May 17. Senate passed, amended, June 16. House agreed to Senate amendment with an amendment July 14. Senate agreed to conference report July 28 (H Rept 98-325). House agreed to conference report July 28. President signed Aug. 5, 1983.

PL 98-68 (S J Res 56) Designate the month of August 1983 as "National Child Support Enforcement Month." Introduced by GRASSLEY, R-Iowa, March 9, 1983. Senate Judiciary reported July 14. Senate passed July 16. House Post Office and Civil Service discharged. House passed July 27. President signed Aug. 5, 1983.

PL 98-69 (S J Res 67) Authorize and request the president to designate the week of Sept. 25-Oct. 1, 1983, as "National Respiratory Therapy Week." Introduced by HEFLIN, D-Ala., March 22, 1983. Senate Judiciary reported May 3. Senate passed May 4. House Post Office and

Civil Service discharged. House passed July 27. President signed Aug. 8, 1983.

PL 98-70 (S 143) Authorize the Twenty-Nine Palms Band of Luiseno Mission Indians to lease for 99 years certain lands held in trust for such band. Introduced by CRANSTON, D-Calif., Jan. 26, 1983. Senate Indian Affairs reported Feb. 23. Senate passed Feb. 24. House Interior and Insular Affairs reported May 4 (H Rept 98-85). House passed, amended, May 17. Senate agreed to House amendments July 26. President signed Aug. 8, 1983.

PL 98-71 (H J Res 139) Designate the week beginning June 24, 1984, as "Federal Credit Union Week." Introduced by OAKAR, D-Ohio, Feb. 10, 1983. House Post Office and Civil Service discharged. House passed July 25. Senate passed July 27. President signed Aug. 11, 1983.

PL 98-72 (S 272) Provide prospective contractors minimum time periods for the solicitation and bidding process on federal contracts. Introduced by PRESSLER, R-S.D., Jan. 27, 1983. Senate Small Business reported Feb. 2. Senate passed Feb. 3. House passed, amended, March 8. Senate agreed to conference report June 27 (H Rept 98-263). House agreed to conference report Aug. 1. President signed Aug. 11, 1983.

PL 98-73 (S 930) Authorize the Smithsonian Institution to purchase land in Santa Cruz, Ariz. Introduced by GOLDWATER, R-Ariz., March 24, 1983. Senate Rules and Administration reported May 16 (S Rept 98-97). Senate passed May 25. House Administration reported July 28 (H Rept 98-330). House passed, under suspension of the rules, Aug. 1. President signed Aug. 11, 1983.

PL 98-74 (S 727) Authorize the secretary of the interior to set aside certain judgment funds of the Three Affiliated Tribes of Fort Berthold Reservation in North Dakota. Introduced by ANDREWS, R-N.D., March 8, 1983. Senate Indian Affairs reported May 17 (S Rept 98-126). Senate passed May 25. House Interior and Insular Affairs reported July 19 (H Rept 98-300). House passed Aug. 1. President signed Aug. 11, 1983.

PL 98-75 (H J Res 321) Proclaim Sept. 3, 1983, as a day of national celebration on the 200th anniversary of the signing of the Treaty of Paris. Introduced by BATEMAN, R-Va., July 14, 1983. House Post Office and Civil Service discharged. House passed July 27. Senate passed July 29. President signed Aug. 11, 1983.

PL 98-76 (HR 1646) Amend the Railroad Retirement Act of 1974 and the Railroad Retirement Tax Act, assuring sufficient resources to pay current and future benefits under the Railroad Retirement Act. Introduced by FLORIO, D-N.J., Feb. 24, 1983. House Energy and Commerce reported March 9 (H Rept 98-30, Part I). House Ways and Means reported July 1 (H Rept 98-30, Part II). House passed Aug. 1. Senate passed Aug. 2. President signed Aug. 12, 1983.

PL 98-77 (HR 2355) Authorize funds for fiscal year 1984 to provide emergency job training and employment assistance programs for wartime veterans. Introduced by LEATH, D-Texas, March 24, 1983. House Veterans' Affairs reported May 13 (H Rept 98-116). House passed, under suspension of the rules, June 7. Senate passed, amended, June 15. House agreed to Senate amendments with amendments Aug. 2. Senate agreed to House amendments Aug. 3. President signed Aug. 15, 1983.

PL 98-78 (HR 3329) Appropriate funds for the Department of Transportation and related agencies for the fiscal year ending Sept. 30, 1984. Introduced by LEHMAN, D-Fla., June 16, 1983. House Appropriations reported June 16 (H Rept 98-246). House passed June 22. Senate Appropriations reported July 14 (S Rept 98-179). Senate passed, amended, July 15. House agreed to conference report Aug. 2 (H Rept 98-318). Senate agreed to conference report Aug. 3. President signed Aug. 15, 1983.

PL 98-79 (HR 3394) Provide additional authority for the consolidation of student loans and make certain other changes in federal student financial assistance. Introduced by SIMON, D-Ill., June 22, 1983. House Education and Labor reported July 27 (H Rept 98-324). House passed, under suspension of the rules, Aug. 1. Senate passed, amended, Aug. 2. House agreed to Senate amendments Aug. 3. President signed Aug. 15, 1983.

PL 98-80 (S 1696) Authorize three additional assistant administrators of the Environmental Protection Agency. Introduced by STAFFORD, R-Vt., July 28, 1983. Senate Environment and Public Works reported July 28 (S Rept 98-196). Senate passed Aug. 3. House passed Aug. 4. President signed Aug. 23, 1983.

PL 98-81 (S 1797) Designate the United States Post Office building to be constructed in Fort Worth, Texas, as the "Jack D. Watson Post Office Building." Introduced by STEVENS, R-Alaska, Aug. 4, 1983. Senate passed Aug. 4. House passed Aug. 4. President signed Aug. 23, 1983.

PL 98-82 (S J Res 85) Designate Sept. 26, 1983, as "National Historically Black Colleges Day." Introduced by THURMOND, R-S.C., April 15, 1983. Senate Judiciary reported July 14. Senate passed July 16. House Post Office and Civil Service discharged. House passed Aug. 4. President signed Aug. 23, 1983.

PL 98-83 (S J Res 98) Designate Oct. 2-9, 1983, as "National Housing

Week." Introduced by TOWER, R-Texas, May 11, 1983. Senate Judiciary reported July 14. Senate passed July 16. House Post Office and Civil Service discharged. House passed Aug. 4. President signed Aug. 23, 1983.

PL 98-84 (S J Res 116) Designate the week of Sept. 4-10, 1983, as "Youth of America Week." Introduced by KASTEN, R-Wis., June 14, 1983. Senate Judiciary reported July 21. Senate passed July 26. House Post Office and Civil Service discharged. House passed Aug. 4. President signed Aug. 23, 1983.

PL 98-85 (HR 2895) Designate the federal building and United States courthouse at 450 Golden Gate Ave., San Francisco, Calif., as the "Phillip Burton Federal Building and United States Courthouse." Introduced by HOWARD, D-N.J., May 4, 1983. House Public Works and Transportation reported May 16 (H Rept 98-152). House passed, under suspension of the rules, May 23. Senate Environment and Public Works reported Aug. 3. Senate passed Aug. 4. President signed Aug. 26, 1983.

PL 98-86 (HR 3232) Amend title 28 of the United States Code, authorizing payment of travel and transportation expenses of newly appointed special agents of the Department of Justice. Introduced by EDWARDS, D-Calif., June 6, 1983. House passed, under suspension of the rules, Aug. 1. Senate passed Aug. 4. President signed Aug. 26, 1983.

PL 98-87 (H J Res 297) Provide for appointment of Jeannine Smith Clark as a citizen regent of the Board of Regents of the Smithsonian Institution. Introduced by BOLAND, D-Mass., June 15, 1983. House Administration reported July 28 (H Rept 98-329). House passed, under suspension of the rules, Aug. 1. Senate passed Aug. 4. President signed Aug. 26, 1983.

PL 98-88 (HR 3190) Establish an improved program for extra long staple cotton. Introduced by DE LA GARZA, D-Texas, June 2, 1983. House Agriculture reported June 22 (H Rept 98-256). House passed, under suspension of the rules, June 27. Senate passed Aug. 4. President signed Aug. 26, 1983.

PL 98-89 (S 46) Consolidate and re-enact certain of the marine safety and seamen's welfare laws of the United States. Introduced by PACKWOOD, R-Ore., Jan. 26, 1983. Senate Commerce, Science and Transportation reported April 12 (S Rept 98-56). Senate passed April 28. House Merchant Marine and Fisheries reported Aug. 1 (H Rept 98-338). House passed, amended, under suspension of the rules, Aug. 1. Senate agreed to House amendment Aug. 3. President signed Aug. 26, 1983.

PL 98-90 (HR 3677) Amend title XVIII of the Social Security Act, increasing the cap amount allowable for reimbursement of hospices under the Medicare program. Introduced by PANETTA, D-Calif., July 27, 1983. House Ways and Means reported July 28 (H Rept 98-333). House passed, under suspension of the rules, Aug. 1. Senate passed Aug. 3. President signed Aug. 29, 1983.

PL 98-91 (HR 3549) Amend the bankruptcy rules with respect to providing notice. Introduced by GLICKMAN, D-Kan., July 13, 1983. House passed Aug. 4. Senate passed Aug. 4. President signed Aug. 30, 1983.

PL 98-92 (HR 3409) Amend the Federal Supplemental Compensation Act of 1982 with respect to the number of weeks of benefits paid in any state. Introduced by SHANNON, D-Mass., June 23, 1983. House Ways and Means reported July 28 (H Rept 98-328). House passed, under suspension of the rules, Aug. 2. Senate passed, amended, Aug. 4. House agreed to Senate amendments Aug. 4. President signed Sept. 2, 1983.

PL 98-93 (S J Res 131) Designate the week of Sept. 18-24, 1983, as "National Cystic Fibrosis Week." Introduced by DOLE, R-Kan., July 14, 1983. Senate Judiciary reported July 21. Senate passed July 26. House Post Office and Civil Service discharged. House passed Sept. 15. President signed Sept. 20, 1983.

PL 98-94 (S 675) Authorize funds for fiscal year 1984 for the Department of Defense. Introduced by TOWER, R-Texas, March 3, 1983. Senate Armed Services reported July 5 (S Rept 98-174). Senate passed July 26. House passed, amended, July 29. Senate agreed to conference report Sept. 13 (H Rept 98-352). House agreed to conference report Sept. 15. President signed Sept. 24, 1983.

PL 98-95 (S 1872) Increase endowment funds for eligible institutions under part C of title III of the Higher Education Act of 1965. Introduced by BAKER, R-Tenn., Sept. 21, 1983. Senate passed Sept. 22. House passed Sept. 26. President signed Sept. 26, 1983.

PL 98-96 (H J Res 132) Designate the week beginning Sept. 25, 1983, as "National Adult Day Care Center Week." Introduced by HERTEL, D-Mich., Feb. 8, 1983. House Post Office and Civil Service discharged. House passed Sept. 15. Senate passed Sept. 20. President signed Sept. 27, 1983.

PL 98-97 (H J Res 218) Designate the month of September 1983 as "National Sewing Month." Introduced by BONER, D-Tenn., March 24, 1983. House Post Office and Civil Service discharged. House passed Aug. 4. Senate Judiciary reported Sept. 15. Senate passed Sept. 20. President signed Sept. 27, 1983.

PL 98-98 (H J Res 353) Condemn the Soviet Union for destruction of the Korean airliner. Introduced by ZABLOCKI, D-Wis., Sept. 13, 1983. House Foreign Affairs discharged. House passed Sept. 14. Senate passed Sept. 15. President signed Sept. 28, 1983.

PL 98-99 (H J Res 229) Authorize and request the president to issue a proclamation designating April 22-28, 1984, as "National Organ Donation Awareness Week." Introduced by MORRISON, R-Wash., April 7, 1983. House Post Office and Civil Service discharged. House passed May 12. Senate Judiciary reported Sept. 15. Senate passed Sept. 20. President signed Sept. 28, 1983.

PL 98-100 (HR 3914) Require the secretary of agriculture to make an earlier announcement of the 1984 crop feed grain program and of the 1985 crop wheat and feed grain program. Introduced by BEDELL, D-Iowa, Sept. 19, 1983. House passed, under suspension of the rules, Sept. 20. Senate passed Sept. 21. President signed Sept. 29, 1983.

PL 98-101 (S 118) Provide for the establishment of a Commission on the Bicentennial of the Constitution. Introduced by HATCH, R-Utah, Jan. 26, 1983. Senate Judiciary reported April 28 (S Rept 98-68). Senate passed July 18. House passed, amended, Aug. 4. Senate agreed to House amendments Sept. 14. President signed Sept. 29, 1983.

PL 98-102 (S J Res 82) Designate November 1983 as "National Alzheimer's Disease Month." Introduced by EAGLETON, D-Mo., April 13, 1983. Senate Judiciary reported April 19. Senate passed April 21. House Post Office and Civil Service discharged. House passed Sept. 15. President signed Sept. 30, 1983.

PL 98-103 (S J Res 119) Designate the week of Dec. 11-17, 1983, as "National Drunk and Drugged Driving Awareness Week." Introduced by HUMPHREY, R-N.H., June 16, 1983. Senate Judiciary reported July 14. Senate passed July 16. House Post Office and Civil Service discharged. House passed Sept. 15. President signed Sept. 30, 1983.

PL 98-104 (S 1625) Amend the District of Columbia Retirement Reform Act. Introduced by EAGLETON, D-Mo., July 15, 1983. Senate Governmental Affairs reported Aug. 2 (S Rept 98-217). Senate passed Aug. 3. House District of Columbia reported Sept. 21 (H Rept 98-372). House passed Sept. 26. President signed Sept. 30, 1983.

PL 98-105 (S 1850) Amend title 38, United States Code, to extend for one year the authority of the Veterans Administration to provide certain contract medical services in Puerto Rico and the Virgin Islands. Introduced by BAKER, R-Tenn., Sept. 15, 1983. Senate passed Sept. 20. House passed Sept. 22. President signed Sept. 30, 1983.

PL 98-106 (H J Res 284) Commemorate the 25th anniversary of the National Aeronautics and Space Administration. Introduced by FUQUA, D-Fla., May 26, 1983. House Post Office and Civil Service discharged. House passed Sept. 27. Senate passed Sept. 29. President signed Oct. 1, 1983.

PL 98-107 (H J Res 368) Make continuing appropriations for fiscal year 1984. Introduced by WHITTEN, D-Miss., Sept. 22, 1983. House passed Sept. 28. Senate passed, amended, Sept. 29. House agreed to conference report Sept. 30 (H Rept 98-397). Senate agreed to conference report Sept. 30. President signed Oct. 1, 1983.

PL 98-108 (HR 3962) Extend the authorities under the Export Administration Act of 1979 until Oct. 14, 1983. Introduced by BONKER, D-Wash., Sept. 22, 1983. House passed, under suspension of the rules, Sept. 27. Senate passed Sept. 30. President signed Oct. 1, 1983.

PL 98-109 (H J Res 366) Provide for the temporary extension of certain insurance programs relating to housing and community development. Introduced by GONZALEZ, D-Texas, Sept. 21, 1983. House passed, under suspension of the rules, Sept. 27. Senate passed, amended, Sept. 29. House agreed to Senate amendment Sept. 30. President signed Oct. 1, 1983.

PL 98-110 (S J Res 81) Authorize and request the president to designate Oct. 16, 1983, as "World Food Day." Introduced by HEINZ, R-Pa., April 13, 1983. Senate Judiciary reported April 19. Senate passed April 21. House Post Office and Civil Service discharged. House passed Sept. 15. President signed Oct. 3, 1983.

PL 98-111 (S 602) Provide federal funding for radio broadcasting to Cuba. Introduced by HAWKINS, R-Fla., Feb. 24, 1983. Senate Foreign Relations reported June 21 (S Rept 98-156). Senate passed Sept. 13. House passed Sept. 29. President signed Oct. 4, 1983.

PL 98-112 (S J Res 142) Designate the week of Oct. 3-9, 1983, as "National Productivity Improvement Week." Introduced by NUNN, D-Ga., Aug. 2, 1983. Senate Judiciary reported Sept. 15. Senate passed Sept. 20. House Post Office and Civil Service discharged. House passed Sept. 30. President signed Oct. 4, 1983.

PL 98-113 (S J Res 140) Designate the week of Oct. 2-8, 1983, as "Myasthenia Gravis Awareness Week." Introduced by METZENBAUM, D-Ohio, July 29, 1983. Senate Judiciary reported Sept. 15. Senate passed Sept. 20. House Post Office and Civil Service discharged. House passed Sept. 30. President signed Oct. 5, 1983.

PL 98-114 (H J Res 137) Authorize and request the president to issue a proclamation designating Oct. 2-8, 1983, as "National Schoolbus Safety Week of 1983." Introduced by CONTE, R-Mass., Feb. 10, 1983.

House Post Office and Civil Service discharged. House passed Sept. 27. Senate passed Sept. 30. President signed Oct. 7, 1983.

PL 98-115 (HR 2972) Authorize certain construction at military installations for fiscal year 1984. Introduced by PRICE, D-Ill., May 11, 1983. House Armed Services reported May 16 (H Rept 98-166). House passed June 21. Senate Armed Services discharged. Senate passed, amended, July 26. House agreed to conference report Sept. 22 (H Rept 98-359). Senate agreed to conference report Sept. 27. President signed Oct. 11, 1983.

PL 98-116 (HR 3263) Appropriate fund for military construction programs of the Department of Defense for the fiscal year ending Sept. 30, 1984. Introduced by HEFNER, D-N.C., June 9, 1983. House Appropriations reported June 9 (H Rept 98-238). House passed June 21. Senate Appropriations reported July 14 (S Rept 98-180). Senate passed, amended, July 27. House agreed to conference report Sept. 27 (H Rept 98-378). Senate agreed to conference report Sept. 28. President signed Oct. 11, 1983.

PL 98-117 (HR 3871) Delay until January 1984, the effective date for recomputing hourly pay rates for certain federal employees. Introduced by FORD, D-Mich., Sept. 13, 1983. House passed, under suspension of the rules, Sept. 20. Senate passed Sept. 27. President signed Oct. 11, 1983.

PL 98-118 (HR 4101) Extend the Federal Supplemental Compensation Act of 1982. Introduced by ROSTENKOWSKI, D-Ill., Oct. 6, 1983. House Post Office and Civil Service discharged. House passed Oct. 6. Senate passed, amended, Oct. 6. House agreed to Senate amendment Oct. 6. President signed Oct. 11, 1983.

PL 98-119 (S J Res 159) Authorize the further participation of U.S. Armed Forces in the multinational peacekeeping force in Lebanon. Introduced by MATHIAS, R-Md., Sept. 12, 1983. Senate Foreign Relations reported Sept. 26 (S Rept 98-242). Senate passed Sept. 29. House passed Sept. 29. President signed Oct. 12, 1983.

PL 98-120 (HR 3813) Extend presidential authority to implement the International Coffee Agreement Act of 1980. Introduced by GUARINI, D-N.J., Aug. 4, 1983. House Ways and Means reported Sept. 22 (H Rept 98-376). House passed, under suspension of the rules, Sept. 27. Senate passed, amended, Sept. 30. House agreed to Senate amendment Sept. 30. President signed Oct. 12, 1983.

PL 98-121 (S 1465) Designate the federal building at Fourth and Cherry Streets, Lafayette, Ind., as the "Charles A. Halleck Federal Building." Introduced by LUGAR, R-Ind., June 14, 1983. Senate Environment and Public Works reported Aug. 3. Senate passed Aug. 4. House Public Works and Transportation discharged. House passed Oct. 3. President signed Oct. 12, 1983.

PL 98-122 (S 1724) Designate the federal building in Las Cruces, N.M., as the "Harold L. Runnels Federal Building." Introduced by DOMENICI, R-N.M., Aug. 2, 1983. Senate Environment and Public Works reported Aug. 3. Senate passed Aug. 4. House Public Works and Transportation discharged. House passed Oct. 3. President signed Oct. 12, 1983.

PL 98-123 (S 884) Provide for the use and distribution of funds awarded the Red Lake Band of Chippewa Indians in docket numbered 15-72 of the U.S. Court of Claims. Introduced by DURENBERGER, R-Minn., March 22, 1983. Senate Indian Affairs reported May 5 (S Rept 98-74). Senate passed May 12. House Interior and Insular Affairs reported Sept. 28 (H Rept 98-389). House passed Oct. 3. President signed Oct. 13, 1983.

PL 98-124 (S 1148) Provide for the use and distribution of funds awarded the Assiniboine Tribe of the Fort Belknap Indian Community, Mont., and the Assiniboine Tribe of the Fort Peck Indian Community, Mont., in docket numbered 10-81L by the U.S. Court of Claims. Introduced by MELCHER, D-Mont., April 26, 1983. Senate Indian Affairs reported July 29 (S Rept 98-204). Senate passed Aug. 3. House Interior and Insular Affairs reported Sept. 28 (H Rept 98-390). House passed Oct. 3. President signed Oct. 13, 1983.

PL 98-125 (HR 3415) Appropriate funds for fiscal year 1984 for the District of Columbia government. Introduced by DIXON, D-Calif., June 23, 1983. House District of Columbia reported June 23 (H Rept 98-265). House passed June 29. Senate Appropriations reported July 19 (S Rept 98-185). Senate passed, amended, July 27. House agreed to conference report Sept. 29 (H Rept 98-379). Senate agreed to conference report Sept. 29. President signed Oct. 13, 1983.

PL 98-126 (S J Res 102) Designate the week of Oct. 16-22, 1983, as "Lupus Awareness Week." Introduced by SPECTER, R-Pa., May 17, 1983. Senate Judiciary reported July 14. Senate passed July 16. House Post Office and Civil Service discharged. House passed Oct. 4. President signed Oct. 13, 1983.

PL 98-127 (S 216) Impose penalties on those individuals who tamper with food, drug, cosmetic and other products with intent to cause personal injury, death or other harm. Introduced by THURMOND, R-S.C., Jan. 27, 1983. Senate Judiciary reported May 2 (S Rept 98-69). Senate passed May 9. House passed, amended, Sept. 29. Senate agreed

to House amendments Sept. 30. President signed Oct. 13, 1983.

PL 98-128 (HR 3379) Name a U.S. Post Office building in the vicinity of Lancaster, Pa., the "Edwin D. Eshleman Post Office Building." Introduced by WALKER, R-Pa., June 21, 1983. House Public Works and Transportation reported Sept. 20 (H Rept 98-361). House passed Oct. 3. Senate passed Oct. 6. President signed Oct. 14, 1983.

PL 98-129 (HR 2840) Provide for the orderly termination of federal management of the Pribilof Islands, Alaska. Introduced by YOUNG, R-Alaska, April 28, 1983. House Merchant Marine and Fisheries reported May 23 (H Rept 98-213). House passed, under suspension of the rules, May 23. Senate Commerce, Science and Transportation reported Aug. 3 (S Rept 98-212). Senate passed, amended, Aug. 4. House agreed to Senate amendment with an amendment Sept. 26. Senate agreed to House amendment Sept. 28. President signed Oct. 14, 1983.

PL 98-130 (S J Res 128) Designate Oct. 22, 1983, as "Metropolitan Opera Day." Introduced by MOYNIHAN, D-N.Y., July 13, 1983. Senate Judiciary reported Sept. 15. Senate passed Sept. 20. House Post Office and Civil Service discharged. House passed Oct. 4. President signed Oct. 14, 1983.

PL 98-131 (HR 3835) Designate the U.S. Post Office building in Oshkosh, Wis., as the "William A. Steiger Post Office Building." Introduced by PETRI, R-Wis., Aug. 4, 1983. House Post Office and Civil Service discharged. House passed Oct. 5. Senate passed Oct. 6. President signed Oct. 17, 1983.

PL 98-132 (S 1894) Designate the Foundation for the Advancement of Military Medicine as the "Henry M. Jackson Foundation for the Advancement of Military Medicine." Introduced by STEVENS, R-Alaska, Sept. 27, 1983. Senate passed Sept. 30. House Armed Services discharged. House passed Oct. 5. President signed Oct. 17, 1983.

PL 98-133 (HR 1556) Authorize the conveyance of the Liberty Ship *John W. Brown* to the John W. Brown Preservation Project. Introduced by BIAGGI, D-N.Y., Feb. 17, 1983. House Merchant Marine and Fisheries reported June 23 (H Rept 98-261). House passed Aug. 2. Senate Commerce, Science and Transportation reported Sept. 26. Senate passed, amended, Sept. 30. House agreed to Senate amendment Oct. 6. President signed Oct. 18, 1983.

PL 98-134 (S 1499) Settle certain claims of the Mashantucket Pequot Indians. Introduced by WEICKER, R-Conn., June 20, 1983. Senate Indian Affairs reported Sept. 14 (S Rept 98-222). Senate passed Sept. 30. House passed Oct. 4. President signed Oct. 18, 1983.

PL 98-135 (HR 3929) Extend the federal supplemental compensation program for 18 months. Introduced by ROSTENKOWSKI, D-Ill., Sept. 20, 1983. House Ways and Means reported Sept. 22 (H Rept 98-377). House passed Sept. 29. Senate passed, amended, Sept. 30. House agreed to conference report Oct. 21 (H Rept 98-428). Senate agreed to conference report Oct. 21. President signed Oct. 24, 1983.

PL 98-136 (HR 3321) Provide for the striking of medals to commemorate the Louisiana World Exposition. Introduced by LIVINGSTON, R-La., June 15, 1983. House passed, under suspension of the rules, Oct. 17. Senate passed Oct. 20. President signed Oct. 24, 1983.

PL 98-137 (HR 1062) Authorize the secretary of the interior to convey, without consideration, certain lands in Lane County, Ore. Introduced by WEAVER, D-Ore., Jan. 27, 1983. House Interior and Insular Affairs reported May 4 (H Rept 98-84). House passed Oct. 3. Senate passed Oct. 6. President vetoed Oct. 19. House passed over veto Oct. 25. Senate passed over veto Oct. 25. Became law without presidential approval Oct. 25, 1983.

PL 98-138 (HR 3044) Grant the consent of Congress to an interstate agreement or compact relating to the restoration of Atlantic salmon in the Connecticut River Basin, and allow the secretaries of commerce and the interior to participate as members of a Connecticut River Atlantic Salmon Commission. Introduced by CONTE, R-Mass., May 18, 1983. House Merchant Marine and Fisheries reported Sept. 28 (H Rept 98-392). House passed, under suspension of the rules, Oct. 4. Senate passed Oct. 19. President signed Oct. 28, 1983.

PL 98-139 (HR 3913) Appropriate funds for fiscal year 1984 for the departments of Labor, Health and Human Services, Education and related agencies. Introduced by NATCHER, D-Ky., Sept. 16, 1983. House Appropriations reported Sept. 16 (H Rept 98-357). House passed Sept. 22. Senate Appropriations reported Sept. 28 (S Rept 98-247). Senate passed, amended, Oct. 4. House agreed to conference report Oct. 20 (H Rept 98-422). Senate agreed to conference report Oct. 20. President signed Oct. 31, 1983.

PL 98-140 (S 96) Establish the Lee Metcalf Wilderness and Management Area in Montana. Introduced by MELCHER, D-Mont., Jan. 26, 1983. Senate Energy and Natural Resources reported March 3 (S Rept 98-16). Senate passed April 13. House Interior and Insular Affairs reported Oct. 5 (H Rept 98-405, Part I). House Agriculture discharged. House passed, amended, Oct. 6. Senate agreed to House amendment Oct. 19. President signed Oct. 31, 1983.

PL 98-141 (HR 1213) Amend certain provisions of law relating to units

of the national park system and other public lands. Introduced by SEIBERLING, D-Ohio, Feb. 2, 1983. House Interior and Insular Affairs reported March 2 (H Rept 98-15). House passed, under suspension of the rules, March 8. Senate Energy and Natural Resources reported May 20 (S Rept 98-141). Senate passed, amended, Oct. 6. House agreed to Senate amendments Oct. 20. President signed Oct. 31, 1983.

PL 98-142 (S J Res 57) Designate the week of Nov. 2-9, 1983, as "National Drug Abuse Education Week." Introduced by CHILES, D-Fla., March 9, 1983. Senate Judiciary reported March 17. Senate passed March 18. House Post Office and Civil Service discharged. House passed, amended, Oct. 26. Senate agreed to House amendments Oct. 31. President signed Nov. 1, 1983.

PL 98-143 (S J Res 189) Extend the expiration date of the Export-Import Bank Act of 1945. Introduced by STEVENS, R-Alaska, Oct. 27, 1983. Senate passed Oct. 28. House passed Oct. 31. President signed Nov. 1, 1983.

PL 98-144 (HR 3706) Amend title 5, U.S.C., making the birthday of Martin Luther King Jr. a legal holiday. Introduced by HALL, D-Ind., July 29, 1983. House passed, under suspension of the rules, Aug. 2. Senate passed Oct. 19. President signed Nov. 2, 1983.

PL 98-145 (S J Res 121) Designate November 1983 as "National Diabetes Month." Introduced by ABDNOR, R-S.D., June 23, 1983. Senate Judiciary reported Sept. 15. Senate passed Sept. 20. House Post Office and Civil Service discharged. House passed Oct. 26. President signed Nov. 3, 1983.

PL 98-146 (HR 3363) Appropriate funds for fiscal year 1984 for the Department of the Interior and certain related agencies. Introduced by YATES, D-Ill., June 21, 1983. House Appropriations reported June 21 (H Rept 98-253). House passed June 28. Senate Appropriations reported July 19 (S Rept 98-184). Senate passed, amended, Sept. 21. House agreed to conference report Oct. 5 (H Rept 98-399). Senate agreed to conference report Oct. 19. House agreed to Senate amendments to House amendments to Senate amendments Oct. 20. President signed Nov. 4, 1983.

PL 98-147 (S J Res 45) Designate the week of Nov. 20-26, 1983, as "National Family Week." Introduced by BURDICK, D-N.D., March 2, 1983. Senate Judiciary reported April 19. Senate passed April 21. House Post Office and Civil Service discharged. House passed Oct. 26. President signed Nov. 4, 1983.

PL 98-148 (S 552) Designate the federal building in Fort Myers, Fla., as the "George W. Whitehurst Federal Building and U.S. Courthouse." Introduced by CHILES, D-Fla., Feb. 22, 1983. Senate Environment and Public Works reported Sept. 29. Senate passed Sept. 30. House Public Works and Transportation discharged. House passed, amended, Oct. 4. Senate agreed to House amendment Oct. 27. President signed Nov. 7, 1983.

PL 98-149 (S 1944) Allow the obsolete submarine U.S.S. *Albacore* to be transferred to the Portsmouth Submarine Memorial Association Inc. before the expiration of the otherwise applicable 60-day congressional review period. Introduced by RUDMAN, R-N.H., Oct. 7, 1983. Senate Armed Services reported Oct. 18. Senate passed Oct. 20. House Armed Services discharged. House passed Oct. 26. President signed Nov. 7, 1983.

PL 98-150 (S 461) Authorize funds through fiscal year 1989 for the Office of Government Ethics. Introduced by COHEN, R-Maine, Feb. 3, 1983. Senate Governmental Affairs reported March 24 (S Rept 98-59). Senate passed April 6. House Post Office and Civil Service and House Judiciary discharged. House passed, amended, Sept. 19. Senate agreed to House amendments with an amendment Sept. 28. House agreed to Senate amendment with amendments Sept. 30. Senate agreed to House amendments Oct. 27. President signed Nov. 11, 1983.

PL 98-151 (H J Res 413) Make further continuing appropriations for fiscal year 1984 for the federal government. Introduced by WHITTEN, D-Miss., Nov. 9, 1983. House passed Nov. 10. Senate passed, amended, Nov. 11. House agreed to conference report Nov. 12 (H Rept 98-540). Senate agreed to conference report Nov. 12. President signed Nov. 14, 1983.

PL 98-152 (H J Res 283) Designate the week beginning Nov. 6, 1983, as "National Disabled Veterans Week." Introduced by BADHAM, R-Calif., May 26, 1983. House Post Office and Civil Service discharged. House passed Sept. 15. Senate Judiciary reported Nov. 3. Senate passed Nov. 10. President signed Nov. 15, 1983.

PL 98-153 (S J Res 122) Designate the week of Nov. 27-Dec. 3, 1983, as "National Home Care Week." Introduced by HATCH, R-Utah, June 23, 1983. Senate Judiciary reported Sept. 30. Senate passed Oct. 4. House Post Office and Civil Service discharged. House passed Nov. 4. President signed Nov. 15, 1983.

PL 98-154 (S J Res 188) Designate November 1983 as "National Christmas Seal Month." Introduced by BYRD, D-W.Va., Oct. 26, 1983. Senate passed Oct. 27. House Post Office and Civil Service discharged. House passed Nov. 4. President signed Nov. 16, 1983.

PL 98-155 (H J Res 408) Designate Nov. 12, 1983, as "Anti-Defamation League Day," in honor of the League's seventieth anniversary. Introduced by PATTERSON, D-Calif., Nov. 1, 1983. House Post Office and Civil Service discharged. House passed Nov. 10. Senate passed Nov. 11. President signed Nov. 16, 1983.

PL 98-156 (H J Res 383) Designate the week beginning Nov. 6, 1983, as "Florence Crittenton Mission Week." Introduced by DANNEMEYER, R-Calif., Oct. 6, 1983. House Post Office and Civil Service discharged. House passed Nov. 4. Senate Judiciary discharged. Senate passed Nov. 10. President signed Nov. 17, 1983.

PL 98-157 (S 448) Authorize rehabilitation of the Belle Fourche irrigation project. Introduced by ABDNOR, R-S.D., Feb. 3, 1983. Senate Energy and Natural Resources reported May 20 (S Rept 98-138). Senate passed June 15. House Interior and Insular Affairs reported Oct. 18 (H Rept 98-415). House passed, amended, under suspension of the rules, Nov. 1. Senate agreed to House amendment Nov. 3. President signed Nov. 17, 1983.

PL 98-158 (S J Res 92) Designate the week beginning May 13, 1984, "Municipal Clerk's Week." Introduced by HAWKINS, R-Fla., May 3, 1983. Senate Judiciary reported May 19. Senate passed May 20. House Post Office and Civil Service discharged. House passed, amended, Sept. 27. Senate agreed to House amendments Nov. 3. President signed Nov. 17, 1983.

PL 98-159 (HR 3348) Honor Congressman Leo J. Ryan and award a special congressional gold medal to the family of the late Honorable Leo J. Ryan. Introduced by LANTOS, D-Calif., June 16, 1983. House Banking, Finance and Urban Affairs discharged. House passed, under suspension of the rules, Oct. 18. Senate Banking, Housing and Urban Affairs reported Nov. 2. Senate passed Nov. 10. President signed Nov. 18, 1983.

PL 98-160 (HR 2920) Amend title 38, U.S. Code, to revise and extend certain health-care programs of the Veterans' Administration. Introduced by EDGAR, D-Pa., May 5, 1983. House Veterans' Affairs reported May 13 (H Rept 98-117). House passed, under suspension of the rules, May 23. Senate passed, amended, June 28. House agreed to Senate amendments with amendments Nov. 2. Senate agreed to House amendments to Senate amendments Nov. 3. President signed Nov. 21, 1983.

PL 98-161 (H J Res 308) Increase the statutory limit on the public debt. Introduced by FOLEY, D-Wash., June 27, 1983. House passed June 27. Senate Finance reported Oct. 25 (S Rept 98-279). Senate defeated Oct. 31. Senate passed, amended, Nov. 17. House disagreed to Senate amendments Nov. 17. Senate agreed to conference report Nov. 17 (H Rept 98-566). House agreed to conference report Nov. 18. President signed Nov. 21.

PL 98-162 (S J Res 139) Commemorate the centennial of Eleanor Roosevelt's birth. Introduced by MOYNIHAN, D-N.Y., July 28, 1983. Senate Energy and Natural Resources discharged. Senate passed Nov. 2. House passed Nov. 4. President signed Nov. 21, 1983.

PL 98-163 (HR 2910) Amend the act of Nov. 2, 1966, regarding leases and contracts affecting land within the Salt River Pima-Maricopa Indian Reservation. Introduced by McCAIN, R-Ariz., May 4, 1983. House Interior and Insular Affairs reported Oct. 20 (H Rept 98-424). House passed Nov. 7. Senate passed Nov. 11. President signed Nov. 22, 1983.

PL 98-164 (HR 2915) Authorize appropriations for fiscal years 1984 and 1985 for the Department of State, the U.S. Information Agency, the Board for International Broadcasting, the Inter-American Foundation, the Asia Foundation, and establish the National Endowment for Democracy. Introduced by FASCELL, D-Fla., May 5, 1983. House Foreign Affairs reported May 16 (H Rept 98-130). House passed June 9. Senate passed, amended, Oct. 20. House disagreed to Senate amendments Oct. 25. House agreed to conference report Nov. 18 (H Rept 98-563). Senate agreed to conference report Nov. 18. President signed Nov. 22, 1983.

PL 98-165 (HR 3885) Provide for the restoration of federal recognition to the Confederated Tribes of the Grand Ronde Community of Oregon. Introduced by AuCOIN, D-Ore., Sept. 14, 1983. House Interior and Insular Affairs reported Nov. 2 (H Rept 98-464). House passed Nov. 7. Senate passed Nov. 11. President signed Nov. 22, 1983.

PL 98-166 (HR 3222) Make appropriations for the Departments of Commerce, Justice, and State, the Judiciary, and related agencies for the fiscal year ending Sept. 30, 1984. Introduced by SMITH, D-Iowa, June 3, 1983. House Appropriations reported June 3 (H Rept 98-232). House passed Sept. 19. Senate passed, amended, Oct. 21. House disagreed to Senate amendments Oct. 31. House agreed to conference report Nov. 9 (H Rept 98-478). Senate agreed to conference report Nov. 15. President signed Nov. 28, 1983.

PL 98-167 (S 376) Amend the Debt Collection Act of 1982 to eliminate the requirement that contracts for collection services to recover indebtedness owed the U.S. be effective only to the extent and in the amount provided in advance appropriation acts. Introduced by

PERCY, R-Ill., Feb. 2, 1983. Senate Governmental Affairs reported May 5 (S Rept 98-75). Senate passed May 20. House Judiciary reported Nov. 4 (H Rept 98-482). House passed, under suspension of the rules, Nov. 14. President signed Nov. 29, 1983.

PL 98-168 (HR 2077) Amend title 5, U.S. Code, to extend the Federal Physicians Comparability Allowance Act of 1978. Introduced by OAKAR, D-Ohio, March 11, 1983. House Post Office and Civil Service discharged. House passed, under suspension of the rules, Sept. 19. Senate Governmental Affairs discharged. Senate passed, amended, Sept. 30. Senate agreed to conference report Nov. 11 (H Rept 98-542). House agreed to conference report Nov. 16. President signed Nov. 29, 1983.

PL 98-169 (HR 2592) Transfer from the director of the Office of Management and Budget to the administrator of General Services the responsibility for publication of the catalog of federal domestic assistance programs. Introduced by BROOKS, D-Texas, April 19, 1983. House Government Operations reported May 12 (H Rept 98-112). House passed, under suspension of the rules, June 1. Senate passed, amended, Oct. 28. House agreed to Senate amendments Nov. 17. President signed Nov. 29, 1983.

PL 98-170 (S 807) Amend the boundaries of the Cumberland Island National Seashore. Introduced by NUNN, D-Ga., March 15, 1983. Senate Energy and Natural Resources reported Sept. 29 (S Rept 98-256). Senate passed Oct. 6. House Interior and Insular Affairs reported Nov. 10 (H Rept 98-529). House passed, under suspension of the rules, Nov. 15. President signed Nov. 29, 1983.

PL 98-171 (HR 2590) Amend the Agricultural Adjustment Act to authorize marketing research and promotion projects, including paid advertising, for filberts. Introduced by AuCOIN, D-Ore., April 19, 1983. House Agriculture reported July 29 (H Rept 98-335). House passed, under suspension of the rules, Aug. 1. Senate Agriculture discharged. Senate passed Nov. 17. President signed Nov. 29, 1983.

PL 98-172 (H J Res 93) Provide for the awarding of a special gold medal to Danny Thomas in recognition of his humanitarian efforts and outstanding work as an American. Introduced by RAHALL, D-W.Va., Jan. 25, 1983. House Banking, Finance and Urban Affairs discharged. House passed, under suspension of the rules, Nov. 7. Senate Banking, Housing and Urban Affairs discharged. Senate passed Nov. 17. President signed Nov. 29, 1983.

PL 98-173 (S 1168) Declare that the U.S. holds certain lands in trust for the Kaw Tribe of Oklahoma. Introduced by BOREN, D-Okla., April 27, 1983. Senate Indian Affairs reported July 11 (S Rept 98-175). Senate passed July 20. House Interior and Insular Affairs reported. House passed Nov. 14. President signed Nov. 29, 1983.

PL 98-174 (S 1837) Designate the federal building in Seattle, Wash., as the "Henry M. Jackson Federal Building." Introduced by GORTON, R-Wash., Sept. 13, 1983. Senate Environment and Public Works reported Sept. 29. Senate passed Sept. 30. House passed Nov. 18. President signed Nov. 29, 1983.

PL 98-175 (HR 24) Make certain land owned by the U.S. in the state of New York part of the Green Mountain National Forest. Introduced by HORTON, R-N.Y., Jan. 3, 1983. House Agriculture reported July 14 (H Rept 98-293). House passed, under suspension of the rules, July 18. Senate Agriculture reported Oct. 31 (S Rept 98-288). Senate passed Nov. 17. President signed Nov. 29, 1983.

PL 98-176 (HR 594) Amend section 1 of the act of June 5, 1920, as amended, to authorize the secretary of commerce to settle claims for damages of less than $2,500 arising by reason of acts for which the National Oceanic and Atmospheric Administration is responsible. Introduced by SAM B. HALL JR., D-Texas, Jan. 6, 1983. House Judiciary reported April 14 (H Rept 98-62). House passed May 3. Senate Judiciary discharged. Senate passed Nov. 15. President signed Nov. 29, 1983.

PL 98-177 (HR 4013) Extend the Small Business Development Center program administered by the Small Business Administration until Jan. 1, 1985. Introduced by MITCHELL, D-Md., Sept. 28, 1983. House Small Business reported Oct. 6 (H Rept 98-406). House passed, under suspension of the rules, Oct. 18. Senate passed Nov. 17. President signed Nov. 29, 1983.

PL 98-178 (H J Res 168) Designate the week beginning May 27, 1984, as "National Tourism Week." Introduced by RITTER, R-Pa., March 2, 1983. House Post Office and Civil Service discharged. House passed June 22. Senate Judiciary reported Nov. 10. Senate passed Nov. 15. President signed Nov. 29, 1983.

PL 98-179 (H J Res 421) Provide for the convening of the second session of the 98th Congress. Introduced by FOLEY, D-Wash., Nov. 16, 1983. House passed Nov. 16. Senate passed Nov. 18. President signed Nov. 29, 1983.

PL 98-180 (HR 3385) Provide equity to cotton producers under the Payment-in-Kind program. Introduced by HUCKABY, D-La., June 22, 1983. House Agriculture reported July 12 (H Rept 98-289). House passed, under suspension of the rules, July 19. Senate passed,

amended, Oct. 7. House agreed to Senate amendments, with amendments, Nov. 9. Senate disagreed to House amendments to Senate amendments Nov. 14. Senate agreed to conference report Nov. 17 (H Rept 98-556). House agreed to conference report Nov. 18. President signed Nov. 29, 1983.

PL 98-181 (HR 3959) Make supplemental appropriations for the fiscal year ending Sept. 30, 1984. Introduced by WHITTEN, D-Miss., Sept. 22, 1983. House Appropriations reported Sept. 22 (H Rept 98-375). House passed Oct. 5. Senate Appropriations reported Oct. 19 (S Rept 98-275). Senate passed, amended, Oct. 27. House disagreed to Senate amendments Nov. 4. House agreed to conference report Nov. 16 (H Rept 98-551). Senate agreed to conference report Nov. 17. House agreed to Senate amendments to House amendments to Senate amendments Nov. 18. President signed Nov. 30, 1983.

PL 98-182 (S J Res 44) Authorize the president to issue a proclamation designating the week beginning March 11, 1984, as "National Surveyors Week." Introduced by THURMOND, R-S.C., March 2, 1983. Senate Judiciary reported March 17. Senate passed March 18. House Post Office and Civil Service discharged. House passed Nov. 17. President signed Nov. 30, 1983.

PL 98-183 (HR 2230) Amend the Civil Rights Act of 1957 to extend the life of the Civil Rights Commission. Introduced by EDWARDS, D-Calif., March 22, 1983. House Judiciary reported May 17 (H Rept 98-197). House passed Aug. 4. Senate passed, amended, Nov. 14. House agreed to Senate amendments Nov. 16. President signed Nov. 30, 1983.

PL 98-184 (HR 2479) Amend the act of March 3, 1969, incorporating the Masonic Mutual Relief Association of the District of Columbia, now known as Acacia Mutual Life Insurance Co. Introduced by SAM B. HALL JR., D-Texas, April 12, 1983. House Judiciary reported Oct. 6 (H Rept 98-408). House passed Nov. 7. Senate Judiciary reported Nov. 17. Senate passed Nov. 18. President signed Nov. 30, 1983.

PL 98-185 (HR 2780) Extend and amend the provisions of title 31, U.S. Code, relating to the general revenue sharing program. Introduced by WEISS, D-N.Y., April 27, 1983. House Government Operations reported May 16 (H Rept 98-179). House passed Aug. 2. Senate passed, amended, Sept. 21. House disagreed to Senate amendments Sept. 29. House agreed to conference report Nov. 17 (H Rept 98-550). Senate agreed to conference report Nov. 17. President signed Nov. 30, 1983.

PL 98-186 (S 450) Amend title 39, U.S. Code, to strengthen the investigatory and enforcement powers of the Postal Service by authorizing certain inspection authority and by providing for civil penalties for violations of orders under section 3005 of such title (pertaining to schemes for obtaining money by false representation or lotteries). Introduced by PRYOR, D-Ark., Feb. 3, 1983. Senate Governmental Affairs reported March 31 (S Rept 98-51). Senate passed Nov. 3. House Post Office and Civil Service discharged. House passed, under suspension of the rules, Nov. 16. President signed Nov. 30, 1983.

PL 98-187 (S J Res 141) Designate the week of Dec. 4-10, 1983, as "Carrier Alert Week." Introduced by BINGAMAN, D-N.M, Aug. 1, 1983. Senate Judiciary reported Nov. 8. Senate passed Nov. 10. House Post Office and Civil Service discharged. House passed Nov. 17. President signed Nov. 30, 1983.

PL 98-188 (H J Res 324) Designate the week beginning Jan. 15, 1984, as "National Fetal Alcohol Syndrome Awareness Week." Introduced by KASICH, R-Ohio, July 19, 1983. House Post Office and Civil Service discharged. House passed Nov. 17. Senate passed Nov. 18. President signed Nov. 30, 1983.

PL 98-189 (HR 2196) Extend the authorization of appropriations of the National Historical Publications and Records Commission for five years. Introduced by BROOKS, D-Texas, March 21, 1983. House Government Operations reported May 16 (H Rept 98-129). House passed, under suspension of the rules, June 1. Senate Governmental Affairs discharged. Senate passed, amended, Nov. 18. House agreed to Senate amendments Nov. 18. President signed Nov. 30, 1983.

PL 98-190 (HR 4294) Name the Veterans' Administration Medical Center in Altoona, Pa., the "James E. Van Zandt Veterans' Administration Medical Center," and name the Veterans' Administration Medical Center in Dublin, Ga., the "Carl Vinson Veterans' Administration Medical Center." Introduced by EDGAR, D-Pa., Nov. 3, 1983. House Veterans' Affairs reported Nov. 3 (H Rept 98-481). House passed, under suspension of the rules, Nov. 8. Senate Veterans' Affairs discharged. Senate passed Nov. 18. President signed Nov. 30, 1983.

PL 98-191 (HR 2293) Amend the Office of Federal Procurement Policy Act. Introduced by BROOKS, D-Texas, March 23, 1983. House Government Operations reported May 16 (H Rept 98-146). House passed, under suspension of the rules, June 1. Senate passed, amended, Nov. 15. House agreed to Senate amendments Nov. 17. President signed Dec. 1, 1983.

PL 98-192 (S 726) Amend and extend the Tribally Controlled Community College Assistance Act of 1978. Introduced by ANDREWS, R-N.D., March 8, 1983. Senate Indian Affairs reported April 26 (S Rept 98-64). Senate passed May 25. House passed, amended, Oct. 20. Sen-

ate disagreed to House amendments Oct. 26. House agreed to conference report Nov. 17 (H Rept 98-505). Senate agreed to conference report Nov. 17. President signed Dec. 1, 1983.

PL 98-193 (S 1046) Clarify the applicability of a provision of law regarding risk retention. Introduced by KASTEN, R-Wis., April 13, 1983. Senate Commerce, Science and Transportation reported July 5 (S Rept 98-172). Senate passed Sept. 27. House passed Nov. 18. President signed Dec. 1, 1983.

PL 98-194 (S 2129) Provide revised reimbursement criteria for small rural health clinics utilizing National Health Service Corps personnel. Introduced by HATCH, R-Utah, Nov. 17, 1983. Senate passed Nov. 18. House passed Nov. 18. President signed Dec. 1, 1983.

PL 98-195 (S 1503) Release the reversionary clause by the federal government on 6.21 acres in the deed to the land conveyed to the state of Delaware Sept. 24, 1954. Introduced by ROTH, R-Del., June 20, 1983. Senate Agriculture reported Oct. 31 (S Rept 98-287). Senate passed Nov. 17. House Agriculture discharged. House passed Nov. 18. President signed Dec. 1, 1983.

PL 98-196 (S 577) Provide for the conveyance of certain federal lands adjacent to Orchard and Lake Shore Drives, Lake Lowell, Boise project, Idaho. Introduced by McCLURE, R-Idaho, Feb. 23, 1983. Senate Energy and Natural Resources reported Feb. 23 (S Rept 98-7). Senate passed March 2. House Interior and Insular Affairs reported June 28 (H Rept 98-269). House passed, amended, July 18. Senate agreed to House amendment Nov. 18. President signed Dec. 1, 1983.

PL 98-197 (H J Res 405) Extend the term of the Presidential Commission for the German-American Tricentennial. Introduced by COURTER, R-N.J., Oct. 28, 1983. House Post Office and Civil Service discharged. House passed Nov. 4. Senate Judiciary discharged. Senate passed Nov. 18. President signed Dec. 1, 1983.

PL 98-198 (S J Res 111) Express the sense of the Congress with respect to international efforts to further a revolution in child health. Introduced by PERCY, R-Ill., May 26, 1983. Senate Foreign Relations reported July 11. Senate passed July 14. House Foreign Affairs discharged. House passed Nov. 17. President signed Dec. 1, 1983.

PL 98-199 (S 1341) Revise and extend the Education of the Handicapped Act. Introduced by HATCH, R-Utah, May 23, 1983. Senate Labor and Human Resources reported May 23 (S Rept 98-191). Senate passed June 27. House Education and Labor discharged. House passed, amended, Nov. 17. Senate agreed to House amendment Nov. 18. President signed Dec. 2, 1983.

PL 98-200 (HR 2395) Extend the Wetlands Loan Act. Introduced by BREAUX, D-La., April 5, 1983. House Merchant Marine and Fisheries reported May 16 (H Rept 98-132). House passed, under suspension of the rules, Oct. 31. Senate Environment and Public Works discharged. Senate passed, amended, Nov. 17. House agreed to Senate amendments Nov. 17. President signed Dec. 2, 1983.

PL 98-201 (HR 2785) Amend the provisions of the Federal Insecticide, Fungicide, and Rodenticide Act relating to the scientific advisory panel and extend the authorization for appropriations for such act. Introduced by BROWN, D-Calif., April 27, 1983. House Agriculture reported May 10 (H Rept 98-104). House passed, under suspension of the rules, May 17. Senate Agriculture discharged. Senate passed Nov. 18. President signed Dec. 2, 1983.

PL 98-202 (HR 2906) Amend the Arms Control and Disarmament Act in order to extend the authorization for appropriations. Introduced by ZABLOCKI, D-Wis., May 4, 1983. House Foreign Affairs reported May 16 (H Rept 98-180). House passed, under suspension of the rules, May 23. Senate passed, amended, Nov. 10. House disagreed to Senate amendments Nov. 14. House agreed to conference report Nov. 17 (H Rept 98-564). Senate agreed to conference report Nov. 18. President signed Dec. 2, 1983.

PL 98-203 (HR 3765) Declare that the U.S. holds certain lands in trust for the Las Vegas Paiute Tribe. Introduced by REID, D-Nev., Aug. 3, 1983. House Interior and Insular Affairs reported Nov. 10 (H Rept 98-530). House passed Nov. 18. Senate passed Nov. 18. President signed Dec. 2, 1983.

PL 98-204 (HR 4252) Repeal the non-cash benefit requirement for the Puerto Rico nutrition assistance program. Introduced by CORRADA, New Prog.-Puerto Rico, Oct. 31, 1983. House Agriculture reported Nov. 11 (H Rept 98-539). House passed, under suspension of the rules, Nov. 15. Senate passed, amended, Nov. 17. House agreed to Senate amendments with an amendment Nov. 17. Senate agreed to House amendment to Senate amendments Nov. 18. President signed Dec. 2, 1983.

PL 98-205 (S 505) Designate the federal building to be constructed in Savannah, Ga., as the "Juliette Gordon Low Federal Building." Introduced by MATTINGLY, R-Ga., Feb. 17, 1983. Senate Environment and Public Works reported May 17 (S Rept 98-123). Senate passed Aug. 3. House passed, amended, Nov. 18. Senate agreed to House amendment Nov. 18. President signed Dec. 2, 1983.

PL 98-206 (H J Res 311) Proclaim March 20, 1984, as "National Agriculture Day." Introduced by DE LA GARZA, D-Texas, June 29, 1983. House Post Office and Civil Service discharged. House passed Sept. 15. Senate Judiciary reported Nov. 17. Senate passed Nov. 18. President signed Dec. 2, 1983.

PL 98-207 (HR 4476) Extend the authorities under the Export Administration Act of 1979. Introduced by BONKER, D-Wash., Nov. 18, 1983. House Foreign Affairs discharged. House passed Nov. 18. Senate passed Nov. 18. President signed Dec. 5, 1983.

PL 98-208 (H J Res 381) Provide for appointment of Samuel Curtis Johnson as a citizen regent of the Board of Regents of the Smithsonian Institution. Introduced by BOLAND, D-Mass., Oct. 4, 1983. House Administration discharged. House passed Nov. 17. Senate passed Nov. 18. President signed Dec. 5, 1983.

PL 98-209 (S 974) Amend chapter 47 of title 10, U.S. Code (the Uniform Code of Military Justice), to improve the quality and efficiency of the military justice system and to revise the laws concerning review of courts-martial. Introduced by JEPSEN, R-Iowa, April 5, 1983. Senate Armed Services reported April 5 (S Rept 98-53). Senate passed April 28. House Armed Services reported Nov. 15 (H Rept 98-549). House passed, amended, under suspension of the rules, Nov. 16. Senate agreed to House amendment Nov. 18. President signed Dec. 6, 1983.

PL 98-210 (S 1099) Consolidate and authorize certain marine fishery programs and functions of the National Oceanic and Atmospheric Administration under the Department of Commerce. Introduced by PACKWOOD, R-Ore., April 19, 1983. Senate Commerce, Science and Transportation reported May 9 (S Rept 98-80). Senate passed June 15. House passed, amended, Nov. 16. Senate agreed to House amendment Nov. 18. President signed Dec. 6, 1983.

PL 98-211 (HR 1035) Make certain technical amendments to improve implementation of the Education Consolidation and Improvement Act of 1981. Introduced by GOODLING, R-Pa., Jan. 27, 1983. House Education and Labor reported April 7 (H Rept 98-51). House passed, under suspension of the rules, April 12. Senate Labor and Human Resources discharged. Senate passed, amended, Oct. 7. House disagreed to Senate amendments Nov. 14. House agreed to conference report Nov. 18 (H Rept 98-574). Senate agreed to conference report Nov. 18. President signed Dec. 8, 1983.

PL 98-212 (HR 4185) Make appropriations for the Department of Defense for the fiscal year ending Sept. 30, 1984. Introduced by ADDABBO, D-N.Y., Oct. 20, 1983. House Appropriations reported Oct. 20 (H Rept 98-427). House passed Nov. 2. Senate passed, amended, Nov. 8. House disagreed to Senate amendments Nov. 15. House agreed to conference report Nov. 18 (H Rept 98-567). Senate agreed to conference report Nov. 18. President signed Dec. 8, 1983.

PL 98-213 (S 589) Amend section 1(a)(1) of PL 95-348 (92 Stat. 487) to authorize the appropriation of $4,038,000 for capital improvement projects on Guam for fiscal year 1984. Introduced by McCLURE, R-Idaho, Feb. 24, 1983. Senate Energy and Natural Resources reported March 31 (S Rept 98-46). Senate passed April 7. House Interior and Insular Affairs reported May 16 (H Rept 98-174). House passed, amended, Oct. 3. Senate agreed to House amendment with an amendment Nov. 17. House agreed to Senate amendments to House amendments Nov. 18. President signed Dec. 8, 1983.

PL 98-214 (HR 2755) Authorize appropriations for the Federal Communications Commission for fiscal years 1984 and 1985. Introduced by WIRTH, D-Colo., April 26, 1983. House Energy and Commerce reported Sept. 15 (H Rept 98-356). House passed Nov. 18. Senate passed Nov. 18. President signed Dec. 8, 1983.

PL 98-215 (HR 2968) Authorize appropriations for fiscal year 1984 for intelligence and intelligence-related activities of the U.S. government, for the Intelligence Community Staff and for the Central Intelligence Agency Retirement and Disability System. Introduced by BOLAND, D-Mass., May 11, 1983. House Intelligence reported May 16 (H Rept 98-189, Part I). House Armed Services reported May 24 (H Rept 98-189, Part II). House passed Oct. 20. Senate passed, amended, Nov. 3. House disagreed to Senate amendments Nov. 9. House agreed to conference report Nov. 18 (H Rept 98-569). Senate agreed to conference report Nov. 18. President signed Dec. 9, 1983. ∎

SENATE ROLL-CALL VOTES

CQ Senate Vote 1

Corresponding to Congressional Record Vote 1

						KEY
	~		~		~	

ALABAMA		**IOWA**		**NEW HAMPSHIRE**		
Denton	Y	*Grassley*	Y	*Humphrey*	Y	
Heflin	Y	*Jepsen*	Y	*Rudman*	Y	
ALASKA		**KANSAS**		**NEW JERSEY**		
Murkowski	Y	*Dole*	Y	Bradley	Y	
Stevens	Y	*Kassebaum*	Y	Lautenberg	Y	
ARIZONA		**KENTUCKY**		**NEW MEXICO**		
Goldwater	Y	Ford	Y	*Domenici*	Y	
DeConcini	Y	Huddleston	Y	Bingaman	Y	
ARKANSAS		**LOUISIANA**		**NEW YORK**		
Bumpers	Y	Johnston	Y	*D'Amato*	Y	
Pryor	Y	Long	Y	Moynihan	Y	
CALIFORNIA		**MAINE**		**NORTH CAROLINA**		
Wilson	Y	*Cohen*	Y	*East*	Y	
Cranston	Y	Mitchell	Y	*Helms*	Y	
COLORADO		**MARYLAND**		**NORTH DAKOTA**		
Armstrong	Y	*Mathias*	Y	*Andrews*	?	
Hart	Y	Sarbanes	Y	Burdick	Y	
CONNECTICUT		**MASSACHUSETTS**		**OHIO**		
Weicker	Y	Kennedy	Y	Glenn	Y	
Dodd	Y	Tsongas	Y	Metzenbaum	Y	
DELAWARE		**MICHIGAN**		**OKLAHOMA**		
Roth	Y	Levin	Y	*Nickles*	Y	
Biden	Y	Riegle	Y	Boren	Y	
FLORIDA		**MINNESOTA**		**OREGON**		
Hawkins	Y	*Boschwitz*	Y	*Hatfield*	Y	
Chiles	Y	*Durenberger*	Y	*Packwood*	Y	
GEORGIA		**MISSISSIPPI**		**PENNSYLVANIA**		
Mattingly	Y	*Cochran*	Y	*Heinz*	Y	
Nunn	Y	Stennis	Y	*Specter*	Y	
HAWAII		**MISSOURI**		**RHODE ISLAND**		
Inouye	+	*Danforth*	?	*Chafee*	Y	
Matsunaga	Y	Eagleton	Y	Pell	Y	
IDAHO		**MONTANA**		**SOUTH CAROLINA**		
McClure	Y	Baucus	Y	*Thurmond*	Y	
Symms	Y	Melcher	Y	Hollings	Y	
ILLINOIS		**NEBRASKA**		**SOUTH DAKOTA**		
Percy	Y	Exon	Y	*Abdnor*	Y	
Dixon	Y	Zorinsky	Y	*Pressler*	Y	
INDIANA		**NEVADA**		**TENNESSEE**		
Lugar	Y	*Hecht*	Y	*Baker*	Y	
Quayle	Y	*Laxalt*	Y	Sasser	Y	

	~
TEXAS	
Tower	Y
Bentsen	Y
UTAH	
Garn	Y
Hatch	Y
VERMONT	
Stafford	Y
Leahy	Y
VIRGINIA	
Trible	Y
Warner	Y
WASHINGTON	
Gorton	Y
Jackson	Y
WEST VIRGINIA	
Byrd	Y
Randolph	Y
WISCONSIN	
Kasten	Y
Proxmire	Y
WYOMING	
Simpson	Y
Wallop	Y

ND - Northern Democrats   SD - Southern Democrats (Southern states - Ala., Ark., Fla., Ga., Ky., La., Miss., N.C., Okla., S.C., Tenn., Texas, Va.)

1. Dole Nomination. Confirmation of President Reagan's nomination of Elizabeth Hanford Dole of Kansas to be secretary of transportation. Confirmed 97-0: R 52-0; D 45-0 (ND 31-0, SD 14-0), Feb. 1, 1983. A "yea" was a vote supporting the president's position.

	2		2		2
ALABAMA		**IOWA**		**NEW HAMPSHIRE**	
Denton	N	*Grassley*	Y	*Humphrey*	Y
Heflin	Y	*Jepsen*	?	*Rudman*	Y
ALASKA		**KANSAS**		**NEW JERSEY**	
Murkowski	?	*Dole*	Y	Bradley	Y
Stevens	?	*Kassebaum*	Y	Lautenberg	Y
ARIZONA		**KENTUCKY**		**NEW MEXICO**	
Goldwater	N	Ford	Y	*Domenici*	Y
DeConcini	?	Huddleston	Y	Bingaman	Y
ARKANSAS		**LOUISIANA**		**NEW YORK**	
Bumpers	Y	Johnston	Y	*D'Amato*	Y
Pryor	Y	Long	Y	Moynihan	Y
CALIFORNIA		**MAINE**		**NORTH CAROLINA**	
Wilson	Y	*Cohen*	Y	*East*	N
Cranston	Y	Mitchell	Y	*Helms*	N
COLORADO		**MARYLAND**		**NORTH DAKOTA**	
Armstrong	?	*Mathias*	Y	*Andrews*	Y
Hart	Y	Sarbanes	Y	Burdick	Y
CONNECTICUT		**MASSACHUSETTS**		**OHIO**	
Weicker	Y	Kennedy	Y	Glenn	Y
Dodd	Y	Tsongas	Y	Metzenbaum	Y
DELAWARE		**MICHIGAN**		**OKLAHOMA**	
Roth	Y	Levin	Y	*Nickles*	Y
Biden	Y	Riegle	Y	Boren	Y
FLORIDA		**MINNESOTA**		**OREGON**	
Hawkins	Y	*Boschwitz*	Y	*Hatfield*	Y
Chiles	Y	*Durenberger*	Y	*Packwood*	Y
GEORGIA		**MISSISSIPPI**		**PENNSYLVANIA**	
Mattingly	Y	*Cochran*	Y	*Heinz*	Y
Nunn	Y	Stennis	N	*Specter*	Y
HAWAII		**MISSOURI**		**RHODE ISLAND**	
Inouye	Y	*Danforth*	Y	*Chafee*	Y
Matsunaga	Y	Eagleton	?	Pell	Y
IDAHO		**MONTANA**		**SOUTH CAROLINA**	
McClure	N	Baucus	Y	*Thurmond*	N
Symms	N	Melcher	Y	Hollings	?
ILLINOIS		**NEBRASKA**		**SOUTH DAKOTA**	
Percy	Y	Exon	Y	*Abdnor*	Y
Dixon	Y	Zorinsky	Y	*Pressler*	Y
INDIANA		**NEVADA**		**TENNESSEE**	
Lugar	Y	*Hecht*	Y	*Baker*	Y
Quayle	Y	*Laxalt*	Y	Sasser	Y

KEY

- **Y** Voted for (yea).
- **#** Paired for.
- **+** Announced for.
- **N** Voted against (nay).
- **X** Paired against.
- **-** Announced against.
- **P** Voted "present".
- **C** Voted "present" to avoid possible conflict of interest.
- **?** Did not vote or otherwise make a position known.

Democrats   *Republicans*

	2
TEXAS	
Tower	Y
Bentsen	Y
UTAH	
Garn	Y
Hatch	N
VERMONT	
Stafford	?
Leahy	Y
VIRGINIA	
Trible	Y
Warner	Y
WASHINGTON	
Gorton	Y
Jackson	Y
WEST VIRGINIA	
Byrd	Y
Randolph	Y
WISCONSIN	
Kasten	N
Proxmire	Y
WYOMING	
Simpson	Y
Wallop	N

ND · Northern Democrats   SD · Southern Democrats (Southern states · Ala., Ark., Fla., Ga., Ky., La., Miss., N.C., Okla., S.C., Tenn., Texas, Va.)

2. Burt Nomination. Confirmation of President Reagan's nomination of Richard R. Burt of the District of Columbia to be assistant secretary of state for European affairs. Confirmed 81-11: R 39-10; D 42-1 (ND 30-0, SD 12-1), Feb. 16, 1983. A "yea" was a vote supporting the president's position.

	3	4	5	6	7	8
ALABAMA						
Denton	N	N	N	N	Y	Y
Heflin	Y	N	N	N	Y	Y
ALASKA						
Murkowski	#	-	-	-	Y	Y
Stevens	Y	N	N	N	Y	Y
ARIZONA						
Goldwater	?	N	N	Y	?	?
DeConcini	Y	Y	N	Y	Y	Y
ARKANSAS						
Bumpers	Y	Y	Y	N	?	?
Pryor	Y	N	N	Y	Y	Y
CALIFORNIA						
Wilson	Y	N	N	Y	?	?
Cranston	?	?	N	Y	Y	Y
COLORADO						
Armstrong	N	Y	N	N	Y	Y
Hart	Y	Y	N	Y	?	?
CONNECTICUT						
Weicker	Y	N	N	Y	?	?
Dodd	N	N	Y	N	Y	Y
DELAWARE						
Roth	N	Y	N	Y	Y	Y
Biden	N	Y	Y	N	Y	Y
FLORIDA						
Hawkins	X	?	Y	N	Y	Y
Chiles	Y	N	N	Y	Y	Y
GEORGIA						
Mattingly	Y	N	N	Y	Y	Y
Nunn	Y	N	N	Y	Y	Y
HAWAII						
Inouye	Y	N	N	Y	?	?
Matsunaga	Y	Y	N	Y	Y	Y
IDAHO						
McClure	Y	N	N	Y	Y	Y
Symms	Y	N	N	Y	Y	Y
ILLINOIS						
Percy	N	N	Y	N	Y	Y
Dixon	N	N	Y	N	Y	Y
INDIANA						
Lugar	N	N	N	Y	Y	Y
Quayle	?	N	N	Y	Y	Y

	3	4	5	6	7	8
IOWA						
Grassley	N	N	N	N	Y	Y
Jepsen	Y	N	N	Y	Y	Y
KANSAS						
Dole	?	?	?	Y	Y	Y
Kassebaum	Y	N	N	Y	?	Y
KENTUCKY						
Ford	Y	N	N	Y	Y	Y
Huddleston	Y	N	N	Y	Y	Y
LOUISIANA						
Johnston	Y	N	N	Y	Y	Y
Long	Y	N	N	Y	?	?
MAINE						
Cohen	Y	N	N	Y	Y	Y
Mitchell	Y	N	N	Y	Y	Y
MARYLAND						
Mathias	Y	N	Y	Y	?	?
Sarbanes	Y	N	N	Y	Y	Y
MASSACHUSETTS						
Kennedy	N	Y	Y	N	Y	Y
Tsongas	Y	Y	Y	N	Y	Y
MICHIGAN						
Levin	N	N	Y	Y	Y	Y
Riegle	Y	N	N	Y	Y	Y
MINNESOTA						
Boschwitz	N	N	N	N	Y	Y
Durenberger	N	Y	N	Y	Y	Y
MISSISSIPPI						
Cochran	?	?	?	?	Y	Y
Stennis	Y	N	?	N	Y	Y
MISSOURI						
Danforth	Y	N	N	Y	Y	Y
Eagleton	Y	N	N	Y	Y	Y
MONTANA						
Baucus	N	Y	Y	N	Y	Y
Melcher	Y	N	N	Y	Y	Y
NEBRASKA						
Exon	Y	N	N	Y	Y	Y
Zorinsky	Y	Y	N	Y	Y	Y
NEVADA						
Hecht	N	N	N	N	Y	Y
Laxalt	N	N	N	N	Y	Y

	3	4	5	6	7	8
NEW HAMPSHIRE						
Humphrey	Y	Y	Y	N	Y	Y
Rudman	Y	N	N	Y	Y	Y
NEW JERSEY						
Bradley	N	N	N	Y	Y	Y
Lautenberg	Y	Y	N	Y	Y	Y
NEW MEXICO						
Domenici	Y	N	N	Y	Y	?
Bingaman	N	Y	Y	N	Y	Y
NEW YORK						
D'Amato	Y	N	N	Y	Y	Y
Moynihan	Y	N	N	Y	?	+
NORTH CAROLINA						
East	N	Y	Y	N	Y	N
Helms	N	N	Y	N	Y	N
NORTH DAKOTA						
Andrews	Y	N	N	Y	Y	Y
Burdick	Y	N	N	Y	Y	Y
OHIO						
Glenn	?	?	?	?	?	?
Metzenbaum	N	Y	Y	N	Y	Y
OKLAHOMA						
Nickles	N	N	Y	N	Y	Y
Boren	N	Y	Y	N	Y	Y
OREGON						
Hatfield	Y	N	N	Y	Y	Y
Packwood	Y	N	N	Y	Y	N
PENNSYLVANIA						
Heinz	Y	N	N	Y	Y	Y
Specter	N	Y	Y	N	Y	Y
RHODE ISLAND						
Chafee	Y	N	N	Y	Y	Y
Pell	N	N	N	Y	Y	Y
SOUTH CAROLINA						
Thurmond	N	N	Y	N	Y	Y
Hollings	Y	N	N	Y	?	?
SOUTH DAKOTA						
Abdnor	Y	N	N	N	Y	Y
Pressler	Y	N	N	N	Y	Y
TENNESSEE						
Baker	Y	N	N	Y	?	?
Sasser	Y	N	N	Y	Y	Y

KEY

Y	Voted for (yea).
#	Paired for.
+	Announced for.
N	Voted against (nay).
X	Paired against.
-	Announced against.
P	Voted "present".
C	Voted "present" to avoid possible conflict of interest.
?	Did not vote or otherwise make a position known.

Democrats *Republicans*

	3	4	5	6	7	8
TEXAS						
Tower	Y	N	N	Y	Y	Y
Bentsen	Y	Y	N	Y	?	Y
UTAH						
Garn	Y	N	N	N	Y	Y
Hatch	N	Y	Y	N	Y	Y
VERMONT						
Stafford	N	N	N	Y	Y	Y
Leahy	N	Y	Y	N	Y	Y
VIRGINIA						
Trible	Y	N	N	Y	Y	Y
Warner	Y	N	N	Y	Y	Y
WASHINGTON						
Gorton	Y	N	N	Y	Y	Y
Jackson	Y	N	N	Y	Y	Y
WEST VIRGINIA						
Byrd	Y	N	N	Y	Y	Y
Randolph	Y	N	N	Y	+	+
WISCONSIN						
Kasten	Y	N	N	Y	Y	Y
Proxmire	N	Y	Y	N	Y	Y
WYOMING						
Simpson	N	N	N	N	Y	Y
Wallop	Y	N	N	Y	?	?

ND - Northern Democrats   SD - Southern Democrats (Southern states - Ala., Ark., Fla., Ga., Ky., La., Miss., N.C., Okla., S.C., Tenn., Texas, Va.)

3. S 47. Shipping Act of 1983. Stevens, R-Alaska, amendment to the Judiciary Committee amendment, to require that ship liner tariffs be filed with and enforced by the Federal Maritime Commission. Adopted 61-31: R 30-18; D 31-13 (ND 18-12, SD 13-1), March 1, 1983. (The committee amendment, which would have eliminated the tariff filing and enforcement requirements, subsequently was adopted as amended by voice vote.) A "nay" was a vote supporting the president's position.

4. S 47. Shipping Act of 1983. Metzenbaum, D-Ohio, amendment to eliminate antitrust immunity for an ocean liner conference setting a rate that included land transportation of goods, such as by truck. Rejected 25-69: R 8-42; D 17-27 (ND 14-16, SD 3-11), March 1, 1983.

5. S 47. Shipping Act of 1983. Metzenbaum, D-Ohio, amendment to eliminate antitrust immunity for rate-fixing and other practices by ocean liner conferences. Rejected 24-71: R 11-40; D 13-31 (ND 11-20, SD 2-11), March 1, 1983.

6. S 47. Shipping Act of 1983. Passage of the bill to provide broad antitrust immunity for rate-fixing and other practices by ocean liner conferences. Passed 64-33: R 33-19; D 31-14 (ND 20-11, SD 11-3), March 1, 1983. A "yea" was a vote supporting the president's position.

7. Treaty Doc 98-1. International Expositions. Adoption of the resolution of ratification of an amendment to the protocol of Nov. 30, 1972, to the Convention of Nov. 22, 1928, concerning International Expositions, to permit the United States and Spain to hold international expositions in 1992 celebrating the 500th anniversary of the discovery of America. Adopted 84-0: R 47-0; D 37-0 (ND 27-0, SD 10-0), March 3, 1983. A two-thirds majority of those present and voting (56 in this case) is required for adoption of resolutions of ratification. A "yea" was a vote supporting the president's position.

8. Heckler Nomination. Confirmation of President Reagan's nomination of Margaret M. Heckler of Massachusetts to be secretary of health and human services. Confirmed 82-3: R 44-3; D 38-0 (ND 27-0, SD 11-0), March 3, 1983. A "yea" was a vote supporting the president's position.

	9	10	11	12	13	14
ALABAMA						
Denton	Y	Y	Y	Y	N	Y
Heflin	N	Y	Y	Y	Y	Y
ALASKA						
Murkowski	Y	Y	Y	Y	Y	N
Stevens	Y	Y	Y	Y	Y	Y
ARIZONA						
Goldwater	Y	Y	Y	N	?	Y
DeConcini	N	N	Y	Y	Y	N
ARKANSAS						
Bumpers	?	?	?	Y	Y	N
Pryor	N	Y	N	Y	Y	N
CALIFORNIA						
Wilson	Y	Y	Y	Y	Y	N
Cranston	Y	N	Y	Y	Y	N
COLORADO						
Armstrong	Y	Y	Y	?	N	N
Hart	Y	?	?	?	?	Y
CONNECTICUT						
Weicker	N	Y	Y	N	Y	N
Dodd	Y	N	Y	?	?	?
DELAWARE						
Roth	N	Y	Y	Y	Y	N
Biden	N	Y	Y	Y	Y	N
FLORIDA						
Hawkins	?	?	?	Y	Y	N
Chiles	N	Y	Y	Y	Y	Y
GEORGIA						
Mattingly	N	Y	Y	Y	N	N
Nunn	?	Y	Y	Y	Y	N
HAWAII						
Inouye	?	?	?	Y	Y	Y
Matsunaga	Y	Y	Y	Y	Y	Y
IDAHO						
McClure	Y	Y	Y	Y	Y	Y
Symms	Y	Y	Y	N	N	N
ILLINOIS						
Percy	Y	Y	Y	Y	Y	Y
Dixon	N	Y	Y	Y	Y	Y
INDIANA						
Lugar	Y	Y	Y	Y	Y	Y
Quayle	Y	Y	Y	N	Y	Y

	9	10	11	12	13	14
IOWA						
Grassley	N	Y	Y	Y	Y	N
Jepsen	Y	Y	Y	Y	Y	N
KANSAS						
Dole	Y	Y	Y	Y	Y	N
Kassebaum	Y	Y	Y	Y	Y	N
KENTUCKY						
Ford	N	Y	Y	Y	Y	Y
Huddleston	N	N	Y	Y	Y	Y
LOUISIANA						
Johnston	N	Y	Y	Y	Y	Y
Long	?	?	?	N	Y	Y
MAINE						
Cohen	N	Y	Y	?	?	N
Mitchell	N	N	N	Y	Y	Y
MARYLAND						
Mathias	Y	Y	Y	Y	Y	Y
Sarbanes	Y	N	Y	Y	Y	Y
MASSACHUSETTS						
Kennedy	N	N	N	Y	Y	Y
Tsongas	Y	N	Y	Y	Y	N
MICHIGAN						
Levin	N	N	N	Y	Y	Y
Riegle	N	N	N	Y	Y	Y
MINNESOTA						
Boschwitz	Y	Y	Y	Y	Y	N
Durenberger	Y	Y	Y	?	?	N
MISSISSIPPI						
Cochran	N	Y	Y	Y	Y	Y
Stennis	N	N	Y	Y	Y	?
MISSOURI						
Danforth	Y	Y	Y	Y	Y	N
Eagleton	N	Y	Y	Y	Y	N
MONTANA						
Baucus	N	Y	Y	Y	Y	N
Melcher	N	Y	N	Y	Y	N
NEBRASKA						
Exon	Y	Y	Y	Y	Y	N
Zorinsky	Y	Y	Y	Y	Y	N
NEVADA						
Hecht	Y	Y	Y	Y	Y	Y
Laxalt	?	?	?	Y	Y	Y

	9	10	11	12	13	14
NEW HAMPSHIRE						
Humphrey	P	Y	Y	Y	N	N
Rudman	Y	Y	Y	Y	Y	Y
NEW JERSEY						
Bradley	Y	Y	Y	Y	Y	N
Lautenberg	N	N	N	Y	Y	-
NEW MEXICO						
Domenici	N	Y	Y	Y	Y	N
Bingaman	N	N	N	Y	Y	N
NEW YORK						
D'Amato	?	?	?	Y	Y	N
Moynihan	Y	N	Y	Y	Y	N
NORTH CAROLINA						
East	N	Y	Y	Y	N	N
Helms	N	Y	Y	N	N	N
NORTH DAKOTA						
Andrews	N	Y	Y	Y	Y	Y
Burdick	Y	Y	Y	Y	Y	N
OHIO						
Glenn	Y	Y	?	?	?	?
Metzenbaum	N	N	N	Y	Y	Y
OKLAHOMA						
Nickles	Y	Y	Y	Y	N	N
Boren	Y	Y	N	Y	Y	N
OREGON						
Hatfield	Y	Y	Y	Y	Y	Y
Packwood	N	Y	Y	Y	Y	Y
PENNSYLVANIA						
Heinz	Y	Y	Y	Y	Y	Y
Specter	Y	Y	Y	Y	Y	Y
RHODE ISLAND						
Chafee	Y	Y	Y	Y	Y	N
Pell	Y	Y	Y	Y	Y	N
SOUTH CAROLINA						
Thurmond	Y	Y	Y	Y	Y	N
Hollings	N	N	?	?	+	?
SOUTH DAKOTA						
Abdnor	Y	Y	Y	Y	Y	N
Pressler	N	Y	Y	Y	Y	N
TENNESSEE						
Baker	N	Y	Y	Y	Y	Y
Sasser	N	N	Y	Y	Y	Y

KEY

Y	Voted for (yea).
#	Paired for.
+	Announced for.
N	Voted against (nay).
X	Paired against.
-	Announced against.
P	Voted "present".
C	Voted "present" to avoid possible conflict of interest.
?	Did not vote or otherwise make a position known.

Democrats   *Republicans*

	9	10	11	12	13	14
TEXAS						
Tower	Y	Y	Y	Y	N	N
Bentsen	N	Y	Y	Y	Y	N
UTAH						
Garn	Y	Y	Y	Y	Y	Y
Hatch	N	Y	Y	Y	Y	Y
VERMONT						
Stafford	N	Y	Y	Y	Y	N
Leahy	N	N	Y	Y	Y	N
VIRGINIA						
Trible	Y	Y	Y	Y	Y	N
Warner	Y	Y	Y	Y	Y	N
WASHINGTON						
Gorton	Y	Y	Y	Y	Y	N
Jackson	Y	Y	Y	Y	Y	Y
WEST VIRGINIA						
Byrd	N	N	N	Y	Y	Y
Randolph	Y	Y	Y	?	+	+
WISCONSIN						
Kasten	Y	Y	Y	Y	Y	N
Proxmire	N	N	N	N	N	Y
WYOMING						
Simpson	Y	Y	Y	Y	N	N
Wallop	N	Y	Y	Y	N	N

ND - Northern Democrats   SD - Southern Democrats (Southern states - Ala., Ark., Fla., Ga., Ky., La., Miss., N.C., Okla., S.C., Tenn., Texas, Va.)

9. Exec B, 95th Cong, 1st Sess, Montreal Aviation Protocols. Adoption of the resolution of ratification regarding Montreal Aviation Protocols Nos. 3 & 4, which would set limits on passenger damage awards in international air crashes. Rejected 50-42: R 34-16; D 16-26 (ND 15-16, SD 1-10), March 8, 1983. A two-thirds majority of those present and voting (62 in this case) is required for adoption of resolutions of ratification. A "yea" was a vote supporting the president's position.

10. Tambs Nomination. Confirmation of President Reagan's nomination of Lewis Arthur Tambs of Arizona to be ambassador to Colombia. Confirmed 73-20: R 51-0; D 22-20 (ND 14-16, SD 8-4), March 8, 1983. A "yea" was a vote supporting the president's position.

11. Svahn Nomination. Confirmation of President Reagan's nomination of John A. Svahn of Maryland to be under secretary of health and human services. Confirmed 80-11: R 51-0; D 29-11 (ND 20-9, SD 9-2), March 8, 1983. A "yea" was a vote supporting the president's position.

12. HR 1718. Emergency Supplemental Appropriations, Fiscal 1983/Jobs. Baker, R-Tenn., motion to instruct the sergeant-at-arms to request the attendance of absent senators. Motion agreed to 87-5: R 48-3; D 39-2 (ND 27-1, SD 12-1), March 9, 1983.

13. HR 1718. Emergency Supplemental Appropriations, Fiscal 1983/Jobs. Bradley, D-N.J., amendment to state the sense of the Senate in opposition to any further reductions in education programs. Adopted 82-10: R 42-9; D 40-1 (ND 27-1, SD 13-0), March 9, 1983.

14. HR 1718. Emergency Supplemental Appropriations, Fiscal 1983/Jobs. Hatfield, R-Ore., motion to table (kill) the Abdnor, R-S.D., amendment to revise the formula for allocating discretionary funds under the bill. The Abdnor amendment would increase the number of states that could receive funds. Motion rejected 43-51: R 23-31; D 20-20 (ND 13-15, SD 7-5), March 9, 1983.

CQ Senate Vote 15

Corresponding to Congressional Record Vote 15

	15		15		15
ALABAMA		**IOWA**		**NEW HAMPSHIRE**	
Denton	N	*Grassley*	Y	*Humphrey*	Y
Heflin	N	*Jepsen*	Y	*Rudman*	N
ALASKA		**KANSAS**		**NEW JERSEY**	
Murkowski	Y	*Dole*	Y	Bradley	Y
Stevens	N	*Kassebaum*	Y	Lautenberg	Y
ARIZONA		**KENTUCKY**		**NEW MEXICO**	
Goldwater	N	Ford	N	*Domenici*	Y
DeConcini	Y	Huddleston	N	Bingaman	N
ARKANSAS		**LOUISIANA**		**NEW YORK**	
Bumpers	N	Johnston	N	*D'Amato*	Y
Pryor	N	Long	N	Moynihan	Y
CALIFORNIA		**MAINE**		**NORTH CAROLINA**	
Wilson	N	*Cohen*	Y	*East*	Y
Cranston	N	Mitchell	Y	*Helms*	Y
COLORADO		**MARYLAND**		**NORTH DAKOTA**	
Armstrong	Y	*Mathias*	N	*Andrews*	?
Hart	N	Sarbanes	N	Burdick	Y
CONNECTICUT		**MASSACHUSETTS**		**OHIO**	
Weicker	Y	Kennedy	N	Glenn	N
Dodd	Y	Tsongas	Y	Metzenbaum	N
DELAWARE		**MICHIGAN**		**OKLAHOMA**	
Roth	Y	Levin	N	*Nickles*	Y
Biden	Y	Riegle	N	Boren	Y
FLORIDA		**MINNESOTA**		**OREGON**	
Hawkins	Y	*Boschwitz*	Y	*Hatfield*	N
Chiles	Y	*Durenberger*	Y	*Packwood*	N
GEORGIA		**MISSISSIPPI**		**PENNSYLVANIA**	
Mattingly	Y	*Cochran*	N	*Heinz*	N
Nunn	Y	Stennis	N	*Specter*	N
HAWAII		**MISSOURI**		**RHODE ISLAND**	
Inouye	N	*Danforth*	Y	*Chafee*	N
Matsunaga	N	Eagleton	Y	Pell	N
IDAHO		**MONTANA**		**SOUTH CAROLINA**	
McClure	Y	Baucus	Y	*Thurmond*	N
Symms	Y	Melcher	Y	Hollings	N
ILLINOIS		**NEBRASKA**		**SOUTH DAKOTA**	
Percy	N	Exon	Y	*Abdnor*	Y
Dixon	N	Zorinsky	Y	*Pressler*	Y
INDIANA		**NEVADA**		**TENNESSEE**	
Lugar	N	*Hecht*	N	*Baker*	N
Quayle	N	*Laxalt*	N	Sasser	N

	15
TEXAS	
Tower	Y
Bentsen	Y
UTAH	
Garn	Y
Hatch	Y
VERMONT	
Stafford	Y
Leahy	Y
VIRGINIA	
Trible	Y
Warner	Y
WASHINGTON	
Gorton	N
Jackson	N
WEST VIRGINIA	
Byrd	N
Randolph	N
WISCONSIN	
Kasten	N
Proxmire	N
WYOMING	
Simpson	N
Wallop	N

KEY

Y	Voted for (yea).
#	Paired for.
+	Announced for.
N	Voted against (nay).
X	Paired against.
-	Announced against.
P	Voted "present".
C	Voted "present" to avoid possible conflict of interest.
?	Did not vote or otherwise make a position known.

Democrats   *Republicans*

ND - Northern Democrats   SD - Southern Democrats (Southern states - Ala., Ark., Fla., Ga., Ky., La., Miss., N.C., Okla., S.C., Tenn., Texas, Va.)

15. HR 1718. Emergency Supplemental Appropriations, Fiscal 1983/Jobs. Abdnor, R-S.D., motion to table (kill) the Hatfield, R-Ore., amendment, to the Abdnor amendment, to establish a three-tier system for distributing $3.2 billion in discretionary funds. One tier would be reserved for 21 states whose average rate of unemployment exceeded the national average for the last six months of 1982. (The Abdnor amendment sought to dilute the targeting formula by making all states eligible for long-term unemployment aid.) Motion rejected 49-50: R 30-23; D 19-27 (ND 15-17, SD 4-10), March 10, 1983. (The Hatfield amendment subsequently was adopted by voice vote.)

	16	17	18	19	20	21	22	23
ALABAMA								
Denton	N	Y	Y	Y	N	Y	Y	N
Heflin	N	Y	N	Y	Y	N	N	N
ALASKA								
Murkowski	N	N	N	N	N	N	Y	Y
Stevens	N	Y	N	Y	Y	N	N	N
ARIZONA								
Goldwater	N	N	Y	N	N	N	Y	Y
DeConcini	N	Y	N	Y	Y	N	N	N
ARKANSAS								
Bumpers	Y	Y	N	Y	Y	N	N	N
Pryor	Y	Y	N	Y	Y	N	N	N
CALIFORNIA								
Wilson	N	N	Y	Y	Y	N	Y	N
Cranston	#	?	?	?	?	?	N	N
COLORADO								
Armstrong	?	?	?	N	N	Y	Y	Y
Hart	?	?	?	Y	Y	N	N	N
CONNECTICUT								
Weicker	?	?	?	Y	Y	N	N	N
Dodd	Y	Y	N	Y	Y	N	N	N
DELAWARE								
Roth	N	Y	N	Y	Y	Y	Y	Y
Biden	Y	Y	N	Y	Y	N	N	N
FLORIDA								
Hawkins	N	Y	N	Y	Y	N	N	N
Chiles	Y	Y	N	Y	Y	N	N	N
GEORGIA								
Mattingly	N	Y	N	Y	N	Y	Y	Y
Nunn	N	Y	N	?	?	?	?	?
HAWAII								
Inouye	Y	Y	N	Y	Y	N	N	N
Matsunaga	?	?	?	?	?	?	?	?
IDAHO								
McClure	N	Y	Y	Y	N	Y	Y	Y
Symms	?	?	?	Y	N	Y	Y	Y
ILLINOIS								
Percy	N	Y	N	Y	Y	N	N	N
Dixon	Y	Y	N	Y	Y	N	N	N
INDIANA								
Lugar	N	N	Y	Y	Y	N	N	N
Quayle	N	Y	Y	Y	Y	N	N	N
IOWA								
Grassley	N	Y	Y	N	Y	N	N	N
Jepsen	N	Y	Y	N	Y	N	N	N
KANSAS								
Dole	?	N	Y	Y	Y	N	N	Y
Kassebaum	N	Y	Y	Y	Y	N	N	N
KENTUCKY								
Ford	Y	Y	N	Y	Y	N	N	N
Huddleston	Y	Y	N	Y	Y	N	N	N
LOUISIANA								
Johnston	?	?	?	Y	Y	N	N	N
Long	Y	Y	N	Y	Y	N	N	N
MAINE								
Cohen	N	Y	N	Y	Y	N	N	N
Mitchell	Y	Y	N	Y	Y	N	N	N
MARYLAND								
Mathias	Y	Y	N	Y	Y	N	N	?
Sarbanes	Y	Y	N	Y	Y	N	N	N
MASSACHUSETTS								
Kennedy	Y	Y	N	?	?	N	N	N
Tsongas	Y	Y	N	?	?	N	?	?
MICHIGAN								
Levin	Y	Y	N	Y	Y	N	N	N
Riegle	Y	Y	N	Y	Y	N	N	N
MINNESOTA								
Boschwitz	N	Y	N	Y	Y	N	N	N
Durenberger	?	?	?	Y	Y	N	N	N
MISSISSIPPI								
Cochran	N	Y	N	+	+	N	N	N
Stennis	N	Y	N	Y	Y	N	N	N
MISSOURI								
Danforth	N	Y	N	Y	Y	N	N	N
Eagleton	Y	Y	N	Y	Y	N	N	N
MONTANA								
Baucus	Y	Y	N	Y	Y	N	N	N
Melcher	Y	Y	N	Y	Y	N	N	N
NEBRASKA								
Exon	N	Y	N	Y	Y	N	N	N
Zorinsky	N	Y	N	N	N	Y	Y	N
NEVADA								
Hecht	N	N	Y	Y	Y	N	N	N
Laxalt	N	N	Y	N	Y	N	N	N
NEW HAMPSHIRE								
Humphrey	N	N	Y	N	N	Y	Y	Y
Rudman	N	?	Y	N	Y	Y	Y	Y
NEW JERSEY								
Bradley	Y	Y	N	Y	Y	N	N	N
Lautenberg	Y	Y	N	Y	Y	N	N	N
NEW MEXICO								
Domenici	N	Y	Y	Y	Y	N	N	N
Bingaman	Y	Y	N	Y	Y	N	N	N
NEW YORK								
D'Amato	N	Y	N	Y	Y	N	N	N
Moynihan	Y	Y	N	Y	Y	N	N	N
NORTH CAROLINA								
East	N	N	Y	Y	N	Y	Y	Y
Helms	N	N	Y	N	N	Y	Y	Y
NORTH DAKOTA								
Andrews	N	Y	N	Y	Y	N	N	N
Burdick	Y	Y	N	Y	Y	N	N	N
OHIO								
Glenn	Y	Y	N	Y	Y	N	N	N
Metzenbaum	Y	Y	N	Y	Y	N	N	N
OKLAHOMA								
Nickles	N	N	Y	N	N	Y	Y	Y
Boren	X	Y	N	N	Y	Y	Y	N
OREGON								
Hatfield	N	N	Y	N	N	Y	N	N
Packwood	N	N	Y	Y	N	Y	N	N
PENNSYLVANIA								
Heinz	N	Y	N	Y	Y	N	N	N
Specter	Y	Y	N	Y	Y	N	N	N
RHODE ISLAND								
Chafee	N	Y	Y	N	Y	N	N	N
Pell	Y	Y	N	N	Y	N	N	N
SOUTH CAROLINA								
Thurmond	N	N	Y	Y	N	Y	Y	Y
Hollings	?	?	?	Y	Y	N	N	N
SOUTH DAKOTA								
Abdnor	N	Y	Y	Y	Y	N	N	N
Pressler	N	Y	N	Y	Y	N	N	N
TENNESSEE								
Baker	N	N	Y	Y	Y	N	N	N
Sasser	Y	Y	N	Y	Y	N	N	N
TEXAS								
Tower	?	?	Y	Y	Y	N	Y	Y
Bentsen	?	?	?	Y	Y	N	N	N
UTAH								
Garn	N	N	Y	Y	Y	N	Y	Y
Hatch	N	Y	Y	Y	Y	Y	Y	N
VERMONT								
Stafford	N	Y	N	Y	Y	N	N	N
Leahy	Y	Y	N	Y	Y	N	N	N
VIRGINIA								
Trible	N	Y	N	Y	Y	N	N	N
Warner	N	Y	N	Y	Y	N	N	N
WASHINGTON								
Gorton	N	N	Y	Y	Y	N	N	N
Jackson	Y	Y	N	Y	Y	N	N	N
WEST VIRGINIA								
Byrd	Y	Y	N	Y	Y	N	N	N
Randolph	Y	Y	N	Y	Y	N	N	N
WISCONSIN								
Kasten	N	Y	N	Y	Y	N	N	N
Proxmire	N	Y	N	N	Y	N	N	Y
WYOMING								
Simpson	N	Y	Y	Y	Y	N	N	N
Wallop	N	N	Y	Y	N	Y	Y	Y

KEY

Y Voted for (yea).
\# Paired for.
\+ Announced for.
N Voted against (nay).
X Paired against.
\- Announced against.
P Voted "present".
C Voted "present" to avoid possible conflict of interest.
? Did not vote or otherwise make a position known.

Democrats   *Republicans*

ND - Northern Democrats   SD - Southern Democrats (Southern states - Ala., Ark., Fla., Ga., Ky., La., Miss., N.C., Okla., S.C., Tenn., Texas, Va.)

16. HR 1718. Emergency Supplemental Appropriations, Fiscal 1983/Jobs. Levin, D-Mich., amendment to add $1.665 billion for job creation, emergency food and shelter assistance and emergency health assistance. Rejected 34-53: R 2-46; D 32-7 (ND 25-4, SD 7-3), March 11, 1983.

17. HR 1718. Emergency Supplemental Appropriations, Fiscal 1983/Jobs. Judgment of the Senate whether the Ford, D-Ky., amendment, to provide federal supplemental unemployment benefits to certain railroad employees with less than 10 years of service, was germane to the bill. Ruled germane 70-18: R 30-18; D 40-0 (ND 29-0, SD 11-0), March 11, 1983.

18. HR 1718. Emergency Supplemental Appropriations, Fiscal 1983/Jobs. Nickles, R-Okla., amendment, to the Ford, D-Ky., amendment, to provide extended unemployment benefits, which would be paid from the Railroad Unemployment Trust Fund — rather than supplemental unemployment benefits, which would be paid by the federal government — for certain railroad employees with less than 10 years of service. Rejected 30-60: R 30-20; D 0-40 (ND 0-29, SD 0-11), March 11, 1983. (The Ford amendment subsequently was adopted by voice vote.)

19. HR 1718. Emergency Supplemental Appropriations, Fiscal 1983/Jobs. Heinz, R-Pa., amendment to accelerate revenue sharing payments to local governments by making allocations at the beginning of each quarter of the calendar year rather than at the end of each quarter. Adopted 73-21: R 38-15; D 35-6 (ND 23-5, SD 12-1), March 14, 1983.

20. HR 1718. Emergency Supplemental Appropriations, Fiscal 1983/Jobs. Eagleton, D-Mo., amendment to add an additional $115 million for health services. Adopted 80-14: R 40-13; D 40-1 (ND 27-1, SD 13-0), March 14, 1983.

21. HR 1718. Emergency Supplemental Appropriations, Fiscal 1983/Jobs. Humphrey, R-N.H., amendment to strike Title I of the bill, providing funding for jobs programs, but retain supplemental appropriations under Title II. Rejected 17-80: R 15-39; D 2-41 (ND 1-29, SD 1-12), March 14, 1983.

22. HR 1718. Emergency Supplemental Appropriations, Fiscal 1983/Jobs. Mattingly, R-Ga., amendment to strike all appropriations under Title I except for $100 million for the Women, Infants and Children (WIC) feeding program, $175 million for the Agriculture Department's surplus food distribution program and $50 million for emergency food and shelter. Rejected 20-77: R 18-36; D 2-41 (ND 1-29, SD 1-12), March 14, 1983.

23. HR 1718. Emergency Supplemental Appropriations, Fiscal 1983/Jobs. Mattingly, R-Ga., amendment to cut $25 million in grants (plus $75 million in loans) from the rural water and waste disposal program; $100 million from Army Corps of Engineers projects; $150 million from social services block grants; and $50 million from the college work-study program. Rejected 16-80: R 15-38; D 1-42 (ND 1-29, SD 0-13), March 14, 1983.

	24	25	26	27	28	29	30	31
ALABAMA								
Denton	N	Y	N	Y	Y	Y	Y	Y
Heflin	N	Y	N	Y	Y	N	Y	N
ALASKA								
Murkowski	N	Y	N	Y	Y	N	N	N
Stevens	N	Y	Y	N	Y	N	Y	N
ARIZONA								
Goldwater	N	Y	N	Y	Y	Y	Y	N
DeConcini	N	Y	P	Y	Y	N	Y	N
ARKANSAS								
Bumpers	Y	Y	N	Y	Y	?	?	?
Pryor	N	Y	N	Y	?	N	Y	N
CALIFORNIA								
Wilson	N	Y	Y	N	Y	N	Y	Y
Cranston	Y	Y	Y	N	Y	N	Y	N
COLORADO								
Armstrong	N	Y	N	Y	Y	Y	Y	N
Hart	N	Y	Y	N	Y	N	Y	?
CONNECTICUT								
Weicker	Y	N	N	Y	N	Y	N	Y
Dodd	Y	Y	Y	N	Y	N	Y	N
DELAWARE								
Roth	Y	Y	Y	?	Y	N	N	N
Biden	Y	Y	Y	Y	Y	Y	Y	N
FLORIDA								
Hawkins	Y	Y	N	Y	N	Y	N	Y
Chiles	Y	Y	Y	N	Y	N	Y	N
GEORGIA								
Mattingly	N	Y	N	Y	Y	Y	Y	Y
Nunn	?	Y	N	Y	N	Y	N	Y
HAWAII								
Inouye	N	Y	N	Y	Y	N	Y	N
Matsunaga	?	Y	N	Y	Y	N	Y	N
IDAHO								
McClure	?	Y	N	Y	N	Y	N	Y
Symms	N	Y	N	Y	Y	Y	N	Y
ILLINOIS								
Percy	Y	Y	Y	N	Y	N	Y	N
Dixon	Y	Y	N	Y	N	Y	N	N
INDIANA								
Lugar	Y	Y	Y	N	Y	N	Y	N
Quayle	Y	N	N	Y	Y	Y	Y	Y

	24	25	26	27	28	29	30	31
IOWA								
Grassley	Y	Y	Y	N	Y	N	Y	Y
Jepsen	Y	Y	N	Y	Y	N	Y	Y
KANSAS								
Dole	N	Y	Y	N	Y	N	Y	N
Kassebaum	N	Y	N	Y	Y	N	Y	N
KENTUCKY								
Ford	N	Y	N	Y	Y	N	Y	N
Huddleston	N	Y	N	Y	Y	Y	N	N
LOUISIANA								
Johnston	N	N	N	Y	Y	N	Y	N
Long	N	N	N	Y	Y	N	Y	N
MAINE								
Cohen	Y	Y	Y	N	Y	N	Y	N
Mitchell	Y	Y	N	Y	Y	N	Y	Y
MARYLAND								
Mathias	Y	Y	Y	N	Y	N	Y	N
Sarbanes	Y	Y	Y	Y	Y	N	Y	N
MASSACHUSETTS								
Kennedy	Y	Y	Y	N	Y	?	Y	N
Tsongas	Y	Y	Y	N	Y	N	Y	N
MICHIGAN								
Levin	Y	Y	Y	N	Y	N	Y	N
Riegle	Y	Y	Y	Y	Y	N	Y	N
MINNESOTA								
Boschwitz	Y	Y	Y	Y	Y	N	Y	Y
Durenberger	Y	Y	Y	N	Y	N	Y	N
MISSISSIPPI								
Cochran	N	Y	N	Y	Y	N	Y	N
Stennis	N	Y	Y	N	Y	N	Y	N
MISSOURI								
Danforth	Y	Y	Y	N	Y	N	Y	N
Eagleton	Y	Y	N	Y	Y	N	Y	N
MONTANA								
Baucus	N	Y	N	Y	Y	N	Y	N
Melcher	N	Y	N	Y	Y	N	Y	N
NEBRASKA								
Exon	Y	Y	N	Y	Y	N	Y	N
Zorinsky	N	Y	N	Y	Y	N	N	N
NEVADA								
Hecht	N	Y	Y	N	Y	N	Y	N
Laxalt	N	Y	Y	N	Y	N	Y	Y

	24	25	26	27	28	29	30	31
NEW HAMPSHIRE								
Humphrey	Y	Y	N	Y	Y	Y	N	Y
Rudman	Y	Y	Y	N	Y	N	N	Y
NEW JERSEY								
Bradley	Y	Y	N	Y	Y	N	Y	N
Lautenberg	+	Y	Y	N	Y	N	Y	N
NEW MEXICO								
Domenici	N	Y	Y	N	Y	N	Y	N
Bingaman	N	Y	Y	Y	Y	N	Y	N
NEW YORK								
D'Amato	Y	Y	Y	Y	+	-	Y	N
Moynihan	Y	Y	Y	N	?	N	Y	N
NORTH CAROLINA								
East	N	Y	N	Y	Y	Y	N	Y
Helms	N	Y	N	Y	Y	Y	N	Y
NORTH DAKOTA								
Andrews	N	Y	Y	Y	Y	N	Y	Y
Burdick	N	Y	Y	N	Y	N	Y	Y
OHIO								
Glenn	Y	?	?	?	Y	N	Y	N
Metzenbaum	Y	Y	Y	N	Y	N	Y	N
OKLAHOMA								
Nickles	N	Y	N	Y	Y	Y	N	Y
Boren	N	Y	N	Y	Y	N	Y	Y
OREGON								
Hatfield	N	Y	Y	N	Y	N	Y	N
Packwood	N	Y	N	Y	Y	N	Y	N
PENNSYLVANIA								
Heinz	Y	Y	Y	N	Y	N	Y	N
Specter	Y	Y	Y	N	Y	N	Y	N
RHODE ISLAND								
Chafee	Y	Y	Y	N	Y	N	Y	N
Pell	Y	Y	Y	Y	Y	N	Y	N
SOUTH CAROLINA								
Thurmond	N	Y	N	Y	Y	N	Y	N
Hollings	Y	Y	N	Y	?	?	?	?
SOUTH DAKOTA								
Abdnor	N	Y	N	Y	Y	N	Y	N
Pressler	N	Y	N	N	Y	N	Y	N
TENNESSEE								
Baker	N	Y	Y	N	Y	N	Y	N
Sasser	N	Y	Y	Y	Y	N	Y	N

KEY

Y Voted for (yea).
\# Paired for.
\+ Announced for.
N Voted against (nay).
\- Announced against.
P Voted "present".
C Voted "present" to avoid possible conflict of interest.
? Did not vote or otherwise make a position known.

Democrats   *Republicans*

	24	25	26	27	28	29	30	31
TEXAS								
Tower	N	Y	Y	N	Y	N	N	N
Bentsen	Y	Y	Y	Y	Y	N	Y	N
UTAH								
Garn	N	Y	N	Y	Y	Y	N	Y
Hatch	N	Y	N	Y	Y	Y	N	Y
VERMONT								
Stafford	Y	Y	Y	N	Y	N	Y	N
Leahy	Y	Y	Y	N	Y	N	Y	N
VIRGINIA								
Trible	Y	Y	N	Y	Y	N	Y	N
Warner	Y	Y	N	Y	Y	N	Y	N
WASHINGTON								
Gorton	N	Y	N	Y	Y	N	Y	N
Jackson	N	Y	N	Y	Y	N	Y	N
WEST VIRGINIA								
Byrd	N	Y	Y	N	Y	N	Y	N
Randolph	N	Y	Y	N	Y	N	Y	N
WISCONSIN								
Kasten	N	Y	N	Y	Y	N	Y	N
Proxmire	Y	N	Y	N	Y	N	Y	N
WYOMING								
Simpson	N	Y	Y	N	Y	N	Y	Y
Wallop	N	Y	Y	N	Y	N	Y	Y

ND - Northern Democrats   SD - Southern Democrats (Southern states - Ala., Ark., Fla., Ga., Ky., La., Miss., N.C., Okla., S.C., Tenn., Texas, Va.)

24. HR 1718. Emergency Supplemental Appropriations, Fiscal 1983/Jobs. Moynihan, D-N.Y., amendment to cut $209.7 million from funding for the Bureau of Reclamation and Corps of Engineers and add $200 million for the Environmental Protection Agency's sewage treatment plan and sewer construction program. Rejected 45-51: R 22-31; D 23-20 (ND 19-11, SD 4-9), March 15, 1983.

25. HR 1718. Emergency Supplemental Appropriations, Fiscal 1983/Jobs. Baker, R-Tenn., motion to instruct the sergeant-at-arms to compel the attendance of absent senators. Motion agreed to 94-5: R 52-2; D 42-3 (ND 30-1, SD 12-2), March 16, 1983.

26. HR 1718. Emergency Supplemental Appropriations, Fiscal 1983/Jobs. Dole, R-Kan.-Baker, R-Tenn., motion to invoke cloture (thus limiting debate) on the bill to provide emergency supplemental funding for jobs and other programs in fiscal 1983. Motion rejected 50-48: R 30-24; D 20-24 (ND 16-14, SD 4-10), March 16, 1983. A three-fifths majority vote (60) of the total Senate is required to invoke cloture.

27. HR 1718. Emergency Supplemental Appropriations, Fiscal 1983/Jobs. Kasten, R-Wis., motion to invoke cloture (thus limiting debate) on the Kasten amendment to repeal requirements for tax withholding on interest and dividend income. Motion rejected 59-39: R 24-29; D 35-10 (ND 22-9, SD 13-1), March 16, 1983. A three-fifths majority vote (60) of the total Senate is required to invoke cloture.

28. HR 1900. Social Security Act Amendments. Armstrong, R-Colo., amendment to permit employers with less than $5,000 in monthly withholding to deposit payroll taxes 15 days after the calendar month in which the taxes were collected. Under existing regulations, only employers with less than $3,000 in monthly withholding were allowed the extra time to deposit the taxes. Adopted 96-0: R 53-0; D 43-0 (ND 31-0, SD 12-0), March 17, 1983.

29. HR 1900. Social Security Act Amendments. Symms, R-Idaho, amendment to increase the retirement age at which full Social Security benefits are paid from 65 to 68 in the year 2020, by raising the age one month a year beginning in 1984. Rejected 12-84: R 12-41; D 0-43 (ND 0-31, SD 0-12), March 17, 1983.

30. HR 1718. Emergency Supplemental Appropriations, Fiscal 1983/Jobs. Passage of the bill to provide $16,340,108,000 in fiscal 1983 supplemental appropriations, including $5.2 billion for emergency jobs and recession relief. Passed 82-16: R 39-15; D 43-1 (ND 31-1, SD 12-0), March 17, 1983. The president had proposed a $4.3 billion jobs program and requested $5,033,000,000 for advances to the unemployment trust fund.

31. HR 1900. Social Security Act Amendments. Symms, R-Idaho, amendment to make effective on Jan. 1, 1983, rather than on Jan. 1, 1988, the provision of the bill that would automatically adjust Social Security cost-of-living increases to a lower level when the system's trust fund reserves fall below a certain level. Rejected 25-72: R 22-32; D 3-40 (ND 1-30, SD 2-10), March 17, 1983.

	32	33	34	35	36	37	38	39
ALABAMA								
Denton	N	N	Y	N	N	N	N	Y
Heflin	N	N	N	Y	N	N	N	Y
ALASKA								
Murkowski	N	N	N	N	Y	P	Y	Y
Stevens	N	N	N	N	Y	N	Y	Y
ARIZONA								
Goldwater	Y	?	N	N	Y	N	Y	Y
DeConcini	N	N	N	Y	N	N	N	N
ARKANSAS								
Bumpers	?	?	?	N	N	N	N	N
Pryor	N	N	N	N	N	N	N	N
CALIFORNIA								
Wilson	N	N	N	Y	Y	Y	Y	Y
Cranston	?	?	?	?	?	?	?	N
COLORADO								
Armstrong	Y	N	N	N	N	N	N	Y
Hart	?	?	?	?	Y	Y	Y	N
CONNECTICUT								
Weicker	N	N	N	Y	Y	Y	Y	Y
Dodd	N	Y	Y	Y	Y	Y	Y	N
DELAWARE								
Roth	N	N	N	Y	Y	Y	Y	Y
Biden	?	?	?	Y	N	N	N	N
FLORIDA								
Hawkins	N	N	N	N	N	N	N	Y
Chiles	N	Y	N	Y	N	?	Y	Y
GEORGIA								
Mattingly	Y	N	N	N	N	N	N	Y
Nunn	N	Y	?	N	N	N	N	Y
HAWAII								
Inouye	N	Y	Y	Y	N	N	N	N
Matsunaga	N	Y	Y	Y	N	N	N	N
IDAHO								
McClure	Y	N	N	N	N	Y	Y	Y
Symms	Y	N	N	N	N	N	N	Y
ILLINOIS								
Percy	N	N	N	N	N	N	N	-
Dixon	N	N	N	N	N	N	N	Y
INDIANA								
Lugar	N	N	Y	N	Y	Y	Y	Y
Quayle	?	?	?	?	N	N	N	Y

	32	33	34	35	36	37	38	39
IOWA								
Grassley	N	N	N	N	Y	Y	Y	Y
Jepsen	N	N	N	N	N	N	N	Y
KANSAS								
Dole	N	N	Y	N	Y	Y	Y	Y
Kassebaum	N	N	Y	N	Y	Y	Y	Y
KENTUCKY								
Ford	N	Y	N	Y	N	N	N	N
Huddleston	N	Y	N	N	N	N	N	N
LOUISIANA								
Johnston	N	N	N	N	N	N	N	Y
Long	N	N	N	N	N	N	N	N
MAINE								
Cohen	N	N	N	N	N	Y	Y	Y
Mitchell	N	Y	Y	Y	N	N	N	N
MARYLAND								
Mathias	?	?	?	?	?	?	Y	Y
Sarbanes	N	Y	Y	Y	N	N	?	?
MASSACHUSETTS								
Kennedy	N	Y	Y	Y	Y	Y	Y	N
Tsongas	N	Y	Y	Y	N	N	N	N
MICHIGAN								
Levin	N	Y	Y	Y	N	N	N	N
Riegle	N	Y	N	Y	N	N	N	N
MINNESOTA								
Boschwitz	N	N	N	N	Y	Y	Y	Y
Durenberger	N	N	Y	N	Y	Y	Y	N
MISSISSIPPI								
Cochran	N	N	N	N	N	N	Y	Y
Stennis	N	N	N	Y	N	Y	N	N
MISSOURI								
Danforth	N	N	Y	N	Y	Y	Y	Y
Eagleton	N	Y	Y	Y	N	N	N	N
MONTANA								
Baucus	N	N	N	N	N	Y	Y	Y
Melcher	N	Y	N	Y	N	N	N	N
NEBRASKA								
Exon	N	N	N	N	N	Y	Y	Y
Zorinsky	N	N	N	Y	N	N	N	Y
NEVADA								
Hecht	N	N	Y	N	Y	Y	Y	Y
Laxalt	Y	N	Y	N	Y	Y	Y	?

	32	33	34	35	36	37	38	39
NEW HAMPSHIRE								
Humphrey	Y	N	N	N	N	N	N	N
Rudman	N	N	N	Y	Y	Y	Y	N
NEW JERSEY								
Bradley	N	Y	Y	Y	N	N	N	N
Lautenberg	N	Y	Y	Y	Y	Y	Y	N
NEW MEXICO								
Domenici	N	N	Y	?	Y	Y	Y	Y
Bingaman	N	Y	Y	Y	Y	N	Y	Y
NEW YORK								
D'Amato	N	N	N	N	N	P	Y	Y
Moynihan	N	Y	Y	N	Y	Y	Y	N
NORTH CAROLINA								
East	Y	N	N	N	N	N	N	Y
Helms	Y	N	N	N	N	N	N	N
NORTH DAKOTA								
Andrews	N	N	N	N	Y	N	N	N
Burdick	N	Y	N	Y	N	N	N	N
OHIO								
Glenn	N	Y	Y	N	Y	Y	Y	N
Metzenbaum	N	Y	Y	Y	Y	Y	Y	N
OKLAHOMA								
Nickles	Y	N	N	N	N	N	N	N
Boren	N	N	N	N	N	N	N	N
OREGON								
Hatfield	N	N	N	Y	Y	Y	Y	Y
Packwood	N	N	N	?	?	Y	Y	Y
PENNSYLVANIA								
Heinz	N	N	Y	N	Y	Y	Y	Y
Specter	N	N	Y	N	Y	Y	Y	N
RHODE ISLAND								
Chafee	N	N	N	Y	Y	Y	Y	Y
Pell	N	Y	Y	Y	N	N	Y	N
SOUTH CAROLINA								
Thurmond	N	N	N	Y	N	Y	Y	Y
Hollings	?	?	?	Y	N	N	N	Y
SOUTH DAKOTA								
Abdnor	N	N	N	N	Y	Y	Y	Y
Pressler	N	N	N	?	N	Y	Y	N
TENNESSEE								
Baker	Y	N	N	N	Y	Y	Y	Y
Sasser	N	N	N	Y	N	N	N	N

	32	33	34	35	36	37	38	39
TEXAS								
Tower	N	N	Y	?	Y	Y	Y	Y
Bentsen	N	Y	Y	N	N	N	Y	Y
UTAH								
Garn	N	N	N	N	Y	Y	Y	Y
Hatch	Y	N	N	N	Y	Y	Y	N
VERMONT								
Stafford	N	N	Y	N	?	?	Y	Y
Leahy	N	Y	N	N	N	?	Y	N
VIRGINIA								
Trible	N	N	N	N	N	N	N	Y
Warner	N	N	N	N	N	N	N	Y
WASHINGTON								
Gorton	N	N	N	N	Y	Y	Y	Y
Jackson	N	Y	Y	Y	N	Y	N	Y
WEST VIRGINIA								
Byrd	N	Y	N	Y	N	N	N	N
Randolph	N	Y	N	Y	N	N	N	N
WISCONSIN								
Kasten	N	N	N	N	N	N	N	N
Proxmire	N	N	Y	N	N	N	N	Y
WYOMING								
Simpson	N	N	Y	N	N	N	?	Y
Wallop	Y	N	N	?	?	?	Y	Y

KEY

Y	Voted for (yea).
#	Paired for.
+	Announced for.
N	Voted against (nay).
X	Paired against.
-	Announced against.
P	Voted "present".
C	Voted "present" to avoid possible conflict of interest.
?	Did not vote or otherwise make a position known.

Democrats   *Republicans*

ND - Northern Democrats   SD - Southern Democrats (Southern states - Ala., Ark., Fla., Ga., Ky., La., Miss., N.C., Okla., S.C., Tenn., Texas, Va.)

32. HR 1900. Social Security Act Amendments. Symms, R-Idaho, amendment to delay the scheduled July 1983 cost-of-living increase for one year. Rejected 13-80: R 13-39; D 0-41 (ND 0-29, SD 0-12), March 18, 1983.

33. HR 1900. Social Security Act Amendments. Kennedy, D-Mass., amendment to provide an additional incentive for states to establish their own Medicaid cost containment programs by removing a current requirement that such programs be established by July 1, 1981, to qualify for larger federal Medicaid payments. Rejected 28-64: R 0-51; D 28-13 (ND 23-6, SD 5-7), March 18, 1983.

34. HR 1900. Social Security Act Amendments. Moynihan, D-N.Y., motion to table (kill) the Nickles, R-Okla., amendment to deny Social Security benefits to aliens who have worked or lived illegally in the United States. Motion rejected 34-58: R 15-37; D 19-21 (ND 18-11, SD 1-10), March 18, 1983. (The amendment subsequently was adopted by voice vote.)

35. HR 1900. Social Security Act Amendments. Bradley, D-N.J., amendment to provide a new disability retirement benefit beginning in the year 2000 for individuals over age 62 who are unable to work until age 66 because they are disabled. Rejected 30-61: R 0-47; D 30-14 (ND 25-5, SD 5-9), March 21, 1983.

36. HR 1900. Social Security Act Amendments. Baker, R-Tenn., motion to table (kill) the Melcher, D-Mont., amendment to delay for six months the July 1, 1983, effective date for a new law requiring tax withholding of interest and dividend income. Motion rejected 37-58: R 27-23; D 10-35 (ND 9-22, SD 1-13), March 21, 1983. A "yea" was a vote supporting the president's position.

37. HR 1900. Social Security Act Amendments. Dole, R-Kan., amendment to the Melcher, D-Mont., amendment, to delay the effective date of the new interest and dividend withholding law until Jan. 1, 1984, only if the average prime interest rate charged by the nation's 10 largest banks is 6 percent or less on June 30, 1983, and the following six months and if the minimum deposit required for money market deposit accounts is lowered from $2,500 to $300. Rejected 35-57: R 29-19; D 6-38 (ND 6-25, SD 0-13), March 21, 1983.

38. HR 1900. Social Security Act Amendments. Moynihan, D-N.Y., motion to table (kill) the Melcher, D-Mont., motion to waive provisions of the Congressional Budget Act that would bar consideration of the Melcher amendment *(see vote 36, above)* to delay tax withholding on interest and dividend income. Motion agreed to 54-43: R 41-12; D 13-31 (ND 10-20, SD 3-11), March 22, 1983. (The Melcher amendment subsequently was ruled out of order.)

39. HR 1900. Social Security Act Amendments. Domenici, R-N.M., motion to table (kill) the Heinz, R-Pa., motion to waive provisions of the Congressional Budget Act that would bar consideration of the Heinz amendment to remove the Social Security trust funds from the unified budget. Motion agreed to 56-41: R 44-8; D 12-33 (ND 5-26, SD 7-7), March 22, 1983. (The Heinz amendment subsequently was ruled out of order.)

CQ Senate Votes 40 - 47

Corresponding to Congressional Record Votes 40, 41, 42, 43, 44, 45, 46, 47

	40	41	42	43	44	45	46	47
ALABAMA								
Denton	Y	+	-	-	+	+	-	N
Heflin	Y	Y	Y	Y	Y	N	Y	Y
ALASKA								
Murkowski	Y	N	N	N	Y	N	Y	N
Stevens	Y	N	N	N	Y	Y	N	Y
ARIZONA								
Goldwater	Y	Y	?	?	?	?	Y	N
DeConcini	N	N	Y	Y	Y	Y	Y	N
ARKANSAS								
Bumpers	N	N	N	N	Y	Y	N	N
Pryor	Y	N	Y	N	Y	N	Y	N
CALIFORNIA								
Wilson	Y	N	N	Y	N	Y	N	N
Cranston	N	N	N	?	Y	N	N	N
COLORADO								
Armstrong	Y	Y	Y	Y	N	Y	N	Y
Hart	N	N	N	N	Y	N	N	N
CONNECTICUT								
Weicker	N	N	N	N	Y	Y	Y	N
Dodd	N	N	N	N	Y	N	N	N
DELAWARE								
Roth	Y	Y	N	Y	N	Y	Y	N
Biden	N	Y	N	Y	Y	N	N	N
FLORIDA								
Hawkins	Y	Y	Y	Y	Y	Y	Y	Y
Chiles	Y	N	Y	N	Y	Y	N	N
GEORGIA								
Mattingly	Y	Y	Y	Y	N	Y	N	Y
Nunn	Y	Y	Y	N	Y	Y	N	N
HAWAII								
Inouye	N	N	N	N	Y	Y	N	N
Matsunaga	N	N	N	N	Y	Y	N	N
IDAHO								
McClure	Y	Y	Y	Y	N	Y	N	Y
Symms	Y	Y	Y	Y	N	+	Y	Y
ILLINOIS								
Percy	?	?	?	?	+	?	N	N
Dixon	Y	N	N	N	Y	Y	N	N
INDIANA								
Lugar	Y	N	N	N	Y	Y	N	N
Quayle	Y	Y	Y	N	Y	Y	N	N

	40	41	42	43	44	45	46	47
IOWA								
Grassley	Y	N	N	N	Y	Y	N	N
Jepsen	Y	Y	Y	N	Y	Y	N	N
KANSAS								
Dole	Y	N	N	N	Y	Y	N	N
Kassebaum	Y	Y	N	N	Y	Y	N	N
KENTUCKY								
Ford	Y	N	Y	N	Y	N	N	N
Huddleston	Y	?	?	N	Y	N	N	N
LOUISIANA								
Johnston	Y	Y	N	N	Y	Y	N	N
Long	Y	N	N	N	Y	Y	Y	N
MAINE								
Cohen	Y	N	Y	N	Y	Y	N	N
Mitchell	N	N	Y	N	Y	N	N	N
MARYLAND								
Mathias	Y	N	Y	N	Y	N	Y	N
Sarbanes	?	?	?	N	Y	N	Y	Y
MASSACHUSETTS								
Kennedy	N	N	N	N	Y	N	?	-
Tsongas	N	N	N	N	Y	N	Y	N
MICHIGAN								
Levin	N	N	N	N	Y	N	N	N
Riegle	N	N	Y	N	Y	N	N	N
MINNESOTA								
Boschwitz	Y	Y	Y	Y	Y	Y	N	N
Durenberger	Y	N	?	N	Y	N	N	N
MISSISSIPPI								
Cochran	Y	Y	N	N	Y	Y	N	N
Stennis	N	N	N	N	Y	Y	Y	N
MISSOURI								
Danforth	Y	N	N	N	Y	Y	N	N
Eagleton	?	?	N	N	Y	Y	Y	N
MONTANA								
Baucus	N	N	N	N	Y	Y	N	N
Melcher	N	Y	Y	N	Y	N	Y	N
NEBRASKA								
Exon	Y	N	N	N	Y	Y	N	N
Zorinsky	Y	Y	Y	N	N	Y	Y	Y
NEVADA								
Hecht	Y	N	Y	N	Y	Y	N	N
Laxalt	Y	N	N	N	Y	Y	N	N

	40	41	42	43	44	45	46	47
NEW HAMPSHIRE								
Humphrey	Y	Y	Y	Y	N	N	Y	N
Rudman	Y	N	N	Y	N	Y	N	N
NEW JERSEY								
Bradley	N	N	N	Y	Y	N	N	N
Lautenberg	N	N	N	N	Y	N	N	N
NEW MEXICO								
Domenici	Y	N	N	Y	N	Y	N	N
Bingaman	Y	N	Y	N	Y	N	Y	N
NEW YORK								
D'Amato	Y	N	Y	Y	Y	N	N	N
Moynihan	N	N	N	N	Y	N	N	N
NORTH CAROLINA								
East	Y	Y	Y	Y	N	N	Y	Y
Helms	Y	Y	Y	Y	N	N	Y	N
NORTH DAKOTA								
Andrews	Y	N	N	N	Y	Y	Y	Y
Burdick	N	N	N	Y	N	Y	N	Y
OHIO								
Glenn	N	?	Y	N	Y	N	N	N
Metzenbaum	N	N	N	N	Y	N	N	N
OKLAHOMA								
Nickles	Y	Y	Y	Y	N	Y	Y	N
Boren	Y	Y	N	Y	Y	Y	Y	N
OREGON								
Hatfield	Y	N	N	N	Y	Y	Y	N
Packwood	Y	N	N	N	Y	?	N	N
PENNSYLVANIA								
Heinz	Y	N	N	N	Y	N	N	N
Specter	Y	N	N	N	Y	N	N	Y
RHODE ISLAND								
Chafee	Y	N	N	N	Y	Y	N	N
Pell	N	N	Y	N	Y	Y	N	N
SOUTH CAROLINA								
Thurmond	Y	N	Y	N	Y	Y	Y	N
Hollings	Y	Y	Y	N	Y	Y	?	?
SOUTH DAKOTA								
Abdnor	Y	N	Y	Y	Y	Y	?	N
Pressler	Y	N	Y	N	Y	Y	N	N
TENNESSEE								
Baker	Y	N	N	Y	Y	Y	Y	N
Sasser	N	N	N	N	Y	N	N	N

	40	41	42	43	44	45	46	47
TEXAS								
Tower	Y	N	N	N	Y	N	N	N
Bentsen	Y	N	?	N	Y	Y	Y	N
UTAH								
Garn	Y	Y	Y	Y	N	Y	N	N
Hatch	Y	Y	Y	Y	N	Y	N	N
VERMONT								
Stafford	Y	N	N	N	Y	?	N	N
Leahy	N	N	N	N	Y	N	N	N
VIRGINIA								
Trible	Y	Y	Y	Y	Y	N	Y	N
Warner	Y	N	Y	Y	Y	Y	N	N
WASHINGTON								
Gorton	Y	N	N	N	Y	Y	N	N
Jackson	N	N	N	N	Y	N	N	N
WEST VIRGINIA								
Byrd	N	N	Y	N	Y	N	Y	N
Randolph	N	N	Y	N	Y	N	Y	N
WISCONSIN								
Kasten	Y	Y	Y	Y	Y	Y	Y	N
Proxmire	Y	N	N	N	Y	Y	N	N
WYOMING								
Simpson	Y	N	N	N	Y	Y	N	N
Wallop	Y	N	N	N	Y	N	Y	N

ND - Northern Democrats   SD - Southern Democrats (Southern states - Ala., Ark., Fla., Ga., Ky., La., Miss., N.C., Okla., S.C., Tenn., Texas, Va.)

40. HR 1900. Social Security Act Amendments. Dole, R-Kan., motion to table (kill) the Riegle, D-Mich., amendment to establish separate budget categories for the Social Security trust funds and stipulate that those funds would not be subject to the reconciliation budget-cutting process. Motion agreed to 68-29: R 52-1; D 16-28 (ND 5-25, SD 11-3), March 22, 1983.

41. HR 1900. Social Security Act Amendments. Armstrong, R-Colo., amendment to eliminate the payroll tax increases in the bill. Rejected 27-67: R 20-32; D 7-35 (ND 2-27, SD 5-8), March 22, 1983.

42. HR 1900. Social Security Act Amendments. Hawkins, R-Fla., amendment to move up by two years the phase-out of the earnings limitation for beneficiaries who have reached retirement age. Rejected 44-49: R 24-26; D 20-23 (ND 13-18, SD 7-5), March 22, 1983.

43. HR 1900. Social Security Act Amendments. Humphrey, R-N.H., amendment to index, or adjust for inflation, the income threshold at which Social Security benefits would be subject to taxation. Rejected 22-74: R 18-33; D 4-41 (ND 3-28, SD 1-13), March 22, 1983.

44. HR 1718. Emergency Supplemental Appropriations, Fiscal 1983/Jobs. Adoption of the conference report on the bill to provide $15,589,034,000 in fiscal 1983 supplemental appropriations, including $4.6 billion for emergency jobs and recession relief. Adopted 82-15: R 37-14; D 45-1 (ND 31-1, SD 14-0), March 22, 1983. The president had requested $10,740,457,000 in supplemental appropriations and had proposed a $4.3 billion jobs program.

45. HR 1718. Emergency Supplemental Appropriations, Fiscal 1983/Jobs. Hatfield, R-Ore., motion to table (kill) the Heinz, R-Pa., appeal of the chair's ruling that a Heinz amendment, offered to an amendment reported in technical disagreement by Senate-House conferees, was out of order. The chair ruled that the Heinz amendment, which would have restored a Senate provision allowing $1.14 billion in accelerated revenue sharing payments, violated requirements of the fiscal 1983 budget resolution. Motion agreed to 62-32: R 42-6; D 20-26 (ND 11-21, SD 9-5), March 22, 1983.

46. HR 1900. Social Security Act Amendments. Boren, D-Okla., amendment to set the income threshold for taxation of Social Security benefits at $20,000 for individuals and $36,000 for married couples, instead of $25,000 for individuals and $32,000 for married couples, as provided in the bill. The amendment was designed to reduce the "marriage penalty" in taxation of Social Security benefits. Rejected 34-62: R 15-37; D 19-25 (ND 11-20, SD 8-5), March 23, 1983.

47. HR 1900. Social Security Act Amendments. Stevens, R-Alaska-Mathias, R-Md., amendment to the Long, D-La., amendment, to strike provisions extending Social Security coverage to federal employees. Rejected 12-86: R 8-46; D 4-40 (ND 3-28, SD 1-12), March 23, 1983. (The Long amendment to provide coverage for newly hired federal workers when a supplemental pension program is in place subsequently was adopted by voice vote.)

	48	49	50	51	52	53
ALABAMA						
Denton	Y	N	N	Y	N	Y
Heflin	N	N	Y	N	N	N
ALASKA						
Murkowski	Y	Y	Y	Y	N	Y
Stevens	Y	Y	Y	Y	N	Y
ARIZONA						
Goldwater	N	Y	?	?	Y	Y
DeConcini	?	N	Y	N	Y	Y
ARKANSAS						
Bumpers	N	N	Y	N	N	Y
Pryor	N	N	Y	N	N	Y
CALIFORNIA						
Wilson	Y	Y	N	Y	Y	Y
Cranston	N	N	Y	?	?	?
COLORADO						
Armstrong	N	Y	Y	Y	Y	Y
Hart	N	N	N	N	N	Y
CONNECTICUT						
Weicker	Y	Y	N	Y	N	Y
Dodd	N	N	Y	N	Y	Y
DELAWARE						
Roth	Y	N	N	Y	N	Y
Biden	N	N	N	N	N	Y
FLORIDA						
Hawkins	?	Y	Y	Y	Y	Y
Chiles	Y	Y	N	N	N	Y
GEORGIA						
Mattingly	Y	Y	N	Y	N	Y
Nunn	N	Y	N	N	N	Y
HAWAII						
Inouye	N	Y	N	Y	N	Y
Matsunaga	N	N	Y	N	N	Y
IDAHO						
McClure	Y	N	N	Y	Y	Y
Symms	Y	N	Y	Y	Y	N
ILLINOIS						
Percy	Y	N	N	Y	N	Y
Dixon	N	N	Y	N	Y	Y
INDIANA						
Lugar	Y	Y	N	Y	N	Y
Quayle	Y	Y	N	Y	Y	Y

	48	49	50	51	52	53
IOWA						
Grassley	Y	Y	N	Y	N	Y
Jepsen	Y	Y	N	Y	Y	Y
KANSAS						
Dole	Y	Y	N	Y	N	Y
Kassebaum	Y	Y	N	Y	N	Y
KENTUCKY						
Ford	N	N	Y	N	N	Y
Huddleston	N	N	Y	N	N	Y
LOUISIANA						
Johnston	N	Y	Y	N	N	N
Long	N	N	Y	N	Y	Y
MAINE						
Cohen	Y	Y	N	Y	N	Y
Mitchell	N	N	N	N	N	Y
MARYLAND						
Mathias	Y	?	?	?	?	+
Sarbanes	N	N	Y	N	N	Y
MASSACHUSETTS						
Kennedy	X	?	?	N	N	Y
Tsongas	N	N	N	N	N	Y
MICHIGAN						
Levin	N	N	N	N	N	Y
Riegle	N	N	Y	N	N	Y
MINNESOTA						
Boschwitz	N	Y	Y	Y	Y	Y
Durenberger	Y	Y	N	Y	N	Y
MISSISSIPPI						
Cochran	N	Y	Y	N	Y	Y
Stennis	N	N	Y	?	?	Y
MISSOURI						
Danforth	Y	Y	N	Y	N	Y
Eagleton	N	N	N	N	N	Y
MONTANA						
Baucus	N	N	Y	N	N	Y
Melcher	N	N	Y	X	N	Y
NEBRASKA						
Exon	N	N	N	N	N	Y
Zorinsky	N	N	Y	Y	Y	N
NEVADA						
Hecht	Y	Y	N	Y	N	Y
Laxalt	Y	Y	N	Y	N	Y

	48	49	50	51	52	53
NEW HAMPSHIRE						
Humphrey	Y	Y	N	Y	Y	Y
Rudman	Y	Y	N	Y	N	Y
NEW JERSEY						
Bradley	Y	N	N	N	N	Y
Lautenberg	Y	N	N	N	N	Y
NEW MEXICO						
Domenici	N	Y	N	Y	N	Y
Bingaman	N	N	Y	N	N	Y
NEW YORK						
D'Amato	N	N	Y	Y	Y	Y
Moynihan	#	N	Y	N	N	Y
NORTH CAROLINA						
East	N	Y	Y	Y	Y	N
Helms	Y	Y	Y	Y	N	N
NORTH DAKOTA						
Andrews	N	N	N	Y	N	Y
Burdick	N	N	Y	N	N	Y
OHIO						
Glenn	N	N	Y	N	?	Y
Metzenbaum	Y	N	N	N	N	Y
OKLAHOMA						
Nickles	Y	Y	N	Y	N	Y
Boren	N	N	N	#	Y	Y
OREGON						
Hatfield	Y	Y	N	Y	N	Y
Packwood	Y'	Y	N	Y	N	Y
PENNSYLVANIA						
Heinz	Y	Y	N	Y	N	Y
Specter	N	N	Y	Y	N	Y
RHODE ISLAND						
Chafee	Y	Y	N	Y	N	Y
Pell	N	N	N	N	N	Y
SOUTH CAROLINA						
Thurmond	Y	Y	Y	Y	Y	Y
Hollings	?	?	?	?	?	?
SOUTH DAKOTA						
Abdnor	Y	N	N	Y	N	Y
Pressler	N	N	Y	N	Y	Y
TENNESSEE						
Baker	Y	Y	N	Y	N	Y
Sasser	N	N	Y	N	N	Y

	48	49	50	51	52	53
TEXAS						
Tower	Y	Y	N	Y	N	Y
Bentsen	N	N	Y	N	N	Y
UTAH						
Garn	Y	Y	N	Y	N	N
Hatch	Y	Y	N	Y	Y	N
VERMONT						
Stafford	Y	Y	N	Y	N	Y
Leahy	N	N	Y	N	N	Y
VIRGINIA						
Trible	N	Y	Y	Y	Y	Y
Warner	N	Y	N	Y	Y	Y
WASHINGTON						
Gorton	Y	Y	N	Y	N	Y
Jackson	N	Y	N	N	N	Y
WEST VIRGINIA						
Byrd	N	N	Y	N	N	Y
Randolph	N	N	Y	N	N	Y
WISCONSIN						
Kasten	Y	Y	Y	N	Y	Y
Proxmire	N	Y	Y	N	Y	Y
WYOMING						
Simpson	Y	Y	N	Y	N	Y
Wallop	Y	Y	N	Y	N	Y

KEY

Y	Voted for (yea).
#	Paired for.
+	Announced for.
N	Voted against (nay).
X	Paired against.
-	Announced against.
P	Voted "present".
C	Voted "present" to avoid possible conflict of interest.
?	Did not vote or otherwise make a position known.

Democrats   *Republicans*

ND - Northern Democrats   SD - Southern Democrats (Southern states - Ala., Ark., Fla., Ga., Ky., La., Miss., N.C., Okla., S.C., Tenn., Texas, Va.)

48. HR 1900. Social Security Act Amendments. Stevens, R-Alaska, amendment to the Long, D-La., amendment, to require the implementation of a supplemental Civil Service retirement plan by Oct. 1, 1985, for new federal workers as of Jan. 1, 1984. Such workers would not have to pay into the Civil Service Retirement System between Jan. 1, 1984, and Oct. 1, 1985, but would receive retirement credit for that period of work. Rejected 45-50: R 41-12; D 4-38 (ND 3-26, SD 1-12), March 23, 1983. (The Long amendment to provide coverage for newly hired federal workers when a supplemental pension program is in place subsequently was adopted by voice vote.)

49. HR 1900. Social Security Act Amendments. Armstrong, R-Colo., amendment to allow local governments covered by Social Security to make their payroll tax payments directly to the Treasury, instead of going through the state government. Adopted 49-48: R 43-10; D 6-38 (ND 3-28, SD 3-10), March 23, 1983.

50. HR 1900. Social Security Act Amendments. Long, D-La., amendment to strike a provision requiring that tax-exempt interest income be included in the calculation used to determine if an individual's Social Security benefits should be taxed. Rejected 44-52: R 15-37; D 29-15 (ND 19-12, SD 10-3), March 23, 1983.

51. HR 1900. Social Security Act Amendments. Quayle, R-Ind., amendment to give those eligible for federal supplemental unemployment benefits the option of receiving vouchers — equal in value to 75 percent of their benefits — which could be turned over to employers in exchange for a job. Employers could use the vouchers to offset tax liability. Adopted 53-40: R 52-0; D 1-40 (ND 1-29, SD 0-11), March 23, 1983.

52. HR 1900. Social Security Act Amendments. Armstrong, R-Colo., amendment to require that only new employees of non-profit organizations, as of Jan. 1, 1984, be covered by Social Security. Rejected 26-69: R 19-34; D 7-35 (ND 5-25, SD 2-10), March 23, 1983.

53. HR 1900. Social Security Act Amendments. Passage of the bill to overhaul the Social Security system, to revamp the way the federal government reimburses hospitals for Medicare, to extend the federal supplemental unemployment benefit program for six months and to increase Supplemental Security Income benefits. Passed 88-9: R 47-6; D 41-3 (ND 30-1, SD 11-2), March 23, 1983.

54		*54*		*54*		KEY
ALABAMA		**IOWA**		**NEW HAMPSHIRE**		Y Voted for (yea).
Denton	Y	*Grassley*	Y	*Humphrey*	Y	# Paired for.
Heflin	?	*Jepsen*	Y	*Rudman*	Y	+ Announced for.
ALASKA		**KANSAS**		**NEW JERSEY**		N Voted against (nay).
Murkowski	+	*Dole*	Y	Bradley	Y	X Paired against.
Stevens	Y	*Kassebaum*	Y	Lautenberg	Y	- Announced against.
ARIZONA		**KENTUCKY**		**NEW MEXICO**		P Voted "present".
Goldwater	+	Ford	Y	*Domenici*	Y	C Voted "present" to avoid possi-
DeConcini	?	Huddleston	?	Bingaman	Y	ble conflict of interest.
ARKANSAS		**LOUISIANA**		**NEW YORK**		? Did not vote or otherwise make a
Bumpers	Y	Johnston	?	*D'Amato*	Y	position known.
Pryor	?	Long	N	Moynihan	Y	
CALIFORNIA		**MAINE**		**NORTH CAROLINA**		Democrats *Republicans*
Wilson	Y	*Cohen*	Y	*East*	N	
Cranston	Y	Mitchell	Y	*Helms*	?	
COLORADO		**MARYLAND**		**NORTH DAKOTA**		*54*
Armstrong	N	*Mathias*	?	*Andrews*	Y	
Hart	?	Sarbanes	?	Burdick	Y	
CONNECTICUT		**MASSACHUSETTS**		**OHIO**		**TEXAS**
Weicker	+	Kennedy	?	Glenn	Y	*Tower*	?
Dodd	Y	Tsongas	Y	Metzenbaum	?	Bentsen	?
DELAWARE		**MICHIGAN**		**OKLAHOMA**		**UTAH**
Roth	?	Levin	Y	*Nickles*	N	*Garn*	N
Biden	Y	Riegle	Y	Boren	N	*Hatch*	N
FLORIDA		**MINNESOTA**		**OREGON**		**VERMONT**
Hawkins	Y	*Boschwitz*	Y	*Hatfield*	?	*Stafford*	?
Chiles	?	*Durenberger*	Y	*Packwood*	?	Leahy	Y
GEORGIA		**MISSISSIPPI**		**PENNSYLVANIA**		**VIRGINIA**
Mattingly	N	*Cochran*	Y	*Heinz*	Y	*Trible*	Y
Nunn	N	Stennis	Y	*Specter*	Y	*Warner*	Y
HAWAII		**MISSOURI**		**RHODE ISLAND**		**WASHINGTON**
Inouye	?	*Danforth*	Y	*Chafee*	Y	*Gorton*	Y
Matsunaga	Y	Eagleton	?	Pell	+	Jackson	Y
IDAHO		**MONTANA**		**SOUTH CAROLINA**		**WEST VIRGINIA**
McClure	N	Baucus	Y	*Thurmond*	Y	Byrd	Y
Symms	N	Melcher	Y	Hollings	N	Randolph	Y
ILLINOIS		**NEBRASKA**		**SOUTH DAKOTA**		**WISCONSIN**
Percy	?	Exon	N	*Abdnor*	Y	*Kasten*	Y
Dixon	Y	Zorinsky	N	*Pressler*	?	Proxmire	Y
INDIANA		**NEVADA**		**TENNESSEE**		**WYOMING**
Lugar	Y	*Hecht*	Y	*Baker*	Y	*Simpson*	Y
Quayle	?	*Laxalt*	?	Sasser	Y	*Wallop*	Y

ND - Northern Democrats   SD - Southern Democrats (Southern states - Ala., Ark., Fla., Ga., Ky., La., Miss., N.C., Okla., S.C., Tenn., Texas, Va.)

54. HR 1900. Social Security Act Amendments. Adoption of the conference report on the bill to overhaul the Social Security system, to revamp the way the federal government reimburses hospitals for Medicare, to extend the federal supplemental unemployment benefit program for six months and to increase Supplemental Security Income benefits. Adopted (thus cleared for the president) 58-14: R 32-8; D 26-6 (ND 22-2, SD 4-4), in the session that began March 24, 1983. A "yea" was a vote supporting the president's position.

	55		55		55	KEY
ALABAMA		**IOWA**		**NEW HAMPSHIRE**		Y Voted for (yea).
Denton	Y	*Grassley*	Y	*Humphrey*	Y	# Paired for.
Heflin	Y	*Jepsen*	Y	*Rudman*	Y	+ Announced for.
ALASKA		**KANSAS**		**NEW JERSEY**		N Voted against (nay).
Murkowski	Y	*Dole*	Y	Bradley	N	X Paired against.
Stevens	Y	*Kassebaum*	Y	Lautenberg	N	- Announced against.
ARIZONA		**KENTUCKY**		**NEW MEXICO**		P Voted "present".
Goldwater	Y	Ford	N	*Domenici*	Y	C Voted "present" to avoid possi-
DeConcini	N	Huddleston	N	Bingaman	N	ble conflict of interest.
ARKANSAS		**LOUISIANA**		**NEW YORK**		? Did not vote or otherwise make a
Bumpers	N	Johnston	Y	*D'Amato*	Y	position known.
Pryor	N	Long	Y	Moynihan	Y	
CALIFORNIA		**MAINE**		**NORTH CAROLINA**		Democrats *Republicans*
Wilson	Y	*Cohen*	Y	*East*	Y	

		55
Cranston	N	Mitchell	N	*Helms*	Y	
COLORADO		**MARYLAND**		**NORTH DAKOTA**		
Armstrong	Y	*Mathias*	N	*Andrews*	N	**TEXAS**	
Hart	N	Sarbanes	N	Burdick	N	*Tower*	Y
CONNECTICUT		**MASSACHUSETTS**		**OHIO**		Bentsen	N
Weicker	Y	Kennedy	N	Glenn	N	**UTAH**	
Dodd	N	Tsongas	N	Metzenbaum	N	*Garn*	Y
DELAWARE		**MICHIGAN**		**OKLAHOMA**		*Hatch*	Y
Roth	Y	Levin	N	*Nickles*	Y	**VERMONT**	
Biden	N	Riegle	N	Boren	N	*Stafford*	Y
FLORIDA		**MINNESOTA**		**OREGON**		Leahy	N
Hawkins	Y	*Boschwitz*	Y	*Hatfield*	Y	**VIRGINIA**	
Chiles	N	*Durenberger*	Y	*Packwood*	?	*Trible*	Y
GEORGIA		**MISSISSIPPI**		**PENNSYLVANIA**		*Warner*	Y
Mattingly	Y	*Cochran*	Y	*Heinz*	Y	**WASHINGTON**	
Nunn	N	Stennis	N	*Specter*	Y	*Gorton*	N
HAWAII		**MISSOURI**		**RHODE ISLAND**		Jackson	Y
Inouye	N	*Danforth*	Y	*Chafee*	Y	**WEST VIRGINIA**	
Matsunaga	N	Eagleton	N	Pell	N	Byrd	N
IDAHO		**MONTANA**		**SOUTH CAROLINA**		Randolph	Y
McClure	Y	Baucus	N	*Thurmond*	Y	**WISCONSIN**	
Symms	Y	Melcher	N	Hollings	N	*Kasten*	Y
ILLINOIS		**NEBRASKA**		**SOUTH DAKOTA**		Proxmire	N
Percy	Y	Exon	N	*Abdnor*	Y	**WYOMING**	
Dixon	Y	Zorinsky	Y	Pressler	N	*Simpson*	Y
INDIANA		**NEVADA**		**TENNESSEE**		*Wallop*	Y
Lugar	Y	*Hecht*	Y	*Baker*	Y	
Quayle	Y	*Laxalt*	Y	Sasser	N	

ND - Northern Democrats   SD - Southern Democrats (Southern states - Ala., Ark., Fla., Ga., Ky., La., Miss., N.C., Okla., S.C., Tenn., Texas, Va.)

55. Adelman Nomination. Confirmation of President Reagan's nomination of Kenneth L. Adelman of Virginia to be director of the Arms Control and Disarmament Agency. Confirmed 57-42: R 49-4; D 8-38 (ND 5-27, SD 3-11), April 14, 1983. A "yea" was a vote supporting the president's position.

	56	57	58	59	60
ALABAMA					
Denton	?	?	N	?	?
Heflin	N	Y	Y	N	Y
ALASKA					
Murkowski	N	N	N	Y	Y
Stevens	Y	N	N	Y	Y
ARIZONA					
Goldwater	Y	N	N	Y	Y
DeConcini	N	Y	Y	N	Y
ARKANSAS					
Bumpers	N	N	Y	N	Y
Pryor	N	Y	Y	N	Y
CALIFORNIA					
Wilson	Y	N	N	Y	Y
Cranston	N	N	N	Y	N
COLORADO					
Armstrong	N	N	N	Y	Y
Hart	N	N	?	?	?
CONNECTICUT					
Weicker	?	?	?	?	?
Dodd	N	N	N	Y	Y
DELAWARE					
Roth	?	?	N	Y	Y
Biden	N	?	Y	N	Y
FLORIDA					
Hawkins	N	N	N	Y	Y
Chiles	N	Y	Y	N	Y
GEORGIA					
Mattingly	N	N	N	Y	Y
Nunn	N	Y	Y	N	Y
HAWAII					
Inouye	N	Y	Y	N	Y
Matsunaga	N	Y	Y	N	Y
IDAHO					
McClure	Y	N	N	Y	Y
Symms	N	N	N	Y	Y
ILLINOIS					
Percy	N	N	N	Y	Y
Dixon	N	Y	Y	N	Y
INDIANA					
Lugar	Y	N	N	Y	Y
Quayle	Y	N	N	Y	Y

	56	57	58	59	60
IOWA					
Grassley	Y	N	N	Y	Y
Jepsen	N	N	N	Y	Y
KANSAS					
Dole	Y	N	N	Y	Y
Kassebaum	N	N	N	Y	Y
KENTUCKY					
Ford	N	Y	Y	N	Y
Huddleston	N	Y	Y	Y	Y
LOUISIANA					
Johnston	N	Y	Y	N	Y
Long	N	Y	Y	N	Y
MAINE					
Cohen	Y	N	N	Y	Y
Mitchell	N	Y	Y	N	Y
MARYLAND					
Mathias	?	?	N	Y	Y
Sarbanes	N	Y	Y	N	Y
MASSACHUSETTS					
Kennedy	Y	N	N	Y	Y
Tsongas	N	?	Y	N	Y
MICHIGAN					
Levin	Y	N	N	Y	Y
Riegle	N	Y	Y	N	Y
MINNESOTA					
Boschwitz	N	N	N	Y	Y
Durenberger	Y	?	N	Y	Y
MISSISSIPPI					
Cochran	N	N	N	Y	Y
Stennis	N	Y	Y	N	Y
MISSOURI					
Danforth	Y	N	N	Y	N
Eagleton	N	Y	Y	Y	Y
MONTANA					
Baucus	N	Y	Y	N	Y
Melcher	N	Y	Y	N	Y
NEBRASKA					
Exon	N	Y	Y	N	Y
Zorinsky	N	Y	Y	N	Y
NEVADA					
Hecht	Y	N	N	Y	Y
Laxalt	Y	?	N	Y	Y

	56	57	58	59	60
NEW HAMPSHIRE					
Humphrey	N	Y	N	Y	Y
Rudman	Y	N	N	Y	Y
NEW JERSEY					
Bradley	N	N	Y	N	Y
Lautenberg	N	N	N	Y	N
NEW MEXICO					
Domenici	Y	N	N	Y	Y
Bingaman	N	N	Y	N	Y
NEW YORK					
D'Amato	N	N	N	Y	Y
Moynihan	N	Y	N	N	Y
NORTH CAROLINA					
East	N	Y	Y	Y	Y
Helms	N	Y	Y	Y	Y
NORTH DAKOTA					
Andrews	Y	N	N	Y	Y
Burdick	N	Y	Y	N	Y
OHIO					
Glenn	N	Y	Y	N	Y
Metzenbaum	Y	N	N	Y	Y
OKLAHOMA					
Nickles	N	N	N	Y	Y
Boren	N	Y	Y	N	Y
OREGON					
Hatfield	?	?	N	Y	Y
Packwood	Y	?	N	Y	Y
PENNSYLVANIA					
Heinz	Y	N	N	Y	Y
Specter	N	N	N	Y	Y
RHODE ISLAND					
Chafee	Y	N	N	Y	Y
Pell	N	Y	Y	N	Y
SOUTH CAROLINA					
Thurmond	Y	N	N	Y	Y
Hollings	N	?	Y	N	Y
SOUTH DAKOTA					
Abdnor	N	N	N	Y	Y
Pressler	N	N	N	Y	Y
TENNESSEE					
Baker	?	N	N	Y	Y
Sasser	N	+	Y	N	Y

KEY

Y	Voted for (yea).
#	Paired for.
+	Announced for.
N	Voted against (nay).
X	Paired against.
-	Announced against.
P	Voted "present".
C	Voted "present" to avoid possible conflict of interest.
?	Did not vote or otherwise make a position known.

Democrats   *Republicans*

	56	57	58	59	60
TEXAS					
Tower	Y	N	N	Y	Y
Bentsen	N	Y	Y	N	Y
UTAH					
Garn	Y	N	N	Y	Y
Hatch	Y	N	N	Y	Y
VERMONT					
Stafford	Y	N	N	Y	Y
Leahy	N	Y	Y	N	Y
VIRGINIA					
Trible	N	N	N	Y	Y
Warner	Y	N	N	Y	Y
WASHINGTON					
Gorton	Y	N	N	Y	Y
Jackson	N	Y	Y	N	Y
WEST VIRGINIA					
Byrd	N	Y	Y	N	Y
Randolph	N	Y	Y	N	Y
WISCONSIN					
Kasten	N	N	N	Y	Y
Proxmire	N	N	N	N	Y
WYOMING					
Simpson	Y	-	N	Y	Y
Wallop	Y	N	N	Y	Y

ND - Northern Democrats   SD - Southern Democrats (Southern states - Ala., Ark., Fla., Ga., Ky., La., Miss., N.C., Okla., S.C., Tenn., Texas, Va.)

56. Procedural Motion. Stevens, R-Alaska, motion that the Senate adjourn, with the effect of delaying a scheduled vote to end debate on a Kasten, R-Wis., amendment, to a trade bill *(see vote 57, below),* that would repeal a new law requiring withholding of interest and dividend income. Motion rejected 31-63: R 28-20; D 3-43 (ND 3-29, SD 0-14), April 19, 1983.

57. S 144. International Trade and Investment Act/Interest and Dividend Withholding. Kasten, R-Wis., motion to invoke cloture (thus limiting debate) on the Kasten amendment to repeal a new law requiring withholding of interest and dividend income. Motion rejected 34-53: R 3-42; D 31-11 (ND 20-10, SD 11-1), April 19, 1983. A three-fifths majority vote (60) of the total Senate is required to invoke cloture.

58. S 144. International Trade and Investment Act/Interest and Dividend Withholding. Kasten, R-Wis., motion to invoke cloture (thus limiting debate) on the Kasten amendment to repeal a new law requiring withholding from inter-est and dividend income. Motion rejected 39-59: R 2-51; D 37-8 (ND 23-8, SD 14-0), April 20, 1983. A three-fifths majority vote (60) of the total Senate is required to invoke cloture.

59. S 144. International Trade and Investment Act/Interest and Dividend Withholding. Dole, R-Kan., motion to table (kill) the Melcher, D-Mont., amendment to the Baker, R-Tenn., motion to waive the relevant sections of the budget act for all bills considered by the Senate during the 98th Congress. Motion agreed to 60-37: R 52-0; D 8-37 (ND 7-24, SD 1-13), April 20, 1983.

60. S 144. International Trade and Investment Act/Interest and Dividend Withholding. Baker, R-Tenn., motion to waive Titles III and IV of the Budget Act for the bill. Motion agreed to 94-3: R 51-1; D 43-2 (ND 29-2, SD 14-0), April 20, 1983.

	61 62 63		61 62 63		61 62 63	KEY
ALABAMA		**IOWA**		**NEW HAMPSHIRE**		Y Voted for (yea).
Denton	Y Y N	*Grassley*	Y Y Y	*Humphrey*	Y Y Y	# Paired for.
Heflin	N Y N	*Jepsen*	Y Y Y	*Rudman*	Y Y Y	+ Announced for.
ALASKA		**KANSAS**		**NEW JERSEY**		N Voted against (nay).
Murkowski	Y Y Y	*Dole*	Y Y Y	Bradley	N Y Y	X Paired against.
Stevens	Y Y Y	*Kassebaum*	Y Y Y	Lautenberg	Y N Y	- Announced against.
ARIZONA		**KENTUCKY**		**NEW MEXICO**		P Voted "present".
Goldwater	Y Y ?	Ford	N Y N	*Domenici*	Y Y Y	C Voted "present" to avoid possible conflict of interest.
DeConcini	N Y Y	Huddleston	N Y N	Bingaman	N Y Y	? Did not vote or otherwise make a position known.
ARKANSAS		**LOUISIANA**		**NEW YORK**		
Bumpers	N Y Y	Johnston	N Y Y	*D'Amato*	Y Y N	Democrats *Republicans*
Pryor	N Y Y	Long	N Y Y	Moynihan	N Y Y	
CALIFORNIA		**MAINE**		**NORTH CAROLINA**		
Wilson	Y Y Y	*Cohen*	Y Y N	*East*	N Y N	61 62 63
Cranston	Y N Y	Mitchell	N Y Y	*Helms*	N Y N	
COLORADO		**MARYLAND**		**NORTH DAKOTA**		
Armstrong	Y Y ?	*Mathias*	Y Y N	*Andrews*	N Y N	**TEXAS**
Hart	? ? ?	Sarbanes	N Y N	Burdick	N Y Y	*Tower* — Y Y Y
CONNECTICUT		**MASSACHUSETTS**		**OHIO**		Bentsen — N Y Y
Weicker	? ? ?	Kennedy	Y N N	Glenn	? ? ?	**UTAH**
Dodd	Y Y N	Tsongas	N Y N	Metzenbaum	Y N ?	*Garn* — Y Y N
DELAWARE		**MICHIGAN**		**OKLAHOMA**		*Hatch* — Y Y Y
Roth	Y Y Y	Levin	Y Y N	*Nickles*	N Y Y	**VERMONT**
Biden	N Y N	Riegle	N Y N	Boren	N Y Y	*Stafford* — Y Y ?
FLORIDA		**MINNESOTA**		**OREGON**		Leahy — N Y Y
Hawkins	Y Y Y	*Boschwitz*	Y Y N	*Hatfield*	Y, Y Y	**VIRGINIA**
Chiles	Y Y Y	*Durenberger*	Y Y Y	*Packwood*	Y Y Y	*Trible* — Y Y Y
GEORGIA		**MISSISSIPPI**		**PENNSYLVANIA**		*Warner* — Y Y Y
Mattingly	Y Y Y	*Cochran*	Y Y ?	*Heinz*	Y Y N	**WASHINGTON**
Nunn	N Y Y	Stennis	N Y Y	*Specter*	Y Y N	*Gorton* — Y Y Y
HAWAII		**MISSOURI**		**RHODE ISLAND**		Jackson — N Y Y
Inouye	N Y N	*Danforth*	Y N Y	*Chafee*	Y Y Y	**WEST VIRGINIA**
Matsunaga	N Y Y	Eagleton	N Y ?	Pell	N Y N	Byrd — N Y N
IDAHO		**MONTANA**		**SOUTH CAROLINA**		Randolph — N Y N
McClure	Y Y Y	Baucus	N Y Y	*Thurmond*	Y Y Y	**WISCONSIN**
Symms	? Y Y	Melcher	N Y N	Hollings	N Y N	*Kasten* — Y Y Y
ILLINOIS		**NEBRASKA**		**SOUTH DAKOTA**		Proxmire — Y Y Y
Percy	Y Y Y	Exon	N Y Y	*Abdnor*	Y Y Y	**WYOMING**
Dixon	N Y N	Zorinsky	N Y N	*Pressler*	Y Y Y	*Simpson* — Y Y Y
INDIANA		**NEVADA**		**TENNESSEE**		*Wallop* — Y Y ?
Lugar	Y Y Y	*Hecht*	Y Y N	*Baker*	? ? ?	
Quayle	Y Y Y	*Laxalt*	Y Y N	Sasser	N Y N	

ND · Northern Democrats   SD - Southern Democrats (Southern states - Ala., Ark., Fla., Ga., Ky., La., Miss., N.C., Okla., S.C., Tenn., Texas, Va.)

61. S 144. International Trade and Investment Act/Interest and Dividend Withholding. Kasten, R-Wis., motion to table (kill) the Long, D-La., amendment to recommit the bill to the Finance Committee with instructions to report the bill with an amendment repealing a new interest and dividend withholding law. Motion agreed to 55-40: R 47-4; D 8-36 (ND 7-23, SD 1-13), April 21, 1983. A "yea" was a vote supporting the president's position.

62. S 144. International Trade and Investment Act/Interest and Dividend Withholding. Dole, R-Kan., amendment to the Kasten, R-Wis., amendment to the Dole motion to recommit the bill to the Finance Committee with instructions to report the bill with an amendment calling for a four-year delay in a new interest and dividend withholding law and to increase reporting requirements on interest and dividend income. Adopted 91-5: R 51-1; D 40-4 (ND 26-4, SD 14-0), April 21, 1983.

63. S 144. International Trade and Investment Act. Danforth, R-Mo., motion to table (kill) the Specter, R-Pa., amendment to allow U.S. federal courts to issue injunctions blocking the import of foreign goods that are being sold on the U.S. market for less than the cost of production, and enabling the courts to award damages to injured U.S. companies. Motion agreed to 57-32: R 34-13; D 23-19 (ND 14-14, SD 9-5), April 21, 1983. A "yea" was a vote supporting the president's position.

	64 65 66 67 68 69 70		64 65 66 67 68 69 70		64 65 66 67 68 69 70
ALABAMA		**IOWA**		**NEW HAMPSHIRE**	
Denton	N N N N N N N	*Grassley*	N N N N N N N	*Humphrey*	N N N Y N N N
Heflin	Y N N N N N Y	*Jepsen*	Y N N Y N N N	*Rudman*	N N N N N N N
ALASKA		**KANSAS**		**NEW JERSEY**	
Murkowski	N N N Y N N N	*Dole*	N N N Y N N N	Bradley	Y N N N N N Y
Stevens	N N N Y N N N	*Kassebaum*	N N N N N N N	Lautenberg	N Y N N N N Y
ARIZONA		**KENTUCKY**		**NEW MEXICO**	
Goldwater	N N ? ? ? ? ?	Ford	N N N N N N Y	*Domenici*	Y N N N N N N
DeConcini	Y Y N N Y N Y	Huddleston	N N N N N N Y	Bingaman	Y Y Y N N N N
ARKANSAS		**LOUISIANA**		**NEW YORK**	
Bumpers	N N Y N N N Y	Johnston	? ? Y N N Y Y	*D'Amato*	Y N N N Y N Y
Pryor	N N Y N N Y Y	Long	N N N N Y Y Y	Moynihan	Y Y N N Y N Y
CALIFORNIA		**MAINE**		**NORTH CAROLINA**	
Wilson	Y Y N Y N N N	*Cohen*	N N N N N N N	*East*	N N N Y N N N
Cranston	Y Y N N N N Y	Mitchell	Y N N N N N Y	*Helms*	N N N Y N N N
COLORADO		**MARYLAND**		**NORTH DAKOTA**	
Armstrong	N N N Y N N N	*Mathias*	N N N N N N N	*Andrews*	N N Y N N Y N
Hart	? ? N N N N Y	Sarbanes	Y ? N N Y N Y	Burdick	? ? N N N N Y
CONNECTICUT		**MASSACHUSETTS**		**OHIO**	
Weicker	Y N N N N N N	Kennedy	Y Y N N Y N Y	Glenn	Y Y N N N N N
Dodd	? ? N N Y N Y	Tsongas	Y Y N N N ? ?	Metzenbaum	Y Y N Y N Y Y
DELAWARE		**MICHIGAN**		**OKLAHOMA**	
Roth	N N N N N N N	Levin	Y Y Y N Y N Y	*Nickles*	N N N N N N N
Biden	? ? N N Y N Y	Riegle	Y N N N N N Y	Boren	Y N Y N N Y N
FLORIDA		**MINNESOTA**		**OREGON**	
Hawkins	N N N N N Y N Y	*Boschwitz*	Y N N N N N N	*Hatfield*	- - N N N N N
Chiles	Y N N N N N Y	*Durenberger*	N N N N N N N	*Packwood*	Y N N N Y Y Y
GEORGIA		**MISSISSIPPI**		**PENNSYLVANIA**	
Mattingly	N N N Y N N N	*Cochran*	N N N N N N N	*Heinz*	Y N N N Y N N
Nunn	Y N Y N N Y N	Stennis	N N N N N N Y	*Specter*	Y N N N N N Y
HAWAII		**MISSOURI**		**RHODE ISLAND**	
Inouye	Y Y Y N N Y Y	*Danforth*	N N N Y N N Y	*Chafee*	Y Y N N N N N
Matsunaga	Y Y N Y N Y	Eagleton	Y N Y N N N Y	Pell	Y Y N N N N Y
IDAHO		**MONTANA**		**SOUTH CAROLINA**	
McClure	? ? N Y N N N	Baucus	N N N N N N Y	*Thurmond*	N N N Y N N N
Symms	Y Y N Y N N N	Melcher	Y Y Y N N N Y	Hollings	? ? Y N N Y Y
ILLINOIS		**NEBRASKA**		**SOUTH DAKOTA**	
Percy	N N ? ? ? ? ?	Exon	Y N Y N Y N Y	*Abdnor*	N N N N N N N
Dixon	Y Y N N Y N Y	Zorinsky	N N N Y Y N Y	*Pressler*	N N N N N N Y
INDIANA		**NEVADA**		**TENNESSEE**	
Lugar	N N N N N N N	*Hecht*	N N N Y N N N	*Baker*	N N N N N N N
Quayle	N N N N N N N	*Laxalt*	N N N Y N N N	Sasser	N N N N N ? ?

	64 65 66 67 68 69 70
TEXAS	
Tower	Y N N Y N N N
Bentsen	Y N N N N N ?
UTAH	
Garn	N N N Y N N N
Hatch	Y N N Y N N N
VERMONT	
Stafford	? ? N N N N N
Leahy	Y Y Y N N N Y
VIRGINIA	
Trible	N N N N N N N
Warner	N N N N N N N
WASHINGTON	
Gorton	N N N N N Y N
Jackson	Y Y N N N N Y
WEST VIRGINIA	
Byrd	N N N N N N Y
Randolph	N N N N N N Y
WISCONSIN	
Kasten	N N N Y N N N
Proxmire	N N Y N N N N
WYOMING	
Simpson	N N N N N N N
Wallop	N N N Y N N N

KEY

Y Voted for (yea).
\# Paired for.
+ Announced for.
N Voted against (nay).
X Paired against.
- Announced against.
P Voted ''present''.
C Voted ''present'' to avoid possible conflict of interest.
? Did not vote or otherwise make a position known.

Democrats   *Republicans*

ND - Northern Democrats   SD - Southern Democrats (Southern states - Ala., Ark., Fla., Ga., Ky., La., Miss., N.C., Okla., S.C., Tenn., Texas, Va.)

64. S 529. Immigration Reform and Control Act. Kennedy, D-Mass., amendment to require termination of the employer sanction provisions after five years if the General Accounting Office finds they have resulted in discrimination, and if Congress adopts a concurrent resolution approving those findings. Rejected 40-51: R 13-38; D 27-13 (ND 22-6, SD 5-7), April 28, 1983.

65. S 529. Immigration Reform and Control Act. Kennedy, D-Mass., amendment to move from Jan. 1, 1980, to Dec. 31, 1981, the date by which an illegal alien had to enter the United States to be eligible for temporary resident status upon enactment of the bill. Rejected 20-70: R 3-48; D 17-22 (ND 17-10, SD 0-12), April 28, 1983.

66. S Con Res 27. First Budget Resolution, Fiscal 1984. Hollings, D-S.C., amendment to freeze domestic spending at current levels, to repeal the scheduled July 1 income tax cut, to repeal the indexing of taxes to inflation, and to allow 3 percent real growth in defense spending. Rejected 16-82: R 2-50; D 14-32 (ND 8-24, SD 6-8), May 4, 1983.

67. S Con Res 27. First Budget Resolution, Fiscal 1984. Hatch, R-Utah, amendment to freeze spending in domestic programs at current levels, to allow a 7.5 percent growth in defense spending for fiscal 1984 and to require no new taxes. Rejected 23-75: R 21-31; D 2-44 (ND 2-30, SD 0-14), May 4, 1983.

68. S Con Res 27. First Budget Resolution, Fiscal 1984. Specter, R-Pa., amendment to allow $650 million in additional budget authority in fiscal years 1984-86 for law enforcement and prison construction. Rejected 17-81: R 5-47; D 12-34 (ND 10-22, SD 2-12), May 4, 1983.

69. S Con Res 27. First Budget Resolution, Fiscal 1984. Johnston, D-La., amendment to raise taxes by $285 billion in fiscal years 1984-88, and to limit real growth in both domestic and defense spending. Rejected 13-83: R 4-48; D 9-35 (ND 3-28, SD 6-7), May 4, 1983.

70. S Con Res 27. First Budget Resolution, Fiscal 1984. Baucus, D-Mont., amendment to provide $400 million in additional funds for Medicare in fiscal 1984. Rejected 45-50: R 5-47; D 40-3 (ND 30-1, SD 10-2), May 4, 1983.

KEY

Y	Voted for (yea).
#	Paired for.
+	Announced for.
N	Voted against (nay).
X	Paired against.
-	Announced against.
P	Voted "present".
C	Voted "present" to avoid possible conflict of interest.
?	Did not vote or otherwise make a position known.

Democrats *Republicans*

State / Senator	71	72	73	74	75
ALABAMA					
Denton	+	N	N	Y	Y
Heflin	N	Y	Y	N	N
ALASKA					
Murkowski	Y	N	Y	Y	Y
Stevens	Y	N	Y	Y	Y
ARIZONA					
Goldwater	Y	N	Y	Y	Y
DeConcini	Y	N	Y	N	N
ARKANSAS					
Bumpers	N	Y	Y	N	N
Pryor	N	N	Y	N	N
CALIFORNIA					
Wilson	Y	N	Y	Y	Y
Cranston	N	Y	Y	N	N
COLORADO					
Armstrong	Y	N	N	Y	Y
Hart	N	Y	Y	N	N
CONNECTICUT					
Weicker	Y	N	Y	Y	Y
Dodd	?	?	?	?	-
DELAWARE					
Roth	Y	N	Y	Y	Y
Biden	N	Y	Y	N	N
FLORIDA					
Hawkins	Y	N	Y	Y	Y
Chiles	Y	N	Y	N	N
GEORGIA					
Mattingly	Y	N	Y	Y	Y
Nunn	Y	N	Y	N	N
HAWAII					
Inouye	N	Y	Y	N	N
Matsunaga	?	Y	Y	N	N
IDAHO					
McClure	Y	N	N	Y	Y
Symms	Y	N	N	Y	Y
ILLINOIS					
Percy	Y	N	Y	Y	Y
Dixon	N	Y	Y	N	N
INDIANA					
Lugar	Y	N	Y	Y	Y
Quayle	Y	N	Y	Y	Y
IOWA					
Grassley	Y	N	Y	Y	Y
Jepsen	Y	N	Y	Y	N
KANSAS					
Dole	Y	N	Y	Y	Y
Kassebaum	Y	N	Y	Y	Y
KENTUCKY					
Ford	N	Y	Y	N	N
Huddleston	N	Y	Y	N	N
LOUISIANA					
Johnston	Y	N	Y	N	N
Long	Y	N	Y	N	N
MAINE					
Cohen	Y	N	Y	N	N
Mitchell	N	Y	Y	N	N
MARYLAND					
Mathias	N	N	Y	Y	Y
Sarbanes	N	Y	Y	N	N
MASSACHUSETTS					
Kennedy	N	Y	Y	-	-
Tsongas	N	Y	Y	N	N
MICHIGAN					
Levin	N	Y	Y	N	N
Riegle	N	Y	Y	N	N
MINNESOTA					
Boschwitz	Y	N	Y	Y	Y
Durenberger	Y	N	Y	Y	Y
MISSISSIPPI					
Cochran	Y	N	Y	N	N
Stennis	N	N	Y	N	N
MISSOURI					
Danforth	Y	N	Y	Y	Y
Eagleton	N	Y	Y	N	N
MONTANA					
Baucus	Y	Y	Y	N	N
Melcher	N	Y	Y	N	N
NEBRASKA					
Exon	Y	N	Y	N	N
Zorinsky	Y	N	Y	N	Y
NEVADA					
Hecht	Y	N	Y	Y	Y
Laxalt	Y	N	Y	Y	Y
NEW HAMPSHIRE					
Humphrey	Y	N	N	Y	Y
Rudman	Y	N	Y	Y	Y
NEW JERSEY					
Bradley	N	Y	Y	N	N
Lautenberg	N	Y	Y	N	N
NEW MEXICO					
Domenici	Y	N	Y	Y	Y
Bingaman	Y	Y	Y	N	N
NEW YORK					
D'Amato	Y	N	Y	N	?
Moynihan	N	Y	Y	N	N
NORTH CAROLINA					
East	Y	N	N	Y	Y
Helms	Y	N	N	Y	Y
NORTH DAKOTA					
Andrews	Y	N	Y	N	N
Burdick	N	Y	Y	N	N
OHIO					
Glenn	N	Y	Y	N	N
Metzenbaum	N	Y	Y	N	N
OKLAHOMA					
Nickles	Y	N	N	Y	Y
Boren	Y	Y	Y	N	N
OREGON					
Hatfield	Y	N	Y	Y	Y
Packwood	Y	N	Y	Y	Y
PENNSYLVANIA					
Heinz	Y	N	Y	Y	Y
Specter	Y	Y	Y	Y	N
RHODE ISLAND					
Chafee	Y	N	Y	Y	Y
Pell	N	Y	Y	N	N
SOUTH CAROLINA					
Thurmond	Y	N	Y	Y	Y
Hollings	N	Y	Y	N	N
SOUTH DAKOTA					
Abdnor	Y	N	Y	Y	Y
Pressler	Y	N	Y	Y	Y
TENNESSEE					
Baker	Y	N	Y	Y	Y
Sasser	N	Y	Y	N	N
TEXAS					
Tower	Y	N	Y	Y	?
Bentsen	Y	Y	Y	?	?
UTAH					
Garn	Y	N	Y	Y	Y
Hatch	Y	N	Y	Y	Y
VERMONT					
Stafford	Y	N	Y	N	N
Leahy	N	Y	Y	N	N
VIRGINIA					
Trible	Y	N	Y	Y	Y
Warner	Y	N	Y	Y	Y
WASHINGTON					
Gorton	Y	N	Y	Y	Y
Jackson	N	Y	Y	Y	N
WEST VIRGINIA					
Byrd	N	Y	Y	N	N
Randolph	N	Y	Y	N	N
WISCONSIN					
Kasten	Y	N	Y	?	?
Proxmire	N	N	Y	N	Y
WYOMING					
Simpson	Y	N	Y	Y	Y
Wallop	Y	N	N	Y	Y

ND - Northern Democrats   SD - Southern Democrats (Southern states - Ala., Ark., Fla., Ga., Ky., La., Miss., N.C., Okla., S.C., Tenn., Texas, Va.)

71. S Con Res 27. First Budget Resolution, Fiscal 1984. Domenici, R-N.M., motion to table (kill) the Metzenbaum, D-Ohio, amendment to provide $1.9 billion in fiscal 1984 for 13 weeks of extended unemployment benefits in states that would no longer be eligible for these benefits after Oct. 1, 1983. Motion agreed to 63-34: R 52-1; D 11-33 (ND 5-25, SD 6-8), May 5, 1983.

72. S Con Res 27. First Budget Resolution, Fiscal 1984. Kennedy, D-Mass., substitute for the Dole, R-Kan., amendment *(see vote 73, below)*, to provide $2.7 billion in fiscal 1984 for health care assistance for the unemployed. Rejected 36-63: R 1-53; D 35-10 (ND 27-4, SD 8-6), May 5, 1983.

73. S Con Res 27. First Budget Resolution, Fiscal 1984. Dole, R-Kan., amendment to provide $1.8 billion in fiscal 1983-85 for health care assistance for the unemployed. Adopted 90-9: R 45-9; D 45-0 (ND 31-0, SD 14-0), May 5, 1983.

74. S Con Res 27. First Budget Resolution, Fiscal 1984. Rudman, R-N.H., amendment to provide an additional $400 million in fiscal 1984 for various education programs. Adopted 50-46: R 48-5; D 2-41 (ND 2-28, SD 0-13), May 5, 1983.

75. S Con Res 27. First Budget Resolution, Fiscal 1984. Domenici, R-N.M., motion to table (kill) the Hollings, D-S.C., amendment to increase fiscal 1984 funding for education $1.5 billion. Motion rejected 46-48: R 45-6; D 1-42 (ND 1-29, SD 0-13), May 5, 1983.

	76	77	78	79	80	81	82	83
ALABAMA								
Denton	Y	N	?	+	Y	Y	Y	Y
Heflin	N	Y	Y	N	Y	Y	Y	N
ALASKA								
Murkowski	+	-	X	+	Y	Y	Y	Y
Stevens	Y	N	N	Y	Y	Y	Y	Y
ARIZONA								
Goldwater	Y	N	N	Y	Y	Y	Y	Y
DeConcini	?	?	?	?	Y	Y	Y	N
ARKANSAS								
Bumpers	N	Y	Y	N	N	N	N	N
Pryor	N	Y	Y	N	N	N	N	N
CALIFORNIA								
Wilson	Y	N	N	Y	Y	Y	Y	Y
Cranston	N	Y	Y	N	N	N	Y	N
COLORADO								
Armstrong	Y	N	N	Y	Y	Y	Y	Y
Hart	N	Y	Y	?	-	X	?	?
CONNECTICUT								
Weicker	Y	N	Y	N	Y	Y	Y	Y
Dodd	N	Y	Y	N	N	Y	Y	Y
DELAWARE								
Roth	Y	N	N	Y	Y	Y	Y	Y
Biden	N	Y	Y	N	N	Y	Y	Y
FLORIDA								
Hawkins	Y	N	Y	Y	Y	Y	Y	Y
Chiles	N	Y	Y	N	N	Y	Y	N
GEORGIA								
Mattingly	Y	N	N	Y	Y	Y	Y	Y
Nunn	N	Y	Y	N	Y	Y	Y	N
HAWAII								
Inouye	N	Y	Y	N	N	N	Y	Y
Matsunaga	N	Y	Y	N	N	N	Y	Y
IDAHO								
McClure	?	?	?	?	Y	Y	Y	Y
Symms	Y	N	N	Y	Y	Y	Y	Y
ILLINOIS								
Percy	Y	N	Y	N	Y	Y	Y	Y
Dixon	-	+	+	?	N	Y	Y	N
INDIANA								
Lugar	Y	N	N	Y	Y	Y	Y	Y
Quayle	Y	N	N	Y	Y	Y	Y	Y

	76	77	78	79	80	81	82	83
IOWA								
Grassley	Y	N	N	Y	N	N	N	N
Jepsen	N	Y	Y	Y	Y	Y	Y	N
KANSAS								
Dole	Y	N	N	Y	Y	Y	Y	Y
Kassebaum	Y	N	N	?	Y	Y	Y	Y
KENTUCKY								
Ford	N	Y	Y	N	N	Y	N	N
Huddleston	-	+	+	?	N	Y	N	N
LOUISIANA								
Johnston	N	Y	Y	N	N	Y	Y	N
Long	N	Y	Y	?	Y	Y	N	N
MAINE								
Cohen	N	Y	Y	?	N	Y	Y	Y
Mitchell	N	Y	Y	N	N	Y	N	N
MARYLAND								
Mathias	?	?	#	?	N	Y	Y	Y
Sarbanes	N	Y	Y	N	N	N	Y	Y
MASSACHUSETTS								
Kennedy	-	+	+	X	X	X	Y	Y
Tsongas	N	Y	Y	N	N	N	Y	Y
MICHIGAN								
Levin	N	Y	Y	N	N	N	Y	N
Riegle	N	Y	Y	N	N	N	Y	N
MINNESOTA								
Boschwitz	Y	N	Y	N	Y	Y	Y	Y
Durenberger	Y	N	N	?	N	Y	Y	Y
MISSISSIPPI								
Cochran	N	Y	Y	Y	Y	Y	Y	N
Stennis	N	Y	Y	Y	Y	N	N	N
MISSOURI								
Danforth	Y	N	Y	N	Y	Y	Y	Y
Eagleton	?	?	?	?	N	#	Y	N
MONTANA								
Baucus	N	Y	Y	-	N	Y	Y	N
Melcher	N	Y	Y	-	N	N	N	N
NEBRASKA								
Exon	N	Y	Y	?	N	Y	N	N
Zorinsky	N	N	Y	Y	Y	Y	Y	N
NEVADA								
Hecht	Y	N	N	Y	Y	Y	Y	Y
Laxalt	Y	N	N	Y	Y	Y	Y	Y

	76	77	78	79	80	81	82	83
NEW HAMPSHIRE								
Humphrey	Y	N	N	Y	Y	Y	N	N
Rudman	Y	N	N	Y	N	Y	Y	Y
NEW JERSEY								
Bradley	N	Y	Y	N	N	Y	N	N
Lautenberg	N	Y	Y	N	N	N	N	Y
NEW MEXICO								
Domenici	Y	N	N	Y	Y	Y	Y	Y
Bingaman	N	Y	Y	N	N	N	Y	N
NEW YORK								
D'Amato	N	Y	Y	Y	Y	Y	Y	Y
Moynihan	N	Y	Y	N	Y	N	Y	Y
NORTH CAROLINA								
East	Y	N	N	Y	Y	Y	Y	Y
Helms	?	?	?	Y	Y	Y	Y	N
NORTH DAKOTA								
Andrews	N	Y	Y	N	Y	Y	Y	N
Burdick	N	Y	Y	N	N	Y	N	N
OHIO								
Glenn	?	?	?	?	?	?	?	?
Metzenbaum	N	Y	Y	N	N	Y	Y	Y
OKLAHOMA								
Nickles	Y	N	N	Y	Y	Y	Y	Y
Boren	N	Y	Y	N	Y	Y	Y	N
OREGON								
Hatfield	?	-	+	?	N	N	Y	Y
Packwood	Y	N	Y	Y	Y	Y	Y	Y
PENNSYLVANIA								
Heinz	Y	N	Y	#	#	#	?	?
Specter	N	Y	Y	N	Y	Y	Y	Y
RHODE ISLAND								
Chafee	Y	N	Y	N	Y	Y	Y	Y
Pell	N	Y	Y	N	N	N	N	Y
SOUTH CAROLINA								
Thurmond	Y	N	Y	Y	Y	Y	Y	Y
Hollings	N	Y	Y	N	N	N	Y	N
SOUTH DAKOTA								
Abdnor	Y	N	Y	Y	Y	Y	Y	Y
Pressler	Y	N	Y	Y	Y	Y	N	N
TENNESSEE								
Baker	Y	N	N	Y	Y	Y	Y	Y
Sasser	N	Y	Y	N	N	N	Y	N

	76	77	78	79	80	81	82	83
TEXAS								
Tower	Y	N	N	Y	Y	Y	Y	Y
Bentsen	N	Y	Y	N	Y	Y	Y	N
UTAH								
Garn	Y	N	N	Y	Y	Y	Y	Y
Hatch	Y	N	N	Y	Y	Y	Y	Y
VERMONT								
Stafford	N	Y	Y	N	Y	N	Y	Y
Leahy	N	Y	Y	N	N	N	N	N
VIRGINIA								
Trible	Y	N	N	Y	Y	Y	Y	Y
Warner	Y	N	N	Y	Y	Y	Y	Y
WASHINGTON								
Gorton	Y	N	N	Y	Y	Y	Y	Y
Jackson	N	Y	Y	N	Y	Y	Y	N
WEST VIRGINIA								
Byrd	N	Y	Y	N	N	Y	Y	N
Randolph	N	Y	Y	N	N	N	N	N
WISCONSIN								
Kasten	?	?	?	+	Y	Y	Y	Y
Proxmire	Y	N	N	Y	N	N	N	N
WYOMING								
Simpson	Y	N	N	Y	Y	Y	Y	Y
Wallop	Y	N	N	Y	Y	Y	Y	Y

ND - Northern Democrats   SD - Southern Democrats (Southern states - Ala., Ark., Fla., Ga., Ky., La., Miss., N.C., Okla., S.C., Tenn., Texas, Va.)

76. S Con Res 27. First Budget Resolution, Fiscal 1984. Hollings, D-S.C., motion to reconsider the vote by which the Domenici, R-N.M., motion to table (kill) the Hollings amendment, to increase fiscal 1984 funding for education by $1.5 billion, was rejected (see vote 75, p. 17-S). Motion rejected 42-46: R 41-7; D 1-39 (ND 1-26, SD 0-13), May 6, 1983. (The amendment subsequently was withdrawn.)

77. S Con Res 27. First Budget Resolution, Fiscal 1984. Hollings, D-S.C., motion to table (kill) the Domenici, R-N.M., amendment to reduce the funding level in the Hollings amendment (see vote 78, below) to $400 million, as provided in the Rudman, R-N.H., amendment (see vote 74, p. 17-S). Motion agreed to 45-43: R 7-41; D 38-2 (ND 25-2, SD 13-0), May 6, 1983.

78. S Con Res 27. First Budget Resolution, Fiscal 1984. Hollings, D-S.C., amendment to increase fiscal 1984 funding for education by $1 billion. Adopted 55-32: R 16-31; D 39-1 (ND 26-1, SD 13-0), May 6, 1983.

79. S Con Res 27. First Budget Resolution, Fiscal 1984. Domenici, R-N.M., motion to table (kill) the Bradley, D-N.J., amendment to state the sense of Congress that the administration should take the lead in pursuing coordinated economic expansion to ensure worldwide economic recovery. Motion agreed to 47-32: R 44-0; D 3-32 (ND 2-21, SD 1-11), May 6, 1983.

80. S Con Res 27. First Budget Resolution, Fiscal 1984. Nunn, D-Ga.-Jackson, D-Wash., amendment to provide a 6.5 percent real increase in defense spending for fiscal 1984. Rejected 48-48: R 38-15; D 10-33 (ND 5-24, SD 5-9), May 10, 1983.

81. S Con Res 27. First Budget Resolution, Fiscal 1984. Domenici, R-N.M., motion to table (kill) the Pryor, D-Ark., amendment to cut fiscal 1984 funding for nuclear warhead production by $2 billion. Motion agreed to 74-21: R 51-2; D 23-19 (ND 13-15, SD 10-4), May 10, 1983.

82. S Con Res 27. First Budget Resolution, Fiscal 1984. Domenici, R-N.M., motion to table (kill) the Pryor, D-Ark., amendment to cut international affairs funding for military assistance programs by $880 million. Motion agreed to 79-18: R 50-3; D 29-15 (ND 21-9, SD 8-6), May 10, 1983.

83. S Con Res 27. First Budget Resolution, Fiscal 1984. Domenici, R-N.M., motion to table (kill) the Melcher, D-Mont., amendment to transfer $100 million from the international affairs function to natural resources and environment for soil conservation programs. Motion agreed to 56-41: R 44-9; D 12-32 (ND 12-18, SD 0-14), May 10, 1983.

	84 85 86		84 85 86		84 85 86
ALABAMA		**IOWA**		**NEW HAMPSHIRE**	
Denton	Y N N	*Grassley*	N N N	*Humphrey*	N N N
Heflin	N N N	*Jepsen*	Y N N	*Rudman*	Y N Y
ALASKA		**KANSAS**		**NEW JERSEY**	
Murkowski	Y N N	*Dole*	Y N N	Bradley	Y Y Y
Stevens	Y N N	*Kassebaum*	Y N Y	Lautenberg	Y Y Y
ARIZONA		**KENTUCKY**		**NEW MEXICO**	
Goldwater	Y N N	Ford	N Y Y	*Domenici*	Y N N
DeConcini	N Y N	Huddleston	N Y Y	Bingaman	Y Y Y
ARKANSAS		**LOUISIANA**		**NEW YORK**	
Bumpers	Y Y N	Johnston	Y Y Y	*D'Amato*	Y N Y
Pryor	N Y ?	Long	Y Y N	Moynihan	Y Y Y
CALIFORNIA		**MAINE**		**NORTH CAROLINA**	
Wilson	Y N N	*Cohen*	Y N N	*East*	N N N
Cranston	Y Y Y	Mitchell	Y Y Y	*Helms*	N N N
COLORADO		**MARYLAND**		**NORTH DAKOTA**	
Armstrong	? N N	*Mathias*	Y Y Y	*Andrews*	Y Y Y
Hart	? Y Y	Sarbanes	Y Y Y	Burdick	N Y N
CONNECTICUT		**MASSACHUSETTS**		**OHIO**	
Weicker	Y Y Y	Kennedy	? Y Y	Glenn	Y Y N
Dodd	Y Y Y	Tsongas	Y Y Y	Metzenbaum	Y Y Y
DELAWARE		**MICHIGAN**		**OKLAHOMA**	
Roth	Y N N	Levin	Y Y N	*Nickles*	N N N
Biden	Y Y Y	Riegle	? Y Y	Boren	N Y N
FLORIDA		**MINNESOTA**		**OREGON**	
Hawkins	Y N N	*Boschwitz*	Y N Y	*Hatfield*	Y Y Y
Chiles	Y Y Y	*Durenberger*	Y N Y	*Packwood*	Y Y Y
GEORGIA		**MISSISSIPPI**		**PENNSYLVANIA**	
Mattingly	Y N N	*Cochran*	Y N N	*Heinz*	Y N Y
Nunn	Y Y N	Stennis	Y Y Y	*Specter*	Y N Y
HAWAII		**MISSOURI**		**RHODE ISLAND**	
Inouye	Y Y Y	*Danforth*	Y N Y	*Chafee*	Y Y Y
Matsunaga	Y Y Y	Eagleton	Y Y Y	Pell	Y Y Y
IDAHO		**MONTANA**		**SOUTH CAROLINA**	
McClure	Y N N	Baucus	N Y N	*Thurmond*	Y N N
Symms	Y N N	Melcher	N Y N	Hollings	Y Y Y
ILLINOIS		**NEBRASKA**		**SOUTH DAKOTA**	
Percy	Y N N	Exon	N Y N	*Abdnor*	Y N N
Dixon	? Y Y	Zorinsky	N Y N	*Pressler*	Y N Y
INDIANA		**NEVADA**		**TENNESSEE**	
Lugar	Y N N	*Hecht*	Y N N	*Baker*	Y N N
Quayle	Y N N	*Laxalt*	Y N N	Sasser	N Y Y

KEY

Y   Voted for (yea).
\#   Paired for.
\+   Announced for.
N   Voted against (nay).
X   Paired against.
-   Announced against.
P   Voted ''present''.
C   Voted ''present'' to avoid possible conflict of interest.
?   Did not vote or otherwise make a position known.

Democrats   *Republicans*

	84 85 86
TEXAS	
Tower	Y N N
Bentsen	Y Y N
UTAH	
Garn	Y N N
Hatch	Y N N
VERMONT	
Stafford	Y Y Y
Leahy	N Y Y
VIRGINIA	
Trible	Y N N
Warner	Y N N
WASHINGTON	
Gorton	Y N Y
Jackson	Y Y Y
WEST VIRGINIA	
Byrd	Y Y Y
Randolph	N Y N
WISCONSIN	
Kasten	Y N N
Proxmire	Y Y N
WYOMING	
Simpson	Y N N
Wallop	Y N N

ND · Northern Democrats   SD · Southern Democrats (Southern states - Ala., Ark., Fla., Ga., Ky., La., Miss., N.C., Okla., S.C., Tenn., Texas, Va.)

84. S Con Res 27. First Budget Resolution, Fiscal 1984.
Domenici, R-N.M., motion to table (kill) the Melcher, D-Mont., amendment, as modified, that sought to limit spending for international affairs to $11.5 billion in fiscal 1983 and $10 billion a year in fiscal 1884-86, notwithstanding any other provision of the resolution; and to express the sense of the Senate that the United States should continue to meet its financial commitments to Israel and Egypt under the Camp David accords. The amendment aimed to curb spending for foreign aid and for U.S. contributions to the International Monetary Fund. Motion agreed to 76-19: R 48-5; D 28-14 (ND 20-8, SD 8-6), May 11, 1983.

85. S Con Res 27. First Budget Resolution, Fiscal 1984.
Chiles, D-Fla., motion to table (kill) the Domenici, R-N.M.-Baker, R-Tenn., amendment to set fiscal 1984 budget targets as follows: budget authority, $918 billion; outlays, $850.4 billion; revenues, $658 billion; and deficit, $192.4 billion. Motion agreed to 52-48: R 7-47; D 45-1 (ND 32-0, SD 13-1), May 12, 1983.

86. S Con Res 27. First Budget Resolution, Fiscal 1984.
Weicker, R-Conn., amendment as modified by Gorton, R-Wash., to set fiscal 1984 budget targets as follows: budget authority, $911.9 billion; outlays, $848.7 billion; revenues, $664.3 billion; and deficit, $184.4 billion. Rejected 46-53: R 17-37; D 29-16 (ND 22-10, SD 7-6), May 12, 1983.

CQ Senate Votes 87 - 94

Corresponding to Congressional Record Votes 87, 88, 89, 90, 91, 92, 93, 94

	87	88	89	90	91	92	93	94
ALABAMA								
Denton	Y	Y	Y	N	Y	N	Y	N
Heflin	Y	Y	Y	Y	Y	Y	Y	N
ALASKA								
Murkowski	Y	Y	N	N	N	N	?	N
Stevens	Y	Y	N	N	N	N	Y	N
ARIZONA								
Goldwater	Y	Y	N	N	N	N	Y	N
DeConcini	?	?	?	?	?	?	?	?
ARKANSAS								
Bumpers	Y	N	Y	N	?	?	?	?
Pryor	Y	N	Y	N	Y	Y	Y	N
CALIFORNIA								
Wilson	Y	Y	N	Y	N	Y	N	Y
Cranston	Y	N	Y	N	N	N	Y	N
COLORADO								
Armstrong	Y	Y	N	Y	N	Y	N	Y
Hart	Y	N	Y	N	N	N	Y	N
CONNECTICUT								
Weicker	Y	Y	Y	N	N	Y	N	Y
Dodd	Y	N	Y	N	N	N	Y	N
DELAWARE								
Roth	Y	Y	N	Y	N	Y	N	Y
Biden	Y	N	Y	N	N	N	Y	N
FLORIDA								
Hawkins	Y	Y	N	N	N	N	Y	Y
Chiles	Y	Y	N	Y	N	Y	N	Y
GEORGIA								
Mattingly	Y	Y	N	N	N	N	Y	N
Nunn	Y	Y	Y	N	Y	Y	Y	N
HAWAII								
Inouye	Y	N	Y	N	N	N	Y	N
Matsunaga	Y	Y	Y	N	N	N	Y	N
IDAHO								
McClure	Y	Y	N	Y	Y	N	Y	Y
Symms	Y	Y	N	Y	Y	N	Y	Y
ILLINOIS								
Percy	Y	Y	N	N	N	N	Y	N
Dixon	Y	Y	Y	N	N	N	Y	N
INDIANA								
Lugar	Y	Y	N	N	N	N	Y	N
Quayle	Y	Y	N	N	N	N	Y	N

	87	88	89	90	91	92	93	94
IOWA								
Grassley	Y	Y	N	N	Y	N	Y	N
Jepsen	Y	Y	N	Y	Y	N	Y	Y
KANSAS								
Dole	Y	Y	N	N	Y	N	Y	Y
Kassebaum	Y	Y	N	N	N	N	Y	N
KENTUCKY								
Ford	Y	Y	Y	Y	Y	?	?	?
Huddleston	Y	Y	Y	N	Y	Y	Y	Y
LOUISIANA								
Johnston	Y	Y	Y	N	Y	Y	Y	Y
Long	Y	Y	Y	Y	Y	Y	Y	Y
MAINE								
Cohen	Y	Y	Y	Y	N	Y	N	Y
Mitchell	Y	N	Y	N	N	N	Y	N
MARYLAND								
Mathias	Y	N	N	N	N	N	Y	N
Sarbanes	Y	N	Y	N	N	N	Y	N
MASSACHUSETTS								
Kennedy	Y	N	Y	N	N	N	Y	N
Tsongas	Y	N	N	N	N	N	Y	N
MICHIGAN								
Levin	Y	N	Y	N	?	N	Y	N
Riegle	Y	N	Y	Y	N	N	Y	N
MINNESOTA								
Boschwitz	Y	Y	N	N	N	N	Y	N
Durenberger	Y	Y	Y	N	N	N	N	N
MISSISSIPPI								
Cochran	Y	Y	N	Y	Y	Y	Y	N
Stennis	Y	Y	Y	Y	N	Y	Y	N
MISSOURI								
Danforth	Y	Y	N	N	N	N	Y	?
Eagleton	Y	N	Y	N	N	N	Y	N
MONTANA								
Baucus	Y	N	Y	N	N	N	Y	N
Melcher	Y	N	Y	N	N	N	Y	N
NEBRASKA								
Exon	Y	Y	Y	Y	Y	N	Y	N
Zorinsky	Y	Y	Y	Y	Y	Y	Y	N
NEVADA								
Hecht	Y	Y	N	N	N	N	Y	N
Laxalt	Y	Y	N	N	N	N	Y	N

	87	88	89	90	91	92	93	94
NEW HAMPSHIRE								
Humphrey	Y	Y	Y	Y	Y	N	N	Y
Rudman	Y	Y	Y	N	N	N	Y	N
NEW JERSEY								
Bradley	Y	N	Y	N	N	N	Y	N
Lautenberg	Y	N	Y	N	N	N	Y	N
NEW MEXICO								
Domenici	Y	Y	N	N	N	N	Y	?
Bingaman	Y	N	Y	N	N	N	Y	N
NEW YORK								
D'Amato	Y	Y	N	N	N	N	Y	Y
Moynihan	Y	N	Y	N	N	N	Y	N
NORTH CAROLINA								
East	Y	Y	Y	Y	Y	Y	Y	N
Helms	Y	Y	Y	Y	Y	Y	Y	N
NORTH DAKOTA								
Andrews	Y	Y	N	N	N	N	Y	N
Burdick	Y	Y	Y	N	N	N	Y	N
OHIO								
Glenn	Y	Y	Y	N	N	N	Y	N
Metzenbaum	Y	N	Y	N	N	N	Y	N
OKLAHOMA								
Nickles	Y	Y	N	Y	N	Y	N	Y
Boren	Y	Y	Y	Y	N	N	Y	N
OREGON								
Hatfield	Y	Y	N	N	N	N	Y	Y
Packwood	Y	Y	Y	N	N	N	Y	Y
PENNSYLVANIA								
Heinz	Y	Y	N	N	-	N	Y	N
Specter	Y	Y	Y	N	Y	N	Y	N
RHODE ISLAND								
Chafee	Y	Y	N	N	N	N	Y	?
Pell	+	+	+	-	-	-	+	+
SOUTH CAROLINA								
Thurmond	Y	Y	N	N	N	N	Y	N
Hollings	?	?	?	?	?	?	?	?
SOUTH DAKOTA								
Abdnor	Y	Y	N	Y	N	Y	N	Y
Pressler	Y	Y	N	Y	N	Y	N	N
TENNESSEE								
Baker	Y	Y	N	N	N	N	Y	N
Sasser	Y	N	Y	N	Y	Y	Y	N

KEY	
Y	Voted for (yea).
#	Paired for.
+	Announced for.
N	Voted against (nay).
X	Paired against.
-	Announced against.
P	Voted "present".
C	Voted "present" to avoid possible conflict of interest.
?	Did not vote or otherwise make a position known.

Democrats   *Republicans*

	87	88	89	90	91	92	93	94
TEXAS								
Tower	Y	Y	N	N	Y	N	Y	Y
Bentsen	Y	N	Y	N	Y	N	Y	N
UTAH								
Garn	Y	Y	N	Y	N	Y	N	Y
Hatch	Y	Y	N	Y	N	Y	N	Y
VERMONT								
Stafford	Y	Y	N	N	N	N	Y	N
Leahy	Y	N	Y	N	N	N	Y	N
VIRGINIA								
Trible	Y	Y	N	N	N	N	Y	N
Warner	Y	Y	N	N	N	N	Y	N
WASHINGTON								
Gorton	Y	Y	N	N	N	N	Y	Y
Jackson	Y	N	Y	N	N	N	Y	N
WEST VIRGINIA								
Byrd	Y	Y	Y	N	Y	Y	Y	N
Randolph	Y	Y	Y	N	N	N	Y	N
WISCONSIN								
Kasten	Y	N	Y	N	Y	N	Y	N
Proxmire	Y	N	Y	N	N	N	Y	N
WYOMING								
Simpson	Y	Y	N	N	N	N	Y	N
Wallop	Y	Y	N	Y	Y	N	Y	N

ND - Northern Democrats   SD - Southern Democrats (Southern states - Ala., Ark., Fla., Ga., Ky., La., Miss., N.C., Okla., S.C., Tenn., Texas, Va.)

---

87. Ruckelshaus Nomination. Confirmation of President Reagan's nomination of William D. Ruckelshaus of Washington to be administrator of the Environmental Protection Agency. Confirmed 97-0: R 54-0; D 43-0 (ND 30-0, SD 13-0), May 17, 1983. A "yea" was a vote supporting the president's position.

88. Regnery Nomination. Confirmation of President Reagan's nomination of Albert S. Regnery of Virginia to be administrator of the Office of Juvenile Justice and Delinquency Prevention. Confirmed 69-28: R 52-2; D 17-26 (ND 8-22, SD 9-4), May 17, 1983. A "yea" was a vote supporting the president's position.

89. S 529. Immigration Reform and Control Act. Bumpers, D-Ark., amendment to delete the visa allotment for immigrants who would invest at least $250,000 and employ at least four persons outside the immigrant's family. Adopted 51-46: R 10-44; D 41-2 (ND 29-1, SD 12-1), May 17, 1983.

90. S 529. Immigration Reform and Control Act. Helms, R-N.C., amendment to strike the section creating a program to grant legal status to millions of aliens already in the United States. Rejected 21-76: R 13-41; D 8-35 (ND 3-27, SD 5-8), May 17, 1983. A "nay" was a vote supporting the president's position.

91. S 529. Immigration Reform and Control Act. Helms, R-N.C., amendment to establish as congressional policy that states are free to deny benefits, including public education, to illegal aliens. Rejected 34-60: R 21-32; D 13-28 (ND 3-26, SD 10-2), May 17, 1983. A "nay" was a vote supporting the president's position.

92. S 529. Immigration Reform and Control Act. Helms, R-N.C., amendment to delete a provision giving Canada and Mexico 40,000 visas each year. Currently, they are allotted 20,000. Rejected 14-81: R 4-50; D 10-31 (ND 2-28, SD 8-3), May 17, 1983. A "nay" was a vote supporting the president's position.

93. S 529. Immigration Reform and Control Act. Baucus, D-Mont., amendment to delete the authority of the attorney general to establish entrance and exit fees for persons entering or leaving the United States. Adopted 91-3: R 50-3; D 41-0 (ND 30-0, SD 11-0), May 17, 1983.

94. S 529. Immigration Reform and Control Act. Wilson, R-Calif., amendment to extend for two years a provision giving agricultural producers three years after enactment to phase out their use of illegal aliens. Rejected 20-72: R 18-33; D 2-39 (ND 0-30, SD 2-9), May 17, 1983. A "nay" was a vote supporting the president's position.

	95 96 97 98 99 100 101		95 96 97 98 99 100 101		95 96 97 98 99 100 101
ALABAMA		**IOWA**		**NEW HAMPSHIRE**	
Denton	N N Y N Y Y Y	*Grassley*	N N N N N N Y	*Humphrey*	N N Y N Y Y N
Heflin	N ? ? ? ? ? ?	*Jepsen*	N N Y N Y Y Y	*Rudman*	N N Y N Y Y Y
ALASKA		**KANSAS**		**NEW JERSEY**	
Murkowski	N N N N Y Y Y	*Dole*	N N Y N Y N Y	Bradley	Y Y N N N N Y
Stevens	N N N N Y Y Y	*Kassebaum*	? N N N N N Y	Lautenberg	Y Y N Y Y Y Y
ARIZONA		**KENTUCKY**		**NEW MEXICO**	
Goldwater	? N N N Y N Y	Ford	? N Y N N Y Y	*Domenici*	? N N N Y Y N
DeConcini	? ? ? ? ? ? X	Huddleston	N N N N N N Y	Bingaman	Y Y N Y Y N N
ARKANSAS		**LOUISIANA**		**NEW YORK**	
Bumpers	? Y Y N Y Y Y	Johnston	Y Y N N N Y Y	*D'Amato*	N Y N Y N Y Y
Pryor	N Y N N Y Y Y	Long	N N Y N N Y Y	Moynihan	Y Y N Y Y Y Y
CALIFORNIA		**MAINE**		**NORTH CAROLINA**	
Wilson	? Y N N Y N N	*Cohen*	N N Y N N N N	*East*	N N Y N Y Y N
Cranston	Y Y N Y N N N	Mitchell	N N N N N N N	*Helms*	N N Y N Y Y N
COLORADO		**MARYLAND**		**NORTH DAKOTA**	
Armstrong	Y N Y N Y N N	*Mathias*	N N N N N N Y	*Andrews*	N Y N N Y Y Y
Hart	Y ? ? ? ? ? ?	Sarbanes	Y Y N Y Y Y Y	Burdick	N Y N N Y Y Y
CONNECTICUT		**MASSACHUSETTS**		**OHIO**	
Weicker	Y N N Y N Y Y	Kennedy	Y N N Y Y Y N	Glenn	Y Y N Y N N Y
Dodd	N Y N N N Y N	Tsongas	N Y N N N N Y	Metzenbaum	Y Y N Y Y Y Y
DELAWARE		**MICHIGAN**		**OKLAHOMA**	
Roth	N N N N Y N Y	Levin	Y Y N Y Y Y Y	*Nickles*	N N Y N Y Y Y
Biden	Y Y N Y Y Y Y	Riegle	Y Y N Y Y Y N	Boren	Y Y Y N Y Y Y
FLORIDA		**MINNESOTA**		**OREGON**	
Hawkins	N Y N N Y Y Y	*Boschwitz*	Y N N Y Y Y Y	*Hatfield*	N N N N Y N Y
Chiles	N Y N N N Y Y	*Durenberger*	Y Y N N N N Y	*Packwood*	Y N N Y N N Y
GEORGIA		**MISSISSIPPI**		**PENNSYLVANIA**	
Mattingly	N N Y N Y N Y	*Cochran*	N N Y N Y Y Y	*Heinz*	N Y N N N Y Y
Nunn	N ? ? N N Y Y	Stennis	N N Y N Y Y Y	*Specter*	Y Y N Y N Y Y
HAWAII		**MISSOURI**		**RHODE ISLAND**	
Inouye	Y Y N Y Y Y #	*Danforth*	? N N N N N Y	*Chafee*	? N N N Y N Y
Matsunaga	Y Y N Y Y Y Y	Eagleton	N N N N N N Y	Pell	+ Y N Y Y N Y
IDAHO		**MONTANA**		**SOUTH CAROLINA**	
McClure	N N Y N Y Y N	Baucus	N N N N Y N Y	*Thurmond*	N N N N N N Y
Symms	N N Y N Y N N	Melcher	Y N N Y Y Y Y	Hollings	? ? ? ? ? ? ?
ILLINOIS		**NEBRASKA**		**SOUTH DAKOTA**	
Percy	N N N N Y Y Y	Exon	Y N Y N Y N Y	*Abdnor*	N N Y N Y Y Y
Dixon	N Y N N Y N Y	Zorinsky	N Y Y N Y N N	*Pressler*	N N N N N Y Y
INDIANA		**NEVADA**		**TENNESSEE**	
Lugar	N N Y N Y Y Y	*Hecht*	N N N N Y N Y	*Baker*	? N Y N ? ? ?
Quayle	N N N N N N Y	*Laxalt*	N N N N Y N Y	Sasser	N Y N N Y Y Y

	95 96 97 98 99 100 101
TEXAS	
Tower	Y Y N N Y Y N
Bentsen	Y Y Y N Y Y Y
UTAH	
Garn	N N Y N Y Y N
Hatch	Y N Y N Y Y N
VERMONT	
Stafford	N ? ? ? N Y Y
Leahy	Y N Y N Y Y Y
VIRGINIA	
Trible	N N Y N Y Y Y
Warner	N N N N Y Y Y
WASHINGTON	
Gorton	N N N N N N Y
Jackson	N Y N N Y Y Y
WEST VIRGINIA	
Byrd	N Y Y N N N Y
Randolph	N Y N N N N Y
WISCONSIN	
Kasten	N N Y N Y Y Y
Proxmire	N N N N N N Y
WYOMING	
Simpson	N N N N N N Y
Wallop	N N Y N Y N Y

KEY

Y	Voted for (yea).
#	Paired for.
+	Announced for.
N	Voted against (nay).
X	Paired against.
-	Announced against.
P	Voted "present".
C	Voted "present" to avoid possible conflict of interest.
?	Did not vote or otherwise make a position known.

Democrats *Republicans*

ND - Northern Democrats   SD - Southern Democrats (Southern states - Ala., Ark., Fla., Ga., Ky., La., Miss., N.C., Okla., S.C., Tenn., Texas, Va.)

95. S 529. Immigration Reform and Control Act. Hart, D-Colo., amendment to provide remedies for persons who believe they encountered discrimination in employment as a result of a new scheme of sanctions against employers who knowingly hire illegal aliens. Rejected 29-59: R 8-39; D 21-20 (ND 18-12, SD 3-8), May 17, 1983.

96. S 529. Immigration Reform and Control Act. Bradley, D-N.J., amendment to provide 100 percent federal reimbursement to states for costs associated with granting legal status to illegal aliens. Rejected 37-57: R 8-45; D 29-12 (ND 22-8, SD 7-4), May 18, 1983. A "nay" was a vote supporting the president's position.

97. S 529. Immigration Reform and Control Act. Humphrey, R-N.H., amendment to deny federal benefits to newly legalized aliens until they become U.S. citizens. Rejected 31-63: R 23-30; D 8-33 (ND 3-27, SD 5-6), May 18, 1983. A "nay" was a vote supporting the president's position.

98. S 529. Immigration Reform and Control Act. Cranston, D-Calif., amendment to allow judicial review of the denial of legalization. Rejected 20-75: R 4-49; D 16-26 (ND 16-14, SD 0-12), May 18, 1983.

99. S 529. Immigration Reform and Control Act. McClure, R-Idaho, amendment to require federal law enforcement officials to obtain warrants before searching open fields. Adopted 62-33: R 34-19; D 28-14 (ND 22-8, SD 6-6), May 18, 1983. A "nay" was a vote supporting the president's position.

100. S 529. Immigration Reform and Control Act. D'Amato, R-N.Y., amendment to require the federal government to reimburse states for costs associated with incarcerating illegal aliens. Adopted 55-40: R 31-22; D 24-18 (ND 14-16, SD 10-2), May 18, 1983.

101. S 529. Immigration Reform and Control Act. Passage of the bill to curb the flow of illegal aliens into the country through a system of sanctions against employers who knowingly hire illegal aliens; to grant legal status to millions of illegal aliens already in the country; to revise and streamline procedures for handling asylum, deportation and exclusion cases; to revise and expand an existing program allowing foreign workers into the country temporarily; and to limit yearly immigration to 425,000 persons. Passed 76-18: R 41-12; D 35-6 (ND 23-6, SD 12-0), May 18, 1983. A "yea" was a vote supporting the president's position.

	102	103	104	105	106	107	108	109
ALABAMA								
Denton	Y	N	Y	Y	Y	Y	N	N
Heflin	N	N	Y	N	N	N	N	Y
ALASKA								
Murkowski	Y	N	Y	Y	Y	Y	N	N
Stevens	Y	N	Y	Y	Y	Y	Y	N
ARIZONA								
Goldwater	Y	N	Y	N	Y	N	N	N
DeConcini	N	N	N	N	Y	N	N	Y
ARKANSAS								
Bumpers	N	N	N	N	N	N	N	Y
Pryor	N	N	Y	N	Y	N	Y	Y
CALIFORNIA								
Wilson	Y	N	Y	Y	Y	Y	N	N
Cranston	N	Y	N	N	N	N	Y	Y
COLORADO								
Armstrong	Y	N	Y	Y	Y	Y	N	N
Hart	N	Y	N	Y	N	N	Y	Y
CONNECTICUT								
Weicker	N	Y	N	Y	N	N	Y	Y
Dodd	N	Y	N	Y	N	N	Y	Y
DELAWARE								
Roth	Y	N	Y	Y	Y	Y	N	N
Biden	N	Y	N	Y	N	N	Y	Y
FLORIDA								
Hawkins	Y	N	Y	Y	Y	Y	N	N
Chiles	N	Y	N	N	N	N	Y	Y
GEORGIA								
Mattingly	Y	N	Y	Y	Y	Y	N	N
Nunn	N	N	Y	N	Y	N	N	Y
HAWAII								
Inouye	N	Y	N	Y	N	N	Y	Y
Matsunaga	N	Y	N	Y	N	N	Y	Y
IDAHO								
McClure	Y	N	Y	N	Y	Y	N	N
Symms	Y	N	Y	N	Y	Y	N	N
ILLINOIS								
Percy	Y	N	Y	Y	Y	Y	N	N
Dixon	N	Y	N	N	N	N	Y	Y
INDIANA								
Lugar	Y	N	Y	Y	Y	Y	N	N
Quayle	Y	N	Y	Y	Y	Y	N	N
IOWA								
Grassley	Y	N	Y	Y	Y	Y	N	N
Jepsen	?	N	Y	N	Y	Y	N	N
KANSAS								
Dole	Y	N	Y	Y	Y	Y	N	N
Kassebaum	Y	Y	N	Y	Y	Y	Y	N
KENTUCKY								
Ford	N	Y	N	N	N	N	Y	Y
Huddleston	N	Y	Y	N	N	N	Y	Y
LOUISIANA								
Johnston	N	N	Y	N	Y	N	N	Y
Long	N	N	Y	N	Y	N	N	Y
MAINE								
Cohen	Y	N	N	N	N	Y	N	Y
Mitchell	N	Y	N	N	N	N	Y	Y
MARYLAND								
Mathias	N	Y	N	Y	N	N	Y	Y
Sarbanes	N	Y	N	Y	N	N	Y	Y
MASSACHUSETTS								
Kennedy	N	Y	N	Y	N	N	Y	Y
Tsongas	N	Y	N	Y	N	N	Y	Y
MICHIGAN								
Levin	N	Y	N	Y	N	N	Y	Y
Riegle	N	Y	N	N	N	N	Y	Y
MINNESOTA								
Boschwitz	Y	Y	N	Y	N	Y	Y	Y
Durenberger	Y	N	Y	N	Y	N	Y	N
MISSISSIPPI								
Cochran	Y	N	N	N	N	Y	N	N
Stennis	N	Y	N	N	N	N	Y	Y
MISSOURI								
Danforth	Y	Y	N	Y	N	Y	Y	N
Eagleton	N	Y	N	N	N	N	Y	Y
MONTANA								
Baucus	N	N	N	N	N	N	N	Y
Melcher	N	N	N	N	N	N	N	Y
NEBRASKA								
Exon	N	N	Y	N	Y	N	N	Y
Zorinsky	N	N	Y	N	Y	N	N	Y
NEVADA								
Hecht	Y	N	Y	Y	Y	Y	N	N
Laxalt	Y	N	Y	Y	Y	Y	N	N
NEW HAMPSHIRE								
Humphrey	Y	N	Y	N	Y	N	N	N
Rudman	Y	Y	Y	Y	Y	Y	Y	N
NEW JERSEY								
Bradley	N	Y	N	Y	N	N	Y	Y
Lautenberg	N	Y	N	N	N	N	Y	Y
NEW MEXICO								
Domenici	Y	N	Y	Y	Y	Y	N	N
Bingaman	N	Y	N	N	N	N	Y	Y
NEW YORK								
D'Amato	Y	Y	N	Y	N	Y	Y	N
Moynihan	N	Y	N	Y	N	N	Y	Y
NORTH CAROLINA								
East	N	N	Y	N	N	N	N	N
Helms	Y	N	Y	N	Y	N	N	N
NORTH DAKOTA								
Andrews	N	Y	N	N	N	N	N	Y
Burdick	N	Y	N	N	N	N	Y	Y
OHIO								
Glenn	N	Y	N	Y	N	N	Y	Y
Metzenbaum	N	Y	N	Y	N	N	Y	Y
OKLAHOMA								
Nickles	N	N	Y	N	Y	N	N	N
Boren	N	N	Y	N	Y	N	N	Y
OREGON								
Hatfield	N	Y	N	Y	N	N	Y	Y
Packwood	N	Y	N	Y	N	N	Y	Y
PENNSYLVANIA								
Heinz	Y	Y	N	Y	N	Y	Y	N
Specter	Y	Y	N	Y	N	Y	Y	N
RHODE ISLAND								
Chafee	N	Y	N	Y	N	N	Y	Y
Pell	N	Y	N	Y	N	N	Y	Y
SOUTH CAROLINA								
Thurmond	Y	N	Y	Y	Y	Y	N	N
Hollings	N	N	N	N	N	N	N	Y
SOUTH DAKOTA								
Abdnor	Y	N	Y	N	Y	Y	Y	N
Pressler	Y	N	Y	N	Y	Y	Y	N
TENNESSEE								
Baker	Y	N	N	Y	N	Y	N	N
Sasser	N	Y	N	N	N	N	Y	Y
TEXAS								
Tower	Y	N	Y	Y	Y	N	N	N
Bentsen	N	Y	Y	Y	Y	N	Y	Y
UTAH								
Garn	Y	N	Y	Y	Y	Y	N	N
Hatch	Y	N	Y	Y	Y	Y	N	N
VERMONT								
Stafford	N	Y	N	Y	N	N	Y	Y
Leahy	N	Y	N	N	N	N	Y	Y
VIRGINIA								
Trible	Y	N	Y	Y	Y	Y	N	N
Warner	N	N	Y	Y	Y	Y	N	N
WASHINGTON								
Gorton	N	Y	N	Y	N	N	Y	Y
Jackson	N	Y	N	N	N	N	Y	Y
WEST VIRGINIA								
Byrd	N	Y	N	N	N	N	Y	Y
Randolph	N	Y	N	N	N	N	Y	Y
WISCONSIN								
Kasten	Y	N	Y	Y	Y	Y	N	N
Proxmire	N	N	Y	N	Y	N	N	Y
WYOMING								
Simpson	Y	N	Y	Y	Y	Y	N	N
Wallop	Y	N	Y	Y	Y	Y	N	N

KEY

Y Voted for (yea).
\# Paired for.
+ Announced for.
N Voted against (nay).
X Paired against.
- Announced against.
P Voted ''present''.
C Voted ''present'' to avoid possible conflict of interest.
? Did not vote or otherwise make a position known.

Democrats   *Republicans*

ND - Northern Democrats   SD - Southern Democrats (Southern states - Ala., Ark., Fla., Ga., Ky., La., Miss., N.C., Okla., S.C., Tenn., Texas, Va.)

102. S Con Res 27. First Budget Resolution, Fiscal 1984. Budget Committee substitute, as modified, to set fiscal 1984 budget targets as follows: budget authority, $918.8 billion; outlays, $851.9 billion; revenues, $658.9 billion; and deficit, $193 billion. Rejected 43-56: R 43-10; D 0-46 (ND 0-32, SD 0-14), May 19, 1983.

103. S Con Res 27. First Budget Resolution, Fiscal 1984. Gorton, R-Wash., substitute to set fiscal 1984 budget targets as follows: budget authority, $914.7 billion; outlays, $849.7 billion; revenues, $671.1 billion; and deficit, $178.6 billion. Rejected 48-52: R 16-38; D 32-14 (ND 26-6, SD 6-8), May 19, 1983.

104. S Con Res 27. First Budget Resolution, Fiscal 1984. Helms, R-N.C., substitute, to the Domenici, R-N.M., substitute *(see vote 107, below)*, to set fiscal 1984 budget targets as follows: budget authority, $875 billion; outlays, $813.1 billion; revenues, $658 billion; and deficits, $155.1 billion. Rejected 41-59: R 30-24; D 11-35 (ND 3-29, SD 8-6), May 19, 1983.

105. S Con Res 27. First Budget Resolution, Fiscal 1984. Domenici, R-N.M., motion to table (kill) the Melcher, D-Mont., amendment to transfer $89 million from the international affairs function to natural resources and environment for soil conservation programs. Motion agreed to 57-43: R 42-12; D 15-31 (ND 14-18, SD 1-13), May 19, 1983.

106. S Con Res 27. First Budget Resolution, Fiscal 1984. Helms, R-N.C., amendment, to the Domenici, R-N.M., substitute *(see vote 107, below)*, to reduce by 5 percent spending totals for all functions other than Social Security and defense, and interest on the national debt, and to reduce the defense function by 0.5 percent. Rejected 45-55: R 35-19; D 10-36 (ND 4-28, SD 6-8), May 19, 1983.

107. S Con Res 27. First Budget Resolution, Fiscal 1984. Domenici, R-N.M., substitute to set fiscal 1984 budget targets as follows: budget authority, $918.8 billion; outlays, $851.9 billion; revenues, $658.9 billion; and deficit, $193 billion. Rejected 43-57: R 43-11; D 0-46 (ND 0-32, SD 0-14), May 19, 1983.

108. S Con Res 27. First Budget Resolution, Fiscal 1984. Baker, R-Tenn., motion to reconsider the vote by which the Gorton, R-Wash., substitute *(see vote 103, above)* was rejected. Motion agreed to 55-45: R 22-32; D 33-13 (ND 26-6, SD 7-7), May 19, 1983.

109. S Con Res 27. First Budget Resolution, Fiscal 1984. Kennedy, D-Mass., motion to table (kill) the Dole, R-Kan., substitute to set fiscal 1984 budget targets as follows: budget authority, $936.6 billion; outlays, $863.6 billion; revenues, $689.1 billion; and deficit, $174.5 billion. Motion agreed to 54-46: R 8-46; D 46-0 (ND 32-0, SD 14-0), May 19, 1983.

Corresponding to Congressional Record Votes 110, 111, 112, 113, 114, 115

	110	111	112	113	114	115
ALABAMA						
Denton	N	N	N	Y	Y	Y
Heflin	N	Y	N	Y	Y	Y
ALASKA						
Murkowski	N	Y	Y	Y	Y	Y
Stevens	Y	N	Y	Y	Y	Y
ARIZONA						
Goldwater	N	?	?	Y	Y	Y
DeConcini	Y	Y	N	Y	N	Y
ARKANSAS						
Bumpers	N	Y	N	N	N	N
Pryor	N	Y	N	N	N	N
CALIFORNIA						
Wilson	N	N	N	Y	Y	Y
Cranston	Y	N	N	N	N	N
COLORADO						
Armstrong	N	Y	N	Y	+	?
Hart	Y	N	Y	N	N	?
CONNECTICUT						
Weicker	Y	N	Y	Y	N	Y
Dodd	Y	N	Y	-	N	Y
DELAWARE						
Roth	N	N	N	Y	Y	Y
Biden	Y	Y	N	Y	N	N
FLORIDA						
Hawkins	N	Y	N	Y	?	Y
Chiles	Y	Y	Y	N	Y	N
GEORGIA						
Mattingly	N	N	N	Y	Y	Y
Nunn	N	N	N	Y	Y	N
HAWAII						
Inouye	Y	N	Y	N	N	N
Matsunaga	Y	Y	Y	N	N	Y
IDAHO						
McClure	N	N	N	Y	Y	Y
Symms	N	Y	N	Y	Y	N
ILLINOIS						
Percy	Y	N	Y	Y	Y	Y
Dixon	Y	Y	Y	N	N	N
INDIANA						
Lugar	N	N	N	Y	Y	Y
Quayle	N	N	N	Y	Y	Y

	110	111	112	113	114	115
IOWA						
Grassley	N	Y	N	Y	Y	N
Jepsen	N	N	N	Y	Y	N
KANSAS						
Dole	N	N	N	Y	Y	Y
Kassebaum	Y	N	Y	Y	Y	Y
KENTUCKY						
Ford	Y	Y	N	X	N	N
Huddleston	Y	Y	Y	N	N	?
LOUISIANA						
Johnston	N	N	N	Y	N	N
Long	N	N	N	N	Y	Y
MAINE						
Cohen	Y	Y	Y	Y	Y	Y
Mitchell	Y	Y	Y	N	N	N
MARYLAND						
Mathias	Y	N	Y	N	Y	Y
Sarbanes	Y	N	Y	N	N	N
MASSACHUSETTS						
Kennedy	Y	N	Y	N	N	Y
Tsongas	Y	N	Y	?	N	N
MICHIGAN						
Levin	Y	Y	Y	N	N	Y
Riegle	Y	Y	Y	N	N	N
MINNESOTA						
Boschwitz	Y	Y	Y	Y	Y	Y
Durenberger	N	Y	N	Y	N	?
MISSISSIPPI						
Cochran	Y	Y	Y	Y	Y	Y
Stennis	Y	N	Y	Y	Y	Y
MISSOURI						
Danforth	Y	N	Y	Y	Y	Y
Eagleton	Y	N	Y	N	N	N
MONTANA						
Baucus	N	Y	N	N	N	N
Melcher	N	Y	N	N	N	N
NEBRASKA						
Exon	N	Y	N	N	N	N
Zorinsky	N	Y	N	Y	Y	N
NEVADA						
Hecht	N	Y	N	Y	Y	Y
Laxalt	N	N	N	Y	Y	Y

	110	111	112	113	114	115
NEW HAMPSHIRE						
Humphrey	N	Y	N	Y	N	N
Rudman	Y	N	Y	Y	Y	Y
NEW JERSEY						
Bradley	Y	N	Y	N	N	Y
Lautenberg	Y	N	Y	N	N	N
NEW MEXICO						
Domenici	N	N	Y	Y	Y	Y
Bingaman	Y	N	Y	N	N	Y
NEW YORK						
D'Amato	Y	Y	Y	?	Y	Y
Moynihan	Y	N	Y	N	N	N
NORTH CAROLINA						
East	N	Y	N	Y	Y	N
Helms	N	Y	N	Y	Y	N
NORTH DAKOTA						
Andrews	Y	Y	Y	Y	N	Y
Burdick	Y	Y	Y	N	N	Y
OHIO						
Glenn	Y	N	Y	N	N	Y
Metzenbaum	Y	Y	Y	N	N	N
OKLAHOMA						
Nickles	N	Y	N	Y	Y	N
Boren	N	Y	N	Y	N	N
OREGON						
Hatfield	Y	N	Y	N	N	Y
Packwood	Y	N	Y	?	Y	?
PENNSYLVANIA						
Heinz	Y	N	Y	N	N	Y
Specter	Y	Y	Y	Y	Y	Y
RHODE ISLAND						
Chafee	Y	N	Y	Y	Y	Y
Pell	Y	N	Y	N	N	Y
SOUTH CAROLINA						
Thurmond	N	Y	N	Y	Y	Y
Hollings	N	N	N	N	?	?
SOUTH DAKOTA						
Abdnor	N	Y	N	Y	Y	Y
Pressler	N	Y	N	Y	Y	Y
TENNESSEE						
Baker	N	N	N	Y	Y	Y
Sasser	Y	N	Y	N	N	N

	110	111	112	113	114	115
TEXAS						
Tower	N	N	N	Y	Y	?
Bentsen	Y	N	Y	Y	Y	N
UTAH						
Garn	N	N	N	Y	Y	Y
Hatch	N	N	N	Y	Y	Y
VERMONT						
Stafford	Y	N	Y	Y	Y	N
Leahy	Y	N	N	N	N	N
VIRGINIA						
Trible	N	Y	N	Y	Y	N
Warner	N	Y	N	Y	Y	N
WASHINGTON						
Gorton	Y	Y	Y	Y	Y	Y
Jackson	Y	Y	Y	Y	Y	Y
WEST VIRGINIA						
Byrd	Y	Y	Y	N	Y	N
Randolph	Y	Y	Y	#	Y	N
WISCONSIN						
Kasten	N	Y	N	Y	Y	Y
Proxmire	N	N	N	N	N	N
WYOMING						
Simpson	Y	Y	Y	Y	Y	Y
Wallop	N	N	N	Y	Y	Y

ND - Northern Democrats   SD - Southern Democrats (Southern states - Ala., Ark., Fla., Ga., Ky., La., Miss., N.C., Okla., S.C., Tenn., Texas, Va.)

110. S Con Res 27. First Budget Resolution, Fiscal 1984. Gorton, R-Wash., substitute to set fiscal 1984 budget targets as follows: budget authority, $914.7 billion; outlays, $849.7 billion; revenues, $671.1 billion; and deficit, $178.6 billion. Adopted 53-47: R 20-34; D 33-13 (ND 27-5, SD 6-8), May 19, 1983. (The Senate previously had rejected the Gorton amendment *(see vote 103, p. 22-S).)*

111. S Con Res 27. First Budget Resolution, Fiscal 1984. Specter, R-Pa., amendment to express the sense of Congress that federal borrowing levels assumed in the resolution should not be used by the International Monetary Fund to provide loans to foreign governments that subsidize exports in unfair competition with goods produced in the United States. Rejected 47-52: R 25-28; D 22-24 (ND 15-17, SD 7-7), May 19, 1983.

112. S Con Res 27. First Budget Resolution, Fiscal 1984. Adoption of the concurrent resolution to set fiscal 1984 budget targets as follows: budget authority, $914.7 billion; outlays, $849.7 billion; revenues, $671.1 billion; and deficit, $178.6 billion. Adopted 50-49: R 21-32; D 29-17 (ND 24-8, SD 5-9), May 19, 1983.

113. S Con Res 26. MX Missile Development. Baker, R-Tenn., motion to table (kill) the Dixon, D-Ill., motion to postpone consideration of the concurrent resolution to permit the use of funds appropriated in fiscal 1983 to develop a basing method for the MX missile and to conduct MX test flights. Motion agreed to 59-35: R 51-1; D 8-34 (ND 2-27, SD 6-7), May 24, 1983. A "yea" was a vote supporting the president's position.

114. S Con Res 26. MX Missile Development. Adoption of the concurrent resolution to permit use of funds appropriated in fiscal 1983 to develop a basing method for the MX missile and to conduct MX test flights. Adopted 59-39: R 47-6; D 12-33 (ND 5-27, SD 7-6), May 25, 1983. A "yea" was a vote supporting the president's position.

115. HR 2990. Debt Limit Increase. Passage of the bill to raise the public debt limit to $1.389 trillion from the previous temporary limit of $1.29 trillion. Passed 51-41: R 39-10; D 12-31 (ND 10-21, SD 2-10), May 25, 1983. A "yea" was a vote supporting the president's position.

	116	117	118	119	120	121	122	123
ALABAMA								
Denton	Y	Y	N	N	Y	Y	N	N
Heflin	?	?	?	N	Y	N	N	N
ALASKA								
Murkowski	+	+	Y	Y	Y	Y	N	N
Stevens	+	+	+	Y	Y	Y	Y	Y
ARIZONA								
Goldwater	?	?	?	?	?	?	?	?
DeConcini	?	?	?	?	?	?	?	?
ARKANSAS								
Bumpers	Y	Y	N	Y	Y	N	Y	Y
Pryor	Y	Y	Y	Y	Y	Y	Y	Y
CALIFORNIA								
Wilson	Y	Y	N	N	N	Y	N	N
Cranston	?	?	?	?	?	?	?	?
COLORADO								
Armstrong	N	N	N	N	Y	N	N	N
Hart	?	?	?	?	?	?	?	?
CONNECTICUT								
Weicker	Y	Y	Y	Y	N	Y	Y	Y
Dodd	?	?	?	?	N	Y	Y	Y
DELAWARE								
Roth	Y	Y	Y	Y	Y	Y	N	Y
Biden	Y	Y	Y	Y	Y	Y	?	?
FLORIDA								
Hawkins	N	N	N	N	Y	N	N	N
Chiles	Y	Y	Y	Y	Y	N	Y	Y
GEORGIA								
Mattingly	Y	Y	N	N	Y	N	N	N
Nunn	Y	Y	Y	Y	Y	N	N	N
HAWAII								
Inouye	Y	Y	Y	Y	Y	N	Y	Y
Matsunaga	Y	Y	Y	Y	Y	Y	Y	Y
IDAHO								
McClure	Y	Y	N	N	Y	Y	N	N
Symms	N	N	N	N	Y	N	N	N
ILLINOIS								
Percy	Y	Y	Y	Y	Y	N	Y	Y
Dixon	Y	Y	Y	Y	Y	Y	Y	Y
INDIANA								
Lugar	Y	Y	Y	Y	N	Y	Y	Y
Quayle	Y	Y	Y	Y	Y	Y	N	Y

	116	117	118	119	120	121	122	123
IOWA								
Grassley	N	N	Y	N	Y	N	N	N
Jepsen	N	N	N	N	Y	N	N	N
KANSAS								
Dole	Y	Y	?	N	Y	Y	N	Y
Kassebaum	N	Y	N	Y	Y	Y	N	Y
KENTUCKY								
Ford	N	Y	N	N	Y	N	N	N
Huddleston	?	?	?	N	Y	Y	Y	Y
LOUISIANA								
Johnston	Y	Y	Y	Y	Y	N	Y	Y
Long	?	?	?	Y	Y	Y	Y	Y
MAINE								
Cohen	N	N	Y	N	Y	N	N	Y
Mitchell	Y	Y	N	Y	Y	Y	Y	Y
MARYLAND								
Mathias	Y	Y	Y	Y	N	Y	Y	Y
Sarbanes	Y	Y	Y	Y	Y	Y	Y	Y
MASSACHUSETTS								
Kennedy	Y	Y	?	Y	N	Y	Y	Y
Tsongas	Y	Y	Y	Y	N	Y	Y	?
MICHIGAN								
Levin	Y	Y	Y	Y	Y	Y	Y	Y
Riegle	Y	Y	Y	Y	Y	Y	Y	Y
MINNESOTA								
Boschwitz	Y	Y	Y	Y	Y	N	N	Y
Durenberger	Y	Y	Y	Y	Y	Y	Y	Y
MISSISSIPPI								
Cochran	Y	Y	N	Y	N	Y	N	Y
Stennis	Y	Y	Y	Y	Y	Y	Y	Y
MISSOURI								
Danforth	Y	Y	Y	Y	N	Y	Y	Y
Eagleton	?	?	?	Y	Y	Y	Y	Y
MONTANA								
Baucus	?	?	?	Y	Y	Y	N	Y
Melcher	N	N	N	Y	Y	Y	N	N
NEBRASKA								
Exon	N	N	Y	Y	Y	Y	N	N
Zorinsky	N	N	N	Y	Y	Y	N	N
NEVADA								
Hecht	Y	Y	Y	Y	Y	Y	Y	Y
Laxalt	Y	Y	N	N	Y	N	N	N

	116	117	118	119	120	121	122	123
NEW HAMPSHIRE								
Humphrey	N	N	N	N	Y	N	N	N
Rudman	Y	Y	Y	N	Y	N	N	N
NEW JERSEY								
Bradley	?	?	?	Y	N	Y	Y	Y
Lautenberg	Y	Y	Y	Y	N	Y	Y	Y
NEW MEXICO								
Domenici	Y	Y	Y	Y	Y	Y	N	Y
Bingaman	Y	Y	Y	Y	Y	Y	Y	Y
NEW YORK								
D'Amato	Y	Y	Y	Y	Y	Y	Y	Y
Moynihan	?	?	?	Y	N	Y	Y	Y
NORTH CAROLINA								
East	N	N	N	N	Y	N	N	N
Helms	N	N	N	N	Y	N	N	N
NORTH DAKOTA								
Andrews	Y	Y	Y	Y	Y	Y	N	N
Burdick	N	N	N	Y	Y	Y	N	N
OHIO								
Glenn	Y	Y	Y	N	Y	Y	Y	Y
Metzenbaum	N	Y	Y	?	?	?	?	?
OKLAHOMA								
Nickles	N	N	N	N	Y	N	N	N
Boren	N	Y	Y	Y	Y	Y	N	Y
OREGON								
Hatfield	Y	Y	Y	Y	Y	Y	Y	Y
Packwood	Y	Y	Y	Y	Y	Y	N	Y
PENNSYLVANIA								
Heinz	Y	Y	Y	Y	Y	Y	Y	Y
Specter	N	Y	?	Y	Y	Y	N	N
RHODE ISLAND								
Chafee	Y	Y	Y	Y	N	Y	Y	Y
Pell	+	+	+	Y	Y	Y	Y	Y
SOUTH CAROLINA								
Thurmond	Y	Y	N	N	Y	N	N	N
Hollings	?	?	?	?	?	?	?	?
SOUTH DAKOTA								
Abdnor	N	N	N	N	Y	N	N	N
Pressler	N	N	N	N	Y	N	N	N
TENNESSEE								
Baker	Y	Y	Y	Y	Y	?	Y	Y
Sasser	Y	Y	Y	Y	Y	Y	Y	Y

	116	117	118	119	120	121	122	123
TEXAS								
Tower	Y	Y	Y	Y	Y	Y	Y	Y
Bentsen	?	?	?	Y	Y	Y	Y	Y
UTAH								
Garn	Y	Y	Y	Y	Y	Y	Y	Y
Hatch	N	Y	N	N	Y	N	N	N
VERMONT								
Stafford	Y	Y	Y	Y	Y	Y	Y	Y
Leahy	N	Y	Y	Y	Y	N	Y	Y
VIRGINIA								
Trible	N	Y	N	Y	N	N	N	N
Warner	N	N	N	Y	N	N	N	N
WASHINGTON								
Gorton	Y	Y	Y	Y	Y	Y	N	Y
Jackson	Y	Y	Y	Y	Y	Y	Y	Y
WEST VIRGINIA								
Byrd	Y	Y	N	Y	N	N	N	N
Randolph	N	N	N	N	Y	N	N	N
WISCONSIN								
Kasten	Y	Y	Y	N	Y	N	N	Y
Proxmire	Y	Y	Y	Y	N	Y	Y	Y
WYOMING								
Simpson	Y	Y	Y	N	Y	N	N	Y
Wallop	Y	Y	Y	N	Y	Y	N	Y

KEY

Y Voted for (yea).
\# Paired for.
\+ Announced for.
N Voted against (nay).
X Paired against.
\- Announced against.
P Voted "present".
C Voted "present" to avoid possible conflict of interest.
? Did not vote or otherwise make a position known.

Democrats   *Republicans*

ND - Northern Democrats   SD - Southern Democrats (Southern states - Ala., Ark., Fla., Ga., Ky., La., Miss., N.C., Okla., S.C., Tenn., Texas, Va.)

116. S 695. International Monetary Fund Authorization. Adoption of the resolution (S Res 146) to waive provisions of the Congressional Budget Act that would bar consideration of the bill to authorize an $8.4 billion increase in the U.S. contribution to the International Monetary Fund. Adopted 57-26: R 34-17; D 23-9 (ND 16-7, SD 7-2), June 7, 1983.

117. S 695. International Monetary Fund Authorization. Baker, R-Tenn., motion to proceed to consideration of the bill to authorize an $8.4 billion increase in the U.S. contribution to the International Monetary Fund. Motion agreed to 65-18: R 38-13; D 27-5 (ND 18-5, SD 9-0), June 7, 1983.

118. S 695. International Monetary Fund Authorization. Heinz, R-Pa., motion to table (kill) the Humphrey, R-N.H., amendment to deny the $8.4 billion increase in the U.S. contribution to the International Monetary Fund (IMF) unless all IMF staff salaries are reduced to $67,000 or less. Motion agreed to 55-26: R 32-18; D 23-8 (ND 16-6, SD 7-2), June 7, 1983.

119. S 695. International Monetary Fund Authorization. Heinz, R-Pa., motion to table (kill) the Humphrey, R-N.H., amendment to deny the increase in the U.S. contribution to the International Monetary Fund (IMF) as long as communist nations remain members of the IMF. Motion agreed to 60-32: R 26-27; D 34-5 (ND 24-2, SD 10-3), June 8, 1983.

120. S 695. International Monetary Fund Authorization. Helms, R-N.C., amendment to encourage the International Monetary Fund to deny loans to nations refusing to eliminate predatory export subsidies for agricultural products. Adopted 81-13: R 48-5; D 33-8 (ND 20-8, SD 13-0), June 8, 1983.

121. S 695. International Monetary Fund Authorization. Heinz, R-Pa., motion to table (kill) the Humphrey, R-N.H., amendment to require the U.S. representative to the International Monetary Fund to oppose loans to certain countries until they agree to hold internationally supervised free elections and allow unrestricted emigration. Motion agreed to 63-30: R 28-24; D 35-6 (ND 27-1, SD 8-5), June 8, 1983.

122. S 695. International Monetary Fund Authorization. Heinz, R-Pa., motion to table (kill) the Armstrong, R-Colo., amendment to express the sense of the Senate that an international monetary conference should be held to investigate monetary problems; that the International Monetary Fund (IMF) should use its gold holdings to raise funds; that IMF loan conditions should encourage growth in developing countries; and that further financial assistance to Third World nations be bilateral. Motion agreed to 47-46: R 19-34; D 28-12 (ND 19-8, SD 9-4), June 8, 1983.

123. S 695. International Monetary Fund Authorization. Heinz, R-Pa., motion to table (kill) the Humphrey, R-N.H., amendment to reduce by 20 percent the new contribution of International Monetary Fund (IMF) members and instead sell IMF gold to raise funds. Motion agreed to 62-30: R 31-22; D 31-8 (ND 20-6, SD 11-2), June 8, 1983.

	124	125	126	127	128	129	130	131
ALABAMA								
Denton	N	Y	Y	N	N	N	N	Y
Heflin	Y	Y	N	C	C	N	Y	Y
ALASKA								
Murkowski	N	N	Y	N	N	N	N	Y
Stevens	N	N	Y	N	N	N	N	Y
ARIZONA								
Goldwater	?	?	-	-	-	-	?	?
DeConcini	?	?	?	?	?	?	?	?
ARKANSAS								
Bumpers	N	N	Y	N	N	N	Y	N
Pryor	N	Y	N	N	N	N	Y	N
CALIFORNIA								
Wilson	N	N	Y	N	N	N	N	Y
Cranston	?	?	?	?	?	?	?	?
COLORADO								
Armstrong	Y	Y	N	N	N	N	N	Y
Hart	?	?	?	?	?	?	?	?
CONNECTICUT								
Weicker	?	?	?	Y	Y	N	N	Y
Dodd	N	N	Y	N	N	N	N	N
DELAWARE								
Roth	N	Y	N	N	N	N	Y	N
Biden	?	?	+	N	N	N	Y	N
FLORIDA								
Hawkins	Y	Y	N	N	N	N	N	Y
Chiles	N	N	Y	Y	N	N	Y	N
GEORGIA								
Mattingly	N	N	Y	N	N	N	Y	N
Nunn	N	N	Y	N	N	N	Y	N
HAWAII								
Inouye	N	N	Y	Y	Y	?	?	?
Matsunaga	N	N	Y	Y	Y	Y	N	Y
IDAHO								
McClure	?	?	N	N	N	N	N	?
Symms	Y	Y	N	N	N	N	N	Y
ILLINOIS								
Percy	N	N	Y	N	N	N	N	Y
Dixon	N	N	Y	N	N	N	N	Y
INDIANA								
Lugar	N	N	Y	N	N	N	N	Y
Quayle	N	N	Y	N	N	N	N	Y
IOWA								
Grassley	Y	Y	N	N	N	N	Y	N
Jepsen	Y	Y	N	N	N	N	Y	Y
KANSAS								
Dole	N	Y	Y	N	N	N	N	Y
Kassebaum	N	Y	N	N	N	N	Y	N
KENTUCKY								
Ford	N	N	Y	C	C	N	Y	N
Huddleston	N	N	N	N	N	N	N	N
LOUISIANA								
Johnston	N	N	Y	N	N	N	N	Y
Long	N	N	Y	N	N	N	Y	Y
MAINE								
Cohen	Y	Y	N	N	N	N	N	Y
Mitchell	N	N	Y	N	N	N	N	Y
MARYLAND								
Mathias	N	N	Y	Y	Y	Y	N	Y
Sarbanes	N	N	Y	Y	N	N	Y	N
MASSACHUSETTS								
Kennedy	N	N	Y	Y	Y	Y	N	Y
Tsongas	?	?	?	N	Y	N	N	N
MICHIGAN								
Levin	N	N	Y	N	N	N	N	Y
Riegle	N	N	Y	C	N	N	Y	N
MINNESOTA								
Boschwitz	N	N	Y	?	?	?	?	?
Durenberger	N	N	?	N	N	N	N	Y
MISSISSIPPI								
Cochran	N	N	Y	N	N	N	N	Y
Stennis	N	N	Y	N	N	N	Y	N
MISSOURI								
Danforth	N	N	Y	N	N	N	N	N
Eagleton	N	N	Y	N	N	N	Y	N
MONTANA								
Baucus	N	N	N	N	N	N	Y	N
Melcher	N	Y	N	Y	Y	N	Y	N
NEBRASKA								
Exon	Y	Y	N	C	N	N	Y	Y
Zorinsky	Y	Y	N	C	N	N	Y	Y
NEVADA								
Hecht	N	N	Y	N	N	N	N	Y
Laxalt	N	Y	N	N	N	N	N	Y
NEW HAMPSHIRE								
Humphrey	Y	Y	N	N	N	N	N	Y
Rudman	N	N	Y	N	N	N	N	Y
NEW JERSEY								
Bradley	N	N	Y	N	N	N	Y	N
Lautenberg	N	N	Y	Y	Y	N	N	N
NEW MEXICO								
Domenici	Y	Y	N	N	N	N	N	Y
Bingaman	N	N	Y	?	?	?	?	-
NEW YORK								
D'Amato	N	Y	N	N	N	N	N	Y
Moynihan	N	N	Y	Y	N	N	Y	N
NORTH CAROLINA								
East	Y	Y	N	N	N	N	Y	Y
Helms	Y	Y	N	N	N	N	Y	Y
NORTH DAKOTA								
Andrews	N	N	N	Y	N	Y	N	Y
Burdick	N	Y	N	Y	N	Y	N	Y
OHIO								
Glenn	N	N	?	?	?	?	?	+
Metzenbaum	?	?	?	Y	N	Y	Y	N
OKLAHOMA								
Nickles	Y	Y	N	N	N	-	Y	Y
Boren	N	Y	N	N	N	N	Y	Y
OREGON								
Hatfield	N	N	Y	N	N	N	N	N
Packwood	N	N	Y	N	N	N	N	Y
PENNSYLVANIA								
Heinz	N	N	Y	N	N	N	N	N
Specter	N	Y	N	N	N	N	Y	Y
RHODE ISLAND								
Chafee	N	N	Y	N	N	Y	N	N
Pell	N	N	Y	N	N	N	Y	N
SOUTH CAROLINA								
Thurmond	Y	Y	N	N	N	N	Y	Y
Hollings	?	?	?	N	N	N	N	N
SOUTH DAKOTA								
Abdnor	Y	Y	N	N	N	N	Y	Y
Pressler	Y	Y	N	N	N	N	Y	N
TENNESSEE								
Baker	N	N	Y	N	N	N	N	Y
Sasser	N	N	Y	C	N	N	Y	Y
TEXAS								
Tower	N	N	Y	N	N	N	N	Y
Bentsen	N	N	Y	Y	N	N	N	Y
UTAH								
Garn	N	N	Y	N	N	N	N	?
Hatch	Y	Y	N	N	N	N	N	Y
VERMONT								
Stafford	N	N	Y	N	N	N	N	Y
Leahy	N	N	Y	N	N	N	Y	N
VIRGINIA								
Trible	N	N	Y	N	N	N	Y	Y
Warner	N	Y	N	N	N	N	Y	Y
WASHINGTON								
Gorton	N	N	Y	N	N	N	N	Y
Jackson	N	N	Y	Y	N	Y	N	Y
WEST VIRGINIA								
Byrd	N	Y	Y	N	N	Y	N	Y
Randolph	Y	Y	N	Y	N	N	Y	Y
WISCONSIN								
Kasten	N	N	Y	N	N	Y	N	Y
Proxmire	N	N	Y	Y	N	Y	N	Y
WYOMING								
Simpson	N	N	N	N	N	N	Y	Y
Wallop	N	Y	N	N	N	N	N	Y

KEY

Y Voted for (yea).
Paired for.
+ Announced for.
N Voted against (nay).
X Paired against.
- Announced against.
P Voted "present".
C Voted "present" to avoid possible conflict of interest.
? Did not vote or otherwise make a position known.

Democrats *Republicans*

ND - Northern Democrats   SD - Southern Democrats (Southern states - Ala., Ark., Fla., Ga., Ky., La., Miss., N.C., Okla., S.C., Tenn., Texas, Va.)

124. S 695. International Monetary Fund Authorization. Helms, R-N.C., amendment to require congressional authorization before the U.S. representative to the International Monetary Fund (IMF) agrees to an increase in Special Drawing Rights, the IMF's international currency used in transactions between governments. Rejected 19-71: R 15-36; D 4-35 (ND 3-23, SD 1-12), June 8, 1983.

125. S 695. International Monetary Fund Authorization. Helms, R-N.C., amendment to make the increase in the U.S. contribution to the International Monetary Fund effective only through fiscal 1984. Rejected 33-57: R 24-27; D 9-30 (ND 6-20, SD 3-10), June 8, 1983.

126. S 695. International Monetary Fund Authorization. Passage of the bill to authorize an $8.4 billion increase in the U.S. contribution to the International Monetary Fund, and to increase regulation of international lending by U.S. banks. Passed 55-34: R 27-24; D 28-10 (ND 19-6, SD 9-4), June 8, 1983. A "yea" was a vote supporting the president's position.

127. HR 3069. Supplemental Appropriations, Fiscal 1983. Jackson, D-Wash., amendment to increase the salary of senators to $69,800, from the existing level of $60,662.50 and limit honoraria income to 30 percent of salary. Rejected 20-67: R 5-47; D 15-20 (ND 13-11, SD 2-9), June 9, 1983.

128. HR 3069. Supplemental Appropriations, Fiscal 1983. Jackson, D-Wash., amendment to allow a senator to choose to accept a $69,800 annual salary along with a 30 percent cap on honoraria income or a $60,662.50 salary with no limit on honoraria. Rejected 13-78: R 4-48; D 9-30 (ND 9-18, SD 0-12), June 9, 1983.

129. HR 3069. Supplemental Appropriations, Fiscal 1983. Jackson, D-Wash., amendment to increase the salary of senators to $69,800, from the existing level of $60,662.50. Rejected 3-88: R 2-49; D 1-39 (ND 1-25, SD 0-14), June 9, 1983.

130. HR 3069. Supplemental Appropriations, Fiscal 1983. Jackson, D-Wash., amendment to limit a senator's honoraria income for speeches, articles or appearances to 30 percent of the existing annual salary of $60,662.50. Adopted 51-41: R 18-34; D 33-7 (ND 22-4, SD 11-3), June 9, 1983.

131. HR 3069. Supplemental Appropriations, Fiscal 1983. Stevens, R-Alaska, amendment to appropriate $185 million for multi-year procurement for the B-1B bomber program and rescind $185 million of previously appropriated funds. Adopted 52-38: R 42-8; D 10-30 (ND 5-21, SD 5-9), June 9, 1983.

State / Senator	132	133	134	135	136	137	138	139
ALABAMA								
Denton	N	N	P	Y	Y	N	N	Y
Heflin	Y	Y	Y	Y	Y	N	N	N
ALASKA								
Murkowski	N	N	Y	Y	N	N	N	Y
Stevens	N	N	N	Y	N	N	N	Y
ARIZONA								
Goldwater	?	?	?	Y	Y	N	N	N
DeConcini	?	?	?	Y	Y	N	Y	N
ARKANSAS								
Bumpers	?	?	?	Y	Y	N	Y	N
Pryor	?	?	?	Y	Y	N	Y	Y
CALIFORNIA								
Wilson	N	N	N	Y	N	N	N	Y
Cranston	?	?	?	?	Y	N	Y	Y
COLORADO								
Armstrong	N	N	N	Y	N	N	N	N
Hart	?	?	?	Y	N	N	Y	Y
CONNECTICUT								
Weicker	Y	N	Y	Y	N	N	N	Y
Dodd	Y	Y	Y	Y	N	N	Y	Y
DELAWARE								
Roth	N	N	N	Y	N	Y	N	Y
Biden	Y	Y	N	Y	Y	N	Y	Y
FLORIDA								
Hawkins	N	N	Y	Y	Y	N	N	N
Chiles	Y	Y	Y	Y	Y	Y	Y	N
GEORGIA								
Mattingly	N	N	Y	Y	N	N	N	N
Nunn	Y	Y	Y	Y	N	N	Y	Y
HAWAII								
Inouye	?	?	?	Y	Y	N	N	Y
Matsunaga	N	Y	Y	Y	N	N	Y	N
IDAHO								
McClure	?	?	?	Y	Y	N	Y	N
Symms	N	N	?	Y	Y	N	N	Y
ILLINOIS								
Percy	N	N	Y	Y	Y	N	Y	Y
Dixon	Y	Y	Y	Y	Y	Y	Y	Y
INDIANA								
Lugar	N	N	Y	Y	Y	N	N	Y
Quayle	N	N	Y	Y	N	N	N	N
IOWA								
Grassley	Y	N	Y	Y	N	N	N	N
Jepsen	N	N	Y	Y	N	N	N	Y
KANSAS								
Dole	N	N	N	?	N	N	N	N
Kassebaum	N	N	Y	Y	N	N	Y	Y
KENTUCKY								
Ford	Y	Y	Y	Y	N	Y	Y	N
Huddleston	Y	Y	Y	Y	N	Y	Y	N
LOUISIANA								
Johnston	?	?	?	Y	N	Y	N	Y
Long	?	Y	Y	Y	Y	Y	Y	Y
MAINE								
Cohen	N	Y	Y	Y	Y	N	N	Y
Mitchell	Y	Y	Y	Y	Y	N	Y	Y
MARYLAND								
Mathias	N	N	N	Y	N	N	N	Y
Sarbanes	Y	Y	Y	Y	Y	Y	Y	Y
MASSACHUSETTS								
Kennedy	Y	Y	Y	Y	N	N	Y	Y
Tsongas	N	Y	Y	Y	N	Y	Y	Y
MICHIGAN								
Levin	Y	Y	?	Y	Y	Y	Y	Y
Riegle	Y	Y	Y	Y	Y	N	Y	?
MINNESOTA								
Boschwitz	?	?	?	Y	Y	Y	Y	N
Durenberger	Y	N	?	Y	Y	N	Y	Y
MISSISSIPPI								
Cochran	N	N	N	Y	N	N	N	N
Stennis	Y	Y	Y	Y	Y	?	Y	Y
MISSOURI								
Danforth	N	N	Y	Y	N	N	N	Y
Eagleton	Y	Y	Y	Y	Y	Y	Y	N
MONTANA								
Baucus	Y	Y	Y	Y	Y	N	Y	N
Melcher	Y	Y	Y	Y	Y	N	Y	Y
NEBRASKA								
Exon	Y	Y	Y	Y	Y	N	N	Y
Zorinsky	Y	Y	Y	Y	Y	N	N	N
NEVADA								
Hecht	N	N	Y	?	?	?	N	Y
Laxalt	N	N	N	Y	N	N	N	Y
NEW HAMPSHIRE								
Humphrey	Y	N	N	Y	N	N	Y	Y
Rudman	N	N	Y	Y	N	N	N	N
NEW JERSEY								
Bradley	N	Y	Y	Y	N	N	Y	Y
Lautenberg	Y	Y	Y	Y	N	N	Y	Y
NEW MEXICO								
Domenici	N	N	Y	Y	Y	N	Y	N
Bingaman	+	?	?	Y	Y	N	Y	Y
NEW YORK								
D'Amato	N	N	Y	Y	N	N	N	N
Moynihan	Y	?	?	Y	N	N	Y	Y
NORTH CAROLINA								
East	N	N	N	Y	N	N	N	N
Helms	N	N	Y	Y	N	N	N	N
NORTH DAKOTA								
Andrews	Y	N	Y	Y	N	N	N	N
Burdick	Y	Y	Y	Y	Y	Y	N	Y
OHIO								
Glenn	?	Y	Y	Y	Y	Y	N	?
Metzenbaum	Y	Y	Y	Y	Y	Y	Y	N
OKLAHOMA								
Nickles	N	N	Y	Y	N	N	N	Y
Boren	Y	Y	Y	Y	N	N	N	N
OREGON								
Hatfield	Y	N	Y	Y	N	N	N	Y
Packwood	?	Y	Y	Y	N	N	Y	Y
PENNSYLVANIA								
Heinz	N	N	N	Y	N	N	N	Y
Specter	N	N	N	Y	N	N	N	N
RHODE ISLAND								
Chafee	N	N	Y	Y	N	N	N	Y
Pell	Y	Y	Y	Y	N	N	Y	Y
SOUTH CAROLINA								
Thurmond	N	N	N	Y	N	N	N	N
Hollings	Y	Y	Y	Y	N	N	Y	Y
SOUTH DAKOTA								
Abdnor	N	N	N	Y	N	N	N	N
Pressler	Y	N	Y	Y	Y	N	N	N
TENNESSEE								
Baker	N	N	N	Y	N	N	N	N
Sasser	Y	Y	Y	Y	Y	Y	N	N
TEXAS								
Tower	N	N	N	Y	N	N	N	Y
Bentsen	Y	Y	Y	Y	N	Y	Y	Y
UTAH								
Garn	?	?	?	Y	N	N	N	Y
Hatch	N	N	N	Y	N	N	N	Y
VERMONT								
Stafford	?	N	?	Y	Y	Y	Y	Y
Leahy	Y	Y	Y	Y	Y	N	Y	Y
VIRGINIA								
Trible	N	N	N	Y	N	N	N	Y
Warner	N	N	N	Y	N	N	N	Y
WASHINGTON								
Gorton	N	N	Y	Y	N	N	N	N
Jackson	N	Y	Y	Y	N	N	N	Y
WEST VIRGINIA								
Byrd	Y	Y	Y	Y	N	N	Y	N
Randolph	Y	Y	Y	Y	N	N	Y	Y
WISCONSIN								
Kasten	N	N	Y	Y	N	N	N	N
Proxmire	Y	N	Y	Y	Y	Y	Y	Y
WYOMING								
Simpson	N	N	Y	Y	N	N	N	Y
Wallop	N	?	?	Y	Y	Y	N	Y

KEY

Y Voted for (yea).
Paired for.
+ Announced for.
N Voted against (nay).
X Paired against.
- Announced against.
P Voted "present".
C Voted "present" to avoid possible conflict of interest.
? Did not vote or otherwise make a position known.

Democrats   *Republicans*

ND - Northern Democrats   SD - Southern Democrats (Southern states - Ala., Ark., Fla., Ga., Ky., La., Miss., N.C., Okla., S.C., Tenn., Texas, Va.)

132. HR 3069. Supplemental Appropriations, Fiscal 1983. Leahy, D-Vt., amendment to cut $376 million for foreign assistance programs. Rejected 39-45: R 7-41; D 32-4 (ND 22-4, SD 10-0), June 9, 1983.

133. HR 3069. Supplemental Appropriations, Fiscal 1983. Kennedy, D-Mass., amendment to appropriate $500,000 for a national summit conference on education. Rejected 38-48: R 2-47; D 36-1 (ND 25-1, SD 11-0), June 9, 1983.

134. HR 3069. Supplemental Appropriations, Fiscal 1983. Bradley, D-N.J., amendment to eliminate a provision that would bar most truck traffic from Route 209, a federally owned road that goes through the Delaware Water Gap National Recreation Area. Adopted 61-20: R 26-19; D 35-1 (ND 24-1, SD 11-0), June 9, 1983.

135. S 66. Cable Telecommunications Act. Abdnor, R-S.D., amendment to reaffirm congressional policy of promoting universal telephone service at reasonable rates and stating that it is in the public interest to ensure that all telecommunications providers share in the obligation of providing universal service. Adopted 97-0: R 52-0; D 45-0 (ND 31-0, SD 14-0), June 14, 1983.

136. S 66. Cable Telecommunications Act. Abdnor, R-S.D., amendment to subject cable companies to the same regulatory restrictions as telephone companies when they offer telecommunications services that could be provided by telephone companies. Rejected 44-55: R 19-34; D 25-21 (ND 18-14, SD 7-7), June 14, 1983.

137. S 66. Cable Telecommunications Act. Bentsen, D-Texas, amendment to grandfather all existing cable contracts with franchising authorities. Rejected 19-79: R 4-49; D 15-30 (ND 8-24, SD 7-6), June 14, 1983.

138. HR 3069. Supplemental Appropriations, Fiscal 1983. Bumpers, D-Ark., amendment to prohibit new coal leasing during the remainder of fiscal 1983. Rejected 48-51: R 10-44; D 38-7 (ND 28-3, SD 10-4), June 14, 1983.

139. HR 3069. Supplemental Appropriations, Fiscal 1983. Percy, R-Ill., amendment to appropriate $4.5 million for voluntary contributions by the United States to the International Atomic Energy Agency. Adopted 65-34: R 35-19; D 30-15 (ND 23-8, SD 7-7), June 14, 1983.

KEY

Y	Voted for (yea).
#	Paired for.
+	Announced for.
N	Voted against (nay).
X	Paired against.
-	Announced against.
P	Voted "present".
C	Voted "present" to avoid possible conflict of interest.
?	Did not vote or otherwise make a position known.

Democrats *Republicans*

	140	141	142	143	144	145	146	147
ALABAMA								
Denton	Y	+	N	Y	Y	Y	N	Y
Heflin	N	Y	N	Y	N	Y	Y	Y
ALASKA								
Murkowski	Y	Y	N	Y	Y	N	Y	N
Stevens	Y	Y	N	Y	Y	Y	Y	N
ARIZONA								
Goldwater	Y	Y	N	Y	N	N	N	?
DeConcini	N	Y	N	Y	Y	Y	Y	Y
ARKANSAS								
Bumpers	N	Y	Y	Y	Y	Y	Y	Y
Pryor	Y	Y	N	Y	Y	Y	Y	Y
CALIFORNIA								
Wilson	Y	Y	N	Y	Y	N	N	N
Cranston	Y	Y	N	Y	Y	Y	Y	N
COLORADO								
Armstrong	N	Y	N	Y	Y	N	N	N
Hart	N	Y	N	Y	?	?	?	?
CONNECTICUT								
Weicker	Y	Y	N	Y	?	?	Y	N
Dodd	N	N	Y	Y	Y	?	Y	N
DELAWARE								
Roth	N	Y	N	Y	Y	Y	N	Y
Biden	N	Y	Y	Y	?	Y	Y	N
FLORIDA								
Hawkins	Y	Y	N	Y	Y	N	Y	Y
Chiles	N	Y	N	Y	Y	N	Y	Y
GEORGIA								
Mattingly	Y	Y	N	Y	Y	N	N	Y
Nunn	N	Y	Y	Y	Y	Y	N	Y
HAWAII								
Inouye	Y	Y	N	Y	Y	Y	N	Y
Matsunaga	N	Y	N	Y	Y	Y	Y	N
IDAHO								
McClure	Y	Y	N	?	Y	N	N	N
Symms	Y	Y	N	Y	?	?	?	+
ILLINOIS								
Percy	N	N	N	Y	Y	Y	N	N
Dixon	N	N	Y	N	Y	Y	Y	N
INDIANA								
Lugar	Y	Y	N	Y	N	Y	N	N
Quayle	Y	Y	N	Y	N	N	Y	N

	140	141	142	143	144	145	146	147
IOWA								
Grassley	N	Y	N	Y	Y	Y	Y	Y
Jepsen	Y	Y	N	Y	Y	Y	Y	Y
KANSAS								
Dole	N	Y	N	Y	Y	N	Y	N
Kassebaum	Y	Y	N	Y	Y	Y	N	N
KENTUCKY								
Ford	N	Y	N	Y	Y	Y	Y	Y
Huddleston	N	Y	?	?	Y	Y	Y	Y
LOUISIANA								
Johnston	N	N	Y	Y	Y	Y	Y	Y
Long	?	?	?	?	Y	Y	N	Y
MAINE								
Cohen	Y	Y	N	Y	Y	Y	Y	Y
Mitchell	Y	Y	Y	Y	Y	Y	Y	Y
MARYLAND								
Mathias	Y	Y	N	Y	Y	Y	Y	N
Sarbanes	Y	N	Y	N	Y	Y	Y	N
MASSACHUSETTS								
Kennedy	N	Y	N	?	Y	Y	Y	N
Tsongas	Y	Y	N	Y	Y	N	Y	N
MICHIGAN								
Levin	N	N	Y	Y	Y	Y	Y	N
Riegle	N	Y	N	Y	Y	Y	Y	N
MINNESOTA								
Boschwitz	Y	Y	N	Y	Y	Y	Y	N
Durenberger	N	Y	N	Y	Y	Y	Y	N
MISSISSIPPI								
Cochran	Y	Y	N	Y	Y	N	Y	Y
Stennis	Y	Y	Y	Y	Y	Y	N	Y
MISSOURI								
Danforth	N	Y	N	Y	Y	Y	Y	N
Eagleton	N	N	Y	Y	Y	Y	Y	N
MONTANA								
Baucus	N	Y	N	Y	Y	Y	Y	Y
Melcher	N	Y	Y	Y	Y	Y	Y	Y
NEBRASKA								
Exon	N	Y	Y	Y	Y	Y	Y	Y
Zorinsky	N	N	Y	Y	Y	Y	N	N
NEVADA								
Hecht	Y	Y	N	Y	Y	N	Y	N
Laxalt	Y	Y	N	Y	Y	Y	Y	N

	140	141	142	143	144	145	146	147
NEW HAMPSHIRE								
Humphrey	Y	Y	Y	Y	Y	N	N	N
Rudman	Y	Y	N	Y	Y	N	N	N
NEW JERSEY								
Bradley	N	N	N	Y	Y	Y	Y	N
Lautenberg	N	Y	N	Y	Y	Y	Y	N
NEW MEXICO								
Domenici	N	Y	N	Y	Y	Y	Y	Y
Bingaman	N	Y	N	Y	Y	Y	Y	Y
NEW YORK								
D'Amato	Y	Y	N	Y	Y	Y	Y	N
Moynihan	N	N	Y	Y	Y	Y	Y	N
NORTH CAROLINA								
East	Y	Y	N	Y	Y	Y	N	+
Helms	Y	Y	N	Y	Y	Y	N	Y
NORTH DAKOTA								
Andrews	Y	Y	N	Y	Y	Y	Y	N
Burdick	N	N	Y	Y	Y	Y	Y	Y
OHIO								
Glenn	N	Y	N	Y	Y	Y	Y	?
Metzenbaum	N	N	Y	N	Y	Y	Y	N
OKLAHOMA								
Nickles	N	Y	N	Y	Y	Y	N	Y
Boren	N	Y	Y	Y	Y	Y	Y	Y
OREGON								
Hatfield	Y	Y	N	Y	Y	N	Y	N
Packwood	Y	Y	N	Y	N	N	Y	N
PENNSYLVANIA								
Heinz	N	Y	N	Y	Y	Y	Y	N
Specter	N	N	N	Y	Y	Y	Y	N
RHODE ISLAND								
Chafee	Y	Y	N	Y	Y	N	Y	N
Pell	Y	Y	Y	Y	Y	N	Y	N
SOUTH CAROLINA								
Thurmond	Y	Y	N	Y	Y	Y	Y	Y
Hollings	N	Y	N	Y	Y	Y	Y	Y
SOUTH DAKOTA								
Abdnor	Y	Y	Y	Y	Y	N	Y	N
Pressler	N	Y	N	Y	Y	Y	N	Y
TENNESSEE								
Baker	N	Y	N	Y	Y	N	Y	N
Sasser	N	N	Y	Y	Y	Y	Y	Y

	140	141	142	143	144	145	146	147
TEXAS								
Tower	Y	Y	N	Y	Y	N	N	N
Bentsen	N	Y	N	Y	Y	N	Y	N
UTAH								
Garn	Y	Y	N	Y	Y	Y	N	N
Hatch	Y	Y	N	Y	Y	Y	Y	N
VERMONT								
Stafford	Y	Y	N	N	Y	Y	Y	N
Leahy	N	N	Y	N	Y	Y	Y	N
VIRGINIA								
Trible	Y	Y	N	Y	?	N	N	Y
Warner	Y	Y	N	Y	Y	Y	Y	Y
WASHINGTON								
Gorton	Y	Y	N	Y	Y	N	N	N
Jackson	N	Y	Y	Y	Y	Y	Y	N
WEST VIRGINIA								
Byrd	N	Y	N	Y	Y	Y	N	N
Randolph	N	Y	N	Y	Y	Y	Y	N
WISCONSIN								
Kasten	Y	Y	N	Y	Y	Y	N	N
Proxmire	N	N	Y	N	N	N	N	N
WYOMING								
Simpson	Y	Y	N	Y	Y	Y	N	N
Wallop	Y	Y	N	Y	Y	Y	N	N

ND - Northern Democrats   SD - Southern Democrats (Southern states - Ala., Ark., Fla., Ga., Ky., La., Miss., N.C., Okla., S.C., Tenn., Texas, Va.)

140. HR 3069. Supplemental Appropriations, Fiscal 1983. Cohen, R-Maine, motion to table (kill) the Metzenbaum, D-Ohio, amendment to prohibit the use of federal funds to indemnify lessors of property to the federal government for tax claims. Motion rejected 49-50: R 41-13; D 8-37 (ND 6-26, SD 2-11), June 14, 1983.

141. S 66. Cable Telecommunications Act. Packwood, R-Ore., motion to table (kill) the Dixon, D-Ill., amendment to place the burden of proof on the cable company seeking franchise renewal to show that it had substantially conformed with applicable law, and to make other changes in the bill's renewal provisions. Motion agreed to 82-16: R 51-2; D 31-14 (ND 20-12, SD 11-2), June 14, 1983.

142. S 66. Cable Telecommunications Act. Dixon, D-Ill., amendment to eliminate a provision that would allow cable companies to automatically raise regulated rates based on the regional consumer price index. Rejected 26-72: R 3-51; D 23-21 (ND 17-15, SD 6-6), June 14, 1983.

143. S 66. Cable Telecommunications Act. Passage of the bill to limit local government regulation of cable television systems. Passed 87-9: R 50-3; D 37-6 (ND 25-6, SD 12-0), June 14, 1983.

144. HR 3069. Supplemental Appropriations, Fiscal 1983. Baker, R-Tenn., motion to instruct the sergeant-at-arms to request the attendance of absent senators. Motion agreed to 91-4: R 49-2; D 42-2 (ND 29-1, SD 13-1), June 15, 1983.

145. HR 3069. Supplemental Appropriations, Fiscal 1983. Melcher, D-Mont., amendment to provide an additional $34.5 million for soil conservation programs. Adopted 67-29: R 28-24; D 39-5 (ND 27-3, SD 12-2), June 15, 1983.

146. HR 3069. Supplemental Appropriations, Fiscal 1983. Moynihan, D-N.Y., amendment to provide $225 million for health care benefits for the unemployed, contingent upon enactment of legislation authorizing such a program. Adopted 75-23: R 34-19; D 41-4 (ND 29-2, SD 12-2), June 15, 1983.

147. HR 3069. Supplemental Appropriations, Fiscal 1983. Judgment of the Senate whether the Bumpers, D-Ark., amendment to alter the formula for distribution of funds under the Chapter I program of compensatory education aid for the disadvantaged was germane. Ruled nongermane 35-60: R 16-35; D 19-25 (ND 7-23, SD 12-2), June 15, 1983.

CQ Senate Votes 148 - 155

Corresponding to Congressional Record Votes 148, 149, 150, 151, 152, 153, 154, 155

KEY

Y Voted for (yea).
Paired for.
+ Announced for.
N Voted against (nay).
X Paired against.
- Announced against.
P Voted "present".
C Voted "present" to avoid possible conflict of interest.
? Did not vote or otherwise make a position known.

Democrats *Republicans*

ND - Northern Democrats   SD - Southern Democrats (Southern states - Ala., Ark., Fla., Ga., Ky., La., Miss., N.C., Okla., S.C., Tenn., Texas, Va.)

	148	149	150	151	152	153	154	155
ALABAMA								
Denton	Y	?	N	N	Y	N	N	?
Heflin	Y	N	N	N	N	N	Y	N
ALASKA								
Murkowski	Y	N	Y	N	Y	Y	N	Y
Stevens	Y	N	Y	?	Y	Y	N	Y
ARIZONA								
Goldwater	N	N	Y	Y	Y	Y	Y	?
DeConcini	Y	N	N	N	Y	Y	Y	N
ARKANSAS								
Bumpers	Y	N	N	N	N	Y	Y	N
Pryor	Y	N	N	N	N	N	Y	N
CALIFORNIA								
Wilson	N	N	N	N	N	Y	N	Y
Cranston	?	?	?	?	?	?	?	?
COLORADO								
Armstrong	N	N	?	N	N	N	N	Y
Hart	?	?	?	?	Y	Y	N	Y
CONNECTICUT								
Weicker	Y	N	Y	Y	N	Y	Y	Y
Dodd	Y	N	N	N	N	N	Y	N
DELAWARE								
Roth	Y	N	N	Y	Y	N	N	Y
Biden	Y	N	N	N	N	N	Y	?
FLORIDA								
Hawkins	Y	N	N	Y	Y	Y	Y	Y
Chiles	Y	N	N	Y	Y	Y	Y	N
GEORGIA								
Mattingly	N	N	N	N	N	Y	N	Y
Nunn	N	N	N	N	N	N	Y	N
HAWAII								
Inouye	Y	N	N	N	?	?	?	?
Matsunaga	N	N	N	N	Y	Y	Y	N
IDAHO								
McClure	N	N	N	N	N	Y	N	Y
Symms	N	N	N	N	N	Y	N	Y
ILLINOIS								
Percy	N	N	N	N	N	N	Y	N
Dixon	N	N	N	N	N	Y	Y	N
INDIANA								
Lugar	N	N	N	N	N	Y	N	Y
Quayle	N	N	N	N	Y	Y	N	Y

	148	149	150	151	152	153	154	155
IOWA								
Grassley	Y	N	N	N	N	N	N	Y
Jepsen	Y	N	N	N	N	N	N	Y
KANSAS								
Dole	N	N	N	N	Y	Y	N	Y
Kassebaum	N	?	N	N	Y	Y	N	Y
KENTUCKY								
Ford	Y	N	N	N	N	N	Y	N
Huddleston	Y	N	N	N	N	Y	Y	N
LOUISIANA								
Johnston	Y	N	N	N	N	Y	Y	N
Long	Y	N	N	Y	Y	Y	Y	N
MAINE								
Cohen	Y	N	N	N	N	N	N	Y
Mitchell	Y	N	N	N	N	N	Y	N
MARYLAND								
Mathias	Y	N	?	?	Y	Y	N	?
Sarbanes	Y	N	N	N	Y	Y	Y	N
MASSACHUSETTS								
Kennedy	Y	N	N	Y	Y	Y	Y	N
Tsongas	Y	N	N	Y	Y	Y	Y	N
MICHIGAN								
Levin	Y	N	N	N	N	Y	Y	N
Riegle	Y	N	N	N	N	Y	Y	N
MINNESOTA								
Boschwitz	Y	N	N	N	N	Y	N	?
Durenberger	Y	N	N	Y	Y	Y	N	Y
MISSISSIPPI								
Cochran	Y	N	N	N	N	Y	N	Y
Stennis	Y	N	N	Y	Y	Y	Y	N
MISSOURI								
Danforth	N	N	N	N	N	N	N	Y
Eagleton	Y	N	N	N	Y	Y	Y	N
MONTANA								
Baucus	Y	N	N	N	N	N	N	Y
Melcher	Y	N	N	N	Y	Y	Y	N
NEBRASKA								
Exon	Y	N	N	P	N	Y	Y	N
Zorinsky	N	N	N	P	N	Y	Y	N
NEVADA								
Hecht	N	N	N	N	N	N	N	Y
Laxalt	N	N	N	N	Y	Y	N	Y

	148	149	150	151	152	153	154	155
NEW HAMPSHIRE								
Humphrey	N	Y	N	N	N	N	N	Y
Rudman	N	N	Y	Y	Y	Y	N	Y
NEW JERSEY								
Bradley	Y	N	N	N	N	N	Y	N
Lautenberg	Y	N	N	Y	Y	Y	Y	N
NEW MEXICO								
Domenici	Y	N	N	N	N	Y	N	Y
Bingaman	Y	N	N	Y	Y	Y	Y	N
NEW YORK								
D'Amato	Y	N	N	N	Y	Y	N	Y
Moynihan	N	N	N	Y	Y	Y	Y	Y
NORTH CAROLINA								
East	N	N	N	N	N	N	N	Y
Helms	N	N	N	N	N	N	N	Y
NORTH DAKOTA								
Andrews	Y	N	N	N	N	Y	N	Y
Burdick	Y	N	N	Y	Y	Y	Y	N
OHIO								
Glenn	?	?	N	Y	Y	Y	Y	N
Metzenbaum	Y	N	N	Y	Y	Y	Y	N
OKLAHOMA								
Nickles	N	N	N	N	N	N	N	Y
Boren	Y	N	N	N	N	Y	Y	N
OREGON								
Hatfield	Y	N	N	Y	Y	Y	N	Y
Packwood	Y	N	N	Y	Y	Y	N	Y
PENNSYLVANIA								
Heinz	Y	N	N	N	N	Y	N	+
Specter	Y	N	N	N	N	N	N	Y
RHODE ISLAND								
Chafee	Y	N	N	Y	Y	Y	N	Y
Pell	Y	N	N	N	Y	Y	Y	Y
SOUTH CAROLINA								
Thurmond	Y	N	N	Y	Y	Y	N	Y
Hollings	Y	N	N	N	N	N	Y	N
SOUTH DAKOTA								
Abdnor	N	N	N	N	Y	N	Y	Y
Pressler	Y	N	N	N	N	N	N	Y
TENNESSEE								
Baker	N	N	N	N	Y	Y	N	Y
Sasser	Y	N	-	-	-	-	+	+

	148	149	150	151	152	153	154	155
TEXAS								
Tower	N	N	N	N	Y	N	Y	N
Bentsen	Y	N	N	N	Y	Y	Y	N
UTAH								
Garn	Y	N	N	N	Y	N	N	Y
Hatch	Y	N	N	N	Y	N	N	Y
VERMONT								
Stafford	Y	N	Y	Y	Y	Y	N	?
Leahy	Y	N	N	N	N	N	Y	N
VIRGINIA								
Trible	N	N	N	N	Y	N	N	Y
Warner	N	N	N	N	N	N	N	Y
WASHINGTON								
Gorton	N	N	N	N	N	Y	N	Y
Jackson	N	N	N	N	Y	Y	Y	N
WEST VIRGINIA								
Byrd	Y	N	N	N	Y	Y	Y	N
Randolph	Y	N	N	N	Y	Y	Y	N
WISCONSIN								
Kasten	N	N	N	N	N	Y	N	Y
Proxmire	N	Y	N	N	N	N	N	Y
WYOMING								
Simpson	Y	N	N	N	N	N	N	Y
Wallop	N	N	N	N	Y	Y	N	Y

148. HR 3069. Supplemental Appropriations, Fiscal 1983. Bumpers, D-Ark., amendment to provide an additional amount, up to $40 million, for the Chapter I program of compensatory education aid for the disadvantaged, to ensure that all states received allocations in fiscal 1983 equal to at least 95 percent of their fiscal 1982 allocation. Adopted 63-34: R 27-27; D 36-7 (ND 23-6, SD 13-1), June 15, 1983.

149. HR 3069. Supplemental Appropriations, Fiscal 1983. Humphrey, R-N.H., amendment to eliminate the authorization for construction of a flood control project on the Pearl River in Mississippi. Rejected 2-93: R 1-51; D 1-42 (ND 1-28, SD 0-14), June 15, 1983.

150. HR 3069. Supplemental Appropriations, Fiscal 1983. Weicker, R-Conn., amendment to raise senators' salaries to $100,000 a year and prohibit the acceptance of honoraria. Rejected 6-89: R 6-46; D 0-43 (ND 0-30, SD 0-13), June 16, 1983.

151. HR 3069. Supplemental Appropriations, Fiscal 1983. Jackson, D-Wash., amendment to raise senators' salaries to $80,100 and prohibit the acceptance of honoraria. Rejected 9-84: R 5-47; D 4-37 (ND 3-25, SD 1-12), June 16, 1983.

152. HR 3069. Supplemental Appropriations, Fiscal 1983. Jackson, D-Wash., amendment to raise senators' salaries to $69,800 beginning July 1, 1983, and, beginning Jan. 1, 1984, to limit the acceptance of honoraria to 30 percent of pay. Adopted 49-47: R 29-25; D 20-22 (ND 16-13, SD 4-9), June 16, 1983.

153. HR 3069. Supplemental Appropriations, Fiscal 1983. Passage of the bill to appropriate $16,058,698,582 in supplemental funds for fiscal 1983. Passed 64-33: R 35-19; D 29-14 (ND 22-8, SD 7-6), June 16, 1983. The president had requested $15,000,005,808.

154. HR 2973. Interest and Dividend Tax Withholding. Long, D-La., motion to table (kill) the Finance Committee amendment to repeal interest and dividend withholding requirements scheduled to take effect July 1, to impose new tax reporting requirements and penalties, to provide trade concessions to certain Central American nations, to strengthen the president's power to retaliate against foreign unfair trading practices, to allow special tax and regulatory relief for businesses in decaying neighborhoods, and to make permanent a current law allowing tax-exempt mortgage revenue bonds. Motion rejected 46-51: R 3-51; D 43-0 (ND 30-0, SD 13-0), June 16, 1983.

155. HR 2973. Interest and Dividend Tax Withholding. Baker, R-Tenn., motion to table (kill) the Pryor, D-Ark., amendment to delete provisions from the Finance Committee amendment that would provide trade concessions to certain Central American nations, strengthen the president's power to retaliate against foreign unfair trading practices, allow special tax and regulatory relief for businesses in decaying neighborhoods, and make permanent a current law allowing tax-exempt mortgage revenue bonds. Motion agreed to 50-40: R 48-0; D 2-40 (ND 2-27, SD 0-13), June 16, 1983. A "yea" was a vote supporting the president's position.

KEY

- Y Voted for (yea).
- # Paired for.
- + Announced for.
- N Voted against (nay).
- X Paired against.
- - Announced against.
- P Voted "present".
- C Voted "present" to avoid possible conflict of interest.
- ? Did not vote or otherwise make a position known.

Democrats   *Republicans*

	156	157	158	159	160	161	162	163
ALABAMA								
Denton	?	Y	Y	Y	Y	Y	N	Y
Heflin	N	Y	Y	Y	Y	Y	N	Y
ALASKA								
Murkowski	Y	Y	Y	Y	Y	Y	Y	Y
Stevens	Y	Y	Y	Y	Y	Y	Y	Y
ARIZONA								
Goldwater	?	?	Y	Y	Y	Y	N	N
DeConcini	N	Y	Y	Y	Y	N	N	Y
ARKANSAS								
Bumpers	N	Y	Y	Y	Y	N	Y	N
Pryor	N	Y	Y	Y	Y	Y	Y	N
CALIFORNIA								
Wilson	Y	Y	Y	Y	Y	Y	Y	N
Cranston	?	?	?	Y	Y	N	Y	N
COLORADO								
Armstrong	Y	Y	Y	Y	Y	Y	N	Y
Hart	N	Y	?	Y	Y	N	Y	-
CONNECTICUT								
Weicker	Y	Y	Y	Y	Y	N	Y	Y
Dodd	N	N	Y	Y	Y	N	Y	Y
DELAWARE								
Roth	Y	Y	Y	Y	Y	Y	N	N
Biden	?	?	Y	Y	Y	N	Y	N
FLORIDA								
Hawkins	Y	Y	Y	Y	Y	N	Y	Y
Chiles	N	Y	Y	Y	Y	Y	Y	Y
GEORGIA								
Mattingly	Y	Y	?	Y	Y	Y	Y	Y
Nunn	N	Y	Y	Y	Y	Y	Y	N
HAWAII								
Inouye	?	?	?	Y	Y	N	Y	Y
Matsunaga	N	Y	?	Y	Y	N	Y	Y
IDAHO								
McClure	Y	Y	Y	Y	Y	Y	Y	Y
Symms	Y	Y	?	N	N	Y	N	Y
ILLINOIS								
Percy	Y	Y	?	Y	Y	Y	Y	N
Dixon	N	Y	Y	Y	Y	N	Y	N
INDIANA								
Lugar	Y	Y	Y	Y	Y	Y	Y	N
Quayle	Y	Y	?	Y	Y	?	?	N

	156	157	158	159	160	161	162	163
IOWA								
Grassley	Y	Y	Y	Y	Y	Y	N	N
Jepsen	Y	Y	Y	Y	Y	Y	Y	N
KANSAS								
Dole	Y	Y	Y	Y	Y	Y	Y	Y
Kassebaum	Y	Y	Y	Y	Y	Y	Y	Y
KENTUCKY								
Ford	N	Y	Y	Y	Y	Y	N	Y
Huddleston	N	Y	?	Y	Y	Y	Y	Y
LOUISIANA								
Johnston	N	Y	Y	Y	Y	N	Y	Y
Long	N	Y	+	Y	Y	?	Y	Y
MAINE								
Cohen	Y	Y	Y	Y	Y	Y	Y	N
Mitchell	N	Y	?	Y	Y	Y	Y	Y
MARYLAND								
Mathias	?	?	Y	Y	Y	N	Y	Y
Sarbanes	N	Y	Y	Y	Y	N	Y	Y
MASSACHUSETTS								
Kennedy	N	N	Y	Y	Y	N	Y	?
Tsongas	N	Y	Y	Y	Y	N	Y	N
MICHIGAN								
Levin	N	Y	+	Y	Y	N	Y	N
Riegle	N	Y	Y	Y	Y	N	Y	Y
MINNESOTA								
Boschwitz	+	+	?	Y	Y	N	Y	N
Durenberger	Y	Y	Y	Y	Y	Y	Y	N
MISSISSIPPI								
Cochran	Y	Y	?	Y	Y	Y	Y	Y
Stennis	N	Y	Y	Y	Y	Y	Y	Y
MISSOURI								
Danforth	Y	Y	Y	Y	Y	?	?	Y
Eagleton	N	Y	Y	Y	Y	N	N	N
MONTANA								
Baucus	N	Y	?	Y	Y	N	Y	N
Melcher	N	Y	Y	Y	Y	N	Y	Y
NEBRASKA								
Exon	N	Y	Y	Y	Y	N	Y	N
Zorinsky	N	Y	Y	Y	Y	Y	Y	Y
NEVADA								
Hecht	Y	Y	Y	Y	Y	Y	Y	Y
Laxalt	Y	Y	Y	Y	Y	Y	Y	Y

	156	157	158	159	160	161	162	163
NEW HAMPSHIRE								
Humphrey	Y	Y	Y	N	Y	Y	N	N
Rudman	Y	Y	Y	Y	Y	Y	Y	N
NEW JERSEY								
Bradley	N	Y	?	Y	Y	N	Y	N
Lautenberg	N	N	Y	Y	Y	N	Y	N
NEW MEXICO								
Domenici	Y	Y	Y	Y	Y	Y	Y	Y
Bingaman	N	Y	Y	Y	Y	N	Y	N
NEW YORK								
D'Amato	Y	Y	Y	Y	Y	N	Y	Y
Moynihan	Y	Y	+	Y	Y	N	Y	Y
NORTH CAROLINA								
East	Y	Y	+	N	N	Y	N	Y
Helms	?	?	Y	N	N	Y	N	Y
NORTH DAKOTA								
Andrews	Y	Y	Y	Y	Y	Y	Y	Y
Burdick	N	Y	Y	Y	Y	N	Y	Y
OHIO								
Glenn	N	Y	?	?	?	?	?	Y
Metzenbaum	N	N	Y	Y	Y	N	Y	N
OKLAHOMA								
Nickles	Y	Y	Y	Y	Y	Y	?	N
Boren	N	Y	Y	Y	Y	N	N	Y
OREGON								
Hatfield	Y	Y	Y	Y	Y	Y	?	Y
Packwood	Y	Y	Y	Y	Y	Y	Y	Y
PENNSYLVANIA								
Heinz	?	?	Y	Y	Y	N	Y	N
Specter	Y	Y	Y	Y	Y	N	Y	Y
RHODE ISLAND								
Chafee	Y	Y	+	Y	Y	Y	Y	N
Pell	N	Y	Y	Y	Y	N	Y	N
SOUTH CAROLINA								
Thurmond	Y	Y	Y	Y	Y	Y	Y	Y
Hollings	N	Y	Y	?	?	?	?	?
SOUTH DAKOTA								
Abdnor	Y	Y	Y	Y	Y	Y	Y	Y
Pressler	Y	Y	?	Y	Y	?	Y	Y
TENNESSEE								
Baker	Y	Y	?	Y	Y	Y	Y	Y
Sasser	-	+	+	Y	Y	N	Y	Y

	156	157	158	159	160	161	162	163
TEXAS								
Tower	Y	Y	Y	Y	Y	Y	Y	Y
Bentsen	N	Y	Y	Y	Y	Y	Y	Y
UTAH								
Garn	Y	Y	?	Y	Y	Y	Y	Y
Hatch	Y	Y	Y	Y	Y	Y	Y	Y
VERMONT								
Stafford	?	?	Y	Y	Y	Y	Y	N
Leahy	N	Y	Y	Y	Y	N	Y	N
VIRGINIA								
Trible	Y	Y	Y	Y	Y	N	N	Y
Warner	Y	Y	Y	Y	Y	Y	Y	Y
WASHINGTON								
Gorton	Y	Y	Y	Y	Y	Y	Y	Y
Jackson	N	Y	Y	Y	Y	N	Y	Y
WEST VIRGINIA								
Byrd	N	Y	Y	Y	Y	N	Y	Y
Randolph	N	Y	+	Y	Y	N	Y	Y
WISCONSIN								
Kasten	Y	Y	Y	Y	Y	N	Y	N
Proxmire	N	Y	Y	Y	Y	N	N	N
WYOMING								
Simpson	Y	Y	Y	Y	Y	Y	Y	Y
Wallop	Y	Y	Y	Y	Y	Y	Y	Y

ND - Northern Democrats   SD - Southern Democrats (Southern states - Ala., Ark., Fla., Ga., Ky., La., Miss., N.C., Okla., S.C., Tenn., Texas, Va.)

156. HR 2973. Interest and Dividend Tax Withholding. Finance Committee substitute to repeal interest and dividend withholding requirements scheduled to take effect July 1, to impose new tax reporting requirements and penalties, to provide trade concessions to certain Central American nations, to strengthen the president's power to retaliate against foreign unfair trading practices, to allow special tax and regulatory relief for businesses in decaying neighborhoods, and to make permanent a current law allowing tax-exempt mortgage revenue bonds. Adopted 48-41: R 47-0; D 1-41 (ND 1-28, SD 0-13), June 16, 1983.

157. HR 2973. Interest and Dividend Tax Withholding. Passage of the bill to repeal interest and dividend withholding requirements scheduled to take effect July 1, to impose new tax reporting requirements and penalties, to provide trade concessions to certain Central American nations, to strengthen the president's power to retaliate against foreign unfair trading practices, to allow special tax and regulatory relief for businesses in decaying neighborhoods, and to make permanent a current law allowing tax-exempt mortgage revenue bonds. Passed 86-4: R 48-0; D 38-4 (ND 25-4, SD 13-0), June 16, 1983.

158. S 336. Labor Management Racketeering Act. Passage of the bill to increase penalties for labor and management officials found to have engaged in bribery and other corrupt practices and to prohibit union officials convicted of crimes from holding union office during appeal of such convictions. Passed 75-0: R 43-0; D 32-0 (ND 21-0, SD 11-0), June 20, 1983.

159. Treaties. Adoption of the resolutions of ratification for **Exec W, 96th Cong, 1st Sess,** Treaty of Friendship with Tuvalu; **Exec A, 96th Cong, 2nd Sess,** Treaty of Friendship with the Republic of Kiribati; **Exec P, 96th Cong, 2nd Sess,** Treaty with the Cook Islands on Friendship and Delimitation of the Maritime Boundary; and **Treaty Doc 97-5,** Treaty with New Zealand on the Delimitation of the Maritime Boundary Between the United States and Tokelau. Adopted en bloc 94-4: R 50-4; D 44-0 (ND 31-0, SD 13-0), June 21, 1983. A two-thirds majority of those present and voting (66 in this case) is required for adoption of resolutions of ratification. A "yea" was a vote supporting the president's position.

160. Treaties. Adoption of the resolutions of ratification for **Treaty Doc 97-19,** the Constitution of the United Nations Industrial Development Organization and **Treaty Doc 97-23,** the International Convention on the Simplification and Harmonization of Customs Procedures. Adopted en bloc 94-4: R 50-4; D 44-0 (ND 31-0, SD 13-0), June 21, 1983. A two-thirds majority of those present and voting (66 in this case) is required for adoption of resolutions of ratification.

161. HR 3133. Department of Housing and Urban Development Appropriations, Fiscal 1984. Garn, R-Utah, motion to table (kill) the Heinz, R-Pa., amendment to establish a mortgage aid program of federal loan guarantees for unemployed homeowners. Motion agreed to 55-39: R 43-8; D 12-31 (ND 4-27, SD 8-4), June 21, 1983.

162. HR 3133. Department of Housing and Urban Development Appropriations, Fiscal 1984. Passage of the bill to appropriate $54,252,397,810 for the Department of Housing and Urban Development, Environmental Protection Agency, Veterans Administration and independent agencies in fiscal 1984. Passed 80-14: R 41-9; D 39-5 (ND 28-3, SD 11-2), June 21, 1983. The president had requested $49,599,358,896 in new budget authority.

163. HR 3132. Energy and Water Development Appropriations, Fiscal 1984. Hatfield, R-Ore., motion to table (kill) the Humphrey, R-N.H., amendment to delete $22.3 million for construction of the Garrison Diversion unit in North Dakota. Motion agreed to 62-35: R 37-17; D 25-18 (ND 15-15, SD 10-3), June 22, 1983.

KEY

- Y Voted for (yea).
- # Paired for.
- + Announced for.
- N Voted against (nay).
- X Paired against.
- - Announced against.
- P Voted "present".
- C Voted "present" to avoid possible conflict of interest.
- ? Did not vote or otherwise make a position known.

Democrats   *Republicans*

	164	165	166	167	168
ALABAMA					
Denton	Y	Y	Y	Y	N
Heflin	Y	N	N	N	N
ALASKA					
Murkowski	Y	+	+	+	#
Stevens	Y	Y	Y	N	Y
ARIZONA					
Goldwater	Y	?	Y	N	N
DeConcini	Y	N	N	N	N
ARKANSAS					
Bumpers	Y	N	Y	N	Y
Pryor	Y	N	Y	N	Y
CALIFORNIA					
Wilson	Y	N	Y	Y	N
Cranston	Y	N	Y	N	Y
COLORADO					
Armstrong	Y	N	N	Y	N
Hart	?	?	?	?	Y
CONNECTICUT					
Weicker	Y	N	Y	N	Y
Dodd	Y	Y	Y	N	Y
DELAWARE					
Roth	Y	N	Y	Y	N
Biden	Y	Y	Y	N	Y
FLORIDA					
Hawkins	Y	Y	N	Y	N
Chiles	Y	N	Y	N	Y
GEORGIA					
Mattingly	Y	Y	Y	Y	N
Nunn	Y	N	Y	Y	N
HAWAII					
Inouye	Y	N	Y	N	Y
Matsunaga	Y	N	Y	N	Y
IDAHO					
McClure	Y	Y	Y	Y	N
Symms	Y	N	N	Y	N
ILLINOIS					
Percy	Y	?	?	?	X
Dixon	Y	N	Y	N	Y
INDIANA					
Lugar	Y	N	Y	Y	N
Quayle	Y	N	N	Y	N

	164	165	166	167	168
IOWA					
Grassley	Y	N	N	?	N
Jepsen	Y	N	Y	N	Y
KANSAS					
Dole	Y	Y	Y	Y	N
Kassebaum	Y	Y	Y	N	Y
KENTUCKY					
Ford	Y	N	Y	N	Y
Huddleston	Y	Y	Y	N	Y
LOUISIANA					
Johnston	Y	N	Y	N	N
Long	Y	N	Y	Y	N
MAINE					
Cohen	Y	Y	?	Y	Y
Mitchell	Y	Y	Y	N	Y
MARYLAND					
Mathias	?	?	?	N	Y
Sarbanes	Y	Y	Y	N	Y
MASSACHUSETTS					
Kennedy	Y	N	Y	N	Y
Tsongas	Y	N	Y	?	?
MICHIGAN					
Levin	Y	N	Y	N	Y
Riegle	Y	Y	Y	N	Y
MINNESOTA					
Boschwitz	Y	N	Y	N	Y
Durenberger	Y	N	Y	Y	N
MISSISSIPPI					
Cochran	Y	N	Y	Y	Y
Stennis	Y	N	Y	N	Y
MISSOURI					
Danforth	Y	N	Y	N	Y
Eagleton	N	N	Y	N	Y
MONTANA					
Baucus	Y	Y	N	Y	N
Melcher	Y	?	Y	Y	N
NEBRASKA					
Exon	Y	N	Y	N	Y
Zorinsky	Y	Y	N	Y	N
NEVADA					
Hecht	Y	Y	Y	Y	N
Laxalt	Y	?	Y	Y	N

	164	165	166	167	168
NEW HAMPSHIRE					
Humphrey	N	N	N	Y	N
Rudman	Y	N	Y	Y	Y
NEW JERSEY					
Bradley	Y	N	Y	N	Y
Lautenberg	Y	N	Y	N	Y
NEW MEXICO					
Domenici	Y	Y	Y	N	Y
Bingaman	Y	N	Y	N	Y
NEW YORK					
D'Amato	Y	Y	Y	Y	Y
Moynihan	N	Y	Y	N	Y
NORTH CAROLINA					
East	Y	N	N	Y	N
Helms	Y	N	N	Y	N
NORTH DAKOTA					
Andrews	Y	N	Y	N	Y
Burdick	Y	N	Y	N	Y
OHIO					
Glenn	Y	N	Y	N	Y
Metzenbaum	Y	N	Y	N	Y
OKLAHOMA					
Nickles	Y	N	N	Y	N
Boren	Y	N	Y	N	N
OREGON					
Hatfield	Y	Y	Y	N	Y
Packwood	Y	Y	Y	N	Y
PENNSYLVANIA					
Heinz	Y	N	Y	Y	Y
Specter	Y	Y	Y	Y	N
RHODE ISLAND					
Chafee	Y	N	Y	N	Y
Pell	N	N	Y	N	Y
SOUTH CAROLINA					
Thurmond	Y	Y	Y	Y	N
Hollings	?	?	?	?	?
SOUTH DAKOTA					
Abdnor	Y	Y	Y	Y	N
Pressler	Y	Y	Y	?	?
TENNESSEE					
Baker	Y	Y	?	Y	Y
Sasser	Y	N	Y	N	Y

	164	165	166	167	168
TEXAS					
Tower	N	Y	Y	N	N
Bentsen	Y	N	Y	N	N
UTAH					
Garn	Y	Y	N	Y	N
Hatch	Y	Y	N	Y	N
VERMONT					
Stafford	Y	N	Y	N	Y
Leahy	Y	Y	Y	N	Y
VIRGINIA					
Trible	Y	N	Y	Y	N
Warner	Y	N	Y	Y	N
WASHINGTON					
Gorton	Y	N	Y	N	Y
Jackson	Y	N	Y	N	Y
WEST VIRGINIA					
Byrd	Y	N	Y	N	Y
Randolph	Y	N	Y	N	Y
WISCONSIN					
Kasten	Y	Y	Y	Y	N
Proxmire	N	N	N	Y	N
WYOMING					
Simpson	Y	Y	Y	?	+
Wallop	Y	Y	Y	Y	N

ND - Northern Democrats   SD - Southern Democrats (Southern states - Ala., Ark., Fla., Ga., Ky., La., Miss., N.C., Okla., S.C., Tenn., Texas, Va.)

164. HR 3132. Energy and Water Development Appropriations, Fiscal 1984. Passage of the bill to appropriate $14,170,853,000 for energy and water development in fiscal 1984. Passed 91-6: R 51-2; D 40-4 (ND 27-4, SD 13-0), June 22, 1983. The president had requested $14,610,671,000 in new budget authority.

165. HR 3135. Legislative Branch Appropriations, Fiscal 1984. Garn, R-Utah, amendment to place a senator's unearned income above 30 percent of his or her annual salary in a restricted trust fund while the senator is in office. Rejected 34-58: R 24-25; D 10-33 (ND 9-21, SD 1-12), June 23, 1983.

166. HR 3135. Legislative Branch Appropriations, Fiscal 1984. Passage of the bill to appropriate $1,475,986,000 for the legislative branch in fiscal 1984. Passed 78-15: R 38-11; D 40-4 (ND 28-3, SD 12-1), June 23, 1983. The president had requested $1,495,478,200 in new budget authority. Traditionally, the president simply requests the amount congressional agencies want included in the budget.

167. H Con Res 91. First Budget Resolution, Fiscal 1984. Dole, R-Kan., amendment to the conference version of the resolution to require the Finance Committee to recommend fiscal 1984-86 revenue increases of $59 billion, rather than $73 billion, and to extend the committee's reporting deadline to Sept. 15. Rejected 41-51: R 34-15; D 7-36 (ND 4-26, SD 3-10), June 23, 1983.

168. H Con Res 91. First Budget Resolution, Fiscal 1984. Baker, R-Tenn., motion to approve the substitute resolution, agreed to by House-Senate conferees but reported in technical disagreement, to set budget targets for the fiscal year ending Sept. 30, 1984, as follows *(totals including reserve fund items in parentheses)*: budget authority, $919.5 billion ($928.725 billion); outlays, $849.5 billion ($858.925 billion); revenues, $679.6 billion; deficit, $169.9 billion ($179.325 billion). The resolution also set preliminary goals for fiscal 1985-86, revised budget levels for fiscal 1983, and included reconciliation instructions requiring House and Senate committees to recommend legislative savings to meet the budget targets. Other provisions established appropriate levels for the public debt and set non-binding limits on federal credit activity. Motion agreed to 51-43: R 19-31; D 32-12 (ND 25-6, SD 7-6), June 23, 1983.

	169	170	171	172	173	174	175	176
ALABAMA								
Denton	Y	N	N	?	Y	N	Y	Y
Heflin	Y	N	N	N	N	N	Y	Y
ALASKA								
Murkowski	Y	N	Y	Y	N	Y	N	?
Stevens	N	N	#	?	?	?	+	+
ARIZONA								
Goldwater	N	N	Y	Y	Y	?	?	+
DeConcini	Y	Y	N	N	N	Y	Y	Y
ARKANSAS								
Bumpers	N	Y	Y	N	N	Y	Y	N
Pryor	N	Y	Y	N	N	Y	Y	Y
CALIFORNIA								
Wilson	N	N	Y	Y	Y	N	Y	Y
Cranston	N	Y	Y	N	N	Y	Y	N
COLORADO								
Armstrong	Y	N	N	Y	Y	Y	N	Y
Hart	N	Y	Y	N	N	N	?	?
CONNECTICUT								
Weicker	N	N	Y	Y	N	N	?	?
Dodd	N	Y	Y	Y	N	Y	Y	Y
DELAWARE								
Roth	N	N	N	Y	N	N	N	Y
Biden	N	Y	Y	Y	N	Y	Y	N
FLORIDA								
Hawkins	Y	N	Y	Y	N	Y	Y	Y
Chiles	Y	Y	Y	Y	N	N	N	N
GEORGIA								
Mattingly	Y	N	Y	Y	N	Y	N	Y
Nunn	Y	Y	N	Y	N	N	N	N
HAWAII								
Inouye	N	Y	Y	?	N	Y	Y	Y
Matsunaga	N	Y	Y	Y	N	Y	Y	Y
IDAHO								
McClure	Y	N	Y	Y	Y	Y	Y	Y
Symms	Y	N	X	Y	Y	Y	Y	N
ILLINOIS								
Percy	N	N	?	Y	N	Y	N	Y
Dixon	N	Y	Y	N	N	N	Y	Y
INDIANA								
Lugar	Y	N	Y	Y	Y	Y	N	Y
Quayle	Y	N	Y	Y	Y	Y	N	Y
IOWA								
Grassley	Y	N	N	N	Y	Y	Y	Y
Jepsen	Y	N	Y	N	N	Y	Y	Y
KANSAS								
Dole	Y	N	Y	Y	N	N	N	Y
Kassebaum	N	N	Y	Y	N	Y	Y	Y
KENTUCKY								
Ford	Y	Y	Y	N	N	Y	Y	Y
Huddleston	Y	Y	Y	N	N	Y	Y	Y
LOUISIANA								
Johnston	Y	N	Y	N	N	Y	Y	Y
Long	Y	Y	Y	N	N	Y	Y	Y
MAINE								
Cohen	N	Y	Y	Y	N	Y	Y	Y
Mitchell	N	Y	Y	Y	N	Y	Y	N
MARYLAND								
Mathias	N	N	Y	Y	N	N	N	N
Sarbanes	N	Y	Y	N	N	Y	N	Y
MASSACHUSETTS								
Kennedy	N	Y	Y	N	Y	N	Y	N
Tsongas	N	Y	Y	Y	N	Y	Y	Y
MICHIGAN								
Levin	N	Y	Y	Y	N	Y	Y	Y
Riegle	N	Y	Y	Y	N	Y	Y	Y
MINNESOTA								
Boschwitz	Y	N	Y	N	?	Y	Y	Y
Durenberger	Y	N	Y	N	N	Y	Y	Y
MISSISSIPPI								
Cochran	Y	N	Y	Y	N	N	Y	Y
Stennis	Y	Y	Y	N	N	N	Y	Y
MISSOURI								
Danforth	Y	N	Y	N	Y	N	Y	N
Eagleton	Y	Y	N	N	N	N	Y	N
MONTANA								
Baucus	N	Y	N	N	N	Y	Y	N
Melcher	Y	Y	Y	N	Y	Y	Y	Y
NEBRASKA								
Exon	Y	Y	Y	N	N	Y	Y	Y
Zorinsky	Y	N	Y	N	Y	N	Y	Y
NEVADA								
Hecht	Y	N	Y	Y	Y	Y	N	N
Laxalt	Y	N	Y	Y	Y	N	Y	Y
NEW HAMPSHIRE								
Humphrey	Y	N	N	Y	Y	Y	N	N
Rudman	N	N	Y	Y	N	Y	Y	Y
NEW JERSEY								
Bradley	N	Y	Y	Y	N	Y	Y	Y
Lautenberg	N	Y	Y	Y	N	Y	Y	Y
NEW MEXICO								
Domenici	Y	N	Y	Y	N	N	Y	Y
Bingaman	N	Y	Y	N	N	Y	Y	Y
NEW YORK								
D'Amato	Y	N	Y	Y	N	Y	Y	Y
Moynihan	N	Y	Y	Y	N	Y	N	Y
NORTH CAROLINA								
East	Y	N	N	Y	Y	N	N	Y
Helms	P	N	N	Y	Y	N	N	Y
NORTH DAKOTA								
Andrews	Y	N	Y	N	N	Y	Y	Y
Burdick	N	Y	Y	N	N	Y	Y	Y
OHIO								
Glenn	N	Y	Y	N	Y	Y	Y	Y
Metzenbaum	N	Y	Y	N	Y	Y	Y	N
OKLAHOMA								
Nickles	Y	N	N	N	Y	N	N	Y
Boren	N	N	N	N	N	Y	Y	Y
OREGON								
Hatfield	Y	N	Y	Y	N	Y	Y	Y
Packwood	N	N	Y	N	Y	Y	Y	Y
PENNSYLVANIA								
Heinz	N	Y	Y	Y	N	N	Y	Y
Specter	N	Y	Y	Y	N	Y	Y	Y
RHODE ISLAND								
Chafee	N	N	Y	Y	N	Y	Y	Y
Pell	N	Y	Y	Y	N	Y	N	N
SOUTH CAROLINA								
Thurmond	Y	N	Y	Y	Y	N	Y	Y
Hollings	N	Y	?	?	?	?	?	?
SOUTH DAKOTA								
Abdnor	Y	N	Y	N	Y	N	Y	Y
Pressler	Y	N	Y	N	N	Y	Y	Y
TENNESSEE								
Baker	Y	N	Y	Y	N	N	Y	Y
Sasser	N	Y	Y	Y	N	Y	Y	Y

	169	170	171	172	173	174	175	176
TEXAS								
Tower	N	N	Y	Y	Y	N	Y	Y
Bentsen	N	Y	Y	N	N	N	Y	Y
UTAH								
Garn	Y	N	Y	Y	N	N	N	Y
Hatch	Y	N	Y	Y	Y	N	Y	Y
VERMONT								
Stafford	N	N	Y	Y	N	N	Y	Y
Leahy	N	Y	N	Y	N	Y	Y	Y
VIRGINIA								
Trible	Y	N	Y	Y	Y	N	N	Y
Warner	Y	N	Y	Y	Y	N	Y	Y
WASHINGTON								
Gorton	N	N	Y	Y	N	Y	N	Y
Jackson	N	Y	Y	N	N	Y	Y	Y
WEST VIRGINIA								
Byrd	N	Y	Y	N	N	Y	Y	Y
Randolph	Y	Y	Y	N	N	Y	Y	Y
WISCONSIN								
Kasten	Y	N	Y	N	Y	N	Y	Y
Proxmire	Y	Y	N	Y	N	N	N	N
WYOMING								
Simpson	N	N	Y	Y	N	Y	N	Y
Wallop	N	N	Y	Y	N	N	N	Y

KEY

- Y Voted for (yea).
- # Paired for.
- + Announced for.
- N Voted against (nay).
- X Paired against.
- - Announced against.
- P Voted "present".
- C Voted "present" to avoid possible conflict of interest.
- ? Did not vote or otherwise make a position known.

Democrats   *Republicans*

ND - Northern Democrats   SD - Southern Democrats (Southern states - Ala., Ark., Fla., Ga., Ky., La., Miss., N.C., Okla., S.C., Tenn., Texas, Va.)

169. S J Res 3. Human Life Federalism Amendment. Passage of the joint resolution to propose an amendment to the Constitution that would overturn the 1973 Supreme Court decision, *Roe v. Wade*, which made abortion legal. Rejected 49-50: R 34-19; D 15-31 (ND 7-25, SD 8-6), June 28, 1983. A two-thirds majority of those present and voting (67 in this case) of both houses is required for passage of a joint resolution proposing an amendment to the Constitution. A "yea" was a vote supporting the president's position.

170. HR 1183. Tax Rate Equity Act. Passage of the bill to place a $720 per family limit on the 10 percent individual income tax cut scheduled for July 1, 1983. Rejected 45-55: R 3-51; D 42-4 (ND 31-1, SD 11-3), June 29, 1983. A "nay" was a vote supporting the president's position.

171. HR 3133. Department of Housing and Urban Development Appropriations, Fiscal 1984. Adoption of the conference report on the bill to appropriate $55,789,340,000 for the Department of Housing and Urban Development and 17 independent agencies in fiscal 1984. Adopted 79-17: R 42-9; D 37-8 (ND 27-5, SD 10-3), June 29, 1983. The president had requested $49,561,458,896 in new budget authority.

172. HR 3223. Agriculture Appropriations, Fiscal 1984. Baker, R-Tenn., motion to table (kill) the Zorinsky, D-Neb., amendment to require the Commodity Credit Corporation to pay farmers, for storage costs on stocks in the producer reserve program, at the same rate that the corporation pays for commercial storage of stocks it owns. Motion agreed to 63-33: R 44-8; D 19-25 (ND 15-16, SD 4-9), June 29, 1983.

173. HR 3223. Agriculture Appropriations, Fiscal 1984. Helms, R-N.C., amendment to strike from the bill the dates by which appropriated funds for child nutrition, women, infants and children (WIC) and food stamp programs would have to be spent. (The effect of the amendment would have been to require that the amounts appropriated for the three programs would be applied for a full fiscal year, instead of the shorter periods provided by the legislation.) Rejected 24-73: R 23-29; D 1-44 (ND 1-31, SD 0-13), June 29, 1983. A "yea" was a vote supporting the president's position.

174. HR 3223. Agriculture Appropriations, Fiscal 1984. Boschwitz, R-Minn.-Boren, D-Okla., amendment to increase funding for Food for Peace (PL 480) programs by $96 million. Adopted 61-36: R 27-25; D 34-11 (ND 26-6, SD 8-5), June 29, 1983.

175. HR 3223. Agriculture Appropriations, Fiscal 1984. Passage of the bill to appropriate $34,804,155,000 for the Agriculture Department, the Food and Drug Administration and the Commodity Futures Trading Commission in fiscal 1984. Passed 77-18: R 38-13; D 39-5 (ND 28-3, SD 11-2), June 29, 1983. The president had requested $34,083,299,000 in new budget authority.

176. HR 3132. Energy and Water Development Appropriations, Fiscal 1984. Adoption of the conference report on the bill to appropriate $14,307,045,000 for energy and water development in fiscal 1984. Adopted (thus cleared for the president) 82-12: R 48-2; D 34-10 (ND 22-9, SD 12-1), June 29, 1983. The president had requested $14,610,671,000 in new budget authority.

	177	178	179	180	181	182	183	184
ALABAMA								
Denton	Y	Y	N	Y	Y	Y	Y	Y
Heflin	Y	Y	Y	Y	Y	N	N	Y
ALASKA								
Murkowski	?	?	?	+	+	-	+	-
Stevens	Y	Y	Y	Y	Y	Y	N	Y
ARIZONA								
Goldwater	N	Y	N	?	?	?	?	?
DeConcini	Y	N	Y	N	Y	N	N	N
ARKANSAS								
Bumpers	Y	N	Y	N	Y	N	N	Y
Pryor	Y	N	Y	N	N	N	N	N
CALIFORNIA								
Wilson	Y	Y	Y	Y	Y	Y	Y	Y
Cranston	Y	N	Y	N	Y	N	N	N
COLORADO								
Armstrong	Y	Y	Y	Y	Y	Y	N	Y
Hart	?	?	?	N	N	N	N	N
CONNECTICUT								
Weicker	?	N	Y	N	Y	N	Y	?
Dodd	Y	N	Y	N	N	N	N	N
DELAWARE								
Roth	Y	Y	Y	N	Y	N	Y	N
Biden	Y	N	Y	N	N	N	N	N
FLORIDA								
Hawkins	Y	N	Y	Y	Y	Y	N	N
Chiles	Y	N	Y	N	Y	N	Y	N
GEORGIA								
Mattingly	Y	Y	Y	Y	Y	Y	Y	Y
Nunn	Y	Y	Y	Y	N	Y	N	Y
HAWAII								
Inouye	Y	N	Y	N	Y	N	N	N
Matsunaga	Y	N	Y	N	N	N	N	N
IDAHO								
McClure	Y	Y	N	Y	Y	Y	Y	Y
Symms	Y	Y	N	Y	Y	Y	Y	Y
ILLINOIS								
Percy	Y	N	Y	N	Y	N	Y	N
Dixon	Y	Y	+	Y	Y	N	N	
INDIANA								
Lugar	Y	Y	Y	Y	Y	Y	Y	Y
Quayle	N	?	?	Y	Y	Y	Y	Y
IOWA								
Grassley	Y	Y	Y	N	Y	Y	Y	N
Jepsen	Y	Y	Y	Y	Y	Y	Y	N
KANSAS								
Dole	N	Y	Y	Y	Y	Y	N	Y
Kassebaum	Y	Y	Y	N	N	Y	Y	N
KENTUCKY								
Ford	Y	Y	Y	N	Y	N	N	N
Huddleston	Y	N	Y	N	Y	N	N	N
LOUISIANA								
Johnston	Y	N	Y	N	Y	N	N	Y
Long	?	?	?	Y	Y	N	Y	N
MAINE								
Cohen	Y	Y	Y	Y	Y	N	Y	N
Mitchell	Y	N	Y	N	N	N	N	N
MARYLAND								
Mathias	Y	N	Y	N	Y	N	N	N
Sarbanes	Y	N	Y	N	N	N	N	N
MASSACHUSETTS								
Kennedy	?	-	+	N	N	N	N	N
Tsongas	Y	N	Y	N	N	N	N	N
MICHIGAN								
Levin	Y	N	Y	N	Y	N	N	N
Riegle	Y	N	Y	N	N	N	N	N
MINNESOTA								
Boschwitz	Y	N	Y	Y	Y	Y	Y	N
Durenberger	Y	N	Y	N	Y	Y	Y	N
MISSISSIPPI								
Cochran	Y	Y	Y	N	Y	N	Y	Y
Stennis	Y	?	?	Y	Y	N	Y	N
MISSOURI								
Danforth	Y	N	Y	N	Y	N	N	N
Eagleton	Y	N	Y	N	N	N	Y	N
MONTANA								
Baucus	Y	N	Y	N	N	N	N	N
Melcher	Y	N	Y	N	Y	N	N	N
NEBRASKA								
Exon	Y	Y	Y	Y	Y	Y	Y	N
Zorinsky	Y	Y	Y	Y	Y	Y	Y	Y
NEVADA								
Hecht	Y	Y	Y	Y	Y	Y	Y	Y
Laxalt	Y	Y	Y	Y	Y	Y	Y	N
NEW HAMPSHIRE								
Humphrey	Y	Y	Y	Y	Y	Y	N	Y
Rudman	Y	Y	Y	Y	Y	Y	Y	Y
NEW JERSEY								
Bradley	Y	N	Y	N	N	N	N	N
Lautenberg	Y	N	Y	N	N	N	Y	N
NEW MEXICO								
Domenici	Y	Y	Y	Y	Y	N	Y	N
Bingaman	Y	N	Y	N	N	N	Y	N
NEW YORK								
D'Amato	Y	Y	Y	Y	Y	Y	N	N
Moynihan	Y	N	Y	N	Y	N	N	N
NORTH CAROLINA								
East	Y	Y	N	Y	Y	Y	Y	Y
Helms	Y	Y	N	Y	Y	Y	Y	Y
NORTH DAKOTA								
Andrews	Y	N	Y	N	Y	N	N	N
Burdick	Y	N	Y	N	Y	N	N	N
OHIO								
Glenn	Y	N	Y	N	Y	N	N	N
Metzenbaum	Y	N	Y	N	Y	N	Y	N
OKLAHOMA								
Nickles	Y	Y	Y	Y	Y	Y	Y	N
Boren	Y	N	Y	N	Y	?	N	N
OREGON								
Hatfield	?	-	?	N	N	Y	N	N
Packwood	Y	N	Y	N	Y	N	Y	N
PENNSYLVANIA								
Heinz	Y	N	Y	N	Y	N	N	N
Specter	Y	N	Y	N	Y	N	N	N
RHODE ISLAND								
Chafee	Y	Y	Y	N	N	N	Y	N
Pell	?	-	+	N	N	N	N	N
SOUTH CAROLINA								
Thurmond	Y	Y	Y	Y	Y	Y	Y	Y
Hollings	?	?	?	Y	N	N	N	N
SOUTH DAKOTA								
Abdnor	Y	Y	Y	Y	Y	Y	Y	Y
Pressler	Y	N	Y	N	N	Y	N	N
TENNESSEE								
Baker	Y	Y	Y	Y	Y	Y	Y	Y
Sasser	Y	N	Y	N	Y	N	N	N
TEXAS								
Tower	Y	Y	Y	Y	Y	Y	Y	Y
Bentsen	Y	Y	Y	Y	Y	N	Y	N
UTAH								
Garn	N	Y	Y	Y	Y	Y	N	Y
Hatch	Y	Y	Y	Y	Y	Y	N	Y
VERMONT								
Stafford	Y	Y	Y	N	Y	N	Y	N
Leahy	Y	N	Y	N	N	N	Y	N
VIRGINIA								
Trible	Y	Y	Y	Y	Y	Y	N	Y
Warner	Y	Y	Y	Y	Y	Y	Y	Y
WASHINGTON								
Gorton	Y	Y	Y	N	Y	N	N	N
Jackson	Y	Y	Y	Y	Y	N	N	N
WEST VIRGINIA								
Byrd	Y	Y	Y	N	N	N	N	N
Randolph	?	-	+	N	Y	N	N	N
WISCONSIN								
Kasten	Y	Y	Y	Y	Y	Y	N	N
Proxmire	N	N	Y	N	N	Y	N	N
WYOMING								
Simpson	Y	Y	Y	Y	Y	Y	Y	Y
Wallop	Y	?	N	Y	Y	Y	Y	Y

KEY

Y Voted for (yea).
\# Paired for.
+ Announced for.
N Voted against (nay).
X Paired against.
- Announced against.
P Voted "present".
C Voted "present" to avoid possible conflict of interest.
? Did not vote or otherwise make a position known.

Democrats *Republicans*

ND - Northern Democrats   SD - Southern Democrats (Southern states - Ala., Ark., Fla., Ga., Ky., La., Miss., N.C., Okla., S.C., Tenn., Texas, Va.)

177. S 675. Omnibus Defense Authorizations. Baker, R-Tenn., motion to instruct the sergeant-at-arms to request the attendance of absent senators. Motion agreed to 86-5: R 47-4; D 39-1 (ND 27-1, SD 12-0), July 12, 1983.

178. S 675. Omnibus Defense Authorizations. Tower, R-Texas, amendment to permit the use of funds to build a production line for a neutron bomb-type artillery shell, if it is certified by the president as being essential to national security. Adopted 47-42: R 38-12; D 9-30 (ND 5-23, SD 4-7), July 12, 1983. A "yea" was a vote supporting the president's position.

179. S 675. Omnibus Defense Authorizations. Specter, R-Pa., amendment providing that it is the sense of the Senate that the U.S. president and the Soviet president should meet as soon as it is practicable to discuss major issues in U.S.-Soviet relations and to work for mutual, equitable and verifiable nuclear arms reductions. Adopted 82-7: R 44-7; D 38-0 (ND 27-0, SD 11-0), July 12, 1983.

180. S 675. Omnibus Defense Authorizations. Tower, R-Texas, motion to table (kill) the Pryor, D-Ark., amendment to prohibit the production of lethal binary chemical munitions and related production facilities. Motion agreed to 50-49: R 35-17; D 14-32 (ND 5-27, SD 9-5), July 13, 1983, with Vice President Bush casting a "yea" vote to break the 49-49 tie. A "yea" was a vote supporting the president's position.

181. S 675. Omnibus Defense Authorizations. Tower, R-Texas, motion to table (kill) the Kennedy, D-Mass., amendment to delete funding for the B-1B bomber and to seek a supplemental budget request for additional funding for the Stealth bomber program. Motion agreed to 68-30: R 47-5; D 21-25 (ND 13-19, SD 8-6), July 13, 1983. A "yea" was a vote supporting the president's position.

182. S 675. Omnibus Defense Authorizations. Tower, R-Texas, motion to table (kill) the Mitchell, D-Maine, amendment to extend for two years the prohibition against contracts for the performance of firefighting and security forces at certain military installations. Motion rejected 44-53: R 40-12; D 4-41 (ND 4-28, SD 0-13), July 13, 1983.

183. S 675. Omnibus Defense Authorizations. Baker, R-Tenn., motion to table (kill) the Armstrong, R-Colo., motion to waive the Congressional Budget Act of 1974 to allow consideration of the Armstrong amendment to provide certain educational benefits for military veterans. Motion agreed to 52-46: R 38-14; D 14-32 (ND 7-25, SD 7-7), July 13, 1983. (The amendment subsequently was ruled not in order because it was in violation of the budget act.) A "yea" was a vote supporting the president's position.

184. S 675. Omnibus Defense Authorizations. Warner, R-Va., motion to table (kill) the Nunn, D-Ga.-Johnston, D-La., amendment to prohibit the use of funds for constructing a production facility for neutron bomb-type artillery shells, but authorizing $50 million for procurement, research and development of improved conventional munitions. Motion rejected 30-67: R 28-23; D 2-44 (ND 1-31, SD 1-13), July 13, 1983. A "yea" was a vote supporting the president's position.

	185	186	187	188	189	190	191
ALABAMA							
Denton	Y	Y	Y	Y	Y	Y	Y
Heflin	Y	N	Y	Y	Y	Y	Y
ALASKA							
Murkowski	+	Y	Y	Y	Y	Y	Y
Stevens	Y	Y	N	Y	Y	Y	Y
ARIZONA							
Goldwater	?	?	?	?	?	?	?
DeConcini	N	Y	Y	Y	Y	N	Y
ARKANSAS							
Bumpers	N	N	Y	Y	Y	N	Y
Pryor	N	N	Y	Y	N	N	Y
CALIFORNIA							
Wilson	Y	Y	Y	Y	Y	Y	Y
Cranston	N	?	?	?	?	?	?
COLORADO							
Armstrong	Y	Y	Y	Y	Y	Y	Y
Hart	N	N	Y	N	N	N	Y
CONNECTICUT							
Weicker	?	Y	Y	N	N	?	?
Dodd	N	N	Y	N	N	N	Y
DELAWARE							
Roth	Y	Y	Y	Y	Y	Y	Y
Biden	N	N	Y	N	Y	N	Y
FLORIDA							
Hawkins	Y	Y	Y	Y	Y	Y	Y
Chiles	N	N	Y	Y	+	N	Y
GEORGIA							
Mattingly	Y	Y	Y	Y	Y	Y	Y
Nunn	Y	N	Y	Y	Y	N	Y
HAWAII							
Inouye	Y	N	Y	N	N	N	Y
Matsunaga	N	N	Y	N	N	N	Y
IDAHO							
McClure	Y	Y	N	Y	Y	Y	Y
Symms	Y	Y	N	Y	Y	Y	Y
ILLINOIS							
Percy	Y	Y	Y	?	?	?	?
Dixon	Y	Y	Y	Y	Y	Y	Y
INDIANA							
Lugar	Y	Y	Y	Y	Y	Y	Y
Quayle	Y	Y	Y	Y	Y	Y	Y
IOWA							
Grassley	N	N	Y	Y	Y	Y	Y
Jepsen	Y	Y	Y	Y	Y	Y	Y
KANSAS							
Dole	Y	Y	Y	Y	Y	Y	Y
Kassebaum	Y	Y	Y	Y	Y	Y	Y
KENTUCKY							
Ford	N	N	Y	N	Y	N	Y
Huddleston	Y	N	Y	Y	Y	N	Y
LOUISIANA							
Johnston	Y	N	Y	Y	Y	Y	Y
Long	?	N	Y	Y	Y	Y	Y
MAINE							
Cohen	Y	Y	Y	Y	Y	Y	Y
Mitchell	N	N	Y	N	N	N	Y
MARYLAND							
Mathias	N	N	Y	N	N	Y	Y
Sarbanes	N	N	Y	N	N	N	Y
MASSACHUSETTS							
Kennedy	N	N	Y	N	N	N	Y
Tsongas	N	N	Y	N	N	N	Y
MICHIGAN							
Levin	N	N	Y	N	N	N	Y
Riegle	N	N	Y	Y	Y	N	Y
MINNESOTA							
Boschwitz	N	Y	Y	Y	Y	Y	Y
Durenberger	N	Y	Y	N	Y	Y	Y
MISSISSIPPI							
Cochran	Y	Y	Y	Y	Y	Y	Y
Stennis	Y	N	Y	Y	Y	Y	Y
MISSOURI							
Danforth	N	N	Y	N	N	Y	Y
Eagleton	N	N	Y	N	Y	N	Y
MONTANA							
Baucus	N	N	Y	N	Y	N	Y
Melcher	N	N	Y	Y	Y	Y	Y
NEBRASKA							
Exon	N	Y	Y	Y	Y	N	Y
Zorinsky	Y	Y	Y	Y	Y	Y	Y
NEVADA							
Hecht	Y	Y	Y	Y	Y	Y	Y
Laxalt	Y	Y	Y	Y	Y	Y	Y
NEW HAMPSHIRE							
Humphrey	Y	Y	Y	Y	Y	Y	Y
Rudman	Y	Y	Y	Y	Y	Y	Y
NEW JERSEY							
Bradley	N	N	Y	N	N	N	Y
Lautenberg	N	N	Y	N	Y	N	Y
NEW MEXICO							
Domenici	Y	Y	Y	Y	Y	Y	Y
Bingaman	Y	N	Y	N	N	N	Y
NEW YORK							
D'Amato	Y	Y	Y	Y	Y	Y	Y
Moynihan	N	N	Y	N	N	N	Y
NORTH CAROLINA							
East	Y	Y	Y	Y	Y	Y	?
Helms	Y	Y	Y	Y	Y	Y	Y
NORTH DAKOTA							
Andrews	Y	Y	Y	Y	Y	Y	Y
Burdick	N	N	Y	Y	Y	Y	Y
OHIO							
Glenn	Y	Y	?	?	?	N	Y
Metzenbaum	N	Y	Y	N	N	N	Y
OKLAHOMA							
Nickles	Y	Y	Y	Y	Y	Y	Y
Boren	Y	Y	Y	Y	Y	N	Y
OREGON							
Hatfield	N	N	Y	N	N	N	Y
Packwood	N	Y	Y	Y	Y	Y	Y
PENNSYLVANIA							
Heinz	N	Y	Y	N	Y	Y	Y
Specter	N	Y	Y	N	N	Y	Y
RHODE ISLAND							
Chafee	Y	N	N	N	N	Y	?
Pell	N	N	Y	N	Y	N	Y
SOUTH CAROLINA							
Thurmond	Y	Y	Y	Y	Y	Y	Y
Hollings	?	?	?	?	?	?	?
SOUTH DAKOTA							
Abdnor	Y	Y	Y	Y	Y	Y	Y
Pressler	Y	N	Y	Y	Y	Y	Y
TENNESSEE							
Baker	Y	Y	Y	Y	Y	Y	Y
Sasser	N	Y	Y	Y	Y	N	Y
TEXAS							
Tower	Y	Y	Y	Y	Y	Y	Y
Bentsen	N	Y	Y	Y	Y	Y	Y
UTAH							
Garn	Y	Y	Y	Y	Y	Y	Y
Hatch	Y	N	Y	Y	Y	Y	Y
VERMONT							
Stafford	?	Y	Y	N	N	Y	Y
Leahy	N	N	Y	N	N	N	Y
VIRGINIA							
Trible	Y	Y	Y	Y	Y	Y	Y
Warner	Y	Y	Y	Y	Y	Y	Y
WASHINGTON							
Gorton	N	Y	Y	Y	Y	Y	Y
Jackson	Y	N	Y	Y	Y	Y	Y
WEST VIRGINIA							
Byrd	Y	N	Y	Y	Y	N	Y
Randolph	N	Y	Y	Y	Y	N	Y
WISCONSIN							
Kasten	Y	Y	Y	Y	Y	Y	Y
Proxmire	N	N	Y	Y	Y	Y	Y
WYOMING							
Simpson	Y	Y	Y	Y	Y	Y	Y
Wallop	Y	Y	N	Y	Y	?	Y

KEY

Y Voted for (yea).
\# Paired for.
\+ Announced for.
N Voted against (nay).
X Paired against.
- Announced against.
P Voted "present".
C Voted "present" to avoid possible conflict of interest.
? Did not vote or otherwise make a position known.

Democrats   *Republicans*

ND - Northern Democrats   SD - Southern Democrats (Southern states - Ala., Ark., Fla., Ga., Ky., La., Miss., N.C., Okla., S.C., Tenn., Texas, Va.)

185. S 675. Omnibus Defense Authorizations. Baker, R-Tenn., motion to table (kill) the Gorton, R-Wash., motion to recommit the bill to the Armed Services Committee with instructions to disregard reduced estimates of inflation in the Pentagon budget that had been authorized by the Office of Management and Budget. The effect of the motion to recommit would have been to require the Armed Services Committee to drop some programs from the bill, but not to reduce the total authorized. Motion agreed to 53-41: R 40-10; D 13-31 (ND 7-25, SD 6-6), July 13, 1983. A "yea" was a vote supporting the president's position.

186. S 675. Omnibus Defense Authorizations. Tower, R-Texas, motion to table (kill) the Nunn, D-Ga., amendment to deny authorization for a multi-year procurement contract for B-1 bombers. Motion agreed to 56-41: R 46-7; D 10-34 (ND 7-24, SD 3-10), July 14, 1983. A "yea" was a vote supporting the president's position.

187. S 675. Omnibus Defense Authorizations. Pryor, D-Ark., amendment to establish an independent weapons testing office within the Department of Defense. Adopted 91-5: R 48-5; D 43-0 (ND 30-0, SD 13-0), July 14, 1983. A "nay" was a vote supporting the president's position.

188. S 675. Omnibus Defense Authorizations. Tower, R-Texas, motion to table (kill) the Stafford, R-Vt., substitute for the Durenberger, R-Minn., amendment, to delay the effective date of a law denying federal education benefits to students who have not registered with the Selective Service System when obligated to do so. Motion agreed to 66-29: R 43-9; D 23-20 (ND 11-19, SD 12-1), July 14, 1983.

189. S 675. Omnibus Defense Authorizations. Tower, R-Texas, motion to table (kill) the Durenberger, R-Minn., amendment to repeal a law denying federal education benefits to students who have not registered with the Selective Service System when obligated to do so. Motion agreed to 71-23: R 44-8; D 27-15 (ND 16-14, SD 11-1), July 14, 1983.

190. S 675. Omnibus Defense Authorizations. Tower, R-Texas, motion to table (kill) the Levin, D-Mich., amendment to add $2.7 billion for various conventional weapons programs and operations and maintenance projects. Motion agreed to 60-34: R 50-0; D 10-34 (ND 6-25, SD 4-9), July 14, 1983.

191. S 675. Omnibus Defense Authorizations. Cohen, R-Maine, amendment to tighten up restrictions on long-term leases of ships and airplanes. Adopted 93-0: R 49-0; D 44-0 (ND 31-0, SD 13-0), July 14, 1983.

CQ Senate Votes 192 - 199

Corresponding to Congressional Record Votes 196, 197, 198, 199, 200, 201, 202, 203

KEY

- Y Voted for (yea).
- # Paired for.
- + Announced for.
- N Voted against (nay).
- X Paired against.
- - Announced against.
- P Voted "present".
- C Voted "present" to avoid possible conflict of interest.
- ? Did not vote or otherwise make a position known.

Democrats   **Republicans**

	192	193	194	195	196	197	198	199
ALABAMA								
Denton	Y	Y	Y	Y	Y	N	Y	Y
Heflin	Y	?	?	?	?	?	Y	Y
ALASKA								
Murkowski	Y	Y	Y	Y	Y	N	Y	Y
Stevens	Y	Y	Y	Y	Y	N	Y	Y
ARIZONA								
Goldwater	?	?	?	?	?	?	?	?
DeConcini	Y	Y	Y	Y	Y	Y	Y	Y
ARKANSAS								
Bumpers	Y	Y	Y	Y	Y	N	?	?
Pryor	Y	Y	Y	Y	Y	N	Y	N
CALIFORNIA								
Wilson	Y	Y	Y	Y	Y	N	Y	Y
Cranston	?	?	?	?	?	?	?	?
COLORADO								
Armstrong	N	Y	Y	?	?	?	?	?
Hart	Y	Y	Y	Y	Y	Y	Y	N
CONNECTICUT								
Weicker	Y	Y	Y	Y	N	N	N	N
Dodd	Y	Y	Y	Y	Y	N	Y	N
DELAWARE								
Roth	Y	Y	Y	Y	Y	N	Y	Y
Biden	Y	Y	Y	Y	Y	N	Y	N
FLORIDA								
Hawkins	Y	Y	Y	Y	Y	N	Y	N
Chiles	Y	Y	Y	Y	Y	N	Y	N
GEORGIA								
Mattingly	Y	Y	Y	Y	Y	N	Y	Y
Nunn	Y	Y	Y	Y	Y	N	Y	N
HAWAII								
Inouye	Y	Y	Y	Y	Y	N	Y	N
Matsunaga	?	Y	Y	Y	Y	N	Y	N
IDAHO								
McClure	Y	Y	Y	Y	Y	N	Y	Y
Symms	?	?	?	?	?	?	?	?
ILLINOIS								
Percy	?	?	?	?	?	?	?	?
Dixon	+	+	+	+	?	?	Y	Y
IOWA								
Grassley	Y	Y	Y	Y	Y	N	Y	Y
Jepsen	Y	Y	Y	Y	Y	N	Y	Y
KANSAS								
Dole	Y	Y	Y	Y	Y	N	Y	Y
Kassebaum	Y	Y	Y	Y	Y	N	Y	N
KENTUCKY								
Ford	Y	Y	Y	Y	Y	N	Y	N
Huddleston	Y	Y	Y	Y	Y	N	Y	N
LOUISIANA								
Johnston	Y	Y	Y	Y	Y	N	Y	Y
Long	Y	Y	Y	Y	Y	N	Y	Y
MAINE								
Cohen	Y	Y	Y	Y	Y	N	Y	Y
Mitchell	Y	Y	Y	Y	Y	N	Y	Y
MARYLAND								
Mathias	Y	Y	Y	Y	Y	N	Y	N
Sarbanes	Y	Y	Y	Y	Y	N	Y	N
MASSACHUSETTS								
Kennedy	Y	Y	Y	Y	?	?	+	-
Tsongas	Y	Y	Y	Y	Y	N	Y	N
MICHIGAN								
Levin	Y	Y	Y	Y	Y	N	Y	N
Riegle	Y	Y	Y	Y	Y	N	Y	N
MINNESOTA								
Boschwitz	Y	Y	Y	Y	Y	N	Y	N
Durenberger	Y	Y	Y	?	N	Y	N	
MISSISSIPPI								
Cochran	Y	Y	Y	Y	Y	N	Y	Y
Stennis	Y	Y	Y	Y	Y	N	Y	Y
MISSOURI								
Danforth	Y	Y	Y	Y	Y	N	Y	N
Eagleton	Y	Y	Y	?	?	?	?	?
MONTANA								
Baucus	Y	Y	Y	Y	Y	Y	Y	Y
Melcher	Y	Y	Y	Y	Y	N	Y	N
NEBRASKA								
Exon	?	Y	Y	Y	Y	N	Y	Y
Zorinsky	Y	?	?	?	?	?	?	?
NEVADA								
Hecht	Y	Y	Y	Y	Y	N	Y	Y
Laxalt	Y	Y	Y	Y	Y	N	Y	Y
NEW HAMPSHIRE								
Humphrey	N	Y	Y	?	?	?	?	?
Rudman	Y	Y	Y	Y	Y	N	Y	Y
NEW JERSEY								
Bradley	Y	Y	Y	Y	Y	N	N	N
Lautenberg	Y	Y	Y	Y	Y	N	Y	N
NEW MEXICO								
Domenici	Y	Y	Y	Y	Y	N	Y	N
Bingaman	Y	Y	Y	Y	Y	N	Y	N
NEW YORK								
D'Amato	Y	Y	Y	Y	Y	N	Y	N
Moynihan	Y	Y	Y	Y	Y	Y	Y	N
NORTH CAROLINA								
East	N	Y	Y	Y	Y	N	Y	Y
Helms	N	Y	Y	Y	Y	N	Y	Y
NORTH DAKOTA								
Andrews	Y	Y	Y	Y	?	?	?	?
Burdick	Y	Y	Y	Y	Y	N	N	N
OHIO								
Glenn	?	?	?	?	?	?	Y	Y
Metzenbaum	Y	Y	Y	Y	Y	N	Y	N
OKLAHOMA								
Nickles	Y	Y	Y	Y	Y	N	Y	Y
Boren	Y	Y	Y	Y	Y	N	Y	?
OREGON								
Hatfield	Y	Y	Y	Y	Y	N	Y	N
Packwood	Y	Y	Y	Y	Y	N	Y	Y
PENNSYLVANIA								
Heinz	Y	Y	Y	Y	?	N	Y	N
Specter	Y	Y	Y	Y	Y	N	Y	N
RHODE ISLAND								
Chafee	Y	Y	Y	Y	Y	N	Y	N
Pell	Y	Y	Y	Y	Y	N	Y	N
SOUTH CAROLINA								
Thurmond	Y	Y	Y	Y	Y	N	Y	Y
Hollings	?	?	?	?	?	?	?	?
SOUTH DAKOTA								
Abdnor	Y	Y	Y	Y	Y	N	Y	Y
Pressler	Y	Y	Y	Y	Y	N	Y	N
TENNESSEE								
Baker	Y	Y	Y	Y	Y	N	Y	Y
Sasser	Y	Y	Y	Y	Y	N	Y	N
TEXAS								
Tower	Y	Y	Y	Y	Y	N	Y	Y
Bentsen	Y	Y	Y	Y	Y	N	Y	Y
UTAH								
Garn	Y	Y	Y	Y	Y	N	Y	Y
Hatch	Y	Y	Y	Y	Y	N	Y	Y
VERMONT								
Stafford	Y	Y	Y	Y	Y	N	N	N
Leahy	Y	Y	Y	Y	Y	N	Y	N
VIRGINIA								
Trible	Y	Y	Y	Y	Y	N	Y	Y
Warner	Y	Y	Y	Y	Y	N	Y	Y
WASHINGTON								
Gorton	Y	Y	Y	Y	Y	N	Y	Y
Jackson	Y	Y	Y	Y	Y	N	Y	Y
WEST VIRGINIA								
Byrd	Y	Y	Y	Y	Y	N	Y	Y
Randolph	Y	Y	Y	Y	Y	N	Y	Y
WISCONSIN								
Kasten	Y	Y	Y	Y	Y	N	Y	Y
Proxmire	N	Y	Y	Y	N	Y	Y	N
WYOMING								
Simpson	Y	Y	Y	Y	Y	N	Y	N
Wallop	Y	Y	Y	Y	Y	N	Y	Y

ND - Northern Democrats   SD - Southern Democrats (Southern states - Ala., Ark., Fla., Ga., Ky., La., Miss., N.C., Okla., S.C., Tenn., Texas, Va.)

192. HR 3329. Transportation Appropriations, Fiscal 1984. Passage of the bill to appropriate $10,853,955,225 for the Transportation Department and related agencies in fiscal 1984. Passed 86-5: R 47-4; D 39-1 (ND 26-1, SD 13-0), July 15, 1983. The president had requested $10,913,472,025 in new budget authority.

193. S 675. Omnibus Defense Authorizations. Mattingly, R-Ga., amendment to restrict the availability of funds to countries not taking adequate measures to control illegal drug trafficking. Adopted 91-0: R 51-0; D 40-0 (ND 28-0, SD 12-0), July 15, 1983.

194. S 675. Omnibus Defense Authorizations. Jepsen, R-Iowa, amendment to provide that one of three new assistant secretaries of defense established by the bill shall be the assistant secretary of defense for reserve affairs. Adopted 91-0: R 51-0; D 40-0 (ND 28-0, SD 12-0), July 15, 1983.

195. S 675. Omnibus Defense Authorizations. Byrd, D-W.Va., amendment to authorize the presentation on behalf of Congress of a specially struck bronze medal to families of U.S. personnel missing or otherwise unaccounted for in Southeast Asia. Adopted 88-0: R 49-0; D 39-0 (ND 27-0, SD 12-0), July 15, 1983.

196. S 675. Omnibus Defense Authorizations. Baker, R-Tenn., motion to instruct the sergeant-at-arms to request the attendance of absent senators. Motion agreed to 81-3: R 44-2; D 37-1 (ND 25-1, SD 12-0), July 15, 1983.

197. S 675. Omnibus Defense Authorizations. Hart, D-Colo., motion to recess the Senate until 7:30 p.m. EDT. Motion rejected 5-81: R 0-48; D 5-33 (ND 5-21, SD 0-12), July 15, 1983.

198. S 675. Omnibus Defense Authorizations. Tower, R-Texas, motion to table (kill) the Tower amendment to provide that no funds authorized by the bill shall be obligated or expended for the MX missile. Motion agreed to 84-4: R 46-2; D 38-2 (ND 26-2, SD 12-0), July 16, 1983.

199. S 675. Omnibus Defense Authorizations. Tower, R-Texas, motion to table (kill) the Mathias, R-Md., amendment expressing the sense of Congress that the president should, as soon as practicable, make every reasonable effort to include in the START talks with the Soviet Union the nuclear-armed sea-launched cruise missile with a view to complete elimination of the weapon by both the United States and the Soviet Union, and should propose a joint moratorium on deployment of the missile for the duration of the START negotiations. Motion agreed to 47-40: R 33-15; D 14-25 (ND 9-19, SD 5-6), July 16, 1983. A "yea" was a vote supporting the president's position.

KEY

- **Y** Voted for (yea).
- **#** Paired for.
- **+** Announced for.
- **N** Voted against (nay).
- **X** Paired against.
- **-** Announced against.
- **P** Voted "present".
- **C** Voted "present" to avoid possible conflict of interest.
- **?** Did not vote or otherwise make a position known.

Democrats *Republicans*

ND - Northern Democrats   SD - Southern Democrats (Southern states - Ala., Ark., Fla., Ga., Ky., La., Miss., N.C., Okla., S.C., Tenn., Texas, Va.)

State / Senator	200	201	202	203	204	205	206	207
ALABAMA								
Denton	Y	Y	Y	Y	Y	Y	N	Y
Heflin	?	?	?	Y	N	N	N	Y
ALASKA								
Murkowski	Y	Y	Y	Y	Y	Y	N	Y
Stevens	N	Y	Y	?	?	Y	Y	Y
ARIZONA								
Goldwater	?	?	?	?	?	?	?	?
DeConcini	N	Y	N	Y	N	N	N	Y
ARKANSAS								
Bumpers	?	?	?	?	?	Y	Y	Y
Pryor	?	?	?	Y	N	N	Y	Y
CALIFORNIA								
Wilson	Y	Y	Y	Y	Y	Y	Y	Y
Cranston	?	?	?	?	?	?	?	Y
COLORADO								
Armstrong	?	?	?	Y	N	Y	N	Y
Hart	N	N	N	Y	N	N	Y	Y
CONNECTICUT								
Weicker	N	Y	Y	Y	N	N	Y	N
Dodd	N	N	Y	Y	N	N	Y	Y
DELAWARE								
Roth	Y	Y	Y	Y	N	N	Y	Y
Biden	N	N	N	Y	N	N	Y	Y
FLORIDA								
Hawkins	N	Y	Y	Y	Y	Y	N	Y
Chiles	Y	Y	N	Y	N	N	Y	Y
GEORGIA								
Mattingly	Y	Y	Y	Y	Y	Y	N	Y
Nunn	Y	Y	Y	Y	N	N	Y	Y
HAWAII								
Inouye	N	Y	?	Y	N	N	Y	Y
Matsunaga	N	N	N	Y	N	N	Y	Y
IDAHO								
McClure	?	?	?	Y	Y	Y	N	Y
Symms	?	?	?	?	Y	Y	N	Y
ILLINOIS								
Percy	?	?	?	Y	N	N	Y	Y
Dixon	Y	Y	Y	Y	N	N	Y	Y
INDIANA								
Lugar	Y	Y	Y	Y	Y	Y	Y	Y
Quayle	Y	Y	Y	Y	Y	Y	Y	N
IOWA								
Grassley	Y	Y	Y	Y	Y	Y	Y	Y
Jepsen	Y	Y	Y	Y	Y	Y	Y	Y
KANSAS								
Dole	N	Y	Y	Y	Y	Y	N	N
Kassebaum	N	Y	?	Y	Y	Y	Y	Y
KENTUCKY								
Ford	N	Y	N	Y	N	N	N	Y
Huddleston	N	Y	Y	Y	N	Y	Y	?
LOUISIANA								
Johnston	Y	Y	Y	Y	N	Y	Y	Y
Long	?	?	?	Y	Y	N	Y	N
MAINE								
Cohen	Y	Y	N	Y	Y	Y	Y	Y
Mitchell	N	N	Y	Y	N	N	Y	Y
MARYLAND								
Mathias	Y	Y	Y	Y	N	N	Y	Y
Sarbanes	N	N	N	Y	N	N	Y	Y
MASSACHUSETTS								
Kennedy	?	?	?	Y	Y	Y	Y	Y
Tsongas	N	N	N	Y	N	N	Y	Y
MICHIGAN								
Levin	#	N	N	Y	Y	Y	Y	Y
Riegle	Y	Y	N	Y	N	N	Y	Y
MINNESOTA								
Boschwitz	N	Y	Y	Y	N	Y	N	Y
Durenberger	N	N	Y	Y	Y	Y	Y	Y
MISSISSIPPI								
Cochran	Y	Y	Y	Y	Y	Y	N	Y
Stennis	Y	Y	Y	Y	Y	Y	Y	Y
MISSOURI								
Danforth	Y	N	Y	Y	Y	Y	Y	Y
Eagleton	?	?	?	Y	N	N	Y	Y
MONTANA								
Baucus	N	N	?	Y	N	N	Y	Y
Melcher	N	Y	N	Y	N	-	+	Y
NEBRASKA								
Exon	Y	Y	Y	Y	N	N	Y	Y
Zorinsky	?	?	?	Y	N	N	Y	Y
NEVADA								
Hecht	Y	Y	Y	Y	Y	Y	N	Y
Laxalt	Y	Y	Y	Y	Y	Y	N	Y
NEW HAMPSHIRE								
Humphrey	?	?	?	Y	Y	Y	N	Y
Rudman	Y	Y	Y	Y	Y	Y	N	Y
NEW JERSEY								
Bradley	Y	N	Y	Y	N	N	Y	Y
Lautenberg	Y	N	N	?	?	N	Y	Y
NEW MEXICO								
Domenici	Y	Y	Y	?	?	?	?	?
Bingaman	Y	Y	N	Y	N	N	Y	Y
NEW YORK								
D'Amato	N	Y	Y	Y	Y	Y	N	Y
Moynihan	Y	Y	Y	Y	Y	Y	N	Y
NORTH CAROLINA								
East	Y	Y	Y	Y	Y	Y	Y	Y
Helms	N	Y	Y	Y	Y	Y	N	Y
NORTH DAKOTA								
Andrews	?	?	?	Y	N	N	N	Y
Burdick	N	Y	?	Y	N	N	Y	Y
OHIO								
Glenn	Y	Y	Y	?	?	?	?	?
Metzenbaum	Y	Y	Y	Y	N	N	Y	Y
OKLAHOMA								
Nickles	Y	Y	Y	Y	Y	Y	N	Y
Boren	X	?	?	Y	N	N	N	Y
OREGON								
Hatfield	N	Y	Y	Y	N	N	Y	?
Packwood	N	Y	Y	?	?	?	?	Y
PENNSYLVANIA								
Heinz	Y	N	Y	Y	N	N	Y	Y
Specter	Y	N	Y	Y	N	N	Y	Y
RHODE ISLAND								
Chafee	Y	Y	Y	Y	N	N	Y	Y
Pell	N	N	Y	Y	N	N	Y	Y
SOUTH CAROLINA								
Thurmond	N	Y	Y	Y	Y	Y	Y	Y
Hollings	?	?	?	Y	N	N	?	Y
SOUTH DAKOTA								
Abdnor	N	Y	?	Y	Y	Y	N	Y
Pressler	N	Y	Y	Y	Y	Y	Y	Y
TENNESSEE								
Baker	Y	Y	Y	Y	Y	Y	?	Y
Sasser	N	N	Y	Y	N	N	Y	Y
TEXAS								
Tower	Y	Y	Y	Y	Y	Y	Y	Y
Bentsen	Y	Y	?	Y	N	N	Y	Y
UTAH								
Garn	Y	Y	Y	Y	Y	Y	N	Y
Hatch	Y	Y	Y	Y	Y	Y	N	Y
VERMONT								
Stafford	Y	N	Y	Y	N	N	Y	Y
Leahy	N	N	Y	Y	N	N	Y	Y
VIRGINIA								
Trible	Y	Y	Y	Y	N	Y	Y	Y
Warner	N	Y	Y	Y	N	?	Y	Y
WASHINGTON								
Gorton	Y	Y	Y	Y	Y	Y	Y	Y
Jackson	Y	Y	Y	Y	N	N	Y	Y
WEST VIRGINIA								
Byrd	N	Y	Y	Y	N	N	N	Y
Randolph	N	Y	Y	Y	N	N	Y	Y
WISCONSIN								
Kasten	N	Y	Y	Y	N	N	Y	Y
Proxmire	Y	Y	Y	Y	N	N	Y	N
WYOMING								
Simpson	Y	Y	Y	Y	Y	N	N	Y
Wallop	Y	Y	Y	Y	Y	Y	N	Y

200. S 675. Omnibus Defense Authorizations. Tower, R-Texas, motion to table (kill) the Pressler, R-S.D., amendment to add funds for operations and maintenance for the Army and Air National Guard. Motion agreed to 47-35: R 31-16; D 16-19 (ND 11-16, SD 5-3), July 16, 1983.

201. S 675. Omnibus Defense Authorizations. Tower, R-Texas, motion to table (kill) the Bradley, D-N.J., amendment to change the method by which it is determined whether students receiving certain educational aid have complied with requirements of the Selective Service Act. Motion agreed to 64-19: R 42-5; D 22-14 (ND 15-13, SD 7-1), July 16, 1983.

202. S 675. Omnibus Defense Authorizations. Tower, R-Texas, motion to table (kill) the Melcher, D-Mont., amendment to provide a 4 percent pay raise, effective April 1, 1984, to enlisted members in pay grade E-1 with less than four months service. Motion agreed to 63-14: R 44-1; D 19-13 (ND 14-11, SD 5-2), July 16, 1983.

203. S 675. Omnibus Defense Authorizations. Tsongas, D-Mass., amendment to prohibit funds for anti-satellite weapons unless the president certifies to Congress progress on a ban of space weapons. Adopted 91-0: R 49-0; D 42-0 (ND 29-0, SD 13-0), July 18, 1983.

204. S 675. Omnibus Defense Authorizations. Tower, R-Texas, motion to table (kill) the Stafford, R-Vt., amendment to extend the period for the transfer of the defense dependents education system to the Department of Education. Motion rejected 42-50: R 36-14; D 6-36 (ND 4-25, SD 2-11), July 18, 1983.

205. S 675. Omnibus Defense Authorizations. Quayle, R-Ind., amendment to the Stafford, R-Vt., amendment, to provide that the defense dependents education system not be transferred to the Department of Education prior to May 4, 1986. (The Stafford amendment would have provided for the transfer of the system no later than that date.) Adopted 47-46: R 39-11; D 8-35 (ND 4-25, SD 4-10), July 19, 1983. (The Stafford amendment, as amended, subsequently was adopted by voice vote.)

206. S 675. Omnibus Defense Authorizations. Tower, R-Texas, motion to table (kill) the Wallop, R-Wyo., amendment to transfer $125 million from other programs to accelerate certain space-based laser development programs. Motion agreed to 65-27: R 28-22; D 37-5 (ND 27-2, SD 10-3), July 19, 1983. A "yea" was a vote supporting the president's position.

207. S 675. Omnibus Defense Authorizations. Baker, R-Tenn., motion to instruct the sergeant-at-arms to request the attendance of absent senators. Motion agreed to 90-5: R 48-3; D 42-2 (ND 30-1, SD 12-1), July 20, 1983.

CQ Senate Votes 208 - 212

Corresponding to Congressional Record Votes 212, 213, 214, 215, 216

	208 209 210 211 212		208 209 210 211 212		208 209 210 211 212	KEY
ALABAMA		**IOWA**		**NEW HAMPSHIRE**		Y Voted for (yea).
Denton	N Y Y Y N	*Grassley*	N Y Y Y N	*Humphrey*	Y Y Y Y N	# Paired for.
Heflin	N Y Y N Y	*Jepsen*	N Y Y Y N	*Rudman*	N Y Y Y N	+ Announced for.
ALASKA		**KANSAS**		**NEW JERSEY**		N Voted against (nay).
Murkowski	N Y Y Y N	*Dole*	N N Y Y Y	Bradley	Y Y N N Y	X Paired against.
Stevens	N Y Y Y N	*Kassebaum*	N Y Y Y N	Lautenberg	N Y N N Y	- Announced against.
ARIZONA		**KENTUCKY**		**NEW MEXICO**		P Voted "present".
Goldwater	? ? ? ? ?	Ford	N Y N N Y	*Domenici*	? ? ? ? ?	C Voted "present" to avoid possible conflict of interest.
DeConcini	N Y Y Y Y	Huddleston	Y ? N N Y	Bingaman	N Y N N Y	? Did not vote or otherwise make a position known.
ARKANSAS		**LOUISIANA**		**NEW YORK**		
Bumpers	N Y N N Y	Johnston	N Y Y Y N	*D'Amato*	N Y Y Y Y	Democrats *Republicans*
Pryor	N Y N N Y	Long	N N N N Y	Moynihan	N Y N N Y	
CALIFORNIA		**MAINE**		**NORTH CAROLINA**		
Wilson	N Y Y Y N	*Cohen*	N Y Y Y N	*East*	N Y Y Y N	
Cranston	N Y N N Y	*Mitchell*	N Y N N Y	*Helms*	N Y Y Y N	
COLORADO		**MARYLAND**		**NORTH DAKOTA**		208 209 210 211 212
Armstrong	N Y Y Y N	*Mathias*	N Y - Y N	*Andrews*	Y Y Y N Y	
Hart	N Y N N Y	Sarbanes	N Y N N Y	Burdick	Y Y N N Y	
CONNECTICUT		**MASSACHUSETTS**		**OHIO**		**TEXAS**	
Weicker	Y N Y N Y	Kennedy	N Y N N Y	Glenn	? Y N N Y	*Tower*	N Y Y Y N
Dodd	N Y N N Y	Tsongas	N Y N N Y	Metzenbaum	N Y N N Y	Bentsen	N Y N N Y
DELAWARE		**MICHIGAN**		**OKLAHOMA**		**UTAH**	
Roth	N Y Y Y N	Levin	N Y N N Y	*Nickles*	N Y Y Y N	*Garn*	N Y Y Y N
Biden	N Y N N Y	Riegle	N Y N N Y	Boren	N Y N N Y	*Hatch*	N Y Y Y N
FLORIDA		**MINNESOTA**		**OREGON**		**VERMONT**	
Hawkins	N Y Y Y N	*Boschwitz*	N Y Y Y N	*Hatfield*	? ? ? ? ?	*Stafford*	N Y Y N Y
Chiles	N Y N N Y	*Durenberger*	N Y Y N Y	*Packwood*	N Y N Y Y	Leahy	N Y N N Y
GEORGIA		**MISSISSIPPI**		**PENNSYLVANIA**		**VIRGINIA**	
Mattingly	N Y Y Y N	*Cochran*	N Y Y Y N	*Heinz*	N Y Y N Y	*Trible*	N Y Y Y N
Nunn	N Y N Y N	Stennis	N Y N N Y	*Specter*	N Y N N Y	*Warner*	N Y Y ? Y
HAWAII		**MISSOURI**		**RHODE ISLAND**		**WASHINGTON**	
Inouye	N Y N N Y	*Danforth*	N Y Y N Y	*Chafee*	N Y Y N Y	*Gorton*	N Y Y Y N
Matsunaga	N Y N N Y	Eagleton	N Y N N Y	Pell	N Y ? N Y	Jackson	N Y Y N Y
IDAHO		**MONTANA**		**SOUTH CAROLINA**		**WEST VIRGINIA**	
McClure	N Y Y Y N	Baucus	N Y N N Y	*Thurmond*	N Y Y Y N	Byrd	N Y N N Y
Symms	N Y Y Y N	Melcher	N Y N N Y	Hollings	N Y N N Y	Randolph	N Y N N Y
ILLINOIS		**NEBRASKA**		**SOUTH DAKOTA**		**WISCONSIN**	
Percy	N Y Y Y Y	Exon	N Y Y Y ?	*Abdnor*	N Y Y Y N	*Kasten*	N Y Y Y N
Dixon	N Y N Y N	Zorinsky	N Y Y Y N	*Pressler*	N Y Y ? N	Proxmire	N N N Y N
INDIANA		**NEVADA**		**TENNESSEE**		**WYOMING**	
Lugar	N Y Y Y N	*Hecht*	N Y Y Y N	*Baker*	N Y Y ? N	*Simpson*	N Y Y Y Y
Quayle	N N Y Y N	*Laxalt*	N Y Y Y N	Sasser	N Y N N Y	*Wallop*	N Y Y Y N

ND - Northern Democrats   SD - Southern Democrats (Southern states - Ala., Ark., Fla., Ga., Ky., La., Miss., N.C., Okla., S.C., Tenn., Texas, Va.)

208. S 675. Omnibus Defense Authorizations. Weicker, R-Conn., motion to table (kill) the Tower, R-Texas, amendment expressing the sense of the Senate commending the President's Commission on Strategic Forces (Scowcroft commission) and endorsing the deployment of MX missiles in existing Minuteman silos. Motion rejected 6-90: R 3-48; D 3-42 (ND 2-29, SD 1-13), July 20, 1983.

209. S 675. Omnibus Defense Authorizations. Baker, R-Tenn., motion to instruct the sergeant-at-arms to request the attendance of absent senators. Motion agreed to 91-5: R 48-3; D 43-2 (ND 31-1, SD 12-1), July 21, 1983.

210. S 675. Omnibus Defense Authorizations. Baker, R-Tenn., motion to invoke cloture (thus limiting debate) on the Armed Services Committee substitute for the bill to authorize appropriations for Defense Department programs in fiscal 1984. Motion rejected 55-41: R 49-2; D 6-39 (ND 4-27, SD 2-12), July 21, 1983. A three-fifths majority vote (60) of the total Senate is required to invoke cloture. A "yea" was a vote supporting the president's position.

211. S 675. Omnibus Defense Authorizations. Mattingly, R-Ga., motion to table (kill) the Moynihan, D-N.Y., amendment to delay until Sept. 30, 1983, the date by which college students required by law to register with the Selective Service System must certify that they have done so in order to be eligible for federal student aid. Motion rejected 46-48: R 39-9; D 7-39 (ND 5-27, SD 2-12), July 21, 1983. (The Moynihan amendment subsequently was adopted *(see vote 212, below).*)

212. S 675. Omnibus Defense Authorizations. Moynihan, D-N.Y., amendment to delay until Sept. 30, 1983, the date by which college students required by law to certify that they have done so in order to be eligible for federal student aid. Adopted 56-40: R 16-35; D 40-5 (ND 28-3, SD 12-2), July 21, 1983.

	213	214	215	216	217	218	219	220
ALABAMA								
Denton	Y	N	N	Y	Y	Y	Y	Y
Heflin	?	N	N	Y	Y	N	Y	N
ALASKA								
Murkowski	?	N	N	Y	Y	Y	Y	Y
Stevens	Y	N	N	Y	Y	Y	Y	Y
ARIZONA								
Goldwater	Y	N	N	N	Y	Y	Y	?
DeConcini	N	N	N	Y	Y	N	Y	Y
ARKANSAS								
Bumpers	N	Y	Y	Y	N	Y	Y	N
Pryor	N	Y	Y	Y	Y	Y	Y	N
CALIFORNIA								
Wilson	Y	N	N	Y	Y	Y	Y	Y
Cranston	?	Y	Y	Y	N	N	Y	N
COLORADO								
Armstrong	Y	N	N	Y	Y	Y	Y	Y
Hart	N	Y	Y	Y	N	Y	Y	?
CONNECTICUT								
Weicker	?	Y	Y	Y	Y	Y	Y	Y
Dodd	N	Y	Y	Y	Y	Y	Y	Y
DELAWARE								
Roth	Y	N	N	Y	Y	Y	Y	Y
Biden	?	Y	Y	Y	Y	Y	Y	Y
FLORIDA								
Hawkins	Y	N	N	Y	Y	N	Y	Y
Chiles	?	N	Y	Y	Y	Y	Y	Y
GEORGIA								
Mattingly	Y	N	N	Y	Y	Y	Y	Y
Nunn	?	N	N	Y	Y	Y	Y	Y
HAWAII								
Inouye	N	Y	Y	Y	Y	Y	Y	N
Matsunaga	N	Y	Y	Y	Y	Y	Y	N
IDAHO								
McClure	Y	N	N	N	Y	N	Y	Y
Symms	Y	N	N	N	Y	N	Y	Y
ILLINOIS								
Percy	Y	N	N	Y	Y	Y	Y	?
Dixon	Y	Y	Y	Y	Y	Y	Y	Y
INDIANA								
Lugar	Y	N	N	Y	Y	Y	Y	Y
Quayle	Y	N	N	Y	Y	Y	Y	Y

	213	214	215	216	217	218	219	220
IOWA								
Grassley	Y	N	N	Y	Y	Y	Y	Y
Jepsen	Y	N	N	Y	Y	Y	Y	Y
KANSAS								
Dole	Y	N	N	Y	Y	Y	Y	Y
Kassebaum	?	N	N	Y	Y	Y	Y	Y
KENTUCKY								
Ford	?	Y	Y	Y	Y	Y	Y	N
Huddleston	N	Y	Y	Y	Y	Y	Y	Y
LOUISIANA								
Johnston	N	N	N	Y	Y	Y	Y	N
Long	?	N	N	Y	Y	Y	Y	N
MAINE								
Cohen	Y	N	N	Y	Y	Y	Y	Y
Mitchell	N	Y	Y	Y	Y	Y	Y	Y
MARYLAND								
Mathias	Y	N	N	Y	Y	Y	Y	Y
Sarbanes	N	Y	Y	Y	Y	Y	Y	N
MASSACHUSETTS								
Kennedy	Y	Y	Y	Y	Y	N	N	Y
Tsongas	N	Y	Y	N	Y	N	Y	Y
MICHIGAN								
Levin	N	Y	Y	Y	N	Y	N	N
Riegle	N	Y	Y	Y	Y	Y	Y	N
MINNESOTA								
Boschwitz	Y	N	N	Y	Y	Y	Y	Y
Durenberger	Y	Y	Y	N	Y	Y	Y	Y
MISSISSIPPI								
Cochran	Y	N	N	Y	Y	Y	Y	?
Stennis	Y	N	N	Y	Y	Y	Y	Y
MISSOURI								
Danforth	Y	N	N	Y	Y	Y	Y	Y
Eagleton	N	Y	Y	Y	Y	Y	Y	N
MONTANA								
Baucus	N	Y	Y	Y	Y	Y	Y	N
Melcher	N	Y	Y	Y	N	N	Y	N
NEBRASKA								
Exon	Y	Y	Y	Y	Y	Y	Y	N
Zorinsky	Y	N	N	Y	Y	Y	Y	N
NEVADA								
Hecht	Y	N	N	Y	Y	Y	Y	Y
Laxalt	Y	N	N	Y	Y	Y	Y	Y

	213	214	215	216	217	218	219	220
NEW HAMPSHIRE								
Humphrey	Y	Y	Y	Y	Y	N	Y	Y
Rudman	?	N	N	Y	Y	Y	Y	Y
NEW JERSEY								
Bradley	Y	Y	Y	Y	Y	Y	Y	Y
Lautenberg	N	Y	Y	Y	Y	Y	Y	Y
NEW MEXICO								
Domenici	?	?	?	?	?	Y	Y	?
Bingaman	N	Y	Y	Y	Y	Y	Y	Y
NEW YORK								
D'Amato	Y	N	N	Y	Y	Y	Y	Y
Moynihan	N	Y	Y	Y	N	Y	Y	Y
NORTH CAROLINA								
East	Y	N	N	N	Y	Y	Y	?
Helms	Y	N	N	N	Y	N	Y	Y
NORTH DAKOTA								
Andrews	Y	Y	Y	Y	Y	Y	Y	N
Burdick	N	Y	Y	Y	Y	Y	Y	N
OHIO								
Glenn	?	Y	Y	Y	Y	Y	Y	Y
Metzenbaum	N	Y	Y	Y	Y	Y	Y	N
OKLAHOMA								
Nickles	Y	N	N	Y	Y	N	Y	N
Boren	?	Y	Y	Y	N	N	Y	N
OREGON								
Hatfield	Y	Y	Y	N	N	Y	Y	Y
Packwood	Y	Y	Y	?	?	Y	Y	Y
PENNSYLVANIA								
Heinz	Y	N	N	Y	Y	Y	Y	Y
Specter	Y	N	N	Y	Y	Y	Y	Y
RHODE ISLAND								
Chafee	Y	N	N	Y	Y	Y	Y	Y
Pell	Y	Y	Y	N	Y	Y	Y	Y
SOUTH CAROLINA								
Thurmond	Y	N	N	Y	Y	Y	Y	Y
Hollings	?	Y	Y	Y	N	Y	Y	N
SOUTH DAKOTA								
Abdnor	Y	N	N	Y	Y	Y	Y	N
Pressler	Y	N	N	Y	Y	Y	Y	N
TENNESSEE								
Baker	Y	N	N	Y	Y	Y	N	Y
Sasser	N	Y	Y	Y	Y	N	Y	N

KEY

Y Voted for (yea).
\# Paired for.
+ Announced for.
N Voted against (nay).
X Paired against.
- Announced against.
P Voted "present".
C Voted "present" to avoid possible conflict of interest.
? Did not vote or otherwise make a position known.

Democrats   *Republicans*

	213	214	215	216	217	218	219	220
TEXAS								
Tower	Y	N	N	Y	Y	Y	Y	?
Bentsen	Y	N	N	Y	Y	Y	Y	Y
UTAH								
Garn	?	N	N	Y	Y	Y	N	Y
Hatch	?	N	N	Y	Y	N	Y	Y
VERMONT								
Stafford	Y	Y	Y	Y	Y	Y	Y	Y
Leahy	N	Y	Y	Y	N	Y	Y	Y
VIRGINIA								
Trible	Y	N	N	Y	Y	Y	Y	Y
Warner	Y	N	N	Y	Y	Y	Y	Y
WASHINGTON								
Gorton	?	N	N	Y	Y	Y	Y	Y
Jackson	Y	N	N	Y	Y	Y	Y	Y
WEST VIRGINIA								
Byrd	N	N	N	Y	Y	Y	Y	Y
Randolph	N	N	N	Y	Y	Y	Y	Y
WISCONSIN								
Kasten	Y	N	N	Y	Y	Y	Y	Y
Proxmire	Y	Y	Y	N	Y	Y	Y	Y
WYOMING								
Simpson	Y	N	N	Y	Y	Y	Y	Y
Wallop	Y	N	N	Y	Y	N	Y	?

ND - Northern Democrats   SD - Southern Democrats (Southern states - Ala., Ark., Fla., Ga., Ky., La., Miss., N.C., Okla., S.C., Tenn., Texas, Va.)

213. S 675. Omnibus Defense Authorizations. Tower, R-Texas, motion to table (kill) the Melcher, D-Mont., amendment to provide a 4 percent pay raise for military recruits with funds transferred from the amount authorized for recruiting. Motion agreed to 56-26: R 46-0; D 10-26 (ND 8-21, SD 2-5), July 25, 1983.

214. S 675. Omnibus Defense Authorizations. Hart, D-Colo., amendment to bar the use of funds for procurement of MX missiles. Rejected 41-58: R 7-46; D 34-12 (ND 27-5, SD 7-7), July 26, 1983. A "nay" was a vote supporting the president's position.

215. S 675. Omnibus Defense Authorizations. Moynihan, D-N.Y., amendment to bar the use of funds to deploy MX missiles. Rejected 42-57: R 7-46; D 35-11 (ND 27-5, SD 8-6), July 26, 1983. A "nay" was a vote supporting the president's position.

216. S 675. Omnibus Defense Authorizations. Levin, D-Mich., amendment expressing the sense of the Senate that the United States and the Soviet Union should both move toward deploying intercontinental ballistic missiles with only one warhead. Adopted 92-6: R 46-6; D 46-0 (ND 32-0, SD 14-0), July 26, 1983.

217. S 675. Omnibus Defense Authorizations. Passage of the bill to authorize $199 billion for weapons procurement, military research and operations, and military construction programs of the Department of Defense and for defense-related programs of the Department of Energy in fiscal 1984. Passed 83-15: R 50-2; D 33-13 (ND 21-11, SD 12-2), July 26, 1983.

218. Volcker Nomination. Confirmation of President Reagan's nomination of Paul A. Volcker of New Jersey to be chairman of the Board of Governors of the Federal Reserve System. Confirmed 84-16: R 46-8; D 38-8 (ND 27-5, SD 11-3), July 27, 1983. A "yea" was a vote supporting the president's position.

219. Treaties. Adoption of the resolutions of ratification for **Exec E, 96th Cong, 1st Sess**, the Revised Nice Agreement Concerning the International Classification of Goods and Services for the Purposes of the Registration of Marks; **Treaty Doc 98-2**, the International Coffee Agreement, 1983; **Exec T, 96th Cong, 1st Sess**, the Convention on Future Multilateral Cooperation in the Northwest Atlantic Fisheries; **Treaty Doc 98-3**, the Eastern Pacific Ocean Tuna Fishing Agreement; **Treaty Doc 97-24**, the Agreement with the People's Republic of China with respect to the mutual exemption from taxation of transportation income from shipping and air transport; **Treaty Doc 97-27**, the Tax Convention with New Zealand; and **Treaty Doc 97-28**, the Tax Convention with Australia. Adopted en bloc 100-0: R 54-0; D 46-0 (ND 32-0, SD 14-0), July 27, 1983. A two-thirds majority of those present and voting (67 in this case) is required for adoption of resolutions of ratification. A "yea" was a vote supporting the president's position.

220. HR 2733. Critical Agricultural Materials Act. Baker, R-Tenn., motion to proceed to the consideration of the resolution (S Res 165) to waive section 402(a) of the Congressional Budget Act of 1974 to permit consideration of the bill to reauthorize federal research and development activities on guayule, and to authorize the secretary of agriculture to keep federal target prices for wheat, feed grains, cotton and rice at fiscal 1983 levels for fiscal 1984 and 1985 (instead of letting them rise automatically as authorized by existing law). Motion agreed to 66-26: R 43-4; D 23-22 (ND 18-13, SD 5-9), July 27, 1983.

	221	222	223	224	225	226	227		221	222	223	224	225	226	227		221	222	223	224	225	226	227
ALABAMA								**IOWA**								**NEW HAMPSHIRE**							
Denton	Y	Y	Y	Y	N	Y	Y	*Grassley*	Y	Y	N	Y	Y	N	N	*Humphrey*	Y	Y	Y	Y	N	Y	Y
Heflin	Y	N	N	Y	N	Y	Y	*Jepsen*	Y	Y	Y	Y	Y	N	N	*Rudman*	Y	Y	Y	Y	N	Y	Y
ALASKA								**KANSAS**								**NEW JERSEY**							
Murkowski	Y	Y	Y	Y	N	Y	Y	*Dole*	N	Y	?	Y	N	Y	Y	Bradley	Y	Y	Y	Y	N	Y	Y
Stevens	Y	Y	Y	Y	N	Y	Y	*Kassebaum*	Y	Y	Y	Y	N	Y	Y	Lautenberg	Y	Y	Y	N	Y	Y	Y
ARIZONA								**KENTUCKY**								**NEW MEXICO**							
Goldwater	?	Y	Y	Y	N	Y	Y	Ford	Y	N	N	Y	Y	N	N	*Domenici*	?	?	?	?	?	?	?
DeConcini	Y	Y	N	Y	N	Y	Y	Huddleston	Y	Y	Y	Y	N	Y	Y	Bingaman	Y	Y	Y	Y	Y	N	N
ARKANSAS								**LOUISIANA**								**NEW YORK**							
Bumpers	Y	N	N	Y	Y	N	N	Johnston	Y	N	N	Y	N	Y	Y	*D'Amato*	Y	Y	Y	Y	N	Y	Y
Pryor	Y	N	N	Y	Y	N	N	Long	N	N	N	Y	N	N	Y	Moynihan	Y	Y	Y	?	N	N
CALIFORNIA								**MAINE**								**NORTH CAROLINA**							
Wilson	Y	Y	Y	Y	N	Y	Y	*Cohen*	?	Y	Y	Y	N	Y	Y	*East*	Y	Y	Y	Y	N	Y	Y
Cranston	Y	N	N	N	?	?	?	Mitchell	Y	Y	Y	Y	Y	N	N	Helms	Y	Y	Y	Y	N	Y	Y
COLORADO								**MARYLAND**								**NORTH DAKOTA**							
Armstrong	Y	Y	Y	Y	N	Y	Y	*Mathias*	Y	Y	N	Y	N	N	N	*Andrews*	Y	N	N	Y	Y	N	N
Hart	?	?	?	?	?	?	?	Sarbanes	Y	N	N	Y	N	Y	Y	Burdick	Y	N	N	Y	N	N	N
CONNECTICUT								**MASSACHUSETTS**								**OHIO**							
Weicker	N	Y	Y	Y	Y	N	N	Kennedy	Y	N	N	N	N	Y	Y	Glenn	?	?	?	?	?	?	?
Dodd	Y	N	Y	N	N	Y	?	Tsongas	Y	Y	Y	Y	Y	N	N	Metzenbaum	Y	N	Y	N	N	Y	Y
DELAWARE								**MICHIGAN**								**OKLAHOMA**							
Roth	Y	Y	Y	Y	N	Y	Y	Levin	Y	N	N	Y	N	Y	Y	*Nickles*	Y	Y	Y	Y	N	Y	Y
Biden	Y	N	N	Y	Y	Y	Y	Riegle	Y	N	N	Y	N	Y	N	Boren	Y	N	N	Y	Y	N	N
FLORIDA								**MINNESOTA**								**OREGON**							
Hawkins	Y	Y	Y	Y	N	Y	Y	*Boschwitz*	Y	Y	Y	Y	N	Y	Y	*Hatfield*	Y	Y	Y	Y	N	Y	Y
Chiles	Y	Y	Y	Y	N	Y	Y	*Durenberger*	Y	Y	Y	Y	N	Y	Y	*Packwood*	Y	Y	Y	Y	N	Y	Y
GEORGIA								**MISSISSIPPI**								**PENNSYLVANIA**							
Mattingly	Y	Y	Y	Y	N	Y	Y	*Cochran*	Y	Y	Y	Y	N	Y	Y	*Heinz*	Y	Y	Y	N	Y	Y	Y
Nunn	Y	Y	Y	Y	N	Y	Y	Stennis	Y	Y	Y	Y	N	N	Y	*Specter*	Y	Y	Y	N	Y	Y	Y
HAWAII								**MISSOURI**								**RHODE ISLAND**							
Inouye	Y	N	N	Y	Y	N	N	*Danforth*	Y	Y	Y	N	Y	N	N	*Chafee*	Y	Y	Y	Y	N	Y	Y
Matsunaga	Y	N	N	Y	N	Y	Y	Eagleton	Y	N	N	Y	N	Y	N	Pell	Y	Y	Y	Y	Y	N	N
IDAHO								**MONTANA**								**SOUTH CAROLINA**							
McClure	Y	Y	Y	Y	N	Y	Y	Baucus	Y	N	N	Y	N	N	N	*Thurmond*	Y	Y	Y	Y	N	Y	Y
Symms	Y	Y	Y	Y	N	Y	Y	Melcher	Y	N	N	Y	N	N	N	Hollings	Y	N	N	Y	?	?	?
ILLINOIS								**NEBRASKA**								**SOUTH DAKOTA**							
Percy	?	?	?	Y	N	Y	Y	Exon	Y	N	N	Y	N	N	N	*Abdnor*	Y	N	N	Y	N	Y	Y
Dixon	Y	Y	Y	Y	Y	N	N	Zorinsky	Y	N	N	Y	N	N	N	*Pressler*	Y	N	N	Y	N	Y	Y
INDIANA								**NEVADA**								**TENNESSEE**							
Lugar	Y	Y	Y	Y	N	Y	Y	*Hecht*	Y	Y	Y	Y	N	Y	Y	*Baker*	Y	Y	Y	Y	N	Y	Y
Quayle	N	Y	Y	Y	N	Y	Y	*Laxalt*	Y	Y	Y	Y	N	Y	Y	Sasser	Y	N	N	Y	N	N	N

	221	222	223	224	225	226	227
TEXAS							
Tower	?	Y	Y	Y	N	Y	Y
Bentsen	Y	Y	Y	Y	N	Y	Y
UTAH							
Garn	Y	Y	Y	Y	N	Y	Y
Hatch	Y	Y	Y	Y	N	Y	Y
VERMONT							
Stafford	Y	Y	Y	Y	Y	Y	Y
Leahy	Y	Y	Y	Y	Y	N	N
VIRGINIA							
Trible	Y	Y	Y	Y	N	Y	Y
Warner	Y	Y	Y	Y	N	Y	Y
WASHINGTON							
Gorton	Y	Y	Y	Y	N	Y	Y
Jackson	Y	N	N	Y	N	Y	Y
WEST VIRGINIA							
Byrd	Y	N	N	Y	N	N	N
Randolph	Y	N	N	Y	N	N	Y
WISCONSIN							
Kasten	Y	N	Y	N	Y	N	Y
Proxmire	N	Y	Y	Y	N	N	N
WYOMING							
Simpson	Y	Y	Y	Y	N	Y	Y
Wallop	Y	Y	Y	Y	N	Y	Y

KEY

Y Voted for (yea).
Paired for.
+ Announced for.
N Voted against (nay).
X Paired against.
- Announced against.
P Voted "present".
C Voted "present" to avoid possible conflict of interest.
? Did not vote or otherwise make a position known.

Democrats *Republicans*

ND - Northern Democrats   SD - Southern Democrats (Southern states - Ala., Ark., Fla., Ga., Ky., La., Miss., N.C., Okla., S.C., Tenn., Texas, Va.)

221. HR 2733. Critical Agricultural Materials Act. Baker, R-Tenn., motion to instruct the sergeant-at-arms to invite the attendance of absent senators. Motion agreed to 88-5: R 46-3; D 42-2 (ND 29-1, SD 13-1), July 27, 1983.

222. HR 2733. Critical Agricultural Materials Act. Baker, R-Tenn., motion to table (kill) the Heflin, D-Ala., motion to recommit to the Agriculture, Nutrition and Forestry Committee the resolution (S Res 165) to waive section 402(a) of the Congressional Budget Act of 1974 to permit consideration of the bill to reauthorize federal research and development activities on guayule, and to authorize the secretary of agriculture to keep federal target prices for wheat, feed grains, cotton and rice at fiscal 1983 levels for fiscal 1984 and 1985 (instead of letting them rise automatically as authorized by existing law). Motion agreed to 64-32: R 48-4; D 16-28 (ND 11-19, SD 5-9), July 27, 1983.

223. HR 2733. Critical Agricultural Materials Act. Adoption of the resolution (S Res 165) to waive section 402(a) of the Congressional Budget Act of 1974 to permit consideration of the bill to reauthorize federal research and development activities on guayule, and to authorize the secretary of agriculture to keep federal target prices for wheat, feed grains, cotton and rice at fiscal 1983 levels for fiscal 1984 and 1985 (instead of letting them rise automatically as authorized by existing law). Adopted 64-31: R 47-4; D 17-27 (ND 12-18, SD 5-9), July 27, 1983.

224. HR 2973. Interest and Dividend Tax Withholding/Caribbean Basin Initiative. Adoption of the conference report on the bill to repeal interest and dividend withholding requirements due to take effect Aug. 5; to impose new tax compliance requirements and penalties; and to provide trade and tax incentives to certain Caribbean nations. Adopted (thus cleared for the president) 90-7: R 51-2; D 39-5 (ND 25-5, SD 14-0), July 28, 1983.

225. S 602. Radio Marti. Weicker, R-Conn., motion to recommit to the Foreign Relations Committee the resolution (S Res 160) waiving section 402(a) of the Congressional Budget Act of 1974 with respect to consideration of the bill to authorize government-sponsored radio broadcasting to Cuba. Motion rejected 33-61: R 9-44; D 24-17 (ND 19-9, SD 5-8), July 28, 1983.

226. S 602. Radio Marti. Symms, R-Idaho, motion to table (kill) the Weicker, R-Conn., motion to recommit to the Budget Committee the resolution (S Res 160) waiving section 402(a) of the Congressional Budget Act of 1974 with respect to consideration of the bill to authorize government-sponsored radio broadcasting to Cuba. Motion agreed to 62-33: R 45-8; D 17-25 (ND 11-18, SD 6-7), July 28, 1983.

227. S 602. Radio Marti. Adoption of the resolution (S Res 160) waiving section 402(a) of the Congressional Budget Act of 1974 with respect to consideration of the bill to authorize government-sponsored radio broadcasting to Cuba. Adopted 64-30: R 45-8; D 19-22 (ND 11-17, SD 8-5), July 28, 1983.

	228	229	230	231	232	233
ALABAMA						
Denton	-	?	Y	N	Y	N
Heflin	?	?	Y	N	Y	Y
ALASKA						
Murkowski	Y	Y	Y	N	N	Y
Stevens	Y	Y	Y	N	Y	Y
ARIZONA						
Goldwater	Y	Y	?	?	?	?
DeConcini	Y	N	Y	Y	Y	Y
ARKANSAS						
Bumpers	?	Y	Y	Y	N	Y
Pryor	?	?	Y	Y	N	Y
CALIFORNIA						
Wilson	Y	Y	Y	N	Y	N
Cranston	?	?	Y	Y	N	?
COLORADO						
Armstrong	Y	Y	Y	N	Y	N
Hart	?	?	Y	Y	Y	Y
CONNECTICUT						
Weicker	Y	Y	?	Y	N	Y
Dodd	?	?	Y	Y	N	Y
DELAWARE						
Roth	N	N	Y	N	Y	Y
Biden	N	N	Y	Y	Y	Y
FLORIDA						
Hawkins	Y	?	Y	Y	Y	Y
Chiles	Y	Y	Y	Y	Y	Y
GEORGIA						
Mattingly	N	Y	Y	N	Y	N
Nunn	N	N	Y	Y	Y	Y
HAWAII						
Inouye	Y	Y	Y	N	Y	Y
Matsunaga	Y	Y	Y	Y	Y	Y
IDAHO						
McClure	?	?	Y	N	Y	N
Symms	N	Y	Y	N	Y	N
ILLINOIS						
Percy	Y	Y	Y	N	Y	Y
Dixon	Y	Y	Y	Y	Y	Y
INDIANA						
Lugar	N	N	Y	N	Y	N
Quayle	Y	Y	Y	N	Y	Y
IOWA						
Grassley	-	?	Y	N	N	Y
Jepsen	N	N	Y	N	N	N
KANSAS						
Dole	N	Y	Y	N	Y	N
Kassebaum	Y	Y	Y	N	N	Y
KENTUCKY						
Ford	Y	Y	Y	N	N	Y
Huddleston	?	?	Y	N	Y	Y
LOUISIANA						
Johnston	?	?	Y	N	N	Y
Long	Y	Y	Y	Y	N	Y
MAINE						
Cohen	N	N	Y	N	Y	Y
Mitchell	N	N	Y	Y	N	Y
MARYLAND						
Mathias	?	?	Y	N	N	Y
Sarbanes	Y	N	Y	Y	Y	Y
MASSACHUSETTS						
Kennedy	?	?	Y	Y	Y	Y
Tsongas	Y	Y	Y	Y	N	Y
MICHIGAN						
Levin	Y	N	Y	Y	N	Y
Riegle	Y	Y	Y	Y	N	Y
MINNESOTA						
Boschwitz	?	?	Y	N	Y	Y
Durenberger	Y	Y	Y	Y	?	?
MISSISSIPPI						
Cochran	Y	Y	Y	N	N	Y
Stennis	Y	Y	?	N	N	Y
MISSOURI						
Danforth	Y	Y	Y	N	Y	Y
Eagleton	Y	Y	Y	N	Y	Y
MONTANA						
Baucus	N	N	Y	N	N	Y
Melcher	Y	N	Y	N	Y	Y
NEBRASKA						
Exon	Y	Y	Y	N	N	Y
Zorinsky	N	N	Y	N	N	N
NEVADA						
Hecht	Y	Y	Y	N	Y	N
Laxalt	?	?	Y	N	Y	N
NEW HAMPSHIRE						
Humphrey	N	Y	Y	Y	Y	N
Rudman	Y	Y	Y	N	Y	N
NEW JERSEY						
Bradley	N	Y	Y	Y	Y	Y
Lautenberg	?	?	Y	Y	Y	Y
NEW MEXICO						
Domenici	?	?	Y	N	Y	?
Bingaman	Y	Y	Y	Y	Y	Y
NEW YORK						
D'Amato	Y	Y	Y	N	Y	Y
Moynihan	?	?	Y	N	N	Y
NORTH CAROLINA						
East	N	N	Y	N	Y	N
Helms	N	N	N	Y	N	N
NORTH DAKOTA						
Andrews	Y	Y	Y	N	N	Y
Burdick	Y	Y	Y	Y	N	Y
OHIO						
Glenn	?	?	Y	?	?	?
Metzenbaum	Y	Y	Y	Y	Y	Y
OKLAHOMA						
Nickles	-	?	N	N	Y	Y
Boren	?	?	Y	N	N	Y
OREGON						
Hatfield	+	+	Y	N	N	Y
Packwood	Y	Y	Y	Y	Y	Y
PENNSYLVANIA						
Heinz	?	?	Y	N	Y	Y
Specter	N	N	Y	N	Y	Y
RHODE ISLAND						
Chafee	Y	?	Y	N	Y	Y
Pell	Y	?	Y	Y	?	Y
SOUTH CAROLINA						
Thurmond	Y	Y	Y	N	Y	Y
Hollings	N	Y	Y	Y	Y	Y
SOUTH DAKOTA						
Abdnor	Y	Y	Y	N	Y	N
Pressler	N	Y	Y	N	Y	Y
TENNESSEE						
Baker	Y	Y	Y	N	Y	Y
Sasser	N	N	Y	Y	Y	Y
TEXAS						
Tower	?	?	Y	N	Y	Y
Bentsen	?	?	Y	Y	Y	?
UTAH						
Garn	N	N	Y	N	Y	Y
Hatch	N	N	Y	N	Y	Y
VERMONT						
Stafford	Y	Y	Y	N	N	Y
Leahy	?	?	Y	Y	N	Y
VIRGINIA						
Trible	Y	Y	Y	Y	Y	Y
Warner	N	N	Y	Y	Y	Y
WASHINGTON						
Gorton	Y	Y	Y	N	Y	Y
Jackson	Y	Y	Y	N	Y	Y
WEST VIRGINIA						
Byrd	Y	N	Y	N	Y	N
Randolph	Y	Y	Y	N	Y	Y
WISCONSIN						
Kasten	Y	Y	Y	+	+	?
Proxmire	N	N	Y	N	Y	N
WYOMING						
Simpson	N	Y	Y	N	Y	Y
Wallop	Y	?	Y	N	Y	N

KEY

Y Voted for (yea).
Paired for.
+ Announced for.
N Voted against (nay).
X Paired against.
- Announced against.
P Voted "present".
C Voted "present" to avoid possible conflict of interest.
? Did not vote or otherwise make a position known.

Democrats *Republicans*

ND - Northern Democrats   SD - Southern Democrats (Southern states - Ala., Ark., Fla., Ga., Ky., La., Miss., N.C., Okla., S.C., Tenn., Texas, Va.)

228. HR 3069. Supplemental Appropriations, Fiscal 1983. Adoption of the conference report on the bill to appropriate $7,038,061,267 in new budget authority for fiscal 1983 supplemental funds for various government agencies. Adopted 49-25: R 27-16; D 22-9 (ND 18-6, SD 4-3), July 29, 1983. The president had requested $15,138,053,808 in supplemental funds for fiscal 1983.

229. HR 3069. Supplemental Appropriations, Fiscal 1983. Stevens, R-Alaska, motion that the Senate concur in a block of amendments adopted by the House. Motion agreed to 49-22: R 30-10; D 19-12 (ND 13-10, SD 6-2), July 29, 1983.

230. HR 1646. Railroad Retirement Solvency. Passage of the bill to increase taxes and change benefits so as to restore solvency to the federal railroad retirement and railroad unemployment compensation programs. Passed 95-2: R 50-2; D 45-0 (ND 32-0, SD 13-0), Aug. 2, 1983.

231. HR 3363. Interior Appropriations, Fiscal 1984. Judgment of the Senate affirming the chair's ruling that the pending Appropriations Committee amendment to the bill relating to the Bonneville Power Administration was out of order. Ruling of the chair rejected 40-57: R 8-44; D 32-13 (ND 24-7, SD 8-6), Aug. 3, 1983.

232. S 602. Radio Marti. Helms, R-N.C., motion to invoke cloture (thus limiting debate) on the Baker, R-Tenn., motion to proceed to the consideration of the bill to authorize creation of a U.S. government radio station, to be called Radio Marti, to broadcast news, information and opinion to Cuba. Motion agreed to 62-33: R 41-10; D 21-23 (ND 14-16, SD 7-7), Aug. 3, 1983. A three-fifths vote (60) of the total Senate is required to invoke cloture.

233. HR 3329. Transportation Appropriations, Fiscal 1984. Mathias, R-Md., motion to concur in a House amendment regarding a reduction in obligations for highway programs, with an amendment prohibiting the use of funds before Oct. 15, 1983, to implement proposed Office of Personnel Management civil service rules. Motion agreed to 75-18: R 33-17; D 42-1 (ND 29-1, SD 13-0), Aug. 3, 1983.

	234	235	236	237	238	239	240	241
ALABAMA								
Denton	Y	Y	Y	Y	Y	Y	Y	Y
Heflin	Y	N	N	N	N	N	N	N
ALASKA								
Murkowski	Y	Y	Y	N	Y	Y	N	N
Stevens	Y	Y	Y	Y	Y	Y	Y	Y
ARIZONA								
Goldwater	Y	Y	Y	Y	Y	Y	Y	Y
DeConcini	Y	N	N	N	Y	N	N	N
ARKANSAS								
Bumpers	Y	Y	Y	N	Y	N	Y	N
Pryor	Y	N	N	N	Y	N	N	N
CALIFORNIA								
Wilson	Y	Y	Y	N	Y	N	Y	N
Cranston	?	?	?	?	?	?	?	?
COLORADO								
Armstrong	Y	N	N	N	N	N	N	N
Hart	X	Y	Y	Y	Y	Y	Y	Y
CONNECTICUT								
Weicker	?	Y	Y	Y	Y	Y	N	N
Dodd	Y	N	Y	N	Y	Y	N	N
DELAWARE								
Roth	Y	Y	Y	Y	Y	Y	Y	Y
Biden	+	Y	N	N	Y	Y	Y	N
FLORIDA								
Hawkins	Y	Y	N	N	Y	N	N	N
Chiles	Y	N	Y	N	Y	N	N	Y
GEORGIA								
Mattingly	Y	Y	N	N	Y	N	N	N
Nunn	Y	Y	Y	Y	Y	Y	Y	Y
HAWAII								
Inouye	#	Y	Y	Y	Y	Y	Y	Y
Matsunaga	Y	Y	Y	Y	Y	Y	Y	Y
IDAHO								
McClure	Y	N	N	Y	N	Y	N	N
Symms	Y	N	N	N	N	N	N	N
ILLINOIS								
Percy	Y	Y	Y	N	Y	Y	Y	Y
Dixon	Y	Y	N	Y	N	Y	Y	N
INDIANA								
Lugar	Y	Y	Y	Y	Y	Y	Y	Y
Quayle	Y	N	Y	Y	Y	Y	N	N

	234	235	236	237	238	239	240	241
IOWA								
Grassley	Y	Y	Y	N	Y	N	Y	N
Jepsen	Y	Y	Y	Y	Y	Y	Y	Y
KANSAS								
Dole	Y	Y	N	Y	N	N	N	Y
Kassebaum	Y	Y	Y	Y	Y	Y	Y	Y
KENTUCKY								
Ford	Y	Y	N	N	Y	N	N	N
Huddleston	Y	N	N	N	Y	N	Y	Y
LOUISIANA								
Johnston	Y	Y	Y	N	Y	N	N	N
Long	?	?	?	?	?	?	?	?
MAINE								
Cohen	Y	Y	Y	N	Y	Y	N	N
Mitchell	Y	N	N	N	Y	N	N	N
MARYLAND								
Mathias	Y	Y	Y	Y	Y	Y	Y	Y
Sarbanes	Y	Y	Y	Y	Y	Y	Y	Y
MASSACHUSETTS								
Kennedy	N	Y	Y	?	Y	Y	Y	Y
Tsongas	N	?	?	Y	Y	Y	Y	Y
MICHIGAN								
Levin	N	N	N	N	Y	Y	N	N
Riegle	Y	Y	Y	N	Y	Y	Y	Y
MINNESOTA								
Boschwitz	Y	Y	Y	Y	Y	Y	Y	Y
Durenberger	Y	Y	Y	Y	Y	Y	Y	Y
MISSISSIPPI								
Cochran	Y	N	N	N	Y	N	Y	N
Stennis	Y	Y	Y	Y	Y	Y	Y	Y
MISSOURI								
Danforth	?	Y	Y	Y	Y	Y	Y	Y
Eagleton	Y	Y	Y	Y	Y	Y	Y	Y
MONTANA								
Baucus	Y	N	Y	N	Y	N	N	N
Melcher	Y	Y	N	Y	N	N	N	N
NEBRASKA								
Exon	Y	Y	Y	N	Y	N	Y	N
Zorinsky	Y	N	N	N	N	N	N	N
NEVADA								
Hecht	Y	Y	Y	Y	Y	Y	Y	Y
Laxalt	Y	Y	Y	N	Y	Y	Y	Y

	234	235	236	237	238	239	240	241
NEW HAMPSHIRE								
Humphrey	Y	N	N	N	N	N	N	N
Rudman	Y	Y	Y	Y	Y	Y	Y	Y
NEW JERSEY								
Bradley	Y	N	N	Y	N	N	N	N
Lautenberg	Y	Y	Y	N	Y	Y	Y	N
NEW MEXICO								
Domenici	Y	Y	Y	Y	Y	Y	Y	Y
Bingaman	Y	Y	Y	Y	Y	Y	Y	Y
NEW YORK								
D'Amato	Y	Y	N	N	Y	N	N	N
Moynihan	Y	Y	Y	Y	Y	Y	Y	Y
NORTH CAROLINA								
East	Y	N	N	N	N	N	N	N
Helms	Y	N	N	N	N	N	N	N
NORTH DAKOTA								
Andrews	Y	Y	Y	Y	Y	Y	Y	Y
Burdick	Y	Y	Y	Y	Y	Y	Y	Y
OHIO								
Glenn	?	Y	Y	N	Y	Y	?	?
Metzenbaum	N	Y	Y	N	Y	Y	Y	Y
OKLAHOMA								
Nickles	Y	N	N	N	N	Y	N	N
Boren	Y	N	Y	N	N	Y	N	N
OREGON								
Hatfield	?	Y	Y	Y	Y	Y	Y	Y
Packwood	Y	Y	Y	N	Y	Y	Y	Y
PENNSYLVANIA								
Heinz	Y	Y	Y	Y	Y	Y	Y	N
Specter	Y	N	N	N	Y	N	N	N
RHODE ISLAND								
Chafee	Y	Y	Y	Y	Y	Y	Y	Y
Pell	N	Y	Y	Y	Y	Y	Y	Y
SOUTH CAROLINA								
Thurmond	Y	Y	Y	Y	Y	Y	Y	Y
Hollings	N	?	?	?	?	?	?	?
SOUTH DAKOTA								
Abdnor	Y	Y	Y	Y	Y	Y	Y	Y
Pressler	Y	?	?	?	?	?	?	?
TENNESSEE								
Baker	Y	Y	Y	Y	Y	Y	Y	Y
Sasser	Y	Y	Y	Y	Y	Y	Y	Y

	234	235	236	237	238	239	240	241
TEXAS								
Tower	Y	Y	Y	Y	Y	Y	Y	Y
Bentsen	Y	N	Y	N	Y	N	Y	N
UTAH								
Garn	Y	Y	N	N	N	N	N	N
Hatch	Y	Y	N	N	N	N	N	N
VERMONT								
Stafford	Y	Y	Y	Y	Y	Y	Y	Y
Leahy	N	Y	Y	Y	Y	Y	Y	Y
VIRGINIA								
Trible	Y	Y	Y	Y	Y	Y	Y	Y
Warner	Y	Y	Y	Y	Y	Y	Y	Y
WASHINGTON								
Gorton	Y	Y	Y	Y	Y	Y	Y	Y
*Evans * †*	Y	Y	Y	Y	Y	Y	Y	Y
WEST VIRGINIA								
Byrd	Y	Y	Y	Y	Y	Y	Y	Y
Randolph	Y	Y	N	Y	Y	Y	Y	N
WISCONSIN								
Kasten	Y	N	N	N	N	N	N	N
Proxmire	N	Y	Y	Y	Y	Y	Y	Y
WYOMING								
Simpson	Y	Y	N	N	N	Y	N	Y
Wallop	Y	N	Y	N	Y	Y	Y	Y

ND - Northern Democrats   SD - Southern Democrats (Southern states - Ala., Ark., Fla., Ga., Ky., La., Miss., N.C., Okla., S.C., Tenn., Texas, Va.)

* *Sen. Henry M. Jackson, D-Wash., died Sept. 1, 1983. The last vote for which he was eligible was CQ vote 233.*

† *Sen. Daniel J. Evans, R-Wash., was sworn in Sept. 12, 1983. He was appointed to fill the seat left vacant by Henry M. Jackson, D-Wash., until a special election is held Nov. 8. The first vote for which he was eligible was CQ vote 234.*

234. S 675. Omnibus Defense Authorizations. Adoption of the conference report on the bill to authorize $187.5 billion for weapons procurement, military research and operations and maintenance of the Department of Defense in fiscal 1984. Adopted 83-8: R 52-0; D 31-8 (ND 19-7, SD 12-1), Sept. 13, 1983.

235. H J Res 353. Korean Plane Resolution. Baker, R-Tenn., motion to table (kill) division 1 of the Helms, R-N.C., amendment stating the sense of Congress that the president should recall the United States ambassador to the Soviet Union for urgent consultations. Motion agreed to 70-25: R 42-12; D 28-13 (ND 22-7, SD 6-6), Sept. 15, 1983. A "yea" was a vote supporting the president's position.

236. H J Res. 353. Korean Plane Resolution. Baker, R-Tenn., motion to table (kill) division 2 of the Helms, R-N.C., amendment stating the sense of Congress that the president should reappraise the complete spectrum of U.S.-Soviet relations, including arms control, human rights, East-West trade and regional issues. Motion agreed to 69-26: R 38-16; D 31-10 (ND 23-6, SD 8-4), Sept. 15, 1983. A "yea" was a vote supporting the president's position.

237. H J Res. 353. Korean Plane Resolution. Baker, R-Tenn., motion to table (kill) division 3 of the Helms, R-N.C., amendment stating the sense of Congress that the president should report to Congress on the record of the Soviet Union's compliance or non-compliance with all existing arms control agreements. Motion agreed to 50-45: R 33-21; D 17-24 (ND 14-15, SD 3-9), Sept. 15, 1983. A "yea" was a vote supporting the president's position.

238. H J Res. 353. Korean Plane Resolution. Baker, R-Tenn., motion to table (kill) division 4 of the Helms, R-N.C.,

amendment stating the sense of Congress that the president should direct the U.S. negotiators at strategic arms reduction talks to link the outcome of those talks with the willingness of the Soviet Union to abide by international law. Motion agreed to 82-14: R 42-12; D 40-2 (ND 29-1, SD 11-1), Sept. 15, 1983. A "yea" was a vote supporting the president's position.

239. H J Res 353. Korean Plane Resolution. Baker, R-Tenn., motion to table (kill) division 5 of the Helms, R-N.C., amendment stating the sense of Congress that the president should re-emphasize the inconsistency of the Soviet military presence in the Western Hemisphere with the Monroe Doctrine. Motion agreed to 60-36: R 35-19; D 25-17 (ND 22-8, SD 3-9), Sept. 15, 1983. A "yea" was a vote supporting the president's position.

240. H J Res 353. Korean Plane Resolution. Baker, R-Tenn., motion to table (kill) division 6 of the Helms, R-N.C., amendment stating the sense of Congress that the president should tighten substantially the foreign policy and military controls over the export of machine tools, high technology products and equipment for the development of Soviet oil and gas resources. Motion agreed to 66-29: R 37-17; D 29-12 (ND 21-8, SD 8-4), Sept. 15, 1983. A "yea" was a vote supporting the president's position.

241. H J Res 353. Korean Plane Resolution. Baker, R-Tenn., motion to table (kill) division 7 of the Helms, R-N.C., amendment stating the sense of Congress that the president should direct the secretary of the Treasury to use existing authority to prevent the importation of any product made in the Soviet Union with forced labor. Motion agreed to 52-43: R 32-22; D 20-21 (ND 15-14, SD 5-7), Sept. 15, 1983. A "yea" was a vote supporting the president's position.

	242	243	244	245	246	247	248	249
ALABAMA								
Denton	Y	Y	N	N	Y	Y	?	N
Heflin	N	Y	Y	Y	Y	Y	Y	N
ALASKA								
Murkowski	Y	Y	N	N	Y	Y	N	Y
Stevens	Y	Y	N	N	Y	Y	N	Y
ARIZONA								
Goldwater	Y	Y	N	N	?	?	?	?
DeConcini	N	Y	Y	Y	Y	Y	N	Y
ARKANSAS								
Bumpers	N	N	Y	Y	N	N	N	Y
Pryor	N	Y	Y	Y	Y	N	Y	N
CALIFORNIA								
Wilson	N	Y	N	N	Y	Y	Y	Y
Cranston	?	+	Y	Y	?	N	N	N
COLORADO								
Armstrong	N	Y	N	N	Y	Y	Y	N
Hart	Y	Y	Y	Y	?	Y	N	Y
CONNECTICUT								
Weicker	Y	Y	N	Y	N	Y	N	Y
Dodd	N	Y	Y	Y	N	N	N	Y
DELAWARE								
Roth	N	Y	N	Y	Y	Y	Y	N
Biden	Y	Y	Y	Y	N	N	N	N
FLORIDA								
Hawkins	N	Y	N	Y	N	Y	Y	Y
Chiles	N	Y	Y	Y	Y	Y	N	Y
GEORGIA								
Mattingly	N	Y	N	Y	Y	Y	Y	N
Nunn	Y	Y	Y	Y	N	N	Y	Y
HAWAII								
Inouye	N	Y	?	?	?	N	N	Y
Matsunaga	Y	Y	Y	Y	?	N	Y	N
IDAHO								
McClure	N	Y	N	N	Y	N	Y	N
Symms	N	Y	N	N	Y	Y	Y	Y
ILLINOIS								
Percy	Y	Y	Y	Y	Y	Y	Y	Y
Dixon	Y	Y	Y	N	Y	N	N	Y
INDIANA								
Lugar	Y	Y	Y	N	Y	Y	N	Y
Quayle	Y	Y	Y	N	Y	Y	Y	N
IOWA								
Grassley	Y	Y	Y	N	Y	Y	Y	N
Jepsen	Y	Y	Y	N	Y	Y	Y	N
KANSAS								
Dole	Y	Y	Y	N	Y	Y	Y	N
Kassebaum	Y	Y	Y	N	Y	Y	N	Y
KENTUCKY								
Ford	N	Y	Y	Y	Y	N	N	Y
Huddleston	N	Y	Y	Y	Y	N	N	Y
LOUISIANA								
Johnston	N	Y	N	Y	Y	Y	N	Y
Long	?	+	Y	Y	Y	Y	Y	Y
MAINE								
Cohen	N	Y	Y	Y	N	Y	N	Y
Mitchell	N	Y	Y	Y	Y	Y	N	Y
MARYLAND								
Mathias	Y	Y	?	Y	Y	?	?	?
Sarbanes	Y	Y	Y	Y	Y	Y	N	Y
MASSACHUSETTS								
Kennedy	N	Y	Y	Y	Y	N	N	Y
Tsongas	Y	Y	Y	Y	Y	N	N	Y
MICHIGAN								
Levin	N	Y	Y	Y	N	N	N	Y
Riegle	N	Y	Y	Y	N	N	Y	Y
MINNESOTA								
Boschwitz	Y	Y	Y	N	Y	N	N	Y
Durenberger	Y	Y	N	Y	Y	N	Y	Y
MISSISSIPPI								
Cochran	N	Y	N	N	Y	N	Y	N
Stennis	Y	Y	Y	Y	?	?	?	?
MISSOURI								
Danforth	Y	Y	Y	Y	Y	N	Y	Y
Eagleton	Y	Y	Y	Y	Y	Y	N	N
MONTANA								
Baucus	N	Y	Y	Y	N	N	Y	Y
Melcher	N	Y	Y	N	N	N	N	Y
NEBRASKA								
Exon	N	Y	Y	Y	N	N	Y	Y
Zorinsky	N	Y	Y	Y	N	N	Y	Y
NEVADA								
Hecht	Y	Y	N	N	Y	Y	Y	Y
Laxalt	?	Y	Y	N	Y	Y	Y	Y
NEW HAMPSHIRE								
Humphrey	N	Y	Y	N	Y	N	Y	N
Rudman	Y	Y	Y	Y	Y	Y	Y	Y
NEW JERSEY								
Bradley	N	Y	Y	Y	N	N	N	Y
Lautenberg	N	Y	Y	Y	Y	N	N	Y
NEW MEXICO								
Domenici	Y	Y	N	N	Y	Y	Y	Y
Bingaman	N	Y	Y	Y	Y	N	N	Y
NEW YORK								
D'Amato	N	Y	Y	Y	Y	Y	Y	Y
Moynihan	Y	Y	Y	Y	Y	Y	N	Y
NORTH CAROLINA								
East	N	Y	N	N	Y	Y	Y	N
Helms	N	Y	N	N	Y	Y	Y	N
NORTH DAKOTA								
Andrews	Y	Y	N	Y	N	Y	N	Y
Burdick	Y	Y	N	Y	N	N	Y	Y
OHIO								
Glenn	?	+	Y	Y	N	N	N	Y
Metzenbaum	N	Y	Y	N	N	N	N	N
OKLAHOMA								
Nickles	N	Y	N	N	Y	N	Y	N
Boren	N	Y	Y	Y	Y	Y	N	Y
OREGON								
Hatfield	Y	Y	Y	N	Y	?	-	+
Packwood	N	Y	Y	Y	Y	Y	N	Y
PENNSYLVANIA								
Heinz	Y	Y	N	Y	Y	Y	Y	Y
Specter	N	Y	Y	Y	Y	Y	Y	Y
RHODE ISLAND								
Chafee	Y	Y	Y	Y	Y	Y	N	Y
Pell	Y	Y	Y	Y	N	N	N	Y
SOUTH CAROLINA								
Thurmond	Y	Y	-	-	+	Y	Y	N
Hollings	?	+	Y	Y	Y	?	?	?
SOUTH DAKOTA								
Abdnor	Y	Y	N	N	Y	Y	Y	Y
Pressler	?	?	N	N	Y	Y	Y	Y
TENNESSEE								
Baker	Y	Y	?	?	?	Y	N	Y
Sasser	N	Y	N	Y	N	Y	N	Y
TEXAS								
Tower	Y	Y	N	N	Y	?	?	?
Bentsen	N	Y	Y	Y	Y	Y	N	Y
UTAH								
Garn	Y	Y	N	N	Y	Y	Y	Y
Hatch	Y	Y	N	N	Y	Y	Y	Y
VERMONT								
Stafford	Y	Y	N	Y	N	Y	N	Y
Leahy	N	Y	Y	Y	Y	Y	N	Y
VIRGINIA								
Trible	Y	Y	N	N	Y	Y	N	N
Warner	Y	Y	N	N	Y	Y	N	N
WASHINGTON								
Gorton	Y	Y	N	N	Y	N	Y	N
Evans	Y	Y	N	N	Y	N	Y	N
WEST VIRGINIA								
Byrd	Y	Y	Y	Y	N	N	Y	Y
Randolph	N	Y	Y	Y	Y	Y	Y	Y
WISCONSIN								
Kasten	N	Y	N	Y	N	Y	N	Y
Proxmire	Y	Y	N	N	N	N	Y	N
WYOMING								
Simpson	Y	Y	N	N	Y	N	Y	N
Wallop	N	Y	N	N	Y	Y	N	Y

KEY

Y Voted for (yea).
\# Paired for.
+ Announced for.
N Voted against (nay).
X Paired against.
- Announced against.
P Voted "present".
C Voted "present" to avoid possible conflict of interest.
? Did not vote or otherwise make a position known.

Democrats *Republicans*

ND - Northern Democrats SD - Southern Democrats (Southern states - Ala., Ark., Fla., Ga., Ky., La., Miss., N.C., Okla., S.C., Tenn., Texas, Va.)

242. H J Res 353. Korean Plane Resolution. Baker, R-Tenn., motion to table (kill) the Huddleston, D-Ky., amendment to require the Soviet Union to reduce "substantially" the number of diplomats stationed in the United States to conform with the number of U.S. diplomats stationed in the Soviet Union. Motion agreed to 49-45: R 35-18; D 14-27 (ND 12-17, SD 2-10), Sept. 15, 1983. A "yea" was a vote supporting the president's position.

243. H J Res 353. Korean Plane Resolution. Passage of the joint resolution to condemn the Soviet Union for its destruction of a Korean civilian airliner. Passed 95-0: R 54-0; D 41-0 (ND 29-0, SD 12-0), Sept. 15, 1983.

244. HR 3363. Interior Appropriations, Fiscal 1984. Bumpers, D-Ark., amendment to ban all further coal leasing on federal lands until 90 days after a special commission created to study the Interior Department's coal leasing policies has completed its report. Adopted 63-33: R 23-29; D 40-4 (ND 29-1, SD 11-3), Sept. 20, 1983.

245. HR 3363. Interior Appropriations, Fiscal 1984. Bradley, D-N.J., amendment to add $1.3 billion to the bill, in the off-budget account, for acquisition of oil to fill the Strategic Petroleum Reserve at a rate of 220,000 barrels per day, the current rate. The president sought a fill rate of 145,000 barrels per day. The amendment also added $370 million in budget authority to build a permanent oil storage facility at Big Hill, Texas. Adopted 54-43: R 12-41; D 42-2 (ND 28-2, SD 14-0), Sept. 20, 1983. A "nay" was a vote supporting the president's position.

246. HR 3363. Interior Appropriations, Fiscal 1984. Judgment of the Senate whether the Domenici, R-N.M.-Bingaman, D-N.M., amendment to provide $450,000 for legal fees of non-Indian litigants in New Mexico water rights litigation was germane. Ruled germane 77-16: R 52-0; D 25-16 (ND 15-13, SD 10-3), Sept. 20, 1983.

248. HR 3363. Interior Appropriations, Fiscal 1984. Nickles, R-Okla., amendment to delete from National Park Service appropriations $650,000 earmarked for the Washington Opera. Rejected 40-53: R 29-21; D 11-32 (ND 7-24, SD 4-8), Sept. 21, 1983.

247. HR 3363. Interior Appropriations, Fiscal 1984. Domenici, R-N.M.-Bingaman, D-N.M., amendment to provide $450,000 for legal fees of non-Indian litigants in New Mexico water rights litigation. Adopted 69-25: R 48-3; D 21-22 (ND 13-18, SD 8-4), Sept. 21, 1983.

249. HR 3363. Interior Appropriations, Fiscal 1984. Passage of the bill to appropriate $8,059,401,000 in fiscal 1984 for the Department of Interior and related agencies. Passed 76-18: R 37-14; D 39-4 (ND 28-3, SD 11-1), Sept. 21, 1983. The president had requested $6,709,628,000 in new budget authority.

CQ Senate Votes 250 - 257

Corresponding to Congressional Record Votes 260, 261, 262, 263, 264, 265, 266, 267

	250	251	252	253	254	255	256	257
ALABAMA								
Denton	N	N	Y	Y	Y	Y	Y	N
Heflin	Y	Y	Y	Y	Y	Y	Y	Y
ALASKA								
Murkowski	N	N	Y	Y	Y	Y	Y	Y
Stevens	N	N	Y	N	N	N	N	Y
ARIZONA								
Goldwater	?	?	?	?	?	?	?	?
DeConcini	N	N	Y	N	N	N	Y	N
ARKANSAS								
Bumpers	Y	Y	Y	Y	N	N	N	Y
Pryor	Y	Y	Y	N	N	N	Y	Y
CALIFORNIA								
Wilson	N	N	Y	N	N	N	Y	Y
Cranston	?	?	?	Y	N	?	?	?
COLORADO								
Armstrong	N	N	N	Y	Y	Y	Y	Y
Hart	Y	Y	?	Y	N	?	?	?
CONNECTICUT								
Weicker	N	Y	Y	Y	N	?	N	Y
Dodd	?	?	?	Y	N	N	?	?
DELAWARE								
Roth	N	N	Y	N	Y	N	Y	Y
Biden	Y	Y	Y	Y	N	Y	Y	Y
FLORIDA								
Hawkins	N	Y	Y	Y	?	?	?	?
Chiles	N	N	Y	N	Y	N	Y	Y
GEORGIA								
Mattingly	N	N	Y	Y	Y	Y	Y	Y
Nunn	N	N	Y	N	Y	N	Y	Y
HAWAII								
Inouye	Y	Y	Y	Y	N	N	N	Y
Matsunaga	Y	Y	Y	Y	N	N	N	Y
IDAHO								
McClure	N	N	Y	Y	Y	Y	Y	Y
Symms	N	N	Y	Y	Y	Y	Y	Y
ILLINOIS								
Percy	N	N	Y	N	N	N	N	Y
Dixon	N	Y	Y	Y	N	N	N	Y
INDIANA								
Lugar	N	N	Y	N	N	N	Y	Y
Quayle	N	N	Y	N	N	N	Y	Y
IOWA								
Grassley	N	N	Y	Y	Y	Y	Y	N
Jepsen	N	N	Y	N	Y	N	Y	N
KANSAS								
Dole	N	N	Y	Y	Y	Y	Y	Y
Kassebaum	N	N	Y	Y	Y	Y	Y	Y
KENTUCKY								
Ford	N	Y	Y	Y	N	N	Y	Y
Huddleston	Y	Y	Y	?	N	N	Y	Y
LOUISIANA								
Johnston	Y	Y	Y	Y	N	N	Y	Y
Long	Y	Y	Y	Y	Y	Y	?	?
MAINE								
Cohen	N	Y	Y	?	?	?	?	?
Mitchell	Y	Y	Y	Y	N	N	N	N
MARYLAND								
Mathias	?	?	?	?	?	?	?	?
Sarbanes	Y	Y	Y	Y	N	N	N	N
MASSACHUSETTS								
Kennedy	Y	Y	Y	Y	N	N	N	N
Tsongas	Y	Y	Y	Y	N	N	N	N
MICHIGAN								
Levin	Y	Y	Y	Y	N	N	N	N
Riegle	Y	Y	Y	Y	N	N	N	N
MINNESOTA								
Boschwitz	N	N	Y	Y	N	N	Y	N
Durenberger	N	N	Y	?	N	N	N	N
MISSISSIPPI								
Cochran	N	N	Y	Y	N	N	Y	Y
Stennis	?	?	?	Y	N	Y	N	?
MISSOURI								
Danforth	N	N	Y	Y	N	N	N	Y
Eagleton	Y	Y	Y	Y	N	N	N	?
MONTANA								
Baucus	N	N	Y	Y	N	Y	Y	N
Melcher	Y	Y	Y	Y	N	Y	Y	N
NEBRASKA								
Exon	N	N	Y	Y	N	Y	Y	Y
Zorinsky	N	N	Y	N	Y	Y	Y	Y
NEVADA								
Hecht	N	N	Y	Y	N	N	Y	Y
Laxalt	N	N	Y	N	N	N	Y	Y
NEW HAMPSHIRE								
Humphrey	N	N	N	Y	Y	Y	Y	Y
Rudman	N	N	Y	Y	N	Y	Y	Y
NEW JERSEY								
Bradley	Y	Y	Y	Y	N	N	Y	N
Lautenberg	Y	Y	Y	Y	N	N	Y	N
NEW MEXICO								
Domenici	N	N	Y	Y	N	Y	Y	Y
Bingaman	Y	Y	Y	Y	N	N	Y	N
NEW YORK								
D'Amato	Y	Y	Y	Y	N	Y	Y	Y
Moynihan	Y	Y	Y	Y	N	N	N	N
NORTH CAROLINA								
East	N	N	Y	Y	Y	Y	Y	Y
Helms	N	N	N	Y	Y	Y	Y	Y
NORTH DAKOTA								
Andrews	N	N	Y	Y	Y	Y	Y	Y
Burdick	Y	Y	Y	Y	N	Y	Y	Y
OHIO								
Glenn	Y	Y	Y	Y	N	N	?	N
Metzenbaum	Y	Y	Y	Y	N	Y	N	N
OKLAHOMA								
Nickles	N	N	N	Y	Y	Y	Y	Y
Boren	N	N	Y	N	Y	Y	Y	Y
OREGON								
Hatfield	N	N	N	?	?	-	-	X
Packwood	N	N	Y	Y	N	N	Y	?
PENNSYLVANIA								
Heinz	N	N	Y	Y	N	N	Y	Y
Specter	N	N	Y	Y	N	N	N	N
RHODE ISLAND								
Chafee	N	N	Y	Y	N	N	N	N
Pell	Y	Y	Y	Y	N	N	N	N
SOUTH CAROLINA								
Thurmond	N	N	Y	Y	Y	Y	Y	Y
Hollings	?	?	?	Y	N	N	N	N
SOUTH DAKOTA								
Abdnor	N	N	Y	Y	Y	Y	Y	Y
Pressler	N	N	Y	Y	Y	Y	Y	Y
TENNESSEE								
Baker	N	N	Y	N	Y	N	N	Y
Sasser	Y	Y	Y	Y	N	N	Y	Y
TEXAS								
Tower	N	N	Y	N	N	N	N	Y
Bentsen	N	N	Y	N	Y	N	Y	?
UTAH								
Garn	N	N	Y	Y	N	Y	N	Y
Hatch	N	N	Y	N	N	Y	Y	Y
VERMONT								
Stafford	N	N	Y	Y	?	?	?	?
Leahy	Y	Y	Y	Y	N	Y	Y	N
VIRGINIA								
Trible	N	N	Y	Y	Y	Y	Y	Y
Warner	N	N	Y	Y	Y	Y	Y	Y
WASHINGTON								
Gorton	N	N	Y	N	N	N	Y	Y
Evans	N	N	Y	N	N	N	N	Y
WEST VIRGINIA								
Byrd	Y	Y	Y	Y	N	N	Y	Y
Randolph	Y	Y	Y	N	Y	Y	Y	Y
WISCONSIN								
Kasten	N	N	Y	Y	N	Y	Y	Y
Proxmire	N	N	N	Y	N	Y	Y	Y
WYOMING								
Simpson	N	N	Y	?	Y	Y	Y	Y
Wallop	N	N	Y	Y	Y	Y	Y	#

KEY

Y Voted for (yea).
\# Paired for.
\+ Announced for.
N Voted against (nay).
X Paired against.
- Announced against.
P Voted "present".
C Voted "present" to avoid possible conflict of interest.
? Did not vote or otherwise make a position known.

Democrats   *Republicans*

ND - Northern Democrats   SD - Southern Democrats (Southern states - Ala., Ark., Fla., Ga., Ky., La., Miss., N.C., Okla., S.C., Tenn., Texas, Va.)

250. S 1426. Revenue Sharing. Moynihan, D-N.Y., amendment to increase the annual authorization in the bill for the revenue sharing program by $450 million per year, to $5 billion. Rejected 30-64: R 1-52; D 29-12 (ND 22-7, SD 7-5), Sept. 21, 1983. A "nay" was a vote supporting the president's position.

251. S 1426. Revenue Sharing. Bradley, D-N.J., amendment to increase the annual authorization in the bill for the revenue sharing program by $225 million per year, to $4.8 billion. Rejected 36-58: R 4-49; D 32-9 (ND 24-5, SD 8-4), Sept. 21, 1983. A "nay" was a vote supporting the president's position.

252. HR 2780. Revenue Sharing. Passage of the bill to authorize $4.6 billion per year in fiscal years 1984-86 for the general revenue sharing program of grants to local governments and communities. Passed 87-6: R 48-5; D 39-1 (ND 27-1, SD 12-0), Sept. 21, 1983. A "yea" was a vote supporting the president's position.

253. S 1342. State Department Authorizations. McClure, R-Idaho, amendment to require the president to report to Congress on Soviet compliance with the letter and spirit of existing arms control agreements. Adopted 93-0: R 49-0; D 44-0 (ND 31-0, SD 13-0), Sept. 22, 1983.

254. S 1342. State Department Authorizations. Helms, R-N.C., amendment to earmark $52.9 million in fiscal 1984 and $95.3 million in fiscal 1985 for the U.S. Information Agency for engineering, site preparation and enhancement of radio transmitter facilities operated by the Voice of America, and to reduce authorizations in the bill for the National Endowment for Democracy program to promote democracy abroad and the Fulbright educational exchange program by total amounts equal to the funds earmarked for the Voice of America. Rejected 26-68: R 24-25; D 2-43 (ND 0-31, SD 2-12), Sept. 22, 1983. A "nay" was a vote supporting the president's position.

255. S 1342. State Department Authorizations. Zorinsky, D-Neb., amendment to delete authorizations of $31.3 million in each of fiscal years 1984 and 1985 for the National Endowment for Democracy program to promote democracy abroad. Rejected 42-49: R 27-21; D 15-28 (ND 10-19, SD 5-9), Sept. 22, 1983. A "nay" was a vote supporting the president's position.

256. S 1342. State Department Authorizations. Kassebaum, R-Kan., amendment to restrict U.S. payments for calendar year 1984 to the United Nations and affiliated organizations to no more than U.S. payments in calendar year 1980, and to reduce such payments in each of calendar years 1985-87 by an amount equal to 10 percent of such U.S. payments in calendar year 1980, for a total reduction estimated at $500 million. Adopted 66-23: R 39-10; D 27-13 (ND 16-11, SD 11-2), Sept. 22, 1983.

257. S 1342. State Department Authorizations. Simpson, R-Wyo., motion to table (kill) the DeConcini, D-Ariz., amendment to express the sense of Congress that the secretary of state should recommend to the attorney general that aliens from El Salvador be granted extended voluntary departure immigration status until the situation in El Salvador permits them to return to their country safely. Motion agreed to 59-26: R 40-7; D 19-19 (ND 9-18, SD 10-1), Sept. 22, 1983.

Corresponding to Congressional Record Votes 268, 269, 270, 271, 272, 273, 274, 275

KEY

- Y Voted for (yea).
- # Paired for.
- + Announced for.
- N Voted against (nay).
- X Paired against.
- - Announced against.
- P Voted "present".
- C Voted "present" to avoid possible conflict of interest.
- ? Did not vote or otherwise make a position known.

Democrats   *Republicans*

	258	259	260	261	262	263	264	265
ALABAMA								
Denton	N	Y	Y	Y	Y	Y	Y	N
Heflin	N	N	N	N	N	Y	N	Y
ALASKA								
Murkowski	?	Y	Y	Y	Y	Y	Y	N
Stevens	Y	Y	Y	Y	Y	Y	Y	N
ARIZONA								
Goldwater	?	Y	Y	Y	Y	Y	Y	N
DeConcini	?	N	N	N	N	N	N	Y
ARKANSAS								
Bumpers	Y	N	N	N	N	N	N	N
Pryor	N	N	N	N	N	N	N	N
CALIFORNIA								
Wilson	N	Y	Y	Y	Y	Y	Y	N
Cranston	Y	N	N	N	N	N	N	?
COLORADO								
Armstrong	N	Y	Y	Y	Y	Y	Y	N
Hart	?	N	Y	N	N	N	N	?
CONNECTICUT								
Weicker	Y	Y	Y	Y	Y	Y	N	?
Dodd	Y	N	Y	N	N	N	Y	N
DELAWARE								
Roth	Y	Y	Y	Y	Y	Y	N	N
Biden	Y	N	Y	N	N	N	N	Y
FLORIDA								
Hawkins	-	Y	Y	Y	Y	Y	Y	N
Chiles	Y	N	Y	N	N	Y	N	Y
GEORGIA								
Mattingly	N	Y	Y	Y	Y	Y	Y	N
Nunn	Y	N	Y	N	N	Y	N	?
HAWAII								
Inouye	Y	N	N	?	N	N	N	Y
Matsunaga	?	N	N	N	N	N	N	Y
IDAHO								
McClure	N	Y	Y	Y	Y	Y	Y	N
Symms	N	Y	Y	Y	Y	Y	Y	N
ILLINOIS								
Percy	Y	Y	Y	Y	Y	Y	Y	N
Dixon	Y	N	N	N	N	Y	N	Y
INDIANA								
Lugar	Y	Y	Y	Y	Y	Y	Y	N
Quayle	Y	Y	Y	Y	Y	Y	Y	N
IOWA								
Grassley	N	Y	Y	Y	Y	Y	Y	N
Jepsen	N	Y	Y	Y	Y	Y	Y	N
KANSAS								
Dole	N	Y	Y	Y	Y	Y	Y	N
Kassebaum	Y	Y	Y	Y	?	Y	Y	N
KENTUCKY								
Ford	N	N	N	N	N	Y	N	Y
Huddleston	Y	N	N	N	N	N	N	Y
LOUISIANA								
Johnston	N	N	N	N	N	Y	N	N
Long	?	N	N	N	N	N	N	N
MAINE								
Cohen	?	Y	Y	Y	Y	Y	Y	N
Mitchell	Y	N	Y	Y	N	Y	Y	N
MARYLAND								
Mathias	Y	Y	N	?	Y	Y	Y	Y
Sarbanes	Y	N	N	N	N	N	N	?
MASSACHUSETTS								
Kennedy	?	N	N	N	N	N	N	Y
Tsongas	?	N	N	N	N	N	N	Y
MICHIGAN								
Levin	Y	N	N	N	N	N	N	Y
Riegle	N	N	N	N	N	N	N	Y
MINNESOTA								
Boschwitz	Y	Y	Y	Y	Y	Y	Y	N
Durenberger	?	Y	Y	Y	Y	Y	Y	N
MISSISSIPPI								
Cochran	?	Y	Y	Y	Y	Y	Y	N
Stennis	?	N	N	N	N	N	N	N
MISSOURI								
Danforth	?	Y	Y	Y	Y	Y	Y	N
Eagleton	Y	N	N	N	N	N	N	Y
MONTANA								
Baucus	?	N	N	N	N	N	N	Y
Melcher	Y	N	N	N	N	N	N	Y
NEBRASKA								
Exon	Y	N	Y	N	N	N	N	Y
Zorinsky	Y	N	Y	N	N	N	N	Y
NEVADA								
Hecht	N	Y	Y	Y	Y	Y	Y	N
Laxalt	N	Y	Y	Y	Y	Y	Y	N
NEW HAMPSHIRE								
Humphrey	N	Y	Y	Y	Y	Y	Y	N
Rudman	N	Y	Y	Y	Y	Y	Y	N
NEW JERSEY								
Bradley	Y	N	N	N	N	N	N	Y
Lautenberg	Y	N	N	N	N	N	N	Y
NEW MEXICO								
Domenici	Y	Y	Y	Y	Y	Y	Y	N
Bingaman	?	N	N	N	N	N	N	Y
NEW YORK								
D'Amato	N	Y	Y	Y	Y	Y	Y	N
Moynihan	?	N	N	N	N	N	N	Y
NORTH CAROLINA								
East	N	Y	Y	Y	Y	Y	Y	N
Helms	N	Y	Y	Y	Y	Y	Y	N
NORTH DAKOTA								
Andrews	Y	Y	Y	Y	Y	Y	Y	N
Burdick	Y	N	N	N	N	N	N	Y
OHIO								
Glenn	?	N	N	N	N	Y	N	Y
Metzenbaum	Y	N	N	N	N	N	N	Y
OKLAHOMA								
Nickles	N	Y	Y	Y	Y	Y	Y	N
Boren	?	N	N	Y	N	Y	N	Y
OREGON								
Hatfield	?	Y	Y	Y	Y	Y	Y	N
Packwood	Y	Y	Y	Y	Y	Y	Y	N
PENNSYLVANIA								
Heinz	Y	Y	Y	Y	Y	Y	Y	N
Specter	Y	Y	Y	N	Y	Y	Y	Y
RHODE ISLAND								
Chafee	Y	Y	Y	Y	Y	Y	Y	N
Pell	Y	N	N	N	N	N	N	Y
SOUTH CAROLINA								
Thurmond	N	Y	Y	Y	Y	Y	Y	N
Hollings	?	N	N	N	N	N	N	Y
SOUTH DAKOTA								
Abdnor	N	Y	Y	Y	Y	Y	Y	N
Pressler	Y	Y	Y	Y	Y	Y	Y	N
TENNESSEE								
Baker	Y	Y	Y	Y	Y	Y	Y	N
Sasser	?	N	Y	N	N	N	N	Y
TEXAS								
Tower	?	Y	Y	Y	Y	Y	Y	?
Bentsen	Y	N	N	N	N	N	N	Y
UTAH								
Garn	Y	Y	Y	Y	Y	Y	Y	N
Hatch	N	Y	Y	Y	Y	Y	Y	N
VERMONT								
Stafford	?	Y	Y	Y	Y	Y	Y	?
Leahy	Y	N	N	N	N	Y	N	Y
VIRGINIA								
Trible	N	Y	Y	Y	Y	Y	Y	N
Warner	N	Y	Y	Y	Y	Y	Y	N
WASHINGTON								
Gorton	Y	Y	Y	Y	Y	Y	Y	N
Evans	Y	Y	Y	Y	Y	Y	Y	N
WEST VIRGINIA								
Byrd	N	N	N	N	N	N	N	Y
Randolph	N	N	N	N	N	N	N	Y
WISCONSIN								
Kasten	N	Y	Y	Y	Y	Y	Y	N
Proxmire	Y	N	N	N	N	N	N	N
WYOMING								
Simpson	?	Y	Y	Y	Y	Y	Y	N
Wallop	Y	Y	Y	Y	Y	Y	Y	N

ND - Northern Democrats   SD - Southern Democrats (Southern states - Ala., Ark., Fla., Ga., Ky., La., Miss., N.C., Okla., S.C., Tenn., Texas, Va.)

258. S 869. Export-Import Bank. Baker, R-Tenn., motion to table (kill) the Helms, R-N.C., amendment to require the United States to oppose loans by the International Monetary Fund to communist dictatorships. Motion agreed to 45-30: R 21-23; D 24-7 (ND 19-3, SD 5-4), Sept. 23, 1983. A "yea" was a vote supporting the president's position.

259. S J Res 159. Multinational Force in Lebanon. Baker, R-Tenn., motion to table (kill) the Byrd, D-W.Va., amendment stating that U.S. Marines in Lebanon became engaged in hostilities on Aug. 29, 1983, requiring the president to submit a report to Congress under section 4(a)(1) of the War Powers Resolution (PL 93-148) concerning those hostilities, and extending for 60 days from the enactment of the resolution the president's authority to keep U.S. forces in Lebanon. Motion agreed to 55-45: R 55-0; D 0-45 (ND 0-31, SD 0-14), Sept. 29, 1983. A "yea" was a vote supporting the president's position.

260. S J Res 159. Multinational Force in Lebanon. Baker, R-Tenn., motion to table (kill) the Pell, D-R.I., amendment to authorize U.S. Marines to remain in Lebanon for an additional six months, rather than an additional 18 months. Motion agreed to 62-38: R 54-1; D 8-37 (ND 5-26, SD 3-11), Sept. 29, 1983. A "yea" was a vote supporting the president's position.

261. S J Res 159. Multinational Force in Lebanon. Baker, R-Tenn., motion to table (kill) the Tsongas, D-Mass., amendment stating that a purpose of the deployment of U.S. Marines in Lebanon was to help the Lebanese government "maintain a secure area" from which it could "restore full control over its own territory." Motion agreed to 56-42: R 53-1; D 3-41 (ND 2-28, SD 1-13), Sept. 29, 1983. A "yea" was a vote supporting the president's position.

262. S J Res 159. Multinational Force in Lebanon. Baker, R-Tenn., motion to table (kill) the Levin, D-Mich., amendment stating that "actual or imminent hostilities involving U.S. armed forces" in Lebanon began on Aug. 29, 1983. Motion agreed to 54-45: R 54-0; D 0-45 (ND 0-31, SD 0-14), Sept. 29, 1983. A "yea" was a vote supporting the president's position.

263. S J Res 159. Multinational Force in Lebanon. Baker, R-Tenn., motion to table (kill) the Eagleton, D-Mo., amendment to allow the United States to take such "defensive" measures as may be necessary to protect the multinational peacekeeping force, rather than such "protective" measures as may be necessary. The amendment also would have required the president to report to Congress periodically on the results of efforts to secure the removal of all foreign forces from Lebanon and to restore full control by the Lebanese government over its own territory. Motion agreed to 66-34: R 55-0; D 11-34 (ND 5-26, SD 6-8), Sept. 29, 1983. A "yea" was a vote supporting the president's position.

264. S J Res 159. Multinational Force in Lebanon. Passage of the joint resolution to provide statutory authorization under the War Powers Resolution for continued U.S. participation in the multinational peacekeeping force in Lebanon for up to 18 months after the enactment of the resolution. Passed 54-46: R 52-3; D 2-43 (ND 2-29, SD 0-14), Sept. 29, 1983. A "yea" was a vote supporting the president's position.

265. S 1887. Federal Supplemental Unemployment Compensation. Moynihan, D-N.Y., amendment to increase for a nine-month period the number of weeks of federal supplemental unemployment compensation available based on a state's unemployment rate and permitting states to use either their insured unemployment rate or the total unemployment rate to determine participation in the federal supplemental unemployment compensation program. Rejected 34-59: R 3-49; D 31-10 (ND 24-4, SD 7-6), Sept. 29, 1983.

Corresponding to Congressional Record Votes 276, 277, 278, 279, 280, 281, 282

	266	267	268	269	270	271	272
ALABAMA							
Denton	N	N	Y	Y	Y	Y	N
Heflin	Y	Y	Y	N	N	N	N
ALASKA							
Murkowski	N	N	Y	Y	Y	Y	Y
Stevens	N	N	Y	Y	Y	Y	Y
ARIZONA							
Goldwater	N	N	Y	Y	Y	Y	?
DeConcini	?	?	?	Y	N	Y	Y
ARKANSAS							
Bumpers	Y	Y	Y	N	N	N	Y
Pryor	Y	N	Y	N	N	N	Y
CALIFORNIA							
Wilson	N	N	Y	Y	Y	Y	Y
Cranston	?	?	?	?	?	?	?
COLORADO							
Armstrong	N	N	Y	?	Y	Y	N
Hart	Y	Y	Y	Y	N	N	N
CONNECTICUT							
Weicker	N	Y	Y	Y	Y	Y	Y
Dodd	?	?	?	Y	N	N	Y
DELAWARE							
Roth	N	N	Y	Y	Y	Y	N
Biden	Y	Y	Y	N	N	-	+
FLORIDA							
Hawkins	N	N	Y	Y	Y	Y	N
Chiles	Y	N	Y	N	N	N	Y
GEORGIA							
Mattingly	N	N	Y	Y	Y	Y	N
Nunn	N	N	Y	Y	N	Y	Y
HAWAII							
Inouye	Y	Y	Y	?	?	?	?
Matsunaga	Y	Y	Y	N	N	N	Y
IDAHO							
McClure	N	N	Y	Y	Y	Y	Y
Symms	N	N	Y	Y	Y	Y	N
ILLINOIS							
Percy	N	N	Y	Y	Y	Y	Y
Dixon	Y	Y	Y	Y	N	N	Y
INDIANA							
Lugar	N	N	Y	Y	Y	N	N
Quayle	N	N	Y	Y	Y	N	Y

	266	267	268	269	270	271	272
IOWA							
Grassley	N	N	Y	Y	Y	Y	N
Jepsen	N	N	Y	Y	Y	Y	Y
KANSAS							
Dole	N	N	Y	Y	Y	Y	N
Kassebaum	N	N	?	Y	Y	Y	Y
KENTUCKY							
Ford	Y	Y	Y	N	N	N	Y
Huddleston	Y	Y	Y	N	N	N	Y
LOUISIANA							
Johnston	?	?	Y	N	N	N	Y
Long	N	N	Y	N	N	Y	Y
MAINE							
Cohen	Y	N	Y	N	N	N	Y
Mitchell	Y	N	Y	N	N	-	+
MARYLAND							
Mathias	Y	N	Y	?	?	?	?
Sarbanes	Y	Y	Y	N	N	N	Y
MASSACHUSETTS							
Kennedy	Y	Y	Y	N	N	N	Y
Tsongas	?	?	Y	N	N	N	Y
MICHIGAN							
Levin	Y	Y	Y	N	N	N	Y
Riegle	Y	Y	Y	-	-	N	Y
MINNESOTA							
Boschwitz	N	N	Y	Y	Y	N	Y
Durenberger	N	N	Y	Y	Y	Y	Y
MISSISSIPPI							
Cochran	N	N	Y	Y	Y	Y	N
Stennis	Y	N	Y	N	N	Y	Y
MISSOURI							
Danforth	N	N	Y	Y	Y	Y	Y
Eagleton	Y	Y	Y	Y	N	N	N
MONTANA							
Baucus	Y	N	Y	?	N	N	N
Melcher	Y	Y	Y	N	N	N	Y
NEBRASKA							
Exon	N	N	?	Y	N	N	N
Zorinsky	N	N	?	Y	N	N	Y
NEVADA							
Hecht	N	N	Y	Y	Y	Y	Y
Laxalt	N	N	Y	Y	Y	Y	N

	266	267	268	269	270	271	272
NEW HAMPSHIRE							
Humphrey	?	?	?	Y	Y	Y	N
Rudman	N	N	Y	Y	Y	Y	Y
NEW JERSEY							
Bradley	Y	Y	Y	N	N	N	Y
Lautenberg	Y	Y	+	N	N	N	Y
NEW MEXICO							
Domenici	N	N	Y	Y	Y	Y	Y
Bingaman	Y	N	Y	N	N	N	Y
NEW YORK							
D'Amato	N	N	Y	Y	Y	Y	Y
Moynihan	Y	Y	Y	N	N	N	Y
NORTH CAROLINA							
East	N	N	Y	Y	Y	Y	N
Helms	N	N	Y	Y	Y	Y	N
NORTH DAKOTA							
Andrews	N	N	Y	Y	Y	Y	N
Burdick	Y	N	Y	N	N	N	Y
OHIO							
Glenn	?	?	?	?	?	N	Y
Metzenbaum	Y	Y	Y	N	N	N	Y
OKLAHOMA							
Nickles	?	?	?	Y	Y	Y	N
Boren	Y	N	Y	N	N	Y	Y
OREGON							
Hatfield	N	N	Y	Y	Y	Y	Y
Packwood	N	N	Y	Y	Y	N	Y
PENNSYLVANIA							
Heinz	Y	N	Y	Y	Y	N	Y
Specter	Y	Y	Y	N	N	Y	Y
RHODE ISLAND							
Chafee	N	N	Y	Y	Y	Y	N
Pell	Y	Y	Y	N	N	N	Y
SOUTH CAROLINA							
Thurmond	N	N	Y	Y	Y	Y	N
Hollings	?	?	?	N	N	N	Y
SOUTH DAKOTA							
Abdnor	N	N	Y	Y	Y	Y	Y
Pressler	N	N	Y	Y	N	Y	Y
TENNESSEE							
Baker	N	?	Y	Y	Y	Y	Y
Sasser	Y	Y	Y	N	N	N	Y

KEY

- **Y** Voted for (yea).
- **#** Paired for.
- **+** Announced for.
- **N** Voted against (nay).
- **X** Paired against.
- **-** Announced against.
- **P** Voted "present".
- **C** Voted "present" to avoid possible conflict of interest.
- **?** Did not vote or otherwise make a position known.

Democrats   *Republicans*

	266	267	268	269	270	271	272
TEXAS							
Tower	N	N	Y	Y	Y	Y	N
Bentsen	Y	N	Y	N	N	N	Y
UTAH							
Garn	N	N	Y	Y	Y	Y	N
Hatch	N	N	Y	Y	Y	N	Y
VERMONT							
Stafford	N	N	Y	N	N	N	Y
Leahy	Y	Y	Y	N	N	-	+
VIRGINIA							
Trible	N	N	Y	Y	Y	Y	N
Warner	N	N	Y	Y	Y	Y	Y
WASHINGTON							
Gorton	N	N	Y	Y	Y	Y	N
Evans	N	N	Y	Y	Y	Y	Y
WEST VIRGINIA							
Byrd	Y	Y	Y	N	N	N	Y
Randolph	Y	Y	Y	N	N	N	Y
WISCONSIN							
Kasten	N	N	Y	Y	Y	Y	N
Proxmire	N	N	Y	Y	Y	Y	N
WYOMING							
Simpson	N	N	Y	Y	Y	Y	Y
Wallop	N	N	Y	Y	Y	Y	N

ND - Northern Democrats   SD - Southern Democrats (Southern states - Ala., Ark., Fla., Ga., Ky., La., Miss., N.C., Okla., S.C., Tenn., Texas, Va.)

266. S 1887. Federal Supplemental Unemployment Compensation. Byrd, D-W.Va., amendment to provide for up to eight additional weeks of benefits for persons who have exhausted all other state and federal benefits. Rejected 37-54: R 4-49; D 33-5 (ND 23-3, SD 10-2), Sept. 30, 1983.

267. S 1887. Federal Supplemental Unemployment Compensation. Levin, D-Mich., amendment to extend benefits in states with long-term unemployment by authorizing up to 10 weeks of extended benefits to any state whose insured unemployment rate since January 1982 had averaged 6 percent or more, and lesser amounts for states whose insured unemployment rates since January 1982 had averaged between 4 percent and 6 percent. Rejected 26-64: R 2-50; D 24-14 (ND 19-7, SD 5-7), Sept. 30, 1983.

268. HR 3929. Federal Supplemental Unemployment Compensation. Passage of the bill to extend for 18 months and modify the program providing federal supplemental unemployment compensation benefits to jobless workers who have exhausted all other state and federal unemployment benefits; and to extend for 60 days authority to continue payments of Social Security disability benefits to a recipient during the recipient's appeal to an administrative law judge of a decision to terminate the recipient's benefits. Passed 89-0: R 52-0; D 37-0 (ND 24-0, SD 13-0), Sept. 30, 1983.

269. HR 3913. Labor, Health and Human Services, Education Appropriations, Fiscal 1984. Weicker, R-Conn., motion to table (kill) the Huddleston, D-Ky., amendment to add $50,000,000 for removal of asbestos from school buildings. Motion agreed to 58-35: R 50-3; D 8-32 (ND 7-19, SD 1-13), Oct. 4, 1983.

270. HR 3913. Labor, Health and Human Services, Education Appropriations, Fiscal 1984. Weicker, R-Conn., motion to table (kill) the Bradley, D-N.J., appeal of the chair's ruling that a Bradley amendment to add $559 million for education programs was out of order because it would have increased funding above authorized levels. Motion agreed to 50-45: R 49-5; D 1-40 (ND 1-26, SD 0-14), Oct. 4, 1983. A "yea" was a vote supporting the president's position.

271. HR 3913. Labor, Health and Human Services, Education Appropriations, Fiscal 1984. Baker, R-Tenn., motion to table (kill) the Quayle, R-Ind., amendment to add $364 million for programs under the Job Training Partnership Act. Motion agreed to 50-44: R 44-10; D 6-34 (ND 2-24, SD 4-10), Oct. 4, 1983.

272. HR 3913. Labor, Health and Human Services, Education Appropriations, Fiscal 1984. Passage of the bill to appropriate $91,084,672,000 in fiscal 1984, $7,772,000,000 in fiscal 1985 and $130,000,000 in fiscal 1986 for the departments of Labor, Health and Human Services, and Education and related agencies. Passed 70-23: R 35-18; D 35-5 (ND 22-4, SD 13-1), Oct. 4, 1983. The president had requested $93,724,144,000 in new budget authority.

	273 274 275 276		273 274 275 276		273 274 275 276
ALABAMA		**IOWA**		**NEW HAMPSHIRE**	
Denton	N Y Y N	*Grassley*	N N Y Y	*Humphrey*	- ? - X
Heflin	Y Y Y N	*Jepsen*	N N Y Y	*Rudman*	N N N N
ALASKA		**KANSAS**		**NEW JERSEY**	
Murkowski	N N N N	*Dole*	Y Y Y Y	Bradley	N N N N
Stevens	Y N Y Y	*Kassebaum*	Y N Y N	Lautenberg	N N N N
ARIZONA		**KENTUCKY**		**NEW MEXICO**	
Goldwater	Y ? Y ?	Ford	Y Y Y Y	*Domenici*	N N Y N
DeConcini	N N N N	Huddleston	Y Y Y Y	Bingaman	Y Y Y Y
ARKANSAS		**LOUISIANA**		**NEW YORK**	
Bumpers	Y Y Y Y	Johnston	N N Y ?	*D'Amato*	Y Y N N
Pryor	Y Y Y Y	Long	X N Y Y	Moynihan	N ? ? ?
CALIFORNIA		**MAINE**		**NORTH CAROLINA**	
Wilson	N N N N	*Cohen*	Y Y N N	East	Y Y Y Y
Cranston	Y ? ? ?	*Mitchell*	Y Y N N	*Helms*	Y Y Y Y
COLORADO		**MARYLAND**		**NORTH DAKOTA**	
Armstrong	N N Y ?	*Mathias*	? ? ? ?	*Andrews*	Y Y Y Y
Hart	Y ? ? ?	Sarbanes	Y Y Y Y	Burdick	Y Y Y Y
CONNECTICUT		**MASSACHUSETTS**		**OHIO**	
Weicker	Y Y N N	Kennedy	# Y Y ?	Glenn	? ? ? ?
Dodd	N N N N	Tsongas	Y N N N	Metzenbaum	Y N N N
DELAWARE		**MICHIGAN**		**OKLAHOMA**	
Roth	N N N N	Levin	Y Y Y N	*Nickles*	Y N N N
Biden	N N N N	Riegle	Y Y N Y	Boren	Y Y Y N
FLORIDA		**MINNESOTA**		**OREGON**	
Hawkins	N N N N	*Boschwitz*	Y Y Y Y	*Hatfield*	N N ? ?
Chiles	Y Y Y Y	*Durenberger*	Y Y Y Y	*Packwood*	N N ? N
GEORGIA		**MISSISSIPPI**		**PENNSYLVANIA**	
Mattingly	N N Y Y	*Cochran*	Y Y Y Y	*Heinz*	Y Y N ?
Nunn	N N Y Y	Stennis	Y ? Y Y	*Specter*	Y Y N Y
HAWAII		**MISSOURI**		**RHODE ISLAND**	
Inouye	? ? ? ?	*Danforth*	Y Y N Y	*Chafee*	N N N N
Matsunaga	Y Y Y Y	Eagleton	Y Y Y Y	Pell	N N N N
IDAHO		**MONTANA**		**SOUTH CAROLINA**	
McClure	Y Y Y Y	Baucus	N N Y N	*Thurmond*	N N Y N
Symms	N N Y N	Melcher	Y Y Y Y	Hollings	? ? ? ?
ILLINOIS		**NEBRASKA**		**SOUTH DAKOTA**	
Percy	N N N Y	Exon	Y Y Y Y	*Abdnor*	Y Y Y Y
Dixon	Y Y N Y	Zorinsky	Y Y Y Y	*Pressler*	Y Y Y Y
INDIANA		**NEVADA**		**TENNESSEE**	
Lugar	N N Y Y	Hecht	Y N Y N	*Baker*	Y Y Y #
Quayle	N N Y N	Laxalt	Y ? Y N	Sasser	Y Y Y Y

	KEY
Y	Voted for (yea).
#	Paired for.
+	Announced for.
N	Voted against (nay).
X	Paired against.
-	Announced against.
P	Voted "present".
C	Voted "present" to avoid possible conflict of interest.
?	Did not vote or otherwise make a position known.

Democrats *Republicans*

	273 274 275 276
TEXAS	
Tower	Y Y Y N
Bentsen	Y Y Y ?
UTAH	
Garn	N N N N
Hatch	N N N N
VERMONT	
Stafford	Y Y N Y
Leahy	Y Y Y Y
VIRGINIA	
Trible	N N Y N
Warner	N N Y N
WASHINGTON	
Gorton	N N N N
Evans	N N N N
WEST VIRGINIA	
Byrd	Y Y Y N
Randolph	Y Y Y Y
WISCONSIN	
Kasten	Y Y N Y
Proxmire	Y Y N Y
WYOMING	
Simpson	N N N Y
Wallop	N N Y Y

ND - Northern Democrats   SD - Southern Democrats (Southern states - Ala., Ark., Fla., Ga., Ky., La., Miss., N.C., Okla., S.C., Tenn., Texas, Va.)

273. S 1529. Dairy and Tobacco Adjustment Act. Baker, R-Tenn., motion to table (kill) the Moynihan, D-N.Y.-Hatch, R-Utah, amendment to do away with the 50 cents per hundredweight assessments on milk production and permit the secretary of agriculture to lower dairy price supports to $11.60 from $13.10 per hundredweight of milk and prevent the Agriculture Department from establishing a program to pay dairy farmers for cutting back milk production. Motion agreed to 56-37: R 26-27; D 30-10 (ND 20-8, SD 10-2), Oct. 6, 1983.

274. S 1529. Dairy and Tobacco Adjustment Act. Huddleston, D-Ky., motion to table (kill) the Hawkins, R-Fla., amendment to do away with the 50 cents per hundredweight assessments on milk production, lower dairy price supports from $13.10 to $12.10 per hundredweight of milk and prevent the Agriculture Department from establishing a program to pay dairy farmers for cutting back milk production. Motion agreed to 47-42: R 21-30; D 26-12 (ND 17-9, SD 9-3), Oct. 6, 1983.

275. S 1529. Dairy and Tobacco Adjustment Act. Baker, R-Tenn., motion to table (kill) the Metzenbaum, D-Ohio, amendment to repeal the federal tobacco price support program. Motion agreed to 57-33: R 30-21; D 27-12 (ND 14-12, SD 13-0), Oct. 6, 1983.

276. S 1529. Dairy and Tobacco Adjustment Act. Baker, R-Tenn., motion to table (kill) the Rudman, R-N.H., amendment to exempt dairy farmers who produce, process and market their own goods from the 50 cents per hundredweight assessments on milk production and programs to pay dairy farmers for cutting back on milk production. Motion agreed to 44-40: R 22-26; D 22-14 (ND 13-12, SD 9-2), Oct. 6, 1983.

Corresponding to Congressional Record Votes 287, 288, 289, 290

	277 278 279 280		277 278 279 280		277 278 279 280	KEY
ALABAMA		**IOWA**		**NEW HAMPSHIRE**		Y Voted for (yea).
Denton	Y Y N ?	*Grassley*	Y N Y Y	*Humphrey*	? ? ? ?	# Paired for.
Heflin	Y N N Y	*Jepsen*	Y Y Y N	*Rudman*	N Y N N	+ Announced for.
ALASKA		**KANSAS**		**NEW JERSEY**		N Voted against (nay).
Murkowski	Y Y N N	*Dole*	Y Y Y Y	Bradley	? ? ? ?	X Paired against.
Stevens	? ? ? ?	*Kassebaum*	N Y Y N	Lautenberg	? ? ? ?	- Announced against.
ARIZONA		**KENTUCKY**		**NEW MEXICO**		P Voted "present".
Goldwater	? Y Y Y	Ford	Y Y Y Y	*Domenici*	? ? ? ?	C Voted "present" to avoid possible conflict of interest.
DeConcini	Y Y N N	Huddleston	Y Y Y Y	Bingaman	Y Y Y Y	? Did not vote or otherwise make a position known.
ARKANSAS		**LOUISIANA**		**NEW YORK**		
Bumpers	Y Y Y ?	Johnston	? ? ? ?	*D'Amato*	Y N N N	*Democrats* *Republicans*
Pryor	? ? ? ?	Long	Y Y N ?	Moynihan	? ? ? ?	
CALIFORNIA		**MAINE**		**NORTH CAROLINA**		
Wilson	N Y N N	*Cohen*	Y Y Y Y	*East*	Y Y Y Y	277 278 279 280
Cranston	? ? ? ?	Mitchell	Y N Y N	*Helms*	Y Y Y Y	
COLORADO		**MARYLAND**		**NORTH DAKOTA**		
Armstrong	? ? ? ?	*Mathias*	? ? ? ?	*Andrews*	Y Y Y Y	
Hart	? ? ? ?	Sarbanes	Y N Y N	Burdick	Y Y ? ?	**TEXAS**
CONNECTICUT		**MASSACHUSETTS**		**OHIO**		*Tower*	Y ? ? ?
Weicker	Y N N Y	Kennedy	Y N Y N	Glenn	? ? ? ?	Bentsen	N Y Y Y
Dodd	? ? ? ?	Tsongas	Y N Y N	Metzenbaum	? ? ? ?	**UTAH**
DELAWARE		**MICHIGAN**		**OKLAHOMA**		*Garn*	Y Y Y Y
Roth	Y Y Y N	Levin	Y N Y Y	*Nickles*	? ? ? ?	*Hatch*	N N ? N
Biden	Y Y Y N	Riegle	Y N Y Y	Boren	? N Y Y	**VERMONT**
FLORIDA		**MINNESOTA**		**OREGON**		*Stafford*	Y Y Y Y
Hawkins	? ? ? ?	*Boschwitz*	Y Y Y N	*Hatfield*	N Y Y N	Leahy	Y Y Y N
Chiles	Y Y Y Y	*Durenberger*	? Y Y N	*Packwood*	Y Y N N	**VIRGINIA**
GEORGIA		**MISSISSIPPI**		**PENNSYLVANIA**		*Trible*	? ? ? ?
Mattingly	Y Y N N	*Cochran*	Y Y Y Y	*Heinz*	Y N Y N	*Warner*	N N N Y
Nunn	Y Y N Y	Stennis	Y Y Y Y	*Specter*	N N N N	**WASHINGTON**
HAWAII		**MISSOURI**		**RHODE ISLAND**		*Gorton*	Y Y Y ?
Inouye	? ? ? ?	*Danforth*	Y Y Y N	*Chafee*	Y Y N N	Evans	? ? ? ?
Matsunaga	Y Y Y Y	Eagleton	? ? ? ?	Pell	Y Y N N	**WEST VIRGINIA**
IDAHO		**MONTANA**		**SOUTH CAROLINA**		Byrd	Y N Y N
McClure	? ? ? ?	Baucus	N N ? ?	*Thurmond*	N N N Y	Randolph	Y Y Y Y
Symms	Y N N Y	Melcher	N N Y Y	Hollings	? ? ? Y	**WISCONSIN**
ILLINOIS		**NEBRASKA**		**SOUTH DAKOTA**		*Kasten*	Y Y Y Y
Percy	+ ? ? -	Exon	Y N Y Y	*Abdnor*	Y N Y Y	Proxmire	Y Y Y Y
Dixon	Y Y N Y	Zorinsky	Y N Y N	*Pressler*	Y N Y N	**WYOMING**
INDIANA		**NEVADA**		**TENNESSEE**		*Simpson*	? ? ? ?
Lugar	Y Y Y N	*Hecht*	N N Y Y	*Baker*	Y Y Y Y	*Wallop*	? ? ? ?
Quayle	Y Y N Y	*Laxalt*	? ? ? ?	Sasser	Y Y Y ?	

ND - Northern Democrats   SD - Southern Democrats (Southern states - Ala., Ark., Fla., Ga., Ky., La., Miss., N.C., Okla., S.C., Tenn., Texas, Va.)

277. S 1529. Dairy and Tobacco Adjustment Act. Baker, R-Tenn., motion to table (kill) the Baucus, D-Mont., amendment to exempt from federal dairy assessments of 50 cents per hundredweight dairy producers living in areas not covered by federal milk marketing orders. Motion agreed to 58-12: R 30-9; D 28-3 (ND 19-2, SD 9-1), Oct. 7, 1983.

278. S 1529. Dairy and Tobacco Adjustment Act. Baker, R-Tenn., motion to table (kill) the Pressler, R-S.D., amendment to extend federal dairy assessments of 15 cents per hundredweight to imported dairy products. Motion agreed to 47-25: R 28-12; D 19-13 (ND 10-11, SD 9-2), Oct. 7, 1983.

279. S 1529. Dairy and Tobacco Adjustment Act. Baker, R-Tenn., motion to table (kill) the D'Amato, R-N.Y., amendment to eliminate the federal dairy assessments of 50 cents per hundred-

weight and reduce the federal price support to $11.85, from $13.10 per hundredweight of milk equivalent, except for fluid milk. Motion agreed to 50-19: R 25-14; D 25-5 (ND 17-2, SD 8-3), Oct. 7, 1983.

280. S 1529. Dairy and Tobacco Adjustment Act. Huddleston, D-Ky., motion to table (kill) the Chafee, R-R.I., amendment to restrict the total payment to an individual producer in the paid diversion program to $85,000, or an amount equal to the total he paid in assessments to support the program, whichever amount was greater. (The assessment total would not include money earmarked for a dairy promotion program.) The amendment also permitted reductions in the minimum production cut required for participation in the paid diversion program. Motion agreed to 36-30: R 19-19; D 17-11 (ND 8-11, SD 9-0), Oct. 7, 1983.

	281 282 283 284 285 286 287 288		281 282 283 284 285 286 287 288		281 282 283 284 285 286 287 288	KEY
ALABAMA		**IOWA**		**NEW HAMPSHIRE**		Y Voted for (yea).
Denton	Y Y Y N Y Y Y Y	*Grassley*	N N Y N Y N N N	*Humphrey*	Y ? ? ? ? ? Y Y	# Paired for.
Heflin	N N N Y N N N N	*Jepsen*	? N Y N Y N N Y	*Rudman*	Y Y Y Y N N Y Y	+ Announced for.
ALASKA		**KANSAS**		**NEW JERSEY**		N Voted against (nay).
Murkowski	N Y N N Y N Y N	*Dole*	N N N N N N N N	Bradley	N N N N N N N N	X Paired against.
Stevens	N N N N N N N N	*Kassebaum*	N N N N N N N N	Lautenberg	N N N N N N N N	- Announced against.
ARIZONA		**KENTUCKY**		**NEW MEXICO**		P Voted "present".
Goldwater	N Y Y Y Y N ? ?	Ford	N N N N N N N N	*Domenici*	N N N N N N N N	C Voted "present" to avoid possible conflict of interest.
DeConcini	N N N Y N N N N	Huddleston	? ? N N N N N N	Bingaman	N N N Y N N N N	
ARKANSAS		**LOUISIANA**		**NEW YORK**		? Did not vote or otherwise make a position known.
Bumpers	N N N N N N N N	Johnston	N N N N N N N N	*D'Amato*	N N N N N N N N	
Pryor	N N N N N N N N	Long	N N N Y N N N N	Moynihan	N N N N N N N N	Democrats *Republicans*
CALIFORNIA		**MAINE**		**NORTH CAROLINA**		
Wilson	N N N N N N N N	*Cohen*	N Y N Y Y N Y N	*East*	Y Y Y P P ? P Y	

						281 282 283 284 285 286 287 288
Cranston	? N N N N N N N	Mitchell	N N N N N N N N	*Helms*	Y Y Y N P Y P Y		
COLORADO		**MARYLAND**		**NORTH DAKOTA**			
Armstrong	N Y Y Y Y N Y N	Mathias	N N N N N ? N N	Andrews	N N N N N N N N	**TEXAS**	
Hart	? ? ? ? ? ? ? ?	Sarbanes	N N N N N N N N	Burdick	N N N N N N N N	*Tower*	N Y N N Y N ? ?
CONNECTICUT		**MASSACHUSETTS**		**OHIO**		Bentsen	N N N N N N N N
Weicker	N N N N N N N N	Kennedy	N N N N N N N N	Glenn	N N N N N N N N	**UTAH**	
Dodd	? - ? ? - - ? ?	Tsongas	N ? N N N N N N	Metzenbaum	N N N N N N N N	*Garn*	Y Y Y Y Y N Y Y
DELAWARE		**MICHIGAN**		**OKLAHOMA**		*Hatch*	Y Y Y Y Y N Y Y
Roth	N N N N N N N N	Levin	N N N N N N N N	*Nickles*	N Y Y N Y N Y N	**VERMONT**	
Biden	N ? N N N N N N	Riegle	N N N N N N - -	Boren	N N N N N N N N	*Stafford*	N N N N N N N N
FLORIDA		**MINNESOTA**		**OREGON**		Leahy	N N N N N N N N
Hawkins	- Y N N N - ? ?	*Boschwitz*	N N N N N N N N	*Hatfield*	N N N N N N N N	**VIRGINIA**	
Chiles	? N N Y N N N N	*Durenberger*	N N N N N N N N	*Packwood*	N N N N N N N N	*Trible*	N N N N N N N N
GEORGIA		**MISSISSIPPI**		**PENNSYLVANIA**		*Warner*	N N N N N N N N
Mattingly	N Y N N N N N N	*Cochran*	N N N N N N N N	*Heinz*	N N N N N N N N	**WASHINGTON**	
Nunn	N N N Y N N N N	Stennis	N N N Y N N N N	*Specter*	N N N Y N N N N	*Gorton*	N N N N N N N N
HAWAII		**MISSOURI**		**RHODE ISLAND**		Evans	N N N N N N ? N
Inouye	N N N N N N N N	*Danforth*	N N N N N N N N	*Chafee*	N N N N N N N N	**WEST VIRGINIA**	
Matsunaga	N N N Y N N N N	Eagleton	N N ? N N N N N	Pell	N N N N N N N N	Byrd	N N N Y N N N N
IDAHO		**MONTANA**		**SOUTH CAROLINA**		Randolph	N N N Y N N N N
McClure	Y Y Y N Y N Y N	Baucus	N N N Y N N N N	*Thurmond*	N N N N N N N N	**WISCONSIN**	
Symms	Y Y Y Y Y Y Y Y	Melcher	N N N Y Y N N N	Hollings	? ? ? ? ? ? N N	*Kasten*	- - N N N N N N
ILLINOIS		**NEBRASKA**		**SOUTH DAKOTA**		Proxmire	N N N N N N N N
Percy	- ? N N N N ? N	Exon	N N N Y N Y N Y	*Abdnor*	Y Y Y N Y N N Y	**WYOMING**	
Dixon	N N N N N N N N	Zorinsky	N N Y N Y N Y N	*Pressler*	Y Y Y Y Y N Y Y	*Simpson*	? Y N Y Y N N N
INDIANA		**NEVADA**		**TENNESSEE**		*Wallop*	N Y Y Y Y N Y N
Lugar	N N N N N N N N	*Hecht*	Y Y Y N Y N N N	*Baker*	N N N N N N N N		
Quayle	N N N Y Y N Y N	*Laxalt*	N Y N N N N N N	Sasser	? ? ? ? ? ? N N		

ND - Northern Democrats   SD - Southern Democrats (Southern states - Ala., Ark., Fla., Ga., Ky., La., Miss., N.C., Okla., S.C., Tenn., Texas, Va.)

281. HR 3706. Martin Luther King Jr. Holiday. Helms, R-N.C., motion to commit to the Judiciary Committee the bill to declare the third Monday in January a legal public holiday honoring Martin Luther King Jr. Motion rejected 12-76: R 12-38; D 0-38 (ND 0-28, SD 0-10), Oct. 18, 1983.

282. HR 3706. Martin Luther King Jr. Holiday. Rudman, R-N.H., amendment to establish a National Equality Day as a legal public holiday, to be observed on Feb. 12 of each year (Lincoln's birthday), instead of making the birthday of Martin Luther King Jr. a holiday. Rejected 22-68: R 22-30; D 0-38 (ND 0-27, SD 0-11), Oct. 18, 1983.

283. HR 3706. Martin Luther King Jr. Holiday. East, R-N.C., amendment to establish a National Civil Rights Day as a non-paid holiday, to be observed on March 16, the birthday of President James Madison, instead of making the birthday of Martin Luther King Jr. a public holiday. Rejected 18-76: R 17-37; D 1-39 (ND 1-27, SD 0-12), Oct. 18, 1983.

284. HR 3706. Martin Luther King Jr. Holiday. Randolph, D-W.Va., amendment to observe the holiday on Jan. 15, the actual birthday of Martin Luther King Jr., rather than on the third Monday in January. Rejected 23-71: R 12-41; D 11-30 (ND 7-22, SD 4-8), Oct. 18, 1983.

285. HR 3706. Martin Luther King Jr. Holiday. Exon, D-Neb., amendment to make Jan. 15, the birthday of Martin Luther King Jr., a national day of observance rather than a paid federal holiday. Rejected 24-69: R 20-32; D 4-37 (ND 3-26, SD 1-11), Oct. 18, 1983.

286. HR 3706. Martin Luther King Jr. Holiday. Helms, R-N.C., amendment to obtain Senate access to all federal records on Martin Luther King Jr. and to postpone a Senate vote on making King's birthday a holiday until after such records have been examined by the Senate or by a select committee appointed for that purpose. Rejected 3-90: R 3-49; D 0-41 (ND 0-29, SD 0-12), Oct. 18, 1983.

287. HR 3706. Martin Luther King Jr. Holiday. Humphrey, R-N.H., amendment to change the date of the proposed holiday from the third Monday in January to the third Sunday in January. Rejected 16-74: R 14-34; D 2-40 (ND 2-26, SD 0-14), Oct. 19, 1983.

288. HR 3706. Martin Luther King Jr. Holiday. Humphrey, R-N.H., amendment to declare the second Sunday in February a national holiday honoring Abraham Lincoln, rather than declaring the third Monday in January a national holiday honoring Martin Luther King Jr. Rejected 11-83: R 11-41; D 0-42 (ND 0-28, SD 0-14), Oct. 19, 1983.

CQ Senate Votes 289 - 294

Corresponding to Congressional Record Votes 299, 300, 301, 302, 303, 304

	289	290	291	292	293	294
ALABAMA						
Denton	Y	Y	N	Y	Y	Y
Heflin	N	N	N	Y	Y	Y
ALASKA						
Murkowski	N	N	N	N	N	Y
Stevens	N	N	N	N	Y	Y
ARIZONA						
Goldwater	Y	N	N	Y	N	Y
DeConcini	N	N	N	N	Y	Y
ARKANSAS						
Bumpers	N	N	N	N	Y	Y
Pryor	N	N	N	Y	Y	Y
CALIFORNIA						
Wilson	N	N	N	N	Y	Y
Cranston	N	N	N	N	Y	?
COLORADO						
Armstrong	N	Y	N	Y	Y	Y
Hart	?	P	N	N	Y	Y
CONNECTICUT						
Weicker	N	N	N	N	Y	Y
Dodd	?	-	?	?	Y	Y
DELAWARE						
Roth	N	N	N	Y	Y	Y
Biden	N	N	N	N	Y	Y
FLORIDA						
Hawkins	-	N	N	Y	Y	Y
Chiles	N	N	N	Y	Y	Y
GEORGIA						
Mattingly	N	N	N	Y	Y	Y
Nunn	N	N	N	Y	Y	Y
HAWAII						
Inouye	N	N	N	N	Y	Y
Matsunaga	N	N	N	Y	Y	Y
IDAHO						
McClure	N	N	N	Y	N	Y
Symms	Y	Y	Y	Y	N	Y
ILLINOIS						
Percy	N	N	N	N	Y	Y
Dixon	N	N	N	N	Y	Y
INDIANA						
Lugar	N	N	N	Y	Y	Y
Quayle	N	N	N	Y	Y	Y
IOWA						
Grassley	N	N	N	Y	N	Y
Jepsen	N	N	N	Y	N	Y
KANSAS						
Dole	N	N	N	N	Y	Y
Kassebaum	N	N	N	Y	Y	Y
KENTUCKY						
Ford	N	N	N	N	Y	Y
Huddleston	N	N	N	N	Y	Y
LOUISIANA						
Johnston	N	N	N	N	Y	Y
Long	N	N	N	Y	Y	Y
MAINE						
Cohen	N	N	N	Y	Y	Y
Mitchell	N	N	N	Y	Y	Y
MARYLAND						
Mathias	N	N	N	Y	Y	Y
Sarbanes	N	N	N	N	Y	Y
MASSACHUSETTS						
Kennedy	N	N	N	N	Y	Y
Tsongas	N	N	N	N	Y	Y
MICHIGAN						
Levin	N	N	N	N	Y	Y
Riegle	-	?	?	?	Y	Y
MINNESOTA						
Boschwitz	N	N	N	Y	Y	Y
Durenberger	N	N	N	Y	Y	Y
MISSISSIPPI						
Cochran	N	N	N	Y	Y	Y
Stennis	N	N	N	N	N	Y
MISSOURI						
Danforth	N	N	N	Y	Y	Y
Eagleton	N	N	N	Y	Y	Y
MONTANA						
Baucus	N	N	N	Y	Y	Y
Melcher	N	N	N	Y	Y	Y
NEBRASKA						
Exon	N	N	N	Y	N	Y
Zorinsky	P	N	N	Y	N	Y
NEVADA						
Hecht	N	N	N	N	N	Y
Laxalt	N	N	N	N	Y	Y
NEW HAMPSHIRE						
Humphrey	Y	P	N	Y	N	Y
Rudman	N	N	N	Y	N	Y
NEW JERSEY						
Bradley	N	N	N	N	Y	Y
Lautenberg	N	N	N	N	Y	Y
NEW MEXICO						
Domenici	N	N	N	Y	Y	Y
Bingaman	N	N	N	Y	Y	Y
NEW YORK						
D'Amato	N	N	N	N	Y	Y
Moynihan	N	N	N	N	Y	Y
NORTH CAROLINA						
East	Y	Y	P	P	N	?
Helms	Y	Y	Y	Y	N	Y
NORTH DAKOTA						
Andrews	N	N	N	Y	Y	Y
Burdick	N	N	N	Y	Y	Y
OHIO						
Glenn	N	N	N	N	Y	Y
Metzenbaum	N	N	N	N	Y	Y
OKLAHOMA						
Nickles	N	N	N	Y	N	Y
Boren	N	N	N	Y	Y	Y
OREGON						
Hatfield	N	N	N	Y	Y	Y
Packwood	N	N	N	Y	Y	Y
PENNSYLVANIA						
Heinz	N	N	N	N	Y	Y
Specter	N	N	N	N	Y	Y
RHODE ISLAND						
Chafee	N	N	N	N	Y	?
Pell	N	N	N	N	Y	Y
SOUTH CAROLINA						
Thurmond	N	N	N	N	Y	Y
Hollings	N	N	N	N	Y	Y
SOUTH DAKOTA						
Abdnor	Y	N	N	N	N	Y
Pressler	N	N	N	N	N	Y
TENNESSEE						
Baker	N	N	N	N	Y	?
Sasser	N	N	N	N	Y	Y
TEXAS						
Tower	?	N	N	Y	N	Y
Bentsen	N	N	N	N	Y	Y
UTAH						
Garn	Y	N	Y	Y	N	Y
Hatch	Y	N	Y	Y	N	Y
VERMONT						
Stafford	N	N	N	N	Y	Y
Leahy	N	N	N	N	Y	Y
VIRGINIA						
Trible	P	N	N	N	Y	Y
Warner	P	N	N	N	Y	Y
WASHINGTON						
Gorton	N	N	N	Y	Y	Y
Evans	N	N	N	Y	Y	Y
WEST VIRGINIA						
Byrd	N	N	N	N	Y	Y
Randolph	N	N	N	Y	N	Y
WISCONSIN						
Kasten	N	N	N	Y	Y	Y
Proxmire	N	N	N	N	Y	Y
WYOMING						
Simpson	N	N	N	Y	Y	Y
Wallop	Y	N	N	Y	N	Y

KEY

Y Voted for (yea).
Paired for.
+ Announced for.
N Voted against (nay).
X Paired against.
- Announced against.
P Voted "present".
C Voted "present" to avoid possible conflict of interest.
? Did not vote or otherwise make a position known.

Democrats   *Republicans*

ND - Northern Democrats   SD - Southern Democrats (Southern states - Ala., Ark., Fla., Ga., Ky., La., Miss., N.C., Okla., S.C., Tenn., Texas, Va.)

289. HR 3706. Martin Luther King Jr. Holiday. Helms, R-N.C., amendment to bar a national holiday honoring Martin Luther King Jr. from taking effect unless a legal public holiday were established honoring Thomas Jefferson and the total number of public holidays remained at nine. Rejected 10-82: R 10-41; D 0-41 (ND 0-27, SD 0-14), Oct. 19, 1983.

290. HR 3706. Martin Luther King Jr. Holiday. Helms, R-N.C., amendment stating the sense of Congress that the president should grant a full pardon to the late Marcus Garvey, a black nationalist leader convicted of fraud in the 1920s. Rejected 5-92: R 5-49; D 0-43 (ND 0-29, SD 0-14), Oct. 19, 1983.

291. HR 3706. Martin Luther King Jr. Holiday. Helms, R-N.C., amendment to bar a national holiday honoring Martin Luther King Jr. from taking effect unless a legal public holiday were established honoring Hispanic Americans and the total number of public holidays remained at nine. Rejected 4-93: R 4-50; D 0-43 (ND 0-29, SD 0-14), Oct. 19, 1983.

292. HR 3706. Martin Luther King Jr. Holiday. Boren, D-Okla., amendment to change the dates of the holidays celebrating George Washington's Birthday, Columbus Day, and Martin Luther King Jr.'s Birthday from Mondays to the actual dates of occurrence (Feb. 22, Oct. 12 and Jan. 15). Rejected 45-52: R 33-21; D 12-31 (ND 7-22, SD 5-9), Oct. 19, 1983.

293. HR 3706. Martin Luther King Jr. Holiday. Passage of the bill to declare the third Monday in January a legal public holiday honoring Martin Luther King Jr. Passed 78-22: R 37-18; D 41-4 (ND 28-3, SD 13-1), Oct. 19, 1983.

294. S 1342. State Department Authorizations. Hawkins, R-Fla., amendment to provide for the suspension of assistance to any country not meeting projected reductions in the production of illicit drugs. Adopted 96-0: R 52-0; D 44-0 (ND 30-0, SD 14-0), Oct. 19, 1983.

	295	296	297	298	299	300
ALABAMA						
Denton	N	N	Y	N	Y	N
Heflin	Y	N	Y	Y	N	Y
ALASKA						
Murkowski	Y	?	?	?	?	?
Stevens	Y	?	?	?	?	?
ARIZONA						
Goldwater	N	?	?	?	?	?
DeConcini	Y	Y	N	Y	N	Y
ARKANSAS						
Bumpers	Y	Y	Y	N	Y	N
Pryor	Y	Y	N	Y	N	Y
CALIFORNIA						
Wilson	N	N	N	Y	Y	N
Cranston	?	?	?	?	?	?
COLORADO						
Armstrong	Y	N	N	Y	N	Y
Hart	Y	Y	Y	Y	N	Y
CONNECTICUT						
Weicker	Y	Y	Y	Y	N	Y
Dodd	Y	?	?	?	?	?
DELAWARE						
Roth	Y	N	N	Y	Y	Y
Biden	Y	Y	Y	Y	N	Y
FLORIDA						
Hawkins	Y	?	?	?	?	?
Chiles	Y	Y	N	Y	N	Y
GEORGIA						
Mattingly	Y	N	N	Y	N	Y
Nunn	Y	Y	N	Y	N	Y
HAWAII						
Inouye	Y	Y	Y	Y	N	Y
Matsunaga	Y	Y	Y	Y	N	Y
IDAHO						
McClure	?	N	N	Y	?	?
Symms	N	N	N	Y	Y	N
ILLINOIS						
Percy	Y	Y	Y	Y	Y	Y
Dixon	Y	Y	N	Y	N	Y
INDIANA						
Lugar	N	Y	N	Y	Y	N
Quayle	N	Y	N	Y	N	Y
IOWA						
Grassley	Y	N	N	Y	N	Y
Jepsen	Y	N	N	Y	N	Y
KANSAS						
Dole	Y	N	?	+	?	?
Kassebaum	Y	Y	Y	Y	N	Y
KENTUCKY						
Ford	Y	Y	N	Y	N	Y
Huddleston	Y	Y	N	Y	Y	Y
LOUISIANA						
Johnston	Y	?	?	?	?	?
Long	Y	?	?	?	?	?
MAINE						
Cohen	Y	Y	Y	Y	N	Y
Mitchell	Y	Y	Y	Y	N	Y
MARYLAND						
Mathias	Y	Y	Y	Y	N	Y
Sarbanes	Y	Y	Y	Y	Y	Y
MASSACHUSETTS						
Kennedy	Y	Y	Y	Y	N	Y
Tsongas	Y	Y	Y	Y	N	Y
MICHIGAN						
Levin	Y	Y	?	Y	N	Y
Riegle	Y	Y	Y	Y	N	Y
MINNESOTA						
Boschwitz	Y	Y	N	Y	N	Y
Durenberger	Y	?	?	?	?	?
MISSISSIPPI						
Cochran	Y	Y	Y	Y	N	Y
Stennis	N	N	Y	Y	Y	Y
MISSOURI						
Danforth	Y	Y	N	Y	N	Y
Eagleton	Y	Y	N	Y	N	Y
MONTANA						
Baucus	Y	Y	N	Y	N	Y
Melcher	Y	Y	N	Y	N	Y
NEBRASKA						
Exon	Y	N	N	Y	N	Y
Zorinsky	Y	N	N	Y	Y	Y
NEVADA						
Hecht	Y	N	Y	Y	N	N
Laxalt	Y	N	Y	Y	Y	N
NEW HAMPSHIRE						
Humphrey	N	N	N	Y	N	Y
Rudman	Y	Y	Y	Y	N	Y
NEW JERSEY						
Bradley	Y	Y	Y	Y	N	Y
Lautenberg	Y	Y	Y	Y	N	Y
NEW MEXICO						
Domenici	Y	Y	N	Y	N	Y
Bingaman	Y	Y	Y	Y	N	Y
NEW YORK						
D'Amato	Y	N	N	Y	N	Y
Moynihan	Y	Y	Y	Y	Y	?
NORTH CAROLINA						
East	N	N	N	P	Y	N
Helms	N	N	N	Y	Y	N
NORTH DAKOTA						
Andrews	Y	Y	Y	Y	N	Y
Burdick	Y	Y	Y	Y	N	Y
OHIO						
Glenn	Y	Y	N	Y	N	Y
Metzenbaum	Y	Y	Y	Y	N	Y
OKLAHOMA						
Nickles	Y	N	N	Y	N	Y
Boren	Y	Y	N	Y	N	Y
OREGON						
Hatfield	Y	Y	Y	Y	N	Y
Packwood	·Y	Y	Y	Y	N	Y
PENNSYLVANIA						
Heinz	?	Y	Y	Y	Y	N
Specter	Y	Y	N	Y	N	Y
RHODE ISLAND						
Chafee	Y	Y	Y	Y	Y	Y
Pell	Y	Y	Y	Y	N	Y
SOUTH CAROLINA						
Thurmond	Y	N	N	Y	Y	N
Hollings	Y	N	Y	Y	Y	Y
SOUTH DAKOTA						
Abdnor	Y	N	N	Y	Y	Y
Pressler	Y	N	N	Y	Y	Y
TENNESSEE						
Baker	Y	N	Y	Y	N	N
Sasser	Y	Y	N	Y	N	Y
TEXAS						
Tower	Y	N	Y	Y	N	N
Bentsen	Y	Y	Y	Y	?	?
UTAH						
Garn	Y	N	N	Y	N	Y
Hatch	N	N	N	Y	Y	N
VERMONT						
Stafford	Y	Y	Y	Y	Y	Y
Leahy	Y	Y	Y	Y	N	Y
VIRGINIA						
Trible	Y	N	Y	Y	N	Y
Warner	Y	N	Y	Y	Y	Y
WASHINGTON						
Gorton	Y	Y	Y	Y	N	Y
Evans	Y	?	?	?	?	?
WEST VIRGINIA						
Byrd	Y	Y	Y	Y	N	Y
Randolph	Y	Y	N	N	N	Y
WISCONSIN						
Kasten	Y	N	N	Y	N	Y
Proxmire	Y	Y	Y	Y	N	Y
WYOMING						
Simpson	Y	N	N	Y	N	N
Wallop	Y	N	N	Y	Y	N

KEY

Y Voted for (yea).
\# Paired for.
\+ Announced for.
N Voted against (nay).
X Paired against.
− Announced against.
P Voted "present".
C Voted "present" to avoid possible conflict of interest.
? Did not vote or otherwise make a position known.

Democrats *Republicans*

ND - Northern Democrats   SD - Southern Democrats (Southern states - Ala., Ark., Fla., Ga., Ky., La., Miss., N.C., Okla., S.C., Tenn., Texas, Va.)

295. S 1342. State Department Authorizations. Byrd, D-W.Va., amendment to revise section 5(c) of the War Powers Resolution (PL 93-148) to require enactment by Congress of a joint resolution, rather than a concurrent resolution, for the removal of U.S. armed forces from hostile situations overseas. To become law, a joint resolution must be signed by the president or passed by Congress over his veto; a concurrent resolution does not require approval by the president. Adopted 86-11: R 43-10; D 43-1 (ND 30-0, SD 13-1), Oct. 20, 1983.

296. S 1342. State Department Authorizations. Mathias, R-Md., amendment to delay implementation until April 15, 1984, of any regulation or executive order that would require former government employees to submit their writings to the government for pre-publication review. Adopted 56-34: R 20-29; D 36-5 (ND 27-2, SD 9-3), Oct. 20, 1983.

297. S 1342. State Department Authorizations. Baker, R-Tenn., motion to table (kill) the Wallop, R-Wyo., amendment to prevent the Soviet Union from occupying new embassy buildings in Washington, D.C., until the president certified to Congress that the United States had acquired a new embassy location in Moscow of "substantially equal character." Motion agreed to 46-42: R 21-27; D 25-15 (ND 20-8, SD 5-7), Oct. 20, 1983.

298. S 1970. Number of Public Holidays. Passage of the bill to limit the number of legal public holidays to 10. Passed 86-2: R 46-1; D 40-1 (ND 28-1, SD 12-0), Oct. 20, 1983.

299. S 1342. State Department Authorizations. Percy, R-Ill., perfecting amendment to the Boschwitz, R-Minn., amendment, to state that the president may allow the export of nuclear supplies or equipment to a foreign country if he determines that such an action is necessary to protect the health and safety of operations of existing civilian nuclear facilities under international safeguards. Rejected 28-59: R 22-25; D 6-34 (ND 3-26, SD 3-8), Oct. 20, 1983. (The Boschwitz amendment, which stated the sense of Congress that the U.S. government should disapprove nuclear exports to the governments of Argentina, India and South Africa until those countries had given the United States stronger nuclear non-proliferation guarantees, subsequently was adopted *(see vote 300, below)*.)

300. S 1342. State Department Authorizations. Boschwitz, R-Minn., amendment stating the sense of Congress that the U.S. government should disapprove nuclear exports to the governments of Argentina, India and South Africa until those countries had given the United States stronger nuclear non-proliferation guarantees. Adopted 70-16: R 31-16; D 39-0 (ND 28-0, SD 11-0), Oct. 20, 1983.

	301	302	303	304	305	306	307
ALABAMA							
Denton	N	+	N	Y	Y	N	Y
Heflin	N	Y	N	Y	N	N	N
ALASKA							
Murkowski	?	?	Y	Y	Y	N	Y
Stevens	?	?	?	?	?	N	Y
ARIZONA							
Goldwater	Y	Y	?	?	?	X	?
DeConcini	N	Y	N	Y	Y	Y	N
ARKANSAS							
Bumpers	?	?	Y	Y	Y	Y	N
Pryor	N	Y	N	Y	Y	Y	N
CALIFORNIA							
Wilson	N	Y	Y	Y	Y	Y	Y
Cranston	?	?	N	Y	Y	Y	N
COLORADO							
Armstrong	N	?	Y	Y	Y	Y	Y
Hart	?	?	Y	Y	Y	Y	N
CONNECTICUT							
Weicker	Y	Y	Y	Y	Y	N	Y
Dodd	?	?	?	Y	Y	Y	N
DELAWARE							
Roth	N	Y	Y	Y	Y	Y	N
Biden	N	N	N	Y	Y	Y	N
FLORIDA							
Hawkins	N	?	+	Y	Y	Y	N
Chiles	?	?	N	Y	Y	Y	N
GEORGIA							
Mattingly	N	?	Y	Y	Y	Y	N
Nunn	N	N	Y	Y	Y	Y	N
HAWAII							
Inouye	?	N	N	Y	Y	Y	N
Matsunaga	Y	Y	?	Y	Y	Y	N
IDAHO							
McClure	?	?	Y	Y	Y	N	Y
Symms	N	Y	Y	Y	Y	N	Y
ILLINOIS							
Percy	Y	Y	Y	Y	Y	Y	N
Dixon	+	?	N	?	+	Y	N
INDIANA							
Lugar	N	Y	N	Y	Y	Y	N
Quayle	N	Y	Y	Y	Y	Y	Y

	301	302	303	304	305	306	307
IOWA							
Grassley	N	Y	Y	Y	Y	N	Y
Jepsen	N	Y	Y	Y	Y	N	Y
KANSAS							
Dole	N	Y	N	Y	Y	N	?
Kassebaum	N	Y	Y	Y	?	Y	Y
KENTUCKY							
Ford	N	?	N	Y	Y	Y	N
Huddleston	N	?	N	Y	Y	N	N
LOUISIANA							
Johnston	?	?	N	Y	Y	N	N
Long	?	?	N	Y	Y	N	Y
MAINE							
Cohen	?	?	Y	Y	Y	Y	N
Mitchell	Y	Y	N	Y	Y	Y	N
MARYLAND							
Mathias	Y	Y	Y	Y	Y	N	Y
Sarbanes	Y	Y	N	Y	Y	Y	N
MASSACHUSETTS							
Kennedy	Y	Y	N	Y	Y	Y	N
Tsongas	Y	N	Y	Y	Y	Y	?
MICHIGAN							
Levin	Y	Y	N	Y	Y	Y	N
Riegle	Y	Y	?	?	?	+	?
MINNESOTA							
Boschwitz	Y	Y	Y	Y	Y	Y	N
Durenberger	Y	Y	N	Y	Y	Y	?
MISSISSIPPI							
Cochran	?	?	Y	Y	Y	N	Y
Stennis	N	N	N	Y	Y	N	Y
MISSOURI							
Danforth	N	Y	Y	Y	Y	N	Y
Eagleton	Y	Y	?	Y	Y	Y	N
MONTANA							
Baucus	Y	N	Y	Y	Y	Y	N
Melcher	N	N	N	Y	Y	Y	N
NEBRASKA							
Exon	?	?	N	Y	Y	Y	N
Zorinsky	N	N	N	Y	Y	N	N
NEVADA							
Hecht	N	Y	Y	Y	Y	N	Y
Laxalt	N	Y	Y	Y	Y	N	Y

	301	302	303	304	305	306	307
NEW HAMPSHIRE							
Humphrey	N	?	Y	Y	Y	Y	N
Rudman	Y	Y	Y	Y	Y	Y	Y
NEW JERSEY							
Bradley	Y	?	Y	Y	Y	Y	N
Lautenberg	Y	?	Y	Y	Y	Y	N
NEW MEXICO							
Domenici	N	Y	Y	Y	Y	N	N
Bingaman	Y	Y	N	Y	Y	Y	N
NEW YORK							
D'Amato	N	?	?	Y	Y	N	N
Moynihan	Y	?	Y	Y	Y	Y	N
NORTH CAROLINA							
East	N	Y	Y	Y	Y	N	Y
Helms	N	Y	Y	Y	Y	N	Y
NORTH DAKOTA							
Andrews	N	N	Y	Y	Y	N	?
Burdick	N	N	Y	Y	Y	N	N
OHIO							
Glenn	?	?	N	Y	Y	N	N
Metzenbaum	Y	N	N	Y	Y	Y	N
OKLAHOMA							
Nickles	N	N	Y	Y	Y	Y	Y
Boren	N	Y	N	Y	Y	Y	N
OREGON							
Hatfield	Y	N	Y	Y	Y	N	N
Packwood	Y	Y	Y	Y	Y	Y	Y
PENNSYLVANIA							
Heinz	Y	Y	N	Y	Y	Y	N
Specter	Y	Y	N	Y	N	N	N
RHODE ISLAND							
Chafee	Y	Y	Y	Y	Y	Y	N
Pell	Y	N	Y	Y	Y	Y	N
SOUTH CAROLINA							
Thurmond	N	Y	Y	Y	Y	N	Y
Hollings	?	?	-	?	?	+	?
SOUTH DAKOTA							
Abdnor	N	Y	Y	Y	Y	N	Y
Pressler	N	Y	N	Y	Y	Y	Y
TENNESSEE							
Baker	N	?	Y	Y	Y	Y	N
Sasser	N	Y	N	Y	Y	N	N

<table>
KEY
Y Voted for (yea).
Paired for.
+ Announced for.
N Voted against (nay).
X Paired against.
- Announced against.
P Voted "present".
C Voted "present" to avoid possible conflict of interest.
? Did not vote or otherwise make a position known.

Democrats   *Republicans*
</table>

	301	302	303	304	305	306	307
TEXAS							
Tower	?	?	+	Y	?	N	Y
Bentsen	N	Y	N	Y	Y	Y	N
UTAH							
Garn	N	Y	Y	Y	Y	N	Y
Hatch	N	Y	Y	Y	Y	N	N
VERMONT							
Stafford	Y	?	Y	Y	Y	#	N
Leahy	Y	Y	Y	Y	Y	Y	N
VIRGINIA							
Trible	N	Y	Y	Y	Y	Y	Y
Warner	N	Y	Y	Y	Y	Y	Y
WASHINGTON							
Gorton	N	Y	Y	Y	Y	N	Y
Evans	?	?	Y	Y	Y	N	Y
WEST VIRGINIA							
Byrd	N	N	N	Y	Y	N	N
Randolph	N	Y	N	Y	Y	N	N
WISCONSIN							
Kasten	N	Y	N	Y	Y	N	Y
Proxmire	N	N	Y	Y	Y	Y	N
WYOMING							
Simpson	N	Y	Y	Y	Y	N	Y
Wallop	N	Y	Y	Y	Y	N	Y

ND - Northern Democrats   SD - Southern Democrats (Southern states - Ala., Ark., Fla., Ga., Ky., La., Miss., N.C., Okla., S.C., Tenn., Texas, Va.)

301. HR 3222. State, Justice, Commerce Appropriations, Fiscal 1984. Baker, R-Tenn., motion to table (kill) the Helms, R-N.C., amendment to bar the Justice Department from spending any funds appropriated in the bill to bring any legal action to require directly or indirectly school busing for desegregation. Motion rejected 29-52: R 13-35; D 16-17 (ND 16-8, SD 0-9), Oct. 21, 1983.

302. HR 3222. State, Justice, Commerce Appropriations, Fiscal 1984. Domenici, R-N.M., amendment to add $450,000 to the Justice Department appropriation to reimburse non-Indian defendants for their legal fees in 17-year-old water rights litigation in New Mexico. Adopted 53-16: R 37-3; D 16-13 (ND 11-11, SD 5-2), Oct. 21, 1983.

303. HR 3103. Surface Transportation Technical Corrections Act. Chafee, R-R.I., motion to table (kill) the Metzenbaum, D-Ohio, amendment to delete the "Buy America" section of the bill and retain provisions contained in the Surface Transportation Assistance Act of 1982. Motion agreed to 55-35: R 43-7; D 12-28 (ND 10-17, SD 2-11), Oct. 25, 1983.

304. HR 1062. Oregon Lands. Passage, over President Reagan's Oct. 19 veto, of the bill to authorize the secretary of the interior to convey, without consideration, certain lands in Lane County, Ore. Passed (thus enacted into law) 95-0: R 53-0; D 42-0 (ND 29-0, SD 13-0), Oct. 25, 1983. A two-thirds majority of those present and voting (64 in this case) of both houses is required to override a veto. A "nay" was a vote supporting the president's position. (The House also voted to override the veto (see vote 386, p. 114-H).)

305. HR 3103. Surface Transportation Technical Corrections Act. Passage of the bill to increase the funding authorized in fiscal 1984 for emergency highway repairs from $100 million to $250 million, to approve certain highway construction cost estimates and to make technical corrections in the Surface Transportation Assistance Act of 1982. Passed 91-2: R 50-1; D 41-1 (ND 29-0, SD 12-1), Oct. 25, 1983.

306. HR 3959. Supplemental Appropriations, Fiscal 1984. Humphrey, R-N.H., motion to table (kill) the Senate Appropriations Committee amendment to add $1.5 billion to the bill to complete the Clinch River breeder reactor in Tennessee. Motion agreed to 56-40: R 23-30; D 33-10 (ND 26-4, SD 7-6), Oct. 26, 1983.

307. HR 3959. Supplemental Appropriations, Fiscal 1984. Thurmond, R-S.C., motion to table (kill) the Biden, D-Del., amendment to create a Cabinet-level Office of the Director of National and International Drug Operations (a "drug czar") and to create a Commission on Drug Interdiction and Enforcement. Motion rejected 40-53: R 38-13; D 2-40 (ND 0-29, SD 2-11), Oct. 26, 1983. (The Biden amendment subsequently was adopted by voice vote.)

	308	309			308	309			308	309
ALABAMA				**IOWA**				**NEW HAMPSHIRE**		
Denton	N	Y		*Grassley*	Y	Y		*Humphrey*	?	Y
Heflin	Y	Y		*Jepsen*	Y	Y		*Rudman*	N	Y
ALASKA				**KANSAS**				**NEW JERSEY**		
Murkowski	Y	Y		*Dole*	N	N		Bradley	N	Y
Stevens	N	N		*Kassebaum*	Y	N		Lautenberg	N	Y
ARIZONA				**KENTUCKY**				**NEW MEXICO**		
Goldwater	?	?		Ford	Y	Y		*Domenici*	Y	Y
DeConcini	N	?		Huddleston	N	Y		Bingaman	Y	Y
ARKANSAS				**LOUISIANA**				**NEW YORK**		
Bumpers	?	?		Johnston	Y	Y		*D'Amato*	Y	Y
Pryor	N	Y		Long	N	Y		Moynihan	Y	Y
CALIFORNIA				**MAINE**				**NORTH CAROLINA**		
Wilson	N	Y		*Cohen*	N	Y		*East*	Y	Y
Cranston	N	?		Mitchell	N	Y		*Helms*	P	Y
COLORADO				**MARYLAND**				**NORTH DAKOTA**		
Armstrong	P	Y		*Mathias*	N	N		*Andrews*	?	?
Hart	N	Y		Sarbanes	N	Y		Burdick	Y	Y
CONNECTICUT				**MASSACHUSETTS**				**OHIO**		
Weicker	?	N		Kennedy	N	?		Glenn	?	?
Dodd	N	Y		Tsongas	?	Y		Metzenbaum	N	Y
DELAWARE				**MICHIGAN**				**OKLAHOMA**		
Roth	N	N		Levin	N	?		*Nickles*	N	Y
Biden	N	+		Riegle	N	Y		Boren	N	Y
FLORIDA				**MINNESOTA**				**OREGON**		
Hawkins	N	Y		*Boschwitz*	N	Y		*Hatfield*	N	?
Chiles	N	Y		*Durenberger*	N	Y		*Packwood*	Y	N
GEORGIA				**MISSISSIPPI**				**PENNSYLVANIA**		
Mattingly	N	Y		*Cochran*	Y	Y		*Heinz*	N	N
Nunn	N	Y		Stennis	N	Y		*Specter*	Y	Y
HAWAII				**MISSOURI**				**RHODE ISLAND**		
Inouye	N	Y		*Danforth*	Y	N		*Chafee*	N	N
Matsunaga	N	Y		Eagleton	Y	Y		Pell	N	Y
IDAHO				**MONTANA**				**SOUTH CAROLINA**		
McClure	N	Y		Baucus	N	Y		*Thurmond*	Y	Y
Symms	N	Y		Melcher	Y	Y		Hollings	?	?
ILLINOIS				**NEBRASKA**				**SOUTH DAKOTA**		
Percy	Y	Y		Exon	Y	Y		*Abdnor*	Y	Y
Dixon	Y	Y		Zorinsky	Y	?		*Pressler*	Y	Y
INDIANA				**NEVADA**				**TENNESSEE**		
Lugar	Y	N		*Hecht*	N	Y		*Baker*	N	?
Quayle	Y	Y		*Laxalt*	N	N		Sasser	Y	Y

	308	309
TEXAS		
Tower	?	?
Bentsen	N	Y
UTAH		
Garn	N	Y
Hatch	N	Y
VERMONT		
Stafford	N	N
Leahy	N	Y
VIRGINIA		
Trible	N	Y
Warner	N	Y
WASHINGTON		
Gorton	N	N
Evans	Y	?
WEST VIRGINIA		
Byrd	N	Y
Randolph	N	Y
WISCONSIN		
Kasten	Y	Y
Proxmire	Y	Y
WYOMING		
Simpson	N	Y
Wallop	N	N

ND - Northern Democrats   SD - Southern Democrats (Southern states - Ala., Ark., Fla., Ga., Ky., La., Miss., N.C., Okla., S.C., Tenn., Texas, Va.)

308. HR 3959. Supplemental Appropriations, Fiscal 1984. Packwood, R-Ore., motion to table (kill) the Stevens, R-Alaska, appeal of the chair's ruling that the Appropriations Committee amendment to block proposed Federal Communications Commission changes in television syndication and financial interest rules was not in order. Motion rejected 32-57: R 19-29; D 13-28 (ND 9-20, SD 4-8), Oct. 27, 1983. (By voice vote, the Senate subsequently voted to reject the ruling of the chair and then to adopt the committee amendment.)

309. H J Res 308. Debt Limit Increase. Armstrong, R-Colo., amendment to reduce the increase of the public debt limit from $1.61 trillion to $1.45 trillion. Adopted 70-15: R 34-15; D 36-0 (ND 24-0, SD 12-0), Oct. 27, 1983.

	310	311	312	313	314	315	316	317
ALABAMA								
Denton	-	-	-	?	X	Y	Y	Y
Heflin	Y	Y	Y	Y	Y	Y	Y	Y
ALASKA								
Murkowski	N	N	Y	Y	Y	Y	Y	Y
Stevens	N	N	Y	Y	N	N	Y	Y
ARIZONA								
Goldwater	?	?	?	?	?	?	Y	Y
DeConcini	?	?	?	?	?	Y	N	Y
ARKANSAS								
Bumpers	Y	Y	Y	Y	Y	Y	N	N
Pryor	N	Y	Y	Y	Y	Y	N	N
CALIFORNIA								
Wilson	N	N	N	?	?	Y	Y	Y
Cranston	?	?	?	?	?	Y	N	N
COLORADO								
Armstrong	N	Y	N	Y	Y	Y	Y	Y
Hart	Y	Y	?	?	?	Y	N	N
CONNECTICUT								
Weicker	Y	Y	?	?	?	Y	N	N
Dodd	Y	Y	Y	Y	?	Y	N	N
DELAWARE								
Roth	N	Y	Y	Y	Y	Y	Y	Y
Biden	Y	Y	?	?	?	Y	N	N
FLORIDA								
Hawkins	?	?	?	?	?	Y	Y	Y
Chiles	Y	?	Y	N	Y	Y	N	Y
GEORGIA								
Mattingly	N	Y	N	Y	N	Y	Y	Y
Nunn	Y	Y	N	Y	Y	C	N	Y
HAWAII								
Inouye	Y	Y	Y	Y	?	N	N	N
Matsunaga	N	Y	Y	N	Y	N	N	N
IDAHO								
McClure	N	N	Y	N	Y	N	Y	Y
Symms	N	N	N	Y	N	Y	Y	Y
ILLINOIS								
Percy	N	Y	?	?	?	Y	Y	Y
Dixon	Y	Y	N	Y	Y	Y	N	N
INDIANA								
Lugar	N	N	N	Y	Y	Y	Y	Y
Quayle	?	?	?	?	?	Y	Y	Y
IOWA								
Grassley	N	Y	Y	Y	Y	Y	Y	Y
Jepsen	N	N	N	Y	N	Y	Y	Y
KANSAS								
Dole	N	Y	Y	Y	Y	N	N	Y
Kassebaum	N	Y	Y	Y	N	Y	N	Y
KENTUCKY								
Ford	Y	Y	Y	Y	Y	Y	N	Y
Huddleston	Y	Y	Y	Y	Y	Y	N	N
LOUISIANA								
Johnston	Y	Y	Y	Y	Y	Y	N	Y
Long	N	Y	Y	Y	N	Y	N	Y
MAINE								
Cohen	N	Y	Y	N	Y	Y	N	Y
Mitchell	N	Y	Y	Y	?	Y	N	N
MARYLAND								
Mathias	Y	Y	?	?	?	?	?	N
Sarbanes	Y	Y	Y	N	Y	N	N	N
MASSACHUSETTS								
Kennedy	Y	Y	Y	N	Y	N	N	N
Tsongas	Y	Y	Y	Y	Y	Y	N	N
MICHIGAN								
Levin	Y	Y	Y	N	Y	Y	N	N
Riegle	Y	Y	Y	Y	Y	Y	N	N
MINNESOTA								
Boschwitz	N	Y	N	Y	Y	Y	?	?
Durenberger	N	Y	Y	Y	N	Y	Y	Y
MISSISSIPPI								
Cochran	?	?	?	?	?	Y	Y	Y
Stennis	N	Y	Y	Y	Y	Y	N	Y
MISSOURI								
Danforth	N	N	Y	Y	Y	Y	N	Y
Eagleton	Y	Y	Y	Y	Y	Y	N	N
MONTANA								
Baucus	N	Y	Y	Y	Y	Y	N	N
Melcher	N	Y	Y	Y	Y	N	N	N
NEBRASKA								
Exon	Y	Y	N	Y	Y	Y	Y	Y
Zorinsky	?	?	?	?	?	Y	Y	Y
NEVADA								
Hecht	N	N	N	Y	N	Y	Y	Y
Laxalt	N	Y	?	?	?	Y	Y	?
NEW HAMPSHIRE								
Humphrey	Y	Y	N	Y	Y	Y	Y	Y
Rudman	N	N	Y	Y	Y	Y	Y	Y
NEW JERSEY								
Bradley	N	Y	Y	Y	?	Y	N	N
Lautenberg	Y	Y	Y	Y	Y	Y	N	N
NEW MEXICO								
Domenici	N	N	Y	N	Y	Y	N	Y
Bingaman	Y	Y	Y	N	Y	Y	N	N
NEW YORK								
D'Amato	N	Y	Y	Y	Y	Y	Y	Y
Moynihan	Y	Y	Y	N	?	Y	N	N
NORTH CAROLINA								
East	N	N	N	Y	N	Y	Y	Y
Helms	N	N	N	Y	N	Y	Y	Y
NORTH DAKOTA								
Andrews	?	?	?	?	?	Y	Y	N
Burdick	Y	Y	Y	Y	Y	Y	N	N
OHIO								
Glenn	?	?	?	?	?	Y	N	N
Metzenbaum	Y	Y	Y	N	?	Y	N	N
OKLAHOMA								
Nickles	N	N	N	Y	N	Y	Y	Y
Boren	N	Y	?	?	?	Y	Y	Y
OREGON								
Hatfield	+	?	?	?	?	Y	N	N
Packwood	N	Y	Y	Y	Y	Y	N	Y
PENNSYLVANIA								
Heinz	N	Y	+	?	+	Y	N	Y
Specter	N	Y	Y	Y	Y	Y	N	N
RHODE ISLAND								
Chafee	N	Y	N	Y	Y	Y	N	N
Pell	Y	Y	Y	Y	Y	N	N	N
SOUTH CAROLINA								
Thurmond	N	N	-	?	+	Y	Y	Y
Hollings	?	?	?	?	?	Y	N	N
SOUTH DAKOTA								
Abdnor	N	N	N	Y	N	Y	Y	Y
Pressler	N	Y	N	Y	Y	Y	Y	Y
TENNESSEE								
Baker	N	Y	Y	Y	Y	N	N	Y
Sasser	Y	Y	Y	Y	Y	Y	N	N
TEXAS								
Tower	?	?	Y	Y	N	Y	?	Y
Bentsen	N	Y	Y	Y	Y	Y	N	Y
UTAH								
Garn	N	N	N	Y	N	Y	Y	Y
Hatch	N	N	N	Y	N	Y	Y	Y
VERMONT								
Stafford	N	Y	Y	Y	Y	Y	N	N
Leahy	Y	Y	Y	Y	Y	Y	N	N
VIRGINIA								
Trible	N	N	N	Y	Y	Y	Y	Y
Warner	N	Y	N	Y	Y	Y	Y	Y
WASHINGTON								
Gorton	N	Y	Y	Y	Y	Y	N	Y
Evans	?	?	?	?	#	Y	N	Y
WEST VIRGINIA								
Byrd	N	Y	Y	N	Y	Y	N	N
Randolph	N	Y	Y	Y	Y	Y	N	N
WISCONSIN								
Kasten	N	Y	N	Y	N	Y	Y	Y
Proxmire	Y	Y	N	Y	Y	Y	Y	N
WYOMING								
Simpson	?	?	N	Y	Y	Y	Y	Y
Wallop	?	N	Y	Y	N	Y	Y	Y

KEY

Y Voted for (yea).
\# Paired for.
+ Announced for.
N Voted against (nay).
X Paired against.
- Announced against.
P Voted "present".
C Voted "present" to avoid possible conflict of interest.
? Did not vote or otherwise make a position known.

Democrats   *Republicans*

ND - Northern Democrats   SD - Southern Democrats (Southern states - Ala., Ark., Fla., Ga., Ky., La., Miss., N.C., Okla., S.C., Tenn., Texas, Va.)

310. H J Res 308. Debt Limit Increase. Chiles, D-Fla., amendment to make the debt limit increase provided by the bill contingent upon enactment of the deficit reduction measures mandated by Congress in the fiscal 1984 budget resolution (H Con Res 91). Rejected 31-53: R 3-41; D 28-12 (ND 20-7, SD 8-5), Oct. 28, 1983.

311. H J Res 308. Debt Limit Increase. Hart, D-Colo., amendment to invoke the War Powers act (PL 93-148) to require the president to withdraw U.S. armed forces from Grenada within 60 days unless Congress authorizes further military involvement there. Adopted 64-20: R 25-20; D 39-0 (ND 27-0, SD 12-0), Oct. 28, 1983.

312. H J Res 308. Debt Limit Increase. Dole, R-Kan., motion to table (kill) the Dixon, D-Ill., amendment to express the sense of the Senate in support of a constitutional amendment permitting the president to veto individual items in appropriations bills. Motion agreed to 53-25: R 20-21; D 33-4 (ND 22-3, SD 11-1), Oct. 29, 1983.

313. H J Res 308. Debt Limit Increase. Long, D-La., amendment to express the sense of the Senate that amendments resulting in increased spending or lower revenues should not be offered or added to debt limit or budget reconciliation bills in 1983. Adopted 66-11: R 38-2; D 28-9 (ND 17-8, SD 11-1), Oct. 29, 1983.

314. H J Res 308. Debt Limit Increase. Riegle, D-Mich., amendment, as modified, to halt U.S. restrictions on press coverage in Grenada as long as such action does not jeopardize the safety or security of U.S. or allied forces or citizens in Grenada. Adopted 53-18: R 23-17; D 30-1 (ND 19-0, SD 11-1), Oct. 29, 1983. (On Oct. 31, the Riegle amendment was reconsidered, further modified and adopted by voice vote. The final modifications prohibited "unreasonable" restrictions on the press in Grenada and stipulated that the amendment did not require the Defense Department to disclose sensitive security information.)

315. H J Res 308. Debt Limit Increase. Baucus, D-Mont., amendment to express the sense of the Senate that the United States should insist that Japan dismantle all non-tariff barriers to the importation of beef. Adopted 92-6: R 51-3; D 41-3 (ND 28-3, SD 13-0), Oct. 31, 1983.

316. H J Res 308. Debt Limit Increase. Kasten, R-Wis., amendment to express the sense of the Senate that no further tax increases should be enacted until Congress reduces spending by $3 for every $1 in revenue raised by the Tax Equity and Fiscal Responsibility Act of 1982 (PL 97-248). Rejected 42-55: R 37-15; D 5-40 (ND 3-28, SD 2-12), Oct. 31, 1983.

317. H J Res 308. Debt Limit Increase. Dole, R-Kan., motion to table (kill) the Kennedy, D-Mass., amendment to call for a mutual and verifiable freeze on and reduction in nuclear weapons. Motion agreed to 58-40: R 46-7; D 12-33 (ND 3-28, SD 9-5), Oct. 31, 1983. A "yea" was a vote supporting the president's position.

	318 319 320 321 322		318 319 320 321 322		318 319 320 321 322
ALABAMA		**IOWA**		**NEW HAMPSHIRE**	
Denton	Y N N Y N	*Grassley*	N N N Y Y	*Humphrey*	N N N Y N
Heflin	N N N Y N	*Jepsen*	N N N Y Y	*Rudman*	N Y N Y Y
ALASKA		**KANSAS**		**NEW JERSEY**	
Murkowski	N Y N Y Y	*Dole*	N Y Y Y Y	Bradley	N Y Y Y N
Stevens	N Y Y Y Y	*Kassebaum*	N Y Y Y Y	Lautenberg	N N N Y N
ARIZONA		**KENTUCKY**		**NEW MEXICO**	
Goldwater	N Y N Y N	Ford	N N N Y N	*Domenici*	N N Y Y Y
DeConcini	N N N Y N	Huddleston	N N N Y N	Bingaman	N N Y Y N
ARKANSAS		**LOUISIANA**		**NEW YORK**	
Bumpers	Y N N N N	Johnston	N N N Y N	*D'Amato*	N N N Y N
Pryor	N N N Y Y	Long	N N N Y N	Moynihan	N N Y Y N
CALIFORNIA		**MAINE**		**NORTH CAROLINA**	
Wilson	N N N Y N	*Cohen*	N Y Y ? ?	*East*	Y N N Y N
Cranston	? ? ? Y N	Mitchell	N N N Y N	*Helms*	Y N N Y N
COLORADO		**MARYLAND**		**NORTH DAKOTA**	
Armstrong	N N N Y Y	*Mathias*	N Y Y ? ?	Andrews	N N Y Y Y
Hart	Y ? ? ? ?	Sarbanes	N N N Y N	Burdick	N N N Y Y
CONNECTICUT		**MASSACHUSETTS**		**OHIO**	
Weicker	? ? ? Y N	Kennedy	N N N Y N	Glenn	Y N Y ? ?
Dodd	Y N Y Y N	Tsongas	N N Y ? N	Metzenbaum	N N N Y N
DELAWARE		**MICHIGAN**		**OKLAHOMA**	
Roth	N Y Y Y Y	Levin	N N Y Y N	*Nickles*	N N N Y Y
Biden	N N N Y Y	Riegle	N N N Y N	Boren	N Y N Y N
FLORIDA		**MINNESOTA**		**OREGON**	
Hawkins	N N N Y Y	*Boschwitz*	? ? ? N Y	*Hatfield*	Y N Y Y Y
Chiles	N N N Y Y	*Durenberger*	N Y Y N Y	*Packwood*	N Y Y Y N
GEORGIA		**MISSISSIPPI**		**PENNSYLVANIA**	
Mattingly	N N N Y Y	*Cochran*	N Y Y Y Y	*Heinz*	N Y Y Y Y
Nunn	N N N Y N	Stennis	N N Y Y N	*Specter*	N N Y Y N
HAWAII		**MISSOURI**		**RHODE ISLAND**	
Inouye	N N N Y N	*Danforth*	N Y Y Y Y	*Chafee*	N Y Y Y Y
Matsunaga	N N Y Y N	Eagleton	Y N Y Y Y	Pell	N N Y Y N
IDAHO		**MONTANA**		**SOUTH CAROLINA**	
McClure	N Y Y Y Y	Baucus	N N N N N	*Thurmond*	N N Y Y N
Symms	Y N N Y N	Melcher	N N N N Y	Hollings	N ? ? ? ?
ILLINOIS		**NEBRASKA**		**SOUTH DAKOTA**	
Percy	N N Y Y Y	Exon	N N N N N	*Abdnor*	N N N Y Y
Dixon	N N N Y N	Zorinsky	N N N Y Y	*Pressler*	N N N Y Y
INDIANA		**NEVADA**		**TENNESSEE**	
Lugar	N Y Y Y Y	*Hecht*	N N N Y Y	*Baker*	N Y N Y Y
Quayle	N Y N Y N	*Laxalt*	N Y Y Y Y	Sasser	N N N Y N

KEY

- **Y** Voted for (yea).
- **#** Paired for.
- **+** Announced for.
- **N** Voted against (nay).
- **X** Paired against.
- **-** Announced against.
- **P** Voted "present".
- **C** Voted "present" to avoid possible conflict of interest.
- **?** Did not vote or otherwise make a position known.

Democrats   *Republicans*

	318 319 320 321 322
TEXAS	
Tower	Y Y N Y N
Bentsen	N N N Y N
UTAH	
Garn	N N Y Y Y
Hatch	N N N Y Y
VERMONT	
Stafford	N Y Y Y Y
Leahy	N N N Y N
VIRGINIA	
Trible	N N N Y Y
Warner	N N N Y Y
WASHINGTON	
Gorton	N Y Y Y Y
Evans	N N Y ? +
WEST VIRGINIA	
Byrd	N N N Y N
Randolph	N N N Y N
WISCONSIN	
Kasten	N N N Y Y
Proxmire	Y N N N Y
WYOMING	
Simpson	N Y Y Y Y
Wallop	Y Y Y Y Y

ND - Northern Democrats   SD - Southern Democrats (Southern states - Ala., Ark., Fla., Ga., Ky., La., Miss., N.C., Okla., S.C., Tenn., Texas, Va.)

318. H J Res 308. Debt Limit Increase. Dole, R-Kan., motion to table (kill) the Cohen, R-Maine, amendment expressing the sense of Congress that Strategic Arms Reduction Talks (START) should seek a reduction in the number of U.S. and Soviet nuclear missiles to equal, lower levels and endorsing the concept of a U.S.-Soviet "build-down" agreement: one requiring the retirement by each country of more existing nuclear warheads than the number of new ones it deploys. Motion rejected 13-84: R 7-46; D 6-38 (ND 5-25, SD 1-13), Oct. 31, 1983. (The amendment subsequently was withdrawn.)

319. H J Res 308. Debt Limit Increase. Baker, R-Tenn., motion to recommit the bill to the Finance Committee with instructions to report the bill back immediately. The effect of the motion would be to strike all amendments adopted during Senate floor debate. Motion rejected 27-68: R 25-28; D 2-40 (ND 1-28, SD 1-12), Oct. 31, 1983.

320. H J Res 308. Debt Limit Increase. Passage of the bill to increase the public debt limit to $1.45 trillion, from $1.389 trillion. Rejected 39-56: R 28-25; D 11-31 (ND 10-19, SD 1-12), Oct. 31, 1983.

321. S 1715. Natural Gas Policy Act Amendments. Baker, R-Tenn., motion to invoke cloture (thus limiting debate) on the Baker motion to proceed to the consideration of the bill to amend the Natural Gas Policy Act of 1978. Motion agreed to 86-7: R 50-2; D 36-5 (ND 24-4, SD 12-1), Nov. 3, 1983. A three-fifths majority vote (60) of the total Senate is required to invoke cloture.

322. HR 4185. Defense Department Appropriations, Fiscal 1984. Stevens, R-Alaska, amendment to delete $168.7 million thus reducing the number of M-1 tanks funded by the bill from 840 to 720. Rejected 45-48: R 38-13; D 7-35 (ND 5-24, SD 2-11), Nov. 3, 1983.

CQ Senate Votes 323 - 330

Corresponding to Congressional Record Votes 333, 334, 335, 336, 337, 338, 339, 340

KEY

Y Voted for (yea).
Paired for.
+ Announced for.
N Voted against (nay).
X Paired against.
- Announced against.
P Voted "present".
C Voted "present" to avoid possible conflict of interest.
? Did not vote or otherwise make a position known.

Democrats   *Republicans*

	323	324	325	326	327	328	329	330
ALABAMA								
Denton	Y	N	N	N	N	Y	N	Y
Heflin	Y	N	N	?	N	Y	N	N
ALASKA								
Murkowski	Y	N	N	Y	N	N	N	Y
Stevens	Y	N	Y	N	N	N	N	Y
ARIZONA								
Goldwater	Y	N	?	?	N	Y	N	Y
DeConcini	Y	X	?	?	?	?	Y	N
ARKANSAS								
Bumpers	Y	N	?	?	Y	Y	Y	N
Pryor	Y	N	N	Y	Y	Y	Y	N
CALIFORNIA								
Wilson	Y	N	N	Y	N	Y	N	Y
Cranston	Y	N	Y	Y	Y	Y	?	Y
COLORADO								
Armstrong	Y	Y	N	Y	N	N	Y	Y
Hart	?	?	?	?	Y	?	?	?
CONNECTICUT								
Weicker	?	?	?	Y	Y	Y	Y	Y
Dodd	Y	N	Y	Y	Y	Y	Y	N
DELAWARE								
Roth	Y	N	Y	N	N	N	N	Y
Biden	Y	N	Y	Y	Y	Y	Y	N
FLORIDA								
Hawkins	Y	N	Y	?	N	N	N	Y
Chiles	?	?	?	?	N	N	Y	Y
GEORGIA								
Mattingly	Y	N	N	N	N	N	N	Y
Nunn	Y	N	Y	N	Y	N	Y	N
HAWAII								
Inouye	?	?	?	?	?	?	?	?
Matsunaga	Y	N	Y	Y	Y	N	Y	N
IDAHO								
McClure	?	N	N	Y	N	N	N	Y
Symms	Y	Y	N	Y	N	Y	N	Y
ILLINOIS								
Percy	?	?	?	?	N	Y	N	Y
Dixon	Y	N	N	+	?	?	?	Y
INDIANA								
Lugar	Y	N	Y	N	N	N	N	Y
Quayle	Y	N	?	?	N	Y	N	Y

	323	324	325	326	327	328	329	330
IOWA								
Grassley	Y	Y	N	Y	N	N	N	Y
Jepsen	Y	Y	N	Y	N	N	N	Y
KANSAS								
Dole	Y	Y	Y	N	N	N	Y	Y
Kassebaum	Y	Y	Y	Y	N	N	Y	Y
KENTUCKY								
Ford	Y	N	Y	Y	Y	N	Y	N
Huddleston	Y	N	Y	Y	Y	N	Y	N
LOUISIANA								
Johnston	Y	N	Y	Y	N	N	Y	Y
Long	Y	N	N	Y	N	Y	N	Y
MAINE								
Cohen	Y	N	Y	N	Y	N	Y	Y
Mitchell	Y	N	Y	Y	Y	Y	Y	Y
MARYLAND								
Mathias	Y	N	Y	N	Y	Y	Y	Y
Sarbanes	Y	N	Y	Y	Y	Y	Y	N
MASSACHUSETTS								
Kennedy	+	?	?	Y	Y	Y	Y	Y
Tsongas	Y	N	Y	Y	Y	Y	Y	N
MICHIGAN								
Levin	Y	N	Y	Y	Y	Y	Y	N
Riegle	Y	N	Y	Y	Y	Y	Y	N
MINNESOTA								
Boschwitz	Y	?	?	?	N	Y	N	Y
Durenberger	Y	N	Y	?	?	?	Y	Y
MISSISSIPPI								
Cochran	?	N	Y	N	Y	N	Y	N
Stennis	Y	N	Y	N	Y	N	Y	N
MISSOURI								
Danforth	Y	N	Y	Y	N	N	N	Y
Eagleton	Y	N	Y	Y	Y	N	Y	N
MONTANA								
Baucus	?	?	?	?	Y	Y	Y	N
Melcher	Y	Y	X	Y	Y	Y	Y	N
NEBRASKA								
Exon	Y	N	N	Y	Y	Y	N	Y
Zorinsky	Y	N	N	Y	N	N	N	Y
NEVADA								
Hecht	Y	Y	N	Y	N	Y	N	Y
Laxalt	Y	Y	Y	?	N	N	N	Y

	323	324	325	326	327	328	329	330
NEW HAMPSHIRE								
Humphrey	Y	Y	N	Y	Y	Y	N	Y
Rudman	Y	N	Y	Y	N	N	N	Y
NEW JERSEY								
Bradley	Y	N	Y	Y	Y	Y	Y	Y
Lautenberg	Y	N	Y	?	+	+	?	?
NEW MEXICO								
Domenici	Y	N	N	N	N	N	N	Y
Bingaman	Y	N	Y	Y	Y	Y	Y	N
NEW YORK								
D'Amato	Y	N	Y	N	Y	N	Y	Y
Moynihan	Y	N	Y	Y	Y	Y	Y	N
NORTH CAROLINA								
East	Y	Y	?	Y	N	Y	N	Y
Helms	Y	Y	N	Y	N	Y	N	Y
NORTH DAKOTA								
Andrews	Y	N	Y	?	Y	Y	Y	Y
Burdick	Y	N	Y	?	Y	N	Y	N
OHIO								
Glenn	?	?	?	?	Y	Y	Y	Y
Metzenbaum	Y	N	Y	Y	Y	N	Y	N
OKLAHOMA								
Nickles	Y	N	N	Y	N	N	N	Y
Boren	Y	N	N	Y	Y	Y	Y	Y
OREGON								
Hatfield	Y	N	Y	Y	Y	N	Y	Y
Packwood	Y	Y	Y	?	?	?	?	?
PENNSYLVANIA								
Heinz	Y	Y	Y	Y	Y	Y	Y	Y
Specter	Y	N	Y	Y	Y	Y	Y	Y
RHODE ISLAND								
Chafee	Y	N	Y	N	Y	N	Y	Y
Pell	Y	N	Y	Y	Y	Y	Y	Y
SOUTH CAROLINA								
Thurmond	Y	N	N	?	N	Y	N	Y
Hollings	?	?	?	?	Y	?	?	?
SOUTH DAKOTA								
Abdnor	Y	?	?	?	N	N	N	Y
Pressler	Y	Y	N	Y	N	Y	Y	Y
TENNESSEE								
Baker	Y	N	Y	Y	N	N	N	Y
Sasser	Y	N	Y	Y	Y	Y	Y	N

	323	324	325	326	327	328	329	330
TEXAS								
Tower	Y	Y	Y	N	N	Y	N	Y
Bentsen	?	?	?	?	N	N	Y	Y
UTAH								
Garn	Y	Y	N	Y	N	N	N	Y
Hatch	Y	Y	N	Y	N	Y	N	Y
VERMONT								
Stafford	Y	Y	Y	Y	Y	Y	Y	Y
Leahy	Y	#	#	+	Y	Y	Y	N
VIRGINIA								
Trible	Y	Y	N	Y	N	Y	N	Y
Warner	Y	N	Y	N	Y	N	Y	Y
WASHINGTON								
Gorton	Y	N	Y	N	Y	N	N	Y
Evans	+	+	+	?	?	?	?	?
WEST VIRGINIA								
Byrd	Y	N	Y	N	Y	N	Y	N
Randolph	Y	N	Y	Y	N	Y	N	N
WISCONSIN								
Kasten	Y	Y	N	Y	N	N	N	Y
Proxmire	Y	N	Y	Y	Y	N	Y	Y
WYOMING								
Simpson	?	?	?	?	N	N	N	Y
Wallop	Y	N	N	N	N	N	N	?

ND - Northern Democrats   SD - Southern Democrats (Southern states - Ala., Ark., Fla., Ga., Ky., La., Miss., N.C., Okla., S.C., Tenn., Texas, Va.)

---

323. HR 4185. Defense Department Appropriations, Fiscal 1984. Metzenbaum, D-Ohio, amendment to provide that up to $100,000 of funds in the bill be available to assist spouses and other close relatives to attend the funeral of armed services personnel who die as a result of injuries incurred in service. Adopted 86-0: R 49-0; D 37-0 (ND 26-0, SD 11-0), Nov. 4, 1983.

324. HR 4185. Defense Department Appropriations, Fiscal 1984. Jepsen, R-Iowa, amendment to delete certain provisions relating to procurement procedures. Rejected 22-62: R 21-28; D 1-34 (ND 1-23, SD 0-11), Nov. 4, 1983.

325. HR 4185. Defense Department Appropriations, Fiscal 1984. Rudman, R-N.H., motion to table (kill) the Helms, R-N.C., amendment expressing the sense of the Senate that no defense program should be constrained to comply with the SALT II U.S.-Soviet arms control treaty, until the Senate has consented to the treaty's ratification. Motion agreed to 50-29: R 24-22; D 26-7 (ND 20-3, SD 6-4), Nov. 4, 1983. A "yea" was a vote supporting the president's position.

326. HR 4185. Defense Department Appropriations, Fiscal 1984. Byrd, D-W.Va., amendment to require the Office of Federal Procurement Policy to review the Defense Department's procedures for purchasing spare parts. Adopted 66-5: R 36-5; D 30-0 (ND 21-0, SD 9-0), Nov. 4, 1983.

327. HR 4185. Defense Department Appropriations, Fiscal 1984. Bumpers, D-Ark., amendment to delete $2.1 billion for 21 MX missiles. Rejected 37-56: R 6-46; D 31-10 (ND 24-3, SD 7-7), Nov. 7, 1983. A "nay" was a vote supporting the president's position.

328. HR 4185. Defense Department Appropriations, Fiscal 1984. Weicker, R-Conn., amendment to add $168 million for components for nuclear-powered attack submarines. Adopted 55-36: R 27-25; D 28-11 (ND 20-6, SD 8-5), Nov. 7, 1983. A "yea" was a vote supporting the president's position.

329. HR 4185. Defense Department Appropriations, Fiscal 1984. Kassebaum, R-Kan., amendment expressing the sense of the Senate that the president should propose to the Soviet government a mutual moratorium of flight tests of ICBMs equipped with multiple warheads (or MIRVs). Rejected 42-50: R 11-42; D 31-8 (ND 22-4, SD 9-4), Nov. 7, 1983. A "nay" was a vote supporting the president's position.

330. HR 4185. Defense Department Appropriations, Fiscal 1984. Jepsen, R-Iowa, motion to table (kill) the Melcher, D-Mont., amendment to require that recruits with less than four months' service receive the 4 percent pay raise due to take effect Jan. 1, 1984, for all other military and federal civilian personnel. Motion agreed to 69-24: R 52-0; D 17-24 (ND 10-18, SD 7-6), Nov. 7, 1983.

	331	332	333	334	335	336
ALABAMA						
Denton	N	Y	N	Y	N	N
Heflin	N	Y	Y	Y	N	N
ALASKA						
Murkowski	?	?	?	?	?	?
Stevens	N	Y	Y	Y	Y	Y
ARIZONA						
Goldwater	N	Y	N	?	N	Y
DeConcini	Y	N	Y	Y	N	N
ARKANSAS						
Bumpers	N	Y	Y	Y	Y	Y
Pryor	Y	N	Y	Y	Y	Y
CALIFORNIA						
Wilson	X	#	N	Y	N	N
Cranston	Y	N	?	?	+	#
COLORADO						
Armstrong	N	Y	N	Y	N	N
Hart	Y	N	?	?	Y	Y
CONNECTICUT						
Weicker	Y	N	Y	Y	Y	Y
Dodd	Y	N	Y	Y	Y	Y
DELAWARE						
Roth	Y	N	Y	Y	Y	Y
Biden	Y	N	Y	Y	N	N
FLORIDA						
Hawkins	N	#	Y	Y	N	N
Chiles	Y	N	Y	Y	Y	Y
GEORGIA						
Mattingly	N	Y	Y	Y	N	N
Nunn	N	Y	N	Y	N	Y
HAWAII						
Inouye	?	X	?	?	Y	Y
Matsunaga	Y	N	Y	Y	Y	Y
IDAHO						
McClure	N	Y	N	Y	N	X
Symms	N	Y	N	Y	N	N
ILLINOIS						
Percy	Y	N	N	Y	?	?
Dixon	N	Y	N	Y	N	N
INDIANA						
Lugar	N	Y	N	Y	N	N
Quayle	N	Y	N	Y	N	N

	331	332	333	334	335	336
IOWA						
Grassley	Y	N	N	Y	N	N
Jepsen	N	Y	N	Y	N	N
KANSAS						
Dole	N	Y	Y	Y	N	N
Kassebaum	Y	N	Y	Y	Y	Y
KENTUCKY						
Ford	N	Y	Y	Y	N	N
Huddleston	Y	N	Y	Y	N	N
LOUISIANA						
Johnston	N	Y	Y	Y	N	N
Long	N	Y	Y	Y	N	X
MAINE						
Cohen	N	Y	N	Y	Y	Y
Mitchell	Y	N	Y	Y	N	N
MARYLAND						
Mathias	Y	N	Y	Y	Y	Y
Sarbanes	Y	N	Y	Y	Y	Y
MASSACHUSETTS						
Kennedy	Y	N	Y	Y	Y	Y
Tsongas	Y	N	Y	Y	Y	Y
MICHIGAN						
Levin	Y	N	N	Y	Y	Y
Riegle	Y	N	Y	Y	Y	Y
MINNESOTA						
Boschwitz	N	Y	N	Y	N	N
Durenberger	Y	N	Y	Y	N	N
MISSISSIPPI						
Cochran	?	X	?	?	N	N
Stennis	N	Y	Y	Y	N	Y
MISSOURI						
Danforth	Y	N	N	Y	N	N
Eagleton	Y	N	Y	Y	N	N
MONTANA						
Baucus	Y	N	Y	N	Y	Y
Melcher	Y	N	Y	N	N	N
NEBRASKA						
Exon	N	Y	N	Y	N	N
Zorinsky	N	Y	Y	Y	N	N
NEVADA						
Hecht	N	Y	N	Y	N	N
Laxalt	N	Y	Y	Y	N	N

	331	332	333	334	335	336
NEW HAMPSHIRE						
Humphrey	N	Y	N	Y	N	N
Rudman	N	Y	Y	Y	Y	Y
NEW JERSEY						
Bradley	Y	N	Y	Y	Y	Y
Lautenberg	Y	N	Y	Y	Y	Y
NEW MEXICO						
Domenici	N	Y	Y	Y	N	N
Bingaman	Y	N	N	Y	Y	Y
NEW YORK						
D'Amato	N	Y	Y	Y	N	N
Moynihan	Y	N	Y	N	Y	Y
NORTH CAROLINA						
East	N	Y	N	Y	N	N
Helms	N	Y	N	Y	N	N
NORTH DAKOTA						
Andrews	Y	N	Y	Y	Y	Y
Burdick	Y	N	Y	Y	Y	Y
OHIO						
Glenn	N	Y	N	Y	N	N
Metzenbaum	Y	N	Y	N	Y	Y
OKLAHOMA						
Nickles	N	Y	N	Y	N	N
Boren	Y	N	Y	Y	N	N
OREGON						
Hatfield	Y	N	Y	N	Y	+
Packwood	Y	N	Y	Y	Y	Y
PENNSYLVANIA						
Heinz	Y	N	Y	Y	Y	Y
Specter	Y	N	Y	Y	Y	Y
RHODE ISLAND						
Chafee	Y	N	Y	Y	Y	Y
Pell	Y	N	Y	Y	Y	Y
SOUTH CAROLINA						
Thurmond	N	Y	N	Y	N	N
Hollings	?	?	?	?	?	?
SOUTH DAKOTA						
Abdnor	N	Y	Y	Y	N	N
Pressler	Y	N	Y	Y	N	N
TENNESSEE						
Baker	N	Y	Y	Y	Y	Y
Sasser	Y	N	Y	Y	Y	Y

	331	332	333	334	335	336
TEXAS						
Tower	N	Y	N	Y	Y	Y
Bentsen	N	Y	N	Y	Y	Y
UTAH						
Garn	N	Y	N	Y	N	N
Hatch	N	Y	N	Y	N	N
VERMONT						
Stafford	Y	N	Y	Y	Y	Y
Leahy	Y	N	Y	Y	Y	Y
VIRGINIA						
Trible	N	Y	N	Y	N	N
Warner	N	Y	N	Y	N	N
WASHINGTON						
Gorton	Y	N	Y	Y	Y	Y
Evans	#	X	?	?	?	#
WEST VIRGINIA						
Byrd	N	#	Y	Y	Y	Y
Randolph	N	Y	Y	Y	N	N
WISCONSIN						
Kasten	N	Y	Y	Y	N	N
Proxmire	Y	N	Y	N	N	N
WYOMING						
Simpson	N	Y	N	Y	Y	Y
Wallop	N	Y	Y	Y	Y	Y

KEY

Y	Voted for (yea).
#	Paired for.
+	Announced for.
N	Voted against (nay).
X	Paired against.
-	Announced against.
P	Voted "present".
C	Voted "present" to avoid possible conflict of interest.
?	Did not vote or otherwise make a position known.

Democrats *Republicans*

ND - Northern Democrats   SD - Southern Democrats (Southern states - Ala., Ark., Fla., Ga., Ky., La., Miss., N.C., Okla., S.C., Tenn., Texas, Va.)

331. HR 4185. Defense Department Appropriations, Fiscal 1984. Hatfield, R-Ore., motion to table (kill) the Tower, R-Texas-Stevens, R-Alaska, amendment to add to the bill $124 million for production of binary chemical munitions. Motion rejected 46-48: R 17-34; D 29-14 (ND 24-6, SD 5-8), Nov. 8, 1983. A "nay" was a vote supporting the president's position. (The Tower-Stevens amendment subsequently was adopted *(see vote 332, below).)*

332. HR 4185. Defense Department Appropriations, Fiscal 1984. Tower, R-Texas-Stevens, R-Alaska, amendment to add to the bill $124 million for production of binary chemical munitions. Adopted 47-46: R 33-17; D 13-29 (ND 5-24, SD 8-5), Nov. 8, 1983, with Vice President Bush casting a "yea" vote to break the 46-46 tie. A "yea" was a vote supporting the president's position.

333. HR 4185. Defense Department Appropriations, Fiscal 1984. Stevens, R-Alaska, motion to table (kill) the Tower, R-Texas, amendment to add $491 million for various programs and delete $900 million for other projects in the bill. Motion agreed to 62-31: R 28-24; D 34-7 (ND 23-5, SD 11-2), Nov. 8, 1983.

334. HR 4185. Defense Department Appropriations, Fiscal 1984. Passage of the bill to appropriate $252,206,037,000 in new budget authority and $839,100,000 in funds appropriated but not spent in prior years for military programs of the Defense Department, for total funding of $253,045,137,000 in fiscal 1984. Passed 86-6: R 50-1; D 36-5 (ND 23-5, SD 13-0), Nov. 8, 1983. The president had requested $260,926,119,000 in new budget authority.

335. S J Res 194. Continuing Appropriations, Fiscal 1984. Weicker, R-Conn., motion to table (kill) the Denton, R-Ala., amendment to prohibit funds in the bill from paying for abortions or for health insurance plans for federal employees if those plans provide benefits or coverage for abortions. Motion rejected 44-51: R 19-33; D 25-18 (ND 20-10, SD 5-8), Nov. 9, 1983.

336. S J Res 194. Continuing Appropriations, Fiscal 1984. Judgment of the Senate affirming the chair's ruling that a portion of the Denton, R-Ala., abortion amendment was out of order because it constituted legislation on an appropriations bill. Ruling of the chair rejected 46-46: R 19-31; D 27-15 (ND 20-10, SD 7-5), Nov. 9, 1983.

	337	338	339	340	341	342	343	344
ALABAMA								
Denton	Y	Y	N	Y	Y	Y	Y	Y
Heflin	Y	N	N	Y	Y	N	N	N
ALASKA								
Murkowski	?	?	?	?	?	?	?	?
Stevens	Y	Y	Y	N	N	Y	Y	Y
ARIZONA								
Goldwater	?	?	?	?	?	?	?	?
DeConcini	Y	Y	N	Y	Y	N	N	Y
ARKANSAS								
Bumpers	Y	N	Y	N	N	N	N	N
Pryor	Y	?	?	?	?	?	?	?
CALIFORNIA								
Wilson	Y	Y	N	Y	Y	Y	Y	Y
Cranston	Y	N	Y	N	N	?	?	?
COLORADO								
Armstrong	Y	Y	N	Y	Y	Y	Y	Y
Hart	Y	N	Y	N	N	?	?	?
CONNECTICUT								
Weicker	?	N	Y	N	N	Y	Y	N
Dodd	Y	?	?	?	?	?	?	?
DELAWARE								
Roth	Y	Y	Y	N	N	Y	Y	Y
Biden	Y	N	N	Y	Y	N	N	N
FLORIDA								
Hawkins	Y	Y	N	Y	Y	Y	Y	Y
Chiles	Y	N	Y	N	N	N	N	Y
GEORGIA								
Mattingly	Y	Y	N	Y	Y	Y	Y	Y
Nunn	Y	Y	Y	N	Y	N	N	Y
HAWAII								
Inouye	Y	?	?	?	?	?	?	?
Matsunaga	Y	N	Y	N	N	N	N	Y
IDAHO								
McClure	?	Y	?	?	?	?	?	?
Symms	Y	Y	N	Y	Y	Y	Y	N
ILLINOIS								
Percy	Y	Y	N	Y	N	N	Y	Y
Dixon	Y	N	N	Y	Y	N	N	N
INDIANA								
Lugar	Y	Y	N	Y	Y	Y	Y	Y
Quayle	N	Y	N	Y	Y	N	Y	Y
IOWA								
Grassley	Y	Y	N	Y	Y	Y	Y	N
Jepsen	Y	Y	N	Y	Y	Y	Y	Y
KANSAS								
Dole	Y	Y	N	Y	N	Y	N	Y
Kassebaum	Y	Y	Y	N	Y	Y	Y	Y
KENTUCKY								
Ford	Y	Y	N	Y	Y	N	N	N
Huddleston	Y	N	N	#	Y	N	N	Y
LOUISIANA								
Johnston	N	N	N	Y	Y	Y	N	Y
Long	Y	N	N	Y	Y	Y	N	Y
MAINE								
Cohen	Y	N	Y	N	N	N	Y	Y
Mitchell	Y	N	N	Y	Y	Y	N	N
MARYLAND								
Mathias	Y	Y	Y	N	N	N	N	N
Sarbanes	Y	N	Y	N	N	N	N	N
MASSACHUSETTS								
Kennedy	Y	N	Y	N	N	N	N	N
Tsongas	Y	N	Y	N	N	N	N	N
MICHIGAN								
Levin	Y	N	Y	N	N	N	N	N
Riegle	Y	N	N	Y	N	N	N	N
MINNESOTA								
Boschwitz	Y	Y	N	Y	Y	Y	Y	Y
Durenberger	Y	Y	X	?	?	?	?	?
MISSISSIPPI								
Cochran	Y	Y	N	Y	Y	Y	Y	Y
Stennis	Y	Y	Y	N	Y	N	Y	Y
MISSOURI								
Danforth	Y	Y	N	Y	Y	Y	Y	Y
Eagleton	Y	N	N	Y	Y	N	N	N
MONTANA								
Baucus	Y	Y	Y	N	N	N	N	N
Melcher	Y	N	N	Y	Y	N	N	N
NEBRASKA								
Exon	Y	Y	N	Y	Y	Y	N	N
Zorinsky	Y	Y	N	Y	Y	N	N	N
NEVADA								
Hecht	Y	Y	N	Y	Y	Y	Y	Y
Laxalt	Y	?	?	?	?	?	?	?
NEW HAMPSHIRE								
Humphrey	Y	Y	N	Y	Y	Y	Y	N
Rudman	Y	Y	Y	N	N	Y	Y	Y
NEW JERSEY								
Bradley	Y	N	Y	N	N	N	N	N
Lautenberg	Y	N	Y	N	N	N	N	N
NEW MEXICO								
Domenici	?	?	?	?	?	?	?	?
Bingaman	Y	N	Y	N	N	N	N	N
NEW YORK								
D'Amato	Y	Y	N	Y	Y	Y	Y	Y
Moynihan	Y	N	Y	N	N	?	?	?
NORTH CAROLINA								
East	Y	Y	N	Y	Y	Y	Y	Y
Helms	Y	Y	N	Y	Y	Y	N	Y
NORTH DAKOTA								
Andrews	Y	N	Y	N	N	Y	Y	N
Burdick	Y	N	Y	N	N	N	N	N
OHIO								
Glenn	?	?	?	X	?	?	?	?
Metzenbaum	Y	N	Y	N	N	N	N	N
OKLAHOMA								
Nickles	Y	Y	N	Y	Y	Y	N	Y
Boren	Y	Y	N	Y	Y	Y	N	N
OREGON								
Hatfield	Y	Y	Y	N	N	Y	Y	N
Packwood	Y	Y	Y	N	N	Y	Y	Y
PENNSYLVANIA								
Heinz	Y	Y	Y	N	N	N	Y	Y
Specter	Y	N	Y	N	N	N	Y	Y
RHODE ISLAND								
Chafee	Y	Y	N	Y	N	Y	Y	Y
Pell	Y	N	Y	N	N	N	N	N
SOUTH CAROLINA								
Thurmond	Y	Y	N	Y	Y	Y	Y	Y
Hollings	?	?	?	?	?	?	?	?
SOUTH DAKOTA								
Abdnor	Y	Y	N	Y	Y	Y	Y	Y
Pressler	Y	Y	N	Y	Y	Y	Y	N
TENNESSEE								
Baker	Y	Y	Y	N	N	Y	Y	Y
Sasser	Y	N	Y	N	N	N	N	N
TEXAS								
Tower	?	Y	Y	N	?	?	?	?
Bentsen	Y	N	Y	N	Y	N	N	N
UTAH								
Garn	N	Y	N	Y	Y	Y	Y	Y
Hatch	Y	Y	N	Y	Y	Y	Y	Y
VERMONT								
Stafford	Y	N	Y	N	N	Y	Y	N
Leahy	Y	N	Y	N	N	N	N	N
VIRGINIA								
Trible	Y	Y	N	Y	Y	Y	Y	Y
Warner	Y	Y	N	Y	Y	Y	Y	Y
WASHINGTON								
Gorton	Y	Y	N	Y	N	Y	Y	Y
Evans	?	+	#	-	?	?	?	?
WEST VIRGINIA								
Byrd	Y	N	Y	N	N	N	N	N
Randolph	Y	N	N	Y	Y	N	N	N
WISCONSIN								
Kasten	Y	Y	N	Y	Y	Y	Y	Y
Proxmire	N	Y	N	Y	Y	Y	N	N
WYOMING								
Simpson	?	?	?	?	?	?	?	?
Wallop	Y	Y	Y	N	N	?	?	Y

KEY

Y Voted for (yea).
\# Paired for.
\+ Announced for.
N Voted against (nay).
X Paired against.
- Announced against.
P Voted "present".
C Voted "present" to avoid possible conflict of interest.
? Did not vote or otherwise make a position known.

Democrats   *Republicans*

ND - Northern Democrats   SD - Southern Democrats (Southern states - Ala., Ark., Fla., Ga., Ky., La., Miss., N.C., Okla., S.C., Tenn., Texas, Va.)

337. Procedural Motion. Hatfield, R-Ore., motion to instruct the sergeant-at-arms to request the attendance of absent senators. Motion agreed to 86-4: R 45-2; D 41-2 (ND 29-1, SD 12-1), Nov. 10, 1983.

338. H J Res 413. Continuing Appropriations, Fiscal 1984. Hatfield, R-Ore., amendment to strike from the bill $954 million added by the House for social programs, including education, health and nutrition, job training and low-income energy assistance. Adopted 53-36: R 44-5; D 9-31 (ND 5-23, SD 4-8), Nov. 10, 1983. A "yea" was a vote supporting the president's position.

339. H J Res 413. Continuing Appropriations, Fiscal 1984. Hatfield, R-Ore., amendment to strike from the bill the House amendment that had the effect of barring federal employees from using federal health insurance plans to pay for abortions. Rejected 43-44: R 19-28; D 24-16 (ND 18-10, SD 6-6), Nov. 10, 1983.

340. H J Res 413. Continuing Appropriations, Fiscal 1984. Nickles, R-Okla., motion to table (kill) the Denton, R-Ala., motion to reconsider the vote by which the Hatfield, R-Ore., amendment was rejected *(see vote 339, above)*. Motion rejected 43-43: R 28-19; D 15-24 (ND 10-18, SD 5-6), Nov. 10, 1983.

341. H J Res 413. Continuing Appropriations, Fiscal 1984. Helms, R-N.C., motion to withdraw the Denton, R-Ala., motion to reconsider the vote by which the Hatfield, R-Ore., amendment was rejected *(see votes 339, 340, above)*. Motion agreed to 45-41: R 28-18; D 17-23 (ND 10-18, SD 7-5), Nov. 10, 1983.

342. H J Res 413. Continuing Appropriations, Fiscal 1984. Judgment of the Senate affirming the chair's ruling that the Riegle, D-Mich., amendment to provide $500 million in health care benefits for the unemployed was out of order because it constituted legislation on an appropriations bill. Ruling of the chair upheld 47-36: R 39-6; D 8-30 (ND 3-23, SD 5-7), Nov. 10, 1983.

343. H J Res 413. Continuing Appropriations, Fiscal 1984. Judgment of the Senate affirming the chair's ruling that the Ford, D-Ky., amendment to require the president annually to submit to Congress a balanced budget for each fiscal year was out of order because it constituted legislation on an appropriations bill. Ruling of the chair upheld 42-40: R 41-4; D 1-36 (ND 0-25, SD 1-11), Nov. 10, 1983.

344. H J Res 413. Continuing Appropriations, Fiscal 1984. Baker, R-Tenn., motion to table (kill) the Mathias, R-Md., amendment to reduce the funds in the bill for military assistance programs from $697 million to $421 million. Motion agreed to 46-37: R 38-8; D 8-29 (ND 2-23, SD 6-6), Nov. 10, 1983.

KEY

- Y Voted for (yea).
- # Paired for.
- + Announced for.
- N Voted against (nay).
- X Paired against.
- − Announced against.
- P Voted "present".
- C Voted "present" to avoid possible conflict of interest.
- ? Did not vote or otherwise make a position known.

Democrats Republicans

	345	346	347	348	349	350	351	352
ALABAMA								
Denton	Y	Y	Y	N	−	?	?	N
Heflin	Y	Y	Y	N	N	Y	N	N
ALASKA								
Murkowski	?	?	?	?	Y	Y	N	N
Stevens	Y	N	N	Y	?	?	?	N
ARIZONA								
Goldwater	?	?	?	?	Y	Y	Y	N
DeConcini	Y	Y	Y	N	N	Y	Y	N
ARKANSAS								
Bumpers	Y	N	Y	Y	Y	Y	Y	N
Pryor	?	?	?	?	?	?	?	N
CALIFORNIA								
Wilson	Y	Y	Y	Y	Y	Y	N	N
Cranston	+	?	?	?	?	?	?	?
COLORADO								
Armstrong	Y	Y	Y	N	N	Y	N	N
Hart	?	?	?	?	?	?	?	Y
CONNECTICUT								
Weicker	Y	N	Y	Y	Y	Y	Y	N
Dodd	?	?	?	?	?	+	+	N
DELAWARE								
Roth	Y	Y	Y	N	N	Y	Y	N
Biden	Y	N	N	Y	Y	Y	Y	Y
FLORIDA								
Hawkins	Y	Y	Y	N	N	Y	Y	N
Chiles	Y	N	N	Y	Y	Y	N	N
GEORGIA								
Mattingly	Y	Y	Y	N	N	Y	N	N
Nunn	Y	Y	Y	Y	?	Y	N	Y
HAWAII								
Inouye	?	?	?	?	?	?	?	?
Matsunaga	Y	N	N	Y	?	?	?	N
IDAHO								
McClure	?	?	?	?	N	Y	Y	N
Symms	N	Y	Y	N	N	N	N	N
ILLINOIS								
Percy	Y	N	Y	Y	?	+	?	N
Dixon	Y	N	N	Y	?	?	?	Y
INDIANA								
Lugar	Y	Y	Y	N	N	Y	Y	N
Quayle	Y	N	Y	N	N	Y	N	N
IOWA								
Grassley	Y	Y	Y	N	N	Y	Y	N
Jepsen	Y	Y	Y	N	N	Y	Y	N
KANSAS								
Dole	Y	?	?	?	Y	Y	Y	N
Kassebaum	Y	N	?	?	?	+	?	N
KENTUCKY								
Ford	Y	N	N	Y	N	Y	Y	Y
Huddleston	Y	Y	Y	Y	Y	Y	N	Y
LOUISIANA								
Johnston	Y	Y	Y	Y	?	?	?	N
Long	Y	?	?	?	?	Y	Y	Y
MAINE								
Cohen	Y	N	N	Y	Y	Y	Y	N
Mitchell	Y	N	N	Y	N	Y	Y	N
MARYLAND								
Mathias	Y	N	N	Y	Y	Y	Y	N
Sarbanes	Y	N	N	Y	Y	Y	Y	N
MASSACHUSETTS								
Kennedy	Y	N	N	Y	Y	Y	Y	N
Tsongas	Y	N	N	Y	Y	Y	Y	Y
MICHIGAN								
Levin	Y	N	N	Y	Y	Y	Y	N
Riegle	Y	N	N	Y	Y	Y	Y	N
MINNESOTA								
Boschwitz	Y	N	N	Y	N	Y	N	N
Durenberger	?	?	?	?	Y	Y	Y	N
MISSISSIPPI								
Cochran	Y	Y	Y	N	Y	Y	Y	N
Stennis	Y	N	?	?	Y	Y	Y	N
MISSOURI								
Danforth	Y	N	Y	Y	N	Y	Y	N
Eagleton	Y	N	N	Y	N	Y	Y	N
MONTANA								
Baucus	Y	Y	Y	Y	Y	Y	Y	Y
Melcher	Y	Y	Y	N	Y	Y	Y	Y
NEBRASKA								
Exon	Y	N	N	Y	N	Y	N	Y
Zorinsky	Y	N	N	N	N	Y	N	Y
NEVADA								
Hecht	Y	Y	Y	N	N	Y	N	N
Laxalt	?	?	?	N	Y	Y	Y	N
NEW HAMPSHIRE								
Humphrey	N	N	Y	N	N	Y	N	Y
Rudman	Y	N	Y	?	?	Y	N	N
NEW JERSEY								
Bradley	Y	N	N	Y	Y	Y	Y	Y
Lautenberg	Y	N	Y	?	?	Y	Y	N
NEW MEXICO								
Domenici	?	?	?	?	Y	Y	Y	N
Bingaman	Y	N	Y	Y	Y	Y	N	N
NEW YORK								
D'Amato	Y	N	N	Y	?	+	?	N
Moynihan	Y	N	N	Y	?	+	?	N
NORTH CAROLINA								
East	N	Y	Y	N	N	N	N	N
Helms	N	Y	Y	N	N	N	N	N
NORTH DAKOTA								
Andrews	Y	N	N	Y	Y	Y	Y	Y
Burdick	Y	N	N	Y	Y	Y	Y	Y
OHIO								
Glenn	?	?	?	?	?	?	?	Y
Metzenbaum	Y	N	N	Y	Y	Y	Y	Y
OKLAHOMA								
Nickles	Y	Y	Y	N	N	Y	N	Y
Boren	Y	Y	Y	N	N	Y	N	N
OREGON								
Hatfield	Y	N	N	Y	?	+	+	Y
Packwood	Y	N	N	Y	Y	Y	Y	N
PENNSYLVANIA								
Heinz	Y	N	Y	N	N	Y	Y	N
Specter	Y	N	N	Y	Y	Y	Y	N
RHODE ISLAND								
Chafee	Y	N	Y	Y	Y	Y	Y	N
Pell	Y	N	N	Y	Y	Y	Y	Y
SOUTH CAROLINA								
Thurmond	Y	Y	Y	N	Y	Y	Y	N
Hollings	?	?	?	?	?	?	?	N
SOUTH DAKOTA								
Abdnor	Y	N	N	N	N	Y	N	N
Pressler	Y	N	N	Y	?	?	?	N
TENNESSEE								
Baker	Y	N	Y	Y	Y	Y	N	N
Sasser	Y	Y	N	Y	N	Y	N	N
TEXAS								
Tower	?	?	?	?	Y	Y	N	N
Bentsen	Y	Y	N	Y	Y	Y	N	N
UTAH								
Garn	N	Y	Y	N	N	Y	N	N
Hatch	Y	Y	Y	N	N	Y	Y	N
VERMONT								
Stafford	Y	N	Y	Y	Y	Y	Y	N
Leahy	Y	N	N	Y	Y	Y	Y	N
VIRGINIA								
Trible	Y	Y	Y	N	N	Y	Y	N
Warner	Y	Y	Y	N	Y	Y	Y	N
WASHINGTON								
Gorton	Y	N	N	Y	Y	Y	Y	N
Evans	+	?	?	?	Y	Y	N	N
WEST VIRGINIA								
Byrd	Y	Y	Y	Y	Y	Y	N	Y
Randolph	Y	N	N	N	N	N	N	N
WISCONSIN								
Kasten	Y	Y	Y	N	?	?	?	N
Proxmire	Y	N	N	Y	N	Y	N	Y
WYOMING								
Simpson	?	?	?	?	?	Y	N	N
Wallop	Y	N	Y	?	Y	Y	Y	N

ND - Northern Democrats   SD - Southern Democrats (Southern states - Ala., Ark., Fla., Ga., Ky., La., Miss., N.C., Okla., S.C., Tenn., Texas, Va.)

345. HR 2230. Civil Rights Commission Act. Specter, R-Pa., amendment to extend the Civil Rights Commission for six years and change it from a presidentially appointed six-member panel to an eight-member panel to which the president and Congress each would make four appointments. Commissioners could be removed only for cause. Adopted 79-5: R 41-5; D 38-0 (ND 26-0, SD 12-0), Nov. 10, 1983.

346. H J Res 413. Continuing Appropriations, Fiscal 1984. Melcher, D-Mont., motion to table (kill) the Metzenbaum, D-Ohio, amendment to provide for termination and extension of certain timber sales contracts. Motion rejected 32-50: R 21-24; D 11-26 (ND 4-22, SD 7-4), Nov. 10, 1983.

347. H J Res 413. Continuing Appropriations, Fiscal 1984. Judgment of the Senate affirming the chair's ruling that the Metzenbaum, D-Ohio, timber amendment *(see vote 346, above)* was out of order because it constituted legislation on an appropriations bill. Ruling of the chair upheld 43-37: R 32-12; D 11-25 (ND 5-21, SD 6-4), Nov. 10, 1983.

348. H J Res 413. Continuing Appropriations, Fiscal 1984. Moynihan, D-N.Y., motion to table (kill) the Helms, R-N.C., amendment to prevent funding of any Internal Revenue Service activity that would deny tax exemptions to schools that discriminate on the basis of race. Motion agreed to 51-28: R 20-23; D 31-5 (ND 23-3, SD 8-2), Nov. 10, 1983.

349. HR 2230. Civil Rights Commission Act. Thurmond, R-S.C., motion to table (kill) the Jepsen, R-Iowa, amendment to make permanent the ban on federal funding of abortion, bar federal insurance coverage for abortion, encourage states to pass new anti-abortion laws, and grant expedited Supreme Court review for challenges to new anti-abortion laws. Motion agreed to 42-34: R 23-22; D 19-12 (ND 14-8, SD 5-4), Nov. 14, 1983.

350. HR 2230. Civil Rights Commission Act. Passage of the bill to extend the Civil Rights Commission for six years and change it from a presidentially appointed six-member panel to an eight-member panel to which the president and Congress each would make four appointments. Commissioners could be removed only for cause. Passed 78-3: R 44-3; D 34-0 (ND 23-0, SD 11-0), Nov. 14, 1983.

351. S Res 269. Senate Day-Care Center. Adoption of the resolution to authorize a day-care center for children of Senate employees. Adopted 50-31: R 29-18; D 21-13 (ND 17-6, SD 4-7), Nov. 14, 1983.

352. HR 3222. State, Justice, Commerce Appropriations, Fiscal 1984. Melcher, D-Mont., motion that the Senate concur in the House amendment to the Senate amendment to the conference report with an additional Melcher amendment striking $450,000 in legal fees for non-Indian defendants in a 17-year-old New Mexico water rights case. Motion rejected 23-75: R 4-51; D 19-24 (ND 15-14, SD 4-10), Nov. 15, 1983.

CQ Senate Votes 353 - 360

Corresponding to Congressional Record Votes 363, 364, 365, 366, 367, 368, 369, 370

	353	354	355	356	357	358	359	360
ALABAMA								
Denton	N	Y	N	N	N	N	Y	Y
Heflin	N	N	Y	N	N	N	N	N
ALASKA								
Murkowski	N	Y	N	N	N	N	Y	Y
Stevens	N	Y	N	Y	Y	N	Y	Y
ARIZONA								
Goldwater	N	Y	N	Y	N	N	N	N
DeConcini	N	N	N	N	Y	N	N	N
ARKANSAS								
Bumpers	Y	N	Y	N	Y	Y	Y	N
Pryor	N	N	Y	N	N	N	Y	N
CALIFORNIA								
Wilson	N	Y	N	Y	N	N	Y	Y
Cranston	?	?	+	?	?	?	?	?
COLORADO								
Armstrong	N	Y	N	N	N	N	N	N
Hart	N	N	Y	N	Y	N	Y	Y
CONNECTICUT								
Weicker	N	Y	Y	N	?	Y	Y	Y
Dodd	Y	N	Y	?	Y	Y	Y	Y
DELAWARE								
Roth	?	?	N	N	N	N	Y	Y
Biden	Y	N	Y	N	Y	N	N	N
FLORIDA								
Hawkins	Y	N	N	Y	N	Y	N	Y
Chiles	N	N	Y	Y	Y	Y	Y	N
GEORGIA								
Mattingly	N	Y	Y	N	N	N	N	N
Nunn	N	N	Y	N	N	N	N	N
HAWAII								
Inouye	?	?	Y	N	Y	Y	Y	Y
Matsunaga	N	Y	N	Y	N	Y	N	Y
IDAHO								
McClure	N	Y	N	N	N	N	N	Y
Symms	N	Y	N	N	N	N	N	N
ILLINOIS								
Percy	N	N	Y	?	?	?	?	?
Dixon	N	N	N	N	Y	Y	Y	Y
INDIANA								
Lugar	N	N	N	Y	N	N	Y	Y
Quayle	N	N	N	Y	N	N	Y	Y
IOWA								
Grassley	N	N	N	N	N	N	N	N
Jepsen	N	N	N	Y	N	N	Y	Y
KANSAS								
Dole	N	N	N	N	N	Y	Y	Y
Kassebaum	Y	N	Y	N	Y	Y	Y	Y
KENTUCKY								
Ford	N	N	Y	N	Y	N	N	N
Huddleston	N	N	N	N	Y	Y	Y	N
LOUISIANA								
Johnston	N	Y	N	Y	N	N	N	N
Long	N	?	N	N	N	N	N	N
MAINE								
Cohen	N	N	N	Y	N	Y	N	Y
Mitchell	N	N	Y	N	Y	Y	Y	N
MARYLAND								
Mathias	Y	N	Y	Y	Y	Y	Y	Y
Sarbanes	Y	N	Y	N	Y	Y	Y	Y
MASSACHUSETTS								
Kennedy	Y	N	Y	N	?	N	Y	Y
Tsongas	Y	N	Y	N	Y	N	Y	Y
MICHIGAN								
Levin	Y	N	Y	N	Y	Y	Y	Y
Riegle	Y	N	Y	N	Y	Y	N	N
MINNESOTA								
Boschwitz	N	N	N	N	N	N	Y	Y
Durenberger	N	N	N	Y	N	Y	N	Y
MISSISSIPPI								
Cochran	N	Y	Y	Y	Y	N	Y	Y
Stennis	N	N	Y	Y	Y	N	Y	Y
MISSOURI								
Danforth	Y	N	N	Y	N	Y	N	N
Eagleton	Y	N	Y	N	Y	N	Y	Y
MONTANA								
Baucus	N	N	Y	N	Y	N	N	N
Melcher	N	N	N	Y	N	N	N	N
NEBRASKA								
Exon	N	?	Y	?	N	N	N	N
Zorinsky	N	N	N	N	N	N	N	N
NEVADA								
Hecht	N	Y	N	Y	N	N	N	Y
Laxalt	N	Y	N	N	N	N	Y	Y
NEW HAMPSHIRE								
Humphrey	N	Y	N	N	N	N	N	N
Rudman	N	Y	Y	N	Y	Y	N	N
NEW JERSEY								
Bradley	Y	N	N	N	Y	N	Y	Y
Lautenberg	Y	N	Y	N	Y	N	Y	Y
NEW MEXICO								
Domenici	N	N	Y	Y	Y	Y	Y	Y
Bingaman	N	N	Y	Y	Y	Y	Y	Y
NEW YORK								
D'Amato	Y	N	N	Y	N	Y	N	Y
Moynihan	Y	N	Y	N	Y	N	Y	Y
NORTH CAROLINA								
East	N	Y	N	N	N	N	N	N
Helms	N	Y	N	N	N	N	N	N
NORTH DAKOTA								
Andrews	Y	N	Y	Y	Y	Y	Y	Y
Burdick	N	N	Y	N	Y	N	Y	N
OHIO								
Glenn	N	N	Y	N	?	N	Y	Y
Metzenbaum	Y	N	Y	N	Y	Y	Y	N
OKLAHOMA								
Nickles	N	Y	Y	N	N	N	N	N
Boren	N	N	Y	N	N	N	N	N
OREGON								
Hatfield	N	N	Y	N	Y	Y	Y	Y
Packwood	N	N	N	N	Y	Y	Y	Y
PENNSYLVANIA								
Heinz	Y	N	?	N	Y	Y	Y	Y
Specter	N	N	Y	N	Y	Y	Y	Y
RHODE ISLAND								
Chafee	Y	N	Y	Y	Y	Y	Y	Y
Pell	Y	N	Y	N	Y	Y	Y	Y
SOUTH CAROLINA								
Thurmond	N	Y	+	Y	N	N	Y	Y
Hollings	N	N	Y	N	Y	N	Y	N
SOUTH DAKOTA								
Abdnor	N	N	Y	N	Y	N	N	Y
Pressler	N	N	Y	N	N	N	N	N
TENNESSEE								
Baker	N	Y	Y	Y	N	Y	Y	Y
Sasser	Y	N	Y	N	Y	Y	Y	N
TEXAS								
Tower	N	Y	N	Y	Y	N	Y	Y
Bentsen	N	N	Y	N	Y	N	Y	Y
UTAH								
Garn	N	Y	Y	N	N	N	Y	Y
Hatch	N	Y	N	N	N	N	N	N
VERMONT								
Stafford	Y	N	Y	Y	Y	Y	Y	Y
Leahy	Y	N	Y	N	Y	N	Y	N
VIRGINIA								
Trible	N	Y	N	N	N	N	Y	N
Warner	N	N	Y	N	N	N	N	N
WASHINGTON								
Gorton	N	N	Y	Y	Y	Y	Y	Y
Evans	N	N	Y	N	Y	N	Y	Y
WEST VIRGINIA								
Byrd	N	N	Y	N	N	N	Y	N
Randolph	N	N	Y	N	Y	N	Y	Y
WISCONSIN								
Kasten	N	N	N	N	N	N	N	N
Proxmire	Y	N	N	Y	N	Y	N	Y
WYOMING								
Simpson	N	Y	Y	N	N	N	Y	Y
Wallop	N	Y	N	Y	N	N	Y	Y

KEY

Y Voted for (yea).
\# Paired for.
\+ Announced for.
N Voted against (nay).
X Paired against.
- Announced against.
P Voted "present".
C Voted "present" to avoid possible conflict of interest.
? Did not vote or otherwise make a position known.

Democrats   *Republicans*

ND - Northern Democrats   SD - Southern Democrats (Southern states - Ala., Ark., Fla., Ga., Ky., La., Miss., N.C., Okla., S.C., Tenn., Texas, Va.)

353. S 1715. Natural Gas Policy Act Amendments. McClure, R-Idaho, amendment (offered on behalf of Kassebaum, R-Kan.), to the McClure amendment, that was the text of S 996, which among other provisions would retain federal price controls on natural gas from wells in production prior to April 1977 and roll other prices back to 1982 levels. Rejected 26-71: R 9-45; D 17-26 (ND 15-14, SD 2-12), Nov. 15, 1983.

354. S 1715. Natural Gas Policy Act Amendments. McClure, R-Idaho, amendment, to the McClure amendment, that was the text of S 1715 which after 44 months would decontrol prices of natural gas from wells in production prior to April 1977 and allow current gas purchase contracts to be adjusted. Rejected 28-67: R 26-28; D 2-39 (ND 1-27, SD 1-12), Nov. 15, 1983.

355. H J Res 290. Olympic Duty Suspension/Tuition Tax Credit. Boren, D-Okla., motion to table (kill) the Dole, R-Kan., amendment to provide tax credits for tuition payments to private elementary and secondary schools. The credits, to be subtracted from taxes owed, would cover 50 percent of tuition payments up to a maximum of $300 a year once the program was fully in force. Motion agreed to 59-38: R 24-29; D 35-9 (ND 24-6, SD 11-3), Nov. 16, 1983. A "nay" was a vote supporting the president's position.

356. S 2062. Omnibus Reconciliation Act. Tower, R-Texas, motion to table (kill) the Humphrey, R-N.H., amendment to express the sense of the Senate in support of U.S. insistence that the government of Lebanon increase security at the Beirut airport. Motion rejected 25-71: R 21-33; D 4-38 (ND 1-27, SD 3-11), Nov. 16, 1983.

357. H J Res 290. Olympic Duty Suspension/Deficit Control. Hatfield, R-Ore., motion to table (kill) the Armstrong, R-Colo., amendment to establish quarterly limits for future increases in the public debt limit and to permit the president to cut back federal spending if necessary to stay within those limits. The president could not use this authority to cut any federal program or activity by more than 20 percent, nor could he reduce current benefit levels for individuals under entitlement programs, which require payments to all who qualify. Motion agreed to 49-46: R 16-37; D 33-9 (ND 25-3, SD 8-6), Nov. 16, 1983.

358. S 2062. Omnibus Reconciliation Act. Domenici, R-N.M., motion to waive the germaneness requirements of the 1974 Congressional Budget Act to permit consideration of the Domenici-Chiles, D-Fla., amendment to increase total three-year reconciliation savings to $87.6 billion. Motion rejected 33-65: R 17-37; D 16-28 (ND 12-18, SD 4-10), Nov. 16, 1983.

359. H J Res 308. Debt Limit Increase. Baker, R-Tenn., motion to reconsider the vote *(see vote 320, p. 53-S)* by which the Senate Oct. 31 rejected the joint resolution to increase the public debt limit to $1.45 trillion, from $1.389 trillion. Motion agreed to 67-31: R 38-16; D 29-15 (ND 21-9, SD 8-6), Nov. 16, 1983.

360. H J Res 308. Debt Limit Increase. Passage of the joint resolution to increase the public debt limit to $1.45 trillion, from $1.389 trillion. Passed 58-40: R 38-16; D 20-24 (ND 18-12, SD 2-12), Nov. 16, 1983.

	361	362	363	364
ALABAMA				
Denton	Y	N	N	N
Heflin	Y	Y	N	N
ALASKA				
Murkowski	Y	Y	Y	Y
Stevens	Y	Y	Y	Y
ARIZONA				
Goldwater	N	N	N	N
DeConcini	Y	N	N	N
ARKANSAS				
Bumpers	Y	Y	N	N
Pryor	Y	Y	N	N
CALIFORNIA				
Wilson	Y	N	Y	Y
Cranston	?	?	?	?
COLORADO				
Armstrong	Y	N	N	N
Hart	Y	Y	Y	Y
CONNECTICUT				
Weicker	N	Y	Y	Y
Dodd	Y	Y	Y	Y
DELAWARE				
Roth	Y	N	N	N
Biden	Y	Y	N	Y
FLORIDA				
Hawkins	Y	Y	N	Y
Chiles	Y	Y	Y	Y
GEORGIA				
Mattingly	Y	Y	N	Y
Nunn	Y	Y	N	Y
HAWAII				
Inouye	Y	Y	Y	Y
Matsunaga	Y	Y	Y	Y
IDAHO				
McClure	Y	Y	N	N
Symms	Y	N	N	N
ILLINOIS				
Percy	Y	Y	Y	Y
Dixon	Y	Y	Y	Y
INDIANA				
Lugar	Y	Y	Y	Y
Quayle	N	Y	Y	Y

	361	362	363	364
IOWA				
Grassley	Y	N	N	N
Jepsen	Y	N	N	N
KANSAS				
Dole	Y	Y	Y	Y
Kassebaum	Y	Y	Y	Y
KENTUCKY				
Ford	Y	Y	N	Y
Huddleston	Y	Y	Y	Y
LOUISIANA				
Johnston	Y	Y	N	Y
Long	Y	Y	Y	Y
MAINE				
Cohen	Y	Y	N	N
Mitchell	Y	Y	Y	Y
MARYLAND				
Mathias	Y	Y	Y	Y
Sarbanes	Y	Y	Y	Y
MASSACHUSETTS				
Kennedy	Y	Y	Y	Y
Tsongas	Y	Y	Y	Y
MICHIGAN				
Levin	Y	Y	N	Y
Riegle	Y	Y	Y	Y
MINNESOTA				
Boschwitz	Y	N	N	Y
Durenberger	Y	Y	Y	Y
MISSISSIPPI				
Cochran	Y	Y	Y	Y
Stennis	Y	Y	Y	Y
MISSOURI				
Danforth	Y	Y	Y	Y
Eagleton	Y	Y	Y	Y
MONTANA				
Baucus	Y	Y	N	N
Melcher	Y	Y	N	N
NEBRASKA				
Exon	Y	N	N	N
Zorinsky	Y	N	N	N
NEVADA				
Hecht	Y	Y	Y	Y
Laxalt	Y	Y	N	Y

	361	362	363	364
NEW HAMPSHIRE				
Humphrey	Y	N	N	N
Rudman	Y	Y	N	Y
NEW JERSEY				
Bradley	Y	Y	Y	Y
Lautenberg	Y	Y	Y	Y
NEW MEXICO				
Domenici	Y	N	Y	N
Bingaman	Y	Y	Y	Y
NEW YORK				
D'Amato	Y	Y	Y	Y
Moynihan	Y	Y	Y	Y
NORTH CAROLINA				
East	?	N	N	N
Helms	Y	N	N	N
NORTH DAKOTA				
Andrews	Y	Y	Y	Y
Burdick	Y	Y	N	Y
OHIO				
Glenn	?	?	?	?
Metzenbaum	Y	Y	N	N
OKLAHOMA				
Nickles	Y	N	N	N
Boren	Y	Y	N	N
OREGON				
Hatfield	Y	Y	Y	Y
Packwood	Y	Y	Y	Y
PENNSYLVANIA				
Heinz	Y	Y	Y	Y
Specter	Y	Y	N	Y
RHODE ISLAND				
Chafee	Y	Y	Y	Y
Pell	Y	Y	Y	Y
SOUTH CAROLINA				
Thurmond	Y	N	N	N
Hollings	?	?	?	?
SOUTH DAKOTA				
Abdnor	Y	N	N	N
Pressler	Y	N	N	N
TENNESSEE				
Baker	Y	Y	Y	Y
Sasser	Y	Y	Y	Y

KEY

- **Y** Voted for (yea).
- **#** Paired for.
- **+** Announced for.
- **N** Voted against (nay).
- **X** Paired against.
- **-** Announced against.
- **P** Voted "present".
- **C** Voted "present" to avoid possible conflict of interest.
- **?** Did not vote or otherwise make a position known.

Democrats   *Republicans*

	361	362	363	364
TEXAS				
Tower	Y	Y	Y	Y
Bentsen	Y	Y	Y	Y
UTAH				
Garn	Y	Y	Y	Y
Hatch	Y	Y	N	Y
VERMONT				
Stafford	Y	Y	Y	Y
Leahy	Y	Y	N	Y
VIRGINIA				
Trible	Y	N	N	N
Warner	Y	N	N	N
WASHINGTON				
Gorton	Y	Y	Y	Y
Evans	Y	Y	Y	Y
WEST VIRGINIA				
Byrd	Y	Y	N	Y
Randolph	Y	Y	N	Y
WISCONSIN				
Kasten	Y	Y	Y	Y
Proxmire	N	Y	Y	Y
WYOMING				
Simpson	Y	N	N	N
Wallop	Y	Y	Y	Y

ND - Northern Democrats   SD - Southern Democrats (Southern states - Ala., Ark., Fla., Ga., Ky., La., Miss., N.C., Okla., S.C., Tenn., Texas, Va.)

361. HR 3959. Supplemental Appropriations, Fiscal 1984. Baker, R-Tenn., motion to instruct the sergeant-at-arms to require the attendance of absent senators. Motion agreed to 92-4: R 51-3; D 41-1 (ND 28-1, SD 13-0), Nov. 17, 1983.

362. HR 3959. Supplemental Appropriations, Fiscal 1984. Garn, R-Utah, motion to table (kill) the Armstrong, R-Colo., amendment to require rental rehabilitation funds to be used only to benefit very low income persons. Motion agreed to 74-23: R 35-20; D 39-3 (ND 26-3, SD 13-0), Nov. 17, 1983.

363. HR 3959. Supplemental Appropriations, Fiscal 1984. Garn, R-Utah, motion to table (kill) the Humphrey, R-N.H., amendment to reduce the U.S. contribution to the International Monetary Fund by $584 million. Motion agreed to 52-45: R 29-26; D 23-19 (ND 17-12, SD 6-7), Nov. 17, 1983.

364. HR 3959. Supplemental Appropriations, Fiscal 1984. Garn, R-Utah, motion to concur in the House amendment to the Senate amendment with the Garn amendment to authorize funds for housing programs, the International Monetary Fund, the Export-Import Bank, and international development banks; reauthorize the Defense Production Act; and appropriate $8.4 billion for the International Monetary Fund. Motion agreed to 67-30: R 35-20; D 32-10 (ND 23-6, SD 9-4), Nov. 17, 1983. A "yea" was a vote supporting the president's position.

CQ Senate Votes 365 - 371
Corresponding to Congressional Record Votes 375, 376, 377, 378, 379, 380, 381

	365	366	367	368	369	370	371
ALABAMA							
Denton	Y	Y	Y	Y	Y	Y	Y
Heflin	N	N	Y	N	Y	Y	Y
ALASKA							
Murkowski	Y	Y	Y	N	Y	Y	Y
Stevens	Y	Y	Y	Y	Y	Y	Y
ARIZONA							
Goldwater	Y	?	?	?	Y	?	?
DeConcini	N	N	N	Y	#	Y	Y
ARKANSAS							
Bumpers	N	N	N	Y	N	Y	Y
Pryor	N	N	N	Y	N	Y	Y
CALIFORNIA							
Wilson	Y	Y	Y	Y	Y	Y	Y
Cranston	?	?	?	?	X	?	?
COLORADO							
Armstrong	Y	Y	Y	Y	Y	Y	Y
Hart	N	N	N	Y	N	N	Y
CONNECTICUT							
Weicker	Y	Y	Y	Y	?	?	?
Dodd	N	N	N	Y	N	?	?
DELAWARE							
Roth	Y	Y	Y	Y	Y	?	?
Biden	N	N	N	Y	N	Y	Y
FLORIDA							
Hawkins	Y	Y	Y	Y	Y	?	?
Chiles	N	N	N	Y	Y	Y	?
GEORGIA							
Mattingly	Y	Y	Y	Y	Y	Y	Y
Nunn	Y	N	Y	Y	Y	Y	Y
HAWAII							
Inouye	N	N	N	N	#	Y	Y
Matsunaga	N	N	N	Y	Y	Y	Y
IDAHO							
McClure	Y	Y	Y	N	Y	Y	Y
Symms	Y	Y	Y	N	Y	Y	Y
ILLINOIS							
Percy	Y	Y	Y	Y	?	?	?
Dixon	N	N	Y	N	N	+	+
INDIANA							
Lugar	Y	Y	Y	Y	Y	Y	Y
Quayle	Y	Y	Y	Y	Y	Y	Y
IOWA							
Grassley	Y	Y	Y	Y	Y	Y	Y
Jepsen	N	Y	Y	Y	Y	Y	Y
KANSAS							
Dole	Y	Y	Y	Y	Y	Y	Y
Kassebaum	N	Y	Y	Y	Y	?	?
KENTUCKY							
Ford	N	N	N	N	N	Y	Y
Huddleston	Y	N	N	N	Y	Y	Y
LOUISIANA							
Johnston	Y	N	N	N	Y	Y	Y
Long	Y	X	Y	N	Y	Y	Y
MAINE							
Cohen	N	?	?	?	Y	Y	Y
Mitchell	N	N	N	Y	N	Y	Y
MARYLAND							
Mathias	Y	Y	Y	Y	Y	Y	Y
Sarbanes	N	N	N	Y	N	?	?
MASSACHUSETTS							
Kennedy	-	?	?	?	?	+	+
Tsongas	N	N	N	Y	N	Y	Y
MICHIGAN							
Levin	N	N	N	Y	N	Y	Y
Riegle	N	N	N	Y	N	Y	Y
MINNESOTA							
Boschwitz	N	N	Y	Y	Y	Y	Y
Durenberger	N	Y	?	Y	Y	Y	Y
MISSISSIPPI							
Cochran	Y	Y	Y	Y	Y	Y	Y
Stennis	Y	N	N	N	Y	Y	Y
MISSOURI							
Danforth	Y	Y	Y	Y	Y	Y	Y
Eagleton	N	N	N	?	N	Y	Y
MONTANA							
Baucus	N	N	N	Y	N	Y	N
Melcher	N	N	N	Y	N	Y	N
NEBRASKA							
Exon	Y	N	N	N	Y	Y	Y
Zorinsky	Y	N	N	Y	Y	Y	Y
NEVADA							
Hecht	Y	Y	Y	Y	Y	Y	Y
Laxalt	Y	Y	Y	Y	Y	Y	?
NEW HAMPSHIRE							
Humphrey	N	N	N	Y	Y	Y	Y
Rudman	N	Y	Y	Y	Y	Y	Y
NEW JERSEY							
Bradley	N	N	N	Y	Y	Y	Y
Lautenberg	N	N	N	Y	N	Y	Y
NEW MEXICO							
Domenici	N	Y	Y	Y	Y	Y	Y
Bingaman	N	N	N	N	Y	Y	Y
NEW YORK							
D'Amato	Y	Y	Y	Y	Y	Y	Y
Moynihan	N	N	N	Y	Y	?	?
NORTH CAROLINA							
East	Y	#	Y	Y	Y	Y	Y
Helms	Y	Y	N	Y	Y	Y	Y
NORTH DAKOTA							
Andrews	N	Y	Y	Y	?	?	?
Burdick	N	N	N	N	Y	Y	Y
OHIO							
Glenn	?	?	?	?	?	?	?
Metzenbaum	N	N	N	Y	N	N	Y
OKLAHOMA							
Nickles	Y	Y	Y	N	Y	Y	Y
Boren	N	N	N	N	Y	Y	Y
OREGON							
Hatfield	Y	Y	Y	Y	Y	N	Y
Packwood	Y	N	Y	Y	Y	Y	Y
PENNSYLVANIA							
Heinz	N	Y	Y	Y	Y	Y	Y
Specter	N	Y	N	Y	Y	Y	Y
RHODE ISLAND							
Chafee	Y	Y	Y	Y	?	?	?
Pell	N	N	N	Y	Y	Y	Y
SOUTH CAROLINA							
Thurmond	Y	Y	Y	Y	Y	+	+
Hollings	?	?	?	?	X	?	?
SOUTH DAKOTA							
Abdnor	Y	Y	Y	Y	Y	Y	Y
Pressler	N	Y	Y	Y	Y	Y	Y
TENNESSEE							
Baker	Y	Y	Y	Y	Y	Y	Y
Sasser	N	N	N	N	Y	Y	Y
TEXAS							
Tower	Y	Y	Y	Y	Y	Y	Y
Bentsen	?	?	?	?	Y	?	?
UTAH							
Garn	Y	Y	Y	Y	Y	Y	Y
Hatch	Y	Y	Y	Y	Y	Y	Y
VERMONT							
Stafford	Y	Y	Y	Y	Y	Y	Y
Leahy	N	N	N	Y	N	Y	Y
VIRGINIA							
Trible	Y	Y	Y	Y	?	?	?
Warner	N	?	Y	?	Y	Y	Y
WASHINGTON							
Gorton	Y	Y	Y	Y	Y	Y	Y
Evans	Y	Y	Y	Y	Y	Y	Y
WEST VIRGINIA							
Byrd	N	N	N	Y	N	Y	Y
Randolph	N	N	N	Y	Y	Y	Y
WISCONSIN							
Kasten	N	Y	Y	Y	Y	Y	Y
Proxmire	Y	N	N	Y	N	N	Y
WYOMING							
Simpson	Y	Y	Y	Y	Y	Y	Y
Wallop	Y	Y	?	N	Y	Y	Y

KEY

- Y Voted for (yea).
- # Paired for.
- + Announced for.
- N Voted against (nay).
- X Paired against.
- − Announced against.
- P Voted "present".
- C Voted "present" to avoid possible conflict of interest.
- ? Did not vote or otherwise make a position known.

Democrats   *Republicans*

ND - Northern Democrats   SD - Southern Democrats (Southern states - Ala., Ark., Fla., Ga., Ky., La., Miss., N.C., Okla., S.C., Tenn., Texas, Va.)

365. HR 3959. Supplemental Appropriations, Fiscal 1984. Garn, R-Utah, motion to table (kill) the Levin, D-Mich., amendment to revise federal procedures for terminating Social Security disability payments to individuals. Motion agreed to 49-46: R 41-14; D 8-32 (ND 3-25, SD 5-7), Nov. 17, 1983.

366. HR 3959. Supplemental Appropriations, Fiscal 1984. Hatfield, R-Ore., motion to table (kill) the Johnston, D-La., amendment to express the sense of the Senate that, upon taking office, Interior Secretary William P. Clark should reverse many of the controversial policies of his predecessor, James G. Watt. Motion agreed to 48-42: R 48-3; D 0-39 (ND 0-28, SD 0-11), Nov. 17, 1983. A "yea" was a vote supporting the president's position.

367. HR 3959. Supplemental Appropriations, Fiscal 1984. Garn, R-Utah, motion to table (kill) the Metzenbaum, D-Ohio, amendment to block through Sept. 30, 1984, a proposal by the Securities and Exchange Commission to limit the disclosure of information pertaining to the corporate benefits of executives. Motion agreed to 51-40: R 48-3; D 3-37 (ND 1-27, SD 2-10), Nov. 17, 1983.

368. HR 3959. Supplemental Appropriations, Fiscal 1984. Hatfield, R-Ore., motion to table (kill) the Johnston, D-La., amendment to relax restrictions in the bill on petroleum production off the coast of Florida. Motion agreed to 71-20: R 47-5; D 24-15 (ND 20-7, SD 4-8), Nov. 17, 1983.

369. Clark Nomination. Confirmation of President Reagan's nomination of William P. Clark of California to be secretary of the interior. Confirmed 71-18: R 50-0; D 21-18 (ND 12-14, SD 9-4), Nov. 18, 1983. A "yea" was a vote supporting the president's position.

370. HR 4185. Defense Department Appropriations, Fiscal 1984. Adoption of the conference report on the bill to provide $249.8 billion for military programs of the Department of Defense in fiscal 1984. Adopted (thus cleared for the president) 75-6: R 44-1; D 31-5 (ND 19-5, SD 12-0), Nov. 18, 1983. The president had requested $260,926,119,000 in new budget authority.

371. HR 3391. Social Security Disability Payments. Passage of the bill to extend to June 7, 1984, from Dec. 7, 1983, the expiration date of the law permitting recipients of Social Security disability payments ruled ineligible for further payments to continue receiving benefits while appealing to an administrative law judge. Passed 80-0: R 44-0; D 36-0 (ND 25-0, SD 11-0), Nov. 18, 1983.

HOUSE ROLL-CALL VOTES

CQ

1. Election of Speaker. For election of the Speaker of the House of Representatives for the 98th Congress, the nominees were Thomas P. O'Neill Jr., D-Mass., the Speaker since 1977, and Robert H. Michel, R-Ill., minority leader since 1981. O'Neill was elected 259-155: R 0-155; D 259-0 (ND 169-0, SD 90-0), Jan. 3, 1983. A "Y" on the chart represents a vote for O'Neill, an "N" a vote for Michel.

2. H Res 5. House Rules. Wright, D-Texas, motion to order the previous question (thus ending debate and the possibility of amendment) on the resolution to adopt the rules of the House of Representatives for the 98th Congress as proposed by the Democratic Caucus. Motion agreed to 249-156: R 0-154; D 249-2 (ND 162-0, SD 87-2), Jan. 3, 1983. (The rules subsequently were adopted by voice vote.)

3. H Res 5. House Rules. Michel, R-Ill., motion to commit the resolution to adopt the rules of the House as proposed by the Democratic Caucus to a select committee for the purpose of removing the rule to limit legislative limitation amendments ("riders") on appropriations bills. Motion rejected 156-250: R 154-0; D 2-250 (ND 0-164, SD 2-86), Jan. 3, 1983. (The rules subsequently were adopted by voice vote.)

All members-elect are eligible to vote on election of the Speaker.

† Not yet sworn in and therefore ineligible for CQ votes 2-3.
‡ Rep.-elect Jack Swigert, R-Colo., died Dec. 27, 1982.
* Rep. Benjamin S. Rosenthal, D-N.Y., died Jan. 4, 1983. The last vote for which he was eligible was CQ vote 1.

KEY

Y Voted for (yea).
\# Paired for.
+ Announced for.
N Voted against (nay).
X Paired against.
- Announced against.
P Voted "present".
C Voted "present" to avoid possible conflict of interest.
? Did not vote or otherwise make a position known.

Democrats   *Republicans*

	1	2	3
ALABAMA			
1 *Edwards*	N	?	?
2 *Dickinson*	N	N	Y
3 Nichols	Y	Y	N
4 Bevill	Y	Y	N
5 Flippo	Y	Y	N
6 Erdreich	Y	Y	?
7 Shelby	Y	Y	N
ALASKA			
AL *Young*	N	N	Y
ARIZONA			
1 *McCain*	N	N	Y
2 Udall	Y	Y	N
3 *Stump*	N	N	Y
4 *Rudd*	N	N	Y
5 McNulty	Y	Y	N
ARKANSAS			
1 Alexander	Y	Y	N
2 *Bethune*	N	N	Y
3 *Hammerschmidt*	N	N	Y
4 Anthony	Y	Y	N
CALIFORNIA			
1 Bosco	Y	Y	N
2 *Chappie*	N	N	Y
3 Matsui	Y	Y	N
4 Fazio†	?		
5 Burton	Y	Y	N
6 Boxer	Y	Y	N
7 Miller	Y	Y	N
8 Dellums	Y	Y	N
9 Stark	Y	Y	N
10 Edwards	Y	Y	N
11 Lantos	Y	Y	N
12 *Zschau*	N	N	Y
13 Mineta	Y	Y	N
14 *Shumway*	N	N	Y
15 Coelho	Y	Y	N
16 Panetta†	?		
17 *Pashayan*	N	N	Y
18 Lehman	Y	Y	N
19 *Lagomarsino*	N	N	Y
20 *Thomas†*	?		
21 *Fiedler*	N	N	Y
22 *Moorhead*	N	N	Y
23 Beilenson	Y	Y	N
24 Waxman	Y	Y	N
25 Roybal	Y	Y	N
26 Berman	Y	Y	N
27 Levine	Y	Y	N
28 Dixon	Y	?	N
29 Hawkins	Y	Y	N
30 Martinez	Y	Y	N
31 Dymally	Y	Y	N
32 Anderson	Y	Y	N
33 *Dreier*	N	N	Y
34 Torres	Y	Y	N
35 *Lewis*	N	N	Y
36 Brown	Y	Y	N
37 *McCandless*	N	N	Y
38 Patterson	Y	Y	N
39 *Dannemeyer*	N	N	Y
40 *Badham†*	?		
41 *Lowery*	N	N	Y
42 *Lungren*	N	N	Y

	1	2	3
43 *Packard*	N	N	Y
44 Bates	Y	Y	N
45 *Hunter*	N	N	Y
COLORADO			
1 Schroeder	Y	Y	N
2 Wirth	Y	Y	N
3 Kogovsek	Y	Y	N
4 *Brown*	N	N	Y
5 *Kramer*	N	N	Y
6 Vacancy‡			
CONNECTICUT			
1 Kennelly	Y	Y	N
2 Gejdenson	Y	Y	N
3 Morrison	Y	Y	N
4 *McKinney*	N	N	Y
5 Ratchford	Y	Y	N
6 *Johnson*	N	N	Y
DELAWARE			
AL Carper	Y	Y	N
FLORIDA			
1 Hutto	Y	Y	N
2 Fuqua	Y	Y	N
3 Bennett	Y	Y	N
4 Chappell	Y	Y	N
5 *McCollum*	N	N	Y
6 MacKay	Y	Y	N
7 Gibbons	Y	Y	N
8 *Young*	N	N	Y
9 *Bilirakis*	N	N	Y
10 Ireland	Y	Y	N
11 Nelson	Y	Y	N
12 *Lewis*	N	N	Y
13 *Mack*	N	N	Y
14 Mica	Y	Y	N
15 *Shaw*	N	N	Y
16 Smith	Y	Y	N
17 Lehman	Y	Y	N
18 Pepper	Y	Y	N
19 Fascell	Y	Y	N
GEORGIA			
1 Thomas	Y	Y	N
2 Hatcher	Y	Y	N
3 Ray	Y	Y	N
4 Levitas	Y	Y	N
5 Fowler	Y	Y	N
6 *Gingrich*	N	N	Y
7 McDonald	?	N	Y
8 Rowland	Y	Y	N
9 Jenkins	Y	Y	N
10 Barnard	Y	Y	N
HAWAII			
1 Heftel†	?		
2 Akaka	Y	Y	N
IDAHO			
1 *Craig*	N	N	Y
2 *Hansen*	N	N	Y
ILLINOIS			
1 Washington	Y	Y	N
2 Savage	Y	Y	N
3 Russo†	?		
4 *O'Brien*	N	N	Y
5 Lipinski	Y	?	N
6 *Hyde*	N	N	Y
7 Collins	Y	Y	N
8 Rostenkowski	Y	Y	N
9 Yates	Y	Y	N
10 *Porter*	N	N	Y
11 Annunzio	Y	Y	N
12 *Crane, P.*	N	N	Y
13 *Erlenborn*	N	N	Y
14 *Corcoran*	N	N	Y
15 *Madigan*	N	N	Y
16 *Martin*	N	N	Y
17 Evans	Y	Y	N
18 *Michel*	C	N	Y
19 *Crane, D.*	N	N	Y
20 Durbin	Y	Y	N
21 Price	Y	Y	N
22 Simon	Y	Y	N
INDIANA			
1 Hall	Y	Y	N
2 Sharp	Y	Y	N
3 *Hiler*	N	N	Y
4 *Coats†*	?		
5 Hillis†	?		

ND - Northern Democrats   SD - Southern Democrats

	1	2	3
6 Burton	N	N	Y
7 Myers	N	N	Y
8 McCloskey	Y	Y	N
9 Hamilton	Y	Y	N
10 Jacobs	Y	P	N
IOWA			
1 Leach	?	N	Y
2 Tauke	N	N	Y
3 Evans	N	N	Y
4 Smith	Y	Y	N
5 Harkin	Y	Y	N
6 Bedell	Y	Y	N
KANSAS			
1 Roberts	N	N	Y
2 Slattery	Y	Y	N
3 Winn	N	N	Y
4 Glickman	Y	Y	N
5 Whittaker	N	N	Y
KENTUCKY			
1 Hubbard	Y	Y	N
2 Natcher	Y	Y	N
3 Mazzoli	Y	Y	N
4 Snyder	N	N	Y
5 Rogers	N	N	Y
6 Hopkins	N	N	Y
7 Perkins	Y	Y	N
LOUISIANA			
1 Livingston	N	N	Y
2 Boggs	Y	Y	N
3 Tauzin	Y	Y	N
4 Roemer	Y	Y	N
5 Huckaby	Y	Y	N
6 Moore	N	N	Y
7 Breaux	Y	Y	N
8 Long	Y	Y	N
MAINE			
1 McKernan	N	N	Y
2 Snowe	N	N	Y
MARYLAND			
1 Dyson	Y	Y	N
2 Long	Y	Y	N
3 Mikulski	Y	Y	N
4 Holt	N	N	Y
5 Hoyer	Y	Y	N
6 Byron	Y	Y	N
7 Mitchell	Y	?	?
8 Barnes	Y	Y	N
MASSACHUSETTS			
1 Conte	N	N	Y
2 Boland	Y	Y	N
3 Early	Y	Y	N
4 Frank	Y	Y	N
5 Shannon	Y	Y	N
6 Mavroules	Y	Y	N
7 Markey	Y	Y	N
8 O'Neill	C		
9 Moakley	Y	Y	N
10 Studds	Y	Y	N
11 Donnelly	Y	Y	N
MICHIGAN			
1 Conyers	Y	?	N
2 Pursell	N	?	?
3 Wolpe	Y	Y	N
4 Siljander	N	N	Y
5 Sawyer	N	N	Y
6 Carr	Y	Y	N
7 Kildee	Y	Y	N
8 Traxler	Y	Y	N
9 Vander Jagt	N	N	Y
10 Albosta	Y	Y	N
11 Davis	N	N	Y
12 Bonior	Y	Y	N
13 Crockett	Y	Y	N
14 Hertel	Y	Y	N
15 Ford	Y	Y	N
16 Dingell	Y	Y	N
17 Levin	Y	Y	N
18 Broomfield	N	N	Y
MINNESOTA			
1 Penny	Y	Y	N
2 Weber	N	N	Y
3 Frenzel	N	N	Y
4 Vento	Y	Y	N
5 Sabo	Y	Y	N
6 Sikorski	Y	Y	N

	1	2	3
7 Stangeland	N	N	Y
8 Oberstar	Y	Y	N
MISSISSIPPI			
1 Whitten	Y	Y	N
2 Franklin	N	N	Y
3 Montgomery	Y	Y	N
4 Dowdy	Y	Y	N
5 Lott	N	N	Y
MISSOURI			
1 Clay	Y	Y	N
2 Young	Y	Y	N
3 Gephardt	Y	Y	N
4 Skelton	Y	Y	N
5 Wheat	Y	Y	N
6 Coleman	N	N	Y
7 Taylor	N	N	Y
8 Emerson	N	N	Y
9 Volkmer	Y	Y	N
MONTANA			
1 Williams	Y	Y	N
2 Marlenee	N	N	Y
NEBRASKA			
1 Bereuter	N	N	Y
2 Daub	N	N	Y
3 Smith	N	N	Y
NEVADA			
1 Reid	Y	Y	N
2 Vucanovich	N	N	Y
NEW HAMPSHIRE			
1 D'Amours†	?		
2 Gregg	N	N	Y
NEW JERSEY			
1 Florio	Y	Y	N
2 Hughes	Y	Y	N
3 Howard	Y	Y	N
4 Smith	N	N	Y
5 Roukema	N	N	Y
6 Dwyer	Y	Y	N
7 Rinaldo	N	N	Y
8 Roe	Y	Y	N
9 Torricelli	Y	?	?
10 Rodino	Y	Y	N
11 Minish	Y	Y	N
12 Courter	N	N	Y
13 Forsythe	N	N	Y
14 Guarini	Y	Y	N
NEW MEXICO			
1 Lujan	N	N	Y
2 Skeen	N	N	Y
3 Richardson	Y	Y	?
NEW YORK			
1 Carney	N	N	Y
2 Downey	Y	Y	N
3 Mrazek	Y	Y	N
4 Lent	N	N	Y
5 McGrath	N	N	Y
6 Addabbo	Y	Y	N
7 Rosenthal†*	?		
8 Scheuer	Y	Y	N
9 Ferraro	Y	Y	N
10 Schumer	Y	Y	N
11 Towns	Y	Y	N
12 Owens	Y	?	?
13 Solarz	Y	Y	N
14 Molinari	N	N	Y
15 Green	N	N	Y
16 Rangel	Y	Y	N
17 Weiss	Y	Y	N
18 Garcia	Y	Y	N
19 Biaggi	Y	Y	N
20 Ottinger†	?		
21 Fish	N	N	Y
22 Gilman	N	N	Y
23 Stratton	Y	Y	N
24 Solomon	N	N	Y
25 Boehlert	N	N	Y
26 Martin	N	N	Y
27 Wortley	N	N	Y
28 McHugh	Y	Y	N
29 Horton	N	N	Y
30 Conable	N	N	Y
31 Kemp	N	N	Y
32 LaFalce	Y	Y	N
33 Nowak	Y	Y	N
34 Lundine	Y	Y	N

	1	2	3
NORTH CAROLINA			
1 Jones	Y	Y	N
2 Valentine	Y	Y	N
3 Whitley	Y	Y	N
4 Andrews	Y	Y	N
5 Neal	Y	Y	N
6 Britt	Y	?	?
7 Rose	Y	Y	N
8 Hefner	Y	Y	N
9 Martin†	?		
10 Broyhill	N	N	Y
11 Clarke	Y	Y	N
NORTH DAKOTA			
AL Dorgan	Y	Y	N
OHIO			
1 Luken	Y	Y	N
2 Gradison	N	N	Y
3 Hall	Y	Y	N
4 Oxley	N	N	Y
5 Latta	N	N	Y
6 McEwen	N	N	Y
7 DeWine	N	N	Y
8 Kindness	N	N	Y
9 Kaptur	Y	Y	N
10 Miller	N	N	Y
11 Eckart	Y	Y	N
12 Kasich	N	N	Y
13 Pease	Y	Y	N
14 Seiberling	Y	Y	N
15 Wylie	N	N	Y
16 Regula	N	N	Y
17 Williams	N	N	Y
18 Applegate	Y	Y	N
19 Feighan	Y	Y	N
20 Oakar	Y	Y	N
21 Stokes	Y	Y	N
OKLAHOMA			
1 Jones	Y	Y	N
2 Synar	Y	Y	N
3 Watkins	Y	Y	N
4 McCurdy	Y	Y	N
5 Edwards†	?		
6 English	Y	Y	N
OREGON			
1 AuCoin	Y	Y	N
2 Smith, B.	N	N	Y
3 Wyden	Y	Y	N
4 Weaver	Y	Y	N
5 Smith D.	N	N	Y
PENNSYLVANIA			
1 Foglietta	Y	Y	N
2 Gray	Y	Y	N
3 Borski	Y	Y	N
4 Kolter	Y	Y	N
5 Schulze	N	N	Y
6 Yatron	Y	Y	N
7 Edgar	Y	Y	N
8 Kostmayer	Y	Y	N
9 Shuster	N	N	Y
10 McDade	N	N	Y
11 Harrison	Y	Y	N
12 Murtha	Y	Y	N
13 Coughlin	N	N	Y
14 Coyne, W.	Y	Y	N
15 Ritter	N	N	Y
16 Walker	N	N	Y
17 Gekas	N	N	Y
18 Walgren	Y	Y	N
19 Goodling	N	N	Y
20 Gaydos	Y	Y	N
21 Ridge	N	N	Y
22 Murphy	Y	Y	N
23 Clinger†	N	N	Y
RHODE ISLAND			
1 St Germain	Y	Y	N
2 Schneider	N	N	Y
SOUTH CAROLINA			
1 Hartnett	N	N	Y
2 Spence	N	N	Y
3 Derrick	Y	Y	N
4 Campbell	N	N	Y
5 Spratt	Y	Y	N
6 Tallon	Y	Y	N
SOUTH DAKOTA			
AL Daschle	Y	Y	N

	1	2	3
TENNESSEE			
1 Quillen	N	N	Y
2 Duncan	N	N	Y
3 Bouquard	Y	Y	N
4 Cooper	Y	?	?
5 Boner	Y	Y	N
6 Gore	Y	Y	N
7 Sundquist	N	N	Y
8 Jones	Y	Y	N
9 Ford	Y	Y	N
TEXAS			
1 Hall, S.	Y	Y	N
2 Wilson	Y	Y	N
3 Bartlett	N	N	Y
4 Hall, R.	Y	Y	N
5 Bryant	Y	Y	N
6 Gramm	Y	N	Y
7 Archer†	?		
8 Fields	N	N	Y
9 Brooks	Y	Y	N
10 Pickle	Y	Y	N
11 Leath	Y	Y	N
12 Wright	Y	Y	N
13 Hightower	Y	Y	N
14 Patman	Y	Y	N
15 de la Garza	Y	Y	N
16 Coleman	Y	Y	N
17 Stenholm	Y	Y	N
18 Leland	Y	Y	N
19 Hance	Y	Y	N
20 Gonzalez	Y	Y	N
21 Loeffler	N	N	Y
22 Paul	N	N	Y
23 Kazen	Y	Y	N
24 Frost	Y	Y	N
25 Andrews	Y	Y	N
26 Vandergriff	Y	Y	N
27 Ortiz	Y	Y	N
UTAH			
1 Hansen	N	N	Y
2 Marriott	N	?	?
3 Nielson	N	N	Y
VERMONT			
AL Jeffords	N	N	Y
VIRGINIA			
1 Bateman	N	N	Y
2 Whitehurst	N	N	Y
3 Bliley	N	N	Y
4 Sisisky	Y	Y	N
5 Daniel, D.	Y	Y	N
6 Olin	Y	Y	N
7 Robinson	N	N	Y
8 Parris	N	N	Y
9 Boucher	Y	Y	N
10 Wolf	N	N	Y
WASHINGTON			
1 Pritchard	N	N	Y
2 Swift	?		
3 Bonker	Y	Y	N
4 Morrison	N	N	Y
5 Foley	Y	Y	N
6 Dicks	Y	Y	N
7 Lowry	Y	Y	N
8 Chandler	N	N	Y
WEST VIRGINIA			
1 Mollohan	Y	Y	N
2 Staggers	Y	Y	N
3 Wise	Y	Y	N
4 Rahall	Y	Y	N
WISCONSIN			
1 Aspin	Y	Y	N
2 Kastenmeier	Y	Y	N
3 Gunderson	N	N	Y
4 Zablocki	Y	Y	N
5 Moody	Y	Y	?
6 Petri	N	N	Y
7 Obey	Y	Y	N
8 Roth	N	N	Y
9 Sensenbrenner	N	N	Y
WYOMING			
AL Cheney	N	N	Y

Southern states · Ala., Ark., Fla., Ga., Ky., La., Miss., N.C., Okla., S.C., Tenn., Texas, Va.

4. H Res 16. Select Committee on Children, Youth and Families. Adoption of the resolution to establish the House Select Committee on Children, Youth and Families, which could hold hearings but would not have legislative jurisdiction. Adopted 312-69: R 89-55; D 223-14 (ND 154-2, SD 69-12), Feb. 2, 1983.

5. H Res 49. Select Committee on Narcotics Abuse and Control. Adoption of the resolution to re-establish the House Select Committee on Narcotics Abuse and Control. Adopted 290-77: R 85-57; D 205-20 (ND 137-13, SD 68-7), Feb. 8, 1983.

KEY

Y   Voted for (yea).
Paired for.
+   Announced for.
N   Voted against (nay).
X   Paired against.
-   Announced against.
P   Voted "present".
C   Voted "present" to avoid possible conflict of interest.
?   Did not vote or otherwise make a position known.

Democrats   *Republicans*

	4	5
ALABAMA		
1 *Edwards*	Y	N
2 *Dickinson*	Y	?
3 Nichols	Y	Y
4 Bevill	Y	Y
5 Flippo	Y	Y
6 Erdreich	Y	Y
7 Shelby	Y	Y
ALASKA		
AL *Young*	Y	Y
ARIZONA		
1 *McCain*	Y	Y
2 Udall	Y	Y
3 *Stump*	N	N
4 *Rudd*	?	Y
5 McNulty	?	?
ARKANSAS		
1 Alexander	Y	?
2 *Bethune*	Y	Y
3 *Hammerschmidt*	Y	Y
4 Anthony	Y	Y
CALIFORNIA		
1 Bosco	?	?
2 *Chappie*	Y	Y
3 Matsui	Y	Y
4 Fazio	Y	Y
5 Burton	?	?
6 Boxer	Y	Y
7 Miller	Y	Y
8 Dellums	Y	?
9 Stark	Y	Y
10 Edwards	?	Y
11 Lantos	Y	?
12 *Zschau*	?	Y
13 Mineta	Y	Y
14 *Shumway*	N	N
15 Coelho	Y	Y
16 Panetta	Y	?
17 *Pashayan*	N	N
18 Lehman	Y	Y
19 *Lagomarsino*	Y	Y
20 *Thomas*	N	N
21 *Fiedler*	Y	Y
22 *Moorhead*	N	N
23 Beilenson	Y	N
24 Waxman	Y	Y
25 Roybal	Y	Y
26 Berman	Y	?
27 Levine	Y	Y
28 Dixon	Y	Y
29 Hawkins	Y	Y
30 Martinez	Y	Y
31 Dymally	Y	Y
32 Anderson	Y	Y
33 *Dreier*	N	?
34 Torres	Y	+
35 *Lewis*	Y	?
36 Brown	Y	Y
37 *McCandless*	Y	Y
38 Patterson	Y	Y
39 *Dannemeyer*	N	N
40 *Badham*	N	N
41 *Lowery*	Y	?
42 Lungren	N	N

	4	5
43 *Packard*	Y	N
44 Bates	Y	Y
45 *Hunter*	Y	Y
COLORADO		
1 Schroeder	Y	Y
2 Wirth	Y	N
3 Kogovsek	Y	Y
4 *Brown*	N	N
5 *Kramer*	N	Y
6 Vacancy		
CONNECTICUT		
1 Kennelly	Y	Y
2 Gejdenson	Y	Y
3 Morrison	Y	Y
4 *McKinney*	?	?
5 Ratchford	Y	N
6 *Johnson*	Y	N
DELAWARE		
AL Carper	Y	?
FLORIDA		
1 Hutto	Y	Y
2 Fuqua	Y	Y
3 Bennett	Y	Y
4 Chappell	?	?
5 *McCollum*	Y	Y
6 MacKay	Y	Y
7 Gibbons	?	?
8 *Young*	?	Y
9 *Bilirakis*	Y	N
10 Ireland	Y	Y
11 Nelson	Y	Y
12 *Lewis*	Y	Y
13 *Mack*	N	Y
14 Mica	Y	Y
15 *Shaw*	Y	Y
16 Smith	Y	Y
17 Lehman	Y	?
18 Pepper	Y	Y
19 Fascell	Y	Y
GEORGIA		
1 Thomas	Y	Y
2 Hatcher	Y	?
3 Ray	Y	?
4 Levitas	Y	Y
5 Fowler	Y	Y
6 *Gingrich*	Y	Y
7 McDonald	N	N
8 Rowland	Y	Y
9 Jenkins	N	Y
10 Barnard	N	N
HAWAII		
1 Heftel	Y	Y
2 Akaka	Y	?
IDAHO		
1 *Craig*	N	?
2 *Hansen*	N	N
ILLINOIS		
1 Washington	?	?
2 Savage	Y	?
3 Russo	Y	Y
4 *O'Brien*	Y	Y
5 Lipinski	?	?
6 *Hyde*	Y	Y
7 Collins	Y	Y
8 Rostenkowski	N	?
9 Yates	Y	Y
10 *Porter*	Y	Y
11 Annunzio	Y	Y
12 *Crane, P.*	N	?
13 *Erlenborn*	N	N
14 *Corcoran*	N	N
15 *Madigan*	Y	?
16 *Martin*	?	N
17 Evans	Y	Y
18 *Michel*	?	N
19 *Crane, D.*	?	?
20 Durbin	Y	Y
21 Price	Y	Y
22 Simon	Y	Y
INDIANA		
1 Hall	Y	Y
2 Sharp	Y	Y
3 *Hiler*	Y	N
4 *Coats*	Y	Y
5 *Hillis*	Y	Y

ND - Northern Democrats   SD - Southern Democrats

	4	5
6 Burton	Y	?
7 Myers	?	Y
8 McCloskey	Y	?
9 Hamilton	Y	Y
10 Jacobs	Y	N
IOWA		
1 Leach	Y	Y
2 Tauke	N	N
3 Evans	?	Y
4 Smith	Y	Y
5 Harkin	Y	Y
6 Bedell	Y	N
KANSAS		
1 Roberts	N	N
2 Slattery	Y	Y
3 Winn	?	?
4 Glickman	Y	Y
5 Whittaker	N	N
KENTUCKY		
1 Hubbard	Y	Y
2 Natcher	Y	Y
3 Mazzoli	Y	Y
4 Snyder	Y	Y
5 Rogers	Y	Y
6 Hopkins	N	N
7 Perkins	Y	Y
LOUISIANA		
1 Livingston	N	Y
2 Boggs	Y	Y
3 Tauzin	Y	Y
4 Roemer	N	N
5 Huckaby	Y	Y
6 Moore	N	N
7 Breaux	Y	Y
8 Long	?	?
MAINE		
1 McKernan	Y	Y
2 Snowe	Y	Y
MARYLAND		
1 Dyson	N	Y
2 Long	Y	Y
3 Mikulski	Y	Y
4 Holt	N	Y
5 Hoyer	Y	?
6 Byron	Y	Y
7 Mitchell	Y	Y
8 Barnes	Y	Y
MASSACHUSETTS		
1 Conte	Y	N
2 Boland	Y	Y
3 Early	Y	N
4 Frank	Y	Y
5 Shannon	Y	Y
6 Mavroules	Y	Y
7 Markey	Y	Y
8 O'Neill		
9 Moakley	Y	Y
10 Studds	Y	Y
11 Donnelly	Y	Y
MICHIGAN		
1 Conyers	?	?
2 Pursell	?	?
3 Wolpe	?	Y
4 Siljander	N	Y
5 Sawyer	Y	N
6 Carr	Y	Y
7 Kildee	Y	Y
8 Traxler	?	Y
9 Vander Jagt	?	Y
10 Albosta	Y	?
11 Davis	Y	N
12 Bonior	Y	Y
13 Crockett	?	Y
14 Hertel	Y	Y
15 Ford	Y	Y
16 Dingell	Y	N
17 Levin	Y	Y
18 Broomfield	?	Y
MINNESOTA		
1 Penny	Y	Y
2 Weber	N	N
3 Frenzel	N	N
4 Vento	Y	Y
5 Sabo	Y	N
6 Sikorski	Y	Y

	4	5
7 Stangeland	?	?
8 Oberstar	Y	N
MISSISSIPPI		
1 Whitten	Y	Y
2 Franklin	Y	Y
3 Montgomery	Y	Y
4 Dowdy	Y	Y
5 Lott	Y	N
MISSOURI		
1 Clay	Y	Y
2 Young	Y	Y
3 Gephardt	Y	Y
4 Skelton	Y	Y
5 Wheat	Y	Y
6 Coleman	Y	Y
7 Taylor	Y	?
8 Emerson	Y	Y
9 Volkmer	Y	Y
MONTANA		
1 Williams	Y	Y
2 Marlenee	N	Y
NEBRASKA		
1 Bereuter	Y	Y
2 Daub	Y	Y
3 Smith	Y	Y
NEVADA		
1 Reid	Y	Y
2 Vucanovich	Y	Y
NEW HAMPSHIRE		
1 D'Amours	?	?
2 Gregg	N	N
NEW JERSEY		
1 Florio	?	?
2 Hughes	Y	Y
3 Howard	Y	?
4 Smith	Y	Y
5 Roukema	Y	Y
6 Dwyer	Y	Y
7 Rinaldo	Y	Y
8 Roe	Y	Y
9 Torricelli	Y	Y
10 Rodino	Y	?
11 Minish	Y	Y
12 Courter	Y	Y
13 Forsythe	Y	Y
14 Guarini	Y	Y
NEW MEXICO		
1 Lujan	Y	Y
2 Skeen	N	N
3 Richardson	Y	Y
NEW YORK		
1 Carney	?	Y
2 Downey	Y	Y
3 Mrazek	Y	Y
4 Lent	Y	Y
5 McGrath	Y	Y
6 Addabbo	Y	Y
7 Vacancy		
8 Scheuer	Y	Y
9 Ferraro	Y	Y
10 Schumer	Y	Y
11 Towns	?	?
12 Owens	Y	Y
13 Solarz	Y	Y
14 Molinari	?	Y
15 Green	N	Y
16 Rangel	Y	Y
17 Weiss	Y	Y
18 Garcia	Y	Y
19 Biaggi	Y	Y
20 Ottinger	Y	Y
21 Fish	Y	Y
22 Gilman	Y	Y
23 Stratton	Y	Y
24 Solomon	N	N
25 Boehlert	Y	Y
26 Martin	?	?
27 Wortley	Y	N
28 McHugh	Y	Y
29 Horton	Y	Y
30 Conable	N	N
31 Kemp	Y	?
32 LaFalce	Y	Y
33 Nowak	Y	?
34 Lundine	?	Y

	4	5
NORTH CAROLINA		
1 Jones	?	Y
2 Valentine	Y	Y
3 Whitley	?	Y
4 Andrews	Y	Y
5 Neal	Y	Y
6 Britt	Y	?
7 Rose	Y	Y
8 Hefner	Y	Y
9 Martin	Y	N
10 Broyhill	N	N
11 Clarke	Y	Y
NORTH DAKOTA		
AL Dorgan	Y	Y
OHIO		
1 Luken	Y	Y
2 Gradison	Y	Y
3 Hall	Y	N
4 Oxley	Y	Y
5 Latta	Y	Y
6 McEwen	Y	Y
7 DeWine	Y	Y
8 Kindness	N	N
9 Kaptur	Y	Y
10 Miller	N	N
11 Eckart	Y	Y
12 Kasich	Y	Y
13 Pease	Y	Y
14 Seiberling	Y	N
15 Wylie	Y	?
16 Regula	Y	Y
17 Williams	Y	?
18 Applegate	Y	N
19 Feighan	Y	Y
20 Oakar	Y	Y
21 Stokes	?	Y
OKLAHOMA		
1 Jones	N	N
2 Synar	Y	Y
3 Watkins	Y	Y
4 McCurdy	Y	Y
5 Edwards	N	Y
6 English	N	Y
OREGON		
1 AuCoin	Y	N
2 Smith, B.	N	N
3 Wyden	Y	Y
4 Weaver	Y	Y
5 Smith, D.	N	?
PENNSYLVANIA		
1 Foglietta	Y	Y
2 Gray	Y	Y
3 Borski	Y	Y
4 Kolter	Y	Y
5 Schulze	?	Y
6 Yatron	Y	Y
7 Edgar	Y	Y
8 Kostmayer	Y	Y
9 Shuster	N	N
10 McDade	Y	Y
11 Harrison	Y	Y
12 Murtha	Y	?
13 Coughlin	N	Y
14 Coyne	Y	Y
15 Ritter	N	N
16 Walker	N	N
17 Gekas	N	N
18 Walgren	Y	Y
19 Goodling	?	Y
20 Gaydos	Y	Y
21 Ridge	Y	Y
22 Murphy	Y	Y
23 Clinger	Y	N
RHODE ISLAND		
1 St Germain	Y	Y
2 Schneider	Y	Y
SOUTH CAROLINA		
1 Hartnett	N	N
2 Spence	Y	Y
3 Derrick	Y	Y
4 Campbell	Y	N
5 Spratt	Y	?
6 Tallon	Y	Y
SOUTH DAKOTA		
AL Daschle	+	Y

	4	5
TENNESSEE		
1 Quillen	Y	Y
2 Duncan	Y	Y
3 Bouquard	Y	?
4 Cooper	Y	Y
5 Boner	Y	?
6 Gore	Y	Y
7 Sundquist	N	N
8 Jones	?	Y
9 Ford	Y	Y
TEXAS		
1 Hall, S.	N	Y
2 Wilson	Y	?
3 Bartlett	N	N
4 Hall, R.	N	Y
5 Bryant	Y	Y
6 Vacancy*		
7 Archer	N	N
8 Fields	N	Y
9 Brooks	Y	Y
10 Pickle	N	N
11 Leath	N	?
12 Wright	Y	Y
13 Hightower	?	Y
14 Patman	Y	Y
15 de la Garza	Y	+
16 Coleman	Y	+
17 Stenholm	?	N
18 Leland	Y	Y
19 Hance	N	Y
20 Gonzalez	Y	Y
21 Loeffler	N	N
22 Paul	N	N
23 Kazen	Y	Y
24 Frost	Y	Y
25 Andrews	?	Y
26 Vandergriff	Y	Y
27 Ortiz	Y	?
UTAH		
1 Hansen	N	?
2 Marriott	?	?
3 Nielson	Y	?
VERMONT		
AL Jeffords	?	Y
VIRGINIA		
1 Bateman	Y	Y
2 Whitehurst	Y	N
3 Bliley	Y	N
4 Sisisky	Y	Y
5 Daniel	N	N
6 Olin	Y	Y
7 Robinson	N	N
8 Parris	Y	Y
9 Boucher	Y	Y
10 Wolf	Y	Y
WASHINGTON		
1 Pritchard	Y	Y
2 Swift	Y	Y
3 Bonker	?	Y
4 Morrison	Y	Y
5 Foley	?	Y
6 Dicks	?	Y
7 Lowry	Y	Y
8 Chandler	Y	Y
WEST VIRGINIA		
1 Mollohan	Y	Y
2 Staggers	Y	Y
3 Wise	Y	Y
4 Rahall	Y	Y
WISCONSIN		
1 Aspin	Y	Y
2 Kastenmeier	?	?
3 Gunderson	N	N
4 Zablocki	Y	Y
5 Moody	Y	Y
6 Petri	Y	Y
7 Obey	Y	Y
8 Roth	Y	Y
9 Sensenbrenner	Y	N
WYOMING		
AL Cheney	N	?

* Rep. Phil Gramm, D-Texas, resigned Jan. 5, 1983. The last vote for which he was eligible was CQ vote 3.

Southern states - Ala., Ark., Fla., Ga., Ky., La., Miss., N.C., Okla., S.C., Tenn., Texas, Va.

KEY

Y Voted for (yea).
Paired for.
+ Announced for.
N Voted against (nay).
X Paired against.
- Announced against.
P Voted "present".
C Voted "present" to avoid possible conflict of interest.
? Did not vote or otherwise make a position known.

———

Democrats   *Republicans*

6. HR 861. Small Business Administration Pilot Program Extension. Mitchell, D-Md., motion to suspend the rules and pass the bill to extend for two years pilot programs in which the Small Business Administration determines which procurement needs of other federal agencies could be met by socially and economically disadvantaged small firms. Motion agreed to 318-5: R 123-4; D 195-1 (ND 125-0, SD 70-1), Feb. 15, 1983. A two-thirds majority of those present and voting (216 in this case) is required for passage under suspension of the rules.

7. HR 1043. Federal Contracting Opportunities. Mitchell, D-Md., motion to suspend the rules and pass the bill to help small businesses compete for federal contracts by creating minimum time periods for contract solicitation notices and for contract bids. Motion agreed to 294-32: R 106-23; D 188-9 (ND 123-3, SD 65-6), Feb. 15, 1983. A two-thirds majority of those present and voting (218 in this case) is required for passage under suspension of the rules.

	6	7
ALABAMA		
1 *Edwards*	Y	Y
2 *Dickinson*	Y	N
3 Nichols	Y	N
4 Bevill	Y	Y
5 Flippo	?	?
6 Erdreich	Y	Y
7 Shelby	Y	?
ALASKA		
AL *Young*	?	?
ARIZONA		
1 *McCain*	Y	Y
2 Udall	Y	Y
3 *Stump*	Y	N
4 *Rudd*	?	?
5 McNulty	Y	Y
ARKANSAS		
1 Alexander	?	?
2 *Bethune*	Y	Y
3 *Hammerschmidt*	Y	Y
4 Anthony	Y	Y
CALIFORNIA		
1 Bosco	?	?
2 *Chappie*	Y	Y
3 Matsui	Y	?
4 Fazio	Y	Y
5 Burton	?	?
6 Boxer	?	?
7 Miller	?	Y
8 Dellums	Y	Y
9 Stark	Y	Y
10 Edwards	Y	Y
11 Lantos	?	?
12 *Zschau*	Y	Y
13 Mineta	?	?
14 *Shumway*	Y	N
15 Coelho	Y	Y
16 Panetta	Y	Y
17 *Pashayan*	?	?
18 Lehman	Y	Y
19 *Lagomarsino*	Y	Y
20 *Thomas*	Y	Y
21 *Fiedler*	Y	Y
22 *Moorhead*	?	?
23 Beilenson	?	?
24 Waxman	?	?
25 Roybal	?	?
26 Berman	?	?
27 Levine	?	?
28 Dixon	?	?
29 Hawkins	Y	Y
30 Martinez	?	?
31 Dymally	?	?
32 Anderson	?	?
33 *Dreier*	?	?
34 Torres	Y	Y
35 *Lewis*	Y	Y
36 Brown	?	Y
37 *McCandless*	Y	Y
38 Patterson	?	?
39 *Dannemeyer*	Y	N
40 *Badham*	?	?
41 *Lowery*	Y	Y
42 *Lungren*	?	?

	6	7
43 *Packard*	Y	N
44 Bates	Y	Y
45 *Hunter*	?	?
COLORADO		
1 Schroeder	Y	Y
2 Wirth	+	+
3 Kogovsek	?	?
4 *Brown*	Y	N
5 *Kramer*	Y	Y
6 Vacancy		
CONNECTICUT		
1 Kennelly	Y	Y
2 Gejdenson	?	?
3 Morrison	Y	Y
4 *McKinney*	?	?
5 Ratchford	Y	Y
6 *Johnson*	Y	Y
DELAWARE		
AL Carper	Y	Y
FLORIDA		
1 Hutto	Y	N
2 Fuqua	?	?
3 Bennett	Y	Y
4 Chappell	Y	Y
5 *McCollum*	?	?
6 MacKay	Y	Y
7 Gibbons	Y	Y
8 *Young*	Y	Y
9 *Bilirakis*	Y	Y
10 Ireland	Y	Y
11 Nelson	Y	Y
12 *Lewis*	Y	Y
13 *Mack*	N	Y
14 Mica	Y	Y
15 *Shaw*	Y	Y
16 Smith	Y	Y
17 Lehman	Y	Y
18 Pepper	Y	Y
19 Fascell	Y	Y
GEORGIA		
1 Thomas	Y	Y
2 Hatcher	Y	Y
3 Ray	Y	Y
4 Levitas	Y	Y
5 Fowler	Y	Y
6 *Gingrich*	Y	Y
7 McDonald	N	N
8 Rowland	Y	Y
9 Jenkins	?	?
10 Barnard	?	?
HAWAII		
1 Heftel	?	?
2 Akaka	Y	Y
IDAHO		
1 *Craig*	?	?
2 *Hansen*	Y	N
ILLINOIS		
1 Washington	?	?
2 Savage	Y	Y
3 Russo	Y	Y
4 *O'Brien*	?	?
5 Lipinski	?	?
6 *Hyde*	Y	Y
7 Collins	?	?
8 Rostenkowski	Y	Y
9 Yates	Y	Y
10 *Porter*	Y	Y
11 Annunzio	Y	Y
12 *Crane, P.*	N	N
13 *Erlenborn*	Y	N
14 *Corcoran*	Y	Y
15 *Madigan*	Y	Y
16 *Martin*	Y	Y
17 Evans	Y	Y
18 *Michel*	?	?
19 *Crane, D.*	Y	N
20 Durbin	Y	Y
21 Price	Y	N
22 Simon	Y	Y
INDIANA		
1 Hall	Y	Y
2 Sharp	Y	Y
3 *Hiler*	Y	Y
4 *Coats*	Y	Y
5 *Hillis*	?	?

ND - Northern Democrats   SD - Southern Democrats

	8	9
6 Burton	Y	N
7 Myers	Y	Y
8 McCloskey	Y	Y
9 Hamilton	Y	Y
10 Jacobs	Y	Y
IOWA		
1 *Leach*	?	?
2 *Tauke*	Y	Y
3 *Evans*	Y	Y
4 Smith	?	?
5 Harkin	Y	Y
6 Bedell	Y	Y
KANSAS		
1 *Roberts*	Y	Y
2 Slattery	Y	Y
3 *Winn*	Y	Y
4 Glickman	Y	Y
5 *Whittaker*	Y	Y
KENTUCKY		
1 Hubbard	Y	Y
2 Natcher	Y	Y
3 Mazzoli	Y	Y
4 *Snyder*	Y	Y
5 *Rogers*	Y	Y
6 *Hopkins*	Y	N
7 Perkins	Y	Y
LOUISIANA		
1 *Livingston*	Y	Y
2 Boggs	Y	Y
3 Tauzin	Y	Y
4 Roemer	Y	Y
5 Huckaby	Y	Y
6 *Moore*	Y	Y
7 Breaux	Y	Y
8 Long	?	?
MAINE		
1 *McKernan*	Y	Y
2 *Snowe*	Y	Y
MARYLAND		
1 Dyson	Y	Y
2 Long	?	?
3 Mikulski	Y	Y
4 *Holt*	Y	N
5 Hoyer	Y	Y
6 Byron	Y	N
7 Mitchell	Y	Y
8 Barnes	?	?
MASSACHUSETTS		
1 *Conte*	Y	Y
2 Boland	Y	Y
3 Early	?	?
4 Frank	Y	Y
5 Shannon	Y	?
6 Mavroules	Y	Y
7 Markey	Y	Y
8 O'Neill		
9 Moakley	?	?
10 Studds	Y	Y
11 Donnelly	Y	Y
MICHIGAN		
1 Conyers	?	?
2 *Pursell*	?	?
3 Wolpe	Y	Y
4 *Siljander*	Y	Y
5 *Sawyer*	Y	Y
6 Carr	?	?
7 Kildee	Y	Y
8 Traxler	?	?
9 *Vander Jagt*	Y	Y
10 Albosta	Y	Y
11 *Davis*	Y	Y
12 Bonior	?	?
13 Crockett	Y	Y
14 Hertel	Y	Y
15 Ford	Y	Y
16 Dingell	Y	Y
17 Levin	Y	Y
18 *Broomfield*	Y	Y
MINNESOTA		
1 Penny	Y	Y
2 *Weber*	Y	Y
3 *Frenzel*	Y	Y
4 Vento	Y	Y
5 Sabo	Y	Y
6 Sikorski	Y	Y

	8	9
7 *Stangeland*	Y	Y
8 Oberstar	Y	Y
MISSISSIPPI		
1 Whitten	Y	Y
2 *Franklin*	Y	Y
3 Montgomery	Y	N
4 Dowdy	Y	Y
5 *Lott*	Y	N
MISSOURI		
1 Clay	Y	Y
2 Young	Y	Y
3 Gephardt	Y	Y
4 Skelton	Y	Y
5 Wheat	Y	Y
6 *Coleman*	Y	Y
7 *Taylor*	?	?
8 *Emerson*	Y	Y
9 Volkmer	Y	Y
MONTANA		
1 Williams	Y	Y
2 *Marlenee*	?	?
NEBRASKA		
1 *Bereuter*	Y	Y
2 *Daub*	Y	Y
3 *Smith*	Y	Y
NEVADA		
1 Reid	Y	Y
2 *Vucanovich*	Y	Y
NEW HAMPSHIRE		
1 D'Amours	?	?
2 *Gregg*	Y	Y
NEW JERSEY		
1 Florio	Y	Y
2 Hughes	Y	Y
3 Howard	Y	Y
4 *Smith*	Y	Y
5 *Roukema*	Y	Y
6 Dwyer	?	?
7 *Rinaldo*	Y	Y
8 Roe	Y	Y
9 Torricelli	Y	Y
10 Rodino	Y	Y
11 Minish	?	?
12 *Courter*	Y	Y
13 *Forsythe*	Y	Y
14 Guarini	Y	Y
NEW MEXICO		
1 *Lujan*	Y	Y
2 *Skeen*	Y	N
3 Richardson	Y	Y
NEW YORK		
1 *Carney*	Y	Y
2 Downey	Y	Y
3 Mrazek	Y	Y
4 *Lent*	?	?
5 *McGrath*	Y	Y
6 Addabbo	Y	Y
7 Vacancy		
8 Scheuer	?	?
9 Ferraro	Y	Y
10 Schumer	Y	Y
11 Towns	Y	Y
12 Owens	?	?
13 Solarz	?	?
14 *Molinari*	Y	Y
15 *Green*	Y	Y
16 Rangel	Y	Y
17 Weiss	Y	Y
18 Garcia	Y	Y
19 Biaggi	Y	Y
20 Ottinger	Y	Y
21 *Fish*	Y	Y
22 Gilman	+	+
23 Stratton	Y	N
24 *Solomon*	Y	N
25 *Boehlert*	Y	Y
26 *Martin*	?	?
27 *Wortley*	Y	Y
28 McHugh	?	?
29 *Horton*	?	?
30 *Conable*	Y	Y
31 *Kemp*	Y	Y
32 LaFalce	Y	Y
33 Nowak	?	Y
34 Lundine	?	?

	8	9
NORTH CAROLINA		
1 Jones	?	?
2 Valentine	Y	Y
3 Whitley	Y	Y
4 Andrews	Y	Y
5 Neal	Y	Y
6 Britt	Y	Y
7 Rose	Y	Y
8 Hefner	?	?
9 *Martin*	Y	Y
10 *Broyhill*	Y	Y
11 Clarke	Y	Y
NORTH DAKOTA		
AL Dorgan	Y	Y
OHIO		
1 Luken	Y	Y
2 *Gradison*	Y	Y
3 Hall	Y	Y
4 *Oxley*	?	?
5 *Latta*	Y	Y
6 *McEwen*	Y	N
7 *DeWine*	Y	Y
8 *Kindness*	Y	Y
9 Kaptur	Y	Y
10 *Miller*	?	?
11 Eckart	Y	Y
12 *Kasich*	Y	Y
13 Pease	Y	Y
14 Seiberling	Y	Y
15 *Wylie*	Y	Y
16 *Regula*	Y	Y
17 *Williams*	?	?
18 Applegate	?	Y
19 Feighan	Y	Y
20 Oakar	Y	Y
21 Stokes	Y	Y
OKLAHOMA		
1 Jones	?	?
2 Synar	Y	Y
3 Watkins	Y	Y
4 *McCurdy*	Y	Y
5 *Edwards*	Y	Y
6 English	Y	Y
OREGON		
1 AuCoin	?	?
2 *Smith, B.*	?	?
3 Wyden	Y	Y
4 Weaver	Y	Y
5 *Smith, D.*	?	?
PENNSYLVANIA		
1 Foglietta	?	?
2 Gray	Y	Y
3 Borski	Y	Y
4 Kolter	Y	Y
5 *Schulze*	Y	Y
6 Yatron	?	?
7 Edgar	Y	Y
8 Kostmayer	Y	Y
9 *Shuster*	Y	Y
10 *McDade*	Y	Y
11 Harrison	?	?
12 Murtha	Y	Y
13 *Coughlin*	Y	Y
14 Coyne	Y	Y
15 *Ritter*	Y	Y
16 *Walker*	Y	Y
17 *Gekas*	Y	Y
18 Walgren	Y	Y
19 *Goodling*	?	?
20 Gaydos	?	?
21 *Ridge*	Y	Y
22 Murphy	Y	Y
23 *Clinger*	Y	Y
RHODE ISLAND		
1 St Germain	Y	Y
2 *Schneider*	?	?
SOUTH CAROLINA		
1 *Hartnett*	?	?
2 *Spence*	Y	N
3 Derrick	Y	Y
4 *Campbell*	?	?
5 Spratt	Y	Y
6 Tallon	Y	Y
SOUTH DAKOTA		
AL Daschle	?	?

	8	9
TENNESSEE		
1 *Quillen*	?	?
2 *Duncan*	Y	Y
3 Bouquard	?	?
4 Cooper	Y	Y
5 Boner	?	?
6 Gore	Y	Y
7 *Sundquist*	Y	Y
8 Jones	?	?
9 Ford	Y	Y
TEXAS		
1 Hall, S.	+	+
2 Wilson	?	?
3 *Bartlett*	Y	Y
4 Hall, R.	Y	Y
5 Bryant	?	?
6 Vacancy		
7 *Archer*	Y	Y
8 *Fields*	?	Y
9 Brooks	Y	Y
10 Pickle	Y	Y
11 Leath	Y	N
12 Wright	Y	Y
13 Hightower	?	?
14 Patman	Y	Y
15 de la Garza	Y	Y
16 Coleman	Y	Y
17 Stenholm	Y	Y
18 Leland	Y	Y
19 Hance	Y	Y
20 Gonzalez	?	?
21 *Loeffler*	Y	Y
22 *Paul*	N	N
23 Kazen	Y	Y
24 Frost	?	Y
25 Andrews	?	?
26 Vandergriff	Y	Y
27 Ortiz	Y	Y
UTAH		
1 Hansen	N	N
2 *Marriott*	+	+
3 *Nielson*	Y	N
VERMONT		
AL *Jeffords*	Y	Y
VIRGINIA		
1 *Bateman*	Y	Y
2 *Whitehurst*	Y	N
3 *Bliley*	Y	Y
4 Sisisky	Y	Y
5 Daniel	Y	N
6 Olin	Y	Y
7 *Robinson*	Y	N
8 *Parris*	Y	Y
9 Boucher	Y	Y
10 *Wolf*	Y	Y
WASHINGTON		
1 *Pritchard*	?	?
2 Swift	Y	Y
3 Bonker	Y	Y
4 *Morrison*	Y	Y
5 Foley	Y	Y
6 Dicks	Y	Y
7 Lowry	Y	Y
8 *Chandler*	?	?
WEST VIRGINIA		
1 Mollohan	Y	Y
2 Staggers	Y	Y
3 Wise	Y	Y
4 Rahall	Y	Y
WISCONSIN		
1 Aspin	?	?
2 Kastenmeier	Y	Y
3 *Gunderson*	Y	Y
4 Zablocki	Y	Y
5 Moody	Y	Y
6 *Petri*	?	?
7 Obey	?	?
8 *Roth*	?	?
9 *Sensenbrenner*	Y	Y
WYOMING		
AL *Cheney*	Y	Y

Southern states · Ala., Ark., Fla., Ga., Ky., La., Miss., N.C., Okla., S.C., Tenn., Texas, Va.

8. HR 999. American Conservation Corps. Seiberling, D-Ohio, motion to suspend the rules and pass the bill to establish an American Conservation Corps to provide conservation jobs for unemployed youth on public and Indian lands. Motion agreed to 301-87: R 70-82; D 231-5 (ND 159-0, SD 72-5), March 1, 1983. A two-thirds majority of those present and voting (259 in this case) is required for passage under suspension of the rules. A "nay" was a vote supporting the president's position.

9. HR 1310. Emergency Mathematics and Science Education Act. Adoption of the rule (H Res 109) providing for House floor consideration of the bill to authorize $325 million in fiscal 1984 and such sums as may be necessary in fiscal 1985 to improve mathematics and science education in U.S. schools, and $100 million in each of fiscal years 1984-1988 to promote a national policy for training engineering, technical and scientific personnel. Adopted 393-0: R 151-0; D 242-0 (ND 163-0, SD 79-0), March 2, 1983.

10. HR 1310. Emergency Mathematics and Science Education Act. Sensenbrenner, R-Wis., amendment to replace the postsecondary assistance provisions in the bill with a "presidential science and mathematics improvement program" providing $50 million in block grants to the states in each of fiscal years 1984 and 1985 for math and science programs. Rejected 92-323: R 89-70; D 3-253 (ND 0-171, SD 3-82), March 2, 1983.

11. HR 1310. Emergency Mathematics and Science Education Act. Coleman, R-Mo., amendment to replace the National Teaching Scholarship Program, which would provide two-year scholarships to train teachers in math, science or a critical foreign language, with a one-year scholarship program to retrain existing teachers in other fields to be math and science teachers. Rejected 138-276: R 137-19; D 1-257 (ND 0-171, SD 1-86), March 2, 1983.

12. HR 1310. Emergency Mathematics and Science Education Act. Passage of the bill to authorize $325 million in fiscal 1984 and such sums as may be necessary in fiscal 1985 to improve mathematics and science education in U.S. schools and $100 million in each of fiscal years 1984-1988 to promote a national policy for training engineering, technical and scientific personnel. Passed 348-54: R 100-54; D 248-0 (ND 163-0, SD 85-0), March 2, 1983.

13. Procedural Motion. Walker, R-Pa., motion to approve the House *Journal* of Wednesday, March 2. Motion agreed to 350-19: R 133-10; D 217-9 (ND 140-8, SD 77-1), March 3, 1983.

14. 1718. Emergency Supplemental Appropriations, Fiscal 1983/Jobs. Bonior, D-Mich., motion to order the previous question (thus ending debate and the possibility of amendment) on the rule (H Res 113) providing for House floor consideration of the bill to appropriate $4.9 billion for emergency jobs and recession relief and $5 billion for the unemployment insurance system in fiscal 1983. Motion agreed to 299-117: R 48-111; D 251-6 (ND 167-2, SD 84-4), March 3, 1983.

15. 1718. Emergency Supplemental Appropriations, Fiscal 1983/Jobs. Adoption of the rule (H Res 113) providing for House floor consideration of the bill to appropriate $4.9 billion for emergency jobs and recession relief and $5 billion for the unemployment insurance system in fiscal 1983. Adopted 300-103: R 64-92; D 236-11 (ND 160-5, SD 76-6), March 3, 1983.

* Rep. Gary L. Ackerman, D-N.Y., was sworn in March 2, 1983. The first vote for which he was eligible was CQ vote 9.

** Rep. Phil Gramm, R-Texas, was sworn in Feb. 22, 1983. The first vote for which he was eligible was CQ vote 8.

KEY

Y	Voted for (yea).
#	Paired for.
+	Announced for.
N	Voted against (nay).
X	Paired against.
-	Announced against.
P	Voted "present".
C	Voted "present" to avoid possible conflict of interest.
?	Did not vote or otherwise make a position known.

Democrats   *Republicans*

Member	8	9	10	11	12	13	14	15
ALABAMA								
1 *Edwards*	Y	?	N	Y	Y	Y	Y	Y
2 *Dickinson*	Y	?	N	Y	Y	N	N	N
3 Nichols	Y	Y	N	N	Y	Y	Y	Y
4 Bevill	Y	Y	N	N	Y	Y	Y	Y
5 Flippo	Y	Y	N	N	Y	Y	Y	Y
6 Erdreich	Y	Y	N	N	Y	Y	Y	Y
7 Shelby	?	Y	N	N	Y	Y	Y	Y
ALASKA								
AL *Young*	Y	Y	N	N	Y	?	Y	Y
ARIZONA								
1 *McCain*	N	Y	Y	Y	Y	Y	Y	Y
2 Udall	Y	Y	N	N	?	?	?	Y
3 *Stump*	N	Y	Y	N	N	N	N	N
4 *Rudd*	N	Y	Y	N	Y	N	N	N
5 McNulty	Y	Y	N	N	Y	Y	Y	?
ARKANSAS								
1 Alexander	Y	Y	N	N	?	Y	Y	Y
2 *Bethune*	Y	Y	N	?	Y	Y	N	N
3 *Hammerschmidt*	Y	Y	N	Y	Y	Y	Y	Y
4 Anthony	Y	Y	N	N	Y	Y	Y	Y
CALIFORNIA								
1 Bosco	Y	Y	N	N	Y	Y	Y	Y
2 *Chappie*	N	Y	Y	Y	Y	Y	N	N
3 Matsui	Y	Y	N	N	Y	Y	Y	Y
4 Fazio	Y	Y	N	N	Y	?	Y	Y
5 Burton	Y	Y	N	N	Y	Y	Y	Y
6 Boxer	Y	Y	N	N	Y	Y	Y	Y
7 Miller	Y	Y	N	N	Y	Y	Y	Y
8 Dellums	Y	Y	?	N	Y	Y	Y	Y
9 Stark	Y	Y	N	?	Y	Y	Y	Y
10 Edwards	Y	Y	N	N	Y	Y	Y	Y
11 Lantos	Y	Y	N	N	Y	Y	Y	Y
12 *Zschau*	N	Y	Y	N	Y	N	N	N
13 Mineta	Y	Y	N	N	Y	Y	Y	Y
14 *Shumway*	N	Y	Y	N	Y	N	N	N
15 Coelho	Y	Y	N	N	Y	Y	Y	Y
16 Panetta	Y	Y	N	N	Y	Y	Y	Y
17 *Pashayan*	Y	Y	Y	N	Y	N	N	Y
18 Lehman	Y	Y	N	N	Y	Y	Y	Y
19 *Lagomarsino*	Y	Y	Y	N	Y	Y	N	N
20 *Thomas*	N	Y	Y	Y	Y	Y	N	N
21 *Fiedler*	Y	Y	Y	Y	Y	Y	N	?
22 *Moorhead*	N	Y	Y	N	Y	N	N	N
23 Beilenson	Y	Y	N	N	Y	Y	Y	Y
24 Waxman	Y	Y	N	N	Y	Y	Y	Y
25 Roybal	Y	Y	N	N	Y	Y	Y	Y
26 Berman	?	Y	N	N	Y	Y	Y	Y
27 Levine	Y	Y	N	N	Y	Y	Y	Y
28 Dixon	Y	Y	N	N	Y	Y	Y	Y
29 Hawkins	Y	Y	N	Y	?	?	Y	Y
30 Martinez	Y	?	N	N	Y	?	Y	Y
31 Dymally	Y	Y	N	N	Y	Y	Y	Y
32 Anderson	Y	Y	N	N	Y	Y	Y	Y
33 *Dreier*	N	Y	Y	Y	N	Y	N	N
34 Torres	Y	Y	N	N	Y	Y	Y	Y
35 *Lewis*	?	Y	Y	Y	N	?	N	N
36 Brown	Y	Y	N	N	Y	Y	Y	Y
37 *McCandless*	N	Y	N	N	N	Y	N	N
38 Patterson	Y	Y	N	N	Y	Y	Y	Y
39 *Dannemeyer*	N	Y	Y	N	Y	N	N	N
40 *Badham*	N	Y	Y	N	Y	N	N	N
41 *Lowery*	Y	Y	Y	Y	?	?	?	?
42 *Lungren*	N	Y	Y	Y	Y	Y	N	N
43 *Packard*	Y	Y	Y	Y	Y	Y	N	N
44 Bates	Y	Y	N	N	Y	N	Y	Y
45 *Hunter*	N	Y	Y	Y	N	Y	N	?
COLORADO								
1 Schroeder	Y	Y	N	N	Y	N	Y	N
2 Wirth	Y	Y	N	N	#	Y	Y	Y
3 Kogovsek	Y	Y	N	N	Y	?	Y	Y
4 *Brown*	N	Y	N	Y	Y	Y	N	N
5 *Kramer*	N	Y	Y	Y	Y	Y	N	N
6 Vacancy								
CONNECTICUT								
1 Kennelly	Y	Y	N	N	Y	Y	Y	Y
2 Gejdenson	Y	Y	N	N	Y	N	Y	Y
3 Morrison	Y	Y	N	N	Y	Y	Y	Y
4 *McKinney*	Y	?	N	Y	Y	?	Y	Y
5 Ratchford	Y	Y	N	N	Y	Y	Y	Y
6 *Johnson*	Y	Y	N	N	Y	Y	Y	Y
DELAWARE								
AL Carper	Y	Y	N	N	Y	?	Y	Y
FLORIDA								
1 Hutto	Y	Y	N	N	Y	Y	Y	Y
2 Fuqua	Y	Y	N	N	Y	Y	Y	Y
3 Bennett	Y	Y	N	N	Y	Y	Y	Y
4 Chappell	Y	Y	?	N	Y	?	Y	Y
5 *McCollum*	N	Y	Y	Y	Y	Y	N	N
6 MacKay	?	Y	N	N	Y	Y	Y	Y
7 Gibbons	?	Y	N	N	Y	?	Y	Y
8 *Young*	Y	Y	N	Y	Y	?	N	N
9 *Bilirakis*	N	Y	Y	?	N	Y	N	N
10 Ireland	N	Y	N	N	Y	Y	Y	Y
11 Nelson	Y	Y	N	N	Y	Y	Y	?
12 *Lewis*	Y	Y	Y	Y	Y	Y	N	N
13 *Mack*	N	Y	Y	Y	N	N	N	N
14 Mica	Y	Y	N	N	Y	Y	Y	Y
15 *Shaw*	N	Y	Y	Y	Y	Y	N	N
16 Smith	Y	Y	N	N	Y	Y	Y	Y
17 Lehman	?	?	N	N	Y	Y	Y	Y
18 Pepper	Y	Y	N	N	Y	Y	Y	Y
19 Fascell	Y	Y	N	N	Y	Y	Y	Y
GEORGIA								
1 Thomas	Y	Y	N	N	Y	Y	Y	Y
2 Hatcher	Y	Y	N	N	Y	Y	Y	Y
3 Ray	Y	Y	N	N	Y	Y	Y	Y
4 Levitas	?	Y	N	N	Y	Y	Y	Y
5 Fowler	?	Y	N	N	Y	Y	Y	Y
6 *Gingrich*	Y	Y	N	Y	Y	Y	N	N
7 McDonald	X	?	#	#	X	Y	N	N
8 Rowland	Y	Y	N	N	Y	Y	Y	Y
9 Jenkins	Y	Y	N	N	Y	Y	Y	Y
10 Barnard	Y	Y	N	N	Y	Y	Y	Y
HAWAII								
1 Heftel	Y	?	N	N	Y	?	?	Y
2 Akaka	Y	Y	N	+	Y	Y	Y	Y
IDAHO								
1 *Craig*	N	Y	N	N	Y	N	N	N
2 *Hansen*	N	Y	?	N	Y	N	N	N
ILLINOIS								
1 Washington	?	?	?	?	?	?	?	?
2 Savage	Y	?	N	N	?	?	?	?
3 Russo	Y	Y	N	N	Y	Y	Y	Y
4 *O'Brien*	Y	?	N	N	Y	Y	Y	Y
5 Lipinski	Y	Y	N	N	Y	Y	Y	Y
6 *Hyde*	Y	Y	N	N	Y	Y	N	Y
7 Collins	Y	Y	N	N	Y	Y	Y	Y
8 Rostenkowski	Y	Y	N	N	Y	Y	Y	Y
9 Yates	Y	Y	N	N	Y	Y	Y	Y
10 *Porter*	N	Y	N	Y	Y	?	N	N
11 Annunzio	Y	Y	N	N	Y	Y	Y	Y
12 *Crane, P.*	N	Y	Y	N	?	N	N	N
13 *Erlenborn*	?	Y	N	Y	N	Y	Y	?
14 *Corcoran*	+	Y	Y	Y	Y	Y	N	N
15 *Madigan*	?	?	N	N	Y	?	Y	Y
16 *Martin*	N	Y	Y	Y	Y	N	N	N
17 Evans	Y	Y	N	N	Y	Y	Y	Y
18 *Michel*	N	Y	N	Y	?	?	Y	Y
19 *Crane, D.*	N	Y	Y	Y	N	Y	N	N
20 Durbin	Y	Y	N	N	Y	Y	Y	Y
21 Price	Y	Y	N	N	Y	Y	Y	Y
22 Simon	Y	Y	N	N	Y	Y	Y	Y
INDIANA								
1 Hall	Y	Y	N	N	Y	Y	Y	Y
2 Sharp	Y	Y	N	N	Y	Y	Y	Y
3 *Hiler*	N	Y	Y	Y	Y	N	N	N
4 *Coats*	N	Y	Y	Y	Y	Y	Y	Y
5 Hillis	Y	Y	N	N	Y	Y	Y	Y

ND - Northern Democrats   SD - Southern Democrats

Corresponding to Congressional Record Votes 10, 11, 12, 13, 14, 15, 16, 17

	8	9	10	11	12	13	14	15
6 *Burton*	N	Y	Y	Y	N	N	N	N
7 *Myers*	N	Y	N	N	Y	Y	Y	Y
8 McCloskey	Y	Y	N	N	Y	Y	Y	Y
9 Hamilton	Y	Y	N	N	Y	Y	Y	Y
10 Jacobs	Y	Y	N	N	Y	N	N	N
IOWA								
1 *Leach*	?	Y	N	Y	Y	Y	Y	N
2 *Tauke*	?	Y	N	Y	Y	Y	N	N
3 *Evans*	?	Y	N	Y	Y	N	Y	Y
4 Smith	Y	Y	N	N	Y	Y	Y	Y
5 Harkin	Y	Y	N	N	Y	N	Y	Y
6 Bedell	Y	Y	N	N	Y	Y	Y	Y
KANSAS								
1 *Roberts*	Y	Y	Y	Y	Y	N	Y	Y
2 Slattery	Y	Y	N	N	Y	?	Y	Y
3 *Winn*	N	Y	Y	Y	Y	Y	N	Y
4 Glickman	Y	Y	N	N	Y	Y	Y	Y
5 *Whittaker*	Y	Y	Y	Y	Y	Y	Y	Y
KENTUCKY								
1 Hubbard	?	Y	N	N	Y	Y	Y	Y
2 Natcher	Y	Y	N	N	Y	Y	Y	Y
3 Mazzoli	Y	Y	N	N	Y	Y	Y	Y
4 *Snyder*	N	Y	Y	Y	Y	Y	N	N
5 *Rogers*	Y	?	N	Y	Y	Y	Y	Y
6 *Hopkins*	Y	Y	N	Y	Y	Y	N	N
7 Perkins	Y	Y	N	N	Y	Y	Y	Y
LOUISIANA								
1 *Livingston*	N	Y	Y	Y	N	Y	N	Y
2 Boggs	Y	Y	N	N	Y	Y	Y	Y
3 Tauzin	Y	Y	N	N	Y	Y	Y	Y
4 Roemer	N	Y	Y	N	Y	N	N	N
5 Huckaby	Y	?	N	N	Y	Y	Y	Y
6 *Moore*	N	Y	Y	Y	N	Y	Y	N
7 Breaux	Y	?	N	N	Y	Y	Y	Y
8 Long	Y	Y	N	N	?	Y	Y	Y
MAINE								
1 *McKernan*	Y	Y	N	Y	Y	Y	N	N
2 *Snowe*	Y	Y	N	Y	Y	Y	N	N
MARYLAND								
1 Dyson	Y	Y	N	N	Y	Y	Y	Y
2 Long	Y	Y	N	N	Y	?	?	?
3 Mikulski	Y	Y	N	N	Y	Y	Y	Y
4 *Holt*	N	Y	N	Y	?	Y	N	N
5 Hoyer	Y	Y	N	N	Y	Y	Y	Y
6 Byron	Y	Y	N	N	Y	?	?	?
7 Mitchell	Y	Y	N	N	Y	N	Y	Y
8 Barnes	Y	Y	N	N	Y	Y	Y	Y
MASSACHUSETTS								
1 *Conte*	Y	Y	N	Y	Y	Y	Y	Y
2 Boland	Y	Y	N	N	Y	Y	Y	Y
3 Early	Y	Y	N	N	Y	Y	Y	Y
4 Frank	Y	Y	N	N	Y	Y	Y	Y
5 Shannon	Y	Y	N	N	Y	Y	Y	Y
6 Mavroules	Y	Y	N	N	Y	Y	Y	Y
7 Markey	Y	Y	N	N	Y	Y	Y	Y
8 O'Neill								
9 Moakley	Y	Y	N	N	Y	Y	Y	Y
10 Studds	Y	Y	N	N	Y	Y	Y	Y
11 Donnelly	?	Y	N	N	Y	?	Y	?
MICHIGAN								
1 Conyers	?	Y	N	N	?	Y	Y	N
2 *Pursell*	Y	?	N	Y	Y	Y	Y	Y
3 Wolpe	Y	Y	N	N	Y	Y	Y	Y
4 *Siljander*	N	Y	Y	Y	N	Y	N	N
5 *Sawyer*	Y	Y	N	Y	?	Y	N	N
6 Carr	Y	Y	N	N	Y	Y	Y	Y
7 Kildee	Y	Y	N	N	Y	Y	Y	Y
8 Traxler	Y	Y	N	N	Y	Y	Y	Y
9 *Vander Jagt*	N	Y	N	Y	Y	Y	N	N
10 Albosta	Y	Y	N	N	Y	N	Y	Y
11 *Davis*	Y	Y	N	Y	?	Y	Y	Y
12 Bonior	Y	Y	N	N	Y	Y	Y	Y
13 Crockett	?	?	N	N	?	?	Y	Y
14 Hertel	Y	Y	N	N	Y	Y	Y	Y
15 Ford	Y	Y	N	N	+	?	Y	Y
16 Dingell	?	Y	N	N	Y	Y	Y	Y
17 Levin	Y	Y	N	N	Y	P	Y	Y
18 *Broomfield*	Y	Y	Y	Y	Y	Y	N	N
MINNESOTA								
1 Penny	Y	Y	N	N	Y	Y	Y	Y
2 *Weber*	Y	Y	Y	Y	N	Y	N	N
3 *Frenzel*	N	Y	N	Y	N	Y	N	N
4 Vento	Y	Y	N	N	Y	Y	Y	Y
5 Sabo	Y	Y	N	N	Y	N	Y	Y
6 Sikorski	+	Y	N	N	Y	Y	Y	Y

	8	9	10	11	12	13	14	15
7 *Stangeland*	Y	?	Y	Y	Y	?	?	?
8 Oberstar	Y	Y	N	N	Y	P	Y	Y
MISSISSIPPI								
1 Whitten	Y	Y	N	N	Y	Y	Y	Y
2 *Franklin*	N	Y	Y	Y	N	Y	N	Y
3 Montgomery	N	Y	N	N	Y	Y	Y	Y
4 Dowdy	Y	Y	N	N	Y	?	Y	Y
5 *Lott*	N	Y	Y	Y	Y	Y	N	Y
MISSOURI								
1 Clay	?	Y	N	N	Y	N	Y	Y
2 Young	Y	?	N	N	Y	Y	Y	Y
3 Gephardt	?	?	N	N	Y	Y	Y	Y
4 Skelton	Y	Y	N	N	Y	?	Y	Y
5 Wheat	Y	Y	N	N	Y	Y	Y	Y
6 *Coleman*	Y	Y	N	Y	Y	Y	Y	Y
7 *Taylor*	N	Y	N	Y	Y	Y	Y	Y
8 *Emerson*	Y	Y	Y	Y	Y	?	Y	Y
9 Volkmer	Y	Y	N	N	Y	Y	Y	Y
MONTANA								
1 Williams	Y	Y	N	N	Y	?	Y	Y
2 *Marlenee*	N	Y	Y	Y	Y	Y	Y	N
NEBRASKA								
1 *Bereuter*	Y	Y	N	N	Y	Y	N	N
2 *Daub*	N	Y	N	Y	Y	Y	N	Y
3 *Smith*	N	Y	N	Y	Y	Y	Y	Y
NEVADA								
1 Reid	Y	Y	N	N	Y	Y	Y	Y
2 *Vucanovich*	N	Y	Y	Y	N	Y	N	Y
NEW HAMPSHIRE								
1 D'Amours	Y	Y	?	N	Y	Y	Y	Y
2 *Gregg*	N	Y	Y	Y	Y	Y	N	N
NEW JERSEY								
1 Florio	Y	Y	N	N	Y	Y	Y	Y
2 Hughes	Y	Y	N	N	Y	Y	N	N
3 Howard	Y	Y	N	N	Y	Y	Y	Y
4 *Smith*	Y	Y	N	Y	Y	Y	Y	Y
5 *Roukema*	N	Y	N	Y	Y	Y	Y	Y
6 Dwyer	Y	Y	N	N	Y	Y	Y	Y
7 *Rinaldo*	Y	Y	N	N	Y	Y	Y	Y
8 Roe	Y	Y	N	N	Y	Y	Y	Y
9 Torricelli	Y	Y	N	N	Y	Y	Y	Y
10 Rodino	Y	Y	N	N	Y	Y	Y	Y
11 Minish	Y	Y	N	N	Y	Y	Y	Y
12 *Courter*	Y	Y	N	N	Y	Y	N	N
13 *Forsythe*	?	?	?	?	?	N	?	?
14 Guarini	#	Y	N	N	Y	Y	Y	Y
NEW MEXICO								
1 *Lujan*	Y	Y	Y	Y	Y	Y	N	N
2 *Skeen*	N	Y	Y	Y	Y	Y	N	N
3 Richardson	Y	Y	N	N	Y	Y	Y	Y
NEW YORK								
1 *Carney*	N	Y	Y	Y	N	Y	N	N
2 Downey	Y	Y	N	N	Y	Y	Y	Y
3 Mrazek	Y	Y	N	N	Y	Y	Y	Y
4 *Lent*	Y	Y	N	Y	Y	Y	N	Y
5 *McGrath*	Y	Y	N	Y	Y	Y	Y	Y
6 Addabbo	Y	Y	N	N	Y	Y	Y	?
7 Ackerman*		Y	N	N	Y	Y	Y	?
8 Scheuer	Y	?	N	N	?	Y	Y	Y
9 Ferraro	Y	Y	N	N	Y	?	Y	Y
10 Schumer	Y	Y	N	N	Y	Y	Y	Y
11 Towns	Y	?	?	?	?	Y	Y	Y
12 Owens	?	?	N	N	Y	Y	Y	Y
13 Solarz	?	Y	N	N	Y	Y	Y	Y
14 *Molinari*	N	Y	Y	?	Y	Y	N	N
15 *Green*	Y	Y	N	Y	Y	Y	Y	Y
16 Rangel	Y	Y	N	N	Y	Y	Y	Y
17 Weiss	Y	Y	N	N	Y	Y	Y	Y
18 Garcia	Y	Y	N	N	Y	Y	Y	Y
19 Biaggi	Y	Y	N	N	Y	Y	Y	Y
20 Ottinger	Y	Y	N	N	Y	P	Y	Y
21 *Fish*	Y	Y	N	Y	Y	Y	N	Y
22 *Gilman*	Y	Y	N	N	Y	+	-	-
23 Stratton	Y	Y	N	N	Y	Y	?	Y
24 *Solomon*	N	Y	Y	Y	Y	N	N	N
25 *Boehlert*	Y	Y	N	N	Y	Y	Y	Y
26 *Martin*	Y	Y	N	Y	Y	?	N	Y
27 *Wortley*	Y	Y	Y	Y	?	Y	Y	Y
28 McHugh	Y	Y	N	N	Y	Y	Y	Y
29 *Horton*	Y	Y	N	N	?	Y	N	N
30 *Conable*	N	Y	Y	Y	N	Y	Y	Y
31 *Kemp*	N	Y	Y	Y	N	Y	Y	Y
32 LaFalce	Y	Y	N	N	Y	Y	Y	Y
33 Nowak	Y	Y	?	?	?	?	Y	Y
34 Lundine	Y	Y	N	N	Y	?	Y	Y

	8	9	10	11	12	13	14	15
NORTH CAROLINA								
1 Jones	?	Y	N	N	Y	?	Y	Y
2 Valentine	Y	Y	N	N	Y	Y	Y	Y
3 Whitley	Y	Y	N	N	Y	?	Y	Y
4 Andrews	Y	?	N	N	Y	Y	Y	Y
5 Neal	?	?	?	?	?	?	?	?
6 Britt	Y	Y	N	N	Y	Y	Y	Y
7 Rose	Y	Y	N	N	Y	Y	Y	Y
8 Hefner	Y	Y	N	N	Y	Y	Y	Y
9 *Martin*	N	Y	Y	Y	Y	Y	N	Y
10 *Broyhill*	N	Y	Y	Y	N	Y	N	Y
11 Clarke	Y	Y	N	N	Y	Y	Y	Y
NORTH DAKOTA								
AL Dorgan	Y	Y	N	N	Y	Y	Y	Y
OHIO								
1 Luken	Y	Y	N	N	Y	Y	Y	Y
2 *Gradison*	Y	Y	Y	Y	N	Y	N	Y
3 Hall	Y	Y	N	?	Y	Y	Y	Y
4 *Oxley*	Y	Y	N	Y	N	Y	N	N
5 *Latta*	N	Y	Y	Y	N	Y	N	N
6 *McEwen*	Y	Y	Y	Y	Y	Y	N	N
7 *DeWine*	N	Y	Y	Y	N	Y	N	N
8 *Kindness*	Y	Y	N	Y	N	Y	N	N
9 Kaptur	Y	Y	N	N	Y	Y	Y	Y
10 *Miller*	N	Y	Y	Y	N	?	N	N
11 Eckart	Y	Y	N	N	Y	Y	Y	Y
12 *Kasich*	N	Y	Y	Y	Y	Y	N	N
13 Pease	Y	Y	N	N	Y	Y	Y	Y
14 Seiberling	Y	Y	N	N	Y	Y	Y	Y
15 *Wylie*	Y	Y	N	N	Y	Y	Y	Y
16 *Regula*	Y	Y	N	Y	Y	Y	Y	Y
17 *Williams*	?	Y	N	Y	Y	Y	Y	Y
18 Applegate	Y	Y	N	N	Y	?	Y	?
19 Feighan	?	Y	N	N	Y	Y	Y	Y
20 Oakar	Y	Y	N	N	Y	?	Y	N
21 Stokes	Y	?	N	N	Y	Y	Y	Y
OKLAHOMA								
1 Jones	Y	Y	N	N	Y	Y	Y	Y
2 Synar	Y	Y	N	N	Y	Y	Y	Y
3 Watkins	Y	?	N	N	Y	Y	Y	Y
4 McCurdy	Y	Y	N	N	Y	Y	Y	Y
5 *Edwards*	N	Y	Y	Y	N	Y	N	N
6 English	Y	Y	N	N	Y	Y	Y	Y
OREGON								
1 AuCoin	Y	Y	N	N	Y	Y	Y	Y
2 *Smith, B.*	N	Y	Y	?	N	Y	N	N
3 Wyden	Y	Y	N	N	Y	Y	Y	Y
4 Weaver	Y	Y	N	?	?	?	?	?
5 *Smith, D.*	?	?	?	?	?	?	?	?
PENNSYLVANIA								
1 Foglietta	Y	Y	N	N	Y	Y	Y	Y
2 Gray	Y	Y	N	N	Y	Y	Y	Y
3 Borski	Y	Y	N	N	Y	Y	Y	Y
4 Kolter	Y	Y	N	N	Y	Y	Y	Y
5 *Schulze*	Y	?	Y	Y	Y	Y	N	Y
6 Yatron	Y	Y	N	N	Y	Y	Y	Y
7 Edgar	Y	Y	N	N	?	?	Y	Y
8 Kostmayer	Y	Y	N	N	Y	Y	Y	Y
9 *Shuster*	N	Y	Y	Y	N	Y	N	N
10 *McDade*	Y	Y	N	N	Y	Y	Y	Y
11 Harrison	Y	Y	N	N	Y	Y	Y	Y
12 Murtha	?	?	N	N	Y	Y	Y	Y
13 *Coughlin*	Y	Y	N	Y	Y	N	Y	Y
14 Coyne	Y	Y	N	N	Y	Y	Y	Y
15 *Ritter*	N	Y	Y	N	Y	?	N	N
16 *Walker*	N	Y	Y	Y	Y	N	N	N
17 *Gekas*	N	Y	Y	Y	Y	?	N	N
18 Walgren	?	Y	N	N	Y	?	Y	Y
19 *Goodling*	Y	Y	N	Y	Y	N	N	Y
20 Gaydos	Y	Y	N	N	Y	Y	Y	Y
21 *Ridge*	Y	?	?	?	Y	?	N	N
22 Murphy	Y	Y	N	N	Y	Y	Y	Y
23 *Clinger*	Y	Y	N	Y	Y	Y	Y	Y
RHODE ISLAND								
1 St Germain	Y	Y	N	N	Y	P	Y	Y
2 *Schneider*	?	Y	N	N	Y	Y	Y	Y
SOUTH CAROLINA								
1 *Hartnett*	N	Y	Y	Y	N	Y	N	N
2 *Spence*	Y	Y	N	Y	Y	Y	N	N
3 Derrick	?	Y	N	N	Y	Y	Y	Y
4 *Campbell*	?	Y	Y	Y	Y	Y	N	N
5 Spratt	Y	?	N	N	Y	Y	Y	?
6 Tallon	Y	?	N	N	Y	Y	Y	Y
SOUTH DAKOTA								
AL Daschle	Y	Y	N	N	Y	Y	Y	Y

	8	9	10	11	12	13	14	15
TENNESSEE								
1 *Quillen*	N	Y	N	N	Y	Y	Y	Y
2 *Duncan*	Y	Y	N	N	Y	Y	Y	Y
3 Bouquard	Y	Y	N	N	Y	Y	Y	Y
4 Cooper	Y	Y	N	N	Y	Y	Y	Y
5 Boner	Y	Y	N	N	Y	Y	Y	Y
6 Gore	Y	Y	N	N	Y	Y	Y	Y
7 *Sundquist*	N	Y	Y	Y	N	Y	Y	N
8 Jones	#	?	?	X	?	?	?	?
9 Ford	Y	Y	N	N	Y	Y	Y	Y
TEXAS								
1 Hall, S.	Y	Y	N	N	Y	Y	Y	Y
2 Wilson	Y	Y	N	N	Y	?	Y	Y
3 *Bartlett*	N	Y	Y	Y	N	Y	N	N
4 Hall, R.	Y	Y	N	N	Y	Y	Y	Y
5 Bryant	Y	Y	N	N	Y	Y	Y	Y
6 *Gramm***	N	Y	Y	Y	N	?	N	N
7 *Archer*	N	Y	Y	Y	N	Y	N	N
8 *Fields*	N	Y	Y	Y	N	Y	N	N
9 Brooks	Y	Y	N	N	Y	?	Y	Y
10 Pickle	Y	Y	N	N	Y	Y	Y	Y
11 Leath	N	Y	Y	N	Y	Y	Y	N
12 Wright	Y	Y	N	N	Y	Y	Y	Y
13 Hightower	Y	Y	N	N	Y	Y	Y	Y
14 Patman	Y	Y	N	N	Y	Y	Y	Y
15 de la Garza	Y	Y	N	N	Y	Y	Y	Y
16 Coleman	Y	Y	N	N	Y	Y	Y	Y
17 Stenholm	N	Y	N	N	Y	Y	N	N
18 Leland	Y	Y	N	N	Y	Y	Y	Y
19 Hance	Y	Y	N	N	Y	Y	Y	Y
20 Gonzalez	?	Y	N	N	Y	Y	Y	N
21 *Loeffler*	N	Y	Y	Y	N	Y	N	N
22 *Paul*	N	Y	Y	Y	N	Y	N	N
23 Kazen	Y	Y	N	N	Y	Y	Y	N
24 Frost	Y	Y	N	N	Y	Y	Y	Y
25 Andrews	Y	Y	N	N	Y	Y	Y	?
26 Vandergriff	Y	Y	N	N	Y	?	Y	Y
27 Ortiz	Y	Y	N	N	Y	?	Y	Y
UTAH								
1 *Hansen*	?	?	?	?	?	?	?	?
2 *Marriott*	Y	Y	N	N	Y	Y	N	N
3 *Nielson*	N	Y	Y	Y	N	Y	N	Y
VERMONT								
AL *Jeffords*	Y	Y	?	?	?	?	N	N
VIRGINIA								
1 *Bateman*	Y	Y	Y	Y	Y	Y	N	Y
2 *Whitehurst*	Y	Y	Y	Y	Y	Y	Y	Y
3 *Bliley*	N	Y	Y	Y	Y	Y	N	Y
4 Sisisky	Y	Y	N	N	Y	Y	Y	?
5 Daniel	Y	Y	Y	Y	Y	Y	Y	Y
6 Olin	Y	Y	N	N	Y	?	Y	?
7 *Robinson*	N	Y	Y	Y	N	Y	N	N
8 *Parris*	N	Y	Y	Y	Y	Y	Y	N
9 Boucher	Y	?	?	N	Y	Y	Y	Y
10 *Wolf*	Y	?	Y	Y	Y	Y	N	Y
WASHINGTON								
1 *Pritchard*	Y	Y	N	Y	Y	Y	N	Y
2 Swift	Y	Y	N	N	Y	Y	Y	Y
3 Bonker	Y	Y	N	N	Y	Y	Y	Y
4 *Morrison*	?	?	?	?	?	?	?	?
5 Foley	Y	Y	N	N	Y	Y	Y	Y
6 Dicks	Y	Y	N	N	Y	Y	Y	Y
7 Lowry	Y	Y	N	N	Y	Y	Y	Y
8 *Chandler*	Y	Y	N	Y	Y	Y	N	Y
WEST VIRGINIA								
1 Mollohan	Y	Y	N	N	Y	Y	Y	Y
2 Staggers	Y	Y	N	N	Y	Y	Y	Y
3 Wise	Y	Y	N	N	Y	Y	Y	Y
4 Rahall	Y	?	X	N	Y	Y	Y	Y
WISCONSIN								
1 Aspin	Y	Y	N	N	Y	Y	Y	Y
2 Kastenmeier	Y	?	N	N	Y	Y	Y	Y
3 *Gunderson*	N	Y	N	Y	Y	Y	N	N
4 Zablocki	Y	Y	N	N	Y	Y	Y	Y
5 Moody	+	Y	N	N	?	Y	Y	Y
6 *Petri*	Y	Y	N	Y	Y	Y	N	N
7 Obey	?	Y	N	N	Y	Y	Y	Y
8 *Roth*	Y	Y	N	Y	Y	Y	N	N
9 *Sensenbrenner*	N	Y	Y	Y	N	Y	N	N
WYOMING								
AL *Cheney*	N	Y	Y	Y	N	Y	N	N

Southern states - Ala., Ark., Fla., Ga., Ky., La., Miss., N.C., Okla., S.C., Tenn., Texas, Va.

16. HR 1718. Emergency Supplemental Appropriations, Fiscal 1983/Jobs. Edgar, D-Pa., amendment to require that 75 percent of the discretionary funding under the bill be spent in areas of high unemployment. Adopted 335-83: R 119-38; D 216-45 (ND 159-14, SD 57-31), March 3, 1983.

17. HR 1718. Emergency Supplemental Appropriations, Fiscal 1983/Jobs. Conte, R-Mass., motion to recommit the bill to the Appropriations Committee with instructions to substitute a GOP alternative that would shift some funds from public works to social programs. Motion rejected 158-256: R 139-20; D 19-236 (ND 15-154, SD 4-82), March 3, 1983.

18. HR 1718. Emergency Supplemental Appropriations, Fiscal 1983/Jobs. Passage of the bill to appropriate $4,898,150,000 for emergency jobs and recession relief and $5,033,000,000 for advances to the unemployment trust fund in fiscal 1983. Passed 324-95: R 77-82; D 247-13 (ND 172-1, SD 75-12), March 3, 1983. The president had proposed a $4.3 billion jobs plan and had requested $5,033,000,000 for advances to the unemployment trust fund.

19. HR 1296. Payment-in-Kind Tax Act. Rostenkowski, D-Ill., motion to suspend the rules and pass the bill to permit farmers to defer income tax payments on commodities received from the 1983 Payment-in-Kind (PIK) program, and to permit land idled under the 1983 program to continue to qualify as active farm land for estate tax purposes. Motion agreed to 401-1: R 155-0; D 246-1 (ND 162-1, SD 84-0), March 8, 1983. A two-thirds majority of those present and voting (268 in this case) is required for passage under suspension of the rules. A "yea" was a vote supporting the president's position.

20. HR 1900. Social Security Act Amendments. Pickle, D-Texas, amendment to gradually raise the normal Social Security retirement age from 65 to 67 after the year 2000, and to delete provisions of the Ways and Means Committee bill that would reduce initial benefit levels beginning in the year 2000 and raise payroll taxes beginning in the year 2015. Adopted 228-202: R 152-14; D 76-188 (ND 23-152, SD 53-36), March 9, 1983. A "yea" was a vote supporting the president's position. (This amendment subsequently was adopted after the House rose from the Committee of the Whole, *see vote 22, below.*)

21. HR 1900. Social Security Act Amendments. Pepper, D-Fla., amendment to substitute a .53 percentage point increase in the payroll tax rate paid by both employers and employees, effective in the year 2010, for the long-term benefit cuts and payroll tax increases in the committee bill. Rejected 132-296: R 1-165; D 131-131 (ND 111-63, SD 20-68), March 9, 1983. A "nay" was a vote supporting the president's position.

22. HR 1900. Social Security Act Amendments. Pickle, D-Texas, amendment to gradually raise the normal Social Security retirement age from 65 to 67 after the year 2000, and to delete provisions that would reduce initial benefit levels beginning in the year 2000 and raise payroll taxes beginning in the year 2015. Adopted 230-200: R 152-14; D 78-186 (ND 23-152, SD 55-34), March 9, 1983. A "yea" was a vote supporting the president's position. (This amendment previously had been adopted in the Committee of the Whole, *see vote 20, above.*)

23. HR 1900. Social Security Act Amendments. Passage of the bill to revise the Social Security retirement program to assure the solvency of the Social Security trust funds; to change the way hospitals are reimbursed for treating Medicare patients; to extend the federal emergency unemployment benefits program; and to revise benefits under the Supplemental Security Income program for the aged, blind and disabled poor. Passed 282-148: R 97-69; D 185-79 (ND 113-62, SD 72-17), March 9, 1983. A "yea" was a vote supporting the president's position.

KEY

- Y Voted for (yea).
- # Paired for.
- + Announced for.
- N Voted against (nay).
- X Paired against.
- - Announced against.
- P Voted "present".
- C Voted "present" to avoid possible conflict of interest.
- ? Did not vote or otherwise make a position known.

Democrats **Republicans**

	16	17	18	19	20	21	22	23
ALABAMA								
1 Edwards	Y	N	Y	Y	Y	N	Y	Y
2 *Dickinson*	N	Y	N	?	Y	N	Y	Y
3 Nichols	Y	N	Y	N	N	N	Y	Y
4 Bevill	Y	N	Y	Y	N	N	N	Y
5 Flippo	Y	N	Y	Y	Y	N	Y	Y
6 Erdreich	Y	N	Y	N	N	N	N	Y
7 Shelby	Y	N	Y	Y	Y	N	Y	Y
ALASKA								
AL *Young*	N	Y	Y	Y	Y	N	Y	N
ARIZONA								
1 *McCain*	N	Y	Y	Y	Y	N	Y	Y
2 Udall	Y	N	Y	Y	Y	N	N	Y
3 *Stump*	N	Y	N	Y	N	Y	N	N
4 *Rudd*	N	N	N	Y	N	Y	N	N
5 McNulty	Y	N	Y	Y	Y	Y	Y	Y
ARKANSAS								
1 Alexander	Y	N	Y	Y	Y	Y	Y	Y
2 *Bethune*	Y	N	Y	Y	N	Y	N	Y
3 *Hammerschmidt*	Y	N	N	Y	N	N	Y	Y
4 Anthony	Y	N	Y	Y	Y	N	Y	Y
CALIFORNIA								
1 Bosco	Y	N	Y	Y	N	N	N	N
2 *Chappie*	N	Y	N	Y	Y	N	Y	Y
3 Matsui	Y	N	Y	Y	Y	N	N	Y
4 Fazio	Y	N	Y	Y	N	N	N	Y
5 Burton	Y	N	Y	N	Y	N	Y	N
6 Boxer	Y	N	Y	Y	N	Y	N	Y
7 Miller	Y	N	Y	?	N	N	N	N
8 Dellums	Y	Y	Y	N	Y	N	N	N
9 Stark	Y	N	Y	Y	Y	Y	Y	Y
10 Edwards	Y	N	Y	Y	N	Y	N	Y
11 Lantos	Y	N	Y	Y	N	N	N	N
12 *Zschau*	Y	Y	Y	Y	Y	Y	N	Y
13 Mineta	Y	N	Y	Y	N	Y	N	Y
14 *Shumway*	Y	Y	N	Y	N	Y	N	N
15 Coelho	Y	N	Y	N	N	Y	N	Y
16 Panetta	Y	N	Y	Y	N	N	N	N
17 *Pashayan*	N	Y	Y	Y	N	Y	N	Y
18 Lehman	Y	N	Y	N	N	N	N	Y
19 *Lagomarsino*	Y	Y	Y	Y	N	N	Y	Y
20 *Thomas*	N	Y	N	Y	N	Y	N	Y
21 *Fiedler*	Y	Y	N	Y	N	Y	N	N
22 *Moorhead*	?	?	X	Y	Y	N	Y	N
23 Beilenson	Y	N	N	Y	N	Y	N	Y
24 Waxman	?	?	?	Y	N	Y	N	N
25 Roybal	Y	?	Y	N	Y	N	Y	Y
26 Berman	Y	N	Y	N	Y	N	N	Y
27 Levine	Y	N	Y	Y	N	Y	N	Y
28 Dixon	Y	N	Y	Y	N	N	N	N
29 Hawkins	?	?	#	Y	N	N	N	N
30 Martinez	Y	N	Y	Y	N	N	N	N
31 Dymally	Y	N	Y	Y	N	N	N	N
32 Anderson	Y	N	Y	N	N	Y	N	Y
33 *Dreier*	N	Y	N	Y	Y	N	Y	N
34 Torres	Y	N	Y	Y	N	N	N	Y
35 *Lewis*	Y	Y	Y	Y	Y	N	Y	N
36 Brown	Y	N	Y	?	N	Y	N	N
37 *McCandless*	Y	Y	N	Y	N	Y	N	Y
38 Patterson	Y	?	Y	Y	N	Y	N	Y
39 *Dannemeyer*	N	Y	N	Y	N	Y	N	N
40 *Badham*	N	Y	N	Y	Y	N	Y	Y
41 *Lowery*	?	?	X	Y	Y	N	Y	N
42 *Lungren*	Y	Y	N	Y	Y	N	Y	N

	16	17	18	19	20	21	22	23
43 *Packard*	Y	Y	Y	Y	Y	N	Y	Y
44 Bates	Y	N	Y	Y	N	N	N	Y
45 *Hunter*	Y	Y	N	Y	Y	N	Y	N
COLORADO								
1 Schroeder	Y	Y	Y	Y	N	N	N	N
2 Wirth	Y	N	Y	N	N	N	N	Y
3 Kogovsek	Y	N	Y	N	Y	N	N	Y
4 *Brown*	Y	Y	N	Y	Y	Y	N	Y
5 *Kramer*	Y	N	Y	Y	N	Y	N	Y
6 Vacancy								
CONNECTICUT								
1 Kennelly	Y	N	Y	Y	N	Y	N	Y
2 Gejdenson	Y	N	Y	N	Y	N	N	N
3 Morrison	Y	N	Y	Y	N	Y	N	N
4 *McKinney*	Y	Y	Y	Y	N	Y	N	Y
5 Ratchford	Y	N	Y	N	Y	N	N	N
6 *Johnson*	Y	Y	Y	Y	N	N	N	Y
DELAWARE								
AL Carper	Y	N	Y	Y	N	Y	N	Y
FLORIDA								
1 Hutto	N	N	Y	Y	N	Y	N	Y
2 Fuqua	Y	N	Y	Y	N	Y	N	Y
3 Bennett	Y	N	Y	Y	N	Y	N	Y
4 Chappell	N	N	N	Y	N	Y	N	Y
5 *McCollum*	Y	Y	N	?	N	Y	N	Y
6 MacKay	N	N	Y	Y	N	Y	N	Y
7 Gibbons	Y	N	Y	Y	N	Y	N	Y
8 *Young*	N	Y	N	Y	N	Y	N	N
9 *Bilirakis*	Y	Y	Y	?	Y	N	Y	N
10 Ireland	Y	Y	Y	Y	N	Y	N	Y
11 Nelson	N	N	Y	Y	N	Y	N	Y
12 *Lewis*	N	Y	Y	N	Y	N	N	Y
13 *Mack*	Y	Y	N	Y	Y	N	Y	N
14 Mica	N	N	Y	Y	N	Y	N	Y
15 *Shaw*	N	Y	N	?	Y	N	Y	Y
16 Smith	Y	N	Y	Y	N	Y	N	Y
17 Lehman	Y	N	Y	N	Y	N	N	Y
18 Pepper	Y	N	Y	Y	N	Y	N	Y
19 Fascell	Y	N	Y	N	Y	N	Y	N
GEORGIA								
1 Thomas	N	N	Y	Y	N	Y	N	Y
2 Hatcher	N	N	Y	Y	N	Y	N	Y
3 Ray	N	N	Y	Y	N	Y	N	Y
4 Levitas	N	N	N	Y	N	Y	N	Y
5 Fowler	N	N	Y	?	N	N	N	Y
6 *Gingrich*	Y	Y	N	Y	N	Y	N	N
7 McDonald	N	?	#	Y	Y	N	Y	N
8 Rowland	N	?	#	Y	Y	N	Y	N
9 Jenkins	N	N	N	?	Y	N	Y	Y
10 Barnard	N	N	N	?	Y	N	Y	Y
HAWAII								
1 Heftel	Y	N	Y	Y	N	Y	N	Y
2 Akaka	Y	N	Y	Y	N	N	N	N
IDAHO								
1 *Craig*	Y	Y	N	Y	N	Y	N	N
2 *Hansen*	N	Y	N	Y	N	Y	N	N
ILLINOIS								
1 Washington	?	?	?	?	?	?	?	X
2 Savage	Y	N	Y	N	Y	N	N	N
3 Russo	Y	N	Y	Y	Y	N	Y	Y
4 *O'Brien*	Y	Y	Y	Y	Y	N	Y	Y
5 Lipinski	Y	N	Y	Y	N	N	N	Y
6 *Hyde*	Y	Y	Y	Y	N	Y	N	Y
7 Collins	Y	N	?	Y	N	N	N	N
8 Rostenkowski	Y	N	Y	Y	N	N	N	Y
9 Yates	Y	N	Y	N	N	N	N	N
10 *Porter*	Y	Y	N	Y	N	Y	N	N
11 Annunzio	Y	N	Y	?	Y	Y	Y	Y
12 *Crane, P.*	Y	Y	N	?	N	Y	N	N
13 *Erlenborn*	Y	Y	Y	Y	Y	N	Y	Y
14 Corcoran	+	+	-	Y	Y	N	Y	N
15 *Madigan*	Y	Y	Y	Y	N	Y	N	Y
16 *Martin*	Y	N	Y	Y	N	Y	N	N
17 Evans	Y	N	Y	N	Y	N	N	Y
18 *Michel*	Y	Y	Y	?	N	Y	N	Y
19 *Crane, D.*	Y	Y	N	Y	N	Y	N	N
20 Durbin	Y	N	Y	N	Y	N	N	Y
21 Price	Y	N	Y	Y	N	Y	N	Y
22 Simon	Y	N	Y	?	N	Y	N	Y
INDIANA								
1 Hall	Y	N	Y	N	Y	N	N	N
2 Sharp	Y	N	Y	Y	Y	N	N	N
3 *Hiler*	Y	Y	N	Y	Y	N	Y	Y
4 *Coats*	Y	Y	Y	Y	N	Y	N	Y
5 *Hillis*	Y	Y	Y	Y	Y	N	Y	Y

ND - Northern Democrats   SD - Southern Democrats

	16	17	18	19	20	21	22	23
6 ***Burton***	Y	Y	N	Y	Y	N	Y	Y
7 ***Myers***	N	Y	Y	Y	Y	N	Y	N
8 McCloskey	Y	N	Y	Y	N	Y	N	Y
9 Hamilton	Y	Y	Y	Y	Y	N	Y	Y
10 Jacobs	Y	Y	Y	Y	N	Y	N	Y
IOWA								
1 ***Leach***	Y	Y	Y	Y	Y	N	Y	Y
2 ***Tauke***	Y	Y	N	Y	Y	N	Y	N
3 ***Evans***	Y	N	Y	Y	Y	N	Y	Y
4 Smith	N	N	Y	Y	N	N	N	Y
5 Harkin	Y	Y	Y	Y	N	N	N	Y
6 Bedell	Y	Y	Y	Y	Y	N	Y	Y
KANSAS								
1 ***Roberts***	N	N	N	Y	Y	N	Y	N
2 Slattery	N	N	Y	Y	Y	N	Y	Y
3 ***Winn***	Y	Y	Y	Y	Y	N	Y	Y
4 Glickman	N	N	Y	Y	Y	N	Y	Y
5 ***Whittaker***	Y	N	Y	Y	Y	N	Y	Y
KENTUCKY								
1 Hubbard	Y	N	Y	Y	N	N	N	N
2 Natcher	Y	N	Y	Y	N	N	N	Y
3 Mazzoli	Y	N	Y	Y	Y	N	Y	Y
4 ***Snyder***	Y	Y	N	Y	N	N	N	Y
5 ***Rogers***	N	Y	Y	Y	Y	N	Y	Y
6 ***Hopkins***	Y	Y	N	Y	Y	N	Y	Y
7 Perkins	Y	N	Y	Y	N	Y	N	N
LOUISIANA								
1 ***Livingston***	N	N	N	Y	Y	N	Y	Y
2 Boggs	Y	N	Y	Y	N	Y	Y	Y
3 Tauzin	N	N	Y	Y	Y	N	Y	Y
4 Roemer	N	N	N	Y	Y	N	Y	N
5 Huckaby	Y	N	Y	Y	N	Y	N	Y
6 ***Moore***	Y	N	N	Y	Y	N	Y	Y
7 Breaux	N	N	Y	Y	Y	N	Y	Y
8 Long	Y	N	Y	Y	N	N	N	Y
MAINE								
1 ***McKernan***	Y	Y	Y	Y	Y	N	Y	N
2 ***Snowe***	Y	Y	Y	Y	Y	N	Y	N
MARYLAND								
1 Dyson	N	N	Y	Y	N	Y	N	Y
2 Long	Y	N	Y	Y	N	N	N	Y
3 Mikulski	Y	N	Y	Y	N	Y	N	Y
4 ***Holt***	Y	Y	N	Y	Y	N	Y	N
5 Hoyer	Y	N	Y	Y	N	Y	N	N
6 Byron	Y	N	Y	Y	Y	N	Y	N
7 Mitchell	Y	N	Y	?	N	Y	N	N
8 Barnes	Y	N	Y	Y	N	Y	N	N
MASSACHUSETTS								
1 ***Conte***	Y	Y	N	Y	N	N	N	Y
2 Boland	Y	N	Y	?	?	?	?	?
3 Early	N	N	Y	Y	N	Y	N	N
4 Frank	Y	N	Y	Y	N	Y	N	N
5 Shannon	N	N	Y	Y	N	Y	N	Y
6 Mavroules	Y	N	Y	Y	N	Y	N	N
7 Markey	Y	N	Y	Y	N	Y	N	N
8 O'Neill								
9 Moakley	Y	N	Y	Y	N	Y	N	Y
10 Studds	Y	Y	Y	Y	Y	N	Y	N
11 Donnelly	Y	N	Y	Y	N	Y	N	N
MICHIGAN								
1 Conyers	Y	N	Y	?	N	Y	N	N
2 ***Pursell***	Y	Y	Y	Y	Y	N	Y	Y
3 Wolpe	Y	N	Y	Y	N	N	N	Y
4 ***Siljander***	Y	Y	Y	Y	Y	N	Y	N
5 ***Sawyer***	Y	Y	Y	Y	Y	N	Y	Y
6 Carr	Y	N	Y	Y	N	Y	N	Y
7 Kildee	Y	N	Y	Y	N	Y	N	N
8 Traxler	Y	N	Y	Y	N	Y	N	N
9 ***Vander Jagt***	Y	Y	Y	Y	Y	N	Y	Y
10 Albosta	Y	N	Y	Y	N	N	N	Y
11 ***Davis***	Y	Y	Y	Y	N	N	N	Y
12 Bonior	Y	N	Y	Y	N	Y	N	Y
13 Crockett	Y	Y	Y	Y	N	Y	N	N
14 Hertel	Y	N	Y	Y	N	Y	N	N
15 Ford	Y	N	Y	Y	N	Y	N	Y
16 Dingell	Y	N	Y	Y	N	?	N	Y
17 Levin	Y	N	Y	Y	N	Y	N	Y
18 ***Broomfield***	Y	Y	Y	Y	Y	N	Y	N
MINNESOTA								
1 Penny	N	N	Y	Y	Y	N	Y	Y
2 ***Weber***	N	Y	N	Y	Y	N	Y	Y
3 ***Frenzel***	N	Y	N	Y	Y	N	Y	Y
4 Vento	Y	Y	Y	Y	N	Y	N	Y
5 Sabo	Y	N	Y	Y	N	N	N	Y
6 Sikorski	Y	N	Y	Y	N	N	N	Y

	16	17	18	19	20	21	22	23
7 ***Stangeland***	Y	Y	N	Y	Y	N	Y	N
8 Oberstar	Y	N	Y	Y	N	Y	N	Y
MISSISSIPPI								
1 Whitten	Y	N	Y	Y	N	N	N	N
2 ***Franklin***	Y	N	Y	Y	Y	N	Y	N
3 Montgomery	Y	N	N	Y	Y	N	Y	Y
4 Dowdy	Y	N	Y	Y	N	Y	N	N
5 ***Lott***	Y	N	N	?	Y	N	Y	N
MISSOURI								
1 Clay	Y	N	Y	Y	N	Y	N	N
2 Young	Y	N	Y	Y	N	Y	N	N
3 Gephardt	Y	N	Y	Y	N	N	N	Y
4 Skelton	Y	N	Y	Y	N	Y	N	Y
5 Wheat	Y	N	Y	Y	N	Y	N	Y
6 ***Coleman***	Y	N	Y	Y	Y	N	Y	Y
7 ***Taylor***	Y	Y	N	Y	Y	N	Y	Y
8 ***Emerson***	Y	N	Y	Y	Y	N	Y	Y
9 Volkmer	N	N	Y	Y	N	N	N	Y
MONTANA								
1 Williams	Y	N	Y	Y	N	N	N	N
2 ***Marlenee***	N	Y	Y	Y	Y	N	Y	N
NEBRASKA								
1 ***Bereuter***	N	Y	N	Y	Y	N	Y	N
2 ***Daub***	Y	Y	N	Y	Y	N	Y	Y
3 ***Smith***	N	Y	Y	Y	Y	N	Y	Y
NEVADA								
1 Reid	Y	N	Y	Y	N	Y	N	Y
2 ***Vucanovich***	Y	Y	N	Y	Y	N	Y	Y
NEW HAMPSHIRE								
1 D'Amours	N	Y	Y	Y	N	Y	N	Y
2 ***Gregg***	Y	Y	N	Y	Y	N	Y	Y
NEW JERSEY								
1 Florio	Y	N	Y	Y	N	N	N	N
2 Hughes	Y	N	Y	Y	N	N	N	Y
3 Howard	Y	N	Y	Y	N	Y	N	N
4 ***Smith***	Y	Y	Y	Y	Y	N	Y	N
5 ***Roukema***	N	Y	Y	Y	Y	N	Y	Y
6 Dwyer	Y	N	Y	?	N	Y	N	Y
7 ***Rinaldo***	N	N	Y	Y	N	N	N	N
8 Roe	Y	N	Y	Y	N	Y	N	N
9 Torricelli	N	N	Y	Y	N	Y	N	N
10 Rodino	Y	N	Y	Y	N	Y	N	Y
11 Minish	Y	N	Y	Y	N	Y	N	N
12 ***Courter***	Y	Y	N	Y	Y	N	Y	Y
13 ***Forsythe***	Y	Y	Y	Y	Y	N	Y	Y
14 Guarini	Y	N	Y	Y	N	Y	N	Y
NEW MEXICO								
1 ***Lujan***	N	Y	Y	Y	Y	N	Y	Y
2 ***Skeen***	N	Y	N	Y	Y	N	Y	Y
3 Richardson	Y	N	Y	Y	N	Y	N	Y
NEW YORK								
1 ***Carney***	N	N	N	Y	Y	N	Y	N
2 Downey	N	N	Y	Y	Y	N	Y	Y
3 Mrazek	N	N	Y	Y	N	N	N	Y
4 ***Lent***	Y	Y	N	Y	Y	N	Y	N
5 ***McGrath***	Y	Y	N	Y	Y	N	Y	N
6 Addabbo	Y	N	Y	Y	N	Y	N	N
7 Ackerman	Y	N	Y	Y	N	Y	N	N
8 Scheuer	Y	N	Y	Y	N	Y	N	Y
9 Ferraro	Y	N	Y	Y	N	Y	N	Y
10 Schumer	Y	N	Y	Y	N	Y	N	Y
11 Towns	Y	N	Y	Y	N	Y	N	N
12 Owens	Y	?	Y	Y	N	Y	N	N
13 Solarz	Y	N	Y	Y	N	Y	N	Y
14 ***Molinari***	Y	Y	N	Y	N	N	N	N
15 ***Green***	Y	Y	Y	Y	Y	N	Y	Y
16 Rangel	Y	N	Y	Y	N	Y	N	Y
17 Weiss	Y	N	Y	Y	N	Y	N	N
18 Garcia	Y	N	Y	Y	N	Y	N	Y
19 Biaggi	Y	N	Y	Y	N	N	N	Y
20 Ottinger	Y	Y	Y	Y	N	Y	N	Y
21 ***Fish***	Y	Y	Y	Y	Y	N	Y	Y
22 ***Gilman***	Y	Y	Y	Y	N	N	N	N
23 Stratton	Y	N	Y	Y	N	Y	Y	Y
24 ***Solomon***	?	Y	N	Y	Y	N	Y	N
25 ***Boehlert***	Y	Y	Y	Y	Y	N	Y	Y
26 ***Martin***	?	Y	Y	Y	Y	N	Y	N
27 ***Wortley***	Y	Y	Y	Y	Y	N	Y	Y
28 McHugh	Y	N	Y	Y	N	N	N	Y
29 ***Horton***	Y	Y	Y	Y	Y	N	Y	N
30 ***Conable***	Y	Y	N	Y	Y	N	Y	Y
31 ***Kemp***	Y	Y	N	Y	Y	N	Y	N
32 LaFalce	Y	N	Y	Y	N	N	N	Y
33 Nowak	Y	N	Y	Y	N	N	N	Y
34 Lundine	Y	N	Y	Y	Y	N	Y	Y

	16	17	18	19	20	21	22	23
NORTH CAROLINA								
1 Jones	Y	?	Y	Y	Y	N	Y	Y
2 Valentine	N	N	Y	Y	Y	N	Y	Y
3 Whitley	N	N	Y	Y	Y	N	Y	Y
4 Andrews	Y	N	Y	Y	N	Y	N	Y
5 Neal	?	?	?	+	?	?	?	#
6 Britt	Y	N	Y	Y	N	N	N	Y
7 Rose	N	N	Y	Y	N	Y	N	Y
8 Hefner	Y	N	Y	Y	Y	N	Y	Y
9 ***Martin***	?	?	?	Y	Y	N	Y	Y
10 ***Broyhill***	Y	Y	N	Y	Y	N	Y	Y
11 Clarke	Y	N	Y	Y	N	Y	Y	Y
NORTH DAKOTA								
AL Dorgan	N	N	Y	Y	N	N	N	Y
OHIO								
1 Luken	Y	N	Y	Y	N	N	N	Y
2 ***Gradison***	Y	Y	Y	Y	Y	N	Y	Y
3 Hall	Y	N	Y	Y	N	Y	N	N
4 ***Oxley***	Y	Y	N	Y	Y	N	Y	Y
5 ***Latta***	Y	Y	N	Y	Y	N	Y	Y
6 ***McEwen***	Y	Y	Y	Y	Y	N	Y	N
7 ***DeWine***	Y	Y	N	Y	Y	N	Y	N
8 ***Kindness***	Y	N	Y	Y	Y	N	Y	N
9 Kaptur	Y	N	Y	?	N	Y	N	Y
10 ***Miller***	Y	Y	Y	Y	N	N	N	Y
11 Eckart	Y	N	Y	Y	N	N	N	Y
12 ***Kasich***	Y	Y	Y	Y	Y	N	Y	Y
13 Pease	Y	N	Y	Y	N	N	N	Y
14 Seiberling	Y	Y	Y	Y	N	Y	N	Y
15 ***Wylie***	Y	Y	Y	Y	Y	N	Y	Y
16 ***Regula***	Y	Y	Y	Y	N	N	N	Y
17 ***Williams***	Y	N	Y	?	N	N	N	Y
18 Applegate	Y	N	Y	Y	N	N	N	Y
19 Feighan	Y	N	Y	Y	N	N	N	N
20 Oakar	Y	N	Y	Y	N	Y	N	N
21 Stokes	Y	N	Y	Y	N	Y	N	N
OKLAHOMA								
1 Jones	N	N	Y	Y	Y	N	Y	Y
2 Synar	N	N	Y	Y	Y	N	Y	Y
3 Watkins	Y	N	Y	Y	Y	N	Y	Y
4 McCurdy	N	N	Y	Y	Y	N	Y	Y
5 ***Edwards***	Y	N	N	?	Y	N	Y	Y
6 English	N	N	Y	Y	Y	N	Y	Y
OREGON								
1 AuCoin	Y	N	Y	Y	Y	N	Y	Y
2 ***Smith, B.***	Y	N	Y	Y	Y	N	Y	Y
3 Wyden	Y	N	Y	Y	N	N	N	Y
4 Weaver	?	?	?	?	N	Y	N	Y
5 ***Smith, D.***	?	?	X	Y	Y	N	Y	N
PENNSYLVANIA								
1 Foglietta	Y	N	Y	Y	N	Y	N	Y
2 Gray	Y	N	Y	?	N	Y	N	N
3 Borski	Y	N	Y	Y	N	Y	N	N
4 Kolter	Y	N	Y	Y	N	Y	N	Y
5 ***Schulze***	Y	Y	Y	Y	Y	N	Y	N
6 Yatron	Y	N	Y	Y	N	N	N	Y
7 Edgar	Y	Y	Y	Y	N	N	N	Y
8 Kostmayer	Y	N	Y	Y	N	Y	N	N
9 ***Shuster***	Y	Y	N	Y	Y	N	Y	N
10 ***McDade***	Y	Y	Y	Y	N	N	N	Y
11 Harrison	Y	N	Y	Y	N	Y	N	Y
12 Murtha	Y	N	Y	Y	N	N	N	Y
13 ***Coughlin***	Y	Y	Y	Y	Y	N	Y	Y
14 Coyne	Y	N	Y	Y	N	Y	N	Y
15 ***Ritter***	Y	Y	Y	Y	Y	N	Y	N
16 ***Walker***	Y	Y	N	Y	Y	N	Y	Y
17 ***Gekas***	Y	Y	N	Y	Y	N	Y	N
18 Walgren	Y	Y	Y	Y	N	Y	N	N
19 ***Goodling***	Y	Y	Y	?	N	N	N	N
20 Gaydos	Y	N	Y	Y	N	N	N	N
21 ***Ridge***	Y	Y	Y	Y	Y	N	Y	Y
22 Murphy	Y	N	Y	Y	N	N	N	N
23 ***Clinger***	Y	Y	Y	Y	Y	N	Y	Y
RHODE ISLAND								
1 St Germain	Y	N	Y	?	N	Y	N	N
2 ***Schneider***	Y	Y	Y	Y	N	Y	N	Y
SOUTH CAROLINA								
1 ***Hartnett***	Y	Y	N	Y	Y	N	Y	N
2 ***Spence***	Y	Y	N	Y	Y	N	Y	N
3 Derrick	Y	N	Y	Y	N	N	N	Y
4 ***Campbell***	Y	Y	N	Y	Y	N	Y	Y
5 Spratt	Y	N	Y	Y	N	Y	N	Y
6 Tallon	Y	N	Y	Y	N	Y	N	Y
SOUTH DAKOTA								
AL Daschle	N	N	Y	Y	Y	N	Y	Y

	16	17	18	19	20	21	22	23
TENNESSEE								
1 ***Quillen***	Y	Y	Y	Y	Y	N	Y	Y
2 ***Duncan***	Y	Y	Y	Y	Y	N	Y	Y
3 Bouquard	Y	N	Y	Y	Y	N	Y	Y
4 Cooper	Y	N	Y	Y	Y	?	Y	Y
5 Boner	Y	N	Y	Y	N	N	N	Y
6 Gore	Y	N	Y	Y	N	N	N	Y
7 ***Sundquist***	Y	Y	Y	Y	Y	N	Y	Y
8 Jones	?	?	#	Y	N	N	N	N
9 Ford	Y	N	Y	Y	N	N	N	Y
TEXAS								
1 Hall, S.	Y	N	Y	Y	Y	N	Y	N
2 Wilson	Y	N	Y	?	Y	N	Y	Y
3 ***Bartlett***	N	Y	N	Y	Y	N	Y	Y
4 Hall, R.	Y	N	Y	Y	Y	N	Y	N
5 Bryant	Y	N	Y	Y	N	Y	N	Y
6 ***Gramm***	N	Y	N	Y	Y	N	Y	Y
7 ***Archer***	N	Y	N	Y	Y	N	Y	N
8 ***Fields***	N	Y	Y	Y	Y	N	Y	Y
9 Brooks	Y	N	Y	Y	Y	N	Y	Y
10 Pickle	Y	N	Y	Y	Y	N	Y	Y
11 Leath	N	N	N	Y	Y	N	Y	N
12 Wright	Y	N	Y	Y	Y	N	Y	Y
13 Hightower	N	N	Y	Y	Y	N	Y	Y
14 Patman	N	N	Y	Y	N	N	N	N
15 de la Garza	Y	N	Y	?	Y	N	Y	Y
16 Coleman	Y	N	Y	Y	Y	N	Y	Y
17 Stenholm	N	N	N	Y	Y	N	Y	N
18 Leland	Y	Y	Y	Y	N	Y	N	N
19 Hance	N	N	Y	Y	Y	N	Y	Y
20 Gonzalez	Y	N	Y	Y	N	Y	N	N
21 ***Loeffler***	N	Y	N	Y	Y	N	Y	N
22 ***Paul***	N	Y	N	Y	Y	N	Y	N
23 Kazen	Y	N	Y	Y	Y	N	Y	N
24 Frost	Y	N	Y	Y	N	Y	N	Y
25 Andrews	Y	N	Y	Y	Y	N	Y	Y
26 Vandergriff	Y	N	Y	Y	Y	N	Y	Y
27 Ortiz	Y	N	Y	Y	Y	N	Y	Y
UTAH								
1 ***Hansen***	?	?	?	Y	Y	N	Y	N
2 ***Marriott***	Y	N	Y	Y	Y	N	Y	N
3 ***Nielson***	Y	Y	Y	Y	Y	N	Y	N
VERMONT								
AL ***Jeffords***	Y	Y	Y	Y	Y	N	Y	Y
VIRGINIA								
1 ***Bateman***	N	Y	N	Y	Y	N	Y	Y
2 ***Whitehurst***	Y	Y	N	Y	Y	N	Y	Y
3 ***Bliley***	N	Y	N	Y	Y	N	Y	Y
4 Sisisky	Y	N	Y	Y	N	Y	N	Y
5 Daniel	N	Y	N	Y	Y	N	Y	N
6 Olin	N	N	Y	Y	Y	N	Y	Y
7 ***Robinson***	N	Y	N	Y	Y	N	Y	Y
8 ***Parris***	Y	Y	N	Y	Y	N	Y	N
9 Boucher	Y	N	Y	Y	N	Y	N	N
10 ***Wolf***	Y	Y	N	Y	Y	N	Y	N
WASHINGTON								
1 ***Pritchard***	Y	Y	Y	Y	Y	N	Y	Y
2 Swift	Y	N	Y	Y	N	Y	N	Y
3 Bonker	Y	N	Y	Y	N	Y	N	Y
4 ***Morrison***	?	?	#	?	Y	N	Y	Y
5 Foley	Y	N	Y	Y	N	Y	N	Y
6 Dicks	Y	N	Y	Y	N	N	N	Y
7 Lowry	Y	N	Y	Y	N	Y	N	Y
8 ***Chandler***	Y	Y	Y	Y	Y	N	Y	Y
WEST VIRGINIA								
1 Mollohan	Y	N	Y	Y	N	Y	N	Y
2 Staggers	Y	N	Y	Y	N	Y	N	Y
3 Wise	Y	N	Y	Y	N	Y	N	Y
4 Rahall	Y	N	Y	Y	N	Y	N	Y
WISCONSIN								
1 Aspin	Y	N	Y	Y	N	Y	N	Y
2 Kastenmeier	Y	N	Y	Y	N	N	N	Y
3 ***Gunderson***	Y	Y	Y	Y	Y	N	Y	Y
4 Zablocki	Y	?	Y	Y	N	Y	N	Y
5 Moody	Y	N	Y	Y	N	Y	N	Y
6 ***Petri***	Y	Y	N	Y	Y	N	Y	Y
7 Obey	Y	N	Y	Y	N	Y	N	Y
8 ***Roth***	Y	Y	N	Y	Y	N	Y	N
9 ***Sensenbrenner***	Y	Y	N	Y	Y	N	Y	N
WYOMING								
AL ***Cheney***	Y	Y	N	Y	Y	N	Y	Y

Southern states - Ala., Ark., Fla., Ga., Ky., La., Miss., N.C., Okla., S.C., Tenn., Texas, Va.

24. H J Res 13. Nuclear Freeze. Adoption of the rule (H Res 138) providing for House floor consideration of the joint resolution to call for a mutual and verifiable freeze on and reductions in nuclear weapons. Adopted 372-35: R 136-25; D 236-10 (ND 160-2, SD 76-8), March 16, 1983.

25. H J Res 13. Nuclear Freeze. Lent, R-N.Y., amendment to require that a negotiated nuclear weapons freeze make provision for verification by on-site inspection, as necessary. Adopted 426-0: R 164-0; D 262-0 (ND 175-0, SD 87-0), March 16, 1983.

26. H J Res 13. Nuclear Freeze. Siljander, R-Mich., amendment to give nuclear weapons reductions an equal priority with a weapons freeze as an objective of arms control negotiations. Rejected 209-215: R 152-11; D 57-204 (ND 8-167, SD 49-37), March 16, 1983.

27. H J Res 13. Nuclear Freeze. Zablocki, D-Wis., motion to limit debate on the Stratton, D-N.Y., amendment stating that nothing in the joint resolution would prevent modernization of U.S. nuclear forces. Motion agreed to 232-173: R 6-150; D 226-23 (ND 152-15, SD 74-8), March 16, 1983.

28. H J Res 13. Nuclear Freeze. Zablocki, D-Wis., amendment to the Stratton, D-N.Y., amendment, stating that, consistent with the overriding goal of a nuclear weapons freeze, nothing in the joint resolution would prevent maintenance of U.S. nuclear forces. Adopted 226-195: R 22-139; D 204-56 (ND 169-6, SD 35-50), March 16, 1983. (The Stratton amendment would have stated that nothing in the joint resolution would prevent modernization of U.S. nuclear forces.)

29. H J Res 13. Nuclear Freeze. Gingrich, R-Ga., motion to strike the enacting clause of the joint resolution to call for a mutual and verifiable freeze on and reductions in nuclear weapons, thus killing the resolution. Motion rejected 172-249: R 139-26; D 33-223 (ND 5-168, SD 28-55), March 16, 1983.

30. H J Res 13. Nuclear Freeze. Zablocki, D-Wis., motion to limit debate on all amendments to the resolving clause of the joint resolution to call for a mutual and verifiable freeze on and reductions in nuclear weapons. Motion rejected 199-209: R 0-159; D 199-50 (ND 151-15, SD 48-35), March 16, 1983.

KEY

Y Voted for (yea).
Paired for.
+ Announced for.
N Voted against (nay).
X Paired against.
- Announced against.
P Voted "present".
C Voted "present" to avoid possible conflict of interest.
? Did not vote or otherwise make a position known.

———

Democrats   *Republicans*

	24	25	26	27	28	29	30
ALABAMA							
1 *Edwards*	Y	Y	Y	N	N	Y	?
2 *Dickinson*	Y	Y	Y	N	N	Y	N
3 Nichols	N	Y	Y	Y	N	Y	N
4 Bevill	Y	Y	Y	Y	N	Y	Y
5 Flippo	Y	.Y	Y	Y	N	Y	Y
6 Erdreich	Y	Y	Y	Y	N	Y	N
7 Shelby	Y	Y	Y	Y	N	Y	N
ALASKA							
AL *Young*	Y	?	Y	N	N	Y	N
ARIZONA							
1 *McCain*	Y	Y	Y	?	?	?	?
2 Udall	Y	Y	N	Y	Y	N	Y
3 *Stump*	N	Y	N	N	N	Y	N
4 *Rudd*	N	Y	Y	N	N	Y	N
5 McNulty	Y	Y	?	Y	Y	N	Y
ARKANSAS							
1 Alexander	Y	Y	N	Y	Y	?	Y
2 *Bethune*	Y	?	Y	N	N	Y	N
3 *Hammerschmidt*	Y	Y	Y	N	N	Y	N
4 Anthony	Y	Y	N	Y	N	Y	Y
CALIFORNIA							
1 Bosco	Y	Y	N	Y	Y	N	Y
2 *Chappie*	Y	Y	Y	?	N	Y	?
3 Matsui	Y	Y	N	Y	Y	N	Y
4 Fazio	?	Y	N	Y	Y	N	Y
5 Burton	Y	Y	N	Y	Y	N	Y
6 Boxer	Y	Y	N	Y	Y	N	Y
7 Miller	Y	Y	N	P	N	N	Y
8 Dellums	?	Y	N	Y	N	N	Y
9 Stark	?	Y	N	Y	N	N	Y
10 Edwards	Y	Y	N	N	N	N	N
11 Lantos	Y	Y	N	Y	Y	N	Y
12 *Zschau*	Y	Y	Y	N	N	Y	N
13 Mineta	Y	Y	N	N	N	N	N
14 *Shumway*	Y	Y	Y	N	N	Y	N
15 Coelho	Y	Y	N	Y	Y	N	Y
16 Panetta	Y	Y	N	Y	Y	N	Y
17 *Pashayan*	Y	Y	Y	N	N	Y	N
18 Lehman	Y	Y	N	Y	Y	N	Y
19 *Lagomarsino*	Y	Y	Y	N	N	Y	N
20 *Thomas*	Y	Y	Y	N	N	Y	N
21 *Fiedler*	Y	Y	Y	N	N	Y	N
22 *Moorhead*	Y	Y	Y	N	N	Y	N
23 Beilenson	?	Y	N	Y	N	N	N
24 Waxman	Y	Y	N	Y	N	Y	?
25 Roybal	Y	Y	N	Y	N	N	Y
26 Berman	Y	Y	N	?	Y	N	?
27 Levine	Y	Y	N	Y	Y	N	Y
28 Dixon	Y	Y	N	?	Y	N	?
29 Hawkins	Y	Y	N	Y	N	N	Y
30 Martinez	Y	Y	N	?	?	?	Y
31 Dymally	Y	Y	N	Y	N	N	Y
32 Anderson	Y	Y	N	Y	Y	N	Y
33 *Dreier*	N	Y	N	Y	N	Y	N
34 Torres	Y	Y	N	Y	N	Y	Y
35 *Lewis*	Y	Y	Y	?	N	Y	?
36 Brown	Y	Y	N	Y	N	N	Y
37 *McCandless*	Y	Y	Y	N	N	Y	N
38 Patterson	Y	Y	N	Y	N	Y	N
39 *Dannemeyer*	Y	Y	Y	N	N	Y	N
40 *Badham*	N	Y	Y	N	N	Y	N
41 *Lowery*	Y	Y	Y	N	N	Y	N
42 *Lungren*	Y	Y	Y	N	N	Y	N

	24	25	26	27	28	29	30
43 *Packard*	Y	Y	Y	N	N	Y	N
44 Bates	Y	Y	N	Y	Y	N	Y
45 *Hunter*	N	Y	Y	N	N	Y	N
COLORADO							
1 Schroeder	Y	Y	N	Y	Y	N	Y
2 Wirth	Y	Y	N	Y	Y	N	Y
3 Kogovsek	Y	Y	N	Y	Y	N	Y
4 *Brown*	Y	Y	Y	N	N	N	N
5 *Kramer*	N	Y	Y	N	N	Y	N
6 Vacancy							
CONNECTICUT							
1 Kennelly	Y	Y	N	Y	Y	N	Y
2 Gejdenson	Y	Y	N	Y	Y	N	Y
3 Morrison	Y	Y	N	Y	Y	N	Y
4 *McKinney*	Y	Y	N	Y	Y	N	?
5 Ratchford	Y	Y	N	Y	Y	N	Y
6 *Johnson*	Y	Y	Y	N	N	Y	N
DELAWARE							
AL Carper	Y	Y	N	Y	Y	N	Y
FLORIDA							
1 Hutto	N	Y	Y	Y	N	Y	N
2 Fuqua	Y	Y	Y	Y	Y	N	Y
3 Bennett	Y	Y	Y	N	N	N	N
4 Chappell	Y	Y	Y	N	N	?	?
5 *McCollum*	Y	Y	Y	N	N	Y	N
6 MacKay	Y	Y	Y	Y	Y	N	Y
7 Gibbons	Y	N	Y	Y	N	N	Y
8 *Young*	?	Y	N	N	N	Y	N
9 *Bilirakis*	?	Y	N	N	N	Y	N
10 Ireland	Y	Y	Y	N	N	Y	N
11 Nelson	Y	Y	Y	N	N	Y	N
12 *Lewis*	Y	Y	N	N	N	Y	N
13 *Mack*	Y	Y	N	N	N	Y	N
14 Mica	Y	Y	N	Y	Y	N	Y
15 *Shaw*	Y	Y	N	N	N	Y	N
16 Smith	?	Y	N	Y	Y	N	Y
17 Lehman	Y	Y	N	Y	Y	N	?
18 Pepper	Y	Y	N	Y	N	N	Y
19 Fascell	Y	Y	N	Y	Y	N	Y
GEORGIA							
1 Thomas	Y	Y	Y	N	N	N	N
2 Hatcher	Y	Y	Y	N	N	N	N
3 Ray	Y	Y	Y	N	N	N	N
4 Levitas	Y	Y	Y	N	N	N	N
5 Fowler	Y	Y	N	Y	N	N	Y
6 *Gingrich*	N	Y	?	N	N	Y	N
7 McDonald	N	Y	N	N	N	Y	N
8 Rowland	Y	Y	Y	N	N	Y	N
9 Jenkins	Y	Y	Y	N	N	N	N
10 Barnard	N	Y	Y	Y	N	Y	N
HAWAII							
1 Heftel	Y	Y	N	Y	Y	N	Y
2 Akaka	Y	Y	N	Y	Y	N	Y
IDAHO							
1 *Craig*	Y	Y	Y	N	N	N	N
2 *Hansen*	N	Y	N	N	N	Y	N
ILLINOIS							
1 Washington	?	?	?	?	?	?	?
2 Savage	?	Y	N	Y	N	N	Y
3 Russo	Y	Y	N	Y	Y	N	Y
4 *O'Brien*	Y	Y	N	N	N	N	N
5 Lipinski	Y	Y	Y	Y	N	N	Y
6 *Hyde*	Y	Y	Y	N	N	Y	N
7 Collins	Y	Y	N	?	Y	N	?
8 Rostenkowski	Y	Y	N	Y	Y	N	Y
9 Yates	Y	Y	N	Y	Y	N	Y
10 *Porter*	Y	Y	Y	N	N	Y	N
11 Annunzio	Y	Y	N	Y	Y	N	Y
12 *Crane, P.*	N	Y	N	N	N	Y	N
13 *Erlenborn*	Y	Y	Y	N	N	Y	N
14 *Corcoran*	Y	Y	Y	N	N	Y	N
15 *Madigan*	Y	Y	Y	?	N	Y	?
16 *Martin*	Y	Y	Y	N	N	Y	N
17 Evans	Y	Y	N	Y	N	N	Y
18 *Michel*	Y	Y	N	N	N	Y	N
19 *Crane, D.*	N	Y	N	N	N	Y	N
20 Durbin	Y	Y	N	Y	Y	N	Y
21 Price	N	Y	Y	Y	N	Y	N
22 Simon	Y	Y	N	Y	Y	N	Y
INDIANA							
1 Hall	Y	Y	N	Y	Y	N	Y
2 Sharp	Y	Y	N	Y	Y	N	Y
3 *Hiler*	Y	Y	Y	N	N	Y	N
4 *Coats*	Y	Y	Y	N	N	Y	N
5 Hillis	Y	Y	Y	N	N	Y	N

ND - Northern Democrats   SD - Southern Democrats

Corresponding to Congressional Record Votes 27, 28, 29, 30, 31, 32, 33

	24	25	26	27	28	29	30
6 ***Burton***	Y	Y	Y	N	N	Y	N
7 ***Myers***	Y	Y	Y	Y	N	Y	N
8 McCloskey	Y	Y	N	Y	Y	N	Y
9 Hamilton	Y	Y	N	Y	Y	N	Y
10 Jacobs	Y	Y	N	N	Y	N	N
IOWA							
1 ***Leach***	Y	Y	Y	N	Y	N	N
2 ***Tauke***	Y	Y	Y	N	Y	N	N
3 ***Evans***	Y	Y	N	N	Y	N	N
4 Smith	Y	Y	N	Y	Y	N	Y
5 Harkin	Y	Y	N	Y	Y	N	Y
6 Bedell	Y	Y	N	Y	Y	N	Y
KANSAS							
1 ***Roberts***	Y	Y	Y	N	N	Y	N
2 Slattery	Y	Y	N	Y	Y	N	Y
3 ***Winn***	Y	Y	Y	N	N	Y	N
4 Glickman	Y	Y	N	Y	Y	N	N
5 ***Whittaker***	Y	Y	Y	N	N	Y	N
KENTUCKY							
1 Hubbard	Y	Y	Y	Y	N	Y	N
2 Natcher	Y	Y	N	Y	Y	N	Y
3 Mazzoli	Y	Y	N	Y	Y	N	Y
4 ***Snyder***	Y	Y	Y	N	N	Y	N
5 ***Rogers***	Y	Y	Y	?	N	Y	N
6 ***Hopkins***	Y	Y	Y	N	N	Y	N
7 Perkins	Y	Y	N	Y	Y	N	Y
LOUISIANA							
1 ***Livingston***	?	Y	Y	N	N	Y	N
2 Boggs	Y	Y	N	?	Y	N	Y
3 Tauzin	Y	Y	Y	Y	N	Y	?
4 Roemer	Y	Y	Y	Y	N	Y	N
5 Huckaby	Y	Y	Y	Y	N	Y	Y
6 ***Moore***	Y	Y	Y	N	N	Y	N
7 Breaux	Y	Y	Y	?	N	Y	N
8 Long	Y	Y	N	?	Y	N	Y
MAINE							
1 ***McKernan***	Y	Y	N	N	Y	N	N
2 ***Snowe***	Y	Y	N	N	Y	N	N
MARYLAND							
1 Dyson	Y	Y	Y	N	N	Y	N
2 Long	Y	Y	N	Y	Y	N	Y
3 Mikulski	?	Y	N	Y	Y	N	Y
4 ***Holt***	N	Y	Y	N	N	Y	N
5 Hoyer	Y	Y	N	Y	Y	N	Y
6 Byron	Y	Y	Y	N	N	Y	N
7 Mitchell	Y	Y	N	Y	Y	N	Y
8 Barnes	Y	Y	N	Y	Y	N	Y
MASSACHUSETTS							
1 ***Conte***	Y	Y	N	N	Y	N	N
2 Boland	Y	Y	N	Y	Y	N	Y
3 Early	Y	Y	N	Y	Y	N	Y
4 Frank	Y	Y	N	Y	Y	N	Y
5 Shannon	Y	Y	N	Y	Y	N	Y
6 Mavroules	Y	Y	N	Y	Y	N	Y
7 Markey	Y	Y	N	Y	Y	N	Y
8 O'Neill							
9 Moakley	Y	Y	N	Y	Y	N	Y
10 Studds	Y	Y	N	Y	Y	N	Y
11 Donnelly	Y	Y	N	Y	Y	N	Y
MICHIGAN							
1 Conyers	Y	Y	N	Y	Y	N	Y
2 ***Pursell***	Y	Y	Y	N	Y	Y	N
3 Wolpe	Y	Y	N	Y	Y	N	Y
4 ***Siljander***	Y	Y	Y	N	N	Y	N
5 ***Sawyer***	Y	Y	Y	N	N	Y	N
6 Carr	Y	Y	N	Y	Y	N	Y
7 Kildee	Y	Y	N	Y	Y	N	Y
8 Traxler	Y	Y	N	Y	Y	N	Y
9 ***Vander Jagt***	Y	Y	Y	N	N	Y	N
10 Albosta	Y	Y	N	Y	Y	N	Y
11 ***Davis***	Y	Y	Y	N	N	N	N
12 Bonior	Y	Y	N	Y	Y	?	Y
13 Crockett	?	?	N	Y	Y	N	Y
14 Hertel	Y	Y	N	Y	Y	N	Y
15 Ford	?	Y	N	Y	Y	N	Y
16 Dingell	?	Y	N	Y	Y	N	Y
17 Levin	Y	Y	N	Y	Y	N	Y
18 ***Broomfield***	Y	Y	Y	N	N	Y	N
MINNESOTA							
1 Penny	Y	Y	N	Y	Y	N	Y
2 ***Weber***	Y	Y	Y	N	N	Y	N
3 ***Frenzel***	?	Y	Y	N	N	Y	N
4 Vento	Y	Y	N	Y	Y	N	Y
5 Sabo	Y	Y	N	Y	Y	N	Y
6 Sikorski	Y	Y	N	Y	Y	N	Y

	24	25	26	27	28	29	30
7 ***Stangeland***	Y	Y	Y	N	N	Y	?
8 Oberstar	Y	Y	N	Y	Y	N	Y
MISSISSIPPI							
1 Whitten	Y	Y	N	Y	N	?	Y
2 ***Franklin***	Y	Y	Y	N	N	Y	N
3 Montgomery	N	Y	Y	N	N	Y	N
4 Dowdy	Y	Y	N	Y	Y	N	Y
5 ***Lott***	Y	Y	Y	N	N	Y	N
MISSOURI							
1 Clay	Y	Y	N	?	Y	N	?
2 Young	Y	Y	N	Y	Y	N	Y
3 Gephardt	Y	Y	N	Y	Y	N	Y
4 Skelton	Y	Y	Y	Y	N	Y	N
5 Wheat	Y	Y	N	Y	Y	N	Y
6 ***Coleman***	Y	Y	Y	N	N	Y	N
7 ***Taylor***	Y	Y	Y	N	N	Y	N
8 ***Emerson***	N	Y	Y	N	N	Y	N
9 Volkmer	Y	Y	N	Y	Y	N	Y
MONTANA							
1 Williams	Y	Y	N	N	Y	N	?
2 ***Marlenee***	Y	Y	Y	Y	N	Y	N
NEBRASKA							
1 ***Bereuter***	Y	Y	Y	N	N	Y	N
2 ***Daub***	Y	Y	Y	N	N	Y	N
3 ***Smith***	Y	Y	Y	N	N	Y	N
NEVADA							
1 Reid	Y	Y	N	Y	Y	N	Y
2 ***Vucanovich***	Y	Y	Y	N	N	Y	N
NEW HAMPSHIRE							
1 D'Amours	Y	Y	N	Y	Y	N	Y
2 ***Gregg***	Y	Y	Y	N	N	Y	N
NEW JERSEY							
1 Florio	Y	Y	N	Y	Y	N	Y
2 Hughes	Y	Y	N	Y	Y	N	N
3 Howard	Y	Y	N	Y	Y	N	Y
4 ***Smith***	Y	Y	Y	N	N	N	N
5 ***Roukema***	Y	Y	Y	N	Y	N	N
6 Dwyer	Y	Y	N	Y	Y	N	Y
7 ***Rinaldo***	Y	Y	N	N	Y	N	N
8 Roe	Y	Y	N	Y	Y	Y	Y
9 Torricelli	Y	Y	N	Y	Y	N	Y
10 Rodino	Y	Y	N	Y	Y	N	Y
11 Minish	Y	Y	N	Y	Y	N	Y
12 ***Courter***	Y	Y	Y	N	N	Y	N
13 ***Forsythe***	Y	Y	?	?	?	N	N
14 Guarini	Y	Y	N	Y	Y	N	Y
NEW MEXICO							
1 ***Lujan***	Y	Y	Y	N	N	Y	N
2 ***Skeen***	Y	Y	Y	?	?	Y	N
3 Richardson	Y	Y	N	Y	Y	N	Y
NEW YORK							
1 ***Carney***	Y	Y	Y	N	N	Y	N
2 Downey	Y	Y	N	Y	Y	N	Y
3 Mrazek	Y	Y	N	Y	Y	N	Y
4 ***Lent***	Y	Y	Y	N	N	Y	N
5 ***McGrath***	Y	Y	Y	N	N	Y	N
6 Addabbo	Y	Y	N	Y	Y	N	Y
7 Ackerman	Y	Y	N	Y	Y	N	Y
8 Scheuer	Y	Y	N	Y	Y	N	Y
9 Ferraro	Y	Y	N	Y	Y	N	Y
10 Schumer	Y	Y	N	Y	Y	N	Y
11 Towns	Y	Y	N	Y	Y	N	Y
12 Owens	?	Y	N	Y	Y	N	Y
13 Solarz	Y	Y	N	Y	Y	N	Y
14 ***Molinari***	Y	Y	Y	N	N	Y	N
15 ***Green***	Y	Y	N	N	Y	N	N
16 Rangel	Y	Y	N	?	Y	N	?
17 Weiss	Y	Y	N	N	Y	N	Y
18 Garcia	Y	Y	N	Y	Y	N	Y
19 Biaggi	Y	Y	N	Y	Y	N	Y
20 Ottinger	Y	Y	N	Y	Y	N	Y
21 ***Fish***	Y	Y	Y	N	Y	Y	N
22 ***Gilman***	Y	Y	Y	N	N	Y	N
23 Stratton	N	Y	Y	N	N	Y	N
24 ***Solomon***	N	Y	Y	N	N	Y	N
25 ***Boehlert***	Y	Y	Y	Y	Y	N	N
26 ***Martin***	N	Y	Y	N	N	Y	N
27 ***Wortley***	N	Y	Y	N	N	Y	N
28 McHugh	Y	Y	N	Y	Y	N	N
29 ***Horton***	Y	Y	N	Y	Y	Y	N
30 ***Conable***	Y	Y	Y	N	N	Y	N
31 ***Kemp***	Y	Y	Y	N	N	Y	N
32 LaFalce	Y	Y	N	Y	Y	N	N
33 Nowak	Y	Y	N	Y	Y	N	Y
34 Lundine	Y	Y	N	Y	Y	N	Y

	24	25	26	27	28	29	30
NORTH CAROLINA							
1 Jones	Y	Y	N	Y	N	N	Y
2 Valentine	Y	Y	Y	Y	N	Y	N
3 Whitley	Y	Y	Y	Y	N	Y	N
4 Andrews	P	Y	N	Y	Y	N	Y
5 Neal	?	+	-	?	+	?	?
6 Britt	Y	Y	N	Y	Y	N	N
7 Rose	Y	Y	N	Y	Y	N	Y
8 Hefner	Y	Y	Y	Y	N	N	Y
9 ***Martin***	Y	Y	Y	N	N	Y	N
10 ***Broyhill***	Y	Y	Y	N	N	Y	N
11 Clarke	Y	Y	N	Y	Y	N	Y
NORTH DAKOTA							
AL Dorgan	Y	Y	N	Y	Y	N	Y
OHIO							
1 Luken	Y	Y	N	Y	Y	N	Y
2 ***Gradison***	Y	Y	Y	N	N	Y	N
3 Hall	Y	Y	N	Y	Y	N	?
4 ***Oxley***	Y	Y	Y	N	N	Y	N
5 ***Latta***	Y	Y	Y	N	N	Y	N
6 ***McEwen***	Y	Y	Y	N	N	Y	N
7 ***DeWine***	Y	Y	Y	N	N	Y	N
8 ***Kindness***	N	Y	Y	N	N	Y	N
9 Kaptur	Y	Y	N	Y	Y	N	Y
10 ***Miller***	Y	Y	Y	N	N	Y	N
11 Eckart	Y	Y	N	Y	Y	N	Y
12 ***Kasich***	Y	Y	Y	N	N	Y	N
13 Pease	Y	Y	N	Y	Y	N	Y
14 Seiberling	Y	Y	N	Y	Y	N	Y
15 ***Wylie***	Y	Y	Y	N	N	Y	N
16 ***Regula***	Y	Y	Y	N	N	N	N
17 ***Williams***	Y	Y	N	?	?	Y	N
18 Applegate	Y	Y	Y	?	Y	N	Y
19 Feighan	?	Y	N	Y	Y	N	Y
20 Oakar	Y	Y	N	Y	Y	N	Y
21 Stokes	Y	Y	N	?	Y	N	?
OKLAHOMA							
1 Jones	Y	Y	Y	Y	Y	N	N
2 Synar	Y	Y	N	Y	Y	N	Y
3 Watkins	Y	Y	Y	Y	N	N	N
4 McCurdy	Y	Y	Y	Y	N	N	Y
5 ***Edwards***	Y	Y	Y	N	N	Y	N
6 English	Y	Y	Y	Y	N	N	Y
OREGON							
1 AuCoin	Y	Y	N	Y	Y	N	Y
2 ***Smith, B.***	Y	Y	Y	N	N	Y	N
3 Wyden	Y	Y	N	Y	Y	N	Y
4 Weaver	Y	Y	N	Y	Y	N	?
5 ***Smith, D.***	N	Y	Y	N	N	Y	N
PENNSYLVANIA							
1 Foglietta	Y	Y	N	Y	Y	N	Y
2 Gray	Y	Y	N	Y	Y	N	Y
3 Borski	Y	Y	N	Y	Y	N	Y
4 Kolter	Y	Y	N	Y	Y	N	Y
5 ***Schulze***	Y	Y	Y	N	N	Y	N
6 Yatron	Y	Y	N	Y	Y	N	Y
7 Edgar	Y	Y	N	Y	Y	N	Y
8 Kostmayer	Y	Y	N	N	Y	N	Y
9 ***Shuster***	Y	Y	Y	N	N	Y	N
10 ***McDade***	Y	Y	Y	N	Y	N	N
11 Harrison	Y	Y	N	Y	Y	N	Y
12 Murtha	Y	Y	Y	Y	N	N	Y
13 ***Coughlin***	Y	Y	Y	N	N	N	N
14 Coyne	Y	Y	N	Y	Y	N	Y
15 ***Ritter***	Y	Y	Y	N	N	Y	N
16 ***Walker***	N	Y	Y	N	N	Y	N
17 ***Gekas***	Y	Y	Y	N	N	Y	N
18 Walgren	Y	Y	N	N	Y	N	Y
19 ***Goodling***	Y	Y	Y	N	Y	N	N
20 Gaydos	Y	Y	N	Y	Y	N	?
21 ***Ridge***	Y	Y	Y	N	N	Y	N
22 Murphy	Y	Y	N	Y	Y	N	Y
23 ***Clinger***	Y	Y	Y	N	N	Y	N
RHODE ISLAND							
1 St Germain	Y	Y	N	Y	Y	N	Y
2 ***Schneider***	Y	Y	N	Y	Y	N	N
SOUTH CAROLINA							
1 ***Hartnett***	N	Y	Y	N	N	Y	N
2 ***Spence***	N	Y	Y	N	N	Y	N
3 Derrick	Y	Y	N	Y	Y	N	Y
4 ***Campbell***	Y	Y	Y	N	N	Y	N
5 Spratt	Y	Y	Y	Y	Y	N	N
6 Tallon	Y	Y	N	Y	Y	N	N
SOUTH DAKOTA							
AL Daschle	?	Y	N	Y	Y	N	Y

	24	25	26	27	28	29	30
TENNESSEE							
1 ***Quillen***	Y	Y	Y	?	N	Y	N
2 ***Duncan***	Y	Y	Y	N	N	Y	N
3 Bouquard	Y	Y	Y	N	N	Y	N
4 Cooper	Y	Y	Y	Y	N	N	Y
5 Boner	?	?	?	?	?	?	?
6 Gore	Y	Y	N	Y	Y	N	Y
7 ***Sundquist***	Y	Y	Y	N	N	Y	N
8 Jones	Y	Y	N	Y	N	N	Y
9 Ford	Y	Y	N	Y	?	N	Y
TEXAS							
1 Hall, S.	Y	Y	Y	Y	N	Y	N
2 Wilson	Y	Y	Y	?	N	Y	Y
3 ***Bartlett***	Y	Y	Y	N	N	Y	N
4 Hall, R.	Y	Y	Y	Y	N	Y	N
5 Bryant	+	+	-	+	+	-	+
6 ***Gramm***	N	Y	Y	N	N	Y	N
7 ***Archer***	Y	Y	Y	N	N	Y	N
8 ***Fields***	N	Y	Y	N	N	Y	N
9 Brooks	Y	Y	N	Y	Y	N	Y
10 Pickle	Y	Y	Y	Y	N	N	Y
11 Leath	N	Y	Y	N	N	Y	N
12 Wright	Y	Y	N	Y	Y	N	Y
13 Hightower	Y	Y	Y	Y	N	N	Y
14 Patman	N	Y	Y	N	N	Y	N
15 de la Garza	Y	Y	?	?	?	?	?
16 Coleman	Y	Y	N	Y	Y	N	Y
17 Stenholm	Y	Y	Y	Y	N	Y	N
18 Leland	Y	Y	N	Y	Y	N	Y
19 Hance	?	Y	Y	Y	N	N	Y
20 Gonzalez	Y	Y	N	Y	Y	N	Y
21 ***Loeffler***	Y	Y	Y	N	N	Y	N
22 ***Paul***	N	Y	Y	N	N	Y	N
23 Kazen	Y	Y	Y	Y	N	N	Y
24 Frost	Y	Y	N	Y	Y	N	Y
25 Andrews	Y	Y	Y	Y	N	N	Y
26 Vandergriff	Y	Y	Y	Y	N	Y	N
27 Ortiz	Y	Y	N	Y	N	?	Y
UTAH							
1 ***Hansen***	N	Y	Y	N	N	Y	N
2 ***Marriott***	Y	Y	Y	N	N	Y	N
3 ***Nielson***	Y	Y	Y	N	N	Y	N
VERMONT							
AL ***Jeffords***	Y	Y	N	N	Y	N	N
VIRGINIA							
1 ***Bateman***	Y	Y	Y	N	N	Y	N
2 ***Whitehurst***	Y	Y	Y	N	N	Y	N
3 ***Bliley***	Y	Y	Y	N	N	Y	N
4 Sisisky	Y	Y	Y	Y	N	Y	Y
5 Daniel	N	Y	Y	N	N	Y	N
6 Olin	Y	Y	N	Y	Y	N	N
7 ***Robinson***	Y	Y	Y	N	N	Y	N
8 ***Parris***	Y	Y	?	?	?	Y	N
9 Boucher	Y	Y	N	Y	Y	N	Y
10 ***Wolf***	Y	Y	Y	N	N	Y	N
WASHINGTON							
1 ***Pritchard***	Y	Y	Y	N	Y	Y	N
2 Swift	Y	Y	N	Y	Y	N	Y
3 Bonker	?	Y	N	Y	Y	N	Y
4 ***Morrison***	Y	Y	Y	N	N	Y	N
5 Foley	Y	Y	N	Y	Y	N	Y
6 Dicks	Y	Y	N	Y	Y	N	Y
7 Lowry	Y	Y	N	N	Y	N	Y
8 ***Chandler***	Y	Y	Y	N	N	Y	N
WEST VIRGINIA							
1 Mollohan	?	Y	N	Y	Y	N	Y
2 Staggers	Y	Y	N	Y	Y	N	Y
3 Wise	Y	Y	N	Y	Y	N	Y
4 Rahall	Y	Y	N	N	Y	N	N
WISCONSIN							
1 Aspin	Y	Y	N	Y	Y	N	Y
2 Kastenmeier	Y	Y	N	Y	Y	N	Y
3 ***Gunderson***	Y	Y	Y	N	Y	N	N
4 Zablocki	Y	Y	N	Y	Y	N	Y
5 Moody	Y	Y	N	Y	Y	N	Y
6 ***Petri***	N	Y	Y	N	N	Y	N
7 Obey	Y	Y	N	Y	Y	N	Y
8 ***Roth***	Y	Y	Y	N	N	Y	N
9 ***Sensenbrenner***	Y	Y	Y	N	N	N	N
WYOMING							
AL ***Cheney***	?	Y	Y	N	N	Y	N

Southern states - Ala., Ark., Fla., Ga., Ky., La., Miss., N.C., Okla., S.C., Tenn., Texas, Va.

KEY

Y Voted for (yea).
Paired for.
+ Announced for.
N Voted against (nay).
X Paired against.
- Announced against.
P Voted "present".
C Voted "present" to avoid possible conflict of interest.
? Did not vote or otherwise make a position known.

Democrats *Republicans*

31. HR 1149. Oregon Wilderness. Adoption of the rule (H Res 141) providing for House floor consideration of the bill to designate 1.13 million acres of national forest land in Oregon as federal wilderness. Adopted 234-84: R 28-82; D 206-2 (ND 130-1, SD 76-1), March 21, 1983.

32. HR 1149. Oregon Wilderness. Denny Smith, R-Ore., substitute to designate no wilderness areas, to exempt from judicial review the Second Roadless Area Review and Evaluation (RARE II) environmental impact statement only for the state of Oregon, and to release all non-wilderness lands in Oregon for other uses. Rejected 58-292: R 53-78; D 5-214 (ND 0-141, SD 5-73), March 21, 1983.

33. HR 1149. Oregon Wilderness. Young, R-Alaska, substitute to exclude from wilderness designation any lands in the 2nd and 5th congressional districts of Oregon. Rejected 91-249: R 82-37; D 9-212 (ND 0-141, SD 9-71), March 21, 1983.

34. HR 1149. Oregon Wilderness. Walker, R-Pa., amendment to allow the secretary of agriculture to waive any provision of the bill shown to cause greater unemployment. Rejected 96-240: R 88-27; D 8-213 (ND 1-141, SD 7-72), March 21, 1983.

35. HR 1149. Oregon Wilderness. Passage of the bill to designate 1.13 million acres of national forest land in Oregon as federal wilderness. Passed 252-93: R 33-87; D 219-6 (ND 145-0, SD 74-6), March 21, 1983. A "nay" was a vote supporting the president's position.

36. Procedural Motion. Loeffler, R-Texas, motion to approve the House *Journal* of Monday, March 21. Motion agreed to 348-21: R 132-15; D 216-6 (ND 139-6, SD 77-0), March 22, 1983.

37. H Res 127. House Committee Funding. Adoption of the resolution to authorize $43.2 million for House committees' "investigative" budgets in 1983. Adopted 262-141: R 21-127; D 241-14 (ND 164-5, SD 77-9), March 22, 1983.

38. H Con Res 91. First Budget Resolution, Fiscal 1984. Adoption of the rule (H Res 144) providing for House floor consideration of the first concurrent budget resolution to set budget targets for the fiscal year ending Sept. 30, 1984, as follows: budget authority, $936.6 billion; outlays, $863.6 billion; revenues, $689.1 billion; deficit, $174.5 billion. The resolution also set preliminary goals for fiscal 1985-86, revised budget levels for fiscal 1983 and included reconciliation instructions requiring House committees to recommend legislative savings to meet the budget targets. Adopted 230-187: R 0-157; D 230-30 (ND 164-8, SD 66-22), March 22, 1983.

	31	32	33	34	35	36	37	38
ALABAMA								
1 *Edwards*	N	Y	Y	Y	N	N	Y	N
2 *Dickinson*	N	Y	Y	Y	N	N	?	N
3 Nichols	Y	N	N	Y	N	Y	Y	N
4 Bevill	Y	N	N	N	Y	Y	Y	Y
5 Flippo	Y	N	N	Y	N	Y	Y	Y
6 Erdreich	Y	N	N	N	Y	Y	Y	Y
7 Shelby	Y	?	Y	N	N	Y	Y	N
ALASKA								
AL *Young*	N	Y	Y	Y	N	N	Y	N
ARIZONA								
1 *McCain*	?	Y	?	Y	N	?	N	N
2 Udall	Y	N	N	N	Y	?	Y	Y
3 *Stump*	N	Y	Y	Y	N	N	N	N
4 *Rudd*	N	Y	Y	Y	N	N	N	N
5 McNulty	Y	?	?	N	Y	Y	?	Y
ARKANSAS								
1 Alexander	Y	N	N	N	Y	Y	Y	Y
2 *Bethune*	?	N	?	?	+	?	N	Y
3 *Hammerschmidt*	?	?	?	Y	N	Y	N	N
4 Anthony	Y	N	N	N	Y	Y	Y	Y
CALIFORNIA								
1 Bosco	?	?	?	?	?	Y	Y	Y
2 *Chappie*	?	?	?	?	X	Y	N	N
3 Matsui	Y	N	N	N	Y	Y	Y	Y
4 Fazio	Y	N	N	N	Y	Y	Y	Y
5 Burton	Y	N	N	N	Y	Y	Y	Y
6 Boxer	Y	N	N	N	Y	Y	Y	Y
7 Miller	?	?	?	?	#	Y	Y	Y
8 Dellums	?	?	?	?	#	?	Y	N
9 Stark	Y	N	N	N	Y	Y	Y	Y
10 Edwards	Y	N	N	N	Y	Y	Y	Y
11 Lantos	Y	N	N	N	Y	Y	Y	Y
12 *Zschau*	Y	N	N	Y	Y	Y	N	N
13 Mineta	Y	N	N	N	Y	Y	Y	Y
14 *Shumway*	N	Y	Y	Y	N	N	N	N
15 Coelho	?	N	N	N	Y	Y	Y	Y
16 Panetta	Y	N	N	N	Y	Y	Y	Y
17 *Pashayan*	?	?	?	?	?	?	?	X
18 Lehman	Y	N	N	N	Y	Y	Y	Y
19 *Lagomarsino*	N	N	Y	Y	N	N	N	N
20 *Thomas*	N	N	Y	Y	N	Y	N	N
21 *Fiedler*	N	N	Y	Y	N	N	N	N
22 *Moorhead*	?	N	Y	Y	N	N	N	N
23 Beilenson	Y	N	N	N	Y	Y	Y	Y
24 Waxman	?	N	N	N	Y	Y	Y	Y
25 Roybal	Y	N	N	N	Y	Y	Y	Y
26 Berman	?	?	?	?	?	Y	Y	Y
27 Levine	Y	N	N	N	Y	Y	Y	Y
28 Dixon	Y	N	N	N	Y	Y	Y	Y
29 Hawkins	Y	N	N	N	Y	Y	Y	Y
30 Martinez	Y	N	N	N	Y	Y	Y	Y
31 Dymally	Y	N	N	N	Y	Y	Y	Y
32 Anderson	Y	N	N	N	Y	Y	Y	Y
33 *Dreier*	N	N	Y	Y	N	N	N	N
34 Torres	+	-	-	-	+	Y	Y	Y
35 *Lewis*	Y	N	Y	Y	N	Y	N	N
36 Brown	Y	N	N	N	Y	Y	Y	Y
37 *McCandless*	N	Y	Y	Y	N	Y	N	N
38 Patterson	?	?	?	?	?	?	Y	#
39 *Dannemeyer*	N	Y	Y	Y	N	N	N	N
40 *Badham*	N	Y	Y	Y	N	N	N	N
41 *Lowery*	?	N	Y	Y	N	Y	?	N
42 *Lungren*	N	N	Y	Y	N	Y	N	N

	31	32	33	34	35	36	37	38
43 *Packard*	N	N	N	Y	N	Y	N	N
44 Bates	Y	N	N	N	Y	?	Y	Y
45 *Hunter*	N	Y	Y	Y	N	Y	N	N
COLORADO								
1 Schroeder	Y	N	N	N	Y	N	Y	N
2 Wirth	?	?	?	?	?	Y	Y	Y
3 Kogovsek	?	N	N	N	Y	?	Y	Y
4 *Brown*	Y	N	Y	Y	N	N	N	N
5 *Kramer*	Y	N	Y	Y	N	N	N	N
6 Vacancy								
CONNECTICUT								
1 Kennelly	Y	N	N	N	Y	Y	Y	Y
2 Gejdenson	Y	N	N	N	Y	N	Y	Y
3 Morrison	?	N	N	N	Y	Y	Y	Y
4 *McKinney*	?	N	N	N	Y	?	N	N
5 Ratchford	Y	N	N	N	Y	Y	Y	Y
6 *Johnson*	?	?	?	?	?	Y	N	N
DELAWARE								
AL Carper	Y	N	N	N	Y	Y	Y	Y
FLORIDA								
1 Hutto	Y	N	N	N	Y	Y	Y	N
2 Fuqua	Y	N	N	N	Y	Y	Y	Y
3 Bennett	Y	N	N	N	Y	Y	Y	Y
4 Chappell	Y	N	N	Y	N	Y	Y	Y
5 *McCollum*	?	N	N	Y	N	Y	N	N
6 MacKay	Y	N	N	N	Y	Y	Y	Y
7 Gibbons	Y	N	N	N	Y	Y	Y	Y
8 *Young*	Y	N	N	Y	Y	Y	?	N
9 *Bilirakis*	?	N	Y	N	N	Y	N	N
10 Ireland	Y	N	N	N	Y	N	N	N
11 Nelson	?	?	?	?	#	Y	Y	Y
12 *Lewis*	N	N	N	N	N	N	N	N
13 *Mack*	N	N	Y	Y	N	N	N	N
14 Mica	Y	N	N	N	Y	Y	Y	Y
15 *Shaw*	?	?	?	?	?	Y	N	N
16 Smith	Y	N	N	N	Y	Y	Y	Y
17 Lehman	Y	N	N	N	Y	?	Y	Y
18 Pepper	Y	N	N	N	Y	Y	Y	Y
19 Fascell	Y	N	N	N	Y	?	Y	Y
GEORGIA								
1 Thomas	Y	N	N	N	Y	Y	Y	Y
2 Hatcher	Y	N	N	N	Y	Y	Y	Y
3 Ray	Y	N	N	N	Y	Y	Y	N
4 Levitas	Y	N	N	N	Y	Y	Y	Y
5 Fowler	Y	N	N	N	Y	Y	Y	Y
6 *Gingrich*	N	N	?	N	Y	N	N	N
7 McDonald	N	Y	Y	N	Y	N	N	N
8 Rowland	Y	N	N	N	Y	Y	Y	Y
9 Jenkins	Y	N	N	N	Y	Y	Y	Y
10 Barnard	Y	N	N	N	Y	?	Y	Y
HAWAII								
1 Heftel	?	?	?	?	?	?	Y	Y
2 Akaka	Y	N	N	N	Y	Y	Y	Y
IDAHO								
1 *Craig*	?	?	?	?	?	X	Y	N
2 *Hansen*	N	Y	Y	Y	N	?	N	N
ILLINOIS								
1 Washington	?	?	?	?	?	?	?	?
2 Savage	Y	N	?	Y	?	?	Y	N
3 Russo	?	?	?	?	?	Y	Y	Y
4 *O'Brien*	?	?	?	?	?	?	?	?
5 Lipinski	?	?	?	?	?	Y	Y	Y
6 *Hyde*	?	?	Y	N	N	?	N	N
7 Collins	Y	?	N	N	Y	Y	Y	Y
8 Rostenkowski	?	?	?	?	?	Y	Y	Y
9 Yates	Y	N	N	N	Y	Y	Y	Y
10 *Porter*	Y	N	N	-	+	Y	N	N
11 Annunzio	Y	N	N	N	Y	Y	Y	Y
12 *Crane, P.*	Y	Y	Y	Y	?	X	N	N
13 *Erlenborn*	Y	N	Y	N	Y	N	Y	N
14 *Corcoran*	-	-	+	-	-	+	X	
15 *Madigan*	N	N	Y	Y	N	Y	N	N
16 *Martin*	N	N	Y	Y	N	Y	N	N
17 Evans	Y	N	N	N	Y	Y	Y	Y
18 *Michel*	N	N	?	?	?	Y	N	N
19 *Crane, D.*	?	?	?	?	?	X	N	N
20 Durbin	?	?	?	?	#	Y	Y	Y
21 Price	Y	N	N	N	Y	Y	Y	Y
22 Simon	Y	N	N	N	Y	Y	?	Y
INDIANA								
1 Hall	+	N	N	N	Y	Y	Y	Y
2 Sharp	Y	N	N	N	Y	Y	Y	Y
3 *Hiler*	N	N	Y	N	N	N	N	N
4 *Coats*	N	N	Y	Y	N	N	N	N
5 Hillis	?	?	?	?	?	?	Y	N

ND - Northern Democrats   SD - Southern Democrats

	31 32 33 34 35 36 37 38
6 Burton	N Y Y Y N N N N
7 Myers	N Y Y Y N Y Y N
8 McCloskey	Y N N Y Y Y Y Y
9 Hamilton	Y N N Y Y Y Y N
10 Jacobs	Y N N N Y N N N
IOWA	
1 *Leach*	Y N N Y Y Y N ?
2 *Tauke*	Y N Y ? ? Y N N
3 *Evans*	? ? ? ? # N N N
4 Smith	Y N N Y Y Y Y Y
5 Harkin	? ? N N Y N Y Y
6 Bedell	Y N N N Y Y Y Y
KANSAS	
1 *Roberts*	N N Y Y N Y N N
2 Slattery	Y N ? N Y Y N Y
3 *Winn*	N N Y Y N Y N N
4 Glickman	Y N N N Y N Y N Y
5 *Whittaker*	N N N ? ? Y N N
KENTUCKY	
1 Hubbard	Y N N N Y Y Y Y
2 Natcher	Y N N N Y Y Y Y
3 Mazzoli	Y N N N Y ? Y Y
4 *Snyder*	N Y Y N Y Y N N
5 *Rogers*	N Y Y Y N Y N N
6 *Hopkins*	N Y Y Y N Y N N
7 Perkins	Y N N N Y Y Y Y
LOUISIANA	
1 Livingston	? N ? ? Y Y N N
2 Boggs	Y N N N Y ? ? #
3 Tauzin	Y N N N Y N N N
4 Roemer	Y N N Y Y N Y N
5 Huckaby	Y N Y N Y N N N
6 *Moore*	? ? ? ? ? Y N N
7 Breaux	? ? ? ? ? ? Y N N
8 Long	Y N N N Y Y Y Y
MAINE	
1 *McKernan*	N N N Y Y Y N N
2 *Snowe*	Y N N Y Y Y N N
MARYLAND	
1 Dyson	Y N N N Y ? Y Y
2 Long	Y N N N Y ? Y Y
3 Mikulski	Y N N N Y Y Y Y
4 *Holt*	N Y Y Y N N N N
5 Hoyer	Y N N N Y Y Y Y
6 Byron	Y N N Y Y Y Y Y
7 Mitchell	Y N N N Y N Y Y
8 Barnes	+ - - - + Y Y Y
MASSACHUSETTS	
1 Conte	Y N N N Y Y Y N N
2 Boland	Y N N N Y Y Y Y
3 Early	? N N N Y Y N Y
4 Frank	Y N N N Y Y Y Y
5 Shannon	Y N N N Y Y Y Y
6 Mavroules	Y N N N Y Y Y Y
7 Markey	Y N N N Y Y ? Y
8 O'Neill	
9 Moakley	Y N N N Y Y Y Y
10 Studds	Y N N N Y Y Y Y
11 Donnelly	? ? ? ? ? ? Y Y
MICHIGAN	
1 Conyers	Y N ? N Y Y Y N
2 *Pursell*	? ? ? ? ? ? Y N N
3 Wolpe	Y N N N Y Y Y Y
4 *Siljander*	? ? ? ? ? Y N N
5 Sawyer	N N N N Y N N N
6 Carr	Y N N N Y Y Y Y
7 Kildee	Y N N N Y Y Y Y
8 Traxler	? ? ? ? ? ? Y Y
9 *Vander Jagt*	N N Y N Y N N N
10 Albosta	? ? ? ? ? Y Y Y
11 *Davis*	N N Y N Y N Y N
12 Bonior	Y N N N Y Y Y Y
13 Crockett	Y N N N Y N ? Y
14 Hertel	Y N N N Y Y Y Y
15 Ford	Y N N N Y Y Y Y
16 Dingell	Y N N N Y ? Y Y
17 Levin	Y N N N Y Y Y Y
18 *Broomfield*	N Y Y Y N Y ? N
MINNESOTA	
1 Penny	Y N N N Y Y Y Y
2 *Weber*	Y N N N Y Y Y N
3 *Frenzel*	? N ? N N N N N
4 Vento	Y N N N Y Y Y Y
5 Sabo	Y N N N Y N Y Y
6 Sikorski	Y N N N Y Y Y Y

	31 32 33 34 35 36 37 38
7 *Stangeland*	? Y Y Y N Y Y N
8 Oberstar	Y N N N Y P Y Y
MISSISSIPPI	
1 Whitten	Y N N N Y Y Y N
2 *Franklin*	N Y Y Y N Y N N
3 Montgomery	Y Y Y N N Y Y N
4 Dowdy	Y N N N Y Y Y Y
5 *Lott*	N Y Y Y N Y N N
MISSOURI	
1 Clay	Y N N N Y ? Y Y
2 Young	Y N N N Y Y Y N
3 Gephardt	Y N N N Y Y Y Y
4 Skelton	Y N N N Y Y Y N
5 Wheat	Y N N ? Y ? Y Y
6 *Coleman*	? N N N Y Y Y N N
7 *Taylor*	N Y Y Y N Y N N
8 *Emerson*	? ? ? ? ? N N N
9 *Volkmer*	Y N N N Y Y Y Y
MONTANA	
1 Williams	Y N N ? Y ? Y Y
2 *Marlenee*	N Y Y Y N Y Y N
NEBRASKA	
1 *Bereuter*	? ? ? ? ? ? N N
2 *Daub*	? Y Y Y N N N N
3 *Smith*	Y N Y N Y Y N
NEVADA	
1 Reid	Y N N N Y Y Y Y
2 *Vucanovich*	N Y Y Y N Y N N
NEW HAMPSHIRE	
1 *D'Amours*	Y N N Y Y Y Y
2 *Gregg*	N N Y N Y N Y N
NEW JERSEY	
1 Florio	? N N N Y Y Y Y
2 Hughes	Y N N N Y Y Y Y
3 Howard	Y N N N Y Y Y Y
4 *Smith*	? N N N Y Y N Y
5 *Roukema*	? ? ? # Y Y N N
6 Dwyer	Y N N N Y Y Y Y
7 *Rinaldo*	Y N ? ? Y Y Y Y
8 Roe	Y N N N Y Y Y Y
9 Torricelli	Y N N N Y Y Y Y
10 Rodino	? N ? ? ? Y Y Y
11 Minish	Y N N N Y Y Y Y
12 *Courter*	? ? ? ? ? Y N Y
13 *Forsythe*	N ? ? ? ? ? ? X
14 Guarini	Y N N N Y Y Y Y
NEW MEXICO	
1 Lujan	Y N Y N Y N N N
2 *Skeen*	N Y Y Y N Y N N
3 Richardson	? ? - - + Y Y Y
NEW YORK	
1 *Carney*	Y Y ? ? N Y Y N
2 Downey	? ? ? ? ? ? ? #
3 Mrazek	Y N N N Y Y Y Y
4 *Lent*	Y N N N Y N N N
5 *McGrath*	N N N - + Y N N
6 Addabbo	Y N N ? Y Y Y Y
7 Ackerman	Y N N N Y ? Y Y
8 Scheuer	Y N N N Y Y Y Y
9 Ferraro	Y N N N Y Y Y Y
10 Schumer	Y N N N Y Y Y Y
11 Towns	? N N N Y Y Y Y
12 Owens	? N N N Y Y Y Y
13 Solarz	Y N N N Y P Y Y
14 *Molinari*	? ? ? ? ? Y Y N
15 *Green*	Y N ? N Y Y N N
16 Rangel	Y N N N Y Y Y ?
17 Weiss	? ? N N Y Y Y Y
18 Garcia	? ? ? ? ? Y Y Y
19 Biaggi	? N N N Y Y Y Y
20 Ottinger	Y N N N Y Y ? Y
21 *Fish*	? N N N Y Y Y N
22 *Gilman*	+ N N N Y Y Y N
23 Stratton	N N N N Y Y Y Y
24 *Solomon*	N Y Y N Y N N N
25 *Boehlert*	? ? ? ? ? ? ? N
26 *Martin*	? ? ? ? ? ? Y N N
27 *Wortley*	N Y Y N Y ? Y N N
28 McHugh	Y ? ? N Y Y Y Y
29 *Horton*	Y ? N N N Y N N
30 *Conable*	N Y Y N N Y N N
31 *Kemp*	? Y ? ? ? ? N
32 LaFalce	Y N N N Y Y Y Y
33 Nowak	Y N N N Y Y Y Y
34 Lundine	Y N N N Y Y Y Y

	31 32 33 34 35 36 37 38
NORTH CAROLINA	
1 Jones	Y N N N Y ? Y Y
2 Valentine	Y N N N Y Y Y Y
3 Whitley	Y N N N Y Y Y N
4 Andrews	Y N N N Y Y Y Y
5 Neal	? ? ? ? ? ? ? Y
6 Britt	Y N N N Y Y Y Y
7 Rose	Y N N N Y Y Y Y
8 Hefner	? ? ? ? ? Y Y Y
9 *Martin*	? ? ? ? ? ? ? X
10 *Broyhill*	? ? Y Y N Y N N
11 *Clarke*	? N N N Y N Y N N
NORTH DAKOTA	
AL Dorgan	Y N N N Y Y Y Y
OHIO	
1 Luken	? N N N Y Y Y Y
2 *Gradison*	Y N ? N Y N N N
3 Hall	Y N N N Y Y Y Y
4 *Oxley*	N Y Y N Y N N N
5 *Latta*	? ? ? Y N Y N N
6 McEwen	N N Y N Y N N N
7 *DeWine*	N N Y N Y N N N
8 *Kindness*	N Y Y N Y N N N
9 Kaptur	? ? ? ? ? Y Y Y
10 *Miller*	Y ·N N N Y N N N
11 Eckart	Y N N N Y Y Y Y
12 *Kasich*	N N N N Y N N N
13 Pease	Y N N N Y Y Y Y
14 Seiberling	Y N N N Y Y Y Y
15 *Wylie*	N N N Y N Y N N
16 *Regula*	Y N N ? Y Y Y N
17 *Williams*	? ? ? ? ? ? ? ?
18 Applegate	Y N N N Y ? Y Y
19 Feighan	Y N N N Y Y Y Y
20 Oakar	Y N N N Y Y Y Y
21 Stokes	Y N N N Y ? Y Y
OKLAHOMA	
1 Jones	Y N N N Y Y Y Y
2 Synar	Y N N N Y Y Y Y
3 Watkins	Y N N N Y Y Y Y
4 McCurdy	? ? ? ? ? Y Y Y
5 *Edwards*	? N Y ? ? ? ? X
6 English	Y ? N N Y Y Y Y
OREGON	
1 AuCoin	Y N N N Y Y Y Y
2 *Smith, B.*	N Y Y N Y N N N
3 Wyden	Y N N N Y Y Y Y
4 Weaver	Y N N N Y ? Y Y
5 *Smith, D.*	N Y Y N N N N N
PENNSYLVANIA	
1 Foglietta	? ? ? ? ? ? Y Y
2 Gray	? ? ? ? ? ? Y Y
3 Borski	Y N N N Y Y Y Y
4 Kolter	Y N N N Y Y Y Y
5 *Schulze*	Y N Y N Y N ? N
6 Yatron	? ? ? ? ? ? ? ?
7 Edgar	Y N N N Y ? ? #
8 Kostmayer	Y N N N Y Y Y Y
9 *Shuster*	N Y Y ? N Y N N
10 *McDade*	? N N N Y N N N
11 Harrison	? ? ? ? ? Y Y Y
12 Murtha	Y N N N Y Y Y Y
13 *Coughlin*	Y N Y N N N Y N
14 Coyne	? ? ? ? ? Y Y Y
15 *Ritter*	Y ? ? ? # Y N N
16 *Walker*	N N Y N N N N N
17 *Gekas*	? ? ? ? ? N N N
18 Walgren	? N N N Y Y Y Y
19 *Goodling*	? N Y ? N N N N
20 Gaydos	? N N N Y Y Y Y
21 *Ridge*	? N N N Y Y N N
22 Murphy	Y N N ? Y Y Y Y
23 *Clinger*	N N Y N Y N Y N
RHODE ISLAND	
1 St Germain	Y N N N Y Y Y Y
2 *Schneider*	Y N N N Y Y N N
SOUTH CAROLINA	
1 *Hartnett*	N Y Y N N N N N
2 Spence	? Y Y Y N Y N N
3 Derrick	Y N N ? Y Y Y Y
4 *Campbell*	? ? ? ? ? Y N N
5 Spratt	Y N N N Y Y Y Y
6 Tallon	Y N N N Y Y Y Y
SOUTH DAKOTA	
AL Daschle	? ? ? ? ? Y Y Y

	31 32 33 34 35 36 37 38
TENNESSEE	
1 *Quillen*	N Y Y Y N Y Y N
2 *Duncan*	N N Y Y Y Y N N
3 Bouquard	? ? ? ? ? Y Y Y
4 Cooper	Y N N N Y Y Y Y
5 Boner	Y N N N Y Y Y Y
6 Gore	Y N ? ? ? Y Y Y
7 *Sundquist*	N Y Y Y N Y N N
8 Jones	Y N N N Y Y Y Y
9 Ford	Y N N N Y Y Y Y
TEXAS	
1 Hall, S.	Y N Y Y Y Y N N
2 Wilson	Y N N Y Y Y ? ? Y
3 *Bartlett*	N Y Y Y N Y N N
4 Hall, R.	Y N N N Y N N N
5 Bryant	Y N N N Y Y Y Y
6 *Gramm*	? Y ? ? N Y N N
7 *Archer*	N Y Y ? X N N N
9 Brooks	Y N N N Y Y Y Y
10 Pickle	Y N N N Y Y Y Y
11 Leath	Y Y Y Y Y Y N N
12 Wright	Y N N N Y Y Y Y
13 Hightower	? ? ? ? ? ? Y Y
14 Patman	Y N N N Y Y Y Y
15 de la Garza	Y N N N Y Y Y #
16 Coleman	Y N N N Y Y Y Y
17 Stenholm	Y Y Y Y Y Y N N
18 Leland	Y ? N N N Y Y Y
19 Hance	Y N N N Y Y Y Y
20 Gonzalez	Y N N N Y Y Y Y
21 *Loeffler*	N Y Y Y N N N N
22 *Paul*	? Y Y Y N Y N N
23 Kazen	? N N N Y Y N N
24 Frost	Y N N N Y ? Y Y
25 Andrews	Y N N N Y Y Y Y
26 *Vandergriff*	Y N N N Y Y Y Y
27 Ortiz	? N N N Y Y Y Y
UTAH	
1 *Hansen*	? ? ? ? X Y N N
2 *Marriott*	N Y ? Y N Y N N
3 *Nielson*	N Y Y Y N ? N N
VERMONT	
AL *Jeffords*	? ? ? ? ? Y N
VIRGINIA	
1 *Bateman*	N Y Y Y N Y N N
2 *Whitehurst*	N N ? ? ? Y N N
3 *Bliley*	N Y Y ? X Y N N
4 Sisisky	Y N N N Y Y Y Y
5 Daniel	Y Y Y Y Y Y N N
6 Olin	? ? ? ? ? Y Y Y
7 *Robinson*	? ? ? ? ? Y N N
8 *Parris*	N N Y N N N N N
9 Boucher	? ? ? ? ? Y Y Y
10 *Wolf*	N N N N Y N N N
WASHINGTON	
1 *Pritchard*	? ? ? ? ? ? N N
2 Swift	Y N N N Y Y Y Y
3 Bonker	Y - - - + Y Y Y
4 *Morrison*	N N N N N Y N N
5 Foley	Y N N N Y Y Y Y
6 Dicks	Y N N N Y Y Y Y
7 Lowry	Y N N N Y Y Y Y
8 *Chandler*	N N Y N Y N N N
WEST VIRGINIA	
1 Mollohan	Y N N N Y Y Y Y
2 Staggers	Y N N N Y Y Y Y
3 Wise	Y N N N Y Y Y Y
4 Rahall	Y N N N Y ? Y Y
WISCONSIN	
1 Aspin	? ? ? ? ? Y Y Y
2 Kastenmeier	? ? ? ? ? Y Y Y
3 *Gunderson*	N N Y N Y N N N
4 Zablocki	? ? N N Y Y Y Y
5 Moody	Y N N N Y Y Y Y
6 *Petri*	Y N N N Y N N N
7 Obey	Y N N N Y Y Y Y
8 Roth	N N N Y Y Y ? ? ?
9 *Sensenbrenner*	? N N N Y N N N
WYOMING	
AL *Cheney*	N Y ? ? ? Y N N

Southern states - Ala., Ark., Fla., Ga., Ky., La., Miss., N.C., Okla., S.C., Tenn., Texas, Va.

39. HR 1718. Emergency Supplemental Appropriations, Fiscal 1983/Jobs. Adoption of the conference report on the bill to provide $15,589,034,000 in fiscal 1983 supplemental appropriations, including $4.6 billion for emergency jobs and recession relief. Adopted 329-86: R 84-71; D 245-15 (ND 169-3, SD 76-12), March 22, 1983. The president had requested $10,740,457,000 in supplemental appropriations and had proposed a $4.3 billion jobs program.

40. HR 1718. Emergency Supplemental Appropriations, Fiscal 1983/Jobs. Whitten, D-Miss., motion that the House recede from its disagreement to the Senate amendment governing the distribution of jobs funds among states, with a further amendment requiring that 75 percent of the discretionary funding under the bill be spent in areas of high unemployment. Motion rejected 132-277: R 46-107; D 86-170 (ND 33-137, SD 53-33), March 22, 1983.

41. Procedural Motion. Walker, R-Pa., motion to approve the House *Journal* of Tuesday, March 22. Motion agreed to 267-33: R 99-23; D 168-10 (ND 107-8, SD 61-2), March 23, 1983.

42. H Con Res 91. First Budget Resolution, Fiscal 1984. Adoption of the first concurrent resolution to set spending and revenue targets for the fiscal year ending Sept. 30, 1984, as follows: budget authority, $936.55 billion; outlays, $863.55 billion; revenues, $689.1 billion; and deficit, $174.45 billion. The resolution also set preliminary goals for fiscal 1985-86, revised budget levels for fiscal 1983 and included reconciliation instructions requiring House committees to recommend legislative savings to meet the budget targets. Adopted 229-196: R 4-160; D 225-36 (ND 168-6, SD 57-30), March 23, 1983.

KEY

Y	Voted for (yea).
#	Paired for.
+	Announced for.
N	Voted against (nay).
X	Paired against.
-	Announced against.
P	Voted "present".
C	Voted "present" to avoid possible conflict of interest.
?	Did not vote or otherwise make a position known.

Democrats   *Republicans*

	39	40	41	42
ALABAMA				
1 *Edwards*	Y	Y	?	N
2 *Dickinson*	Y	N	N	N
3 Nichols	Y	Y	Y	N
4 Bevill	Y	Y	Y	Y
5 Flippo	Y	Y	Y	Y
6 Erdreich	Y	N	Y	N
7 Shelby	Y	N	Y	N
ALASKA				
AL *Young*	Y	N	?	N
ARIZONA				
1 *McCain*	Y	Y	Y	N
2 Udall	Y	Y	Y	Y
3 *Stump*	N	Y	Y	N
4 *Rudd*	N	Y	Y	N
5 McNulty	?	N	?	Y
ARKANSAS				
1 Alexander	Y	Y	Y	Y
2 *Bethune*	N	N	N	N
3 *Hammerschmidt*	Y	N	?	N
4 Anthony	Y	N	?	Y
CALIFORNIA				
1 Bosco	Y	N	Y	Y
2 *Chappie*	Y	Y	Y	N
3 Matsui	Y	N	?	Y
4 Fazio	Y	Y	Y	Y
5 Burton	Y	Y	Y	Y
6 Boxer	Y	N	Y	Y
7 Miller	Y	Y	Y	Y
8 Dellums	Y	N	Y	Y
9 Stark	Y	N	?	Y
10 Edwards	Y	Y	Y	Y
11 Lantos	Y	Y	Y	Y
12 *Zschau*	Y	N	?	N
13 Mineta	Y	Y	Y	Y
14 *Shumway*	N	N	Y	N
15 Coelho	Y	N	Y	Y
16 Panetta	Y	Y	Y	Y
17 *Pashayan*	?	?	Y	N
18 Lehman	Y	N	Y	Y
19 *Lagomarsino*	Y	Y	Y	N
20 *Thomas*	Y	Y	Y	N
21 *Fiedler*	Y	N	Y	N
22 *Moorhead*	N	Y	Y	N
23 Beilenson	N	N	?	Y
24 Waxman	Y	Y	Y	Y
25 Roybal	Y	Y	Y	Y
26 Berman	Y	Y	Y	Y
27 Levine	Y	N	?	Y
28 Dixon	Y	N	Y	Y
29 Hawkins	Y	N	Y	Y
30 Martinez	Y	N	Y	Y
31 Dymally	Y	N	Y	Y
32 Anderson	N	N	Y	Y
33 *Dreier*	N	Y	N	N
34 Torres	Y	N	Y	Y
35 *Lewis*	N	Y	N	N
36 Brown	Y	N	Y	Y
37 *McCandless*	Y	Y	?	N
38 Patterson	Y	N	Y	Y
39 *Dannemeyer*	N	Y	N	N
40 *Badham*	N	N	?	N
41 *Lowery*	Y	Y	?	N
42 Lungren	N	N	N	N

	39	40	41	42
43 *Packard*	Y	Y	Y	N
44 Bates	Y	N	Y	Y
45 *Hunter*	N	N	Y	N
COLORADO				
1 Schroeder	Y	N	N	Y
2 Wirth	Y	N	Y	Y
3 Kogovsek	Y	N	Y	Y
4 *Brown*	N	Y	N	N
5 *Kramer*	N	N	Y	N
6 Vacancy				
CONNECTICUT				
1 Kennelly	Y	N	Y	Y
2 Gejdenson	Y	N	N	Y
3 Morrison	Y	N	Y	Y
4 *McKinney*	Y	N	?	N
5 Ratchford	Y	Y	Y	Y
6 *Johnson*	Y	N	Y	N
DELAWARE				
AL Carper	Y	N	?	Y
FLORIDA				
1 Hutto	Y	Y	Y	N
2 Fuqua	Y	Y	?	Y
3 Bennett	Y	N	Y	N
4 Chappell	N	Y	?	N
5 *McCollum*	N	N	Y	N
6 MacKay	N	Y	Y	Y
7 Gibbons	Y	Y	Y	Y
8 *Young*	N	Y	N	N
9 *Bilirakis*	Y	N	?	N
10 Ireland	Y	Y	Y	N
11 Nelson	Y	Y	Y	Y
12 *Lewis*	Y	N	+	N
13 *Mack*	N	N	?	N
14 Mica	Y	Y	Y	Y
15 *Shaw*	N	N	Y	N
16 Smith	Y	N	?	Y
17 Lehman	Y	Y	Y	Y
18 Pepper	Y	N	Y	Y
19 Fascell	Y	Y	?	Y
GEORGIA				
1 Thomas	Y	Y	Y	N
2 Hatcher	Y	Y	Y	N
3 Ray	N	Y	?	N
4 Levitas	N	Y	Y	N
5 Fowler	Y	N	Y	Y
6 *Gingrich*	N	N	Y	N
7 McDonald	N	Y	N	N
8 Rowland	Y	Y	Y	N
9 Jenkins	N	Y	Y	Y
10 Barnard	N	Y	Y	N
HAWAII				
1 Heftel	Y	Y	?	Y
2 Akaka	Y	Y	Y	Y
IDAHO				
1 *Craig*	N	N	Y	N
2 *Hansen*	X	N	Y	N
ILLINOIS				
1 Washington	?	?	?	#
2 Savage	Y	N	?	N
3 Russo	Y	N	Y	N
4 *O'Brien*	?	?	?	N
5 Lipinski	Y	N	?	Y
6 *Hyde*	?	N	Y	N
7 Collins	Y	N	Y	Y
8 Rostenkowski	Y	N	Y	Y
9 Yates	Y	N	N	Y
10 *Porter*	Y	N	?	N
11 Annunzio	Y	N	Y	Y
12 *Crane, P.*	N	N	?	N
13 *Erlenborn*	Y	N	Y	N
14 *Corcoran*	X	X	Y	N
15 *Madigan*	Y	?	?	N
16 *Martin*	Y	N	N	N
17 Evans	Y	N	?	Y
18 *Michel*	Y	N	Y	N
19 *Crane, D.*	N	N	?	N
20 Durbin	Y	N	?	Y
21 Price	Y	Y	?	Y
22 Simon	Y	N	?	Y
INDIANA				
1 Hall	Y	N	Y	N
2 Sharp	Y	N	Y	Y
3 *Hiler*	Y	N	N	N
4 *Coats*	Y	N	N	N
5 Hillis	Y	N	Y	N

ND - Northern Democrats   SD - Southern Democrats

	39	40	41	42
6 Burton	N	N	Y	N
7 Myers	Y	Y	Y	N
8 McCloskey	Y	N	Y	Y
9 Hamilton	Y	N	Y	Y
10 Jacobs	Y	N	N	Y
IOWA				
1 Leach	Y	N	Y	N
2 Tauke	N	N	Y	N
3 Evans	Y	N	N	N
4 Smith	Y	Y	Y	N
5 Harkin	Y	N	N	Y
6 Bedell	Y	N	Y	Y
KANSAS				
1 Roberts	N	Y	?	N
2 Slattery	Y	N	?	Y
3 Winn	Y	N	?	N
4 Glickman	Y	Y	Y	Y
5 Whittaker	Y	Y	?	N
KENTUCKY				
1 Hubbard	Y	Y	Y	Y
2 Natcher	Y	Y	Y	Y
3 Mazzoli	Y	Y	Y	Y
4 Snyder	N	N	Y	N
5 Rogers	Y	Y	?	N
6 Hopkins	N	Y	Y	N
7 Perkins	Y	Y	Y	Y
LOUISIANA				
1 Livingston	N	Y	Y	N
2 Boggs	?	N	?	Y
3 Tauzin	Y	Y	Y	N
4 Roemer	N	N	N	N
5 Huckaby	Y	Y	?	N
6 Moore	N	N	Y	N
7 Breaux	Y	N	Y	N
8 Long	Y	N	?	Y
MAINE				
1 McKernan	Y	N	?	N
2 Snowe	Y	N	Y	N
MARYLAND				
1 Dyson	Y	N	Y	N
2 Long	Y	N	?	Y
3 Mikulski	Y	X	?	Y
4 Holt	Y	?	?	N
5 Hoyer	Y	Y	Y	Y
6 Byron	Y	?	?	N
7 Mitchell	Y	N	N	Y
8 Barnes	Y	?	Y	Y
MASSACHUSETTS				
1 Conte	Y	N	Y	N
2 Boland	Y	N	?	Y
3 Early	Y	Y	?	Y
4 Frank	Y	N	Y	Y
5 Shannon	Y	Y	?	Y
6 Mavroules	Y	N	?	Y
7 Markey	Y	N	+	Y
8 O'Neill				
9 Moakley	Y	N	Y	Y
10 Studds	Y	N	Y	Y
11 Donnelly	Y	N	?	Y
MICHIGAN				
1 Conyers	Y	N	Y	Y
2 Pursell	Y	N	Y	N
3 Wolpe	Y	N	Y	Y
4 Siljander	N	N	Y	N
5 Sawyer	Y	N	?	N
6 Carr	Y	N	Y	Y
7 Kildee	Y	N	Y	Y
8 Traxler	N	N	Y	Y
9 Vander Jagt	Y	N	?	N
10 Albosta	Y	N	?	Y
11 Davis	Y	N	Y	N
12 Bonior	Y	N	?	Y
13 Crockett	Y	N	?	Y
14 Hertel	Y	N	?	Y
15 Ford	Y	N	?	Y
16 Dingell	?	N	?	Y
17 Levin	Y	N	Y	Y
18 Broomfield	Y	?	Y	N
MINNESOTA				
1 Penny	Y	Y	Y	Y
2 Weber	N	Y	N	N
3 Frenzel	N	N	N	N
4 Vento	Y	N	Y	Y
5 Sabo	Y	Y	Y	Y
6 Sikorski	Y	N	Y	Y

	39	40	41	42
7 Stangeland	N	#	Y	N
8 Oberstar	Y	N	P	Y
MISSISSIPPI				
1 Whitten	Y	Y	Y	Y
2 Franklin	Y	Y	Y	N
3 Montgomery	N	Y	Y	N
4 Dowdy	Y	Y	?	Y
5 Lott	N	Y	?	N
MISSOURI				
1 Clay	Y	N	?	Y
2 Young	Y	Y	Y	Y
3 Gephardt	Y	Y	Y	Y
4 Skelton	Y	Y	Y	N
5 Wheat	Y	N	Y	Y
6 Coleman	Y	N	Y	N
7 Taylor	N	Y	N	N
8 Emerson	Y	Y	N	N
9 Volkmer	Y	Y	Y	Y
MONTANA				
1 Williams	Y	Y	Y	Y
2 Marlenee	Y	Y	Y	N
NEBRASKA				
1 Bereuter	N	Y	Y	N
2 Daub	N	N	N	N
3 Smith	Y	Y	Y	N
NEVADA				
1 Reid	Y	N	?	Y
2 Vucanovich	N	N	?	N
NEW HAMPSHIRE				
1 D'Amours	Y	Y	Y	Y
2 Gregg	N	Y	Y	N
NEW JERSEY				
1 Florio	Y	N	?	Y
2 Hughes	Y	N	Y	Y
3 Howard	Y	N	?	Y
4 Smith	Y	N	Y	N
5 Roukema	Y	N	Y	N
6 Dwyer	Y	N	Y	Y
7 Rinaldo	Y	N	?	Y
8 Roe	Y	N	Y	Y
9 Torricelli	Y	N	Y	Y
10 Rodino	Y	N	Y	Y
11 Minish	Y	N	Y	Y
12 Courter	N	N	Y	N
13 Forsythe	#	?	?	N
14 Guarini	Y	N	Y	Y
NEW MEXICO				
1 Lujan	N	Y	Y	N
2 Skeen	Y	Y	Y	N
3 Richardson	Y	N	Y	Y
NEW YORK				
1 Carney	N	Y	?	N
2 Downey	?	?	?	Y
3 Mrazek	Y	Y	?	Y
4 Lent	N	N	Y	N
5 McGrath	N	Y	Y	N
6 Addabbo	Y	N	Y	Y
7 Ackerman	Y	N	?	Y
8 Scheuer	Y	N	?	Y
9 Ferraro	Y	N	Y	Y
10 Schumer	Y	N	?	Y
11 Towns	Y	N	?	Y
12 Owens	Y	N	?	Y
13 Solarz	Y	N	?	Y
14 Molinari	N	Y	?	N
15 Green	Y	N	Y	Y
16 Rangel	Y	N	Y	Y
17 Weiss	Y	N	Y	Y
18 Garcia	Y	N	?	Y
19 Biaggi	Y	N	Y	Y
20 Ottinger	Y	N	P	Y
21 Fish	Y	N	Y	N
22 Gilman	Y	N	Y	N
23 Stratton	Y	N	Y	N
24 Solomon	N	N	?	N
25 Boehlert	Y	N	Y	N
26 Martin	Y	N	Y	N
27 Wortley	Y	N	Y	N
28 McHugh	Y	N	?	Y
29 Horton	Y	N	Y	N
30 Conable	N	Y	N	N
31 Kemp	N	N	?	N
32 LaFalce	Y	N	Y	Y
33 Nowak	Y	N	Y	Y
34 Lundine	Y	N	Y	Y

	39	40	41	42
NORTH CAROLINA				
1 Jones	?	?	?	Y
2 Valentine	Y	Y	?	N
3 Whitley	Y	Y	Y	N
4 Andrews	Y	Y	Y	Y
5 Neal	Y	?	?	#
6 Britt	Y	N	?	Y
7 Rose	Y	?	Y	Y
8 Hefner	Y	Y	?	Y
9 Martin	?	?	?	N
10 Broyhill	N	N	Y	N
11 Clarke	Y	N	Y	Y
NORTH DAKOTA				
AL Dorgan	Y	Y	Y	Y
OHIO				
1 Luken	Y	N	Y	Y
2 Gradison	Y	N	Y	N
3 Hall	Y	N	Y	Y
4 Oxley	N	N	Y	N
5 Latta	N	N	Y	N
6 McEwen	N	N	Y	N
7 DeWine	N	N	Y	N
8 Kindness	Y	N	?	N
9 Kaptur	Y	N	?	Y
10 Miller	Y	N	N	N
11 Eckart	Y	N	Y	Y
12 Kasich	Y	N	Y	N
13 Pease	Y	N	Y	Y
14 Seiberling	Y	N	?	Y
15 Wylie	Y	N	Y	N
16 Regula	Y	N	Y	N
17 Williams	?	?	?	X
18 Applegate	Y	N	?	Y
19 Feighan	Y	N	?	Y
20 Oakar	Y	N	Y	Y
21 Stokes	Y	N	Y	Y
OKLAHOMA				
1 Jones	Y	Y	Y	Y
2 Synar	Y	Y	Y	Y
3 Watkins	Y	Y	Y	Y
4 McCurdy	Y	Y	Y	Y
5 Edwards	?	?	?	X
6 English	Y	Y	?	N
OREGON				
1 AuCoin	Y	N	?	Y
2 Smith, B.	Y	N	Y	N
3 Wyden	Y	N	Y	Y
4 Weaver	Y	N	?	Y
5 Smith, D.	N	N	N	N
PENNSYLVANIA				
1 Foglietta	Y	N	Y	Y
2 Gray	Y	N	?	Y
3 Borski	Y	N	Y	Y
4 Kolter	Y	N	Y	Y
5 Schulze	Y	N	Y	N
6 Yatron	?	?	?	?
7 Edgar	Y	N	?	Y
8 Kostmayer	Y	N	Y	Y
9 Shuster	N	N	N	N
10 McDade	Y	N	?	N
11 Harrison	Y	N	Y	Y
12 Murtha	Y	N	Y	Y
13 Coughlin	Y	N	N	N
14 Coyne	Y	N	?	Y
15 Ritter	Y	N	Y	N
16 Walker	N	N	N	N
17 Gekas	N	N	?	N
18 Walgren	Y	N	?	Y
19 Goodling	Y	N	N	N
20 Gaydos	Y	N	Y	?
21 Ridge	Y	N	Y	N
22 Murphy	Y	N	N	Y
23 Clinger	Y	N	Y	N
RHODE ISLAND				
1 St Germain	Y	N	?	Y
2 Schneider	Y	N	Y	Y
SOUTH CAROLINA				
1 Hartnett	N	N	N	N
2 Spence	N	N	Y	N
3 Derrick	Y	N	Y	Y
4 Campbell	Y	N	?	N
5 Spratt	Y	N	Y	Y
6 Tallon	Y	N	Y	Y
SOUTH DAKOTA				
AL Daschle	Y	Y	Y	Y

	39	40	41	42
TENNESSEE				
1 Quillen	Y	N	Y	N
2 Duncan	Y	N	Y	N
3 Bouquard	Y	?	Y	Y
4 Cooper	Y	N	Y	Y
5 Boner	Y	N	Y	Y
6 Gore	Y	N	Y	Y
7 Sundquist	Y	N	Y	N
8 Jones	Y	Y	Y	Y
9 Ford	Y	N	Y	Y
TEXAS				
1 Hall, S.	Y	N	Y	N
2 Wilson	Y	Y	Y	X
3 Bartlett	N	Y	Y	N
4 Hall, R.	Y	N	?	N
5 Bryant	Y	N	Y	Y
6 Gramm	N	Y	?	N
7 Archer	N	#	Y	N
8 Fields	Y	Y	?	N
9 Brooks	Y	N	Y	#
10 Pickle	Y	N	Y	Y
11 Leath	N	Y	?	N
12 Wright	Y	Y	Y	Y
13 Hightower	Y	Y	Y	Y
14 Patman	Y	Y	?	Y
15 de la Garza	Y	Y	?	Y
16 Coleman	Y	Y	Y	Y
17 Stenholm	N	N	N	N
18 Leland	Y	N	Y	Y
19 Hance	Y	Y	Y	N
20 Gonzalez	Y	Y	Y	Y
21 Loeffler	N	Y	Y	N
22 Paul	N	Y	Y	N
23 Kazen	Y	N	Y	Y
24 Frost	Y	N	Y	Y
25 Andrews	Y	N	?	Y
26 Vandergriff	Y	Y	Y	N
27 Ortiz	Y	Y	?	Y
UTAH				
1 Hansen	N	N	?	N
2 Marriott	Y	N	Y	N
3 Nielson	N	N	Y	N
VERMONT				
AL Jeffords	Y	N	Y	Y
VIRGINIA				
1 Bateman	#	?	Y	N
2 Whitehurst	Y	Y	Y	N
3 Bliley	N	N	Y	N
4 Sisisky	Y	N	?	Y
5 Daniel	N	Y	Y	N
6 Olin	Y	N	P	Y
7 Robinson	N	Y	Y	N
8 Parris	N	N	Y	N
9 Boucher	Y	N	?	Y
10 Wolf	N	N	Y	N
WASHINGTON				
1 Pritchard	Y	N	?	N
2 Swift	Y	?	?	Y
3 Bonker	Y	N	?	Y
4 Morrison	Y	Y	Y	Y
5 Foley	Y	Y	Y	Y
6 Dicks	Y	N	P	Y
7 Lowry	Y	N	Y	Y
8 Chandler	Y	N	Y	N
WEST VIRGINIA				
1 Mollohan	Y	N	Y	Y
2 Staggers	Y	N	Y	Y
3 Wise	Y	N	+	Y
4 Rahall	Y	N	Y	Y
WISCONSIN				
1 Aspin	Y	N	Y	Y
2 Kastenmeier	Y	Y	Y	Y
3 Gunderson	Y	N	Y	N
4 Zablocki	Y	N	?	Y
5 Moody	Y	N	Y	Y
6 Petri	Y	N	Y	N
7 Obey	Y	N	Y	Y
8 Roth	?	N	?	N
9 Sensenbrenner	N	N	Y	N
WYOMING				
AL Cheney	N	N	Y	N

Southern states · Ala., Ark., Fla., Ga., Ky., La., Miss., N.C., Okla., S.C., Tenn., Texas, Va.

	43
43 *Packard*	Y
44 Bates	Y
45 *Hunter*	N
COLORADO	
1 Schroeder	Y
2 Wirth	Y
3 Kogovsek	Y
4 *Brown*	N
5 *Kramer*	N
6 Vacancy	
CONNECTICUT	
1 Kennelly	Y
2 Gejdenson	N
3 Morrison	N
4 *McKinney*	?
5 Ratchford	N
6 *Johnson*	Y
DELAWARE	
AL Carper	Y
FLORIDA	
1 Hutto	Y
2 Fuqua	Y
3 Bennett	Y
4 Chappell	#
5 *McCollum*	Y
6 MacKay	Y
7 Gibbons	Y
8 *Young*	Y
9 *Bilirakis*	Y
10 Ireland	Y
11 Nelson	Y
12 *Lewis*	#
13 *Mack*	Y
14 Mica	Y
15 *Shaw*	Y
16 Smith	Y
17 Lehman	Y
18 Pepper	Y
19 Fascell	?
GEORGIA	
1 Thomas	Y
2 Hatcher	Y
3 Ray	Y
4 Levitas	Y
5 Fowler	?
6 *Gingrich*	N
7 McDonald	N
8 Rowland	Y
9 Jenkins	?
10 Barnard	?
HAWAII	
1 Heftel	Y
2 Akaka	?
IDAHO	
1 *Craig*	?
2 *Hansen*	N
ILLINOIS	
1 Washington	?
2 Savage	?
3 Russo	Y
4 *O'Brien*	Y
5 Lipinski	Y
6 *Hyde*	Y
7 Collins	N
8 Rostenkowski	Y
9 Yates	?
10 *Porter*	X
11 Annunzio	Y
12 *Crane, P.*	X
13 *Erlenborn*	Y
14 *Corcoran*	+
15 *Madigan*	Y
16 *Martin*	N
17 Evans	N
18 *Michel*	Y
19 *Crane, D.*	N
20 Durbin	Y
21 Price	?
22 Simon	Y
INDIANA	
1 Hall	N
2 Sharp	Y
3 *Hiler*	Y
4 *Coats*	Y
5 *Hillis*	Y

KEY

Y Voted for (yea).
Paired for.
+ Announced for.
N Voted against (nay).
X Paired against.
- Announced against.
P Voted "present".
C Voted "present" to avoid possible conflict of interest.
? Did not vote or otherwise make a position known.

Democrats   *Republicans*

43. HR 1900. Social Security Act Amendments. Adoption of the conference report on the bill to overhaul the Social Security system, to revamp the way the federal government reimburses hospitals for Medicare, to extend the federal supplemental unemployment benefit program for six months and to increase Supplemental Security Income benefits. Adopted 243-102: R 80-48; D 163-54 (ND 106-42, SD 57-12), March 24, 1983. A "yea" was a vote supporting the president's position.

	43
ALABAMA	
1 *Edwards*	?
2 *Dickinson*	?
3 Nichols	#
4 Bevill	Y
5 Flippo	#
6 Erdreich	Y
7 Shelby	Y
ALASKA	
AL *Young*	X
ARIZONA	
1 *McCain*	Y
2 Udall	Y
3 *Stump*	N
4 *Rudd*	N
5 McNulty	Y
ARKANSAS	
1 Alexander	Y
2 *Bethune*	N
3 *Hammerschmidt*	Y
4 Anthony	?
CALIFORNIA	
1 Bosco	N
2 *Chappie*	Y
3 Matsui	Y
4 Fazio	Y
5 Burton	#
6 Boxer	Y
7 Miller	Y
8 Dellums	N
9 Stark	Y
10 Edwards	Y
11 Lantos	X
12 *Zschau*	Y
13 Mineta	Y
14 *Shumway*	N
15 Coelho	Y
16 Panetta	N
17 *Pashayan*	Y
18 Lehman	Y
19 *Lagomarsino*	N
20 *Thomas*	Y
21 *Fiedler*	N
22 *Moorhead*	N
23 Beilenson	Y
24 Waxman	N
25 Roybal	Y
26 Berman	#
27 Levine	X
28 Dixon	Y
29 Hawkins	?
30 Martinez	N
31 Dymally	?
32 Anderson	Y
33 *Dreier*	N
34 Torres	Y
35 *Lewis*	N
36 Brown	N
37 *McCandless*	Y
38 Patterson	Y
39 *Dannemeyer*	X
40 *Badham*	Y
41 *Lowery*	Y
42 *Lungren*	N

ND - Northern Democrats   SD - Southern Democrats

	43
6 Burton	Y
7 Myers	?
8 McCloskey	Y
9 Hamilton	Y
10 Jacobs	Y
IOWA	
1 Leach	Y
2 Tauke	N
3 Evans	Y
4 Smith	?
5 Harkin	?
6 Bedell	Y
KANSAS	
1 Roberts	N
2 Slattery	Y
3 Winn	Y
4 Glickman	Y
5 Whittaker	Y
KENTUCKY	
1 Hubbard	Y
2 Natcher	Y
3 Mazzoli	Y
4 Snyder	Y
5 Rogers	Y
6 Hopkins	Y
7 Perkins	N
LOUISIANA	
1 Livingston	#
2 Boggs	Y
3 Tauzin	Y
4 Roemer	N
5 Huckaby	?
6 Moore	Y
7 Breaux	Y
8 Long	?
MAINE	
1 McKernan	N
2 Snowe	N
MARYLAND	
1 Dyson	Y
2 Long	Y
3 Mikulski	Y
4 Holt	N
5 Hoyer	N
6 Byron	N
7 Mitchell	N
8 Barnes	N
MASSACHUSETTS	
1 Conte	Y
2 Boland	Y
3 Early	N
4 Frank	N
5 Shannon	Y
6 Mavroules	N
7 Markey	N
8 O'Neill	
9 Moakley	Y
10 Studds	N
11 Donnelly	N
MICHIGAN	
1 Conyers	?
2 Pursell	#
3 Wolpe	Y
4 Siljander	N
5 Sawyer	Y
6 Carr	Y
7 Kildee	N
8 Traxler	N
9 Vander Jagt	?
10 Albosta	Y
11 Davis	#
12 Bonior	Y
13 Crockett	Y
14 Hertel	N
15 Ford	Y
16 Dingell	Y
17 Levin	Y
18 Broomfield	N
MINNESOTA	
1 Penny	Y
2 Weber	Y
3 Frenzel	Y
4 Vento	Y
5 Sabo	Y
6 Sikorski	Y

	43
7 Stangeland	N
8 Oberstar	Y
MISSISSIPPI	
1 Whitten	N
2 Franklin	X
3 Montgomery	Y
4 Dowdy	Y
5 Lott	Y
MISSOURI	
1 Clay	N
2 Young	Y
3 Gephardt	Y
4 Skelton	Y
5 Wheat	Y
6 Coleman	Y
7 Taylor	Y
8 Emerson	?
9 Volkmer	Y
MONTANA	
1 Williams	N
2 Marlenee	?
NEBRASKA	
1 Bereuter	N
2 Daub	Y
3 Smith	Y
NEVADA	
1 Reid	Y
2 Vucanovich	Y
NEW HAMPSHIRE	
1 D'Amours	?
2 Gregg	?
NEW JERSEY	
1 Florio	N
2 Hughes	Y
3 Howard	Y
4 Smith	N
5 Roukema	Y
6 Dwyer	Y
7 Rinaldo	N
8 Roe	N
9 Torricelli	X
10 Rodino	Y
11 Minish	N
12 Courter	Y
13 Forsythe	?
14 Guarini	Y
NEW MEXICO	
1 Lujan	?
2 Skeen	Y
3 Richardson	Y
NEW YORK	
1 Carney	N
2 Downey	Y
3 Mrazek	Y
4 Lent	N
5 McGrath	N
6 Addabbo	X
7 Ackerman	N
8 Scheuer	Y
9 Ferraro	?
10 Schumer	Y
11 Towns	N
12 Owens	N
13 Solarz	Y
14 Molinari	N
15 Green	#
16 Rangel	Y
17 Weiss	N
18 Garcia	Y
19 Biaggi	Y
20 Ottinger	?
21 Fish	Y
22 Gilman	N
23 Stratton	Y
24 Solomon	N
25 Boehlert	Y
26 Martin	N
27 Wortley	Y
28 McHugh	Y
29 Horton	X
30 Conable	Y
31 Kemp	N
32 LaFalce	Y
33 Nowak	Y
34 Lundine	Y

	43
NORTH CAROLINA	
1 Jones	?
2 Valentine	Y
3 Whitley	Y
4 Andrews	Y
5 Neal	?
6 Britt	Y
7 Rose	?
8 Hefner	Y
9 Martin	Y
10 Broyhill	?
11 Clarke	Y
NORTH DAKOTA	
AL Dorgan	Y
OHIO	
1 Luken	?
2 Gradison	Y
3 Hall	N
4 Oxley	Y
5 Latta	Y
6 McEwen	N
7 DeWine	N
8 Kindness	N
9 Kaptur	Y
10 Miller	Y
11 Eckart	Y
12 Kasich	Y
13 Pease	Y
14 Seiberling	Y
15 Wylie	Y
16 Regula	Y
17 Williams	?
18 Applegate	?
19 Feighan	N
20 Oakar	N
21 Stokes	N
OKLAHOMA	
1 Jones	Y
2 Synar	Y
3 Watkins	Y
4 McCurdy	Y
5 Edwards	?
6 English	?
OREGON	
1 AuCoin	Y
2 Smith, B.	Y
3 Wyden	Y
4 Weaver	?
5 Smith, D.	X
PENNSYLVANIA	
1 Foglietta	Y
2 Gray	N
3 Borski	N
4 Kolter	Y
5 Schulze	?
6 Yatron	?
7 Edgar	Y
8 Kostmayer	N
9 Shuster	?
10 McDade	Y
11 Harrison	Y
12 Murtha	Y
13 Coughlin	Y
14 Coyne	Y
15 Ritter	N
16 Walker	Y
17 Gekas	N
18 Walgren	N
19 Goodling	N
20 Gaydos	?
21 Ridge	Y
22 Murphy	X
23 Clinger	Y
RHODE ISLAND	
1 St Germain	?
2 Schneider	Y
SOUTH CAROLINA	
1 Hartnett	?
2 Spence	N
3 Derrick	Y
4 Campbell	Y
5 Spratt	Y
6 Tallon	Y
SOUTH DAKOTA	
AL Daschle	Y

	43
TENNESSEE	
1 Quillen	Y
2 Duncan	N
3 Bouquard	Y
4 Cooper	#
5 Boner	Y
6 Gore	?
7 Sundquist	Y
8 Jones	N
9 Ford	Y
TEXAS	
1 Hall, S.	N
2 Wilson	Y
3 Bartlett	Y
4 Hall, R.	N
5 Bryant	Y
6 Gramm	Y
7 Archer	N
8 Fields	Y
9 Brooks	?
10 Pickle	Y
11 Leath	N
12 Wright	Y
13 Hightower	Y
14 Patman	N
15 de la Garza	Y
16 Coleman	Y
17 Stenholm	?
18 Leland	X
19 Hance	#
20 Gonzalez	N
21 Loeffler	?
22 Paul	?
23 Kazen	N
24 Frost	Y
25 Andrews	Y
26 Vandergriff	Y
27 Ortiz	Y
UTAH	
1 Hansen	?
2 Marriott	?
3 Nielson	?
VERMONT	
AL Jeffords	?
VIRGINIA	
1 Bateman	Y
2 Whitehurst	Y
3 Bliley	Y
4 Sisisky	Y
5 Daniel	?
6 Olin	Y
7 Robinson	?
8 Parris	N
9 Boucher	N
10 Wolf	N
WASHINGTON	
1 Pritchard	Y
2 Swift	Y
3 Bonker	?
4 Morrison	Y
5 Foley	Y
6 Dicks	Y
7 Lowry	Y
8 Chandler	Y
WEST VIRGINIA	
1 Mollohan	Y
2 Staggers	Y
3 Wise	Y
4 Rahall	#
WISCONSIN	
1 Aspin	?
2 Kastenmeier	Y
3 Gunderson	Y
4 Zablocki	Y
5 Moody	Y
6 Petri	Y
7 Obey	Y
8 Roth	?
9 Sensenbrenner	N
WYOMING	
AL Cheney	Y

Southern states · Ala., Ark., Fla., Ga., Ky., La., Miss., N.C., Okla., S.C., Tenn., Texas, Va.

44. HR 1071. Kodiak National Wildlife Refuge. Seiberling, D-Ohio, motion to suspend the rules and pass the bill to provide for acquisition by the United States, by exchange, of certain native-owned lands or interests in lands in Alaska. Motion agreed to 366-18: R 153-7; D 213-11 (ND 147-5, SD 66-6), April 12, 1983. A two-thirds majority of those present and voting (257 in this case) is required for passage under suspension of the rules.

45. HR 1437. California Wilderness Act. Walker, R-Pa., amendment to the Interior and Insular Affairs Committee substitute, to authorize the agriculture secretary, upon application by the state of California, to waive provisions of the bill shown to increase unemployment. Rejected 121-272: R 111-49; D 10-223 (ND 2-152, SD 8-71), April 12, 1983.

46. HR 1437. California Wilderness Act. Shumway, R-Calif., amendment to the Interior and Insular Affairs Committee substitute, to substitute provisions designating as federal wilderness about 1,278,000 acres of national forest land in California, approximately equivalent to the amount recommended by the U.S. Forest Service. Rejected 136-257: R 123-35; D 13-222 (ND 0-157, SD 13-65), April 12, 1983.

47. HR 1437. California Wilderness Act. Passage of the bill to designate as federal wilderness approximately 2.33 million acres of national forest land in California. Passed 297-96: R 75-85; D 222-11 (ND 153-1, SD 69-10), April 12, 1983.

48. Procedural Motion. Walker, R-Pa., motion to approve the House *Journal* of Tuesday, April 12. Motion agreed to 361-16: R 146-9; D 215-7 (ND 140-6, SD 75-1), April 13, 1983.

49. H J Res 13. Nuclear Freeze. Levitas, D-Ga., amendment to make the goal of U.S.-Soviet arms control negotiations an agreement to scrap two existing nuclear warheads for each new one deployed, instead of seeking a freeze on nuclear weapons. Rejected 190-229: R 140-22; D 50-207 (ND 7-166, SD 43-41), April 13, 1983.

50. H J Res 13. Nuclear Freeze. Leach, R-Iowa, amendment to the Brown, R-Colo., amendment, to make a nuclear arms freeze a more immediate priority than arms reductions. The Brown amendment would have given the two goals equal priority. Adopted 219-195: R 18-144; D 201-51 (ND 163-7, SD 38-44), April 13, 1983. (The Brown amendment, as amended, subsequently was adopted by voice vote.)

* Phillip Burton, D-Calif., died April 10, 1983. The last vote for which he was eligible was CQ vote 43.

** Daniel L. Schaefer, R-Colo., was sworn in April 7, 1983. The first vote for which he was eligible was CQ vote 44.

*** Marilyn Lloyd, D-Tenn., was formerly known as Marilyn Lloyd Bouquard.

KEY

Y	Voted for (yea).
#	Paired for.
+	Announced for.
N	Voted against (nay).
X	Paired against.
-	Announced against.
P	Voted "present".
C	Voted "present" to avoid possible conflict of interest.
?	Did not vote or otherwise make a position known.

Democrats   *Republicans*

	44	45	46	47	48	49	50
ALABAMA							
1 *Edwards*	Y	N	Y	Y	Y	Y	N
2 *Dickinson*	Y	N	Y	N	N	Y	N
3 Nichols	Y	N	N	Y	Y	Y	N
4 Bevill	Y	N	N	Y	Y	Y	N
5 Flippo	Y	N	N	Y	Y	Y	N
6 Erdreich	Y	N	N	Y	Y	Y	N
7 Shelby	Y	Y	Y	N	Y	Y	?
ALASKA							
AL *Young*	Y	Y	Y	N	?	Y	?
ARIZONA							
1 *McCain*	Y	Y	Y	N	Y	Y	?
2 Udall	Y	N	N	Y	Y	N	Y
3 *Stump*	N	Y	N	Y	N	N	N
4 *Rudd*	N	Y	Y	N	Y	N	Y
5 McNulty	Y	N	N	Y	Y	N	Y
ARKANSAS							
1 Alexander	?	N	N	Y	Y	N	Y
2 *Bethune*	N	N	N	Y	?	+	N
3 *Hammerschmidt*	Y	Y	Y	N	Y	Y	N
4 Anthony	Y	N	Y	N	Y	Y	N
CALIFORNIA							
1 Bosco	Y	N	N	N	Y	N	Y
2 *Chappie*	Y	Y	Y	N	Y	Y	N
3 Matsui	Y	N	N	Y	Y	N	Y
4 Fazio	Y	N	N	Y	Y	N	Y
5 Vacancy*							
6 Boxer	Y	N	N	Y	Y	N	Y
7 Miller	Y	N	N	Y	Y	N	Y
8 Dellums	Y	N	N	Y	?	N	Y
9 Stark	Y	N	N	Y	Y	N	Y
10 Edwards	Y	N	N	Y	Y	N	Y
11 Lantos	Y	N	N	Y	Y	N	Y
12 *Zschau*	Y	N	N	Y	Y	N	N
13 Mineta	Y	N	N	Y	Y	N	Y
14 *Shumway*	Y	Y	Y	N	Y	Y	N
15 Coelho	Y	N	N	Y	Y	N	Y
16 Panetta	N	N	N	Y	Y	N	Y
17 *Pashayan*	?	Y	Y	N	Y	Y	N
18 Lehman	Y	N	N	Y	?	N	Y
19 *Lagomarsino*	Y	N	Y	N	Y	Y	N
20 *Thomas*	Y	Y	N	Y	Y	Y	N
21 *Fiedler*	Y	N	Y	Y	Y	Y	N
22 *Moorhead*	Y	Y	Y	N	Y	Y	N
23 Beilenson	Y	N	N	Y	Y	N	Y
24 Waxman	Y	N	N	Y	Y	N	Y
25 Roybal	Y	N	N	Y	?	N	Y
26 Berman	Y	N	N	Y	Y	N	Y
27 Levine	Y	N	N	Y	Y	N	Y
28 Dixon	Y	N	N	Y	Y	N	Y
29 Hawkins	Y	N	N	Y	Y	N	Y
30 Martinez	Y	N	N	Y	Y	N	Y
31 Dymally	?	N	N	Y	Y	N	Y
32 Anderson	Y	N	N	Y	Y	N	Y
33 *Dreier*	Y	Y	Y	N	Y	Y	N
34 Torres	Y	N	N	Y	Y	N	Y
35 *Lewis*	Y	Y	Y	N	Y	Y	N
36 Brown	Y	N	N	Y	Y	N	Y
37 *McCandless*	Y	Y	Y	N	Y	Y	N
38 Patterson	Y	N	N	Y	Y	N	Y
39 *Dannemeyer*	Y	Y	Y	N	Y	Y	N
40 *Badham*	Y	N	Y	N	?	?	N
41 *Lowery*	Y	Y	Y	Y	Y	Y	N
42 *Lungren*	Y	Y	Y	N	Y	Y	N

	44	45	46	47	48	49	50
43 *Packard*	Y	Y	Y	N	Y	Y	N
44 Bates	Y	N	N	Y	Y	N	Y
45 *Hunter*	Y	Y	Y	Y	Y	Y	N
COLORADO							
1 Schroeder	Y	N	N	Y	N	N	Y
2 Wirth	?	?	?	?	Y	N	Y
3 Kogovsek	Y	N	N	Y	Y	N	Y
4 *Brown*	Y	Y	Y	Y	Y	Y	N
5 *Kramer*	Y	Y	Y	N	Y	Y	N
6 *Schaefer* *	Y	Y	Y	N	Y	Y	N
CONNECTICUT							
1 Kennelly	Y	N	N	Y	N	Y	N
2 Gejdenson	Y	N	N	N	N	N	Y
3 Morrison	Y	N	N	Y	N	N	Y
4 *McKinney*	Y	?	?	Y	Y	N	Y
5 Ratchford	Y	N	N	Y	N	Y	N
6 *Johnson*	Y	Y	N	Y	N	N	N
DELAWARE							
AL Carper	Y	N	N	Y	Y	N	Y
FLORIDA							
1 Hutto	Y	?	?	?	?	Y	N
2 Fuqua	Y	N	N	Y	N	Y	N
3 Bennett	Y	N	N	Y	Y	N	N
4 Chappell	?	N	N	Y	P	?	N
5 *McCollum*	Y	Y	Y	Y	Y	Y	N
6 MacKay	-	N	N	Y	Y	N	Y
7 Gibbons	?	?	?	?	Y	N	Y
8 *Young*	Y	Y	Y	Y	N	N	N
9 *Bilirakis*	Y	Y	N	Y	Y	N	N
10 Ireland	Y	N	N	Y	Y	N	Y
11 Nelson	Y	N	N	Y	Y	N	Y
12 *Lewis*	Y	Y	Y	Y	Y	Y	N
13 *Mack*	Y	Y	Y	Y	Y	Y	N
14 Mica	Y	N	N	Y	N	N	Y
15 *Shaw*	Y	Y	Y	Y	Y	Y	N
16 Smith	Y	N	N	Y	Y	N	Y
17 Lehman	Y	N	?	Y	P	N	Y
18 Pepper	Y	N	N	Y	N	N	Y
19 Fascell	Y	N	N	Y	Y	N	Y
GEORGIA							
1 Thomas	Y	N	N	Y	Y	Y	N
2 Hatcher	Y	N	N	Y	Y	Y	N
3 Ray	N	N	N	Y	Y	Y	N
4 Levitas	Y	N	N	Y	Y	Y	N
5 Fowler	Y	N	N	+	Y	N	Y
6 *Gingrich*	?	Y	Y	Y	Y	Y	N
7 McDonald	N	Y	Y	N	Y	N	N
8 Rowland	Y	N	N	Y	Y	Y	N
9 Jenkins	Y	N	Y	Y	Y	Y	N
10 Barnard	Y	N	Y	Y	Y	Y	N
HAWAII							
1 Heftel	Y	N	N	Y	?	N	Y
2 Akaka	Y	N	N	Y	Y	N	Y
IDAHO							
1 *Craig*	Y	Y	Y	N	Y	Y	N
2 *Hansen*	Y	Y	Y	N	?	?	N
ILLINOIS							
1 Washington	?	?	?	?	?	?	#
2 Savage	?	?	?	?	Y	N	Y
3 Russo	Y	N	N	Y	Y	N	Y
4 *O'Brien*	Y	N	Y	?	Y	Y	N
5 Lipinski	?	?	?	?	?	Y	N
6 *Hyde*	Y	N	N	Y	N	N	Y
7 Collins	X	?	?	?	?	N	Y
8 Rostenkowski	?	?	?	?	Y	N	Y
9 Yates	Y	N	N	Y	?	N	Y
10 *Porter*	Y	N	N	Y	Y	Y	N
11 Annunzio	?	X	?	?	?	N	Y
12 *Crane, P.*	Y	Y	Y	N	Y	Y	N
13 *Erlenborn*	Y	Y	Y	Y	Y	Y	N
14 *Corcoran*	Y	Y	N	Y	Y	Y	N
15 *Madigan*	Y	N	Y	Y	Y	Y	N
16 *Martin*	Y	N	Y	Y	Y	Y	Y
17 Evans	Y	N	N	Y	Y	N	Y
18 *Michel*	Y	N	Y	Y	Y	Y	N
19 *Crane, D.*	Y	Y	Y	N	Y	Y	N
20 Durbin	Y	N	N	Y	Y	N	Y
21 Price	Y	N	N	Y	Y	Y	Y
22 Simon	Y	N	N	Y	Y	N	?
INDIANA							
1 Hall	?	?	?	?	?	N	Y
2 Sharp	Y	N	N	Y	Y	N	Y
3 *Hiler*	Y	Y	Y	N	Y	N	Y
4 *Coats*	Y	Y	Y	Y	Y	Y	N
5 Hillis	Y	Y	Y	N	Y	N	Y

ND - Northern Democrats   SD - Southern Democrats

Corresponding to Congressional Record Votes 48, 49, 50, 51, 52, 53, 54

	44	45	46	47	48	49	50
6 ***Burton***	Y	Y	Y	N	Y	Y	N
7 ***Myers***	Y	Y	Y	N	Y	Y	N
8 McCloskey	?	N	N	Y	Y	N	Y
9 Hamilton	Y	N	N	Y	Y	N	Y
10 Jacobs	Y	N	N	Y	N	N	Y
IOWA							
1 ***Leach***	Y	N	N	Y	Y	N	Y
2 ***Tauke***	Y	Y	N	Y	Y	N	Y
3 ***Evans***	Y	Y	N	Y	?	N	Y
4 Smith	Y	N	N	Y	Y	N	Y
5 Harkin	Y	N	N	Y	N	N	Y
6 Bedell	Y	N	N	Y	Y	N	Y
KANSAS							
1 ***Roberts***	Y	N	Y	Y	Y	Y	N
2 Slattery	?	N	N	Y	Y	N	N
3 ***Winn***	Y	Y	Y	Y	Y	Y	N
4 Glickman	Y	N	N	Y	Y	N	Y
5 ***Whittaker***	Y	Y	Y	Y	Y	Y	N
KENTUCKY							
1 Hubbard	Y	N	N	Y	Y	Y	N
2 Natcher	Y	N	N	Y	Y	N	Y
3 Mazzoli	+	-	-	-	Y	N	Y
4 ***Snyder***	Y	Y	Y	N	Y	Y	N
5 ***Rogers***	Y	Y	Y	Y	Y	Y	N
6 ***Hopkins***	Y	Y	Y	Y	Y	Y	N
7 Perkins	Y	N	N	Y	Y	N	Y
LOUISIANA							
1 ***Livingston***	Y	Y	Y	Y	Y	Y	N
2 Boggs	Y	N	N	Y	Y	N	Y
3 Tauzin	Y	N	N	Y	Y	Y	N
4 Roemer	Y	N	N	Y	N	Y	N
5 Huckaby	?	N	N	Y	Y	Y	N
6 ***Moore***	Y	Y	Y	Y	Y	Y	N
7 Breaux	Y	?	?	?	?	Y	N
8 Long	Y	N	N	Y	Y	N	Y
MAINE							
1 ***McKernan***	Y	N	N	Y	Y	N	Y
2 ***Snowe***	Y	N	N	Y	Y	N	Y
MARYLAND							
1 Dyson	Y	N	N	Y	Y	Y	N
2 Long	Y	N	N	?	?	N	Y
3 Mikulski	Y	N	N	Y	Y	N	Y
4 ***Holt***	Y	N	Y	N	Y	Y	N
5 Hoyer	Y	N	N	Y	Y	N	Y
6 Byron	Y	N	N	Y	Y	Y	N
7 Mitchell	Y	N	N	Y	N	N	Y
8 Barnes	Y	N	N	Y	Y	N	Y
MASSACHUSETTS							
1 ***Conte***	Y	N	N	Y	Y	N	Y
2 Boland	Y	N	N	+	Y	N	Y
3 Early	Y	N	N	Y	Y	N	Y
4 Frank	Y	N	N	Y	Y	N	Y
5 Shannon	Y	N	N	Y	Y	N	Y
6 Mavroules	Y	N	N	Y	?	N	Y
7 Markey	Y	N	N	Y	Y	N	Y
8 O'Neill							
9 Moakley	Y	N	N	Y	Y	N	Y
10 Studds	Y	N	N	Y	Y	N	Y
11 Donnelly	N	N	N	Y	Y	N	Y
MICHIGAN							
1 Conyers	?	?	?	?	?	N	Y
2 ***Pursell***	Y	N	N	Y	Y	N	Y
3 Wolpe	Y	N	N	Y	Y	N	Y
4 ***Siljander***	Y	Y	Y	N	Y	Y	N
5 ***Sawyer***	Y	N	Y	Y	Y	Y	N
6 Carr	Y	N	N	Y	Y	N	Y
7 Kildee	Y	N	N	Y	Y	N	Y
8 Traxler	Y	N	N	Y	?	N	Y
9 ***Vander Jagt***	?	N	Y	Y	Y	Y	N
10 Albosta	Y	N	N	Y	Y	N	Y
11 ***Davis***	Y	Y	Y	N	Y	Y	Y
12 Bonior	?	?	?	?	Y	N	Y
13 Crockett	Y	N	N	Y	Y	N	?
14 Hertel	N	N	N	Y	Y	N	?
15 Ford	Y	N	N	Y	?	N	Y
16 Dingell	Y	N	N	Y	?	N	Y
17 Levin	Y	N	N	Y	Y	N	Y
18 ***Broomfield***	Y	Y	Y	N	Y	Y	N
MINNESOTA							
1 Penny	Y	N	N	Y	Y	N	Y
2 ***Weber***	Y	N	N	Y	Y	Y	N
3 ***Frenzel***	N	N	Y	N	Y	Y	N
4 Vento	Y	N	N	Y	Y	N	Y
5 Sabo	Y	N	N	Y	N	N	Y
6 Sikorski	Y	N	N	Y	Y	N	Y
7 ***Stangeland***	Y	Y	Y	N	Y	Y	N
8 Oberstar	Y	N	N	Y	P	N	Y
MISSISSIPPI							
1 Whitten	N	N	N	Y	?	N	N
2 ***Franklin***	?	#	?	?	Y	Y	N
3 Montgomery	Y	Y	Y	N	Y	Y	N
4 Dowdy	Y	N	N	Y	Y	N	N
5 ***Lott***	Y	Y	Y	N	Y	Y	N
MISSOURI							
1 Clay	Y	?	?	?	?	N	Y
2 Young	Y	N	N	Y	Y	N	Y
3 Gephardt	Y	N	N	Y	?	?	Y
4 Skelton	Y	N	N	Y	?	Y	?
5 Wheat	Y	N	N	Y	Y	N	Y
6 ***Coleman***	Y	N	N	Y	Y	Y	N
7 ***Taylor***	Y	Y	Y	N	Y	Y	N
8 ***Emerson***	Y	Y	Y	N	N	Y	N
9 Volkmer	Y	N	-	+	Y	N	Y
MONTANA							
1 Williams	?	?	?	?	Y	N	Y
2 ***Marlenee***	Y	Y	Y	N	Y	Y	N
NEBRASKA							
1 ***Bereuter***	Y	N	N	Y	Y	Y	N
2 ***Daub***	Y	Y	Y	Y	Y	Y	N
3 ***Smith***	Y	Y	Y	Y	Y	Y	N
NEVADA							
1 Reid	?	N	N	Y	Y	N	Y
2 ***Vucanovich***	Y	Y	Y	N	Y	Y	N
NEW HAMPSHIRE							
1 D'Amours	Y	N	N	Y	Y	N	Y
2 ***Gregg***	Y	Y	Y	Y	Y	Y	N
NEW JERSEY							
1 Florio	Y	?	N	Y	Y	N	Y
2 Hughes	?	N	N	Y	Y	N	Y
3 Howard	Y	N	N	Y	Y	N	Y
4 ***Smith***	Y	N	N	Y	Y	N	Y
5 ***Roukema***	Y	N	N	Y	Y	N	N
6 Dwyer	Y	N	N	Y	Y	N	Y
7 ***Rinaldo***	Y	N	N	Y	Y	N	Y
8 Roe	Y	N	N	Y	Y	N	Y
9 Torricelli	Y	N	N	Y	Y	N	Y
10 Rodino	?	X	?	?	?	N	Y
11 Minish	Y	N	N	Y	Y	N	Y
12 ***Courter***	Y	N	N	Y	Y	Y	N
13 ***Forsythe***	Y	Y	Y	N	N	N	Y
14 Guarini	Y	N	N	Y	Y	N	Y
NEW MEXICO							
1 ***Lujan***	Y	Y	Y	N	Y	Y	N
2 ***Skeen***	Y	Y	Y	N	Y	Y	N
3 Richardson	Y	N	N	Y	Y	N	Y
NEW YORK							
1 ***Carney***	Y	Y	Y	N	Y	Y	N
2 Downey	Y	N	N	Y	Y	N	Y
3 Mrazek	Y	N	N	Y	Y	N	Y
4 ***Lent***	Y	N	Y	Y	Y	Y	N
5 ***McGrath***	Y	Y	Y	Y	Y	Y	N
6 Addabbo	Y	X	?	?	Y	N	Y
7 Ackerman	Y	N	N	Y	Y	N	Y
8 Scheuer	Y	N	N	Y	Y	N	Y
9 Ferraro	N	N	N	Y	Y	N	Y
10 Schumer	Y	N	N	Y	Y	N	Y
11 Towns	Y	N	N	Y	Y	N	N
12 Owens	?	?	?	?	?	N	Y
13 Solarz	Y	N	N	Y	Y	N	Y
14 ***Molinari***	Y	Y	Y	N	Y	Y	N
15 ***Green***	Y	N	N	Y	Y	N	Y
16 Rangel	Y	N	N	Y	Y	N	Y
17 Weiss	Y	N	N	Y	Y	N	Y
18 Garcia	?	N	N	Y	Y	N	Y
19 Biaggi	Y	N	N	Y	Y	N	Y
20 Ottinger	Y	-	?	+	P	-	Y
21 ***Fish***	?	?	?	?	Y	Y	Y
22 ***Gilman***	Y	N	N	Y	Y	Y	N
23 Stratton	Y	N	N	Y	Y	Y	N
24 ***Solomon***	Y	Y	Y	N	N	Y	N
25 ***Boehlert***	Y	N	N	Y	Y	N	Y
26 ***Martin***	Y	Y	Y	N	Y	Y	N
27 ***Wortley***	Y	Y	Y	N	Y	Y	N
28 McHugh	Y	N	N	Y	?	N	Y
29 ***Horton***	?	?	?	?	?	?	?
30 ***Conable***	N	N	Y	N	Y	Y	N
31 ***Kemp***	Y	Y	Y	N	Y	Y	N
32 LaFalce	Y	N	N	Y	Y	N	Y
33 Nowak	Y	?	N	Y	Y	N	Y
34 Lundine	Y	N	N	Y	Y	N	Y
NORTH CAROLINA							
1 Jones	?	?	?	?	?	?	?
2 Valentine	Y	N	N	Y	Y	Y	X
3 Whitley	Y	N	N	Y	Y	Y	N
4 Andrews	Y	N	N	Y	Y	N	Y
5 Neal	?	?	?	?	?	?	?
6 Britt	Y	N	N	Y	Y	N	Y
7 Rose	Y	N	N	Y	Y	N	Y
8 Hefner	N	N	N	Y	Y	N	Y
9 ***Martin***	Y	Y	Y	N	Y	Y	N
10 ***Broyhill***	Y	#	?	?	?	Y	N
11 Clarke	Y	N	N	Y	Y	N	Y
NORTH DAKOTA							
AL Dorgan	Y	N	N	Y	Y	N	Y
OHIO							
1 Luken	Y	N	N	Y	Y	N	Y
2 ***Gradison***	Y	N	N	Y	Y	Y	N
3 Hall	Y	N	N	Y	Y	N	Y
4 ***Oxley***	Y	Y	Y	N	Y	Y	N
5 ***Latta***	Y	Y	Y	N	Y	Y	N
6 ***McEwen***	Y	Y	Y	Y	Y	Y	N
7 ***DeWine***	Y	Y	N	Y	?	Y	N
8 ***Kindness***	Y	#	?	?	Y	Y	N
9 Kaptur	Y	N	N	Y	Y	N	Y
10 ***Miller***	Y	Y	Y	N	N	Y	N
11 Eckart	Y	N	N	Y	Y	N	Y
12 ***Kasich***	Y	Y	Y	N	Y	Y	N
13 Pease	Y	N	N	Y	Y	N	Y
14 Seiberling	Y	N	N	Y	Y	N	Y
15 ***Wylie***	Y	N	N	Y	Y	Y	N
16 ***Regula***	Y	Y	Y	Y	Y	Y	N
17 ***Williams***	Y	N	?	Y	?	?	?
18 Applegate	Y	N	N	Y	?	N	Y
19 Feighan	Y	N	N	Y	Y	N	Y
20 Oakar	Y	N	N	Y	Y	N	Y
21 Stokes	Y	N	N	?	Y	N	Y
OKLAHOMA							
1 Jones	N	N	N	Y	Y	N	N
2 Synar	Y	N	N	Y	Y	N	Y
3 Watkins	Y	N	N	Y	Y	Y	Y
4 McCurdy	Y	N	N	Y	Y	Y	N
5 ***Edwards***	?	Y	N	Y	Y	Y	N
6 English	?	N	N	Y	Y	Y	Y
OREGON							
1 AuCoin	Y	?	N	Y	Y	N	Y
2 ***Smith, R.***	Y	Y	Y	N	Y	Y	N
3 Wyden	Y	N	N	Y	Y	N	Y
4 Weaver	Y	N	N	Y	Y	N	Y
5 ***Smith, D.***	Y	Y	Y	N	Y	Y	N
PENNSYLVANIA							
1 Foglietta	Y	N	N	Y	Y	N	Y
2 Gray	?	?	?	?	Y	N	Y
3 Borski	Y	N	N	Y	Y	N	Y
4 Kolter	Y	Y	N	Y	Y	N	Y
5 ***Schulze***	Y	#	?	?	Y	Y	N
6 Yatron	Y	N	N	Y	Y	N	Y
7 Edgar	Y	N	N	Y	Y	N	Y
8 Kostmayer	Y	N	N	Y	?	N	Y
9 ***Shuster***	Y	Y	Y	N	Y	Y	N
10 ***McDade***	Y	Y	N	Y	Y	Y	N
11 Harrison	Y	N	N	Y	Y	N	Y
12 Murtha	N	N	N	Y	Y	Y	N
13 ***Coughlin***	Y	N	N	Y	N	N	N
14 Coyne	Y	N	N	Y	Y	N	Y
15 ***Ritter***	Y	Y	Y	N	Y	Y	N
16 ***Walker***	Y	Y	Y	N	N	Y	N
17 ***Gekas***	Y	Y	Y	N	Y	Y	N
18 Walgren	Y	N	N	Y	Y	N	Y
19 ***Goodling***	Y	Y	Y	Y	?	N	N
20 Gaydos	Y	Y	N	Y	Y	N	Y
21 ***Ridge***	Y	N	Y	Y	Y	Y	N
22 Murphy	?	?	N	Y	?	N	Y
23 ***Clinger***	Y	Y	N	Y	Y	Y	N
RHODE ISLAND							
1 St Germain	Y	N	N	Y	Y	N	?
2 ***Schneider***	Y	N	N	Y	Y	N	?
SOUTH CAROLINA							
1 ***Hartnett***	N	Y	Y	N	Y	Y	N
2 ***Spence***	Y	Y	Y	N	Y	Y	N
3 Derrick	Y	N	N	Y	Y	N	Y
4 ***Campbell***	Y	Y	Y	N	Y	Y	N
5 Spratt	Y	N	N	Y	Y	Y	Y
6 Tallon	?	N	N	Y	Y	N	Y
SOUTH DAKOTA							
AL Daschle	?	N	N	Y	Y	N	Y
TENNESSEE							
1 ***Quillen***	Y	Y	Y	N	Y	Y	N
2 ***Duncan***	Y	N	Y	Y	Y	Y	N
3 Lloyd***	?	?	?	?	?	?	?
4 Cooper	Y	N	N	Y	Y	N	N
5 Boner	?	N	N	Y	Y	N	Y
6 Gore	Y	N	N	Y	Y	N	Y
7 ***Sundquist***	Y	Y	Y	N	Y	Y	N
8 Jones	?	?	?	?	?	?	?
9 Ford	?	?	?	?	Y	N	Y
TEXAS							
1 Hall, S.	Y	Y	Y	N	Y	Y	N
2 Wilson	?	?	?	?	?	?	?
3 ***Bartlett***	Y	Y	Y	N	Y	Y	N
4 Hall, R.	Y	Y	Y	N	Y	Y	N
5 Bryant	Y	N	N	Y	Y	N	Y
6 ***Gramm***	N	Y	Y	N	Y	Y	N
7 ***Archer***	Y	Y	Y	N	Y	Y	N
8 ***Fields***	Y	Y	Y	N	Y	Y	N
9 Brooks	Y	N	N	Y	Y	N	Y
10 Pickle	Y	N	Y	Y	Y	Y	Y
11 Leath	N	Y	Y	N	Y	Y	N
12 Wright	Y	N	N	Y	Y	N	Y
13 Hightower	Y	N	Y	Y	Y	Y	N
14 Patman	Y	N	N	N	Y	Y	N
15 de la Garza	Y	N	N	Y	Y	N	?
16 Coleman	Y	N	N	Y	Y	N	Y
17 Stenholm	Y	Y	Y	N	Y	Y	N
18 Leland	?	?	?	Y	?	N	Y
19 Hance	Y	N	N	Y	Y	Y	N
20 Gonzalez	P	N	N	Y	Y	N	Y
21 ***Loeffler***	Y	Y	Y	N	Y	Y	N
22 ***Paul***	N	Y	Y	N	Y	Y	N
23 Kazen	Y	N	N	Y	Y	Y	N
24 Frost	Y	N	N	Y	Y	N	Y
25 Andrews	Y	N	N	Y	Y	Y	N
26 Vandergriff	Y	N	N	Y	?	Y	N
27 Ortiz	?	N	N	Y	?	N	N
UTAH							
1 ***Hansen***	Y	Y	Y	N	Y	Y	N
2 ***Marriott***	Y	Y	Y	N	Y	Y	N
3 ***Nielson***	Y	Y	Y	N	Y	Y	N
VERMONT							
AL ***Jeffords***	Y	N	?	Y	Y	N	Y
VIRGINIA							
1 ***Bateman***	Y	Y	Y	N	Y	Y	N
2 ***Whitehurst***	Y	Y	Y	N	Y	Y	N
3 ***Bliley***	Y	Y	Y	N	Y	Y	N
4 Sisisky	Y	N	N	Y	Y	Y	N
5 Daniel	Y	Y	Y	N	?	Y	N
6 Olin	Y	N	N	Y	Y	N	Y
7 ***Robinson***	Y	Y	Y	N	Y	Y	N
8 ***Parris***	Y	N	Y	N	Y	Y	N
9 Boucher	Y	N	N	Y	Y	N	N
10 ***Wolf***	Y	Y	Y	Y	Y	Y	N
WASHINGTON							
1 ***Pritchard***	Y	N	Y	?	Y	Y	N
2 Swift	Y	N	N	Y	Y	N	Y
3 Bonker	Y	N	N	Y	?	N	Y
4 ***Morrison***	Y	Y	Y	N	Y	Y	N
5 Foley	Y	N	N	Y	Y	N	Y
6 Dicks	Y	N	N	Y	?	N	Y
7 Lowry	Y	N	N	Y	Y	N	Y
8 ***Chandler***	Y	N	Y	N	Y	Y	N
WEST VIRGINIA							
1 Mollohan	Y	?	?	?	?	N	Y
2 Staggers	Y	N	N	Y	Y	N	Y
3 Wise	Y	N	N	Y	Y	N	Y
4 Rahall	Y	N	N	Y	Y	N	Y
WISCONSIN							
1 Aspin	Y	N	N	Y	Y	N	Y
2 Kastenmeier	?	N	N	Y	Y	N	Y
3 ***Gunderson***	Y	N	Y	Y	Y	Y	Y
4 Zablocki	Y	N	N	Y	Y	N	Y
5 Moody	Y	N	N	Y	Y	N	Y
6 ***Petri***	Y	N	N	Y	Y	Y	N
7 Obey	Y	N	N	Y	Y	N	Y
8 ***Roth***	Y	N	N	Y	Y	Y	N
9 ***Sensenbrenner***	Y	N	N	Y	Y	Y	N
WYOMING							
AL ***Cheney***	Y	Y	Y	N	?	Y	N

Southern states - Ala., Ark., Fla., Ga., Ky., La., Miss., N.C., Okla., S.C., Tenn., Texas, Va.

51. Procedural Motion. Fiedler, R-Calif., motion to approve the House *Journal* of Monday, April 18. Motion agreed to 350-18: R 140-10; D 210-8 (ND 142-7, SD 68-1), April 19, 1983.

52. H J Res 13. Nuclear Freeze. Martin, R-N.C., amendment to require that any freeze negotiation take account of the relative age and obsolescence of nuclear weapons. Rejected 204-211: R 142-21; D 62-190 (ND 10-157, SD 52-33), April 20, 1983.

53. H J Res 13. Nuclear Freeze. Stratton, D-N.Y., amendment to require that any freeze provide for vigorous programs of research and development and safety-related improvements in U.S. weapons. Adopted 407-3: R 160-0; D 247-3 (ND 160-3, SD 87-0), April 20, 1983.

54. Procedural Motion. Siljander, R-Mich., motion to approve the House *Journal* of Wednesday, April 20. Motion agreed to 375-18: R 147-10; D 228-8 (ND 150-7, SD 78-1), April 21, 1983.

55. H J Res 13. Nuclear Freeze. Zablocki, D-Wis., substitute for the Carney, R-N.Y., amendment, to provide that, unless a freeze agreement were negotiated, nothing in the resolution would impede U.S. compliance with the 1979 NATO decision to deploy new missiles in Europe. The Carney amendment provided that the freeze would not impede U.S. compliance with the 1979 agreement. Adopted 221-195: R 19-143; D 202-52 (ND 163-9, SD 39-43), April 21, 1983.

56. H J Res 13. Nuclear Freeze. Zablocki, D-Wis., motion to end the debate on the text of the joint resolution at 3:30 p.m. April 21. Motion agreed to 214-194: R 0-160; D 214-34 (ND 162-5, SD 52-29), April 21, 1983.

57. H J Res 13. Nuclear Freeze. Dicks, D-Wash., substitute for the Stratton, D-N.Y., amendment, to require that the president ensure that any freeze agreement be adequately verifiable. The Stratton amendment would not require a president to negotiate a freeze agreement if he certified that it would not be verifiable. Adopted 221-171: R 30-125; D 191-46 (ND 156-6, SD 35-40), April 21, 1983.

58. H J Res 13. Nuclear Freeze. Stratton, D-N.Y., amendment as amended by the Dicks, D-Wash., amendment *(see vote 57, above)*, to require that the president ensure that any freeze agreement be adequately verifiable. Adopted 374-6: R 147-3; D 227-3 (ND 155-0, SD 72-3), April 21, 1983.

KEY

Y Voted for (yea).
Paired for.
+ Announced for.
N Voted against (nay).
X Paired against.
- Announced against.
P Voted "present".
C Voted "present" to avoid possible conflict of interest.
? Did not vote or otherwise make a position known.

Democrats   *Republicans*

	51	52	53	54	55	56	57	58
ALABAMA								
1 *Edwards*	?	Y	?	?	X	?	?	?
2 *Dickinson*	?	Y	Y	N	N	N	N	?
3 Nichols	?	Y	Y	N	Y	N	Y	Y
4 Bevill	Y	Y	Y	Y	N	Y	N	Y
5 Flippo	Y	Y	Y	?	?	?	?	?
6 Erdreich	Y	Y	Y	Y	N	N	N	Y
7 Shelby	Y	Y	Y	Y	N	N	N	Y
ALASKA								
AL *Young*	N	Y	Y	N	N	N	N	Y
ARIZONA								
1 *McCain*	Y	Y	Y	?	N	N	N	N
2 Udall	Y	N	Y	Y	Y	Y	Y	Y
3 *Stump*	Y	Y	Y	N	N	N	N	Y
4 *Rudd*	?	Y	Y	N	N	N	N	Y
5 McNulty	Y	N	?	?	Y	Y	Y	Y
ARKANSAS								
1 Alexander	?	?	Y	Y	Y	Y	Y	Y
2 *Bethune*	Y	Y	Y	N	N	N	N	Y
3 *Hammerschmidt*	Y	Y	Y	Y	N	N	N	Y
4 Anthony	Y	Y	Y	?	Y	Y	Y	Y
CALIFORNIA								
1 Bosco	Y	N	Y	Y	Y	Y	Y	Y
2 *Chappie*	Y	Y	Y	Y	N	N	N	Y
3 Matsui	?	N	Y	Y	Y	Y	Y	Y
4 Fazio	Y	N	Y	Y	Y	Y	Y	?
5 Vacancy								
6 Boxer	Y	N	Y	?	Y	Y	Y	Y
7 Miller	Y	N	Y	Y	Y	Y	Y	Y
8 Dellums	?	N	Y	?	Y	Y	Y	?
9 Stark	Y	N	Y	Y	Y	Y	Y	Y
10 Edwards	Y	N	Y	Y	Y	N	Y	Y
11 Lantos	Y	N	Y	Y	Y	Y	Y	Y
12 Zschau	Y	Y	Y	Y	Y	N	Y	Y
13 Mineta	Y	N	Y	Y	Y	Y	Y	Y
14 *Shumway*	Y	Y	Y	Y	N	N	N	N
15 Coelho	Y	N	?	?	Y	Y	Y	Y
16 Panetta	Y	N	Y	Y	Y	Y	Y	Y
17 *Pashayan*	Y	Y	Y	Y	N	N	N	Y
18 Lehman	Y	N	Y	Y	Y	Y	Y	Y
19 *Lagomarsino*	Y	Y	Y	Y	N	N	N	Y
20 *Thomas*	Y	Y	Y	Y	N	N	N	Y
21 *Fiedler*	Y	Y	Y	Y	N	N	N	Y
22 *Moorhead*	Y	Y	Y	Y	N	N	N	Y
23 Beilenson	Y	N	Y	Y	Y	Y	Y	Y
24 Waxman	Y	N	Y	Y	Y	Y	Y	Y
25 Roybal	Y	N	Y	Y	Y	Y	Y	Y
26 Berman	Y	N	Y	Y	Y	Y	Y	Y
27 Levine	Y	N	Y	Y	Y	Y	Y	Y
28 Dixon	?	N	Y	Y	Y	Y	#	?
29 Hawkins	Y	N	Y	Y	Y	Y	Y	Y
30 Martinez	Y	?	?	Y	Y	Y	Y	?
31 Dymally	?	X	?	?	#	?	#	?
32 Anderson	Y	N	Y	Y	Y	Y	Y	Y
33 *Dreier*	Y	Y	Y	Y	N	N	N	Y
34 Torres	Y	N	Y	Y	Y	Y	Y	Y
35 *Lewis*	Y	Y	Y	Y	N	N	N	Y
36 Brown	Y	N	Y	Y	Y	Y	Y	Y
37 *McCandless*	N	Y	Y	Y	N	N	N	Y
38 Patterson	P	N	Y	Y	Y	Y	Y	Y
39 *Dannemeyer*	Y	Y	Y	Y	N	N	N	N
40 *Badham*	Y	Y	Y	Y	N	N	N	Y
41 *Lowery*	Y	Y	Y	Y	N	N	N	Y
42 Lungren	Y	Y	Y	N	N	N	N	?

	51	52	53	54	55	56	57	58
43 *Packard*	?	Y	Y	N	N	N	N	?
44 Bates	Y	N	Y	?	Y	Y	Y	Y
45 *Hunter*	Y	Y	Y	N	N	N	N	Y
COLORADO								
1 Schroeder	N	N	Y	N	Y	Y	Y	Y
2 Wirth	Y	N	Y	Y	Y	Y	Y	Y
3 Kogovsek	Y	N	Y	Y	Y	Y	Y	Y
4 *Brown*	Y	Y	Y	Y	N	Y	N	Y
5 *Kramer*	Y	Y	Y	Y	N	N	N	Y
6 *Schaefer*	Y	Y	Y	N	N	N	N	Y
CONNECTICUT								
1 Kennelly	Y	N	Y	Y	Y	Y	Y	Y
2 Gejdenson	N	N	Y	N	Y	Y	Y	Y
3 Morrison	?	?	?	Y	Y	Y	Y	Y
4 *McKinney*	?	N	Y	?	Y	?	Y	Y
5 Ratchford	Y	N	Y	Y	Y	Y	Y	Y
6 *Johnson*	Y	N	Y	Y	N	N	Y	Y
DELAWARE								
AL Carper	Y	N	Y	Y	Y	Y	Y	Y
FLORIDA								
1 Hutto	Y	Y	Y	Y	N	N	N	Y
2 Fuqua	Y	Y	Y	Y	Y	Y	Y	Y
3 Bennett	Y	Y	Y	N	N	N	N	Y
4 Chappell	Y	Y	Y	?	?	?	N	Y
5 *McCollum*	Y	Y	Y	N	N	N	N	Y
6 MacKay	Y	N	Y	Y	Y	Y	Y	Y
7 Gibbons	Y	Y	Y	Y	Y	Y	Y	Y
8 *Young*	Y	Y	Y	N	N	N	N	Y
9 *Bilirakis*	?	Y	Y	N	N	N	N	Y
10 Ireland	Y	Y	Y	N	N	N	N	Y
11 Nelson	Y	Y	Y	N	Y	N	N	N
12 *Lewis*	Y	Y	Y	N	N	N	N	Y
13 *Mack*	?	Y	?	N	N	N	N	Y
14 Mica	Y	N	Y	Y	Y	Y	Y	Y
15 *Shaw*	?	Y	Y	N	N	N	N	Y
16 Smith	Y	N	Y	Y	Y	Y	Y	Y
17 Lehman	Y	N	Y	Y	Y	Y	Y	Y
18 Pepper	?	N	Y	Y	Y	Y	Y	Y
19 Fascell	?	N	Y	Y	Y	Y	Y	Y
GEORGIA								
1 Thomas	?	Y	Y	N	Y	N	Y	Y
2 Hatcher	Y	Y	Y	N	N	N	N	Y
3 Ray	Y	Y	Y	N	N	N	N	N
4 Levitas	?	N	Y	N	N	N	N	Y
5 Fowler	Y	N	Y	Y	Y	Y	Y	Y
6 *Gingrich*	Y	Y	Y	N	N	N	N	Y
7 McDonald	Y	Y	Y	N	N	N	N	Y
8 Rowland	Y	Y	Y	N	N	N	N	Y
9 Jenkins	Y	Y	Y	Y	N	Y	N	Y
10 Barnard	Y	Y	Y	N	N	N	?	?
HAWAII								
1 Heftel	?	N	Y	Y	N	Y	Y	Y
2 Akaka	Y	N	Y	Y	Y	Y	Y	Y
IDAHO								
1 *Craig*	Y	Y	Y	Y	N	N	N	Y
2 *Hansen*	Y	?	?	?	X	?	X	?
ILLINOIS								
1 Washington	?	X	?	?	#	?	#	?
2 Savage	?	N	Y	?	Y	Y	Y	Y
3 Russo	Y	N	Y	Y	Y	Y	Y	Y
4 *O'Brien*	Y	Y	Y	Y	N	N	N	Y
5 Lipinski	?	Y	Y	N	Y	N	Y	Y
6 *Hyde*	Y	Y	Y	N	N	N	N	Y
7 Collins	Y	N	Y	N	Y	Y	Y	Y
8 Rostenkowski	Y	N	Y	Y	Y	Y	Y	Y
9 Yates	N	N	Y	N	Y	Y	Y	Y
10 *Porter*	Y	Y	Y	Y	Y	Y	Y	Y
11 Annunzio	Y	N	Y	Y	Y	Y	Y	Y
12 *Crane, P.*	Y	Y	Y	Y	N	N	N	?
13 *Erlenborn*	Y	Y	Y	Y	N	N	N	Y
14 *Corcoran*	Y	Y	Y	Y	N	N	N	Y
15 *Madigan*	Y	Y	Y	Y	N	N	N	Y
16 *Martin*	Y	Y	Y	Y	N	Y	N	Y
17 Evans	Y	N	Y	Y	Y	Y	Y	Y
18 *Michel*	Y	#	Y	Y	N	N	N	Y
19 *Crane, D.*	Y	Y	Y	N	N	N	N	Y
20 Durbin	Y	N	Y	Y	Y	Y	Y	Y
21 Price	Y	Y	Y	Y	N	Y	N	Y
22 Simon	Y	N	Y	Y	Y	?	?	?
INDIANA								
1 Hall	Y	N	Y	Y	Y	?	?	Y
2 Sharp	Y	N	Y	Y	Y	Y	Y	Y
3 *Hiler*	N	N	Y	N	N	N	N	Y
4 *Coats*	N	N	Y	N	N	N	N	Y
5 Hillis	Y	Y	Y	N	N	N	?	?

ND - Northern Democrats   SD - Southern Democrats

Corresponding to Congressional Record Votes 55, 56, 57, 58, 59, 60, 62, 63

	51	52	53	54	55	56	57	58
6 ***Burton***	Y	Y	Y	Y	N	N	N	Y
7 ***Myers***	Y	Y	Y	?	N	N	N	Y
8 McCloskey	Y	N	Y	Y	Y	Y	Y	Y
9 Hamilton	Y	N	Y	Y	Y	Y	Y	Y
10 Jacobs	N	N	Y	N	Y	N	Y	Y
IOWA								
1 ***Leach***	Y	N	Y	Y	Y	N	Y	Y
2 ***Tauke***	Y	N	Y	Y	N	N	Y	Y
3 ***Evans***	N	N	Y	N	N	N	Y	Y
4 Smith	Y	N	Y	Y	Y	Y	Y	Y
5 Harkin	N	N	Y	N	Y	Y	Y	Y
6 Bedell	Y	N	Y	Y	Y	Y	Y	Y
KANSAS								
1 ***Roberts***	Y	Y	Y	N	N	N	?	?
2 Slattery	?	?	?	?	?	?	?	?
3 ***Winn***	Y	Y	Y	Y	N	N	?	?
4 Glickman	Y	N	Y	Y	N	Y	Y	Y
5 ***Whittaker***	Y	Y	Y	Y	N	N	N	Y
KENTUCKY								
1 Hubbard	Y	Y	Y	Y	N	Y	N	Y
2 Natcher	Y	N	Y	Y	Y	Y	Y	Y
3 Mazzoli	Y	N	Y	Y	Y	Y	Y	Y
4 ***Snyder***	Y	Y	Y	Y	N	N	N	Y
5 ***Rogers***	Y	Y	Y	Y	N	N	N	Y
6 ***Hopkins***	Y	Y	Y	Y	N	N	N	Y
7 Perkins	?	N	Y	Y	Y	Y	?	?
LOUISIANA								
1 ***Livingston***	Y	Y	Y	Y	N	N	N	Y
2 Boggs	Y	Y	Y	?	#	?	#	?
3 Tauzin	Y	Y	Y	Y	N	?	N	Y
4 Roemer	N	Y	Y	N	N	N	N	Y
5 Huckaby	Y	Y	Y	Y	N	N	N	Y
6 ***Moore***	Y	Y	Y	Y	N	N	N	Y
7 Breaux	Y	Y	Y	Y	N	N	N	Y
8 Long	?	?	Y	Y	Y	Y	Y	Y
MAINE								
1 ***McKernan***	Y	N	Y	Y	Y	N	Y	Y
2 ***Snowe***	Y	N	Y	Y	N	N	Y	Y
MARYLAND								
1 Dyson	Y	Y	Y	Y	N	N	N	Y
2 Long	Y	N	Y	Y	Y	Y	Y	Y
3 Mikulski	Y	N	Y	Y	Y	Y	Y	Y
4 ***Holt***	Y	Y	?	N	N	N	N	N
5 Hoyer	Y	N	Y	Y	Y	Y	Y	Y
6 Byron	Y	Y	Y	Y	N	N	N	Y
7 Mitchell	?	N	Y	N	Y	Y	?	Y
8 Barnes	Y	N	Y	Y	Y	Y	Y	Y
MASSACHUSETTS								
1 ***Conte***	Y	N	Y	Y	Y	N	Y	Y
2 Boland	Y	N	Y	Y	Y	Y	Y	Y
3 Early	Y	N	Y	Y	Y	Y	Y	Y
4 Frank	Y	N	Y	Y	Y	Y	Y	Y
5 Shannon	?	N	Y	Y	Y	Y	Y	Y
6 Mavroules	Y	N	Y	Y	Y	Y	Y	Y
7 Markey	Y	N	Y	Y	Y	Y	Y	Y
8 O'Neill								
9 Moakley	Y	N	Y	Y	Y	Y	Y	Y
10 Studds	Y	N	Y	Y	Y	Y	Y	Y
11 Donnelly	Y	N	Y	Y	Y	Y	Y	Y
MICHIGAN								
1 Conyers	Y	N	N	Y	Y	Y	Y	Y
2 ***Pursell***	Y	N	Y	Y	N	N	N	Y
3 Wolpe	Y	N	Y	Y	Y	Y	Y	Y
4 ***Siljander***	Y	Y	Y	Y	N	N	N	Y
5 ***Sawyer***	Y	Y	Y	Y	N	N	N	Y
6 Carr	Y	N	Y	Y	Y	Y	Y	Y
7 Kildee	Y	N	Y	Y	Y	Y	Y	Y
8 Traxler	Y	N	Y	Y	Y	Y	?	?
9 ***Vander Jagt***	Y	Y	Y	Y	N	N	N	Y
10 Albosta	Y	N	Y	Y	Y	Y	Y	Y
11 ***Davis***	Y	Y	Y	Y	N	N	Y	Y
12 Bonior	Y	N	?	Y	Y	Y	Y	Y
13 Crockett	Y	N	Y	Y	?	Y	Y	Y
14 Hertel	Y	N	Y	Y	Y	Y	Y	Y
15 Ford	?	N	Y	?	Y	Y	Y	Y
16 Dingell	Y	N	?	?	Y	Y	Y	Y
17 Levin	Y	N	Y	Y	Y	Y	Y	Y
18 ***Broomfield***	Y	Y	Y	Y	N	N	N	Y
MINNESOTA								
1 Penny	Y	·	Y	Y	Y	Y	Y	Y
2 ***Weber***	Y	Y	Y	Y	N	N	N	Y
3 ***Frenzel***	Y	Y	Y	Y	N	N	N	Y
4 Vento	Y	N	Y	Y	Y	Y	Y	Y
5 Sabo	N	N	Y	N	Y	Y	Y	Y
6 Sikorski	Y	N	Y	Y	Y	Y	Y	Y
7 ***Stangeland***	Y	Y	Y	Y	N	N	N	Y
8 Oberstar	?	N	Y	P	Y	Y	Y	Y
MISSISSIPPI								
1 Whitten	Y	Y	Y	Y	Y	Y	Y	Y
2 ***Franklin***	Y	Y	Y	Y	N	N	N	Y
3 Montgomery	Y	Y	Y	Y	N	N	N	Y
4 Dowdy	Y	Y	Y	Y	N	?	Y	Y
5 ***Lott***	Y	Y	Y	?	N	N	N	Y
MISSOURI								
1 Clay	N	N	Y	?	Y	Y	Y	Y
2 Young	?	N	Y	Y	Y	Y	?	?
3 Gephardt	Y	N	Y	Y	Y	Y	Y	Y
4 Skelton	Y	Y	Y	Y	N	Y	N	Y
5 Wheat	Y	N	Y	Y	Y	Y	Y	Y
6 ***Coleman***	Y	Y	Y	Y	N	N	N	Y
7 ***Taylor***	Y	Y	Y	Y	N	N	N	Y
8 ***Emerson***	N	Y	Y	N	N	N	N	Y
9 Volkmer	Y	N	Y	Y	Y	Y	Y	Y
MONTANA								
1 Williams	Y	N	Y	Y	Y	?	Y	?
2 ***Marlenee***	?	Y	Y	?	X	?	N	Y
NEBRASKA								
1 ***Bereuter***	Y	Y	Y	Y	N	N	Y	Y
2 ***Daub***	Y	Y	Y	Y	N	N	N	Y
3 ***Smith***	Y	Y	Y	Y	N	N	N	Y
NEVADA								
1 Reid	Y	N	Y	Y	Y	Y	Y	Y
2 ***Vucanovich***	Y	Y	Y	Y	N	N	N	Y
NEW HAMPSHIRE								
1 D'Amours	Y	N	?	?	Y	Y	?	Y
2 ***Gregg***	Y	Y	Y	Y	N	N	N	Y
NEW JERSEY								
1 Florio	Y	N	Y	Y	Y	Y	Y	Y
2 Hughes	Y	Y	Y	Y	N	Y	Y	Y
3 Howard	Y	N	Y	Y	Y	Y	Y	Y
4 ***Smith***	Y	N	Y	Y	N	N	N	Y
5 ***Roukema***	Y	N	Y	Y	N	N	Y	Y
6 Dwyer	Y	N	Y	Y	Y	Y	Y	Y
7 ***Rinaldo***	Y	N	Y	Y	Y	N	Y	Y
8 Roe	Y	N	Y	Y	Y	Y	Y	Y
9 Torricelli	Y	N	Y	Y	Y	Y	Y	Y
10 Rodino	?	N	Y	Y	Y	Y	Y	Y
11 Minish	Y	N	Y	Y	Y	Y	Y	Y
12 ***Courter***	Y	Y	?	Y	N	N	N	Y
13 ***Forsythe***	N	N	?	?	?	?	?	?
14 Guarini	Y	N	Y	Y	Y	Y	Y	Y
NEW MEXICO								
1 ***Lujan***	Y	Y	Y	Y	N	N	N	Y
2 ***Skeen***	Y	Y	Y	Y	N	N	N	Y
3 Richardson	Y	N	Y	Y	Y	Y	Y	Y
NEW YORK								
1 ***Carney***	?	Y	Y	Y	N	N	N	Y
2 Downey	Y	N	Y	Y	Y	Y	Y	Y
3 Mrazek	Y	N	Y	?	Y	Y	Y	Y
4 ***Lent***	Y	Y	Y	Y	N	N	?	Y
5 ***McGrath***	Y	Y	Y	Y	N	N	N	Y
6 Addabbo	?	N	Y	?	Y	Y	Y	Y
7 Ackerman	Y	N	Y	Y	Y	Y	Y	+
8 Scheuer	Y	N	Y	Y	Y	Y	Y	Y
9 Ferraro	Y	N	Y	Y	Y	Y	Y	Y
10 Schumer	Y	N	Y	Y	Y	Y	Y	Y
11 Towns	Y	N	Y	Y	Y	?	Y	Y
12 Owens	Y	?	Y	Y	Y	?	Y	Y
13 Solarz	Y	N	Y	Y	Y	Y	Y	Y
14 ***Molinari***	Y	Y	Y	Y	N	N	N	Y
15 ***Green***	Y	N	Y	Y	Y	N	Y	Y
16 Rangel	Y	N	Y	?	Y	Y	Y	Y
17 Weiss	Y	N	Y	Y	Y	Y	Y	Y
18 Garcia	Y	N	Y	Y	Y	Y	Y	Y
19 Biaggi	Y	N	Y	Y	Y	Y	Y	Y
20 Ottinger	?	N	Y	P	Y	Y	Y	Y
21 ***Fish***	?	Y	Y	Y	N	N	Y	Y
22 ***Gilman***	?	Y	Y	Y	N	N	N	Y
23 Stratton	Y	Y	Y	Y	N	N	N	Y
24 ***Solomon***	Y	Y	Y	Y	N	N	N	Y
25 ***Boehlert***	Y	N	Y	Y	Y	N	Y	Y
26 ***Martin***	Y	Y	Y	Y	N	N	N	Y
27 ***Wortley***	Y	Y	Y	Y	N	N	N	Y
28 McHugh	Y	N	Y	Y	Y	Y	Y	Y
29 ***Horton***	Y	N	Y	Y	Y	N	Y	Y
30 ***Conable***	Y	Y	Y	Y	N	N	N	Y
31 ***Kemp***	?	Y	Y	Y	N	N	N	Y
32 LaFalce	Y	N	Y	Y	Y	?	?	?
33 Nowak	Y	N	Y	Y	Y	Y	Y	?
34 Lundine	?	N	Y	Y	Y	Y	Y	?
NORTH CAROLINA								
1 Jones	?	N	Y	?	Y	Y	N	Y
2 Valentine	?	Y	Y	Y	N	N	N	?
3 Whitley	Y	Y	Y	Y	N	N	?	?
4 Andrews	Y	N	Y	?	Y	Y	Y	Y
5 Neal	?	?	?	?	?	?	?	?
6 Britt	Y	N	Y	Y	Y	Y	Y	Y
7 Rose	?	N	Y	Y	?	?	?	?
8 Hefner	Y	Y	Y	Y	Y	Y	?	?
9 ***Martin***	Y	Y	Y	Y	N	N	N	Y
10 ***Broyhill***	Y	Y	Y	Y	N	N	Y	Y
11 Clarke	Y	N	Y	Y	Y	Y	Y	Y
NORTH DAKOTA								
AL Dorgan	?	N	Y	Y	Y	Y	Y	Y
OHIO								
1 Luken	Y	N	Y	Y	Y	Y	Y	Y
2 ***Gradison***	Y	Y	Y	Y	N	N	N	Y
3 Hall	Y	N	Y	Y	Y	Y	Y	Y
4 ***Oxley***	?	Y	Y	Y	N	N	N	Y
5 ***Latta***	Y	#	Y	Y	N	N	X	Y
6 ***McEwen***	Y	Y	Y	Y	N	N	N	Y
7 ***DeWine***	Y	Y	Y	Y	N	N	N	Y
8 ***Kindness***	Y	Y	Y	Y	N	N	N	Y
9 Kaptur	Y	N	Y	Y	Y	Y	Y	Y
10 ***Miller***	N	Y	Y	N	N	N	N	Y
11 Eckart	?	N	Y	Y	Y	Y	Y	Y
12 ***Kasich***	Y	Y	Y	Y	N	N	N	Y
13 Pease	Y	N	Y	Y	Y	Y	Y	Y
14 Seiberling	Y	N	Y	Y	Y	Y	Y	Y
15 ***Wylie***	Y	Y	Y	Y	N	N	N	Y
16 ***Regula***	Y	Y	Y	Y	N	N	N	Y
17 ***Williams***	Y	Y	Y	Y	Y	N	Y	Y
18 Applegate	?	Y	Y	?	Y	Y	Y	Y
19 Feighan	Y	N	Y	Y	Y	Y	Y	Y
20 Oakar	Y	N	Y	Y	Y	Y	Y	Y
21 Stokes	Y	N	Y	Y	Y	Y	Y	Y
OKLAHOMA								
1 Jones	?	N	Y	Y	Y	Y	Y	Y
2 Synar	Y	N	Y	Y	Y	Y	+	+
3 Watkins	Y	Y	Y	Y	N	Y	Y	Y
4 McCurdy	Y	?	Y	Y	N	?	N	N
5 ***Edwards***	Y	Y	Y	Y	N	N	N	Y
6 English	Y	Y	Y	Y	N	Y	Y	Y
OREGON								
1 AuCoin	Y	N	Y	Y	Y	Y	Y	Y
2 ***Smith, R.***	Y	Y	Y	Y	N	N	N	Y
3 Wyden	Y	N	Y	Y	Y	Y	Y	Y
4 Weaver	?	N	Y	Y	Y	Y	Y	Y
5 ***Smith, D.***	Y	Y	Y	Y	N	N	N	Y
PENNSYLVANIA								
1 Foglietta	?	N	Y	Y	Y	Y	Y	Y
2 Gray	Y	N	Y	Y	Y	Y	Y	Y
3 Borski	Y	N	N	Y	Y	Y	Y	Y
4 Kolter	Y	N	Y	Y	Y	Y	Y	Y
5 ***Schulze***	Y	Y	Y	Y	N	N	N	?
6 Yatron	Y	N	Y	Y	Y	Y	?	?
7 Edgar	Y	N	Y	Y	Y	Y	Y	Y
8 Kostmayer	Y	N	Y	Y	Y	Y	Y	Y
9 ***Shuster***	?	Y	Y	Y	N	N	N	Y
10 ***McDade***	Y	Y	?	Y	N	N	Y	Y
11 Harrison	Y	N	Y	Y	Y	Y	Y	Y
12 Murtha	Y	Y	?	Y	Y	Y	Y	Y
13 ***Coughlin***	N	Y	Y	Y	Y	N	Y	?
14 Coyne	Y	N	Y	Y	Y	Y	Y	Y
15 ***Ritter***	Y	Y	Y	Y	N	N	Y	Y
16 ***Walker***	N	Y	Y	N	N	N	N	Y
17 ***Gekas***	Y	Y	Y	Y	N	N	N	Y
18 Walgren	Y	N	Y	Y	Y	Y	Y	Y
19 ***Goodling***	N	N	Y	N	Y	N	Y	Y
20 Gaydos	Y	N	Y	Y	Y	Y	?	?
21 ***Ridge***	?	Y	Y	Y	N	N	N	?
22 Murphy	Y	N	Y	Y	Y	Y	Y	?
23 ***Clinger***	Y	Y	Y	Y	N	N	N	Y
RHODE ISLAND								
1 St Germain	?	N	Y	Y	Y	Y	?	?
2 ***Schneider***	Y	N	Y	Y	Y	N	Y	Y
SOUTH CAROLINA								
1 ***Hartnett***	?	Y	Y	Y	N	N	N	N
2 ***Spence***	Y	Y	Y	Y	N	N	N	Y
3 Derrick	Y	N	?	Y	Y	Y	Y	Y
4 ***Campbell***	Y	Y	Y	Y	N	N	N	Y
5 Spratt	Y	Y	Y	Y	Y	Y	Y	Y
6 Tallon	?	N	Y	Y	Y	Y	Y	Y
SOUTH DAKOTA								
AL Daschle	Y	Y	Y	Y	Y	Y	Y	Y
TENNESSEE								
1 ***Quillen***	Y	Y	Y	Y	N	?	X	?
2 ***Duncan***	Y	?	Y	Y	N	N	N	Y
3 Lloyd	Y	Y	Y	Y	N	N	N	Y
4 Cooper	Y	Y	Y	Y	N	Y	N	Y
5 Boner	Y	N	Y	Y	Y	Y	Y	Y
6 Gore	Y	N	Y	Y	Y	Y	Y	Y
7 ***Sundquist***	Y	Y	Y	Y	N	N	N	Y
8 Jones	Y	Y	Y	Y	Y	Y	N	Y
9 Ford	Y	N	Y	Y	Y	?	Y	Y
TEXAS								
1 Hall, S.	?	Y	Y	Y	N	N	N	Y
2 Wilson	Y	Y	Y	Y	N	N	N	Y
3 ***Bartlett***	Y	Y	Y	Y	N	N	N	Y
4 Hall, R.	?	Y	Y	Y	N	N	N	Y
5 Bryant	?	N	Y	Y	Y	Y	?	Y
6 ***Gramm***	Y	Y	Y	Y	N	N	N	Y
7 ***Archer***	Y	Y	Y	Y	N	N	N	?
8 ***Fields***	Y	Y	Y	Y	N	N	N	Y
9 Brooks	Y	Y	Y	Y	Y	Y	Y	Y
10 Pickle	Y	Y	Y	Y	Y	Y	Y	Y
11 Leath	Y	Y	Y	Y	N	N	N	Y
12 Wright	Y	N	Y	Y	Y	Y	?	?
13 Hightower	Y	Y	Y	Y	N	N	N	Y
14 Patman	Y	Y	Y	Y	N	N	N	Y
15 de la Garza	Y	N	Y	Y	?	Y	N	Y
16 Coleman	Y	N	Y	Y	Y	Y	?	?
17 Stenholm	Y	Y	Y	Y	N	N	N	Y
18 Leland	?	N	Y	Y	#	Y	Y	Y
19 Hance	Y	Y	Y	Y	N	Y	?	?
20 Gonzalez	Y	N	Y	Y	Y	Y	Y	Y
21 ***Loeffler***	Y	Y	Y	Y	N	N	N	Y
22 ***Paul***	Y	Y	Y	Y	Y	N	?	?
23 Kazen	Y	Y	Y	Y	N	N	?	?
24 Frost	?	N	Y	Y	Y	Y	Y	Y
25 Andrews	Y	Y	Y	Y	?	Y	N	Y
26 Vandergriff	?	Y	Y	?	N	N	N	Y
27 Ortiz	?	N	Y	?	N	Y	?	?
UTAH								
1 ***Hansen***	Y	Y	Y	?	X	?	X	?
2 ***Marriott***	Y	Y	Y	Y	N	N	N	Y
3 ***Nielson***	Y	Y	Y	Y	N	N	N	Y
VERMONT								
AL ***Jeffords***	Y	N	Y	Y	N	N	Y	Y
VIRGINIA								
1 ***Bateman***	Y	Y	Y	Y	N	N	N	Y
2 ***Whitehurst***	Y	Y	Y	Y	N	N	N	Y
3 ***Bliley***	Y	Y	Y	Y	N	N	N	Y
4 Sisisky	Y	#	?	Y	N	N	N	Y
5 Daniel	Y	Y	Y	?	N	N	N	Y
6 Olin	Y	N	Y	Y	Y	N	Y	Y
7 ***Robinson***	Y	Y	Y	Y	N	N	N	Y
8 ***Parris***	Y	Y	Y	Y	N	N	N	Y
9 Boucher	Y	N	Y	Y	Y	Y	Y	Y
10 ***Wolf***	Y	Y	Y	Y	N	N	N	Y
WASHINGTON								
1 ***Pritchard***	Y	N	Y	Y	Y	N	N	Y
2 Swift	Y	N	Y	Y	Y	Y	Y	Y
3 Bonker	Y	N	Y	Y	Y	Y	Y	Y
4 ***Morrison***	Y	Y	Y	Y	N	N	N	Y
5 Foley	Y	?	?	Y	Y	Y	Y	Y
6 Dicks	Y	N	Y	Y	Y	Y	Y	Y
7 Lowry	Y	N	Y	Y	Y	Y	Y	Y
8 ***Chandler***	Y	Y	Y	Y	Y	N	N	Y
WEST VIRGINIA								
1 Mollohan	Y	N	Y	Y	Y	Y	Y	Y
2 Staggers	Y	N	Y	Y	Y	Y	Y	Y
3 Wise	Y	N	Y	Y	Y	Y	Y	Y
4 Rahall	Y	X	Y	Y	Y	Y	#	?
WISCONSIN								
1 Aspin	?	N	Y	Y	Y	Y	Y	Y
2 Kastenmeier	Y	N	N	Y	Y	Y	Y	Y
3 ***Gunderson***	Y	N	Y	Y	N	N	Y	Y
4 Zablocki	Y	N	Y	Y	Y	Y	Y	Y
5 Moody	Y	N	Y	Y	Y	Y	Y	Y
6 ***Petri***	Y	Y	Y	Y	N	N	N	Y
7 Obey	Y	N	?	Y	Y	Y	Y	Y
8 ***Roth***	Y	Y	Y	Y	N	N	N	Y
9 ***Sensenbrenner***	Y	Y	Y	Y	N	N	N	Y
WYOMING								
AL ***Cheney***	Y	Y	Y	Y	N	N	X	Y

Southern states - Ala., Ark., Fla., Ga., Ky., La., Miss., N.C., Okla., S.C., Tenn., Texas, Va.

59. HR 1190. Emergency Agricultural Credit Act. Derrick, D-S.C., motion to order the previous question (thus ending debate and the possibility of amendment) on the rule (H Res 158) providing for House floor consideration of the bill to revise federal agricultural credit programs and permit farmers, in certain circumstances, to postpone repayment of Farmers Home Administration loans. Motion agreed to 262-133: R 26-130; D 236-3 (ND 158-1, SD 78-2), April 27, 1983.

60. HR 1190. Emergency Agricultural Credit Act. Adoption of the rule (H Res 158) providing for House floor consideration of the bill to revise federal agricultural credit programs and permit farmers, in certain circumstances, to postpone repayment of Farmers Home Administration loans. Adopted 341-60: R 97-59; D 244-1 (ND 163-0, SD 81-1), April 27, 1983.

61. HR 1190. Emergency Agricultural Credit Act. Derrick, D-S.C., motion to table (kill) the de la Garza, D-Texas, motion to reconsider the vote by which the rule (H Res 158) was adopted *(see vote 60, above)*. Motion agreed to 292-111: R 48-109; D 244-2 (ND 165-0, SD 79-2), April 27, 1983.

62. HR 1190. Emergency Agricultural Credit Act. Bedell, D-Iowa, amendment to eliminate two sections of the bill that increased limits on the size of Farmers Home Administration loans to individuals for farm operating and ownership expenses. Adopted 284-121: R 96-63; D 188-58 (ND 149-14, SD 39-44), April 27, 1983.

63. Procedural Motion. Sundquist, R-Tenn., motion to approve the House *Journal* of Wednesday, April 27. Motion agreed to 358-21: R 140-13; D 218-8 (ND 140-7, SD 78-1), April 28, 1983.

64. H Res 176. House Records Subpoena. Sensenbrenner, R-Wis., motion to refer to the Judiciary Committee the resolution directing the House clerk not to comply with a subpoena for records concerning a 1978 investigation by the Select Committee on Aging. Motion rejected 21-389: R 19-140; D 2-249 (ND 0-166, SD 2-83), April, 28, 1983.

65. H Res 176. House Records Subpoena. Adoption of the resolution directing the House clerk not to comply with a subpoena for records concerning a 1978 investigation by the Select Committee on Aging. Adopted 386-22: R 137-21; D 249-1 (ND 166-0, SD 83-1), April, 28, 1983.

66. H J Res 13. Nuclear Freeze. AuCoin, D-Ore., motion that the Committee of the Whole rise and report the joint resolution back to the House with the recommendation that the resolving clause be stricken out. Motion rejected 135-269: R 106-54; D 29-215 (ND 4-161, SD 25-54), April 28, 1983.

KEY

Y	Voted for (yea).
#	Paired for.
+	Announced for.
N	Voted against (nay).
X	Paired against.
-	Announced against.
P	Voted "present".
C	Voted "present" to avoid possible conflict of interest.
?	Did not vote or otherwise make a position known.

Democrats   *Republicans*

	59	60	61	62	63	64	65	66
ALABAMA								
1 *Edwards*	N	Y	Y	N	?	N	Y	Y
2 *Dickinson*	Y	Y	N	Y	Y	N	Y	Y
3 Nichols	Y	Y	?	N	Y	N	Y	Y
4 Bevill	Y	Y	Y	N	Y	N	Y	N
5 Flippo	Y	Y	Y	N	Y	N	Y	N
6 Erdreich	Y	Y	Y	Y	Y	N	Y	N
7 Shelby	Y	Y	Y	N	Y	N	Y	Y
ALASKA								
AL *Young*	Y	?	Y	Y	N	N	Y	Y
ARIZONA								
1 *McCain*	N	Y	N	N	Y	N	Y	Y
2 Udall	Y	Y	Y	Y	Y	N	Y	N
3 *Stump*	N	N	N	N	Y	N	Y	Y
4 *Rudd*	N	Y	N	Y	Y	N	Y	Y
5 McNulty	Y	Y	Y	Y	Y	N	Y	N
ARKANSAS								
1 Alexander	Y	Y	Y	Y	Y	N	Y	N
2 *Bethune*	N	N	N	N	Y	N	Y	Y
3 *Hammerschmidt*	N	Y	Y	Y	Y	N	Y	Y
4 Anthony	Y	Y	Y	N	Y	N	Y	?
CALIFORNIA								
1 Bosco	?	Y	Y	N	Y	N	Y	N
2 *Chappie*	N	N	N	N	P	N	N	Y
3 Matsui	Y	Y	Y	N	Y	N	Y	N
4 Fazio	Y	Y	Y	N	Y	N	Y	N
5 Vacancy								
6 Boxer	Y	Y	Y	Y	Y	N	Y	N
7 Miller	Y	Y	?	?	N	N	Y	N
8 Dellums	Y	Y	Y	Y	N	N	Y	N
9 Stark	Y	Y	Y	Y	N	N	Y	N
10 Edwards	Y	Y	Y	N	Y	N	Y	N
11 Lantos	Y	Y	Y	N	Y	N	Y	N
12 *Zschau*	N	Y	N	N	Y	Y	Y	N
13 Mineta	?	Y	Y	N	Y	N	Y	N
14 *Shumway*	N	N	N	?	Y	N	Y	Y
15 Coelho	Y	Y	Y	N	Y	N	Y	N
16 Panetta	Y	Y	Y	N	Y	N	Y	N
17 *Pashayan*	N	Y	N	?	Y	N	Y	N
18 Lehman	Y	Y	Y	N	Y	N	Y	N
19 *Lagomarsino*	N	N	N	N	Y	N	Y	N
20 *Thomas*	N	Y	N	Y	N	N	N	Y
21 *Fiedler*	N	N	N	N	Y	N	Y	N
22 *Moorhead*	N	N	N	N	Y	N	Y	Y
23 Beilenson	Y	Y	Y	Y	N	N	Y	N
24 Waxman	Y	Y	Y	N	?	N	Y	N
25 Roybal	Y	Y	Y	Y	Y	N	Y	N
26 Berman	Y	Y	?	Y	Y	N	Y	-
27 Levine	Y	Y	Y	Y	Y	N	Y	N
28 Dixon	Y	Y	Y	Y	Y	N	Y	N
29 Hawkins	?	?	?	?	?	?	?	X
30 Martinez	?	?	Y	Y	N	Y	N	?
31 Dymally	Y	Y	Y	Y	Y	N	Y	N
32 Anderson	N	Y	Y	Y	Y	N	Y	N
33 *Dreier*	N	N	N	Y	N	N	Y	Y
34 Torres	Y	Y	Y	Y	Y	N	Y	N
35 *Lewis*	N	N	?	N	Y	Y	Y	Y
36 Brown	?	?	Y	Y	Y	N	Y	?
37 *McCandless*	N	Y	N	Y	?	N	Y	Y
38 Patterson	Y	Y	Y	Y	Y	N	Y	N
39 *Dannemeyer*	N	N	N	N	Y	N	Y	N
40 *Badham*	N	N	N	N	Y	N	Y	Y
41 *Lowery*	N	Y	N	N	Y	N	Y	Y
42 *Lungren*	N	Y	N	N	Y	Y	Y	Y

	59	60	61	62	63	64	65	66
43 *Packard*	N	N	N	Y	Y	N	Y	Y
44 Bates	Y	Y	Y	N	Y	N	?	N
45 *Hunter*	N	Y	N	Y	Y	N	Y	Y
COLORADO								
1 Schroeder	Y	Y	Y	Y	N	N	Y	N
2 Wirth	Y	Y	Y	Y	Y	N	Y	N
3 Kogovsek	Y	Y	Y	Y	Y	N	Y	N
4 *Brown*	Y	Y	Y	N	Y	N	N	N
5 *Kramer*	N	N	N	Y	Y	N	Y	N
6 *Schaefer*	N	N	N	N	Y	N	N	Y
CONNECTICUT								
1 Kennelly	Y	Y	Y	Y	Y	N	Y	N
2 Gejdenson	Y	Y	Y	Y	N	N	Y	N
3 Morrison	Y	Y	Y	Y	N	N	Y	N
4 *McKinney*	?	Y	N	?	?	N	Y	N
5 Ratchford	Y	Y	Y	Y	N	N	Y	N
6 *Johnson*	N	N	N	Y	N	N	Y	N
DELAWARE								
AL Carper	Y	Y	Y	Y	Y	N	Y	N
FLORIDA								
1 Hutto	Y	Y	Y	Y	Y	N	Y	Y
2 Fuqua	Y	Y	?	Y	Y	N	Y	N
3 Bennett	Y	Y	Y	Y	Y	N	Y	N
4 Chappell	?	?	?	?	?	?	?	?
5 *McCollum*	N	N	N	N	Y	N	Y	Y
6 MacKay	Y	Y	Y	Y	Y	N	Y	?
7 Gibbons	Y	Y	Y	Y	Y	N	Y	N
8 *Young*	N	Y	?	Y	Y	N	Y	Y
9 *Bilirakis*	N	Y	N	N	Y	N	Y	Y
10 Ireland	Y	Y	Y	Y	N	N	Y	Y
11 Nelson	?	?	?	Y	Y	N	Y	N
12 *Lewis*	N	Y	N	Y	N	N	Y	Y
13 *Mack*	N	Y	N	Y	N	Y	Y	Y
14 Mica	Y	Y	Y	Y	Y	N	Y	N
15 *Shaw*	N	Y	N	Y	N	N	N	Y
16 Smith	Y	Y	Y	N	Y	N	Y	N
17 Lehman	Y	Y	Y	Y	N	N	Y	N
18 Pepper	?	?	?	?	?	?	?	X
19 Fascell	Y	Y	Y	Y	N	N	Y	N
GEORGIA								
1 Thomas	Y	Y	Y	N	Y	N	Y	N
2 Hatcher	Y	Y	Y	N	Y	N	Y	N
3 Ray	Y	Y	Y	N	Y	Y	Y	Y
4 Levitas	Y	Y	Y	Y	N	N	Y	N
5 Fowler	Y	Y	Y	Y	Y	N	Y	N
6 *Gingrich*	?	?	N	N	Y	N	Y	Y
7 McDonald	N	N	N	Y	N	N	Y	Y
8 Rowland	Y	Y	N	Y	N	N	Y	N
9 Jenkins	Y	Y	Y	Y	Y	N	Y	N
10 Barnard	Y	Y	N	?	Y	Y	Y	Y
HAWAII								
1 Heftel	Y	Y	Y	Y	Y	N	Y	N
2 Akaka	Y	Y	Y	N	Y	N	Y	N
IDAHO								
1 *Craig*	N	N	N	Y	Y	N	Y	N
2 *Hansen*	N	Y	N	Y	Y	N	Y	Y
ILLINOIS								
1 Washington	?	?	?	?	?	?	?	?
2 Savage	Y	Y	Y	?	?	?	?	?
3 Russo	Y	Y	Y	Y	Y	N	Y	N
4 *O'Brien*	N	Y	N	N	?	Y	N	N
5 Lipinski	?	?	Y	Y	P	N	Y	Y
6 *Hyde*	?	?	?	?	Y	N	Y	Y
7 Collins	Y	Y	Y	Y	N	N	Y	N
8 Rostenkowski	?	?	?	?	Y	N	Y	N
9 Yates	Y	Y	Y	Y	N	N	Y	N
10 *Porter*	N	Y	Y	Y	N	N	Y	N
11 Annunzio	Y	Y	Y	Y	Y	N	Y	N
12 *Crane, P.*	N	N	N	Y	N	Y	Y	Y
13 *Erlenborn*	N	Y	Y	Y	?	?	?	Y
14 *Corcoran*	N	N	N	N	Y	N	Y	Y
15 *Madigan*	N	N	N	N	Y	N	Y	Y
16 *Martin*	N	N	N	Y	Y	N	Y	Y
17 Evans	Y	Y	Y	N	Y	N	Y	N
18 *Michel*	N	Y	N	N	Y	N	Y	Y
19 *Crane, D.*	N	N	N	N	Y	N	Y	Y
20 Durbin	Y	Y	Y	Y	Y	N	Y	N
21 Price	Y	Y	Y	Y	Y	N	Y	N
22 Simon	Y	Y	Y	Y	Y	N	Y	N
INDIANA								
1 Hall	Y	Y	Y	Y	?	N	Y	N
2 Sharp	Y	Y	Y	Y	Y	N	Y	N
3 *Hiler*	N	Y	N	N	N	N	Y	Y
4 *Coats*	N	Y	N	N	N	N	Y	Y
5 Hillis	N	Y	N	Y	Y	N	Y	Y

ND - Northern Democrats   SD - Southern Democrats

Corresponding to Congressional Record Votes 64, 65, 66, 68, 69, 70, 71, 72

	59	60	61	62	63	64	65	66
6 ***Burton***	N	N	N	N	Y	N	Y	Y
7 ***Myers***	Y	Y	Y	N	?	N	Y	Y
8 McCloskey	Y	Y	Y	Y	Y	N	Y	N
9 Hamilton	Y	Y	Y	Y	Y	N	Y	N
10 Jacobs	Y	Y	Y	Y	N	N	Y	N
IOWA								
1 ***Leach***	Y	Y	Y	Y	Y	N	Y	N
2 ***Tauke***	N	N	N	Y	Y	N	Y	N
3 ***Evans***	N	N	N	Y	N	N	Y	N
4 Smith	Y	Y	Y	Y	Y	N	Y	N
5 Harkin	Y	Y	Y	Y	N	N	Y	?
6 Bedell	Y	Y	Y	Y	?	N	Y	N
KANSAS								
1 ***Roberts***	Y	Y	Y	Y	Y	N	Y	N
2 Slattery	Y	Y	Y	Y	Y	N	Y	N
3 ***Winn***	N	Y	Y	Y	Y	N	Y	Y
4 Glickman	Y	Y	Y	Y	Y	N	Y	N
5 ***Whittaker***	Y	Y	Y	Y	Y	N	Y	N
KENTUCKY								
1 Hubbard	Y	Y	Y	Y	Y	N	Y	N
2 Natcher	Y	Y	Y	Y	Y	N	Y	N
3 Mazzoli	Y	Y	Y	Y	Y	N	Y	N
4 ***Snyder***	N	N	N	Y	Y	N	Y	Y
5 ***Rogers***	N	Y	N	Y	Y	N	Y	Y
6 ***Hopkins***	N	N	N	N	Y	N	Y	N
7 Perkins	Y	Y	Y	Y	Y	N	Y	N
LOUISIANA								
1 ***Livingston***	N	Y	N	N	Y	N	N	Y
2 Boggs	?	?	?	?	?	?	?	?
3 Tauzin	Y	Y	Y	N	Y	N	Y	Y
4 Roemer	N	Y	Y	N	N	N	Y	Y
5 Huckaby	Y	Y	Y	N	Y	N	Y	Y
6 ***Moore***	Y	Y	Y	N	Y	N	N	Y
7 Breaux	Y	?	Y	N	P	N	Y	?
8 Long	Y	Y	Y	Y	Y	N	Y	N
MAINE								
1 ***McKernan***	N	Y	N	N	Y	N	Y	N
2 ***Snowe***	N	Y	Y	Y	Y	N	Y	N
MARYLAND								
1 Dyson	Y	Y	Y	N	Y	N	Y	N
2 Long	Y	Y	Y	Y	Y	N	Y	N
3 Mikulski	Y	Y	Y	Y	Y	N	Y	N
4 ***Holt***	N	N	N	N	Y	N	?	Y
5 Hoyer	?	?	?	Y	Y	N	Y	N
6 Byron	Y	Y	Y	Y	Y	N	Y	Y
7 Mitchell	Y	Y	Y	Y	?	N	?	N
8 Barnes	Y	Y	Y	Y	Y	N	Y	N
MASSACHUSETTS								
1 ***Conte***	Y	Y	Y	Y	Y	N	Y	N
2 Boland	Y	Y	Y	Y	Y	N	Y	N
3 Early	Y	Y	Y	Y	Y	N	Y	N
4 Frank	Y	Y	Y	Y	Y	N	Y	N
5 Shannon	Y	Y	Y	Y	Y	N	Y	N
6 Mavroules	Y	Y	?	Y	?	?	Y	N
7 Markey	Y	Y	Y	Y	Y	N	Y	N
8 O'Neill								
9 Moakley	Y	Y	Y	Y	Y	N	Y	N
10 Studds	Y	Y	Y	Y	Y	N	Y	N
11 Donnelly	Y	Y	Y	Y	Y	N	Y	N
MICHIGAN								
1 Conyers	Y	Y	Y	Y	?	?	?	?
2 ***Pursell***	Y	Y	Y	Y	Y	N	?	N
3 Wolpe	Y	Y	Y	Y	Y	N	Y	N
4 ***Siljander***	N	N	N	Y	Y	N	Y	N
5 ***Sawyer***	Y	Y	Y	Y	Y	Y	N	Y
6 Carr	Y	Y	Y	Y	Y	N	Y	N
7 Kildee	Y	Y	Y	Y	Y	N	Y	N
8 Traxler	Y	Y	Y	Y	Y	N	Y	N
9 ***Vander Jagt***	?	Y	Y	Y	?	N	Y	N
10 Albosta	Y	Y	Y	Y	Y	N	Y	N
11 ***Davis***	N	Y	N	Y	Y	N	Y	N
12 Bonior	Y	Y	Y	Y	Y	?	Y	N
13 Crockett	Y	Y	Y	?	?	N	Y	N
14 Hertel	Y	Y	Y	Y	Y	N	Y	N
15 Ford	Y	Y	Y	?	?	N	Y	N
16 Dingell	?	?	?	Y	Y	N	Y	N
17 Levin	Y	Y	Y	Y	Y	N	Y	N
18 ***Broomfield***	N	N	N	Y	Y	N	Y	Y
MINNESOTA								
1 Penny	Y	Y	Y	Y	Y	N	Y	N
2 ***Weber***	?	?	Y	Y	N	N	Y	Y
3 ***Frenzel***	N	N	N	N	?	?	?	#
4 Vento	Y	Y	Y	Y	Y	N	Y	N
5 Sabo	Y	Y	Y	Y	N	N	Y	N
6 Sikorski	?	?	Y	Y	Y	N	Y	N
7 ***Stangeland***	?	?	?	Y	Y	Y	Y	N
8 Oberstar	Y	Y	Y	Y	P	N	Y	N
MISSISSIPPI								
1 Whitten	Y	Y	Y	N	Y	N	Y	N
2 ***Franklin***	Y	Y	N	N	Y	N	Y	Y
3 Montgomery	?	Y	Y	N	Y	N	Y	Y
4 Dowdy	Y	Y	?	N	Y	N	Y	N
5 ***Lott***	N	Y	N	N	Y	N	Y	Y
MISSOURI								
1 Clay	Y	Y	Y	?	N	N	Y	N
2 Young	Y	Y	Y	Y	Y	?	?	?
3 Gephardt	Y	Y	Y	Y	Y	N	Y	N
4 Skelton	Y	Y	Y	N	?	N	Y	Y
5 Wheat	Y	Y	Y	Y	Y	N	Y	N
6 ***Coleman***	Y	Y	Y	N	Y	N	Y	N
7 ***Taylor***	N	Y	N	?	?	?	?	#
8 ***Emerson***	Y	Y	Y	Y	N	N	Y	Y
9 Volkmer	Y	Y	Y	Y	Y	N	Y	N
MONTANA								
1 Williams	Y	Y	Y	Y	?	N	Y	N
2 ***Marlenee***	Y	Y	Y	?	Y	N	Y	Y
NEBRASKA								
1 ***Bereuter***	N	Y	Y	Y	Y	N	Y	Y
2 ***Daub***	N	N	N	Y	Y	N	N	Y
3 ***Smith***	N	Y	Y	Y	Y	N	Y	Y
NEVADA								
1 Reid	Y	Y	Y	Y	Y	N	Y	N
2 ***Vucanovich***	N	N	N	N	Y	N	Y	Y
NEW HAMPSHIRE								
1 D'Amours	Y	Y	Y	Y	Y	N	Y	N
2 ***Gregg***	N	Y	N	N	Y	N	Y	N
NEW JERSEY								
1 Florio	Y	Y	Y	Y	Y	N	Y	N
2 Hughes	Y	Y	Y	Y	Y	N	Y	N
3 Howard	Y	Y	Y	Y	Y	N	Y	N
4 ***Smith***	N	Y	Y	Y	Y	N	N	N
5 ***Roukema***	N	Y	N	Y	Y	N	Y	N
6 Dwyer	Y	Y	Y	Y	Y	N	Y	N
7 ***Rinaldo***	N	Y	Y	Y	Y	N	Y	N
8 Roe	Y	Y	Y	Y	Y	N	Y	N
9 Torricelli	?	?	Y	Y	Y	N	Y	N
10 Rodino	?	?	?	Y	Y	N	Y	N
11 Minish	Y	Y	Y	Y	Y	N	Y	N
12 ***Courter***	N	Y	Y	N	Y	N	Y	N
13 ***Forsythe***	N	N	N	N	N	N	Y	X
.14 Guarini	Y	Y	Y	Y	Y	N	Y	N
NEW MEXICO								
1 ***Lujan***	Y	?	?	Y	Y	Y	N	Y
2 ***Skeen***	N	N	N	N	Y	N	Y	Y
3 Richardson	Y	Y	Y	Y	Y	N	Y	N
NEW YORK								
1 ***Carney***	N	N	N	Y	Y	Y	N	Y
2 Downey	Y	Y	Y	Y	Y	N	Y	N
3 Mrazek	Y	Y	Y	?	Y	N	Y	N
4 ***Lent***	N	N	N	Y	Y	N	Y	Y
5 ***McGrath***	N	N	N	Y	Y	N	Y	Y
6 Addabbo	Y	Y	Y	Y	Y	N	Y	N
7 Ackerman	Y	Y	Y	Y	Y	N	Y	N
8 Scheuer	Y	Y	?	Y	Y	N	Y	N
9 Ferraro	Y	Y	Y	Y	Y	N	Y	N
10 Schumer	Y	?	Y	Y	Y	N	Y	N
11 Towns	Y	Y	Y	Y	Y	N	Y	N
12 Owens	Y	Y	Y	Y	Y	?	?	?
13 Solarz	Y	Y	Y	Y	Y	N	Y	N
14 ***Molinari***	?	?	?	Y	Y	N	Y	Y
15 ***Green***	N	N	N	Y	Y	N	Y	N
16 Rangel	Y	Y	Y	Y	Y	N	Y	N
17 Weiss	Y	Y	Y	Y	Y	N	Y	N
18 Garcia	Y	Y	Y	Y	Y	N	Y	N
19 Biaggi	Y	Y	Y	Y	Y	N	Y	N
20 Ottinger	Y	Y	Y	Y	?	N	Y	N
21 ***Fish***	N	Y	N	Y	Y	N	Y	N
22 ***Gilman***	Y	Y	Y	N	Y	N	Y	Y
23 Stratton	Y	Y	Y	Y	Y	N	Y	Y
24 ***Solomon***	N	N	N	Y	Y	N	Y	Y
25 ***Boehlert***	?	?	?	?	?	?	?	X
26 ***Martin***	N	Y	N	Y	Y	N	Y	Y
27 ***Wortley***	N	N	N	N	Y	N	Y	Y
28 McHugh	?	Y	Y	Y	Y	N	Y	N
29 ***Horton***	Y	Y	Y	Y	Y	N	Y	N
30 ***Conable***	N	N	N	Y	Y	?	?	Y
31 ***Kemp***	N	Y	Y	N	Y	N	Y	Y
32 LaFalce	Y	Y	Y	?	Y	N	Y	N
33 Nowak	Y	Y	Y	Y	Y	N	Y	N
34 Lundine	Y	Y	Y	Y	?	N	Y	N
NORTH CAROLINA								
1 Jones	Y	Y	Y	Y	?	N	N	N
2 Valentine	Y	Y	Y	Y	?	N	Y	N
3 Whitley	Y	Y	Y	N	Y	N	Y	N
4 Andrews	Y	Y	Y	N	?	N	Y	?
5 Neal	?	?	?	?	?	N	Y	N
6 Britt	Y	Y	Y	Y	Y	N	Y	N
7 Rose	?	Y	Y	?	Y	N	Y	N
8 Hefner	?	Y	Y	N	Y	N	Y	N
9 ***Martin***	N	N	N	Y	Y	?	Y	N
10 ***Broyhill***	Y	Y	N	Y	Y	N	Y	Y
11 Clarke	?	?	?	Y	Y	N	Y	N
NORTH DAKOTA								
AL Dorgan	Y	Y	Y	Y	Y	N	Y	N
OHIO								
1 Luken	Y	Y	Y	Y	?	?	?	?
2 ***Gradison***	N	Y	N	N	Y	N	Y	Y
3 Hall	Y	Y	Y	Y	?	N	Y	N
4 ***Oxley***	N	Y	Y	N	Y	N	Y	Y
5 ***Latta***	N	N	N	N	Y	N	N	Y
6 ***McEwen***	N	Y	Y	Y	Y	N	Y	Y
7 ***DeWine***	N	N	N	Y	Y	Y	N	Y
8 ***Kindness***	N	Y	Y	N	Y	Y	Y	Y
9 Kaptur	Y	Y	Y	Y	Y	N	Y	X
10 ***Miller***	Y	Y	Y	Y	N	N	N	N
11 Eckart	Y	Y	Y	Y	Y	N	Y	N
12 ***Kasich***	N	Y	N	N	Y	N	Y	Y
13 Pease	Y	Y	Y	Y	Y	N	Y	N
14 Seiberling	Y	Y	Y	Y	Y	N	Y	N
15 ***Wylie***	N	N	N	N	Y	N	Y	N
16 ***Regula***	N	Y	Y	Y	Y	N	Y	N
17 ***Williams***	Y	Y	Y	Y	Y	N	Y	N
18 Applegate	Y	Y	Y	Y	Y	N	Y	N
19 Feighan	Y	Y	Y	Y	?	N	Y	N
20 Oakar	Y	Y	Y	Y	Y	N	Y	N
21 Stokes	Y	Y	Y	Y	Y	N	Y	N
OKLAHOMA								
1 Jones	Y	Y	Y	Y	Y	N	Y	N
2 Synar	Y	Y	Y	Y	Y	N	Y	N
3 Watkins	Y	Y	Y	Y	Y	N	Y	N
4 McCurdy	Y	Y	Y	N	Y	N	Y	N
5 ***Edwards***	N	Y	Y	N	Y	Y	N	Y
6 English	Y	Y	Y	N	?	N	Y	N
OREGON								
1 AuCoin	Y	Y	Y	?	Y	N	Y	N
2 ***Smith, R.***	N	?	?	N	Y	N	Y	Y
3 Wyden	Y	Y	Y	Y	Y	N	Y	N
4 Weaver	Y	Y	Y	Y	Y	N	Y	N
5 ***Smith, D.***	N	N	N	Y	Y	N	Y	Y
PENNSYLVANIA								
1 Foglietta	Y	Y	Y	Y	Y	N	Y	N
2 Gray	Y	Y	Y	Y	?	N	Y	N
3 Borski	Y	Y	Y	Y	Y	N	Y	N
4 Kolter	Y	Y	Y	Y	Y	N	Y	N
5 ***Schulze***	?	Y	N	N	Y	Y	N	Y
6 Yatron	Y	Y	Y	Y	Y	N	Y	N
7 Edgar	Y	Y	Y	Y	Y	N	Y	N
8 Kostmayer	Y	Y	Y	Y	Y	N	Y	N
9 ***Shuster***	N	Y	N	Y	Y	N	Y	Y
10 ***McDade***	N	Y	Y	Y	Y	N	Y	N
11 Harrison	Y	Y	Y	Y	Y	N	Y	N
12 Murtha	Y	Y	Y	Y	?	N	Y	N
13 ***Coughlin***	?	N	N	Y	?	N	N	N
14 Coyne	Y	Y	Y	Y	?	N	Y	N
15 ***Ritter***	N	Y	N	Y	Y	N	Y	Y
16 ***Walker***	N	N	N	Y	N	Y	Y	Y
17 ***Gekas***	N	N	N	Y	Y	N	Y	Y
18 Walgren	Y	Y	Y	Y	Y	N	?	N
19 ***Goodling***	Y	Y	N	Y	N	N	Y	N
20 Gaydos	?	Y	Y	Y	?	N	Y	N
21 ***Ridge***	N	Y	Y	N	Y	N	Y	N
22 Murphy	Y	Y	?	Y	?	N	Y	N
23 ***Clinger***	N	N	Y	Y	Y	N	Y	N
RHODE ISLAND								
1 St Germain	Y	Y	Y	Y	P	N	Y	N
2 ***Schneider***	N	Y	N	Y	Y	N	Y	N
SOUTH CAROLINA								
1 ***Hartnett***	N	Y	Y	N	Y	N	Y	Y
2 ***Spence***	N	Y	N	N	Y	N	Y	Y
3 Derrick	Y	Y	Y	Y	Y	N	Y	N
4 ***Campbell***	N	Y	N	N	Y	N	Y	Y
5 Spratt	Y	Y	Y	Y	Y	N	Y	N
6 Tallon	Y	Y	Y	N	Y	N	Y	N
SOUTH DAKOTA								
AL Daschle	Y	Y	Y	Y	Y	?	Y	N
TENNESSEE								
1 ***Quillen***	Y	Y	Y	Y	Y	N	Y	Y
2 ***Duncan***	N	Y	Y	Y	Y	Y	Y	Y
3 Lloyd	Y	Y	Y	N	Y	N	Y	Y
4 Cooper	Y	Y	Y	N	Y	N	Y	Y
5 Boner	Y	Y	Y	N	Y	N	Y	N
6 Gore	Y	Y	Y	Y	Y	N	Y	N
7 ***Sundquist***	Y	Y	Y	N	Y	Y	Y	Y
8 Jones	Y	Y	Y	N	Y	?	?	?
9 Ford	Y	Y	Y	N	Y	N	Y	N
TEXAS								
1 Hall, S.	Y	Y	Y	N	Y	N	Y	Y
2 Wilson	?	?	?	Y	?	N	Y	?
3 ***Bartlett***	N	Y	Y	Y	Y	N	Y	Y
4 Hall, R.	Y	Y	Y	N	Y	N	Y	Y
5 Bryant	Y	Y	Y	N	Y	N	?	N
6 ***Gramm***	N	N	N	N	Y	Y	Y	Y
7 ***Archer***	N	?	N	Y	Y	Y	Y	Y
8 ***Fields***	N	N	N	Y	N	N	Y	Y
9 Brooks	Y	Y	Y	Y	Y	N	Y	N
10 Pickle	Y	Y	Y	Y	Y	N	Y	N
11 Leath	Y	Y	Y	N	Y	N	Y	Y
12 Wright	Y	Y	Y	Y	Y	N	Y	N
13 Hightower	Y	Y	Y	N	Y	N	Y	Y
14 Patman	Y	Y	Y	N	Y	N	Y	Y
15 de la Garza	Y	Y	Y	N	Y	N	Y	N
16 Coleman	Y	Y	Y	N	Y	N	Y	N
17 Stenholm	Y	Y	Y	N	Y	N	Y	Y
18 Leland	Y	Y	Y	N	Y	N	Y	?
19 Hance	Y	Y	Y	N	Y	?	?	?
20 Gonzalez	Y	Y	Y	N	Y	N	Y	N
21 ***Loeffler***	N	N	N	N	Y	N	Y	Y
22 ***Paul***	N	N	N	Y	?	?	?	#
23 Kazen	Y	Y	Y	N	Y	N	Y	Y
24 Frost	Y	Y	Y	?	Y	N	Y	N
25 Andrews	Y	Y	Y	N	Y	N	Y	Y
26 Vandergriff	Y	Y	Y	N	Y	N	Y	N
27 Ortiz	Y	Y	Y	N	Y	N	Y	N
UTAH								
1 ***Hansen***	N	Y	N	Y	Y	N	Y	Y
2 ***Marriott***	N	Y	N	Y	Y	N	Y	+
3 ***Nielson***	N	Y	N	Y	Y	N	Y	Y
VERMONT								
AL ***Jeffords***	Y	Y	?	Y	Y	N	Y	N
VIRGINIA								
1 ***Bateman***	?	?	?	?	?	?	?	#
2 ***Whitehurst***	N	Y	N	Y	Y	N	Y	Y
3 ***Bliley***	N	Y	N	Y	Y	N	Y	Y
4 Sisisky	Y	Y	Y	Y	Y	N	Y	N
5 Daniel	Y	Y	N	Y	Y	N	Y	Y
6 Olin	Y	Y	Y	Y	Y	N	Y	N
7 ***Robinson***	N	Y	N	Y	Y	N	Y	Y
8 ***Parris***	N	Y	N	Y	Y	N	Y	Y
9 Boucher	Y	Y	Y	Y	Y	N	Y	N
10 ***Wolf***	N	Y	N	N	Y	N	Y	Y
WASHINGTON								
1 ***Pritchard***	N	Y	N	N	Y	N	Y	N
2 Swift	Y	Y	Y	Y	Y	N	Y	N
3 Bonker	Y	Y	Y	Y	Y	N	Y	N
4 ***Morrison***	N	Y	N	N	Y	N	Y	N
5 Foley	?	?	?	?	Y	N	Y	N
6 Dicks	Y	Y	Y	Y	Y	N	Y	N
7 Lowry	Y	Y	Y	Y	Y	N	Y	N
8 ***Chandler***	N	Y	N	Y	Y	N	Y	N
WEST VIRGINIA								
1 Mollohan	Y	Y	Y	Y	Y	N	Y	N
2 Staggers	Y	Y	Y	Y	Y	N	Y	N
3 Wise	Y	Y	Y	Y	Y	N	Y	N
4 Rahall	Y	Y	Y	Y	Y	N	Y	N
WISCONSIN								
1 Aspin	Y	Y	Y	Y	Y	N	Y	N
2 Kastenmeier	Y	Y	Y	Y	Y	N	Y	N
3 ***Gunderson***	Y	Y	N	Y	Y	N	Y	N
4 Zablocki	Y	Y	Y	Y	Y	N	Y	N
5 Moody	?	Y	Y	Y	Y	N	Y	N
6 ***Petri***	N	N	N	Y	Y	N	Y	N
7 Obey	Y	Y	Y	Y	Y	N	Y	N
8 ***Roth***	N	N	N	Y	Y	N	Y	Y
9 ***Sensenbrenner***	N	N	N	Y	Y	Y	N	N
WYOMING								
AL ***Cheney***	N	N	N	N	Y	N	Y	Y

Southern states - Ala., Ark., Fla., Ga., Ky., La., Miss., N.C., Okla., S.C., Tenn., Texas, Va.

67. H J Res 13. Nuclear Freeze. Leach, R-Iowa, amendment to the Siljander, R-Mich., amendment, to require that a nuclear freeze be sought first as a goal of arms control negotiations, to be followed by reductions in nuclear arms. Adopted 215-194: R 18-142; D 197-52 (ND 160-8, SD 37-44), April 28, 1983. (The Siljander amendment, as amended, subsequently was rejected by voice vote. The amendment would have set an arms control goal of a freeze and reductions in nuclear weapons.)

68. H J Res 13. Nuclear Freeze. Martin, R-N.C., amendment to require that negotiators for a nuclear freeze try to maintain the essential equivalence of U.S. and Soviet nuclear forces now and in the future. Adopted 397-0: R 154-0; D 243-0 (ND 166-0, SD 77-0), April 28, 1983.

69. HR 2307. Tribally Controlled Community Colleges. Simon, D-Ill., motion to suspend the rules and pass the bill to authorize assistance to community colleges operated by Indian tribes in fiscal 1985-87, as follows: $33.2 million a year for basic operating grants and technical assistance, $5 million a year for endowments and such sums as necessary for construction and renovation of buildings. Motion rejected 255-148: R 28-127; D 227-21 (ND 160-2, SD 67-19), May 3, 1983. A two-thirds majority of those present and voting (269 in this case) is required for passage under suspension of the rules. A "nay" was a vote supporting the president's position.

70. HR 1190. Emergency Agricultural Credit Act. Smith, D-Iowa, amendment to specify that interest on Farmers Home Administration water and waste disposal facility loans would be at the rate in effect when the loan was approved or the rate when the borrower actually received the money, whichever was lower. Adopted 399-1: R 156-1; D 243-0 (ND 157-0, SD 86-0), May 3, 1983.

71. HR 1190. Emergency Agricultural Credit Act. Watkins, D-Okla., amendment to authorize grants to nonprofit organizations for centers on rural technology. Adopted 383-8: R 146-5; D 237-3 (ND 153-2, SD 84-1), May 3, 1983. (This vote subsequently was vacated, *see vote 72, below*.)

72. HR 1190. Emergency Agricultural Credit Act. Watkins, D-Okla., amendment to authorize grants to nonprofit organizations for centers on rural technology. Adopted 398-3: R 151-1; D 247-2 (ND 160-1, SD 87-1), May 3, 1983. (Previous vote on the Watkins amendment was vacated, *see vote 71, above*).

73. HR 1190. Emergency Agricultural Credit Act. Passage of the bill to revise federal agricultural credit programs and permit farmers, in certain circumstances, to postpone repayment of Farmers Home Administration loans. Passed 378-35: R 132-28; D 246-7 (ND 160-5, SD 86-2), May 3, 1983.

74. Procedural Motion. Hartnett, R-S.C., motion to approve the House *Journal* of Tuesday, May 3. Motion agreed to 361-21: R 133-12; D 228-9 (ND 149-8, SD 79-1), May 4, 1983.

KEY

Y Voted for (yea).
Paired for.
+ Announced for.
N Voted against (nay).
X Paired against.
- Announced against.
P Voted "present".
C Voted "present" to avoid possible conflict of interest.
? Did not vote or otherwise make a position known.

Democrats   *Republicans*

	67	68	69	70	71	72	73	74
ALABAMA								
1 *Edwards*	N	Y	Y	?	?	?	Y	Y
2 *Dickinson*	X	?	N	Y	Y	Y	Y	N
3 Nichols	X	?	Y	Y	Y	Y	Y	Y
4 Bevill	N	Y	Y	Y	Y	Y	Y	Y
5 Flippo	N	Y	Y	Y	Y	Y	Y	Y
6 Erdreich	N	Y	Y	Y	Y	Y	Y	Y
7 Shelby	N	Y	N	Y	Y	Y	Y	Y
ALASKA								
AL *Young*	N	Y	N	Y	Y	Y	Y	N
ARIZONA								
1 *McCain*	N	Y	?	?	?	?	?	Y
2 Udall	Y	Y	Y	Y	Y	Y	Y	Y
3 *Stump*	N	Y	N	Y	Y	Y	N	Y
4 *Rudd*	N	?	Y	Y	Y	Y	N	Y
5 McNulty	Y	Y	Y	Y	Y	?	Y	Y
ARKANSAS								
1 Alexander	Y	Y	Y	Y	Y	Y	Y	?
2 *Bethune*	N	Y	Y	Y	Y	Y	N	?
3 *Hammerschmidt*	N	Y	Y	Y	Y	Y	Y	Y
4 Anthony	Y	Y	Y	Y	Y	Y	Y	Y
CALIFORNIA								
1 Bosco	Y	Y	Y	Y	Y	Y	Y	Y
2 *Chappie*	N	Y	N	?	N	Y	N	Y
3 Matsui	Y	Y	Y	Y	Y	Y	Y	Y
4 Fazio	Y	Y	Y	Y	Y	Y	Y	Y
5 Vacancy								
6 Boxer	Y	Y	Y	Y	Y	Y	Y	Y
7 Miller	Y	Y	?	?	Y	Y	?	Y
8 Dellums	Y	Y	Y	Y	Y	Y	Y	Y
9 Stark	Y	Y	Y	Y	Y	N	Y	N
10 Edwards	Y	Y	Y	Y	Y	Y	Y	Y
11 Lantos	Y	Y	?	?	?	?	?	Y
12 *Zschau*	N	Y	N	N	Y	Y	N	?
13 Mineta	Y	Y	Y	Y	Y	Y	Y	Y
14 *Shumway*	N	Y	N	Y	Y	Y	N	Y
15 Coelho	Y	Y	?	?	Y	?	Y	Y
16 Panetta	Y	Y	Y	Y	Y	Y	Y	Y
17 *Pashayan*	N	Y	N	Y	Y	Y	Y	Y
18 Lehman	Y	Y	Y	Y	Y	Y	Y	Y
19 *Lagomarsino*	N	Y	N	Y	Y	Y	Y	Y
20 *Thomas*	N	Y	N	Y	Y	Y	Y	?
21 *Fiedler*	N	Y	N	Y	Y	Y	Y	?
22 *Moorhead*	N	Y	N	Y	Y	Y	Y	?
23 Beilenson	Y	Y	Y	Y	Y	Y	Y	Y
24 Waxman	Y	Y	Y	?	Y	Y	Y	?
25 Roybal	Y	Y	Y	Y	Y	Y	Y	Y
26 Berman	Y	Y	Y	Y	Y	Y	Y	Y
27 Levine	Y	Y	Y	Y	Y	Y	Y	Y
28 Dixon	Y	?	Y	Y	Y	Y	Y	Y
29 Hawkins	#	?	Y	Y	Y	Y	Y	Y
30 Martinez	Y	Y	Y	Y	Y	Y	Y	Y
31 Dymally	Y	Y	Y	Y	Y	Y	Y	Y
32 Anderson	Y	Y	Y	Y	Y	Y	Y	N
33 *Dreier*	N	Y	N	N	Y	N	Y	N
34 Torres	Y	Y	Y	Y	Y	Y	?	Y
35 *Lewis*	N	Y	N	Y	N	Y	N	Y
36 Brown	Y	Y	Y	Y	Y	Y	Y	Y
37 *McCandless*	N	Y	N	Y	N	Y	N	Y
38 Patterson	Y	Y	Y	Y	?	Y	Y	Y
39 *Dannemeyer*	N	Y	N	Y	Y	Y	N	Y
40 *Badham*	N	Y	N	Y	Y	Y	N	Y
41 *Lowery*	N	Y	?	Y	Y	Y	Y	Y
42 *Lungren*	N	Y	N	Y	Y	Y	N	Y

	67	68	69	70	71	72	73	74
43 *Packard*	N	Y	N	Y	Y	Y	N	Y
44 Bates	Y	Y	Y	Y	Y	Y	Y	Y
45 *Hunter*	N	Y	Y	Y	Y	Y	Y	Y
COLORADO								
1 Schroeder	Y	Y	Y	Y	Y	Y	Y	N
2 Wirth	?	Y	#	Y	Y	Y	Y	Y
3 Kogovsek	Y	Y	Y	?	Y	Y	Y	Y
4 *Brown*	N	Y	N	Y	Y	Y	Y	Y
5 *Kramer*	N	Y	N	Y	Y	Y	Y	Y
6 *Schaefer*	N	Y	N	Y	Y	Y	N	?
CONNECTICUT								
1 Kennelly	Y	Y	Y	Y	Y	Y	Y	Y
2 Gejdenson	Y	Y	Y	Y	Y	Y	Y	N
3 Morrison	Y	Y	Y	Y	Y	Y	Y	Y
4 *McKinney*	Y	Y	?	?	?	?	?	Y
5 Ratchford	Y	Y	Y	Y	Y	Y	Y	Y
6 *Johnson*	N	Y	?	?	?	?	?	Y
DELAWARE								
AL Carper	Y	Y	Y	Y	Y	Y	Y	Y
FLORIDA								
1 Hutto	N	Y	N	Y	Y	Y	Y	Y
2 Fuqua	Y	Y	Y	Y	Y	Y	Y	Y
3 Bennett	N	Y	Y	Y	Y	Y	Y	Y
4 Chappell	?	?	?	Y	Y	Y	Y	Y
5 *McCollum*	N	Y	N	Y	Y	Y	Y	Y
6 MacKay	Y	Y	Y	Y	Y	Y	N	Y
7 Gibbons	Y	Y	N	?	Y	Y	Y	Y
8 *Young*	N	Y	N	Y	Y	Y	Y	Y
9 *Bilirakis*	N	Y	N	Y	Y	Y	Y	?
10 Ireland	N	Y	N	Y	?	Y	Y	Y
11 Nelson	N	Y	Y	Y	Y	Y	Y	Y
12 *Lewis*	N	Y	N	Y	Y	Y	Y	Y
13 *Mack*	N	Y	N	Y	Y	Y	N	Y
14 Mica	Y	Y	Y	Y	Y	Y	Y	Y
15 *Shaw*	N	Y	N	Y	Y	Y	Y	Y
16 Smith	Y	Y	Y	Y	Y	Y	Y	Y
17 Lehman	Y	?	Y	Y	Y	Y	Y	Y
18 Pepper	#	?	Y	Y	Y	Y	Y	Y
19 Fascell	Y	Y	Y	Y	Y	Y	Y	Y
GEORGIA								
1 Thomas	Y	Y	Y	Y	Y	Y	Y	Y
2 Hatcher	N	Y	?	?	?	Y	Y	?
3 Ray	N	Y	N	Y	Y	Y	Y	Y
4 Levitas	N	Y	Y	Y	Y	Y	Y	Y
5 Fowler	Y	Y	Y	Y	Y	Y	Y	Y
6 *Gingrich*	N	Y	N	Y	Y	Y	Y	Y
7 McDonald	N	Y	N	N	N	N	N	Y
8 Rowland	N	Y	Y	Y	Y	Y	Y	Y
9 Jenkins	N	Y	N	Y	Y	Y	Y	Y
10 Barnard	N	Y	?	?	?	?	?	?
HAWAII								
1 Heftel	Y	Y	Y	Y	Y	Y	Y	Y
2 Akaka	Y	Y	Y	Y	Y	Y	Y	Y
IDAHO								
1 *Craig*	N	Y	N	Y	N	Y	N	Y
2 *Hansen*	N	?	?	Y	Y	?	Y	Y
ILLINOIS								
1 Washington *	#	?						
2 Savage	?	?	?	Y	Y	Y	Y	Y
3 Russo	Y	Y	Y	Y	Y	Y	Y	Y
4 *O'Brien*	N	Y	N	Y	Y	Y	Y	Y
5 Lipinski	N	Y	Y	Y	Y	Y	Y	Y
6 *Hyde*	N	Y	N	Y	Y	Y	Y	Y
7 Collins	Y	Y	?	Y	Y	Y	Y	Y
8 Rostenkowski	Y	Y	Y	Y	Y	Y	Y	Y
9 Yates	Y	?	Y	Y	Y	Y	Y	?
10 *Porter*	N	Y	Y	Y	Y	Y	Y	Y
11 Annunzio	Y	Y	#	?	?	?	?	?
12 *Crane, P.*	N	Y	X	Y	Y	N	?	?
13 *Erlenborn*	N	Y	N	Y	?	Y	Y	Y
14 *Corcoran*	N	Y	N	Y	Y	Y	Y	Y
15 *Madigan*	N	Y	N	Y	Y	Y	Y	?
16 *Martin*	N	Y	N	Y	Y	N	N	Y
17 Evans	Y	Y	Y	Y	Y	Y	Y	Y
18 *Michel*	N	Y	N	Y	?	Y	Y	Y
19 *Crane, D.*	N	Y	N	Y	Y	N	Y	Y
20 Durbin	Y	Y	Y	Y	Y	Y	Y	Y
21 Price	N	Y	Y	Y	Y	Y	Y	Y
22 Simon	Y	Y	Y	Y	Y	Y	Y	Y
INDIANA								
1 Hall	Y	Y	?	?	?	?	?	?
2 Sharp	Y	Y	Y	Y	Y	Y	Y	Y
3 *Hiler*	N	Y	N	Y	Y	Y	Y	N
4 *Coats*	N	Y	N	Y	Y	?	Y	Y
5 *Hillis*	N	Y	N	Y	Y	Y	Y	Y

ND - Northern Democrats   SD - Southern Democrats

	67	68	69	70	71	72	73	74
6 ***Burton***	N	Y	N	Y	Y	Y	Y	Y
7 ***Myers***	N	Y	N	Y	Y	Y	Y	Y
8 McCloskey	Y	Y	Y	Y	Y	Y	Y	Y
9 Hamilton	Y	Y	Y	Y	Y	Y	Y	Y
10 Jacobs	Y	Y	Y	Y	Y	Y	Y	N
IOWA								
1 ***Leach***	Y	Y	Y	Y	Y	Y	Y	?
2 ***Tauke***	Y	Y	N	Y	Y	Y	Y	Y
3 ***Evans***	Y	Y	N	Y	Y	Y	Y	N
4 Smith	Y	Y	Y	Y	Y	Y	Y	Y
5 Harkin	Y	Y	Y	?	?	Y	Y	N
6 Bedell	Y	Y	Y	Y	Y	Y	Y	Y
KANSAS								
1 ***Roberts***	N	Y	N	Y	?	?	Y	Y
2 Slattery	N	Y	Y	Y	Y	Y	Y	Y
3 ***Winn***	N	Y	Y	Y	Y	Y	Y	Y
4 Glickman	Y	Y	Y	Y	Y	Y	Y	Y
5 ***Whittaker***	N	Y	N	Y	Y	Y	Y	Y
KENTUCKY								
1 Hubbard	N	Y	N	Y	Y	Y	Y	Y
2 Natcher	Y	Y	Y	Y	Y	Y	Y	Y
3 Mazzoli	Y	Y	Y	Y	Y	Y	Y	Y
4 ***Snyder***	N	Y	N	Y	Y	Y	Y	Y
5 ***Rogers***	N	Y	N	Y	Y	Y	Y	Y
6 ***Hopkins***	N	Y	N	Y	Y	Y	Y	Y
7 Perkins	Y	Y	Y	Y	Y	Y	Y	Y
LOUISIANA								
1 ***Livingston***	N	Y	N	Y	Y	Y	Y	?
2 Boggs	?	?	Y	Y	?	Y	Y	Y
3 Tauzin	N	Y	Y	Y	Y	Y	Y	Y
4 Roemer	N	Y	N	Y	Y	Y	Y	N
5 Huckaby	N	Y	Y	Y	Y	Y	Y	?
6 ***Moore***	N	Y	N	Y	Y	Y	Y	Y
7 Breaux	?	?	N	Y	Y	Y	Y	Y
8 Long	Y	Y	Y	Y	Y	Y	Y	Y
MAINE								
1 ***McKernan***	Y	Y	Y	Y	Y	Y	Y	Y
2 ***Snowe***	Y	Y	N	Y	Y	Y	Y	Y
MARYLAND								
1 Dyson	N	Y	Y	Y	Y	Y	Y	Y
2 Long	Y	Y	Y	?	Y	Y	Y	Y
3 Mikulski	Y	Y	Y	Y	Y	Y	Y	?
4 ***Holt***	N	Y	N	Y	Y	Y	N	N
5 Hoyer	Y	Y	Y	Y	Y	Y	Y	Y
6 Byron	N	Y	N	Y	Y	Y	Y	N
7 Mitchell	Y	Y	Y	Y	Y	Y	Y	?
8 Barnes	Y	Y	Y	Y	Y	Y	Y	Y
MASSACHUSETTS								
1 ***Conte***	Y	Y	N	Y	Y	Y	Y	Y
2 Boland	#	Y	Y	Y	Y	Y	Y	Y
3 Early	Y	Y	Y	Y	Y	Y	Y	Y
4 Frank	Y	Y	Y	Y	Y	Y	Y	Y
5 Shannon	Y	Y	Y	Y	Y	Y	Y	Y
6 Mavroules	Y	Y	Y	Y	Y	Y	Y	Y
7 Markey	Y	Y	Y	Y	Y	Y	Y	Y
8 O'Neill								
9 Moakley	Y	Y	Y	?	?	?	Y	Y
10 Studds	Y	Y	Y	Y	Y	Y	Y	Y
11 Donnelly	Y	Y	Y	Y	Y	Y	Y	Y
MICHIGAN								
1 Conyers	#	?	Y	Y	Y	Y	Y	Y
2 ***Pursell***	Y	Y	N	Y	Y	Y	Y	?
3 Wolpe	Y	Y	Y	Y	Y	Y	Y	Y
4 ***Siljander***	N	Y	N	Y	Y	Y	Y	Y
5 ***Sawyer***	N	Y	Y	Y	Y	Y	Y	Y
6 Carr	Y	Y	Y	Y	Y	?	Y	Y
7 Kildee	Y	Y	Y	Y	Y	Y	Y	Y
8 Traxler	Y	Y	Y	Y	Y	Y	Y	Y
9 ***Vander Jagt***	N	Y	?	?	?	?	?	?
10 Albosta	Y	Y	Y	Y	Y	Y	Y	Y
11 ***Davis***	Y	Y	Y	Y	Y	Y	Y	Y
12 Bonior	Y	Y	Y	Y	Y	Y	Y	Y
13 Crockett	Y	Y	Y	Y	Y	Y	Y	Y
14 Hertel	Y	Y	Y	Y	Y	Y	Y	Y
15 Ford	Y	Y	Y	Y	?	Y	Y	?
16 Dingell	Y	Y	Y	Y	Y	Y	Y	?
17 Levin	Y	Y	Y	Y	Y	Y	Y	Y
18 ***Broomfield***	N	Y	N	Y	Y	Y	Y	Y
MINNESOTA								
1 Penny	Y	Y	Y	Y	Y	Y	Y	Y
2 ***Weber***	N	Y	N	Y	Y	Y	Y	Y
3 ***Frenzel***	X	?	N	Y	Y	Y	Y	Y
4 Vento	Y	Y	Y	?	N	N	Y	Y
5 Sabo	Y	Y	Y	Y	Y	Y	Y	N
6 Sikorski	Y	Y	Y	Y	Y	Y	Y	Y

	67	68	69	70	71	72	73	74
7 ***Stangeland***	N	Y	N	Y	Y	Y	Y	?
8 Oberstar	Y	Y	Y	Y	Y	Y	Y	P
MISSISSIPPI								
1 Whitten	N	Y	N	?	Y	Y	Y	Y
2 ***Franklin***	N	Y	N	Y	Y	Y	Y	Y
3 Montgomery	N	Y	N	Y	Y	Y	Y	Y
4 Dowdy	Y	Y	Y	Y	Y	Y	Y	Y
5 ***Lott***	N	Y	?	Y	Y	Y	Y	Y
MISSOURI								
1 Clay	Y	Y	Y	Y	Y	Y	Y	N
2 Young	?	?	Y	Y	Y	Y	Y	Y
3 Gephardt	Y	Y	Y	Y	Y	Y	Y	Y
4 Skelton	N	Y	N	Y	Y	Y	Y	Y
5 Wheat	Y	Y	Y	Y	Y	Y	Y	Y
6 ***Coleman***	N	Y	Y	Y	?	Y	Y	Y
7 ***Taylor***	X	?	Y	Y	Y	Y	?	?
8 ***Emerson***	N	Y	N	Y	Y	Y	Y	Y
9 Volkmer	Y	Y	Y	Y	Y	Y	Y	Y
MONTANA								
1 Williams	Y	Y	Y	Y	Y	Y	Y	?
2 ***Marlenee***	N	Y	Y	Y	Y	?	Y	Y
NEBRASKA								
1 ***Bereuter***	N	Y	Y	Y	?	Y	Y	Y
2 ***Daub***	N	Y	N	Y	Y	Y	Y	Y
3 ***Smith***	N	Y	N	Y	Y	Y	Y	Y
NEVADA								
1 Reid	Y	Y	Y	Y	Y	Y	N	Y
2 ***Vucanovich***	N	Y	N	Y	Y	Y	N	Y
NEW HAMPSHIRE								
1 D'Amours	Y	Y	Y	Y	Y	Y	Y	Y
2 ***Gregg***	N	Y	N	Y	Y	Y	N	Y
NEW JERSEY								
1 Florio	Y	Y	Y	Y	Y	Y	Y	Y
2 Hughes	Y	Y	Y	Y	Y	Y	Y	Y
3 Howard	Y	Y	Y	Y	Y	Y	Y	Y
4 ***Smith***	N	Y	Y	Y	Y	Y	Y	Y
5 ***Roukema***	N	Y	N	Y	Y	Y	Y	Y
6 Dwyer	Y	Y	Y	Y	Y	Y	Y	Y
7 ***Rinaldo***	Y	Y	N	Y	?	Y	Y	Y
8 Roe	Y	Y	Y	Y	Y	Y	Y	Y
9 Torricelli	Y	Y	Y	Y	Y	Y	Y	Y
10 Rodino	Y	Y	Y	Y	Y	Y	Y	Y
11 Minish	Y	Y	Y	Y	Y	Y	Y	Y
12 ***Courter***	N	Y	N	Y	Y	Y	Y	Y
13 ***Forsythe***	N	Y	N	Y	?	Y	Y	N
14 Guarini	Y	Y	Y	Y	Y	Y	Y	Y
NEW MEXICO								
1 ***Lujan***	N	Y	Y	Y	Y	Y	Y	Y
2 ***Skeen***	N	Y	Y	Y	Y	Y	Y	Y
3 Richardson	Y	Y	Y	Y	Y	Y	Y	Y
NEW YORK								
1 ***Carney***	N	Y	N	Y	Y	Y	Y	Y
2 Downey	Y	Y	Y	Y	Y	Y	Y	Y
3 Mrazek	Y	Y	Y	Y	?	?	Y	Y
4 ***Lent***	N	Y	N	Y	Y	Y	Y	Y
5 ***McGrath***	N	Y	N	Y	Y	Y	Y	Y
6 Addabbo	Y	?	Y	?	?	Y	Y	Y
7 Ackerman	Y	Y	Y	Y	Y	Y	Y	Y
8 Scheuer	Y	Y	Y	Y	Y	Y	Y	Y
9 Ferraro	Y	Y	Y	Y	Y	Y	Y	Y
10 Schumer	Y	Y	?	?	?	?	?	Y
11 Towns	Y	Y	?	?	?	?	?	?
12 Owens	?	?	Y	?	?	Y	Y	Y
13 Solarz	Y	Y	?	?	?	?	?	Y
14 ***Molinari***	N	Y	N	Y	?	Y	Y	Y
15 ***Green***	Y	Y	N	Y	Y	Y	Y	Y
16 Rangel	Y	Y	Y	Y	Y	Y	Y	Y
17 Weiss	Y	Y	Y	Y	N	Y	Y	Y
18 Garcia	Y	Y	Y	Y	Y	Y	Y	Y
19 Biaggi	Y	Y	Y	Y	Y	Y	Y	Y
20 Ottinger	Y	Y	Y	Y	Y	Y	N	?
21 ***Fish***	Y	Y	N	?	Y	Y	Y	Y
22 ***Gilman***	N	Y	Y	Y	Y	Y	Y	Y
23 Stratton	N	Y	Y	Y	Y	Y	?	N
24 ***Solomon***	N	Y	N	Y	Y	Y	Y	N
25 ***Boehlert***	#	?	Y	Y	Y	Y	Y	Y
26 ***Martin***	N	Y	N	Y	Y	Y	?	?
27 ***Wortley***	N	Y	N	Y	Y	?	Y	Y
28 McHugh	Y	Y	Y	Y	Y	Y	Y	Y
29 ***Horton***	Y	Y	Y	Y	Y	Y	Y	Y
30 ***Conable***	N	Y	N	Y	Y	Y	N	N
31 ***Kemp***	N	Y	N	Y	Y	Y	Y	?
32 LaFalce	Y	Y	Y	Y	?	Y	Y	Y
33 Nowak	Y	Y	Y	Y	Y	Y	Y	Y
34 Lundine	Y	Y	?	Y	Y	?	Y	Y

	67	68	69	70	71	72	73	74
NORTH CAROLINA								
1 Jones	Y	Y	Y	Y	Y	Y	Y	?
2 Valentine	N	Y	Y	Y	Y	Y	Y	Y
3 Whitley	N	Y	Y	Y	Y	Y	Y	Y
4 Andrews	Y	Y	Y	Y	Y	Y	Y	Y
5 Neal	Y	Y	Y	Y	Y	Y	Y	?
6 Britt	Y	Y	Y	Y	Y	Y	Y	Y
7 Rose	Y	Y	Y	Y	Y	Y	Y	?
8 Hefner	Y	Y	Y	Y	Y	Y	Y	?
9 ***Martin***	N	?	N	Y	Y	Y	Y	Y
10 ***Broyhill***	N	Y	N	?	Y	Y	Y	Y
11 Clarke	Y	Y	Y	Y	Y	Y	Y	Y
NORTH DAKOTA								
AL Dorgan	Y	Y	Y	Y	Y	Y	Y	Y
OHIO								
1 Luken	Y	Y	Y	Y	Y	Y	Y	Y
2 ***Gradison***	N	Y	N	Y	Y	Y	Y	Y
3 Hall	Y	Y	Y	Y	Y	?	N	Y
4 ***Oxley***	N	Y	N	Y	?	Y	Y	Y
5 ***Latta***	N	?	N	Y	Y	Y	Y	Y
6 ***McEwen***	N	Y	N	Y	Y	Y	Y	?
7 ***DeWine***	N	Y	N	Y	Y	Y	Y	Y
8 ***Kindness***	N	?	?	?	Y	Y	Y	Y
9 Kaptur	Y	Y	Y	Y	Y	Y	Y	Y
10 ***Miller***	N	Y	N	Y	Y	Y	Y	N
11 Eckart	Y	Y	Y	Y	Y	Y	+	Y
12 ***Kasich***	N	Y	N	Y	Y	Y	Y	Y
13 Pease	Y	Y	Y	Y	Y	Y	Y	Y
14 Seiberling	Y	Y	Y	Y	Y	Y	Y	Y
15 ***Wylie***	N	Y	N	Y	Y	Y	Y	Y
16 ***Regula***	N	Y	N	Y	Y	Y	Y	Y
17 ***Williams***	N	Y	Y	Y	Y	Y	Y	Y
18 Applegate	Y	Y	Y	Y	Y	Y	Y	?
19 Feighan	Y	Y	Y	Y	Y	Y	Y	Y
20 Oakar	Y	Y	Y	Y	Y	Y	Y	Y
21 Stokes	Y	?	Y	Y	Y	Y	Y	Y
OKLAHOMA								
1 Jones	N	Y	Y	Y	Y	Y	Y	Y
2 Synar	Y	+	Y	Y	Y	Y	Y	Y
3 Watkins	N	Y	Y	Y	Y	Y	Y	Y
4 McCurdy	N	Y	Y	Y	Y	Y	Y	Y
5 ***Edwards***	N	Y	N	Y	Y	Y	Y	Y
6 English	N	Y	Y	Y	Y	Y	Y	Y
OREGON								
1 AuCoin	Y	Y	Y	Y	Y	Y	Y	Y
2 ***Smith, R.***	N	Y	Y	Y	Y	Y	Y	Y
3 Wyden	Y	Y	Y	Y	Y	Y	Y	Y
4 Weaver	Y	Y	Y	Y	Y	Y	Y	Y
5 ***Smith, D.***	N	Y	N	Y	Y	Y	N	Y
PENNSYLVANIA								
1 Foglietta	Y	Y	Y	Y	Y	Y	Y	Y
2 Gray	Y	Y	Y	Y	Y	Y	Y	Y
3 Borski	Y	Y	Y	Y	Y	Y	Y	Y
4 Kolter	Y	Y	Y	Y	Y	Y	Y	Y
5 ***Schulze***	N	Y	N	Y	Y	Y	Y	Y
6 Yatron	Y	Y	Y	Y	?	Y	Y	Y
7 Edgar	Y	Y	Y	Y	Y	Y	Y	Y
8 Kostmayer	Y	Y	Y	Y	Y	Y	Y	Y
9 ***Shuster***	N	Y	N	Y	Y	Y	Y	Y
10 ***McDade***	N	Y	N	Y	Y	Y	Y	Y
11 Harrison	Y	Y	Y	Y	Y	Y	Y	Y
12 Murtha	N	Y	Y	Y	Y	Y	Y	Y
13 ***Coughlin***	N	Y	N	Y	Y	?	Y	N
14 Coyne	Y	Y	Y	Y	Y	Y	Y	Y
15 ***Ritter***	N	Y	N	Y	Y	Y	Y	Y
16 ***Walker***	N	Y	N	Y	?	Y	Y	N
17 ***Gekas***	N	Y	N	Y	Y	Y	Y	Y
18 Walgren	Y	Y	Y	Y	?	Y	Y	Y
19 ***Goodling***	Y	?	?	Y	Y	Y	Y	N
20 Gaydos	Y	Y	Y	Y	?	Y	Y	Y
21 ***Ridge***	?	Y	N	Y	Y	Y	Y	Y
22 Murphy	Y	Y	Y	Y	Y	Y	Y	?
23 ***Clinger***	N	Y	N	Y	Y	Y	Y	Y
RHODE ISLAND								
1 St Germain	Y	Y	Y	Y	?	Y	Y	P
2 ***Schneider***	Y	Y	Y	Y	Y	Y	N	Y
SOUTH CAROLINA								
1 ***Hartnett***	N	Y	N	Y	Y	Y	Y	Y
2 ***Spence***	N	Y	N	Y	Y	Y	Y	Y
3 Derrick	N	?	Y	Y	Y	Y	Y	Y
4 ***Campbell***	N	Y	?	?	?	?	?	?
5 Spratt	Y	Y	Y	Y	Y	Y	Y	Y
6 Tallon	Y	Y	Y	Y	Y	Y	Y	Y
SOUTH DAKOTA								
AL Daschle	Y	Y	?	?	Y	Y	+	Y

	67	68	69	70	71	72	73	74
TENNESSEE								
1 ***Quillen***	N	Y	N	Y	Y	Y	Y	Y
2 ***Duncan***	N	Y	N	Y	Y	Y	Y	Y
3 Lloyd	N	Y	N	Y	Y	Y	Y	Y
4 Cooper	N	Y	Y	Y	Y	Y	Y	Y
5 Boner	Y	Y	Y	Y	Y	Y	Y	Y
6 Gore	?	?	Y	Y	Y	Y	Y	Y
7 ***Sundquist***	N	Y	N	Y	Y	Y	Y	Y
8 Jones	?	?	Y	Y	Y	Y	Y	Y
9 Ford	Y	Y	Y	Y	Y	Y	Y	Y
TEXAS								
1 Hall, S.	N	Y	N	Y	Y	Y	Y	Y
2 Wilson	?	?	?	?	Y	Y	Y	Y
3 ***Bartlett***	N	Y	N	Y	Y	Y	Y	Y
4 Hall, R.	N	Y	Y	Y	Y	Y	Y	Y
5 Bryant	Y	Y	Y	Y	Y	Y	Y	Y
6 ***Gramm***	N	Y	N	Y	Y	Y	Y	Y
7 ***Archer***	N	Y	N	Y	Y	Y	N	Y
8 ***Fields***	N	Y	N	Y	Y	Y	N	Y
9 Brooks	Y	Y	Y	Y	Y	Y	Y	Y
10 Pickle	N	Y	Y	Y	Y	Y	Y	Y
11 Leath	N	Y	N	Y	Y	Y	Y	Y
12 Wright	Y	Y	Y	Y	Y	?	?	Y
13 Hightower	N	Y	Y	Y	Y	Y	Y	Y
14 Patman	N	Y	N	Y	Y	Y	Y	Y
15 de la Garza	N	Y	Y	Y	Y	Y	Y	Y
16 Coleman	Y	Y	Y	Y	Y	Y	Y	Y
17 Stenholm	N	Y	N	Y	Y	Y	Y	Y
18 Leland	Y	?	Y	Y	Y	Y	Y	?
19 Hance	?	?	N	Y	Y	Y	Y	Y
20 Gonzalez	Y	Y	Y	Y	Y	Y	Y	Y
21 ***Loeffler***	N	Y	N	Y	Y	Y	Y	?
22 ***Paul***	X	?	N	Y	N	N	N	Y
23 Kazen	N	Y	Y	Y	Y	Y	Y	Y
24 Frost	Y	Y	Y	Y	Y	Y	Y	Y
25 Andrews	N	Y	Y	Y	Y	Y	Y	Y
26 Vandergriff	N	Y	Y	Y	Y	Y	Y	?
27 Ortiz	N	Y	Y	Y	Y	Y	Y	Y
UTAH								
1 ***Hansen***	N	Y	N	Y	Y	Y	N	Y
2 ***Marriott***	N	+	N	Y	Y	Y	Y	Y
3 ***Nielson***	N	Y	?	Y	Y	Y	N	Y
VERMONT								
AL ***Jeffords***	Y	Y	Y	Y	Y	Y	Y	Y
VIRGINIA								
1 ***Bateman***	X	?	N	Y	Y	Y	Y	Y
2 ***Whitehurst***	N	Y	N	Y	Y	Y	Y	Y
3 ***Bliley***	N	Y	N	Y	Y	Y	Y	Y
4 Sisisky	N	Y	Y	Y	Y	Y	Y	Y
5 Daniel	N	Y	N	Y	Y	Y	Y	Y
6 Olin	Y	Y	Y	Y	Y	Y	Y	Y
7 ***Robinson***	N	Y	N	Y	Y	Y	Y	Y
8 ***Parris***	N	Y	N	Y	Y	Y	Y	Y
9 Boucher	Y	Y	Y	Y	Y	Y	Y	Y
10 ***Wolf***	N	Y	Y	Y	Y	Y	Y	Y
WASHINGTON								
1 ***Pritchard***	N	Y	N	Y	Y	Y	Y	Y
2 Swift	Y	Y	Y	Y	Y	Y	Y	Y
3 Bonker	Y	Y	Y	Y	Y	Y	Y	Y
4 ***Morrison***	N	Y	Y	Y	Y	Y	Y	Y
5 Foley	Y	Y	Y	Y	Y	Y	Y	Y
6 Dicks	Y	Y	Y	Y	?	Y	Y	Y
7 Lowry	Y	Y	Y	Y	Y	Y	Y	Y
8 ***Chandler***	N	Y	Y	Y	Y	Y	Y	Y
WEST VIRGINIA								
1 Mollohan	Y	Y	Y	Y	Y	Y	Y	Y
2 Staggers	Y	Y	Y	Y	Y	Y	Y	Y
3 Wise	Y	Y	Y	Y	Y	Y	Y	+
4 Rahall	Y	Y	Y	Y	Y	Y	Y	Y
WISCONSIN								
1 Aspin	Y	Y	Y	?	Y	Y	Y	Y
2 Kastenmeier	Y	Y	Y	Y	Y	Y	Y	Y
3 ***Gunderson***	Y	Y	Y	Y	Y	Y	Y	Y
4 Zablocki	Y	Y	Y	Y	Y	Y	Y	Y
5 Moody	Y	Y	Y	Y	Y	Y	Y	Y
6 ***Petri***	N	Y	N	Y	Y	Y	Y	?
7 Obey	Y	Y	Y	Y	Y	Y	Y	Y
8 ***Roth***	N	Y	N	Y	Y	Y	Y	Y
9 ***Sensenbrenner***	N	Y	N	Y	Y	Y	Y	Y
WYOMING								
AL ***Cheney***	N	Y	N	Y	Y	Y	Y	Y

** Rep. Harold Washington, D-Ill., resigned April 30, 1983. The last vote for which he was eligible was CQ vote 68.*

Southern states - Ala., Ark., Fla., Ga., Ky., La., Miss., N.C., Okla., S.C., Tenn., Texas, Va.

KEY

Y   Voted for (yea).
\#   Paired for.
\+   Announced for.
N   Voted against (nay).
X   Paired against.
\-   Announced against.
P   Voted "present".
C   Voted "present" to avoid possible conflict of interest.
?   Did not vote or otherwise make a position known.

Democrats   *Republicans*

75. H J Res 13. Nuclear Freeze. Pepper, D-Fla., motion to order the previous question (thus ending debate and the possibility of amendment) on the rule (H Res 179) providing for further House floor consideration of the joint resolution calling for a mutual and verifiable freeze on and reductions in nuclear weapons. Motion agreed to 269-150: R 19-144; D 250-6 (ND 169-1, SD 81-5), May 4, 1983.

76. H J Res 13. Nuclear Freeze. Adoption of the rule (H Res 179) providing for further House floor consideration of the joint resolution calling for a mutual and verifiable freeze on and reductions in nuclear weapons. Adopted 270-149: R 22-138; D 248-11 (ND 168-3, SD 80-8), May 4, 1983.

77. H J Res 13. Nuclear Freeze. Zablocki, D-Wis., amendment to the Courter, R-N.J., substitute for the Lungren, R-Calif., amendment, to provide that nothing in the resolution shall be construed to supersede the treaty-making powers of the president. Adopted 234-183: R 27-136; D 207-47 (ND 161-9, SD 46-38), May 4, 1983. (The Courter amendment and Lungren amendment, as amended, subsequently were adopted by voice votes. The amendments would have provided in slightly different words that nothing in the resolution would bind the president or his negotiators in the formation of strategy, instructions or positions in the conduct of the Strategic Arms Reduction Talks.)

78. H J Res 13. Nuclear Freeze. Solarz, D-N.Y., amendment to the Levitas, D-Ga., amendment, to provide that it would be a goal of U.S. arms control policy that nuclear arms reductions be achieved as soon as possible after the achievement of a nuclear weapons freeze. Rejected 210-214: R 14-151; D 196-63 (ND 161-10, SD 35-53), May 4, 1983.

79. H J Res 13. Nuclear Freeze. Hyde, R-Ill., amendment to the Dicks, D-Wash., substitute for the Levitas, D-Ga., amendment, to provide that an agreement to freeze nuclear weapons would include a specified, reasonable period of time within which reductions in U.S. and Soviet nuclear weapons would be agreed to. Adopted 221-203: R 155-11; D 66-192 (ND 12-158, SD 54-34), May 4, 1983. (The Hyde amendment restored the original language of the Levitas amendment. The Dicks amendment would have provided that negotiators would seek arms reductions immediately after agreement on a freeze.)

	75	76	77	78	79
ALABAMA					
1 *Edwards*	N	N	N	N	Y
2 *Dickinson*	N	N	N	N	Y
3 Nichols	Y	Y	N	N	Y
4 Bevill	Y	Y	Y	N	Y
5 Flippo	Y	Y	N	N	Y
6 Erdreich	Y	Y	N	N	Y
7 Shelby	N	N	N	N	Y
ALASKA					
AL *Young*	N	N	N	N	Y
ARIZONA					
1 *McCain*	N	N	N	N	Y
2 Udall	Y	Y	Y	Y	N
3 *Stump*	N	N	N	N	Y
4 *Rudd*	N	N	N	N	Y
5 McNulty	Y	Y	Y	Y	N
ARKANSAS					
1 Alexander	Y	?	Y	Y	N
2 *Bethune*	N	N	N	N	Y
3 *Hammerschmidt*	N	N	N	N	Y
4 Anthony	Y	Y	Y	Y	N
CALIFORNIA					
1 Bosco	Y	Y	Y	Y	N
2 *Chappie*	N	N	N	N	Y
3 Matsui	Y	Y	Y	Y	N
4 Fazio	Y	Y	Y	Y	N
5 Vacancy					
6 Boxer	Y	Y	Y	Y	N
7 Miller	Y	Y	?	Y	N
8 Dellums	Y	Y	Y	Y	N
9 Stark	?	Y	Y	Y	N
10 Edwards	Y	Y	Y	Y	N
11 Lantos	Y	Y	Y	Y	-
12 Zschau	N	N	N	N	Y
13 Mineta	Y	Y	Y	Y	N
14 *Shumway*	N	N	N	N	Y
15 Coelho	Y	Y	Y	Y	N
16 Panetta	Y	Y	Y	Y	N
17 *Pashayan*	N	N	N	N	Y
18 Lehman	Y	Y	Y	Y	N
19 *Lagomarsino*	N	N	N	N	Y
20 *Thomas*	N	N	N	N	Y
21 *Fiedler*	N	N	N	N	Y
22 *Moorhead*	N	N	N	N	Y
23 Beilenson	Y	Y	Y	Y	N
24 Waxman	#	#	#	?	?
25 Roybal	Y	Y	Y	Y	N
26 Berman	Y	Y	Y	Y	N
27 Levine	Y	Y	Y	Y	N
28 Dixon	Y	Y	Y	Y	?
29 Hawkins	Y	Y	Y	Y	N
30 Martinez	Y	Y	Y	Y	N
31 Dymally	Y	Y	Y	Y	N
32 Anderson	Y	Y	Y	Y	N
33 *Dreier*	N	N	N	N	Y
34 Torres	Y	Y	Y	Y	N
35 *Lewis*	N	N	N	N	Y
36 Brown	Y	Y	Y	Y	N
37 *McCandless*	N	N	N	N	Y
38 Patterson	Y	Y	Y	Y	N
39 *Dannemeyer*	N	N	N	N	Y
40 *Badham*	N	N	N	N	Y
41 *Lowery*	N	N	N	N	Y
42 *Lungren*	N	N	N	N	Y

	75	76	77	78	79
43 *Packard*	N	N	N	N	Y
44 Bates	Y	Y	Y	Y	N
45 *Hunter*	N	N	N	N	Y
COLORADO					
1 Schroeder	Y	Y	Y	Y	N
2 Wirth	Y	Y	Y	Y	N
3 Kogovsek	Y	Y	Y	Y	N
4 *Brown*	Y	Y	N	N	Y
5 *Kramer*	N	N	N	N	Y
6 *Schaefer*	N	N	N	N	Y
CONNECTICUT					
1 Kennelly	Y	Y	Y	Y	N
2 Gejdenson	Y	Y	Y	Y	N
3 Morrison	Y	Y	Y	Y	N
4 *McKinney*	Y	Y	Y	Y	N
5 Ratchford	Y	Y	Y	Y	N
6 *Johnson*	N	?	Y	N	Y
DELAWARE					
AL Carper	Y	Y	Y	Y	N
FLORIDA					
1 Hutto	Y	N	N	N	Y
2 Fuqua	Y	Y	Y	N	Y
3 Bennett	Y	Y	N	N	Y
4 Chappell	Y	N	N	N	Y
5 *McCollum*	N	N	N	N	Y
6 MacKay	Y	Y	Y	#	X
7 Gibbons	Y	Y	Y	Y	N
8 *Young*	N	N	N	N	Y
9 *Bilirakis*	N	N	N	N	Y
10 Ireland	Y	N	N	N	Y
11 Nelson	Y	Y	N	N	Y
12 *Lewis*	N	N	N	N	Y
13 *Mack*	N	N	N	N	Y
14 Mica	Y	Y	Y	N	Y
15 *Shaw*	N	N	N	N	Y
16 Smith	Y	Y	Y	Y	N
17 Lehman	Y	Y	Y	Y	N
18 Pepper	Y	Y	#	Y	N
19 Fascell	Y	Y	Y	Y	N
GEORGIA					
1 Thomas	Y	Y	Y	N	Y
2 Hatcher	Y	Y	?	?	?
3 Ray	Y	N	N	N	Y
4 Levitas	Y	Y	Y	N	Y
5 Fowler	Y	Y	Y	Y	N
6 *Gingrich*	N	N	N	N	Y
7 McDonald	N	N	N	N	Y
8 Rowland	Y	Y	N	N	Y
9 Jenkins	Y	Y	N	N	Y
10 Barnard	Y	Y	N	N	Y
HAWAII					
1 Heftel	Y	Y	Y	Y	N
2 Akaka	Y	Y	Y	Y	N
IDAHO					
1 *Craig*	N	N	N	N	Y
2 *Hansen*	X	X	X	N	Y
ILLINOIS					
1 Vacancy					
2 Savage	Y	Y	Y	Y	N
3 Russo	Y	Y	Y	Y	N
4 *O'Brien*	Y	Y	Y	Y	N
5 Lipinski	Y	Y	N	N	Y
6 *Hyde*	N	N	N	N	Y
7 Collins	Y	Y	Y	Y	N
8 Rostenkowski	Y	Y	Y	Y	N
9 Yates	Y	Y	Y	Y	N
10 *Porter*	N	N	N	N	Y
11 Annunzio	Y	Y	Y	Y	N
12 *Crane, P.*	N	N	N	N	Y
13 *Erlenborn*	N	N	N	N	Y
14 *Corcoran*	N	N	N	N	Y
15 *Madigan*	N	N	N	N	Y
16 *Martin*	N	N	Y	N	Y
17 Evans	Y	Y	Y	Y	N
18 *Michel*	N	N	N	N	Y
19 *Crane, D.*	N	N	N	N	Y
20 Durbin	Y	Y	Y	Y	N
21 Price	Y	Y	Y	Y	N
22 Simon	Y	Y	Y	Y	N
INDIANA					
1 Hall	?	?	Y	Y	N
2 Sharp	Y	Y	Y	Y	N
3 *Hiler*	N	N	N	N	Y
4 *Coats*	N	N	N	N	Y
5 Hillis	N	N	N	N	Y

ND - Northern Democrats   SD - Southern Democrats

	75	76	77	78	79
6 Burton	N	N	N	N	Y
7 Myers	N	N	N	N	Y
8 McCloskey	Y	Y	Y	Y	N
9 Hamilton	Y	Y	Y	Y	N
10 Jacobs	Y	Y	Y	Y	N
IOWA					
1 Leach	Y	Y	Y	Y	N
2 Tauke	Y	Y	Y	Y	N
3 Evans	N	Y	Y	Y	N
4 Smith	Y	Y	Y	Y	N
5 Harkin	Y	Y	Y	Y	N
6 Bedell	Y	Y	Y	Y	N
KANSAS					
1 Roberts	N	Y	N	N	Y
2 Slattery	Y	Y	N	N	Y
3 Winn	N	N	N	N	Y
4 Glickman	Y	Y	N	Y	Y
5 Whittaker	N	Y	N	N	Y
KENTUCKY					
1 Hubbard	Y	Y	N	N	Y
2 Natcher	Y	Y	Y	N	N
3 Mazzoli	Y	Y	Y	Y	N
4 Snyder	N	N	N	N	Y
5 Rogers	N	N	N	N	Y
6 Hopkins	N	Y	N	N	Y
7 Perkins	Y	Y	Y	Y	N
LOUISIANA					
1 Livingston	N	N	N	N	Y
2 Boggs	Y	Y	N	N	N
3 Tauzin	Y	Y	N	N	Y
4 Roemer	Y	Y	N	N	Y
5 Huckaby	Y	Y	N	N	Y
6 Moore	N	N	N	N	Y
7 Breaux	Y	Y	N	N	Y
8 Long	Y	Y	Y	Y	N
MAINE					
1 McKernan	N	N	Y	Y	N
2 Snowe	N	N	Y	Y	N
MARYLAND					
1 Dyson	Y	Y	N	N	Y
2 Long	Y	Y	Y	Y	N
3 Mikulski	Y	Y	Y	Y	N
4 Holt	N	N	N	N	Y
5 Hoyer	Y	Y	Y	Y	N
6 Byron	Y	N	N	N	Y
7 Mitchell	Y	Y	Y	Y	N
8 Barnes	Y	Y	Y	Y	N
MASSACHUSETTS					
1 Conte	Y	Y	Y	Y	Y
2 Boland	#	Y	Y	Y	N
3 Early	Y	Y	Y	Y	N
4 Frank	Y	Y	Y	Y	N
5 Shannon	Y	Y	Y	Y	N
6 Mavroules	Y	Y	Y	Y	N
7 Markey	Y	Y	Y	Y	N
8 O'Neill					
9 Moakley	Y	Y	Y	Y	N
10 Studds	Y	Y	Y	Y	N
11 Donnelly	Y	Y	Y	Y	N
MICHIGAN					
1 Conyers	Y	Y	Y	Y	N
2 Pursell	N	Y	N	N	Y
3 Wolpe	Y	Y	Y	Y	N
4 Siljander	N	N	N	N	Y
5 Sawyer	N	N	N	N	Y
6 Carr	Y	Y	Y	Y	N
7 Kildee	Y	Y	Y	Y	N
8 Traxler	Y	Y	Y	Y	N
9 Vander Jagt	N	N	N	N	Y
10 Albosta	Y	Y	Y	Y	N
11 Davis	N	N	Y	N	Y
12 Bonior	Y	Y	Y	Y	N
13 Crockett	Y	Y	Y	Y	N
14 Hertel	Y	Y	Y	Y	N
15 Ford	Y	#	Y	Y	N
16 Dingell	Y	Y	Y	Y	N
17 Levin	Y	Y	Y	Y	N
18 Broomfield	Y	Y	N	N	Y
MINNESOTA					
1 Penny	Y	Y	Y	Y	N
2 Weber	N	N	N	N	Y
3 Frenzel	X	X	N	N	Y
4 Vento	Y	Y	Y	Y	N
5 Sabo	Y	Y	Y	Y	N
6 Sikorski	?	Y	Y	Y	N

	75	76	77	78	79
7 Stangeland	N	N	N	N	Y
8 Oberstar	Y	Y	Y	Y	N
MISSISSIPPI					
1 Whitten	Y	Y	Y	N	N
2 Franklin	N	N	N	N	Y
3 Montgomery	Y	Y	N	N	Y
4 Dowdy	Y	Y	Y	Y	Y
5 Lott	N	N	N	N	Y
MISSOURI					
1 Clay	Y	Y	Y	Y	N
2 Young	Y	Y	Y	Y	N
3 Gephardt	Y	Y	Y	Y	N
4 Skelton	Y	Y	N	N	Y
5 Wheat	Y	Y	Y	Y	N
6 Coleman	N	N	N	N	Y
7 Taylor	N	N	N	N	Y
8 Emerson	N	N	N	N	Y
9 Volkmer	Y	Y	N	N	Y
MONTANA					
1 Williams	Y	Y	Y	Y	N
2 Marlenee	N	N	N	N	Y
NEBRASKA					
1 Bereuter	N	N	N	N	Y
2 Daub	N	N	N	N	Y
3 Smith	N	N	N	N	Y
NEVADA					
1 Reid	Y	Y	Y	Y	N
2 Vucanovich	N	N	N	N	Y
NEW HAMPSHIRE					
1 D'Amours	Y	Y	Y	Y	N
2 Gregg	N	N	N	N	Y
NEW JERSEY					
1 Florio	Y	Y	Y	Y	N
2 Hughes	Y	Y	N	Y	N
3 Howard	Y	Y	Y	Y	N
4 Smith	Y	Y	Y	Y	N
5 Roukema	Y	Y	Y	Y	N
6 Dwyer	Y	Y	Y	Y	N
7 Rinaldo	Y	Y	Y	?	Y
8 Roe	Y	Y	Y	Y	Y
9 Torricelli	Y	Y	Y	Y	N
10 Rodino	Y	Y	Y	Y	N
11 Minish	Y	Y	Y	Y	N
12 Courter	N	N	N	N	Y
13 Forsythe	N	N	N	N	Y
14 Guarini	Y	Y	Y	Y	N
NEW MEXICO					
1 Lujan	N	N	N	N	Y
2 Skeen	N	N	N	N	Y
3 Richardson	Y	Y	Y	Y	N
NEW YORK					
1 Carney	N	N	N	N	Y
2 Downey	Y	Y	Y	Y	N
3 Mrazek	Y	Y	Y	Y	N
4 Lent	N	N	N	N	Y
5 McGrath	N	N	N	N	Y
6 Addabbo	Y	Y	Y	Y	N
7 Ackerman	Y	Y	Y	Y	N
8 Scheuer	Y	Y	Y	Y	N
9 Ferraro	Y	Y	Y	Y	N
10 Schumer	Y	Y	Y	Y	N
11 Towns	#	#	#	?	?
12 Owens	Y	Y	Y	Y	N
13 Solarz	Y	Y	Y	Y	N
14 Molinari	N	X	N	N	Y
15 Green	Y	Y	Y	Y	N
16 Rangel	Y	Y	#	Y	N
17 Weiss	Y	Y	Y	Y	N
18 Garcia	Y	Y	?	Y	N
19 Biaggi	Y	Y	Y	Y	N
20 Ottinger	Y	Y	Y	Y	N
21 Fish	N	N	Y	N	Y
22 Gilman	N	N	N	N	Y
23 Stratton	N	N	N	N	Y
24 Solomon	N	N	N	N	Y
25 Boehlert	Y	Y	Y	Y	Y
26 Martin	X	?	X	N	Y
27 Wortley	N	N	N	N	Y
28 McHugh	Y	Y	Y	Y	N
29 Horton	N	N	Y	N	Y
30 Conable	N	N	N	N	Y
31 Kemp	N	N	N	N	Y
32 LaFalce	Y	Y	Y	Y	N
33 Nowak	Y	Y	Y	Y	N
34 Lundine	Y	Y	Y	Y	N

	75	76	77	78	79
NORTH CAROLINA					
1 Jones	?	#	?	Y	Y
2 Valentine	Y	Y	N	N	Y
3 Whitley	Y	Y	N	N	Y
4 Andrews	Y	Y	Y	Y	Y
5 Neal	Y	Y	Y	Y	N
6 Britt	Y	Y	Y	Y	N
7 Rose	Y	Y	Y	Y	N
8 Hefner	?	Y	Y	Y	N
9 Martin	N	N	N	N	Y
10 Broyhill	N	N	N	N	Y
11 Clarke	Y	Y	Y	Y	N
NORTH DAKOTA					
AL Dorgan	Y	Y	Y	Y	N
OHIO					
1 Luken	Y	Y	Y	Y	N
2 Gradison	N	N	N	N	Y
3 Hall	N	Y	Y	N	N
4 Oxley	N	N	N	N	Y
5 Latta	N	N	N	N	Y
6 McEwen	X	X	X	X	#
7 DeWine	N	N	N	N	Y
8 Kindness	N	N	N	N	Y
9 Kaptur	Y	Y	Y	Y	N
10 Miller	N	N	N	N	Y
11 Eckart	Y	Y	Y	Y	N
12 Kasich	N	N	N	N	Y
13 Pease	Y	Y	Y	Y	N
14 Seiberling	Y	Y	Y	Y	N
15 Wylie	N	N	N	N	Y
16 Regula	N	N	N	N	Y
17 Williams	Y	Y	Y	Y	Y
18 Applegate	Y	Y	Y	Y	N
19 Feighan	Y	Y	Y	Y	N
20 Oakar	Y	Y	Y	Y	N
21 Stokes	Y	Y	Y	Y	N
OKLAHOMA					
1 Jones	Y	Y	Y	N	Y
2 Synar	Y	Y	Y	N	N
3 Watkins	#	Y	Y	N	Y
4 McCurdy	Y	Y	N	N	Y
5 Edwards	N	N	N	N	Y
6 English	Y	Y	N	N	Y
OREGON					
1 AuCoin	Y	Y	Y	Y	N
2 Smith, R.	N	N	N	N	Y
3 Wyden	Y	Y	Y	Y	N
4 Weaver	Y	Y	Y	Y	N
5 Smith, D.	N	N	N	N	Y
PENNSYLVANIA					
1 Foglietta	Y	Y	Y	Y	N
2 Gray	Y	Y	Y	Y	N
3 Borski	Y	Y	Y	Y	N
4 Kolter	Y	Y	Y	Y	N
5 Schulze	N	N	N	N	Y
6 Yatron	Y	Y	Y	Y	N
7 Edgar	Y	Y	Y	Y	N
8 Kostmayer	Y	Y	Y	Y	N
9 Shuster	N	N	N	N	Y
10 McDade	Y	N	N	N	Y
11 Harrison	Y	Y	Y	Y	N
12 Murtha	Y	Y	Y	?	Y
13 Coughlin	Y	Y	Y	N	Y
14 Coyne	Y	Y	Y	Y	N
15 Ritter	N	N	N	N	Y
16 Walker	N	N	N	N	Y
17 Gekas	N	N	N	N	Y
18 Walgren	Y	Y	Y	Y	N
19 Goodling	Y	Y	N	N	N
20 Gaydos	Y	Y	Y	?	?
21 Ridge	N	N	N	N	Y
22 Murphy	Y	Y	Y	Y	N
23 Clinger	N	Y	N	N	Y
RHODE ISLAND					
1 St Germain	Y	Y	Y	Y	N
2 Schneider	Y	Y	Y	Y	N
SOUTH CAROLINA					
1 Hartnett	N	N	N	N	Y
2 Spence	N	N	N	N	Y
3 Derrick	Y	Y	?	Y	N
4 Campbell	N	N	N	N	Y
5 Spratt	Y	Y	Y	N	Y
6 Tallon	Y	Y	Y	Y	N
SOUTH DAKOTA					
AL Daschle	Y	Y	Y	Y	Y

	75	76	77	78	79
TENNESSEE					
1 Quillen	N	N	N	N	Y
2 Duncan	N	N	N	N	Y
3 Lloyd	Y	N	N	N	Y
4 Cooper	Y	Y	N	N	Y
5 Boner	Y	Y	Y	Y	Y
6 Gore	Y	Y	Y	Y	N
7 Sundquist	N	N	N	N	Y
8 Jones	Y	Y	Y	Y	N
9 Ford	Y	Y	Y	Y	N
TEXAS					
1 Hall, S.	Y	Y	?	N	Y
2 Wilson	N	Y	N	N	Y
3 Bartlett	N	N	N	N	Y
4 Hall, R.	Y	Y	N	N	Y
5 Bryant	Y	Y	Y	Y	N
6 Gramm	N	N	X	N	Y
7 Archer	N	N	N	N	Y
8 Fields	N	N	N	N	Y
9 Brooks	Y	Y	Y	Y	N
10 Pickle	?	Y	Y	N	Y
11 Leath	Y	N	N	N	Y
12 Wright	Y	Y	Y	Y	N
13 Hightower	Y	Y	N	N	Y
14 Patman	N	N	N	N	Y
15 de la Garza	Y	Y	?	Y	N
16 Coleman	Y	Y	Y	Y	N
17 Stenholm	Y	Y	N	N	Y
18 Leland	Y	Y	Y	Y	N
19 Hance	Y	Y	Y	N	Y
20 Gonzalez	Y	Y	Y	Y	N
21 Loeffler	N	N	N	N	Y
22 Paul	N	N	N	N	Y
23 Kazen	Y	Y	N	N	Y
24 Frost	Y	Y	Y	Y	N
25 Andrews	Y	Y	Y	Y	N
26 Vandergriff	N	Y	N	N	Y
27 Ortiz	Y	Y	Y	N	Y
UTAH					
1 Hansen	N	N	N	N	Y
2 Marriott	N	N	N	N	Y
3 Nielson	N	N	N	N	Y
VERMONT					
AL Jeffords	N	N	Y	Y	N
VIRGINIA					
1 Bateman	N	N	N	N	Y
2 Whitehurst	N	N	N	N	Y
3 Bliley	N	N	N	N	Y
4 Sisisky	Y	Y	N	N	Y
5 Daniel	Y	Y	N	N	Y
6 Olin	Y	Y	Y	Y	N
7 Robinson	N	N	N	N	Y
8 Parris	N	N	N	N	Y
9 Boucher	Y	Y	Y	Y	N
10 Wolf	N	N	N	N	Y
WASHINGTON					
1 Pritchard	Y	?	Y	N	Y
2 Swift	Y	Y	Y	Y	N
3 Bonker	Y	Y	Y	Y	N
4 Morrison	N	N	Y	N	Y
5 Foley	Y	Y	Y	Y	N
6 Dicks	Y	Y	Y	Y	N
7 Lowry	Y	Y	Y	Y	N
8 Chandler	Y	N	Y	N	Y
WEST VIRGINIA					
1 Mollohan	Y	Y	Y	Y	N
2 Staggers	Y	Y	Y	Y	N
3 Wise	Y	Y	Y	Y	N
4 Rahall	Y	Y	Y	Y	N
WISCONSIN					
1 Aspin	Y	Y	Y	Y	N
2 Kastenmeier	Y	Y	Y	Y	N
3 Gunderson	N	N	Y	N	Y
4 Zablocki	Y	Y	Y	Y	N
5 Moody	Y	Y	Y	Y	N
6 Petri	N	N	N	N	Y
7 Obey	Y	Y	Y	Y	N
8 Roth	N	N	N	N	Y
9 Sensenbrenner	N	N	N	N	Y
WYOMING					
AL Cheney	N	N	N	N	Y

Southern states - Ala., Ark., Fla., Ga., Ky., La., Miss., N.C., Okla., S.C., Tenn., Texas, Va.

80. H J Res 13. Nuclear Freeze. Dicks, D-Wash., substitute, as amended by the Hyde, R-Ill., amendment *(see vote 79, p. 28-H)*, for the Levitas, D-Ga., amendment, to provide that an agreement to freeze nuclear weapons would include a specified, reasonable period of time within which reductions in U.S. and Soviet nuclear weapons would be agreed to. Adopted 225-191: R 154-11; D 71-180 (ND 14-153, SD 57-27), May 4, 1983.

81. H J Res 13. Nuclear Freeze. Solarz, D-N.Y., amendment to the Hunter, R-Calif., amendment, to provide that nothing in the resolution would prevent safety-related improvements in strategic bombers. Adopted 227-189: R 21-143; D 206-46 (ND 158-9, SD 48-37), May 4, 1983. (The Hunter amendment would have provided that nothing in the resolution would prevent the replacement of B-52 bombers with B-1 bombers if required for the safety of U.S. bomber crews.)

82. H J Res 13. Nuclear Freeze. Broomfield, R-Mich., motion to recommit the joint resolution calling for a mutual and verifiable freeze on and reduction in nuclear weapons to the Foreign Affairs Committee. Motion rejected 175-247: R 132-34; D 43-213 (ND 4-165, SD 39-48), May 4, 1983.

83. H J Res 13. Nuclear Freeze. Passage of the joint resolution calling for a mutual and verifiable freeze on and reduction in nuclear weapons. Passed 278-149: R 60-106; D 218-43 (ND 168-4, SD 50-39), May 4, 1983. A "nay" was a vote supporting the president's position.

KEY

Y Voted for (yea).
\# Paired for.
+ Announced for.
N Voted against (nay).
X Paired against.
- Announced against.
P Voted "present".
C Voted "present" to avoid possible conflict of interest.
? Did not vote or otherwise make a position known.

Democrats *Republicans*

	80	81	82	83
ALABAMA				
1 *Edwards*	Y	N	Y	N
2 *Dickinson*	Y	N	Y	N
3 Nichols	Y	N	Y	N
4 Bevill	Y	N	Y	N
5 Flippo	Y	N	Y	N
6 Erdreich	Y	N	Y	N
7 Shelby	Y	N	Y	N
ALASKA				
AL *Young*	Y	N	Y	Y
ARIZONA				
1 *McCain*	Y	N	Y	N
2 Udall	N	Y	N	Y
3 *Stump*	Y	N	Y	N
4 *Rudd*	Y	N	Y	N
5 McNulty	N	Y	N	Y
ARKANSAS				
1 Alexander	?	?	N	Y
2 *Bethune*	Y	N	Y	N
3 *Hammerschmidt*	Y	N	Y	N
4 Anthony	N	Y	N	Y
CALIFORNIA				
1 Bosco	N	?	?	Y
2 *Chappie*	Y	N	Y	N
3 Matsui	N	Y	N	Y
4 Fazio	N	Y	N	Y
5 Vacancy				
6 Boxer	N	Y	N	Y
7 Miller	N	Y	N	Y
8 Dellums	N	Y	N	Y
9 Stark	N	Y	N	Y
10 Edwards	N	Y	N	Y
11 Lantos	-	+	-	+
12 *Zschau*	Y	N	Y	N
13 Mineta	N	Y	N	Y
14 *Shumway*	Y	N	Y	N
15 Coelho	N	Y	N	Y
16 Panetta	N	Y	N	Y
17 *Pashayan*	Y	?	Y	N
18 Lehman	N	Y	N	Y
19 *Lagomarsino*	Y	N	Y	Y
20 *Thomas*	Y	N	Y	Y
21 *Fiedler*	Y	N	Y	Y
22 *Moorhead*	Y	N	Y	N
23 Beilenson	N	Y	N	Y
24 Waxman	?	?	?	?
25 Roybal	N	Y	N	Y
26 Berman	N	Y	N	Y
27 Levine	N	Y	N	Y
28 Dixon	N	Y	N	Y
29 Hawkins	N	?	N	Y
30 Martinez	N	Y	N	Y
31 Dymally	N	Y	N	Y
32 Anderson	N	N	N	Y
33 *Dreier*	Y	N	Y	N
34 Torres	N	Y	N	Y
35 *Lewis*	Y	N	Y	N
36 Brown	N	Y	N	Y
37 *McCandless*	Y	N	Y	N
38 Patterson	N	Y	N	Y
39 *Dannemeyer*	Y	N	Y	N
40 *Badham*	Y	N	Y	N
41 *Lowery*	Y	N	Y	N
42 *Lungren*	Y	N	Y	N

	80	81	82	83
43 *Packard*	Y	N	Y	N
44 Bates	N	Y	N	Y
45 *Hunter*	Y	N	Y	N
COLORADO				
1 Schroeder	N	Y	N	Y
2 Wirth	N	Y	N	Y
3 Kogovsek	N	Y	N	Y
4 *Brown*	Y	N	N	Y
5 *Kramer*	Y	N	Y	N
6 *Schaefer*	Y	N	Y	N
CONNECTICUT				
1 Kennelly	N	Y	N	Y
2 Gejdenson	N	Y	N	Y
3 Morrison	N	Y	N	Y
4 *McKinney*	N	Y	N	Y
5 Ratchford	N	Y	N	Y
6 *Johnson*	Y	Y	N	Y
DELAWARE				
AL Carper	N	Y	N	Y
FLORIDA				
1 Hutto	Y	N	Y	N
2 Fuqua	Y	Y	N	Y
3 Bennett	Y	N	Y	N
4 Chappell	Y	N	Y	N
5 *McCollum*	Y	N	Y	N
6 MacKay	?	+	-	Y
7 Gibbons	N	Y	N	Y
8 *Young*	Y	N	Y	N
9 *Bilirakis*	Y	N	Y	N
10 Ireland	Y	N	Y	N
11 Nelson	Y	+	+	Y
12 *Lewis*	Y	N	Y	N
13 *Mack*	Y	N	Y	N
14 Mica	N	Y	N	Y
15 *Shaw*	Y	N	Y	N
16 Smith	N	Y	N	Y
17 Lehman	N	Y	N	Y
18 Pepper	N	Y	N	Y
19 Fascell	N	Y	N	Y
GEORGIA				
1 Thomas	Y	N	N	N
2 Hatcher	?	?	?	?
3 Ray	Y	N	Y	N
4 Levitas	Y	Y	Y	Y
5 Fowler	N	Y	N	Y
6 *Gingrich*	?	N	Y	N
7 McDonald	Y	N	Y	N
8 Rowland	Y	N	Y	N
9 Jenkins	Y	N	Y	N
10 Barnard	Y	N	Y	N
HAWAII				
1 Heftel	Y	Y	N	Y
2 Akaka	N	Y	N	Y
IDAHO				
1 *Craig*	Y	N	Y	N
2 *Hansen*	Y	N	Y	N
ILLINOIS				
1 Vacancy				
2 Savage	N	Y	N	Y
3 Russo	N	Y	N	Y
4 *O'Brien*	Y	N	Y	N
5 Lipinski	Y	N	Y	N
6 *Hyde*	Y	N	Y	N
7 Collins	N	Y	N	Y
8 Rostenkowski	N	Y	N	Y
9 Yates	?	Y	N	Y
10 *Porter*	Y	Y	N	Y
11 Annunzio	N	Y	N	Y
12 *Crane, P.*	Y	N	Y	N
13 *Erlenborn*	Y	N	Y	N
14 *Corcoran*	Y	N	Y	N
15 *Madigan*	Y	N	Y	Y
16 *Martin*	Y	N	Y	N
17 Evans	N	Y	N	Y
18 *Michel*	Y	N	Y	N
19 *Crane, D.*	Y	N	Y	N
20 Durbin	N	Y	N	Y
21 Price	Y	N	Y	N
22 Simon	N	Y	N	Y
INDIANA				
1 Hall	N	Y	N	Y
2 Sharp	N	Y	N	Y
3 *Hiler*	Y	N	Y	N
4 *Coats*	Y	N	Y	N
5 Hillis	Y	N	Y	N

ND - Northern Democrats   SD - Southern Democrats

	80	81	82	83
6 Burton	Y	N	Y	N
7 Myers	Y	N	Y	N
8 McCloskey	N	Y	N	Y
9 Hamilton	N	Y	N	Y
10 Jacobs	N	Y	N	Y
IOWA				
1 Leach	N	Y	N	Y
2 Tauke	N	Y	N	Y
3 Evans	N	Y	N	Y
4 Smith	N	Y	N	Y
5 Harkin	N	Y	N	Y
6 Bedell	N	Y	N	Y
KANSAS				
1 Roberts	Y	N	Y	N
2 Slattery	Y	Y	N	Y
3 Winn	Y	N	Y	N
4 Glickman	Y	Y	N	Y
5 Whittaker	Y	N	N	Y
KENTUCKY				
1 Hubbard	Y	N	Y	N
2 Natcher	N	Y	N	Y
3 Mazzoli	Y	Y	N	Y
4 Snyder	Y	N	Y	N
5 Rogers	Y	N	Y	N
6 Hopkins	Y	N	Y	Y
7 Perkins	N	Y	N	Y
LOUISIANA				
1 Livingston	Y	N	Y	N
2 Boggs	Y	Y	N	Y
3 Tauzin	Y	N	Y	N
4 Roemer	Y	N	Y	N
5 Huckaby	Y	N	Y	N
6 Moore	Y	N	Y	N
7 Breaux	Y	N	Y	N
8 Long	Y	Y	N	Y
MAINE				
1 McKernan	N	Y	N	Y
2 Snowe	N	Y	N	Y
MARYLAND				
1 Dyson	Y	N	Y	N
2 Long	N	Y	N	Y
3 Mikulski	N	Y	N	Y
4 Holt	Y	N	Y	N
5 Hoyer	N	Y	N	Y
6 Byron	Y	N	Y	N
7 Mitchell	N	Y	N	Y
8 Barnes	N	Y	N	Y
MASSACHUSETTS				
1 Conte	Y	Y	N	Y
2 Boland	N	Y	N	Y
3 Early	N	Y	N	Y
4 Frank	N	Y	N	Y
5 Shannon	N	Y	N	Y
6 Mavroules	N	Y	N	Y
7 Markey	N	Y	N	Y
8 O'Neill				
9 Moakley	N	Y	N	Y
10 Studds	N	Y	N	Y
11 Donnelly	N	Y	?	Y
MICHIGAN				
1 Conyers	?	Y	N	Y
2 Pursell	Y	Y	N	Y
3 Wolpe	N	Y	N	Y
4 Siljander	Y	N	Y	N
5 Sawyer	Y	N	Y	Y
6 Carr	N	Y	N	Y
7 Kildee	N	Y	N	Y
8 Traxler	N	Y	N	Y
9 Vander Jagt	Y	N	Y	Y
10 Albosta	N	Y	N	Y
11 Davis	Y	N	N	Y
12 Bonior	N	Y	N	Y
13 Crockett	?	?	?	?
14 Hertel	N	Y	N	Y
15 Ford	N	Y	N	Y
16 Dingell	N	Y	N	Y
17 Levin	N	Y	N	Y
18 Broomfield	Y	N	Y	N
MINNESOTA				
1 Penny	N	Y	N	Y
2 Weber	Y	N	Y	N
3 Frenzel	Y	N	Y	Y
4 Vento	N	Y	N	Y
5 Sabo	N	Y	N	Y
6 Sikorski	N	Y	N	Y

	80	81	82	83
7 Stangeland	Y	N	Y	Y
8 Oberstar	N	Y	N	Y
MISSISSIPPI				
1 Whitten	N	N	N	Y
2 Franklin	Y	N	Y	N
3 Montgomery	Y	N	Y	N
4 Dowdy	Y	Y	N	Y
5 Lott	Y	N	Y	N
MISSOURI				
1 Clay	N	Y	N	Y
2 Young	N	Y	N	Y
3 Gephardt	N	Y	N	Y
4 Skelton	Y	N	N	Y
5 Wheat	N	Y	N	Y
6 Coleman	Y	N	Y	N
7 Taylor	Y	N	Y	N
8 Emerson	Y	N	Y	N
9 Volkmer	N	Y	N	Y
MONTANA				
1 Williams	Y	Y	N	Y
2 Marlenee	Y	N	Y	N
NEBRASKA				
1 Bereuter	Y	N	Y	N
2 Daub	Y	N	Y	N
3 Smith	Y	N	Y	N
NEVADA				
1 Reid	N	Y	N	Y
2 Vucanovich	Y	N	Y	N
NEW HAMPSHIRE				
1 D'Amours	N	?	N	Y
2 Gregg	Y	N	N	Y
NEW JERSEY				
1 Florio	N	Y	N	Y
2 Hughes	N	Y	N	Y
3 Howard	N	Y	N	Y
4 Smith	Y	N	N	Y
5 Roukema	N	Y	N	Y
6 Dwyer	N	Y	N	Y
7 Rinaldo	Y	N	N	Y
8 Roe	Y	Y	N	Y
9 Torricelli	N	Y	N	Y
10 Rodino	N	Y	N	Y
11 Minish	N	Y	N	Y
12 Courter	Y	N	Y	N
13 Forsythe	Y	?	?	?
14 Guarini	N	Y	N	Y
NEW MEXICO				
1 Lujan	Y	N	Y	N
2 Skeen	Y	N	Y	N
3 Richardson	N	Y	N	Y
NEW YORK				
1 Carney	Y	N	Y	N
2 Downey	N	Y	N	Y
3 Mrazek	N	Y	N	Y
4 Lent	Y	N	Y	N
5 McGrath	Y	N	Y	Y
6 Addabbo	N	Y	N	Y
7 Ackerman	N	Y	N	Y
8 Scheuer	N	Y	N	Y
9 Ferraro	N	Y	N	Y
10 Schumer	N	Y	N	Y
11 Towns	N	Y	N	Y
12 Owens	?	N	Y	Y
13 Solarz	N	Y	N	Y
14 Molinari	Y	N	Y	N
15 Green	N	Y	N	Y
16 Rangel	N	Y	N	Y
17 Weiss	N	Y	N	Y
18 Garcia	N	Y	N	Y
19 Biaggi	N	Y	N	Y
20 Ottinger	N	Y	N	Y
21 Fish	Y	Y	N	Y
22 Gilman	Y	N	Y	N
23 Stratton	Y	N	Y	N
24 Solomon	Y	N	Y	N
25 Boehlert	Y	Y	N	Y
26 Martin	Y	N	Y	N
27 Wortley	Y	N	Y	N
28 McHugh	N	Y	N	Y
29 Horton	Y	Y	N	Y
30 Conable	Y	N	Y	N
31 Kemp	Y	N	Y	N
32 LaFalce	N	Y	N	Y
33 Nowak	N	Y	N	Y
34 Lundine	N	Y	N	Y

	80	81	82	83
NORTH CAROLINA				
1 Jones	Y	Y	N	Y
2 Valentine	Y	N	Y	N
3 Whitley	Y	N	Y	N
4 Andrews	N	Y	N	Y
5 Neal	Y	Y	N	Y
6 Britt	N	Y	N	Y
7 Rose	N	Y	N	Y
8 Hefner	Y	Y	N	Y
9 Martin	Y	N	Y	N
10 Broyhill	Y	N	Y	Y
11 Clarke	N	Y	N	Y
NORTH DAKOTA				
AL Dorgan	N	Y	N	Y
OHIO				
1 Luken	N	N	N	Y
2 Gradison	Y	N	Y	N
3 Hall	N	Y	N	Y
4 Oxley	Y	N	Y	N
5 Latta	Y	N	Y	N
6 McEwen	?	N	Y	N
7 DeWine	Y	N	Y	N
8 Kindness	Y	N	Y	N
9 Kaptur	N	Y	N	Y
10 Miller	Y	N	Y	N
11 Eckart	N	Y	N	Y
12 Kasich	Y	N	Y	N
13 Pease	N	Y	N	Y
14 Seiberling	N	Y	N	Y
15 Wylie	Y	N	Y	Y
16 Regula	Y	N	Y	Y
17 Williams	Y	N	N	Y
18 Applegate	N	Y	N	Y
19 Feighan	N	Y	N	Y
20 Oakar	N	Y	N	Y
21 Stokes	N	Y	N	Y
OKLAHOMA				
1 Jones	Y	Y	N	Y
2 Synar	N	Y	N	Y
3 Watkins	Y	Y	N	Y
4 McCurdy	Y	Y	Y	N
5 Edwards	Y	N	Y	N
6 English	Y	Y	Y	N
OREGON				
1 AuCoin	N	Y	N	Y
2 Smith, R.	Y	N	Y	Y
3 Wyden	N	Y	N	Y
4 Weaver	N	Y	N	Y
5 Smith, D.	Y	N	Y	N
PENNSYLVANIA				
1 Foglietta	N	Y	N	Y
2 Gray	N	Y	N	Y
3 Borski	N	Y	N	Y
4 Kolter	Y	Y	N	Y
5 Schulze	Y	N	Y	Y
6 Yatron	N	Y	N	Y
7 Edgar	N	Y	N	Y
8 Kostmayer	N	Y	N	Y
9 Shuster	Y	N	Y	N
10 McDade	Y	N	N	Y
11 Harrison	N	Y	N	Y
12 Murtha	Y	N	N	Y
13 Coughlin	Y	Y	N	Y
14 Coyne	N	Y	N	Y
15 Ritter	Y	N	Y	N
16 Walker	Y	N	Y	N
17 Gekas	Y	N	Y	N
18 Walgren	N	Y	N	Y
19 Goodling	N	Y	N	Y
20 Gaydos	?	Y	N	Y
21 Ridge	Y	N	N	Y
22 Murphy	Y	Y	N	Y
23 Clinger	Y	N	Y	Y
RHODE ISLAND				
1 St Germain	N	Y	N	Y
2 Schneider	N	Y	N	Y
SOUTH CAROLINA				
1 Hartnett	Y	N	Y	N
2 Spence	Y	N	Y	N
3 Derrick	?	Y	N	Y
4 Campbell	Y	N	Y	N
5 Spratt	Y	Y	N	Y
6 Tallon	N	Y	N	Y
SOUTH DAKOTA				
AL Daschle	?	?	?	Y

	80	81	82	83
TENNESSEE				
1 Quillen	Y	?	Y	N
2 Duncan	Y	N	Y	N
3 Lloyd	Y	N	Y	N
4 Cooper	Y	Y	N	N
5 Boner	Y	Y	N	Y
6 Gore	N	Y	N	Y
7 Sundquist	Y	N	Y	N
8 Jones	N	Y	N	Y
9 Ford	N	Y	N	Y
TEXAS				
1 Hall, S.	Y	N	Y	N
2 Wilson	?	Y	N	Y
3 Bartlett	Y	N	Y	N
4 Hall, R.	Y	N	Y	N
5 Bryant	N	Y	N	Y
6 Gramm	Y	N	Y	N
7 Archer	Y	N	Y	N
8 Fields	Y	N	Y	N
9 Brooks	N	Y	N	Y
10 Pickle	Y	N	N	Y
11 Leath	Y	N	Y	N
12 Wright	N	Y	N	Y
13 Hightower	Y	N	Y	N
14 Patman	Y	N	Y	N
15 de la Garza	Y	Y	N	Y
16 Coleman	N	Y	N	Y
17 Stenholm	Y	N	Y	N
18 Leland	N	Y	N	Y
19 Hance	Y	Y	Y	N
20 Gonzalez	?	Y	N	Y
21 Loeffler	Y	N	Y	N
22 Paul	Y	N	Y	N
23 Kazen	Y	N	Y	Y
24 Frost	N	Y	N	Y
25 Andrews	Y	N	Y	N
26 Vandergriff	Y	Y	Y	Y
27 Ortiz	Y	N	N	N
UTAH				
1 Hansen	Y	N	Y	N
2 Marriott	Y	N	Y	N
3 Nielson	Y	N	Y	N
VERMONT				
AL Jeffords	N	Y	N	Y
VIRGINIA				
1 Bateman	Y	N	Y	N
2 Whitehurst	Y	N	Y	N
3 Bliley	Y	N	Y	N
4 Sisisky	Y	?	Y	N
5 Daniel	Y	N	Y	N
6 Olin	Y	Y	N	Y
7 Robinson	Y	N	Y	N
8 Parris	Y	N	Y	N
9 Boucher	N	Y	N	Y
10 Wolf	Y	N	Y	N
WASHINGTON				
1 Pritchard	Y	Y	N	Y
2 Swift	N	Y	N	Y
3 Bonker	N	Y	N	Y
4 Morrison	Y	N	N	Y
5 Foley	N	Y	N	Y
6 Dicks	N	Y	N	Y
7 Lowry	N	Y	N	Y
8 Chandler	Y	N	N	Y
WEST VIRGINIA				
1 Mollohan	N	Y	N	Y
2 Staggers	N	Y	N	Y
3 Wise	N	Y	N	Y
4 Rahall	N	Y	N	Y
WISCONSIN				
1 Aspin	N	Y	N	Y
2 Kastenmeier	N	Y	N	Y
3 Gunderson	Y	Y	N	Y
4 Zablocki	N	Y	N	Y
5 Moody	N	?	N	Y
6 Petri	Y	N	Y	Y
7 Obey	N	Y	N	Y
8 Roth	Y	N	Y	Y
9 Sensenbrenner	Y	N	Y	Y
WYOMING				
AL Cheney	Y	N	Y	N

Southern states - Ala., Ark., Fla., Ga., Ky., La., Miss., N.C., Okla., S.C., Tenn., Texas, Va.

KEY

Y Voted for (yea).
Paired for.
+ Announced for.
N Voted against (nay).
X Paired against.
- Announced against.
P Voted "present".
C Voted "present" to avoid possible conflict of interest.
? Did not vote or otherwise make a position known.

Democrats   *Republicans*

84. HR 2357. Congressional Award Board. Murphy, D-Pa., motion to suspend the rules and pass the bill to increase the number of members on the Congressional Award Board, which administers an award program for young adults. Motion agreed to 275-2: R 111-0; D 164-2 (ND 106-2, SD 58-0), May 9, 1983. A two-thirds majority of those present and voting (185 in this case) is required for passage under suspension of the rules.

85. HR 2173. Drug Dependent Federal Offenders. Hughes, D-N.J., motion to suspend the rules and pass the bill to reauthorize for three years a drug treatment program for federal offenders. Motion agreed to 275-8: R 107-7; D 168-1 (ND 111-0, SD 57-1), May 9, 1983. A two-thirds majority of those present and voting (189 in this case) is required for passage under suspension of the rules.

86. HR 2174. Consumer Products Tampering. Hughes, D-N.J., motion to suspend the rules and pass the bill to make it a federal felony to tamper with consumer products such as food, drugs and cosmetics. Motion agreed to 292-0: R 115-0; D 177-0 (ND 117-0, SD 60-0), May 9, 1983. A two-thirds majority of those present and voting (195 in this case) is required for passage under suspension of the rules.

87. S 653. Military Medicine Foundation. Montgomery, D-Miss., motion to suspend the rules and pass the bill to establish a non-profit, charitable corporation to receive grants, legacies and private donations on behalf of the Uniformed Services University of the Health Sciences. Motion agreed to 295-0: R 115-0; D 180-0 (ND 119-0, SD 61-0), May 9, 1983: A two-thirds majority of those present and voting (197 in this case) is required for passage under suspension of the rules.

88. HR 2175. Justice Assistance Act of 1983. Adoption of the rule (H Res 184) providing for House floor consideration of the bill to create a three-year, $170 million grant program to help states combat crime. Adopted 267-32: R 89-28; D 178-4 (ND 120-0, SD 58-4), May 9, 1983.

89. Procedural Motion. Hunter, R-Calif., motion to approve the House *Journal* of Monday, May 9. Motion agreed to 368-22: R 143-11; D 225-11 (ND 146-10, SD 79-1), May 10, 1983.

90. HR 2175. Justice Assistance Act of 1983. Walker, R-Pa., amendment to make programs aimed at fighting crimes against the elderly eligible for federal matching funds. Adopted 401-5: R 151-0; D 250-5 (ND 165-3, SD 85-2), May 10, 1983.

91. HR 2175. Justice Assistance Act of 1983. Passage of the bill to authorize a grant program funded at $170 million annually for fiscal 1983-86 to help states combat crime. Passed 399-16: R 143-14; D 256-2 (ND 168-1, SD 88-1), May 10, 1983.

	84	85	86	87	88	89	90	91
ALABAMA								
1 *Edwards*	?	?	?	?	Y	Y	Y	Y
2 *Dickinson*	Y	Y	Y	N	N	N	Y	Y
3 Nichols	Y	Y	Y	Y	Y	Y	Y	Y
4 Bevill	?	?	Y	Y	Y	Y	Y	Y
5 Flippo	Y	Y	Y	Y	Y	Y	Y	Y
6 Erdreich	+	+	#	+	Y	Y	Y	Y
7 Shelby	Y	Y	Y	Y	Y	Y	Y	Y
ALASKA								
AL *Young*	Y	Y	Y	Y	N	N	Y	Y
ARIZONA								
1 *McCain*	?	?	?	?	?	Y	?	Y
2 Udall	Y	Y	Y	Y	Y	Y	Y	Y
3 *Stump*	Y	N	Y	N	Y	N	Y	N
4 *Rudd*	?	?	?	?	?	Y	Y	Y
5 McNulty	Y	?	Y	Y	Y	Y	Y	Y
ARKANSAS								
1 Alexander	?	?	?	?	?	?	Y	Y
2 *Bethune*	Y	Y	Y	Y	Y	Y	Y	?
3 *Hammerschmidt*	Y	Y	Y	N	Y	N	Y	Y
4 Anthony	?	?	?	?	?	?	Y	Y
CALIFORNIA								
1 Bosco	?	?	?	?	?	Y	Y	Y
2 *Chappie*	Y	Y	Y	N	Y	N	Y	Y
3 Matsui	Y	Y	Y	Y	Y	Y	Y	Y
4 Fazio	Y	Y	Y	Y	Y	Y	Y	Y
5 Vacancy								
6 Boxer	Y	Y	Y	Y	Y	Y	Y	Y
7 Miller	?	?	?	?	?	Y	Y	Y
8 Dellums	Y	Y	Y	Y	Y	Y	Y	Y
9 Stark	Y	Y	Y	Y	?	Y	Y	Y
10 Edwards	Y	Y	Y	Y	Y	Y	Y	Y
11 Lantos	Y	Y	Y	Y	Y	Y	Y	Y
12 Zschau	Y	Y	Y	Y	Y	Y	Y	Y
13 Mineta	Y	Y	Y	Y	Y	Y	Y	Y
14 *Shumway*	Y	Y	Y	N	N	Y	Y	N
15 *Coelho*	?	?	?	?	?	Y	Y	Y
16 Panetta	?	?	?	?	?	Y	Y	Y
17 *Pashayan*	?	?	?	?	?	?	Y	Y
18 Lehman	?	?	?	?	N	Y	Y	Y
19 *Lagomarsino*	Y	Y	Y	Y	Y	Y	Y	Y
20 *Thomas*	Y	Y	Y	Y	Y	Y	Y	Y
21 *Fiedler*	Y	Y	Y	Y	Y	Y	Y	Y
22 *Moorhead*	Y	Y	Y	N	Y	N	Y	Y
23 Beilenson	Y	Y	Y	Y	Y	Y	Y	Y
24 Waxman	?	?	?	?	Y	Y	Y	Y
25 Roybal	?	?	?	?	?	Y	Y	Y
26 Berman	?	?	?	?	?	Y	Y	Y
27 Levine	?	?	Y	Y	Y	Y	Y	Y
28 Dixon	Y	Y	Y	?	Y	?	Y	Y
29 Hawkins	Y	Y	Y	?	?	Y	Y	Y
30 Martinez	?	?	?	?	Y	?	?	?
31 Dymally	Y	Y	Y	Y	Y	Y	Y	Y
32 Anderson	Y	Y	Y	Y	Y	Y	Y	Y
33 *Dreier*	Y	N	Y	N	Y	N	Y	N
34 Torres	+	+	+	+	+	Y	Y	Y
35 *Lewis*	Y	Y	Y	Y	Y	Y	Y	Y
36 Brown	Y	Y	Y	Y	Y	Y	Y	Y
37 *McCandless*	Y	Y	Y	N	Y	N	Y	Y
38 Patterson	?	?	?	?	?	N	Y	Y
39 *Dannemeyer*	Y	N	Y	N	Y	?	N	N
40 *Badham*	Y	Y	Y	Y	N	Y	Y	Y
41 *Lowery*	Y	Y	Y	Y	Y	Y	Y	Y
42 *Lungren*	Y	Y	Y	Y	Y	Y	Y	Y

	84	85	86	87	88	89	90	91
43 *Packard*	Y	Y	Y	Y	Y	Y	Y	Y
44 Bates	Y	Y	Y	Y	Y	?	Y	Y
45 *Hunter*	?	?	Y	Y	Y	Y	Y	Y
COLORADO								
1 Schroeder	N	Y	Y	Y	Y	N	Y	Y
2 Wirth	Y	Y	Y	Y	Y	Y	Y	Y
3 Kogovsek	?	?	?	?	?	?	Y	Y
4 *Brown*	Y	N	Y	N	Y	N	Y	N
5 *Kramer*	Y	Y	Y	Y	Y	Y	Y	Y
6 *Schaefer*	?	?	?	?	?	Y	Y	Y
CONNECTICUT								
1 Kennelly	Y	Y	Y	Y	Y	Y	Y	Y
2 Gejdenson	Y	Y	Y	Y	Y	N	Y	Y
3 Morrison	Y	Y	Y	Y	Y	Y	Y	Y
4 *McKinney*	Y	Y	Y	Y	Y	Y	?	Y
5 Ratchford	Y	Y	Y	Y	Y	Y	Y	Y
6 *Johnson*	?	?	?	?	?	Y	Y	Y
DELAWARE								
AL Carper	Y	Y	Y	Y	Y	Y	Y	Y
FLORIDA								
1 Hutto	Y	Y	Y	Y	Y	Y	Y	Y
2 Fuqua	Y	Y	Y	Y	Y	Y	Y	Y
3 Bennett	Y	Y	Y	Y	Y	Y	Y	Y
4 Chappell	?	?	?	?	?	Y	Y	Y
5 *McCollum*	?	?	?	?	?	N	Y	Y
6 MacKay	+	+	+	+	?	?	Y	Y
7 Gibbons	Y	Y	Y	Y	Y	Y	Y	Y
8 *Young*	Y	Y	Y	Y	Y	Y	Y	Y
9 *Bilirakis*	?	?	?	?	?	Y	Y	Y
10 Ireland	Y	Y	Y	Y	Y	Y	Y	Y
11 Nelson	+	+	+	+	+	Y	Y	Y
12 *Lewis*	Y	Y	Y	Y	Y	Y	Y	Y
13 *Mack*	Y	Y	Y	Y	N	Y	Y	Y
14 Mica	?	?	?	?	?	Y	Y	Y
15 *Shaw*	Y	Y	Y	Y	Y	Y	Y	Y
16 Smith	Y	Y	Y	Y	Y	Y	Y	Y
17 Lehman	?	?	?	?	?	Y	Y	Y
18 Pepper	+	+	#	+	+	Y	Y	Y
19 Fascell	Y	Y	Y	Y	Y	Y	Y	Y
GEORGIA								
1 Thomas	Y	Y	Y	Y	Y	Y	Y	Y
2 Hatcher	?	?	?	?	?	Y	Y	Y
3 Ray	Y	Y	Y	Y	Y	Y	Y	Y
4 Levitas	Y	Y	Y	Y	Y	Y	Y	Y
5 Fowler	Y	Y	Y	Y	Y	Y	Y	Y
6 *Gingrich*	?	?	?	?	?	Y	Y	Y
7 McDonald	Y	N	Y	N	Y	N	Y	N
8 Rowland	Y	Y	Y	Y	Y	Y	Y	Y
9 Jenkins	Y	Y	Y	?	Y	?	Y	Y
10 Barnard	Y	Y	Y	Y	Y	Y	Y	?
HAWAII								
1 Heftel	?	?	?	?	?	?	?	?
2 Akaka	?	Y	Y	Y	Y	Y	Y	Y
IDAHO								
1 *Craig*	?	?	?	?	?	?	?	?
2 *Hansen*	Y	Y	Y	N	?	?	?	?
ILLINOIS								
1 Vacancy								
2 Savage	?	?	?	?	?	?	?	Y
3 Russo	Y	Y	Y	Y	Y	?	Y	Y
4 *O'Brien*	?	?	?	?	?	Y	Y	Y
5 Lipinski	Y	Y	Y	Y	Y	Y	Y	Y
6 *Hyde*	Y	Y	Y	Y	Y	Y	Y	Y
7 Collins	Y	Y	Y	Y	Y	Y	Y	Y
8 Rostenkowski	Y	Y	Y	Y	Y	Y	Y	Y
9 Yates	?	Y	Y	Y	Y	Y	Y	Y
10 *Porter*	?	Y	Y	Y	Y	Y	Y	Y
11 Annunzio	?	?	?	?	?	Y	Y	Y
12 *Crane, P.*	?	?	?	?	?	Y	Y	N
13 *Erlenborn*	Y	Y	Y	Y	Y	Y	Y	Y
14 *Corcoran*	Y	Y	Y	N	Y	N	Y	Y
15 *Madigan*	?	?	?	?	?	Y	Y	Y
16 *Martin*	Y	Y	Y	Y	Y	Y	Y	Y
17 Evans	Y	Y	Y	Y	Y	Y	Y	Y
18 *Michel*	Y	Y	Y	Y	Y	?	?	?
19 *Crane, D.*	?	?	?	?	?	Y	Y	N
20 Durbin	Y	Y	Y	Y	Y	N	Y	Y
21 Price	Y	Y	Y	Y	Y	Y	Y	Y
22 Simon	?	Y	Y	?	Y	Y	Y	Y
INDIANA								
1 Hall	Y	Y	Y	Y	Y	Y	Y	Y
2 Sharp	Y	Y	Y	Y	Y	Y	Y	Y
3 *Hiler*	Y	Y	Y	Y	N	Y	Y	Y
4 *Coats*	+	+	+	+	+	+	+	+
5 Hillis	Y	Y	Y	Y	Y	Y	Y	Y

ND - Northern Democrats   SD - Southern Democrats

Corresponding to Congressional Record Votes 90, 91, 92, 93, 94, 95, 97, 98

	84	85	86	87	88	89	90	91
6 ***Burton***	Y	Y	Y	Y	Y	Y	Y	Y
7 ***Myers***	Y	Y	Y	Y	N	Y	Y	Y
8 McCloskey	Y	Y	Y	Y	Y	Y	Y	Y
9 Hamilton	Y	Y	Y	Y	Y	Y	Y	Y
10 Jacobs	?	?	?	?	?	N	Y	Y
IOWA								
1 ***Leach***	Y	Y	Y	Y	Y	Y	Y	Y
2 ***Tauke***	Y	Y	Y	Y	Y	Y	Y	Y
3 ***Evans***	Y	Y	Y	Y	Y	N	Y	Y
4 Smith	?	?	?	?	?	Y	Y	Y
5 Harkin	?	?	?	?	?	N	Y	Y
6 Bedell	Y	Y	Y	Y	Y	Y	Y	Y
KANSAS								
1 ***Roberts***	?	?	?	?	?	Y	Y	Y
2 Slattery	Y	Y	Y	Y	Y	Y	Y	Y
3 ***Winn***	Y	Y	Y	Y	Y	Y	Y	Y
4 Glickman	Y	Y	Y	Y	Y	Y	Y	Y
5 ***Whittaker***	Y	Y	Y	Y	Y	Y	Y	Y
KENTUCKY								
1 Hubbard	Y	Y	Y	Y	N	Y	Y	Y
2 Natcher	Y	Y	Y	Y	Y	Y	Y	Y
3 Mazzoli	+	+	+	+	+	Y	Y	Y
4 ***Snyder***	?	?	?	?	?	Y	Y	Y
5 ***Rogers***	Y	Y	Y	Y	N	Y	Y	Y
6 ***Hopkins***	Y	Y	Y	Y	N	Y	Y	Y
7 Perkins	Y	Y	Y	Y	Y	Y	Y	Y
LOUISIANA								
1 ***Livingston***	Y	Y	Y	Y	Y	Y	Y	Y
2 Boggs	Y	Y	Y	Y	Y	Y	Y	Y
3 Tauzin	Y	Y	Y	Y	N	Y	?	Y
4 Roemer	Y	Y	Y	Y	N	N	Y	Y
5 Huckaby	?	?	?	?	?	?	?	Y
6 ***Moore***	Y	Y	Y	Y	Y	Y	Y	Y
7 Breaux	Y	Y	Y	Y	Y	Y	Y	Y
8 Long	Y	Y	Y	Y	Y	Y	Y	Y
MAINE								
1 ***McKernan***	?	?	?	?	?	Y	Y	Y
2 ***Snowe***	Y	Y	Y	Y	Y	Y	Y	Y
MARYLAND								
1 Dyson	Y	Y	Y	Y	Y	Y	Y	Y
2 Long	?	?	+	?	Y	Y	Y	Y
3 Mikulski	?	?	?	?	?	Y	N	Y
4 ***Holt***	Y	Y	Y	Y	Y	Y	Y	Y
5 Hoyer	?	?	?	?	Y	Y	Y	Y
6 Byron	?	?	?	?	?	Y	Y	Y
7 Mitchell	Y	Y	Y	Y	Y	?	N	Y
8 Barnes	?	?	?	Y	Y	Y	Y	Y
MASSACHUSETTS								
1 ***Conte***	?	?	?	?	?	Y	Y	Y
2 Boland	Y	Y	Y	Y	?	Y	Y	Y
3 Early	?	?	?	?	?	Y	Y	Y
4 Frank	Y	Y	Y	Y	Y	Y	Y	Y
5 Shannon	Y	Y	Y	Y	Y	Y	Y	Y
6 Mavroules	Y	Y	Y	Y	Y	?	?	Y
7 Markey	Y	Y	Y	Y	Y	Y	Y	Y
8 O'Neill								
9 Moakley	Y	Y	Y	Y	Y	Y	Y	Y
10 Studds	?	?	?	?	?	Y	Y	Y
11 Donnelly	Y	Y	Y	Y	Y	Y	Y	Y
MICHIGAN								
1 Conyers	?	?	X	?	?	?	?	?
2 ***Pursell***	?	?	?	?	?	Y	Y	Y
3 Wolpe	Y	Y	Y	Y	Y	Y	Y	Y
4 ***Siljander***	Y	Y	Y	Y	Y	Y	Y	Y
5 ***Sawyer***	Y	Y	Y	Y	Y	Y	Y	Y
6 Carr	Y	Y	Y	Y	Y	Y	Y	Y
7 Kildee	Y	Y	Y	Y	Y	Y	Y	Y
8 Traxler	Y	Y	Y	Y	Y	Y	Y	Y
9 ***Vander Jagt***	Y	Y	Y	Y	Y	Y	Y	Y
10 Albosta	Y	Y	Y	Y	Y	Y	Y	Y
11 ***Davis***	Y	Y	Y	Y	Y	Y	Y	Y
12 Bonior	?	?	?	?	?	?	Y	Y
13 Crockett	?	?	X	?	?	Y	Y	Y
14 Hertel	Y	Y	Y	Y	Y	Y	Y	Y
15 Ford	?	?	?	?	Y	Y	Y	Y
16 Dingell	?	?	?	?	?	?	Y	Y
17 Levin	Y	Y	Y	Y	Y	Y	Y	Y
18 ***Broomfield***	Y	Y	Y	Y	Y	Y	Y	Y
MINNESOTA								
1 Penny	Y	Y	Y	Y	Y	Y	Y	Y
2 ***Weber***	Y	Y	Y	Y	Y	Y	Y	Y
3 ***Frenzel***	Y	Y	Y	Y	Y	Y	Y	N
4 Vento	Y	Y	Y	Y	Y	Y	Y	Y
5 Sabo	?	?	?	?	Y	N	Y	Y
6 Sikorski	Y	Y	Y	Y	Y	Y	Y	Y

	84	85	86	87	88	89	90	91
7 ***Stangeland***	?	?	?	?	Y	Y	?	Y
8 Oberstar	Y	Y	Y	Y	Y	P	Y	Y
MISSISSIPPI								
1 Whitten	Y	Y	Y	Y	Y	Y	Y	Y
2 ***Franklin***	Y	Y	Y	Y	Y	Y	Y	Y
3 Montgomery	Y	Y	Y	Y	Y	Y	Y	Y
4 Dowdy	?	?	?	?	?	Y	Y	Y
5 ***Lott***	Y	Y	Y	Y	Y	Y	Y	?
MISSOURI								
1 Clay	Y	Y	Y	Y	Y	N	Y	Y
2 Young	?	?	?	?	?	Y	Y	Y
3 Gephardt	Y	Y	Y	Y	Y	Y	Y	Y
4 Skelton	Y	Y	Y	Y	?	Y	Y	Y
5 Wheat	Y	Y	Y	Y	Y	Y	Y	Y
6 ***Coleman***	Y	Y	Y	Y	Y	Y	Y	Y
7 ***Taylor***	?	?	?	?	?	?	?	?
8 ***Emerson***	?	?	?	?	?	N	Y	Y
9 Volkmer	Y	Y	Y	Y	Y	Y	Y	Y
MONTANA								
1 Williams	N	Y	Y	Y	Y	?	Y	Y
2 ***Marlenee***	?	?	?	?	?	?	?	?
NEBRASKA								
1 ***Bereuter***	Y	Y	Y	Y	Y	Y	Y	Y
2 ***Daub***	+	+	+	+	+	N	Y	Y
3 ***Smith***	Y	Y	Y	Y	Y	Y	Y	Y
NEVADA								
1 Reid	?	?	?	?	?	Y	Y	Y
2 ***Vucanovich***	Y	Y	Y	Y	Y	Y	Y	N
NEW HAMPSHIRE								
1 D'Amours	Y	Y	Y	Y	?	Y	Y	Y
2 ***Gregg***	?	?	?	?	?	Y	Y	Y
NEW JERSEY								
1 Florio	Y	Y	Y	Y	Y	?	Y	Y
2 Hughes	Y	Y	Y	Y	Y	Y	Y	Y
3 Howard	?	?	?	?	?	Y	Y	Y
4 ***Smith***	Y	Y	Y	Y	Y	Y	Y	Y
5 ***Roukema***	Y	Y	Y	Y	Y	Y	Y	Y
6 Dwyer	Y	Y	Y	Y	Y	Y	Y	Y
7 ***Rinaldo***	?	?	Y	Y	Y	Y	Y	Y
8 Roe	Y	Y	Y	Y	Y	Y	Y	Y
9 Torricelli	Y	Y	Y	Y	Y	Y	Y	Y
10 Rodino	?	?	?	?	?	Y	Y	Y
11 Minish	Y	Y	Y	Y	Y	Y	Y	Y
12 ***Courter***	Y	Y	Y	Y	Y	Y	Y	Y
13 ***Forsythe***	Y	Y	Y	Y	?	N	?	Y
14 Guarini	?	?	Y	Y	Y	Y	Y	Y
NEW MEXICO								
1 ***Lujan***	Y	Y	Y	Y	Y	Y	Y	Y
2 ***Skeen***	Y	Y	Y	Y	Y	Y	Y	Y
3 Richardson	Y	Y	?	Y	Y	Y	Y	Y
NEW YORK								
1 ***Carney***	Y	Y	Y	Y	Y	Y	Y	Y
2 Downey	Y	Y	Y	Y	Y	Y	Y	Y
3 Mrazek	?	?	?	?	?	Y	Y	Y
4 ***Lent***	Y	Y	Y	Y	N	Y	Y	Y
5 ***McGrath***	?	?	?	?	?	Y	Y	Y
6 Addabbo	?	?	#	?	?	Y	Y	Y
7 Ackerman	Y	Y	Y	Y	Y	Y	Y	Y
8 Scheuer	Y	Y	Y	Y	Y	?	Y	Y
9 Ferraro	+	+	+	+	+	Y	Y	Y
10 Schumer	Y	Y	Y	Y	Y	Y	Y	Y
11 Towns	Y	Y	Y	Y	Y	Y	?	Y
12 Owens	?	?	?	?	?	?	Y	Y
13 Solarz	Y	Y	Y	Y	Y	Y	Y	Y
14 ***Molinari***	Y	Y	Y	Y	Y	Y	Y	Y
15 ***Green***	Y	Y	Y	Y	Y	Y	Y	Y
16 Rangel	?	?	?	?	?	Y	Y	Y
17 Weiss	Y	Y	Y	Y	Y	Y	Y	Y
18 Garcia	?	?	Y	Y	Y	Y	Y	Y
19 Biaggi	?	?	?	?	?	Y	Y	Y
20 Ottinger	Y	Y	Y	Y	Y	?	Y	Y
21 ***Fish***	Y	Y	Y	Y	Y	Y	?	Y
22 ***Gilman***	+	+	+	+	+	Y	Y	Y
23 Stratton	Y	Y	Y	Y	Y	Y	Y	Y
24 ***Solomon***	?	?	?	?	?	?	Y	Y
25 ***Boehlert***	?	?	?	?	?	Y	Y	Y
26 ***Martin***	?	?	?	?	?	?	?	?
27 ***Wortley***	?	?	?	?	?	Y	Y	Y
28 McHugh	?	?	?	?	?	?	Y	Y
29 ***Horton***	Y	Y	Y	Y	Y	Y	Y	Y
30 ***Conable***	Y	Y	Y	Y	N	Y	Y	Y
31 ***Kemp***	Y	Y	Y	Y	Y	Y	?	Y
32 LaFalce	Y	Y	Y	Y	Y	Y	Y	Y
33 Nowak	?	Y	Y	Y	Y	Y	Y	Y
34 Lundine	?	?	?	?	Y	Y	Y	Y

	84	85	86	87	88	89	90	91
NORTH CAROLINA								
1 Jones	Y	Y	Y	Y	Y	?	Y	Y
2 Valentine	Y	Y	Y	Y	Y	Y	Y	Y
3 Whitley	?	?	Y	Y	Y	Y	Y	Y
4 Andrews	?	?	?	?	?	Y	Y	Y
5 Neal	Y	Y	Y	Y	Y	Y	Y	Y
6 Britt	Y	Y	Y	Y	Y	Y	Y	Y
7 Rose	Y	Y	Y	Y	Y	Y	Y	Y
8 Hefner	?	?	?	?	?	Y	Y	Y
9 ***Martin***	Y	Y	Y	Y	N	Y	Y	Y
10 ***Broyhill***	Y	Y	Y	Y	?	Y	Y	Y
11 Clarke	+	+	+	+	+	Y	N	Y
NORTH DAKOTA								
AL Dorgan	Y	Y	Y	Y	Y	Y	Y	N
OHIO								
1 Luken	Y	Y	Y	Y	Y	Y	Y	Y
2 ***Gradison***	Y	Y	Y	Y	Y	Y	Y	Y
3 Hall	?	?	?	?	?	Y	Y	Y
4 ***Oxley***	+	+	+	+	+	Y	Y	Y
5 ***Latta***	?	?	?	?	?	Y	Y	Y
6 ***McEwen***	Y	Y	Y	Y	Y	Y	Y	Y
7 ***DeWine***	Y	Y	Y	Y	N	Y	Y	Y
8 ***Kindness***	Y	Y	Y	Y	Y	Y	Y	Y
9 Kaptur	Y	Y	Y	Y	Y	Y	Y	Y
10 ***Miller***	?	?	?	?	?	N	Y	Y
11 Eckart	?	?	Y	Y	Y	Y	Y	Y
12 ***Kasich***	Y	Y	Y	Y	Y	Y	Y	Y
13 Pease	Y	Y	Y	Y	Y	Y	Y	Y
14 Seiberling	Y	Y	Y	Y	Y	Y	Y	Y
15 ***Wylie***	Y	Y	Y	Y	Y	Y	Y	Y
16 ***Regula***	Y	Y	Y	Y	Y	Y	Y	Y
17 ***Williams***	?	?	?	?	Y	Y	Y	Y
18 Applegate	?	?	?	?	?	?	Y	Y
19 Feighan	?	?	#	?	?	Y	Y	Y
20 Oakar	Y	Y	Y	Y	Y	Y	Y	Y
21 Stokes	?	?	?	?	?	Y	Y	Y
OKLAHOMA								
1 Jones	Y	Y	Y	Y	Y	Y	Y	Y
2 Synar	+	+	+	+	+	Y	Y	Y
3 Watkins	?	?	?	?	?	Y	Y	Y
4 McCurdy	?	?	?	?	?	Y	Y	Y
5 ***Edwards***	?	?	?	?	?	Y	Y	Y
6 English	Y	Y	Y	Y	Y	Y	Y	Y
OREGON								
1 AuCoin	?	?	?	?	?	N	Y	Y
2 ***Smith, R.***	Y	Y	Y	Y	Y	?	?	?
3 Wyden	?	?	?	?	?	Y	Y	Y
4 Weaver	?	?	?	?	?	Y	Y	Y
5 ***Smith, D.***	?	?	?	?	?	Y	Y	Y
PENNSYLVANIA								
1 Foglietta	?	?	?	?	?	Y	Y	Y
2 Gray	?	?	?	?	?	?	?	?
3 Borski	Y	Y	Y	Y	Y	Y	Y	Y
4 Kolter	?	?	?	?	?	Y	Y	Y
5 ***Schulze***	?	?	?	?	?	Y	Y	Y
6 Yatron	Y	Y	Y	Y	Y	Y	Y	Y
7 Edgar	Y	Y	Y	Y	Y	Y	Y	Y
8 Kostmayer	Y	Y	Y	Y	Y	Y	Y	Y
9 ***Shuster***	?	?	?	?	?	Y	Y	Y
10 ***McDade***	Y	Y	Y	Y	Y	Y	?	Y
11 Harrison	?	Y	Y	Y	Y	Y	Y	Y
12 Murtha	Y	Y	Y	Y	Y	Y	Y	Y
13 ***Coughlin***	Y	Y	Y	Y	Y	?	Y	Y
14 Coyne	Y	Y	Y	Y	?	Y	Y	Y
15 ***Ritter***	?	Y	Y	Y	Y	Y	Y	Y
16 ***Walker***	Y	Y	Y	Y	Y	N	Y	Y
17 ***Gekas***	Y	N	Y	Y	N	Y	Y	Y
18 Walgren	Y	Y	Y	Y	Y	Y	Y	Y
19 ***Goodling***	?	?	?	?	?	N	Y	Y
20 Gaydos	Y	Y	Y	Y	Y	Y	N	?
21 ***Ridge***	?	?	?	?	?	Y	Y	Y
22 Murphy	Y	Y	Y	Y	Y	Y	Y	Y
23 ***Clinger***	Y	Y	Y	Y	Y	Y	Y	Y
RHODE ISLAND								
1 St Germain	Y	Y	Y	Y	Y	Y	Y	Y
2 ***Schneider***	Y	Y	Y	Y	Y	Y	Y	Y
SOUTH CAROLINA								
1 ***Hartnett***	Y	N	Y	Y	N	Y	Y	Y
2 ***Spence***	Y	Y	Y	Y	Y	Y	Y	Y
3 Derrick	Y	Y	Y	Y	Y	Y	Y	Y
4 ***Campbell***	?	?	?	?	?	Y	Y	Y
5 Spratt	Y	Y	Y	Y	Y	?	Y	Y
6 Tallon	?	?	?	?	?	?	Y	Y
SOUTH DAKOTA								
AL Daschle	?	?	Y	Y	Y	Y	Y	Y

	84	85	86	87	88	89	90	91
TENNESSEE								
1 ***Quillen***	?	?	?	?	?	Y	Y	Y
2 ***Duncan***	Y	Y	Y	Y	Y	Y	Y	Y
3 Lloyd	Y	Y	Y	Y	Y	Y	Y	Y
4 Cooper	Y	Y	Y	Y	Y	Y	Y	Y
5 Boner	Y	Y	Y	Y	Y	Y	Y	Y
6 Gore	Y	Y	Y	Y	?	Y	Y	Y
7 ***Sundquist***	Y	Y	Y	Y	Y	Y	Y	Y
8 Jones	Y	Y	Y	Y	Y	Y	Y	Y
9 Ford	Y	Y	Y	Y	Y	Y	Y	Y
TEXAS								
1 Hall, S.	Y	Y	Y	Y	Y	Y	Y	Y
2 Wilson	?	?	?	?	?	Y	Y	Y
3 ***Bartlett***	?	?	?	?	?	Y	Y	N
4 Hall, R.	?	?	?	?	Y	Y	Y	Y
5 Bryant	Y	Y	Y	Y	Y	Y	Y	Y
6 ***Gramm***	?	?	?	?	?	?	Y	N
7 ***Archer***	Y	Y	Y	Y	N	Y	Y	Y
8 ***Fields***	?	?	?	?	?	Y	Y	Y
9 Brooks	Y	Y	Y	Y	Y	Y	Y	Y
10 Pickle	?	?	?	?	?	?	Y	Y
11 Leath	?	?	?	?	?	Y	Y	Y
12 Wright	Y	Y	Y	Y	Y	Y	Y	Y
13 Hightower	Y	Y	Y	Y	Y	Y	Y	Y
14 Patman	Y	Y	Y	Y	Y	Y	Y	Y
15 de la Garza	?	?	?	?	Y	Y	Y	Y
16 Coleman	?	?	?	?	?	Y	Y	Y
17 Stenholm	?	?	?	?	?	Y	Y	Y
18 Leland	?	?	?	?	?	Y	Y	Y
19 Hance	Y	Y	Y	Y	Y	Y	Y	Y
20 Gonzalez	Y	Y	Y	Y	Y	Y	N	Y
21 ***Loeffler***	Y	Y	Y	Y	Y	Y	Y	Y
22 ***Paul***	?	N	Y	Y	N	Y	Y	N
23 Kazen	Y	Y	Y	Y	Y	Y	Y	Y
24 Frost	Y	Y	Y	Y	Y	Y	Y	Y
25 Andrews	Y	Y	Y	Y	Y	Y	Y	Y
26 Vandergriff	Y	Y	Y	Y	Y	?	Y	Y
27 Ortiz	Y	Y	Y	Y	Y	?	Y	Y
UTAH								
1 ***Hansen***	?	?	?	?	?	Y	Y	Y
2 ***Marriott***	Y	Y	Y	Y	Y	Y	Y	Y
3 ***Nielson***	Y	Y	Y	Y	Y	Y	Y	Y
VERMONT								
AL ***Jeffords***	?	?	?	?	?	?	Y	Y
VIRGINIA								
1 ***Bateman***	Y	Y	Y	?	Y	Y	Y	Y
2 ***Whitehurst***	Y	Y	Y	Y	Y	Y	Y	Y
3 ***Bliley***	Y	Y	Y	Y	Y	Y	Y	Y
4 Sisisky	Y	Y	Y	Y	Y	Y	Y	Y
5 Daniel	?	?	?	?	?	Y	Y	Y
6 Olin	Y	Y	Y	Y	Y	Y	Y	Y
7 ***Robinson***	Y	Y	Y	Y	Y	Y	Y	Y
8 ***Parris***	?	?	?	?	?	Y	Y	Y
9 Boucher	?	?	?	Y	Y	Y	Y	Y
10 ***Wolf***	Y	Y	Y	Y	Y	Y	Y	Y
WASHINGTON								
1 ***Pritchard***	Y	Y	?	Y	Y	Y	Y	Y
2 Swift	Y	Y	Y	Y	Y	Y	Y	Y
3 Bonker	?	?	?	Y	Y	Y	Y	Y
4 ***Morrison***	Y	Y	Y	Y	Y	Y	Y	Y
5 Foley	Y	Y	Y	Y	Y	Y	Y	?
6 Dicks	Y	Y	Y	Y	Y	Y	Y	Y
7 Lowry	Y	Y	Y	Y	Y	Y	Y	Y
8 ***Chandler***	Y	Y	Y	Y	Y	Y	Y	Y
WEST VIRGINIA								
1 Mollohan	?	?	?	?	Y	Y	Y	Y
2 Staggers	?	?	?	?	?	Y	Y	Y
3 Wise	Y	Y	Y	Y	Y	Y	Y	Y
4 Rahall	Y	Y	Y	Y	Y	Y	Y	Y
WISCONSIN								
1 Aspin	?	?	?	?	?	Y	Y	Y
2 Kastenmeier	Y	Y	Y	Y	Y	Y	Y	Y
3 ***Gunderson***	Y	Y	Y	Y	Y	Y	Y	Y
4 Zablocki	Y	Y	Y	Y	Y	Y	Y	Y
5 Moody	Y	Y	Y	Y	Y	Y	Y	Y
6 ***Petri***	Y	Y	Y	Y	Y	Y	Y	Y
7 Obey	Y	Y	Y	Y	Y	Y	Y	Y
8 ***Roth***	Y	Y	Y	Y	Y	Y	Y	Y
9 ***Sensenbrenner***	Y	Y	Y	Y	N	Y	Y	N
WYOMING								
AL ***Cheney***	?	?	?	?	N	Y	Y	N

Southern states - Ala., Ark., Fla., Ga., Ky., La., Miss., N.C., Okla., S.C., Tenn., Texas, Va.

92. HR 2066. National Science Foundation Authorization. Adoption of the rule (H Res 183) providing for House floor consideration of the bill to authorize appropriations for the National Science Foundation for fiscal 1984. Adopted 408-1: R 154-0; D 254-1 (ND 166-0, SD 88-1), May 10, 1983.

93. HR 2587. Department of Energy Civilian Research and Development Programs. Adoption of the rule (H Res 185) providing for House floor consideration of the bill to authorize appropriations for civilian research and development programs of the Department of Energy for fiscal 1984. Adopted 409-2: R 152-1; D 257-1 (ND 169-0, SD 88-1), May 10, 1983.

94. HR 1983. Emergency Housing Assistance Act. Roemer, D-La., amendment to the Gonzalez, D-Texas, substitute for the Wylie, R-Ohio, amendment, to strike the $760 million mortgage relief program. The Roemer amendment would retain provisions relaxing federal bank regulations to make it easier for lenders to practice forbearance, authorizing $100 million for the homeless in fiscal 1984 and encouraging a payment moratorium on Farmers Home Administration home loans. Rejected 197-220: R 160-4; D 37-216 (ND 5-163, SD 32-53), May 11, 1983. A "yea" was a vote supporting the president's position. (The Gonzalez amendment and the Wylie amendment, as amended by Gonzalez, subsequently were adopted by voice votes. The Gonzalez amendment substituted new provisions, including new eligibility standards for mortgage aid. The Wylie amendment was identical to the Roemer amendment.)

95. HR 1983. Emergency Housing Assistance Act. Walker, R-Pa., amendment to the Gonzalez, D-Texas, substitute for the Wylie, R-Ohio, amendment *(see vote 94, above)*, to prohibit expenditure of funds in violation of balanced budget requirements. Rejected 157-254: R 135-26; D 22-228 (ND 4-163, SD 18-65), May 11, 1983.

96. HR 1983. Emergency Housing Assistance Act. Bartlett, R-Texas, amendment to the Gonzalez, D-Texas, substitute for the Wylie, R-Ohio, amendment *(see vote 94, above)*, to require mortgage aid applicants to file a wage earner's plan under Chapter 13 of federal bankruptcy law. Rejected 154-254: R 142-19; D 12-235 (ND 2-163, SD 10-72), May 11, 1983.

97. HR 1983. Emergency Housing Assistance Act. Bethune, R-Ark., amendment to the Gonzalez, D-Texas, substitute for the Wylie, R-Ohio, amendment *(see vote 94, above)*, to prohibit activation of the emergency mortgage program in any area where federal officials determine the program would reduce lender forbearance or increase mortgage foreclosures. Rejected 175-234: R 159-3; D 16-231 (ND 1-163, SD 15-68), May 11, 1983.

98. HR 1983. Emergency Housing Assistance Act. Passage of the bill to authorize $760 million in fiscal 1983 for a temporary loan program to help unemployed homeowners make their mortgage payments, and $100 million in fiscal 1984 for emergency shelter for the homeless. Passed 216-196: R 6-155; D 210-41 (ND 158-8, SD 52-33), May 11, 1983. A "nay" was a vote supporting the president's position.

KEY

Y Voted for (yea).
\# Paired for.
+ Announced for.
N Voted against (nay).
X Paired against.
- Announced against.
P Voted "present".
C Voted "present" to avoid possible conflict of interest.
? Did not vote or otherwise make a position known.

Democrats   *Republicans*

	92	93	94	95	96	97	98
ALABAMA							
1 *Edwards*	Y	Y	Y	N	N	N	N
2 *Dickinson*	Y	Y	Y	Y	Y	Y	X
3 Nichols	Y	-	Y	N	Y	N	N
4 Bevill	Y	Y	N	N	N	N	Y
5 Flippo	Y	Y	Y	N	N	N	Y
6 Erdreich	Y	Y	N	N	N	N	Y
7 Shelby	Y	Y	Y	N	Y	Y	Y
ALASKA							
AL *Young*	Y	Y	Y	Y	Y	Y	N
ARIZONA							
1 *McCain*	Y	Y	Y	Y	Y	Y	N
2 Udall	Y	Y	N	N	N	N	Y
3 *Stump*	Y	Y	Y	Y	Y	Y	N
4 *Rudd*	Y	Y	Y	Y	Y	Y	N
5 McNulty	?	Y	N	N	N	?	N
ARKANSAS							
1 Alexander	Y	N	N	N	N	N	Y
2 *Bethune*	?	?	Y	N	Y	N	N
3 *Hammerschmidt*	Y	Y	Y	Y	Y	Y	N
4 Anthony	Y	Y	Y	?	?	?	N
CALIFORNIA							
1 Bosco	Y	N	N	N	N	N	Y
2 *Chappie*	Y	Y	Y	Y	Y	Y	N
3 Matsui	Y	N	N	N	N	N	Y
4 Fazio	Y	N	N	N	N	N	Y
5 Vacancy							
6 Boxer	Y	N	N	N	N	N	Y
7 Miller	Y	N	N	N	N	N	Y
8 Dellums	Y	N	N	N	N	N	Y
9 Stark	Y	N	N	N	N	N	Y
10 Edwards	Y	N	N	N	N	N	Y
11 Lantos	Y	N	N	?	?	?	#
12 *Zschau*	Y	Y	Y	Y	Y	Y	N
13 Mineta	Y	N	N	N	N	N	Y
14 *Shumway*	Y	Y	Y	Y	Y	Y	N
15 Coelho	Y	N	N	N	N	N	Y
16 Panetta	Y	N	N	N	N	N	Y
17 *Pashayan*	Y	Y	Y	Y	Y	Y	N
18 Lehman	Y	N	N	N	N	N	Y
19 *Lagomarsino*	Y	Y	Y	Y	Y	Y	N
20 *Thomas*	Y	Y	Y	Y	Y	Y	N
21 *Fiedler*	Y	Y	Y	Y	Y	Y	N
22 *Moorhead*	Y	Y	Y	Y	Y	Y	N
23 Beilenson	Y	N	N	N	N	N	Y
24 Waxman	Y	N	N	N	N	N	Y
25 Roybal	Y	N	N	N	N	N	Y
26 Berman	Y	N	N	N	N	N	Y
27 Levine	Y	N	N	N	N	N	Y
28 Dixon	Y	Y	X	?	?	X	#
29 Hawkins	?	Y	N	N	N	N	Y
30 Martinez	?	?	?	?	?	?	?
31 Dymally	Y	N	N	N	N	N	Y
32 Anderson	Y	N	N	N	N	N	Y
33 *Dreier*	?	Y	Y	Y	Y	Y	N
34 Torres	Y	N	N	N	N	N	Y
35 *Lewis*	Y	N	Y	Y	Y	Y	N
36 Brown	Y	N	N	N	N	N	Y
37 *McCandless*	Y	Y	Y	Y	Y	Y	N
38 Patterson	Y	N	N	N	N	N	Y
39 *Dannemeyer*	Y	Y	Y	Y	Y	Y	X
40 *Badham*	Y	Y	Y	Y	Y	Y	N
41 *Lowery*	Y	Y	Y	Y	Y	Y	N
42 *Lungren*	Y	Y	Y	Y	Y	Y	N
43 *Packard*	Y	Y	Y	Y	Y	Y	N
44 Bates	Y	Y	N	N	N	N	Y
45 *Hunter*	Y	Y	Y	Y	Y	Y	N
COLORADO							
1 Schroeder	Y	N	N	N	N	N	N
2 Wirth	Y	N	N	N	N	N	Y
3 Kogovsek	Y	N	N	N	N	N	Y
4 *Brown*	Y	Y	Y	Y	Y	Y	N
5 *Kramer*	Y	Y	Y	Y	N	Y	N
6 *Schaefer*	Y	Y	Y	Y	Y	Y	N
CONNECTICUT							
1 Kennelly	Y	Y	N	N	N	N	Y
2 Gejdenson	Y	Y	N	N	N	N	Y
3 Morrison	Y	N	N	N	N	N	Y
4 *McKinney*	Y	Y	Y	N	Y	Y	N
5 Ratchford	Y	N	N	N	N	N	Y
6 *Johnson*	Y	Y	Y	Y	Y	Y	N
DELAWARE							
AL Carper	Y	Y	N	N	N	N	Y
FLORIDA							
1 Hutto	Y	Y	Y	N	N	N	N
2 Fuqua	Y	Y	Y	N	N	N	Y
3 Bennett	Y	Y	N	N	N	N	N
4 Chappell	Y	Y	Y	N	N	N	N
5 *McCollum*	Y	Y	Y	Y	Y	Y	N
6 MacKay	Y	Y	Y	N	N	N	Y
7 Gibbons	Y	Y	Y	N	N	N	N
8 *Young*	Y	Y	Y	Y	Y	Y	N
9 *Bilirakis*	Y	Y	Y	Y	Y	Y	N
10 Ireland	Y	Y	Y	Y	Y	Y	N
11 Nelson	Y	Y	N	N	N	N	Y
12 *Lewis*	Y	Y	Y	Y	Y	Y	N
13 *Mack*	Y	Y	Y	Y	Y	Y	N
14 Mica	Y	Y	N	N	N	N	Y
15 *Shaw*	Y	Y	Y	Y	Y	Y	N
16 Smith	Y	Y	N	N	N	N	Y
17 Lehman	Y	Y	N	N	N	N	Y
18 Pepper	Y	Y	N	N	N	N	Y
19 Fascell	Y	Y	N	N	N	N	Y
GEORGIA							
1 Thomas	Y	Y	N	N	N	N	Y
2 Hatcher	Y	Y	N	N	N	N	Y
3 Ray	Y	Y	N	Y	Y	Y	N
4 Levitas	Y	Y	N	N	N	N	Y
5 Fowler	Y	Y	N	N	N	N	Y
6 *Gingrich*	Y	Y	Y	Y	Y	Y	N
7 McDonald	N	N	N	N	N	N	N
8 Rowland	Y	Y	N	N	N	N	Y
9 Jenkins	Y	Y	N	N	N	N	N
10 Barnard	Y	Y	Y	N	Y	Y	N
HAWAII							
1 Heftel	?	?	?	?	?	?	?
2 Akaka	Y	N	N	?	N	N	Y
IDAHO							
1 *Craig*	?	?	Y	Y	Y	Y	Y
2 *Hansen*	?	?	Y	?	Y	Y	N
ILLINOIS							
1 Vacancy							
2 Savage	?	?	N	N	N	N	N
3 Russo	Y	Y	N	N	N	N	Y
4 *O'Brien*	Y	Y	Y	Y	Y	Y	N
5 Lipinski	Y	Y	N	N	N	N	Y
6 *Hyde*	Y	Y	Y	Y	Y	Y	N
7 Collins	Y	N	N	N	N	N	Y
8 Rostenkowski	Y	Y	N	N	N	N	Y
9 Yates	Y	N	N	N	N	N	Y
10 *Porter*	Y	Y	Y	Y	Y	Y	N
11 Annunzio	Y	Y	N	N	N	N	Y
12 *Crane, P.*	Y	Y	Y	Y	Y	Y	N
13 *Erlenborn*	Y	Y	Y	Y	Y	Y	N
14 *Corcoran*	Y	Y	Y	Y	Y	Y	N
15 *Madigan*	Y	Y	Y	Y	N	Y	N
16 *Martin*	Y	Y	Y	Y	Y	Y	N
17 Evans	Y	Y	N	N	N	N	Y
18 *Michel*	?	?	#	?	?	#	X
19 *Crane, D.*	Y	Y	Y	Y	Y	Y	N
20 Durbin	Y	Y	N	N	N	N	Y
21 Price	Y	Y	N	N	N	N	Y
22 Simon	Y	Y	N	N	N	N	Y
INDIANA							
1 Hall	Y	Y	N	N	N	N	Y
2 Sharp	Y	Y	N	N	N	N	Y
3 *Hiler*	Y	Y	Y	Y	Y	Y	N
4 *Coats*	+	+	Y	Y	Y	Y	N
5 *Hillis*	Y	Y	Y	Y	Y	Y	N

ND - Northern Democrats   SD - Southern Democrats

Corresponding to Congressional Record Votes 99, 100, 102, 103, 104, 105, 106

	92	93	94	95	96	97	98
6 ***Burton***	Y	Y	Y	Y	Y	Y	N
7 ***Myers***	Y	Y	Y	Y	Y	Y	N
8 McCloskey	Y	Y	N	N	N	N	Y
9 Hamilton	Y	Y	Y	N	N	N	N
10 Jacobs	Y	Y	N	Y	N	N	Y
IOWA							
1 ***Leach***	Y	Y	Y	N	Y	Y	N
2 ***Tauke***	Y	Y	Y	N	N	Y	N
3 ***Evans***	Y	Y	Y	N	Y	Y	N
4 Smith	Y	Y	N	N	N	N	Y
5 Harkin	Y	Y	N	N	N	N	Y
6 Bedell	Y	Y	N	N	N	N	Y
KANSAS							
1 ***Roberts***	Y	Y	Y	Y	Y	Y	N
2 Slattery	Y	Y	Y	N	Y	Y	N
3 ***Winn***	Y	Y	Y	Y	Y	Y	N
4 Glickman	Y	Y	N	N	?	?	N
5 ***Whittaker***	Y	Y	Y	Y	Y	Y	N
KENTUCKY							
1 Hubbard	Y	Y	?	?	N	N	Y
2 Natcher	Y	Y	N	N	N	N	Y
3 Mazzoli	Y	Y	N	N	N	N	Y
4 ***Snyder***	Y	Y	Y	Y	Y	Y	N
5 ***Rogers***	Y	Y	Y	Y	Y	Y	N
6 ***Hopkins***	Y	Y	Y	Y	Y	Y	N
7 Perkins	Y	Y	N	N	N	N	Y
LOUISIANA							
1 ***Livingston***	Y	Y	Y	?	Y	Y	N
2 Boggs	Y	Y	N	N	N	N	Y
3 Tauzin	Y	Y	Y	Y	N	Y	N
4 Roemer	Y	Y	Y	Y	N	Y	N
5 Huckaby	Y	Y	Y	N	N	N	N
6 ***Moore***	Y	Y	Y	Y	Y	Y	N
7 Breaux	Y	Y	Y	Y	N	Y	N
8 Long	Y	Y	N	N	N	N	Y
MAINE							
1 ***McKernan***	Y	Y	Y	N	N	Y	N
2 ***Snowe***	Y	Y	Y	N	N	Y	N
MARYLAND							
1 Dyson	Y	Y	N	N	N	N	Y
2 Long	Y	Y	N	N	N	N	Y
3 Mikulski	Y	Y	N	N	N	N	Y
4 ***Holt***	Y	Y	Y	Y	Y	Y	N
5 Hoyer	Y	Y	N	N	N	N	Y
6 Byron	Y	Y	Y	N	N	N	N
7 Mitchell	Y	Y	N	N	N	N	Y
8 Barnes	Y	Y	N	N	N	N	Y
MASSACHUSETTS							
1 ***Conte***	Y	Y	Y	N	N	N	N
2 Boland	Y	Y	N	N	N	N	Y
3 Early	Y	Y	?	?	?	?	?
4 Frank	Y	Y	N	N	N	N	Y
5 Shannon	Y	Y	N	N	N	N	Y
6 Mavroules	Y	Y	N	N	N	N	Y
7 Markey	Y	Y	N	N	N	N	Y
8 O'Neill							
9 Moakley	Y	Y	N	N	N	N	Y
10 Studds	Y	Y	N	N	N	N	Y
11 Donnelly	Y	Y	N	N	N	N	Y
MICHIGAN							
1 Conyers	Y	Y	N	N	N	N	Y
2 ***Pursell***	Y	Y	Y	Y	Y	Y	N
3 Wolpe	Y	Y	N	N	N	N	Y
4 ***Siljander***	Y	Y	Y	Y	Y	Y	N
5 ***Sawyer***	?	Y	Y	Y	Y	Y	N
6 Carr	Y	Y	N	N	N	N	Y
7 Kildee	Y	Y	N	N	N	N	Y
8 Traxler	Y	Y	N	N	N	N	Y
9 ***Vander Jagt***	Y	Y	Y	Y	N	Y	N
10 Albosta	Y	Y	N	N	N	N	Y
11 ***Davis***	Y	Y	Y	N	N	Y	Y
12 Bonior	Y	Y	N	N	N	N	Y
13 Crockett	Y	Y	N	N	N	N	Y
14 Hertel	Y	Y	N	N	N	N	Y
15 Ford	Y	Y	N	N	N	N	Y
16 Dingell	?	Y	N	N	N	N	Y
17 Levin	Y	Y	N	N	N	N	Y
18 ***Broomfield***	Y	Y	Y	Y	Y	Y	N
MINNESOTA							
1 Penny	Y	Y	N	N	N	N	Y
2 ***Weber***	Y	Y	Y	Y	Y	Y	N
3 ***Frenzel***	Y	Y	Y	Y	Y	Y	N
4 Vento	Y	Y	N	N	N	N	Y
5 Sabo	Y	Y	N	N	N	N	Y
6 Sikorski	Y	Y	N	N	N	N	Y
7 ***Stangeland***	Y	Y	Y	Y	Y	Y	N
8 Oberstar	Y	Y	N	N	N	N	Y
MISSISSIPPI							
1 Whitten	Y	Y	N	N	N	N	Y
2 ***Franklin***	Y	Y	Y	Y	Y	Y	N
3 Montgomery	Y	Y	Y	Y	N	N	N
4 Dowdy	Y	Y	N	N	N	N	Y
5 ***Lott***	?	Y	Y	Y	?	Y	N
MISSOURI							
1 Clay	Y	Y	N	N	N	N	Y
2 Young	Y	Y	N	N	N	N	Y
3 Gephardt	Y	Y	N	N	N	N	Y
4 Skelton	Y	Y	?	?	N	N	Y
5 Wheat	Y	Y	N	N	N	N	Y
6 ***Coleman***	Y	Y	Y	Y	Y	Y	N
7 ***Taylor***	?	?	Y	Y	Y	Y	N
8 ***Emerson***	Y	Y	Y	Y	Y	Y	N
9 Volkmer	Y	Y	N	Y	N	N	Y
MONTANA							
1 Williams	?	Y	N	N	N	?	Y
2 ***Marlenee***	?	?	#	?	?	#	X
NEBRASKA							
1 ***Bereuter***	Y	Y	Y	Y	Y	Y	N
2 ***Daub***	Y	Y	Y	Y	Y	Y	N
3 ***Smith***	Y	Y	Y	Y	Y	Y	N
NEVADA							
1 Reid	Y	Y	N	N	N	N	Y
2 ***Vucanovich***	Y	Y	Y	Y	Y	Y	N
NEW HAMPSHIRE							
1 D'Amours	Y	Y	N	N	N	N	Y
2 ***Gregg***	Y	Y	Y	Y	Y	Y	N
NEW JERSEY							
1 Florio	Y	Y	N	N	N	N	Y
2 Hughes	Y	Y	N	N	N	N	Y
3 Howard	Y	Y	N	N	N	N	Y
4 ***Smith***	Y	Y	N	N	N	N	Y
5 ***Roukema***	Y	Y	Y	N	Y	Y	N
6 Dwyer	Y	Y	N	N	N	N	#
7 ***Rinaldo***	Y	Y	N	N	N	Y	Y
8 Roe	Y	Y	N	N	N	N	Y
9 Torricelli	Y	Y	N	N	N	N	Y
10 Rodino	Y	Y	N	N	N	N	Y
11 Minish	Y	Y	N	N	N	N	Y
12 ***Courter***	Y	Y	Y	Y	?	Y	N
13 ***Forsythe***	?	?	Y	Y	Y	Y	N
14 Guarini	Y	Y	N	N	N	N	Y
NEW MEXICO							
1 ***Lujan***	Y	Y	Y	Y	Y	Y	N
2 ***Skeen***	Y	Y	Y	Y	Y	Y	N
3 Richardson	Y	Y	N	N	N	N	Y
NEW YORK							
1 ***Carney***	Y	Y	Y	Y	Y	Y	N
2 Downey	Y	Y	N	N	N	N	Y
3 Mrazek	Y	Y	Y	N	Y	N	N
4 ***Lent***	Y	Y	Y	Y	Y	Y	N
5 ***McGrath***	Y	Y	Y	Y	Y	Y	N
6 Addabbo	Y	Y	N	N	N	N	Y
7 Ackerman	Y	Y	N	N	N	N	Y
8 Scheuer	Y	Y	N	N	N	N	Y
9 Ferraro	Y	Y	N	N	N	N	Y
10 Schumer	Y	Y	N	N	N	N	Y
11 Towns	Y	Y	N	N	N	N	Y
12 Owens	Y	?	?	?	?	?	?
13 Solarz	Y	Y	N	N	N	N	Y
14 ***Molinari***	Y	Y	Y	Y	Y	Y	N
15 ***Green***	Y	Y	Y	N	Y	Y	N
16 Rangel	Y	Y	N	N	N	N	Y
17 Weiss	Y	Y	N	N	N	N	Y
18 Garcia	Y	Y	N	N	N	N	Y
19 Biaggi	Y	Y	N	N	N	N	Y
20 Ottinger	Y	Y	N	N	N	N	Y
21 ***Fish***	Y	Y	Y	N	N	Y	N
22 ***Gilman***	Y	Y	Y	N	N	Y	N
23 Stratton	Y	Y	N	N	N	N	Y
24 ***Solomon***	Y	Y	Y	Y	Y	Y	N
25 ***Boehlert***	Y	Y	Y	N	N	Y	N
26 ***Martin***	?	?	Y	Y	Y	Y	N
27 ***Wortley***	Y	Y	Y	Y	Y	Y	N
28 McHugh	Y	Y	N	?	N	N	Y
29 ***Horton***	Y	Y	Y	N	Y	Y	N
30 ***Conable***	Y	Y	Y	N	N	Y	N
31 ***Kemp***	Y	Y	Y	Y	Y	Y	N
32 LaFalce	Y	Y	N	N	?	?	?
33 Nowak	Y	Y	N	N	N	N	Y
34 Lundine	Y	Y	N	N	N	N	Y
NORTH CAROLINA							
1 Jones	Y	Y	N	N	N	N	Y
2 Valentine	Y	Y	Y	N	N	N	N
3 Whitley	Y	Y	N	N	N	N	Y
4 Andrews	Y	Y	Y	N	N	N	N
5 Neal	Y	Y	N	N	N	N	Y
6 Britt	Y	Y	N	N	N	N	Y
7 Rose	Y	Y	N	N	N	N	Y
8 Hefner	?	?	X	?	?	X	#
9 ***Martin***	Y	?	Y	Y	Y	Y	N
10 ***Broyhill***	Y	Y	Y	Y	Y	Y	N
11 Clarke	Y	Y	N	N	N	N	N
NORTH DAKOTA							
AL Dorgan	Y	Y	Y	N	N	N	N
OHIO							
1 Luken	Y	Y	N	N	N	N	Y
2 ***Gradison***	Y	Y	Y	Y	Y	Y	N
3 Hall	Y	Y	N	N	N	N	Y
4 ***Oxley***	Y	Y	Y	Y	Y	Y	N
5 ***Latta***	Y	Y	Y	Y	Y	Y	N
6 ***McEwen***	Y	Y	Y	Y	Y	Y	N
7 ***DeWine***	Y	Y	Y	Y	Y	Y	N
8 ***Kindness***	Y	Y	Y	Y	Y	Y	N
9 Kaptur	Y	Y	N	N	N	N	Y
10 ***Miller***	Y	Y	Y	Y	Y	Y	N
11 Eckart	Y	Y	N	N	N	N	Y
12 ***Kasich***	Y	Y	Y	Y	Y	Y	N
13 Pease	Y	Y	N	N	N	N	Y
14 Seiberling	Y	Y	N	N	N	N	Y
15 ***Wylie***	Y	Y	Y	Y	Y	Y	N
16 ***Regula***	Y	Y	Y	Y	Y	Y	N
17 ***Williams***	Y	Y	N	N	N	Y	Y
18 Applegate	Y	Y	N	N	N	N	Y
19 Feighan	Y	Y	N	N	N	N	Y
20 Oakar	Y	Y	N	N	N	N	Y
21 Stokes	Y	Y	N	N	N	N	Y
OKLAHOMA							
1 Jones	Y	Y	N	N	N	N	N
2 Synar	Y	Y	N	N	N	N	Y
3 Watkins	Y	Y	N	N	N	N	Y
4 McCurdy	Y	Y	Y	N	N	N	N
5 ***Edwards***	Y	Y	Y	Y	Y	Y	N
6 English	Y	Y	Y	N	N	N	N
OREGON							
1 AuCoin	Y	Y	N	N	N	N	Y
2 ***Smith, R.***	?	?	#	?	?	#	X
3 Wyden	Y	Y	N	N	N	N	Y
4 Weaver	Y	Y	N	N	N	N	Y
5 ***Smith, D.***	Y	Y	Y	Y	Y	Y	N
PENNSYLVANIA							
1 Foglietta	Y	Y	N	N	N	N	Y
2 Gray	?	?	N	N	N	N	Y
3 Borski	Y	Y	N	N	N	N	Y
4 Kolter	Y	Y	N	N	N	N	Y
5 ***Schulze***	Y	Y	Y	Y	Y	Y	N
6 Yatron	Y	Y	N	N	N	N	Y
7 Edgar	Y	Y	-	-	-	-	+
8 Kostmayer	Y	Y	N	N	N	N	Y
9 ***Shuster***	Y	Y	Y	Y	Y	Y	N
10 ***McDade***	Y	?	Y	?	?	?	?
11 Harrison	Y	Y	N	N	N	N	Y
12 Murtha	Y	Y	N	N	N	N	Y
13 ***Coughlin***	Y	Y	Y	N	Y	Y	N
14 Coyne	Y	Y	N	N	N	N	Y
15 ***Ritter***	Y	Y	Y	N	N	Y	N
16 ***Walker***	Y	Y	Y	Y	Y	Y	N
17 ***Gekas***	Y	Y	Y	Y	Y	Y	N
18 Walgren	Y	Y	N	N	N	N	Y
19 ***Goodling***	Y	Y	Y	Y	Y	Y	N
20 Gaydos	?	?	N	N	N	N	Y
21 ***Ridge***	Y	Y	Y	N	Y	Y	Y
22 Murphy	Y	Y	N	N	N	N	Y
23 ***Clinger***	Y	Y	Y	Y	Y	Y	N
RHODE ISLAND							
1 St Germain	Y	Y	N	N	N	N	Y
2 ***Schneider***	Y	Y	N	N	Y	Y	Y
SOUTH CAROLINA							
1 ***Hartnett***	Y	Y	Y	Y	Y	Y	N
2 ***Spence***	Y	Y	Y	Y	Y	Y	N
3 Derrick	Y	Y	N	N	N	N	N
4 ***Campbell***	Y	Y	Y	Y	Y	Y	N
5 Spratt	Y	Y	N	?	?	?	?
6 Tallon	Y	Y	N	N	Y	N	N
SOUTH DAKOTA							
AL Daschle	Y	Y	N	N	N	N	Y
TENNESSEE							
1 ***Quillen***	Y	Y	Y	Y	Y	Y	N
2 ***Duncan***	Y	Y	Y	Y	Y	Y	N
3 Lloyd	Y	Y	N	N	N	N	N
4 Cooper	Y	Y	Y	Y	Y	Y	N
5 Boner	Y	Y	N	N	N	N	Y
6 Gore	Y	Y	N	N	N	N	Y
7 ***Sundquist***	Y	Y	Y	Y	Y	Y	N
8 Jones	Y	Y	N	N	N	N	Y
9 Ford	Y	Y	X	?	?	X	#
TEXAS							
1 Hall, S.	Y	Y	N	Y	Y	N	Y
2 Wilson	Y	Y	N	?	?	?	?
3 ***Bartlett***	Y	Y	Y	Y	Y	Y	N
4 Hall, R.	Y	Y	Y	Y	N	Y	Y
5 Bryant	Y	Y	N	N	N	N	Y
6 ***Gramm***	Y	Y	Y	Y	Y	Y	N
7 ***Archer***	Y	Y	Y	Y	Y	Y	N
8 ***Fields***	Y	Y	Y	Y	Y	Y	N
9 Brooks	Y	Y	N	N	N	N	Y
10 Pickle	Y	Y	N	N	?	N	N
11 Leath	Y	Y	?	?	?	?	?
12 Wright	Y	Y	N	N	N	N	Y
13 Hightower	Y	Y	Y	N	N	Y	Y
14 Patman	Y	Y	N	N	N	N	Y
15 de la Garza	Y	Y	N	N	N	N	Y
16 Coleman	Y	Y	N	Y	N	N	Y
17 Stenholm	Y	Y	Y	Y	N	Y	N
18 Leland	Y	Y	N	N	N	N	Y
19 Hance	Y	Y	N	Y	N	Y	Y
20 Gonzalez	Y	Y	N	N	N	N	Y
21 ***Loeffler***	Y	Y	Y	Y	Y	Y	N
22 ***Paul***	Y	Y	Y	Y	Y	Y	N
23 Kazen	Y	Y	N	Y	N	N	Y
24 Frost	Y	Y	N	N	N	N	Y
25 Andrews	Y	Y	N	N	Y	N	Y
26 Vandergriff	Y	Y	?	N	N	N	N
27 Ortiz	Y	Y	N	N	N	N	Y
UTAH							
1 ***Hansen***	Y	?	Y	Y	Y	Y	N
2 ***Marriott***	Y	Y	Y	Y	Y	Y	N
3 ***Nielson***	Y	Y	Y	Y	Y	Y	N
VERMONT							
AL ***Jeffords***	Y	Y	Y	N	N	Y	N
VIRGINIA							
1 ***Bateman***	Y	Y	Y	Y	Y	Y	N
2 ***Whitehurst***	Y	Y	Y	Y	Y	Y	N
3 ***Bliley***	Y	Y	Y	Y	Y	Y	N
4 Sisisky	Y	Y	N	Y	N	N	Y
5 Daniel	Y	Y	Y	Y	Y	Y	N
6 Olin	Y	Y	Y	N	?	?	N
7 ***Robinson***	Y	Y	Y	Y	Y	Y	N
8 ***Parris***	Y	?	Y	Y	Y	Y	N
9 Boucher	Y	Y	N	N	N	N	Y
10 ***Wolf***	Y	Y	Y	Y	Y	Y	N
WASHINGTON							
1 ***Pritchard***	Y	Y	Y	N	Y	?	N
2 Swift	Y	Y	N	N	N	N	Y
3 Bonker	Y	Y	N	N	N	N	Y
4 ***Morrison***	Y	Y	Y	Y	Y	Y	N
5 Foley	Y	Y	N	N	N	N	Y
6 Dicks	Y	Y	N	N	N	N	Y
7 Lowry	Y	Y	N	N	N	N	Y
8 ***Chandler***	Y	Y	Y	Y	Y	Y	N
WEST VIRGINIA							
1 Mollohan	Y	Y	N	N	N	N	Y
2 Staggers	Y	Y	N	N	N	N	Y
3 Wise	Y	Y	N	N	N	N	Y
4 Rahall	Y	Y	N	N	N	N	Y
WISCONSIN							
1 Aspin	Y	Y	N	N	N	N	Y
2 Kastenmeier	Y	Y	N	N	N	N	Y
3 ***Gunderson***	Y	Y	Y	Y	Y	Y	N
4 Zablocki	Y	Y	N	N	N	N	Y
5 Moody	Y	Y	N	N	N	N	Y
6 ***Petri***	Y	Y	Y	Y	Y	Y	N
7 Obey	Y	Y	N	N	N	N	Y
8 ***Roth***	Y	Y	Y	Y	Y	Y	N
9 ***Sensenbrenner***	Y	Y	Y	Y	Y	Y	N
WYOMING							
AL ***Cheney***	Y	Y	Y	Y	Y	Y	N

Southern states - Ala., Ark., Fla., Ga., Ky., La., Miss., N.C., Okla., S.C., Tenn., Texas, Va.

KEY

Y Voted for (yea).
Paired for.
+ Announced for.
N Voted against (nay).
X Paired against.
- Announced against.
P Voted "present".
C Voted "present" to avoid possible conflict of interest.
? Did not vote or otherwise make a position known.

———

Democrats ***Republicans***

99. Procedural Motion. Hunter, R-Calif., motion to approve the House *Journal* of Wednesday, May 11. Motion agreed to 362-20: R 140-12; D 222-8 (ND 147-7, SD 75-1), May 12, 1983.

100. HR 2066. National Science Foundation Authorization. Brown, D-Calif., amendment to increase by $49 million the bill's $50 million authorization for a new high-technology instrumentation program. Rejected 150-255: R 8-150; D 142-105 (ND 129-36, SD 13-69), May 12, 1983.

101. HR 2066. National Science Foundation Authorization. Winn, R-Kan., amendment to delete from the bill a $50 million authorization for a new high-technology instrumentation program. Rejected 150-257: R 139-21; D 11-236 (ND 2-165, SD 9-71), May 12, 1983.

102. HR 2066. National Science Foundation Authorization. Gregg, R-N.H., amendment to earmark $25 million in high-technology instrumentation funds for elementary and secondary schools. Rejected 150-251: R 133-23; D 17-228 (ND 9-158, SD 8-70), May 12, 1983.

103. HR 2066. National Science Foundation Authorization. Passage of the bill to authorize $1.34 billion for the National Science Foundation in fiscal year 1984, including $50 million for a new high-technology instrumentation program. Passed 297-111: R 60-101; D 237-10 (ND 167-2, SD 70-8), May 12, 1983.

104. HR 2587. Department of Energy Civilian Research and Development Programs. Science and Technology Committee amendment to deauthorize fiscal 1984 funding for the continuation or termination of the Clinch River Breeder Reactor Project. Adopted 388-1: R 148-1; D 240-0 (ND 161-0, SD 79-0), May 12, 1983.

105. HR 2587. Department of Energy Civilian Research and Development Programs. Mineta, D-Calif., amendment to redirect $5 million of construction funds for a vitreous state laboratory at Catholic University of America. Adopted 261-113: R 42-100; D 219-13 (ND 152-3, SD 67-10), May 12, 1983.

106. HR 2587. Department of Energy Civilian Research and Development Programs. Winn, R-Kan., substitute to reduce total authorizations in the bill to $2.97 billion, from $3.29 billion. Rejected 140-228: R 119-21; D 21-207 (ND 5-148, SD 16-59), May 12, 1983.

	99	100	101	102	103	104	105	106
ALABAMA								
1 *Edwards*	Y	N	?	Y	Y	?	N	N
2 *Dickinson*	N	N	Y	N	Y	Y	N	Y
3 Nichols	Y	N	N	N	Y	Y	Y	Y
4 Bevill	Y	N	N	?	Y	Y	Y	N
5 Flippo	?	N	N	N	Y	Y	Y	N
6 Erdreich	Y	N	N	-	+	+	+	-
7 Shelby	Y	N	N	N	Y	Y	Y	Y
ALASKA								
AL *Young*	N	N	Y	Y	Y	Y	Y	Y
ARIZONA								
1 *McCain*	?	N	Y	N	Y	N	Y	Y
2 Udall	Y	Y	N	N	Y	Y	Y	N
3 *Stump*	Y	N	Y	N	Y	N	Y	Y
4 *Rudd*	Y	N	Y	N	Y	N	Y	Y
5 McNulty	Y	Y	N	N	Y	?	?	?
ARKANSAS								
1 Alexander	Y	?	?	?	?	Y	?	?
2 *Bethune*	Y	N	Y	?	N	Y	N	Y
3 *Hammerschmidt*	Y	N	N	N	Y	Y	Y	Y
4 Anthony	?	N	N	N	Y	Y	Y	N
CALIFORNIA								
1 Bosco	Y	N	N	N	Y	Y	Y	N
2 *Chappie*	P	N	Y	Y	N	?	?	?
3 Matsui	Y	Y	N	N	Y	Y	Y	N
4 Fazio	Y	Y	N	N	Y	Y	Y	N
5 Vacancy								
6 Boxer	Y	Y	N	N	Y	Y	Y	N
7 Miller	Y	Y	N	N	Y	Y	Y	N
8 Dellums	?	Y	N	N	Y	Y	Y	N
9 Stark	Y	Y	N	N	Y	Y	Y	N
10 Edwards	Y	Y	N	N	Y	Y	Y	N
11 Lantos	?	Y	N	N	Y	Y	Y	N
12 Zschau	Y	N	Y	N	Y	Y	N	N
13 Mineta	Y	Y	N	N	Y	Y	Y	N
14 *Shumway*	Y	N	Y	N	Y	N	Y	Y
15 Coelho	Y	?	?	?	Y	Y	?	?
16 Panetta	Y	Y	N	N	Y	Y	Y	N
17 *Pashayan*	Y	N	Y	?	?	Y	N	Y
18 Lehman	Y	Y	N	N	Y	Y	Y	N
19 *Lagomarsino*	P	N	Y	N	Y	N	Y	Y
20 *Thomas*	Y	N	Y	Y	N	?	?	?
21 *Fiedler*	Y	N	Y	Y	Y	Y	N	Y
22 *Moorhead*	Y	N	Y	N	Y	?	?	?
23 Beilenson	Y	Y	N	N	Y	Y	Y	N
24 Waxman	Y	Y	N	N	Y	Y	Y	N
25 Roybal	Y	Y	N	N	Y	Y	Y	N
26 Berman	Y	Y	N	N	Y	?	?	?
27 Levine	Y	Y	N	N	Y	?	?	?
28 Dixon	?	#	?	?	?	?	?	?
29 Hawkins	Y	Y	?	N	Y	Y	Y	N
30 Martinez	?	?	?	?	?	?	?	?
31 Dymally	Y	Y	N	N	Y	?	?	?
32 Anderson	Y	Y	N	N	Y	Y	Y	N
33 *Dreier*	Y	N	Y	N	Y	N	Y	Y
34 Torres	?	Y	N	N	Y	Y	Y	N
35 *Lewis*	Y	N	Y	N	N	N	N	Y
36 Brown	Y	Y	N	N	Y	Y	Y	N
37 *McCandless*	Y	N	Y	Y	Y	Y	N	?
38 Patterson	?	Y	N	N	Y	Y	N	N
39 *Dannemeyer*	Y	N	Y	Y	N	N	Y	Y
40 *Badham*	Y	N	Y	N	?	?	?	?
41 *Lowery*	?	N	Y	Y	Y	Y	N	Y
42 *Lungren*	Y	N	Y	Y	N	Y	N	Y

	99	100	101	102	103	104	105	106
43 *Packard*	Y	N	Y	Y	N	Y	N	Y
44 Bates	Y	Y	N	N	Y	Y	Y	N
45 *Hunter*	Y	N	Y	Y	N	Y	N	Y
COLORADO								
1 Schroeder	N	Y	N	N	Y	Y	Y	N
2 Wirth	Y	Y	N	?	?	?	?	?
3 Kogovsek	Y	Y	N	N	Y	Y	Y	N
4 *Brown*	N	N	Y	Y	Y	Y	N	Y
5 *Kramer*	Y	N	Y	N	Y	Y	Y	Y
6 *Schaefer*	Y	N	Y	N	Y	N	Y	Y
CONNECTICUT								
1 Kennelly	Y	Y	N	N	Y	Y	Y	N
2 Gejdenson	N	Y	N	N	Y	Y	Y	N
3 Morrison	Y	Y	N	N	Y	Y	Y	N
4 *McKinney*	Y	Y	N	Y	Y	Y	Y	N
5 Ratchford	Y	Y	N	N	Y	Y	Y	N
6 *Johnson*	Y	N	N	?	Y	Y	N	Y
DELAWARE								
AL Carper	Y	N	N	N	Y	Y	Y	N
FLORIDA								
1 Hutto	Y	N	N	N	Y	Y	Y	N
2 Fuqua	Y	N	N	Y	Y	Y	Y	N
3 Bennett	Y	N	N	N	Y	Y	Y	N
4 Chappell	Y	N	N	N	Y	Y	Y	N
5 *McCollum*	Y	N	Y	Y	N	N	Y	Y
6 MacKay	Y	Y	?	?	?	?	?	?
7 Gibbons	Y	N	N	N	Y	Y	Y	?
8 *Young*	Y	N	Y	N	Y	N	Y	Y
9 *Bilirakis*	Y	N	Y	N	Y	N	Y	Y
10 Ireland	Y	N	Y	Y	Y	Y	N	Y
11 Nelson	Y	N	N	N	Y	Y	Y	N
12 *Lewis*	Y	N	N	Y	Y	Y	Y	N
13 *Mack*	Y	N	Y	N	Y	N	Y	Y
14 Mica	Y	N	N	N	Y	Y	Y	N
15 *Shaw*	Y	N	Y	N	Y	N	Y	Y
16 Smith	Y	N	N	N	Y	Y	Y	N
17 Lehman	?	?	?	?	?	?	?	?
18 Pepper	Y	Y	N	-	#	+	+	-
19 Fascell	Y	N	N	N	Y	Y	Y	N
GEORGIA								
1 Thomas	Y	N	N	N	Y	Y	Y	N
2 Hatcher	Y	N	N	N	Y	Y	Y	N
3 Ray	Y	N	N	N	Y	Y	Y	Y
4 Levitas	Y	N	N	N	Y	Y	Y	N
5 Fowler	Y	N	N	N	Y	Y	N	Y
6 *Gingrich*	Y	N	Y	Y	Y	Y	Y	N
7 McDonald	Y	N	Y	N	Y	N	Y	Y
8 Rowland	Y	N	N	N	Y	Y	Y	N
9 Jenkins	Y	N	N	N	Y	Y	Y	N
10 Barnard	Y	N	N	N	Y	Y	Y	N
HAWAII								
1 Heftel	?	?	?	?	?	?	?	?
2 Akaka	Y	N	N	N	Y	Y	Y	N
IDAHO								
1 *Craig*	Y	N	Y	N	Y	N	Y	Y
2 *Hansen*	?	?	?	?	X	?	?	?
ILLINOIS								
1 Vacancy								
2 Savage	?	Y	N	N	Y	Y	Y	N
3 Russo	?	N	N	N	Y	Y	Y	?
4 *O'Brien*	Y	N	Y	N	Y	N	Y	Y
5 Lipinski	?	Y	N	N	Y	Y	Y	N
6 *Hyde*	Y	N	Y	N	Y	N	Y	N
7 Collins	Y	Y	N	N	Y	Y	Y	N
8 Rostenkowski	Y	N	N	N	Y	Y	Y	N
9 Yates	N	Y	N	N	Y	Y	Y	N
10 *Porter*	Y	N	Y	Y	N	Y	Y	N
11 Annunzio	Y	N	N	N	Y	Y	Y	N
12 *Crane, P.*	Y	N	Y	N	Y	N	Y	Y
13 *Erlenborn*	?	N	Y	N	N	Y	N	Y
14 *Corcoran*	Y	N	Y	N	+	-	+	
15 *Madigan*	Y	N	Y	Y	Y	Y	Y	N
16 *Martin*	Y	N	Y	Y	Y	Y	Y	Y
17 Evans	Y	Y	N	N	Y	Y	Y	N
18 *Michel*	?	?	?	?	X	?	?	?
19 *Crane, D.*	Y	N	Y	N	Y	N	Y	Y
20 Durbin	N	N	N	N	Y	Y	Y	?
21 Price	Y	N	N	N	Y	Y	Y	N
22 Simon	?	N	N	N	Y	Y	Y	N
INDIANA								
1 Hall	Y	N	N	N	Y	Y	Y	N
2 Sharp	Y	N	N	N	Y	Y	Y	N
3 *Hiler*	N	N	Y	N	Y	N	Y	Y
4 *Coats*	Y	N	Y	N	Y	N	Y	Y
5 Hillis	Y	N	Y	Y	Y	Y	N	Y

ND - Northern Democrats   SD - Southern Democrats

Corresponding to Congressional Record Votes 107, 108, 109, 110, 111, 112, 113, 114

	99	100	101	102	103	104	105	106
6 ***Burton***	Y	N	Y	Y	N	Y	N	Y
7 ***Myers***	Y	N	Y	Y	N	Y	Y	Y
8 McCloskey	Y	?	N	N	Y	Y	Y	N
9 Hamilton	Y	N	N	N	Y	Y	Y	N
10 Jacobs	P	N	N	N	Y	Y	Y	Y
IOWA								
1 ***Leach***	?	Y	N	N	Y	Y	Y	Y
2 ***Tauke***	Y	N	N	Y	Y	Y	N	N
3 ***Evans***	N	Y	N	N	Y	Y	N	N
4 Smith	Y	Y	N	N	Y	Y	Y	N
5 Harkin	N	Y	N	N	Y	Y	Y	N
6 Bedell	Y	Y	N	N	Y	Y	Y	N
KANSAS								
1 ***Roberts***	Y	N	Y	Y	N	Y	N	Y
2 Slattery	Y	N	N	N	Y	Y	Y	N
3 ***Winn***	Y	N	Y	Y	N	Y	N	Y
4 Glickman	Y	N	N	N	Y	Y	Y	N
5 ***Whittaker***	Y	N	Y	Y	N	Y	N	Y
KENTUCKY								
1 Hubbard	Y	N	Y	Y	N	Y	Y	Y
2 Natcher	Y	N	N	N	Y	Y	Y	N
3 Mazzoli	Y	N	N	N	Y	Y	Y	N
4 ***Snyder***	Y	N	Y	Y	Y	Y	Y	Y
5 ***Rogers***	Y	N	Y	Y	Y	Y	N	Y
6 ***Hopkins***	Y	N	Y	Y	N	Y	N	Y
7 Perkins	Y	N	N	N	Y	Y	Y	N
LOUISIANA								
1 ***Livingston***	Y	N	Y	Y	N	Y	Y	Y
2 Boggs	Y	Y	N	N	Y	Y	Y	N
3 Tauzin	Y	N	Y	Y	N	Y	Y	Y
4 Roemer	N	N	Y	N	N	Y	N	Y
5 Huckaby	Y	N	?	?	?	Y	?	?
6 ***Moore***	Y	N	Y	Y	N	Y	Y	Y
7 Breaux	Y	N	N	N	Y	Y	Y	N
8 Long	Y	Y	N	N	Y	Y	Y	N
MAINE								
1 ***McKernan***	Y	N	N	Y	Y	Y	N	N
2 ***Snowe***	Y	N	Y	Y	Y	Y	Y	N
MARYLAND								
1 Dyson	Y	N	N	N	Y	Y	Y	N
2 Long	Y	Y	N	N	Y	Y	?	?
3 Mikulski	Y	N	N	Y	Y	Y	Y	N
4 ***Holt***	Y	N	Y	N	N	Y	N	Y
5 Hoyer	Y	Y	N	N	Y	Y	Y	N
6 Byron	Y	N	Y	Y	Y	Y	Y	Y
7 Mitchell	?	?	N	N	Y	Y	Y	N
8 Barnes	Y	Y	N	N	Y	Y	Y	N
MASSACHUSETTS								
1 ***Conte***	Y	N	N	N	Y	Y	Y	N
2 Boland	Y	N	N	N	Y	Y	Y	N
3 Early	Y	Y	N	N	Y	Y	Y	N
4 Frank	Y	Y	N	?	Y	Y	Y	N
5 Shannon	Y	Y	N	N	Y	Y	Y	N
6 Mavroules	Y	N	N	N	Y	Y	Y	N
7 Markey	Y	Y	N	N	Y	Y	Y	N
8 O'Neill								
9 Moakley	Y	?	N	N	Y	Y	Y	N
10 Studds	Y	Y	N	N	Y	Y	Y	N
11 Donnelly	Y	Y	N	N	Y	Y	Y	N
MICHIGAN								
1 Conyers	Y	Y	?	N	Y	Y	Y	N
2 ***Pursell***	Y	N	Y	Y	Y	Y	N	Y
3 Wolpe	Y	Y	N	N	Y	Y	Y	N
4 ***Siljander***	Y	N	Y	Y	Y	Y	N	Y
5 ***Sawyer***	Y	N	Y	N	Y	Y	Y	Y
6 Carr	Y	Y	N	N	Y	Y	Y	N
7 Kildee	Y	Y	N	N	Y	Y	Y	N
8 Traxler	Y	Y	N	N	Y	?	?	?
9 ***Vander Jagt***	Y	N	Y	Y	Y	Y	?	?
10 Albosta	Y	N	N	N	Y	Y	Y	N
11 ***Davis***	N	N	N	Y	Y	Y	N	Y
12 Bonior	Y	Y	N	N	Y	Y	Y	N
13 Crockett	?	?	N	N	Y	Y	Y	N
14 Hertel	Y	Y	N	N	Y	?	?	?
15 Ford	?	Y	N	N	Y	Y	Y	N
16 Dingell	Y	Y	N	N	Y	Y	Y	N
17 Levin	Y	Y	N	N	Y	Y	Y	N
18 ***Broomfield***	Y	N	Y	Y	N	Y	N	Y
MINNESOTA								
1 Penny	Y	Y	N	N	Y	Y	Y	N
2 ***Weber***	Y	N	Y	Y	N	Y	N	Y
3 ***Frenzel***	Y	N	Y	Y	N	Y	N	Y
4 Vento	Y	Y	N	Y	Y	Y	Y	N
5 Sabo	N	Y	N	N	Y	Y	Y	N
6 Sikorski	Y	Y	N	N	Y	Y	Y	N

	99	100	101	102	103	104	105	106
7 ***Stangeland***	Y	?	Y	Y	N	Y	?	Y
8 Oberstar	P	Y	N	N	Y	Y	Y	N
MISSISSIPPI								
1 Whitten	Y	N	N	Y	Y	Y	Y	N
2 ***Franklin***	Y	N	Y	Y	N	Y	Y	?
3 Montgomery	Y	N	Y	N	N	Y	Y	Y
4 Dowdy	Y	N	N	N	Y	Y	Y	N
5 ***Lott***	Y	N	Y	Y	N	?	?	?
MISSOURI								
1 Clay	N	Y	N	N	Y	Y	Y	N
2 Young	Y	N	N	N	Y	Y	Y	N
3 Gephardt	?	Y	N	N	Y	Y	Y	N
4 Skelton	Y	N	N	N	N	Y	Y	N
5 Wheat	Y	Y	N	N	Y	Y	Y	N
6 ***Coleman***	Y	N	N	N	Y	Y	N	Y
7 ***Taylor***	Y	N	Y	Y	N	Y	N	Y
8 ***Emerson***	N	N	Y	Y	N	Y	N	Y
9 Volkmer	Y	Y	N	N	Y	Y	Y	N
MONTANA								
1 Williams	?	Y	N	Y	Y	Y	?	N
2 ***Marlenee***	?	?	?	?	?	?	?	?
NEBRASKA								
1 ***Bereuter***	Y	N	N	Y	Y	Y	N	?
2 ***Daub***	Y	N	Y	Y	N	Y	N	Y
3 ***Smith***	Y	N	Y	Y	N	Y	?	?
NEVADA								
1 Reid	Y	Y	N	N	Y	Y	Y	N
2 ***Vucanovich***	Y	N	Y	Y	N	Y	N	Y
NEW HAMPSHIRE								
1 D'Amours	Y	Y	N	N	Y	Y	Y	N
2 ***Gregg***	Y	N	Y	Y	N	Y	N	Y
NEW JERSEY								
1 Florio	Y	Y	N	N	Y	Y	Y	N
2 Hughes	Y	N	N	N	Y	Y	Y	Y
3 Howard	Y	Y	N	N	Y	Y	Y	N
4 ***Smith***	Y	N	Y	N	Y	Y	Y	Y
5 ***Roukema***	Y	N	Y	Y	N	Y	N	Y
6 Dwyer	Y	Y	N	N	Y	Y	?	?
7 ***Rinaldo***	Y	N	Y	N	Y	Y	Y	Y
8 Roe	Y	Y	N	N	Y	Y	Y	N
9 Torricelli	Y	Y	N	N	Y	Y	Y	?
10 Rodino	Y	Y	N	N	Y	Y	Y	N
11 Minish	Y	Y	N	N	Y	Y	Y	N
12 ***Courter***	Y	N	Y	Y	N	Y	N	Y
13 ***Forsythe***	N	N	Y	Y	N	Y	N	Y
14 Guarini	Y	Y	N	N	Y	Y	Y	N
NEW MEXICO								
1 ***Lujan***	Y	N	Y	Y	Y	Y	Y	?
2 ***Skeen***	Y	N	Y	Y	Y	Y	?	?
3 Richardson	Y	Y	N	N	Y	Y	Y	N
NEW YORK								
1 ***Carney***	Y	N	Y	Y	N	Y	N	Y
2 Downey	Y	Y	N	N	Y	Y	Y	N
3 Mrazek	Y	N	N	N	Y	Y	Y	N
4 ***Lent***	Y	N	?	Y	Y	Y	Y	N
5 ***McGrath***	Y	N	Y	Y	Y	Y	Y	Y
6 Addabbo	Y	Y	N	N	Y	Y	#	?
7 Ackerman	Y	Y	N	N	Y	Y	Y	N
8 Scheuer	Y	Y	N	N	Y	Y	Y	N
9 Ferraro	Y	Y	N	N	Y	Y	Y	N
10 Schumer	Y	Y	N	N	Y	Y	Y	N
11 Towns	Y	N	N	N	Y	Y	Y	N
12 Owens	?	?	?	?	?	?	?	?
13 Solarz	Y	Y	N	Y	Y	Y	Y	N
14 ***Molinari***	Y	N	Y	Y	Y	Y	Y	N
15 ***Green***	Y	N	N	Y	Y	Y	Y	N
16 Rangel	Y	N	N	N	Y	Y	Y	N
17 Weiss	Y	Y	N	N	Y	Y	Y	N
18 Garcia	Y	Y	N	N	Y	Y	Y	N
19 Biaggi	Y	Y	N	N	Y	Y	Y	N
20 Ottinger	?	Y	N	N	Y	Y	Y	N
21 ***Fish***	Y	N	N	Y	Y	Y	Y	N
22 ***Gilman***	Y	Y	N	N	Y	Y	Y	N
23 Stratton	Y	N	N	N	Y	Y	Y	N
24 ***Solomon***	N	N	Y	Y	N	Y	N	Y
25 ***Boehlert***	Y	Y	N	N	Y	Y	N	Y
26 ***Martin***	Y	N	Y	Y	Y	Y	Y	Y
27 ***Wortley***	Y	Y	Y	Y	Y	Y	Y	Y
28 McHugh	Y	Y	N	N	Y	Y	Y	N
29 ***Horton***	Y	N	N	N	Y	Y	?	?
30 ***Conable***	Y	N	Y	Y	N	Y	N	Y
31 ***Kemp***	?	?	Y	Y	N	Y	N	Y
32 LaFalce	Y	Y	N	N	Y	Y	Y	N
33 Nowak	Y	Y	N	N	Y	Y	Y	N
34 Lundine	Y	Y	N	N	Y	Y	Y	N

	99	100	101	102	103	104	105	106
NORTH CAROLINA								
1 Jones	?	N	N	N	Y	Y	Y	N
2 Valentine	Y	N	N	N	Y	Y	Y	N
3 Whitley	Y	N	N	N	Y	Y	Y	N
4 Andrews	?	Y	N	N	Y	Y	N	N
5 Neal	Y	N	N	N	Y	Y	?	?
6 Britt	Y	N	N	N	Y	Y	Y	N
7 Rose	Y	N	?	N	Y	Y	Y	N
8 Hefner	?	?	?	?	?	?	?	?
9 ***Martin***	?	Y	N	N	Y	Y	N	Y
10 ***Broyhill***	Y	N	Y	Y	N	Y	Y	Y
11 Clarke	Y	N	N	N	Y	Y	Y	N
NORTH DAKOTA								
AL Dorgan	Y	Y	N	N	Y	Y	Y	N
OHIO								
1 Luken	Y	N	N	N	Y	Y	Y	N
2 ***Gradison***	Y	N	Y	Y	N	Y	N	Y
3 Hall	Y	N	N	N	N	Y	N	N
4 ***Oxley***	Y	N	Y	Y	N	Y	N	Y
5 ***Latta***	Y	N	Y	Y	N	Y	Y	Y
6 ***McEwen***	Y	N	Y	Y	N	Y	Y	Y
7 ***DeWine***	Y	N	Y	Y	N	Y	N	Y
8 ***Kindness***	Y	N	Y	N	N	Y	Y	Y
9 Kaptur	Y	Y	N	N	Y	Y	Y	N
10 ***Miller***	N	N	Y	Y	N	Y	N	Y
11 Eckart	Y	Y	N	Y	Y	Y	Y	N
12 ***Kasich***	Y	N	Y	Y	N	Y	N	Y
13 Pease	Y	Y	N	N	Y	Y	Y	N
14 Seiberling	Y	Y	N	N	Y	Y	Y	N
15 ***Wylie***	Y	N	Y	?	Y	?	?	?
16 ***Regula***	Y	N	Y	Y	N	Y	Y	Y
17 ***Williams***	Y	N	Y	N	Y	Y	?	Y
18 Applegate	Y	N	Y	Y	Y	Y	N	Y
19 Feighan	Y	Y	N	N	Y	Y	Y	N
20 Oakar	Y	Y	N	Y	Y	Y	Y	N
21 Stokes	Y	Y	N	N	Y	Y	Y	N
OKLAHOMA								
1 Jones	Y	N	N	N	Y	Y	Y	?
2 Synar	Y	N	N	N	Y	Y	Y	N
3 Watkins	Y	N	N	N	Y	Y	Y	N
4 McCurdy	Y	N	N	N	Y	Y	Y	N
5 ***Edwards***	Y	N	Y	Y	N	Y	Y	N
6 English	Y	N	N	N	Y	Y	Y	Y
OREGON								
1 AuCoin	Y	Y	N	N	Y	Y	Y	N
2 ***Smith, R.***	?	?	?	?	X	?	?	?
3 Wyden	Y	Y	N	N	Y	Y	Y	N
4 Weaver	Y	Y	N	N	Y	Y	Y	N
5 ***Smith, D.***	Y	N	Y	Y	N	Y	N	Y
PENNSYLVANIA								
1 Foglietta	Y	Y	N	N	Y	Y	Y	N
2 Gray	Y	Y	N	N	Y	Y	Y	N
3 Borski	Y	Y	N	N	Y	Y	Y	N
4 Kolter	Y	Y	N	N	Y	Y	Y	N
5 ***Schulze***	Y	N	Y	Y	N	Y	?	Y
6 Yatron	Y	N	N	N	Y	Y	Y	N
7 Edgar	Y	Y	N	N	Y	Y	Y	N
8 Kostmayer	Y	Y	N	N	Y	Y	Y	N
9 ***Shuster***	Y	N	Y	Y	N	Y	Y	Y
10 ***McDade***	?	?	?	?	?	?	?	?
11 Harrison	?	Y	N	N	Y	Y	Y	N
12 Murtha	Y	N	N	N	Y	Y	Y	N
13 ***Coughlin***	N	N	Y	Y	Y	Y	Y	Y
14 Coyne	Y	Y	N	N	Y	Y	Y	N
15 ***Ritter***	Y	N	Y	N	Y	?	?	?
16 ***Walker***	N	N	Y	Y	N	Y	N	Y
17 ***Gekas***	Y	N	Y	Y	N	Y	N	Y
18 Walgren	Y	Y	N	N	Y	Y	Y	N
19 ***Goodling***	?	N	Y	Y	N	Y	N	Y
20 Gaydos	Y	Y	N	N	Y	Y	Y	N
21 ***Ridge***	?	N	N	?	Y	Y	Y	Y
22 Murphy	Y	N	N	N	Y	?	?	?
23 ***Clinger***	Y	N	N	N	Y	Y	Y	Y
RHODE ISLAND								
1 St Germain	Y	Y	N	Y	Y	Y	Y	N
2 ***Schneider***	Y	N	Y	Y	Y	Y	N	N
SOUTH CAROLINA								
1 ***Hartnett***	Y	N	Y	Y	N	Y	N	Y
2 ***Spence***	Y	N	Y	Y	Y	Y	N	Y
3 Derrick	?	X	N	N	Y	Y	Y	N
4 ***Campbell***	Y	N	Y	Y	N	Y	N	Y
5 Spratt	Y	Y	N	N	#	?	X	?
6 Tallon	Y	N	N	N	Y	Y	Y	N
SOUTH DAKOTA								
AL Daschle	Y	?	?	?	?	?	?	?

	99	100	101	102	103	104	105	106
TENNESSEE								
1 ***Quillen***	Y	N	Y	Y	Y	?	?	?
2 ***Duncan***	Y	N	N	N	Y	Y	Y	N
3 Lloyd	Y	N	N	N	Y	Y	Y	N
4 Cooper	?	?	?	?	?	?	?	?
5 Boner	Y	N	N	N	Y	Y	Y	N
6 Gore	Y	Y	N	N	Y	?	Y	N
7 ***Sundquist***	Y	N	Y	Y	N	Y	Y	Y
8 Jones	Y	N	N	N	Y	Y	Y	N
9 Ford	?	?	?	?	?	?	?	?
TEXAS								
1 Hall, S.	Y	N	N	N	N	Y	N	Y
2 Wilson	?	N	N	N	Y	Y	Y	N
3 ***Bartlett***	Y	N	Y	Y	N	Y	N	Y
4 Hall, R.	Y	N	N	N	Y	Y	N	N
5 Bryant	Y	Y	N	N	Y	Y	Y	N
6 ***Gramm***	Y	N	Y	N	N	Y	N	Y
7 ***Archer***	Y	N	Y	Y	N	?	?	?
8 ***Fields***	Y	N	Y	Y	N	Y	N	Y
9 Brooks	Y	N	N	N	Y	Y	Y	N
10 Pickle	Y	N	N	N	Y	Y	Y	N
11 Leath	?	?	?	?	?	?	?	?
12 Wright	Y	N	N	N	Y	Y	Y	N
13 Hightower	Y	N	N	N	Y	Y	N	Y
14 Patman	Y	N	N	N	Y	Y	Y	Y
15 de la Garza	Y	Y	N	N	Y	Y	Y	N
16 Coleman	Y	Y	N	Y	Y	Y	Y	N
17 Stenholm	Y	N	Y	N	N	Y	N	Y
18 Leland	?	Y	N	N	Y	Y	Y	N
19 Hance	Y	?	?	?	#	?	?	?
20 Gonzalez	Y	N	N	N	Y	Y	Y	N
21 ***Loeffler***	Y	?	Y	Y	N	Y	N	Y
22 ***Paul***	Y	N	Y	Y	N	Y	N	Y
23 Kazen	Y	N	N	N	Y	Y	Y	N
24 Frost	Y	N	N	N	Y	Y	Y	N
25 Andrews	Y	N	N	N	Y	Y	Y	N
26 Vandergriff	?	N	N	N	Y	Y	Y	N
27 Ortiz	?	N	N	N	Y	Y	Y	N
UTAH								
1 ***Hansen***	Y	N	Y	Y	N	Y	N	Y
2 ***Marriott***	Y	N	Y	?	N	Y	N	Y
3 ***Nielson***	Y	N	Y	Y	N	Y	N	Y
VERMONT								
AL ***Jeffords***	Y	Y	N	Y	Y	Y	N	N
VIRGINIA								
1 ***Bateman***	Y	N	Y	Y	Y	Y	N	Y
2 ***Whitehurst***	Y	N	Y	Y	Y	?	?	?
3 ***Bliley***	Y	N	Y	Y	Y	Y	Y	Y
4 Sisisky	Y	N	Y	N	Y	Y	Y	N
5 Daniel	Y	N	Y	Y	Y	Y	N	Y
6 Olin	Y	N	N	N	Y	Y	Y	N
7 ***Robinson***	Y	N	Y	Y	N	Y	N	Y
8 ***Parris***	Y	N	Y	Y	N	Y	Y	Y
9 Boucher	Y	Y	N	N	Y	Y	Y	N
10 ***Wolf***	Y	N	Y	Y	N	Y	N	N
WASHINGTON								
1 ***Pritchard***	Y	N	Y	N	Y	Y	N	Y
2 Swift	Y	Y	N	N	Y	?	?	?
3 Bonker	Y	Y	N	N	Y	Y	Y	N
4 ***Morrison***	Y	?	Y	Y	N	Y	N	N
5 Foley	Y	Y	N	N	Y	Y	Y	N
6 Dicks	Y	N	N	N	Y	Y	Y	N
7 Lowry	Y	Y	N	N	Y	Y	Y	N
8 ***Chandler***	Y	N	Y	Y	N	Y	N	Y
WEST VIRGINIA								
1 Mollohan	Y	Y	N	N	Y	Y	Y	N
2 Staggers	Y	Y	N	N	Y	Y	Y	N
3 Wise	Y	Y	N	N	Y	Y	Y	N
4 Rahall	Y	Y	N	N	Y	Y	?	N
WISCONSIN								
1 Aspin	Y	Y	N	N	Y	Y	Y	N
2 Kastenmeier	Y	Y	N	N	Y	Y	Y	N
3 ***Gunderson***	Y	N	Y	Y	N	Y	N	N
4 Zablocki	Y	N	N	N	Y	Y	Y	N
5 Moody	Y	Y	N	N	Y	Y	Y	N
6 ***Petri***	Y	N	Y	N	N	Y	N	N
7 Obey	Y	Y	N	N	Y	Y	Y	N
8 ***Roth***	Y	N	Y	Y	Y	Y	Y	Y
9 ***Sensenbrenner***	Y	N	Y	Y	N	Y	N	Y
WYOMING								
AL ***Cheney***	Y	N	Y	Y	N	?	?	?

Southern states - Ala., Ark., Fla., Ga., Ky., La., Miss., N.C., Okla., S.C., Tenn., Texas, Va.

107. HR 2587. Department of Energy Civilian Research and Development Programs. Rangel, D-N.Y., amendment to redirect $5 million for construction of a chemical research center at Columbia University. Adopted 215-150: R 19-121; D 196-29 (ND 145-8, SD 51-21), May 12, 1983.

108. HR 2587. Department of Energy Civilian Research and Development Programs. Passage of the bill to authorize $3,288,271,000 for civilian research and development programs of the Department of Energy in fiscal 1984. Passed 230-132: R 32-109; D 198-23 (ND 142-7, SD 56-16), May 12, 1983.

109. HR 2733. Critical Agricultural Materials. Brown, D-Calif., motion to suspend the rules and pass the bill to continue, through Sept. 30, 1988, research and development programs on production of guayule rubber, to expand the program to include other agricultural crops that have a potential for producing materials of strategic or industrial importance, and to authorize a total of $50 million for the activities. Motion agreed to 326-96: R 73-91; D 253-5 (ND 168-1, SD 85-4), May 17, 1983. A two-thirds majority of those present and voting (282 in this case) is required for passage under suspension of the rules.

110. H J Res 265. Temporary Extension of Certain Federal Housing Programs. Gonzalez, D-Texas, motion to suspend the rules and pass the joint resolution to continue most of the housing and community development programs of the Department of Housing and Urban Development, the Farmers Home Administration and other agencies through Sept. 30, 1983. Motion agreed to 418-6: R 160-5; D 258-1 (ND 170-0, SD 88-1), May 17, 1983. A two-thirds majority of those present and voting (283 in this case) is required for passage under suspension of the rules.

111. HR 1416. Securities and Exchange Commission Authorization. Wirth, D-Colo., motion to suspend the rules and pass the bill to authorize $102.3 million in fiscal 1984 and $111.1 million in fiscal 1985 for the Securities and Exchange Commission. Motion agreed to 322-100: R 88-76; D 234-24 (ND 163-7, SD 71-17), May 17, 1983. A two-thirds majority of those present and voting (282 in this case) is required for passage under suspension of the rules.

112. HR 2681. Securities Exchange Act Amendments. Wirth, D-Colo., motion to suspend the rules and pass the bill to make technical changes in the Securities Exchange Act of 1934. Motion agreed to 361-63: R 129-37; D 232-26 (ND 149-20, SD 83-6), May 17, 1983. A two-thirds majority of those present and voting (283 in this case) is required for passage under suspension of the rules.

113. HR 2936. Veterans' Appeals Board Expansion. Montgomery, D-Miss., motion to suspend the rules and pass the bill to increase from 50 to 65 the authorized number of members of the Board of Veterans' Appeals in the Veterans Administration. Motion agreed to 423-2: R 165-1; D 258-1 (ND 170-1, SD 88-0), May 17, 1983. A two-thirds majority of those present and voting (284 in this case) is required for passage under suspension of the rules.

114. HR 2602. Trade Programs Authorizations. Gibbons, D-Fla., motion to suspend the rules and pass the bill to authorize $21.2 million for the U.S. International Trade Commission, $627.8 million for the U.S. Customs Service, and $11.9 million for the Office of the U.S. Trade Representative in fiscal 1984. Motion agreed to 380-45: R 131-34; D 249-11 (ND 167-4, SD 82-7), May 17, 1983. A two-thirds majority of those present and voting (284 in this case) is required for passage under suspension of the rules.

KEY

Y	Voted for (yea).
#	Paired for.
+	Announced for.
N	Voted against (nay).
X	Paired against.
-	Announced against.
P	Voted "present".
C	Voted "present" to avoid possible conflict of interest.
?	Did not vote or otherwise make a position known.

Democrats **Republicans**

	107	108	109	110	111	112	113	114
ALABAMA								
1 *Edwards*	N	N	Y	Y	Y	Y	Y	Y
2 *Dickinson*	N	N	N	Y	Y	Y	Y	Y
3 Nichols	N	Y	?	?	?	?	?	?
4 Bevill	Y	Y	Y	Y	Y	Y	Y	Y
5 Flippo	Y	Y	Y	Y	Y	Y	Y	Y
6 Erdreich	+	Y	Y	Y	Y	Y	Y	Y
7 Shelby	N	N	N	Y	Y	Y	Y	Y
ALASKA								
AL *Young*	N	N	Y	Y	Y	Y	Y	Y
ARIZONA								
1 *McCain*	N	N	N	Y	Y	Y	Y	Y
2 Udall	Y	Y	Y	Y	Y	Y	Y	Y
3 *Stump*	N	N	N	N	N	N	Y	N
4 *Rudd*	N	N	N	Y	N	Y	Y	Y
5 McNulty	?	?	Y	Y	Y	Y	Y	Y
ARKANSAS								
1 Alexander	?	Y	Y	Y	Y	Y	Y	Y
2 *Bethune*	N	N	N	Y	Y	Y	Y	Y
3 *Hammerschmidt*	N	N	N	Y	Y	Y	Y	Y
4 Anthony	Y	Y	Y	Y	Y	Y	Y	Y
CALIFORNIA								
1 Bosco	N	Y	Y	Y	Y	Y	Y	Y
2 *Chappie*	?	?	Y	N	Y	Y	Y	Y
3 Matsui	Y	Y	Y	Y	Y	Y	Y	Y
4 Fazio	Y	Y	Y	Y	Y	Y	Y	Y
5 Vacancy								
6 Boxer	Y	Y	Y	Y	Y	Y	Y	Y
7 Miller	Y	Y	Y	Y	Y	Y	Y	Y
8 Dellums	Y	Y	?	Y	Y	Y	Y	Y
9 Stark	Y	Y	Y	Y	Y	Y	Y	Y
10 Edwards	Y	Y	Y	Y	Y	Y	Y	Y
11 Lantos	Y	Y	Y	Y	Y	Y	Y	Y
12 *Zschau*	N	N	Y	Y	Y	Y	Y	Y
13 Mineta	Y	Y	Y	Y	Y	Y	Y	Y
14 *Shumway*	N	N	N	Y	N	N	Y	N
15 Coelho	?	Y	Y	Y	Y	Y	Y	Y
16 Panetta	Y	Y	Y	Y	Y	Y	Y	Y
17 *Pashayan*	N	N	Y	Y	Y	Y	Y	Y
18 Lehman	Y	Y	Y	Y	Y	Y	Y	Y
19 *Lagomarsino*	N	N	N	Y	N	Y	Y	Y
20 *Thomas*	?	X	N	Y	Y	Y	Y	Y
21 *Fiedler*	N	N	Y	N	Y	Y	Y	Y
22 *Moorhead*	?	?	N	Y	Y	Y	Y	Y
23 Beilenson	N	Y	Y	Y	Y	Y	Y	Y
24 Waxman	Y	Y	Y	Y	Y	Y	Y	Y
25 Roybal	Y	Y	Y	Y	Y	Y	Y	Y
26 Berman	?	#	Y	Y	Y	Y	Y	Y
27 Levine	?	#	Y	Y	Y	Y	Y	Y
28 Dixon	?	?	Y	Y	Y	Y	Y	Y
29 Hawkins	Y	Y	Y	Y	Y	Y	Y	Y
30 Martinez	?	?	?	?	?	?	?	?
31 Dymally	?	?	?	?	?	?	?	?
32 Anderson	Y	Y	Y	Y	Y	Y	Y	Y
33 *Dreier*	N	N	N	Y	N	N	N	N
34 Torres	Y	Y	Y	Y	Y	Y	Y	Y
35 *Lewis*	N	N	Y	Y	N	Y	Y	Y
36 Brown	Y	Y	Y	Y	Y	Y	Y	Y
37 *McCandless*	?	?	Y	Y	Y	Y	Y	Y
38 Patterson	Y	Y	Y	Y	Y	Y	Y	Y
39 *Dannemeyer*	N	N	N	N	Y	N	Y	N
40 *Badham*	?	X	N	Y	N	Y	Y	N
41 *Lowery*	N	N	N	Y	N	Y	Y	Y
42 *Lungren*	N	N	N	Y	N	Y	Y	Y

	107	108	109	110	111	112	113	114
43 *Packard*	N	N	N	Y	Y	Y	Y	Y
44 Bates	Y	N	Y	Y	Y	Y	Y	Y
45 *Hunter*	N	N	?	Y	Y	Y	Y	Y
COLORADO								
1 Schroeder	Y	Y	Y	Y	Y	Y	Y	Y
2 Wirth	?	?	Y	Y	Y	Y	Y	Y
3 Kogovsek	Y	Y	Y	Y	Y	Y	Y	Y
4 *Brown*	N	N	N	Y	N	N	Y	N
5 *Kramer*	N	N	N	Y	N	Y	N	Y
6 *Schaefer*	N	N	N	Y	N	N	Y	N
CONNECTICUT								
1 Kennelly	Y	Y	Y	Y	Y	Y	Y	Y
2 Gejdenson	Y	Y	Y	Y	Y	Y	Y	Y
3 Morrison	Y	Y	Y	Y	Y	Y	Y	Y
4 *McKinney*	Y	Y	Y	Y	Y	Y	Y	Y
5 Ratchford	Y	Y	Y	Y	Y	Y	Y	Y
6 *Johnson*	N	Y	N	Y	Y	Y	Y	Y
DELAWARE								
AL Carper	N	Y	Y	Y	Y	Y	Y	Y
FLORIDA								
1 Hutto	Y	Y	Y	Y	Y	Y	Y	Y
2 Fuqua	Y	?	Y	Y	Y	Y	Y	Y
3 Bennett	Y	Y	Y	Y	N	N	Y	Y
4 Chappell	Y	Y	Y	Y	Y	Y	Y	Y
5 *McCollum*	N	N	N	Y	N	Y	Y	Y
6 MacKay	?	?	Y	Y	Y	Y	Y	Y
7 Gibbons	?	?	Y	Y	Y	Y	Y	Y
8 *Young*	N	N	N	Y	N	N	Y	Y
9 *Bilirakis*	N	N	N	N	N	N	Y	Y
10 Ireland	N	N	N	Y	Y	Y	Y	Y
11 Nelson	Y	Y	Y	Y	Y	Y	Y	Y
12 *Lewis*	N	N	N	Y	N	Y	Y	Y
13 *Mack*	N	N	N	Y	N	Y	Y	Y
14 Mica	Y	Y	Y	Y	Y	Y	Y	Y
15 *Shaw*	N	N	N	Y	N	Y	Y	Y
16 Smith	Y	Y	Y	Y	Y	Y	Y	Y
17 Lehman	?	?	Y	Y	Y	Y	Y	Y
18 Pepper	+	+	Y	Y	Y	Y	Y	Y
19 Fascell	Y	Y	Y	Y	Y	Y	Y	Y
GEORGIA								
1 Thomas	Y	Y	Y	Y	Y	Y	Y	Y
2 Hatcher	?	?	Y	Y	Y	Y	Y	Y
3 Ray	N	N	Y	Y	Y	Y	Y	Y
4 Levitas	Y	Y	Y	Y	N	Y	Y	Y
5 Fowler	Y	Y	Y	Y	Y	Y	Y	Y
6 *Gingrich*	N	N	Y	Y	Y	Y	Y	N
7 McDonald	N	N	N	N	N	N	N	Y
8 Rowland	N	Y	Y	Y	Y	Y	Y	Y
9 Jenkins	N	?	Y	Y	N	Y	Y	Y
10 Barnard	N	N	Y	Y	Y	Y	Y	Y
HAWAII								
1 Heftel	?	?	?	?	?	?	?	?
2 Akaka	Y	Y	Y	Y	Y	Y	Y	Y
IDAHO								
1 *Craig*	N	N	?	?	?	N	Y	Y
2 *Hansen*	N	N	N	N	N	N	Y	N
ILLINOIS								
1 Vacancy								
2 Savage	Y	Y	Y	Y	Y	Y	Y	Y
3 Russo	?	?	Y	Y	Y	Y	Y	Y
4 *O'Brien*	?	?	Y	Y	Y	N	Y	Y
5 Lipinski	?	?	Y	Y	Y	Y	Y	Y
6 *Hyde*	N	N	N	Y	N	Y	Y	Y
7 Collins	Y	Y	Y	Y	Y	Y	Y	Y
8 Rostenkowski	Y	Y	Y	Y	Y	Y	Y	Y
9 Yates	Y	Y	Y	Y	Y	Y	Y	Y
10 *Porter*	N	N	N	Y	N	Y	Y	Y
11 Annunzio	Y	Y	Y	Y	Y	Y	Y	Y
12 *Crane, P.*	N	N	N	N	N	N	Y	N
13 *Erlenborn*	N	N	Y	Y	Y	Y	Y	Y
14 Corcoran	-	X	Y	Y	Y	Y	Y	Y
15 *Madigan*	N	N	Y	N	Y	Y	Y	Y
16 *Martin*	N	N	Y	N	N	Y	N	Y
17 Evans	Y	Y	Y	Y	Y	Y	Y	Y
18 *Michel*	?	?	Y	Y	Y	Y	Y	Y
19 *Crane, D.*	N	N	N	N	N	N	N	N
20 Durbin	?	#	Y	Y	Y	Y	Y	Y
21 Price	Y	Y	Y	Y	Y	Y	Y	Y
22 Simon	?	Y	Y	Y	Y	Y	Y	Y
INDIANA								
1 Hall	Y	Y	Y	Y	Y	Y	Y	Y
2 Sharp	Y	Y	Y	Y	Y	Y	Y	Y
3 *Hiler*	N	N	N	Y	N	N	Y	Y
4 *Coats*	N	N	Y	N	Y	N	Y	Y
5 Hillis	N	Y	Y	Y	Y	Y	Y	Y

ND - Northern Democrats   SD - Southern Democrats

Corresponding to Congressional Record Votes 115, 116, 117, 118, 119, 120, 121, 122

	107	108	109	110	111	112	113	114
6 *Burton*	N	N	N	Y	N	N	Y	N
7 *Myers*	Y	Y	Y	Y	Y	Y	Y	Y
8 McCloskey	Y	Y	Y	Y	?	Y	Y	Y
9 Hamilton	Y	Y	Y	Y	Y	Y	Y	Y
10 Jacobs	Y	N	N	Y	N	Y	N	Y
IOWA								
1 *Leach*	?	N	Y	Y	Y	Y	Y	Y
2 *Tauke*	N	N	N	Y	Y	Y	Y	Y
3 *Evans*	N	Y	Y	Y	Y	Y	Y	Y
4 Smith	Y	Y	Y	Y	Y	Y	Y	Y
5 Harkin	Y	Y	Y	Y	Y	Y	Y	Y
6 Bedell	Y	Y	Y	Y	Y	N	Y	Y
KANSAS								
1 *Roberts*	N	N	Y	Y	N	N	Y	N
2 Slattery	N	N	Y	Y	N	Y	Y	N
3 *Winn*	N	N	Y	Y	Y	Y	Y	Y
4 Glickman	Y	Y	Y	Y	Y	Y	Y	Y
5 *Whittaker*	N	N	N	Y	Y	Y	Y	Y
KENTUCKY								
1 Hubbard	N	N	Y	Y	N	N	Y	N
2 Natcher	Y	Y	Y	Y	Y	Y	Y	Y
3 Mazzoli	Y	Y	Y	Y	Y	Y	Y	Y
4 *Snyder*	N	?	N	Y	Y	Y	Y	Y
5 *Rogers*	N	N	N	Y	N	Y	Y	Y
6 *Hopkins*	N	N	N	Y	N	N	Y	N
7 Perkins	Y	Y	Y	Y	Y	Y	Y	Y
LOUISIANA								
1 *Livingston*	N	N	Y	Y	N	Y	Y	Y
2 Boggs	Y	Y	Y	Y	Y	Y	Y	Y
3 Tauzin	Y	N	Y	Y	N	Y	Y	Y
4 Roemer	N	N	N	Y	N	Y	Y	Y
5 Huckaby	?	N	Y	Y	Y	Y	Y	Y
6 *Moore*	N	N	N	Y	Y	Y	Y	Y
7 Breaux	Y	N	Y	Y	Y	Y	Y	Y
8 Long	Y	Y	Y	Y	Y	Y	Y	Y
MAINE								
1 *McKernan*	N	Y	Y	Y	Y	Y	Y	Y
2 *Snowe*	N	Y	Y	Y	Y	Y	Y	Y
MARYLAND								
1 Dyson	Y	N	Y	Y	Y	Y	Y	N
2 Long	?	?	Y	Y	Y	Y	Y	Y
3 Mikulski	Y	Y	Y	Y	Y	Y	Y	Y
4 *Holt*	N	N	N	Y	N	Y	Y	Y
5 Hoyer	Y	Y	Y	Y	Y	Y	Y	Y
6 Byron	N	N	Y	Y	Y	N	Y	N
7 Mitchell	Y	Y	Y	Y	Y	Y	Y	Y
8 Barnes	Y	Y	Y	Y	Y	Y	Y	Y
MASSACHUSETTS								
1 *Conte*	Y	Y	Y	Y	Y	Y	Y	Y
2 Boland	Y	Y	Y	Y	Y	Y	Y	Y
3 Early	Y	Y	Y	Y	Y	Y	Y	Y
4 Frank	Y	Y	Y	Y	Y	Y	Y	Y
5 Shannon	Y	Y	Y	Y	Y	Y	Y	Y
6 Mavroules	Y	Y	Y	Y	Y	Y	Y	Y
7 Markey	Y	Y	Y	Y	Y	Y	Y	Y
8 O'Neill								
9 Moakley	Y	Y	Y	Y	Y	Y	Y	Y
10 Studds	Y	?	Y	Y	Y	Y	Y	Y
11 Donnelly	Y	Y	Y	Y	Y	Y	Y	Y
MICHIGAN								
1 Conyers	Y	Y	?	?	Y	Y	Y	Y
2 *Pursell*	N	N	Y	Y	Y	Y	Y	Y
3 Wolpe	Y	Y	Y	Y	Y	Y	Y	Y
4 *Siljander*	N	N	Y	Y	N	Y	Y	N
5 *Sawyer*	N	N	Y	Y	Y	Y	Y	Y
6 Carr	Y	Y	Y	Y	Y	Y	Y	Y
7 Kildee	Y	Y	Y	Y	Y	Y	Y	Y
8 Traxler	?	?	Y	Y	Y	Y	Y	Y
9 *Vander Jagt*	?	?	Y	Y	Y	Y	Y	Y
10 Albosta	Y	Y	Y	Y	Y	Y	Y	Y
11 *Davis*	N	Y	Y	Y	Y	Y	Y	Y
12 Bonior	Y	Y	Y	Y	Y	Y	Y	Y
13 Crockett	Y	Y	Y	Y	Y	Y	Y	Y
14 Hertel	?	?	Y	Y	Y	Y	Y	Y
15 Ford	Y	Y	Y	Y	Y	Y	Y	Y
16 Dingell	Y	Y	Y	Y	Y	Y	Y	Y
17 Levin	Y	Y	Y	Y	Y	Y	Y	Y
18 *Broomfield*	N	N	Y	Y	Y	Y	Y	Y
MINNESOTA								
1 Penny	Y	Y	Y	Y	Y	?	Y	Y
2 *Weber*	N	N	N	Y	N	N	Y	N
3 *Frenzel*	N	N	N	Y	N	Y	Y	Y
4 Vento	Y	Y	Y	Y	Y	Y	Y	Y
5 Sabo	Y	Y	Y	Y	Y	Y	Y	Y
6 Sikorski	Y	Y	Y	Y	Y	Y	Y	Y
7 *Stangeland*	N	N	Y	Y	N	Y	Y	Y
8 Oberstar	Y	Y	Y	Y	Y	Y	Y	Y
MISSISSIPPI								
1 Whitten	Y	Y	Y	Y	Y	Y	Y	Y
2 *Franklin*	?	N	Y	Y	Y	Y	Y	Y
3 Montgomery	N	N	Y	Y	N	Y	Y	Y
4 Dowdy	Y	Y	Y	Y	Y	Y	Y	Y
5 *Lott*	?	?	Y	Y	Y	Y	Y	Y
MISSOURI								
1 Clay	Y	Y	Y	Y	Y	Y	Y	Y
2 Young	Y	Y	Y	Y	Y	Y	Y	Y
3 Gephardt	Y	Y	Y	Y	Y	Y	Y	Y
4 Skelton	Y	Y	Y	Y	Y	N	Y	N
5 Wheat	Y	Y	Y	Y	Y	Y	Y	Y
6 *Coleman*	N	N	Y	Y	?	Y	Y	Y
7 *Taylor*	N	N	N	Y	Y	Y	Y	Y
8 *Emerson*	N	N	Y	Y	N	N	Y	N
9 Volkmer	N	Y	Y	Y	Y	Y	Y	Y
MONTANA								
1 Williams	Y	Y	Y	Y	Y	N	Y	Y
2 *Marlenee*	?	?	Y	Y	Y	Y	Y	Y
NEBRASKA								
1 *Bereuter*	?	?	N	Y	N	Y	Y	Y
2 *Daub*	N	N	N	Y	N	Y	Y	N
3 *Smith*	?	?	N	Y	N	Y	Y	N
NEVADA								
1 Reid	Y	Y	Y	Y	Y	Y	Y	Y
2 *Vucanovich*	N	N	N	Y	N	Y	Y	Y
NEW HAMPSHIRE								
1 D'Amours	Y	Y	Y	Y	Y	Y	Y	Y
2 *Gregg*	N	N	Y	Y	N	Y	Y	Y
NEW JERSEY								
1 Florio	Y	Y	Y	Y	Y	Y	Y	Y
2 Hughes	Y	N	Y	Y	Y	Y	Y	Y
3 Howard	Y	Y	Y	Y	Y	Y	Y	Y
4 *Smith*	N	Y	Y	Y	Y	Y	Y	Y
5 *Roukema*	N	N	Y	Y	Y	Y	Y	Y
6 Dwyer	?	#	Y	Y	Y	Y	Y	Y
7 *Rinaldo*	Y	Y	Y	Y	Y	Y	Y	Y
8 Roe	Y	Y	Y	Y	Y	Y	Y	Y
9 Torricelli	?	?	Y	Y	Y	Y	Y	Y
10 Rodino	Y	Y	Y	Y	Y	Y	Y	Y
11 Minish	Y	Y	Y	Y	Y	Y	Y	Y
12 *Courter*	N	N	Y	Y	Y	Y	Y	Y
13 *Forsythe*	N	N	Y	Y	Y	Y	Y	Y
14 Guarini	Y	Y	Y	Y	Y	Y	Y	Y
NEW MEXICO								
1 *Lujan*	?	?	Y	Y	Y	Y	Y	Y
2 *Skeen*	?	?	Y	Y	N	Y	Y	Y
3 Richardson	Y	Y	Y	Y	Y	Y	Y	Y
NEW YORK								
1 *Carney*	N	N	Y	Y	N	Y	Y	Y
2 Downey	Y	#	Y	Y	Y	Y	Y	Y
3 Mrazek	Y	?	Y	Y	N	N	Y	Y
4 *Lent*	Y	Y	Y	Y	Y	Y	Y	Y
5 *McGrath*	Y	Y	Y	Y	Y	Y	Y	Y
6 Addabbo	?	#	Y	Y	Y	Y	Y	Y
7 Ackerman	Y	Y	Y	Y	Y	Y	Y	Y
8 Scheuer	Y	?	Y	Y	Y	Y	Y	Y
9 Ferraro	Y	Y	Y	Y	Y	Y	Y	Y
10 Schumer	Y	Y	Y	Y	Y	Y	Y	Y
11 Towns	Y	Y	Y	Y	Y	Y	Y	Y
12 Owens	?	?	Y	Y	Y	Y	Y	Y
13 Solarz	Y	Y	Y	Y	Y	Y	Y	Y
14 *Molinari*	Y	Y	Y	Y	Y	Y	Y	Y
15 *Green*	Y	Y	Y	Y	Y	Y	Y	Y
16 Rangel	Y	Y	Y	Y	Y	Y	Y	Y
17 Weiss	Y	Y	Y	Y	Y	N	Y	Y
18 Garcia	Y	Y	Y	Y	Y	Y	Y	Y
19 Biaggi	Y	Y	+	+	+	+	+	+
20 Ottinger	Y	Y	Y	Y	Y	Y	Y	Y
21 *Fish*	Y	Y	Y	Y	Y	Y	Y	Y
22 *Gilman*	Y	Y	Y	Y	Y	Y	Y	?
23 Stratton	Y	Y	Y	Y	Y	Y	Y	Y
24 *Solomon*	N	N	N	Y	N	Y	Y	N
25 *Boehlert*	Y	Y	Y	Y	Y	Y	Y	Y
26 *Martin*	?	?	N	Y	Y	Y	Y	Y
27 *Wortley*	Y	Y	N	Y	N	Y	Y	Y
28 McHugh	Y	Y	Y	Y	Y	Y	Y	Y
29 *Horton*	?	?	Y	Y	Y	Y	Y	Y
30 *Conable*	N	N	Y	Y	N	N	Y	Y
31 *Kemp*	Y	N	Y	Y	Y	Y	Y	Y
32 LaFalce	Y	Y	Y	Y	Y	Y	Y	Y
33 Nowak	Y	Y	Y	Y	Y	Y	Y	Y
34 Lundine	Y	Y	Y	Y	Y	Y	Y	Y
NORTH CAROLINA								
1 Jones	Y	Y	Y	Y	Y	Y	Y	Y
2 Valentine	N	Y	Y	Y	Y	Y	Y	Y
3 Whitley	Y	Y	Y	Y	Y	Y	Y	Y
4 Andrews	N	Y	Y	Y	Y	Y	Y	Y
5 Neal	?	?	Y	Y	Y	Y	Y	Y
6 Britt	Y	Y	Y	Y	Y	Y	Y	Y
7 Rose	Y	Y	Y	Y	Y	Y	Y	Y
8 Hefner	?	?	Y	Y	Y	Y	Y	Y
9 *Martin*	N	N	N	Y	N	Y	Y	Y
10 *Broyhill*	N	N	N	Y	Y	Y	Y	Y
11 Clarke	Y	Y	Y	Y	Y	Y	Y	Y
NORTH DAKOTA								
AL Dorgan	Y	Y	Y	Y	Y	Y	Y	Y
OHIO								
1 Luken	Y	Y	Y	Y	Y	N	Y	Y
2 *Gradison*	N	N	N	Y	N	N	Y	Y
3 Hall	N	Y	Y	Y	N	Y	Y	Y
4 *Oxley*	N	N	?	?	?	?	?	?
5 *Latta*	Y	N	N	Y	N	N	Y	Y
6 *McEwen*	N	N	N	Y	Y	Y	Y	Y
7 *DeWine*	N	N	N	Y	N	Y	Y	N
8 *Kindness*	N	N	N	Y	N	Y	Y	Y
9 Kaptur	Y	Y	Y	Y	Y	N	Y	Y
10 *Miller*	N	N	N	Y	N	N	Y	Y
11 Eckart	Y	Y	Y	Y	Y	Y	Y	Y
12 *Kasich*	N	N	N	Y	N	Y	Y	Y
13 Pease	N	Y	Y	Y	Y	N	Y	Y
14 Seiberling	Y	Y	Y	Y	Y	N	Y	Y
15 *Wylie*	?	?	N	Y	N	N	Y	Y
16 *Regula*	N	N	N	Y	Y	N	Y	Y
17 *Williams*	N	Y	Y	Y	?	Y	Y	Y
18 Applegate	Y	N	Y	Y	Y	N	Y	Y
19 Feighan	Y	Y	Y	Y	Y	Y	Y	Y
20 Oakar	Y	Y	Y	Y	Y	Y	Y	Y
21 Stokes	Y	Y	Y	Y	Y	?	Y	Y
OKLAHOMA								
1 Jones	?	#	Y	Y	N	Y	Y	N
2 Synar	Y	Y	Y	Y	Y	Y	Y	Y
3 Watkins	Y	Y	Y	Y	N	N	Y	N
4 McCurdy	Y	Y	Y	Y	N	Y	Y	Y
5 *Edwards*	Y	Y	N	Y	N	N	Y	Y
6 English	Y	Y	Y	Y	N	Y	Y	Y
OREGON								
1 AuCoin	Y	Y	Y	Y	Y	Y	Y	Y
2 *Smith, R.*	?	X	N	Y	Y	Y	Y	Y
3 Wyden	Y	Y	Y	Y	Y	Y	Y	Y
4 Weaver	Y	Y	Y	Y	N	N	Y	Y
5 *Smith, D.*	N	N	N	Y	N	N	Y	N
PENNSYLVANIA								
1 Foglietta	Y	Y	Y	Y	Y	Y	Y	Y
2 Gray	Y	Y	Y	Y	Y	Y	Y	Y
3 Borski	Y	Y	Y	Y	Y	Y	Y	Y
4 Kolter	Y	Y	Y	Y	Y	Y	Y	Y
5 *Schulze*	N	N	N	Y	Y	Y	Y	Y
6 Yatron	Y	Y	Y	Y	Y	N	Y	Y
7 Edgar	Y	Y	Y	Y	Y	Y	Y	Y
8 Kostmayer	Y	Y	Y	Y	Y	Y	Y	Y
9 *Shuster*	N	N	N	Y	N	Y	Y	N
10 *McDade*	?	?	Y	Y	Y	Y	Y	Y
11 Harrison	Y	Y	Y	Y	Y	Y	Y	Y
12 Murtha	Y	Y	Y	Y	Y	N	Y	Y
13 *Coughlin*	N	Y	N	Y	N	N	Y	Y
14 Coyne	Y	Y	Y	Y	Y	Y	Y	Y
15 *Ritter*	?	?	Y	Y	N	Y	Y	Y
16 *Walker*	N	N	N	Y	N	Y	Y	N
17 *Gekas*	N	N	N	Y	N	Y	Y	N
18 Walgren	Y	Y	Y	Y	Y	N	Y	Y
19 *Goodling*	N	N	N	Y	Y	Y	Y	Y
20 Gaydos	Y	Y	Y	Y	Y	N	Y	Y
21 *Ridge*	N	Y	Y	Y	Y	Y	Y	Y
22 Murphy	?	?	Y	Y	Y	N	Y	Y
23 *Clinger*	Y	Y	N	Y	Y	Y	Y	Y
RHODE ISLAND								
1 St Germain	Y	Y	Y	Y	Y	Y	Y	Y
2 *Schneider*	Y	Y	N	Y	Y	Y	Y	Y
SOUTH CAROLINA								
1 *Hartnett*	N	N	N	Y	N	Y	Y	N
2 *Spence*	N	N	N	Y	N	Y	Y	Y
3 Derrick	?	?	Y	Y	Y	Y	Y	Y
4 *Campbell*	Y	N	Y	Y	N	Y	Y	Y
5 Spratt	?	?	Y	Y	Y	Y	Y	Y
6 Tallon	Y	Y	Y	Y	Y	Y	Y	Y
SOUTH DAKOTA								
AL Daschle	?	?	Y	Y	Y	Y	Y	Y
TENNESSEE								
1 *Quillen*	?	?	Y	Y	N	N	Y	Y
2 *Duncan*	Y	Y	Y	Y	Y	Y	Y	Y
3 Lloyd	?	?	Y	Y	Y	Y	Y	Y
4 Cooper	?	?	Y	Y	Y	Y	?	Y
5 Boner	Y	Y	Y	Y	Y	Y	Y	Y
6 Gore	Y	Y	Y	Y	Y	Y	Y	Y
7 *Sundquist*	N	N	N	Y	N	Y	Y	Y
8 Jones	Y	Y	Y	Y	Y	Y	Y	Y
9 Ford	?	?	Y	Y	Y	Y	Y	Y
TEXAS								
1 Hall, S.	N	N	Y	Y	Y	Y	Y	N
2 Wilson	Y	Y	Y	Y	Y	Y	Y	Y
3 *Bartlett*	N	N	N	Y	N	N	Y	Y
4 Hall, R.	N	Y	Y	Y	N	N	Y	N
5 Bryant	Y	Y	Y	Y	Y	Y	Y	Y
6 *Gramm*	N	N	N	Y	N	N	Y	N
7 *Archer*	?	?	N	Y	N	N	Y	Y
8 *Fields*	N	N	N	Y	N	Y	Y	Y
9 Brooks	Y	Y	Y	Y	Y	Y	Y	Y
10 Pickle	Y	Y	Y	Y	Y	Y	Y	Y
11 Leath	?	?	Y	Y	N	Y	Y	Y
12 Wright	Y	Y	Y	Y	Y	Y	Y	Y
13 Hightower	N	N	Y	Y	Y	Y	Y	Y
14 Patman	N	N	Y	Y	Y	Y	Y	Y
15 de la Garza	Y	Y	Y	Y	Y	Y	Y	Y
16 Coleman	Y	Y	Y	Y	Y	Y	Y	Y
17 Stenholm	N	N	Y	Y	N	Y	Y	N
18 Leland	Y	Y	Y	Y	Y	Y	Y	Y
19 Hance	?	X	Y	Y	N	Y	Y	Y
20 Gonzalez	Y	Y	Y	Y	Y	Y	Y	Y
21 *Loeffler*	N	N	Y	Y	N	Y	Y	Y
22 *Paul*	N	N	N	N	N	N	N	N
23 Kazen	N	Y	Y	Y	Y	Y	Y	Y
24 Frost	Y	Y	Y	Y	Y	Y	Y	Y
25 Andrews	Y	Y	Y	Y	Y	Y	Y	Y
26 Vandergriff	N	Y	Y	Y	?	Y	Y	Y
27 Ortiz	Y	Y	Y	Y	Y	Y	Y	Y
UTAH								
1 *Hansen*	N	N	N	Y	N	N	Y	N
2 *Marriott*	N	N	N	Y	Y	Y	Y	Y
3 *Nielson*	N	N	N	Y	Y	Y	Y	Y
VERMONT								
AL *Jeffords*	N	Y	Y	Y	Y	Y	Y	Y
VIRGINIA								
1 *Bateman*	N	Y	Y	Y	Y	Y	Y	Y
2 *Whitehurst*	?	X	N	Y	Y	Y	Y	Y
3 *Bliley*	N	N	N	Y	Y	Y	Y	Y
4 Sisisky	Y	Y	Y	Y	Y	Y	Y	Y
5 Daniel	N	N	N	Y	N	Y	Y	Y
6 Olin	Y	Y	Y	Y	Y	Y	Y	Y
7 *Robinson*	N	N	N	Y	Y	Y	Y	Y
8 *Parris*	N	Y	N	Y	Y	Y	Y	N
9 Boucher	Y	Y	Y	Y	Y	Y	Y	Y
10 *Wolf*	N	Y	Y	Y	Y	Y	Y	Y
WASHINGTON								
1 *Pritchard*	N	Y	Y	Y	Y	N	Y	Y
2 Swift	?	?	Y	Y	Y	Y	Y	Y
3 Bonker	Y	Y	Y	Y	Y	Y	Y	Y
4 *Morrison*	N	Y	Y	Y	Y	Y	Y	Y
5 Foley	Y	Y	Y	Y	Y	Y	Y	Y
6 Dicks	Y	Y	Y	Y	Y	Y	Y	Y
7 Lowry	Y	Y	Y	Y	Y	N	Y	Y
8 *Chandler*	N	N	Y	Y	Y	Y	Y	Y
WEST VIRGINIA								
1 Mollohan	Y	Y	Y	Y	N	N	Y	Y
2 Staggers	Y	Y	Y	Y	Y	Y	Y	Y
3 Wise	Y	Y	Y	Y	Y	Y	Y	Y
4 Rahall	Y	Y	Y	Y	N	N	Y	Y
WISCONSIN								
1 Aspin	Y	Y	Y	Y	Y	Y	Y	Y
2 Kastenmeier	Y	Y	Y	Y	Y	Y	Y	Y
3 *Gunderson*	N	N	Y	Y	Y	Y	Y	Y
4 Zablocki	Y	Y	Y	Y	Y	Y	Y	Y
5 Moody	Y	Y	Y	Y	Y	Y	Y	Y
6 *Petri*	N	N	N	Y	N	N	N	N
7 Obey	Y	Y	Y	Y	Y	Y	Y	Y
8 *Roth*	N	N	N	Y	Y	N	Y	Y
9 *Sensenbrenner*	N	N	N	Y	N	N	Y	N
WYOMING								
AL *Cheney*	?	X	N	Y	N	Y	Y	N

Southern states - Ala., Ark., Fla., Ga., Ky., La., Miss., N.C., Okla., S.C., Tenn., Texas, Va.

KEY

Y Voted for (yea).
Paired for.
+ Announced for.
N Voted against (nay).
X Paired against.
- Announced against.
P Voted "present".
C Voted "present" to avoid possible conflict of interest.
? Did not vote or otherwise make a position known.

Democrats   *Republicans*

115. HR 2973. Interest and Dividend Tax Withholding. Rostenkowski, D-Ill., motion to suspend the rules and pass the bill to repeal provisions of 1982 legislation (PL 97-248) requiring banks and financial institutions to begin withholding taxes from interest and dividend income on July 1, 1983. Motion agreed to 382-41: R 157-9; D 225-32 (ND 141-29, SD 84-3), May 17, 1983. A two-thirds majority of those present and voting (282 in this case) is required for passage under suspension of the rules. A "nay" was a vote supporting the president's position.

116. S J Res 51. Andrei Sakharov Day. Passage of the joint resolution to designate May 21, 1983, as "National Andrei Sakharov Day" in honor of the 62nd birthday of the dissident Soviet physicist who was exiled in the city of Gorky and refused permission to emigrate. Passed 420-0: R 165-0; D 255-0 (ND 167-0, SD 88-0), May 17, 1983.

117. H J Res 226. Digestive Diseases Awareness Week. Passage of the joint resolution to designate the week of May 22-28, 1983, as "National Digestive Diseases Awareness Week." Passed 408-13: R 160-5; D 248-8 (ND 164-4, SD 84-4), May 17, 1983.

118. Procedural Motion. Whittaker, R-Kan., motion to approve the House *Journal* of Tuesday, May 17. Motion agreed to 367-17: R 143-8; D 224-9 (ND 142-8, SD 82-1), May 18, 1983.

119. H Res 200. Lavelle Contempt of Congress Resolution. Adoption of the resolution to cite Rita M. Lavelle, former assistant administrator of the Environmental Protection Agency, for contempt of Congress for refusing to testify in response to a subpoena of the House Energy and Commerce Subcommittee on Oversight and Investigations. Adopted 413-0: R 158-0; D 255-0 (ND 170-0, SD 85-0), May 18, 1983.

120. HR 2990. Debt Limit Extension. Frost, D-Texas, motion to order the previous question (thus ending debate and the possibility of amendment) on the rule (H Res 196) providing for House floor consideration of the bill to raise the public debt limit to $1.389 trillion through Sept. 30, 1983. Motion agreed to 249-171: R 1-162; D 248-9 (ND 169-2, SD 79-7), May 18, 1983.

121. HR 2990. Debt Limit Extension. Adoption of the rule (H Res 196) providing for House floor consideration of the bill to raise the public debt limit to $1.389 trillion through Sept. 30, 1983. Adopted 263-156: R 23-141; D 240-15 (ND 167-3, SD 73-12), May 18, 1983. (The bill subsequently was passed by voice vote.)

	115	116	117	118	119	120	121
ALABAMA							
1 *Edwards*	N	Y	Y	?	Y	N	Y
2 *Dickinson*	Y	Y	Y	N	Y	N	N
3 Nichols	?	?	?	?	?	?	?
4 Bevill	Y	Y	Y	Y	Y	Y	Y
5 Flippo	Y	Y	Y	Y	Y	Y	Y
6 Erdreich	Y	Y	Y	Y	Y	Y	Y
7 Shelby	Y	Y	Y	Y	Y	N	N
ALASKA							
AL *Young*	Y	Y	Y	?	Y	N	N
ARIZONA							
1 *McCain*	Y	Y	Y	Y	Y	N	N
2 Udall	Y	Y	Y	Y	Y	Y	Y
3 *Stump*	Y	Y	N	Y	Y	N	N
4 *Rudd*	Y	Y	Y	Y	Y	N	N
5 McNulty	Y	Y	Y	Y	Y	Y	Y
ARKANSAS							
1 Alexander	Y	Y	Y	Y	Y	Y	Y
2 *Bethune*	Y	Y	Y	Y	Y	N	N
3 *Hammerschmidt*	Y	Y	Y	Y	Y	N	N
4 Anthony	Y	Y	Y	Y	Y	Y	Y
CALIFORNIA							
1 Bosco	Y	Y	Y	Y	Y	Y	Y
2 *Chappie*	Y	Y	Y	Y	Y	N	N
3 Matsui	N	Y	Y	Y	Y	Y	Y
4 Fazio	Y	Y	Y	Y	Y	Y	Y
5 Vacancy							
6 Boxer	Y	Y	Y	Y	Y	Y	Y
7 Miller	N	Y	Y	Y	Y	Y	Y
8 Dellums	Y	Y	Y	Y	Y	Y	Y
9 Stark	N	Y	Y	?	Y	Y	Y
10 Edwards	N	Y	Y	Y	Y	Y	Y
11 Lantos	Y	Y	Y	Y	Y	Y	Y
12 *Zschau*	Y	Y	Y	Y	Y	N	Y
13 Mineta	Y	Y	Y	Y	Y	Y	Y
14 *Shumway*	Y	Y	Y	Y	Y	N	N
15 Coelho	Y	Y	?	Y	Y	Y	Y
16 Panetta	N	Y	Y	Y	Y	Y	Y
17 *Pashayan*	Y	Y	Y	Y	Y	N	N
18 Lehman	Y	Y	Y	Y	Y	Y	Y
19 *Lagomarsino*	Y	Y	Y	Y	Y	N	N
20 *Thomas*	Y	?	Y	Y	Y	N	Y
21 *Fiedler*	Y	Y	Y	Y	Y	N	N
22 *Moorhead*	Y	Y	Y	Y	Y	N	N
23 Beilenson	N	Y	Y	Y	Y	Y	Y
24 Waxman	N	Y	Y	Y	Y	Y	Y
25 Roybal	Y	Y	Y	Y	Y	Y	Y
26 Berman	N	Y	Y	Y	Y	Y	Y
27 Levine	Y	Y	Y	Y	Y	Y	Y
28 Dixon	Y	Y	Y	Y	Y	Y	Y
29 Hawkins	Y	Y	Y	Y	Y	Y	Y
30 Martinez	?	?	?	?	?	?	?
31 Dymally	?	?	?	?	?	?	?
32 Anderson	Y	Y	Y	Y	Y	Y	Y
33 *Dreier*	Y	Y	Y	Y	Y	N	N
34 Torres	Y	?	Y	Y	Y	Y	Y
35 *Lewis*	Y	Y	Y	Y	Y	N	N
36 Brown	Y	Y	Y	Y	Y	Y	Y
37 *McCandless*	Y	Y	Y	Y	Y	N	N
38 Patterson	Y	Y	Y	Y	Y	Y	Y
39 *Dannemeyer*	Y	Y	Y	Y	Y	N	N
40 *Badham*	Y	Y	Y	Y	Y	N	N
41 *Lowery*	Y	Y	Y	Y	Y	N	N
42 *Lungren*	Y	Y	Y	Y	Y	N	N
43 *Packard*	Y	Y	Y	Y	Y	N	N
44 Bates	Y	Y	Y	Y	Y	Y	Y
45 *Hunter*	Y	Y	Y	Y	Y	N	N
COLORADO							
1 Schroeder	Y	Y	Y	N	Y	N	N
2 Wirth	Y	Y	Y	Y	Y	Y	Y
3 Kogovsek	Y	Y	Y	Y	Y	Y	Y
4 *Brown*	Y	Y	Y	N	Y	N	N
5 *Kramer*	Y	Y	Y	Y	Y	N	N
6 *Schaefer*	Y	Y	Y	Y	Y	N	N
CONNECTICUT							
1 Kennelly	Y	Y	Y	Y	Y	Y	Y
2 Gejdenson	Y	Y	Y	N	Y	Y	Y
3 Morrison	Y	Y	Y	Y	Y	Y	Y
4 *McKinney*	Y	Y	Y	Y	Y	Y	Y
5 Ratchford	Y	Y	Y	Y	Y	Y	Y
6 *Johnson*	Y	Y	Y	?	Y	N	Y
DELAWARE							
AL Carper	+	Y	Y	Y	Y	Y	Y
FLORIDA							
1 Hutto	Y	Y	Y	Y	Y	Y	Y
2 Fuqua	Y	Y	Y	Y	Y	Y	Y
3 Bennett	N	Y	Y	Y	Y	Y	Y
4 Chappell	Y	Y	Y	?	Y	Y	Y
5 *McCollum*	Y	Y	Y	Y	Y	N	N
6 MacKay	Y	Y	Y	Y	Y	Y	Y
7 Gibbons	Y	Y	Y	Y	Y	?	?
8 *Young*	Y	Y	Y	Y	Y	N	N
9 *Bilirakis*	Y	Y	Y	Y	Y	N	N
10 Ireland	Y	Y	Y	Y	Y	Y	Y
11 Nelson	Y	Y	Y	Y	Y	Y	Y
12 *Lewis*	Y	Y	Y	Y	Y	N	N
13 *Mack*	Y	Y	Y	Y	Y	N	N
14 Mica	Y	Y	Y	Y	Y	Y	Y
15 *Shaw*	Y	Y	Y	Y	Y	N	N
16 Smith	Y	Y	Y	Y	Y	Y	Y
17 Lehman	Y	Y	Y	Y	Y	Y	Y
18 Pepper	Y	Y	Y	Y	Y	Y	Y
19 Fascell	Y	Y	Y	Y	Y	Y	Y
GEORGIA							
1 Thomas	Y	Y	Y	Y	Y	Y	Y
2 Hatcher	Y	Y	Y	Y	Y	Y	Y
3 Ray	+	Y	Y	Y	Y	Y	Y
4 Levitas	Y	Y	Y	Y	Y	Y	Y
5 Fowler	Y	Y	Y	Y	Y	Y	Y
6 *Gingrich*	Y	Y	Y	Y	Y	N	N
7 McDonald	Y	Y	N	?	Y	N	N
8 Rowland	Y	Y	Y	Y	Y	Y	Y
9 Jenkins	Y	Y	Y	Y	Y	Y	Y
10 Barnard	Y	Y	Y	Y	Y	Y	Y
HAWAII							
1 Heftel	?	?	?	?	?	?	?
2 Akaka	Y	Y	Y	Y	Y	Y	Y
IDAHO							
1 *Craig*	Y	Y	Y	Y	Y	N	N
2 *Hansen*	Y	Y	N	?	?	N	N
ILLINOIS							
1 Vacancy							
2 Savage	Y	Y	Y	Y	Y	Y	Y
3 Russo	Y	Y	Y	Y	Y	Y	Y
4 *O'Brien*	Y	Y	Y	Y	Y	N	N
5 Lipinski	Y	Y	Y	Y	Y	Y	Y
6 *Hyde*	Y	Y	Y	Y	Y	N	Y
7 Collins	Y	Y	Y	Y	Y	Y	Y
8 Rostenkowski	N	Y	Y	Y	Y	Y	Y
9 Yates	N	Y	Y	N	Y	Y	Y
10 *Porter*	Y	Y	Y	Y	Y	N	N
11 Annunzio	Y	Y	Y	Y	Y	Y	Y
12 *Crane, P.*	Y	Y	Y	Y	Y	N	N
13 *Erlenborn*	N	Y	N	Y	Y	N	Y
14 *Corcoran*	Y	Y	Y	Y	Y	N	N
15 *Madigan*	Y	Y	Y	Y	Y	N	N
16 *Martin*	N	Y	Y	Y	Y	N	N
17 Evans	Y	Y	Y	Y	Y	Y	Y
18 *Michel*	Y	Y	Y	?	?	?	?
19 *Crane, D.*	Y	Y	Y	Y	Y	N	N
20 Durbin	Y	Y	Y	N	Y	Y	Y
21 Price	Y	Y	Y	Y	Y	Y	Y
22 Simon	Y	?	Y	?	Y	Y	Y
INDIANA							
1 Hall	Y	Y	Y	Y	Y	Y	Y
2 Sharp	Y	Y	Y	Y	Y	Y	Y
3 *Hiler*	Y	Y	Y	Y	Y	N	N
4 *Coats*	Y	Y	Y	Y	Y	N	N
5 *Hillis*	Y	Y	Y	Y	Y	N	N

ND - Northern Democrats   SD - Southern Democrats

Corresponding to Congressional Record Votes 123, 124, 125, 126, 127, 128, 129

	115	116	117	118	119	120	121
6 ***Burton***	Y	Y	Y	?	Y	N	N
7 ***Myers***	Y	Y	Y	Y	Y	N	N
8 McCloskey	Y	Y	Y	Y	Y	Y	Y
9 Hamilton	Y	Y	Y	Y	Y	Y	Y
10 Jacobs	Y	Y	Y	P	Y	N	N
IOWA							
1 ***Leach***	Y	Y	Y	Y	?	N	N
2 ***Tauke***	Y	Y	Y	Y	Y	N	Y
3 ***Evans***	Y	Y	Y	N	Y	N	N
4 Smith	Y	Y	Y	Y	Y	Y	Y
5 Harkin	Y	Y	Y	?	Y	Y	Y
6 Bedell	Y	Y	N	Y	Y	Y	Y
KANSAS							
1 ***Roberts***	Y	Y	Y	Y	Y	N	N
2 Slattery	Y	Y	N	Y	Y	Y	Y
3 ***Winn***	Y	Y	Y	Y	Y	N	N
4 Glickman	Y	Y	Y	Y	Y	Y	Y
5 ***Whittaker***	Y	Y	Y	Y	Y	N	N
KENTUCKY							
1 Hubbard	Y	Y	Y	?	?	?	?
2 Natcher	Y	Y	Y	Y	Y	Y	Y
3 Mazzoli	N	Y	Y	Y	Y	Y	Y
4 ***Snyder***	Y	Y	Y	Y	Y	N	N
5 ***Rogers***	Y	Y	Y	Y	Y	N	N
6 ***Hopkins***	Y	Y	Y	Y	Y	N	N
7 Perkins	Y	Y	Y	Y	Y	Y	Y
LOUISIANA							
1 ***Livingston***	Y	Y	Y	Y	Y	N	N
2 Boggs	Y	Y	Y	Y	Y	Y	Y
3 Tauzin	Y	Y	Y	Y	Y	N	N
4 Roemer	Y	Y	Y	N	Y	N	N
5 Huckaby	Y	Y	Y	Y	Y	N	N
6 ***Moore***	Y	Y	Y	Y	Y	N	N
7 Breaux	Y	Y	Y	Y	Y	Y	Y
8 Long	Y	Y	Y	Y	Y	Y	Y
MAINE							
1 ***McKernan***	Y	Y	Y	Y	Y	N	N
2 ***Snowe***	Y	Y	Y	Y	Y	N	Y
MARYLAND							
1 Dyson	Y	Y	Y	Y	Y	Y	Y
2 Long	Y	Y	Y	Y	Y	Y	Y
3 Mikulski	Y	Y	Y	Y	Y	Y	Y
4 ***Holt***	Y	Y	Y	Y	Y	N	N
5 Hoyer	Y	Y	Y	Y	Y	Y	Y
6 Byron	Y	Y	N	Y	Y	Y	Y
7 Mitchell	Y	Y	Y	N	Y	Y	Y
8 Barnes	Y	Y	Y	Y	Y	Y	Y
MASSACHUSETTS							
1 ***Conte***	Y	Y	Y	Y	Y	N	Y
2 Boland	N	Y	Y	Y	Y	Y	?
3 Early	N	Y	Y	Y	Y	Y	Y
4 Frank	Y	Y	Y	Y	Y	Y	Y
5 Shannon	N	?	?	?	?	Y	Y
6 Mavroules	Y	Y	Y	Y	Y	Y	Y
7 Markey	N	Y	Y	Y	Y	Y	Y
8 O'Neill							
9 Moakley	Y	Y	Y	+	Y	Y	Y
10 Studds	Y	Y	Y	Y	Y	Y	Y
11 Donnelly	Y	Y	Y	Y	Y	Y	Y
MICHIGAN							
1 Conyers	N	Y	Y	?	Y	Y	Y
2 ***Pursell***	Y	Y	Y	Y	Y	N	N
3 Wolpe	Y	Y	Y	Y	Y	Y	Y
4 ***Siljander***	Y	Y	Y	Y	Y	N	N
5 ***Sawyer***	N	Y	Y	Y	Y	N	Y
6 Carr	Y	Y	Y	?	?	?	?
7 Kildee	Y	Y	Y	Y	Y	Y	Y
8 Traxler	Y	Y	Y	Y	Y	Y	Y
9 ***Vander Jagt***	Y	Y	Y	Y	Y	N	N
10 Albosta	Y	Y	Y	Y	Y	Y	Y
11 ***Davis***	Y	Y	Y	Y	Y	N	Y
12 Bonior	Y	Y	Y	Y	Y	Y	Y
13 Crockett	N	Y	Y	Y	Y	Y	Y
14 Hertel	Y	Y	Y	Y	Y	Y	Y
15 Ford	Y	Y	Y	Y	Y	Y	Y
16 Dingell	Y	Y	Y	Y	Y	Y	Y
17 Levin	N	Y	Y	Y	Y	Y	Y
18 ***Broomfield***	Y	Y	Y	Y	Y	N	N
MINNESOTA							
1 Penny	Y	Y	Y	Y	Y	Y	Y
2 ***Weber***	Y	Y	Y	Y	Y	N	N
3 ***Frenzel***	Y	Y	Y	Y	Y	N	Y
4 Vento	Y	Y	Y	Y	Y	Y	Y
5 Sabo	N	Y	Y	N	Y	Y	Y
6 Sikorski	Y	Y	Y	Y	Y	Y	Y
7 ***Stangeland***	Y	Y	Y	?	Y	N	N
8 Oberstar	Y	Y	Y	?	Y	Y	Y
MISSISSIPPI							
1 Whitten	Y	Y	Y	Y	Y	Y	Y
2 ***Franklin***	Y	Y	Y	Y	Y	N	N
3 Montgomery	Y	Y	Y	Y	Y	Y	N
4 Dowdy	Y	Y	Y	Y	Y	Y	Y
5 ***Lott***	Y	Y	Y	?	Y	N	Y
MISSOURI							
1 Clay	Y	Y	Y	?	Y	Y	Y
2 Young	Y	Y	Y	Y	Y	Y	Y
3 Gephardt	Y	Y	Y	Y	Y	Y	Y
4 Skelton	Y	Y	Y	Y	Y	Y	Y
5 Wheat	Y	Y	Y	Y	Y	Y	Y
6 ***Coleman***	Y	Y	Y	Y	Y	N	N
7 ***Taylor***	Y	Y	Y	Y	Y	N	N
8 ***Emerson***	Y	Y	Y	N	Y	N	N
9 Volkmer	Y	Y	Y	Y	Y	Y	Y
MONTANA							
1 Williams	Y	Y	Y	?	Y	Y	Y
2 ***Marlenee***	Y	Y	Y	?	?	N	N
NEBRASKA							
1 ***Bereuter***	Y	Y	Y	Y	Y	N	N
2 ***Daub***	Y	Y	Y	Y	Y	N	N
3 ***Smith***	Y	Y	Y	Y	Y	N	N
NEVADA							
1 Reid	Y	Y	Y	Y	Y	Y	Y
2 ***Vucanovich***	Y	Y	Y	Y	Y	N	N
NEW HAMPSHIRE							
1 D'Amours	Y	Y	Y	?	Y	Y	Y
2 ***Gregg***	Y	Y	Y	Y	Y	N	N
NEW JERSEY							
1 Florio	Y	Y	Y	Y	Y	Y	Y
2 Hughes	Y	Y	Y	Y	Y	Y	Y
3 Howard	Y	Y	Y	?	Y	Y	Y
4 ***Smith***	Y	Y	Y	Y	Y	N	N
5 ***Roukema***	Y	Y	Y	Y	Y	N	Y
6 Dwyer	Y	Y	Y	Y	Y	Y	Y
7 ***Rinaldo***	Y	Y	Y	Y	Y	N	N
8 Roe	Y	Y	Y	Y	Y	Y	Y
9 Torricelli	Y	Y	Y	Y	Y	Y	Y
10 Rodino	Y	Y	Y	?	Y	Y	Y
11 Minish	Y	Y	Y	Y	Y	Y	Y
12 ***Courter***	Y	Y	Y	Y	Y	N	N
13 ***Forsythe***	Y	Y	Y	N	Y	N	N
14 Guarini	Y	Y	Y	Y	Y	Y	Y
NEW MEXICO							
1 ***Lujan***	Y	Y	Y	Y	Y	N	N
2 ***Skeen***	Y	Y	Y	Y	Y	N	N
3 Richardson	Y	Y	Y	Y	Y	Y	Y
NEW YORK							
1 ***Carney***	Y	Y	Y	Y	Y	N	N
2 Downey	N	Y	Y	Y	Y	Y	Y
3 Mrazek	Y	Y	Y	Y	Y	Y	Y
4 ***Lent***	Y	Y	Y	Y	Y	N	N
5 ***McGrath***	Y	Y	Y	Y	Y	N	N
6 Addabbo	Y	Y	Y	Y	Y	Y	Y
7 Ackerman	Y	Y	Y	Y	Y	Y	Y
8 Scheuer	Y	Y	Y	Y	Y	Y	Y
9 Ferraro	Y	Y	Y	Y	Y	Y	Y
10 Schumer	Y	Y	Y	Y	Y	Y	Y
11 Towns	Y	Y	Y	Y	Y	Y	Y
12 Owens	Y	Y	Y	?	Y	Y	Y
13 Solarz	N	Y	Y	Y	Y	Y	Y
14 ***Molinari***	Y	Y	Y	Y	Y	N	N
15 ***Green***	Y	Y	Y	Y	Y	N	N
16 Rangel	N	Y	Y	Y	Y	Y	Y
17 Weiss	N	Y	Y	Y	Y	Y	Y
18 Garcia	Y	Y	Y	?	Y	Y	Y
19 Biaggi	+	+	+	Y	Y	Y	Y
20 Ottinger	Y	Y	Y	P	Y	Y	Y
21 ***Fish***	Y	Y	Y	Y	Y	N	N
22 ***Gilman***	Y	Y	Y	Y	Y	N	N
23 Stratton	Y	Y	Y	Y	Y	Y	Y
24 ***Solomon***	Y	Y	Y	N	Y	N	N
25 ***Boehlert***	N	Y	Y	Y	Y	N	Y
26 ***Martin***	Y	Y	Y	Y	Y	N	N
27 ***Wortley***	Y	Y	Y	Y	P	N	N
28 McHugh	N	Y	Y	Y	Y	Y	Y
29 ***Horton***	Y	Y	Y	Y	Y	N	Y
30 ***Conable***	N	Y	Y	Y	Y	N	Y
31 ***Kemp***	Y	Y	?	Y	Y	N	N
32 LaFalce	Y	Y	Y	Y	Y	Y	Y
33 Nowak	Y	Y	Y	Y	Y	Y	Y
34 Lundine	Y	Y	Y	Y	Y	Y	Y
NORTH CAROLINA							
1 Jones	Y	Y	Y	Y	Y	Y	Y
2 Valentine	Y	Y	Y	Y	Y	Y	Y
3 Whitley	Y	Y	Y	Y	Y	Y	Y
4 Andrews	Y	Y	Y	?	?	?	?
5 Neal	Y	Y	Y	Y	Y	Y	Y
6 Britt	Y	Y	Y	Y	Y	Y	Y
7 Rose	+	Y	Y	Y	Y	Y	Y
8 Hefner	Y	Y	Y	Y	Y	Y	Y
9 ***Martin***	Y	Y	Y	Y	Y	N	Y
10 ***Broyhill***	Y	Y	Y	Y	Y	N	N
11 Clarke	Y	Y	Y	Y	Y	Y	Y
NORTH DAKOTA							
AL Dorgan	Y	Y	Y	Y	Y	Y	Y
OHIO							
1 Luken	Y	Y	Y	Y	Y	Y	Y
2 ***Gradison***	Y	Y	Y	?	Y	N	Y
3 Hall	Y	Y	Y	Y	Y	Y	Y
4 ***Oxley***	?	?	?	?	?	?	#
5 ***Latta***	Y	Y	Y	Y	Y	N	N
6 ***McEwen***	Y	Y	Y	Y	Y	N	N
7 ***DeWine***	Y	Y	Y	Y	Y	N	N
8 ***Kindness***	Y	Y	Y	Y	Y	N	N
9 Kaptur	Y	?	Y	Y	Y	Y	Y
10 ***Miller***	Y	Y	Y	N	Y	N	N
11 Eckart	Y	Y	Y	Y	Y	Y	Y
12 ***Kasich***	Y	Y	Y	Y	Y	N	N
13 Pease	Y	Y	Y	Y	Y	Y	Y
14 Seiberling	N	Y	N	?	Y	Y	Y
15 ***Wylie***	Y	Y	Y	Y	Y	N	N
16 ***Regula***	Y	Y	Y	Y	Y	N	N
17 ***Williams***	Y	Y	Y	Y	Y	N	N
18 Applegate	Y	Y	Y	Y	Y	Y	Y
19 Feighan	Y	Y	Y	Y	Y	Y	Y
20 Oakar	Y	Y	Y	Y	Y	Y	Y
21 Stokes	Y	Y	Y	Y	Y	Y	Y
OKLAHOMA							
1 Jones	Y	Y	N	Y	Y	Y	Y
2 Synar	Y	Y	Y	Y	Y	Y	Y
3 Watkins	Y	Y	Y	Y	Y	Y	Y
4 McCurdy	Y	Y	Y	Y	Y	Y	Y
5 ***Edwards***	Y	Y	Y	Y	Y	N	N
6 English	Y	Y	Y	Y	Y	Y	N
OREGON							
1 AuCoin	Y	Y	Y	?	Y	Y	Y
2 ***Smith, R.***	Y	Y	Y	Y	Y	N	N
3 Wyden	Y	Y	Y	Y	Y	Y	Y
4 Weaver	Y	Y	Y	Y	Y	Y	N
5 ***Smith, D.***	Y	Y	Y	Y	Y	N	N
PENNSYLVANIA							
1 Foglietta	Y	Y	Y	?	Y	Y	Y
2 Gray	Y	Y	Y	Y	Y	Y	Y
3 Borski	Y	Y	Y	Y	Y	Y	Y
4 Kolter	Y	Y	Y	Y	Y	Y	Y
5 ***Schulze***	Y	Y	Y	Y	Y	N	N
6 Yatron	Y	Y	Y	Y	Y	Y	Y
7 Edgar	Y	Y	Y	Y	Y	Y	Y
8 Kostmayer	Y	Y	Y	Y	Y	Y	Y
9 ***Shuster***	Y	Y	Y	Y	Y	N	N
10 ***McDade***	Y	Y	Y	Y	Y	N	N
11 Harrison	Y	Y	Y	Y	Y	Y	Y
12 Murtha	N	Y	Y	Y	Y	Y	Y
13 ***Coughlin***	Y	Y	Y	Y	Y	N	N
14 Coyne	N	Y	Y	Y	Y	Y	Y
15 ***Ritter***	Y	Y	Y	Y	Y	N	N
16 ***Walker***	Y	Y	Y	N	Y	N	N
17 ***Gekas***	Y	Y	Y	Y	Y	N	N
18 Walgren	Y	Y	Y	Y	Y	Y	Y
19 ***Goodling***	N	Y	Y	P	Y	N	N
20 Gaydos	Y	Y	Y	?	Y	Y	Y
21 ***Ridge***	Y	Y	Y	Y	Y	N	N
22 Murphy	Y	Y	Y	Y	Y	Y	Y
23 ***Clinger***	Y	Y	Y	Y	Y	N	N
RHODE ISLAND							
1 St Germain	Y	Y	Y	Y	Y	Y	Y
2 ***Schneider***	Y	Y	Y	Y	Y	N	N
SOUTH CAROLINA							
1 ***Hartnett***	Y	Y	Y	Y	Y	N	N
2 ***Spence***	Y	Y	Y	Y	Y	N	N
3 Derrick	Y	Y	Y	Y	Y	Y	Y
4 ***Campbell***	Y	Y	Y	Y	Y	N	Y
5 Spratt	Y	Y	Y	Y	Y	Y	Y
6 Tallon	Y	Y	Y	Y	Y	Y	Y
SOUTH DAKOTA							
AL Daschle	Y	Y	Y	Y	Y	Y	Y
TENNESSEE							
1 ***Quillen***	Y	Y	Y	Y	Y	N	N
2 ***Duncan***	Y	Y	Y	Y	Y	N	Y
3 Lloyd	Y	Y	Y	Y	Y	Y	N
4 Cooper	Y	Y	Y	Y	Y	Y	Y
5 Boner	Y	Y	Y	Y	Y	Y	Y
6 Gore	Y	Y	Y	Y	Y	Y	Y
7 ***Sundquist***	Y	Y	Y	Y	Y	N	N
8 Jones	Y	Y	Y	Y	Y	Y	Y
9 Ford	Y	Y	Y	Y	?	Y	Y
TEXAS							
1 Hall, S.	Y	Y	N	?	Y	Y	N
2 Wilson	Y	Y	Y	Y	Y	Y	Y
3 ***Bartlett***	Y	Y	Y	Y	Y	N	N
4 Hall, R.	Y	Y	Y	Y	Y	N	N
5 Bryant	Y	Y	Y	Y	Y	Y	Y
6 ***Gramm***	Y	Y	Y	P	Y	N	N
7 ***Archer***	Y	Y	Y	Y	?	N	N
8 ***Fields***	Y	Y	Y	Y	Y	N	N
9 Brooks	Y	?	Y	?	?	Y	Y
10 Pickle	N	Y	Y	Y	Y	Y	Y
11 Leath	Y	Y	Y	Y	Y	Y	Y
12 Wright	Y	Y	Y	Y	Y	Y	Y
13 Hightower	Y	Y	Y	Y	Y	Y	?
14 Patman	Y	Y	Y	Y	Y	Y	Y
15 de la Garza	Y	Y	Y	Y	Y	Y	Y
16 Coleman	Y	Y	Y	Y	Y	Y	Y
17 Stenholm	Y	Y	Y	Y	Y	N	N
18 Leland	Y	Y	Y	Y	Y	Y	Y
19 Hance	Y	Y	Y	Y	Y	Y	Y
20 Gonzalez	Y	Y	Y	Y	Y	Y	Y
21 ***Loeffler***	Y	Y	Y	Y	Y	N	N
22 ***Paul***	Y	Y	N	Y	Y	N	N
23 Kazen	Y	Y	Y	Y	Y	Y	Y
24 Frost	Y	Y	Y	Y	Y	Y	Y
25 Andrews	Y	Y	Y	Y	Y	Y	Y
26 Vandergriff	Y	Y	?	Y	Y	Y	Y
27 Ortiz	Y	Y	Y	Y	Y	Y	Y
UTAH							
1 ***Hansen***	Y	Y	Y	Y	Y	N	N
2 ***Marriott***	Y	Y	Y	Y	Y	N	N
3 ***Nielson***	Y	Y	Y	Y	+	-	X
VERMONT							
AL ***Jeffords***	N	Y	Y	?	?	N	N
VIRGINIA							
1 ***Bateman***	Y	Y	Y	Y	Y	N	N
2 ***Whitehurst***	Y	Y	Y	Y	Y	N	N
3 ***Bliley***	Y	Y	Y	Y	Y	N	N
4 Sisisky	Y	Y	Y	Y	Y	Y	Y
5 Daniel	Y	Y	N	Y	Y	Y	Y
6 Olin	Y	Y	Y	Y	Y	Y	Y
7 ***Robinson***	Y	Y	Y	Y	Y	N	N
8 ***Parris***	Y	Y	Y	Y	Y	N	N
9 Boucher	Y	Y	Y	Y	Y	Y	Y
10 ***Wolf***	Y	Y	Y	Y	Y	N	N
WASHINGTON							
1 ***Pritchard***	N	Y	Y	?	Y	?	Y
2 Swift	Y	Y	Y	Y	Y	Y	Y
3 Bonker	Y	Y	Y	Y	Y	Y	Y
4 ***Morrison***	Y	Y	Y	?	Y	N	N
5 Foley	N	Y	Y	Y	Y	Y	Y
6 Dicks	Y	Y	Y	Y	Y	Y	Y
7 Lowry	N	Y	Y	N	Y	Y	Y
8 ***Chandler***	Y	Y	Y	Y	Y	N	N
WEST VIRGINIA							
1 Mollohan	Y	Y	Y	Y	Y	Y	Y
2 Staggers	Y	Y	Y	N	Y	Y	Y
3 Wise	Y	Y	Y	Y	Y	Y	Y
4 Rahall	Y	Y	Y	Y	Y	Y	Y
WISCONSIN							
1 Aspin	Y	Y	Y	?	Y	Y	Y
2 Kastenmeier	Y	Y	Y	Y	Y	Y	Y
3 ***Gunderson***	Y	Y	Y	Y	Y	N	N
4 Zablocki	Y	Y	Y	Y	Y	Y	Y
5 Moody	Y	Y	Y	Y	Y	Y	Y
6 ***Petri***	Y	Y	Y	Y	Y	N	N
7 Obey	N	Y	P	Y	Y	Y	Y
8 ***Roth***	Y	Y	Y	Y	Y	N	N
9 ***Sensenbrenner***	Y	Y	N	Y	Y	N	N
WYOMING							
AL ***Cheney***	Y	Y	Y	Y	Y	N	N

Southern states - Ala., Ark., Fla., Ga., Ky., La., Miss., N.C., Okla., S.C., Tenn., Texas, Va.

122. Procedural Motion. McGrath, R-N.Y., motion to approve the House *Journal* of Monday, May 23. Motion agreed to 370-17: R 145-12; D 225-5 (ND 146-4, SD 79-1), May 24, 1983.

123. H Con Res 113. MX Missile Development. Adoption of the concurrent resolution to permit use of funds appropriated in fiscal 1983 to develop a basing method for the MX missile and to conduct MX test flights. Adopted 239-186: R 148-18; D 91-168 (ND 23-147, SD 68-21), May 24, 1983. A "yea" was a vote supporting the president's position.

124. HR 2948. Veterans' Housing Benefits Amendments. Montgomery, D-Miss., motion to suspend the rules and pass the bill as amended to provide financial assistance to unemployed veterans facing foreclosure on home mortgages guaranteed by the Veterans Administration. Motion agreed to 394-23: R 140-22; D 254-1 (ND 168-0, SD 86-1), May 24, 1983. A two-thirds majority of those present and voting (278 in this case) is required for passage under suspension of the rules.

125. HR 2807. Meals for Older Americans. Andrews, D-N.C., motion to suspend the rules and pass the bill to increase authorized funding levels for meals served under the Older Americans Act by $6.8 million in fiscal 1982, $16 million in fiscal 1983 and such sums as may be necessary in fiscal 1984. Under existing law, spending ceilings for the program were $93.2 million in fiscal 1982, $100 million in 1983 and $105 million in 1984. Motion agreed to 386-31: R 133-30; D 253-1 (ND 168-0, SD 85-1), May 24, 1983. A two-thirds majority of those present and voting (278 in this case) is required for passage under suspension of the rules. A "nay" was a vote supporting the president's position.

126. HR 1707. National Traffic Safety Board Authorization. Mineta, D-Calif., motion to suspend the rules and pass the bill to authorize the National Traffic Safety Board to spend $22.6 million for fiscal 1984. Motion agreed to 372-43: R 128-34; D 244-9 (ND 165-2, SD 79-7), May 24, 1983. A two-thirds majority of those present and voting (277 in this case) is required for passage under suspension of the rules. (The House subsequently vacated passage of the bill and passed by voice vote S 967, a similar Senate-passed bill, thus clearing the measure for the president.)

127. Procedural Motion. Oxley, R-Ohio, motion to approve the House *Journal* of Tuesday, May 24. Motion agreed to 351-22: R 140-11; D 211-11 (ND 131-10, SD 80-1), May 25, 1983.

128. H Res 203. Lebanon-Israel Agreement. Adoption of the resolution to support the May 17, 1983, agreement between Israel and Lebanon on the withdrawal of Israeli military forces from Lebanon, and calling on Syria and the Palestine Liberation Organization to withdraw their forces from Lebanon. Adopted 408-0: R 159-0; D 249-0 (ND 162-0, SD 87-0), May 25, 1983.

129. HR 3069. Supplemental Appropriations, Fiscal 1983. Adoption of the rule (H Res 209) providing for House floor consideration of the bill to make $4.8 billion in supplemental appropriations for fiscal 1983. Adopted 212-195: R 30-128; D 182-67 (ND 119-44, SD 63-23), May 25, 1983.

KEY

Y Voted for (yea).
\# Paired for.
\+ Announced for.
N Voted against (nay).
X Paired against.
\- Announced against.
P Voted "present".
C Voted "present" to avoid possible conflict of interest.
? Did not vote or otherwise make a position known.

Democrats   *Republicans*

	122	123	124	125	126	127	128	129
ALABAMA								
1 *Edwards*	Y	Y	Y	Y	Y	Y	Y	Y
2 *Dickinson*	N	Y	Y	Y	Y	N	Y	N
3 Nichols	Y	Y	Y	Y	Y	Y	Y	Y
4 Bevill	Y	Y	Y	Y	Y	Y	Y	Y
5 Flippo	Y	Y	Y	Y	Y	Y	Y	Y
6 Erdreich	Y	Y	Y	Y	Y	Y	Y	Y
7 Shelby	Y	Y	Y	Y	Y	Y	Y	N
ALASKA								
AL *Young*	N	Y	Y	Y	Y	?	Y	Y
ARIZONA								
1 *McCain*	Y	Y	Y	Y	Y	Y	Y	N
2 Udall	Y	N	Y	Y	Y	Y	Y	Y
3 *Stump*	Y	Y	Y	N	Y	N	Y	N
4 *Rudd*	Y	Y	Y	N	N	Y	Y	N
5 McNulty	Y	N	Y	Y	Y	Y	Y	Y
ARKANSAS								
1 Alexander	Y	Y	Y	Y	Y	Y	Y	Y
2 *Bethune*	Y	Y	?	Y	Y	Y	Y	N
3 *Hammerschmidt*	Y	Y	Y	Y	Y	Y	Y	Y
4 Anthony	Y	N	Y	Y	Y	Y	Y	N
CALIFORNIA								
1 Bosco	Y	N	Y	Y	Y	Y	Y	Y
2 *Chappie*	Y	Y	Y	Y	Y	Y	Y	N
3 Matsui	Y	N	Y	Y	Y	Y	Y	N
4 Fazio	Y	Y	Y	Y	Y	Y	Y	Y
5 Vacancy								
6 Boxer	Y	N	Y	Y	Y	Y	Y	Y
7 Miller	Y	N	Y	Y	Y	Y	Y	N
8 Dellums	Y	N	Y	Y	Y	Y	Y	N
9 Stark	Y	N	Y	Y	Y	?	Y	N
10 Edwards	?	N	Y	Y	Y	Y	Y	Y
11 Lantos	Y	N	Y	Y	Y	Y	Y	Y
12 *Zschau*	Y	Y	N	Y	N	Y	Y	N
13 Mineta	Y	N	Y	Y	Y	?	Y	Y
14 *Shumway*	Y	Y	N	N	N	Y	Y	N
15 Coelho	Y	N	Y	Y	Y	Y	Y	N
16 Panetta	Y	N	Y	Y	Y	Y	Y	Y
17 *Pashayan*	Y	Y	Y	Y	Y	Y	Y	N
18 Lehman	Y	N	Y	Y	Y	Y	Y	Y
19 *Lagomarsino*	Y	Y	Y	Y	N	Y	Y	N
20 *Thomas*	Y	Y	Y	Y	Y	Y	Y	N
21 *Fiedler*	Y	Y	Y	Y	Y	Y	Y	N
22 *Moorhead*	Y	Y	?	?	?	?	?	?
23 Beilenson	Y	N	Y	Y	Y	Y	Y	Y
24 Waxman	Y	N	Y	Y	Y	Y	Y	Y
25 Roybal	Y	N	Y	Y	Y	Y	Y	Y
26 Berman	Y	N	Y	Y	Y	Y	Y	Y
27 Levine	Y	N	Y	Y	Y	Y	Y	Y
28 Dixon	?	N	Y	Y	Y	?	Y	Y
29 Hawkins	Y	N	Y	Y	N	Y	Y	Y
30 Martinez	?	?	?	?	?	?	?	?
31 Dymally	Y	Y	Y	Y	Y	Y	Y	Y
32 Anderson	Y	Y	Y	Y	Y	Y	Y	Y
33 *Dreier*	Y	Y	N	N	N	Y	Y	N
34 Torres	Y	N	Y	Y	Y	Y	Y	Y
35 *Lewis*	Y	Y	Y	Y	Y	Y	Y	N
36 Brown	Y	N	Y	Y	Y	Y	Y	Y
37 *McCandless*	Y	Y	Y	Y	Y	Y	Y	N
38 Patterson	Y	N	Y	Y	Y	Y	Y	Y
39 *Dannemeyer*	Y	Y	N	N	N	Y	Y	N
40 *Badham*	?	Y	Y	N	Y	Y	Y	N
41 *Lowery*	Y	Y	Y	Y	Y	Y	Y	N
42 *Lungren*	Y	Y	N	N	N	Y	Y	N

	122	123	124	125	126	127	128	129
43 *Packard*	Y	Y	N	N	Y	Y	Y	N
44 Bates	Y	N	Y	Y	Y	Y	Y	?
45 *Hunter*	Y	Y	Y	Y	Y	Y	Y	N
COLORADO								
1 Schroeder	?	N	Y	Y	Y	N	Y	N
2 Wirth	Y	N	Y	Y	Y	Y	Y	Y
3 Kogovsek	Y	N	Y	Y	Y	Y	Y	Y
4 *Brown*	N	Y	N	N	Y	Y	Y	N
5 *Kramer*	Y	Y	Y	Y	Y	Y	Y	N
6 *Schaefer*	Y	Y	Y	Y	N	Y	Y	N
CONNECTICUT								
1 Kennelly	Y	N	Y	Y	Y	Y	Y	N
2 Gejdenson	N	N	Y	Y	Y	N	Y	Y
3 Morrison	Y	N	Y	Y	Y	Y	Y	N
4 *McKinney*	Y	N	Y	Y	Y	Y	Y	Y
5 Ratchford	Y	N	Y	Y	Y	Y	Y	Y
6 *Johnson*	Y	N	Y	Y	Y	Y	Y	N
DELAWARE								
AL Carper	Y	N	Y	Y	Y	Y	Y	Y
FLORIDA								
1 Hutto	Y	Y	Y	Y	Y	Y	Y	Y
2 Fuqua	?	Y	Y	Y	Y	Y	Y	Y
3 Bennett	Y	N	Y	Y	Y	Y	Y	Y
4 Chappell	Y	Y	Y	Y	Y	?	?	Y
5 *McCollum*	Y	Y	Y	Y	Y	Y	Y	N
6 MacKay	Y	N	Y	Y	Y	Y	Y	Y
7 Gibbons	Y	N	Y	Y	Y	Y	Y	Y
8 *Young*	Y	Y	Y	Y	Y	Y	Y	N
9 *Bilirakis*	Y	Y	Y	Y	Y	Y	Y	N
10 Ireland	Y	Y	Y	Y	Y	Y	Y	N
11 Nelson	Y	Y	Y	Y	Y	Y	Y	N
12 *Lewis*	Y	Y	Y	Y	Y	Y	Y	N
13 *Mack*	Y	Y	N	Y	N	Y	Y	N
14 Mica	Y	Y	Y	Y	Y	Y	Y	N
15 *Shaw*	Y	Y	Y	Y	Y	Y	Y	N
16 Smith	Y	N	Y	Y	Y	Y	Y	Y
17 Lehman	Y	N	Y	Y	Y	Y	Y	Y
18 Pepper	Y	Y	Y	Y	Y	Y	Y	Y
19 Fascell	Y	N	Y	Y	Y	?	Y	Y
GEORGIA								
1 Thomas	Y	Y	Y	Y	Y	Y	Y	Y
2 Hatcher	Y	Y	Y	Y	Y	Y	Y	Y
3 Ray	?	Y	Y	Y	Y	Y	Y	Y
4 Levitas	Y	Y	Y	Y	Y	Y	Y	N
5 Fowler	Y	N	Y	Y	Y	Y	Y	Y
6 *Gingrich*	Y	Y	Y	Y	Y	Y	Y	N
7 McDonald	?	Y	Y	N	N	Y	N	N
8 Rowland	Y	Y	Y	Y	Y	Y	Y	Y
9 Jenkins	Y	Y	Y	Y	Y	Y	Y	Y
10 Barnard	Y	Y	Y	Y	Y	Y	Y	N
HAWAII								
1 Heftel	?	?	?	?	?	?	?	?
2 Akaka	Y	N	Y	Y	Y	Y	Y	Y
IDAHO								
1 *Craig*	Y	Y	Y	Y	N	Y	Y	N
2 *Hansen*	?	Y	Y	N	N	?	Y	N
ILLINOIS								
1 Vacancy								
2 Savage	Y	N	Y	Y	Y	Y	Y	Y
3 Russo	Y	N	Y	Y	Y	Y	Y	N
4 *O'Brien*	Y	Y	Y	Y	Y	Y	Y	N
5 Lipinski	Y	Y	Y	Y	Y	Y	Y	N
6 *Hyde*	Y	Y	Y	Y	Y	Y	Y	N
7 Collins	Y	N	Y	Y	Y	Y	Y	Y
8 Rostenkowski	Y	N	Y	Y	Y	Y	Y	Y
9 Yates	Y	N	Y	Y	Y	N	Y	Y
10 *Porter*	Y	Y	Y	Y	Y	Y	Y	?
11 Annunzio	Y	N	Y	Y	Y	Y	Y	Y
12 *Crane, P.*	Y	Y	N	N	N	Y	Y	N
13 *Erlenborn*	Y	Y	Y	Y	Y	Y	Y	N
14 *Corcoran*	Y	Y	Y	Y	Y	Y	Y	N
15 *Madigan*	Y	Y	Y	Y	Y	Y	Y	N
16 *Martin*	Y	Y	Y	Y	Y	Y	Y	N
17 Evans	Y	N	Y	Y	Y	Y	Y	Y
18 *Michel*	Y	Y	Y	Y	Y	Y	Y	N
19 *Crane, D.*	Y	N	N	N	N	Y	Y	N
20 Durbin	?	N	Y	Y	Y	N	Y	N
21 Price	Y	Y	Y	Y	Y	Y	Y	Y
22 Simon	Y	N	Y	Y	Y	Y	Y	Y
INDIANA								
1 Hall	Y	N	Y	Y	Y	?	Y	Y
2 Sharp	Y	N	Y	Y	Y	Y	Y	Y
3 *Hiler*	Y	Y	N	Y	Y	Y	Y	N
4 *Coats*	Y	Y	Y	Y	Y	Y	Y	N
5 Hillis	Y	Y	Y	Y	Y	Y	Y	N

ND - Northern Democrats   SD - Southern Democrats

Corresponding to Congressional Record Votes 130, 131, 132, 133, 134, 135, 136, 137

	122	123	124	125	126	127	128	129
6 ***Burton***	Y	Y	Y	Y	Y	?	Y	N
7 ***Myers***	Y	Y	Y	Y	Y	Y	Y	Y
8 McCloskey	Y	N	Y	Y	Y	Y	Y	Y
9 Hamilton	Y	Y	Y	Y	Y	Y	Y	N
10 Jacobs	P	N	Y	Y	Y	P	Y	N
IOWA								
1 ***Leach***	?	N	Y	Y	Y	Y	Y	N
2 ***Tauke***	Y	N	Y	Y	Y	Y	Y	N
3 ***Evans***	N	N	Y	Y	Y	?	?	?
4 Smith	Y	N	Y	Y	Y	Y	Y	Y
5 Harkin	N	N	Y	Y	Y	N	Y	N
6 Bedell	Y	N	Y	Y	Y	Y	Y	N
KANSAS								
1 ***Roberts***	Y	Y	Y	Y	Y	N	Y	N
2 Slattery	Y	N	Y	Y	N	Y	Y	Y
3 ***Winn***	Y	Y	Y	Y	Y	Y	Y	N
4 Glickman	Y	Y	Y	Y	Y	Y	Y	Y
5 ***Whittaker***	Y	Y	Y	Y	Y	Y	Y	N
KENTUCKY								
1 Hubbard	Y	Y	Y	Y	Y	Y	Y	Y
2 Natcher	Y	N	Y	Y	Y	Y	Y	Y
3 Mazzoli	Y	N	Y	Y	Y	Y	Y	Y
4 ***Snyder***	Y	Y	Y	Y	Y	Y	Y	Y
5 ***Rogers***	Y	Y	Y	Y	Y	Y	Y	Y
6 ***Hopkins***	Y	Y	Y	Y	Y	Y	Y	N
7 Perkins	Y	N	Y	Y	Y	Y	Y	Y
LOUISIANA								
1 ***Livingston***	Y	Y	Y	N	Y	Y	Y	N
2 Boggs	Y	Y	Y	Y	Y	Y	Y	?
3 Tauzin	Y	Y	Y	Y	Y	Y	Y	?
4 Roemer	N	Y	N	Y	N	N	Y	N
5 Huckaby	Y	Y	Y	Y	Y	Y	Y	Y
6 ***Moore***	Y	Y	Y	N	Y	Y	Y	Y
7 Breaux	Y	Y	Y	Y	Y	Y	Y	Y
8 Long	Y	Y	Y	Y	Y	Y	Y	Y
MAINE								
1 ***McKernan***	Y	Y	Y	Y	Y	Y	Y	N
2 ***Snowe***	Y	Y	Y	Y	Y	Y	Y	N
MARYLAND								
1 Dyson	Y	N	Y	Y	Y	Y	Y	Y
2 Long	Y	N	Y	Y	Y	Y	Y	Y
3 Mikulski	Y	N	Y	Y	Y	?	Y	Y
4 ***Holt***	Y	Y	Y	N	Y	?	Y	N
5 Hoyer	Y	Y	Y	Y	Y	Y	Y	Y
6 Byron	Y	Y	Y	Y	Y	?	?	?
7 Mitchell	N	N	Y	Y	Y	N	Y	Y
8 Barnes	Y	N	Y	Y	Y	Y	Y	Y
MASSACHUSETTS								
1 ***Conte***	Y	N	Y	Y	Y	Y	Y	Y
2 Boland	Y	N	Y	Y	Y	Y	Y	Y
3 Early	Y	N	Y	Y	Y	Y	Y	Y
4 Frank	Y	N	Y	Y	Y	Y	Y	Y
5 Shannon	Y	N	Y	Y	Y	Y	Y	N
6 Mavroules	Y	N	Y	Y	Y	Y	Y	N
7 Markey	Y	N	Y	Y	Y	Y	Y	N
8 O'Neill								
9 Moakley	Y	N	Y	Y	Y	Y	Y	Y
10 Studds	Y	N	Y	Y	Y	Y	Y	Y
11 Donnelly	Y	N	Y	Y	Y	Y	Y	Y
MICHIGAN								
1 Conyers	?	N	Y	Y	N	Y	Y	Y
2 ***Pursell***	Y	Y	Y	Y	Y	Y	Y	Y
3 Wolpe	Y	N	Y	Y	Y	Y	Y	N
4 ***Siljander***	Y	Y	Y	Y	N	Y	Y	N
5 ***Sawyer***	?	#	?	?	?	?	?	?
6 Carr	Y	N	Y	Y	Y	Y	Y	Y
7 Kildee	Y	N	Y	Y	Y	Y	Y	N
8 Traxler	Y	N	Y	Y	Y	Y	Y	Y
9 ***Vander Jagt***	Y	Y	Y	Y	Y	Y	Y	N
10 Albosta	Y	N	Y	Y	Y	Y	Y	Y
11 ***Davis***	Y	Y	Y	Y	Y	Y	Y	N
12 Bonior	Y	N	Y	Y	Y	Y	Y	N
13 Crockett	?	X	?	?	?	?	?	?
14 Hertel	Y	N	Y	Y	Y	Y	Y	Y
15 Ford	?	N	Y	Y	Y	?	Y	Y
16 Dingell	Y	N	?	Y	Y	?	Y	Y
17 Levin	Y	N	Y	Y	Y	Y	Y	Y
18 ***Broomfield***	Y	Y	Y	Y	Y	Y	Y	N
MINNESOTA								
1 Penny	Y	N	Y	Y	Y	Y	Y	Y
2 ***Weber***	Y	Y	Y	Y	?	Y	Y	N
3 ***Frenzel***	Y	Y	N	N	N	Y	Y	N
4 Vento	Y	N	Y	Y	Y	Y	Y	N
5 Sabo	N	N	Y	Y	Y	N	Y	Y
6 Sikorski	Y	N	Y	Y	Y	Y	Y	Y
7 ***Stangeland***	Y	Y	Y	Y	Y	Y	Y	N
8 Oberstar	Y	N	Y	Y	Y	P	Y	Y
MISSISSIPPI								
1 Whitten	Y	N	Y	Y	Y	Y	Y	Y
2 ***Franklin***	Y	Y	Y	Y	Y	Y	Y	N
3 Montgomery	Y	Y	Y	Y	Y	Y	Y	Y
4 Dowdy	?	Y	Y	Y	Y	Y	Y	Y
5 ***Lott***	Y	Y	Y	Y	Y	Y	Y	N
MISSOURI								
1 Clay	?	N	Y	Y	Y	?	Y	Y
2 Young	Y	N	Y	Y	Y	Y	Y	N
3 Gephardt	Y	Y	Y	Y	Y	Y	Y	N
4 Skelton	Y	Y	Y	Y	Y	Y	Y	Y
5 Wheat	Y	N	Y	Y	Y	Y	Y	Y
6 ***Coleman***	Y	Y	Y	Y	Y	Y	Y	N
7 ***Taylor***	Y	Y	Y	Y	Y	Y	Y	Y
8 ***Emerson***	N	Y	Y	Y	Y	N	Y	N
9 Volkmer	Y	Y	Y	Y	Y	Y	Y	N
MONTANA								
1 Williams	?	N	Y	Y	Y	?	Y	Y
2 ***Marlenee***	Y	Y	Y	Y	Y	Y	Y	N
NEBRASKA								
1 ***Bereuter***	Y	N	Y	Y	Y	Y	Y	N
2 ***Daub***	Y	Y	Y	Y	Y	Y	Y	N
3 ***Smith***	Y	N	Y	Y	Y	Y	Y	Y
NEVADA								
1 Reid	Y	Y	Y	Y	Y	Y	Y	Y
2 ***Vucanovich***	Y	Y	Y	Y	Y	Y	Y	N
NEW HAMPSHIRE								
1 D'Amours	Y	N	Y	Y	Y	Y	Y	Y
2 ***Gregg***	Y	Y	N	N	N	Y	Y	N
NEW JERSEY								
1 Florio	Y	N	Y	Y	Y	Y	Y	Y
2 Hughes	Y	N	Y	Y	Y	Y	Y	Y
3 Howard	?	?	?	?	?	Y	Y	N
4 ***Smith***	Y	N	Y	Y	Y	?	Y	N
5 ***Roukema***	Y	Y	Y	Y	Y	Y	Y	N
6 Dwyer	Y	N	Y	Y	Y	Y	Y	Y
7 ***Rinaldo***	Y	Y	Y	Y	Y	Y	Y	N
8 Roe	Y	N	Y	Y	Y	Y	Y	N
9 Torricelli	Y	N	Y	Y	Y	?	Y	Y
10 Rodino	?	N	Y	Y	Y	Y	Y	Y
11 Minish	Y	N	Y	Y	Y	Y	Y	Y
12 ***Courter***	Y	Y	Y	Y	Y	Y	Y	N
13 ***Forsythe***	N	N	Y	N	Y	N	Y	N
14 Guarini	Y	N	Y	Y	Y	Y	Y	N
NEW MEXICO								
1 ***Lujan***	Y	Y	Y	Y	Y	Y	Y	N
2 ***Skeen***	Y	Y	Y	Y	Y	Y	Y	N
3 Richardson	Y	N	Y	Y	Y	Y	Y	Y
NEW YORK								
1 ***Carney***	Y	Y	Y	Y	Y	Y	Y	Y
2 Downey	Y	N	Y	Y	Y	Y	Y	N
3 Mrazek	Y	N	Y	Y	Y	Y	Y	Y
4 ***Lent***	Y	Y	Y	Y	Y	Y	Y	N
5 ***McGrath***	Y	Y	Y	Y	Y	Y	Y	N
6 Addabbo	Y	N	Y	Y	Y	Y	Y	Y
7 Ackerman	Y	N	Y	Y	Y	Y	Y	Y
8 Scheuer	Y	N	Y	Y	Y	Y	Y	N
9 Ferraro	Y	N	Y	Y	Y	Y	Y	N
10 Schumer	Y	N	Y	Y	Y	Y	Y	N
11 Towns	Y	N	Y	Y	Y	Y	Y	Y
12 Owens	Y	N	Y	Y	Y	?	?	?
13 Solarz	?	N	Y	?	?	?	Y	Y
14 ***Molinari***	Y	Y	Y	Y	Y	Y	Y	N
15 ***Green***	?	N	Y	Y	Y	Y	Y	Y
16 Rangel	Y	N	Y	Y	Y	?	Y	N
17 Weiss	Y	N	Y	Y	Y	Y	Y	N
18 Garcia	?	N	Y	Y	Y	?	?	Y
19 Biaggi	Y	N	Y	Y	Y	Y	Y	Y
20 Ottinger	P	N	Y	Y	Y	?	Y	Y
21 ***Fish***	Y	Y	?	?	?	?	?	?
22 ***Gilman***	Y	Y	Y	Y	Y	+	+	-
23 Stratton	Y	Y	Y	Y	Y	Y	Y	Y
24 ***Solomon***	N	Y	Y	Y	Y	N	Y	N
25 ***Boehlert***	Y	Y	Y	Y	Y	Y	Y	Y
26 ***Martin***	Y	Y	Y	Y	Y	Y	Y	N
27 ***Wortley***	Y	Y	Y	Y	Y	?	Y	Y
28 McHugh	?	N	Y	Y	Y	?	Y	Y
29 ***Horton***	Y	Y	Y	Y	Y	Y	Y	N
30 ***Conable***	Y	Y	N	N	N	Y	Y	N
31 ***Kemp***	Y	Y	Y	Y	N	Y	Y	Y
32 LaFalce	Y	N	Y	Y	Y	Y	Y	N
33 Nowak	Y	N	Y	Y	Y	Y	Y	Y
34 Lundine	Y	N	Y	Y	Y	?	?	?
NORTH CAROLINA								
1 Jones	Y	Y	Y	Y	Y	Y	Y	Y
2 Valentine	?	Y	Y	Y	Y	Y	Y	Y
3 Whitley	Y	Y	Y	Y	Y	Y	Y	Y
4 Andrews	?	Y	Y	Y	Y	?	?	?
5 Neal	Y	Y	Y	Y	Y	Y	Y	Y
6 Britt	Y	Y	Y	Y	Y	Y	Y	Y
7 Rose	Y	Y	?	?	?	Y	Y	Y
8 Hefner	Y	Y	Y	Y	Y	Y	Y	Y
9 ***Martin***	?	Y	Y	N	Y	Y	Y	N
10 ***Broyhill***	Y	Y	Y	Y	Y	Y	Y	N
11 Clarke	Y	N	Y	Y	Y	Y	Y	N
NORTH DAKOTA								
AL Dorgan	Y	N	Y	Y	Y	N	Y	N
OHIO								
1 Luken	Y	N	Y	Y	Y	N	Y	Y
2 ***Gradison***	Y	N	Y	Y	Y	Y	Y	N
3 Hall	Y	N	Y	Y	Y	Y	Y	Y
4 ***Oxley***	Y	Y	Y	Y	Y	N	Y	N
5 ***Latta***	Y	Y	Y	Y	N	?	Y	N
6 ***McEwen***	Y	Y	Y	Y	Y	Y	Y	Y
7 ***DeWine***	Y	Y	Y	Y	N	Y	Y	N
8 ***Kindness***	Y	Y	Y	N	Y	Y	Y	N
9 Kaptur	Y	N	Y	Y	Y	?	Y	Y
10 ***Miller***	N	Y	Y	Y	Y	N	Y	N
11 Eckart	Y	N	Y	Y	Y	Y	Y	N
12 ***Kasich***	Y	Y	Y	Y	Y	Y	Y	N
13 Pease	Y	N	Y	Y	Y	Y	Y	N
14 Seiberling	Y	N	Y	Y	Y	Y	Y	Y
15 ***Wylie***	Y	Y	N	Y	N	Y	Y	N
16 ***Regula***	Y	Y	Y	Y	Y	Y	Y	N
17 ***Williams***	Y	Y	Y	Y	Y	Y	Y	Y
18 Applegate	Y	Y	Y	Y	Y	?	?	?
19 Feighan	Y	N	Y	Y	Y	Y	Y	Y
20 Oakar	Y	N	Y	Y	Y	Y	Y	N
21 Stokes	Y	N	Y	Y	Y	Y	Y	Y
OKLAHOMA								
1 Jones	?	?	?	?	?	Y	Y	N
2 Synar	Y	N	Y	Y	Y	Y	Y	Y
3 Watkins	Y	Y	Y	Y	Y	Y	Y	Y
4 McCurdy	Y	Y	Y	Y	Y	Y	Y	Y
5 ***Edwards***	Y	Y	Y	Y	Y	Y	Y	N
6 English	Y	Y	Y	Y	Y	Y	Y	Y
OREGON								
1 AuCoin	Y	N	Y	Y	Y	Y	Y	Y
2 ***Smith, R.***	Y	Y	Y	Y	Y	?	?	?
3 Wyden	Y	N	Y	Y	Y	Y	Y	Y
4 Weaver	Y	N	Y	Y	Y	Y	Y	Y
5 ***Smith, D.***	Y	Y	N	N	N	Y	Y	N
PENNSYLVANIA								
1 Foglietta	?	N	Y	Y	Y	Y	Y	Y
2 Gray	?	N	Y	Y	Y	Y	Y	Y
3 Borski	Y	N	Y	Y	Y	Y	Y	Y
4 Kolter	?	?	?	?	?	?	?	?
5 ***Schulze***	Y	Y	Y	Y	Y	Y	Y	N
6 Yatron	Y	Y	Y	Y	Y	Y	Y	Y
7 Edgar	Y	N	Y	Y	Y	?	?	-
8 Kostmayer	Y	N	Y	Y	Y	Y	Y	Y
9 ***Shuster***	Y	Y	Y	Y	Y	Y	Y	N
10 ***McDade***	Y	Y	Y	Y	Y	?	Y	Y
11 Harrison	Y	N	Y	Y	Y	Y	Y	Y
12 Murtha	Y	Y	Y	Y	Y	?	Y	Y
13 ***Coughlin***	N	Y	Y	Y	Y	N	Y	Y
14 Coyne	Y	N	Y	Y	Y	Y	Y	Y
15 ***Ritter***	Y	Y	Y	Y	Y	Y	Y	N
16 ***Walker***	N	Y	N	N	N	N	Y	N
17 ***Gekas***	Y	Y	Y	Y	Y	Y	Y	N
18 Walgren	Y	N	Y	Y	Y	Y	Y	N
19 ***Goodling***	N	N	Y	Y	Y	N	Y	N
20 Gaydos	Y	N	Y	Y	Y	?	Y	Y
21 ***Ridge***	Y	N	Y	Y	N	?	Y	N
22 Murphy	?	N	Y	Y	Y	?	Y	Y
23 ***Clinger***	Y	Y	Y	Y	Y	Y	Y	Y
RHODE ISLAND								
1 St Germain	P	N	Y	Y	?	?	Y	N
2 ***Schneider***	Y	N	Y	Y	Y	Y	Y	Y
SOUTH CAROLINA								
1 ***Hartnett***	Y	Y	N	N	N	Y	Y	N
2 ***Spence***	Y	Y	Y	Y	Y	Y	Y	N
3 Derrick	Y	Y	Y	Y	Y	Y	Y	Y
4 ***Campbell***	Y	Y	Y	Y	N	Y	Y	N
5 Spratt	Y	Y	Y	Y	Y	Y	Y	Y
6 Tallon	Y	Y	Y	Y	Y	Y	Y	Y
SOUTH DAKOTA								
AL Daschle	Y	N	Y	Y	Y	Y	Y	Y
TENNESSEE								
1 ***Quillen***	Y	Y	Y	Y	Y	Y	Y	N
2 ***Duncan***	Y	Y	Y	Y	Y	Y	Y	Y
3 Lloyd	Y	Y	Y	Y	Y	Y	Y	N
4 Cooper	Y	Y	Y	Y	Y	?	Y	Y
5 Boner	Y	Y	Y	Y	Y	Y	Y	Y
6 Gore	Y	Y	Y	Y	Y	Y	Y	Y
7 ***Sundquist***	Y	Y	Y	Y	Y	Y	Y	N
8 Jones	Y	Y	Y	Y	Y	Y	Y	Y
9 Ford	Y	N	Y	Y	Y	Y	Y	N
TEXAS								
1 Hall, S.	Y	Y	Y	Y	Y	?	Y	N
2 Wilson	Y	Y	Y	Y	Y	Y	Y	Y
3 ***Bartlett***	Y	Y	N	Y	N	Y	Y	Y
4 Hall, R.	Y	Y	Y	Y	N	Y	Y	N
5 Bryant	Y	N	Y	Y	Y	Y	Y	Y
6 ***Gramm***	?	Y	Y	Y	N	Y	Y	N
7 ***Archer***	Y	Y	Y	N	N	Y	Y	N
8 ***Fields***	N	Y	Y	Y	Y	Y	Y	N
9 Brooks	Y	N	Y	Y	Y	Y	Y	Y
10 Pickle	Y	Y	?	?	?	?	?	?
11 Leath	Y	Y	Y	Y	Y	Y	Y	N
12 Wright	Y	Y	Y	Y	Y	?	Y	Y
13 Hightower	Y	Y	Y	Y	Y	Y	Y	Y
14 Patman	Y	Y	Y	Y	Y	Y	Y	Y
15 de la Garza	Y	Y	Y	Y	Y	Y	Y	Y
16 Coleman	Y	Y	Y	Y	Y	Y	Y	Y
17 Stenholm	Y	Y	Y	Y	N	Y	Y	N
18 Leland	Y	N	Y	Y	Y	?	Y	Y
19 Hance	?	Y	Y	Y	N	Y	Y	Y
20 Gonzalez	Y	N	Y	Y	Y	Y	Y	Y
21 ***Loeffler***	Y	Y	Y	Y	Y	Y	Y	Y
22 ***Paul***	Y	N	N	N	N	Y	Y	N
23 Kazen	Y	Y	Y	Y	N	Y	Y	N
24 Frost	Y	Y	Y	?	?	?	Y	Y
25 Andrews	Y	Y	Y	Y	Y	Y	Y	Y
26 Vandergriff	?	Y	Y	Y	Y	Y	Y	N
27 Ortiz	?	Y	Y	Y	Y	Y	Y	Y
UTAH								
1 ***Hansen***	Y	Y	N	N	N	Y	Y	N
2 ***Marriott***	Y	Y	Y	Y	Y	Y	Y	N
3 ***Nielson***	Y	Y	N	N	N	Y	Y	N
VERMONT								
AL ***Jeffords***	Y	N	Y	Y	Y	N	Y	N
VIRGINIA								
1 ***Bateman***	?	Y	?	?	?	?	?	?
2 ***Whitehurst***	Y	Y	Y	Y	Y	Y	Y	N
3 ***Bliley***	Y	Y	Y	Y	Y	Y	Y	N
4 Sisisky	Y	N	Y	Y	Y	Y	Y	Y
5 Daniel	Y	Y	Y	Y	N	Y	Y	N
6 Olin	Y	Y	Y	Y	Y	Y	Y	N
7 ***Robinson***	Y	Y	Y	N	Y	Y	Y	Y
8 ***Parris***	Y	Y	Y	Y	Y	Y	Y	Y
9 Boucher	Y	N	Y	Y	Y	Y	Y	Y
10 ***Wolf***	Y	Y	Y	Y	Y	Y	Y	N
WASHINGTON								
1 ***Pritchard***	?	Y	Y	Y	Y	Y	Y	N
2 Swift	Y	N	Y	Y	Y	Y	Y	Y
3 Bonker	P	N	Y	Y	Y	Y	Y	N
4 ***Morrison***	Y	Y	Y	Y	Y	Y	Y	N
5 Foley	?	Y	Y	Y	Y	?	Y	Y
6 Dicks	Y	Y	Y	Y	Y	Y	Y	Y
7 Lowry	Y	N	Y	Y	Y	Y	Y	Y
8 ***Chandler***	Y	Y	Y	Y	Y	Y	Y	N
WEST VIRGINIA								
1 Mollohan	Y	Y	Y	Y	Y	Y	Y	Y
2 Staggers	Y	Y	Y	Y	Y	Y	Y	Y
3 Wise	Y	N	Y	Y	Y	Y	Y	Y
4 Rahall	Y	N	Y	Y	Y	Y	Y	Y
WISCONSIN								
1 Aspin	Y	Y	Y	Y	Y	?	?	Y
2 Kastenmeier	Y	N	?	?	?	?	?	?
3 ***Gunderson***	Y	Y	Y	Y	Y	Y	Y	N
4 Zablocki	Y	Y	Y	Y	Y	Y	Y	Y
5 Moody	Y	N	Y	Y	Y	Y	Y	?
6 ***Petri***	Y	N	Y	Y	Y	Y	Y	N
7 Obey	Y	N	Y	Y	Y	Y	Y	Y
8 ***Roth***	Y	Y	Y	Y	Y	Y	Y	N
9 ***Sensenbrenner***	Y	Y	Y	N	N	Y	Y	N
WYOMING								
AL ***Cheney***	Y	Y	Y	Y	Y	Y	Y	N

Southern states - Ala., Ark., Fla., Ga., Ky., La., Miss., N.C., Okla., S.C., Tenn., Texas, Va.

130. HR 3069. Supplemental Appropriations, Fiscal 1983. Roybal, D-Calif., amendment to reduce the funds in the bill for restoration and expansion of the West Front of the Capitol from $70.5 million to $49 million and allow only restoration, not expansion. Adopted 325-86: R 134-26; D 191-60 (ND 122-42, SD 69-18), May 25, 1983.

131. HR 3069. Supplemental Appropriations, Fiscal 1983. Passage of the bill to appropriate $4,809,430,665 in supplemental funds for fiscal 1983. Passed 309-92: R 94-64; D 215-28 (ND 142-15, SD 73-13), May 25, 1983.

132. Procedural Motion. DeWine, R-Ohio, motion to approve the House *Journal* of Wednesday, May 25. Motion agreed to 331-23: R 135-12; D 196-11 (ND 120-10, SD 76-1), May 26, 1983.

133. S Con Res 26. MX Missile Development. Adoption of the concurrent resolution to permit use of funds appropriated in fiscal 1983 to develop a basing method for the MX missile and to conduct MX test flights. Adopted 223-167: R 139-18; D 84-149 (ND 23-129, SD 61-20), May 26, 1983. A "yea" was a vote supporting the president's position.

134. H Res 177. Disapproving Energy Conservation Deferral. Adoption of the resolution to disapprove the president's proposed deferral of $4,500,000 in fiscal 1983 budget authority for energy conservation programs. Adopted 280-107: R 60-94; D 220-13 (ND 150-1, SD 70-12), May 26, 1983. A "nay" was a vote supporting the president's position.

135. H Res 178. Disapproving Fossil Energy Research and Development Deferral. Adoption of the resolution to disapprove the president's proposed deferral of $8,750,000 in fiscal 1983 budget authority for fossil energy research and development programs. Adopted 265-121: R 51-103; D 214-18 (ND 146-4, SD 68-14), May 26, 1983. A "nay" was a vote supporting the president's position.

136. H Res 181. Disapproving Mariana Islands Hospital Deferral. Adoption of the resolution to disapprove the deferral of $3.2 million appropriated for the construction of a hospital in the Northern Mariana Islands. Adopted 266-116: R 58-95; D 208-21 (ND 142-6, SD 66-15), May 26, 1983. A "nay" was a vote supporting the president's position.

137. HR 3133. Housing and Urban Development Department Appropriations, Fiscal 1984. Adoption of the rule (H Res 211) providing for House floor consideration of the bill to authorize appropriations for the Department of Housing and Urban Development and 17 independent agencies through fiscal 1984. Adopted 274-99: R 57-93; D 217-6 (ND 139-1, SD 78-5), May 26, 1983.

KEY

Y Voted for (yea).
\# Paired for.
\+ Announced for.
N Voted against (nay).
X Paired against.
- Announced against.
P Voted "present".
C Voted "present" to avoid possible conflict of interest.
? Did not vote or otherwise make a position known.

Democrats *Republicans*

	130	131	132	133	134	135	136	137
ALABAMA								
1 *Edwards*	Y	Y	Y	Y	Y	Y	Y	Y
2 *Dickinson*	N	Y	N	Y	N	N	N	N
3 Nichols	Y	Y	Y	Y	Y	Y	Y	Y
4 Bevill	N	Y	Y	Y	Y	Y	Y	Y
5 Flippo	N	Y	?	?	?	?	?	?
6 Erdreich	Y	Y	Y	Y	Y	Y	Y	Y
7 Shelby	Y	Y	Y	Y	N	N	N	Y
ALASKA								
AL *Young*	Y	Y	?	Y	Y	N	Y	Y
ARIZONA								
1 *McCain*	N	N	Y	N	N	N	N	N
2 Udall	Y	Y	Y	N	Y	Y	Y	Y
3 *Stump*	N	N	Y	N	N	N	N	N
4 *Rudd*	N	Y	Y	Y	Y	Y	N	Y
5 McNulty	Y	Y	Y	N	Y	Y	Y	Y
ARKANSAS								
1 Alexander	N	Y	?	?	?	?	?	?
2 *Bethune*	Y	?	Y	N	Y	N	Y	Y
3 *Hammerschmidt*	Y	Y	Y	Y	Y	N	Y	Y
4 Anthony	Y	Y	Y	N	Y	Y	Y	Y
CALIFORNIA								
1 Bosco	N	Y	N	Y	Y	Y	Y	Y
2 *Chappie*	Y	N	Y	Y	?	?	?	?
3 Matsui	N	Y	Y	N	Y	Y	Y	Y
4 Fazio	N	Y	Y	Y	Y	Y	Y	Y
5 Vacancy								
6 Boxer	Y	Y	?	N	Y	Y	Y	Y
7 Miller	Y	Y	?	N	Y	Y	Y	Y
8 Dellums	Y	N	Y	N	Y	Y	?	Y
9 Stark	Y	N	Y	N	Y	Y	Y	Y
10 Edwards	Y	Y	N	Y	N	Y	Y	Y
11 Lantos	Y	Y	Y	N	Y	Y	Y	Y
12 *Zschau*	Y	N	Y	Y	Y	N	N	N
13 Mineta	Y	Y	?	N	Y	Y	Y	Y
14 *Shumway*	Y	N	Y	N	Y	N	N	N
15 Coelho	N	Y	Y	N	Y	Y	Y	Y
16 Panetta	Y	Y	Y	N	Y	Y	Y	Y
17 *Pashayan*	Y	Y	Y	N	N	N	N	Y
18 Lehman	N	Y	Y	N	Y	Y	Y	Y
19 *Lagomarsino*	Y	Y	Y	Y	N	N	N	N
20 *Thomas*	N	Y	Y	N	N	N	N	N
21 *Fiedler*	Y	Y	Y	N	N	N	N	N
22 *Moorhead*	?	?	?	?	?	?	?	?
23 Beilenson	Y	Y	Y	N	Y	Y	Y	Y
24 Waxman	Y	Y	?	X	?	?	?	?
25 Roybal	Y	Y	Y	N	Y	Y	Y	Y
26 Berman	N	Y	Y	N	Y	Y	Y	Y
27 Levine	Y	Y	Y	N	Y	Y	Y	?
28 Dixon	N	Y	Y	N	Y	Y	Y	Y
29 Hawkins	N	Y	N	N	Y	Y	Y	Y
30 Martinez	?	?	?	?	?	?	?	?
31 Dymally	Y	Y	Y	Y	Y	Y	Y	Y
32 Anderson	Y	N	Y	Y	Y	Y	Y	Y
33 *Dreier*	Y	N	Y	N	N	N	N	N
34 Torres	Y	Y	Y	N	Y	Y	Y	Y
35 *Lewis*	N	N	Y	N	N	N	N	Y
36 Brown	Y	Y	Y	N	Y	Y	Y	Y
37 *McCandless*	N	N	Y	N	N	N	N	N
38 Patterson	Y	Y	?	N	Y	Y	Y	Y
39 *Dannemeyer*	Y	N	Y	N	N	N	N	N
40 *Badham*	N	N	Y	N	N	N	N	N
41 *Lowery*	Y	Y	Y	Y	N	N	N	Y
42 *Lungren*	Y	N	Y	N	N	N	N	N
43 *Packard*	N	N	Y	Y	N	N	N	N
44 Bates	Y	Y	Y	N	Y	Y	N	Y
45 *Hunter*	Y	N	Y	Y	N	N	N	Y
COLORADO								
1 Schroeder	Y	N	N	Y	Y	Y	Y	Y
2 Wirth	Y	Y	Y	N	Y	Y	Y	Y
3 Kogovsek	Y	Y	Y	N	Y	Y	Y	Y
4 *Brown*	N	N	N	N	N	N	N	N
5 *Kramer*	Y	Y	Y	N	N	N	N	N
6 *Schaefer*	Y	N	Y	Y	?	?	?	?
CONNECTICUT								
1 Kennelly	Y	Y	Y	N	Y	Y	Y	Y
2 Gejdenson	N	Y	N	N	Y	Y	Y	Y
3 Morrison	Y	N	Y	N	N	Y	N	Y
4 *McKinney*	Y	Y	Y	N	Y	Y	Y	Y
5 Ratchford	Y	Y	Y	Y	Y	Y	Y	Y
6 *Johnson*	Y	?	Y	N	Y	N	N	N
DELAWARE								
AL Carper	Y	Y	?	N	Y	Y	Y	Y
FLORIDA								
1 Hutto	Y	Y	Y	Y	Y	Y	Y	Y
2 Fuqua	Y	Y	Y	Y	Y	Y	Y	Y
3 Bennett	Y	Y	Y	Y	Y	Y	Y	Y
4 Chappell	N	Y	Y	Y	Y	Y	Y	Y
5 *McCollum*	Y	N	Y	Y	N	N	N	N
6 MacKay	Y	N	Y	N	Y	Y	Y	Y
7 Gibbons	N	Y	Y	N	N	N	N	Y
8 *Young*	Y	Y	Y	N	N	N	Y	Y
9 *Bilirakis*	Y	Y	Y	N	N	Y	N	N
10 Ireland	Y	N	Y	N	N	N	N	Y
11 Nelson	Y	Y	Y	Y	Y	Y	Y	Y
12 *Lewis*	Y	Y	Y	N	N	N	N	N
13 *Mack*	Y	N	Y	N	N	N	N	N
14 Mica	Y	Y	Y	Y	Y	Y	Y	Y
15 *Shaw*	Y	Y	Y	N	N	N	N	N
16 Smith	Y	Y	Y	N	Y	Y	Y	Y
17 Lehman	Y	Y	Y	N	Y	Y	Y	Y
18 Pepper	Y	Y	Y	Y	Y	Y	Y	Y
19 Fascell	N	Y	Y	N	Y	Y	Y	Y
GEORGIA								
1 Thomas	Y	Y	Y	Y	Y	Y	Y	Y
2 Hatcher	Y	Y	Y	Y	Y	Y	Y	Y
3 Ray	Y	N	Y	N	Y	N	N	N
4 Levitas	Y	N	Y	Y	Y	Y	Y	N
5 Fowler	Y	Y	Y	N	Y	Y	Y	Y
6 *Gingrich*	Y	Y	Y	N	N	N	N	N
7 McDonald	Y	N	Y	Y	N	N	N	N
8 Rowland	Y	Y	Y	Y	Y	Y	Y	Y
9 Jenkins	N	N	?	?	?	?	?	?
10 Barnard	N	N	Y	Y	N	Y	Y	Y
HAWAII								
1 Heftel	?	?	?	?	?	?	?	?
2 Akaka	N	Y	Y	X	?	?	?	?
IDAHO								
1 *Craig*	Y	N	?	#	?	?	?	?
2 *Hansen*	Y	N	?	Y	N	N	N	N
ILLINOIS								
1 Vacancy								
2 Savage	Y	Y	Y	N	Y	Y	Y	Y
3 Russo	?	?	?	X	?	?	?	?
4 *O'Brien*	Y	Y	Y	Y	Y	Y	Y	Y
5 Lipinski	Y	Y	Y	Y	Y	Y	Y	Y
6 *Hyde*	Y	Y	Y	Y	N	N	Y	?
7 Collins	Y	Y	Y	Y	Y	Y	Y	Y
8 Rostenkowski	?	?	Y	N	Y	Y	Y	Y
9 Yates	Y	Y	Y	N	Y	Y	Y	Y
10 *Porter*	N	Y	Y	Y	N	Y	N	N
11 Annunzio	N	Y	Y	N	Y	Y	Y	Y
12 *Crane, P.*	Y	N	?	Y	N	N	N	N
13 *Erlenborn*	N	Y	?	#	?	?	?	?
14 *Corcoran*	Y	N	Y	Y	N	N	N	N
15 *Madigan*	Y	Y	?	Y	N	N	Y	Y
16 *Martin*	Y	N	Y	Y	Y	Y	Y	N
17 Evans	Y	Y	Y	Y	Y	Y	Y	Y
18 *Michel*	Y	Y	Y	Y	Y	Y	Y	Y
19 *Crane, D.*	Y	N	Y	#	?	?	?	?
20 Durbin	Y	Y	N	Y	Y	Y	Y	Y
21 Price	N	Y	Y	Y	Y	Y	Y	Y
22 Simon	?	?	?	?	?	?	?	?
INDIANA								
1 Hall	N	Y	?	N	Y	Y	Y	Y
2 Sharp	Y	N	Y	N	Y	Y	Y	Y
3 *Hiler*	Y	N	Y	Y	N	N	N	N
4 *Coats*	Y	N	N	Y	N	N	N	N
5 Hillis	Y	Y	Y	Y	N	N	N	N

ND - Northern Democrats   SD - Southern Democrats

Corresponding to Congressional Record Votes 138, 139, 140, 141, 142, 143, 144, 145

	130	131	132	133	134	135	136	137
6 ***Burton***	Y	Y	Y	Y	N	N	N	N
7 ***Myers***	N	N	Y	Y	Y	Y	Y	Y
8 McCloskey	Y	Y	Y	N	Y	Y	Y	Y
9 Hamilton	N	N	Y	Y	Y	Y	Y	Y
10 Jacobs	Y	N	P	N	Y	N	N	Y
IOWA								
1 ***Leach***	Y	Y	Y	N	N	N	N	Y
2 ***Tauke***	N	N	Y	N	Y	N	N	N
3 ***Evans***	Y	Y	N	N	N	Y	N	Y
4 Smith	N	Y	Y	N	Y	Y	Y	Y
5 Harkin	N	Y	N	N	Y	Y	Y	Y
6 Bedell	N	Y	Y	N	Y	Y	Y	Y
KANSAS								
1 ***Roberts***	Y	Y	N	Y	N	N	N	N
2 Slattery	Y	N	Y	N	Y	Y	N	Y
3 ***Winn***	Y	Y	Y	Y	N	N	N	N
4 Glickman	Y	Y	Y	Y	Y	Y	Y	Y
5 ***Whittaker***	Y	Y	Y	Y	Y	N	N	N
KENTUCKY								
1 Hubbard	?	?	?	?	?	?	?	?
2 Natcher	N	Y	Y	N	Y	Y	Y	Y
3 Mazzoli	Y	Y	Y	N	Y	Y	Y	Y
4 ***Snyder***	Y	Y	Y	Y	N	N	N	Y
5 ***Rogers***	N	Y	Y	Y	N	Y	N	Y
6 ***Hopkins***	Y	Y	Y	Y	Y	Y	Y	N
7 Perkins	N	Y	Y	N	Y	Y	Y	Y
LOUISIANA								
1 ***Livingston***	Y	Y	?	Y	Y	Y	Y	Y
2 Boggs	Y	Y	Y	Y	Y	Y	Y	Y
3 Tauzin	Y	Y	Y	Y	N	N	N	Y
4 Roemer	Y	N	N	Y	N	N	N	N
5 Huckaby	Y	Y	Y	Y	Y	Y	Y	Y
6 ***Moore***	Y	Y	Y	Y	N	N	N	Y
7 Breaux	Y	Y	?	Y	N	Y	Y	Y
8 Long	N	Y	Y	Y	Y	Y	Y	Y
MAINE								
1 ***McKernan***	Y	Y	Y	Y	Y	Y	Y	N
2 ***Snowe***	Y	Y	Y	Y	Y	Y	Y	Y
MARYLAND								
1 Dyson	Y	Y	Y	N	Y	Y	Y	Y
2 Long	Y	Y	Y	N	Y	Y	Y	Y
3 Mikulski	Y	Y	Y	N	Y	Y	Y	Y
4 ***Holt***	Y	Y	Y	Y	N	N	N	Y
5 Hoyer	N	Y	Y	Y	Y	Y	Y	Y
6 Byron	Y	Y	Y	Y	N	Y	N	Y
7 Mitchell	Y	Y	N	N	Y	Y	Y	Y
8 Barnes	Y	Y	Y	N	Y	Y	Y	Y
MASSACHUSETTS								
1 ***Conte***	Y	Y	Y	N	Y	Y	Y	Y
2 Boland	Y	Y	Y	N	Y	Y	Y	?
3 Early	Y	Y	Y	N	Y	Y	Y	Y
4 Frank	N	Y	Y	N	Y	Y	Y	Y
5 Shannon	Y	Y	Y	N	Y	Y	Y	Y
6 Mavroules	Y	Y	Y	N	Y	Y	Y	?
7 Markey	N	Y	Y	N	Y	Y	Y	Y
8 O'Neill								
9 Moakley	N	Y	Y	N	Y	Y	Y	Y
10 Studds	Y	Y	Y	N	Y	Y	Y	Y
11 Donnelly	N	Y	Y	N	Y	Y	Y	Y
MICHIGAN								
1 Conyers	Y	Y	?	?	?	?	?	?
2 ***Pursell***	Y	N	Y	Y	Y	N	N	?
3 Wolpe	Y	Y	Y	N	Y	Y	Y	Y
4 ***Siljander***	Y	N	Y	Y	Y	N	N	N
5 ***Sawyer***	?	?	?	#	?	?	?	?
6 Carr	Y	Y	Y	N	Y	Y	Y	Y
7 Kildee	Y	Y	Y	N	Y	Y	Y	Y
8 Traxler	N	Y	Y	N	Y	Y	Y	Y
9 ***Vander Jagt***	Y	Y	?	#	?	?	?	?
10 Albosta	Y	Y	Y	N	Y	Y	Y	Y
11 ***Davis***	Y	Y	Y	Y	Y	Y	Y	Y
12 Bonior	N	Y	?	N	Y	Y	Y	Y
13 Crockett	?	?	?	X	?	?	?	?
14 Hertel	Y	Y	Y	N	Y	Y	Y	Y
15 Ford	N	Y	?	N	Y	Y	Y	Y
16 Dingell	N	Y	?	N	Y	Y	Y	Y
17 Levin	Y	Y	Y	N	Y	Y	Y	Y
18 ***Broomfield***	Y	N	Y	Y	Y	Y	Y	Y
MINNESOTA								
1 Penny	Y	Y	Y	N	Y	Y	Y	Y
2 ***Weber***	Y	N	Y	Y	N	N	N	N
3 ***Frenzel***	N	N	Y	Y	N	N	Y	N
4 Vento	Y	Y	Y	N	Y	Y	Y	Y
5 Sabo	N	Y	N	N	Y	Y	Y	Y
6 Sikorski	Y	Y	Y	N	Y	Y	Y	Y
7 ***Stangeland***	N	Y	Y	Y	Y	Y	Y	Y
8 Oberstar	Y	Y	P	N	Y	Y	Y	Y
MISSISSIPPI								
1 Whitten	N	Y	?	?	Y	Y	Y	Y
2 ***Franklin***	Y	Y	Y	Y	N	N	N	N
3 Montgomery	N	Y	Y	Y	Y	Y	N	Y
4 Dowdy	Y	Y	Y	Y	Y	Y	Y	Y
5 ***Lott***	Y	Y	Y	Y	N	N	N	N
MISSOURI								
1 Clay	N	Y	?	N	Y	Y	Y	?
2 Young	Y	Y	Y	N	Y	Y	Y	Y
3 Gephardt	Y	Y	Y	Y	Y	Y	Y	?
4 Skelton	N	Y	Y	Y	Y	Y	Y	Y
5 Wheat	Y	Y	Y	N	Y	Y	Y	Y
6 ***Coleman***	Y	Y	Y	Y	Y	Y	Y	Y
7 ***Taylor***	Y	Y	Y	Y	?	?	?	?
8 ***Emerson***	Y	Y	N	Y	N	N	N	N
9 Volkmer	Y	Y	Y	Y	Y	Y	Y	Y
MONTANA								
1 Williams	Y	Y	?	X	?	?	?	?
2 ***Marlenee***	Y	N	Y	Y	N	Y	N	N
NEBRASKA								
1 ***Bereuter***	Y	Y	Y	N	Y	N	Y	N
2 ***Daub***	Y	Y	Y	Y	N	N	N	N
3 ***Smith***	Y	Y	Y	N	Y	Y	Y	Y
NEVADA								
1 Reid	Y	Y	Y	Y	?	?	?	?
2 ***Vucanovich***	Y	N	Y	Y	N	N	N	N
NEW HAMPSHIRE								
1 D'Amours	Y	Y	?	N	Y	Y	?	Y
2 ***Gregg***	N	N	Y	Y	N	N	N	N
NEW JERSEY								
1 Florio	Y	Y	Y	N	Y	Y	Y	Y
2 Hughes	Y	N	Y	N	Y	Y	Y	Y
3 Howard	N	Y	Y	N	Y	Y	Y	Y
4 ***Smith***	N	Y	Y	N	Y	Y	Y	Y
5 ***Roukema***	Y	Y	Y	Y	Y	Y	Y	Y
6 Dwyer	Y	Y	Y	N	Y	Y	Y	Y
7 ***Rinaldo***	Y	Y	Y	Y	Y	Y	Y	Y
8 Roe	N	Y	Y	N	Y	Y	Y	Y
9 Torricelli	Y	Y	Y	N	Y	Y	Y	?
10 Rodino	Y	Y	Y	N	Y	Y	Y	Y
11 Minish	Y	Y	Y	N	Y	Y	Y	Y
12 ***Courter***	Y	N	Y	Y	Y	N	N	Y
13 ***Forsythe***	N	N	N	N	N	N	N	N
14 Guarini	Y	Y	Y	N	Y	Y	Y	Y
NEW MEXICO								
1 ***Lujan***	Y	N	Y	Y	N	N	Y	Y
2 ***Skeen***	Y	Y	Y	Y	N	N	N	N
3 Richardson	Y	Y	Y	N	Y	Y	Y	Y
NEW YORK								
1 ***Carney***	Y	Y	Y	Y	N	N	Y	Y
2 Downey	Y	Y	Y	N	Y	Y	Y	Y
3 Mrazek	Y	Y	?	N	Y	Y	Y	Y
4 ***Lent***	Y	Y	Y	Y	Y	Y	Y	Y
5 ***McGrath***	Y	Y	Y	Y	N	Y	Y	N
6 Addabbo	Y	Y	Y	N	Y	Y	Y	Y
7 Ackerman	Y	Y	Y	N	Y	Y	Y	Y
8 Scheuer	Y	Y	Y	N	Y	Y	Y	Y
9 Ferraro	Y	Y	Y	N	Y	Y	Y	Y
10 Schumer	Y	Y	Y	N	Y	N	Y	Y
11 Towns	Y	Y	Y	N	Y	Y	Y	Y
12 Owens	Y	?	P	N	Y	Y	Y	?
13 Solarz	Y	?	?	?	?	?	?	?
14 ***Molinari***	Y	Y	Y	Y	Y	Y	Y	N
15 ***Green***	Y	Y	Y	N	Y	Y	Y	Y
16 Rangel	Y	Y	?	X	?	?	?	?
17 Weiss	Y	+	+	-	+	+	+	+
18 Garcia	N	Y	Y	N	?	?	?	?
19 Biaggi	Y	Y	?	X	?	?	?	?
20 Ottinger	Y	N	?	N	Y	Y	Y	Y
21 ***Fish***	?	?	?	#	?	?	?	?
22 ***Gilman***	Y	Y	Y	Y	Y	Y	Y	Y
23 Stratton	Y	Y	Y	Y	Y	N	N	Y
24 ***Solomon***	Y	N	N	Y	N	N	?	N
25 ***Boehlert***	Y	Y	Y	Y	Y	Y	Y	Y
26 ***Martin***	Y	Y	Y	Y	N	N	N	N
27 ***Wortley***	Y	Y	Y	Y	N	N	Y	N
28 McHugh	Y	Y	?	N	Y	Y	Y	?
29 ***Horton***	Y	Y	Y	Y	Y	Y	Y	?
30 ***Conable***	Y	N	Y	Y	N	N	Y	N
31 ***Kemp***	N	Y	?	Y	N	N	N	?
32 LaFalce	Y	Y	Y	N	Y	Y	Y	Y
33 Nowak	Y	Y	Y	N	Y	Y	Y	Y
34 Lundine	?	?	P	N	Y	Y	Y	Y
NORTH CAROLINA								
1 Jones	Y	Y	Y	Y	Y	Y	Y	Y
2 Valentine	Y	Y	Y	Y	Y	Y	Y	Y
3 Whitley	Y	Y	Y	Y	Y	Y	Y	Y
4 Andrews	?	?	?	?	?	?	?	?
5 Neal	Y	Y	?	Y	Y	Y	Y	Y
6 Britt	Y	Y	Y	Y	Y	Y	Y	Y
7 Rose	Y	Y	Y	?	Y	Y	Y	Y
8 Hefner	Y	Y	Y	Y	Y	Y	Y	Y
9 ***Martin***	Y	N	Y	Y	N	N	N	N
10 ***Broyhill***	N	N	Y	Y	N	N	N	N
11 Clarke	Y	Y	Y	N	Y	Y	Y	Y
NORTH DAKOTA								
AL Dorgan	Y	N	N	N	Y	Y	Y	?
OHIO								
1 Luken	Y	Y	Y	N	Y	Y	Y	Y
2 ***Gradison***	Y	Y	Y	N	Y	N	N	Y
3 Hall	Y	N	Y	N	Y	Y	?	Y
4 ***Oxley***	Y	N	Y	Y	N	N	N	N
5 ***Latta***	Y	N	Y	Y	N	N	N	N
6 ***McEwen***	Y	Y	Y	Y	N	N	N	N
7 ***DeWine***	Y	Y	Y	Y	N	N	N	N
8 ***Kindness***	Y	N	Y	Y	N	N	N	N
9 Kaptur	Y	Y	Y	N	Y	Y	Y	Y
10 ***Miller***	Y	N	N	Y	N	Y	N	N
11 Eckart	Y	Y	Y	N	Y	Y	Y	Y
12 ***Kasich***	Y	Y	Y	Y	N	N	N	N
13 Pease	Y	Y	Y	N	Y	Y	Y	Y
14 Seiberling	N	N	Y	N	Y	Y	Y	?
15 ***Wylie***	Y	Y	Y	Y	Y	Y	Y	N
16 ***Regula***	Y	Y	Y	Y	Y	Y	Y	Y
17 ***Williams***	Y	Y	Y	Y	Y	Y	N	Y
18 Applegate	Y	Y	?	Y	Y	Y	Y	Y
19 Feighan	Y	Y	?	?	Y	Y	Y	Y
20 Oakar	Y	Y	Y	N	Y	Y	Y	Y
21 Stokes	N	Y	?	N	Y	Y	Y	Y
OKLAHOMA								
1 Jones	Y	Y	Y	Y	N	N	N	Y
2 Synar	Y	Y	Y	N	Y	Y	Y	Y
3 Watkins	Y	Y	Y	Y	Y	Y	Y	Y
4 McCurdy	Y	Y	Y	Y	Y	N	N	Y
5 ***Edwards***	Y	Y	Y	Y	Y	N	N	Y
6 English	Y	Y	Y	Y	Y	N	Y	Y
OREGON								
1 AuCoin	Y	Y	?	N	Y	Y	Y	Y
2 ***Smith, R.***	?	?	?	#	?	?	?	?
3 Wyden	Y	Y	Y	N	Y	Y	Y	Y
4 Weaver	?	?	?	?	?	?	?	?
5 ***Smith, D.***	Y	N	Y	Y	N	N	N	N
PENNSYLVANIA								
1 Foglietta	Y	?	?	?	?	?	?	?
2 Gray	N	Y	?	?	?	?	?	?
3 Borski	Y	?	?	X	?	?	?	?
4 Kolter	?	?	?	?	?	?	?	?
5 ***Schulze***	N	N	Y	Y	Y	Y	N	N
6 Yatron	N	Y	Y	Y	Y	Y	Y	Y
7 Edgar	+	-	?	?	?	?	?	?
8 Kostmayer	Y	?	?	X	?	?	?	?
9 ***Shuster***	N	N	?	#	?	?	?	?
10 ***McDade***	N	Y	?	Y	Y	Y	Y	Y
11 Harrison	Y	Y	Y	N	Y	Y	Y	Y
12 Murtha	N	Y	Y	Y	Y	Y	Y	Y
13 ***Coughlin***	N	Y	N	Y	Y	N	N	Y
14 Coyne	Y	?	?	?	?	?	?	?
15 ***Ritter***	Y	N	Y	Y	N	Y	N	Y
16 ***Walker***	Y	N	N	Y	N	N	N	N
17 ***Gekas***	Y	N	?	Y	N	N	Y	N
18 Walgren	Y	N	Y	N	Y	Y	N	Y
19 ***Goodling***	Y	N	N	N	Y	N	N	N
20 Gaydos	Y	Y	Y	N	Y	Y	Y	Y
21 ***Ridge***	Y	Y	?	N	Y	Y	Y	Y
22 Murphy	N	Y	Y	N	Y	Y	Y	Y
23 ***Clinger***	Y	Y	Y	Y	Y	Y	Y	Y
RHODE ISLAND								
1 St Germain	N	Y	P	N	Y	Y	Y	N
2 ***Schneider***	?	?	Y	N	Y	Y	Y	Y
SOUTH CAROLINA								
1 ***Hartnett***	Y	N	Y	Y	N	N	N	N
2 ***Spence***	Y	Y	Y	Y	N	Y	Y	N
3 Derrick	Y	Y	Y	Y	Y	N	?	Y
4 ***Campbell***	Y	Y	Y	Y	N	N	N	N
5 Spratt	Y	Y	Y	Y	Y	Y	Y	Y
6 Tallon	Y	Y	Y	Y	Y	Y	Y	Y
SOUTH DAKOTA								
AL Daschle	Y	Y	Y	N	Y	Y	Y	Y
TENNESSEE								
1 ***Quillen***	N	Y	Y	Y	N	N	N	Y
2 ***Duncan***	Y	Y	Y	Y	N	Y	Y	Y
3 Lloyd	Y	Y	Y	Y	Y	Y	Y	Y
4 Cooper	Y	Y	Y	Y	Y	Y	N	Y
5 Boner	Y	Y	Y	Y	Y	Y	Y	Y
6 Gore	Y	Y	?	Y	Y	Y	Y	Y
7 ***Sundquist***	Y	Y	Y	Y	Y	Y	Y	N
8 Jones	Y	Y	Y	Y	Y	Y	Y	Y
9 Ford	Y	Y	Y	N	Y	Y	Y	Y
TEXAS								
1 Hall, S.	Y	Y	Y	Y	Y	Y	N	Y
2 Wilson	Y	Y	?	Y	Y	Y	Y	Y
3 ***Bartlett***	Y	Y	Y	Y	N	N	N	N
4 Hall, R.	Y	N	Y	Y	Y	Y	N	Y
5 Bryant	Y	Y	Y	N	Y	Y	Y	Y
6 ***Gramm***	Y	N	Y	Y	N	N	N	N
7 ***Archer***	Y	N	Y	Y	N	N	N	N
8 ***Fields***	Y	N	?	Y	N	N	N	N
9 Brooks	Y	Y	Y	N	Y	Y	Y	Y
10 Pickle	?	?	?	#	?	?	?	?
11 Leath	N	Y	Y	Y	N	N	Y	Y
12 Wright	N	Y	Y	Y	Y	Y	Y	Y
13 Hightower	N	Y	Y	Y	Y	Y	Y	Y
14 Patman	Y	N	Y	Y	N	Y	N	Y
15 de la Garza	Y	Y	Y	Y	Y	Y	Y	Y
16 Coleman	Y	Y	Y	Y	Y	Y	Y	Y
17 Stenholm	N	N	Y	Y	N	N	N	N
18 Leland	Y	Y	?	N	Y	Y	Y	Y
19 Hance	Y	?	?	?	?	?	?	?
20 Gonzalez	Y	Y	Y	N	Y	Y	Y	Y
21 ***Loeffler***	Y	Y	Y	Y	N	N	N	N
22 ***Paul***	Y	N	Y	N	N	N	N	N
23 Kazen	Y	Y	Y	Y	Y	Y	Y	Y
24 Frost	N	Y	Y	Y	Y	Y	Y	Y
25 Andrews	Y	Y	Y	Y	Y	Y	Y	Y
26 Vandergriff	Y	Y	Y	Y	?	?	?	Y
27 Ortiz	Y	Y	Y	Y	Y	Y	Y	Y
UTAH								
1 ***Hansen***	Y	N	Y	Y	N	N	Y	N
2 ***Marriott***	?	?	?	#	?	?	?	?
3 ***Nielson***	Y	N	Y	Y	N	N	Y	N
VERMONT								
AL ***Jeffords***	Y	Y	Y	N	Y	Y	Y	N
VIRGINIA								
1 ***Bateman***	Y	Y	Y	Y	N	N	N	N
2 ***Whitehurst***	Y	Y	Y	Y	N	N	N	Y
3 ***Bliley***	Y	Y	?	Y	N	N	N	N
4 Sisisky	Y	Y	Y	N	Y	Y	N	Y
5 Daniel	Y	Y	Y	Y	Y	N	N	N
6 Olin	Y	N	Y	Y	Y	Y	Y	Y
7 ***Robinson***	Y	Y	Y	Y	Y	N	N	Y
8 ***Parris***	Y	Y	Y	Y	Y	Y	Y	N
9 Boucher	Y	Y	Y	N	Y	Y	Y	Y
10 ***Wolf***	Y	Y	Y	Y	Y	Y	Y	N
WASHINGTON								
1 ***Pritchard***	Y	N	Y	Y	Y	Y	Y	Y
2 Swift	Y	Y	Y	N	Y	Y	Y	Y
3 Bonker	Y	Y	Y	N	Y	?	Y	Y
4 ***Morrison***	Y	Y	Y	Y	Y	Y	N	N
5 Foley	N	Y	Y	Y	Y	Y	Y	Y
6 Dicks	Y	Y	Y	Y	Y	Y	Y	Y
7 Lowry	Y	Y	N	N	Y	Y	Y	Y
8 ***Chandler***	Y	Y	Y	Y	Y	Y	Y	N
WEST VIRGINIA								
1 Mollohan	Y	Y	Y	Y	Y	Y	Y	Y
2 Staggers	Y	Y	N	Y	Y	Y	Y	Y
3 Wise	Y	Y	Y	N	Y	Y	Y	Y
4 Rahall	Y	Y	Y	N	Y	Y	Y	Y
WISCONSIN								
1 Aspin	Y	Y	Y	Y	Y	Y	Y	Y
2 Kastenmeier	?	?	?	X	?	?	?	?
3 ***Gunderson***	Y	N	Y	Y	Y	Y	Y	N
4 Zablocki	N	Y	Y	Y	Y	Y	Y	Y
5 Moody	Y	Y	Y	N	Y	Y	Y	?
6 ***Petri***	Y	N	Y	N	Y	Y	Y	N
7 Obey	N	Y	Y	N	Y	Y	Y	Y
8 ***Roth***	Y	Y	Y	Y	N	N	N	Y
9 ***Sensenbrenner***	Y	N	Y	Y	N	N	N	N
WYOMING								
AL ***Cheney***	?	?	Y	Y	N	N	N	N

Southern states - Ala., Ark., Fla., Ga., Ky., La., Miss., N.C., Okla., S.C., Tenn., Texas, Va.

138. HR 3133. Department of Housing and Urban Development Appropriations, Fiscal 1984. Boland, D-Mass., motion that the House resolve itself into the Committee of the Whole for consideration of the bill to make fiscal 1984 appropriations for the Department of Housing and Urban Development and 17 independent agencies. Motion agreed to 324-2: R 130-1; D 194-1 (ND 126-0, SD 68-1), June 2, 1983.

139. HR 3133. Department of Housing and Urban Development Appropriations, Fiscal 1984. Wirth, D-Colo., amendments offered *en bloc* to increase fiscal 1984 funding levels for the Environmental Protection Agency by $219.7 million. Adopted 200-167: R 36-107; D 164-60 (ND 126-20, SD 38-40), June 2, 1983.

140. HR 3133. Department of Housing and Urban Development Appropriations, Fiscal 1984. Boland, D-Mass., motion that the Committee of the Whole rise and report the bill back to the House with amendments. Motion rejected 144-225: R 5-136; D 139-89 (ND 85-64, SD 54-25), June 2, 1983. (Rejection of the motion was required under a new House rule in order to attach riders to the bill *(see vote 141, below).*)

141. HR 3133. Department of Housing and Urban Development Appropriations, Fiscal 1984. Dannemeyer, R-Calif., amendment to prohibit the Environmental Protection Agency from using any funds provided by the bill to impose sanctions during fiscal 1984 on any area for failing to attain any national ambient air quality standard established under the Clean Air Act. Adopted 227-136: R 89-50; D 138-86 (ND 88-58, SD 50-28), June 2, 1983.

142. HR 3133. Department of Housing and Urban Development Appropriations, Fiscal 1984. Boland, D-Mass., motion that the Committee of the Whole rise and report the bill back to the House with amendments, recommending passage of the bill. Motion agreed to 241-120: R 24-113; D 217-7 (ND 144-2, SD 73-5), June 2, 1983.

143. HR 3133. Department of Housing and Urban Development Appropriations, Fiscal 1984. Passage of the bill to appropriate $54,426,088,000 for the Department of Housing and Urban Development and 17 independent agencies in fiscal 1984. Passed 216-143: R 32-103; D 184-40 (ND 132-15, SD 52-25), June 2, 1983. The president had requested $44,729,258,896 in new budget authority.

144. HR 3135. Legislative Branch Appropriations, Fiscal 1984. Walker, R-Pa., amendment to reduce by $1.1 million the bill's funding for the staffs of House committees. Rejected 142-213: R 109-22; D 33-191 (ND 12-135, SD 21-56), June 2, 1983.

145. S 639. Lebanon Aid. Hamilton, D-Ind., motion to suspend the rules and pass the bill to authorize $101 million in military aid and $150 million in economic aid for Lebanon in fiscal 1983 and to require the president to seek authorization from Congress for the expansion of U.S. participation in a multinational peacekeeping force in Lebanon. Motion agreed to 276-76: R 89-42; D 187-34 (ND 132-14, SD 55-20), June 2, 1983. A two-thirds majority of those present and voting (235 in this case) is required for passage under suspension of the rules. A "yea" was a vote supporting the president's position.

KEY

Y Voted for (yea).
Paired for.
+ Announced for.
N Voted against (nay).
X Paired against.
- Announced against.
P Voted "present".
C Voted "present" to avoid possible conflict of interest.
? Did not vote or otherwise make a position known.

Democrats **Republicans**

	138	139	140	141	142	143	144	145
ALABAMA								
1 Edwards	?	?	N	Y	Y	N	N	Y
2 Dickinson	?	?	?	?	?	?	?	?
3 Nichols	Y	N	Y	N	Y	N	N	N
4 Bevill	Y	N	Y	Y	Y	Y	N	?
5 Flippo	Y	Y	Y	Y	Y	Y	N	Y
6 Erdreich	Y	Y	N	Y	Y	Y	N	Y
7 Shelby	Y	Y	N	N	Y	N	N	N
ALASKA								
AL Young	?	?	?	?	?	?	?	?
ARIZONA								
1 McCain	?	?	?	?	?	X	?	?
2 Udall	?	Y	Y	Y	Y	Y	N	Y
3 Stump	?	N	N	N	N	N	Y	N
4 Rudd	Y	N	N	Y	N	Y	N	Y
5 McNulty	Y	Y	Y	Y	Y	?	N	Y
ARKANSAS								
1 Alexander	Y	Y	Y	?	?	Y	N	Y
2 Bethune	Y	N	?	Y	N	Y	N	N
3 Hammerschmidt	Y	N	N	Y	N	Y	N	Y
4 Anthony	Y	N	Y	N	Y	Y	N	Y
CALIFORNIA								
1 Bosco	Y	Y	N	N	Y	Y	N	Y
2 Chappie	?	X	?	?	?	X	?	?
3 Matsui	Y	Y	N	Y	Y	Y	N	Y
4 Fazio	Y	Y	N	Y	Y	Y	N	Y
5 Vacancy								
6 Boxer	Y	Y	N	Y	Y	Y	N	Y
7 Miller	Y	Y	N	Y	Y	Y	N	Y
8 Dellums	Y	Y	N	Y	Y	Y	N	N
9 Stark	?	Y	N	Y	Y	Y	N	Y
10 Edwards	Y	Y	N	Y	Y	Y	N	Y
11 Lantos	Y	Y	N	Y	Y	Y	N	Y
12 Zschau	Y	N	N	Y	N	N	Y	Y
13 Mineta	Y	Y	N	Y	Y	Y	N	Y
14 Shumway	Y	N	N	Y	?	?	?	?
15 Coelho	Y	Y	Y	Y	Y	Y	N	Y
16 Panetta	+	+	-	+	+	+	+	+
17 Pashayan	?	?	?	?	?	?	?	?
18 Lehman	Y	Y	Y	Y	Y	Y	N	Y
19 Lagomarsino	Y	N	N	Y	N	N	Y	Y
20 Thomas	Y	N	N	Y	N	N	Y	Y
21 Fiedler	Y	N	N	Y	N	N	Y	Y
22 Moorhead	Y	N	N	Y	N	N	N	Y
23 Beilenson	Y	Y	Y	N	Y	Y	N	Y
24 Waxman	Y	N	Y	N	Y	Y	N	Y
25 Roybal	Y	N	Y	N	Y	N	Y	Y
26 Berman	?	?	?	?	?	?	?	?
27 Levine	+	?	?	+	?	+	?	+
28 Dixon	Y	Y	N	?	?	?	?	?
29 Hawkins	?	#	?	?	?	#	?	?
30 Martinez	?	?	?	?	?	?	?	?
31 Dymally	Y	N	Y	N	Y	Y	N	Y
32 Anderson	Y	Y	Y	Y	Y	Y	N	N
33 Dreier	Y	N	N	Y	N	N	Y	Y
34 Torres	+	+	+	+	+	+	-	+
35 Lewis	?	N	N	Y	N	Y	N	Y
36 Brown	Y	Y	N	Y	N	Y	N	Y
37 McCandless	Y	N	N	Y	N	N	Y	Y
38 Patterson	Y	Y	N	Y	Y	Y	N	Y
39 Dannemeyer	Y	N	N	Y	N	N	Y	N
40 Badham	?	X	?	?	?	X	?	?
41 Lowery	Y	N	N	Y	N	N	Y	Y
42 Lungren	Y	N	N	Y	N	N	Y	Y
43 Packard	Y	N	N	Y	N	N	Y	Y
44 Bates	?	Y	Y	Y	Y	Y	N	Y
45 Hunter	Y	N	N	Y	N	N	Y	Y
COLORADO								
1 Schroeder	Y	Y	N	Y	?	Y	N	Y
2 Wirth	Y	Y	N	Y	Y	Y	N	Y
3 Kogovsek	Y	Y	N	Y	Y	Y	N	Y
4 Brown	Y	N	N	N	N	N	N	Y
5 Kramer	Y	N	N	Y	N	N	Y	Y
6 Schaefer	Y	N	N	Y	N	N	Y	N
CONNECTICUT								
1 Kennelly	?	Y	Y	N	Y	Y	N	Y
2 Gejdenson	Y	Y	N	Y	N	Y	N	Y
3 Morrison	Y	Y	N	Y	Y	Y	N	Y
4 McKinney	Y	Y	N	Y	N	Y	N	Y
5 Ratchford	Y	Y	N	Y	Y	Y	N	Y
6 Johnson	Y	Y	N	N	Y	Y	Y	Y
DELAWARE								
AL Carper	Y	Y	Y	N	Y	Y	N	Y
FLORIDA								
1 Hutto	?	N	N	Y	Y	N	+	+
2 Fuqua	Y	N	Y	N	Y	Y	N	Y
3 Bennett	Y	N	Y	N	Y	Y	N	Y
4 Chappell	?	?	Y	Y	Y	Y	N	Y
5 McCollum	Y	Y	N	Y	N	N	Y	Y
6 MacKay	Y	Y	N	Y	Y	Y	N	Y
7 Gibbons	?	?	?	?	Y	Y	N	Y
8 Young	?	N	N	Y	N	N	N	Y
9 Bilirakis	Y	N	N	Y	N	N	Y	Y
10 Ireland	Y	N	Y	Y	N	N	Y	?
11 Nelson	Y	Y	Y	N	Y	#	-	+
12 Lewis	Y	N	N	Y	N	N	Y	Y
13 Mack	Y	N	N	N	N	N	N	Y
14 Mica	?	?	?	?	?	?	?	?
15 Shaw	Y	N	N	Y	N	N	Y	Y
16 Smith	Y	Y	N	?	?	?	?	?
17 Lehman	?	?	?	?	?	?	?	?
18 Pepper	Y	Y	Y	N	Y	Y	N	Y
19 Fascell	Y	Y	Y	Y	Y	Y	N	Y
GEORGIA								
1 Thomas	Y	Y	N	Y	N	Y	N	Y
2 Hatcher	?	N	Y	N	Y	Y	N	Y
3 Ray	Y	N	N	Y	N	Y	N	N
4 Levitas	Y	Y	Y	N	Y	Y	N	Y
5 Fowler	Y	Y	N	Y	N	N	N	Y
6 Gingrich	Y	N	N	Y	N	N	Y	Y
7 McDonald	N	N	N	N	N	N	N	N
8 Rowland	Y	Y	N	?	?	#	?	?
9 Jenkins	Y	N	Y	N	N	N	N	N
10 Barnard	Y	N	Y	N	Y	N	N	N
HAWAII								
1 Heftel	?	?	?	?	?	?	?	?
2 Akaka	Y	N	Y	N	Y	N	Y	N
IDAHO								
1 Craig	?	X	?	?	?	X	?	?
2 Hansen	?	N	N	Y	N	N	Y	N
ILLINOIS								
1 Vacancy								
2 Savage	Y	Y	Y	Y	Y	Y	N	N
3 Russo	Y	N	N	N	N	N	N	Y
4 O'Brien	Y	N	N	Y	N	N	Y	Y
5 Lipinski	?	Y	Y	N	Y	N	Y	Y
6 Hyde	Y	N	N	Y	N	N	?	?
7 Collins	?	?	?	?	?	#	?	?
8 Rostenkowski	Y	Y	Y	N	Y	Y	N	Y
9 Yates	Y	Y	Y	Y	Y	Y	N	Y
10 Porter	Y	N	N	N	N	N	N	Y
11 Annunzio	Y	N	N	Y	N	N	N	Y
12 Crane, P.	Y	N	N	Y	N	Y	N	Y
13 Erlenborn	Y	N	N	Y	N	N	Y	Y
14 Corcoran	Y	N	N	N	N	N	Y	Y
15 Madigan	?	N	N	Y	N	N	N	Y
16 Martin	Y	N	N	N	N	N	Y	Y
17 Evans	Y	Y	Y	Y	Y	Y	N	Y
18 Michel	Y	N	N	Y	N	N	Y	Y
19 Crane, D.	Y	N	N	Y	N	N	Y	N
20 Durbin	Y	Y	Y	Y	Y	Y	N	N
21 Price	?	?	?	?	?	?	?	?
22 Simon	Y	Y	Y	?	?	?	?	?
INDIANA								
1 Hall	?	Y	Y	Y	Y	Y	N	Y
2 Sharp	?	Y	N	Y	Y	Y	N	Y
3 Hiler	Y	N	N	N	N	N	Y	Y
4 Coats	Y	N	N	N	N	N	Y	N
5 Hillis	Y	N	N	Y	N	N	Y	Y

ND - Northern Democrats   SD - Southern Democrats

Corresponding to Congressional Record Votes 146, 147, 148, 149, 150, 151, 152, 153

	138	139	140	141	142	143	144	145
6 ***Burton***	Y	N	N	Y	N	N	Y	Y
7 ***Myers***	Y	N	Y	Y	Y	N	N	N
8 McCloskey	Y	Y	N	N	Y	Y	N	Y
9 Hamilton	Y	Y	N	Y	Y	Y	Y	Y
10 Jacobs	Y	N	N	Y	Y	Y	Y	N
IOWA								
1 ***Leach***	Y	Y	?	?	?	?	?	?
2 ***Tauke***	Y	Y	N	N	N	N	Y	Y
3 ***Evans***	Y	Y	N	N	N	N	Y	N
4 Smith	Y	N	Y	N	Y	Y	N	Y
5 Harkin	?	?	?	?	?	?	?	?
6 Bedell	Y	Y	N	N	Y	Y	N	Y
KANSAS								
1 ***Roberts***	Y	N	N	N	N	N	Y	N
2 Slattery	Y	Y	Y	N	Y	Y	N	N
3 ***Winn***	Y	N	N	N	N	N	Y	Y
4 Glickman	Y	Y	Y	N	Y	Y	Y	Y
5 ***Whittaker***	Y	N	N	N	N	N	Y	Y
KENTUCKY								
1 Hubbard	Y	N	Y	Y	Y	N	Y	N
2 Natcher	Y	N	Y	N	Y	Y	N	Y
3 Mazzoli	Y	Y	Y	N	Y	Y	N	Y
4 ***Snyder***	Y	N	N	Y	N	N	N	N
5 ***Rogers***	Y	N	N	Y	N	N	Y	Y
6 ***Hopkins***	?	N	N	N	N	N	Y	N
7 Perkins	Y	Y	Y	N	Y	Y	N	Y
LOUISIANA								
1 ***Livingston***	Y	N	N	N	N	N	N	Y
2 Boggs	?	N	?	Y	Y	Y	N	Y
3 Tauzin	?	N	N	N	Y	N	Y	N
4 Roemer	Y	N	N	N	Y	N	Y	N
5 Huckaby	Y	N	Y	N	Y	N	Y	Y
6 ***Moore***	Y	N	N	N	N	N	Y	N
7 Breaux	Y	N	Y	N	Y	N	N	Y
8 Long	Y	Y	Y	Y	Y	Y	N	Y
MAINE								
1 ***McKernan***	Y	Y	N	N	N	Y	Y	Y
2 ***Snowe***	Y	Y	N	N	Y	Y	Y	Y
MARYLAND								
1 Dyson	Y	N	Y	Y	Y	N	N	Y
2 Long	Y	Y	Y	?	Y	Y	N	?
3 Mikulski	Y	Y	N	Y	Y	Y	N	Y
4 ***Holt***	?	X	?	?	?	?	?	?
5 Hoyer	Y	N	Y	N	Y	Y	N	Y
6 Byron	?	N	N	Y	Y	N	N	N
7 Mitchell	Y	#	Y	N	Y	Y	N	Y
8 Barnes	Y	Y	N	Y	Y	Y	N	Y
MASSACHUSETTS								
1 ***Conte***	?	?	?	?	?	?	?	?
2 Boland	Y	N	Y	N	Y	Y	N	Y
3 Early	Y	N	Y	N	Y	Y	Y	Y
4 Frank	?	#	N	Y	Y	Y	N	Y
5 Shannon	Y	Y	Y	N	Y	Y	N	Y
6 Mavroules	Y	N	Y	N	Y	Y	N	Y
7 Markey	?	Y	Y	Y	Y	Y	N	Y
8 O'Neill								
9 Moakley	Y	Y	Y	N	Y	Y	N	Y
10 Studds	Y	Y	Y	N	Y	Y	N	Y
11 Donnelly	?	Y	Y	N	Y	Y	N	Y
MICHIGAN								
1 Conyers	?	?	?	?	?	?	?	?
2 ***Pursell***	?	?	?	?	?	?	?	?
3 Wolpe	Y	Y	Y	Y	Y	Y	N	Y
4 ***Siljander***	?	X	?	?	?	X	?	?
5 ***Sawyer***	Y	N	N	Y	N	Y	N	Y
6 Carr	Y	Y	Y	N	Y	Y	N	Y
7 Kildee	Y	Y	Y	N	Y	Y	N	Y
8 Traxler	?	?	?	?	?	?	?	?
9 ***Vander Jagt***	?	?	N	N	N	Y	Y	Y
10 Albosta	Y	N	Y	N	Y	Y	N	Y
11 ***Davis***	Y	Y	N	N	N	Y	N	Y
12 Bonior	Y	Y	Y	N	Y	Y	N	Y
13 Crockett	?	#	?	?	?	?	?	?
14 Hertel	Y	Y	Y	N	Y	Y	N	Y
15 Ford	?	Y	Y	N	Y	Y	N	Y
16 Dingell	Y	Y	Y	N	Y	Y	N	Y
17 Levin	Y	Y	Y	Y	Y	Y	N	Y
18 ***Broomfield***	Y	Y	N	N	N	N	Y	Y
MINNESOTA								
1 Penny	Y	Y	N	Y	Y	Y	N	N
2 ***Weber***	?	Y	N	N	N	N	Y	Y
3 ***Frenzel***	Y	N	N	?	?	X	?	?
4 Vento	Y	Y	Y	Y	Y	Y	N	Y
5 Sabo	?	?	?	?	?	?	?	?
6 Sikorski	Y	Y	N	Y	Y	Y	N	Y

	138	139	140	141	142	143	144	145
7 ***Stangeland***	Y	N	N	Y	N	N	N	Y
8 Oberstar	+	Y	Y	Y	Y	Y	N	Y
MISSISSIPPI								
1 Whitten	Y	N	Y	N	Y	Y	N	Y
2 ***Franklin***	Y	N	N	Y	N	N	Y	Y
3 Montgomery	?	N	Y	Y	N	N	N	N
4 Dowdy	?	Y	Y	Y	Y	Y	N	Y
5 ***Lott***	Y	N	N	Y	N	N	Y	Y
MISSOURI								
1 Clay	?	?	?	?	?	?	?	?
2 Young	Y	N	Y	Y	Y	Y	N	Y
3 Gephardt	Y	Y	Y	Y	Y	Y	N	Y
4 Skelton	Y	Y	Y	?	?	?	?	?
5 Wheat	Y	Y	Y	Y	Y	Y	N	Y
6 ***Coleman***	Y	Y	N	N	N	Y	Y	Y
7 ***Taylor***	Y	N	N	Y	N	Y	Y	N
8 ***Emerson***	Y	N	N	Y	N	Y	Y	N
9 Volkmer	Y	Y	Y	Y	Y	Y	N	N
MONTANA								
1 Williams	?	Y	N	Y	Y	Y	N	Y
2 ***Marlenee***	?	?	?	?	?	?	?	?
NEBRASKA								
1 ***Bereuter***	Y	N	N	N	N	N	Y	Y
2 ***Daub***	?	N	N	Y	N	N	Y	Y
3 ***Smith***	Y	N	N	Y	Y	Y	N	Y
NEVADA								
1 Reid	Y	Y	Y	Y	Y	Y	N	Y
2 ***Vucanovich***	+	X	-	+	-	X	+	-
NEW HAMPSHIRE								
1 D'Amours	Y	Y	Y	N	Y	Y	N	N
2 ***Gregg***	Y	Y	N	Y	N	N	Y	Y
NEW JERSEY								
1 Florio	+	+	-	+	+	#	-	+
2 Hughes	Y	N	Y	N	Y	N	N	Y
3 Howard	?	#	?	?	?	Y	N	Y
4 ***Smith***	Y	Y	N	N	N	Y	Y	Y
5 ***Roukema***	Y	Y	N	N	Y	Y	Y	Y
6 Dwyer	Y	N	Y	N	Y	Y	N	Y
7 ***Rinaldo***	Y	Y	N	N	Y	Y	N	Y
8 Roe	Y	Y	Y	N	Y	Y	N	Y
9 Torricelli	Y	Y	N	Y	Y	Y	N	Y
10 Rodino	?	#	Y	N	Y	Y	N	Y
11 Minish	Y	Y	Y	N	Y	Y	N	Y
12 ***Courter***	Y	Y	N	N	N	Y	Y	N
13 ***Forsythe***	Y	N	N	+	-	-	-	-
14 Guarini	Y	Y	Y	N	Y	Y	N	Y
NEW MEXICO								
1 ***Lujan***	Y	N	N	Y	N	Y	Y	Y
2 ***Skeen***	Y	N	N	Y	N	N	Y	Y
3 Richardson	Y	Y	N	Y	Y	Y	N	Y
NEW YORK								
1 ***Carney***	?	?	?	?	?	?	?	?
2 Downey	Y	Y	N	N	Y	Y	N	Y
3 Mrazek	Y	Y	Y	N	Y	N	Y	Y
4 ***Lent***	Y	N	N	N	N	N	?	?
5 ***McGrath***	Y	Y	N	N	N	N	?	?
6 Addabbo	Y	Y	Y	Y	Y	Y	?	?
7 Ackerman	Y	Y	Y	N	Y	Y	N	Y
8 Scheuer	Y	Y	N	Y	Y	Y	Y	Y
9 Ferraro	Y	Y	Y	N	Y	Y	N	Y
10 Schumer	Y	Y	N	Y	Y	Y	N	Y
11 Towns	Y	Y	?	N	Y	Y	N	Y
12 Owens	Y	Y	Y	N	Y	Y	?	?
13 Solarz	?	Y	N	Y	Y	Y	N	Y
14 ***Molinari***	Y	Y	N	N	N	Y	N	Y
15 ***Green***	Y	N	Y	N	Y	Y	N	Y
16 Rangel	Y	Y	N	Y	Y	Y	N	Y
17 Weiss	+	+	-	+	+	+	-	+
18 Garcia	Y	Y	Y	N	Y	Y	N	Y
19 Biaggi	Y	Y	N	Y	Y	Y	N	Y
20 Ottinger	?	Y	N	Y	Y	Y	N	Y
21 ***Fish***	Y	Y	Y	Y	N	Y	N	Y
22 ***Gilman***	Y	Y	N	Y	Y	Y	N	Y
23 Stratton	?	?	?	?	?	?	?	?
24 ***Solomon***	N	N	N	N	N	N	Y	N
25 ***Boehlert***	Y	Y	N	N	N	Y	Y	Y
26 ***Martin***	Y	N	N	N	N	N	Y	Y
27 ***Wortley***	Y	N	N	Y	N	?	?	?
28 McHugh	?	Y	Y	Y	Y	Y	N	Y
29 ***Horton***	Y	Y	N	Y	Y	Y	N	Y
30 ***Conable***	Y	N	N	Y	N	N	Y	Y
31 ***Kemp***	?	N	N	Y	N	N	Y	Y
32 LaFalce	Y	Y	N	Y	Y	Y	N	Y
33 Nowak	Y	Y	N	Y	Y	Y	N	Y
34 Lundine	?	Y	N	Y	Y	N	N	Y

	138	139	140	141	142	143	144	145
NORTH CAROLINA								
1 Jones	Y	N	Y	N	Y	Y	N	N
2 Valentine	Y	Y	Y	Y	Y	Y	Y	N
3 Whitley	Y	Y	Y	Y	Y	Y	N	Y
4 Andrews	?	?	Y	Y	Y	Y	N	Y
5 Neal	Y	Y	N	Y	Y	N	N	Y
6 Britt	Y	Y	Y	N	Y	Y	N	Y
7 Rose	?	N	Y	Y	Y	Y	N	Y
8 Hefner	Y	Y	Y	Y	Y	Y	N	Y
9 ***Martin***	Y	N	N	Y	N	N	Y	Y
10 ***Broyhill***	Y	N	N	Y	N	N	Y	N
11 Clarke	Y	N	Y	N	Y	Y	N	Y
NORTH DAKOTA								
AL Dorgan	Y	Y	Y	Y	Y	N	N	N
OHIO								
1 Luken	?	Y	N	N	Y	Y	N	Y
2 ***Gradison***	?	?	?	?	?	?	?	?
3 Hall	Y	Y	N	Y	Y	Y	N	Y
4 ***Oxley***	Y	N	N	Y	N	N	Y	Y
5 ***Latta***	Y	N	N	Y	N	N	Y	N
6 ***McEwen***	Y	N	N	Y	N	N	Y	N
7 ***DeWine***	Y	Y	N	N	N	N	Y	Y
8 ***Kindness***	Y	N	N	N	N	N	Y	Y
9 Kaptur	Y	Y	N	N	Y	Y	Y	Y
10 ***Miller***	Y	N	N	Y	Y	N	Y	N
11 Eckart	Y	Y	N	Y	Y	N	N	Y
12 ***Kasich***	Y	N	N	Y	N	N	Y	Y
13 Pease	Y	Y	Y	Y	Y	Y	N	Y
14 Seiberling	Y	N	Y	Y	Y	Y	N	Y
15 ***Wylie***	?	N	N	N	N	N	Y	Y
16 ***Regula***	Y	N	N	N	N	N	Y	N
17 ***Williams***	Y	N	N	N	Y	Y	Y	Y
18 Applegate	?	N	N	Y	N	N	N	N
19 Feighan	Y	Y	N	Y	Y	N	N	Y
20 Oakar	Y	Y	N	Y	Y	Y	N	Y
21 Stokes	Y	N	Y	N	Y	Y	N	Y
OKLAHOMA								
1 Jones	Y	N	Y	Y	Y	Y	Y	Y
2 Synar	Y	Y	Y	Y	Y	Y	N	Y
3 Watkins	Y	N	Y	Y	Y	Y	N	N
4 McCurdy	Y	Y	Y	Y	Y	N	Y	Y
5 ***Edwards***	Y	N	N	Y	N	N	N	N
6 English	Y	N	Y	Y	Y	N	N	N
OREGON								
1 AuCoin	?	?	?	?	?	?	?	?
2 ***Smith, R.***	Y	N	N	Y	N	N	Y	N
3 Wyden	Y	Y	N	Y	Y	Y	N	Y
4 Weaver	Y	Y	N	Y	Y	Y	N	N
5 ***Smith, D.***	?	X	?	?	?	?	?	?
PENNSYLVANIA								
1 Foglietta	?	?	?	?	?	?	?	?
2 Gray	?	Y	Y	N	Y	Y	N	Y
3 Borski	Y	Y	Y	Y	Y	Y	N	Y
4 Kolter	?	?	?	?	?	?	?	?
5 ***Schulze***	Y	N	N	?	?	?	?	?
6 Yatron	Y	Y	N	Y	Y	Y	Y	Y
7 Edgar	?	Y	Y	N	Y	Y	N	Y
8 Kostmayer	?	#	?	?	?	?	?	?
9 ***Shuster***	?	X	?	?	?	?	?	?
10 ***McDade***	?	Y	?	N	Y	Y	N	Y
11 Harrison	Y	Y	Y	Y	Y	Y	N	Y
12 Murtha	Y	N	Y	Y	Y	Y	N	Y
13 ***Coughlin***	Y	Y	N	N	N	Y	Y	Y
14 Coyne	Y	Y	Y	N	Y	Y	N	Y
15 ***Ritter***	Y	N	N	N	N	Y	Y	N
16 ***Walker***	Y	N	N	N	N	N	Y	N
17 ***Gekas***	Y	N	N	Y	N	N	Y	Y
18 Walgren	Y	Y	N	Y	Y	Y	Y	Y
19 ***Goodling***	Y	N	N	Y	N	N	Y	N
20 Gaydos	Y	Y	N	Y	Y	Y	N	Y
21 ***Ridge***	Y	Y	?	Y	Y	Y	Y	Y
22 Murphy	Y	N	Y	Y	Y	Y	N	Y
23 ***Clinger***	Y	Y	N	N	N	N	Y	Y
RHODE ISLAND								
1 St Germain	Y	Y	Y	N	Y	Y	N	Y
2 ***Schneider***	Y	Y	N	?	?	#	?	?
SOUTH CAROLINA								
1 ***Hartnett***	?	?	N	Y	N	N	Y	Y
2 ***Spence***	Y	N	N	Y	N	N	Y	Y
3 Derrick	?	#	?	?	?	#	?	?
4 ***Campbell***	Y	N	N	Y	N	N	Y	Y
5 Spratt	?	Y	Y	Y	Y	Y	N	Y
6 Tallon	Y	Y	Y	Y	Y	Y	N	Y
SOUTH DAKOTA								
AL Daschle	Y	Y	Y	Y	Y	Y	N	N

	138	139	140	141	142	143	144	145
TENNESSEE								
1 ***Quillen***	Y	N	N	Y	?	?	?	?
2 ***Duncan***	Y	N	N	?	?	?	?	?
3 Lloyd	?	#	?	?	?	?	?	?
4 Cooper	Y	Y	Y	N	Y	Y	N	Y
5 Boner	Y	Y	N	Y	Y	?	N	Y
6 Gore	Y	Y	N	Y	Y	Y	N	Y
7 ***Sundquist***	Y	N	N	Y	N	N	Y	Y
8 Jones	?	?	?	?	?	?	?	?
9 Ford	Y	Y	Y	Y	Y	Y	N	Y
TEXAS								
1 Hall, S.	Y	N	N	Y	N	N	Y	N
2 Wilson	?	?	?	?	?	?	?	?
3 ***Bartlett***	Y	N	N	Y	N	N	Y	Y
4 Hall, R.	Y	N	N	Y	N	N	Y	N
5 Bryant	Y	Y	N	Y	Y	Y	N	Y
6 ***Gramm***	Y	N	N	Y	N	N	Y	N
7 ***Archer***	Y	N	N	Y	N	N	Y	N
8 ***Fields***	Y	N	N	Y	N	Y	Y	N
9 Brooks	Y	N	Y	Y	Y	Y	N	Y
10 Pickle	Y	N	Y	N	Y	Y	N	Y
11 Leath	Y	N	Y	Y	Y	N	Y	Y
12 Wright	Y	N	Y	Y	Y	Y	N	Y
13 Hightower	Y	N	Y	N	Y	Y	Y	Y
14 Patman	Y	Y	N	Y	Y	Y	Y	N
15 de la Garza	Y	N	Y	N	Y	Y	N	Y
16 Coleman	Y	N	N	Y	Y	Y	N	Y
17 Stenholm	Y	N	N	Y	Y	N	Y	N
18 Leland	Y	Y	N	Y	Y	Y	N	Y
19 Hance	Y	N	Y	Y	Y	N	Y	N
20 Gonzalez	Y	Y	N	Y	Y	Y	N	N
21 ***Loeffler***	Y	N	N	Y	N	N	Y	N
22 ***Paul***	Y	N	N	Y	N	N	Y	N
23 Kazen	?	?	?	?	?	?	?	?
24 Frost	?	?	?	?	?	?	?	?
25 Andrews	Y	Y	N	Y	Y	Y	Y	Y
26 Vandergriff	Y	Y	N	Y	Y	N	Y	Y
27 Ortiz	Y	Y	Y	Y	Y	Y	N	Y
UTAH								
1 ***Hansen***	?	X	?	?	?	X	?	?
2 ***Marriott***	Y	N	N	Y	Y	N	N	Y
3 ***Nielson***	+	X	-	+	-	X	+	+
VERMONT								
AL ***Jeffords***	Y	Y	N	N	N	Y	N	Y
VIRGINIA								
1 ***Bateman***	Y	N	N	Y	N	N	Y	Y
2 ***Whitehurst***	Y	N	N	Y	N	N	Y	Y
3 ***Bliley***	Y	N	N	Y	N	N	Y	Y
4 Sisisky	?	X	?	?	?	#	?	?
5 Daniel	Y	N	N	Y	N	N	Y	Y
6 Olin	Y	N	Y	N	Y	Y	Y	Y
7 ***Robinson***	Y	N	N	Y	N	N	Y	Y
8 ***Parris***	Y	N	N	N	N	N	Y	Y
9 Boucher	?	Y	N	Y	Y	Y	N	Y
10 ***Wolf***	Y	N	N	N	N	N	Y	Y
WASHINGTON								
1 ***Pritchard***	?	?	?	?	?	?	?	?
2 Swift	Y	Y	N	Y	Y	Y	N	Y
3 Bonker	+	#	-	+	+	#	-	+
4 ***Morrison***	+	+	-	+	-	+	+	+
5 Foley	Y	Y	Y	Y	Y	Y	N	Y
6 Dicks	?	?	Y	Y	Y	Y	N	Y
7 Lowry	Y	Y	N	Y	Y	N	N	Y
8 ***Chandler***	Y	Y	N	Y	N	N	Y	Y
WEST VIRGINIA								
1 Mollohan	Y	Y	N	Y	Y	Y	N	Y
2 Staggers	Y	Y	Y	Y	Y	Y	N	Y
3 Wise	Y	Y	N	Y	Y	Y	Y	Y
4 Rahall	?	#	?	?	?	#	N	Y
WISCONSIN								
1 Aspin	Y	Y	N	Y	Y	Y	N	Y
2 Kastenmeier	Y	Y	N	N	Y	Y	N	Y
3 ***Gunderson***	Y	Y	N	N	Y	N	Y	Y
4 Zablocki	Y	Y	Y	Y	Y	Y	N	Y
5 Moody	Y	Y	Y	Y	Y	N	N	Y
6 ***Petri***	Y	Y	N	N	N	N	Y	N
7 Obey	Y	Y	Y	Y	Y	Y	N	Y
8 ***Roth***	Y	Y	N	Y	N	N	?	?
9 ***Sensenbrenner***	Y	Y	N	Y	N	N	Y	N
WYOMING								
AL ***Cheney***	?	N	?	?	?	X	?	?

Southern states - Ala., Ark., Fla., Ga., Ky., La., Miss., N.C., Okla., S.C., Tenn., Texas, Va.

CQ House Votes 146 - 153

146. Procedural Motion. Sensenbrenner, R-Wis., motion to approve the House *Journal* of Thursday, June 2. Motion agreed to 283-21: R 108-13; D 175-8 (ND 112-6, SD 63-2), June 3, 1983.

147. HR 3135. Legislative Branch Appropriations, Fiscal 1984. Fazio, D-Calif., motion that the House resolve itself into the Committee of the Whole for consideration of the bill to make fiscal 1984 appropriations for the legislative branch. Motion agreed to 301-10: R 114-8; D 187-2 (ND 122-1, SD 65-1), June 3, 1983.

148. HR 3135. Legislative Branch Appropriations, Fiscal 1984. Gregg, R-N.H., amendment to reduce funding for House committees by $6 million, from $44 million to $38 million. Rejected 133-189: R 108-17; D 25-172 (ND 8-121, SD 17-51), June 3, 1983.

149. HR 3135. Legislative Branch Appropriations, Fiscal 1984. Bartlett, R-Texas, amendment to cut $6.9 million from the recommended $67 million for members' expense accounts. Rejected 156-160: R 106-16; D 50-144 (ND 19-109, SD 31-35), June 3, 1983.

150. HR 3135. Legislative Branch Appropriations, Fiscal 1984. Hunter, R-Calif., amendment to cut $9.3 million from official congressional mail costs, reducing the amount from $107.1 million to $97.8 million. Rejected 134-173: R 104-15; D 30-158 (ND 12-112, SD 18-46), June 3, 1983.

151. HR 3135. Legislative Branch Appropriations, Fiscal 1984. Hiler, R-Ind., amendment to reduce funds for the Congressional Budget Office by $733,850, from $16.3 million to $15.6 million. Rejected 141-164: R 118-2; D 23-162 (ND 8-113, SD 15-49), June 3, 1983.

152. HR 3135. Legislative Branch Appropriations, Fiscal 1984. Brown, R-Colo., amendment to reduce by $169,876 the bill's funding for 14 operators of automatic elevators in House office buildings, thus eliminating their positions. Rejected 101-193: R 82-36; D 19-157 (ND 5-107, SD 14-50), June 3, 1983.

153. HR 3135. Legislative Branch Appropriations, Fiscal 1984. Passage of the bill to appropriate $1,208,397,750 for the legislative branch in fiscal 1984. Passed 184-104: R 34-82; D 150-22 (ND 104-8, SD 46-14), June 3, 1983. The president had requested $1,227,335,200 in new budget authority. Traditionally, the president simply requests the amount congressional agencies want included in the budget.

KEY

- Y Voted for (yea).
- # Paired for.
- + Announced for.
- N Voted against (nay).
- X Paired against.
- - Announced against.
- P Voted "present".
- C Voted "present" to avoid possible conflict of interest.
- ? Did not vote or otherwise make a position known.

Democrats *Republicans*

	146	147	148	149	150	151	152	153
ALABAMA								
1 *Edwards*	Y	?	?	?	?	?	?	?
2 *Dickinson*	?	?	?	?	?	?	?	?
3 Nichols	?	?	#	#	#	?	?	X
4 Bevill	?	?	?	?	#	?	?	?
5 Flippo	Y	Y	N	N	N	N	N	N
6 Erdreich	Y	Y	Y	Y	Y	N	N	X
7 Shelby	Y	Y	N	Y	N	N	N	Y
ALASKA								
AL *Young*	?	?	?	?	?	?	?	?
ARIZONA								
1 *McCain*	?	?	?	?	?	?	?	X
2 Udall	Y	Y	N	N	N	N	N	Y
3 *Stump*	Y	Y	Y	Y	Y	Y	Y	N
4 *Rudd*	?	Y	Y	N	Y	Y	N	Y
5 McNulty	Y	Y	N	Y	Y	N	N	Y
ARKANSAS								
1 Alexander	Y	Y	N	?	?	?	?	?
2 *Bethune*	Y	Y	Y	Y	Y	Y	Y	N
3 *Hammerschmidt*	Y	Y	Y	Y	Y	Y	N	N
4 Anthony	Y	Y	N	N	N	N	N	Y
CALIFORNIA								
1 Bosco	Y	?	N	N	N	N	N	Y
2 *Chappie*	?	?	#	?	?	?	?	X
3 Matsui	Y	Y	N	N	N	N	N	Y
4 Fazio	Y	Y	N	N	N	N	N	Y
5 Vacancy								
6 Boxer	Y	Y	N	N	N	N	N	Y
7 Miller	Y	Y	N	N	N	N	N	Y
8 Dellums	?	?	N	N	N	N	?	Y
9 Stark	Y	Y	N	N	N	N	N	Y
10 Edwards	Y	Y	N	N	N	N	N	Y
11 Lantos	Y	Y	N	N	N	N	N	Y
12 Zschau	Y	Y	Y	Y	Y	Y	Y	Y
13 Mineta	Y	Y	N	N	N	N	N	Y
14 *Shumway*	?	?	?	?	?	?	?	?
15 Coelho	?	?	?	?	?	?	?	?
16 Panetta	+	+	+	+	+	-	-	-
17 *Pashayan*	?	?	#	?	?	?	?	X
18 Lehman	Y	Y	N	N	N	N	N	Y
19 *Lagomarsino*	Y	Y	Y	Y	N	Y	Y	N
20 *Thomas*	Y	Y	Y	Y	Y	Y	Y	Y
21 *Fiedler*	Y	Y	Y	Y	Y	Y	N	N
22 *Moorhead*	Y	Y	Y	Y	Y	Y	Y	N
23 Beilenson	Y	Y	N	N	N	N	N	Y
24 Waxman	Y	Y	N	N	N	N	N	Y
25 Roybal	Y	Y	N	N	N	N	N	Y
26 Berman	?	?	?	?	?	?	?	?
27 Levine	?	?	?	?	?	?	?	+
28 Dixon	?	?	X	?	?	?	?	#
29 Hawkins	?	?	X	?	X	?	?	#
30 Martinez	?	?	?	?	?	?	?	?
31 Dymally	?	?	X	?	?	?	?	#
32 Anderson	Y	Y	N	N	Y	Y	Y	Y
33 *Dreier*	Y	Y	Y	Y	Y	Y	Y	N
34 Torres	+	+	-	-	-	-	-	+
35 *Lewis*	Y	Y	N	N	N	Y	N	Y
36 Brown	?	?	?	?	?	?	?	?
37 *McCandless*	Y	Y	Y	Y	Y	Y	Y	N
38 Patterson	Y	Y	Y	N	N	N	N	Y
39 *Dannemeyer*	Y	Y	Y	Y	Y	Y	Y	N
40 *Badham*	?	?	#	?	?	?	?	X
41 *Lowery*	Y	Y	Y	Y	Y	Y	N	N
42 *Lungren*	?	Y	Y	Y	Y	Y	Y	N
43 *Packard*	Y	Y	Y	Y	?	Y	Y	N
44 Bates	Y	Y	N	N	N	N	N	Y
45 *Hunter*	Y	Y	Y	Y	Y	Y	Y	N
COLORADO								
1 Schroeder	N	Y	N	Y	N	Y	N	Y
2 Wirth	?	?	?	?	?	?	?	?
3 Kogovsek	Y	Y	N	Y	N	Y	N	Y
4 *Brown*	N	Y	Y	N	Y	Y	N	Y
5 *Kramer*	Y	Y	Y	Y	Y	Y	Y	N
6 *Schaefer*	Y	Y	Y	Y	Y	Y	Y	N
CONNECTICUT								
1 Kennelly	Y	Y	N	N	N	N	N	Y
2 Gejdenson	N	Y	N	N	N	N	N	Y
3 Morrison	?	?	?	X	?	?	?	#
4 *McKinney*	?	?	?	?	?	?	?	?
5 Ratchford	Y	Y	N	N	?	?	?	#
6 *Johnson*	Y	Y	Y	?	?	?	?	?
DELAWARE								
AL Carper	Y	Y	Y	Y	N	N	N	Y
FLORIDA								
1 Hutto	?	?	+	+	+	+	+	+
2 Fuqua	Y	Y	N	N	N	N	N	Y
3 Bennett	Y	Y	Y	Y	Y	Y	Y	N
4 Chappell	Y	Y	N	N	N	N	N	Y
5 *McCollum*	N	Y	Y	Y	Y	Y	N	N
6 MacKay	Y	Y	N	Y	N	N	N	Y
7 Gibbons	Y	Y	N	N	N	Y	N	Y
8 *Young*	?	Y	Y	Y	Y	Y	Y	N
9 *Bilirakis*	Y	Y	Y	Y	Y	Y	Y	N
10 Ireland	?	?	?	?	?	?	?	?
11 Nelson	+	?	X	X	X	X	X	?
12 *Lewis*	?	?	?	#	#	?	?	X
13 *Mack*	N	Y	Y	Y	Y	Y	Y	N
14 Mica	?	?	?	?	?	?	?	#
15 *Shaw*	?	?	#	?	?	?	?	#
16 Smith	?	?	X	?	?	?	?	#
17 Lehman	?	?	?	?	?	?	N	Y
18 Pepper	?	?	X	?	?	?	?	#
19 Fascell	Y	Y	N	N	N	N	N	Y
GEORGIA								
1 Thomas	Y	Y	N	Y	N	N	N	Y
2 Hatcher	Y	Y	N	Y	N	N	N	Y
3 Ray	Y	Y	N	Y	Y	N	N	Y
4 Levitas	Y	Y	N	Y	N	N	N	Y
5 Fowler	?	?	?	?	?	?	?	?
6 *Gingrich*	Y	Y	Y	Y	Y	Y	Y	N
7 McDonald	Y	N	Y	N	N	N	N	N
8 Rowland	Y	Y	N	Y	N	N	N	Y
9 Jenkins	Y	Y	N	N	N	N	N	Y
10 Barnard	Y	Y	N	Y	Y	Y	Y	Y
HAWAII								
1 Heftel	?	?	?	?	?	?	?	?
2 Akaka	Y	Y	N	N	N	N	N	Y
IDAHO								
1 *Craig*	?	?	?	#	#	#	?	X
2 *Hansen*	?	?	Y	Y	Y	Y	?	N
ILLINOIS								
1 Vacancy								
2 Savage	Y	Y	N	N	N	N	N	Y
3 Russo	?	?	?	?	?	?	?	?
4 *O'Brien*	Y	Y	Y	Y	Y	Y	Y	N
5 Lipinski	?	?	?	?	?	?	?	?
6 *Hyde*	Y	Y	Y	Y	Y	Y	Y	N
7 Collins	?	?	?	?	?	?	?	?
8 Rostenkowski	Y	Y	N	N	N	N	N	?
9 Yates	N	Y	N	Y	N	N	N	Y
10 *Porter*	Y	Y	Y	Y	N	Y	N	Y
11 Annunzio	Y	Y	N	N	N	N	N	Y
12 *Crane, P.*	Y	Y	Y	Y	Y	Y	Y	N
13 *Erlenborn*	Y	Y	Y	Y	Y	Y	Y	N
14 *Corcoran*	+	+	+	#	#	#	+	X
15 *Madigan*	Y	Y	Y	N	Y	Y	Y	Y
16 *Martin*	Y	Y	Y	Y	Y	Y	Y	Y
17 Evans	Y	Y	N	N	N	?	?	#
18 *Michel*	Y	Y	Y	Y	Y	Y	Y	Y
19 *Crane, D.*	Y	Y	Y	Y	Y	Y	Y	N
20 Durbin	N	Y	N	Y	?	?	?	#
21 Price	?	?	?	?	?	?	?	?
22 Simon	Y	Y	N	N	N	N	N	Y
INDIANA								
1 Hall	?	?	?	?	?	?	?	#
2 Sharp	Y	Y	N	Y	N	N	N	Y
3 *Hiler*	N	Y	Y	Y	Y	Y	Y	X
4 *Coats*	Y	N	Y	Y	Y	Y	Y	N
5 *Hillis*	Y	Y	Y	?	?	?	?	?

ND - Northern Democrats   SD - Southern Democrats

	146	147	148	149	150	151	152	153
6 ***Burton***	Y	Y	Y	Y	Y	Y	Y	N
7 ***Myers***	Y	Y	N	N	N	Y	N	Y
8 McCloskey	Y	Y	N	N	N	N	N	Y
9 Hamilton	Y	Y	N	N	N	N	N	Y
10 Jacobs	P	Y	Y	Y	Y	Y	N	N
IOWA								
1 ***Leach***	?	?	?	?	?	?	?	?
2 ***Tauke***	Y	Y	Y	Y	Y	Y	Y	N
3 ***Evans***	N	Y	Y	Y	Y	Y	Y	N
4 Smith	Y	Y	N	N	N	N	N	Y
5 Harkin	?	?	?	?	?	?	?	?
6 Bedell	Y	Y	N	N	N	N	N	Y
KANSAS								
1 ***Roberts***	N	Y	Y	Y	Y	Y	Y	N
2 Slattery	?	?	?	?	?	?	?	?
3 ***Winn***	?	?	Y	Y	Y	Y	Y	N
4 Glickman	?	?	?	#	?	?	?	?
5 ***Whittaker***	Y	Y	Y	Y	Y	Y	Y	N
KENTUCKY								
1 Hubbard	Y	Y	Y	Y	Y	Y	Y	N
2 Natcher	Y	Y	N	N	N	N	N	Y
3 Mazzoli	Y	Y	N	N	N	N	N	Y
4 ***Snyder***	Y	Y	N	Y	N	Y	Y	Y
5 ***Rogers***	Y	Y	Y	Y	Y	Y	Y	N
6 ***Hopkins***	Y	Y	Y	Y	Y	Y	Y	?
7 Perkins	Y	Y	N	N	N	N	N	Y
LOUISIANA								
1 ***Livingston***	Y	Y	Y	Y	N	Y	N	N
2 Boggs	Y	Y	N	N	N	N	N	Y
3 Tauzin	Y	Y	Y	Y	Y	N	Y	N
4 Roemer	N	Y	Y	Y	Y	N	Y	N
5 Huckaby	?	?	?	?	?	?	?	?
6 ***Moore***	Y	Y	Y	Y	Y	Y	Y	N
7 Breaux	Y	Y	Y	N	N	N	N	Y
8 Long	Y	Y	N	N	N	N	N	Y
MAINE								
1 ***McKernan***	Y	Y	Y	Y	Y	Y	N	?
2 ***Snowe***	Y	Y	Y	Y	Y	Y	?	?
MARYLAND								
1 Dyson	Y	Y	N	N	N	N	N	N
2 Long	Y	Y	N	N	N	N	N	Y
3 Mikulski	Y	Y	N	N	N	N	N	?
4 ***Holt***	?	?	?	?	?	?	?	?
5 Hoyer	Y	Y	N	N	N	N	N	Y
6 Byron	?	Y	N	Y	N	Y	N	N
7 Mitchell	N	Y	N	N	N	N	N	Y
8 Barnes	Y	Y	N	N	N	N	N	Y
MASSACHUSETTS								
1 ***Conte***	?	?	?	?	?	?	?	?
2 Boland	Y	Y	N	X	X	?	?	#
3 Early	Y	Y	Y	Y	N	N	?	Y
4 Frank	Y	Y	N	N	N	N	N	Y
5 Shannon	?	?	?	?	?	?	?	?
6 Mavroules	Y	Y	N	N	N	?	?	?
7 Markey	Y	?	N	N	N	N	N	Y
8 O'Neill								
9 Moakley	Y	Y	N	N	N	N	N	Y
10 Studds	Y	Y	N	N	N	N	?	?
11 Donnelly	Y	Y	N	N	N	N	N	Y
MICHIGAN								
1 Conyers	?	?	?	?	?	?	?	?
2 ***Pursell***	?	?	?	?	?	?	?	?
3 Wolpe	Y	Y	N	N	N	N	?	?
4 ***Siljander***	?	?	#	?	?	?	?	X
5 ***Sawyer***	Y	Y	N	N	N	?	N	Y
6 Carr	Y	Y	N	N	N	N	N	Y
7 Kildee	Y	Y	N	N	N	N	N	Y
8 Traxler	Y	Y	N	N	N	N	?	?
9 ***Vander Jagt***	?	?	Y	Y	Y	Y	Y	Y
10 Albosta	Y	Y	N	N	N	Y	?	?
11 ***Davis***	Y	Y	N	N	Y	Y	N	Y
12 Bonior	Y	Y	N	N	?	?	?	?
13 Crockett	?	?	?	?	?	?	?	?
14 Hertel	Y	Y	N	N	N	N	N	Y
15 Ford	?	Y	N	N	N	N	N	Y
16 Dingell	Y	Y	N	N	N	N	?	Y
17 Levin	Y	Y	N	N	N	N	N	Y
18 ***Broomfield***	Y	Y	N	Y	Y	Y	N	N
MINNESOTA								
1 Penny	Y	Y	N	Y	Y	N	N	Y
2 ***Weber***	Y	Y	Y	Y	Y	Y	Y	N
3 ***Frenzel***	?	?	?	?	?	?	?	X
4 Vento	Y	Y	N	N	N	N	N	Y
5 Sabo	?	?	?	?	?	?	?	?
6 Sikorski	?	?	?	?	?	?	?	?

	146	147	148	149	150	151	152	153
7 ***Stangeland***	Y	Y	N	N	Y	Y	N	Y
8 Oberstar	P	Y	N	N	N	N	N	Y
MISSISSIPPI								
1 Whitten	Y	Y	N	N	N	N	N	Y
2 ***Franklin***	Y	Y	Y	Y	Y	Y	N	N
3 Montgomery	Y	Y	N	Y	?	?	?	?
4 Dowdy	Y	Y	N	N	N	N	N	Y
5 ***Lott***	Y	Y	Y	?	?	?	?	?
MISSOURI								
1 Clay	?	?	?	?	?	?	?	?
2 Young	Y	Y	N	N	N	N	N	Y
3 Gephardt	Y	Y	N	N	N	N	N	Y
4 Skelton	?	?	?	?	?	?	?	?
5 Wheat	Y	Y	N	N	N	N	N	Y
6 ***Coleman***	Y	Y	Y	Y	N	Y	Y	N
7 ***Taylor***	Y	Y	Y	N	N	Y	N	Y
8 ***Emerson***	N	N	Y	Y	Y	Y	Y	N
9 Volkmer	Y	Y	Y	Y	N	Y	N	Y
MONTANA								
1 Williams	?	?	?	?	?	?	?	?
2 ***Marlenee***	?	?	?	?	?	?	?	?
NEBRASKA								
1 ***Bereuter***	Y	Y	Y	Y	Y	Y	N	N
2 ***Daub***	Y	Y	Y	Y	Y	Y	Y	N
3 ***Smith***	Y	Y	Y	Y	Y	Y	Y	Y
NEVADA								
1 Reid	Y	Y	N	N	N	N	N	Y
2 ***Vucanovich***	+	+	#	+	+	+	+	#
NEW HAMPSHIRE								
1 D'Amours	Y	Y	N	Y	Y	?	?	?
2 ***Gregg***	Y	N	Y	Y	Y	Y	Y	N
NEW JERSEY								
1 Florio	+	+	-	-	-	X	-	#
2 Hughes	Y	Y	N	N	Y	N	?	Y
3 Howard	Y	Y	N	N	N	N	?	?
4 ***Smith***	Y	Y	N	Y	N	Y	N	Y
5 ***Roukema***	Y	Y	Y	Y	Y	Y	N	N
6 Dwyer	Y	Y	N	N	N	N	N	Y
7 ***Rinaldo***	Y	Y	N	N	Y	Y	N	Y
8 Roe	Y	Y	N	N	N	N	N	Y
9 Torricelli	?	?	?	?	?	?	?	?
10 Rodino	Y	Y	N	N	N	N	N	Y
11 Minish	Y	Y	N	N	N	N	N	Y
12 ***Courter***	Y	Y	Y	Y	Y	Y	Y	N
13 ***Forsythe***	-	+	-	-	-	-	+	+
14 Guarini	Y	Y	N	N	N	N	N	Y
NEW MEXICO								
1 ***Lujan***	Y	N	Y	Y	Y	Y	Y	N
2 ***Skeen***	Y	Y	Y	Y	Y	Y	Y	N
3 Richardson	?	?	?	?	?	?	?	?
NEW YORK								
1 ***Carney***	?	?	?	?	?	?	?	X
2 Downey	Y	?	N	N	N	N	N	Y
3 Mrazek	Y	Y	N	N	N	N	N	Y
4 ***Lent***	?	?	?	?	?	?	?	?
5 ***McGrath***	?	?	?	?	?	?	?	?
6 Addabbo	?	?	X	X	X	X	?	#
7 Ackerman	Y	Y	N	N	N	N	N	Y
8 Scheuer	Y	Y	N	N	N	N	N	Y
9 Ferraro	Y	Y	N	N	N	N	N	Y
10 Schumer	Y	Y	N	N	N	N	N	Y
11 Towns	Y	Y	N	N	N	N	N	Y
12 Owens	?	?	N	N	N	N	N	Y
13 Solarz	Y	Y	N	N	N	N	N	Y
14 ***Molinari***	Y	Y	Y	N	Y	Y	Y	Y
15 ***Green***	Y	Y	N	N	N	Y	N	Y
16 Rangel	?	?	X	N	N	N	N	Y
17 Weiss	+	+	-	-	-	-	-	+
18 Garcia	?	?	X	?	?	?	?	#
19 Biaggi	?	?	?	?	?	?	?	?
20 Ottinger	P	P	N	N	N	N	N	Y
21 ***Fish***	Y	Y	Y	Y	Y	Y	N	Y
22 ***Gilman***	Y	Y	N	Y	Y	Y	Y	Y
23 Stratton	?	?	?	?	?	?	?	?
24 ***Solomon***	N	N	Y	Y	Y	Y	Y	N
25 ***Boehlert***	Y	Y	Y	Y	N	Y	Y	N
26 ***Martin***	?	?	?	?	?	?	?	?
27 ***Wortley***	?	?	#	?	?	?	?	#
28 McHugh	Y	Y	N	N	N	N	N	?
29 ***Horton***	Y	Y	N	N	N	N	N	Y
30 ***Conable***	Y	Y	Y	Y	Y	Y	Y	N
31 ***Kemp***	Y	Y	Y	Y	Y	Y	N	N
32 LaFalce	Y	Y	N	N	N	N	?	?
33 Nowak	Y	Y	N	N	Y	N	N	Y
34 Lundine	?	Y	N	N	N	N	N	Y

	146	147	148	149	150	151	152	153
NORTH CAROLINA								
1 Jones	?	Y	N	N	N	N	N	Y
2 Valentine	Y	Y	Y	Y	Y	Y	Y	N
3 Whitley	Y	Y	N	N	N	N	N	?
4 Andrews	Y	Y	N	N	N	N	N	Y
5 Neal	?	Y	N	N	N	N	N	Y
6 Britt	Y	Y	N	Y	N	N	N	Y
7 Rose	Y	Y	N	N	N	N	N	?
8 Hefner	Y	Y	N	N	N	N	N	Y
9 ***Martin***	Y	Y	Y	Y	Y	Y	Y	N
10 ***Broyhill***	Y	Y	Y	Y	?	Y	Y	N
11 Clarke	Y	Y	N	N	N	N	N	Y
NORTH DAKOTA								
AL Dorgan	N	N	N	N	N	N	N	Y
OHIO								
1 Luken	Y	Y	N	N	N	N	N	Y
2 ***Gradison***	?	?	?	?	?	?	?	?
3 Hall	?	?	X	?	?	?	?	?
4 ***Oxley***	Y	Y	Y	Y	Y	Y	Y	N
5 ***Latta***	Y	Y	Y	Y	Y	Y	Y	X
6 ***McEwen***	Y	Y	Y	Y	Y	Y	Y	N
7 ***DeWine***	Y	Y	Y	Y	Y	Y	Y	N
8 ***Kindness***	Y	Y	Y	Y	Y	Y	N	N
9 Kaptur	Y	Y	N	N	N	?	N	Y
10 ***Miller***	N	Y	Y	Y	Y	Y	Y	N
11 Eckart	Y	Y	Y	Y	N	N	N	Y
12 ***Kasich***	Y	Y	Y	Y	Y	Y	Y	N
13 Pease	Y	Y	N	N	N	N	Y	Y
14 Seiberling	Y	Y	N	N	N	N	N	Y
15 ***Wylie***	Y	Y	Y	Y	Y	Y	Y	N
16 ***Regula***	Y	Y	Y	Y	Y	Y	Y	Y
17 ***Williams***	Y	Y	Y	Y	Y	N	N	Y
18 Applegate	?	Y	Y	Y	N	Y	N	N
19 Feighan	Y	Y	N	N	N	N	N	Y
20 Oakar	Y	Y	N	N	N	N	N	Y
21 Stokes	Y	Y	N	N	?	N	N	Y
OKLAHOMA								
1 Jones	Y	Y	N	Y	N	N	N	Y
2 Synar	Y	Y	N	N	N	N	N	Y
3 Watkins	Y	Y	N	?	?	?	?	?
4 McCurdy	Y	Y	N	Y	N	N	N	Y
5 ***Edwards***	Y	Y	Y	Y	Y	Y	Y	N
6 English	Y	Y	N	Y	N	Y	N	Y
OREGON								
1 AuCoin	?	?	?	?	?	?	?	?
2 ***Smith, R.***	Y	Y	Y	Y	Y	Y	Y	N
3 Wyden	Y	Y	N	N	N	N	N	Y
4 Weaver	Y	Y	N	N	N	N	N	Y
5 ***Smith, D.***	?	?	#	?	?	?	?	X
PENNSYLVANIA								
1 Foglietta	?	?	?	?	?	?	?	?
2 Gray	?	Y	N	N	N	N	N	Y
3 Borski	Y	Y	N	N	N	N	Y	Y
4 Kolter	?	?	?	?	?	?	?	?
5 ***Schulze***	Y	Y	Y	?	?	?	?	?
6 Yatron	Y	Y	N	Y	Y	Y	N	Y
7 Edgar	Y	Y	N	N	N	N	N	Y
8 Kostmayer	?	?	?	?	?	?	?	?
9 ***Shuster***	?	?	?	?	?	?	?	X
10 ***McDade***	Y	Y	N	N	N	Y	N	Y
11 Harrison	Y	Y	N	N	N	N	N	Y
12 Murtha	Y	Y	N	N	N	N	N	Y
13 ***Coughlin***	N	Y	Y	Y	Y	Y	N	N
14 Coyne	Y	Y	N	N	N	N	N	Y
15 ***Ritter***	Y	N	Y	Y	Y	Y	Y	N
16 ***Walker***	N	Y	Y	Y	Y	Y	Y	N
17 ***Gekas***	Y	Y	Y	Y	Y	Y	Y	N
18 Walgren	?	Y	Y	Y	N	N	N	Y
19 ***Goodling***	N	Y	Y	Y	Y	Y	N	N
20 Gaydos	?	?	?	?	?	?	?	?
21 ***Ridge***	Y	Y	Y	Y	Y	Y	Y	Y
22 Murphy	Y	Y	N	N	N	N	N	N
23 ***Clinger***	Y	Y	Y	Y	Y	Y	N	N
RHODE ISLAND								
1 St Germain	?	?	?	?	?	?	?	?
2 ***Schneider***	?	?	?	?	?	?	?	?
SOUTH CAROLINA								
1 ***Hartnett***	N	N	Y	Y	Y	Y	Y	N
2 ***Spence***	Y	?	?	Y	Y	Y	N	N
3 Derrick	?	?	?	?	?	?	?	#
4 ***Campbell***	Y	Y	Y	?	?	?	?	X
5 Spratt	Y	Y	N	N	N	N	Y	Y
6 Tallon	Y	Y	N	N	Y	N	N	Y
SOUTH DAKOTA								
AL Daschle	Y	Y	N	N	N	N	N	Y

	146	147	148	149	150	151	152	153
TENNESSEE								
1 ***Quillen***	?	?	#	?	?	?	?	X
2 ***Duncan***	Y	Y	Y	Y	Y	Y	?	Y
3 Lloyd	?	?	?	?	?	?	?	?
4 Cooper	Y	Y	N	Y	Y	N	N	Y
5 Boner	Y	Y	N	N	N	N	N	Y
6 Gore	?	?	?	?	?	?	?	?
7 ***Sundquist***	Y	Y	Y	Y	Y	Y	Y	N
8 Jones	?	?	?	?	?	?	?	?
9 Ford	Y	Y	N	N	N	N	N	?
TEXAS								
1 Hall, S.	Y	Y	Y	Y	N	Y	N	N
2 Wilson	?	?	?	?	?	?	?	?
3 ***Bartlett***	Y	Y	Y	Y	Y	Y	Y	N
4 Hall, R.	Y	Y	Y	Y	N	Y	Y	N
5 Bryant	?	?	?	?	?	?	?	?
6 ***Gramm***	?	?	#	?	?	?	?	X
7 ***Archer***	Y	Y	Y	Y	Y	Y	Y	N
8 ***Fields***	?	?	+	+	+	+	+	?
9 Brooks	Y	Y	N	N	N	N	N	Y
10 Pickle	Y	Y	N	Y	N	Y	N	Y
11 Leath	Y	Y	Y	Y	Y	Y	Y	N
12 Wright	Y	Y	N	N	?	?	?	?
13 Hightower	?	?	?	?	?	?	?	?
14 Patman	Y	Y	Y	N	N	N	N	Y
15 de la Garza	Y	Y	N	N	N	N	N	Y
16 Coleman	Y	Y	N	N	N	N	N	Y
17 Stenholm	N	Y	Y	Y	Y	Y	Y	N
18 Leland	?	Y	N	N	N	N	N	Y
19 Hance	?	?	?	?	?	?	?	?
20 Gonzalez	Y	Y	N	N	N	N	N	Y
21 ***Loeffler***	Y	Y	Y	Y	Y	Y	Y	N
22 ***Paul***	Y	Y	Y	Y	Y	Y	Y	N
23 Kazen	?	?	?	?	?	?	?	?
24 Frost	?	?	?	?	?	?	?	?
25 Andrews	Y	Y	Y	Y	Y	Y	?	?
26 Vandergriff	Y	?	N	Y	Y	N	N	Y
27 Ortiz	Y	Y	N	Y	N	N	N	Y
UTAH								
1 ***Hansen***	?	?	?	?	?	?	?	?
2 ***Marriott***	Y	Y	N	Y	Y	Y	N	Y
3 ***Nielson***	+	+	+	+	+	+	+	X
VERMONT								
AL ***Jeffords***	Y	Y	N	N	Y	Y	N	Y
VIRGINIA								
1 ***Bateman***	Y	Y	Y	Y	N	Y	Y	N
2 ***Whitehurst***	?	?	?	?	?	?	?	?
3 ***Bliley***	Y	Y	Y	Y	Y	Y	Y	N
4 Sisisky	?	?	?	?	?	X	?	#
5 Daniel	Y	?	Y	Y	Y	Y	N	N
6 Olin	Y	Y	Y	Y	Y	Y	Y	N
7 ***Robinson***	Y	Y	Y	Y	Y	Y	Y	Y
8 ***Parris***	Y	Y	N	N	Y	Y	Y	N
9 Boucher	Y	Y	N	N	N	N	N	Y
10 ***Wolf***	Y	Y	Y	N	Y	Y	Y	Y
WASHINGTON								
1 ***Pritchard***	?	?	?	?	?	?	?	?
2 Swift	Y	Y	N	N	N	N	N	Y
3 Bonker	+	+	X	-	-	-	-	#
4 ***Morrison***	+	+	+	-	-	-	-	-
5 Foley	Y	Y	N	N	N	N	N	Y
6 Dicks	Y	Y	N	N	N	N	N	Y
7 Lowry	Y	Y	N	N	N	N	N	Y
8 ***Chandler***	?	?	?	?	?	?	?	?
WEST VIRGINIA								
1 Mollohan	Y	Y	N	Y	Y	Y	N	Y
2 Staggers	Y	Y	N	?	?	?	?	#
3 Wise	Y	Y	N	Y	Y	N	N	N
4 Rahall	Y	Y	N	N	N	N	N	Y
WISCONSIN								
1 Aspin	Y	Y	N	N	N	N	N	Y
2 Kastenmeier	Y	Y	N	N	N	N	N	Y
3 ***Gunderson***	Y	Y	Y	Y	Y	Y	N	N
4 Zablocki	Y	Y	N	N	N	N	N	Y
5 Moody	Y	Y	N	N	N	N	N	?
6 ***Petri***	Y	Y	Y	Y	Y	Y	Y	N
7 Obey	Y	Y	N	N	N	N	N	Y
8 ***Roth***	Y	Y	Y	Y	Y	Y	Y	N
9 ***Sensenbrenner***	Y	N	Y	Y	Y	Y	Y	N
WYOMING								
AL ***Cheney***	?	?	?	?	?	?	?	X

Southern states - Ala., Ark., Fla., Ga., Ky., La., Miss., N.C., Okla., S.C., Tenn., Texas, Va.

KEY

- **Y** Voted for (yea).
- **#** Paired for.
- **+** Announced for.
- **N** Voted against (nay).
- **X** Paired against.
- **-** Announced against.
- **P** Voted "present".
- **C** Voted "present" to avoid possible conflict of interest.
- **?** Did not vote or otherwise make a position known.

Democrats *Republicans*

---

154. HR 3132. Energy and Water Development Appropriations, Fiscal 1984. Adoption of the rule (H Res 210) to waive certain points of order during House floor consideration of the bill to make fiscal 1984 appropriations for energy and water development. Adopted 271-92: R 59-78; D 212-14 (ND 131-13, SD 81-1), June 6, 1983.

155. HR 3132. Energy and Water Development Appropriations, Fiscal 1984. Bevill, D-Ala., motion that the House resolve itself into the Committee of the Whole for consideration of the bill to make fiscal 1984 appropriations for energy and water development. Motion agreed to 337-30: R 111-28; D 226-2 (ND 145-1, SD 81-1), June 6, 1983.

156. HR 3132. Energy and Water Development Appropriations, Fiscal 1984. Wise, D-W.Va., amendment to delete $26 million in the bill for construction of the Stonewall Jackson Dam in West Virginia. Adopted 213-161: R 79-61; D 134-100 (ND 109-42, SD 25-58), June 6, 1983.

157. Procedural Motion. Lott, R-Miss., motion to approve the House *Journal* of Monday, June 6. Motion agreed to 377-21: R 146-9; D 231-12 (ND 147-10, SD 84-2), June 7, 1983.

158. HR 3132. Energy and Water Development Appropriations, Fiscal 1984. Edgar, D-Pa., amendment to delete $56 million in the bill for the Dolores and Dallas Creek water projects in Colorado. Rejected 140-257: R 73-78; D 67-179 (ND 56-107, SD 11-72), June 7, 1983.

159. HR 3132. Energy and Water Development Appropriations, Fiscal 1984. Sensenbrenner, R-Wis., amendment to reduce the appropriation for the Department of Energy's energy supply, research and development activities by $10 million. Rejected 105-312: R 91-69; D 14-243 (ND 2-167, SD 12-76), June 7, 1983.

160. HR 3132. Energy and Water Development Appropriations, Fiscal 1984. Passage of the bill to appropriate $14,179,223,000 for energy and water development for fiscal 1984. Passed 379-39: R 137-24; D 242-15 (ND 155-14, SD 87-1), June 7, 1983. The president had requested $14,610,671,000 in new budget authority.

161. HR 1271. El Salvador Aid Certification. Barnes, D-Md., motion to suspend the rules and pass the bill to require the president, in his July 1983 certification report to Congress on El Salvador's eligibility for continued U.S. military aid, to report on whether the government had made "good faith efforts" to bring to justice those responsible for the murders of eight U.S. citizens. Motion agreed to 416-2: R 159-2; D 257-0 (ND 169-0, SD 88-0), June 7, 1983. A two-thirds majority of those present and voting (279 in this case) is required for passage under suspension of the rules.

	154	155	156	157	158	159	160	161
ALABAMA								
1 *Edwards*	Y	Y	N	?	?	N	Y	Y
2 *Dickinson*	Y	Y	N	N	?	N	Y	Y
3 Nichols	?	?	?	Y	N	Y	Y	Y
4 Bevill	Y	Y	N	Y	N	N	N	Y
5 Flippo	Y	Y	N	N	N	N	Y	Y
6 Erdreich	Y	Y	N	N	N	N	Y	Y
7 Shelby	Y	Y	N	N	N	N	Y	Y
ALASKA								
AL *Young*	?	?	?	?	N	N	Y	Y
ARIZONA								
1 *McCain*	Y	Y	N	Y	N	N	Y	Y
2 Udall	Y	Y	N	Y	N	N	Y	Y
3 *Stump*	Y	Y	N	Y	N	N	Y	N
4 *Rudd*	Y	Y	N	Y	N	N	Y	Y
5 McNulty	Y	Y	N	Y	N	N	Y	Y
ARKANSAS								
1 Alexander	Y	Y	N	Y	N	N	Y	Y
2 *Bethune*	N	Y	N	Y	Y	N	Y	Y
3 *Hammerschmidt*	Y	Y	N	Y	N	N	Y	Y
4 Anthony	Y	Y	N	Y	N	N	Y	Y
CALIFORNIA								
1 Bosco	?	Y	Y	?	N	N	Y	Y
2 *Chappie*	N	Y	N	Y	N	Y	Y	Y
3 Matsui	Y	Y	Y	N	N	N	Y	Y
4 Fazio	Y	Y	N	Y	?	N	Y	Y
5 Vacancy								
6 Boxer	?	?	?	Y	N	N	N	Y
7 Miller	?	?	?	Y	N	Y	N	Y
8 Dellums	Y	Y	Y	Y	N	N	N	Y
9 Stark	?	?	?	?	Y	N	N	Y
10 Edwards	Y	Y	Y	Y	Y	N	Y	Y
11 Lantos	Y	Y	Y	N	N	N	Y	Y
12 *Zschau*	N	Y	Y	?	N	Y	Y	Y
13 Mineta	Y	Y	Y	Y	N	N	Y	Y
14 *Shumway*	N	Y	Y	Y	Y	Y	Y	Y
15 Coelho	Y	Y	N	Y	N	N	Y	Y
16 Panetta	Y	Y	N	Y	N	N	Y	Y
17 *Pashayan*	?	?	?	Y	N	Y	Y	Y
18 Lehman	?	?	?	Y	N	Y	N	Y
19 *Lagomarsino*	N	Y	Y	Y	N	N	Y	Y
20 *Thomas*	N	Y	N	Y	N	Y	Y	Y
21 *Fiedler*	N	Y	Y	Y	N	N	Y	Y
22 *Moorhead*	N	Y	Y	Y	N	Y	N	Y
23 Beilenson	Y	Y	Y	Y	Y	N	N	Y
24 Waxman	?	?	?	Y	N	Y	N	Y
25 Roybal	Y	Y	N	Y	N	N	Y	Y
26 Berman	Y	Y	Y	Y	Y	N	N	Y
27 Levine	Y	Y	Y	Y	N	N	Y	Y
28 Dixon	Y	Y	N	Y	N	N	Y	Y
29 Hawkins	Y	Y	?	N	N	N	N	Y
30 Martinez	?	?	?	?	?	?	?	?
31 Dymally	Y	Y	Y	Y	N	N	Y	Y
32 Anderson	Y	Y	Y	Y	N	N	Y	Y
33 *Dreier*	N	N	Y	Y	Y	Y	N	Y
34 Torres	Y	Y	Y	Y	N	N	Y	Y
35 *Lewis*	?	?	N	Y	N	N	Y	Y
36 Brown	?	?	?	Y	Y	N	?	?
37 *McCandless*	Y	Y	N	Y	N	Y	Y	Y
38 Patterson	Y	Y	Y	Y	N	N	Y	Y
39 *Dannemeyer*	N	N	Y	Y	Y	Y	N	Y
40 *Badham*	?	?	?	?	X	?	?	?
41 *Lowery*	Y	Y	N	Y	N	Y	N	Y
42 *Lungren*	N	Y	Y	Y	Y	Y	Y	Y

	154	155	156	157	158	159	160	161
43 *Packard*	N	Y	N	Y	N	Y	Y	Y
44 Bates	Y	Y	Y	?	Y	N	Y	Y
45 *Hunter*	Y	Y	N	Y	N	N	Y	?
COLORADO								
1 Schroeder	N	Y	Y	N	N	N	N	Y
2 Wirth	Y	Y	Y	N	N	N	Y	Y
3 Kogovsek	Y	Y	N	Y	N	N	Y	Y
4 *Brown*	N	Y	N	Y	N	Y	Y	Y
5 *Kramer*	N	Y	N	Y	N	Y	Y	Y
6 *Schaefer*	N	N	N	Y	N	Y	Y	Y
CONNECTICUT								
1 Kennelly	Y	Y	Y	N	N	N	Y	Y
2 Gejdenson	+	Y	Y	N	N	N	N	Y
3 Morrison	Y	Y	Y	N	N	N	Y	Y
4 *McKinney*	N	?	?	Y	N	Y	N	Y
5 Ratchford	Y	Y	Y	N	N	N	Y	Y
6 *Johnson*	?	?	Y	Y	Y	Y	Y	Y
DELAWARE								
AL Carper	Y	Y	Y	Y	Y	Y	Y	Y
FLORIDA								
1 Hutto	Y	Y	N	Y	N	N	N	Y
2 Fuqua	Y	Y	N	N	N	N	Y	Y
3 Bennett	Y	Y	N	Y	N	N	Y	Y
4 Chappell	?	?	N	?	N	N	Y	Y
5 *McCollum*	N	N	Y	N	Y	Y	Y	Y
6 MacKay	Y	Y	N	Y	N	N	Y	Y
7 Gibbons	Y	Y	N	N	N	N	Y	Y
8 *Young*	Y	Y	N	Y	N	Y	N	Y
9 *Bilirakis*	N	N	?	N	Y	N	Y	Y
10 Ireland	Y	Y	N	Y	N	N	N	Y
11 Nelson	Y	Y	Y	N	N	N	Y	Y
12 *Lewis*	Y	Y	N	Y	N	N	Y	Y
13 *Mack*	?	?	?	?	Y	Y	Y	N
14 Mica	Y	Y	N	Y	N	N	Y	Y
15 *Shaw*	N	N	Y	Y	Y	Y	Y	Y
16 Smith	Y	Y	N	Y	N	N	Y	Y
17 Lehman	Y	Y	N	N	N	N	Y	Y
18 Pepper	Y	Y	N	Y	N	N	Y	Y
19 Fascell	Y	Y	N	Y	?	N	Y	Y
GEORGIA								
1 Thomas	Y	Y	N	Y	N	Y	N	Y
2 Hatcher	Y	Y	Y	N	N	N	Y	Y
3 Ray	Y	Y	N	Y	N	Y	N	Y
4 Levitas	?	?	?	Y	N	Y	Y	Y
5 Fowler	Y	Y	N	Y	N	N	Y	Y
6 *Gingrich*	N	N	?	N	Y	N	Y	Y
7 McDonald	N	N	Y	Y	Y	Y	Y	N
8 Rowland	Y	Y	N	Y	N	N	Y	Y
9 Jenkins	Y	Y	N	Y	N	N	Y	Y
10 Barnard	Y	Y	N	Y	N	N	Y	Y
HAWAII								
1 Heftel	?	?	?	?	?	?	?	?
2 Akaka	Y	Y	N	Y	N	N	Y	Y
IDAHO								
1 *Craig*	N	Y	Y	N	Y	N	N	Y
2 *Hansen*	N	Y	Y	?	N	?	Y	Y
ILLINOIS								
1 Vacancy								
2 Savage	Y	Y	Y	Y	N	N	Y	Y
3 Russo	Y	Y	Y	Y	N	N	Y	Y
4 *O'Brien*	N	Y	N	Y	N	N	Y	Y
5 Lipinski	Y	Y	Y	Y	N	N	Y	Y
6 *Hyde*	N	Y	Y	Y	#	Y	Y	Y
7 Collins	?	?	?	?	?	X	?	?
8 Rostenkowski	Y	Y	N	Y	N	N	Y	Y
9 Yates	Y	Y	Y	Y	N	N	Y	Y
10 *Porter*	N	Y	Y	Y	N	Y	N	Y
11 Annunzio	Y	Y	N	Y	N	N	Y	Y
12 *Crane, P.*	?	?	?	?	#	#	?	?
13 *Erlenborn*	N	Y	Y	Y	Y	Y	Y	Y
14 *Corcoran*	N	N	Y	Y	Y	Y	N	Y
15 *Madigan*	Y	Y	Y	Y	N	N	Y	Y
16 *Martin*	?	N	Y	Y	N	Y	N	Y
17 Evans	Y	Y	Y	Y	N	N	Y	Y
18 *Michel*	N	Y	N	Y	N	N	Y	Y
19 *Crane, D.*	N	Y	Y	Y	N	Y	Y	Y
20 Durbin	Y	Y	Y	Y	N	N	Y	Y
21 Price	Y	Y	N	Y	N	N	Y	Y
22 Simon	Y	Y	Y	Y	N	N	Y	Y
INDIANA								
1 Hall	Y	Y	Y	Y	N	N	Y	Y
2 Sharp	Y	Y	Y	Y	N	N	Y	Y
3 *Hiler*	N	N	Y	Y	Y	Y	Y	Y
4 *Coats*	N	Y	Y	Y	N	Y	Y	Y
5 Hillis	Y	Y	Y	Y	N	N	Y	Y

ND - Northern Democrats   SD - Southern Democrats

Corresponding to Congressional Record Votes 162, 163, 164, 165, 166, 167, 168, 169

	154	155	156	157	158	159	160	161
6 ***Burton***	N	N	N	Y	Y	Y	Y	Y
7 ***Myers***	Y	Y	N	?	N	N	Y	Y
8 McCloskey	Y	Y	Y	Y	N	N	Y	Y
9 Hamilton	Y	Y	N	Y	?	N	Y	Y
10 Jacobs	Y	Y	Y	P	Y	N	N	Y
IOWA								
1 ***Leach***	N	Y	Y	Y	Y	N	N	Y
2 ***Tauke***	N	Y	Y	Y	Y	Y	N	Y
3 ***Evans***	Y	Y	N	N	Y	Y	N	Y
4 Smith	Y	Y	N	Y	N	N	Y	Y
5 Harkin	Y	Y	Y	N	Y	N	Y	Y
6 Bedell	N	Y	Y	Y	Y	N	Y	Y
KANSAS								
1 ***Roberts***	?	?	?	Y	N	Y	Y	Y
2 Slattery	Y	Y	Y	Y	N	N	Y	Y
3 ***Winn***	N	Y	N	Y	N	Y	Y	Y
4 Glickman	Y	Y	Y	Y	Y	N	Y	Y
5 ***Whittaker***	N	Y	N	Y	N	Y	Y	Y
KENTUCKY								
1 Hubbard	?	?	?	?	?	?	?	?
2 Natcher	Y	Y	N	Y	N	N	Y	Y
3 Mazzoli	Y	Y	N	Y	N	N	Y	Y
4 ***Snyder***	Y	Y	N	Y	N	N	Y	Y
5 ***Rogers***	Y	Y	N	Y	N	N	Y	Y
6 ***Hopkins***	Y	Y	N	Y	N	Y	Y	Y
7 Perkins	Y	Y	N	Y	N	N	Y	Y
LOUISIANA								
1 ***Livingston***	Y	Y	N	Y	N	N	Y	Y
2 Boggs	Y	Y	N	Y	N	N	Y	Y
3 Tauzin	Y	Y	N	Y	N	N	Y	Y
4 Roemer	Y	Y	Y	N	Y	Y	Y	Y
5 Huckaby	Y	Y	N	Y	N	N	Y	Y
6 ***Moore***	Y	Y	N	Y	N	N	Y	Y
7 Breaux	Y	Y	N	Y	N	N	Y	Y
8 Long	Y	Y	N	Y	N	N	Y	Y
MAINE								
1 ***McKernan***	N	N	Y	Y	Y	Y	Y	Y
2 ***Snowe***	Y	Y	Y	Y	Y	Y	Y	Y
MARYLAND								
1 Dyson	?	?	?	Y	N	N	Y	Y
2 Long	Y	Y	N	Y	N	N	Y	Y
3 Mikulski	Y	Y	Y	Y	Y	N	Y	Y
4 ***Holt***	N	Y	?	Y	X	N	Y	Y
5 Hoyer	Y	Y	Y	Y	N	N	Y	Y
6 Byron	Y	Y	?	Y	N	N	Y	Y
7 Mitchell	Y	Y	Y	N	Y	N	Y	Y
8 Barnes	Y	Y	Y	Y	N	N	Y	Y
MASSACHUSETTS								
1 ***Conte***	Y	Y	Y	Y	Y	N	Y	Y
2 Boland	?	?	?	Y	Y	N	Y	Y
3 Early	Y	Y	Y	Y	Y	N	Y	Y
4 Frank	N	Y	Y	Y	Y	N	Y	Y
5 Shannon	Y	Y	Y	Y	N	N	Y	Y
6 Mavroules	Y	Y	Y	Y	N	N	Y	Y
7 Markey	Y	Y	Y	Y	Y	N	Y	Y
8 O'Neill								
9 Moakley	Y	Y	Y	Y	N	N	Y	Y
10 Studds	N	N	Y	Y	Y	N	N	Y
11 Donnelly	Y	Y	N	Y	N	N	Y	Y
MICHIGAN								
1 Conyers	?	Y	Y	Y	Y	N	Y	Y
2 ***Pursell***	Y	Y	Y	Y	N	N	Y	Y
3 Wolpe	Y	Y	Y	Y	Y	N	N	Y
4 ***Siljander***	Y	Y	Y	Y	Y	Y	Y	Y
5 ***Sawyer***	Y	Y	Y	Y	Y	Y	Y	Y
6 Carr	Y	Y	N	Y	N	N	Y	Y
7 Kildee	Y	Y	Y	Y	Y	N	Y	Y
8 Traxler	Y	Y	Y	Y	N	N	Y	Y
9 ***Vander Jagt***	N	Y	Y	Y	N	N	Y	Y
10 Albosta	Y	Y	N	Y	N	N	Y	Y
11 ***Davis***	Y	Y	N	Y	N	N	Y	Y
12 Bonior	Y	Y	Y	Y	P	N	N	Y
13 Crockett	Y	Y	Y	Y	Y	N	Y	Y
14 Hertel	N	Y	Y	Y	Y	N	N	Y
15 Ford	Y	Y	N	Y	N	N	Y	Y
16 Dingell	Y	Y	Y	Y	N	N	Y	Y
17 Levin	Y	Y	Y	Y	N	N	Y	Y
18 ***Broomfield***	Y	Y	Y	Y	?	Y	Y	Y
MINNESOTA								
1 Penny	N	Y	Y	Y	Y	N	Y	Y
2 ***Weber***	N	N	Y	Y	Y	Y	N	Y
3 ***Frenzel***	N	N	Y	Y	Y	Y	N	Y
4 Vento	N	Y	Y	Y	Y	N	Y	Y
5 Sabo	?	?	?	N	N	N	Y	Y
6 Sikorski	?	Y	Y	Y	Y	N	Y	Y
7 ***Stangeland***	Y	Y	N	Y	N	Y	Y	Y
8 Oberstar	Y	Y	Y	P	N	N	Y	Y
MISSISSIPPI								
1 Whitten	Y	Y	N	Y	N	N	Y	Y
2 ***Franklin***	Y	Y	Y	Y	N	Y	Y	Y
3 Montgomery	Y	Y	N	Y	N	Y	Y	Y
4 Dowdy	Y	Y	N	Y	N	N	Y	Y
5 ***Lott***	Y	Y	N	Y	N	Y	Y	Y
MISSOURI								
1 Clay	Y	Y	Y	N	Y	N	Y	Y
2 Young	Y	Y	N	Y	N	N	Y	Y
3 Gephardt	Y	Y	Y	?	N	N	Y	Y
4 Skelton	Y	Y	N	Y	N	N	Y	Y
5 Wheat	Y	Y	N	Y	N	N	Y	Y
6 ***Coleman***	Y	Y	N	Y	Y	Y	Y	Y
7 ***Taylor***	Y	Y	N	Y	N	Y	Y	Y
8 ***Emerson***	Y	Y	N	Y	N	N	Y	Y
9 Volkmer	Y	Y	N	Y	N	N	Y	Y
MONTANA								
1 Williams	N	Y	Y	?	N	N	Y	Y
2 ***Marlenee***	?	?	?	N	N	Y	Y	Y
NEBRASKA								
1 ***Bereuter***	N	Y	Y	Y	N	Y	Y	Y
2 ***Daub***	N	Y	N	Y	N	Y	Y	Y
3 ***Smith***	Y	Y	Y	Y	N	N	Y	Y
NEVADA								
1 Reid	Y	Y	Y	Y	N	N	Y	Y
2 ***Vucanovich***	N	Y	N	+	-	+	-	+
NEW HAMPSHIRE								
1 D'Amours	Y	Y	Y	Y	Y	N	Y	Y
2 ***Gregg***	N	Y	Y	Y	Y	Y	Y	Y
NEW JERSEY								
1 Florio	Y	Y	Y	Y	Y	N	Y	Y
2 Hughes	Y	Y	N	Y	N	N	Y	Y
3 Howard	?	?	?	Y	N	N	Y	Y
4 ***Smith***	Y	Y	Y	Y	Y	N	Y	Y
5 ***Roukema***	Y	Y	Y	Y	Y	Y	Y	Y
6 Dwyer	Y	Y	N	Y	N	N	Y	Y
7 ***Rinaldo***	Y	Y	N	Y	Y	N	Y	Y
8 Roe	Y	Y	N	Y	N	N	Y	Y
9 Torricelli	?	Y	Y	Y	N	N	Y	Y
10 Rodino	?	?	N	Y	Y	N	Y	Y
11 Minish	Y	Y	Y	Y	Y	N	Y	Y
12 ***Courter***	?	?	Y	Y	Y	N	N	Y
13 ***Forsythe***	N	N	Y	N	Y	Y	Y	Y
14 Guarini	Y	Y	Y	Y	N	N	Y	Y
NEW MEXICO								
1 ***Lujan***	Y	Y	?	Y	N	N	Y	Y
2 ***Skeen***	N	Y	N	Y	N	Y	Y	Y
3 Richardson	Y	Y	Y	Y	N	N	Y	Y
NEW YORK								
1 ***Carney***	?	?	?	?	#	X	?	?
2 Downey	?	?	Y	Y	N	N	Y	Y
3 Mrazek	?	Y	Y	Y	N	N	Y	Y
4 ***Lent***	?	?	?	Y	Y	N	Y	Y
5 ***McGrath***	?	?	?	Y	Y	N	Y	Y
6 Addabbo	Y	Y	Y	Y	N	N	Y	Y
7 Ackerman	Y	Y	Y	Y	N	N	Y	Y
8 Scheuer	Y	Y	Y	Y	N	N	Y	Y
9 Ferraro	+	+	+	?	N	?	?	?
10 Schumer	N	Y	Y	?	?	?	Y	Y
11 Towns	Y	Y	Y	Y	N	N	Y	Y
12 Owens	?	?	Y	Y	N	N	Y	Y
13 Solarz	Y	Y	Y	Y	Y	N	Y	Y
14 ***Molinari***	N	Y	Y	Y	Y	N	Y	Y
15 ***Green***	Y	Y	Y	Y	Y	N	Y	Y
16 Rangel	Y	Y	N	Y	N	N	Y	Y
17 Weiss	N	Y	Y	Y	Y	N	N	Y
18 Garcia	Y	Y	Y	Y	N	N	Y	Y
19 Biaggi	Y	Y	N	Y	N	N	Y	Y
20 Ottinger	N	P	Y	P	Y	N	Y	Y
21 ***Fish***	Y	Y	Y	Y	Y	N	Y	Y
22 ***Gilman***	Y	Y	Y	Y	Y	N	Y	Y
23 Stratton	Y	Y	N	Y	N	N	Y	Y
24 ***Solomon***	N	N	Y	N	?	Y	N	Y
25 ***Boehlert***	Y	Y	Y	Y	Y	N	Y	Y
26 ***Martin***	N	Y	Y	Y	N	N	Y	Y
27 ***Wortley***	N	Y	Y	Y	Y	N	Y	Y
28 McHugh	Y	Y	Y	Y	N	N	Y	Y
29 ***Horton***	Y	Y	N	Y	N	N	Y	Y
30 ***Conable***	Y	Y	Y	Y	Y	Y	Y	Y
31 ***Kemp***	?	?	N	Y	Y	N	Y	Y
32 LaFalce	Y	Y	Y	Y	Y	N	Y	Y
33 Nowak	Y	Y	N	Y	N	N	Y	Y
34 Lundine	Y	?	Y	Y	Y	N	Y	Y
NORTH CAROLINA								
1 Jones	Y	Y	N	Y	N	N	Y	Y
2 Valentine	Y	Y	Y	Y	N	N	Y	Y
3 Whitley	Y	Y	N	Y	N	N	Y	Y
4 Andrews	Y	Y	N	Y	N	N	Y	Y
5 Neal	Y	Y	?	Y	N	N	Y	Y
6 Britt	Y	Y	Y	Y	N	N	Y	Y
7 Rose	Y	Y	?	Y	N	N	Y	Y
8 Hefner	Y	Y	N	Y	N	N	Y	Y
9 ***Martin***	N	N	?	Y	?	Y	N	Y
10 ***Broyhill***	N	N	Y	Y	Y	Y	N	Y
11 Clarke	Y	Y	Y	Y	N	N	Y	Y
NORTH DAKOTA								
AL Dorgan	Y	Y	N	N	N	N	Y	Y
OHIO								
1 Luken	Y	Y	N	Y	N	N	Y	Y
2 ***Gradison***	N	Y	Y	Y	Y	Y	N	Y
3 Hall	?	?	?	?	Y	Y	N	Y
4 ***Oxley***	N	N	Y	Y	N	N	Y	Y
5 ***Latta***	N	N	N	Y	Y	N	N	Y
6 ***McEwen***	?	?	N	Y	N	N	Y	Y
7 ***DeWine***	N	N	Y	Y	N	Y	N	Y
8 ***Kindness***	?	?	?	Y	Y	Y	Y	Y
9 Kaptur	Y	Y	Y	Y	N	N	Y	Y
10 ***Miller***	Y	Y	N	N	Y	Y	Y	Y
11 Eckart	Y	Y	Y	Y	Y	N	Y	Y
12 ***Kasich***	N	N	Y	Y	Y	Y	Y	Y
13 Pease	Y	Y	Y	Y	Y	N	Y	Y
14 Seiberling	Y	Y	Y	Y	N	N	Y	Y
15 ***Wylie***	N	N	Y	Y	Y	N	Y	Y
16 ***Regula***	Y	Y	Y	Y	N	N	Y	Y
17 ***Williams***	?	?	Y	Y	N	N	Y	Y
18 Applegate	?	?	?	?	N	N	Y	Y
19 Feighan	Y	Y	Y	Y	N	N	Y	Y
20 Oakar	?	Y	N	Y	N	N	Y	Y
21 Stokes	Y	Y	Y	?	N	N	Y	Y
OKLAHOMA								
1 Jones	Y	Y	Y	Y	N	N	Y	Y
2 Synar	Y	Y	Y	Y	N	N	Y	Y
3 Watkins	Y	Y	N	Y	N	N	Y	Y
4 McCurdy	Y	Y	N	Y	N	N	Y	Y
5 ***Edwards***	N	Y	N	Y	?	Y	Y	Y
6 English	Y	Y	Y	Y	N	N	Y	Y
OREGON								
1 AuCoin	Y	Y	Y	Y	Y	N	N	Y
2 ***Smith, R.***	N	Y	Y	Y	N	Y	Y	Y
3 Wyden	Y	Y	Y	Y	N	N	Y	Y
4 Weaver	Y	Y	Y	Y	Y	N	N	Y
5 ***Smith, D.***	N	Y	Y	Y	N	Y	N	Y
PENNSYLVANIA								
1 Foglietta	Y	Y	Y	Y	Y	N	Y	Y
2 Gray	Y	Y	Y	Y	N	N	Y	Y
3 Borski	Y	Y	Y	Y	N	N	Y	Y
4 Kolter	?	?	?	?	?	?	?	?
5 ***Schulze***	?	?	?	Y	Y	N	Y	Y
6 Yatron	?	?	?	Y	Y	N	Y	Y
7 Edgar	N	Y	Y	Y	Y	N	N	Y
8 Kostmayer	Y	Y	Y	Y	Y	N	Y	Y
9 ***Shuster***	?	?	N	Y	Y	N	Y	Y
10 ***McDade***	?	?	?	Y	N	N	Y	Y
11 Harrison	Y	Y	N	Y	N	N	Y	Y
12 Murtha	Y	?	N	Y	N	N	Y	Y
13 ***Coughlin***	N	Y	Y	N	Y	N	Y	Y
14 Coyne	Y	Y	N	Y	N	N	Y	Y
15 ***Ritter***	N	Y	Y	Y	Y	Y	N	Y
16 ***Walker***	N	N	Y	N	Y	Y	Y	Y
17 ***Gekas***	N	N	?	Y	Y	Y	Y	Y
18 Walgren	?	?	?	Y	Y	N	Y	Y
19 ***Goodling***	N	N	?	?	?	?	?	?
20 Gaydos	Y	Y	N	Y	N	N	Y	Y
21 ***Ridge***	N	Y	Y	Y	Y	Y	Y	Y
22 Murphy	Y	?	Y	Y	Y	N	Y	Y
23 ***Clinger***	Y	Y	Y	Y	Y	N	Y	Y
RHODE ISLAND								
1 St Germain	?	?	?	?	N	N	Y	Y
2 ***Schneider***	?	Y	Y	Y	Y	N	Y	Y
SOUTH CAROLINA								
1 ***Hartnett***	N	Y	N	Y	Y	Y	N	Y
2 ***Spence***	Y	Y	N	Y	Y	Y	Y	Y
3 Derrick	Y	Y	Y	Y	N	N	Y	Y
4 ***Campbell***	N	Y	?	Y	N	Y	Y	Y
5 Spratt	?	?	?	Y	Y	N	Y	Y
6 Tallon	Y	Y	Y	?	?	N	Y	Y
SOUTH DAKOTA								
AL Daschle	Y	Y	Y	N	N	N	Y	Y
TENNESSEE								
1 ***Quillen***	Y	Y	N	Y	N	N	Y	Y
2 ***Duncan***	Y	Y	N	Y	N	N	Y	Y
3 Lloyd	Y	Y	N	Y	N	N	Y	Y
4 Cooper	Y	Y	Y	Y	Y	N	Y	Y
5 Boner	Y	Y	N	Y	N	N	Y	Y
6 Gore	Y	Y	N	Y	?	N	Y	Y
7 ***Sundquist***	?	Y	Y	Y	Y	Y	Y	Y
8 Jones	Y	Y	N	Y	N	N	Y	Y
9 Ford	Y	Y	N	Y	N	N	Y	Y
TEXAS								
1 Hall, S.	Y	Y	N	Y	N	Y	Y	Y
2 Wilson	?	?	?	Y	?	N	Y	Y
3 ***Bartlett***	?	?	?	Y	Y	Y	Y	Y
4 Hall, R.	?	?	N	Y	N	Y	Y	Y
5 Bryant	Y	Y	N	Y	Y	N	Y	Y
6 ***Gramm***	N	N	Y	Y	N	Y	Y	Y
7 ***Archer***	N	Y	Y	Y	Y	Y	Y	Y
8 ***Fields***	?	?	Y	Y	N	Y	Y	Y
9 Brooks	Y	Y	N	Y	N	N	Y	Y
10 Pickle	?	?	N	Y	N	N	Y	Y
11 Leath	Y	Y	N	Y	N	Y	Y	Y
12 Wright	Y	Y	N	Y	?	N	Y	Y
13 Hightower	Y	Y	N	Y	N	Y	Y	Y
14 Patman	Y	Y	N	Y	Y	N	Y	Y
15 de la Garza	Y	Y	N	?	?	?	?	?
16 Coleman	Y	Y	N	Y	N	N	Y	Y
17 Stenholm	Y	Y	Y	Y	N	Y	Y	Y
18 Leland	Y	Y	Y	Y	N	N	Y	Y
19 Hance	Y	Y	Y	Y	N	N	Y	Y
20 Gonzalez	Y	Y	N	Y	N	N	Y	Y
21 ***Loeffler***	Y	Y	N	Y	N	Y	Y	Y
22 ***Paul***	?	?	?	?	?	#	N	N
23 Kazen	Y	Y	N	Y	N	N	Y	Y
24 Frost	Y	Y	Y	Y	N	N	Y	Y
25 Andrews	Y	Y	Y	Y	Y	Y	Y	Y
26 Vandergriff	Y	Y	Y	Y	N	N	Y	Y
27 Ortiz	Y	Y	N	Y	N	N	Y	Y
UTAH								
1 ***Hansen***	N	Y	N	Y	N	Y	Y	Y
2 ***Marriott***	?	?	?	Y	N	N	Y	Y
3 ***Nielson***	N	Y	N	Y	N	Y	Y	Y
VERMONT								
AL ***Jeffords***	?	?	Y	Y	Y	Y	Y	Y
VIRGINIA								
1 ***Bateman***	Y	Y	N	Y	N	N	Y	Y
2 ***Whitehurst***	Y	Y	Y	Y	N	N	Y	Y
3 ***Bliley***	Y	Y	N	Y	N	N	Y	Y
4 Sisisky	Y	Y	Y	Y	N	N	Y	Y
5 Daniel	Y	Y	N	Y	N	Y	Y	Y
6 Olin	Y	Y	Y	Y	Y	Y	Y	Y
7 ***Robinson***	Y	Y	N	Y	N	N	Y	Y
8 ***Parris***	N	Y	N	Y	N	Y	Y	Y
9 Boucher	Y	Y	Y	Y	N	N	Y	Y
10 ***Wolf***	N	Y	Y	Y	N	N	Y	Y
WASHINGTON								
1 ***Pritchard***	?	?	?	Y	X	Y	?	Y
2 Swift	?	?	?	Y	N	N	Y	Y
3 Bonker	Y	Y	Y	Y	N	N	Y	Y
4 ***Morrison***	Y	Y	N	Y	N	Y	Y	Y
5 Foley	Y	Y	?	Y	?	N	Y	Y
6 Dicks	Y	Y	N	Y	?	N	Y	Y
7 Lowry	Y	Y	Y	Y	N	N	Y	Y
8 ***Chandler***	?	?	?	Y	N	Y	Y	Y
WEST VIRGINIA								
1 Mollohan	Y	Y	N	Y	N	N	Y	Y
2 Staggers	Y	Y	N	Y	N	N	Y	Y
3 Wise	Y	Y	Y	Y	Y	N	Y	Y
4 Rahall	Y	Y	N	Y	N	N	Y	Y
WISCONSIN								
1 Aspin	Y	Y	Y	Y	?	N	Y	Y
2 Kastenmeier	N	Y	Y	Y	Y	N	Y	Y
3 ***Gunderson***	Y	Y	N	Y	Y	Y	Y	Y
4 Zablocki	Y	Y	N	Y	?	N	Y	Y
5 Moody	Y	Y	Y	Y	Y	N	Y	Y
6 ***Petri***	Y	Y	Y	Y	Y	Y	Y	Y
7 Obey	Y	Y	Y	Y	N	N	Y	Y
8 ***Roth***	Y	Y	Y	Y	Y	N	Y	Y
9 ***Sensenbrenner***	N	Y	Y	Y	Y	Y	N	Y
WYOMING								
AL ***Cheney***	N	N	N	Y	N	Y	Y	Y

Southern states - Ala., Ark., Fla., Ga., Ky., La., Miss., N.C., Okla., S.C., Tenn., Texas, Va.

162. HR 2207. Emergency School Aid Act. Perkins, D-Ky., motion to suspend the rules and pass the bill to authorize a program of grants to local school districts in fiscal 1984-86 to help them offset the costs of school desegregation. Motion agreed to 299-120: R 60-103; D 239-17 (ND 159-9, SD 80-8), June 7, 1983. A two-thirds majority of those present and voting (280 in this case) is required for passage under suspension of the rules. A "nay" was a vote supporting the president's position.

163. HR 2355. Vietnam Veterans' Training Act. Leath, D-Texas, motion to suspend the rules and pass the bill to establish a $325 million job training program for unemployed and disabled Vietnam-era veterans. Motion agreed to 407-10: R 155-8; D 252-2 (ND 167-0, SD 85-2), June 7, 1983. A two-thirds majority of those present and voting (278 in this case) is required for passage under suspension of the rules.

164. HR 2148. Follow Through Amendments. Andrews, D-N.C., motion to suspend the rules and pass the bill to extend the Follow Through program through fiscal 1985. The program provides educational, health, nutritional and social services to disadvantaged children previously enrolled in such preschool programs as Head Start. Motion agreed to 288-132: R 46-117; D 242-15 (ND 165-4, SD 77-11), June 7, 1983. A two-thirds majority of those present and voting (280 in this case) is required for passage under suspension of the rules. A "nay" was a vote supporting the president's position.

165. HR 2943. Washington Workshops Foundation Authorization. Perkins, D-Ky., motion to suspend the rules and pass the bill to authorize $1.5 million in each of fiscal years 1983-85 for the Allen J. Ellender Fellowship program; $100,000 in fiscal 1983 for the Washington Workshops Foundation, and $2 million in each of fiscal years 1984-85 for several law-related education programs. Motion rejected 230-190: R 28-135; D 202-55 (ND 137-32, SD 65-23), June 7, 1983. A two-thirds majority of those present and voting (280 in this case) is required for passage under suspension of the rules. A "nay" was a vote supporting the president's position.

166. HR 3223. Agriculture Appropriations, Fiscal 1984. Adoption of the rule (H Res 220) providing for House floor consideration of the bill to make fiscal 1984 appropriations for the Agriculture Department, the Food and Drug Administration and the Commodity Futures Trading Commission. Adopted 339-66: R 96-59; D 243-7 (ND 157-6, SD 86-1), June 8, 1983.

167. HR 3223. Agriculture Appropriations, Fiscal 1984. Passage of the bill to appropriate $34,029,527,000 in fiscal 1984 for the Agriculture Department, the Food and Drug Administration and the Commodity Futures Trading Commission. Passed 297-115: R 68-92; D 229-23 (ND 151-14, SD 78-9), June 8, 1983. The president had requested $34,083,299,000 in new budget authority.

168. HR 3191. Treasury, Postal Service and General Government Appropriations, Fiscal 1984. Adoption of the rule (H Res 222) providing for House floor consideration of the bill to make fiscal 1984 appropriations for the Treasury Department, U.S. Postal Service, executive offices and certain independent agencies. Adopted 229-183: R 132-30; D 97-153 (ND 50-113, SD 47-40), June 8, 1983.

169. HR 3191. Treasury, Postal Service and General Government Appropriations, Fiscal 1984. Jacobs, D-Ind., amendment to eliminate from the bill $910,700 for the office expenses of former Presidents Richard M. Nixon, Gerald R. Ford and Jimmy Carter, leaving $260,300 for pensions for them and for the widow of former President Lyndon B. Johnson. Adopted 244-169: R 83-79; D 161-90 (ND 105-59, SD 56-31), June 8, 1983.

KEY

Y	Voted for (yea).
#	Paired for.
+	Announced for.
N	Voted against (nay).
X	Paired against.
-	Announced against.
P	Voted "present".
C	Voted "present" to avoid possible conflict of interest.
?	Did not vote or otherwise make a position known.

Democrats   *Republicans*

	162	163	164	165	166	167	168	169
ALABAMA								
1 *Edwards*	N	Y	N	N	Y	N	N	N
2 *Dickinson*	Y	Y	N	?	Y	Y	Y	Y
3 Nichols	Y	Y	Y	Y	Y	Y	Y	Y
4 Bevill	Y	Y	Y	Y	Y	Y	Y	Y
5 Flippo	Y	Y	Y	Y	Y	Y	Y	N
6 Erdreich	Y	Y	Y	Y	Y	Y	Y	Y
7 Shelby	Y	Y	Y	N	Y	Y	Y	Y
ALASKA								
AL *Young*	Y	Y	Y	Y	Y	Y	Y	N
ARIZONA								
1 *McCain*	N	Y	N	N	Y	N	Y	N
2 Udall	Y	Y	Y	Y	Y	Y	N	Y
3 *Stump*	N	Y	N	N	Y	N	Y	Y
4 *Rudd*	N	Y	N	N	Y	N	Y	Y
5 McNulty	Y	Y	Y	Y	Y	Y	Y	Y
ARKANSAS								
1 Alexander	Y	Y	Y	Y	Y	Y	N	Y
2 *Bethune*	Y	Y	N	N	Y	N	Y	Y
3 *Hammerschmidt*	Y	Y	N	Y	Y	Y	Y	Y
4 Anthony	Y	Y	Y	Y	Y	Y	N	Y
CALIFORNIA								
1 Bosco	Y	Y	Y	N	Y	Y	N	Y
2 *Chappie*	N	Y	N	N	Y	Y	Y	Y
3 Matsui	Y	Y	Y	Y	Y	Y	N	Y
4 Fazio	Y	Y	Y	Y	Y	Y	N	N
5 Vacancy								
6 Boxer	Y	Y	Y	Y	Y	Y	N	Y
7 Miller	Y	Y	Y	N	N	N	N	Y
8 Dellums	Y	Y	Y	Y	Y	Y	N	Y
9 Stark	Y	Y	Y	Y	Y	Y	N	?
10 Edwards	Y	Y	Y	Y	Y	N	N	N
11 Lantos	Y	Y	Y	Y	Y	Y	N	N
12 *Zschau*	Y	Y	N	N	?	N	Y	
13 Mineta	Y	Y	Y	Y	Y	Y	N	N
14 *Shumway*	N	N	N	N	N	N	Y	Y
15 Coelho	Y	Y	Y	Y	Y	Y	N	Y
16 Panetta	Y	Y	Y	Y	Y	Y	N	Y
17 *Pashayan*	Y	N	Y	N	Y	?	Y	N
18 Lehman	Y	Y	Y	N	Y	Y	N	Y
19 *Lagomarsino*	N	Y	N	N	N	N	Y	N
20 *Thomas*	N	Y	N	N	Y	N	N	N
21 *Fiedler*	N	Y	N	N	N	N	N	N
22 *Moorhead*	N	Y	N	N	N	N	Y	Y
23 Beilenson	Y	Y	Y	N	Y	Y	N	?
24 Waxman	Y	Y	Y	Y	Y	Y	N	N
25 Roybal	Y	Y	Y	Y	Y	Y	N	N
26 Berman	Y	Y	Y	Y	Y	Y	?	Y
27 Levine	Y	Y	Y	Y	Y	Y	N	Y
28 Dixon	Y	Y	Y	?	?	?	Y	?
29 Hawkins	Y	Y	Y	Y	Y	Y	N	N
30 Martinez	?	?	?	?	?	?	?	?
31 Dymally	Y	Y	Y	Y	Y	Y	N	Y
32 Anderson	Y	Y	Y	Y	Y	N	N	N
33 *Dreier*	N	Y	N	N	N	N	N	Y
34 Torres	Y	Y	Y	Y	Y	Y	N	N
35 *Lewis*	Y	Y	N	N	?	?	?	?
36 Brown	?	?	?	?	Y	Y	?	Y
37 *McCandless*	N	Y	N	N	Y	N	Y	Y
38 Patterson	Y	Y	Y	Y	Y	Y	N	Y
39 *Dannemeyer*	N	N	N	N	N	N	N	Y
40 *Badham*	?	#	?	?	?	?	?	?
41 *Lowery*	N	Y	N	N	Y	N	Y	N
42 *Lungren*	N	Y	N	N	N	N	Y	Y
43 *Packard*	N	Y	N	N	N	N	Y	Y
44 Bates	Y	Y	Y	N	Y	Y	N	Y
45 *Hunter*	Y	Y	N	N	Y	N	Y	N
COLORADO								
1 Schroeder	Y	Y	Y	Y	Y	Y	N	N
2 Wirth	Y	Y	Y	Y	Y	Y	N	Y
3 Kogovsek	Y	Y	Y	Y	Y	Y	N	Y
4 *Brown*	N	Y	N	N	N	N	N	Y
5 *Kramer*	N	Y	N	N	N	N	Y	Y
6 *Schaefer*	N	Y	N	N	N	N	Y	Y
CONNECTICUT								
1 Kennelly	Y	Y	Y	Y	Y	Y	N	Y
2 Gejdenson	Y	Y	Y	Y	Y	Y	N	Y
3 Morrison	Y	Y	Y	Y	?	N	N	Y
4 *McKinney*	Y	Y	Y	Y	?	N	N	
5 Ratchford	Y	Y	Y	Y	Y	Y	Y	Y
6 *Johnson*	Y	Y	Y	N	Y	Y	N	N
DELAWARE								
AL Carper	Y	Y	Y	N	Y	N	N	Y
FLORIDA								
1 Hutto	Y	Y	Y	N	Y	Y	Y	Y
2 Fuqua	Y	Y	Y	N	Y	Y	N	Y
3 Bennett	Y	Y	Y	N	Y	Y	N	N
4 Chappell	Y	Y	Y	N	Y	Y	Y	N
5 *McCollum*	N	Y	N	N	N	N	Y	Y
6 MacKay	Y	Y	Y	N	Y	Y	N	Y
7 Gibbons	Y	Y	Y	Y	Y	Y	N	N
8 *Young*	Y	Y	Y	N	Y	Y	Y	N
9 *Bilirakis*	N	Y	N	N	N	N	Y	Y
10 Ireland	Y	Y	Y	N	Y	Y	N	Y
11 Nelson	Y	Y	Y	N	Y	Y	N	Y
12 *Lewis*	N	Y	N	N	N	Y	Y	Y
13 *Mack*	N	Y	N	N	N	N	Y	Y
14 Mica	Y	Y	Y	N	Y	Y	N	Y
15 *Shaw*	N	Y	N	N	N	N	Y	N
16 Smith	Y	Y	Y	Y	Y	Y	N	Y
17 Lehman	Y	Y	Y	Y	Y	Y	N	Y
18 Pepper	Y	Y	Y	Y	Y	Y	N	N
19 Fascell	Y	Y	Y	Y	Y	Y	N	N
GEORGIA								
1 Thomas	Y	Y	Y	Y	Y	Y	N	N
2 Hatcher	Y	Y	Y	Y	Y	Y	N	N
3 Ray	N	N	N	Y	Y	Y	Y	N
4 Levitas	Y	Y	Y	N	Y	Y	N	N
5 Fowler	Y	Y	Y	Y	Y	Y	N	Y
6 *Gingrich*	N	Y	N	N	N	N	Y	Y
7 McDonald	N	N	N	N	N	N	N	Y
8 Rowland	Y	Y	Y	Y	Y	Y	N	N
9 Jenkins	Y	Y	N	N	Y	Y	N	Y
10 Barnard	N	Y	N	N	Y	N	Y	N
HAWAII								
1 Heftel	?	?	?	?	?	?	?	?
2 Akaka	Y	Y	Y	Y	Y	N	N	N
IDAHO								
1 *Craig*	N	Y	N	N	N	N	Y	Y
2 *Hansen*	N	Y	N	N	?	N	Y	Y
ILLINOIS								
1 Vacancy								
2 Savage	Y	Y	Y	Y	Y	Y	N	Y
3 Russo	Y	Y	Y	Y	N	Y	N	Y
4 *O'Brien*	Y	Y	Y	Y	Y	Y	N	Y
5 Lipinski	Y	Y	Y	Y	Y	Y	Y	N
6 *Hyde*	N	Y	N	N	N	N	N	Y
7 Collins	#	#	?	?	Y	Y	N	Y
8 Rostenkowski	Y	Y	Y	Y	Y	Y	N	Y
9 Yates	Y	Y	Y	Y	Y	Y	N	Y
10 *Porter*	Y	Y	Y	Y	N	N	N	N
11 Annunzio	Y	Y	Y	Y	Y	Y	N	Y
12 *Crane, P.*	?	?	?	?	N	N	Y	Y
13 *Erlenborn*	N	Y	N	N	N	N	N	N
14 *Corcoran*	N	N	N	N	N	N	N	N
15 *Madigan*	N	Y	N	N	N	N	Y	N
16 *Martin*	Y	Y	N	N	Y	N	Y	N
17 Evans	Y	Y	Y	Y	Y	Y	N	Y
18 *Michel*	N	Y	N	N	N	?	N	N
19 *Crane, D.*	N	Y	N	N	N	N	N	Y
20 Durbin	Y	Y	Y	Y	Y	Y	N	Y
21 Price	Y	Y	Y	Y	?	Y	Y	Y
22 Simon	Y	Y	Y	Y	Y	?	N	Y
INDIANA								
1 Hall	?	?	Y	Y	Y	Y	N	Y
2 Sharp	Y	Y	Y	N	Y	N	Y	N
3 *Hiler*	N	Y	N	N	N	N	N	Y
4 *Coats*	N	N	N	N	N	N	Y	Y
5 Hillis	N	Y	N	N	Y	Y	Y	Y

Corresponding to Congressional Record Votes 170, 171, 172, 173, 174, 175, 176, 177

	162	163	164	165	166	167	168	169
6 ***Burton***	N	Y	N	N	N	N	Y	Y
7 ***Myers***	N	Y	N	N	Y	Y	Y	N
8 McCloskey	Y	Y	Y	Y	Y	Y	N	Y
9 Hamilton	Y	Y	Y	Y	Y	Y	Y	Y
10 Jacobs	Y	Y	Y	N	Y	N	Y	Y
IOWA								
1 ***Leach***	Y	Y	Y	Y	Y	Y	Y	Y
2 ***Tauke***	N	Y	N	N	Y	N	Y	N
3 ***Evans***	N	Y	Y	Y	Y	N	Y	Y
4 Smith	Y	Y	Y	Y	Y	Y	N	N
5 Harkin	Y	Y	Y	Y	Y	Y	N	?
6 Bedell	Y	Y	Y	N	Y	Y	N	Y
KANSAS								
1 ***Roberts***	N	Y	N	N	Y	N	Y	Y
2 Slattery	Y	Y	Y	N	Y	Y	N	Y
3 ***Winn***	N	Y	N	N	Y	Y	Y	Y
4 Glickman	Y	Y	Y	Y	Y	Y	N	Y
5 ***Whittaker***	N	Y	N	N	Y	Y	Y	Y
KENTUCKY								
1 Hubbard	?	?	?	?	?	?	?	?
2 Natcher	Y	Y	Y	Y	Y	Y	Y	N
3 Mazzoli	Y	Y	Y	Y	Y	Y	Y	N
4 ***Snyder***	N	Y	N	N	Y	N	Y	Y
5 ***Rogers***	N	Y	N	N	Y	Y	Y	N
6 ***Hopkins***	Y	Y	N	N	Y	N	Y	Y
7 Perkins	Y	Y	Y	Y	Y	Y	Y	N
LOUISIANA								
1 ***Livingston***	Y	Y	N	Y	Y	N	Y	N
2 Boggs	Y	Y	Y	Y	?	Y	Y	N
3 Tauzin	Y	Y	Y	Y	Y	N	Y	Y
4 Roemer	Y	Y	N	Y	Y	N	Y	Y
5 Huckaby	Y	Y	Y	Y	Y	Y	Y	Y
6 ***Moore***	Y	Y	Y	N	Y	N	Y	N
7 Breaux	Y	Y	Y	Y	Y	Y	Y	N
8 Long	Y	Y	Y	Y	Y	Y	Y	Y
MAINE								
1 ***McKernan***	Y	Y	Y	Y	N	Y	N	N
2 ***Snowe***	Y	Y	Y	N	Y	Y	N	N
MARYLAND								
1 Dyson	Y	Y	Y	Y	Y	Y	?	Y
2 Long	Y	Y	Y	Y	Y	Y	N	N
3 Mikulski	Y	Y	Y	Y	Y	Y	N	Y
4 ***Holt***	N	Y	N	N	N	N	Y	N
5 Hoyer	Y	Y	Y	Y	Y	Y	N	N
6 Byron	N	Y	N	N	Y	Y	Y	Y
7 Mitchell	Y	Y	Y	Y	Y	Y	N	Y
8 Barnes	Y	Y	Y	Y	Y	Y	N	N
MASSACHUSETTS								
1 ***Conte***	Y	Y	Y	Y	Y	Y	Y	N
2 Boland	Y	Y	Y	Y	Y	Y	N	N
3 Early	Y	Y	Y	Y	Y	Y	N	N
4 Frank	Y	Y	Y	N	Y	N	N	Y
5 Shannon	Y	Y	Y	Y	Y	Y	N	Y
6 Mavroules	Y	Y	Y	Y	Y	Y	Y	Y
7 Markey	Y	Y	Y	Y	Y	Y	N	Y
8 O'Neill								
9 Moakley	Y	Y	Y	Y	Y	Y	Y	N
10 Studds	Y	Y	Y	Y	Y	Y	N	Y
11 Donnelly	Y	Y	Y	Y	Y	Y	Y	Y
MICHIGAN								
1 Conyers	Y	Y	Y	Y	?	?	?	?
2 ***Pursell***	Y	Y	N	N	Y	Y	N	Y
3 Wolpe	Y	Y	Y	Y	Y	Y	N	Y
4 ***Siljander***	N	Y	N	N	Y	Y	Y	Y
5 ***Sawyer***	Y	Y	N	Y	Y	Y	N	N
6 Carr	Y	Y	Y	Y	Y	Y	N	Y
7 Kildee	Y	Y	Y	Y	Y	Y	Y	Y
8 Traxler	Y	Y	Y	Y	Y	Y	Y	Y
9 ***Vander Jagt***	Y	Y	Y	N	Y	Y	Y	N
10 Albosta	Y	Y	Y	Y	Y	Y	Y	Y
11 ***Davis***	Y	Y	Y	Y	Y	Y	Y	Y
12 Bonior	Y	Y	Y	Y	Y	Y	Y	N
13 Crockett	Y	Y	Y	Y	Y	Y	N	Y
14 Hertel	Y	Y	Y	Y	Y	Y	Y	N
15 Ford	Y	Y	Y	Y	Y	Y	N	N
16 Dingell	Y	Y	Y	N	Y	Y	Y	Y
17 Levin	Y	Y	Y	Y	Y	Y	N	Y
18 ***Broomfield***	N	Y	N	N	?	N	Y	N
MINNESOTA								
1 Penny	Y	Y	N	Y	Y	Y	Y	Y
2 ***Weber***	N	Y	Y	N	Y	Y	Y	Y
3 ***Frenzel***	N	Y	N	Y	?	N	N	N
4 Vento	Y	Y	Y	Y	Y	Y	N	Y
5 Sabo	Y	Y	Y	Y	Y	Y	N	N
6 Sikorski	Y	Y	Y	Y	Y	Y	Y	Y
7 ***Stangeland***	N	Y	N	N	Y	Y	Y	Y
8 Oberstar	Y	Y	Y	Y	Y	Y	Y	N
MISSISSIPPI								
1 Whitten	Y	Y	Y	Y	Y	Y	Y	N
2 ***Franklin***	N	Y	N	Y	Y	Y	Y	N
3 Montgomery	N	Y	N	Y	Y	Y	Y	Y
4 Dowdy	Y	Y	Y	Y	Y	Y	N	Y
5 ***Lott***	N	Y	N	N	?	N	Y	N
MISSOURI								
1 Clay	Y	Y	Y	Y	Y	Y	N	Y
2 Young	N	Y	Y	Y	Y	Y	Y	N
3 Gephardt	Y	Y	Y	Y	Y	?	N	Y
4 Skelton	N	Y	Y	N	Y	Y	Y	Y
5 Wheat	Y	Y	Y	Y	Y	Y	N	N
6 ***Coleman***	N	Y	Y	N	Y	Y	Y	N
7 ***Taylor***	N	Y	N	N	Y	Y	Y	N
8 ***Emerson***	N	Y	Y	N	Y	Y	Y	Y
9 Volkmer	N	Y	Y	N	Y	Y	Y	Y
MONTANA								
1 Williams	Y	Y	Y	Y	Y	Y	?	Y
2 ***Marlenee***	Y	Y	Y	N	Y	Y	Y	N
NEBRASKA								
1 ***Bereuter***	Y	Y	Y	Y	Y	Y	Y	Y
2 ***Daub***	N	Y	N	N	Y	Y	Y	Y
3 ***Smith***	N	Y	N	N	Y	Y	Y	Y
NEVADA								
1 Reid	Y	Y	Y	Y	N	Y	Y	Y
2 ***Vucanovich***	X	X	-	-	N	N	Y	N
NEW HAMPSHIRE								
1 D'Amours	N	Y	Y	N	Y	N	Y	Y
2 ***Gregg***	N	Y	N	N	N	N	Y	Y
NEW JERSEY								
1 Florio	Y	Y	Y	Y	Y	Y	Y	N
2 Hughes	Y	Y	Y	Y	Y	N	N	Y
3 Howard	Y	Y	Y	Y	Y	Y	N	N
4 ***Smith***	Y	Y	Y	Y	Y	Y	Y	Y
5 ***Roukema***	N	Y	N	N	Y	N	N	N
6 Dwyer	Y	Y	Y	Y	Y	Y	N	N
7 ***Rinaldo***	Y	Y	Y	Y	Y	Y	Y	Y
8 Roe	Y	Y	Y	Y	Y	Y	Y	N
9 Torricelli	Y	Y	Y	Y	Y	Y	N	Y
10 Rodino	Y	Y	Y	Y	Y	Y	Y	N
11 Minish	Y	Y	Y	Y	Y	Y	N	N
12 ***Courter***	Y	Y	N	N	N	N	Y	N
13 ***Forsythe***	N	Y	N	N	N	N	N	N
14 Guarini	Y	Y	Y	Y	Y	Y	N	Y
NEW MEXICO								
1 ***Lujan***	N	Y	N	N	Y	N	Y	Y
2 ***Skeen***	N	Y	N	N	N	Y	Y	N
3 Richardson	Y	Y	Y	Y	Y	Y	N	Y
NEW YORK								
1 ***Carney***	#	?	?	?	?	?	?	?
2 Downey	Y	Y	Y	Y	Y	Y	N	N
3 Mrazek	Y	Y	Y	Y	Y	Y	N	Y
4 ***Lent***	N	Y	Y	N	Y	Y	Y	N
5 ***McGrath***	N	Y	Y	N	N	N	Y	Y
6 Addabbo	Y	Y	Y	Y	Y	Y	Y	N
7 Ackerman	Y	Y	Y	Y	Y	Y	N	N
8 Scheuer	Y	Y	Y	N	Y	Y	N	Y
9 Ferraro	?	?	?	?	Y	Y	N	N
10 Schumer	Y	Y	Y	Y	Y	N	N	N
11 Towns	Y	Y	Y	Y	Y	Y	N	Y
12 Owens	Y	Y	Y	Y	?	?	?	?
13 Solarz	Y	Y	Y	Y	Y	Y	N	N
14 ***Molinari***	N	Y	N	N	Y	N	Y	N
15 ***Green***	Y	Y	N	Y	Y	N	N	N
16 Rangel	Y	Y	Y	Y	Y	Y	N	N
17 Weiss	Y	Y	Y	Y	Y	Y	N	N
18 Garcia	Y	Y	Y	Y	Y	Y	N	N
19 Biaggi	Y	Y	Y	Y	Y	Y	Y	N
20 Ottinger	Y	Y	Y	Y	N	N	N	Y
21 ***Fish***	Y	Y	Y	Y	Y	Y	Y	N
22 ***Gilman***	Y	Y	Y	Y	Y	Y	N	N
23 Stratton	Y	+	Y	N	Y	Y	Y	Y
24 ***Solomon***	N	Y	N	N	Y	Y	Y	Y
25 ***Boehlert***	Y	Y	Y	N	Y	Y	N	N
26 ***Martin***	Y	Y	Y	N	Y	Y	Y	Y
27 ***Wortley***	Y	Y	Y	N	N	Y	Y	Y
28 McHugh	Y	Y	Y	Y	?	Y	N	N
29 ***Horton***	Y	Y	Y	Y	Y	Y	Y	Y
30 ***Conable***	Y	Y	N	N	N	N	N	Y
31 ***Kemp***	Y	Y	Y	Y	?	N	Y	N
32 LaFalce	Y	Y	Y	N	Y	Y	N	N
33 Nowak	Y	Y	Y	Y	Y	Y	Y	Y
34 Lundine	Y	Y	Y	Y	Y	Y	N	N
NORTH CAROLINA								
1 Jones	Y	Y	Y	N	Y	Y	N	Y
2 Valentine	Y	Y	Y	Y	Y	Y	N	Y
3 Whitley	Y	Y	Y	Y	Y	Y	N	Y
4 Andrews	Y	?	Y	Y	Y	Y	N	Y
5 Neal	Y	Y	Y	Y	Y	Y	N	Y
6 Britt	Y	Y	Y	Y	Y	Y	N	Y
7 Rose	Y	Y	Y	Y	Y	Y	N	Y
8 Hefner	Y	Y	Y	Y	Y	Y	N	Y
9 ***Martin***	N	Y	N	N	N	N	N	N
10 ***Broyhill***	N	Y	N	Y	N	N	Y	N
11 Clarke	Y	Y	Y	Y	Y	Y	N	Y
NORTH DAKOTA								
AL Dorgan	Y	Y	Y	Y	Y	Y	N	Y
OHIO								
1 Luken	Y	Y	N	N	Y	N	Y	N
2 ***Gradison***	N	Y	N	N	Y	N	Y	N
3 Hall	Y	Y	Y	N	Y	N	Y	Y
4 ***Oxley***	N	Y	N	N	Y	N	Y	N
5 ***Latta***	N	Y	N	N	Y	N	Y	N
6 ***McEwen***	N	Y	N	N	N	Y	Y	Y
7 ***DeWine***	N	Y	N	N	N	N	Y	N
8 ***Kindness***	N	Y	N	[illegible]	Y	Y	Y	N
9 Kaptur	Y	Y	Y	N	Y	Y	N	Y
10 ***Miller***	N	Y	N	N	Y	N	Y	N
11 Eckart	N	Y	Y	Y	Y	Y	Y	Y
12 ***Kasich***	N	Y	N	N	Y	N	Y	Y
13 Pease	Y	Y	N	N	Y	Y	N	Y
14 Seiberling	Y	Y	Y	Y	Y	Y	N	Y
15 ***Wylie***	N	Y	N	N	?	N	Y	N
16 ***Regula***	Y	Y	Y	N	Y	Y	Y	N
17 ***Williams***	Y	Y	Y	Y	Y	Y	Y	Y
18 Applegate	Y	Y	Y	Y	Y	Y	Y	Y
19 Feighan	N	Y	Y	Y	Y	Y	N	Y
20 Oakar	N	Y	Y	Y	Y	Y	Y	Y
21 Stokes	Y	Y	Y	Y	Y	Y	N	Y
OKLAHOMA								
1 Jones	Y	Y	Y	Y	Y	N	N	N
2 Synar	Y	Y	Y	Y	Y	Y	N	Y
3 Watkins	Y	Y	Y	N	Y	Y	Y	Y
4 McCurdy	Y	Y	Y	Y	Y	Y	Y	Y
5 ***Edwards***	Y	Y	Y	N	Y	Y	Y	Y
6 English	Y	Y	Y	Y	Y	Y	Y	Y
OREGON								
1 AuCoin	Y	Y	Y	N	Y	N	N	Y
2 ***Smith, R.***	N	Y	N	N	Y	N	Y	Y
3 Wyden	Y	Y	Y	Y	Y	Y	N	Y
4 Weaver	Y	Y	Y	N	N	N	N	Y
5 ***Smith, D.***	N	Y	N	N	N	N	Y	Y
PENNSYLVANIA								
1 Foglietta	Y	Y	Y	Y	Y	Y	N	Y
2 Gray	Y	Y	Y	Y	Y	Y	N	N
3 Borski	Y	Y	Y	N	Y	Y	Y	Y
4 Kolter	?	?	?	?	?	?	?	?
5 ***Schulze***	Y	Y	N	N	N	Y	Y	N
6 Yatron	Y	Y	Y	N	Y	Y	Y	Y
7 Edgar	Y	Y	Y	Y	N	Y	N	Y
8 Kostmayer	Y	Y	Y	Y	?	?	?	N
9 ***Shuster***	N	Y	N	N	N	N	Y	Y
10 ***McDade***	Y	Y	Y	Y	Y	Y	Y	N
11 Harrison	Y	Y	Y	Y	Y	Y	Y	N
12 Murtha	Y	Y	Y	N	Y	Y	Y	N
13 ***Coughlin***	Y	Y	N	N	N	N	N	N
14 Coyne	Y	Y	Y	Y	Y	Y	N	N
15 ***Ritter***	N	Y	N	N	Y	N	Y	Y
16 ***Walker***	N	Y	N	N	N	N	Y	Y
17 ***Gekas***	N	Y	N	N	N	N	N	Y
18 Walgren	Y	Y	Y	Y	Y	?	?	?
19 ***Goodling***	Y	Y	Y	N	Y	N	Y	?
20 Gaydos	N	Y	Y	N	Y	Y	Y	Y
21 ***Ridge***	Y	Y	Y	Y	Y	Y	N	N
22 Murphy	Y	Y	Y	N	Y	Y	Y	Y
23 ***Clinger***	Y	Y	Y	N	Y	Y	Y	N
RHODE ISLAND								
1 St Germain	Y	Y	Y	Y	Y	Y	Y	N
2 ***Schneider***	Y	Y	Y	Y	Y	Y	N	Y
SOUTH CAROLINA								
1 ***Hartnett***	N	N	N	N	N	N	Y	Y
2 ***Spence***	N	Y	N	N	Y	Y	Y	N
3 Derrick	Y	Y	Y	N	Y	Y	Y	Y
4 ***Campbell***	N	Y	N	N	Y	Y	Y	N
5 Spratt	Y	Y	Y	Y	Y	Y	N	N
6 Tallon	Y	Y	Y	Y	Y	Y	Y	Y
SOUTH DAKOTA								
AL Daschle	Y	Y	Y	Y	Y	Y	N	Y
TENNESSEE								
1 ***Quillen***	N	Y	Y	N	Y	Y	Y	N
2 ***Duncan***	Y	Y	N	N	?	?	Y	Y
3 Lloyd	Y	Y	Y	N	Y	Y	Y	Y
4 Cooper	Y	Y	Y	Y	Y	Y	N	Y
5 Boner	Y	Y	Y	Y	Y	Y	N	N
6 Gore	Y	Y	Y	Y	Y	Y	Y	N
7 ***Sundquist***	N	Y	N	N	Y	Y	Y	N
8 Jones	Y	Y	Y	Y	Y	Y	N	Y
9 Ford	Y	Y	Y	Y	Y	Y	N	N
TEXAS								
1 Hall, S.	Y	Y	Y	Y	Y	Y	Y	Y
2 Wilson	Y	Y	Y	N	Y	Y	Y	?
3 ***Bartlett***	N	N	N	N	N	N	Y	Y
4 Hall, R.	Y	Y	Y	Y	Y	Y	Y	Y
5 Bryant	Y	Y	Y	Y	Y	Y	N	Y
6 ***Gramm***	N	Y	N	N	N	N	Y	Y
7 ***Archer***	N	Y	N	N	N	N	Y	Y
8 ***Fields***	N	Y	N	N	N	N	Y	Y
9 Brooks	Y	Y	Y	N	Y	Y	N	N
10 Pickle	Y	Y	Y	Y	Y	Y	N	N
11 Leath	N	Y	N	Y	Y	N	Y	Y
12 Wright	Y	Y	Y	Y	Y	Y	Y	N
13 Hightower	N	Y	Y	N	Y	Y	Y	Y
14 Patman	Y	Y	Y	N	Y	Y	Y	Y
15 de la Garza	?	?	?	?	?	?	?	?
16 Coleman	Y	Y	Y	Y	Y	Y	N	Y
17 Stenholm	N	Y	N	Y	Y	N	Y	Y
18 Leland	Y	Y	Y	Y	Y	Y	N	Y
19 Hance	Y	Y	Y	Y	Y	Y	N	Y
20 Gonzalez	Y	Y	Y	Y	Y	Y	N	N
21 ***Loeffler***	N	Y	N	N	Y	N	Y	N
22 ***Paul***	N	N	N	N	N	N	Y	Y
23 Kazen	Y	Y	Y	Y	Y	Y	Y	Y
24 Frost	Y	Y	Y	Y	Y	Y	Y	N
25 Andrews	Y	Y	Y	N	Y	Y	N	Y
26 Vandergriff	Y	Y	Y	Y	Y	Y	N	N
27 Ortiz	Y	Y	Y	Y	Y	Y	Y	N
UTAH								
1 ***Hansen***	N	N	N	N	N	N	Y	Y
2 ***Marriott***	Y	Y	Y	N	Y	Y	Y	Y
3 ***Nielson***	N	N	N	N	N	N	Y	Y
VERMONT								
AL ***Jeffords***	Y	Y	Y	N	Y	Y	N	N
VIRGINIA								
1 ***Bateman***	N	Y	N	N	Y	Y	Y	N
2 ***Whitehurst***	Y	Y	N	N	Y	N	?	Y
3 ***Bliley***	N	Y	N	N	Y	Y	Y	Y
4 Sisisky	Y	Y	Y	Y	Y	Y	N	Y
5 Daniel	N	Y	N	N	Y	Y	Y	N
6 Olin	Y	Y	N	N	Y	Y	Y	N
7 ***Robinson***	N	Y	N	N	Y	Y	Y	N
8 ***Parris***	Y	Y	N	N	Y	Y	?	?
9 Boucher	Y	Y	Y	Y	Y	+	?	Y
10 ***Wolf***	Y	Y	N	N	Y	Y	Y	N
WASHINGTON								
1 ***Pritchard***	Y	Y	N	N	Y	N	N	N
2 Swift	Y	Y	Y	Y	Y	Y	N	?
3 Bonker	Y	Y	Y	Y	Y	Y	Y	Y
4 ***Morrison***	N	Y	Y	N	N	Y	N	N
5 Foley	Y	Y	Y	Y	?	Y	N	N
6 Dicks	Y	Y	Y	Y	Y	Y	N	Y
7 Lowry	Y	Y	Y	N	Y	Y	N	Y
8 ***Chandler***	N	Y	N	N	Y	Y	N	N
WEST VIRGINIA								
1 Mollohan	Y	Y	Y	Y	Y	Y	Y	Y
2 Staggers	Y	Y	Y	Y	Y	Y	Y	Y
3 Wise	Y	Y	Y	Y	Y	Y	N	Y
4 Rahall	Y	Y	Y	Y	Y	Y	N	Y
WISCONSIN								
1 Aspin	Y	Y	Y	Y	Y	Y	Y	Y
2 Kastenmeier	Y	Y	Y	Y	Y	Y	N	N
3 ***Gunderson***	Y	Y	N	N	Y	Y	Y	N
4 Zablocki	Y	Y	Y	Y	?	Y	Y	N
5 Moody	Y	Y	Y	Y	Y	Y	N	Y
6 ***Petri***	Y	Y	N	N	N	Y	Y	Y
7 Obey	Y	Y	Y	Y	Y	Y	N	Y
8 ***Roth***	Y	Y	N	N	N	Y	Y	Y
9 ***Sensenbrenner***	Y	Y	N	N	N	N	Y	Y
WYOMING								
AL ***Cheney***	N	Y	N	N	N	N	Y	N

Southern states - Ala., Ark., Fla., Ga., Ky., La., Miss., N.C., Okla., S.C., Tenn., Texas, Va.

170. HR 3191. Treasury, Postal Service and General Government Appropriations, Fiscal 1984. Smith, R-N.J., amendment to prohibit the use of federal health benefit funds to pay for abortions unless the life of the mother is endangered. Adopted 226-182: R 128-33; D 98-149 (ND 55-106, SD 43-43), June 8, 1983. A "yea" was a vote supporting the president's position.

171. HR 3191. Treasury, Postal Service and General Government Appropriations, Fiscal 1984. Passage of the bill to appropriate $11,907,652,300 for the Treasury Department, U.S. Postal Service, executive offices and certain independent agencies in fiscal 1984. Rejected 149-259: R 31-129; D 118-130 (ND 80-82, SD 38-48), June 8, 1983. The president had requested $11,576,298,000 in new budget authority.

172. Procedural Motion. Gekas, R-Pa., motion to approve the House *Journal* of Wednesday, June 8. Motion agreed to 363-32: R 140-16; D 223-16 (ND 142-14, SD 81-2), June 9, 1983.

173. HR 2915. State Department Authorizations. Adoption of the rule (H Res 198) providing for House floor consideration of the bill to make supplemental authorizations in fiscal year 1983 and regular authorizations in fiscal years 1984-85 for the State Department, the United States Information Agency, the Board for International Broadcasting and the Inter-American Foundation. Adopted 373-37: R 121-36; D 252-1 (ND 168-1, SD 84-0), June 9, 1983.

174. HR 2915. State Department Authorizations. Brown, R-Colo., amendment to delete Title VI, establishing a National Endowment for Democracy. Rejected 194-215: R 89-68; D 105-147 (ND 65-102, SD 40-45), June 9, 1983. A "nay" was a vote supporting the president's position.

175. HR 2915. State Department Authorizations. Brown, R-Colo., amendment to delete references in the section establishing a National Endowment for Democracy to participation in the endowment by the "two major American political parties." Adopted 267-136: R 100-54; D 167-82 (ND 114-50, SD 53-32), June 9, 1983. A "nay" was a vote supporting the president's position. (By voice vote, the House later adopted a related Brown amendment to delete funding in the bill for grants by the National Endowment for Democracy to private institutes established by the Republican and Democratic parties.)

176. HR 1590. Emergency Food Assistance. Adoption of the rule (H Res 207) providing for House floor consideration of the bill to promote the distribution of surplus, federally owned commodities to emergency feeding programs. The program would be authorized from Oct. 1, 1983, to Sept. 30, 1985. Adopted 346-51: R 107-44; D 239-7 (ND 158-3, SD 81-4), June 9, 1983.

KEY

Y	Voted for (yea).
#	Paired for.
+	Announced for.
N	Voted against (nay).
X	Paired against.
-	Announced against.
P	Voted "present".
C	Voted "present" to avoid possible conflict of interest.
?	Did not vote or otherwise make a position known.

Democrats   *Republicans*

	170	171	172	173	174	175	176
ALABAMA							
1 *Edwards*	N	N	Y	Y	Y	Y	Y
2 *Dickinson*	N	N	N	?	Y	N	Y
3 Nichols	Y	N	Y	Y	Y	Y	Y
4 Bevill	Y	Y	Y	Y	Y	Y	Y
5 Flippo	Y	N	Y	Y	Y	Y	Y
6 Erdreich	Y	Y	Y	Y	Y	Y	Y
7 Shelby	Y	N	Y	Y	N	Y	N
ALASKA							
AL *Young*	Y	Y	?	Y	N	Y	Y
ARIZONA							
1 *McCain*	Y	N	Y	?	Y	Y	?
2 Udall	N	Y	Y	Y	N	N	Y
3 *Stump*	Y	N	Y	Y	Y	Y	N
4 *Rudd*	Y	Y	Y	Y	Y	N	Y
5 McNulty	N	N	Y	Y	N	Y	Y
ARKANSAS							
1 Alexander	N	Y	Y	?	N	N	Y
2 *Bethune*	Y	N	Y	Y	Y	Y	N
3 *Hammerschmidt*	Y	N	Y	Y	Y	Y	Y
4 Anthony	N	N	Y	Y	Y	Y	Y
CALIFORNIA							
1 Bosco	N	Y	Y	Y	N	N	Y
2 *Chappie*	N	N	Y	N	Y	Y	N
3 Matsui	N	N	Y	Y	N	Y	Y
4 Fazio	N	Y	Y	Y	N	N	?
5 Vacancy							
6 Boxer	N	N	Y	Y	N	N	Y
7 Miller	N	N	Y	Y	Y	Y	Y
8 Dellums	N	N	Y	Y	Y	Y	Y
9 Stark	?	?	Y	Y	Y	Y	Y
10 Edwards	N	N	Y	Y	Y	Y	Y
11 Lantos	N	Y	Y	Y	N	?	Y
12 Zschau	N	N	Y	Y	N	Y	Y
13 Mineta	N	N	Y	Y	Y	Y	Y
14 *Shumway*	Y	N	Y	N	Y	N	N
15 Coelho	N	N	Y	Y	N	N	Y
16 Panetta	N	N	Y	Y	Y	Y	Y
17 *Pashayan*	Y	N	Y	N	N	Y	Y
18 Lehman	N	Y	?	Y	N	Y	Y
19 *Lagomarsino*	Y	N	Y	N	N	Y	Y
20 *Thomas*	N	N	Y	N	N	N	N
21 *Fiedler*	N	N	Y	N	N	N	Y
22 *Moorhead*	Y	N	Y	Y	Y	Y	N
23 Beilenson	?	?	?	?	?	?	?
24 Waxman	N	N	Y	Y	N	N	Y
25 Roybal	N	Y	Y	Y	N	N	Y
26 Berman	N	N	Y	Y	N	N	Y
27 Levine	N	N	Y	Y	Y	Y	Y
28 Dixon	?	?	?	Y	N	N	Y
29 Hawkins	N	N	N	N	Y	N	Y
30 Martinez	?	?	?	?	?	?	?
31 Dymally	N	N	N	?	N	N	Y
32 Anderson	N	N	Y	Y	N	Y	Y
33 *Dreier*	Y	N	Y	N	Y	Y	N
34 Torres	N	N	Y	Y	N	N	Y
35 *Lewis*	?	?	Y	Y	N	N	Y
36 Brown	N	Y	Y	Y	Y	Y	Y
37 *McCandless*	N	N	Y	Y	Y	Y	N
38 Patterson	N	N	Y	Y	Y	Y	Y
39 *Dannemeyer*	Y	N	N	N	Y	Y	N
40 *Badham*	?	?	?	?	#	#	?
41 *Lowery*	Y	N	Y	Y	Y	Y	Y
42 *Lungren*	Y	N	Y	Y	Y	Y	N

	170	171	172	173	174	175	176
43 *Packard*	Y	N	Y	Y	Y	Y	Y
44 Bates	N	N	Y	Y	Y	Y	Y
45 *Hunter*	Y	Y	?	Y	Y	Y	Y
COLORADO							
1 Schroeder	N	N	N	Y	Y	Y	Y
2 Wirth	N	N	Y	Y	Y	Y	Y
3 Kogovsek	N	N	?	Y	Y	Y	Y
4 *Brown*	N	N	N	N	Y	N	N
5 *Kramer*	Y	N	Y	Y	Y	Y	Y
6 *Schaefer*	Y	N	Y	?	Y	Y	Y
CONNECTICUT							
1 Kennelly	N	Y	Y	Y	Y	Y	Y
2 Gejdenson	N	N	N	Y	Y	Y	Y
3 Morrison	N	N	Y	Y	Y	Y	Y
4 *McKinney*	N	N	Y	N	N	N	Y
5 Ratchford	N	Y	N	Y	Y	Y	Y
6 *Johnson*	N	N	Y	Y	Y	N	Y
DELAWARE							
AL Carper	N	N	Y	Y	Y	Y	Y
FLORIDA							
1 Hutto	Y	N	Y	N	N	Y	Y
2 Fuqua	Y	Y	?	Y	N	N	Y
3 Bennett	Y	N	Y	N	N	N	Y
4 Chappell	Y	Y	Y	N	N	Y	Y
5 *McCollum*	Y	N	Y	Y	Y	Y	N
6 MacKay	N	N	Y	Y	Y	Y	?
7 Gibbons	Y	Y	Y	N	N	Y	?
8 *Young*	Y	Y	Y	N	N	Y	Y
9 *Bilirakis*	Y	N	Y	N	N	N	Y
10 Ireland	Y	N	Y	N	N	Y	Y
11 Nelson	Y	Y	Y	N	N	Y	Y
12 *Lewis*	N	N	Y	N	N	Y	Y
13 *Mack*	Y	N	Y	N	Y	Y	N
14 Mica	N	Y	Y	N	N	Y	Y
15 *Shaw*	Y	Y	Y	Y	Y	N	N
16 Smith	N	N	Y	N	N	N	Y
17 Lehman	N	Y	Y	N	N	N	Y
18 Pepper	N	Y	Y	Y	N	N	Y
19 Fascell	N	Y	Y	N	N	N	Y
GEORGIA							
1 Thomas	Y	N	Y	Y	Y	Y	Y
2 Hatcher	Y	Y	Y	N	Y	Y	Y
3 Ray	Y	N	Y	Y	Y	Y	Y
4 Levitas	N	N	Y	Y	Y	Y	Y
5 Fowler	N	N	Y	N	N	Y	Y
6 *Gingrich*	Y	N	Y	N	N	N	N
7 McDonald	Y	N	Y	Y	Y	Y	N
8 Rowland	Y	Y	Y	Y	Y	Y	Y
9 Jenkins	Y	N	Y	Y	Y	Y	Y
10 Barnard	Y	N	Y	Y	Y	Y	Y
HAWAII							
1 Heftel	?	?	?	?	?	?	?
2 Akaka	N	Y	Y	Y	N	Y	Y
IDAHO							
1 *Craig*	Y	N	Y	Y	Y	Y	N
2 *Hansen*	Y	N	?	?	?	?	N
ILLINOIS							
1 Vacancy							
2 Savage	N	N	Y	Y	Y	Y	Y
3 Russo	Y	N	Y	Y	N	N	Y
4 *O'Brien*	Y	Y	Y	N	N	Y	Y
5 Lipinski	Y	Y	Y	N	N	Y	Y
6 *Hyde*	Y	Y	Y	Y	N	N	?
7 Collins	N	Y	Y	N	Y	Y	Y
8 Rostenkowski	Y	N	?	Y	N	N	Y
9 Yates	N	Y	N	Y	N	Y	Y
10 *Porter*	Y	N	Y	Y	Y	Y	N
11 Annunzio	Y	Y	Y	Y	N	N	Y
12 *Crane, P.*	Y	N	Y	N	Y	Y	?
13 *Erlenborn*	Y	N	Y	Y	N	N	Y
14 *Corcoran*	Y	N	Y	Y	N	N	Y
15 *Madigan*	N	N	Y	Y	Y	Y	Y
16 *Martin*	N	N	Y	Y	N	N	Y
17 Evans	N	N	Y	Y	N	N	Y
18 *Michel*	Y	N	Y	N	N	N	Y
19 *Crane, D.*	Y	N	Y	N	Y	Y	N
20 Durbin	Y	N	Y	Y	Y	Y	Y
21 Price	N	Y	Y	Y	N	N	Y
22 Simon	N	Y	Y	N	N	N	Y
INDIANA							
1 Hall	N	N	Y	Y	Y	Y	Y
2 Sharp	Y	N	Y	Y	Y	Y	Y
3 *Hiler*	Y	N	Y	N	Y	Y	N
4 *Coats*	Y	N	Y	N	Y	Y	Y
5 *Hillis*	Y	N	Y	Y	Y	Y	Y

ND - Northern Democrats   SD - Southern Democrats

Corresponding to Congressional Record Votes 178, 179, 180, 181, 182, 183, 184

	170	171	172	173	174	175	176
6 ***Burton***	Y	N	Y	N	Y	Y	N
7 ***Myers***	Y	Y	Y	Y	Y	Y	Y
8 McCloskey	N	N	Y	Y	Y	Y	Y
9 Hamilton	Y	N	Y	Y	Y	Y	Y
10 Jacobs	N	N	P	Y	Y	Y	Y
IOWA							
1 ***Leach***	Y	N	Y	Y	Y	Y	Y
2 ***Tauke***	Y	N	Y	Y	Y	Y	Y
3 ***Evans***	Y	N	N	Y	Y	Y	Y
4 Smith	N	Y	Y	Y	N	N	Y
5 Harkin	?	?	?	Y	Y	Y	Y
6 Bedell	Y	Y	Y	Y	Y	Y	Y
KANSAS							
1 ***Roberts***	Y	N	N	Y	Y	Y	N
2 Slattery	Y	N	Y	Y	Y	Y	Y
3 ***Winn***	Y	N	Y	Y	Y	Y	Y
4 Glickman	N	N	Y	Y	Y	Y	Y
5 ***Whittaker***	N	N	Y	Y	Y	Y	Y
KENTUCKY							
1 Hubbard	?	?	?	?	?	?	?
2 Natcher	Y	Y	Y	Y	N	Y	Y
3 Mazzoli	Y	Y	Y	Y	N	Y	Y
4 ***Snyder***	Y	N	Y	Y	Y	Y	Y
5 ***Rogers***	Y	Y	Y	Y	Y	Y	Y
6 ***Hopkins***	Y	Y	Y	Y	Y	Y	Y
7 Perkins	Y	Y	Y	Y	N	Y	Y
LOUISIANA							
1 ***Livingston***	Y	N	Y	Y	N	N	Y
2 Boggs	Y	Y	Y	Y	N	N	Y
3 Tauzin	Y	N	Y	Y	Y	Y	Y
4 Roemer	Y	N	N	Y	Y	Y	N
5 Huckaby	N	N	Y	Y	N	N	Y
6 ***Moore***	Y	N	Y	Y	Y	Y	Y
7 Breaux	Y	N	Y	Y	Y	Y	Y
8 Long	Y	Y	Y	Y	Y	N	Y
MAINE							
1 ***McKernan***	N	N	Y	N	Y	Y	N
2 ***Snowe***	N	N	Y	Y	Y	Y	Y
MARYLAND							
1 Dyson	Y	N	Y	Y	N	Y	Y
2 Long	N	Y	Y	Y	N	Y	Y
3 Mikulski	N	Y	Y	Y	Y	Y	Y
4 ***Holt***	Y	N	Y	Y	N	N	N
5 Hoyer	N	Y	Y	Y	N	N	Y
6 Byron	Y	N	Y	Y	Y	Y	Y
7 Mitchell	N	Y	N	Y	N	Y	Y
8 Barnes	N	Y	Y	Y	N	N	Y
MASSACHUSETTS							
1 ***Conte***	Y	Y	Y	Y	N	N	Y
2 Boland	Y	Y	Y	Y	?	?	?
3 Early	Y	Y	Y	Y	Y	?	?
4 Frank	N	N	Y	Y	Y	Y	Y
5 Shannon	N	N	Y	Y	Y	Y	Y
6 Mavroules	Y	Y	Y	Y	N	?	?
7 Markey	?	Y	Y	Y	N	Y	Y
8 O'Neill							
9 Moakley	Y	Y	Y	Y	N	N	Y
10 Studds	N	N	Y	Y	Y	Y	?
11 Donnelly	Y	Y	Y	Y	N	Y	Y
MICHIGAN							
1 Conyers	?	?	?	?	?	?	?
2 ***Pursell***	N	N	Y	Y	N	?	?
3 Wolpe	N	N	Y	Y	?	Y	Y
4 ***Siljander***	Y	N	Y	N	N	N	N
5 ***Sawyer***	Y	N	Y	Y	N	Y	Y
6 Carr	N	Y	Y	Y	N	Y	Y
7 Kildee	Y	Y	Y	Y	N	Y	Y
8 Traxler	Y	Y	Y	Y	Y	Y	Y
9 ***Vander Jagt***	Y	N	Y	Y	N	N	Y
10 Albosta	Y	Y	Y	Y	N	Y	Y
11 ***Davis***	Y	Y	Y	Y	N	Y	Y
12 Bonior	Y	Y	Y	Y	N	Y	Y
13 Crockett	N	Y	?	Y	Y	Y	Y
14 Hertel	Y	Y	Y	Y	N	Y	Y
15 Ford	N	Y	Y	Y	?	?	?
16 Dingell	N	Y	Y	Y	N	N	Y
17 Levin	N	N	Y	Y	N	N	Y
18 ***Broomfield***	Y	N	Y	Y	N	N	N
MINNESOTA							
1 Penny	Y	N	Y	Y	N	Y	Y
2 ***Weber***	Y	N	Y	N	Y	Y	?
3 ***Frenzel***	N	N	N	X	X	X	?
4 Vento	N	Y	Y	Y	Y	Y	Y
5 Sabo	N	Y	N	Y	N	N	Y
6 Sikorski	Y	Y	Y	Y	N	Y	Y
7 ***Stangeland***	Y	N	Y	Y	N	N	Y
8 Oberstar	Y	Y	P	Y	N	N	Y
MISSISSIPPI							
1 Whitten	Y	Y	Y	Y	Y	Y	Y
2 ***Franklin***	Y	N	Y	Y	X	X	?
3 Montgomery	Y	N	Y	Y	Y	Y	Y
4 Dowdy	Y	Y	Y	Y	N	Y	Y
5 ***Lott***	Y	N	Y	Y	Y	Y	Y
MISSOURI							
1 Clay	N	N	N	Y	Y	Y	Y
2 Young	Y	Y	Y	Y	N	Y	Y
3 Gephardt	Y	Y	Y	Y	N	Y	Y
4 Skelton	Y	Y	Y	Y	N	Y	Y
5 Wheat	N	N	Y	Y	N	N	Y
6 ***Coleman***	Y	N	Y	Y	?	N	Y
7 ***Taylor***	Y	N	Y	Y	Y	Y	Y
8 ***Emerson***	Y	N	N	N	Y	Y	Y
9 Volkmer	Y	Y	N	Y	Y	Y	Y
MONTANA							
1 Williams	N	N	Y	Y	N	N	Y
2 ***Marlenee***	N	N	Y	Y	Y	Y	Y
NEBRASKA							
1 ***Bereuter***	Y	N	Y	Y	N	Y	Y
2 ***Daub***	Y	N	Y	Y	Y	Y	Y
3 ***Smith***	Y	Y	Y	Y	Y	Y	Y
NEVADA							
1 Reid	Y	N	Y	Y	N	N	Y
2 ***Vucanovich***	Y	N	Y	Y	Y	Y	N
NEW HAMPSHIRE							
1 D'Amours	Y	N	Y	Y	Y	Y	Y
2 ***Gregg***	Y	N	N	N	Y	Y	N
NEW JERSEY							
1 Florio	Y	Y	Y	Y	Y	Y	Y
2 Hughes	N	N	Y	Y	Y	Y	Y
3 Howard	N	Y	Y	Y	N	N	Y
4 ***Smith***	Y	Y	?	Y	N	N	Y
5 ***Roukema***	N	N	Y	Y	N	Y	Y
6 Dwyer	Y	Y	Y	Y	N	Y	Y
7 ***Rinaldo***	Y	Y	Y	Y	N	N	Y
8 Roe	Y	Y	Y	Y	N	Y	Y
9 Torricelli	N	N	Y	Y	N	N	Y
10 Rodino	N	Y	Y	Y	N	N	Y
11 Minish	Y	Y	Y	Y	N	Y	Y
12 ***Courter***	Y	N	Y	Y	Y	N	Y
13 ***Forsythe***	N	N	N	N	Y	Y	Y
14 Guarini	N	Y	Y	Y	Y	Y	Y
NEW MEXICO							
1 ***Lujan***	Y	N	Y	Y	Y	Y	Y
2 ***Skeen***	Y	N	Y	Y	Y	Y	Y
3 Richardson	N	Y	Y	Y	N	Y	Y
NEW YORK							
1 ***Carney***	#	?	Y	Y	Y	Y	Y
2 Downey	N	N	Y	Y	N	Y	Y
3 Mrazek	N	N	Y	Y	N	Y	Y
4 ***Lent***	Y	N	Y	Y	N	N	Y
5 ***McGrath***	Y	N	Y	N	Y	Y	N
6 Addabbo	N	Y	Y	Y	N	N	?
7 Ackerman	N	N	Y	Y	N	N	Y
8 Scheuer	?	?	Y	Y	N	N	Y
9 Ferraro	N	N	Y	Y	N	N	Y
10 Schumer	N	N	Y	Y	N	Y	Y
11 Towns	N	N	Y	Y	N	Y	Y
12 Owens	?	?	?	Y	N	N	Y
13 Solarz	N	N	Y	Y	N	N	Y
14 ***Molinari***	Y	Y	Y	N	Y	Y	Y
15 ***Green***	N	N	Y	Y	N	Y	Y
16 Rangel	N	N	Y	Y	N	N	Y
17 Weiss	N	N	Y	Y	Y	Y	Y
18 Garcia	N	Y	?	Y	N	N	Y
19 Biaggi	N	Y	Y	Y	N	N	Y
20 Ottinger	N	N	P	Y	Y	Y	N
21 ***Fish***	Y	Y	Y	Y	N	?	?
22 ***Gilman***	N	Y	Y	Y	N	N	Y
23 Stratton	Y	Y	Y	Y	N	Y	Y
24 ***Solomon***	Y	N	N	Y	N	Y	Y
25 ***Boehlert***	N	N	Y	Y	N	Y	Y
26 ***Martin***	Y	N	Y	Y	Y	Y	Y
27 ***Wortley***	Y	Y	Y	Y	Y	Y	Y
28 McHugh	Y	Y	Y	Y	N	Y	Y
29 ***Horton***	N	Y	Y	Y	N	N	Y
30 ***Conable***	N	N	N	N	Y	Y	Y
31 ***Kemp***	Y	?	Y	N	N	N	Y
32 LaFalce	Y	Y	Y	Y	Y	Y	N
33 Nowak	Y	Y	Y	Y	N	N	?
34 Lundine	N	N	Y	Y	N	Y	Y
NORTH CAROLINA							
1 Jones	N	Y	?	Y	?	N	Y
2 Valentine	N	N	?	Y	N	Y	Y
3 Whitley	N	N	Y	Y	N	N	Y
4 Andrews	N	N	Y	Y	?	Y	Y
5 Neal	N	N	Y	?	N	N	Y
6 Britt	N	N	Y	Y	N	N	Y
7 Rose	N	Y	?	Y	N	Y	Y
8 Hefner	N	Y	Y	Y	Y	Y	Y
9 ***Martin***	N	N	Y	Y	Y	Y	Y
10 ***Broyhill***	N	N	Y	Y	Y	Y	Y
11 Clarke	N	Y	Y	Y	N	N	Y
NORTH DAKOTA							
AL Dorgan	Y	Y	Y	Y	Y	Y	Y
OHIO							
1 Luken	Y	Y	Y	Y	N	Y	Y
2 ***Gradison***	Y	N	Y	Y	Y	Y	Y
3 Hall	Y	Y	Y	Y	N	Y	Y
4 ***Oxley***	Y	N	Y	Y	Y	Y	Y
5 ***Latta***	Y	N	Y	N	N	Y	Y
6 ***McEwen***	Y	N	Y	Y	Y	Y	Y
7 ***DeWine***	Y	Y	Y	N	Y	Y	N
8 ***Kindness***	Y	N	Y	Y	Y	N	Y
9 Kaptur	Y	N	Y	Y	Y	Y	Y
10 ***Miller***	Y	Y	N	N	Y	Y	Y
11 Eckart	N	N	Y	Y	N	Y	Y
12 ***Kasich***	Y	N	Y	N	Y	Y	Y
13 Pease	N	Y	Y	Y	Y	Y	Y
14 Seiberling	N	N	Y	Y	Y	Y	Y
15 ***Wylie***	Y	N	Y	Y	N	N	Y
16 ***Regula***	Y	Y	Y	Y	Y	?	?
17 ***Williams***	Y	N	Y	Y	N	?	?
18 Applegate	Y	N	?	Y	Y	Y	Y
19 Feighan	N	N	Y	Y	Y	Y	Y
20 Oakar	Y	N	Y	Y	Y	Y	Y
21 Stokes	N	N	Y	Y	N	Y	Y
OKLAHOMA							
1 Jones	Y	N	Y	Y	Y	Y	Y
2 Synar	N	N	Y	Y	Y	Y	Y
3 Watkins	Y	Y	Y	Y	Y	Y	Y
4 McCurdy	N	N	Y	Y	Y	Y	Y
5 ***Edwards***	Y	Y	Y	Y	N	Y	N
6 English	Y	N	Y	Y	Y	Y	Y
OREGON							
1 AuCoin	X	X	?	Y	Y	Y	Y
2 ***Smith, R.***	Y	N	Y	Y	Y	Y	Y
3 Wyden	N	N	N	Y	Y	Y	Y
4 Weaver	N	N	Y	Y	Y	Y	Y
5 ***Smith, D.***	Y	N	Y	N	Y	Y	N
PENNSYLVANIA							
1 Foglietta	Y	Y	Y	Y	N	Y	Y
2 Gray	N	N	Y	Y	N	?	Y
3 Borski	Y	Y	Y	Y	N	Y	Y
4 Kolter	?	?	?	?	?	?	?
5 ***Schulze***	Y	N	Y	N	N	N	Y
6 Yatron	Y	Y	Y	Y	N	Y	Y
7 Edgar	N	N	N	N	Y	Y	N
8 Kostmayer	N	N	Y	Y	N	N	Y
9 ***Shuster***	Y	N	Y	N	Y	Y	Y
10 ***McDade***	Y	Y	Y	Y	N	Y	Y
11 Harrison	Y	N	Y	Y	N	Y	Y
12 Murtha	Y	Y	Y	Y	N	Y	Y
13 ***Coughlin***	Y	N	N	N	N	N	Y
14 Coyne	N	Y	Y	Y	N	N	Y
15 ***Ritter***	Y	N	Y	Y	N	N	Y
16 ***Walker***	Y	N	N	N	Y	Y	N
17 ***Gekas***	N	N	Y	Y	N	Y	Y
18 Walgren	?	?	Y	Y	Y	Y	Y
19 ***Goodling***	Y	N	N	Y	N	N	N
20 Gaydos	Y	Y	Y	Y	N	Y	Y
21 ***Ridge***	Y	Y	Y	Y	N	Y	Y
22 Murphy	Y	Y	N	Y	N	Y	Y
23 ***Clinger***	Y	N	Y	Y	N	N	Y
RHODE ISLAND							
1 St Germain	Y	Y	?	Y	N	N	Y
2 ***Schneider***	N	N	Y	Y	N	N	?
SOUTH CAROLINA							
1 ***Hartnett***	?	?	?	?	?	?	?
2 ***Spence***	Y	N	Y	Y	N	Y	Y
3 Derrick	N	N	Y	Y	N	N	Y
4 ***Campbell***	Y	N	Y	Y	N	N	Y
5 Spratt	N	N	Y	Y	Y	Y	Y
6 Tallon	N	N	Y	Y	N	N	Y
SOUTH DAKOTA							
AL Daschle	N	N	Y	Y	Y	Y	Y
TENNESSEE							
1 ***Quillen***	Y	Y	Y	Y	N	N	Y
2 ***Duncan***	Y	Y	Y	Y	Y	Y	Y
3 Lloyd	Y	N	?	?	?	?	?
4 Cooper	N	Y	Y	Y	N	Y	Y
5 Boner	Y	Y	Y	Y	Y	Y	Y
6 Gore	?	?	Y	Y	N	Y	Y
7 ***Sundquist***	Y	N	Y	Y	Y	Y	Y
8 Jones	Y	Y	Y	Y	Y	?	Y
9 Ford	N	N	Y	Y	N	?	Y
TEXAS							
1 Hall, S.	Y	N	Y	Y	Y	Y	Y
2 Wilson	?	?	?	?	?	?	?
3 ***Bartlett***	Y	N	Y	Y	Y	Y	Y
4 Hall, R.	Y	N	Y	Y	Y	Y	Y
5 Bryant	N	N	Y	Y	N	Y	Y
6 ***Gramm***	Y	N	?	N	Y	Y	N
7 ***Archer***	Y	N	Y	N	Y	Y	N
8 ***Fields***	Y	N	Y	N	Y	Y	N
9 Brooks	N	N	Y	Y	N	N	Y
10 Pickle	N	Y	Y	Y	N	N	Y
11 Leath	Y	N	Y	Y	Y	Y	Y
12 Wright	N	Y	Y	Y	N	N	Y
13 Hightower	Y	Y	Y	Y	Y	Y	Y
14 Patman	Y	Y	Y	Y	Y	Y	Y
15 de la Garza	?	?	Y	Y	N	N	Y
16 Coleman	N	Y	Y	Y	Y	Y	Y
17 Stenholm	Y	N	N	Y	Y	Y	Y
18 Leland	N	N	Y	?	Y	Y	Y
19 Hance	N	Y	Y	Y	N	N	Y
20 Gonzalez	N	Y	Y	Y	N	N	Y
21 ***Loeffler***	Y	N	Y	Y	Y	Y	Y
22 ***Paul***	Y	N	Y	N	?	?	?
23 Kazen	Y	Y	Y	Y	N	Y	Y
24 Frost	N	N	Y	Y	N	Y	Y
25 Andrews	N	N	Y	Y	Y	Y	Y
26 Vandergriff	N	N	Y	Y	N	Y	Y
27 Ortiz	Y	Y	Y	Y	N	N	Y
UTAH							
1 ***Hansen***	Y	N	N	Y	Y	Y	Y
2 ***Marriott***	Y	N	Y	Y	N	N	Y
3 ***Nielson***	Y	N	Y	N	Y	Y	N
VERMONT							
AL ***Jeffords***	?	?	?	?	?	?	?
VIRGINIA							
1 ***Bateman***	Y	N	?	?	#	#	N
2 ***Whitehurst***	Y	N	Y	Y	N	N	Y
3 ***Bliley***	Y	N	Y	Y	N	N	Y
4 Sisisky	N	N	Y	Y	Y	Y	?
5 Daniel	Y	N	Y	Y	Y	Y	N
6 Olin	N	N	Y	Y	Y	Y	Y
7 ***Robinson***	Y	Y	?	Y	N	N	Y
8 ***Parris***	?	#	Y	Y	N	N	Y
9 Boucher	N	Y	Y	Y	N	N	Y
10 ***Wolf***	Y	Y	Y	Y	N	N	Y
WASHINGTON							
1 ***Pritchard***	N	N	Y	Y	N	N	Y
2 Swift	N	Y	Y	Y	Y	Y	Y
3 Bonker	N	Y	Y	Y	N	N	Y
4 ***Morrison***	N	N	Y	Y	N	N	Y
5 Foley	N	N	Y	Y	N	Y	Y
6 Dicks	N	N	Y	Y	N	Y	Y
7 Lowry	N	N	Y	Y	Y	Y	Y
8 ***Chandler***	N	N	Y	Y	N	Y	Y
WEST VIRGINIA							
1 Mollohan	Y	Y	Y	Y	N	N	Y
2 Staggers	N	Y	Y	Y	Y	Y	Y
3 Wise	N	N	Y	Y	Y	Y	Y
4 Rahall	Y	Y	Y	Y	Y	Y	Y
WISCONSIN							
1 Aspin	?	?	Y	Y	N	N	Y
2 Kastenmeier	N	Y	Y	Y	Y	Y	Y
3 ***Gunderson***	Y	Y	Y	Y	N	N	Y
4 Zablocki	Y	Y	Y	Y	N	N	Y
5 Moody	N	N	Y	Y	Y	Y	Y
6 ***Petri***	Y	N	Y	Y	N	N	N
7 Obey	N	N	Y	Y	N	N	Y
8 ***Roth***	Y	N	Y	Y	N	N	Y
9 ***Sensenbrenner***	Y	N	Y	Y	Y	Y	N
WYOMING							
AL ***Cheney***	Y	N	?	#	?	?	?

Southern states - Ala., Ark., Fla., Ga., Ky., La., Miss., N.C., Okla., S.C., Tenn., Texas, Va.

177. Procedural Motion. Fields, R-Texas, motion to approve the House *Journal* of Monday, June 13. Motion agreed to 375-20: R 147-9; D 228-11 (ND 142-10, SD 86-1), June 14, 1983.

178. HR 1076. Elimination of Jones Act Exemption. Jones, D-N.C., motion to suspend the rules and pass the bill designed to strengthen U.S. domestic waterborne commerce. Motion agreed to 373-44: R 122-39; D 251-5 (ND 167-2, SD 84-3), June 14, 1983. A two-thirds majority of those present and voting (278 in this case) is required for passage under suspension of the rules.

179. HR 2062. National Marine Sanctuaries. Jones, D-N.C., motion to suspend the rules and pass the bill to authorize $2.26 million in fiscal 1984, $2.5 million in fiscal 1985 and $2.75 million in fiscal 1986 for Title III of the Marine Protection, Research and Sanctuaries Act, to provide protection for nationally significant areas of the marine environment. Motion agreed to 379-38: R 127-34; D 252-4 (ND 166-2, SD 86-2), June 14, 1983. A two-thirds majority of those present and voting (278 in this case) is required for passage under suspension of the rules.

180. HR 2969. Department of Defense Authorization. Brown, D-Calif., amendment to delete $19.4 million for procurement of an anti-satellite missile (ASAT). Rejected 177-243: R 13-150; D 164-93 (ND 144-23, SD 20-70), June 14, 1983. A "nay" was a vote supporting the president's position.

181. HR 2969. Department of Defense Authorization. McCloskey, D-Ind., amendment to bar multi-year procurement contracts for the B-1 bomber. Rejected 171-252: R 17-147; D 154-105 (ND 130-39, SD 24-66), June 14, 1983. A "nay" was a vote supporting the president's position.

182. HR 2969. Department of Defense Authorization. Levine, D-Calif., amendment to bar expenditure of funds authorized for the M-2 fighting vehicle until the vehicle is subjected to certain tests. Rejected 124-283: R 9-151; D 115-132 (ND 101-61, SD 14-71), June 14, 1983. A "nay" was a vote supporting the president's position.

183. Procedural Motion. Parris, R-Va., motion to approve the House *Journal* of Tuesday, June 14. Motion agreed to 367-25: R 146-13; D 221-12 (ND 136-9, SD 85-3), June 15, 1983.

184. HR 2969. Department of Defense Authorization. Smith, D-Fla., amendment to delete $671 million for procurement of Divad anti-aircraft guns. Rejected 134-283: R 12-150; D 122-133 (ND 106-59, SD 16-74), June 15, 1983. A "nay" was a vote supporting the president's position.

KEY	
Y	Voted for (yea).
#	Paired for.
+	Announced for.
N	Voted against (nay).
X	Paired against.
-	Announced against.
P	Voted "present".
C	Voted "present" to avoid possible conflict of interest.
?	Did not vote or otherwise make a position known.

Democrats *Republicans*

	177	178	179	180	181	182	183	184
ALABAMA								
1 *Edwards*	Y	Y	Y	N	N	N	Y	N
2 *Dickinson*	N	Y	Y	N	N	N	N	N
3 Nichols	Y	Y	Y	N	N	N	N	N
4 Bevill	Y	Y	Y	N	N	N	N	N
5 Flippo	?	Y	Y	N	N	Y	N	N
6 Erdreich	Y	Y	Y	N	Y	N	N	N
7 Shelby	Y	Y	Y	N	N	N	N	N
ALASKA								
AL *Young*	N	Y	N	N	N	N	N	N
ARIZONA								
1 *McCain*	Y	Y	N	N	N	N	Y	N
2 Udall	?	Y	Y	Y	Y	Y	Y	Y
3 *Stump*	Y	N	N	N	N	N	Y	N
4 *Rudd*	Y	N	N	N	N	N	Y	N
5 McNulty	Y	Y	Y	Y	Y	N	Y	Y
ARKANSAS								
1 Alexander	Y	Y	Y	N	N	?	?	N
2 *Bethune*	Y	Y	Y	N	N	N	?	N
3 *Hammerschmidt*	Y	Y	N	N	N	N	Y	N
4 Anthony	Y	?	?	N	N	N	Y	N
CALIFORNIA								
1 Bosco	Y	Y	Y	Y	Y	Y	Y	N
2 *Chappie*	Y	Y	N	N	N	N	Y	N
3 Matsui	Y	Y	Y	Y	N	N	Y	N
4 Fazio	Y	Y	Y	Y	Y	N	Y	N
5 Vacancy								
6 Boxer	Y	Y	Y	Y	Y	Y	Y	Y
7 Miller	N	Y	Y	Y	Y	Y	Y	Y
8 Dellums	Y	Y	Y	Y	Y	Y	Y	Y
9 Stark	Y	Y	Y	Y	Y	Y	Y	Y
10 Edwards	Y	Y	Y	Y	Y	N	Y	Y
11 Lantos	Y	Y	Y	Y	N	N	Y	N
12 Zschau	Y	N	Y	N	N	N	Y	N
13 Mineta	Y	Y	Y	N	Y	N	Y	N
14 *Shumway*	Y	Y	N	N	N	N	N	N
15 Coelho	Y	Y	Y	Y	N	N	Y	N
16 Panetta	Y	Y	Y	Y	N	Y	Y	N
17 *Pashayan*	Y	Y	Y	N	N	N	Y	N
18 Lehman	Y	Y	Y	Y	Y	Y	Y	Y
19 *Lagomarsino*	Y	Y	Y	N	N	N	Y	N
20 *Thomas*	Y	N	Y	N	N	N	?	X
21 *Fiedler*	?	Y	Y	N	N	N	Y	N
22 *Moorhead*	Y	Y	N	N	N	N	Y	N
23 Beilenson	Y	Y	Y	Y	Y	Y	Y	Y
24 Waxman	Y	Y	Y	Y	Y	Y	Y	Y
25 Roybal	Y	Y	Y	Y	Y	Y	Y	Y
26 Berman	?	?	?	Y	Y	Y	?	#
27 Levine	Y	Y	Y	N	Y	Y	Y	Y
28 Dixon	Y	Y	Y	Y	N	Y	?	Y
29 Hawkins	?	Y	Y	#	N	Y	N	Y
30 Martinez	?	?	?	?	?	?	?	?
31 Dymally	Y	Y	Y	Y	N	Y	N	Y
32 Anderson	Y	Y	Y	N	N	Y	N	N
33 *Dreier*	Y	N	N	N	N	N	N	N
34 Torres	Y	Y	Y	Y	Y	Y	Y	Y
35 *Lewis*	Y	Y	?	N	N	N	Y	N
36 Brown	Y	Y	Y	Y	Y	Y	Y	Y
37 *McCandless*	Y	Y	N	N	N	N	Y	N
38 Patterson	Y	Y	Y	Y	N	Y	Y	N
39 *Dannemeyer*	Y	Y	N	N	N	N	N	N
40 *Badham*	Y	Y	N	N	N	N	Y	N
41 *Lowery*	Y	Y	Y	N	N	N	Y	N
42 *Lungren*	Y	N	Y	N	N	N	N	N

	177	178	179	180	181	182	183	184
43 *Packard*	Y	Y	N	N	N	N	Y	N
44 Bates	Y	Y	Y	Y	Y	Y	?	Y
45 *Hunter*	Y	Y	Y	N	N	N	Y	N
COLORADO								
1 Schroeder	?	?	?	?	Y	Y	N	Y
2 Wirth	Y	Y	Y	Y	Y	Y	Y	Y
3 Kogovsek	Y	Y	Y	Y	Y	N	Y	Y
4 *Brown*	Y	N	Y	N	Y	N	Y	N
5 *Kramer*	Y	Y	Y	N	N	N	Y	N
6 *Schaefer*	Y	Y	N	N	N	N	Y	N
CONNECTICUT								
1 Kennelly	Y	Y	Y	Y	Y	N	?	?
2 Gejdenson	N	Y	Y	Y	Y	Y	?	Y
3 Morrison	Y	Y	Y	Y	Y	Y	Y	N
4 *McKinney*	?	?	?	#	#	#	?	?
5 Ratchford	Y	Y	Y	Y	Y	N	Y	N
6 *Johnson*	Y	Y	Y	N	N	Y	N	N
DELAWARE								
AL Carper	Y	Y	Y	Y	Y	Y	Y	N
FLORIDA								
1 Hutto	?	Y	Y	N	N	N	Y	N
2 Fuqua	Y	?	?	N	N	N	Y	N
3 Bennett	Y	Y	Y	N	N	N	Y	N
4 Chappell	Y	Y	Y	N	N	N	?	N
5 *McCollum*	Y	Y	Y	N	N	N	Y	N
6 MacKay	Y	Y	Y	Y	Y	Y	Y	N
7 Gibbons	Y	N	Y	N	Y	N	Y	N
8 *Young*	?	Y	Y	N	N	N	Y	N
9 *Bilirakis*	Y	Y	Y	N	N	N	Y	N
10 Ireland	Y	Y	Y	N	N	N	Y	N
11 Nelson	Y	Y	Y	N	N	N	Y	N
12 *Lewis*	Y	Y	Y	N	N	N	Y	N
13 *Mack*	Y	Y	Y	N	N	N	Y	N
14 Mica	Y	Y	Y	N	N	N	Y	N
15 *Shaw*	Y	Y	Y	N	N	N	Y	N
16 Smith	Y	Y	Y	Y	Y	Y	Y	Y
17 Lehman	Y	Y	Y	Y	Y	Y	Y	Y
18 Pepper	Y	Y	Y	N	Y	N	Y	N
19 Fascell	Y	Y	Y	Y	Y	N	Y	N
GEORGIA								
1 Thomas	Y	Y	N	N	Y	N	Y	N
2 Hatcher	Y	Y	N	N	N	N	Y	N
3 Ray	Y	Y	N	N	N	N	Y	N
4 Levitas	Y	Y	Y	N	Y	Y	Y	Y
5 Fowler	Y	Y	Y	Y	N	N	Y	N
6 *Gingrich*	Y	Y	Y	N	N	N	Y	N
7 McDonald	Y	N	N	N	N	N	Y	N
8 Rowland	Y	Y	N	N	N	N	Y	N
9 Jenkins	Y	Y	Y	N	N	N	Y	N
10 Barnard	Y	Y	N	N	?	?	Y	N
HAWAII								
1 Heftel	?	?	?	?	?	?	?	?
2 Akaka	Y	Y	Y	Y	N	N	Y	N
IDAHO								
1 *Craig*	N	Y	N	N	N	N	N	N
2 *Hansen*	?	?	?	X	N	N	Y	?
ILLINOIS								
1 Vacancy								
2 Savage	Y	Y	Y	Y	Y	Y	Y	Y
3 Russo	Y	Y	Y	Y	Y	Y	Y	Y
4 *O'Brien*	Y	Y	Y	N	N	N	?	N
5 Lipinski	Y	Y	N	N	N	N	Y	N
6 *Hyde*	Y	Y	N	N	N	N	Y	N
7 Collins	?	Y	Y	Y	Y	Y	Y	Y
8 Rostenkowski	Y	Y	Y	N	N	N	Y	N
9 Yates	N	Y	Y	Y	?	?	?	Y
10 *Porter*	Y	Y	Y	N	N	?	Y	N
11 Annunzio	Y	Y	Y	N	N	Y	N	N
12 *Crane, P.*	Y	N	N	N	N	N	N	N
13 Erlenborn	N	N	N	N	N	N	N	N
14 *Corcoran*	+	+	+	X	?	-	Y	N
15 *Madigan*	Y	Y	N	N	N	N	Y	N
16 *Martin*	Y	Y	N	N	N	N	Y	N
17 Evans	Y	Y	Y	Y	Y	Y	Y	Y
18 *Michel*	Y	Y	N	N	N	N	Y	N
19 *Crane, D.*	Y	N	N	N	N	N	N	N
20 Durbin	N	Y	Y	Y	Y	N	Y	N
21 Price	Y	Y	Y	N	N	N	Y	N
22 Simon	Y	Y	Y	?	Y	Y	Y	N
INDIANA								
1 Hall	Y	Y	Y	Y	Y	N	Y	N
2 Sharp	Y	Y	Y	N	Y	N	Y	N
3 *Hiler*	Y	N	Y	N	N	N	Y	N
4 *Coats*	Y	Y	Y	N	N	N	Y	N
5 Hillis	Y	Y	N	N	N	N	Y	N

ND - Northern Democrats   SD - Southern Democrats

Corresponding to Congressional Record Votes 185, 186, 187, 188, 189, 190, 191, 193

	177	178	179	180	181	182	183	184
6 ***Burton***	Y	N	N	N	N	N	Y	N
7 ***Myers***	Y	Y	Y	N	N	N	Y	N
8 McCloskey	Y	Y	Y	N	Y	N	Y	N
9 Hamilton	Y	Y	Y	Y	Y	N	Y	N
10 Jacobs	P	Y	Y	Y	Y	N	P	N
IOWA								
1 ***Leach***	?	N	Y	Y	Y	N	Y	N
2 ***Tauke***	Y	N	Y	N	Y	N	Y	N
3 ***Evans***	N	N	Y	N	N	N	N	Y
4 Smith	Y	Y	Y	Y	Y	N	Y	N
5 Harkin	N	Y	Y	Y	Y	?	N	Y
6 Bedell	Y	Y	Y	Y	Y	Y	Y	Y
KANSAS								
1 ***Roberts***	Y	N	Y	N	N	N	N	N
2 Slattery	Y	Y	N	N	N	Y	Y	Y
3 ***Winn***	Y	Y	Y	N	N	N	Y	N
4 Glickman	Y	Y	Y	Y	N	Y	Y	Y
5 ***Whittaker***	Y	Y	Y	N	N	N	Y	N
KENTUCKY								
1 Hubbard	Y	Y	Y	N	N	N	Y	N
2 Natcher	Y	Y	Y	N	N	N	Y	N
3 Mazzoli	Y	N	Y	N	Y	N	Y	N
4 ***Snyder***	Y	Y	Y	N	N	N	Y	N
5 ***Rogers***	Y	Y	Y	N	N	N	Y	N
6 ***Hopkins***	Y	Y	Y	N	N	N	Y	N
7 Perkins	Y	Y	Y	N	N	N	Y	N
LOUISIANA								
1 ***Livingston***	Y	Y	Y	N	N	N	Y	N
2 Boggs	Y	Y	Y	N	N	N	Y	N
3 Tauzin	Y	Y	Y	N	N	N	Y	N
4 Roemer	N	Y	Y	N	N	Y	N	Y
5 Huckaby	Y	Y	Y	N	N	N	Y	N
6 ***Moore***	Y	Y	Y	N	N	N	Y	N
7 Breaux	Y	Y	Y	N	N	N	N	Y
8 Long	Y	Y	Y	Y	N	Y	Y	Y
MAINE								
1 ***McKernan***	Y	Y	Y	N	N	N	Y	N
2 ***Snowe***	Y	Y	Y	N	N	Y	Y	Y
MARYLAND								
1 Dyson	Y	Y	Y	N	N	N	Y	N
2 Long	Y	Y	Y	Y	Y	N	Y	N
3 Mikulski	Y	Y	Y	Y	Y	Y	?	N
4 ***Holt***	Y	Y	Y	N	N	N	Y	N
5 Hoyer	Y	Y	Y	Y	N	N	Y	N
6 Byron	Y	Y	Y	N	N	N	Y	N
7 Mitchell	?	Y	Y	Y	Y	Y	N	Y
8 Barnes	Y	Y	Y	Y	Y	Y	Y	Y
MASSACHUSETTS								
1 ***Conte***	Y	Y	Y	Y	Y	N	Y	N
2 Boland	Y	Y	Y	Y	Y	Y	Y	N
3 Early	Y	Y	Y	Y	Y	Y	Y	Y
4 Frank	Y	N	Y	Y	Y	Y	?	Y
5 Shannon	Y	Y	Y	Y	Y	Y	Y	N
6 Mavroules	Y	Y	Y	Y	Y	N	Y	-
7 Markey	?	Y	?	Y	Y	Y	Y	Y
8 O'Neill								
9 Moakley	Y	Y	Y	Y	Y	Y	Y	Y
10 Studds	Y	Y	Y	Y	?	?	Y	Y
11 Donnelly	Y	Y	Y	Y	Y	N	Y	Y
MICHIGAN								
1 Conyers	?	Y	Y	Y	Y	Y	?	Y
2 ***Pursell***	Y	Y	Y	N	Y	?	Y	N
3 Wolpe	Y	Y	Y	Y	Y	Y	Y	N
4 ***Siljander***	Y	Y	Y	N	N	N	Y	N
5 ***Sawyer***	Y	Y	Y	N	N	N	Y	N
6 Carr	Y	Y	Y	Y	Y	N	Y	N
7 Kildee	Y	Y	Y	Y	Y	Y	Y	Y
8 Traxler	Y	Y	Y	Y	Y	N	Y	?
9 ***Vander Jagt***	Y	Y	Y	N	N	N	Y	N
10 Albosta	Y	Y	Y	Y	Y	N	Y	N
11 ***Davis***	Y	Y	Y	N	N	N	Y	N
12 Bonior	Y	Y	Y	Y	Y	Y	Y	Y
13 Crockett	?	Y	Y	Y	Y	Y	?	Y
14 Hertel	Y	Y	Y	Y	Y	N	Y	N
15 Ford	Y	Y	Y	Y	Y	Y	?	Y
16 Dingell	Y	Y	Y	Y	Y	N	?	Y
17 Levin	Y	Y	Y	Y	Y	N	Y	Y
18 ***Broomfield***	Y	Y	Y	N	N	N	Y	N
MINNESOTA								
1 Penny	N	Y	Y	Y	Y	Y	Y	Y
2 ***Weber***	Y	N	Y	N	Y	N	Y	Y
3 ***Frenzel***	Y	N	Y	X	Y	Y	Y	Y
4 Vento	Y	Y	Y	Y	Y	Y	Y	N
5 Sabo	N	Y	Y	Y	Y	Y	N	Y
6 Sikorski	N	Y	Y	Y	Y	Y	Y	Y

	177	178	179	180	181	182	183	184
7 ***Stangeland***	Y	Y	Y	N	N	N	Y	N
8 Oberstar	P	Y	Y	Y	Y	Y	P	Y
MISSISSIPPI								
1 Whitten	Y	Y	Y	N	N	N	Y	N
2 ***Franklin***	Y	Y	Y	N	N	N	Y	N
3 Montgomery	Y	Y	Y	N	N	N	Y	N
4 Dowdy	?	Y	Y	N	N	N	Y	N
5 ***Lott***	Y	Y	Y	N	N	N	Y	N
MISSOURI								
1 Clay	N	Y	Y	Y	Y	Y	?	Y
2 Young	Y	Y	Y	N	N	N	Y	Y
3 Gephardt	Y	Y	Y	Y	Y	Y	Y	N
4 Skelton	Y	Y	Y	N	N	N	Y	N
5 Wheat	Y	Y	Y	Y	Y	Y	Y	Y
6 ***Coleman***	Y	Y	Y	N	N	N	N	N
7 ***Taylor***	Y	Y	Y	N	N	N	Y	N
8 ***Emerson***	N	N	N	N	N	N	N	N
9 Volkmer	Y	Y	Y	N	N	Y	Y	Y
MONTANA								
1 Williams	Y	Y	Y	Y	Y	Y	?	Y
2 ***Marlenee***	Y	Y	Y	N	N	N	Y	N
NEBRASKA								
1 ***Bereuter***	Y	Y	Y	N	N	N	Y	N
2 ***Daub***	Y	Y	Y	N	N	N	Y	N
3 ***Smith***	Y	N	Y	N	N	N	Y	N
NEVADA								
1 Reid	Y	Y	Y	Y	Y	Y	Y	Y
2 ***Vucanovich***	Y	Y	N	N	N	N	Y	N
NEW HAMPSHIRE								
1 D'Amours	Y	Y	Y	Y	N	?	?	N
2 ***Gregg***	Y	N	Y	N	N	N	Y	N
NEW JERSEY								
1 Florio	Y	Y	Y	Y	Y	Y	Y	Y
2 Hughes	Y	Y	Y	N	N	Y	Y	Y
3 Howard	Y	Y	Y	Y	Y	Y	Y	Y
4 ***Smith***	Y	Y	Y	N	N	N	?	N
5 ***Roukema***	Y	N	Y	Y	Y	N	Y	N
6 Dwyer	Y	Y	Y	Y	Y	Y	Y	Y
7 ***Rinaldo***	Y	Y	Y	N	N	N	?	N
8 Roe	Y	Y	Y	N	N	N	Y	Y
9 Torricelli	Y	Y	Y	N	Y	Y	Y	Y
10 Rodino	?	?	?	#	?	?	?	?
11 Minish	Y	Y	Y	Y	Y	N	Y	N
12 ***Courter***	?	Y	Y	N	N	?	Y	?
13 ***Forsythe***	N	Y	Y	Y	Y	?	N	Y
14 Guarini	Y	Y	Y	Y	Y	Y	Y	Y
NEW MEXICO								
1 ***Lujan***	Y	N	N	N	N	N	Y	N
2 ***Skeen***	?	Y	N	N	N	N	Y	N
3 Richardson	N	Y	Y	Y	N	N	Y	Y
NEW YORK								
1 ***Carney***	Y	Y	Y	N	N	N	Y	N
2 Downey	Y	Y	Y	Y	Y	Y	Y	N
3 Mrazek	Y	Y	Y	Y	Y	N	Y	N
4 ***Lent***	Y	Y	Y	N	N	N	Y	N
5 ***McGrath***	Y	Y	Y	N	N	N	Y	N
6 Addabbo	Y	Y	Y	Y	Y	?	Y	Y
7 Ackerman	Y	Y	Y	Y	Y	Y	Y	Y
8 Scheuer	Y	Y	Y	Y	Y	Y	Y	Y
9 Ferraro	Y	Y	Y	Y	Y	Y	Y	Y
10 Schumer	Y	Y	Y	Y	Y	?	Y	Y
11 Towns	Y	Y	Y	Y	Y	Y	Y	Y
12 Owens	Y	Y	Y	Y	Y	Y	Y	Y
13 Solarz	Y	Y	Y	Y	Y	Y	Y	Y
14 ***Molinari***	Y	Y	Y	N	N	N	Y	N
15 ***Green***	Y	N	Y	N	Y	Y	Y	N
16 Rangel	Y	Y	Y	Y	Y	Y	Y	Y
17 Weiss	Y	Y	Y	Y	Y	Y	Y	Y
18 Garcia	Y	Y	Y	Y	Y	Y	?	Y
19 Biaggi	Y	Y	Y	Y	Y	N	Y	Y
20 Ottinger	P	Y	Y	Y	Y	Y	P	Y
21 ***Fish***	Y	Y	N	N	Y	N	Y	N
22 ***Gilman***	Y	Y	Y	N	N	N	Y	N
23 Stratton	Y	Y	Y	N	N	N	Y	N
24 ***Solomon***	N	Y	N	N	N	N	N	N
25 ***Boehlert***	Y	Y	Y	N	N	N	Y	N
26 ***Martin***	Y	Y	Y	N	N	N	Y	N
27 ***Wortley***	Y	Y	Y	N	N	N	Y	N
28 McHugh	Y	Y	Y	Y	Y	Y	?	Y
29 ***Horton***	Y	Y	Y	N	Y	N	Y	N
30 ***Conable***	Y	N	Y	N	N	N	Y	Y
31 ***Kemp***	Y	Y	Y	N	N	N	Y	N
32 LaFalce	?	Y	Y	Y	Y	N	Y	Y
33 Nowak	Y	Y	Y	Y	Y	Y	Y	Y
34 Lundine	P	Y	Y	Y	Y	N	Y	N

	177	178	179	180	181	182	183	184
NORTH CAROLINA								
1 Jones	Y	Y	Y	N	N	N	Y	N
2 Valentine	Y	Y	Y	N	N	N	Y	Y
3 Whitley	Y	Y	Y	N	N	N	Y	N
4 Andrews	Y	Y	Y	N	N	N	Y	N
5 Neal	Y	Y	Y	N	N	N	Y	N
6 Britt	Y	Y	Y	Y	Y	?	Y	N
7 Rose	Y	Y	Y	N	N	?	Y	N
8 Hefner	Y	Y	Y	N	N	N	Y	N
9 ***Martin***	?	?	?	N	N	N	Y	N
10 ***Broyhill***	Y	N	Y	N	N	N	Y	N
11 Clarke	Y	Y	Y	Y	N	N	Y	N
NORTH DAKOTA								
AL Dorgan	Y	?	?	Y	N	Y	N	Y
OHIO								
1 Luken	Y	Y	Y	Y	N	N	N	N
2 ***Gradison***	Y	N	Y	N	N	N	Y	N
3 Hall	Y	Y	Y	Y	N	?	Y	N
4 ***Oxley***	Y	N	Y	N	N	N	Y	N
5 ***Latta***	Y	Y	Y	N	N	N	Y	N
6 ***McEwen***	Y	Y	Y	N	N	N	Y	N
7 ***DeWine***	Y	N	Y	N	N	N	Y	N
8 ***Kindness***	Y	Y	N	N	N	N	Y	N
9 Kaptur	Y	Y	Y	Y	Y	Y	Y	Y
10 ***Miller***	Y	Y	Y	Y	N	N	N	N
11 Eckart	Y	Y	Y	Y	N	Y	Y	Y
12 ***Kasich***	Y	Y	Y	N	N	N	Y	N
13 Pease	Y	Y	Y	Y	Y	Y	Y	Y
14 Seiberling	Y	Y	Y	Y	Y	Y	Y	N
15 ***Wylie***	Y	Y	Y	N	N	N	Y	N
16 ***Regula***	Y	Y	Y	N	N	N	Y	N
17 ***Williams***	Y	Y	Y	N	N	N	Y	N
18 Applegate	?	Y	N	N	N	N	Y	N
19 Feighan	Y	Y	Y	Y	N	N	Y	Y
20 Oakar	Y	Y	Y	Y	N	N	Y	N
21 Stokes	Y	Y	Y	Y	Y	Y	Y	Y
OKLAHOMA								
1 Jones	Y	Y	N	Y	N	N	Y	Y
2 Synar	Y	Y	Y	Y	N	Y	Y	Y
3 Watkins	Y	Y	Y	Y	N	N	Y	N
4 McCurdy	Y	Y	Y	N	Y	N	Y	N
5 ***Edwards***	Y	Y	N	N	N	N	Y	N
6 English	Y	Y	Y	N	N	N	Y	N
OREGON								
1 AuCoin	Y	Y	Y	Y	Y	Y	P	Y
2 ***Smith, R.***	Y	Y	N	N	N	N	Y	N
3 Wyden	Y	Y	Y	Y	Y	Y	Y	Y
4 Weaver	Y	Y	Y	Y	Y	Y	Y	Y
5 ***Smith, D.***	Y	N	N	N	N	N	Y	N
PENNSYLVANIA								
1 Foglietta	Y	Y	Y	Y	Y	N	Y	N
2 Gray	Y	Y	Y	Y	Y	Y	Y	Y
3 Borski	Y	Y	Y	Y	Y	Y	Y	Y
4 Kolter	?	Y	Y	Y	Y	N	?	?
5 ***Schulze***	Y	Y	Y	N	N	N	Y	N
6 Yatron	Y	Y	Y	N	Y	Y	Y	Y
7 Edgar	P	Y	Y	Y	Y	Y	Y	Y
8 Kostmayer	Y	Y	Y	Y	Y	?	Y	Y
9 ***Shuster***	Y	Y	Y	N	N	N	Y	N
10 ***McDade***	Y	Y	Y	N	N	N	?	?
11 Harrison	Y	Y	Y	N	Y	Y	Y	Y
12 Murtha	Y	Y	Y	N	N	N	Y	N
13 ***Coughlin***	Y	?	?	Y	Y	Y	N	N
14 Coyne	Y	Y	Y	Y	Y	N	Y	Y
15 ***Ritter***	Y	Y	Y	N	N	N	Y	N
16 ***Walker***	N	Y	Y	N	N	N	N	N
17 ***Gekas***	Y	Y	Y	N	N	N	Y	N
18 Walgren	Y	Y	Y	Y	Y	Y	Y	Y
19 ***Goodling***	?	Y	Y	Y	N	N	N	N
20 Gaydos	?	Y	Y	N	N	N	Y	N
21 ***Ridge***	Y	?	Y	N	N	Y	Y	Y
22 Murphy	?	Y	Y	N	N	Y	Y	N
23 ***Clinger***	Y	N	Y	N	N	N	Y	Y
RHODE ISLAND								
1 St Germain	P	Y	Y	?	Y	Y	P	Y
2 ***Schneider***	Y	Y	Y	Y	Y	N	Y	Y
SOUTH CAROLINA								
1 ***Hartnett***	Y	Y	Y	N	N	N	Y	N
2 ***Spence***	Y	Y	Y	N	N	N	Y	N
3 Derrick	Y	Y	Y	N	N	X	Y	N
4 ***Campbell***	Y	Y	Y	N	N	N	Y	N
5 Spratt	Y	Y	Y	Y	N	N	Y	N
6 Tallon	Y	Y	Y	N	Y	N	Y	N
SOUTH DAKOTA								
AL Daschle	Y	Y	Y	Y	N	N	Y	N

	177	178	179	180	181	182	183	184
TENNESSEE								
1 ***Quillen***	Y	Y	Y	N	N	N	Y	N
2 ***Duncan***	Y	Y	Y	N	X	?	Y	N
3 Lloyd	Y	Y	Y	N	N	N	Y	N
4 Cooper	Y	Y	Y	Y	Y	Y	Y	Y
5 Boner	Y	Y	Y	N	N	N	Y	N
6 Gore	Y	Y	Y	Y	Y	Y	Y	Y
7 ***Sundquist***	?	Y	Y	N	N	N	Y	N
8 Jones	Y	Y	Y	N	N	N	Y	N
9 Ford	Y	Y	Y	Y	Y	Y	Y	Y
TEXAS								
1 Hall, S.	Y	Y	Y	N	N	N	Y	N
2 Wilson	Y	Y	Y	N	N	N	Y	N
3 ***Bartlett***	Y	N	N	N	N	N	Y	N
4 Hall, R.	Y	Y	Y	N	N	N	Y	N
5 Bryant	Y	Y	Y	N	N	Y	Y	N
6 ***Gramm***	Y	N	N	N	N	N	Y	N
7 ***Archer***	Y	Y	Y	N	N	N	Y	N
8 ***Fields***	N	Y	N	N	N	N	N	N
9 Brooks	Y	Y	Y	N	Y	N	Y	Y
10 Pickle	Y	Y	Y	N	N	N	Y	N
11 Leath	Y	Y	Y	N	N	N	Y	N
12 Wright	Y	?	Y	N	N	N	Y	N
13 Hightower	Y	Y	Y	N	Y	N	Y	N
14 Patman	Y	Y	Y	N	N	N	Y	N
15 de la Garza	Y	Y	Y	N	N	N	Y	N
16 Coleman	Y	Y	Y	N	Y	N	Y	N
17 Stenholm	Y	Y	Y	N	N	N	Y	N
18 Leland	Y	Y	Y	Y	Y	Y	Y	Y
19 Hance	Y	Y	Y	N	N	N	Y	N
20 Gonzalez	Y	Y	Y	N	N	N	Y	N
21 ***Loeffler***	Y	N	Y	N	N	N	Y	N
22 ***Paul***	Y	N	N	N	Y	Y	Y	Y
23 Kazen	Y	Y	Y	N	N	N	Y	N
24 Frost	Y	Y	Y	N	N	N	Y	N
25 Andrews	Y	Y	Y	Y	Y	N	Y	N
26 Vandergriff	Y	Y	Y	N	N	N	Y	N
27 Ortiz	Y	Y	Y	N	N	N	Y	N
UTAH								
1 ***Hansen***	Y	N	N	N	N	N	Y	N
2 ***Marriott***	Y	Y	Y	N	N	N	Y	N
3 ***Nielson***	Y	N	N	N	N	N	Y	N
VERMONT								
AL ***Jeffords***	Y	Y	Y	Y	Y	N	Y	Y
VIRGINIA								
1 ***Bateman***	Y	Y	N	N	N	N	Y	N
2 ***Whitehurst***	Y	Y	Y	N	N	N	Y	N
3 ***Bliley***	Y	Y	Y	N	N	N	Y	N
4 Sisisky	Y	Y	Y	N	N	N	Y	N
5 Daniel	Y	Y	Y	N	N	N	Y	N
6 Olin	Y	Y	Y	Y	Y	Y	Y	Y
7 ***Robinson***	Y	Y	Y	N	N	N	Y	N
8 ***Parris***	Y	Y	Y	N	N	N	Y	N
9 Boucher	Y	Y	Y	Y	N	Y	Y	N
10 ***Wolf***	Y	Y	Y	N	N	N	Y	N
WASHINGTON								
1 ***Pritchard***	Y	Y	Y	Y	Y	N	?	Y
2 Swift	Y	Y	Y	Y	Y	Y	?	N
3 Bonker	Y	Y	Y	?	Y	Y	Y	Y
4 ***Morrison***	Y	Y	Y	N	N	N	Y	N
5 Foley	Y	Y	Y	Y	Y	N	?	?
6 Dicks	Y	Y	Y	Y	N	N	Y	Y
7 Lowry	Y	Y	Y	Y	Y	Y	Y	Y
8 ***Chandler***	Y	Y	Y	Y	N	N	Y	N
WEST VIRGINIA								
1 Mollohan	Y	Y	Y	N	N	N	Y	N
2 Staggers	Y	Y	Y	Y	Y	N	Y	N
3 Wise	Y	Y	Y	Y	Y	Y	Y	N
4 Rahall	Y	Y	Y	Y	?	?	?	N
WISCONSIN								
1 Aspin	Y	Y	Y	Y	Y	Y	Y	Y
2 Kastenmeier	Y	N	Y	Y	Y	Y	Y	Y
3 ***Gunderson***	Y	Y	Y	N	N	N	Y	N
4 Zablocki	Y	Y	Y	N	N	N	Y	N
5 Moody	Y	Y	Y	Y	Y	Y	?	?
6 ***Petri***	Y	N	Y	N	N	Y	Y	N
7 Obey	Y	Y	Y	Y	Y	Y	Y	Y
8 ***Roth***	Y	Y	Y	N	N	N	Y	N
9 ***Sensenbrenner***	Y	Y	Y	N	N	N	Y	N
WYOMING								
AL ***Cheney***	Y	N	N	N	N	N	Y	N

Southern states - Ala., Ark., Fla., Ga., Ky., La., Miss., N.C., Okla., S.C., Tenn., Texas, Va.

185. HR 2969. Department of Defense Authorization. Dellums, D-Calif., amendment to delete $6.2 billion for procurement of B-1 bombers. Rejected 164-255: R 19-144; D 145-111 (ND 129-37, SD 16-74), June 15, 1983. A "nay" was a vote supporting the president's position.

186. HR 2969. Department of Defense Authorization. Leath, D-Texas, amendment to the Zablocki, D-Wis., amendment, to permit the use of funds in the bill to manufacture components of binary chemical weapons, but barring their final assembly until after Oct. 1, 1985. Rejected 202-216: R 117-47; D 85-169 (ND 21-145, SD 64-24), June 15, 1983. A "yea" was a vote supporting the president's position. (The Zablocki amendment would delete from the bill $114.6 million for procurement of binary munitions.)

187. HR 2969. Department of Defense Authorization. Bethune, R-Ark., substitute for the Zablocki, D-Wis., amendment, to delete $114.6 million for binary chemical munitions and prohibiting the procurement of binary munitions or their components. Adopted 256-161: R 62-101; D 194-60 (ND 156-11, SD 38-49), June 15, 1983. (The Zablocki amendment would delete from the bill $114.6 million for procurement of binary munitions. The Zablocki amendment, as modified by Bethune, subsequently was adopted by voice vote.)

188. Procedural Motion. Corcoran, R-Ill., motion to approve the House *Journal* of Wednesday, June 15. Motion agreed to 364-22: R 144-12; D 220-10 (ND 141-9, SD 79-1), June 16, 1983.

189. HR 1590. Emergency Food Assistance. Passage of the bill to require the secretary of agriculture to make available, to emergency food organizations and certain other agencies, federally owned farm commodities that are not obligated to other programs and to authorize funds for processing, transportation and administrative costs associated with distribution. Passed 389-18: R 142-16; D 247-2 (ND 161-0, SD 86-2), June 16, 1983.

190. HR 2668. Consumer Product Safety Act. Adoption of the rule (H Res 227) providing for House floor consideration of the bill to reauthorize the Consumer Product Safety Commission through fiscal 1988. Adopted 390-2: R 150-1; D 240-1 (ND 158-0, SD 82-1), June 16, 1983.

191. HR 2972. Military Construction Authorization. Adoption of the rule (H Res 229) providing for House floor consideration of the bill to authorize appropriations for military construction in fiscal 1984. Adopted 397-0: R 156-0; D 241-0 (ND 159-0, SD 82-0), June 16, 1983.

192. HR 2969. Department of Defense Authorization. Dellums, D-Calif., amendment to delete from the authorization all funds, amounting to $432.8 million, for procurement of Pershing II missiles. Rejected 73-319: R 4-152; D 69-167 (ND 67-88, SD 2-79), June 16, 1983. A "nay" was a vote supporting the president's position.

KEY

Y   Voted for (yea).
Paired for.
+   Announced for.
N   Voted against (nay).
X   Paired against.
-   Announced against.
P   Voted "present".
C   Voted "present" to avoid possible conflict of interest.
?   Did not vote or otherwise make a position known.

Democrats   *Republicans*

	185	186	187	188	189	190	191	192
ALABAMA								
1 *Edwards*	N	Y	N	Y	Y	Y	Y	N
2 *Dickinson*	N	Y	N	N	Y	Y	Y	N
3 Nichols	N	Y	N	Y	Y	Y	Y	N
4 Bevill	N	Y	N	Y	Y	Y	Y	N
5 Flippo	N	Y	N	Y	Y	Y	Y	N
6 Erdreich	N	N	Y	Y	Y	Y	Y	N
7 Shelby	N	Y	N	Y	Y	Y	Y	N
ALASKA								
AL *Young*	N	Y	N	?	?	?	?	?
ARIZONA								
1 *McCain*	N	Y	N	Y	N	Y	Y	N
2 Udall	N	N	Y	Y	Y	Y	?	?
3 *Stump*	N	Y	N	N	N	Y	Y	N
4 *Rudd*	N	Y	N	Y	Y	Y	Y	?
5 McNulty	Y	Y	Y	Y	Y	Y	Y	N
ARKANSAS								
1 Alexander	N	Y	N	Y	Y	Y	?	?
2 *Bethune*	N	N	Y	Y	Y	Y	Y	N
3 *Hammerschmidt*	N	Y	N	P	Y	Y	Y	N
4 Anthony	N	Y	N	?	Y	Y	Y	N
CALIFORNIA								
1 Bosco	Y	Y	N	Y	Y	Y	?	Y
2 *Chappie*	N	Y	N	Y	Y	Y	Y	N
3 Matsui	N	Y	Y	Y	Y	Y	Y	N
4 Fazio	Y	Y	Y	Y	Y	Y	Y	N
5 Vacancy								
6 Boxer	Y	N	Y	?	?	?	?	#
7 Miller	Y	?	?	?	?	?	?	#
8 Dellums	Y	N	Y	Y	Y	Y	Y	Y
9 Stark	Y	N	Y	?	?	?	?	#
10 Edwards	Y	N	Y	Y	Y	Y	Y	Y
11 Lantos	Y	N	Y	Y	Y	Y	Y	N
12 *Zschau*	N	Y	Y	Y	Y	Y	Y	N
13 Mineta	Y	N	Y	Y	Y	Y	Y	N
14 *Shumway*	N	Y	N	Y	N	Y	Y	N
15 Coelho	N	Y	Y	Y	Y	Y	Y	N
16 Panetta	Y	N	Y	Y	Y	Y	Y	N
17 *Pashayan*	N	Y	N	Y	Y	Y	Y	N
18 Lehman	Y	N	Y	Y	Y	Y	Y	Y
19 *Lagomarsino*	N	Y	N	Y	Y	Y	Y	N
20 *Thomas*	X	Y	N	Y	Y	?	Y	N
21 *Fiedler*	N	Y	N	Y	Y	Y	Y	N
22 *Moorhead*	N	Y	N	Y	Y	Y	Y	N
23 Beilenson	Y	N	Y	Y	Y	Y	Y	Y
24 Waxman	Y	N	Y	Y	Y	Y	Y	Y
25 Roybal	Y	N	Y	Y	Y	Y	Y	Y
26 Berman	Y	N	Y	Y	Y	Y	Y	Y
27 Levine	N	N	Y	Y	Y	Y	Y	N
28 Dixon	P	N	Y	Y	Y	Y	Y	Y
29 Hawkins	N	N	Y	Y	Y	Y	Y	Y
30 Martinez	?	?	?	?	?	?	?	?
31 Dymally	?	N	Y	Y	Y	Y	Y	Y
32 Anderson	N	N	Y	Y	Y	Y	?	N
33 *Dreier*	N	Y	N	Y	N	Y	Y	N
34 Torres	N	N	Y	Y	Y	Y	Y	Y
35 *Lewis*	N	Y	N	Y	Y	Y	Y	N
36 Brown	N	N	Y	?	Y	Y	Y	Y
37 *McCandless*	N	Y	N	Y	Y	Y	Y	N
38 Patterson	N	N	Y	?	?	?	?	X
39 *Dannemeyer*	N	Y	N	N	N	N	Y	N
40 *Badham*	N	Y	N	N	Y	N	Y	N
41 *Lowery*	N	Y	N	Y	Y	Y	Y	N
42 *Lungren*	N	Y	Y	Y	Y	?	?	N

	185	186	187	188	189	190	191	192
43 *Packard*	N	Y	N	Y	Y	Y	Y	N
44 Bates	Y	N	Y	Y	Y	Y	Y	?
45 *Hunter*	N	Y	N	Y	Y	Y	Y	N
COLORADO								
1 Schroeder	Y	N	Y	N	Y	Y	Y	Y
2 Wirth	Y	N	Y	Y	Y	Y	Y	Y
3 Kogovsek	Y	N	Y	Y	Y	Y	Y	N
4 *Brown*	N	Y	N	Y	Y	Y	Y	N
5 *Kramer*	N	Y	N	Y	Y	Y	Y	?
6 *Schaefer*	N	Y	N	Y	Y	Y	Y	N
CONNECTICUT								
1 Kennelly	?	?	?	Y	Y	Y	Y	Y
2 Gejdenson	Y	N	Y	N	Y	Y	Y	Y
3 Morrison	Y	N	Y	Y	Y	Y	Y	Y
4 *McKinney*	?	?	?	?	?	?	?	N
5 Ratchford	Y	Y	Y	Y	Y	Y	Y	Y
6 *Johnson*	N	N	Y	Y	Y	Y	Y	N
DELAWARE								
AL Carper	Y	N	Y	Y	Y	Y	Y	N
FLORIDA								
1 Hutto	N	Y	N	Y	Y	Y	Y	N
2 Fuqua	N	Y	N	Y	Y	Y	Y	N
3 Bennett	N	Y	N	Y	Y	Y	Y	N
4 Chappell	N	Y	N	Y	?	?	Y	N
5 *McCollum*	N	Y	N	Y	Y	Y	Y	N
6 MacKay	Y	N	Y	Y	Y	Y	Y	N
7 Gibbons	N	Y	N	Y	Y	Y	Y	N
8 *Young*	N	Y	N	Y	Y	Y	Y	N
9 *Bilirakis*	N	Y	N	Y	Y	Y	Y	N
10 Ireland	N	Y	N	?	Y	Y	?	?
11 Nelson	N	Y	N	Y	Y	Y	Y	N
12 *Lewis*	N	Y	N	Y	Y	Y	Y	N
13 *Mack*	N	Y	N	N	Y	N	Y	N
14 Mica	N	Y	N	Y	Y	Y	Y	N
15 *Shaw*	N	Y	N	Y	Y	Y	Y	N
16 Smith	N	N	Y	Y	Y	Y	Y	N
17 Lehman	Y	N	Y	Y	Y	Y	Y	Y
18 Pepper	N	N	Y	Y	Y	Y	Y	Y
19 Fascell	Y	N	Y	Y	Y	Y	Y	N
GEORGIA								
1 Thomas	N	Y	N	Y	Y	Y	Y	N
2 Hatcher	N	Y	N	Y	Y	Y	Y	N
3 Ray	N	Y	N	Y	N	Y	Y	N
4 Levitas	N	Y	N	Y	Y	Y	Y	N
5 Fowler	Y	N	Y	Y	Y	Y	Y	N
6 *Gingrich*	N	Y	N	?	?	?	?	N
7 McDonald	N	Y	N	?	N	N	Y	X
8 Rowland	N	Y	N	Y	Y	Y	Y	N
9 Jenkins	Y	N	Y	Y	Y	Y	Y	N
10 Barnard	N	Y	N	Y	Y	Y	?	N
HAWAII								
1 Heftel	?	?	?	?	?	?	?	?
2 Akaka	N	N	Y	Y	?	?	?	N
IDAHO								
1 *Craig*	N	Y	N	Y	Y	Y	Y	N
2 *Hansen*	N	Y	N	?	Y	Y	?	?
ILLINOIS								
1 Vacancy								
2 Savage	Y	N	Y	Y	Y	Y	Y	Y
3 Russo	Y	N	Y	?	Y	Y	Y	N
4 *O'Brien*	N	Y	N	Y	Y	Y	Y	N
5 Lipinski	Y	N	Y	N	Y	Y	Y	N
6 *Hyde*	N	Y	N	Y	Y	Y	Y	N
7 Collins	Y	?	Y	Y	Y	Y	Y	Y
8 Rostenkowski	N	Y	N	Y	Y	Y	Y	N
9 Yates	Y	?	?	?	?	?	?	?
10 *Porter*	N	N	Y	Y	Y	Y	Y	N
11 Annunzio	N	N	Y	Y	Y	Y	Y	N
12 *Crane, P.*	N	Y	N	Y	N	Y	N	N
13 Erlenborn	N	Y	N	Y	Y	Y	Y	?
14 *Corcoran*	N	Y	N	Y	Y	+	Y	N
15 *Madigan*	N	Y	?	?	Y	Y	Y	N
16 *Martin*	N	N	Y	Y	Y	Y	Y	N
17 Evans	Y	N	Y	Y	Y	?	Y	N
18 *Michel*	N	N	Y	Y	Y	?	Y	N
19 *Crane, D.*	N	Y	N	Y	N	Y	N	N
20 Durbin	Y	N	Y	N	Y	Y	Y	N
21 Price	N	N	Y	Y	Y	Y	Y	N
22 Simon	Y	N	Y	?	?	?	Y	?
INDIANA								
1 Hall	Y	N	Y	?	?	?	?	?
2 Sharp	Y	N	Y	Y	Y	Y	Y	N
3 *Hiler*	N	N	Y	Y	Y	Y	Y	N
4 *Coats*	N	N	Y	+	+	+	+	-
5 Hillis	N	Y	N	Y	Y	Y	Y	N

ND - Northern Democrats   SD - Southern Democrats

Corresponding to Congressional Record Votes 195, 196, 197, 198, 199, 200, 201, 202

	185	186	187	188	189	190	191	192
6 ***Burton***	N	Y	N	Y	N	Y	Y	N
7 ***Myers***	N	Y	N	Y	Y	Y	Y	N
8 McCloskey	Y	N	Y	Y	Y	Y	Y	?
9 Hamilton	Y	N	Y	Y	Y	Y	Y	N
10 Jacobs	Y	N	Y	P	Y	Y	Y	N
IOWA								
1 ***Leach***	Y	N	Y	Y	Y	Y	Y	N
2 ***Tauke***	Y	N	Y	Y	Y	Y	Y	N
3 ***Evans***	N	Y	Y	N	Y	Y	Y	N
4 Smith	Y	N	Y	Y	Y	Y	Y	N
5 Harkin	Y	N	Y	?	?	?	?	?
6 Bedell	Y	N	Y	Y	Y	Y	Y	Y
KANSAS								
1 ***Roberts***	N	N	Y	Y	Y	Y	Y	N
2 Slattery	Y	N	Y	?	Y	Y	Y	N
3 ***Winn***	N	Y	N	Y	Y	Y	Y	N
4 Glickman	N	N	Y	Y	Y	Y	Y	N
5 ***Whittaker***	N	N	Y	Y	Y	Y	Y	N
KENTUCKY								
1 Hubbard	N	Y	N	Y	Y	Y	Y	N
2 Natcher	N	Y	Y	Y	Y	Y	Y	N
3 Mazzoli	Y	N	Y	Y	Y	Y	Y	N
4 ***Snyder***	N	Y	N	Y	Y	Y	Y	N
5 ***Rogers***	N	Y	N	Y	Y	Y	Y	N
6 ***Hopkins***	N	Y	Y	Y	Y	Y	Y	N
7 Perkins	N	Y	Y	Y	Y	Y	Y	N
LOUISIANA								
1 ***Livingston***	N	Y	N	Y	+	+	+	N
2 Boggs	N	N	Y	Y	Y	?	?	N
3 Tauzin	N	Y	N	Y	Y	Y	Y	N
4 Roemer	N	N	Y	N	Y	Y	Y	N
5 Huckaby	N	Y	Y	Y	Y	Y	Y	N
6 ***Moore***	N	Y	N	Y	Y	Y	Y	N
7 Breaux	N	Y	N	Y	Y	Y	Y	N
8 Long	N	N	Y	Y	Y	Y	Y	N
MAINE								
1 ***McKernan***	N	N	Y	Y	Y	Y	Y	N
2 ***Snowe***	N	N	Y	Y	Y	Y	Y	N
MARYLAND								
1 Dyson	N	Y	N	Y	Y	Y	Y	N
2 Long	Y	Y	N	Y	Y	Y	Y	N
3 Mikulski	Y	N	Y	Y	Y	Y	Y	N
4 ***Holt***	N	Y	N	N	Y	Y	Y	N
5 Hoyer	N	N	Y	Y	Y	Y	Y	N
6 Byron	N	Y	N	Y	Y	Y	Y	N
7 Mitchell	Y	N	Y	?	Y	Y	Y	Y
8 Barnes	Y	N	Y	Y	Y	Y	Y	N
MASSACHUSETTS								
1 ***Conte***	Y	N	Y	Y	Y	Y	Y	Y
2 Boland	Y	N	Y	Y	Y	Y	Y	N
3 Early	Y	N	Y	Y	Y	Y	Y	Y
4 Frank	Y	N	Y	?	Y	Y	Y	Y
5 Shannon	Y	N	Y	Y	Y	Y	Y	Y
6 Mavroules	Y	N	Y	Y	Y	Y	Y	Y
7 Markey	Y	N	Y	Y	Y	Y	+	Y
8 O'Neill								
9 Moakley	Y	N	Y	Y	Y	Y	Y	Y
10 Studds	Y	N	Y	Y	Y	Y	Y	Y
11 Donnelly	Y	Y	Y	Y	Y	Y	Y	N
MICHIGAN								
1 Conyers	Y	N	Y	?	Y	Y	Y	Y
2 ***Pursell***	Y	?	?	Y	Y	Y	Y	N
3 Wolpe	Y	N	Y	Y	Y	Y	Y	Y
4 ***Siljander***	N	Y	N	Y	Y	Y	Y	N
5 ***Sawyer***	N	Y	N	Y	Y	Y	Y	N
6 Carr	Y	N	Y	Y	Y	Y	Y	Y
7 Kildee	Y	N	Y	Y	Y	Y	Y	Y
8 Traxler	Y	N	Y	Y	Y	Y	Y	N
9 ***Vander Jagt***	N	Y	N	Y	Y	Y	Y	N
10 Albosta	Y	N	Y	Y	Y	Y	Y	N
11 ***Davis***	N	Y	N	Y	Y	Y	Y	N
12 Bonior	Y	N	Y	Y	Y	Y	Y	Y
13 Crockett	Y	N	Y	Y	Y	Y	Y	#
14 Hertel	Y	N	Y	Y	Y	Y	Y	N
15 Ford	Y	N	Y	Y	Y	Y	Y	N
16 Dingell	Y	N	Y	?	Y	Y	Y	N
17 Levin	Y	N	Y	Y	Y	Y	Y	N
18 ***Broomfield***	N	Y	Y	Y	Y	Y	Y	N
MINNESOTA								
1 Penny	Y	N	Y	Y	Y	Y	Y	Y
2 ***Weber***	Y	N	Y	Y	Y	Y	Y	N
3 ***Frenzel***	Y	N	Y	Y	Y	Y	Y	N
4 Vento	Y	N	Y	N	Y	Y	Y	Y
5 Sabo	Y	N	Y	N	Y	Y	Y	Y
6 Sikorski	Y	N	Y	Y	Y	Y	Y	Y
7 ***Stangeland***	N	N	Y	?	Y	Y	Y	N
8 Oberstar	Y	N	Y	?	Y	Y	Y	Y
MISSISSIPPI								
1 Whitten	N	Y	Y	Y	Y	Y	Y	N
2 ***Franklin***	N	Y	N	N	Y	Y	Y	N
3 Montgomery	N	Y	N	Y	Y	Y	Y	N
4 Dowdy	N	N	Y	Y	Y	Y	Y	N
5 ***Lott***	N	Y	N	Y	Y	Y	Y	N
MISSOURI								
1 Clay	Y	N	Y	N	Y	Y	Y	Y
2 Young	N	Y	N	Y	Y	Y	Y	N
3 Gephardt	Y	N	Y	Y	Y	Y	Y	N
4 Skelton	N	Y	N	Y	Y	Y	Y	N
5 Wheat	Y	N	Y	Y	Y	Y	Y	Y
6 ***Coleman***	N	Y	N	Y	Y	Y	Y	N
7 ***Taylor***	N	Y	N	Y	Y	Y	Y	N
8 ***Emerson***	N	Y	N	N	Y	Y	Y	N
9 Volkmer	N	Y	Y	Y	Y	Y	Y	N
MONTANA								
1 Williams	Y	N	Y	?	Y	Y	Y	Y
2 ***Marlenee***	N	Y	N	P	Y	Y	Y	N
NEBRASKA								
1 ***Bereuter***	N	Y	N	Y	Y	Y	Y	N
2 ***Daub***	N	Y	Y	Y	Y	Y	Y	N
3 ***Smith***	N	Y	Y	Y	Y	Y	Y	N
NEVADA								
1 Reid	Y	N	Y	Y	Y	Y	Y	N
2 ***Vucanovich***	N	Y	N	Y	Y	Y	Y	N
NEW HAMPSHIRE								
1 D'Amours	Y	N	Y	Y	Y	Y	Y	N
2 ***Gregg***	N	N	Y	Y	Y	Y	Y	N
NEW JERSEY								
1 Florio	Y	N	Y	Y	Y	Y	Y	X
2 Hughes	Y	Y	Y	Y	Y	Y	Y	N
3 Howard	Y	N	Y	Y	Y	Y	Y	N
4 ***Smith***	N	N	Y	Y	Y	Y	Y	N
5 ***Roukema***	N	N	Y	Y	Y	Y	Y	N
6 Dwyer	Y	N	Y	Y	Y	Y	Y	N
7 ***Rinaldo***	N	N	Y	Y	Y	Y	Y	N
8 Roe	N	N	Y	Y	Y	Y	Y	?
9 Torricelli	Y	N	Y	Y	Y	Y	Y	Y
10 Rodino	#	N	Y	Y	Y	Y	Y	Y
11 Minish	Y	N	Y	Y	Y	Y	Y	N
12 ***Courter***	?	?	?	?	?	?	?	?
13 ***Forsythe***	Y	N	Y	N	Y	Y	Y	Y
14 Guarini	Y	N	Y	Y	Y	Y	Y	N
NEW MEXICO								
1 ***Lujan***	N	Y	Y	Y	Y	Y	Y	N
2 ***Skeen***	N	Y	N	Y	Y	Y	Y	N
3 Richardson	N	N	Y	Y	Y	Y	Y	N
NEW YORK								
1 ***Carney***	N	N	Y	Y	Y	Y	Y	N
2 Downey	Y	?	?	Y	Y	Y	Y	Y
3 Mrazek	Y	N	Y	Y	Y	Y	Y	N
4 ***Lent***	N	Y	N	Y	Y	Y	Y	N
5 ***McGrath***	N	N	Y	Y	Y	Y	Y	N
6 Addabbo	Y	N	Y	Y	Y	Y	Y	Y
7 Ackerman	Y	N	Y	Y	Y	Y	Y	Y
8 Scheuer	Y	N	Y	Y	Y	Y	Y	Y
9 Ferraro	Y	N	Y	Y	Y	Y	Y	N
10 Schumer	Y	N	Y	Y	Y	Y	Y	Y
11 Towns	Y	N	Y	Y	Y	Y	Y	Y
12 Owens	?	?	?	?	?	?	?	?
13 Solarz	Y	N	Y	Y	Y	Y	Y	N
14 ***Molinari***	N	Y	Y	Y	Y	Y	Y	N
15 ***Green***	Y	N	Y	Y	Y	Y	Y	N
16 Rangel	Y	N	Y	Y	Y	Y	Y	Y
17 Weiss	Y	N	Y	Y	Y	Y	Y	Y
18 Garcia	Y	N	Y	Y	?	?	Y	Y
19 Biaggi	Y	N	Y	Y	Y	Y	Y	N
20 Ottinger	Y	N	Y	P	Y	Y	Y	Y
21 ***Fish***	Y	N	Y	Y	Y	Y	Y	N
22 ***Gilman***	N	Y	N	Y	Y	Y	Y	N
23 Stratton	N	Y	N	Y	Y	Y	Y	N
24 ***Solomon***	N	Y	N	N	Y	Y	?	N
25 ***Boehlert***	N	N	Y	Y	Y	Y	Y	N
26 ***Martin***	N	Y	N	Y	Y	Y	Y	N
27 ***Wortley***	N	N	Y	Y	Y	Y	Y	N
28 McHugh	Y	N	Y	Y	Y	Y	Y	N
29 ***Horton***	Y	N	Y	Y	Y	Y	Y	N
30 ***Conable***	N	Y	N	Y	Y	Y	Y	N
31 ***Kemp***	N	Y	N	Y	Y	Y	Y	N
32 LaFalce	Y	N	Y	Y	Y	Y	Y	Y
33 Nowak	Y	N	Y	Y	Y	Y	Y	?
34 Lundine	Y	N	Y	Y	Y	Y	Y	Y
NORTH CAROLINA								
1 Jones	N	Y	N	Y	Y	Y	Y	N
2 Valentine	N	Y	N	Y	Y	Y	Y	N
3 Whitley	N	Y	N	Y	Y	Y	Y	N
4 Andrews	N	N	Y	P	Y	Y	Y	N
5 Neal	N	Y	Y	Y	Y	Y	Y	N
6 Britt	Y	N	Y	Y	Y	Y	?	N
7 Rose	N	Y	N	?	Y	Y	Y	?
8 Hefner	N	Y	Y	Y	Y	Y	Y	N
9 ***Martin***	N	N	Y	Y	Y	Y	Y	N
10 ***Broyhill***	N	N	Y	Y	Y	Y	Y	N
11 Clarke	N	Y	Y	Y	Y	?	Y	N
NORTH DAKOTA								
AL Dorgan	N	N	Y	N	Y	Y	Y	N
OHIO								
1 Luken	N	N	Y	Y	Y	Y	Y	N
2 ***Gradison***	N	N	Y	Y	Y	Y	Y	N
3 Hall	N	N	Y	Y	Y	Y	Y	Y
4 ***Oxley***	N	N	Y	Y	Y	Y	Y	N
5 ***Latta***	N	Y	N	Y	Y	Y	Y	N
6 ***McEwen***	N	Y	N	Y	Y	Y	Y	N
7 ***DeWine***	N	Y	N	Y	Y	Y	Y	N
8 ***Kindness***	N	Y	N	Y	Y	Y	Y	N
9 Kaptur	Y	N	Y	Y	Y	Y	Y	N
10 ***Miller***	N	Y	Y	N	Y	Y	Y	N
11 Eckart	N	N	Y	Y	Y	Y	Y	N
12 ***Kasich***	N	Y	N	Y	Y	Y	Y	N
13 Pease	Y	N	Y	Y	Y	Y	Y	N
14 Seiberling	Y	N	Y	Y	Y	Y	?	Y
15 ***Wylie***	N	Y	N	Y	Y	Y	Y	N
16 ***Regula***	N	Y	N	Y	Y	Y	Y	N
17 ***Williams***	N	N	Y	Y	Y	Y	Y	N
18 Applegate	N	N	Y	?	Y	Y	Y	N
19 Feighan	Y	N	Y	Y	Y	Y	Y	N
20 Oakar	N	N	Y	Y	Y	Y	Y	N
21 Stokes	Y	N	Y	Y	Y	Y	Y	Y
OKLAHOMA								
1 Jones	N	Y	Y	Y	Y	Y	Y	N
2 Synar	N	N	Y	Y	Y	Y	Y	N
3 Watkins	N	Y	Y	Y	Y	Y	Y	?
4 McCurdy	N	Y	Y	Y	Y	Y	Y	N
5 ***Edwards***	N	N	Y	Y	Y	Y	Y	N
6 English	N	Y	Y	Y	Y	Y	Y	N
OREGON								
1 AuCoin	Y	N	Y	P	Y	Y	Y	Y
2 ***Smith, R.***	N	Y	Y	Y	Y	Y	Y	N
3 Wyden	Y	N	Y	Y	Y	Y	Y	Y
4 Weaver	Y	N	Y	Y	Y	Y	Y	Y
5 ***Smith, D.***	N	Y	N	Y	N	Y	Y	N
PENNSYLVANIA								
1 Foglietta	Y	N	Y	Y	Y	Y	Y	N
2 Gray	Y	N	Y	Y	Y	Y	Y	Y
3 Borski	Y	N	Y	Y	Y	Y	Y	N
4 Kolter	?	N	Y	?	Y	Y	Y	N
5 ***Schulze***	N	Y	N	Y	Y	Y	Y	N
6 Yatron	N	N	Y	Y	Y	Y	Y	N
7 Edgar	Y	N	Y	?	?	?	Y	Y
8 Kostmayer	Y	N	Y	Y	Y	Y	Y	N
9 ***Shuster***	N	Y	Y	Y	Y	Y	Y	N
10 ***McDade***	?	N	Y	?	?	?	?	?
11 Harrison	Y	N	Y	Y	Y	Y	Y	N
12 Murtha	N	Y	N	Y	Y	Y	Y	N
13 ***Coughlin***	Y	N	Y	Y	Y	Y	Y	N
14 Coyne	Y	N	Y	Y	Y	?	Y	Y
15 ***Ritter***	N	Y	N	Y	Y	?	Y	N
16 ***Walker***	N	N	Y	N	Y	Y	Y	N
17 ***Gekas***	N	Y	Y	Y	Y	Y	Y	N
18 Walgren	Y	N	Y	Y	Y	Y	Y	?
19 ***Goodling***	N	N	Y	N	Y	Y	Y	Y
20 Gaydos	N	N	Y	Y	Y	Y	Y	N
21 ***Ridge***	N	Y	N	Y	Y	Y	Y	N
22 Murphy	N	N	Y	Y	Y	Y	Y	N
23 ***Clinger***	Y	N	Y	Y	Y	Y	Y	N
RHODE ISLAND								
1 St Germain	Y	N	Y	P	Y	Y	Y	?
2 ***Schneider***	Y	N	Y	Y	Y	Y	Y	?
SOUTH CAROLINA								
1 ***Hartnett***	N	Y	N	Y	N	Y	Y	N
2 ***Spence***	N	Y	N	Y	Y	Y	Y	N
3 Derrick	Y	N	Y	Y	Y	Y	Y	N
4 ***Campbell***	N	Y	N	Y	Y	Y	Y	N
5 Spratt	N	N	Y	Y	Y	Y	Y	N
6 Tallon	Y	N	Y	Y	Y	Y	Y	N
SOUTH DAKOTA								
AL Daschle	?	N	Y	Y	Y	Y	Y	N
TENNESSEE								
1 ***Quillen***	N	Y	N	Y	Y	Y	Y	N
2 ***Duncan***	N	Y	N	Y	Y	Y	Y	N
3 Lloyd	N	Y	N	Y	Y	Y	Y	N
4 Cooper	Y	?	?	?	?	?	?	X
5 Boner	N	Y	N	Y	Y	Y	Y	N
6 Gore	Y	N	Y	Y	Y	Y	Y	N
7 ***Sundquist***	N	Y	N	Y	Y	Y	Y	?
8 Jones	N	Y	N	Y	Y	Y	Y	N
9 Ford	Y	N	Y	Y	Y	Y	?	N
TEXAS								
1 Hall, S.	N	Y	N	Y	Y	Y	Y	N
2 Wilson	N	Y	N	Y	Y	Y	Y	N
3 ***Bartlett***	N	Y	N	Y	N	Y	Y	N
4 Hall, R.	N	Y	N	Y	Y	Y	Y	N
5 Bryant	N	Y	N	?	Y	Y	Y	N
6 ***Gramm***	N	Y	N	Y	N	Y	Y	N
7 ***Archer***	N	Y	N	Y	Y	Y	Y	N
8 ***Fields***	N	Y	N	N	Y	Y	Y	N
9 Brooks	Y	Y	N	Y	Y	Y	Y	N
10 Pickle	N	N	Y	Y	Y	Y	Y	N
11 Leath	N	Y	N	Y	Y	Y	Y	N
12 Wright	N	Y	Y	Y	Y	Y	Y	N
13 Hightower	N	Y	N	Y	Y	Y	Y	N
14 Patman	N	Y	N	Y	Y	Y	Y	N
15 de la Garza	N	Y	?	Y	Y	Y	Y	N
16 Coleman	N	Y	N	?	Y	Y	Y	?
17 Stenholm	N	Y	N	Y	Y	Y	Y	N
18 Leland	Y	N	Y	Y	Y	Y	Y	#
19 Hance	N	Y	N	Y	Y	Y	Y	N
20 Gonzalez	N	N	Y	Y	Y	Y	Y	Y
21 ***Loeffler***	N	Y	N	Y	Y	Y	Y	N
22 ***Paul***	Y	N	Y	Y	N	Y	Y	Y
23 Kazen	N	Y	N	Y	Y	Y	Y	N
24 Frost	N	Y	Y	Y	Y	Y	Y	N
25 Andrews	Y	Y	N	?	?	?	?	X
26 Vandergriff	N	Y	N	Y	Y	Y	Y	N
27 Ortiz	N	Y	N	Y	Y	Y	Y	N
UTAH								
1 ***Hansen***	N	Y	N	Y	Y	Y	Y	N
2 ***Marriott***	N	Y	N	Y	Y	Y	Y	N
3 ***Nielson***	N	Y	N	?	?	?	?	?
VERMONT								
AL ***Jeffords***	Y	N	Y	Y	Y	Y	Y	N
VIRGINIA								
1 ***Bateman***	N	Y	N	Y	?	?	Y	N
2 ***Whitehurst***	N	Y	N	Y	Y	Y	Y	N
3 ***Bliley***	N	Y	N	Y	Y	Y	Y	N
4 Sisisky	N	Y	N	Y	Y	Y	Y	N
5 Daniel	N	Y	N	Y	Y	Y	Y	N
6 Olin	N	N	Y	Y	Y	Y	Y	N
7 ***Robinson***	N	Y	N	Y	Y	Y	Y	N
8 ***Parris***	N	N	Y	Y	Y	Y	Y	N
9 Boucher	N	?	?	Y	Y	Y	Y	N
10 ***Wolf***	N	Y	N	Y	Y	Y	Y	N
WASHINGTON								
1 ***Pritchard***	Y	N	Y	Y	Y	Y	Y	N
2 Swift	Y	N	Y	Y	Y	Y	Y	Y
3 Bonker	Y	N	Y	Y	Y	?	Y	N
4 ***Morrison***	N	Y	N	Y	Y	Y	Y	N
5 Foley	N	N	Y	Y	Y	Y	Y	N
6 Dicks	N	Y	Y	Y	Y	Y	Y	N
7 Lowry	Y	N	Y	Y	Y	Y	Y	Y
8 ***Chandler***	N	Y	N	Y	Y	Y	Y	N
WEST VIRGINIA								
1 Mollohan	N	Y	N	Y	Y	Y	Y	N
2 Staggers	Y	N	Y	Y	Y	Y	Y	N
3 Wise	Y	Y	N	Y	Y	Y	Y	N
4 Rahall	Y	?	?	Y	Y	Y	Y	N
WISCONSIN								
1 Aspin	Y	N	Y	Y	Y	Y	Y	N
2 Kastenmeier	Y	N	Y	Y	Y	Y	Y	Y
3 ***Gunderson***	Y	N	Y	Y	Y	Y	Y	N
4 Zablocki	N	N	Y	Y	Y	Y	Y	N
5 Moody	Y	N	Y	Y	Y	Y	Y	Y
6 ***Petri***	Y	Y	N	Y	Y	Y	Y	N
7 Obey	Y	N	Y	Y	Y	Y	Y	N
8 ***Roth***	N	Y	N	Y	Y	Y	Y	N
9 ***Sensenbrenner***	N	N	Y	Y	Y	Y	Y	N
WYOMING								
AL ***Cheney***	N	Y	N	Y	N	?	Y	N

Southern states - Ala., Ark., Fla., Ga., Ky., La., Miss., N.C., Okla., S.C., Tenn., Texas, Va.

193. HR 1492. Christopher Columbus Quincentenary. Garcia, D-N.Y., motion to suspend the rules and pass the bill to establish a Christopher Columbus Quincentenary Jubilee Commission and authorize funding of $200,000 for fiscal 1984, $250,000 a year in fiscal 1985-92 and an additional $50,000 for the period of Oct. 1-Nov. 15, 1992. Motion agreed to 288-123: R 74-85; D 214-38 (ND 154-13, SD 60-25), June 21, 1983. A two-thirds majority of those present and voting (274 in this case) is required for passage under suspension of the rules.

194. HR 3329. Transportation Appropriations, Fiscal 1984. Adoption of the resolution (H Res 238) to waive certain points of order against consideration of the bill to appropriate funds for the Transportation Department and related agencies in fiscal 1984. Adopted 373-41: R 123-38; D 250-3 (ND 163-2, SD 87-1), June 22, 1983.

195. HR 3329. Transportation Appropriations, Fiscal 1984. Fiedler, R-Calif., amendment to delete $127.5 million for a Los Angeles subway. Rejected 139-280: R 117-43; D 22-237 (ND 9-160, SD 13-77), June 22, 1983.

196. HR 3329. Transportation Appropriations, Fiscal 1984. Glickman, D-Kan., amendment to strike a provision prohibiting the use of funds to develop or implement a federal regulation that would lower the number of passengers or air carrier slots at National Airport in Washington, D.C. Rejected 170-249: R 83-77; D 87-172 (ND 59-110, SD 28-62), June 22, 1983.

197. HR 3329. Transportation Appropriations, Fiscal 1984. Lehman, D-Fla., motion that the Committee of the Whole rise and report the bill back to the House with sundry amendments, with the recommendation that the amendments be adopted and the bill passed. Motion agreed to 275-139: R 37-121; D 238-18 (ND 164-5, SD 74-13), June 22, 1983.

198. HR 3329. Transportation Appropriations, Fiscal 1984. Coughlin, R-Pa., motion to recommit the bill to the Appropriations Committee with instructions to cut all programs by 4 percent except for mandatory appropriations, rescissions and appropriations to liquidate obligations already incurred. Motion rejected 191-223: R 154-6; D 37-217 (ND 12-154, SD 25-63), June 22, 1983.

199. HR 3329. Transportation Appropriations, Fiscal 1984. Passage of the bill to appropriate $11,299,897,225 for the Transportation Department and related agencies in fiscal 1984. Passed 250-156: R 35-123; D 215-33 (ND 154-8, SD 61-25), June 22, 1983. The president had requested $10,913,472,025 in new budget authority.

KEY

Y Voted for (yea).
\# Paired for.
+ Announced for.
N Voted against (nay).
X Paired against.
- Announced against.
P Voted "present".
C Voted "present" to avoid possible conflict of interest.
? Did not vote or otherwise make a position known.

Democrats   *Republicans*

	193	194	195	196	197	198	199
ALABAMA							
1 *Edwards*	Y	Y	Y	Y	Y	Y	Y
2 *Dickinson*	Y	Y	Y	N	Y	Y	N
3 Nichols	Y	Y	Y	N	Y	Y	N
4 Bevill	Y	Y	N	Y	Y	N	Y
5 Flippo	Y	Y	N	N	Y	N	Y
6 Erdreich	Y	Y	N	Y	Y	Y	Y
7 Shelby	Y	Y	Y	Y	Y	N	N
ALASKA							
AL *Young*	?	Y	Y	Y	Y	Y	N
ARIZONA							
1 *McCain*	N	Y	N	Y	N	Y	N
2 Udall	Y	Y	N	Y	N	Y	N
3 *Stump*	N	Y	Y	N	N	Y	N
4 *Rudd*	Y	Y	N	N	Y	Y	N
5 McNulty	Y	Y	N	Y	N	Y	Y
ARKANSAS							
1 Alexander	Y	Y	N	N	?	?	?
2 *Bethune*	Y	Y	?	Y	?	?	?
3 *Hammerschmidt*	N	Y	N	N	N	Y	N
4 Anthony	Y	Y	N	N	Y	N	Y
CALIFORNIA							
1 Bosco	Y	Y	N	N	Y	N	Y
2 *Chappie*	Y	Y	N	N	Y	Y	N
3 Matsui	Y	Y	N	N	Y	N	Y
4 Fazio	Y	Y	N	N	Y	N	Y
5 Vacancy							
6 Boxer	Y	Y	N	Y	Y	N	Y
7 Miller	Y	Y	N	Y	Y	N	Y
8 Dellums	Y	Y	N	Y	N	Y	Y
9 Stark	Y	Y	Y	N	Y	N	Y
10 Edwards	Y	Y	N	N	Y	N	Y
11 Lantos	Y	Y	N	Y	Y	N	Y
12 *Zschau*	N	N	N	Y	N	Y	Y
13 Mineta	Y	Y	N	Y	Y	N	Y
14 *Shumway*	N	N	N	Y	N	Y	N
15 Coelho	Y	Y	N	N	Y	N	Y
16 Panetta	Y	Y	N	Y	Y	N	Y
17 *Pashayan*	Y	Y	N	Y	N	Y	N
18 Lehman	Y	Y	N	Y	N	Y	Y
19 *Lagomarsino*	Y	Y	Y	Y	N	Y	N
20 *Thomas*	Y	N	Y	X	?	Y	X
21 *Fiedler*	N	Y	Y	Y	N	Y	N
22 *Moorhead*	N	Y	N	Y	N	Y	N
23 Beilenson	Y	Y	N	Y	N	Y	Y
24 Waxman	Y	Y	N	Y	Y	N	Y
25 Roybal	Y	Y	N	Y	N	Y	Y
26 Berman	Y	Y	N	N	Y	N	Y
27 Levine	Y	Y	N	N	Y	N	Y
28 Dixon	Y	Y	N	N	Y	N	Y
29 Hawkins	Y	Y	N	N	Y	N	Y
30 Martinez	?	?	?	?	?	?	?
31 Dymally	Y	Y	N	Y	Y	N	Y
32 Anderson	Y	Y	N	N	Y	N	Y
33 *Dreier*	N	N	N	Y	N	Y	N
34 Torres	Y	Y	N	N	Y	N	Y
35 *Lewis*	Y	Y	N	N	Y	Y	Y
36 Brown	Y	Y	N	N	Y	N	Y
37 *McCandless*	N	Y	N	N	Y	Y	N
38 Patterson	Y	?	X	?	?	?	#
39 *Dannemeyer*	N	N	Y	N	N	Y	N
40 *Badham*	N	Y	N	N	Y	N	Y
41 *Lowery*	N	N	Y	Y	N	Y	N
42 *Lungren*	N	N	Y	Y	N	Y	N

	193	194	195	196	197	198	199
43 *Packard*	N	N	N	Y	N	Y	N
44 Bates	Y	Y	N	N	Y	N	Y
45 *Hunter*	N	Y	Y	Y	N	Y	N
COLORADO							
1 Schroeder	Y	Y	N	Y	Y	Y	N
2 Wirth	Y	Y	N	N	Y	N	Y
3 Kogovsek	Y	Y	N	Y	Y	N	Y
4 *Brown*	N	N	Y	N	Y	N	Y
5 *Kramer*	N	Y	Y	Y	N	Y	N
6 *Schaefer*	N	Y	Y	Y	N	Y	N
CONNECTICUT							
1 Kennelly	Y	Y	N	N	Y	N	Y
2 Gejdenson	Y	Y	N	N	Y	N	Y
3 Morrison	Y	Y	N	N	Y	N	Y
4 *McKinney*	Y	Y	Y	Y	Y	Y	N
5 Ratchford	Y	Y	N	N	Y	N	Y
6 *Johnson*	N	Y	#	#	?	?	?
DELAWARE							
AL *Carper*	N	Y	Y	Y	Y	Y	Y
FLORIDA							
1 Hutto	Y	Y	N	N	Y	N	N
2 Fuqua	Y	Y	N	N	Y	N	Y
3 Bennett	Y	Y	N	N	Y	N	Y
4 Chappell	Y	Y	N	N	Y	N	Y
5 *McCollum*	Y	Y	Y	N	N	Y	N
6 MacKay	Y	Y	N	N	Y	N	Y
7 Gibbons	Y	Y	N	N	Y	N	Y
8 *Young*	Y	Y	Y	N	N	Y	N
9 *Bilirakis*	N	Y	Y	N	N	Y	N
10 Ireland	Y	Y	N	N	Y	N	Y
11 Nelson	Y	Y	N	N	N	N	N
12 *Lewis*	Y	Y	Y	N	N	Y	N
13 *Mack*	N	N	Y	N	Y	N	Y
14 Mica	Y	Y	N	N	Y	N	Y
15 *Shaw*	Y	Y	Y	N	N	Y	N
16 Smith	Y	Y	N	Y	Y	N	Y
17 Lehman	Y	Y	N	N	Y	N	Y
18 Pepper	Y	Y	N	N	Y	N	Y
19 Fascell	Y	Y	N	N	Y	N	Y
GEORGIA							
1 Thomas	N	Y	N	N	Y	N	Y
2 Hatcher	N	Y	N	Y	N	Y	Y
3 Ray	N	Y	N	Y	N	Y	Y
4 Levitas	N	Y	N	N	Y	N	Y
5 Fowler	Y	Y	N	N	Y	N	Y
6 *Gingrich*	N	Y	Y	N	N	Y	N
7 McDonald	N	N	Y	N	N	Y	N
8 Rowland	N	Y	N	N	Y	N	Y
9 Jenkins	N	Y	N	N	Y	N	Y
10 Barnard	Y	Y	N	N	Y	N	Y
HAWAII							
1 Heftel	?	?	?	?	?	?	?
2 Akaka	?	Y	X	N	Y	N	Y
IDAHO							
1 *Craig*	N	N	Y	Y	N	Y	N
2 *Hansen*	?	?	Y	?	?	Y	N
ILLINOIS							
1 Vacancy							
2 Savage	Y	Y	N	N	Y	N	Y
3 Russo	Y	Y	N	N	Y	N	Y
4 *O'Brien*	Y	Y	N	N	Y	Y	Y
5 Lipinski	Y	Y	N	N	Y	Y	Y
6 *Hyde*	Y	Y	Y	N	Y	N	Y
7 Collins	Y	Y	N	N	Y	N	Y
8 Rostenkowski	Y	?	?	?	?	?	?
9 Yates	?	?	N	N	Y	N	Y
10 *Porter*	Y	Y	N	N	Y	N	Y
11 Annunzio	Y	Y	N	N	Y	N	Y
12 *Crane, P.*	N	N	Y	N	N	Y	N
13 *Erlenborn*	?	?	#	?	?	?	X
14 *Corcoran*	Y	Y	Y	N	N	Y	N
15 *Madigan*	Y	?	Y	Y	N	Y	N
16 *Martin*	Y	Y	Y	Y	Y	Y	N
17 Evans	Y	Y	N	Y	Y	N	?
18 *Michel*	Y	Y	Y	Y	Y	Y	N
19 *Crane, D.*	N	N	Y	N	N	Y	N
20 Durbin	Y	Y	N	Y	Y	Y	Y
21 Price	Y	Y	N	N	Y	Y	Y
22 Simon	Y	Y	?	?	?	?	#
INDIANA							
1 Hall	Y	Y	N	N	Y	N	Y
2 Sharp	N	Y	Y	N	N	Y	Y
3 *Hiler*	N	N	Y	N	Y	N	Y
4 *Coats*	N	Y	Y	Y	N	Y	N
5 Hillis	Y	Y	N	N	Y	N	Y

ND - Northern Democrats   SD - Southern Democrats

	193	194	195	196	197	198	199
6 ***Burton***	N	N	Y	Y	N	Y	N
7 ***Myers***	Y	Y	Y	N	N	Y	Y
8 McCloskey	Y	Y	N	N	Y	N	Y
9 Hamilton	Y	Y	N	Y	Y	Y	Y
10 Jacobs	N	Y	Y	Y	Y	Y	N
IOWA							
1 ***Leach***	N	Y	Y	Y	Y	Y	N
2 ***Tauke***	N	Y	N	Y	Y	Y	N
3 ***Evans***	N	Y	Y	N	Y	Y	N
4 Smith	Y	Y	N	N	Y	N	Y
5 Harkin	Y	Y	N	Y	Y	N	Y
6 Bedell	N	Y	Y	N	Y	N	Y
KANSAS							
1 ***Roberts***	N	Y	Y	Y	N	Y	N
2 Slattery	N	Y	Y	Y	Y	Y	N
3 ***Winn***	N	Y	Y	N	N	Y	X
4 Glickman	N	Y	N	Y	Y	N	Y
5 ***Whittaker***	N	Y	Y	N	N	Y	N
KENTUCKY							
1 Hubbard	N	Y	Y	Y	N	N	N
2 Natcher	Y	Y	N	N	Y	N	Y
3 Mazzoli	Y	Y	N	N	Y	N	Y
4 ***Snyder***	Y	Y	N	N	N	Y	Y
5 ***Rogers***	N	Y	Y	Y	N	Y	N
6 ***Hopkins***	N	Y	Y	N	N	Y	N
7 Perkins	Y	Y	N	N	Y	N	Y
LOUISIANA							
1 ***Livingston***	N	?	N	N	N	Y	Y
2 Boggs	Y	Y	N	N	?	N	Y
3 Tauzin	N	Y	N	Y	Y	Y	N
4 Roemer	N	Y	Y	Y	Y	Y	N
5 Huckaby	Y	Y	N	N	Y	Y	N
6 ***Moore***	N	Y	Y	N	N	Y	N
7 Breaux	N	Y	N	Y	Y	Y	N
8 Long	Y	Y	N	N	Y	N	Y
MAINE							
1 ***McKernan***	Y	N	Y	Y	N	Y	N
2 ***Snowe***	Y	Y	Y	N	Y	Y	N
MARYLAND							
1 Dyson	Y	Y	Y	Y	N	N	N
2 Long	Y	Y	N	Y	Y	N	Y
3 Mikulski	Y	Y	N	Y	Y	N	Y
4 ***Holt***	N	Y	Y	Y	?	?	?
5 Hoyer	Y	Y	N	Y	Y	N	Y
6 Byron	N	Y	Y	Y	Y	Y	N
7 Mitchell	Y	Y	N	N	Y	N	Y
8 Barnes	Y	Y	N	Y	Y	N	Y
MASSACHUSETTS							
1 ***Conte***	Y	Y	N	Y	Y	Y	Y
2 Boland	Y	Y	N	N	Y	N	Y
3 Early	Y	Y	N	N	Y	N	Y
4 Frank	Y	Y	N	Y	Y	N	?
5 Shannon	Y	Y	N	N	Y	N	Y
6 Mavroules	Y	Y	N	N	Y	N	Y
7 Markey	Y	Y	N	Y	Y	N	Y
8 O'Neill							
9 Moakley	Y	Y	N	N	Y	N	Y
10 Studds	?	?	N	Y	Y	N	Y
11 Donnelly	Y	Y	N	N	Y	N	Y
MICHIGAN							
1 Conyers	Y	Y	N	Y	Y	N	Y
2 ***Pursell***	N	Y	N	Y	Y	Y	Y
3 Wolpe	Y	Y	N	N	Y	N	Y
4 ***Siljander***	N	Y	N	Y	N	Y	N
5 ***Sawyer***	Y	Y	Y	N	N	Y	N
6 Carr	Y	Y	N	N	Y	N	Y
7 Kildee	Y	Y	N	Y	Y	N	Y
8 Traxler	Y	Y	N	N	Y	N	Y
9 ***Vander Jagt***	Y	N	?	Y	N	Y	Y
10 Albosta	Y	Y	N	N	Y	N	Y
11 ***Davis***	Y	Y	Y	Y	N	Y	Y
12 Bonior	Y	Y	N	N	Y	N	Y
13 Crockett	Y	Y	N	N	Y	N	Y
14 Hertel	Y	Y	N	N	Y	N	N
15 Ford	Y	Y	N	N	Y	N	Y
16 Dingell	Y	Y	N	N	Y	N	Y
17 Levin	Y	Y	N	N	Y	N	Y
18 ***Broomfield***	Y	Y	Y	Y	N	Y	N
MINNESOTA							
1 Penny	N	Y	N	N	Y	N	Y
2 ***Weber***	N	N	Y	N	N	Y	N
3 ***Frenzel***	N	N	Y	N	N	Y	N
4 Vento	Y	Y	N	N	Y	N	Y
5 Sabo	Y	Y	N	N	Y	N	Y
6 Sikorski	Y	Y	N	N	Y	N	Y

	193	194	195	196	197	198	199
7 ***Stangeland***	N	Y	N	N	Y	Y	Y
8 Oberstar	Y	Y	N	N	Y	N	Y
MISSISSIPPI							
1 Whitten	Y	Y	N	N	Y	N	Y
2 ***Franklin***	N	Y	Y	Y	N	Y	N
3 Montgomery	N	Y	Y	N	Y	Y	N
4 Dowdy	Y	Y	N	N	Y	N	Y
5 ***Lott***	Y	Y	Y	N	N	Y	N
MISSOURI							
1 Clay	Y	Y	N	N	Y	N	Y
2 Young	Y	Y	N	N	Y	N	Y
3 Gephardt	Y	Y	N	N	Y	N	Y
4 Skelton	N	Y	N	Y	Y	Y	N
5 Wheat	Y	Y	N	N	Y	N	Y
6 ***Coleman***	Y	Y	Y	N	N	Y	Y
7 ***Taylor***	Y	Y	Y	N	N	Y	N
8 ***Emerson***	Y	Y	Y	Y	N	Y	N
9 Volkmer	N	Y	N	N	Y	Y	Y
MONTANA							
1 Williams	?	Y	N	Y	Y	N	Y
2 ***Marlenee***	N	Y	Y	N	Y	Y	N
NEBRASKA							
1 ***Bereuter***	N	Y	Y	Y	Y	Y	Y
2 ***Daub***	Y	Y	Y	Y	N	Y	N
3 ***Smith***	N	Y	Y	Y	Y	Y	N
NEVADA							
1 Reid	Y	Y	N	N	Y	N	Y
2 ***Vucanovich***	N	Y	Y	Y	N	Y	Y
NEW HAMPSHIRE							
1 D'Amours	?	Y	N	Y	Y	N	Y
2 ***Gregg***	N	N	Y	N	N	Y	N
NEW JERSEY							
1 Florio	Y	Y	N	N	?	?	#
2 Hughes	Y	Y	N	N	Y	N	Y
3 Howard	Y	Y	N	N	Y	N	Y
4 ***Smith***	Y	Y	Y	Y	N	N	Y
5 ***Roukema***	?	Y	Y	N	Y	Y	N
6 Dwyer	Y	Y	N	N	Y	N	Y
7 ***Rinaldo***	Y	Y	N	N	Y	N	Y
8 Roe	Y	Y	N	N	Y	N	Y
9 Torricelli	Y	Y	N	N	Y	N	Y
10 Rodino	Y	Y	N	N	Y	N	Y
11 Minish	Y	Y	N	N	Y	N	Y
12 ***Courter***	Y	Y	Y	N	N	Y	N
13 ***Forsythe***	Y	Y	Y	N	N	Y	N
14 Guarini	Y	Y	N	N	Y	N	Y
NEW MEXICO							
1 ***Lujan***	Y	?	Y	N	N	Y	N
2 ***Skeen***	N	Y	N	Y	N	Y	N
3 Richardson	Y	?	N	N	Y	N	Y
NEW YORK							
1 ***Carney***	Y	Y	Y	N	N	Y	N
2 Downey	Y	Y	N	N	Y	N	Y
3 Mrazek	Y	Y	N	N	Y	N	Y
4 ***Lent***	Y	Y	Y	N	N	Y	Y
5 ***McGrath***	Y	N	Y	Y	N	Y	N
6 Addabbo	Y	Y	N	N	Y	N	Y
7 Ackerman	Y	Y	N	Y	Y	N	Y
8 Scheuer	Y	Y	N	N	Y	N	Y
9 Ferraro	Y	Y	N	N	Y	N	Y
10 Schumer	Y	?	N	Y	Y	?	?
11 Towns	Y	Y	N	N	Y	N	Y
12 Owens	Y	Y	N	N	Y	N	Y
13 Solarz	Y	Y	N	Y	Y	N	Y
14 ***Molinari***	Y	Y	Y	N	Y	N	Y
15 ***Green***	Y	Y	Y	N	Y	N	Y
16 Rangel	Y	Y	N	Y	Y	N	Y
17 Weiss	Y	Y	N	Y	Y	N	Y
18 Garcia	Y	?	N	N	Y	N	Y
19 Biaggi	Y	Y	N	N	Y	N	#
20 Ottinger	Y	Y	N	N	Y	N	Y
21 ***Fish***	Y	Y	N	Y	N	Y	Y
22 ***Gilman***	Y	Y	N	N	Y	Y	Y
23 Stratton	Y	Y	N	N	N	N	Y
24 ***Solomon***	Y	N	Y	N	Y	Y	N
25 ***Boehlert***	Y	Y	N	Y	Y	Y	Y
26 ***Martin***	Y	Y	?	X	?	Y	N
27 ***Wortley***	Y	Y	Y	N	N	Y	N
28 McHugh	Y	Y	N	Y	Y	N	Y
29 ***Horton***	Y	Y	Y	N	Y	Y	Y
30 ***Conable***	N	N	Y	N	N	Y	N
31 ***Kemp***	?	Y	N	N	N	Y	N
32 LaFalce	Y	N	N	?	Y	N	Y
33 Nowak	Y	Y	N	N	Y	N	Y
34 Lundine	Y	Y	N	Y	Y	N	Y

	193	194	195	196	197	198	199
NORTH CAROLINA							
1 Jones	Y	Y	N	N	Y	N	Y
2 Valentine	Y	Y	N	Y	Y	Y	Y
3 Whitley	Y	Y	N	N	Y	N	Y
4 Andrews	?	Y	N	N	Y	Y	Y
5 Neal	Y	Y	N	N	Y	Y	N
6 Britt	Y	Y	N	N	Y	Y	Y
7 Rose	Y	Y	N	N	Y	N	Y
8 Hefner	Y	Y	N	N	Y	N	Y
9 ***Martin***	N	N	Y	N	N	Y	N
10 ***Broyhill***	N	N	Y	N	N	Y	N
11 Clarke	Y	Y	N	Y	Y	N	Y
NORTH DAKOTA							
AL Dorgan	N	Y	N	N	Y	N	Y
OHIO							
1 Luken	Y	Y	N	N	Y	N	Y
2 ***Gradison***	N	Y	Y	Y	N	Y	N
3 Hall	N	Y	Y	N	Y	N	Y
4 ***Oxley***	Y	Y	N	N	N	Y	N
5 ***Latta***	N	Y	Y	N	N	Y	N
6 ***McEwen***	N	Y	Y	N	N	Y	Y
7 ***DeWine***	N	N	Y	Y	N	Y	N
8 ***Kindness***	Y	Y	Y	N	N	Y	N
9 Kaptur	Y	Y	N	N	Y	N	Y
10 ***Miller***	N	Y	Y	Y	Y	Y	N
11 Eckart	Y	Y	N	Y	Y	N	Y
12 ***Kasich***	Y	N	Y	N	N	Y	N
13 Pease	Y	Y	N	Y	Y	N	Y
14 Seiberling	Y	Y	N	Y	Y	N	Y
15 ***Wylie***	Y	Y	Y	Y	N	Y	N
16 ***Regula***	Y	Y	Y	N	Y	Y	N
17 ***Williams***	Y	Y	N	N	Y	Y	N
18 Applegate	Y	Y	N	N	Y	N	Y
19 Feighan	Y	Y	N	Y	Y	N	Y
20 Oakar	Y	Y	N	N	Y	N	Y
21 Stokes	Y	Y	N	Y	Y	N	Y
OKLAHOMA							
1 Jones	N	Y	N	Y	Y	N	?
2 Synar	Y	Y	N	N	Y	N	Y
3 Watkins	N	Y	N	N	Y	N	Y
4 McCurdy	N	Y	Y	Y	Y	N	Y
5 ***Edwards***	Y	N	N	N	N	Y	N
6 English	?	Y	Y	Y	Y	N	Y
OREGON							
1 AuCoin	Y	Y	N	N	Y	N	Y
2 ***Smith, R.***	N	?	?	#	?	?	X
3 Wyden	Y	Y	N	Y	Y	N	Y
4 Weaver	Y	Y	N	Y	Y	N	N
5 ***Smith, D.***	N	N	Y	Y	N	Y	N
PENNSYLVANIA							
1 Foglietta	Y	Y	N	N	Y	?	?
2 Gray	Y	Y	N	N	Y	N	Y
3 Borski	Y	Y	N	N	Y	N	?
4 Kolter	Y	Y	N	N	N	N	Y
5 ***Schulze***	Y	Y	Y	N	N	Y	N
6 Yatron	Y	Y	N	Y	Y	N	Y
7 Edgar	Y	N	N	N	Y	N	Y
8 Kostmayer	Y	Y	N	Y	Y	N	Y
9 ***Shuster***	N	Y	?	?	?	?	?
10 ***McDade***	Y	Y	N	Y	N	Y	Y
11 Harrison	Y	Y	N	N	Y	N	Y
12 Murtha	Y	Y	N	N	Y	N	Y
13 ***Coughlin***	Y	Y	Y	Y	Y	Y	N
14 Coyne	Y	Y	N	Y	Y	N	Y
15 ***Ritter***	Y	Y	Y	N	N	Y	N
16 ***Walker***	N	N	Y	N	N	Y	N
17 ***Gekas***	Y	Y	Y	Y	N	Y	N
18 Walgren	Y	Y	N	Y	N	N	Y
19 ***Goodling***	N	Y	Y	Y	N	Y	N
20 Gaydos	Y	Y	N	N	Y	N	Y
21 ***Ridge***	Y	Y	Y	Y	N	Y	Y
22 Murphy	Y	Y	N	N	Y	Y	Y
23 ***Clinger***	Y	Y	N	N	Y	Y	Y
RHODE ISLAND							
1 St Germain	Y	Y	N	N	Y	N	Y
2 ***Schneider***	Y	Y	N	Y	N	Y	Y
SOUTH CAROLINA							
1 ***Hartnett***	N	N	Y	N	N	Y	N
2 ***Spence***	N	Y	N	N	N	Y	N
3 Derrick	N	Y	N	N	Y	N	Y
4 ***Campbell***	?	Y	N	N	N	Y	N
5 Spratt	Y	Y	N	N	Y	N	Y
6 Tallon	Y	Y	N	N	Y	N	Y
SOUTH DAKOTA							
AL Daschle	Y	Y	N	N	Y	?	?

	193	194	195	196	197	198	199
TENNESSEE							
1 ***Quillen***	N	Y	Y	N	N	Y	N
2 ***Duncan***	Y	Y	Y	N	N	Y	N
3 Lloyd	Y	Y	N	N	N	N	N
4 Cooper	Y	Y	N	Y	Y	N	Y
5 Boner	Y	Y	N	N	Y	N	Y
6 Gore	Y	Y	N	Y	Y	N	Y
7 ***Sundquist***	N	Y	Y	Y	N	Y	N
8 Jones	Y	Y	N	N	N	N	N
9 Ford	Y	Y	N	N	Y	N	Y
TEXAS							
1 Hall, S.	N	Y	Y	N	N	Y	N
2 Wilson	Y	?	N	N	Y	?	?
3 ***Bartlett***	N	Y	N	Y	N	Y	N
4 Hall, R.	N	Y	N	N	?	Y	N
5 Bryant	Y	Y	N	N	Y	N	Y
6 ***Gramm***	N	N	Y	Y	N	Y	N
7 ***Archer***	N	Y	N	N	N	Y	N
8 ***Fields***	N	Y	N	N	N	Y	N
9 Brooks	Y	Y	N	Y	Y	N	?
10 Pickle	Y	Y	N	Y	Y	Y	Y
11 Leath	Y	Y	Y	Y	N	Y	N
12 Wright	Y	Y	N	Y	Y	N	Y
13 Hightower	Y	Y	Y	Y	Y	Y	N
14 Patman	N	Y	N	N	N	Y	N
15 de la Garza	Y	Y	N	N	Y	N	Y
16 Coleman	?	Y	N	Y	Y	N	Y
17 Stenholm	N	Y	Y	Y	N	Y	N
18 Leland	?	Y	N	N	Y	N	Y
19 Hance	N	Y	N	Y	Y	Y	N
20 Gonzalez	Y	Y	N	N	Y	N	Y
21 ***Loeffler***	N	Y	Y	Y	N	Y	N
22 ***Paul***	N	N	Y	N	N	Y	N
23 Kazen	Y	Y	N	N	N	Y	N
24 Frost	?	Y	N	N	Y	N	Y
25 Andrews	N	Y	N	N	N	N	Y
26 Vandergriff	Y	Y	N	Y	N	Y	N
27 Ortiz	Y	?	N	Y	Y	N	Y
UTAH							
1 ***Hansen***	N	N	Y	Y	N	Y	N
2 ***Marriott***	N	Y	Y	Y	N	Y	N
3 ***Nielson***	?	N	Y	Y	N	Y	N
VERMONT							
AL ***Jeffords***	Y	Y	Y	Y	Y	Y	Y
VIRGINIA							
1 ***Bateman***	Y	N	N	Y	Y	Y	N
2 ***Whitehurst***	N	Y	N	N	N	Y	N
3 ***Bliley***	N	Y	N	Y	N	Y	N
4 Sisisky	N	Y	N	Y	Y	N	Y
5 Daniel	N	Y	Y	N	N	Y	N
6 Olin	N	Y	N	N	Y	N	Y
7 ***Robinson***	Y	Y	Y	Y	N	Y	N
8 ***Parris***	?	Y	Y	Y	Y	N	Y
9 Boucher	Y	Y	N	Y	Y	N	Y
10 ***Wolf***	Y	Y	N	Y	Y	N	Y
WASHINGTON							
1 ***Pritchard***	Y	Y	Y	Y	Y	Y	?
2 Swift	N	Y	N	N	Y	N	Y
3 Bonker	?	Y	N	Y	Y	N	Y
4 ***Morrison***	N	Y	Y	N	N	Y	N
5 Foley	Y	Y	N	N	Y	N	Y
6 Dicks	Y	Y	N	N	Y	N	Y
7 Lowry	Y	Y	N	N	Y	N	Y
8 ***Chandler***	N	Y	Y	Y	N	Y	N
WEST VIRGINIA							
1 Mollohan	Y	Y	N	Y	Y	Y	Y
2 Staggers	Y	Y	N	Y	Y	N	Y
3 Wise	Y	Y	N	Y	Y	N	Y
4 Rahall	Y	Y	N	Y	Y	N	Y
WISCONSIN							
1 Aspin	Y	?	N	N	Y	N	Y
2 Kastenmeier	Y	Y	N	N	Y	N	Y
3 ***Gunderson***	N	Y	Y	Y	N	Y	N
4 Zablocki	Y	Y	N	N	Y	N	Y
5 Moody	Y	Y	N	N	Y	N	Y
6 ***Petri***	N	Y	Y	Y	N	Y	Y
7 Obey	Y	Y	N	N	Y	N	Y
8 ***Roth***	N	Y	Y	N	N	Y	N
9 ***Sensenbrenner***	N	N	Y	N	N	Y	N
WYOMING							
AL ***Cheney***	N	N	Y	Y	N	Y	N

Southern states - Ala., Ark., Fla., Ga., Ky., La., Miss., N.C., Okla., S.C., Tenn., Texas, Va.

200. Procedural Motion. Coats, R-Ind., motion to approve the House *Journal* of Wednesday, June 22. Motion agreed to 355-34: R 135-22; D 220-12 (ND 138-11, SD 82-1), June 23, 1983.

201. H Con Res 91. First Budget Resolution, Fiscal 1984. Adoption of the rule (H Res 243) providing for House floor consideration of the conference version of the resolution to set budget targets for the fiscal year ending Sept. 30, 1984. Adopted 265-150: R 11-149; D 254-1 (ND 166-0, SD 88-1), June 23, 1983.

202. HR 1183. Tax Rate Equity Act. Bonior, D-Mich., motion to order the previous question (thus ending debate and the possibility of amendment) on the rule (H Res 242) providing for House floor consideration of the bill to place a $720 per family limit on the 10 percent individual income tax cut scheduled for July 1, 1983. Motion agreed to 255-165: R 0-163; D 255-2 (ND 169-1, SD 86-1), June 23, 1983.

203. HR 1183. Tax Rate Equity Act. Adoption of the rule (H Res 242) providing for House floor consideration of the bill to place a $720 per family limit on the 10 percent individual income tax cut scheduled for July 1, 1983. Adopted 253-166: R 0-162; D 253-4 (ND 167-2, SD 86-2), June 23, 1983.

204. H Con Res 91. First Budget Resolution, Fiscal 1984. Jones, D-Okla., motion to approve the substitute resolution, agreed to by House-Senate conferees but reported in technical disagreement, to set budget targets for the fiscal year ending Sept. 30, 1984, as follows *(totals including reserve fund items in parentheses)*: budget authority, $919.5 billion ($928.725 billion); outlays, $849.5 billion ($858.925 billion); revenues, $679.6 billion; deficit, $169.9 billion ($179.325 billion). The resolution also set preliminary goals for fiscal 1985-86, revised budget levels for fiscal 1983, and included reconciliation instructions requiring House and Senate committees to recommend legislative savings to meet the budget targets. Motion agreed to 239-186: R 10-153; D 229-33 (ND 164-9, SD 65-24), June 23, 1983.

205. HR 1183. Tax Rate Equity Act. McCurdy, D-Okla., amendment to call for a reduction in fiscal 1984 spending by at least the amount that is expected to be raised by placing a $720 per family limit on the individual income tax cut scheduled for July 1, 1983. Adopted 267-155: R 11-152; D 256-3 (ND 170-2, SD 86-1), June 23, 1983.

206. HR 1183. Tax Rate Equity Act. Frenzel, R-Minn., motion to recommit the bill to the Ways and Means Committee with instructions to strike the $720 tax-cut limit and replace it with language calling for legislation to reduce fiscal 1984 spending by at least $12 billion. Motion rejected 181-241: R 163-0; D 18-241 (ND 3-169, SD 15-72), June 23, 1983.

207. HR 1183. Tax Rate Equity Act. Passage of the bill to place a $720 per family limit on the 10 percent individual income tax cut scheduled for July 1, 1983. Passed 229-191: R 0-162; D 229-29 (ND 161-11, SD 68-18), June 23, 1983. A "nay" was a vote supporting the president's position.

KEY

Y	Voted for (yea).
#	Paired for.
+	Announced for.
N	Voted against (nay).
X	Paired against.
-	Announced against.
P	Voted "present".
C	Voted "present" to avoid possible conflict of interest.
?	Did not vote or otherwise make a position known.

Democrats **Republicans**

	200	201	202	203	204	205	206	207
ALABAMA								
1 *Edwards*	Y	N	N	N	N	N	Y	N
2 *Dickinson*	N	N	N	N	N	N	Y	N
3 Nichols	Y	Y	Y	N	Y	N	Y	Y
4 Bevill	Y	Y	Y	Y	Y	Y	Y	Y
5 Flippo	Y	Y	Y	Y	Y	Y	Y	Y
6 Erdreich	Y	Y	Y	Y	Y	Y	N	Y
7 Shelby	Y	Y	Y	N	Y	Y	N	N
ALASKA								
AL *Young*	N	N	N	N	N	N	Y	N
ARIZONA								
1 *McCain*	Y	N	N	N	N	N	Y	N
2 Udall	Y	Y	Y	Y	Y	Y	N	Y
3 *Stump*	Y	N	N	N	N	N	Y	N
4 *Rudd*	Y	N	N	N	N	N	Y	N
5 McNulty	Y	Y	Y	Y	Y	Y	N	Y
ARKANSAS								
1 Alexander	?	#	#	#	#	Y	N	Y
2 *Bethune*	?	?	N	N	N	N	Y	N
3 *Hammerschmidt*	N	N	N	N	N	N	Y	N
4 Anthony	?	Y	Y	Y	Y	Y	N	Y
CALIFORNIA								
1 Bosco	?	Y	Y	Y	Y	Y	N	N
2 *Chappie*	Y	N	N	N	N	N	Y	N
3 Matsui	Y	Y	Y	Y	Y	Y	N	Y
4 Fazio	Y	Y	Y	Y	Y	Y	N	Y
5 Vacancy								
6 Boxer	Y	Y	Y	Y	Y	N	N	Y
7 Miller	N	Y	Y	Y	Y	N	N	Y
8 Dellums	?	Y	Y	Y	N	Y	N	Y
9 Stark	Y	Y	Y	N	Y	N	N	Y
10 Edwards	Y	Y	Y	Y	Y	N	N	Y
11 Lantos	Y	Y	Y	Y	Y	Y	N	Y
12 Zschau	Y	N	N	N	N	N	Y	N
13 Mineta	Y	Y	Y	Y	Y	N	N	Y
14 *Shumway*	Y	N	N	N	N	N	Y	N
15 Coelho	Y	Y	Y	Y	Y	Y	N	Y
16 Panetta	Y	Y	Y	Y	Y	Y	N	Y
17 *Pashayan*	Y	N	N	N	N	N	Y	N
18 Lehman	Y	Y	Y	Y	Y	Y	N	Y
19 *Lagomarsino*	Y	N	N	N	N	N	Y	N
20 *Thomas*	?	X	X	X	X	X	#	X
21 *Fiedler*	Y	N	N	N	N	N	Y	N
22 *Moorhead*	Y	N	N	N	N	N	Y	N
23 Beilenson	Y	Y	Y	Y	Y	Y	N	Y
24 Waxman	Y	Y	Y	Y	Y	Y	N	Y
25 Roybal	Y	Y	Y	Y	Y	Y	N	Y
26 Berman	Y	Y	Y	Y	Y	Y	N	Y
27 Levine	Y	Y	Y	Y	Y	Y	N	Y
28 Dixon	Y	Y	Y	Y	Y	Y	N	Y
29 Hawkins	Y	Y	Y	Y	Y	Y	N	Y
30 Martinez	?	?	?	?	?	?	?	?
31 Dymally	Y	Y	Y	Y	Y	Y	N	Y
32 Anderson	?	Y	Y	Y	Y	Y	N	Y
33 *Dreier*	Y	N	N	N	N	N	Y	N
34 Torres	Y	Y	Y	Y	Y	Y	N	Y
35 *Lewis*	N	N	N	N	N	N	Y	N
36 Brown	?	Y	Y	Y	Y	Y	N	Y
37 *McCandless*	Y	N	N	N	N	N	Y	N
38 Patterson	Y	Y	Y	Y	Y	Y	N	Y
39 *Dannemeyer*	Y	N	N	N	N	N	Y	N
40 *Badham*	Y	N	N	N	N	N	Y	N
41 *Lowery*	Y	N	N	N	N	N	Y	N
42 *Lungren*	Y	N	N	N	N	N	Y	N

	200	201	202	203	204	205	206	207
43 *Packard*	Y	N	N	N	N	N	Y	N
44 Bates	Y	Y	Y	Y	Y	Y	N	Y
45 *Hunter*	Y	N	N	N	N	N	Y	N
COLORADO								
1 Schroeder	N	Y	Y	Y	Y	Y	N	Y
2 Wirth	?	?	Y	Y	Y	Y	N	Y
3 Kogovsek	Y	Y	Y	Y	Y	Y	N	Y
4 *Brown*	N	N	N	N	N	N	Y	N
5 *Kramer*	Y	N	N	N	N	N	Y	N
6 *Schaefer*	N	N	N	N	N	N	Y	N
CONNECTICUT								
1 Kennelly	Y	Y	Y	Y	Y	Y	N	Y
2 Gejdenson	N	Y	Y	Y	Y	Y	N	Y
3 Morrison	Y	Y	Y	Y	Y	Y	N	Y
4 *McKinney*	Y	Y	N	N	Y	N	Y	N
5 Ratchford	Y	Y	Y	Y	Y	Y	N	Y
6 *Johnson*	Y	N	N	N	Y	N	Y	N
DELAWARE								
AL Carper	Y	Y	Y	Y	Y	Y	N	Y
FLORIDA								
1 Hutto	Y	Y	Y	N	Y	N	Y	N
2 Fuqua	Y	Y	Y	Y	Y	Y	N	Y
3 Bennett	Y	Y	Y	Y	Y	Y	N	Y
4 Chappell	Y	Y	Y	N	Y	N	Y	N
5 *McCollum*	Y	N	N	N	N	N	Y	N
6 MacKay	Y	Y	Y	Y	Y	Y	N	Y
7 Gibbons	Y	Y	Y	Y	Y	Y	N	Y
8 *Young*	Y	N	N	N	N	N	Y	N
9 *Bilirakis*	N	N	N	N	N	N	Y	N
10 Ireland	Y	Y	Y	Y	N	Y	Y	N
11 Nelson	Y	Y	Y	Y	Y	Y	N	Y
12 *Lewis*	N	N	N	N	N	N	Y	N
13 *Mack*	N	N	N	N	N	N	Y	N
14 Mica	Y	Y	Y	Y	Y	Y	N	Y
15 *Shaw*	N	N	N	N	N	N	Y	N
16 Smith	Y	Y	Y	Y	Y	Y	N	Y
17 Lehman	Y	Y	Y	Y	Y	Y	N	Y
18 Pepper	?	Y	Y	Y	Y	Y	N	Y
19 Fascell	Y	Y	Y	Y	Y	Y	N	Y
GEORGIA								
1 Thomas	Y	Y	Y	Y	Y	Y	N	Y
2 Hatcher	Y	Y	Y	Y	Y	Y	N	Y
3 Ray	Y	Y	Y	Y	N	Y	Y	Y
4 Levitas	Y	Y	Y	Y	Y	Y	N	N
5 Fowler	Y	Y	Y	Y	Y	Y	N	Y
6 *Gingrich*	Y	N	N	N	N	N	Y	N
7 *McDonald*	Y	N	N	N	N	N	Y	N
8 Rowland	Y	Y	Y	Y	Y	Y	N	Y
9 Jenkins	Y	Y	Y	Y	Y	Y	N	Y
10 Barnard	Y	Y	Y	Y	N	Y	Y	N
HAWAII								
1 Heftel	?	#	#	#	#	#	X	#
2 Akaka	Y	Y	Y	Y	Y	Y	N	Y
IDAHO								
1 *Craig*	N	N	N	N	N	N	Y	N
2 *Hansen*	?	X	N	N	N	N	Y	N
ILLINOIS								
1 Vacancy								
2 Savage	Y	Y	Y	Y	Y	Y	N	Y
3 Russo	Y	Y	Y	Y	Y	Y	N	N
4 *O'Brien*	Y	N	N	N	N	N	Y	N
5 Lipinski	N	Y	Y	Y	Y	Y	N	Y
6 *Hyde*	Y	N	N	N	N	N	Y	N
7 Collins	Y	Y	Y	Y	Y	Y	N	Y
8 Rostenkowski	Y	Y	Y	Y	Y	Y	N	Y
9 Yates	N	Y	Y	Y	Y	Y	N	Y
10 *Porter*	Y	N	N	N	N	N	Y	N
11 Annunzio	Y	Y	Y	Y	Y	Y	N	Y
12 *Crane, P.*	Y	N	N	N	N	N	Y	N
13 *Erlenborn*	?	X	X	X	?	?	?	X
14 *Corcoran*	Y	N	N	N	N	N	Y	-
15 *Madigan*	Y	N	N	N	N	N	Y	N
16 *Martin*	N	N	N	N	N	N	Y	N
17 Evans	Y	Y	Y	Y	Y	Y	N	Y
18 *Michel*	Y	N	N	N	N	N	Y	N
19 *Crane, D.*	N	N	N	N	N	N	Y	N
20 Durbin	N	Y	Y	Y	Y	Y	N	Y
21 Price	Y	Y	Y	Y	Y	Y	N	Y
22 Simon	?	?	Y	Y	Y	Y	N	Y
INDIANA								
1 Hall	Y	Y	Y	Y	Y	Y	N	Y
2 Sharp	Y	Y	Y	Y	Y	Y	N	Y
3 *Hiler*	N	N	N	N	N	N	Y	N
4 *Coats*	N	N	N	N	N	N	Y	N
5 Hillis	Y	N	N	N	N	N	Y	N

ND - Northern Democrats   SD - Southern Democrats

Corresponding to Congressional Record Votes 210, 211, 212, 213, 214, 216, 217, 218

	200	201	202	203	204	205	206	207
6 ***Burton***	N	N	N	N	N	N	Y	N
7 ***Myers***	Y	N	N	N	N	N	Y	N
8 McCloskey	Y	Y	Y	Y	Y	Y	N	N
9 Hamilton	Y	Y	Y	Y	Y	Y	N	Y
10 Jacobs	P	Y	N	N	N	#	X	#
IOWA								
1 ***Leach***	Y	?	N	?	N	N	Y	N
2 ***Tauke***	Y	Y	N	N	N	N	Y	N
3 ***Evans***	N	N	N	N	N	N	Y	N
4 Smith	Y	Y	Y	Y	N	Y	N	N
5 Harkin	N	Y	Y	Y	Y	Y	N	Y
6 Bedell	Y	Y	Y	Y	Y	Y	N	Y
KANSAS								
1 ***Roberts***	N	N	N	N	N	N	Y	N
2 Slattery	Y	Y	Y	Y	Y	Y	N	Y
3 ***Winn***	Y	N	N	N	N	N	Y	N
4 Glickman	Y	Y	Y	Y	Y	Y	N	Y
5 ***Whittaker***	Y	N	N	N	N	N	Y	N
KENTUCKY								
1 Hubbard	Y	Y	Y	Y	Y	Y	N	Y
2 Natcher	Y	Y	Y	Y	Y	Y	N	N
3 Mazzoli	Y	Y	Y	Y	Y	N	N	N
4 ***Snyder***	Y	N	N	N	N	Y	Y	N
5 ***Rogers***	Y	N	N	N	N	N	Y	N
6 ***Hopkins***	Y	N	N	N	N	Y	Y	N
7 Perkins	Y	Y	Y	Y	Y	Y	N	Y
LOUISIANA								
1 ***Livingston***	Y	N	N	N	N	N	Y	N
2 Boggs	Y	Y	Y	Y	Y	Y	N	Y
3 Tauzin	Y	Y	Y	Y	N	Y	Y	N
4 Roemer	N	Y	Y	Y	N	Y	Y	N
5 Huckaby	Y	Y	Y	Y	N	Y	N	Y
6 ***Moore***	Y	N	N	N	N	N	Y	N
7 Breaux	?	Y	Y	Y	N	Y	N	Y
8 Long	Y	Y	Y	Y	Y	Y	N	Y
MAINE								
1 ***McKernan***	Y	N	N	N	N	N	Y	N
2 ***Snowe***	Y	Y	N	N	N	N	Y	N
MARYLAND								
1 Dyson	Y	Y	Y	Y	N	Y	N	Y
2 Long	Y	Y	Y	N	Y	Y	Y	N
3 Mikulski	Y	Y	Y	Y	Y	Y	N	Y
4 ***Holt***	N	N	N	N	N	N	Y	N
5 Hoyer	Y	Y	Y	Y	Y	Y	N	Y
6 Byron	Y	Y	Y	Y	N	Y	Y	N
7 Mitchell	?	Y	Y	Y	Y	Y	N	Y
8 Barnes	Y	Y	Y	Y	Y	Y	N	Y
MASSACHUSETTS								
1 ***Conte***	Y	N	N	N	N	N	Y	N
2 Boland	Y	Y	Y	Y	Y	Y	N	Y
3 Early	Y	Y	Y	Y	Y	Y	N	Y
4 Frank	Y	Y	Y	Y	Y	N	N	Y
5 Shannon	Y	Y	Y	Y	Y	Y	N	Y
6 Mavroules	Y	Y	Y	Y	Y	Y	N	Y
7 Markey	Y	Y	Y	Y	Y	Y	N	Y
8 O'Neill								
9 Moakley	Y	Y	Y	Y	Y	Y	N	Y
10 Studds	Y	Y	Y	Y	Y	N	N	Y
11 Donnelly	Y	Y	Y	Y	Y	Y	N	Y
MICHIGAN								
1 Conyers	Y	Y	Y	Y	Y	Y	N	Y
2 ***Pursell***	Y	N	N	N	N	N	Y	N
3 Wolpe	Y	Y	Y	Y	Y	Y	N	Y
4 ***Siljander***	Y	N	N	N	N	N	Y	N
5 ***Sawyer***	Y	N	N	N	N	N	Y	N
6 Carr	Y	Y	Y	Y	Y	Y	N	N
7 Kildee	Y	Y	Y	Y	Y	Y	N	Y
8 Traxler	Y	Y	Y	Y	Y	Y	N	Y
9 ***Vander Jagt***	Y	N	N	N	N	N	Y	N
10 Albosta	Y	Y	Y	Y	Y	Y	N	Y
11 ***Davis***	Y	N	N	N	N	N	Y	N
12 Bonior	Y	Y	Y	Y	Y	Y	N	Y
13 Crockett	?	Y	Y	Y	Y	Y	N	Y
14 Hertel	Y	Y	Y	Y	Y	Y	N	Y
15 Ford	?	Y	Y	Y	Y	Y	N	Y
16 Dingell	?	Y	Y	Y	Y	Y	N	Y
17 Levin	Y	Y	Y	Y	Y	Y	N	Y
18 ***Broomfield***	Y	N	N	N	N	N	Y	N
MINNESOTA								
1 Penny	Y	Y	Y	Y	Y	Y	N	Y
2 ***Weber***	Y	N	N	N	N	N	Y	N
3 ***Frenzel***	N	N	N	N	N	N	Y	N
4 Vento	Y	Y	Y	Y	Y	Y	N	Y
5 Sabo	N	Y	Y	Y	Y	Y	N	Y
6 Sikorski	N	Y	Y	Y	Y	Y	N	Y
7 ***Stangeland***	Y	N	N	N	N	N	Y	N
8 Oberstar	P	Y	Y	Y	Y	Y	N	Y
MISSISSIPPI								
1 Whitten	Y	Y	Y	Y	Y	Y	N	Y
2 ***Franklin***	Y	N	N	N	N	N	Y	N
3 Montgomery	Y	Y	Y	Y	N	Y	N	Y
4 Dowdy	Y	Y	Y	Y	Y	Y	N	Y
5 ***Lott***	Y	N	N	N	N	N	Y	N
MISSOURI								
1 Clay	N	Y	Y	Y	Y	Y	N	Y
2 Young	Y	Y	Y	Y	Y	Y	Y	N
3 Gephardt	Y	Y	Y	Y	Y	Y	N	Y
4 Skelton	Y	Y	Y	Y	N	Y	N	Y
5 Wheat	Y	Y	Y	Y	Y	Y	N	Y
6 ***Coleman***	Y	N	N	N	N	N	Y	N
7 ***Taylor***	Y	N	N	N	N	N	Y	N
8 ***Emerson***	N	N	N	N	N	N	Y	N
9 Volkmer	Y	Y	Y	Y	Y	Y	N	Y
MONTANA								
1 Williams	Y	Y	Y	Y	Y	Y	N	Y
2 ***Marlenee***	Y	N	N	N	N	N	Y	N
NEBRASKA								
1 ***Bereuter***	Y	N	N	N	N	N	Y	N
2 ***Daub***	N	N	N	N	N	Y	Y	N
3 ***Smith***	Y	N	N	N	N	N	Y	N
NEVADA								
1 Reid	Y	Y	Y	Y	Y	Y	N	Y
2 ***Vucanovich***	Y	N	N	N	N	N	Y	N
NEW HAMPSHIRE								
1 D'Amours	Y	Y	Y	Y	Y	Y	N	Y
2 ***Gregg***	Y	N	N	N	N	N	Y	N
NEW JERSEY								
1 Florio	Y	Y	Y	Y	Y	Y	N	Y
2 Hughes	Y	Y	Y	Y	Y	Y	N	Y
3 Howard	Y	Y	Y	Y	Y	Y	N	Y
4 ***Smith***	Y	Y	N	N	Y	N	Y	N
5 ***Roukema***	Y	Y	X	N	Y	Y	Y	N
6 Dwyer	Y	Y	Y	Y	Y	Y	N	Y
7 ***Rinaldo***	Y	Y	N	N	Y	N	Y	N
8 Roe	Y	Y	Y	Y	Y	Y	N	Y
9 Torricelli	Y	Y	Y	Y	Y	Y	N	Y
10 Rodino	Y	Y	Y	Y	Y	Y	N	Y
11 Minish	Y	Y	Y	Y	Y	Y	N	Y
12 ***Courter***	Y	N	N	N	N	N	Y	N
13 ***Forsythe***	?	N	N	N	N	N	Y	N
14 Guarini	Y	Y	Y	Y	Y	Y	N	Y
NEW MEXICO								
1 ***Lujan***	Y	N	N	N	N	Y	Y	N
2 ***Skeen***	Y	N	N	N	N	N	Y	N
3 Richardson	Y	Y	Y	Y	Y	Y	N	Y
NEW YORK								
1 ***Carney***	Y	N	N	N	N	N	Y	N
2 Downey	Y	Y	Y	Y	Y	Y	N	N
3 Mrazek	Y	Y	Y	Y	Y	Y	N	Y
4 ***Lent***	Y	N	N	N	N	N	Y	N
5 ***McGrath***	Y	N	N	N	N	N	Y	N
6 Addabbo	Y	Y	Y	Y	Y	Y	N	Y
7 Ackerman	Y	Y	Y	Y	Y	Y	N	Y
8 Scheuer	Y	Y	Y	Y	Y	Y	N	Y
9 Ferraro	Y	Y	Y	Y	Y	Y	N	Y
10 Schumer	?	?	?	?	Y	Y	N	Y
11 Towns	?	#	#	#	Y	Y	N	Y
12 Owens	Y	Y	Y	Y	Y	Y	N	Y
13 Solarz	Y	Y	Y	Y	Y	Y	N	Y
14 ***Molinari***	Y	N	N	N	N	N	Y	N
15 ***Green***	Y	Y	N	N	Y	N	Y	N
16 Rangel	?	#	Y	Y	Y	Y	N	Y
17 Weiss	Y	Y	Y	Y	Y	Y	N	Y
18 Garcia	?	#	#	#	Y	Y	N	Y
19 Biaggi	Y	Y	Y	Y	Y	Y	N	Y
20 Ottinger	P	Y	Y	Y	Y	Y	N	Y
21 ***Fish***	Y	N	N	N	N	N	Y	N
22 ***Gilman***	Y	Y	N	N	N	N	Y	N
23 Stratton	Y	Y	Y	Y	Y	Y	N	Y
24 ***Solomon***	?	N	N	N	N	N	Y	N
25 ***Boehlert***	Y	N	N	N	N	N	Y	N
26 ***Martin***	Y	N	N	N	N	N	Y	N
27 ***Wortley***	Y	N	N	N	N	N	Y	N
28 McHugh	Y	Y	Y	Y	Y	Y	N	Y
29 ***Horton***	Y	Y	N	N	N	N	Y	N
30 ***Conable***	Y	N	N	N	N	N	Y	N
31 ***Kemp***	?	N	N	X	N	N	Y	N
32 LaFalce	Y	Y	Y	Y	Y	Y	N	Y
33 Nowak	Y	Y	Y	Y	Y	Y	N	Y
34 Lundine	Y	Y	Y	Y	Y	Y	N	Y
NORTH CAROLINA								
1 Jones	Y	Y	Y	Y	Y	Y	N	Y
2 Valentine	Y	Y	Y	?	Y	Y	N	Y
3 Whitley	Y	Y	Y	Y	Y	Y	N	Y
4 Andrews	Y	Y	Y	Y	Y	Y	N	Y
5 Neal	Y	Y	?	Y	N	Y	N	Y
6 Britt	Y	Y	Y	Y	Y	Y	N	Y
7 Rose	Y	Y	Y	Y	Y	?	?	?
8 Hefner	Y	Y	Y	Y	Y	Y	N	Y
9 ***Martin***	Y	N	N	N	N	N	Y	N
10 ***Broyhill***	Y	N	N	N	N	N	Y	N
11 Clarke	Y	Y	Y	Y	Y	Y	N	Y
NORTH DAKOTA								
AL Dorgan	Y	Y	Y	Y	Y	Y	N	Y
OHIO								
1 Luken	Y	Y	Y	Y	Y	Y	N	Y
2 ***Gradison***	Y	N	N	N	N	N	Y	N
3 Hall	Y	Y	Y	Y	Y	Y	N	Y
4 ***Oxley***	Y	N	N	N	N	N	Y	N
5 ***Latta***	Y	N	N	N	N	N	Y	N
6 ***McEwen***	Y	N	N	N	N	Y	Y	N
7 ***DeWine***	Y	N	N	N	N	N	Y	N
8 ***Kindness***	Y	N	N	N	N	Y	Y	N
9 Kaptur	Y	Y	Y	Y	Y	Y	N	Y
10 ***Miller***	N	N	N	N	N	Y	Y	N
11 Eckart	N	Y	Y	Y	Y	Y	N	Y
12 ***Kasich***	Y	N	N	N	N	N	Y	N
13 Pease	Y	Y	Y	Y	Y	Y	N	Y
14 Seiberling	Y	Y	Y	Y	Y	Y	N	Y
15 ***Wylie***	Y	N	N	N	N	N	Y	N
16 ***Regula***	Y	N	N	N	N	N	Y	N
17 ***Williams***	Y	N	N	N	Y	Y	Y	N
18 Applegate	Y	Y	Y	Y	N	Y	N	N
19 Feighan	?	?	Y	Y	Y	Y	N	Y
20 Oakar	Y	Y	Y	Y	Y	Y	N	Y
21 Stokes	?	Y	Y	Y	Y	Y	N	Y
OKLAHOMA								
1 Jones	Y	Y	Y	Y	Y	Y	N	Y
2 Synar	Y	Y	Y	Y	Y	Y	N	Y
3 Watkins	Y	Y	Y	Y	Y	Y	N	Y
4 McCurdy	Y	Y	Y	Y	Y	Y	N	Y
5 ***Edwards***	Y	N	N	N	N	N	Y	N
6 English	Y	Y	?	Y	N	Y	Y	Y
OREGON								
1 AuCoin	?	Y	Y	Y	Y	Y	N	Y
2 ***Smith, R.***	?	X	X	X	X	X	#	X
3 Wyden	Y	Y	Y	Y	Y	Y	N	Y
4 Weaver	Y	Y	Y	Y	Y	Y	N	Y
5 ***Smith, D.***	Y	N	N	N	N	N	Y	N
PENNSYLVANIA								
1 Foglietta	Y	Y	Y	Y	Y	Y	N	Y
2 Gray	Y	Y	Y	Y	Y	Y	N	Y
3 Borski	Y	Y	Y	Y	Y	Y	N	Y
4 Kolter	?	Y	Y	Y	Y	Y	N	Y
5 ***Schulze***	Y	N	N	N	N	N	Y	N
6 Yatron	Y	Y	Y	Y	Y	Y	N	Y
7 Edgar	Y	Y	Y	Y	Y	Y	N	Y
8 Kostmayer	Y	Y	Y	Y	Y	Y	N	Y
9 ***Shuster***	Y	N	N	N	N	N	Y	N
10 ***McDade***	Y	N	N	N	N	N	Y	N
11 Harrison	Y	Y	Y	Y	Y	Y	N	Y
12 Murtha	Y	Y	Y	Y	Y	Y	N	Y
13 ***Coughlin***	N	N	N	N	N	N	Y	N
14 Coyne	Y	Y	Y	Y	Y	Y	N	Y
15 ***Ritter***	Y	N	N	N	N	N	Y	N
16 ***Walker***	N	N	N	N	N	N	Y	N
17 ***Gekas***	Y	N	N	N	N	N	Y	N
18 Walgren	Y	Y	Y	Y	Y	Y	N	Y
19 ***Goodling***	N	N	N	N	N	N	Y	N
20 Gaydos	Y	Y	Y	Y	Y	Y	N	Y
21 ***Ridge***	Y	N	N	N	N	N	Y	N
22 Murphy	Y	Y	Y	Y	Y	Y	N	Y
23 ***Clinger***	Y	N	N	N	N	N	Y	N
RHODE ISLAND								
1 St Germain	P	Y	Y	Y	Y	Y	N	Y
2 ***Schneider***	Y	Y	N	N	Y	N	Y	N
SOUTH CAROLINA								
1 ***Hartnett***	N	N	N	N	N	N	Y	N
2 ***Spence***	Y	N	N	N	N	N	Y	N
3 Derrick	Y	Y	Y	Y	Y	Y	N	Y
4 ***Campbell***	Y	N	N	N	N	N	Y	N
5 Spratt	Y	Y	Y	Y	Y	Y	N	Y
6 Tallon	Y	Y	Y	Y	Y	Y	N	Y
SOUTH DAKOTA								
AL Daschle	Y	Y	Y	Y	Y	Y	N	Y
TENNESSEE								
1 ***Quillen***	Y	N	N	N	N	N	Y	N
2 ***Duncan***	Y	N	N	N	N	N	Y	N
3 Lloyd	Y	Y	Y	Y	N	Y	N	Y
4 Cooper	Y	Y	Y	Y	Y	Y	N	Y
5 Boner	Y	Y	Y	Y	Y	Y	N	Y
6 Gore	Y	Y	Y	Y	Y	?	?	#
7 ***Sundquist***	?	X	N	N	N	N	Y	N
8 Jones	Y	Y	Y	Y	Y	Y	N	Y
9 Ford	?	Y	Y	Y	Y	Y	N	Y
TEXAS								
1 Hall, S.	Y	Y	Y	Y	N	Y	Y	X
2 Wilson	Y	Y	Y	Y	N	Y	N	Y
3 ***Bartlett***	Y	N	N	N	N	N	Y	N
4 Hall, R.	Y	Y	Y	Y	N	Y	Y	N
5 Bryant	?	Y	Y	Y	Y	Y	N	Y
6 ***Gramm***	Y	N	N	N	N	N	Y	N
7 ***Archer***	Y	N	N	N	N	N	Y	N
8 ***Fields***	N	N	N	N	N	N	Y	N
9 Brooks	Y	Y	Y	Y	Y	Y	N	Y
10 Pickle	Y	Y	Y	Y	Y	Y	N	Y
11 Leath	Y	Y	Y	Y	N	Y	Y	N
12 Wright	Y	Y	Y	Y	Y	Y	N	Y
13 Hightower	Y	Y	Y	Y	Y	Y	Y	N
14 Patman	Y	Y	Y	Y	Y	Y	N	N
15 de la Garza	?	Y	Y	Y	Y	Y	N	Y
16 Coleman	Y	Y	Y	Y	Y	Y	N	Y
17 Stenholm	Y	Y	Y	Y	N	Y	Y	Y
18 Leland	Y	Y	Y	Y	Y	?	?	#
19 Hance	Y	Y	Y	Y	Y	Y	N	Y
20 Gonzalez	Y	Y	Y	Y	Y	Y	N	Y
21 ***Loeffler***	Y	N	N	N	N	N	Y	N
22 ***Paul***	Y	N	N	N	N	N	Y	N
23 Kazen	Y	Y	Y	Y	Y	Y	N	Y
24 Frost	Y	Y	Y	Y	Y	Y	N	Y
25 Andrews	Y	Y	Y	Y	Y	Y	N	Y
26 Vandergriff	Y	Y	Y	Y	N	Y	Y	Y
27 Ortiz	Y	Y	Y	Y	Y	Y	N	Y
UTAH								
1 ***Hansen***	Y	N	N	N	N	N	Y	N
2 ***Marriott***	Y	N	N	N	-	N	Y	N
3 ***Nielson***	Y	N	N	N	N	-	+	?
VERMONT								
AL ***Jeffords***	Y	N	N	N	Y	N	Y	N
VIRGINIA								
1 ***Bateman***	Y	N	N	N	N	N	Y	N
2 ***Whitehurst***	Y	N	N	N	N	N	Y	N
3 ***Bliley***	Y	N	N	N	N	N	Y	N
4 Sisisky	Y	Y	Y	Y	Y	Y	N	Y
5 Daniel	Y	Y	Y	Y	N	Y	Y	N
6 Olin	Y	Y	Y	Y	Y	Y	N	Y
7 ***Robinson***	Y	N	N	N	N	N	Y	N
8 ***Parris***	N	N	N	N	N	N	Y	N
9 Boucher	Y	Y	Y	Y	Y	Y	N	Y
10 ***Wolf***	Y	N	N	N	N	N	Y	N
WASHINGTON								
1 ***Pritchard***	?	Y	N	N	Y	N	Y	N
2 Swift	Y	Y	Y	Y	Y	Y	N	Y
3 Bonker	Y	Y	Y	Y	Y	Y	N	Y
4 ***Morrison***	Y	N	N	N	N	N	Y	N
5 Foley	Y	Y	Y	Y	Y	Y	N	Y
6 Dicks	Y	Y	Y	?	Y	Y	N	Y
7 Lowry	Y	Y	Y	Y	Y	Y	N	Y
8 ***Chandler***	Y	N	N	N	N	N	Y	N
WEST VIRGINIA								
1 Mollohan	Y	Y	Y	Y	Y	Y	N	Y
2 Staggers	Y	Y	Y	Y	Y	Y	N	Y
3 Wise	Y	Y	Y	Y	Y	Y	N	Y
4 Rahall	Y	Y	Y	Y	Y	Y	N	Y
WISCONSIN								
1 Aspin	?	Y	Y	Y	Y	Y	N	Y
2 Kastenmeier	Y	Y	Y	Y	N	Y	N	Y
3 ***Gunderson***	Y	N	N	N	N	Y	Y	N
4 Zablocki	Y	Y	Y	Y	Y	Y	N	Y
5 Moody	Y	Y	Y	Y	Y	Y	N	Y
6 ***Petri***	Y	N	N	N	N	N	Y	N
7 Obey	?	Y	Y	Y	Y	Y	N	Y
8 ***Roth***	Y	N	N	N	N	N	Y	N
9 ***Sensenbrenner***	Y	N	N	N	N	N	Y	N
WYOMING								
AL ***Cheney***	Y	N	N	N	N	N	Y	N

Southern states - Ala., Ark., Fla., Ga., Ky., La., Miss., N.C., Okla., S.C., Tenn., Texas, Va.

208. HR 3132. Energy and Water Development Appropriations, Fiscal 1984. Conte, R-Mass., motion to instruct conferees on the fiscal 1984 energy and water development appropriations bill to insist on the House position not including funds for construction on the Garrison Diversion unit in North Dakota. Motion rejected 150-215: R 89-57; D 61-158 (ND 49-94, SD 12-64), June 23, 1983.

209. Procedural Motion. Walker, R-Pa., motion to approve the House *Journal* of Monday, June 27. Motion agreed to 366-22: R 147-10; D 219-12 (ND 141-11, SD 78-1), June 28, 1983.

210. HR 3363. Interior Appropriations, Fiscal 1984. Hiler, R-Ind., amendments offered *en bloc* to reduce appropriations in the bill for the National Endowment for the Arts and National Endowment for the Humanities by $40 million, returning them to fiscal 1983 levels. Rejected 150-271: R 118-47; D 32-224 (ND 6-164, SD 26-60), June 28, 1983.

211. HR 3363. Interior Appropriations, Fiscal 1984. McDade, R-Pa., amendment to reduce program funding contained in the bill by 4 percent across-the-board, with certain exceptions. Adopted 211-209: R 164-1; D 47-208 (ND 14-155, SD 33-53), June 28, 1983. (This amendment subsequently was defeated after the House rose from the Committee of the Whole (*see vote 212, below*).)

212. HR 3363. Interior Appropriations, Fiscal 1984. McDade, R-Pa., amendment to reduce program funding contained in the bill by 4 percent across-the-board, with certain exceptions. Rejected 206-213: R 164-0; D 42-213 (ND 10-159, SD 32-54), June 28, 1983. (This amendment previously had been adopted in the Committee of the Whole (*see vote 211, above*).)

213. HR 3363. Interior Appropriations, Fiscal 1984. Passage of the bill to appropriate $8,081,974,000 for the Interior Department and related agencies in fiscal 1984. Passed 272-144: R 49-114; D 223-30 (ND 163-4, SD 60-26), June 28, 1983. The president had requested $6,700,928,000 in new budget authority.

214. HR 3398. Omnibus Minor Tariff Amendments. Gibbons, D-Fla., motion to suspend the rules and pass the bill to make 23 minor changes in tariff and customs laws. Motion agreed to 368-43: R 137-25; D 231-18 (ND 150-15, SD 81-3), June 28, 1983. A two-thirds majority of those present and voting (274 in this case) is required for passage under suspension of the rules.

215. HR 3133. Department of Housing and Urban Development Appropriations, Fiscal 1984. Adoption of the conference report on the bill to appropriate $55,789,340,000 for the Department of Housing and Urban Development and 17 independent agencies in fiscal 1984. Adopted 314-99: R 84-76; D 230-23 (ND 158-7, SD 72-16), June 29, 1983. The president had requested $49,561,458,896 in new budget authority.

KEY

Y Voted for (yea).
\# Paired for.
\+ Announced for.
N Voted against (nay).
X Paired against.
\- Announced against.
P Voted "present".
C Voted "present" to avoid possible conflict of interest.
? Did not vote or otherwise make a position known.

Democrats *Republicans*

	208	209	210	211	212	213	214	215
ALABAMA								
1 *Edwards*	N	Y	N	Y	Y	Y	Y	Y
2 *Dickinson*	N	N	Y	Y	Y	N	Y	Y
3 Nichols	N	Y	Y	Y	Y	N	Y	Y
4 Bevill	N	Y	Y	N	N	Y	Y	Y
5 Flippo	?	Y	Y	N	N	N	Y	Y
6 Erdreich	?	Y	N	Y	N	Y	N	Y
7 Shelby	N	Y	N	Y	Y	N	Y	N
ALASKA								
AL *Young*	N	N	N	Y	Y	Y	Y	Y
ARIZONA								
1 *McCain*	N	Y	N	N	Y	N	Y	Y
2 Udall	N	Y	N	N	N	Y	Y	Y
3 *Stump*	N	Y	Y	Y	Y	N	N	N
4 *Rudd*	N	Y	Y	Y	Y	N	N	N
5 McNulty	?	Y	N	N	N	Y	Y	Y
ARKANSAS								
1 Alexander	N	Y	?	?	?	?	?	Y
2 *Bethune*	N	Y	Y	Y	Y	N	Y	Y
3 *Hammerschmidt*	N	Y	N	Y	Y	Y	Y	Y
4 Anthony	N	Y	N	Y	Y	Y	Y	Y
CALIFORNIA								
1 Bosco	?	Y	N	N	N	Y	Y	Y
2 *Chappie*	Y	Y	Y	Y	Y	N	N	Y
3 Matsui	N	Y	N	N	N	Y	Y	Y
4 Fazio	?	Y	N	N	N	Y	Y	Y
5 Burton *			N	N	N	Y	Y	Y
6 Boxer	?	Y	N	N	N	Y	Y	Y
7 Miller	?	Y	N	N	N	Y	Y	Y
8 Dellums	Y	Y	N	N	N	Y	Y	Y
9 Stark	N	Y	N	N	N	Y	Y	Y
10 Edwards	Y	Y	N	N	N	Y	Y	Y
11 Lantos	Y	Y	N	N	N	Y	Y	Y
12 *Zschau*	Y	Y	N	Y	Y	N	Y	N
13 Mineta	N	Y	N	N	N	Y	Y	Y
14 *Shumway*	N	Y	Y	Y	Y	N	Y	N
15 Coelho	N	Y	N	N	N	Y	Y	Y
16 Panetta	N	Y	N	N	N	Y	Y	Y
17 *Pashayan*	N	Y	Y	Y	Y	Y	N	Y
18 Lehman	N	Y	N	N	N	Y	Y	Y
19 *Lagomarsino*	Y	Y	Y	Y	Y	N	Y	N
20 *Thomas*	?	Y	Y	Y	Y	N	Y	Y
21 *Fiedler*	Y	Y	Y	Y	Y	Y	Y	Y
22 *Moorhead*	Y	Y	Y	Y	Y	N	Y	N
23 Beilenson	N	Y	N	N	N	Y	Y	Y
24 Waxman	?	?	N	N	N	Y	Y	Y
25 Roybal	N	Y	N	N	N	Y	Y	Y
26 Berman	?	Y	N	N	N	Y	Y	Y
27 Levine	Y	Y	N	N	N	Y	Y	Y
28 Dixon	N	?	N	N	N	Y	Y	Y
29 Hawkins	?	N	N	N	N	Y	Y	Y
30 Martinez	?	?	?	?	?	?	?	?
31 Dymally	N	Y	N	N	N	Y	Y	?
32 Anderson	N	Y	N	N	N	Y	Y	Y
33 *Dreier*	Y	Y	Y	Y	Y	N	Y	N
34 Torres	N	Y	N	N	N	Y	Y	Y
35 *Lewis*	Y	Y	N	Y	Y	Y	Y	Y
36 Brown	?	Y	N	N	N	Y	Y	Y
37 *McCandless*	N	Y	Y	Y	Y	Y	N	X
38 Patterson	N	Y	N	N	N	Y	Y	Y
39 *Dannemeyer*	Y	Y	Y	Y	Y	N	Y	N
40 *Badham*	N	Y	Y	Y	Y	Y	N	Y
41 *Lowery*	Y	Y	N	Y	Y	N	Y	?
42 *Lungren*	Y	Y	Y	Y	Y	N	Y	N

	208	209	210	211	212	213	214	215
43 *Packard*	Y	Y	N	Y	Y	N	Y	N
44 Bates	Y	Y	N	N	N	Y	Y	Y
45 *Hunter*	Y	Y	Y	Y	Y	N	N	N
COLORADO								
1 Schroeder	?	N	N	N	N	Y	Y	N
2 Wirth	Y	Y	N	N	N	Y	Y	Y
3 Kogovsek	N	Y	N	N	N	Y	Y	Y
4 *Brown*	N	Y	Y	Y	Y	N	N	N
5 *Kramer*	?	Y	Y	Y	Y	N	Y	?
6 *Schaefer*	N	Y	Y	Y	Y	N	N	N
CONNECTICUT								
1 Kennelly	N	Y	N	N	N	Y	Y	Y
2 Gejdenson	?	?	N	N	N	Y	Y	Y
3 Morrison	Y	Y	-	-	-	+	+	Y
4 *McKinney*	Y	Y	N	Y	Y	Y	Y	Y
5 Ratchford	N	Y	N	N	N	Y	Y	Y
6 *Johnson*	#	Y	N	Y	Y	Y	Y	Y
DELAWARE								
AL Carper	Y	Y	Y	Y	Y	Y	Y	Y
FLORIDA								
1 Hutto	N	Y	N	N	N	Y	Y	Y
2 Fuqua	N	Y	N	N	N	Y	Y	Y
3 Bennett	N	Y	Y	Y	Y	N	Y	Y
4 Chappell	N	N	N	N	Y	Y	Y	Y
5 *McCollum*	Y	Y	Y	Y	Y	N	Y	N
6 MacKay	Y	Y	N	N	N	Y	N	Y
7 Gibbons	N	Y	Y	N	N	Y	Y	Y
8 *Young*	Y	Y	Y	Y	Y	N	Y	N
9 *Bilirakis*	Y	Y	Y	Y	Y	N	Y	N
10 Ireland	?	Y	Y	Y	Y	N	Y	N
11 Nelson	N	Y	N	N	N	Y	Y	Y
12 *Lewis*	X	Y	Y	Y	Y	Y	Y	Y
13 *Mack*	Y	Y	Y	Y	Y	N	Y	N
14 Mica	N	Y	N	N	N	Y	Y	Y
15 *Shaw*	Y	Y	Y	Y	Y	N	Y	N
16 Smith	Y	N	N	N	N	Y	Y	Y
17 Lehman	N	Y	N	N	N	Y	Y	Y
18 Pepper	N	Y	N	N	N	Y	Y	Y
19 Fascell	N	Y	N	N	N	Y	Y	Y
GEORGIA								
1 Thomas	Y	Y	N	N	N	Y	Y	Y
2 Hatcher	?	Y	N	N	N	Y	Y	Y
3 Ray	N	Y	Y	Y	Y	N	Y	Y
4 Levitas	N	?	N	N	N	Y	N	Y
5 Fowler	N	Y	N	N	N	Y	Y	Y
6 *Gingrich*	?	Y	Y	Y	Y	N	?	N
7 McDonald	Y	Y	Y	Y	Y	N	Y	N
8 Rowland	N	Y	N	Y	Y	Y	Y	Y
9 Jenkins	N	Y	N	Y	N	Y	Y	Y
10 Barnard	N	?	Y	Y	Y	Y	Y	N
HAWAII								
1 Heftel	?	?	?	?	?	?	?	?
2 Akaka	N	Y	N	N	N	Y	Y	Y
IDAHO								
1 *Craig*	Y	Y	Y	Y	Y	N	Y	N
2 *Hansen*	N	?	Y	Y	Y	N	Y	X
ILLINOIS								
1 Vacancy								
2 Savage	Y	Y	N	N	N	Y	Y	Y
3 Russo	N	Y	N	N	N	Y	Y	Y
4 *O'Brien*	Y	Y	N	Y	Y	Y	Y	Y
5 Lipinski	N	N	N	N	N	Y	Y	Y
6 *Hyde*	N	Y	Y	Y	Y	N	Y	Y
7 Collins	N	?	N	N	N	Y	Y	Y
8 Rostenkowski	N	Y	N	N	N	Y	Y	Y
9 Yates	Y	Y	N	N	N	Y	Y	Y
10 *Porter*	#	Y	N	Y	Y	Y	Y	Y
11 Annunzio	?	Y	N	N	N	Y	Y	Y
12 *Crane, P.*	Y	Y	Y	Y	Y	N	Y	N
13 *Erlenborn*	?	?	?	?	?	?	?	?
14 *Corcoran*	#	Y	Y	Y	Y	N	Y	N
15 *Madigan*	Y	Y	Y	Y	Y	N	Y	N
16 *Martin*	Y	Y	N	Y	Y	N	Y	N
17 Evans	Y	Y	N	N	N	Y	Y	Y
18 *Michel*	Y	Y	Y	Y	Y	N	Y	N
19 *Crane, D.*	Y	Y	Y	Y	Y	N	Y	N
20 Durbin	Y	N	N	N	N	Y	Y	Y
21 Price	N	Y	N	N	N	Y	?	Y
22 Simon	N	?	N	N	N	Y	Y	Y
INDIANA								
1 Hall	N	Y	N	N	N	Y	Y	Y
2 Sharp	N	Y	N	N	N	Y	Y	Y
3 *Hiler*	Y	Y	Y	Y	Y	N	Y	N
4 *Coats*	Y	Y	Y	Y	Y	N	Y	N
5 Hillis	Y	?	N	Y	Y	N	Y	Y

ND - Northern Democrats   SD - Southern Democrats

	208	209	210	211	212	213	214	215
6 ***Burton***	Y	Y	Y	Y	Y	N	N	N
7 ***Myers***	N	Y	N	Y	Y	Y	Y	Y
8 McCloskey	N	Y	N	N	N	Y	Y	Y
9 Hamilton	Y	Y	N	Y	Y	Y	Y	Y
10 Jacobs	?	P	N	Y	Y	N	Y	Y
IOWA								
1 ***Leach***	Y	Y	N	Y	Y	N	Y	Y
2 ***Tauke***	Y	Y	N	Y	Y	N	N	N
3 ***Evans***	Y	N	Y	Y	Y	N	Y	N
4 Smith	N	Y	N	N	N	Y	Y	Y
5 Harkin	N	N	N	N	N	?	?	Y
6 Bedell	Y	?	N	N	N	Y	Y	Y
KANSAS								
1 ***Roberts***	N	Y	Y	Y	Y	N	Y	N
2 Slattery	Y	Y	Y	Y	Y	N	Y	N
3 ***Winn***	N	Y	Y	Y	Y	N	Y	Y
4 Glickman	N	Y	N	N	N	Y	Y	Y
5 ***Whittaker***	N	Y	Y	Y	Y	N	Y	N
KENTUCKY								
1 Hubbard	?	Y	Y	Y	N	N	N	N
2 Natcher	N	Y	N	N	N	Y	Y	Y
3 Mazzoli	N	Y	N	N	N	Y	Y	Y
4 ***Snyder***	N	Y	Y	Y	Y	N	Y	N
5 ***Rogers***	N	Y	Y	Y	Y	Y	N	N
6 ***Hopkins***	N	Y	Y	Y	Y	N	Y	N
7 Perkins	N	Y	N	N	N	Y	Y	Y
LOUISIANA								
1 ***Livingston***	N	?	Y	Y	Y	N	N	Y
2 Boggs	N	Y	N	N	N	Y	Y	Y
3 Tauzin	Y	Y	?	?	?	?	?	?
4 Roemer	Y	N	Y	Y	Y	N	Y	N
5 Huckaby	N	Y	Y	N	N	Y	Y	Y
6 ***Moore***	Y	Y	Y	Y	Y	N	Y	Y
7 Breaux	N	?	Y	N	N	Y	Y	Y
8 Long	N	Y	N	N	N	Y	Y	Y
MAINE								
1 ***McKernan***	Y	Y	N	Y	Y	Y	Y	Y
2 ***Snowe***	Y	Y	N	Y	Y	Y	Y	Y
MARYLAND								
1 Dyson	N	Y	N	N	N	Y	Y	Y
2 Long	?	?	N	N	N	?	?	Y
3 Mikulski	N	Y	N	N	N	Y	Y	Y
4 ***Holt***	N	Y	Y	Y	Y	N	Y	Y
5 Hoyer	N	Y	N	N	N	Y	Y	Y
6 Byron	Y	Y	N	N	N	Y	Y	?
7 Mitchell	N	N	N	N	N	Y	Y	#
8 Barnes	Y	Y	N	N	N	Y	Y	Y
MASSACHUSETTS								
1 ***Conte***	Y	Y	N	Y	Y	Y	Y	Y
2 Boland	N	Y	N	N	N	Y	N	Y
3 Early	N	Y	N	N	N	Y	Y	Y
4 Frank	Y	Y	N	N	N	Y	Y	Y
5 Shannon	N	Y	N	N	N	Y	Y	Y
6 Mavroules	N	?	N	N	N	Y	Y	Y
7 Markey	Y	Y	N	N	N	Y	Y	Y
8 O'Neill								
9 Moakley	?	Y	N	N	Y	Y	Y	Y
10 Studds	Y	Y	N	N	N	Y	Y	Y
11 Donnelly	N	N	N	N	N	Y	Y	Y
MICHIGAN								
1 Conyers	Y	Y	N	?	?	?	Y	Y
2 ***Pursell***	Y	?	Y	Y	Y	N	Y	Y
3 Wolpe	Y	Y	N	N	N	Y	Y	Y
4 ***Siljander***	Y	Y	Y	Y	Y	N	Y	N
5 ***Sawyer***	N	Y	Y	Y	Y	N	Y	Y
6 Carr	N	Y	N	N	N	Y	Y	Y
7 Kildee	Y	Y	N	N	N	Y	Y	Y
8 Traxler	?	Y	N	N	N	Y	Y	Y
9 ***Vander Jagt***	Y	Y	Y	Y	Y	Y	Y	Y
10 Albosta	?	Y	N	N	N	Y	Y	Y
11 ***Davis***	N	Y	N	Y	Y	Y	Y	Y
12 Bonior	Y	Y	N	N	N	Y	Y	Y
13 Crockett	?	Y	N	N	N	Y	Y	?
14 Hertel	Y	Y	N	N	N	Y	N	Y
15 Ford	?	Y	?	?	?	?	?	?
16 Dingell	Y	Y	N	N	N	Y	Y	?
17 Levin	N	Y	N	N	N	Y	Y	Y
18 ***Broomfield***	Y	Y	Y	Y	Y	N	N	Y
MINNESOTA								
1 Penny	N	Y	N	N	N	Y	Y	Y
2 ***Weber***	Y	Y	Y	Y	Y	N	Y	N
3 ***Frenzel***	Y	Y	Y	Y	Y	N	Y	N
4 Vento	Y	Y	N	N	N	Y	Y	Y
5 Sabo	N	N	N	N	N	Y	Y	Y
6 Sikorski	Y	N	N	N	N	Y	Y	Y
7 ***Stangeland***	N	Y	Y	Y	Y	N	Y	N
8 Oberstar	Y	P	N	N	N	Y	Y	Y
MISSISSIPPI								
1 Whitten	N	Y	N	N	N	Y	Y	Y
2 ***Franklin***	N	Y	Y	Y	Y	N	Y	N
3 Montgomery	N	Y	Y	Y	Y	N	Y	N
4 Dowdy	?	Y	N	N	N	Y	Y	Y
5 ***Lott***	N	Y	Y	Y	Y	N	Y	N
MISSOURI								
1 Clay	N	?	N	N	N	Y	Y	Y
2 Young	N	?	N	N	N	Y	Y	Y
3 Gephardt	N	Y	N	N	N	Y	Y	Y
4 Skelton	N	Y	N	N	N	Y	Y	Y
5 Wheat	N	Y	N	N	N	Y	Y	Y
6 ***Coleman***	Y	Y	Y	Y	Y	Y	Y	Y
7 ***Taylor***	N	Y	Y	Y	Y	Y	Y	N
8 ***Emerson***	N	N	Y	Y	Y	N	Y	Y
9 Volkmer	N	Y	N	N	N	N	Y	Y
MONTANA								
1 Williams	N	Y	N	N	N	Y	N	Y
2 ***Marlenee***	N	Y	Y	Y	Y	N	Y	Y
NEBRASKA								
1 ***Bereuter***	N	Y	N	Y	Y	N	Y	N
2 ***Daub***	N	Y	Y	Y	Y	N	Y	Y
3 ***Smith***	N	Y	Y	Y	Y	Y	Y	Y
NEVADA								
1 Reid	N	Y	N	N	N	Y	Y	Y
2 ***Vucanovich***	N	Y	Y	Y	Y	Y	N	N
NEW HAMPSHIRE								
1 D'Amours	Y	Y	N	N	N	Y	Y	Y
2 ***Gregg***	?	?	Y	Y	Y	N	Y	Y
NEW JERSEY								
1 Florio	N	Y	N	N	N	Y	N	Y
2 Hughes	N	Y	N	Y	Y	Y	Y	Y
3 Howard	N	Y	N	N	N	Y	Y	Y
4 ***Smith***	Y	Y	N	Y	Y	Y	Y	Y
5 ***Roukema***	Y	Y	Y	Y	Y	N	Y	Y
6 Dwyer	N	Y	N	N	N	Y	Y	Y
7 ***Rinaldo***	Y	Y	N	Y	Y	Y	Y	Y
8 Roe	N	Y	N	N	N	Y	N	Y
9 Torricelli	Y	Y	N	N	N	Y	Y	Y
10 Rodino	Y	Y	N	N	N	Y	Y	Y
11 Minish	Y	Y	N	N	N	Y	Y	Y
12 ***Courter***	Y	Y	Y	Y	Y	N	Y	Y
13 ***Forsythe***	Y	?	Y	Y	Y	N	Y	N
14 Guarini	N	Y	N	N	N	Y	Y	Y
NEW MEXICO								
1 ***Lujan***	N	Y	N	Y	Y	N	Y	Y
2 ***Skeen***	N	Y	Y	Y	Y	N	Y	N
3 Richardson	N	Y	N	N	N	Y	Y	N
NEW YORK								
1 ***Carney***	N	Y	Y	Y	Y	N	Y	N
2 Downey	?	Y	N	N	N	Y	Y	Y
3 Mrazek	?	Y	N	N	N	Y	Y	Y
4 ***Lent***	?	Y	N	Y	Y	Y	Y	Y
5 ***McGrath***	Y	Y	N	Y	Y	Y	Y	Y
6 Addabbo	?	Y	N	N	N	Y	Y	Y
7 Ackerman	N	Y	N	-	-	+	+	Y
8 Scheuer	N	?	N	N	N	Y	Y	Y
9 Ferraro	N	Y	N	N	N	Y	Y	Y
10 Schumer	?	Y	N	N	N	Y	Y	Y
11 Towns	N	?	N	N	N	Y	Y	Y
12 Owens	N	?	N	N	N	Y	?	Y
13 Solarz	?	Y	N	N	N	Y	Y	Y
14 ***Molinari***	Y	Y	N	Y	Y	Y	Y	Y
15 ***Green***	Y	Y	N	Y	Y	Y	Y	Y
16 Rangel	N	Y	N	N	N	Y	Y	Y
17 Weiss	Y	Y	N	N	N	Y	Y	Y
18 Garcia	N	Y	N	N	N	Y	Y	Y
19 Biaggi	Y	Y	N	N	N	Y	?	Y
20 Ottinger	Y	?	N	N	N	Y	N	Y
21 ***Fish***	?	?	N	Y	Y	Y	Y	Y
22 ***Gilman***	+	Y	N	Y	Y	Y	Y	Y
23 Stratton	Y	Y	N	Y	Y	Y	Y	Y
24 ***Solomon***	Y	N	Y	Y	Y	N	N	N
25 ***Boehlert***	Y	Y	N	Y	Y	Y	Y	Y
26 ***Martin***	Y	Y	Y	Y	Y	N	N	Y
27 ***Wortley***	Y	Y	N	Y	Y	N	Y	Y
28 McHugh	N	?	N	N	N	Y	Y	Y
29 ***Horton***	Y	Y	N	Y	Y	Y	Y	Y
30 ***Conable***	Y	Y	Y	Y	Y	N	Y	N
31 ***Kemp***	?	?	Y	Y	Y	N	Y	Y
32 LaFalce	?	Y	N	N	N	Y	Y	Y
33 Nowak	N	Y	N	N	N	Y	Y	Y
34 Lundine	Y	P	N	N	N	Y	Y	Y
NORTH CAROLINA								
1 Jones	N	?	N	N	N	Y	Y	Y
2 Valentine	Y	Y	Y	Y	Y	Y	Y	N
3 Whitley	N	Y	Y	Y	Y	Y	Y	Y
4 Andrews	N	Y	N	Y	Y	Y	Y	N
5 Neal	N	Y	N	Y	Y	Y	Y	N
6 Britt	N	Y	N	Y	Y	Y	Y	Y
7 Rose	?	Y	?	?	?	?	?	Y
8 Hefner	N	Y	N	N	N	Y	Y	Y
9 ***Martin***	Y	Y	Y	Y	Y	N	Y	N
10 ***Broyhill***	Y	Y	Y	Y	Y	N	Y	N
11 Clarke	Y	Y	N	N	N	Y	Y	Y
NORTH DAKOTA								
AL Dorgan	N	Y	N	N	N	Y	Y	Y
OHIO								
1 Luken	N	Y	N	N	N	Y	Y	Y
2 ***Gradison***	Y	Y	Y	Y	Y	N	Y	N
3 Hall	Y	?	Y	Y	N	Y	N	Y
4 ***Oxley***	Y	Y	Y	Y	Y	N	N	N
5 ***Latta***	X	Y	N	Y	Y	N	Y	N
6 ***McEwen***	N	Y	Y	Y	Y	N	N	N
7 ***DeWine***	Y	Y	Y	Y	Y	N	N	N
8 ***Kindness***	N	Y	Y	Y	Y	N	N	N
9 Kaptur	Y	Y	Y	Y	Y	Y	Y	Y
10 ***Miller***	Y	N	Y	Y	Y	N	N	N
11 Eckart	Y	N	N	N	N	Y	N	Y
12 ***Kasich***	Y	Y	Y	Y	Y	N	N	Y
13 Pease	Y	Y	N	N	N	Y	Y	Y
14 Seiberling	Y	Y	N	N	N	Y	N	Y
15 ***Wylie***	Y	Y	Y	Y	Y	N	Y	Y
16 ***Regula***	N	Y	N	Y	Y	Y	Y	Y
17 ***Williams***	Y	Y	N	Y	Y	Y	Y	#
18 Applegate	?	?	N	N	N	Y	N	N
19 Feighan	?	Y	N	Y	Y	Y	Y	Y
20 Oakar	N	Y	N	N	N	Y	Y	Y
21 Stokes	N	Y	N	N	N	Y	Y	Y
OKLAHOMA								
1 Jones	N	?	N	Y	Y	N	Y	Y
2 Synar	+	Y	N	N	N	Y	Y	Y
3 Watkins	N	Y	N	N	N	Y	?	Y
4 McCurdy	?	Y	N	Y	Y	N	Y	Y
5 ***Edwards***	N	Y	N	Y	Y	Y	N	N
6 English	N	Y	N	Y	Y	N	N	Y
OREGON								
1 AuCoin	Y	Y	N	N	N	Y	Y	Y
2 ***Smith, R.***	?	?	?	?	?	?	?	X
3 Wyden	?	Y	N	N	N	Y	Y	Y
4 Weaver	Y	Y	N	N	N	Y	N	Y
5 ***Smith, D.***	N	Y	Y	Y	Y	N	Y	N
PENNSYLVANIA								
1 Foglietta	N	Y	N	N	N	Y	Y	Y
2 Gray	?	Y	N	N	N	Y	Y	?
3 Borski	N	Y	N	N	N	Y	Y	Y
4 Kolter	N	Y	N	Y	N	N	Y	Y
5 ***Schulze***	Y	Y	Y	Y	Y	Y	Y	Y
6 Yatron	N	Y	N	Y	N	Y	Y	Y
7 Edgar	Y	Y	N	N	N	Y	Y	Y
8 Kostmayer	?	Y	N	N	N	Y	Y	Y
9 ***Shuster***	N	Y	Y	Y	Y	N	Y	N
10 ***McDade***	N	Y	N	Y	Y	Y	Y	Y
11 Harrison	N	Y	?	?	?	?	?	?
12 Murtha	N	Y	N	N	N	Y	Y	Y
13 ***Coughlin***	Y	N	N	Y	Y	Y	Y	Y
14 Coyne	N	Y	N	N	N	Y	Y	Y
15 ***Ritter***	Y	Y	Y	Y	Y	N	Y	Y
16 ***Walker***	Y	N	Y	Y	Y	N	Y	N
17 ***Gekas***	?	Y	Y	Y	Y	Y	Y	N
18 Walgren	Y	Y	N	Y	Y	Y	Y	Y
19 ***Goodling***	Y	N	Y	Y	Y	N	Y	N
20 Gaydos	N	Y	N	Y	N	Y	N	Y
21 ***Ridge***	Y	Y	N	Y	Y	Y	Y	Y
22 Murphy	N	Y	Y	Y	N	Y	N	Y
23 ***Clinger***	Y	Y	N	Y	Y	Y	N	Y
RHODE ISLAND								
1 St Germain	N	P	N	N	N	Y	Y	Y
2 ***Schneider***	?	Y	N	Y	Y	Y	Y	Y
SOUTH CAROLINA								
1 ***Hartnett***	Y	Y	Y	Y	Y	N	Y	N
2 ***Spence***	Y	Y	Y	Y	Y	N	Y	Y
3 Derrick	Y	Y	N	N	N	Y	Y	Y
4 ***Campbell***	N	Y	Y	Y	Y	N	Y	Y
5 Spratt	N	Y	N	Y	Y	Y	Y	Y
6 Tallon	N	Y	N	N	N	Y	Y	Y
SOUTH DAKOTA								
AL Daschle	N	Y	N	N	N	Y	Y	Y
TENNESSEE								
1 ***Quillen***	?	Y	Y	Y	Y	N	Y	Y
2 ***Duncan***	N	Y	Y	Y	Y	Y	Y	Y
3 Lloyd	N	Y	N	N	N	Y	Y	Y
4 Cooper	?	Y	N	N	N	Y	Y	Y
5 Boner	?	Y	N	N	N	Y	Y	Y
6 Gore	?	Y	N	N	N	Y	Y	N
7 ***Sundquist***	Y	Y	Y	Y	Y	N	Y	Y
8 Jones	N	Y	N	N	N	Y	Y	Y
9 Ford	N	?	N	N	N	Y	Y	Y
TEXAS								
1 Hall, S.	N	Y	Y	Y	Y	N	Y	Y
2 Wilson	N	?	N	N	N	Y	Y	Y
3 ***Bartlett***	Y	Y	Y	Y	Y	N	Y	N
4 Hall, R.	N	?	Y	Y	Y	N	Y	Y
5 Bryant	Y	Y	N	N	N	Y	Y	Y
6 ***Gramm***	Y	N	Y	Y	Y	N	Y	N
7 ***Archer***	Y	Y	Y	Y	Y	N	Y	Y
8 ***Fields***	Y	Y	Y	Y	Y	N	Y	Y
9 Brooks	N	?	?	?	?	?	?	Y
10 Pickle	N	?	N	N	N	Y	Y	Y
11 Leath	N	Y	Y	Y	Y	N	Y	?
12 Wright	N	Y	N	N	N	Y	Y	Y
13 Hightower	N	Y	N	N	N	Y	Y	Y
14 Patman	N	Y	Y	Y	Y	N	Y	Y
15 de la Garza	?	?	N	N	N	Y	Y	Y
16 Coleman	N	Y	N	N	N	Y	Y	Y
17 Stenholm	N	Y	Y	Y	Y	N	Y	N
18 Leland	?	Y	N	N	N	Y	?	Y
19 Hance	N	Y	Y	Y	Y	N	Y	N
20 Gonzalez	N	Y	N	N	N	Y	N	Y
21 ***Loeffler***	N	Y	Y	Y	Y	N	Y	N
22 ***Paul***	Y	Y	Y	Y	Y	N	Y	N
23 Kazen	N	Y	N	N	N	Y	Y	Y
24 Frost	N	Y	N	N	N	Y	Y	Y
25 Andrews	Y	Y	Y	Y	Y	N	Y	Y
26 Vandergriff	N	Y	N	N	N	Y	Y	Y
27 Ortiz	N	Y	N	N	N	Y	Y	Y
UTAH								
1 ***Hansen***	N	Y	Y	Y	Y	N	Y	N
2 ***Marriott***	N	Y	N	Y	Y	N	Y	Y
3 ***Nielson***	X	Y	N	Y	Y	N	Y	N
VERMONT								
AL ***Jeffords***	Y	Y	N	N	Y	?	Y	Y
VIRGINIA								
1 ***Bateman***	N	Y	Y	Y	Y	Y	Y	Y
2 ***Whitehurst***	?	Y	Y	Y	Y	N	N	Y
3 ***Bliley***	N	Y	Y	Y	Y	N	Y	Y
4 Sisisky	N	Y	Y	Y	Y	N	Y	Y
5 Daniel	N	Y	Y	Y	Y	N	Y	Y
6 Olin	N	Y	Y	Y	Y	N	Y	Y
7 ***Robinson***	N	Y	Y	Y	Y	N	Y	Y
8 ***Parris***	Y	Y	Y	Y	Y	Y	?	Y
9 Boucher	N	Y	N	N	N	Y	Y	Y
10 ***Wolf***	Y	Y	Y	Y	?	?	?	Y
WASHINGTON								
1 ***Pritchard***	?	Y	N	Y	Y	Y	Y	N
2 Swift	N	Y	N	N	N	Y	Y	Y
3 Bonker	N	Y	N	N	N	Y	Y	Y
4 ***Morrison***	N	Y	Y	Y	Y	Y	Y	Y
5 Foley	N	Y	?	N	N	Y	Y	Y
6 Dicks	N	Y	N	N	N	Y	Y	Y
7 Lowry	N	Y	N	N	N	Y	Y	Y
8 ***Chandler***	Y	Y	N	Y	Y	Y	Y	Y
WEST VIRGINIA								
1 Mollohan	N	Y	Y	N	N	Y	Y	#
2 Staggers	N	Y	N	N	N	Y	Y	Y
3 Wise	Y	Y	N	N	N	Y	Y	Y
4 Rahall	N	Y	N	N	N	Y	N	Y
WISCONSIN								
1 Aspin	N	Y	N	N	N	Y	Y	Y
2 Kastenmeier	N	Y	N	N	N	Y	Y	Y
3 ***Gunderson***	Y	Y	Y	Y	Y	N	Y	N
4 Zablocki	N	Y	N	N	N	Y	Y	Y
5 Moody	Y	Y	N	N	N	Y	Y	N
6 ***Petri***	Y	Y	Y	Y	Y	N	Y	N
7 Obey	N	Y	N	N	N	Y	Y	Y
8 ***Roth***	Y	Y	Y	Y	Y	N	Y	N
9 ***Sensenbrenner***	Y	Y	Y	Y	Y	N	N	N
WYOMING								
AL ***Cheney***	N	Y	Y	Y	Y	N	Y	N

* *Rep. Sala Burton, D-Calif., was sworn in June 28, 1983. The first vote for which she was eligible was CQ vote 210.*

Southern states - Ala., Ark., Fla., Ga., Ky., La., Miss., N.C., Okla., S.C., Tenn., Texas, Va.

216. H Res 245. Hearing Transcript Investigation. Wright, D-Texas, motion to refer to the Rules Committee the resolution to create a select committee to investigate alterations of hearing transcripts. Motion agreed to 256-161: R 0-157; D 256-4 (ND 169-2, SD 87-2), June 29, 1983.

217. HR 3135. Legislative Branch Appropriations, Fiscal 1984. Adoption of the conference report on the bill to appropriate $1,473,359,000 for Congress and its agencies in fiscal 1984. Adopted 241-175: R 40-120; D 201-55 (ND 145-23, SD 56-32), June 29, 1983. The president had requested $1,495,478,200 in new budget authority. Traditionally, the president simply requests the amount congressional agencies want included in the budget.

218. HR 3132. Energy and Water Development Appropriations, Fiscal 1984. Adoption of the conference report on the bill to appropriate $14,307,045,000 for energy and water development in fiscal 1984. Adopted 337-82: R 115-46; D 222-36 (ND 135-34, SD 87-2), June 29, 1983. The president had requested $14,610,671,000 in new budget authority.

219. HR 3415. District of Columbia Appropriations, Fiscal 1984. Passage of the bill to appropriate $544,590,000 in federal funds for the District of Columbia in fiscal 1984, and $2,122,013,000 in funds from the District's own treasury. Passed 296-124: R 71-90; D 225-34 (ND 157-13, SD 68-21), June 29, 1983. The president had requested $569,590,000 in federal funds and $2,122,013,000 in District funds.

220. HR 2668. Consumer Product Safety Act Authorization. Shelby, D-Ala., substitute to authorize $35.7 million for the Consumer Product Safety Commission in fiscal 1984, $37.485 million in fiscal 1985 and $39.36 million in fiscal 1986. Adopted 238-177: R 152-9; D 86-168 (ND 20-146, SD 66-22), June 29, 1983. (The bill, as amended, subsequently was passed by voice vote.)

221. H Res 254. Hearing Transcript Investigation. Long, D-La., motion to order the previous question (thus ending debate and the possibility of amendment) on the resolution to authorize the Committee on Standards of Official Conduct to begin an investigation of alleged alterations of hearing transcripts. Motion agreed to 250-151: R 8-148; D 242-3 (ND 162-1, SD 80-2), June 30, 1983.

222. H Res 254. Hearing Transcript Investigation. Adoption of the resolution to authorize the Committee on Standards of Official Conduct to begin an investigation of alleged alterations of hearing transcripts. Adopted 409-0: R 159-0; D 250-0 (ND 166-0, SD 84-0), June 30, 1983.

223. HR 1. Housing and Urban-Rural Recovery Act. Adoption of the rule (H Res 248) providing for House floor consideration of the bill to authorize $24.6 billion for the Department of Housing and Urban Development in fiscal 1984. Adopted 291-110: R 51-107; D 240-3 (ND 162-1, SD 78-2), June 30, 1983.

KEY

Y Voted for (yea).
Paired for.
+ Announced for.
N Voted against (nay).
X Paired against.
- Announced against.
P Voted "present".
C Voted "present" to avoid possible conflict of interest.
? Did not vote or otherwise make a position known.

Democrats   *Republicans*

	216	217	218	219	220	221	222	223
ALABAMA								
1 Edwards	N	Y	Y	Y	Y	N	Y	N
2 Dickinson	N	Y	Y	N	Y	?	Y	Y
3 Nichols	Y	N	Y	N	Y	Y	Y	Y
4 Bevill	Y	Y	Y	Y	Y	?	Y	Y
5 Flippo	Y	Y	N	Y	Y	Y	Y	Y
6 Erdreich	Y	N	Y	Y	Y	Y	Y	Y
7 Shelby	Y	N	Y	N	Y	Y	Y	Y
ALASKA								
AL *Young*	N	Y	Y	Y	Y	N	Y	N
ARIZONA								
1 *McCain*	N	N	Y	N	Y	N	Y	N
2 Udall	Y	Y	Y	Y	N	Y	Y	Y
3 *Stump*	N	N	Y	N	Y	N	Y	N
4 *Rudd*	N	Y	Y	N	Y	N	Y	N
5 McNulty	Y	Y	Y	Y	N	Y	Y	Y
ARKANSAS								
1 Alexander	Y	Y	Y	Y	N	Y	Y	Y
2 *Bethune*	N	N	Y	N	Y	N	Y	N
3 *Hammerschmidt*	N	N	Y	N	Y	N	Y	Y
4 Anthony	Y	Y	Y	N	Y	Y	Y	Y
CALIFORNIA								
1 Bosco	Y	?	?	Y	N	Y	Y	Y
2 *Chappie*	N	N	?	N	Y	N	Y	Y
3 Matsui	Y	Y	Y	Y	N	Y	Y	Y
4 Fazio	Y	Y	Y	Y	N	Y	Y	Y
5 Burton	Y	Y	Y	Y	N	Y	Y	Y
6 Boxer	Y	Y	Y	Y	N	Y	Y	Y
7 Miller	Y	Y	Y	Y	N	Y	Y	Y
8 Dellums	Y	Y	N	Y	N	Y	Y	Y
9 Stark	Y	Y	Y	Y	N	Y	Y	Y
10 Edwards	Y	Y	Y	Y	N	Y	Y	Y
11 Lantos	Y	Y	Y	Y	N	Y	Y	Y
12 *Zschau*	N	N	Y	N	Y	N	Y	N
13 Mineta	Y	Y	Y	Y	N	Y	Y	Y
14 *Shumway*	N	N	Y	N	Y	N	Y	N
15 Coelho	Y	Y	Y	Y	N	Y	Y	Y
16 Panetta	Y	N	Y	Y	N	Y	Y	Y
17 *Pashayan*	N	N	N	Y	N	Y	N	N
18 Lehman	Y	Y	Y	Y	N	#	?	?
19 *Lagomarsino*	N	N	Y	Y	N	Y	N	N
20 *Thomas*	N	N	Y	Y	N	Y	N	N
21 *Fiedler*	N	N	Y	Y	N	Y	N	N
22 *Moorhead*	N	N	N	N	Y	N	Y	N
23 Beilenson	Y	Y	Y	Y	N	Y	Y	Y
24 Waxman	Y	Y	Y	Y	N	Y	Y	Y
25 Roybal	Y	Y	Y	Y	N	Y	Y	Y
26 Berman	Y	Y	Y	Y	N	Y	Y	Y
27 Levine	Y	Y	Y	Y	N	Y	Y	Y
28 Dixon	Y	Y	Y	Y	N	Y	Y	Y
29 Hawkins	Y	Y	Y	Y	N	Y	Y	Y
30 Martinez	Y	?	?	?	?	?	?	?
31 Dymally	Y	Y	Y	Y	N	#	?	Y
32 Anderson	Y	N	Y	Y	N	Y	Y	Y
33 *Dreier*	N	N	N	N	#	?	?	?
34 Torres	Y	Y	Y	Y	N	Y	Y	Y
35 *Lewis*	N	Y	Y	Y	N	Y	N	N
36 Brown	Y	Y	Y	Y	N	Y	Y	Y
37 *McCandless*	X	X	?	?	#	X	?	?
38 Patterson	Y	Y	Y	Y	N	Y	Y	Y
39 *Dannemeyer*	N	N	N	N	Y	N	Y	N
40 *Badham*	?	?	?	?	?	X	?	?
41 *Lowery*	N	Y	Y	Y	N	Y	N	Y
42 *Lungren*	N	N	Y	Y	N	Y	N	N

	216	217	218	219	220	221	222	223
43 *Packard*	N	N	Y	Y	Y	N	Y	N
44 Bates	Y	Y	Y	Y	N	Y	Y	Y
45 *Hunter*	?	?	Y	N	Y	N	Y	N
COLORADO								
1 Schroeder	Y	Y	N	N	N	Y	Y	Y
2 Wirth	Y	Y	Y	Y	N	Y	Y	Y
3 Kogovsek	Y	Y	Y	Y	N	Y	Y	Y
4 *Brown*	N	N	N	N	Y	N	Y	N
5 *Kramer*	N	N	Y	Y	N	Y	N	N
6 *Schaefer*	N	N	Y	N	Y	N	Y	N
CONNECTICUT								
1 Kennelly	Y	Y	Y	Y	N	Y	Y	Y
2 Gejdenson	Y	Y	Y	Y	N	Y	Y	Y
3 Morrison	Y	Y	N	Y	N	Y	Y	Y
4 *McKinney*	N	Y	N	Y	N	Y	Y	Y
5 Ratchford	Y	Y	N	Y	N	Y	Y	Y
6 *Johnson*	N	N	Y	Y	N	Y	N	Y
DELAWARE								
AL Carper	Y	Y	Y	Y	Y	Y	Y	Y
FLORIDA								
1 Hutto	Y	N	Y	Y	Y	Y	Y	Y
2 Fuqua	Y	Y	Y	Y	?	?	?	?
3 Bennett	Y	N	Y	Y	Y	Y	Y	Y
4 Chappell	Y	Y	Y	Y	Y	Y	Y	Y
5 *McCollum*	N	?	Y	N	Y	N	Y	N
6 MacKay	Y	N	Y	Y	N	Y	Y	Y
7 Gibbons	?	?	Y	N	Y	N	Y	Y
8 *Young*	N	Y	Y	N	Y	N	Y	N
9 *Bilirakis*	N	N	N	N	Y	N	Y	N
10 Ireland	Y	N	Y	Y	Y	Y	Y	Y
11 Nelson	Y	N	Y	Y	Y	Y	Y	Y
12 *Lewis*	N	Y	Y	Y	N	Y	N	N
13 *Mack*	N	N	N	N	Y	N	Y	N
14 Mica	Y	Y	Y	Y	Y	Y	Y	Y
15 *Shaw*	N	Y	Y	?	Y	N	Y	N
16 Smith	Y	Y	Y	Y	N	Y	Y	Y
17 Lehman	Y	Y	Y	Y	N	Y	Y	Y
18 Pepper	Y	Y	Y	Y	N	Y	Y	?
19 Fascell	Y	Y	Y	Y	N	Y	Y	Y
GEORGIA								
1 Thomas	Y	Y	Y	Y	Y	Y	Y	Y
2 Hatcher	Y	Y	Y	Y	Y	Y	Y	Y
3 Ray	Y	N	Y	Y	Y	Y	Y	Y
4 Levitas	Y	N	Y	Y	Y	Y	Y	Y
5 Fowler	Y	Y	Y	Y	N	Y	Y	Y
6 *Gingrich*	N	N	Y	Y	Y	N	Y	N
7 *McDonald*	N	N	N	N	N	N	Y	N
8 Rowland	Y	Y	Y	Y	N	Y	Y	Y
9 Jenkins	Y	N	Y	Y	N	Y	Y	Y
10 Barnard	Y	N	Y	Y	Y	Y	Y	Y
HAWAII								
1 Heftel	#	#	?	?	?	?	#	?
2 Akaka	Y	Y	Y	Y	Y	Y	Y	Y
IDAHO								
1 *Craig*	N	N	Y	N	Y	N	Y	N
2 *Hansen*	N	N	Y	N	Y	?	?	?
ILLINOIS								
1 Vacancy								
2 Savage	Y	Y	Y	Y	N	Y	Y	Y
3 Russo	Y	N	Y	N	Y	N	Y	Y
4 *O'Brien*	N	Y	Y	Y	Y	Y	Y	Y
5 Lipinski	Y	Y	Y	Y	N	Y	Y	Y
6 *Hyde*	N	N	Y	Y	N	Y	N	N
7 Collins	Y	Y	Y	Y	N	Y	Y	?
8 Rostenkowski	Y	Y	Y	Y	N	Y	Y	Y
9 Yates	Y	Y	Y	Y	N	Y	Y	Y
10 *Porter*	N	Y	Y	Y	N	Y	N	N
11 Annunzio	Y	Y	Y	Y	N	Y	Y	Y
12 *Crane, P.*	N	N	N	N	Y	N	N	N
13 *Erlenborn*	?	?	?	?	?	?	?	?
14 *Corcoran*	N	N	N	N	Y	N	Y	N
15 *Madigan*	?	N	Y	N	Y	N	Y	N
16 *Martin*	N	N	N	N	N	N	Y	N
17 Evans	Y	Y	Y	Y	N	Y	Y	Y
18 *Michel*	N	Y	Y	N	Y	N	Y	N
19 *Crane, D.*	N	N	N	N	N	N	Y	N
20 Durbin	Y	Y	Y	Y	N	Y	Y	Y
21 Price	Y	Y	Y	Y	Y	Y	Y	Y
22 Simon	Y	Y	Y	Y	N	Y	Y	Y
INDIANA								
1 Hall	Y	Y	Y	Y	N	Y	Y	Y
2 Sharp	Y	N	Y	Y	N	Y	Y	Y
3 *Hiler*	N	N	N	N	Y	N	Y	N
4 *Coats*	N	N	Y	N	Y	N	Y	N
5 Hillis	N	Y	Y	Y	N	Y	N	N

	216	217	218	219	220	221	222	223
6 ***Burton***	N	N	N	N	Y	N	Y	N
7 ***Myers***	P	Y	Y	Y	Y	N	Y	Y
8 McCloskey	Y	Y	Y	Y	Y	Y	Y	Y
9 Hamilton	Y	Y	Y	Y	Y	Y	Y	Y
10 Jacobs	Y	N	N	Y	Y	N	Y	Y
IOWA								
1 ***Leach***	N	N	N	N	N	?	?	?
2 ***Tauke***	N	N	N	N	Y	N	Y	Y
3 ***Evans***	N	N	N	N	Y	N	Y	N
4 Smith	N	Y	Y	Y	?	?	?	?
5 Harkin	Y	?	Y	Y	N	Y	Y	Y
6 Bedell	Y	Y	N	Y	Y	?	?	?
KANSAS								
1 ***Roberts***	N	N	Y	N	Y	N	Y	N
2 Slattery	Y	N	Y	N	Y	Y	Y	Y
3 ***Winn***	N	Y	Y	N	Y	N	Y	N
4 Glickman	Y	N	Y	N	Y	Y	Y	Y
5 ***Whittaker***	N	N	Y	N	Y	N	Y	N
KENTUCKY								
1 Hubbard	Y	N	Y	N	Y	Y	Y	N
2 Natcher	Y	Y	Y	Y	Y	Y	Y	Y
3 Mazzoli	N	Y	Y	Y	Y	N	Y	Y
4 ***Snyder***	N	Y	Y	N	Y	Y	Y	N
5 ***Rogers***	N	Y	Y	Y	Y	N	Y	Y
6 ***Hopkins***	N	N	Y	N	Y	N	Y	Y
7 Perkins	Y	Y	Y	Y	N	Y	Y	Y
LOUISIANA								
1 ***Livingston***	N	N	Y	Y	Y	N	Y	Y
2 Boggs	Y	Y	Y	Y	N	Y	Y	Y
3 Tauzin	Y	N	Y	Y	Y	Y	Y	Y
4 Roemer	Y	N	Y	Y	Y	Y	Y	Y
5 Huckaby	Y	N	?	Y	Y	Y	Y	Y
6 ***Moore***	N	N	Y	Y	Y	N	Y	Y
7 Breaux	Y	N	Y	Y	Y	Y	Y	Y
8 Long	Y	Y	Y	Y	N	Y	Y	Y
MAINE								
1 ***McKernan***	N	N	Y	Y	N	N	Y	N
2 ***Snowe***	N	N	Y	N	Y	N	Y	Y
MARYLAND								
1 Dyson	Y	Y	Y	Y	Y	Y	Y	Y
2 Long	Y	Y	Y	Y	?	Y	Y	Y
3 Mikulski	Y	Y	Y	Y	N	Y	Y	Y
4 ***Holt***	N	N	Y	Y	Y	N	Y	N
5 Hoyer	Y	Y	Y	Y	N	Y	Y	Y
6 Byron	Y	Y	Y	N	?	?	?	?
7 Mitchell	Y	Y	Y	Y	N	Y	Y	Y
8 Barnes	Y	Y	N	Y	N	Y	Y	Y
MASSACHUSETTS								
1 ***Conte***	N	Y	N	Y	N	N	Y	Y
2 Boland	Y	Y	Y	Y	N	Y	Y	?
3 Early	Y	Y	N	Y	N	Y	Y	Y
4 Frank	Y	Y	N	Y	N	Y	Y	Y
5 Shannon	Y	Y	N	Y	N	Y	Y	Y
6 Mavroules	Y	Y	Y	Y	N	?	?	?
7 Markey	Y	Y	N	Y	N	Y	Y	Y
8 O'Neill								
9 Moakley	Y	Y	Y	Y	N	Y	Y	Y
10 Studds	Y	Y	N	Y	N	Y	Y	Y
11 Donnelly	Y	Y	Y	Y	N	Y	Y	Y
MICHIGAN								
1 Conyers	?	Y	N	Y	N	?	Y	Y
2 ***Pursell***	N	N	Y	N	Y	N	Y	N
3 Wolpe	Y	N	N	Y	N	Y	Y	Y
4 ***Siljander***	N	N	Y	Y	Y	N	Y	N
5 ***Sawyer***	N	Y	N	N	Y	N	Y	N
6 Carr	Y	N	Y	Y	N	Y	Y	Y
7 Kildee	Y	Y	N	Y	N	Y	Y	Y
8 Traxler	Y	Y	Y	Y	N	Y	Y	Y
9 ***Vander Jagt***	N	Y	Y	Y	Y	N	Y	Y
10 Albosta	Y	Y	?	N	N	Y	Y	Y
11 ***Davis***	N	Y	Y	Y	Y	N	Y	Y
12 Bonior	Y	Y	Y	Y	N	Y	Y	Y
13 Crockett	Y	Y	N	Y	N	Y	Y	Y
14 Hertel	Y	N	N	Y	N	Y	Y	Y
15 Ford	#	#	?	?	X	Y	Y	Y
16 Dingell	?	?	Y	Y	N	Y	Y	Y
17 Levin	Y	Y	Y	Y	N	Y	Y	Y
18 ***Broomfield***	N	N	N	N	Y	N	Y	N
MINNESOTA								
1 Penny	Y	N	Y	Y	Y	Y	Y	Y
2 ***Weber***	N	N	N	N	Y	N	Y	N
3 ***Frenzel***	N	N	N	N	Y	N	Y	N
4 Vento	Y	Y	N	Y	N	Y	Y	Y
5 Sabo	Y	Y	Y	Y	N	Y	Y	Y
6 Sikorski	Y	N	N	Y	N	Y	Y	Y
7 ***Stangeland***	N	N	Y	Y	Y	N	Y	N
8 Oberstar	Y	Y	Y	Y	N	Y	Y	Y
MISSISSIPPI								
1 Whitten	Y	Y	Y	Y	Y	?	?	?
2 ***Franklin***	N	N	Y	N	Y	N	Y	N
3 Montgomery	Y	N	Y	N	Y	Y	Y	Y
4 Dowdy	Y	Y	Y	Y	?	?	?	?
5 ***Lott***	N	N	Y	N	Y	N	Y	N
MISSOURI								
1 Clay	Y	Y	Y	Y	N	Y	Y	Y
2 Young	Y	Y	Y	Y	Y	Y	Y	Y
3 Gephardt	Y	Y	Y	Y	N	Y	Y	Y
4 Skelton	Y	N	Y	Y	Y	Y	Y	Y
5 Wheat	Y	Y	Y	Y	N	Y	Y	Y
6 ***Coleman***	N	N	Y	N	Y	N	Y	Y
7 ***Taylor***	N	N	Y	N	Y	N	Y	Y
8 ***Emerson***	N	N	Y	N	Y	N	Y	N
9 Volkmer	Y	N	Y	N	Y	Y	Y	Y
MONTANA								
1 Williams	Y	Y	Y	Y	N	?	Y	Y
2 ***Marlenee***	N	N	N	N	Y	N	Y	Y
NEBRASKA								
1 ***Bereuter***	N	N	Y	Y	Y	N	Y	N
2 ***Daub***	N	N	Y	N	Y	N	Y	N
3 ***Smith***	N	Y	Y	Y	Y	N	Y	Y
NEVADA								
1 Reid	Y	Y	Y	Y	N	Y	Y	Y
2 ***Vucanovich***	N	N	Y	N	Y	N	Y	N
NEW HAMPSHIRE								
1 D'Amours	N	Y	Y	Y	N	Y	Y	Y
2 ***Gregg***	N	N	N	N	Y	N	Y	N
NEW JERSEY								
1 Florio	Y	Y	?	Y	X	Y	Y	Y
2 Hughes	Y	Y	Y	N	N	Y	Y	Y
3 Howard	Y	Y	Y	Y	N	Y	Y	Y
4 ***Smith***	N	Y	Y	Y	N	N	Y	Y
5 ***Roukema***	N	Y	N	Y	Y	N	Y	Y
6 Dwyer	Y	Y	Y	Y	N	Y	Y	Y
7 ***Rinaldo***	N	Y	Y	Y	N	N	Y	Y
8 Roe	Y	Y	Y	Y	N	Y	Y	Y
9 Torricelli	Y	Y	Y	Y	N	Y	Y	Y
10 Rodino	Y	Y	Y	Y	N	Y	Y	Y
11 Minish	Y	Y	Y	Y	N	Y	Y	Y
12 ***Courter***	N	N	N	N	Y	N	Y	Y
13 ***Forsythe***	P	N	Y	Y	Y	Y	Y	Y
14 Guarini	Y	Y	Y	Y	N	Y	Y	Y
NEW MEXICO								
1 ***Lujan***	N	N	Y	Y	Y	N	Y	Y
2 ***Skeen***	N	N	Y	N	Y	N	Y	N
3 Richardson	Y	N	Y	Y	N	Y	Y	Y
NEW YORK								
1 ***Carney***	N	N	Y	Y	Y	N	Y	Y
2 Downey	Y	Y	Y	Y	N	Y	Y	Y
3 Mrazek	Y	N	Y	Y	N	#	?	Y
4 ***Lent***	N	Y	Y	N	Y	N	Y	N
5 ***McGrath***	N	N	Y	N	Y	N	Y	N
6 Addabbo	Y	Y	Y	Y	N	Y	Y	Y
7 Ackerman	Y	Y	Y	Y	N	Y	Y	Y
8 Scheuer	Y	Y	Y	Y	N	Y	Y	Y
9 Ferraro	Y	Y	Y	Y	N	Y	Y	Y
10 Schumer	Y	Y	N	Y	N	Y	Y	Y
11 Towns	Y	Y	Y	Y	N	Y	Y	Y
12 Owens	Y	Y	Y	Y	N	Y	Y	Y
13 Solarz	Y	Y	Y	Y	N	Y	Y	Y
14 ***Molinari***	N	Y	N	Y	Y	Y	Y	Y
15 ***Green***	N	Y	N	Y	N	N	Y	Y
16 Rangel	Y	Y	Y	Y	N	Y	Y	Y
17 Weiss	Y	Y	N	Y	N	Y	Y	Y
18 Garcia	Y	Y	Y	Y	N	Y	Y	Y
19 Biaggi	Y	Y	Y	Y	N	Y	Y	Y
20 Ottinger	Y	Y	Y	Y	N	Y	Y	Y
21 ***Fish***	N	N	N	Y	Y	N	Y	Y
22 ***Gilman***	N	Y	Y	N	N	N	Y	Y
23 Stratton	Y	Y	Y	Y	Y	Y	Y	Y
24 ***Solomon***	N	N	N	N	Y	N	Y	N
25 ***Boehlert***	N	N	Y	Y	Y	N	Y	Y
26 ***Martin***	N	N	Y	Y	Y	Y	Y	N
27 ***Wortley***	N	N	Y	Y	Y	N	Y	Y
28 McHugh	Y	Y	Y	Y	N	Y	Y	Y
29 ***Horton***	N	Y	Y	Y	Y	Y	Y	Y
30 ***Conable***	N	N	N	Y	Y	N	Y	N
31 ***Kemp***	N	N	Y	Y	?	?	?	?
32 LaFalce	Y	Y	Y	Y	N	Y	Y	Y
33 Nowak	Y	Y	Y	Y	N	Y	Y	Y
34 Lundine	Y	Y	N	Y	N	Y	Y	Y
NORTH CAROLINA								
1 Jones	Y	?	Y	Y	Y	?	Y	?
2 Valentine	Y	N	Y	Y	Y	Y	Y	Y
3 Whitley	Y	Y	Y	Y	Y	Y	Y	Y
4 Andrews	Y	Y	Y	Y	Y	Y	Y	Y
5 Neal	Y	Y	Y	Y	Y	Y	Y	Y
6 Britt	Y	Y	Y	Y	Y	Y	Y	Y
7 Rose	Y	Y	Y	Y	Y	Y	Y	Y
8 Hefner	Y	Y	Y	Y	Y	Y	Y	Y
9 ***Martin***	N	N	N	Y	Y	N	Y	N
10 ***Broyhill***	N	N	?	N	Y	N	Y	N
11 Clarke	Y	Y	Y	Y	Y	Y	Y	Y
NORTH DAKOTA								
AL Dorgan	Y	Y	Y	Y	N	Y	Y	Y
OHIO								
1 Luken	Y	Y	Y	Y	Y	Y	Y	Y
2 ***Gradison***	N	N	N	Y	Y	N	Y	N
3 Hall	Y	Y	N	?	N	Y	Y	?
4 ***Oxley***	N	N	Y	N	Y	N	Y	N
5 ***Latta***	N	N	N	N	Y	N	Y	N
6 ***McEwen***	N	N	Y	N	Y	N	Y	N
7 ***DeWine***	N	N	N	N	Y	N	Y	N
8 ***Kindness***	N	N	Y	N	Y	N	Y	N
9 Kaptur	Y	N	Y	Y	N	Y	Y	Y
10 ***Miller***	N	N	Y	N	Y	N	Y	Y
11 Eckart	Y	N	N	N	N	Y	Y	Y
12 ***Kasich***	N	N	Y	N	Y	N	Y	N
13 Pease	Y	Y	Y	Y	N	Y	Y	Y
14 Seiberling	Y	Y	Y	Y	N	Y	Y	Y
15 ***Wylie***	N	N	Y	Y	Y	N	Y	Y
16 ***Regula***	N	N	Y	Y	Y	N	Y	Y
17 ***Williams***	N	?	Y	Y	Y	N	Y	Y
18 Applegate	Y	N	N	N	Y	Y	Y	Y
19 Feighan	Y	Y	N	Y	N	Y	Y	Y
20 Oakar	Y	N	Y	Y	N	Y	Y	Y
21 Stokes	Y	Y	Y	Y	N	Y	Y	Y
OKLAHOMA								
1 Jones	Y	Y	Y	Y	Y	Y	Y	Y
2 Synar	Y	Y	Y	Y	N	Y	Y	Y
3 Watkins	Y	Y	Y	N	Y	Y	Y	Y
4 McCurdy	Y	N	Y	Y	Y	Y	Y	Y
5 ***Edwards***	N	N	Y	N	Y	N	Y	N
6 English	Y	N	Y	Y	N	Y	Y	Y
OREGON								
1 AuCoin	Y	Y	Y	N	N	Y	Y	Y
2 ***Smith, R.***	X	X	?	?	?	X	?	?
3 Wyden	Y	Y	Y	Y	N	Y	Y	Y
4 Weaver	Y	Y	N	N	N	?	Y	?
5 ***Smith, D.***	N	N	N	N	Y	X	Y	N
PENNSYLVANIA								
1 Foglietta	Y	Y	Y	Y	N	Y	Y	Y
2 Gray	Y	Y	Y	Y	N	Y	Y	Y
3 Borski	Y	Y	Y	Y	N	Y	Y	Y
4 Kolter	Y	N	Y	Y	N	Y	Y	Y
5 ***Schulze***	N	N	Y	N	Y	N	Y	N
6 Yatron	Y	Y	Y	Y	N	Y	Y	Y
7 Edgar	Y	Y	N	Y	N	Y	Y	N
8 Kostmayer	Y	Y	Y	Y	N	Y	Y	Y
9 ***Shuster***	N	N	Y	N	Y	N	Y	N
10 ***McDade***	N	Y	Y	Y	Y	X	Y	Y
11 Harrison	?	?	?	?	?	?	?	?
12 Murtha	Y	Y	Y	Y	N	Y	Y	Y
13 ***Coughlin***	N	Y	N	Y	Y	N	Y	N
14 Coyne	Y	Y	Y	Y	N	Y	Y	Y
15 ***Ritter***	N	N	N	N	Y	N	Y	N
16 ***Walker***	N	N	Y	N	Y	N	Y	N
17 ***Gekas***	N	N	Y	Y	Y	N	Y	N
18 Walgren	Y	Y	Y	Y	N	Y	Y	Y
19 ***Goodling***	N	N	Y	N	Y	N	Y	N
20 Gaydos	Y	Y	Y	Y	N	Y	Y	Y
21 ***Ridge***	N	N	Y	Y	Y	N	Y	Y
22 Murphy	Y	Y	Y	Y	Y	Y	Y	Y
23 ***Clinger***	N	N	Y	Y	Y	N	Y	N
RHODE ISLAND								
1 St Germain	Y	Y	Y	?	N	Y	Y	Y
2 ***Schneider***	N	Y	N	Y	N	N	Y	Y
SOUTH CAROLINA								
1 ***Hartnett***	N	N	N	N	Y	N	Y	N
2 ***Spence***	P	N	Y	N	Y	Y	Y	N
3 Derrick	Y	Y	Y	Y	Y	Y	Y	Y
4 ***Campbell***	N	N	Y	N	Y	N	Y	Y
5 Spratt	Y	Y	Y	Y	Y	Y	Y	Y
6 Tallon	Y	Y	Y	Y	Y	Y	Y	Y
SOUTH DAKOTA								
AL Daschle	Y	?	Y	Y	?	Y	Y	Y
TENNESSEE								
1 ***Quillen***	N	N	Y	N	Y	Y	Y	Y
2 ***Duncan***	N	N	Y	N	Y	N	Y	N
3 Lloyd	Y	N	Y	N	Y	Y	Y	Y
4 Cooper	Y	Y	Y	Y	Y	Y	Y	Y
5 Boner	Y	Y	Y	Y	Y	#	?	?
6 Gore	Y	Y	Y	N	N	Y	Y	Y
7 ***Sundquist***	N	N	Y	N	Y	N	Y	Y
8 Jones	Y	Y	Y	N	Y	Y	Y	Y
9 Ford	Y	Y	Y	Y	N	Y	Y	?
TEXAS								
1 Hall, S.	Y	N	Y	N	Y	Y	Y	Y
2 Wilson	Y	Y	Y	Y	Y	Y	Y	Y
3 ***Bartlett***	N	N	Y	Y	Y	N	Y	N
4 Hall, R.	Y	N	Y	N	Y	Y	Y	Y
5 Bryant	Y	Y	N	Y	N	Y	Y	Y
6 ***Gramm***	N	N	Y	N	Y	N	Y	N
7 ***Archer***	N	N	N	N	Y	N	Y	N
8 ***Fields***	N	N	N	N	Y	N	Y	N
9 Brooks	Y	Y	Y	Y	N	Y	Y	Y
10 Pickle	Y	Y	Y	Y	Y	Y	Y	Y
11 Leath	Y	N	Y	N	Y	Y	Y	Y
12 Wright	Y	Y	Y	Y	Y	Y	Y	?
13 Hightower	Y	Y	Y	Y	Y	Y	Y	Y
14 Patman	Y	Y	Y	N	Y	Y	Y	Y
15 de la Garza	Y	Y	Y	Y	N	Y	Y	Y
16 Coleman	Y	Y	Y	Y	Y	Y	Y	Y
17 Stenholm	Y	N	Y	N	Y	Y	Y	Y
18 Leland	Y	Y	Y	Y	N	Y	Y	Y
19 Hance	Y	N	Y	N	Y	?	?	?
20 Gonzalez	Y	Y	Y	Y	N	Y	Y	Y
21 ***Loeffler***	N	N	Y	N	Y	N	Y	N
22 ***Paul***	N	N	N	N	Y	N	Y	N
23 Kazen	Y	Y	Y	Y	Y	Y	Y	Y
24 Frost	Y	Y	Y	?	N	Y	Y	Y
25 Andrews	Y	N	Y	Y	Y	Y	Y	Y
26 Vandergriff	Y	N	Y	Y	Y	Y	Y	Y
27 Ortiz	Y	Y	Y	Y	N	Y	Y	Y
UTAH								
1 ***Hansen***	P	N	Y	N	Y	N	Y	Y
2 ***Marriott***	N	Y	Y	Y	Y	N	Y	Y
3 ***Nielson***	N	N	Y	N	Y	N	Y	N
VERMONT								
AL ***Jeffords***	N	Y	N	Y	N	N	Y	Y
VIRGINIA								
1 ***Bateman***	N	N	Y	Y	Y	N	Y	N
2 ***Whitehurst***	N	Y	Y	Y	Y	N	Y	N
3 ***Bliley***	N	N	Y	Y	Y	N	Y	N
4 Sisisky	Y	Y	Y	Y	Y	Y	Y	Y
5 Daniel	Y	N	Y	N	Y	?	?	?
6 Olin	Y	N	Y	Y	Y	Y	Y	Y
7 ***Robinson***	N	Y	Y	Y	Y	N	Y	N
8 ***Parris***	N	Y	Y	Y	Y	N	Y	Y
9 Boucher	Y	Y	Y	Y	Y	Y	Y	Y
10 ***Wolf***	N	Y	Y	Y	Y	N	Y	N
WASHINGTON								
1 ***Pritchard***	N	N	N	?	Y	N	Y	?
2 Swift	Y	Y	Y	Y	N	Y	Y	?
3 Bonker	Y	Y	Y	Y	N	Y	Y	Y
4 ***Morrison***	N	N	Y	N	Y	N	Y	Y
5 Foley	Y	Y	Y	Y	?	Y	Y	Y
6 Dicks	Y	Y	Y	N	N	Y	Y	Y
7 Lowry	Y	Y	N	Y	N	Y	Y	Y
8 ***Chandler***	N	N	Y	N	Y	N	Y	Y
WEST VIRGINIA								
1 Mollohan	Y	Y	Y	Y	Y	Y	Y	Y
2 Staggers	Y	Y	Y	Y	N	Y	Y	Y
3 Wise	Y	N	Y	Y	N	Y	Y	Y
4 Rahall	Y	Y	Y	Y	Y	Y	Y	Y
WISCONSIN								
1 Aspin	Y	N	Y	Y	N	Y	Y	Y
2 Kastenmeier	Y	Y	N	Y	N	Y	Y	Y
3 ***Gunderson***	N	N	Y	Y	Y	N	Y	N
4 Zablocki	Y	Y	Y	Y	N	Y	Y	Y
5 Moody	Y	Y	N	Y	N	Y	Y	Y
6 ***Petri***	N	N	N	N	Y	N	Y	N
7 Obey	Y	Y	Y	Y	N	Y	Y	Y
8 ***Roth***	N	N	N	N	Y	N	Y	N
9 ***Sensenbrenner***	N	N	N	N	Y	N	Y	N
WYOMING								
AL ***Cheney***	N	N	Y	N	Y	N	Y	N

Southern states - Ala., Ark., Fla., Ga., Ky., La., Miss., N.C., Okla., S.C., Tenn., Texas, Va.

224. H Con Res 126. Harry S Truman Centennial Commemoration. Adoption of the concurrent resolution providing for the commemoration of the 100th anniversary of the birth of the late President Harry S Truman. Adopted 382-5: R 147-4; D 235-1 (ND 158-0, SD 77-1), June 30, 1983.

225. S 273. Small Business Pilot Programs. Adoption of the conference report on the bill to authorize in fiscal 1984-85 two minority enterprise pilot programs conducted by the Small Business Administration. Adopted (thus cleared for the president) 367-6: R 143-4; D 224-2 (ND 157-0, SD 67-2), June 30, 1983.

KEY

Y Voted for (yea).
Paired for.
+ Announced for.
N Voted against (nay).
X Paired against.
- Announced against.
P Voted "present".
C Voted "present" to avoid possible conflict of interest.
? Did not vote or otherwise make a position known.

Democrats   *Republicans*

	224	225
ALABAMA		
1 *Edwards*	Y	Y
2 *Dickinson*	Y	Y
3 Nichols	Y	Y
4 Bevill	Y	Y
5 Flippo	Y	Y
6 Erdreich	Y	Y
7 Shelby	Y	Y
ALASKA		
AL *Young*	?	Y
ARIZONA		
1 *McCain*	Y	Y
2 Udall	Y	Y
3 *Stump*	Y	Y
4 *Rudd*	Y	Y
5 McNulty	Y	Y
ARKANSAS		
1 Alexander	Y	Y
2 *Bethune*	Y	Y
3 *Hammerschmidt*	Y	Y
4 Anthony	Y	Y
CALIFORNIA		
1 Bosco	Y	Y
2 *Chappie*	Y	Y
3 Matsui	Y	Y
4 Fazio	Y	Y
5 Burton	Y	Y
6 Boxer	Y	Y
7 Miller	Y	Y
8 Dellums	Y	Y
9 Stark	Y	Y
10 Edwards	?	Y
11 Lantos	Y	Y
12 *Zschau*	Y	Y
13 Mineta	Y	Y
14 *Shumway*	Y	Y
15 Coelho	?	Y
16 Panetta	Y	Y
17 *Pashayan*	Y	Y
18 Lehman	?	?
19 *Lagomarsino*	Y	Y
20 *Thomas*	Y	Y
21 *Fiedler*	Y	Y
22 *Moorhead*	Y	Y
23 Beilenson	Y	Y
24 Waxman	Y	Y
25 Roybal	Y	Y
26 Berman	Y	Y
27 Levine	Y	Y
28 Dixon	Y	Y
29 Hawkins	Y	Y
30 Martinez	?	?
31 Dymally	Y	Y
32 Anderson	Y	Y
33 *Dreier*	?	?
34 Torres	Y	Y
35 *Lewis*	Y	?
36 Brown	Y	Y
37 *McCandless*	?	?
38 Patterson	Y	Y
39 *Dannemeyer*	?	?
40 *Badham*	?	?
41 Lowery	Y	Y
42 Lungren	Y	Y

	224	225
43 *Packard*	Y	Y
44 Bates	Y	Y
45 *Hunter*	Y	Y
COLORADO		
1 Schroeder	Y	Y
2 Wirth	Y	Y
3 Kogovsek	Y	Y
4 *Brown*	Y	Y
5 *Kramer*	Y	Y
6 *Schaefer*	Y	Y
CONNECTICUT		
1 Kennelly	Y	Y
2 Gejdenson	Y	Y
3 Morrison	Y	Y
4 *McKinney*	?	Y
5 Ratchford	Y	Y
6 *Johnson*	?	Y
DELAWARE		
AL Carper	Y	Y
FLORIDA		
1 Hutto	Y	Y
2 Fuqua	?	?
3 Bennett	Y	Y
4 Chappell	?	?
5 *McCollum*	Y	Y
6 MacKay	Y	Y
7 Gibbons	Y	Y
8 *Young*	Y	Y
9 *Bilirakis*	Y	Y
10 Ireland	Y	?
11 Nelson	Y	Y
12 *Lewis*	Y	Y
13 *Mack*	Y	Y
14 Mica	Y	Y
15 *Shaw*	Y	Y
16 Smith	Y	Y
17 Lehman	Y	Y
18 Pepper	?	?
19 Fascell	Y	Y
GEORGIA		
1 Thomas	Y	Y
2 Hatcher	Y	Y
3 Ray	Y	Y
4 Levitas	Y	Y
5 Fowler	Y	Y
6 *Gingrich*	Y	Y
7 McDonald	N	N
8 Rowland	Y	Y
9 Jenkins	Y	Y
10 Barnard	Y	Y
HAWAII		
1 Heftel	?	?
2 Akaka	Y	Y
IDAHO		
1 *Craig*	Y	Y
2 *Hansen*	?	Y
ILLINOIS		
1 Vacancy		
2 Savage	Y	Y
3 Russo	Y	Y
4 *O'Brien*	Y	Y
5 Lipinski	Y	Y
6 *Hyde*	Y	Y
7 Collins	?	?
8 Rostenkowski	Y	?
9 Yates	Y	Y
10 *Porter*	Y	Y
11 Annunzio	Y	Y
12 *Crane, P.*	N	N
13 *Erlenborn*	?	?
14 *Corcoran*	Y	Y
15 *Madigan*	Y	Y
16 *Martin*	Y	Y
17 Evans	Y	Y
18 *Michel*	?	?
19 *Crane, D.*	N	N
20 Durbin	Y	Y
21 Price	Y	Y
22 Simon	?	Y
INDIANA		
1 Hall	Y	Y
2 Sharp	Y	Y
3 *Hiler*	Y	Y
4 *Coats*	Y	Y
5 *Hillis*	?	?

ND - Northern Democrats   SD - Southern Democrats

	224	225
6 Burton	Y	Y
7 Myers	Y	Y
8 McCloskey	Y	Y
9 Hamilton	Y	Y
10 Jacobs	Y	Y
IOWA		
1 Leach	?	?
2 Tauke	Y	Y
3 Evans	Y	Y
4 Smith	?	?
5 Harkin	Y	Y
6 Bedell	Y	Y
KANSAS		
1 Roberts	Y	Y
2 Slattery	Y	Y
3 Winn	Y	Y
4 Glickman	Y	Y
5 Whittaker	Y	Y
KENTUCKY		
1 Hubbard	Y	Y
2 Natcher	Y	Y
3 Mazzoli	Y	Y
4 Snyder	Y	Y
5 Rogers	Y	Y
6 Hopkins	Y	Y
7 Perkins	Y	Y
LOUISIANA		
1 Livingston	Y	Y
2 Boggs	Y	Y
3 Tauzin	Y	Y
4 Roemer	Y	Y
5 Huckaby	Y	Y
6 Moore	Y	Y
7 Breaux	Y	?
8 Long	Y	Y
MAINE		
1 McKernan	Y	Y
2 Snowe	Y	Y
MARYLAND		
1 Dyson	Y	Y
2 Long	Y	Y
3 Mikulski	Y	Y
4 Holt	Y	Y
5 Hoyer	Y	Y
6 Byron	?	?
7 Mitchell	Y	Y
8 Barnes	Y	Y
MASSACHUSETTS		
1 Conte	Y	Y
2 Boland	?	?
3 Early	Y	Y
4 Frank	Y	Y
5 Shannon	Y	Y
6 Mavroules	?	?
7 Markey	?	Y
8 O'Neill		
9 Moakley	Y	Y
10 Studds	Y	Y
11 Donnelly	Y	Y
MICHIGAN		
1 Conyers	Y	?
2 Pursell	Y	?
3 Wolpe	Y	Y
4 Siljander	Y	Y
5 Sawyer	Y	Y
6 Carr	Y	Y
7 Kildee	Y	Y
8 Traxler	Y	?
9 Vander Jagt	Y	Y
10 Albosta	Y	Y
11 Davis	Y	?
12 Bonior	Y	?
13 Crockett	Y	Y
14 Hertel	Y	Y
15 Ford	Y	Y
16 Dingell	Y	Y
17 Levin	Y	Y
18 Broomfield	Y	Y
MINNESOTA		
1 Penny	Y	Y
2 Weber	Y	Y
3 Frenzel	Y	Y
4 Vento	Y	Y
5 Sabo	Y	Y
6 Sikorski	Y	Y

	224	225
7 Stangeland	Y	Y
8 Oberstar	Y	Y
MISSISSIPPI		
1 Whitten	?	?
2 Franklin	Y	?
3 Montgomery	Y	?
4 Dowdy	?	?
5 Lott	Y	Y
MISSOURI		
1 Clay	?	?
2 Young	Y	Y
3 Gephardt	Y	Y
4 Skelton	Y	Y
5 Wheat	Y	Y
6 Coleman	Y	Y
7 Taylor	Y	Y
8 Emerson	Y	Y
9 Volkmer	Y	Y
MONTANA		
1 Williams	Y	Y
2 Marlenee	Y	N
NEBRASKA		
1 Bereuter	Y	Y
2 Daub	Y	Y
3 Smith	Y	Y
NEVADA		
1 Reid	Y	Y
2 Vucanovich	Y	Y
NEW HAMPSHIRE		
1 D'Amours	Y	Y
2 Gregg	Y	Y
NEW JERSEY		
1 Florio	Y	Y
2 Hughes	Y	Y
3 Howard	Y	Y
4 Smith	Y	Y
5 Roukema	Y	Y
6 Dwyer	?	?
7 Rinaldo	Y	Y
8 Roe	Y	Y
9 Torricelli	Y	Y
10 Rodino	Y	Y
11 Minish	Y	Y
12 Courter	Y	Y
13 Forsythe	Y	Y
14 Guarini	Y	Y
NEW MEXICO		
1 Lujan	Y	Y
2 Skeen	Y	Y
3 Richardson	Y	Y
NEW YORK		
1 Carney	Y	Y
2 Downey	Y	Y
3 Mrazek	Y	Y
4 Lent	Y	Y
5 McGrath	Y	Y
6 Addabbo	Y	Y
7 Ackerman	Y	Y
8 Scheuer	Y	Y
9 Ferraro	Y	Y
10 Schumer	Y	Y
11 Towns	Y	Y
12 Owens	Y	Y
13 Solarz	Y	Y
14 Molinari	Y	Y
15 Green	Y	Y
16 Rangel	Y	Y
17 Weiss	Y	Y
18 Garcia	Y	Y
19 Biaggi	Y	Y
20 Ottinger	Y	Y
21 Fish	Y	Y
22 Gilman	Y	Y
23 Stratton	Y	Y
24 Solomon	Y	Y
25 Boehlert	Y	Y
26 Martin	Y	Y
27 Wortley	Y	Y
28 McHugh	Y	Y
29 Horton	Y	Y
30 Conable	Y	?
31 Kemp	?	?
32 LaFalce	Y	Y
33 Nowak	Y	Y
34 Lundine	Y	Y

	224	225
NORTH CAROLINA		
1 Jones	?	?
2 Valentine	Y	Y
3 Whitley	Y	Y
4 Andrews	Y	Y
5 Neal	Y	Y
6 Britt	Y	Y
7 Rose	Y	Y
8 Hefner	Y	Y
9 Martin	Y	Y
10 Broyhill	Y	Y
11 Clarke	Y	Y
NORTH DAKOTA		
AL Dorgan	Y	Y
OHIO		
1 Luken	Y	Y
2 Gradison	Y	Y
3 Hall	Y	Y
4 Oxley	Y	Y
5 Latta	Y	Y
6 McEwen	Y	Y
7 DeWine	Y	Y
8 Kindness	Y	Y
9 Kaptur	Y	Y
10 Miller	Y	Y
11 Eckart	Y	Y
12 Kasich	Y	Y
13 Pease	Y	Y
14 Seiberling	Y	Y
15 Wylie	Y	Y
16 Regula	Y	Y
17 Williams	Y	Y
18 Applegate	Y	Y
19 Feighan	Y	Y
20 Oakar	Y	Y
21 Stokes	Y	Y
OKLAHOMA		
1 Jones	Y	Y
2 Synar	Y	Y
3 Watkins	Y	?
4 McCurdy	Y	Y
5 Edwards	Y	Y
6 English	Y	Y
OREGON		
1 AuCoin	Y	Y
2 Smith, R.	?	?
3 Wyden	Y	Y
4 Weaver	?	?
5 Smith, D.	Y	Y
PENNSYLVANIA		
1 Foglietta	Y	Y
2 Gray	Y	Y
3 Borski	Y	Y
4 Kolter	Y	Y
5 Schulze	Y	Y
6 Yatron	Y	Y
7 Edgar	Y	Y
8 Kostmayer	Y	Y
9 Shuster	Y	Y
10 McDade	Y	Y
11 Harrison	?	?
12 Murtha	Y	Y
13 Coughlin	Y	Y
14 Coyne	Y	Y
15 Ritter	Y	Y
16 Walker	Y	Y
17 Gekas	Y	Y
18 Walgren	Y	Y
19 Goodling	?	?
20 Gaydos	Y	Y
21 Ridge	Y	Y
22 Murphy	Y	Y
23 Clinger	Y	Y
RHODE ISLAND		
1 St Germain	?	?
2 Schneider	Y	Y
SOUTH CAROLINA		
1 Hartnett	Y	?
2 Spence	Y	Y
3 Derrick	Y	Y
4 Campbell	Y	Y
5 Spratt	Y	Y
6 Tallon	Y	Y
SOUTH DAKOTA		
AL Daschle	Y	Y

	224	225
TENNESSEE		
1 Quillen	Y	Y
2 Duncan	Y	Y
3 Lloyd	Y	Y
4 Cooper	Y	Y
5 Boner	?	?
6 Gore	Y	Y
7 Sundquist	Y	?
8 Jones	?	?
9 Ford	Y	Y
TEXAS		
1 Hall, S.	Y	Y
2 Wilson	Y	Y
3 Bartlett	Y	Y
4 Hall, R.	Y	Y
5 Bryant	Y	Y
6 Gramm	Y	Y
7 Archer	N	Y
8 Fields	Y	Y
9 Brooks	Y	?
10 Pickle	Y	Y
11 Leath	Y	N
12 Wright	?	?
13 Hightower	Y	?
14 Patman	Y	Y
15 de la Garza	Y	?
16 Coleman	Y	?
17 Stenholm	?	?
18 Leland	Y	+
19 Hance	?	?
20 Gonzalez	Y	Y
21 Loeffler	Y	Y
22 Paul	N	N
23 Kazen	Y	Y
24 Frost	Y	Y
25 Andrews	Y	Y
26 Vandergriff	Y	Y
27 Ortiz	Y	Y
UTAH		
1 Hansen	Y	Y
2 Marriott	Y	Y
3 Nielson	Y	Y
VERMONT		
AL Jeffords	Y	Y
VIRGINIA		
1 Bateman	Y	Y
2 Whitehurst	?	?
3 Bliley	Y	Y
4 Sisisky	Y	Y
5 Daniel	?	?
6 Olin	Y	Y
7 Robinson	Y	Y
8 Parris	Y	Y
9 Boucher	Y	Y
10 Wolf	Y	Y
WASHINGTON		
1 Pritchard	Y	Y
2 Swift	Y	Y
3 Bonker	Y	Y
4 Morrison	Y	?
5 Foley	Y	Y
6 Dicks	Y	?
7 Lowry	Y	Y
8 Chandler	Y	Y
WEST VIRGINIA		
1 Mollohan	Y	Y
2 Staggers	Y	Y
3 Wise	Y	Y
4 Rahall	Y	Y
WISCONSIN		
1 Aspin	?	?
2 Kastenmeier	Y	Y
3 Gunderson	Y	Y
4 Zablocki	Y	Y
5 Moody	Y	Y
6 Petri	Y	Y
7 Obey	Y	Y
8 Roth	Y	Y
9 Sensenbrenner	Y	Y
WYOMING		
AL Cheney	Y	Y

Southern states · Ala., Ark., Fla., Ga., Ky., La., Miss., N.C., Okla., S.C., Tenn., Texas, Va.

226. HR 10. National Development Investment Act. Walker, R-Pa., amendment to require the secretary of commerce to study whether adhering to federal rules or regulations affecting funding in the bill, such as the Davis-Bacon Act requiring that prevailing local wages be paid on federal construction projects, would reduce job opportunities in affected areas of the country. Rejected 170-245: R 139-22; D 31-223 (ND 2-165, SD 29-58), July 12, 1983.

227. HR 10. National Development Investment Act. Walker, R-Pa., amendment to permit the secretary of commerce, upon application by an Economic Development Administration grant recipient, to waive federal rules or regulations affecting funding in the bill, such as the Davis-Bacon Act requiring that prevailing local wages be paid on federal construction projects, if the waiver would increase job opportunities in the affected area. Rejected 148-270: R 124-38; D 24-232 (ND 1-168, SD 23-64), July 12, 1983.

228. HR 10. National Development Investment Act. Passage of the bill to authorize $500 million in each of fiscal years 1984-86 for Economic Development Administration grants to state and local governments and other entities to foster economic development by improving roads, bridges and other infrastructure items and by making loans to save or start small businesses; and to authorize continued funding for Appalachian Regional Commission projects at various levels in fiscal years 1984-91. Passed 306-113: R 64-98; D 242-15 (ND 166-4, SD 76-11), July 12, 1983. A "nay" was a vote supporting the president's position.

229. HR 1. Housing and Urban-Rural Recovery Act. Wylie, R-Ohio, amendment to prevent federal funds for a new $900 million multifamily rental housing production program from going to areas or communities that place rent control on projects built after the date of enactment. Rejected 206-208: R 149-10; D 57-198 (ND 18-150, SD 39-48), July 12, 1983.

230. Procedural Motion. Archer, R-Texas, motion to approve the House *Journal* of Tuesday, July 12. Motion agreed to 374-34: R 143-18; D 231-16 (ND 146-14, SD 85-2), July 13, 1983.

231. HR 1. Housing and Urban-Rural Recovery Act. Bartlett, R-Texas, amendment to allow the interest rates on Federal Housing Administration insured mortgage loans to be negotiated between the lender and the buyer. Adopted 223-201: R 156-8; D 67-193 (ND 18-154, SD 49-39), July 13, 1983. (This amendment subsequently was adopted after the House rose from the Committee of the Whole *(see vote 233 below)*.)

232. HR 1. Housing and Urban-Rural Recovery Act. Bartlett, R-Texas, amendment to eliminate $900 million for a new multifamily rental rehabilitation program and $167 million for the Section 235 homeownership program for low- and moderate-income people and transfer the money to the Section 8 rental assistance program for existing housing. Rejected 120-300: R 118-43; D 2-257 (ND 1-170, SD 1-87), July 13, 1983.

233. HR 1. Housing and Urban-Rural Recovery Act. Bartlett, R-Texas, amendment to allow the interest rates on Federal Housing Administration insured mortgage loans to be negotiated between the lender and the buyer. Adopted 228-194: R 157-6; D 71-188 (ND 18-154, SD 53-34), July 13, 1983. (This amendment previously had been adopted in the Committee of the Whole *(see vote 231, above)*.)

KEY

Y	Voted for (yea).
#	Paired for.
+	Announced for.
N	Voted against (nay).
X	Paired against.
-	Announced against.
P	Voted "present".
C	Voted "present" to avoid possible conflict of interest.
?	Did not vote or otherwise make a position known.

Democrats   *Republicans*

	226	227	228	229	230	231	232	233
ALABAMA								
1 *Edwards*	Y	Y	Y	Y	Y	Y	Y	Y
2 *Dickinson*	Y	Y	N	Y	N	Y	Y	Y
3 Nichols	N	N	Y	N	Y	Y	N	N
4 Bevill	N	N	Y	N	Y	N	N	N
5 Flippo	N	N	Y	?	Y	Y	N	Y
6 Erdreich	N	N	Y	Y	Y	Y	N	Y
7 Shelby	Y	N	Y	Y	Y	Y	N	Y
ALASKA								
AL *Young*	Y	N	Y	N	Y	N	Y	N
ARIZONA								
1 *McCain*	Y	Y	N	Y	Y	Y	Y	Y
2 Udall	N	N	Y	N	Y	N	N	N
3 *Stump*	Y	Y	N	Y	N	Y	Y	Y
4 *Rudd*	Y	Y	N	Y	Y	Y	Y	Y
5 McNulty	N	N	Y	N	Y	N	N	N
ARKANSAS								
1 Alexander	N	N	Y	N	Y	N	N	N
2 *Bethune*	Y	N	Y	Y	Y	Y	Y	Y
3 *Hammerschmidt*	Y	N	Y	?	?	?	?	?
4 Anthony	Y	N	Y	Y	Y	Y	N	Y
CALIFORNIA								
1 Bosco	N	N	Y	N	Y	?	N	N
2 *Chappie*	Y	Y	N	Y	Y	Y	Y	Y
3 Matsui	N	N	Y	N	Y	N	N	N
4 Fazio	N	N	Y	N	Y	Y	N	Y
5 Burton	N	N	Y	N	Y	N	N	N
6 Boxer	N	N	Y	N	Y	N	N	N
7 Miller	N	N	Y	N	Y	N	N	Y
8 Dellums	N	N	?	N	Y	N	N	N
9 Stark	N	N	Y	N	?	N	N	N
10 Edwards	N	N	Y	N	Y	N	N	N
11 Lantos	N	N	Y	N	Y	N	N	N
12 *Zschau*	Y	Y	N	Y	Y	Y	Y	Y
13 Mineta	N	N	Y	N	Y	N	N	N
14 *Shumway*	Y	Y	N	Y	?	?	?	?
15 Coelho	N	N	Y	N	Y	N	N	N
16 Panetta	N	N	Y	N	Y	N	N	N
17 *Pashayan*	Y	N	Y	Y	Y	Y	Y	Y
18 Lehman	N	N	Y	N	Y	N	N	N
19 *Lagomarsino*	Y	N	Y	Y	Y	Y	Y	Y
20 *Thomas*	Y	Y	N	Y	Y	Y	Y	Y
21 *Fiedler*	Y	Y	Y	Y	Y	Y	Y	Y
22 *Moorhead*	Y	Y	N	Y	Y	Y	Y	Y
23 Beilenson	N	N	Y	N	Y	N	N	N
24 Waxman	N	N	Y	N	Y	N	?	N
25 Roybal	N	N	Y	N	Y	N	N	N
26 Berman	N	N	Y	N	Y	N	N	N
27 Levine	N	N	Y	N	Y	N	N	N
28 Dixon	N	?	Y	N	Y	N	N	N
29 Hawkins	?	?	Y	X	?	?	?	?
30 Martinez	N	N	Y	N	Y	N	N	N
31 Dymally	N	N	Y	N	P	N	N	N
32 Anderson	N	N	Y	N	Y	N	N	Y
33 *Dreier*	Y	Y	N	Y	N	Y	N	Y
34 Torres	N	N	Y	N	Y	N	N	N
35 *Lewis*	Y	N	N	Y	N	Y	Y	Y
36 Brown	N	N	Y	N	Y	N	N	N
37 *McCandless*	Y	Y	N	Y	Y	Y	Y	Y
38 Patterson	N	N	Y	N	Y	N	N	N
39 *Dannemeyer*	?	?	?	?	Y	Y	Y	Y
40 *Badham*	Y	Y	N	Y	Y	Y	Y	Y
41 *Lowery*	Y	Y	N	?	Y	Y	Y	Y
42 *Lungren*	Y	Y	N	Y	Y	Y	Y	Y

	226	227	228	229	230	231	232	233
43 *Packard*	Y	Y	Y	Y	Y	Y	N	N
44 Bates	N	N	Y	N	Y	N	N	N
45 *Hunter*	Y	Y	N	Y	Y	Y	Y	Y
COLORADO								
1 Schroeder	N	N	Y	N	N	N	N	N
2 Wirth	N	N	Y	N	Y	Y	N	Y
3 Kogovsek	N	N	Y	N	Y	N	N	N
4 *Brown*	Y	Y	N	Y	Y	Y	Y	Y
5 *Kramer*	Y	Y	N	Y	N	Y	Y	Y
6 *Schaefer*	Y	Y	N	Y	N	Y	Y	Y
CONNECTICUT								
1 Kennelly	N	N	Y	N	Y	N	N	N
2 Gejdenson	N	N	Y	N	N	N	N	N
3 Morrison	N	N	Y	N	Y	N	N	N
4 *McKinney*	N	N	Y	Y	Y	Y	Y	Y
5 Ratchford	N	N	Y	N	Y	N	N	N
6 *Johnson*	Y	N	Y	Y	Y	N	N	N
DELAWARE								
AL Carper	Y	N	N	Y	Y	N	N	N
FLORIDA								
1 Hutto	Y	Y	Y	Y	Y	Y	N	Y
2 Fuqua	N	N	Y	N	Y	N	N	N
3 Bennett	N	N	Y	N	Y	N	N	N
4 Chappell	N	Y	Y	N	Y	N	N	Y
5 *McCollum*	Y	Y	N	Y	Y	Y	Y	Y
6 MacKay	N	N	Y	N	Y	N	N	N
7 Gibbons	Y	N	Y	N	Y	N	N	Y
8 *Young*	Y	Y	Y	Y	Y	Y	N	Y
9 *Bilirakis*	Y	Y	N	Y	Y	Y	N	Y
10 Ireland	Y	Y	N	Y	Y	Y	N	Y
11 Nelson	Y	Y	Y	Y	Y	Y	N	Y
12 *Lewis*	Y	Y	Y	Y	Y	Y	N	Y
13 *Mack*	Y	Y	N	Y	Y	Y	Y	Y
14 Mica	N	N	Y	N	Y	N	N	N
15 *Shaw*	Y	Y	Y	Y	Y	Y	Y	Y
16 Smith	N	N	Y	N	Y	N	N	Y
17 Lehman	N	N	Y	N	Y	N	N	N
18 Pepper	N	N	Y	N	Y	N	N	N
19 Fascell	N	N	Y	N	Y	N	N	N
GEORGIA								
1 Thomas	N	N	Y	Y	Y	Y	N	Y
2 Hatcher	N	N	Y	N	Y	N	N	N
3 Ray	Y	N	Y	Y	N	Y	N	N
4 Levitas	Y	N	Y	Y	Y	N	N	N
5 Fowler	N	N	Y	N	Y	N	N	N
6 *Gingrich*	Y	Y	Y	Y	Y	Y	Y	Y
7 McDonald	Y	Y	N	Y	Y	Y	Y	Y
8 Rowland	N	N	Y	N	Y	N	N	Y
9 Jenkins	Y	Y	Y	Y	Y	Y	N	Y
10 Barnard	Y	Y	Y	Y	Y	Y	N	Y
HAWAII								
1 Heftel	?	?	?	?	?	?	?	?
2 Akaka	N	N	Y	N	Y	N	N	N
IDAHO								
1 *Craig*	Y	Y	N	Y	N	Y	Y	Y
2 *Hansen*	Y	Y	N	?	?	Y	Y	Y
ILLINOIS								
1 Vacancy								
2 Savage	N	N	Y	N	?	N	N	N
3 Russo	N	N	Y	N	Y	N	N	N
4 *O'Brien*	Y	N	Y	Y	Y	Y	N	Y
5 Lipinski	N	N	Y	N	N	N	N	N
6 *Hyde*	Y	Y	N	Y	Y	Y	N	Y
7 Collins	N	N	Y	N	Y	N	N	N
8 Rostenkowski	N	N	Y	N	Y	N	N	N
9 Yates	N	N	Y	N	Y	N	N	N
10 *Porter*	Y	Y	N	Y	Y	Y	Y	Y
11 Annunzio	N	N	Y	N	Y	N	N	N
12 *Crane, P.*	Y	Y	N	Y	Y	Y	Y	Y
13 *Erlenborn*	Y	Y	N	Y	Y	Y	?	Y
14 *Corcoran*	Y	Y	N	Y	Y	Y	N	Y
15 *Madigan*	N	N	Y	N	Y	N	Y	Y
16 *Martin*	Y	N	Y	Y	Y	Y	N	Y
17 Evans	N	N	Y	N	Y	N	N	N
18 *Michel*	Y	N	Y	Y	Y	Y	Y	Y
19 *Crane, D.*	Y	Y	N	Y	Y	Y	Y	Y
20 Durbin	N	N	Y	N	Y	N	N	N
21 Price	N	N	Y	N	Y	N	N	N
22 Simon	N	N	Y	N	Y	N	N	N
INDIANA								
1 Hall	N	N	Y	N	Y	N	N	N
2 Sharp	N	N	Y	N	Y	N	N	N
3 *Hiler*	Y	Y	N	Y	Y	Y	Y	Y
4 *Coats*	Y	Y	Y	Y	Y	Y	Y	Y
5 Hillis	Y	Y	N	Y	?	Y	N	Y

Corresponding to Congressional Record Votes 238, 239, 240, 241, 242, 243, 244, 245

	226	227	228	229	230	231	232	233
6 ***Burton***	Y	N	N	Y	Y	Y	Y	Y
7 ***Myers***	Y	Y	N	Y	Y	Y	N	Y
8 McCloskey	N	N	Y	N	Y	N	N	N
9 Hamilton	N	N	Y	N	Y	N	N	N
10 Jacobs	N	N	Y	N	P	N	N	N
IOWA								
1 ***Leach***	Y	Y	N	Y	Y	Y	Y	Y
2 ***Tauke***	Y	Y	N	Y	Y	Y	Y	Y
3 ***Evans***	N	Y	N	Y	N	Y	Y	Y
4 Smith	N	N	Y	Y	Y	N	N	N
5 Harkin	N	N	Y	Y	N	N	N	N
6 Bedell	N	N	Y	Y	Y	N	N	N
KANSAS								
1 ***Roberts***	Y	Y	N	Y	N	Y	Y	Y
2 Slattery	N	N	N	N	Y	Y	N	Y
3 ***Winn***	Y	Y	N	Y	Y	Y	Y	Y
4 Glickman	N	N	Y	Y	Y	N	N	N
5 ***Whittaker***	Y	Y	N	Y	Y	Y	Y	Y
KENTUCKY								
1 Hubbard	N	N	Y	Y	Y	N	N	N
2 Natcher	N	N	Y	N	Y	N	N	N
3 Mazzoli	N	N	Y	N	Y	N	N	N
4 ***Snyder***	Y	Y	Y	Y	Y	Y	N	Y
5 ***Rogers***	Y	Y	Y	Y	Y	Y	Y	Y
6 ***Hopkins***	Y	Y	N	Y	Y	Y	Y	Y
7 Perkins	N	N	Y	N	Y	N	N	N
LOUISIANA								
1 ***Livingston***	Y	Y	Y	Y	Y	Y	+	+
2 Boggs	N	N	Y	N	Y	N	N	N
3 Tauzin	Y	Y	N	Y	Y	Y	N	Y
4 Roemer	Y	Y	N	Y	N	Y	N	Y
5 Huckaby	Y	Y	Y	Y	Y	Y	N	Y
6 ***Moore***	Y	Y	N	Y	Y	Y	Y	Y
7 Breaux	#	#	X	#	?	?	?	?
8 Long	N	N	Y	N	Y	N	N	N
MAINE								
1 ***McKernan***	N	Y	Y	Y	Y	Y	N	Y
2 ***Snowe***	N	Y	Y	Y	Y	N	N	N
MARYLAND								
1 Dyson	N	N	Y	N	Y	Y	N	Y
2 Long	Y	N	Y	Y	Y	N	N	N
3 Mikulski	N	N	Y	N	Y	N	N	N
4 ***Holt***	?	?	?	?	Y	Y	N	Y
5 Hoyer	N	N	Y	N	Y	N	N	N
6 Byron	N	Y	Y	Y	N	Y	N	Y
7 Mitchell	N	N	Y	N	N	N	N	N
8 Barnes	N	N	Y	?	Y	Y	N	Y
MASSACHUSETTS								
1 ***Conte***	N	N	Y	N	N	Y	N	Y
2 Boland	N	N	Y	N	Y	N	N	N
3 Early	N	N	Y	N	Y	N	N	N
4 Frank	N	N	Y	N	Y	N	N	N
5 Shannon	N	N	Y	N	Y	N	N	N
6 Mavroules	N	N	Y	N	Y	N	N	N
7 Markey	N	N	Y	N	Y	N	N	N
8 O'Neill								
9 Moakley	N	N	Y	N	Y	N	N	N
10 Studds	N	N	Y	N	Y	N	N	N
11 Donnelly	N	N	Y	N	Y	N	N	N
MICHIGAN								
1 Conyers	N	N	Y	N	?	N	N	N
2 ***Pursell***	Y	Y	Y	Y	Y	Y	N	Y
3 Wolpe	N	N	Y	N	Y	N	N	N
4 ***Siljander***	Y	Y	N	Y	Y	Y	Y	Y
5 ***Sawyer***	Y	Y	Y	Y	Y	Y	N	Y
6 Carr	N	N	Y	N	Y	N	N	N
7 Kildee	N	N	Y	N	Y	N	N	N
8 Traxler	N	N	Y	N	Y	N	N	N
9 ***Vander Jagt***	Y	Y	Y	Y	Y	Y	Y	Y
10 Albosta	N	N	Y	Y	Y	N	N	N
11 ***Davis***	N	N	Y	Y	Y	N	Y	Y
12 Bonior	N	N	Y	N	Y	N	N	N
13 Crockett	?	?	?	X	Y	N	N	?
14 Hertel	N	N	Y	N	Y	N	N	N
15 Ford	N	N	Y	N	?	N	N	N
16 Dingell	N	N	Y	N	Y	N	N	N
17 Levin	N	N	Y	N	Y	N	N	N
18 ***Broomfield***	Y	Y	N	Y	Y	Y	N	Y
MINNESOTA								
1 Penny	N	N	Y	N	Y	Y	N	Y
2 ***Weber***	Y	Y	N	Y	Y	Y	Y	Y
3 ***Frenzel***	Y	Y	N	Y	Y	Y	Y	Y
4 Vento	N	N	Y	N	Y	N	N	N
5 Sabo	N	N	Y	N	N	N	N	N
6 Sikorski	N	N	Y	N	N	Y	N	Y
7 ***Stangeland***	Y	Y	Y	Y	Y	Y	Y	Y
8 Oberstar	N	N	Y	N	P	N	N	N
MISSISSIPPI								
1 Whitten	N	N	Y	N	Y	N	N	N
2 ***Franklin***	Y	Y	Y	Y	Y	Y	Y	Y
3 Montgomery	Y	Y	Y	Y	Y	Y	N	Y
4 Dowdy	N	N	Y	N	Y	Y	N	Y
5 ***Lott***	Y	Y	Y	Y	Y	Y	Y	Y
MISSOURI								
1 Clay	N	N	Y	N	N	N	N	N
2 Young	N	N	Y	Y	Y	N	N	N
3 Gephardt	N	N	Y	N	Y	N	N	N
4 Skelton	N	N	Y	Y	Y	N	N	N
5 Wheat	N	N	Y	N	Y	N	N	N
6 ***Coleman***	Y	Y	Y	Y	Y	Y	N	Y
7 ***Taylor***	Y	Y	Y	Y	Y	Y	N	Y
8 ***Emerson***	Y	Y	Y	Y	N	Y	N	Y
9 Volkmer	N	N	Y	Y	Y	N	N	N
MONTANA								
1 Williams	N	N	Y	N	Y	N	N	N
2 ***Marlenee***	Y	Y	N	Y	Y	N	N	N
NEBRASKA								
1 ***Bereuter***	Y	Y	N	Y	Y	Y	Y	Y
2 ***Daub***	Y	Y	N	Y	Y	Y	N	Y
3 ***Smith***	Y	Y	N	Y	Y	Y	Y	Y
NEVADA								
1 Reid	N	N	Y	N	Y	N	N	N
2 ***Vucanovich***	Y	Y	N	Y	Y	Y	Y	Y
NEW HAMPSHIRE								
1 D'Amours	N	N	Y	N	Y	N	N	N
2 ***Gregg***	Y	Y	N	Y	Y	Y	Y	Y
NEW JERSEY								
1 Florio	N	N	Y	N	Y	N	N	N
2 Hughes	N	N	Y	N	Y	N	Y	N
3 Howard	N	N	Y	N	Y	N	N	N
4 ***Smith***	N	N	Y	N	Y	Y	N	Y
5 ***Roukema***	N	N	N	N	Y	N	Y	N
6 Dwyer	N	N	Y	N	Y	N	N	N
7 ***Rinaldo***	N	N	Y	N	Y	Y	N	Y
8 Roe	N	N	Y	N	Y	N	N	N
9 Torricelli	?	?	?	?	?	?	?	?
10 Rodino	X	X	#	?	Y	N	N	N
11 Minish	N	N	Y	N	Y	N	N	N
12 ***Courter***	N	N	N	Y	Y	Y	N	Y
13 ***Forsythe***	Y	Y	N	Y	N	Y	?	Y
14 Guarini	N	N	Y	N	Y	N	N	N
NEW MEXICO								
1 ***Lujan***	?	Y	Y	Y	Y	Y	Y	Y
2 ***Skeen***	Y	Y	N	Y	Y	Y	Y	Y
3 Richardson	N	N	Y	N	Y	Y	N	Y
NEW YORK								
1 ***Carney***	Y	Y	Y	Y	Y	Y	Y	Y
2 Downey	N	N	Y	N	Y	N	N	N
3 Mrazek	N	N	N	N	Y	Y	N	Y
4 ***Lent***	N	N	Y	Y	Y	Y	Y	Y
5 ***McGrath***	N	N	Y	Y	Y	Y	Y	Y
6 Addabbo	N	N	Y	N	Y	N	N	N
7 Ackerman	-	N	Y	N	Y	N	N	N
8 Scheuer	N	N	Y	N	Y	N	N	N
9 Ferraro	N	N	Y	N	Y	N	N	N
10 Schumer	N	N	Y	N	Y	N	N	N
11 Towns	N	N	Y	N	Y	N	N	N
12 Owens	N	N	Y	N	Y	N	N	N
13 Solarz	N	N	Y	N	Y	N	N	N
14 ***Molinari***	N	Y	Y	N	Y	Y	N	Y
15 ***Green***	Y	N	Y	N	Y	Y	N	Y
16 Rangel	N	N	Y	N	Y	N	N	N
17 Weiss	N	N	Y	N	?	N	N	N
18 Garcia	N	N	Y	N	Y	N	N	N
19 Biaggi	N	N	Y	N	Y	N	N	N
20 Ottinger	N	N	Y	N	P	N	N	N
21 ***Fish***	N	N	Y	N	Y	Y	N	Y
22 ***Gilman***	N	N	Y	N	Y	Y	N	Y
23 Stratton	N	N	Y	N	N	N	N	N
24 ***Solomon***	Y	Y	N	Y	N	Y	Y	Y
25 ***Boehlert***	N	N	Y	N	Y	Y	N	Y
26 ***Martin***	Y	Y	Y	Y	Y	Y	Y	Y
27 ***Wortley***	Y	Y	N	Y	Y	Y	Y	Y
28 McHugh	N	N	Y	N	Y	N	N	N
29 ***Horton***	N	N	Y	N	Y	Y	N	Y
30 ***Conable***	Y	N	N	Y	Y	Y	Y	Y
31 ***Kemp***	Y	N	N	Y	?	Y	Y	Y
32 LaFalce	N	N	Y	N	?	N	N	N
33 Nowak	N	N	Y	N	Y	N	N	N
34 Lundine	N	N	Y	N	Y	N	N	N
NORTH CAROLINA								
1 Jones	N	N	Y	N	Y	N	N	N
2 Valentine	N	Y	Y	N	Y	Y	N	Y
3 Whitley	N	N	Y	N	Y	Y	N	Y
4 Andrews	Y	Y	Y	N	Y	N	N	Y
5 Neal	N	N	Y	N	Y	Y	N	Y
6 Britt	N	N	Y	N	Y	N	N	N
7 Rose	N	N	Y	N	Y	N	N	N
8 Hefner	N	N	Y	N	Y	N	N	Y
9 ***Martin***	Y	Y	Y	Y	Y	Y	N	Y
10 ***Broyhill***	?	?	?	?	?	?	?	?
11 Clarke	N	N	Y	Y	Y	Y	N	Y
NORTH DAKOTA								
AL Dorgan	N	N	Y	N	N	N	N	N
OHIO								
1 Luken	N	N	Y	N	Y	N	N	N
2 ***Gradison***	Y	Y	Y	Y	Y	Y	Y	Y
3 Hall	N	N	Y	Y	Y	N	N	Y
4 ***Oxley***	Y	Y	N	Y	Y	Y	N	Y
5 ***Latta***	Y	Y	N	Y	Y	Y	Y	Y
6 ***McEwen***	Y	Y	Y	Y	Y	Y	Y	Y
7 ***DeWine***	Y	Y	N	Y	Y	Y	Y	Y
8 ***Kindness***	Y	Y	N	Y	Y	Y	Y	Y
9 Kaptur	N	N	Y	N	Y	N	N	N
10 ***Miller***	Y	Y	Y	Y	N	Y	Y	Y
11 Eckart	N	N	Y	N	N	Y	N	N
12 ***Kasich***	Y	Y	Y	Y	Y	Y	Y	Y
13 Pease	N	N	Y	N	Y	N	N	N
14 Seiberling	N	N	Y	N	Y	N	N	N
15 ***Wylie***	Y	N	N	Y	Y	Y	Y	Y
16 ***Regula***	Y	N	N	Y	Y	Y	Y	Y
17 ***Williams***	N	N	Y	?	Y	Y	N	Y
18 Applegate	N	N	Y	N	Y	N	?	N
19 Feighan	N	N	Y	N	Y	N	N	N
20 Oakar	N	N	Y	N	Y	N	N	N
21 Stokes	N	N	Y	N	Y	N	N	N
OKLAHOMA								
1 Jones	Y	N	Y	N	Y	Y	N	Y
2 Synar	N	N	Y	N	Y	Y	N	Y
3 Watkins	N	N	Y	N	Y	Y	N	Y
4 McCurdy	Y	N	Y	N	Y	Y	N	Y
5 ***Edwards***	Y	Y	N	Y	Y	Y	Y	Y
6 English	Y	N	N	N	Y	Y	N	Y
OREGON								
1 AuCoin	N	N	N	Y	Y	N	N	N
2 ***Smith, R.***	Y	Y	N	Y	Y	Y	Y	Y
3 Wyden	N	N	Y	N	Y	N	N	N
4 Weaver	?	N	Y	N	Y	N	N	N
5 ***Smith, D.***	Y	Y	N	Y	Y	Y	Y	Y
PENNSYLVANIA								
1 Foglietta	N	N	Y	N	Y	N	N	N
2 Gray	N	N	Y	N	Y	N	N	N
3 Borski	N	N	Y	N	Y	N	N	N
4 Kolter	N	N	Y	Y	?	N	N	N
5 ***Schulze***	Y	Y	N	Y	Y	Y	Y	Y
6 Yatron	N	N	Y	N	Y	N	N	N
7 Edgar	N	N	Y	N	Y	N	N	N
8 Kostmayer	N	N	Y	N	Y	N	N	N
9 ***Shuster***	Y	Y	Y	Y	Y	Y	Y	Y
10 ***McDade***	?	?	?	?	Y	N	Y	N
11 Harrison	-	-	+	-	Y	N	N	N
12 Murtha	N	N	Y	N	Y	N	N	N
13 ***Coughlin***	Y	Y	Y	Y	N	Y	Y	Y
14 Coyne	N	N	Y	N	Y	N	N	N
15 ***Ritter***	Y	N	Y	Y	Y	Y	Y	Y
16 ***Walker***	Y	Y	N	Y	N	Y	Y	Y
17 ***Gekas***	Y	Y	Y	Y	Y	Y	Y	Y
18 Walgren	N	N	Y	N	Y	N	N	N
19 ***Goodling***	Y	Y	Y	Y	N	Y	Y	Y
20 Gaydos	N	N	Y	Y	Y	N	N	N
21 ***Ridge***	Y	N	Y	Y	Y	Y	Y	Y
22 Murphy	N	N	Y	N	Y	Y	N	Y
23 ***Clinger***	N	N	Y	Y	Y	Y	Y	Y
RHODE ISLAND								
1 St Germain	N	N	Y	N	P	N	N	N
2 ***Schneider***	N	N	Y	Y	Y	Y	N	Y
SOUTH CAROLINA								
1 ***Hartnett***	Y	Y	N	Y	Y	N	Y	N
2 ***Spence***	Y	Y	N	Y	Y	Y	Y	Y
3 Derrick	N	Y	Y	Y	Y	N	N	N
4 ***Campbell***	Y	Y	Y	Y	Y	Y	Y	Y
5 Spratt	N	N	Y	N	?	Y	N	Y
6 Tallon	N	N	Y	Y	Y	Y	N	Y
SOUTH DAKOTA								
AL Daschle	N	N	Y	Y	Y	Y	N	Y
TENNESSEE								
1 ***Quillen***	Y	Y	Y	Y	Y	Y	Y	Y
2 ***Duncan***	Y	Y	Y	Y	Y	Y	Y	Y
3 Lloyd	N	N	Y	Y	Y	Y	N	Y
4 Cooper	N	N	Y	N	Y	N	N	N
5 Boner	N	N	Y	?	?	?	?	?
6 Gore	?	?	?	Y	Y	N	N	N
7 ***Sundquist***	Y	Y	Y	Y	Y	Y	Y	Y
8 Jones	N	N	Y	N	Y	Y	N	Y
9 Ford	?	?	?	N	Y	N	N	N
TEXAS								
1 Hall, S.	Y	Y	Y	Y	Y	Y	N	Y
2 Wilson	N	N	Y	Y	Y	N	N	N
3 ***Bartlett***	Y	Y	N	Y	Y	Y	Y	Y
4 Hall, R.	Y	Y	Y	Y	Y	Y	N	Y
5 Bryant	N	N	Y	Y	Y	Y	N	Y
6 ***Gramm***	Y	Y	N	Y	Y	Y	N	Y
7 ***Archer***	Y	Y	N	Y	Y	Y	Y	Y
8 ***Fields***	Y	Y	N	Y	Y	Y	Y	Y
9 Brooks	N	N	Y	N	Y	N	N	N
10 Pickle	N	N	Y	N	Y	Y	N	Y
11 Leath	Y	Y	Y	Y	Y	Y	N	Y
12 Wright	N	N	Y	N	Y	N	N	N
13 Hightower	Y	Y	Y	Y	Y	Y	N	Y
14 Patman	Y	N	Y	Y	Y	N	N	N
15 de la Garza	N	N	Y	N	Y	N	N	N
16 Coleman	N	N	Y	N	Y	Y	N	Y
17 Stenholm	Y	Y	N	Y	Y	Y	N	Y
18 Leland	N	N	Y	N	Y	N	N	-
19 Hance	Y	Y	N	Y	N	Y	N	Y
20 Gonzalez	N	N	Y	N	Y	N	N	N
21 ***Loeffler***	Y	Y	N	Y	Y	Y	N	Y
22 ***Paul***	Y	Y	N	Y	Y	Y	Y	Y
23 Kazen	N	Y	Y	N	Y	Y	N	Y
24 Frost	N	N	Y	N	Y	N	N	N
25 Andrews	Y	N	Y	Y	Y	Y	N	Y
26 Vandergriff	N	N	Y	Y	Y	Y	N	Y
27 Ortiz	N	N	Y	N	Y	Y	N	Y
UTAH								
1 ***Hansen***	Y	Y	N	Y	Y	Y	Y	Y
2 ***Marriott***	Y	Y	N	Y	Y	Y	Y	Y
3 ***Nielson***	Y	Y	N	Y	Y	Y	Y	Y
VERMONT								
AL ***Jeffords***	N	N	Y	Y	N	Y	Y	Y
VIRGINIA								
1 ***Bateman***	Y	Y	N	Y	Y	Y	Y	Y
2 ***Whitehurst***	Y	Y	N	Y	Y	Y	Y	Y
3 ***Bliley***	Y	Y	N	Y	Y	Y	Y	Y
4 Sisisky	N	N	Y	N	Y	Y	N	Y
5 Daniel	Y	Y	N	Y	Y	Y	N	Y
6 Olin	N	N	Y	N	Y	Y	N	Y
7 ***Robinson***	Y	Y	N	Y	Y	Y	Y	Y
8 ***Parris***	Y	N	N	Y	Y	Y	N	Y
9 Boucher	N	N	Y	N	Y	N	N	N
10 ***Wolf***	Y	Y	Y	Y	Y	Y	N	Y
WASHINGTON								
1 ***Pritchard***	Y	Y	Y	Y	Y	N	N	Y
2 Swift	N	N	Y	N	Y	N	N	N
3 Bonker	N	N	Y	N	?	N	N	N
4 ***Morrison***	Y	Y	Y	Y	Y	Y	Y	Y
5 Foley	N	N	Y	N	Y	N	N	N
6 Dicks	N	N	Y	N	Y	N	N	N
7 Lowry	N	N	Y	N	N	N	N	N
8 ***Chandler***	?	?	?	?	Y	Y	Y	Y
WEST VIRGINIA								
1 Mollohan	N	N	Y	Y	Y	Y	N	Y
2 Staggers	N	N	Y	N	Y	N	N	N
3 Wise	N	N	Y	N	Y	N	N	N
4 Rahall	N	N	Y	#	Y	N	N	N
WISCONSIN								
1 Aspin	N	N	Y	N	Y	N	N	N
2 Kastenmeier	N	N	Y	N	Y	N	N	N
3 ***Gunderson***	N	Y	Y	Y	Y	Y	Y	Y
4 Zablocki	N	N	Y	N	Y	N	N	N
5 Moody	?	N	Y	N	Y	Y	N	Y
6 ***Petri***	Y	N	N	Y	Y	Y	Y	Y
7 Obey	N	N	Y	N	Y	N	N	N
8 ***Roth***	Y	Y	N	Y	Y	Y	Y	Y
9 ***Sensenbrenner***	Y	Y	N	Y	Y	Y	Y	Y
WYOMING								
AL ***Cheney***	Y	Y	N	Y	Y	Y	Y	Y

Southern states · Ala., Ark., Fla., Ga., Ky., La., Miss., N.C., Okla., S.C., Tenn., Texas, Va.

234. HR 1. Housing and Urban-Rural Recovery Act.
Wylie, R-Ohio, motion to recommit the bill to the Banking, Finance and Urban Affairs Committee with instructions to bar communities that place rent control on projects built after enactment from receiving federal funds from a new $900 million multifamily rental housing production program. Motion rejected 205-217: R 152-10; D 53-207 (ND 14-159, SD 39-48), July 13, 1983.

235. HR 1. Housing and Urban-Rural Recovery Act.
Passage of the bill to authorize $15.64 billion in fiscal 1984 for federal housing programs and to establish a new $900 million multifamily rental housing production program. Passed 263-158: R 28-135; D 235-23 (ND 167-5, SD 68-18), July 13, 1983. A "nay" was a vote supporting the president's position.

236. HR 2769. Caribbean Basin Initiative. Adoption of the rule (H Res 246) providing for House floor consideration of the bill to provide trade and tax preferences to the nations of the Caribbean region. The rule allowed no amendments except those offered by the Ways and Means Committee. Adopted 212-204: R 131-30; D 81-174 (ND 23-146, SD 58-28), July 13, 1983.

237. HR 2769. Caribbean Basin Initiative. Passage of the bill to provide trade and tax preferences to the nations of the Caribbean region. Passed 289-129: R 145-16; D 144-113 (ND 79-90, SD 65-23), July 14, 1983. A "yea" was a vote supporting the president's position.

238. HR 2350. Health Research Extension Act. Adoption of the rule (H Res 208) providing for House floor consideration of the bill to authorize programs at the National Cancer Institute, National Heart, Lung and Blood Institute and other agencies through fiscal 1986. Adopted 388-15: R 137-13; D 251-2 (ND 166-1, SD 85-1), July 14, 1983.

239. HR 1398. Daylight-Saving Time. Coats, R-Ind., amendment to allow states to exempt themselves from the additional two months of daylight-saving time. Adopted 221-187: R 114-45; D 107-142 (ND 51-112, SD 56-30), July 14, 1983.

240. HR 1398. Daylight-Saving Time. Passage of the bill to extend daylight-saving time by beginning it on the first Sunday in March rather than the last Sunday in April. Rejected 199-211: R 62-96; D 137-115 (ND 108-57, SD 29-58), July 14, 1983.

KEY

Y	Voted for (yea).
#	Paired for.
+	Announced for.
N	Voted against (nay).
X	Paired against.
-	Announced against.
P	Voted "present".
C	Voted "present" to avoid possible conflict of interest.
?	Did not vote or otherwise make a position known.

Democrats *Republicans*

	234	235	236	237	238	239	240
ALABAMA							
1 *Edwards*	Y	N	Y	Y	Y	N	N
2 *Dickinson*	Y	Y	Y	Y	Y	Y	Y
3 Nichols	Y	Y	Y	Y	Y	Y	N
4 Bevill	N	Y	N	N	Y	N	N
5 Flippo	Y	Y	Y	N	Y	N	Y
6 Erdreich	Y	Y	N	N	Y	Y	Y
7 Shelby	Y	Y	Y	N	Y	N	Y
ALASKA							
AL *Young*	Y	N	Y	Y	Y	Y	N
ARIZONA							
1 *McCain*	Y	N	Y	Y	Y	Y	N
2 Udall	N	Y	N	Y	Y	N	N
3 *Stump*	Y	N	Y	N	Y	N	N
4 *Rudd*	Y	N	Y	Y	Y	Y	N
5 McNulty	N	Y	N	Y	Y	Y	N
ARKANSAS							
1 Alexander	N	Y	Y	Y	Y	?	Y
2 *Bethune*	Y	?	N	Y	Y	Y	?
3 *Hammerschmidt*	?	?	?	Y	?	Y	N
4 Anthony	Y	Y	Y	Y	Y	Y	N
CALIFORNIA							
1 Bosco	N	Y	N	Y	Y	Y	N
2 *Chappie*	Y	N	Y	Y	Y	Y	N
3 Matsui	N	#	N	N	Y	N	N
4 Fazio	N	Y	N	?	?	?	?
5 Burton	N	Y	N	N	Y	N	Y
6 Boxer	N	Y	N	N	Y	N	Y
7 Miller	N	Y	N	N	Y	N	Y
8 Dellums	N	Y	N	N	Y	N	Y
9 Stark	N	Y	?	Y	Y	N	Y
10 Edwards	N	Y	N	N	Y	N	Y
11 Lantos	N	Y	N	N	Y	N	Y
12 *Zschau*	Y	N	Y	Y	Y	Y	Y
13 Mineta	N	Y	N	N	Y	N	Y
14 *Shumway*	?	?	?	Y	Y	Y	Y
15 Coelho	N	Y	N	Y	Y	N	N
16 Panetta	N	Y	N	N	Y	N	Y
17 *Pashayan*	Y	N	Y	Y	Y	Y	N
18 Lehman	N	Y	N	Y	Y	Y	N
19 *Lagomarsino*	Y	N	Y	Y	Y	N	Y
20 *Thomas*	Y	N	Y	Y	Y	N	Y
21 *Fiedler*	Y	N	Y	Y	Y	Y	Y
22 *Moorhead*	Y	N	Y	Y	Y	N	Y
23 Beilenson	N	Y	Y	Y	Y	N	Y
24 Waxman	N	Y	N	Y	Y	N	Y
25 Roybal	N	Y	N	N	Y	N	Y
26 Berman	N	Y	Y	Y	Y	N	Y
27 Levine	N	Y	N	Y	Y	?	?
28 Dixon	N	Y	N	N	Y	N	Y
29 Hawkins	?	?	?	N	Y	N	Y
30 Martinez	N	Y	N	Y	Y	N	Y
31 Dymally	N	Y	Y	Y	Y	N	Y
32 Anderson	Y	Y	N	N	Y	N	Y
33 *Dreier*	Y	N	Y	N	Y	N	Y
34 Torres	N	Y	N	Y	Y	N	Y
35 *Lewis*	Y	N	Y	Y	Y	Y	Y
36 Brown	N	Y	N	Y	Y	?	?
37 *McCandless*	Y	N	Y	Y	Y	N	Y
38 Patterson	N	Y	N	N	Y	N	Y
39 *Dannemeyer*	Y	N	Y	N	N	Y	Y
40 *Badham*	Y	N	Y	#	?	?	#
41 *Lowery*	Y	N	Y	Y	Y	N	Y
42 *Lungren*	Y	N	Y	Y	N	N	Y

	234	235	236	237	238	239	240
43 *Packard*	Y	N	?	?	?	?	?
44 Bates	N	Y	N	N	Y	N	Y
45 *Hunter*	Y	N	Y	Y	Y	Y	Y
COLORADO							
1 Schroeder	N	Y	N	N	Y	N	N
2 Wirth	N	Y	Y	Y	Y	Y	Y
3 Kogovsek	N	Y	N	Y	Y	Y	Y
4 *Brown*	Y	N	N	Y	Y	Y	Y
5 *Kramer*	Y	N	Y	Y	Y	Y	Y
6 *Schaefer*	Y	N	Y	Y	Y	Y	Y
CONNECTICUT							
1 Kennelly	N	Y	Y	Y	Y	N	Y
2 Gejdenson	N	Y	N	Y	Y	N	Y
3 Morrison	N	Y	N	N	Y	N	Y
4 *McKinney*	Y	Y	N	Y	Y	N	N
5 Ratchford	N	Y	N	Y	Y	N	N
6 *Johnson*	N	Y	Y	Y	Y	Y	Y
DELAWARE							
AL Carper	N	Y	N	Y	Y	Y	Y
FLORIDA							
1 Hutto	Y	Y	Y	Y	Y	N	Y
2 Fuqua	N	Y	Y	Y	Y	Y	N
3 Bennett	Y	Y	Y	Y	Y	Y	Y
4 Chappell	Y	Y	Y	Y	Y	Y	N
5 *McCollum*	Y	N	Y	Y	Y	N	Y
6 MacKay	Y	Y	Y	Y	Y	Y	N
7 Gibbons	Y	Y	Y	Y	Y	N	N
8 *Young*	Y	N	Y	Y	Y	N	Y
9 *Bilirakis*	Y	N	N	Y	Y	Y	Y
10 Ireland	Y	N	?	?	Y	N	Y
11 Nelson	Y	+	Y	Y	Y	N	Y
12 *Lewis*	Y	N	Y	N	Y	Y	Y
13 *Mack*	Y	N	Y	N	Y	Y	Y
14 Mica	Y	Y	Y	Y	Y	N	Y
15 *Shaw*	Y	N	Y	Y	Y	N	Y
16 Smith	N	Y	Y	Y	Y	N	Y
17 Lehman	N	Y	Y	Y	Y	N	Y
18 Pepper	N	Y	Y	Y	Y	N	Y
19 Fascell	N	Y	Y	Y	Y	N	Y
GEORGIA							
1 Thomas	Y	Y	Y	Y	Y	N	Y
2 Hatcher	N	Y	Y	Y	Y	Y	N
3 Ray	Y	N	Y	N	Y	N	N
4 Levitas	Y	N	N	Y	Y	Y	N
5 Fowler	N	Y	Y	Y	Y	N	N
6 *Gingrich*	Y	N	Y	Y	Y	Y	N
7 McDonald	Y	N	N	N	N	Y	N
8 Rowland	N	Y	Y	Y	Y	Y	N
9 Jenkins	N	Y	Y	Y	Y	N	N
10 Barnard	Y	N	Y	N	Y	?	?
HAWAII							
1 Heftel	?	?	?	X	?	?	?
2 Akaka	N	Y	N	N	Y	N	N
IDAHO							
1 *Craig*	Y	N	Y	Y	Y	Y	N
2 *Hansen*	Y	N	Y	Y	Y	Y	N
ILLINOIS							
1 Vacancy							
2 Savage	N	Y	N	N	Y	N	Y
3 Russo	N	Y	Y	Y	Y	N	Y
4 *O'Brien*	Y	Y	Y	Y	?	Y	Y
5 Lipinski	N	Y	N	Y	Y	N	N
6 *Hyde*	Y	N	Y	Y	Y	N	Y
7 Collins	N	Y	N	N	Y	N	Y
8 Rostenkowski	N	Y	Y	Y	Y	N	N
9 Yates	N	Y	N	N	Y	N	N
10 *Porter*	Y	Y	Y	Y	Y	Y	Y
11 Annunzio	N	Y	N	Y	Y	N	Y
12 *Crane, P.*	Y	N	N	Y	Y	Y	Y
13 *Erlenborn*	Y	N	Y	Y	Y	N	Y
14 *Corcoran*	Y	N	Y	Y	Y	N	Y
15 *Madigan*	Y	N	Y	Y	Y	N	N
16 *Martin*	Y	N	N	Y	Y	N	N
17 Evans	N	Y	N	N	Y	N	Y
18 *Michel*	Y	N	Y	Y	?	Y	Y
19 *Crane, D.*	Y	N	N	?	?	?	?
20 Durbin	N	Y	N	N	Y	N	Y
21 Price	N	Y	Y	Y	Y	N	Y
22 Simon	N	Y	N	Y	Y	N	Y
INDIANA							
1 Hall	N	Y	N	N	Y	N	N
2 Sharp	N	Y	N	Y	Y	Y	N
3 *Hiler*	Y	N	Y	Y	Y	Y	N
4 *Coats*	Y	N	Y	Y	Y	Y	N
5 Hillis	Y	N	Y	Y	?	Y	N

ND · Northern Democrats   SD · Southern Democrats

	234	235	236	237	238	239	240
6 ***Burton***	Y	N	Y	Y	N	Y	N
7 ***Myers***	Y	N	Y	Y	Y	Y	N
8 McCloskey	N	Y	N	Y	Y	Y	Y
9 Hamilton	N	Y	N	Y	Y	Y	N
10 Jacobs	N	Y	N	Y	?	Y	Y
IOWA							
1 ***Leach***	Y	N	N	Y	Y	Y	N
2 ***Tauke***	Y	N	Y	Y	Y	Y	N
3 ***Evans***	Y	N	Y	Y	Y	Y	N
4 Smith	Y	Y	N	Y	Y	Y	N
5 Harkin	Y	Y	N	N	Y	Y	N
6 Bedell	Y	Y	P	Y	Y	Y	N
KANSAS							
1 ***Roberts***	Y	N	Y	Y	Y	Y	N
2 Slattery	N	Y	N	N	Y	Y	N
3 ***Winn***	Y	N	Y	Y	Y	Y	N
4 Glickman	Y	Y	N	Y	Y	N	N
5 ***Whittaker***	Y	N	Y	Y	Y	Y	N
KENTUCKY							
1 Hubbard	Y	Y	N	N	Y	Y	N
2 Natcher	N	Y	N	N	Y	Y	N
3 Mazzoli	N	Y	Y	Y	Y	N	Y
4 ***Snyder***	Y	N	N	N	Y	Y	N
5 ***Rogers***	Y	N	N	N	Y	Y	N
6 ***Hopkins***	?	N	N	N	Y	Y	N
7 Perkins	N	Y	Y	N	Y	Y	N
LOUISIANA							
1 ***Livingston***	+	N	Y	Y	Y	Y	Y
2 Boggs	N	Y	?	Y	Y	Y	Y
3 Tauzin	Y	N	N	Y	Y	Y	N
4 Roemer	Y	N	N	Y	Y	Y	N
5 Huckaby	Y	N	Y	Y	Y	Y	Y
6 ***Moore***	Y	N	Y	Y	Y	N	Y
7 Breaux	?	X	?	Y	Y	Y	Y
8 Long	N	Y	Y	Y	Y	Y	N
MAINE							
1 ***McKernan***	Y	Y	Y	Y	Y	N	N
2 ***Snowe***	N	Y	Y	Y	Y	N	N
MARYLAND							
1 Dyson	N	Y	N	N	Y	Y	N
2 Long	N	Y	N	Y	Y	N	Y
3 Mikulski	N	Y	N	N	N	Y	N
4 ***Holt***	Y	N	Y	Y	Y	Y	N
5 Hoyer	N	Y	N	Y	Y	N	Y
6 Byron	Y	N	N	Y	Y	Y	N
7 Mitchell	N	Y	N	N	?	N	Y
8 Barnes	N	Y	N	Y	Y	N	Y
MASSACHUSETTS							
1 ***Conte***	N	Y	N	Y	Y	N	Y
2 Boland	N	Y	N	Y	Y	N	Y
3 Early	N	Y	N	N	Y	?	?
4 Frank	N	Y	N	N	Y	Y	Y
5 Shannon	N	Y	N	N	Y	N	Y
6 Mavroules	N	Y	N	N	Y	N	Y
7 Markey	N	Y	Y	Y	Y	N	Y
8 O'Neill							
9 Moakley	N	Y	Y	Y	Y	N	Y
10 Studds	N	Y	N	?	?	?	Y
11 Donnelly	N	Y	N	N	Y	N	Y
MICHIGAN							
1 Conyers	N	Y	N	?	?	?	?
2 ***Pursell***	Y	N	Y	Y	Y	Y	N
3 Wolpe	N	Y	N	Y	Y	Y	N
4 ***Siljander***	Y	N	Y	Y	Y	Y	N
5 ***Sawyer***	Y	N	Y	Y	Y	Y	Y
6 Carr	N	Y	N	N	Y	Y	N
7 Kildee	N	Y	N	N	Y	N	Y
8 Traxler	N	Y	N	N	Y	Y	N
9 ***Vander Jagt***	Y	N	Y	Y	Y	Y	Y
10 Albosta	N	Y	Y	Y	Y	Y	N
11 ***Davis***	Y	Y	Y	N	Y	Y	N
12 Bonior	N	Y	Y	Y	Y	N	Y
13 Crockett	N	Y	N	N	Y	N	Y
14 Hertel	N	Y	N	N	Y	N	N
15 Ford	N	Y	N	N	Y	N	Y
16 Dingell	N	Y	N	N	Y	N	Y
17 Levin	N	Y	N	Y	Y	Y	Y
18 ***Broomfield***	Y	N	Y	Y	Y	Y	Y
MINNESOTA							
1 Penny	N	N	N	N	Y	Y	N
2 ***Weber***	Y	N	Y	Y	N	Y	N
3 ***Frenzel***	Y	N	Y	Y	Y	N	Y
4 Vento	N	Y	N	N	Y	N	Y
5 Sabo	N	Y	N	Y	Y	N	Y
6 Sikorski	N	Y	N	N	Y	Y	N

	234	235	236	237	238	239	240
7 ***Stangeland***	Y	N	Y	?	Y	Y	N
8 Oberstar	N	Y	N	N	Y	N	N
MISSISSIPPI							
1 Whitten	N	Y	N	N	Y	Y	N
2 ***Franklin***	Y	N	Y	Y	Y	Y	N
3 Montgomery	Y	N	Y	Y	Y	N	Y
4 Dowdy	N	Y	N	N	Y	N	Y
5 ***Lott***	Y	N	Y	Y	Y	Y	N
MISSOURI							
1 Clay	N	Y	N	N	Y	N	Y
2 Young	Y	Y	N	N	Y	Y	N
3 Gephardt	N	Y	N	N	Y	?	?
4 Skelton	Y	Y	N	N	Y	Y	N
5 Wheat	N	Y	N	N	Y	N	Y
6 ***Coleman***	Y	N	Y	Y	?	Y	N
7 ***Taylor***	Y	N	Y	N	Y	Y	N
8 ***Emerson***	Y	N	Y	N	Y	Y	N
9 Volkmer	Y	Y	N	N	Y	Y	N
MONTANA							
1 Williams	N	Y	N	Y	Y	N	N
2 ***Marlenee***	Y	N	N	Y	Y	Y	N
NEBRASKA							
1 ***Bereuter***	Y	N	Y	Y	Y	Y	N
2 ***Daub***	Y	N	N	Y	Y	Y	N
3 ***Smith***	Y	N	Y	Y	Y	Y	N
NEVADA							
1 Reid	N	Y	N	Y	Y	Y	Y
2 ***Vucanovich***	Y	N	Y	Y	Y	Y	N
NEW HAMPSHIRE							
1 D'Amours	N	Y	N	Y	Y	N	Y
2 ***Gregg***	Y	N	Y	Y	Y	N	Y
NEW JERSEY							
1 Florio	N	Y	N	Y	Y	N	Y
2 Hughes	N	Y	N	Y	Y	N	Y
3 Howard	N	Y	N	N	Y	N	Y
4 ***Smith***	N	Y	Y	Y	Y	Y	Y
5 ***Roukema***	N	N	Y	Y	Y	N	Y
6 Dwyer	N	Y	N	Y	Y	N	Y
7 ***Rinaldo***	N	Y	N	Y	?	N	Y
8 Roe	N	Y	N	Y	Y	N	Y
9 Torricelli	?	?	?	N	Y	N	Y
10 Rodino	N	Y	N	?	?	?	?
11 Minish	N	Y	N	N	Y	N	Y
12 ***Courter***	Y	N	Y	Y	Y	N	Y
13 ***Forsythe***	Y	N	Y	Y	Y	N	N
14 Guarini	N	Y	N	Y	Y	N	Y
NEW MEXICO							
1 ***Lujan***	Y	N	Y	Y	Y	?	?
2 ***Skeen***	Y	N	Y	Y	Y	Y	N
3 Richardson	N	Y	N	Y	Y	Y	Y
NEW YORK							
1 ***Carney***	Y	N	N	Y	Y	Y	Y
2 Downey	N	Y	Y	Y	Y	N	Y
3 Mrazek	N	Y	N	Y	Y	N	Y
4 ***Lent***	Y	N	Y	Y	?	Y	Y
5 ***McGrath***	Y	N	N	Y	Y	Y	Y
6 Addabbo	N	Y	Y	Y	Y	?	#
7 Ackerman	N	Y	N	N	Y	N	N
8 Scheuer	N	Y	N	N	Y	N	N
9 Ferraro	N	Y	N	Y	Y	N	Y
10 Schumer	N	Y	N	Y	Y	N	Y
11 Towns	N	Y	N	Y	Y	N	Y
12 Owens	N	Y	N	Y	Y	N	Y
13 Solarz	N	Y	N	Y	Y	Y	N
14 ***Molinari***	Y	N	Y	Y	Y	N	Y
15 ***Green***	N	Y	Y	Y	?	N	Y
16 Rangel	N	Y	Y	Y	Y	N	Y
17 Weiss	N	Y	N	Y	Y	N	Y
18 Garcia	N	Y	N	Y	Y	N	Y
19 Biaggi	N	Y	N	Y	Y	N	Y
20 Ottinger	N	Y	N	Y	Y	N	Y
21 ***Fish***	N	Y	N	Y	Y	N	Y
22 ***Gilman***	N	Y	N	Y	Y	N	Y
23 Stratton	N	Y	N	Y	Y	N	Y
24 ***Solomon***	Y	N	Y	Y	Y	Y	N
25 ***Boehlert***	Y	N	Y	Y	Y	Y	N
26 ***Martin***	Y	N	Y	Y	Y	Y	N
27 ***Wortley***	Y	N	N	Y	Y	Y	N
28 McHugh	N	Y	N	N	Y	N	Y
29 ***Horton***	N	Y	N	N	Y	N	N
30 ***Conable***	Y	N	Y	Y	Y	N	Y
31 ***Kemp***	Y	N	Y	Y	Y	Y	N
32 LaFalce	N	Y	N	Y	Y	N	Y
33 Nowak	N	Y	N	N	Y	N	Y
34 ***Lundine***	N	Y	N	N	Y	Y	N

	234	235	236	237	238	239	240
NORTH CAROLINA							
1 Jones	N	Y	N	N	?	N	N
2 Valentine	Y	Y	Y	N	Y	Y	N
3 Whitley	N	Y	N	N	Y	N	N
4 Andrews	Y	Y	Y	Y	Y	N	N
5 Neal	N	Y	N	Y	Y	Y	Y
6 Britt	N	Y	Y	Y	Y	N	N
7 Rose	N	Y	Y	N	Y	?	?
8 Hefner	N	Y	N	N	Y	Y	N
9 ***Martin***	Y	N	Y	Y	?	N	N
10 ***Broyhill***	?	?	?	?	?	?	X
11 Clarke	N	Y	Y	Y	Y	N	N
NORTH DAKOTA							
AL Dorgan	N	N	?	Y	Y	Y	N
OHIO							
1 Luken	N	Y	N	N	Y	N	Y
2 ***Gradison***	Y	Y	Y	Y	Y	Y	N
3 Hall	Y	Y	Y	N	Y	N	Y
4 ***Oxley***	Y	N	Y	Y	Y	Y	N
5 ***Latta***	Y	N	Y	Y	Y	Y	N
6 ***McEwen***	Y	N	Y	N	Y	Y	N
7 ***DeWine***	Y	N	Y	Y	Y	Y	N
8 ***Kindness***	Y	N	Y	Y	Y	Y	N
9 Kaptur	N	Y	N	N	Y	N	Y
10 ***Miller***	Y	N	Y	N	Y	N	N
11 Eckart	N	Y	N	N	Y	N	N
12 ***Kasich***	Y	N	N	Y	Y	Y	N
13 Pease	N	Y	Y	Y	Y	N	N
14 Seiberling	N	Y	N	Y	Y	N	Y
15 ***Wylie***	Y	N	Y	N	?	N	N
16 ***Regula***	Y	N	Y	Y	Y	N	N
17 ***Williams***	Y	Y	?	N	Y	?	?
18 Applegate	N	N	N	N	Y	Y	N
19 Feighan	N	Y	N	N	Y	Y	N
20 Oakar	N	Y	N	N	Y	N	N
21 Stokes	N	Y	N	N	Y	N	Y
OKLAHOMA							
1 Jones	N	Y	Y	Y	Y	N	Y
2 Synar	N	Y	N	Y	Y	N	Y
3 Watkins	N	Y	N	Y	Y	Y	N
4 McCurdy	N	N	Y	Y	Y	Y	N
5 ***Edwards***	Y	N	Y	Y	Y	Y	N
6 English	N	N	N	Y	Y	Y	N
OREGON							
1 AuCoin	Y	Y	-	N	Y	Y	Y
2 ***Smith, R.***	Y	N	Y	Y	Y	Y	N
3 Wyden	N	Y	N	N	Y	N	Y
4 Weaver	N	Y	N	N	Y	Y	Y
5 ***Smith, D.***	Y	N	Y	Y	N	Y	Y
PENNSYLVANIA							
1 Foglietta	N	Y	N	N	Y	N	Y
2 Gray	N	Y	N	N	Y	N	Y
3 Borski	N	Y	N	N	Y	N	Y
4 Kolter	N	Y	N	N	Y	Y	N
5 ***Schulze***	Y	N	Y	Y	Y	?	X
6 Yatron	Y	Y	N	N	Y	Y	N
7 Edgar	N	Y	N	N	Y	N	Y
8 Kostmayer	N	Y	N	Y	Y	N	Y
9 ***Shuster***	Y	N	Y	Y	Y	Y	N
10 ***McDade***	Y	Y	N	Y	Y	Y	N
11 Harrison	N	Y	N	N	Y	Y	N
12 Murtha	N	Y	Y	N	Y	N	N
13 ***Coughlin***	Y	Y	Y	Y	Y	N	Y
14 Coyne	N	Y	N	Y	Y	N	Y
15 ***Ritter***	Y	N	Y	Y	?	N	N
16 ***Walker***	Y	N	N	N	N	Y	N
17 ***Gekas***	Y	N	Y	Y	Y	N	N
18 Walgren	N	Y	N	N	Y	Y	Y
19 ***Goodling***	Y	N	Y	Y	Y	Y	N
20 Gaydos	N	Y	N	N	Y	Y	N
21 ***Ridge***	Y	Y	N	Y	Y	N	N
22 Murphy	Y	Y	N	N	Y	N	Y
23 ***Clinger***	Y	Y	Y	Y	Y	Y	N
RHODE ISLAND							
1 St Germain	N	Y	Y	?	?	?	?
2 ***Schneider***	Y	Y	N	Y	Y	N	N
SOUTH CAROLINA							
1 ***Hartnett***	Y	N	Y	Y	Y	Y	N
2 ***Spence***	Y	N	Y	Y	Y	Y	N
3 Derrick	N	Y	Y	N	Y	Y	Y
4 ***Campbell***	Y	N	Y	Y	?	Y	N
5 Spratt	N	Y	Y	Y	Y	Y	N
6 Tallon	Y	Y	N	Y	Y	Y	N
SOUTH DAKOTA							
AL Daschle	N	Y	N	N	Y	Y	N

	234	235	236	237	238	239	240
TENNESSEE							
1 ***Quillen***	Y	Y	Y	Y	Y	Y	N
2 ***Duncan***	Y	Y	Y	N	Y	Y	N
3 Lloyd	Y	Y	N	N	Y	Y	N
4 Cooper	N	Y	N	N	Y	Y	Y
5 Boner	?	?	?	N	Y	Y	Y
6 Gore	N	Y	N	N	Y	N	N
7 ***Sundquist***	Y	Y	N	Y	Y	Y	N
8 Jones	N	Y	N	N	Y	N	N
9 Ford	N	Y	Y	Y	Y	N	N
TEXAS							
1 Hall, S.	Y	N	Y	Y	Y	Y	N
2 Wilson	Y	Y	Y	Y	?	Y	N
3 ***Bartlett***	Y	N	Y	Y	Y	Y	Y
4 Hall, R.	Y	N	Y	Y	Y	Y	N
5 Bryant	N	Y	N	Y	Y	N	Y
6 ***Gramm***	Y	N	?	Y	N	Y	N
7 ***Archer***	Y	N	Y	Y	Y	Y	Y
8 ***Fields***	Y	N	Y	Y	N	Y	N
9 Brooks	N	Y	Y	Y	Y	Y	Y
10 Pickle	N	Y	Y	Y	Y	N	N
11 Leath	Y	N	Y	Y	Y	Y	N
12 Wright	N	Y	Y	Y	Y	Y	N
13 Hightower	Y	Y	N	Y	Y	Y	N
14 Patman	Y	Y	N	Y	Y	Y	N
15 de la Garza	N	Y	Y	Y	Y	Y	N
16 Coleman	N	Y	Y	Y	Y	Y	N
17 Stenholm	Y	N	Y	Y	Y	Y	N
18 Leland	-	+	-	-	+	-	-
19 Hance	Y	N	Y	Y	Y	Y	N
20 Gonzalez	N	Y	Y	N	Y	Y	N
21 ***Loeffler***	Y	N	Y	Y	Y	Y	N
22 ***Paul***	Y	N	N	N	N	Y	Y
23 Kazen	N	Y	Y	Y	Y	Y	N
24 Frost	N	Y	Y	N	Y	N	N
25 Andrews	Y	N	Y	Y	Y	Y	Y
26 Vandergriff	Y	N	N	N	Y	Y	N
27 Ortiz	Y	Y	Y	Y	Y	Y	N
UTAH							
1 ***Hansen***	Y	N	Y	Y	Y	Y	N
2 ***Marriott***	Y	N	Y	Y	Y	N	Y
3 ***Nielson***	Y	N	Y	Y	N	Y	N
VERMONT							
AL ***Jeffords***	Y	Y	N	Y	Y	Y	Y
VIRGINIA							
1 ***Bateman***	Y	N	Y	Y	Y	N	N
2 ***Whitehurst***	Y	N	Y	Y	Y	N	N
3 ***Bliley***	Y	N	Y	Y	Y	Y	Y
4 Sisisky	N	Y	Y	Y	Y	N	N
5 Daniel	Y	N	Y	Y	Y	N	N
6 Olin	N	Y	Y	Y	Y	Y	N
7 ***Robinson***	Y	N	Y	Y	Y	Y	N
8 ***Parris***	Y	N	Y	Y	Y	Y	Y
9 Boucher	N	Y	N	Y	Y	N	N
10 ***Wolf***	Y	N	Y	Y	Y	Y	Y
WASHINGTON							
1 ***Pritchard***	Y	Y	Y	?	?	?	?
2 Swift	N	Y	N	Y	Y	N	Y
3 Bonker	N	Y	N	Y	Y	N	Y
4 ***Morrison***	Y	N	Y	Y	Y	Y	Y
5 Foley	N	Y	Y	Y	Y	N	Y
6 Dicks	N	Y	N	?	?	?	?
7 Lowry	N	Y	N	Y	Y	N	Y
8 ***Chandler***	Y	N	Y	Y	Y	N	N
WEST VIRGINIA							
1 Mollohan	N	Y	N	N	Y	Y	N
2 Staggers	N	Y	N	N	Y	Y	N
3 Wise	N	Y	N	N	Y	Y	N
4 Rahall	Y	Y	N	N	Y	Y	N
WISCONSIN							
1 Aspin	N	Y	N	Y	Y	Y	Y
2 Kastenmeier	N	Y	N	N	Y	N	Y
3 ***Gunderson***	Y	N	Y	Y	Y	Y	N
4 Zablocki	N	Y	Y	Y	Y	N	Y
5 Moody	N	N	Y	Y	Y	N	Y
6 ***Petri***	Y	N	Y	Y	Y	Y	N
7 Obey	N	Y	N	N	Y	?	N
8 ***Roth***	Y	N	Y	Y	Y	Y	N
9 ***Sensenbrenner***	Y	N	Y	Y	Y	Y	Y
WYOMING							
AL ***Cheney***	Y	N	Y	Y	Y	Y	N

Southern states - Ala., Ark., Fla., Ga., Ky., La., Miss., N.C., Okla., S.C., Tenn., Texas, Va.

KEY

Y Voted for (yea).
Paired for.
+ Announced for.
N Voted against (nay).
X Paired against.
- Announced against.
P Voted "present".
C Voted "present" to avoid possible conflict of interest.
? Did not vote or otherwise make a position known.

Democrats   *Republicans*

241. HR 3385. Upland Cotton PIK Program. De la Garza, D-Texas, motion to suspend the rules and pass the bill to require the secretary of agriculture to take bids from cotton producers for federal acquisition of cotton under price support loans for use in the 1983 cotton Payment-in-Kind (PIK) program and to specify that bids meeting certain criteria must be accepted. Motion agreed to 312-97: R 96-70; D 216-27 (ND 134-26, SD 82-1), July 19, 1983. A two-thirds majority of those present and voting (274 in this case) is required for passage under suspension of the rules. A "nay" was a vote supporting the president's position.

242. H Res 268. Committee Election. Adoption of the resolution to elect Rep. Sala Burton, D-Calif., to the Committee on Education and Labor and the Committee on Interior and Insular Affairs. Adopted 298-112: R 52-112; D 246-0 (ND 162-0, SD 84-0), July 19, 1983.

243. H Res 266. Daniel B. Crane Censure. Michel, R-Ill., motion to recommit the resolution to the Committee on Standards of Official Conduct with instructions that the committee report a recommendation of censure instead of merely a reprimand. Motion agreed to 289-136: R 129-37; D 160-99 (ND 85-85, SD 75-14), July 20, 1983.

244. H Res 266. Daniel B. Crane Censure. Adoption of the resolution to censure Rep. Daniel B. Crane, R-Ill. Adopted 421-3: R 165-0; D 256-3 (ND 167-3, SD 89-0), July 20, 1983.

245. H Res 265. Gerry E. Studds Censure. Michel, R-Ill., motion to recommit the resolution to the Committee on Standards of Official Conduct with instructions that the committee report a recommendation of censure instead of merely a reprimand. Motion agreed to 338-87: R 158-8; D 180-79 (ND 96-74, SD 84-5), July 20, 1983.

246. H Res 265. Gerry E. Studds Censure. Adoption of the resolution to censure Rep. Gerry E. Studds, D-Mass. Adopted 420-3: R 164-0; D 256-3 (ND 167-3, SD 89-0), July 20, 1983.

247. HR 2969. Department of Defense Authorization. Dicks, D-Wash., amendment to remove from the bill a ban on seeking a second production source for the gas turbine engine of the M-1 tank. Rejected 187-241: R 70-97; D 117-144 (ND 90-83, SD 27-61), July 20, 1983.

248. HR 2969. Department of Defense Authorization. Bennett, D-Fla., amendment to delete $2.6 billion for procurement of 27 MX missiles. Rejected 207-220: R 18-147; D 189-73 (ND 157-16, SD 32-57), July 20, 1983. A "nay" was a vote supporting the president's position.

	241	242	243	244	245	246	247	248
ALABAMA								
1 *Edwards*	Y	N	Y	Y	Y	Y	N	N
2 *Dickinson*	Y	N	Y	Y	Y	Y	N	N
3 Nichols	Y	Y	Y	Y	Y	Y	N	N
4 Bevill	Y	N	Y	Y	Y	Y	N	N
5 Flippo	Y	N	Y	Y	Y	Y	N	N
6 Erdreich	Y	Y	Y	Y	Y	Y	Y	N
7 Shelby	Y	Y	Y	Y	Y	Y	Y	N
ALASKA								
AL *Young*	Y	N	N	N	Y	Y	Y	N
ARIZONA								
1 *McCain*	Y	N	Y	Y	Y	Y	Y	N
2 Udall	Y	Y	Y	Y	Y	Y	Y	Y
3 *Stump*	Y	Y	Y	Y	Y	Y	Y	N
4 *Rudd*	Y	Y	Y	Y	Y	Y	Y	N
5 McNulty	Y	Y	Y	Y	Y	Y	Y	Y
ARKANSAS								
1 Alexander	Y	Y	Y	Y	Y	Y	N	N
2 *Bethune*	Y	N	Y	Y	Y	Y	N	N
3 *Hammerschmidt*	Y	Y	Y	Y	Y	Y	N	N
4 Anthony	Y	Y	Y	Y	Y	Y	Y	Y
CALIFORNIA								
1 Bosco	Y	Y	N	Y	N	Y	N	Y
2 *Chappie*	N	Y	N	Y	N	Y	N	N
3 Matsui	Y	Y	N	Y	N	Y	N	Y
4 Fazio	Y	Y	N	Y	N	Y	N	Y
5 Burton	Y	Y	N	Y	N	Y	N	Y
6 Boxer	Y	Y	Y	Y	Y	Y	Y	Y
7 Miller	N	Y	N	Y	N	Y	Y	Y
8 Dellums	N	Y	?	?	?	?	Y	Y
9 Stark	N	?	N	Y	N	Y	N	Y
10 Edwards	Y	Y	N	Y	N	Y	N	Y
11 Lantos	Y	Y	N	Y	N	Y	Y	Y
12 *Zschau*	N	Y	Y	Y	Y	Y	Y	N
13 Mineta	Y	Y	N	Y	N	Y	N	Y
14 *Shumway*	N	Y	Y	Y	Y	Y	N	N
15 Coelho	Y	Y	Y	Y	Y	Y	N	Y
16 Panetta	Y	Y	Y	Y	Y	Y	Y	Y
17 *Pashayan*	Y	N	Y	Y	Y	Y	N	N
18 Lehman	Y	Y	N	Y	N	Y	N	Y
19 *Lagomarsino*	N	Y	Y	Y	Y	Y	N	N
20 *Thomas*	Y	N	Y	Y	Y	Y	N	N
21 *Fiedler*	Y	Y	Y	Y	Y	Y	N	N
22 *Moorhead*	N	Y	Y	Y	Y	Y	N	N
23 Beilenson	N	Y	N	Y	N	Y	Y	Y
24 Waxman	N	Y	N	Y	N	Y	Y	Y
25 Roybal	Y	Y	N	Y	N	Y	N	Y
26 Berman	?	Y	N	Y	N	Y	N	Y
27 Levine	Y	Y	N	Y	N	Y	N	Y
28 Dixon	Y	Y	N	Y	N	Y	N	Y
29 Hawkins	?	?	N	Y	N	Y	N	Y
30 Martinez	Y	Y	N	Y	N	Y	N	Y
31 Dymally	Y	Y	N	N	N	N	Y	Y
32 Anderson	N	Y	Y	Y	Y	Y	Y	N
33 *Dreier*	N	Y	Y	Y	Y	Y	N	N
34 Torres	Y	Y	N	Y	N	Y	N	Y
35 *Lewis*	Y	Y	N	Y	N	Y	N	N
36 Brown	Y	Y	N	Y	N	Y	Y	Y
37 *McCandless*	Y	Y	Y	Y	Y	Y	N	N
38 Patterson	Y	Y	Y	Y	Y	Y	Y	Y
39 *Dannemeyer*	N	N	Y	Y	Y	Y	N	N
40 *Badham*	N	Y	N	Y	N	Y	N	N
41 *Lowery*	Y	Y	Y	Y	Y	Y	Y	N
42 *Lungren*	N	N	Y	Y	Y	Y	Y	N

	241	242	243	244	245	246	247	248
43 *Packard*	N	Y	Y	Y	Y	Y	Y	N
44 Bates	N	Y	Y	Y	Y	Y	Y	Y
45 *Hunter*	Y	Y	Y	Y	Y	Y	N	N
COLORADO								
1 Schroeder	Y	Y	Y	Y	Y	Y	N	Y
2 Wirth	Y	Y	Y	Y	Y	Y	Y	Y
3 Kogovsek	Y	Y	Y	Y	Y	Y	Y	Y
4 *Brown*	N	N	N	N	N	N	N	N
5 *Kramer*	N	Y	N	Y	N	Y	N	N
6 *Schaefer*	N	N	Y	Y	Y	Y	N	N
CONNECTICUT								
1 Kennelly	Y	Y	N	Y	N	Y	N	Y
2 Gejdenson	Y	Y	N	Y	N	Y	N	Y
3 Morrison	N	Y	N	Y	N	Y	N	Y
4 *McKinney*	Y	N	N	Y	N	Y	N	Y
5 Ratchford	Y	Y	N	Y	N	Y	N	Y
6 Johnson	Y	N	Y	Y	Y	Y	N	Y
DELAWARE								
AL Carper	N	Y	Y	Y	Y	Y	Y	Y
FLORIDA								
1 Hutto	Y	Y	Y	Y	Y	Y	N	N
2 Fuqua	Y	Y	Y	Y	Y	Y	Y	N
3 Bennett	Y	Y	Y	Y	Y	Y	Y	N
4 Chappell	Y	Y	Y	Y	Y	Y	N	N
5 *McCollum*	Y	N	Y	Y	Y	Y	N	N
6 MacKay	Y	Y	Y	Y	Y	Y	Y	Y
7 Gibbons	Y	Y	Y	Y	Y	Y	N	N
8 *Young*	Y	?	Y	Y	Y	Y	N	N
9 *Bilirakis*	Y	N	Y	Y	Y	Y	N	N
10 Ireland	Y	Y	Y	Y	Y	Y	N	N
11 Nelson	N	Y	Y	Y	Y	Y	N	N
12 *Lewis*	Y	N	Y	Y	Y	Y	N	N
13 *Mack*	Y	N	Y	Y	Y	Y	N	N
14 Mica	Y	Y	Y	Y	Y	Y	N	N
15 *Shaw*	Y	N	Y	Y	Y	Y	N	N
16 Smith	Y	Y	Y	Y	Y	Y	Y	Y
17 Lehman	Y	Y	N	Y	N	Y	N	Y
18 Pepper	Y	Y	N	Y	N	Y	Y	N
19 Fascell	Y	Y	Y	Y	Y	Y	N	Y
GEORGIA								
1 Thomas	Y	Y	Y	Y	Y	Y	N	N
2 Hatcher	Y	Y	N	Y	N	Y	N	N
3 Ray	Y	Y	Y	Y	Y	Y	N	N
4 Levitas	Y	Y	Y	Y	Y	Y	N	N
5 Fowler	Y	Y	N	Y	N	Y	Y	Y
6 *Gingrich*	Y	N	Y	Y	Y	Y	N	N
7 McDonald	X	-	N	Y	Y	Y	N	N
8 Rowland	Y	Y	Y	Y	Y	Y	N	N
9 Jenkins	Y	Y	N	Y	N	Y	N	N
10 Barnard	Y	Y	N	Y	N	Y	N	N
HAWAII								
1 Heftel	?	?	?	?	?	?	?	X
2 Akaka	Y	Y	Y	Y	Y	Y	N	Y
IDAHO								
1 *Craig*	N	N	Y	Y	Y	Y	N	N
2 *Hansen*	Y	N	Y	Y	Y	Y	N	N
ILLINOIS								
1 Vacancy								
2 Savage	Y	Y	N	Y	N	Y	Y	Y
3 Russo	Y	Y	N	Y	N	Y	Y	Y
4 *O'Brien*	Y	Y	Y	Y	Y	Y	N	?
5 Lipinski	N	Y	Y	Y	Y	Y	N	N
6 *Hyde*	N	N	N	Y	N	Y	N	N
7 Collins	?	Y	Y	Y	Y	Y	Y	Y
8 Rostenkowski	Y	Y	Y	Y	Y	Y	N	N
9 Yates	N	Y	Y	Y	Y	?	Y	Y
10 *Porter*	N	N	N	Y	N	Y	Y	N
11 Annunzio	Y	Y	N	Y	N	Y	N	Y
12 *Crane, P.*	N	N	N	C	Y	Y	N	N
13 *Erlenborn*	N	N	Y	Y	Y	Y	N	N
14 *Corcoran*	N	N	N	Y	N	Y	N	N
15 *Madigan*	Y	N	Y	Y	Y	Y	N	N
16 *Martin*	N	N	Y	Y	Y	Y	Y	N
17 Evans	Y	Y	Y	Y	Y	Y	N	N
18 *Michel*	N	N	Y	Y	Y	Y	N	N
19 *Crane, D.*	N	N	C	Y	C	C	N	N
20 Durbin	Y	Y	N	Y	N	Y	N	Y
21 Price	Y	Y	N	Y	Y	Y	N	N
22 Simon	?	?	?	?	?	?	?	Y
INDIANA								
1 Hall	?	Y	Y	Y	Y	Y	Y	Y
2 Sharp	Y	Y	?	?	?	Y	Y	Y
3 *Hiler*	N	N	Y	Y	Y	Y	N	N
4 *Coats*	Y	N	Y	Y	Y	Y	N	N
5 Hillis	Y	N	Y	Y	Y	Y	N	N

ND - Northern Democrats   SD - Southern Democrats

Corresponding to Congressional Record Votes 254, 255, 257, 258, 259, 260, 261, 262

	241	242	243	244	245	246	247	248
6 ***Burton***	N	N	N	Y	Y	Y	N	N
7 ***Myers***	Y	N	N	Y	Y	Y	N	N
8 McCloskey	Y	Y	Y	Y	Y	Y	Y	Y
9 Hamilton	Y	Y	Y	Y	Y	Y	Y	Y
10 Jacobs	N	Y	Y	Y	Y	Y	Y	Y
IOWA								
1 ***Leach***	N	N	Y	Y	Y	Y	Y	Y
2 ***Tauke***	N	N	Y	Y	Y	Y	Y	Y
3 ***Evans***	N	N	N	Y	Y	Y	Y	Y
4 Smith	Y	Y	Y	Y	Y	Y	Y	Y
5 Harkin	Y	Y	Y	Y	Y	Y	Y	Y
6 Bedell	Y	Y	Y	Y	Y	Y	Y	Y
KANSAS								
1 ***Roberts***	Y	N	N	Y	Y	Y	Y	N
2 Slattery	Y	Y	Y	Y	Y	Y	Y	Y
3 ***Winn***	Y	N	N	Y	Y	Y	Y	N
4 Glickman	Y	Y	Y	Y	Y	Y	Y	Y
5 ***Whittaker***	Y	N	Y	Y	Y	Y	Y	N
KENTUCKY								
1 Hubbard	Y	Y	Y	Y	Y	Y	Y	N
2 Natcher	Y	Y	Y	Y	Y	Y	N	Y
3 Mazzoli	Y	Y	Y	Y	Y	Y	Y	Y
4 ***Snyder***	Y	N	Y	Y	Y	Y	Y	N
5 ***Rogers***	Y	N	Y	Y	Y	Y	Y	N
6 ***Hopkins***	Y	Y	Y	Y	Y	Y	Y	N
7 Perkins	Y	Y	Y	Y	Y	Y	N	Y
LOUISIANA								
1 ***Livingston***	Y	N	N	Y	Y	Y	N	N
2 Boggs	Y	Y	Y	Y	Y	Y	N	N
3 Tauzin	Y	Y	Y	Y	Y	Y	N	N
4 Roemer	P	Y	Y	Y	Y	Y	Y	N
5 Huckaby	Y	Y	Y	Y	Y	Y	N	N
6 ***Moore***	Y	N	Y	Y	Y	Y	N	N
7 Breaux	Y	Y	Y	Y	Y	Y	N	N
8 Long	Y	Y	Y	Y	Y	Y	N	Y
MAINE								
1 ***McKernan***	N	N	Y	Y	Y	Y	Y	N
2 ***Snowe***	N	Y	Y	Y	Y	Y	Y	N
MARYLAND								
1 Dyson	Y	Y	N	Y	N	Y	Y	Y
2 Long	Y	?	Y	Y	Y	Y	N	Y
3 Mikulski	Y	Y	N	Y	N	Y	Y	Y
4 ***Holt***	N	N	Y	?	Y	Y	N	N
5 Hoyer	Y	Y	N	Y	N	Y	N	N
6 Byron	Y	Y	Y	Y	Y	Y	N	N
7 Mitchell	?	?	N	N	N	N	Y	Y
8 Barnes	Y	Y	Y	Y	Y	Y	N	Y
MASSACHUSETTS								
1 ***Conte***	N	Y	N	Y	N	Y	N	Y
2 Boland	Y	Y	N	Y	N	Y	N	Y
3 Early	Y	Y	N	Y	N	Y	N	Y
4 Frank	N	Y	N	Y	N	Y	N	Y
5 Shannon	?	?	N	Y	N	Y	N	Y
6 Mavroules	Y	Y	N	Y	N	Y	N	Y
7 Markey	Y	Y	N	Y	N	Y	N	Y
8 O'Neill								
9 Moakley	Y	Y	N	Y	N	Y	N	Y
10 Studds	Y	Y	C	C	C	C	N	Y
11 Donnelly	Y	Y	N	Y	N	Y	N	Y
MICHIGAN								
1 Conyers	?	Y	N	Y	N	Y	Y	?
2 ***Pursell***	N	N	Y	Y	Y	Y	N	N
3 Wolpe	Y	Y	N	Y	N	Y	Y	Y
4 ***Siljander***	Y	N	Y	Y	Y	Y	Y	N
5 ***Sawyer***	Y	Y	N	Y	Y	Y	N	N
6 Carr	Y	Y	Y	Y	Y	Y	Y	Y
7 Kildee	Y	Y	Y	Y	Y	Y	Y	Y
8 Traxler	Y	Y	Y	Y	Y	Y	Y	Y
9 ***Vander Jagt***	Y	N	N	Y	Y	Y	Y	?
10 Albosta	Y	Y	Y	Y	Y	Y	N	Y
11 ***Davis***	Y	Y	N	Y	Y	Y	N	N
12 Bonior	Y	Y	N	Y	N	Y	N	Y
13 Crockett	Y	Y	N	Y	N	Y	Y	Y
14 Hertel	N	Y	Y	Y	Y	Y	N	Y
15 Ford	?	Y	N	Y	N	Y	N	Y
16 Dingell	Y	Y	Y	Y	Y	Y	Y	Y
17 Levin	Y	Y	Y	Y	Y	Y	N	Y
18 ***Broomfield***	N	N	Y	Y	Y	Y	Y	N
MINNESOTA								
1 Penny	Y	Y	Y	Y	Y	Y	N	Y
2 ***Weber***	Y	N	Y	Y	Y	Y	N	N
3 ***Frenzel***	N	Y	Y	Y	Y	Y	Y	N
4 Vento	Y	Y	N	Y	Y	Y	Y	Y
5 Sabo	Y	Y	N	Y	N	Y	N	Y
6 Sikorski	Y	Y	Y	Y	Y	Y	Y	Y
7 ***Stangeland***	Y	N	Y	Y	Y	Y	Y	N
8 Oberstar	Y	Y	Y	Y	Y	Y	Y	Y
MISSISSIPPI								
1 Whitten	Y	Y	Y	Y	Y	Y	N	Y
2 ***Franklin***	Y	N	Y	Y	Y	Y	N	N
3 Montgomery	Y	Y	N	Y	Y	Y	N	N
4 Dowdy	Y	Y	Y	Y	Y	Y	N	Y
5 ***Lott***	Y	N	Y	Y	Y	Y	N	N
MISSOURI								
1 Clay	?	?	N	N	N	N	Y	Y
2 Young	Y	Y	Y	Y	Y	Y	Y	Y
3 Gephardt	Y	Y	Y	Y	Y	Y	Y	Y
4 Skelton	Y	Y	Y	Y	Y	Y	N	N
5 Wheat	Y	Y	Y	Y	Y	Y	N	Y
6 ***Coleman***	Y	Y	Y	Y	Y	Y	N	N
7 ***Taylor***	Y	Y	Y	Y	Y	Y	Y	N
8 ***Emerson***	Y	N	Y	Y	Y	Y	N	N
9 Volkmer	Y	Y	Y	Y	Y	Y	Y	Y
MONTANA								
1 Williams	Y	Y	Y	Y	Y	Y	N	Y
2 ***Marlenee***	Y	N	N	Y	N	Y	N	N
NEBRASKA								
1 ***Bereuter***	Y	Y	Y	Y	Y	Y	Y	Y
2 ***Daub***	Y	N	Y	Y	Y	+	N	N
3 ***Smith***	Y	N	Y	Y	Y	Y	N	Y
NEVADA								
1 Reid	Y	Y	Y	Y	Y	Y	Y	N
2 ***Vucanovich***	N	N	Y	Y	Y	Y	N	N
NEW HAMPSHIRE								
1 D'Amours	N	Y	Y	Y	Y	Y	N	Y
2 ***Gregg***	N	N	Y	Y	Y	Y	N	N
NEW JERSEY								
1 Florio	N	Y	Y	Y	Y	Y	Y	Y
2 Hughes	N	Y	Y	Y	Y	Y	N	Y
3 Howard	Y	Y	N	Y	N	Y	N	Y
4 ***Smith***	Y	Y	Y	Y	Y	Y	N	Y
5 ***Roukema***	N	Y	Y	Y	Y	Y	N	Y
6 Dwyer	Y	Y	N	Y	N	Y	N	Y
7 ***Rinaldo***	N	Y	Y	Y	Y	Y	Y	N
8 Roe	Y	Y	Y	Y	Y	Y	N	Y
9 Torricelli	Y	?	N	Y	N	Y	N	Y
10 Rodino	#	?	?	?	?	?	?	#
11 Minish	N	Y	Y	Y	Y	Y	Y	Y
12 ***Courter***	N	N	Y	Y	Y	Y	N	N
13 ***Forsythe***	N	Y	N	Y	Y	Y	N	Y
14 Guarini	Y	Y	Y	Y	Y	Y	N	Y
NEW MEXICO								
1 ***Lujan***	Y	N	Y	Y	Y	Y	Y	N
2 ***Skeen***	Y	N	N	Y	Y	Y	N	N
3 Richardson	Y	Y	Y	Y	Y	Y	Y	Y
NEW YORK								
1 ***Carney***	N	Y	N	Y	N	Y	N	N
2 Downey	?	?	N	Y	N	Y	Y	Y
3 Mrazek	N	Y	Y	Y	Y	Y	Y	Y
4 ***Lent***	Y	Y	Y	Y	Y	Y	N	N
5 ***McGrath***	Y	Y	Y	Y	Y	Y	N	N
6 Addabbo	Y	Y	N	Y	N	Y	N	Y
7 Ackerman	Y	Y	N	Y	N	Y	N	Y
8 Scheuer	Y	Y	N	Y	N	Y	N	Y
9 Ferraro	Y	Y	Y	Y	Y	Y	N	Y
10 Schumer	Y	Y	N	Y	N	Y	N	Y
11 Towns	Y	Y	N	Y	N	Y	Y	Y
12 Owens	Y	Y	N	Y	N	Y	Y	Y
13 Solarz	Y	Y	N	Y	N	Y	Y	Y
14 ***Molinari***	Y	N	Y	Y	Y	Y	N	N
15 ***Green***	N	Y	Y	Y	Y	Y	N	Y
16 Rangel	?	?	N	Y	Y	Y	N	Y
17 Weiss	Y	Y	N	Y	N	Y	Y	Y
18 Garcia	Y	Y	N	Y	N	Y	N	Y
19 Biaggi	?	?	Y	Y	Y	Y	N	Y
20 Ottinger	N	Y	N	Y	N	Y	N	Y
21 ***Fish***	Y	N	Y	Y	Y	Y	N	N
22 ***Gilman***	Y	Y	Y	Y	Y	Y	Y	N
23 Stratton	N	Y	Y	Y	Y	Y	N	N
24 ***Solomon***	N	N	Y	Y	Y	Y	N	N
25 ***Boehlert***	Y	N	Y	Y	Y	Y	N	N
26 ***Martin***	Y	N	Y	Y	Y	Y	N	N
27 ***Wortley***	Y	N	Y	Y	Y	Y	N	N
28 McHugh	Y	Y	Y	Y	Y	Y	N	Y
29 ***Horton***	Y	Y	N	Y	N	Y	Y	N
30 ***Conable***	N	Y	N	Y	Y	Y	N	N
31 ***Kemp***	Y	N	Y	Y	Y	Y	N	N
32 LaFalce	Y	Y	N	Y	N	Y	N	Y
33 Nowak	Y	Y	Y	Y	Y	Y	N	Y
34 Lundine	Y	Y	N	Y	N	Y	Y	Y
NORTH CAROLINA								
1 Jones	Y	Y	Y	Y	Y	Y	?	Y
2 Valentine	Y	Y	Y	Y	Y	Y	N	Y
3 Whitley	Y	Y	Y	Y	Y	Y	N	N
4 Andrews	?	?	Y	Y	Y	Y	N	Y
5 Neal	Y	Y	Y	Y	Y	Y	Y	N
6 Britt	Y	Y	Y	Y	Y	Y	N	N
7 Rose	Y	Y	Y	Y	Y	Y	Y	Y
8 Hefner	?	?	?	?	?	?	?	N
9 ***Martin***	Y	N	Y	Y	Y	Y	N	N
10 ***Broyhill***	Y	N	Y	Y	Y	Y	Y	N
11 Clarke	Y	Y	Y	Y	Y	Y	Y	Y
NORTH DAKOTA								
AL Dorgan	Y	Y	Y	Y	Y	Y	N	Y
OHIO								
1 Luken	Y	Y	Y	Y	Y	Y	N	Y
2 ***Gradison***	N	Y	N	Y	Y	Y	N	Y
3 Hall	Y	Y	N	Y	Y	Y	N	Y
4 ***Oxley***	N	N	Y	Y	Y	Y	Y	N
5 ***Latta***	Y	Y	Y	Y	Y	Y	Y	N
6 ***McEwen***	Y	N	Y	Y	Y	Y	Y	N
7 ***DeWine***	N	N	Y	Y	Y	Y	N	N
8 ***Kindness***	N	N	N	Y	Y	Y	Y	N
9 Kaptur	Y	Y	N	Y	N	Y	Y	Y
10 ***Miller***	N	N	Y	Y	Y	Y	Y	N
11 Eckart	N	Y	Y	Y	Y	Y	Y	Y
12 ***Kasich***	N	N	Y	Y	Y	Y	N	N
13 Pease	Y	Y	N	Y	N	Y	N	Y
14 Seiberling	Y	Y	N	Y	N	Y	Y	Y
15 ***Wylie***	N	N	Y	Y	Y	Y	Y	N
16 ***Regula***	Y	Y	Y	Y	Y	Y	Y	N
17 ***Williams***	Y	Y	Y	Y	Y	Y	N	N
18 Applegate	Y	Y	Y	Y	Y	Y	N	Y
19 Feighan	Y	Y	Y	Y	Y	Y	Y	Y
20 Oakar	Y	Y	Y	Y	Y	Y	Y	Y
21 Stokes	Y	Y	N	Y	N	Y	N	Y
OKLAHOMA								
1 Jones	Y	Y	Y	Y	Y	Y	Y	N
2 Synar	Y	Y	Y	Y	Y	Y	Y	Y
3 Watkins	Y	Y	Y	Y	Y	Y	N	N
4 McCurdy	Y	Y	Y	Y	Y	Y	N	N
5 ***Edwards***	Y	Y	Y	Y	Y	Y	N	N
6 English	Y	Y	Y	Y	Y	Y	N	N
OREGON								
1 AuCoin	Y	Y	Y	Y	Y	Y	N	Y
2 ***Smith, R.***	N	Y	Y	Y	Y	Y	Y	N
3 Wyden	Y	Y	Y	Y	Y	Y	N	Y
4 Weaver	Y	Y	N	Y	N	Y	N	Y
5 ***Smith, D.***	N	N	Y	Y	Y	Y	Y	N
PENNSYLVANIA								
1 Foglietta	N	Y	N	Y	N	Y	N	Y
2 Gray	Y	Y	Y	Y	Y	Y	Y	Y
3 Borski	?	?	Y	Y	Y	Y	Y	Y
4 Kolter	Y	Y	Y	Y	Y	Y	Y	Y
5 ***Schulze***	Y	N	Y	Y	Y	Y	N	N
6 Yatron	Y	Y	Y	Y	Y	Y	Y	N
7 Edgar	N	Y	N	Y	N	Y	Y	Y
8 Kostmayer	Y	Y	N	Y	N	Y	Y	Y
9 ***Shuster***	N	N	Y	Y	Y	Y	N	N
10 ***McDade***	N	N	N	Y	Y	+	Y	N
11 Harrison	Y	Y	Y	Y	Y	Y	N	Y
12 Murtha	Y	Y	N	Y	Y	Y	N	N
13 ***Coughlin***	N	N	Y	Y	Y	Y	Y	N
14 Coyne	Y	Y	N	Y	N	Y	N	Y
15 ***Ritter***	N	N	Y	Y	Y	Y	Y	N
16 ***Walker***	N	N	Y	Y	Y	Y	Y	N
17 ***Gekas***	N	N	Y	Y	Y	Y	N	N
18 Walgren	N	Y	Y	Y	Y	Y	Y	Y
19 ***Goodling***	?	?	Y	Y	Y	Y	N	Y
20 Gaydos	Y	Y	Y	Y	Y	Y	N	Y
21 ***Ridge***	Y	N	Y	Y	Y	Y	N	Y
22 Murphy	Y	Y	Y	Y	Y	Y	Y	Y
23 ***Clinger***	Y	N	Y	Y	Y	Y	Y	N
RHODE ISLAND								
1 St Germain	Y	Y	Y	Y	Y	Y	N	Y
2 ***Schneider***	N	N	Y	Y	Y	Y	N	Y
SOUTH CAROLINA								
1 ***Hartnett***	Y	N	Y	Y	Y	Y	N	N
2 ***Spence***	Y	Y	N	Y	N	Y	N	N
3 Derrick	Y	Y	Y	Y	Y	Y	N	Y
4 ***Campbell***	Y	N	Y	Y	Y	Y	N	N
5 Spratt	Y	Y	Y	Y	Y	Y	N	Y
6 Tallon	Y	Y	N	Y	N	Y	N	Y
SOUTH DAKOTA								
AL Daschle	Y	Y	Y	Y	Y	Y	N	Y
TENNESSEE								
1 ***Quillen***	Y	Y	Y	Y	Y	Y	N	N
2 ***Duncan***	Y	Y	Y	Y	Y	Y	N	N
3 Lloyd	Y	Y	Y	Y	Y	Y	N	N
4 Cooper	Y	Y	Y	Y	Y	Y	N	N
5 Boner	Y	Y	Y	Y	Y	Y	N	N
6 Gore	?	?	Y	Y	Y	Y	N	N
7 ***Sundquist***	Y	Y	Y	Y	Y	Y	N	N
8 Jones	#	?	Y	Y	Y	Y	N	N
9 Ford	Y	Y	N	Y	N	Y	N	?
TEXAS								
1 Hall, S.	?	?	Y	Y	Y	Y	N	N
2 Wilson	Y	Y	N	Y	N	Y	N	N
3 ***Bartlett***	Y	N	Y	Y	Y	Y	Y	N
4 Hall, R.	Y	Y	Y	Y	Y	Y	Y	N
5 Bryant	Y	Y	Y	Y	Y	Y	N	Y
6 ***Gramm***	Y	N	Y	Y	Y	Y	N	N
7 ***Archer***	N	N	Y	Y	Y	Y	N	N
8 ***Fields***	N	N	Y	Y	Y	Y	N	N
9 Brooks	Y	Y	Y	Y	Y	Y	Y	Y
10 Pickle	Y	Y	Y	Y	Y	Y	Y	N
11 Leath	Y	Y	Y	Y	Y	Y	N	N
12 Wright	Y	Y	Y	Y	Y	Y	N	Y
13 Hightower	Y	Y	Y	Y	Y	Y	Y	N
14 Patman	Y	Y	Y	Y	Y	Y	Y	N
15 de la Garza	Y	Y	Y	Y	Y	Y	N	N
16 Coleman	Y	Y	Y	Y	Y	Y	Y	Y
17 Stenholm	Y	Y	Y	Y	Y	Y	N	N
18 Leland	Y	Y	N	Y	N	Y	N	Y
19 Hance	Y	Y	Y	Y	Y	Y	N	N
20 Gonzalez	Y	Y	Y	Y	Y	Y	N	Y
21 ***Loeffler***	Y	N	Y	Y	Y	Y	N	N
22 ***Paul***	N	N	N	Y	Y	Y	Y	Y
23 Kazen	Y	Y	Y	Y	Y	Y	N	N
24 Frost	Y	Y	Y	Y	Y	Y	N	N
25 Andrews	Y	Y	Y	Y	Y	Y	Y	N
26 Vandergriff	Y	Y	Y	Y	Y	Y	N	N
27 Ortiz	Y	Y	Y	Y	Y	Y	N	N
UTAH								
1 ***Hansen***	N	N	N	Y	Y	Y	Y	N
2 ***Marriott***	N	Y	Y	Y	Y	Y	Y	N
3 ***Nielson***	N	N	Y	Y	Y	Y	N	N
VERMONT								
AL ***Jeffords***	Y	P	N	Y	N	Y	Y	Y
VIRGINIA								
1 ***Bateman***	N	N	Y	Y	Y	Y	Y	N
2 ***Whitehurst***	Y	N	Y	Y	Y	Y	N	N
3 ***Bliley***	Y	N	Y	Y	Y	Y	N	N
4 Sisisky	Y	Y	Y	Y	Y	Y	N	Y
5 Daniel	Y	Y	Y	Y	Y	Y	N	N
6 Olin	Y	Y	Y	Y	Y	Y	N	N
7 ***Robinson***	Y	N	Y	Y	Y	Y	N	N
8 ***Parris***	Y	N	Y	Y	Y	Y	N	N
9 Boucher	Y	Y	Y	Y	Y	Y	N	Y
10 ***Wolf***	Y	N	Y	Y	Y	Y	Y	N
WASHINGTON								
1 ***Pritchard***	N	Y	Y	Y	Y	Y	Y	N
2 Swift	Y	Y	N	Y	N	Y	Y	Y
3 Bonker	Y	Y	Y	Y	Y	Y	Y	Y
4 ***Morrison***	Y	N	Y	Y	Y	Y	Y	N
5 Foley	Y	Y	N	Y	Y	Y	Y	N
6 Dicks	Y	Y	Y	Y	Y	Y	Y	N
7 Lowry	Y	Y	N	Y	N	Y	Y	Y
8 ***Chandler***	Y	N	Y	Y	Y	Y	Y	N
WEST VIRGINIA								
1 Mollohan	Y	Y	Y	Y	Y	Y	Y	N
2 Staggers	Y	Y	Y	Y	Y	Y	Y	Y
3 Wise	Y	Y	Y	Y	Y	Y	N	Y
4 Rahall	Y	Y	N	Y	N	Y	Y	Y
WISCONSIN								
1 Aspin	Y	Y	N	Y	N	Y	Y	N
2 Kastenmeier	Y	Y	Y	Y	Y	Y	Y	Y
3 ***Gunderson***	Y	N	Y	Y	Y	Y	N	N
4 Zablocki	Y	Y	N	Y	Y	Y	N	N
5 Moody	N	Y	N	Y	N	Y	Y	Y
6 ***Petri***	N	Y	N	Y	Y	Y	Y	N
7 Obey	Y	Y	N	Y	N	Y	Y	Y
8 ***Roth***	Y	Y	N	Y	Y	Y	Y	N
9 ***Sensenbrenner***	N	N	Y	Y	Y	Y	Y	N
WYOMING								
AL ***Cheney***	N	N	Y	Y	Y	Y	N	N

Southern states - Ala., Ark., Fla., Ga., Ky., La., Miss., N.C., Okla., S.C., Tenn., Texas, Va.

249. Procedural Motion. Solomon, R-N.Y., motion to approve the House *Journal* of Wednesday, July 20. Motion agreed to 349-30: R 139-15; D 210-15 (ND 134-14, SD 76-1), July 21, 1983.

250. HR 2969. Department of Defense Authorization. Seiberling, D-Ohio, amendment to bar flight tests of anti-satellite weapons until separately authorized by law. Rejected 142-275: R 9-155; D 133-120 (ND 118-48, SD 15-72), July 21, 1983. A "nay" was a vote supporting the president's position.

251. HR 2957. International Recovery and Financial Stability Act. Adoption of the rule (H Res 249) providing for House floor consideration of the bill to increase U.S. participation in the International Monetary Fund by $8.4 billion, to extend authority for the Export-Import Bank and to provide multilateral development assistance. Adopted 369-42: R 131-28; D 238-14 (ND 160-5, SD 78-9), July 21, 1983.

KEY

- **Y** Voted for (yea).
- **#** Paired for.
- **+** Announced for.
- **N** Voted against (nay).
- **X** Paired against.
- **-** Announced against.
- **P** Voted "present".
- **C** Voted "present" to avoid possible conflict of interest.
- **?** Did not vote or otherwise make a position known.

Democrats *Republicans*

	249	250	251
ALABAMA			
1 *Edwards*	Y	N	Y
2 *Dickinson*	N	N	N
3 Nichols	Y	N	Y
4 Bevill	Y	N	N
5 Flippo	Y	N	N
6 Erdreich	Y	N	N
7 Shelby	Y	N	?
ALASKA			
AL *Young*	?	N	Y
ARIZONA			
1 *McCain*	?	N	Y
2 Udall	Y	Y	Y
3 *Stump*	Y	N	N
4 *Rudd*	Y	N	Y
5 McNulty	Y	Y	Y
ARKANSAS			
1 Alexander	Y	N	Y
2 *Bethune*	?	N	Y
3 *Hammerschmidt*	Y	N	Y
4 Anthony	?	N	Y
CALIFORNIA			
1 Bosco	Y	Y	Y
2 *Chappie*	Y	N	?
3 Matsui	Y	N	Y
4 Fazio	Y	Y	Y
5 Burton	Y	Y	Y
6 Boxer	?	Y	Y
7 Miller	Y	Y	Y
8 Dellums	Y	Y	Y
9 Stark	Y	Y	?
10 Edwards	Y	Y	Y
11 Lantos	Y	Y	Y
12 *Zschau*	Y	Y	Y
13 Mineta	Y	Y	Y
14 *Shumway*	Y	N	Y
15 Coelho	Y	?	N
16 Panetta	Y	Y	Y
17 *Pashayan*	Y	N	Y
18 Lehman	Y	Y	Y
19 *Lagomarsino*	Y	N	Y
20 *Thomas*	Y	N	Y
21 *Fiedler*	Y	N	Y
22 *Moorhead*	Y	N	Y
23 Beilenson	Y	Y	Y
24 Waxman	Y	Y	Y
25 Roybal	Y	Y	Y
26 Berman	Y	Y	Y
27 Levine	Y	Y	Y
28 Dixon	Y	?	?
29 Hawkins	Y	#	Y
30 Martinez	Y	Y	Y
31 Dymally	P	Y	Y
32 Anderson	Y	N	N
33 *Dreier*	Y	N	Y
34 Torres	Y	N	Y
35 *Lewis*	N	N	?
36 Brown	?	Y	Y
37 *McCandless*	Y	N	Y
38 Patterson	?	N	Y
39 *Dannemeyer*	Y	N	N
40 *Badham*	Y	N	Y
41 *Lowery*	?	N	Y
42 *Lungren*	Y	N	Y
43 *Packard*	Y	N	Y
44 Bates	Y	Y	Y
45 *Hunter*	Y	N	Y
COLORADO			
1 Schroeder	N	Y	Y
2 Wirth	Y	Y	Y
3 Kogovsek	Y	Y	Y
4 *Brown*	Y	N	N
5 *Kramer*	Y	N	N
6 *Schaefer*	Y	N	Y
CONNECTICUT			
1 Kennelly	Y	Y	Y
2 Gejdenson	N	N	Y
3 Morrison	Y	Y	Y
4 *McKinney*	Y	Y	Y
5 Ratchford	Y	Y	Y
6 *Johnson*	Y	N	Y
DELAWARE			
AL Carper	Y	Y	Y
FLORIDA			
1 Hutto	P	N	N
2 Fuqua	Y	N	Y
3 Bennett	Y	N	Y
4 Chappell	Y	N	Y
5 *McCollum*	?	N	N
6 MacKay	Y	N	Y
7 Gibbons	Y	N	Y
8 *Young*	Y	N	Y
9 *Bilirakis*	Y	N	N
10 Ireland	Y	N	Y
11 Nelson	Y	N	Y
12 Lewis	Y	N	Y
13 *Mack*	Y	N	N
14 Mica	Y	N	Y
15 *Shaw*	?	X	?
16 Smith	Y	N	Y
17 Lehman	Y	Y	Y
18 Pepper	Y	N	Y
19 Fascell	?	?	Y
GEORGIA			
1 Thomas	Y	N	Y
2 Hatcher	Y	N	Y
3 Ray	Y	N	Y
4 Levitas	Y	N	Y
5 Fowler	Y	N	Y
6 *Gingrich*	Y	N	Y
7 McDonald	?	N	N
8 Rowland	Y	N	Y
9 Jenkins	Y	N	Y
10 Barnard	?	N	Y
HAWAII			
1 Heftel	?	X	?
2 Akaka	Y	N	Y
IDAHO			
1 *Craig*	?	N	N
2 *Hansen*	?	N	?
ILLINOIS			
1 Vacancy			
2 Savage	Y	Y	Y
3 Russo	Y	Y	Y
4 *O'Brien*	Y	N	Y
5 Lipinski	N	N	Y
6 *Hyde*	Y	N	Y
7 Collins	Y	Y	Y
8 Rostenkowski	Y	N	Y
9 Yates	Y	Y	Y
10 *Porter*	Y	N	Y
11 Annunzio	Y	N	Y
12 *Crane, P.*	Y	N	N
13 *Erlenborn*	N	N	Y
14 *Corcoran*	N	N	Y
15 *Madigan*	?	N	Y
16 *Martin*	Y	N	Y
17 Evans	Y	Y	Y
18 *Michel*	Y	N	Y
19 *Crane, D.*	Y	N	?
20 Durbin	N	Y	Y
21 Price	Y	N	Y
22 Simon	?	?	?
INDIANA			
1 Hall	Y	Y	Y
2 Sharp	Y	N	Y
3 *Hiler*	Y	N	Y
4 *Coats*	N	N	N
5 Hillis	Y	N	Y

ND - Northern Democrats   SD - Southern Democrats

	249	250	251
6 Burton	N	N	Y
7 Myers	Y	N	Y
8 McCloskey	Y	N	Y
9 Hamilton	Y	N	Y
10 Jacobs	P	N	Y
IOWA			
1 Leach	Y	Y	Y
2 Tauke	Y	N	Y
3 Evans	N	N	Y
4 Smith	Y	N	Y
5 Harkin	N	Y	Y
6 Bedell	Y	Y	Y
KANSAS			
1 Roberts	Y	N	Y
2 Slattery	?	N	Y
3 Winn	Y	N	Y
4 Glickman	Y	N	Y
5 Whittaker	Y	N	Y
KENTUCKY			
1 Hubbard	Y	N	Y
2 Natcher	Y	N	Y
3 Mazzoli	Y	N	Y
4 Snyder	Y	N	N
5 Rogers	Y	N	Y
6 Hopkins	Y	N	Y
7 Perkins	Y	?	Y
LOUISIANA			
1 Livingston	Y	N	Y
2 Boggs	Y	Y	Y
3 Tauzin	?	N	Y
4 Roemer	N	N	Y
5 Huckaby	Y	N	?
6 Moore	Y	N	Y
7 Breaux	Y	N	Y
8 Long	Y	Y	Y
MAINE			
1 McKernan	Y	N	Y
2 Snowe	Y	Y	Y
MARYLAND			
1 Dyson	Y	N	Y
2 Long	?	N	N
3 Mikulski	Y	Y	Y
4 Holt	Y	N	Y
5 Hoyer	Y	Y	Y
6 Byron	Y	N	Y
7 Mitchell	?	Y	Y
8 Barnes	Y	Y	Y
MASSACHUSETTS			
1 Conte	Y	N	Y
2 Boland	Y	N	Y
3 Early	Y	Y	Y
4 Frank	Y	Y	Y
5 Shannon	?	N	Y
6 Mavroules	Y	Y	Y
7 Markey	Y	Y	Y
8 O'Neill			
9 Moakley	Y	Y	Y
10 Studds	Y	Y	Y
11 Donnelly	N	Y	Y
MICHIGAN			
1 Conyers	?	Y	Y
2 Pursell	Y	N	Y
3 Wolpe	Y	Y	Y
4 Siljander	Y	N	Y
5 Sawyer	Y	N	Y
6 Carr	Y	Y	Y
7 Kildee	Y	Y	Y
8 Traxler	N	Y	N
9 Vander Jagt	Y	N	?
10 Albosta	Y	Y	Y
11 Davis	Y	N	Y
12 Bonior	Y	Y	Y
13 Crockett	?	Y	Y
14 Hertel	Y	Y	Y
15 Ford	?	Y	Y
16 Dingell	?	?	?
17 Levin	Y	Y	Y
18 Broomfield	Y	N	Y
MINNESOTA			
1 Penny	Y	Y	Y
2 Weber	Y	N	N
3 Frenzel	Y	N	Y
4 Vento	N	Y	Y
5 Sabo	N	Y	Y
6 Sikorski	N	Y	Y

	249	250	251
7 Stangeland	Y	N	Y
8 Oberstar	P	Y	Y
MISSISSIPPI			
1 Whitten	Y	N	Y
2 Franklin	Y	N	Y
3 Montgomery	Y	N	Y
4 Dowdy	?	?	?
5 Lott	Y	N	Y
MISSOURI			
1 Clay	N	Y	Y
2 Young	Y	N	Y
3 Gephardt	?	Y	Y
4 Skelton	Y	N	Y
5 Wheat	Y	Y	Y
6 Coleman	Y	N	N
7 Taylor	Y	N	Y
8 Emerson	N	N	Y
9 Volkmer	Y	Y	N
MONTANA			
1 Williams	Y	Y	Y
2 Marlenee	Y	N	?
NEBRASKA			
1 Bereuter	Y	N	Y
2 Daub	Y	N	N
3 Smith	Y	N	Y
NEVADA			
1 Reid	Y	N	Y
2 Vucanovich	Y	N	Y
NEW HAMPSHIRE			
1 D'Amours	Y	Y	Y
2 Gregg	Y	N	N
NEW JERSEY			
1 Florio	Y	N	Y
2 Hughes	Y	N	Y
3 Howard	Y	Y	Y
4 Smith	Y	N	Y
5 Roukema	Y	Y	Y
6 Dwyer	Y	Y	Y
7 Rinaldo	Y	N	Y
8 Roe	Y	Y	Y
9 Torricelli	?	N	Y
10 Rodino	?	#	?
11 Minish	Y	Y	Y
12 Courter	Y	N	Y
13 Forsythe	N	Y	Y
14 Guarini	Y	Y	Y
NEW MEXICO			
1 Lujan	Y	N	N
2 Skeen	Y	N	Y
3 Richardson	Y	Y	Y
NEW YORK			
1 Carney	?	N	Y
2 Downey	Y	Y	Y
3 Mrazek	Y	Y	Y
4 Lent	Y	N	Y
5 McGrath	Y	N	Y
6 Addabbo	Y	Y	Y
7 Ackerman	Y	Y	Y
8 Scheuer	Y	Y	Y
9 Ferraro	Y	Y	Y
10 Schumer	Y	Y	Y
11 Towns	Y	Y	Y
12 Owens	Y	Y	?
13 Solarz	Y	Y	Y
14 Molinari	Y	N	Y
15 Green	Y	N	Y
16 Rangel	Y	Y	?
17 Weiss	Y	Y	Y
18 Garcia	Y	Y	Y
19 Biaggi	Y	Y	Y
20 Ottinger	?	Y	Y
21 Fish	Y	N	Y
22 Gilman	Y	N	Y
23 Stratton	Y	N	Y
24 Solomon	N	N	N
25 Boehlert	Y	N	Y
26 Martin	Y	N	Y
27 Wortley	Y	N	Y
28 McHugh	Y	Y	Y
29 Horton	Y	N	Y
30 Conable	Y	N	Y
31 Kemp	Y	N	Y
32 LaFalce	?	?	?
33 Nowak	Y	N	Y
34 Lundine	?	?	?

	249	250	251
NORTH CAROLINA			
1 Jones	?	Y	Y
2 Valentine	Y	N	Y
3 Whitley	Y	N	Y
4 Andrews	Y	N	Y
5 Neal	?	Y	Y
6 Britt	Y	N	Y
7 Rose	Y	N	Y
8 Hefner	?	N	Y
9 Martin	Y	N	Y
10 Broyhill	Y	N	N
11 Clarke	Y	Y	Y
NORTH DAKOTA			
AL Dorgan	N	Y	Y
OHIO			
1 Luken	Y	N	Y
2 Gradison	Y	N	Y
3 Hall	Y	Y	Y
4 Oxley	Y	N	Y
5 Latta	Y	N	Y
6 McEwen	Y	N	Y
7 DeWine	Y	N	Y
8 Kindness	Y	N	Y
9 Kaptur	Y	Y	Y
10 Miller	N	N	Y
11 Eckart	Y	N	Y
12 Kasich	?	N	N
13 Pease	Y	Y	Y
14 Seiberling	?	Y	Y
15 Wylie	Y	N	Y
16 Regula	Y	N	Y
17 Williams	?	?	Y
18 Applegate	?	N	Y
19 Feighan	?	N	Y
20 Oakar	Y	N	Y
21 Stokes	Y	Y	Y
OKLAHOMA			
1 Jones	Y	Y	Y
2 Synar	Y	Y	Y
3 Watkins	Y	Y	Y
4 McCurdy	Y	N	Y
5 Edwards	Y	N	Y
6 English	?	N	Y
OREGON			
1 AuCoin	?	Y	?
2 Smith, R.	Y	N	Y
3 Wyden	Y	Y	Y
4 Weaver	Y	Y	Y
5 Smith, D.	Y	N	Y
PENNSYLVANIA			
1 Foglietta	Y	Y	Y
2 Gray	Y	Y	Y
3 Borski	Y	Y	Y
4 Kolter	?	N	Y
5 Schulze	Y	N	Y
6 Yatron	Y	N	Y
7 Edgar	Y	Y	Y
8 Kostmayer	Y	Y	Y
9 Shuster	Y	N	Y
10 McDade	Y	N	Y
11 Harrison	Y	N	Y
12 Murtha	Y	N	Y
13 Coughlin	N	Y	Y
14 Coyne	Y	Y	Y
15 Ritter	Y	N	N
16 Walker	N	N	N
17 Gekas	Y	N	Y
18 Walgren	Y	Y	Y
19 Goodling	N	N	Y
20 Gaydos	Y	N	Y
21 Ridge	Y	N	Y
22 Murphy	N	N	Y
23 Clinger	Y	N	Y
RHODE ISLAND			
1 St Germain	P	N	Y
2 Schneider	Y	Y	Y
SOUTH CAROLINA			
1 Hartnett	Y	N	Y
2 Spence	Y	N	Y
3 Derrick	Y	N	Y
4 Campbell	Y	N	Y
5 Spratt	Y	N	Y
6 Tallon	Y	N	Y
SOUTH DAKOTA			
AL Daschle	Y	?	Y

	249	250	251
TENNESSEE			
1 Quillen	Y	N	Y
2 Duncan	Y	N	Y
3 Lloyd	Y	N	Y
4 Cooper	Y	Y	Y
5 Boner	Y	N	Y
6 Gore	Y	Y	Y
7 Sundquist	Y	N	Y
8 Jones	Y	N	Y
9 Ford	Y	Y	Y
TEXAS			
1 Hall, S.	Y	N	Y
2 Wilson	?	N	Y
3 Bartlett	Y	N	Y
4 Hall, R.	Y	N	N
5 Bryant	Y	N	Y
6 Gramm	Y	N	N
7 Archer	Y	N	N
8 Fields	Y	N	N
9 Brooks	Y	N	Y
10 Pickle	Y	N	Y
11 Leath	Y	N	Y
12 Wright	Y	N	Y
13 Hightower	Y	N	Y
14 Patman	Y	N	N
15 de la Garza	Y	N	Y
16 Coleman	Y	N	Y
17 Stenholm	?	N	N
18 Leland	Y	Y	Y
19 Hance	Y	N	N
20 Gonzalez	Y	N	Y
21 Loeffler	Y	N	Y
22 Paul	N	?	?
23 Kazen	Y	N	Y
24 Frost	Y	N	Y
25 Andrews	Y	N	Y
26 Vandergriff	Y	N	Y
27 Ortiz	Y	N	Y
UTAH			
1 Hansen	Y	N	Y
2 Marriott	Y	N	Y
3 Nielson	Y	N	Y
VERMONT			
AL Jeffords	Y	Y	Y
VIRGINIA			
1 Bateman	Y	N	N
2 Whitehurst	Y	N	Y
3 Bliley	Y	N	Y
4 Sisisky	Y	N	Y
5 Daniel	Y	N	Y
6 Olin	Y	Y	Y
7 Robinson	Y	N	Y
8 Parris	Y	N	Y
9 Boucher	Y	Y	Y
10 Wolf	Y	N	Y
WASHINGTON			
1 Pritchard	Y	N	Y
2 Swift	Y	Y	Y
3 Bonker	Y	N	Y
4 Morrison	Y	N	Y
5 Foley	Y	N	Y
6 Dicks	Y	N	Y
7 Lowry	N	Y	Y
8 Chandler	?	N	Y
WEST VIRGINIA			
1 Mollohan	Y	N	Y
2 Staggers	Y	N	Y
3 Wise	Y	Y	Y
4 Rahall	Y	Y	Y
WISCONSIN			
1 Aspin	Y	Y	Y
2 Kastenmeier	Y	Y	Y
3 Gunderson	Y	N	Y
4 Zablocki	Y	N	Y
5 Moody	Y	Y	Y
6 Petri	Y	N	N
7 Obey	Y	Y	Y
8 Roth	Y	N	Y
9 Sensenbrenner	Y	N	N
WYOMING			
AL Cheney	Y	N	Y

Southern states · Ala., Ark., Fla., Ga., Ky., La., Miss., N.C., Okla., S.C., Tenn., Texas, Va.

252. HR 622. Death Benefits for Policemen and Firefighters. Kildee, D-Mich., motion to suspend the rules and pass the bill to provide a $50,000 lump sum death benefit to survivors of federal law enforcement officers and firefighters killed in the line of duty. Motion agreed to 390-33: R 134-31; D 256-2 (ND 169-1, SD 87-1), July 26, 1983. A two-thirds majority of those present and voting (282 in this case) is required for passage under suspension of the rules.

253. HR 2498. Congressional Advisory Commission on Boxing. Florio, D-N.J., motion to suspend the rules and pass the bill to establish a commission to advise Congress on the need to establish a federal agency to regulate professional boxing and set national standards for licensing and regulating the industry. Motion rejected 167-254: R 29-135; D 138-119 (ND 121-49, SD 17-70), July 26, 1983. A two-thirds majority of those present and voting (281 in this case) is required for passage under suspension of the rules.

254. HR 2957. International Recovery and Financial Stability Act. Schumer, D-N.Y., amendment to require the U.S. representative to the International Monetary Fund (IMF) to vote for plans imposing lower interest rates and longer maturities on private bank debt when that debt is being restructured under IMF direction. Rejected 157-268: R 25-140; D 132-128 (ND 116-56, SD 16-72), July 26, 1983.

255. HR 2969. Department of Defense Authorization. Skelton, D-Mo., substitute to the Schroeder, D-Colo., amendment, expressing the sense of Congress that U.S. allies should pay more of the cost of alliance defense. Adopted 329-82: R 154-7; D 175-75 (ND 95-70, SD 80-5), July 26, 1983. (The Schroeder amendment would have reduced the number of U.S. troops stationed abroad to the level so deployed at the end of fiscal 1980.)

256. HR 2969. Department of Defense Authorization. Shannon, D-Mass., amendment to limit the number of U.S. military advisers in El Salvador to 55 and to limit the number of active duty U.S. military personnel in El Salvador to the number present on July 25, 1983. Rejected 170-247: R 16-147; D 154-100 (ND 141-26, SD 13-74), July 26, 1983. A "nay" was a vote supporting the president's position.

257. HR 2969. Department of Defense Authorization. Price, D-Ill., motion to end debate on the Markey, D-Mass., amendment and all amendments thereto in 20 minutes. Motion agreed to 213-195: R 106-52; D 107-143 (ND 43-119, SD 64-24), July 26, 1983. (The Markey amendment, to bar the deployment of U.S. combat troops to El Salvador, Nicaragua, Honduras, Guatemala or Costa Rica unless authorized by joint resolution, intended to evacuate U.S. citizens or to respond to a clear and present danger of military attack on the United States, subsequently was rejected *(see vote 258, below).)*

258. HR 2969. Department of Defense Authorization. Markey, D-Mass., amendment to bar the deployment of U.S. combat troops to El Salvador, Nicaragua, Honduras, Guatemala or Costa Rica unless authorized by joint resolution, intended to evacuate U.S. citizens or to respond to a clear and present danger of military attack on the United States. Rejected 165-259: R 9-155; D 156-104 (ND 141-30, SD 15-74), July 26, 1983. A "nay" was a vote supporting the president's position.

259. HR 2969. Department of Defense Authorization. Dellums, D-Calif., amendment to bar deployment in Europe of Pershing II missiles before Dec. 31, 1984. Rejected 101-320: R 4-159; D 97-161 (ND 93-77, SD 4-84), July 26, 1983. A "nay" was a vote supporting the president's position.

KEY

Y	Voted for (yea).
#	Paired for.
+	Announced for.
N	Voted against (nay).
X	Paired against.
-	Announced against.
P	Voted "present".
C	Voted "present" to avoid possible conflict of interest.
?	Did not vote or otherwise make a position known.

Democrats   **Republicans**

	252	253	254	255	256	257	258	259
ALABAMA								
1 *Edwards*	Y	N	N	Y	N	N	N	N
2 *Dickinson*	Y	N	N	Y	N	Y	N	N
3 Nichols	Y	N	N	Y	N	Y	N	N
4 Bevill	Y	N	N	?	N	Y	N	N
5 Flippo	Y	N	N	?	N	Y	N	N
6 Erdreich	Y	N	N	Y	N	Y	N	N
7 Shelby	Y	N	N	Y	N	N	N	N
ALASKA								
AL *Young*	Y	Y	N	Y	N	Y	N	?
ARIZONA								
1 *McCain*	Y	N	N	Y	N	N	N	N
2 Udall	Y	Y	Y	N	?	Y	Y	N
3 *Stump*	N	N	N	Y	N	N	N	N
4 *Rudd*	N	N	N	Y	N	N	N	N
5 McNulty	Y	Y	Y	N	Y	Y	Y	N
ARKANSAS								
1 Alexander	?	?	?	?	?	?	Y	N
2 *Bethune*	Y	N	N	Y	N	N	N	N
3 *Hammerschmidt*	Y	N	N	Y	N	?	N	N
4 Anthony	Y	N	Y	Y	N	Y	N	N
CALIFORNIA								
1 Bosco	Y	N	N	Y	Y	?	Y	Y
2 *Chappie*	Y	N	N	Y	N	N	N	N
3 Matsui	Y	Y	Y	Y	Y	N	Y	Y
4 Fazio	Y	Y	N	Y	N	Y	N	Y
5 Burton	Y	Y	Y	N	Y	Y	Y	Y
6 Boxer	Y	Y	Y	N	Y	Y	N	Y
7 Miller	Y	Y	Y	Y	Y	N	Y	Y
8 Dellums	Y	Y	Y	N	Y	N	Y	Y
9 Stark	Y	Y	Y	Y	Y	N	Y	Y
10 Edwards	Y	Y	N	Y	?	Y	Y	Y
11 Lantos	Y	Y	N	Y	Y	N	Y	Y
12 *Zschau*	Y	N	N	?	N	Y	N	N
13 Mineta	Y	Y	Y	Y	Y	N	Y	Y
14 *Shumway*	Y	N	N	Y	N	Y	N	N
15 Coelho	Y	N	Y	?	Y	N	Y	Y
16 Panetta	Y	Y	Y	Y	Y	N	Y	Y
17 *Pashayan*	Y	N	Y	Y	N	Y	N	N
18 Lehman	Y	N	Y	N	Y	N	Y	Y
19 *Lagomarsino*	Y	N	N	Y	N	Y	N	N
20 *Thomas*	Y	N	N	Y	N	N	N	N
21 *Fiedler*	Y	N	N	Y	N	Y	N	N
22 *Moorhead*	Y	N	N	Y	N	Y	N	N
23 Beilenson	N	Y	Y	Y	Y	N	Y	Y
24 Waxman	Y	Y	Y	Y	Y	N	Y	Y
25 Roybal	Y	Y	N	N	Y	N	Y	Y
26 Berman	Y	Y	Y	Y	Y	N	Y	Y
27 Levine	Y	Y	Y	N	Y	N	Y	Y
28 Dixon	Y	N	Y	?	Y	N	Y	?
29 Hawkins	Y	Y	Y	?	Y	N	Y	Y
30 Martinez	Y	Y	N	N	Y	N	Y	Y
31 Dymally	Y	Y	Y	N	Y	N	Y	Y
32 Anderson	Y	Y	Y	Y	Y	N	Y	Y
33 *Dreier*	N	N	N	Y	N	Y	N	N
34 Torres	Y	Y	Y	Y	Y	N	Y	Y
35 *Lewis*	Y	Y	?	?	?	?	?	?
36 Brown	Y	Y	Y	Y	Y	N	Y	Y
37 *McCandless*	Y	N	N	Y	N	N	N	N
38 Patterson	Y	N	N	Y	N	Y	N	N
39 *Dannemeyer*	N	N	N	Y	N	Y	N	N
40 *Badham*	N	N	N	Y	N	N	N	N
41 *Lowery*	Y	N	N	Y	N	Y	N	N
42 *Lungren*	Y	N	N	Y	N	Y	N	N

	252	253	254	255	256	257	258	259
43 *Packard*	Y	N	Y	Y	N	Y	N	N
44 Bates	Y	Y	Y	N	Y	N	Y	?
45 *Hunter*	Y	Y	N	Y	N	Y	N	N
COLORADO								
1 Schroeder	Y	N	Y	N	Y	N	Y	Y
2 Wirth	Y	Y	Y	Y	Y	N	Y	Y
3 Kogovsek	Y	Y	N	N	Y	N	Y	Y
4 *Brown*	N	N	N	N	N	N	N	N
5 *Kramer*	Y	N	N	Y	N	N	N	N
6 *Schaefer*	Y	N	N	Y	N	Y	N	N
CONNECTICUT								
1 Kennelly	Y	Y	N	Y	Y	N	Y	Y
2 Gejdenson	Y	Y	Y	N	Y	N	Y	Y
3 Morrison	Y	Y	Y	Y	Y	N	Y	Y
4 *McKinney*	Y	N	Y	N	?	Y	Y	Y
5 Ratchford	Y	Y	Y	Y	Y	N	Y	Y
6 *Johnson*	Y	N	N	N	N	Y	N	N
DELAWARE								
AL Carper	Y	N	Y	N	N	N	N	N
FLORIDA								
1 Hutto	Y	N	N	Y	N	N	N	N
2 Fuqua	Y	N	N	Y	N	Y	N	N
3 Bennett	Y	Y	Y	Y	N	Y	N	N
4 Chappell	Y	N	N	Y	N	N	N	N
5 *McCollum*	Y	N	N	Y	N	Y	N	N
6 MacKay	Y	N	N	Y	N	Y	N	N
7 Gibbons	Y	N	Y	Y	Y	Y	Y	N
8 *Young*	Y	N	N	Y	N	N	N	N
9 *Bilirakis*	Y	N	N	Y	N	N	N	N
10 Ireland	Y	N	N	Y	N	N	N	N
11 Nelson	Y	N	N	Y	N	N	N	N
12 *Lewis*	Y	N	N	Y	N	N	N	N
13 *Mack*	Y	N	N	Y	N	N	N	N
14 Mica	Y	N	N	Y	N	Y	N	N
15 *Shaw*	Y	N	Y	Y	N	N	N	N
16 Smith	Y	N	Y	Y	Y	N	Y	N
17 Lehman	Y	N	Y	N	Y	N	Y	Y
18 Pepper	Y	Y	Y	Y	N	Y	N	Y
19 Fascell	Y	N	N	Y	N	N	N	N
GEORGIA								
1 Thomas	Y	N	Y	Y	N	Y	N	N
2 Hatcher	Y	N	N	Y	N	N	N	N
3 Ray	Y	N	N	Y	N	Y	N	N
4 Levitas	Y	N	N	N	N	Y	N	N
5 Fowler	Y	N	Y	N	N	Y	N	N
6 *Gingrich*	Y	N	N	Y	N	N	N	N
7 McDonald	N	N	N	N	N	N	N	N
8 Rowland	Y	N	N	Y	N	N	N	N
9 Jenkins	Y	N	N	Y	N	Y	N	N
10 Barnard	Y	N	N	Y	N	Y	N	N
HAWAII								
1 Heftel	?	?	?	?	?	?	?	?
2 Akaka	Y	N	N	Y	N	Y	N	N
IDAHO								
1 *Craig*	Y	N	N	Y	N	N	N	N
2 *Hansen*	N	N	N	Y	N	?	N	?
ILLINOIS								
1 Vacancy								
2 Savage	Y	Y	Y	N	+	?	+	+
3 Russo	Y	Y	Y	Y	Y	Y	Y	N
4 *O'Brien*	Y	Y	N	Y	N	Y	N	N
5 Lipinski	Y	Y	Y	Y	Y	Y	N	N
6 *Hyde*	Y	N	N	Y	N	N	N	N
7 Collins	Y	Y	Y	N	Y	N	Y	Y
8 Rostenkowski	Y	Y	Y	N	Y	N	N	N
9 Yates	Y	N	Y	N	Y	N	Y	Y
10 *Porter*	Y	N	N	N	N	N	N	N
11 Annunzio	Y	N	Y	N	Y	N	Y	N
12 *Crane, P.*	N	N	N	N	N	N	N	N
13 *Erlenborn*	N	N	N	Y	N	N	N	N
14 *Corcoran*	Y	N	N	N	N	N	N	N
15 *Madigan*	Y	N	N	Y	N	Y	N	N
16 *Martin*	Y	N	Y	Y	N	Y	N	N
17 Evans	Y	Y	Y	N	?	N	Y	Y
18 *Michel*	Y	N	Y	Y	N	N	N	N
19 *Crane, D.*	N	N	N	N	N	N	N	N
20 Durbin	Y	N	Y	N	Y	N	Y	Y
21 Price	Y	N	Y	N	Y	N	N	N
22 Simon	Y	N	Y	N	Y	Y	Y	N
INDIANA								
1 Hall	Y	Y	Y	N	Y	N	Y	Y
2 Sharp	Y	N	N	Y	N	N	N	N
3 *Hiler*	Y	N	N	Y	N	N	N	N
4 *Coats*	N	N	Y	N	N	N	N	N
5 *Hillis*	Y	Y	Y	Y	N	Y	N	N

ND - Northern Democrats   SD - Southern Democrats

	252	253	254	255	256	257	258	259
6 ***Burton***	Y	N	N	Y	N	N	N	N
7 ***Myers***	Y	N	N	Y	N	Y	N	N
8 McCloskey	Y	N	N	N	Y	N	Y	N
9 Hamilton	Y	N	N	Y	N	Y	N	N
10 Jacobs	Y	N	N	N	Y	N	Y	Y
IOWA								
1 ***Leach***	Y	Y	N	N	Y	N	Y	Y
2 ***Tauke***	N	N	N	Y	Y	N	N	N
3 ***Evans***	Y	Y	N	Y	N	Y	N	N
4 Smith	Y	N	N	Y	Y	Y	N	N
5 Harkin	Y	Y	N	N	Y	N	Y	Y
6 Bedell	Y	Y	N	N	Y	N	Y	Y
KANSAS								
1 ***Roberts***	Y	N	N	Y	N	Y	N	N
2 Slattery	Y	N	Y	Y	N	N	N	N
3 ***Winn***	Y	N	N	Y	N	?	N	N
4 Glickman	Y	N	Y	Y	N	N	N	N
5 ***Whittaker***	Y	N	N	Y	N	Y	N	N
KENTUCKY								
1 Hubbard	Y	N	N	Y	N	Y	N	N
2 Natcher	Y	N	N	Y	N	Y	N	N
3 Mazzoli	Y	N	N	Y	N	Y	N	N
4 ***Snyder***	Y	N	N	Y	N	Y	N	N
5 ***Rogers***	Y	N	N	Y	N	Y	N	N
6 ***Hopkins***	Y	N	N	Y	N	N	N	N
7 Perkins	Y	N	N	Y	N	Y	N	N
LOUISIANA								
1 ***Livingston***	Y	N	N	Y	N	N	N	N
2 Boggs	Y	Y	N	Y	N	Y	Y	N
3 Tauzin	Y	Y	N	Y	N	Y	N	N
4 Roemer	Y	N	N	Y	N	N	Y	N
5 Huckaby	Y	Y	N	Y	N	Y	N	N
6 ***Moore***	Y	N	N	Y	N	N	N	N
7 Breaux	Y	Y	N	Y	N	Y	N	N
8 Long	Y	Y	N	Y	Y	Y	Y	N
MAINE								
1 ***McKernan***	Y	Y	N	Y	Y	N	N	N
2 ***Snowe***	Y	N	Y	Y	Y	N	N	N
MARYLAND								
1 Dyson	Y	Y	Y	Y	N	Y	N	N
2 Long	Y	N	N	Y	Y	Y	Y	N
3 Mikulski	Y	Y	Y	Y	Y	N	Y	N
4 ***Holt***	Y	N	N	Y	N	Y	N	N
5 Hoyer	Y	Y	N	Y	Y	N	N	N
6 Byron	Y	N	N	Y	N	Y	N	N
7 Mitchell	Y	N	Y	N	Y	N	Y	Y
8 Barnes	Y	N	N	Y	Y	N	Y	N
MASSACHUSETTS								
1 ***Conte***	Y	Y	Y	Y	Y	Y	Y	N
2 Boland	?	Y	Y	Y	Y	N	Y	N
3 Early	Y	Y	Y	N	Y	N	Y	Y
4 Frank	Y	Y	Y	N	Y	N	Y	Y
5 Shannon	Y	N	Y	N	Y	N	Y	Y
6 Mavroules	Y	Y	Y	Y	Y	N	Y	Y
7 Markey	Y	Y	Y	N	Y	N	Y	Y
8 O'Neill								
9 Moakley	Y	Y	Y	N	Y	N	Y	Y
10 Studds	Y	Y	Y	N	Y	N	Y	Y
11 Donnelly	Y	Y	Y	Y	Y	N	Y	N
MICHIGAN								
1 Conyers	?	?	?	?	?	?	?	?
2 ***Pursell***	Y	N	N	Y	N	Y	N	N
3 Wolpe	Y	Y	Y	Y	Y	N	Y	Y
4 ***Siljander***	Y	N	N	Y	N	Y	N	N
5 ***Sawyer***	Y	N	N	Y	N	Y	N	N
6 Carr	Y	N	N	Y	Y	N	Y	Y
7 Kildee	Y	Y	Y	N	Y	N	Y	Y
8 Traxler	?	?	N	Y	Y	N	Y	N
9 ***Vander Jagt***	Y	N	N	?	N	Y	N	N
10 Albosta	Y	N	N	Y	Y	Y	Y	N
11 ***Davis***	Y	Y	Y	Y	N	Y	N	N
12 Bonior	Y	Y	N	?	Y	Y	Y	Y
13 Crockett	Y	N	Y	N	Y	Y	Y	Y
14 Hertel	Y	Y	Y	Y	Y	N	Y	N
15 Ford	Y	Y	N	N	Y	N	Y	Y
16 Dingell	Y	Y	Y	Y	N	Y	N	N
17 Levin	Y	Y	N	Y	N	N	Y	N
18 ***Broomfield***	Y	N	N	Y	N	Y	N	N
MINNESOTA								
1 Penny	Y	N	Y	Y	Y	N	Y	N
2 ***Weber***	N	N	N	Y	N	Y	N	N
3 ***Frenzel***	?	?	N	Y	?	Y	N	N
4 Vento	Y	Y	Y	N	Y	N	Y	Y
5 Sabo	Y	Y	N	N	Y	Y	Y	Y
6 Sikorski	Y	Y	N	N	Y	N	Y	Y
7 ***Stangeland***	Y	N	N	Y	N	Y	N	N
8 Oberstar	Y	N	Y	N	Y	N	Y	Y
MISSISSIPPI								
1 Whitten	Y	N	N	Y	N	Y	N	N
2 ***Franklin***	Y	N	N	Y	N	Y	N	N
3 Montgomery	Y	N	N	Y	N	Y	N	N
4 Dowdy	Y	Y	N	Y	N	Y	N	N
5 ***Lott***	Y	N	N	Y	N	Y	N	N
MISSOURI								
1 Clay	Y	N	Y	N	Y	?	Y	Y
2 Young	Y	Y	Y	Y	N	Y	N	N
3 Gephardt	Y	N	Y	?	?	?	N	N
4 Skelton	Y	N	N	Y	N	Y	N	N
5 Wheat	Y	Y	N	Y	Y	N	Y	Y
6 ***Coleman***	Y	N	N	Y	N	Y	N	N
7 ***Taylor***	Y	N	Y	Y	N	Y	N	N
8 ***Emerson***	Y	N	N	Y	N	Y	N	N
9 Volkmer	Y	N	Y	Y	Y	Y	N	N
MONTANA								
1 Williams	Y	Y	Y	Y	Y	?	Y	N
2 ***Marlenee***	Y	Y	N	Y	N	Y	N	N
NEBRASKA								
1 ***Bereuter***	N	N	N	Y	Y	N	N	N
2 ***Daub***	Y	N	N	Y	N	Y	N	N
3 ***Smith***	N	N	N	Y	N	Y	N	N
NEVADA								
1 Reid	Y	N	Y	Y	Y	N	Y	N
2 ***Vucanovich***	Y	N	N	Y	N	N	N	N
NEW HAMPSHIRE								
1 D'Amours	Y	N	Y	Y	Y	Y	N	N
2 ***Gregg***	N	N	N	Y	N	N	N	N
NEW JERSEY								
1 Florio	Y	Y	N	Y	Y	Y	Y	N
2 Hughes	Y	Y	Y	Y	N	N	N	N
3 Howard	Y	Y	Y	N	Y	Y	Y	N
4 ***Smith***	Y	?	N	Y	N	Y	N	N
5 ***Roukema***	Y	Y	N	Y	Y	N	N	N
6 Dwyer	Y	Y	Y	N	Y	N	Y	N
7 ***Rinaldo***	Y	Y	N	Y	N	N	N	N
8 Roe	Y	Y	N	Y	Y	Y	Y	N
9 Torricelli	Y	?	Y	Y	Y	N	Y	Y
10 Rodino	Y	Y	Y	N	Y	N	Y	Y
11 Minish	Y	Y	Y	Y	Y	Y	Y	N
12 ***Courter***	Y	Y	N	Y	N	N	N	N
13 ***Forsythe***	Y	N	N	Y	N	+	-	+
14 Guarini	Y	Y	Y	#	Y	N	Y	N
NEW MEXICO								
1 ***Lujan***	Y	N	N	Y	N	Y	N	N
2 ***Skeen***	Y	N	N	Y	N	Y	N	N
3 Richardson	Y	Y	Y	Y	Y	N	Y	N
NEW YORK								
1 ***Carney***	N	N	N	Y	N	Y	N	N
2 Downey	Y	Y	Y	Y	Y	N	Y	Y
3 Mrazek	Y	Y	Y	Y	Y	N	Y	N
4 ***Lent***	Y	Y	N	Y	?	Y	N	N
5 ***McGrath***	Y	Y	N	Y	N	N	N	N
6 Addabbo	Y	Y	Y	N	Y	N	Y	Y
7 Ackerman	Y	Y	Y	Y	Y	N	Y	Y
8 Scheuer	Y	Y	Y	Y	Y	N	Y	Y
9 Ferraro	Y	Y	Y	N	Y	Y	Y	N
10 Schumer	Y	Y	Y	Y	Y	N	Y	Y
11 Towns	Y	Y	Y	N	Y	N	Y	Y
12 Owens	Y	Y	Y	N	Y	?	?	Y
13 Solarz	Y	Y	Y	Y	Y	N	N	N
14 ***Molinari***	Y	N	N	Y	N	N	N	N
15 ***Green***	Y	Y	N	Y	N	N	N	N
16 Rangel	Y	Y	Y	X	?	N	Y	Y
17 Weiss	Y	Y	Y	N	Y	N	Y	Y
18 Garcia	Y	Y	Y	N	Y	Y	Y	Y
19 Biaggi	Y	Y	Y	N	?	?	N	Y
20 Ottinger	Y	Y	Y	N	Y	N	Y	Y
21 ***Fish***	Y	N	Y	Y	Y	N	N	N
22 ***Gilman***	Y	Y	Y	Y	N	N	N	N
23 Stratton	Y	N	N	Y	N	Y	N	N
24 ***Solomon***	Y	N	N	Y	N	Y	N	N
25 ***Boehlert***	Y	Y	Y	Y	Y	N	Y	N
26 ***Martin***	Y	N	N	Y	N	Y	N	N
27 ***Wortley***	Y	Y	N	Y	N	Y	N	N
28 McHugh	Y	Y	N	Y	Y	Y	N	N
29 ***Horton***	Y	Y	N	Y	Y	Y	Y	N
30 ***Conable***	N	N	N	Y	N	Y	N	N
31 ***Kemp***	Y	N	N	Y	N	N	N	N
32 LaFalce	Y	Y	Y	N	Y	N	Y	Y
33 Nowak	Y	Y	N	Y	Y	N	Y	Y
34 Lundine	Y	Y	N	N	Y	Y	Y	N
NORTH CAROLINA								
1 Jones	Y	N	Y	Y	N	Y	N	N
2 Valentine	Y	N	N	Y	N	Y	N	N
3 Whitley	Y	N	N	Y	N	Y	N	N
4 Andrews	Y	N	N	Y	N	Y	N	?
5 Neal	Y	N	N	Y	Y	N	N	N
6 Britt	Y	N	N	Y	N	Y	N	N
7 Rose	Y	N	N	Y	N	Y	Y	N
8 Hefner	Y	N	N	Y	N	Y	N	N
9 ***Martin***	Y	N	N	Y	N	Y	N	N
10 ***Broyhill***	Y	N	N	Y	N	Y	N	N
11 Clarke	Y	N	N	Y	Y	Y	N	N
NORTH DAKOTA								
AL Dorgan	Y	Y	N	N	Y	N	Y	N
OHIO								
1 Luken	Y	N	N	Y	Y	N	Y	N
2 ***Gradison***	Y	N	N	Y	N	Y	N	N
3 Hall	Y	N	Y	N	Y	N	Y	N
4 ***Oxley***	Y	N	N	Y	N	Y	N	N
5 ***Latta***	Y	N	Y	Y	N	Y	N	N
6 ***McEwen***	Y	N	N	Y	N	Y	N	N
7 ***DeWine***	Y	N	N	Y	N	N	N	N
8 ***Kindness***	N	N	N	Y	N	Y	N	N
9 Kaptur	Y	N	N	N	Y	N	Y	Y
10 ***Miller***	N	N	Y	Y	N	N	N	N
11 Eckart	Y	Y	Y	N	Y	N	Y	Y
12 ***Kasich***	Y	N	N	Y	N	N	N	N
13 Pease	Y	N	Y	Y	Y	N	Y	Y
14 Seiberling	Y	Y	Y	N	Y	N	Y	Y
15 ***Wylie***	Y	N	Y	Y	N	N	N	N
16 ***Regula***	Y	N	Y	Y	N	Y	N	N
17 ***Williams***	Y	N	N	?	?	?	?	N
18 Applegate	Y	Y	N	Y	Y	?	Y	N
19 Feighan	Y	Y	Y	Y	Y	N	Y	Y
20 Oakar	Y	N	Y	N	Y	N	Y	Y
21 Stokes	Y	N	Y	N	Y	?	Y	Y
OKLAHOMA								
1 Jones	Y	N	N	Y	N	N	N	N
2 Synar	Y	Y	N	Y	N	N	N	N
3 Watkins	Y	N	N	?	N	N	N	N
4 McCurdy	Y	N	N	Y	N	N	N	N
5 ***Edwards***	Y	N	N	Y	N	N	N	N
6 English	Y	N	N	Y	N	Y	N	N
OREGON								
1 AuCoin	Y	Y	Y	N	Y	Y	Y	Y
2 ***Smith, R.***	Y	N	N	Y	N	Y	N	N
3 Wyden	Y	Y	N	Y	Y	N	Y	Y
4 Weaver	Y	Y	Y	N	Y	N	Y	Y
5 ***Smith, D.***	N	N	N	Y	N	?	N	N
PENNSYLVANIA								
1 Foglietta	Y	Y	Y	N	Y	N	Y	Y
2 Gray	Y	Y	Y	N	Y	N	Y	Y
3 Borski	Y	Y	Y	Y	Y	N	Y	N
4 Kolter	Y	N	N	Y	Y	Y	Y	N
5 ***Schulze***	?	?	?	?	N	Y	N	N
6 Yatron	Y	Y	N	Y	Y	N	Y	N
7 Edgar	Y	Y	N	N	Y	N	Y	Y
8 Kostmayer	Y	N	Y	Y	Y	N	Y	Y
9 ***Shuster***	Y	N	N	Y	N	Y	N	N
10 ***McDade***	Y	Y	Y	Y	N	Y	N	N
11 Harrison	Y	N	Y	Y	Y	N	Y	N
12 Murtha	Y	Y	Y	Y	N	Y	N	N
13 ***Coughlin***	Y	N	N	N	N	N	Y	N
14 Coyne	Y	Y	Y	N	N	N	Y	Y
15 ***Ritter***	N	Y	N	Y	N	N	N	N
16 ***Walker***	Y	N	N	Y	N	N	N	N
17 ***Gekas***	Y	N	Y	Y	N	N	N	N
18 Walgren	Y	N	N	Y	Y	N	Y	Y
19 ***Goodling***	Y	N	N	Y	Y	Y	N	N
20 Gaydos	Y	Y	N	Y	N	?	N	N
21 ***Ridge***	Y	N	N	Y	N	N	N	N
22 Murphy	Y	Y	N	Y	Y	Y	Y	N
23 ***Clinger***	Y	N	N	Y	N	Y	N	N
RHODE ISLAND								
1 St Germain	Y	Y	Y	N	Y	Y	Y	N
2 ***Schneider***	Y	N	Y	Y	Y	Y	Y	Y
SOUTH CAROLINA								
1 ***Hartnett***	Y	N	N	Y	N	Y	N	N
2 ***Spence***	Y	N	N	Y	N	Y	N	N
3 Derrick	Y	N	N	Y	Y	Y	N	N
4 ***Campbell***	Y	N	N	Y	N	Y	N	N
5 Spratt	Y	N	N	Y	N	Y	N	N
6 Tallon	Y	N	Y	Y	N	Y	N	N
SOUTH DAKOTA								
AL Daschle	Y	Y	N	Y	Y	N	Y	N
TENNESSEE								
1 ***Quillen***	Y	N	N	Y	N	?	N	N
2 ***Duncan***	Y	Y	N	Y	N	Y	N	N
3 Lloyd	Y	N	N	Y	N	Y	N	N
4 Cooper	Y	N	N	Y	N	Y	N	N
5 Boner	Y	Y	N	Y	N	Y	N	N
6 Gore	Y	N	N	Y	N	Y	N	N
7 ***Sundquist***	Y	N	N	Y	N	Y	N	N
8 Jones	Y	N	N	Y	N	Y	N	N
9 Ford	Y	Y	Y	N	?	N	Y	Y
TEXAS								
1 Hall, S.	Y	N	N	Y	N	Y	N	N
2 Wilson	?	?	N	?	?	?	?	?
3 ***Bartlett***	Y	N	N	Y	N	Y	N	N
4 Hall, R.	Y	N	N	Y	N	Y	N	N
5 Bryant	Y	Y	Y	Y	Y	N	Y	N
6 ***Gramm***	Y	N	N	Y	N	Y	N	N
7 ***Archer***	N	N	N	Y	N	Y	N	N
8 ***Fields***	N	N	N	Y	N	Y	N	N
9 Brooks	Y	N	N	Y	Y	Y	N	N
10 Pickle	Y	N	Y	Y	N	N	N	N
11 Leath	Y	N	N	Y	N	Y	N	N
12 Wright	Y	Y	Y	Y	N	Y	N	N
13 Hightower	Y	N	N	Y	N	Y	N	N
14 Patman	Y	N	N	Y	N	N	N	N
15 de la Garza	Y	Y	N	Y	N	N	N	N
16 Coleman	Y	N	N	N	N	N	Y	N
17 Stenholm	Y	N	?	Y	N	Y	N	N
18 Leland	Y	?	Y	N	Y	N	Y	Y
19 Hance	Y	N	N	Y	N	Y	N	N
20 Gonzalez	Y	N	N	Y	Y	N	Y	Y
21 ***Loeffler***	Y	N	N	Y	N	Y	N	N
22 ***Paul***	N	N	N	N	Y	N	Y	Y
23 Kazen	Y	N	N	Y	N	Y	N	N
24 Frost	Y	N	Y	Y	N	N	N	N
25 Andrews	Y	N	N	Y	N	Y	N	N
26 Vandergriff	Y	N	N	Y	N	Y	N	N
27 Ortiz	Y	Y	Y	Y	Y	N	N	N
UTAH								
1 ***Hansen***	N	N	N	Y	N	Y	N	N
2 ***Marriott***	Y	N	N	Y	N	Y	N	N
3 ***Nielson***	N	N	N	Y	N	Y	N	N
VERMONT								
AL ***Jeffords***	N	Y	Y	Y	Y	N	N	N
VIRGINIA								
1 ***Bateman***	Y	N	Y	Y	N	Y	N	N
2 ***Whitehurst***	Y	N	N	Y	N	Y	N	N
3 ***Bliley***	Y	N	N	Y	N	Y	N	N
4 Sisisky	Y	N	N	Y	N	Y	N	N
5 Daniel	Y	N	N	Y	N	Y	N	N
6 Olin	Y	N	N	Y	N	N	N	N
7 ***Robinson***	Y	N	N	Y	N	Y	N	N
8 ***Parris***	Y	N	N	Y	N	Y	N	N
9 Boucher	Y	Y	N	Y	Y	N	Y	N
10 ***Wolf***	Y	Y	N	Y	N	N	N	N
WASHINGTON								
1 ***Pritchard***	Y	N	N	?	Y	Y	N	N
2 Swift	Y	Y	Y	Y	Y	Y	Y	Y
3 Bonker	Y	Y	N	Y	Y	Y	Y	Y
4 ***Morrison***	Y	N	N	Y	N	Y	N	N
5 Foley	?	?	?	?	?	?	?	?
6 Dicks	Y	N	Y	Y	N	N	N	N
7 Lowry	Y	Y	Y	N	Y	N	Y	Y
8 ***Chandler***	Y	N	N	Y	N	Y	N	N
WEST VIRGINIA								
1 Mollohan	Y	N	N	Y	N	Y	Y	N
2 Staggers	Y	Y	Y	Y	N	N	Y	Y
3 Wise	+	-	+	Y	Y	N	Y	N
4 Rahall	Y	N	N	Y	Y	N	Y	N
WISCONSIN								
1 Aspin	Y	Y	Y	Y	N	N	N	N
2 Kastenmeier	Y	Y	Y	N	Y	N	Y	Y
3 ***Gunderson***	N	N	Y	Y	N	Y	N	N
4 Zablocki	Y	Y	Y	Y	N	Y	N	N
5 Moody	Y	Y	Y	Y	Y	Y	Y	Y
6 ***Petri***	N	N	N	N	N	N	N	N
7 Obey	Y	N	Y	?	Y	Y	Y	N
8 ***Roth***	Y	N	Y	Y	N	N	N	N
9 ***Sensenbrenner***	Y	N	N	Y	N	N	N	N
WYOMING								
AL ***Cheney***	N	N	N	Y	N	Y	N	N

Southern states - Ala., Ark., Fla., Ga., Ky., La., Miss., N.C., Okla., S.C., Tenn., Texas, Va.

260. HR 2969. Department of Defense Authorization. Hertel, D-Mich., amendment to allow the allocation of up to $7 billion worth of defense procurement contracts to firms in areas of high unemployment. Adopted 218-201: R 62-99; D 156-102 (ND 146-24, SD 10-78), July 26, 1983.

261. HR 2969. Department of Defense Authorization. Passage of the bill to authorize $187.4 billion for weapons procurement, military research and operations in fiscal 1984. Passed 305-114: R 136-26; D 169-88 (ND 84-85, SD 85-3), July 26, 1983.

262. H Res 267. Committee Funds. Adoption of the resolution to provide not more than $200,000 from the contingent fund of the House for further expenses of investigations by the Committee on Standards of Official Conduct. The money would be used to continue the ethics committee's examination of drug use at the Capitol. Adopted 407-3: R 157-3; D 250-0 (ND 168-0, SD 82-0), July 28, 1983.

263. HR 2973. Interest and Dividend Tax Withholding/Caribbean Basin Initiative. Adoption of the conference report on the bill to repeal interest and dividend withholding requirements due to take effect Aug. 5; to impose new tax compliance requirements and penalties; and to provide trade and tax incentives to certain Caribbean nations. Adopted 392-18: R 158-2; D 234-16 (ND 150-16, SD 84-0), July 28, 1983.

264. HR 2760. Prohibition on Covert Action in Nicaragua. Barnes, D-Md., amendment to the Young, R-Fla., amendment, to retain the prohibition in the bill on U.S. covert action in Nicaragua and to state the sense of Congress that the government of Nicaragua should enter into agreements with other countries in Central America to halt support for anti-government forces in the region. Rejected 213-214: R 7-158; D 206-56 (ND 166-8, SD 40-48), July 28, 1983. A "nay" was a vote supporting the president's position. (The Young amendment, as amended by subsequent amendments, was later deleted by the Wright, D-Texas, substitute amendment.)

265. HR 2760. Prohibition on Covert Action in Nicaragua. Boland, D-Mass., amendment to the Mica, D-Fla., amendment to the Young, R-Fla., amendment, to terminate U.S. covert action in Nicaragua for 30 days, after which the president could submit a new plan to Congress for resuming such covert action, and Congress could approve such a plan by passing a joint resolution. Adopted 221-205: R 10-156; D 211-49 (ND 165-8, SD 46-41), July 28, 1983. (The Young amendment, as amended by this and subsequent amendments, was later deleted by the Wright, D-Texas, substitute amendment.)

266. HR 2760. Prohibition on Covert Action in Nicaragua. Broomfield, R-Mich., amendment (offered on behalf of Mica, D-Fla.), to the Young, R-Fla., amendment, to permit U.S. covert action in Nicaragua to continue if the president submitted to Congress a new plan for interdiction of arms being shipped from or through Nicaragua to anti-government forces in El Salvador. Rejected 203-223: R 156-9; D 47-214 (ND 7-166, SD 40-48), July 28, 1983. A "yea" was a vote supporting the president's position. (The Young amendment, as amended, was later deleted by the Wright, D-Texas, substitute amendment.)

267. HR 2760. Prohibition on Covert Action in Nicaragua. Hyde, R-Ill., amendment to the Wright, D-Texas, amendment, to make the prohibition on U.S. covert action in Nicaragua effective 30 days after the House Armed Services, Foreign Affairs and Intelligence committees had held hearings on the feasibility of section 802 of the bill, which authorized overt aid to countries in Central America for the interdiction of cross-border arms shipments. Rejected 194-229: R 155-7; D 39-222 (ND 8-166, SD 31-56), July 28, 1983. (The Wright amendment subsequently was adopted by voice vote.)

KEY

Y Voted for (yea).
Paired for.
+ Announced for.
N Voted against (nay).
X Paired against.
- Announced against.
P Voted "present".
C Voted "present" to avoid possible conflict of interest.
? Did not vote or otherwise make a position known.

Democrats   *Republicans*

	260	261	262	263	264	265	266	267
ALABAMA								
1 *Edwards*	N	Y	Y	Y	N	N	Y	Y
2 *Dickinson*	N	Y	N	Y	N	N	Y	Y
3 Nichols	N	Y	Y	Y	N	N	Y	Y
4 Bevill	N	Y	Y	Y	N	Y	N	Y
5 Flippo	N	Y	Y	Y	N	N	Y	N
6 Erdreich	N	Y	Y	Y	N	N	Y	Y
7 Shelby	N	Y	Y	Y	N	N	Y	Y
ALASKA								
AL *Young*	?	?	Y	Y	N	N	Y	Y
ARIZONA								
1 *McCain*	N	Y	Y	Y	N	N	Y	Y
2 Udall	N	Y	Y	Y	Y	Y	N	N
3 *Stump*	N	Y	Y	Y	N	N	Y	Y
4 *Rudd*	N	Y	Y	Y	N	Y	Y	Y
5 McNulty	Y	Y	Y	Y	Y	Y	N	N
ARKANSAS								
1 Alexander	N	Y	?	Y	Y	Y	N	N
2 *Bethune*	N	N	Y	Y	N	N	Y	Y
3 *Hammerschmidt*	?	?	Y	Y	N	N	Y	Y
4 Anthony	N	Y	Y	Y	Y	Y	N	N
CALIFORNIA								
1 Bosco	Y	N	Y	Y	Y	Y	N	N
2 *Chappie*	N	Y	?	?	X	X	?	?
3 Matsui	Y	Y	Y	N	Y	Y	N	N
4 Fazio	Y	Y	Y	Y	Y	Y	N	N
5 Burton	Y	N	Y	Y	Y	Y	N	N
6 Boxer	Y	N	Y	Y	Y	Y	N	N
7 Miller	N	N	Y	Y	Y	Y	N	N
8 Dellums	Y	N	P	P	Y	Y	N	N
9 Stark	Y	N	Y	Y	Y	Y	N	N
10 Edwards	Y	N	Y	N	Y	Y	N	N
11 Lantos	Y	Y	Y	Y	Y	Y	N	N
12 *Zschau*	N	Y	Y	Y	N	N	Y	Y
13 Mineta	Y	N	Y	Y	Y	Y	N	N
14 *Shumway*	N	Y	Y	Y	N	N	Y	Y
15 Coelho	Y	Y	Y	Y	Y	Y	N	N
16 Panetta	Y	N	Y	N	Y	Y	N	N
17 *Pashayan*	N	Y	Y	Y	N	N	Y	Y
18 Lehman	Y	Y	Y	Y	Y	Y	N	N
19 *Lagomarsino*	N	Y	Y	Y	N	N	Y	Y
20 *Thomas*	N	N	Y	Y	N	N	Y	Y
21 *Fiedler*	N	Y	Y	Y	N	N	Y	Y
22 *Moorhead*	N	Y	Y	Y	N	Y	Y	Y
23 Beilenson	Y	N	Y	Y	Y	Y	N	N
24 Waxman	Y	N	Y	Y	Y	Y	N	N
25 Roybal	Y	N	Y	N	Y	Y	N	N
26 Berman	Y	N	Y	Y	Y	Y	N	N
27 Levine	N	Y	Y	Y	Y	Y	N	N
28 Dixon	Y	N	?	?	#	#	N	N
29 Hawkins	Y	Y	Y	Y	Y	Y	N	N
30 Martinez	Y	N	Y	Y	Y	Y	N	N
31 Dymally	Y	N	Y	Y	Y	Y	N	N
32 Anderson	Y	Y	Y	Y	Y	Y	N	N
33 *Dreier*	N	Y	Y	Y	N	N	Y	Y
34 Torres	Y	Y	Y	Y	Y	Y	N	N
35 *Lewis*	?	?	Y	Y	N	N	Y	Y
36 Brown	Y	N	Y	Y	Y	Y	N	N
37 *McCandless*	N	N	Y	Y	N	N	Y	Y
38 Patterson	N	Y	Y	Y	Y	Y	N	N
39 *Dannemeyer*	N	Y	Y	Y	N	N	Y	Y
40 *Badham*	N	Y	N	Y	N	N	Y	Y
41 *Lowery*	N	Y	Y	Y	N	N	Y	Y
42 *Lungren*	N	Y	Y	Y	N	N	Y	Y

	260	261	262	263	264	265	266	267
43 *Packard*	N	Y	Y	Y	N	N	Y	Y
44 Bates	Y	N	Y	N	Y	Y	N	N
45 *Hunter*	N	Y	?	Y	N	N	Y	Y
COLORADO								
1 Schroeder	N	N	Y	Y	Y	Y	N	N
2 Wirth	Y	N	Y	Y	Y	Y	N	N
3 Kogovsek	Y	N	Y	Y	Y	Y	N	N
4 *Brown*	N	N	?	Y	N	N	Y	Y
5 *Kramer*	N	Y	Y	Y	N	N	Y	Y
6 *Schaefer*	N	Y	Y	Y	N	N	Y	Y
CONNECTICUT								
1 Kennelly	Y	Y	Y	Y	Y	Y	N	N
2 Gejdenson	Y	Y	Y	Y	Y	Y	N	N
3 Morrison	Y	N	Y	Y	Y	Y	N	N
4 *McKinney*	Y	N	Y	Y	Y	Y	N	Y
5 Ratchford	Y	Y	Y	Y	Y	Y	N	N
6 Johnson	Y	Y	Y	Y	N	N	Y	Y
DELAWARE								
AL Carper	N	Y	Y	Y	Y	Y	N	Y
FLORIDA								
1 Hutto	N	Y	Y	Y	N	N	Y	N
2 Fuqua	N	Y	Y	Y	N	N	Y	N
3 Bennett	N	Y	Y	Y	Y	Y	N	N
4 Chappell	N	Y	Y	Y	N	N	Y	N
5 *McCollum*	N	Y	Y	Y	N	N	Y	Y
6 MacKay	N	Y	Y	Y	N	Y	N	N
7 Gibbons	N	Y	Y	Y	N	N	Y	N
8 *Young*	Y	Y	Y	Y	N	N	Y	N
9 *Bilirakis*	N	Y	Y	Y	N	N	Y	Y
10 Ireland	N	Y	Y	Y	N	N	Y	N
11 Nelson	N	Y	Y	Y	N	Y	N	N
12 *Lewis*	N	Y	Y	Y	N	N	Y	Y
13 *Mack*	N	Y	Y	Y	N	N	Y	Y
14 Mica	N	Y	Y	Y	N	N	Y	N
15 *Shaw*	N	Y	Y	+	N	N	Y	Y
16 Smith	N	Y	Y	Y	N	N	Y	N
17 Lehman	N	N	Y	Y	Y	Y	N	N
18 Pepper	N	Y	Y	Y	Y	Y	N	N
19 Fascell	N	Y	Y	Y	N	N	Y	N
GEORGIA								
1 Thomas	N	Y	Y	Y	N	N	Y	Y
2 Hatcher	N	Y	Y	Y	N	N	Y	Y
3 Ray	N	Y	Y	Y	N	N	Y	Y
4 Levitas	N	Y	Y	Y	Y	Y	N	N
5 Fowler	N	Y	Y	Y	Y	Y	N	N
6 *Gingrich*	N	Y	?	Y	N	N	Y	Y
7 McDonald	N	Y	Y	N	N	N	Y	Y
8 Rowland	N	Y	Y	Y	N	N	Y	N
9 Jenkins	N	Y	Y	Y	N	N	Y	N
10 Barnard	N	Y	Y	Y	N	N	Y	Y
HAWAII								
1 Heftel	?	#	?	?	?	?	?	?
2 Akaka	Y	Y	Y	P	Y	Y	N	N
IDAHO								
1 *Craig*	N	Y	Y	Y	N	N	Y	Y
2 *Hansen*	N	Y	?	?	N	N	Y	Y
ILLINOIS								
1 Vacancy								
2 Savage	+	X	Y	Y	Y	Y	N	N
3 Russo	Y	N	Y	Y	Y	Y	N	N
4 *O'Brien*	Y	Y	Y	Y	N	N	Y	Y
5 Lipinski	Y	Y	Y	Y	Y	Y	N	N
6 *Hyde*	Y	Y	Y	Y	N	N	Y	Y
7 Collins	Y	N	Y	Y	Y	Y	N	N
8 Rostenkowski	N	Y	Y	Y	Y	Y	N	N
9 Yates	Y	N	Y	N	Y	Y	N	N
10 *Porter*	Y	Y	Y	Y	N	N	Y	Y
11 Annunzio	Y	Y	Y	Y	Y	Y	N	N
12 *Crane, P.*	N	Y	Y	Y	N	N	Y	Y
13 *Erlenborn*	Y	Y	Y	Y	N	N	Y	Y
14 *Corcoran*	Y	Y	Y	Y	N	N	Y	Y
15 *Madigan*	?	?	Y	Y	N	N	Y	Y
16 *Martin*	Y	Y	N	Y	N	N	Y	Y
17 Evans	Y	Y	Y	Y	Y	Y	N	N
18 *Michel*	Y	Y	Y	Y	N	N	Y	Y
19 *Crane, D.*	N	Y	Y	Y	N	N	Y	Y
20 Durbin	Y	Y	Y	Y	Y	Y	N	N
21 Price	Y	Y	Y	Y	Y	Y	N	N
22 Simon	Y	Y	Y	+	Y	Y	N	N
INDIANA								
1 Hall	Y	N	Y	Y	Y	Y	N	N
2 Sharp	Y	Y	Y	Y	Y	Y	N	N
3 *Hiler*	Y	Y	Y	Y	N	N	Y	Y
4 *Coats*	Y	Y	Y	Y	N	N	Y	Y
5 *Hillis*	N	Y	Y	Y	N	N	Y	Y

ND - Northern Democrats   SD - Southern Democrats

Corresponding to Congressional Record Votes 274, 275, 277, 278, 279, 280, 281, 282

	260	261	262	263	264	265	266	267
6 ***Burton***	Y	Y	Y	Y	N	N	Y	Y
7 ***Myers***	N	Y	Y	Y	N	N	Y	Y
8 McCloskey	Y	Y	Y	Y	Y	Y	N	N
9 Hamilton	Y	Y	Y	Y	Y	Y	N	N
10 Jacobs	Y	Y	Y	Y	Y	Y	N	N
IOWA								
1 ***Leach***	Y	N	Y	Y	Y	Y	N	N
2 ***Tauke***	Y	N	Y	Y	N	N	Y	Y
3 ***Evans***	Y	N	Y	Y	N	N	Y	Y
4 Smith	N	N	Y	Y	Y	Y	N	N
5 Harkin	Y	N	Y	P	Y	Y	N	N
6 Bedell	Y	N	Y	Y	Y	Y	N	N
KANSAS								
1 ***Roberts***	N	Y	Y	Y	N	N	Y	Y
2 Slattery	N	Y	Y	Y	Y	Y	N	N
3 ***Winn***	N	Y	Y	Y	N	N	Y	Y
4 Glickman	N	Y	Y	Y	Y	Y	N	N
5 ***Whittaker***	N	Y	Y	Y	N	N	Y	Y
KENTUCKY								
1 Hubbard	N	Y	Y	Y	N	N	Y	Y
2 Natcher	Y	Y	Y	Y	Y	Y	N	N
3 Mazzoli	N	Y	Y	Y	N	Y	N	Y
4 ***Snyder***	N	Y	Y	Y	N	N	Y	Y
5 ***Rogers***	N	Y	Y	Y	N	N	Y	Y
6 ***Hopkins***	N	Y	Y	Y	N	N	Y	Y
7 Perkins	Y	Y	Y	Y	Y	Y	N	N
LOUISIANA								
1 ***Livingston***	N	Y	Y	Y	N	N	Y	Y
2 Boggs	N	Y	Y	Y	Y	Y	N	N
3 Tauzin	N	Y	Y	Y	N	N	Y	Y
4 Roemer	N	N	Y	Y	N	N	Y	Y
5 Huckaby	N	Y	Y	Y	N	N	Y	Y
6 ***Moore***	N	Y	Y	Y	N	N	Y	Y
7 Breaux	N	Y	Y	Y	N	N	Y	Y
8 Long	N	Y	Y	Y	Y	Y	N	N
MAINE								
1 ***McKernan***	Y	Y	Y	Y	N	Y	Y	Y
2 ***Snowe***	Y	Y	Y	Y	N	Y	Y	N
MARYLAND								
1 Dyson	Y	Y	Y	Y	N	N	Y	Y
2 Long	Y	Y	Y	N	Y	Y	N	N
3 Mikulski	Y	N	Y	Y	Y	Y	N	N
4 ***Holt***	N	Y	Y	Y	N	N	Y	Y
5 Hoyer	N	Y	Y	Y	Y	Y	N	N
6 Byron	Y	Y	Y	Y	N	N	Y	Y
7 Mitchell	Y	N	Y	Y	Y	Y	N	N
8 Barnes	N	Y	Y	Y	Y	Y	N	N
MASSACHUSETTS								
1 ***Conte***	Y	Y	Y	Y	Y	Y	N	N
2 Boland	Y	Y	Y	Y	Y	Y	N	N
3 Early	Y	N	Y	N	Y	Y	N	N
4 Frank	Y	N	Y	Y	Y	Y	N	N
5 Shannon	Y	N	Y	N	Y	Y	N	N
6 Mavroules	Y	Y	Y	Y	Y	Y	N	N
7 Markey	Y	N	Y	N	Y	Y	N	N
8 O'Neill					Y			
9 Moakley	Y	N	Y	Y	Y	Y	N	N
10 Studds	Y	N	Y	Y	Y	Y	N	N
11 Donnelly	Y	N	Y	Y	Y	Y	N	N
MICHIGAN								
1 Conyers	?	?	?	?	Y	Y	N	N
2 ***Pursell***	Y	Y	Y	Y	N	N	Y	Y
3 Wolpe	Y	N	Y	Y	Y	Y	N	N
4 ***Siljander***	Y	Y	Y	Y	N	N	Y	Y
5 ***Sawyer***	Y	Y	Y	Y	N	N	Y	Y
6 Carr	Y	Y	Y	Y	Y	Y	N	N
7 Kildee	Y	N	Y	Y	Y	Y	N	N
8 Traxler	Y	Y	Y	Y	Y	Y	N	N
9 ***Vander Jagt***	Y	Y	Y	Y	N	N	Y	Y
10 Albosta	Y	Y	Y	Y	Y	Y	N	N
11 ***Davis***	Y	Y	Y	Y	N	N	Y	Y
12 Bonior	Y	N	Y	Y	Y	Y	N	N
13 Crockett	Y	N	Y	Y	Y	Y	N	N
14 Hertel	Y	N	Y	Y	Y	Y	N	N
15 Ford	Y	Y	Y	N	Y	Y	N	N
16 Dingell	Y	Y	Y	Y	Y	Y	N	N
17 Levin	Y	N	Y	Y	Y	Y	N	N
18 ***Broomfield***	Y	Y	Y	Y	N	N	Y	Y
MINNESOTA								
1 Penny	Y	N	Y	Y	Y	Y	N	N
2 ***Weber***	N	N	Y	Y	N	N	Y	Y
3 ***Frenzel***	N	N	N	Y	N	N	Y	Y
4 Vento	Y	N	Y	Y	Y	Y	N	N
5 Sabo	Y	N	Y	Y	Y	Y	N	N
6 Sikorski	Y	N	Y	Y	Y	Y	N	N
7 ***Stangeland***	N	N	Y	Y	N	N	Y	?
8 Oberstar	Y	N	?	N	Y	Y	N	N
MISSISSIPPI								
1 Whitten	N	Y	Y	Y	Y	Y	N	N
2 ***Franklin***	N	Y	Y	Y	N	N	Y	?
3 Montgomery	N	Y	Y	Y	N	N	Y	Y
4 Dowdy	N	Y	?	?	?	?	#	?
5 ***Lott***	N	Y	Y	Y	N	N	Y	Y
MISSOURI								
1 Clay	Y	?	Y	Y	Y	Y	N	N
2 Young	Y	Y	Y	Y	Y	Y	N	N
3 Gephardt	Y	Y	Y	Y	Y	Y	N	N
4 Skelton	N	Y	Y	Y	N	N	Y	Y
5 Wheat	Y	N	Y	Y	Y	Y	N	N
6 ***Coleman***	N	?	Y	Y	N	N	Y	Y
7 ***Taylor***	N	Y	Y	Y	N	N	Y	Y
8 ***Emerson***	N	Y	Y	Y	N	N	Y	Y
9 Volkmer	N	Y	Y	Y	Y	Y	N	N
MONTANA								
1 Williams	Y	N	Y	Y	Y	Y	N	N
2 ***Marlenee***	N	Y	Y	Y	N	N	Y	Y
NEBRASKA								
1 ***Bereuter***	N	Y	Y	Y	N	N	Y	Y
2 ***Daub***	N	Y	Y	Y	N	N	Y	Y
3 ***Smith***	N	Y	Y	Y	N	N	Y	Y
NEVADA								
1 Reid	Y	Y	Y	Y	Y	Y	N	N
2 ***Vucanovich***	N	Y	Y	Y	N	N	Y	Y
NEW HAMPSHIRE								
1 D'Amours	Y	Y	Y	Y	Y	Y	N	N
2 ***Gregg***	N	N	Y	Y	N	N	Y	Y
NEW JERSEY								
1 Florio	Y	?	Y	Y	Y	Y	X	N
2 Hughes	Y	N	Y	Y	N	Y	N	N
3 Howard	Y	Y	Y	Y	Y	Y	N	N
4 ***Smith***	Y	Y	Y	Y	N	N	Y	Y
5 ***Roukema***	N	N	Y	Y	Y	Y	N	N
6 Dwyer	Y	Y	Y	Y	Y	Y	N	N
7 ***Rinaldo***	Y	Y	?	?	N	N	Y	Y
8 Roe	Y	Y	Y	Y	Y	Y	N	N
9 Torricelli	Y	N	Y	Y	Y	Y	N	N
10 Rodino	Y	N	Y	?	Y	Y	N	N
11 Minish	Y	Y	Y	Y	Y	Y	N	N
12 ***Courter***	Y	Y	Y	Y	N	N	Y	Y
13 ***Forsythe***	+	-	Y	Y	?	N	Y	Y
14 Guarini	Y	N	Y	Y	Y	Y	X	N
NEW MEXICO								
1 ***Lujan***	Y	Y	Y	Y	N	N	Y	Y
2 ***Skeen***	N	Y	Y	Y	N	N	Y	Y
3 Richardson	N	Y	Y	Y	Y	Y	N	N
NEW YORK								
1 ***Carney***	Y	Y	Y	Y	N	N	Y	Y
2 Downey	Y	Y	Y	Y	Y	Y	N	N
3 Mrazek	Y	Y	Y	Y	Y	Y	N	N
4 ***Lent***	Y	Y	Y	Y	N	N	Y	Y
5 ***McGrath***	Y	Y	Y	Y	N	N	Y	Y
6 Addabbo	Y	Y	Y	Y	Y	Y	N	X
7 Ackerman	Y	N	Y	Y	Y	Y	N	N
8 Scheuer	Y	Y	Y	Y	Y	Y	N	N
9 Ferraro	Y	Y	Y	Y	Y	Y	N	N
10 Schumer	Y	Y	Y	Y	Y	Y	N	N
11 Towns	Y	N	Y	Y	Y	Y	N	N
12 Owens	Y	N	Y	Y	Y	Y	N	N
13 Solarz	Y	Y	Y	Y	Y	Y	N	N
14 ***Molinari***	Y	Y	Y	Y	N	N	Y	#
15 ***Green***	Y	N	Y	Y	Y	Y	N	N
16 Rangel	Y	N	Y	Y	Y	Y	N	N
17 Weiss	Y	N	Y	P	Y	N	N	N
18 Garcia	Y	N	?	Y	Y	Y	N	N
19 Biaggi	Y	Y	Y	Y	Y	Y	N	Y
20 Ottinger	Y	N	Y	Y	Y	Y	N	N
21 ***Fish***	Y	Y	Y	Y	N	N	Y	Y
22 ***Gilman***	Y	Y	+	+	N	N	Y	Y
23 Stratton	Y	Y	Y	Y	N	N	Y	Y
24 ***Solomon***	Y	Y	Y	Y	N	N	Y	Y
25 ***Boehlert***	Y	Y	Y	Y	N	Y	N	N
26 ***Martin***	Y	Y	Y	Y	N	N	Y	Y
27 ***Wortley***	Y	Y	Y	Y	N	N	Y	Y
28 McHugh	Y	N	Y	N	Y	Y	N	N
29 ***Horton***	Y	N	Y	Y	N	N	Y	Y
30 ***Conable***	Y	N	Y	Y	N	N	Y	Y
31 ***Kemp***	Y	Y	Y	Y	N	N	Y	Y
32 LaFalce	?	?	Y	Y	Y	Y	N	N
33 Nowak	Y	Y	Y	Y	Y	Y	N	N
34 Lundine	Y	Y	Y	Y	Y	Y	N	N
NORTH CAROLINA								
1 Jones	N	Y	?	?	N	Y	N	N
2 Valentine	N	Y	Y	Y	N	Y	N	N
3 Whitley	N	Y	Y	Y	N	Y	N	N
4 Andrews	?	?	Y	Y	Y	?	N	N
5 Neal	N	Y	?	Y	Y	Y	N	N
6 Britt	N	Y	Y	Y	Y	Y	N	N
7 Rose	N	Y	Y	Y	Y	Y	N	N
8 Hefner	N	Y	Y	Y	N	Y	N	N
9 ***Martin***	N	Y	Y	Y	N	N	Y	Y
10 ***Broyhill***	N	Y	Y	Y	N	N	Y	Y
11 Clarke	N	Y	Y	Y	Y	Y	N	N
NORTH DAKOTA								
AL Dorgan	N	N	Y	Y	Y	Y	N	N
OHIO								
1 Luken	Y	Y	Y	Y	Y	Y	N	N
2 ***Gradison***	N	Y	Y	Y	N	N	Y	Y
3 Hall	Y	Y	Y	Y	Y	Y	N	N
4 ***Oxley***	N	Y	Y	Y	N	N	Y	Y
5 ***Latta***	Y	Y	Y	Y	N	N	Y	Y
6 ***McEwen***	N	Y	Y	Y	N	N	Y	Y
7 ***DeWine***	N	Y	Y	Y	N	N	Y	Y
8 ***Kindness***	Y	Y	Y	?	N	N	Y	Y
9 Kaptur	Y	N	Y	Y	Y	Y	N	N
10 ***Miller***	Y	Y	Y	Y	N	N	Y	Y
11 Eckart	Y	Y	Y	Y	Y	Y	N	N
12 ***Kasich***	Y	Y	Y	Y	N	N	Y	Y
13 Pease	Y	Y	Y	Y	Y	Y	N	N
14 Seiberling	Y	N	Y	Y	Y	Y	N	N
15 ***Wylie***	Y	N	Y	Y	N	N	Y	Y
16 ***Regula***	Y	Y	Y	Y	N	N	Y	Y
17 ***Williams***	Y	Y	Y	Y	N	N	Y	Y
18 Applegate	Y	N	Y	Y	Y	Y	N	N
19 Feighan	Y	N	?	Y	Y	Y	N	N
20 Oakar	Y	Y	Y	Y	Y	Y	N	N
21 Stokes	Y	N	Y	Y	Y	Y	N	N
OKLAHOMA								
1 Jones	N	Y	Y	Y	Y	Y	N	N
2 Synar	N	Y	Y	Y	Y	Y	N	N
3 Watkins	N	Y	Y	Y	Y	Y	N	N
4 McCurdy	N	Y	Y	Y	Y	Y	N	N
5 ***Edwards***	N	Y	Y	Y	N	N	Y	Y
6 English	N	Y	Y	Y	N	Y	N	N
OREGON								
1 AuCoin	N	N	Y	Y	Y	Y	N	N
2 ***Smith, R.***	N	Y	Y	Y	N	N	Y	Y
3 Wyden	N	N	Y	Y	Y	Y	N	N
4 Weaver	N	N	Y	Y	Y	Y	N	N
5 ***Smith, D.***	N	Y	Y	Y	N	N	Y	Y
PENNSYLVANIA								
1 Foglietta	Y	Y	Y	Y	Y	Y	N	N
2 Gray	Y	N	Y	Y	Y	Y	N	N
3 Borski	Y	Y	Y	Y	Y	Y	N	N
4 Kolter	Y	N	Y	Y	Y	Y	N	N
5 ***Schulze***	Y	Y	Y	Y	N	N	Y	Y
6 Yatron	Y	Y	Y	Y	Y	Y	N	N
7 Edgar	Y	N	Y	Y	Y	Y	N	N
8 Kostmayer	Y	N	Y	Y	Y	Y	N	N
9 ***Shuster***	Y	Y	Y	Y	N	N	Y	Y
10 ***McDade***	Y	Y	Y	Y	N	N	#	?
11 Harrison	Y	Y	Y	Y	Y	Y	N	N
12 Murtha	Y	Y	Y	N	N	N	Y	N
13 ***Coughlin***	Y	N	Y	Y	N	N	Y	Y
14 Coyne	Y	Y	Y	Y	Y	Y	N	N
15 ***Ritter***	Y	Y	Y	Y	N	N	Y	Y
16 ***Walker***	Y	Y	Y	Y	N	N	Y	Y
17 ***Gekas***	Y	Y	Y	Y	N	N	Y	Y
18 Walgren	Y	N	Y	Y	Y	Y	N	N
19 ***Goodling***	N	N	Y	Y	N	N	Y	Y
20 Gaydos	Y	Y	Y	Y	N	N	Y	N
21 ***Ridge***	Y	Y	Y	Y	N	N	Y	Y
22 Murphy	Y	N	Y	Y	Y	Y	N	N
23 ***Clinger***	Y	Y	Y	Y	N	N	Y	Y
RHODE ISLAND								
1 St Germain	N	Y	Y	Y	Y	Y	N	N
2 ***Schneider***	Y	N	Y	Y	Y	Y	N	Y
SOUTH CAROLINA								
1 ***Hartnett***	N	Y	Y	Y	N	N	Y	Y
2 ***Spence***	N	Y	Y	Y	N	N	Y	Y
3 Derrick	N	Y	Y	Y	Y	Y	N	N
4 ***Campbell***	N	Y	Y	Y	N	N	Y	Y
5 Spratt	N	Y	Y	Y	Y	Y	N	N
6 Tallon	N	Y	Y	Y	N	N	N	N
SOUTH DAKOTA								
AL Daschle	Y	Y	Y	Y	Y	Y	N	N
TENNESSEE								
1 ***Quillen***	N	Y	Y	Y	N	N	Y	Y
2 ***Duncan***	N	Y	Y	Y	N	N	Y	Y
3 Lloyd	N	Y	Y	Y	N	N	Y	Y
4 Cooper	N	Y	Y	Y	Y	Y	N	N
5 Boner	N	Y	Y	Y	Y	Y	Y	N
6 Gore	N	Y	?	?	Y	Y	N	N
7 ***Sundquist***	N	Y	Y	Y	N	N	Y	Y
8 Jones	N	Y	?	?	?	?	?	?
9 Ford	Y	Y	Y	Y	Y	Y	N	N
TEXAS								
1 Hall, S.	Y	Y	Y	Y	N	N	Y	Y
2 Wilson	?	?	?	Y	N	N	Y	Y
3 ***Bartlett***	N	Y	Y	Y	N	N	Y	Y
4 Hall, R.	N	Y	Y	Y	N	N	Y	Y
5 Bryant	N	Y	Y	Y	Y	Y	N	N
6 ***Gramm***	N	Y	Y	Y	N	N	Y	Y
7 ***Archer***	N	Y	Y	Y	N	N	Y	Y
8 ***Fields***	N	Y	Y	Y	N	N	Y	Y
9 Brooks	N	Y	Y	Y	N	N	N	N
10 Pickle	N	Y	Y	Y	Y	Y	N	N
11 Leath	N	Y	Y	Y	N	N	Y	Y
12 Wright	N	Y	Y	Y	Y	Y	N	N
13 Hightower	N	Y	Y	Y	N	N	Y	Y
14 Patman	N	Y	Y	Y	N	N	Y	Y
15 de la Garza	Y	Y	?	Y	N	Y	N	N
16 Coleman	N	Y	Y	Y	Y	Y	N	N
17 Stenholm	N	Y	Y	Y	N	N	Y	Y
18 Leland	Y	N	Y	Y	Y	Y	N	N
19 Hance	N	Y	Y	Y	N	N	Y	N
20 Gonzalez	Y	Y	Y	P	Y	Y	N	N
21 ***Loeffler***	N	Y	Y	Y	N	N	Y	Y
22 ***Paul***	N	N	Y	N	N	N	Y	Y
23 Kazen	Y	Y	Y	Y	N	N	Y	Y
24 Frost	N	Y	Y	Y	Y	Y	N	N
25 Andrews	N	Y	Y	Y	N	Y	N	N
26 Vandergriff	N	Y	Y	Y	N	N	Y	Y
27 Ortiz	Y	Y	Y	Y	N	Y	N	N
UTAH								
1 ***Hansen***	N	Y	Y	Y	N	N	Y	Y
2 ***Marriott***	N	Y	Y	Y	N	N	Y	Y
3 ***Nielson***	N	Y	Y	Y	N	N	Y	Y
VERMONT								
AL ***Jeffords***	Y	N	Y	Y	N	Y	N	N
VIRGINIA								
1 ***Bateman***	N	Y	Y	Y	N	N	Y	Y
2 ***Whitehurst***	N	Y	Y	Y	N	N	Y	Y
3 ***Bliley***	N	Y	Y	Y	N	N	Y	Y
4 Sisisky	N	Y	Y	Y	N	N	Y	Y
5 Daniel	N	Y	Y	Y	N	N	Y	Y
6 Olin	N	Y	Y	Y	Y	Y	N	N
7 ***Robinson***	N	Y	Y	Y	N	N	Y	Y
8 ***Parris***	N	Y	Y	Y	N	N	Y	Y
9 Boucher	Y	Y	Y	Y	Y	Y	N	?
10 ***Wolf***	N	Y	Y	Y	N	N	Y	Y
WASHINGTON								
1 ***Pritchard***	?	Y	Y	P	N	N	Y	Y
2 Swift	N	N	Y	Y	Y	Y	N	N
3 Bonker	Y	N	Y	Y	Y	Y	N	N
4 ***Morrison***	N	Y	Y	Y	N	N	Y	Y
5 Foley	?	?	?	?	?	?	N	N
6 Dicks	N	Y	Y	Y	Y	Y	N	N
7 Lowry	N	N	Y	N	Y	Y	N	N
8 ***Chandler***	N	Y	Y	Y	N	N	Y	Y
WEST VIRGINIA								
1 Mollohan	Y	Y	Y	Y	Y	Y	N	N
2 Staggers	Y	Y	Y	Y	Y	Y	N	N
3 Wise	Y	Y	Y	Y	Y	Y	N	N
4 Rahall	Y	N	Y	Y	Y	Y	N	N
WISCONSIN								
1 Aspin	N	Y	Y	Y	Y	Y	N	N
2 Kastenmeier	Y	N	Y	Y	Y	Y	N	N
3 ***Gunderson***	Y	N	Y	Y	N	N	Y	Y
4 Zablocki	Y	Y	Y	Y	Y	Y	N	N
5 Moody	?	N	Y	Y	Y	Y	N	N
6 ***Petri***	Y	N	Y	Y	N	N	Y	Y
7 Obey	Y	N	Y	N	Y	Y	N	N
8 ***Roth***	Y	N	Y	Y	N	N	Y	Y
9 ***Sensenbrenner***	Y	N	Y	Y	N	N	Y	Y
WYOMING								
AL ***Cheney***	N	Y	Y	Y	N	N	Y	Y

Southern states - Ala., Ark., Fla., Ga., Ky., La., Miss., N.C., Okla., S.C., Tenn., Texas, Va.

268. HR 2760. Prohibition on Covert Action in Nicaragua. Bereuter, R-Neb., substitute for the Wright, D-Texas, substitute, to prohibit U.S. covert action in Nicaragua after Oct. 1, 1983, unless before that date the president submits to Congress a new plan for interdiction of arms transfers from Nicaragua to guerrillas in El Salvador. The new plan would not be implemented, and the covert action prohibition would take effect, if the president or the Organization of American States verifies that the government of Nicaragua had ceased to aid anti-government groups elsewhere in Central America and had taken steps to carry out the promises it made to the Organization of American States in July 1979. Rejected 196-228: R 151-11; D 45-217 (ND 5-169, SD 40-48), July 28, 1983. (The Wright substitute subsequently was adopted by voice vote.)

269. HR 2760. Prohibition on Covert Action in Nicaragua. Broomfield, R-Mich., motion to recommit the bill to the Foreign Affairs and Intelligence committees. Motion rejected 189-234: R 151-10; D 38-224 (ND 3-171, SD 35-53), July 28, 1983.

270. HR 2760. Prohibition on Covert Action in Nicaragua. Passage of the bill to prohibit, at a classified date specified by the House Intelligence Committee, support by U.S. intelligence agencies for military or paramilitary operations in Nicaragua and to authorize $30 million in fiscal 1983 and $50 million in fiscal 1984 to help friendly countries in Central America interdict cross-border shipments of arms to anti-government forces in the region. The bill also directed the president to seek action by the Organization of American States to resolve the conflicts in Central America and to seek an agreement by the government of Nicaragua to halt its support for anti-government forces in the region. Passed 228-195: R 18-145; D 210-50 (ND 163-9, SD 47-41), July 28, 1983. A "nay" was a vote supporting the president's position.

271. HR 3069. Supplemental Appropriations, Fiscal 1983. Adoption of the rule (H Res 284) providing for House floor consideration of the conference report on the bill to provide supplemental appropriations for fiscal 1983. Adopted 267-138: R 28-132; D 239-6 (ND 159-4, SD 80-2), July 28, 1983.

272. HR 3069. Supplemental Appropriations, Fiscal 1983. Frost, D-Texas, motion to table (kill) the Gephardt, D-Mo., motion to reconsider the vote by which the rule, providing for House floor consideration of the conference report on the bill to provide supplemental appropriations for fiscal 1983, was adopted *(see vote 271, above)*. Motion agreed to 271-125: R 37-121; D 234-4 (ND 155-2, SD 79-2), July 28, 1983.

273. HR 3069. Supplemental Appropriations, Fiscal 1983. Adoption of the conference report on the bill to appropriate $7,038,061,267 in new budget authority for supplemental funds for various government programs in fiscal 1983. Adopted 257-133: R 56-98; D 201-35 (ND 139-17, SD 62-18), July 28, 1983. The president had requested $15,138,053,808 in new budget authority for fiscal 1983 supplemental funds.

274. HR 2957. International Recovery and Financial Stability Act. St Germain, D-R.I., motion to limit debate on the bill to increase U.S. participation in the International Monetary Fund by $8.4 billion, including $5.8 billion in the U.S. quota in the fund and $2.6 billion in the General Arrangements to Borrow; to extend authority for the Export-Import Bank; and to provide multilateral development assistance. Motion agreed to 242-145: R 44-110; D 198-35 (ND 132-20, SD 66-15), July 29, 1983.

275. HR 2957. International Recovery and Financial Stability Act. St Germain, D-R.I., amendment to require the U.S. executive director to the International Monetary Fund to negotiate lower interest rates and longer maturities on private loans in debt restructuring agreements, to give other new instructions to the director, and to place restrictions on international lending by U.S. banks. Adopted 332-76: R 114-44; D 218-32 (ND 155-11, SD 63-21), July 29, 1983.

KEY

Y Voted for (yea).
Paired for.
+ Announced for.
N Voted against (nay).
X Paired against.
- Announced against.
P Voted "present".
C Voted "present" to avoid possible conflict of interest.
? Did not vote or otherwise make a position known.

Democrats *Republicans*

	268	269	270	271	272	273	274	275
ALABAMA								
1 *Edwards*	Y	Y	N	Y	Y	Y	Y	Y
2 *Dickinson*	Y	Y	N	N	N	Y	Y	Y
3 Nichols	Y	Y	N	Y	N	Y	Y	Y
4 Bevill	Y	Y	N	Y	Y	Y	Y	N
5 Flippo	Y	Y	N	?	?	Y	Y	N
6 Erdreich	Y	Y	N	Y	Y	Y	Y	Y
7 Shelby	Y	Y	N	Y	Y	Y	N	Y
ALASKA								
AL *Young*	Y	Y	N	?	?	?	N	Y
ARIZONA								
1 *McCain*	Y	Y	N	N	N	N	N	Y
2 Udall	N	N	Y	Y	Y	Y	?	Y
3 *Stump*	Y	Y	N	N	N	N	Y	N
4 *Rudd*	Y	Y	N	N	N	N	N	N
5 McNulty	N	N	Y	Y	Y	Y	Y	Y
ARKANSAS								
1 Alexander	N	N	Y	Y	Y	?	Y	Y
2 *Bethune*	Y	Y	N	N	N	N	N	N
3 *Hammerschmidt*	Y	Y	N	Y	N	Y	Y	N
4 Anthony	N	N	Y	?	?	N	Y	Y
CALIFORNIA								
1 Bosco	N	N	Y	?	?	Y	Y	Y
2 *Chappie*	?	?	?	?	?	?	?	?
3 Matsui	N	N	Y	Y	Y	Y	Y	Y
4 Fazio	N	N	Y	Y	Y	Y	Y	Y
5 Burton	N	N	Y	C	Y	C	Y	Y
6 Boxer	N	N	Y	Y	Y	Y	Y	Y
7 Miller	N	N	Y	Y	Y	N	Y	Y
8 Dellums	N	N	Y	Y	N	?	?	Y
9 Stark	N	N	Y	Y	Y	Y	Y	Y
10 Edwards	N	N	Y	Y	Y	Y	Y	Y
11 Lantos	N	N	Y	Y	Y	Y	Y	Y
12 Zschau	Y	Y	N	N	Y	N	N	Y
13 Mineta	N	N	Y	Y	Y	Y	Y	Y
14 Shumway	Y	Y	N	N	N	N	?	?
15 Coelho	N	N	Y	Y	Y	Y	Y	Y
16 Panetta	N	N	Y	Y	Y	Y	Y	Y
17 *Pashayan*	Y	Y	N	N	N	N	N	Y
18 Lehman	N	N	Y	Y	Y	Y	Y	Y
19 *Lagomarsino*	Y	Y	N	N	N	N	N	Y
20 *Thomas*	Y	Y	N	N	N	N	N	Y
21 *Fiedler*	Y	Y	N	N	N	N	N	N
22 *Moorhead*	Y	Y	N	N	N	N	N	N
23 Beilenson	N	N	Y	Y	Y	Y	Y	Y
24 Waxman	N	N	Y	?	?	?	Y	Y
25 Roybal	N	N	Y	Y	Y	Y	Y	Y
26 Berman	N	N	Y	Y	Y	Y	Y	Y
27 Levine	N	N	Y	Y	Y	Y	Y	Y
28 Dixon	N	N	Y	Y	Y	Y	Y	Y
29 Hawkins	N	N	Y	Y	Y	?	Y	Y
30 Martinez	N	N	Y	Y	Y	Y	Y	Y
31 Dymally	N	N	Y	Y	Y	Y	Y	Y
32 Anderson	N	N	Y	N	N	N	Y	Y
33 *Dreier*	Y	Y	N	N	N	N	N	N
34 Torres	N	N	Y	Y	Y	Y	Y	Y
35 *Lewis*	Y	Y	N	N	N	N	N	Y
36 Brown	N	N	Y	Y	Y	Y	Y	Y
37 *McCandless*	Y	Y	N	N	N	N	N	Y
38 Patterson	N	N	Y	Y	Y	Y	Y	Y
39 *Dannemeyer*	Y	Y	N	N	N	N	?	X
40 *Badham*	Y	Y	N	N	N	N	N	Y
41 *Lowery*	Y	Y	N	N	N	N	Y	Y
42 *Lungren*	Y	Y	N	N	N	N	N	N

	268	269	270	271	272	273	274	275
43 *Packard*	Y	Y	N	N	N	Y	N	Y
44 Bates	N	N	Y	Y	Y	Y	?	Y
45 *Hunter*	Y	Y	N	N	N	N	?	N
COLORADO								
1 Schroeder	N	N	Y	Y	Y	Y	-	-
2 Wirth	N	N	Y	Y	Y	Y	Y	Y
3 Kogovsek	N	N	Y	Y	Y	Y	Y	Y
4 *Brown*	Y	Y	N	N	N	N	N	N
5 *Kramer*	Y	Y	N	N	N	?	?	?
6 *Schaefer*	Y	Y	N	N	N	N	N	Y
CONNECTICUT								
1 Kennelly	N	N	Y	Y	Y	Y	Y	Y
2 Gejdenson	N	N	Y	Y	Y	Y	Y	Y
3 Morrison	N	N	Y	Y	Y	Y	Y	Y
4 *McKinney*	N	N	Y	Y	?	Y	Y	Y
5 Ratchford	N	N	Y	Y	Y	Y	Y	Y
6 *Johnson*	Y	Y	N	Y	Y	Y	Y	Y
DELAWARE								
AL Carper	N	N	Y	Y	Y	Y	Y	Y
FLORIDA								
1 Hutto	Y	Y	N	Y	N	Y	N	Y
2 Fuqua	Y	Y	N	Y	Y	Y	?	?
3 Bennett	N	N	Y	Y	Y	Y	N	Y
4 Chappell	Y	Y	N	Y	Y	Y	?	Y
5 *McCollum*	Y	Y	N	N	N	N	N	Y
6 MacKay	N	N	Y	Y	Y	Y	N	Y
7 Gibbons	N	N	Y	?	Y	Y	Y	Y
8 *Young*	Y	Y	N	Y	Y	Y	Y	Y
9 *Bilirakis*	Y	Y	N	N	N	N	N	N
10 Ireland	Y	Y	N	?	?	?	Y	Y
11 Nelson	Y	Y	N	Y	Y	Y	Y	Y
12 *Lewis*	Y	Y	N	N	N	N	N	N
13 *Mack*	Y	Y	N	N	N	N	N	N
14 Mica	Y	Y	N	Y	Y	Y	Y	Y
15 *Shaw*	Y	Y	N	N	N	N	N	Y
16 Smith	N	N	Y	Y	Y	Y	Y	Y
17 Lehman	N	N	Y	?	Y	Y	Y	Y
18 Pepper	N	N	Y	Y	Y	Y	Y	Y
19 Fascell	Y	N	Y	Y	Y	Y	?	Y
GEORGIA								
1 Thomas	Y	N	Y	Y	Y	Y	Y	Y
2 Hatcher	Y	Y	N	Y	Y	Y	?	?
3 Ray	Y	Y	N	Y	N	Y	Y	Y
4 Levitas	Y	N	Y	Y	Y	Y	N	Y
5 Fowler	N	N	Y	Y	Y	Y	Y	Y
6 *Gingrich*	Y	Y	N	N	N	N	N	Y
7 McDonald	Y	Y	N	N	N	N	N	N
8 Rowland	Y	N	Y	Y	Y	Y	Y	Y
9 Jenkins	Y	Y	N	?	?	?	Y	Y
10 Barnard	Y	Y	N	Y	N	Y	Y	Y
HAWAII								
1 Heftel	?	?	?	?	?	?	?	?
2 Akaka	N	N	Y	Y	Y	Y	Y	N
IDAHO								
1 *Craig*	Y	Y	N	N	N	N	N	N
2 *Hansen*	Y	Y	N	N	N	N	N	N
ILLINOIS								
1 Vacancy								
2 Savage	N	N	Y	Y	?	Y	Y	Y
3 Russo	N	N	Y	Y	Y	Y	Y	Y
4 *O'Brien*	Y	Y	N	N	N	N	N	Y
5 Lipinski	Y	Y	N	Y	Y	Y	Y	Y
6 *Hyde*	Y	Y	N	N	N	?	N	Y
7 Collins	N	N	Y	Y	Y	Y	Y	Y
8 Rostenkowski	N	N	Y	Y	Y	Y	Y	Y
9 Yates	N	N	Y	Y	Y	Y	Y	Y
10 *Porter*	Y	Y	N	?	N	Y	N	Y
11 Annunzio	N	N	Y	Y	Y	?	?	?
12 *Crane, P.*	Y	Y	N	N	N	N	N	N
13 *Erlenborn*	Y	Y	N	N	N	N	N	N
14 *Corcoran*	Y	Y	N	N	N	N	N	N
15 *Madigan*	Y	Y	N	N	N	N	?	Y
16 *Martin*	N	Y	N	N	N	N	Y	Y
17 Evans	N	N	Y	Y	Y	Y	Y	Y
18 *Michel*	Y	Y	N	Y	Y	Y	Y	Y
19 *Crane, D.*	Y	Y	N	N	N	N	N	N
20 Durbin	N	N	Y	Y	Y	Y	Y	Y
21 Price	N	N	Y	Y	Y	Y	Y	Y
22 Simon	N	N	Y	Y	Y	Y	?	?
INDIANA								
1 Hall	N	N	Y	Y	Y	Y	Y	Y
2 Sharp	N	N	Y	N	?	N	Y	Y
3 *Hiler*	Y	Y	N	N	N	N	N	Y
4 *Coats*	Y	Y	N	Y	N	Y	N	Y
5 *Hillis*	Y	Y	N	Y	N	Y	N	Y

ND - Northern Democrats   SD - Southern Democrats

Corresponding to Congressional Record Votes 283, 284, 285, 286, 287, 288, 289, 290

	268	269	270	271	272	273	274	275
6 ***Burton***	Y	Y	N	N	N	N	N	N
7 ***Myers***	Y	Y	N	Y	Y	Y	?	?
8 McCloskey	N	N	Y	Y	Y	Y	Y	N
9 Hamilton	N	N	Y	Y	Y	Y	Y	Y
10 Jacobs	N	N	Y	Y	Y	N	N	N
IOWA								
1 ***Leach***	N	N	Y	Y	Y	Y	?	Y
2 ***Tauke***	Y	Y	N	N	Y	N	N	Y
3 ***Evans***	Y	Y	Y	N	N	Y	N	Y
4 Smith	N	N	Y	Y	Y	Y	Y	Y
5 Harkin	N	N	Y	Y	?	Y	N	Y
6 Bedell	N	N	Y	Y	Y	Y	N	Y
KANSAS								
1 ***Roberts***	Y	Y	N	N	N	N	N	Y
2 Slattery	N	N	Y	Y	Y	N	?	N
3 ***Winn***	Y	Y	N	N	N	Y	N	N
4 Glickman	N	N	Y	Y	Y	Y	N	Y
5 ***Whittaker***	Y	Y	N	N	N	?	N	Y
KENTUCKY								
1 Hubbard	Y	Y	N	Y	Y	N	Y	Y
2 Natcher	N	N	Y	Y	Y	Y	Y	N
3 Mazzoli	N	N	Y	Y	Y	Y	N	Y
4 ***Snyder***	Y	Y	N	Y	Y	Y	N	N
5 ***Rogers***	Y	Y	N	N	N	Y	N	N
6 ***Hopkins***	Y	Y	N	N	N	N	N	N
7 Perkins	N	N	Y	Y	Y	Y	Y	N
LOUISIANA								
1 ***Livingston***	Y	Y	N	Y	N	N	N	Y
2 Boggs	N	N	Y	Y	Y	Y	Y	Y
3 Tauzin	Y	Y	N	Y	Y	N	N	N
4 Roemer	Y	Y	N	Y	Y	N	N	N
5 Huckaby	Y	Y	N	Y	Y	Y	N	Y
6 ***Moore***	Y	Y	N	Y	Y	N	N	Y
7 Breaux	Y	Y	N	Y	Y	N	Y	Y
8 Long	N	N	Y	Y	Y	Y	Y	Y
MAINE								
1 ***McKernan***	N	Y	Y	N	N	Y	N	Y
2 ***Snowe***	N	N	Y	N	N	Y	Y	Y
MARYLAND								
1 Dyson	Y	N	N	Y	Y	Y	Y	Y
2 Long	N	N	Y	Y	Y	Y	Y	N
3 Mikulski	N	N	Y	Y	?	?	N	Y
4 ***Holt***	Y	Y	N	N	N	N	?	?
5 Hoyer	N	N	#	?	?	Y	Y	Y
6 Byron	Y	N	N	Y	Y	Y	Y	Y
7 Mitchell	N	N	Y	Y	Y	Y	Y	Y
8 Barnes	N	N	Y	Y	Y	Y	Y	Y
MASSACHUSETTS								
1 ***Conte***	N	N	Y	N	Y	Y	Y	Y
2 Boland	N	N	Y	Y	Y	Y	Y	Y
3 Early	N	N	Y	Y	Y	Y	?	N
4 Frank	N	N	Y	Y	Y	Y	?	Y
5 Shannon	N	N	Y	Y	Y	Y	Y	Y
6 Mavroules	N	N	Y	Y	Y	Y	Y	Y
7 Markey	N	N	Y	Y	Y	Y	Y	Y
8 O'Neill								
9 Moakley	N	N	Y	Y	Y	Y	Y	Y
10 Studds	N	N	Y	Y	Y	Y	Y	Y
11 Donnelly	N	N	Y	Y	Y	Y	Y	N
MICHIGAN								
1 Conyers	N	N	Y	?	?	?	?	Y
2 ***Pursell***	Y	Y	N	Y	Y	N	N	Y
3 Wolpe	N	N	Y	Y	Y	Y	Y	Y
4 ***Siljander***	Y	Y	N	N	N	N	N	Y
5 ***Sawyer***	Y	Y	N	N	N	N	N	Y
6 Carr	N	N	Y	?	?	?	?	?
7 Kildee	N	N	Y	Y	Y	Y	Y	Y
8 Traxler	N	N	Y	Y	Y	Y	N	N
9 ***Vander Jagt***	Y	Y	N	?	?	?	N	Y
10 Albosta	N	N	Y	Y	Y	Y	Y	Y
11 ***Davis***	Y	Y	N	Y	Y	Y	N	Y
12 Bonior	N	N	Y	Y	?	?	Y	Y
13 Crockett	N	N	N	?	?	?	?	Y
14 Hertel	N	N	Y	Y	Y	N	Y	Y
15 Ford	N	N	Y	Y	Y	Y	Y	Y
16 Dingell	N	N	Y	?	Y	Y	?	Y
17 Levin	N	N	Y	Y	Y	Y	Y	Y
18 ***Broomfield***	Y	Y	N	N	N	N	Y	?
MINNESOTA								
1 Penny	N	N	Y	Y	Y	Y	Y	Y
2 ***Weber***	Y	Y	N	N	N	N	N	Y
3 ***Frenzel***	Y	Y	N	N	N	N	Y	Y
4 Vento	N	N	Y	Y	Y	Y	Y	Y
5 Sabo	N	N	Y	Y	Y	Y	Y	Y
6 Sikorski	N	N	Y	Y	Y	Y	Y	Y
7 ***Stangeland***	?	?	?	N	N	N	N	Y
8 Oberstar	N	N	Y	Y	Y	Y	Y	Y
MISSISSIPPI								
1 Whitten	N	N	Y	Y	Y	Y	Y	N
2 ***Franklin***	?	?	N	N	Y	N	N	N
3 Montgomery	Y	Y	N	Y	Y	?	?	N
4 Dowdy	?	?	?	?	?	?	?	?
5 ***Lott***	Y	Y	N	N	N	N	N	Y
MISSOURI								
1 Clay	N	N	Y	Y	Y	Y	Y	Y
2 Young	N	N	Y	Y	?	?	Y	Y
3 Gephardt	N	N	Y	Y	Y	Y	Y	Y
4 Skelton	Y	Y	N	Y	Y	Y	Y	Y
5 Wheat	N	N	Y	Y	Y	Y	Y	Y
6 ***Coleman***	Y	Y	N	N	N	Y	N	Y
7 ***Taylor***	Y	Y	N	N	Y	N	Y	Y
8 ***Emerson***	Y	Y	N	N	N	N	Y	Y
9 Volkmer	N	N	Y	Y	Y	N	N	Y
MONTANA								
1 Williams	N	N	Y	Y	Y	N	Y	Y
2 ***Marlenee***	Y	Y	N	N	N	N	N	N
NEBRASKA								
1 ***Bereuter***	Y	Y	N	N	Y	N	Y	Y
2 ***Daub***	Y	Y	N	N	N	N	N	N
3 ***Smith***	Y	Y	N	Y	Y	Y	N	Y
NEVADA								
1 Reid	N	N	Y	Y	Y	Y	Y	Y
2 ***Vucanovich***	Y	Y	N	N	N	Y	N	N
NEW HAMPSHIRE								
1 D'Amours	N	N	Y	Y	Y	Y	Y	N
2 ***Gregg***	Y	Y	N	N	N	N	N	Y
NEW JERSEY								
1 Florio	N	N	Y	Y	Y	Y	Y	N
2 Hughes	N	N	Y	N	Y	Y	N	Y
3 Howard	N	N	Y	Y	Y	Y	Y	Y
4 ***Smith***	Y	Y	N	Y	Y	Y	Y	Y
5 ***Roukema***	N	N	Y	N	N	Y	Y	Y
6 Dwyer	N	N	Y	Y	Y	Y	Y	Y
7 ***Rinaldo***	Y	Y	N	Y	Y	Y	N	Y
8 Roe	N	N	Y	Y	?	?	Y	Y
9 Torricelli	N	N	Y	Y	Y	Y	?	Y
10 Rodino	N	N	Y	Y	Y	Y	Y	Y
11 Minish	N	N	Y	Y	Y	Y	Y	Y
12 ***Courter***	Y	Y	N	N	N	N	N	N
13 ***Forsythe***	Y	Y	N	N	N	?	Y	Y
14 Guarini	N	N	Y	Y	Y	Y	Y	Y
NEW MEXICO								
1 ***Lujan***	Y	Y	N	Y	N	N	Y	Y
2 ***Skeen***	Y	Y	N	N	N	N	N	Y
3 Richardson	N	N	Y	Y	Y	Y	Y	Y
NEW YORK								
1 ***Carney***	Y	Y	N	N	N	Y	N	Y
2 Downey	N	N	Y	Y	N	Y	N	Y
3 Mrazek	N	N	Y	Y	Y	N	Y	Y
4 ***Lent***	Y	Y	N	N	N	Y	N	Y
5 ***McGrath***	Y	Y	N	N	N	Y	N	N
6 Addabbo	X	X	#	?	?	?	?	?
7 Ackerman	N	N	Y	Y	Y	Y	Y	Y
8 Scheuer	N	N	Y	Y	Y	Y	Y	Y
9 Ferraro	N	N	Y	Y	Y	Y	Y	Y
10 Schumer	N	N	Y	Y	Y	Y	Y	Y
11 Towns	N	N	Y	Y	Y	Y	Y	Y
12 Owens	N	N	Y	Y	Y	Y	?	Y
13 Solarz	N	N	+	Y	Y	?	Y	Y
14 ***Molinari***	#	#	X	?	?	?	?	Y
15 ***Green***	N	N	Y	Y	Y	Y	Y	Y
16 Rangel	N	N	Y	Y	Y	Y	Y	Y
17 Weiss	N	N	Y	Y	Y	Y	Y	Y
18 Garcia	N	N	Y	Y	Y	Y	?	?
19 Biaggi	N	N	Y	Y	Y	Y	Y	Y
20 Ottinger	N	N	Y	Y	Y	?	Y	Y
21 ***Fish***	Y	Y	Y	Y	?	?	N	Y
22 ***Gilman***	Y	Y	N	N	N	Y	N	Y
23 Stratton	Y	Y	N	Y	Y	Y	Y	Y
24 ***Solomon***	Y	Y	N	N	N	N	N	N
25 ***Boehlert***	N	N	Y	Y	Y	Y	Y	Y
26 ***Martin***	Y	Y	N	N	Y	Y	N	Y
27 ***Wortley***	Y	Y	N	N	N	Y	Y	Y
28 McHugh	N	N	Y	Y	Y	Y	Y	Y
29 ***Horton***	Y	Y	Y	Y	Y	Y	Y	Y
30 ***Conable***	Y	Y	N	N	N	N	Y	Y
31 ***Kemp***	Y	Y	N	N	N	Y	N	N
32 LaFalce	N	N	Y	Y	Y	Y	Y	Y
33 Nowak	N	N	Y	Y	Y	Y	Y	Y
34 Lundine	N	N	Y	?	?	Y	Y	Y
NORTH CAROLINA								
1 Jones	N	N	Y	Y	?	?	Y	Y
2 Valentine	N	N	Y	Y	Y	Y	Y	Y
3 Whitley	N	N	Y	Y	Y	Y	Y	Y
4 Andrews	N	N	Y	Y	Y	Y	Y	Y
5 Neal	N	N	Y	Y	?	?	Y	Y
6 Britt	N	N	Y	Y	Y	Y	Y	Y
7 Rose	N	N	Y	Y	Y	Y	Y	Y
8 Hefner	N	N	Y	Y	Y	Y	Y	Y
9 ***Martin***	Y	Y	N	?	?	?	N	Y
10 ***Broyhill***	Y	Y	N	N	Y	N	Y	Y
11 Clarke	N	N	Y	Y	Y	Y	Y	Y
NORTH DAKOTA								
AL Dorgan	N	N	Y	Y	Y	N	?	?
OHIO								
1 Luken	N	N	Y	Y	Y	Y	Y	Y
2 ***Gradison***	Y	Y	N	N	N	Y	Y	Y
3 Hall	N	N	Y	Y	Y	?	Y	Y
4 ***Oxley***	Y	Y	N	N	N	N	N	Y
5 ***Latta***	Y	Y	N	N	N	N	Y	Y
6 ***McEwen***	Y	Y	N	N	N	N	N	Y
7 ***DeWine***	Y	Y	N	N	N	N	N	Y
8 ***Kindness***	Y	Y	N	N	N	N	N	Y
9 Kaptur	N	N	Y	Y	Y	Y	N	Y
10 ***Miller***	Y	Y	N	Y	Y	N	N	Y
11 Eckart	N	N	Y	Y	Y	Y	N	N
12 ***Kasich***	Y	Y	N	N	N	N	N	N
13 Pease	N	N	Y	Y	Y	Y	Y	Y
14 Seiberling	N	N	Y	Y	Y	Y	?	Y
15 ***Wylie***	Y	Y	N	N	N	?	Y	Y
16 ***Regula***	Y	Y	N	Y	Y	Y	Y	Y
17 ***Williams***	Y	Y	Y	Y	?	Y	?	N
18 Applegate	N	N	N	Y	Y	N	?	Y
19 Feighan	N	N	Y	Y	Y	N	Y	Y
20 Oakar	N	N	Y	Y	Y	Y	Y	Y
21 Stokes	N	N	Y	Y	Y	Y	Y	Y
OKLAHOMA								
1 Jones	N	N	Y	Y	Y	N	N	Y
2 Synar	N	N	Y	Y	Y	Y	Y	Y
3 Watkins	N	N	Y	Y	Y	Y	Y	N
4 McCurdy	N	N	Y	Y	Y	Y	N	Y
5 ***Edwards***	Y	Y	N	N	N	Y	N	N
6 English	N	N	Y	Y	Y	Y	Y	Y
OREGON								
1 AuCoin	N	N	Y	Y	?	N	?	Y
2 ***Smith, R.***	Y	Y	N	N	N	Y	N	Y
3 Wyden	N	N	Y	Y	Y	N	Y	Y
4 Weaver	N	N	Y	Y	Y	N	N	Y
5 ***Smith, D.***	Y	Y	N	N	N	N	N	N
PENNSYLVANIA								
1 Foglietta	N	N	Y	Y	Y	Y	Y	Y
2 Gray	N	N	Y	Y	Y	Y	Y	Y
3 Borski	N	N	Y	Y	Y	Y	Y	Y
4 Kolter	N	N	Y	Y	Y	Y	Y	Y
5 ***Schulze***	Y	Y	N	N	N	N	Y	Y
6 Yatron	N	N	Y	Y	Y	Y	Y	Y
7 Edgar	N	N	Y	N	Y	Y	Y	Y
8 Kostmayer	N	N	Y	Y	Y	Y	Y	Y
9 ***Shuster***	Y	Y	N	N	N	N	Y	N
10 ***McDade***	?	?	?	?	?	?	?	#
11 Harrison	N	N	Y	Y	Y	Y	Y	Y
12 Murtha	N	N	N	Y	Y	Y	Y	Y
13 ***Coughlin***	Y	N	Y	Y	Y	Y	N	?
14 Coyne	N	N	Y	Y	Y	Y	Y	Y
15 ***Ritter***	Y	Y	N	N	N	N	N	N
16 ***Walker***	Y	Y	N	N	N	N	N	Y
17 ***Gekas***	Y	Y	N	N	N	N	N	Y
18 Walgren	N	N	Y	Y	Y	N	N	Y
19 ***Goodling***	Y	Y	N	N	N	N	N	Y
20 Gaydos	N	N	N	Y	Y	Y	Y	Y
21 ***Ridge***	Y	Y	Y	N	N	Y	N	Y
22 Murphy	N	N	Y	Y	Y	Y	Y	Y
23 ***Clinger***	Y	Y	N	N	Y	Y	Y	Y
RHODE ISLAND								
1 St Germain	N	N	Y	Y	Y	Y	Y	Y
2 ***Schneider***	N	N	Y	N	N	Y	N	Y
SOUTH CAROLINA								
1 ***Hartnett***	Y	Y	N	N	N	N	Y	Y
2 ***Spence***	Y	Y	N	N	N	N	N	Y
3 Derrick	N	N	Y	Y	Y	Y	N	Y
4 ***Campbell***	Y	Y	N	N	N	N	N	Y
5 Spratt	N	N	Y	Y	Y	Y	Y	Y
6 Tallon	N	N	N	Y	Y	Y	Y	Y
SOUTH DAKOTA								
AL Daschle	N	N	Y	Y	Y	Y	Y	Y
TENNESSEE								
1 ***Quillen***	Y	Y	N	Y	Y	Y	Y	Y
2 ***Duncan***	Y	Y	N	Y	Y	Y	Y	Y
3 Lloyd	Y	Y	N	Y	Y	Y	Y	N
4 Cooper	N	N	Y	Y	Y	Y	Y	?
5 Boner	Y	N	N	Y	Y	Y	Y	Y
6 Gore	N	N	Y	Y	Y	Y	Y	Y
7 ***Sundquist***	Y	?	N	N	N	Y	N	N
8 Jones	?	?	X	?	?	?	?	?
9 Ford	N	N	Y	Y	Y	Y	Y	Y
TEXAS								
1 Hall, S.	Y	Y	N	Y	Y	Y	?	N
2 Wilson	Y	Y	N	Y	Y	Y	Y	Y
3 ***Bartlett***	Y	Y	N	N	N	N	Y	Y
4 Hall, R.	Y	Y	N	Y	Y	Y	Y	N
5 Bryant	N	N	Y	Y	Y	Y	Y	Y
6 ***Gramm***	Y	Y	N	N	N	N	N	N
7 ***Archer***	Y	Y	N	N	N	N	N	Y
8 ***Fields***	Y	Y	N	N	N	N	N	N
9 Brooks	N	N	Y	Y	Y	Y	Y	Y
10 Pickle	N	N	Y	Y	Y	Y	Y	Y
11 Leath	Y	Y	N	?	Y	N	Y	Y
12 Wright	N	N	Y	Y	Y	Y	Y	Y
13 Hightower	Y	Y	N	Y	Y	Y	Y	Y
14 Patman	Y	Y	N	N	N	N	N	N
15 de la Garza	N	N	Y	Y	Y	Y	N	Y
16 Coleman	N	N	Y	Y	Y	Y	Y	Y
17 Stenholm	Y	Y	N	Y	Y	N	Y	N
18 Leland	N	N	Y	Y	Y	Y	Y	Y
19 Hance	Y	Y	N	Y	Y	Y	Y	Y
20 Gonzalez	N	N	Y	Y	Y	Y	N	N
21 ***Loeffler***	Y	Y	N	N	N	N	N	Y
22 ***Paul***	Y	Y	N	N	N	N	N	N
23 Kazen	Y	Y	N	Y	Y	Y	Y	N
24 Frost	N	N	Y	Y	Y	Y	?	?
25 Andrews	N	N	Y	Y	Y	Y	Y	Y
26 Vandergriff	Y	Y	N	Y	Y	N	N	Y
27 Ortiz	N	N	Y	Y	Y	Y	Y	Y
UTAH								
1 ***Hansen***	Y	Y	N	N	N	N	Y	Y
2 ***Marriott***	Y	Y	N	N	N	N	Y	Y
3 ***Nielson***	Y	Y	N	N	N	N	N	Y
VERMONT								
AL ***Jeffords***	N	N	Y	Y	Y	Y	Y	Y
VIRGINIA								
1 ***Bateman***	Y	Y	N	N	Y	N	N	Y
2 ***Whitehurst***	Y	Y	N	N	?	?	Y	Y
3 ***Bliley***	Y	Y	N	N	N	Y	Y	N
4 Sisisky	Y	Y	N	Y	Y	Y	Y	Y
5 Daniel	Y	Y	N	Y	Y	N	Y	N
6 Olin	N	N	Y	Y	Y	N	N	Y
7 ***Robinson***	Y	Y	N	N	N	N	Y	N
8 ***Parris***	Y	Y	N	N	N	Y	Y	Y
9 Boucher	N	N	Y	Y	Y	Y	Y	Y
10 ***Wolf***	Y	Y	N	N	N	Y	N	Y
WASHINGTON								
1 ***Pritchard***	Y	Y	Y	N	N	N	N	Y
2 Swift	N	N	Y	?	?	Y	Y	Y
3 Bonker	N	N	Y	Y	Y	Y	Y	Y
4 ***Morrison***	Y	Y	N	N	N	N	N	Y
5 Foley	N	N	Y	Y	Y	?	?	?
6 Dicks	N	N	Y	Y	Y	?	Y	Y
7 Lowry	N	N	Y	Y	Y	Y	Y	Y
8 ***Chandler***	Y	Y	N	Y	N	N	N	Y
WEST VIRGINIA								
1 Mollohan	N	N	Y	Y	Y	Y	Y	Y
2 Staggers	N	N	Y	Y	Y	Y	N	Y
3 Wise	N	N	Y	Y	Y	Y	N	Y
4 Rahall	N	N	Y	Y	Y	Y	N	Y
WISCONSIN								
1 Aspin	N	N	Y	Y	Y	?	Y	Y
2 Kastenmeier	N	N	Y	Y	Y	Y	N	Y
3 ***Gunderson***	Y	Y	N	N	Y	N	N	Y
4 Zablocki	N	N	Y	Y	Y	Y	Y	Y
5 Moody	N	N	Y	?	?	?	Y	Y
6 ***Petri***	Y	Y	N	N	N	N	N	N
7 Obey	N	N	Y	Y	Y	Y	Y	Y
8 ***Roth***	Y	Y	N	N	N	N	N	Y
9 ***Sensenbrenner***	Y	Y	N	N	N	N	N	N
WYOMING								
AL ***Cheney***	Y	Y	N	N	N	N	Y	Y

Southern states - Ala., Ark., Fla., Ga., Ky., La., Miss., N.C., Okla., S.C., Tenn., Texas, Va.

276. HR 2957. International Recovery and Financial Stability Act. McCollum, R-Fla., amendment to strike the $5.8 billion increase in the U.S. quota in the International Monetary Fund. Rejected 181-226: R 91-68; D 90-158 (ND 46-119, SD 44-39), July 29, 1983. A "nay" was a vote supporting the president's position.

277. HR 2957. International Recovery and Financial Stability Act. Patman, D-Texas, amendment to strike the portion of the bill increasing the U.S. participation in the International Monetary Fund. Rejected 178-226: R 89-71; D 89-155 (ND 46-117, SD 43-38), July 29, 1983. A "nay" was a vote supporting the president's position.

278. HR 3069. Supplemental Appropriations, Fiscal 1983. Whitten, D-Miss., motion that the House recede from its disagreement to the Senate amendment striking House language to make rented land eligible for the Payment-in-Kind (PIK) acreage reduction program and concur with an amendment that restored the language and directed the agriculture secretary to reopen bids for cotton producers to sell their 1983 crop to the federal government for the PIK program. Motion agreed to 204-191: R 43-111; D 161-80 (ND 88-73, SD 73-7), July 29, 1983. A "nay" was a vote supporting the president's position.

279. HR 3069. Supplemental Appropriations, Fiscal 1983. Conte, R-Mass., motion that the House recede from its disagreement to the Senate amendment appropriating $8,464,008,776 for the International Monetary Fund and concur with an amendment to reduce the amount by $40 million. Motion rejected 165-213: R 55-91; D 110-122 (ND 83-78, SD 27-44), July 29, 1983.

280. HR 3069. Supplemental Appropriations, Fiscal 1983. Whitten, D-Miss., motion that the House recede from its disagreement to the Senate amendment to raise senators' pay by 15 percent to $69,800 a year and cap, effective Jan. 1, 1984, the amount of outside earned income a senator may receive at 30 percent of salary. Motion agreed to 225-106: R 72-60; D 153-46 (ND 112-24, SD 41-22), July 29, 1983.

281. H Con Res 153. District Work Period. Adoption of the concurrent resolution to provide for the recess of the House and Senate until Sept. 12 or two days after members are notified, whichever comes first. Adopted 291-0: R 115-0; D 176-0 (ND 117-0, SD 59-0), July 29, 1983.

282. HR 1646. Railroad Retirement Solvency. Passage of the bill to increase taxes and change benefits so as to restore solvency to the federal railroad retirement and railroad unemployment compensation programs. Passed 398-5: R 157-4; D 241-1 (ND 162-0, SD 79-1), Aug. 1, 1983.

283. H Res 256. Most Favored Nation Status for Romania. Frenzel, R-Minn., motion to postpone indefinitely consideration of the resolution to disapprove renewal of most favored nation trade status for Romania. Motion agreed to 279-126: R 73-88; D 206-38 (ND 152-11, SD 54-27), Aug. 1, 1983.

KEY

Y	Voted for (yea).
#	Paired for.
+	Announced for.
N	Voted against (nay).
X	Paired against.
-	Announced against.
P	Voted "present".
C	Voted "present" to avoid possible conflict of interest.
?	Did not vote or otherwise make a position known.

Democrats   *Republicans*

	276	277	278	279	280	281	282	283
ALABAMA								
1 *Edwards*	N	N	Y	Y	Y	Y	?	Y
2 *Dickinson*	N	N	Y	Y	?	?	Y	N
3 Nichols	Y	Y	Y	X	?	Y	Y	N
4 Bevill	Y	Y	Y	N	Y	Y	?	?
5 Flippo	Y	Y	Y	N	N	Y	Y	Y
6 Erdreich	Y	Y	Y	-	-	+	Y	Y
7 Shelby	Y	Y	Y	N	N	Y	Y	N
ALASKA								
AL *Young*	Y	Y	Y	N	Y	N	Y	N
ARIZONA								
1 *McCain*	Y	Y	Y	N	Y	Y	Y	Y
2 Udall	N	N	Y	Y	Y	Y	Y	Y
3 *Stump*	Y	Y	Y	N	Y	N	Y	N
4 *Rudd*	Y	Y	Y	N	Y	?	Y	N
5 McNulty	N	N	Y	Y	Y	Y	Y	Y
ARKANSAS								
1 Alexander	?	?	Y	Y	Y	Y	Y	?
2 *Bethune*	Y	Y	Y	N	N	Y	Y	N
3 *Hammerschmidt*	Y	Y	Y	N	?	Y	Y	
4 Anthony	N	N	Y	Y	Y	Y	Y	Y
CALIFORNIA								
1 Bosco	N	Y	N	N	N	?	Y	Y
2 *Chappie*	?	?	?	?	?	?	?	?
3 Matsui	N	N	Y	Y	Y	Y	Y	Y
4 Fazio	N	N	Y	Y	Y	Y	Y	Y
5 Burton	N	N	N	Y	Y	Y	Y	Y
6 Boxer	N	N	Y	Y	Y	Y	Y	Y
7 Miller	N	N	?	N	Y	Y	Y	Y
8 Dellums	?	?	?	?	?	?	?	?
9 Stark	N	N	N	N	Y	Y	Y	Y
10 Edwards	N	N	Y	Y	Y	Y	Y	Y
11 Lantos	N	N	Y	N	Y	Y	Y	Y
12 *Zschau*	N	N	N	Y	Y	Y	Y	Y
13 Mineta	N	N	Y	?	?	Y	Y	Y
14 *Shumway*	?	?	?	?	?	Y	Y	N
15 Coelho	N	N	Y	Y	Y	Y	Y	Y
16 Panetta	N	N	Y	Y	N	?	Y	Y
17 *Pashayan*	?	Y	Y	N	Y	Y	N	Y
18 Lehman	N	N	Y	Y	?	?	Y	Y
19 *Lagomarsino*	N	N	N	Y	N	Y	Y	Y
20 *Thomas*	N	Y	Y	Y	?	?	Y	N
21 *Fiedler*	Y	Y	N	Y	N	Y	Y	Y
22 *Moorhead*	Y	Y	N	N	N	Y	Y	Y
23 Beilenson	N	N	N	Y	Y	Y	Y	Y
24 Waxman	N	?	N	Y	Y	?	Y	Y
25 Roybal	N	N	Y	Y	Y	Y	Y	Y
26 Berman	N	N	N	Y	Y	Y	Y	?
27 Levine	N	N	N	Y	Y	Y	Y	Y
28 Dixon	N	N	N	Y	Y	Y	Y	Y
29 Hawkins	N	N	Y	Y	Y	?	Y	Y
30 Martinez	N	N	Y	N	Y	Y	Y	Y
31 Dymally	N	N	N	Y	Y	Y	Y	Y
32 Anderson	Y	Y	N	N	N	Y	Y	Y
33 *Dreier*	Y	Y	N	Y	N	Y	Y	N
34 Torres	N	N	Y	Y	Y	?	Y	Y
35 *Lewis*	Y	Y	Y	N	N	Y	Y	N
36 Brown	N	N	N	Y	N	Y	Y	Y
37 *McCandless*	N	N	Y	Y	Y	Y	Y	Y
38 Patterson	N	N	Y	Y	Y	Y	Y	Y
39 *Dannemeyer*	#	?	?	X	?	?	N	N
40 *Badham*	Y	N	?	?	?	?	Y	N
41 *Lowery*	N	N	Y	Y	Y	Y	Y	Y
42 *Lungren*	Y	Y	N	Y	N	Y	Y	Y

	276	277	278	279	280	281	282	283
43 *Packard*	Y	Y	N	N	Y	Y	Y	N
44 *Bates*	Y	Y	N	Y	?	Y	Y	
45 *Hunter*	Y	Y	Y	N	N	Y	Y	N
COLORADO								
1 Schroeder	+	+	-	.	.	.	+	Y	Y
2 Wirth	N	N	N	Y	?	?	Y	Y
3 Kogovsek	N	N	Y	Y	?	?	Y	Y
4 *Brown*	Y	Y	N	N	N	Y	Y	N
5 *Kramer*	?	?	?	?	?	?	Y	Y
6 *Schaefer*	Y	Y	N	?	?	?	Y	N
CONNECTICUT								
1 Kennelly	N	N	Y	Y	Y	Y	Y	Y
2 Gejdenson	N	N	Y	Y	Y	Y	Y	Y
3 Morrison	N	N	N	N	Y	?	Y	Y
4 *McKinney*	N	N	N	Y	?	?	Y	Y
5 Ratchford	N	N	Y	Y	Y	?	Y	Y
6 *Johnson*	N	N	N	Y	?	?	Y	Y
DELAWARE								
AL Carper	N	N	N	Y	Y	Y	Y	Y
FLORIDA								
1 Hutto	Y	Y	Y	?	?	?	Y	Y
2 Fuqua	?	?	?	X	?	Y	Y	
3 Bennett	Y	Y	N	Y	N	N	Y	Y
4 Chappell	Y	Y	Y	Y	?	Y	Y	
5 *McCollum*	Y	Y	N	N	N	Y	Y	N
6 MacKay	N	N	N	#	?	?	Y	Y
7 Gibbons	N	N	N	Y	Y	Y	Y	Y
8 *Young*	N	N	N	Y	Y	Y	?	?
9 *Bilirakis*	Y	Y	N	N	N	Y	Y	Y
10 Ireland	N	N	Y	Y	Y	Y	Y	Y
11 Nelson	Y	Y	N	-	-	+	Y	Y
12 *Lewis*	Y	Y	Y	N	Y	?	Y	Y
13 *Mack*	Y	Y	N	N	N	Y	Y	N
14 Mica	N	N	?	?	?	?	Y	Y
15 *Shaw*	Y	Y	N	N	N	Y	Y	N
16 Smith	N	N	Y	N	?	?	Y	Y
17 Lehman	N	N	Y	Y	Y	Y	Y	Y
18 Pepper	N	N	Y	Y	Y	Y	Y	Y
19 Fascell	N	N	Y	?	?	?	Y	Y
GEORGIA								
1 Thomas	Y	Y	Y	N	Y	Y	Y	Y
2 Hatcher	?	?	?	#	?	?	Y	Y
3 Ray	Y	Y	Y	N	Y	Y	Y	Y
4 Levitas	Y	Y	Y	N	N	Y	Y	Y
5 Fowler	N	N	Y	Y	N	?	+	Y
6 *Gingrich*	Y	Y	N	N	Y	Y	Y	N
7 McDonald	Y	Y	N	N	N	Y	N	N
8 Rowland	Y	Y	?	N	Y	Y	Y	Y
9 Jenkins	Y	?	?	?	Y	Y	Y	Y
10 Barnard	N	N	?	?	?	?	Y	N
HAWAII								
1 Heftel	?	?	?	?	?	?	?	?
2 Akaka	N	N	Y	N	Y	Y	Y	Y
IDAHO								
1 *Craig*	Y	Y	N	N	?	?	Y	N
2 *Hansen*	Y	Y	N	Y	N	Y	Y	N
ILLINOIS								
1 Vacancy								
2 Savage	N	N	Y	N	?	?	Y	Y
3 Russo	Y	Y	Y	N	Y	Y	Y	Y
4 *O'Brien*	N	N	N	Y	N	Y	Y	Y
5 Lipinski	Y	Y	N	Y	N	Y	Y	Y
6 *Hyde*	Y	N	N	Y	N	Y	Y	Y
7 Collins	N	N	Y	Y	Y	Y	Y	Y
8 Rostenkowski	N	N	Y	?	?	Y	Y	Y
9 Yates	N	N	Y	Y	Y	Y	Y	Y
10 *Porter*	N	N	N	Y	?	?	Y	Y
11 Annunzio	?	?	?	X	?	?	Y	Y
12 *Crane, P.*	Y	Y	N	?	?	?	N	N
13 *Erlenborn*	N	N	N	Y	Y	Y	Y	Y
14 *Corcoran*	Y	Y	N	N	Y	Y	Y	?
15 *Madigan*	N	N	N	?	?	?	Y	Y
16 *Martin*	Y	Y	N	N	Y	Y	Y	Y
17 Evans	Y	Y	Y	N	Y	Y	Y	Y
18 *Michel*	N	N	N	Y	Y	Y	Y	Y
19 *Crane, D.*	Y	Y	N	N	?	N	N	
20 Durbin	Y	Y	N	Y	N	Y	Y	Y
21 Price	N	N	Y	Y	Y	Y	Y	Y
22 Simon	?	?	?	?	?	?	Y	Y
INDIANA								
1 Hall	N	N	Y	Y	Y	Y	Y	Y
2 Sharp	Y	Y	N	Y	N	Y	Y	Y
3 *Hiler*	Y	Y	N	N	N	Y	Y	N
4 *Coats*	Y	Y	N	N	Y	Y	Y	N
5 Hillis	N	N	N	Y	?	?	Y	Y

ND - Northern Democrats   SD - Southern Democrats

Corresponding to Congressional Record Votes 291, 292, 293, 294, 295, 296, 297, 298

	276	277	278	279	280	281	282	283
6 ***Burton***	Y	Y	N	N	N	Y	Y	N
7 ***Myers***	?	?	?	?	?	?	Y	N
8 McCloskey	Y	Y	Y	N	?	?	Y	Y
9 Hamilton	N	N	Y	Y	Y	Y	Y	Y
10 Jacobs	Y	Y	N	N	N	Y	Y	Y
IOWA								
1 ***Leach***	N	N	N	Y	N	Y	Y	Y
2 ***Tauke***	N	N	N	Y	Y	Y	Y	Y
3 ***Evans***	Y	N	N	Y	N	Y	Y	Y
4 Smith	N	N	Y	N	Y	Y	Y	Y
5 Harkin	Y	Y	?	?	?	?	?	?
6 Bedell	N	N	Y	Y	Y	Y	Y	Y
KANSAS								
1 ***Roberts***	Y	Y	Y	N	N	Y	Y	Y
2 Slattery	Y	Y	Y	N	N	Y	Y	Y
3 ***Winn***	N	Y	Y	N	N	Y	Y	Y
4 Glickman	N	N	Y	Y	N	?	Y	Y
5 ***Whittaker***	Y	Y	Y	N	?	?	Y	Y
KENTUCKY								
1 Hubbard	N	N	Y	Y	N	Y	Y	Y
2 Natcher	Y	Y	Y	N	Y	Y	Y	Y
3 Mazzoli	N	N	N	N	Y	Y	Y	Y
4 ***Snyder***	Y	Y	N	N	N	Y	Y	N
5 ***Rogers***	Y	Y	Y	N	N	Y	Y	N
6 ***Hopkins***	Y	Y	Y	N	N	Y	Y	N
7 Perkins	Y	Y	Y	N	Y	?	Y	Y
LOUISIANA								
1 ***Livingston***	N	N	Y	Y	Y	Y	Y	N
2 Boggs	N	N	Y	Y	Y	Y	Y	Y
3 Tauzin	Y	Y	Y	N	N	Y	?	?
4 Roemer	Y	Y	C	N	N	Y	Y	N
5 Huckaby	N	N	Y	?	?	?	Y	N
6 ***Moore***	Y	Y	Y	N	Y	Y	Y	Y
7 Breaux	Y	?	Y	N	Y	Y	?	Y
8 Long	N	N	Y	Y	Y	Y	Y	Y
MAINE								
1 ***McKernan***	N	N	N	Y	N	Y	Y	Y
2 ***Snowe***	N	N	N	Y	Y	?	Y	Y
MARYLAND								
1 Dyson	Y	Y	Y	N	N	Y	Y	Y
2 Long	Y	Y	Y	N	Y	Y	Y	Y
3 Mikulski	Y	Y	N	N	Y	?	Y	Y
4 ***Holt***	?	?	?	?	?	?	Y	N
5 Hoyer	N	N	Y	Y	Y	Y	Y	Y
6 Byron	Y	Y	Y	N	N	Y	Y	Y
7 Mitchell	N	?	N	N	Y	Y	Y	Y
8 Barnes	N	N	Y	Y	Y	Y	Y	Y
MASSACHUSETTS								
1 ***Conte***	N	N	N	Y	Y	Y	Y	Y
2 Boland	N	N	Y	Y	Y	?	?	?
3 Early	Y	Y	Y	N	?	?	Y	N
4 Frank	N	N	N	N	Y	Y	Y	Y
5 Shannon	N	N	Y	Y	Y	Y	Y	Y
6 Mavroules	N	N	N	Y	?	?	Y	Y
7 Markey	N	N	N	Y	Y	Y	Y	Y
8 O'Neill								
9 Moakley	N	N	Y	Y	?	?	Y	Y
10 Studds	N	N	N	Y	Y	Y	Y	Y
11 Donnelly	Y	Y	N	N	Y	Y	Y	Y
MICHIGAN								
1 Conyers	N	N	Y	Y	Y	?	?	?
2 ***Pursell***	N	N	N	Y	Y	Y	Y	Y
3 Wolpe	N	N	Y	Y	N	Y	Y	Y
4 ***Siljander***	Y	Y	N	N	N	Y	?	?
5 ***Sawyer***	N	N	N	Y	Y	Y.	Y	Y
6 Carr	?	?	?	?	?	?	Y	Y
7 Kildee	N	N	N	Y	N	Y	Y	Y
8 Traxler	Y	Y	Y	N	?	?	Y	Y
9 ***Vander Jagt***	Y	Y	N	N	Y	Y	Y	Y
10 Albosta	Y	Y	Y	N	Y	Y	?	?
11 ***Davis***	Y	N	N	N	N	Y	Y	Y
12 Bonior	N	N	Y	Y	Y	Y	Y	Y
13 Crockett	N	N	N	N	Y	?	?	?
14 Hertel	Y	N	N	N	N	Y	Y	Y
15 Ford	N	N	N	N	Y	Y	Y	Y
16 Dingell	?	?	?	Y	?	?	Y	Y
17 Levin	N	N	N	N	Y	Y	Y	Y
18 ***Broomfield***	Y	Y	N	N	?	?	Y	Y
MINNESOTA								
1 Penny	Y	Y	Y	N	N	Y	Y	Y
2 ***Weber***	Y	Y	Y	N	N	Y	Y	Y
3 ***Frenzel***	N	N	N	Y	Y	Y	Y	Y
4 Vento	N	N	N	Y	Y	?	Y	Y
5 Sabo	N	N	Y	Y	Y	Y	Y	Y
6 Sikorski	N	N	Y	Y	Y	Y	Y	Y
7 ***Stangeland***	N	N	Y	Y	N	Y	Y	Y
8 Oberstar	Y	N	Y	N	Y	Y	Y	Y
MISSISSIPPI								
1 Whitten	Y	Y	Y	N	Y	Y	?	?
2 ***Franklin***	Y	Y	?	X	?	?	Y	N
3 Montgomery	Y	Y	Y	N	N	Y	Y	N
4 Dowdy	?	?	?	?	?	?	?	?
5 ***Lott***	Y	Y	Y	X	?	?	Y	N
MISSOURI								
1 Clay	N	N	N	N	Y	Y	Y	Y
2 Young	N	N	Y	Y	Y	Y	Y	Y
3 Gephardt	N	N	Y	-	+	+	Y	Y
4 Skelton	Y	Y	Y	N	Y	Y	Y	Y
5 Wheat	Y	Y	N	N	Y	Y	Y	Y
6 ***Coleman***	Y	Y	N	N	Y	Y	Y	Y
7 ***Taylor***	Y	Y	N	X	?	?	Y	Y
8 ***Emerson***	Y	Y	Y	N	N	Y	Y	Y
9 Volkmer	Y	Y	Y	N	N	Y	Y	N
MONTANA								
1 Williams	N	N	Y	Y	Y	Y	Y	Y
2 ***Marlenee***	Y	Y	Y	N	Y	Y	Y	Y
NEBRASKA								
1 ***Bereuter***	N	N	N	Y	N	Y	Y	Y
2 ***Daub***	Y	Y	N	N	N	Y	Y	N
3 ***Smith***	Y	Y	N	N	N	Y	Y	Y
NEVADA								
1 Reid	Y	Y	Y	N	Y	Y	Y	Y
2 ***Vucanovich***	Y	Y	Y	N	Y	Y	Y	N
NEW HAMPSHIRE								
1 D'Amours	Y	Y	N	N	?	Y	Y	Y
2 ***Gregg***	Y	Y	N	?	?	?	Y	N
NEW JERSEY								
1 Florio	Y	N	N	N	Y	Y	Y	Y
2 Hughes	N	Y	N	N	Y	Y	Y	Y
3 Howard	N	N	N	Y	?	?	Y	Y
4 ***Smith***	N	N	Y	Y	N	Y	Y	Y
5 ***Roukema***	N	N	N	Y	Y	Y	Y	Y
6 Dwyer	N	N	Y	Y	?	?	Y	Y
7 ***Rinaldo***	Y	N	N	N	Y	Y	Y	Y
8 Roe	N	N	Y	Y	Y	Y	Y	Y
9 Torricelli	N	N	N	Y	Y	Y	Y	Y
10 Rodino	N	N	N	Y	Y	Y	Y	Y
11 Minish	N	N	N	N	N	?	Y	Y
12 ***Courter***	Y	Y	N	N	N	Y	Y	N
13 ***Forsythe***	N	N	N	Y	Y	Y	Y	Y
14 Guarini	N	N	N	Y	Y	Y	Y	Y
NEW MEXICO								
1 ***Lujan***	Y	Y	N	N	Y	Y	Y	N
2 ***Skeen***	Y	Y	Y	N	Y	Y	Y	Y
3 Richardson	Y	Y	Y	N	Y	Y	Y	Y
NEW YORK								
1 ***Carney***	Y	Y	N	N	Y	Y	Y	N
2 Downey	N	N	N	N	Y	Y	Y	Y
3 Mrazek	Y	Y	N	N	Y	Y	Y	N
4 ***Lent***	N	N	N	?	?	?	Y	Y
5 ***McGrath***	Y	Y	N	N	Y	Y	Y	N
6 Addabbo	?	?	?	#	?	?	Y	Y
7 Ackerman	N	N	N	Y	Y	+	Y	Y
8 Scheuer	N	N	N	Y	Y	?	Y	Y
9 Ferraro	N	N	N	N	Y	?	Y	Y
10 Schumer	N	N	N	Y	Y	Y	Y	Y
11 Towns	N	N	Y	Y	Y	Y	?	?
12 Owens	N	N	N	N	Y	?	Y	Y
13 Solarz	N	N	Y	Y	Y	Y	Y	Y
14 ***Molinari***	N	N	N	Y	Y	Y	Y	Y
15 ***Green***	N	N	N	Y	Y	Y	?	N
16 Rangel	N	N	N	Y	Y	Y	Y	Y
17 Weiss	N	N	N	Y	Y	Y	Y	Y
18 Garcia	?	?	?	#	?	?	Y	Y
19 Biaggi	N	N	N	Y	N	?	Y	N
20 Ottinger	N	N	N	Y	Y	?	Y	Y
21 ***Fish***	N	N	N	Y	Y	Y	Y	Y
22 ***Gilman***	N	N	N	Y	N	Y	Y	Y
23 Stratton	Y	N	N	Y	Y	Y	Y	Y
24 ***Solomon***	Y	Y	N	N	?	?	Y	N
25 ***Boehlert***	N	N	?	#	?	?	Y	Y
26 ***Martin***	N	N	N	Y	Y	Y	Y	N
27 ***Wortley***	N	N	N	Y	Y	?	Y	N
28 McHugh	N	N	Y	Y	Y	Y	Y	Y
29 ***Horton***	N	N	?	#	?	?	Y	Y
30 ***Conable***	N	N	N	Y	Y	?	Y	Y
31 ***Kemp***	Y	Y	N	N	Y	Y	Y	N
32 LaFalce	N	N	N	?	?	?	Y	Y
33 Nowak	N	N	Y	?	?	?	Y	Y
34 Lundine	N	N	Y	Y	Y	Y	Y	Y
NORTH CAROLINA								
1 Jones	Y	Y	Y	Y	?	?	Y	Y
2 Valentine	Y	Y	Y	N	Y	Y	Y	N
3 Whitley	Y	Y	Y	N	Y	Y	Y	N
4 Andrews	N	N	Y	Y	?	?	Y	N
5 Neal	N	N	Y	Y	Y	Y	?	?
6 Britt	N	N	Y	Y	N	Y	Y	N
7 Rose	N	N	Y	Y	Y	Y	?	?
8 Hefner	Y	Y	Y	N	Y	Y	Y	N
9 ***Martin***	N	N	Y	Y	Y	Y	Y	Y
10 ***Broyhill***	Y	N	N	N	N	?	Y	N
11 Clarke	N	N	N	Y	Y	+	Y	N
NORTH DAKOTA								
AL Dorgan	?	?	?	X	?	?	Y	Y
OHIO								
1 Luken	Y	N	N	N	Y	Y	?	?
2 ***Gradison***	N	N	N	N	?	?	Y	Y
3 Hall	Y	Y	N	N	Y	Y	Y	Y
4 ***Oxley***	N	N	N	Y	Y	Y	Y	N
5 ***Latta***	N	N	N	Y	Y	Y	Y	N
6 ***McEwen***	Y	Y	Y	N	Y	?	Y	N
7 ***DeWine***	N	N	N	N	N	Y	Y	N
8 ***Kindness***	N	N	N	N	Y	Y	Y	N
9 Kaptur	Y	Y	N	N	N	Y	Y	Y
10 ***Miller***	Y	Y	N	N	N	Y	Y	N
11 Eckart	Y	Y	N	N	N	Y	Y	Y
12 ***Kasich***	Y	Y	N	N	N	Y	Y	N
13 Pease	N	N	Y	Y	?	?	Y	Y
14 Seiberling	N	N	Y	Y	?	?	Y	Y
15 ***Wylie***	N	N	N	Y	Y	Y	Y	Y
16 ***Regula***	N	N	N	Y	N	Y	Y	Y
17 ***Williams***	Y	Y	N	N	N	Y	Y	Y
18 Applegate	Y	Y	Y	N	Y	?	Y	N
19 Feighan	N	N	Y	N	Y	Y	Y	Y
20 Oakar	N	N	N	Y	Y	Y	Y	Y
21 Stokes	N	N	N	N	Y	Y	Y	Y
OKLAHOMA								
1 Jones	N	N	Y	N	Y	Y	Y	Y
2 Synar	N	N	Y	N	Y	Y	Y	Y
3 Watkins	Y	Y	Y	N	?	?	Y	N
4 McCurdy	Y	Y	Y	N	N	Y	Y	N
5 ***Edwards***	Y	Y	Y	N	Y	Y	Y	N
6 English	Y	Y	Y	N	N	Y	Y	N
OREGON								
1 AuCoin	N	N	Y	Y	Y	Y	Y	Y
2 ***Smith, R.***	Y	Y	N	N	N	Y	Y	N
3 Wyden	N	N	N	N	N	Y	Y	Y
4 Weaver	Y	Y	N	N	Y	Y	?	?
5 ***Smith, D.***	Y	Y	N	N	N	Y	Y	N
PENNSYLVANIA								
1 Foglietta	N	N	N	Y	Y	Y	Y	Y
2 Gray	N	N	N	N	Y	Y	Y	Y
3 Borski	N	N	N	N	Y	Y	Y	Y
4 Kolter	N	Y	Y	N	Y	Y	Y	Y
5 ***Schulze***	Y	Y	N	?	?	?	Y	N
6 Yatron	Y	Y	Y	N	N	Y	Y	Y
7 Edgar	N	N	N	Y	?	?	+	?
8 Kostmayer	N	N	N	Y	Y	Y	Y	Y
9 ***Shuster***	Y	Y	N	N	N	Y	Y	N
10 ***McDade***	X	?	?	#	?	?	Y	Y
11 Harrison	Y	Y	Y	N	Y	Y	Y	Y
12 Murtha	N	N	Y	Y	?	?	Y	Y
13 ***Coughlin***	N	N	N	Y	Y	Y	Y	Y
14 Coyne	N	N	N	Y	Y	Y	Y	Y
15 ***Ritter***	Y	Y	N	N	N	Y	Y	N
16 ***Walker***	Y	Y	N	N	N	Y	Y	N
17 ***Gekas***	N	N	N	Y	N	Y	Y	Y
18 Walgren	Y	Y	N	N	Y	Y	Y	Y
19 ***Goodling***	N	N	N	Y	N	Y	Y	Y
20 Gaydos	N	N	N	Y	?	?	Y	N
21 ***Ridge***	N	N	N	N	Y	Y	Y	Y
22 Murphy	N	Y	Y	N	Y	Y	Y	N
23 ***Clinger***	N	N	N	Y	N	+	Y	Y
RHODE ISLAND								
1 St Germain	N	N	Y	Y	?	Y	?	?
2 ***Schneider***	N	N	?	?	?	?	Y	Y
SOUTH CAROLINA								
1 ***Hartnett***	N	Y	Y	?	?	?	Y	N
2 ***Spence***	Y	Y	Y	N	?	?	Y	?
3 Derrick	N	N	Y	Y	?	?	Y	Y
4 ***Campbell***	Y	Y	Y	N	Y	Y	Y	N
5 Spratt	N	N	Y	Y	Y	Y	Y	Y
6 Tallon	Y	Y	Y	N	Y	Y	Y	N
SOUTH DAKOTA								
AL Daschle	Y	Y	Y	N	Y	Y	?	?
TENNESSEE								
1 ***Quillen***	N	N	?	?	?	?	Y	N
2 ***Duncan***	Y	Y	Y	N	Y	Y	Y	N
3 Lloyd	Y	Y	Y	N	N	?	Y	N
4 Cooper	?	?	?	#	?	?	Y	Y
5 Boner	N	N	Y	N	Y	Y	Y	N
6 Gore	N	N	Y	Y	?	?	?	?
7 ***Sundquist***	Y	Y	Y	N	N	Y	Y	N
8 Jones	?	?	?	?	?	?	Y	N
9 Ford	N	N	Y	Y	Y	Y	Y	Y
TEXAS								
1 Hall, S.	Y	Y	Y	N	N	Y	Y	N
2 Wilson	N	N	Y	Y	Y	Y	Y	Y
3 ***Bartlett***	N	N	Y	Y	Y	Y	Y	N
4 Hall, R.	Y	Y	Y	N	N	Y	Y	N
5 Bryant	N	N	Y	?	?	?	Y	Y
6 ***Gramm***	Y	Y	N	N	N	Y	Y	N
7 ***Archer***	Y	Y	N	N	?	?	Y	Y
8 ***Fields***	Y	Y	N	N	N	Y	Y	N
9 Brooks	N	Y	Y	N	Y	Y	Y	Y
10 Pickle	Y	N	Y	?	?	?	Y	Y
11 Leath	Y	?	?	?	?	?	Y	N
12 Wright	N	N	Y	?	?	?	Y	Y
13 Hightower	Y	Y	Y	N	N	Y	Y	Y
14 Patman	Y	Y	Y	N	N	Y	Y	N
15 de la Garza	N	Y	Y	N	?	?	Y	Y
16 Coleman	N	N	Y	Y	Y	Y	Y	Y
17 Stenholm	Y	Y	Y	N	N	Y	Y	N
18 Leland	N	N	Y	Y	Y	Y	Y	Y
19 Hance	Y	Y	Y	N	N	Y	?	?
20 Gonzalez	Y	Y	Y	N	Y	Y	Y	Y
21 ***Loeffler***	Y	Y	Y	N	N	Y	?	?
22 ***Paul***	Y	Y	N	N	N	Y	N	N
23 Kazen	Y	Y	Y	N	N	Y	Y	Y
24 Frost	?	?	?	#	?	?	Y	Y
25 Andrews	N	N	Y	Y	N	Y	Y	Y
26 Vandergriff	N	Y	Y	N	Y	Y	Y	N
27 Ortiz	Y	Y	Y	N	Y	Y	Y	Y
UTAH								
1 ***Hansen***	Y	Y	N	N	Y	?	Y	N
2 ***Marriott***	N	N	N	N	Y	?	Y	N
3 ***Nielson***	Y	N	N	N	N	Y	Y	N
VERMONT								
AL ***Jeffords***	N	N	N	Y	Y	Y	Y	N
VIRGINIA								
1 ***Bateman***	N	N	N	Y	Y	Y	Y	Y
2 ***Whitehurst***	N	N	N	Y	Y	?	Y	N
3 ***Bliley***	Y	Y	N	N	Y	Y	Y	N
4 Sisisky	N	N	Y	Y	Y	Y	Y	Y
5 Daniel	Y	Y	Y	N	Y	Y	Y	N
6 Olin	Y	N	Y	N	Y	Y	Y	Y
7 ***Robinson***	Y	Y	N	N	Y	Y	Y	N
8 ***Parris***	N	Y	Y	N	?	?	Y	N
9 Boucher	N	N	Y	Y	Y	Y	Y	Y
10 ***Wolf***	N	N	N	Y	Y	Y	Y	N
WASHINGTON								
1 ***Pritchard***	N	N	N	Y	N	?	Y	Y
2 Swift	N	N	?	N	Y	Y	Y	Y
3 Bonker	N	N	N	Y	?	?	Y	Y
4 ***Morrison***	N	N	N	Y	Y	Y	Y	N
5 Foley	?	?	?	?	?	?	Y	Y
6 Dicks	N	N	N	Y	?	?	Y	Y
7 Lowry	N	N	N	N	Y	Y	Y	Y
8 ***Chandler***	N	N	N	Y	Y	?	Y	Y
WEST VIRGINIA								
1 Mollohan	Y	Y	Y	N	Y	Y	Y	N
2 Staggers	Y	Y	Y	N	N	Y	Y	N
3 Wise	Y	Y	Y	N	N	Y	Y	N
4 Rahall	Y	Y	Y	N	Y	Y	Y	N
WISCONSIN								
1 Aspin	N	N	?	?	?	?	Y	Y
2 Kastenmeier	N	Y	Y	N	Y	Y	Y	Y
3 ***Gunderson***	Y	Y	N	N	N	Y	Y	Y
4 Zablocki	N	N	N	Y	Y	Y	Y	Y
5 Moody	N	N	N	Y	?	Y	Y	Y
6 ***Petri***	Y	Y	N	N	N	Y	Y	Y
7 Obey	N	N	Y	N	Y	?	Y	Y
8 ***Roth***	Y	Y	N	N	N	Y	Y	N
9 ***Sensenbrenner***	Y	Y	N	N	N	Y	Y	Y
WYOMING								
AL ***Cheney***	N	N	N	Y	Y	?	Y	Y

Southern states - Ala., Ark., Fla., Ga., Ky., La., Miss., N.C., Okla., S.C., Tenn., Texas, Va.

284. S 675. Omnibus Defense Authorizations. Price, D-Ill., motion to close the conference committee meetings on the bill to authorize appropriations for Defense Department programs in fiscal 1984. Motion agreed to 396-10: R 161-0; D 235-10 (ND 152-10, SD 83-0), Aug. 1, 1983.

285. HR 3409. Federal Supplemental Unemployment Compensation. Rostenkowski, D-Ill., motion to suspend the rules and pass the bill to limit the number of weeks of unemployment compensation any state could lose as a result of strictures in the extended supplemental unemployment compensation program that took effect April 1, 1983. Motion agreed to 338-84: R 86-78; D 252-6 (ND 170-0, SD 82-6), Aug. 2, 1983. A two-thirds majority of those present and voting (282 in this case) is required for passage under suspension of the rules.

286. HR 3564. Early Agriculture Program Announcements. De la Garza, D-Texas, motion to suspend the rules and pass the bill to change dates for required federal announcements of crop acreage limitations or set-aside programs, as follows: for 1984 and 1985 feed grain crops, the announcement must be made by Sept. 30 (instead of Nov. 15) of the year before that in which the crop is harvested; for the 1985 wheat crop, announcement must be made by July 1, 1984 (instead of Aug. 15, 1984). Motion agreed to 329-93: R 82-80; D 247-13 (ND 160-11, SD 87-2), Aug. 2, 1983. A two-thirds majority of those present and voting (282 in this case) is required for passage under suspension of the rules.

287. H Con Res 40. Federal Nutrition Programs. De la Garza, D-Texas, motion to suspend the rules and adopt the concurrent resolution expressing the sense of Congress that federal nutrition programs should be protected from budget cuts, that the supplemental food program for women, infants and children (WIC) should be funded to maintain the number of cases carried at the end of fiscal 1983, and that the federal government should maintain current efforts in nutrition programs to prevent increases in domestic hunger. Motion agreed to 407-16: R 150-14; D 257-2 (ND 170-0, SD 87-2), Aug. 2, 1983. A two-thirds majority of those present and voting (282 in this case) is required for adoption under suspension of the rules.

288. S 64. Irish Wilderness. Seiberling, D-Ohio, motion to suspend the rules and pass the bill to establish as federal wilderness and protect from development the Irish Wilderness Area of about 15,500 acres in the Mark Twain National Forest, Missouri. Motion agreed to 406-18: R 151-13; D 255-5 (ND 170-1, SD 85-4), Aug. 2, 1983. A two-thirds majority of those present and voting (283 in this case) is required for passage under suspension of the rules.

289. HR 3706. Martin Luther King Jr. Holiday. Hall, D-Ind., motion to suspend the rules and pass the bill to designate the third Monday of every January as a federal holiday in honor of the late civil rights leader the Rev. Dr. Martin Luther King Jr. Motion agreed to 338-90: R 89-77; D 249-13 (ND 171-1, SD 78-12), Aug. 2, 1983. A two-thirds majority of those present and voting (286 in this case) is required for passage under suspension of the rules.

290. HR 2780. Revenue Sharing. Horton, R-N.Y., amendment to reauthorize the general revenue sharing program for three years, through Sept. 30, 1986, rather than five years in the bill as reported. Adopted 226-202: R 138-27; D 88-175 (ND 39-134, SD 49-41), Aug. 2, 1983. A "yea" was a vote supporting the president's position.

291. HR 2780. Revenue Sharing. McCandless, R-Calif., amendment, to the Horton, R-N.Y., amendment (see vote 292, p. 88-H), to reduce entitlement funding for local governments from $5.02 billion annually as proposed by the Horton amendment to $4.6 billion, the level requested by the president. Rejected 176-248: R 123-41; D 53-207 (ND 16-156, SD 37-51), Aug. 2, 1983. A "yea" was a vote supporting the president's position.

KEY

Y Voted for (yea).
Paired for.
+ Announced for.
N Voted against (nay).
X Paired against.
- Announced against.
P Voted "present".
C Voted "present" to avoid possible conflict of interest.
? Did not vote or otherwise make a position known.

Democrats   *Republicans*

	284	285	286	287	288	289	290	291
ALABAMA								
1 *Edwards*	Y	Y	N	Y	Y	Y	Y	Y
2 *Dickinson*	Y	Y	Y	Y	Y	N	Y	Y
3 Nichols	Y	Y	Y	Y	Y	N	N	N
4 Bevill	Y	Y	Y	Y	Y	Y	N	N
5 Flippo	Y	Y	Y	Y	Y	Y	N	N
6 Erdreich	Y	Y	Y	Y	Y	N	N	N
7 Shelby	Y	Y	Y	Y	Y	N	N	N
ALASKA								
AL *Young*	Y	Y	Y	Y	N	N	Y	N
ARIZONA								
1 *McCain*	Y	Y	N	Y	Y	N	Y	Y
2 Udall	Y	Y	Y	Y	Y	Y	Y	N
3 *Stump*	Y	N	N	N	N	Y	Y	Y
4 *Rudd*	N	N	N	N	N	Y	Y	Y
5 McNulty	N	Y	Y	Y	Y	Y	Y	N
ARKANSAS								
1 Alexander	Y	Y	Y	Y	Y	Y	N	N
2 *Bethune*	Y	Y	Y	Y	Y	Y	Y	Y
3 *Hammerschmidt*	Y	Y	Y	Y	Y	N	Y	N
4 Anthony	Y	Y	Y	Y	Y	Y	Y	Y
CALIFORNIA								
1 Bosco	Y	Y	Y	Y	Y	Y	N	?
2 *Chappie*	?	N	Y	Y	Y	Y	Y	Y
3 Matsui	Y	Y	Y	Y	Y	Y	N	N
4 Fazio	Y	Y	Y	Y	Y	Y	N	N
5 Burton	Y	Y	Y	Y	Y	Y	N	N
6 Boxer	Y	Y	Y	Y	Y	Y	N	N
7 Miller	Y	Y	Y	Y	Y	?	N	N
8 Dellums	?	Y	Y	Y	Y	Y	N	N
9 Stark	Y	?	Y	Y	Y	Y	N	N
10 Edwards	Y	Y	Y	Y	Y	Y	N	N
11 Lantos	Y	Y	Y	Y	Y	Y	N	N
12 *Zschau*	Y	N	N	Y	Y	Y	Y	N
13 Mineta	Y	Y	Y	Y	Y	Y	N	N
14 *Shumway*	Y	N	N	N	N	Y	N	Y
15 Coelho	Y	Y	Y	Y	Y	Y	N	N
16 Panetta	Y	Y	Y	Y	Y	Y	Y	Y
17 *Pashayan*	Y	Y	N	Y	Y	N	N	N
18 Lehman	Y	Y	Y	Y	Y	Y	N	N
19 *Lagomarsino*	Y	N	N	Y	Y	N	Y	Y
20 *Thomas*	Y	N	N	Y	Y	Y	Y	Y
21 *Fiedler*	Y	Y	Y	Y	Y	N	Y	N
22 *Moorhead*	Y	N	N	Y	Y	N	Y	Y
23 Beilenson	Y	Y	Y	Y	Y	Y	N	Y
24 Waxman	Y	Y	N	Y	Y	Y	N	N
25 Roybal	Y	Y	Y	Y	Y	Y	N	N
26 Berman	Y	Y	Y	Y	Y	Y	present	
27 Levine	Y	N	Y	Y	Y	N	N	N
28 Dixon	Y	Y	Y	Y	Y	Y	N	N
29 Hawkins	Y	Y	Y	Y	Y	Y	N	N
30 Martinez	Y	Y	N	Y	Y	Y	N	N
31 Dymally	Y	Y	Y	Y	Y	Y	N	N
32 Anderson	Y	N	Y	Y	Y	Y	N	N
33 *Dreier*	Y	N	N	Y	Y	N	Y	Y
34 Torres	Y	Y	Y	Y	Y	Y	N	N
35 *Lewis*	Y	Y	?	Y	Y	Y	N	N
36 Brown	Y	Y	Y	Y	Y	Y	N	N
37 *McCandless*	Y	N	N	Y	Y	N	Y	Y
38 Patterson	N	Y	Y	Y	Y	Y	N	N
39 *Dannemeyer*	Y	N	N	Y	N	N	Y	Y
40 *Badham*	Y	N	N	Y	N	N	Y	Y
41 *Lowery*	Y	N	N	Y	Y	Y	Y	Y
42 *Lungren*	Y	N	N	Y	Y	Y	Y	Y
43 *Packard*	Y	N	N	Y	N	Y	N	Y
44 Bates	Y	Y	Y	Y	Y	Y	Y	N
45 *Hunter*	Y	N	Y	Y	Y	Y	Y	Y
COLORADO								
1 Schroeder	N	Y	Y	Y	Y	N	N	Y
2 Wirth	?	Y	Y	Y	Y	Y	Y	Y
3 Kogovsek	Y	Y	Y	Y	Y	Y	N	N
4 *Brown*	Y	N	Y	Y	N	Y	N	Y
5 *Kramer*	Y	Y	Y	Y	N	Y	Y	Y
6 *Schaefer*	Y	N	N	Y	N	Y	N	Y
CONNECTICUT								
1 Kennelly	Y	Y	Y	Y	Y	N	N	N
2 Gejdenson	Y	Y	Y	Y	Y	N	N	N
3 Morrison	Y	Y	Y	Y	Y	N	N	N
4 *McKinney*	Y	N	Y	Y	Y	Y	Y	N
5 Ratchford	Y	Y	Y	Y	Y	N	N	N
6 *Johnson*	Y	Y	Y	Y	Y	N	N	N
DELAWARE								
AL Carper	Y	Y	Y	Y	Y	Y	N	
FLORIDA								
1 Hutto	Y	Y	Y	Y	Y	N	Y	Y
2 Fuqua	Y	Y	Y	Y	Y	Y	Y	Y
3 Bennett	Y	Y	Y	Y	Y	Y	Y	Y
4 Chappell	Y	Y	Y	Y	Y	Y	Y	Y
5 *McCollum*	Y	N	N	Y	N	Y	Y	Y
6 MacKay	Y	Y	Y	Y	Y	Y	N	N
7 Gibbons	Y	Y	Y	Y	Y	Y	Y	Y
8 *Young*	?	Y	Y	Y	N	Y	Y	Y
9 *Bilirakis*	Y	N	Y	Y	N	Y	Y	Y
10 Ireland	Y	Y	Y	Y	Y	Y	Y	Y
11 Nelson	Y	Y	Y	Y	Y	Y	Y	Y
12 *Lewis*	Y	N	N	Y	Y	Y	Y	Y
13 *Mack*	Y	N	N	Y	Y	Y	Y	Y
14 Mica	Y	Y	Y	Y	Y	Y	Y	Y
15 *Shaw*	Y	N	N	Y	Y	Y	Y	Y
16 Smith	Y	Y	Y	Y	Y	Y	N	N
17 Lehman	Y	Y	Y	Y	Y	Y	N	N
18 Pepper	Y	Y	Y	Y	Y	Y	N	Y
19 Fascell	Y	Y	Y	Y	Y	Y	Y	Y
GEORGIA								
1 Thomas	Y	Y	Y	Y	Y	Y	N	N
2 Hatcher	Y	Y	Y	Y	Y	Y	Y	N
3 Ray	Y	N	Y	Y	N	Y	Y	Y
4 Levitas	Y	Y	Y	Y	Y	N	Y	Y
5 Fowler	Y	Y	Y	Y	Y	N	N	N
6 *Gingrich*	Y	N	Y	Y	N	Y	Y	Y
7 McDonald	N	N	N	N	N	N	Y	Y
8 Rowland	Y	Y	Y	Y	Y	N	N	N
9 Jenkins	Y	Y	Y	Y	Y	N	N	Y
10 Barnard	Y	Y	Y	Y	Y	Y	N	N
HAWAII								
1 Heftel	?	?	?	?	?	?	?	?
2 Akaka	Y	Y	Y	Y	Y	Y	Y	N
IDAHO								
1 *Craig*	Y	Y	Y	Y	Y	N	Y	Y
2 *Hansen*	Y	?	?	?	?	?	?	?
ILLINOIS								
1 Vacancy								
2 Savage	Y	Y	Y	?	?	Y	N	N
3 Russo	Y	Y	Y	Y	Y	Y	N	N
4 *O'Brien*	Y	N	Y	Y	Y	N	Y	N
5 Lipinski	Y	Y	Y	Y	Y	Y	N	N
6 *Hyde*	Y	N	N	Y	Y	Y	Y	Y
7 Collins	Y	Y	Y	Y	Y	Y	N	N
8 Rostenkowski	Y	Y	Y	Y	Y	Y	N	N
9 Yates	Y	Y	Y	Y	Y	Y	N	N
10 *Porter*	Y	Y	Y	Y	Y	Y	N	N
11 Annunzio	Y	Y	Y	Y	Y	Y	N	N
12 *Crane, P.*	Y	N	N	N	N	N	Y	Y
13 *Erlenborn*	?	Y	N	Y	Y	N	Y	?
14 *Corcoran*	Y	Y	N	Y	Y	N	Y	Y
15 *Madigan*	Y	Y	N	Y	Y	Y	N	Y
16 *Martin*	Y	Y	Y	Y	Y	N	Y	Y
17 Evans	Y	Y	Y	Y	Y	Y	N	N
18 *Michel*	Y	Y	Y	Y	Y	Y	N	Y
19 *Crane, D.*	Y	N	N	N	N	N	Y	Y
20 Durbin	Y	Y	Y	Y	Y	Y	N	N
21 Price	Y	Y	Y	Y	Y	Y	N	N
22 Simon	Y	Y	Y	Y	Y	Y	N	N
INDIANA								
1 Hall	Y	Y	Y	Y	Y	N	N	N
2 Sharp	Y	Y	Y	Y	Y	Y	N	Y
3 *Hiler*	Y	Y	Y	Y	Y	Y	Y	Y
4 *Coats*	Y	Y	Y	Y	Y	Y	N	Y
5 Hillis	Y	Y	Y	Y	Y	Y	Y	Y

ND - Northern Democrats   SD - Southern Democrats

Corresponding to Congressional Record Votes 299, 300, 301, 302, 303, 304, 306, 307

	284	285	286	287	288	289	290	291
6 ***Burton***	Y	Y	N	Y	Y	Y	Y	Y
7 ***Myers***	Y	Y	Y	Y	Y	Y	N	Y
8 McCloskey	Y	Y	Y	Y	Y	Y	N	N
9 Hamilton	Y	Y	Y	Y	Y	Y	N	N
10 Jacobs	Y	Y	Y	Y	N	Y	Y	Y
IOWA								
1 ***Leach***	Y	Y	Y	Y	Y	Y	N	Y
2 ***Tauke***	Y	Y	Y	Y	Y	N	N	N
3 ***Evans***	Y	Y	Y	Y	Y	Y	N	Y
4 Smith	Y	Y	Y	Y	Y	Y	N	N
5 Harkin	?	Y	Y	Y	Y	Y	N	N
6 Bedell	Y	Y	Y	Y	Y	Y	Y	N
KANSAS								
1 ***Roberts***	Y	Y	Y	Y	Y	Y	Y	Y
2 Slattery	Y	Y	Y	Y	Y	Y	Y	Y
3 ***Winn***	Y	N	Y	Y	Y	N	Y	Y
4 Glickman	Y	Y	Y	Y	Y	Y	Y	Y
5 ***Whittaker***	Y	Y	Y	Y	Y	Y	Y	Y
KENTUCKY								
1 Hubbard	Y	Y	Y	Y	Y	Y	N	N
2 Natcher	Y	Y	Y	Y	Y	Y	N	N
3 Mazzoli	Y	Y	Y	Y	Y	Y	Y	N
4 ***Snyder***	Y	Y	N	Y	Y	N	Y	Y
5 ***Rogers***	Y	Y	Y	Y	Y	N	N	N
6 ***Hopkins***	Y	Y	Y	Y	Y	Y	Y	N
7 Perkins	Y	Y	Y	Y	Y	Y	N	N
LOUISIANA								
1 ***Livingston***	Y	N	N	Y	Y	Y	Y	Y
2 Boggs	Y	Y	Y	Y	Y	Y	N	N
3 Tauzin	?	Y	Y	Y	Y	Y	N	N
4 Roemer	Y	Y	Y	Y	Y	Y	Y	Y
5 Huckaby	Y	Y	Y	Y	Y	Y	Y	Y
6 ***Moore***	Y	N	N	Y	Y	N	N	N
7 Breaux	Y	Y	Y	Y	Y	Y	N	N
8 Long	Y	Y	Y	Y	Y	Y	N	N
MAINE								
1 ***McKernan***	Y	Y	Y	Y	Y	Y	Y	N
2 ***Snowe***	Y	Y	Y	Y	Y	Y	Y	N
MARYLAND								
1 Dyson	Y	Y	Y	Y	Y	Y	N	N
2 Long	Y	Y	Y	Y	Y	Y	Y	Y
3 Mikulski	Y	Y	Y	Y	Y	Y	N	N
4 ***Holt***	Y	N	N	Y	Y	N	Y	Y
5 Hoyer	Y	Y	Y	Y	Y	Y	N	N
6 Byron	Y	Y	Y	Y	Y	Y	Y	N
7 Mitchell	N	Y	Y	Y	Y	Y	N	N
8 Barnes	Y	Y	Y	Y	Y	Y	N	N
MASSACHUSETTS								
1 ***Conte***	Y	Y	N	Y	Y	Y	Y	Y
2 Boland	?	Y	Y	Y	Y	Y	Y	N
3 Early	Y	Y	Y	Y	Y	Y	N	N
4 Frank	Y	Y	Y	Y	Y	Y	N	N
5 Shannon	Y	Y	Y	Y	Y	Y	N	N
6 Mavroules	Y	Y	Y	Y	Y	Y	N	N
7 Markey	Y	Y	Y	Y	Y	Y	N	N
8 O'Neill								
9 Moakley	Y	Y	Y	Y	Y	Y	N	N
10 Studds	Y	Y	Y	Y	Y	Y	N	N
11 Donnelly	Y	Y	Y	Y	Y	Y	Y	N
MICHIGAN								
1 Conyers	?	Y	Y	Y	Y	Y	N	N
2 ***Pursell***	Y	Y	Y	Y	Y	N	Y	N
3 Wolpe	Y	Y	Y	Y	Y	Y	N	N
4 ***Siljander***	?	?	?	?	?	Y	Y	Y
5 ***Sawyer***	Y	Y	Y	Y	Y	Y	N	Y
6 Carr	Y	Y	Y	Y	Y	Y	N	N
7 Kildee	Y	Y	Y	Y	Y	Y	N	N
8 Traxler	Y	Y	Y	Y	Y	Y	N	N
9 ***Vander Jagt***	Y	Y	N	Y	Y	Y	Y	Y
10 Albosta	?	Y	Y	Y	Y	Y	Y	N
11 ***Davis***	Y	Y	Y	Y	Y	Y	N	N
12 Bonior	Y	Y	Y	Y	Y	Y	N	N
13 Crockett	?	Y	Y	Y	Y	Y	Y	N
14 Hertel	Y	Y	Y	Y	Y	Y	Y	N
15 Ford	Y	Y	Y	Y	Y	Y	Y	Y
16 Dingell	Y	Y	Y	Y	Y	Y	Y	Y
17 Levin	Y	Y	Y	Y	Y	Y	N	N
18 ***Broomfield***	Y	Y	Y	Y	Y	Y	Y	Y
MINNESOTA								
1 Penny	Y	Y	Y	Y	Y	Y	N	N
2 ***Weber***	Y	N	Y	Y	Y	Y	Y	Y
3 ***Frenzel***	Y	N	Y	Y	Y	N	Y	Y
4 Vento	Y	Y	Y	Y	Y	Y	Y	N
5 Sabo	Y	Y	Y	Y	Y	Y	Y	N
6 Sikorski	Y	Y	Y	Y	Y	Y	N	N

	284	285	286	287	288	289	290	291
7 ***Stangeland***	Y	Y	Y	Y	Y	N	Y	N
8 Oberstar	Y	Y	Y	Y	Y	Y	N	N
MISSISSIPPI								
1 Whitten	?	Y	Y	Y	Y	Y	N	N
2 ***Franklin***	Y	N	Y	Y	Y	N	Y	Y
3 Montgomery	Y	Y	Y	Y	Y	N	Y	Y
4 Dowdy	?	?	Y	Y	Y	Y	N	N
5 ***Lott***	Y	N	N	Y	Y	N	?	Y
MISSOURI								
1 Clay	Y	Y	Y	Y	Y	Y	N	N
2 Young	Y	Y	Y	Y	Y	Y	N	N
3 Gephardt	Y	Y	Y	Y	Y	Y	N	N
4 Skelton	Y	Y	Y	Y	Y	Y	Y	N
5 Wheat	Y	Y	Y	Y	Y	Y	N	N
6 ***Coleman***	Y	Y	Y	Y	Y	Y	Y	Y
7 ***Taylor***	Y	Y	Y	Y	Y	N	Y	Y
8 ***Emerson***	Y	Y	Y	Y	Y	Y	Y	Y
9 Volkmer	Y	Y	Y	Y	Y	Y	N	N
MONTANA								
1 Williams	Y	Y	Y	Y	Y	Y	N	N
2 ***Marlenee***	Y	Y	Y	Y	Y	N	N	N
NEBRASKA								
1 ***Bereuter***	Y	N	Y	Y	Y	Y	N	Y
2 ***Daub***	Y	N	Y	Y	Y	Y	Y	Y
3 ***Smith***	Y	N	Y	Y	Y	N	Y	Y
NEVADA								
1 Reid	Y	Y	Y	Y	Y	Y	N	N
2 ***Vucanovich***	Y	N	N	Y	Y	N	Y	Y
NEW HAMPSHIRE								
1 D'Amours	Y	Y	N	Y	Y	Y	Y	Y
2 ***Gregg***	Y	N	N	Y	Y	N	Y	Y
NEW JERSEY								
1 Florio	Y	Y	N	Y	Y	Y	N	N
2 Hughes	Y	Y	N	Y	Y	Y	Y	Y
3 Howard	Y	Y	Y	Y	Y	Y	Y	N
4 ***Smith***	Y	Y	Y	Y	Y	Y	Y	N
5 ***Roukema***	Y	Y	N	Y	Y	Y	Y	N
6 Dwyer	Y	Y	Y	Y	Y	Y	Y	N
7 ***Rinaldo***	Y	Y	N	Y	Y	Y	N	N
8 Roe	Y	Y	Y	Y	Y	Y	N	N
9 Torricelli	Y	Y	Y	?	Y	Y	N	N
10 Rodino	Y	Y	Y	Y	Y	Y	N	N
11 Minish	Y	Y	N	Y	Y	Y	Y	N
12 ***Courter***	Y	Y	N	Y	Y	Y	Y	Y
13 ***Forsythe***	Y	N	N	Y	N	Y	Y	Y
14 Guarini	Y	Y	?	Y	Y	Y	N	N
NEW MEXICO								
1 ***Lujan***	Y	N	N	Y	Y	N	Y	Y
2 ***Skeen***	Y	N	Y	Y	N	Y	Y	Y
3 Richardson	Y	Y	Y	Y	Y	Y	N	N
NEW YORK								
1 ***Carney***	Y	N	N	Y	Y	N	N	N
2 Downey	Y	Y	Y	Y	Y	Y	N	N
3 Mrazek	Y	Y	Y	Y	Y	Y	N	N
4 ***Lent***	Y	Y	N	Y	Y	Y	N	N
5 ***McGrath***	Y	Y	N	Y	Y	Y	N	N
6 Addabbo	Y	Y	Y	Y	Y	Y	N	N
7 Ackerman	Y	Y	Y	Y	Y	Y	N	N
8 Scheuer	Y	Y	Y	Y	Y	?	N	N
9 Ferraro	Y	Y	Y	Y	Y	Y	N	N
10 Schumer	N	Y	Y	Y	Y	Y	N	N
11 Towns	?	Y	Y	Y	Y	Y	N	N
12 Owens	Y	Y	Y	Y	Y	Y	N	N
13 Solarz	Y	Y	Y	Y	Y	Y	N	N
14 ***Molinari***	Y	N	Y	Y	Y	N	N	Y
15 ***Green***	Y	N	N	Y	Y	Y	N	N
16 Rangel	Y	Y	Y	Y	Y	Y	N	N
17 Weiss	Y	Y	Y	Y	Y	Y	N	N
18 Garcia	N	Y	Y	Y	Y	Y	N	?
19 Biaggi	Y	Y	Y	Y	Y	Y	N	N
20 Ottinger	N	Y	Y	Y	Y	Y	N	N
21 ***Fish***	Y	Y	N	Y	Y	Y	Y	N
22 ***Gilman***	?	Y	Y	Y	Y	Y	N	N
23 Stratton	Y	Y	Y	Y	Y	Y	Y	N
24 ***Solomon***	Y	N	Y	Y	Y	N	Y	Y
25 ***Boehlert***	Y	Y	N	Y	Y	Y	Y	N
26 ***Martin***	Y	N	Y	Y	Y	N	Y	N
27 ***Wortley***	Y	N	Y	Y	Y	Y	Y	N
28 McHugh	Y	Y	Y	Y	Y	Y	N	N
29 ***Horton***	Y	Y	N	Y	Y	Y	Y	N
30 ***Conable***	Y	N	N	Y	Y	N	Y	Y
31 ***Kemp***	Y	Y	N	Y	Y	Y	Y	Y
32 LaFalce	Y	Y	Y	Y	Y	Y	Y	N
33 Nowak	Y	Y	Y	Y	Y	Y	N	N
34 Lundine	N	?	?	?	?	Y	N	N

	284	285	286	287	288	289	290	291
NORTH CAROLINA								
1 Jones	Y	Y	Y	Y	Y	Y	Y	N
2 Valentine	Y	Y	Y	Y	Y	Y	Y	Y
3 Whitley	Y	Y	Y	Y	Y	Y	Y	N
4 Andrews	Y	Y	Y	Y	Y	Y	Y	N
5 Neal	?	Y	Y	Y	Y	Y	Y	Y
6 Britt	Y	Y	Y	Y	Y	Y	N	N
7 Rose	?	?	?	?	?	Y	N	N
8 Hefner	Y	Y	Y	Y	Y	Y	Y	N
9 ***Martin***	Y	Y	N	Y	Y	N	N	Y
10 ***Broyhill***	Y	Y	Y	Y	Y	Y	Y	Y
11 Clarke	Y	Y	Y	Y	Y	Y	Y	Y
NORTH DAKOTA								
AL Dorgan	Y	Y	Y	Y	Y	Y	N	N
OHIO								
1 Luken	?	Y	N	Y	Y	Y	N	N
2 ***Gradison***	Y	Y	N	Y	Y	Y	Y	Y
3 Hall	Y	Y	Y	Y	Y	Y	N	N
4 ***Oxley***	Y	Y	N	Y	Y	Y	Y	Y
5 ***Latta***	Y	Y	N	Y	N	N	Y	Y
6 ***McEwen***	Y	Y	N	Y	Y	Y	Y	Y
7 ***DeWine***	Y	Y	Y	Y	Y	Y	Y	Y
8 ***Kindness***	Y	Y	N	N	Y	N	Y	Y
9 Kaptur	Y	Y	Y	Y	Y	Y	N	N
10 ***Miller***	Y	Y	N	Y	Y	N	Y	N
11 Eckart	Y	Y	Y	Y	Y	Y	N	N
12 ***Kasich***	Y	Y	N	Y	Y	Y	Y	Y
13 Pease	Y	Y	Y	Y	Y	Y	Y	N
14 Seiberling	Y	Y	Y	Y	Y	Y	Y	N
15 ***Wylie***	Y	Y	N	Y	Y	Y	Y	N
16 ***Regula***	Y	Y	N	Y	Y	Y	Y	Y
17 ***Williams***	Y	Y	N	Y	Y	Y	Y	N
18 Applegate	Y	Y	Y	Y	Y	N	Y	N
19 Feighan	Y	Y	Y	Y	Y	Y	N	Y
20 Oakar	Y	Y	Y	Y	Y	Y	N	N
21 Stokes	Y	Y	Y	Y	Y	Y	N	N
OKLAHOMA								
1 Jones	Y	Y	Y	Y	Y	Y	Y	Y
2 Synar	Y	Y	Y	Y	Y	Y	Y	N
3 Watkins	Y	Y	Y	Y	Y	Y	Y	Y
4 McCurdy	Y	Y	Y	Y	Y	Y	Y	Y
5 ***Edwards***	Y	N	Y	Y	Y	Y	Y	Y
6 English	Y	Y	Y	Y	Y	Y	Y	Y
OREGON								
1 AuCoin	Y	Y	Y	Y	Y	Y	N	N
2 ***Smith, R.***	Y	Y	Y	Y	Y	N	Y	Y
3 Wyden	Y	Y	N	Y	Y	Y	N	N
4 Weaver	?	?	?	?	?	?	?	?
5 ***Smith, D.***	Y	N	Y	N	N	N	Y	Y
PENNSYLVANIA								
1 Foglietta	Y	Y	Y	Y	Y	Y	N	N
2 Gray	Y	?	Y	Y	Y	Y	N	N
3 Borski	Y	Y	Y	Y	Y	Y	N	N
4 Kolter	Y	Y	Y	Y	Y	Y	N	N
5 ***Schulze***	Y	N	N	Y	Y	Y	Y	Y
6 Yatron	Y	Y	Y	Y	Y	Y	N	N
7 Edgar	?	Y	Y	Y	Y	Y	N	N
8 Kostmayer	Y	Y	Y	Y	Y	Y	N	N
9 ***Shuster***	Y	N	N	N	Y	N	Y	Y
10 ***McDade***	Y	N	N	Y	Y	Y	Y	Y
11 Harrison	Y	Y	Y	Y	Y	Y	N	N
12 Murtha	Y	Y	Y	Y	Y	Y	Y	N
13 ***Coughlin***	Y	N	Y	Y	Y	Y	Y	N
14 Coyne	Y	Y	Y	Y	Y	Y	N	N
15 ***Ritter***	Y	N	N	Y	Y	Y	Y	Y
16 ***Walker***	Y	N	N	Y	Y	Y	N	Y
17 ***Gekas***	Y	N	Y	Y	Y	Y	Y	Y
18 Walgren	Y	Y	Y	Y	Y	Y	N	N
19 ***Goodling***	Y	?	?	?	?	N	Y	Y
20 Gaydos	Y	Y	Y	Y	Y	Y	N	N
21 ***Ridge***	Y	Y	Y	Y	Y	Y	Y	N
22 Murphy	Y	Y	Y	Y	Y	Y	Y	N
23 ***Clinger***	Y	Y	N	Y	Y	N	N	N
RHODE ISLAND								
1 St Germain	?	?	?	?	?	?	Y	N
2 ***Schneider***	Y	Y	N	Y	Y	Y	Y	N
SOUTH CAROLINA								
1 ***Hartnett***	Y	N	Y	N	N	Y	Y	Y
2 ***Spence***	Y	N	Y	Y	Y	N	Y	Y
3 Derrick	Y	Y	Y	Y	Y	Y	N	N
4 ***Campbell***	Y	Y	Y	Y	Y	N	Y	Y
5 Spratt	Y	Y	Y	Y	Y	Y	N	N
6 Tallon	Y	Y	Y	Y	Y	Y	Y	N
SOUTH DAKOTA								
AL Daschle	?	Y	Y	Y	Y	Y	N	N

	284	285	286	287	288	289	290	291
TENNESSEE								
1 ***Quillen***	Y	N	N	Y	Y	N	Y	Y
2 ***Duncan***	Y	Y	Y	Y	Y	Y	N	Y
3 Lloyd	Y	Y	Y	Y	Y	Y	N	N
4 Cooper	Y	Y	Y	Y	Y	Y	Y	N
5 Boner	Y	Y	Y	Y	Y	Y	Y	N
6 Gore	?	Y	Y	Y	Y	Y	N	N
7 ***Sundquist***	Y	Y	Y	Y	Y	N	N	N
8 Jones	Y	Y	Y	Y	Y	Y	Y	N
9 Ford	Y	Y	Y	Y	Y	Y	N	N
TEXAS								
1 Hall, S.	Y	Y	Y	Y	Y	N	Y	Y
2 Wilson	Y	Y	Y	Y	Y	Y	Y	?
3 ***Bartlett***	Y	N	Y	Y	Y	N	N	Y
4 Hall, R.	Y	Y	Y	Y	N	Y	N	N
5 Bryant	Y	Y	Y	Y	Y	Y	N	N
6 ***Gramm***	Y	N	Y	N	N	N	Y	Y
7 ***Archer***	Y	N	N	Y	Y	N	Y	Y
8 ***Fields***	Y	N	Y	Y	Y	N	Y	Y
9 Brooks	Y	Y	Y	Y	Y	Y	Y	Y
10 Pickle	Y	Y	Y	Y	Y	Y	Y	Y
11 Leath	Y	N	Y	N	N	N	Y	Y
12 Wright	Y	Y	Y	Y	Y	Y	Y	?
13 Hightower	Y	Y	Y	Y	Y	Y	Y	Y
14 Patman	Y	Y	Y	Y	N	Y	N	Y
15 de la Garza	Y	Y	Y	Y	Y	Y	N	N
16 Coleman	Y	Y	Y	Y	Y	Y	N	Y
17 Stenholm	Y	N	Y	Y	Y	N	Y	Y
18 Leland	Y	Y	Y	Y	Y	Y	N	N
19 Hance	?	Y	Y	Y	Y	Y	N	N
20 Gonzalez	Y	Y	Y	Y	Y	Y	N	N
21 ***Loeffler***	?	N	Y	Y	N	N	Y	Y
22 ***Paul***	Y	N	Y	N	N	N	Y	Y
23 Kazen	Y	Y	Y	Y	Y	Y	N	N
24 Frost	Y	Y	Y	Y	Y	Y	Y	N
25 Andrews	Y	Y	Y	Y	Y	Y	Y	Y
26 Vandergriff	Y	Y	Y	Y	Y	Y	N	N
27 Ortiz	Y	Y	Y	Y	Y	Y	Y	N
UTAH								
1 ***Hansen***	Y	N	Y	N	Y	N	Y	Y
2 ***Marriott***	Y	N	N	Y	Y	N	Y	Y
3 ***Nielson***	Y	N	N	Y	Y	N	Y	Y
VERMONT								
AL ***Jeffords***	Y	Y	Y	Y	Y	N	N	?
VIRGINIA								
1 ***Bateman***	Y	N	N	Y	Y	N	Y	N
2 ***Whitehurst***	Y	Y	N	Y	Y	N	Y	Y
3 ***Bliley***	Y	N	?	Y	Y	Y	Y	Y
4 Sisisky	Y	Y	Y	Y	Y	Y	Y	N
5 Daniel	Y	N	Y	Y	Y	N	Y	Y
6 Olin	Y	N	Y	Y	Y	Y	Y	Y
7 ***Robinson***	Y	N	Y	Y	Y	N	Y	Y
8 ***Parris***	Y	Y	N	Y	Y	Y	Y	Y
9 Boucher	Y	Y	Y	Y	Y	Y	N	N
10 ***Wolf***	Y	Y	N	Y	Y	Y	Y	Y
WASHINGTON								
1 ***Pritchard***	Y	N	N	Y	Y	Y	Y	Y
2 Swift	Y	Y	Y	Y	Y	Y	N	N
3 Bonker	Y	Y	Y	Y	Y	Y	N	N
4 ***Morrison***	Y	N	Y	Y	Y	Y	Y	N
5 Foley	Y	Y	Y	Y	Y	Y	N	N
6 Dicks	Y	Y	Y	Y	Y	Y	N	N
7 Lowry	N	Y	Y	Y	Y	Y	N	N
8 ***Chandler***	Y	N	Y	Y	Y	Y	Y	N
WEST VIRGINIA								
1 Mollohan	Y	Y	Y	Y	Y	Y	N	N
2 Staggers	Y	Y	Y	Y	Y	Y	N	N
3 Wise	Y	Y	Y	Y	Y	Y	N	N
4 Rahall	Y	Y	Y	Y	Y	Y	N	N
WISCONSIN								
1 Aspin	Y	Y	Y	Y	Y	Y	N	N
2 Kastenmeier	N	Y	Y	Y	Y	Y	N	N
3 ***Gunderson***	Y	Y	Y	Y	Y	Y	N	Y
4 Zablocki	Y	Y	Y	Y	Y	Y	N	N
5 Moody	Y	Y	Y	Y	Y	Y	Y	N
6 ***Petri***	Y	Y	Y	Y	Y	N	Y	Y
7 Obey	Y	Y	Y	Y	Y	Y	Y	Y
8 ***Roth***	Y	Y	Y	Y	Y	N	Y	Y
9 ***Sensenbrenner***	Y	Y	Y	Y	Y	N	Y	Y
WYOMING								
AL ***Cheney***	Y	N	Y	N	Y	Y	Y	Y

Southern states - Ala., Ark., Fla., Ga., Ky., La., Miss., N.C., Okla., S.C., Tenn., Texas, Va.

292. HR 2780. Revenue Sharing. Horton, R-N.Y., amendment to reduce entitlement funding for local governments to $5.02 billion annually, the level assumed in the first fiscal 1984 budget resolution (H Con Res 91), from the $5.3 billion under the bill as reported. Adopted 381-43: R 159-4; D 222-39 (ND 138-35, SD 84-4), Aug. 2, 1983.

293. HR 2780. Revenue Sharing. Williams, R-Ohio, amendment to distribute any increase in funding over $4.6 billion only to localities in counties where the unemployment rate was equal to or greater than the national unemployment rate for the previous year, the formula to be weighted to the advantage of counties with the highest unemployment rates. Rejected 154-259: R 48-111; D 106-148 (ND 92-75, SD 14-73), Aug. 2, 1983.

294. HR 2780. Revenue Sharing. McCandless, R-Calif., amendment to delete from the bill an annual authorization of $2.3 billion in revenue sharing for state governments that applied for funds and received an appropriation of them from Congress. Adopted 218-193: R 113-46; D 105-147 (ND 40-126, SD 65-21), Aug. 2, 1983.

295. HR 2780. Revenue Sharing. Levin, D-Mich., amendment to change the factors used in the formula for allocating revenue sharing funds among the states for distribution to local governments so as to take into account all potential revenue available in each state, rather than just personal income. Rejected 192-220: R 55-100; D 137-120 (ND 123-48, SD 14-72), Aug. 2, 1983.

296. HR 2780. Revenue Sharing. Passage of the bill to reauthorize the general revenue sharing program from Oct. 1, 1983, through Sept. 30, 1986, and entitle governments eligible to receive such funds to share $5.02 billion per year. Passed 381-35: R 134-24; D 247-11 (ND 168-3, SD 79-8), Aug. 2, 1983.

297. Procedural Motion. Bartlett, R-Texas, motion to approve the House *Journal* of Tuesday, Aug. 2. Motion agreed to 356-24: R 137-12; D 219-12 (ND 141-10, SD 78-2), Aug. 3, 1983.

298. HR 3021. Unemployment Health Insurance. Adoption of the rule (H Res 276) providing for House floor consideration of the bill to authorize $4 billion in fiscal 1983-85, for block grants to states for health insurance plans for the unemployed, and for grants to hospitals caring for needy, uninsured people. The bill also required certain changes in employment-based private group health insurance plans to continue coverage for laid-off workers. Adopted 227-196: R 0-165; D 227-31 (ND 164-10, SD 63-21), Aug. 3, 1983.

299. HR 3021. Unemployment Health Insurance. Tauke, R-Iowa, motion to recommit the bill to the Energy and Commerce Committee with instructions to substitute a $1.8 billion authorization for block grants to states for health insurance plans for the unemployed, with funding contingent on appropriations and without mandated state contributions and certain other requirements. Motion rejected 171-255: R 153-12; D 18-243 (ND 3-169, SD 15-74), Aug. 3, 1983.

KEY

Y Voted for (yea).
Paired for.
+ Announced for.
N Voted against (nay).
X Paired against.
- Announced against.
P Voted "present".
C Voted "present" to avoid possible conflict of interest.
? Did not vote or otherwise make a position known.

Democrats   *Republicans*

	292	293	294	295	296	297	298	299
ALABAMA								
1 Edwards	Y	N	N	N	Y	?	N	Y
2 Dickinson	Y	N	N	N	Y	N	N	X
3 Nichols	Y	Y	N	N	Y	N	Y	N
4 Bevill	Y	Y	Y	N	Y	Y	Y	N
5 Flippo	Y	N	Y	N	Y	Y	N	N
6 Erdreich	Y	Y	N	Y	Y	Y	Y	N
7 Shelby	Y	Y	N	Y	Y	Y	N	N
ALASKA								
AL Young	?	N	Y	N	Y	?	N	N
ARIZONA								
1 McCain	Y	N	Y	N	Y	Y	Y	N
2 Udall	Y	N	Y	Y	Y	Y	Y	N
3 Stump	Y	N	Y	N	Y	N	Y	N
4 Rudd	Y	N	Y	Y	Y	Y	Y	N
5 McNulty	Y	N	Y	Y	Y	Y	N	N
ARKANSAS								
1 Alexander	Y	N	Y	N	Y	Y	?	N
2 Bethune	Y	N	Y	N	Y	N	N	Y
3 Hammerschmidt	Y	N	N	N	Y	Y	N	Y
4 Anthony	Y	N	N	N	Y	?	Y	N
CALIFORNIA								
1 Bosco	?	?	?	Y	Y	Y	Y	N
2 Chappie	Y	N	Y	N	Y	?	N	Y
3 Matsui	Y	Y	N	Y	Y	Y	Y	N
4 Fazio	Y	N	N	Y	Y	Y	Y	N
5 Burton	N	N	N	N	Y	Y	N	N
6 Boxer	N	N	N	N	Y	N	N	N
7 Miller	Y	Y	Y	N	Y	Y	Y	N
8 Dellums	N	Y	N	Y	Y	N	N	N
9 Stark	Y	?	?	Y	Y	Y	N	N
10 Edwards	N	N	N	N	Y	Y	Y	N
11 Lantos	Y	N	Y	Y	Y	Y	Y	N
12 Zschau	Y	N	Y	N	Y	Y	N	Y
13 Mineta	Y	?	?	N	Y	Y	Y	N
14 Shumway	Y	N	Y	N	Y	Y	N	Y
15 Coelho	Y	Y	Y	Y	Y	Y	Y	N
16 Panetta	Y	N	N	N	Y	Y	Y	N
17 Pashayan	Y	N	N	N	Y	Y	N	Y
18 Lehman	Y	N	N	Y	Y	Y	Y	N
19 Lagomarsino	Y	N	Y	N	Y	Y	N	Y
20 Thomas	Y	N	N	N	Y	Y	N	Y
21 Fiedler	Y	N	Y	N	Y	?	N	Y
22 Moorhead	Y	?	Y	N	Y	Y	N	Y
23 Beilenson	Y	N	N	Y	Y	Y	Y	N
24 Waxman	Y	N	N	Y	Y	Y	Y	N
25 Roybal	Y	N	N	N	Y	Y	Y	N
26 Berman	N	Y	Y	Y	Y	Y	Y	N
27 Levine	Y	N	N	N	Y	Y	Y	N
28 Dixon	Y	Y	?	Y	Y	Y	Y	N
29 Hawkins	Y	Y	Y	Y	Y	Y	Y	N
30 Martinez	Y	N	N	N	Y	?	Y	N
31 Dymally	N	Y	N	Y	Y	P	Y	N
32 Anderson	N	N	Y	Y	Y	Y	Y	?
33 Dreier	Y	N	Y	N	N	Y	N	Y
34 Torres	Y	Y	N	N	Y	Y	Y	N
35 Lewis	Y	?	Y	N	Y	Y	N	Y
36 Brown	N	Y	Y	Y	Y	?	Y	N
37 McCandless	Y	N	Y	N	Y	Y	N	Y
38 Patterson	Y	N	N	N	Y	Y	Y	N
39 Dannemeyer	Y	N	Y	N	N	Y	N	Y
40 Badham	Y	N	Y	N	Y	N	Y	N
41 Lowery	Y	N	Y	?	?	Y	N	Y
42 Lungren	Y	N	Y	N	N	Y	N	Y

	292	293	294	295	296	297	298	299
43 Packard	Y	N	Y	N	Y	Y	N	Y
44 Bates	Y	Y	Y	Y	Y	Y	Y	N
45 Hunter	Y	N	Y	N	Y	Y	N	Y
COLORADO								
1 Schroeder	Y	Y	Y	N	Y	N	N	N
2 Wirth	Y	N	Y	N	Y	Y	Y	N
3 Kogovsek	Y	Y	N	N	Y	Y	Y	N
4 Brown	Y	N	Y	N	N	N	N	Y
5 Kramer	Y	N	Y	N	Y	Y	N	Y
6 Schaefer	Y	N	Y	N	Y	Y	N	Y
CONNECTICUT								
1 Kennelly	Y	N	Y	Y	Y	Y	Y	N
2 Gejdenson	N	N	N	Y	N	Y	N	N
3 Morrison	Y	N	Y	N	Y	Y	Y	N
4 McKinney	Y	N	Y	Y	Y	Y	Y	N
5 Ratchford	Y	N	Y	Y	Y	Y	Y	N
6 Johnson	N	N	N	N	Y	?	N	Y
DELAWARE								
AL Carper	Y	N	Y	N	Y	Y	Y	N
FLORIDA								
1 Hutto	Y	N	Y	N	Y	Y	Y	N
2 Fuqua	Y	N	Y	N	Y	Y	Y	N
3 Bennett	Y	N	Y	N	Y	N	Y	N
4 Chappell	Y	N	Y	N	Y	Y	Y	N
5 McCollum	Y	N	Y	N	Y	Y	?	N
6 MacKay	Y	N	N	N	Y	?	Y	N
7 Gibbons	Y	N	Y	N	Y	Y	Y	N
8 Young	Y	N	Y	N	Y	Y	Y	N
9 Bilirakis	Y	N	Y	N	Y	Y	Y	N
10 Ireland	Y	N	Y	N	Y	?	?	Y
11 Nelson	Y	N	Y	N	Y	Y	Y	N
12 Lewis	Y	N	Y	N	Y	Y	Y	N
13 Mack	Y	N	Y	N	N	Y	N	Y
14 Mica	Y	N	Y	N	Y	?	Y	N
15 Shaw	Y	N	Y	N	Y	Y	N	Y
16 Smith	Y	N	N	N	Y	Y	Y	N
17 Lehman	Y	N	Y	N	Y	Y	Y	N
18 Pepper	Y	N	?	N	Y	Y	Y	N
19 Fascell	Y	N	Y	N	Y	Y	Y	N
GEORGIA								
1 Thomas	Y	N	N	N	Y	N	N	N
2 Hatcher	Y	N	N	N	Y	Y	Y	N
3 Ray	Y	N	Y	N	Y	Y	Y	N
4 Levitas	Y	N	N	N	Y	Y	Y	N
5 Fowler	Y	N	N	N	Y	Y	Y	N
6 Gingrich	Y	N	?	?	Y	Y	N	Y
7 McDonald	Y	N	Y	N	Y	N	Y	N
8 Rowland	Y	N	Y	N	Y	Y	N	N
9 Jenkins	Y	N	Y	N	Y	Y	N	N
10 Barnard	Y	N	Y	Y	Y	Y	N	Y
HAWAII								
1 Heftel	?	?	?	?	?	?	?	?
2 Akaka	Y	N	N	Y	Y	Y	Y	N
IDAHO								
1 Craig	Y	N	Y	N	Y	Y	N	Y
2 Hansen	?	?	?	?	?	?	N	Y
ILLINOIS								
1 Vacancy								
2 Savage	N	Y	N	Y	Y	Y	Y	N
3 Russo	N	Y	N	Y	Y	Y	Y	N
4 O'Brien	Y	Y	?	?	Y	Y	Y	N
5 Lipinski	Y	N	?	?	?	N	Y	N
6 Hyde	Y	N	Y	Y	Y	Y	N	Y
7 Collins	N	Y	N	Y	Y	Y	Y	N
8 Rostenkowski	Y	Y	Y	Y	Y	Y	Y	N
9 Yates	Y	N	Y	Y	Y	Y	Y	N
10 Porter	Y	N	Y	N	Y	Y	Y	N
11 Annunzio	Y	Y	Y	Y	Y	Y	Y	N
12 Crane, P.	Y	N	N	N	N	Y	N	Y
13 Erlenborn	?	?	?	?	?	Y	N	Y
14 Corcoran	Y	Y	Y	?	Y	Y	N	Y
15 Madigan	Y	Y	Y	Y	Y	N	N	N
16 Martin	Y	Y	Y	Y	Y	?	N	Y
17 Evans	Y	Y	N	Y	Y	Y	Y	N
18 Michel	Y	Y	Y	Y	Y	Y	N	Y
19 Crane, D.	Y	Y	Y	N	Y	N	Y	N
20 Durbin	Y	Y	N	Y	Y	Y	Y	N
21 Price	Y	Y	Y	Y	Y	Y	Y	N
22 Simon	Y	?	Y	Y	Y	Y	Y	N
INDIANA								
1 Hall	Y	Y	N	Y	Y	Y	Y	N
2 Sharp	Y	Y	Y	Y	Y	Y	Y	N
3 Hiler	Y	N	Y	N	Y	N	Y	N
4 Coats	Y	Y	Y	N	Y	Y	N	Y
5 Hillis	Y	Y	Y	N	Y	Y	N	Y

ND - Northern Democrats   SD - Southern Democrats

Corresponding to Congressional Record Votes 308, 309, 310, 311, 312, 313, 314, 315

	292	293	294	295	296	297	298	299
6 ***Burton***	Y	Y	Y	N	Y	Y	N	Y
7 ***Myers***	Y	N	Y	N	Y	Y	N	Y
8 McCloskey	Y	N	N	Y	Y	?	Y	N
9 Hamilton	Y	N	N	Y	Y	Y	Y	N
10 Jacobs	Y	Y	Y	Y	N	P	N	N
IOWA								
1 ***Leach***	Y	N	Y	N	Y	Y	N	Y
2 ***Tauke***	Y	Y	N	N	Y	Y	N	Y
3 ***Evans***	Y	N	Y	N	Y	N	N	Y
4 Smith	Y	N	Y	N	Y	Y	Y	N
5 Harkin	Y	N	Y	N	Y	N	Y	N
6 Bedell	Y	N	Y	Y	Y	Y	Y	N
KANSAS								
1 ***Roberts***	Y	N	Y	N	N	N	N	Y
2 Slattery	Y	N	Y	N	Y	Y	Y	N
3 ***Winn***	Y	N	Y	N	Y	?	N	Y
4 Glickman	Y	N	Y	N	N	Y	Y	N
5 ***Whittaker***	Y	N	Y	N	Y	Y	N	Y
KENTUCKY								
1 Hubbard	Y	N	Y	N	Y	Y	Y	N
2 Natcher	Y	N	N	N	Y	Y	Y	N
3 Mazzoli	Y	N	N	N	Y	Y	Y	N
4 ***Snyder***	Y	N	Y	N	Y	Y	N	Y
5 ***Rogers***	Y	Y	Y	N	Y	Y	N	Y
6 ***Hopkins***	Y	N	Y	N	Y	Y	N	Y
7 Perkins	N	Y	N	N	Y	Y	Y	N
LOUISIANA								
1 ***Livingston***	Y	Y	Y	N	Y	Y	N	Y
2 Boggs	Y	N	Y	N	Y	Y	Y	N
3 Tauzin	Y	N	Y	N	Y	Y	N	Y
4 Roemer	Y	N	Y	N	N	N	N	Y
5 Huckaby	Y	N	Y	N	Y	Y	N	Y
6 ***Moore***	Y	N	Y	N	Y	Y	N	Y
7 Breaux	Y	N	Y	N	Y	Y	Y	Y
8 Long	Y	Y	Y	N	Y	Y	Y	N
MAINE								
1 ***McKernan***	Y	N	N	Y	Y	Y	N	Y
2 ***Snowe***	Y	N	N	Y	Y	?	N	Y
MARYLAND								
1 Dyson	Y	N	N	Y	Y	?	Y	N
2 Long	Y	?	Y	Y	Y	Y	Y	N
3 Mikulski	Y	Y	N	Y	Y	?	Y	N
4 ***Holt***	Y	N	Y	Y	N	Y	N	Y
5 Hoyer	Y	N	N	Y	Y	Y	Y	N
6 Byron	Y	N	Y	Y	Y	?	Y	N
7 Mitchell	N	Y	N	Y	Y	?	Y	N
8 Barnes	Y	N	N	Y	Y	Y	Y	N
MASSACHUSETTS								
1 ***Conte***	Y	Y	N	Y	Y	Y	N	Y
2 Boland	Y	N	N	Y	Y	Y	Y	N
3 Early	N	N	N	Y	Y	Y	Y	N
4 Frank	N	N	?	Y	Y	Y	Y	N
5 Shannon	N	N	N	Y	Y	?	Y	N
6 Mavroules	Y	N	N	Y	Y	Y	Y	N
7 Markey	N	N	N	Y	Y	N	Y	N
8 O'Neill								
9 Moakley	Y	N	N	Y	Y	Y	Y	N
10 Studds	N	N	N	Y	Y	Y	Y	N
11 Donnelly	Y	N	Y	Y	Y	Y	Y	N
MICHIGAN								
1 Conyers	N	Y	N	Y	Y	?	Y	N
2 ***Pursell***	Y	Y	N	N	Y	Y	N	Y
3 Wolpe	Y	Y	N	Y	Y	Y	Y	N
4 ***Siljander***	Y	Y	Y	Y	Y	Y	N	Y
5 ***Sawyer***	Y	Y	N	Y	Y	Y	N	Y
6 Carr	Y	Y	N	Y	Y	Y	Y	N
7 Kildee	Y	Y	N	Y	Y	Y	Y	N
8 Traxler	Y	Y	N	Y	Y	Y	Y	N
9 ***Vander Jagt***	Y	Y	Y	Y	Y	Y	N	Y
10 Albosta	Y	Y	Y	Y	Y	Y	Y	N
11 ***Davis***	N	Y	N	Y	Y	Y	N	N
12 Bonior	Y	Y	N	Y	Y	Y	Y	N
13 Crockett	Y	Y	N	Y	Y	Y	Y	N
14 Hertel	Y	Y	N	Y	Y	Y	Y	N
15 Ford	Y	Y	N	Y	Y	?	Y	N
16 Dingell	Y	Y	N	Y	Y	?	Y	N
17 Levin	Y	Y	N	Y	Y	Y	Y	N
18 ***Broomfield***	Y	Y	Y	Y	Y	Y	N	Y
MINNESOTA								
1 Penny	Y	N	Y	Y	Y	Y	Y	Y
2 ***Weber***	Y	N	?	?	?	Y	N	Y
3 ***Frenzel***	Y	N	Y	N	Y	N	N	Y
4 Vento	Y	N	Y	Y	Y	Y	Y	N
5 Sabo	Y	N	N	Y	Y	?	Y	N
6 Sikorski	Y	N	Y	Y	Y	N	Y	N
7 ***Stangeland***	Y	N	Y	N	Y	Y	N	Y
8 Oberstar	Y	Y	N	Y	Y	P	Y	N
MISSISSIPPI								
1 Whitten	Y	N	Y	N	Y	Y	Y	N
2 ***Franklin***	Y	N	Y	N	Y	Y	N	Y
3 Montgomery	Y	N	Y	N	Y	Y	Y	Y
4 Dowdy	Y	N	Y	N	Y	Y	Y	N
5 ***Lott***	Y	N	Y	N	Y	Y	N	Y
MISSOURI								
1 Clay	Y	Y	N	Y	Y	?	Y	N
2 Young	Y	N	N	N	Y	Y	N	N
3 Gephardt	Y	N	N	Y	Y	Y	Y	N
4 Skelton	Y	N	Y	N	Y	Y	Y	N
5 Wheat	N	N	N	Y	Y	Y	Y	N
6 ***Coleman***	Y	N	Y	N	Y	Y	N	Y
7 ***Taylor***	Y	N	Y	N	Y	Y	N	Y
8 ***Emerson***	Y	N	Y	N	Y	N	N	Y
9 Volkmer	Y	N	Y	N	Y	Y	N	N
MONTANA								
1 Williams	Y	Y	N	N	Y	Y	Y	N
2 ***Marlenee***	N	N	N	N	Y	Y	N	Y
NEBRASKA								
1 ***Bereuter***	Y	N	N	N	Y	Y	N	Y
2 ***Daub***	Y	N	N	N	Y	Y	N	Y
3 ***Smith***	Y	N	N	N	Y	Y	N	Y
NEVADA								
1 Reid	Y	Y	N	N	Y	Y	Y	N
2 ***Vucanovich***	Y	N	Y	N	Y	Y	N	Y
NEW HAMPSHIRE								
1 D'Amours	Y	N	Y	N	Y	Y	Y	N
2 ***Gregg***	Y	N	Y	N	N	Y	N	Y
NEW JERSEY								
1 Florio	N	Y	N	Y	Y	Y	Y	N
2 Hughes	Y	Y	N	Y	N	Y	Y	Y
3 Howard	N	Y	N	Y	Y	Y	Y	N
4 ***Smith***	Y	N	N	Y	Y	Y	N	N
5 ***Roukema***	Y	N	N	Y	Y	?	N	Y
6 Dwyer	Y	N	N	Y	Y	Y	Y	N
7 ***Rinaldo***	Y	N	N	Y	Y	Y	N	N
8 Roe	N	Y	N	Y	Y	Y	Y	N
9 Torricelli	Y	N	N	Y	Y	Y	Y	N
10 Rodino	N	Y	N	Y	Y	Y	Y	N
11 Minish	Y	Y	N	Y	Y	Y	Y	N
12 ***Courter***	Y	Y	N	Y	Y	Y	N	Y
13 ***Forsythe***	Y	?	?	Y	Y	N	N	Y
14 Guarini	Y	Y	N	Y	Y	Y	Y	N
NEW MEXICO								
1 ***Lujan***	Y	N	Y	N	Y	Y	N	Y
2 ***Skeen***	Y	N	Y	N	Y	Y	N	Y
3 Richardson	Y	Y	N	N	Y	Y	Y	N
NEW YORK								
1 ***Carney***	Y	N	N	Y	Y	Y	N	Y
2 Downey	Y	N	N	Y	Y	Y	Y	N
3 Mrazek	Y	N	N	Y	Y	Y	N	N
4 ***Lent***	Y	N	N	Y	Y	Y	N	Y
5 ***McGrath***	Y	N	N	Y	Y	Y	N	Y
6 Addabbo	Y	N	N	N	Y	Y	Y	N
7 Ackerman	Y	N	N	N	Y	Y	Y	·
8 Scheuer	Y	N	N	Y	Y	Y	Y	N
9 Ferraro	Y	N	N	N	Y	Y	Y	N
10 Schumer	N	N	N	N	Y	Y	Y	N
11 Towns	Y	Y	N	N	Y	Y	Y	N
12 Owens	Y	Y	N	N	Y	?	Y	N
13 Solarz	Y	N	N	Y	Y	Y	Y	N
14 ***Molinari***	Y	N	N	N	Y	Y	N	Y
15 ***Green***	N	N	N	Y	Y	Y	N	Y
16 Rangel	Y	Y	N	N	Y	Y	Y	N
17 Weiss	Y	N	N	N	Y	Y	Y	N
18 Garcia	Y	N	N	N	Y	Y	Y	N
19 Biaggi	N	?	?	?	?	Y	Y	N
20 Ottinger	Y	N	N	N	Y	?	Y	N
21 ***Fish***	Y	N	N	Y	Y	Y	N	Y
22 ***Gilman***	Y	N	N	Y	Y	Y	N	N
23 Stratton	Y	N	Y	N	Y	Y	Y	N
24 ***Solomon***	Y	N	Y	N	Y	Y	N	Y
25 ***Boehlert***	Y	N	N	Y	Y	Y	N	N
26 ***Martin***	Y	N	N	Y	Y	Y	N	Y
27 ***Wortley***	Y	N	N	Y	Y	Y	N	Y
28 McHugh	Y	N	N	Y	Y	?	Y	N
29 ***Horton***	Y	N	N	N	Y	Y	N	Y
30 ***Conable***	Y	N	Y	Y	Y	Y	N	Y
31 ***Kemp***	Y	Y	Y	?	?	Y	N	Y
32 LaFalce	Y	Y	N	Y	Y	Y	Y	N
33 Nowak	N	Y	N	Y	Y	Y	Y	N
34 Lundine	Y	?	Y	Y	Y	Y	Y	N
NORTH CAROLINA								
1 Jones	Y	N	Y	N	Y	Y	?	N
2 Valentine	Y	N	Y	N	Y	Y	Y	N
3 Whitley	Y	N	Y	N	Y	Y	Y	N
4 Andrews	Y	N	Y	N	Y	Y	Y	N
5 Neal	Y	N	Y	N	Y	Y	Y	N
6 Britt	Y	N	N	N	Y	Y	Y	N
7 Rose	Y	?	?	?	#	?	?	N
8 Hefner	Y	N	Y	N	Y	Y	Y	N
9 ***Martin***	Y	N	N	N	Y	?	N	?
10 ***Broyhill***	Y	N	Y	N	Y	Y	N	Y
11 Clarke	Y	N	Y	N	Y	Y	Y	N
NORTH DAKOTA								
AL Dorgan	Y	N	N	N	Y	N	Y	N
OHIO								
1 Luken	Y	Y	N	Y	Y	Y	Y	N
2 ***Gradison***	Y	Y	Y	Y	Y	Y	N	Y
3 Hall	Y	Y	N	Y	Y	Y	Y	N
4 ***Oxley***	Y	Y	Y	N	Y	Y	N	Y
5 ***Latta***	Y	Y	Y	Y	Y	N	N	Y
6 ***McEwen***	Y	Y	Y	Y	Y	Y	N	Y
7 ***DeWine***	Y	Y	Y	N	Y	Y	N	Y
8 ***Kindness***	Y	Y	Y	Y	Y	Y	N	Y
9 Kaptur	Y	Y	N	Y	Y	Y	Y	N
10 ***Miller***	Y	Y	Y	Y	Y	N	N	Y
11 Eckart	Y	Y	N	Y	Y	N	Y	N
12 ***Kasich***	Y	Y	Y	N	Y	Y	N	Y
13 Pease	Y	Y	Y	Y	Y	Y	Y	N
14 Seiberling	Y	Y	N	Y	Y	Y	Y	N
15 ***Wylie***	Y	Y	Y	N	Y	Y	N	Y
16 ***Regula***	Y	Y	Y	N	Y	Y	N	Y
17 ***Williams***	Y	Y	N	Y	Y	?	N	N
18 Applegate	N	Y	Y	Y	Y	Y	Y	N
19 Feighan	Y	Y	N	Y	Y	?	Y	N
20 Oakar	Y	Y	N	Y	Y	Y	Y	N
21 Stokes	Y	Y	N	Y	Y	?	?	#
OKLAHOMA								
1 Jones	Y	N	Y	N	N	Y	Y	N
2 Synar	Y	N	Y	N	Y	Y	Y	N
3 Watkins	Y	N	Y	N	Y	Y	?	N
4 McCurdy	Y	N	Y	N	N	?	Y	Y
5 ***Edwards***	Y	N	Y	?	?	Y	N	Y
6 English	Y	N	Y	N	N	Y	Y	Y
OREGON								
1 AuCoin	Y	Y	Y	N	Y	Y	N	N
2 ***Smith, R.***	Y	N	Y	N	Y	?	N	Y
3 Wyden	Y	Y	N	Y	Y	Y	Y	N
4 Weaver	?	?	?	?	?	?	Y	N
5 ***Smith, D.***	Y	N	Y	N	N	N	N	Y
PENNSYLVANIA								
1 Foglietta	N	Y	N	Y	Y	Y	Y	N
2 Gray	N	Y	N	Y	Y	Y	Y	N
3 Borski	Y	Y	N	Y	Y	Y	Y	N
4 Kolter	Y	Y	N	Y	Y	Y	Y	N
5 ***Schulze***	Y	Y	N	Y	Y	Y	N	Y
6 Yatron	Y	Y	N	Y	Y	Y	Y	N
7 Edgar	N	N	N	Y	Y	Y	Y	N
8 Kostmayer	N	Y	N	Y	Y	Y	Y	N
9 ***Shuster***	Y	Y	Y	Y	N	Y	N	Y
10 ***McDade***	Y	Y	Y	Y	Y	Y	N	N
11 Harrison	Y	Y	N	Y	Y	Y	Y	N
12 Murtha	Y	Y	Y	Y	Y	Y	Y	N
13 ***Coughlin***	Y	Y	Y	Y	Y	Y	N	Y
14 Coyne	N	Y	N	Y	Y	Y	Y	N
15 ***Ritter***	Y	Y	N	Y	Y	Y	N	N
16 ***Walker***	Y	N	Y	N	Y	Y	N	Y
17 ***Gekas***	Y	Y	N	Y	Y	Y	N	Y
18 Walgren	Y	N	N	Y	Y	Y	Y	N
19 ***Goodling***	Y	Y	Y	Y	N	N	N	Y
20 Gaydos	Y	Y	N	Y	Y	Y	Y	N
21 ***Ridge***	Y	Y	N	Y	Y	Y	N	Y
22 Murphy	Y	Y	Y	Y	Y	N	Y	N
23 ***Clinger***	Y	Y	N	Y	Y	Y	N	Y
RHODE ISLAND								
1 St Germain	Y	N	?	?	?	?	Y	N
2 ***Schneider***	Y	N	N	Y	Y	?	N	Y
SOUTH CAROLINA								
1 ***Hartnett***	Y	N	Y	N	N	Y	N	Y
2 ***Spence***	Y	N	Y	N	Y	Y	N	Y
3 Derrick	Y	N	Y	Y	Y	Y	Y	N
4 ***Campbell***	Y	N	Y	?	?	Y	N	Y
5 Spratt	Y	N	Y	Y	Y	Y	N	N
6 Tallon	Y	N	N	Y	Y	Y	Y	N
SOUTH DAKOTA								
AL Daschle	Y	N	N	N	Y	Y	Y	N
TENNESSEE								
1 ***Quillen***	Y	N	N	N	Y	Y	N	Y
2 ***Duncan***	Y	Y	N	N	Y	Y	N	Y
3 Lloyd	Y	N	Y	Y	Y	Y	N	Y
4 Cooper	Y	N	Y	Y	Y	Y	N	N
5 Boner	Y	N	Y	Y	Y	Y	Y	N
6 Gore	Y	N	Y	Y	Y	Y	Y	N
7 ***Sundquist***	Y	Y	N	N	Y	Y	N	Y
8 Jones	Y	N	Y	Y	Y	Y	Y	N
9 Ford	N	Y	N	Y	Y	Y	Y	N
TEXAS								
1 Hall, S.	Y	N	Y	N	Y	Y	Y	N
2 Wilson	?	?	?	?	?	?	Y	N
3 ***Bartlett***	Y	N	Y	N	Y	Y	N	Y
4 Hall, R.	Y	N	Y	N	Y	?	?	?
5 Bryant	Y	N	Y	N	Y	Y	Y	N
6 ***Gramm***	Y	N	Y	N	N	Y	?	Y
7 ***Archer***	Y	N	Y	N	N	Y	N	Y
8 ***Fields***	Y	Y	Y	N	N	Y	N	Y
9 Brooks	Y	N	Y	N	N	Y	Y	N
10 Pickle	Y	N	Y	N	N	Y	Y	N
11 Leath	Y	N	Y	N	Y	?	N	N
12 Wright	?	?	?	N	Y	Y	Y	N
13 Hightower	Y	N	Y	N	Y	Y	N	Y
14 Patman	Y	N	Y	N	Y	?	N	N
15 de la Garza	Y	Y	Y	N	Y	Y	Y	N
16 Coleman	Y	N	N	?	Y	Y	Y	N
17 Stenholm	Y	N	Y	N	X	N	N	Y
18 Leland	N	Y	N	N	Y	Y	Y	N
19 Hance	Y	Y	Y	N	Y	Y	Y	N
20 Gonzalez	Y	Y	N	N	Y	Y	Y	N
21 ***Loeffler***	Y	N	Y	N	N	Y	N	Y
22 ***Paul***	Y	Y	Y	N	N	Y	N	Y
23 Kazen	N	Y	N	N	Y	Y	N	N
24 Frost	Y	N	Y	N	Y	Y	Y	N
25 Andrews	Y	N	Y	N	Y	Y	Y	N
26 Vandergriff	Y	N	Y	N	Y	Y	Y	N
27 Ortiz	Y	Y	N	N	Y	Y	Y	N
UTAH								
1 ***Hansen***	Y	N	Y	N	N	Y	N	Y
2 ***Marriott***	Y	N	Y	N	Y	Y	N	Y
3 ***Nielson***	Y	N	Y	N	Y	Y	N	Y
VERMONT								
AL ***Jeffords***	?	?	?	?	?	?	?	N
VIRGINIA								
1 ***Bateman***	Y	N	Y	N	Y	Y	N	Y
2 ***Whitehurst***	Y	N	Y	N	Y	Y	N	Y
3 ***Bliley***	Y	N	Y	N	Y	Y	N	Y
4 Sisisky	Y	N	N	Y	Y	Y	Y	N
5 Daniel	Y	N	Y	N	Y	Y	Y	Y
6 Olin	Y	N	Y	N	Y	Y	Y	N
7 ***Robinson***	Y	N	Y	N	Y	Y	N	Y
8 ***Parris***	Y	?	?	Y	Y	?	N	Y
9 Boucher	Y	Y	N	?	Y	Y	Y	N
10 ***Wolf***	Y	N	Y	N	Y	Y	N	Y
WASHINGTON								
1 ***Pritchard***	Y	?	?	?	Y	Y	N	Y
2 Swift	Y	Y	N	N	Y	Y	Y	N
3 Bonker	Y	Y	Y	Y	Y	Y	Y	N
4 ***Morrison***	Y	N	Y	Y	Y	?	N	Y
5 Foley	Y	Y	N	Y	Y	Y	Y	N
6 Dicks	Y	Y	Y	Y	Y	Y	Y	N
7 Lowry	Y	Y	N	N	Y	Y	Y	N
8 ***Chandler***	Y	N	Y	Y	Y	Y	N	Y
WEST VIRGINIA								
1 Mollohan	N	Y	N	N	Y	Y	Y	N
2 Staggers	Y	Y	N	N	Y	Y	Y	N
3 Wise	Y	Y	N	N	Y	Y	Y	N
4 Rahall	N	Y	N	N	Y	Y	Y	N
WISCONSIN								
1 Aspin	Y	N	N	Y	Y	Y	Y	N
2 Kastenmeier	Y	Y	N	Y	Y	Y	Y	N
3 ***Gunderson***	Y	N	N	Y	Y	Y	N	Y
4 Zablocki	Y	Y	N	N	Y	Y	Y	N
5 Moody	Y	Y	N	Y	Y	Y	Y	N
6 ***Petri***	Y	Y	N	Y	Y	Y	N	Y
7 Obey	Y	Y	N	Y	Y	P	Y	N
8 ***Roth***	Y	N	Y	Y	Y	Y	N	Y
9 ***Sensenbrenner***	Y	Y	Y	Y	Y	Y	N	Y
WYOMING								
AL ***Cheney***	Y	N	Y	N	N	Y	N	Y

Southern states - Ala., Ark., Fla., Ga., Ky., La., Miss., N.C., Okla., S.C., Tenn., Texas, Va.

300. HR 3021. Unemployment Health Insurance. Passage of the bill to authorize $4 billion in fiscal 1983-85 for block grants to states for health insurance plans for the unemployed, and for grants to hospitals caring for needy, uninsured people. The bill also required certain changes in employment-based private group health insurance plans to continue coverage for laid-off workers. Passed 252-174: R 37-129; D 215-45 (ND 170-3, SD 45-42), Aug. 3, 1983. A "nay" was a vote supporting the president's position.

301. HR 2957. International Recovery and Financial Stability Act. Gramm, R-Texas, amendment to instruct the U.S. representative to the International Monetary Fund to oppose loans to communist dictatorships. Adopted 242-185: R 140-27; D 102-158 (ND 36-136, SD 66-22), Aug. 3, 1983.

302. HR 2957. International Recovery and Financial Stability Act. St Germain, D-R.I., amendment to the Burton, R-Ind., amendment, instructing the U.S. representative to the International Monetary Fund (IMF) to support policies to bring IMF interest rates in line with market rates. St Germain's amendment effectively gutted the Burton amendment, which would have required the United States to oppose any IMF loan with a rate of interest that is less than the average rate of interest for similar loans guaranteed by the Small Business Administration. Adopted 286-136: R 68-96; D 218-40 (ND 155-15, SD 63-25), Aug. 3, 1983.

303. HR 2957. International Recovery and Financial Stability Act. Corcoran, R-Ill., amendment to strike the increase in the U.S. quota in the International Monetary Fund (IMF) and direct the secretary of the Treasury to encourage the IMF to help foreign countries renegotiate their bank loans on more favorable terms. Rejected 174-249: R 92-72; D 82-177 (ND 49-122, SD 33-55), Aug. 3, 1983. A "nay" was a vote supporting the president's position.

304. HR 2957. International Recovery and Financial Stability Act. Passage of the bill to authorize an $8.4 billion increase in U.S. participation in the International Monetary Fund, extend for two years with some changes the authority for the Export-Import Bank, and provide multilateral development aid. Passed 217-211: R 72-94; D 145-117 (ND 106-68, SD 39-49), Aug. 3, 1983. A "yea" was a vote supporting the president's position.

KEY

Y Voted for (yea).
Paired for.
+ Announced for.
N Voted against (nay).
X Paired against.
- Announced against.
P Voted "present".
C Voted "present" to avoid possible conflict of interest.
? Did not vote or otherwise make a position known.

Democrats   *Republicans*

	300	301	302	303	304
ALABAMA					
1 *Edwards*	N	Y	Y	?	Y
2 *Dickinson*	#	Y	N	Y	N
3 Nichols	Y	Y	N	Y	N
4 Bevill	Y	Y	Y	Y	N
5 Flippo	Y	Y	N	Y	N
6 Erdreich	Y	Y	N	Y	N
7 Shelby	Y	Y	N	Y	N
ALASKA					
AL *Young*	Y	Y	Y	Y	N
ARIZONA					
1 *McCain*	N	Y	Y	Y	N
2 Udall	Y	?	?	N	Y
3 *Stump*	N	Y	N	Y	N
4 *Rudd*	N	Y	N	Y	N
5 McNulty	Y	N	Y	N	Y
ARKANSAS					
1 Alexander	Y	N	Y	N	Y
2 *Bethune*	N	Y	N	Y	N
3 *Hammerschmidt*	N	Y	N	Y	N
4 Anthony	N	Y	Y	N	Y
CALIFORNIA					
1 Bosco	Y	N	Y	N	N
2 *Chappie*	N	Y	N	Y	N
3 Matsui	Y	N	Y	N	Y
4 Fazio	Y	N	Y	N	Y
5 Burton	Y	N	Y	N	Y
6 Boxer	Y	N	Y	N	Y
7 Miller	Y	N	Y	N	Y
8 Dellums	Y	N	Y	N	N
9 Stark	Y	N	Y	?	N
10 Edwards	Y	N	Y	N	Y
11 Lantos	Y	N	Y	N	Y
12 *Zschau*	N	N	Y	N	Y
13 Mineta	Y	N	Y	N	Y
14 *Shumway*	N	Y	N	Y	N
15 Coelho	Y	N	Y	N	Y
16 Panetta	Y	N	Y	N	Y
17 *Pashayan*	N	Y	N	Y	N
18 Lehman	Y	N	Y	N	Y
19 *Lagomarsino*	N	Y	Y	N	Y
20 *Thomas*	N	Y	N	Y	N
21 *Fiedler*	N	Y	N	Y	N
22 *Moorhead*	N	Y	N	Y	N
23 Beilenson	Y	N	Y	N	Y
24 Waxman	Y	N	?	N	Y
25 Roybal	Y	N	Y	N	Y
26 Berman	Y	N	Y	N	Y
27 Levine	Y	N	Y	N	Y
28 Dixon	Y	N	Y	N	Y
29 Hawkins	Y	N	Y	N	Y
30 Martinez	Y	N	Y	N	Y
31 Dymally	Y	N	Y	N	Y
32 Anderson	Y	N	Y	N	N
33 *Dreier*	N	Y	N	Y	N
34 Torres	Y	N	Y	N	Y
35 *Lewis*	N	Y	N	Y	N
36 Brown	Y	N	Y	N	Y
37 *McCandless*	N	Y	N	N	Y
38 Patterson	Y	N	Y	N	Y
39 *Dannemeyer*	N	Y	N	Y	N
40 *Badham*	N	Y	Y	N	Y
41 *Lowery*	N	Y	Y	Y	Y
42 *Lungren*	N	Y	N	Y	N

	300	301	302	303	304
43 *Packard*	N	Y	N	Y	N
44 Bates	Y	N	Y	N	N
45 *Hunter*	N	Y	N	Y	N
COLORADO					
1 Schroeder	Y	Y	Y	N	N
2 Wirth	Y	N	Y	N	Y
3 Kogovsek	Y	Y	Y	Y	N
4 *Brown*	N	Y	N	Y	N
5 *Kramer*	N	Y	N	Y	N
6 *Schaefer*	N	Y	N	Y	N
CONNECTICUT					
1 Kennelly	Y	N	Y	N	Y
2 Gejdenson	Y	N	Y	N	Y
3 Morrison	Y	N	Y	N	Y
4 *McKinney*	Y	N	Y	N	Y
5 Ratchford	Y	N	Y	N	Y
6 *Johnson*	Y	N	Y	N	Y
DELAWARE					
AL Carper	Y	N	Y	N	Y
FLORIDA					
1 Hutto	N	Y	Y	Y	N
2 Fuqua	N	Y	Y	N	N
3 Bennett	Y	Y	N	Y	N
4 Chappell	N	Y	Y	Y	N
5 *McCollum*	N	Y	?	?	X
6 MacKay	N	Y	Y	N	Y
7 Gibbons	Y	N	Y	N	Y
8 *Young*	N	Y	Y	Y	N
9 *Bilirakis*	N	Y	N	Y	N
10 Ireland	N	Y	N	Y	N
11 Nelson	N	Y	Y	Y	Y
12 *Lewis*	N	Y	Y	Y	N
13 *Mack*	N	Y	Y	Y	N
14 Mica	Y	Y	N	Y	N
15 *Shaw*	N	Y	Y	Y	N
16 Smith	Y	N	Y	N	Y
17 Lehman	Y	N	Y	N	Y
18 Pepper	Y	N	Y	N	Y
19 Fascell	Y	N	Y	N	Y
GEORGIA					
1 Thomas	N	Y	Y	N	N
2 Hatcher	N	Y	Y	N	Y
3 Ray	N	Y	Y	N	N
4 Levitas	Y	Y	N	Y	N
5 Fowler	Y	Y	Y	N	Y
6 *Gingrich*	N	Y	N	Y	N
7 McDonald	N	Y	N	Y	N
8 Rowland	Y	Y	Y	Y	N
9 Jenkins	N	Y	N	Y	N
10 Barnard	N	N	Y	N	Y
HAWAII					
1 Heftel	?	?	?	?	?
2 Akaka	Y	N	Y	N	Y
IDAHO					
1 *Craig*	N	Y	N	Y	N
2 *Hansen*	N	Y	N	Y	N
ILLINOIS					
1 Vacancy					
2 Savage	Y	N	Y	N	N
3 Russo	Y	Y	N	Y	N
4 *O'Brien*	Y	Y	Y	N	Y
5 Lipinski	Y	Y	N	Y	N
6 *Hyde*	N	N	N	N	Y
7 Collins	Y	N	Y	N	N
8 Rostenkowski	Y	N	Y	N	Y
9 Yates	Y	N	Y	N	Y
10 *Porter*	N	N	Y	N	Y
11 Annunzio	Y	Y	Y	N	N
12 *Crane, P.*	N	Y	N	Y	N
13 *Erlenborn*	N	N	Y	N	Y
14 *Corcoran*	N	Y	Y	Y	N
15 *Madigan*	Y	N	N	N	Y
16 *Martin*	Y	N	Y	N	Y
17 Evans	Y	N	Y	N	Y
18 *Michel*	N	N	Y	N	Y
19 *Crane, D.*	N	Y	N	Y	N
20 Durbin	Y	N	Y	N	Y
21 Price	Y	N	Y	N	Y
22 Simon	Y	N	Y	N	Y
INDIANA					
1 Hall	Y	N	Y	N	Y
2 Sharp	Y	Y	Y	N	Y
3 *Hiler*	N	Y	N	Y	N
4 *Coats*	N	Y	N	Y	N
5 *Hillis*	N	Y	Y	N	Y

ND - Northern Democrats   SD - Southern Democrats

	300	301	302	303	304
6 Burton	N	Y	N	Y	N
7 Myers	N	Y	N	Y	N
8 McCloskey	Y	Y	Y	Y	N
9 Hamilton	Y	Y	Y	N	Y
10 Jacobs	Y	Y	?	Y	N
IOWA					
1 Leach	Y	N	Y	N	Y
2 Tauke	N	N	Y	N	Y
3 Evans	N	Y	Y	N	Y
4 Smith	Y	N	Y	N	Y
5 Harkin	Y	N	Y	Y	N
6 Bedell	Y	N	Y	N	Y
KANSAS					
1 Roberts	N	Y	N	Y	N
2 Slattery	N	Y	N	Y	N
3 Winn	N	Y	N	Y	N
4 Glickman	Y	Y	Y	N	Y
5 Whittaker	Y	Y	Y	N	Y
KENTUCKY					
1 Hubbard	Y	Y	N	N	Y
2 Natcher	Y	Y	Y	N	N
3 Mazzoli	Y	Y	Y	Y	N
4 Snyder	N	Y	N	N	Y
5 Rogers	N	Y	N	Y	N
6 Hopkins	N	Y	N	Y	N
7 Perkins	Y	Y	N	Y	N
LOUISIANA					
1 Livingston	N	Y	N	N	Y
2 Boggs	?	N	Y	N	Y
3 Tauzin	N	Y	N	Y	N
4 Roemer	N	Y	N	Y	N
5 Huckaby	N	Y	N	N	Y
6 Moore	N	Y	N	Y	N
7 Breaux	Y	Y	N	Y	N
8 Long	Y	N	Y	?	Y
MAINE					
1 McKernan	Y	Y	Y	N	Y
2 Snowe	Y	Y	Y	N	Y
MARYLAND					
1 Dyson	Y	Y	N	Y	N
2 Long	Y	Y	N	Y	N
3 Mikulski	Y	N	Y	N	N
4 Holt	N	Y	N	N	N
5 Hoyer	Y	N	Y	N	Y
6 Byron	N	Y	N	Y	N
7 Mitchell	Y	N	Y	N	N
8 Barnes	Y	N	Y	N	Y
MASSACHUSETTS					
1 Conte	Y	N	Y	N	Y
2 Boland	Y	N	Y	N	Y
3 Early	Y	Y	N	Y	N
4 Frank	Y	N	Y	N	Y
5 Shannon	Y	N	Y	N	Y
6 Mavroules	Y	N	Y	N	Y
7 Markey	Y	N	Y	N	Y
8 O'Neill					
9 Moakley	Y	N	Y	N	Y
10 Studds	Y	N	Y	N	Y
11 Donnelly	Y	N	Y	Y	N
MICHIGAN					
1 Conyers	Y	N	Y	Y	N
2 Pursell	N	Y	N	Y	N
3 Wolpe	Y	N	Y	N	Y
4 Siljander	Y	Y	N	Y	N
5 Sawyer	N	Y	N	Y	N
6 Carr	Y	N	Y	N	Y
7 Kildee	Y	N	Y	N	Y
8 Traxler	Y	Y	Y	N	Y
9 Vander Jagt	N	Y	?	Y	Y
10 Albosta	Y	Y	Y	N	Y
11 Davis	Y	Y*	N	Y	N
12 Bonior	Y	N	Y	N	Y
13 Crockett	Y	N	Y	N	Y
14 Hertel	Y	N	Y	N	Y
15 Ford	Y	N	Y	?	N
16 Dingell	Y	N	Y	N	Y
17 Levin	Y	N	Y	N	Y
18 Broomfield	N	Y	Y	N	Y
MINNESOTA					
1 Penny	Y	Y	Y	N	Y
2 Weber	N	Y	N	Y	N
3 Frenzel	N	N	Y	N	Y
4 Vento	Y	N	Y	N	Y
5 Sabo	Y	N	N	N	Y
6 Sikorski	Y	N	Y	N	Y

	300	301	302	303	304
7 Stangeland	Y	Y	N	N	Y
8 Oberstar	Y	N	Y	Y	N
MISSISSIPPI					
1 Whitten	Y	Y	?	N	N
2 Franklin	N	Y	N	Y	N
3 Montgomery	N	Y	N	Y	N
4 Dowdy	Y	Y	N	Y	N
5 Lott	N	Y	N	Y	N
MISSOURI					
1 Clay	Y	N	Y	N	Y
2 Young	Y	N	Y	N	Y
3 Gephardt	Y	N	Y	N	N
4 Skelton	Y	Y	Y	N	N
5 Wheat	Y	N	Y	N	N
6 Coleman	Y	Y	Y	Y	N
7 Taylor	N	Y	N	Y	N
8 Emerson	N	Y	N	Y	N
9 Volkmer	Y	Y	N	Y	N
MONTANA					
1 Williams	N	Y	Y	N	Y
2 Marlenee	N	Y	N	Y	N
NEBRASKA					
1 Bereuter	N	Y	Y	N	Y
2 Daub	N	Y	N	Y	N
3 Smith	N	Y	N	Y	N
NEVADA					
1 Reid	Y	Y	Y	N	N
2 Vucanovich	N	Y	N	Y	N
NEW HAMPSHIRE					
1 D'Amours	Y	Y	Y	Y	N
2 Gregg	N	Y	N	Y	N
NEW JERSEY					
1 Florio	Y	Y	Y	Y	N
2 Hughes	Y	Y	Y	Y	N
3 Howard	Y	N	Y	N	N
4 Smith	Y	Y	N	N	Y
5 Roukema	N	N	Y	N	Y
6 Dwyer	Y	N	Y	N	Y
7 Rinaldo	Y	Y	Y	Y	N
8 Roe	Y	N	Y	N	Y
9 Torricelli	Y	N	Y	N	Y
10 Rodino	Y	N	Y	N	Y
11 Minish	Y	N	Y	N	Y
12 Courter	N	Y	Y	N	Y
13 Forsythe	N	N	Y	?	Y
14 Guarini	Y	N	Y	N	Y
NEW MEXICO					
1 Lujan	N	Y	N	Y	N
2 Skeen	N	Y	N	N	Y
3 Richardson	Y	N	Y	N	Y
NEW YORK					
1 Carney	N	Y	N	Y	N
2 Downey	Y	N	Y	N	Y
3 Mrazek	Y	Y	Y	N	Y
4 Lent	N	Y	Y	N	Y
5 McGrath	N	N	Y	N	Y
6 Addabbo	Y	N	Y	N	N
7 Ackerman	+	N	Y	N	Y
8 Scheuer	Y	N	Y	N	Y
9 Ferraro	Y	N	Y	N	N
10 Schumer	Y	N	Y	N	Y
11 Towns	Y	N	Y	N	Y
12 Owens	Y	N	Y	N	Y
13 Solarz	Y	N	Y	N	Y
14 Molinari	N	Y	N	Y	N
15 Green	Y	N	Y	N	Y
16 Rangel	Y	N	Y	N	Y
17 Weiss	Y	N	Y	N	Y
18 Garcia	Y	N	Y	N	Y
19 Biaggi	Y	N	Y	?	N
20 Ottinger	Y	N	Y	N	Y
21 Fish	Y	N	Y	N	Y
22 Gilman	Y	Y	Y	N	Y
23 Stratton	Y	N	Y	N	Y
24 Solomon	N	Y	N	Y	N
25 Boehlert	Y	Y	N	Y	N
26 Martin	N	Y	N	Y	N
27 Wortley	Y	Y	N	Y	N
28 McHugh	Y	N	Y	N	Y
29 Horton	Y	N	Y	N	Y
30 Conable	N	N	Y	N	Y
31 Kemp	N	Y	N	Y	N
32 LaFalce	Y	N	Y	N	Y
33 Nowak	Y	Y	N	Y	N
34 Lundine	Y	N	Y	N	Y

	300	301	302	303	304
NORTH CAROLINA					
1 Jones	N	?	Y	N	N
2 Valentine	N	Y	N	Y	N
3 Whitley	N	Y	N	N	N
4 Andrews	N	Y	Y	N	Y
5 Neal	N	Y	Y	N	Y
6 Britt	Y	Y	Y	Y	N
7 Rose	Y	Y	Y	N	N
8 Hefner	N	Y	N	N	N
9 Martin	N	Y	Y	N	Y
10 Broyhill	N	Y	Y	Y	N
11 Clarke	N	Y	Y	N	N
NORTH DAKOTA					
AL Dorgan	Y	Y	?	Y	N
OHIO					
1 Luken	Y	N	Y	N	Y
2 Gradison	N	Y	Y	N	Y
3 Hall	Y	N	Y	Y	N
4 Oxley	N	Y	Y	N	Y
5 Latta	N	Y	N	N	Y
6 McEwen	N	Y	N	Y	N
7 DeWine	N	Y	Y	N	Y
8 Kindness	N	Y	Y	N	Y
9 Kaptur	Y	N	Y	N	N
10 Miller	Y	Y	Y	Y	N
11 Eckart	Y	Y	Y	Y	N
12 Kasich	N	Y	N	Y	N
13 Pease	Y	Y	Y	N	Y
14 Seiberling	Y	N	Y	N	Y
15 Wylie	N	N	Y	N	Y
16 Regula	N	Y	Y	N	Y
17 Williams	Y	Y	Y	N	Y
18 Applegate	Y	N	Y	N	Y
19 Feighan	Y	N	Y	N	N
20 Oakar	Y	N	Y	N	Y
21 Stokes	X	?	?	?	#
OKLAHOMA					
1 Jones	N	Y	N	Y	N
2 Synar	Y	N	Y	N	Y
3 Watkins	Y	Y	N	Y	N
4 McCurdy	N	Y	Y	N	N
5 Edwards	N	Y	Y	N	Y
6 English	N	Y	Y	N	Y
OREGON					
1 AuCoin	Y	Y	Y	N	Y
2 Smith, R.	N	Y	N	N	N
3 Wyden	Y	N	Y	Y	Y
4 Weaver	Y	?	N	Y	N
5 Smith, D.	N	Y	N	Y	N
PENNSYLVANIA					
1 Foglietta	Y	N	Y	N	Y
2 Gray	Y	N	Y	N	Y
3 Borski	Y	N	Y	N	Y
4 Kolter	Y	Y	Y	N	N
5 Schulze	Y	Y	Y	N	Y
6 Yatron	Y	N	Y	N	N
7 Edgar	Y	N	Y	N	Y
8 Kostmayer	Y	N	Y	N	Y
9 Shuster	N	Y	N	Y	N
10 McDade	Y	N	Y	N	Y
11 Harrison	Y	N	Y	N	Y
12 Murtha	Y	N	Y	N	Y
13 Coughlin	N	Y	N	Y	N
14 Coyne	Y	N	Y	N	Y
15 Ritter	Y	Y	N	Y	N
16 Walker	N	Y	N	Y	N
17 Gekas	Y	Y	N	Y	N
18 Walgren	Y	N	Y	N	Y
19 Goodling	N	Y	Y	N	Y
20 Gaydos	Y	Y	Y	N	Y
21 Ridge	Y	Y	N	Y	N
22 Murphy	Y	Y	Y	Y	N
23 Clinger	Y	N	Y	N	Y
RHODE ISLAND					
1 St Germain	Y	N	Y	N	Y
2 Schneider	Y	Y	Y	N	Y
SOUTH CAROLINA					
1 Hartnett	N	Y	N	Y	N
2 Spence	N	Y	N	Y	N
3 Derrick	N	Y	Y	N	Y
4 Campbell	N	Y	N	N	Y
5 Spratt	N	N	Y	N	Y
6 Tallon	?	Y	Y	Y	N
SOUTH DAKOTA					
AL Daschle	Y	N	Y	Y	N

	300	301	302	303	304
TENNESSEE					
1 Quillen	N	Y	Y	N	Y
2 Duncan	N	Y	N	Y	N
3 Lloyd	N	Y	N	Y	N
4 Cooper	Y	N	Y	N	Y
5 Boner	Y	Y	Y	N	Y
6 Gore	Y	N	Y	N	Y
7 Sundquist	N	Y	N	Y	N
8 Jones	N	N	Y	N	Y
9 Ford	Y	N	Y	N	Y
TEXAS					
1 Hall, S.	Y	Y	N	Y	N
2 Wilson	Y	Y	Y	N	?
3 Bartlett	N	Y	N	Y	N
4 Hall, R.	?	?	?	?	?
5 Bryant	N	Y	N	Y	N
6 Gramm	N	Y	N	Y	N
7 Archer	N	Y	N	Y	N
8 Fields	N	Y	N	Y	N
9 Brooks	Y	Y	N	Y	N
10 Pickle	Y	Y	Y	N	N
11 Leath	N	Y	N	Y	N
12 Wright	Y	N	Y	N	Y
13 Hightower	N	Y	N	Y	N
14 Patman	Y	Y	N	Y	N
15 de la Garza	N	N	Y	N	N
16 Coleman	Y	N	Y	N	Y
17 Stenholm	Y	N	Y	N	N
18 Leland	Y	N	Y	N	Y
19 Hance	Y	Y	N	Y	N
20 Gonzalez	Y	Y	Y	N	Y
21 Loeffler	N	Y	N	Y	N
22 Paul	N	N	Y	N	Y
23 Kazen	N	Y	Y	N	Y
24 Frost	Y	Y	N	Y	N
25 Andrews	N	Y	Y	N	Y
26 Vandergriff	N	Y	Y	N	Y
27 Ortiz	Y	N	Y	N	Y
UTAH					
1 Hansen	N	Y	N	Y	N
2 Marriott	N	Y	N	Y	N
3 Nielson	N	Y	Y	N	Y
VERMONT					
AL Jeffords	Y	N	Y	N	Y
VIRGINIA					
1 Bateman	N	Y	Y	N	Y
2 Whitehurst	N	Y	N	Y	N
3 Bliley	N	Y	N	Y	N
4 Sisisky	N	Y	N	N	Y
5 Daniel	N	Y	N	N	N
6 Olin	N	N	Y	N	Y
7 Robinson	N	Y	N	Y	N
8 Parris	N	Y	Y	N	N
9 Boucher	Y	N	Y	N	Y
10 Wolf	N	Y	N	N	N
WASHINGTON					
1 Pritchard	N	N	?	N	Y
2 Swift	Y	N	Y	N	Y
3 Bonker	Y	N	Y	N	Y
4 Morrison	N	N	N	N	Y
5 Foley	Y	N	Y	N	Y
6 Dicks	Y	N	Y	N	Y
7 Lowry	Y	N	Y	N	Y
8 Chandler	N	N	Y	N	Y
WEST VIRGINIA					
1 Mollohan	Y	Y	N	Y	N
2 Staggers	Y	N	Y	N	Y
3 Wise	Y	N	Y	N	Y
4 Rahall	Y	N	Y	N	Y
WISCONSIN					
1 Aspin	Y	N	Y	N	Y
2 Kastenmeier	Y	N	N	N	N
3 Gunderson	Y	Y	N	Y	N
4 Zablocki	Y	N	Y	N	Y
5 Moody	Y	N	Y	N	Y
6 Petri	Y	Y	N	Y	N
7 Obey	Y	N	Y	N	Y
8 Roth	Y	Y	N	Y	N
9 Sensenbrenner	Y	Y	N	Y	N
WYOMING					
AL Cheney	N	Y	Y	N	Y

Southern states · Ala., Ark., Fla., Ga., Ky., La., Miss., N.C., Okla., S.C., Tenn., Texas, Va.

305. Procedural Motion. Bateman, R-Va., motion to approve the House *Journal* of Wednesday, Aug. 3. Motion agreed to 342-42: R 131-23; D 211-19 (ND 137-16, SD 74-3), Aug. 4, 1983.

306. HR 2230. U.S. Commission on Civil Rights. Edwards, D-Calif., amendment (part 1) to extend the life of the commission for five years, rather than 15 years as provided in the bill. Adopted 400-24: R 140-23; D 260-1 (ND 171-1, SD 89-0), Aug. 4, 1983.

307. HR 2230. U.S. Commission on Civil Rights. Edwards, D-Calif., amendment (part 2) to permit removal of members of the Civil Rights Commission only for neglect of duty or malfeasance in office. Adopted 286-128: R 41-119; D 245-9 (ND 166-3, SD 79-6), Aug. 4, 1983.

308. HR 2867. Hazardous Waste Control. Florio, D-N.J., amendment to the Shelby, D-Ala., amendment, to require generators of 25 or more kilograms per month of hazardous wastes to notify transporters the wastes are hazardous. Adopted 236-180: R 37-124; D 199-56 (ND 155-15, SD 44-41), Aug. 4, 1983. (The Shelby amendment, which would have raised the notification threshold from the committee-approved 25 kg/mo. to 100 kg/mo., subsequently was adopted by voice vote.)

309. HR 2867. Hazardous Waste Control. Hiler, R-Ind., amendment to the Shelby, D-Ala., amendment, to lengthen to 810 days the phase-in period for requirements on generators of small quantities of hazardous wastes. Adopted 218-192: R 144-16; D 74-176 (ND 25-140, SD 49-36), Aug. 4, 1983. (The Shelby amendment, as modified by the Florio, D-N.J., amendment *(see vote 308, above)*, would have imposed the small-generator requirements in 180 days. It subsequently was adopted by voice vote.)

310. HR 3520. Rehabilitation Act Amendments. Adoption of the rule (H Res 283) providing for House floor consideration of the bill to amend and reauthorize through fiscal 1988 the Rehabilitation Act, which provides grants for vocational rehabilitation programs; authorizes several other educational programs for handicapped persons; and increases authorizations for 10 other educational, arts and welfare programs. Adopted 251-137: R 28-125; D 223-12 (ND 155-2, SD 68-10), Aug. 4, 1983.

311. HR 3391. Trade Adjustment Assistance. Adoption of the rule (H Res 299) providing for House floor consideration of the bill to reauthorize and amend trade adjustment assistance programs for workers and firms. Adopted 233-132: R 24-120; D 209-12 (ND 143-1, SD 66-11), Aug. 4, 1983.

KEY

Y Voted for (yea).
Paired for.
+ Announced for.
N Voted against (nay).
X Paired against.
- Announced against.
P Voted "present".
C Voted "present" to avoid possible conflict of interest.
? Did not vote or otherwise make a position known.

Democrats   *Republicans*

	305	306	307	308	309	310	311
ALABAMA							
1 *Edwards*	Y	Y	N	N	Y	Y	N
2 *Dickinson*	N	Y	N	N	Y	Y	N
3 Nichols	?	Y	N	N	Y	Y	Y
4 Bevill	Y	Y	Y	N	Y	Y	Y
5 Flippo	Y	Y	Y	N	Y	Y	?
6 Erdreich	Y	Y	Y	N	Y	Y	Y
7 Shelby	N	Y	N	N	Y	Y	Y
ALASKA							
AL *Young*	N	Y	N	?	?	?	?
ARIZONA							
1 *McCain*	Y	Y	Y	N	Y	N	N
2 Udall	Y	Y	Y	Y	Y	Y	Y
3 *Stump*	Y	N	N	N	Y	N	N
4 *Rudd*	Y	N	N	N	Y	N	N
5 McNulty	Y	Y	Y	Y	Y	Y	?
ARKANSAS							
1 Alexander	?	Y	Y	?	N	Y	Y
2 *Bethune*	Y	N	N	N	Y	N	N
3 *Hammerschmidt*	Y	Y	N	N	Y	N	N
4 Anthony	?	Y	Y	N	Y	Y	Y
CALIFORNIA							
1 Bosco	Y	Y	Y	Y	?	?	?
2 *Chappie*	Y	N	N	N	Y	N	N
3 Matsui	Y	Y	Y	N	Y	Y	Y
4 Fazio	Y	Y	Y	N	Y	Y	Y
5 Burton	Y	Y	Y	N	Y	Y	Y
6 Boxer	?	Y	Y	N	?	?	?
7 Miller	Y	Y	Y	N	Y	Y	Y
8 Dellums	?	Y	Y	N	Y	Y	Y
9 Stark	Y	Y	Y	N	Y	Y	Y
10 Edwards	Y	Y	Y	?	?	?	?
11 Lantos	Y	Y	Y	N	Y	Y	Y
12 *Zschau*	Y	Y	N	N	Y	N	N
13 Mineta	Y	Y	Y	N	Y	Y	Y
14 Shumway	N	N	N	N	Y	N	N
15 Coelho	Y	Y	Y	N	Y	Y	Y
16 Panetta	Y	Y	Y	N	Y	N	Y
17 *Pashayan*	Y	Y	?	N	Y	N	Y
18 Lehman	Y	Y	?	N	Y	N	Y
19 *Lagomarsino*	P	Y	N	N	Y	N	N
20 *Thomas*	Y	N	N	N	N	N	N
21 *Fiedler*	Y	Y	N	N	Y	?	?
22 *Moorhead*	Y	Y	N	N	Y	N	N
23 Beilenson	Y	Y	Y	N	Y	Y	Y
24 Waxman	?	Y	Y	Y	N	Y	?
25 Roybal	?	Y	Y	N	Y	N	Y
26 Berman	Y	?	Y	N	Y	N	Y
27 Levine	Y	Y	Y	N	Y	N	Y
28 Dixon	N	Y	Y	N	Y	N	?
29 Hawkins	N	Y	Y	N	Y	N	Y
30 Martinez	Y	Y	Y	N	Y	N	Y
31 Dymally	P	Y	Y	?	?	?	?
32 Anderson	Y	Y	Y	Y	?	?	?
33 *Dreier*	N	Y	N	N	Y	N	N
34 Torres	Y	Y	Y	N	N	Y	Y
35 *Lewis*	N	N	N	N	Y	N	N
36 Brown	Y	Y	Y	Y	N	Y	?
37 *McCandless*	Y	N	N	N	Y	N	N
38 Patterson	Y	Y	Y	N	Y	N	Y
39 *Dannemeyer*	N	N	N	N	Y	N	N
40 *Badham*	Y	N	N	N	Y	N	N
41 *Lowery*	Y	Y	N	N	Y	N	N
42 Lungren	Y	N	N	N	Y	N	N

	305	306	307	308	309	310	311
43 *Packard*	Y	N	N	N	Y	N	N
44 Bates	Y	Y	Y	Y	N	?	Y
45 *Hunter*	Y	Y	N	N	Y	N	N
COLORADO							
1 Schroeder	N	Y	Y	Y	N	Y	Y
2 Wirth	Y	Y	Y	Y	?	Y	Y
3 Kogovsek	Y	Y	Y	Y	N	Y	Y
4 *Brown*	Y	Y	N	N	Y	N	N
5 *Kramer*	Y	Y	N	N	Y	N	N
6 *Schaefer*	N	N	N	N	Y	N	N
CONNECTICUT							
1 Kennelly	Y	Y	Y	Y	N	Y	Y
2 Gejdenson	N	Y	Y	Y	N	Y	Y
3 Morrison	Y	Y	Y	Y	N	?	?
4 *McKinney*	Y	Y	Y	Y	N	Y	N
5 Ratchford	Y	Y	Y	N	Y	Y	Y
6 *Johnson*	Y	Y	Y	Y	N	N	N
DELAWARE							
AL Carper	Y	Y	Y	Y	N	Y	Y
FLORIDA							
1 Hutto	Y	Y	N	N	Y	Y	N
2 Fuqua	Y	Y	Y	N	Y	?	?
3 Bennett	Y	Y	Y	N	Y	Y	Y
4 Chappell	?	Y	N	N	Y	Y	Y
5 *McCollum*	?	?	?	?	Y	?	X
6 MacKay	Y	Y	?	N	N	N	Y
7 Gibbons	Y	Y	Y	N	Y	N	Y
8 *Young*	Y	Y	N	Y	Y	N	?
9 *Bilirakis*	Y	Y	N	N	Y	N	N
10 Ireland	Y	Y	N	N	Y	N	N
11 Nelson	Y	Y	Y	Y	N	Y	Y
12 *Lewis*	Y	N	N	N	Y	N	N
13 *Mack*	N	N	N	N	Y	N	N
14 Mica	Y	Y	Y	N	Y	Y	Y
15 *Shaw*	Y	Y	N	Y	Y	N	N
16 Smith	Y	Y	?	N	Y	N	Y
17 Lehman	Y	Y	Y	N	Y	Y	Y
18 Pepper	?	Y	Y	N	Y	Y	Y
19 Fascell	Y	Y	Y	N	Y	Y	Y
GEORGIA							
1 Thomas	Y	Y	Y	N	Y	Y	Y
2 Hatcher	Y	Y	?	N	Y	Y	Y
3 Ray	Y	Y	Y	N	Y	Y	Y
4 Levitas	Y	Y	Y	N	Y	Y	Y
5 Fowler	Y	Y	Y	N	Y	Y	Y
6 *Gingrich*	?	Y	N	N	Y	N	N
7 McDonald	?	Y	N	N	?	?	?
8 Rowland	Y	Y	Y	N	Y	Y	Y
9 Jenkins	Y	Y	Y	Y	Y	Y	Y
10 Barnard	Y	Y	Y	Y	Y	Y	Y
HAWAII							
1 Heftel	?	?	?	?	?	?	?
2 Akaka	Y	Y	Y	N	Y	N	Y
IDAHO							
1 *Craig*	N	Y	N	N	Y	N	N
2 *Hansen*	Y	Y	N	N	Y	N	N
ILLINOIS							
1 Vacancy							
2 Savage	Y	Y	Y	Y	N	Y	Y
3 Russo	Y	Y	Y	Y	N	Y	?
4 *O'Brien*	Y	Y	N	N	Y	N	N
5 Lipinski	N	Y	Y	N	Y	N	Y
6 *Hyde*	Y	N	N	N	Y	N	N
7 Collins	Y	Y	Y	N	Y	N	N
8 Rostenkowski	Y	Y	Y	N	Y	N	Y
9 Yates	N	Y	Y	N	Y	Y	Y
10 *Porter*	?	Y	Y	N	Y	N	N
11 Annunzio	Y	Y	Y	N	Y	N	Y
12 *Crane, P.*	Y	N	N	N	Y	N	N
13 *Erlenborn*	Y	N	N	N	Y	N	N
14 *Corcoran*	Y	N	N	N	Y	N	N
15 *Madigan*	Y	N	Y	N	Y	N	N
16 *Martin*	Y	Y	Y	N	Y	N	N
17 Evans	Y	Y	Y	Y	N	Y	Y
18 *Michel*	N	N	N	N	Y	N	N
19 *Crane, D.*	Y	N	N	?	?	?	?
20 Durbin	N	Y	Y	Y	Y	Y	Y
21 Price	Y	Y	Y	Y	N	Y	Y
22 Simon	Y	Y	Y	N	Y	Y	Y
INDIANA							
1 Hall	Y	Y	?	Y	N	Y	Y
2 Sharp	Y	Y	Y	N	Y	N	Y
3 *Hiler*	Y	Y	N	N	Y	N	N
4 *Coats*	N	Y	N	N	Y	N	Y
5 Hillis	?	Y	N	Y	N	Y	Y

ND - Northern Democrats   SD - Southern Democrats

Corresponding to Congressional Record Votes 321, 322, 323, 324, 325, 326, 327

	305	306	307	308	309	310	311
6 ***Burton***	N	Y	N	N	Y	N	N
7 ***Myers***	Y	Y	N	N	Y	Y	?
8 McCloskey	Y	Y	Y	Y	N	Y	?
9 Hamilton	Y	Y	Y	Y	N	Y	Y
10 Jacobs	P	Y	?	Y	Y	Y	N
IOWA							
1 ***Leach***	N	Y	Y	Y	Y	N	N
2 ***Tauke***	Y	Y	Y	Y	Y	N	N
3 ***Evans***	N	Y	Y	Y	N	N	N
4 Smith	Y	Y	Y	Y	N	Y	Y
5 Harkin	N	Y	Y	Y	N	Y	Y
6 Bedell	Y	Y	Y	Y	N	Y	Y
KANSAS							
1 ***Roberts***	N	Y	N	N	Y	N	N
2 Slattery	Y	Y	Y	Y	N	Y	Y
3 ***Winn***	Y	Y	N	N	Y	N	?
4 Glickman	Y	Y	Y	Y	N	Y	Y
5 ***Whittaker***	Y	Y	N	N	Y	N	N
KENTUCKY							
1 Hubbard	Y	Y	Y	N	Y	Y	Y
2 Natcher	Y	Y	Y	Y	N	Y	Y
3 Mazzoli	Y	Y	Y	N	Y	Y	Y
4 ***Snyder***	Y	Y	N	N	Y	Y	?
5 ***Rogers***	N	Y	N	N	Y	N	Y
6 ***Hopkins***	Y	Y	N	N	Y	Y	N
7 Perkins	Y	Y	Y	Y	N	Y	Y
LOUISIANA							
1 ***Livingston***	Y	Y	N	Y	N	N	?
2 Boggs	?	Y	Y	Y	N	Y	Y
3 Tauzin	Y	Y	Y	Y	N	Y	N
4 Roemer	N	Y	Y	Y	N	N	N
5 Huckaby	Y	Y	Y	Y	N	N	Y
6 ***Moore***	Y	Y	N	Y	Y	N	N
7 Breaux	Y	Y	Y	Y	N	Y	N
8 Long	Y	Y	Y	Y	N	Y	Y
MAINE							
1 ***McKernan***	Y	Y	Y	Y	N	N	N
2 ***Snowe***	Y	Y	Y	Y	N	Y	Y
MARYLAND							
1 Dyson	Y	Y	Y	N	Y	Y	Y
2 Long	Y	Y	Y	Y	N	Y	Y
3 Mikulski	Y	Y	Y	Y	N	Y	Y
4 ***Holt***	Y	Y	N	N	Y	N	N
5 Hoyer	Y	Y	P	Y	N	Y	Y
6 Byron	Y	Y	N	N	Y	Y	Y
7 Mitchell	?	Y	Y	?	?	Y	Y
8 Barnes	Y	Y	Y	Y	N	Y	Y
MASSACHUSETTS							
1 ***Conte***	P	Y	Y	Y	N	Y	N
2 Boland	Y	Y	Y	Y	N	Y	Y
3 Early	Y	Y	Y	?	?	?	?
4 Frank	Y	Y	Y	Y	N	Y	?
5 Shannon	Y	Y	Y	Y	N	Y	Y
6 Mavroules	Y	Y	Y	Y	N	Y	Y
7 Markey	N	Y	Y	Y	N	Y	Y
8 O'Neill							
9 Moakley	Y	Y	Y	Y	N	Y	Y
10 Studds	Y	Y	Y	Y	N	Y	Y
11 Donnelly	Y	Y	N	Y	Y	N	Y
MICHIGAN							
1 Conyers	Y	Y	Y	Y	Y	Y	Y
2 ***Pursell***	Y	Y	Y	Y	Y	?	?
3 Wolpe	Y	Y	Y	Y	N	Y	Y
4 ***Siljander***	Y	Y	N	N	Y	Y	?
5 ***Sawyer***	Y	Y	N	N	Y	N	Y
6 Carr	Y	Y	Y	Y	N	Y	Y
7 Kildee	Y	Y	Y	Y	N	Y	Y
8 Traxler	?	Y	Y	Y	N	?	?
9 ***Vander Jagt***	Y	Y	N	N	Y	N	Y
10 Albosta	Y	Y	Y	Y	Y	Y	Y
11 ***Davis***	Y	Y	Y	Y	Y	Y	Y
12 Bonior	?	Y	Y	Y	N	Y	Y
13 Crockett	Y	Y	Y	Y	N	Y	Y
14 Hertel	Y	Y	Y	Y	N	Y	Y
15 Ford	?	Y	Y	Y	N	Y	Y
16 Dingell	Y	N	Y	N	N	Y	Y
17 Levin	Y	Y	Y	Y	N	Y	Y
18 ***Broomfield***	Y	Y	N	N	Y	?	?
MINNESOTA							
1 Penny	Y	Y	Y	N	Y	Y	Y
2 ***Weber***	?	?	?	?	?	?	?
3 ***Frenzel***	N	Y	Y	N	Y	N	N
4 Vento	Y	Y	Y	Y	N	?	?
5 Sabo	N	Y	Y	Y	N	Y	Y
6 Sikorski	N	Y	Y	Y	N	Y	Y
7 ***Stangeland***	Y	Y	N	N	Y	N	N
8 Oberstar	P	Y	Y	Y	N	Y	Y
MISSISSIPPI							
1 Whitten	Y	Y	?	N	Y	?	?
2 ***Franklin***	Y	Y	N	N	Y	N	N
3 Montgomery	Y	Y	Y	N	Y	Y	N
4 Dowdy	Y	Y	Y	N	Y	?	?
5 ***Lott***	Y	Y	N	N	Y	N	N
MISSOURI							
1 Clay	?	Y	Y	Y	N	Y	?
2 Young	Y	Y	Y	Y	Y	Y	Y
3 Gephardt	Y	Y	Y	Y	N	N	Y
4 Skelton	Y	Y	Y	N	Y	Y	Y
5 Wheat	Y	Y	Y	Y	N	Y	Y
6 ***Coleman***	Y	Y	N	Y	N	N	N
7 ***Taylor***	Y	Y	N	N	Y	N	N
8 ***Emerson***	N	Y	N	N	Y	N	N
9 Volkmer	Y	Y	Y	Y	N	Y	Y
MONTANA							
1 Williams	?	Y	Y	Y	N	Y	Y
2 ***Marlenee***	Y	Y	N	N	Y	N	N
NEBRASKA							
1 ***Bereuter***	Y	Y	Y	N	Y	N	N
2 ***Daub***	Y	Y	N	N	Y	N	N
3 ***Smith***	Y	Y	N	N	Y	N	N
NEVADA							
1 Reid	Y	Y	Y	Y	N	Y	Y
2 ***Vucanovich***	Y	N	N	N	Y	N	N
NEW HAMPSHIRE							
1 D'Amours	Y	Y	Y	Y	Y	?	?
2 ***Gregg***	?	?	?	?	?	?	?
NEW JERSEY							
1 Florio	Y	Y	Y	Y	N	Y	?
2 Hughes	Y	Y	Y	Y	N	Y	Y
3 Howard	Y	Y	Y	Y	N	Y	Y
4 ***Smith***	?	Y	N	Y	N	Y	Y
5 ***Roukema***	Y	Y	N	Y	Y	N	N
6 Dwyer	?	Y	Y	Y	N	Y	?
7 ***Rinaldo***	Y	Y	Y	Y	N	Y	Y
8 Roe	Y	Y	Y	Y	N	Y	Y
9 Torricelli	Y	Y	Y	Y	N	Y	Y
10 Rodino	Y	Y	Y	Y	N	Y	Y
11 Minish	Y	Y	Y	Y	N	Y	Y
12 ***Courter***	Y	Y	Y	Y	N	N	N
13 ***Forsythe***	N	N	N	Y	Y	?	?
14 Guarini	Y	Y	Y	Y	N	Y	Y
NEW MEXICO							
1 ***Lujan***	Y	Y	?	N	Y	N	N
2 ***Skeen***	Y	Y	N	N	Y	N	N
3 Richardson	N	Y	Y	Y	N	Y	Y
NEW YORK							
1 ***Carney***	Y	Y	N	N	Y	N	N
2 Downey	?	Y	Y	Y	N	Y	Y
3 Mrazek	Y	Y	Y	Y	N	Y	Y
4 ***Lent***	Y	Y	Y	N	Y	N	N
5 ***McGrath***	Y	Y	Y	Y	Y	N	N
6 Addabbo	Y	Y	Y	Y	N	Y	#
7 Ackerman	?	Y	Y	Y	N	Y	?
8 Scheuer	Y	Y	Y	Y	N	Y	Y
9 Ferraro	Y	Y	Y	Y	N	Y	Y
10 Schumer	Y	Y	Y	Y	N	?	?
11 Towns	Y	Y	Y	Y	N	Y	Y
12 Owens	Y	Y	Y	Y	N	?	?
13 Solarz	Y	Y	Y	Y	N	Y	Y
14 ***Molinari***	Y	Y	N	Y	N	N	N
15 ***Green***	Y	Y	Y	Y	N	Y	N
16 Rangel	Y	Y	Y	Y	N	Y	Y
17 Weiss	Y	Y	Y	Y	N	Y	Y
18 Garcia	Y	Y	Y	Y	N	Y	Y
19 Biaggi	Y	Y	Y	Y	N	Y	Y
20 Ottinger	?	Y	Y	Y	N	Y	Y
21 ***Fish***	Y	Y	Y	Y	Y	N	N
22 ***Gilman***	Y	Y	Y	Y	N	Y	Y
23 Stratton	Y	Y	Y	N	Y	Y	Y
24 ***Solomon***	Y	N	N	N	Y	N	?
25 ***Boehlert***	Y	Y	Y	Y	Y	Y	Y
26 ***Martin***	P	Y	N	N	Y	N	N
27 ***Wortley***	Y	Y	N	N	Y	N	N
28 McHugh	Y	Y	Y	Y	N	Y	Y
29 ***Horton***	Y	Y	Y	Y	Y	Y	N
30 ***Conable***	N	Y	Y	N	Y	N	N
31 ***Kemp***	Y	Y	Y	N	Y	Y	Y
32 LaFalce	Y	Y	N	Y	N	Y	Y
33 Nowak	Y	Y	Y	Y	Y	Y	Y
34 Lundine	Y	Y	Y	Y	?	?	?
NORTH CAROLINA							
1 Jones	Y	Y	Y	Y	?	?	?
2 Valentine	Y	Y	Y	N	Y	Y	Y
3 Whitley	Y	Y	Y	N	Y	?	?
4 Andrews	?	Y	Y	N	N	Y	Y
5 Neal	?	Y	Y	Y	Y	Y	Y
6 Britt	Y	Y	Y	N	Y	Y	Y
7 Rose	Y	Y	Y	N	?	Y	Y
8 Hefner	Y	Y	Y	N	Y	Y	Y
9 ***Martin***	Y	Y	N	Y	Y	N	N
10 ***Broyhill***	Y	Y	Y	N	Y	N	N
11 Clarke	Y	Y	Y	Y	N	Y	Y
NORTH DAKOTA							
AL Dorgan	N	Y	Y	N	Y	Y	Y
OHIO							
1 Luken	Y	Y	Y	N	Y	Y	Y
2 ***Gradison***	Y	Y	Y	N	Y	N	N
3 Hall	Y	Y	Y	Y	N	Y	Y
4 ***Oxley***	Y	Y	N	N	Y	N	N
5 ***Latta***	Y	Y	N	N	Y	N	N
6 ***McEwen***	Y	Y	Y	N	Y	Y	Y
7 ***DeWine***	Y	N	N	Y	Y	N	N
8 ***Kindness***	Y	Y	N	N	Y	N	N
9 Kaptur	Y	Y	Y	Y	N	?	?
10 ***Miller***	N	Y	N	N	Y	N	Y
11 Eckart	N	Y	Y	Y	N	Y	Y
12 ***Kasich***	Y	Y	N	N	Y	N	Y
13 Pease	Y	Y	Y	Y	N	Y	Y
14 Seiberling	?	Y	Y	Y	N	Y	Y
15 ***Wylie***	Y	Y	N	Y	Y	N	Y
16 ***Regula***	Y	Y	Y	Y	Y	Y	Y
17 ***Williams***	?	Y	N	N	Y	Y	Y
18 Applegate	?	Y	Y	Y	N	Y	Y
19 Feighan	Y	Y	Y	Y	N	Y	Y
20 Oakar	Y	Y	Y	Y	N	Y	Y
21 Stokes	?	?	?	?	?	?	?
OKLAHOMA							
1 Jones	Y	Y	Y	Y	N	N	Y
2 Synar	Y	Y	Y	Y	N	Y	Y
3 Watkins	?	Y	Y	Y	Y	?	Y
4 McCurdy	Y	Y	Y	Y	N	Y	Y
5 ***Edwards***	Y	Y	N	N	Y	N	N
6 English	Y	Y	Y	N	Y	N	N
OREGON							
1 AuCoin	Y	Y	Y	Y	N	Y	Y
2 ***Smith, R.***	Y	Y	N	N	Y	?	?
3 Wyden	Y	Y	Y	Y	N	Y	Y
4 Weaver	Y	Y	Y	Y	N	Y	Y
5 ***Smith, D.***	N	Y	N	N	?	?	?
PENNSYLVANIA							
1 Foglietta	Y	Y	Y	Y	N	Y	Y
2 Gray	Y	Y	Y	Y	N	Y	Y
3 Borski	Y	Y	Y	Y	N	Y	Y
4 Kolter	Y	Y	Y	Y	Y	Y	Y
5 ***Schulze***	Y	Y	?	N	Y	N	N
6 Yatron	Y	Y	Y	N	N	Y	Y
7 Edgar	Y	Y	Y	Y	N	?	Y
8 Kostmayer	Y	Y	Y	Y	N	Y	Y
9 ***Shuster***	Y	Y	N	N	Y	N	N
10 ***McDade***	?	Y	N	Y	Y	Y	Y
11 Harrison	Y	Y	Y	Y	N	Y	?
12 Murtha	Y	Y	Y	Y	N	Y	?
13 ***Coughlin***	N	Y	?	N	N	N	N
14 Coyne	Y	Y	Y	Y	N	Y	Y
15 ***Ritter***	Y	Y	N	N	Y	N	?
16 ***Walker***	N	N	Y	N	Y	N	N
17 ***Gekas***	Y	Y	Y	N	Y	N	N
18 Walgren	Y	Y	Y	Y	N	Y	Y
19 ***Goodling***	N	Y	N	Y	Y	N	N
20 Gaydos	Y	Y	Y	N	Y	Y	Y
21 ***Ridge***	Y	Y	Y	N	Y	N	N
22 Murphy	N	Y	Y	Y	Y	Y	Y
23 ***Clinger***	Y	Y	Y	N	Y	Y	Y
RHODE ISLAND							
1 St Germain	?	?	?	?	?	?	?
2 ***Schneider***	Y	?	Y	Y	N	Y	Y
SOUTH CAROLINA							
1 ***Hartnett***	Y	N	N	N	Y	?	?
2 ***Spence***	Y	Y	N	N	Y	Y	N
3 Derrick	Y	Y	Y	N	N	Y	Y
4 ***Campbell***	Y	Y	N	N	Y	N	N
5 Spratt	Y	Y	Y	Y	Y	Y	Y
6 Tallon	Y	Y	Y	N	Y	Y	N
SOUTH DAKOTA							
AL Daschle	Y	Y	Y	N	Y	Y	Y
TENNESSEE							
1 ***Quillen***	Y	N	N	N	Y	Y	N
2 ***Duncan***	Y	Y	N	N	Y	Y	Y
3 Lloyd	Y	Y	Y	N	Y	Y	Y
4 Cooper	Y	Y	Y	?	Y	Y	Y
5 Boner	Y	?	?	?	?	?	?
6 Gore	Y	Y	Y	Y	N	Y	Y
7 ***Sundquist***	Y	N	N	N	Y	Y	N
8 Jones	Y	Y	Y	N	Y	Y	Y
9 Ford	?	Y	Y	?	N	?	Y
TEXAS							
1 Hall, S.	Y	Y	Y	Y	Y	Y	Y
2 Wilson	?	Y	Y	Y	Y	Y	Y
3 ***Bartlett***	Y	Y	N	N	Y	N	N
4 Hall, R.	Y	Y	Y	N	Y	Y	Y
5 Bryant	Y	Y	Y	Y	N	?	?
6 ***Gramm***	Y	Y	N	N	Y	N	N
7 ***Archer***	Y	Y	N	N	Y	N	N
8 ***Fields***	N	Y	N	N	Y	N	Y
9 Brooks	Y	Y	Y	Y	N	Y	Y
10 Pickle	Y	Y	Y	Y	Y	Y	Y
11 Leath	Y	Y	Y	N	Y	Y	Y
12 Wright	Y	Y	Y	Y	N	Y	Y
13 Hightower	Y	Y	Y	?	?	?	?
14 Patman	N	Y	Y	Y	N	Y	N
15 de la Garza	Y	Y	Y	Y	Y	Y	Y
16 Coleman	Y	Y	Y	Y	N	?	?
17 Stenholm	Y	Y	Y	N	Y	N	N
18 Leland	Y	Y	Y	Y	N	Y	Y
19 Hance	Y	Y	Y	Y	Y	Y	Y
20 Gonzalez	Y	Y	Y	Y	N	Y	Y
21 ***Loeffler***	Y	Y	N	N	Y	N	N
22 ***Paul***	Y	Y	N	N	Y	N	N
23 Kazen	Y	Y	Y	N	Y	Y	Y
24 Frost	Y	Y	Y	Y	N	Y	Y
25 Andrews	Y	Y	Y	Y	N	N	Y
26 Vandergriff	Y	Y	Y	N	Y	Y	Y
27 Ortiz	Y	Y	Y	Y	N	Y	?
UTAH							
1 ***Hansen***	Y	Y	N	N	Y	N	N
2 ***Marriott***	Y	Y	N	N	Y	?	?
3 ***Nielson***	Y	N	N	N	Y	N	Y
VERMONT							
AL ***Jeffords***	Y	Y	Y	Y	N	N	N
VIRGINIA							
1 ***Bateman***	Y	N	N	N	Y	N	N
2 ***Whitehurst***	Y	Y	N	N	Y	Y	?
3 ***Bliley***	Y	Y	N	?	?	?	?
4 Sisisky	Y	Y	Y	N	Y	Y	Y
5 Daniel	Y	Y	N	N	Y	Y	N
6 Olin	P	Y	Y	N	Y	N	Y
7 ***Robinson***	Y	Y	N	N	Y	N	N
8 ***Parris***	Y	Y	N	N	Y	N	N
9 Boucher	Y	Y	Y	Y	N	Y	Y
10 ***Wolf***	Y	Y	N	N	Y	N	N
WASHINGTON							
1 ***Pritchard***	?	Y	Y	N	N	N	N
2 Swift	Y	Y	Y	Y	N	Y	Y
3 Bonker	Y	Y	Y	Y	N	Y	Y
4 ***Morrison***	Y	Y	N	N	Y	N	N
5 Foley	Y	Y	Y	Y	N	Y	Y
6 Dicks	Y	Y	Y	Y	N	Y	Y
7 Lowry	Y	Y	Y	Y	N	Y	Y
8 ***Chandler***	Y	Y	N	N	Y	N	N
WEST VIRGINIA							
1 Mollohan	Y	Y	Y	Y	Y	Y	Y
2 Staggers	N	Y	Y	Y	N	Y	Y
3 Wise	P	Y	Y	Y	N	Y	Y
4 Rahall	Y	Y	Y	N	Y	Y	Y
WISCONSIN							
1 Aspin	Y	Y	Y	Y	N	Y	Y
2 Kastenmeier	Y	Y	Y	Y	N	Y	Y
3 ***Gunderson***	Y	Y	N	N	Y	N	N
4 Zablocki	Y	Y	Y	Y	N	Y	?
5 Moody	Y	Y	Y	Y	Y	Y	Y
6 ***Petri***	Y	Y	Y	N	Y	N	N
7 Obey	Y	Y	Y	Y	N	Y	Y
8 ***Roth***	Y	Y	N	N	Y	N	N
9 ***Sensenbrenner***	Y	N	N	N	Y	N	N
WYOMING							
AL ***Cheney***	Y	Y	N	N	Y	N	N

Southern states - Ala., Ark., Fla., Ga., Ky., La., Miss., N.C., Okla., S.C., Tenn., Texas, Va.

312. Procedural Motion. Bliley, R-Va., motion to approve the House *Journal* of Monday, Sept. 12. Motion agreed to 298-18: R 114-8; D 184-10 (ND 113-9, SD 71-1), Sept. 13, 1983.

313. HR 3520. Rehabilitation Act Amendments. Bartlett, R-Texas, amendment to delete the section of the bill increasing authorization levels for 10 education and social services programs. Rejected 124-283: R 117-40; D 7-243 (ND 0-166, SD 7-77), Sept. 13, 1983.

314. HR 3520. Rehabilitation Act Amendments. Moorhead, R-Calif., amendment to revise the formula for distribution of funds for energy assistance to low-income people. Adopted 226-174: R 93-60; D 133-114 (ND 54-109, SD 79-5), Sept. 13, 1983.

315. HR 3520. Rehabilitation Act Amendments. Erlenborn, R-Ill., motion to recommit the bill to the Education and Labor Committee with instructions to amend the bill to prohibit funds authorized by Title IV of the bill from being spent by any school district or other political subdivision responsible for education unless that body has a procedure for determining functional literacy as a condition for high school graduation. Motion rejected 128-275: R 121-33; D 7-242 (ND 0-166, SD 7-76), Sept. 13, 1983.

316. HR 3520. Rehabilitation Act Amendments. Passage of the bill to authorize fiscal 1984 appropriations of $1,037,800,000 for state grant vocational rehabilitation programs, with increases for fiscal 1985-88 according to a formula and such sums as necessary for other Rehabilitation Act programs for fiscal 1984-88; to create a federal program to assist in the education of immigrant children for fiscal 1984-86 and authorize such sums as necessary; and increase fiscal 1984 authorizations for 11 other educational, arts and welfare programs from $9,474,700,000 to $11,092,700,000. Passed 324-79: R 78-75; D 246-4 (ND 167-0, SD 79-4), Sept. 13, 1983. A "nay" was a vote supporting the president's position.

317. HR 5. Ocean and Coastal Resources Management. Passage of the bill to share up to $300 million annually in federal offshore oil and gas leasing revenues with coastal and Great Lakes states as block grants for certain ocean and coastal resource programs. Passed 301-93: R 68-83; D 233-10 (ND 155-6, SD 78-4), Sept. 14, 1983. A "nay" was a vote supporting the president's position.

318. HR 3391. Trade Adjustment Assistance. Frenzel, R-Minn., amendment, to the Ways and Means Committee amendment, to lower the percentage of customs duties to be set aside in a special account for trade adjustment assistance, thereby bringing the program into conformity with the fiscal 1984 budget resolution, and to delete language authorizing additional funds if necessary to meet the bill's requirements. Rejected 176-234: R 142-17; D 34-217 (ND 8-160, SD 26-57), Sept. 14, 1983.

319. HR 3391. Trade Adjustment Assistance. Frenzel, R-Minn., amendment to eliminate a provision extending trade adjustment assistance to workers in firms that supply parts and services to industries damaged by import competition. Rejected 154-255: R 125-30; D 29-225 (ND 8-162, SD 21-63), Sept. 14, 1983.

* Rep. Larry P. McDonald, D-Ga., died Sept. 1, 1983, Tokyo time. The last vote for which he was eligible was CQ vote 311.

** Rep. Charles A. Hayes, D-Ill., was sworn in Sept. 12, 1983. The first vote for which he was eligible was CQ vote 312.

KEY

Y Voted for (yea).
Paired for.
+ Announced for.
N Voted against (nay).
X Paired against.
- Announced against.
P Voted "present".
C Voted "present" to avoid possible conflict of interest.
? Did not vote or otherwise make a position known.

Democrats *Republicans*

	312	313	314	315	316	317	318	319
ALABAMA								
1 *Edwards*	Y	Y	Y	Y	Y	Y	Y	Y
2 *Dickinson*	N	Y	Y	N	Y	N	Y	Y
3 Nichols	Y	N	Y	N	Y	Y	Y	Y
4 Bevill	Y	N	N	N	Y	Y	N	N
5 Flippo	?	?	?	?	?	Y	N	N
6 Erdreich	Y	N	Y	N	Y	Y	N	Y
7 Shelby	Y	N	Y	N	Y	Y	N	N
ALASKA								
AL *Young*	?	X	X	?	?	?	?	?
ARIZONA								
1 *McCain*	P	Y	Y	Y	Y	N	Y	Y
2 Udall	?	N	Y	N	Y	Y	N	N
3 *Stump*	?	?	#	?	?	?	?	?
4 *Rudd*	Y	Y	Y	Y	N	N	Y	Y
5 McNulty	Y	N	Y	N	Y	Y	N	N
ARKANSAS								
1 Alexander	Y	N	Y	N	Y	?	N	N
2 *Bethune*	Y	N	Y	N	?	Y	Y	?
3 *Hammerschmidt*	Y	Y	Y	N	Y	Y	Y	Y
4 Anthony	Y	N	Y	N	Y	Y	?	N
CALIFORNIA								
1 Bosco	Y	N	Y	N	Y	Y	N	N
2 *Chappie*	Y	Y	Y	Y	Y	N	Y	Y
3 Matsui	Y	N	Y	N	Y	Y	N	N
4 Fazio	Y	N	Y	N	Y	Y	N	N
5 Burton	Y	N	?	N	Y	Y	N	N
6 Boxer	Y	N	Y	N	Y	Y	N	N
7 Miller	?	N	Y	N	Y	Y	N	N
8 Dellums	?	?	?	?	#	?	X	?
9 Stark	Y	N	N	N	Y	Y	N	N
10 Edwards	Y	N	Y	N	Y	Y	N	N
11 Lantos	Y	N	Y	N	Y	Y	N	N
12 *Zschau*	Y	Y	Y	Y	N	Y	Y	Y
13 Mineta	?	N	Y	N	Y	Y	N	N
14 *Shumway*	Y	Y	Y	Y	N	N	Y	Y
15 Coelho	Y	N	?	?	?	Y	N	N
16 Panetta	Y	N	Y	N	Y	Y	N	N
17 *Pashayan*	?	#	#	#	?	?	#	#
18 Lehman	Y	N	Y	N	Y	Y	N	N
19 *Lagomarsino*	Y	Y	Y	Y	N	Y	Y	Y
20 *Thomas*	Y	Y	Y	Y	N	Y	Y	Y
21 *Fiedler*	Y	Y	Y	Y	Y	Y	Y	Y
22 *Moorhead*	Y	Y	Y	Y	N	Y	Y	Y
23 Beilenson	Y	N	N	N	Y	N	N	N
24 Waxman	Y	N	Y	N	Y	Y	N	N
25 Roybal	Y	N	Y	N	Y	Y	N	N
26 Berman	Y	N	N	N	Y	Y	N	N
27 Levine	Y	N	N	N	Y	Y	N	N
28 Dixon	Y	N	Y	N	Y	Y	N	N
29 Hawkins	Y	N	Y	N	Y	Y	N	N
30 Martinez	?	N	N	N	Y	Y	N	N
31 Dymally	?	N	Y	N	Y	Y	N	N
32 Anderson	Y	N	Y	N	Y	Y	N	N
33 *Dreier*	Y	Y	Y	Y	N	N	Y	Y
34 Torres	Y	N	Y	N	Y	Y	N	N
35 *Lewis*	?	Y	Y	Y	Y	N	Y	Y
36 Brown	Y	N	N	N	Y	Y	N	N
37 *McCandless*	Y	Y	Y	Y	N	Y	Y	Y
38 Patterson	?	?	?	?	?	Y	N	N
39 *Dannemeyer*	Y	Y	Y	Y	N	Y	Y	Y
40 *Badham*	Y	Y	Y	Y	N	Y	Y	Y
41 *Lowery*	?	Y	Y	Y	Y	N	Y	Y
42 *Lungren*	Y	Y	Y	Y	N	Y	Y	Y

	312	313	314	315	316	317	318	319
43 *Packard*	Y	Y	Y	N	Y	N	Y	Y
44 Bates	Y	N	N	Y	Y	N	N	N
45 *Hunter*	Y	Y	Y	Y	N	N	Y	Y
COLORADO								
1 Schroeder	N	N	N	Y	Y	N	N	N
2 Wirth	Y	N	N	Y	Y	N	N	N
3 Kogovsek	Y	N	N	N	Y	Y	N	N
4 *Brown*	Y	Y	Y	Y	Y	N	Y	Y
5 *Kramer*	Y	Y	Y	N	Y	Y	Y	Y
6 *Schaefer*	Y	Y	Y	Y	N	N	Y	Y
CONNECTICUT								
1 Kennelly	Y	N	N	N	Y	Y	N	N
2 Gejdenson	N	N	N	N	Y	Y	N	N
3 Morrison	?	N	N	Y	Y	Y	N	N
4 *McKinney*	Y	N	N	Y	Y	Y	Y	Y
5 Ratchford	Y	N	N	N	Y	Y	N	N
6 *Johnson*	?	N	N	Y	Y	N	N	N
DELAWARE								
AL Carper	Y	N	Y	N	Y	Y	Y	Y
FLORIDA								
1 Hutto	Y	N	Y	Y	Y	Y	Y	Y
2 Fuqua	Y	N	Y	N	Y	Y	N	N
3 Bennett	Y	N	Y	N	Y	Y	N	N
4 Chappell	Y	N	Y	N	Y	?	N	N
5 *McCollum*	Y	Y	Y	Y	N	Y	Y	Y
6 MacKay	Y	N	Y	N	Y	Y	N	N
7 Gibbons	?	N	Y	N	Y	N	N	N
8 *Young*	?	N	Y	Y	Y	Y	Y	Y
9 *Bilirakis*	?	Y	Y	Y	Y	N	Y	Y
10 Ireland	Y	N	N	N	Y	Y	Y	Y
11 Nelson	Y	N	Y	N	Y	Y	N	N
12 *Lewis*	Y	Y	Y	Y	Y	Y	Y	Y
13 *Mack*	Y	Y	Y	Y	N	Y	Y	Y
14 Mica	P	N	Y	N	Y	?	N	Y
15 *Shaw*	Y	Y	Y	Y	N	N	Y	Y
16 Smith	Y	N	Y	N	Y	Y	N	N
17 Lehman	Y	N	N	N	Y	Y	N	N
18 Pepper	?	N	Y	N	Y	Y	N	N
19 Fascell	Y	N	Y	N	Y	N	N	N
GEORGIA								
1 Thomas	Y	N	N	Y	Y	Y	Y	Y
2 Hatcher	Y	N	Y	N	Y	Y	N	N
3 Ray	Y	N	Y	N	Y	Y	N	N
4 Levitas	?	N	Y	N	Y	Y	Y	Y
5 Fowler	Y	N	Y	N	Y	N	N	N
6 *Gingrich*	?	?	#	?	?	?	Y	Y
7 Vacancy *								
8 Rowland	Y	N	Y	N	Y	Y	N	N
9 Jenkins	Y	N	Y	N	Y	Y	N	N
10 Barnard	?	N	Y	N	Y	N	N	N
HAWAII								
1 Heftel	?	?	?	?	?	?	?	?
2 Akaka	?	N	Y	N	Y	Y	N	N
IDAHO								
1 *Craig*	?	#	#	X	X	?	#	?
2 *Hansen*	?	Y	Y	Y	N	N	Y	Y
ILLINOIS								
1 Hayes **	?	N	N	N	Y	N	N	N
2 Savage	Y	N	N	N	Y	N	N	N
3 Russo	Y	N	Y	N	Y	N	N	N
4 *O'Brien*	Y	Y	Y	?	?	N	N	N
5 Lipinski	?	N	Y	N	Y	Y	N	N
6 *Hyde*	Y	Y	Y	Y	N	Y	N	N
7 Collins	?	N	N	?	?	Y	N	N
8 Rostenkowski	?	?	?	?	?	?	?	?
9 Yates	N	N	N	N	Y	Y	N	N
10 *Porter*	P	Y	Y	Y	N	N	Y	Y
11 Annunzio	Y	N	Y	N	Y	Y	N	N
12 *Crane, P.*	Y	Y	Y	Y	N	N	Y	Y
13 *Erlenborn*	Y	N	Y	N	N	N	Y	Y
14 Corcoran	?	#	#	#	X	N	Y	Y
15 *Madigan*	?	Y	Y	Y	#	?	?	?
16 *Martin*	?	?	#	?	?	N	Y	Y
17 Evans	Y	N	Y	N	Y	Y	N	N
18 *Michel*	Y	Y	Y	N	N	Y	Y	Y
19 *Crane, D.*	?	Y	Y	Y	N	N	Y	Y
20 Durbin	N	N	Y	N	Y	Y	N	N
21 Price	Y	N	Y	N	Y	Y	N	N
22 Simon	?	N	Y	N	Y	Y	N	N
INDIANA								
1 Hall	Y	N	N	N	Y	Y	N	N
2 Sharp	Y	N	Y	N	Y	Y	N	N
3 *Hiler*	Y	Y	Y	Y	N	N	Y	Y
4 *Coats*	Y	Y	Y	N	N	Y	Y	Y
5 Hillis	Y	Y	Y	Y	Y	N	N	N

ND - Northern Democrats   SD - Southern Democrats

	312	313	314	315	316	317	318	319
6 ***Burton***	?	Y	#	Y	N	N	Y	Y
7 ***Myers***	Y	Y	Y	Y	N	N	Y	Y
8 McCloskey	Y	N	Y	N	Y	Y	N	N
9 Hamilton	Y	N	Y	N	Y	Y	N	N
10 Jacobs	N	N	Y	N	Y	Y	N	N
IOWA								
1 ***Leach***	Y	N	N	N	?	N	Y	Y
2 ***Tauke***	?	X	X	?	?	N	Y	Y
3 ***Evans***	N	N	N	Y	Y	N	Y	Y
4 Smith	Y	N	N	N	Y	Y	N	N
5 Harkin	N	N	N	?	Y	N	N	N
6 Bedell	Y	N	N	N	Y	Y	Y	N
KANSAS								
1 ***Roberts***	N	Y	Y	Y	N	N	Y	?
2 Slattery	?	N	Y	N	Y	N	Y	Y
3 ***Winn***	Y	Y	Y	Y	N	N	Y	Y
4 Glickman	Y	N	Y	N	Y	N	Y	N
5 ***Whittaker***	Y	Y	Y	Y	N	N	Y	Y
KENTUCKY								
1 Hubbard	?	?	?	?	?	?	?	?
2 Natcher	Y	N	Y	N	Y	Y	N	N
3 Mazzoli	Y	N	Y	N	Y	Y	N	N
4 ***Snyder***	?	Y	Y	N	Y	N	Y	Y
5 ***Rogers***	?	?	?	?	?	N	Y	Y
6 ***Hopkins***	Y	Y	Y	Y	N	N	Y	Y
7 Perkins	Y	N	Y	N	Y	Y	N	N
LOUISIANA								
1 ***Livingston***	Y	Y	Y	Y	Y	Y	Y	?
2 Boggs	Y	N	Y	N	Y	Y	N	N
3 Tauzin	Y	Y	Y	Y	Y	Y	Y	N
4 Roemer	N	Y	Y	Y	N	Y	Y	Y
5 Huckaby	Y	Y	Y	N	Y	Y	Y	N
6 ***Moore***	Y	Y	Y	Y	Y	Y	Y	Y
7 Breaux	?	Y	Y	Y	Y	Y	Y	Y
8 Long	Y	N	Y	N	Y	Y	N	N
MAINE								
1 ***McKernan***	Y	N	N	Y	Y	Y	Y	N
2 ***Snowe***	Y	N	N	N	Y	Y	N	N
MARYLAND								
1 Dyson	?	N	Y	N	Y	Y	N	N
2 Long	?	N	Y	N	Y	Y	N	N
3 Mikulski	?	?	?	X	#	Y	N	N
4 ***Holt***	?	?	?	?	?	?	?	?
5 Hoyer	Y	N	N	N	Y	Y	N	N
6 Byron	Y	N	Y	N	Y	Y	N	N
7 Mitchell	N	N	N	N	Y	Y	N	N
8 Barnes	?	N	N	N	Y	Y	N	N
MASSACHUSETTS								
1 ***Conte***	Y	N	N	Y	Y	Y	N	N
2 Boland	Y	N	N	N	Y	Y	N	N
3 Early	Y	N	N	N	Y	Y	N	N
4 Frank	Y	N	N	N	Y	Y	N	N
5 Shannon	?	N	N	N	Y	Y	N	N
6 Mavroules	Y	N	N	N	Y	Y	N	N
7 Markey	Y	N	N	N	Y	?	N	N
8 O'Neill								
9 Moakley	Y	N	N	N	Y	Y	N	N
10 Studds	Y	N	N	N	Y	Y	N	N
11 Donnelly	?	N	N	N	Y	Y	Y	Y
MICHIGAN								
1 Conyers	?	N	?	N	Y	Y	N	N
2 ***Pursell***	Y	N	Y	N	Y	N	N	N
3 Wolpe	Y	N	Y	N	Y	Y	N	N
4 ***Siljander***	Y	Y	Y	Y	N	Y	Y	N
5 ***Sawyer***	Y	Y	Y	Y	N	Y	Y	N
6 Carr	Y	N	Y	N	Y	Y	N	N
7 Kildee	Y	N	Y	N	Y	Y	N	N
8 Traxler	Y	N	Y	N	Y	Y	N	?
9 ***Vander Jagt***	?	Y	Y	Y	Y	?	?	?
10 Albosta	Y	N	Y	N	Y	Y	N	N
11 ***Davis***	Y	N	Y	N	Y	Y	N	N
12 Bonior	Y	N	N	N	Y	Y	N	N
13 Crockett	?	N	N	N	Y	?	N	N
14 Hertel	Y	N	Y	N	Y	Y	N	N
15 Ford	?	N	Y	N	Y	?	N	N
16 Dingell	Y	N	N	N	Y	Y	N	N
17 Levin	Y	N	N	N	Y	Y	N	N
18 ***Broomfield***	Y	Y	Y	Y	Y	?	Y	N
MINNESOTA								
1 Penny	Y	N	N	N	Y	Y	N	N
2 ***Weber***	Y	Y	N	Y	Y	?	Y	Y
3 ***Frenzel***	Y	Y	N	N	N	N	Y	Y
4 Vento	Y	N	N	N	Y	Y	N	N
5 Sabo	N	N	N	N	Y	Y	N	N
6 Sikorski	N	N	N	N	Y	Y	N	N
7 ***Stangeland***	?	Y	N	Y	Y	Y	Y	Y
8 Oberstar	?	N	N	N	Y	Y	N	N
MISSISSIPPI								
1 Whitten	Y	N	Y	?	?	Y	?	?
2 ***Franklin***	?	Y	Y	Y	N	Y	Y	Y
3 Montgomery	Y	Y	Y	Y	N	Y	Y	Y
4 Dowdy	Y	N	Y	N	Y	Y	N	N
5 ***Lott***	Y	Y	Y	Y	N	Y	Y	Y
MISSOURI								
1 Clay	?	?	?	?	?	Y	N	N
2 Young	Y	N	N	N	Y	Y	N	X
3 Gephardt	?	N	N	N	Y	Y	N	N
4 Skelton	Y	N	N	N	Y	Y	N	N
5 Wheat	Y	N	N	N	Y	Y	N	N
6 ***Coleman***	Y	Y	N	Y	Y	?	Y	N
7 ***Taylor***	Y	Y	N	N	Y	N	Y	Y
8 ***Emerson***	N	Y	N	Y	Y	N	Y	Y
9 Volkmer	Y	N	N	N	Y	Y	N	Y
MONTANA								
1 Williams	?	N	N	N	Y	Y	N	N
2 ***Marlenee***	?	Y	N	N	Y	N	Y	Y
NEBRASKA								
1 ***Bereuter***	Y	N	N	Y	Y	-	Y	Y
2 ***Daub***	Y	N	N	Y	Y	N	Y	Y
3 ***Smith***	Y	N	N	Y	Y	N	Y	Y
NEVADA								
1 Reid	Y	N	Y	N	Y	N	Y	Y
2 ***Vucanovich***	?	Y	Y	Y	N	N	Y	Y
NEW HAMPSHIRE								
1 D'Amours	?	N	N	N	Y	Y	N	N
2 ***Gregg***	Y	Y	N	Y	N	Y	Y	Y
NEW JERSEY								
1 Florio	?	N	N	N	Y	Y	X	N
2 Hughes	Y	N	N	N	Y	Y	Y	N
3 Howard	?	?	X	X	?	Y	N	N
4 ***Smith***	Y	N	N	N	Y	Y	N	N
5 ***Roukema***	?	N	N	N	Y	Y	Y	Y
6 Dwyer	Y	N	N	N	Y	Y	N	N
7 ***Rinaldo***	?	N	N	N	Y	Y	N	N
8 Roe	?	?	X	X	?	Y	N	N
9 Torricelli	?	N	N	N	Y	Y	N	N
10 Rodino	Y	N	N	N	Y	Y	N	N
11 Minish	Y	N	N	N	Y	Y	N	N
12 ***Courter***	Y	Y	N	N	N	Y	Y	Y
13 ***Forsythe***	N	Y	X	Y	N	Y	Y	Y
14 Guarini	?	N	N	N	Y	Y	N	N
NEW MEXICO								
1 ***Lujan***	Y	Y	N	Y	Y	N	Y	Y
2 ***Skeen***	?	Y	N	Y	Y	N	Y	Y
3 Richardson	Y	N	Y	N	Y	Y	N	N
NEW YORK								
1 ***Carney***	Y	N	N	Y	Y	Y	Y	Y
2 Downey	Y	N	N	N	Y	Y	N	N
3 Mrazek	Y	N	N	N	Y	?	N	N
4 ***Lent***	?	N	N	Y	Y	Y	Y	Y
5 ***McGrath***	?	N	N	Y	Y	Y	Y	Y
6 Addabbo	Y	N	N	N	Y	Y	N	N
7 Ackerman	Y	N	N	N	Y	Y	N	N
8 Scheuer	Y	N	N	N	Y	?	?	?
9 Ferraro	Y	N	N	N	Y	Y	N	N
10 Schumer	?	N	N	N	Y	Y	N	N
11 Towns	?	N	N	N	Y	Y	N	N
12 Owens	Y	N	N	N	Y	Y	N	N
13 Solarz	Y	N	N	N	Y	Y	N	N
14 ***Molinari***	Y	N	N	Y	Y	Y	Y	Y
15 ***Green***	?	N	N	Y	Y	Y	Y	Y
16 Rangel	?	N	N	N	Y	Y	N	N
17 Weiss	Y	N	N	N	Y	Y	N	N
18 Garcia	Y	N	N	N	Y	Y	N	N
19 Biaggi	Y	N	N	N	Y	?	N	?
20 Ottinger	?	N	N	N	Y	Y	?	N
21 ***Fish***	Y	N	N	Y	Y	Y	Y	Y
22 ***Gilman***	+	N	N	N	Y	Y	N	N
23 Stratton	Y	N	N	N	Y	Y	N	N
24 ***Solomon***	Y	Y	N	Y	N	Y	Y	?
25 ***Boehlert***	Y	N	N	N	Y	Y	N	N
26 ***Martin***	Y	N	N	Y	Y	Y	Y	N
27 ***Wortley***	Y	Y	N	Y	N	Y	Y	Y
28 McHugh	?	N	N	N	Y	Y	N	N
29 ***Horton***	Y	N	N	N	Y	Y	N	N
30 ***Conable***	Y	Y	N	Y	N	N	Y	Y
31 ***Kemp***	?	Y	N	Y	N	Y	Y	N
32 LaFalce	Y	N	N	N	Y	Y	N	Y
33 Nowak	Y	N	N	N	Y	Y	N	N
34 Lundine	Y	?	N	N	Y	Y	?	N
NORTH CAROLINA								
1 Jones	?	N	?	N	Y	Y	N	?
2 Valentine	Y	N	Y	N	Y	Y	N	N
3 Whitley	Y	N	Y	N	Y	Y	N	N
4 Andrews	?	?	Y	N	Y	Y	N	N
5 Neal	?	N	Y	N	Y	Y	N	N
6 Britt	Y	N	Y	N	Y	Y	N	Y
7 Rose	Y	N	Y	N	Y	Y	N	N
8 Hefner	Y	N	Y	N	Y	Y	N	N
9 ***Martin***	Y	Y	Y	Y	Y	Y	Y	Y
10 ***Broyhill***	?	Y	Y	Y	N	Y	Y	Y
11 Clarke	Y	N	Y	-	+	+	N	N
NORTH DAKOTA								
AL Dorgan	Y	N	N	N	Y	Y	N	N
OHIO								
1 Luken	Y	N	Y	N	Y	Y	N	N
2 ***Gradison***	Y	Y	Y	Y	Y	N	Y	Y
3 Hall	Y	N	Y	N	Y	Y	N	N
4 ***Oxley***	?	Y	Y	Y	Y	N	Y	Y
5 ***Latta***	Y	Y	Y	Y	N	?	Y	Y
6 ***McEwen***	Y	Y	Y	Y	Y	Y	N	Y
7 ***DeWine***	Y	Y	Y	N	N	N	Y	Y
8 ***Kindness***	Y	Y	Y	Y	Y	N	Y	N
9 Kaptur	Y	N	Y	N	Y	Y	N	N
10 ***Miller***	N	Y	Y	Y	N	N	Y	Y
11 Eckart	?	N	Y	N	Y	Y	N	N
12 ***Kasich***	Y	Y	Y	N	Y	N	Y	Y
13 Pease	Y	N	Y	N	Y	Y	N	N
14 Seiberling	?	N	N	N	Y	?	N	N
15 ***Wylie***	Y	Y	Y	Y	Y	N	Y	Y
16 ***Regula***	Y	Y	Y	Y	Y	N	N	Y
17 ***Williams***	Y	N	Y	N	Y	Y	N	N
18 Applegate	?	N	Y	N	Y	Y	N	N
19 Feighan	?	N	Y	N	Y	Y	N	N
20 Oakar	Y	N	Y	N	Y	Y	N	N
21 Stokes	?	N	N	N	Y	Y	N	N
OKLAHOMA								
1 Jones	Y	N	Y	N	Y	N	Y	Y
2 Synar	Y	N	Y	N	Y	Y	N	N
3 Watkins	Y	N	Y	N	Y	N	N	N
4 McCurdy	Y	N	Y	N	Y	Y	?	Y
5 ***Edwards***	Y	Y	Y	Y	N	N	Y	Y
6 English	Y	N	Y	N	Y	Y	Y	Y
OREGON								
1 AuCoin	?	N	N	N	Y	Y	N	N
2 ***Smith, R.***	Y	Y	N	Y	N	Y	Y	Y
3 Wyden	Y	N	?	N	Y	Y	N	N
4 Weaver	Y	N	N	N	Y	Y	N	N
5 ***Smith, D.***	Y	Y	N	Y	N	N	Y	Y
PENNSYLVANIA								
1 Foglietta	?	N	N	N	Y	Y	N	N
2 Gray	?	N	N	N	Y	Y	N	N
3 Borski	Y	N	N	N	Y	Y	N	N
4 Kolter	?	N	N	N	Y	?	N	N
5 ***Schulze***	Y	Y	X	#	?	N	Y	Y
6 Yatron	?	N	N	N	Y	Y	N	N
7 Edgar	Y	N	N	N	Y	?	N	N
8 Kostmayer	Y	N	N	N	Y	Y	N	N
9 ***Shuster***	Y	Y	N	Y	N	N	Y	Y
10 ***McDade***	?	N	X	Y	Y	N	N	N
11 Harrison	Y	N	N	N	Y	Y	N	N
12 Murtha	Y	N	N	N	Y	?	N	N
13 ***Coughlin***	N	N	N	Y	Y	Y	Y	N
14 Coyne	Y	N	N	N	Y	Y	N	N
15 ***Ritter***	Y	Y	N	Y	N	N	Y	N
16 ***Walker***	N	Y	N	Y	N	N	Y	Y
17 ***Gekas***	Y	Y	N	Y	N	N	Y	Y
18 Walgren	Y	N	N	N	Y	Y	N	N
19 ***Goodling***	?	Y	N	Y	Y	Y	Y	Y
20 Gaydos	Y	N	N	N	Y	Y	N	N
21 ***Ridge***	?	N	N	Y	Y	Y	Y	N
22 Murphy	Y	N	N	N	Y	Y	N	N
23 ***Clinger***	Y	Y	N	Y	Y	Y	Y	Y
RHODE ISLAND								
1 St Germain	?	?	N	N	Y	Y	N	N
2 ***Schneider***	Y	N	N	N	Y	Y	Y	N
SOUTH CAROLINA								
1 ***Hartnett***	?	Y	Y	Y	N	N	Y	Y
2 ***Spence***	Y	Y	Y	Y	Y	Y	?	Y
3 Derrick	?	X	?	X	?	?	?	?
4 ***Campbell***	?	Y	Y	Y	Y	Y	Y	Y
5 Spratt	Y	N	Y	N	Y	Y	N	N
6 Tallon	Y	N	Y	N	Y	Y	N	N
SOUTH DAKOTA								
AL Daschle	Y	N	N	N	Y	Y	N	N
TENNESSEE								
1 ***Quillen***	Y	N	Y	N	Y	N	Y	Y
2 ***Duncan***	Y	N	Y	N	Y	N	Y	N
3 Lloyd	?	N	Y	N	Y	Y	Y	Y
4 Cooper	Y	N	Y	N	Y	Y	Y	N
5 Boner	Y	N	Y	N	Y	Y	N	N
6 Gore	Y	N	Y	N	Y	Y	N	N
7 ***Sundquist***	Y	N	Y	N	Y	N	Y	Y
8 Jones	Y	N	Y	N	Y	Y	N	N
9 Ford	Y	N	N	N	Y	Y	N	N
TEXAS								
1 Hall, S.	Y	N	Y	N	Y	Y	N	N
2 Wilson	Y	N	Y	N	Y	N	N	N
3 ***Bartlett***	Y	Y	Y	Y	N	N	Y	Y
4 Hall, R.	Y	N	Y	N	Y	Y	N	N
5 Bryant	?	N	Y	Y	Y	Y	N	N
6 ***Gramm***	?	Y	Y	Y	N	?	Y	Y
7 ***Archer***	Y	Y	Y	Y	N	N	Y	Y
8 ***Fields***	Y	Y	Y	Y	N	N	N	N
9 Brooks	Y	N	Y	N	Y	Y	N	N
10 Pickle	Y	N	Y	N	Y	Y	N	N
11 Leath	Y	N	Y	N	Y	Y	N	N
12 Wright	Y	N	Y	N	Y	Y	N	N
13 Hightower	Y	N	Y	N	Y	Y	Y	N
14 Patman	Y	N	Y	N	Y	Y	Y	Y
15 de la Garza	Y	N	Y	N	Y	Y	N	N
16 Coleman	Y	N	Y	N	Y	Y	N	N
17 Stenholm	Y	Y	Y	Y	N	Y	Y	Y
18 Leland	?	N	N	N	Y	Y	N	N
19 Hance	?	?	?	?	?	?	?	?
20 Gonzalez	Y	N	Y	N	Y	Y	N	N
21 ***Loeffler***	Y	Y	Y	Y	N	N	Y	Y
22 ***Paul***	?	Y	Y	Y	N	N	Y	Y
23 Kazen	Y	N	Y	N	Y	Y	N	N
24 Frost	Y	N	Y	N	Y	Y	N	N
25 Andrews	Y	N	Y	N	Y	Y	Y	N
26 Vandergriff	Y	N	Y	N	Y	Y	Y	N
27 Ortiz	?	N	Y	N	Y	Y	N	N
UTAH								
1 ***Hansen***	Y	Y	N	Y	N	N	Y	Y
2 ***Marriott***	Y	Y	Y	Y	N	N	Y	Y
3 ***Nielson***	Y	Y	Y	Y	N	N	Y	Y
VERMONT								
AL ***Jeffords***	Y	Y	N	N	N	N	Y	?
VIRGINIA								
1 ***Bateman***	Y	Y	Y	Y	N	Y	Y	Y
2 ***Whitehurst***	Y	Y	Y	Y	N	Y	Y	Y
3 ***Bliley***	Y	Y	Y	Y	N	N	Y	Y
4 Sisisky	Y	N	Y	N	Y	Y	N	N
5 Daniel	Y	Y	Y	N	N	N	Y	Y
6 Olin	Y	N	Y	N	Y	Y	Y	Y
7 ***Robinson***	Y	Y	Y	Y	N	N	Y	Y
8 ***Parris***	Y	Y	Y	Y	Y	Y	Y	Y
9 Boucher	Y	N	Y	N	Y	Y	N	N
10 ***Wolf***	Y	N	Y	Y	Y	N	Y	Y
WASHINGTON								
1 ***Pritchard***	?	N	N	N	Y	Y	Y	Y
2 Swift	?	N	N	N	Y	Y	N	Y
3 Bonker	Y	N	N	N	Y	Y	N	N
4 ***Morrison***	Y	N	N	N	Y	Y	Y	Y
5 Foley	Y	N	?	N	Y	?	N	N
6 Dicks	Y	N	N	N	Y	Y	N	N
7 Lowry	?	N	N	N	Y	Y	N	N
8 ***Chandler***	Y	N	N	N	Y	Y	Y	Y
WEST VIRGINIA								
1 Mollohan	Y	N	N	N	Y	Y	N	N
2 Staggers	Y	?	N	N	Y	Y	N	N
3 Wise	Y	N	N	N	Y	Y	N	N
4 Rahall	Y	N	N	N	Y	Y	N	N
WISCONSIN								
1 Aspin	?	N	N	N	Y	Y	?	N
2 Kastenmeier	Y	N	N	N	Y	Y	N	N
3 ***Gunderson***	Y	Y	N	N	Y	Y	Y	N
4 Zablocki	Y	N	N	N	Y	?	?	N
5 Moody	Y	N	N	N	Y	?	N	N
6 ***Petri***	Y	N	N	N	Y	?	Y	Y
7 Obey	P	N	N	N	Y	Y	N	N
8 ***Roth***	Y	Y	N	Y	Y	Y	Y	Y
9 ***Sensenbrenner***	Y	Y	N	Y	N	Y	Y	Y
WYOMING								
AL ***Cheney***	Y	Y	Y	Y	N	N	Y	Y

Southern states - Ala., Ark., Fla., Ga., Ky., La., Miss., N.C., Okla., S.C., Tenn., Texas, Va.

320. H J Res 353. Korean Plane Resolution. Passage of the joint resolution to condemn the Soviet Union for its destruction of a Korean civilian airliner. Passed 416-0: R 159-0; D 257-0 (ND 172-0, SD 85-0), Sept. 14, 1983.

321. Procedural Motion. Rogers, R-Ky., motion to approve the House *Journal* of Wednesday, Sept. 14. Motion agreed to 361-23: R 141-11; D 220-12 (ND 141-11, SD 79-1), Sept. 15, 1983.

322. S 675. Omnibus Defense Authorizations. Adoption of the conference report on the bill to authorize $187.5 billion for weapons procurement, military research and operations and maintenance of the Department of Defense in fiscal 1984. Adopted 266-152: R 133-28; D 133-124 (ND 54-119, SD 79-5), Sept. 15, 1983.

323. HR 3391. Trade Adjustment Assistance. Frenzel, R-Minn., amendment to eliminate the special fund that would finance benefits from a percentage of annual customs duties, and replace it with a regular authorization. Rejected 173-231: R 135-25; D 38-206 (ND 11-151, SD 27-55), Sept. 15, 1983.

324. HR 3391. Trade Adjustment Assistance. Frenzel, R-Minn., motion to recommit the bill to the Ways and Means Committee with instructions to amend the bill so that the amount authorized for trade adjustment assistance could not exceed the amount provided in Congress' 1984 budget resolution. Motion rejected 194-218: R 142-16; D 52-202 (ND 13-156, SD 39-46), Sept. 15, 1983.

KEY

Y Voted for (yea).
\# Paired for.
+ Announced for.
N Voted against (nay).
X Paired against.
− Announced against.
P Voted "present".
C Voted "present" to avoid possible conflict of interest.
? Did not vote or otherwise make a position known.

Democrats *Republicans*

	320	321	322	323	324
ALABAMA					
1 *Edwards*	Y	?	Y	Y	Y
2 *Dickinson*	Y	N	Y	Y	Y
3 Nichols	Y	Y	Y	Y	Y
4 Bevill	Y	Y	N	N	N
5 Flippo	Y	Y	Y	N	N
6 Erdreich	Y	Y	Y	N	N
7 Shelby	Y	Y	Y	N	N
ALASKA					
AL *Young*	?	?	?	#	?
ARIZONA					
1 *McCain*	Y	Y	Y	Y	Y
2 Udall	Y	Y	N	N	N
3 *Stump*	?	?	Y	Y	Y
4 *Rudd*	Y	Y	Y	Y	Y
5 McNulty	Y	Y	Y	N	N
ARKANSAS					
1 Alexander	Y	Y	Y	N	N
2 *Bethune*	Y	Y	N	Y	Y
3 *Hammerschmidt*	Y	Y	Y	Y	Y
4 Anthony	Y	Y	Y	N	N
CALIFORNIA					
1 Bosco	Y	?	N	N	N
2 *Chappie*	Y	Y	Y	Y	Y
3 Matsui	Y	Y	Y	N	N
4 Fazio	Y	Y	N	N	N
5 Burton	Y	Y	N	N	N
6 Boxer	Y	Y	N	N	N
7 Miller	Y	N	?	?	
8 Dellums	?	?	X	X	X
9 Stark	Y	Y	N	?	?
10 Edwards	Y	N	N	N	N
11 Lantos	Y	Y	N	N	N
12 *Zschau*	Y	Y	N	Y	Y
13 Mineta	Y	Y	N	N	N
14 *Shumway*	Y	Y	Y	Y	Y
15 Coelho	Y	Y	Y	?	N
16 Panetta	Y	Y	Y	N	N
17 *Pashayan*	?	?	?	#	?
18 Lehman	Y	Y	N	−	N
19 *Lagomarsino*	Y	Y	Y	Y	Y
20 *Thomas*	Y	Y	Y	Y	Y
21 *Fiedler*	Y	Y	Y	Y	Y
22 *Moorhead*	Y	Y	Y	Y	Y
23 Beilenson	Y	Y	N	Y	N
24 Waxman	Y	N	N	N	N
25 Roybal	Y	Y	?	N	N
26 Berman	Y	Y	N	N	N
27 Levine	Y	N	N	N	N
28 Dixon	Y	Y	N	N	N
29 Hawkins	Y	N	N	N	N
30 Martinez	Y	?	N	N	N
31 Dymally	Y	P	N	N	N
32 Anderson	Y	Y	N	N	N
33 *Dreier*	Y	Y	Y	Y	Y
34 Torres	Y	Y	N	N	N
35 *Lewis*	Y	Y	Y	Y	Y
36 Brown	Y	N	N	N	N
37 *McCandless*	Y	Y	Y	Y	Y
38 Patterson	Y	Y	N	?	N
39 *Dannemeyer*	Y	Y	Y	Y	Y
40 *Badham*	Y	Y	Y	Y	Y
41 *Lowery*	Y	Y	Y	Y	Y
42 Lungren	Y	Y	Y	Y	Y

	320	321	322	323	324
43 *Packard*	Y	Y	Y	Y	Y
44 Bates	Y	Y	N	N	?
45 *Hunter*	Y	Y	Y	Y	Y
COLORADO					
1 Schroeder	Y	N	N	N	N
2 Wirth	Y	Y	N	N	Y
3 Kogovsek	Y	Y	N	N	N
4 *Brown*	Y	N	N	Y	Y
5 *Kramer*	Y	Y	Y	Y	Y
6 *Schaefer*	?	Y	Y	Y	Y
CONNECTICUT					
1 Kennelly	Y	Y	Y	N	N
2 Gejdenson	Y	N	N	N	N
3 Morrison	Y	N	N	N	N
4 *McKinney*	Y	Y	N	Y	Y
5 Ratchford	Y	Y	N	N	N
6 *Johnson*	Y	Y	Y	Y	N
DELAWARE					
AL Carper	Y	Y	Y	Y	Y
FLORIDA					
1 Hutto	Y	Y	Y	N	Y
2 Fuqua	Y	Y	N	N	N
3 Bennett	Y	Y	Y	N	N
4 Chappell	Y	Y	Y	N	Y
5 *McCollum*	Y	Y	Y	Y	Y
6 MacKay	Y	Y	N	N	N
7 Gibbons	Y	Y	Y	N	N
8 *Young*	Y	Y	Y	Y	Y
9 *Bilirakis*	Y	Y	Y	Y	Y
10 Ireland	Y	Y	Y	Y	Y
11 Nelson	Y	Y	N	Y	Y
12 *Lewis*	Y	Y	Y	Y	Y
13 *Mack*	Y	Y	Y	Y	#
14 Mica	Y	Y	Y	Y	N
15 *Shaw*	Y	Y	Y	Y	Y
16 Smith	Y	Y	N	N	N
17 Lehman	Y	N	N	N	N
18 Pepper	Y	?	N	N	N
19 Fascell	Y	N	N	N	N
GEORGIA					
1 Thomas	Y	Y	Y	Y	N
2 Hatcher	Y	Y	Y	N	N
3 Ray	Y	Y	Y	Y	Y
4 Levitas	Y	Y	Y	Y	Y
5 Fowler	Y	Y	Y	N	N
6 *Gingrich*	Y	?	Y	Y	Y
7 Vacancy					
8 Rowland	Y	Y	Y	Y	Y
9 Jenkins	Y	Y	?	Y	Y
10 Barnard	Y	Y	Y	Y	Y
HAWAII					
1 Heftel	?	?	?	?	?
2 Akaka	Y	Y	Y	N	N
IDAHO					
1 *Craig*	?	Y	Y	Y	Y
2 *Hansen*	Y	?	Y	Y	Y
ILLINOIS					
1 Hayes	Y	N	N	N	N
2 Savage	Y	N	N	N	N
3 Russo	Y	Y	N	N	N
4 *O'Brien*	Y	Y	N	N	N
5 Lipinski	Y	N	N	N	N
6 *Hyde*	Y	Y	Y	Y	Y
7 Collins	Y	N	N	N	N
8 Rostenkowski	?	Y	N	N	N
9 Yates	Y	N	N	N	N
10 *Porter*	Y	Y	N	Y	Y
11 Annunzio	Y	Y	N	N	N
12 *Crane, P.*	Y	?	Y	Y	Y
13 *Erlenborn*	Y	?	Y	Y	Y
14 *Corcoran*	Y	?	Y	Y	Y
15 *Madigan*	Y	N	Y	Y	Y
16 *Martin*	Y	Y	Y	Y	Y
17 Evans	Y	Y	N	N	N
18 *Michel*	Y	Y	Y	Y	Y
19 *Crane, D.*	Y	Y	Y	Y	Y
20 Durbin	Y	N	Y	N	N
21 Price	Y	Y	Y	N	N
22 Simon	?	?	N	N	N
INDIANA					
1 Hall	Y	N	N	N	N
2 Sharp	Y	Y	Y	N	N
3 *Hiler*	Y	Y	Y	Y	Y
4 *Coats*	Y	Y	Y	N	N
5 *Hillis*	Y	Y	Y	N	N

ND - Northern Democrats   SD - Southern Democrats

	320	321	322	323	324
6 Burton	Y	Y	Y	Y	Y
7 Myers	Y	Y	Y	Y	Y
8 McCloskey	Y	?	Y	N	N
9 Hamilton	Y	Y	Y	N	N
10 Jacobs	Y	N	Y	N	N
IOWA					
1 Leach	Y	Y	N	N	Y
2 Tauke	Y	Y	N	Y	Y
3 Evans	Y	N	N	Y	Y
4 Smith	Y	Y	N	N	N
5 Harkin	N	N	N	N	N
6 Bedell	Y	Y	N	N	Y
KANSAS					
1 Roberts	Y	N	Y	Y	Y
2 Slattery	Y	Y	Y	Y	Y
3 Winn	Y	Y	Y	Y	Y
4 Glickman	Y	Y	Y	Y	Y
5 Whittaker	Y	Y	Y	Y	Y
KENTUCKY					
1 Hubbard	Y	Y	Y	N	Y
2 Natcher	Y	Y	Y	N	N
3 Mazzoli	Y	Y	Y	N	Y
4 Snyder	Y	Y	Y	Y	Y
5 Rogers	Y	Y	Y	Y	Y
6 Hopkins	Y	Y	Y	Y	Y
7 Perkins	Y	Y	Y	N	N
LOUISIANA					
1 Livingston	Y	Y	Y	Y	Y
2 Boggs	Y	Y	Y	N	N
3 Tauzin	Y	Y	Y	Y	Y
4 Roemer	Y	N	N	Y	Y
5 Huckaby	Y	Y	Y	?	Y
6 Moore	Y	Y	Y	Y	Y
7 Breaux	Y	Y	Y	Y	Y
8 Long	Y	Y	Y	N	N
MAINE					
1 McKernan	Y	Y	N	N	Y
2 Snowe	Y	Y	N	N	N
MARYLAND					
1 Dyson	Y	Y	Y	N	N
2 Long	Y	Y	Y	N	N
3 Mikulski	Y	Y	N	N	N
4 Holt	?	?	?	?	?
5 Hoyer	Y	Y	Y	N	N
6 Byron	Y	Y	Y	N	N
7 Mitchell	Y	N	N	N	N
8 Barnes	Y	Y	N	N	N
MASSACHUSETTS					
1 Conte	Y	Y	N	N	Y
2 Boland	Y	Y	N	N	N
3 Early	Y	Y	N	N	N
4 Frank	Y	Y	N	?	N
5 Shannon	Y	Y	N	N	N
6 Mavroules	Y	?	Y	N	N
7 Markey	Y	Y	N	N	N
8 O'Neill	Y				
9 Moakley	Y	Y	N	N	N
10 Studds	Y	Y	N	N	N
11 Donnelly	Y	Y	N	Y	Y
MICHIGAN					
1 Conyers	P	?	N	?	N
2 Pursell	Y	Y	N	Y	Y
3 Wolpe	Y	Y	N	N	N
4 Siljander	Y	Y	Y	Y	Y
5 Sawyer	Y	Y	Y	N	Y
6 Carr	Y	Y	N	N	N
7 Kildee	Y	Y	N	N	N
8 Traxler	Y	Y	N	N	N
9 Vander Jagt	Y	Y	Y	Y	Y
10 Albosta	Y	Y	Y	N	N
11 Davis	Y	Y	N	N	N
12 Bonior	Y	Y	N	N	N
13 Crockett	P	?	N	N	N
14 Hertel	Y	Y	N	N	N
15 Ford	Y	?	N	N	N
16 Dingell	Y	?	N	N	N
17 Levin	Y	Y	N	N	N
18 Broomfield	Y	Y	Y	Y	?
MINNESOTA					
1 Penny	Y	Y	N	N	N
2 Weber	Y	Y	N	Y	Y
3 Frenzel	Y	N	Y	Y	Y
4 Vento	Y	Y	N	N	N
5 Sabo	Y	N	N	N	N
6 Sikorski	Y	N	N	N	N

	320	321	322	323	324
7 Stangeland	Y	Y	Y	Y	Y
8 Oberstar	Y	?	N	N	N
MISSISSIPPI					
1 Whitten	Y	Y	Y	N	N
2 Franklin	Y	Y	Y	Y	Y
3 Montgomery	Y	Y	Y	Y	Y
4 Dowdy	Y	?	Y	N	N
5 Lott	Y	Y	Y	Y	Y
MISSOURI					
1 Clay	Y	N	N	N	N
2 Young	Y	?	Y	N	N
3 Gephardt	Y	Y	Y	N	N
4 Skelton	Y	Y	N	N	N
5 Wheat	Y	Y	N	N	N
6 Coleman	Y	?	?	?	?
7 Taylor	Y	Y	Y	Y	Y
8 Emerson	Y	N	Y	Y	Y
9 Volkmer	Y	Y	N	N	N
MONTANA					
1 Williams	Y	?	N	N	N
2 Marlenee	Y	Y	Y	Y	Y
NEBRASKA					
1 Bereuter	Y	Y	Y	Y	Y
2 Daub	Y	Y	Y	Y	Y
3 Smith	Y	Y	Y	Y	Y
NEVADA					
1 Reid	Y	Y	Y	Y	Y
2 Vucanovich	Y	Y	Y	Y	Y
NEW HAMPSHIRE					
1 D'Amours	Y	Y	N	Y	Y
2 Gregg	Y	Y	N	N	N
NEW JERSEY					
1 Florio	Y	Y	Y	N	N
2 Hughes	Y	Y	Y	N	N
3 Howard	Y	Y	Y	N	N
4 Smith	Y	Y	Y	N	N
5 Roukema	Y	Y	N	Y	Y
6 Dwyer	Y	Y	Y	N	N
7 Rinaldo	Y	Y	Y	N	N
8 Roe	Y	Y	Y	N	N
9 Torricelli	Y	Y	N	N	N
10 Rodino	Y	Y	N	N	N
11 Minish	Y	Y	Y	N	N
12 Courter	Y	Y	Y	Y	Y
13 Forsythe	Y	N	N	Y	Y
14 Guarini	Y	Y	Y	N	N
NEW MEXICO					
1 Lujan	Y	Y	Y	Y	Y
2 Skeen	Y	Y	Y	Y	Y
3 Richardson	Y	Y	Y	N	N
NEW YORK					
1 Carney	Y	Y	Y	Y	Y
2 Downey	Y	Y	N	N	N
3 Mrazek	Y	Y	Y	N	N
4 Lent	Y	Y	Y	Y	Y
5 McGrath	Y	Y	Y	Y	Y
6 Addabbo	Y	Y	N	N	N
7 Ackerman	Y	Y	N	N	N
8 Scheuer	Y	Y	N	N	N
9 Ferraro	Y	Y	N	N	N
10 Schumer	Y	Y	N	N	N
11 Towns	Y	?	N	N	N
12 Owens	Y	Y	N	N	N
13 Solarz	Y	Y	N	X	X
14 Molinari	Y	Y	Y	Y	Y
15 Green	Y	Y	N	Y	Y
16 Rangel	Y	Y	N	N	N
17 Weiss	Y	Y	N	N	N
18 Garcia	Y	Y	N	N	N
19 Biaggi	Y	Y	?	N	N
20 Ottinger	Y	P	N	N	N
21 Fish	Y	Y	N	Y	Y
22 Gilman	Y	Y	Y	N	N
23 Stratton	Y	Y	Y	N	N
24 Solomon	Y	?	Y	Y	Y
25 Boehlert	Y	Y	Y	N	N
26 Martin	Y	Y	Y	N	N
27 Wortley	Y	Y	Y	Y	Y
28 McHugh	Y	Y	N	N	N
29 Horton	Y	Y	N	N	Y
30 Conable	Y	Y	Y	Y	Y
31 Kemp	Y	Y	Y	Y	Y
32 LaFalce	Y	Y	Y	N	N
33 Nowak	Y	Y	N	N	N
34 Lundine	Y	P	N	N	N

	320	321	322	323	324
NORTH CAROLINA					
1 Jones	?	?	?	?	?
2 Valentine	Y	Y	Y	Y	Y
3 Whitley	Y	Y	Y	N	Y
4 Andrews	Y	Y	Y	N	Y
5 Neal	Y	Y	Y	Y	Y
6 Britt	Y	Y	Y	Y	Y
7 Rose	Y	Y	Y	N	Y
8 Hefner	Y	Y	Y	?	Y
9 Martin	Y	Y	Y	Y	Y
10 Broyhill	Y	Y	Y	Y	Y
11 Clarke	Y	Y	Y	N	N
NORTH DAKOTA					
AL Dorgan	Y	Y	N	Y	Y
OHIO					
1 Luken	Y	Y	N	N	N
2 Gradison	Y	Y	Y	Y	Y
3 Hall	Y	Y	N	N	N
4 Oxley	Y	Y	Y	Y	Y
5 Latta	Y	Y	Y	#	Y
6 McEwen	Y	Y	Y	Y	Y
7 DeWine	Y	Y	Y	Y	Y
8 Kindness	Y	Y	Y	Y	Y
9 Kaptur	Y	?	N	X	N
10 Miller	Y	N	Y	Y	Y
11 Eckart	Y	?	N	N	N
12 Kasich	Y	Y	Y	Y	Y
13 Pease	Y	N	N	N	N
14 Seiberling	Y	?	N	N	N
15 Wylie	?	Y	Y	Y	Y
16 Regula	Y	Y	Y	Y	Y
17 Williams	Y	Y	Y	N	N
18 Applegate	Y	?	N	N	N
19 Feighan	Y	N	N	N	N
20 Oakar	Y	Y	N	N	N
21 Stokes	Y	Y	N	N	N
OKLAHOMA					
1 Jones	Y	Y	Y	Y	Y
2 Synar	Y	Y	Y	Y	N
3 Watkins	Y	Y	Y	Y	Y
4 McCurdy	Y	Y	Y	Y	Y
5 Edwards	Y	Y	Y	Y	Y
6 English	Y	Y	Y	Y	Y
OREGON					
1 AuCoin	Y	?	N	N	N
2 Smith, R.	Y	Y	Y	Y	Y
3 Wyden	Y	Y	N	N	N
4 Weaver	Y	N	N	N	N
5 Smith, D.	Y	Y	Y	Y	Y
PENNSYLVANIA					
1 Foglietta	Y	N	N	N	N
2 Gray	Y	N	N	N	N
3 Borski	Y	N	N	N	N
4 Kolter	Y	Y	N	N	N
5 Schulze	Y	Y	Y	Y	Y
6 Yatron	Y	Y	N	N	N
7 Edgar	Y	Y	N	?	?
8 Kostmayer	Y	N	N	N	N
9 Shuster	Y	Y	Y	Y	Y
10 McDade	Y	Y	Y	N	Y
11 Harrison	Y	N	N	N	N
12 Murtha	Y	Y	N	N	N
13 Coughlin	Y	?	X	Y	Y
14 Coyne	Y	Y	N	N	N
15 Ritter	Y	Y	Y	Y	Y
16 Walker	Y	N	Y	Y	Y
17 Gekas	Y	Y	Y	Y	Y
18 Walgren	Y	Y	N	N	N
19 Goodling	Y	?	N	Y	Y
20 Gaydos	Y	Y	N	N	N
21 Ridge	Y	Y	Y	Y	Y
22 Murphy	Y	Y	Y	N	N
23 Clinger	Y	Y	N	Y	Y
RHODE ISLAND					
1 St Germain	Y	?	?	?	?
2 Schneider	Y	Y	N	N	N
SOUTH CAROLINA					
1 Hartnett	Y	Y	Y	Y	Y
2 Spence	Y	Y	Y	Y	Y
3 Derrick	?	?	?	?	?
4 Campbell	+	Y	Y	Y	Y
5 Spratt	Y	Y	N	N	N
6 Tallon	Y	Y	Y	N	Y
SOUTH DAKOTA					
AL Daschle	Y	Y	Y	Y	Y

	320	321	322	323	324
TENNESSEE					
1 Quillen	Y	Y	Y	Y	#
2 Duncan	Y	Y	Y	N	Y
3 Lloyd	Y	Y	Y	Y	Y
4 Cooper	Y	Y	Y	N	Y
5 Boner	Y	Y	#	X	X
6 Gore	Y	Y	Y	N	N
7 Sundquist	Y	Y	Y	N	N
8 Jones	Y	Y	Y	N	N
9 Ford	Y	Y	N	N	N
TEXAS					
1 Hall, S.	Y	Y	Y	N	N
2 Wilson	Y	?	Y	N	N
3 Bartlett	Y	Y	Y	N	N
4 Hall, R.	Y	Y	Y	N	N
5 Bryant	Y	Y	Y	N	N
6 Gramm	Y	Y	Y	Y	Y
7 Archer	Y	Y	Y	Y	Y
8 Fields	Y	N	Y	N	N
9 Brooks	Y	?	Y	N	N
10 Pickle	Y	Y	N	N	N
11 Leath	Y	Y	N	N	N
12 Wright	Y	Y	N	N	N
13 Hightower	Y	Y	N	N	N
14 Patman	Y	Y	Y	N	N
15 de la Garza	?	?	Y	N	N
16 Coleman	Y	Y	N	N	N
17 Stenholm	Y	Y	?	Y	Y
18 Leland	Y	N	N	N	N
19 Hance	+	?	?	?	?
20 Gonzalez	Y	Y	N	N	N
21 Loeffler	Y	Y	Y	Y	Y
22 Paul	Y	N	Y	N	Y
23 Kazen	Y	Y	N	N	N
24 Frost	Y	Y	N	N	N
25 Andrews	Y	Y	Y	Y	Y
26 Vandergriff	Y	P	Y	Y	Y
27 Ortiz	Y	Y	N	N	N
UTAH					
1 Hansen	Y	Y	Y	Y	Y
2 Marriott	Y	Y	Y	Y	Y
3 Nielson	Y	Y	Y	Y	Y
VERMONT					
AL Jeffords	Y	Y	N	N	Y
VIRGINIA					
1 Bateman	Y	Y	Y	Y	Y
2 Whitehurst	Y	Y	Y	Y	Y
3 Bliley	Y	Y	Y	Y	Y
4 Sisisky	Y	Y	Y	N	N
5 Daniel	Y	Y	Y	Y	Y
6 Olin	Y	Y	Y	N	N
7 Robinson	Y	Y	Y	Y	Y
8 Parris	Y	?	#	#	#
9 Boucher	Y	Y	Y	N	N
10 Wolf	Y	Y	Y	Y	Y
WASHINGTON					
1 Pritchard	Y	Y	N	Y	Y
2 Swift	Y	Y	N	N	N
3 Bonker	Y	Y	N	N	N
4 Morrison	Y	Y	Y	N	N
5 Foley	Y	Y	N	N	N
6 Dicks	Y	Y	N	N	N
7 Lowry	Y	Y	N	N	N
8 Chandler	Y	Y	Y	Y	Y
WEST VIRGINIA					
1 Mollohan	Y	Y	Y	N	N
2 Staggers	Y	?	Y	N	N
3 Wise	Y	Y	N	N	N
4 Rahall	Y	Y	N	N	N
WISCONSIN					
1 Aspin	Y	Y	Y	N	N
2 Kastenmeier	Y	Y	N	?	N
3 Gunderson	Y	Y	Y	Y	Y
4 Zablocki	Y	Y	Y	N	N
5 Moody	Y	Y	N	N	N
6 Petri	Y	Y	N	Y	Y
7 Obey	Y	Y	N	N	N
8 Roth	Y	Y	Y	?	?
9 Sensenbrenner	Y	Y	Y	Y	Y
WYOMING					
AL Cheney	Y	Y	Y	Y	Y

Southern states · Ala., Ark., Fla., Ga., Ky., La., Miss., N.C., Okla., S.C., Tenn., Texas, Va.

325. HR 3222. State, Justice, Commerce Appropriations, Fiscal 1984. Smith, D-Iowa, motion that the Committee of the Whole rise and report the bill back to the House with amendments, thereby barring any legislative riders such as a prohibition on use of Justice Department funds to block programs of "voluntary" school prayer. Motion agreed to 245-120: R 34-112; D 211-8 (ND 146-1, SD 65-7), Sept. 19, 1983.

326. HR 3222. State, Justice, Commerce Appropriations, Fiscal 1984. Passage of the bill to provide $6,717,926,000 in fiscal 1984 for the State, Justice and Commerce departments and the federal judiciary. Passed 228-142: R 41-106; D 187-36 (ND 142-9, SD 45-27), Sept. 19, 1983. The president had requested $9,744,502,000 in new budget authority.

327. HR 1036. Community Renewal Employment Act. Adoption of the rule (H Res 302) providing for House floor consideration of the bill to authorize federal grants to local communities for projects to provide public service jobs in areas of high unemployment. Adopted 309-108: R 56-104; D 253-4 (ND 172-0, SD 81-4), Sept. 20, 1983.

328. HR 1036. Community Renewal Employment Act. Hawkins, D-Calif., amendment to delete the $5 billion fiscal 1983 authorization in the bill and instead authorize $3.5 billion in fiscal 1984 for the jobs program. Adopted 414-0: R 164-0; D 250-0 (ND 163-0, SD 87-0), Sept. 21, 1983.

329. HR 1036. Community Renewal Employment Act. Hawkins, D-Calif., amendment to the Jeffords, R-Vt., amendment, to terminate the bill's authorization if unemployment rates fall below 4 percent while continuing authorization of funds for areas where unemployment was at least 6.5 percent. Rejected 208-210: R 4-158; D 204-52 (ND 160-10, SD 44-42), Sept. 21, 1983. (The Jeffords amendment, which would phase down the authorization levels as unemployment declines and eliminate it if unemployment falls below 6 percent, subsequently was adopted by voice vote.)

330. HR 1036. Community Renewal Employment Act. Gekas, R-Pa., amendment to prohibit authorization of the funds in the bill if spending those funds would result in deficit spending by the federal government. Rejected 166-258: R 134-30; D 32-228 (ND 6-166, SD 26-62), Sept. 21, 1983.

331. HR 1036. Community Renewal Employment Act. Walker, R-Pa., amendment to require that all of the jobs created under the bill go to people who had been unemployed at least six weeks before the bill is enacted. Rejected 142-279: R 129-34; D 13-245 (ND 0-172, SD 13-73), Sept. 21, 1983.

332. HR 1036. Community Renewal Employment Act. Walker, R-Pa., amendment to, in effect, waive the Davis-Bacon Act, which requires that the prevailing local wage be paid on federal construction projects, as applied to revenue sharing projects, if such a waiver would result in a substantial increase in employment for minority youths. Rejected 92-327: R 89-73; D 3-254 (ND 0-169, SD 3-85), Sept. 21, 1983.

KEY

Y Voted for (yea).
\# Paired for.
+ Announced for.
N Voted against (nay).
X Paired against.
- Announced against.
P Voted "present".
C Voted "present" to avoid possible conflict of interest.
? Did not vote or otherwise make a position known.

Democrats *Republicans*

	325	326	327	328	329	330	331	332
ALABAMA								
1 *Edwards*	N	N	N	Y	N	N	N	N
2 *Dickinson*	Y	N	N	Y	N	Y	N	N
3 Nichols	?	X	Y	Y	N	N	N	N
4 Bevill	?	?	Y	Y	Y	N	N	N
5 Flippo	Y	N	Y	Y	Y	N	N	N
6 Erdreich	Y	N	Y	Y	N	Y	N	N
7 Shelby	Y	N	Y	Y	?	Y	Y	N
ALASKA								
AL *Young*	?	X	Y	Y	N	Y	Y	Y
ARIZONA								
1 *McCain*	N	N	N	Y	N	Y	Y	Y
2 Udall	Y	Y	Y	?	Y	N	N	N
3 *Stump*	Y	N	N	Y	N	Y	Y	Y
4 *Rudd*	N	Y	N	Y	N	Y	Y	Y
5 McNulty	Y	Y	Y	Y	Y	N	N	N
ARKANSAS								
1 Alexander	Y	?	Y	Y	Y	N	N	N
2 *Bethune*	N	Y	N	Y	N	Y	Y	Y
3 *Hammerschmidt*	N	Y	Y	Y	N	Y	Y	Y
4 Anthony	Y	Y	?	Y	#	N	N	N
CALIFORNIA								
1 Bosco	?	?	Y	Y	Y	N	N	N
2 *Chappie*	?	Y	N	Y	N	Y	Y	Y
3 Matsui	Y	Y	?	Y	Y	N	N	N
4 Fazio	Y	Y	?	Y	Y	N	N	N
5 Burton	?	?	Y	Y	Y	N	N	N
6 Boxer	Y	Y	Y	Y	Y	N	N	N
7 Miller	Y	Y	Y	Y	Y	N	N	N
8 Dellums	Y	Y	Y	Y	Y	N	N	N
9 Stark	Y	N	Y	Y	?	N	N	?
10 Edwards	Y	Y	Y	Y	Y	N	N	N
11 Lantos	Y	Y	?	Y	Y	N	N	N
12 *Zschau*	Y	Y	N	Y	N	Y	Y	Y
13 Mineta	Y	Y	Y	Y	Y	N	N	N
14 *Shumway*	N	N	N	Y	N	Y	Y	Y
15 Coelho	?	Y	Y	Y	Y	N	N	N
16 Panetta	Y	Y	Y	Y	Y	N	N	N
17 *Pashayan*	N	N	N	Y	N	?	?	Y
18 Lehman	Y	Y	Y	Y	Y	N	N	N
19 *Lagomarsino*	N	N	N	Y	N	Y	Y	Y
20 *Thomas*	N	N	N	Y	N	Y	Y	Y
21 *Fiedler*	N	N	N	Y	N	Y	Y	Y
22 *Moorhead*	N	N	N	Y	N	Y	Y	Y
23 Beilenson	Y	Y	Y	Y	Y	N	N	N
24 Waxman	Y	Y	Y	Y	Y	N	N	N
25 Roybal	Y	Y	Y	Y	Y	N	N	N
26 Berman	Y	Y	Y	?	Y	N	N	N
27 Levine	Y	Y	Y	Y	Y	N	N	N
28 Dixon	Y	Y	Y	Y	Y	N	N	N
29 Hawkins	Y	Y	Y	Y	Y	N	N	N
30 Martinez	Y	Y	Y	Y	Y	N	N	N
31 Dymally	Y	Y	Y	Y	Y	N	N	N
32 Anderson	Y	Y	Y	Y	Y	N	N	N
33 *Dreier*	N	N	N	Y	N	Y	Y	Y
34 Torres	Y	Y	Y	Y	Y	N	N	N
35 *Lewis*	N	Y	N	Y	N	Y	Y	Y
36 Brown	Y	Y	Y	Y	Y	N	N	N
37 *McCandless*	N	N	N	Y	N	Y	Y	Y
38 Patterson	Y	Y	Y	Y	Y	N	N	N
39 *Dannemeyer*	N	N	N	Y	N	Y	Y	Y
40 *Badham*	N	N	N	Y	N	Y	Y	Y
41 *Lowery*	N	N	N	Y	N	Y	Y	Y
42 *Lungren*	N	N	N	Y	N	Y	Y	Y
43 *Packard*	N	N	N	Y	N	Y	Y	Y
44 Bates	Y	N	Y	Y	N	N	N	N
45 *Hunter*	N	Y	N	Y	N	Y	Y	Y
COLORADO								
1 Schroeder	Y	Y	Y	Y	Y	N	N	N
2 Wirth	Y	Y	Y	Y	Y	N	N	N
3 Kogovsek	Y	Y	Y	Y	Y	N	N	N
4 *Brown*	N	N	N	Y	N	Y	Y	N
5 *Kramer*	N	N	N	Y	N	Y	Y	Y
6 *Schaefer*	N	N	N	Y	N	Y	Y	Y
CONNECTICUT								
1 Kennelly	Y	Y	Y	Y	Y	N	N	N
2 Gejdenson	Y	Y	Y	Y	Y	N	N	N
3 Morrison	Y	Y	Y	?	#	X	N	N
4 *McKinney*	Y	Y	Y	Y	Y	N	N	N
5 Ratchford	Y	Y	Y	Y	Y	N	N	N
6 *Johnson*	Y	Y	Y	Y	N	N	N	N
DELAWARE								
AL Carper	Y	Y	Y	Y	N	Y	N	N
FLORIDA								
1 Hutto	Y	N	Y	Y	N	N	Y	N
2 Fuqua	Y	Y	Y	Y	Y	N	N	N
3 Bennett	Y	Y	Y	Y	N	N	N	N
4 Chappell	Y	Y	Y	Y	N	N	N	N
5 *McCollum*	N	N	N	Y	N	Y	Y	Y
6 MacKay	?	#	Y	N	Y	N	N	N
7 Gibbons	Y	Y	Y	Y	Y	N	N	N
8 *Young*	N	N	N	Y	N	Y	Y	Y
9 *Bilirakis*	N	N	N	Y	N	Y	Y	Y
10 Ireland	?	?	Y	Y	Y	N	N	N
11 Nelson	Y	Y	Y	Y	Y	N	N	N
12 *Lewis*	N	Y	Y	Y	N	Y	Y	Y
13 *Mack*	N	N	N	Y	N	Y	Y	Y
14 Mica	Y	Y	Y	Y	N	N	N	N
15 *Shaw*	N	N	N	Y	N	Y	Y	Y
16 Smith	Y	Y	Y	Y	N	N	N	N
17 Lehman	Y	Y	Y	Y	N	N	N	N
18 Pepper	N	Y	?	Y	Y	N	N	N
19 Fascell	Y	Y	Y	Y	N	N	N	N
GEORGIA								
1 Thomas	Y	Y	Y	Y	N	N	N	N
2 Hatcher	?	?	Y	Y	N	N	N	N
3 Ray	Y	Y	Y	Y	N	Y	Y	Y
4 Levitas	Y	N	Y	Y	N	N	N	N
5 Fowler	Y	N	Y	Y	N	N	N	N
6 *Gingrich*	?	?	Y	Y	N	Y	Y	Y
7 Vacancy								
8 Rowland	Y	Y	Y	Y	N	N	N	N
9 Jenkins	Y	N	Y	N	N	N	N	N
10 Barnard	Y	N	?	?	?	?	?	N
HAWAII								
1 Heftel	?	?	?	?	?	?	?	?
2 Akaka	?	?	Y	Y	Y	N	N	N
IDAHO								
1 *Craig*	N	N	N	Y	N	Y	Y	N
2 *Hansen*	N	N	N	Y	N	Y	Y	N
ILLINOIS								
1 Hayes	?	Y	Y	Y	Y	N	N	N
2 Savage	Y	Y	Y	Y	Y	N	N	N
3 Russo	Y	Y	Y	Y	N	N	N	N
4 O'Brien	Y	Y	Y	Y	N	N	N	N
5 Lipinski	Y	Y	Y	Y	N	N	N	N
6 *Hyde*	N	N	N	Y	N	Y	Y	Y
7 Collins	?	Y	Y	Y	N	N	N	N
8 Rostenkowski	?	?	Y	?	N	N	N	N
9 Yates	Y	Y	Y	Y	Y	N	N	N
10 *Porter*	N	Y	Y	Y	N	Y	Y	N
11 Annunzio	Y	Y	Y	Y	N	N	N	N
12 *Crane, P.*	N	N	N	X	Y	Y	Y	Y
13 *Erlenborn*	N	N	N	X	Y	Y	Y	Y
14 *Corcoran*	?	X	N	Y	N	Y	Y	Y
15 *Madigan*	N	N	Y	Y	N	Y	Y	Y
16 *Martin*	?	X	Y	Y	N	Y	Y	Y
17 Evans	Y	Y	Y	Y	Y	N	N	N
18 *Michel*	N	N	N	Y	N	Y	Y	Y
19 *Crane, D.*	?	N	N	Y	N	Y	Y	Y
20 Durbin	Y	Y	Y	Y	Y	N	N	N
21 Price	Y	Y	Y	Y	Y	N	N	N
22 Simon	?	#	Y	Y	Y	N	N	N
INDIANA								
1 Hall	Y	Y	Y	?	Y	N	N	N
2 Sharp	Y	N	Y	Y	N	Y	N	N
3 *Hiler*	?	?	N	Y	N	Y	Y	Y
4 *Coats*	N	N	N	Y	N	Y	Y	Y
5 Hillis	Y	N	Y	Y	N	Y	Y	Y

Corresponding to Congressional Record Votes 342, 343, 344, 346, 347, 348, 349, 350

	325	326	327	328	329	330	331	332
6 ***Burton***	N	N	N	Y	N	Y	Y	Y
7 ***Myers***	N	Y	N	Y	N	Y	Y	N
8 McCloskey	Y	Y	Y	Y	Y	N	N	N
9 Hamilton	Y	Y	Y	Y	Y	N	N	N
10 Jacobs	Y	N	Y	Y	Y	N	N	N
IOWA								
1 ***Leach***	N	Y	Y	Y	N	N	N	N
2 ***Tauke***	N	N	N	Y	N	Y	N	N
3 ***Evans***	N	N	N	Y	N	N	N	N
4 Smith	Y	Y	Y	Y	Y	N	N	N
5 Harkin	Y	Y	Y	Y	?	N	N	N
6 Bedell	Y	Y	Y	Y	Y	N	N	N
KANSAS								
1 ***Roberts***	N	N	N	Y	N	Y	Y	Y
2 Slattery	Y	N	Y	Y	N	N	N	N
3 ***Winn***	N	N	Y	Y	N	Y	Y	Y
4 Glickman	Y	Y	Y	Y	Y	Y	N	N
5 ***Whittaker***	?	?	N	Y	N	Y	Y	Y
KENTUCKY								
1 Hubbard	N	N	Y	Y	N	Y	N	N
2 Natcher	Y	Y	Y	Y	Y	N	N	N
3 Mazzoli	N	Y	Y	Y	N	N	N	N
4 ***Snyder***	N	N	N	Y	N	Y	Y	N
5 ***Rogers***	N	N	Y	Y	N	Y	Y	N
6 ***Hopkins***	N	N	Y	Y	N	Y	Y	Y
7 Perkins	Y	Y	Y	Y	Y	N	N	N
LOUISIANA								
1 ***Livingston***	N	N	N	Y	N	Y	Y	Y
2 Boggs	Y	Y	Y	Y	Y	N	N	N
3 Tauzin	Y	N	Y	Y	N	Y	Y	N
4 Roemer	?	N	Y	Y	N	Y	Y	N
5 Huckaby	Y	N	Y	Y	N	N	Y	N
6 ***Moore***	N	N	Y	Y	N	Y	Y	N
7 Breaux	N	N	Y	Y	N	Y	Y	N
8 Long	Y	Y	Y	Y	Y	N	N	N
MAINE								
1 ***McKernan***	Y	Y	N	Y	N	N	Y	N
2 ***Snowe***	Y	Y	Y	Y	N	N	Y	N
MARYLAND								
1 Dyson	Y	Y	Y	Y	Y	N	N	N
2 Long	Y	Y	Y	Y	Y	N	N	N
3 Mikulski	Y	Y	Y	Y	Y	N	N	N
4 ***Holt***	N	N	?	Y	N	Y	Y	Y
5 Hoyer	Y	Y	Y	Y	Y	N	N	N
6 Byron	Y	N	Y	Y	N	N	N	N
7 Mitchell	Y	Y	Y	Y	Y	N	N	N
8 Barnes	Y	Y	Y	Y	Y	N	N	N
MASSACHUSETTS								
1 ***Conte***	Y	Y	Y	Y	N	N	N	N
2 Boland	Y	Y	Y	Y	Y	N	N	N
3 Early	Y	Y	Y	Y	Y	N	N	N
4 Frank	Y	Y	Y	Y	Y	N	N	N
5 Shannon	?	?	Y	Y	Y	N	N	N
6 Mavroules	Y	Y	Y	Y	Y	N	N	N
7 Markey	Y	Y	Y	Y	Y	N	N	N
8 O'Neill								
9 Moakley	?	?	Y	Y	Y	N	?	?
10 Studds	Y	Y	Y	Y	Y	N	N	N
11 Donnelly	Y	Y	Y	Y	Y	N	N	N
MICHIGAN								
1 Conyers	?	?	Y	Y	Y	N	N	N
2 ***Pursell***	?	#	Y	Y	N	N	N	N
3 Wolpe	Y	Y	Y	Y	Y	N	N	N
4 ***Siljander***	N	N	N	Y	N	Y	Y	Y
5 ***Sawyer***	Y	N	Y	Y	N	Y	N	N
6 Carr	Y	Y	Y	Y	Y	N	N	N
7 Kildee	Y	Y	Y	Y	Y	N	N	N
8 Traxler	Y	Y	Y	Y	Y	N	N	N
9 ***Vander Jagt***	N	Y	N	Y	N	Y	Y	Y
10 Albosta	Y	Y	Y	Y	Y	N	N	N
11 ***Davis***	Y	Y	Y	Y	N	N	N	N
12 Bonior	Y	Y	Y	Y	Y	N	N	N
13 Crockett	Y	Y	Y	Y	Y	?	N	N
14 Hertel	Y	Y	Y	Y	Y	N	N	N
15 Ford	?	?	Y	Y	Y	N	N	N
16 Dingell	?	#	Y	Y	Y	N	N	N
17 Levin	Y	Y	Y	Y	Y	N	N	N
18 ***Broomfield***	Y	N	Y	Y	N	Y	Y	Y
MINNESOTA								
1 Penny	Y	Y	Y	Y	N	Y	N	N
2 ***Weber***	N	N	N	Y	N	Y	Y	Y
3 ***Frenzel***	Y	X	N	Y	N	#	Y	N
4 Vento	Y	Y	Y	Y	Y	N	N	N
5 Sabo	Y	Y	Y	Y	Y	N	N	N
6 Sikorski	Y	Y	Y	Y	Y	N	N	N

	325	326	327	328	329	330	331	332
7 ***Stangeland***	N	N	N	Y	N	N	Y	Y
8 Oberstar	Y	Y	Y	Y	Y	N	N	N
MISSISSIPPI								
1 Whitten	?	?	Y	Y	Y	N	N	N
2 ***Franklin***	N	N	N	Y	N	Y	Y	N
3 Montgomery	Y	N	N	Y	N	Y	Y	N
4 Dowdy	Y	Y	Y	Y	Y	N	N	N
5 ***Lott***	N	N	N	Y	N	Y	Y	N
MISSOURI								
1 Clay	Y	Y	Y	Y	Y	N	N	N
2 Young	Y	Y	Y	Y	Y	N	N	N
3 Gephardt	Y	Y	Y	Y	Y	N	N	N
4 Skelton	Y	N	Y	Y	Y	N	N	N
5 Wheat	Y	Y	Y	Y	Y	N	N	N
6 ***Coleman***	Y	Y	Y	Y	N	Y	Y	N
7 ***Taylor***	?	?	N	Y	N	Y	?	N
8 ***Emerson***	N	N	N	Y	N	Y	Y	N
9 Volkmer	N	Y	Y	Y	Y	N	N	N
MONTANA								
1 Williams	?	Y	Y	Y	Y	N	N	?
2 ***Marlenee***	N	N	N	Y	N	Y	Y	N
NEBRASKA								
1 ***Bereuter***	N	N	N	Y	N	Y	N	N
2 ***Daub***	N	N	N	Y	N	Y	Y	N
3 ***Smith***	Y	Y	N	Y	N	Y	Y	Y
NEVADA								
1 Reid	Y	Y	Y	Y	Y	Y	N	N
2 ***Vucanovich***	N	N	N	Y	N	Y	Y	Y
NEW HAMPSHIRE								
1 D'Amours	?	?	Y	Y	N	N	N	N
2 ***Gregg***	N	N	Y	Y	N	Y	Y	Y
NEW JERSEY								
1 Florio	Y	Y	Y	Y	Y	N	N	N
2 Hughes	Y	Y	Y	Y	Y	N	N	N
3 Howard	?	#	Y	Y	Y	N	N	N
4 ***Smith***	Y	Y	Y	Y	N	N	N	N
5 ***Roukema***	Y	N	Y	Y	N	N	N	N
6 Dwyer	Y	Y	Y	Y	Y	N	N	N
7 ***Rinaldo***	N	Y	Y	Y	Y	N	N	N
8 Roe	Y	Y	Y	Y	Y	N	N	N
9 Torricelli	?	?	Y	Y	Y	N	N	N
10 Rodino	Y	Y	Y	Y	Y	N	N	N
11 Minish	Y	Y	Y	Y	Y	N	N	N
12 ***Courter***	N	N	Y	Y	N	N	Y	N
13 ***Forsythe***	N	Y	N	Y	N	Y	Y	Y
14 Guarini	?	#	Y	Y	Y	N	N	N
NEW MEXICO								
1 ***Lujan***	N	N	N	Y	N	Y	Y	Y
2 ***Skeen***	N	N	N	Y	N	Y	Y	Y
3 Richardson	Y	Y	Y	Y	Y	N	N	N
NEW YORK								
1 ***Carney***	N	N	N	Y	X	Y	Y	N
2 Downey	Y	Y	Y	Y	Y	N	N	N
3 Mrazek	Y	Y	Y	?	Y	N	N	N
4 ***Lent***	N	Y	Y	Y	N	Y	Y	N
5 ***McGrath***	N	Y	Y	Y	N	Y	Y	N
6 Addabbo	Y	Y	Y	Y	Y	N	N	N
7 Ackerman	Y	Y	Y	Y	Y	N	N	N
8 Scheuer	Y	Y	Y	+	Y	N	N	N
9 Ferraro	Y	Y	Y	+	+	-	N	N
10 Schumer	Y	Y	?	?	#	N	N	N
11 Towns	?	?	Y	?	Y	N	N	N
12 Owens	?	?	Y	Y	Y	N	N	N
13 Solarz	?	?	Y	Y	Y	N	N	N
14 ***Molinari***	N	Y	N	Y	N	Y	Y	N
15 ***Green***	?	#	Y	Y	N	N	N	N
16 Rangel	?	#	Y	Y	Y	N	N	N
17 Weiss	Y	Y	Y	Y	Y	N	N	N
18 Garcia	Y	Y	Y	Y	Y	N	N	N
19 Biaggi	Y	Y	Y	Y	Y	N	?	N
20 Ottinger	Y	Y	Y	Y	Y	N	N	N
21 ***Fish***	Y	Y	?	Y	N	N	N	N
22 ***Gilman***	Y	Y	?	Y	Y	N	N	N
23 Stratton	Y	Y	Y	Y	Y	N	N	N
24 ***Solomon***	N	N	N	Y	N	Y	Y	Y
25 ***Boehlert***	Y	Y	Y	Y	N	N	N	N
26 ***Martin***	N	N	N	?	N	N	N	N
27 ***Wortley***	N	N	N	Y	N	Y	?	N
28 McHugh	Y	Y	Y	Y	Y	N	N	N
29 ***Horton***	Y	Y	Y	Y	?	N	N	N
30 ***Conable***	N	N	N	Y	N	Y	Y	N
31 ***Kemp***	N	N	Y	Y	N	Y	Y	?
32 LaFalce	Y	Y	Y	?	Y	N	N	N
33 Nowak	Y	Y	Y	Y	Y	N	N	N
34 Lundine	Y	Y	Y	Y	N	N	N	N

	325	326	327	328	329	330	331	332
NORTH CAROLINA								
1 Jones	Y	Y	Y	Y	Y	N	N	N
2 Valentine	Y	Y	Y	Y	N	Y	N	N
3 Whitley	?	?	Y	Y	N	N	N	N
4 Andrews	?	?	Y	Y	N	N	N	N
5 Neal	?	?	Y	Y	Y	N	N	N
6 Britt	Y	Y	Y	Y	Y	Y	N	N
7 Rose	?	?	?	Y	Y	N	N	N
8 Hefner	?	?	Y	Y	Y	N	N	N
9 ***Martin***	N	N	N	Y	N	Y	Y	Y
10 ***Broyhill***	Y	N	N	Y	N	Y	Y	Y
11 Clarke	Y	Y	Y	Y	N	N	N	N
NORTH DAKOTA								
AL Dorgan	Y	N	Y	Y	Y	N	N	N
OHIO								
1 Luken	Y	Y	Y	Y	Y	N	N	N
2 ***Gradison***	Y	Y	Y	Y	N	Y	Y	N
3 Hall	?	?	Y	Y	Y	N	N	?
4 ***Oxley***	N	N	N	Y	N	Y	Y	N
5 ***Latta***	N	N	N	Y	N	Y	Y	Y
6 ***McEwen***	?	?	Y	Y	N	Y	Y	N
7 ***DeWine***	N	N	Y	Y	N	Y	Y	Y
8 ***Kindness***	N	N	N	Y	N	Y	N	N
9 Kaptur	Y	Y	Y	Y	Y	N	N	N
10 ***Miller***	Y	N	Y	Y	N	Y	Y	N
11 Eckart	Y	Y	Y	Y	Y	N	N	N
12 ***Kasich***	N	N	N	Y	N	Y	Y	Y
13 Pease	Y	Y	Y	Y	N	N	N	N
14 Seiberling	Y	Y	Y	Y	Y	N	N	N
15 ***Wylie***	N	N	N	Y	N	Y	Y	N
16 ***Regula***	N	N	Y	Y	N	Y	N	N
17 ***Williams***	Y	Y	Y	Y	Y	N	N	?
18 Applegate	Y	Y	Y	Y	Y	N	N	N
19 Feighan	Y	Y	Y	Y	Y	N	N	N
20 Oakar	Y	Y	Y	Y	Y	N	N	N
21 Stokes	Y	Y	Y	?	Y	N	N	N
OKLAHOMA								
1 Jones	Y	N	Y	Y	N	N	N	N
2 Synar	Y	Y	Y	Y	N	N	N	N
3 Watkins	Y	Y	Y	Y	N	N	N	N
4 McCurdy	Y	N	Y	Y	N	N	N	N
5 ***Edwards***	N	N	N	Y	N	Y	Y	Y
6 English	Y	N	Y	Y	N	Y	N	N
OREGON								
1 AuCoin	Y	Y	Y	Y	N	N	N	N
2 ***Smith, R.***	?	?	Y	Y	N	Y	Y	Y
3 Wyden	Y	Y	Y	Y	Y	N	N	N
4 Weaver	Y	N	Y	Y	Y	N	N	N
5 ***Smith, D.***	N	N	N	Y	N	Y	Y	Y
PENNSYLVANIA								
1 Foglietta	Y	Y	Y	Y	Y	N	N	N
2 Gray	Y	Y	Y	Y	Y	N	N	N
3 Borski	Y	Y	Y	Y	Y	N	N	N
4 Kolter	Y	Y	Y	Y	Y	N	N	N
5 ***Schulze***	?	?	N	Y	N	Y	Y	Y
6 Yatron	Y	Y	Y	Y	Y	N	N	N
7 Edgar	Y	Y	Y	Y	Y	N	N	N
8 Kostmayer	Y	Y	Y	Y	Y	N	N	N
9 ***Shuster***	Y	N	N	Y	N	Y	Y	Y
10 ***McDade***	Y	Y	Y	Y	Y	N	N	N
11 Harrison	Y	Y	Y	Y	Y	N	N	N
12 Murtha	Y	Y	Y	Y	Y	N	N	N
13 ***Coughlin***	N	Y	Y	Y	N	Y	Y	N
14 Coyne	Y	Y	Y	Y	Y	N	N	N
15 ***Ritter***	N	N	N	Y	N	Y	Y	N
16 ***Walker***	N	N	N	Y	N	Y	Y	Y
17 ***Gekas***	N	N	N	Y	N	Y	Y	Y
18 Walgren	Y	Y	Y	Y	Y	N	N	N
19 ***Goodling***	N	Y	N	Y	N	Y	Y	Y
20 Gaydos	Y	Y	Y	?	Y	N	N	N
21 ***Ridge***	Y	Y	Y	Y	N	N	N	?
22 Murphy	Y	Y	Y	Y	Y	N	N	N
23 ***Clinger***	Y	N	Y	Y	N	Y	N	N
RHODE ISLAND								
1 St Germain	?	?	Y	Y	Y	N	N	N
2 ***Schneider***	Y	Y	Y	Y	N	N	N	N
SOUTH CAROLINA								
1 ***Hartnett***	N	N	?	Y	N	Y	Y	Y
2 ***Spence***	N	N	?	Y	N	Y	Y	Y
3 Derrick	Y	Y	Y	?	N	N	N	N
4 ***Campbell***	N	N	?	Y	N	Y	Y	Y
5 Spratt	Y	Y	Y	Y	N	N	N	N
6 Tallon	Y	Y	Y	Y	Y	N	N	N
SOUTH DAKOTA								
AL Daschle	Y	Y	Y	Y	Y	?	N	N

	325	326	327	328	329	330	331	332
TENNESSEE								
1 ***Quillen***	N	N	N	Y	N	Y	Y	N
2 ***Duncan***	?	X	Y	Y	N	Y	Y	N
3 Lloyd	N	Y	Y	Y	N	N	N	N
4 Cooper	Y	Y	Y	Y	N	N	N	N
5 Boner	?	?	Y	Y	N	N	N	N
6 Gore	Y	Y	Y	Y	Y	N	?	N
7 ***Sundquist***	N	N	Y	Y	N	Y	Y	Y
8 Jones	Y	Y	Y	Y	Y	N	N	N
9 Ford	?	#	Y	Y	Y	N	N	N
TEXAS								
1 Hall, S.	Y	N	N	Y	N	Y	N	N
2 Wilson	Y	N	Y	Y	Y	N	N	N
3 ***Bartlett***	?	X	N	Y	N	Y	Y	Y
4 Hall, R.	N	N	Y	Y	N	Y	Y	N
5 Bryant	Y	Y	Y	Y	Y	N	N	N
6 ***Gramm***	N	N	N	Y	N	Y	Y	?
7 ***Archer***	N	N	N	Y	N	Y	Y	Y
8 ***Fields***	N	N	N	?	N	Y	Y	Y
9 Brooks	?	?	Y	Y	Y	N	N	N
10 Pickle	Y	Y	Y	Y	Y	N	N	N
11 Leath	Y	N	Y	Y	N	N	N	N
12 Wright	Y	Y	Y	Y	Y	N	N	N
13 Hightower	Y	Y	Y	Y	Y	Y	N	N
14 Patman	Y	N	Y	Y	Y	N	N	N
15 de la Garza	Y	Y	Y	Y	Y	N	N	N
16 Coleman	Y	Y	Y	Y	Y	Y	N	?
17 Stenholm	N	N	N	Y	N	Y	Y	Y
18 Leland	?	?	Y	Y	Y	N	?	N
19 Hance	Y	N	Y	Y	Y	N	N	N
20 Gonzalez	Y	Y	Y	Y	Y	N	N	N
21 ***Loeffler***	N	N	N	Y	N	Y	Y	Y
22 ***Paul***	N	N	N	Y	N	Y	Y	Y
23 Kazen	Y	Y	Y	Y	Y	Y	N	N
24 Frost	?	?	Y	Y	Y	N	N	N
25 Andrews	Y	N	Y	Y	N	Y	N	N
26 Vandergriff	Y	N	Y	Y	N	Y	N	N
27 Ortiz	Y	Y	Y	Y	Y	N	N	N
UTAH								
1 ***Hansen***	?	X	N	Y	N	Y	Y	N
2 ***Marriott***	?	X	Y	Y	N	Y	Y	N
3 ***Nielson***	N	N	N	Y	N	Y	Y	N
VERMONT								
AL ***Jeffords***	Y	Y	Y	Y	N	N	N	N
VIRGINIA								
1 ***Bateman***	N	Y	N	Y	N	Y	Y	Y
2 ***Whitehurst***	N	N	Y	Y	N	Y	Y	Y
3 ***Bliley***	N	N	N	Y	N	Y	Y	N
4 Sisisky	Y	Y	Y	Y	Y	N	N	N
5 Daniel	Y	N	N	Y	N	Y	Y	N
6 Olin	Y	Y	Y	Y	N	N	N	N
7 ***Robinson***	N	N	N	Y	N	Y	Y	Y
8 ***Parris***	?	X	Y	Y	N	N	Y	Y
9 Boucher	Y	Y	Y	Y	Y	N	N	N
10 ***Wolf***	N	Y	Y	Y	N	Y	Y	Y
WASHINGTON								
1 ***Pritchard***	?	?	?	?	?	?	?	?
2 Swift	Y	Y	Y	Y	Y	N	N	N
3 Bonker	?	?	Y	Y	Y	N	N	?
4 ***Morrison***	Y	N	N	Y	N	Y	Y	Y
5 Foley	Y	Y	Y	Y	Y	N	N	N
6 Dicks	?	?	Y	Y	Y	N	?	?
7 Lowry	Y	Y	Y	Y	Y	N	N	N
8 ***Chandler***	Y	N	N	Y	N	Y	Y	N
WEST VIRGINIA								
1 Mollohan	Y	Y	Y	Y	Y	N	N	N
2 Staggers	Y	Y	Y	Y	Y	N	N	N
3 Wise	+	+	Y	Y	Y	N	N	N
4 Rahall	?	#	Y	Y	Y	N	N	N
WISCONSIN								
1 Aspin	?	?	Y	Y	Y	N	?	?
2 Kastenmeier	Y	Y	Y	Y	Y	N	N	N
3 ***Gunderson***	N	N	Y	Y	N	N	N	N
4 Zablocki	Y	Y	Y	Y	Y	N	N	N
5 Moody	Y	Y	Y	Y	Y	N	N	N
6 ***Petri***	?	?	N	Y	N	N	N	N
7 Obey	Y	Y	Y	Y	Y	N	N	N
8 ***Roth***	N	N	N	Y	N	Y	N	Y
9 ***Sensenbrenner***	N	N	N	Y	N	Y	Y	Y
WYOMING								
AL ***Cheney***	N	N	N	Y	N	Y	Y	Y

Southern states - Ala., Ark., Fla., Ga., Ky., La., Miss., N.C., Okla., S.C., Tenn., Texas, Va.

KEY

Y Voted for (yea).
Paired for.
+ Announced for.
N Voted against (nay).
X Paired against.
- Announced against.
P Voted "present".
C Voted "present" to avoid possible conflict of interest.
? Did not vote or otherwise make a position known.

Democrats   *Republicans*

333. HR 1036. Community Renewal Employment Act. Passage of the bill to authorize $3.5 billion in fiscal 1984, and funds in future years according to a formula based on levels of unemployment, to provide grants to local governments to finance repairs and renovation of community facilities and public schools for the purpose of creating jobs. Passed 246-178: R 19-144; D 227-34 (ND 167-6, SD 60-28), Sept. 21, 1983.

334. HR 3913. Labor, Health and Human Services, Education Appropriations, Fiscal 1984. Conte, R-Mass., amendment to prohibit use of funds in the bill to pay for abortions. Adopted 231-184: R 131-30; D 100-154 (ND 59-109, SD 41-45), Sept. 22, 1983.

335. HR 3913. Labor, Health and Human Services, Education Appropriations, Fiscal 1984. Wright, D-Texas, amendment to add $300 million to the bill for job training and education programs. (The amendment was originally to add $400 million but was reduced to $300 million.) Adopted 302-111: R 56-101; D 246-10 (ND 168-1, SD 78-9), Sept. 22, 1983.

336. HR 3913. Labor, Health and Human Services, Education Appropriations, Fiscal 1984. Passage of the bill to appropriate $96,466,088,000 in fiscal 1984 for the departments of Labor, Health and Human Services, and Education and related agencies. Passed 310-101: R 81-75; D 229-26 (ND 149-19, SD 80-7), Sept. 22, 1983. The president had requested $93,714,144,000 in new budget authority.

	333	334	335	336
ALABAMA				
1 *Edwards*	N	Y	Y	Y
2 *Dickinson*	N	Y	Y	Y
3 Nichols	Y	Y	Y	Y
4 Bevill	Y	Y	Y	Y
5 Flippo	Y	N	Y	Y
6 Erdreich	Y	Y	Y	Y
7 Shelby	Y	Y	Y	N
ALASKA				
AL *Young*	Y	Y	Y	Y
ARIZONA				
1 *McCain*	N	Y	N	N
2 Udall	Y	N	Y	Y
3 *Stump*	N	Y	N	N
4 *Rudd*	N	Y	N	N
5 McNulty	Y	N	Y	Y
ARKANSAS				
1 Alexander	Y	N	Y	Y
2 *Bethune*	N	Y	?	?
3 *Hammerschmidt*	N	Y	N	N
4 Anthony	Y	N	Y	Y
CALIFORNIA				
1 Bosco	Y	N	Y	Y
2 *Chappie*	N	Y	Y	N
3 Matsui	Y	N	Y	Y
4 Fazio	Y	N	Y	Y
5 Burton	Y	N	Y	N
6 Boxer	Y	N	Y	N
7 Miller	Y	N	Y	N
8 Dellums	Y	N	Y	N
9 Stark	Y	N	Y	Y
10 Edwards	Y	N	Y	Y
11 Lantos	Y	N	Y	Y
12 *Zschau*	N	N	N	Y
13 Mineta	Y	N	Y	Y
14 *Shumway*	N	Y	N	N
15 Coelho	Y	N	Y	Y
16 Panetta	Y	N	Y	N
17 *Pashayan*	N	Y	N	Y
18 Lehman	Y	N	Y	Y
19 *Lagomarsino*	N	Y	N	Y
20 *Thomas*	N	N	N	Y
21 *Fiedler*	N	N	N	N
22 *Moorhead*	N	Y	N	N
23 Beilenson	Y	N	Y	Y
24 Waxman	Y	N	?	Y
25 Roybal	Y	N	Y	Y
26 Berman	Y	N	Y	Y
27 Levine	Y	N	Y	Y
28 Dixon	Y	N	Y	Y
29 Hawkins	Y	N	Y	Y
30 Martinez	Y	?	?	?
31 Dymally	Y	X	Y	N
32 Anderson	Y	N	Y	Y
33 *Dreier*	N	Y	N	N
34 Torres	Y	N	Y	Y
35 *Lewis*	N	X	X	X
36 Brown	Y	N	Y	Y
37 *McCandless*	N	N	N	N
38 Patterson	Y	N	Y	Y
39 *Dannemeyer*	N	Y	N	N
40 *Badham*	N	Y	N	N
41 *Lowery*	N	Y	N	N
42 *Lungren*	N	Y	N	N

	333	334	335	336
43 *Packard*	N	Y	N	N
44 Bates	Y	N	Y	Y
45 *Hunter*	N	Y	N	N
COLORADO				
1 Schroeder	Y	N	Y	N
2 Wirth	Y	N	Y	Y
3 Kogovsek	Y	N	Y	Y
4 *Brown*	N	N	Y	Y
5 *Kramer*	N	Y	N	Y
6 *Schaefer*	N	Y	N	Y
CONNECTICUT				
1 Kennelly	Y	N	Y	Y
2 Gejdenson	Y	N	Y	N
3 Morrison	Y	N	Y	Y
4 *McKinney*	Y	N	Y	Y
5 Ratchford	Y	N	Y	Y
6 *Johnson*	Y	N	Y	Y
DELAWARE				
AL Carper	N	Y	Y	Y
FLORIDA				
1 Hutto	N	Y	Y	Y
2 Fuqua	Y	Y	Y	Y
3 Bennett	Y	Y	N	Y
4 Chappell	Y	Y	Y	Y
5 *McCollum*	N	Y	N	Y
6 MacKay	N	N	Y	Y
7 Gibbons	Y	Y	Y	Y
8 *Young*	N	Y	Y	Y
9 *Bilirakis*	N	Y	Y	Y
10 Ireland	N	Y	N	Y
11 Nelson	N	Y	Y	Y
12 *Lewis*	N	Y	Y	Y
13 *Mack*	N	Y	N	N
14 Mica	N	N	Y	Y
15 *Shaw*	N	Y	N	N
16 Smith	Y	N	Y	Y
17 Lehman	Y	N	Y	Y
18 Pepper	Y	N	Y	Y
19 Fascell	Y	N	Y	Y
GEORGIA				
1 Thomas	N	N	Y	Y
2 Hatcher	Y	N	Y	Y
3 Ray	N	Y	Y	Y
4 Levitas	N	N	Y	Y
5 Fowler	Y	N	Y	Y
6 *Gingrich*	N	Y	N	N
7 Vacancy				
8 Rowland	N	N	Y	Y
9 Jenkins	N	N	Y	Y
10 Barnard	N	Y	Y	Y
HAWAII				
1 Heftel	?	?	?	?
2 Akaka	Y	N	Y	Y
IDAHO				
1 *Craig*	N	Y	N	N
2 *Hansen*	N	Y	N	N
ILLINOIS				
1 Hayes	Y	X	Y	Y
2 Savage	Y	N	Y	Y
3 Russo	Y	Y	Y	Y
4 *O'Brien*	Y	Y	N	Y
5 Lipinski	Y	Y	Y	Y
6 *Hyde*	N	Y	N	Y
7 Collins	Y	N	Y	Y
8 Rostenkowski	Y	Y	Y	Y
9 Yates	Y	N	Y	Y
10 *Porter*	N	Y	N	Y
11 Annunzio	Y	Y	Y	Y
12 *Crane, P.*	N	Y	N	N
13 *Erlenborn*	N	Y	N	N
14 *Corcoran*	N	Y	X	-
15 *Madigan*	N	Y	N	N
16 *Martin*	N	N	N	N
17 Evans	Y	N	Y	N
18 *Michel*	N	Y	N	N
19 *Crane, D.*	N	Y	N	N
20 Durbin	Y	Y	Y	Y
21 Price	Y	Y	Y	Y
22 Simon	Y	X	?	?
INDIANA				
1 Hall	Y	N	Y	Y
2 Sharp	Y	Y	?	?
3 *Hiler*	N	Y	N	N
4 *Coats*	N	Y	N	N
5 *Hillis*	N	?	?	?

ND - Northern Democrats   SD - Southern Democrats

	333	334	335	336
6 Burton	N	Y	N	N
7 Myers	N	Y	Y	Y
8 McCloskey	Y	N	Y	Y
9 Hamilton	Y	Y	Y	Y
10 Jacobs	Y	N	Y	Y
IOWA				
1 Leach	Y	Y	Y	N
2 Tauke	N	Y	Y	N
3 Evans	N	Y	Y	Y
4 Smith	Y	N	Y	Y
5 Harkin	Y	N	Y	Y
6 Bedell	Y	Y	Y	Y
KANSAS				
1 Roberts	N	Y	N	N
2 Slattery	Y	Y	N	N
3 Winn	N	Y	N	N
4 Glickman	Y	N	Y	N
5 Whittaker	N	N	N	N
KENTUCKY				
1 Hubbard	Y	Y	Y	Y
2 Natcher	Y	Y	Y	Y
3 Mazzoli	Y	Y	Y	Y
4 Snyder	N	Y	N	Y
5 Rogers	N	Y	Y	Y
6 Hopkins	N	Y	Y	Y
7 Perkins	Y	Y	Y	Y
LOUISIANA				
1 Livingston	N	Y	?	?
2 Boggs	Y	Y	Y	Y
3 Tauzin	Y	Y	N	Y
4 Roemer	Y	Y	N	N
5 Huckaby	Y	N	N	Y
6 Moore	N	Y	N	Y
7 Breaux	Y	Y	N	Y
8 Long	Y	Y	Y	Y
MAINE				
1 McKernan	N	N	Y	Y
2 Snowe	N	N	Y	Y
MARYLAND				
1 Dyson	Y	Y	Y	Y
2 Long	Y	N	Y	Y
3 Mikulski	Y	N	Y	Y
4 Holt	N	Y	N	N
5 Hoyer	Y	N	Y	Y
6 Byron	Y	Y	Y	Y
7 Mitchell	Y	N	Y	Y
8 Barnes	Y	N	Y	Y
MASSACHUSETTS				
1 Conte	Y	Y	Y	Y
2 Boland	Y	Y	Y	Y
3 Early	Y	Y	Y	Y
4 Frank	Y	N	Y	Y
5 Shannon	Y	N	Y	Y
6 Mavroules	Y	Y	Y	?
7 Markey	Y	Y	Y	Y
8 O'Neill				
9 Moakley	Y	Y	Y	Y
10 Studds	Y	N	Y	Y
11 Donnelly	Y	Y	Y	Y
MICHIGAN				
1 Conyers	Y	N	Y	Y
2 Pursell	N	N	Y	Y
3 Wolpe	Y	N	Y	Y
4 Siljander	N	Y	N	N
5 Sawyer	N	Y	Y	Y
6 Carr	Y	N	Y	Y
7 Kildee	Y	Y	Y	Y
8 Traxler	Y	Y	Y	Y
9 Vander Jagt	N	Y	Y	Y
10 Albosta	Y	Y	Y	Y
11 Davis	Y	Y	Y	#
12 Bonior	Y	Y	Y	Y
13 Crockett	Y	N	Y	Y
14 Hertel	Y	Y	Y	Y
15 Ford	Y	N	Y	Y
16 Dingell	?	N	Y	Y
17 Levin	Y	N	Y	Y
18 Broomfield	N	Y	N	Y
MINNESOTA				
1 Penny	N	Y	Y	Y
2 Weber	N	Y	Y	N
3 Frenzel	N	N	N	N
4 Vento	Y	Y	Y	Y
5 Sabo	Y	N	Y	Y
6 Sikorski	Y	Y	Y	Y

	333	334	335	336
7 Stangeland	N	Y	N	N
8 Oberstar	Y	Y	Y	Y
MISSISSIPPI				
1 Whitten	Y	Y	Y	Y
2 Franklin	N	Y	N	N
3 Montgomery	N	Y	N	N
4 Dowdy	Y	Y	Y	Y
5 Lott	N	#	N	N
MISSOURI				
1 Clay	Y	N	Y	Y
2 Young	Y	Y	Y	Y
3 Gephardt	Y	Y	Y	Y
4 Skelton	Y	Y	Y	Y
5 Wheat	Y	N	Y	N
6 Coleman	N	N	Y	Y
7 Taylor	N	Y	N	Y
8 Emerson	N	Y	N	Y
9 Volkmer	Y	Y	Y	Y
MONTANA				
1 Williams	Y	N	Y	Y
2 Marlenee	?	Y	N	N
NEBRASKA				
1 Bereuter	N	Y	Y	Y
2 Daub	N	Y	N	Y
3 Smith	N	Y	N	Y
NEVADA				
1 Reid	Y	Y	Y	Y
2 Vucanovich	N	Y	N	N
NEW HAMPSHIRE				
1 D'Amours	N	Y	Y	Y
2 Gregg	N	Y	N	N
NEW JERSEY				
1 Florio	Y	N	Y	Y
2 Hughes	Y	N	Y	Y
3 Howard	Y	N	#	?
4 Smith	Y	Y	Y	Y
5 Roukema	N	N	N	Y
6 Dwyer	Y	N	Y	Y
7 Rinaldo	Y	Y	Y	Y
8 Roe	Y	Y	Y	Y
9 Torricelli	Y	N	Y	Y
10 Rodino	Y	?	Y	Y
11 Minish	Y	Y	Y	Y
12 Courter	N	Y	Y	Y
13 Forsythe	N	N	N	N
14 Guarini	Y	N	Y	Y
NEW MEXICO				
1 Lujan	N	#	N	Y
2 Skeen	N	Y	N	Y
3 Richardson	Y	N	Y	Y
NEW YORK				
1 Carney	N	Y	Y	Y
2 Downey	Y	N	Y	N
3 Mrazek	N	N	Y	Y
4 Lent	N	Y	Y	Y
5 McGrath	N	Y	Y	Y
6 Addabbo	Y	N	Y	Y
7 Ackerman	Y	N	Y	Y
8 Scheuer	Y	N	Y	Y
9 Ferraro	Y	N	Y	N
10 Schumer	Y	N	Y	Y
11 Towns	Y	N	Y	N
12 Owens	Y	N	Y	Y
13 Solarz	Y	N	Y	Y
14 Molinari	N	Y	Y	Y
15 Green	N	N	Y	Y
16 Rangel	Y	N	Y	Y
17 Weiss	Y	N	Y	N
18 Garcia	Y	N	Y	Y
19 Biaggi	Y	N	Y	Y
20 Ottinger	Y	N	Y	Y
21 Fish	Y	Y	Y	Y
22 Gilman	Y	N	Y	Y
23 Stratton	Y	Y	Y	Y
24 Solomon	N	Y	N	N
25 Boehlert	Y	N	Y	Y
26 Martin	Y	Y	Y	Y
27 Wortley	N	Y	N	Y
28 McHugh	Y	Y	Y	Y
29 Horton	Y	N	Y	Y
30 Conable	N	N	N	N
31 Kemp	N	Y	N	Y
32 LaFalce	Y	Y	Y	Y
33 Nowak	Y	Y	Y	Y
34 Lundine	?	N	Y	Y

	333	334	335	336
NORTH CAROLINA				
1 Jones	Y	Y	Y	Y
2 Valentine	N	N	Y	Y
3 Whitley	Y	N	Y	Y
4 Andrews	Y	N	Y	Y
5 Neal	Y	N	Y	Y
6 Britt	N	N	Y	Y
7 Rose	Y	N	Y	Y
8 Hefner	Y	N	Y	Y
9 Martin	N	N	N	N
10 Broyhill	N	N	N	N
11 Clarke	Y	N	Y	Y
NORTH DAKOTA				
AL Dorgan	N	Y	Y	N
OHIO				
1 Luken	Y	Y	Y	Y
2 Gradison	N	Y	N	Y
3 Hall	Y	Y	Y	Y
4 Oxley	N	Y	N	N
5 Latta	N	Y	N	N
6 McEwen	N	Y	N	Y
7 DeWine	N	Y	N	N
8 Kindness	N	Y	N	N
9 Kaptur	Y	Y	Y	Y
10 Miller	N	Y	N	N
11 Eckart	Y	?	Y	Y
12 Kasich	N	Y	N	N
13 Pease	Y	N	Y	Y
14 Seiberling	Y	N	Y	Y
15 Wylie	N	Y	N	N
16 Regula	N	Y	Y	Y
17 Williams	Y	Y	Y	Y
18 Applegate	Y	Y	Y	Y
19 Feighan	Y	N	Y	Y
20 Oakar	Y	Y	Y	Y
21 Stokes	Y	N	Y	Y
OKLAHOMA				
1 Jones	N	N	Y	N
2 Synar	N	N	Y	Y
3 Watkins	Y	N	Y	Y
4 McCurdy	N	N	Y	Y
5 Edwards	N	Y	?	?
6 English	N	Y	Y	Y
OREGON				
1 AuCoin	N	N	Y	Y
2 Smith, R.	N	Y	N	Y
3 Wyden	Y	N	Y	Y
4 Weaver	Y	N	Y	N
5 Smith, D.	N	Y	N	N
PENNSYLVANIA				
1 Foglietta	Y	N	Y	Y
2 Gray	Y	X	Y	Y
3 Borski	Y	Y	Y	Y
4 Kolter	Y	Y	Y	Y
5 Schulze	N	Y	?	?
6 Yatron	Y	Y	Y	Y
7 Edgar	Y	N	Y	Y
8 Kostmayer	Y	N	Y	Y
9 Shuster	N	Y	N	N
10 McDade	Y	Y	Y	Y
11 Harrison	Y	Y	Y	Y
12 Murtha	Y	Y	Y	Y
13 Coughlin	N	N	Y	Y
14 Coyne	Y	Y	Y	Y
15 Ritter	N	Y	N	N
16 Walker	N	Y	N	N
17 Gekas	N	N	N	N
18 Walgren	Y	N	Y	Y
19 Goodling	N	Y	N	Y
20 Gaydos	Y	Y	Y	?
21 Ridge	Y	N	Y	Y
22 Murphy	Y	Y	Y	Y
23 Clinger	N	Y	Y	Y
RHODE ISLAND				
1 St Germain	Y	Y	Y	Y
2 Schneider	Y	N	Y	Y
SOUTH CAROLINA				
1 Hartnett	N	Y	N	N
2 Spence	N	Y	N	N
3 Derrick	Y	N	Y	Y
4 Campbell	N	Y	N	N
5 Spratt	Y	N	Y	Y
6 Tallon	Y	N	Y	Y
SOUTH DAKOTA				
AL Daschle	Y	Y	Y	N

	333	334	335	336
TENNESSEE				
1 Quillen	N	Y	N	N
2 Duncan	N	Y	Y	Y
3 Lloyd	Y	Y	Y	Y
4 Cooper	Y	Y	Y	Y
5 Boner	Y	Y	Y	Y
6 Gore	Y	Y	Y	Y
7 Sundquist	N	Y	Y	Y
8 Jones	Y	Y	Y	Y
9 Ford	?	N	Y	Y
TEXAS				
1 Hall, S.	N	Y	Y	Y
2 Wilson	Y	N	Y	Y
3 Bartlett	N	Y	N	N
4 Hall, R.	Y	Y	Y	Y
5 Bryant	Y	N	Y	Y
6 Gramm	?	#	?	?
7 Archer	N	Y	N	N
8 Fields	N	Y	N	N
9 Brooks	Y	N	Y	Y
10 Pickle	N	N	Y	N
11 Leath	N	Y	N	Y
12 Wright	Y	?	Y	Y
13 Hightower	N	Y	Y	Y
14 Patman	Y	Y	Y	Y
15 de la Garza	Y	Y	Y	Y
16 Coleman	Y	N	Y	Y
17 Stenholm	N	Y	N	N
18 Leland	Y	N	Y	Y
19 Hance	N	?	#	?
20 Gonzalez	Y	N	Y	Y
21 Loeffler	N	Y	N	N
22 Paul	N	#	X	X
23 Kazen	Y	Y	Y	Y
24 Frost	Y	N	Y	Y
25 Andrews	N	N	Y	Y
26 Vandergriff	N	N	Y	N
27 Ortiz	Y	Y	Y	Y
UTAH				
1 Hansen	N	Y	N	N
2 Marriott	N	Y	N	Y
3 Nielson	N	Y	N	N
VERMONT				
AL Jeffords	Y	N	Y	Y
VIRGINIA				
1 Bateman	N	Y	N	Y
2 Whitehurst	N	Y	N	Y
3 Bliley	N	Y	N	N
4 Sisisky	Y	N	Y	Y
5 Daniel	N	?	?	?
6 Olin	N	N	Y	Y
7 Robinson	N	Y	N	N
8 Parris	N	Y	Y	Y
9 Boucher	Y	N	Y	Y
10 Wolf	N	Y	N	Y
WASHINGTON				
1 Pritchard	?	?	?	?
2 Swift	Y	N	Y	Y
3 Bonker	?	N	Y	Y
4 Morrison	N	N	Y	Y
5 Foley	Y	N	Y	Y
6 Dicks	Y	N	Y	Y
7 Lowry	Y	?	?	?
8 Chandler	N	N	Y	Y
WEST VIRGINIA				
1 Mollohan	Y	Y	Y	Y
2 Staggers	Y	Y	Y	Y
3 Wise	Y	N	Y	Y
4 Rahall	Y	N	#	#
WISCONSIN				
1 Aspin	Y	N	Y	Y
2 Kastenmeier	Y	N	Y	Y
3 Gunderson	N	Y	Y	Y
4 Zablocki	Y	Y	Y	Y
5 Moody	Y	N	Y	Y
6 Petri	N	Y	Y	Y
7 Obey	Y	N	Y	Y
8 Roth	?	Y	Y	Y
9 Sensenbrenner	N	Y	N	N
WYOMING				
AL Cheney	N	Y	N	N

Southern states · Ala., Ark., Fla., Ga., Ky., La., Miss., N.C., Okla., S.C., Tenn., Texas, Va.

337. HR 3962. Export Administration Act. Bonker, D-Wash., motion to suspend the rules and pass the bill to extend authority under the Export Administration Act of 1979 from Sept. 30 until Oct. 14, 1983. Motion agreed to 410-0: R 158-0; D 252-0 (ND 167-0, SD 85-0), Sept. 27, 1983. A two-thirds majority of those present and voting (274 in this case) is required for passage under suspension of the rules.

338. HR 1010. Coal Pipeline Act. Vento, D-Minn., amendment to mandate that affected states establish an interstate compact to determine the sale or diversion of water to coal slurry pipelines and to clarify rights of downstream states. Rejected 162-257: R 35-125; D 127-132 (ND 103-70, SD 24-62), Sept. 27, 1983.

339. HR 1010. Coal Pipeline Act. Passage of the bill to grant federal power of eminent domain to certified coal slurry pipeline companies. Rejected 182-235: R 85-75; D 97-160 (ND 52-120, SD 45-40), Sept. 27, 1983.

340. H J Res 364. Multinational Force in Lebanon. Adoption of the rule (H Res 318) providing for House floor consideration of the joint resolution to provide statutory authorization under the War Powers Resolution for continued U.S. participation in the multinational peacekeeping force in Lebanon for up to 18 months after enactment of the resolution. Adopted 306-91: R 111-30; D 195-61 (ND 120-47, SD 75-14), Sept. 28, 1983.

341. H J Res 364. Multinational Force in Lebanon. Long, D-Md., substitute to require the president to invoke the War Powers Resolution by the end of November, or at the end of any month thereafter, unless he certified to Congress that a cease-fire was in effect and was being observed by all parties, and that significant progress was being made in negotiations to broaden the base of the Lebanese government and to achieve a political resolution of existing differences. Rejected 158-272: R 12-154; D 146-118 (ND 113-62, SD 33-56), Sept. 28, 1983. A "nay" was a vote supporting the president's position.

342. H J Res 364. Multinational Force in Lebanon. Passage of the joint resolution to provide statutory authorization under the War Powers Resolution for continued U.S. participation in the multinational peacekeeping force in Lebanon for up to 18 months after the enactment of the resolution. Passed 270-161: R 140-27; D 130-134 (ND 70-105, SD 60-29), Sept. 28, 1983. A "yea" was a vote supporting the president's position.

343. H J Res 368. Continuing Appropriations, Fiscal 1984. Passage of the joint resolution to provide continued funding, through Nov. 15, 1983, for government agencies whose regular fiscal 1984 appropriations bills had not been enacted. Passed 261-160: R 74-92; D 187-68 (ND 116-53, SD 71-15), Sept. 28, 1983.

KEY

Y	Voted for (yea).
#	Paired for.
+	Announced for.
N	Voted against (nay).
X	Paired against.
-	Announced against.
P	Voted "present".
C	Voted "present" to avoid possible conflict of interest.
?	Did not vote or otherwise make a position known.

Democrats *Republicans*

	337	338	339	340	341	342	343
ALABAMA							
1 *Edwards*	Y	N	N	Y	?	Y	Y
2 *Dickinson*	?	N	N	N	N	Y	Y
3 Nichols	Y	N	N	N	N	N	Y
4 Bevill	Y	Y	N	N	Y	N	Y
5 Flippo	Y	N	N	Y	N	N	Y
6 Erdreich	Y	Y	N	N	N	Y	Y
7 Shelby	Y	Y	N	Y	N	Y	Y
ALASKA							
AL *Young*	Y	Y	Y	Y	N	Y	Y
ARIZONA							
1 *McCain*	Y	N	Y	Y	N	N	Y
2 Udall	Y	N	Y	?	Y	N	Y
3 *Stump*	Y	Y	N	?	N	Y	N
4 *Rudd*	Y	N	Y	N	Y	N	Y
5 McNulty	Y	N	Y	Y	Y	N	Y
ARKANSAS							
1 Alexander	Y	N	Y	Y	N	Y	Y
2 *Bethune*	Y	N	Y	N	Y	N	N
3 *Hammerschmidt*	Y	Y	N	Y	N	Y	Y
4 Anthony	Y	N	N	Y	N	Y	Y
CALIFORNIA							
1 Bosco	Y	N	Y	N	N	N	N
2 *Chappie*	Y	N	Y	N	Y	N	Y
3 Matsui	?	Y	N	Y	N	Y	Y
4 Fazio	Y	Y	N	Y	Y	Y	Y
5 Burton	Y	Y	N	Y	N	Y	Y
6 Boxer	Y	Y	N	N	N	N	N
7 Miller	Y	Y	N	N	N	N	N
8 Dellums	Y	Y	N	N	Y	N	Y
9 Stark	Y	Y	N	N	N	Y	?
10 Edwards	Y	Y	N	N	N	Y	Y
11 Lantos	Y	Y	N	Y	N	Y	Y
12 Zschau	Y	N	Y	Y	N	Y	N
13 Mineta	Y	N	Y	Y	Y	Y	Y
14 *Shumway*	Y	N	Y	?	N	Y	N
15 Coelho	Y	N	Y	?	?	?	?
16 Panetta	Y	Y	Y	Y	Y	Y	Y
17 *Pashayan*	Y	?	?	Y	N	Y	Y
18 Lehman	Y	Y	N	Y	N	Y	Y
19 *Lagomarsino*	Y	N	Y	N	N	Y	N
20 *Thomas*	Y	N	Y	Y	N	Y	N
21 *Fiedler*	Y	N	Y	N	N	Y	Y
22 *Moorhead*	Y	N	Y	?	N	Y	N
23 Beilenson	Y	N	Y	N	Y	N	Y
24 Waxman	Y	Y	N	?	Y	N	Y
25 Roybal	Y	Y	N	Y	N	Y	Y
26 Berman	Y	N	N	Y	N	Y	Y
27 Levine	Y	N	Y	Y	Y	Y	Y
28 Dixon	Y	N	N	Y	N	Y	N
29 Hawkins	Y	N	Y	Y	Y	Y	Y
30 Martinez	Y	N	Y	?	Y	N	?
31 Dymally	Y	N	N	P	Y	N	Y
32 Anderson	Y	N	Y	Y	N	Y	N
33 *Dreier*	Y	N	Y	N	N	Y	N
34 Torres	Y	N	N	Y	N	Y	Y
35 *Lewis*	Y	N	N	N	N	Y	Y
36 Brown	Y	Y	Y	Y	Y	Y	Y
37 *McCandless*	Y	N	Y	Y	N	Y	N
38 Patterson	Y	N	N	Y	Y	Y	Y
39 *Dannemeyer*	Y	N	Y	N	N	Y	N
40 *Badham*	Y	N	Y	N	N	N	N
41 *Lowery*	Y	N	Y	Y	N	Y	N
42 *Lungren*	Y	N	Y	N	N	Y	N

	337	338	339	340	341	342	343
43 *Packard*	Y	N	Y	Y	N	Y	N
44 Bates	Y	N	Y	Y	Y	N	N
45 *Hunter*	Y	N	Y	Y	N	Y	N
COLORADO							
1 Schroeder	Y	Y	N	N	Y	N	N
2 Wirth	Y	Y	N	N	Y	N	N
3 Kogovsek	Y	N	N	Y	N	Y	Y
4 *Brown*	Y	N	Y	N	N	N	N
5 *Kramer*	Y	Y	Y	N	Y	N	Y
6 *Schaefer*	Y	N	Y	N	N	Y	N
CONNECTICUT							
1 Kennelly	Y	Y	N	Y	Y	N	Y
2 Gejdenson	Y	Y	N	Y	N	Y	Y
3 Morrison	Y	Y	N	N	Y	N	Y
4 *McKinney*	Y	?	N	Y	N	Y	Y
5 Ratchford	Y	Y	N	Y	Y	N	Y
6 *Johnson*	Y	N	Y	Y	N	Y	Y
DELAWARE							
AL Carper	Y	Y	N	Y	Y	N	N
FLORIDA							
1 Hutto	Y	N	Y	N	Y	N	Y
2 Fuqua	Y	N	Y	N	Y	N	Y
3 Bennett	Y	N	Y	N	Y	N	Y
4 Chappell	Y	N	N	N	N	N	Y
5 *McCollum*	Y	N	N	N	N	N	N
6 MacKay	Y	N	Y	N	Y	N	N
7 Gibbons	Y	?	?	N	Y	N	Y
8 *Young*	Y	N	Y	N	N	N	Y
9 *Bilirakis*	Y	N	Y	N	N	Y	N
10 Ireland	Y	N	Y	N	Y	N	Y
11 Nelson	Y	N	Y	N	Y	N	N
12 *Lewis*	Y	N	Y	N	Y	N	N
13 *Mack*	Y	N	Y	N	Y	N	N
14 Mica	Y	N	Y	N	Y	Y	Y
15 *Shaw*	Y	N	Y	N	N	N	N
16 Smith	Y	N	Y	N	Y	Y	Y
17 Lehman	Y	N	Y	N	Y	Y	Y
18 Pepper	Y	Y	N	Y	N	Y	Y
19 Fascell	Y	N	Y	N	Y	N	Y
GEORGIA							
1 Thomas	Y	N	N	N	N	Y	Y
2 Hatcher	Y	N	N	N	N	Y	Y
3 Ray	Y	Y	N	Y	N	Y	Y
4 Levitas	Y	Y	Y	N	Y	N	Y
5 Fowler	Y	Y	N	Y	N	Y	?
6 *Gingrich*	Y	Y	Y	Y	N	Y	N
7 Vacancy							
8 Rowland	Y	N	Y	N	Y	N	Y
9 Jenkins	Y	Y	N	Y	N	Y	Y
10 Barnard	Y	N	N	Y	N	Y	Y
HAWAII							
1 Heftel	?	?	?	?	?	?	?
2 Akaka	Y	N	Y	Y	N	Y	Y
IDAHO							
1 *Craig*	Y	N	N	?	N	Y	N
2 *Hansen*	Y	N	N	N	N	N	N
ILLINOIS							
1 Hayes	Y	N	Y	N	Y	N	Y
2 Savage	Y	Y	N	N	N	Y	Y
3 Russo	Y	Y	N	Y	N	N	N
4 *O'Brien*	Y	N	N	Y	N	Y	Y
5 Lipinski	Y	Y	N	Y	N	Y	Y
6 *Hyde*	Y	N	N	?	N	Y	Y
7 Collins	Y	N	Y	N	Y	N	Y
8 Rostenkowski	Y	Y	N	Y	N	Y	Y
9 Yates	Y	Y	N	N	Y	N	Y
10 *Porter*	Y	N	Y	N	Y	N	N
11 Annunzio	Y	N	Y	N	Y	N	Y
12 *Crane, P.*	Y	N	N	N	N	N	N
13 *Erlenborn*	Y	N	Y	Y	N	Y	Y
14 *Corcoran*	+	-	X	Y	N	Y	N
15 *Madigan*	Y	N	N	Y	N	Y	N
16 *Martin*	Y	Y	N	Y	N	Y	N
17 Evans	Y	Y	N	N	Y	N	N
18 *Michel*	Y	N	Y	?	N	Y	Y
19 *Crane, D.*	Y	N	N	N	N	N	N
20 Durbin	Y	Y	N	Y	N	Y	Y
21 Price	Y	N	N	Y	N	Y	Y
22 Simon	Y	Y	N	?	N	Y	Y
INDIANA							
1 Hall	Y	Y	N	Y	N	N	Y
2 Sharp	Y	N	Y	N	Y	N	N
3 *Hiler*	Y	N	Y	N	Y	N	N
4 *Coats*	Y	N	Y	Y	N	Y	N
5 *Hillis*	Y	N	N	?	N	N	Y

ND - Northern Democrats   SD - Southern Democrats

	337	338	339	340	341	342	343
6 ***Burton***	Y	N	Y	Y	N	Y	N
7 ***Myers***	Y	N	?	Y	N	N	Y
8 McCloskey	Y	Y	N	N	Y	N	Y
9 Hamilton	Y	Y	N	Y	N	Y	Y
10 Jacobs	Y	Y	N	N	N	N	N
IOWA							
1 ***Leach***	Y	Y	N	N	Y	Y	N
2 ***Tauke***	?	?	?	Y	N	N	N
3 ***Evans***	Y	Y	N	Y	N	Y	N
4 Smith	Y	Y	Y	N	N	N	Y
5 Harkin	Y	Y	N	N	Y	N	Y
6 Bedell	Y	Y	N	Y	Y	N	Y
KANSAS							
1 ***Roberts***	Y	Y	N	?	N	Y	N
2 Slattery	Y	Y	N	Y	N	Y	N
3 ***Winn***	Y	Y	N	Y	N	Y	Y
4 Glickman	Y	Y	N	Y	Y	Y	N
5 ***Whittaker***	Y	Y	N	Y	N	Y	N
KENTUCKY							
1 Hubbard	Y	Y	N	Y	Y	N	N
2 Natcher	Y	Y	N	Y	N	N	Y
3 Mazzoli	Y	N	N	Y	Y	N	Y
4 ***Snyder***	Y	N	N	N	Y	N	N
5 ***Rogers***	Y	N	N	Y	N	Y	Y
6 ***Hopkins***	?	?	#	N	N	N	N
7 Perkins	Y	Y	N	Y	Y	N	Y
LOUISIANA							
1 ***Livingston***	Y	N	Y	Y	N	Y	Y
2 Boggs	Y	N	Y	Y	N	Y	Y
3 Tauzin	Y	N	Y	Y	Y	Y	N
4 Roemer	Y	N	Y	Y	Y	N	N
5 Huckaby	Y	N	Y	Y	N	Y	Y
6 ***Moore***	Y	N	Y	N	N	Y	N
7 Breaux	Y	N	Y	Y	N	Y	Y
8 Long	Y	N	Y	Y	N	Y	Y
MAINE							
1 ***McKernan***	Y	N	Y	Y	N	Y	Y
2 ***Snowe***	Y	N	Y	Y	N	Y	N
MARYLAND							
1 Dyson	Y	N	N	Y	N	Y	Y
2 Long	Y	Y	N	N	Y	N	Y
3 Mikulski	Y	Y	N	N	Y	Y	Y
4 ***Holt***	Y	N	Y	Y	N	Y	Y
5 Hoyer	Y	N	N	Y	N	Y	Y
6 Byron	Y	N	N	Y	N	N	Y
7 Mitchell	Y	Y	N	N	Y	N	Y
8 Barnes	Y	Y	N	?	N	Y	Y
MASSACHUSETTS							
1 ***Conte***	Y	N	N	Y	N	N	Y
2 Boland	Y	N	Y	Y	N	Y	Y
3 Early	Y	N	Y	N	Y	N	N
4 Frank	Y	N	Y	N	Y	N	N
5 Shannon	Y	N	Y	Y	Y	N	N
6 Mavroules	Y	N	Y	Y	N	Y	Y
7 Markey	Y	Y	N	Y	Y	Y	N
8 O'Neill							
9 Moakley	Y	Y	N	Y	N	Y	Y
10 Studds	Y	Y	N	N	Y	N	N
11 Donnelly	Y	Y	Y	Y	Y	N	N
MICHIGAN							
1 Conyers	Y	Y	Y	Y	Y	N	N
2 ***Pursell***	Y	N	Y	Y	N	Y	N
3 Wolpe	Y	Y	?	N	Y	N	N
4 ***Siljander***	?	Y	N	Y	N	Y	N
5 ***Sawyer***	Y	?	Y	Y	N	Y	Y
6 Carr	?	Y	N	Y	Y	Y	N
7 Kildee	Y	Y	N	N	Y	N	N
8 Traxler	Y	Y	N	N	Y	N	N
9 ***Vander Jagt***	Y	N	Y	Y	N	Y	Y
10 Albosta	Y	N	Y	Y	Y	N	?
11 ***Davis***	Y	N	Y	Y	N	Y	Y
12 Bonior	?	Y	N	Y	N	Y	Y
13 Crockett	Y	Y	N	Y	Y	N	Y
14 Hertel	Y	Y	N	N	N	N	N
15 Ford	Y	Y	N	Y	Y	N	N
16 Dingell	?	Y	Y	Y	Y	N	Y
17 Levin	Y	Y	N	Y	N	Y	N
18 ***Broomfield***	Y	N	N	Y	N	Y	Y
MINNESOTA							
1 Penny	Y	Y	N	Y	Y	N	N
2 ***Weber***	Y	Y	N	Y	Y	N	N
3 ***Frenzel***	Y	Y	?	?	N	Y	N
4 Vento	Y	Y	N	N	Y	N	Y
5 Sabo	Y	Y	N	Y	Y	N	Y
6 Sikorski	Y	Y	N	N	Y	N	N
7 ***Stangeland***	?	Y	N	Y	N	Y	N
8 Oberstar	Y	Y	N	N	Y	N	N
MISSISSIPPI							
1 Whitten	Y	N	N	Y	N	Y	Y
2 ***Franklin***	Y	N	Y	Y	N	Y	Y
3 Montgomery	Y	N	Y	Y	Y	Y	Y
4 Dowdy	Y	Y	N	Y	Y	N	Y
5 ***Lott***	Y	N	Y	Y	N	Y	Y
MISSOURI							
1 Clay	Y	Y	N	Y	Y	N	Y
2 Young	Y	N	Y	N	Y	N	Y
3 Gephardt	Y	N	N	Y	N	Y	Y
4 Skelton	Y	Y	N	N	N	N	Y
5 Wheat	Y	Y	N	Y	Y	N	Y
6 ***Coleman***	Y	Y	N	?	N	Y	Y
7 ***Taylor***	Y	N	N	?	N	Y	N
8 ***Emerson***	Y	Y	N	?	N	Y	N
9 Volkmer	Y	Y	N	N	N	N	Y
MONTANA							
1 Williams	Y	N	N	Y	Y	Y	Y
2 ***Marlenee***	Y	N	N	Y	N	Y	N
NEBRASKA							
1 ***Bereuter***	Y	Y	N	N	N	N	Y
2 ***Daub***	Y	Y	N	N	N	Y	N
3 ***Smith***	Y	Y	N	Y	N	Y	Y
NEVADA							
1 Reid	Y	N	N	Y	N	Y	N
2 ***Vucanovich***	Y	N	Y	Y	N	Y	N
NEW HAMPSHIRE							
1 D'Amours	Y	Y	N	Y	N	Y	Y
2 ***Gregg***	Y	N	Y	N	N	Y	N
NEW JERSEY							
1 Florio	Y	Y	N	Y	Y	N	Y
2 Hughes	Y	Y	N	N	N	Y	N
3 Howard	Y	N	Y	N	Y	N	Y
4 ***Smith***	Y	N	N	Y	N	Y	Y
5 ***Roukema***	Y	N	Y	Y	N	Y	Y
6 Dwyer	Y	N	Y	Y	Y	Y	Y
7 ***Rinaldo***	?	N	N	Y	N	Y	Y
8 Roe	Y	N	Y	Y	Y	Y	Y
9 Torricelli	Y	N	N	Y	Y	Y	Y
10 Rodino	Y	N	Y	Y	Y	N	Y
11 Minish	Y	Y	N	Y	Y	Y	Y
12 ***Courter***	Y	N	Y	N	N	Y	N
13 ***Forsythe***	Y	N	Y	Y	N	Y	Y
14 Guarini	Y	N	Y	Y	Y	N	Y
NEW MEXICO							
1 ***Lujan***	Y	N	Y	Y	N	Y	Y
2 ***Skeen***	Y	N	N	Y	N	Y	Y
3 Richardson	Y	N	N	Y	Y	N	Y
NEW YORK							
1 ***Carney***	Y	N	Y	N	N	Y	Y
2 Downey	Y	Y	N	Y	Y	N	Y
3 Mrazek	Y	N	N	Y	N	Y	Y
4 ***Lent***	Y	N	N	Y	N	Y	Y
5 ***McGrath***	Y	N	Y	Y	N	Y	Y
6 Addabbo	Y	N	N	Y	Y	N	Y
7 Ackerman	Y	N	Y	Y	N	Y	Y
8 Scheuer	Y	Y	N	Y	N	Y	Y
9 Ferraro	Y	N	Y	Y	Y	N	Y
10 Schumer	Y	N	Y	Y	N	Y	Y
11 Towns	Y	N	Y	Y	Y	N	?
12 Owens	Y	Y	N	N	Y	N	Y
13 Solarz	Y	N	Y	Y	N	Y	?
14 ***Molinari***	Y	N	N	Y	N	Y	Y
15 ***Green***	Y	N	Y	N	N	Y	Y
16 Rangel	Y	N	Y	Y	Y	N	Y
17 Weiss	Y	N	Y	N	Y	N	N
18 Garcia	Y	Y	N	Y	N	N	Y
19 Biaggi	?	?	?	Y	N	Y	Y
20 Ottinger	Y	Y	N	N	Y	N	Y
21 ***Fish***	Y	N	Y	Y	N	Y	Y
22 ***Gilman***	Y	N	N	Y	N	Y	Y
23 Stratton	Y	Y	N	N	N	N	Y
24 ***Solomon***	Y	N	N	Y	N	Y	N
25 ***Boehlert***	Y	Y	N	Y	N	Y	Y
26 ***Martin***	Y	N	Y	?	N	Y	N
27 ***Wortley***	Y	N	Y	Y	N	Y	Y
28 McHugh	Y	Y	N	Y	Y	N	Y
29 ***Horton***	Y	N	N	Y	N	N	Y
30 ***Conable***	Y	N	Y	?	N	Y	Y
31 ***Kemp***	Y	N	N	?	N	Y	Y
32 LaFalce	?	Y	N	N	N	N	Y
33 Nowak	Y	Y	N	Y	Y	N	Y
34 Lundine	Y	N	Y	Y	Y	N	N
NORTH CAROLINA							
1 Jones	Y	Y	Y	Y	N	Y	Y
2 Valentine	Y	N	Y	Y	N	Y	?
3 Whitley	Y	Y	N	Y	N	Y	Y
4 Andrews	Y	N	Y	Y	Y	N	Y
5 Neal	Y	N	Y	N	N	N	Y
6 Britt	Y	Y	Y	Y	N	Y	N
7 Rose	Y	N	Y	Y	Y	Y	Y
8 Hefner	Y	Y	N	Y	N	Y	Y
9 ***Martin***	Y	N	Y	Y	N	Y	N
10 ***Broyhill***	Y	N	Y	Y	N	Y	N
11 Clarke	Y	N	Y	Y	N	Y	Y
NORTH DAKOTA							
AL Dorgan	Y	N	N	Y	Y	N	N
OHIO							
1 Luken	?	?	?	Y	Y	N	N
2 ***Gradison***	Y	N	Y	Y	Y	N	Y
3 Hall	Y	Y	N	Y	Y	Y	Y
4 ***Oxley***	Y	Y	N	Y	N	Y	Y
5 ***Latta***	Y	N	N	Y	N	Y	N
6 ***McEwen***	Y	N	N	N	N	Y	N
7 ***DeWine***	Y	N	N	?	N	Y	N
8 ***Kindness***	Y	N	Y	N	Y	Y	Y
9 Kaptur	Y	Y	N	Y	Y	N	N
10 ***Miller***	Y	Y	N	?	N	N	N
11 Eckart	Y	Y	N	N	Y	N	N
12 ***Kasich***	Y	Y	N	Y	Y	N	N
13 Pease	Y	Y	N	Y	Y	N	N
14 Seiberling	Y	N	Y	N	Y	Y	Y
15 ***Wylie***	Y	N	N	?	N	Y	Y
16 ***Regula***	Y	N	N	?	N	Y	N
17 ***Williams***	Y	N	N	Y	N	Y	Y
18 Applegate	Y	N	N	Y	Y	N	N
19 Feighan	Y	Y	N	Y	Y	Y	N
20 Oakar	?	Y	N	Y	N	Y	N
21 Stokes	Y	Y	N	Y	Y	N	Y
OKLAHOMA							
1 Jones	Y	N	Y	Y	Y	N	Y
2 Synar	Y	N	Y	Y	N	Y	+
3 Watkins	Y	N	Y	Y	Y	N	Y
4 McCurdy	Y	N	Y	N	Y	N	N
5 ***Edwards***	Y	N	Y	Y	Y	Y	N
6 English	Y	N	Y	Y	Y	N	N
OREGON							
1 AuCoin	Y	Y	N	Y	Y	N	N
2 ***Smith, R.***	Y	N	Y	Y	N	Y	?
3 Wyden	Y	N	N	Y	Y	N	N
4 Weaver	Y	N	N	N	Y	N	N
5 ***Smith, D.***	Y	N	Y	N	N	N	N
PENNSYLVANIA							
1 Foglietta	Y	Y	Y	Y	N	Y	Y
2 Gray	Y	Y	Y	Y	Y	N	Y
3 Borski	Y	N	Y	Y	N	Y	Y
4 Kolter	Y	N	N	Y	N	Y	Y
5 ***Schulze***	Y	N	Y	Y	N	N	Y
6 Yatron	Y	N	N	Y	N	Y	Y
7 Edgar	Y	Y	N	N	Y	N	N
8 Kostmayer	Y	N	Y	N	Y	N	N
9 ***Shuster***	Y	N	N	Y	N	Y	N
10 ***McDade***	Y	N	N	Y	N	Y	Y
11 Harrison	?	?	X	?	N	Y	Y
12 Murtha	Y	N	N	Y	N	Y	Y
13 ***Coughlin***	Y	Y	N	Y	Y	Y	Y
14 Coyne	Y	Y	N	Y	N	Y	Y
15 ***Ritter***	Y	N	Y	Y	N	Y	N
16 ***Walker***	Y	Y	N	?	N	N	N
17 ***Gekas***	Y	N	N	Y	N	Y	N
18 Walgren	Y	Y	Y	Y	Y	N	N
19 ***Goodling***	Y	N	N	Y	N	Y	N
20 Gaydos	Y	N	N	N	N	N	Y
21 ***Ridge***	Y	Y	N	Y	N	Y	Y
22 Murphy	Y	Y	N	Y	Y	N	Y
23 ***Clinger***	Y	N	Y	Y	N	Y	Y
RHODE ISLAND							
1 St Germain	Y	Y	Y	Y	Y	N	Y
2 ***Schneider***	Y	Y	N	Y	Y	Y	Y
SOUTH CAROLINA							
1 ***Hartnett***	?	?	X	?	N	Y	N
2 ***Spence***	Y	N	N	Y	N	Y	N
3 Derrick	Y	N	N	Y	Y	N	Y
4 ***Campbell***	Y	N	N	Y	N	Y	N
5 Spratt	Y	Y	N	N	N	Y	Y
6 Tallon	Y	Y	N	N	N	Y	Y
SOUTH DAKOTA							
AL Daschle	Y	N	Y	Y	Y	N	Y
TENNESSEE							
1 ***Quillen***	Y	Y	N	Y	N	Y	Y
2 ***Duncan***	Y	N	N	Y	N	Y	Y
3 Lloyd	?	N	N	Y	N	Y	Y
4 Cooper	Y	Y	N	Y	Y	Y	Y
5 Boner	Y	N	N	Y	N	Y	Y
6 Gore	Y	Y	N	Y	N	Y	Y
7 ***Sundquist***	Y	N	Y	Y	N	Y	N
8 Jones	Y	N	N	Y	N	Y	Y
9 Ford	?	?	?	Y	Y	Y	Y
TEXAS							
1 Hall, S.	Y	N	Y	Y	Y	N	N
2 Wilson	Y	N	Y	Y	N	Y	Y
3 ***Bartlett***	Y	N	Y	?	N	Y	N
4 Hall, R.	Y	N	N	Y	Y	N	N
5 Bryant	Y	N	N	N	Y	N	N
6 ***Gramm***	Y	N	Y	?	N	Y	N
7 ***Archer***	Y	N	Y	Y	N	N	N
8 ***Fields***	Y	N	Y	Y	N	N	N
9 Brooks	Y	N	#	Y	Y	N	Y
10 Pickle	Y	N	Y	Y	N	Y	Y
11 Leath	Y	N	Y	Y	N	Y	Y
12 Wright	Y	N	Y	Y	N	Y	Y
13 Hightower	Y	N	Y	Y	N	Y	Y
14 Patman	Y	N	Y	Y	Y	N	N
15 de la Garza	Y	N	Y	Y	Y	Y	Y
16 Coleman	Y	Y	N	Y	N	Y	Y
17 Stenholm	Y	N	Y	N	Y	N	N
18 Leland	Y	N	Y	Y	Y	N	Y
19 Hance	?	N	Y	Y	N	N	N
20 Gonzalez	Y	N	Y	N	Y	N	Y
21 ***Loeffler***	Y	N	Y	?	N	Y	N
22 ***Paul***	?	Y	N	N	Y	N	N
23 Kazen	Y	N	Y	Y	N	Y	Y
24 Frost	Y	N	N	Y	Y	Y	Y
25 Andrews	Y	N	Y	Y	Y	Y	N
26 Vandergriff	?	?	#	Y	N	Y	Y
27 Ortiz	Y	N	Y	Y	N	Y	Y
UTAH							
1 ***Hansen***	Y	N	Y	?	N	Y	Y
2 ***Marriott***	Y	N	Y	Y	N	Y	N
3 ***Nielson***	Y	N	Y	N	N	Y	N
VERMONT							
AL ***Jeffords***	Y	N	N	Y	N	Y	Y
VIRGINIA							
1 ***Bateman***	Y	N	N	Y	N	Y	Y
2 ***Whitehurst***	Y	N	N	Y	N	Y	Y
3 ***Bliley***	Y	N	N	Y	N	Y	Y
4 Sisisky	Y	N	N	Y	N	Y	Y
5 Daniel	Y	Y	N	Y	N	Y	Y
6 Olin	Y	N	N	Y	N	Y	Y
7 ***Robinson***	Y	N	Y	Y	N	Y	Y
8 ***Parris***	Y	N	Y	Y	N	Y	Y
9 Boucher	Y	N	N	Y	Y	Y	Y
10 ***Wolf***	Y	N	Y	Y	N	Y	Y
WASHINGTON							
1 ***Pritchard***	Y	N	Y	Y	N	Y	Y
2 Swift	Y	Y	N	Y	Y	N	Y
3 Bonker	Y	Y	N	Y	N	Y	Y
4 ***Morrison***	Y	N	N	Y	N	Y	N
5 Foley	Y	N	N	Y	N	Y	Y
6 Dicks	Y	N	N	Y	N	Y	Y
7 Lowry	Y	Y	N	Y	Y	N	N
8 ***Chandler***	Y	N	Y	?	N	Y	N
WEST VIRGINIA							
1 Mollohan	Y	Y	N	Y	N	Y	Y
2 Staggers	Y	Y	N	Y	Y	Y	Y
3 Wise	Y	N	N	Y	Y	N	Y
4 Rahall	Y	Y	N	Y	N	Y	Y
WISCONSIN							
1 Aspin	Y	Y	N	?	N	Y	N
2 Kastenmeier	Y	Y	N	N	Y	N	Y
3 ***Gunderson***	Y	Y	N	Y	Y	N	Y
4 Zablocki	Y	Y	Y	Y	N	Y	Y
5 Moody	Y	N	Y	Y	Y	N	Y
6 ***Petri***	Y	N	Y	N	Y	N	N
7 Obey	Y	Y	N	Y	Y	N	Y
8 ***Roth***	Y	N	Y	N	Y	N	N
9 ***Sensenbrenner***	Y	Y	N	Y	Y	N	N
WYOMING							
AL ***Cheney***	Y	N	Y	Y	N	Y	N

Southern states - Ala., Ark., Fla., Ga., Ky., La., Miss., N.C., Okla., S.C., Tenn., Texas, Va.

344. HR 3929. Federal Supplemental Unemployment Compensation. Campbell, R-S.C., motion to recommit the bill to the Committee on Ways and Means with instructions to extend the current program of federal supplemental unemployment compensation for 18 months, with maximum benefits going to states with the highest unemployment rates. Motion rejected 141-278: R 125-35; D 16-243 (ND 0-174, SD 16-69), Sept. 29, 1983.

345. HR 3929. Federal Supplemental Unemployment Compensation. Passage of the bill to extend for 45 days and modify the program providing federal supplemental unemployment compensation benefits to jobless workers who have exhausted all other state and federal unemployment benefits, and to extend for 45 days authority to continue payments of Social Security disability benefits to a recipient during the recipient's appeal to an administrative law judge of a decision to terminate the recipient's benefits. Passed 327-92: R 78-81; D 249-11 (ND 174-0, SD 75-11), Sept. 29, 1983.

346. S 602. Radio Marti. Passage of the bill to establish a service under the Voice of America, to be called "Radio Marti," to broadcast news and information to Cuba, and authorizing $14 million in fiscal year 1984 and $11 million in fiscal 1985 for the station's operations. The bill also authorized $54.8 million each year for modernization of Voice of America broadcast facilities. Passed 302-109: R 151-4; D 151-105 (ND 80-91, SD 71-14), Sept. 29, 1983.

347. HR 3415. District of Columbia Appropriations, Fiscal 1984. Adoption of the conference report on the bill to appropriate $600,811,600 in federal funds for the District of Columbia in fiscal 1984, and $2,178,086,600 from the District's own treasury. Adopted 231-177: R 42-115; D 189-62 (ND 140-27, SD 49-35), Sept. 29, 1983. The president had requested $569,590,000 in federal funds and $2,147,013,000 in District funds.

348. HR 3231. Export Administration Act. Bonker, D-Wash., substitute, for the Hughes, D-N.J., amendment (see vote 349, below), to maintain most of the new law enforcement authority granted to the Department of Commerce under the bill, but prohibit Commerce officers to make arrests without a warrant. Rejected 164-246: R 81-75; D 83-171 (ND 63-107, SD 20-64), Sept. 29, 1983.

349. HR 3231. Export Administration Act. Hughes, D-N.J., amendment to strike provisions of the bill granting new law enforcement authority to the Department of Commerce. Rejected 160-243: R 27-129; D 133-114 (ND 84-81, SD 49-33), Sept. 29, 1983.

350. S J Res 159. Multinational Force in Lebanon. Passage of the joint resolution, conforming to the Senate version, to provide statutory authorization under the War Powers Resolution for continued U.S. participation in the multinational peacekeeping force in Lebanon for up to 18 months after the enactment of the resolution. Passed 253-156: R 130-27; D 123-129 (ND 67-101, SD 56-28), Sept. 29, 1983.

KEY

Y	Voted for (yea).
#	Paired for.
+	Announced for.
N	Voted against (nay).
X	Paired against.
-	Announced against.
P	Voted "present".
C	Voted "present" to avoid possible conflict of interest.
?	Did not vote or otherwise make a position known.

Democrats   *Republicans*

	344	345	346	347	348	349	350
ALABAMA							
1 *Edwards*	Y	Y	Y	Y	Y	N	Y
2 *Dickinson*	Y	N	Y	N	Y	N	Y
3 Nichols	N	Y	Y	N	N	Y	N
4 Bevill	N	Y	Y	Y	N	Y	Y
5 Flippo	N	Y	Y	N	N	Y	N
6 Erdreich	N	Y	Y	N	N	Y	Y
7 Shelby	N	Y	Y	N	N	Y	N
ALASKA							
AL *Young*	N	Y	?	?	?	N	?
ARIZONA							
1 *McCain*	Y	N	Y	N	N	N	N
2 Udall	N	Y	Y	?	Y	Y	N
3 *Stump*	Y	N	Y	N	N	N	N
4 *Rudd*	?	X	?	?	?	?	?
5 McNulty	N	Y	N	Y	Y	Y	N
ARKANSAS							
1 Alexander	?	Y	Y	Y	Y	Y	Y
2 *Bethune*	Y	?	?	N	N	Y	Y
3 *Hammerschmidt*	Y	N	N	N	Y	N	Y
4 Anthony	N	Y	N	N	N	N	Y
CALIFORNIA							
1 Bosco	N	Y	Y	?	N	N	N
2 *Chappie*	Y	N	Y	N	Y	N	Y
3 Matsui	N	Y	Y	Y	Y	Y	Y
4 Fazio	N	Y	Y	N	Y	N	Y
5 Burton	N	Y	Y	N	Y	N	Y
6 Boxer	N	Y	N	Y	N	Y	N
7 Miller	N	Y	N	N	N	N	N
8 Dellums	N	Y	N	Y	N	N	N
9 Stark	N	Y	N	Y	N	Y	N
10 Edwards	N	Y	N	Y	N	N	N
11 Lantos	N	Y	Y	Y	Y	N	Y
12 *Zschau*	Y	N	Y	Y	Y	N	Y
13 Mineta	N	Y	N	Y	N	N	N
14 *Shumway*	Y	N	Y	N	Y	N	Y
15 Coelho	N	Y	Y	?	?	?	?
16 Panetta	N	Y	N	N	Y	N	Y
17 *Pashayan*	Y	Y	Y	Y	Y	N	Y
18 Lehman	N	Y	Y	Y	N	N	Y
19 *Lagomarsino*	Y	N	Y	N	Y	N	Y
20 *Thomas*	Y	N	Y	N	Y	N	Y
21 *Fiedler*	Y	Y	Y	Y	N	N	Y
22 *Moorhead*	Y	N	Y	N	N	N	Y
23 Beilenson	N	Y	N	Y	Y	N	Y
24 Waxman	N	Y	?	?	N	Y	N
25 Roybal	N	Y	N	Y	N	Y	N
26 Berman	N	Y	N	Y	N	Y	N
27 Levine	N	Y	N	Y	N	Y	Y
28 Dixon	N	Y	N	Y	N	Y	N
29 Hawkins	N	Y	N	Y	?	?	?
30 Martinez	N	Y	N	Y	N	Y	N
31 Dymally	N	Y	N	Y	N	N	N
32 Anderson	N	Y	N	Y	N	N	Y
33 *Dreier*	Y	N	Y	N	N	N	Y
34 Torres	N	Y	N	Y	N	N	Y
35 Lewis	Y	N	Y	N	Y	N	Y
36 Brown	N	Y	N	Y	N	N	Y
37 *McCandless*	Y	N	Y	N	Y	N	Y
38 Patterson	N	Y	Y	Y	N	Y	Y
39 *Dannemeyer*	Y	N	Y	N	N	N	N
40 *Badham*	Y	N	Y	N	N	Y	?
41 *Lowery*	Y	N	Y	N	Y	N	Y
42 *Lungren*	?	X	?	?	?	?	?

	344	345	346	347	348	349	350
43 *Packard*	Y	N	Y	N	Y	N	Y
44 Bates	N	Y	N	Y	N	N	N
45 *Hunter*	Y	N	Y	N	N	Y	Y
COLORADO							
1 Schroeder	N	Y	N	Y	N	Y	N
2 Wirth	N	Y	N	Y	N	Y	N
3 Kogovsek	N	Y	N	Y	N	Y	Y
4 *Brown*	Y	N	Y	N	Y	N	Y
5 *Kramer*	Y	N	Y	N	Y	N	Y
6 *Schaefer*	Y	N	Y	N	Y	N	Y
CONNECTICUT							
1 Kennelly	N	Y	Y	Y	N	N	N
2 Gejdenson	N	Y	N	Y	Y	N	Y
3 Morrison	N	Y	N	?	N	Y	N
4 *McKinney*	Y	Y	Y	Y	N	Y	Y
5 Ratchford	N	Y	N	N	N	N	N
6 *Johnson*	?	Y	Y	Y	Y	N	Y
DELAWARE							
AL Carper	N	Y	Y	N	N	Y	N
FLORIDA							
1 Hutto	N	Y	Y	Y	N	Y	Y
2 Fuqua	N	Y	Y	Y	N	Y	Y
3 Bennett	N	Y	Y	Y	N	Y	Y
4 Chappell	N	Y	Y	Y	Y	N	Y
5 *McCollum*	Y	N	Y	N	N	Y	Y
6 MacKay	N	Y	Y	N	Y	Y	Y
7 Gibbons	N	Y	Y	Y	?	?	?
8 *Young*	Y	N	Y	N	Y	N	Y
9 *Bilirakis*	Y	N	Y	N	Y	N	Y
10 Ireland	Y	N	Y	N	Y	N	Y
11 Nelson	Y	N	Y	N	-	-	#
12 *Lewis*	Y	Y	Y	N	N	N	Y
13 *Mack*	Y	N	Y	N	Y	N	Y
14 Mica	N	Y	Y	N	Y	N	Y
15 *Shaw*	Y	N	Y	N	Y	N	Y
16 Smith	N	Y	Y	Y	N	Y	Y
17 Lehman	N	Y	Y	Y	N	Y	Y
18 Pepper	N	Y	Y	Y	N	Y	Y
19 Fascell	N	Y	Y	Y	N	Y	Y
GEORGIA							
1 Thomas	Y	Y	Y	N	N	Y	Y
2 Hatcher	Y	Y	Y	N	N	Y	Y
3 Ray	Y	N	Y	N	N	Y	N
4 Levitas	Y	Y	Y	N	N	Y	Y
5 Fowler	N	Y	Y	?	?	?	?
6 *Gingrich*	Y	N	Y	N	Y	N	Y
7 Vacancy							
8 Rowland	Y	Y	Y	Y	N	Y	Y
9 Jenkins	Y	Y	Y	N	N	Y	Y
10 Barnard	Y	N	Y	N	N	N	Y
HAWAII							
1 Heftel	?	?	?	?	?	?	?
2 Akaka	N	Y	Y	Y	N	Y	Y
IDAHO							
1 *Craig*	Y	Y	Y	N	N	N	Y
2 *Hansen*	Y	N	Y	N	N	N	Y
ILLINOIS							
1 Hayes	N	Y	N	Y	N	N	N
2 Savage	N	Y	N	Y	N	Y	N
3 Russo	N	Y	N	Y	N	Y	N
4 *O'Brien*	N	Y	?	Y	N	Y	Y
5 Lipinski	N	Y	Y	Y	N	Y	N
6 *Hyde*	Y	N	Y	N	Y	N	Y
7 Collins	N	Y	N	Y	N	N	N
8 Rostenkowski	N	Y	Y	Y	N	Y	Y
9 Yates	N	Y	N	Y	N	Y	N
10 *Porter*	Y	Y	Y	Y	N	Y	Y
11 Annunzio	N	Y	Y	Y	Y	Y	Y
12 *Crane, P.*	Y	N	Y	N	N	N	N
13 *Erlenborn*	Y	N	Y	N	Y	N	Y
14 *Corcoran*	N	Y	Y	N	-	-	+
15 *Madigan*	N	Y	Y	Y	N	Y	Y
16 *Martin*	N	Y	Y	Y	N	Y	Y
17 Evans	N	Y	N	Y	N	Y	N
18 *Michel*	N	Y	Y	Y	N	Y	Y
19 *Crane, D.*	Y	N	Y	N	N	N	N
20 Durbin	N	Y	N	Y	N	Y	Y
21 Price	N	Y	Y	Y	Y	N	Y
22 Simon	N	Y	Y	Y	Y	N	Y
INDIANA							
1 Hall	?	?	?	?	N	N	N
2 Sharp	N	Y	Y	Y	N	N	N
3 *Hiler*	Y	Y	Y	N	Y	N	Y
4 *Coats*	Y	Y	Y	N	Y	N	Y
5 *Hillis*	?	?	?	?	Y	N	N

ND - Northern Democrats   SD - Southern Democrats

Corresponding to Congressional Record Votes 363, 364, 365, 366, 368, 369, 370

	344	345	346	347	348	349	350
6 ***Burton***	Y	Y	Y	N	N	N	Y
7 ***Myers***	Y	Y	Y	N	N	N	N
8 McCloskey	N	Y	Y	Y	N	Y	N
9 Hamilton	N	Y	Y	N	Y	N	Y
10 Jacobs	N	Y	N	?	Y	N	N
IOWA							
1 ***Leach***	N	?	Y	N	Y	N	Y
2 ***Tauke***	N	Y	Y	N	Y	N	N
3 ***Evans***	N	Y	Y	N	Y	N	Y
4 Smith	N	Y	N	Y	Y	N	N
5 Harkin	N	Y	N	Y	Y	N	N
6 Bedell	N	Y	N	Y	Y	Y	N
KANSAS							
1 ***Roberts***	Y	N	Y	N	Y	N	Y
2 Slattery	N	Y	Y	N	N	N	Y
3 ***Winn***	Y	N	Y	N	Y	N	Y
4 Glickman	?	?	?	?	N	N	Y
5 ***Whittaker***	Y	N	Y	N	Y	N	Y
KENTUCKY							
1 Hubbard	N	Y	Y	Y	N	N	N
2 Natcher	N	Y	Y	Y	N	N	N
3 Mazzoli	N	Y	Y	Y	N	Y	N
4 ***Snyder***	Y	Y	Y	N	N	Y	N
5 ***Rogers***	Y	Y	Y	Y	N	Y	Y
6 ***Hopkins***	Y	Y	Y	N	N	Y	N
7 Perkins	N	Y	Y	Y	N	N	N
LOUISIANA							
1 ***Livingston***	Y	Y	Y	N	N	N	Y
2 Boggs	N	Y	Y	Y	Y	Y	Y
3 Tauzin	Y	Y	Y	N	Y	N	Y
4 Roemer	Y	N	Y	N	Y	N	N
5 Huckaby	N	Y	Y	N	N	Y	Y
6 ***Moore***	N	Y	Y	N	Y	N	Y
7 Breaux	Y	Y	Y	N	Y	N	Y
8 Long	N	Y	Y	Y	Y	Y	Y
MAINE							
1 ***McKernan***	N	Y	Y	Y	N	N	Y
2 ***Snowe***	N	Y	Y	N	Y	N	Y
MARYLAND							
1 Dyson	N	Y	Y	Y	N	Y	Y
2 Long	N	Y	N	Y	N	N	N
3 Mikulski	N	Y	Y	Y	N	Y	Y
4 ***Holt***	Y	N	Y	Y	N	Y	Y
5 Hoyer	N	Y	Y	Y	N	Y	Y
6 Byron	N	Y	Y	N	N	Y	N
7 Mitchell	N	Y	N	Y	Y	N	N
8 Barnes	N	Y	Y	Y	Y	N	Y
MASSACHUSETTS							
1 ***Conte***	N	Y	Y	Y	N	Y	N
2 Boland	N	Y	Y	Y	Y	N	Y
3 Early	N	Y	Y	Y	N	Y	N
4 Frank	N	Y	Y	Y	Y	N	N
5 Shannon	N	Y	N	Y	N	Y	N
6 Mavroules	N	Y	Y	Y	N	Y	Y
7 Markey	N	Y	N	Y	Y	?	Y
8 O'Neill							
9 Moakley	N	Y	Y	Y	N	Y	Y
10 Studds	N	Y	N	Y	N	Y	N
11 Donnelly	N	Y	Y	Y	Y	Y	N
MICHIGAN							
1 Conyers	N	Y	N	Y	N	N	N
2 ***Pursell***	N	Y	Y	N	N	N	Y
3 Wolpe	N	Y	N	Y	Y	N	N
4 ***Siljander***	Y	Y	Y	N	N	N	Y
5 ***Sawyer***	N	Y	Y	Y	N	Y	Y
6 Carr	N	Y	N	Y	N	Y	Y
7 Kildee	N	Y	N	Y	N	Y	N
8 Traxler	N	Y	Y	Y	Y	N	N
9 ***Vander Jagt***	Y	Y	Y	N	N	N	?
10 Albosta	N	Y	Y	N	Y	N	N
11 ***Davis***	N	Y	Y	Y	N	N	Y
12 Bonior	N	Y	?	Y	?	?	?
13 Crockett	N	Y	N	Y	N	N	N
14 Hertel	N	Y	N	Y	N	Y	N
15 Ford	N	Y	N	Y	N	Y	N
16 Dingell	N	Y	N	?	Y	N	N
17 Levin	N	Y	N	Y	N	Y	Y
18 ***Broomfield***	N	Y	?	?	?	?	?
MINNESOTA							
1 Penny	N	Y	N	Y	N	N	N
2 ***Weber***	Y	N	Y	N	?	?	Y
3 ***Frenzel***	Y	N	Y	N	Y	N	Y
4 Vento	N	Y	N	Y	N	Y	N
5 Sabo	N	Y	N	Y	Y	N	N
6 Sikorski	N	Y	N	Y	Y	N	N

	344	345	346	347	348	349	350
7 ***Stangeland***	Y	N	Y	N	N	N	Y
8 Oberstar	N	Y	N	Y	N	N	N
MISSISSIPPI							
1 Whitten	N	Y	Y	Y	N	N	Y
2 ***Franklin***	Y	N	Y	N	Y	?	?
3 Montgomery	Y	N	Y	N	N	Y	Y
4 Dowdy	N	Y	Y	Y	N	Y	N
5 ***Lott***	Y	N	Y	N	Y	N	Y
MISSOURI							
1 Clay	N	Y	N	Y	?	?	?
2 Young	N	Y	Y	Y	?	?	?
3 Gephardt	N	Y	Y	Y	N	Y	Y
4 Skelton	N	Y	Y	N	?	?	?
5 Wheat	N	Y	Y	Y	N	Y	N
6 ***Coleman***	Y	Y	Y	N	Y	N	Y
7 ***Taylor***	Y	N	Y	N	Y	N	Y
8 ***Emerson***	N	Y	Y	N	Y	N	Y
9 Volkmer	N	Y	Y	N	Y	N	N
MONTANA							
1 Williams	N	Y	Y	N	Y	N	Y
2 ***Marlenee***	Y	Y	?	N	Y	Y	Y
NEBRASKA							
1 ***Bereuter***	Y	N	Y	N	Y	N	N
2 ***Daub***	Y	N	Y	N	Y	N	Y
3 ***Smith***	?	N	Y	N	Y	N	Y
NEVADA							
1 Reid	N	Y	Y	Y	N	Y	Y
2 ***Vucanovich***	Y	N	Y	N	Y	N	Y
NEW HAMPSHIRE							
1 D'Amours	N	Y	Y	N	Y	N	Y
2 ***Gregg***	Y	N	Y	N	Y	N	Y
NEW JERSEY							
1 Florio	N	Y	Y	Y	N	N	N
2 Hughes	N	Y	N	N	N	Y	Y
3 Howard	N	Y	Y	Y	N	Y	N
4 ***Smith***	N	Y	Y	Y	N	N	Y
5 ***Roukema***	Y	Y	N	N	N	N	Y
6 Dwyer	N	Y	Y	Y	N	Y	Y
7 ***Rinaldo***	N	Y	Y	Y	N	N	Y
8 Roe	N	Y	Y	Y	N	?	?
9 Torricelli	N	Y	Y	N	N	N	Y
10 Rodino	N	Y	Y	Y	N	Y	N
11 Minish	N	Y	Y	Y	Y	N	Y
12 ***Courter***	N	Y	Y	Y	N	Y	Y
13 ***Forsythe***	Y	N	?	?	N	Y	Y
14 Guarini	N	Y	Y	Y	N	Y	N
NEW MEXICO							
1 ***Lujan***	Y	N	Y	N	Y	N	Y
2 ***Skeen***	Y	N	Y	N	Y	N	Y
3 Richardson	N	Y	Y	Y	N	Y	N
NEW YORK							
1 ***Carney***	Y	N	Y	Y	Y	N	Y
2 Downey	N	Y	N	Y	N	Y	N
3 Mrazek	N	Y	N	Y	N	N	Y
4 ***Lent***	Y	Y	Y	N	N	Y	Y
5 ***McGrath***	Y	Y	Y	N	N	Y	Y
6 Addabbo	N	Y	N	Y	N	Y	N
7 Ackerman	N	Y	Y	Y	N	Y	Y
8 Scheuer	N	Y	N	Y	N	Y	Y
9 Ferraro	N	Y	Y	Y	N	Y	N
10 Schumer	N	Y	N	Y	N	Y	Y
11 Towns	N	Y	N	Y	N	Y	N
12 Owens	N	Y	N	Y	N	Y	N
13 Solarz	N	Y	Y	Y	Y	N	Y
14 ***Molinari***	Y	N	Y	Y	N	Y	Y
15 ***Green***	N	Y	Y	Y	Y	N	Y
16 Rangel	N	Y	N	Y	N	Y	N
17 Weiss	N	Y	N	Y	N	Y	N
18 Garcia	N	Y	Y	Y	N	Y	N
19 Biaggi	N	Y	N	Y	N	N	Y
20 Ottinger	N	Y	N	Y	N	Y	N
21 ***Fish***	N	Y	Y	Y	N	Y	Y
22 ***Gilman***	N	Y	Y	N	N	Y	Y
23 Stratton	N	Y	Y	Y	N	N	N
24 ***Solomon***	Y	?	Y	N	N	N	Y
25 ***Boehlert***	N	Y	Y	Y	N	N	Y
26 ***Martin***	Y	Y	Y	Y	N	N	Y
27 ***Wortley***	Y	N	Y	N	N	Y	Y
28 McHugh	N	Y	N	Y	N	N	N
29 ***Horton***	N	Y	Y	?	Y	N	N
30 ***Conable***	Y	Y	Y	N	Y	N	Y
31 ***Kemp***	Y	Y	Y	Y	Y	Y	Y
32 LaFalce	N	Y	Y	N	Y	N	N
33 Nowak	N	Y	N	Y	N	Y	N
34 Lundine	N	Y	N	Y	Y	N	N

	344	345	346	347	348	349	350
NORTH CAROLINA							
1 Jones	N	Y	?	Y	N	Y	Y
2 Valentine	N	Y	Y	Y	N	?	Y
3 Whitley	N	Y	Y	Y	N	Y	Y
4 Andrews	N	Y	N	?	N	?	N
5 Neal	N	Y	Y	Y	N	N	N
6 Britt	N	Y	Y	Y	N	Y	Y
7 Rose	N	Y	N	Y	N	Y	Y
8 Hefner	N	Y	Y	Y	N	Y	Y
9 ***Martin***	Y	N	Y	N	N	N	Y
10 ***Broyhill***	Y	N	Y	N	N	N	Y
11 Clarke	N	Y	Y	Y	N	Y	Y
NORTH DAKOTA							
AL Dorgan	N	Y	N	Y	N	?	N
OHIO							
1 Luken	N	Y	N	N	Y	Y	N
2 ***Gradison***	Y	Y	Y	Y	Y	N	N
3 Hall	N	Y	N	N	N	Y	Y
4 ***Oxley***	Y	Y	Y	N	?	N	Y
5 ***Latta***	Y	N	Y	N	Y	N	Y
6 ***McEwen***	N	Y	Y	N	?	?	?
7 ***DeWine***	Y	Y	Y	N	N	Y	Y
8 ***Kindness***	Y	Y	Y	N	N	Y	Y
9 Kaptur	N	Y	Y	Y	N	Y	N
10 ***Miller***	Y	Y	Y	N	N	Y	N
11 Eckart	N	Y	N	N	N	N	N
12 ***Kasich***	Y	Y	Y	N	N	N	N
13 Pease	N	Y	Y	Y	Y	?	N
14 Seiberling	N	Y	N	Y	N	Y	Y
15 ***Wylie***	Y	N	Y	N	Y	N	Y
16 ***Regula***	N	Y	Y	N	Y	N	Y
17 ***Williams***	N	Y	Y	Y	N	N	Y
18 Applegate	N	Y	N	N	N	Y	N
19 Feighan	N	Y	Y	N	Y	N	Y
20 Oakar	N	Y	Y	Y	N	Y	Y
21 Stokes	N	Y	N	Y	N	?	X
OKLAHOMA							
1 Jones	N	Y	Y	N	Y	N	N
2 Synar	N	Y	Y	Y	N	Y	Y
3 Watkins	N	Y	Y	N	Y	N	N
4 McCurdy	N	Y	Y	N	Y	N	N
5 ***Edwards***	Y	N	Y	N	N	N	Y
6 English	N	Y	Y	N	Y	N	N
OREGON							
1 AuCoin	N	Y	N	N	Y	N	N
2 ***Smith, R.***	Y	Y	Y	N	N	N	Y
3 Wyden	N	Y	N	Y	Y	N	N
4 Weaver	N	Y	N	N	N	N	N
5 ***Smith, D.***	Y	N	Y	N	N	?	N
PENNSYLVANIA							
1 Foglietta	N	Y	Y	Y	N	Y	Y
2 Gray	N	Y	N	Y	N	Y	N
3 Borski	N	Y	Y	Y	N	Y	Y
4 Kolter	N	Y	Y	Y	Y	Y	Y
5 ***Schulze***	Y	N	Y	N	?	?	N
6 Yatron	N	Y	N	Y	N	N	Y
7 Edgar	N	Y	N	Y	Y	Y	N
8 Kostmayer	N	Y	N	Y	N	Y	Y
9 ***Shuster***	Y	N	Y	N	Y	N	Y
10 ***McDade***	N	Y	Y	Y	N	N	Y
11 Harrison	N	Y	Y	Y	N	Y	Y
12 Murtha	N	Y	N	Y	N	Y	Y
13 ***Coughlin***	Y	Y	Y	Y	Y	N	Y
14 Coyne	N	Y	Y	Y	N	N	Y
15 ***Ritter***	N	Y	Y	N	N	N	Y
16 ***Walker***	Y	N	Y	N	N	N	N
17 ***Gekas***	Y	Y	Y	Y	N	Y	Y
18 Walgren	N	Y	Y	Y	Y	N	N
19 ***Goodling***	Y	Y	Y	N	N	N	Y
20 Gaydos	N	Y	N	N	N	N	N
21 ***Ridge***	N	Y	Y	Y	Y	N	Y
22 Murphy	N	Y	Y	Y	N	Y	N
23 ***Clinger***	N	Y	Y	N	Y	N	Y
RHODE ISLAND							
1 St Germain	N	Y	?	Y	N	Y	N
2 ***Schneider***	N	Y	?	?	Y	N	Y
SOUTH CAROLINA							
1 ***Hartnett***	Y	N	Y	N	N	N	Y
2 ***Spence***	Y	N	Y	N	N	N	Y
3 Derrick	N	Y	Y	Y	Y	Y	N
4 ***Campbell***	Y	N	Y	N	Y	N	Y
5 Spratt	N	Y	Y	Y	N	Y	Y
6 Tallon	N	Y	N	Y	N	Y	Y
SOUTH DAKOTA							
AL Daschle	N	Y	N	Y	N	Y	N

	344	345	346	347	348	349	350
TENNESSEE							
1 ***Quillen***	Y	N	Y	N	Y	N	Y
2 ***Duncan***	N	Y	Y	N	Y	N	Y
3 Lloyd	N	Y	N	N	N	Y	Y
4 Cooper	N	Y	N	N	N	Y	Y
5 Boner	N	Y	Y	Y	N	N	Y
6 Gore	N	Y	Y	Y	N	Y	Y
7 ***Sundquist***	Y	N	Y	Y	Y	N	Y
8 Jones	?	#	X	N	N	Y	Y
9 Ford	N	Y	N	Y	?	?	?
TEXAS							
1 Hall, S.	N	Y	N	N	N	Y	N
2 Wilson	N	Y	Y	Y	N	N	Y
3 ***Bartlett***	Y	N	Y	N	Y	N	Y
4 Hall, R.	N	Y	N	N	N	N	N
5 Bryant	N	Y	Y	Y	N	Y	N
6 ***Gramm***	Y	N	?	?	Y	N	Y
7 ***Archer***	Y	N	Y	N	?	N	N
8 ***Fields***	Y	N	Y	N	Y	N	N
9 Brooks	N	Y	Y	Y	N	Y	N
10 Pickle	?	?	?	?	Y	N	Y
11 Leath	N	N	Y	N	N	Y	Y
12 Wright	N	Y	Y	Y	Y	N	Y
13 Hightower	N	Y	Y	N	N	N	Y
14 Patman	N	Y	N	N	N	N	N
15 de la Garza	N	Y	Y	?	N	Y	N
16 Coleman	N	Y	Y	Y	Y	N	Y
17 Stenholm	Y	N	Y	N	Y	N	N
18 Leland	N	Y	N	Y	N	Y	N
19 Hance	?	#	#	?	?	?	?
20 Gonzalez	N	Y	N	Y	N	N	N
21 ***Loeffler***	Y	N	Y	N	Y	N	Y
22 ***Paul***	Y	N	N	N	Y	N	N
23 Kazen	N	Y	N	N	N	Y	Y
24 Frost	N	Y	N	Y	N	N	Y
25 Andrews	N	Y	Y	Y	N	N	Y
26 Vandergriff	Y	N	Y	N	N	Y	Y
27 Ortiz	N	Y	Y	Y	N	Y	Y
UTAH							
1 ***Hansen***	Y	N	Y	N	N	N	Y
2 ***Marriott***	Y	Y	Y	Y	N	N	Y
3 ***Nielson***	Y	N	Y	N	Y	N	Y
VERMONT							
AL ***Jeffords***	?	?	Y	Y	N	Y	Y
VIRGINIA							
1 ***Bateman***	Y	N	Y	Y	Y	N	Y
2 ***Whitehurst***	Y	N	Y	N	N	N	Y
3 ***Bliley***	Y	N	Y	Y	N	N	Y
4 Sisisky	N	Y	Y	Y	N	Y	Y
5 Daniel	N	N	Y	N	N	N	Y
6 Olin	Y	N	Y	Y	N	Y	Y
7 ***Robinson***	Y	N	Y	N	N	N	Y
8 ***Parris***	Y	N	N	Y	N	N	Y
9 Boucher	N	Y	Y	Y	N	Y	Y
10 ***Wolf***	Y	Y	Y	Y	N	N	Y
WASHINGTON							
1 ***Pritchard***	?	?	?	?	?	?	?
2 Swift	N	Y	N	Y	Y	N	N
3 Bonker	N	Y	Y	Y	Y	N	Y
4 ***Morrison***	Y	Y	Y	N	Y	N	Y
5 Foley	N	Y	N	Y	Y	N	Y
6 Dicks	N	Y	N	N	Y	N	Y
7 Lowry	N	Y	N	Y	Y	N	N
8 ***Chandler***	Y	Y	Y	N	Y	N	Y
WEST VIRGINIA							
1 Mollohan	N	Y	Y	Y	N	Y	Y
2 Staggers	N	Y	Y	Y	Y	N	Y
3 Wise	N	Y	Y	Y	Y	N	N
4 Rahall	N	Y	Y	N	N	Y	Y
WISCONSIN							
1 Aspin	N	Y	Y	Y	N	Y	Y
2 Kastenmeier	N	Y	N	Y	N	Y	N
3 ***Gunderson***	Y	Y	Y	N	Y	N	N
4 Zablocki	N	Y	Y	Y	Y	N	Y
5 Moody	N	Y	N	Y	Y	Y	N
6 ***Petri***	Y	Y	Y	N	Y	N	N
7 Obey	N	Y	Y	N	N	Y	N
8 ***Roth***	Y	N	Y	N	Y	N	N
9 ***Sensenbrenner***	Y	Y	Y	N	N	N	N
WYOMING							
AL ***Cheney***	Y	N	Y	N	Y	N	Y

Southern states - Ala., Ark., Fla., Ga., Ky., La., Miss., N.C., Okla., S.C., Tenn., Texas, Va.

351. HR 2912. Justice Department Authorization. Adoption of the rule (H Res 239) providing for House floor consideration of the bill to authorize $3.43 billion for programs of the Justice Department. Adopted 341-43: R 108-41; D 233-2 (ND 154-1, SD 79-1), Sept. 30, 1983.

352. HR 3231. Export Administration Act. Roth, R-Wis., amendment to the Wolpe, D-Mich., amendment *(see vote 353, below)*, to prohibit the export of goods or technologies likely to be used in a nuclear production facility to any country that does not maintain International Atomic Energy Agency safeguards on all its peaceful nuclear activities, unless those goods or technologies are readily available from foreign sources. Rejected 163-220: R 128-20; D 35-200 (ND 9-147, SD 26-53), Sept. 30, 1983.

353. HR 3231. Export Administration Act. Wolpe, D-Mich., amendment to prohibit export licenses for goods or technologies likely to be used in a nuclear production facility to any country that does not maintain International Atomic Energy Agency safeguards. Adopted 196-189: R 15-134; D 181-55 (ND 142-15, SD 39-40), Sept. 30, 1983. A "nay" was a vote supporting the president's position.

354. H J Res 368. Continuing Appropriations, Fiscal 1984. Adoption of the conference report on the joint resolution to provide continued funding, through Nov. 10, 1983, for government agencies whose regular fiscal 1984 appropriations bills had not been enacted. Adopted 232-136: R 66-75; D 166-61 (ND 101-49, SD 65-12), Sept. 30, 1983.

355. H J Res 368. Continuing Appropriations, Fiscal 1984. Whitten, D-Miss., motion that the House recede from its disagreement to the Senate amendment No. 7 and concur therein with a substitute amendment. The substitute was the compromise that conferees had reached on defense spending for fiscal 1984. Motion agreed to 232-65: R 113-11; D 119-54 (ND 64-51, SD 55-3), Sept. 30, 1983.

356. Procedural Motion. Dreier, R-Calif., motion to approve the House *Journal* of Monday, Oct. 3. Motion agreed to 339-23: R 132-10; D 207-13 (ND 131-12, SD 76-1), Oct. 4, 1983.

357. HR 2379. Park System Protection. Hansen, R-Utah, amendment to the Udall, D-Ariz., substitute, to delete provisions requiring the interior secretary to delay exercise of his authority to lease, permit any use of, sell or dispose of lands adjacent to national park units until he has determined such action will have no significant adverse effect on park values. Rejected 160-245: R 120-39; D 40-206 (ND 7-157, SD 33-49), Oct. 4, 1983.

358. HR 2379. Park System Protection. Passage of the bill to require the interior secretary to identify threats to the national park system, both inside and outside park unit boundaries, together with measures for alleviating them, in a biennial "State of the Parks Report" to Congress, and to review beforehand proposed actions by the Interior Department and other federal agencies on lands inside and adjacent to park units that may adversely affect park values. Passed 321-82: R 92-65; D 229-17 (ND 160-3, SD 69-14), Oct. 4, 1983. A "nay" was a vote supporting the president's position.

KEY

- Y Voted for (yea).
- # Paired for.
- + Announced for.
- N Voted against (nay).
- X Paired against.
- - Announced against.
- P Voted "present".
- C Voted "present" to avoid possible conflict of interest.
- ? Did not vote or otherwise make a position known.

Democrats **Republicans**

	351	352	353	354	355	356	357	358
ALABAMA								
1 *Edwards*	Y	Y	N	Y	Y	Y	?	N
2 *Dickinson*	Y	Y	N	N	Y	Y	Y	N
3 Nichols	?	#	?	#	?	Y	N	Y
4 Bevill	?	?	?	?	?	Y	Y	Y
5 Flippo	Y	N	N	Y	?	Y	Y	Y
6 Erdreich	Y	N	N	Y	Y	Y	N	Y
7 Shelby	Y	Y	N	Y	Y	Y	Y	Y
ALASKA								
AL *Young*	Y	Y	N	Y	Y	N	Y	N
ARIZONA								
1 *McCain*	Y	Y	N	N	Y	Y	Y	N
2 Udall	Y	N	Y	Y	Y	Y	N	Y
3 *Stump*	Y	Y	N	N	Y	Y	Y	N
4 *Rudd*	?	?	?	#	?	Y	Y	N
5 McNulty	Y	N	Y	Y	Y	?	?	?
ARKANSAS								
1 Alexander	Y	?	?	?	?	Y	N	Y
2 *Bethune*	?	Y	N	N	N	Y	N	Y
3 *Hammerschmidt*	Y	Y	N	?	?	Y	Y	N
4 Anthony	Y	N	N	Y	?	Y	Y	Y
CALIFORNIA								
1 Bosco	Y	N	Y	Y	Y	Y	N	Y
2 *Chappie*	N	Y	N	N	Y	Y	Y	N
3 Matsui	Y	N	Y	Y	Y	Y	N	Y
4 Fazio	Y	N	Y	?	?	N	Y	Y
5 Burton	Y	N	Y	Y	?	Y	X	?
6 Boxer	Y	N	Y	?	?	Y	N	Y
7 Miller	?	?	?	?	?	?	?	?
8 Dellums	Y	N	Y	N	Y	N	Y	Y
9 Stark	Y	?	Y	N	N	N	Y	Y
10 Edwards	Y	N	Y	Y	Y	Y	N	Y
11 Lantos	Y	N	Y	Y	Y	Y	N	Y
12 *Zschau*	N	N	N	N	Y	Y	Y	Y
13 Mineta	Y	N	Y	Y	Y	Y	N	Y
14 Shumway	Y	Y	N	N	Y	Y	Y	N
15 Coelho	?	N	N	Y	?	N	Y	Y
16 Panetta	Y	N	Y	Y	Y	N	Y	Y
17 *Pashayan*	Y	Y	N	?	?	Y	Y	Y
18 Lehman	Y	N	Y	?	?	Y	N	Y
19 *Lagomarsino*	Y	Y	N	N	Y	Y	Y	N
20 *Thomas*	?	?	?	X	?	P	Y	N
21 *Fiedler*	N	Y	N	Y	?	Y	Y	Y
22 *Moorhead*	Y	Y	N	N	Y	Y	Y	N
23 Beilenson	Y	N	Y	N	Y	N	Y	Y
24 Waxman	?	N	Y	?	?	N	Y	Y
25 Roybal	Y	N	Y	Y	?	P	N	Y
26 Berman	Y	N	Y	N	Y	N	Y	Y
27 Levine	Y	N	Y	N	Y	N	Y	Y
28 Dixon	Y	N	Y	Y	Y	Y	N	Y
29 Hawkins	Y	N	Y	Y	Y	Y	?	?
30 Martinez	Y	N	Y	Y	Y	Y	N	Y
31 Dymally	P	N	Y	?	?	P	N	Y
32 Anderson	Y	N	Y	?	?	Y	N	Y
33 *Dreier*	N	Y	N	N	Y	Y	Y	N
34 Torres	Y	N	Y	N	Y	N	Y	Y
35 *Lewis*	Y	Y	N	Y	?	Y	N	Y
36 Brown	Y	N	Y	?	?	Y	N	Y
37 *McCandless*	Y	Y	N	X	?	Y	Y	N
38 Patterson	Y	N	Y	Y	Y	Y	N	Y
39 *Dannemeyer*	N	Y	N	N	Y	Y	Y	N
40 *Badham*	Y	Y	N	N	Y	?	#	?
41 *Lowery*	Y	Y	N	N	Y	Y	Y	N
42 *Lungren*	?	?	?	?	?	Y	Y	N

	351	352	353	354	355	356	357	358
43 *Packard*	Y	Y	N	N	Y	Y	Y	N
44 Bates	Y	N	Y	N	N	?	N	Y
45 *Hunter*	Y	N	Y	N	Y	?	Y	N
COLORADO								
1 Schroeder	Y	N	Y	N	N	N	N	Y
2 Wirth	Y	N	Y	N	Y	N	X	?
3 Kogovsek	Y	N	Y	Y	Y	Y	N	Y
4 *Brown*	N	Y	N	N	N	Y	Y	N
5 *Kramer*	?	?	?	X	?	Y	Y	Y
6 *Schaefer*	N	Y	N	N	Y	Y	Y	N
CONNECTICUT								
1 Kennelly	?	N	Y	Y	Y	?	N	Y
2 Gejdenson	Y	N	Y	N	N	N	N	Y
3 Morrison	Y	N	Y	N	Y	N	N	Y
4 *McKinney*	Y	N	Y	Y	Y	Y	N	Y
5 Ratchford	Y	N	Y	?	?	Y	N	Y
6 *Johnson*	Y	N	N	Y	Y	Y	N	Y
DELAWARE								
AL Carper	Y	N	Y	N	Y	Y	N	Y
FLORIDA								
1 Hutto	Y	Y	N	Y	Y	Y	N	Y
2 Fuqua	Y	N	N	Y	?	Y	N	Y
3 Bennett	N	Y	Y	Y	Y	Y	N	Y
4 Chappell	Y	Y	N	Y	?	Y	N	Y
5 *McCollum*	Y	Y	N	N	Y	Y	Y	Y
6 MacKay	Y	N	Y	N	Y	Y	N	Y
7 Gibbons	?	?	?	?	?	Y	N	Y
8 *Young*	Y	Y	?	Y	Y	?	?	?
9 *Bilirakis*	N	Y	N	N	Y	Y	Y	Y
10 Ireland	Y	N	N	Y	?	N	Y	Y
11 Nelson	+	#	X	N	Y	N	N	Y
12 *Lewis*	Y	N	N	Y	Y	Y	Y	Y
13 *Mack*	N	Y	N	N	Y	N	Y	N
14 Mica	Y	N	Y	Y	Y	N	Y	Y
15 *Shaw*	N	Y	N	N	?	Y	Y	Y
16 Smith	Y	N	Y	Y	Y	Y	N	Y
17 Lehman	Y	N	Y	N	Y	N	Y	Y
18 Pepper	+	X	+	#	+	+	-	+
19 Fascell	Y	N	Y	Y	Y	?	?	?
GEORGIA								
1 Thomas	Y	N	Y	Y	Y	Y	Y	Y
2 Hatcher	Y	N	Y	Y	Y	Y	N	Y
3 Ray	Y	N	Y	Y	Y	Y	N	Y
4 Levitas	Y	N	N	Y	Y	?	?	#
5 Fowler	?	N	Y	?	Y	?	N	Y
6 *Gingrich*	Y	Y	N	?	?	Y	Y	Y
7 VACANCY								
8 Rowland	Y	N	Y	?	?	Y	Y	Y
9 Jenkins	Y	N	Y	?	?	Y	Y	Y
10 Barnard	Y	N	Y	Y	Y	Y	Y	Y
HAWAII								
1 Heftel	?	?	?	?	?	?	?	?
2 Akaka	Y	N	N	Y	Y	Y	N	Y
IDAHO								
1 *Craig*	?	Y	N	N	Y	Y	Y	N
2 *Hansen*	N	Y	N	Y	?	Y	Y	N
ILLINOIS								
1 Hayes	Y	N	Y	N	N	Y	N	Y
2 Savage	Y	N	Y	N	?	P	N	Y
3 Russo	Y	N	Y	N	N	Y	N	Y
4 *O'Brien*	Y	N	Y	Y	?	?	?	?
5 Lipinski	Y	N	Y	N	Y	?	N	Y
6 *Hyde*	Y	N	Y	N	Y	Y	N	Y
7 Collins	Y	N	Y	Y	Y	Y	N	Y
8 Rostenkowski	Y	N	Y	N	Y	Y	N	Y
9 Yates	Y	N	Y	?	N	N	N	Y
10 *Porter*	Y	Y	Y	N	Y	Y	N	Y
11 Annunzio	Y	N	Y	Y	Y	Y	N	Y
12 *Crane, P.*	N	Y	N	N	Y	Y	Y	N
13 *Erlenborn*	Y	Y	N	?	?	Y	Y	N
14 *Corcoran*	+	-	X	+	+	N	Y	N
15 *Madigan*	Y	N	Y	Y	Y	?	?	?
16 *Martin*	N	Y	N	N	?	#	?	?
17 Evans	Y	N	N	Y	N	Y	N	Y
18 *Michel*	Y	N	Y	Y	Y	Y	N	Y
19 *Crane, D.*	N	Y	N	X	?	Y	Y	N
20 Durbin	Y	N	N	Y	N	N	N	Y
21 Price	Y	Y	Y	Y	Y	Y	Y	Y
22 Simon	?	?	?	?	?	Y	?	?
INDIANA								
1 Hall	?	N	Y	Y	Y	Y	N	Y
2 Sharp	Y	N	Y	N	Y	N	Y	Y
3 *Hiler*	N	Y	N	N	Y	N	Y	N
4 *Coats*	N	Y	N	N	Y	Y	Y	N
5 *Hillis*	Y	N	Y	Y	Y	Y	Y	N

ND - Northern Democrats   SD - Southern Democrats

Corresponding to Congressional Record Votes 371, 372, 373, 374, 375, 376, 377, 378

	351	352	353	354	355	356	357	358
6 ***Burton***	N	Y	N	N	Y	Y	Y	N
7 ***Myers***	Y	Y	N	Y	Y	Y	Y	N
8 McCloskey	Y	N	Y	Y	N	Y	N	Y
9 Hamilton	Y	N	Y	?	?	Y	N	Y
10 Jacobs	?	?	?	?	?	N	N	Y
IOWA								
1 ***Leach***	Y	N	Y	N	N	Y	N	Y
2 ***Tauke***	Y	N	Y	N	Y	Y	N	Y
3 ***Evans***	N	Y	N	N	Y	N	N	Y
4 Smith	Y	Y	N	Y	Y	Y	N	Y
5 Harkin	Y	N	Y	N	Y	N	N	Y
6 Bedell	Y	N	Y	?	?	Y	N	Y
KANSAS								
1 ***Roberts***	N	Y	N	N	?	N	Y	Y
2 Slattery	Y	Y	Y	N	N	Y	N	Y
3 ***Winn***	Y	Y	N	Y	Y	Y	Y	Y
4 Glickman	Y	N	Y	N	Y	Y	N	Y
5 ***Whittaker***	N	Y	N	N	?	Y	Y	Y
KENTUCKY								
1 Hubbard	N	Y	N	N	Y	Y	Y	N
2 Natcher	Y	N	N	Y	Y	Y	Y	Y
3 Mazzoli	Y	N	Y	Y	Y	Y	N	Y
4 ***Snyder***	Y	Y	N	N	Y	Y	Y	Y
5 ***Rogers***	Y	Y	N	Y	Y	Y	Y	N
6 ***Hopkins***	Y	Y	N	N	Y	Y	Y	N
7 Perkins	Y	N	Y	Y	Y	Y	N	Y
LOUISIANA								
1 ***Livingston***	Y	Y	N	Y	Y	Y	Y	N
2 Boggs	?	N	Y	Y	Y	Y	?	Y
3 Tauzin	Y	N	Y	N	Y	Y	Y	Y
4 Roemer	Y	N	Y	N	Y	N	N	Y
5 Huckaby	Y	N	Y	Y	?	Y	Y	Y
6 ***Moore***	Y	Y	N	N	Y	Y	Y	N
7 Breaux	Y	Y	N	Y	Y	Y	Y	Y
8 Long	Y	N	Y	Y	?	Y	N	Y
MAINE								
1 ***McKernan***	Y	N	Y	Y	Y	?	N	Y
2 ***Snowe***	Y	Y	N	N	Y	?	N	Y
MARYLAND								
1 Dyson	Y	Y	N	Y	Y	Y	Y	Y
2 Long	Y	N	Y	Y	?	Y	N	Y
3 Mikulski	Y	N	Y	Y	Y	Y	N	Y
4 ***Holt***	Y	?	N	Y	Y	Y	Y	Y
5 Hoyer	Y	N	Y	Y	Y	?	N	Y
6 Byron	?	?	?	Y	Y	?	N	Y
7 Mitchell	Y	N	Y	Y	Y	N	N	Y
8 Barnes	Y	N	Y	Y	Y	Y	N	Y
MASSACHUSETTS								
1 ***Conte***	Y	Y	N	Y	Y	Y	N	Y
2 Boland	Y	?	?	?	?	Y	N	Y
3 Early	Y	N	Y	N	Y	Y	N	Y
4 Frank	Y	N	Y	N	?	Y	N	Y
5 Shannon	Y	N	Y	N	N	Y	N	Y
6 Mavroules	Y	N	Y	Y	Y	Y	N	Y
7 Markey	Y	N	Y	N	N	Y	N	Y
8 O'Neill								
9 Moakley	?	?	?	?	?	Y	N	Y
10 Studds	Y	N	?	?	?	Y	N	Y
11 Donnelly	Y	N	Y	N	N	Y	N	Y
MICHIGAN								
1 Conyers	Y	N	Y	N	N	?	N	Y
2 ***Pursell***	Y	N	N	X	?	?	Y	Y
3 Wolpe	Y	N	Y	N	N	Y	N	Y
4 ***Siljander***	N	Y	N	N	Y	Y	Y	Y
5 ***Sawyer***	Y	Y	N	Y	Y	Y	N	Y
6 Carr	Y	N	Y	N	Y	Y	N	Y
7 Kildee	Y	N	Y	N	N	Y	N	Y
8 Traxler	Y	N	Y	?	?	N	N	Y
9 ***Vander Jagt***	Y	Y	N	Y	Y	Y	Y	Y
10 Albosta	Y	N	Y	?	?	Y	N	Y
11 ***Davis***	Y	?	?	?	?	Y	Y	Y
12 Bonior	?	X	#	#	?	Y	N	Y
13 Crockett	?	N	Y	Y	N	?	N	Y
14 Hertel	Y	N	Y	N	N	Y	N	Y
15 Ford	?	?	?	Y	?	?	N	Y
16 Dingell	?	?	?	?	?	?	?	?
17 Levin	Y	N	Y	Y	N	Y	N	Y
18 ***Broomfield***	?	?	?	#	?	Y	Y	Y
MINNESOTA								
1 Penny	Y	N	Y	N	N	Y	N	Y
2 ***Weber***	N	N	Y	N	?	Y	N	Y
3 ***Frenzel***	N	N	N	N	Y	Y	Y	Y
4 Vento	Y	N	Y	Y	Y	Y	N	Y
5 Sabo	Y	N	Y	Y	N	N	N	Y
6 Sikorski	Y	N	Y	N	N	N	N	Y
7 ***Stangeland***	N	Y	N	N	?	Y	Y	N
8 Oberstar	Y	N	Y	Y	N	P	N	Y
MISSISSIPPI								
1 Whitten	Y	N	N	Y	Y	Y	Y	Y
2 ***Franklin***	?	?	N	Y	Y	Y	Y	Y
3 Montgomery	Y	Y	N	Y	?	Y	Y	Y
4 Dowdy	Y	N	N	Y	Y	Y	N	Y
5 ***Lott***	Y	Y	N	Y	Y	Y	Y	Y
MISSOURI								
1 Clay	?	?	?	?	?	N	N	Y
2 Young	Y	N	N	Y	?	Y	N	Y
3 Gephardt	Y	N	Y	Y	Y	Y	N	Y
4 Skelton	?	?	?	#	?	Y	N	Y
5 Wheat	Y	N	Y	Y	Y	Y	N	Y
6 ***Coleman***	Y	Y	N	N	Y	Y	Y	Y
7 ***Taylor***	Y	Y	N	Y	Y	Y	Y	Y
8 ***Emerson***	Y	Y	N	N	Y	?	Y	N
9 Volkmer	Y	N	Y	N	Y	Y	N	Y
MONTANA								
1 Williams	Y	N	Y	Y	N	Y	N	Y
2 ***Marlenee***	Y	Y	N	N	Y	Y	Y	N
NEBRASKA								
1 ***Bereuter***	Y	Y	N	Y	Y	Y	N	Y
2 ***Daub***	Y	Y	N	N	Y	Y	Y	Y
3 ***Smith***	Y	Y	N	Y	Y	Y	Y	N
NEVADA								
1 Reid	Y	N	Y	N	?	Y	Y	Y
2 ***Vucanovich***	N	Y	N	N	Y	Y	Y	N
NEW HAMPSHIRE								
1 D'Amours	Y	N	Y	Y	Y	?	X	?
2 ***Gregg***	?	?	?	?	?	Y	Y	Y
NEW JERSEY								
1 Florio	?	N	Y	Y	?	Y	N	Y
2 Hughes	Y	N	Y	N	Y	Y	N	Y
3 Howard	Y	N	Y	Y	Y	Y	N	Y
4 ***Smith***	Y	N	Y	Y	Y	Y	N	Y
5 ***Roukema***	Y	Y	N	Y	Y	Y	N	Y
6 Dwyer	Y	N	Y	Y	?	Y	N	Y
7 ***Rinaldo***	Y	N	Y	Y	Y	Y	N	Y
8 Roe	?	N	Y	Y	?	?	N	Y
9 Torricelli	Y	N	Y	Y	Y	Y	N	Y
10 Rodino	Y	N	Y	Y	Y	Y	N	Y
11 Minish	Y	N	Y	Y	?	Y	N	Y
12 ***Courter***	Y	Y	Y	Y	Y	Y	N	Y
13 ***Forsythe***	N	Y	Y	Y	?	N	Y	Y
14 Guarini	Y	N	Y	Y	Y	Y	N	Y
NEW MEXICO								
1 ***Lujan***	Y	Y	N	Y	Y	Y	Y	Y
2 ***Skeen***	N	Y	N	Y	Y	Y	Y	N
3 Richardson	Y	N	Y	N	?	Y	N	Y
NEW YORK								
1 ***Carney***	Y	Y	N	Y	Y	Y	Y	Y
2 Downey	Y	N	Y	Y	?	Y	N	Y
3 Mrazek	Y	N	Y	Y	N	Y	N	Y
4 ***Lent***	Y	Y	N	Y	Y	Y	Y	Y
5 ***McGrath***	Y	Y	N	Y	Y	?	?	?
6 Addabbo	Y	N	Y	#	?	Y	N	Y
7 Ackerman	Y	N	Y	Y	N	Y	N	Y
8 Scheuer	Y	N	Y	Y	Y	Y	N	Y
9 Ferraro	Y	N	Y	Y	?	Y	N	Y
10 Schumer	Y	?	Y	Y	N	Y	N	Y
11 Towns	Y	N	Y	N	N	Y	N	Y
12 Owens	Y	N	Y	Y	?	Y	N	Y
13 Solarz	Y	N	Y	Y	Y	?	?	?
14 ***Molinari***	Y	Y	N	Y	Y	Y	N	Y
15 ***Green***	Y	Y	N	Y	N	Y	N	Y
16 Rangel	Y	N	Y	Y	N	Y	N	Y
17 Weiss	Y	N	Y	N	N	Y	N	Y
18 Garcia	Y	N	Y	Y	N	Y	N	Y
19 Biaggi	Y	N	?	?	?	Y	N	Y
20 Ottinger	Y	N	Y	Y	N	P	N	Y
21 ***Fish***	Y	?	?	Y	Y	Y	N	Y
22 ***Gilman***	Y	Y	N	Y	?	Y	N	Y
23 Stratton	Y	Y	N	Y	Y	Y	N	Y
24 ***Solomon***	?	Y	N	N	Y	Y	Y	?
25 ***Boehlert***	?	?	?	Y	Y	Y	N	Y
26 ***Martin***	Y	Y	N	?	Y	Y	Y	N
27 ***Wortley***	Y	Y	N	Y	Y	Y	Y	Y
28 McHugh	Y	N	Y	Y	Y	Y	N	Y
29 ***Horton***	Y	Y	?	Y	Y	Y	N	Y
30 ***Conable***	N	Y	N	#	?	Y	Y	Y
31 ***Kemp***	Y	Y	N	Y	Y	Y	N	Y
32 LaFalce	Y	N	Y	Y	?	Y	N	Y
33 Nowak	Y	N	Y	Y	?	?	N	Y
34 Lundine	Y	N	Y	N	N	Y	N	Y
NORTH CAROLINA								
1 Jones	Y	N	Y	Y	?	Y	N	Y
2 Valentine	Y	Y	N	Y	Y	Y	N	Y
3 Whitley	Y	Y	N	Y	?	Y	N	Y
4 Andrews	Y	Y	N	Y	Y	?	N	Y
5 Neal	Y	N	Y	Y	Y	?	N	Y
6 Britt	Y	?	?	?	?	Y	N	Y
7 Rose	Y	N	Y	Y	Y	?	?	?
8 Hefner	Y	N	N	Y	?	Y	N	Y
9 ***Martin***	?	Y	N	N	Y	Y	N	Y
10 ***Broyhill***	Y	Y	N	N	Y	Y	N	Y
11 Clarke	Y	N	Y	Y	Y	Y	N	Y
NORTH DAKOTA								
AL Dorgan	Y	N	Y	N	N	Y	Y	Y
OHIO								
1 Luken	Y	N	Y	?	?	Y	N	Y
2 ***Gradison***	Y	N	N	Y	Y	Y	Y	Y
3 Hall	Y	N	Y	N	N	?	?	?
4 ***Oxley***	Y	Y	N	Y	Y	Y	Y	N
5 ***Latta***	?	?	?	X	?	Y	Y	N
6 ***McEwen***	Y	Y	N	N	Y	Y	N	Y
7 ***DeWine***	Y	Y	N	N	Y	Y	Y	Y
8 ***Kindness***	Y	Y	N	Y	Y	Y	Y	N
9 Kaptur	Y	N	Y	N	N	Y	N	Y
10 ***Miller***	N	Y	N	N	Y	N	Y	Y
11 Eckart	Y	N	Y	N	Y	Y	N	Y
12 ***Kasich***	N	N	N	N	Y	Y	Y	Y
13 Pease	Y	N	Y	N	Y	Y	N	Y
14 Seiberling	Y	N	Y	Y	?	Y	N	Y
15 ***Wylie***	Y	Y	N	#	?	Y	N	Y
16 ***Regula***	Y	Y	N	Y	?	Y	N	Y
17 ***Williams***	Y	Y	N	#	?	Y	N	Y
18 Applegate	Y	N	Y	N	?	?	N	Y
19 Feighan	Y	N	Y	N	N	Y	N	Y
20 Oakar	Y	?	?	N	Y	Y	N	Y
21 Stokes	?	?	?	?	?	Y	N	Y
OKLAHOMA								
1 Jones	Y	N	N	?	?	Y	Y	Y
2 Synar	Y	N	Y	Y	Y	Y	N	Y
3 Watkins	Y	N	Y	Y	Y	?	Y	N
4 McCurdy	Y	N	Y	N	?	Y	Y	N
5 ***Edwards***	N	Y	N	N	Y	?	Y	N
6 English	Y	N	Y	N	Y	Y	Y	N
OREGON								
1 AuCoin	?	?	?	X	?	Y	N	Y
2 ***Smith, R.***	Y	Y	N	N	Y	Y	Y	N
3 Wyden	Y	N	Y	N	N	Y	N	Y
4 Weaver	N	N	Y	N	?	Y	N	Y
5 ***Smith, D.***	N	Y	N	N	Y	N	Y	N
PENNSYLVANIA								
1 Foglietta	Y	N	Y	Y	?	Y	N	Y
2 Gray	Y	N	Y	Y	Y	Y	N	Y
3 Borski	Y	N	Y	Y	Y	Y	N	Y
4 Kolter	Y	N	N	Y	?	Y	N	Y
5 ***Schulze***	Y	Y	N	N	?	Y	Y	N
6 Yatron	Y	N	N	Y	Y	Y	N	Y
7 Edgar	Y	N	Y	N	?	Y	N	Y
8 Kostmayer	Y	N	Y	N	N	Y	N	Y
9 ***Shuster***	Y	Y	N	X	?	Y	Y	Y
10 ***McDade***	?	?	N	Y	Y	?	N	Y
11 Harrison	Y	N	Y	Y	Y	Y	N	Y
12 Murtha	Y	Y	N	Y	?	?	N	Y
13 ***Coughlin***	Y	N	Y	Y	N	N	N	Y
14 Coyne	Y	N	Y	Y	Y	Y	N	Y
15 ***Ritter***	Y	N	N	N	N	Y	Y	Y
16 ***Walker***	N	Y	N	N	Y	N	Y	N
17 ***Gekas***	N	Y	N	N	?	?	Y	N
18 Walgren	Y	N	Y	N	N	Y	N	Y
19 ***Goodling***	Y	N	N	N	N	?	Y	Y
20 Gaydos	Y	Y	N	Y	?	Y	N	Y
21 ***Ridge***	Y	Y	N	Y	Y	Y	N	Y
22 Murphy	Y	Y	N	Y	Y	P	N	Y
23 ***Clinger***	N	Y	N	Y	Y	Y	Y	Y
RHODE ISLAND								
1 St Germain	Y	?	?	?	?	P	N	Y
2 ***Schneider***	Y	N	Y	Y	N	Y	N	Y
SOUTH CAROLINA								
1 ***Hartnett***	N	Y	N	X	?	Y	Y	N
2 ***Spence***	Y	Y	N	N	Y	Y	Y	Y
3 Derrick	Y	N	Y	#	?	Y	N	Y
4 ***Campbell***	Y	Y	N	Y	Y	Y	Y	N
5 Spratt	Y	N	N	Y	N	Y	N	Y
6 Tallon	Y	N	Y	Y	?	Y	N	Y
SOUTH DAKOTA								
AL Daschle	?	?	?	?	?	?	?	?
TENNESSEE								
1 ***Quillen***	Y	?	?	#	?	Y	Y	N
2 ***Duncan***	Y	Y	N	Y	Y	Y	Y	Y
3 Lloyd	Y	Y	N	Y	Y	Y	Y	Y
4 Cooper	Y	N	Y	Y	?	Y	N	Y
5 Boner	Y	N	N	Y	?	Y	N	Y
6 Gore	Y	N	Y	Y	Y	Y	N	Y
7 ***Sundquist***	Y	Y	N	Y	Y	Y	Y	Y
8 Jones	Y	N	N	Y	Y	Y	N	Y
9 Ford	?	?	?	?	?	?	?	?
TEXAS								
1 Hall, S.	Y	Y	N	Y	?	Y	Y	N
2 Wilson	Y	Y	N	Y	Y	Y	Y	N
3 ***Bartlett***	Y	Y	N	N	?	?	Y	N
4 Hall, R.	Y	Y	N	N	Y	Y	Y	N
5 Bryant	Y	N	Y	N	Y	Y	N	Y
6 ***Gramm***	?	?	?	?	?	Y	Y	N
7 ***Archer***	Y	Y	N	N	Y	Y	Y	N
8 ***Fields***	Y	Y	N	N	Y	N	Y	N
9 Brooks	Y	N	Y	Y	Y	?	?	?
10 Pickle	Y	?	?	?	?	Y	N	Y
11 Leath	Y	Y	N	Y	?	Y	Y	N
12 Wright	Y	N	Y	Y	Y	Y	N	Y
13 Hightower	Y	Y	N	Y	Y	Y	Y	Y
14 Patman	Y	Y	N	N	Y	Y	Y	N
15 de la Garza	Y	N	N	Y	?	?	N	Y
16 Coleman	Y	N	Y	Y	Y	Y	N	Y
17 Stenholm	Y	Y	N	N	Y	Y	Y	N
18 Leland	Y	N	Y	N	N	Y	N	Y
19 Hance	?	?	?	X	?	Y	Y	N
20 Gonzalez	Y	N	Y	Y	Y	Y	N	Y
21 ***Loeffler***	Y	Y	N	N	Y	Y	Y	N
22 ***Paul***	N	Y	N	X	?	Y	Y	N
23 Kazen	Y	Y	N	Y	Y	Y	N	Y
24 Frost	Y	N	Y	Y	Y	Y	N	Y
25 Andrews	Y	N	Y	Y	Y	Y	N	Y
26 Vandergriff	Y	Y	N	Y	Y	Y	Y	N
27 Ortiz	Y	Y	Y	Y	Y	?	Y	Y
UTAH								
1 ***Hansen***	N	Y	N	N	?	Y	Y	N
2 ***Marriott***	Y	?	?	?	?	Y	Y	N
3 ***Nielson***	N	Y	N	N	Y	Y	Y	N
VERMONT								
AL ***Jeffords***	Y	N	Y	Y	N	Y	N	Y
VIRGINIA								
1 ***Bateman***	Y	Y	N	Y	Y	Y	Y	Y
2 ***Whitehurst***	Y	Y	N	Y	?	?	?	?
3 ***Bliley***	Y	Y	N	Y	Y	Y	Y	?
4 Sisisky	Y	Y	N	Y	Y	Y	N	Y
5 Daniel	Y	Y	N	Y	Y	Y	Y	N
6 Olin	Y	Y	N	Y	Y	Y	Y	N
7 ***Robinson***	Y	Y	N	Y	Y	Y	Y	N
8 ***Parris***	Y	Y	N	Y	?	Y	#	?
9 Boucher	Y	N	Y	Y	?	Y	N	Y
10 ***Wolf***	Y	Y	N	Y	Y	Y	Y	Y
WASHINGTON								
1 ***Pritchard***	?	?	?	#	?	?	?	?
2 Swift	Y	N	N	Y	Y	Y	N	N
3 Bonker	Y	N	N	Y	Y	Y	N	Y
4 ***Morrison***	Y	Y	N	Y	Y	?	Y	N
5 Foley	Y	?	Y	Y	Y	?	N	Y
6 Dicks	Y	N	Y	Y	Y	?	N	Y
7 Lowry	Y	N	Y	N	N	?	N	Y
8 ***Chandler***	Y	Y	N	Y	Y	Y	Y	Y
WEST VIRGINIA								
1 Mollohan	Y	N	Y	Y	Y	Y	Y	Y
2 Staggers	Y	N	Y	Y	N	Y	N	Y
3 Wise	Y	N	Y	Y	Y	Y	N	Y
4 Rahall	Y	N	Y	N	?	Y	Y	X
WISCONSIN								
1 Aspin	Y	?	?	?	?	?	N	Y
2 Kastenmeier	Y	N	Y	Y	N	Y	N	Y
3 ***Gunderson***	N	Y	N	N	N	Y	Y	Y
4 Zablocki	Y	N	N	Y	Y	?	?	?
5 Moody	Y	Y	Y	Y	Y	?	N	Y
6 ***Petri***	Y	Y	N	N	N	Y	Y	Y
7 Obey	Y	N	Y	Y	N	Y	N	Y
8 ***Roth***	Y	Y	N	N	Y	Y	Y	N
9 ***Sensenbrenner***	Y	Y	N	N	Y	Y	N	Y
WYOMING								
AL ***Cheney***	?	?	?	X	?	Y	Y	N

Southern states - Ala., Ark., Fla., Ga., Ky., La., Miss., N.C., Okla., S.C., Tenn., Texas, Va.

359. S 1852. Defense Production Act Extension. La-Falce, D-N.Y., motion to suspend the rules and pass the bill to extend the Defense Production Act for two years, through Sept. 30, 1985. Motion rejected 233-168: R 59-97; D 174-71 (ND 110-52, SD 64-19), Oct. 4, 1983. A two-thirds majority of those present and voting (268 in this case) is required for passage under suspension of the rules.

360. HR 3363. Interior Appropriations, Fiscal 1984. Adoption of the conference report on the bill to appropriate $7,953,783,000 in fiscal 1984 for the Interior Department and related agencies. Adopted 296-95: R 71-82; D 225-13 (ND 157-3, SD 68-10), Oct. 5, 1983. The president had requested $6,709,628,000 in new budget authority.

361. HR 3958. Energy and Water Supplemental Appropriations, Fiscal 1984. Adoption of the rule (H Res 331) providing for House floor consideration of the bill to provide $119 million in fiscal 1984 supplemental appropriations for 43 water resource projects. The rule waived points of order against the bill for making appropriations without authorizing legislation. Adopted 270-124: R 71-82; D 199-42 (ND 126-35, SD 73-7), Oct. 5, 1983.

362. HR 3959. Supplemental Appropriations, Fiscal 1984. Adoption of the rule (H Res 332) providing for House floor consideration of the bill to make supplemental appropriations for fiscal 1984. Adopted 308-83: R 99-52; D 209-31 (ND 134-26, SD 75-5), Oct. 5, 1983.

363. HR 3959. Supplemental Appropriations, Fiscal 1984. Passage of the bill to appropriate $444,740,800 in supplemental funds for fiscal 1984. Passed 363-30: R 124-27; D 239-3 (ND 160-2, SD 79-1), Oct. 5, 1983.

364. HR 3958. Energy and Water Supplemental Appropriations, Fiscal 1984. Edgar, D-Pa., amendment to delete 20 unauthorized projects from the bill to provide $119 million in fiscal 1984 supplemental appropriations for 43 water resource projects. Rejected 133-271: R 68-89; D 65-182 (ND 53-112, SD 12-70), Oct. 6, 1983. A "yea" was a vote supporting the president's position.

365. HR 3648. Amtrak Improvement Act. Florio, D-N.J., amendment to direct Amtrak to issue preferred stock to the secretary of transportation to discharge Amtrak's debt on loans guaranteed by the secretary. Rejected 151-198: R 7-136; D 144-62 (ND 119-15, SD 25-47), Oct. 6, 1983.

KEY

- Y Voted for (yea).
- # Paired for.
- + Announced for.
- N Voted against (nay).
- X Paired against.
- − Announced against.
- P Voted "present".
- C Voted "present" to avoid possible conflict of interest.
- ? Did not vote or otherwise make a position known.

Democrats *Republicans*

	359	360	361	362	363	364	365
ALABAMA							
1 *Edwards*	Y	Y	Y	Y	Y	N	N
2 Dickinson	Y	Y	Y	Y	Y	N	?
3 Nichols	N	Y	Y	Y	Y	N	N
4 Bevill	Y	Y	Y	Y	Y	N	N
5 Flippo	Y	Y	Y	Y	Y	N	?
6 Erdreich	Y	Y	Y	Y	Y	N	N
7 Shelby	Y	Y	Y	Y	Y	N	N
ALASKA							
AL *Young*	Y	N	Y	Y	Y	N	N
ARIZONA							
1 *McCain*	Y	N	Y	Y	Y	N	N
2 Udall	Y	Y	Y	Y	Y	N	Y
3 *Stump*	Y	N	N	Y	Y	N	N
4 *Rudd*	N	Y	Y	Y	Y	N	N
5 McNulty	?	?	?	?	?	?	?
ARKANSAS							
1 Alexander	Y	Y	Y	Y	Y	N	Y
2 *Bethune*	N	N	Y	Y	Y	N	?
3 *Hammerschmidt*	N	Y	Y	Y	Y	N	N
4 Anthony	Y	Y	Y	Y	Y	N	Y
CALIFORNIA							
1 Bosco	N	Y	Y	Y	Y	N	?
2 *Chappie*	N	N	Y	Y	Y	N	?
3 Matsui	N	Y	Y	Y	Y	N	Y
4 Fazio	N	Y	Y	Y	Y	N	Y
5 Burton	?	?	?	?	?	?	?
6 Boxer	N	Y	N	Y	N	Y	?
7 Miller	?	Y	Y	Y	N	Y	Y
8 Dellums	N	?	N	N	Y	N	Y
9 Stark	N	Y	N	Y	Y	Y	Y
10 Edwards	N	Y	Y	Y	Y	?	?
11 Lantos	N	Y	Y	Y	Y	Y	Y
12 *Zschau*	N	N	N	Y	Y	Y	N
13 Mineta	N	Y	Y	Y	Y	Y	Y
14 *Shumway*	Y	N	N	Y	N	Y	N
15 Coelho	Y	Y	Y	Y	Y	?	?
16 Panetta	N	Y	Y	Y	Y	Y	Y
17 *Pashayan*	N	N	N	N	Y	N	N
18 Lehman	Y	Y	Y	Y	Y	N	?
19 *Lagomarsino*	Y	Y	N	Y	Y	N	N
20 *Thomas*	Y	N	N	N	Y	N	N
21 *Fiedler*	Y	Y	N	Y	Y	N	N
22 *Moorhead*	Y	N	N	Y	N	Y	N
23 Beilenson	Y	Y	Y	Y	Y	Y	Y
24 Waxman	N	?	Y	Y	Y	Y	Y
25 Roybal	N	Y	?	Y	Y	N	?
26 Berman	N	Y	Y	Y	Y	Y	Y
27 Levine	N	Y	Y	N	Y	N	Y
28 Dixon	Y	Y	Y	Y	Y	N	#
29 Hawkins	?	Y	Y	Y	Y	N	Y
30 Martinez	Y	Y	Y	Y	Y	N	Y
31 Dymally	Y	Y	Y	Y	Y	N	Y
32 Anderson	Y	Y	N	Y	Y	N	Y
33 *Dreier*	N	N	N	N	N	Y	N
34 Torres	Y	Y	Y	Y	Y	N	?
35 *Lewis*	N	N	Y	Y	Y	N	N
36 Brown	Y	Y	Y	?	Y	N	Y
37 *McCandless*	N	N	N	Y	N	Y	N
38 Patterson	N	Y	Y	Y	Y	N	Y
39 *Dannemeyer*	N	N	N	N	Y	N	?
40 *Badham*	?	?	?	?	?	?	X
41 *Lowery*	Y	Y	N	Y	N	Y	N
42 *Lungren*	N	N	N	N	Y	Y	N

	359	360	361	362	363	364	365
43 *Packard*	Y	Y	C	P	Y	C	N
44 Bates	N	Y	N	Y	Y	Y	Y
45 *Hunter*	N	Y	N	Y	Y	N	N
COLORADO							
1 Schroeder	N	+	−	−	−	N	N
2 Wirth	?	Y	Y	Y	Y	N	?
3 Kogovsek	Y	Y	Y	Y	Y	N	?
4 *Brown*	N	Y	N	N	N	N	N
5 *Kramer*	Y	Y	Y	Y	Y	N	N
6 *Schaefer*	Y	N	Y	Y	N	N	N
CONNECTICUT							
1 Kennelly	N	Y	Y	N	Y	Y	Y
2 Gejdenson	Y	+	Y	Y	Y	Y	Y
3 Morrison	Y	Y	Y	Y	Y	Y	Y
4 *McKinney*	Y	Y	N	N	Y	Y	Y
5 Ratchford	Y	Y	Y	Y	Y	Y	Y
6 *Johnson*	Y	Y	N	Y	Y	N	N
DELAWARE							
AL Carper	Y	Y	N	Y	Y	Y	N
FLORIDA							
1 Hutto	Y	Y	Y	Y	Y	N	N
2 Fuqua	Y	Y	Y	Y	Y	N	N
3 Bennett	Y	Y	Y	Y	Y	N	N
4 Chappell	Y	Y	Y	Y	Y	N	N
5 *McCollum*	N	N	N	N	Y	N	N
6 MacKay	Y	Y	Y	Y	Y	N	N
7 Gibbons	N	Y	Y	Y	N	N	N
8 *Young*	?	Y	N	Y	Y	N	Y
9 *Bilirakis*	N	?	N	Y	Y	Y	Y
10 Ireland	Y	N	Y	Y	Y	N	N
11 Nelson	Y	Y	Y	Y	Y	N	N
12 *Lewis*	N	N	N	N	Y	N	N
13 *Mack*	N	N	Y	Y	N	N	N
14 Mica	Y	Y	Y	Y	Y	N	N
15 *Shaw*	N	Y	N	N	Y	N	N
16 Smith	Y	Y	Y	Y	Y	N	Y
17 Lehman	N	Y	Y	Y	Y	N	Y
18 Pepper	+	+	+	+	+	−	+
19 Fascell	?	?	?	?	?	?	?
GEORGIA							
1 Thomas	Y	Y	Y	Y	Y	Y	Y
2 Hatcher	Y	Y	Y	Y	Y	N	N
3 Ray	N	Y	N	Y	Y	N	N
4 Levitas	?	?	?	?	?	?	?
5 Fowler	Y	Y	Y	Y	Y	N	N
6 *Gingrich*	N	Y	N	Y	Y	N	N
7 Vacancy							
8 Rowland	Y	Y	Y	Y	Y	N	Y
9 Jenkins	N	Y	Y	Y	Y	N	N
10 Barnard	Y	Y	Y	Y	Y	N	N
HAWAII							
1 Heftel	?	?	?	?	?	?	?
2 Akaka	Y	Y	Y	Y	Y	N	Y
IDAHO							
1 *Craig*	N	Y	Y	Y	N	N	N
2 *Hansen*	N	Y	Y	Y	Y	N	N
ILLINOIS							
1 Hayes	N	Y	Y	Y	N	Y	Y
2 Savage	N	Y	Y	Y	N	Y	Y
3 Russo	Y	Y	Y	Y	Y	?	?
4 *O'Brien*	?	?	?	?	?	?	?
5 Lipinski	Y	Y	Y	Y	Y	N	?
6 *Hyde*	Y	N	N	?	Y	Y	N
7 Collins	Y	Y	Y	Y	Y	N	Y
8 Rostenkowski	Y	Y	Y	Y	Y	N	Y
9 Yates	Y	Y	Y	Y	Y	N	Y
10 *Porter*	N	Y	N	N	Y	N	Y
11 Annunzio	Y	Y	Y	Y	Y	N	Y
12 *Crane, P.*	N	?	?	?	?	Y	N
13 *Erlenborn*	N	N	N	N	Y	N	N
14 *Corcoran*	N	N	−	+	−	−	−
15 *Madigan*	Y	Y	Y	Y	Y	N	N
16 *Martin*	?	?	?	?	?	?	?
17 Evans	N	Y	N	N	Y	Y	Y
18 *Michel*	Y	Y	Y	Y	Y	N	N
19 *Crane, D.*	N	N	N	N	N	Y	N
20 Durbin	N	Y	Y	Y	Y	N	Y
21 Price	Y	Y	Y	Y	Y	N	Y
22 Simon	?	?	?	?	?	?	?
INDIANA							
1 Hall	Y	Y	Y	Y	Y	N	Y
2 Sharp	Y	Y	N	N	Y	Y	Y
3 *Hiler*	N	N	N	N	N	Y	N
4 *Coats*	N	N	N	N	Y	N	N
5 Hillis	Y	N	Y	Y	Y	N	N

Corresponding to Congressional Record Votes 379, 380, 381, 382, 383, 384, 386

	359	360	361	362	363	364	365
6 ***Burton***	N	N	N	N	N	Y	N
7 ***Myers***	N	Y	Y	Y	Y	N	N
8 McCloskey	Y	Y	Y	Y	Y	N	?
9 Hamilton	Y	Y	Y	Y	Y	N	Y
10 Jacobs	N	Y	N	N	Y	Y	Y
IOWA							
1 ***Leach***	N	N	N	N	Y	Y	N
2 ***Tauke***	N	N	N	Y	Y	Y	N
3 ***Evans***	Y	N	N	Y	Y	Y	N
4 Smith	Y	Y	Y	Y	Y	N	?
5 Harkin	N	Y	Y	Y	Y	Y	N
6 Bedell	N	Y	N	N	Y	Y	N
KANSAS							
1 ***Roberts***	N	N	Y	N	Y	N	N
2 Slattery	N	N	N	N	Y	Y	N
3 ***Winn***	Y	Y	Y	N	Y	N	N
4 Glickman	Y	Y	N	Y	Y	Y	N
5 ***Whittaker***	N	Y	Y	N	Y	N	N
KENTUCKY							
1 Hubbard	Y	N	N	Y	Y	N	N
2 Natcher	Y	Y	Y	Y	Y	N	N
3 Mazzoli	N	Y	Y	Y	Y	N	N
4 ***Snyder***	N	N	Y	Y	Y	N	N
5 ***Rogers***	N	N	Y	Y	Y	N	N
6 ***Hopkins***	N	N	N	Y	Y	N	N
7 Perkins	Y	Y	Y	Y	Y	N	Y
LOUISIANA							
1 ***Livingston***	N	N	Y	Y	Y	N	N
2 Boggs	Y	Y	Y	Y	Y	N	Y
3 Tauzin	Y	?	N	N	Y	N	N
4 Roemer	N	N	Y	N	Y	N	N
5 Huckaby	Y	?	?	?	?	N	N
6 ***Moore***	N	Y	Y	Y	Y	N	N
7 Breaux	Y	Y	Y	Y	Y	N	N
8 Long	Y	Y	Y	Y	Y	N	N
MAINE							
1 ***McKernan***	N	Y	N	Y	Y	Y	N
2 ***Snowe***	N	Y	N	Y	Y	Y	N
MARYLAND							
1 Dyson	Y	Y	Y	Y	Y	N	N
2 Long	Y	Y	Y	Y	Y	N	N
3 Mikulski	Y	Y	Y	Y	Y	N	?
4 ***Holt***	N	N	Y	Y	Y	N	N
5 Hoyer	Y	Y	Y	Y	Y	N	Y
6 Byron	Y	Y	Y	Y	Y	N	N
7 Mitchell	Y	Y	N	Y	Y	?	Y
8 Barnes	N	Y	N	N	Y	Y	Y
MASSACHUSETTS							
1 ***Conte***	Y	Y	N	Y	Y	Y	N
2 Boland	Y	Y	Y	Y	Y	N	Y
3 Early	N	Y	N	Y	Y	Y	?
4 Frank	Y	Y	N	N	Y	Y	Y
5 Shannon	N	Y	Y	Y	Y	Y	Y
6 Mavroules	N	Y	Y	Y	Y	Y	?
7 Markey	Y	?	Y	N	Y	Y	#
8 O'Neill							
9 Moakley	Y	Y	Y	Y	Y	N	Y
10 Studds	N	Y	N	Y	Y	Y	Y
11 Donnelly	Y	Y	N	N	Y	Y	Y
MICHIGAN							
1 Conyers	N	Y	Y	N	Y	N	Y
2 ***Pursell***	N	Y	N	Y	Y	N	?
3 Wolpe	Y	Y	N	Y	Y	Y	Y
4 ***Siljander***	Y	N	Y	Y	Y	N	N
5 ***Sawyer***	N	N	N	Y	Y	Y	N
6 Carr	Y	Y	Y	Y	?	N	Y
7 Kildee	N	Y	N	Y	Y	Y	Y
8 Traxler	Y	Y	Y	Y	Y	N	?
9 ***Vander Jagt***	Y	Y	N	Y	Y	Y	?
10 Albosta	Y	Y	Y	Y	Y	N	Y
11 ***Davis***	Y	Y	Y	Y	Y	N	N
12 Bonior	N	Y	Y	Y	Y	Y	Y
13 Crockett	N	Y	Y	N	Y	N	Y
14 Hertel	Y	Y	N	Y	Y	Y	Y
15 Ford	Y	Y	Y	Y	Y	N	Y
16 Dingell	?	?	?	?	?	N	Y
17 Levin	Y	Y	N	Y	Y	Y	Y
18 ***Broomfield***	N	N	Y	N	N	Y	N
MINNESOTA							
1 Penny	Y	Y	Y	Y	Y	N	N
2 ***Weber***	N	N	N	N	Y	Y	N
3 ***Frenzel***	N	N	N	N	N	Y	N
4 Vento	Y	Y	N	Y	Y	Y	Y
5 Sabo	Y	Y	Y	Y	Y	N	Y
6 Sikorski	Y	Y	N	Y	Y	Y	N

	359	360	361	362	363	364	365
7 ***Stangeland***	N	N	Y	Y	Y	N	?
8 Oberstar	Y	Y	Y	Y	Y	N	Y
MISSISSIPPI							
1 Whitten	Y	Y	Y	Y	Y	N	N
2 ***Franklin***	N	N	Y	Y	Y	N	N
3 Montgomery	Y	Y	Y	Y	Y	N	?
4 Dowdy	Y	Y	Y	Y	Y	N	Y
5 ***Lott***	N	N	Y	Y	Y	N	N
MISSOURI							
1 Clay	Y	Y	Y	Y	Y	N	Y
2 Young	Y	Y	Y	Y	Y	N	?
3 Gephardt	Y	Y	Y	Y	Y	N	Y
4 Skelton	Y	Y	Y	Y	Y	N	N
5 Wheat	N	Y	Y	Y	Y	N	Y
6 ***Coleman***	N	Y	Y	Y	Y	N	N
7 ***Taylor***	N	Y	Y	Y	Y	N	N
8 ***Emerson***	N	Y	Y	Y	Y	N	N
9 Volkmer	Y	Y	Y	Y	Y	N	Y
MONTANA							
1 Williams	N	?	?	Y	Y	Y	Y
2 ***Marlenee***	Y	N	Y	?	Y	N	?
NEBRASKA							
1 ***Bereuter***	Y	Y	N	N	Y	N	N
2 ***Daub***	N	N	N	N	Y	N	N
3 ***Smith***	Y	Y	Y	Y	Y	N	N
NEVADA							
1 Reid	Y	Y	Y	Y	Y	N	Y
2 ***Vucanovich***	N	Y	Y	Y	Y	N	N
NEW HAMPSHIRE							
1 D'Amours	Y	Y	N	?	Y	N	Y
2 ***Gregg***	N	N	N	N	Y	Y	?
NEW JERSEY							
1 Florio	Y	Y	N	Y	Y	Y	Y
2 Hughes	Y	N	Y	N	Y	N	Y
3 Howard	Y	Y	Y	Y	Y	N	?
4 ***Smith***	Y	Y	Y	Y	Y	N	N
5 ***Roukema***	N	Y	N	Y	?	Y	N
6 Dwyer	Y	Y	Y	Y	Y	N	?
7 ***Rinaldo***	Y	Y	Y	Y	Y	N	N
8 Roe	Y	Y	Y	Y	Y	N	?
9 Torricelli	Y	Y	Y	Y	Y	?	Y
10 Rodino	Y	Y	Y	Y	Y	N	Y
11 Minish	Y	Y	Y	Y	Y	Y	Y
12 ***Courter***	N	Y	N	N	N	Y	N
13 ***Forsythe***	N	Y	N	N	Y	Y	N
14 Guarini	Y	Y	Y	Y	Y	N	Y
NEW MEXICO							
1 ***Lujan***	Y	Y	Y	Y	Y	N	N
2 ***Skeen***	Y	Y	N	N	Y	N	N
3 Richardson	Y	Y	Y	Y	Y	Y	Y
NEW YORK							
1 ***Carney***	Y	N	Y	Y	Y	N	N
2 Downey	Y	Y	Y	Y	Y	Y	?
3 Mrazek	N	Y	Y	Y	Y	N	Y
4 ***Lent***	Y	Y	Y	Y	Y	Y	N
5 ***McGrath***	?	?	?	?	?	?	?
6 Addabbo	Y	Y	Y	Y	Y	N	?
7 Ackerman	-	Y	Y	Y	+	Y	Y
8 Scheuer	N	Y	Y	N	Y	N	Y
9 Ferraro	N	Y	Y	Y	Y	N	?
10 Schumer	Y	Y	Y	Y	Y	Y	?
11 Towns	Y	Y	Y	Y	Y	N	Y
12 Owens	Y	Y	Y	Y	Y	N	Y
13 Solarz	?	?	?	?	?	N	?
14 ***Molinari***	N	?	?	?	?	Y	Y
15 ***Green***	?	Y	N	Y	Y	Y	N
16 Rangel	N	Y	Y	Y	Y	N	Y
17 Weiss	N	Y	N	Y	Y	Y	Y
18 Garcia	Y	Y	Y	Y	Y	N	Y
19 Biaggi	Y	Y	Y	Y	?	N	Y
20 Ottinger	?	Y	N	N	Y	Y	?
21 ***Fish***	N	Y	N	Y	?	Y	N
22 ***Gilman***	Y	Y	N	Y	Y	N	Y
23 Stratton	N	Y	Y	Y	Y	N	Y
24 ***Solomon***	?	?	?	?	?	?	?
25 ***Boehlert***	N	Y	N	Y	Y	Y	N
26 ***Martin***	N	N	N	Y	Y	?	N
27 ***Wortley***	Y	Y	Y	Y	Y	Y	N
28 McHugh	Y	Y	Y	Y	Y	Y	Y
29 ***Horton***	Y	Y	Y	Y	Y	N	N
30 ***Conable***	N	N	N	N	N	Y	N
31 ***Kemp***	N	Y	Y	Y	Y	N	?
32 LaFalce	Y	N	Y	N	Y	Y	Y
33 Nowak	Y	Y	Y	Y	Y	N	Y
34 Lundine	Y	Y	Y	Y	Y	Y	Y

	359	360	361	362	363	364	365
NORTH CAROLINA							
1 Jones	Y	?	Y	Y	Y	N	Y
2 Valentine	Y	Y	Y	Y	Y	N	N
3 Whitley	Y	Y	Y	Y	Y	N	N
4 Andrews	Y	Y	Y	Y	Y	N	N
5 Neal	Y	Y	N	Y	Y	N	N
6 Britt	Y	Y	Y	Y	Y	N	Y
7 Rose	?	?	?	?	?	?	?
8 Hefner	Y	Y	Y	Y	Y	N	Y
9 ***Martin***	Y	N	N	Y	N	Y	N
10 ***Broyhill***	Y	N	Y	Y	N	Y	N
11 Clarke	Y	Y	Y	Y	Y	N	Y
NORTH DAKOTA							
AL Dorgan	Y	Y	Y	Y	Y	N	?
OHIO							
1 Luken	Y	Y	Y	Y	Y	N	Y
2 ***Gradison***	Y	N	N	Y	Y	Y	N
3 Hall	?	?	?	?	?	?	?
4 ***Oxley***	N	N	N	N	Y	Y	N
5 ***Latta***	N	N	N	N	N	N	N
6 ***McEwen***	N	N	Y	Y	Y	N	N
7 ***DeWine***	N	Y	N	N	Y	Y	N
8 ***Kindness***	Y	N	Y	Y	Y	N	N
9 Kaptur	Y	Y	Y	N	Y	N	?
10 ***Miller***	Y	N	Y	Y	Y	N	N
11 Eckart	Y	?	?	?	Y	N	Y
12 ***Kasich***	Y	N	N	Y	Y	N	N
13 Pease	Y	Y	Y	Y	Y	N	Y
14 Seiberling	Y	Y	N	Y	Y	Y	Y
15 ***Wylie***	Y	?	?	?	?	?	?
16 ***Regula***	N	Y	N	N	Y	N	N
17 ***Williams***	Y	Y	Y	Y	Y	?	Y
18 Applegate	Y	Y	Y	Y	Y	N	Y
19 Feighan	Y	?	?	?	?	N	Y
20 Oakar	Y	Y	Y	Y	Y	N	Y
21 Stokes	Y	Y	Y	Y	Y	N	?
OKLAHOMA							
1 Jones	N	Y	Y	N	Y	N	N
2 Synar	Y	Y	N	Y	Y	Y	-
3 Watkins	N	Y	Y	Y	Y	N	N
4 McCurdy	N	Y	Y	Y	Y	N	N
5 ***Edwards***	N	Y	Y	Y	Y	N	N
6 English	N	Y	Y	Y	Y	Y	N
OREGON							
1 AuCoin	Y	Y	Y	Y	N	N	?
2 ***Smith, R.***	N	Y	Y	Y	Y	N	N
3 Wyden	N	Y	Y	Y	Y	N	Y
4 Weaver	N	Y	N	N	N	Y	Y
5 ***Smith, D.***	N	N	N	N	N	N	?
PENNSYLVANIA							
1 Foglietta	Y	Y	N	Y	Y	N	Y
2 Gray	Y	Y	Y	Y	Y	N	Y
3 Borski	Y	Y	Y	N	Y	N	Y
4 Kolter	Y	Y	Y	Y	Y	N	Y
5 ***Schulze***	Y	Y	Y	Y	Y	Y	N
6 Yatron	Y	Y	Y	Y	Y	Y	Y
7 Edgar	N	Y	N	N	Y	Y	Y
8 Kostmayer	N	Y	N	Y	Y	N	Y
9 ***Shuster***	N	N	Y	Y	Y	N	N
10 ***McDade***	N	Y	Y	Y	Y	Y	N
11 Harrison	Y	Y	Y	Y	Y	N	Y
12 Murtha	Y	Y	Y	Y	Y	N	Y
13 ***Coughlin***	N	Y	N	N	Y	Y	N
14 Coyne	Y	Y	Y	Y	Y	N	Y
15 ***Ritter***	Y	N	N	Y	?	Y	N
16 ***Walker***	N	N	N	N	N	Y	N
17 ***Gekas***	N	N	N	Y	Y	N	N
18 Walgren	N	Y	Y	Y	Y	N	Y
19 ***Goodling***	N	?	N	N	Y	Y	N
20 Gaydos	Y	Y	Y	Y	Y	N	Y
21 ***Ridge***	Y	Y	N	Y	Y	Y	N
22 Murphy	Y	Y	Y	Y	Y	N	Y
23 ***Clinger***	Y	N	Y	Y	Y	N	N
RHODE ISLAND							
1 St Germain	Y	Y	Y	Y	Y	?	?
2 ***Schneider***	N	Y	N	Y	Y	Y	Y
SOUTH CAROLINA							
1 ***Hartnett***	Y	N	N	N	N	N	N
2 ***Spence***	Y	N	Y	N	Y	N	N
3 Derrick	Y	?	?	?	?	Y	Y
4 ***Campbell***	Y	?	?	?	?	N	N
5 Spratt	N	Y	Y	Y	Y	Y	Y
6 Tallon	Y	Y	Y	Y	Y	N	Y
SOUTH DAKOTA							
AL Daschle	?	Y	Y	Y	Y	N	?

	359	360	361	362	363	364	365
TENNESSEE							
1 ***Quillen***	N	Y	N	Y	Y	N	N
2 ***Duncan***	N	Y	Y	Y	Y	N	N
3 Lloyd	N	Y	Y	Y	Y	N	N
4 Cooper	Y	Y	Y	Y	Y	N	Y
5 Boner	Y	Y	Y	Y	Y	N	N
6 Gore	N	Y	Y	Y	Y	N	Y
7 ***Sundquist***	N	Y	N	Y	Y	N	?
8 Jones	Y	Y	Y	Y	Y	N	N
9 Ford	?	?	?	?	?	?	?
TEXAS							
1 Hall, S.	Y	Y	Y	Y	Y	N	N
2 Wilson	Y	Y	Y	Y	Y	N	N
3 ***Bartlett***	N	N	N	N	Y	Y	?
4 Hall, R.	Y	N	Y	Y	Y	N	N
5 Bryant	N	Y	Y	Y	Y	Y	Y
6 ***Gramm***	N	N	N	Y	Y	Y	N
7 ***Archer***	N	N	N	N	N	N	N
8 ***Fields***	N	N	Y	N	Y	N	?
9 Brooks	?	?	?	?	?	?	?
10 Pickle	Y	Y	Y	Y	Y	N	N
11 Leath	N	N	Y	Y	Y	N	?
12 Wright	Y	Y	Y	Y	Y	N	Y
13 Hightower	Y	Y	Y	Y	Y	N	N
14 Patman	Y	N	Y	Y	Y	N	N
15 de la Garza	Y	?	?	?	?	?	?
16 Coleman	Y	Y	Y	Y	Y	N	Y
17 Stenholm	Y	N	N	N	Y	N	N
18 Leland	Y	Y	Y	N	Y	N	Y
19 Hance	Y	N	Y	Y	Y	N	?
20 Gonzalez	Y	Y	Y	Y	Y	N	P
21 ***Loeffler***	N	N	N	N	Y	N	N
22 ***Paul***	N	N	N	N	N	Y	?
23 Kazen	Y	Y	Y	Y	Y	N	N
24 Frost	Y	Y	Y	Y	Y	N	Y
25 Andrews	Y	Y	Y	Y	Y	N	N
26 Vandergriff	N	N	Y	Y	Y	N	N
27 Ortiz	Y	Y	Y	Y	Y	N	X
UTAH							
1 ***Hansen***	Y	N	Y	Y	N	N	N
2 ***Marriott***	Y	Y	N	Y	Y	N	?
3 ***Nielson***	N	N	N	Y	N	Y	N
VERMONT							
AL ***Jeffords***	N	Y	N	N	Y	Y	N
VIRGINIA							
1 ***Bateman***	N	Y	Y	Y	Y	N	N
2 ***Whitehurst***	?	?	?	?	?	N	N
3 ***Bliley***	?	N	Y	Y	Y	N	N
4 Sisisky	Y	Y	Y	Y	Y	N	N
5 Daniel	N	N	Y	Y	Y	Y	N
6 Olin	N	Y	Y	Y	N	Y	?
7 ***Robinson***	N	N	Y	Y	Y	N	N
8 ***Parris***	?	N	Y	Y	Y	N	N
9 Boucher	Y	Y	Y	Y	Y	N	Y
10 ***Wolf***	N	Y	Y	Y	Y	N	N
WASHINGTON							
1 ***Pritchard***	?	?	?	?	?	Y	N
2 Swift	Y	Y	Y	Y	Y	N	Y
3 Bonker	Y	Y	Y	Y	Y	N	Y
4 ***Morrison***	Y	Y	Y	N	Y	N	N
5 Foley	Y	Y	?	?	Y	N	Y
6 Dicks	Y	Y	?	?	?	N	N
7 Lowry	Y	Y	N	?	Y	N	N
8 ***Chandler***	N	?	?	?	?	N	N
WEST VIRGINIA							
1 Mollohan	Y	Y	Y	Y	Y	N	Y
2 Staggers	Y	Y	N	Y	Y	N	Y
3 Wise	Y	Y	Y	Y	Y	N	Y
4 Rahall	?	?	?	?	?	N	Y
WISCONSIN							
1 Aspin	Y	Y	Y	Y	Y	Y	Y
2 Kastenmeier	N	Y	N	Y	Y	Y	Y
3 ***Gunderson***	N	N	Y	N	Y	Y	N
4 Zablocki	?	?	?	?	?	?	?
5 Moody	N	Y	Y	Y	Y	Y	Y
6 ***Petri***	Y	N	N	N	N	Y	N
7 Obey	N	Y	N	Y	Y	Y	Y
8 ***Roth***	Y	N	N	N	N	Y	N
9 ***Sensenbrenner***	N	N	N	N	N	Y	N
WYOMING							
AL ***Cheney***	Y	N	Y	Y	N	N	?

Southern states - Ala., Ark., Fla., Ga., Ky., La., Miss., N.C., Okla., S.C., Tenn., Texas, Va.

366. Procedural Motion. McCain, R-Ariz., motion to approve the House *Journal* of Monday, Oct. 17. Motion agreed to 373-22: R 148-10; D 225-12 (ND 143-11, SD 82-1), Oct. 18, 1983.

367. HR 1870. Vietnam Veterans Medal. Annunzio, D-Ill., motion to suspend the rules and pass the bill to require the secretary of the Treasury to coin and sell a national medal in honor of the members and former members of the armed forces who served in the Vietnam War. Motion agreed to 410-0: R 159-0; D 251-0 (ND 168-0, SD 83-0), Oct. 18, 1983. A two-thirds majority vote of those present and voting (274 in this case) is required for passage under suspension of the rules.

368. HR 3231. Export Administration Act. Hutto, D-Fla., amendment to the Bonker, D-Wash., substitute *(see vote 369, below)* for the Roth, R-Wis., amendment *(see vote 370, below)*, to allow the president to continue to require licenses for exports to allied nations that participate in Coordinating Committee (COCOM) export controls, if those goods are likely to be diverted to a Soviet-bloc nation. Adopted 237-175: R 127-36; D 110-139 (ND 43-124, SD 67-15), Oct. 18, 1983.

369. HR 3231. Export Administration Act. Bonker, D-Wash., substitute, as amended by Hutto, D-Fla. *(see vote 368, above)*, to the Roth, R-Wis., amendment *(see vote 370, below)*. Bonker's substitute originally would have allowed the president to control exports to particular persons or companies in Coordinating Committee (COCOM) nations that are likely to divert those exports to Soviet-bloc nations. As amended by Hutto, the substitute allowed the president to control any product likely to be diverted to the Soviet bloc, and was opposed by Bonker. Adopted 240-173: R 128-35; D 112-138 (ND 43-123, SD 69-15), Oct. 18, 1983.

370. HR 3231. Export Administration Act. Roth, R-Wis., amendment, as amended *(see votes 368, 369, above)*, to allow the president to continue to require licenses for exports to Coordinating Committee (COCOM) nations. Adopted 239-171: R 128-33; D 111-138 (ND 40-125, SD 71-13), Oct. 18, 1983.

371. HR 3385. Upland Cotton PIK Program. De la Garza, D-Texas, motion to disagree with the Senate amendments to and request a conference on the bill to establish a temporary paid diversion program for dairy producers, financed by a 50-cents-per-hundredweight assessment on dairy products, to repeal a second 50-cent assessment and to reduce the price support level in the federal dairy program; also to freeze price support levels in the federal tobacco program, revise the program's acreage allotment and marketing quota system and make other changes. The bill also included revisions in the Payment-in-Kind (PIK) program for cotton that had already been enacted as part of other legislation. Motion rejected 188-208: R 32-126; D 156-82 (ND 86-69, SD 70-13), Oct. 18, 1983.

372. HR 3231. Export Administration Act. Frenzel, R-Minn., amendment to prohibit the president from imposing foreign policy controls that break existing contracts. Rejected 172-237: R 71-89; D 101-148 (ND 61-106, SD 40-42), Oct. 19, 1983.

373. HR 3231. Export Administration Act. Hunter, R-Calif., amendment to the Solomon, R-N.Y., substitute for the Bonker, D-Wash., perfecting amendment to the Courter, R-N.J., amendment to the section of the bill providing for decontrol of exports that are readily available from foreign sources. The Hunter amendment would have allowed the president to continue to control a technology that is available from foreign sources indefinitely, if he determined the transfer would damage U.S. national security. Rejected 137-285: R 105-59; D 32-226 (ND 10-163, SD 22-63), Oct. 19, 1983.

KEY

Y	Voted for (yea).
#	Paired for.
+	Announced for.
N	Voted against (nay).
X	Paired against.
-	Announced against.
P	Voted "present".
C	Voted "present" to avoid possible conflict of interest.
?	Did not vote or otherwise make a position known.

Democrats   *Republicans*

	366	367	368	369	370	371	372	373
ALABAMA								
1 *Edwards*	Y	Y	Y	Y	Y	N	N	N
2 *Dickinson*	N	Y	Y	Y	Y	N	N	Y
3 Nichols	Y	Y	Y	Y	Y	N	Y	?
4 Bevill	Y	Y	Y	Y	Y	Y	N	N
5 Flippo	Y	Y	Y	Y	Y	Y	Y	N
6 Erdreich	Y	Y	Y	Y	Y	Y	N	Y
7 Shelby	Y	Y	?	Y	Y	Y	N	Y
ALASKA								
AL *Young*	?	?	?	?	?	?	?	?
ARIZONA								
1 *McCain*	Y	Y	Y	Y	Y	N	N	N
2 Udall	Y	Y	?	?	?	Y	N	Y
3 *Stump*	Y	Y	Y	Y	Y	N	N	Y
4 *Rudd*	Y	Y	Y	Y	Y	N	N	Y
5 McNulty	Y	Y	Y	Y	Y	Y	N	N
ARKANSAS								
1 Alexander	Y	Y	N	N	N	Y	N	N
2 *Bethune*	Y	Y	N	N	N	N	Y	N
3 *Hammerschmidt*	Y	Y	Y	Y	Y	Y	Y	Y
4 Anthony	Y	Y	Y	Y	Y	Y	Y	N
CALIFORNIA								
1 Bosco	Y	?	Y	Y	N	?	N	N
2 *Chappie*	Y	Y	Y	Y	Y	N	N	Y
3 Matsui	Y	Y	N	N	N	N	N	N
4 Fazio	Y	Y	N	N	N	Y	N	N
5 Burton	Y	N	N	N	N	N	N	N
6 Boxer	Y	Y	N	N	N	N	N	N
7 Miller	?	?	?	?	?	?	?	N
8 Dellums	Y	Y	N	N	N	N	N	?
9 Stark	Y	Y	N	N	N	N	N	N
10 Edwards	Y	Y	N	N	N	N	N	N
11 Lantos	Y	Y	N	N	N	N	N	N
12 *Zschau*	Y	Y	N	N	N	N	N	Y
13 Mineta	Y	Y	N	N	N	N	N	N
14 *Shumway*	Y	Y	Y	Y	Y	N	N	Y
15 Coelho	Y	Y	N	N	N	Y	N	N
16 Panetta	Y	Y	N	N	N	Y	N	N
17 *Pashayan*	Y	Y	Y	Y	Y	Y	N	Y
18 Lehman	Y	Y	N	N	N	Y	N	N
19 *Lagomarsino*	Y	Y	Y	Y	Y	N	N	Y
20 *Thomas*	?	Y	Y	Y	N	Y	N	Y
21 *Fiedler*	Y	Y	N	Y	N	N	N	Y
22 *Moorhead*	Y	Y	Y	Y	Y	N	N	Y
23 Beilenson	Y	Y	N	N	N	N	N	N
24 Waxman	Y	Y	N	N	N	?	N	N
25 Roybal	Y	Y	N	N	N	Y	N	N
26 Levine	Y	Y	N	N	N	?	N	N
27 Levine	Y	Y	N	N	N	Y	N	N
28 Dixon	Y	Y	N	N	N	Y	N	N
29 Hawkins	?	?	?	?	?	?	?	?
30 Martinez	Y	Y	N	N	N	Y	N	N
31 Dymally	P	Y	N	N	N	Y	N	N
32 Anderson	Y	Y	Y	Y	Y	Y	N	N
33 *Dreier*	Y	Y	Y	Y	Y	N	N	Y
34 Torres	Y	Y	N	N	N	Y	N	N
35 *Lewis*	Y	Y	Y	Y	Y	N	N	Y
36 Brown	Y	Y	N	N	N	N	N	N
37 *McCandless*	Y	Y	Y	Y	Y	N	N	Y
38 Patterson	Y	Y	N	N	N	N	N	N
39 *Dannemeyer*	Y	Y	Y	Y	Y	N	N	Y
40 *Badham*	Y	Y	Y	Y	Y	N	N	Y
41 *Lowery*	Y	Y	Y	Y	Y	N	N	Y
42 *Lungren*	Y	Y	Y	Y	Y	N	N	Y

	366	367	368	369	370	371	372	373
43 *Packard*	Y	Y	Y	Y	Y	N	N	Y
44 Bates	Y	Y	N	N	N	N	?	N
45 *Hunter*	Y	Y	Y	Y	Y	N	N	Y
COLORADO								
1 Schroeder	N	Y	N	N	N	N	N	N
2 Wirth	Y	Y	N	N	N	?	N	N
3 Kogovsek	?	Y	N	N	N	?	?	N
4 *Brown*	Y	Y	Y	Y	Y	N	Y	Y
5 *Kramer*	Y	Y	Y	Y	Y	N	N	N
6 *Schaefer*	Y	Y	Y	Y	Y	N	N	Y
CONNECTICUT								
1 Kennelly	Y	Y	N	N	N	Y	N	N
2 Gejdenson	N	Y	N	N	N	N	N	N
3 Morrison	?	Y	N	N	N	N	N	N
4 *McKinney*	Y	Y	Y	Y	Y	N	Y	N
5 Ratchford	Y	Y	N	N	N	N	N	N
6 *Johnson*	Y	Y	N	N	N	?	Y	N
DELAWARE								
AL Carper	Y	Y	N	N	N	N	Y	N
FLORIDA								
1 Hutto	Y	Y	Y	Y	Y	Y	N	Y
2 Fuqua	Y	Y	Y	Y	Y	Y	?	N
3 Bennett	Y	Y	Y	Y	Y	Y	Y	Y
4 Chappell	Y	Y	Y	Y	Y	Y	Y	N
5 *McCollum*	Y	Y	Y	Y	Y	N	N	Y
6 MacKay	Y	Y	Y	Y	Y	Y	Y	N
7 Gibbons	Y	Y	N	N	N	Y	N	Y
8 *Young*	Y	Y	Y	Y	Y	N	Y	N
9 *Bilirakis*	Y	Y	Y	Y	Y	N	Y	N
10 Ireland	?	?	?	?	?	?	N	Y
11 Nelson	Y	Y	Y	Y	Y	Y	N	N
12 *Lewis*	Y	Y	Y	Y	Y	N	N	Y
13 *Mack*	Y	Y	Y	Y	Y	N	N	Y
14 Mica	Y	N	N	N	N	N	N	N
15 *Shaw*	Y	Y	Y	Y	Y	N	Y	N
16 Smith	Y	?	N	N	N	Y	N	?
17 Lehman	Y	Y	N	N	N	N	N	N
18 Pepper	Y	Y	N	Y	N	-	?	?
19 Fascell	Y	Y	N	N	N	N	N	N
GEORGIA								
1 Thomas	Y	Y	Y	Y	Y	Y	Y	N
2 Hatcher	Y	Y	Y	Y	Y	Y	N	N
3 Ray	Y	Y	Y	Y	Y	Y	N	Y
4 Levitas	Y	Y	Y	Y	Y	Y	N	N
5 Fowler	Y	Y	Y	Y	Y	Y	N	N
6 *Gingrich*	Y	Y	Y	Y	Y	N	N	Y
7 Vacancy								
8 Rowland	Y	Y	Y	Y	Y	Y	Y	N
9 Jenkins	Y	Y	Y	Y	Y	Y	N	N
10 Barnard	Y	Y	Y	Y	Y	Y	Y	N
HAWAII								
1 Heftel	?	Y	Y	N	Y	N	Y	N
2 Akaka	Y	Y	Y	Y	Y	Y	?	N
IDAHO								
1 *Craig*	Y	Y	Y	Y	N	Y	Y	Y
2 *Hansen*	Y	Y	Y	Y	N	?	?	Y
ILLINOIS								
1 Hayes	?	Y	N	N	N	N	N	N
2 Savage	Y	Y	N	N	N	N	N	N
3 Russo	Y	Y	Y	Y	N	N	N	N
4 *O'Brien*	Y	Y	Y	Y	Y	Y	N	N
5 Lipinski	N	Y	N	Y	N	N	N	N
6 *Hyde*	Y	Y	Y	Y	N	N	N	Y
7 Collins	Y	N	N	N	N	N	N	N
8 Rostenkowski	Y	Y	N	N	N	N	N	N
9 Yates	Y	Y	N	N	N	N	N	N
10 *Porter*	Y	Y	N	N	N	N	N	N
11 Annunzio	Y	Y	N	N	N	N	N	N
12 *Crane, P.*	Y	Y	Y	Y	Y	N	Y	Y
13 *Erlenborn*	P	Y	Y	Y	Y	N	N	?
14 *Corcoran*	Y	Y	Y	Y	Y	N	N	Y
15 *Madigan*	Y	Y	N	N	N	N	N	N
16 *Martin*	Y	Y	Y	Y	Y	N	Y	N
17 Evans	Y	Y	N	N	N	Y	N	N
18 *Michel*	Y	Y	Y	Y	Y	N	N	N
19 *Crane, D.*	Y	Y	Y	Y	Y	N	N	Y
20 Durbin	N	Y	Y	Y	Y	N	N	N
21 Price	Y	N	N	N	N	N	N	N
22 Simon	Y	Y	?	?	?	?	Y	N
INDIANA								
1 Hall	Y	Y	?	?	?	Y	Y	N
2 Sharp	Y	Y	N	N	N	N	Y	N
3 *Hiler*	Y	Y	Y	Y	N	N	N	Y
4 *Coats*	Y	Y	Y	Y	Y	N	N	Y
5 Hillis	Y	?	Y	Y	?	N	N	Y

ND - Northern Democrats   SD - Southern Democrats

Corresponding to Congressional Record Votes 387, 388, 390, 391, 392, 393, 395, 397

	366	367	368	369	370	371	372	373
6 ***Burton***	Y	Y	Y	Y	Y	N	N	Y
7 ***Myers***	Y	Y	Y	Y	Y	N	Y	N
8 McCloskey	Y	Y	Y	N	Y	N	N	N
9 Hamilton	Y	Y	N	N	N	N	?	N
10 Jacobs	N	Y	N	N	N	N	Y	N
IOWA								
1 ***Leach***	Y	Y	N	N	N	N	Y	N
2 ***Tauke***	Y	Y	N	N	N	N	Y	N
3 ***Evans***	N	Y	Y	N	N	N	Y	N
4 Smith	Y	Y	N	N	N	Y	Y	N
5 Harkin	N	Y	N	N	N	Y	Y	N
6 Bedell	Y	Y	N	N	N	Y	Y	N
KANSAS								
1 ***Roberts***	N	Y	N	N	N	N	Y	N
2 Slattery	Y	Y	N	N	N	N	Y	N
3 ***Winn***	Y	Y	Y	Y	Y	N	?	Y
4 Glickman	Y	Y	N	N	N	Y	Y	N
5 ***Whittaker***	Y	Y	Y	Y	Y	N	Y	Y
KENTUCKY								
1 Hubbard	Y	Y	Y	Y	Y	Y	Y	Y
2 Natcher	Y	Y	Y	Y	Y	Y	Y	N
3 Mazzoli	Y	Y	Y	Y	Y	N	Y	N
4 ***Snyder***	Y	Y	Y	Y	Y	Y	N	Y
5 ***Rogers***	Y	Y	Y	Y	Y	Y	N	Y
6 ***Hopkins***	Y	Y	Y	Y	Y	Y	N	Y
7 Perkins	Y	Y	Y	N	Y	Y	Y	N
LOUISIANA								
1 ***Livingston***	Y	Y	Y	Y	Y	N	N	Y
2 Boggs	Y	Y	Y	N	Y	N	?	N
3 Tauzin	Y	Y	Y	Y	Y	N	Y	N
4 Roemer	N	Y	Y	Y	Y	N	Y	N
5 Huckaby	Y	Y	Y	Y	Y	Y	Y	Y
6 ***Moore***	Y	Y	N	N	N	N	Y	N
7 Breaux	Y	?	Y	Y	Y	N	Y	N
8 Long	Y	Y	Y	N	N	N	N	N
MAINE								
1 ***McKernan***	Y	Y	N	N	N	Y	N	N
2 ***Snowe***	Y	Y	Y	Y	Y	Y	N	N
MARYLAND								
1 Dyson	Y	Y	Y	Y	Y	Y	Y	Y
2 Long	Y	Y	N	N	Y	Y	N	N
3 Mikulski	Y	Y	?	?	?	?	N	N
4 ***Holt***	Y	Y	Y	Y	Y	N	N	N
5 Hoyer	Y	Y	N	N	N	Y	N	N
6 Byron	Y	Y	Y	Y	Y	Y	N	Y
7 Mitchell	N	Y	N	N	N	N	N	N
8 Barnes	Y	Y	N	N	N	N	N	N
MASSACHUSETTS								
1 ***Conte***	Y	Y	Y	Y	Y	N	Y	N
2 Boland	Y	Y	N	N	N	N	Y	N
3 Early	Y	Y	N	N	N	N	Y	N
4 Frank	Y	Y	N	N	N	N	Y	N
5 Shannon	Y	Y	N	N	N	N	N	N
6 Mavroules	Y	Y	N	N	N	N	Y	N
7 Markey	Y	Y	N	N	N	N	N	N
8 O'Neill								
9 Moakley	Y	Y	N	N	N	N	Y	N
10 Studds	Y	Y	N	N	N	N	N	N
11 Donnelly	Y	Y	N	Y	N	N	N	N
MICHIGAN								
1 Conyers	Y	Y	N	N	N	N	N	N
2 ***Pursell***	Y	Y	Y	Y	Y	N	N	Y
3 Wolpe	Y	Y	N	N	N	Y	N	N
4 ***Siljander***	?	?	Y	Y	Y	N	N	Y
5 ***Sawyer***	Y	Y	Y	Y	Y	N	N	Y
6 Carr	Y	Y	Y	Y	Y	Y	N	Y
7 Kildee	Y	Y	Y	Y	Y	Y	Y	N
8 Traxler	Y	Y	Y	Y	Y	Y	Y	N
9 ***Vander Jagt***	Y	Y	N	N	Y	N	Y	N
10 Albosta	Y	Y	Y	Y	Y	?	Y	N
11 ***Davis***	Y	Y	Y	Y	Y	Y	N	Y
12 Bonior	Y	Y	Y	Y	Y	Y	N	N
13 Crockett	?	Y	N	N	N	?	N	N
14 Hertel	Y	Y	Y	Y	Y	Y	N	N
15 Ford	?	?	?	?	?	?	Y	N
16 Dingell	Y	Y	Y	Y	Y	Y	N	N
17 Levin	?	Y	Y	Y	Y	N	N	N
18 ***Broomfield***	Y	Y	Y	Y	Y	N	N	Y
MINNESOTA								
1 Penny	Y	Y	N	N	N	Y	Y	N
2 ***Weber***	Y	Y	N	N	N	Y	Y	N
3 ***Frenzel***	Y	Y	N	N	N	Y	Y	N
4 Vento	Y	Y	N	N	N	Y	Y	N
5 Sabo	Y	Y	N	N	N	Y	Y	N
6 Sikorski	N	Y	N	N	N	Y	Y	N
7 ***Stangeland***	Y	Y	N	N	N	Y	Y	Y
8 Oberstar	P	Y	N	N	N	N	N	N
MISSISSIPPI								
1 Whitten	Y	Y	Y	Y	Y	Y	Y	N
2 ***Franklin***	Y	Y	Y	Y	Y	N	Y	Y
3 Montgomery	Y	Y	Y	Y	Y	Y	N	Y
4 Dowdy	Y	Y	Y	Y	Y	Y	N	Y
5 ***Lott***	Y	Y	Y	Y	Y	Y	N	Y
MISSOURI								
1 Clay	N	Y	N	N	N	Y	N	N
2 Young	Y	Y	N	Y	Y	Y	Y	N
3 Gephardt	Y	Y	N	N	N	Y	Y	N
4 Skelton	Y	Y	Y	Y	Y	N	Y	Y
5 Wheat	Y	Y	N	N	N	Y	Y	N
6 ***Coleman***	Y	Y	N	N	N	Y	Y	N
7 ***Taylor***	Y	+	Y	Y	Y	Y	Y	Y
8 ***Emerson***	N	Y	N	N	N	N	Y	Y
9 Volkmer	Y	Y	Y	Y	Y	Y	-	N
MONTANA								
1 Williams	?	Y	N	N	N	N	Y	N
2 ***Marlenee***	?	?	?	?	?	?	Y	Y
NEBRASKA								
1 ***Bereuter***	Y	Y	N	N	N	N	Y	N
2 ***Daub***	Y	Y	N	Y	N	N	N	N
3 ***Smith***	Y	Y	N	N	N	N	Y	N
NEVADA								
1 Reid	Y	Y	N	Y	N	Y	N	N
2 ***Vucanovich***	Y	Y	N	N	N	N	N	Y
NEW HAMPSHIRE								
1 D'Amours	Y	Y	Y	Y	Y	N	N	?
2 ***Gregg***	Y	Y	N	N	N	N	N	Y
NEW JERSEY								
1 Florio	N	Y	Y	Y	Y	?	N	Y
2 Hughes	Y	Y	Y	Y	Y	N	N	N
3 Howard	Y	Y	N	Y	N	Y	N	N
4 ***Smith***	Y	Y	Y	Y	Y	N	N	Y
5 ***Roukema***	Y	Y	N	N	N	N	N	N
6 Dwyer	Y	Y	N	N	N	N	N	N
7 ***Rinaldo***	Y	Y	Y	Y	Y	N	N	Y
8 Roe	Y	Y	Y	Y	Y	N	N	Y
9 Torricelli	Y	Y	Y	Y	Y	N	N	Y
10 Rodino	Y	Y	N	N	N	Y	?	?
11 Minish	Y	Y	Y	Y	Y	?	Y	N
12 ***Courter***	Y	Y	Y	Y	Y	N	N	Y
13 ***Forsythe***	N	Y	Y	Y	?	N	Y	N
14 Guarini	Y	Y	Y	Y	Y	N	N	N
NEW MEXICO								
1 ***Lujan***	Y	Y	Y	Y	Y	N	?	Y
2 ***Skeen***	Y	Y	Y	Y	Y	N	Y	Y
3 Richardson	Y	Y	Y	Y	N	Y	N	N
NEW YORK								
1 ***Carney***	Y	Y	Y	Y	Y	N	N	Y
2 Downey	Y	Y	N	N	N	N	N	N
3 Mrazek	Y	Y	N	N	N	N	N	N
4 ***Lent***	Y	Y	Y	Y	Y	N	N	Y
5 ***McGrath***	Y	Y	Y	Y	Y	N	N	Y
6 Addabbo	Y	Y	N	N	N	Y	N	N
7 Ackerman	Y	Y	N	N	N	?	-	N
8 Scheuer	Y	Y	N	N	N	Y	N	N
9 Ferraro	Y	Y	N	N	N	?	Y	N
10 Schumer	Y	Y	N	N	N	Y	N	N
11 Towns	Y	Y	N	N	N	Y	N	N
12 Owens	Y	Y	N	N	N	N	N	N
13 Solarz	?	?	N	N	N	Y	N	N
14 ***Molinari***	Y	Y	Y	N	Y	N	N	Y
15 ***Green***	Y	Y	N	N	N	N	Y	N
16 Rangel	Y	Y	N	N	N	Y	N	N
17 Weiss	Y	Y	N	-	-	-	N	N
18 Garcia	Y	Y	N	N	N	Y	N	N
19 Biaggi	?	?	?	?	?	?	N	N
20 Ottinger	P	Y	N	N	N	N	N	N
21 ***Fish***	Y	Y	Y	Y	Y	Y	N	Y
22 ***Gilman***	Y	Y	Y	Y	Y	Y	N	Y
23 Stratton	Y	Y	Y	Y	Y	N	N	N
24 ***Solomon***	Y	Y	Y	Y	Y	N	N	Y
25 ***Boehlert***	Y	Y	N	N	N	N	Y	N
26 ***Martin***	Y	Y	Y	Y	Y	N	Y	Y
27 ***Wortley***	Y	Y	Y	N	Y	N	Y	Y
28 McHugh	Y	Y	N	N	N	Y	N	N
29 ***Horton***	Y	Y	Y	Y	Y	N	Y	N
30 ***Conable***	Y	Y	N	N	N	N	Y	N
31 ***Kemp***	Y	Y	Y	Y	Y	?	Y	N
32 LaFalce	Y	Y	N	N	N	N	N	N
33 Nowak	Y	Y	Y	N	N	?	N	N
34 Lundine	?	?	N	N	N	Y	Y	N
NORTH CAROLINA								
1 Jones	?	Y	Y	Y	Y	Y	N	N
2 Valentine	Y	Y	Y	Y	Y	Y	N	Y
3 Whitley	Y	Y	Y	Y	Y	Y	N	N
4 Andrews	?	Y	Y	Y	Y	Y	N	N
5 Neal	Y	Y	Y	Y	Y	Y	N	N
6 Britt	Y	Y	Y	Y	Y	Y	N	N
7 Rose	Y	Y	Y	Y	Y	Y	N	N
8 Hefner	Y	Y	Y	Y	Y	Y	N	N
9 ***Martin***	?	Y	Y	Y	Y	Y	N	Y
10 ***Broyhill***	Y	Y	Y	Y	Y	N	N	Y
11 Clarke	Y	Y	Y	Y	Y	Y	N	Y
NORTH DAKOTA								
AL Dorgan	Y	Y	Y	Y	Y	Y	Y	N
OHIO								
1 Luken	?	Y	Y	N	N	Y	N	N
2 ***Gradison***	Y	Y	Y	Y	Y	N	N	Y
3 Hall	Y	Y	Y	Y	Y	N	N	N
4 ***Oxley***	Y	Y	Y	Y	Y	N	N	Y
5 ***Latta***	Y	Y	Y	Y	Y	N	N	Y
6 ***McEwen***	Y	Y	Y	Y	Y	N	Y	Y
7 ***DeWine***	Y	Y	Y	Y	Y	N	N	Y
8 ***Kindness***	Y	Y	N	N	N	Y	Y	N
9 Kaptur	Y	Y	N	N	N	N	N	N
10 ***Miller***	N	Y	Y	Y	Y	N	N	Y
11 Eckart	N	Y	Y	N	N	Y	Y	N
12 ***Kasich***	Y	Y	Y	Y	Y	N	N	Y
13 Pease	Y	Y	N	N	N	Y	Y	N
14 Seiberling	?	Y	N	N	N	Y	N	N
15 ***Wylie***	?	?	?	?	?	?	Y	N
16 ***Regula***	Y	Y	Y	Y	Y	Y	N	Y
17 ***Williams***	Y	Y	Y	Y	Y	?	N	N
18 Applegate	?	Y	Y	Y	Y	Y	N	N
19 Feighan	Y	Y	N	N	N	N	N	N
20 Oakar	Y	Y	Y	Y	N	N	N	N
21 Stokes	Y	Y	N	N	?	N	N	N
OKLAHOMA								
1 Jones	Y	Y	N	N	N	Y	Y	N
2 Synar	Y	Y	N	N	N	N	Y	N
3 Watkins	?	Y	Y	Y	Y	Y	Y	Y
4 McCurdy	Y	Y	Y	Y	Y	Y	Y	Y
5 ***Edwards***	Y	Y	Y	Y	Y	N	Y	Y
6 English	Y	Y	Y	Y	Y	Y	Y	N
OREGON								
1 AuCoin	Y	Y	N	N	N	N	Y	N
2 ***Smith, R.***	Y	Y	Y	Y	Y	N	Y	Y
3 Wyden	Y	Y	N	N	N	N	Y	N
4 Weaver	Y	Y	Y	Y	Y	Y	N	N
5 ***Smith, D.***	Y	Y	Y	Y	Y	N	Y	Y
PENNSYLVANIA								
1 Foglietta	Y	Y	N	N	N	N	N	N
2 Gray	Y	Y	N	N	N	Y	N	N
3 Borski	Y	Y	N	N	N	N	N	N
4 Kolter	Y	Y	N	N	Y	Y	N	N
5 ***Schulze***	Y	Y	Y	Y	Y	N	N	Y
6 Yatron	Y	Y	N	N	N	N	N	N
7 Edgar	Y	Y	N	N	N	N	Y	N
8 Kostmayer	Y	Y	?	?	?	?	Y	N
9 ***Shuster***	Y	Y	Y	Y	Y	N	N	Y
10 ***McDade***	?	Y	Y	Y	Y	N	?	Y
11 Harrison	?	Y	N	N	N	Y	N	N
12 Murtha	Y	Y	Y	Y	Y	Y	N	N
13 ***Coughlin***	N	Y	Y	Y	Y	N	N	N
14 Coyne	Y	Y	N	N	N	N	N	N
15 ***Ritter***	Y	Y	Y	Y	Y	N	N	Y
16 ***Walker***	N	Y	Y	Y	Y	N	N	Y
17 ***Gekas***	Y	Y	Y	Y	Y	Y	N	Y
18 Walgren	Y	Y	N	N	N	Y	N	N
19 ***Goodling***	N	?	Y	Y	Y	?	N	N
20 Gaydos	Y	Y	N	N	N	Y	?	N
21 ***Ridge***	Y	Y	Y	Y	Y	N	Y	N
22 Murphy	?	?	?	?	?	Y	N	N
23 ***Clinger***	Y	Y	N	N	N	N	Y	N
RHODE ISLAND								
1 St Germain	?	Y	Y	Y	Y	N	N	N
2 ***Schneider***	Y	Y	Y	Y	Y	?	?	N
SOUTH CAROLINA								
1 ***Hartnett***	Y	Y	Y	Y	Y	N	Y	Y
2 ***Spence***	Y	Y	Y	Y	Y	N	Y	N
3 Derrick	Y	Y	Y	Y	Y	N	Y	N
4 ***Campbell***	Y	Y	Y	Y	Y	N	Y	N
5 Spratt	Y	Y	Y	Y	Y	N	N	N
6 Tallon	Y	Y	Y	Y	Y	Y	Y	N
SOUTH DAKOTA								
AL Daschle	Y	Y	N	N	N	Y	Y	N
TENNESSEE								
1 ***Quillen***	Y	Y	Y	Y	Y	Y	N	N
2 ***Duncan***	Y	Y	Y	Y	Y	Y	N	N
3 Lloyd	Y	Y	Y	Y	Y	Y	N	Y
4 Cooper	Y	Y	Y	Y	Y	Y	Y	Y
5 Boner	Y	Y	Y	Y	Y	Y	?	?
6 Gore	Y	Y	Y	Y	Y	Y	Y	N
7 ***Sundquist***	Y	Y	Y	Y	Y	Y	N	Y
8 Jones	Y	Y	Y	Y	Y	Y	Y	N
9 Ford	Y	Y	?	N	N	Y	N	N
TEXAS								
1 Hall, S.	Y	Y	Y	Y	Y	Y	N	N
2 Wilson	Y	Y	?	Y	Y	Y	N	N
3 ***Bartlett***	Y	Y	N	N	N	N	Y	N
4 Hall, R.	?	?	?	?	?	?	N	N
5 Bryant	Y	Y	Y	Y	Y	Y	N	N
6 ***Gramm***	Y	Y	Y	Y	Y	N	Y	N
7 ***Archer***	Y	Y	Y	Y	Y	N	Y	Y
8 ***Fields***	N	Y	Y	Y	Y	N	N	Y
9 Brooks	Y	Y	N	Y	N	Y	N	N
10 Pickle	Y	Y	Y	Y	Y	Y	N	N
11 Leath	Y	Y	Y	Y	Y	?	Y	Y
12 Wright	Y	Y	N	Y	Y	Y	N	N
13 Hightower	?	?	?	?	?	?	?	?
14 Patman	Y	Y	Y	Y	Y	Y	Y	Y
15 de la Garza	Y	Y	Y	Y	Y	Y	?	N
16 Coleman	Y	Y	Y	N	Y	Y	N	N
17 Stenholm	Y	Y	N	Y	Y	Y	Y	N
18 Leland	Y	Y	N	N	N	Y	N	N
19 Hance	Y	Y	Y	Y	Y	N	Y	N
20 Gonzalez	Y	Y	N	P	P	Y	N	N
21 ***Loeffler***	Y	Y	Y	Y	Y	Y	Y	Y
22 ***Paul***	Y	Y	Y	Y	Y	N	Y	N
23 Kazen	Y	Y	Y	Y	Y	Y	N	Y
24 Frost	Y	Y	Y	Y	Y	Y	N	N
25 Andrews	Y	Y	Y	Y	Y	Y	N	N
26 Vandergriff	Y	Y	Y	Y	Y	Y	Y	N
27 Ortiz	Y	Y	Y	Y	Y	Y	N	N
UTAH								
1 ***Hansen***	Y	Y	Y	Y	Y	N	N	Y
2 ***Marriott***	Y	Y	N	Y	Y	N	N	Y
3 ***Nielson***	Y	Y	N	N	N	N	N	N
VERMONT								
AL ***Jeffords***	Y	Y	Y	Y	N	Y	Y	N
VIRGINIA								
1 ***Bateman***	Y	Y	Y	Y	Y	N	Y	N
2 ***Whitehurst***	Y	Y	Y	Y	Y	N	N	Y
3 ***Bliley***	Y	Y	Y	Y	Y	Y	N	Y
4 Sisisky	Y	Y	Y	Y	Y	Y	N	Y
5 Daniel	Y	Y	?	?	?	?	N	Y
6 Olin	Y	Y	Y	Y	Y	Y	Y	N
7 ***Robinson***	Y	Y	Y	Y	Y	N	N	Y
8 ***Parris***	Y	Y	Y	Y	Y	N	N	Y
9 Boucher	Y	Y	N	N	Y	Y	N	N
10 ***Wolf***	Y	Y	Y	Y	Y	N	Y	Y
WASHINGTON								
1 ***Pritchard***	?	?	?	?	?	?	?	?
2 Swift	Y	Y	N	N	N	N	Y	N
3 Bonker	Y	Y	N	N	N	?	Y	N
4 ***Morrison***	Y	Y	N	N	N	N	Y	Y
5 Foley	Y	Y	N	N	N	Y	Y	N
6 Dicks	Y	Y	N	N	N	N	Y	N
7 Lowry	Y	Y	N	N	N	N	Y	N
8 ***Chandler***	Y	Y	N	N	N	N	Y	Y
WEST VIRGINIA								
1 Mollohan	Y	Y	N	N	N	Y	Y	N
2 Staggers	Y	Y	Y	Y	Y	Y	Y	N
3 Wise	Y	Y	Y	Y	Y	Y	N	Y
4 Rahall	Y	Y	N	N	N	Y	Y	Y
WISCONSIN								
1 Aspin	?	?	N	Y	Y	Y	N	N
2 Kastenmeier	Y	Y	N	N	N	Y	Y	N
3 ***Gunderson***	Y	Y	N	N	N	Y	Y	N
4 Zablocki	Y	Y	N	N	N	Y	Y	N
5 Moody	Y	Y	N	Y	N	N	N	N
6 ***Petri***	Y	Y	Y	Y	Y	Y	N	Y
7 Obey	Y	Y	N	N	N	Y	N	N
8 ***Roth***	Y	Y	Y	Y	Y	Y	N	Y
9 ***Sensenbrenner***	Y	Y	Y	Y	Y	Y	N	Y
WYOMING								
AL ***Cheney***	Y	Y	Y	Y	Y	N	N	Y

Southern states - Ala., Ark., Fla., Ga., Ky., La., Miss., N.C., Okla., S.C., Tenn., Texas, Va.

374. HR 3231. Export Administration Act. Erlenborn, R-Ill., amendment to strike the provision prohibiting the application of foreign policy controls to companies outside the United States. Rejected 199-215: R 130-33; D 69-182 (ND 35-132, SD 34-50), Oct. 19, 1983. A "yea" was a vote supporting the president's position.

375. HR 2968. Intelligence Authorizations. Adoption of the rule (H Res 329) providing for House floor consideration of the bill to authorize appropriations for U.S. intelligence agencies in fiscal 1984 and prohibiting U.S. aid for "covert" military or paramilitary operations in Nicaragua. Adopted 232-179: R 6-154; D 226-25 (ND 163-5, SD 63-20), Oct. 19, 1983.

376. Procedural Motion. McCain, R-Ariz., motion to approve the House *Journal* of Wednesday, Oct. 19. Motion agreed to 361-28: R 139-16; D 222-12 (ND 144-11, SD 78-1), Oct. 20, 1983.

377. HR 2968. Intelligence Authorizations. Boland, D-Mass., amendment to prohibit, at a classified date specified by the House Intelligence Committee, support by U.S. intelligence agencies for military or paramilitary operations in Nicaragua; to authorize $50 million in fiscal 1984 to help friendly countries in Central America interdict cross-border shipments of arms to anti-government forces in the region; and to direct the president to seek action by the Organization of American States to resolve the conflicts in Central America and to seek an agreement by the government of Nicaragua to halt its support for anti-government forces in the region. Adopted 227-194: R 18-146; D 209-48 (ND 166-8, SD 43-40), Oct. 20, 1983. A "nay" was a vote supporting the president's position.

378. HR 2968. Intelligence Authorizations. Robinson, R-Va., motion to recommit the bill to the House Intelligence Committee with instructions to insert a provision to prohibit, 60 days after enactment of the bill, support by U.S. intelligence agencies for military or paramilitary operations in Nicaragua if the government of Nicaragua had reaffirmed the commitments it made to the Organization of American States in July 1979, had concluded peace agreements with other countries in Central America, and had ceased all support for military and paramilitary operations against other governments in Central America and the Caribbean. Motion rejected 193-223: R 147-16; D 46-207 (ND 7-164, SD 39-43), Oct. 20, 1983. A "yea" was a vote supporting the president's position.

379. HR 2968. Intelligence Authorizations. Passage of the bill to make authorizations for U.S. intelligence agencies in fiscal year 1984. The bill also prohibited, at a classified date specified by the House Intelligence Committee, support by U.S. intelligence agencies for military or paramilitary operations in Nicaragua; authorized $50 million in fiscal 1984 to help friendly countries in Central America interdict cross-border shipments of arms to anti-government forces in the region; and directed the president to seek action by the Organization of American States to resolve the conflicts in Central America and to seek an agreement by the government of Nicaragua to halt its support for anti-government forces in the region. Passed 243-171: R 28-134; D 215-37 (ND 156-15, SD 59-22), Oct. 20, 1983.

380. HR 3913. Labor, Health and Human Services, Education Appropriations, Fiscal 1984. Adoption of the conference report on the bill to appropriate $96,531,883,000 in fiscal 1984 and $7,902,000,000 in fiscal 1985-86 for the departments of Labor, Health and Human Services, and Education and related agencies. Adopted 323-79: R 93-66; D 230-13 (ND 166-4, SD 64-9), Oct. 20, 1983. The Senate subsequently adopted the conference report by voice vote Oct. 20, clearing the bill for the president, who had requested $95,215,687,000 in new budget authority.

KEY

Y	Voted for (yea).
#	Paired for.
+	Announced for.
N	Voted against (nay).
X	Paired against.
-	Announced against.
P	Voted "present".
C	Voted "present" to avoid possible conflict of interest.
?	Did not vote or otherwise make a position known.

Democrats *Republicans*

	374	375	376	377	378	379	380
ALABAMA							
1 Edwards	N	N	N	Y	N	Y	Y
2 *Dickinson*	Y	N	N	N	Y	N	Y
3 Nichols	Y	Y	Y	N	Y	N	?
4 Bevill	Y	Y	?	X	#	?	?
5 Flippo	Y	Y	Y	N	Y	Y	Y
6 Erdreich	Y	Y	Y	N	Y	Y	Y
7 Shelby	N	N	?	N	Y	N	Y
ALASKA							
AL *Young*	?	?	?	X	#	?	?
ARIZONA							
1 *McCain*	Y	N	Y	N	Y	N	Y
2 Udall	N	Y	Y	Y	N	Y	Y
3 *Stump*	Y	N	Y	N	Y	N	N
4 *Rudd*	Y	N	Y	N	Y	N	Y
5 McNulty	N	Y	Y	Y	N	Y	Y
ARKANSAS							
1 Alexander	N	Y	Y	Y	N	Y	Y
2 *Bethune*	N	N	Y	N	Y	?	Y
3 *Hammerschmidt*	Y	N	Y	N	Y	N	Y
4 Anthony	N	Y	Y	N	Y	N	Y
CALIFORNIA							
1 Bosco	N	Y	Y	Y	N	Y	Y
2 *Chappie*	Y	N	Y	N	Y	N	Y
3 Matsui	N	Y	Y	Y	N	Y	Y
4 Fazio	N	Y	Y	N	Y	Y	Y
5 Burton	N	Y	Y	Y	?	Y	Y
6 Boxer	N	Y	Y	Y	N	Y	N
7 Miller	N	Y	Y	Y	N	Y	Y
8 Dellums	N	Y	Y	N	N	Y	Y
9 Stark	N	Y	Y	Y	N	Y	?
10 Edwards	N	Y	Y	Y	N	Y	Y
11 Lantos	N	?	?	Y	N	Y	Y
12 Zschau	N	N	Y	N	N	N	Y
13 Mineta	N	Y	Y	Y	N	Y	Y
14 *Shumway*	Y	N	Y	N	Y	N	N
15 Coelho	N	Y	Y	Y	N	Y	Y
16 Panetta	N	Y	Y	N	Y	N	Y
17 *Pashayan*	Y	N	?	N	Y	N	Y
18 Lehman	N	Y	Y	Y	N	Y	Y
19 *Lagomarsino*	Y	N	Y	N	Y	N	Y
20 *Thomas*	N	N	Y	N	Y	N	Y
21 *Fiedler*	Y	N	Y	N	N	N	N
22 *Moorhead*	Y	N	Y	N	Y	N	N
23 Beilenson	N	Y	Y	Y	N	Y	Y
24 Waxman	Y	Y	Y	Y	N	Y	Y
25 Roybal	N	Y	Y	Y	N	Y	Y
26 Berman	Y	Y	Y	Y	X	?	Y
27 Levine	N	Y	Y	Y	N	Y	Y
28 Dixon	?	Y	?	?	?	?	?
29 Hawkins	?	?	Y	Y	N	Y	Y
30 Martinez	N	Y	Y	Y	N	Y	Y
31 Dymally	N	Y	P	Y	N	Y	Y
32 Anderson	N	Y	Y	N	Y	N	Y
33 *Dreier*	Y	N	Y	N	Y	N	?
34 Torres	N	Y	Y	Y	N	Y	Y
35 *Lewis*	Y	N	Y	N	Y	N	Y
36 Brown	N	Y	Y	Y	N	Y	Y
37 *McCandless*	Y	N	Y	N	Y	N	Y
38 Patterson	N	Y	?	Y	N	Y	Y
39 *Dannemeyer*	Y	N	N	N	Y	N	N
40 *Badham*	Y	N	Y	N	Y	N	N
41 *Lowery*	N	N	Y	N	Y	N	N
42 *Lungren*	?	N	Y	N	Y	N	N

	374	375	376	377	378	379	380
43 *Packard*	Y	N	Y	N	Y	N	N
44 Bates	N	Y	Y	Y	N	Y	Y
45 *Hunter*	Y	N	Y	N	Y	N	N
COLORADO							
1 Schroeder	N	Y	N	Y	N	N	N
2 Wirth	N	Y	Y	Y	N	Y	Y
3 Kogovsek	N	Y	Y	N	N	N	Y
4 *Brown*	Y	N	Y	N	Y	N	Y
5 *Kramer*	Y	N	Y	N	Y	N	Y
6 *Schaefer*	Y	N	Y	N	Y	N	N
CONNECTICUT							
1 Kennelly	N	Y	Y	Y	N	Y	Y
2 Gejdenson	N	Y	N	Y	N	Y	Y
3 Morrison	N	Y	Y	Y	N	Y	Y
4 *McKinney*	N	N	Y	N	N	Y	Y
5 Ratchford	N	Y	Y	Y	N	Y	Y
6 *Johnson*	N	N	Y	N	N	Y	Y
DELAWARE							
AL Carper	N	Y	Y	Y	N	Y	Y
FLORIDA							
1 Hutto	Y	Y	P	N	Y	N	Y
2 Fuqua	?	?	?	N	Y	N	Y
3 Bennett	Y	Y	Y	N	Y	N	Y
4 Chappell	Y	Y	Y	N	Y	N	Y
5 *McCollum*	Y	N	Y	N	Y	N	N
6 MacKay	Y	Y	Y	#	X	?	?
7 Gibbons	N	Y	Y	N	Y	N	Y
8 *Young*	Y	N	Y	N	Y	N	Y
9 *Bilirakis*	Y	N	Y	N	Y	N	Y
10 Ireland	Y	Y	Y	N	Y	N	Y
11 Nelson	N	N	Y	N	Y	N	Y
12 *Lewis*	Y	N	Y	N	N	N	N
13 *Mack*	Y	N	Y	N	Y	N	N
14 Mica	N	Y	Y	N	Y	Y	?
15 *Shaw*	Y	N	Y	N	Y	N	N
16 Smith	N	Y	Y	N	Y	N	Y
17 Lehman	N	Y	Y	N	Y	N	Y
18 Pepper	?	?	?	?	?	?	?
19 Fascell	N	?	Y	N	Y	Y	Y
GEORGIA							
1 Thomas	Y	N	Y	N	Y	N	Y
2 Hatcher	Y	Y	Y	N	Y	Y	Y
3 Ray	Y	N	Y	N	Y	N	N
4 Levitas	Y	Y	Y	N	Y	Y	Y
5 Fowler	?	Y	Y	Y	N	Y	Y
6 *Gingrich*	Y	N	Y	N	Y	N	Y
7 Vacancy							
8 Rowland	Y	Y	Y	N	Y	Y	Y
9 Jenkins	Y	Y	Y	N	Y	Y	Y
10 Barnard	Y	N	Y	N	Y	Y	?
HAWAII							
1 Heftel	Y	Y	?	Y	N	Y	Y
2 Akaka	N	Y	Y	Y	N	Y	Y
IDAHO							
1 *Craig*	Y	N	Y	N	N	N	N
2 *Hansen*	Y	N	Y	N	N	N	N
ILLINOIS							
1 Hayes	?	Y	Y	Y	N	Y	N
2 Savage	N	Y	Y	N	N	Y	Y
3 Russo	N	Y	Y	N	Y	N	Y
4 *O'Brien*	Y	N	Y	N	Y	N	Y
5 Lipinski	Y	N	Y	N	N	N	Y
6 *Hyde*	Y	N	Y	N	Y	N	Y
7 Collins	N	Y	Y	#	X	?	?
8 Rostenkowski	Y	Y	Y	N	Y	N	Y
9 Yates	N	Y	Y	N	N	Y	Y
10 *Porter*	Y	N	Y	N	Y	N	Y
11 Annunzio	N	Y	Y	N	Y	N	Y
12 *Crane, P.*	Y	N	Y	N	Y	N	N
13 *Erlenborn*	Y	N	Y	N	Y	N	Y
14 *Corcoran*	Y	N	Y	N	Y	N	-
15 *Madigan*	Y	?	?	N	Y	N	Y
16 *Martin*	Y	N	Y	N	Y	N	N
17 Evans	N	Y	Y	Y	N	Y	Y
18 *Michel*	N	N	Y	N	Y	N	N
19 *Crane, D.*	Y	N	Y	N	Y	N	N
20 Durbin	Y	Y	N	Y	N	Y	Y
21 Price	N	Y	Y	Y	N	Y	Y
22 Simon	N	Y	Y	Y	N	Y	?
INDIANA							
1 Hall	?	?	Y	Y	N	Y	Y
2 Sharp	Y	Y	Y	Y	N	Y	Y
3 *Hiler*	Y	N	N	N	N	N	N
4 *Coats*	Y	N	Y	N	Y	N	Y
5 *Hillis*	Y	N	Y	N	Y	N	N

ND - Northern Democrats   SD - Southern Democrats

Corresponding to Congressional Record Votes 399, 400, 401, 403, 404, 405, 406

	374	375	376	377	378	379	380
6 ***Burton***	Y	N	N	N	Y	N	N
7 ***Myers***	N	N	Y	N	Y	N	Y
8 McCloskey	Y	Y	Y	Y	N	Y	Y
9 Hamilton	N	Y	Y	Y	N	Y	Y
10 Jacobs	?	N	N	Y	N	N	Y
IOWA							
1 ***Leach***	N	N	Y	Y	N	Y	Y
2 ***Tauke***	N	N	Y	N	Y	N	Y
3 ***Evans***	Y	N	N	Y	N	N	Y
4 Smith	N	Y	Y	Y	N	Y	Y
5 Harkin	N	Y	N	Y	N	Y	Y
6 Bedell	N	Y	Y	Y	N	Y	Y
KANSAS							
1 ***Roberts***	N	N	N	N	Y	N	N
2 Slattery	N	Y	Y	Y	N	Y	Y
3 ***Winn***	Y	N	Y	N	Y	N	Y
4 Glickman	N	Y	Y	Y	N	Y	Y
5 ***Whittaker***	N	N	Y	N	Y	N	Y
KENTUCKY							
1 Hubbard	N	Y	Y	N	Y	N	?
2 Natcher	N	Y	Y	Y	N	Y	Y
3 Mazzoli	N	N	Y	Y	N	Y	Y
4 ***Snyder***	Y	N	Y	N	Y	N	N
5 ***Rogers***	Y	N	Y	N	Y	N	Y
6 ***Hopkins***	Y	N	Y	N	Y	N	Y
7 Perkins	N	Y	Y	Y	N	Y	Y
LOUISIANA							
1 ***Livingston***	N	N	Y	N	Y	N	Y
2 Boggs	N	Y	Y	Y	N	Y	Y
3 Tauzin	N	N	Y	N	Y	N	?
4 Roemer	Y	N	N	N	Y	N	N
5 Huckaby	N	N	Y	N	Y	N	N
6 ***Moore***	N	N	Y	N	Y	N	Y
7 Breaux	N	Y	?	N	Y	N	?
8 Long	N	Y	Y	Y	N	Y	Y
MAINE							
1 ***McKernan***	Y	N	Y	Y	N	Y	Y
2 ***Snowe***	Y	N	Y	Y	N	Y	Y
MARYLAND							
1 Dyson	Y	Y	Y	N	Y	N	Y
2 Long	N	Y	Y	Y	N	?	Y
3 Mikulski	N	Y	Y	Y	N	Y	Y
4 ***Holt***	Y	N	Y	N	Y	N	N
5 Hoyer	N	Y	Y	Y	N	Y	Y
6 Byron	Y	N	Y	N	Y	N	Y
7 Mitchell	N	Y	?	Y	N	Y	Y
8 Barnes	N	Y	?	Y	N	Y	Y
MASSACHUSETTS							
1 ***Conte***	N	N	Y	Y	N	Y	Y
2 Boland	N	Y	Y	Y	N	Y	Y
3 Early	N	Y	Y	Y	N	Y	Y
4 Frank	N	N	Y	Y	N	Y	Y
5 Shannon	N	Y	Y	Y	N	Y	Y
6 Mavroules	N	Y	Y	Y	N	Y	Y
7 Markey	N	Y	Y	Y	N	Y	Y
8 O'Neill							
9 Moakley	N	Y	Y	Y	N	Y	Y
10 Studds	N	Y	Y	Y	N	Y	Y
11 Donnelly	N	Y	Y	Y	N	Y	Y
MICHIGAN							
1 Conyers	N	Y	Y	Y	N	N	Y
2 ***Pursell***	Y	N	Y	Y	N	Y	Y
3 Wolpe	N	Y	Y	Y	N	Y	Y
4 ***Siljander***	Y	?	Y	N	Y	N	N
5 ***Sawyer***	Y	N	Y	N	Y	N	Y
6 Carr	N	Y	P	Y	?	?	?
7 Kildee	N	Y	Y	Y	N	Y	Y
8 Traxler	N	Y	Y	Y	N	Y	Y
9 ***Vander Jagt***	N	?	Y	N	Y	N	?
10 Albosta	N	Y	Y	Y	N	Y	Y
11 ***Davis***	Y	N	Y	N	Y	N	Y
12 Bonior	N	Y	Y	Y	N	Y	Y
13 Crockett	N	Y	Y	N	N	N	Y
14 Hertel	Y	Y	Y	Y	N	Y	Y
15 Ford	N	Y	?	Y	N	Y	Y
16 Dingell	N	Y	?	Y	N	Y	Y
17 Levin	N	Y	Y	Y	N	Y	Y
18 ***Broomfield***	Y	N	Y	N	Y	N	?
MINNESOTA							
1 Penny	N	Y	Y	Y	N	Y	Y
2 ***Weber***	N	?	Y	N	Y	N	N
3 ***Frenzel***	N	N	N	N	Y	N	N
4 Vento	N	Y	Y	Y	N	Y	Y
5 Sabo	N	Y	N	Y	N	Y	Y
6 Sikorski	N	Y	N	Y	N	Y	Y
7 ***Stangeland***	Y	N	Y	N	Y	N	N
8 Oberstar	N	Y	?	#	X	Y	Y
MISSISSIPPI							
1 Whitten	N	Y	Y	Y	N	Y	Y
2 ***Franklin***	Y	N	P	N	Y	N	N
3 Montgomery	Y	Y	Y	N	Y	N	N
4 Dowdy	Y	Y	?	N	Y	N	Y
5 ***Lott***	Y	N	Y	N	Y	Y	N
MISSOURI							
1 Clay	Y	Y	N	Y	N	Y	Y
2 Young	N	Y	Y	Y	N	Y	Y
3 Gephardt	N	Y	Y	Y	N	Y	Y
4 Skelton	Y	Y	Y	N	Y	Y	Y
5 Wheat	N	Y	Y	Y	N	Y	Y
6 ***Coleman***	Y	N	Y	N	Y	N	Y
7 ***Taylor***	Y	N	Y	N	Y	N	Y
8 ***Emerson***	Y	N	N	N	Y	N	Y
9 Volkmer	Y	Y	Y	Y	N	Y	Y
MONTANA							
1 Williams	N	?	?	Y	N	N	?
2 ***Marlenee***	Y	Y	Y	N	Y	N	N
NEBRASKA							
1 ***Bereuter***	N	N	Y	N	Y	N	Y
2 ***Daub***	Y	N	Y	N	Y	N	Y
3 ***Smith***	N	N	Y	N	Y	N	Y
NEVADA							
1 Reid	N	Y	Y	Y	N	Y	Y
2 ***Vucanovich***	Y	N	Y	N	Y	N	N
NEW HAMPSHIRE							
1 D'Amours	Y	Y	Y	Y	N	Y	Y
2 ***Gregg***	Y	N	Y	N	Y	N	N
NEW JERSEY							
1 Florio	Y	Y	Y	Y	N	Y	Y
2 Hughes	Y	Y	Y	Y	N	Y	Y
3 Howard	N	Y	Y	Y	N	Y	Y
4 ***Smith***	Y	N	Y	N	Y	N	Y
5 ***Roukema***	N	N	Y	Y	N	Y	Y
6 Dwyer	N	Y	Y	Y	N	Y	Y
7 ***Rinaldo***	Y	N	Y	N	Y	Y	Y
8 Roe	Y	Y	Y	Y	N	Y	Y
9 Torricelli	Y	Y	Y	Y	N	Y	Y
10 Rodino	?	?	?	Y	N	Y	Y
11 Minish	Y	Y	Y	Y	N	Y	Y
12 ***Courter***	Y	N	Y	N	Y	Y	Y
13 ***Forsythe***	Y	N	?	N	+	-	-
14 Guarini	Y	Y	Y	Y	N	Y	Y
NEW MEXICO							
1 ***Lujan***	Y	N	Y	N	Y	N	Y
2 ***Skeen***	Y	N	Y	N	Y	N	Y
3 Richardson	N	Y	Y	Y	N	Y	Y
NEW YORK							
1 ***Carney***	Y	N	Y	N	Y	N	Y
2 Downey	N	Y	Y	Y	N	Y	Y
3 Mrazek	N	Y	Y	Y	N	Y	Y
4 ***Lent***	Y	N	Y	N	Y	N	Y
5 ***McGrath***	Y	N	Y	N	Y	N	Y
6 Addabbo	N	?	Y	Y	N	Y	Y
7 Ackerman	N	Y	Y	Y	N	Y	Y
8 Scheuer	N	Y	Y	Y	N	Y	Y
9 Ferraro	N	Y	Y	Y	N	Y	Y
10 Schumer	N	Y	Y	Y	N	Y	Y
11 Towns	N	Y	?	Y	N	Y	Y
12 Owens	N	N	Y	Y	N	Y	Y
13 Solarz	N	Y	Y	Y	N	Y	Y
14 ***Molinari***	Y	N	Y	N	Y	Y	Y
15 ***Green***	N	N	Y	Y	N	Y	Y
16 Rangel	?	Y	Y	Y	N	Y	Y
17 Weiss	N	Y	Y	Y	N	Y	Y
18 Garcia	?	Y	Y	Y	N	Y	?
19 Biaggi	Y	?	Y	Y	N	Y	Y
20 Ottinger	N	Y	P	Y	N	Y	Y
21 ***Fish***	Y	N	Y	Y	N	Y	Y
22 ***Gilman***	Y	Y	Y	N	Y	N	Y
23 Stratton	N	N	Y	N	Y	N	Y
24 ***Solomon***	Y	N	Y	N	Y	N	N
25 ***Boehlert***	Y	N	Y	Y	N	Y	Y
26 ***Martin***	Y	N	Y	N	Y	N	Y
27 ***Wortley***	Y	N	Y	N	Y	N	Y
28 McHugh	N	Y	Y	Y	N	Y	Y
29 ***Horton***	Y	Y	Y	Y	N	Y	Y
30 ***Conable***	N	N	Y	N	Y	N	N
31 ***Kemp***	Y	N	Y	N	Y	N	Y
32 LaFalce	Y	Y	Y	Y	N	Y	Y
33 Nowak	Y	Y	Y	Y	N	Y	Y
34 Lundine	N	Y	?	Y	N	Y	Y
NORTH CAROLINA							
1 Jones	N	?	P	Y	N	Y	Y
2 Valentine	Y	Y	Y	Y	N	Y	?
3 Whitley	N	Y	Y	Y	Y	Y	Y
4 Andrews	Y	Y	Y	Y	N	Y	Y
5 Neal	Y	Y	Y	Y	N	Y	Y
6 Britt	N	Y	Y	Y	N	Y	Y
7 Rose	N	Y	Y	Y	N	Y	Y
8 Hefner	N	Y	Y	Y	N	Y	Y
9 ***Martin***	Y	N	Y	N	Y	N	N
10 ***Broyhill***	Y	N	Y	N	Y	N	N
11 Clarke	N	Y	Y	Y	N	Y	Y
NORTH DAKOTA							
AL Dorgan	Y	Y	Y	Y	N	N	N
OHIO							
1 Luken	N	Y	N	Y	N	Y	Y
2 ***Gradison***	Y	N	Y	N	Y	Y	Y
3 Hall	Y	Y	Y	Y	N	Y	Y
4 ***Oxley***	Y	N	Y	N	Y	N	Y
5 ***Latta***	Y	N	Y	N	Y	N	N
6 ***McEwen***	Y	N	Y	N	Y	N	N
7 ***DeWine***	Y	N	Y	N	Y	N	N
8 ***Kindness***	N	N	Y	N	Y	N	N
9 Kaptur	N	Y	Y	Y	N	Y	Y
10 ***Miller***	Y	N	N	N	Y	N	N
11 Eckart	Y	Y	N	Y	N	Y	Y
12 ***Kasich***	Y	N	Y	N	Y	N	Y
13 Pease	N	Y	Y	Y	N	Y	Y
14 Seiberling	N	Y	Y	Y	N	Y	Y
15 ***Wylie***	Y	N	Y	N	Y	N	Y
16 ***Regula***	Y	N	Y	N	Y	Y	Y
17 ***Williams***	Y	N	Y	Y	Y	Y	Y
18 Applegate	Y	Y	?	Y	N	Y	Y
19 Feighan	Y	Y	?	Y	N	Y	Y
20 Oakar	N	Y	Y	Y	N	Y	Y
21 Stokes	?	Y	Y	Y	N	Y	Y
OKLAHOMA							
1 Jones	N	Y	Y	Y	N	Y	Y
2 Synar	N	Y	Y	Y	N	Y	Y
3 Watkins	N	Y	Y	Y	N	Y	Y
4 McCurdy	N	Y	Y	Y	N	Y	Y
5 ***Edwards***	Y	N	N	N	Y	Y	N
6 English	N	Y	Y	Y	N	Y	Y
OREGON							
1 AuCoin	N	Y	Y	Y	N	Y	Y
2 ***Smith, R.***	Y	N	Y	N	Y	N	Y
3 Wyden	N	Y	Y	Y	N	Y	Y
4 Weaver	Y	Y	Y	Y	N	Y	N
5 ***Smith, D.***	Y	N	Y	N	Y	N	N
PENNSYLVANIA							
1 Foglietta	N	Y	Y	Y	N	Y	Y
2 Gray	?	Y	Y	Y	N	Y	Y
3 Borski	N	Y	Y	Y	N	Y	Y
4 Kolter	N	Y	Y	Y	N	Y	Y
5 ***Schulze***	Y	N	Y	N	Y	N	Y
6 Yatron	N	Y	Y	Y	N	Y	Y
7 Edgar	N	Y	Y	Y	N	Y	Y
8 Kostmayer	N	?	Y	Y	N	Y	Y
9 ***Shuster***	Y	N	Y	N	Y	N	Y
10 ***McDade***	Y	N	Y	N	Y	Y	Y
11 Harrison	Y	Y	Y	Y	N	Y	Y
12 Murtha	Y	Y	Y	N	Y	Y	Y
13 ***Coughlin***	N	N	N	Y	Y	Y	Y
14 Coyne	N	Y	?	Y	N	Y	Y
15 ***Ritter***	Y	N	?	N	Y	N	N
16 ***Walker***	Y	N	N	N	Y	N	N
17 ***Gekas***	Y	N	Y	N	Y	N	N
18 Walgren	Y	Y	Y	Y	N	Y	Y
19 ***Goodling***	Y	N	N	N	Y	N	Y
20 Gaydos	N	Y	?	N	N	N	Y
21 ***Ridge***	Y	N	Y	Y	Y	Y	Y
22 Murphy	N	Y	Y	Y	Y	Y	Y
23 ***Clinger***	N	N	Y	N	Y	N	Y
RHODE ISLAND							
1 St Germain	N	Y	P	Y	N	Y	Y
2 ***Schneider***	N	Y	?	Y	N	Y	Y
SOUTH CAROLINA							
1 ***Hartnett***	Y	N	Y	N	Y	N	N
2 ***Spence***	Y	N	Y	N	Y	N	N
3 Derrick	N	Y	Y	Y	N	Y	Y
4 ***Campbell***	Y	N	Y	N	Y	N	N
5 Spratt	N	Y	Y	Y	N	Y	Y
6 Tallon	N	Y	Y	N	Y	Y	Y
SOUTH DAKOTA							
AL Daschle	N	?	Y	Y	N	Y	Y
TENNESSEE							
1 ***Quillen***	?	Y	Y	N	Y	N	Y
2 ***Duncan***	Y	N	Y	N	Y	N	Y
3 Lloyd	Y	N	Y	N	Y	N	Y
4 Cooper	N	Y	Y	Y	N	Y	Y
5 Boner	?	?	Y	N	?	?	?
6 Gore	N	Y	Y	Y	N	Y	Y
7 ***Sundquist***	Y	N	Y	N	Y	N	Y
8 Jones	N	Y	Y	N	N	Y	Y
9 Ford	N	Y	Y	#	?	?	?
TEXAS							
1 Hall, S.	Y	N	Y	N	Y	Y	N
2 Wilson	N	N	Y	N	Y	?	Y
3 ***Bartlett***	Y	N	Y	N	Y	N	N
4 Hall, R.	Y	N	Y	N	Y	N	N
5 Bryant	Y	Y	Y	Y	N	Y	Y
6 ***Gramm***	N	N	?	N	Y	N	N
7 ***Archer***	N	N	Y	N	Y	N	N
8 ***Fields***	Y	N	N	N	Y	N	Y
9 Brooks	Y	Y	?	Y	N	Y	Y
10 Pickle	N	Y	Y	Y	N	Y	Y
11 Leath	Y	Y	Y	N	Y	N	Y
12 Wright	N	Y	Y	Y	N	Y	Y
13 Hightower	?	?	?	?	?	?	?
14 Patman	Y	N	Y	N	Y	N	Y
15 de la Garza	N	Y	Y	Y	N	Y	Y
16 Coleman	N	Y	Y	Y	N	Y	Y
17 Stenholm	N	N	Y	N	Y	N	N
18 Leland	N	Y	Y	Y	N	Y	Y
19 Hance	Y	N	Y	X	#	?	?
20 Gonzalez	N	Y	Y	Y	N	Y	Y
21 ***Loeffler***	Y	N	Y	N	Y	N	N
22 ***Paul***	N	N	?	?	?	?	?
23 Kazen	Y	N	Y	N	Y	Y	Y
24 Frost	Y	Y	Y	Y	N	Y	Y
25 Andrews	N	Y	Y	Y	N	Y	Y
26 Vandergriff	N	N	Y	N	Y	N	N
27 Ortiz	N	Y	Y	N	Y	Y	Y
UTAH							
1 ***Hansen***	Y	N	?	N	Y	N	N
2 ***Marriott***	Y	N	Y	N	Y	N	N
3 ***Nielson***	Y	N	Y	N	Y	N	N
VERMONT							
AL ***Jeffords***	Y	N	Y	Y	N	Y	Y
VIRGINIA							
1 ***Bateman***	Y	N	Y	N	Y	N	N
2 ***Whitehurst***	Y	N	Y	N	Y	N	Y
3 ***Bliley***	Y	N	Y	N	Y	N	N
4 Sisisky	Y	N	Y	N	Y	N	Y
5 Daniel	Y	N	Y	N	Y	N	N
6 Olin	N	Y	Y	Y	N	Y	Y
7 ***Robinson***	Y	Y	Y	N	Y	N	Y
8 ***Parris***	Y	?	N	N	Y	N	Y
9 Boucher	N	Y	Y	Y	N	Y	Y
10 ***Wolf***	Y	N	N	N	Y	N	Y
WASHINGTON							
1 ***Pritchard***	?	?	?	X	#	?	?
2 Swift	N	Y	Y	Y	N	+	Y
3 Bonker	N	Y	Y	Y	N	Y	Y
4 ***Morrison***	N	N	Y	N	Y	Y	Y
5 Foley	N	Y	?	Y	N	Y	Y
6 Dicks	N	Y	Y	Y	N	Y	Y
7 Lowry	N	Y	Y	Y	N	Y	Y
8 ***Chandler***	N	N	Y	Y	N	Y	Y
WEST VIRGINIA							
1 Mollohan	N	Y	Y	Y	N	Y	Y
2 Staggers	N	Y	Y	Y	N	Y	Y
3 Wise	Y	Y	Y	Y	N	Y	Y
4 Rahall	N	Y	Y	Y	N	Y	Y
WISCONSIN							
1 Aspin	Y	Y	Y	Y	N	Y	Y
2 Kastenmeier	N	Y	Y	Y	N	N	Y
3 ***Gunderson***	Y	N	Y	N	Y	N	Y
4 Zablocki	N	Y	Y	Y	N	Y	Y
5 Moody	N	Y	Y	Y	N	Y	Y
6 ***Petri***	Y	N	Y	N	Y	N	Y
7 Obey	Y	Y	Y	Y	N	Y	Y
8 ***Roth***	Y	N	Y	N	Y	N	Y
9 ***Sensenbrenner***	Y	N	Y	N	Y	N	N
WYOMING							
AL ***Cheney***	Y	N	?	N	Y	N	N

Southern states - Ala., Ark., Fla., Ga., Ky., La., Miss., N.C., Okla., S.C., Tenn., Texas, Va.

381. HR 3324. Close Up Foundation Grants. Erlenborn, R-Ill., amendment to retain the Department of Education's law-related education program in the state block grant. (The bill shifted the program to the secretary's discretionary fund and mandated that $500,000 be made available.) Rejected 136-173: R 116-4; D 20-169 (ND 5-124, SD 15-45), Oct. 21, 1983.

382. HR 3324. Close Up Foundation Grants. Passage of the bill to authorize $1.5 million annually for fiscal 1983-85 for Allen J. Ellender Fellowships to allow low-income high school students to participate in seminars conducted by the Close Up Foundation. The bill also increased the annual authorization level in fiscal 1984 and 1985 for the law school clinical experience program to $2 million, removed the program from the state education block grant and instead earmarked $500,000 within the secretary of education's discretionary fund for the program. Passed 233-78: R 49-74; D 184-4 (ND 130-0, SD 54-4), Oct. 21, 1983. A "nay" was a vote supporting the president's position.

383. HR 3929. Federal Supplemental Unemployment Compensation. Adoption of the conference report on the bill to extend until March 31, 1985, the program of federal supplemental unemployment compensation payments for a minimum of eight weeks and up to a maximum of 14 weeks to unemployed persons who have exhausted all other state and federal unemployment benefits. Adopted 300-5: R 113-5; D 187-0 (ND 128-0, SD 59-0), Oct. 21, 1983.

384. Procedural Motion. Hansen, R-Utah, motion to approve the House *Journal* of Monday, Oct. 24. Motion agreed to 360-19: R 138-11; D 222-8 (ND 141-7, SD 81-1), Oct. 25, 1983.

385. HR 1062. Oregon Lands. Udall, D-Ariz., motion to table (kill) the Lujan, R-N.M., motion to refer to the Interior and Insular Affairs Committee, together with President Reagan's Oct. 19 veto message, the bill to authorize the secretary of the interior to convey, without consideration, certain lands in Lane County, Ore. Motion agreed to 273-144: R 20-141; D 253-3 (ND 170-0, SD 83-3), Oct. 25, 1983. A "nay" was a vote supporting the president's position.

386. HR 1062. Oregon Lands. Passage, over President Reagan's Oct. 19 veto, of the bill to authorize the secretary of the interior to convey, without consideration, certain lands in Lane County, Ore. Passed 297-125: R 42-121; D 255-4 (ND 170-2, SD 85-2), Oct. 25, 1983. A two-thirds majority of those present and voting (282 in this case) of both houses is required to override a veto. A "nay" was a vote supporting the president's position. (Subsequently, the Senate also voted to override the veto *(see vote 304, p. 50-S),* thus the bill was enacted into law.)

387. HR 4091. School Lunch and Child Nutrition Amendments. Perkins, D-Ky., motion to suspend the rules and pass the bill to raise income eligibility standards and reduce student prices for federally subsidized lunches and breakfasts and to make other changes in federal child nutrition programs. Motion agreed to 306-114: R 53-110; D 253-4 (ND 169-0, SD 84-4), Oct. 25, 1983. A two-thirds majority of those present and voting (280 in this case) is required for passage under suspension of the rules. A "nay" was a vote supporting the president's position.

388. H Con Res 187. Aquino Assassination. Solarz, D-N.Y., motion to suspend the rules and adopt the concurrent resolution deploring the assassination of opposition leader Benigno S. Aquino Jr. in the Philippines, stating the sense of Congress that all steps should be taken toward a full investigation of the assassination, stating that U.S. policy should support genuine, free and fair elections in the Philippines in May 1984, and stating that the United States should take the outcome of the Aquino assassination investigation and the May 1984 elections into account in conducting its relations with the Philippines. Motion agreed to 413-3: R 156-2; D 257-1 (ND 170-0, SD 87-1), Oct. 25, 1983. A two-thirds majority of those present and voting (281 in this case) is required for adoption under suspension of the rules.

KEY

Y	Voted for (yea).
#	Paired for.
+	Announced for.
N	Voted against (nay).
X	Paired against.
-	Announced against.
P	Voted "present".
C	Voted "present" to avoid possible conflict of interest.
?	Did not vote or otherwise make a position known.

Democrats   *Republicans*

	381	382	383	384	385	386	387	388
ALABAMA								
1 *Edwards*	?	?	?	?	N	N	N	Y
2 *Dickinson*	Y	N	?	N	N	N	N	Y
3 Nichols	?	?	?	Y	Y	Y	Y	Y
4 Bevill	N	Y	Y	Y	Y	?	?	Y
5 Flippo	?	?	?	Y	Y	Y	Y	Y
6 Erdreich	N	Y	Y	Y	Y	Y	Y	Y
7 Shelby	?	?	?	Y	N	Y	Y	Y
ALASKA								
AL *Young*	?	?	?	?	N	N	Y	N
ARIZONA								
1 *McCain*	Y	N	Y	N	N	N	N	P
2 Udall	N	Y	Y	Y	Y	Y	Y	Y
3 *Stump*	#	?	?	Y	N	N	N	N
4 *Rudd*	#	X	?	Y	N	N	N	N
5 McNulty	N	Y	Y	Y	Y	Y	Y	Y
ARKANSAS								
1 Alexander	N	Y	Y	Y	Y	Y	Y	Y
2 *Bethune*	?	?	?	?	Y	Y	Y	Y
3 *Hammerschmidt*	Y	N	Y	N	N	Y	N	Y
4 Anthony	?	?	?	Y	Y	Y	Y	Y
CALIFORNIA								
1 Bosco	N	Y	Y	Y	?	Y	Y	Y
2 *Chappie*	Y	Y	N	N	N	Y	N	Y
3 Matsui	N	Y	Y	Y	Y	Y	Y	Y
4 Fazio	?	?	?	Y	Y	Y	Y	Y
5 Burton	?	?	?	Y	Y	Y	Y	Y
6 Boxer	N	Y	Y	Y	Y	Y	Y	Y
7 Miller	N	Y	Y	Y	Y	Y	Y	Y
8 Dellums	N	Y	Y	Y	Y	Y	Y	Y
9 Stark	X	?	?	Y	Y	Y	Y	Y
10 Edwards	N	Y	Y	Y	Y	Y	Y	Y
11 Lantos	N	Y	Y	Y	Y	Y	Y	Y
12 *Zschau*	Y	N	Y	N	N	N	N	Y
13 Mineta	N	Y	Y	Y	Y	Y	Y	Y
14 *Shumway*	?	?	?	Y	N	N	N	Y
15 Coelho	?	?	?	Y	Y	Y	Y	Y
16 Panetta	N	Y	Y	Y	Y	Y	Y	Y
17 *Pashayan*	Y	N	Y	N	N	N	N	Y
18 Lehman	N	Y	Y	Y	Y	Y	Y	Y
19 *Lagomarsino*	Y	N	Y	Y	N	N	N	Y
20 *Thomas*	Y	N	Y	N	N	N	N	Y
21 *Fiedler*	?	?	?	Y	Y	Y	Y	Y
22 *Moorhead*	Y	N	Y	N	N	N	N	Y
23 Beilenson	N	Y	Y	Y	Y	Y	?	Y
24 Waxman	N	Y	Y	Y	Y	Y	Y	Y
25 Roybal	X	?	?	Y	N	Y	Y	Y
26 Berman	N	Y	Y	Y	Y	Y	Y	Y
27 Levine	N	Y	Y	Y	Y	Y	Y	Y
28 Dixon	X	?	?	Y	Y	Y	Y	Y
29 Hawkins	N	Y	Y	Y	Y	Y	Y	Y
30 Martinez	N	Y	?	Y	Y	Y	Y	Y
31 Dymally	N	Y	Y	P	Y	Y	Y	Y
32 Anderson	?	?	?	Y	Y	Y	Y	Y
33 *Dreier*	Y	N	N	Y	N	N	N	N
34 Torres	N	Y	Y	Y	Y	Y	Y	Y
35 *Lewis*	Y	Y	Y	N	N	Y	N	P
36 Brown	N	Y	Y	Y	Y	Y	Y	Y
37 *McCandless*	Y	N	Y	N	N	N	N	Y
38 Patterson	N	Y	Y	Y	Y	Y	Y	Y
39 *Dannemeyer*	#	?	?	Y	N	N	N	N
40 *Badham*	#	?	?	Y	N	N	N	N
41 *Lowery*	Y	Y	Y	Y	N	N	N	Y
42 *Lungren*	Y	N	Y	N	N	N	N	Y
43 *Packard*	Y	N	Y	N	N	N	Y	Y
44 Bates	N	Y	Y	Y	Y	Y	Y	?
45 *Hunter*	?	?	?	Y	N	Y	N	Y
COLORADO								
1 Schroeder	N	Y	Y	N	Y	Y	Y	Y
2 Wirth	N	Y	Y	Y	Y	Y	Y	Y
3 Kogovsek	N	Y	Y	Y	Y	Y	Y	Y
4 *Brown*	Y	Y	Y	Y	N	Y	N	Y
5 *Kramer*	Y	N	Y	N	Y	N	N	Y
6 *Schaefer*	Y	N	N	Y	N	N	N	Y
CONNECTICUT								
1 Kennelly	N	Y	Y	Y	Y	Y	Y	Y
2 Gejdenson	N	Y	Y	N	Y	Y	Y	Y
3 Morrison	N	Y	Y	Y	Y	Y	Y	Y
4 *McKinney*	?	#	?	Y	N	N	Y	Y
5 Ratchford	N	Y	Y	Y	Y	Y	Y	Y
6 *Johnson*	Y	Y	Y	N	Y	Y	Y	Y
DELAWARE								
AL Carper	Y	Y	Y	Y	Y	Y	Y	Y
FLORIDA								
1 Hutto	Y	N	Y	Y	Y	Y	Y	Y
2 Fuqua	?	?	?	Y	Y	Y	Y	Y
3 Bennett	Y	Y	Y	Y	Y	Y	Y	Y
4 Chappell	Y	+	Y	Y	Y	Y	Y	Y
5 *McCollum*	?	X	?	Y	N	N	N	Y
6 MacKay	X	?	?	Y	Y	Y	Y	Y
7 Gibbons	?	?	?	Y	Y	Y	Y	Y
8 *Young*	Y	N	Y	Y	N	N	N	Y
9 *Bilirakis*	Y	N	Y	N	N	Y	Y	Y
10 Ireland	?	?	?	Y	Y	Y	Y	Y
11 Nelson	N	Y	Y	Y	Y	Y	Y	Y
12 Lewis	Y	Y	Y	N	N	N	Y	Y
13 *Mack*	#	?	?	?	N	N	N	Y
14 Mica	?	?	?	?	Y	Y	Y	Y
15 *Shaw*	Y	Y	Y	N	N	N	N	Y
16 Smith	?	?	?	Y	Y	Y	Y	Y
17 Lehman	?	?	?	Y	Y	Y	Y	Y
18 Pepper	X	?	?	?	Y	Y	Y	Y
19 Fascell	N	Y	Y	Y	Y	Y	Y	Y
GEORGIA								
1 Thomas	Y	Y	Y	Y	Y	Y	Y	Y
2 Hatcher	?	?	?	?	?	Y	Y	Y
3 Ray	N	Y	Y	Y	Y	N	Y	Y
4 Levitas	Y	Y	Y	Y	Y	Y	Y	Y
5 Fowler	N	Y	Y	Y	Y	Y	Y	Y
6 *Gingrich*	Y	Y	Y	?	N	Y	N	Y
7 Vacancy								
8 Rowland	N	Y	Y	Y	Y	Y	Y	Y
9 Jenkins	N	Y	Y	Y	Y	Y	Y	Y
10 Barnard	?	?	?	Y	?	Y	Y	Y
HAWAII								
1 Heftel	?	?	?	?	?	Y	Y	Y
2 Akaka	N	Y	Y	Y	Y	Y	Y	Y
IDAHO								
1 *Craig*	Y	N	Y	N	N	N	N	Y
2 *Hansen*	Y	N	Y	N	N	N	N	Y
ILLINOIS								
1 Hayes	N	Y	Y	Y	Y	Y	Y	Y
2 Savage	N	Y	Y	Y	Y	Y	Y	Y
3 Russo	?	?	?	Y	Y	Y	Y	Y
4 *O'Brien*	?	?	?	N	Y	Y	Y	Y
5 Lipinski	?	?	?	N	Y	Y	Y	Y
6 *Hyde*	Y	Y	Y	Y	N	Y	N	Y
7 Collins	N	Y	Y	Y	Y	Y	Y	Y
8 Rostenkowski	?	?	?	Y	Y	Y	Y	Y
9 Yates	N	Y	Y	Y	Y	Y	Y	Y
10 *Porter*	?	?	?	N	Y	Y	Y	Y
11 Annunzio	N	Y	Y	Y	Y	Y	Y	Y
12 *Crane, P.*	Y	N	N	?	N	Y	N	Y
13 *Erlenborn*	Y	N	Y	N	N	N	N	Y
14 *Corcoran*	#	X	+	Y	N	N	N	Y
15 *Madigan*	Y	N	Y	N	N	N	N	Y
16 *Martin*	Y	N	Y	N	Y	N	N	Y
17 Evans	N	Y	Y	Y	Y	Y	Y	Y
18 *Michel*	#	?	?	Y	N	N	N	Y
19 *Crane, D.*	Y	N	N	N	N	N	N	Y
20 Durbin	N	Y	N	Y	Y	Y	Y	Y
21 Price	N	Y	Y	Y	Y	Y	Y	Y
22 Simon	?	?	?	Y	Y	Y	Y	Y
INDIANA								
1 Hall	N	Y	Y	Y	Y	Y	Y	Y
2 Sharp	N	Y	Y	Y	Y	Y	Y	Y
3 *Hiler*	Y	N	Y	N	N	N	N	Y
4 *Coats*	Y	N	Y	N	N	N	N	Y
5 *Hillis*	?	?	?	Y	N	N	N	Y

ND - Northern Democrats   SD - Southern Democrats

Corresponding to Congressional Record Votes 408, 409, 410, 411, 412, 413, 414, 415

	381	382	383	384	385	386	387	388
6 ***Burton***	Y	N	Y	Y	N	N	N	Y
7 ***Myers***	Y	Y	Y	Y	N	N	N	Y
8 McCloskey	N	Y	Y	Y	Y	Y	Y	Y
9 Hamilton	N	Y	Y	Y	Y	Y	Y	Y
10 Jacobs	N	Y	Y	?	?	?	?	?
IOWA								
1 ***Leach***	?	?	?	Y	Y	Y	Y	Y
2 ***Tauke***	Y	N	Y	Y	Y	Y	N	Y
3 ***Evans***	N	Y	Y	N	N	N	Y	?
4 Smith	N	Y	Y	Y	Y	Y	Y	Y
5 Harkin	N	Y	Y	N	Y	Y	Y	Y
6 Bedell	N	Y	Y	Y	Y	Y	Y	Y
KANSAS								
1 ***Roberts***	Y	N	Y	N	N	N	N	Y
2 Slattery	N	Y	Y	Y	Y	Y	Y	Y
3 ***Winn***	#	?	?	Y	N	N	N	Y
4 Glickman	Y	Y	Y	?	Y	Y	Y	Y
5 ***Whittaker***	Y	Y	Y	Y	N	N	N	Y
KENTUCKY								
1 Hubbard	?	?	?	Y	Y	Y	Y	Y
2 Natcher	N	Y	Y	Y	Y	Y	Y	Y
3 Mazzoli	N	Y	Y	Y	Y	Y	Y	Y
4 ***Snyder***	?	?	?	Y	N	N	N	Y
5 ***Rogers***	Y	Y	Y	Y	N	N	Y	Y
6 ***Hopkins***	Y	N	Y	Y	N	N	N	Y
7 Perkins	N	Y	?	Y	Y	Y	Y	Y
LOUISIANA								
1 ***Livingston***	?	#	?	Y	N	N	N	Y
2 Boggs	N	Y	Y	Y	Y	Y	Y	Y
3 Tauzin	?	?	?	Y	Y	Y	Y	Y
4 Roemer	Y	Y	Y	N	Y	Y	Y	Y
5 Huckaby	N	Y	Y	Y	Y	Y	Y	Y
6 ***Moore***	Y	Y	Y	Y	Y	Y	N	Y
7 Breaux	Y	Y	Y	Y	Y	Y	Y	Y
8 Long	N	Y	Y	Y	Y	Y	Y	Y
MAINE								
1 ***McKernan***	Y	Y	Y	Y	Y	Y	Y	Y
2 ***Snowe***	N	Y	Y	Y	Y	Y	Y	Y
MARYLAND								
1 Dyson	Y	Y	Y	Y	Y	Y	Y	Y
2 Long	?	?	?	Y	Y	Y	Y	?
3 Mikulski	N	Y	Y	Y	Y	Y	Y	Y
4 ***Holt***	Y	N	Y	?	?	N	N	Y
5 Hoyer	N	Y	Y	Y	Y	Y	Y	Y
6 Byron	Y	Y	Y	Y	Y	Y	Y	Y
7 Mitchell	X	?	?	?	?	Y	Y	Y
8 Barnes	N	Y	Y	Y	Y	Y	Y	Y
MASSACHUSETTS								
1 ***Conte***	?	?	?	Y	N	Y	Y	Y
2 Boland	?	?	?	Y	Y	Y	Y	Y
3 Early	?	?	?	Y	Y	Y	Y	Y
4 Frank	?	?	?	Y	Y	Y	Y	Y
5 Shannon	N	Y	Y	Y	Y	Y	Y	Y
6 Mavroules	?	?	?	Y	Y	Y	Y	Y
7 Markey	N	Y	?	P	Y	Y	Y	Y
8 O'Neill								
9 Moakley	N	Y	Y	Y	Y	Y	Y	Y
10 Studds	N	Y	Y	Y	Y	Y	Y	Y
11 Donnelly	N	Y	Y	Y	Y	Y	Y	Y
MICHIGAN								
1 Conyers	N	Y	Y	?	Y	Y	Y	Y
2 ***Pursell***	N	N	Y	Y	N	N	Y	Y
3 Wolpe	X	?	?	Y	Y	Y	Y	Y
4 ***Siljander***	#	?	?	?	N	N	N	Y
5 ***Sawyer***	Y	Y	Y	Y	N	Y	Y	Y
6 Carr	N	Y	Y	Y	Y	Y	Y	Y
7 Kildee	N	Y	Y	Y	Y	Y	Y	Y
8 Traxler	?	?	?	Y	Y	Y	Y	Y
9 ***Vander Jagt***	Y	Y	Y	P	N	N	Y	Y
10 Albosta	?	?	?	Y	Y	Y	Y	Y
11 ***Davis***	Y	Y	Y	Y	N	N	?	Y
12 Bonior	N	Y	Y	?	Y	Y	Y	Y
13 Crockett	N	Y	Y	?	Y	Y	?	Y
14 Hertel	N	Y	Y	Y	Y	Y	Y	Y
15 Ford	N	Y	Y	?	Y	Y	Y	Y
16 Dingell	N	Y	Y	?	Y	N	Y	Y
17 Levin	N	Y	Y	Y	Y	Y	Y	Y
18 ***Broomfield***	#	?	?	Y	N	N	N	Y
MINNESOTA								
1 Penny	N	Y	Y	Y	Y	Y	Y	Y
2 ***Weber***	Y	N	Y	Y	Y	Y	N	Y
3 ***Frenzel***	Y	Y	Y	Y	N	Y	Y	Y
4 Vento	X	?	?	Y	Y	Y	Y	Y
5 Sabo	N	Y	Y	N	Y	Y	Y	Y
6 Sikorski	N	Y	Y	N	Y	Y	Y	Y

	381	382	383	384	385	386	387	388
7 ***Stangeland***	Y	Y	Y	Y	N	N	Y	Y
8 Oberstar	-	+	+	?	Y	Y	Y	Y
MISSISSIPPI								
1 Whitten	N	Y	Y	Y	Y	Y	Y	Y
2 ***Franklin***	Y	Y	Y	Y	N	N	N	Y
3 Montgomery	Y	N	Y	Y	Y	Y	N	Y
4 Dowdy	N	?	Y	Y	Y	Y	Y	Y
5 ***Lott***	#	?	?	Y	N	N	N	Y
MISSOURI								
1 Clay	?	?	?	?	Y	Y	Y	Y
2 Young	X	?	?	Y	Y	Y	Y	Y
3 Gephardt	N	Y	Y	Y	Y	Y	?	Y
4 Skelton	Y	Y	Y	Y	Y	Y	Y	Y
5 Wheat	N	Y	Y	Y	Y	Y	Y	Y
6 ***Coleman***	Y	Y	Y	Y	N	Y	Y	Y
7 ***Taylor***	Y	N	Y	Y	N	N	Y	Y
8 ***Emerson***	Y	N	Y	?	N	N	Y	Y
9 Volkmer	N	Y	Y	Y	Y	Y	Y	Y
MONTANA								
1 Williams	?	?	?	?	Y	Y	Y	Y
2 ***Marlenee***	Y	Y	Y	Y	N	N	N	P
NEBRASKA								
1 ***Bereuter***	Y	Y	Y	?	N	N	N	Y
2 ***Daub***	Y	Y	Y	Y	N	N	N	Y
3 ***Smith***	Y	Y	Y	Y	N	N	N	Y
NEVADA								
1 Reid	N	Y	Y	Y	Y	Y	Y	Y
2 ***Vucanovich***	#	X	?	Y	N	N	N	Y
NEW HAMPSHIRE								
1 D'Amours	?	?	?	?	?	?	?	?
2 ***Gregg***	Y	N	Y	Y	N	N	Y	Y
NEW JERSEY								
1 Florio	X	?	?	Y	Y	Y	Y	Y
2 Hughes	N	Y	Y	Y	Y	Y	Y	Y
3 Howard	N	Y	Y	Y	Y	Y	Y	Y
4 ***Smith***	Y	Y	Y	Y	Y	N	Y	Y
5 ***Roukema***	Y	N	Y	?	?	N	N	Y
6 Dwyer	N	Y	Y	Y	Y	Y	Y	Y
7 ***Rinaldo***	Y	Y	Y	Y	Y	N	Y	Y
8 Roe	N	Y	Y	Y	Y	Y	Y	Y
9 Torricelli	N	Y	Y	Y	Y	Y	Y	Y
10 Rodino	X	?	?	?	?	?	?	?
11 Minish	N	Y	Y	Y	Y	Y	Y	Y
12 ***Courter***	Y	Y	Y	Y	Y	N	N	Y
13 ***Forsythe***	#	#	+	N	N	N	N	Y
14 Guarini	X	?	?	Y	Y	Y	Y	Y
NEW MEXICO								
1 ***Lujan***	Y	N	Y	Y	N	N	Y	Y
2 ***Skeen***	?	?	?	Y	N	N	N	Y
3 Richardson	N	Y	Y	Y	Y	Y	Y	Y
NEW YORK								
1 ***Carney***	Y	N	Y	Y	N	N	N	Y
2 Downey	N	Y	Y	Y	Y	Y	Y	Y
3 Mrazek	X	?	?	Y	Y	Y	Y	Y
4 ***Lent***	?	Y	Y	?	?	?	?	?
5 ***McGrath***	Y	N	Y	Y	N	Y	Y	Y
6 Addabbo	X	#	?	Y	Y	Y	Y	Y
7 Ackerman	N	Y	Y	Y	Y	Y	Y	Y
8 Scheuer	N	Y	Y	Y	Y	Y	Y	Y
9 Ferraro	N	Y	Y	Y	Y	Y	Y	Y
10 Schumer	N	Y	Y	Y	Y	Y	Y	Y
11 Towns	N	Y	Y	?	Y	Y	Y	Y
12 Owens	N	Y	Y	Y	Y	Y	Y	Y
13 Solarz	?	?	?	?	?	?	?	?
14 ***Molinari***	Y	Y	Y	Y	N	N	N	Y
15 ***Green***	?	?	?	Y	Y	N	N	Y
16 Rangel	N	Y	Y	?	Y	Y	Y	Y
17 Weiss	N	Y	Y	Y	Y	Y	Y	Y
18 Garcia	X	?	?	Y	Y	Y	Y	Y
19 Biaggi	?	?	?	Y	Y	Y	Y	Y
20 Ottinger	N	Y	Y	P	Y	Y	Y	Y
21 ***Fish***	?	?	?	Y	Y	N	Y	Y
22 ***Gilman***	N	Y	Y	Y	N	N	Y	Y
23 Stratton	N	Y	Y	Y	Y	Y	Y	Y
24 ***Solomon***	Y	N	Y	Y	N	Y	N	?
25 ***Boehlert***	#	#	?	Y	N	N	Y	Y
26 ***Martin***	Y	Y	?	?	N	Y	Y	Y
27 ***Wortley***	Y	N	Y	Y	N	N	Y	Y
28 McHugh	N	Y	Y	Y	Y	Y	Y	Y
29 ***Horton***	Y	Y	Y	Y	Y	Y	Y	Y
30 ***Conable***	Y	N	Y	Y	N	?	N	Y
31 ***Kemp***	?	?	?	Y	N	N	N	Y
32 LaFalce	N	Y	Y	Y	Y	Y	Y	Y
33 Nowak	?	?	?	Y	Y	Y	Y	Y
34 Lundine	?	?	?	Y	Y	Y	Y	Y

	381	382	383	384	385	386	387	388
NORTH CAROLINA								
1 Jones	N	Y	Y	Y	Y	Y	Y	Y
2 Valentine	N	Y	Y	Y	Y	Y	Y	P
3 Whitley	N	Y	Y	Y	Y	Y	Y	Y
4 Andrews	N	Y	Y	Y	Y	Y	Y	Y
5 Neal	?	?	?	Y	Y	Y	Y	Y
6 Britt	N	Y	Y	Y	Y	Y	Y	Y
7 Rose	N	Y	Y	Y	Y	Y	Y	Y
8 Hefner	N	Y	Y	Y	Y	Y	Y	Y
9 ***Martin***	Y	N	Y	Y	N	Y	N	Y
10 ***Broyhill***	Y	N	Y	Y	N	Y	N	Y
11 Clarke	-	+	+	Y	Y	Y	Y	Y
NORTH DAKOTA								
AL Dorgan	?	?	?	Y	Y	Y	Y	Y
OHIO								
1 Luken	N	Y	Y	Y	Y	Y	Y	Y
2 ***Gradison***	Y	N	Y	Y	N	Y	N	Y
3 Hall	N	Y	Y	Y	Y	Y	Y	Y
4 ***Oxley***	Y	Y	Y	Y	N	N	N	Y
5 ***Latta***	Y	N	Y	Y	N	N	N	Y
6 ***McEwen***	Y	N	Y	Y	N	N	N	Y
7 ***DeWine***	Y	N	Y	Y	Y	Y	N	Y
8 ***Kindness***	Y	N	?	Y	N	N	N	Y
9 Kaptur	N	Y	Y	Y	Y	Y	Y	Y
10 ***Miller***	Y	N	Y	N	N	N	N	Y
11 Eckart	N	Y	Y	Y	Y	Y	Y	Y
12 ***Kasich***	Y	N	Y	Y	N	N	N	Y
13 Pease	N	Y	Y	Y	Y	Y	Y	Y
14 Seiberling	N	Y	Y	?	Y	Y	Y	Y
15 ***Wylie***	Y	Y	Y	Y	N	N	N	Y
16 ***Regula***	Y	N	Y	Y	Y	Y	Y	Y
17 ***Williams***	?	?	?	?	?	?	?	?
18 Applegate	N	Y	Y	?	Y	Y	Y	Y
19 Feighan	N	Y	Y	Y	Y	Y	Y	Y
20 Oakar	N	Y	Y	Y	Y	Y	Y	Y
21 Stokes	X	?	?	?	Y	Y	Y	Y
OKLAHOMA								
1 Jones	N	Y	Y	Y	Y	Y	Y	Y
2 Synar	N	Y	+	Y	Y	Y	Y	Y
3 Watkins	N	Y	Y	Y	Y	Y	Y	Y
4 McCurdy	X	?	Y	?	?	Y	Y	Y
5 ***Edwards***	Y	Y	Y	N	Y	Y	N	Y
6 English	?	?	?	Y	Y	Y	Y	Y
OREGON								
1 AuCoin	?	?	?	Y	Y	Y	Y	Y
2 ***Smith, R.***	Y	Y	Y	Y	N	N	Y	Y
3 Wyden	N	Y	Y	Y	Y	Y	Y	Y
4 Weaver	?	Y	Y	Y	Y	Y	Y	Y
5 ***Smith, D.***	Y	N	N	Y	N	Y	N	Y
PENNSYLVANIA								
1 Foglietta	N	Y	Y	Y	Y	Y	Y	Y
2 Gray	N	Y	Y	?	Y	Y	Y	Y
3 Borski	N	Y	Y	Y	Y	Y	Y	Y
4 Kolter	N	Y	Y	Y	Y	Y	Y	Y
5 ***Schulze***	Y	N	Y	Y	N	N	N	Y
6 Yatron	N	Y	Y	Y	Y	Y	Y	Y
7 Edgar	N	Y	Y	Y	Y	Y	Y	Y
8 Kostmayer	N	Y	Y	Y	Y	Y	Y	Y
9 ***Shuster***	Y	N	Y	Y	N	N	N	Y
10 ***McDade***	Y	Y	Y	Y	N	N	Y	Y
11 Harrison	N	Y	Y	Y	Y	Y	Y	Y
12 Murtha	N	Y	Y	?	?	?	?	?
13 ***Coughlin***	?	?	?	Y	N	N	Y	Y
14 Coyne	?	?	?	Y	Y	Y	Y	Y
15 ***Ritter***	Y	N	Y	Y	N	Y	N	Y
16 ***Walker***	Y	N	Y	N	N	N	N	Y
17 ***Gekas***	Y	N	Y	Y	N	N	Y	Y
18 Walgren	?	?	?	Y	Y	Y	Y	Y
19 ***Goodling***	Y	Y	Y	?	?	N	Y	Y
20 Gaydos	N	Y	Y	Y	Y	Y	Y	Y
21 ***Ridge***	?	+	+	Y	Y	N	Y	Y
22 Murphy	N	Y	Y	Y	Y	Y	Y	Y
23 ***Clinger***	Y	Y	Y	Y	N	Y	Y	Y
RHODE ISLAND								
1 St Germain	?	?	?	?	Y	Y	Y	Y
2 ***Schneider***	X	Y	Y	Y	Y	Y	Y	Y
SOUTH CAROLINA								
1 ***Hartnett***	#	?	?	Y	N	N	N	Y
2 ***Spence***	Y	N	Y	Y	N	N	N	Y
3 Derrick	N	Y	Y	?	Y	Y	Y	Y
4 ***Campbell***	Y	Y	Y	Y	N	N	N	Y
5 Spratt	?	?	?	Y	Y	Y	Y	Y
6 Tallon	N	Y	Y	Y	Y	Y	Y	Y
SOUTH DAKOTA								
AL Daschle	?	?	?	Y	Y	Y	Y	Y

	381	382	383	384	385	386	387	388
TENNESSEE								
1 ***Quillen***	Y	Y	Y	Y	N	N	Y	Y
2 ***Duncan***	#	?	?	Y	N	N	Y	Y
3 Lloyd	N	N	Y	Y	Y	Y	Y	Y
4 Cooper	N	Y	Y	Y	Y	Y	Y	Y
5 Boner	?	?	?	Y	Y	Y	Y	Y
6 Gore	N	Y	Y	Y	Y	Y	Y	Y
7 ***Sundquist***	Y	Y	Y	Y	N	N	N	Y
8 Jones	N	Y	Y	Y	Y	Y	Y	Y
9 Ford	?	?	?	Y	Y	Y	Y	Y
TEXAS								
1 Hall, S.	Y	Y	Y	Y	Y	Y	Y	Y
2 Wilson	Y	Y	Y	Y	Y	?	Y	Y
3 ***Bartlett***	?	?	?	Y	N	N	N	Y
4 Hall, R.	Y	Y	Y	Y	Y	Y	Y	Y
5 Bryant	N	Y	Y	Y	Y	Y	Y	Y
6 ***Gramm***	#	?	?	Y	N	N	N	Y
7 ***Archer***	#	Y	Y	Y	N	N	N	Y
8 ***Fields***	Y	N	?	Y	N	N	N	Y
9 Brooks	?	?	?	Y	Y	Y	Y	Y
10 Pickle	N	Y	Y	Y	Y	Y	Y	Y
11 Leath	?	?	?	Y	Y	Y	N	Y
12 Wright	N	Y	Y	?	Y	Y	Y	Y
13 Hightower	?	?	?	Y	Y	Y	Y	Y
14 Patman	Y	Y	Y	Y	N	Y	Y	N
15 de la Garza	N	Y	Y	?	Y	Y	Y	Y
16 Coleman	?	?	?	Y	Y	Y	Y	Y
17 Stenholm	Y	Y	Y	Y	Y	Y	N	Y
18 Leland	N	Y	Y	Y	Y	Y	Y	Y
19 Hance	?	?	?	Y	Y	Y	Y	Y
20 Gonzalez	N	Y	Y	Y	Y	Y	Y	Y
21 ***Loeffler***	Y	N	Y	Y	N	N	N	Y
22 ***Paul***	?	?	?	Y	N	N	N	P
23 Kazen	?	?	?	Y	Y	Y	Y	Y
24 Frost	N	Y	Y	Y	Y	Y	Y	Y
25 Andrews	N	Y	Y	Y	Y	Y	Y	Y
26 Vandergriff	N	Y	Y	Y	Y	Y	Y	Y
27 Ortiz	N	Y	Y	Y	Y	Y	Y	Y
UTAH								
1 ***Hansen***	#	X	?	Y	N	N	N	Y
2 ***Marriott***	Y	N	Y	Y	N	N	Y	Y
3 ***Nielson***	Y	N	Y	Y	N	N	N	Y
VERMONT								
AL ***Jeffords***	Y	Y	Y	Y	N	Y	Y	Y
VIRGINIA								
1 ***Bateman***	Y	N	Y	Y	N	N	N	Y
2 ***Whitehurst***	?	?	?	Y	N	N	N	Y
3 ***Bliley***	Y	N	Y	Y	N	N	N	Y
4 Sisisky	N	Y	Y	Y	Y	Y	Y	Y
5 Daniel	Y	N	Y	Y	N	N	N	Y
6 Olin	Y	Y	Y	Y	Y	Y	Y	Y
7 ***Robinson***	Y	N	Y	Y	N	N	N	Y
8 ***Parris***	Y	N	Y	Y	N	Y	N	Y
9 Boucher	N	Y	Y	Y	Y	Y	Y	Y
10 ***Wolf***	Y	N	Y	Y	N	Y	N	Y
WASHINGTON								
1 ***Pritchard***	?	?	?	?	?	?	?	?
2 Swift	N	Y	Y	Y	Y	Y	Y	Y
3 Bonker	N	Y	Y	Y	Y	Y	Y	Y
4 ***Morrison***	Y	N	Y	Y	N	Y	Y	Y
5 Foley	?	?	?	?	Y	Y	Y	Y
6 Dicks	N	Y	Y	Y	Y	Y	Y	Y
7 Lowry	N	Y	Y	Y	Y	Y	Y	Y
8 ***Chandler***	Y	N	Y	Y	N	Y	Y	Y
WEST VIRGINIA								
1 Mollohan	N	Y	Y	Y	Y	Y	Y	Y
2 Staggers	N	Y	Y	Y	Y	Y	Y	Y
3 Wise	+	+	+	Y	Y	Y	Y	Y
4 Rahall	X	?	?	?	Y	Y	Y	Y
WISCONSIN								
1 Aspin	N	Y	Y	Y	Y	Y	Y	Y
2 Kastenmeier	N	Y	Y	Y	Y	Y	Y	Y
3 ***Gunderson***	Y	N	Y	Y	Y	N	Y	Y
4 Zablocki	N	Y	Y	Y	Y	Y	Y	Y
5 Moody	N	Y	Y	Y	Y	Y	Y	Y
6 ***Petri***	Y	N	Y	Y	N	N	Y	Y
7 Obey	N	Y	Y	?	Y	Y	Y	Y
8 ***Roth***	Y	N	Y	Y	N	N	N	Y
9 ***Sensenbrenner***	Y	N	Y	Y	N	N	N	Y
WYOMING								
AL ***Cheney***	Y	Y	Y	Y	N	N	N	Y

Southern states - Ala., Ark., Fla., Ga., Ky., La., Miss., N.C., Okla., S.C., Tenn., Texas, Va.

389. HR 4169. Budget Reconciliation. Adoption of the rule (H Res 344) providing for House floor consideration of the bill to reduce projected federal spending by $8.5 billion over fiscal 1984-86 in partial compliance with reconciliation instructions in the fiscal 1984 budget resolution. Adopted 224-198: R 88-76; D 136-122 (ND 98-72, SD 38-50), Oct. 25, 1983.

390. HR 4169. Budget Reconciliation. Jones, D-Okla., amendment to delay the planned 4 percent pay raise for federal civilian employees from Oct. 1, 1983, to Jan. 1, 1984, thus increasing total three-year savings under the bill to $10.3 billion. Adopted 245-176: R 133-32; D 112-144 (ND 55-115, SD 57-29), Oct. 25, 1983. (The amendment previously had been adopted by voice vote in the Committee of the Whole. The bill, as amended, subsequently was passed by voice vote.)

391. HR 4185. Defense Department Appropriations, Fiscal 1984. Montgomery, D-Miss., amendment to add $81.7 million to the bill for the purchase of aircraft for the Army and for initial procurement of a new radar system. Adopted 219-193: R 96-66; D 123-127 (ND 54-108, SD 69-19), Oct. 26, 1983.

392. HR 4185. Defense Department Appropriations, Fiscal 1984. Addabbo, D-N.Y., amendment to provide $218 million for the Navy's frigate construction program. The money would not be a new appropriation but would come from shipbuilding funds appropriated in previous years. Adopted 287-140: R 66-99; D 221-41 (ND 165-10, SD 56-31), Oct. 26, 1983.

393. HR 4185. Defense Department Appropriations, Fiscal 1984. Bennett, D-Fla., amendment to add $355.5 million for the Navy shipbuilding program. Rejected 85-342: R 49-116; D 36-226 (ND 8-165, SD 28-61), Oct. 26, 1983.

KEY

- Y Voted for (yea).
- # Paired for.
- + Announced for.
- N Voted against (nay).
- X Paired against.
- - Announced against.
- P Voted "present".
- C Voted "present" to avoid possible conflict of interest.
- ? Did not vote or otherwise make a position known.

Democrats   *Republicans*

	389	390	391	392	393
ALABAMA					
1 *Edwards*	Y	Y	N	Y	N
2 *Dickinson*	Y	Y	Y	N	Y
3 Nichols	Y	Y	Y	N	Y
4 Bevill	Y	Y	Y	Y	N
5 Flippo	Y	Y	Y	N	N
6 Erdreich	N	Y	N	N	N
7 Shelby	Y	Y	Y	N	N
ALASKA					
AL *Young*	Y	N	Y	Y	N
ARIZONA					
1 *McCain*	Y	Y	Y	N	Y
2 Udall	Y	N	N	Y	N
3 *Stump*	N	N	Y	N	Y
4 *Rudd*	Y	Y	Y	N	Y
5 McNulty	N	Y	N	Y	N
ARKANSAS					
1 Alexander	Y	N	N	?	N
2 *Bethune*	N	Y	Y	N	Y
3 *Hammerschmidt*	Y	Y	Y	N	N
4 Anthony	Y	Y	N	N	N
CALIFORNIA					
1 Bosco	Y	N	?	Y	N
2 *Chappie*	Y	Y	Y	N	N
3 Matsui	Y	N	N	Y	N
4 Fazio	Y	N	N	Y	N
5 Burton	Y	N	N	Y	N
6 Boxer	N	N	N	Y	N
7 Miller	N	Y	N	Y	N
8 Dellums	-N	N	N	Y	N
9 Stark	N	N	Y	Y	N
10 Edwards	N	N	N	Y	N
11 Lantos	Y	N	N	Y	?
12 *Zschau*	Y	Y	N	N	N
13 Mineta	Y	N	?	Y	N
14 *Shumway*	N	Y	Y	N	Y
15 Coelho	N	N	N	Y	?
16 Panetta	Y	Y	Y	Y	Y
17 *Pashayan*	N	Y	Y	Y	Y
18 Lehman	?	N	?	Y	N
19 *Lagomarsino*	N	N	Y	N	Y
20 *Thomas*	Y	Y	Y	N	N
21 *Fiedler*	N	N	Y	N	N
22 *Moorhead*	N	Y	Y	N	Y
23 Beilenson	Y	Y	N	Y	N
24 Waxman	Y	N	N	Y	N
25 Roybal	Y	Y	N	Y	N
26 Berman	Y	Y	N	Y	N
27 Levine	N	Y	N	Y	N
28 Dixon	Y	N	N	Y	N
29 Hawkins	Y	N	N	N	N
30 Martinez	Y	N	N	Y	N
31 Dymally	Y	N	N	Y	N
32 Anderson	N	N	Y	Y	N
33 *Dreier*	N	Y	Y	N	Y
34 Torres	N	N	N	Y	N
35 *Lewis*	Y	N	?	Y	Y
36 Brown	Y	N	Y	Y	N
37 *McCandless*	N	Y	N	N	N
38 Patterson	Y	Y	Y	Y	N
39 *Dannemeyer*	N	Y	Y	N	Y
40 *Badham*	Y	Y	Y	N	Y
41 *Lowery*	Y	Y	Y	N	Y
42 Lungren	N	Y	Y	N	Y

	389	390	391	392	393
43 *Packard*	N	Y	Y	N	Y
44 Bates	N	N	N	Y	N
45 *Hunter*	N	Y	Y	N	Y
COLORADO					
1 Schroeder	N	Y	N	Y	N
2 Wirth	Y	Y	N	Y	N
3 Kogovsek	Y	Y	N	Y	N
4 *Brown*	N	Y	N	N	N
5 *Kramer*	N	Y	Y	Y	N
6 *Schaefer*	Y	N	Y	N	N
CONNECTICUT					
1 Kennelly	Y	N	Y	Y	N
2 Gejdenson	N	N	N	Y	N
3 Morrison	N	Y	N	Y	N
4 *McKinney*	Y	N	N	Y	N
5 Ratchford	N	N	Y	Y	N
6 *Johnson*	N	Y	Y	N	N
DELAWARE					
AL Carper	N	Y	N	Y	N
FLORIDA					
1 Hutto	N	Y	Y	N	Y
2 Fuqua	N	Y	N	Y	N
3 Bennett	N	Y	Y	N	Y
4 Chappell	N	?	Y	N	Y
5 *McCollum*	N	Y	Y	N	N
6 MacKay	N	Y	Y	?	N
7 Gibbons	Y	Y	N	Y	N
8 *Young*	N	Y	N	Y	N
9 *Bilirakis*	N	Y	N	N	N
10 Ireland	N	Y	Y	N	Y
11 Nelson	N	Y	N	Y	N
12 *Lewis*	N	Y	N	N	N
13 *Mack*	N	N	N	N	N
14 Mica	N	Y	Y	Y	Y
15 *Shaw*	N	Y	N	N	N
16 Smith	Y	N	N	Y	N
17 Lehman	N	N	N	Y	N
18 Pepper	Y	Y	Y	Y	Y
19 Fascell	N	Y	N	Y	Y
GEORGIA					
1 Thomas	N	Y	Y	Y	N
2 Hatcher	Y	Y	Y	N	Y
3 Ray	N	Y	N	Y	N
4 Levitas	N	Y	Y	Y	N
5 Fowler	N	N	N	N	N
6 *Gingrich*	Y	Y	Y	N	N
7 Vacancy					
8 Rowland	N	N	Y	N	N
9 Jenkins	Y	Y	Y	N	N
10 Barnard	N	N	Y	N	Y
HAWAII					
1 Heftel	Y	N	Y	N	N
2 Akaka	Y	N	Y	Y	N
IDAHO					
1 *Craig*	N	Y	Y	N	N
2 *Hansen*	N	Y	Y	N	N
ILLINOIS					
1 Hayes	N	N	X	Y	N
2 Savage	N	N	N	Y	N
3 Russo	N	N	N	Y	N
4 *O'Brien*	Y	Y	N	Y	N
5 Lipinski	Y	N	Y	N	N
6 *Hyde*	Y	Y	Y	N	N
7 Collins	Y	N	?	Y	N
8 Rostenkowski	Y	?	N	Y	N
9 Yates	Y	N	N	Y	N
10 *Porter*	Y	Y	N	Y	N
11 Annunzio	Y	N	N	Y	N
12 *Crane, P.*	N	Y	Y	N	Y
13 *Erlenborn*	Y	?	Y	N	N
14 *Corcoran*	Y	Y	#	-	+
15 *Madigan*	Y	Y	Y	N	N
16 *Martin*	Y	Y	N	Y	N
17 Evans	N	N	Y	Y	N
18 *Michel*	Y	Y	N	Y	N
19 *Crane, D.*	N	Y	Y	N	Y
20 Durbin	N	Y	Y	Y	N
21 Price	Y	N	Y	N	Y
22 Simon	Y	?	Y	Y	N
INDIANA					
1 Hall	Y	N	N	Y	N
2 Sharp	N	Y	N	Y	N
3 *Hiler*	N	Y	N	Y	N
4 *Coats*	N	Y	N	Y	N
5 *Hillis*	Y	Y	Y	N	Y

	389	390	391	392	393
6 Burton	N	Y	Y	N	Y
7 Myers	Y	Y	N	Y	N
8 McCloskey	Y	N	N	Y	N
9 Hamilton	N	Y	N	Y	N
10 Jacobs	?	?	?	Y	N
IOWA					
1 Leach	N	Y	N	Y	N
2 Tauke	N	Y	N	Y	N
3 Evans	N	Y	N	N	N
4 Smith	Y	N	Y	N	N
5 Harkin	N	N	Y	Y	N
6 Bedell	N	Y	Y	Y	N
KANSAS					
1 Roberts	Y	Y	N	Y	N
2 Slattery	N	Y	N	Y	N
3 Winn	Y	Y	N	N	N
4 Glickman	N	Y	N	Y	N
5 Whittaker	Y	Y	Y	Y	N
KENTUCKY					
1 Hubbard	N	N	Y	N	N
2 Natcher	N	N	N	Y	N
3 Mazzoli	Y	Y	N	Y	N
4 Snyder	N	Y	N	Y	N
5 Rogers	Y	Y	Y	N	N
6 Hopkins	N	Y	Y	N	N
7 Perkins	N	N	N	Y	N
LOUISIANA					
1 Livingston	Y	Y	Y	N	?
2 Boggs	Y	N	Y	Y	Y
3 Tauzin	N	Y	Y	Y	N
4 Roemer	N	Y	Y	Y	Y
5 Huckaby	N	Y	Y	N	N
6 Moore	N	Y	N	Y	N
7 Breaux	N	Y	Y	Y	N
8 Long	Y	N	Y	Y	N
MAINE					
1 McKernan	Y	Y	N	N	Y
2 Snowe	Y	Y	N	N	Y
MARYLAND					
1 Dyson	Y	N	Y	N	Y
2 Long	Y	N	N	Y	N
3 Mikulski	Y	N	N	Y	N
4 Holt	Y	N	Y	N	Y
5 Hoyer	Y	N	N	Y	N
6 Byron	N	N	Y	Y	N
7 Mitchell	Y	N	-	-	?
8 Barnes	Y	N	N	Y	N
MASSACHUSETTS					
1 Conte	Y	Y	N	Y	N
2 Boland	Y	Y	?	Y	N
3 Early	N	N	?	Y	N
4 Frank	N	N	Y	N	N
5 Shannon	Y	N	?	Y	N
6 Mavroules	Y	N	Y	Y	N
7 Markey	Y	N	N	Y	N
8 O'Neill					
9 Moakley	Y	N	?	Y	N
10 Studds	N	N	N	Y	N
11 Donnelly	Y	Y	N	Y	N
MICHIGAN					
1 Conyers	Y	N	N	Y	N
2 Pursell	Y	Y	N	N	N
3 Wolpe	N	Y	N	Y	N
4 Siljander	N	Y	Y	N	Y
5 Sawyer	Y	Y	N	Y	N
6 Carr	Y	N	Y	N	N
7 Kildee	N	N	N	Y	N
8 Traxler	Y	N	N	Y	N
9 Vander Jagt	Y	Y	Y	N	N
10 Albosta	Y	Y	Y	Y	N
11 Davis	Y	N	Y	N	Y
12 Bonior	Y	N	?	Y	N
13 Crockett	Y	N	N	Y	N
14 Hertel	N	N	N	N	Y
15 Ford	Y	N	N	Y	N
16 Dingell	Y	N	Y	N	N
17 Levin	N	Y	N	Y	N
18 Broomfield	Y	Y	N	N	N
MINNESOTA					
1 Penny	N	Y	N	Y	N
2 Weber	N	Y	Y	N	N
3 Frenzel	N	Y	N	N	N
4 Vento	N	N	N	Y	N
5 Sabo	Y	N	Y	N	N
6 Sikorski	N	N	N	Y	N

	389	390	391	392	393
7 Stangeland	N	N	N	N	N
8 Oberstar	N	N	N	Y	N
MISSISSIPPI					
1 Whitten	N	N	N	Y	N
2 Franklin	Y	Y	Y	N	N
3 Montgomery	Y	Y	Y	Y	N
4 Dowdy	Y	N	Y	N	N
5 Lott	Y	Y	Y	N	Y
MISSOURI					
1 Clay	Y	N	N	Y	N
2 Young	Y	Y	Y	Y	N
3 Gephardt	Y	Y	Y	Y	N
4 Skelton	N	N	Y	Y	N
5 Wheat	Y	N	Y	Y	N
6 Coleman	Y	Y	Y	N	N
7 Taylor	Y	Y	Y	N	N
8 Emerson	N	Y	Y	Y	N
9 Volkmer	N	Y	Y	Y	N
MONTANA					
1 Williams	Y	Y	Y	Y	N
2 Marlenee	Y	Y	Y	N	Y
NEBRASKA					
1 Bereuter	N	Y	Y	Y	N
2 Daub	N	Y	N	Y	N
3 Smith	N	Y	N	Y	N
NEVADA					
1 Reid	N	N	Y	Y	N
2 Vucanovich	N	Y	Y	Y	Y
NEW HAMPSHIRE					
1 D'Amours	?	Y	Y	Y	N
2 Gregg	N	Y	N	Y	N
NEW JERSEY					
1 Florio	Y	N	Y	N	N
2 Hughes	N	Y	N	Y	N
3 Howard	Y	?	N	Y	N
4 Smith	Y	N	Y	N	Y
5 Roukema	N	Y	N	Y	N
6 Dwyer	Y	N	N	Y	N
7 Rinaldo	N	N	Y	Y	N
8 Roe	Y	N	N	Y	N
9 Torricelli	Y	N	N	Y	N
10 Rodino	#	?	N	Y	N
11 Minish	Y	N	N	Y	N
12 Courter	N	N	Y	N	N
13 Forsythe	Y	Y	N	?	N
14 Guarini	Y	N	Y	N	N
NEW MEXICO					
1 Lujan	Y	Y	Y	Y	N
2 Skeen	Y	Y	Y	Y	N
3 Richardson	N	Y	Y	Y	N
NEW YORK					
1 Carney	Y	N	Y	N	Y
2 Downey	Y	N	N	Y	N
3 Mrazek	N	N	N	Y	N
4 Lent	Y	N	Y	N	N
5 McGrath	Y	N	Y	N	Y
6 Addabbo	Y	N	N	Y	N
7 Ackerman	X	-	N	Y	N
8 Scheuer	N	N	N	Y	N
9 Ferraro	Y	N	N	Y	N
10 Schumer	Y	N	N	Y	N
11 Towns	N	N	N	Y	N
12 Owens	N	N	N	Y	N
13 Solarz	?	N	N	Y	N
14 Molinari	Y	N	Y	N	Y
15 Green	Y	N	N	Y	N
16 Rangel	Y	N	N	Y	N
17 Weiss	Y	N	N	Y	N
18 Garcia	Y	N	N	Y	N
19 Biaggi	Y	N	Y	N	N
20 Ottinger	N	N	N	Y	N
21 Fish	Y	Y	Y	N	N
22 Gilman	N	N	Y	N	Y
23 Stratton	Y	Y	Y	Y	N
24 Solomon	N	Y	Y	N	Y
25 Boehlert	Y	N	N	Y	N
26 Martin	Y	N	Y	N	Y
27 Wortley	Y	Y	?	N	Y
28 McHugh	Y	Y	Y	Y	N
29 Horton	Y	N	N	N	N
30 Conable	N	Y	N	Y	N
31 Kemp	Y	Y	Y	N	Y
32 LaFalce	Y	N	Y	N	N
33 Nowak	N	N	Y	N	Y
34 Lundine	N	Y	N	Y	N

	389	390	391	392	393
NORTH CAROLINA					
1 Jones	?	Y	Y	Y	N
2 Valentine	N	Y	Y	Y	N
3 Whitley	N	N	N	Y	N
4 Andrews	Y	Y	Y	Y	N
5 Neal	Y	Y	Y	Y	Y
6 Britt	N	Y	N	Y	N
7 Rose	Y	Y	Y	Y	N
8 Hefner	Y	?	N	Y	N
9 Martin	Y	Y	Y	Y	N
10 Broyhill	Y	Y	N	Y	N
11 Clarke	N	Y	Y	Y	N
NORTH DAKOTA					
AL Dorgan	N	Y	Y	Y	N
OHIO					
1 Luken	N	N	N	Y	N
2 Gradison	Y	Y	N	Y	N
3 Hall	Y	N	N	N	N
4 Oxley	Y	Y	Y	N	N
5 Latta	Y	Y	Y	N	N
6 McEwen	N	Y	Y	N	Y
7 DeWine	Y	N	Y	N	Y
8 Kindness	Y	Y	Y	N	N
9 Kaptur	Y	Y	Y	Y	N
10 Miller	N	Y	N	Y	N
11 Eckart	N	Y	Y	Y	N
12 Kasich	N	Y	N	Y	N
13 Pease	Y	Y	Y	Y	N
14 Seiberling	N	N	N	Y	N
15 Wylie	Y	Y	Y	N	N
16 Regula	Y	Y	Y	N	N
17 Williams	?	Y	Y	Y	N
18 Applegate	N	Y	Y	Y	N
19 Feighan	N	Y	Y	Y	N
20 Oakar	Y	N	Y	N	N
21 Stokes	Y	N	N	Y	N
OKLAHOMA					
1 Jones	Y	Y	Y	N	N
2 Synar	N	Y	Y	Y	N
3 Watkins	N	Y	Y	Y	N
4 McCurdy	N	?	Y	N	N
5 Edwards	Y	Y	Y	N	N
6 English	N	Y	Y	Y	N
OREGON					
1 AuCoin	N	Y	N	Y	N
2 Smith, R.	Y	Y	N	N	N
3 Wyden	N	Y	N	Y	N
4 Weaver	N	Y	Y	Y	N
5 Smith, D.	N	Y	Y	N	N
PENNSYLVANIA					
1 Foglietta	Y	N	N	N	Y
2 Gray	Y	N	N	Y	N
3 Borski	N	N	Y	N	N
4 Kolter	N	N	Y	Y	N
5 Schulze	Y	Y	N	N	N
6 Yatron	N	N	Y	N	N
7 Edgar	N	N	N	Y	Y
8 Kostmayer	Y	N	N	Y	?
9 Shuster	N	N	Y	N	N
10 McDade	Y	N	N	Y	N
11 Harrison	Y	N	?	Y	N
12 Murtha	?	?	?	?	N
13 Coughlin	Y	Y	N	Y	N
14 Coyne	Y	N	?	Y	N
15 Ritter	Y	Y	N	Y	N
16 Walker	N	Y	N	N	N
17 Gekas	?	Y	N	Y	N
18 Walgren	N	Y	N	Y	N
19 Goodling	N	N	N	Y	N
20 Gaydos	N	N	N	Y	N
21 Ridge	N	N	Y	N	N
22 Murphy	N	Y	Y	Y	N
23 Clinger	N	Y	N	Y	N
RHODE ISLAND					
1 St Germain	Y	N	Y	N	N
2 Schneider	Y	Y	N	Y	Y
SOUTH CAROLINA					
1 Hartnett	N	N	Y	N	Y
2 Spence	Y	N	Y	N	Y
3 Derrick	Y	Y	Y	Y	N
4 Campbell	N	Y	Y	Y	N
5 Spratt	N	Y	Y	Y	N
6 Tallon	Y	N	Y	Y	N
SOUTH DAKOTA					
AL Daschle	N	Y	Y	Y	N

	389	390	391	392	393
TENNESSEE					
1 Quillen	Y	Y	Y	N	Y
2 Duncan	Y	Y	Y	N	N
3 Lloyd	Y	Y	Y	N	Y
4 Cooper	N	Y	N	Y	N
5 Boner	N	N	Y	Y	N
6 Gore	N	N	Y	Y	N
7 Sundquist	N	Y	Y	Y	N
8 Jones	Y	N	Y	Y	N
9 Ford	Y	N	N	N	N
TEXAS					
1 Hall, S.	N	Y	Y	Y	N
2 Wilson	Y	Y	N	Y	N
3 Bartlett	Y	Y	Y	Y	N
4 Hall, R.	N	N	Y	Y	Y
5 Bryant	N	Y	Y	Y	Y
6 Gramm	N	Y	Y	N	N
7 Archer	Y	Y	Y	Y	N
8 Fields	N	Y	?	Y	N
9 Brooks	Y	Y	N	Y	N
10 Pickle	Y	Y	Y	Y	N
11 Leath	Y	N	Y	N	N
12 Wright	Y	Y	Y	Y	N
13 Hightower	N	Y	N	Y	N
14 Patman	N	Y	Y	Y	Y
15 de la Garza	Y	Y	Y	Y	N
16 Coleman	N	N	Y	N	Y
17 Stenholm	N	Y	Y	Y	N
18 Leland	Y	N	N	N	N
19 Hance	Y	N	Y	Y	N
20 Gonzalez	Y	N	?	Y	N
21 Loeffler	N	Y	Y	Y	N
22 Paul	N	Y	N	Y	N
23 Kazen	N	N	Y	Y	N
24 Frost	Y	Y	Y	Y	N
25 Andrews	N	Y	Y	Y	N
26 Vandergriff	N	N	Y	N	Y
27 Ortiz	N	Y	Y	Y	Y
UTAH					
1 Hansen	N	Y	Y	Y	N
2 Marriott	Y	Y	Y	Y	N
3 Nielson	N	Y	N	N	N
VERMONT					
AL Jeffords	N	Y	N	N	N
VIRGINIA					
1 Bateman	Y	Y	Y	N	Y
2 Whitehurst	Y	N	Y	N	Y
3 Bliley	Y	Y	Y	Y	N
4 Sisisky	N	N	Y	N	Y
5 Daniel	Y	Y	Y	N	Y
6 Olin	N	Y	Y	Y	N
7 Robinson	Y	Y	Y	N	N
8 Parris	N	N	Y	N	N
9 Boucher	Y	N	Y	Y	N
10 Wolf	N	N	N	N	N
WASHINGTON					
1 Pritchard	?	?	?	Y	N
2 Swift	Y	Y	N	Y	N
3 Bonker	Y	Y	N	Y	N
4 Morrison	Y	N	Y	N	N
5 Foley	Y	N	Y	Y	N
6 Dicks	Y	N	N	Y	N
7 Lowry	Y	N	Y	Y	N
8 Chandler	Y	Y	N	Y	N
WEST VIRGINIA					
1 Mollohan	N	N	Y	Y	Y
2 Staggers	N	N	Y	Y	N
3 Wise	N	Y	Y	Y	N
4 Rahall	Y	N	N	Y	N
WISCONSIN					
1 Aspin	Y	Y	Y	Y	N
2 Kastenmeier	N	N	N	Y	N
3 Gunderson	N	Y	Y	Y	N
4 Zablocki	Y	N	Y	Y	N
5 Moody	N	Y	Y	N	N
6 Petri	N	N	Y	N	N
7 Obey	Y	Y	N	Y	N
8 Roth	N	N	N	N	Y
9 Sensenbrenner	N	N	Y	Y	N
WYOMING					
AL Cheney	Y	Y	Y	N	N

Southern states · Ala., Ark., Fla., Ga., Ky., La., Miss., N.C., Okla., S.C., Tenn., Texas, Va.

KEY

Y Voted for (yea).
Paired for.
+ Announced for.
N Voted against (nay).
X Paired against.
- Announced against.
P Voted "present".
C Voted "present" to avoid possible conflict of interest.
? Did not vote or otherwise make a position known.

Democrats   *Republicans*

394. Procedural Motion. Solomon, R-N.Y., motion to approve the House *Journal* of Wednesday, Oct. 26. Motion agreed to 350-27: R 136-15; D 214-12 (ND 134-11, SD 80-1), Oct. 27, 1983.

395. HR 4139. Treasury, Postal Service, General Government Appropriations, Fiscal 1984. Frank, D-Mass., amendment to strike a section barring the Office of Management and Budget from reviewing agricultural marketing orders. Rejected 97-319: R 35-128; D 62-191 (ND 57-113, SD 5-78), Oct. 27, 1983.

396. HR 4139. Treasury, Postal Service, General Government Appropriations, Fiscal 1984. Roybal, D-Calif., motion that the Committee of the Whole rise and report back to the House the bill to make appropriations for the Treasury Department, Postal Service, executive offices and certain independent agencies in fiscal 1984. Motion rejected 193-229: R 28-135; D 165-94 (ND 115-58, SD 50-36), Oct. 27, 1983. (Agreement to the motion would have barred further amendments limiting expenditure of appropriated funds.)

397. HR 3231. Export Administration Act. Roth, R-Wis., amendment, as amended, to allow the president to continue to require licenses for exports to Coordinating Committee (COCOM) nations. Rejected 188-223: R 105-52; D 83-171 (ND 30-140, SD 53-31), Oct. 27, 1983. (This amendment previously had been adopted in the Committee of the Whole *(see vote 369, p. 110-H).)*

398. HR 3231. Export Administration Act. Erlenborn, R-Ill., motion to recommit the bill to the Foreign Affairs Committee with instructions to amend it to permit the president to continue to exercise export controls over subsidiaries of U.S. firms operating abroad. Motion rejected 124-285: R 104-53; D 20-232 (ND 10-159, SD 10-73), Oct. 27, 1983. A "yea" was a vote supporting the president's position.

	394	395	396	397	398
ALABAMA					
1 *Edwards*	Y	N	Y	N	N
2 *Dickinson*	N	N	N	Y	Y
3 Nichols	Y	N	N	Y	N
4 Bevill	Y	N	N	Y	N
5 Flippo	Y	N	Y	Y	N
6 Erdreich	Y	N	N	Y	N
7 Shelby	Y	N	N	Y	N
ALASKA					
AL *Young*	?	N	N	Y	Y
ARIZONA					
1 *McCain*	Y	N	N	Y	Y
2 Udall	?	N	Y	N	N
3 *Stump*	Y	N	N	Y	Y
4 *Rudd*	Y	N	N	Y	Y
5 McNulty	Y	N	Y	N	N
ARKANSAS					
1 Alexander	Y	N	Y	N	N
2 *Bethune*	Y	N	N	N	N
3 *Hammerschmidt*	Y	N	N	Y	N
4 Anthony	Y	N	Y	N	N
CALIFORNIA					
1 Bosco	Y	N	Y	N	N
2 *Chappie*	N	N	N	Y	Y
3 Matsui	Y	N	Y	N	N
4 Fazio	Y	N	Y	N	N
5 Burton	Y	Y	Y	?	?
6 Boxer	Y	N	N	N	N
7 Miller	Y	Y	Y	N	N
8 Dellums	Y	N	Y	N	N
9 Stark	?	Y	N	Y	N
10 Edwards	Y	Y	Y	N	N
11 Lantos	?	N	Y	N	N
12 *Zschau*	Y	N	N	N	N
13 Mineta	Y	?	Y	N	N
14 *Shumway*	Y	N	N	Y	N
15 Coelho	Y	N	N	N	N
16 Panetta	Y	N	Y	N	N
17 *Pashayan*	Y	N	N	Y	N
18 Lehman	Y	N	Y	N	N
19 *Lagomarsino*	Y	N	N	Y	Y
20 *Thomas*	Y	N	N	N	N
21 *Fiedler*	Y	N	Y	Y	Y
22 *Moorhead*	Y	N	N	Y	Y
23 Beilenson	Y	Y	Y	N	N
24 Waxman	Y	N	Y	N	N
25 Roybal	Y	N	Y	N	N
26 Berman	Y	N	Y	N	Y
27 Levine	Y	N	Y	N	N
28 Dixon	?	N	Y	N	N
29 Hawkins	?	N	Y	N	N
30 Martinez	?	N	Y	N	N
31 Dymally	P	N	Y	N	N
32 Anderson	Y	Y	Y	Y	N
33 *Dreier*	Y	N	N	Y	Y
34 Torres	Y	N	Y	N	N
35 *Lewis*	Y	N	N	N	N
36 Brown	Y	N	Y	N	N
37 *McCandless*	Y	N	Y	Y	Y
38 Patterson	Y	N	Y	N	N
39 *Dannemeyer*	Y	Y	N	Y	Y
40 *Badham*	Y	N	N	Y	Y
41 Lowery	?	N	N	N	N
42 Lungren	Y	Y	N	Y	Y

	394	395	396	397	398
43 *Packard*	Y	N	N	Y	Y
44 Bates	Y	N	Y	N	N
45 *Hunter*	Y	N	N	Y	Y
COLORADO					
1 Schroeder	N	N	Y	N	N
2 Wirth	Y	N	Y	N	N
3 Kogovsek	Y	N	Y	N	N
4 *Brown*	N	N	N	N	N
5 *Kramer*	Y	Y	N	Y	Y
6 *Schaefer*	Y	N	N	Y	Y
CONNECTICUT					
1 Kennelly	Y	Y	Y	N	N
2 Gejdenson	N	Y	Y	N	N
3 Morrison	Y	Y	X	?	
4 *McKinney*	Y	N	Y	N	N
5 Ratchford	Y	Y	Y	N	N
6 *Johnson*	Y	Y	Y	N	N
DELAWARE					
AL Carper	Y	Y	Y	N	N
FLORIDA					
1 Hutto	Y	N	N	Y	Y
2 Fuqua	Y	N	N	Y	N
3 Bennett	Y	N	N	Y	N
4 Chappell	?	N	N	Y	N
5 *McCollum*	Y	N	N	Y	Y
6 MacKay	Y	N	N	Y	N
7 Gibbons	Y	Y	N	N	N
8 *Young*	?	N	N	Y	Y
9 *Bilirakis*	Y	N	N	Y	Y
10 Ireland	Y	N	N	Y	Y
11 Nelson	Y	N	N	Y	N
12 *Lewis*	Y	Y	N	Y	N
13 *Mack*	Y	Y	N	Y	Y
14 Mica	Y	N	N	N	N
15 *Shaw*	Y	N	N	Y	N
16 Smith	Y	N	Y	N	N
17 Lehman	?	?	Y	N	N
18 Pepper	Y	N	Y	N	N
19 Fascell	Y	Y	Y	N	N
GEORGIA					
1 Thomas	Y	N	Y	Y	N
2 Hatcher	Y	N	Y	Y	N
3 Ray	N	N	Y	Y	Y
4 Levitas	Y	Y	Y	?	?
5 Fowler	Y	N	Y	N	N
6 *Gingrich*	?	N	N	Y	Y
7 Vacancy					
8 Rowland	?	N	Y	Y	N
9 Jenkins	Y	N	Y	N	N
10 Barnard	Y	N	N	Y	N
HAWAII					
1 Heftel	?	N	Y	N	N
2 Akaka	Y	N	Y	N	N
IDAHO					
1 *Craig*	Y	N	N	Y	Y
2 *Hansen*	?	N	N	Y	Y
ILLINOIS					
1 Hayes	Y	N	Y	N	N
2 Savage	Y	Y	Y	N	N
3 Russo	Y	Y	N	Y	N
4 *O'Brien*	?	?	?	?	?
5 Lipinski	N	N	N	Y	?
6 *Hyde*	Y	Y	N	Y	N
7 Collins	Y	Y	Y	N	N
8 Rostenkowski	Y	N	N	N	N
9 Yates	Y	Y	Y	Y	N
10 *Porter*	Y	N	N	Y	N
11 Annunzio	Y	N	N	N	N
12 *Crane, P.*	?	N	N	Y	Y
13 *Erlenborn*	?	?	N	Y	Y
14 *Corcoran*	Y	Y	N	#	#
15 *Madigan*	?	N	N	N	N
16 *Martin*	Y	N	Y	Y	Y
17 Evans	P	N	Y	N	N
18 *Michel*	Y	N	N	?	?
19 *Crane, D.*	Y	N	N	Y	N
20 Durbin	N	N	N	N	N
21 Price	Y	N	N	N	N
22 Simon	Y	Y	Y	?	?
INDIANA					
1 Hall	Y	N	Y	N	N
2 Sharp	Y	N	N	N	N
3 *Hiler*	Y	Y	N	Y	Y
4 *Coats*	Y	N	N	N	Y
5 *Hillis*	Y	N	N	Y	N

ND - Northern Democrats   SD - Southern Democrats

	394	395	396	397	398
6 Burton	Y	N	N	Y	Y
7 Myers	Y	N	N	N	N
8 McCloskey	Y	Y	Y	Y	N
9 Hamilton	Y	N	N	N	N
10 Jacobs	N	N	Y	N	N
IOWA					
1 Leach	Y	N	N	N	N
2 Tauke	Y	N	N	N	N
3 Evans	N	N	N	N	Y
4 Smith	Y	N	Y	N	N
5 Harkin	N	N	N	N	N
6 Bedell	Y	N	N	N	N
KANSAS					
1 Roberts	N	N	N	N	N
2 Slattery	Y	N	Y	N	N
3 Winn	Y	N	Y	N	N
4 Glickman	Y	N	Y	N	N
5 Whittaker	Y	N	Y	Y	N
KENTUCKY					
1 Hubbard	Y	N	N	Y	Y
2 Natcher	Y	N	N	Y	N
3 Mazzoli	Y	Y	N	Y	N
4 Snyder	Y	N	N	N	Y
5 Rogers	Y	N	Y	Y	Y
6 Hopkins	Y	N	Y	Y	Y
7 Perkins	Y	N	N	Y	N
LOUISIANA					
1 Livingston	?	N	N	?	?
2 Boggs	Y	N	N	Y	N
3 Tauzin	Y	N	N	Y	N
4 Roemer	N	Y	N	Y	N
5 Huckaby	Y	N	Y	Y	N
6 Moore	N	N	N	N	N
7 Breaux	Y	N	Y	N	?
8 Long	?	N	N	N	N
MAINE					
1 McKernan	Y	N	Y	N	Y
2 Snowe	Y	N	Y	N	N
MARYLAND					
1 Dyson	Y	N	N	Y	N
2 Long	?	N	N	Y	N
3 Mikulski	Y	N	Y	N	N
4 Holt	N	N	N	?	?
5 Hoyer	Y	N	Y	N	N
6 Byron	Y	N	Y	Y	Y
7 Mitchell	?	?	?	?	?
8 Barnes	Y	Y	Y	N	N
MASSACHUSETTS					
1 Conte	Y	Y	N	Y	N
2 Boland	Y	Y	N	N	N
3 Early	Y	Y	N	N	N
4 Frank	Y	Y	Y	N	N
5 Shannon	Y	Y	Y	N	N
6 Mavroules	Y	Y	N	N	N
7 Markey	N	Y	Y	N	N
8 O'Neill					
9 Moakley	?	#	?	X	X
10 Studds	Y	Y	Y	N	N
11 Donnelly	Y	Y	N	N	N
MICHIGAN					
1 Conyers	P	Y	Y	N	N
2 Pursell	Y	Y	Y	Y	Y
3 Wolpe	Y	N	Y	N	N
4 Siljander	Y	N	N	Y	N
5 Sawyer	Y	N	Y	Y	N
6 Carr	Y	X	Y	X	N
7 Kildee	Y	N	N	Y	N
8 Traxler	Y	N	N	Y	N
9 Vander Jagt	Y	N	N	N	N
10 Albosta	Y	N	N	Y	N
11 Davis	Y	N	N	Y	Y
12 Bonior	Y	N	N	N	N
13 Crockett	?	Y	Y	N	N
14 Hertel	Y	N	N	Y	N
15 Ford	?	N	Y	N	N
16 Dingell	Y	N	Y	N	N
17 Levin	Y	Y	Y	N	N
18 Broomfield	Y	Y	N	N	Y
MINNESOTA					
1 Penny	Y	N	N	N	N
2 Weber	Y	Y	N	N	N
3 Frenzel	Y	Y	Y	N	N
4 Vento	Y	Y	Y	N	N
5 Sabo	N	N	Y	N	N
6 Sikorski	N	N	N	N	N

	394	395	396	397	398
7 Stangeland	Y	?	N	N	N
8 Oberstar	P	N	N	N	N
MISSISSIPPI					
1 Whitten	Y	N	N	N	N
2 Franklin	Y	N	N	Y	Y
3 Montgomery	Y	N	N	Y	Y
4 Dowdy	Y	N	?	?	?
5 Lott	Y	N	N	Y	Y
MISSOURI					
1 Clay	?	N	Y	N	N
2 Young	Y	N	N	Y	N
3 Gephardt	?	?	?	N	N
4 Skelton	?	N	Y	N	N
5 Wheat	Y	N	Y	N	N
6 Coleman	Y	N	N	Y	N
7 Taylor	Y	N	N	Y	N
8 Emerson	N	N	N	N	N
9 Volkmer	Y	N	N	Y	N
MONTANA					
1 Williams	?	N	Y	N	N
2 Marlenee	Y	N	Y	Y	Y
NEBRASKA					
1 Bereuter	Y	N	N	N	N
2 Daub	Y	N	N	Y	Y
3 Smith	?	N	N	N	N
NEVADA					
1 Reid	Y	N	N	N	N
2 Vucanovich	Y	N	N	N	N
NEW HAMPSHIRE					
1 D'Amours	Y	Y	N	Y	Y
2 Gregg	?	Y	N	N	N
NEW JERSEY					
1 Florio	Y	N	N	Y	N
2 Hughes	Y	Y	N	Y	Y
3 Howard	Y	?	?	?	?
4 Smith	Y	N	N	Y	Y
5 Roukema	Y	Y	Y	N	N
6 Dwyer	Y	Y	N	N	N
7 Rinaldo	Y	Y	N	Y	N
8 Roe	Y	N	N	Y	N
9 Torricelli	Y	Y	Y	Y	N
10 Rodino	Y	Y	N	N	N
11 Minish	Y	Y	N	Y	N
12 Courter	Y	Y	N	Y	Y
13 Forsythe	N	N	Y	N	Y
14 Guarini	Y	Y	Y	Y	N
NEW MEXICO					
1 Lujan	Y	N	N	Y	Y
2 Skeen	Y	N	N	Y	Y
3 Richardson	Y	N	Y	N	N
NEW YORK					
1 Carney	Y	N	N	Y	Y
2 Downey	Y	N	Y	N	N
3 Mrazek	?	N	Y	N	N
4 Lent	Y	Y	N	Y	Y
5 McGrath	Y	Y	N	Y	Y
6 Addabbo	?	Y	Y	N	N
7 Ackerman	Y	Y	Y	N	N
8 Scheuer	Y	Y	Y	N	N
9 Ferraro	Y	Y	Y	N	N
10 Schumer	Y	N	N	N	N
11 Towns	Y	N	N	N	N
12 Owens	Y	Y	Y	N	N
13 Solarz	?	?	Y	N	N
14 Molinari	Y	Y	N	Y	N
15 Green	Y	Y	Y	N	N
16 Rangel	?	Y	Y	N	N
17 Weiss	Y	Y	Y	N	N
18 Garcia	Y	Y	Y	N	N
19 Biaggi	Y	Y	N	N	N
20 Ottinger	P	Y	Y	N	N
21 Fish	Y	N	N	Y	N
22 Gilman	Y	N	Y	Y	Y
23 Stratton	Y	N	N	N	N
24 Solomon	N	N	N	Y	Y
25 Boehlert	Y	N	N	Y	N
26 Martin	P	N	N	Y	Y
27 Wortley	Y	N	N	Y	N
28 McHugh	Y	N	N	N	N
29 Horton	Y	N	Y	N	N
30 Conable	Y	?	?	N	N
31 Kemp	Y	N	N	N	N
32 LaFalce	Y	N	N	Y	N
33 Nowak	Y	N	N	N	N
34 Lundine	Y	N	Y	N	N

	394	395	396	397	398
NORTH CAROLINA					
1 Jones	?	N	Y	Y	N
2 Valentine	Y	N	Y	Y	Y
3 Whitley	Y	N	Y	N	N
4 Andrews	Y	N	Y	N	N
5 Neal	Y	N	Y	Y	Y
6 Britt	Y	N	Y	N	N
7 Rose	Y	?	?	?	?
8 Hefner	Y	N	N	N	N
9 Martin	Y	N	Y	Y	Y
10 Broyhill	Y	N	Y	Y	Y
11 Clarke	Y	N	Y	N	N
NORTH DAKOTA					
AL Dorgan	N	N	N	Y	N
OHIO					
1 Luken	Y	Y	N	N	N
2 Gradison	Y	Y	N	Y	Y
3 Hall	?	N	N	Y	N
4 Oxley	Y	N	N	Y	Y
5 Latta	Y	N	N	Y	N
6 McEwen	Y	N	N	Y	Y
7 DeWine	Y	N	N	Y	Y
8 Kindness	Y	N	N	Y	N
9 Kaptur	Y	N	N	Y	N
10 Miller	N	Y	N	Y	Y
11 Eckart	N	N	N	Y	N
12 Kasich	Y	N	Y	Y	Y
13 Pease	Y	Y	Y	N	N
14 Seiberling	Y	N	Y	N	N
15 Wylie	Y	N	N	?	?
16 Regula	Y	N	Y	Y	Y
17 Williams	Y	Y	N	Y	N
18 Applegate	?	N	N	Y	Y
19 Feighan	?	N	Y	N	N
20 Oakar	Y	N	N	N	N
21 Stokes	Y	N	Y	N	N
OKLAHOMA					
1 Jones	Y	N	Y	N	N
2 Synar	Y	N	Y	N	N
3 Watkins	Y	N	Y	Y	Y
4 McCurdy	Y	?	Y	Y	N
5 Edwards	N	N	?	Y	Y
6 English	Y	N	Y	N	N
OREGON					
1 AuCoin	Y	N	Y	N	N
2 Smith, R.	Y	N	N	Y	Y
3 Wyden	Y	N	Y	N	N
4 Weaver	Y	N	Y	N	N
5 Smith, D.	Y	N	Y	Y	Y
PENNSYLVANIA					
1 Foglietta	Y	Y	Y	N	N
2 Gray	Y	N	Y	N	N
3 Borski	Y	Y	N	N	N
4 Kolter	Y	N	Y	N	N
5 Schulze	Y	N	Y	N	N
6 Yatron	Y	N	Y	N	N
7 Edgar	?	Y	Y	N	N
8 Kostmayer	Y	Y	Y	N	N
9 Shuster	Y	N	N	Y	N
10 McDade	P	N	N	Y	N
11 Harrison	Y	N	N	?	?
12 Murtha	Y	N	N	Y	N
13 Coughlin	N	N	Y	N	N
14 Coyne	Y	N	Y	N	N
15 Ritter	Y	Y	Y	Y	Y
16 Walker	N	N	N	Y	N
17 Gekas	P	N	Y	N	Y
18 Walgren	?	Y	Y	N	Y
19 Goodling	N	N	N	Y	N
20 Gaydos	Y	N	N	N	N
21 Ridge	Y	N	N	N	N
22 Murphy	Y	N	Y	N	N
23 Clinger	Y	N	N	N	N
RHODE ISLAND					
1 St Germain	P	N	N	N	N
2 Schneider	Y	Y	Y	N	N
SOUTH CAROLINA					
1 Hartnett	Y	N	N	Y	Y
2 Spence	Y	N	Y	N	Y
3 Derrick	Y	N	Y	N	N
4 Campbell	Y	N	Y	Y	Y
5 Spratt	Y	N	Y	N	N
6 Tallon	Y	N	Y	Y	N
SOUTH DAKOTA					
AL Daschle	Y	N	Y	N	N

	394	395	396	397	398
TENNESSEE					
1 Quillen	Y	N	N	N	N
2 Duncan	Y	N	N	Y	Y
3 Lloyd	Y	N	N	Y	Y
4 Cooper	Y	N	Y	Y	N
5 Boner	Y	N	N	N	N
6 Gore	Y	N	N	?	?
7 Sundquist	Y	N	N	Y	Y
8 Jones	Y	N	N	N	N
9 Ford	Y	?	Y	N	N
TEXAS					
1 Hall, S.	?	N	N	Y	N
2 Wilson	Y	N	N	Y	N
3 Bartlett	Y	Y	N	N	N
4 Hall, R.	Y	N	N	Y	N
5 Bryant	Y	N	Y	N	N
6 Gramm	Y	N	?	#	?
7 Archer	Y	N	N	Y	N
8 Fields	N	N	N	Y	N
9 Brooks	Y	N	N	Y	N
10 Pickle	Y	N	N	Y	N
11 Leath	Y	N	N	Y	N
12 Wright	Y	N	Y	N	N
13 Hightower	Y	N	Y	Y	N
14 Patman	Y	N	N	Y	N
15 de la Garza	Y	N	Y	Y	N
16 Coleman	Y	N	Y	Y	N
17 Stenholm	Y	N	N	Y	N
18 Leland	Y	?	Y	N	N
19 Hance	Y	?	?	?	?
20 Gonzalez	Y	N	N	N	N
21 Loeffler	Y	N	N	Y	Y
22 Paul	Y	Y	N	Y	N
23 Kazen	Y	N	Y	N	N
24 Frost	Y	N	Y	N	N
25 Andrews	Y	N	Y	N	N
26 Vandergriff	Y	N	N	N	N
27 Ortiz	Y	N	Y	N	N
UTAH					
1 Hansen	Y	N	N	Y	Y
2 Marriott	Y	N	N	?	?
3 Nielson	Y	N	N	N	N
VERMONT					
AL Jeffords	Y	N	Y	N	N
VIRGINIA					
1 Bateman	Y	N	N	N	N
2 Whitehurst	Y	N	N	Y	Y
3 Bliley	Y	N	N	Y	N
4 Sisisky	Y	N	Y	Y	N
5 Daniel	Y	N	N	Y	N
6 Olin	P	N	Y	Y	N
7 Robinson	Y	N	N	Y	N
8 Parris	?	N	N	?	?
9 Boucher	Y	N	Y	Y	N
10 Wolf	Y	N	N	Y	N
WASHINGTON					
1 Pritchard	Y	Y	Y	?	?
2 Swift	Y	N	N	Y	N
3 Bonker	Y	N	Y	N	N
4 Morrison	Y	N	Y	Y	N
5 Foley	Y	N	Y	N	N
6 Dicks	Y	N	Y	N	N
7 Lowry	Y	N	Y	N	N
8 Chandler	Y	N	N	Y	N
WEST VIRGINIA					
1 Mollohan	Y	N	N	N	N
2 Staggers	Y	N	N	Y	N
3 Wise	Y	N	Y	Y	N
4 Rahall	?	N	N	N	N
WISCONSIN					
1 Aspin	Y	N	N	Y	N
2 Kastenmeier	Y	N	Y	N	N
3 Gunderson	Y	N	Y	Y	N
4 Zablocki	N	N	N	N	N
5 Moody	Y	N	N	Y	N
6 Petri	Y	Y	N	Y	Y
7 Obey	N	N	N	N	N
8 Roth	Y	N	N	Y	Y
9 Sensenbrenner	Y	N	N	Y	Y
WYOMING					
AL Cheney	Y	Y	N	Y	Y

Southern states · Ala., Ark., Fla., Ga., Ky., La., Miss., N.C., Okla., S.C., Tenn., Texas, Va.

399. Procedural Motion. Bethune, R-Ark., motion to approve the House *Journal* of Thursday, Oct. 27. Motion agreed to 298-21: R 120-9; D 178-12 (ND 115-10, SD 63-2), Oct. 28, 1983.

400. HR 2655. Domestic Volunteer Service Act Amendments. Bartlett, R-Texas, amendment to strike language setting a $25 million authorization floor for Volunteers in Service to America (VISTA). Rejected 132-215: R 119-18; D 13-197 (ND 3-139, SD 10-58), Oct. 28, 1983. A "yea" was a vote supporting the president's position.

401. HR 2655. Domestic Volunteer Service Act Amendments. Passage of the bill to reauthorize volunteer programs administered by ACTION for three years through fiscal 1986. Passed 312-30: R 103-30; D 209-0 (ND 141-0, SD 68-0), Oct. 28, 1983.

402. HR 3222. State, Justice, Commerce Appropriations, Fiscal 1984. O'Brien, R-Ill., motion to order the previous question on the O'Brien motion to instruct conferees to insist on the House position that $70.15 million of the funds in the bill be earmarked for juvenile justice programs. Motion rejected 123-182: R 31-90; D 92-92 (ND 76-46, SD 16-46), Oct. 31, 1983.

403. HR 3222. State, Justice, Commerce Appropriations, Fiscal 1984. Brown, R-Colo., amendment to the O'Brien, R-Ill., motion *(see vote 402, above)*, to further instruct conferees to insist on the House position that not more than $21.3 million of the funds in the bill be appropriated for the Endowment for Democracy, and that no endowment funds be given to any entity related to a U.S. political party or party official or employee. Adopted 234-103: R 100-29; D 134-74 (ND 76-59, SD 58-15), Oct. 31, 1983.

404. HR 2867. Hazardous Waste Control. Judiciary Committee amendment to strike provisions allowing the Environmental Protection Agency (EPA) to file civil actions in cases where the Justice Department fails to act within a specified time on EPA requests for litigation under the Resource Conservation and Recovery Act. Adopted 215-165: R 127-22; D 88-143 (ND 44-107, SD 44-36), Oct. 31, 1983.

405. Procedural Motion. Lewis, R-Fla., motion to approve the House *Journal* of Monday, Oct. 31. Motion agreed to 376-32: R 143-18; D 233-14 (ND 151-12, SD 82-2), Nov. 1, 1983.

406. S 448. Belle Fourche Project. Kazen, D-Texas, motion to suspend the rules and pass the bill to authorize $42 million in appropriations for the rehabilitation of the Belle Fourche Reclamation Project in South Dakota. Motion agreed to 373-51: R 116-47; D 257-4 (ND 170-4, SD 87-0), Nov. 1, 1983. A two-thirds majority of those present and voting (283 in this case) is required for passage under suspension of the rules.

KEY

- Y Voted for (yea).
- # Paired for.
- + Announced for.
- N Voted against (nay).
- X Paired against.
- - Announced against.
- P Voted "present".
- C Voted "present" to avoid possible conflict of interest.
- ? Did not vote or otherwise make a position known.

Democrats *Republicans*

	399	400	401	402	403	404	405	406
ALABAMA								
1 *Edwards*	?	Y	Y	N	Y	Y	Y	Y
2 *Dickinson*	N	Y	Y	?	?	Y	Y	N
3 Nichols	Y	Y	Y	?	Y	Y	Y	Y
4 Bevill	Y	N	Y	N	Y	Y	?	Y
5 Flippo	Y	N	Y	N	Y	Y	Y	Y
6 Erdreich	Y	N	Y	N	Y	Y	Y	Y
7 Shelby	Y	N	Y	?	?	N	Y	Y
ALASKA								
AL *Young*	?	N	Y	N	Y	N	Y	N
ARIZONA								
1 *McCain*	Y	Y	Y	N	Y	Y	Y	Y
2 Udall	Y	N	Y	N	Y	N	Y	Y
3 *Stump*	?	#	?	N	Y	Y	Y	Y
4 *Rudd*	Y	Y	N	Y	Y	Y	Y	Y
5 McNulty	Y	N	Y	N	Y	N	Y	Y
ARKANSAS								
1 Alexander	Y	N	Y	N	Y	N	Y	Y
2 *Bethune*	Y	Y	N	N	?	N	Y	Y
3 *Hammerschmidt*	?	?	?	N	Y	Y	Y	Y
4 Anthony	?	N	Y	N	Y	N	?	Y
CALIFORNIA								
1 Bosco	?	?	?	?	?	?	Y	Y
2 *Chappie*	Y	Y	Y	N	Y	Y	N	Y
3 Matsui	Y	N	Y	N	N	N	Y	Y
4 Fazio	Y	N	Y	N	Y	N	Y	Y
5 Burton	?	?	?	?	?	?	Y	Y
6 Boxer	Y	N	Y	?	?	?	Y	Y
7 Miller	Y	N	Y	?	?	#	Y	Y
8 Dellums	Y	N	Y	N	N	N	?	Y
9 Stark	?	?	?	Y	N	Y	Y	Y
10 Edwards	Y	N	Y	Y	Y	Y	Y	Y
11 Lantos	Y	N	Y	?	?	Y	Y	Y
12 *Zschau*	Y	Y	N	N	Y	Y	N	N
13 Mineta	Y	N	Y	?	?	Y	Y	Y
14 *Shumway*	Y	Y	N	N	Y	Y	N	N
15 Coelho	Y	N	Y	?	N	N	Y	Y
16 Panetta	Y	N	Y	N	Y	N	Y	Y
17 *Pashayan*	Y	Y	Y	?	?	Y	Y	Y
18 Lehman	Y	N	Y	?	?	?	?	?
19 *Lagomarsino*	Y	Y	Y	N	N	N	Y	Y
20 *Thomas*	Y	Y	N	?	?	Y	Y	Y
21 *Fiedler*	Y	Y	Y	N	Y	Y	N	Y
22 *Moorhead*	Y	Y	Y	N	Y	Y	N	N
23 Beilenson	Y	N	Y	N	N	N	Y	Y
24 Waxman	Y	N	Y	?	?	?	?	Y
25 Roybal	Y	N	Y	?	?	N	Y	Y
26 Berman	Y	N	Y	N	N	Y	Y	Y
27 Levine	Y	N	Y	N	N	Y	Y	Y
28 Dixon	?	X	Y	Y	N	Y	Y	Y
29 Hawkins	Y	N	Y	N	N	Y	Y	Y
30 Martinez	?	N	Y	Y	N	N	?	Y
31 Dymally	P	N	Y	N	Y	N	P	Y
32 Anderson	Y	N	Y	N	Y	N	Y	Y
33 *Dreier*	Y	Y	N	N	Y	Y	N	N
34 Torres	Y	N	Y	N	N	N	Y	Y
35 *Lewis*	Y	Y	Y	Y	Y	Y	Y	Y
36 Brown	Y	N	Y	N	N	?	Y	?
37 *McCandless*	Y	Y	Y	?	?	?	Y	Y
38 Patterson	Y	N	Y	N	Y	N	Y	Y
39 *Dannemeyer*	Y	Y	N	N	Y	N	N	N
40 *Badham*	Y	Y	N	N	Y	Y	Y	Y
41 *Lowery*	?	Y	Y	?	?	?	Y	Y
42 Lungren	Y	Y	N	N	Y	Y	Y	Y

	399	400	401	402	403	404	405	406
43 *Packard*	Y	Y	Y	N	Y	Y	Y	Y
44 *Bates*	Y	N	Y	?	?	?	Y	Y
45 *Hunter*	?	Y	Y	N	Y	Y	Y	Y
COLORADO								
1 Schroeder	N	N	Y	N	Y	N	N	Y
2 Wirth	Y	N	Y	N	Y	N	Y	Y
3 Kogovsek	Y	N	Y	N	Y	N	Y	Y
4 *Brown*	Y	Y	N	N	Y	N	Y	Y
5 *Kramer*	?	?	?	?	?	Y	Y	Y
6 *Schaefer*	?	?	?	?	?	Y	Y	Y
CONNECTICUT								
1 Kennelly	Y	N	Y	N	Y	N	Y	Y
2 Gejdenson	N	N	Y	N	N	N	Y	Y
3 Morrison	Y	N	Y	?	?	N	Y	Y
4 *McKinney*	Y	N	Y	?	Y	Y	Y	Y
5 Ratchford	Y	N	Y	?	Y	N	Y	Y
6 *Johnson*	Y	Y	N	N	N	Y	Y	Y
DELAWARE								
AL Carper	Y	Y	Y	N	Y	N	Y	Y
FLORIDA								
1 Hutto	?	?	?	?	N	Y	Y	Y
2 Fuqua	Y	N	Y	?	Y	Y	Y	Y
3 Bennett	Y	N	Y	N	Y	N	Y	Y
4 Chappell	?	N	Y	N	N	N	Y	?
5 *McCollum*	Y	Y	Y	N	Y	Y	Y	N
6 MacKay	?	?	?	?	?	Y	Y	Y
7 Gibbons	?	?	?	?	?	N	Y	Y
8 *Young*	Y	Y	?	?	Y	Y	Y	Y
9 *Bilirakis*	Y	Y	Y	?	?	#	N	N
10 Ireland	Y	Y	Y	N	N	Y	Y	Y
11 Nelson	Y	N	Y	N	Y	N	Y	Y
12 *Lewis*	Y	Y	Y	-	+	Y	Y	N
13 *Mack*	Y	Y	N	Y	N	Y	Y	N
14 Mica	Y	N	Y	N	Y	N	Y	Y
15 *Shaw*	?	?	?	?	?	Y	Y	Y
16 Smith	Y	N	Y	?	?	?	Y	Y
17 Lehman	Y	N	Y	?	Y	Y	Y	Y
18 Pepper	Y	X	?	?	?	?	Y	Y
19 Fascell	Y	N	Y	N	N	N	Y	Y
GEORGIA								
1 Thomas	Y	N	Y	N	Y	N	Y	Y
2 Hatcher	Y	N	Y	?	?	?	Y	?
3 Ray	Y	N	Y	N	Y	Y	Y	Y
4 Levitas	Y	N	Y	N	N	N	Y	Y
5 Fowler	Y	N	Y	?	?	N	Y	Y
6 *Gingrich*	Y	Y	Y	N	?	Y	Y	Y
7 Vacancy								
8 Rowland	Y	N	Y	N	Y	N	Y	Y
9 Jenkins	Y	N	Y	N	Y	N	Y	Y
10 Barnard	Y	N	Y	N	N	N	Y	Y
HAWAII								
1 Heftel	?	?	?	?	?	Y	Y	Y
2 Akaka	Y	N	Y	N	Y	N	Y	Y
IDAHO								
1 *Craig*	Y	Y	N	N	Y	Y	Y	Y
2 *Hansen*	Y	Y	N	N	Y	Y	Y	Y
ILLINOIS								
1 Hayes	?	?	?	?	?	?	Y	Y
2 Savage	Y	N	Y	N	Y	Y	Y	Y
3 Russo	?	?	?	N	Y	N	Y	Y
4 *O'Brien*	?	?	?	Y	N	Y	N	Y
5 Lipinski	?	?	Y	N	N	N	Y	Y
6 *Hyde*	Y	Y	Y	N	Y	Y	Y	Y
7 Collins	?	?	Y	?	?	N	?	Y
8 Rostenkowski	?	?	N	Y	?	N	?	Y
9 Yates	N	N	Y	N	N	N	Y	Y
10 *Porter*	Y	Y	Y	?	?	N	Y	N
11 Annunzio	Y	N	Y	N	Y	N	Y	Y
12 *Crane, P.*	Y	Y	N	?	?	Y	Y	N
13 *Erlenborn*	Y	Y	N	?	Y	Y	Y	Y
14 *Corcoran*	+	#	+	+	-	+	?	?
15 *Madigan*	Y	?	?	?	Y	Y	Y	Y
16 *Martin*	Y	Y	Y	N	Y	Y	Y	Y
17 Evans	Y	N	Y	Y	Y	Y	Y	Y
18 *Michel*	Y	?	?	Y	N	Y	Y	Y
19 *Crane, D.*	Y	Y	N	?	?	Y	Y	N
20 Durbin	N	N	Y	N	N	N	Y	Y
21 Price	Y	N	Y	N	Y	Y	Y	Y
22 Simon	?	?	?	?	?	?	Y	Y
INDIANA								
1 Hall	Y	N	Y	?	?	N	Y	Y
2 Sharp	Y	N	Y	N	Y	N	Y	Y
3 *Hiler*	Y	Y	Y	N	Y	Y	Y	N
4 *Coats*	Y	Y	Y	N	Y	Y	Y	N
5 *Hillis*	Y	Y	Y	N	Y	Y	Y	Y

ND - Northern Democrats   SD - Southern Democrats

Corresponding to Congressional Record Votes 427, 429, 430, 431, 432, 434, 435, 436

	399	400	401	402	403	404	405	406
6 ***Burton***	Y	Y	Y	N	Y	Y	Y	N
7 ***Myers***	Y	Y	Y	Y	N	Y	Y	Y
8 McCloskey	Y	N	Y	N	Y	N	Y	Y
9 Hamilton	Y	N	Y	N	Y	N	Y	Y
10 Jacobs	N	N	Y	N	Y	N	P	Y
IOWA								
1 ***Leach***	?	?	?	N	Y	N	Y	N
2 ***Tauke***	Y	Y	Y	?	?	?	Y	N
3 ***Evans***	N	Y	Y	N	Y	N	N	N
4 Smith	Y	N	Y	Y	N	N	Y	Y
5 Harkin	N	N	Y	Y	N	N	N	Y
6 Bedell	Y	N	Y	N	Y	N	Y	N
KANSAS								
1 ***Roberts***	N	Y	?	N	Y	Y	N	Y
2 Slattery	Y	Y	Y	N	Y	N	Y	Y
3 ***Winn***	Y	Y	Y	N	Y	Y	Y	Y
4 Glickman	Y	Y	Y	N	Y	Y	Y	Y
5 ***Whittaker***	Y	Y	Y	N	Y	Y	Y	Y
KENTUCKY								
1 Hubbard	Y	Y	Y	?	?	?	Y	Y
2 Natcher	Y	N	Y	Y	N	N	Y	Y
3 Mazzoli	+	-	+	?	Y	Y	Y	Y
4 ***Snyder***	Y	Y	Y	N	Y	Y	Y	Y
5 ***Rogers***	Y	Y	Y	N	N	Y	Y	Y
6 ***Hopkins***	?	?	?	N	Y	Y	Y	N
7 Perkins	Y	N	?	Y	N	N	Y	Y
LOUISIANA								
1 ***Livingston***	?	?	?	Y	N	Y	Y	Y
2 Boggs	?	?	?	?	N	N	Y	Y
3 Tauzin	Y	N	Y	N	Y	N	Y	Y
4 Roemer	N	N	Y	N	Y	Y	N	Y
5 Huckaby	Y	N	Y	N	Y	Y	Y	Y
6 ***Moore***	Y	Y	Y	N	Y	Y	Y	Y
7 Breaux	?	?	?	N	Y	N	Y	Y
8 Long	Y	N	Y	?	?	N	Y	Y
MAINE								
1 ***McKernan***	Y	N	Y	?	?	Y	Y	Y
2 ***Snowe***	Y	N	Y	?	?	Y	Y	Y
MARYLAND								
1 Dyson	?	X	?	N	Y	Y	Y	Y
2 Long	?	N	Y	Y	N	N	Y	Y
3 Mikulski	?	N	Y	N	Y	N	Y	Y
4 ***Holt***	?	?	?	Y	Y	Y	Y	Y
5 Hoyer	Y	N	Y	?	N	N	Y	Y
6 Byron	?	?	Y	?	?	Y	Y	Y
7 Mitchell	?	X	+	-	-	?	?	+
8 Barnes	Y	N	Y	Y	N	N	Y	Y
MASSACHUSETTS								
1 ***Conte***	?	?	?	Y	N	N	Y	N
2 Boland	?	X	?	Y	N	N	Y	Y
3 Early	?	?	?	Y	N	N	Y	Y
4 Frank	Y	N	Y	Y	N	N	Y	Y
5 Shannon	Y	?	?	Y	N	N	Y	Y
6 Mavroules	Y	N	Y	Y	N	N	Y	Y
7 Markey	N	N	Y	-	+	N	Y	Y
8 O'Neill								
9 Moakley	?	X	?	?	X	X	Y	Y
10 Studds	Y	N	Y	?	?	N	Y	Y
11 Donnelly	Y	N	Y	?	?	?	Y	Y
MICHIGAN								
1 Conyers	?	N	Y	Y	N	Y	Y	Y
2 ***Pursell***	?	?	?	N	Y	N	Y	Y
3 Wolpe	Y	N	Y	N	Y	N	Y	Y
4 ***Siljander***	Y	Y	Y	Y	N	Y	Y	Y
5 ***Sawyer***	?	?	?	N	N	Y	Y	?
6 Carr	Y	N	Y	Y	N	Y	Y	Y
7 Kildee	Y	N	Y	Y	Y	N	Y	N
8 Traxler	?	?	?	?	N	N	Y	Y
9 ***Vander Jagt***	Y	Y	Y	N	N	Y	Y	?
10 Albosta	Y	N	Y	N	Y	N	Y	Y
11 ***Davis***	Y	Y	Y	?	?	?	P	Y
12 Bonior	Y	N	Y	Y	?	N	Y	Y
13 Crockett	?	N	Y	N	Y	Y	Y	Y
14 Hertel	Y	N	Y	Y	Y	?	Y	Y
15 Ford	?	N	Y	?	?	?	Y	Y
16 Dingell	?	N	Y	?	Y	N	Y	Y
17 Levin	Y	N	Y	Y	N	N	Y	Y
18 ***Broomfield***	Y	Y	Y	Y	N	Y	Y	Y
MINNESOTA								
1 Penny	Y	N	Y	?	N	N	Y	Y
2 ***Weber***	Y	Y	N	N	Y	N	Y	N
3 ***Frenzel***	Y	Y	Y	N	Y	Y	Y	N
4 Vento	Y	N	Y	Y	Y	N	Y	N
5 Sabo	N	N	Y	Y	N	N	N	Y
6 Sikorski	N	N	Y	Y	Y	N	N	Y
7 ***Stangeland***	?	#	?	N	Y	Y	Y	Y
8 Oberstar	?	N	Y	Y	Y	-	P	Y
MISSISSIPPI								
1 Whitten	Y	Y	Y	Y	Y	Y	Y	Y
2 ***Franklin***	Y	Y	Y	N	Y	Y	Y	Y
3 Montgomery	?	?	?	N	Y	?	Y	Y
4 Dowdy	?	?	?	N	Y	N	Y	Y
5 ***Lott***	?	Y	Y	N	Y	Y	Y	Y
MISSOURI								
1 Clay	?	?	?	?	?	?	N	Y
2 Young	Y	N	Y	Y	Y	Y	Y	Y
3 Gephardt	?	?	?	Y	Y	N	Y	Y
4 Skelton	?	?	?	N	Y	N	Y	Y
5 Wheat	Y	N	Y	Y	Y	N	Y	Y
6 ***Coleman***	Y	Y	Y	Y	N	N	Y	Y
7 ***Taylor***	Y	Y	Y	N	Y	Y	Y	Y
8 ***Emerson***	N	Y	Y	N	Y	Y	N	Y
9 Volkmer	Y	N	Y	N	Y	N	Y	Y
MONTANA								
1 Williams	?	?	?	?	N	N	Y	Y
2 ***Marlenee***	Y	N	Y	?	?	?	Y	Y
NEBRASKA								
1 ***Bereuter***	Y	Y	Y	N	Y	Y	Y	Y
2 ***Daub***	?	#	+	N	Y	Y	Y	Y
3 ***Smith***	Y	Y	Y	Y	Y	Y	Y	Y
NEVADA								
1 Reid	Y	N	Y	Y	Y	N	Y	Y
2 ***Vucanovich***	?	Y	Y	?	?	?	Y	Y
NEW HAMPSHIRE								
1 D'Amours	Y	N	Y	N	Y	N	Y	Y
2 ***Gregg***	Y	Y	Y	?	?	?	N	N
NEW JERSEY								
1 Florio	?	N	Y	?	Y	N	Y	Y
2 Hughes	Y	N	Y	Y	N	Y	Y	Y
3 Howard	?	?	?	Y	N	N	Y	Y
4 ***Smith***	Y	N	Y	Y	N	Y	Y	Y
5 ***Roukema***	Y	Y	Y	N	Y	#	Y	N
6 Dwyer	Y	N	Y	Y	N	N	Y	Y
7 ***Rinaldo***	?	N	Y	Y	N	Y	Y	N
8 Roe	?	?	?	Y	N	N	Y	Y
9 Torricelli	Y	N	Y	Y	Y	N	Y	Y
10 Rodino	Y	N	Y	Y	N	Y	Y	Y
11 Minish	Y	N	Y	N	Y	N	Y	Y
12 ***Courter***	Y	Y	Y	Y	Y	N	Y	Y
13 ***Forsythe***	N	?	?	N	?	Y	N	N
14 Guarini	Y	N	Y	?	?	Y	Y	Y
NEW MEXICO								
1 ***Lujan***	?	?	?	N	Y	Y	Y	Y
2 ***Skeen***	Y	Y	N	N	Y	Y	Y	Y
3 Richardson	+	-	+	Y	Y	N	Y	Y
NEW YORK								
1 ***Carney***	Y	Y	Y	N	Y	Y	Y	Y
2 Downey	Y	N	Y	Y	N	N	Y	Y
3 Mrazek	?	?	?	Y	Y	N	Y	Y
4 ***Lent***	?	N	Y	N	Y	Y	Y	Y
5 ***McGrath***	Y	N	Y	N	Y	N	Y	Y
6 Addabbo	?	X	?	?	?	N	Y	Y
7 Ackerman	Y	N	Y	Y	N	N	Y	Y
8 Scheuer	Y	N	Y	Y	N	N	Y	Y
9 Ferraro	+	+	+	?	?	Y	Y	Y
10 Schumer	?	?	?	Y	N	Y	Y	Y
11 Towns	Y	N	Y	?	?	N	Y	Y
12 Owens	Y	N	Y	?	?	Y	Y	Y
13 Solarz	?	?	?	?	?	?	Y	Y
14 ***Molinari***	?	?	?	N	Y	N	Y	Y
15 ***Green***	Y	Y	Y	?	Y	N	Y	N
16 Rangel	Y	N	Y	?	Y	Y	Y	Y
17 Weiss	Y	N	Y	N	Y	Y	Y	Y
18 Garcia	?	?	?	?	?	?	Y	Y
19 Biaggi	Y	N	Y	?	?	?	Y	Y
20 Ottinger	P	N	Y	N	Y	N	P	Y
21 ***Fish***	Y	N	Y	?	Y	Y	Y	N
22 ***Gilman***	Y	N	Y	+	-	N	Y	Y
23 Stratton	Y	N	Y	N	Y	Y	Y	Y
24 ***Solomon***	Y	Y	Y	N	Y	Y	N	N
25 ***Boehlert***	Y	N	Y	N	Y	Y	Y	Y
26 ***Martin***	?	?	?	?	Y	Y	Y	Y
27 ***Wortley***	Y	Y	?	N	Y	Y	Y	Y
28 McHugh	?	N	Y	Y	Y	N	Y	Y
29 ***Horton***	Y	N	Y	?	N	N	Y	Y
30 ***Conable***	Y	Y	Y	N	Y	Y	Y	N
31 ***Kemp***	Y	Y	Y	Y	N	?	Y	Y
32 LaFalce	Y	N	Y	N	Y	Y	Y	Y
33 Nowak	Y	N	Y	?	Y	N	Y	Y
34 Lundine	Y	N	Y	Y	Y	N	Y	Y
NORTH CAROLINA								
1 Jones	?	N	Y	Y	N	Y	Y	Y
2 Valentine	Y	N	Y	N	Y	Y	N	Y
3 Whitley	Y	N	Y	N	Y	Y	Y	Y
4 Andrews	Y	N	Y	?	?	N	Y	Y
5 Neal	?	?	Y	?	N	N	Y	Y
6 Britt	Y	N	Y	Y	N	Y	Y	Y
7 Rose	?	?	?	?	?	Y	Y	Y
8 Hefner	Y	N	Y	N	Y	Y	Y	Y
9 ***Martin***	Y	Y	Y	N	Y	Y	Y	Y
10 ***Broyhill***	Y	Y	N	Y	Y	Y	Y	N
11 Clarke	Y	N	Y	+	-	-	Y	Y
NORTH DAKOTA								
AL Dorgan	?	N	Y	?	Y	N	N	Y
OHIO								
1 Luken	Y	N	?	N	Y	N	Y	Y
2 ***Gradison***	Y	Y	?	N	Y	Y	Y	N
3 Hall	Y	N	Y	Y	Y	N	Y	Y
4 ***Oxley***	?	#	?	N	Y	Y	Y	Y
5 ***Latta***	Y	?	?	?	?	?	N	N
6 ***McEwen***	Y	Y	Y	N	Y	Y	Y	Y
7 ***DeWine***	Y	Y	Y	N	Y	Y	Y	N
8 ***Kindness***	Y	Y	Y	N	Y	Y	Y	Y
9 Kaptur	Y	N	Y	?	?	X	Y	Y
10 ***Miller***	N	Y	Y	Y	Y	Y	N	N
11 Eckart	N	N	Y	N	Y	N	Y	Y
12 ***Kasich***	Y	Y	Y	N	Y	Y	Y	N
13 Pease	Y	N	Y	Y	Y	Y	Y	Y
14 Seiberling	Y	N	Y	Y	Y	N	Y	Y
15 ***Wylie***	Y	Y	Y	Y	N	Y	Y	Y
16 ***Regula***	Y	Y	Y	N	Y	Y	Y	Y
17 ***Williams***	?	N	Y	?	?	N	Y	Y
18 Applegate	?	N	Y	?	?	N	?	Y
19 Feighan	Y	N	Y	?	Y	Y	Y	Y
20 Oakar	Y	N	Y	?	?	N	Y	Y
21 Stokes	?	?	?	Y	Y	Y	?	Y
OKLAHOMA								
1 Jones	N	Y	Y	?	Y	Y	Y	Y
2 Synar	Y	-	+	N	Y	Y	Y	Y
3 Watkins	?	?	?	N	Y	N	Y	Y
4 McCurdy	?	?	Y	N	Y	Y	Y	Y
5 ***Edwards***	N	Y	Y	?	Y	Y	N	Y
6 English	Y	Y	Y	N	Y	N	Y	Y
OREGON								
1 AuCoin	Y	N	Y	N	Y	?	Y	Y
2 ***Smith, R.***	Y	Y	N	N	Y	Y	Y	Y
3 Wyden	?	?	?	N	Y	N	Y	Y
4 Weaver	Y	N	Y	?	?	?	Y	Y
5 ***Smith, D.***	?	#	?	-	+	Y	Y	Y
PENNSYLVANIA								
1 Foglietta	Y	N	Y	Y	Y	N	Y	Y
2 Gray	Y	N	?	?	?	?	Y	Y
3 Borski	Y	N	Y	Y	Y	Y	Y	Y
4 Kolter	Y	N	Y	Y	N	N	Y	Y
5 ***Schulze***	Y	Y	?	?	Y	Y	Y	Y
6 Yatron	Y	N	Y	N	N	N	Y	Y
7 Edgar	Y	N	Y	N	Y	N	Y	Y
8 Kostmayer	Y	N	Y	Y	N	N	Y	Y
9 ***Shuster***	Y	Y	N	N	Y	Y	Y	Y
10 ***McDade***	Y	N	Y	?	N	Y	Y	Y
11 Harrison	?	?	?	?	Y	Y	Y	Y
12 Murtha	?	N	Y	Y	Y	N	Y	Y
13 ***Coughlin***	N	N	Y	?	?	?	?	Y
14 Coyne	Y	N	Y	Y	N	N	Y	Y
15 ***Ritter***	Y	Y	Y	?	N	Y	Y	N
16 ***Walker***	N	Y	N	N	Y	Y	N	N
17 ***Gekas***	Y	Y	Y	?	Y	Y	Y	Y
18 Walgren	Y	N	Y	?	?	N	Y	Y
19 ***Goodling***	?	Y	Y	?	?	N	N	Y
20 Gaydos	Y	N	Y	Y	N	N	Y	Y
21 ***Ridge***	Y	Y	Y	N	Y	N	Y	N
22 Murphy	Y	N	Y	?	?	N	Y	Y
23 ***Clinger***	Y	Y	Y	Y	N	Y	Y	Y
RHODE ISLAND								
1 St Germain	P	N	Y	Y	N	N	P	Y
2 ***Schneider***	Y	N	Y	Y	N	N	Y	Y
SOUTH CAROLINA								
1 ***Hartnett***	?	?	?	?	Y	Y	Y	N
2 ***Spence***	Y	Y	Y	?	Y	Y	Y	Y
3 Derrick	Y	N	Y	Y	Y	Y	Y	Y
4 ***Campbell***	Y	Y	Y	Y	Y	Y	Y	Y
5 Spratt	Y	N	Y	Y	Y	Y	Y	Y
6 Tallon	Y	N	Y	?	Y	Y	?	Y
SOUTH DAKOTA								
AL Daschle	Y	N	Y	N	Y	Y	N	Y
TENNESSEE								
1 ***Quillen***	Y	Y	Y	N	N	Y	Y	Y
2 ***Duncan***	Y	Y	Y	Y	Y	Y	Y	Y
3 Lloyd	Y	N	?	N	Y	Y	Y	Y
4 Cooper	Y	N	Y	N	Y	N	Y	Y
5 Boner	Y	N	Y	N	Y	N	Y	Y
6 Gore	?	?	?	N	Y	N	Y	Y
7 ***Sundquist***	Y	Y	Y	N	Y	Y	Y	N
8 Jones	Y	N	Y	Y	Y	N	Y	Y
9 Ford	Y	N	Y	?	?	Y	Y	Y
TEXAS								
1 Hall, S.	?	?	?	N	Y	Y	Y	Y
2 Wilson	?	?	?	?	N	N	Y	Y
3 ***Bartlett***	Y	Y	N	N	Y	Y	Y	N
4 Hall, R.	Y	N	Y	N	Y	Y	Y	Y
5 Bryant	?	N	Y	N	Y	N	P	Y
6 ***Gramm***	?	#	?	N	Y	Y	Y	N
7 ***Archer***	Y	Y	N	N	Y	Y	Y	N
8 ***Fields***	Y	Y	N	?	?	Y	N	N
9 Brooks	Y	N	Y	N	Y	Y	Y	Y
10 Pickle	Y	N	Y	?	?	?	?	Y
11 Leath	Y	N	Y	N	Y	?	Y	Y
12 Wright	?	?	?	Y	Y	N	Y	Y
13 Hightower	Y	N	Y	?	Y	Y	Y	Y
14 Patman	Y	N	Y	N	Y	N	Y	Y
15 de la Garza	Y	N	Y	?	?	Y	Y	Y
16 Coleman	Y	N	Y	Y	Y	N	Y	Y
17 Stenholm	Y	Y	Y	N	Y	Y	Y	Y
18 Leland	?	N	Y	?	#	?	Y	Y
19 Hance	?	#	?	N	Y	Y	Y	Y
20 Gonzalez	Y	N	Y	N	N	N	Y	Y
21 ***Loeffler***	Y	Y	N	N	Y	Y	Y	Y
22 ***Paul***	Y	Y	N	?	?	?	Y	N
23 Kazen	Y	N	Y	N	Y	Y	Y	Y
24 Frost	?	?	?	Y	Y	N	Y	Y
25 Andrews	Y	N	Y	N	Y	N	Y	Y
26 Vandergriff	Y	Y	Y	N	Y	Y	Y	Y
27 Ortiz	?	X	?	N	Y	N	Y	Y
UTAH								
1 ***Hansen***	?	?	?	N	Y	Y	Y	Y
2 ***Marriott***	?	?	?	N	Y	Y	Y	Y
3 ***Nielson***	?	Y	N	N	Y	Y	Y	Y
VERMONT								
AL ***Jeffords***	Y	Y	Y	?	?	?	Y	Y
VIRGINIA								
1 ***Bateman***	Y	Y	Y	N	Y	Y	Y	Y
2 ***Whitehurst***	Y	Y	Y	?	?	?	?	?
3 ***Bliley***	Y	Y	Y	N	Y	Y	Y	Y
4 Sisisky	Y	N	Y	N	Y	Y	Y	Y
5 Daniel	Y	Y	Y	N	Y	Y	Y	Y
6 Olin	Y	Y	Y	N	Y	Y	Y	Y
7 ***Robinson***	Y	Y	Y	N	Y	Y	Y	Y
8 ***Parris***	Y	N	Y	?	?	?	?	Y
9 Boucher	Y	N	Y	?	Y	Y	Y	Y
10 ***Wolf***	Y	Y	Y	N	N	Y	Y	Y
WASHINGTON								
1 ***Pritchard***	?	?	?	Y	N	?	Y	Y
2 Swift	?	N	Y	N	Y	N	Y	Y
3 Bonker	Y	N	?	N	Y	N	Y	Y
4 ***Morrison***	Y	Y	Y	N	N	Y	Y	Y
5 Foley	Y	N	Y	Y	N	Y	Y	Y
6 Dicks	Y	N	Y	?	?	?	Y	Y
7 Lowry	Y	N	Y	?	?	X	Y	Y
8 ***Chandler***	Y	Y	Y	N	Y	Y	Y	Y
WEST VIRGINIA								
1 Mollohan	Y	N	Y	Y	N	Y	Y	Y
2 Staggers	Y	N	Y	Y	Y	N	N	Y
3 Wise	Y	N	Y	N	Y	N	Y	Y
4 Rahall	Y	N	Y	Y	N	Y	Y	Y
WISCONSIN								
1 Aspin	?	N	Y	Y	N	N	Y	Y
2 Kastenmeier	Y	N	Y	Y	N	Y	Y	Y
3 ***Gunderson***	Y	Y	Y	Y	N	Y	Y	Y
4 Zablocki	Y	N	Y	Y	N	N	Y	Y
5 Moody	Y	N	Y	Y	N	N	Y	Y
6 ***Petri***	Y	Y	Y	Y	N	Y	Y	Y
7 Obey	Y	N	Y	Y	N	Y	Y	Y
8 ***Roth***	Y	Y	Y	Y	N	Y	Y	Y
9 ***Sensenbrenner***	Y	Y	N	?	?	Y	Y	Y
WYOMING								
AL ***Cheney***	Y	Y	N	N	Y	Y	Y	Y

Southern states - Ala., Ark., Fla., Ga., Ky., La., Miss., N.C., Okla., S.C., Tenn., Texas, Va.

407. H J Res 402. War Powers Resolution. Zablocki, D-Wis., motion to suspend the rules and pass the bill to declare that the section of the War Powers Resolution (PL 93-148) requiring that the president withdraw U.S. troops from hostile situations within 60 days unless Congress grants an extension took effect as of Oct. 25, 1983, with the introduction of U.S. armed forces onto the island of Grenada. Motion agreed to 403-23: R 147-16; D 256-7 (ND 173-2, SD 83-5), Nov. 1, 1983. A two-thirds majority of those present and voting (284 in this case) is required for passage under suspension of the rules.

408. HR 4185. Defense Department Appropriations, Fiscal 1984. Addabbo, D-N.Y., amendment to delete multi-year procurement funds for the B-1 bomber. Rejected 175-247: R 18-144; D 157-103 (ND 137-35, SD 20-68), Nov. 1, 1983. A "nay" was a vote supporting the president's position.

409. HR 4185. Defense Department Appropriations, Fiscal 1984. Addabbo, D-N.Y., amendment to delete $2.1 billion for procurement of 21 MX missiles. Rejected 208-217: R 18-145; D 190-72 (ND 156-18, SD 34-54), Nov. 1, 1983. A "nay" was a vote supporting the president's position.

410. Procedural Motion. Hartnett, R-S.C., motion to approve the House *Journal* of Tuesday, Nov. 1. Motion agreed to 376-27: R 149-12; D 227-15 (ND 145-14, SD 82-1), Nov. 2, 1983.

411. HR 4185. Defense Department Appropriations, Fiscal 1984. Long, D-Md., amendment to prohibit use of funds in the bill for the deployment of U.S. armed forces participating in the multinational peacekeeping force in Lebanon after March 1, 1984. Rejected 153-274: R 17-148; D 136-126 (ND 113-62, SD 23-64), Nov. 2, 1983. A "nay" was a vote supporting the president's position.

412. HR 4185. Defense Department Appropriations, Fiscal 1984. Edwards, R-Ala., motion that the Committee of the Whole rise and report the bill, as amended, to the House. Motion agreed to 233-195: R 124-41; D 109-154 (ND 40-135, SD 69-19), Nov. 2, 1983.

413. HR 4185. Defense Department Appropriations, Fiscal 1984. Passage of the bill to appropriate $247,318,091,000 for military programs of the Department of Defense in fiscal 1984. Passed 328-97: R 152-11; D 176-86 (ND 91-83, SD 85-3), Nov. 2, 1983. The president had requested $260,926,119,000 in new budget authority.

KEY

Y Voted for (yea).
\# Paired for.
+ Announced for.
N Voted against (nay).
X Paired against.
- Announced against.
P Voted "present".
C Voted "present" to avoid possible conflict of interest.
? Did not vote or otherwise make a position known.

Democrats **Republicans**

	407	408	409	410	411	412	413
ALABAMA							
1 *Edwards*	Y	N	N	Y	N	Y	Y
2 *Dickinson*	Y	N	N	N	N	Y	Y
3 Nichols	Y	N	N	Y	N	Y	Y
4 Bevill	Y	N	N	Y	N	Y	Y
5 Flippo	Y	N	N	Y	N	Y	Y
6 Erdreich	Y	Y	N	Y	N	Y	Y
7 Shelby	Y	N	N	Y	N	Y	Y
ALASKA							
AL *Young*	Y	N	N	N	N	Y	Y
ARIZONA							
1 *McCain*	Y	N	N	Y	N	Y	Y
2 Udall	Y	?	Y	Y	Y	N	Y
3 *Stump*	N	N	N	Y	N	Y	Y
4 *Rudd*	N	N	N	Y	N	Y	Y
5 *McNulty*	Y	Y	Y	Y	N	Y	Y
ARKANSAS							
1 Alexander	Y	N	N	Y	N	Y	Y
2 Bethune	Y	N	N	N	N	Y	Y
3 *Hammerschmidt*	Y	N	N	N	N	N	Y
4 Anthony	Y	N	Y	Y	N	N	N
CALIFORNIA							
1 Bosco	Y	Y	Y	Y	Y	N	N
2 *Chappie*	Y	N	N	Y	N	Y	Y
3 Matsui	Y	N	Y	Y	N	Y	Y
4 Fazio	Y	Y	N	Y	N	Y	Y
5 Burton	Y	Y	Y	Y	N	N	N
6 Boxer	Y	Y	Y	Y	N	N	N
7 Miller	Y	Y	Y	Y	N	N	N
8 Dellums	Y	Y	Y	Y	N	N	N
9 Stark	Y	Y	Y	Y	N	N	N
10 Edwards	Y	Y	Y	Y	N	N	N
11 Lantos	Y	Y	Y	N	Y	N	N
12 *Zschau*	Y	N	N	Y	N	Y	Y
13 Mineta	Y	Y	Y	Y	N	N	N
14 *Shumway*	Y	N	N	Y	N	Y	Y
15 Coelho	Y	N	Y	N	N	Y	Y
16 Panetta	Y	Y	Y	Y	N	N	N
17 *Pashayan*	Y	N	N	Y	N	Y	Y
18 Lehman	?	\#	?	Y	N	Y	Y
19 *Lagomarsino*	Y	N	N	Y	N	N	Y
20 *Thomas*	Y	N	N	Y	N	Y	Y
21 *Fiedler*	Y	N	N	Y	N	Y	Y
22 *Moorhead*	Y	N	N	Y	N	Y	Y
23 Beilenson	Y	Y	Y	N	N	N	N
24 Waxman	Y	Y	Y	Y	N	N	N
25 Roybal	Y	Y	Y	Y	N	N	N
26 Berman	Y	Y	Y	N	N	N	N
27 Levine	Y	N	Y	Y	N	Y	Y
28 Dixon	Y	Y	Y	Y	N	N	N
29 Hawkins	Y	N	Y	Y	N	N	N
30 Martinez	Y	Y	Y	Y	N	N	N
31 Dymally	Y	Y	?	P	Y	N	N
32 Anderson	Y	N	N	Y	N	N	Y
33 *Dreier*	N	N	N	Y	N	Y	Y
34 Torres	Y	Y	Y	Y	N	N	N
35 *Lewis*	Y	N	N	Y	N	Y	Y
36 Brown	Y	X	Y	N	N	N	N
37 *McCandless*	Y	N	N	Y	N	Y	Y
38 Patterson	Y	N	Y	Y	Y	N	Y
39 *Dannemeyer*	Y	N	N	Y	N	Y	Y
40 *Badham*	Y	N	N	Y	N	N	Y
41 *Lowery*	Y	N	N	Y	N	Y	Y
42 *Lungren*	Y	N	N	N	N	Y	Y
43 *Packard*	Y	N	N	Y	N	Y	Y
44 Bates	Y	?	Y	Y	Y	N	N
45 *Hunter*	Y	N	N	Y	N	N	Y
COLORADO							
1 Schroeder	Y	Y	Y	N	Y	N	N
2 Wirth	Y	Y	Y	Y	Y	N	N
3 Kogovsek	Y	Y	Y	N	N	N	N
4 *Brown*	Y	Y	N	Y	N	N	N
5 *Kramer*	N	N	N	Y	Y	Y	Y
6 *Schaefer*	Y	N	N	Y	N	Y	Y
CONNECTICUT							
1 Kennelly	Y	Y	Y	Y	Y	N	Y
2 Gejdenson	Y	Y	Y	N	Y	N	Y
3 Morrison	Y	Y	Y	Y	Y	N	N
4 *McKinney*	Y	Y	Y	Y	N	N	N
5 Ratchford	Y	Y	Y	Y	N	Y	Y
6 *Johnson*	Y	N	Y	Y	N	N	N
DELAWARE							
AL Carper	Y	Y	Y	Y	Y	Y	Y
FLORIDA							
1 Hutto	Y	N	N	Y	N	Y	Y
2 Fuqua	Y	N	N	Y	N	Y	Y
3 Bennett	Y	N	Y	Y	N	Y	Y
4 Chappell	Y	N	N	Y	N	Y	Y
5 *McCollum*	Y	N	N	Y	N	Y	Y
6 MacKay	Y	Y	Y	Y	N	Y	Y
7 Gibbons	Y	Y	Y	Y	N	N	Y
8 *Young*	Y	N	N	Y	N	Y	Y
9 *Bilirakis*	Y	N	N	Y	N	Y	Y
10 Ireland	Y	N	N	Y	N	Y	Y
11 Nelson	Y	N	N	Y	N	Y	Y
12 *Lewis*	Y	N	N	Y	N	Y	Y
13 *Mack*	Y	N	N	Y	N	N	Y
14 Mica	Y	N	Y	N	N	Y	Y
15 *Shaw*	Y	N	N	Y	N	Y	Y
16 Smith	Y	Y	Y	?	N	N	Y
17 Lehman	Y	Y	Y	Y	Y	N	N
18 Pepper	Y	Y	Y	?	N	Y	Y
19 Fascell	Y	Y	Y	Y	N	Y	Y
GEORGIA							
1 Thomas	Y	N	N	Y	N	Y	Y
2 Hatcher	?	N	N	Y	N	Y	Y
3 Ray	Y	N	N	Y	N	Y	Y
4 Levitas	Y	N	Y	Y	N	Y	Y
5 Fowler	Y	Y	Y	Y	N	Y	Y
6 *Gingrich*	Y	N	N	Y	N	N	N
7 Vacancy							
8 Rowland	Y	N	N	Y	N	Y	Y
9 Jenkins	Y	N	N	Y	N	Y	Y
10 Barnard	Y	?	?	?	N	Y	Y
HAWAII							
1 Heftel	Y	N	Y	?	N	Y	Y
2 Akaka	Y	Y	Y	Y	N	Y	Y
IDAHO							
1 *Craig*	N	N	N	Y	Y	Y	Y
2 *Hansen*	N	N	N	Y	N	Y	\#
ILLINOIS							
1 Hayes	Y	Y	Y	?	Y	N	N
2 Savage	Y	Y	Y	Y	N	N	N
3 Russo	Y	Y	Y	Y	N	N	N
4 *O'Brien*	Y	N	N	Y	N	Y	Y
5 Lipinski	Y	Y	N	Y	N	Y	Y
6 *Hyde*	Y	N	N	Y	N	N	N
7 Collins	Y	Y	Y	Y	N	N	N
8 Rostenkowski	Y	Y	Y	Y	N	N	Y
9 Yates	Y	Y	Y	Y	N	N	N
10 *Porter*	Y	N	N	Y	N	N	N
11 Annunzio	Y	Y	Y	Y	N	N	Y
12 *Crane, P.*	Y	N	N	Y	N	Y	Y
13 *Erlenborn*	Y	N	N	Y	N	Y	Y
14 *Corcoran*	?	?	X	?	N	Y	Y
15 *Madigan*	Y	N	N	Y	N	Y	Y
16 *Martin*	Y	N	Y	Y	Y	Y	Y
17 Evans	Y	Y	Y	Y	N	Y	Y
18 *Michel*	Y	N	N	Y	N	Y	Y
19 *Crane, D.*	Y	N	N	Y	N	Y	Y
20 Durbin	Y	Y	Y	N	Y	N	Y
21 Price	Y	N	N	Y	N	Y	Y
22 Simon	Y	Y	\#	Y	N	N	Y
INDIANA							
1 Hall	Y	Y	Y	Y	Y	N	Y
2 Sharp	Y	Y	Y	?	Y	Y	Y
3 *Hiler*	Y	N	N	Y	N	N	N
4 *Coats*	Y	N	N	Y	N	N	N
5 *Hillis*	Y	N	N	Y	Y	Y	Y

Corresponding to Congressional Record Votes 437, 438, 439, 440, 441, 442, 443

	407	408	409	410	411	412	413
6 ***Burton***	N	N	N	Y	N	Y	Y
7 ***Myers***	Y	N	N	Y	N	Y	Y
8 McCloskey	Y	Y	Y	Y	Y	N	Y
9 Hamilton	Y	Y	Y	Y	N	Y	Y
10 Jacobs	Y	Y	Y	?	Y	N	Y
IOWA							
1 ***Leach***	Y	Y	Y	Y	Y	N	N
2 ***Tauke***	Y	Y	Y	Y	Y	N	N
3 ***Evans***	Y	X	#	N	N	N	N
4 Smith	Y	Y	Y	Y	Y	Y	N
5 Harkin	Y	Y	Y	N	Y	N	N
6 Bedell	Y	Y	Y	Y	Y	N	N
KANSAS							
1 ***Roberts***	Y	N	N	N	N	Y	Y
2 Slattery	Y	N	Y	Y	N	Y	Y
3 ***Winn***	Y	N	N	Y	N	Y	Y
4 Glickman	Y	N	Y	Y	Y	Y	Y
5 ***Whittaker***	Y	N	N	Y	N	Y	Y
KENTUCKY							
1 Hubbard	N	N	N	Y	N	Y	Y
2 Natcher	Y	N	Y	Y	N	Y	Y
3 Mazzoli	Y	Y	Y	Y	N	N	Y
4 ***Snyder***	Y	N	N	Y	N	N	Y
5 ***Rogers***	Y	N	N	Y	N	Y	Y
6 ***Hopkins***	N	N	N	Y	N	N	Y
7 Perkins	Y	N	Y	Y	Y	N	Y
LOUISIANA							
1 ***Livingston***	Y	N	N	Y	N	Y	Y
2 Boggs	Y	N	N	Y	N	Y	Y
3 Tauzin	Y	N	N	Y	N	Y	Y
4 Roemer	Y	N	N	N	Y	Y	Y
5 Huckaby	Y	N	N	Y	N	Y	Y
6 ***Moore***	Y	N	N	Y	N	N	Y
7 Breaux	Y	N	N	Y	N	N	Y
8 Long	Y	N	Y	Y	N	Y	Y
MAINE							
1 ***McKernan***	Y	N	N	Y	N	Y	Y
2 ***Snowe***	Y	N	N	Y	N	Y	Y
MARYLAND							
1 Dyson	Y	N	Y	Y	N	Y	Y
2 Long	Y	Y	Y	Y	Y	Y	Y
3 Mikulski	Y	Y	Y	Y	N	Y	Y
4 ***Holt***	Y	N	N	Y	N	Y	Y
5 Hoyer	Y	N	N	Y	N	Y	Y
6 Byron	Y	N	N	Y	N	Y	Y
7 Mitchell	+	#	Y	?	+	-	X
8 Barnes	Y	Y	Y	Y	N	N	Y
MASSACHUSETTS							
1 ***Conte***	Y	Y	Y	Y	Y	N	Y
2 Boland	Y	Y	Y	Y	N	N	Y
3 Early	Y	Y	Y	Y	Y	N	N
4 Frank	Y	Y	Y	Y	Y	N	N
5 Shannon	Y	Y	Y	Y	Y	N	N
6 Mavroules	Y	Y	Y	Y	N	N	Y
7 Markey	Y	Y	Y	Y	N	N	N
8 O'Neill							
9 Moakley	Y	Y	Y	Y	N	N	N
10 Studds	Y	Y	Y	Y	Y	N	N
11 Donnelly	Y	Y	Y	Y	Y	N	N
MICHIGAN							
1 Conyers	Y	Y	Y	?	Y	N	N
2 ***Pursell***	Y	Y	N	Y	N	Y	Y
3 Wolpe	Y	Y	Y	Y	Y	N	N
4 ***Siljander***	Y	N	N	Y	N	Y	Y
5 ***Sawyer***	?	?	?	Y	N	Y	Y
6 Carr	Y	N	Y	Y	Y	N	Y
7 Kildee	Y	Y	Y	Y	Y	N	N
8 Traxler	Y	Y	Y	Y	Y	N	Y
9 ***Vander Jagt***	?	?	X	Y	N	Y	Y
10 Albosta	Y	Y	Y	Y	N	N	Y
11 ***Davis***	Y	N	N	Y	N	Y	Y
12 Bonior	Y	Y	Y	Y	N	N	N
13 Crockett	Y	Y	Y	?	Y	N	N
14 Hertel	Y	Y	Y	Y	Y	N	N
15 Ford	Y	Y	Y	?	Y	N	Y
16 Dingell	Y	Y	Y	?	Y	N	Y
17 Levin	Y	Y	Y	Y	N	N	N
18 ***Broomfield***	Y	N	N	Y	N	Y	Y
MINNESOTA							
1 Penny	Y	Y	Y	Y	Y	N	N
2 ***Weber***	Y	N	N	Y	N	N	Y
3 ***Frenzel***	Y	Y	N	Y	N	N	N
4 Vento	Y	Y	Y	Y	Y	N	N
5 Sabo	Y	Y	Y	N	Y	N	N
6 Sikorski	Y	Y	Y	N	Y	N	N

	407	408	409	410	411	412	413
7 ***Stangeland***	Y	N	N	Y	N	Y	Y
8 Oberstar	Y	Y	Y	P	Y	N	N
MISSISSIPPI							
1 Whitten	Y	N	Y	Y	N	Y	Y
2 ***Franklin***	N	N	N	Y	N	Y	Y
3 Montgomery	Y	N	N	Y	N	Y	Y
4 Dowdy	Y	N	Y	Y	Y	Y	Y
5 ***Lott***	Y	N	N	Y	N	Y	Y
MISSOURI							
1 Clay	Y	Y	Y	N	Y	N	N
2 Young	Y	N	Y	Y	Y	N	Y
3 Gephardt	Y	Y	Y	Y	N	Y	Y
4 Skelton	Y	N	N	Y	Y	Y	Y
5 Wheat	Y	Y	Y	?	Y	N	N
6 ***Coleman***	Y	N	N	Y	N	Y	Y
7 ***Taylor***	Y	N	N	Y	N	Y	Y
8 ***Emerson***	Y	N	N	N	N	Y	Y
9 Volkmer	Y	N	Y	Y	Y	N	Y
MONTANA							
1 Williams	Y	Y	Y	?	N	N	N
2 ***Marlenee***	N	N	N	Y	N	Y	Y
NEBRASKA							
1 ***Bereuter***	Y	N	Y	Y	N	N	Y
2 ***Daub***	Y	N	N	Y	N	Y	Y
3 ***Smith***	Y	N	Y	Y	N	N	Y
NEVADA							
1 Reid	Y	N	N	Y	N	N	Y
2 ***Vucanovich***	Y	N	N	Y	N	N	Y
NEW HAMPSHIRE							
1 D'Amours	Y	Y	Y	Y	N	N	Y
2 ***Gregg***	Y	N	N	Y	N	N	Y
NEW JERSEY							
1 Florio	Y	Y	Y	Y	Y	Y	N
2 Hughes	Y	Y	Y	Y	N	N	Y
3 Howard	Y	Y	Y	Y	N	Y	Y
4 ***Smith***	Y	N	Y	Y	N	N	Y
5 ***Roukema***	Y	N	Y	Y	N	Y	Y
6 Dwyer	Y	Y	Y	Y	N	N	Y
7 ***Rinaldo***	Y	N	N	Y	N	N	Y
8 Roe	Y	Y	Y	Y	N	N	Y
9 Torricelli	Y	Y	Y	Y	Y	N	Y
10 Rodino	Y	Y	Y	Y	Y	N	N
11 Minish	Y	Y	Y	Y	Y	Y	Y
12 ***Courter***	Y	N	N	Y	N	Y	Y
13 ***Forsythe***	Y	Y	Y	N	N	Y	N
14 Guarini	Y	Y	Y	N	#	N	Y
NEW MEXICO							
1 ***Lujan***	Y	N	N	Y	N	Y	Y
2 ***Skeen***	Y	N	N	Y	N	Y	Y
3 Richardson	Y	N	Y	Y	Y	N	Y
NEW YORK							
1 ***Carney***	Y	N	N	Y	N	Y	Y
2 Downey	Y	Y	Y	Y	Y	N	Y
3 Mrazek	Y	Y	Y	Y	Y	N	Y
4 ***Lent***	Y	N	N	?	N	Y	Y
5 ***McGrath***	Y	N	N	Y	N	Y	Y
6 Addabbo	Y	Y	Y	Y	Y	N	Y
7 Ackerman	Y	Y	Y	Y	N	N	Y
8 Scheuer	Y	Y	Y	Y	N	N	Y
9 Ferraro	Y	Y	Y	Y	Y	N	Y
10 Schumer	Y	Y	Y	Y	N	N	Y
11 Towns	Y	Y	Y	Y	Y	N	N
12 Owens	Y	Y	Y	Y	Y	N	N
13 Solarz	Y	Y	Y	Y	N	N	Y
14 ***Molinari***	Y	N	N	Y	N	Y	Y
15 ***Green***	Y	Y	Y	Y	N	N	N
16 Rangel	Y	Y	Y	Y	Y	N	N
17 Weiss	N	Y	Y	Y	Y	N	N
18 Garcia	Y	Y	N	Y	Y	N	N
19 Biaggi	Y	Y	Y	?	N	Y	Y
20 Ottinger	Y	Y	Y	P	Y	N	X
21 ***Fish***	Y	N	N	Y	N	N	Y
22 ***Gilman***	Y	N	N	Y	N	N	Y
23 Stratton	N	N	N	Y	Y	Y	Y
24 ***Solomon***	Y	N	N	Y	N	Y	Y
25 ***Boehlert***	Y	N	N	Y	N	N	Y
26 ***Martin***	Y	N	N	Y	N	Y	Y
27 ***Wortley***	Y	N	N	Y	N	Y	Y
28 McHugh	Y	Y	Y	Y	N	N	Y
29 ***Horton***	Y	Y	N	Y	Y	Y	Y
30 ***Conable***	Y	N	N	?	X	#	#
31 ***Kemp***	N	N	N	Y	N	Y	Y
32 LaFalce	Y	Y	Y	Y	Y	Y	N
33 Nowak	Y	Y	Y	Y	Y	N	N
34 Lundine	Y	Y	Y	Y	Y	Y	?

	407	408	409	410	411	412	413
NORTH CAROLINA							
1 Jones	Y	N	N	?	N	Y	Y
2 Valentine	Y	Y	Y	Y	N	Y	Y
3 Whitley	Y	N	N	Y	N	Y	Y
4 Andrews	Y	Y	Y	Y	Y	Y	Y
5 Neal	Y	N	N	?	N	N	Y
6 Britt	Y	Y	N	Y	N	Y	Y
7 Rose	Y	N	Y	Y	Y	Y	Y
8 Hefner	Y	N	N	Y	Y	Y	Y
9 ***Martin***	Y	?	N	Y	N	Y	Y
10 ***Broyhill***	Y	N	N	Y	N	Y	Y
11 Clarke	Y	N	Y	Y	N	N	Y
NORTH DAKOTA							
AL Dorgan	Y	Y	Y	N	Y	N	N
OHIO							
1 Luken	Y	N	Y	Y	Y	Y	N
2 ***Gradison***	Y	N	Y	Y	N	Y	Y
3 Hall	Y	N	Y	Y	Y	N	N
4 ***Oxley***	Y	N	N	Y	N	Y	Y
5 ***Latta***	Y	N	N	Y	N	Y	Y
6 ***McEwen***	Y	N	N	Y	N	Y	Y
7 ***DeWine***	Y	N	N	Y	N	Y	Y
8 ***Kindness***	Y	N	N	Y	N	Y	Y
9 Kaptur	Y	Y	Y	Y	N	N	N
10 ***Miller***	Y	N	N	N	N	Y	Y
11 Eckart	Y	N	Y	N	Y	N	Y
12 ***Kasich***	Y	N	N	Y	Y	N	Y
13 Pease	Y	Y	Y	Y	Y	N	Y
14 Seiberling	Y	Y	Y	Y	Y	N	N
15 ***Wylie***	Y	N	N	Y	N	Y	Y
16 ***Regula***	Y	N	N	Y	N	Y	Y
17 ***Williams***	Y	N	N	Y	N	Y	Y
18 Applegate	Y	N	Y	Y	Y	N	N
19 Feighan	Y	N	Y	Y	N	N	Y
20 Oakar	Y	N	Y	Y	N	N	Y
21 Stokes	Y	Y	Y	Y	Y	N	N
OKLAHOMA							
1 Jones	Y	N	N	Y	Y	Y	Y
2 Synar	Y	N	Y	Y	N	N	Y
3 Watkins	Y	N	N	Y	Y	Y	Y
4 McCurdy	Y	N	N	Y	+	Y	Y
5 ***Edwards***	Y	N	N	N	N	Y	Y
6 English	Y	N	N	Y	N	Y	Y
OREGON							
1 AuCoin	Y	Y	Y	?	Y	N	N
2 ***Smith, R.***	Y	N	N	Y	N	Y	Y
3 Wyden	Y	Y	Y	Y	Y	N	N
4 Weaver	Y	Y	Y	Y	Y	N	N
5 ***Smith, D.***	Y	N	N	Y	N	Y	Y
PENNSYLVANIA							
1 Foglietta	Y	Y	Y	Y	N	N	Y
2 Gray	Y	Y	Y	Y	Y	N	N
3 Borski	Y	Y	Y	Y	N	Y	Y
4 Kolter	Y	Y	Y	N	Y	Y	Y
5 ***Schulze***	Y	N	N	Y	N	Y	Y
6 Yatron	Y	N	N	Y	N	Y	Y
7 Edgar	Y	Y	Y	Y	Y	N	N
8 Kostmayer	Y	Y	Y	Y	Y	N	N
9 ***Shuster***	Y	N	N	Y	N	Y	Y
10 ***McDade***	Y	N	N	Y	N	Y	Y
11 Harrison	Y	Y	Y	Y	N	Y	Y
12 Murtha	Y	N	N	Y	N	Y	Y
13 ***Coughlin***	Y	Y	N	N	N	N	Y
14 Coyne	Y	Y	Y	Y	N	N	Y
15 ***Ritter***	Y	N	N	Y	N	N	N
16 ***Walker***	Y	N	N	N	N	N	Y
17 ***Gekas***	Y	N	N	Y	N	Y	?
18 Walgren	Y	Y	Y	Y	Y	N	N
19 ***Goodling***	Y	N	N	Y	N	N	N
20 Gaydos	Y	N	N	Y	Y	Y	Y
21 ***Ridge***	Y	Y	Y	?	N	N	Y
22 Murphy	Y	N	Y	Y	Y	N	Y
23 ***Clinger***	Y	Y	N	Y	N	N	Y
RHODE ISLAND							
1 St Germain	Y	Y	Y	P	Y	N	N
2 ***Schneider***	Y	Y	Y	?	#	X	X
SOUTH CAROLINA							
1 ***Hartnett***	N	N	N	Y	N	Y	Y
2 ***Spence***	Y	N	N	Y	N	Y	Y
3 Derrick	Y	N	Y	Y	Y	Y	Y
4 ***Campbell***	Y	N	N	Y	N	Y	Y
5 Spratt	Y	Y	Y	Y	N	Y	Y
6 Tallon	Y	Y	Y	Y	N	Y	Y
SOUTH DAKOTA							
AL Daschle	Y	N	Y	N	Y	N	Y

	407	408	409	410	411	412	413
TENNESSEE							
1 ***Quillen***	Y	N	N	Y	N	Y	Y
2 ***Duncan***	Y	N	N	Y	N	Y	Y
3 Lloyd	Y	N	N	Y	N	Y	Y
4 Cooper	Y	N	N	Y	N	N	Y
5 Boner	Y	N	N	Y	N	Y	Y
6 Gore	Y	N	N	Y	N	Y	Y
7 ***Sundquist***	Y	N	N	Y	N	Y	Y
8 Jones	Y	N	N	Y	N	Y	Y
9 Ford	Y	Y	Y	Y	N	N	Y
TEXAS							
1 Hall, S.	Y	N	N	Y	Y	Y	Y
2 Wilson	N	N	N	?	N	Y	Y
3 ***Bartlett***	Y	N	N	Y	N	Y	Y
4 Hall, R.	N	N	N	Y	N	Y	Y
5 Bryant	Y	N	Y	Y	Y	N	Y
6 ***Gramm***	N	N	N	Y	N	Y	Y
7 ***Archer***	Y	N	N	Y	Y	Y	Y
8 ***Fields***	Y	N	N	N	Y	Y	Y
9 Brooks	Y	Y	Y	Y	Y	Y	Y
10 Pickle	Y	N	N	Y	N	Y	Y
11 Leath	N	N	N	Y	N	Y	Y
12 Wright	Y	N	Y	Y	N	Y	Y
13 Hightower	Y	N	N	Y	N	Y	Y
14 Patman	Y	N	N	Y	Y	Y	Y
15 de la Garza	Y	N	N	Y	Y	Y	Y
16 Coleman	Y	N	Y	Y	N	Y	Y
17 Stenholm	Y	N	N	Y	Y	Y	Y
18 Leland	Y	Y	Y	Y	Y	N	N
19 Hance	Y	N	N	Y	X	?	#
20 Gonzalez	Y	Y	Y	Y	Y	N	Y
21 ***Loeffler***	N	N	N	Y	N	Y	Y
22 ***Paul***	Y	Y	Y	Y	Y	Y	N
23 Kazen	Y	N	N	Y	N	Y	Y
24 Frost	Y	N	N	Y	N	Y	Y
25 Andrews	Y	N	N	Y	N	Y	Y
26 Vandergriff	Y	N	N	Y	N	Y	Y
27 Ortiz	Y	N	N	Y	N	Y	Y
UTAH							
1 ***Hansen***	N	N	N	Y	N	Y	Y
2 ***Marriott***	Y	N	N	Y	N	Y	Y
3 ***Nielson***	Y	N	N	Y	N	Y	Y
VERMONT							
AL ***Jeffords***	Y	Y	Y	Y	N	N	Y
VIRGINIA							
1 ***Bateman***	Y	N	N	Y	N	Y	Y
2 ***Whitehurst***	?	N	N	Y	N	Y	Y
3 ***Bliley***	Y	N	N	Y	N	Y	Y
4 Sisisky	Y	N	Y	Y	N	Y	Y
5 Daniel	N	N	N	Y	N	Y	Y
6 Olin	Y	N	Y	Y	Y	N	Y
7 ***Robinson***	Y	N	N	Y	N	Y	Y
8 ***Parris***	Y	N	N	Y	N	Y	Y
9 Boucher	Y	N	Y	Y	Y	Y	Y
10 ***Wolf***	Y	N	N	Y	N	Y	Y
WASHINGTON							
1 ***Pritchard***	Y	Y	N	?	N	Y	Y
2 Swift	Y	Y	Y	Y	Y	N	N
3 Bonker	Y	Y	Y	Y	N	N	N
4 ***Morrison***	Y	N	N	Y	N	Y	Y
5 Foley	Y	N	N	Y	N	Y	Y
6 Dicks	Y	N	N	Y	N	Y	Y
7 Lowry	Y	Y	Y	Y	Y	?	N
8 ***Chandler***	Y	N	N	Y	N	Y	Y
WEST VIRGINIA							
1 Mollohan	Y	N	N	Y	N	Y	Y
2 Staggers	Y	Y	Y	Y	Y	N	Y
3 Wise	Y	Y	Y	Y	Y	Y	Y
4 Rahall	Y	Y	Y	Y	N	Y	N
WISCONSIN							
1 Aspin	Y	Y	N	Y	N	Y	Y
2 Kastenmeier	Y	Y	Y	?	Y	N	N
3 ***Gunderson***	Y	N	N	Y	N	Y	Y
4 Zablocki	Y	N	N	Y	N	Y	Y
5 Moody	Y	Y	Y	Y	Y	N	N
6 ***Petri***	Y	Y	Y	Y	N	Y	Y
7 Obey	Y	Y	Y	Y	Y	N	N
8 ***Roth***	Y	N	N	Y	Y	N	Y
9 ***Sensenbrenner***	Y	N	N	Y	Y	N	Y
WYOMING							
AL ***Cheney***	N	N	N	Y	N	Y	Y

Southern states - Ala., Ark., Fla., Ga., Ky., La., Miss., N.C., Okla., S.C., Tenn., Texas, Va.

414. Procedural Motion. Broyhill, R-N.C., motion to approve the House *Journal* of Wednesday, Nov. 2. Motion agreed to 371-27: R 147-9; D 224-18 (ND 140-17, SD 84-1), Nov. 3, 1983.

415. HR 1234. Auto Domestic Content Requirement. Coats, R-Ind., amendment to prohibit auto domestic content requirements from being enforced if they violate U.S. trade obligations under the General Agreement on Tariffs and Trade (GATT) and would lead to retaliation by other countries. The amendment also would give U.S. federal courts the authority to resolve trade disputes arising under the bill. Rejected 178-232: R 136-26; D 42-206 (ND 6-159, SD 36-47), Nov. 3, 1983.

416. HR 1234. Auto Domestic Content Requirement. Pease, D-Ohio, amendment to the McNulty, D-Ariz., amendment, to impose a sunset provision on the domestic content bill. The provisions of the bill would lapse six years after date of enactment if the secretary of transportation certified that the U.S. auto industry no longer was injured by foreign car imports. The McNulty amendment would have simply terminated the bill's provisions on Sept. 30, 1992. Adopted 214-196: R 26-138; D 188-58 (ND 150-14, SD 38-44), Nov. 3, 1983. (The McNulty amendment, as amended, subsequently was adopted by voice vote.)

417. HR 1234. Auto Domestic Content Requirement. Passage of the bill to require fixed levels of U.S. labor and parts in automobiles sold in the United States by foreign car manufacturers. The bill would phase in domestic content levels beginning in 1985 and reaching maximum levels in 1987. Passed 219-199: R 32-131; D 187-68 (ND 150-22, SD 37-46), Nov. 3, 1983. A "nay" was a vote supporting the president's position.

418. HR 2867. Hazardous Waste Control. Hughes, D-N.J., amendment to the Judiciary Committee amendment, to direct the attorney general, upon request of the Environmental Protection Agency (EPA) administrator and upon a showing of need, to deputize qualified EPA employees as special deputy U.S. marshals for criminal investigations into violations of this act. The Judiciary Committee amendment would strike from the bill provisions authorizing EPA employees to carry firearms, serve warrants and subpoenas, administer oaths and make arrests. Adopted 292-125: R 146-17; D 146-108 (ND 87-84, SD 59-24), Nov. 3, 1983.

419. HR 2867. Hazardous Waste Control. Levitas, D-Ga., amendment to require approval of a joint resolution by both houses of Congress and by the president before any final rule promulgated by the Environmental Protection Agency shall take effect pertaining to generators of small quantities of hazardous waste if such rule will have an annual economic impact of at least $100 million. Adopted 198-195: R 131-22; D 67-173 (ND 21-142, SD 46-31), Nov. 3, 1983. (The House subsequently rejected the amendment after rising from the Committee of the Whole *(see vote 420, below)*.)

420. HR 2867. Hazardous Waste Control. Levitas, D-Ga., amendment to require approval of a joint resolution by both houses of Congress and by the president before any final rule promulgated by the Environmental Protection Agency shall take effect pertaining to generators of small quantities of hazardous waste if such rule will have an annual economic impact of at least $100 million. Rejected 189-204: R 131-21; D 58-183 (ND 13-151, SD 45-32), Nov. 3, 1983. (The amendment previously was adopted in the Committee of the Whole *(see vote 419, above)*.)

KEY

Y Voted for (yea).
Paired for.
+ Announced for.
N Voted against (nay).
X Paired against.
- Announced against.
P Voted "present".
C Voted "present" to avoid possible conflict of interest.
? Did not vote or otherwise make a position known.

Democrats *Republicans*

	414	415	416	417	418	419	420
ALABAMA							
1 *Edwards*	Y	Y	N	N	Y	Y	Y
2 *Dickinson*	N	Y	N	N	N	?	?
3 Nichols	Y	Y	N	Y	Y	Y	Y
4 Bevill	Y	N	Y	N	Y	Y	Y
5 Flippo	Y	N	Y	Y	Y	Y	Y
6 Erdreich	Y	N	Y	Y	Y	Y	Y
7 Shelby	Y	N	Y	N	Y	N	Y
ALASKA							
AL *Young*	?	N	N	Y	Y	Y	Y
ARIZONA							
1 *McCain*	Y	Y	N	N	Y	Y	Y
2 Udall	Y	N	Y	Y	N	N	N
3 *Stump*	Y	Y	N	N	Y	Y	Y
4 *Rudd*	Y	Y	N	N	Y	Y	Y
5 McNulty	Y	N	Y	Y	Y	N	N
ARKANSAS							
1 Alexander	Y	N	Y	N	N	N	Y
2 *Bethune*	Y	Y	N	N	Y	Y	Y
3 *Hammerschmidt*	Y	Y	N	N	Y	N	N
4 Anthony	Y	Y	N	N	Y	N	Y
CALIFORNIA							
1 Bosco	Y	N	N	N	N	N	N
2 *Chappie*	N	Y	N	N	Y	Y	Y
3 Matsui	Y	N	Y	Y	N	N	N
4 Fazio	Y	N	Y	Y	N	N	N
5 Burton	Y	N	Y	Y	N	N	N
6 Boxer	Y	N	Y	Y	N	N	N
7 Miller	N	N	Y	Y	N	N	N
8 Dellums	?	?	?	Y	N	N	N
9 Stark	Y	N	Y	Y	N	N	N
10 Edwards	Y	N	Y	Y	N	N	N
11 Lantos	Y	N	Y	Y	Y	N	N
12 Zschau	Y	Y	N	N	Y	Y	Y
13 Mineta	Y	N	Y	Y	N	N	N
14 Shumway	Y	Y	N	N	Y	Y	Y
15 Coelho	?	?	?	?	?	?	?
16 Panetta	Y	N	Y	N	N	N	N
17 *Pashayan*	Y	Y	N	N	Y	?	?
18 Lehman	Y	N	Y	Y	N	N	N
19 *Lagomarsino*	Y	Y	N	N	Y	Y	Y
20 *Thomas*	Y	Y	N	N	Y	Y	Y
21 *Fiedler*	Y	Y	N	Y	Y	Y	Y
22 *Moorhead*	Y	Y	N	N	Y	Y	Y
23 Beilenson	N	N	Y	N	Y	N	N
24 Waxman	Y	N	Y	N	N	N	N
25 Roybal	Y	N	Y	Y	N	N	N
26 Berman	Y	N	Y	Y	Y	N	N
27 Levine	N	N	N	Y	N	N	N
28 Dixon	Y	N	Y	Y	N	N	N
29 Hawkins	N	N	Y	N	N	N	N
30 Martinez	Y	N	Y	Y	N	N	N
31 Dymally	?	?	?	Y	Y	N	N
32 Anderson	Y	Y	N	N	N	N	N
33 *Dreier*	Y	Y	N	N	Y	Y	Y
34 Torres	Y	N	Y	Y	N	N	N
35 *Lewis*	Y	Y	N	N	Y	Y	Y
36 Brown	?	N	Y	N	N	N	N
37 *McCandless*	Y	Y	N	N	Y	Y	Y
38 Patterson	Y	N	N	Y	N	N	N
39 *Dannemeyer*	Y	Y	N	N	Y	?	?
40 *Badham*	Y	Y	N	N	Y	Y	Y
41 *Lowery*	Y	Y	N	N	Y	Y	Y
42 *Lungren*	Y	Y	N	N	Y	Y	Y

	414	415	416	417	418	419	420
43 *Packard*	Y	Y	N	N	Y	?	?
44 Bates	Y	N	Y	N	Y	N	N
45 *Hunter*	Y	Y	Y	Y	Y	Y	Y
COLORADO							
1 Schroeder	N	N	Y	Y	N	N	N
2 Wirth	Y	N	Y	Y	N	N	N
3 Kogovsek	Y	N	Y	Y	Y	?	?
4 *Brown*	Y	Y	N	N	Y	Y	Y
5 *Kramer*	Y	Y	N	N	Y	Y	Y
6 *Schaefer*	Y	Y	N	N	Y	Y	Y
CONNECTICUT							
1 Kennelly	Y	N	Y	Y	N	N	N
2 Gejdenson	N	N	Y	N	N	N	N
3 Morrison	Y	N	Y	Y	N	N	N
4 *McKinney*	Y	Y	Y	Y	N	N	N
5 Ratchford	Y	N	Y	Y	N	N	N
6 *Johnson*	Y	N	Y	Y	N	N	N
DELAWARE							
AL Carper	Y	N	N	Y	Y	N	N
FLORIDA							
1 Hutto	Y	Y	N	N	Y	Y	Y
2 Fuqua	Y	N	N	N	Y	Y	Y
3 Bennett	Y	N	N	N	N	N	N
4 Chappell	Y	Y	Y	N	?	#	#
5 *McCollum*	Y	Y	N	N	Y	Y	Y
6 MacKay	Y	N	N	N	Y	Y	Y
7 Gibbons	Y	N	N	N	N	N	N
8 *Young*	?	Y	N	N	Y	Y	Y
9 *Bilirakis*	Y	Y	N	N	Y	Y	Y
10 Ireland	Y	Y	N	N	Y	Y	Y
11 Nelson	Y	N	N	Y	N	Y	Y
12 *Lewis*	Y	Y	N	N	Y	Y	Y
13 *Mack*	Y	Y	N	N	Y	Y	Y
14 Mica	Y	N	N	N	N	N	N
15 *Shaw*	Y	N	N	N	Y	Y	Y
16 Smith	Y	N	Y	N	N	N	N
17 Lehman	Y	C	C	C	Y	N	N
18 Pepper	Y	N	Y	Y	N	N	N
19 Fascell	Y	N	Y	Y	N	N	N
GEORGIA							
1 Thomas	Y	Y	N	N	Y	Y	Y
2 Hatcher	Y	N	N	N	Y	?	?
3 Ray	Y	Y	N	N	Y	Y	Y
4 Levitas	Y	N	N	N	N	Y	Y
5 Fowler	Y	N	Y	N	Y	N	N
6 *Gingrich*	Y	N	N	Y	N	Y	Y
7 Vacancy							
8 Rowland	Y	Y	N	N	Y	Y	Y
9 Jenkins	Y	N	?	N	Y	Y	Y
10 Barnard	Y	Y	N	N	Y	?	?
HAWAII							
1 Heftel	?	N	Y	N	N	N	N
2 Akaka	Y	?	?	Y	Y	N	N
IDAHO							
1 *Craig*	Y	Y	N	N	Y	Y	Y
2 *Hansen*	?	Y	N	N	Y	Y	Y
ILLINOIS							
1 Hayes	?	N	Y	Y	Y	N	N
2 Savage	?	?	?	Y	Y	?	?
3 Russo	Y	N	Y	Y	N	N	N
4 *O'Brien*	Y	N	Y	Y	Y	N	N
5 Lipinski	N	N	Y	Y	N	N	N
6 *Hyde*	Y	Y	N	N	Y	Y	Y
7 Collins	Y	N	Y	N	N	N	N
8 Rostenkowski	Y	Y	N	Y	N	N	N
9 Yates	N	N	Y	Y	N	N	N
10 *Porter*	Y	Y	N	Y	Y	Y	Y
11 Annunzio	Y	N	Y	Y	N	N	N
12 *Crane, P.*	Y	Y	N	N	Y	Y	Y
13 *Erlenborn*	Y	Y	N	N	Y	Y	Y
14 *Corcoran*	Y	Y	N	N	Y	Y	Y
15 *Madigan*	?	N	Y	N	Y	N	Y
16 *Martin*	Y	Y	Y	Y	Y	Y	Y
17 Evans	Y	N	?	Y	Y	N	N
18 *Michel*	Y	Y	N	N	#	Y	Y
19 *Crane, D.*	Y	Y	N	Y	Y	Y	Y
20 Durbin	N	N	Y	Y	N	N	N
21 Price	Y	N	?	Y	Y	N	N
22 Simon	Y	N	Y	Y	N	N	N
INDIANA							
1 Hall	Y	N	Y	Y	Y	N	N
2 Sharp	Y	N	Y	N	N	N	N
3 *Hiler*	Y	Y	N	N	Y	Y	Y
4 *Coats*	Y	Y	N	N	Y	Y	Y
5 Hillis	Y	N	Y	Y	Y	Y	Y

ND - Northern Democrats   SD - Southern Democrats

Corresponding to Congressional Record Votes 444, 445, 447, 448, 450, 451, 452

	414	415	416	417	418	419	420
6 ***Burton***	Y	N	Y	Y	Y	Y	Y
7 ***Myers***	Y	Y	N	N	Y	Y	Y
8 McCloskey	Y	N	Y	Y	Y	N	N
9 Hamilton	Y	N	Y	Y	N	N	N
10 Jacobs	N	N	Y	?	Y	N	N
IOWA							
1 ***Leach***	Y	Y	Y	Y	Y	N	N
2 ***Tauke***	Y	Y	N	N	Y	Y	Y
3 ***Evans***	N	Y	N	N	Y	N	N
4 Smith	Y	N	N	N	Y	?	?
5 Harkin	?	N	Y	Y	Y	N	N
6 Bedell	Y	N	Y	N	N	N	N
KANSAS							
1 ***Roberts***	?	Y	N	N	Y	Y	Y
2 Slattery	Y	N	Y	N	N	Y	Y
3 ***Winn***	Y	Y	N	N	Y	Y	Y
4 Glickman	Y	N	N	N	Y	N	N
5 ***Whittaker***	Y	Y	N	N	Y	Y	Y
KENTUCKY							
1 Hubbard	Y	N	Y	Y	Y	Y	Y
2 Natcher	Y	N	Y	Y	Y	N	N
3 Mazzoli	Y	Y	N	N	Y	N	N
4 ***Snyder***	Y	N	Y	Y	Y	Y	Y
5 ***Rogers***	Y	N	Y	Y	Y	Y	Y
6 ***Hopkins***	Y	Y	N	N	Y	Y	Y
7 Perkins	Y	N	Y	Y	N	N	N
LOUISIANA							
1 ***Livingston***	Y	Y	N	N	Y	Y	Y
2 Boggs	?	N	N	Y	N	N	N
3 Tauzin	Y	N	Y	Y	Y	Y	Y
4 Roemer	N	N	Y	Y	Y	Y	Y
5 Huckaby	Y	Y	N	N	Y	Y	Y
6 ***Moore***	Y	Y	N	N	Y	Y	Y
7 Breaux	Y	Y	N	N	N	Y	Y
8 Long	Y	N	Y	Y	N	N	N
MAINE							
1 ***McKernan***	Y	Y	N	N	Y	N	N
2 ***Snowe***	Y	Y	Y	N	N	N	N
MARYLAND							
1 Dyson	Y	N	Y	Y	N	Y	Y
2 Long	?	N	Y	Y	N	Y	N
3 Mikulski	Y	N	Y	Y	N	N	N
4 ***Holt***	Y	Y	N	N	N	Y	Y
5 Hoyer	Y	N	Y	Y	N	N	N
6 Byron	Y	N	N	N	N	Y	Y
7 Mitchell	N	N	Y	Y	Y	N	N
8 Barnes	Y	N	Y	Y	N	N	N
MASSACHUSETTS							
1 ***Conte***	Y	N	Y	Y	Y	N	N
2 Boland	Y	N	Y	Y	Y	N	N
3 Early	Y	N	Y	Y	?	?	?
4 Frank	Y	N	Y	Y	Y	N	N
5 Shannon	Y	N	Y	Y	N	N	N
6 Mavroules	Y	N	Y	Y	Y	N	N
7 Markey	N	N	Y	Y	N	N	N
8 O'Neill							
9 Moakley	Y	N	Y	Y	Y	N	N
10 Studds	Y	N	Y	Y	N	N	N
11 Donnelly	Y	N	Y	Y	Y	N	N
MICHIGAN							
1 Conyers	?	?	?	Y	Y	N	N
2 ***Pursell***	Y	N	Y	N	Y	Y	Y
3 Wolpe	Y	N	Y	Y	N	N	N
4 ***Siljander***	Y	Y	N	Y	Y	Y	Y
5 ***Sawyer***	Y	N	Y	Y	Y	Y	Y
6 Carr	Y	N	Y	Y	Y	N	N
7 Kildee	Y	N	Y	Y	N	N	N
8 Traxler	Y	N	Y	Y	N	N	N
9 ***Vander Jagt***	Y	Y	N	N	Y	Y	Y
10 Albosta	Y	N	Y	Y	N	Y	Y
11 ***Davis***	Y	N	Y	Y	Y	Y	Y
12 Bonior	Y	N	Y	Y	N	N	N
13 Crockett	?	N	Y	Y	Y	N	N
14 Hertel	Y	N	Y	Y	N	N	N
15 Ford	?	N	Y	Y	N	N	N
16 Dingell	Y	N	Y	Y	N	N	N
17 Levin	Y	N	Y	Y	N	N	N
18 ***Broomfield***	Y	Y	N	N	Y	Y	Y
MINNESOTA							
1 Penny	Y	N	Y	Y	N	Y	N
2 ***Weber***	Y	Y	N	N	N	N	N
3 ***Frenzel***	Y	Y	N	N	Y	Y	Y
4 Vento	Y	N	Y	Y	N	N	N
5 Sabo	N	N	Y	Y	Y	N	N
6 Sikorski	N	N	Y	Y	N	N	N
7 ***Stangeland***	Y	Y	N	N	Y	Y	Y
8 Oberstar	P	N	Y	Y	Y	Y	N
MISSISSIPPI							
1 Whitten	Y	?	?	?	?	?	?
2 ***Franklin***	Y	Y	N	N	?	#	#
3 Montgomery	Y	Y	N	N	Y	Y	Y
4 Dowdy	Y	?	?	?	?	?	?
5 ***Lott***	Y	Y	N	N	Y	Y	Y
MISSOURI							
1 Clay	N	N	Y	Y	Y	N	N
2 Young	Y	N	Y	Y	Y	Y	Y
3 Gephardt	Y	N	Y	Y	N	N	N
4 Skelton	Y	N	Y	Y	N	Y	Y
5 Wheat	Y	N	Y	Y	N	N	N
6 ***Coleman***	Y	Y	N	Y	N	Y	Y
7 ***Taylor***	Y	Y	N	N	Y	Y	Y
8 ***Emerson***	N	Y	N	N	Y	Y	Y
9 Volkmer	Y	N	Y	Y	Y	N	N
MONTANA							
1 Williams	?	N	Y	Y	Y	?	N
2 ***Marlenee***	Y	Y	N	N	N	Y	Y
NEBRASKA							
1 ***Bereuter***	Y	Y	N	N	Y	Y	Y
2 ***Daub***	Y	Y	N	N	Y	Y	Y
3 ***Smith***	Y	Y	N	N	Y	Y	Y
NEVADA							
1 Reid	Y	N	Y	N	Y	N	N
2 ***Vucanovich***	Y	?	N	N	Y	Y	Y
NEW HAMPSHIRE							
1 D'Amours	Y	N	Y	Y	N	N	N
2 ***Gregg***	Y	Y	N	N	N	Y	Y
NEW JERSEY							
1 Florio	Y	N	Y	Y	N	N	N
2 Hughes	Y	N	Y	Y	Y	N	N
3 Howard	Y	N	Y	Y	N	N	N
4 ***Smith***	Y	N	Y	Y	Y	N	N
5 ***Roukema***	Y	Y	N	N	Y	N	N
6 Dwyer	Y	N	Y	Y	N	N	N
7 ***Rinaldo***	Y	N	Y	Y	N	N	N
8 Roe	Y	N	Y	Y	N	N	N
9 Torricelli	Y	N	Y	Y	N	N	N
10 Rodino	Y	N	?	Y	Y	N	N
11 Minish	Y	N	Y	Y	Y	N	N
12 ***Courter***	Y	Y	N	N	Y	N	N
13 ***Forsythe***	N	Y	N	N	Y	?	?
14 Guarini	N	N	Y	Y	Y	X	X
NEW MEXICO							
1 ***Lujan***	Y	Y	N	N	Y	Y	Y
2 ***Skeen***	Y	Y	N	N	Y	Y	Y
3 Richardson	Y	N	Y	Y	N	N	N
NEW YORK							
1 ***Carney***	Y	Y	N	N	Y	Y	Y
2 Downey	Y	N	Y	Y	N	?	?
3 Mrazek	Y	N	Y	Y	N	N	N
4 ***Lent***	Y	Y	N	N	N	N	N
5 ***McGrath***	Y	Y	N	N	N	N	N
6 Addabbo	Y	N	Y	Y	Y	N	N
7 Ackerman	Y	N	Y	Y	Y	N	N
8 Scheuer	Y	N	Y	Y	Y	N	N
9 Ferraro	Y	N	Y	Y	Y	N	N
10 Schumer	Y	N	Y	Y	Y	N	N
11 Towns	Y	?	?	Y	Y	N	N
12 Owens	?	?	?	Y	Y	X	X
13 Solarz	?	?	?	#	?	?	?
14 ***Molinari***	Y	Y	N	N	N	?	?
15 ***Green***	Y	Y	N	N	N	N	N
16 Rangel	Y	N	Y	Y	N	N	N
17 Weiss	Y	N	Y	Y	Y	N	N
18 Garcia	Y	N	Y	Y	Y	N	N
19 Biaggi	?	N	Y	Y	N	N	N
20 Ottinger	P	N	Y	Y	N	N	N
21 ***Fish***	Y	N	Y	Y	Y	N	?
22 ***Gilman***	Y	N	Y	Y	Y	Y	Y
23 Stratton	Y	N	Y	Y	Y	N	N
24 ***Solomon***	Y	Y	N	Y	Y	Y	Y
25 ***Boehlert***	Y	Y	N	N	Y	N	N
26 ***Martin***	Y	Y	N	N	Y	Y	Y
27 ***Wortley***	Y	?	N	N	Y	Y	Y
28 McHugh	Y	N	Y	N	Y	N	N
29 ***Horton***	Y	N	?	#	Y	N	N
30 ***Conable***	Y	Y	N	N	Y	N	N
31 ***Kemp***	Y	Y	N	N	Y	Y	Y
32 LaFalce	Y	N	Y	Y	N	N	N
33 Nowak	Y	N	Y	Y	N	Y	Y
34 Lundine	Y	N	Y	Y	?	?	?
NORTH CAROLINA							
1 Jones	?	N	N	N	Y	N	N
2 Valentine	Y	Y	N	N	Y	Y	Y
3 Whitley	Y	N	Y	N	Y	Y	Y
4 Andrews	Y	N	Y	N	N	Y	Y
5 Neal	Y	Y	N	N	N	N	N
6 Britt	Y	N	Y	Y	Y	Y	Y
7 Rose	Y	N	Y	Y	?	?	?
8 Hefner	Y	N	Y	N	Y	Y	Y
9 ***Martin***	Y	Y	N	N	Y	Y	Y
10 ***Broyhill***	Y	Y	N	N	Y	Y	Y
11 Clarke	Y	N	N	N	N	N	N
NORTH DAKOTA							
AL Dorgan	N	N	Y	N	N	Y	Y
OHIO							
1 Luken	Y	N	Y	Y	N	?	?
2 ***Gradison***	Y	Y	N	N	Y	N	N
3 Hall	Y	N	Y	Y	Y	N	N
4 ***Oxley***	Y	Y	N	N	Y	Y	Y
5 ***Latta***	Y	N	N	Y	Y	Y	Y
6 ***McEwen***	Y	N	N	Y	Y	Y	Y
7 ***DeWine***	Y	Y	N	N	Y	Y	Y
8 ***Kindness***	Y	Y	N	Y	Y	Y	Y
9 Kaptur	Y	N	Y	Y	Y	Y	N
10 ***Miller***	N	Y	Y	N	Y	Y	Y
11 Eckart	Y	N	Y	Y	N	N	N
12 ***Kasich***	Y	Y	N	N	Y	Y	Y
13 Pease	Y	N	Y	Y	Y	N	N
14 Seiberling	Y	N	Y	Y	N	N	N
15 ***Wylie***	?	?	?	?	Y	Y	Y
16 ***Regula***	Y	N	Y	Y	Y	Y	Y
17 ***Williams***	Y	N	Y	Y	Y	?	?
18 Applegate	Y	N	Y	Y	Y	Y	Y
19 Feighan	Y	N	Y	Y	Y	N	N
20 Oakar	Y	N	Y	Y	Y	N	N
21 Stokes	Y	?	Y	Y	Y	N	N
OKLAHOMA							
1 Jones	Y	Y	N	N	Y	N	N
2 Synar	Y	Y	N	N	Y	N	N
3 Watkins	Y	Y	N	Y	Y	Y	Y
4 McCurdy	?	?	?	?	?	?	?
5 ***Edwards***	N	Y	N	N	Y	Y	Y
6 English	Y	Y	N	Y	Y	Y	Y
OREGON							
1 AuCoin	Y	Y	N	N	N	N	N
2 ***Smith, R.***	Y	Y	N	N	Y	Y	Y
3 Wyden	Y	Y	N	N	N	N	N
4 Weaver	Y	N	Y	Y	Y	N	N
5 ***Smith, D.***	Y	Y	N	N	Y	?	?
PENNSYLVANIA							
1 Foglietta	Y	N	Y	Y	N	N	N
2 Gray	Y	N	Y	#	Y	N	N
3 Borski	Y	N	Y	Y	N	N	N
4 Kolter	Y	N	Y	Y	N	N	N
5 ***Schulze***	Y	Y	N	N	Y	Y	Y
6 Yatron	Y	N	Y	Y	N	Y	Y
7 Edgar	Y	N	Y	Y	-	-	?
8 Kostmayer	Y	N	Y	Y	Y	N	N
9 ***Shuster***	Y	Y	N	N	Y	Y	Y
10 ***McDade***	Y	?	Y	Y	Y	Y	Y
11 Harrison	Y	N	Y	Y	Y	N	N
12 Murtha	Y	N	Y	Y	N	N	N
13 ***Coughlin***	N	N	Y	Y	Y	Y	Y
14 Coyne	Y	N	Y	Y	N	N	N
15 ***Ritter***	Y	N	Y	#	N	Y	Y
16 ***Walker***	N	Y	N	N	Y	Y	Y
17 ***Gekas***	?	Y	N	N	Y	Y	Y
18 Walgren	Y	N	Y	Y	Y	N	N
19 ***Goodling***	?	Y	N	Y	Y	Y	Y
20 Gaydos	Y	N	Y	Y	N	Y	N
21 ***Ridge***	Y	Y	N	N	Y	Y	Y
22 Murphy	Y	N	Y	Y	N	Y	N
23 ***Clinger***	Y	Y	N	N	Y	Y	Y
RHODE ISLAND							
1 St Germain	P	N	Y	Y	N	N	N
2 ***Schneider***	Y	N	N	Y	Y	N	N
SOUTH CAROLINA							
1 ***Hartnett***	Y	Y	N	N	Y	?	?
2 ***Spence***	Y	Y	N	N	Y	Y	Y
3 Derrick	Y	N	N	N	Y	?	?
4 ***Campbell***	?	Y	N	N	Y	Y	Y
5 Spratt	Y	N	N	N	N	Y	Y
6 Tallon	Y	Y	Y	X	Y	Y	Y
SOUTH DAKOTA							
AL Daschle	Y	N	Y	N	Y	N	N
TENNESSEE							
1 ***Quillen***	Y	Y	N	N	Y	Y	Y
2 ***Duncan***	Y	Y	N	N	Y	Y	Y
3 Lloyd	Y	Y	N	N	Y	Y	Y
4 Cooper	Y	?	N	N	N	Y	N
5 Boner	Y	N	Y	Y	N	Y	Y
6 Gore	Y	Y	N	N	N	N	N
7 ***Sundquist***	Y	Y	N	N	Y	?	?
8 Jones	Y	N	Y	Y	Y	N	N
9 Ford	Y	N	?	Y	N	?	?
TEXAS							
1 Hall, S.	Y	Y	Y	Y	Y	N	N
2 Wilson	Y	N	Y	Y	Y	Y	Y
3 ***Bartlett***	Y	Y	N	N	Y	Y	Y
4 Hall, R.	Y	N	Y	Y	Y	Y	Y
5 Bryant	Y	N	Y	Y	N	N	N
6 ***Gramm***	Y	Y	N	N	Y	Y	Y
7 ***Archer***	Y	Y	N	N	Y	Y	Y
8 ***Fields***	Y	Y	N	N	Y	Y	Y
9 Brooks	Y	N	Y	Y	Y	N	N
10 Pickle	Y	Y	N	N	Y	N	N
11 Leath	Y	Y	N	N	Y	Y	Y
12 Wright	Y	N	Y	Y	Y	Y	Y
13 Hightower	Y	Y	N	N	Y	Y	Y
14 Patman	Y	Y	N	N	N	Y	Y
15 de la Garza	Y	N	Y	N	Y	?	?
16 Coleman	Y	N	Y	Y	Y	N	N
17 Stenholm	Y	Y	N	N	Y	Y	Y
18 Leland	Y	N	Y	Y	N	N	N
19 Hance	?	?	?	X	X	#	#
20 Gonzalez	Y	N	Y	Y	Y	N	N
21 ***Loeffler***	?	Y	N	N	Y	Y	Y
22 ***Paul***	?	?	?	X	?	?	?
23 Kazen	Y	N	N	N	Y	?	?
24 Frost	Y	N	Y	Y	N	Y	N
25 Andrews	Y	Y	N	N	N	N	N
26 Vandergriff	Y	N	Y	Y	Y	Y	Y
27 Ortiz	Y	N	Y	Y	Y	N	N
UTAH							
1 ***Hansen***	Y	Y	N	N	Y	?	?
2 ***Marriott***	Y	Y	N	N	Y	?	?
3 ***Nielson***	Y	Y	N	N	Y	Y	Y
VERMONT							
AL ***Jeffords***	Y	Y	N	N	Y	N	N
VIRGINIA							
1 ***Bateman***	Y	Y	N	N	N	Y	Y
2 ***Whitehurst***	Y	Y	N	N	Y	Y	Y
3 ***Bliley***	Y	Y	N	N	Y	Y	Y
4 Sisisky	Y	N	Y	Y	Y	Y	Y
5 Daniel	Y	Y	N	N	Y	Y	Y
6 Olin	Y	N	N	N	Y	Y	Y
7 ***Robinson***	Y	Y	N	N	Y	Y	Y
8 ***Parris***	Y	Y	N	N	Y	Y	Y
9 Boucher	Y	Y	N	N	Y	N	N
10 ***Wolf***	Y	Y	N	N	Y	Y	Y
WASHINGTON							
1 ***Pritchard***	Y	Y	N	N	Y	Y	Y
2 Swift	Y	N	Y	Y	N	N	N
3 Bonker	Y	Y	N	N	N	N	N
4 ***Morrison***	Y	Y	N	N	Y	Y	Y
5 Foley	Y	Y	N	N	Y	N	N
6 Dicks	Y	N	Y	N	N	N	N
7 Lowry	?	?	?	X	?	X	X
8 ***Chandler***	Y	Y	N	N	Y	Y	Y
WEST VIRGINIA							
1 Mollohan	Y	N	Y	Y	N	Y	Y
2 Staggers	Y	N	Y	Y	Y	Y	N
3 Wise	Y	N	Y	Y	N	N	N
4 Rahall	Y	N	Y	Y	N	Y	Y
WISCONSIN							
1 Aspin	Y	?	Y	Y	N	N	N
2 Kastenmeier	Y	N	Y	Y	Y	N	N
3 ***Gunderson***	Y	Y	N	N	Y	Y	Y
4 Zablocki	Y	N	Y	Y	N	N	N
5 Moody	Y	N	Y	Y	Y	N	N
6 ***Petri***	Y	Y	N	N	Y	Y	Y
7 Obey	Y	N	Y	Y	Y	N	N
8 ***Roth***	Y	Y	N	N	Y	Y	Y
9 ***Sensenbrenner***	Y	Y	N	N	Y	Y	Y
WYOMING							
AL ***Cheney***	Y	Y	N	N	Y	Y	Y

Southern states - Ala., Ark., Fla., Ga., Ky., La., Miss., N.C., Okla., S.C., Tenn., Texas, Va.

421. Procedural Motion. Kasich, R-Ohio, motion to approve the House *Journal* of Thursday, Nov. 3. Motion agreed to 280-24: R 112-13; D 168-11 (ND 104-10, SD 64-1), Nov. 4, 1983.

422. HR 4196. Dairy Production Stabilization. Adoption of the rule (H Res 355) providing for House floor consideration of the bill to authorize a paid diversion program for dairy producers, a producer-financed dairy promotion program, reductions in the federal dairy price support and to retain an existing 50 cents per hundred pounds assessment on milk to help finance the diversion program, and to repeal a second 50-cent assessment. Adopted 319-3: R 125-3; D 194-0 (ND 128-0, SD 66-0), Nov. 4, 1983.

423. HR 2114. Maritime Programs Authorization. Passage of the bill to authorize $486,807,000 in fiscal 1984 for maritime programs of the Department of Transportation. Passed 281-35: R 97-29; D 184-6 (ND 122-5, SD 62-1), Nov. 4, 1983.

424. Procedural Motion. Lungren, R-Calif., motion that the House adjourn. Motion rejected 99-120: R 87-1; D 12-119 (ND 4-84, SD 8-35), Nov. 4, 1983. (Although legislative business for the day had finished, Lungren's motion would have prevented a planned speech by Rep. Henry B. Gonzalez, D-Texas. Lungren said he was not trying to cut Gonzalez off but was protesting what he felt was unfair treatment of Republicans by Rules Committee adoption of a rule providing for floor consideration of a joint resolution making stopgap, continuing appropriations for federal agencies. That rule (H Res 362) subsequently was adopted by the House *(see vote 425, below)*, but the continuing resolution (H J Res 308) was rejected Nov. 8 *(see vote 436, p. 128-H).)*

425. H J Res 403. Continuing Appropriations, Fiscal 1984. Adoption of the rule (H Res 362) providing for House floor consideration of the bill to provide temporary funding to government agencies whose regular appropriations bills had not been enacted. Adopted 233-169: R 3-152; D 230-17 (ND 159-5, SD 71-12), Nov. 8, 1983.

426. H J Res 403. Continuing Appropriations, Fiscal 1984. Long, D-Md., amendment as amended by Zablocki, D-Wis., to increase the bill's total for foreign aid. The Zablocki amendment provided fiscal 1984 authorization for foreign assistance programs. Adopted 262-150: R 70-87; D 192-63 (ND 144-27, SD 48-36), Nov. 8, 1983.

427. H J Res 403. Continuing Appropriations, Fiscal 1984. Portion of the Wright, D-Texas, amendment *(see vote 434, p. 128-H)* to appropriate $145 million for the education of immigrant children. Adopted 208-203: R 11-146; D 197-57 (ND 148-21, SD 49-36), Nov. 8, 1983.

428. H J Res 403. Continuing Appropriations, Fiscal 1984. Portion of the Wright, D-Texas, amendment *(see vote 434, p. 128-H)* to appropriate $43.3 million for construction of engineering or computer facilities at three universities. Rejected 122-286: R 3-152; D 119-134 (ND 97-71, SD 22-63), Nov. 8, 1983.

KEY

- Y Voted for (yea).
- # Paired for.
- + Announced for.
- N Voted against (nay).
- X Paired against.
- - Announced against.
- P Voted "present".
- C Voted "present" to avoid possible conflict of interest.
- ? Did not vote or otherwise make a position known.

Democrats   *Republicans*

Member	421	422	423	424	425	426	427	428
ALABAMA								
1 *Edwards*	?	?	?	?	N	Y	N	N
2 *Dickinson*	?	?	?	?	N	N	N	N
3 Nichols	?	?	?	?	Y	N	N	N
4 Bevill	Y	Y	Y	N	Y	N	N	Y
5 Flippo	?	?	?	?	Y	N	N	N
6 Erdreich	Y	Y	Y	N	Y	N	Y	N
7 Shelby	Y	Y	Y	N	Y	N	N	N
ALASKA								
AL *Young*	?	Y	Y	Y	X	?	?	?
ARIZONA								
1 *McCain*	?	?	?	?	N	Y	N	N
2 Udall	?	?	?	?	Y	Y	Y	Y
3 *Stump*	Y	Y	N	?	N	N	N	N
4 *Rudd*	?	?	?	?	N	Y	N	N
5 McNulty	Y	Y	Y	N	Y	Y	Y	N
ARKANSAS								
1 Alexander	?	?	?	?	Y	Y	Y	Y
2 *Bethune*	Y	Y	Y	N	N	N	N	N
3 *Hammerschmidt*	Y	Y	Y	N	N	Y	N	N
4 Anthony	?	Y	Y	Y	Y	Y	N	N
CALIFORNIA								
1 Bosco	Y	Y	Y	N	Y	Y	Y	Y
2 *Chappie*	P	Y	Y	Y	N	N	N	N
3 Matsui	?	?	?	?	Y	Y	Y	Y
4 Fazio	Y	Y	Y	N	Y	Y	Y	Y
5 Burton	Y	Y	Y	N	Y	Y	Y	Y
6 Boxer	?	Y	Y	?	Y	Y	Y	Y
7 Miller	Y	Y	Y	N	Y	N	Y	N
8 Dellums	?	?	?	?	?	Y	Y	Y
9 Stark	?	Y	Y	N	Y	Y	Y	Y
10 Edwards	Y	Y	Y	Y	Y	Y	Y	?
11 Lantos	Y	Y	Y	N	Y	Y	Y	Y
12 Zschau	Y	Y	Y	Y	N	N	N	N
13 Mineta	Y	Y	Y	N	Y	Y	Y	Y
14 *Shumway*	Y	Y	Y	?	N	N	N	N
15 Coelho	?	?	?	?	Y	Y	Y	Y
16 Panetta	?	?	?	?	Y	N	Y	N
17 *Pashayan*	?	?	?	?	N	N	N	N
18 Lehman	Y	Y	Y	N	Y	Y	Y	Y
19 *Lagomarsino*	Y	Y	Y	?	N	N	N	N
20 *Thomas*	Y	Y	Y	?	N	N	N	N
21 *Fiedler*	Y	Y	Y	N	Y	N	N	N
22 *Moorhead*	Y	Y	Y	N	Y	N	N	N
23 Beilenson	?	Y	Y	N	Y	Y	Y	Y
24 Waxman	?	?	?	?	Y	Y	Y	Y
25 Roybal	Y	Y	Y	N	Y	Y	Y	Y
26 Berman	?	?	?	?	Y	Y	Y	Y
27 Levine	N	Y	Y	N	Y	Y	Y	Y
28 Dixon	Y	Y	Y	N	Y	?	Y	Y
29 Hawkins	N	Y	Y	N	Y	Y	Y	Y
30 Martinez	Y	Y	Y	?	Y	Y	Y	Y
31 Dymally	P	Y	?	?	Y	Y	Y	Y
32 Anderson	Y	Y	Y	N	Y	Y	Y	N
33 *Dreier*	N	Y	N	Y	N	N	N	N
34 Torres	?	?	?	?	Y	Y	Y	Y
35 *Lewis*	Y	Y	Y	Y	N	Y	N	N
36 Brown	Y	Y	Y	?	Y	Y	Y	Y
37 *McCandless*	Y	Y	Y	Y	N	N	N	N
38 Patterson	?	?	?	?	Y	Y	Y	N
39 *Dannemeyer*	?	?	?	?	Y	N	N	N
40 *Badham*	Y	Y	Y	?	N	N	N	N
41 *Lowery*	Y	Y	Y	Y	N	Y	N	N
42 *Lungren*	Y	Y	Y	N	N	N	N	N
43 *Packard*	?	?	?	?	N	N	N	N
44 Bates	Y	Y	Y	?	Y	N	Y	N
45 *Hunter*	Y	Y	Y	N	Y	N	Y	N
COLORADO								
1 Schroeder	-	+	-	-	Y	Y	Y	N
2 Wirth	?	?	?	?	Y	Y	Y	Y
3 Kogovsek	?	?	?	?	Y	Y	Y	Y
4 *Brown*	N	N	N	N	N	N	N	N
5 *Kramer*	Y	Y	Y	N	N	N	N	N
6 *Schaefer*	Y	Y	N	Y	N	Y	N	N
CONNECTICUT								
1 Kennelly	Y	Y	Y	?	Y	Y	Y	Y
2 Gejdenson	N	Y	Y	N	Y	Y	Y	Y
3 Morrison	?	?	?	?	Y	Y	Y	Y
4 *McKinney*	Y	Y	Y	?	N	Y	N	N
5 Ratchford	Y	Y	Y	N	Y	Y	Y	Y
6 *Johnson*	?	?	?	Y	Y	Y	Y	Y
DELAWARE								
AL Carper	Y	Y	Y	?	N	Y	Y	N
FLORIDA								
1 Hutto	Y	Y	Y	?	Y	Y	Y	N
2 Fuqua	Y	?	?	?	Y	Y	Y	N
3 Bennett	Y	Y	Y	N	Y	N	Y	N
4 Chappell	?	?	?	?	Y	Y	Y	N
5 *McCollum*	Y	Y	Y	N	Y	N	N	N
6 MacKay	?	?	?	?	Y	Y	Y	N
7 Gibbons	Y	N	N	N	N	N	N	N
8 *Young*	Y	Y	Y	?	X	N	Y	N
9 *Bilirakis*	Y	Y	Y	N	N	N	N	N
10 Ireland	Y	Y	Y	N	Y	N	N	N
11 Nelson	Y	Y	Y	N	Y	N	Y	N
12 *Lewis*	Y	Y	Y	?	N	N	N	N
13 *Mack*	Y	Y	Y	?	N	N	N	N
14 Mica	Y	Y	Y	N	Y	N	Y	N
15 *Shaw*	Y	Y	Y	N	Y	N	N	N
16 Smith	Y	Y	Y	?	Y	Y	Y	Y
17 Lehman	Y	Y	Y	?	Y	Y	Y	Y
18 Pepper	Y	Y	Y	N	Y	Y	Y	Y
19 Fascell	Y	Y	Y	N	Y	Y	Y	Y
GEORGIA								
1 Thomas	Y	Y	Y	N	Y	N	Y	N
2 Hatcher	?	?	?	?	Y	N	Y	N
3 Ray	Y	Y	Y	N	N	N	N	N
4 Levitas	Y	Y	Y	?	Y	Y	Y	N
5 Fowler	Y	Y	Y	?	Y	Y	Y	Y
6 *Gingrich*	Y	?	Y	Y	N	N	N	N
7 Vacancy								
8 Rowland	Y	Y	Y	N	Y	N	Y	N
9 Jenkins	?	?	?	?	?	?	?	?
10 Barnard	?	?	?	Y	N	N	N	N
HAWAII								
1 Heftel	?	?	?	N	Y	Y	Y	N
2 Akaka	?	?	?	?	Y	Y	Y	Y
IDAHO								
1 *Craig*	N	Y	N	?	N	N	N	N
2 *Hansen*	?	?	?	?	N	N	N	N
ILLINOIS								
1 Hayes	Y	Y	Y	?	Y	N	Y	N
2 Savage	?	?	?	?	Y	N	Y	N
3 Russo	Y	Y	Y	?	Y	Y	Y	N
4 *O'Brien*	Y	Y	Y	?	N	Y	N	?
5 Lipinski	?	?	?	?	Y	Y	Y	N
6 *Hyde*	Y	Y	Y	?	Y	N	Y	N
7 Collins	Y	Y	Y	?	Y	Y	Y	Y
8 Rostenkowski	?	?	?	?	Y	Y	Y	Y
9 Yates	Y	Y	N	N	Y	Y	Y	Y
10 *Porter*	Y	Y	Y	Y	N	N	N	N
11 Annunzio	Y	Y	Y	N	Y	Y	Y	N
12 *Crane, P.*	?	N	N	N	N	N	N	N
13 *Erlenborn*	Y	Y	Y	?	N	N	N	N
14 *Corcoran*	Y	Y	Y	N	N	N	N	N
15 *Madigan*	Y	Y	Y	N	N	N	N	N
16 *Martin*	Y	Y	N	?	N	N	N	N
17 Evans	Y	Y	Y	?	Y	Y	Y	Y
18 *Michel*	?	?	?	?	N	N	N	N
19 *Crane, D.*	?	?	?	?	N	N	N	N
20 Durbin	N	Y	Y	?	Y	Y	Y	Y
21 Price	Y	Y	Y	N	Y	Y	Y	Y
22 Simon	?	?	?	?	Y	Y	Y	Y
INDIANA								
1 Hall	Y	Y	Y	?	#	Y	Y	Y
2 Sharp	Y	Y	N	Y	Y	Y	N	N
3 *Hiler*	?	?	?	?	N	N	N	N
4 *Coats*	Y	Y	Y	N	N	N	N	N
5 *Hillis*	?	?	?	?	N	N	N	N

ND - Northern Democrats   SD - Southern Democrats

Corresponding to Congressional Record Votes 453, 454, 455, 456, 457, 459, 461, 462

	421	422	423	424	425	426	427	428
6 ***Burton***	Y	Y	N	?	N	Y	N	N
7 ***Myers***	Y	Y	N	Y	N	N	N	N
8 McCloskey	Y	Y	Y	N	N	Y	Y	Y
9 Hamilton	Y	Y	N	?	Y	Y	Y	N
10 Jacobs	P	Y	N	N	N	N	Y	Y
IOWA								
1 ***Leach***	Y	N	N	Y	N	Y	Y	N
2 ***Tauke***	Y	Y	N	Y	N	N	N	N
3 ***Evans***	N	Y	N	Y	N	N	N	N
4 Smith	?	?	?	?	Y	N	N	N
5 Harkin	N	Y	Y	N	Y	Y	N	N
6 Bedell	Y	Y	Y	N	Y	N	N	N
KANSAS								
1 ***Roberts***	N	Y	?	?	N	N	N	N
2 Slattery	Y	Y	Y	N	N	N	N	N
3 ***Winn***	Y	Y	Y	Y	X	?	?	?
4 Glickman	Y	Y	Y	N	Y	Y	N	N
5 ***Whittaker***	?	?	?	?	N	N	N	N
KENTUCKY								
1 Hubbard	Y	Y	Y	N	Y	N	Y	N
2 Natcher	Y	Y	Y	N	Y	N	N	N
3 Mazzoli	Y	+	+	+	Y	N	N	N
4 ***Snyder***	Y	Y	Y	?	N	N	N	N
5 ***Rogers***	Y	Y	Y	Y	N	N	N	N
6 ***Hopkins***	Y	Y	Y	Y	N	N	N	N
7 Perkins	Y	Y	Y	N	Y	N	Y	Y
LOUISIANA								
1 ***Livingston***	?	Y	Y	Y	N	Y	N	N
2 Boggs	?	Y	Y	?	Y	Y	Y	N
3 Tauzin	Y	Y	Y	N	N	Y	N	N
4 Roemer	N	Y	Y	N	N	N	N	N
5 Huckaby	Y	Y	Y	Y	N	N	N	N
6 ***Moore***	Y	Y	Y	Y	N	Y	N	N
7 Breaux	?	?	?	?	N	Y	N	N
8 Long	Y	Y	Y	N	Y	Y	Y	Y
MAINE								
1 ***McKernan***	Y	Y	Y	Y	N	Y	N	N
2 ***Snowe***	Y	Y	Y	Y	N	Y	N	N
MARYLAND								
1 Dyson	Y	Y	Y	N	Y	Y	N	N
2 Long	Y	Y	Y	?	Y	Y	Y	Y
3 Mikulski	Y	Y	Y	N	Y	Y	Y	Y
4 ***Holt***	Y	Y	Y	?	Y	N	N	N
5 Hoyer	Y	Y	Y	P	Y	Y	Y	Y
6 Byron	Y	Y	Y	N	Y	N	N	N
7 Mitchell	?	Y	Y	N	Y	Y	Y	Y
8 Barnes	+	+	+	-	Y	Y	Y	Y
MASSACHUSETTS								
1 ***Conte***	Y	Y	Y	Y	N	N	N	N
2 Boland	?	?	?	?	Y	Y	Y	N
3 Early	?	?	?	?	?	?	?	?
4 Frank	Y	Y	Y	N	Y	Y	Y	Y
5 Shannon	Y	Y	Y	N	Y	Y	Y	N
6 Mavroules	Y	Y	Y	?	Y	Y	Y	Y
7 Markey	N	Y	Y	N	Y	Y	Y	Y
8 O'Neill								
9 Moakley	Y	Y	Y	?	Y	Y	Y	Y
10 Studds	Y	Y	Y	?	Y	Y	Y	Y
11 Donnelly	Y	Y	Y	N	#	Y	Y	Y
MICHIGAN								
1 Conyers	?	Y	Y	?	Y	N	Y	?
2 ***Pursell***	Y	?	Y	?	N	N	N	N
3 Wolpe	Y	Y	Y	?	Y	Y	Y	N
4 ***Siljander***	Y	Y	Y	?	N	Y	N	N
5 ***Sawyer***	?	?	?	?	N	Y	N	N
6 Carr	P	Y	Y	N	Y	Y	Y	N
7 Kildee	Y	Y	Y	N	Y	Y	Y	Y
8 Traxler	Y	Y	Y	N	Y	Y	Y	N
9 ***Vander Jagt***	P	Y	Y	Y	N	Y	N	N
10 Albosta	Y	Y	Y	?	Y	Y	Y	N
11 ***Davis***	Y	Y	Y	?	N	N	N	N
12 Bonior	Y	Y	Y	N	Y	N	Y	Y
13 Crockett	?	?	?	?	Y	N	Y	Y
14 Hertel	Y	Y	Y	N	Y	Y	Y	Y
15 Ford	?	?	Y	?	Y	Y	Y	Y
16 Dingell	?	?	?	?	Y	Y	Y	Y
17 Levin	Y	Y	Y	N	Y	Y	Y	N
18 ***Broomfield***	?	?	?	?	N	Y	N	N
MINNESOTA								
1 Penny	Y	Y	Y	N	Y	N	Y	N
2 ***Weber***	Y	Y	N	Y	N	Y	N	N
3 ***Frenzel***	N	Y	N	Y	N	Y	N	N
4 Vento	Y	Y	Y	?	Y	Y	Y	Y
5 Sabo	N	Y	Y	N	Y	Y	Y	Y
6 Sikorski	N	Y	Y	N	Y	Y	Y	N
7 ***Stangeland***	Y	Y	Y	?	N	N	N	N
8 Oberstar	?	Y	Y	N	Y	Y	Y	Y
MISSISSIPPI								
1 Whitten	Y	Y	Y	Y	Y	N	N	N
2 ***Franklin***	?	?	+	?	N	Y	N	N
3 Montgomery	Y	?	Y	Y	N	N	N	N
4 Dowdy	?	?	?	N	Y	Y	N	Y
5 ***Lott***	?	?	?	?	N	N	N	N
MISSOURI								
1 Clay	?	?	?	?	Y	Y	Y	Y
2 Young	?	?	?	?	Y	Y	N	N
3 Gephardt	Y	Y	Y	?	Y	Y	Y	N
4 Skelton	?	?	?	?	Y	Y	N	Y
5 Wheat	Y	Y	Y	N	Y	Y	Y	Y
6 ***Coleman***	Y	Y	Y	Y	N	Y	N	N
7 ***Taylor***	Y	Y	Y	Y	N	N	N	N
8 ***Emerson***	N	Y	Y	Y	N	N	N	N
9 Volkmer	Y	Y	Y	N	Y	N	Y	N
MONTANA								
1 Williams	?	?	?	?	Y	N	Y	Y
2 ***Marlenee***	Y	Y	N	Y	N	N	N	N
NEBRASKA								
1 ***Bereuter***	Y	Y	Y	Y	N	Y	N	N
2 ***Daub***	+	+	+	?	N	N	N	N
3 ***Smith***	Y	Y	Y	Y	N	N	N	N
NEVADA								
1 Reid	Y	Y	Y	N	Y	Y	Y	N
2 ***Vucanovich***	Y	Y	Y	Y	N	Y	N	N
NEW HAMPSHIRE								
1 D'Amours	Y	Y	?	?	Y	Y	N	N
2 ***Gregg***	Y	Y	N	?	N	N	N	N
NEW JERSEY								
1 Florio	Y	Y	Y	N	Y	Y	Y	N
2 Hughes	Y	Y	Y	Y	Y	N	N	N
3 Howard	Y	?	?	?	#	?	?	?
4 ***Smith***	Y	Y	Y	Y	N	Y	N	N
5 ***Roukema***	Y	Y	Y	Y	N	Y	N	N
6 Dwyer	Y	Y	Y	?	Y	Y	Y	N
7 ***Rinaldo***	?	?	?	?	N	Y	N	N
8 Roe	Y	Y	Y	?	?	Y	Y	Y
9 Torricelli	Y	Y	Y	N	Y	Y	Y	N
10 Rodino	Y	Y	Y	N	Y	Y	Y	Y
11 Minish	Y	Y	Y	?	Y	Y	Y	N
12 ***Courter***	Y	Y	N	Y	N	Y	N	N
13 ***Forsythe***	N	Y	Y	?	N	Y	N	N
14 Guarini	N	Y	Y	N	Y	Y	Y	Y
NEW MEXICO								
1 ***Lujan***	Y	Y	Y	Y	N	Y	N	Y
2 ***Skeen***	Y	Y	Y	?	N	N	Y	Y
3 Richardson	Y	Y	Y	N	Y	Y	Y	Y
NEW YORK								
1 ***Carney***	Y	Y	Y	Y	X	Y	N	N
2 Downey	?	?	?	?	Y	Y	Y	Y
3 Mrazek	?	?	?	?	Y	Y	Y	N
4 ***Lent***	Y	Y	Y	Y	N	Y	N	N
5 ***McGrath***	Y	Y	Y	?	N	Y	N	N
6 Addabbo	?	?	?	?	Y	Y	Y	Y
7 Ackerman	Y	Y	Y	?	Y	Y	Y	Y
8 Scheuer	Y	Y	Y	Y	Y	Y	Y	Y
9 Ferraro	Y	Y	Y	?	Y	Y	Y	N
10 Schumer	Y	Y	Y	N	Y	Y	Y	Y
11 Towns	Y	Y	Y	N	#	Y	Y	Y
12 Owens	Y	Y	Y	N	#	Y	Y	Y
13 Solarz	?	?	?	?	Y	Y	Y	Y
14 ***Molinari***	?	?	?	?	X	?	?	?
15 ***Green***	Y	Y	Y	Y	N	Y	Y	N
16 Rangel	Y	Y	Y	N	Y	?	Y	Y
17 Weiss	Y	Y	Y	N	Y	Y	Y	N
18 Garcia	?	?	?	?	Y	Y	?	?
19 Biaggi	?	?	?	?	Y	Y	Y	N
20 Ottinger	P	Y	Y	N	Y	Y	Y	N
21 ***Fish***	?	?	?	?	N	Y	N	N
22 ***Gilman***	Y	Y	Y	?	N	Y	Y	N
23 Stratton	?	?	?	?	Y	Y	?	?
24 ***Solomon***	N	Y	N	Y	N	N	N	N
25 ***Boehlert***	Y	Y	Y	Y	N	Y	Y	N
26 ***Martin***	Y	Y	?	?	N	Y	N	N
27 ***Wortley***	Y	Y	Y	Y	N	Y	N	N
28 McHugh	Y	Y	?	?	Y	Y	Y	N
29 ***Horton***	Y	Y	Y	Y	N	Y	Y	N
30 ***Conable***	Y	Y	N	?	N	N	N	N
31 ***Kemp***	Y	Y	?	?	N	Y	N	N
32 LaFalce	Y	Y	Y	N	Y	Y	Y	Y
33 Nowak	Y	Y	Y	N	Y	Y	Y	Y
34 Lundine	?	?	?	?	Y	Y	Y	Y
NORTH CAROLINA								
1 Jones	Y	Y	Y	?	Y	N	Y	N
2 Valentine	Y	Y	Y	?	Y	N	N	N
3 Whitley	?	?	?	?	Y	N	Y	N
4 Andrews	?	?	?	?	Y	N	Y	N
5 Neal	?	Y	Y	N	Y	Y	N	N
6 Britt	Y	Y	Y	?	Y	Y	Y	N
7 Rose	?	?	?	?	Y	Y	Y	Y
8 Hefner	Y	Y	Y	N	#	X	?	?
9 ***Martin***	?	?	?	?	N	?	N	N
10 ***Broyhill***	Y	Y	N	Y	N	N	N	N
11 Clarke	Y	Y	+	-	Y	Y	Y	N
NORTH DAKOTA								
AL Dorgan	Y	Y	Y	N	Y	Y	Y	N
OHIO								
1 Luken	Y	Y	Y	N	?	?	?	?
2 ***Gradison***	Y	Y	N	Y	N	N	N	N
3 Hall	Y	Y	Y	N	Y	Y	?	Y
4 ***Oxley***	Y	Y	Y	?	N	N	N	N
5 ***Latta***	?	?	?	?	N	N	N	N
6 ***McEwen***	Y	Y	Y	Y	N	N	N	N
7 ***DeWine***	Y	Y	N	Y	N	?	?	?
8 ***Kindness***	?	?	?	?	N	N	N	N
9 Kaptur	Y	Y	Y	?	Y	Y	Y	N
10 ***Miller***	N	Y	Y	Y	N	N	N	N
11 Eckart	Y	Y	Y	N	Y	Y	N	N
12 ***Kasich***	Y	Y	Y	Y	N	Y	N	N
13 Pease	Y	Y	Y	N	Y	N	Y	N
14 Seiberling	Y	Y	Y	N	Y	Y	Y	Y
15 ***Wylie***	Y	Y	Y	Y	N	N	N	N
16 ***Regula***	Y	Y	Y	Y	N	N	N	N
17 ***Williams***	?	?	?	?	?	?	?	?
18 Applegate	?	Y	Y	?	Y	N	N	N
19 Feighan	?	?	?	?	?	Y	Y	N
20 Oakar	Y	Y	Y	?	Y	N	Y	Y
21 Stokes	?	?	?	?	Y	Y	Y	Y
OKLAHOMA								
1 Jones	Y	Y	Y	N	Y	N	N	N
2 Synar	Y	Y	Y	-	Y	Y	Y	N
3 Watkins	Y	Y	Y	N	Y	N	N	Y
4 McCurdy	Y	Y	Y	N	Y	N	N	N
5 ***Edwards***	N	Y	N	Y	N	Y	?	?
6 English	Y	Y	Y	Y	Y	N	N	N
OREGON								
1 AuCoin	?	?	?	N	Y	N	N	N
2 ***Smith, R.***	Y	Y	Y	Y	N	N	N	N
3 Wyden	Y	Y	Y	?	Y	Y	Y	N
4 Weaver	Y	Y	Y	N	Y	N	Y	Y
5 ***Smith, D.***	?	?	?	?	N	N	N	N
PENNSYLVANIA								
1 Foglietta	Y	Y	Y	N	?	Y	Y	Y
2 Gray	Y	Y	Y	N	Y	Y	Y	Y
3 Borski	Y	Y	Y	?	Y	Y	Y	Y
4 Kolter	Y	Y	Y	?	Y	Y	N	Y
5 ***Schulze***	Y	Y	Y	?	N	N	N	N
6 Yatron	Y	Y	Y	?	Y	Y	N	N
7 Edgar	?	?	+	?	Y	Y	?	?
8 Kostmayer	+	+	+	-	Y	Y	Y	N
9 ***Shuster***	Y	Y	Y	?	N	N	N	N
10 ***McDade***	Y	Y	Y	?	N	N	N	N
11 Harrison	?	Y	Y	?	Y	Y	Y	Y
12 Murtha	Y	Y	Y	?	Y	Y	Y	N
13 ***Coughlin***	?	?	?	Y	X	Y	N	N
14 Coyne	Y	Y	Y	N	Y	Y	Y	Y
15 ***Ritter***	Y	Y	Y	?	N	N	N	N
16 ***Walker***	N	Y	N	Y	N	N	N	N
17 ***Gekas***	Y	Y	N	Y	N	Y	N	N
18 Walgren	Y	Y	Y	N	Y	Y	Y	N
19 ***Goodling***	N	Y	Y	?	N	N	N	N
20 Gaydos	Y	Y	Y	?	Y	N	N	Y
21 ***Ridge***	Y	Y	Y	?	N	Y	N	N
22 Murphy	?	Y	Y	?	Y	N	N	Y
23 ***Clinger***	Y	Y	Y	+	N	N	N	N
RHODE ISLAND								
1 St Germain	P	Y	Y	N	Y	Y	Y	N
2 ***Schneider***	Y	Y	Y	Y	N	Y	N	N
SOUTH CAROLINA								
1 ***Hartnett***	?	?	?	?	N	Y	N	N
2 ***Spence***	Y	Y	?	?	N	Y	N	N
3 Derrick	?	?	?	?	?	?	Y	N
4 ***Campbell***	Y	Y	Y	Y	N	N	N	N
5 Spratt	?	Y	Y	N	Y	Y	Y	N
6 Tallon	Y	Y	?	?	Y	Y	Y	N
SOUTH DAKOTA								
AL Daschle	?	?	?	?	Y	Y	Y	N
TENNESSEE								
1 ***Quillen***	Y	Y	Y	?	N	N	N	N
2 ***Duncan***	Y	Y	Y	?	N	N	N	?
3 Lloyd	Y	Y	Y	?	Y	N	N	N
4 Cooper	Y	Y	Y	N	Y	Y	N	N
5 Boner	Y	Y	?	?	Y	Y	N	Y
6 Gore	?	?	?	?	Y	Y	N	N
7 ***Sundquist***	?	?	?	?	N	Y	N	N
8 Jones	Y	?	?	?	Y	N	N	N
9 Ford	?	?	?	?	Y	Y	Y	Y
TEXAS								
1 Hall, S.	Y	Y	Y	Y	Y	N	N	N
2 Wilson	?	Y	Y	N	Y	Y	Y	Y
3 ***Bartlett***	Y	Y	N	Y	N	Y	Y	N
4 Hall, R.	Y	Y	?	?	N	N	Y	N
5 Bryant	Y	Y	Y	N	Y	Y	Y	Y
6 ***Gramm***	Y	Y	N	Y	X	?	?	?
7 ***Archer***	Y	Y	Y	Y	N	N	N	N
8 ***Fields***	Y	Y	Y	?	N	N	N	N
9 Brooks	Y	Y	Y	N	Y	N	Y	Y
10 Pickle	Y	Y	Y	?	Y	Y	Y	N
11 Leath	Y	Y	Y	N	?	?	?	?
12 Wright	Y	Y	Y	?	Y	Y	Y	Y
13 Hightower	Y	Y	Y	?	Y	N	Y	N
14 Patman	Y	Y	Y	N	N	N	Y	N
15 de la Garza	?	?	?	?	Y	N	Y	Y
16 Coleman	Y	Y	Y	N	Y	Y	Y	Y
17 Stenholm	Y	Y	Y	?	N	N	Y	N
18 Leland	Y	Y	Y	?	#	+	?	?
19 Hance	?	?	?	?	Y	Y	Y	N
20 Gonzalez	Y	Y	Y	N	Y	Y	Y	N
21 ***Loeffler***	Y	Y	N	Y	N	N	Y	N
22 ***Paul***	?	?	?	?	X	?	?	?
23 Kazen	?	?	?	?	Y	Y	Y	N
24 Frost	Y	Y	Y	?	Y	Y	Y	Y
25 Andrews	Y	Y	Y	?	#	Y	Y	N
26 Vandergriff	Y	Y	Y	N	Y	Y	Y	N
27 Ortiz	Y	Y	Y	?	Y	Y	Y	Y
UTAH								
1 ***Hansen***	?	?	?	?	N	N	N	N
2 ***Marriott***	?	?	?	?	N	N	N	N
3 ***Nielson***	Y	Y	N	Y	N	N	N	N
VERMONT								
AL ***Jeffords***	Y	Y	Y	Y	N	Y	N	Y
VIRGINIA								
1 ***Bateman***	Y	Y	Y	Y	N	Y	N	N
2 ***Whitehurst***	Y	Y	Y	?	N	Y	N	N
3 ***Bliley***	?	?	?	?	N	Y	N	N
4 Sisisky	Y	Y	Y	N	Y	Y	N	N
5 Daniel	Y	Y	Y	Y	Y	N	N	N
6 Olin	Y	Y	Y	?	Y	N	Y	N
7 ***Robinson***	?	?	?	?	N	N	N	N
8 ***Parris***	Y	Y	Y	?	N	N	N	N
9 Boucher	Y	Y	Y	?	Y	Y	Y	N
10 ***Wolf***	Y	Y	Y	Y	?	Y	N	N
WASHINGTON								
1 ***Pritchard***	?	?	?	?	?	?	?	?
2 Swift	Y	Y	Y	N	Y	Y	Y	N
3 Bonker	?	?	?	?	Y	Y	Y	Y
4 ***Morrison***	Y	Y	Y	Y	N	Y	Y	N
5 Foley	?	?	?	?	Y	Y	Y	Y
6 Dicks	?	?	?	?	Y	Y	Y	N
7 Lowry	?	?	?	?	#	#	?	?
8 ***Chandler***	Y	Y	Y	Y	N	Y	Y	N
WEST VIRGINIA								
1 Mollohan	Y	Y	Y	N	Y	Y	Y	Y
2 Staggers	N	Y	Y	N	Y	Y	Y	Y
3 Wise	Y	Y	Y	?	Y	Y	Y	Y
4 Rahall	Y	Y	Y	Y	N	N	Y	N
WISCONSIN								
1 Aspin	P	Y	Y	N	Y	Y	Y	N
2 Kastenmeier	Y	Y	N	N	Y	N	Y	Y
3 ***Gunderson***	Y	Y	Y	?	N	N	N	N
4 Zablocki	Y	Y	Y	N	Y	Y	Y	Y
5 Moody	Y	Y	Y	N	Y	Y	Y	Y
6 ***Petri***	Y	Y	Y	Y	N	N	N	N
7 Obey	Y	Y	Y	N	Y	N	Y	N
8 ***Roth***	Y	Y	Y	Y	N	Y	N	N
9 ***Sensenbrenner***	Y	Y	Y	?	N	N	N	N
WYOMING								
AL ***Cheney***	?	?	?	?	X	?	?	?

Southern states - Ala., Ark., Fla., Ga., Ky., La., Miss., N.C., Okla., S.C., Tenn., Texas, Va.

KEY

Y Voted for (yea).
\# Paired for.
\+ Announced for.
N Voted against (nay).
X Paired against.
- Announced against.
P Voted "present".
C Voted "present" to avoid possible conflict of interest.
? Did not vote or otherwise make a position known.

Democrats   *Republicans*

429. H J Res 403. Continuing Appropriations, Fiscal 1984. Portion of the Wright, D-Texas, amendment *(see vote 434, below)* to appropriate $20 million for work-study programs under title IV of the Higher Education Act of 1965. Adopted 336-72: R 90-64; D 246-8 (ND 166-3, SD 80-5), Nov. 8, 1983.

430. H J Res 403. Continuing Appropriations, Fiscal 1984. Portion of the Wright, D-Texas, amendment *(see vote 434, below)* to appropriate $10 million for supplemental educational opportunity grants under title IV of the Higher Education Act of 1965. Adopted 328-78: R 82-71; D 246-7 (ND 168-0, SD 78-7), Nov. 8, 1983.

431. H J Res 403. Continuing Appropriations, Fiscal 1984. Portion of the Wright, D-Texas, amendment *(see vote 434, below)* to appropriate $20 million for community health centers. Adopted 267-141: R 33-121; D 234-20 (ND 162-7, SD 72-13), Nov. 8, 1983.

432. H J Res 403. Continuing Appropriations, Fiscal 1984. Portion of the Wright, D-Texas, amendment *(see vote 434, below)* to appropriate $75.4 million for job training programs. Adopted 257-150: R 32-121; D 225-29 (ND 163-6, SD 62-23), Nov. 8, 1983.

433. H J Res 403. Continuing Appropriations, Fiscal 1984. Portion of the Wright, D-Texas, amendment *(see vote 434, below)* to postpone an administrative requirement — called monthly reporting and retrospective budgeting — that households receiving food stamps submit monthly reports on income and other factors affecting eligibility. Adopted 210-201: R 5-151; D 205-50 (ND 154-16, SD 51-34), Nov. 8, 1983.

434. H J Res 403. Continuing Appropriations, Fiscal 1984. Wright, D-Texas, amendment to increase funding in the bill by approximately $955 million for an assortment of programs, most of them concerning education. Adopted 254-155: R 22-134; D 232-21 (ND 162-7, SD 70-14), Nov. 8, 1983. A "nay" was a vote supporting the president's position.

435. H J Res 403. Continuing Appropriations, Fiscal 1984. Conte, R-Mass., motion to recommit the joint resolution to the Appropriations Committee with instructions to remove all the amendments that had been added by the House. Motion rejected 166-244: R 141-15; D 25-229 (ND 4-165, SD 21-64), Nov. 8, 1983.

436. H J Res 403. Continuing Appropriations, Fiscal 1984. Passage of the joint resolution to make further continuing appropriations for government agencies for fiscal 1984. Rejected 203-206: R 16-139; D 187-67 (ND 137-32, SD 50-35), Nov. 8, 1983. (The House subsequently passed a nearly identical resolution, H J Res 413, on Nov. 10.)

	429	430	431	432	433	434	435	436
ALABAMA								
1 Edwards	Y	Y	Y	N	N	N	Y	N
2 *Dickinson*	N	Y	N	N	N	N	Y	N
3 Nichols	Y	Y	Y	N	N	N	Y	N
4 Bevill	Y	Y	Y	Y	Y	Y	N	Y
5 Flippo	Y	Y	Y	Y	Y	Y	N	Y
6 Erdreich	Y	Y	Y	Y	N	Y	Y	N
7 Shelby	Y	N	Y	N	Y	N	Y	N
ALASKA								
AL *Young*	?	?	?	?	?	?	?	?
ARIZONA								
1 *McCain*	N	Y	N	N	N	N	Y	N
2 Udall	Y	Y	Y	Y	Y	Y	N	Y
3 *Stump*	N	N	N	N	N	N	Y	N
4 *Rudd*	N	N	N	N	N	N	Y	N
5 McNulty	Y	Y	Y	Y	Y	Y	N	Y
ARKANSAS								
1 Alexander	Y	Y	Y	Y	Y	Y	N	Y
2 *Bethune*	Y	Y	N	N	N	N	Y	N
3 *Hammerschmidt*	Y	Y	N	N	N	N	Y	N
4 Anthony	Y	Y	Y	Y	Y	Y	N	Y
CALIFORNIA								
1 Bosco	Y	Y	Y	Y	Y	Y	N	Y
2 *Chappie*	Y	N	N	N	N	N	Y	N
3 Matsui	Y	Y	Y	Y	Y	Y	N	Y
4 Fazio	Y	Y	Y	Y	Y	Y	N	Y
5 Burton	Y	Y	Y	Y	Y	Y	N	Y
6 Boxer	Y	Y	Y	Y	Y	Y	N	Y
7 Miller	Y	Y	Y	Y	Y	Y	N	Y
8 Dellums	Y	Y	Y	Y	Y	Y	N	Y
9 Stark	Y	Y	Y	Y	Y	Y	N	Y
10 Edwards	?	?	?	?	Y	Y	Y	N
11 Lantos	Y	Y	Y	Y	Y	Y	N	Y
12 *Zschau*	N	N	N	N	N	N	N	N
13 Mineta	Y	Y	Y	Y	Y	Y	N	Y
14 *Shumway*	N	N	N	N	N	N	Y	N
15 Coelho	Y	Y	Y	Y	Y	Y	N	Y
16 Panetta	Y	Y	Y	Y	Y	Y	N	Y
17 *Pashayan*	Y	Y	Y	Y	N	N	N	Y
18 Lehman	Y	Y	Y	Y	Y	Y	N	Y
19 *Lagomarsino*	Y	N	N	N	N	N	Y	N
20 *Thomas*	N	?	?	?	N	N	Y	N
21 *Fiedler*	Y	Y	N	N	N	N	Y	N
22 *Moorhead*	N	N	N	N	N	N	Y	N
23 Beilenson	Y	Y	Y	Y	Y	Y	Y	N
24 Waxman	Y	Y	Y	Y	Y	Y	N	Y
25 Roybal	Y	Y	Y	Y	Y	Y	N	Y
26 Berman	Y	Y	Y	Y	Y	Y	N	Y
27 Levine	Y	Y	Y	Y	Y	Y	N	Y
28 Dixon	Y	Y	Y	Y	Y	Y	N	Y
29 Hawkins	Y	Y	Y	Y	Y	Y	N	Y
30 Martinez	Y	Y	Y	Y	Y	Y	N	Y
31 Dymally	Y	Y	Y	Y	Y	Y	N	Y
32 Anderson	Y	Y	Y	Y	Y	Y	N	Y
33 *Dreier*	N	N	N	N	N	N	N	N
34 Torres	Y	Y	Y	Y	Y	Y	N	Y
35 *Lewis*	N	N	N	N	N	N	Y	N
36 Brown	Y	Y	Y	Y	Y	Y	N	Y
37 *McCandless*	N	N	N	N	N	N	Y	N
38 Patterson	Y	Y	Y	Y	Y	Y	N	Y
39 *Dannemeyer*	N	N	N	N	N	N	Y	N
40 *Badham*	N	N	N	N	N	N	Y	N
41 *Lowery*	Y	N	N	N	N	N	Y	N
42 *Lungren*	N	N	N	N	N	N	Y	N
43 *Packard*	Y	Y	N	N	N	N	Y	N
44 Bates	Y	Y	Y	Y	N	Y	N	N
45 *Hunter*	N	N	N	N	N	N	Y	N
COLORADO								
1 Schroeder	Y	Y	Y	Y	Y	Y	N	N
2 Wirth	Y	Y	Y	Y	Y	Y	N	Y
3 Kogovsek	Y	Y	Y	Y	Y	Y	N	Y
4 *Brown*	N	N	N	N	N	N	Y	N
5 *Kramer*	N	N	N	N	N	N	Y	N
6 *Schaefer*	N	N	N	N	N	N	Y	N
CONNECTICUT								
1 Kennelly	Y	Y	Y	Y	Y	Y	N	Y
2 Gejdenson	Y	Y	Y	Y	Y	Y	N	Y
3 Morrison	Y	Y	Y	Y	Y	Y	N	Y
4 *McKinney*	Y	Y	Y	N	N	N	Y	N
5 Ratchford	Y	Y	Y	Y	Y	Y	N	Y
6 *Johnson*	Y	Y	Y	Y	Y	Y	N	Y
DELAWARE								
AL Carper	Y	Y	Y	N	Y	N	N	N
FLORIDA								
1 Hutto	Y	Y	Y	N	N	Y	N	Y
2 Fuqua	Y	Y	Y	N	Y	N	N	Y
3 Bennett	Y	Y	N	N	N	N	Y	N
4 Chappell	Y	Y	Y	N	N	N	Y	N
5 *McCollum*	N	N	N	N	N	N	Y	N
6 MacKay	Y	Y	Y	Y	Y	N	N	N
7 Gibbons	Y	Y	Y	N	N	N	N	N
8 *Young*	N	N	N	N	N	N	Y	N
9 *Bilirakis*	Y	Y	N	Y	N	Y	N	N
10 Ireland	Y	Y	N	N	N	N	Y	N
11 Nelson	Y	Y	Y	N	N	N	N	Y
12 *Lewis*	Y	Y	Y	Y	Y	Y	N	N
13 *Mack*	N	N	N	N	N	N	Y	N
14 Mica	Y	Y	Y	Y	Y	N	N	Y
15 *Shaw*	N	N	N	N	N	N	Y	N
16 Smith	Y	Y	Y	N	Y	N	N	Y
17 Lehman	Y	Y	Y	Y	Y	Y	N	Y
18 Pepper	Y	Y	Y	Y	Y	Y	N	Y
19 Fascell	Y	Y	Y	Y	Y	Y	N	Y
GEORGIA								
1 Thomas	Y	Y	Y	N	Y	N	Y	N
2 Hatcher	Y	Y	Y	Y	Y	Y	N	Y
3 Ray	N	N	N	N	Y	N	Y	N
4 Levitas	Y	Y	Y	Y	Y	Y	N	Y
5 Fowler	Y	Y	Y	Y	Y	Y	N	Y
6 *Gingrich*	Y	N	N	N	N	N	Y	N
7 Vacancy								
8 Rowland	Y	Y	Y	Y	Y	Y	N	Y
9 Jenkins	?	?	?	?	?	?	?	?
10 Barnard	N	Y	N	N	Y	N	Y	N
HAWAII								
1 Heftel	Y	Y	Y	Y	N	Y	N	Y
2 Akaka	Y	Y	Y	Y	Y	Y	N	Y
IDAHO								
1 *Craig*	N	N	N	N	N	N	Y	N
2 *Hansen*	N	N	N	N	N	N	Y	N
ILLINOIS								
1 Hayes	Y	Y	Y	Y	Y	Y	N	Y
2 Savage	Y	Y	Y	Y	Y	Y	N	Y
3 Russo	Y	Y	Y	Y	Y	Y	N	N
4 *O'Brien*	?	?	?	?	?	?	?	?
5 Lipinski	Y	Y	Y	Y	Y	Y	N	Y
6 *Hyde*	N	N	N	N	N	N	Y	N
7 Collins	Y	Y	Y	Y	Y	Y	N	Y
8 Rostenkowski	Y	Y	Y	Y	Y	Y	N	Y
9 Yates	Y	Y	Y	Y	Y	Y	N	Y
10 *Porter*	Y	N	N	N	N	N	Y	N
11 Annunzio	Y	Y	Y	Y	Y	Y	N	Y
12 *Crane, P.*	N	N	N	N	N	N	Y	N
13 *Erlenborn*	N	N	N	N	N	N	Y	N
14 *Corcoran*	Y	Y	N	N	N	N	Y	N
15 *Madigan*	?	N	N	Y	N	N	Y	N
16 *Martin*	Y	N	N	N	N	N	Y	N
17 Evans	Y	Y	Y	Y	Y	Y	N	Y
18 *Michel*	Y	N	N	N	N	N	Y	N
19 *Crane, D.*	N	N	N	N	N	N	Y	N
20 Durbin	Y	Y	Y	Y	Y	Y	N	Y
21 Price	Y	Y	Y	Y	Y	Y	N	Y
22 Simon	Y	Y	Y	Y	Y	Y	N	Y
INDIANA								
1 Hall	Y	Y	Y	Y	Y	Y	N	Y
2 Sharp	Y	Y	Y	Y	N	Y	N	Y
3 *Hiler*	N	N	N	N	N	N	Y	N
4 *Coats*	N	N	N	N	N	N	Y	N
5 Hillis	Y	Y	N	Y	N	N	Y	N

	429	430	431	432	433	434	435	436
6 ***Burton***	N	N	N	N	N	N	Y	N
7 ***Myers***	Y	Y	N	N	N	N	Y	N
8 McCloskey	Y	Y	Y	Y	Y	Y	N	N
9 Hamilton	Y	Y	Y	Y	N	Y	N	Y
10 Jacobs	Y	Y	Y	Y	N	Y	N	N
IOWA								
1 ***Leach***	Y	Y	Y	N	N	Y	Y	N
2 ***Tauke***	N	N	N	N	N	N	Y	N
3 ***Evans***	Y	Y	Y	Y	Y	Y	Y	N
4 Smith	Y	Y	N	N	Y	N	Y	Y
5 Harkin	Y	Y	Y	Y	Y	Y	N	Y
6 Bedell	Y	Y	N	N	Y	Y	Y	N
KANSAS								
1 ***Roberts***	N	N	N	N	N	N	Y	N
2 Slattery	Y	Y	Y	N	Y	N	Y	N
3 ***Winn***	?	?	?	?	?	?	?	?
4 Glickman	N	Y	Y	N	Y	N	N	Y
5 ***Whittaker***	N	N	Y	N	N	N	Y	N
KENTUCKY								
1 Hubbard	Y	Y	Y	Y	N	Y	N	N
2 Natcher	Y	Y	Y	Y	N	N	N	Y
3 Mazzoli	Y	Y	Y	Y	N	Y	N	Y
4 ***Snyder***	Y	Y	N	N	N	N	Y	N
5 ***Rogers***	Y	Y	Y	Y	N	N	Y	N
6 ***Hopkins***	Y	Y	N	N	N	N	Y	N
7 Perkins	Y	Y	Y	Y	Y	Y	N	Y
LOUISIANA								
1 ***Livingston***	Y	Y	N	N	N	N	Y	N
2 Boggs	Y	Y	Y	Y	Y	Y	N	Y
3 Tauzin	Y	Y	Y	Y	N	N	Y	N
4 Roemer	N	Y	N	N	N	N	Y	N
5 Huckaby	Y	Y	Y	N	N	N	Y	N
6 ***Moore***	Y	Y	N	N	N	N	Y	N
7 Breaux	Y	Y	Y	N	N	N	Y	N
8 Long	Y	Y	Y	Y	Y	Y	N	Y
MAINE								
1 ***McKernan***	Y	Y	Y	Y	Y	Y	N	Y
2 ***Snowe***	Y	Y	Y	N	N	Y	Y	N
MARYLAND								
1 Dyson	Y	Y	Y	Y	N	N	N	Y
2 Long	Y	Y	Y	Y	Y	Y	N	Y
3 Mikulski	Y	Y	Y	Y	Y	Y	N	Y
4 ***Holt***	Y	N	N	N	N	N	Y	N
5 Hoyer	Y	Y	Y	Y	Y	Y	N	Y
6 Byron	Y	Y	N	Y	N	Y	N	N
7 Mitchell	Y	Y	Y	Y	Y	Y	N	Y
8 Barnes	Y	Y	Y	Y	Y	Y	N	Y
MASSACHUSETTS								
1 ***Conte***	Y	Y	Y	N	N	N	Y	N
2 Boland	Y	Y	Y	Y	Y	Y	N	Y
3 Early	?	?	?	?	?	?	?	?
4 Frank	Y	Y	Y	Y	Y	Y	N	Y
5 Shannon	Y	Y	Y	Y	Y	Y	N	Y
6 Mavroules	Y	Y	Y	Y	Y	Y	N	Y
7 Markey	Y	Y	Y	Y	Y	Y	N	Y
8 O'Neill								
9 Moakley	Y	Y	Y	Y	Y	Y	N	Y
10 Studds	Y	Y	Y	Y	Y	Y	N	Y
11 Donnelly	Y	Y	Y	Y	Y	Y	N	Y
MICHIGAN								
1 Conyers	Y	Y	Y	Y	Y	Y	N	Y
2 ***Pursell***	N	Y	N	N	N	N	Y	N
3 Wolpe	Y	Y	Y	Y	Y	Y	N	Y
4 ***Siljander***	Y	N	N	N	N	N	Y	N
5 ***Sawyer***	Y	Y	N	Y	N	N	Y	N
6 Carr	Y	Y	Y	Y	N	Y	N	Y
7 Kildee	Y	Y	Y	Y	Y	Y	N	Y
8 Traxler	Y	Y	Y	Y	Y	Y	N	Y
9 ***Vander Jagt***	N	Y	N	N	N	N	Y	N
10 Albosta	Y	Y	Y	Y	Y	Y	N	Y
11 ***Davis***	Y	Y	Y	Y	N	Y	N	Y
12 Bonior	Y	Y	Y	Y	Y	Y	N	Y
13 Crockett	Y	Y	Y	Y	Y	Y	N	N
14 Hertel	Y	Y	Y	Y	Y	Y	N	Y
15 Ford	Y	Y	Y	Y	Y	Y	N	Y
16 Dingell	Y	Y	Y	Y	Y	Y	N	Y
17 Levin	Y	Y	Y	Y	Y	Y	N	N
18 ***Broomfield***	N	Y	N	N	N	N	Y	N
MINNESOTA								
1 Penny	Y	Y	Y	Y	Y	Y	N	N
2 ***Weber***	N	Y	N	N	N	N	Y	N
3 ***Frenzel***	N	N	N	N	N	N	Y	N
4 Vento	Y	Y	Y	Y	Y	Y	N	Y
5 Sabo	Y	Y	Y	Y	Y	Y	N	Y
6 Sikorski	Y	Y	Y	Y	Y	Y	N	Y

	429	430	431	432	433	434	435	436
7 ***Stangeland***	Y	Y	N	N	N	N	Y	N
8 Oberstar	Y	Y	Y	Y	Y	Y	N	Y
MISSISSIPPI								
1 Whitten	Y	Y	Y	Y	Y	Y	N	Y
2 ***Franklin***	Y	Y	N	N	N	N	Y	N
3 Montgomery	Y	N	N	N	N	N	Y	N
4 Dowdy	Y	Y	Y	Y	Y	Y	N	Y
5 ***Lott***	Y	N	N	N	N	N	Y	N
MISSOURI								
1 Clay	Y	Y	Y	Y	Y	Y	N	Y
2 Young	N	Y	N	Y	N	Y	N	Y
3 Gephardt	Y	Y	Y	Y	Y	Y	N	Y
4 Skelton	N	Y	N	Y	N	Y	N	Y
5 Wheat	Y	Y	Y	Y	Y	Y	N	Y
6 ***Coleman***	Y	Y	N	Y	N	N	Y	N
7 ***Taylor***	Y	N	N	N	N	N	Y	N
8 ***Emerson***	Y	Y	N	N	N	N	Y	N
9 Volkmer	Y	Y	N	N	N	Y	N	N
MONTANA								
1 Williams	Y	Y	Y	Y	Y	Y	N	Y
2 ***Marlenee***	Y	Y	N	Y	N	N	Y	N
NEBRASKA								
1 ***Bereuter***	Y	Y	N	N	N	N	Y	N
2 ***Daub***	Y	Y	N	N	N	N	Y	N
3 ***Smith***	Y	Y	N	N	N	N	Y	N
NEVADA								
1 Reid	Y	Y	Y	Y	Y	Y	N	N
2 ***Vucanovich***	Y	Y	N	N	N	N	Y	N
NEW HAMPSHIRE								
1 D'Amours	Y	Y	Y	Y	N	Y	N	Y
2 ***Gregg***	N	N	N	N	N	N	Y	N
NEW JERSEY								
1 Florio	Y	Y	Y	Y	Y	?	?	?
2 Hughes	Y	Y	Y	Y	N	N	N	N
3 Howard	?	?	?	?	?	?	?	?
4 ***Smith***	Y	Y	Y	Y	N	Y	N	Y
5 ***Roukema***	Y	Y	Y	N	N	Y	Y	N
6 Dwyer	Y	Y	Y	Y	Y	Y	N	Y
7 ***Rinaldo***	Y	Y	Y	Y	Y	Y	N	Y
8 Roe	Y	Y	Y	Y	Y	Y	N	Y
9 Torricelli	Y	Y	Y	Y	Y	Y	N	Y
10 Rodino	Y	Y	Y	Y	Y	Y	N	Y
11 Minish	Y	Y	Y	Y	Y	Y	N	Y
12 ***Courter***	Y	Y	Y	N	N	N	Y	N
13 ***Forsythe***	N	N	N	N	N	N	Y	N
14 Guarini	Y	Y	Y	Y	Y	Y	N	Y
NEW MEXICO								
1 ***Lujan***	Y	Y	Y	N	N	N	Y	N
2 ***Skeen***	N	N	N	N	N	N	Y	N
3 Richardson	Y	Y	Y	Y	Y	Y	N	N
NEW YORK								
1 ***Carney***	Y	Y	N	N	N	N	Y	N
2 Downey	Y	Y	Y	Y	Y	Y	N	Y
3 Mrazek	Y	Y	Y	Y	Y	Y	N	Y
4 ***Lent***	Y	Y	N	N	N	N	Y	N
5 ***McGrath***	Y	Y	N	N	N	N	N	Y
6 Addabbo	Y	Y	Y	Y	Y	Y	N	Y
7 Ackerman	Y	Y	Y	Y	Y	Y	N	Y
8 Scheuer	Y	Y	Y	Y	Y	Y	N	Y
9 Ferraro	Y	Y	Y	Y	Y	Y	N	Y
10 Schumer	Y	Y	Y	Y	Y	Y	N	Y
11 Towns	Y	Y	Y	Y	Y	Y	N	Y
12 Owens	Y	Y	Y	Y	Y	Y	N	Y
13 Solarz	Y	Y	Y	Y	Y	Y	N	Y
14 ***Molinari***	?	?	?	?	?	?	?	?
15 ***Green***	Y	Y	Y	N	N	Y	N	Y
16 Rangel	Y	Y	Y	Y	Y	Y	N	Y
17 Weiss	Y	Y	Y	Y	Y	Y	N	Y
18 Garcia	?	?	?	?	?	?	?	?
19 Biaggi	Y	Y	Y	Y	Y	Y	N	Y
20 Ottinger	Y	Y	Y	Y	Y	Y	N	Y
21 ***Fish***	Y	Y	Y	?	N	N	Y	N
22 ***Gilman***	Y	Y	Y	Y	N	Y	N	Y
23 Stratton	?	?	?	?	?	?	?	?
24 ***Solomon***	N	N	N	N	N	N	Y	N
25 ***Boehlert***	Y	Y	Y	Y	N	Y	N	Y
26 ***Martin***	Y	Y	Y	N	N	N	Y	N
27 ***Wortley***	Y	Y	Y	N	N	N	Y	N
28 McHugh	Y	Y	Y	Y	Y	Y	N	Y
29 ***Horton***	Y	Y	Y	Y	N	Y	N	Y
30 ***Conable***	N	N	N	N	N	N	Y	N
31 ***Kemp***	N	N	N	N	N	N	Y	N
32 LaFalce	Y	Y	Y	Y	Y	Y	N	Y
33 Nowak	Y	Y	Y	Y	Y	Y	N	Y
34 Lundine	Y	Y	Y	Y	Y	Y	N	Y

	429	430	431	432	433	434	435	436
NORTH CAROLINA								
1 Jones	Y	Y	Y	Y	Y	Y	N	Y
2 Valentine	Y	Y	Y	Y	Y	Y	N	Y
3 Whitley	Y	Y	Y	Y	Y	Y	N	Y
4 Andrews	Y	Y	Y	Y	Y	Y	N	Y
5 Neal	Y	Y	Y	Y	Y	Y	N	Y
6 Britt	Y	Y	Y	Y	Y	Y	N	N
7 Rose	Y	Y	Y	Y	Y	Y	N	Y
8 Hefner	?	?	?	?	?	?	?	?
9 ***Martin***	Y	N	N	N	N	N	Y	N
10 ***Broyhill***	Y	N	N	N	N	N	Y	?
11 Clarke	Y	Y	N	Y	Y	Y	N	Y
NORTH DAKOTA								
AL Dorgan	Y	Y	Y	N	Y	Y	N	N
OHIO								
1 Luken	?	?	?	?	?	?	?	?
2 ***Gradison***	N	N	N	N	N	N	Y	N
3 Hall	Y	Y	Y	Y	Y	Y	N	Y
4 ***Oxley***	N	N	N	N	N	N	Y	N
5 ***Latta***	N	N	N	N	N	N	Y	N
6 ***McEwen***	N	Y	Y	N	N	N	Y	N
7 ***DeWine***	?	?	?	?	?	?	?	?
8 ***Kindness***	Y	N	N	N	N	N	Y	N
9 Kaptur	Y	Y	Y	Y	Y	Y	N	N
10 ***Miller***	N	N	N	N	N	N	Y	N
11 Eckart	Y	Y	Y	Y	Y	Y	N	N
12 ***Kasich***	Y	Y	N	N	N	N	Y	N
13 Pease	Y	Y	Y	Y	Y	Y	N	Y
14 Seiberling	Y	Y	Y	Y	Y	Y	N	Y
15 ***Wylie***	Y	Y	N	N	N	N	Y	N
16 ***Regula***	Y	Y	Y	Y	N	N	Y	N
17 ***Williams***	?	?	?	?	?	?	?	?
18 Applegate	Y	Y	Y	Y	Y	Y	N	N
19 Feighan	Y	Y	Y	Y	Y	Y	N	N
20 Oakar	Y	Y	Y	Y	Y	Y	N	N
21 Stokes	Y	Y	Y	Y	Y	Y	N	Y
OKLAHOMA								
1 Jones	Y	Y	Y	N	Y	Y	N	N
2 Synar	Y	Y	Y	Y	Y	Y	N	Y
3 Watkins	Y	Y	Y	Y	N	Y	N	Y
4 McCurdy	Y	Y	Y	N	Y	Y	N	N
5 ***Edwards***	?	?	?	?	?	?	?	?
6 English	Y	Y	Y	N	N	Y	N	N
OREGON								
1 AuCoin	Y	Y	N	Y	N	N	Y	N
2 ***Smith, R.***	N	N	N	N	N	N	Y	N
3 Wyden	Y	Y	Y	Y	Y	Y	N	Y
4 Weaver	Y	Y	Y	Y	Y	Y	N	N
5 ***Smith, D.***	N	N	N	N	N	N	Y	N
PENNSYLVANIA								
1 Foglietta	Y	Y	Y	Y	Y	Y	N	Y
2 Gray	Y	Y	Y	Y	Y	Y	N	Y
3 Borski	Y	Y	Y	Y	Y	Y	N	Y
4 Kolter	Y	Y	Y	Y	Y	Y	N	Y
5 ***Schulze***	Y	?	?	?	N	N	Y	N
6 Yatron	Y	Y	Y	Y	Y	Y	N	N
7 Edgar	?	?	?	?	?	+	+	-
8 Kostmayer	Y	Y	Y	Y	Y	Y	N	Y
9 ***Shuster***	N	N	N	N	N	N	Y	N
10 ***McDade***	Y	Y	Y	Y	N	N	Y	N
11 Harrison	Y	Y	Y	Y	Y	Y	N	Y
12 Murtha	Y	Y	Y	Y	Y	Y	N	Y
13 ***Coughlin***	Y	Y	Y	Y	N	Y	Y	N
14 Coyne	Y	Y	Y	Y	Y	Y	N	Y
15 ***Ritter***	Y	N	N	Y	N	N	Y	N
16 ***Walker***	Y	N	N	N	N	N	Y	N
17 ***Gekas***	N	N	N	N	N	N	Y	N
18 Walgren	Y	Y	Y	Y	Y	Y	N	Y
19 ***Goodling***	Y	Y	Y	Y	N	N	Y	N
20 Gaydos	Y	Y	Y	Y	Y	Y	N	Y
21 ***Ridge***	Y	Y	Y	Y	N	Y	Y	Y
22 Murphy	Y	Y	Y	Y	Y	Y	N	N
23 ***Clinger***	Y	Y	N	Y	N	N	Y	N
RHODE ISLAND								
1 St Germain	Y	P	Y	Y	Y	Y	N	Y
2 ***Schneider***	Y	Y	Y	Y	N	Y	N	Y
SOUTH CAROLINA								
1 ***Hartnett***	N	N	N	N	N	N	Y	N
2 ***Spence***	Y	Y	N	N	N	N	Y	N
3 Derrick	Y	Y	Y	Y	N	Y	N	Y
4 ***Campbell***	Y	Y	N	N	N	N	Y	N
5 Spratt	Y	Y	Y	Y	N	Y	N	N
6 Tallon	Y	Y	Y	Y	Y	Y	N	Y
SOUTH DAKOTA								
AL Daschle	Y	Y	Y	Y	Y	Y	N	Y

	429	430	431	432	433	434	435	436
TENNESSEE								
1 ***Quillen***	N	Y	N	N	N	N	Y	N
2 ***Duncan***	?	?	N	N	N	N	Y	N
3 Lloyd	Y	Y	Y	Y	N	Y	N	N
4 Cooper	Y	Y	Y	Y	N	Y	Y	N
5 Boner	Y	Y	Y	Y	Y	Y	N	Y
6 Gore	Y	Y	Y	Y	Y	Y	N	Y
7 ***Sundquist***	Y	Y	N	N	N	N	Y	N
8 Jones	Y	Y	Y	Y	Y	Y	N	Y
9 Ford	Y	Y	Y	Y	Y	?	N	Y
TEXAS								
1 Hall, S.	Y	N	N	N	N	N	Y	N
2 Wilson	Y	Y	Y	Y	Y	Y	N	Y
3 ***Bartlett***	N	N	N	N	N	N	Y	N
4 Hall, R.	Y	N	Y	N	N	Y	Y	N
5 Bryant	Y	Y	Y	Y	Y	Y	N	Y
6 ***Gramm***	?	?	?	?	?	?	?	?
7 ***Archer***	N	N	N	N	N	N	Y	N
8 ***Fields***	N	N	N	Y	N	N	Y	N
9 Brooks	Y	Y	Y	Y	Y	Y	N	Y
10 Pickle	Y	Y	N	Y	Y	Y	N	Y
11 Leath	?	?	?	?	?	?	?	?
12 Wright	Y	Y	Y	Y	Y	Y	N	Y
13 Hightower	Y	Y	N	N	N	Y	N	N
14 Patman	Y	Y	Y	Y	N	Y	Y	N
15 de la Garza	Y	Y	Y	Y	Y	Y	N	Y
16 Coleman	Y	Y	Y	Y	Y	Y	N	Y
17 Stenholm	N	N	Y	N	N	N	Y	N
18 Leland	?	?	?	?	?	?	?	?
19 Hance	Y	Y	Y	Y	Y	Y	N	Y
20 Gonzalez	Y	Y	Y	Y	Y	Y	N	Y
21 ***Loeffler***	N	N	N	N	N	N	Y	N
22 ***Paul***	?	?	?	?	?	?	?	?
23 Kazen	Y	Y	Y	Y	Y	Y	N	Y
24 Frost	Y	Y	Y	Y	Y	Y	N	Y
25 Andrews	Y	Y	Y	N	N	Y	N	N
26 Vandergriff	Y	Y	N	N	N	Y	Y	N
27 Ortiz	Y	Y	Y	Y	Y	Y	N	Y
UTAH								
1 ***Hansen***	N	N	N	N	N	N	Y	N
2 ***Marriott***	Y	N	N	N	N	N	Y	N
3 ***Nielson***	N	N	N	N	N	N	Y	N
VERMONT								
AL ***Jeffords***	Y	Y	Y	Y	Y	Y	N	Y
VIRGINIA								
1 ***Bateman***	N	N	N	N	N	N	Y	N
2 ***Whitehurst***	Y	Y	N	N	N	N	Y	N
3 ***Bliley***	Y	Y	N	N	N	N	Y	N
4 Sisisky	Y	Y	Y	Y	Y	Y	N	N
5 Daniel	N	N	N	N	N	N	Y	N
6 Olin	Y	Y	Y	N	Y	Y	N	N
7 ***Robinson***	N	N	N	N	N	N	Y	N
8 ***Parris***	Y	Y	N	N	N	N	Y	N
9 Boucher	Y	Y	Y	Y	Y	Y	N	Y
10 ***Wolf***	Y	Y	N	N	N	N	Y	N
WASHINGTON								
1 ***Pritchard***	?	?	?	?	?	?	?	?
2 Swift	Y	Y	Y	Y	Y	Y	N	Y
3 Bonker	Y	Y	Y	Y	Y	Y	N	Y
4 ***Morrison***	Y	Y	N	N	N	Y	N	Y
5 Foley	Y	Y	Y	Y	Y	Y	N	Y
6 Dicks	Y	Y	Y	Y	Y	Y	N	Y
7 Lowry	?	?	?	?	?	?	?	?
8 ***Chandler***	Y	Y	N	N	N	Y	Y	Y
WEST VIRGINIA								
1 Mollohan	Y	Y	Y	Y	Y	Y	N	Y
2 Staggers	Y	Y	Y	Y	Y	Y	N	N
3 Wise	Y	Y	Y	Y	Y	Y	N	Y
4 Rahall	Y	Y	Y	Y	Y	Y	N	N
WISCONSIN								
1 Aspin	Y	Y	Y	Y	Y	Y	N	Y
2 Kastenmeier	Y	Y	Y	Y	Y	Y	N	Y
3 ***Gunderson***	Y	N	N	Y	N	N	Y	N
4 Zablocki	Y	Y	Y	Y	Y	Y	N	Y
5 Moody	Y	Y	Y	Y	Y	Y	N	N
6 ***Petri***	Y	Y	N	Y	N	N	Y	N
7 Obey	Y	Y	Y	Y	Y	Y	N	Y
8 ***Roth***	Y	Y	N	N	N	N	Y	N
9 ***Sensenbrenner***	N	Y	N	N	N	N	Y	N
WYOMING								
AL ***Cheney***	?	?	?	?	?	?	?	?

Southern states - Ala., Ark., Fla., Ga., Ky., La., Miss., N.C., Okla., S.C., Tenn., Texas, Va.

437. Procedural Motion. Bliley, R-Va., motion to approve the House *Journal* of Tuesday, Nov. 8. Motion agreed to 368-25: R 140-12; D 228-13 (ND 145-12, SD 83-1), Nov. 9, 1983.

438. HR 4196. Dairy Production Stabilization. Harkin, D-Iowa, amendment to authorize the secretary of agriculture to make adjustments in the paid diversion program to mitigate its impact on fresh meat markets, and to require such adjustments if the average price received by beef producers drops by 10 percent during 10 consecutive days. Adopted 348-71: R 106-55; D 242-16 (ND 154-15, SD 88-1), Nov. 9, 1983.

439. HR 4196. Dairy Production Stabilization. Skeen, R-N.M., amendment to exempt dairy farmers who sell directly to consumers ("producer-handlers") from the paid diversion program, from an existing 50-cent assessment to be used to finance the program and from the 15-cent assessment for the national dairy promotion program authorized by the bill. Rejected 162-249: R 107-52; D 55-197 (ND 39-128, SD 16-69), Nov. 9, 1983.

440. HR 4196. Dairy Production Stabilization. Oberstar, D-Minn., amendment to extend the 15-month paid diversion program to 21 months and to revise dates for authorized changes in federal dairy price supports. Rejected 93-325: R 19-142; D 74-183 (ND 69-102, SD 5-81), Nov. 9, 1983.

441. HR 4196. Dairy Production Stabilization. Conable, R-N.Y., substitute to authorize the secretary of agriculture to reduce the existing $13.10 (per hundred pounds) federal dairy support by as much as $1.50, and to repeal two existing dairy assessments, each 50 cents per hundred pounds. Rejected 174-250: R 97-65; D 77-185 (ND 52-122, SD 25-63), Nov. 9, 1983. A "yea" was a vote supporting the president's position.

442. HR 4196. Dairy Production Stabilization. Clinger, R-Pa., amendment to exempt from the 50-cent assessment those dairy producers who did not increase production after the paid diversion program began. Rejected 159-255: R 101-59; D 58-196 (ND 48-119, SD 10-77), Nov. 9, 1983.

443. HR 4196. Dairy Production Stabilization. Passage of the bill to authorize a paid diversion program for dairy producers, a producer-financed dairy promotion program, reductions in the federal dairy price support, and also to retain an existing 50 cents per hundred pounds assessment on milk to help finance the diversion program, and to repeal a second 50-cent assessment. Passed 325-91: R 99-62; D 226-29 (ND 144-26, SD 82-3), Nov. 9, 1983. A "nay" was a vote supporting the president's position.

444. HR 3222. State, Justice, Commerce Appropriations, Fiscal 1984. Adoption of the conference report on the bill to provide $10,499,665,000 in fiscal 1984 for the State, Justice and Commerce Departments and the federal judiciary. Adopted 281-133: R 62-97; D 219-36 (ND 159-12, SD 60-24), Nov. 9, 1983. The president had requested $10,026,318,000 in new budget authority.

KEY

Y Voted for (yea).
\# Paired for.
+ Announced for.
N Voted against (nay).
X Paired against.
- Announced against.
P Voted "present".
C Voted "present" to avoid possible conflict of interest.
? Did not vote or otherwise make a position known.

Democrats   *Republicans*

Member	437	438	439	440	441	442	443	444
ALABAMA								
1 Edwards	?	Y	Y	N	N	Y	Y	Y
2 *Dickinson*	N	Y	N	N	N	Y	Y	Y
3 Nichols	Y	Y	N	N	N	Y	N	N
4 Bevill	Y	Y	N	N	Y	Y	Y	Y
5 Flippo	Y	Y	N	N	N	Y	N	Y
6 Erdreich	Y	Y	N	N	Y	Y	Y	N
7 Shelby	Y	Y	N	Y	N	Y	Y	N
ALASKA								
AL *Young*	N	Y	Y	N	N	?	N	Y
ARIZONA								
1 *McCain*	Y	N	Y	N	Y	Y	N	N
2 Udall	?	?	?	?	Y	?	?	?
3 *Stump*	Y	Y	Y	N	Y	N	N	N
4 *Rudd*	Y	Y	Y	N	Y	N	N	N
5 McNulty	Y	N	Y	N	Y	N	N	Y
ARKANSAS								
1 Alexander	Y	Y	N	N	N	N	Y	Y
2 *Bethune*	Y	Y	Y	Y	Y	Y	Y	N
3 *Hammerschmidt*	Y	Y	Y	Y	Y	Y	Y	Y
4 Anthony	Y	Y	N	N	Y	N	Y	Y
CALIFORNIA								
1 Bosco	Y	Y	Y	N	N	Y	Y	Y
2 *Chappie*	Y	N	Y	N	Y	Y	Y	N
3 Matsui	Y	Y	N	N	N	N	Y	Y
4 Fazio	Y	Y	Y	Y	N	Y	Y	Y
5 Burton	Y	Y	N	N	N	N	Y	Y
6 Boxer	Y	Y	?	N	N	Y	Y	Y
7 Miller	Y	N	Y	N	N	N	Y	Y
8 Dellums	Y	?	N	Y	Y	?	Y	Y
9 Stark	Y	Y	N	N	N	Y	N	Y
10 Edwards	Y	C	N	Y	N	N	Y	Y
11 Lantos	Y	Y	N	N	N	N	Y	Y
12 *Zschau*	Y	Y	Y	N	Y	N	N	N
13 Mineta	Y	Y	N	N	N	N	Y	Y
14 *Shumway*	Y	N	Y	N	Y	Y	N	N
15 Coelho	Y	Y	Y	N	N	Y	Y	Y
16 Panetta	Y	Y	N	N	N	N	Y	Y
17 *Pashayan*	Y	Y	Y	N	Y	Y	Y	N
18 Lehman	Y	Y	Y	N	N	Y	N	Y
19 *Lagomarsino*	Y	Y	Y	N	Y	Y	N	Y
20 *Thomas*	Y	N	Y	N	Y	N	N	N
21 *Fiedler*	Y	Y	Y	N	Y	N	Y	Y
22 *Moorhead*	Y	N	Y	N	Y	N	N	N
23 Beilenson	Y	Y	N	Y	N	N	Y	Y
24 Waxman	Y	N	N	?	Y	?	N	Y
25 Roybal	Y	Y	N	Y	N	Y	N	Y
26 Berman	Y	Y	N	Y	N	Y	Y	Y
27 Levine	Y	Y	N	Y	N	Y	N	Y
28 Dixon	?	Y	N	Y	N	N	Y	Y
29 Hawkins	Y	Y	N	N	N	Y	N	Y
30 Martinez	Y	Y	Y	Y	Y	N	N	Y
31 Dymally	P	Y	?	Y	Y	Y	Y	Y
32 Anderson	Y	N	Y	N	N	Y	N	N
33 *Dreier*	Y	N	Y	N	Y	N	N	N
34 Torres	Y	Y	Y	Y	Y	Y	N	Y
35 *Lewis*	Y	N	Y	N	Y	N	N	Y
36 Brown	Y	N	?	N	Y	N	Y	N
37 *McCandless*	Y	N	Y	N	Y	N	N	N
38 Patterson	Y	Y	N	N	N	N	Y	N
39 *Dannemeyer*	N	N	N	N	Y	N	N	N
40 *Badham*	N	N	Y	N	N	Y	N	N
41 *Lowery*	Y	N	Y	N	N	Y	N	N
42 *Lungren*	?	N	Y	N	Y	N	N	N
43 *Packard*	Y	N	Y	N	Y	Y	N	N
44 Bates	Y	Y	N	Y	N	N	N	Y
45 *Hunter*	Y	Y	Y	N	Y	N	N	N
COLORADO								
1 Schroeder	N	Y	N	Y	Y	N	N	Y
2 Wirth	Y	Y	N	Y	N	?	Y	Y
3 Kogovsek	Y	Y	N	N	N	N	Y	Y
4 *Brown*	Y	N	Y	N	N	N	N	N
5 *Kramer*	Y	N	N	N	N	Y	N	N
6 *Schaefer*	Y	Y	N	N	N	Y	N	N
CONNECTICUT								
1 Kennelly	Y	Y	Y	Y	N	N	Y	Y
2 Gejdenson	N	Y	Y	N	N	Y	N	Y
3 Morrison	Y	Y	Y	Y	N	Y	N	Y
4 *McKinney*	Y	N	N	N	Y	N	Y	Y
5 Ratchford	Y	Y	Y	N	Y	N	?	Y	Y
6 *Johnson*	Y	Y	N	N	N	Y	Y	Y
DELAWARE								
AL Carper	Y	Y	N	N	Y	N	N	Y
FLORIDA								
1 Hutto	Y	Y	N	N	N	Y	Y	Y
2 Fuqua	Y	Y	N	N	N	Y	Y	Y
3 Bennett	Y	Y	N	N	N	Y	Y	Y
4 Chappell	Y	Y	Y	?	Y	N	Y	Y
5 *McCollum*	Y	Y	Y	N	N	Y	N	N
6 MacKay	Y	Y	N	N	N	N	Y	Y
7 Gibbons	Y	Y	Y	Y	N	Y	Y	Y
8 *Young*	Y	N	Y	Y	N	Y	Y	N
9 *Bilirakis*	Y	N	N	N	N	N	Y	N
10 Ireland	Y	Y	N	Y	N	Y	Y	Y
11 Nelson	Y	Y	N	Y	N	Y	Y	Y
12 *Lewis*	Y	N	N	N	N	Y	Y	N
13 *Mack*	Y	N	Y	N	Y	Y	N	N
14 Mica	Y	N	N	N	N	Y	N	N
15 *Shaw*	Y	Y	N	Y	Y	N	N	N
16 Smith	Y	N	N	N	N	Y	N	Y
17 Lehman	Y	Y	N	N	N	N	Y	Y
18 Pepper	Y	Y	?	N	N	N	Y	Y
19 Fascell	Y	Y	N	N	N	N	Y	Y
GEORGIA								
1 Thomas	Y	Y	N	N	N	N	Y	Y
2 Hatcher	Y	Y	N	N	N	N	Y	N
3 Ray	Y	Y	N	N	N	N	Y	Y
4 Levitas	Y	Y	N	N	N	N	Y	N
5 Fowler	Y	Y	Y	N	N	N	Y	Y
6 *Gingrich*	Y	Y	Y	N	N	?	?	?
7 Vacancy								
8 Rowland	Y	Y	N	N	N	N	Y	Y
9 Jenkins	?	Y	Y	N	N	N	Y	Y
10 Barnard	Y	Y	?	N	N	Y	Y	Y
HAWAII								
1 Heftel	?	?	Y	Y	N	Y	Y	Y
2 Akaka	Y	Y	X	N	N	N	N	Y
IDAHO								
1 *Craig*	Y	Y	N	N	Y	N	N	N
2 *Hansen*	Y	Y	Y	N	Y	N	N	N
ILLINOIS								
1 Hayes	Y	Y	N	N	N	Y	Y	Y
2 Savage	Y	Y	N	Y	N	N	N	Y
3 Russo	Y	Y	N	N	N	N	Y	Y
4 *O'Brien*	Y	N	Y	N	Y	N	Y	Y
5 Lipinski	N	Y	N	N	N	Y	Y	Y
6 *Hyde*	Y	N	Y	N	Y	N	N	N
7 Collins	Y	Y	N	N	N	N	Y	Y
8 Rostenkowski	Y	Y	N	N	N	N	Y	Y
9 Yates	Y	N	N	N	N	N	Y	Y
10 *Porter*	Y	Y	N	Y	N	Y	N	Y
11 Annunzio	Y	Y	N	N	N	N	Y	Y
12 *Crane, P.*	Y	N	Y	N	Y	N	N	N
13 *Erlenborn*	N	N	N	N	N	Y	N	N
14 *Corcoran*	Y	N	Y	N	N	N	N	N
15 *Madigan*	Y	N	Y	N	Y	N	N	N
16 *Martin*	Y	Y	Y	Y	Y	Y	Y	Y
17 Evans	Y	Y	N	N	N	N	Y	Y
18 *Michel*	Y	N	Y	N	N	N	N	N
19 *Crane, D.*	Y	N	Y	N	Y	N	N	N
20 Durbin	N	Y	N	N	N	N	Y	Y
21 Price	Y	Y	N	N	N	N	Y	Y
22 Simon	Y	Y	Y	N	N	N	Y	Y
INDIANA								
1 Hall	Y	Y	N	N	N	N	Y	Y
2 Sharp	Y	Y	N	N	N	N	Y	Y
3 *Hiler*	N	Y	N	Y	N	Y	Y	N
4 *Coats*	Y	Y	Y	N	N	Y	Y	N
5 Hillis	Y	N	Y	N	Y	N	Y	Y

ND - Northern Democrats   SD - Southern Democrats

Corresponding to Congressional Record Votes 471, 473, 474, 475, 476, 477, 478, 479

	437	438	439	440	441	442	443	444
6 ***Burton***	Y	Y	Y	N	N	Y	Y	N
7 ***Myers***	Y	Y	N	N	N	Y	Y	Y
8 McCloskey	Y	Y	Y	N	Y	Y	Y	Y
9 Hamilton	Y	Y	N	N	N	N	Y	Y
10 Jacobs	P	Y	N	N	N	N	N	N
IOWA								
1 ***Leach***	?	Y	N	N	Y	Y	N	Y
2 ***Tauke***	Y	Y	N	N	N	N	Y	N
3 ***Evans***	?	Y	N	N	Y	N	Y	N
4 Smith	Y	Y	N	Y	N	N	Y	Y
5 Harkin	N	Y	N	Y	N	N	Y	Y
6 Bedell	Y	Y	N	Y	N	N	Y	Y
KANSAS								
1 ***Roberts***	N	Y	Y	N	Y	N	N	N
2 Slattery	Y	Y	N	N	N	N	Y	N
3 ***Winn***	?	?	?	?	?	?	?	?
4 Glickman	Y	Y	N	N	Y	N	Y	Y
5 ***Whittaker***	Y	Y	Y	N	Y	N	Y	N
KENTUCKY								
1 Hubbard	Y	Y	N	N	N	N	Y	N
2 Natcher	Y	Y	N	N	N	N	Y	Y
3 Mazzoli	Y	N	N	N	Y	N	Y	Y
4 ***Snyder***	Y	Y	N	N	N	N	Y	N
5 ***Rogers***	Y	Y	N	N	N	N	Y	Y
6 ***Hopkins***	Y	Y	N	N	N	N	Y	N
7 Perkins	Y	Y	N	N	N	N	Y	Y
LOUISIANA								
1 ***Livingston***	Y	Y	Y	N	Y	Y	Y	N
2 Boggs	?	Y	N	N	N	N	Y	Y
3 Tauzin	Y	Y	N	N	N	N	Y	N
4 Roemer	N	Y	Y	N	Y	N	Y	N
5 Huckaby	Y	Y	N	N	N	N	Y	N
6 ***Moore***	Y	Y	Y	N	Y	Y	Y	N
7 Breaux	Y	Y	N	N	N	N	Y	Y
8 Long	Y	Y	N	N	Y	N	N	Y
MAINE								
1 ***McKernan***	Y	Y	Y	N	N	Y	Y	Y
2 ***Snowe***	Y	Y	N	N	N	Y	Y	Y
MARYLAND								
1 Dyson	Y	Y	N	N	Y	N	Y	Y
2 Long	Y	Y	N	N	N	N	Y	?
3 Mikulski	?	Y	N	N	N	N	Y	Y
4 ***Holt***	N	N	Y	N	Y	Y	N	N
5 Hoyer	Y	Y	N	N	N	N	Y	Y
6 Byron	?	Y	Y	N	N	Y	Y	Y
7 Mitchell	N	Y	N	Y	Y	N	?	Y
8 Barnes	Y	Y	N	N	Y	N	N	Y
MASSACHUSETTS								
1 ***Conte***	Y	Y	Y	N	Y	Y	Y	Y
2 Boland	Y	Y	Y	N	Y	Y	Y	Y
3 Early	?	?	?	?	?	?	?	?
4 Frank	Y	N	Y	N	Y	Y	N	Y
5 Shannon	Y	Y	Y	N	Y	Y	Y	Y
6 Mavroules	Y	Y	Y	N	Y	Y	Y	Y
7 Markey	N	N	Y	N	Y	Y	N	Y
8 O'Neill								
9 Moakley	Y	Y	Y	N	Y	Y	Y	Y
10 Studds	Y	Y	Y	N	Y	N	N	Y
11 Donnelly	Y	Y	Y	N	Y	Y	Y	Y
MICHIGAN								
1 Conyers	Y	Y	N	Y	N	N	Y	Y
2 ***Pursell***	Y	Y	Y	N	N	Y	Y	N
3 Wolpe	Y	Y	N	Y	N	N	Y	Y
4 ***Siljander***	Y	Y	N	N	N	N	Y	N
5 ***Sawyer***	Y	Y	Y	N	N	Y	Y	Y
6 Carr	Y	Y	?	N	N	N	Y	Y
7 Kildee	Y	Y	N	N	N	N	Y	Y
8 Traxler	Y	Y	N	N	N	N	Y	Y
9 ***Vander Jagt***	Y	Y	?	N	Y	Y	Y	Y
10 Albosta	Y	Y	N	Y	N	N	Y	Y
11 ***Davis***	Y	Y	N	Y	N	Y	Y	Y
12 Bonior	Y	Y	N	N	N	N	Y	Y
13 Crockett	?	Y	N	Y	N	N	Y	Y
14 Hertel	Y	Y	N	N	N	N	Y	N
15 Ford	?	Y	N	Y	N	N	Y	Y
16 Dingell	Y	Y	N	N	N	N	Y	Y
17 Levin	Y	Y	N	N	N	N	Y	Y
18 ***Broomfield***	Y	N	N	N	Y	Y	N	Y
MINNESOTA								
1 Penny	Y	Y	N	Y	N	Y	Y	Y
2 ***Weber***	Y	Y	Y	Y	N	Y	Y	N
3 ***Frenzel***	Y	Y	N	N	N	N	Y	N
4 Vento	Y	Y	N	Y	N	Y	Y	Y
5 Sabo	N	Y	N	Y	N	N	Y	Y
6 Sikorski	N	Y	N	Y	N	Y	Y	Y
7 ***Stangeland***	Y	Y	Y	Y	N	Y	Y	N
8 Oberstar	P	Y	N	Y	N	Y	Y	Y
MISSISSIPPI								
1 Whitten	Y	Y	N	N	N	Y	Y	Y
2 ***Franklin***	Y	Y	Y	N	Y	Y	N	N
3 Montgomery	Y	Y	N	N	Y	Y	Y	Y
4 Dowdy	Y	Y	N	N	N	N	Y	Y
5 ***Lott***	Y	Y	Y	N	N	Y	Y	N
MISSOURI								
1 Clay	Y	Y	N	N	N	N	Y	Y
2 Young	Y	Y	N	N	N	N	Y	Y
3 Gephardt	Y	Y	N	N	N	N	Y	Y
4 Skelton	Y	Y	N	N	N	N	Y	N
5 Wheat	Y	Y	N	N	N	N	Y	Y
6 ***Coleman***	Y	Y	Y	N	N	Y	Y	Y
7 ***Taylor***	Y	Y	Y	N	N	Y	Y	Y
8 ***Emerson***	Y	Y	Y	N	N	N	Y	N
9 Volkmer	Y	Y	Y	N	N	Y	Y	N
MONTANA								
1 Williams	Y	Y	N	Y	N	Y	Y	Y
2 ***Marlenee***	Y	Y	N	Y	N	N	Y	N
NEBRASKA								
1 ***Bereuter***	Y	Y	Y	N	N	Y	Y	N
2 ***Daub***	Y	Y	N	N	N	N	Y	N
3 ***Smith***	Y	Y	N	N	Y	N	N	Y
NEVADA								
1 Reid	Y	Y	N	N	N	N	Y	Y
2 ***Vucanovich***	Y	N	Y	N	Y	N	N	N
NEW HAMPSHIRE								
1 D'Amours	Y	N	Y	N	Y	N	N	Y
2 ***Gregg***	Y	N	Y	N	Y	N	N	N
NEW JERSEY								
1 Florio	Y	N	N	N	N	N	Y	Y
2 Hughes	Y	Y	N	N	N	N	Y	Y
3 Howard	?	Y	N	N	Y	N	Y	Y
4 ***Smith***	Y	N	Y	N	Y	Y	Y	Y
5 ***Roukema***	Y	N	Y	N	Y	Y	N	Y
6 Dwyer	Y	Y	Y	Y	Y	N	Y	Y
7 ***Rinaldo***	Y	N	N	N	N	N	Y	Y
8 Roe	Y	N	N	Y	Y	Y	Y	Y
9 Torricelli	Y	Y	N	N	N	N	Y	Y
10 Rodino	Y	Y	N	Y	N	N	Y	Y
11 Minish	Y	N	N	N	Y	N	N	Y
12 ***Courter***	Y	N	N	N	Y	N	N	N
13 ***Forsythe***	?	N	N	Y	N	N	Y	N
14 Guarini	Y	Y	N	N	N	N	?	?
NEW MEXICO								
1 ***Lujan***	Y	Y	Y	N	Y	N	Y	Y
2 ***Skeen***	Y	Y	Y	N	Y	N	Y	Y
3 Richardson	Y	Y	N	N	N	N	Y	Y
NEW YORK								
1 ***Carney***	Y	N	Y	N	Y	N	N	N
2 Downey	Y	Y	N	N	Y	N	Y	Y
3 Mrazek	?	Y	N	?	Y	N	Y	Y
4 ***Lent***	Y	N	N	N	Y	Y	N	Y
5 ***McGrath***	Y	N	N	N	Y	Y	N	N
6 Addabbo	Y	Y	N	N	N	N	Y	Y
7 Ackerman	Y	Y	Y	N	Y	N	Y	Y
8 Scheuer	Y	Y	N	N	N	Y	Y	Y
9 Ferraro	Y	Y	N	N	N	N	Y	Y
10 Schumer	Y	Y	N	N	Y	N	Y	Y
11 Towns	Y	Y	N	N	N	N	Y	Y
12 Owens	Y	Y	N	N	N	N	Y	Y
13 Solarz	?	?	?	?	?	?	?	?
14 ***Molinari***	?	?	?	?	?	?	?	?
15 ***Green***	Y	N	Y	N	Y	N	N	Y
16 Rangel	Y	Y	N	N	Y	N	Y	Y
17 Weiss	Y	N	N	N	Y	N	-	Y
18 Garcia	?	Y	N	N	N	N	Y	Y
19 Biaggi	Y	Y	N	N	Y	N	Y	Y
20 Ottinger	N	Y	N	Y	Y	N	N	Y
21 ***Fish***	Y	Y	N	N	N	Y	Y	Y
22 ***Gilman***	Y	Y	N	N	N	Y	Y	Y
23 Stratton	?	Y	N	N	N	N	Y	Y
24 ***Solomon***	N	N	?	N	N	Y	Y	N
25 ***Boehlert***	Y	Y	Y	Y	N	Y	Y	Y
26 ***Martin***	Y	N	N	N	Y	Y	Y	Y
27 ***Wortley***	Y	N	Y	N	Y	Y	Y	Y
28 McHugh	Y	Y	N	Y	N	Y	Y	Y
29 ***Horton***	Y	Y	N	N	N	Y	Y	Y
30 ***Conable***	Y	N	Y	N	Y	N	N	N
31 ***Kemp***	?	Y	Y	N	Y	Y	N	N
32 LaFalce	Y	Y	N	Y	Y	Y	Y	Y
33 Nowak	Y	Y	Y	Y	Y	Y	N	Y
34 Lundine	Y	Y	Y	N	N	Y	Y	Y
NORTH CAROLINA								
1 Jones	?	Y	N	Y	N	N	?	?
2 Valentine	Y	Y	N	N	N	N	Y	N
3 Whitley	Y	Y	N	N	N	N	Y	?
4 Andrews	Y	Y	N	N	N	N	Y	Y
5 Neal	?	Y	N	N	N	N	Y	Y
6 Britt	Y	Y	N	N	Y	N	Y	Y
7 Rose	Y	Y	N	N	N	N	Y	Y
8 Hefner	Y	Y	N	N	N	N	Y	Y
9 ***Martin***	Y	Y	Y	N	Y	Y	Y	N
10 ***Broyhill***	Y	Y	Y	Y	Y	Y	N	N
11 Clarke	Y	Y	N	N	Y	N	Y	Y
NORTH DAKOTA								
AL Dorgan	Y	Y	N	Y	N	N	Y	N
OHIO								
1 Luken	Y	Y	N	N	Y	N	N	N
2 ***Gradison***	Y	N	N	N	Y	Y	Y	Y
3 Hall	?	Y	N	N	Y	N	N	Y
4 ***Oxley***	Y	Y	N	N	N	Y	Y	N
5 ***Latta***	Y	Y	Y	N	Y	Y	N	N
6 ***McEwen***	Y	Y	N	Y	N	Y	Y	N
7 ***DeWine***	Y	Y	N	N	N	N	Y	N
8 ***Kindness***	Y	Y	Y	?	N	N	Y	N
9 Kaptur	Y	Y	N	N	N	N	Y	Y
10 ***Miller***	N	N	N	N	N	Y	Y	Y
11 Eckart	Y	Y	N	N	N	N	Y	Y
12 ***Kasich***	Y	N	N	N	N	Y	Y	N
13 Pease	Y	Y	N	Y	N	Y	Y	Y
14 Seiberling	Y	N	N	Y	N	N	Y	Y
15 ***Wylie***	Y	N	N	N	N	Y	Y	Y
16 ***Regula***	Y	Y	N	N	N	Y	Y	Y
17 ***Williams***	Y	Y	N	N	N	Y	Y	Y
18 Applegate	Y	Y	Y	Y	N	Y	Y	Y
19 Feighan	Y	Y	N	N	N	N	Y	Y
20 Oakar	Y	Y	N	Y	N	N	Y	Y
21 Stokes	Y	N	N	Y	Y	?	Y	Y
OKLAHOMA								
1 Jones	Y	Y	Y	N	N	N	Y	Y
2 Synar	Y	Y	N	N	N	N	Y	Y
3 Watkins	Y	Y	Y	N	Y	N	Y	N
4 McCurdy	Y	Y	Y	N	N	N	Y	N
5 ***Edwards***	?	?	?	N	Y	Y	N	N
6 English	Y	Y	Y	N	N	N	Y	N
OREGON								
1 AuCoin	N	Y	Y	N	N	N	Y	Y
2 ***Smith, R.***	P	Y	Y	N	Y	Y	N	N
3 Wyden	Y	Y	N	N	N	N	Y	Y
4 Weaver	Y	Y	N	N	N	N	Y	N
5 ***Smith, D.***	Y	Y	N	N	Y	Y	N	?
PENNSYLVANIA								
1 Foglietta	Y	Y	N	N	Y	Y	Y	Y
2 Gray	Y	Y	N	Y	N	N	Y	Y
3 Borski	Y	Y	N	N	N	Y	Y	Y
4 Kolter	Y	Y	Y	N	N	Y	Y	Y
5 ***Schulze***	Y	N	N	N	N	Y	Y	?
6 Yatron	Y	Y	Y	Y	N	Y	Y	Y
7 Edgar	?	+	?	Y	N	Y	Y	Y
8 Kostmayer	Y	Y	Y	N	N	Y	Y	Y
9 ***Shuster***	Y	Y	Y	N	N	Y	Y	N
10 ***McDade***	Y	N	Y	Y	N	Y	Y	Y
11 Harrison	Y	Y	N	Y	N	Y	Y	Y
12 Murtha	Y	Y	Y	Y	N	Y	Y	Y
13 ***Coughlin***	N	N	Y	N	Y	Y	N	Y
14 Coyne	Y	Y	N	N	Y	Y	Y	Y
15 ***Ritter***	Y	N	Y	N	N	Y	Y	N
16 ***Walker***	N	N	Y	N	Y	Y	Y	N
17 ***Gekas***	Y	Y	Y	N	N	Y	Y	N
18 Walgren	Y	Y	N	Y	Y	Y	Y	N
19 ***Goodling***	N	Y	Y	N	N	Y	Y	N
20 Gaydos	Y	Y	N	Y	N	Y	Y	Y
21 ***Ridge***	?	N	Y	Y	N	Y	Y	Y
22 Murphy	Y	Y	N	Y	N	Y	Y	N
23 ***Clinger***	Y	N	Y	Y	N	Y	Y	Y
RHODE ISLAND								
1 St Germain	P	Y	Y	Y	Y	Y	N	Y
2 ***Schneider***	Y	Y	Y	N	Y	N	Y	Y
SOUTH CAROLINA								
1 ***Hartnett***	Y	N	Y	N	Y	Y	N	N
2 ***Spence***	Y	Y	Y	N	Y	Y	Y	N
3 Derrick	Y	Y	N	N	Y	N	Y	Y
4 ***Campbell***	Y	Y	Y	N	Y	N	Y	N
5 Spratt	Y	Y	N	N	Y	Y	Y	Y
6 Tallon	Y	Y	N	N	N	N	Y	Y
SOUTH DAKOTA								
AL Daschle	Y	Y	N	Y	N	N	Y	Y
TENNESSEE								
1 ***Quillen***	Y	Y	N	N	N	N	Y	N
2 ***Duncan***	Y	Y	Y	N	N	Y	Y	Y
3 Lloyd	Y	Y	N	N	N	N	Y	Y
4 Cooper	Y	Y	N	N	N	N	Y	Y
5 Boner	Y	Y	?	?	N	N	Y	Y
6 Gore	Y	Y	N	N	N	N	Y	Y
7 ***Sundquist***	Y	Y	N	N	N	N	Y	N
8 Jones	Y	Y	N	N	N	N	Y	Y
9 Ford	P	Y	N	N	N	N	Y	Y
TEXAS								
1 Hall, S.	Y	Y	N	N	N	N	Y	N
2 Wilson	Y	Y	N	N	N	?	?	?
3 ***Bartlett***	Y	Y	N	N	Y	N	Y	N
4 Hall, R.	Y	Y	N	N	Y	N	Y	N
5 Bryant	Y	Y	N	N	N	N	Y	Y
6 ***Gramm***	?	?	?	?	?	?	?	?
7 ***Archer***	Y	Y	Y	N	Y	N	N	N
8 ***Fields***	Y	Y	Y	N	Y	N	N	N
9 Brooks	Y	Y	N	N	Y	N	Y	Y
10 Pickle	Y	Y	Y	N	Y	N	Y	Y
11 Leath	Y	Y	N	N	N	N	Y	N
12 Wright	Y	Y	N	Y	N	N	Y	Y
13 Hightower	Y	Y	Y	N	Y	N	Y	Y
14 Patman	Y	Y	N	N	Y	N	N	N
15 de la Garza	Y	Y	N	N	N	N	Y	Y
16 Coleman	Y	Y	Y	N	Y	N	Y	Y
17 Stenholm	Y	Y	N	N	N	N	Y	N
18 Leland	Y	Y	Y	Y	N	N	Y	Y
19 Hance	Y	Y	#	?	?	?	?	?
20 Gonzalez	Y	Y	N	Y	N	N	Y	Y
21 ***Loeffler***	Y	Y	Y	N	Y	N	Y	N
22 ***Paul***	?	?	?	?	?	?	?	?
23 Kazen	Y	Y	N	N	Y	N	Y	Y
24 Frost	Y	Y	N	N	N	N	Y	Y
25 Andrews	Y	Y	N	N	N	N	Y	Y
26 Vandergriff	Y	Y	Y	N	N	N	Y	N
27 Ortiz	Y	Y	N	N	Y	N	Y	Y
UTAH								
1 ***Hansen***	Y	Y	Y	N	Y	Y	Y	N
2 ***Marriott***	Y	Y	Y	N	Y	N	N	Y
3 ***Nielson***	Y	Y	Y	N	Y	Y	Y	N
VERMONT								
AL ***Jeffords***	Y	Y	N	N	N	N	Y	Y
VIRGINIA								
1 ***Bateman***	Y	Y	N	N	Y	Y	Y	Y
2 ***Whitehurst***	Y	Y	Y	N	Y	Y	Y	Y
3 ***Bliley***	Y	Y	Y	N	Y	N	Y	Y
4 Sisisky	Y	Y	N	N	N	N	Y	?
5 Daniel	Y	Y	Y	N	N	Y	Y	N
6 Olin	Y	Y	N	N	Y	N	Y	Y
7 ***Robinson***	Y	N	Y	N	Y	Y	Y	Y
8 ***Parris***	Y	Y	Y	N	Y	Y	Y	Y
9 Boucher	Y	Y	N	N	N	N	Y	Y
10 ***Wolf***	Y	Y	Y	N	Y	Y	Y	Y
WASHINGTON								
1 ***Pritchard***	?	?	?	?	?	?	?	?
2 Swift	Y	Y	N	Y	N	N	Y	Y
3 Bonker	Y	Y	N	N	N	?	Y	Y
4 ***Morrison***	Y	Y	Y	Y	N	N	Y	Y
5 Foley	Y	Y	N	N	N	N	Y	Y
6 Dicks	Y	Y	Y	N	N	N	Y	Y
7 Lowry	?	?	?	?	?	?	?	?
8 ***Chandler***	Y	Y	Y	N	Y	N	Y	Y
WEST VIRGINIA								
1 Mollohan	Y	Y	N	N	N	N	Y	Y
2 Staggers	Y	Y	N	N	N	Y	Y	Y
3 Wise	Y	Y	N	N	Y	Y	N	Y
4 Rahall	N	Y	N	N	N	Y	Y	Y
WISCONSIN								
1 Aspin	Y	Y	Y	Y	N	N	Y	Y
2 Kastenmeier	Y	Y	N	Y	N	Y	Y	Y
3 ***Gunderson***	Y	Y	N	Y	N	N	Y	N
4 Zablocki	Y	Y	N	Y	N	Y	Y	Y
5 Moody	Y	Y	N	Y	Y	Y	N	Y
6 ***Petri***	Y	Y	Y	Y	N	Y	Y	N
7 Obey	Y	Y	N	Y	N	Y	Y	Y
8 ***Roth***	Y	Y	Y	Y	N	Y	Y	N
9 ***Sensenbrenner***	Y	Y	N	Y	N	N	Y	N
WYOMING								
AL ***Cheney***	?	Y	Y	N	Y	N	N	N

Southern states - Ala., Ark., Fla., Ga., Ky., La., Miss., N.C., Okla., S.C., Tenn., Texas, Va.

445. HR 3222. State, Justice, Commerce Appropriations, Fiscal 1984. Smith, D-Iowa, motion that the House recede from its disagreement and accept a Senate amendment, as amended by the conference committee, to provide $240 million in economic development assistance through the Economic Development Administration. Motion agreed to 305-107: R 61-98; D 244-9 (ND 170-0, SD 74-9), Nov. 9, 1983.

446. HR 3222. State, Justice, Commerce Appropriations, Fiscal 1984. Smith, D-Iowa, motion that the House recede from its disagreement and accept a Senate amendment, as amended by the conference committee, barring the Federal Trade Commission from issuing final rules until its authorization cleared Congress or until the first session of the 98th Congress adjourned. Motion agreed to 214-192: R 21-133; D 193-59 (ND 153-15, SD 40-44), Nov. 9, 1983.

447. HR 3222. State, Justice, Commerce Appropriations, Fiscal 1984. Smith, D-Iowa, motion that the House recede from its disagreement and accept a Senate amendment, as amended by the conference committee, providing $11.89 million for the U.S. Civil Rights Commission. Motion rejected 170-235: R 129-24; D 41-211 (ND 14-153, SD 27-58), Nov. 9, 1983.

448. HR 4102. Universal Telephone Service. Adoption of the rule (H Res 363) providing for House floor consideration of the bill to prohibit the Federal Communications Commission from imposing a monthly access charge on residential and small business telephone users for the right to use long-distance service. Adopted 249-149: R 18-135; D 231-14 (ND 155-6, SD 76-8), Nov. 9, 1983.

449. Procedural Motion. Nielson, R-Utah, motion to approve the House *Journal* of Wednesday, Nov. 9. Motion agreed to 351-31: R 136-14; D 215-17 (ND 135-16, SD 80-1), Nov. 10, 1983.

450. H J Res 413. Continuing Appropriations, Fiscal 1984. Adoption of the rule (H Res 367) providing for House floor consideration of the bill to make further continuing appropriations for fiscal 1984. Adopted 238-177: R 0-157; D 238-20 (ND 168-5, SD 70-15), Nov. 10, 1983.

451. H J Res 413. Continuing Appropriations, Fiscal 1984. Wright, D-Texas, substitute as amended by the Hoyer, D-Md., amendment. The Wright amendment consisted of the contents of the version of H J Res 403, as amended prior to the House rejection of the measure Nov. 8 *(see vote 436, p. 128-H)*. Adopted 235-181: R 19-138; D 216-43 (ND 156-17, SD 60-26), Nov. 10, 1983. A "nay" was a vote supporting the president's position.

452. H J Res 413. Continuing Appropriations, Fiscal 1984. Passage of the joint resolution to make further continuing appropriations for fiscal 1984 for those government agencies whose regular appropriations bills had not cleared. Passed 224-189: R 14-140; D 210-49 (ND 156-17, SD 54-32), Nov. 10, 1983.

KEY

Y Voted for (yea).
\# Paired for.
\+ Announced for.
N Voted against (nay).
X Paired against.
- Announced against.
P Voted "present".
C Voted "present" to avoid possible conflict of interest.
? Did not vote or otherwise make a position known.

Democrats   ***Republicans***

	445	446	447	448	449	450	451	452
ALABAMA								
1 *Edwards*	Y	N	Y	Y	Y	N	N	N
2 *Dickinson*	N	N	?	N	N	N	N	N
3 Nichols	Y	N	Y	Y	Y	Y	N	N
4 Bevill	Y	Y	Y	Y	Y	Y	Y	Y
5 Flippo	Y	N	Y	Y	Y	Y	N	N
6 Erdreich	Y	N	N	Y	Y	Y	Y	N
7 Shelby	Y	N	Y	Y	Y	Y	N	N
ALASKA								
AL *Young*	N	N	Y	N	?	N	N	N
ARIZONA								
1 *McCain*	N	N	N	N	Y	N	N	N
2 Udall	?	?	?	?	Y	Y	Y	Y
3 *Stump*	N	N	Y	N	N	N	N	N
4 *Rudd*	N	N	Y	N	Y	N	N	N
5 McNulty	Y	Y	N	Y	Y	Y	Y	Y
ARKANSAS								
1 Alexander	Y	Y	Y	Y	Y	Y	Y	Y
2 *Bethune*	N	N	N	N	Y	N	N	N
3 *Hammerschmidt*	Y	N	Y	N	N	N	N	N
4 Anthony	Y	N	?	?	Y	Y	Y	Y
CALIFORNIA								
1 Bosco	Y	Y	N	Y	Y	Y	Y	Y
2 *Chappie*	N	N	Y	N	Y	N	N	N
3 Matsui	Y	Y	N	Y	Y	Y	Y	Y
4 Fazio	Y	Y	N	Y	Y	Y	Y	Y
5 Burton	Y	Y	N	Y	Y	Y	Y	Y
6 Boxer	Y	Y	N	Y	Y	Y	Y	Y
7 Miller	Y	Y	N	Y	Y	Y	Y	Y
8 Dellums	Y	Y	?	Y	?	Y	Y	Y
9 Stark	Y	?	N	?	Y	\#	\#	\#
10 Edwards	Y	Y	N	Y	Y	Y	Y	Y
11 Lantos	Y	Y	N	Y	Y	Y	Y	Y
12 *Zschau*	N	N	N	N	Y	N	N	N
13 Mineta	Y	Y	N	Y	Y	Y	Y	Y
14 *Shumway*	N	N	Y	N	Y	N	N	N
15 Coelho	Y	Y	N	Y	Y	Y	Y	Y
16 Panetta	Y	Y	N	Y	Y	Y	Y	Y
17 *Pashayan*	N	N	Y	N	Y	N	N	N
18 Lehman	Y	Y	N	Y	Y	Y	Y	Y
19 *Lagomarsino*	N	N	Y	N	Y	N	N	N
20 *Thomas*	N	N	Y	N	Y	N	N	N
21 *Fiedler*	N	N	Y	N	Y	N	N	N
22 *Moorhead*	N	N	Y	N	N	N	N	N
23 Beilenson	Y	Y	N	Y	N	Y	Y	Y
24 Waxman	Y	Y	N	Y	Y	Y	Y	Y
25 Roybal	Y	Y	Y	Y	Y	Y	Y	Y
26 Berman	Y	Y	N	?	Y	Y	Y	Y
27 Levine	Y	Y	N	Y	Y	Y	Y	Y
28 Dixon	Y	Y	N	Y	Y	Y	Y	Y
29 Hawkins	Y	Y	N	?	N	Y	Y	Y
30 Martinez	Y	Y	N	?	?	Y	Y	Y
31 Dymally	Y	Y	N	Y	P	Y	Y	Y
32 Anderson	Y	Y	N	Y	Y	Y	Y	Y
33 *Dreier*	N	N	Y	N	Y	N	N	N
34 Torres	Y	Y	N	Y	Y	Y	Y	Y
35 *Lewis*	N	N	Y	N	N	N	N	N
36 Brown	Y	Y	N	Y	?	\#	\#	\#
37 *McCandless*	N	N	Y	N	Y	N	N	N
38 Patterson	Y	Y	N	Y	Y	Y	Y	Y
39 *Dannemeyer*	N	N	Y	N	Y	N	N	N
40 *Badham*	N	N	Y	N	Y	N	N	N
41 Lowery	N	N	Y	N	Y	N	N	N
42 Lungren	N	N	Y	N	Y	N	N	N
43 *Packard*	N	N	Y	N	Y	N	N	N
44 Bates	Y	Y	N	Y	Y	Y	Y	N
45 *Hunter*	N	N	Y	N	Y	N	N	N
COLORADO								
1 Schroeder	Y	Y	N	Y	N	Y	Y	Y
2 Wirth	Y	Y	N	Y	Y	Y	Y	Y
3 Kogovsek	Y	Y	N	Y	Y	Y	Y	Y
4 *Brown*	N	N	N	N	N	N	N	N
5 *Kramer*	N	N	Y	N	Y	N	N	N
6 *Schaefer*	N	N	N	N	Y	N	N	N
CONNECTICUT								
1 Kennelly	Y	Y	N	Y	Y	Y	Y	Y
2 Gejdenson	Y	Y	N	?	?	Y	Y	Y
3 Morrison	Y	Y	N	Y	Y	Y	Y	Y
4 *McKinney*	Y	N	Y	N	Y	N	N	N
5 Ratchford	Y	Y	N	Y	Y	Y	Y	Y
6 *Johnson*	Y	Y	N	Y	N	Y	N	+
DELAWARE								
AL Carper	Y	Y	N	Y	Y	Y	Y	N
FLORIDA								
1 Hutto	Y	N	N	Y	Y	Y	Y	Y
2 Fuqua	Y	N	N	Y	Y	Y	Y	Y
3 Bennett	Y	Y	Y	Y	Y	Y	N	N
4 Chappell	Y	Y	Y	Y	Y	Y	Y	N
5 *McCollum*	N	N	Y	N	Y	N	N	N
6 MacKay	Y	?	N	Y	Y	Y	Y	N
7 Gibbons	Y	Y	Y	Y	Y	Y	N	N
8 *Young*	N	N	Y	N	Y	N	N	N
9 *Bilirakis*	N	N	Y	N	Y	N	Y	N
10 Ireland	Y	N	Y	N	N	N	N	N
11 Nelson	N	N	Y	N	Y	N	N	N
12 *Lewis*	Y	N	Y	N	Y	N	Y	N
13 *Mack*	N	N	Y	N	N	N	N	N
14 Mica	Y	Y	Y	Y	Y	Y	Y	Y
15 *Shaw*	Y	N	Y	N	N	N	N	N
16 Smith	Y	N	Y	N	Y	N	N	N
17 Lehman	?	Y	N	Y	Y	Y	Y	Y
18 Pepper	Y	Y	N	Y	Y	Y	Y	Y
19 Fascell	Y	Y	N	Y	?	Y	Y	Y
GEORGIA								
1 Thomas	Y	N	N	Y	Y	Y	Y	Y
2 Hatcher	Y	N	N	N	Y	Y	Y	Y
3 Ray	Y	N	Y	N	Y	N	N	N
4 Levitas	Y	N	Y	Y	Y	Y	Y	N
5 Fowler	Y	N	Y	Y	Y	Y	N	N
6 *Gingrich*	?	?	?	?	Y	Y	N	N
7 Darden*					Y	Y	N	N
8 Rowland	Y	N	Y	Y	Y	Y	Y	Y
9 Jenkins	Y	N	N	Y	?	?	?	X
10 Barnard	Y	N	Y	N	Y	N	N	N
HAWAII								
1 Heftel	Y	Y	Y	Y	?	\#	N	Y
2 Akaka	Y	Y	N	Y	Y	Y	Y	Y
IDAHO								
1 *Craig*	N	N	Y	N	N	N	N	N
2 *Hansen*	N	N	Y	N	Y	N	N	?
ILLINOIS								
1 Hayes	Y	Y	N	Y	N	Y	Y	Y
2 Savage	Y	Y	N	Y	Y	Y	Y	Y
3 Russo	Y	N	Y	N	Y	Y	Y	N
4 *O'Brien*	Y	Y	Y	?	?	X	X	X
5 Lipinski	Y	N	N	Y	Y	Y	Y	Y
6 *Hyde*	N	N	Y	N	N	N	N	N
7 Collins	Y	Y	N	Y	?	Y	Y	Y
8 Rostenkowski	Y	Y	N	Y	Y	Y	Y	Y
9 Yates	Y	Y	N	Y	Y	Y	Y	Y
10 *Porter*	N	Y	N	N	N	N	N	N
11 Annunzio	Y	Y	Y	?	Y	Y	Y	Y
12 *Crane, P.*	N	N	Y	N	?	N	N	N
13 *Erlenborn*	N	N	Y	N	N	N	N	N
14 *Corcoran*	N	N	Y	N	N	N	N	N
15 *Madigan*	N	?	Y	N	N	N	N	N
16 *Martin*	Y	N	N	N	N	N	N	N
17 Evans	Y	Y	N	Y	Y	Y	Y	Y
18 *Michel*	Y	N	Y	N	N	N	N	N
19 *Crane, D.*	N	N	Y	N	N	N	N	N
20 Durbin	Y	Y	N	Y	N	Y	Y	Y
21 Price	Y	Y	N	Y	Y	Y	Y	Y
22 Simon	Y	Y	N	Y	?	Y	Y	Y
INDIANA								
1 Hall	Y	Y	N	Y	Y	Y	Y	Y
2 Sharp	Y	Y	N	Y	Y	Y	Y	N
3 *Hiler*	N	N	Y	N	N	N	N	N
4 *Coats*	N	N	Y	N	N	N	N	N
5 *Hillis*	Y	N	Y	N	Y	N	N	N

ND - Northern Democrats   SD - Southern Democrats

Corresponding to Congressional Record Votes 480, 481, 482, 483, 484, 485, 486, 487

	445	446	447	448	449	450	451	452
6 ***Burton***	N	N	Y	N	?	?	?	?
7 ***Myers***	Y	Y	Y	N	Y	N	N	N
8 McCloskey	Y	Y	N	Y	Y	Y	Y	Y
9 Hamilton	Y	N	N	Y	Y	Y	Y	Y
10 Jacobs	Y	Y	N	N	P	N	N	N
IOWA								
1 ***Leach***	N	Y	N	N	Y	N	Y	N
2 ***Tauke***	N	N	Y	N	Y	N	N	N
3 ***Evans***	N	N	N	N	N	N	N	N
4 Smith	Y	Y	Y	Y	Y	N	N	Y
5 Harkin	Y	Y	N	Y	N	Y	Y	Y
6 Bedell	?	?	?	?	Y	Y	N	N
KANSAS								
1 ***Roberts***	N	N	Y	N	N	N	N	N
2 Slattery	Y	Y	N	Y	?	Y	N	N
3 ***Winn***	?	?	?	?	?	?	?	?
4 Glickman	Y	Y	N	Y	Y	Y	N	Y
5 ***Whittaker***	N	N	Y	N	Y	N	N	N
KENTUCKY								
1 Hubbard	Y	N	N	Y	Y	Y	N	N
2 Natcher	Y	Y	Y	Y	Y	Y	Y	Y
3 Mazzoli	Y	Y	Y	Y	Y	Y	Y	Y
4 ***Snyder***	N	N	Y	Y	Y	N	N	N
5 ***Rogers***	Y	N	Y	N	Y	N	N	N
6 ***Hopkins***	N	N	Y	N	Y	N	N	N
7 Perkins	Y	Y	N	Y	Y	Y	Y	Y
LOUISIANA								
1 ***Livingston***	Y	N	Y	N	Y	N	N	N
2 Boggs	Y	Y	N	?	?	?	Y	Y
3 Tauzin	Y	N	N	Y	Y	N	N	N
4 Roemer	N	N	N	Y	N	N	N	N
5 Huckaby	Y	N	N	N	Y	N	N	N
6 ***Moore***	Y	N	Y	N	Y	N	N	N
7 Breaux	Y	N	Y	Y	Y	N	N	N
8 Long	Y	Y	N	Y	Y	Y	Y	Y
MAINE								
1 ***McKernan***	Y	Y	N	N	Y	N	Y	Y
2 ***Snowe***	Y	N	N	Y	Y	N	N	N
MARYLAND								
1 Dyson	Y	Y	Y	Y	Y	Y	Y	Y
2 Long	?	?	?	?	Y	Y	Y	Y
3 Mikulski	Y	Y	N	Y	Y	Y	Y	Y
4 ***Holt***	Y	N	Y	N	Y	N	N	N
5 Hoyer	Y	Y	N	Y	Y	Y	Y	Y
6 Byron	Y	N	Y	Y	N	Y	N	N
7 Mitchell	Y	Y	N	Y	N	Y	Y	Y
8 Barnes	Y	Y	N	Y	Y	Y	Y	Y
MASSACHUSETTS								
1 ***Conte***	Y	Y	N	N	Y	N	N	N
2 Boland	Y	Y	N	Y	Y	Y	Y	Y
3 Early	?	?	?	?	?	?	?	?
4 Frank	Y	Y	N	Y	Y	Y	Y	Y
5 Shannon	Y	Y	N	N	Y	Y	Y	Y
6 Mavroules	Y	Y	N	N	Y	Y	Y	Y
7 Markey	Y	Y	N	Y	N	Y	Y	Y
8 O'Neill								
9 Moakley	Y	Y	N	Y	Y	Y	Y	Y
10 Studds	Y	Y	N	Y	Y	Y	Y	Y
11 Donnelly	Y	Y	N	N	Y	Y	Y	Y
MICHIGAN								
1 Conyers	Y	Y	N	Y	Y	Y	Y	Y
2 ***Pursell***	Y	Y	?	?	Y	N	N	N
3 Wolpe	Y	Y	N	Y	Y	Y	Y	Y
4 ***Siljander***	N	N	Y	N	Y	N	N	N
5 ***Sawyer***	Y	N	Y	N	Y	N	N	N
6 Carr	Y	Y	N	N	Y	Y	Y	Y
7 Kildee	Y	Y	N	Y	Y	Y	Y	Y
8 Traxler	Y	Y	N	Y	Y	Y	Y	Y
9 ***Vander Jagt***	Y	N	Y	N	Y	N	N	N
10 Albosta	Y	N	N	Y	Y	Y	Y	Y
11 ***Davis***	Y	N	Y	N	?	N	Y	Y
12 Bonior	Y	Y	N	Y	?	Y	Y	Y
13 Crockett	Y	Y	N	Y	?	Y	Y	N
14 Hertel	Y	Y	N	Y	Y	Y	Y	Y
15 Ford	Y	Y	N	Y	?	Y	Y	Y
16 Dingell	Y	Y	N	Y	?	Y	Y	Y
17 Levin	Y	Y	N	Y	Y	Y	Y	Y
18 ***Broomfield***	N	N	Y	Y	?	X	X	X
MINNESOTA								
1 Penny	Y	Y	N	Y	Y	Y	Y	Y
2 ***Weber***	N	N	Y	N	Y	N	N	N
3 ***Frenzel***	N	N	Y	N	N	N	N	N
4 Vento	Y	Y	N	Y	Y	Y	Y	Y
5 Sabo	Y	Y	N	Y	N	Y	Y	Y
6 Sikorski	Y	Y	N	Y	N	Y	Y	Y

	445	446	447	448	449	450	451	452
7 ***Stangeland***	N	N	Y	N	Y	N	N	N
8 Oberstar	Y	Y	N	Y	P	Y	Y	Y
MISSISSIPPI								
1 Whitten	Y	Y	Y	Y	Y	Y	Y	Y
2 ***Franklin***	Y	N	Y	N	Y	N	N	N
3 Montgomery	N	N	N	Y	Y	N	N	N
4 Dowdy	Y	Y	N	Y	?	?	?	?
5 ***Lott***	N	N	Y	N	?	N	N	N
MISSOURI								
1 Clay	Y	Y	N	?	N	Y	Y	Y
2 Young	Y	N	N	Y	Y	Y	Y	Y
3 Gephardt	Y	Y	N	Y	Y	Y	Y	Y
4 Skelton	Y	N	N	Y	Y	Y	Y	Y
5 Wheat	Y	Y	N	Y	Y	Y	Y	Y
6 ***Coleman***	Y	?	Y	N	Y	N	N	N
7 ***Taylor***	N	N	Y	Y	Y	N	N	N
8 ***Emerson***	N	N	Y	N	N	N	N	N
9 Volkmer	Y	N	N	Y	Y	Y	N	N
MONTANA								
1 Williams	Y	Y	N	Y	Y	Y	Y	Y
2 ***Marlenee***	N	N	Y	N	Y	N	N	N
NEBRASKA								
1 ***Bereuter***	N	+	-	Y	Y	N	N	N
2 ***Daub***	N	N	Y	N	Y	N	N	N
3 ***Smith***	N	Y	Y	N	Y	N	N	?
NEVADA								
1 Reid	Y	Y	N	Y	Y	Y	Y	Y
2 ***Vucanovich***	N	N	Y	N	Y	N	N	N
NEW HAMPSHIRE								
1 D'Amours	Y	Y	N	Y	Y	Y	Y	Y
2 ***Gregg***	N	N	Y	N	Y	N	N	N
NEW JERSEY								
1 Florio	Y	Y	N	Y	Y	Y	Y	Y
2 Hughes	Y	Y	N	Y	Y	Y	N	N
3 Howard	Y	Y	N	Y	Y	Y	Y	Y
4 ***Smith***	Y	N	Y	N	Y	N	Y	Y
5 ***Roukema***	Y	N	Y	Y	Y	N	N	N
6 Dwyer	Y	Y	N	Y	Y	Y	Y	Y
7 ***Rinaldo***	Y	N	Y	N	Y	N	Y	Y
8 Roe	Y	Y	N	Y	Y	Y	Y	Y
9 Torricelli	Y	Y	N	Y	Y	Y	Y	Y
10 Rodino	Y	Y	N	Y	Y	Y	Y	Y
11 Minish	Y	Y	N	Y	Y	Y	Y	Y
12 ***Courter***	Y	N	Y	N	Y	N	N	N
13 ***Forsythe***	N	N	Y	N	N	N	N	N
14 Guarini	?	?	?	?	N	Y	Y	Y
NEW MEXICO								
1 ***Lujan***	Y	N	Y	N	Y	N	N	N
2 ***Skeen***	N	N	Y	N	Y	N	N	N
3 Richardson	Y	Y	Y	Y	Y	Y	Y	Y
NEW YORK								
1 ***Carney***	Y	N	Y	N	Y	N	N	N
2 Downey	Y	Y	N	Y	Y	Y	Y	Y
3 Mrazek	Y	Y	N	Y	Y	Y	Y	Y
4 ***Lent***	N	N	Y	N	Y	N	N	N
5 ***McGrath***	Y	N	Y	N	Y	N	Y	Y
6 Addabbo	Y	Y	N	Y	Y	Y	Y	Y
7 Ackerman	Y	Y	N	Y	Y	Y	Y	Y
8 Scheuer	Y	Y	N	Y	Y	Y	Y	Y
9 Ferraro	Y	Y	N	Y	Y	Y	Y	Y
10 Schumer	Y	Y	N	Y	Y	Y	Y	Y
11 Towns	Y	Y	N	Y	Y	Y	Y	Y
12 Owens	Y	Y	N	Y	Y	Y	Y	Y
13 Solarz	?	?	?	?	?	Y	Y	Y
14 ***Molinari***	?	?	?	?	?	?	?	?
15 ***Green***	Y	Y	Y	N	Y	N	Y	Y
16 Rangel	Y	Y	N	Y	Y	Y	#	Y
17 Weiss	Y	Y	N	Y	Y	Y	Y	Y
18 Garcia	Y	Y	N	?	?	Y	Y	Y
19 Biaggi	Y	N	N	Y	Y	Y	Y	Y
20 Ottinger	Y	Y	N	Y	?	Y	Y	Y
21 ***Fish***	Y	Y	N	?	Y	N	N	N
22 ***Gilman***	Y	Y	N	N	Y	N	N	N
23 Stratton	Y	N	Y	Y	Y	Y	Y	Y
24 ***Solomon***	N	N	N	N	N	N	N	N
25 ***Boehlert***	Y	Y	N	N	Y	N	Y	Y
26 ***Martin***	Y	N	Y	?	Y	N	N	N
27 ***Wortley***	Y	N	Y	N	Y	N	N	N
28 McHugh	Y	Y	N	Y	Y	Y	Y	Y
29 ***Horton***	Y	?	Y	Y	Y	N	Y	Y
30 ***Conable***	N	N	N	N	Y	N	N	N
31 ***Kemp***	Y	N	Y	Y	?	N	N	N
32 LaFalce	Y	Y	Y	Y	?	Y	Y	Y
33 Nowak	Y	Y	N	Y	Y	Y	Y	Y
34 Lundine	Y	Y	N	?	Y	Y	Y	Y

	445	446	447	448	449	450	451	452
NORTH CAROLINA								
1 Jones	Y	Y	Y	Y	Y	Y	Y	Y
2 Valentine	?	?	N	Y	Y	Y	N	N
3 Whitley	Y	N	N	Y	Y	Y	Y	Y
4 Andrews	Y	Y	N	Y	Y	Y	Y	Y
5 Neal	Y	Y	N	Y	?	Y	Y	Y
6 Britt	Y	N	N	N	Y	Y	Y	Y
7 Rose	Y	Y	N	Y	Y	Y	Y	Y
8 Hefner	Y	Y	N	Y	Y	Y	Y	Y
9 ***Martin***	N	N	?	N	?	?	?	?
10 ***Broyhill***	N	N	Y	N	Y	N	N	N
11 Clarke	Y	Y	N	Y	Y	Y	Y	Y
NORTH DAKOTA								
AL Dorgan	Y	Y	N	Y	Y	Y	Y	Y
OHIO								
1 Luken	Y	N	N	Y	Y	Y	Y	Y
2 ***Gradison***	Y	Y	Y	N	Y	N	N	N
3 Hall	Y	Y	N	Y	Y	Y	Y	Y
4 ***Oxley***	N	?	?	?	Y	N	N	N
5 ***Latta***	N	N	Y	N	Y	N	N	N
6 ***McEwen***	Y	N	Y	N	Y	N	N	N
7 ***DeWine***	N	N	Y	N	Y	N	N	N
8 ***Kindness***	N	N	?	?	Y	N	N	N
9 Kaptur	Y	Y	N	Y	Y	Y	Y	N
10 ***Miller***	N	Y	Y	N	N	N	N	N
11 Eckart	Y	Y	N	Y	Y	Y	Y	Y
12 ***Kasich***	Y	N	Y	N	?	N	N	N
13 Pease	Y	Y	N	Y	Y	Y	Y	Y
14 Seiberling	Y	Y	N	Y	Y	Y	Y	Y
15 ***Wylie***	Y	N	Y	N	Y	N	N	N
16 ***Regula***	Y	N	Y	N	Y	N	N	N
17 ***Williams***	Y	N	N	N	Y	N	Y	Y
18 Applegate	Y	N	N	Y	?	N	N	N
19 Feighan	Y	Y	N	Y	Y	Y	Y	Y
20 Oakar	Y	Y	N	Y	P	N	N	N
21 Stokes	Y	Y	N	Y	Y	Y	Y	Y
OKLAHOMA								
1 Jones	Y	N	N	Y	Y	Y	Y	N
2 Synar	Y	Y	N	Y	Y	Y	Y	Y
3 Watkins	Y	Y	Y	Y	Y	Y	Y	Y
4 McCurdy	Y	N	N	Y	Y	Y	Y	N
5 ***Edwards***	N	N	Y	N	N	N	N	N
6 English	N	N	N	Y	Y	Y	N	N
OREGON								
1 AuCoin	Y	Y	Y	Y	Y	Y	N	-
2 ***Smith, R.***	Y	N	Y	N	Y	N	N	N
3 Wyden	Y	Y	N	Y	Y	Y	Y	Y
4 Weaver	Y	Y	N	Y	Y	Y	Y	N
5 ***Smith, D.***	?	?	?	?	?	X	X	?
PENNSYLVANIA								
1 Foglietta	Y	Y	N	Y	Y	Y	Y	Y
2 Gray	Y	Y	N	Y	N	Y	Y	Y
3 Borski	Y	Y	N	Y	Y	Y	Y	Y
4 Kolter	Y	Y	N	Y	Y	Y	Y	Y
5 ***Schulze***	?	?	?	?	?	X	?	?
6 Yatron	Y	Y	N	N	Y	Y	Y	Y
7 Edgar	Y	Y	N	Y	Y	Y	Y	Y
8 Kostmayer	Y	Y	N	Y	Y	Y	Y	Y
9 ***Shuster***	N	N	Y	N	Y	N	N	N
10 ***McDade***	Y	Y	Y	N	Y	N	N	N
11 Harrison	Y	Y	N	Y	Y	Y	Y	Y
12 Murtha	Y	Y	Y	Y	Y	Y	Y	Y
13 ***Coughlin***	N	N	N	N	N	N	N	N
14 Coyne	Y	Y	N	Y	Y	Y	Y	Y
15 ***Ritter***	Y	N	Y	N	Y	N	N	N
16 ***Walker***	N	N	Y	N	N	N	N	N
17 ***Gekas***	N	N	Y	N	Y	N	N	N
18 Walgren	Y	Y	Y	Y	Y	Y	Y	Y
19 ***Goodling***	N	N	Y	N	N	N	N	N
20 Gaydos	Y	?	Y	Y	Y	Y	Y	Y
21 ***Ridge***	Y	Y	N	N	Y	N	Y	Y
22 Murphy	Y	Y	N	Y	N	Y	Y	Y
23 ***Clinger***	Y	N	N	N	Y	N	N	N
RHODE ISLAND								
1 St Germain	Y	Y	N	Y	P	Y	Y	Y
2 ***Schneider***	Y	Y	N	Y	Y	N	Y	N
SOUTH CAROLINA								
1 ***Hartnett***	N	N	Y	N	Y	N	N	N
2 ***Spence***	Y	N	Y	N	Y	N	N	N
3 Derrick	Y	Y	N	Y	Y	Y	Y	Y
4 ***Campbell***	Y	N	Y	N	Y	N	N	N
5 Spratt	?	Y	N	Y	Y	Y	Y	Y
6 Tallon	Y	Y	N	Y	Y	Y	Y	Y
SOUTH DAKOTA								
AL Daschle	Y	N	?	Y	N	Y	Y	Y

	445	446	447	448	449	450	451	452
TENNESSEE								
1 ***Quillen***	Y	N	Y	Y	Y	N	N	N
2 ***Duncan***	Y	N	Y	Y	Y	N	N	N
3 Lloyd	Y	N	N	Y	?	N	N	N
4 Cooper	Y	N	N	Y	Y	Y	Y	Y
5 Boner	Y	N	N	Y	Y	Y	Y	Y
6 Gore	Y	Y	N	Y	Y	Y	Y	Y
7 ***Sundquist***	Y	N	Y	N	Y	N	N	N
8 Jones	Y	N	N	Y	Y	Y	N	Y
9 Ford	Y	Y	N	N	Y	Y	Y	Y
TEXAS								
1 Hall, S.	N	N	Y	Y	Y	N	N	N
2 Wilson	?	N	N	Y	?	Y	Y	Y
3 ***Bartlett***	N	N	Y	N	Y	N	N	N
4 Hall, R.	N	N	Y	Y	Y	N	N	N
5 Bryant	Y	Y	N	Y	Y	Y	Y	Y
6 ***Gramm***	?	?	?	?	?	?	?	?
7 ***Archer***	N	N	Y	N	Y	N	N	N
8 ***Fields***	N	N	Y	N	Y	N	N	N
9 Brooks	Y	Y	N	Y	Y	Y	Y	Y
10 Pickle	Y	Y	N	Y	Y	Y	Y	Y
11 Leath	Y	N	Y	Y	Y	Y	Y	Y
12 Wright	Y	N	N	Y	Y	Y	Y	Y
13 Hightower	Y	N	Y	Y	Y	Y	N	N
14 Patman	Y	N	Y	Y	Y	N	N	N
15 de la Garza	Y	?	?	?	?	?	?	?
16 Coleman	Y	Y	N	Y	Y	Y	Y	Y
17 Stenholm	N	N	Y	N	Y	N	N	N
18 Leland	Y	Y	N	Y	Y	Y	Y	Y
19 Hance	?	?	?	?	?	#	#	#
20 Gonzalez	Y	Y	N	Y	Y	Y	Y	Y
21 ***Loeffler***	N	N	Y	N	Y	N	N	N
22 ***Paul***	?	?	?	?	?	?	X	?
23 Kazen	Y	N	N	Y	Y	Y	Y	Y
24 Frost	Y	N	N	Y	Y	Y	Y	Y
25 Andrews	Y	N	N	Y	Y	Y	Y	N
26 Vandergriff	N	N	Y	Y	Y	N	N	N
27 Ortiz	Y	Y	N	Y	Y	Y	Y	Y
UTAH								
1 ***Hansen***	N	N	Y	N	Y	N	N	N
2 ***Marriott***	Y	N	Y	N	Y	N	N	N
3 ***Nielson***	N	N	Y	N	Y	N	N	N
VERMONT								
AL ***Jeffords***	Y	Y	N	Y	Y	N	Y	Y
VIRGINIA								
1 ***Bateman***	Y	N	Y	N	Y	N	N	N
2 ***Whitehurst***	N	N	Y	N	Y	N	N	N
3 ***Bliley***	N	N	Y	N	Y	N	N	N
4 Sisisky	?	?	?	?	Y	Y	Y	Y
5 Daniel	N	N	Y	N	Y	N	N	N
6 Olin	Y	Y	N	Y	Y	Y	Y	Y
7 ***Robinson***	N	N	Y	N	Y	N	N	N
8 ***Parris***	N	N	Y	N	?	N	N	N
9 Boucher	Y	Y	N	Y	Y	Y	Y	Y
10 ***Wolf***	N	N	Y	N	Y	N	N	N
WASHINGTON								
1 ***Pritchard***	?	?	?	?	Y	N	Y	Y
2 Swift	Y	Y	N	Y	Y	Y	Y	Y
3 Bonker	Y	Y	N	Y	?	Y	Y	Y
4 ***Morrison***	Y	N	Y	N	Y	N	Y	Y
5 Foley	Y	Y	N	Y	Y	Y	Y	Y
6 Dicks	Y	Y	N	?	Y	Y	Y	Y
7 Lowry	?	?	?	?	?	Y	Y	Y
8 ***Chandler***	Y	N	Y	N	Y	N	Y	Y
WEST VIRGINIA								
1 Mollohan	Y	N	N	Y	Y	Y	Y	Y
2 Staggers	Y	Y	N	Y	Y	Y	Y	Y
3 Wise	Y	Y	N	Y	Y	Y	Y	Y
4 Rahall	Y	N	?	Y	Y	N	N	N
WISCONSIN								
1 Aspin	Y	Y	N	Y	Y	Y	Y	Y
2 Kastenmeier	Y	Y	N	Y	Y	Y	N	Y
3 ***Gunderson***	N	N	N	Y	Y	N	N	N
4 Zablocki	Y	Y	Y	Y	Y	Y	Y	Y
5 Moody	Y	Y	N	Y	Y	Y	N	N
6 ***Petri***	N	Y	Y	Y	Y	N	N	N
7 Obey	Y	Y	N	Y	Y	Y	Y	Y
8 ***Roth***	N	N	Y	N	Y	N	N	N
9 ***Sensenbrenner***	N	N	Y	N	Y	N	N	N
WYOMING								
AL ***Cheney***	N	N	Y	N	Y	N	N	N

** Rep. George W. "Buddy" Darden, D-Ga., was sworn in Nov. 10, 1983. The first vote for which he was eligible was CQ vote 449.*

Southern states - Ala., Ark., Fla., Ga., Ky., La., Miss., N.C., Okla., S.C., Tenn., Texas, Va.

453. HR 4102. Universal Telephone Service. Tauke, R-Iowa, substitute to phase in, rather than ban, the Federal Communications Commission plan to impose an access charge on residential and small business telephone users for the right to long-distance service, but only as of Jan. 1, 1985, rather than April 3, 1984, and at levels of no more than $1 a month the first year, rather than $2, rising to $4 a month by 1988. Rejected 142-264: R 134-19; D 8-245 (ND 1-169, SD 7-76), Nov. 10, 1983.

454. HR 4102. Universal Telephone Service. Rinaldo, R-N.J., amendment to phase in, rather than ban, the Federal Communications Commission plan to impose an access charge on residential and small business telephone users for the right to long-distance service, but only as of Jan. 1, 1985, rather than April 3, 1984, at levels of up to $2 a month the first year but no more than $4 in years after 1985, and only if necessary to preserve universal telephone service. Rejected 122-270: R 113-40; D 9-230 (ND 5-158, SD 4-72), Nov. 10, 1983.

455. H J Res 413. Continuing Appropriations, Fiscal 1984. Adoption of the conference report on the joint resolution to provide further continuing appropriations through Sept. 30, 1984, for federal agencies whose regular fiscal 1984 appropriations have not been enacted. Adopted 173-136: R 51-65; D 122-71 (ND 85-43, SD 37-28), Nov. 12, 1983.

456. HR 3635. Child Protection Act. Sawyer, R-Mich., demand for a second on the Hughes, D-N.J., motion to suspend the rules and pass the bill to strengthen federal laws against production and distribution of pornographic materials involving children. Second ordered 280-0: R 106-0; D 174-0 (ND 112-0, SD 62-0), Nov. 14, 1983.

457. Procedural Motion. Sensenbrenner, R-Wis., motion that the House adjourn. Motion rejected 121-258: R 120-29; D 1-229 (ND 0-151, SD 1-78), Nov. 14, 1983.

458. Procedural Motion. Gingrich, R-Ga., motion that the House adjourn. Motion rejected 100-261: R 98-42; D 2-219 (ND 1-142, SD 1-77), Nov. 14, 1983.

459. HR 3635. Child Protection Act. Hughes, D-N.J., motion to suspend the rules and pass the bill to strengthen federal laws against production and distribution of pornographic materials involving children. Motion agreed to 400-1: R 154-0; D 246-1 (ND 162-1, SD 84-0), Nov. 14, 1983. A two-thirds majority of those present and voting (268 in this case) is required for passage under suspension of the rules.

460. HR 3729. Refugee Assistance Extension Act. Mazzoli, D-Ky., motion to suspend the rules and pass the bill to extend for two years refugee resettlement programs. Motion agreed to 300-99: R 89-64; D 211-35 (ND 156-6, SD 55-29), Nov. 14, 1983. A two-thirds majority of those present and voting (266 in this case) is required for passage under suspension of the rules.

KEY

Y Voted for (yea).
Paired for.
+ Announced for.
N Voted against (nay).
X Paired against.
- Announced against.
P Voted "present".
C Voted "present" to avoid possible conflict of interest.
? Did not vote or otherwise make a position known.

Democrats *Republicans*

	453	454	455	456	457	458	459	460
43 *Packard*	Y	Y	N	Y	Y	Y	Y	Y
44 Bates	N	N	Y	N	?	Y	Y	
45 *Hunter*	N	N	Y	?	Y	Y	Y	Y
COLORADO								
1 Schroeder	N	N	Y	N	N	N	Y	
2 Wirth	N	N	?	Y	N	N	Y	
3 Kogovsek	N	N	Y	N	N	N	Y	
4 *Brown*	Y	Y	N	Y	Y	Y	Y	N
5 *Kramer*	?	Y	?	Y	Y	Y	Y	N
6 *Schaefer*	Y	Y	N	?	Y	Y	Y	N
CONNECTICUT								
1 Kennelly	N	N	Y	N	N	N	Y	
2 Gejdenson	N	N	Y	?	?	N	Y	
3 Morrison	N	N	Y	?	N	N	Y	
4 *McKinney*	Y	Y	Y	N	N	Y	Y	
5 Ratchford	N	N	Y	N	N	N	Y	
6 *Johnson*	Y	Y	Y	Y	Y	Y	Y	Y
DELAWARE								
AL Carper	Y	Y	N	Y	N	N	Y	
FLORIDA								
1 Hutto	N	N	Y	N	N	N	Y	
2 Fuqua	Y	N	?	Y	N	N	Y	
3 Bennett	N	N	N	N	N	N	Y	
4 Chappell	N	N	?	?	?	?	?	
5 *McCollum*	Y	Y	N	Y	Y	Y	Y	Y
6 MacKay	N	N	?	N	N	Y	Y	
7 Gibbons	N	N	N	Y	N	N	Y	
8 *Young*	N	N	?	N	N	N	Y	
9 *Bilirakis*	N	N	Y	Y	Y	Y	Y	Y
10 Ireland	N	N	N	N	N	N	Y	
11 Nelson	N	N	X	?	N	N	Y	
12 *Lewis*	#	#	X	Y	Y	Y	Y	Y
13 *Mack*	Y	Y	N	Y	Y	Y	Y	Y
14 Mica	X	?	Y	N	N	Y	Y	
15 *Shaw*	Y	Y	N	Y	Y	Y	Y	Y
16 Smith	N	N	Y	N	N	N	Y	
17 Lehman	N	?	Y	N	N	N	Y	
18 Pepper	N	N	Y	N	N	N	Y	
19 Fascell	N	N	?	Y	N	N	Y	
GEORGIA								
1 Thomas	Y	N	Y	N	N	N	Y	
2 Hatcher	N	?	Y	?	N	N	Y	
3 Ray	Y	N	N	Y	N	N	Y	N
4 Levitas	N	N	N	?	?	?	Y	
5 Fowler	N	N	Y	Y	N	N	Y	
6 *Gingrich*	Y	Y	N	Y	Y	Y	Y	Y
7 Darden	N	?	Y	N	N	Y	Y	
8 Rowland	Y	N	Y	N	N	N	Y	
9 Jenkins	?	?	N	?	?	?	Y	N
10 Barnard	Y	N	N	N	N	Y	Y	
HAWAII								
1 Heftel	N	N	N	?	?	N	Y	
2 Akaka	N	N	Y	N	N	N	Y	
IDAHO								
1 *Craig*	Y	Y	N	Y	Y	Y	Y	N
2 *Hansen*	Y	Y	N	Y	Y	Y	Y	N
ILLINOIS								
1 Hayes	N	N	?	N	N	N	Y	
2 Savage	N	N	N	N	N	N	Y	
3 Russo	?	?	?	N	?	N	Y	
4 *O'Brien*	#	#	#	Y	Y	Y	Y	Y
5 Lipinski	N	N	?	N	N	N	Y	
6 *Hyde*	Y	Y	Y	Y	Y	Y	Y	Y
7 Collins	N	N	Y	?	N	N	Y	
8 Rostenkowski	N	N	?	?	?	?	Y	
9 Yates	N	N	Y	N	N	N	Y	
10 *Porter*	Y	Y	Y	Y	Y	Y	Y	Y
11 Annunzio	N	N	Y	N	N	N	Y	
12 *Crane, P.*	Y	Y	?	?	Y	Y	Y	N
13 *Erlenborn*	Y	Y	Y	Y	Y	Y	Y	N
14 *Corcoran*	Y	Y	#	?	?	?	?	?
15 *Madigan*	Y	Y	N	N	Y	Y	Y	
16 *Martin*	Y	Y	N	Y	N	Y	Y	
17 Evans	N	N	?	Y	N	N	Y	
18 *Michel*	Y	Y	Y	?	Y	Y	N	A
19 *Crane, D.*	Y	Y	?	Y	Y	?	Y	N
20 Durbin	N	N	Y	?	?	?	+	+
21 Price	N	N	Y	N	N	N	Y	
22 Simon	X	?	?	?	N	N	Y	Y
INDIANA								
1 Hall	N	N	Y	N	N	N	Y	
2 Sharp	N	N	N	Y	N	N	Y	
3 *Hiler*	Y	Y	X	Y	Y	Y	Y	Y
4 *Coats*	Y	Y	N	Y	N	N	Y	
5 Hillis	Y	Y	?	Y	Y	Y	Y	N

ALABAMA	453	454	455	456	457	458	459	460
1 *Edwards*	Y	Y	?	?	N	N	Y	N
2 *Dickinson*	?	Y	?	?	N	N	Y	
3 Nichols	N	N	X	Y	N	N	Y	N
4 Bevill	N	N	Y	N	N	N	Y	
5 Flippo	N	N	N	N	N	N	Y	
6 Erdreich	N	-	N	?	N	N	Y	
7 Shelby	N	?	N	Y	N	N	Y	N
ALASKA								
AL *Young*	Y	N	#	Y	Y	Y	Y	Y
ARIZONA								
1 *McCain*	Y	Y	?	Y	Y	Y	Y	Y
2 Udall	N	?	Y	N	N	N	Y	
3 *Stump*	Y	Y	N	Y	Y	Y	Y	N
4 *Rudd*	Y	Y	Y	Y	Y	Y	Y	N
5 McNulty	N	N	Y	N	N	N	Y	Y
ARKANSAS								
1 Alexander	N	N	?	?	?	?	Y	Y
2 *Bethune*	Y	N	N	?	Y	Y	Y	Y
3 *Hammerschmidt*	Y	N	N	N	N	Y	Y	Y
4 Anthony	N	N	?	+	-	-	+	+
CALIFORNIA								
1 Bosco	N	N	?	Y	N	?	Y	Y
2 *Chappie*	Y	N	N	Y	Y	Y	Y	Y
3 Matsui	N	N	Y	Y	N	N	Y	
4 Fazio	N	Y	Y	N	N	N	Y	
5 Burton	N	N	Y	N	N	N	Y	
6 Boxer	N	N	N	Y	N	N	Y	
7 Miller	N	N	N	N	N	N	Y	
8 Dellums	N	N	N	?	?	N	Y	
9 Stark	X	X	?	?	?	N	Y	Y
10 Edwards	N	N	Y	N	N	N	Y	
11 Lantos	N	N	Y	N	N	N	Y	
12 *Zschau*	Y	Y	?	Y	N	N	Y	
13 Mineta	N	N	Y	N	N	N	Y	
14 *Shumway*	Y	Y	N	Y	Y	Y	Y	N
15 Coelho	N	N	?	Y	N	N	Y	
16 Panetta	N	N	Y	N	N	N	Y	
17 *Pashayan*	Y	Y	N	Y	?	?	Y	Y
18 Lehman	N	N	?	?	?	?	?	?
19 *Lagomarsino*	Y	N	Y	Y	Y	Y	Y	Y
20 *Thomas*	Y	Y	N	?	Y	Y	Y	Y
21 *Fiedler*	Y	N	Y	?	N	N	Y	Y
22 *Moorhead*	Y	Y	N	Y	Y	Y	Y	Y
23 Beilenson	N	N	?	?	N	N	Y	
24 Waxman	N	N	?	Y	?	N	Y	
25 Roybal	N	N	?	N	N	N	Y	
26 Berman	N	N	Y	?	N	N	Y	
27 Levine	N	N	#	?	?	?	Y	Y
28 Dixon	N	?	Y	Y	N	N	Y	
29 Hawkins	N	?	N	Y	N	N	Y	
30 Martinez	N	?	+	Y	N	N	Y	
31 Dymally	N	?	?	Y	N	N	Y	
32 Anderson	N	N	?	Y	N	N	Y	
33 *Dreier*	Y	Y	N	?	Y	Y	Y	N
34 Torres	N	N	Y	+	-	-	+	+
35 *Lewis*	Y	Y	Y	Y	Y	Y	Y	Y
36 Brown	?	?	?	Y	N	Y	?	?
37 *McCandless*	Y	Y	N	Y	Y	Y	Y	N
38 Patterson	N	N	?	Y	N	N	Y	
39 *Dannemeyer*	Y	Y	N	Y	Y	Y	Y	N
40 *Badham*	Y	?	Y	?	Y	Y	Y	
41 *Lowery*	Y	Y	Y	?	Y	Y	Y	Y
42 *Lungren*	Y	Y	N	Y	Y	Y	Y	Y

ND - Northern Democrats   SD - Southern Democrats

Corresponding to Congressional Record Votes 488, 489, 490, 491, 492, 493, 494, 495

	453	454	455	456	457	458	459	460
6 ***Burton***	?	?	X	?	?	?	?	?
7 ***Myers***	Y	Y	?	Y	Y	Y	Y	N
8 McCloskey	N	N	Y	Y	N	N	Y	Y
9 Hamilton	N	N	Y	Y	N	N	Y	Y
10 Jacobs	N	N	?	Y	?	N	Y	Y
IOWA								
1 ***Leach***	Y	Y	N	Y	N	N	Y	Y
2 ***Tauke***	Y	Y	N	?	Y	?	Y	N
3 ***Evans***	Y	Y	N	Y	Y	N	Y	N
4 Smith	N	N	Y	Y	N	N	Y	Y
5 Harkin	N	N	N	Y	N	N	Y	Y
6 Bedell	N	N	N	?	N	N	Y	Y
KANSAS								
1 ***Roberts***	Y	Y	N	Y	Y	Y	Y	N
2 Slattery	N	N	N	Y	N	N	Y	Y
3 ***Winn***	#	?	?	Y	Y	Y	Y	Y
4 Glickman	N	N	?	Y	N	N	Y	Y
5 ***Whittaker***	Y	Y	N	Y	Y	N	Y	N
KENTUCKY								
1 Hubbard	N	N	N	?	N	N	Y	N
2 Natcher	N	N	Y	Y	N	N	Y	Y
3 Mazzoli	N	N	Y	Y	N	N	Y	Y
4 ***Snyder***	N	N	?	Y	Y	N	Y	N
5 ***Rogers***	Y	N	Y	Y	Y	Y	Y	N
6 ***Hopkins***	Y	N	N	Y	Y	Y	Y	N
7 Perkins	N	N	?	Y	N	N	Y	Y
LOUISIANA								
1 ***Livingston***	Y	Y	Y	?	?	?	?	?
2 Boggs	N	N	#	?	?	?	Y	Y
3 Tauzin	N	N	Y	Y	N	?	Y	N
4 Roemer	N	N	N	Y	Y	Y	Y	N
5 Huckaby	Y	Y	N	Y	N	N	Y	N
6 ***Moore***	Y	N	Y	Y	Y	Y	Y	N
7 Breaux	N	N	Y	?	N	N	Y	N
8 Long	N	N	Y	Y	N	N	Y	Y
MAINE								
1 ***McKernan***	N	N	Y	Y	Y	?	Y	Y
2 ***Snowe***	N	N	N	Y	Y	Y	Y	Y
MARYLAND								
1 Dyson	N	N	N	?	N	N	Y	Y
2 Long	N	N	Y	?	N	N	Y	Y
3 Mikulski	N	N	?	Y	N	N	Y	Y
4 ***Holt***	Y	Y	N	Y	N	N	Y	N
5 Hoyer	N	N	Y	Y	N	N	Y	Y
6 Byron	N	?	?	?	?	?	?	?
7 Mitchell	N	N	N	Y	?	N	Y	Y
8 Barnes	N	N	Y	Y	N	?	Y	Y
MASSACHUSETTS								
1 ***Conte***	Y	N	Y	Y	Y	N	Y	Y
2 Boland	N	N	?	?	N	N	Y	Y
3 Early	?	?	?	?	N	N	Y	Y
4 Frank	N	N	N	Y	N	N	Y	Y
5 Shannon	N	N	Y	Y	N	N	Y	Y
6 Mavroules	?	?	?	?	?	?	?	?
7 Markey	N	N	N	?	N	?	Y	Y
8 O'Neill								
9 Moakley	N	X	Y	Y	N	N	Y	Y
10 Studds	N	N	Y	?	N	N	Y	Y
11 Donnelly	N	N	X	?	N	N	Y	Y
MICHIGAN								
1 Conyers	N	N	Y	Y	N	N	Y	Y
2 ***Pursell***	N	N	?	?	Y	N	Y	Y
3 Wolpe	N	N	Y	?	N	N	Y	Y
4 ***Siljander***	Y	Y	N	?	Y	Y	Y	Y
5 ***Sawyer***	N	N	?	Y	Y	Y	Y	Y
6 Carr	N	N	Y	Y	N	N	Y	Y
7 Kildee	N	N	N	Y	N	N	Y	Y
8 Traxler	N	N	?	?	N	N	Y	Y
9 ***Vander Jagt***	Y	?	Y	Y	Y	Y	Y	Y
10 Albosta	N	N	?	Y	N	N	Y	Y
11 ***Davis***	Y	N	?	?	Y	?	Y	Y
12 Bonior	N	Y	?	?	N	N	Y	Y
13 Crockett	N	N	?	Y	N	N	?	?
14 Hertel	N	N	N	Y	N	N	Y	Y
15 Ford	N	N	N	?	?	?	?	?
16 Dingell	N	N	Y	Y	N	?	Y	Y
17 Levin	N	N	Y	Y	N	N	Y	Y
18 ***Broomfield***	?	?	Y	Y	Y	Y	Y	Y
MINNESOTA								
1 Penny	N	N	Y	Y	N	N	Y	Y
2 ***Weber***	N	N	N	?	Y	Y	Y	Y
3 ***Frenzel***	Y	Y	X	?	N	N	Y	Y
4 Vento	N	N	Y	Y	N	N	Y	Y
5 Sabo	N	N	Y	Y	N	?	Y	Y
6 Sikorski	N	N	Y	Y	N	N	Y	Y
7 ***Stangeland***	N	N	N	?	Y	Y	Y	N
8 Oberstar	N	N	N	+	-	-	+	+
MISSISSIPPI								
1 Whitten	N	N	Y	Y	N	N	Y	Y
2 ***Franklin***	Y	Y	N	?	?	?	?	?
3 Montgomery	?	?	?	?	N	N	Y	N
4 Dowdy	N	N	Y	Y	N	N	Y	N
5 ***Lott***	Y	Y	?	?	?	?	Y	N
MISSOURI								
1 Clay	N	N	N	Y	N	N	Y	Y
2 Young	N	N	Y	Y	N	N	Y	Y
3 Gephardt	N	N	Y	Y	N	N	Y	Y
4 Skelton	N	N	N	Y	N	N	Y	N
5 Wheat	N	N	Y	Y	N	N	Y	Y
6 ***Coleman***	N	N	N	?	Y	Y	Y	Y
7 ***Taylor***	Y	N	X	?	?	?	Y	N
8 ***Emerson***	Y	N	N	Y	Y	Y	Y	N
9 Volkmer	N	N	N	Y	N	N	Y	Y
MONTANA								
1 Williams	N	N	N	?	N	?	Y	Y
2 ***Marlenee***	N	N	N	Y	Y	N	Y	N
NEBRASKA								
1 ***Bereuter***	Y	Y	?	?	?	?	?	?
2 ***Daub***	Y	Y	N	Y	Y	Y	Y	Y
3 ***Smith***	#	?	?	Y	Y	Y	Y	Y
NEVADA								
1 Reid	N	N	Y	Y	N	N	Y	Y
2 ***Vucanovich***	Y	Y	N	Y	Y	Y	Y	Y
NEW HAMPSHIRE								
1 D'Amours	N	N	Y	Y	N	?	Y	Y
2 ***Gregg***	Y	Y	?	?	Y	Y	Y	Y
NEW JERSEY								
1 Florio	N	N	Y	?	?	?	Y	Y
2 Hughes	N	Y	N	Y	N	N	Y	Y
3 Howard	N	N	Y	Y	N	N	Y	Y
4 ***Smith***	Y	Y	Y	Y	Y	Y	Y	Y
5 ***Roukema***	Y	Y	#	?	N	N	Y	?
6 Dwyer	N	N	Y	Y	N	N	Y	Y
7 ***Rinaldo***	Y	Y	?	?	Y	Y	Y	Y
8 Roe	N	N	Y	Y	N	N	Y	Y
9 Torricelli	N	N	Y	?	?	?	?	?
10 Rodino	N	N	Y	Y	N	N	Y	Y
11 Minish	N	N	#	?	?	?	?	?
12 ***Courter***	Y	Y	?	Y	Y	Y	Y	Y
13 ***Forsythe***	Y	Y	Y	Y	N	N	Y	Y
14 Guarini	N	N	Y	Y	N	N	Y	Y
NEW MEXICO								
1 ***Lujan***	Y	Y	Y	Y	Y	Y	Y	N
2 ***Skeen***	Y	N	N	?	Y	Y	Y	Y
3 Richardson	N	N	Y	?	N	N	Y	Y
NEW YORK								
1 ***Carney***	Y	Y	Y	Y	Y	Y	Y	N
2 Downey	N	N	Y	?	N	?	Y	Y
3 Mrazek	N	N	Y	Y	N	?	Y	Y
4 ***Lent***	Y	Y	?	Y	N	N	Y	Y
5 ***McGrath***	Y	Y	?	Y	N	N	Y	Y
6 Addabbo	N	Y	Y	?	N	N	Y	Y
7 Ackerman	N	N	?	Y	N	N	Y	Y
8 Scheuer	N	N	Y	Y	N	N	Y	Y
9 Ferraro	N	N	?	?	N	N	Y	Y
10 Schumer	N	N	Y	?	N	N	Y	Y
11 Towns	N	N	Y	Y	N	N	Y	Y
12 Owens	N	N	Y	?	?	?	Y	Y
13 Solarz	X	X	Y	Y	?	?	?	?
14 ***Molinari***	?	?	#	?	?	?	?	?
15 ***Green***	Y	Y	Y	Y	N	N	Y	Y
16 Rangel	N	N	Y	?	?	?	Y	Y
17 Weiss	N	N	Y	Y	N	N	N	Y
18 Garcia	N	N	#	?	?	N	Y	Y
19 Biaggi	N	Y	?	?	N	?	Y	Y
20 Ottinger	N	N	Y	?	N	N	Y	Y
21 ***Fish***	Y	Y	Y	Y	N	N	Y	Y
22 ***Gilman***	Y	Y	Y	+	N	N	Y	Y
23 Stratton	N	N	Y	Y	N	N	Y	Y
24 ***Solomon***	Y	Y	N	Y	Y	?	Y	N
25 ***Boehlert***	Y	Y	Y	?	N	N	Y	Y
26 ***Martin***	#	#	?	?	?	?	?	?
27 ***Wortley***	Y	Y	Y	Y	Y	Y	Y	Y
28 McHugh	N	N	Y	Y	N	N	Y	Y
29 ***Horton***	Y	Y	Y	?	Y	?	Y	Y
30 ***Conable***	Y	Y	?	?	?	?	?	?
31 ***Kemp***	Y	Y	Y	Y	Y	Y	Y	Y
32 LaFalce	N	N	?	Y	N	N	Y	Y
33 Nowak	N	N	N	?	N	N	Y	Y
34 Lundine	N	N	?	?	N	N	Y	Y
NORTH CAROLINA								
1 Jones	N	N	Y	?	N	N	Y	Y
2 Valentine	N	N	N	?	?	?	?	?
3 Whitley	N	N	?	Y	N	?	Y	Y
4 Andrews	N	N	?	Y	N	N	Y	N
5 Neal	N	N	?	Y	N	N	Y	Y
6 Britt	?	+	?	?	?	?	?	?
7 Rose	N	N	?	Y	N	N	Y	Y
8 Hefner	N	N	Y	Y	N	N	Y	Y
9 ***Martin***	Y	Y	?	?	?	?	?	?
10 ***Broyhill***	Y	Y	?	Y	Y	Y	Y	Y
11 Clarke	N	N	Y	Y	N	N	Y	Y
NORTH DAKOTA								
AL Dorgan	N	N	N	Y	N	N	Y	?
OHIO								
1 Luken	N	N	N	?	N	N	Y	Y
2 ***Gradison***	Y	N	?	Y	N	N	Y	Y
3 Hall	N	N	N	Y	?	N	Y	Y
4 ***Oxley***	Y	Y	N	?	Y	Y	Y	Y
5 ***Latta***	Y	Y	N	?	Y	Y	Y	N
6 ***McEwen***	Y	Y	?	Y	Y	Y	Y	N
7 ***DeWine***	Y	Y	N	Y	Y	Y	Y	Y
8 ***Kindness***	Y	Y	N	Y	Y	Y	Y	Y
9 Kaptur	N	N	?	?	N	N	Y	Y
10 ***Miller***	Y	Y	?	?	?	?	Y	N
11 Eckart	N	N	Y	Y	N	N	Y	Y
12 ***Kasich***	Y	Y	Y	Y	Y	Y	Y	N
13 Pease	N	N	N	Y	N	N	Y	Y
14 Seiberling	N	N	?	Y	N	N	Y	Y
15 ***Wylie***	Y	Y	Y	Y	N	N	Y	N
16 ***Regula***	Y	N	?	Y	Y	Y	Y	Y
17 ***Williams***	N	N	Y	?	Y	N	Y	N
18 Applegate	N	N	N	Y	N	?	Y	N
19 Feighan	N	N	Y	?	N	N	Y	Y
20 Oakar	N	N	N	?	N	N	Y	Y
21 Stokes	N	N	N	?	N	N	Y	Y
OKLAHOMA								
1 Jones	N	N	N	Y	N	N	Y	Y
2 Synar	N	-	Y	Y	N	N	Y	Y
3 Watkins	N	N	Y	Y	N	N	Y	N
4 McCurdy	N	N	N	?	?	?	?	?
5 ***Edwards***	Y	Y	N	Y	Y	Y	Y	Y
6 English	N	N	N	Y	N	N	Y	Y
OREGON								
1 AuCoin	N	N	N	?	N	N	Y	Y
2 ***Smith, R.***	N	N	N	Y	Y	Y	Y	N
3 Wyden	N	N	Y	Y	N	N	Y	Y
4 Weaver	N	N	N	Y	N	N	Y	Y
5 ***Smith, D.***	?	?	X	?	Y	Y	Y	N
PENNSYLVANIA								
1 Foglietta	N	N	?	Y	N	N	Y	Y
2 Gray	N	N	Y	Y	N	N	Y	Y
3 Borski	N	N	Y	Y	N	N	Y	Y
4 Kolter	N	N	Y	Y	N	N	Y	N
5 ***Schulze***	?	?	Y	Y	Y	N	Y	N
6 Yatron	N	N	?	Y	N	N	Y	Y
7 Edgar	N	N	N	?	N	N	Y	Y
8 Kostmayer	N	N	Y	Y	N	N	Y	Y
9 ***Shuster***	Y	Y	?	?	Y	N	Y	N
10 ***McDade***	N	Y	Y	?	N	N	Y	Y
11 Harrison	N	N	Y	?	N	N	Y	Y
12 Murtha	N	N	N	Y	N	N	Y	Y
13 ***Coughlin***	Y	Y	Y	?	Y	Y	Y	N
14 Coyne	N	N	Y	?	N	N	Y	Y
15 ***Ritter***	Y	Y	N	?	Y	Y	Y	Y
16 ***Walker***	Y	Y	N	Y	Y	Y	Y	Y
17 ***Gekas***	Y	Y	Y	Y	N	N	,	Y
18 Walgren	N	N	N	?	N	N	Y	Y
19 ***Goodling***	Y	Y	N	?	N	N	Y	Y
20 Gaydos	N	N	?	Y	N	N	Y	N
21 ***Ridge***	N	N	Y	?	Y	?	Y	Y
22 Murphy	N	N	N	?	N	?	Y	N
23 ***Clinger***	Y	Y	Y	+	Y	Y	Y	Y
RHODE ISLAND								
1 St Germain	N	N	?	?	N	N	Y	Y
2 ***Schneider***	Y	Y	Y	?	N	N	Y	Y
SOUTH CAROLINA								
1 ***Hartnett***	Y	Y	N	?	?	?	?	?
2 ***Spence***	Y	Y	N	?	N	N	Y	N
3 Derrick	N	N	Y	Y	N	N	Y	Y
4 ***Campbell***	Y	Y	?	?	?	?	?	?
5 Spratt	N	N	Y	Y	N	N	Y	Y
6 Tallon	N	N	Y	?	N	N	Y	N
SOUTH DAKOTA								
AL Daschle	N	N	Y	Y	N	N	Y	Y
TENNESSEE								
1 ***Quillen***	Y	Y	N	?	Y	N	Y	N
2 ***Duncan***	Y	N	Y	Y	Y	N	Y	N
3 Lloyd	N	N	N	Y	N	N	Y	N
4 Cooper	N	N	Y	?	N	N	Y	Y
5 Boner	N	N	Y	?	N	N	Y	N
6 Gore	N	N	?	Y	N	N	Y	Y
7 ***Sundquist***	Y	N	Y	Y	Y	Y	Y	N
8 Jones	N	N	Y	?	N	N	Y	Y
9 Ford	N	N	?	Y	N	N	Y	Y
TEXAS								
1 Hall, S.	N	Y	N	Y	N	N	Y	N
2 Wilson	N	?	Y	Y	N	N	Y	N
3 ***Bartlett***	Y	Y	?	Y	Y	Y	Y	N
4 Hall, R.	N	N	N	Y	N	N	Y	N
5 Bryant	N	N	?	?	N	N	Y	Y
6 ***Gramm***	?	?	?	?	?	?	?	?
7 ***Archer***	Y	Y	?	Y	Y	Y	Y	N
8 ***Fields***	Y	Y	N	Y	Y	Y	Y	N
9 Brooks	N	N	Y	Y	N	N	Y	N
10 Pickle	N	N	?	?	N	N	Y	Y
11 Leath	N	N	Y	Y	N	N	Y	N
12 Wright	N	N	Y	Y	N	N	Y	Y
13 Hightower	N	N	N	?	N	N	Y	Y
14 Patman	N	N	N	Y	N	N	Y	N
15 de la Garza	?	?	?	Y	?	N	Y	Y
16 Coleman	N	N	Y	Y	N	N	Y	Y
17 Stenholm	?	?	?	Y	N	N	Y	N
18 Leland	N	N	#	Y	N	N	Y	Y
19 Hance	X	?	?	?	?	?	?	?
20 Gonzalez	N	N	N	Y	N	N	Y	Y
21 ***Loeffler***	Y	N	?	Y	Y	Y	Y	N
22 ***Paul***	?	?	?	?	?	?	?	?
23 Kazen	N	N	?	Y	N	N	Y	Y
24 Frost	N	N	?	Y	N	N	Y	N
25 Andrews	N	N	N	Y	N	N	Y	Y
26 Vandergriff	N	N	N	Y	N	N	Y	Y
27 Ortiz	N	N	?	?	N	N	Y	Y
UTAH								
1 ***Hansen***	Y	Y	N	Y	Y	Y	Y	N
2 ***Marriott***	Y	Y	N	Y	Y	?	Y	N
3 ***Nielson***	Y	Y	N	Y	Y	Y	Y	N
VERMONT								
AL ***Jeffords***	N	N	Y	?	?	?	Y	Y
VIRGINIA								
1 ***Bateman***	Y	Y	Y	Y	Y	Y	Y	N
2 ***Whitehurst***	Y	Y	?	Y	Y	Y	Y	Y
3 ***Bliley***	Y	Y	Y	Y	Y	Y	Y	N
4 Sisisky	N	N	Y	Y	N	N	Y	Y
5 Daniel	Y	Y	N	Y	N	N	Y	N
6 Olin	N	N	Y	Y	N	N	Y	Y
7 ***Robinson***	Y	Y	Y	Y	Y	Y	Y	Y
8 ***Parris***	Y	Y	Y	Y	Y	Y	Y	N
9 Boucher	N	N	Y	Y	N	N	Y	Y
10 ***Wolf***	Y	Y	Y	Y	Y	Y	Y	Y
WASHINGTON								
1 ***Pritchard***	Y	Y	?	?	N	N	Y	Y
2 Swift	N	N	Y	Y	N	?	Y	Y
3 Bonker	N	N	Y	Y	N	N	Y	Y
4 ***Morrison***	Y	Y	Y	Y	Y	N	Y	Y
5 Foley	N	N	Y	Y	N	N	Y	Y
6 Dicks	N	N	?	?	N	?	Y	Y
7 Lowry	N	N	Y	Y	N	N	Y	Y
8 ***Chandler***	Y	Y	Y	Y	Y	?	Y	Y
WEST VIRGINIA								
1 Mollohan	N	N	Y	Y	N	N	Y	Y
2 Staggers	N	N	Y	Y	N	?	Y	Y
3 Wise	N	N	Y	+	-	N	Y	Y
4 Rahall	N	N	X	Y	N	N	Y	N
WISCONSIN								
1 Aspin	N	N	?	?	N	?	?	?
2 Kastenmeier	N	N	?	Y	N	N	Y	Y
3 ***Gunderson***	N	N	N	?	Y	Y	Y	Y
4 Zablocki	N	N	?	Y	N	N	Y	Y
5 Moody	N	N	N	?	?	?	?	?
6 ***Petri***	N	N	N	Y	Y	Y	Y	Y
7 Obey	N	N	N	Y	N	N	Y	Y
8 ***Roth***	Y	Y	N	Y	Y	Y	Y	N
9 ***Sensenbrenner***	Y	N	N	Y	Y	Y	Y	N
WYOMING								
AL ***Cheney***	Y	N	N	Y	Y	Y	Y	N

Southern states - Ala., Ark., Fla., Ga., Ky., La., Miss., N.C., Okla., S.C., Tenn., Texas, Va.

461. S 376. Debt Collection Act. Sam B. Hall Jr., D-Texas, motion to suspend the rules and pass the bill to permit federal agencies to contract with private agencies for debt collection services on a contingency fee basis. Motion agreed to (thus cleared for the president) 397-3: R 154-0; D 243-3 (ND 161-2, SD 82-1), Nov. 14, 1983. A two-thirds majority of those present and voting (267 in this case) is required for passage under suspension of the rules.

462. HR 1095. 369th Veterans' Association. Sam B. Hall Jr., D-Texas, motion to suspend the rules and pass the bill to grant a federal charter to the 369th Veterans' Association. Motion agreed to 406-0: R 156-0; D 250-0 (ND 165-0, SD 85-0), Nov. 14, 1983. A two-thirds majority of those present and voting (271 in this case) is required for passage under suspension of the rules.

463. HR 29. Polish Legion of American Veterans. Sam B. Hall Jr., D-Texas, motion to suspend the rules and pass the bill to grant a federal charter to the Polish Legion of American Veterans. Motion agreed to 404-0: R 156-0; D 248-0 (ND 163-0, SD 85-0), Nov. 14, 1983. A two-thirds majority of those present and voting (270 in this case) is required for passage under suspension of the rules.

464. HR 3249. National Academy of Public Administration. Sam B. Hall Jr., D-Texas, motion to suspend the rules and pass the bill to grant a federal charter to the National Academy of Public Administration. Motion agreed to 401-2: R 155-1; D 246-1 (ND 161-1, SD 85-0), Nov. 14, 1983. A two-thirds majority of those present and voting (269 in this case) is required for passage under suspension of the rules.

465. H Con Res 190. Satellite-Directed Navigation. Glickman, D-Kan., motion to suspend the rules and adopt the concurrent resolution expressing the sense of Congress that the secretary of transportation should report to the Congress on the steps being taken to make a satellite-directed navigational system available to civilian aviation. Motion agreed to 402-0: R 152-0; D 250-0 (ND 165-0, SD 85-0), Nov. 14, 1983. A two-thirds majority of those present and voting (268 in this case) is required for adoption under suspension of the rules.

466. H Con Res 168. Weather Satellite Systems. Fuqua, D-Fla., motion to suspend the rules and adopt the concurrent resolution expressing the sense of Congress that it is inappropriate at this time to sell or transfer weather satellite systems to the private sector. Motion agreed to 377-28: R 128-27; D 249-1 (ND 165-1, SD 84-0), Nov. 14, 1983. A two-thirds majority of those present and voting (270 in this case) is required for adoption under suspension of the rules.

467. Procedural Motion. Foley, D-Wash., motion that the House adjourn. Motion agreed to 240-156: R 10-140; D 230-16 (ND 160-3, SD 70-13), Nov. 14, 1983.

468. Procedural Motion. Bliley, R-Va., motion to approve the House *Journal* of Monday, Nov 14. Motion agreed to 284-120: R 49-110; D 235-10 (ND 156-5, SD 79-5), Nov. 15, 1983.

KEY

Y	Voted for (yea).
#	Paired for.
+	Announced for.
N	Voted against (nay).
X	Paired against.
-	Announced against.
P	Voted "present".
C	Voted "present" to avoid possible conflict of interest.
?	Did not vote or otherwise make a position known.

Democrats *Republicans*

	461	462	463	464	465	466	467	468
ALABAMA								
1 *Edwards*	Y	Y	Y	Y	?	?	?	Y
2 *Dickinson*	Y	Y	Y	Y	Y	Y	N	N
3 Nichols	Y	Y	Y	Y	Y	Y	Y	?
4 Bevill	Y	Y	Y	Y	Y	Y	Y	Y
5 Flippo	Y	Y	Y	Y	Y	Y	Y	?
6 Erdreich	Y	Y	Y	Y	Y	Y	Y	Y
7 Shelby	Y	Y	Y	Y	Y	Y	Y	?
ALASKA								
AL *Young*	Y	Y	Y	Y	Y	Y	N	N
ARIZONA								
1 *McCain*	Y	Y	Y	Y	Y	Y	N	N
2 Udall	Y	Y	Y	Y	Y	Y	?	Y
3 *Stump*	Y	Y	Y	Y	N	N	N	N
4 *Rudd*	Y	Y	Y	Y	?	Y	N	N
5 McNulty	Y	Y	Y	Y	Y	Y	Y	Y
ARKANSAS								
1 Alexander	Y	Y	Y	Y	Y	Y	Y	Y
2 *Bethune*	Y	Y	Y	Y	Y	Y	N	N
3 *Hammerschmidt*	Y	Y	Y	Y	Y	Y	N	N
4 Anthony	+	+	+	+	+	+	Y	Y
CALIFORNIA								
1 Bosco	Y	Y	Y	Y	Y	Y	Y	Y
2 *Chappie*	Y	Y	Y	Y	Y	Y	N	N
3 Matsui	Y	Y	Y	Y	Y	Y	Y	Y
4 Fazio	Y	Y	Y	Y	Y	Y	Y	Y
5 Burton	Y	Y	Y	Y	Y	Y	Y	Y
6 Boxer	Y	Y	Y	Y	N	N	N	Y
7 Miller	Y	Y	Y	Y	Y	Y	Y	Y
8 Dellums	Y	Y	Y	Y	Y	Y	Y	Y
9 Stark	Y	Y	Y	Y	Y	Y	Y	Y
10 Edwards	Y	Y	Y	Y	Y	Y	Y	Y
11 Lantos	Y	Y	Y	Y	Y	Y	Y	Y
12 Zschau	Y	Y	Y	Y	Y	Y	N	Y
13 Mineta	Y	Y	Y	Y	Y	Y	Y	Y
14 *Shumway*	Y	Y	Y	Y	Y	N	N	N
15 Coelho	Y	Y	Y	Y	Y	Y	Y	Y
16 Panetta	Y	Y	Y	Y	Y	Y	Y	Y
17 *Pashayan*	Y	Y	Y	Y	Y	Y	N	N
18 Lehman	?	?	?	?	+	Y	Y	Y
19 *Lagomarsino*	Y	Y	Y	Y	Y	Y	N	N
20 *Thomas*	Y	Y	Y	Y	Y	Y	N	N
21 *Fiedler*	Y	Y	Y	Y	Y	N	N	N
22 *Moorhead*	Y	Y	Y	Y	N	N	N	N
23 Beilenson	Y	Y	Y	Y	Y	Y	Y	Y
24 Waxman	Y	Y	Y	Y	Y	Y	Y	Y
25 Roybal	Y	Y	Y	?	Y	Y	Y	Y
26 Berman	Y	Y	Y	Y	Y	Y	Y	Y
27 Levine	Y	Y	Y	Y	Y	Y	Y	Y
28 Dixon	Y	Y	Y	Y	Y	Y	Y	Y
29 Hawkins	Y	Y	Y	Y	Y	Y	Y	Y
30 Martinez	Y	Y	Y	Y	Y	Y	Y	Y
31 Dymally	Y	Y	Y	Y	Y	Y	Y	Y
32 Anderson	Y	Y	Y	Y	Y	N	N	Y
33 *Dreier*	Y	Y	Y	Y	N	N	N	N
34 Torres	+	+	+	+	+	+	+	Y
35 *Lewis*	Y	Y	Y	?	Y	Y	Y	Y
36 Brown	?	?	?	?	?	?	?	Y
37 *McCandless*	Y	Y	Y	Y	Y	Y	N	Y
38 Patterson	Y	Y	Y	Y	Y	Y	N	Y
39 *Dannemeyer*	Y	Y	Y	Y	N	N	N	N
40 *Badham*	Y	Y	Y	Y	N	N	N	N
41 *Lowery*	Y	Y	Y	Y	Y	Y	N	N
42 Lungren	Y	Y	Y	N	Y	Y	N	N

	461	462	463	464	465	466	467	468
43 *Packard*	Y	Y	Y	Y	Y	Y	N	N
44 Bates	Y	Y	Y	?	Y	Y	Y	Y
45 *Hunter*	Y	Y	Y	Y	Y	Y	N	Y
COLORADO								
1 Schroeder	Y	Y	Y	Y	Y	Y	Y	Y
2 Wirth	Y	Y	Y	Y	Y	Y	Y	Y
3 Kogovsek	Y	Y	Y	Y	Y	Y	Y	Y
4 *Brown*	Y	Y	Y	Y	Y	N	N	N
5 *Kramer*	Y	Y	Y	Y	Y	N	N	N
6 *Schaefer*	Y	Y	Y	Y	N	N	N	N
CONNECTICUT								
1 Kennelly	Y	Y	Y	Y	Y	Y	Y	Y
2 Gejdenson	Y	Y	Y	Y	Y	Y	N	Y
3 Morrison	Y	Y	Y	Y	Y	Y	Y	Y
4 *McKinney*	Y	Y	Y	Y	Y	Y	Y	Y
5 Ratchford	Y	Y	Y	Y	Y	Y	Y	Y
6 *Johnson*	Y	Y	Y	Y	Y	Y	Y	Y
DELAWARE								
AL Carper	Y	Y	Y	Y	Y	Y	?	Y
FLORIDA								
1 Hutto	Y	Y	Y	Y	Y	Y	N	Y
2 Fuqua	Y	Y	Y	Y	Y	Y	Y	Y
3 Bennett	Y	Y	Y	Y	Y	Y	Y	Y
4 Chappell	?	Y	Y	Y	Y	Y	?	Y
5 *McCollum*	Y	Y	Y	Y	Y	Y	N	N
6 MacKay	Y	Y	Y	Y	Y	Y	Y	Y
7 Gibbons	Y	Y	Y	Y	Y	Y	Y	Y
8 *Young*	Y	Y	Y	Y	Y	Y	Y	Y
9 *Bilirakis*	Y	Y	Y	Y	Y	Y	N	N
10 Ireland	Y	Y	Y	Y	Y	Y	Y	Y
11 Nelson	Y	Y	Y	Y	Y	Y	Y	Y
12 *Lewis*	Y	Y	Y	Y	Y	Y	N	N
13 *Mack*	Y	Y	Y	Y	Y	Y	N	N
14 Mica	Y	Y	Y	Y	Y	Y	Y	Y
15 *Shaw*	Y	Y	Y	Y	Y	Y	N	N
16 Smith	Y	Y	Y	Y	Y	Y	Y	Y
17 Lehman	Y	Y	Y	Y	Y	Y	Y	Y
18 Pepper	Y	Y	Y	Y	Y	Y	Y	Y
19 Fascell	Y	Y	Y	Y	Y	Y	Y	Y
GEORGIA								
1 Thomas	Y	Y	Y	Y	Y	Y	Y	Y
2 Hatcher	Y	Y	Y	Y	Y	Y	Y	Y
3 Ray	Y	Y	Y	Y	Y	Y	Y	Y
4 Levitas	Y	Y	Y	Y	Y	Y	Y	N
5 Fowler	Y	Y	Y	Y	Y	Y	Y	Y
6 *Gingrich*	Y	Y	Y	Y	Y	Y	N	N
7 Darden	Y	Y	Y	Y	Y	Y	Y	Y
8 Rowland	Y	Y	Y	Y	Y	Y	Y	Y
9 Jenkins	Y	Y	Y	Y	Y	Y	Y	?
10 Barnard	Y	Y	Y	Y	Y	Y	Y	Y
HAWAII								
1 Heftel	Y	Y	Y	Y	Y	Y	Y	Y
2 Akaka	Y	Y	Y	Y	Y	Y	Y	Y
IDAHO								
1 *Craig*	Y	Y	Y	Y	N	N	N	N
2 *Hansen*	Y	Y	Y	Y	N	N	N	N
ILLINOIS								
1 Hayes	Y	Y	Y	Y	Y	Y	Y	Y
2 Savage	Y	Y	Y	Y	Y	Y	Y	Y
3 Russo	Y	Y	Y	Y	Y	Y	Y	Y
4 *O'Brien*	Y	Y	Y	Y	Y	Y	N	Y
5 Lipinski	Y	Y	Y	Y	Y	Y	Y	Y
6 *Hyde*	Y	Y	Y	Y	Y	N	Y	N
7 Collins	Y	Y	Y	Y	Y	Y	Y	Y
8 Rostenkowski	Y	Y	Y	Y	Y	Y	Y	Y
9 Yates	Y	Y	Y	Y	Y	Y	Y	Y
10 *Porter*	Y	Y	Y	Y	Y	N	Y	Y
11 Annunzio	Y	Y	Y	Y	Y	Y	Y	Y
12 *Crane, P.*	Y	Y	Y	Y	N	N	N	N
13 *Erlenborn*	Y	Y	Y	Y	Y	Y	?	N
14 *Corcoran*	?	?	?	?	?	?	?	Y
15 *Madigan*	Y	Y	Y	Y	Y	N	N	N
16 *Martin*	Y	Y	Y	Y	Y	Y	N	N
17 Evans	Y	Y	Y	Y	Y	Y	Y	Y
18 *Michel*	Y	Y	Y	Y	Y	Y	N	Y
19 *Crane, D.*	Y	Y	Y	Y	N	N	N	N
20 Durbin	+	+	+	+	+	+	?	N
21 Price	Y	Y	Y	Y	Y	Y	Y	Y
22 Simon	Y	Y	Y	Y	Y	Y	?	Y
INDIANA								
1 Hall	Y	Y	Y	Y	Y	Y	Y	Y
2 Sharp	Y	Y	Y	Y	Y	Y	Y	Y
3 *Hiler*	Y	Y	Y	Y	Y	Y	N	N
4 *Coats*	Y	Y	Y	Y	Y	Y	N	N
5 *Hillis*	Y	Y	Y	Y	Y	Y	N	Y

ND - Northern Democrats   SD - Southern Democrats

Corresponding to Congressional Record Votes 496, 497, 498, 499, 500, 501, 502, 503

	461	462	463	464	465	466	467	468
6 ***Burton***	?	?	?	?	?	?	?	Y
7 ***Myers***	Y	Y	Y	Y	Y	Y	N	Y
8 McCloskey	Y	Y	Y	Y	Y	Y	Y	Y
9 Hamilton	Y	Y	Y	Y	Y	Y	Y	Y
10 Jacobs	?	Y	Y	Y	Y	Y	Y	P
IOWA								
1 ***Leach***	Y	Y	Y	Y	Y	Y	N	Y
2 ***Tauke***	Y	Y	Y	Y	Y	Y	N	N
3 ***Evans***	Y	Y	Y	Y	Y	Y	N	N
4 Smith	Y	Y	Y	Y	Y	Y	Y	Y
5 Harkin	Y	Y	Y	Y	Y	Y	Y	N
6 Bedell	Y	Y	Y	Y	Y	Y	Y	Y
KANSAS								
1 ***Roberts***	Y	Y	Y	Y	Y	Y	N	N
2 Slattery	Y	Y	Y	Y	Y	Y	Y	Y
3 ***Winn***	Y	Y	Y	Y	Y	Y	N	N
4 Glickman	Y	Y	Y	Y	Y	Y	Y	Y
5 ***Whittaker***	Y	Y	Y	Y	Y	Y	N	N
KENTUCKY								
1 Hubbard	Y	Y	Y	Y	Y	Y	N	Y
2 Natcher	Y	Y	Y	Y	Y	Y	Y	Y
3 Mazzoli	Y	Y	Y	Y	Y	Y	Y	Y
4 ***Snyder***	Y	Y	Y	Y	Y	Y	N	Y
5 ***Rogers***	Y	Y	Y	Y	Y	Y	N	N
6 ***Hopkins***	Y	Y	Y	Y	Y	Y	N	Y
7 Perkins	Y	Y	Y	Y	Y	Y	Y	Y
LOUISIANA								
1 ***Livingston***	?	?	?	?	?	?	?	N
2 Boggs	Y	Y	Y	Y	Y	Y	Y	Y
3 Tauzin	Y	Y	Y	Y	Y	Y	N	N
4 Roemer	Y	Y	Y	Y	Y	Y	N	N
5 Huckaby	Y	Y	Y	Y	Y	Y	Y	Y
6 ***Moore***	Y	Y	Y	Y	Y	Y	N	Y
7 Breaux	Y	Y	Y	Y	Y	Y	Y	?
8 Long	Y	Y	Y	Y	Y	Y	?	Y
MAINE								
1 ***McKernan***	Y	Y	Y	Y	Y	Y	N	Y
2 ***Snowe***	Y	Y	Y	Y	Y	Y	N	Y
MARYLAND								
1 Dyson	Y	Y	Y	Y	Y	Y	Y	Y
2 Long	Y	Y	Y	Y	Y	Y	Y	?
3 Mikulski	Y	Y	Y	Y	Y	Y	Y	Y
4 ***Holt***	Y	Y	Y	Y	Y	Y	Y	Y
5 Hoyer	Y	Y	Y	Y	Y	Y	Y	Y
6 Byron	?	?	?	?	?	?	?	?
7 Mitchell	Y	Y	Y	Y	Y	Y	Y	Y
8 Barnes	Y	Y	Y	Y	Y	Y	Y	Y
MASSACHUSETTS								
1 ***Conte***	Y	Y	Y	Y	Y	Y	Y	Y
2 Boland	Y	Y	Y	Y	Y	Y	Y	Y
3 Early	Y	Y	Y	Y	Y	Y	Y	Y
4 Frank	Y	Y	Y	Y	Y	Y	Y	?
5 Shannon	Y	Y	Y	Y	Y	Y	Y	Y
6 Mavroules	?	?	?	?	?	?	?	Y
7 Markey	Y	Y	Y	Y	Y	Y	Y	Y
8 O'Neill								
9 Moakley	Y	Y	Y	Y	Y	Y	Y	Y
10 Studds	Y	Y	Y	Y	Y	Y	Y	Y
11 Donnelly	Y	Y	Y	Y	Y	Y	Y	?
MICHIGAN								
1 Conyers	Y	Y	Y	Y	Y	Y	Y	?
2 ***Pursell***	Y	Y	Y	Y	Y	Y	Y	Y
3 Wolpe	Y	Y	Y	Y	Y	Y	Y	Y
4 ***Siljander***	Y	Y	Y	Y	Y	Y	N	N
5 ***Sawyer***	Y	Y	Y	Y	Y	Y	N	?
6 Carr	Y	Y	Y	Y	Y	Y	Y	Y
7 Kildee	Y	Y	Y	Y	Y	Y	Y	Y
8 Traxler	Y	Y	Y	Y	Y	Y	Y	Y
9 ***Vander Jagt***	Y	Y	Y	Y	Y	Y	N	N
10 Albosta	Y	Y	Y	Y	Y	Y	Y	Y
11 ***Davis***	Y	Y	Y	Y	Y	Y	N	N
12 Bonior	Y	Y	Y	Y	Y	Y	Y	Y
13 Crockett	Y	Y	Y	Y	Y	Y	Y	?
14 Hertel	Y	Y	Y	Y	Y	Y	Y	Y
15 Ford	?	?	?	?	?	?	?	?
16 Dingell	Y	Y	Y	Y	Y	Y	Y	Y
17 Levin	Y	Y	Y	Y	Y	Y	Y	Y
18 ***Broomfield***	Y	Y	Y	Y	Y	N	N	N
MINNESOTA								
1 Penny	Y	Y	Y	Y	Y	Y	Y	Y
2 ***Weber***	Y	Y	Y	Y	Y	Y	N	N
3 ***Frenzel***	Y	Y	Y	Y	Y	N	N	N
4 Vento	Y	Y	Y	Y	Y	Y	Y	Y
5 Sabo	Y	Y	Y	Y	Y	Y	Y	Y
6 Sikorski	Y	Y	Y	Y	Y	Y	Y	N
7 ***Stangeland***	Y	Y	Y	Y	Y	Y	N	N
8 Oberstar	+	+	+	+	+	+	+	?
MISSISSIPPI								
1 Whitten	Y	Y	Y	Y	Y	Y	Y	Y
2 ***Franklin***	?	?	?	?	?	?	?	N
3 Montgomery	Y	Y	Y	Y	Y	Y	Y	Y
4 Dowdy	Y	Y	Y	Y	Y	Y	Y	Y
5 ***Lott***	Y	Y	Y	Y	Y	Y	N	N
MISSOURI								
1 Clay	Y	Y	Y	Y	Y	Y	Y	Y
2 Young	Y	Y	Y	Y	Y	Y	Y	Y
3 Gephardt	Y	Y	?	Y	Y	Y	Y	Y
4 Skelton	Y	Y	Y	Y	Y	Y	Y	Y
5 Wheat	Y	Y	Y	Y	Y	Y	Y	Y
6 ***Coleman***	Y	Y	Y	Y	Y	Y	?	N
7 ***Taylor***	Y	Y	Y	Y	Y	Y	N	N
8 ***Emerson***	Y	Y	Y	Y	Y	Y	N	N
9 Volkmer	Y	Y	Y	Y	Y	Y	Y	Y
MONTANA								
1 Williams	N	Y	Y	Y	Y	Y	Y	?
2 ***Marlenee***	Y	Y	Y	Y	Y	Y	N	N
NEBRASKA								
1 ***Bereuter***	?	Y	Y	Y	Y	Y	N	N
2 ***Daub***	Y	Y	Y	Y	Y	Y	N	N
3 ***Smith***	Y	Y	Y	Y	Y	Y	N	Y
NEVADA								
1 Reid	Y	Y	Y	Y	Y	Y	Y	Y
2 ***Vucanovich***	Y	Y	Y	Y	Y	N	N	N
NEW HAMPSHIRE								
1 D'Amours	Y	Y	Y	Y	Y	Y	Y	Y
2 ***Gregg***	Y	Y	Y	Y	Y	Y	N	Y
NEW JERSEY								
1 Florio	Y	Y	Y	Y	Y	Y	Y	Y
2 Hughes	Y	Y	Y	Y	Y	Y	N	Y
3 Howard	Y	Y	Y	Y	Y	Y	Y	Y
4 ***Smith***	Y	Y	Y	Y	Y	Y	N	N
5 ***Roukema***	Y	Y	Y	Y	Y	Y	N	Y
6 Dwyer	Y	Y	Y	Y	Y	Y	Y	Y
7 ***Rinaldo***	Y	Y	Y	Y	Y	Y	N	N
8 Roe	Y	Y	Y	Y	Y	Y	Y	Y
9 Torricelli	?	Y	Y	Y	Y	Y	Y	Y
10 Rodino	Y	Y	Y	Y	Y	Y	Y	Y
11 Minish	?	?	?	?	?	?	?	Y
12 ***Courter***	Y	Y	Y	Y	Y	Y	N	N
13 ***Forsythe***	Y	Y	Y	Y	Y	Y	Y	N
14 Guarini	Y	Y	Y	Y	Y	Y	Y	Y
NEW MEXICO								
1 ***Lujan***	Y	Y	Y	Y	Y	Y	N	Y
2 ***Skeen***	Y	Y	Y	Y	Y	Y	N	N
3 Richardson	Y	Y	Y	Y	Y	Y	Y	Y
NEW YORK								
1 ***Carney***	Y	Y	Y	Y	Y	Y	N	N
2 Downey	Y	Y	?	Y	Y	Y	Y	Y
3 Mrazek	Y	Y	Y	Y	Y	Y	Y	Y
4 ***Lent***	Y	Y	Y	Y	Y	Y	N	?
5 ***McGrath***	Y	Y	Y	Y	Y	Y	N	N
6 Addabbo	Y	Y	Y	Y	Y	Y	Y	Y
7 Ackerman	Y	Y	Y	Y	Y	Y	Y	Y
8 Scheuer	Y	?	?	?	?	?	?	Y
9 Ferraro	Y	Y	Y	Y	Y	Y	Y	Y
10 Schumer	Y	Y	Y	Y	Y	Y	Y	Y
11 Towns	Y	Y	Y	Y	Y	Y	Y	Y
12 Owens	Y	Y	Y	Y	Y	Y	Y	Y
13 Solarz	?	?	?	?	?	?	?	?
14 ***Molinari***	?	?	?	?	?	?	?	?
15 ***Green***	Y	Y	Y	Y	Y	Y	?	Y
16 Rangel	Y	Y	Y	Y	Y	Y	Y	Y
17 Weiss	Y	Y	Y	Y	Y	Y	Y	Y
18 Garcia	Y	Y	Y	Y	Y	Y	Y	?
19 Biaggi	Y	Y	Y	Y	Y	Y	Y	Y
20 Ottinger	Y	Y	Y	Y	Y	Y	Y	P
21 ***Fish***	Y	Y	Y	Y	Y	Y	N	N
22 ***Gilman***	Y	Y	Y	Y	Y	Y	N	Y
23 Stratton	Y	Y	Y	Y	Y	Y	Y	Y
24 ***Solomon***	Y	Y	Y	Y	Y	N	N	N
25 ***Boehlert***	Y	Y	Y	Y	Y	Y	N	Y
26 ***Martin***	?	?	?	?	?	?	?	Y
27 ***Wortley***	Y	Y	Y	Y	Y	Y	N	Y
28 McHugh	Y	Y	Y	Y	Y	Y	Y	Y
29 ***Horton***	Y	Y	Y	Y	Y	Y	N	Y
30 ***Conable***	?	?	?	?	?	?	?	N
31 ***Kemp***	Y	Y	Y	Y	Y	Y	N	N
32 LaFalce	Y	Y	Y	Y	Y	Y	Y	Y
33 Nowak	Y	Y	Y	Y	Y	Y	Y	Y
34 Lundine	Y	Y	Y	Y	Y	Y	Y	Y
NORTH CAROLINA								
1 Jones	Y	Y	Y	Y	Y	Y	Y	Y
2 Valentine	?	?	?	?	?	?	?	Y
3 Whitley	Y	Y	Y	Y	Y	Y	Y	Y
4 Andrews	Y	Y	Y	Y	Y	Y	Y	Y
5 Neal	Y	Y	Y	Y	Y	Y	Y	Y
6 Britt	?	?	?	?	?	?	?	Y
7 Rose	Y	Y	Y	Y	Y	Y	Y	Y
8 Hefner	Y	Y	Y	Y	Y	Y	Y	Y
9 ***Martin***	?	Y	Y	Y	Y	Y	N	N
10 ***Broyhill***	Y	Y	Y	Y	Y	Y	N	Y
11 Clarke	Y	Y	Y	Y	Y	Y	Y	Y
NORTH DAKOTA								
AL Dorgan	?	Y	Y	Y	Y	Y	Y	Y
OHIO								
1 Luken	Y	Y	Y	Y	Y	Y	Y	Y
2 ***Gradison***	Y	Y	Y	Y	Y	Y	N	N
3 Hall	Y	Y	Y	?	Y	Y	Y	Y
4 ***Oxley***	Y	Y	Y	Y	Y	Y	N	N
5 ***Latta***	Y	Y	Y	Y	Y	Y	N	N
6 ***McEwen***	Y	Y	Y	Y	Y	Y	N	Y
7 ***DeWine***	Y	Y	Y	Y	Y	Y	N	N
8 ***Kindness***	Y	Y	Y	Y	Y	Y	N	N
9 Kaptur	Y	Y	Y	Y	Y	Y	Y	Y
10 ***Miller***	Y	Y	Y	Y	Y	Y	N	N
11 Eckart	Y	Y	Y	Y	Y	Y	Y	Y
12 ***Kasich***	Y	Y	Y	Y	Y	N	N	N
13 Pease	Y	Y	Y	Y	Y	Y	Y	Y
14 Seiberling	Y	Y	Y	Y	Y	Y	Y	?
15 ***Wylie***	Y	Y	Y	Y	Y	Y	N	Y
16 ***Regula***	Y	Y	Y	Y	Y	Y	N	N
17 ***Williams***	Y	Y	Y	Y	Y	Y	?	Y
18 Applegate	Y	Y	Y	Y	Y	Y	N	?
19 Feighan	Y	Y	Y	Y	Y	Y	Y	Y
20 Oakar	Y	Y	Y	Y	Y	Y	Y	Y
21 Stokes	Y	Y	Y	Y	Y	Y	Y	Y
OKLAHOMA								
1 Jones	Y	Y	Y	Y	Y	Y	Y	Y
2 Synar	Y	Y	Y	Y	Y	Y	Y	Y
3 Watkins	Y	Y	Y	Y	Y	Y	N	Y
4 McCurdy	?	?	?	?	?	?	?	Y
5 ***Edwards***	Y	Y	Y	Y	Y	N	N	N
6 English	Y	Y	Y	Y	Y	Y	Y	Y
OREGON								
1 AuCoin	Y	Y	Y	Y	Y	Y	Y	Y
2 ***Smith, R.***	Y	Y	Y	Y	Y	Y	N	N
3 Wyden	Y	Y	Y	Y	Y	Y	Y	Y
4 Weaver	Y	Y	Y	Y	Y	Y	Y	Y
5 ***Smith, D.***	Y	Y	Y	Y	Y	Y	N	N
PENNSYLVANIA								
1 Foglietta	Y	Y	Y	Y	Y	Y	Y	Y
2 Gray	Y	Y	Y	Y	Y	Y	Y	Y
3 Borski	Y	Y	Y	Y	Y	Y	Y	Y
4 Kolter	Y	Y	Y	Y	Y	Y	Y	Y
5 ***Schulze***	Y	Y	Y	Y	Y	Y	N	N
6 Yatron	Y	Y	Y	Y	Y	Y	Y	Y
7 Edgar	Y	Y	Y	Y	Y	Y	Y	Y
8 Kostmayer	Y	Y	Y	Y	Y	Y	Y	Y
9 ***Shuster***	Y	Y	Y	Y	Y	N	N	N
10 ***McDade***	Y	Y	Y	Y	Y	Y	N	Y
11 Harrison	Y	Y	Y	Y	Y	Y	Y	Y
12 Murtha	Y	Y	Y	Y	Y	Y	Y	Y
13 ***Coughlin***	Y	Y	Y	Y	Y	Y	N	N
14 Coyne	Y	Y	Y	Y	Y	Y	Y	Y
15 ***Ritter***	Y	Y	Y	Y	Y	N	N	N
16 ***Walker***	Y	Y	Y	Y	Y	N	N	N
17 ***Gekas***	Y	Y	Y	Y	Y	Y	N	N
18 Walgren	Y	Y	Y	Y	Y	Y	Y	Y
19 ***Goodling***	Y	Y	Y	Y	Y	Y	Y	?
20 Gaydos	Y	Y	Y	Y	Y	Y	Y	Y
21 ***Ridge***	Y	Y	Y	Y	Y	Y	N	N
22 Murphy	N	Y	Y	N	Y	N	Y	N
23 ***Clinger***	Y	Y	Y	Y	Y	Y	N	N
RHODE ISLAND								
1 St Germain	Y	Y	Y	Y	Y	Y	Y	P
2 ***Schneider***	Y	Y	Y	Y	Y	Y	N	Y
SOUTH CAROLINA								
1 ***Hartnett***	?	?	?	?	?	?	?	?
2 ***Spence***	Y	Y	Y	Y	Y	Y	N	Y
3 Derrick	Y	Y	Y	Y	Y	Y	Y	Y
4 ***Campbell***	?	?	?	?	?	?	?	N
5 Spratt	Y	Y	Y	Y	Y	?	?	Y
6 Tallon	Y	Y	Y	Y	Y	Y	Y	Y
SOUTH DAKOTA								
AL Daschle	Y	Y	Y	Y	Y	Y	Y	Y
TENNESSEE								
1 ***Quillen***	Y	Y	Y	Y	Y	Y	N	Y
2 ***Duncan***	Y	Y	Y	Y	Y	Y	Y	Y
3 Lloyd	Y	Y	Y	Y	Y	Y	N	N
4 Cooper	Y	Y	Y	Y	Y	Y	Y	Y
5 Boner	Y	Y	Y	Y	Y	Y	Y	Y
6 Gore	Y	Y	Y	Y	Y	Y	Y	Y
7 ***Sundquist***	Y	Y	Y	Y	Y	Y	N	N
8 Jones	Y	Y	Y	Y	Y	Y	Y	N
9 Ford	Y	Y	Y	Y	Y	Y	Y	Y
TEXAS								
1 Hall, S.	Y	Y	Y	Y	Y	Y	N	Y
2 Wilson	Y	Y	Y	Y	Y	Y	Y	Y
3 ***Bartlett***	Y	Y	Y	Y	Y	Y	N	Y
4 Hall, R.	Y	Y	Y	Y	Y	Y	Y	Y
5 Bryant	Y	Y	Y	Y	Y	Y	Y	Y
6 ***Gramm***	?	?	?	?	?	?	?	N
7 ***Archer***	Y	Y	Y	Y	Y	N	N	Y
8 ***Fields***	Y	Y	Y	Y	Y	Y	N	N
9 Brooks	Y	Y	Y	Y	Y	Y	Y	Y
10 Pickle	N	Y	Y	Y	Y	Y	N	Y
11 Leath	Y	Y	Y	Y	Y	Y	Y	Y
12 Wright	Y	Y	Y	Y	Y	Y	Y	Y
13 Hightower	Y	Y	Y	Y	Y	Y	N	Y
14 Patman	Y	Y	Y	Y	Y	Y	N	Y
15 de la Garza	Y	Y	Y	Y	Y	Y	Y	Y
16 Coleman	Y	Y	Y	Y	Y	Y	Y	Y
17 Stenholm	Y	Y	Y	Y	Y	Y	N	Y
18 Leland	+	Y	Y	Y	Y	Y	Y	Y
19 Hance	?	?	?	?	?	?	?	?
20 Gonzalez	Y	Y	Y	Y	Y	Y	N	Y
21 ***Loeffler***	Y	Y	Y	Y	Y	Y	N	N
22 ***Paul***	?	?	?	?	?	?	?	?
23 Kazen	Y	Y	Y	Y	Y	Y	N	Y
24 Frost	Y	Y	Y	Y	Y	Y	Y	Y
25 Andrews	Y	Y	Y	Y	Y	Y	Y	Y
26 Vandergriff	Y	Y	Y	Y	Y	Y	Y	Y
27 Ortiz	Y	Y	Y	Y	Y	Y	Y	Y
UTAH								
1 ***Hansen***	Y	Y	Y	Y	Y	Y	N	N
2 ***Marriott***	Y	Y	Y	Y	Y	Y	N	Y
3 ***Nielson***	Y	Y	Y	Y	Y	N	N	N
VERMONT								
AL ***Jeffords***	Y	Y	Y	Y	Y	Y	N	Y
VIRGINIA								
1 ***Bateman***	Y	Y	Y	Y	Y	Y	N	Y
2 ***Whitehurst***	Y	Y	Y	Y	Y	Y	N	N
3 ***Bliley***	Y	Y	Y	Y	Y	Y	N	N
4 Sisisky	Y	Y	Y	Y	Y	Y	Y	Y
5 Daniel	Y	Y	Y	Y	Y	Y	Y	Y
6 Olin	Y	Y	Y	Y	Y	Y	Y	Y
7 ***Robinson***	Y	Y	Y	Y	Y	Y	N	N
8 ***Parris***	Y	Y	Y	Y	Y	Y	N	N
9 Boucher	Y	Y	Y	Y	Y	Y	Y	Y
10 ***Wolf***	Y	Y	Y	Y	Y	Y	N	N
WASHINGTON								
1 ***Pritchard***	Y	Y	Y	Y	?	Y	?	?
2 Swift	Y	Y	Y	Y	Y	Y	Y	Y
3 Bonker	Y	Y	Y	Y	Y	Y	Y	Y
4 ***Morrison***	Y	Y	Y	Y	Y	Y	Y	N
5 Foley	Y	Y	Y	Y	Y	Y	Y	Y
6 Dicks	Y	Y	Y	Y	Y	Y	Y	Y
7 Lowry	Y	Y	Y	Y	Y	Y	Y	Y
8 ***Chandler***	Y	Y	Y	Y	Y	Y	Y	Y
WEST VIRGINIA								
1 Mollohan	Y	Y	Y	Y	Y	Y	Y	Y
2 Staggers	Y	Y	Y	Y	Y	Y	Y	Y
3 Wise	Y	Y	Y	Y	Y	Y	Y	Y
4 Rahall	Y	Y	Y	Y	Y	Y	Y	Y
WISCONSIN								
1 Aspin	Y	Y	Y	Y	Y	Y	Y	Y
2 Kastenmeier	Y	Y	Y	Y	Y	Y	Y	Y
3 ***Gunderson***	Y	Y	Y	Y	Y	Y	N	Y
4 Zablocki	Y	Y	Y	Y	Y	Y	Y	Y
5 Moody	?	?	?	?	?	?	?	Y
6 ***Petri***	Y	Y	Y	Y	Y	N	N	Y
7 Obey	Y	Y	Y	Y	Y	Y	Y	Y
8 ***Roth***	Y	Y	Y	Y	Y	Y	N	N
9 ***Sensenbrenner***	Y	Y	Y	Y	Y	N	N	N
WYOMING								
AL ***Cheney***	Y	Y	Y	Y	Y	N	N	N

Southern states - Ala., Ark., Fla., Ga., Ky., La., Miss., N.C., Okla., S.C., Tenn., Texas, Va.

KEY

Y Voted for (yea).
Paired for.
+ Announced for.
N Voted against (nay).
X Paired against.
- Announced against.
P Voted "present".
C Voted "present" to avoid possible conflict of interest.
? Did not vote or otherwise make a position known.

Democrats   ***Republicans***

469. H J Res 1. Equal Rights Amendment. Rodino, D-N.J., motion to suspend the rules and pass the joint resolution to propose an amendment to the Constitution declaring, "Equality of rights under the law shall not be denied or abridged by the United States or by any state on account of sex." Motion rejected 278-147: R 53-109; D 225-38 (ND 164-13, SD 61-25), Nov. 15, 1983. A two-thirds majority of those present and voting (284 in this case) is required for passage under suspension of the rules. A "nay" was a vote supporting the president's position.

470. HR 4185. Defense Department Appropriations, Fiscal 1984. Young, R-Fla., motion to order the previous question on the Young motion to instruct the House conferees to insist upon the House provision barring the use of animals by the Department of Defense in certain medical experiments. Motion rejected 164-256: R 100-62; D 64-194 (ND 13-158, SD 51-36), Nov. 15, 1983. (Agreement to the motion would have prevented a vote on the Porter, R-Ill., amendment *(see vote 471, below)*.)

471. HR 4185. Defense Department Appropriations, Fiscal 1984. Porter, R-Ill., amendment, to the Young, R-Fla., motion to instruct House conferees, to insist on the House position, namely opposition to $124.4 million for production facilities for and procurement of chemical munitions. Motion agreed to 258-166: R 60-103; D 198-63 (ND 162-12, SD 36-51), Nov. 15, 1983. A "nay" was a vote supporting the president's position.

472. HR 4185. Defense Department Appropriations, Fiscal 1984. Addabbo, D-N.Y., motion that conference committee meetings on the bill be closed to the public when classified national security information is under consideration. Motion agreed to 419-0: R 159-0; D 260-0 (ND 172-0, SD 88-0), Nov. 15, 1983.

473. Procedural Motion. Walker, R-Pa., motion to approve the House *Journal* of Tuesday, Nov. 15. Motion agreed to 335-59: R 113-40; D 222-19 (ND 139-17, SD 83-2), Nov. 16, 1983.

474. HR 3222. State, Justice, Commerce Appropriations, Fiscal 1984. Smith, D-Iowa, motion to take the bill from the Speaker's table and have the House concur in the remaining Senate amendment that provided $11.89 million for the U.S. Civil Rights Commission. Motion agreed to 417-3: R 155-3; D 262-0 (ND 174-0, SD 88-0), Nov. 16, 1983. (This cleared the $10,499,665,000 bill for the president. The president had requested $10,026,318,000 in new budget authority.)

475. HR 3959. Supplemental Appropriations, Fiscal 1984. Adoption of the conference report on the bill to appropriate $302,213,600 in supplemental appropriations for several federal agencies for fiscal 1984. Adopted 372-51: R 126-35; D 246-16 (ND 164-11, SD 82-5), Nov. 16, 1983.

	469	470	471	472	473	474	475
ALABAMA							
1 *Edwards*	N	Y	N	Y	Y	Y	Y
2 *Dickinson*	N	Y	N	Y	?	Y	Y
3 Nichols	N	Y	N	Y	Y	Y	Y
4 Bevill	Y	Y	N	Y	Y	Y	Y
5 Flippo	Y	N	Y	Y	Y	Y	Y
6 Erdreich	Y	N	Y	Y	Y	Y	Y
7 Shelby	N	Y	N	Y	Y	Y	Y
ALASKA							
AL *Young*	Y	Y	N	?	?	Y	Y
ARIZONA							
1 *McCain*	N	Y	N	Y	Y	Y	Y
2 Udall	Y	N	Y	Y	Y	Y	Y
3 *Stump*	N	Y	N	Y	Y	Y	N
4 *Rudd*	N	Y	N	Y	Y	Y	Y
5 McNulty	Y	N	Y	Y	Y	Y	Y
ARKANSAS							
1 Alexander	Y	?	N	Y	Y	Y	Y
2 *Bethune*	N	Y	N	Y	Y	Y	Y
3 *Hammerschmidt*	N	Y	N	Y	Y	Y	Y
4 Anthony	+	Y	N	Y	Y	Y	?
CALIFORNIA							
1 Bosco	Y	?	Y	Y	Y	?	Y
2 *Chappie*	Y	Y	N	Y	N	Y	Y
3 Matsui	Y	N	Y	Y	Y	Y	Y
4 Fazio	Y	Y	?	?	Y	Y	Y
5 Burton	Y	?	Y	Y	Y	Y	Y
6 Boxer	Y	N	Y	Y	Y	Y	Y
7 Miller	Y	N	Y	Y	Y	Y	Y
8 Dellums	Y	N	Y	Y	Y	Y	Y
9 Stark	Y	N	Y	Y	?	Y	Y
10 Edwards	Y	N	Y	Y	Y	Y	Y
11 Lantos	Y	N	Y	Y	Y	Y	Y
12 *Zschau*	Y	N	Y	Y	Y	Y	Y
13 Mineta	Y	N	Y	Y	Y	Y	Y
14 *Shumway*	N	Y	N	Y	N	Y	N
15 Coelho	Y	?	Y	Y	Y	Y	Y
16 Panetta	Y	N	Y	Y	Y	Y	Y
17 *Pashayan*	N	Y	N	Y	N	Y	Y
18 Lehman	Y	N	Y	Y	Y	Y	Y
19 *Lagomarsino*	N	Y	N	Y	Y	Y	Y
20 *Thomas*	Y	Y	N	Y	Y	Y	Y
21 *Fiedler*	Y	Y	N	Y	?	Y	Y
22 *Moorhead*	N	Y	N	Y	Y	Y	N
23 Beilenson	Y	N	Y	Y	Y	Y	Y
24 Waxman	Y	N	Y	?	Y	?	Y
25 Roybal	Y	N	?	?	Y	Y	Y
26 Berman	Y	N	Y	Y	Y	Y	Y
27 Levine	Y	N	Y	Y	Y	Y	Y
28 Dixon	Y	N	Y	Y	Y	Y	Y
29 Hawkins	Y	N	Y	Y	N	Y	Y
30 Martinez	Y	N	Y	Y	Y	Y	Y
31 Dymally	Y	N	Y	Y	P	Y	Y
32 Anderson	Y	N	Y	Y	Y	Y	Y
33 *Dreier*	N	Y	N	Y	Y	Y	Y
34 Torres	Y	N	Y	Y	Y	Y	Y
35 *Lewis*	?	?	?	?	?	?	?
36 Brown	Y	N	Y	Y	Y	Y	Y
37 *McCandless*	N	Y	N	Y	Y	Y	N
38 Patterson	Y	N	Y	Y	Y	Y	Y
39 *Dannemeyer*	N	Y	N	Y	N	Y	N
40 *Badham*	N	Y	N	Y	Y	Y	Y
41 *Lowery*	N	Y	N	Y	Y	Y	Y
42 *Lungren*	N	Y	N	Y	Y	Y	Y
43 *Packard*	N	Y	N	Y	Y	Y	Y
44 Bates	Y	N	Y	Y	Y	Y	Y
45 *Hunter*	N	Y	N	Y	Y	Y	Y
COLORADO							
1 Schroeder	Y	N	Y	Y	N	Y	N
2 Wirth	Y	N	Y	Y	Y	Y	Y
3 Kogovsek	Y	N	Y	Y	Y	Y	Y
4 *Brown*	Y	N	Y	Y	Y	Y	N
5 *Kramer*	N	Y	N	Y	Y	Y	Y
6 *Schaefer*	N	N	Y	N	Y	Y	Y
CONNECTICUT							
1 Kennelly	Y	N	Y	Y	Y	Y	Y
2 Gejdenson	Y	N	Y	Y	N	Y	Y
3 Morrison	Y	N	Y	Y	Y	Y	Y
4 *McKinney*	Y	N	Y	Y	Y	Y	Y
5 Ratchford	Y	N	Y	Y	Y	Y	Y
6 *Johnson*	Y	N	Y	Y	Y	Y	?
DELAWARE							
AL Carper	Y	N	Y	Y	Y	Y	Y
FLORIDA							
1 Hutto	N	Y	N	Y	Y	Y	Y
2 Fuqua	N	Y	N	Y	Y	Y	Y
3 Bennett	N	Y	N	Y	Y	Y	Y
4 Chappell	N	Y	N	Y	Y	Y	Y
5 *McCollum*	N	Y	N	Y	Y	Y	Y
6 MacKay	Y	N	Y	Y	Y	Y	Y
7 Gibbons	Y	Y	Y	?	Y	Y	Y
8 *Young*	N	Y	N	?	?	?	?
9 *Bilirakis*	N	Y	N	Y	Y	Y	Y
10 Ireland	N	Y	N	Y	Y	Y	Y
11 Nelson	Y	N	Y	Y	Y	Y	Y
12 *Lewis*	Y	N	Y	Y	N	Y	Y
13 *Mack*	Y	N	Y	Y	Y	Y	Y
14 Mica	Y	N	Y	Y	Y	Y	Y
15 *Shaw*	N	Y	N	Y	Y	Y	Y
16 Smith	Y	N	Y	Y	Y	Y	Y
17 Lehman	Y	N	Y	Y	Y	Y	Y
18 Pepper	Y	N	Y	Y	Y	Y	Y
19 Fascell	Y	N	Y	Y	Y	Y	Y
GEORGIA							
1 Thomas	N	Y	N	Y	Y	Y	Y
2 Hatcher	Y	N	Y	Y	Y	Y	Y
3 Ray	N	Y	N	Y	Y	Y	Y
4 Levitas	Y	N	Y	Y	Y	Y	N
5 Fowler	Y	N	Y	Y	Y	Y	Y
6 *Gingrich*	N	Y	N	Y	Y	Y	Y
7 Darden	Y	N	Y	Y	Y	Y	Y
8 Rowland	N	Y	N	Y	Y	Y	Y
9 Jenkins	?	?	?	?	Y	Y	Y
10 Barnard	N	Y	N	Y	Y	Y	Y
HAWAII							
1 Heftel	Y	N	Y	Y	?	Y	Y
2 Akaka	Y	N	Y	Y	Y	Y	Y
IDAHO							
1 *Craig*	N	Y	N	Y	N	?	N
2 *Hansen*	N	Y	N	Y	?	Y	N
ILLINOIS							
1 Hayes	Y	N	Y	N	Y	N	Y
2 Savage	Y	N	Y	N	Y	N	Y
3 Russo	N	N	Y	N	Y	N	Y
4 *O'Brien*	Y	N	Y	N	Y	N	Y
5 Lipinski	N	N	Y	N	Y	N	Y
6 *Hyde*	N	Y	N	Y	N	Y	Y
7 Collins	Y	N	Y	Y	Y	Y	Y
8 Rostenkowski	Y	N	Y	Y	Y	Y	Y
9 Yates	Y	N	Y	Y	Y	Y	Y
10 *Porter*	Y	N	Y	Y	Y	+	Y
11 Annunzio	Y	N	Y	Y	Y	Y	Y
12 *Crane, P.*	N	Y	N	Y	N	Y	N
13 *Erlenborn*	N	Y	N	Y	Y	Y	Y
14 *Corcoran*	N	Y	N	Y	Y	Y	Y
15 *Madigan*	N	Y	N	Y	Y	Y	Y
16 *Martin*	Y	N	Y	N	Y	N	Y
17 *Evans*	Y	N	Y	Y	Y	Y	Y
18 *Michel*	N	?	N	Y	Y	Y	Y
19 *Crane, D.*	N	Y	N	Y	Y	Y	N
20 Durbin	Y	N	Y	N	Y	Y	Y
21 Price	Y	Y	Y	Y	Y	Y	Y
22 Simon	Y	N	Y	Y	?	Y	Y
INDIANA							
1 Hall	Y	N	Y	Y	?	Y	Y
2 Sharp	Y	N	Y	Y	Y	Y	Y
3 *Hiler*	N	N	Y	N	Y	Y	Y
4 *Coats*	N	N	Y	N	Y	N	Y
5 *Hillis*	N	Y	N	Y	Y	Y	Y

ND - Northern Democrats   SD - Southern Democrats

	469	470	471	472	473	474	475
6 ***Burton***	N	Y	N	Y	Y	Y	N
7 ***Myers***	N	Y	N	Y	Y	Y	Y
8 McCloskey	Y	N	Y	Y	Y	Y	Y
9 Hamilton	Y	N	Y	Y	Y	Y	Y
10 Jacobs	Y	N	Y	Y	P	Y	N
IOWA							
1 ***Leach***	Y	N	Y	Y	Y	Y	Y
2 ***Tauke***	N	N	Y	Y	Y	Y	N
3 ***Evans***	Y	N	Y	Y	?	Y	Y
4 Smith	Y	N	Y	Y	Y	Y	Y
5 Harkin	Y	N	Y	Y	N	Y	Y
6 Bedell	N	N	Y	Y	Y	Y	N
KANSAS							
1 ***Roberts***	N	N	Y	Y	N	Y	Y
2 Slattery	Y	Y	Y	Y	Y	Y	Y
3 ***Winn***	N	Y	N	Y	Y	?	Y
4 Glickman	Y	N	Y	Y	Y	Y	Y
5 ***Whittaker***	N	N	Y	Y	N	Y	Y
KENTUCKY							
1 Hubbard	N	Y	N	Y	Y	Y	N
2 Natcher	Y	N	Y	Y	Y	Y	Y
3 Mazzoli	N	N	Y	Y	Y	Y	Y
4 ***Snyder***	N	N	N	Y	Y	Y	Y
5 ***Rogers***	N	N	N	Y	N	Y	Y
6 ***Hopkins***	Y	N	Y	Y	Y	Y	N
7 Perkins	Y	N	Y	Y	Y	Y	Y
LOUISIANA							
1 ***Livingston***	N	Y	N	Y	?	Y	N
2 Boggs	Y	N	Y	Y	Y	Y	Y
3 Tauzin	Y	Y	N	Y	Y	Y	Y
4 Roemer	N	Y	Y	Y	N	Y	Y
5 Huckaby	Y	Y	Y	Y	Y	Y	Y
6 ***Moore***	N	Y	N	Y	Y	Y	Y
7 Breaux	Y	Y	N	Y	P	Y	N
8 Long	Y	N	Y	Y	Y	Y	Y
MAINE							
1 ***McKernan***	Y	N	Y	Y	Y	Y	Y
2 ***Snowe***	Y	N	Y	Y	Y	Y	Y
MARYLAND							
1 Dyson	Y	Y	N	Y	Y	Y	Y
2 Long	Y	Y	N	Y	Y	Y	Y
3 Mikulski	Y	N	Y	Y	?	Y	Y
4 ***Holt***	Y	Y	N	Y	N	Y	N
5 Hoyer	Y	N	Y	Y	Y	Y	Y
6 Byron	Y	Y	N	Y	Y	Y	Y
7 Mitchell	Y	N	Y	Y	N	Y	Y
8 Barnes	Y	N	Y	Y	Y	Y	Y
MASSACHUSETTS							
1 ***Conte***	Y	N	Y	Y	Y	Y	Y
2 Boland	Y	N	Y	Y	Y	Y	Y
3 Early	Y	N	Y	Y	Y	Y	Y
4 Frank	Y	N	Y	Y	Y	Y	Y
5 Shannon	Y	N	Y	Y	Y	Y	Y
6 Mavroules	Y	N	Y	Y	Y	Y	Y
7 Markey	Y	N	Y	Y	Y	Y	Y
8 O'Neill	Y						
9 Moakley	Y	N	Y	Y	Y	Y	Y
10 Studds	Y	N	Y	Y	Y	Y	Y
11 Donnelly	Y	Y	N	Y	Y	Y	Y
MICHIGAN							
1 Conyers	Y	N	Y	Y	Y	Y	Y
2 ***Pursell***	Y	N	Y	?	Y	Y	N
3 Wolpe	Y	N	Y	Y	Y	Y	Y
4 ***Siljander***	N	Y	N	Y	?	Y	N
5 ***Sawyer***	?	?	?	?	?	?	?
6 Carr	Y	N	Y	Y	Y	Y	Y
7 Kildee	Y	N	Y	Y	Y	Y	Y
8 Traxler	Y	N	Y	Y	Y	Y	Y
9 ***Vander Jagt***	N	Y	Y	Y	Y	Y	Y
10 Albosta	Y	N	Y	Y	Y	Y	Y
11 ***Davis***	N	Y	N	Y	N	Y	Y
12 Bonior	Y	?	Y	Y	Y	Y	Y
13 Crockett	Y	N	Y	Y	Y	Y	Y
14 Hertel	Y	N	Y	Y	Y	Y	N
15 Ford	Y	N	Y	Y	?	Y	Y
16 Dingell	Y	N	Y	Y	Y	Y	Y
17 Levin	Y	N	Y	Y	Y	Y	Y
18 ***Broomfield***	N	Y	Y	Y	P	Y	Y
MINNESOTA							
1 Penny	Y	N	Y	Y	Y	Y	Y
2 ***Weber***	N	N	Y	Y	N	Y	N
3 ***Frenzel***	Y	N	Y	Y	N	Y	N
4 Vento	Y	N	Y	Y	Y	Y	N
5 Sabo	Y	N	Y	Y	N	Y	Y
6 Sikorski	Y	N	Y	Y	N	Y	Y
7 ***Stangeland***	N	Y	N	Y	Y	Y	Y
8 Oberstar	Y	N	Y	Y	P	Y	Y
MISSISSIPPI							
1 Whitten	Y	N	Y	Y	Y	Y	Y
2 ***Franklin***	N	Y	N	Y	Y	+	Y
3 Montgomery	N	Y	N	Y	Y	Y	Y
4 Dowdy	Y	Y	N	Y	Y	Y	Y
5 ***Lott***	N	Y	N	Y	Y	?	Y
MISSOURI							
1 Clay	Y	N	Y	Y	N	Y	Y
2 Young	N	?	N	Y	Y	Y	Y
3 Gephardt	Y	N	Y	Y	Y	Y	?
4 Skelton	N	Y	N	Y	Y	Y	Y
5 Wheat	Y	N	Y	Y	Y	Y	Y
6 ***Coleman***	N	Y	N	Y	Y	Y	Y
7 ***Taylor***	N	Y	N	Y	Y	Y	Y
8 ***Emerson***	N	Y	N	Y	N	Y	Y
9 Volkmer	Y	N	Y	Y	Y	Y	Y
MONTANA							
1 Williams	Y	N	Y	?	Y	Y	Y
2 ***Marlenee***	N	Y	N	Y	Y	Y	Y
NEBRASKA							
1 ***Bereuter***	Y	Y	N	Y	Y	Y	Y
2 ***Daub***	Y	N	Y	Y	N	Y	Y
3 ***Smith***	Y	Y	N	Y	Y	Y	Y
NEVADA							
1 Reid	N	N	Y	Y	Y	Y	Y
2 ***Vucanovich***	N	Y	N	Y	Y	Y	Y
NEW HAMPSHIRE							
1 D'Amours	Y	N	Y	Y	Y	Y	Y
2 ***Gregg***	Y	N	Y	Y	Y	Y	Y
NEW JERSEY							
1 Florio	Y	N	Y	Y	Y	Y	Y
2 Hughes	Y	N	N	Y	Y	Y	Y
3 Howard	Y	N	Y	Y	Y	Y	Y
4 ***Smith***	N	N	Y	Y	Y	Y	Y
5 ***Roukema***	Y	N	Y	Y	Y	Y	Y
6 Dwyer	Y	N	Y	Y	Y	Y	Y
7 ***Rinaldo***	Y	N	Y	Y	Y	Y	Y
8 Roe	Y	N	Y	Y	Y	Y	Y
9 Torricelli	Y	N	Y	Y	Y	Y	Y
10 Rodino	Y	N	Y	Y	Y	Y	Y
11 Minish	Y	N	Y	Y	Y	Y	Y
12 ***Courter***	Y	Y	N	Y	N	Y	Y
13 ***Forsythe***	N	N	Y	Y	N	Y	Y
14 Guarini	Y	N	Y	Y	N	Y	Y
NEW MEXICO							
1 ***Lujan***	Y	Y	N	Y	Y	Y	N
2 ***Skeen***	N	Y	N	Y	N	Y	Y
3 Richardson	Y	N	Y	Y	N	Y	Y
NEW YORK							
1 ***Carney***	N	N	Y	Y	Y	Y	Y
2 Downey	Y	N	Y	Y	Y	Y	Y
3 Mrazek	Y	N	Y	Y	?	Y	Y
4 ***Lent***	?	Y	N	Y	Y	Y	Y
5 ***McGrath***	N	N	Y	Y	Y	Y	Y
6 Addabbo	Y	N	Y	Y	Y	Y	Y
7 Ackerman	Y	N	Y	Y	?	Y	Y
8 Scheuer	Y	N	Y	Y	Y	Y	Y
9 Ferraro	Y	N	Y	Y	Y	Y	Y
10 Schumer	Y	N	Y	Y	Y	Y	Y
11 Towns	Y	N	Y	Y	Y	Y	Y
12 Owens	Y	N	Y	Y	Y	Y	Y
13 Solarz	Y	N	Y	Y	?	?	?
14 ***Molinari***	?	?	?	?	N	Y	Y
15 ***Green***	Y	N	Y	Y	Y	Y	Y
16 Rangel	Y	N	Y	Y	Y	Y	Y
17 Weiss	Y	N	Y	Y	Y	Y	Y
18 Garcia	#	N	Y	Y	Y	Y	Y
19 Biaggi	Y	N	Y	Y	Y	Y	Y
20 Ottinger	Y	N	Y	Y	P	Y	Y
21 ***Fish***	N	N	Y	Y	Y	Y	Y
22 ***Gilman***	Y	Y	N	Y	Y	Y	Y
23 Stratton	Y	Y	N	Y	Y	Y	Y
24 ***Solomon***	N	Y	N	Y	N	Y	Y
25 ***Boehlert***	Y	N	Y	Y	Y	Y	Y
26 ***Martin***	N	Y	N	Y	N	Y	Y
27 ***Wortley***	Y	N	Y	Y	Y	Y	Y
28 McHugh	Y	N	Y	Y	Y	Y	Y
29 ***Horton***	Y	N	Y	?	Y	Y	Y
30 ***Conable***	Y	Y	N	Y	Y	Y	N
31 ***Kemp***	N	Y	N	Y	Y	Y	Y
32 LaFalce	Y	N	Y	Y	Y	Y	Y
33 Nowak	N	N	Y	Y	Y	Y	Y
34 Lundine	Y	N	Y	Y	?	Y	Y
NORTH CAROLINA							
1 Jones	Y	N	Y	?	Y	Y	Y
2 Valentine	N	Y	N	Y	Y	Y	Y
3 Whitley	Y	Y	N	Y	Y	Y	Y
4 Andrews	Y	N	N	Y	Y	Y	Y
5 Neal	Y	N	Y	Y	Y	Y	N
6 Britt	Y	N	Y	Y	Y	Y	Y
7 Rose	Y	N	N	Y	Y	Y	Y
8 Hefner	Y	Y	N	Y	Y	Y	Y
9 ***Martin***	N	N	Y	Y	Y	Y	Y
10 ***Broyhill***	N	N	Y	Y	Y	Y	N
11 Clarke	Y	Y	N	Y	Y	Y	Y
NORTH DAKOTA							
AL Dorgan	Y	N	Y	Y	N	Y	N
OHIO							
1 Luken	N	N	Y	?	Y	Y	Y
2 ***Gradison***	Y	N	Y	Y	Y	Y	Y
3 Hall	Y	N	Y	Y	?	Y	Y
4 ***Oxley***	N	N	Y	Y	Y	Y	N
5 ***Latta***	N	Y	N	Y	N	Y	Y
6 ***McEwen***	N	Y	N	Y	Y	Y	Y
7 ***DeWine***	N	Y	N	Y	N	Y	Y
8 ***Kindness***	N	Y	N	Y	Y	Y	Y
9 Kaptur	Y	N	Y	Y	Y	Y	Y
10 ***Miller***	N	N	Y	Y	N	Y	Y
11 Eckart	Y	N	Y	Y	Y	Y	Y
12 ***Kasich***	N	Y	N	Y	N	Y	Y
13 Pease	Y	N	Y	Y	Y	Y	Y
14 Seiberling	Y	N	Y	?	?	Y	Y
15 ***Wylie***	N	N	N	Y	Y	Y	Y
16 ***Regula***	Y	N	Y	Y	Y	Y	Y
17 ***Williams***	Y	N	Y	Y	Y	Y	Y
18 Applegate	Y	N	Y	Y	?	Y	Y
19 Feighan	Y	N	Y	Y	Y	Y	Y
20 Oakar	Y	N	Y	Y	Y	Y	Y
21 Stokes	Y	N	Y	Y	Y	Y	Y
OKLAHOMA							
1 Jones	Y	Y	N	Y	Y	Y	Y
2 Synar	Y	N	Y	Y	Y	Y	Y
3 Watkins	Y	N	Y	Y	Y	Y	Y
4 McCurdy	Y	N	Y	Y	Y	Y	Y
5 ***Edwards***	N	N	Y	Y	N	Y	Y
6 English	Y	N	Y	Y	Y	Y	Y
OREGON							
1 AuCoin	Y	N	Y	Y	Y	Y	N
2 ***Smith, R.***	N	N	Y	Y	Y	Y	Y
3 Wyden	Y	N	Y	Y	Y	Y	Y
4 Weaver	Y	N	Y	Y	Y	Y	N
5 ***Smith, D.***	N	Y	N	Y	Y	Y	N
PENNSYLVANIA							
1 Foglietta	Y	N	Y	Y	Y	Y	Y
2 Gray	Y	N	Y	Y	N	Y	Y
3 Borski	Y	N	Y	Y	Y	Y	Y
4 Kolter	Y	N	Y	Y	Y	Y	Y
5 ***Schulze***	N	Y	N	Y	Y	Y	Y
6 Yatron	N	Y	Y	Y	Y	Y	Y
7 Edgar	Y	N	Y	Y	N	Y	N
8 Kostmayer	Y	N	Y	Y	Y	Y	Y
9 ***Shuster***	N	Y	N	Y	Y	Y	Y
10 ***McDade***	N	N	N	Y	Y	Y	Y
11 Harrison	Y	N	Y	Y	Y	Y	Y
12 Murtha	N	Y	N	Y	Y	Y	Y
13 ***Coughlin***	Y	N	Y	Y	N	Y	Y
14 Coyne	Y	N	Y	Y	Y	Y	Y
15 ***Ritter***	N	Y	N	Y	Y	Y	N
16 ***Walker***	N	N	Y	Y	N	Y	N
17 ***Gekas***	Y	N	Y	Y	N	Y	Y
18 Walgren	Y	N	Y	Y	Y	Y	Y
19 ***Goodling***	Y	N	Y	Y	P	Y	Y
20 Gaydos	N	Y	N	Y	Y	Y	Y
21 ***Ridge***	Y	Y	N	Y	Y	Y	Y
22 Murphy	Y	N	Y	Y	N	Y	N
23 ***Clinger***	Y	N	Y	Y	Y	Y	Y
RHODE ISLAND							
1 St Germain	N	N	Y	Y	P	Y	Y
2 ***Schneider***	Y	N	Y	Y	Y	Y	Y
SOUTH CAROLINA							
1 ***Hartnett***	N	Y	N	Y	N	Y	N
2 ***Spence***	N	Y	N	Y	Y	Y	Y
3 Derrick	Y	N	Y	Y	Y	Y	Y
4 ***Campbell***	N	Y	N	Y	Y	Y	Y
5 Spratt	Y	N	Y	Y	Y	Y	Y
6 Tallon	Y	N	Y	Y	Y	Y	Y
SOUTH DAKOTA							
AL Daschle	Y	N	Y	Y	N	Y	Y
TENNESSEE							
1 ***Quillen***	N	Y	N	Y	Y	Y	Y
2 ***Duncan***	N	Y	Y	Y	Y	Y	Y
3 Lloyd	N	Y	N	Y	Y	Y	Y
4 Cooper	N	Y	Y	Y	Y	Y	Y
5 Boner	Y	Y	N	Y	Y	Y	Y
6 Gore	Y	N	Y	Y	Y	Y	Y
7 ***Sundquist***	N	Y	N	Y	?	Y	Y
8 Jones	N	Y	N	Y	Y	Y	Y
9 Ford	Y	N	Y	Y	Y	Y	Y
TEXAS							
1 Hall, S.	N	Y	N	Y	Y	Y	Y
2 Wilson	Y	Y	N	Y	Y	Y	Y
3 ***Bartlett***	N	Y	N	Y	Y	Y	Y
4 Hall, R.	Y	Y	N	Y	Y	Y	Y
5 Bryant	Y	N	Y	Y	Y	Y	Y
6 ***Gramm***	N	Y	N	Y	Y	Y	Y
7 ***Archer***	N	Y	N	Y	Y	Y	Y
8 ***Fields***	N	Y	N	Y	N	Y	Y
9 Brooks	Y	Y	N	Y	Y	Y	Y
10 Pickle	Y	N	Y	Y	Y	Y	Y
11 Leath	N	Y	N	Y	Y	Y	Y
12 Wright	Y	Y	N	Y	Y	Y	Y
13 Hightower	X	Y	N	Y	Y	Y	Y
14 Patman	Y	Y	N	Y	Y	Y	N
15 de la Garza	Y	Y	N	Y	Y	Y	Y
16 Coleman	Y	Y	N	Y	Y	Y	Y
17 Stenholm	N	Y	N	Y	Y	Y	Y
18 Leland	Y	N	Y	Y	Y	Y	Y
19 Hance	#	?	?	?	?	?	?
20 Gonzalez	Y	N	Y	Y	Y	Y	Y
21 ***Loeffler***	N	Y	N	Y	N	Y	N
22 ***Paul***	?	?	?	?	Y	N	N
23 Kazen	N	Y	N	Y	Y	Y	Y
24 Frost	Y	N	Y	Y	Y	Y	Y
25 Andrews	Y	Y	N	Y	Y	Y	Y
26 Vandergriff	N	Y	N	Y	Y	Y	Y
27 Ortiz	Y	N	N	Y	Y	Y	Y
UTAH							
1 ***Hansen***	N	Y	N	Y	Y	Y	N
2 ***Marriott***	N	Y	N	Y	Y	Y	Y
3 ***Nielson***	N	Y	N	Y	Y	Y	N
VERMONT							
AL ***Jeffords***	Y	N	Y	Y	Y	Y	Y
VIRGINIA							
1 ***Bateman***	N	Y	N	Y	Y	Y	Y
2 ***Whitehurst***	Y	Y	N	Y	Y	Y	Y
3 ***Bliley***	N	Y	N	Y	Y	Y	Y
4 Sisisky	Y	Y	N	Y	Y	Y	Y
5 Daniel	N	Y	N	Y	N	Y	Y
6 Olin	Y	N	Y	Y	?	?	?
7 ***Robinson***	N	Y	N	Y	N	Y	Y
8 ***Parris***	Y	N	Y	Y	Y	Y	Y
9 Boucher	Y	N	?	Y	Y	Y	Y
10 ***Wolf***	N	N	N	Y	Y	Y	?
WASHINGTON							
1 ***Pritchard***	Y	N	Y	Y	?	?	?
2 Swift	Y	N	Y	Y	Y	Y	Y
3 Bonker	Y	N	Y	Y	?	Y	Y
4 ***Morrison***	Y	Y	N	Y	Y	Y	Y
5 Foley	Y	?	Y	Y	Y	Y	Y
6 Dicks	Y	N	Y	Y	Y	Y	Y
7 Lowry	Y	N	Y	Y	Y	Y	N
8 ***Chandler***	Y	Y	N	Y	Y	Y	Y
WEST VIRGINIA							
1 Mollohan	N	Y	N	Y	Y	Y	Y
2 Staggers	Y	N	Y	Y	Y	Y	Y
3 Wise	Y	N	Y	Y	Y	Y	Y
4 Rahall	Y	N	Y	Y	Y	Y	Y
WISCONSIN							
1 Aspin	Y	N	Y	Y	Y	Y	Y
2 Kastenmeier	Y	N	Y	Y	Y	Y	Y
3 ***Gunderson***	Y	N	Y	Y	Y	Y	Y
4 Zablocki	Y	N	Y	Y	Y	Y	Y
5 Moody	Y	N	?	Y	Y	Y	Y
6 ***Petri***	Y	Y	N	Y	N	Y	Y
7 Obey	Y	N	Y	Y	P	Y	Y
8 ***Roth***	N	Y	N	Y	Y	Y	Y
9 ***Sensenbrenner***	N	N	Y	Y	Y	Y	N
WYOMING							
AL ***Cheney***	N	Y	N	Y	N	Y	N

Southern states - Ala., Ark., Fla., Ga., Ky., La., Miss., N.C., Okla., S.C., Tenn., Texas, Va.

476. HR 4325. Child Support Enforcement. Rostenkowski, D-Ill., motion to suspend the rules and pass the bill to amend the Social Security Act to require that states institute mandatory procedures for withholding payments from the wages of those in arrears in child support and to make all child support recipients eligible for state assistance in collecting payments. Motion agreed to 422-0: R 161-0; D 261-0 (ND 174-0, SD 87-0), Nov. 16, 1983. A two-thirds majority of those present and voting (282 in this case) is required for passage under suspension of the rules.

477. HR 1264. Select Commission on Voluntary Service Opportunities. Murphy, D-Pa., motion to suspend the rules and pass the bill to establish a commission to assess voluntary service opportunities. Motion rejected 179-245: R 17-145; D 162-100 (ND 127-47, SD 35-53), Nov. 16, 1983. A two-thirds majority of those present and voting (283 in this case) is required for passage under suspension of the rules.

478. H J Res 190. Guidelines for Equal Opportunity in Education. Simon, D-Ill., motion to suspend the rules and pass the joint resolution expressing the sense of Congress that Title IX of the Education Amendments of 1972 prohibiting discrimination by educational institutions on the basis of sex, should be broadly interpreted. Motion agreed to 414-8: R 153-8; D 261-0 (ND 174-0, SD 87-0), Nov. 16, 1983. A two-thirds majority of those present and voting (282 in this case) is required for passage under suspension of the rules.

479. HR 3922. Postal Savings System Statute of Limitations. Sam B. Hall Jr., D-Texas, motion to suspend the rules and pass the bill to establish a one-year limitation on the filing of claims for unpaid accounts formerly maintained in the Postal Savings System. Motion agreed to 410-11: R 159-1; D 251-10 (ND 164-9, SD 87-1), Nov. 16, 1983. A two-thirds majority of those present and voting (281 in this case) is required for passage under suspension of the rules.

480. HR 3622. Credit Card Protection. Annunzio, D-Ill., motion to suspend the rules and pass the bill to restrict disclosures of credit card numbers, make it a federal crime to possess more than five fraudulent credit cards or other payment devices, and make it a federal crime to steal $1,000 or more in a single year through the fraudulent use of credit cards or other payment devices. Motion agreed to 422-0: R 162-0; D 260-0 (ND 173-0, SD 87-0), Nov. 16, 1983. A two-thirds majority of those present and voting (282 in this case) is required for passage under suspension of the rules.

481. HR 4278. Extending Ban on Credit Card Surcharges. Annunzio, D-Ill., motion to suspend the rules and pass the bill to extend to July 31, 1984, from Feb. 27, 1984, the ban on imposing surcharges on purchases made with credit cards. Motion agreed to 349-73: R 101-61; D 248-12 (ND 172-1, SD 76-11), Nov. 16, 1983. A two-thirds majority of those present and voting (282 in this case) is required for passage under suspension of the rules.

482. HR 3960. North Carolina Wilderness Act. Seiberling, D-Ohio, motion to suspend the rules and pass the bill to designate 68,750 acres of national forest land in North Carolina as federally protected wilderness and to set aside an additional 25,816 acres for further wilderness study. Motion agreed to 398-21: R 141-20; D 257-1 (ND 171-0, SD 86-1), Nov. 16, 1983. A two-thirds majority of those present and voting (280 in this case) is required for passage under suspension of the rules.

483. HR 3578. Wisconsin Wilderness Act. Seiberling, D-Ohio, motion to suspend the rules and pass the bill to designate 24,339 acres of national forest land in Wisconsin as federally protected wilderness. Motion agreed to 402-17: R 145-16; D 257-1 (ND 171-0, SD 86-1), Nov. 16, 1983. A two-thirds majority of those present and voting (280 in this case) is required for passage under suspension of the rules.

KEY

Y Voted for (yea).
\# Paired for.
\+ Announced for.
N Voted against (nay).
X Paired against.
\- Announced against.
P Voted "present".
C Voted "present" to avoid possible conflict of interest.
? Did not vote or otherwise make a position known.

Democrats *Republicans*

	476	477	478	479	480	481	482	483
ALABAMA								
1 *Edwards*	Y	N	Y	Y	Y	N	Y	Y
2 *Dickinson*	Y	N	Y	Y	Y	Y	N	Y
3 Nichols	Y	N	Y	Y	Y	Y	Y	Y
4 Bevill	Y	N	Y	Y	Y	Y	Y	Y
5 Flippo	Y	N	Y	Y	Y	Y	Y	Y
6 Erdreich	Y	N	Y	Y	Y	Y	Y	Y
7 Shelby	Y	N	Y	Y	Y	N	Y	Y
ALASKA								
AL *Young*	Y	N	Y	Y	Y	Y	Y	Y
ARIZONA								
1 *McCain*	Y	N	Y	Y	Y	N	Y	Y
2 Udall	Y	Y	Y	Y	Y	Y	Y	Y
3 *Stump*	Y	N	Y	Y	Y	N	N	N
4 *Rudd*	Y	N	Y	Y	Y	N	Y	Y
5 McNulty	Y	Y	Y	Y	Y	Y	Y	Y
ARKANSAS								
1 Alexander	Y	Y	Y	Y	?	?	?	?
2 *Bethune*	Y	N	Y	Y	Y	Y	Y	Y
3 *Hammerschmidt*	Y	N	Y	Y	Y	N	Y	N
4 Anthony	Y	Y	Y	Y	Y	Y	Y	Y
CALIFORNIA								
1 Bosco	Y	Y	Y	Y	Y	Y	Y	Y
2 *Chappie*	Y	N	Y	Y	Y	Y	Y	Y
3 Matsui	Y	Y	Y	Y	Y	Y	Y	Y
4 Fazio	Y	Y	Y	Y	Y	Y	Y	Y
5 Burton	Y	Y	Y	Y	Y	Y	Y	Y
6 Boxer	Y	Y	Y	Y	Y	Y	Y	Y
7 Miller	Y	Y	Y	Y	Y	Y	Y	Y
8 Dellums	Y	Y	Y	Y	Y	Y	Y	Y
9 Stark	Y	N	Y	Y	Y	Y	Y	Y
10 Edwards	Y	Y	Y	Y	Y	Y	Y	Y
11 Lantos	Y	Y	Y	Y	Y	Y	Y	Y
12 *Zschau*	Y	Y	Y	Y	Y	N	Y	Y
13 Mineta	Y	Y	Y	Y	Y	Y	Y	Y
14 *Shumway*	?	?	?	?	?	?	?	?
15 Coelho	Y	Y	Y	Y	Y	Y	Y	Y
16 Panetta	Y	Y	Y	Y	Y	Y	Y	Y
17 *Pashayan*	Y	N	Y	Y	Y	Y	Y	Y
18 Lehman	Y	Y	Y	Y	Y	Y	Y	Y
19 *Lagomarsino*	Y	N	Y	Y	Y	Y	Y	Y
20 *Thomas*	Y	N	Y	Y	Y	N	Y	Y
21 *Fiedler*	Y	N	Y	Y	Y	N	Y	Y
22 *Moorhead*	Y	N	Y	Y	Y	N	Y	Y
23 Beilenson	Y	Y	Y	Y	Y	Y	Y	Y
24 Waxman	Y	Y	Y	Y	Y	Y	Y	Y
25 Roybal	Y	Y	Y	Y	Y	Y	Y	Y
26 Berman	Y	Y	Y	Y	Y	Y	Y	Y
27 Levine	Y	Y	Y	Y	Y	Y	Y	Y
28 Dixon	Y	Y	Y	Y	Y	Y	Y	Y
29 Hawkins	Y	Y	Y	?	?	?	?	?
30 Martinez	?	?	?	?	?	?	?	?
31 Dymally	Y	Y	Y	Y	Y	Y	Y	Y
32 Anderson	Y	Y	Y	Y	Y	Y	Y	Y
33 *Dreier*	Y	N	Y	Y	Y	N	N	N
34 Torres	Y	Y	Y	Y	Y	Y	Y	Y
35 *Lewis*	?	?	?	?	?	?	?	?
36 Brown	Y	Y	Y	Y	Y	Y	Y	Y
37 *McCandless*	Y	N	Y	Y	Y	N	Y	Y
38 Patterson	Y	Y	Y	Y	Y	Y	Y	Y
39 *Dannemeyer*	Y	N	N	Y	N	N	N	N
40 *Badham*	Y	N	Y	Y	Y	N	N	N
41 *Lowery*	Y	N	Y	Y	Y	Y	Y	Y
42 *Lungren*	Y	N	Y	Y	Y	N	Y	Y

	476	477	478	479	480	481	482	483
43 *Packard*	Y	N	Y	Y	Y	N	Y	Y
44 Bates	Y	Y	Y	Y	Y	Y	Y	Y
45 *Hunter*	Y	N	Y	Y	Y	N	Y	Y
COLORADO								
1 Schroeder	Y	N	Y	Y	Y	Y	Y	Y
2 Wirth	Y	Y	Y	Y	Y	Y	Y	Y
3 Kogovsek	Y	Y	Y	Y	Y	Y	Y	Y
4 *Brown*	Y	N	Y	Y	Y	N	Y	Y
5 *Kramer*	Y	N	Y	Y	Y	N	Y	Y
6 *Schaefer*	Y	N	Y	Y	Y	N	Y	Y
CONNECTICUT								
1 Kennelly	Y	Y	Y	Y	Y	Y	Y	Y
2 Gejdenson	Y	Y	Y	Y	Y	Y	Y	Y
3 Morrison	Y	Y	Y	Y	Y	Y	Y	Y
4 *McKinney*	Y	N	Y	Y	Y	Y	Y	Y
5 Ratchford	Y	Y	Y	Y	Y	Y	Y	Y
6 *Johnson*	Y	N	Y	Y	Y	Y	Y	Y
DELAWARE								
AL *Carper*	Y	N	Y	Y	Y	Y	Y	Y
FLORIDA								
1 Hutto	Y	N	Y	Y	Y	Y	Y	Y
2 Fuqua	Y	N	Y	Y	Y	Y	Y	Y
3 Bennett	Y	N	Y	Y	Y	Y	Y	Y
4 Chappell	Y	N	Y	Y	Y	Y	Y	Y
5 *McCollum*	Y	N	Y	Y	Y	N	Y	Y
6 MacKay	?	N	Y	Y	Y	Y	Y	Y
7 Gibbons	Y	N	Y	Y	Y	Y	Y	Y
8 *Young*	Y	N	Y	Y	Y	N	Y	Y
9 *Bilirakis*	Y	N	Y	Y	Y	N	Y	Y
10 Ireland	Y	N	Y	Y	Y	N	Y	Y
11 Nelson	Y	Y	Y	Y	Y	Y	Y	Y
12 *Lewis*	Y	N	Y	Y	Y	Y	Y	Y
13 *Mack*	Y	N	Y	Y	Y	N	Y	Y
14 Mica	Y	Y	Y	Y	Y	Y	Y	Y
15 *Shaw*	Y	N	Y	Y	Y	Y	Y	Y
16 Smith	Y	Y	Y	Y	Y	Y	Y	Y
17 Lehman	Y	Y	Y	Y	Y	Y	Y	Y
18 Pepper	Y	N	Y	Y	Y	Y	Y	Y
19 Fascell	Y	Y	Y	Y	Y	Y	Y	Y
GEORGIA								
1 Thomas	Y	N	Y	Y	Y	Y	Y	Y
2 Hatcher	Y	Y	Y	Y	Y	Y	Y	Y
3 Ray	Y	N	?	Y	Y	Y	Y	Y
4 Levitas	Y	Y	Y	Y	Y	Y	Y	Y
5 Fowler	Y	Y	Y	Y	Y	Y	Y	Y
6 *Gingrich*	Y	N	Y	Y	Y	N	Y	Y
7 Darden	Y	N	Y	Y	Y	Y	Y	Y
8 Rowland	Y	N	Y	Y	Y	Y	Y	Y
9 Jenkins	Y	N	Y	Y	Y	Y	Y	Y
10 Barnard	Y	N	Y	Y	Y	N	Y	Y
HAWAII								
1 Heftel	Y	Y	Y	N	Y	Y	Y	Y
2 Akaka	Y	N	Y	Y	Y	Y	Y	Y
IDAHO								
1 *Craig*	Y	N	Y	Y	Y	N	N	N
2 *Hansen*	Y	N	N	Y	Y	N	N	N
ILLINOIS								
1 Hayes	Y	Y	Y	Y	Y	Y	Y	Y
2 Savage	Y	Y	Y	Y	Y	Y	Y	Y
3 Russo	Y	N	Y	Y	Y	Y	Y	Y
4 *O'Brien*	?	Y	Y	Y	Y	Y	Y	Y
5 Lipinski	Y	Y	Y	Y	Y	Y	Y	Y
6 *Hyde*	Y	N	Y	Y	Y	Y	Y	Y
7 Collins	Y	Y	Y	Y	Y	Y	Y	Y
8 Rostenkowski	Y	Y	Y	Y	Y	Y	Y	Y
9 Yates	Y	Y	Y	Y	Y	Y	Y	Y
10 *Porter*	Y	N	Y	Y	Y	N	Y	Y
11 Annunzio	Y	Y	Y	Y	Y	Y	Y	Y
12 *Crane, P.*	Y	N	N	N	Y	N	N	N
13 *Erlenborn*	Y	N	N	Y	Y	N	Y	Y
14 *Corcoran*	?	?	?	?	?	?	?	?
15 *Madigan*	Y	N	Y	Y	Y	N	Y	Y
16 *Martin*	Y	N	Y	Y	Y	N	Y	Y
17 Evans	Y	Y	Y	Y	Y	Y	Y	Y
18 *Michel*	Y	N	Y	Y	Y	N	Y	Y
19 *Crane, D.*	Y	N	Y	Y	Y	N	N	N
20 Durbin	Y	Y	Y	Y	Y	Y	Y	Y
21 Price	Y	Y	Y	Y	Y	Y	Y	Y
22 Simon	Y	Y	Y	Y	Y	Y	Y	Y
INDIANA								
1 Hall	Y	Y	Y	Y	Y	Y	Y	Y
2 Sharp	Y	N	Y	Y	Y	Y	Y	Y
3 *Hiler*	Y	N	Y	Y	Y	N	Y	Y
4 *Coats*	Y	N	Y	Y	Y	Y	Y	Y
5 *Hillis*	Y	N	Y	Y	Y	N	Y	Y

ND - Northern Democrats SD - Southern Democrats

	476	477	478	479	480	481	482	483
6 ***Burton***	Y	N	Y	Y	Y	N	N	Y
7 ***Myers***	Y	N	Y	Y	Y	N	N	Y
8 McCloskey	Y	Y	Y	Y	Y	Y	Y	Y
9 Hamilton	Y	N	Y	Y	Y	Y	Y	Y
10 Jacobs	Y	N	Y	Y	Y	Y	Y	Y
IOWA								
1 ***Leach***	Y	Y	Y	Y	Y	Y	Y	Y
2 ***Tauke***	Y	N	Y	Y	Y	Y	Y	Y
3 ***Evans***	Y	Y	Y	Y	Y	Y	Y	Y
4 Smith	Y	Y	Y	Y	Y	Y	Y	Y
5 Harkin	Y	Y	Y	Y	Y	Y	Y	Y
6 Bedell	Y	Y	Y	Y	Y	Y	Y	Y
KANSAS								
1 ***Roberts***	Y	N	Y	Y	Y	Y	Y	Y
2 Slattery	Y	N	Y	Y	Y	Y	Y	Y
3 ***Winn***	Y	N	Y	Y	Y	Y	Y	Y
4 Glickman	Y	N	Y	Y	Y	Y	Y	Y
5 ***Whittaker***	Y	N	Y	Y	Y	Y	Y	Y
KENTUCKY								
1 Hubbard	Y	N	Y	Y	Y	Y	Y	Y
2 Natcher	Y	N	Y	Y	Y	Y	Y	Y
3 Mazzoli	Y	N	Y	Y	Y	Y	Y	Y
4 ***Snyder***	Y	N	Y	Y	Y	Y	Y	Y
5 ***Rogers***	Y	N	Y	Y	Y	Y	Y	Y
6 ***Hopkins***	Y	N	Y	Y	Y	N	N	Y
7 Perkins	Y	Y	Y	Y	Y	Y	Y	Y
LOUISIANA								
1 ***Livingston***	Y	N	Y	Y	Y	N	Y	Y
2 Boggs	Y	Y	Y	Y	Y	Y	Y	Y
3 Tauzin	Y	N	Y	Y	Y	Y	Y	Y
4 Roemer	Y	N	Y	Y	Y	N	Y	Y
5 Huckaby	Y	N	Y	Y	Y	Y	Y	Y
6 ***Moore***	Y	N	Y	Y	Y	Y	Y	Y
7 Breaux	Y	N	Y	Y	Y	Y	Y	Y
8 Long	Y	Y	Y	Y	Y	Y	Y	Y
MAINE								
1 ***McKernan***	Y	N	Y	Y	Y	Y	Y	Y
2 ***Snowe***	Y	N	Y	Y	Y	Y	Y	Y
MARYLAND								
1 Dyson	Y	N	Y	Y	Y	Y	Y	Y
2 Long	Y	Y	Y	Y	Y	Y	Y	Y
3 Mikulski	Y	N	Y	Y	Y	Y	Y	Y
4 ***Holt***	Y	N	Y	Y	Y	N	Y	Y
5 Hoyer	Y	Y	Y	Y	Y	Y	Y	Y
6 Byron	Y	Y	Y	Y	Y	Y	Y	Y
7 Mitchell	Y	N	Y	Y	Y	Y	Y	Y
8 Barnes	Y	Y	Y	Y	Y	Y	Y	Y
MASSACHUSETTS								
1 ***Conte***	Y	Y	Y	Y	Y	Y	Y	Y
2 Boland	Y	N	Y	Y	Y	Y	Y	Y
3 Early	Y	N	Y	Y	Y	Y	Y	Y
4 Frank	Y	Y	Y	Y	Y	N	?	?
5 Shannon	Y	N	Y	Y	Y	Y	Y	Y
6 Mavroules	Y	Y	Y	Y	Y	Y	Y	Y
7 Markey	Y	Y	Y	Y	Y	Y	Y	Y
8 O'Neill								
9 Moakley	Y	Y	Y	Y	Y	Y	Y	Y
10 Studds	Y	Y	Y	Y	Y	Y	Y	Y
11 Donnelly	Y	Y	Y	Y	Y	Y	Y	Y
MICHIGAN								
1 Conyers	Y	Y	Y	Y	Y	Y	Y	Y
2 ***Pursell***	Y	N	Y	Y	Y	Y	Y	Y
3 Wolpe	Y	Y	Y	Y	Y	Y	Y	Y
4 ***Siljander***	Y	N	Y	Y	Y	Y	Y	Y
5 ***Sawyer***	?	?	?	?	?	?	?	?
6 Carr	Y	N	Y	Y	Y	Y	Y	Y
7 Kildee	Y	Y	Y	N	Y	Y	Y	Y
8 Traxler	Y	Y	Y	Y	Y	Y	Y	Y
9 ***Vander Jagt***	Y	N	Y	Y	Y	Y	Y	Y
10 Albosta	Y	N	Y	Y	Y	Y	Y	Y
11 ***Davis***	Y	Y	Y	Y	Y	Y	N	N
12 Bonior	Y	Y	Y	Y	Y	Y	Y	Y
13 Crockett	Y	Y	Y	Y	Y	Y	Y	Y
14 Hertel	Y	Y	Y	Y	Y	Y	Y	Y
15 Ford	Y	Y	Y	Y	Y	Y	Y	Y
16 Dingell	Y	N	Y	Y	Y	Y	Y	Y
17 Levin	Y	Y	Y	Y	Y	Y	Y	Y
18 ***Broomfield***	Y	N	Y	Y	Y	Y	Y	Y
MINNESOTA								
1 Penny	Y	Y	Y	Y	Y	Y	Y	Y
2 ***Weber***	Y	N	Y	Y	Y	Y	Y	Y
3 ***Frenzel***	Y	N	Y	Y	Y	N	Y	Y
4 Vento	Y	Y	Y	N	Y	Y	Y	Y
5 Sabo	Y	Y	Y	Y	Y	Y	Y	Y
6 Sikorski	Y	Y	Y	Y	Y	Y	Y	Y
7 ***Stangeland***	Y	N	Y	Y	Y	Y	Y	Y
8 Oberstar	Y	N	Y	Y	Y	Y	Y	Y
MISSISSIPPI								
1 Whitten	Y	N	Y	Y	Y	Y	Y	Y
2 ***Franklin***	Y	N	Y	Y	Y	N	Y	Y
3 Montgomery	Y	N	Y	Y	Y	Y	Y	Y
4 Dowdy	?	?	?	?	?	?	?	?
5 ***Lott***	Y	N	Y	Y	Y	N	Y	Y
MISSOURI								
1 Clay	Y	Y	Y	Y	Y	Y	Y	Y
2 Young	Y	N	Y	Y	Y	Y	Y	Y
3 Gephardt	Y	N	Y	Y	Y	Y	Y	Y
4 Skelton	Y	N	Y	Y	Y	Y	Y	Y
5 Wheat	Y	Y	Y	Y	Y	Y	Y	Y
6 ***Coleman***	Y	N	Y	Y	Y	Y	Y	Y
7 ***Taylor***	Y	N	Y	Y	Y	Y	Y	Y
8 ***Emerson***	Y	N	Y	Y	Y	Y	Y	Y
9 Volkmer	Y	N	Y	Y	Y	Y	Y	Y
MONTANA								
1 Williams	Y	N	Y	N	Y	Y	Y	Y
2 ***Marlenee***	Y	N	Y	Y	Y	Y	Y	Y
NEBRASKA								
1 ***Bereuter***	Y	Y	Y	Y	Y	Y	Y	Y
2 ***Daub***	Y	N	Y	Y	Y	Y	Y	Y
3 ***Smith***	Y	N	Y	Y	Y	Y	Y	Y
NEVADA								
1 Reid	Y	Y	Y	Y	Y	Y	Y	Y
2 ***Vucanovich***	Y	N	Y	Y	Y	N	Y	Y
NEW HAMPSHIRE								
1 D'Amours	Y	N	Y	Y	Y	Y	Y	Y
2 ***Gregg***	Y	N	Y	?	Y	Y	Y	Y
NEW JERSEY								
1 Florio	Y	N	Y	Y	Y	Y	Y	Y
2 Hughes	Y	Y	Y	Y	Y	Y	Y	Y
3 Howard	Y	Y	Y	Y	Y	Y	Y	Y
4 ***Smith***	Y	N	Y	Y	Y	Y	Y	Y
5 ***Roukema***	Y	N	Y	Y	Y	Y	Y	Y
6 Dwyer	Y	Y	Y	Y	Y	Y	Y	Y
7 ***Rinaldo***	Y	N	Y	Y	Y	Y	Y	Y
8 Roe	Y	Y	Y	Y	Y	Y	Y	Y
9 Torricelli	Y	Y	Y	Y	Y	Y	Y	Y
10 Rodino	Y	Y	Y	Y	Y	Y	Y	Y
11 Minish	Y	N	Y	Y	Y	Y	Y	Y
12 ***Courter***	Y	N	Y	Y	Y	N	Y	Y
13 ***Forsythe***	Y	N	Y	Y	Y	Y	Y	Y
14 Guarini	Y	Y	Y	Y	Y	Y	Y	Y
NEW MEXICO								
1 ***Lujan***	Y	N	Y	Y	Y	N	Y	Y
2 ***Skeen***	Y	N	Y	Y	Y	Y	Y	Y
3 Richardson	Y	Y	Y	Y	Y	Y	Y	Y
NEW YORK								
1 ***Carney***	Y	N	Y	Y	Y	Y	Y	Y
2 Downey	Y	Y	Y	Y	Y	Y	Y	Y
3 Mrazek	Y	N	Y	Y	Y	Y	Y	Y
4 ***Lent***	Y	N	Y	Y	Y	Y	Y	Y
5 ***McGrath***	Y	N	Y	Y	Y	Y	Y	Y
6 Addabbo	Y	Y	Y	Y	Y	Y	Y	Y
7 Ackerman	Y	Y	Y	Y	Y	Y	?	?
8 Scheuer	Y	N	Y	Y	Y	Y	Y	Y
9 Ferraro	Y	Y	Y	Y	Y	Y	Y	Y
10 Schumer	Y	Y	Y	Y	Y	Y	Y	Y
11 Towns	Y	Y	Y	Y	Y	Y	Y	Y
12 Owens	Y	Y	Y	Y	Y	Y	Y	Y
13 Solarz	?	?	?	?	?	?	?	?
14 ***Molinari***	Y	N	Y	Y	Y	Y	Y	Y
15 ***Green***	Y	N	Y	Y	Y	Y	Y	Y
16 Rangel	?	?	?	?	?	?	?	?
17 Weiss	Y	Y	Y	Y	Y	Y	Y	Y
18 Garcia	Y	Y	Y	Y	Y	Y	Y	Y
19 Biaggi	Y	Y	Y	Y	Y	Y	Y	Y
20 Ottinger	Y	Y	Y	Y	Y	Y	Y	Y
21 ***Fish***	Y	Y	Y	Y	Y	Y	Y	Y
22 ***Gilman***	Y	Y	Y	Y	Y	Y	Y	Y
23 Stratton	Y	N	Y	Y	Y	Y	Y	Y
24 ***Solomon***	Y	N	Y	Y	Y	N	Y	Y
25 ***Boehlert***	Y	Y	Y	Y	Y	Y	Y	Y
26 ***Martin***	Y	N	Y	Y	Y	Y	Y	Y
27 ***Wortley***	Y	N	Y	Y	Y	Y	Y	Y
28 McHugh	Y	Y	Y	Y	Y	Y	Y	Y
29 ***Horton***	Y	N	Y	Y	Y	Y	Y	Y
30 ***Conable***	Y	N	?	Y	Y	N	Y	Y
31 ***Kemp***	Y	N	Y	Y	Y	Y	?	?
32 LaFalce	Y	Y	Y	Y	Y	Y	Y	Y
33 Nowak	Y	Y	Y	Y	Y	Y	Y	Y
34 Lundine	Y	Y	Y	Y	Y	Y	Y	Y
NORTH CAROLINA								
1 Jones	Y	N	Y	Y	Y	Y	Y	Y
2 Valentine	Y	N	Y	Y	Y	Y	Y	Y
3 Whitley	Y	N	Y	Y	Y	Y	Y	Y
4 Andrews	Y	N	Y	Y	Y	Y	Y	Y
5 Neal	Y	Y	Y	Y	Y	Y	Y	Y
6 Britt	Y	Y	Y	Y	Y	Y	Y	Y
7 Rose	Y	Y	Y	Y	Y	Y	Y	Y
8 Hefner	Y	Y	Y	Y	Y	Y	Y	Y
9 ***Martin***	Y	N	Y	Y	Y	N	Y	Y
10 ***Broyhill***	Y	N	Y	Y	Y	N	Y	Y
11 Clarke	Y	Y	Y	Y	Y	Y	Y	Y
NORTH DAKOTA								
AL Dorgan	Y	N	Y	Y	Y	Y	Y	Y
OHIO								
1 Luken	Y	Y	Y	Y	Y	Y	Y	Y
2 ***Gradison***	Y	Y	Y	Y	Y	Y	Y	Y
3 Hall	Y	Y	Y	Y	Y	Y	Y	Y
4 ***Oxley***	Y	N	Y	Y	Y	N	Y	Y
5 ***Latta***	Y	N	Y	Y	Y	Y	N	Y
6 ***McEwen***	Y	N	Y	Y	Y	Y	Y	Y
7 ***DeWine***	Y	N	Y	Y	Y	N	Y	Y
8 ***Kindness***	Y	N	Y	Y	Y	N	Y	Y
9 Kaptur	Y	Y	Y	Y	Y	Y	Y	Y
10 ***Miller***	Y	N	Y	Y	Y	Y	Y	Y
11 Eckart	Y	N	Y	Y	Y	Y	Y	Y
12 ***Kasich***	Y	N	Y	Y	Y	Y	Y	Y
13 Pease	Y	Y	Y	Y	Y	Y	Y	Y
14 Seiberling	Y	Y	Y	Y	Y	Y	Y	Y
15 ***Wylie***	Y	N	Y	Y	Y	Y	Y	Y
16 ***Regula***	Y	N	Y	Y	Y	Y	Y	Y
17 ***Williams***	Y	Y	Y	Y	Y	Y	Y	Y
18 Applegate	Y	N	Y	N	Y	Y	Y	Y
19 Feighan	Y	Y	Y	Y	Y	Y	Y	Y
20 Oakar	Y	Y	Y	Y	Y	Y	Y	Y
21 Stokes	Y	Y	Y	Y	Y	Y	Y	Y
OKLAHOMA								
1 Jones	Y	N	Y	Y	Y	Y	Y	Y
2 Synar	Y	N	Y	Y	Y	Y	Y	Y
3 Watkins	Y	N	Y	Y	Y	Y	Y	Y
4 McCurdy	Y	N	Y	Y	Y	Y	Y	Y
5 ***Edwards***	Y	N	Y	Y	Y	Y	Y	Y
6 English	Y	N	Y	Y	Y	Y	Y	Y
OREGON								
1 AuCoin	Y	N	Y	Y	Y	Y	Y	Y
2 ***Smith, R.***	Y	N	Y	Y	Y	Y	Y	Y
3 Wyden	Y	N	Y	Y	Y	Y	Y	Y
4 Weaver	Y	N	Y	Y	Y	Y	Y	Y
5 ***Smith, D.***	Y	N	Y	Y	Y	N	N	N
PENNSYLVANIA								
1 Foglietta	Y	Y	Y	Y	Y	Y	Y	Y
2 Gray	Y	Y	Y	Y	Y	Y	Y	Y
3 Borski	Y	Y	Y	Y	Y	Y	Y	Y
4 Kolter	Y	N	Y	N	Y	Y	Y	Y
5 ***Schulze***	Y	N	Y	N	Y	Y	Y	Y
6 Yatron	Y	N	Y	Y	Y	Y	Y	Y
7 Edgar	Y	Y	Y	Y	Y	Y	Y	Y
8 Kostmayer	Y	Y	Y	Y	Y	Y	Y	Y
9 ***Shuster***	Y	N	Y	Y	Y	N	Y	Y
10 ***McDade***	Y	N	Y	Y	Y	Y	Y	Y
11 Harrison	Y	Y	Y	Y	Y	Y	Y	Y
12 Murtha	Y	N	Y	Y	Y	Y	Y	Y
13 ***Coughlin***	Y	N	Y	Y	Y	N	Y	Y
14 Coyne	Y	Y	Y	Y	Y	Y	Y	Y
15 ***Ritter***	Y	N	Y	Y	Y	Y	Y	Y
16 ***Walker***	Y	N	Y	Y	Y	N	Y	Y
17 ***Gekas***	Y	N	Y	Y	Y	Y	Y	Y
18 Walgren	Y	Y	Y	Y	Y	Y	Y	Y
19 ***Goodling***	Y	N	Y	Y	Y	Y	Y	Y
20 Gaydos	Y	N	Y	N	Y	Y	Y	Y
21 ***Ridge***	Y	N	N	?	Y	Y	Y	Y
22 Murphy	Y	Y	Y	N	Y	Y	Y	Y
23 ***Clinger***	Y	N	Y	Y	Y	Y	Y	Y
RHODE ISLAND								
1 St Germain	Y	Y	Y	Y	Y	Y	Y	Y
2 ***Schneider***	Y	N	Y	Y	Y	Y	Y	Y
SOUTH CAROLINA								
1 ***Hartnett***	Y	N	Y	Y	Y	N	Y	Y
2 ***Spence***	Y	N	Y	Y	Y	Y	Y	Y
3 Derrick	Y	Y	Y	Y	Y	Y	Y	Y
4 ***Campbell***	Y	N	Y	Y	Y	N	Y	Y
5 Spratt	Y	Y	Y	Y	Y	N	Y	Y
6 Tallon	Y	Y	Y	Y	Y	Y	Y	Y
SOUTH DAKOTA								
AL Daschle	Y	N	Y	Y	Y	Y	Y	Y
TENNESSEE								
1 ***Quillen***	Y	N	Y	Y	Y	N	Y	Y
2 ***Duncan***	Y	N	Y	Y	Y	Y	Y	Y
3 Lloyd	Y	N	Y	Y	Y	Y	Y	Y
4 Cooper	Y	Y	Y	Y	Y	N	Y	Y
5 Boner	Y	Y	Y	Y	Y	Y	Y	Y
6 Gore	Y	Y	Y	Y	Y	Y	Y	Y
7 ***Sundquist***	Y	N	Y	Y	Y	N	Y	Y
8 Jones	Y	N	Y	Y	Y	Y	Y	Y
9 Ford	Y	Y	Y	Y	Y	Y	Y	Y
TEXAS								
1 Hall, S.	Y	N	Y	Y	Y	N	Y	Y
2 Wilson	Y	N	Y	Y	Y	Y	Y	Y
3 ***Bartlett***	Y	N	Y	Y	Y	N	Y	Y
4 Hall, R.	Y	N	Y	Y	Y	Y	Y	Y
5 Bryant	Y	Y	Y	Y	Y	Y	Y	Y
6 ***Gramm***	Y	N	Y	Y	Y	N	N	N
7 ***Archer***	Y	N	Y	Y	Y	N	Y	Y
8 ***Fields***	Y	N	Y	Y	Y	N	Y	Y
9 Brooks	Y	Y	Y	Y	Y	Y	Y	Y
10 Pickle	Y	N	Y	Y	Y	Y	Y	Y
11 Leath	Y	N	Y	Y	Y	N	Y	Y
12 Wright	Y	Y	Y	Y	Y	Y	Y	Y
13 Hightower	Y	N	Y	Y	Y	Y	Y	Y
14 Patman	Y	N	Y	N	Y	Y	N	N
15 de la Garza	Y	Y	Y	Y	Y	Y	Y	Y
16 Coleman	Y	N	Y	Y	Y	Y	Y	Y
17 Stenholm	Y	N	Y	Y	Y	N	Y	Y
18 Leland	Y	Y	Y	Y	Y	Y	Y	Y
19 Hance	?	?	?	?	?	?	?	?
20 Gonzalez	Y	Y	Y	Y	Y	Y	Y	Y
21 ***Loeffler***	Y	N	Y	Y	Y	Y	N	N
22 ***Paul***	Y	N	N	Y	Y	N	N	N
23 Kazen	Y	N	Y	Y	Y	Y	Y	Y
24 Frost	Y	Y	Y	Y	Y	Y	Y	Y
25 Andrews	Y	Y	Y	Y	Y	Y	Y	Y
26 Vandergriff	Y	N	Y	Y	Y	Y	Y	Y
27 Ortiz	Y	Y	Y	Y	Y	Y	Y	Y
UTAH								
1 ***Hansen***	Y	N	N	Y	Y	N	N	N
2 ***Marriott***	Y	Y	Y	Y	Y	N	Y	Y
3 ***Nielson***	Y	N	N	Y	Y	N	Y	Y
VERMONT								
AL ***Jeffords***	Y	Y	Y	Y	Y	Y	Y	Y
VIRGINIA								
1 ***Bateman***	Y	Y	Y	Y	Y	Y	Y	Y
2 ***Whitehurst***	Y	N	Y	Y	Y	Y	Y	Y
3 ***Bliley***	Y	N	Y	Y	Y	N	Y	Y
4 Sisisky	Y	N	Y	Y	Y	Y	Y	Y
5 Daniel	Y	N	Y	Y	Y	N	Y	Y
6 Olin	Y	Y	Y	Y	Y	N	Y	Y
7 ***Robinson***	Y	N	Y	Y	Y	Y	Y	Y
8 ***Parris***	Y	N	Y	Y	Y	Y	Y	Y
9 Boucher	Y	Y	Y	Y	Y	Y	Y	Y
10 ***Wolf***	Y	Y	Y	Y	Y	Y	Y	Y
WASHINGTON								
1 ***Pritchard***	?	?	?	?	?	?	?	?
2 Swift	Y	Y	Y	Y	Y	Y	Y	Y
3 Bonker	Y	Y	Y	Y	Y	Y	Y	Y
4 ***Morrison***	Y	N	Y	Y	Y	Y	Y	Y
5 Foley	Y	N	Y	Y	Y	Y	Y	Y
6 Dicks	Y	N	Y	Y	Y	Y	Y	Y
7 Lowry	Y	Y	Y	N	Y	Y	Y	Y
8 ***Chandler***	Y	N	Y	Y	Y	Y	Y	Y
WEST VIRGINIA								
1 Mollohan	Y	N	Y	Y	Y	Y	Y	Y
2 Staggers	Y	Y	Y	Y	Y	Y	Y	Y
3 Wise	Y	Y	Y	Y	Y	Y	Y	Y
4 Rahall	Y	N	Y	Y	Y	Y	Y	Y
WISCONSIN								
1 Aspin	Y	Y	Y	Y	Y	Y	Y	Y
2 Kastenmeier	Y	Y	Y	Y	Y	Y	Y	Y
3 ***Gunderson***	Y	Y	Y	Y	Y	Y	Y	Y
4 Zablocki	Y	Y	Y	Y	Y	Y	Y	Y
5 Moody	Y	Y	Y	Y	Y	Y	Y	Y
6 ***Petri***	Y	N	Y	Y	Y	Y	Y	Y
7 Obey	Y	Y	Y	Y	Y	Y	Y	Y
8 ***Roth***	Y	N	Y	Y	Y	Y	Y	Y
9 ***Sensenbrenner***	Y	N	Y	Y	Y	Y	Y	Y
WYOMING								
AL ***Cheney***	Y	N	Y	Y	Y	N	N	N

Southern states - Ala., Ark., Fla., Ga., Ky., La., Miss., N.C., Okla., S.C., Tenn., Texas, Va.

484. HR 2077. Federal Physicians Comparability Allowance Act. Adoption of the conference report on the bill to extend the federal physicians comparability allowance act for four years, and to provide for an interim retirement system for federal workers hired after Jan. 1, 1984. Adopted 244-127: R 69-82; D 175-45 (ND 122-23, SD 53-22), Nov. 16, 1983.

485. Procedural Motion. Solomon, R-N.Y., motion to approve the House *Journal* of Wednesday, Nov. 16. Motion agreed to 356-34: R 130-22; D 226-12 (ND 145-11, SD 81-1), Nov. 17, 1983.

486. H Con Res 220. Cyprus. Adoption of the concurrent resolution to condemn the declaration of independence on Nov. 15, 1983, by the Turkish Federation of Cyprus. Adopted 423-1: R 163-1; D 260-0 (ND 174-0, SD 86-0), Nov. 17, 1983.

487. HR 3435. Education of the Handicapped. Passage of the bill to authorize $163.8 million in fiscal 1984, $171.6 million in fiscal 1985 and $179.6 million in fiscal 1986 for discretionary programs of the Education of the Handicapped Act; $1.038 billion in fiscal 1984 and additional sums for fiscal 1985 and 1986 for state block grant programs of the Rehabilitation Act; and $117.1 million plus such sums as may be necessary for fiscal 1984 for discretionary programs of the Rehabilitation Act. Passed 415-1: R 159-1; D 256-0 (ND 171-0, SD 85-0), Nov. 17, 1983.

488. HR 2755. Federal Communications Commission Authorization. Adoption of the rule (H Res 364) providing for House floor consideration of the bill to authorize $91.2 million for the Federal Communications Commission in fiscal 1984 and 1985, to increase the fiscal 1984-86 authorization for the Corporation for Public Broadcasting and to impose financial controls on National Public Radio. Adopted 258-160: R 24-137; D 234-23 (ND 166-7, SD 68-16), Nov. 17, 1983.

489. HR 2755. Federal Communications Commission Authorization. Oxley, R-Ohio, amendment to reduce the authorization for the Corporation for Public Broadcasting by $11 million in fiscal 1984, $15 million in fiscal 1985 and $20 million in fiscal 1986. Rejected 141-277: R 119-44; D 22-233 (ND 4-166, SD 18-67), Nov. 17, 1983.

490. HR 4170. Tax Reform Act. Adoption of the rule (H Res 376) providing for House floor consideration of the bill to raise $8 billion in revenues over fiscal 1984-86 through a variety of changes in tax law. The main elements of the bill dealt with mortgage revenue bonds, industrial development bonds, fringe benefits, tax simplification, curbs on sale/lease-back schemes by non-profit groups and the taxation of life insurance companies. The bill also made substantial savings in the Medicare program and revised administration of the Social Security Disability Insurance program. Rejected 204-214: R 13-149; D 191-65 (ND 147-23, SD 44-42), Nov. 17, 1983.

491. HR 2350. Health Research Extension. Dingell, D-Mich., amendment, to the Shelby, D-Ala., substitute, to transfer the National Institute for Occupational Safety and Health to the National Institutes of Health, from the Centers for Disease Control. Rejected 186-206: R 18-136; D 168-70 (ND 138-16, SD 30-54), Nov. 17, 1983.

KEY

Y Voted for (yea).
Paired for.
+ Announced for.
N Voted against (nay).
X Paired against.
- Announced against.
P Voted "present".
C Voted "present" to avoid possible conflict of interest.
? Did not vote or otherwise make a position known.

Democrats   *Republicans*

ND - Northern Democrats   SD - Southern Democrats

	484	485	486	487	488	489	490	491
ALABAMA								
1 *Edwards*	?	Y	Y	Y	Y	N	N	?
2 *Dickinson*	Y	N	Y	Y	N	Y	N	Y
3 Nichols	Y	Y	Y	Y	Y	N	N	N
4 Bevill	Y	Y	Y	Y	Y	N	Y	N
5 Flippo	Y	Y	Y	Y	Y	N	Y	?
6 Erdreich	Y	Y	Y	Y	Y	N	N	N
7 Shelby	N	?	Y	Y	Y	N	N	N
ALASKA								
AL *Young*	?	?	Y	Y	Y	?	N	N	Y
ARIZONA								
1 *McCain*	N	Y	Y	Y	N	N	N	Y
2 Udall	Y	?	Y	Y	Y	N	Y	?
3 *Stump*	N	Y	Y	Y	N	N	N	N
4 *Rudd*	N	Y	Y	N	Y	N	Y	?
5 McNulty	N	Y	Y	Y	Y	N	Y	N
ARKANSAS								
1 Alexander	?	Y	Y	Y	?	N	Y	Y
2 *Bethune*	?	Y	Y	Y	N	Y	N	N
3 *Hammerschmidt*	N	Y	Y	N	N	N	N	N
4 Anthony	Y	Y	Y	Y	Y	N	Y	Y
CALIFORNIA								
1 Bosco	?	Y	Y	Y	?	N	Y	Y
2 *Chappie*	N	Y	Y	Y	N	Y	N	?
3 Matsui	Y	Y	Y	Y	Y	N	Y	Y
4 Fazio	?	Y	Y	?	Y	N	Y	Y
5 Burton	Y	Y	Y	Y	Y	N	Y	Y
6 Boxer	Y	Y	Y	Y	Y	N	Y	Y
7 Miller	Y	Y	Y	Y	Y	N	Y	Y
8 Dellums	Y	Y	Y	Y	N	N	Y	Y
9 Stark	?	?	Y	Y	Y	N	Y	Y
10 Edwards	Y	Y	Y	Y	Y	N	Y	Y
11 Lantos	Y	Y	Y	Y	Y	N	Y	Y
12 *Zschau*	N	Y	Y	Y	N	N	N	N
13 Mineta	Y	Y	Y	Y	Y	N	Y	Y
14 *Shumway*	?	Y	Y	Y	N	Y	N	N
15 Coelho	Y	Y	Y	Y	Y	N	Y	Y
16 Panetta	Y	Y	Y	Y	Y	N	Y	Y
17 *Pashayan*	N	N	Y	Y	N	Y	N	N
18 Lehman	Y	Y	Y	Y	Y	N	Y	Y
19 *Lagomarsino*	N	Y	Y	N	Y	N	N	N
20 *Thomas*	Y	Y	Y	N	Y	N	Y	?
21 *Fiedler*	Y	Y	Y	Y	N	Y	N	N
22 *Moorhead*	N	Y	Y	N	N	N	N	N
23 Beilenson	Y	Y	Y	Y	Y	N	Y	Y
24 Waxman	Y	Y	Y	Y	N	N	Y	Y
25 Roybal	Y	Y	Y	Y	Y	N	Y	N
26 Berman	Y	Y	Y	Y	Y	N	Y	Y
27 Levine	Y	Y	Y	Y	Y	N	Y	Y
28 Dixon	Y	?	Y	Y	Y	N	Y	Y
29 Hawkins	?	N	Y	Y	?	#	#
30 Martinez	?	?	?	?	?	N	Y	Y
31 Dymally	?	P	Y	Y	N	#	?
32 Anderson	N	Y	Y	N	N	N	Y	Y
33 *Dreier*	N	Y	Y	Y	N	Y	N	N
34 Torres	Y	Y	Y	Y	Y	N	Y	Y
35 *Lewis*	?	?	?	?	?	?	X	?
36 Brown	?	Y	Y	Y	Y	N	Y	?
37 *McCandless*	N	Y	Y	N	N	N	N	N
38 Patterson	N	Y	Y	Y	Y	N	N	Y
39 *Dannemeyer*	N	N	Y	Y	N	Y	N	N
40 *Badham*	?	Y	Y	Y	N	Y	N	N
41 Lowery	Y	Y	Y	Y	N	?	N	N
42 *Lungren*	Y	Y	Y	Y	N	Y	N	N

	484	485	486	487	488	489	490	491
43 *Packard*	N	Y	Y	Y	N	Y	N	N
44 Bates	?	Y	Y	Y	Y	N	Y	Y
45 *Hunter*	N	Y	Y	Y	N	Y	N	N
COLORADO								
1 Schroeder	N	N	Y	Y	Y	N	N	Y
2 Wirth	Y	Y	Y	Y	Y	N	Y	Y
3 Kogovsek	N	Y	Y	Y	Y	N	Y	?
4 *Brown*	N	Y	Y	Y	N	N	N	N
5 *Kramer*	N	Y	Y	Y	N	Y	N	N
6 *Schaefer*	N	N	Y	Y	N	Y	N	N
CONNECTICUT								
1 Kennelly	Y	Y	Y	Y	Y	N	Y	Y
2 Gejdenson	Y	N	Y	Y	Y	N	Y	Y
3 Morrison	Y	Y	Y	Y	Y	N	Y	?
4 *McKinney*	Y	Y	Y	Y	N	Y	Y	Y
5 Ratchford	Y	Y	Y	Y	Y	N	Y	Y
6 *Johnson*	Y	Y	Y	Y	N	Y	Y	Y
DELAWARE								
AL *Carper*	Y	Y	Y	Y	Y	N	N	N
FLORIDA								
1 Hutto	Y	Y	Y	Y	Y	N	Y	N
2 Fuqua	?	Y	Y	Y	Y	N	N	Y
3 Bennett	Y	Y	Y	Y	Y	N	N	N
4 Chappell	?	Y	Y	Y	Y	N	Y	N
5 *McCollum*	Y	Y	Y	N	N	Y	N	N
6 MacKay	Y	Y	Y	Y	Y	N	Y	N
7 Gibbons	N	Y	?	Y	Y	N	Y	Y
8 *Young*	N	Y	Y	N	N	Y	N	N
9 *Bilirakis*	Y	Y	Y	Y	N	Y	N	N
10 Ireland	N	?	Y	Y	?	N	N	N
11 Nelson	Y	Y	Y	Y	Y	N	Y	Y
12 *Lewis*	Y	Y	Y	N	N	Y	N	N
13 *Mack*	N	?	Y	Y	N	Y	N	N
14 Mica	Y	Y	Y	Y	Y	N	N	Y
15 *Shaw*	N	Y	Y	Y	Y	N	N	N
16 Smith	Y	?	Y	Y	N	Y	N	N
17 Lehman	Y	Y	Y	Y	Y	N	Y	?
18 Pepper	Y	Y	Y	?	Y	N	Y	Y
19 Fascell	Y	Y	Y	Y	?	N	Y	Y
GEORGIA								
1 Thomas	Y	Y	Y	Y	N	N	N	N
2 Hatcher	?	Y	Y	?	Y	N	Y	N
3 Ray	N	Y	Y	Y	Y	?	X	X
4 Levitas	N	Y	Y	N	N	N	N	N
5 Fowler	?	Y	Y	Y	N	N	Y	N
6 *Gingrich*	N	?	Y	Y	N	Y	N	N
7 Darden	Y	Y	Y	N	N	N	N	N
8 Rowland	Y	Y	Y	N	N	N	N	N
9 Jenkins	?	?	?	?	?	?	?	?
10 Barnard	Y	Y	Y	N	N	N	N	N
HAWAII								
1 Heftel	Y	?	Y	Y	Y	N	Y	Y
2 Akaka	Y	Y	Y	Y	Y	N	Y	Y
IDAHO								
1 *Craig*	N	Y	Y	Y	N	Y	N	N
2 *Hansen*	N	Y	Y	Y	N	N	N	N
ILLINOIS								
1 Hayes	Y	Y	Y	Y	N	N	Y	Y
2 Savage	Y	Y	Y	Y	N	N	Y	Y
3 Russo	Y	Y	Y	Y	N	N	N	N
4 *O'Brien*	Y	Y	Y	Y	N	N	N	N
5 Lipinski	Y	N	Y	Y	Y	N	Y	N
6 *Hyde*	Y	Y	Y	N	N	N	N	N
7 Collins	Y	?	?	?	?	?	?	?
8 Rostenkowski	?	Y	Y	Y	N	N	Y	Y
9 Yates	Y	Y	Y	Y	Y	N	Y	Y
10 *Porter*	Y	Y	Y	N	N	N	N	N
11 Annunzio	?	Y	Y	Y	N	N	Y	N
12 *Crane, P.*	N	N	Y	N	Y	N	N	N
13 *Erlenborn*	N	Y	Y	N	N	N	N	?
14 *Corcoran*	?	?	Y	N	N	N	N	N
15 *Madigan*	?	?	Y	N	N	N	N	Y
16 *Martin*	N	Y	Y	N	Y	N	N	Y
17 Evans	Y	Y	Y	N	Y	N	N	N
18 *Michel*	Y	Y	Y	N	N	N	N	N
19 *Crane, D.*	N	Y	Y	N	Y	N	N	N
20 Durbin	Y	N	Y	Y	N	N	Y	N
21 Price	Y	Y	Y	Y	N	Y	N	?
22 Simon	Y	Y	Y	?	Y	N	?	?
INDIANA								
1 Hall	Y	Y	Y	Y	Y	N	Y	Y
2 Sharp	N	Y	Y	Y	Y	N	Y	Y
3 *Hiler*	N	N	Y	Y	N	N	N	N
4 *Coats*	N	Y	Y	N	N	N	N	N
5 Hillis	Y	Y	Y	?	N	N	N	N

Corresponding to Congressional Record Votes 519, 520, 521, 522, 523, 524, 525, 526

	484	485	486	487	488	489	490	491
6 ***Burton***	N	Y	Y	Y	N	Y	N	N
7 ***Myers***	Y	Y	Y	Y	N	Y	N	N
8 McCloskey	Y	Y	Y	Y	Y	N	Y	Y
9 Hamilton	N	Y	Y	Y	Y	N	Y	N
10 Jacobs	N	P	Y	Y	N	N	Y	N
IOWA								
1 ***Leach***	N	Y	Y	Y	N	?	?	?
2 ***Tauke***	N	Y	Y	Y	N	N	N	Y
3 ***Evans***	N	N	Y	Y	N	N	N	Y
4 Smith	Y	Y	Y	Y	Y	N	N	Y
5 Harkin	Y	Y	Y	Y	Y	N	N	Y
6 Bedell	Y	Y	Y	Y	Y	N	N	N
KANSAS								
1 ***Roberts***	Y	N	Y	Y	N	Y	N	N
2 Slattery	Y	Y	Y	Y	Y	Y	Y	Y
3 ***Winn***	Y	Y	Y	Y	N	Y	N	N
4 Glickman	N	Y	Y	?	Y	N	Y	N
5 ***Whittaker***	Y	Y	Y	Y	N	Y	N	N
KENTUCKY								
1 Hubbard	Y	Y	Y	Y	Y	N	N	Y
2 Natcher	Y	Y	Y	Y	Y	N	N	N
3 Mazzoli	Y	Y	Y	Y	Y	N	Y	N
4 ***Snyder***	Y	Y	Y	Y	N	Y	N	N
5 ***Rogers***	N	Y	Y	Y	N	Y	N	N
6 ***Hopkins***	N	Y	Y	Y	N	Y	N	N
7 Perkins	Y	Y	Y	Y	Y	N	N	Y
LOUISIANA								
1 ***Livingston***	Y	Y	Y	?	N	Y	N	N
2 Boggs	Y	?	Y	Y	Y	N	N	N
3 Tauzin	N	Y	Y	Y	Y	N	N	N
4 Roemer	N	N	Y	Y	N	Y	N	N
5 Huckaby	N	Y	Y	Y	N	N	N	N
6 ***Moore***	N	?	Y	Y	N	Y	Y	N
7 Breaux	Y	Y	Y	Y	Y	Y	N	N
8 Long	Y	Y	Y	Y	Y	N	Y	Y
MAINE								
1 ***McKernan***	Y	Y	Y	Y	N	N	N	Y
2 ***Snowe***	?	Y	Y	Y	N	N	N	Y
MARYLAND								
1 Dyson	N	Y	Y	Y	Y	N	N	N
2 Long	Y	Y	Y	Y	Y	N	Y	Y
3 Mikulski	Y	Y	Y	Y	Y	N	N	Y
4 ***Holt***	N	Y	Y	Y	N	Y	N	N
5 Hoyer	Y	Y	Y	Y	Y	N	Y	Y
6 Byron	Y	Y	Y	Y	Y	N	N	Y
7 Mitchell	Y	?	Y	Y	N	N	Y	Y
8 Barnes	Y	Y	Y	Y	Y	N	Y	Y
MASSACHUSETTS								
1 ***Conte***	Y	Y	Y	Y	Y	N	N	N
2 Boland	Y	Y	Y	Y	Y	N	Y	Y
3 Early	Y	Y	Y	Y	Y	N	N	N
4 Frank	?	Y	Y	Y	Y	N	Y	Y
5 Shannon	Y	Y	Y	Y	Y	N	Y	Y
6 Mavroules	Y	Y	Y	Y	Y	N	Y	Y
7 Markey	Y	Y	Y	Y	Y	N	Y	Y
8 O'Neill								
9 Moakley	Y	?	Y	Y	Y	N	Y	Y
10 Studds	Y	Y	Y	Y	Y	N	Y	Y
11 Donnelly	Y	Y	Y	Y	Y	N	Y	Y
MICHIGAN								
1 Conyers	?	Y	Y	Y	Y	N	Y	Y
2 ***Pursell***	N	Y	Y	Y	Y	Y	N	N
3 Wolpe	Y	Y	Y	Y	Y	N	Y	Y
4 ***Siljander***	N	Y	Y	Y	N	Y	N	N
5 ***Sawyer***	?	?	Y	Y	N	N	N	N
6 Carr	N	Y	Y	Y	Y	?	N	Y
7 Kildee	N	Y	Y	Y	Y	N	Y	Y
8 Traxler	?	Y	Y	Y	Y	N	Y	Y
9 ***Vander Jagt***	?	?	?	?	?	Y	Y	N
10 Albosta	Y	Y	Y	Y	Y	N	N	Y
11 ***Davis***	Y	Y	Y	Y	Y	N	N	N
12 Bonior	Y	Y	Y	Y	Y	N	Y	Y
13 Crockett	?	?	Y	Y	Y	N	Y	?
14 Hertel	N	Y	Y	Y	Y	N	Y	Y
15 Ford	Y	?	Y	Y	Y	N	Y	Y
16 Dingell	Y	Y	Y	Y	Y	N	Y	Y
17 Levin	Y	Y	Y	Y	Y	N	Y	Y
18 ***Broomfield***	?	N	Y	Y	N	Y	N	?
MINNESOTA								
1 Penny	Y	Y	Y	Y	Y	N	Y	Y
2 ***Weber***	N	N	Y	Y	N	Y	N	N
3 ***Frenzel***	N	N	Y	Y	N	Y	Y	N
4 Vento	Y	Y	Y	Y	Y	N	Y	Y
5 Sabo	Y	N	Y	Y	Y	N	Y	Y
6 Sikorski	Y	N	Y	Y	Y	N	Y	Y

	484	485	486	487	488	489	490	491
7 ***Stangeland***	N	Y	Y	Y	Y	Y	N	N
8 Oberstar	Y	P	Y	Y	Y	N	N	?
MISSISSIPPI								
1 Whitten	Y	Y	Y	Y	Y	N	N	N
2 ***Franklin***	Y	Y	Y	Y	N	Y	N	N
3 Montgomery	Y	Y	Y	Y	Y	Y	N	N
4 Dowdy	?	?	?	?	?	?	?	Y
5 ***Lott***	Y	Y	Y	Y	N	Y	N	N
MISSOURI								
1 Clay	?	N	Y	Y	Y	?	?	?
2 Young	?	Y	Y	Y	Y	N	N	Y
3 Gephardt	Y	Y	Y	Y	Y	N	Y	Y
4 Skelton	N	Y	Y	Y	Y	N	N	Y
5 Wheat	Y	Y	Y	Y	Y	N	Y	Y
6 ***Coleman***	Y	Y	Y	Y	N	Y	N	N
7 ***Taylor***	Y	Y	Y	Y	N	Y	N	N
8 ***Emerson***	N	N	Y	Y	N	Y	N	N
9 Volkmer	N	Y	Y	Y	N	N	Y	N
MONTANA								
1 Williams	Y	Y	Y	Y	Y	N	Y	Y
2 ***Marlenee***	Y	?	Y	Y	N	Y	N	N
NEBRASKA								
1 ***Bereuter***	Y	Y	Y	Y	N	N	N	N
2 ***Daub***	Y	Y	Y	Y	N	Y	N	N
3 ***Smith***	Y	Y	Y	Y	N	Y	N	N
NEVADA								
1 Reid	Y	Y	Y	Y	Y	N	Y	Y
2 ***Vucanovich***	N	Y	Y	Y	N	Y	N	N
NEW HAMPSHIRE								
1 D'Amours	Y	Y	Y	Y	Y	N	N	Y
2 ***Gregg***	N	Y	Y	Y	N	Y	N	N
NEW JERSEY								
1 Florio	Y	Y	Y	Y	Y	N	Y	Y
2 Hughes	Y	Y	Y	Y	Y	Y	Y	Y
3 Howard	Y	Y	Y	Y	Y	N	Y	?
4 ***Smith***	Y	Y	Y	Y	N	N	N	Y
5 ***Roukema***	N	Y	Y	Y	Y	N	Y	N
6 Dwyer	?	Y	Y	Y	Y	N	Y	Y
7 ***Rinaldo***	Y	Y	Y	Y	Y	Y	N	Y
8 Roe	Y	Y	Y	Y	Y	N	Y	Y
9 Torricelli	N	Y	Y	Y	Y	N	Y	Y
10 Rodino	?	Y	Y	Y	Y	N	Y	Y
11 Minish	?	Y	Y	Y	Y	N	Y	Y
12 ***Courter***	Y	N	Y	Y	N	Y	N	Y
13 ***Forsythe***	Y	N	Y	Y	N	Y	N	?
14 Guarini	?	N	Y	Y	Y	N	Y	Y
NEW MEXICO								
1 ***Lujan***	N	Y	Y	Y	N	N	N	N
2 ***Skeen***	Y	N	Y	Y	N	Y	N	N
3 Richardson	Y	Y	Y	Y	Y	N	N	Y
NEW YORK								
1 ***Carney***	Y	Y	Y	Y	N	Y	N	N
2 Downey	Y	Y	Y	Y	Y	N	Y	Y
3 Mrazek	N	Y	Y	Y	Y	N	Y	Y
4 ***Lent***	Y	?	Y	Y	N	Y	N	Y
5 ***McGrath***	Y	Y	Y	Y	N	Y	N	N
6 Addabbo	Y	Y	Y	Y	Y	N	Y	Y
7 Ackerman	?	Y	Y	Y	Y	N	Y	Y
8 Scheuer	Y	Y	Y	Y	Y	N	Y	Y
9 Ferraro	Y	Y	Y	Y	Y	N	Y	Y
10 Schumer	Y	Y	Y	Y	Y	N	Y	Y
11 Towns	?	Y	Y	Y	Y	N	Y	Y
12 Owens	Y	Y	Y	Y	Y	N	Y	?
13 Solarz	?	?	?	?	?	?	?	?
14 ***Molinari***	Y	Y	Y	Y	N	N	N	N
15 ***Green***	Y	Y	Y	Y	N	N	N	Y
16 Rangel	?	Y	Y	Y	Y	N	Y	Y
17 Weiss	Y	?	Y	Y	Y	N	Y	Y
18 Garcia	?	Y	Y	Y	Y	N	Y	Y
19 Biaggi	Y	Y	Y	Y	Y	N	N	Y
20 Ottinger	Y	?	Y	Y	Y	N	Y	Y
21 ***Fish***	?	Y	Y	Y	Y	Y	N	N
22 ***Gilman***	Y	Y	Y	Y	Y	N	N	Y
23 Stratton	Y	Y	Y	Y	Y	N	Y	Y
24 ***Solomon***	N	N	Y	Y	N	Y	N	N
25 ***Boehlert***	Y	Y	Y	Y	N	N	N	N
26 ***Martin***	N	Y	Y	Y	N	N	N	N
27 ***Wortley***	N	Y	Y	Y	N	N	N	N
28 McHugh	?	Y	Y	Y	Y	N	Y	?
29 ***Horton***	Y	Y	Y	Y	Y	N	N	?
30 ***Conable***	N	Y	Y	?	N	Y	Y	N
31 ***Kemp***	?	Y	Y	Y	N	Y	?	?
32 LaFalce	?	Y	Y	?	Y	N	Y	Y
33 Nowak	Y	Y	Y	Y	Y	N	Y	Y
34 Lundine	Y	Y	Y	Y	Y	N	N	Y

	484	485	486	487	488	489	490	491
NORTH CAROLINA								
1 Jones	?	Y	Y	Y	Y	N	N	N
2 Valentine	Y	Y	Y	Y	Y	N	Y	N
3 Whitley	Y	Y	Y	Y	Y	N	Y	N
4 Andrews	Y	Y	Y	Y	Y	N	Y	?
5 Neal	N	Y	Y	Y	Y	N	Y	N
6 Britt	N	Y	Y	Y	Y	N	Y	N
7 Rose	Y	Y	Y	Y	Y	N	Y	N
8 Hefner	N	Y	Y	Y	Y	N	Y	N
9 ***Martin***	N	Y	Y	Y	Y	Y	N	N
10 ***Broyhill***	Y	Y	Y	Y	N	Y	N	N
11 Clarke	?	Y	Y	Y	Y	N	Y	N
NORTH DAKOTA								
AL Dorgan	N	Y	Y	Y	Y	?	#	?
OHIO								
1 Luken	?	Y	Y	Y	Y	N	Y	Y
2 ***Gradison***	N	Y	Y	Y	Y	Y	N	N
3 Hall	Y	Y	Y	Y	Y	N	Y	Y
4 ***Oxley***	Y	Y	Y	Y	N	Y	N	N
5 ***Latta***	Y	N	Y	Y	N	Y	N	N
6 ***McEwen***	N	Y	Y	Y	N	Y	N	N
7 ***DeWine***	N	Y	Y	Y	N	Y	N	N
8 ***Kindness***	Y	Y	Y	Y	N	Y	N	N
9 Kaptur	Y	Y	Y	Y	Y	N	Y	Y
10 ***Miller***	N	N	Y	Y	?	Y	N	N
11 Eckart	N	Y	Y	Y	Y	N	Y	Y
12 ***Kasich***	N	Y	Y	Y	N	Y	N	N
13 Pease	Y	Y	Y	Y	Y	N	Y	Y
14 Seiberling	Y	Y	Y	Y	Y	N	Y	Y
15 ***Wylie***	N	Y	Y	Y	N	Y	Y	N
16 ***Regula***	N	Y	Y	Y	N	Y	N	N
17 ***Williams***	Y	Y	Y	Y	Y	N	N	N
18 Applegate	Y	?	Y	Y	Y	Y	Y	Y
19 Feighan	?	?	Y	Y	Y	N	Y	Y
20 Oakar	Y	Y	Y	Y	Y	N	Y	Y
21 Stokes	Y	Y	Y	Y	Y	N	Y	Y
OKLAHOMA								
1 Jones	Y	Y	Y	Y	Y	N	Y	Y
2 Synar	Y	Y	Y	Y	Y	N	N	Y
3 Watkins	N	Y	Y	Y	Y	Y	N	N
4 McCurdy	?	Y	Y	Y	Y	N	Y	N
5 ***Edwards***	N	Y	Y	Y	N	Y	N	N
6 English	N	Y	Y	Y	Y	N	N	N
OREGON								
1 AuCoin	N	Y	Y	Y	Y	N	N	Y
2 ***Smith, R.***	N	Y	Y	Y	N	Y	N	N
3 Wyden	N	?	Y	Y	Y	N	N	Y
4 Weaver	N	Y	Y	Y	Y	N	N	Y
5 ***Smith, D.***	N	Y	Y	Y	N	Y	N	N
PENNSYLVANIA								
1 Foglietta	Y	Y	Y	Y	Y	N	Y	?
2 Gray	Y	Y	Y	Y	Y	N	Y	Y
3 Borski	Y	Y	Y	Y	Y	N	Y	Y
4 Kolter	Y	Y	Y	Y	Y	N	Y	?
5 ***Schulze***	N	Y	Y	Y	N	Y	N	N
6 Yatron	Y	Y	Y	Y	Y	N	Y	Y
7 Edgar	Y	Y	Y	Y	Y	N	Y	Y
8 Kostmayer	Y	Y	Y	Y	Y	N	Y	Y
9 ***Shuster***	N	Y	Y	Y	N	Y	N	N
10 ***McDade***	Y	?	Y	Y	N	N	N	Y
11 Harrison	Y	Y	Y	Y	Y	N	Y	N
12 Murtha	?	Y	Y	Y	Y	N	Y	Y
13 ***Coughlin***	Y	N	Y	Y	N	N	N	N
14 Coyne	Y	Y	Y	Y	Y	N	Y	Y
15 ***Ritter***	Y	Y	Y	Y	N	N	N	Y
16 ***Walker***	N	N	Y	Y	N	Y	N	N
17 ***Gekas***	Y	Y	Y	Y	N	N	N	N
18 Walgren	Y	Y	Y	Y	Y	N	Y	Y
19 ***Goodling***	Y	N	Y	Y	N	Y	N	N
20 Gaydos	Y	Y	Y	Y	Y	N	Y	Y
21 ***Ridge***	N	?	Y	Y	N	N	N	N
22 Murphy	N	P	Y	Y	N	Y	Y	Y
23 ***Clinger***	Y	+	Y	Y	N	N	N	N
RHODE ISLAND								
1 St Germain	?	P	Y	Y	Y	N	Y	Y
2 ***Schneider***	N	?	Y	Y	Y	N	N	N
SOUTH CAROLINA								
1 ***Hartnett***	N	Y	Y	Y	N	Y	N	N
2 ***Spence***	Y	Y	Y	Y	N	Y	N	N
3 Derrick	Y	Y	Y	Y	Y	N	Y	Y
4 ***Campbell***	Y	Y	Y	Y	N	Y	N	N
5 Spratt	Y	Y	Y	Y	Y	N	Y	N
6 Tallon	Y	Y	Y	Y	Y	Y	N	Y
SOUTH DAKOTA								
AL Daschle	Y	N	Y	Y	Y	N	N	Y

	484	485	486	487	488	489	490	491
TENNESSEE								
1 ***Quillen***	Y	Y	Y	Y	Y	Y	Y	N
2 ***Duncan***	N	Y	Y	Y	Y	Y	Y	N
3 Lloyd	N	Y	Y	Y	N	N	N	N
4 Cooper	Y	Y	Y	Y	Y	N	Y	N
5 Boner	?	Y	Y	Y	Y	N	N	N
6 Gore	Y	Y	Y	Y	Y	N	N	Y
7 ***Sundquist***	N	Y	Y	Y	N	Y	Y	N
8 Jones	Y	Y	Y	Y	Y	N	N	Y
9 Ford	Y	Y	Y	Y	Y	N	Y	Y
TEXAS								
1 Hall, S.	N	Y	Y	Y	Y	Y	Y	N
2 Wilson	?	Y	Y	Y	Y	N	Y	Y
3 ***Bartlett***	N	Y	Y	Y	N	Y	N	N
4 Hall, R.	N	Y	Y	Y	N	Y	N	N
5 Bryant	Y	?	Y	Y	Y	N	Y	Y
6 ***Gramm***	N	N	Y	Y	N	Y	N	N
7 ***Archer***	N	Y	Y	Y	N	Y	N	N
8 ***Fields***	N	Y	Y	Y	N	Y	N	N
9 Brooks	Y	Y	Y	Y	Y	N	N	Y
10 Pickle	N	Y	Y	Y	Y	N	Y	N
11 Leath	?	Y	Y	Y	N	Y	N	N
12 Wright	?	Y	Y	Y	Y	N	Y	Y
13 Hightower	Y	Y	Y	Y	Y	Y	N	N
14 Patman	N	Y	Y	Y	N	Y	N	N
15 de la Garza	Y	Y	Y	Y	Y	Y	Y	Y
16 Coleman	Y	Y	Y	Y	Y	N	Y	Y
17 Stenholm	N	Y	Y	Y	N	Y	N	N
18 Leland	Y	Y	Y	Y	Y	N	Y	Y
19 Hance	?	?	?	?	?	?	?	?
20 Gonzalez	Y	Y	Y	Y	N	N	N	Y
21 ***Loeffler***	N	Y	Y	Y	N	Y	N	N
22 ***Paul***	N	Y	N	N	N	Y	N	N
23 Kazen	Y	Y	Y	Y	Y	Y	N	N
24 Frost	Y	Y	Y	Y	Y	N	N	Y
25 Andrews	N	Y	Y	Y	Y	N	Y	N
26 Vandergriff	N	Y	Y	Y	N	Y	N	N
27 Ortiz	Y	Y	Y	Y	Y	N	Y	Y
UTAH								
1 ***Hansen***	N	Y	Y	Y	N	Y	X	?
2 ***Marriott***	Y	Y	Y	Y	N	Y	N	N
3 ***Nielson***	N	Y	Y	Y	N	Y	N	N
VERMONT								
AL ***Jeffords***	N	Y	Y	Y	Y	N	N	Y
VIRGINIA								
1 ***Bateman***	Y	Y	Y	Y	N	N	N	N
2 ***Whitehurst***	?	Y	Y	Y	N	N	N	N
3 ***Bliley***	Y	Y	Y	Y	Y	Y	N	N
4 Sisisky	Y	Y	Y	Y	Y	Y	Y	N
5 Daniel	N	Y	Y	Y	N	Y	N	N
6 Olin	Y	Y	Y	Y	Y	N	Y	Y
7 ***Robinson***	Y	Y	Y	Y	N	Y	N	N
8 ***Parris***	Y	Y	Y	Y	Y	Y	N	N
9 Boucher	Y	Y	Y	Y	Y	N	N	Y
10 ***Wolf***	Y	Y	Y	Y	N	Y	N	N
WASHINGTON								
1 ***Pritchard***	?	?	?	?	?	?	?	?
2 Swift	Y	Y	Y	Y	Y	N	Y	Y
3 Bonker	Y	Y	Y	Y	Y	N	Y	Y
4 ***Morrison***	Y	Y	Y	Y	N	N	N	N
5 Foley	Y	Y	Y	Y	Y	N	Y	?
6 Dicks	?	Y	Y	Y	Y	N	Y	Y
7 Lowry	Y	N	Y	Y	Y	N	Y	Y
8 ***Chandler***	Y	Y	Y	Y	Y	N	N	N
WEST VIRGINIA								
1 Mollohan	Y	Y	Y	Y	Y	N	Y	Y
2 Staggers	Y	Y	Y	Y	Y	N	Y	N
3 Wise	Y	Y	Y	Y	Y	N	Y	N
4 Rahall	Y	Y	Y	Y	Y	N	Y	?
WISCONSIN								
1 Aspin	Y	Y	Y	Y	Y	N	Y	?
2 Kastenmeier	Y	Y	Y	Y	Y	N	Y	Y
3 ***Gunderson***	N	Y	Y	Y	N	Y	N	N
4 Zablocki	Y	Y	Y	Y	Y	N	Y	Y
5 Moody	Y	Y	Y	Y	Y	N	Y	Y
6 ***Petri***	N	Y	Y	Y	N	Y	Y	N
7 Obey	Y	Y	Y	Y	Y	N	Y	Y
8 ***Roth***	Y	Y	Y	Y	N	Y	N	N
9 ***Sensenbrenner***	N	Y	Y	Y	N	Y	N	N
WYOMING								
AL ***Cheney***	Y	Y	Y	?	N	Y	N	?

Southern states - Ala., Ark., Fla., Ga., Ky., La., Miss., N.C., Okla., S.C., Tenn., Texas, Va.

492. Procedural Motion.
Solomon, R-N.Y., motion to approve the House *Journal* of Thursday, Nov. 17. Motion agreed to 335-33: R 126-22; D 209-11 (ND 134-10, SD 75-1), Nov. 18, 1983.

493. HR 2915. State Department Authorization.
Adoption of the conference report on the bill to make authorizations for fiscal years 1984-85 for the State Department, the United States Information Agency, the Board for International Broadcasting and related agencies. Adopted 254-146: R 91-66; D 163-80 (ND 120-42, SD 43-38), Nov. 18, 1983.

494. H Con Res 100. Forced Labor in the Soviet Union.
Adoption of the concurrent resolution to call upon the Soviet Union to end its policy of using forced labor. Adopted 402-0: R 159-0; D 243-0 (ND 160-0, SD 83-0), Nov. 18, 1983.

495. H Con Res 100. Forced Labor in the Soviet Union.
Foley, D-Wash., motion to table (kill) the Levitas, D-Ga., motion to reconsider the vote by which the concurrent resolution was adopted *(see vote 494, above)*. Motion agreed to 390-0: R 151-0; D 239-0 (ND 158-0, SD 81-0), Nov. 18, 1983.

496. HR 4185. Defense Department Appropriations, Fiscal 1984.
Adoption of the conference report on the bill to provide $249,820,875,000 for military programs of the Department of Defense in fiscal 1984. Adopted 311-99: R 143-16; D 168-83 (ND 85-81, SD 83-2), Nov. 18, 1983. The president had requested $260,926,119,000 in new budget authority.

497. HR 3959. Supplemental Appropriations, Fiscal 1984.
Adoption of the rule (H Res 379) that, when adopted, had the effect of providing House approval to the Senate (Garn, R-Utah) amendment adding a $15.6 billion reauthorization of housing programs, an $8.4 billion reauthorization and appropriation for the International Monetary Fund and a reauthorization of U.S. participation in international development banks. Adopted (thus cleared for the president) 226-186: R 69-90; D 157-96 (ND 115-52, SD 42-44), Nov. 18, 1983. A "yea" was a vote supporting the president's position.

498. H J Res 308. Debt Limit Increase.
Adoption of the conference report on the joint resolution to increase the public debt limit to $1.49 trillion, from $1.389 trillion. Adopted (thus cleared for the president) 214-186: R 60-92; D 154-94 (ND 114-50, SD 40-44), Nov. 18, 1983. A "yea" was a vote supporting the president's position.

KEY

Y	Voted for (yea).
#	Paired for.
+	Announced for.
N	Voted against (nay).
X	Paired against.
-	Announced against.
P	Voted "present".
C	Voted "present" to avoid possible conflict of interest.
?	Did not vote or otherwise make a position known.

Democrats   **Republicans**

	492	493	494	495	496	497	498
ALABAMA							
1 *Edwards*	?	Y	Y	Y	Y	Y	Y
2 *Dickinson*	N	N	Y	Y	Y	Y	Y
3 Nichols	?	?	?	?	Y	X	X
4 Bevill	Y	N	Y	Y	Y	X	?
5 Flippo	Y	N	Y	Y	Y	Y	Y
6 Erdreich	Y	N	Y	Y	Y	N	N
7 Shelby	?	N	Y	Y	Y	N	N
ALASKA							
AL *Young*	?	N	Y	Y	Y	N	N
ARIZONA							
1 *McCain*	Y	N	Y	?	Y	N	Y
2 Udall	?	Y	Y	Y	Y	Y	Y
3 *Stump*	Y	N	Y	Y	Y	N	N
4 *Rudd*	?	?	?	?	?	?	?
5 McNulty	Y	Y	Y	Y	Y	Y	Y
ARKANSAS							
1 Alexander	?	Y	Y	Y	Y	Y	Y
2 *Bethune*	Y	N	Y	Y	Y	N	N
3 *Hammerschmidt*	Y	Y	Y	Y	Y	N	N
4 Anthony	?	?	Y	Y	Y	Y	Y
CALIFORNIA							
1 Bosco	Y	Y	Y	Y	N	N	N
2 *Chappie*	N	N	Y	Y	Y	N	N
3 Matsui	Y	Y	Y	Y	Y	Y	Y
4 Fazio	Y	Y	Y	Y	Y	Y	Y
5 Burton	Y	Y	Y	Y	N	Y	Y
6 Boxer	Y	Y	Y	N	N	Y	Y
7 Miller	Y	N	Y	Y	N	N	N
8 Dellums	?	Y	Y	Y	N	Y	Y
9 Stark	Y	N	Y	Y	N	Y	Y
10 Edwards	Y	Y	Y	Y	N	Y	Y
11 Lantos	Y	Y	Y	Y	Y	Y	N
12 Zschau	Y	Y	Y	Y	Y	N	N
13 Mineta	Y	Y	Y	Y	N	Y	Y
14 *Shumway*	Y	N	Y	Y	Y	N	N
15 Coelho	Y	Y	Y	Y	Y	Y	Y
16 Panetta	Y	N	Y	Y	N	N	Y
17 *Pashayan*	N	Y	Y	Y	Y	N	N
18 Lehman	Y	N	Y	Y	Y	Y	Y
19 *Lagomarsino*	Y	Y	Y	Y	Y	N	Y
20 *Thomas*	Y	Y	Y	Y	Y	N	N
21 *Fiedler*	Y	Y	Y	Y	Y	N	N
22 *Moorhead*	Y	Y	Y	Y	Y	N	N
23 Beilenson	Y	Y	Y	Y	N	Y	Y
24 Waxman	Y	Y	?	?	N	Y	Y
25 Roybal	Y	Y	Y	Y	N	Y	Y
26 Berman	?	#	?	?	N	Y	Y
27 Levine	Y	Y	Y	Y	Y	Y	Y
28 Dixon	?	?	?	?	X	Y	Y
29 Hawkins	?	?	?	?	X	#	#
30 Martinez	?	Y	Y	Y	?	?	#
31 Dymally	?	?	?	?	X	#	?
32 Anderson	Y	Y	Y	Y	N	N	N
33 *Dreier*	Y	Y	Y	Y	Y	N	N
34 Torres	Y	?	Y	Y	Y	Y	Y
35 *Lewis*	?	?	?	?	?	?	?
36 Brown	Y	Y	Y	Y	N	Y	Y
37 *McCandless*	Y	Y	Y	Y	Y	Y	N
38 Patterson	Y	Y	Y	Y	Y	Y	N
39 *Dannemeyer*	N	N	Y	Y	Y	N	N
40 *Badham*	Y	N	Y	Y	Y	N	N
41 *Lowery*	Y	Y	Y	Y	Y	Y	Y
42 Lungren	Y	N	Y	?	Y	N	N

	492	493	494	495	496	497	498
43 *Packard*	Y	Y	Y	Y	Y	N	N
44 Bates	Y	Y	Y	N	N	N	N
45 *Hunter*	Y	Y	Y	?	Y	N	N
COLORADO							
1 Schroeder	N	N	Y	N	Y	N	N
2 Wirth	Y	Y	Y	Y	N	Y	Y
3 Kogovsek	Y	N	Y	Y	N	Y	Y
4 *Brown*	Y	N	Y	Y	N	N	N
5 *Kramer*	Y	Y	Y	Y	Y	N	N
6 *Schaefer*	N	N	Y	Y	Y	N	N
CONNECTICUT							
1 Kennelly	Y	Y	Y	Y	Y	Y	Y
2 Gejdenson	N	Y	Y	Y	Y	Y	Y
3 Morrison	Y	N	Y	Y	N	Y	Y
4 *McKinney*	Y	Y	Y	Y	N	Y	Y
5 Ratchford	Y	Y	Y	Y	Y	Y	Y
6 *Johnson*	Y	Y	Y	Y	Y	Y	Y
DELAWARE							
AL Carper	?	Y	Y	Y	Y	Y	N
FLORIDA							
1 Hutto	Y	Y	Y	Y	N	N	N
2 Fuqua	Y	Y	Y	Y	Y	Y	Y
3 Bennett	Y	N	Y	Y	Y	N	N
4 Chappell	Y	N	Y	Y	N	N	N
5 *McCollum*	Y	Y	Y	Y	N	N	N
6 MacKay	Y	N	Y	Y	Y	Y	Y
7 Gibbons	?	Y	Y	Y	Y	Y	Y
8 *Young*	Y	N	Y	Y	N	N	N
9 *Bilirakis*	Y	N	Y	Y	N	N	N
10 Ireland	Y	Y	Y	Y	N	N	N
11 Nelson	Y	N	Y	Y	N	N	N
12 *Lewis*	Y	N	Y	Y	N	N	N
13 *Mack*	Y	N	?	Y	?	?	X
14 Mica	Y	Y	Y	Y	Y	Y	Y
15 *Shaw*	?	?	Y	Y	Y	N	N
16 Smith	Y	Y	Y	Y	Y	Y	Y
17 Lehman	Y	Y	Y	Y	N	Y	?
18 Pepper	Y	Y	?	Y	Y	Y	Y
19 Fascell	Y	Y	Y	Y	Y	Y	Y
GEORGIA							
1 Thomas	Y	Y	Y	Y	Y	N	Y
2 Hatcher	Y	Y	Y	Y	Y	Y	Y
3 Ray	Y	N	Y	Y	Y	N	N
4 Levitas	Y	Y	Y	Y	Y	N	N
5 Fowler	?	?	?	?	?	Y	N
6 *Gingrich*	Y	Y	Y	?	Y	N	Y
7 Darden	Y	Y	Y	Y	Y	N	N
8 Rowland	Y	Y	Y	Y	Y	N	Y
9 Jenkins	?	?	?	?	Y	N	Y
10 Barnard	Y	N	Y	Y	Y	N	N
HAWAII							
1 Heftel	?	?	?	?	Y	Y	Y
2 Akaka	Y	Y	Y	Y	Y	Y	Y
IDAHO							
1 *Craig*	Y	N	Y	Y	N	N	N
2 *Hansen*	?	?	Y	Y	N	N	N
ILLINOIS							
1 Hayes	Y	Y	Y	Y	N	Y	Y
2 Savage	Y	N	Y	N	Y	Y	Y
3 Russo	Y	N	Y	N	N	N	N
4 *O'Brien*	?	Y	Y	Y	Y	Y	Y
5 Lipinski	N	Y	Y	Y	N	N	N
6 *Hyde*	Y	Y	Y	Y	Y	Y	Y
7 Collins	?	Y	Y	N	Y	Y	Y
8 Rostenkowski	Y	Y	Y	?	Y	Y	Y
9 Yates	Y	Y	Y	Y	N	Y	Y
10 *Porter*	Y	Y	Y	Y	Y	Y	Y
11 Annunzio	Y	Y	Y	Y	Y	?	?
12 *Crane, P.*	?	N	Y	Y	Y	N	N
13 *Erlenborn*	Y	Y	Y	Y	Y	?	Y
14 *Corcoran*	?	?	?	?	?	?	?
15 *Madigan*	Y	Y	Y	Y	Y	N	#
16 *Martin*	Y	N	Y	Y	Y	N	N
17 Evans	Y	Y	Y	Y	Y	N	Y
18 *Michel*	Y	Y	Y	Y	Y	Y	Y
19 *Crane, D.*	Y	N	Y	Y	Y	N	N
20 Durbin	N	N	Y	Y	Y	N	N
21 Price	Y	Y	Y	Y	Y	Y	Y
22 Simon	?	?	?	?	?	?	?
INDIANA							
1 Hall	Y	Y	Y	Y	N	Y	Y
2 Sharp	Y	Y	Y	Y	N	Y	?
3 *Hiler*	Y	Y	Y	Y	N	N	N
4 *Coats*	Y	Y	Y	Y	N	N	N
5 Hillis	Y	Y	Y	Y	Y	Y	Y

ND - Northern Democrats   SD - Southern Democrats

Corresponding to Congressional Record Votes 527, 528, 529, 530, 531, 532, 533

	492	493	494	495	496	497	498
6 ***Burton***	Y	N	Y	Y	Y	N	N
7 ***Myers***	Y	Y	Y	Y	Y	N	N
8 McCloskey	Y	Y	Y	Y	Y	N	Y
9 Hamilton	Y	Y	Y	Y	Y	Y	Y
10 Jacobs	P	N	Y	Y	Y	N	N
IOWA							
1 ***Leach***	Y	Y	Y	Y	N	Y	N
2 ***Tauke***	Y	N	Y	Y	N	Y	N
3 ***Evans***	N	N	Y	Y	N	Y	N
4 Smith	Y	Y	Y	Y	N	Y	Y
5 Harkin	N	Y	Y	Y	N	Y	N
6 Bedell	Y	Y	Y	Y	N	Y	Y
KANSAS							
1 ***Roberts***	N	N	Y	Y	N	N	N
2 Slattery	Y	N	Y	Y	Y	N	N
3 ***Winn***	Y	Y	Y	Y	Y	N	N
4 Glickman	Y	N	Y	Y	Y	Y	Y
5 ***Whittaker***	N	N	Y	Y	Y	N	N
KENTUCKY							
1 Hubbard	Y	N	Y	Y	Y	Y	N
2 Natcher	Y	N	Y	Y	Y	Y	N
3 Mazzoli	Y	Y	Y	Y	Y	Y	Y
4 ***Snyder***	Y	N	Y	Y	Y	N	N
5 ***Rogers***	Y	N	Y	Y	Y	N	N
6 ***Hopkins***	Y	N	Y	Y	Y	N	N
7 Perkins	Y	N	Y	Y	Y	N	Y
LOUISIANA							
1 ***Livingston***	Y	Y	Y	Y	Y	Y	Y
2 Boggs	?	Y	Y	Y	Y	Y	Y
3 Tauzin	Y	N	Y	Y	Y	N	N
4 Roemer	N	N	Y	Y	Y	N	N
5 Huckaby	Y	N	Y	Y	Y	N	N
6 ***Moore***	Y	Y	Y	Y	Y	N	N
7 Breaux	?	?	?	?	Y	N	Y
8 Long	Y	Y	Y	Y	Y	Y	Y
MAINE							
1 ***McKernan***	Y	Y	Y	Y	Y	Y	Y
2 ***Snowe***	Y	Y	Y	Y	Y	Y	Y
MARYLAND							
1 Dyson	Y	N	Y	Y	Y	N	N
2 Long	Y	Y	Y	Y	Y	N	N
3 Mikulski	?	N	Y	Y	Y	N	Y
4 ***Holt***	?	?	?	?	?	?	?
5 Hoyer	Y	Y	Y	Y	Y	Y	Y
6 Byron	Y	N	Y	Y	Y	N	N
7 Mitchell	N	N	Y	Y	N	Y	Y
8 Barnes	Y	Y	Y	Y	Y	Y	Y
MASSACHUSETTS							
1 ***Conte***	Y	Y	Y	Y	Y	Y	Y
2 Boland	Y	Y	Y	Y	Y	Y	Y
3 Early	Y	N	Y	Y	N	N	N
4 Frank	Y	N	Y	Y	N	Y	Y
5 Shannon	Y	N	Y	Y	N	N	Y
6 Mavroules	Y	N	Y	Y	Y	Y	Y
7 Markey	Y	Y	Y	Y	N	Y	Y
8 O'Neill							
9 Moakley	Y	Y	Y	Y	N	Y	Y
10 Studds	Y	Y	Y	Y	N	Y	Y
11 Donnelly	Y	N	Y	Y	N	N	Y
MICHIGAN							
1 Conyers	?	?	?	Y	N	Y	Y
2 ***Pursell***	Y	Y	Y	Y	Y	Y	N
3 Wolpe	Y	Y	Y	Y	Y	Y	N
4 ***Siljander***	Y	Y	Y	Y	Y	N	N
5 ***Sawyer***	Y	Y	Y	Y	Y	Y	Y
6 Carr	Y	Y	Y	Y	Y	N	N
7 Kildee	Y	N	Y	Y	N	N	Y
8 Traxler	Y	Y	Y	Y	Y	N	N
9 ***Vander Jagt***	Y	Y	Y	Y	Y	Y	Y
10 Albosta	?	Y	Y	Y	Y	N	N
11 ***Davis***	Y	Y	Y	Y	Y	Y	N
12 Bonior	Y	Y	Y	Y	N	Y	Y
13 Crockett	Y	Y	Y	Y	N	Y	Y
14 Hertel	Y	N	Y	Y	N	N	N
15 Ford	?	?	?	?	#	?	?
16 Dingell	?	Y	Y	Y	Y	Y	Y
17 Levin	Y	Y	Y	Y	N	Y	Y
18 ***Broomfield***	N	Y	Y	Y	Y	N	Y
MINNESOTA							
1 Penny	Y	N	Y	Y	N	N	N
2 ***Weber***	N	N	Y	?	Y	N	N
3 ***Frenzel***	N	N	Y	Y	N	Y	Y
4 Vento	Y	Y	Y	Y	N	Y	Y
5 Sabo	N	Y	Y	Y	N	Y	Y
6 Sikorski	N	N	Y	Y	N	Y	N
7 ***Stangeland***	Y	N	Y	Y	Y	Y	Y
8 Oberstar	?	Y	Y	Y	N	Y	Y
MISSISSIPPI							
1 Whitten	Y	Y	Y	Y	Y	Y	Y
2 ***Franklin***	Y	N	Y	Y	Y	N	N
3 Montgomery	Y	N	Y	Y	Y	N	N
4 Dowdy	Y	N	Y	Y	Y	N	N
5 ***Lott***	Y	N	Y	Y	Y	N	Y
MISSOURI							
1 Clay	?	?	?	?	X	?	?
2 Young	Y	Y	Y	Y	Y	Y	Y
3 Gephardt	Y	Y	Y	Y	Y	Y	Y
4 Skelton	Y	N	Y	Y	Y	N	Y
5 Wheat	Y	Y	Y	Y	N	Y	Y
6 ***Coleman***	Y	Y	Y	Y	Y	N	N
7 ***Taylor***	Y	Y	Y	Y	Y	N	X
8 ***Emerson***	N	N	Y	Y	Y	N	X
9 Volkmer	?	N	Y	Y	Y	N	Y
MONTANA							
1 Williams	?	?	?	?	?	X	?
2 ***Marlenee***	N	Y	Y	Y	Y	N	N
NEBRASKA							
1 ***Bereuter***	Y	Y	Y	Y	Y	Y	N
2 ***Daub***	Y	N	Y	Y	Y	N	N
3 ***Smith***	Y	N	Y	Y	Y	N	Y
NEVADA							
1 Reid	Y	Y	Y	Y	Y	N	Y
2 ***Vucanovich***	Y	Y	Y	?	Y	N	N
NEW HAMPSHIRE							
1 D'Amours	Y	Y	Y	Y	Y	N	X
2 ***Gregg***	Y	Y	Y	Y	N	N	Y
NEW JERSEY							
1 Florio	Y	Y	Y	Y	N	N	N
2 Hughes	Y	N	Y	Y	N	N	N
3 Howard	Y	Y	Y	Y	Y	Y	Y
4 ***Smith***	?	Y	Y	Y	Y	Y	Y
5 ***Roukema***	Y	Y	Y	Y	Y	Y	?
6 Dwyer	Y	Y	Y	Y	Y	Y	Y
7 ***Rinaldo***	?	Y	Y	Y	Y	?	?
8 Roe	Y	Y	Y	Y	Y	Y	Y
9 Torricelli	Y	Y	Y	Y	Y	Y	N
10 Rodino	Y	Y	Y	Y	N	Y	Y
11 Minish	Y	Y	Y	Y	#	#	#
12 ***Courter***	N	Y	Y	Y	Y	N	N
13 ***Forsythe***	N	Y	Y	Y	N	Y	Y
14 Guarini	N	N	Y	Y	Y	Y	Y
NEW MEXICO							
1 ***Lujan***	Y	Y	?	Y	Y	Y	N
2 ***Skeen***	N	Y	Y	Y	Y	N	N
3 Richardson	Y	Y	Y	Y	Y	N	N
NEW YORK							
1 ***Carney***	Y	N	Y	Y	Y	N	N
2 Downey	Y	Y	Y	Y	Y	Y	Y
3 Mrazek	?	Y	Y	Y	Y	N	N
4 ***Lent***	Y	Y	Y	Y	Y	Y	Y
5 ***McGrath***	Y	Y	Y	Y	Y	N	N
6 Addabbo	Y	Y	Y	Y	Y	Y	Y
7 Ackerman	?	Y	Y	Y	N	Y	Y
8 Scheuer	Y	Y	Y	Y	Y	Y	Y
9 Ferraro	Y	Y	Y	Y	?	?	?
10 Schumer	Y	Y	Y	Y	N	Y	Y
11 Towns	Y	Y	Y	Y	N	Y	Y
12 Owens	Y	Y	Y	Y	N	Y	N
13 Solarz	Y	Y	Y	Y	Y	Y	Y
14 ***Molinari***	Y	Y	Y	Y	Y	N	N
15 ***Green***	Y	Y	Y	Y	N	Y	Y
16 Rangel	Y	Y	Y	Y	N	Y	Y
17 Weiss	Y	Y	Y	Y	N	Y	Y
18 Garcia	?	Y	Y	Y	N	Y	Y
19 Biaggi	Y	Y	?	Y	Y	Y	N
20 Ottinger	P	Y	Y	Y	N	Y	Y
21 ***Fish***	Y	Y	Y	Y	Y	Y	Y
22 ***Gilman***	Y	Y	Y	Y	Y	Y	N
23 Stratton	Y	Y	Y	Y	Y	Y	Y
24 ***Solomon***	N	N	Y	Y	Y	N	N
25 ***Boehlert***	Y	Y	Y	Y	Y	Y	Y
26 ***Martin***	Y	Y	Y	Y	Y	Y	N
27 ***Wortley***	Y	Y	Y	Y	Y	Y	N
28 McHugh	Y	Y	Y	?	N	Y	Y
29 ***Horton***	Y	Y	Y	Y	Y	Y	Y
30 ***Conable***	N	Y	Y	Y	N	Y	Y
31 ***Kemp***	Y	Y	Y	Y	Y	N	Y
32 LaFalce	Y	Y	Y	Y	Y	Y	Y
33 Nowak	Y	Y	Y	Y	Y	Y	Y
34 Lundine	Y	Y	Y	Y	N	Y	Y
NORTH CAROLINA							
1 Jones	Y	Y	Y	Y	Y	Y	Y
2 Valentine	Y	N	Y	Y	Y	N	N
3 Whitley	Y	N	Y	Y	Y	N	Y
4 Andrews	Y	N	Y	Y	Y	Y	Y
5 Neal	Y	Y	Y	Y	Y	Y	N
6 Britt	Y	Y	Y	Y	Y	Y	N
7 Rose	Y	Y	Y	Y	Y	Y	Y
8 Hefner	Y	N	Y	Y	Y	N	Y
9 ***Martin***	Y	N	Y	Y	Y	Y	Y
10 ***Broyhill***	Y	N	Y	Y	Y	N	Y
11 Clarke	Y	Y	Y	Y	Y	Y	Y
NORTH DAKOTA							
AL Dorgan	?	?	?	?	N	N	N
OHIO							
1 Luken	Y	N	Y	Y	N	Y	N
2 ***Gradison***	Y	Y	Y	Y	Y	Y	Y
3 Hall	Y	Y	Y	?	N	N	Y
4 ***Oxley***	Y	Y	Y	Y	Y	Y	Y
5 ***Latta***	Y	Y	Y	Y	Y	Y	N
6 ***McEwen***	Y	N	Y	Y	Y	Y	N
7 ***DeWine***	Y	Y	Y	Y	Y	Y	N
8 ***Kindness***	Y	Y	Y	Y	Y	Y	Y
9 Kaptur	Y	Y	Y	Y	N	Y	Y
10 ***Miller***	?	?	?	?	?	?	?
11 Eckart	Y	N	Y	Y	N	N	N
12 ***Kasich***	Y	Y	Y	Y	Y	N	N
13 Pease	Y	Y	Y	Y	N	Y	Y
14 Seiberling	?	Y	?	?	N	Y	Y
15 ***Wylie***	Y	Y	Y	Y	Y	Y	Y
16 ***Regula***	Y	N	Y	Y	Y	Y	N
17 ***Williams***	Y	Y	Y	Y	Y	Y	Y
18 Applegate	?	N	Y	?	N	N	N
19 Feighan	Y	N	Y	Y	Y	N	N
20 Oakar	Y	N	Y	Y	N	Y	N
21 Stokes	Y	Y	Y	Y	N	Y	Y
OKLAHOMA							
1 Jones	Y	N	Y	Y	Y	N	N
2 Synar	Y	N	Y	Y	Y	Y	Y
3 Watkins	Y	N	Y	Y	Y	N	N
4 McCurdy	Y	N	Y	Y	Y	N	N
5 ***Edwards***	N	N	Y	Y	Y	N	N
6 English	Y	N	Y	Y	Y	N	N
OREGON							
1 AuCoin	Y	Y	Y	Y	N	Y	N
2 ***Smith, R.***	Y	N	Y	Y	Y	N	N
3 Wyden	Y	N	Y	Y	N	Y	N
4 Weaver	Y	N	Y	Y	N	N	N
5 ***Smith, D.***	?	N	Y	Y	Y	N	N
PENNSYLVANIA							
1 Foglietta	?	?	?	?	Y	Y	Y
2 Gray	Y	Y	Y	Y	N	Y	Y
3 Borski	Y	Y	Y	Y	Y	Y	Y
4 Kolter	Y	N	Y	Y	Y	N	N
5 ***Schulze***	Y	N	Y	Y	Y	N	N
6 Yatron	Y	Y	Y	Y	Y	N	N
7 Edgar	Y	Y	Y	Y	N	Y	Y
8 Kostmayer	Y	Y	Y	Y	Y	Y	Y
9 ***Shuster***	Y	N	Y	Y	Y	N	N
10 ***McDade***	Y	Y	Y	Y	Y	Y	Y
11 Harrison	Y	Y	Y	Y	Y	Y	Y
12 Murtha	Y	Y	Y	Y	Y	Y	Y
13 ***Coughlin***	N	Y	Y	Y	N	Y	N
14 Coyne	Y	Y	Y	Y	Y	Y	Y
15 ***Ritter***	Y	N	Y	Y	N	N	N
16 ***Walker***	N	N	Y	Y	Y	N	N
17 ***Gekas***	Y	N	Y	Y	Y	Y	N
18 Walgren	Y	Y	Y	Y	N	N	?
19 ***Goodling***	N	Y	Y	Y	Y	N	N
20 Gaydos	?	Y	Y	Y	Y	Y	N
21 ***Ridge***	Y	Y	Y	Y	Y	Y	?
22 Murphy	N	N	Y	Y	Y	N	N
23 ***Clinger***	Y	Y	Y	Y	Y	Y	Y
RHODE ISLAND							
1 St Germain	P	Y	Y	Y	Y	Y	Y
2 ***Schneider***	Y	Y	Y	?	N	Y	Y
SOUTH CAROLINA							
1 ***Hartnett***	Y	N	Y	Y	Y	N	N
2 ***Spence***	Y	N	Y	Y	Y	N	N
3 Derrick	?	?	?	?	#	Y	Y
4 ***Campbell***	?	X	Y	Y	Y	Y	Y
5 Spratt	Y	Y	Y	Y	Y	Y	Y
6 Tallon	Y	Y	Y	Y	Y	N	N
SOUTH DAKOTA							
AL Daschle	?	?	?	?	Y	N	N
TENNESSEE							
1 ***Quillen***	Y	N	Y	Y	Y	Y	Y
2 ***Duncan***	Y	N	Y	Y	Y	N	Y
3 Lloyd	Y	N	Y	Y	Y	N	N
4 Cooper	Y	Y	Y	Y	Y	Y	#
5 Boner	Y	Y	Y	Y	Y	Y	N
6 Gore	Y	Y	Y	Y	Y	Y	Y
7 ***Sundquist***	Y	Y	Y	Y	Y	N	Y
8 Jones	Y	Y	Y	Y	Y	N	N
9 Ford	?	?	?	?	?	Y	Y
TEXAS							
1 Hall, S.	Y	N	Y	Y	Y	N	N
2 Wilson	?	Y	Y	Y	Y	N	N
3 ***Bartlett***	?	Y	Y	Y	Y	Y	N
4 Hall, R.	Y	N	Y	Y	Y	N	N
5 Bryant	?	Y	Y	Y	Y	N	N
6 ***Gramm***	?	N	Y	Y	Y	N	N
7 ***Archer***	Y	N	Y	Y	Y	N	N
8 ***Fields***	Y	N	Y	Y	Y	N	N
9 Brooks	Y	Y	Y	?	Y	N	Y
10 Pickle	Y	Y	Y	Y	Y	N	Y
11 Leath	Y	N	Y	Y	Y	N	N
12 Wright	Y	Y	Y	Y	Y	Y	Y
13 Hightower	Y	N	Y	Y	Y	Y	Y
14 Patman	Y	N	Y	Y	Y	N	N
15 de la Garza	Y	Y	Y	Y	?	Y	Y
16 Coleman	Y	Y	Y	Y	Y	Y	N
17 Stenholm	Y	N	Y	Y	Y	N	N
18 Leland	Y	Y	Y	Y	N	Y	Y
19 Hance	?	?	?	?	?	?	?
20 Gonzalez	Y	P	Y	Y	Y	N	N
21 ***Loeffler***	Y	N	Y	Y	Y	N	Y
22 ***Paul***	Y	N	Y	Y	N	N	?
23 Kazen	Y	N	Y	Y	Y	N	Y
24 Frost	Y	Y	Y	Y	Y	Y	Y
25 Andrews	Y	N	Y	Y	Y	Y	N
26 Vandergriff	Y	Y	Y	Y	Y	N	N
27 Ortiz	Y	Y	Y	Y	Y	?	?
UTAH							
1 ***Hansen***	?	?	?	?	?	?	X
2 ***Marriott***	Y	Y	Y	Y	Y	Y	N
3 ***Nielson***	Y	N	Y	Y	Y	N	N
VERMONT							
AL ***Jeffords***	Y	Y	Y	Y	Y	Y	Y
VIRGINIA							
1 ***Bateman***	Y	Y	Y	Y	Y	Y	Y
2 ***Whitehurst***	Y	Y	Y	Y	Y	Y	Y
3 ***Bliley***	Y	N	Y	Y	Y	N	Y
4 Sisisky	Y	N	Y	Y	Y	N	Y
5 Daniel	Y	N	Y	Y	Y	N	N
6 Olin	Y	Y	Y	Y	Y	N	Y
7 ***Robinson***	Y	N	Y	Y	Y	N	Y
8 ***Parris***	Y	Y	Y	?	Y	N	Y
9 Boucher	Y	Y	Y	Y	Y	Y	N
10 ***Wolf***	Y	Y	Y	Y	Y	N	Y
WASHINGTON							
1 ***Pritchard***	?	?	?	?	Y	Y	#
2 Swift	Y	Y	Y	Y	N	Y	Y
3 Bonker	Y	Y	Y	Y	Y	Y	Y
4 ***Morrison***	Y	Y	Y	Y	Y	Y	Y
5 Foley	Y	Y	Y	Y	Y	Y	Y
6 Dicks	Y	Y	Y	Y	Y	Y	Y
7 Lowry	Y	N	Y	Y	N	Y	N
8 ***Chandler***	Y	Y	Y	Y	Y	Y	Y
WEST VIRGINIA							
1 Mollohan	Y	Y	Y	Y	Y	N	Y
2 Staggers	Y	Y	Y	Y	Y	N	Y
3 Wise	Y	Y	Y	Y	Y	N	N
4 Rahall	?	?	?	?	#	N	Y
WISCONSIN							
1 Aspin	Y	Y	Y	Y	Y	Y	Y
2 Kastenmeier	Y	N	Y	Y	N	N	N
3 ***Gunderson***	Y	N	Y	Y	Y	N	N
4 Zablocki	Y	Y	Y	Y	Y	Y	Y
5 Moody	Y	Y	Y	Y	N	Y	N
6 ***Petri***	Y	N	Y	Y	Y	N	N
7 Obey	Y	N	Y	Y	N	Y	N
8 ***Roth***	Y	Y	Y	Y	Y	N	N
9 ***Sensenbrenner***	Y	N	Y	Y	Y	N	N
WYOMING							
AL ***Cheney***	Y	N	Y	Y	Y	Y	N

Southern states - Ala., Ark., Fla., Ga., Ky., La., Miss., N.C., Okla., S.C., Tenn., Texas, Va.

HOUSE ROLL-CALL VOTES

	CQ Roll-Call No.	Page

AGRICULTURE
Critical agricultural materials............109 ....38-H
Dairy production stabilization ... 422, 438-443 ......126-H, 130-H
Early agriculture program announcements . 286 ....86-H
Emergency Agricultural Credit
   Act........................ 59-62, 70-73 ....24-H, 26-H
Federal nutrition programs ....287 ....86-H
Payment-in-Kind Tax Act ....19 ....10-H
Upland cotton PIK program .... 241, 371 ......74-H, 110-H

APPROPRIATIONS
FY 1983
   Emergency supplemental .... 14-15 ....8-H
   Emergency supplemental/Jobs..... 16-18, ...10-H, 16-H
   39-40
   Supplemental 129-131, 271-273, 278-280 ....42-H—44-H,
   82-H, 84-H
FY 1984
   Agriculture .... 166-167 ....52-H
   Continuing ..... 343, 354-355, 425-436, ...102-H, 106-H,
   450-452, 455   126-H—128-H,
   132-H, 134-H
   Defense 391-393, 408-413, 470-472, 496 .....116-H, 122-H,
   138-H, 144-H
   District of Columbia......... 219, 347 ......66-H, 104-H
   Energy and water development.. 154-160, ... 50-H, 64-H, 66-H
   208, 218
   Energy and water supplemental 361, 364 ....108-H
   HUD/Independent agencies..... 137-143, .. 44-H—46-H, 64-H
   215
   Interior .... 210-213, 360 ......64-H, 108-H
   Labor-HHS-Education ...... 334-336, 380 ......100-H, 112-H
   Legislative branch.... 144, 147-153, 217 ... 46-H, 48-H, 66-H
   State, Justice, Commerce 325-326, 402-403, ... 98-H, 120-H,
   444-447, 474-475 130-H—132-H, 138-H
   Supplemental .... 362-363, 497 ......108-H, 144-H
   Transportation .... 194-199 ....60-H
   Treasury, Postal Service and General
   Government .... 168-171, 395-396 . 52-H—54-H, 118-H

COMMUNICATIONS
Universal telephone service ..... 448, 453-454 ......132-H, 134-H

CONGRESSIONAL AFFAIRS
Committee election....................242 ....74-H
Committee funds......................262 ....80-H
Congressional Advisory Commission on
   Boxing ....253 ....78-H
Congressional Award Board .... 84 ....32-H
Daniel B. Crane censure .... 243-244 ....74-H
District work period.................281 ....84-H
Election of Speaker ....1 ....2-H
Gerry E. Studds censure .... 245-246 ....74-H
Hearing transcript investigation . 216, 221-222 ....66-H
House committee funding.............. 37 ....14-H
House records subpoena .... 64-65 ....24-H
House rules .... 2-3 ....2-H
Procedural motion 13, 36, 41, 48, 51, 63, 74, .. 8-H, 14-H, 16-H,
   89, 99, 118, 122, 146, 177, 200, 209, 20-H, 22-H, 24-H,
   249, 394, 399, 421, 457, 467, 485 26-H, 32-H, 36-H,
   40-H, 42-H, 48-H,
   56-H, 62-H, 64-H,
   76-H, 118-H, 120-H,
   126-H, 134-H, 136-H,
   142-H

Select Committee on Children, Youth and
   Families ....4 ....4-H

	CQ Roll-Call No.	Page

Select Committee on Narcotics Abuse and
   Control..........................5 ....4-H

DEFENSE
Defense authorization. 180-182, 184-187, 192, ...56-H—58-H,
   247-248, 250, 255-261 74-H, 76-H, 78-H—
   80-H
Intelligence authorizations .... 377-379 ....112-H
Military construction authorization........191 ....58-H
Multinational Force in Lebanon .. 340-342, 350 ......102-H, 104-H
MX development .... 123, 133 ......42-H, 44-H
Nuclear freeze .... 24-30, 49-50, 52-58, .. 12-H, 20-H, 22-H,
   66-68, 75-83 24-H—26-H,
   28-H—30-H
Omnibus defense authorizations .... 284, 322 ......86-H, 96-H
Polish Legion of American Veterans ......463 ....136-H
Veterans' Association ....462 ....136-H
Vietnam veterans medal...............367 ....110-H

ECONOMIC AFFAIRS/LABOR
American Conservation Corps .... 8 ....8-H
Budget reconciliation .... 389-390 ....116-H
Community Renewal Employment
   Act .... 327-333 ...... 98-H—100-H
Debt limit extension .... 120-121 ....40-H
Debt limit increase ....498 ....144-H
Defense Production Act extension ....359 ....108-H
Federal supplemental unemployment
   compensation .... 285, 383 .... 86-H, 114-H
First budget resolution, FY 1984 . 38, 42, 201, ... 14-H, 16-H, 62-H
   204
Interest and dividend tax withholding...115 ....40-H
Interest and dividend tax withholding/
   Caribbean Basin Initiative ....263 ....80-H
International Recovery and Financial
   Stability Act.......... 251, 254, 274-277 .... 76-H, 78-H,
   82-H—84-H
National Development Investment Act. 226-228 ....70-H
Railroad retirement solvency ....282 ....84-H
Revenue sharing................. 290-296 ...... 86-H—88-H
Social Security Act Amendments .... 20-23, 43 ...... 10-H, 18-H
Tax Rate Equity Act....... 202-203, 205-207 ....62-H
Tax Reform Act ....490 ....142-H
Trade adjustment assistance.............311 ....92-H
Unemployment compensation supple-
   mental .... 344-345 ....104-H

ENERGY/ENVIRONMENT
Belle Fourche project .... 406 ....120-H
California Wilderness Act .... 45-47 ....20-H
Coal Pipeline Act.....................339 ....102-H
Dept. of Energy civilian research and devel-
   opment programs .... 93, 104-108 .. 34-H, 36-H—38-H
Disapproving energy conservation deferral . 134 ....44-H
Disapproving fossil energy research deferral. 135 ....44-H
Hazardous waste control...... 308-309, 404, ... 92-H, 120-H,
   418-420 124-H
Irish wilderness......................288 ....86-H
Kodiak National Wildlife Refuge .... 44 ....20-H
Lavelle contempt of Congress resolution ...119 ....40-H
National Marine Sanctuaries ....179 ....56-H
North Carolina Wilderness Act ....482 ....140-H
Ocean and coastal resources management. 317 ....94-H
Oregon lands................... 385-386 ....114-H
Oregon wilderness................. 31-35 ....14-H
Park system protection........... 357-358 ....106-H
Wisconsin Wilderness Act ....483 ....140-H

	CQ Roll-Call No.	Page
FOREIGN AFFAIRS		
Andrei Sakharov Day	116	40-H
Aquino assassination	388	114-H
Auto domestic content requirement	415-417	124-H
Caribbean Basin Initiative	236-237	72-H
Cyprus	486	142-H
El Salvador aid certification	161	50-H
Export Administration Act	337, 348-349, 352-353, 368-374, 397-398	102-H, 104-H, 106-H, 110-H—112-H, 118-H
Forced labor in the Soviet Union	494-495	144-H
International Recovery and Financial Stability Act	302-304	90-H
Korean plane resolution	320	96-H
Lebanon aid	145	46-H
Lebanon-Israel agreement	128	42-H
Most-favored nation status for Romania	283	84-H
Prohibition on covert action in Nicaragua	264-270	80-H—82-H
Radio broadcasting to Cuba	346	104-H
State Department authorizations	173-175, 493	54-H, 144-H
Trade adjustment assistance	318-319, 323-324	94-H, 96-H
Trade programs authorizations	114	38-H
War Powers Resolution	407	122-H
GOVERNMENT OPERATIONS		
Christopher Columbus Quincentenary	193	60-H
Death benefits for policemen and firefighters	252	78-H
Debt Collection Act	461	136-H
Federal contracting opportunities	7	6-H
Federal Physicians Comparability Allowance Act	484	142-H
Follow Through Amendments	164	52-H
Harry S Truman Centennial Commemoration	224	68-H
Martin Luther King Jr. holiday	289	
National Academy of Public Administration	464	136-H
National Science Foundation authorization	92, 100-103	34-H, 36-H
Omnibus Minor Tariff Amendments	214	64-H
Postal Savings System Statute of Limitations	479	140-H
Securities and Exchange Act Amendments	112	38-H
Securities and Exchange Commission authorization	111	38-H
Select Commission on Voluntary Service Opportunities	477	140-H
Small Business Administration pilot program extension	6, 225	6-H, 68-H
Tribally controlled community colleges	69	26-H
Veterans' Appeals Board expansion	113	38-H
Veterans' housing benefits	124	42-H
Vietnam Veterans' Training Act	163	52-H
Washington Workshops Foundation authorization	165	52-H
Weather satellite systems	466	136-H

	CQ Roll-Call No.	Page
HEALTH/EDUCATION/WELFARE		
Child support enforcement	476	140-H
Close Up Foundation	381-382	114-H
Digestive diseases awareness week	117	40-H
Disapproving Mariana Islands hospital deferral	136	44-H
Domestic Volunteer Service Act Amendments	400-401	120-H
Education of the handicapped	487	142-H
Emergency food assistance	176, 189	54-H, 58-H
Emergency Mathematics and Science Education Act	9-12	8-H
Emergency School Aid Act	162	52-H
Guidelines for Equal Opportunity in Education	478	140-H
Health Research Extension Act	238, 491	72-H, 142-H
Meals for Older Americans	125	42-H
Military Medicine Foundation	87	32-H
Rehabilitation Act Amendments	310, 313-316	92-H, 94-H
School lunch and child nutrition amendments	387	114-H
Unemployment health insurance	298-300	88-H—90-H
HOUSING/COMMUNITY DEVELOPMENT		
Emergency Housing Assistance Act	95-98	34-H
Housing and Urban-Rural Recovery Act	223, 229-235	66-H, 70-H—72-H
Temporary extension of certain housing programs	110	38-H
LAW ENFORCEMENT/JUDICIARY		
Child Protection Act	456, 459	134-H
Consumer Products Tampering	86	32-H
Drug Dependent Federal Offenders	85	32-H
Equal Rights Amendment	469	138-H
Justice Assistance Act of 1983	88-91	32-H
Justice Department authorization	351	106-H
Refugee Assistance Act	460	134-H
U.S. Commission on Civil Rights	307	92-H
TRANSPORTATION/COMMERCE		
Amtrak Improvement Act	365	108-H
Consumer Product Safety Act	190, 220	58-H, 66-H
Credit card protection	480	140-H
Credit card surcharges ban extension	481	140-H
Daylight-saving time	239-240	72-H
Elimination of Jones Act exemption	178	56-H
Federal Communications Commission authorization	488-489	142-H
Maritime authorization	423	126-H
National Transportation Safety Board authorization	126	42-H
Satellite-directed navigation	465	136-H

SENATE ROLL-CALL VOTES

	CQ Roll-Call No.	Page
AGRICULTURE		
Critical Agricultural Materials Act	220-223	37-S—38-S
Dairy and Tobacco Adjustment Act	273-280	45-S—46-S
APPROPRIATIONS		
FY 1983		
Emergency supplemental/Jobs	12-27, 30-31, 44-45	5-S—8-S, 10-S
Supplemental	127-134, 138-140, 144-153, 228-229	25-S—28-S, 39-S

	CQ Roll-Call No.	Page
FY 1984		
Agriculture	172-175	31-S
Continuing	335-344, 346-348	55-S—56-S, 57-S
Defense	322-334, 370	53-S—55-S, 60-S
Energy and water development	163-164, 176	29-S—30-S, 31-S
HUD/Independent agencies	161-162, 171	29-S, 31-S
Interior	231, 244-249	39-S, 41-S

	CQ Roll-Call No.	Page
Labor-HHS-Education	269-272	44-S
Legislative branch	165-166	30-S
State, Justice, Commerce	301-302, 352	50-S, 57-S
Supplemental	306-308, 361-364, 365-368	50-S — 51-S, 59-S, 60-S
Transportation	192, 233	34-S, 39-S

CONGRESSIONAL AFFAIRS

Procedural motion	56, 337	14-S, 56-S
Senate day-care center	351	57-S

DEFENSE

MX development	113-115	23-S
Multinational Force in Lebanon	259-264	43-S
Omnibus defense authorizations	177-191, 193-217, 234	32-S — 33-S, 34-S — 37-S, 40-S

ECONOMIC AFFAIRS/LABOR

Budget

First resolution, FY 1984	66-86, 102-122, 167-168	16-S — 19-S, 22-S — 23-S, 30-S
Omnibus Reconciliation Act	356, 358	58-S
Debt limit increase	309-320, 359-360	51-S — 53-S, 58-S
Export-Import Bank	258	43-S
Interest and dividend tax withholding	57-63, 156-157	14-S — 15-S, 29-S
Interest and dividend tax withholding/Caribbean Basin Initiative	224	38-S
Jobs supplemental, FY 1983	12-27, 30, 44, 45	5-S — 8-S, 10-S
Korean plane resolution	242-243	41-S
Labor Management Racketeering Act	158	29-S
Oregon lands	304	50-S
Railroad retirement solvency	230	39-S
Revenue sharing	250-252	42-S
Social Security Act Amendments	28-29, 32-43, 46-54	8-S, 9-S — 12-S
Tax Rate Equity Act	170	31-S
Unemployment compensation supplemental	265-268	43-S — 44-S
Volcker nomination	218	37-S

EDUCATION

Olympic duty suspension/Tuition tax credit	355, 357	58-S

	CQ Roll-Call No.	Page

ENERGY/ENVIRONMENT

Natural Gas Policy Act Amendments	321, 353-354	53-S, 58-S

FOREIGN POLICY

International Monetary Fund authorization	116-126	24-S — 25-S
Korean plane resolution	235-241	40-S
Radio Marti	225-227, 232	38-S, 39-S
State Department authorizations	253-257, 294, 295-300	42-S, 48-S, 49-S
Treaties	159-160, 219	29-S, 37-S
Treaty (Doc 97-5), Maritime boundaries	159	29-S
Treaty (Doc 98-1), 1992 International expositions	7	4-S

HEALTH

Social Security disability payments	371	60-S

GOVERNMENT OPERATIONS

Martin Luther King Jr. holiday	281-293	47-S — 48-S
Number of public holidays	298	49-S

LAW ENFORCEMENT/JUDICIARY

Civil Rights Commission Act	345, 349-350	57-S
Human Life Federalism Amendment	169	31-S
Immigration reform	64-65, 89-101	16-S, 20-S — 21-S
Montreal Aviation Protocols	9	5-S

NOMINATIONS

Adelman	55	13-S
Burt	2	3-S
Clark	369	60-S
Dole	1	2-S
Heckler	8	4-S
Regnery	88	20-S
Ruckelshaus	87	20-S
Svahn	11	5-S
Tambs	10	5-S

TRANSPORTATION/COMMERCE

Cable Telecommunications Act	135-137, 141-143	26-S, 27-S
Shipping Act of 1983	3-6	4-S
Surface Transportation Technical Corrections Act	303, 305	50-S

INDEX

A

Abandoned Mine Reclamation Fund - 511

Abdnor, James, R-S.D.
Appropriations - 455, 534
Cable television deregulation - 553
Committees - 44-62, 99-100
Congressional voting studies - 3-C-42-C
Martin Luther King holiday - 601
MX debate - 198
Roll call votes - 2-S-60-S

Abortion
Amendment efforts - 308-311
Appropriations - 507, 508
Equal Rights Amendment issue - 296, 297
Federal employee health plans - 530, 533, 535
Fetal research - 409
Funding restrictions (box) - 310
Key votes - 4-C
Legislative summary - 25
Supreme Court decisions - 306-308, 3-A, 10-A-11-A

Abram, Morris - 293-295

Abscam investigation
Background - 585-586
Censure proceedings - 582
Prison convictions - 585-586

Acid rain
Administration policy - 340-341
Congressional action - 151

Ackerman, Gary, D-N.Y. (7)
Acid rain - 340-341
Committees - 63-98, 101-105
Congressional voting studies - 3-C-42-C
Election results - 6-B
Roll call votes - 2-H-145-H

Acquired Immune Deficiency Syndrome (AIDS)
Emergency health fund - 417
Research appropriations - 506, 510, 511, 513

ACTION. *(See also Peace Corps.)*
Appropriations - 505, 508, 509
Authorization - 398

Addabbo, Joseph P., D-N.Y. (6)
Appropriations - 478, 484, 513
Committees - 63-98, 101-105
Congressional voting studies - 3-C-42-C
MX debate - 198
Nicaragua covert aid - 132
Pershing II deployment - 207
Roll call votes - 2-H-145-H

Adelman, Kenneth L.
Confirmation - 173, 23-A, 25-A
Legislative summary - 16

Administration of Foreign Affairs - 473 (chart)

Adolescents. *See Youth.*

Adult and continuing education
Appropriations - 505 (chart)
Vocational - 507

Aegis cruisers - 482, 487, 493

Aerojet-General Corp. - 332, 333

Affirmative action
Education - 10-A
Employment - 9-A-10-A
Sex discrimination - 4-A, 10-A

AFL-CIO - 145, 148 (box)

Africa. *(See also Middle East; names of individual countries.)*
Development funds - 241, 242, 247, 522 (chart)
Foreign aid - 144

African Development Fund
Appropriations - 522 (chart)
Authorization - 241, 242, 247

Aged persons. *(See also Medicaid; Medicare; Retirement and pensions; Social security programs; Supplemental Security Income.)*

Community service - 504, 506
Employment discrimination - 4-A
Employment programs - 433, 449 (chart), 504, 506
Food assistance program - 415, 418
Health care - 504
Housing programs - 279
Housing project mortgages - 495-500
Nutrition programs - 510

Agency for International Development (AID)
Appropriations - 511, 522 (chart), 526
Foreign aid - 145
Nominations and confirmations - 28-A

Agent Orange - 536, 537

Agricultural Adjustment Act - 456

Agricultural commerce. *See Agricultural price supports; Agricultural trade.*

Agricultural Cooperative Service - 516

Agricultural Credit Insurance Fund - 453

Agricultural Marketing Agreement Act - 532

Agricultural price supports
Appropriations - 517
Dairy program - 13, 375-380, 10-C
Grain - 14
Key votes - 10-C
PIK payments - 381
Target price freeze - 376, 383-384
Tobacco program - 13, 375-380
Wheat industry - 14, 383

Agricultural Research Service
Appropriations - 448 (chart), 453, 454, 457, 516 (chart), 517-518
Budget - 430

Agricultural Stabilization and Conservation Service (ASCS)
Appropriations - 516 (chart), 517
Tobacco quotas - 379

Agricultural trade. *(See also Food for Peace.)*
Dairy surplus - 14
Export subsidies - 384, 385 (box)
Export markets - 381
Meat imports - 380
Produce trade - 388
Tobacco imports - 380
U.S. Soviet grain pact (box) - 387

Agriculture and farming. *(See also Agriculture Department; Farm income stabilization and aid programs; Food and nutrition; Forests and forestry; Migrant farmworkers; Rural affairs.)*
Acreage reduction program - 380-383, 386-387, 509, 510
Appropriations - 448 (chart), 453, 454, 457, 509, 510
Budget - 430, 433, 445 (chart)
Drought aid, impact - 374, 378, 387-388
Farm recession relief - 384-386
Food assistance programs - 412-416
Food stamp program - 509
Illegal alien labor - 287-290
Legislative summary - 13-14
Loan repayments - 13
Overview, 1983 - 373-374
Mortgage foreclosure relief - 444
Payment-in-Kind program (PIK)
Appropriations - 509, 510, 517, 519
Background - 373-374, 380-381
Budget - 433
Provisions - 381
Tax changes - 381-383
Target price freeze - 383-384
Tobacco program
Legislative summary - 13
Licensing system (box) - 369
Price-support freeze - 375, 377, 378 (box)
Provisions - 375-376
Soil conservation bill - 14, 387

Agriculture Department (USDA). *(See also Forest Service, U.S.)*
Appropriations
FY 1983 supplemental - 448 (chart), 453, 454, 457, 509, 510
FY 1984 continuing resolution - 516-520, 529
Budget - 434
Dairy assessment delay veto - 35-E-36-E
Dairy program - 10-C
Farm announcements veto - 34-E-35-E
Food assistance programs - 412-416
Food stamps - 509, 516-518
Nominations and confirmations - 25-A
OMB review - 531, 535
Payment-in-Kind program (PIK) - 373-374, 509, 510, 517, 519

AID. *See Agency for International Development.*

Aid to Families with Dependent Children (AFDC)
Budget - 433, 438
Child support enforcement - 300, 418
Refugee assistance - 305

Air bags - 544, 3-A

Air Force. *(See also Aircraft; Weapons.)*
Appropriations - 479-494, 510
Authorization - 175-178, 183-185, 192
Military construction funds - 193-195, 469-472

Air National Guard
Appropriation - 481
Authorization - 183, 189

Air pollution
Acid rain
Administration policy - 340-341
Congressional action - 151
Appropriations - 497-500
Clean Air Act proposals
Background - 339
Legislative summary - 20
Sanctions - 339-340, 498, 8-C

Air Transport Association - 301, 543

Air transportation. *(See also Aircraft; Airports.)*
Air disaster treaty - 300-301
Air traffic controllers - 460
Airline industry - 543
Appropriations - 457-462, 459 (chart)
Budget - 430 (chart), 434
Korean airline downing - 136-137, 175, 190, 257

Aircraft. *(See also Space and space programs.)*
Commercial
DC-10 - 178, 185
Korean airline downing - 136-137, 175, 190, 257
Military
Appropriations - 479-494, 488 (chart), 511
Authorization - 175-193
B-1 bomber - 175, 179, 187, 190, 485, 486, 491, 510, 513, 515
Cargo - 185, 481, 483, 486
Carrier - 486
Fighter planes - 177, 184, 192, 482, 486, 488 (chart)
Helicopters - 176, 178, 191, 192, 481, 483, 487, 488 (chart)
Sales - 133-134
Spare parts - 178, 193
Stealth bomber - 175
Tanker - 185, 190
Transports - 178, 192

Airline Deregulation Act - 461

Airlines. *See Air transportation.*

Airport and Airway Trust Fund - 458, 460

Airports
Appropriations
FY 1983 supplemental - 448 (chart), 453, 456

FY 1984 - 457-462
Baltimore-Washington International (BWI) Airport - 462
Dulles Airport - 462
National Airport - 461-462

Akaka, Daniel K., D-Hawaii (2)
Committees - 63-98, 101-105
Congressional voting studies - 3-C-42-C
Housing authorization - 283
Roll call votes - 2-H-145-H

Alabama
Employment funds - 455
Highway construction bill - 536
Wilderness areas - 342

Alaska. *(See also Indians and Alaskan natives.)*
Hunting bill - 347-348
Park system - 347-348

Alaska National Interest Lands Conservation Act - 347

Alaska Power Administration - 501

Albosta, Donald J., D-Mich. (10)
Carter briefing papers - 564, 594
Committees - 63-98, 101-105
Congressional voting studies - 3-C-42-C
Roll call votes - 2-H-145-H

Alcohol, Drug Abuse and Mental Health Administration - 505

Alcoholic beverages. *(See also Alcoholism; Bureau of Alcohol, Tobacco and Firearms.)*
Imported rum - 253

Alcoholism. *(See also Drugs, drug abuse.)*
Block grants - 505, 506
Drunk driving legislation - 321
Research
Appropriations - 449 (chart), 454
Education programs - 402

Alexander, Bill, D-Ark. (1)
Appropriations - 527, 537
Committees - 63-98, 101-105
Congressional voting studies - 3-C-42-C
Drought aid - 388
Peacekeeping forces in Lebanon - 123
Roll call votes - 2-H-145-H

Aliens. *(See also Refugees.)*
Asylum review - 289, 290
Bilingual education - 505, 507
Employment - 287-290
Immigration reform bill - 287-292
Supreme Court rulings - 11-A

All Volunteer Force
Education benefits - 418-419
Reductions - 480

Allain, Bill - 4-B

Allen, Richard V. - 330

Alternative fuels. *See Solar and renewable energies; Synthetic fuels.*

Alzheimer's disease - 409

Ambassador confirmations - 27-A

Amendments, constitutional
Anti-abortion - 308-311
Balanced Budget - 238
Equal Rights - 296-298, 11-C
First Amendment
Church and State - 168-169, 4-A, 12-A
Freedom of speech - 298, 12-A
Freedom of the press - 5-A, 12-A
Supreme Court rulings - 12-A
Tenth Amendment - 5-A, 17-A-18-A

American Academy of Pediatrics - 419

American Association of Retired Persons (AARP) - 222

American Association of University Women (AAUW) - 299

American Bank & Trust Co. v. Dallas County - 18-A

American Bankers Association - 263

American Bar Association
Air crash liability - 301
Insanity defense revisions - 314

Judicial nominee ratings - 303, 304
American Battle Monuments Commission - 496, 499
American Civil Liberties Union (ACLU)
Human rights issues - 165-167
Immigration reform bill - 289
School prayer - 301
American Conservation Corps - 229, 230
American Farm Bureau Federation - 378
American Federation of State, County and Municipal Employees (AFSCME) - 268
American Hospital Association - 392
American Indians. See Indians and Alaskan natives.
American Legion - 599
American Medical Association
Medicare revisions - 392
Regulation of professionals - 473, 561
American Paper Institute Inc. v. American Electric Power Service Corp., Federal Energy Regulatory Commission (FERC) v. American Electric Power Service Corp. - 16-A
American Public Health Association - 419
American Psychiatric Association (APA) - 314
American Telephone & Telegraph Co. (AT&T)
Cable television deregulation - 15, 552-554
Divestiture - 544
Telephone rates - 545-549, 10-C, 13
American Trucking Association - 543
Amtrak
Appropriations
FY 1983 supplemental - 448 (chart), 451, 453, 456
FY 1984 - 458, 460, 461
Authorization - 544, 561-562
Budget - 434
Legislative summary - 27
Rerouting - 461
Anderson, Glenn M., D-Calif. (32)
Committees - 63-98, 101-105
Congressional voting studies - 3-C-42-C
Maritime antitrust bill - 556
NIH authorization - 410
Roll call votes - 2-H-145-H
Anderson v. Celebrezze - 13-A
Andrews, Ike, D-N.C. (4)
Committees - 63-98, 101-105
Congressional voting studies - 3-C-42-C
Roll call votes - 2-H-145-H
Andrews, Mark, R-N.D.
Appropriations - 461, 494, 503, 520
Budget - 439, 440
Committees - 44-62, 99-100
Congressional voting studies - 3-C-42-C
Food assistance programs - 414
Indian colleges aid - 396
Roll call votes - 2-S-60-S
Water projects - 355
Andrews, Michael A., D-Texas (25)
Adelman nomination - 213
Committees - 63-98, 101-105
Congressional voting studies - 3-C-42-C
MX debate - 196
Roll call votes - 2-H-145-H
Andropov, Yuri - 480
Animals. (See also Wildlife and wildlife refuges.)
Alaska sport hunting bill - 347
Research monitoring - 409
Wild horses and burros management - 347
Annunzio, Frank, D-Ill. (11)
Appropriations - 534
Committees - 63-98, 101-105
Congressional voting studies - 3-C-42-C

Credit card surcharges - 267
Roll call votes - 2-H-145-H
Anthony, Beryl Jr., D-Ark. (4)
Committees - 63-98, 101-105
Congressional voting studies - 3-C-42-C
Roll call votes - 2-H-145-H
Antiballistic missile system (ABM) - 176
Anti-recession aid. See Countercyclical aid and targeted fiscal assistance.
Anti-satellite missiles (ASAT)
Appropriations - 479, 480, 483, 494
Authorization - 181, 188, 191
Antigua - 135
Antitrust and competition
Maritime antitrust bill - 27, 544, 554-557
Oil industry - 19, 371
Price fixing - 477, 478
Supreme Court decisions - 13-A
Trucking industry - 543, 559-560
Appalachian Regional Commission
Appropriations - 501, 536, 537
Authorization - 229-230
Applegate, Douglas, D-Ohio (18)
Committees - 63-98, 101-105
Congressional voting studies - 3-C-42-C
Roll call votes - 2-H-145-H
Appointments, presidential. See Nominations and confirmations.
Appropriations. (See also Budget, U.S.)
FY 1983 supplementals
Agriculture - 509-515
Commerce - 509-515
Congressional action - 511-515
Defense - 509-515
Education - 509-515
Employment - 447
Energy - 509-515
Foreign aid - 509-515, 524
Health and Human Services - 447-457, 509-515
Housing and Urban Development - 495-500, 509-515
Interior - 509-515
Labor - 509-515
Provisions - 448-449 (chart)
Transportation - 509-515
Treasury - 496, 499
Veto threat - 514
FY 1984
Agriculture - 516-520
Commerce - 472-479
Continuing resolutions
First - 526-528
Second - 528-531
Defense - 479-494
District of Columbia - 494-495
Education - 504-509
Energy - 500-503
Environment - 495, 496
Executive branch - 531-536
Foreign aid - 521-526, 522 (chart)
Health and Human Services - 504-509
Housing and Urban Development - 495-500
Independent agencies - 495-500
Interior - 20, 462-469
Judiciary - 472-479
Justice - 472-479
Labor - 504-509
Legislative branch - 539-542
Military construction - 469-472
Postal Service - 531-536
State - 472-479
Summary, end of session (chart) - 422
Transportation - 457-462
Treasury - 531-536
Veterans Administration - 496-500
Water projects - 500-503
House rule changes - 596-597

Legislative summary - 14
Aquatic Resources Trust Fund - 562
Arkansas National Wildlife Refuge - 345
Aravaipa Canyon - 341
Archer, Bill, R-Texas (7)
Committees - 63-98, 101-105
Congressional voting studies - 3-C-42-C
Roll call votes - 2-H-145-H
Social Security rescue bill - 221-222
Architect of the Capitol - 540, 542
Architectural and Transportation Barriers Compliance Board - 459
Argentina
Foreign aid - 143
U.S. technology transfer - 150, 152
Arizona
Abortion laws - 308
Coal slurry pipelines - 550
Employment funds - 455
Indian water rights - 587
Unemployment benefits - 275
Water projects - 520-521
Wilderness area - 341, 464
Arizona Governing Committee for Tax Deferred Annuity and Deferred Compensation Plans v. Norris - 10-A
Arizona v. California - 19-A
Arizona v. San Carlos Apache Tribe of Arizona, Montana v. Northern Cheyenne Tribe of the Northern Cheyenne Indian Reservation - 18-A
Arkansas - 455
Arkansas Electric Cooperative Corp. v. Arkansas Public Commission - 16-A
Arleigh Burke (ship) - 178, 185, 487, 493
Armed services. See Defense Department; Military personnel issues; Veterans affairs; individual branches: Air Force; Army; Coast Guard; Marine Corps; National Guard; Navy; Reserves, military.
"Armed Resistance Unit" - 30
Armored combat vehicles. See Tanks (military).
Arms, military. See Weapons.
Arms control. (See also Nuclear nonproliferation.)
Adelman nomination - 213
Arms talks - 173-174, 200-201, 210-211, 214, 479, 484
Defense authorization - 175, 180
Joint Statement of Agreed Principles for Disarmament Negotiations - 210
Legislative summary - 16
MX missile deployment - 175, 180
Nuclear freeze resolution
Congressional action - 205-212
Text - 210-211
Legislative summary - 6-C, 8-C
Nuclear deterrence debate (box) - 202-203
Overview, 1983 - 173-174
Presidential messages (text) - 21-E, 22-E-25-E, 32-E-34-E
Scowcroft Commission report - 195-196, 203 (box), 204
Strategic Arms Limitation Treaty (SALT II)
Nuclear freeze resolution - 214
Presidential messages (text) - 27-E
Strategic Arms Reduction Talks (START)
Nuclear freeze resolution - 173-174
Presidential messages (text) - 27-E-28-E, 33-E-34-E
Revised proposals - 200-201
Scowcroft Commission - 197
Arms Control and Disarmament Agency (ACDA)
Appropriations - 473 (chart), 475, 477 (chart), 509
Nominations and confirmations - 25-A, 30-A

Arms Export Control Act - 563, 569
Arms sales
Guatemala - 137-138
Israel - 133-134
Jordan - 134-135
Legislative veto - 569
"Sensitive technology" items - 144
Armstrong, William L., R-Colo.
Appropriations - 539
Budget - 438, 439
Budget control proposal - 238
Coal leasing ban - 354
Committees - 44-62, 99-100
Congressional voting studies - 3-C-42-C
Debt limit increase - 240
Deficit reduction proposals - 231
Housing authorization - 281
IMF Funding - 243
Roll call votes - 2-S-60-S
Social Security rescue bill - 221-222, 224
Soil conservation - 387
Tax proposals - 237
Army. (See also Military personnel issues; National Guard; Reserves, military; Selective service system; Veterans affairs; Weapons.)
Appropriations
FY 1983 supplemental - 448 (chart), 452, 509, 510
FY 1984 - 500-503, 500 (chart)
Army cemeterial expenses - 496, 499
Authorization - 177, 178, 180, 183-186, 191-195
Grenada invasion - 135
Military construction - 193-195, 469-472
Nominations and confirmations - 26-A
Army Corps of Engineers
Appropriations - 500-503, 520-521
Authorization bill - 354-359
Cost sharing - 358
ASAT. See Anti-satellite missiles (ASAT).
Ashbrook, John M. - 530
Asia. (See also Middle East; names of individual countries.)
Asia Foundation
Appropriations - 473 (chart), 475
Authorization - 146, 148 (box)
Asian Development Bank
Appropriations - 522 (chart), 537
Authorization - 241, 242, 247
Aspin, Les, D-Wis. (1)
Appropriations - 484
Committees - 63-98, 101-105
Congressional voting studies - 3-C-42-C
Defense authorization - 180, 181
MX debate - 197, 202-204
Peacekeeping forces in Lebanon - 123
Roll call votes - 2-H-145-H
Associated General Contractors of California Inc. v. California State Council of Carpenters - 13-A
Associated Milk Producers Inc.(AMPI) - 376
Association of Trial Lawyers of America - 301
Athletics. See Sports and recreation.
Atlantic Alliance. See North Atlantic Treaty Organization.
Atomic energy. See Nuclear energy.
Atomic Energy Act - 5-A
AuCoin, Les, D-Ore. (1)
Appropriations - 507
Committees - 63-98, 101-105
Congressional voting studies - 3-C-42-C
Defense authorization - 190
MX debate - 198, 200
Nuclear freeze resolution - 208-209, 212
Roll call votes - 2-H-145-H
Wilderness areas - 343
Automobiles and automobile industry. (See also Gasoline; Highways and roads.)

Domestic content bill - 257-259
Drunk driving legislation - 321
Passive restraints - 544, 3-A

B

B-1 bomber
  Appropriations - 485, 486, 488 (chart),
    491, 510, 513, 515
  Authorization - 175, 179, 187, 190
  Budget - 432
"Baby Doe" controversy - 390
Badham, Robert E., R-Calif. (40)
  Committees - 63-98, 101-105
  Congressional voting studies - 3-C-42-C
  Roll call votes - 2-H-145-H
Baker, Howard H. Jr., R-Tenn.
  Adelman nomination - 214
  Air crash liability treaty - 301
  Appropriations - 454, 478, 527, 530-
    531, 536, 538, 541
  Budget - 438, 442, 444, 447
  Capitol bombing - 593
  Carter briefing papers - 594
  Civil Rights Commission - 292-293, 295
  Clinch River breeder reactor - 364,
    365, 6-C
  Committees - 44-62, 99-100
  Congressional voting studies - 3-C-42-C
  Debt limit increase - 240
  El Salvador aid - 161
  Grenada invasion - 122, 135
  Housing authorization - 281
  Korean airline downing - 137
  Lebanon resolution - 5-C
  Legislative veto - 569-570
  Martin Luther King holiday - 601, 6-C
  Peacekeeping forces in Lebanon - 118-
    119, 122, 9-C
  Presidential support - 20-C
  Politics - 12
  Roll call votes - 2-S-60-S
  Senate rule changes proposals - 598
  Senate television coverage - 15, 595-
    596, 598
  Social Security rescue bill - 221, 225
  Tuition tax credits - 395
  Watt resignation - 150
  Withholding tax revisions - 263
Baker, James A. III - 438
Baker v. Carr - 5-B
Balanced Budget Amendment - 238
Baldrige, Malcolm - 250
**Baltimore-Washington International
  (BWI) Airport** - 462
BankAmerica Corp. v. United States -
  14-A
Bankruptcy
  Airline - 543
  Consumer bill - 318-321
  Courts - 286, 318-320
  Grain elevators - 311
  Legislative summary - 25
  Shopping center bankruptcy - 321
  Supreme Court decisions - 14-A
Banks and banking. *(See also Coins
  and currency; Credit; Federal Reserve
  Board; International development banks;
  Stocks, bonds and securities.)*
  Credit card surcharges - 267
  Deregulation - 15
  Farm program - 385
  Industrial policy proposals - 251
  Key votes - 5-C
  South African loans - 256, 257
  Supreme Court decision - 14-A
  Trade reciprocity bill - 250
  Withholding of interest income - 17,
    261-264
Barclay v. Florida - 8-A
Barefoot v. Estelle - 5-A, 8-A

Barnard, Doug Jr., D-Ga. (10)
  Committees - 63-98, 101-105
  Congressional voting studies - 3-C-42-C
  IMF funding - 244
  Roll call votes - 2-H-145-H
Barnes, Michael D., D-Md. (8)
  Committees - 63-98, 101-105
  Congressional voting studies - 3-C-42-C
  El Salvador aid - 155, 162, 166, 168-
    62
  El Salvador certification - 156
  El Salvador human rights - 164
  Grenada invasion - 136
  Guatemalan foreign aid - 138
  Guatemalan human rights - 137
  Nicaragua covert aid - 130
  Roll call votes - 2-H-145-H
Bartlett, Steve, R-Texas (3)
  Appropriations - 541
  Committees - 63-98, 101-105
  Congressional voting studies - 3-C-42-C
  Handicapped education - 404
  Housing authorization - 283
  Mortgage assistance - 268
  Roll call votes - 2-H-145-H
  VISTA authorization - 398
Basic Educational Opportunity Grants.
  See Pell grants.
Bateman, Herbert H., R-Va. (1)
  Committees - 63-98, 101-105
  Congressional voting studies - 3-C-42-C
  Roll call votes - 2-H-145-H
Bates, Jim, D-Calif. (44)
  Committees - 63-98, 101-105
  Congressional voting studies - 3-C-42-C
  Energy Committee appointment - 340
  Roll call votes - 2-H-145-H
Baucus, Max, D-Mont.
  Anti-crime proposal - 317
  Committees - 44-62, 99-100
  Congressional voting studies - 3-C-42-C
  Japan trade barriers - 241
  Roll call votes - 2-S-60-S
Baxter, William F. - 477
Bayh, Birch - 334
Beardon v. Georgia - 8-A
Beaverhead National Forest - 343
Bedell, Berkley, D-Iowa (6)
  Committees - 63-98, 101-105
  Congressional voting studies - 3-C-42-C
  Equal Rights Amendment - 297
  FmHA programs - 385
  Roll call votes - 2-H-145-H
Beilenson, Anthony C., D-Calif. (23)
  Committees - 63-98, 101-105
  Congressional voting studies - 3-C-42-C
  Roll call votes - 2-H-145-H
Belgium - 195
Belize - 157
Belknap Inc. v. Hale - 16-A
Bell, Terrel H.
  Draft registration requirement - 399
  Endowment aid - 398
  Education commission, proposals - 389,
    397
Bell v. New Jersey - 17-A
Bell v. United States - 8-A
Bennett, Charles E., D-Fla. (3)
  Appropriations - 484
  Committees - 63-98, 101-105
  Congressional voting studies - 3-C-42-C
  Defense authorization - 180
  Roll call votes - 2-H-145-H
Bentsen, Lloyd, D-Texas
  Appropriations - 476, 489
  Cable television deregulation - 553
  Child health care plan - 420
  Committees - 44-62, 99-100
  Congressional voting studies - 3-C-42-C
  Drought - 378
  El Salvador aid - 170
  Nicaragua covert aid - 126
  Peacekeeping forces in Lebanon - 115,
    120

Roll call votes - 2-S-60-S
  Withholding tax revisions - 264
BEOGs. *See Pell grants.*
Bereuter, Douglas K., R-Neb. (1)
  Committees - 63-98, 101-105
  Congressional voting studies - 3-C-42-C
  Export controls - 255, 256
  Foreign aid authorization - 143
  Peacekeeping forces in Lebanon - 118
  Roll call votes - 2-H-145-H
Berman, Howard L., D-Calif. (26)
  Committees - 63-98, 101-105
  Congressional voting studies - 3-C-42-C
  Equal Rights Amendment - 296
  Export control bill - 254
  Roll call votes - 2-H-145-H
Berry, Mary Frances - 292-295
Bethune, Ed, R-Ark. (2)
  Committees - 63-98, 101-105
  Congressional voting studies - 3-C-42-C
  Defense authorization - 179, 189, 190
  IMF funding - 245-246
  Mortgage assistance - 268
  Roll call votes - 2-H-145-H
Bevill, Tom, D-Ala. (4)
  Appropriations - 502, 536-537
  Committees - 63-98, 101-105
  Congressional voting studies - 3-C-42-C
  Roll call votes - 2-H-145-H
Biaggi, Mario, D-N.Y. (19)
  Committees - 63-98, 101-105
  Congressional voting studies - 3-C-42-C
  Housing authorization - 283
  Roll call votes - 2-H-145-H
Biden, Joseph R. Jr., D-Del.
  Abortion Amendment - 309
  Anti-crime bill - 315, 317
  Appropriations - 538
  Budget - 439
  Central American intelligence activities -
    131
  Civil Rights Commission - 294, 295
  Committees - 44-62, 99-100
  Congressional voting studies - 3-C-42-C
  Nuclear freeze resolution - 213
  Peacekeeping forces in Lebanon - 120
  Roll call votes - 2-S-60-S
  School prayer - 302
Bieber, Owen F. - 258
Bighorn National Forest - 344
**Bilateral Science and Technology
  Agreements, U.S.** - 473
Bilingual education - 505, 507
Bilirakis, Michael, R-Fla. (9)
  Committees - 63-98, 101-105
  Congressional voting studies - 3-C-42-C
  Roll call votes -2-H-145-H
Bill of Rights - 324
*Bill Johnson's Restaurants Inc. v. Na-
  tional Labor Relations Board* - 15-A
Binary munitions. *See Chemical and
  biological weapons.*
Bingaman, Jeff, D-N.M.
  Committees - 44-62, 99-100
  Congressional voting studies - 3-C-42-C
  Immigration reform bill - 289
  Roll call votes - 2-S-60-S
Biomedical research. *See Health, re-
  search and development.*
Birth control
  Foreign aid - 522
  "Squeal" rule - 390
Black lung disability benefits - 505,
  506, 510, 511, 513
Blackmun, Harry A.
  Abortion - 307
  Legislative veto - 567
  Supreme Court term, 1982-83 - 3-A-22-
    A
Blacks. *(See also Civil rights.)*
  Black college endowment aid - 397-398
  Infant mortality rates - 419
  Judicial appointments - 302-304

Martin Luther King holiday - 601-602
Bliley, Thomas J. Jr., R-Va. (3)
  Child health care plan - 420
  Committees - 63-96, 101-105
  Congressional voting studies - 3-C-42-C
  Roll call votes - 2-H-145-H
Block, John R.
  Agricultural price support - 10-C
  Dairy, tobacco programs - 375, 378,
    380
  Energy loan program - 14
  FmHA program - 385
  PIK program - 380-381
  Target price freeze - 383-384
  U.S. Soviet grain pact (box) - 387
Block v. Neal - 20-A
Block v. North Dakota - 17-A
**Blue Cross and Blue Shield Associa-
  tions** - 392
**Board for International Broadcasting
  (BIB)**
  Appropriations - 473 (chart), 477
    (chart), 509
  Authorization - 145, 146 (box)
Boats, boating
  Excise tax - 562
  Safety programs - 511, 562
*Bob Jones University v. United States,
  Goldsboro Christian Schools v. United
  States* - 10-A
Bob Marshall Wilderness - 328
Boehlert, Sherwood, R-N.Y. (25)
  Committees - 63-98, 101-105
  Congressional voting studies - 3-C-42-C
  Nicaragua covert aid - 130
  Roll call votes - 2-H-145-H
Boggs, Lindy (Mrs. Hale), D-La. (2)
  Committees - 63-98, 101-105
  Congressional voting studies - 3-C-42-C
  Roll call votes - 2-H-145-H
Boland, Edward P., D-Mass. (2)
  Appropriations - 450, 496, 498
  Central American involvement - 125-
    126
  Clean Air Act - 340
  Committees - 63-98, 101-105
  Congressional voting studies - 3-C-42-C
  Nicaragua covert aid - 123-124, 127-
    130, 132
  Roll call votes - 2-H-145-H
Bolger v. Youngs Drug Products Corp. -
  12-A
Bolivia - 144
Bonds. *See Stocks, bonds and securities.*
Boner, Bill, D-Tenn. (5)
  Appropriations - 512
  Committees - 63-98, 101-105
  Congressional voting studies - 3-C-42-C
  Roll call votes - 2-H-145-H
Bonior, David E., D-Mich. (12)
  Committees - 63-98, 101-105
  Congressional voting studies - 3-C-42-C
  Hazardous waste disposal - 338
  Roll call votes - 2-H-145-H
Bonker, Don, D-Wash. (3)
  Committees - 63-98, 101-105
  Congressional voting studies - 3-C-42-C
  Export control bill - 254, 256
  International trade department pro-
    posal - 250
  Roll call votes - 2-H-145-H
Bonneville Power Administration -
  466, 501
Boren, David L., D-Okla.
  Clinch River project - 365
  Coal slurry piplines - 550
  Committees - 44-62, 99-100
  Congressional voting studies - 3-C-42-C
  Legislative veto - 571-572
  Martin Luther King holiday - 602
  Roll call votes - 2-S-60-S
  Target price freeze - 384
  Tax cap bill - 250

Tuition tax credits - 395
Borski, Robert A., D-Pa. (3)
  Committees - 63-98, 101-105
  Congressional voting studies - 3-C-42-C
  Roll call votes - 2-H-145-H
Boschwitz, Rudy, R-Minn.
  Appropriations - 489, 520
  Budget - 439
  Clark confirmation - 331
  Committees - 44-62, 99-100
  Congressional voting studies - 3-C-42-C
  El Salvador aid - 161
  Foreign aid - 141
  Roll call votes - 2-S-60-S
  U.S. technology transfer - 150
Bosco, Douglas H., D-Calif. (1)
  Committees - 63-98, 101-105
  Congressional voting studies - 3-C-42-C
  Roll call votes - 2-H-145-H
Boston Firefighters Union, Local 718, v. Boston Chapter, NAACP, Boston Police Patrolmen's Association v. Castro, Beecher v. Boston Chapter, NAACP - 9-A
Botanic Gardens - 540, 541
Boucher, Frederick C., D-Va. (9)
  Committees - 63-98, 101-105
  Congressional voting studies - 3-C-42-C
  Roll call votes - 2-H-145-H
Bouquard, Marilyn Lloyd, D-Tenn. (3). *(See also Lloyd, Marilyn, D-Tenn. (3).)*
  Committees - 63-98, 101-105
Bowen v. United States Postal Service - 15-A
Bowsher v. Merch & Co., Merck & Co. v. Bowsher - 20-A
Boxer, Barbara, D-Calif. (6)
  Appropriations - 535
  Committees - 63-98, 101-105
  Congressional voting studies - 3-C-42-C
  Equal Rights Amendment - 297
  Roll call votes - 2-H-145-H
Bradley, Bill, D-N.J.
  Abortion amendment - 310
  Appropriations - 455, 467, 508
  Committees - 44-62, 99-100
  Congressional voting studies - 3-C-42-C
  Dam safety repairs - 349
  Defense authorization - 189
  Education spending - 6-C
  IMF funding - 243-244
  Immigration reform bill - 289
  Martin Luther King holiday - 601
  Natural gas pricing - 367
  Revenue sharing - 229
  Roll call votes - 2-S-60-S
  Tax cap bill - 250
Brazil - 241
Breaux, John B., D-La. (7)
  Appropriations - 469
  Coal slurry pipelines - 550
  Committees - 63-98, 101-105
  Congressional voting studies - 3-C-42-C
  House rule changes - 597
  Roll call votes - 2-H-145-H
Breeder Reactor Corp. - 365
Breeder reactors - 362-365
Brennan, William J. Jr.
  Abortion - 307
  Legislative veto - 567
  Redistricting - 5-B
  Supreme Court term, 1982-83 - 3-A-22-A
Brewington, Percy Jr. - 364
Bribery of congressional members. *See Congressional ethics.*
Bribery of government officials. *See Ethics in government.*
Bridger-Teton National Forest - 344
Briscoe v. Lahue - 8-A
Britain. *See Great Britain.*
Britt, Robin, D-N.C. (6)
  Committees - 63-98, 101-105

Congressional voting studies - 3-C-42-C
  Roll call votes - 2-H-145-H
Broadcasting. *(See also Board for International Broadcasting; Federal Communications Commission; Radio; Television.)*
  Broadcast deregulation - 551-552
  Cable television rights - 552-554
  International service - 138-140
  Public broadcasting - 558
  Senate television coverage - 15
  Television deregulation - 552-554
  Television syndication rights - 560-561
Brock, William E. III
  International trade department proposal - 251
  Project Democracy (box) - 148
  Trade reciprocity bill - 259
  U.S. Soviet grain pact (box) - 387
Brooks, Jack, D-Texas (9)
  Committees - 63-98, 101-105
  Committee transcript alterations - 583
  Congressional voting studies - 3-C-42-C
  Legal Services Corporation - 323
  Paperwork reduction - 591
  Revenue sharing - 227-229
  Roll call votes - 2-H-145-H
Broomfield, William S., R-Mich. (18)
  Committees - 63-98, 101-105
  Congressional voting studies - 3-C-42-C
  El Salvador aid - 170
  Equal Rights Amendment - 297
  Nicaragua covert aid - 128, 130
  Nuclear freeze resolution - 206
  Roll call votes - 2-H-145-H
Brown, Edmund G. Jr. - 332
Brown, George E. Jr., D-Calif. (36)
  Appropriations - 535
  Clinch River project - 365
  Committees - 63-98, 101-105
  Congressional voting studies - 3-C-42-C
  Defense authorization - 179
  NSF authorization - 604
  Roll call votes - 2-H-145-H
  Target price freeze - 384
Brown, Hank, R-Colo. (4)
  Appropriations - 541
  Committees - 63-98, 101-105
  Congressional voting studies - 3-C-42-C
  Nuclear freeze resolution - 208
  Roll call votes - 2-H-145-H
  State Department authorization - 147
Brown, Harold - 197
Brown, John Y. - 4-B
Brown v. Socialist Workers '74 Campaign Committee (Ohio) - 13-A
Brown v. Thomson - 5-B
Broyhill, James T., R-N.C. (10)
  Acid rain - 340
  Clean Air Act - 340
  Committees - 63-98, 101-105
  Congressional voting studies - 3-C-42-C
  CPSC authorization - 557
  Environmental Protection Agency - 14-E
  Roll call votes - 2-H-145-H
  Telephone rates - 547
Bryant, John, D-Texas (5)
  Committees - 63-98, 101-105
  Congressional voting studies - 3-C-42-C
  Energy Committee appointment - 340
  Roll call votes - 2-H-145-H
Brzezinski, Zbigniew - 330
Buckley, Esther Gonzalez-Arroyo - 293
Buckley, James L. - 152
Budget Act. *See Congressional Budget and Impoundment Control Act of 1974.*
Budget, U.S. *(See also Appropriations; Taxes, taxation.)*
  Administration plans - 425-434
  Authority and outlay charts, FY 1984
    By agency - 434
    By function - 430-431
    Percent growth in outlays - 432
    Reconciliation requirements - 446

Summary, end of session - 424
  Balanced Budget Amendment - 238
  Baseline budget projections - 429, 432
  Budget dollar (chart) - 427
  Budget process
    Overview - 423
    Reagan administration - 435
    Reconciliation requirements - 446
  Continuing resolutions
    Congressional action - 527-528, 529-531
    Provisions - 526-529
  Debt
    Collection - 591
    Debt limit increases - 231, 239, 7-C
  Deficits
    Administration proposals - 427
    Chart - 232
    Economic forecast (box) - 429
    Interest - 431
    Key votes - 7-C
    Presidential messages (text) - 3-E-4-E
    Reconciliation instructions - 423
    Reduction plans - 429, 231-239
  Economic forecasts and assumptions - 428, 429, 446
  First resolution - 435-447
    Background - 423
    Budget targets - 435-436
    Conference action - 444, 447
    House action - 436-438
    Reconciliation instructions - 435, 441, 446
    Senate action - 438-444
    Targets (chart) - 445
  Freeze proposal - 441
  Key votes - 4-C, 7-C
  Legislative veto provisions - 566
  Legislative summary - 18
  Presidential messages (text)
    Budget message - 7-E-12-E
    Economic message - 13-E
  Receipts, FY 1974-86 (chart) - 433
  Receipts by source (chart) - 427
  Reconciliation process - 435, 438, 446
  Reserve fund - 444
  Revisions, FY 1983 - 427
  Senate rule change proposals - 598
  Spending freeze - 425
  Tax reconciliation - 231-239
  Terminology (box) - 426
  Totals charts
    Fiscal 1977-1983 - 424
    Fiscal 1982-1986 - 425, 440, 9-E
Buildings, public. *See Public buildings.*
Bumpers, Dale, D-Ark.
  Appropriations - 467, 489, 500, 515
  Clark confirmation - 329, 331
  Coal leasing ban - 350, 352-354, 5-C
  Committees - 44-62, 99-100
  Congressional voting studies - 3-C-42-C
  Immigration reform bill - 290
  MX debate - 198, 200, 7-C
  Natural gas pricing - 367
  Roll call votes - 2-S-60-S
Burdick, Quentin N., D-N.D.
  Appropriations - 503
  Committees - 44-62, 99-100
  Congressional voting studies - 3-C-42-C
  Garrison Diversion project - 356
  MX debate - 198
  Roll call votes - 2-S-60-S
Bureau of Alcohol, Tobacco and Firearms (BATF) - 532
Bureau of Government Financial Operations - 532
Bureau of Indian Affairs (BIA)
  Appropriations, FY 1983 supplemental - 448 (chart), 453
  Appropriations, FY 1984 - 463 (chart), 464
Bureau of Justice Statistics - 27-A
Bureau of Labor Statistics (BLS) - 504
Bureau of Land Management (BLM)

Appropriations - 463 (chart), 464, 466
  Oil and gas leasing - 462-469
  Public lands jurisdiction - 341
  Public lands use - 345
  Wilderness study areas - 464
Bureau of Mines - 463 (chart)
Bureau of Reclamation
  Appropriations - 448 (chart), 452, 453, 500-503, 501 (chart), 520-521
  Authorization bill - 354-359
  Dam safety repairs - 349
Bureau of the Census. *See Census Bureau.*
Bureau of the Mint - 532
Burford, Anne M.
  Clean air sanctions - 339
  Contempt charges - 333-334
  Resignation - 325, 327, 332-335, 496
Burger, Warren E.
  Abortions - 307
  Bankruptcy laws - 319
  Legislative veto - 567-568, 20-A-21-A
  New Appeals court proposal - 311
  Redistricting - 5-B
  Supreme Court term, 1982-83 - 3-A-22-A
Burlington Northern Inc. v. United States - 14-A
Burton, Dan L., R-Ind. (6)
  Committees - 63-98, 101-105
  Congressional voting studies - 3-C-42-C
  Grenada invasion - 135-136
  Roll call votes - 2-H-145-H
  State Department authorization - 147
Burton, John L. - 15
Burton, Phillip, D-Calif. (5)
  Committees - 63-98, 101-105
  Congressional voting studies - 3-C-42-C
  Death - 13
  Labor reform bills - 271
  Roll call votes - 2-H-145-H
  Wilderness preservation - 342
Burton, Sala, D-Calif. (5)
  Election results - 7-B
  Committees - 63-98, 101-105
  Congressional voting studies - 3-C-42-C
  Roll call votes - 2-H-145-H
Bus systems, local. *See Mass transit.*
Bush, George
  Chemical weapons - 186-187, 480, 489, 491, 3-C-5-C
  El Salvador death squads - 154
  Social Security rescue bill - 225
Bush v. Lucas - 12-A
Business and industry. *(See also Advertising; Antitrust and competition; Automobiles and automobile industry; Business taxes; Business interests, lobbying; Chemicals industry; Commerce Department; Foreign trade; Minority business; Oil industry; Patents and trademarks; Small business.)*
  Auto domestic content bill - 257-259
  "Buy America" restrictions - 510
  Defense production - 265-266
  Economic outlook - 13-E
  Enterprise zones - 14-E-15-E, 17-E
  Foreign affairs
    Caribbean Basin initiative - 252-253
    Export controls - 253-257
  Funeral home regulation - 562
  Government contracts - 590
  Industrial development bonds - 235
  Industrial policy proposals - 250-251
  International trade department proposal - 250-251
  Loans - 386
  Presidential messages (text) - 14-E-15-E, 17-E
  Price fixing - 472, 477, 478
  Relocation assistance - 587
  Supreme Court decisions - 13-A-15-A
  Trade adjustment assistance - 251-252

Trade reciprocity bill - 259-260
Weather satellites - 477, 588-589
Business interests, lobbying
Antitrust proposals - 554-557
Lobby registrations - 3-D-55-D
Withholding of interest income - 261-264
Business taxes. *(See also Taxes, taxation.)*
Budget
Administration plans - 426, 432
Federal deficit - 427
Overview, 1983 - 217
Reconciliation proposals - 231-239
Resolution proposals - 439, 442, 444
Caribbean trade incentives - 252-253
Employer tax credits - 17-E
Enterprise Zone proposal - 14-E-15-E
Excise taxes
Coal - 511
Boating - 562
Fishing - 562
Oil windfall - 4-A
Legislative summary - 17
Payment-in-Kind program - 13, 381-383
Presidential messages (text) - 10-E, 15-E
Supreme Court decisions - 14-A, 18-A
Tax leasing veto - 34-E
Busing, school. *See School busing.*
Byrd, Robert C., D-W.Va.
Appropriations - 489, 490, 503, 514, 536
Budget - 447
Capitol bombing - 592, 593
Clinch River project - 365
Committees - 44-62, 99-100
Congressional voting studies - 3-C-42-C
Debt limit increase - 240
MX debate - 198
Nicaragua covert aid - 129
Peacekeeping forces in Lebanon - 114
Roll call votes - 2-S-60-S
Unemployment benefits - 275
Wars powers - 147
Watt resignation - 150
Byron, Beverly B., D-Md. (6)
Committees - 63-98, 101-105
Congressional voting studies - 3-C-42-C
Roll call votes - 2-H-145-H

C

CAB. *See Civil Aeronautics Board (CAB).*
Cabinet
List - 11
Nominations and confirmations - 23-A, 25-A-27-A
Cable television
Deregulation - 15, 552-554
Syndication rights - 560-561
Caccia, Charles L. - 341
Califano, Joseph A. - 581, 582
California
Abortion funding - 306
Earthquake damage funds - 511
Election results, 1983 - 6-B
Employment funds - 455
Nuclear power plant construction - 5-A
Offshore oil and gas leasing - 462-469
Redistricting - 5-B (box)
Wilderness areas - 342-343
California v. Ramos - 8-A
California Zephyr - 461
Cambodia. *See Kampuchea.*
Campaign financing.
Supreme Court decisions - 5-A, 13-A
Union dues - 594
Campbell, Carroll A. Jr., R-S.C. (4)
Committees - 63-98, 101-105

Congressional voting studies - 3-C-42-C
Roll call votes - 2-H-145-H
Canada
Acid rain controversy - 341
U.S. immigration quotas - 288
Cancer. *(See also Hazardous substances.)*
Research reauthorization proposal - 409-410
Saccharin ban - 401-402
Capital punishment - 8-A
Capitol building
Bomb explosion - 592-594
Restoration - 511, 512, 540
Capitol Architect. *See Architect of the Capitol.*
Carcinogens. *See Hazardous substances.*
Caribbean Basin Initiative (CBI)
Background - 253
El Salvador aid - 157
Legislative summary - 26
Legislative veto - 570
Provisions - 252-253
Tax incentives - 252, 261, 264
Caribbean countries. *See Latin America and the Caribbean.*
Carnegie Foundation - 389, 400
Carney, William, R-N.Y. (1)
Committees - 63-98, 101-105
Congressional voting studies - 3-C-42-C
Roll call votes - 2-H-145-H
Carper, Thomas R., D-Del. (AL)
Committees - 63-98, 101-105
Congressional voting studies - 3-C-42-C
IMF funding - 248
Roll call votes - 2-H-145-H
Carr, Bob, D-Mich. (6)
Committees - 63-98, 101-105
Congressional voting studies - 3-C-42-C
Roll call votes - 2-H-145-H
Carter, Jimmy
Briefing papers - 563, 594
Clinch River project - 362
Grain embargo (box) - 387
Guatemalan foreign aid - 138
Judicial appointments - 302-304
Nuclear arms treaty - 490
Presidential support (box) - 19-C
Public lands - 347
Staff funding - 534, 535
U.S.-Vatican ties - 169
Water projects - 520, 355
Women appointees - 23-A
Casey, William J.
Central American intelligence activities - 125, 131
Project Democracy (box) - 149
Castro, Fidel
Grenada invasion - 135
Kissinger Commission - 170
Radio broadcasts - 138
Cemeteries - 496, 499
Census Bureau
Appropriations - 472, 475
Reorganization proposal - 250-251
Center for Disease Control - 417, 449, 504
Central America. *See Latin America and the Caribbean and specific country.*
Central Intelligence Agency (CIA)
Authorization - 130-132
Central American involvement - 123-132
Chafee, John H., R-R.I.
Appropriations - 467
Budget - 442
Central American intelligence activities - 131
Clark confirmation - 331
Clean Water Act - 361
Coal leasing ban - 354
Committees - 44-62, 99-100
Congressional voting studies - 3-C-42-C
Roll call votes - 2-S-60-S

Chamber of Commerce, U.S.
Immigration reform bill - 290
Project Democracy - 145, 148-149 (box)
Chandler, Rod, R-Wash (8)
Committees - 63-98, 101-105
Congressional voting studies - 3-C-42-C
NIH authorization - 410
Roll call votes - 2-H-145-H
Channel Islands - 464
Chappell, Bill Jr., D-Fla. (4)
Committees - 63-98, 101-105
Congressional voting studies - 3-C-42-C
Roll call votes - 2-H-145-H
Chappell v. Wallace - 9-A
Chappie, Gene, R-Calif. (2)
Committees - 63-98, 101-105
Congressional voting studies - 3-C-42-C
Roll call votes - 2-H-145-H
Chardon v. Soto - 9-A
Chemical and biological weapons
Appropriations - 479, 480, 489, 491
Authorization - 175, 177-179, 186-187, 189-190
Key votes - 11-C
Legislative summary - 16
Chemical wastes management. *See Hazardous wastes management.*
Chemicals, toxic. *See Hazardous substances.*
Cheney, Dick, R-Wyo. (AL)
Coal slurry pipelines - 550
Committees - 63-98, 101-105
Congressional voting studies - 3-C-42-C
Roll call votes - 2-H-145-H
Chicago, Rock Island and Pacific Railroad. *See Rock Island Railroad.*
Child abuse
Appropriations - 454, 457
Pornography - 318
Child and maternal health programs. *(See also Child nutrition programs.)*
Appropriations - 449
Child health plan - 419-420
Child Health Assurance Program - 419-420
Child nutrition programs
Appropriations - 510, 516 (chart), 518-519
Budget - 433, 438
Eligibility levels - 417
School lunch and milk programs - 412, 414-415
Women, infants and children (WIC) program - 449 (chart), 452, 516 (chart)
Children. *(See also Aid to Families with Dependent Children; Child abuse; Day care programs; Elementary and secondary education; Youth.)*
Adoption services - 454, 457
Child pornography bill - 318
Child support enforcement - 28, 300, 418, 505, 506
Handicapped infant care - 390
Illegitimate children, Supreme Court rulings - 11-A
Mortality rates - 306, 419
Children's Defense Fund - 419
Chile - 143
Chiles, Lawton, D-Fla.
Appropriations - 465, 489
Budget - 439, 447
Committees - 44-62, 99-100
Congressional voting studies - 3-C-42-C
Debt limit increase - 241
Defense authorization - 172, 186
Deficit reduction proposals - 233
Illegal aliens - 241
MX debate - 198
Roll call votes - 2-S-60-S
Tax proposals - 237
China, People's Republic. *See People's Republic of China.*

Chamber of Commerce, U.S.
Christian Broadcasting Network - 302
Chrysler Corporation Loan Guarantee Program - 473
Church and state separation. *See Freedom of religion.*
Churches. *See Religion, religious organizations.*
Cigarettes - 22, 408-409
Circuit Courts, U.S.
Bankruptcy laws - 320
Nominations and confirmations - 30-A-31-A
Cities (urban affairs). *See Community development; Mass transit; State and local government.*
Citizen/Labor Energy Coalition (CLEC) - 366, 367
Citizenship rights. *See Civil rights.*
City government. *See State and local government.*
City of Akron v. Akron Center for Reproductive Health Inc., Akron Center for Reproductive Health Inc. v. City of Akron - 306-308, 10-A
City of Lockhart, Texas v. United States - 13-A
City of Los Angeles v. Lyons - 19-A
City of Port Arthur, Texas v. United States - 13-A
City of Revere v. Massachusetts General Hospital - 17-A
Civil Aeronautics Board (CAB)
Appropriations - 458, 459 (chart), 461
Nominations and confirmations - 29-A, 24-A
Civil defense. *(See also Emergency preparedness.)*
Authorization - 191
Budget - 434
Civil rights. *(See also Commission on Civil Rights, U.S.; Equal employment opportunity; First Amendment; Freedom of information; School desegregation; Sex discrimination.)*
Appropriations - 473 (chart), 474, 477 (chart), 478-479
Desegregation aid - 404
Desegregation funds veto - 35-E
Education - 3-A, 4-A, 10-A
Equal Rights Amendment - 296-298
Illegal alien workers - 289
Legislative summary - 25
Lobby registrations - 3-D-55-D
Presidential messages (text) - 5-E, 38-E-39-E
Supreme Court decisions - 3-A, 4-A, 8-A-11-A
Tax-exempt private schools - 3-A, 4-A, 10-A
Civil Rights Act of 1964 - 4-A
Civil Service Commission. *See Merit Systems Protection Board; Office of Personnel Management.*
Civil Service Retirement and Disability Fund
Appropriations - 511
Federal contribution - 574-575
Social Security rescue plan - 222
Civil Service System. *See Federal employees.*
Civilian Conservation Corps (CCC) - 230
Clark, William P.
Family employment - 146
Profile (box) - 330
Nominations and confirmations - 326, 327, 23-A
Clarke, James McClure, D-N.C. (11)
Committees - 63-96, 101-105
Congressional voting studies - 3-C-42-C
Roll call votes - 2-H-145-H
Clay, William, D-Mo. (1)
Committees - 63-96, 101-105

Congressional voting studies - 3-C-42-C
Labor reform bills - 271
Phase II jobs bill - 268
Roll call votes - 2-H-145-H
Clean Air Act - 20, 339-340, 498, 8-C
Clean Water Act - 20, 360-361
Climate. *See Weather.*
Clinch River breeder reactor
   Appropriations - 500, 502, 538
   Background - 362-364
   Funding proposals - 364-365
   Key votes - 6-C
Clinger, William F. Jr., R-Pa. (23)
   Committees - 63-96, 101-105
   Congressional voting studies - 3-C-42-C
   Roll call votes - 2-H-145-H
Cloture votes. *See Filibusters and cloture votes.*
Coal. *(See also Mines and mining.)*
   Buy American provisions - 494
   Coal slurry pipelines - 26, 544, 549-551, 9-C
   Leasing ban - 329, 350-354, 462, 464-465, 467-468, 511, 515, 573
Court of Appeals, U.S. - 288
Coast Guard
   Anti-crime proposal - 317
   Appropriations - 458, 459 (chart), 460, 485, 490
   Boating safety - 562
Costa Rica - 144
Coastal Zone Management Program - 360
Coastal zones
   Marine sanctuaries - 359
   Revenue sharing - 359-360
Coats, Dan, R-Ind. (4)
   Auto domestic content bill - 259
   Committees - 63-96, 101-105
   Congressional voting studies - 3-C-42-C
   Roll call votes - 2-H-145-H
Cochran, Thad, R-Miss.
   Appropriations - 520
   Committees - 44-62, 99-101
   Congressional voting studies - 3-C-42-C
   MX debate - 198
   Roll call votes - 2-S-60-S
COCOM. *See Coordinating Committee on Export Controls (COCOM).*
Coelho, Tony, D-Calif. (15)
   Committees - 63-96, 101-105
   Congressional voting studies - 3-C-42-C
   Roll call votes - 2-H-145-H
Cohen, William S., R-Maine
   Committees - 44-62, 99-101
   Congressional voting studies - 3-C-42-C
   Federal contracts - 590
   Government ethics office - 584
   International trade department proposal - 251
   MX debate - 197-198, 201, 203, 204
   Nuclear freeze resolution - 212-213
   Procurement office - 590
   Roll call votes - 2-S-60-S
   Tax cap bill - 250
Coins and currency. *(See also Monetary policy.)*
   Foreign currency program - 481
   South African gold coins - 257
   Soviet gold coins - 257
   Special Drawing Rights - 241
Coleman, E. Thomas, R-Mo. (6)
   Committees - 63-96, 101-105
   Congressional voting studies - 3-C-42-C
   Math-science education proposals - 397
   Roll call votes - 2-H-145-H
Coleman, Ron, D-Texas (16)
   Committees - 63-96, 101-105
   Congressional voting studies - 3-C-42-C
   Roll call votes - 2-H-145-H
Collective bargaining. *See Labor, labor unions.*
Colleges. *See Postsecondary education.*

Collins, Cardiss, D-Ill. (7)
   Committees - 63-96, 101-105
   Congressional voting studies - 3-C-42-C
   Roll call votes - 2-H-145-H
Collins, Martha L. - 4-B
Colorado
   Amtrak rerouting - 461
   Abortion funding - 306
   Election results, 1983 - 6-B
   Forest areas - 349
   Water projects - 502, 520-521
Colorado v. New Mexico - 18-A
Commerce. *(See also Agricultural trade; Banks and banking; Business and industry; Commerce Department; Consumer affairs; Federal Trade Commission; Foreign trade; Interstate Commerce Commission; Transportation.)*
   Appropriations - 472-479, 527
   Budget - 430, 445 (chart)
   Federal contracts - 587-588
   Industrial policy proposals - 250-251
   Legislative summary - 13
   Overview, 1983 - 543-544
   Trade reciprocity proposal - 259-260
Commerce Business Daily - 588, 590
Commerce Department. *(See also Economic Development Administration.)*
   Appropriations
      FY 1983 supplemental - 509, 510
      FY 1984 continuing resolution - 472-479, 529
   Nominations and confirmations - 26-A
Commission for Security and Cooperation in Europe - 473 (chart), 477 (chart)
Commission on Civil Rights
   Appropriations - 473, 474, 477, 478-479
   Nominations and confirmations - 23-A, 25-A
   Reconstitution
      Background - 286, 293-295
      Presidential messages - 38-E-39-E
   Report on women - 299
Commission on Congressional Mailing Standards - 579
Commissioner of Internal Revenue v. Tufts - 15-A
Committees, House and Senate. *For committee action on a bill, see the topic of the legislation.*
   House
      Assignments - 63-96, 101-105
      Background - 42-43
      Joint - 97-98
      Leadership - 4-8
   Senate
      Assignments - 44-63, 99-100
      Background - 42-43
      Joint - 97-98
      Leadership - 4
Commodity Credit Corporation (CCC)
   Appropriations - 449 (chart), 453, 456, 516 (chart), 517
   Budget - 429
   Food surplus distribution - 412-413, 416
   Nominations and confirmations - 26-A
   Target price freeze - 384
Commodity Futures Trading Commission (CFTC)
   Appropriations - 517 (chart), 518-519
   Nominations and confirmations - 29-A, 24-A
Commodity Supplemental Food Program - 415
Common Cause - 578
Communications and telecommunications. *(See also Broadcasting; Federal Communications Commission; Information Agency, U.S.; Print media and publishing.)*
   Cable television deregulation - 15, 553

   Rural telephone systems - 14, 388
   Telephone rates - 14, 545-549, 10-C-11-C
   Trade reciprocity bill - 260
Communications Satellite Corp. (COMSAT) - 589
Community development. *(See also Countercyclical aid and targeted fiscal assistance; Economic Development Administration; Housing and Urban Development Department; Trade adjustment assistance.)*
   Appropriations
      FY 1983 supplemental - 448 (chart), 450, 451, 453, 509, 511
      FY 1984 - 495-500
   Budget - 430, 445 (chart)
   Housing - 277-283
   Infrastructure repairs - 230
   Legislative summary - 23
   Presidential messages - 14-E-15-E, 17-E
   Urban enterprise zones - 14-E-15-E, 17-E
   Urban development, homesteading - 278
Community Development Block Grants (CDGBs)
   Appropriations
      FY 1983 supplemental - 448 (chart), 450, 451, 453, 456
      FY 1984 - 495, 497, 499, 506
   Authorization - 278, 283
Community Television of Southern California v. Gottfried, Federal Communications Commission (FCC) v. Gottfried - 11-A
Competition (business and industry). *See Antitrust and competition.*
Conable, Barber B. Jr., R-N.Y. (30)
   Agricultural price supports - 10-C
   Committees - 63-96, 101-105
   Congressional voting studies - 3-C-42-C
   Dairy, tobacco program - 377-378, 380
   Debt limit increase - 239
   Deficit reduction proposals - 233
   Roll call votes - 2-H-145-H
   Withholding tax revisions - 264
Conference of Mayors, U.S. - 416
Confirmation of nominations. *See Nominations and confirmations.*
Conflicts of interest in Congress. *See Congressional ethics.*
Conflicts of interest in federal government. *See Ethics in government.*
Congress. *(See also Congressional elections; Congressional employees; Congressional ethics; Congressional votes; House of Representatives; Legislation; Legislative veto; Senate.)*
   Budget - 434
   Budget control procedures - 238
   Capitol building
      Bomb explosion - 592-594
      Map - 106
      Restoration - 511, 512, 540
   Committees
      Background - 42-43
      House - 63-96
      Index - 99-105
      Joint - 97-98
      Senate - 44-62
   Contempt power - 334
   First session summary (box) - 12
   Foreign policy role (box) - 142
   Franking privileges - 540, 541, 578-580
   Glossary of congressional terms - xiii-xxiii
   How a bill becomes law - xxiv
   Leadership (box) - 3
   Legislative branch funds
      FY 1983 supplemental appropriations - 510, 511

      FY 1984 - 539-542
   Legislative process in brief - xxv-xxviii
   Legislative summary - 12-28
   Legislative veto - 4-A, 19-A, 20-A-22-A (text)
   Membership
      Changes, 98th Congress (box) - 5
      Characteristics of 98th Congress - 29-38
      Leadership - 3-9
      Master list - 10-11
      Seniority - 38-41
   Pay and expenses
      Appropriations - 510, 511, 539-542
      Honoraria - 541
      Office and travel funds - 541
      Pay raise - 15-16, 539, 577-578
   Presidential support
      Key votes - 3-C-17-C
      Legislative summary - 12-28
      Voting participation - 32-C-36-C
   Redistricting decisions - 4-A, 5-A, 12-A
   Rules changes - 596-599
   Social Security coverage - 219, 573, 576-577
   Television coverage - 15
Congressional Budget and Impoundment Control Act of 1974
   Legislative veto - 563, 565
   Presidential powers - 238,429
   Reconciliation process - 231
Congressional Budget Office (CBO)
   Appointment - 443
   Appropriations - 540
   Child health care plan - 420
   Economic projections - 429
   King holiday cost - 600
   Unemployment projections - 432
Congressional elections. *(See also Campaign financing.)*
   Political report - 3-B-7-B
      House elections - 6-B-7-B
      Senate elections - 4-B-5-B
      Redistricting - 4-A, 5-A, 5-B (box)
Congressional employees
   Appropriations - 531-536
   Page system - 15, 580-583
Congressional ethics
   Abscam - 585-586
   Censure proceedings - 581 (box)
   Drug investigation - 15, 595
   Financial disclosure - 592
   Hansen indictment - 592
   Legislative summary - 15
   Page sex charges - 15, 580-583, 595
   Transcript alterations - 583
Congressional Research Service (CRS) - 540
Congressional veto. *See Legislative veto.*
Congressional votes. *(See also Filibusters and cloture votes.)*
   Key votes - 3-C-17-C
   Party unity - 26-C-31-C
   Presidential support - 18-C-25-C
   Roll call votes
      House roll call votes - 2-H-145-H
      Senate roll call votes - 2-S-60-S
   Voting participation - 32-C-42-C
Connecticut
   Abortion funding - L-22
   Indian land claim veto - 586-587
Connecticut v. Johnson - 7-A
Connick v. Myers - 5-A, 12-A
Conrail - 562
Conservation. *(See also Energy conservation; Wilderness preservation areas; Wildlife and wildlife refuges.)*
   Appropriations - 448
   Soil conservation plan - 14, 387
   Youth employment - 229-231
Constitution, U.S.
   Amendments
      Anti-abortion - 308-311

Balanced Budget Amendment - 238
Equal Rights Amendment - 296-298, 11-C
First Amendment - 168-169, 298, 4-A, 5-A, 12-A
Fourth Amendment - 6-A
Tenth Amendment - 5-A, 17-A-18-A
Bankruptcy court - 318
Bicentennial - 324
Consular posts. *See Embassies and consulates.*
Consultants, federal. *See Federal contractors and consultants.*
Consumer affairs (general). *(See also Consumer interests, lobbying; Credit; Labeling and packaging.)*
Anti-tampering bill - 313
Appropriations - 496, 499
Bankruptcy courts - 286, 318-321
Boating safety - 562
Cigarette labeling - 22, 408-409
Commission authorization - 557
Credit card surcharges - 267
FTC used car rule - 562
Legislative summary - 14-15
Natural gas pricing - 366-370
Overview, 1983 - 543-544
Physician regulation - 473
Price fixing - 472, 477
Record rentals - 313
Safety - 431
Telephone rates - 14
Withholding of interest income - 17, 261-264
Consumer Information Center - 496, 499
Consumer interests, lobbying
Air crash liability treaty - 301
Cigarette labeling - 408-409
Lobby registrations - 3-D-55-D
Natural gas pricing - 367
Sex-based insurance programs - 300
Consumer Price Index (CPI)
Budget - 426, 428 (chart)
Cost-of-living adjustments - 219
Consumer product safety
Anti-tampering bill - 313-314
Tylenol tragedy - 313
Consumer Product Safety Commission (CPSC)
Appropriations - 496-497, 499
Authorization - 557
Legislative veto - 570
Nominations and confirmations - 29-A, 24-A
Container Corporation of America v. Franchise Tax Board - 18-A
Conte, Silvio O., R-Mass. (1)
Appropriations - 450, 456, 503, 508, 512, 529, 533, 535, 537, 542
Committees - 63-98, 101-105
Garrison Diversion project - 356-357
MX debate - 199
Roll call votes - 2-H-145-H
Senate honoraria - 577
Water projects - 520
Continental Airlines - 543
Continuing education. *See Adult and continuing education.*
Contractors, federal. *See Federal contractors and consultants.*
Conyers, John Jr., D-Mich. (1)
Committees - 63-98, 101-105
Congressional voting studies - 3-C-42-C
Insanity defense - 315
Martin Luther King holiday - 601
Roll call votes - 2-H-145-H
Cooper, Jim, D-Tenn. (4)
Committees - 63-98, 101-105
Congressional voting studies - 3-C-42-C
Roll call votes - 2-H-145-H
Coordinating Committee on Export Controls (COCOM) - 152, 254-257
Copyright Royalty Tribunal - 540

Copyrights
Caribbean trade provisions - 252
Protection of U.S. rights - 260
Record rentals - 313
Corcoran, Tom, R-Ill. (14)
Committees - 63-98, 101-105
Congressional voting studies - 3-C-42-C
Natural gas pricing - 369
Roll call votes - 2-H-145-H
Telephone rates - 547
Corn. *See Grains.*
Corporation for Public Broadcasting
Appropriations - 505
Authorization - 558
Corps of Engineers. *See Army Corps of Engineers.*
Correctional institutions. *See Prisons and prisoners.*
Cosmetics - 313
Cost-of-living adjustments (COLAs)
Federal employee pay - 219, 576-577
Federal employee retirement pay - 577
Social Security programs - 219-226, 425
Costa Rica - 157
Cotton
PIK program (box) - 382
Specialty cotton program - 388
Target price freeze - 383-384
Coughlin, Lawrence, R-Pa. (13)
Appropriations - 459
Committees - 63-98, 101-105
Congressional voting studies - 3-C-42-C
MX debate - 199
Roll call votes - 2-H-145-H
Council for a Livable World - 491
Council of Economic Advisers - 532 (chart)
Council on Environmental Quality (CEQ)
Appropriations - 496, 499
Nominations and confirmations - 25-A
Countercyclical aid and targeted fiscal assistance. *(See also Impact aid.)*
Economic development bill - 229-231
Industrial development bonds - 235-236
Key votes - 4-C
Public works jobs plan - 270
Court of Appeals, U.S.
Appointments - 302-304
Appropriations - 473 (chart)
Judgeship proposal - 320
Court of International Trade, U.S.
Appropriations - 473 (chart)
Nominations and confirmations - 31-A
Court of Military Appeals, U.S. - 311
Court trials. *See Trial procedures.*
Courter, Jim, R-N.J. (12)
Committees - 63-98, 101-105
Congressional voting studies - 3-C-42-C
Defense authorization - 181
Export controls - 256, 257
Nuclear freeze resolution - 212
Roll call votes - 2-H-145-H
Courts. *(See also District Courts, U.S.; Judiciary; Law profession and law practice; Supreme Court; Trial procedures.)*
Appeals court proposal - 311-312
Appropriations - 473 (chart), 475
Bankruptcy - 286, 318-320
Federal court jurisdiction - 19-A
Military - 311
State courts - 18-A
Supreme Court decisions - 3-A-22-A
Tax court
Appropriations - 532
Nominations and confirmations - 31-A
Courts, U.S. *See Courts.*
Covert action. *See Intelligence affairs.*
Coyne, William J., D-Pa. (14)
Committees - 63-98, 101-105

Congressional voting studies - 3-C-42-C
Roll call votes - 2-H-145-H
Cox, Archibald - 334
Craig, Larry E., R-Idaho (1)
Committees - 63-98, 101-105
Congressional voting studies - 3-C-42-C
Roll call votes - 2-H-145-H
Crane, Daniel B., R-Ill. (19)
Censure - 563, 580-583
Committees - 63-98, 101-105
Congressional voting studies - 3-C-42-C
Page sex scandal - 15, 595
Profile - 582
Roll call votes - 2-H-145-H
Crane, Philip M., R-Ill. (12)
Committees - 63-98, 101-105
Congressional voting studies - 3-C-42-C
El Salvador aid - 158
IMF funding - 245
Roll call votes - 2-H-145-H
Social Security rescue bill - 222
Cranston, Alan, D-Calif.
Abscam investigation - 586
Appropriations - 468
Committees - 44-62, 99-100
Congressional voting studies - 3-C-42-C
Immigration reform bill - 289
Peace-keeping forces in Lebanon - 118
Roll call votes - 2-S-60-S
Veteran's counseling centers - 410
Veteran's job training program - 600
VISTA authorization - 398
Voting scores (box) - 18-C
Withholding tax revisions - 263
Credit. *(See also Farm income stabilization and aid programs; Mortgages and home loans.)*
Consumer bankruptcy issues - 318-322
Credit card surcharges - 267
Crime and criminal justice. *(See also Capital punishment; Drug trafficking; Ethics in government; Federal Bureau of Investigation; Fraud and abuse in government programs; Judiciary; Law profession and law practice; Prisons and prisoners; Trial procedures.)*
Abscam investigation - 585-586
Anti-crime grant program - 312
Anti-crime proposals - 315-317
Appropriations - 472-479
Bail reform - 316
Budget - 431
Cruel and unusual punishment decisions - 8-A
Drug offenders - 311
Exclusionary rule - 315, 317
Food and drug tampering - 313-314
Insanity defense - 314, 316, 5-A, 7-A
Juvenile justice programs - 472
Legislative summary - 25
Labor racketeering - 316
Pornography - 318
Presidential messages (text) - 19-E
Right to counsel - 7-A
Search and seizure - 6-A
Sentencing reform - 316
State and local government judicial assistance - 316
Supreme Court decisions - 5-A, 6-A-8-A
Threats and crimes against public officials - 316
Criminal trials. *See Trial procedures.*
Crockett, George W. Jr., D-Mich. (13)
Committees - 63-98, 101-105
Congressional voting studies - 3-C-42-C
El Salvador aid - 163, 169
Nicaragua covert war - 128
Peacekeeping forces in Lebanon - 118
Project Democracy - 148
Roll call votes - 2-H-145-H
Crop insurance - 519
Crown, Cork & Seal Co. v. Parker - 9-A
Cruise missiles

Appropriations - 470, 471, 482
Air-launched (ALCM) - 175, 182
Ground-launched (GLCM) - 175, 181, 183, 190-191, 195
Sea-launched - 188
Cuba
El Salvador aid - 157
Grenada presence - 135
Illegal aliens - 241
Radio Marti - 138
U.S. radio broadcasts - 473 (chart), 476, 477 (chart)
Customs Court, U.S. *See Court of International Trade, U.S.*
Customs duties. *See Tariffs and duties.*
Customs Service, U.S. - 449 (chart), 454, 457, 532, 533
Cyprus - 141-142, 144, 514 (box)

D

D.C. General Hospital - 495
Dam, Kenneth W. - 117
D'Amato, Alfonse M., R-N.Y.
Appropriations - 467, 541
Coal leasing ban - 354
Committees - 44-62, 99-100
Congressional voting studies - 3-C-42-C
El Salvador aid - 159
Housing authorization - 281
Military sales to Jordan - 134
MX debate - 198
Roll call votes - 2-S-60-S
Withholding tax revisions - 262
D'Amours, Norman E., D-N.H. (1)
Committees - 63-98, 101-105
Congressional voting studies - 3-C-42-C
Roll call votes - 2-H-145-H
Withholding tax revisions - 263
D'Aubuisson, Roberto - 166
Dairy programs
Assessments - 376 (box), 377-378
Egg marketing - 376
Industry lobbying - 378
Key votes - 10-C
Legislative summary - 13
Provisions - 375-376
Dams - 349
Danforth, John C., R-Mo.
Appropriations - 508, 509
Bankruptcy laws - 321
Committees - 44-62, 99-100
Congressional voting studies - 3-C-42-C
Deficit reduction proposals - 231
Immigration reform bill - 290
Natural gas pricing - 368
Roll call votes - 2-S-60-S
Trade reciprocity bill - 259
Withholding tax revisions - 263
Daniel, Dan, D-Va. (5)
Committees - 63-98, 101-105
Congressional voting studies - 3-C-42-C
Party unity votes - 27-C
Presidential support - 21-C
Roll call votes - 2-H-145-H
Dannemeyer, William E., R-Calif. (39)
Appropriations - 460, 498
Budget - 437
Clean Air Act sanctions - 339, 8-C
Committees - 63-98, 101-105
Federal employee social security coverage - 577
IMF funding - 245
Martin Luther King holiday - 600
NIH authorization - 410
Roll call votes - 2-H-145-H
Darden, George "Buddy" - 7-B
Daschle, Thomas A., D-S.D. (AL)
Committees - 63-98, 101-105
Congressional voting studies - 3-C-42-C
Franking privilege - 580

Roll call votes - 2-H-145-H
Daub, Hal, R-Neb. (2)
  Committees - 63-98, 101-105
  Congressional voting studies - 3-C-42-C
  Roll call votes - 2-H-145-H
Davis, Robert W., R-Mich. (11)
  Committees - 63-98, 101-105
  Congressional voting studies - 3-C-42-C
  Equal Rights Amendment - 297
  Grenada invasion - 135
  Roll call votes - 2-H-145-H
Davis-Bacon Act - 229, 269
Day care programs
  Assistance programs - 414
  Jobs bill - 451, 454, 457
  Senate facilities - 594
Daylight-saving time - 551
Death penalty. See Capital punishment.
Debategate - 594
DeConcini, Dennis, D-Ariz.
  Appropriations - 455, 534
  Committees - 44-62, 99-100
  Congressional voting studies - 3-C-42-C
  Drug enforcement - 317
  El Salvador aid - 159
  Immigration reform bill - 288
  Legislative veto - 573
  MX debate - 198
  Roll call votes - 2-S-60-S
  Volcker confirmation - 266
Defense. (See also Aircraft, Military aircraft; Defense Department; Foreign affairs, Foreign aid, Military aid, Intelligence affairs; Joint Chiefs of Staff; Military construction; Military personnel issues; North Atlantic Treaty Organization; Weapons, individual branches of the armed services: Air Force, Army, Coast Guard, Marine Corps, National Guard, Navy, Reserves, military.)
  Appropriations - 479-494, 509-515
  Arms control
    Arms talks - 479, 484
    Defense authorization - 175, 180
    MX missile construction, deployment - 175, 180, 195-205
    Nuclear deterrence debate (box) - 202-203
    Nuclear freeze resolution - 205, 212, 6-C, 8-C
    Presidential messages (text) - 21-E, 22-E-25-E, 32-E-34-E
  Authorizations - 175-193
  Budget
    Administration plan - 425-426, 430 (chart), 432, 434 (chart)
    First resolution - 438, 439-441, 444, 445 (chart)
    Overview - 171-172
  Civil defense - 434 (chart)
  Defense production - 265-266
  Employee pre-publication review - 148, 152
  Export controls - 254-255
  Grenada invasion - 121, 122
  Key votes - 4-C-5-C, 7-C, 8-C-9-C
  Lebanon peacekeeping forces
    Congressional resolution - 113-123, 5-C
    Marine headquarters attack - 121-123
    Presidential message - 36-E-38-E
  Legislative summary - 16
  Legislative veto provisions - 566
  Military advisers - 215
  National Security directive - 148, 152
  Nicaragua covert aid - 123-132
  Nominations and confirmations - 26-A
  Nuclear deterrence debate (box) - 202-203
  Overview, 1983 - 171-174
  Peace Academy proposal - 399
  Presidential messages (text) - 21-E, 22-E-25-E

Procurement - 172-173, 181-182, 481, 490
  Rapid Deployment Forces (RDF) - 194
Defense Department (DOD)
  Appropriations - 479-494
  Authorization - 175-193, 527, 528
  Budget - 432, 434, 440
  Education, armed forces - 418-419
  Export controls - 255
  Joint Chiefs of Staff reorganization - 215
  Military construction
    Appropriations - 469-472
    Continuing resolution - 526
  Procurement - 172-173, 181-182, 481, 490
Defense Production Act - 241, 242, 265-266, 537
de la Garza, E.'Kika', D-Texas (15)
  Committees - 63-98, 101-105
  Congressional voting studies - 3-C-42-C
  Dairy, tobacco program - 376, 378, 380
  Handicapped education - 403
  Immigration reform bill - 291
  Roll call votes - 2-H-145-H
DeLauer, Richard D. - 189
Delaware - 275
Delaware River Basin Commission - 501
DelCostello v. International Brotherhood of Teamsters, United Steelworkers of America v. Flowers - 15-A
Dellums, Ronald V., D-Calif. (8)
  Appropriations - 513
  Budget - 447
  Committees - 63-98, 101-105
  Congressional voting studies - 3-C-42-C
  Defense authorization - 179, 181
  Drug probe - 15, 595
  Grenada invasion - 136
  Military construction funds - 194
  Pershing II deployment - 207
  Roll call votes - 2-H-145-H
Democratic Party. (See also Elections and politics.)
  Budget - 437-438
  Conservative coalition - 37-C-42-C
  Political report - 3-B-7-B
  Presidential support - 18-C-25-C
  Voting unity - 26-C-31-C, 33-C
Democratic Revolutionary Alliance - 128
Democracy Program - 145, 148 (box)
Denmark - 472
Dense pack - 176, 193, 195, 199, 203
Dental research - 504
Denton, Jeremiah, R-Ala.
  Abortion Amendment - 309
  Abortion funding - 530
  Appropriations - 536
  Capitol bombing - 593
  Committees - 44-62, 99-100
  Congressional voting studies - 3-C-42-C
  Legal Services Corporation - 323
  Martin Luther King holiday - 602
  Roll call votes - 2-S-60-S
  School prayer - 301
Department. See other part of agency name, e.g. Agriculture Department.
Deregulation
  Airline - 461, 543
  Banking - 15
  Broadcasting - 15, 551-552
  Cable television - 15, 552-554
  Trucking industry - 543, 559-560
Derrick, Butler, D-S.C. (3)
  Committees - 63-98, 101-105
  Congressional voting studies - 3-C-42-C
  Roll call votes - 2-H-145-H
Desegregation, schools. See School desegregation.
Destro, Robert - 293, 294

Developing countries, aid to. See Foreign aid.
DeWine, Michael, R-Ohio (7)
  Committees - 63-98, 101-105
  Congressional voting studies - 3-C-42-C
  Equal Rights Amendment - 297
  Roll call votes - 2-H-145-H
Dickerson v. New Banner Institute Inc. - 8-A
Dickinson, William L., R-Ala. (2)
  Committees - 63-98, 101-105
  Congressional voting studies - 3-C-42-C
  Defense authorization - 190
  Roll call votes - 2-H-145-H
Dicks, Norman D., D-Wash. (6)
  Appropriations - 484
  Arms control letter - 32-E-33-E
  Committees - 63-98, 101-105
  Congressional voting studies - 3-C-42-C
  Defense authorization - 181
  MX debate - 197-199, 202-203
  Nuclear freeze resolution - 208
  Roll call votes - 2-H-145-H
Diego Garcia - 194, 470
Dingell, John D., D-Mich. (16)
  Amtrak authorization - 562
  Appropriations - 467
  Broadcast deregulation - 552
  Budget control proposals - 238
  Clean Air Act - 339-340
  Committees - 63-98, 99-101
  Congressional voting studies - 3-C-42-C
  EPA investigation - 332, 14-E
  Hazardous waste disposal - 338
  Natural gas pricing - 369
  NIH authorization - 410
  Roll call votes - 2-H-145-H
  Sex-based insurance plans - 300, 558
  Telephone rates - 545, 547
Director, Office of Workers' Compensation Program v. Perini North River Associates - 16-A
Dirks v. Securities and Exchange Commission - 14-A
Disabled American Veterans - 599
Disabled persons. See Handicapped persons.
Disability insurance. See Social Security Disability Insurance (SSDI).
Disaster relief. (See also Earthquakes; Emergency preparedness; Floods and flood control; Foreign aid; Impact aid; Insurance.)
  Budget - 430
  Drought relief - 375, 378, 387-388
  Farm disaster relief - 384-386
  International disaster relief - 522
Discrimination. See Civil rights.
Disease prevention. See Preventive medicine.
District Courts, U.S.
  Appropriations - 473 (chart), 475, 476
  Bankruptcy laws - 320
  Judges - 318
  Nominations and confirmations - 302-304, 31-A
  Supreme Court decisions - 19-A
District of Columbia
  Appropriations - 494-495, 511
  Continuing resolution - 526
  National trails - 346
  Prison overcrowding - 495
  Unemployment payments - 447
District of Columbia Court of Appeals v. Feldman - 19-A
Dixon, Alan J., D-Ill.
  Appropriations - 455
  Cable television deregulation - 553
  Coal leasing ban - 352
  Committees - 44-62, 99-100
  Congressional voting studies - 3-C-42-C
  Countercyclical aid - 4-C
  Debt limit increase - 241
  Export control bill - 254-255

Peacekeeping forces in Lebanon - 122
  Roll call votes - 2-S-60-S
Dixon, Julian C., D-Calif. (28)
  Committees - 63-98, 101-105
  Congressional voting studies - 3-C-42-C
  Roll call votes - 2-H-145-H
Doctors, medical. See Physicians.
Dodd, Christopher J., D-Conn.
  Central American involvement - 125, 31-E-32-E
  Committees - 44-62, 99-100
  Congressional voting studies - 3-C-42-C
  El Salvador aid - 158, 159, 161
  El Salvador certification - 156
  El Salvador human rights - 164
  Export control bill - 254
  Roll call votes - 2-S-60-S
Dole, Elizabeth Hanford
  Amtrak authorization - 562
  Deregulation - 543
  Federal employee social security coverage - 576
  Maritime antitrust bill - 556
  Martin Luther King holiday - 602
  Trucking deregulation proposals - 560
  Nominations and confirmations - 23-A
Dole, Robert, R-Kan.
  Appropriations - 454, 489, 512
  Bankruptcy laws - 321
  Budget - 442, 444, 447
  Civil Rights Commission - 293, 295
  Committee chairmanship - 151
  Committees - 44-62, 99-100
  Congressional voting studies - 3-C-42-C
  Debt limit increase - 240
  Deficit reduction proposals - 231, 237
  Food assistance programs - 412, 416
  Health insurance proposal - 390, 405
  Medicare revisions - 392
  Pension equity bill - 276
  PIK tax provisions - 382
  Presidential support - 21-C
  Revenue sharing - 227
  Roll call votes - 2-S-60-S
  Social Security rescue bill - 221, 224-225
  Tax proposals - 217, 237
  Tuition tax credits - 395
  Unemployment benefits - 276
  Watt resignation - 327
  Withholding tax revisions - 261-262
Domenici, Pete V., R-N.M.
  Appropriations - 468, 478, 508
  Budget - 423, 435, 438, 439, 441, 443, 446-447, 4-C
  Budget control proposal - 238
  Budget resolution - 3-C
  Committees - 44-62, 99-100
  Congressional voting studies - 3-C-42-C
  Defense authorization - 187
  Deficit reduction proposals - 231
  El Salvador aid - 170
  IMF funding - 244
  Immigration reform bill - 289
  MX debate - 198
  Presidential support - 21-C
  Roll call votes - 2-S-60-S
  Tax proposals - 217, 237
  Water projects - 355
Domestic social programs. See Welfare and social services.
Dominica - 135
Donnelly, Brian J., D-Mass. (11)
  Budget - 436
  Committees - 63-98, 101-105
  Congressional voting studies - 3-C-42-C
  Roll call votes - 2-H-145-H
Dorgan, Byron L., D-N.D. (AL)
  Auto domestic content bill - 258
  Committees - 63-98, 101-105
  Congressional voting studies - 3-C-42-C
  Garrison Diversion project - 356-357

IMF funding - 245
Roll call votes - 2-H-145-H
Dowdy, Wayne, D-Miss. (4)
Committees - 63-98, 101-105
Congressional voting studies - 3-C-42-C
Energy Committee appointment - 340
Roll call votes - 2-H-145-H
Downey, Thomas J., D-N.Y. (2)
Appropriations - 484
Committees - 63-98, 101-105
Congressional voting studies - 3-C-42-C
MX debate - 200
Roll call votes - 2-H-145-H
Tax cap bill - 249
Withholding tax revisions - 263
Draft, military. See Selective service system.
Dreier, David, R-Calif. (33)
Appropriations - 484
Committees - 63-98, 101-105
Congressional voting studies - 3-C-42-C
Party unity votes - 27-C
Roll call votes - 2-H-145-H
Drug Enforcement Administration
(DEA)
Anti-crime proposal - 317
Appropriations - 473
Nominations and confirmations - 27-A
Drug industry. (See also Food and Drug Administration.)
Anti-tampering bill - 313-314
''Orphan'' drug development - 409
Drug trafficking. (See also Drug Enforcement Administration.)
Appropriations - 454, 522
Caribbean trade provisions - 252
Drug czar proposal - 538, 539
Foreign aid provisions - 145, 151
Drugs, drug abuse. (See also Alcohol, Drug Abuse, and Mental Health Administration; Alcoholism.)
Anti-tampering bill - 313-314
Appropriations - 449, 454, 473, 474
Authorization bill - 402
Block grants - 506
Congressional probe - 15, 595
Drug czar proposal - 317
Forane - 313, 314
Military code - 311
Research and information programs - 402
Treatment and monitoring program - 314
Druse Moslems - 114
Due process - 7-A, 11-A
Dulles Airport - 462
Duncan, John J., R-Tenn. (2)
Committees - 63-98, 101-105
Congressional voting studies - 3-C-42-C
Roll call votes - 2-H-145-H
Durbin, Dick, D-Ill. (20)
Committees - 63-98, 101-105
Congressional voting studies - 3-C-42-C
Housing authorization - 283
Jobs bill, phase II program - 269
Roll call votes - 2-H-145-H
Durenberger, Dave, R-Minn.
Appropriations - 467
Clark confirmation - 331
Clean Water Act- 361
Committees - 44-62, 99-100
Congressional voting studies - 3-C-42-C
Defense authorization - 189
Revenue sharing - 227, 229
Roll call votes - 2-S-60-S
Youth job programs - 230
Dwyer, Bernard J., D-N.J. (6)
Committees - 63-98, 101-105
Congressional voting studies - 3-C-42-C
Roll call votes - 2-H-145-H
Dymally, Mervyn M., D-Calif. (31)
Committees - 63-98, 101-105
Congressional voting studies - 3-C-42-C

Nicaragua covert aid - 128
Peacekeeping forces in Lebanon - 118
Roll call votes - 2-H-145-H
Dyson, Roy, D-Md. (1)
Committees - 63-98, 101-105
Congressional voting studies - 3-C-42-C
Roll call votes - 2-H-145-H
Maritime authorization - 549

E

Eagleton, Thomas F., D-Mo.
Anti-Abortion Amendment - 308
Appropriations - 455, 476, 508
Cigarette labeling - 408
Committees - 44-62, 99-100
Congressional voting studies - 3-C-42-C
Education funding - 18
International trade department proposal - 250
Legal Services Corporation - 322, 324
Math-science education proposals - 396
MX debate - 198
National Security directive - 148
Peacekeeping forces in Lebanon - 120, 122
Roll call votes - 2-S-60-S
Early, Joseph D., D-Mass. (3)
Committees - 63-98, 101-105
Congressional voting studies - 3-C-42-C
Roll call votes - 2-H-145-H
Earthquake Hazards Reduction Act - 591
Earthquakes - 511, 591
East, John P., R-N.C.
Bankruptcy laws - 320, 321
Civil Rights Commission - 295
Committees - 44-62, 99-100
Congressional voting studies - 3-C-42-C
Immigration reform bill - 288, 289
Martin Luther King holiday - 601
Nominations and confirmations - 23-A
Roll call votes - 2-S-60-S
Eckart, Dennis E., D-Ohio (11)
Appropriations - 539
Auto domestic content bill - 258
Committees - 63-98, 101-105
Congressional voting studies - 3-C-42-C
Energy Committee appointment - 340
IMF funding - 248
Roll call votes - 2-H-145-H
Economic affairs. (See also Agricultural price supports; Budget, U.S.; Community development; Countercyclical aid and targeted fiscal assistance; Employment and unemployment; Taxes and taxation.)
Budget issues
Deficits - 231-239, 427, 3-E-4-E
Economic forecasts and assumptions - 428 (chart), 446
Economic outlook - 426
Defense production - 438, 439-441, 265-266
Economic Report - 12-E-14-E
Economic summit - 217, 7-E-12-E
Fiscal policy - 426-427, 429, 432
Inflation
Administration budget plans - 426
Overview, 1983 - 218
Presidential messages (text) - 8-E, 12-E
Interest rates
Administration budget plans - 426
Presidential message - 13-E
Key votes - 4-C
Legislative summary - 16, 18
Monetary policy - 217-218, 446
Nominations and confirmations - 23-A
Overview, 1983 - 217-218
Presidential messages (text) - 4-E, 12-E-14-E

Social Security rescue bill - 219-226
Economic and Statistical Analysis - 472
Economic development (domestic). See Community development.
Economic Development Act - 604
Economic Development Administration (EDA)
Appropriations
FY 1983 supplemental - 448 (chart), 451, 453, 456
FY 1984 - 472, 474, 475
Background - 229-231
Economic development, foreign aid. See Foreign aid.
Economic impact aid. See Impact aid.
Economic Recovery Tax Act of 1981 - 603
Economic Support Fund (ESF)
Appropriations - 522 (chart), 524
Authorization - 141, 524
El Salvador - 154, 157, 159
Lebanon aid - 116-117 (box)
Economics, Statistics and Cooperatives Service. See Agricultural Cooperative Service.
Economy, U. S. See Economic affairs.
Ecuador - 144
Edgar, Bob D-Pa. (7)
Appropriations - 450, 502, 536
Committees - 63-98, 101-105
Congressional voting studies - 3-C-42-C
Garrison Diversion project - 357
Roll call votes - 2-H-145-H
Veterans' counseling centers - 410
Water projects - 521
Education. (See also Adult and continuing education; Education Department; Elementary and secondary education; Postsecondary education; Student aid; Vocational education.)
Academic facilities construction - 511
Appropriations
FY 1983 supplemental - 509-515
FY 1984 continuing resolution- 504-509, 527, 528
Armed forces - 418-419
Budget - 431, 434, 441, 442, 445 (chart)
Bilingual - 505, 507
Desegregation aid - 404-405
Disadvantaged children - 506, 507, 511
Education savings accounts - 10-E, 20-E
El Salvador aid - 162
Federal responsibilities - 9-E-10-E
Foreign aid - 522 (chart)
Foreign exchange programs - 152
Handicapped education - 18, 404, 434, 449, 505, 507, 511
Impact aid payments - 505
Indian education
Appropriations- 463
Tribal colleges - 395-396
Key votes - 6-C
Legislative summary - 18
Legislative veto provisions - 566
Math-science education
Legislative summary - 18
Proposals - 396-397
Merit pay proposals - 389
Military dependents - 189
Non-resident students - 5-A
Nutrition education - 414
Overview, 1983 - 389-390
Page school - 582
Presidential messages (text) - 5-E, 20-E-21-E
Reports, recommendations - 18, 389-390, 396
School prayer - 301-302
Sex discrimination - 300
Tax breaks for education savings - 432
Tax-exempt private schools - 3-A, 10-A

Tuition tax credit - 18, 395, 432, 3-A, 4-A, 10-E
Veterans
GI bill - 418-419
Vocational education - 599-600
Education Commission of the States - 389
Education Consolidation and Improvement Act (ECIA) - 400, 507
Education Department (ED)
Appropriations
FY 1983 supplemental - 509-515
FY 1984 - 504-509
Budget - 390, 434
Dismantlement proposals - 390
Draft registration requirement - 399
Nominations and confirmations - 26-A
Student aid programs - 449, 454, 457
Education, elementary and secondary. See Elementary and secondary education.
Education, higher. See Postsecondary education.
Education, postsecondary. See Postsecondary education.
Educational loans. See Student aid.
Edward J. DeBartolo Corp. v. National Labor Relations Board - 15-A-16-A
Edwards, Don, D-Calif. (10)
Appropriations - 479
Bankruptcy laws - 319
Civil Rights Commission - 294
Committees - 63-98, 101-105
Congressional voting studies - 3-C-42-C
Equal Rights Amendment - 286, 296
Justice authorization - 312
Records rentals/copyrights - 313
Refugee programs - 305
Roll call votes - 2-H-145-H
Edwards, Edwin W., - 3-B
Edwards, Jack, R-Ala. (1)
Appropriations - 480, 485
Committees - 63-98, 101-105
Congressional voting studies - 3-C-42-C
Roll call votes - 2-H-145-H
Edwards, Mickey, R-Okla. (5)
Appropriations - 480, 533
Committees - 63-98, 101-105
Congressional voting studies - 3-C-42-C
Roll call votes - 2-H-145-H
Eggs - 13, 376
Egypt
Foreign aid - 149, 514 (box), 525
Military aid - 144
Military construction funds - 194, 470-472
Eisenhower, Dwight D.
Civil Rights Commission -293
Congressional support - 19-C
El Salvador
CIA involvement - 125
Congressional Democrats' policy - 31-E-32-E
Foreign aid - 160
Appropriations - 142 (box), 164, 510, 513, 514 (box), 523-524
Authorization - 160
Chart, 1981-84 - 162
Legislative summary - 20
Foreign policy overview - 111
Human rights - 154, 156, 160, 164
Certification - 111
Death squads - 154, 161, 165
Political prisoners - 160
Reports - 164-168
Land reform - 165, 168
Military aid - 20, 125, 126, 144
Murdered Americans - 167
Presidential message (text) - 28-E-31-E
Refugee assistance - 150, 152
Elderly Feeding Program - 415
Elderly persons. See Aged persons.
Elections and politics. (See also Campaign financing; Congressional elections; Democratic Party; Federal Election Commission; Republican Party.)

Budget impact - 423
Campaign financing - 5-A, 13-A
Carter briefing papers - 563-564
Congressional partnership - 12-A-13-A
Franking regulations - 579
Gender gap politics - 299
Gubernatorial elections - 3-B-4-B
Political association - 13-A
Political report - 3-B-7-B
Redistricting - 4-A, 5-A, 12-A
Supreme Court decisions - 4-A, 5-A, 12-A-13-A
Voting rights - 13-A
Electric power utilities. See Utilities.
Elementary and secondary education.
(See also Bilingual education; Education Department; Private and parochial schools; School desegregation; School lunch and milk programs; School prayer.)
Access for religious groups - 302
Appropriations - 434, 511
Budget - 434
Disadvantaged children - 434, 511
Federal aid revisions - 400
Government fellowship program - 405
Handicapped persons - 511
High school graduation requirements - 389
Non-resident students - 5-A
Military dependents - 189
Page school - 582
Science education - 18, 390, 396-397
Tuition tax credits - 395, 3-A, 10-E
Weatherization - 449
Embassies and consulates
Appropriations - 509, 510
Construction contracts - 152
Lebanon bombing - 435, 509, 510
Soviet embassy site in U.S.- 150
Emergency preparedness. (See also Civil defense; Disaster relief; Federal Emergency Management Agency)
Appropriations - 496-497, 499-500
Budget - 430 (chart)
Earthquake housing standards - 591
Oil allocations - 371, 372, 462, 463, 466-469, 515
Emerson, Bill, R-Mo. (8)
Committees - 63-98, 101-105
Congressional voting studies - 3-C-42-C
Roll call votes - 2-H-145-H
Employee Retirement Income Security Act (ERISA) of 1974 - 271, 276
Employment and Training Administration - 504, 505
Employment and training programs.
(See also Rehabilitation programs; Vocational education.)
Agriculture worker program - 287
Appropriations
FY 1983 supplemental - 447-457, 448 (chart), 504, 505, 506
FY 1984 - 495-500
Budget - 431, 433, 441, 444
Discrimination - 9-A
Dislocated workers program - 433, 17-E
Elderly employment - 433, 449 (chart), 504 (chart)
Emergency jobs bill
Chart - 448-449
House action - 450-454
Senate action - 454-456
Targeting - 450-454
Women's issues - 298-299
Job Training Partnership Act - 17-E
Jobs bill, phase II program - 268-270
Presidential message (text) - 14-E
Public works jobs plan - 270
Veterans - 444, 495-500, 599-600
Voucher plan - 432
Youth - 432, 18-E

Women - 298-299
Work incentive program - 433, 506
Employment and unemployment. (See also Community development; Countercyclical aid and targeted fiscal assistance; Employment and training programs; Equal employment opportunity; Federal employees; Labor, labor unions; Occupational safety and health; Retirement and pensions; Trade adjustment assistance; Unemployment compensation; Wages and salaries.)
Aid for dislocated workers - 270-271
Appropriations - 447-457, 504, 505, 506
Budget - 431, 432
Defense contract targeting - 182
Economic forecasts and assumptions - 426, 428 (chart)
Enterprise Zone program - 14-E-15-E, 17-E
Health insurance coverage - 405-408
Illegal aliens - 287-292
Jobs bill, phase II program - 268-270
Legislative summary - 24
Presidential messages (text) - 4-E, 11-E, 16-E-19-E
Public works jobs plan - 270
Structural unemployment - 16-E-19-E
Trade adjustment benefits - 251-252
Veterans - 599
Employment Standards Administration - 504
Enders, Thomas O. - 126, 138, 165
Energy. (See also Coal; Energy conservation; Energy Department; Federal Energy Regulatory Commission; Fuel aid to poor; Gasoline; Natural gas; Nuclear energy; Oil; Solar and renewable energies; Utilities.)
Appropriations
FY 1983 supplemental - 509, 510
FY 1984 - 462-469, 500-503
Budget - 430, 433, 434 (chart), 445 (chart)
Congressional policy - 325
Energy preparedness bill - 371
Foreign aid - 522 (chart)
Fossil fuels research and development - 465
Geothermal - 501
Key votes - 6-C
Legislative summary - 18-19
Industrial policy - 18
Legislative veto provisions - 567
Low-income assistance - 505, 506
Nomination and confirmation - 26-A
Overview, 1983 - 325-326
Research and development - 465
Solar research - 502-503
Strategic Petroleum Reserve - 371, 372, 462, 463, 466-469, 515
Supreme Court decisions - 16-A-17-A
Energy conservation
Appropriations - 463, 496-500
Budget - 430
Energy preparedness - 371
Home weatherization - 433, 449 (chart), 452, 454, 457, 465, 466
Oil reserves - 371, 372, 462, 463, 466-469, 515
Research and development - 365
Energy Department (DOE). (See also Federal Energy Regulatory Commission.)
Appropriations
FY 1983 supplemental - 509, 510
FY 1984 - 463 (chart), 465, 466, 500-503
Atomic energy activities - 537
Budget - 433, 434 (chart)
Clinch River project - 364-365
Research and development
Civilian - 365

Fossil fuels - 465
Solar energy - 502-503
Energy Reserves Group Inc. v. Kansas Power & Light Co., Inc. - 16-A
Engineering. See Science and technology.
England. See Great Britain.
English, Glenn, D-Okla. (6)
Committees - 63-98, 101-105
Congressional voting studies - 3-C-42-C
Roll call votes - 2-H-145-H
Enterprise Zone program
Employment assistance - 17-E
Legislative summary - 23
Presidential messages (text) - 14-E-15-E, 17-E
Small business assistance - 14-E-15-E
State and local roles - 15-E
Tax provisions - 15-E
Entitlement programs funding
Budget - 425, 438, 441, 442, 443
Presidential message (text) - 9-E
Environment (See also Conservation; Council on Environmental Quality; Environmental health; Environmental interests, lobbying; Environmental Protection Agency; Forests and forestry; Land and land use; Pollution; Water resources; Wildlife and wildlife refuges.)
Acid rain - 151
Administration policies - 327-331
Air quality standards - 339-340, 8-C
Appropriations - 497-499
Budget - 430 (chart), 433, 445 (chart)
Clean Air Act sanctions - 339-340, 8-C
Congressional policy - 325-326
Earthquakes - 511
Foreign exchange program - 152
Hazardous waste legislation - 335-339
Interior Department changes - 327-331
Legislative summary - 19
Oil and gas leasing ban - 327-331
Overview, 1983 - 325-326
Pesticide regulation program - 14, 335, 386
Research and development - 433
Supreme Court decisions - 17-A
Water
Conservation - 448
Pollution control act - 360-361
Project impact studies - 358
Wilderness bills - 341-344
Environmental health
Clean Air Act proposals - 339-340
Pesticide regulation - 335
Superfund enforcement - 335
Environmental interests, lobbying
Alaska sport hunting bill - 347-348
Clean air sanctions - 339-340
Clinch River nuclear breeder reactor - 365
Hazardous waste disposal - 332-339
Lobby registrations - 3-D-55-D
Pesticide regulation - 14, 386
Superfund enforcement - 335
Wilderness oil and gas leases - 327-331
Environmental Protection Agency (EPA)
Agency investigation - 332-335, 16-E
Appropriations
FY 1983 supplemental - 509
FY 1984 - 495-500
Budget - 434
Burford resignation - 332-335
Clean Air Act proposals - 339-340
Document agreement - 16-E
Hazardous waste disposal
Agency investigation - 332-335
Legislation - 335-339
Legislative summary - 19
Nominations and confirmations - 334, 25-A, 29-A
Pesticide regulation program - 335, 386

Presidential message - 16-E
Ruckelshaus confirmation (box) - 334, 25-A
Equal education opportunity. See Affirmative action; School desegregation.
Equal employment opportunity
Age discrimination - 4-A
Sex discrimination - 10-A
Supreme Court rulings - 9-A-10-A
Equal Employment Opportunity Commission (EEOC) - 473 (chart), 477 (chart)
Equal Employment Opportunity Commission v. Wyoming - 5-A, 17-A
Equal rights. See Civil Rights.
Equal Rights Amendment - 25, 285-286, 296-298, 11-C
Erdreich, Ben, D-Ala. (6)
Committees - 63-98, 101-105
Congressional voting studies - 3-C-42-C
Roll call votes - 2-H-145-H
Erlenborn, John N., R-Ill. (13)
Boxing commission proposal - 586
Committees - 63-98, 101-105
Congressional contempt procedure - 334
Congressional voting studies - 3-C-42-C
Fellowship program - 405
Jobs bill, phase II program - 270
Math-science education proposals - 397
Roll call votes - 2-H-145-H
Student aid eligibility - 401
VISTA authorization - 398
ESF. See Economic Support Fund (ESF).
Estonia - 153
Ethics in Government Act of 1978 - 592, 594
Ethics in government. (See also Congressional ethics; Fraud and abuse in government programs.)
Ethics office - 584
Financial disclosure - 584
Outside earned income - 584
Conflict-of-interest laws - 22
Evans, Cooper, R-Iowa (3)
Committees - 63-98, 101-105
Congressional voting studies - 3-C-42-C
Roll call votes - 2-H-145-H
Evans, Daniel J. - 4-B-5-B
Evans, Lane, D-Ill. (17)
Committees - 63-98, 101-105
Congressional voting studies - 3-C-42-C
Presidential support - 21-C
Roll call votes - 2-H-145-H
Executive branch. (See also Cabinet; Nominations and confirmations; Reagan, President Ronald; Vetoes.)
Appropriations - 531-536
Budget - 434
Executive privilege - 334
Financial disclosure - 584
Presidential budget control - 238
Executive Office of the President
Appropriations - 532 (chart)
Budget - 431, 434 (charts)
Executive privilege - 334
Legislative veto - 147, 565-566, 569, 573
Nominations and confirmations - 25-A
Reorganization Act renewal - 588
War powers
Grenada invasion - 121, 135-136, 240
Legislative veto - 147, 563, 565-566, 569, 573
Peacekeeping forces in Lebanon - 113-123, 5-C, 9-C
Exon, J. James, D-Neb.
Appropriations - 467, 489
Budget - 439, 440
Coal leasing ban - 354
Committees - 44-62, 99-100
Congressional voting studies - 3-C-42-C

Martin Luther King holiday - 602
MX debate - 196
Peacekeeping forces in Lebanon - 114
Roll call votes - 2-S-60-S

Export Administration Act - 253, 567
Export-Import Bank. *(See also International development banks.)*
Administration budget plan - 429
Appropriation - 522 (chart), 525
Authorization - 241-248
Budget - 432
Functions - 245 (box)
Exports and imports. *See Foreign trade.*
Exxon Corp. v. Eagerton, Exchange Oil and Gas Corp. v. Eagerton - 18-A

F

Falls City Industries Inc. v. Vanco Beverage, Inc. - 13-A
Family and marital issues. *(See also Aid to Families with Dependent Children; Military dependents.)*
Child support enforcement - 300, 418
Family services - 506
Parental consent for minor's abortion - 307
Supreme Court rulings - 307, 10-A
Farm income stabilization and aid programs. *(See also Agricultural price supports; Crop insurance; Farmers Home Administration.)*
Budget - 429
Farm loans - 384-386
Farmers Home Administration (FmHA)
Appropriations - 448 (chart), 452, 516 (chart), 518-519
Authorization bill - 278, 279-280
Budget - 429
Drought aid - 388
Loan repayment - 13, 384-386
Farming. *See Agriculture and farming.*
Fascell, Dante B., D-Fla. (19)
Committees - 63-98, 101-105
Committee chairmanship - 145, 151
Congressional voting studies - 3-C-42-C
El Salvador aid - 161, 162, 163
Foreign affairs - 109
IMF funding - 248
Nicaragua covert aid - 128
Nuclear freeze resolution - 206
Project Democracy - 148-149 (box)
Roll call votes - 2-H-145-H
State Department authorization - 147
Fazio, Vic, D-Calif. (4)
Appropriations - 527, 537, 539, 541
Committees - 63-98, 101-105
Congressional voting studies - 3-C-42-C
Franking privilege - 579
MX debate - 199
Page sex charges - 583
Roll call votes - 2-H-145-H
Fed, The. *See Federal Reserve Board.*
Federal agencies (general). *See Federal government (general).*
Federal Aviation Administration (FAA)
Appropriations, FY 1983 supplemental - 510, 511
Appropriations, FY 1984 - 458-461, 459 (chart)
Federal buildings
Capitol - 511, 512, 540, 592-594
Repairs - 451
Federal Bureau of Investigation (FBI)
Abscam role - 585-586
Appropriations - 473 (chart), 474, 476
Martin Luther King investigation - 601
Federal Communications Commission (FCC)
Appropriations - 473, 474, 477
Broadcast deregulation - 551

Cable television regulations - 552
Nominations and confirmations - 24-A
Radio Marti bill - 140
Syndication rights - 538, 539
Telephone rates - 13, 544, 545, 10-C
Television syndication rights - 544, 560-561
Federal contractors and consultants. *(See also Davis-Bacon Act; Minority contractors; Small business.)*
Competitive bidding - 590
Procurement office - 22
Procurement policy - 589-590
Small business procurement - 587-588
Federal courts. *See Courts.*
Federal Crop Insurance Corporation (FCIC) - 516 (chart)
Federal debt. *See Budget, U.S.*
Federal Debt Collection Act of 1982 - 591
Federal Election Commission (FEC)
Appropriations - 532, 533
Nominations and confirmations - 24-A, 29-A
Federal Election Commission v. National Right to Work Committee - 13-A
Federal Emergency Management Agency (FEMA)
Appropriations - 496-497, 499-500
Authorization - 594
Earthquake reduction - 591
Nominations and confirmations - 30-A
Federal employees. *(See also Congressional employees; Federal retirement benefits; Merit Systems Protection Board; Military personnel issues; Office of Personnel Management.)*
Employment regulations - 22, 512, 513
Ethics office - 22, 584
Pay and benefits - 576-577, 584
Outside earned income - 584
Abortion payments - 528, 530, 533, 535
Appropriations - 511
Budget - 428 (chart), 441
Legislative veto - 573
Merit pay - 602-603
Pay raises - 22, 192, 233, 428, 441, 511, 532, 535, 576-578
Performance regulations - 602-603
Personnel rules - 602-603
Pre-publication review - 148, 152
Social Security coverage - 219-226, 573-576, 574 (box), 578
Federal Energy Regulatory Commission (FERC)
Appropriations - 501
Construction charges - 372
Legislative veto provisions - 570
Natural gas pricing - 367, 370
Nominations and confirmations - 24-A, 26-A
Federal Financing Bank (FFB) - 561
Federal government (general). *(See also Ethics in government; Federal contractors and consultants; Federal employees; Fraud and abuse in government programs; General Services Administration; Regulatory process, agencies.)*
Appropriations - 510
Budget - 431, 445 (chart)
Historical publications - 595
Legislative summary - 21-22
Lobby registrations - 3-D-55-D
Paperwork reduction - 590-591
Procurement policy - 589-590
Federal Grain Inspection Service (FGIS) - 516 (chart)
Federal Highway Administration (FHWA) - 458-460, 510
Federal Home Loan Bank Board (FHLBB) - 30-A

Federal Housing Administration (FHA)
Appropriations - 495, 497
Budget - 429
Insurance programs - 280
Federal information management - 590-591
Federal Insecticide, Fungicide and Rodenticide Act (FIFRA) - 386
Federal Judicial Center - 473 (chart)
Federal Labor Relations Authority - 532
Federal Land Policy and Management Act of 1976 - 345, 464, 567
Federal lands. *See Public lands.*
Federal Law Enforcement Training Center - 532
Federal Maritime Commission (FMC)
Appropriations - 473 (chart), 474, 477 (chart), 478
Authorization - 549
Maritime antitrust bill - 554-557
Nominations and confirmations - 30-A
Federal Mediation and Conciliation Service - 505
Federal Mine Safety and Health Review Commission - 505
Federal pay and benefits. *See Federal employees, Pay and benefits; Federal retirement benefits.*
Federal Prison System - 473 (chart)
Federal Railroad Administration (FRA)
Appropriations - 458, 459 (chart), 460
Nominations and confirmations - 28-A
Federal Reserve Board
Budget objectives - 437
Monetary policy - 217-218
Nominations and confirmations - 23-A, 24-A
Volcker confirmation - 266-267, 23-A
Federal Reserve System. *See Federal Reserve Board.*
Federal retirement benefits. *(See also Military retirement benefits.)*
Budget - 431
Cost-of-living adjustments - 233
Disability benefits - 431
Social Security coverage - 573-576
Federal Trade Commission (FTC)
Appropriations - 473, 474, 477 (chart)
Authorization bill - 561
Funeral home regulation - 562
Legislative veto provisions - 570
Maritime antitrust bill - 555
Nominations and confirmations - 24-A, 30-A
Regulation of professionals - 473, 561
Used-car rule - 562
Federal Trade Commission v. Grolier Inc. - 20-A
Federation of American Hospitals - 392
Feed grain. *See Grains.*
Feighan, Edward F., D-Ohio (19)
Committees - 63-98, 101-105
Congressional voting studies - 3-C-42-C
Roll call votes - 2-H-145-H
Feldstein, Martin S.
Budget - 426
Tax proposals - 217
Ferraro, Geraldine A., D-N.Y. (9)
Abortion amendment - 310
Committees - 63-98, 101-105
Congressional voting studies - 3-C-42-C
Roll call votes - 2-H-145-H
Women's economic equity bills - 298
Fiedler, Bobbi, R-Calif. (21)
Appropriations - 460
Committee assignments - 63-98, 101-105
Congressional voting studies - 3-C-42-C
Equal Rights Amendment - 297
Roll call votes - 2-H-145-H
Fielding, Fred F. - 14-E
Fields, Jack, R-Texas (8)
Committees - 63-98, 101-105

Congressional voting studies - 3-C-42-C
Roll call votes - 2-H-145-H
Water pollution - 360
Filibusters and cloture votes
Martin Luther King holiday - 601
Natural gas pricing - 368
Senate cloture votes (box) - 7
Senate rule change proposals - 598
Financial aid to students. *See Student aid.*
Financial institutions. *See Banks and banking.*
First Amendment rights
Equal Rights Amendment issues - 298
Religious freedom - 169
Supreme Court decisions - 4-A-5-A, 12-A
First National City Bank v. Banco Para El Comercio Exterior de Cuba - 14-A
Fish and fishing - 562
Fish and Wildlife Service, U.S.
Appropriations, FY 1983 supplemental - 448 (chart), 452
Appropriations, FY 1984 - 463 (chart), 464, 466
Fish, Hamilton Jr., R-N.Y. (21)
Anti-crime proposal - 317
Bankruptcy laws - 319
Committees - 63-98, 101-105
Congressional voting studies - 3-C-42-C
Equal Rights Amendment - 297
Refugee resettlement programs - 305, 306
Roll call votes - 2-H-145-H
Fission - 362
Flemming, Arthur S. - 293
Flippo, Ronnie G., D-Ala. (5)
Committees - 63-98, 101-105
Congressional voting studies - 3-C-42-C
Roll call votes - 2-H-145-H
Wilderness areas - 342
Floods and flood control. *(See also Water projects.)*
Appropriations - 448 (chart), 452, 453, 456, 510
Garrison Diversion Act - 357
Florida
Fish research facility - 511
Judicial appointments - 302
Military construction - 469
National trails - 346
Offshore drilling - 462, 464, 465, 468-469
Teacher merit pay system - 389
Wilderness areas - 343
Florida v. Casal - 6-A
Florida v. Royer - 6-A
Florio, James J., D-N.J. (1)
Amtrak authorization - 562
Auto domestic content bill - 258
Boxing commission proposal - 586
Committees - 63-98, 101-105
Congressional voting studies - 3-C-42-C
EPA investigation - 333
Hazardous waste disposal - 336, 339
Railroad retirement bill - 272
Roll call votes - 2-H-145-H
Telephone rates - 548
FmHA. *See Farmers Home Administration.*
Foglietta, Thomas M., D-Pa. (1)
Committees - 63-98, 101-105
Congressional voting studies - 3-C-42-C
Roll call votes - 2-H-145-H
Foley, Thomas S., D-Wash. (5)
Appropriations - 450
Budget - 438
Committees - 63-98, 101-105
Congressional voting studies - 3-C-42-C
Dairy, tobacco program - 380
Defense authorization - 180
Grenada invasion - 135
MX debate - 199

Roll call votes - 2-H-145-H
Wheat target prices - 386
Food and Drug Administration (FDA)
　Appropriations - 448 (chart), 510, 517 (chart), 518
　Generic drug market clearance - 4-A
　Saccharin ban - 401-402
Food and nutrition. *(See also Agriculture and farming; Child nutrition programs; Food for Peace; Food stamps.)*
　Aged persons - 415, 418
　Anti-tampering bill - 313, 314
　Appropriations - 509, 510, 516-520
　Assistance programs
　　Administration proposals - 415-416
　　Background - 413-414
　　Provisions - 412-413
　Elderly feeding program - 510
　Export controls - 256
　Foreign aid programs - 154
　Surplus distribution - 449, 457
Food for Peace
　Appropriations - 517 (chart), 519
　El Salvador aid - 157
　Export aid bill (box) - 385
Food Research and Action Center (FRAC) - 413
Food Safety and Inspection Service - 516
Food stamps
　Appropriations - 509, 516 (chart), 517-519
　Budget - 414, 433, 438, 444
　　Eligibility - 414
　Food donations - 413
　Fraud - 416
Forane - 313, 314
Ford, Gerald
　Authorization bill - 354-359
　Judicial appointments - 303
　Legislative veto - 569
　Presidential support - 19-C
　Staff funding - 534
　U.S.-Vatican ties - 169
Ford, Harold E., D-Tenn. (9)
　Committees - 63-98, 101-105
　Congressional voting studies - 3-C-42-C
　Roll call votes - 2-H-145-H
Ford, Wendell H., D-Ky.
　Appropriations - 455
　Clark confirmation - 331
　Coal slurry pipelines - 550
　Committees - 44-62, 99-100
　Congressional voting studies - 3-C-42-C
　Natural gas pricing - 367-368
　Roll call votes - 2-S-60-S
　Senate rule change proposals - 598
　Senate television broadcasting - 596
　Wild horses and burros management - 346
Ford, William D., D-Mich. (15)
　Committees - 63-98, 101-105
　Congressional voting studies - 3-C-42-C
　Franking privilege - 579
　Roll call votes - 2-H-145-H
Foreign affairs. *(See also Embassies and consulates; Foreign aid; Foreign trade; Human rights; Immigration and emigration; Defense; State Department; Treaties and international agreements; names of individual countries.)*
　Air crash liability treaty - 300-301
　Appropriations - 521-526
　Authorization - 145-153
　Budget - 430, 432, 445 (chart)
　Central America
　　Congressional Democrats' policy - 31-E-32-E
　　El Salvador aid - 154-164
　　Nicaragua covert aid - 123-132
　　Presidential message (text) - 28-E-31-E
　Export controls - 254-255

　Grenada invasion - 135-136
　Israel-U.S. Accord - 133
　Lebanon policy - 113-123
　Legislative veto
　　Implications - 569
　　Provisions - 566
　Lobby registrations - 3-D-55-D
　Middle East
　　Israel-U.S. Accord - 133
　　Lebanon policy - 113-123
　Nominations and confirmations - 25-A
　　Peacekeeping forces in Lebanon - 113-123, 5-C
　　Presidential message (text) - 36-E-38-E
　Overview, 1983 - 109-112
Foreign Agricultural Service - 517 (chart)
Foreign aid. *(See also Agency for International Development; Arms sales; Economic Support Fund; Food for Peace; International development banks.)*
　Appropriations
　　FY 1983 supplemental - 509-515, 524
　　FY 1984 continuing resolution - 521-526, 522 (chart), 528, 529
　Arms vs. development - 153, 523-524
　Authorization - 140-145, 521-526
　Budget - 432
　Caribbean Basin Initiative
　　Background - 253
　　Legislative summary - 26
　　Provisions - 252-253
　Carlucci Commission - 153
　Economic aid - 144-145
　Guatemala - 137-138
　Kissinger Commission - 169-170
　Lebanon emergency aid - 116-117 (box)
　Legislative summary - 20
　Military aid
　　Appropriations - 116-117 (box), 509-515, 522 (chart)
　　Authorizations - 143-144
　　Buy American provisions - 144-145
　　Foreign aid commission report - 153
　　Israel increase - 132-134
　　Kissinger Commission - 169-170
　Overview, 1983 - 109-112
Foreign Military Sales (FMS)
　Appropriations - 522 (chart), 524
　Authorization - 141
　El Salvador - 154, 157, 162
　Foreign aid - 144
　Israel - 132
　Jordan - 134
　Lebanon aid - 116-117 (box)
Foreign Service, U.S. *(See also Embassies and consulates.)*
　Appropriations - 522
　Danger pay - 151
　USIA merger - 152
Foreign trade. *(See also Agricultural trade; Arms sales; Customs Service, U.S.; Drug trafficking; Export-Import Bank; International Trade Commission, U.S.; Office of the U.S. Trade Representative; Oil imports; Tariffs and duties; Trade adjustment assistance.)*
　Automobile imports - 26
　Caribbean Basin Initiative
　　Background - 253
　　Legislative summary - 26
　Chinese trade status - 264-265
　Coffee - 26
　Domestic content - 26, 257-259
　Export controls bill
　　Background - 253-254
　　Congressional action - 254-257
　　Legislative summary - 26
　　Provisions - 257

　Hungarian trade status - 264-265
　International development banks - 241-248
　International trade court - 31-A
　International trade department proposal - 250
　Jackson-Vanik amendment - 265
　Legislative veto provisions - 567
　Most-favored-nation status - 264-265
　Overview, 1983 - 218
　Presidential messages (text) - 4-E-5-E, 13-E
　Special Drawing Rights - 241, 245
　Trade adjustment aid - 251-252
　Trade deficit - 13-E-14-E
　Trade reciprocity bill - 26, 259-260, 454
Forest Service, U.S.
　Appropriations
　　FY 1983 supplemental - 448 (chart), 452
　　FY 1984 - 463
　　Timber sales - 464
Forests and forestry. *(See also National forests; Wilderness preservation areas.)*
　Federal seedling donations - 388
　Timber sales - 464
　Wilderness areas - 342
　Wilderness-study-area leasing - 464
Forsythe, Edwin B., R-N.J. (13)
　Committees - 63-98, 101-105
　Congressional voting studies - 3-C-42-C
　Equal Rights Amendment - 297
　Roll call votes - 2-H-145-H
Fort Sill - 469
Fort Union - 467
Fossil fuels. *See Coal; Gasoline; Natural gas; Oil.*
Fowler, Wyche Jr., D-Ga. (5)
　Committees - 63-98, 101-105
　Congressional voting studies - 3-C-42-C
　Nicaragua covert aid - 127, 129
　Roll call votes - 2-H-145-H
　Tax cap bill - 249
France - 114
Franchise Tax Board of California v. Construction Laborers Vacation Trust for Southern California - 19-A
Frank, Barney, D-Mass. (4)
　Appropriations - 535
　Committees - 63-98, 101-105
　Contempt procedures - 334
　Congressional voting studies - 3-C-42-C
　Dairy program - 377
　Election - 390
　Housing authorization - 282
　Immigration reform bill - 290
　Nominations and confirmations - 23-A
　Revenue sharing - 227
　Roll call votes - 2-H-145-H
Franking privileges, congressional - 540, 541, 578-580
Franklin, Webb, R-Miss. (2)
　Committees - 63-98, 101-105
　Congressional voting studies - 3-C-42-C
　Roll call votes - 2-H-145-H
Fraud and abuse in government programs. *(See also Ethics in government.)*
　Medicare program - 393
　Presidential messages - 11-E-12-E
Free enterprise system. *See Antitrust and competition.*
Free Trade Union Institute - 148-149 (box)
Freedom of information
　Administration proposals - 22
　Executive privilege - 334
　Supreme Court rulings - 12-A
Freedom of religion. *(See also Private and parochial schools; School prayer.)*
　Supreme Court decisions - 4-A, 12-A
　U.S.-Vatican relations - 152, 168-169
Freedom of speech - 298, 12-A

Freedom of the press - 5-A, 12-A
Frenzel, Bill, R-Minn. (3)
　Appropriations - 518, 534
　Auto domestic content bill - 258
　Budget - 437
　Committees - 63-98, 101-105
　Congressional voting studies - 3-C-42-C
　Debt limit increase - 239
　Export controls - 257
　IMF funding - 248
　Page sex charges - 583
　Roll call votes - 2-H-145-H
　Social Security rescue bill - 223
　Trade adjustment assistance - 252
Frost, Martin, D-Texas (24)
　Committees - 63-98, 101-105
　Coal slurry pipelines - 550
　Congressional voting studies - 3-C-42-C
　Roll call votes - 2-H-145-H
FTC. *See Federal Trade Commission.*
Fuel aid to poor. *(See also Home weatherization.)*
　Budget - 433
Fuels. *See Coal; Gasoline; Natural gas; Nuclear energy; Oil; Solar and renewable energies.*
Fuqua, Don, D-Fla. (2)
　Clinch River project - 365
　Committees - 63-98, 101-105
　Congressional voting studies - 3-C-42-C
　Math-science education proposals - 396
　Roll call votes - 2-H-145-H
Fur Seal Act of 1966 - 345

G

GAO. *See General Accounting Office.*
Gallatin National Forest - 343
Garcia, Robert, D-N.Y. (18)
　Committees - 63-98, 101-105
　Congressional voting studies - 3-C-42-C
　Roll call votes - 2-H-145-H
Garn, Jake, R-Utah
　Appropriations - 499, 536, 539, 541, 542
　Banking deregulation - 15
　Civil Rights Commission - 295
　Committees - 44-62, 99-100
　Congressional voting studies - 3-C-42-C
　Export control bill - 254
　Honoraria limit - 515
　Housing authorization - 281
　IMF funding - 243-244, 248
　Mortgage assistance - 267
　MX debate - 198
　Roll call votes - 2-S-60-S
　Senate honoraria - 577
　Tobacco program - 378
　Volcker confirmation - 266
　Water projects - 355
Garrison Diversion project - 356-357, 500, 502, 503
GATT. *See General Agreement on Tariffs and Trade (GATT).*
Gas. *See Natural gas.*
Gasoline
　Industry antitrust exemptions - 371
　Motorboat fuel taxes - 562
　Oil glut - 326
　Oil leases - 328, 344, 462-469
Gaydos, Joseph M., D-Pa. (20)
　Appropriations - 465
　Committees - 63-98, 101-105
　Congressional voting studies - 3-C-42-C
　Roll call votes - 2-H-145-H
Gejdenson, Sam, D-Conn. (2)
　Committees - 63-98, 101-105
　Congressional voting studies - 3-C-42-C
　Indian land claim veto - 586
　Party unity votes - 27-C
　Roll call votes - 2-H-145-H

Gekas, George W., R-Pa. (17)
Committees - 63-98, 101-105
Congressional voting studies - 3-C-42-C
Equal Rights Amendment - 297
Insanity defense - 315
Jobs bill, phase II program - 269
Roll call votes - 2-H-145-H
General Accounting Office (GAO)
Appropriations - 540
Bankruptcy - 320
Coal leasing bids - 352
Paperwork reduction - 591
PIK payments - 383
General Agreement on Tariffs and Trade (GATT)
Domestic content requirements - 259
IMF funding - 244
Trade reciprocity bill - 260
General Motors Corp. v. Devex Corp. - 14-A
General revenue sharing. *See Revenue sharing.*
General Services Administration (GSA)
Appropriations - 449, 496, 499, 532 (chart)
Coal sales - 467
Consumer Information Center - 496, 499
Federal program catalog - 591
Paperwork reduction - 590-591
Genetic engineering - 409
Geological Survey - 463
Georges Bank - 462, 465, 468
Georgia - 7-B
Geothermal energy - 501
Gephardt, Richard A., D-Mo. (3)
Caribbean trade plan - 253
Committees - 63-98, 101-105
Congressional voting studies - 3-C-42-C
Natural gas pricing - 367
Roll call votes - 2-H-145-H
Geriatric concerns. *See Aged persons.*
Germany, West. *See West Germany.*
Giannelli, William R. - 331, 355-356
Gibbons, Sam, D-Fla. (7)
Appropriations - 536
Committees - 63-98, 101-105
Congressional voting studies - 3-C-42-C
Most-favored-nation trade status - 265
Peacekeeping forces in Lebanon - 119
Roll call votes - 2-H-145-H
Tax cap bill - 249
Trade reciprocity bill - 260
Gillette Company v. Miner - 18-A
Gilman, Benjamin A., R-N.Y. (22)
Committees - 63-98, 101-105
Roll call votes - 2-H-145-H
Gingrich, Newt, R-Ga. (6)
Censure proceedings - 580, 582
Committees - 63-98, 101-105
Congressional voting studies - 3-C-42-C
Equal Rights Amendment - 297
Nuclear freeze resolution - 212
Roll call votes - 2-H-145-H
Glenn, John, D-Ohio
Committees - 44-62, 99-100
Congressional voting studies - 3-C-42-C
El Salvador aid - 161
Roll call votes - 2-S-60-S
"Sensitive technology" items - 144
Voting scores (box) - 18-C
Glickman, Dan, D-Kan. (4)
Appropriations - 460
Committees - 63-98, 101-105
Congressional voting studies - 3-C-42-C
Defense authorization - 181
Immigration reform bill - 291
Legal Services Corporation - 323
Natural gas pricing - 367
Peace Academy proposal - 399
Roll call votes - 2-H-145-H
Glossary of congressional terms - xiii-xxiii

GNP. *See Gross National Product.*
Goldwater, Barry, R-Ariz.
Arizona wilderness area - 341
Central American intelligence activities - 131
Committees - 44-62, 99-100
Congressional voting studies - 3-C-42-C
Drug probe - 15, 595
National Security directive - 148
Nicaragua covert aid - 126, 130, 132
Peacekeeping forces in Lebanon - 115, 120
Roll call votes - 2-S-60-S
Telephone rates - 545, 548-549
Television deregulation - 552
War powers - 147
Water projects - 355
Gonzalez, Henry B., D-Texas (20)
Committees - 63-98, 101-105
Congressional voting studies - 3-C-42-C
Housing authorization - 282-283
Mortgage assistance - 268
Roll call votes - 2-H-145-H
Goodling, Bill, R-Pa. (19)
Child nutrition programs - 417
Committees - 63-98, 101-105
Congressional voting studies - 3-C-42-C
Roll call votes - 2-H-145-H
Goodman, Robert O. - 113
Gore, Albert Jr., D-Tenn. (6)
Appropriations - 484, 485
Committees - 63-98, 101-105
Congressional voting studies - 3-C-42-C
Defense authorization - 181, 190
Hazardous waste disposal - 338
MX debate - 197-198, 202, 203
Natural gas pricing - 367
Roll call votes - 2-H-145-H
Telephone rates - 548
Gorsuch, Anne M. *See Burford, Anne M.*
Gorton, Slade, R-Wash.
Adelman nomination - 214
Appropriations - 455, 467
Budget - 439-441, 443
Coal leasing ban - 354
Committees - 44-62, 99-100
Congressional voting studies - 3-C-42-C
Defense authorization - 187
Maritime antitrust bill - 554-555
Natural gas pricing - 368
NRC authorization - 370
Roll call votes - 2-S-60-S
Telephone rates - 549
Water projects - 355
Government contractors and consultants. *See Federal contractors and consultants.*
Government, local. *See State and local government.*
Government National Mortgage Association (GNMA) - 495, 497, 500
Government operations (federal). *See Federal government (general).*
Government Printing Office (GPO) - 540, 541
Government, state. *See State and local government.*
Governors
Elections, 1983 - 3-B-4-B
Master list - 11
GPO. *See Government Printing Office.*
Gradison, Bill, R-Ohio (2)
Committees - 63-98, 101-105
Congressional voting studies - 3-C-42-C
Health insurance proposal - 406-407
Politics - 12
Roll call votes - 2-H-145-H
Social Security rescue bill - 222
Tuition tax credits - 395
Grains
Acreage reduction programs - 380-383, 386-387
Grain elevator bankruptcies - 311

International emergency reserve - 413
Pesticides, pest control - 14
Price supports - 436
Target price freeze - 383-384
U.S. Soviet pact (box) - 387
Wheat program - 386-387
Gramm, Phil, R-Texas (6)
Budget - 436
Clinch River project - 364
Committees - 63-98, 101-105
Congressional voting studies - 3-C-42-C
Election results, 1983 - 6-B
House rule changes - 596
IMF funding - 245
Nicaragua covert aid - 129
Roll call votes - 2-H-145-H
Grassley, Charles E., R-Iowa
Appropriations - 467
Budget - 438, 439, 441
Coal leasing ban - 354
Committees - 44-62, 99-100
Congressional voting studies - 3-C-42-C
Debt limit increase - 241
Legislative veto - 570, 572
Martin Luther King holiday - 602
Radio Marti - 140
Roll call votes - 2-S-60-S
School prayer - 302
Gray, L. Patrick - 334
Gray, William H. III, D-Pa. (2)
Committees - 63-98, 101-105
Congressional voting studies - 3-C-42-C
Export controls - 256
Roll call votes - 2-H-145-H
Great Britain
Missile deployment - 195
Peacekeeping forces in Lebanon - 114
Great Lakes - 358
Greece - 141-143, 514, 525
Green, Bill, R-N.Y. (15)
Appropriations - 498
Budget - 437
Committees - 63-98, 101-105
Congressional voting studies - 3-C-42-C
MX debate - 199
Roll call votes - 2-H-145-H
Green Mountain National Forest - 344
Greenspan, Alan - 221
Gregg, Judd, R-N.H. (2)
Appropriations - 534, 541
Committees - 63-98, 101-105
Congressional voting studies - 3-C-42-C
Handicapped education - 403
Roll call votes - 2-H-145-H
Grenada
Economic aid - 525-526
Foreign aid - 136
Foreign policy overview - 112
U.S. Capitol bombing - 593
U.S. invasion - 121, 122, 135-136
War Powers Resolution - 135-136, 240
Grisham, Wayne - 241
Gross National Product (GNP)
Economic projections - 426, 428 (chart)
Overview, 1983 - 218
Grove City College v. Bell - 300, 397 (box)
Guaranteed Student Loans - 400-401
Guaranty Reserve Fund - 144
Guardians Association v. Civil Service Commission of City of New York - 9-A
Guarini, Frank J., D-N.J. (14)
Committees - 63-98, 101-105
Congressional voting studies - 3-C-42-C
Roll call votes - 2-H-145-H
Guatemala
Economic aid - 526
Foreign aid - 137-138, 143, 514, 524
Foreign policy overview - 111
Human rights - 137
Guess, Francis F. - 293, 295
Gulf of Mexico - 462-469
Gunderson, Steve, R-Wis. (3)

Committees - 63-98, 101-105
Congressional voting studies - 3-C-42-C
Educational summit proposal - 400
Roll call votes - 2-H-145-H
Guns
Federal criminal use - 316
Sport hunting bill - 347-348

H

Haig, Alexander M. Jr. - 146, 330
Hall, Katie, D-Ind. (1)
Committees - 63-98, 101-105
Congressional voting studies - 3-C-42-C
IMF funding - 248
Martin Luther King holiday - 600
Roll call votes - 2-H-145-H
Hall, Ralph M., D-Texas (4)
Committees - 63-98, 101-105
Congressional voting studies - 3-C-42-C
Roll call votes - 2-H-145-H
Hall, Sam B. Jr., D-Texas (1)
Bankruptcy laws - 320
Committees - 63-98, 101-105
Congressional voting studies - 3-C-42-C
Equal Rights Amendment - 296, 297
Immigration review bill - 288
Legal Services Corporation - 323
Legislative veto - 572
Roll call votes - 2-H-145-H
Hall, Tony P., D-Ohio (3)
Appropriations - 465
Coal slurry pipelines - 550
Committees - 63-98, 101-105
Congressional voting studies - 3-C-42-C
Roll call votes - 2-H-145-H
Hamilton, Lee H., D-Ind. (9)
Committees - 63-98, 101-105
Congressional voting studies - 3-C-42-C
Export controls - 255-256
El Salvador aid - 162
Foreign aid - 142
Lebanon foreign aid - 116-117 (box)
MX debate - 199
Nicaragua covert aid - 127, 129
Peacekeeping forces in Lebanon - 118-119, 122-123
Roll call votes - 2-H-145-H
Hammerschmidt, John Paul, R-Ark. (3)
Coal slurry pipelines - 550
Committees - 63-98, 101-105
Congressional voting studies - 3-C-42-C
Roll call votes - 2-H-145-H
Hance, Kent, D-Texas (19)
Committees - 63-98, 101-105
Congressional voting studies - 3-C-42-C
Roll call votes - 2-H-145-H
Social Security rescue bill - 223
Handicapped persons. *(See also Supplemental Security Income; Rehabilitation programs.)*
Education
Appropriations - 449, 505, 507, 511
Authorization - 18, 402
Budget - 434
Legislative summary - 18
Housing programs - 279
Infant care - 390
Medicare revisions - 391-394
Research programs - 409
Supreme Court decisions - 11-A
Hansen, George, R-Idaho (2)
Committees - 63-98, 101-105
Congressional voting studies - 3-C-42-C
Roll call votes - 2-H-145-H
Hansen, James V., R-Utah (1)
Committees - 63-98, 101-105
Congressional voting studies - 3-C-42-C
Indictment - 592
Park protection bill - 348
Roll call votes - 2-H-145-H

Harbors and ports
Authorization bill - 359
Budget message - 10-E
Longshoremen and harbor workers - 16-A
Hargrove, John - 302
Haring v. Prosise - 9-A
Harkin, Tom, D-Iowa (5)
Committees - 63-98, 101-105
Congressional voting studies - 3-C-42-C
Guatemalan foreign aid - 138
Natural gas pricing - 367
Roll call votes - 2-H-145-H
Harrison, Frank, D-Pa. (11)
Committees - 63-98, 101-105
Congressional voting studies - 3-C-42-C
Roll call votes - 2-H-145-H
Hart, Gary, D-Colo.
Budget - 443, 447
Committees - 44-62, 99-100
Congressional voting studies - 3-C-42-C
Defense authorization - 186
Immigration reform bill - 289
MX debate - 203
Roll call votes - 2-S-60-S
Voting scores (box) - 18-C
Hartnett, Thomas F., R-S.C. (1)
Appropriations - 541
Committees - 63-98, 101-105
Congressional voting studies - 3-C-42-C
Defense authorization - 180
El Salvador aid - 168
Roll call votes - 2-H-145-H
Hatch, Orrin G., R-Utah
Abortion - 4-C
Aid for dislocated workers - 270
Anti-abortion Amendment - 308-309
Appropriations - 455, 476
Bankruptcy laws - 321
Budget - 440, 441
Cigarette labeling - 408
Civil Rights Commission - 294
Committees - 44-62, 99-100
Congressional voting studies - 3-C-42-C
Desegregation aid - 404
Education funding - 18
Equal Rights Amendment - 296, 298
Handicapped education - 403
Legal Services Corporation - 323
Maritime antitrust bill - 555
Math-science education proposals - 396
Peace Academy proposal - 399
Records rentals/copyrights - 313
Roll call votes - 2-S-60-S
Saccharin ban - 402
School prayer - 301-302
Tax cap bill - 250
Water projects - 355
Hatcher, Charles, D-Ga. (2)
Committees - 63-98, 101-105
Congressional voting studies - 3-C-42-C
Roll call votes - 2-H-145-H
Hatfield, Mark O., R-Ore.
Anti-abortion Amendment - 309
Appropriations - 447, 450, 455, 467, 489, 514, 527, 530, 536, 538-539
Budget - 442
Budget control proposal - 238
Clark confirmation - 331
Coal leasing ban - 354
Committees - 44-62, 99-100
Congressional voting studies - 3-C-42-C
Defense authorization - 186
El Salvador aid - 159
MX debate - 198
Nuclear freeze resolution - 205
Peacekeeping forces in Lebanon - 118
Roll call votes - 2-S-60-S
Senate television broadcasting - 596
School prayer - 301
Hawaii
Abortion funding - 306

Hawkins, Augustus F., D-Calif. (29)
Committees - 63-98, 101-105
Congressional voting studies - 3-C-42-C
Immigration reform bill - 292
Phase II jobs bill - 268-269
Roll call votes - 2-H-145-H
Hawkins, Paula, R-Fla.
Appropriations - 467, 469
Clinch River project - 365
Coal leasing ban - 354
Committees - 44-62, 99-100
Congressional voting studies - 3-C-42-C
Housing authorization - 281
Immigration reform bill - 290
Radio Marti - 139-140
Roll call votes - 2-S-60-S
Hayes, Charles A., D-Ill. (1)
Committees - 63-98, 101-105
Congressional voting studies - 3-C-42-C
Election results - 7-B
Roll call votes - 2-H-145-H
Hazardous Substance Response Trust Fund - 497, 500
Hazardous substances. *(See also Environmental health; Hazardous wastes management; Nuclear waste and radioactive materials management; Pesticides, pest control; Pollution.)*
Acid rain - 340-341
Appropriations - 497, 500
Black lung compensation - 505, 506, 510, 511, 513
Cigarette labeling - 22, 408-409
Hazardous waste management
Appropriations - 497-500
Authorization bill - 335-339
Budget - 433
Burford contempt citation - 333
Container specifications - 336
Enforcement - 337-338
EPA investigation - 332-335
Legislative summary - 19-20
Legislative veto - 338-339
Superfund tax - 335
Head Start - 449 (chart), 507
Health. *(See also Abortion; Alcoholism; Child and maternal health programs; Drugs, drug abuse; Drug industry; Hazardous substances; Health and Human Services Department; Health insurance; Hospitals; Child and maternal health programs; Medicaid, Medicare; Mental health and illness; Military personnel issues, Health; National Institutes of Health; Nurses and nursing; Physicians; Preventive medicine.)*
Appropriations
FY 1983 supplemental - 452, 454, 510, 511, 512
FY 1984 - 504-509
Budget - 431, 433, 441, 442, 445 (chart)
Cigarette labeling - 408-409
Emergency fund - 417
Food and drug tampering - 313-314
Foreign aid - 522 (chart)
Genetic engineering - 409
Handicapped infant care - 390
Health planning system - 420-421
Hospice care - 398-399
Indian facilities - 457
Jobless health benefits - 512
Legislative summary - 20
Migrant-worker facilities - 457
Overview, 1983 - 389-390
Research and development - 23, 452, 454, 504-512
Saccharin ban - 401-402
Veterans programs
Agent Orange research - 536, 537
Counseling centers - 410-412

Veterans hospitals - 451, 453
Health and Human Services Department (HHS). *(See also Food and Drug Administration; National Institutes of Health.)*
Appropriations
FY 1983 supplemental - 510
FY 1984 continuing resolution - 504-509, 527, 528
Budget - 434
Heckler nomination - 23-A, 26-A
Hospital infant care regulations - 390
Nominations and confirmations - 23-A, 26-A
''Squeal'' rule - 390
Health Care Financing Administration (HCFA) - 505
Health, Education and Welfare Department (HEW). *See Education Department (ED); Health and Human Services Department (HHS).*
Health insurance. *(See also Health Maintenance Organizations; Medicaid, Medicare.)*
Budget - 425, 444, 445 (chart)
Employer-based programs - 390
Jobless health program proposal - 405-408
Health Maintenance Organizations (HMOs) - 392
Health promotion. *See Preventive medicine.*
Health research - 431, 504-505
Heckler, Margaret M.
Health emergency fund - 417
Nominations and confirmations - 390, 23-A, 26-A
Heckler v. Campbell - 20-A
Hecht, Chic, R-Nev.
Committees - 44-62, 99-100
Congressional voting studies - 3-C-42-C
Roll call votes - 2-S-60-S
Water projects - 355
Heflin, Howell, D-Ala.
Anti-abortion Amendment - 309
Anti-crime proposal - 316
Bankruptcy laws - 320
Coal leasing ban - 354
Committees - 44-62, 99-100
Congressional voting studies - 3-C-42-C
Immigration reform bill - 288
Roll call votes - 2-S-60-S
Tax cap bill - 250
Trade reciprocity bill - 259
Hefner, W.G.'Bill', D-N.C. (8)
Committees - 63-98, 101-105
Congressional voting studies - 3-C-42-C
Roll call votes - 2-H-145-H
Heftel, Cecil, D-Hawaii (1)
Committees - 63-98, 101-105
Congressional voting studies - 3-C-42-C
Roll call votes - 2-H-145-H
Heinz, John, R-Pa.
Appropriations - 455, 500, 508
Banking deregulation - 15
Committees - 44-62, 99-100
Congressional voting studies - 3-C-42-C
Export control bill - 254
Housing authorization - 281
IMF funding - 243
Mortgage assistance - 267
Revenue sharing - 229
Roll call votes - 2-S-60-S
Social Security rescue bill - 224
Tax cap bill - 250
Helicopters, military - 481, 483, 487
Helms, Jesse, R-N.C.
Anti-abortion Amendment - 25, 308-309
Abortion - 306-311, 566
Appropriations - 478, 490
Bankruptcy laws - 321
Budget - 444

Campaign financing - 594
Civil Rights Commission - 295
Committees - 44-62, 99-100
Congressional voting studies - 3-C-42-C
Dairy, tobacco program - 380
El Salvador aid - 158, 161, 169
Food assistance programs - 412, 417
Foreign aid - 145
Heckler nomination - 23-A
IMF funding - 243
Immigration reform bill - 289
Korean airline downing - 137
Martin Luther King Holiday - 600-601, 6-C
Most-favored-nation trade status - 265
Project Democracy - 149
Roll call votes - 2-S-60-S
Tax leasing plan - 603
Tobacco program - 13, 375
United Nations authorization - 150
Helsinki Commission - 151
Hensley v. Eckerhart -9-A
Heritage Foundation - 364
Herman & MacLean v. Huddleston, Huddleston v. Herman & MacLean - 14-A
Hertel, Dennis M., D-Mich. (14)
Committees - 63-98, 101-105
Congressional voting studies - 3-C-42-C
Defense authorization - 181
Roll call votes - 2-H-145-H
Hesburgh, Theodore M. - 293
Hewitt v. Helms - 11-A
High schools. *See Elementary and secondary education.*
Higher education. *See Postsecondary education.*
Hightower, Jack, D-Texas (13)
Committees - 63-98, 101-105
Congressional voting studies - 3-C-42-C
Roll call votes - 2-H-145-H
Highway Trust Fund
Appropriations
FY 1983 supplemental - 451, 453, 458, 459
FY 1984 - 460-461
Budget - 434
Highways and roads
Appalachian Regional Commission highway - 536
Appropriations - 448 (chart), 451, 453, 456
Authorization - 544, 559
Budget - 434
Construction, repair bill - 544, 559
Hiler, John, R-Ind. (3)
Appropriations - 465, 541
Committees - 63-98, 101-105
Congressional voting studies - 3-C-42-C
Roll call votes - 2-H-145-H
Hillis, Elwood, R-Ind. (5)
Committees - 63-98, 101-105
Roll call votes - 2-H-145-H
Hillsboro National Bank v. Commissioner of Internal Revenue, United States v. Bliss Dairy - 14-A
Hinckley, John W. Jr., - 314
Hispanics. *(See also Bilingual education; Minority groups.)*
Immigration reform bill - 287, 290
Judicial appointments - 302-304
Hodel, Donald P.
Acid rain - 340
Clinch River breeder reactor - 538
Emergency preparedness - 466
Hollings, Ernest F., D-S.C.
Air crash liability treaty - 300
Appropriations - 508
Budget - 438, 441, 443
Committees - 44-62, 99-100
Congressional voting studies - 3-C-42-C
Education spending - 6-C
MX debate - 198

Roll call votes - 2-S-60-S
Voting scores (box) - 18-C
Holt, Marjorie S., R-Md. (4)
    Committees - 63-98, 101-105
    Congressional tenure - 298
    Congressional voting studies - 3-C-42-C
    Roll call votes - 2-H-145-H
Home weatherization - 433, 449
(chart), 452, 454, 457, 465, 466
Honduras
    Foreign aid - 143, 157, 514 (box)
    Military aid - 144
    Military construction funds - 470-472
Honoraria - 511, 512, 514, 515, 4-C
Hooks, Benjamin L. - 601
Hoover, Herbert - 565
Hopkins, Larry J., R-Ky. (6)
    Committees - 63-98, 101-105
    Congressional voting studies - 3-C-42-C
    Roll call votes - 2-H-145-H
Horton, Frank, R-N.Y. (29)
    Committees - 63-98, 101-105
    Congressional voting studies - 3-C-42-C
    Procurement office - 590
    Revenue sharing - 227-228
    Roll call votes - 2-H-145-H
Horton, John P. - 333
Hospice care - 398-399
Hospital insurance trust fund - 391
Hospitalization insurance. See Health
insurance.
Hospitals
    Foreign aid - 522 (chart)
    Handicapped infant care - 390
    Jobless health insurance proposal -
    405-408
    Medicare revisions - 391-394
    Veterans hospitals - 451, 453
    Weatherization program - 449
House committees (general). (For com-
mittee action on a specific bill, see the
topic of the legislation.)
    Assignments - 63-96, 101-105
    Background - 42-43
    Joint - 97-98
House of Representatives. (See also
Congressional elections.)
    Congressional employees
        Appropriations - 539-542
        Page sex charges - 580-583
    Ethics
        Abscam investigation - 585-586
        Censure proceedings - 581 (box)
        Drug investigation - 595
        Page sex charges - 580-583
        Transcript alterations - 583
    Franking privileges - 578-580
    Hansen indictment - 592
    Honoraria limit - 511, 512, 514, 515
    House rules - 8-9, 563
    Leadership - 3-9
    Legislative branch appropriations -
    539-542
    Membership
        Changes, 98th Congress (box) - 5
            Characteristics of 98th Congress -
            31-38
            Leadership - 3-9
            Master list - 10-11
            Seniority - 39-41
    Party switches - 9, 597
    Pay and expenses - 577
        Appropriations - 539-542
        Office, travel allowances - 541
        Pay, key vote - 4-C
        Pay raises - 577-578
    Political report - 3-B-7-B
    Rule changes - 8-9, 596-597
    Secret hearings - 597
    Seniority - 39-41
    Social security coverage - 577
    Tax jurisdiction - 9
    Votes

Conservative coalition - 37-C-42-C
    Key votes - 7-C-11-C
    Party unity - 26-C-31-C
    Presidential support - 18-C-25-C
    Roll call votes - 2-H-145-H
    Voting participation - 32-C-35-C
Housing. (See also Community development; Housing and Urban Development
Department; Mortgages and home
loans; Public housing and housing assistance.)
    Appropriations
        FY 1983 supplemental - 448 (chart),
        511
        FY 1984 - 495-500
        Authorization - 277-283, 536
    Budget - 434
    College programs - 496
    Earthquake standards - 591
    Elderly and handicapped - 279, 495,
    496
    Home weatherization - 449 (chart)
    Indian housing - 282, 448, 495
    Legislative summary - 23
    Military family housing - 449
    Mortgage revenue bonds - 276-277
    Mortgage subsidies - 495-500
    Relocation assistance - 587
    Rural development - 278, 279-280
Housing Act of 1959 - 500
**Housing and Urban Development De-
partment (HUD).** (See also Federal
Housing Administration.)
    Appropriations
        FY 1984 - 495-500
        FY 1984 continuing resolution - 529
    Budget - 434
    Nominations and confirmations - 27-A
Housing subsidies. See Public housing
and housing assistance.
How a bill becomes law
    Chart - xxiv
    Glossary - xiii-xxiii
    Legislative process - xxv-xxviii
Howard, James J., D-N.J. (3)
    Appropriations - 452, 456, 531
    Committees - 63-98, 101-105
    Congressional contempt procedure -
    334
    Congressional voting studies - 3-C-42-C
    Roll call votes - 2-H-145-H
    Trucking deregulation proposals - 560
Howard University - 397
Hoyer, Steny H., D-Md. (5)
    Appropriations - 530
    Committees - 63-98, 101-105
    Congressional voting studies - 3-C-42-C
    Federal personnel rules - 603
    MX debate - 199
    Roll call votes - 2-H-145-H
Hubbard, Carroll Jr., D-Ky. (1)
    Appropriations - 465
    Committees - 63-98, 101-105
    Roll call votes - 2-H-145-H
Huckaby, Jerry, D-La. (5)
    Committees - 63-98, 101-105
    Congressional voting studies - 3-C-42-C
    Roll call votes - 2-H-145-H
Huddleston, Walter D., D-Ky.
    Appropriations - 508
    Committees - 44-62, 99-100
    Congressional voting studies - 3-C-42-C
    Korean airline downing - 137
    MX debate - 198, 200
    Roll call votes - 2-S-60-S
    U.S.-Soviet relations - 150
Hughes, William J., D-N.J. (2)
    Anti-crime grant program - 313
    Bankruptcy laws - 319
    Committees - 63-98, 101-105
    Congressional voting studies - 3-C-42-C
    El Salvador aid - 160
    Export controls - 257

Hazardous waste disposal - 338
    Legal Services Corporation - 323
    Roll call votes - 2-H-145-H
Human development services. See
Welfare and social services.
Human rights
    Central America - 128
    El Salvador
        Certification - 111
        Death squads - 154, 161, 165
        Political prisoners - 160
        Reports - 164-168
    Guatemala - 137-138
    South Africa - 152
    Turkey - 142
Humphrey, Gordon J., R-N.H.
    Air crash liability treaty - 300
    Appropriations - 455, 490, 503, 539
    Civil Rights Commission - 295
    Clark confirmation - 331
    Clinch River project - 364
    Committees - 44-62, 99-100
    Congressional voting studies - 3-C-42-C
    Garrison Diversion project - 357
    IMF funding - 243, 248
    Martin Luther King holiday - 602
    MX debate - 200
    Peace Academy proposal - 399
    Presidential support - 21-C
    Revenue sharing - 229
    Roll call votes - 2-S-60-S
Hungary - 264-265
Hunter, Duncan L., R-Calif. (45)
    Appropriations - 541
    Committees - 63-98, 101-105
    Congressional voting studies - 3-C-42-C
    Franking privilege - 579
    Roll call votes - 2-H-145-H
Hussein, King - 135
Hutto, Earl, D-Fla. (1)
    Appropriations - 469
    Committees - 63-98, 101-105
    Congressional voting studies - 3-C-42-C
    Export controls - 256, 257
    Roll call votes - 2-H-145-H
Hyde, Henry J., R-Ill. (6)
    Anti-abortion Amendment - 308
    Bankruptcy laws - 319
    Committees - 63-98, 101-105
    Congressional voting studies - 3-C-42-C
    El Salvador aid - 162
    Equal Rights Amendment - 296-298
    Nicaragua covert aid - 129
    Nuclear freeze resolution - 206, 208,
    212
    Peacekeeping forces in Lebanon - 120
    Roll call votes - 2-H-145-H

I

Idaho - 308
Idaho v. Oregon and Washington - 19-
A
Illinois
    Abortion laws - 308
    Election results, 1983 - 7-B
    Employment funds - 455
    Sulphuric emissions - 341
Illinois v. Abbott & Associates - 13-A
Illinois v. Andreas - 6-A
Illinois v. Gates - 5-A, 6-A
Illinois v. Lafayette - 6-A
IMF. See International Monetary Fund
(IMF).
Immigration and emigration. (See also
Aliens; Refugees.)
    Asylum review - 289, 290
    Quotas - 288
    Reform bill - 285, 287-292
**Immigration and Naturalization Ser-
vice** - 473 (chart), 474

*Immigration and Naturalization Ser-
vice v. Chadha, United States House
of Representatives v. Chadha,
United States Senate v. Chadha* -
566-568, 570, 4-A, 19-A, 20-A, 22-A
Impact aid. (See also Countercyclical aid
and targeted fiscal assistance; Trade
adjustment assistance.)
    Appropriations - 449 (chart)
    Education impact aid - 505
Imports and exports. See Foreign trade.
Income security programs. See Welfare
and social services.
Income taxes
    Budget - 426, 432
    Presidential messages - 7-E
    Tax credits
        Investment - 15-E
        Tuition - 395, 3-A, 10-E
India - 150, 152
Indian lands
    Water rights - 478
    Youth conservation jobs - 230
Indian Ocean. See Middle East.
Indiana
    Abortion laws - 308
    Employment funds - 455
    Land claim veto - 586-587
    Sulphuric emissions - 341
    Water rights - 587
Indians and Alaskan natives. (See also
Bureau of Indian Affairs; Indian lands.)
    Appropriations
        FY 1983 supplemental - 448 (chart),
        453, 510
        FY 1984 - 463 (chart), 464, 495
    Education programs - 463
    Food assistance program - 415
    Health programs, facilities - 457, 463,
    510, 511
    Housing programs - 282, 448 (chart),
    495
    Human services - 506
    Indian tribal colleges - 395
Individual Retirement Accounts (IRAs)
- 235, 300
Individual rights. See Civil rights.
Industrial Development Bonds - 235,
15-E
Industrial policy - 18
Industry. See Business and industry.
Inflation. See Economic affairs.
Information Agency, U.S. (USIA)
    Appropriations
        FY 1983 supplemental - 509, 510
        FY 1984 - 473 (chart), 475, 477
        (chart)
    Authorization - 146-147
    Education exchange programs - 152
    Foreign Service merger - 152
    Project Democracy - 145, 146
Information management. See Librar-
ies.
Inland Waterways Trust Fund - 358
Inouye, Daniel K., D-Hawaii
    Appropriations - 513
    Committees - 44-62, 99-100
    Congressional voting studies - 3-C-42-C
    El Salvador aid - 159, 170
    Military sales to Jordan - 134
    MX debate - 198
    Roll call votes - 2-S-60-S
Inspector General - 459, 516 (chart)
Institutionalized, rights. See Rights of
institutionalized.
Insurance. (See also Crop insurance;
Health insurance; Social Security Disabil-
ity Insurance; Unemployment compensa-
tion.)
    Air crash liability treaty - 300-301
    Disaster - 430
    Life insurance taxation - 235
    Retirement insurance - 431

Sex-based insurance plans - 15, 300, 558

Trade reciprocity bill - 260

Intelligence affairs. (See also Central Intelligence Agency; Federal Bureau of Investigation.)
Authorization - 130-132
Central American activities - 123-132

Interagency Law Enforcement - 473 (chart)

Inter-American Development Bank (IADB)
Appropriations - 522 (chart), 537
Authorization - 241, 242, 247

Inter-American Foundation
Appropriations - 522 (chart)
Authorization - 146 (box)

Interest groups. See Lobbies, lobbying.

Interest rates
Administration budget plans - 426
Presidential messages - 13-E-14-E

Intergovernmental Fiscal Assistance. See Countercyclical aid and targeted fiscal assistance.

Interior Department. (See also Bureau of Indian Affairs; Bureau of Land Management; Bureau of Mines; Fish and Wildlife Service, U.S.; National Park Service.)
Appropriations
FY 1983 supplemental - 452, 510, 511
FY 1984 continuing resolution - 527
FY 1984 - 20, 462-469
Budget - 434
Clark confirmation - 23-A
Coal leasing moratorium - 350-354
Nominations and confirmations - 23-A, 27-A

Intermediate-range Nuclear Forces (INF) talks - 206, 479

Internal Revenue Service (IRS)
Appropriations - 532
PIK tax provisions - 381
Tax-exempt private schools - 3-A, 4-A, 10-A
Withholding taxes - 261

International affairs. See Foreign affairs.

International Atomic Energy Agency (IAEA) - 510

International Bank for Reconstruction and Development. See World Bank.

International Brotherhood of Teamsters - 271-272

International Communications Agency (ICA) See Information Agency, U.S. (USIA).

International Coffee Agreement - 26

International Development Association (IDA)
Appropriations - 510, 513
Foreign aid - 524

International development banks. (See also Export-Import Bank; International Monetary Fund.)
Appropriations - 509, 510, 513, 522 (chart), 525, 536-538, 540
Funding increase
Background - 241-243
Congressional action - 243-248

International Energy Agency (IEA)
Energy preparedness legislation - 371
Oil industry participation - 19

International Fund for Agricultural Development - 510

International Longshoremen's and Warehousemen's Union (ILWU) - 271

International Longshoremen's Association (ILA) - 271

International Military Education and Training (IMET) - 154

International Monetary Fund (IMF)

Appropriations - 509, 513
Funding increase - 241-248
Background - 242-243
Congressional action - 243-248, 536-538, 540
Key votes - 9-C

International organizations. (See also International development banks; names of individual organizations.)
Appropriations - 473 (chart), 522 (chart)
Authorizations - 146 (box)
Central American intervention - 159
South African human rights - 152

International Trade Administration
Appropriations - 472, 474
Nominations and confirmations - 30-A

International Trade Commission, U.S. (USITC) - 259

Interstate Commerce Commission (ICC)
Appropriations - 459 (chart), 461
Trucking industry deregulation - 543
Nominations and confirmations - 24-A

Interstate Commission on the Potomac River Basin - 501

Interstate disputes - 18-A-19-A

Interstate Highway System
Appropriations - 458
Repair funding - 559

Investments. See Stocks, bonds and securities.

IRA. See Individual Retirement Accounts (IRAs).

Ireland, Andy, D-Fla. (10)
Committees - 63-98, 101-105
Congressional voting studies - 3-C-42-C
Nicaragua covert aid - 128
Roll call votes - 2-H-145-H

Irish Wilderness - 343

Irrigation projects
Dams- 349
Garrison Diversion Project - 356-357, 500, 503, 511

Islamic Revolutionary Movement - 121

Israel
Foreign aid - 132-134, 144, 149, 432, 514 (box), 525
Invasion of Lebanon - 133, 134
Military forces in Lebanon - 119

Italy
Economic aid - 525
Missile deployment - 195
Peacekeeping forces in Lebanon - 114

Izaak Walton League - 347

J

Jackson, Henry M., D-Wash.
Committees - 44-62, 99-100
Congressional voting studies - 3-C-42-C
Death - 13
Defense authorization - 188
El Salvador aid - 169
Honoraria limit - 514, 515, 4-C
Legislative veto - 569
Roll call votes - 2-S-60-S
Senate honoraria - 577
Window payments - 537

Jackson, Jesse - 113

Jackson, Robert H. - 3-A

Jacobs, Andrew Jr., D-Ind. (10)
Committees - 63-98, 101-105
Congressional voting studies - 3-C-42-C
Federal employee social security coverage - 575
IMF funding - 245
Legislative veto - 571
Roll call votes - 2-H-145-H

Japan
Auto domestic content bill - 258

Military construction funds - 472
Non-tariff trade barriers - 241

Japan-United States Friendship Commission - 473 (chart)

Javits, Jacob K. - 508

Javits National Graduate Fellowships - 508

Jefferson County Pharmaceutical Association Inc. v. Abbott Laboratories - 13-A

Jeffords, James M., R-Vt. (AL)
Appropriations - 465
Budget - 437
Committees - 63-98, 101-105
Congressional voting studies - 3-C-42-C
Dairy, tobacco program - 376, 380
Jobs bill, Democrats "phase II" program - 269
Price freeze - 383
Roll call votes - 2-H-145-H
Tax-exempt bonds - 401

Jenkins, Ed, D-Ga. (9)
Caribbean trade plan - 253
Committees - 63-98, 101-105
Congressional voting studies - 3-C-42-C
Roll call votes - 2-H-145-H

Jenrette, John W. Jr. - 585

Jepsen, Roger W., R-Iowa
Anti-abortion Amendment - 308
Appropriations - 467
Clinch River project - 365
Committees - 44-62, 99-100
Coal leasing ban - 354
Congressional voting studies - 3-C-42-C
Defense authorization - 189
Radio Marti - 139
Roll call votes - 2-S-60-S

Jim McNeff Inc.v. Todd - 15-A

Job Corps - 452, 454

Job discrimination. See Equal employment opportunity.

Job safety. See Occupational safety and health.

Job Training and Partnership Act
Appropriations - 507
Presidential message - 17-E-18-E
Veterans - 27

Johnson, Harold T. - 346

Johnson, Lyndon B.
Judicial appointments - 303
Poverty programs - 416
Presidential support (box) - 19-C
Staff funding - 534, 535

Johnson, Nancy L., R-Conn. (6)
Committees - 63-98, 101-105
Congressional voting studies - 3-C-42-C
Roll call votes - 2-H-145-H

Johnson, Norma Holloway - 294

Johnston, J. Bennett, D-La.
Appropriations - 469, 489, 490, 513, 539
Budget - 439-441
Clark confirmation - 331
Coal slurry pipeline - 551, 9-C
Committees - 44-62, 99-100
Congressional voting studies - 3-C-42-C
Defense authorization - 187
El Salvador aid - 159
MX debate - 198
Natural gas pricing - 368
Roll call votes - 2-S-60-S
Tax cap bill - 250

Joint Chiefs of Staff - 215

Joint Statement of Agreed Principles for Disarmament Negotiations - 210

Jones, David C. - 215

Jones, Ed, D-Tenn. (8)
Committees - 63-98, 101-105
Congressional voting studies - 3-C-42-C
Roll call votes - 2-H-145-H
Target price freeze - 384

Jones, James R., D-Okla. (1)
Budget - 436, 447

Committees - 63-98, 101-105
Congressional voting studies - 3-C-42-C
Debt limit increase - 239
Deficit reduction proposals - 233
Federal deficit - 12
Roll call votes - 2-H-145-H
Trade reciprocity bill - 260

Jones, Walter B., D-N.C. (1)
Censure proceedings - 580
Committees - 63-98, 101-105
Congressional voting studies - 3-C-42-C
Roll call votes - 2-H-145-H

Jones & Laughlin Steel Corp. v. Pfeifer - 16-A

Jones v. Barnes - 8-A

Jones v. United States - 7-A

Jordan - 134-135, 241, 513, 514 (box), 524

Judiciary. (See also Courts; Crime and criminal justice; Supreme Court.)
Appropriations
FY 1983 supplemental - 509
FY 1984 - 472-479
Authorization - 312
Bankruptcy courts - 286, 318-320
Budget - 434, 445 (chart)
Immigration legislation review - 288
Judgeship proposal - 320
Legal assistance - 316
Legislative summary - 25
Nominations and confirmations
List - 30-A-31-A
Reagan appointments - 286, 302-304
Overview, 1983 - 285-286

Justice Department. (See also Drug Enforcement Administration; Federal Bureau of Investigation; Immigration and Naturalization Service; Office of Justice Assistance, Research and Statistics.)
Appropriations
FY 1983 supplemental - 509, 510
FY 1984 continuing resolution - 472-479, 527, 529
Authorization - 312
Budget - 434
Child pornography - 318
Congressional drug investigation - 595
Draft registration requirement - 399
EPA investigation - 333
Legal Services Corporation - 323
Nominations and confirmations - 27-A
Telephone rates - 14
Wilderness leasing - 329

Juveniles. See Children; Youth.

K

Kampuchea - 150, 153

Kansas - 275

Kaptur, Marcy, D-Ohio (9)
Committees - 63-98, 101-105
Congressional voting studies - 3-C-42-C
Roll call votes - 2-H-145-H

Karcher v. Daggett - 12-A, 5-B

Kasich, John R., R-Ohio (12)
Committees - 63-98, 101-105
Congressional voting studies - 3-C-42-C
Peacekeeping forces in Lebanon - 122
Roll call votes - 2-H-145-H

Kassebaum, Nancy Landon, R-Kan.
Abortion amendment - 310
Air crash liability treaty - 300
Appropriations - 489
Budget - 439
Committees - 44-62, 99-100
Congressional voting studies - 3-C-42-C
El Salvador aid - 159, 161
Gender gap politics - 299
MX debate - 205
Natural gas pricing - 367, 369

Roll call votes - 2-S-60-S
United Nations authorization - 147, 150
USIA authorization - 146
Kasten, Bob, R-Wis.
  Appropriations - 454, 467, 476
  Bankruptcy laws - 319, 320
  Coal leasing ban - 354
  Committees - 44-62, 99-100
  Congressional voting studies - 3-C-42-C
  Debt limit increase - 241
  El Salvador aid - 158, 159
  Foreign aid - 525
  MX debate - 198
  PIK tax provisions - 382
  Roll call votes - 2-S-60-S
  Withholding tax revisions - 262
Kastenmeier, Robert W., D-Wis. (2)
  Anti-crime proposal - 317
  Committees - 63-98, 101-105
  Congressional voting studies - 3-C-42-C
  Immigration reform bill - 290
  Legal Services Corporation - 322, 323
  Roll call votes - 2-H-145-H
Kazen, Abraham Jr., D-Texas (23)
  Committees - 63-98, 101-105
  Congressional voting studies - 3-C-42-C
  Roll call votes - 2-H-145-H
Kelly, Richard - 585
Kelly, Gen. Paul X. - 121-123
Kemp, Jack F., R-N.Y. (31)
  Appropriations - 529
  Budget - 436
  Committees - 63-98, 101-105
  Congressional voting studies - 3-C-42-C
  El Salvador aid - 169, 170
  Martin Luther King holiday - 600
  Roll call votes - 2-H-145-H
Kennedy, Edward M., D-Mass.
  Abortion amendment - 310
  Anti-crime proposal - 315, 317
  Appropriations - 476, 490, 508, 515
  Committees - 44-62, 99-100
  Congressional voting studies - 3-C-42-C
  Defense authorization - 187
  Immigration reform bill - 288, 289
  Martin Luther King holiday - 601-602
  Nuclear freeze resolution - 205, 213
  Peacekeeping forces in Lebanon - 122
  Refugee resettlement programs - 305
  Roll call votes - 2-S-60-S
  Withholding tax revisions - 262-263
Kennedy, John F. - 19-C
Kennelly, Barbara B., D-Conn. (1)
  Child support enforcement - 300, 418
  Committees - 63-98, 101-105
  Congressional voting studies - 3-C-42-C
  Party unity votes - 27-C
  Roll call votes - 2-H-145-H
Kentucky
  Abortion laws - 308
  Election results, 1983 - 4-B
  Employment funds - 455
Key votes - 3-C-17-C
Khmer Rouge - 150, 153
Kidney disease - 409
Kildee, Dale E., D-Mich. (7)
  Committees - 63-98, 101-105
  Congressional voting studies - 3-C-42-C
  Roll call votes - 2-H-145-H
Kindness, Thomas N., R-Ohio (8)
  Bankruptcy laws - 320
  Committees - 63-98, 101-105
  Congressional voting studies - 3-C-42-C
  Equal Rights Amendment - 297
  Immigration reform bill - 290
  Roll call votes - 2-H-145-H
King, Coretta Scott - 601
King, Martin Luther Jr. - 21, 600-602, 6-C
Kirkland, Lane
  Federal employee social security coverage - 574

Social Security rescue bill - 221
Kirkpatrick, Jeane J. - 170
Kissinger Commission - 110
Kissinger, Henry A. - 110, 169, 330
Kogovsek, Ray, D-Colo. (3)
  Appropriations - 502
  Committees - 63-98, 101-105
  Congressional voting studies - 3-C-42-C
  Roll call votes - 2-H-145-H
Kolender v. Lawson - 11-A
Kolter, Joe, D-Pa. (4)
  Appropriations - 465
  Committees - 63-98, 101-105
  Congressional voting studies - 3-C-42-C
  Roll call votes - 2-H-145-H
Korea, South. See South Korea.
Korean Airline disaster - 20, 136-137, 190, 257
Korean War - 599
Kostmayer, Peter H., D-Pa. (8)
  Committees - 63-98, 101-105
  Congressional voting studies - 3-C-42-C
  Foreign aid - 145
  Nuclear freeze resolution - 206
  Peacekeeping forces in Lebanon - 118
  Roll call votes - 2-H-145-H
Kramer, Ken, R-Colo. (5)
  Committees - 63-98, 101-105
  Congressional voting studies - 3-C-42-C
  Roll call votes - 2-H-145-H
Kush v. Rutledge - 9-A

L

Labeling and packaging - 408-409
Labor Department. (See also Mine Safety and Health Administration; Occupational Safety and Health Administration.)
  Appropriations
    FY 1983 supplemental - 504-509
    FY 1984 continuing resolution - 527, 528
  Budget - 434
  Nominations and confirmations - 27-A
Labor interests, lobbying
  Auto domestic content bill - 257-259
  Immigration reform bill - 287-292
  Lobby registrations - 3-D-55-D
  Natural gas pricing - 367
  Trade reciprocity bill - 259-260
Labor, labor unions. (See also AFL-CIO; Employment and unemployment; International Brotherhood of Teamsters; Labor interests, lobbying; National Labor Relations Board; Political action committees; United Auto Workers; Wages and salaries.)
  Buy American campaign - 148
  Immigration reform bill - 287-292
  Labor racketeering - 316
  Legislative summary - 24-25
  Lobby registrations - 3-D-55-D
  Longshoremen's compensation program - 271-272
  Phase II Jobs bill - 268-270
  Political contributions - 594
  Supreme Court decisions - 15-A-16-A
  Union corruption bill - 271-272
Labor-management relations. See Labor, labor unions.
Labor-Management Relations Act of 1947. See Taft-Hartley Act.
Labor-Management Services Administration - 504
LaFalce, John J., D-N.Y. (32)
  Committees - 63-98, 101-105
  Congressional voting studies - 3-C-42-C
  Defense production - 266
  Handicapped education - 403
  IMF funding - 244

Industrial policy proposals - 251
  Roll call votes - 2-H-145-H
Lagomarsino, Robert J., R-Calif. (19)
  Committees - 63-98, 101-105
  Congressional voting studies - 3-C-42-C
  El Salvador aid - 156
  Export controls - 256
  Nicaragua covert aid - 129
  Roll call votes - 2-H-145-H
Land and land use. (See also Coastal zones; Public lands.)
  Acreage reduction program - 13, 380-383, 386-387
  Hazardous waste disposal - 336-338
  Indian land claim veto - 586-587
  Marine sanctuaries - 359
  Soil conservation - 14, 387
  Wilderness bills - 341-344
Land and Water Conservation Fund - 463
Landon v. Plasencia - 11-A
Landrum-Griffin Act - 271
Lantos, Tom, D-Calif. (11)
  Committees - 63-98, 101-105
  Congressional voting studies - 3-C-42-C
  Nicaragua covert aid - 128
  Roll call votes - 2-H-145-H
Larkin v. Grendel's Den - 12-A
Latin America and the Caribbean. (See also Inter-American Development Bank; Organization of American States; names of individual countries.)
  Caribbean Basin Initiative
    Background - 253
    Provisions - 252-253
  El Salvador aid
    CIA involvement - 125
    Congressional Democrats' policy - 31-E-32-E
    Foreign aid - 142, 160, 162 (chart), 164, 510, 513, 514 (box)
    Human rights - 111, 154, 156, 160, 161, 164-168
    Land reform - 165, 168
    Military aid - 20, 125, 126, 144
    Presidential messages - 28-E-31-E
  Foreign aid - 143, 144
  Foreign policy overview - 110-112
  Grenada involvement
    Foreign aid - 136, 525-526
    U.S. invasion - 121, 122, 135-136
  Kissinger Commission - 110, 169-170
  Nicaragua covert aid
    Background - 124-126
    Congressional action - 126-132
    Provision - 124
    Refugees - 150, 152, 305
    U.S. intelligence activities - 130-132
Latta, Delbert L., R-Ohio (5)
  Appropriations - 452
  Budget - 446
  Committees - 63-98, 101-105
  Congressional voting studies - 3-C-42-C
  Roll call votes - 2-H-145-H
Latvia - 153
Lautenberg, Frank R., D-N.J.
  Committees - 44-62, 99-100
  Congressional voting studies - 3-C-42-C
  Roll call votes - 2-S-60-S
  Telephone rates - 548-549
  Withholding tax revisions - 263
Lavelle, Rita M. - 332-333
Law enforcement. See Crime and criminal justice.
Law Enforcement Assistance Administration (LEAA) - 312
Law profession and law practice - 322-324
Laws, public. See Legislation (general); Public laws.
Laxalt, Paul, R-Nev.
  Anti-crime proposal - 315
  Appropriations - 478

Clark confirmation - 329
  Committees - 44-62, 99-100
  Congressional voting studies - 3-C-42-C
  MX debate - 198
  Roll call votes - 2-S-60-S
  Water projects - 355
Leach, Jim, R-Iowa (1)
  Committees - 63-98, 101-105
  Congressional voting studies - 3-C-42-C
  El Salvador aid - 159
  Foreign aid - 525
  IMF funding - 244
  Nicaragua covert aid - 128
  Nuclear freeze resolution - 208-209
  Peace Corps authorization - 145
  Roll call votes - 2-H-145-H
Leadership Conference on Civil Rights - 294
League of Conservation Voters - 340
League of Women Voters - 299
Leahy, Patrick J., D-Vt.
  Anti-crime proposal - 317
  Appropriations - 466, 499, 515, 538
  Central American intelligence activities - 131
  Committees - 44-62, 99-100
  Congressional voting studies - 3-C-42-C
  Legislative veto - 570
  MX debate - 198
  Nuclear freeze resolution - 213
  Peacekeeping forces in Lebanon - 121, 132
  Roll call votes - 2-S-60-S
Leath, Marvin, D-Texas (11)
  Committees - 63-98, 101-105
  Congressional voting studies - 3-C-42-C
  Defense authorization - 179, 190
  Roll call votes - 2-H-145-H
  Veterans' emergency job training program - 599
Lebanon
  Congressional resolution - 113-123
    Background - 114
    Congressional action - 114-123
    Presidential message - 36-E-38-E
    Provisions - 113-114
  Foreign aid - 116-117 (box), 432, 513, 514 (box), 524
  Israeli invasion - 133, 134
  Legislative summary - 21
  Refugee assistance - 150
  U.S. Capitol bombing - 593
  U.S. Embassy
    Bombing - 114
    Reconstruction - 509, 510
  U.S. peacekeeping troops - 484, 569, 9-C
Lederer, Raymond F. - 585-586
Legal Services Corporation (LSC)
  Appropriations - 322-324, 472-478, 477 (chart)
  Budget - 434
  Lobbying investigation - 323
  Nominations and confirmations - 23-A, 324
  Provisions - 322
Legislation (general). (See also Congressional votes; Vetoes.)
  Glossary of terms - xiii-xxiii
  How a bill becomes law (chart) - xxiv
  Key votes - 3-C-42-C
  Legislative process in brief - xxv-xxviii
  Public laws - 3-F-10-F
  Summary of major legislation - 12-28
Legislative branch. See Congress.
Legislative veto
  Background - 565-566
  Congressional response - 570-573
  Foreign policy implications - 569
  Hazardous waste disposal - 338-339
  Legislative summary - 16
  Provisions - 566-567
  Supreme Court decision - 566-568, 570

War powers - 147
Wilderness leasing - 328-329
Supreme Court decision - 4-A, 19-A, 20-A-22-A (text)
Lehman, John F. Jr. - 482
Lehman, Richard H., D-Calif. (18)
Committees - 63-98, 101-105
Congressional voting studies - 3-C-42-C
Roll call votes - 2-H-145-H
Lehman, William, D-Fla. (17)
Auto domestic content bill - 258
Appropriations - 456, 459
Committees - 63-98, 101-105
Congressional voting studies - 3-C-42-C
Roll call votes - 2-H-145-H
Lehr v. Robertson - 11-A
Leland, Mickey, D-Texas (18)
Committees - 63-98, 101-105
Congressional voting studies - 3-C-42-C
Radio Marti - 140
Roll call votes - 2-H-145-H
Telephone rates - 547
Lent, Norman F., R-N.Y. (4)
Committee assignments - 63-98, 101-105
Congressional voting studies - 3-C-42-C
Nuclear freeze resolution - 212
Roll call votes - 2-H-145-H
Levin, Carl, D-Mich.
Appropriations - 455, 490, 520, 539
Committees - 44-62, 99-100
Congressional voting studies - 3-C-42-C
Countercyclical aid - 4-C
Defense authorization - 186
Immigration reform bill - 289
International trade department proposal - 250
Legislative veto - 570-571
Peacekeeping forces in Lebanon - 120
Roll call votes - 2-S-60-S
Levin, Sander M., D-Mich. (17)
Committees - 63-98, 101-105
Congressional voting studies - 3-C-42-C
Housing authorization - 283
Revenue sharing - 228
Roll call votes - 2-H-145-H
Levine, Mel, D-Calif. (27)
Committees - 63-98, 101-105
Congressional voting studies - 3-C-42-C
Defense authorization - 180
Roll call votes - 2-H-145-H
Levitas, Elliott H., D-Ga. (4)
Appropriations - 479
Coal slurry pipelines - 550
Committees - 63-98, 101-105
Congressional voting studies - 3-C-42-C
CPSC authorization - 557
EPA investigation - 333-334
Hazardous waste disposal - 338
Legislative veto - 565
Nuclear freeze resolution - 207, 211
Paperwork reduction - 591
Revenue sharing - 227
Roll call votes - 2-H-145-H
Lewis, Jerry, R-Calif. (35)
Committees - 63-98, 101-105
Congressional voting studies - 3-C-42-C
Roll call votes - 2-H-145-H
Lewis, Tom, R-Fla. (12)
Committee assignments - 63-98, 101-105
Congressional voting studies - 3-C-42-C
Roll call votes - 2-H-145-H
Liberia - 144
Libraries
Appropriations - 449 (chart), 505, 507
Medical - 409
Library of Congress - 540
Lichenstein, Charles M. - 147
Liebengood, Howard S. - 580
Limited Test Ban Treaty - 214
Linowes Commission - 352
Linowes, David F. - 350

Lipinski, William O., D-Ill. (5)
Committees - 63-98, 101-105
Congressional voting studies - 3-C-42-C
Roll call votes - 2-H-145-H
Liquor. See Alcoholic beverages.
Lithuania - 153
Litigation. See Courts, U.S.; Trial procedures.
Livingston, Bob, R-La. (1)
Committees - 63-98, 101-105
Congressional voting studies - 3-C-42-C
El Salvador aid - 160
Roll call votes - 2-H-145-H
Lloyd, Marilyn, D-Tenn. (3)
Clinch River project - 364
Committees (listed under Bouquard, Marilyn) - 63-98, 101-105
Congressional voting studies - 3-C-42-C
Equal Rights Amendment - 297
Roll call votes 2-H-145-H
Lobbies, lobbying. *(See also Business interests, lobbying; Consumer interests, lobbying; Environmental interests, lobbying; Labor interests, lobbying; Political action committees; Religion and religious organizations; names of specific groups.)*
Capitol building repairs - 512
Civil Rights Commission - 292
Clinch River project - 365
Dairy program - 376, 378
El Salvador aid - 155
Equal Rights Amendment - 296-298
Federal employee social security coverage - 575
Immigration reform bill - 287-292
Legal profession - 322
Legal Services Corporation - 323
Lobby registrations
Index - 55-D-66-D
List by month - 3-D-55-D
Nuclear freeze - 205
PIK program - 382
Sex-based insurance - 558
Social Security rescue bill - 222
Telephone rates - 545
Television syndication rights - 538
Local government. See State and local government.
Local Public Works program - 270
Local 926, International Union of Operating Engineers, AFL-CIO v. Jones - 18-A
Lockheed Aircraft Corp. v. United States - 20-A
Loeffler, Tom, R-Texas (21)
Appropriations - 468, 527
Budget - 436
Committees - 63-98, 101-105
Congressional voting studies - 3-C-42-C
Drought aid - 388
Roll call votes - 2-H-145-H
Long, Clarence D., D-Md. (2)
Appropriations - 484, 521, 529, 539
Committees - 63-98, 101-105
Congressional voting studies - 3-C-42-C
El Salvador aid - 155, 159, 160
Federal employee social security coverage - 575
Foreign aid - 521
IMF funding - 248
Peacekeeping forces in Lebanon - 115, 119
Roll call votes - 2-H-145-H
Long, Gillis W., D-La. (8)
Appropriations - 537
Committees - 63-98, 101-105
Congressional voting studies - 3-C-42-C
Dairy program - 377
Roll call votes - 2-H-145-H
Long, Russell B., D-La.
Budget - 238, 447
Committees - 44-62, 99-100
Congressional voting studies - 3-C-42-C

Debt limit increase - 240-241
Deficit reduction proposals - 231
Revenue sharing - 228
Roll call votes - 2-S-60-S
Senate television broadcasting - 596
Social Security rescue bill - 224
Tax proposals - 237
Trade reciprocity bill - 259
Withholding tax revisions - 262-263
Longshoremen's and Harbor Workers' Compensation Act - 271
Los Angeles. (ship) - 493
Lott, Trent, R-Miss. (5)
Bankruptcy laws - 320
Clinch River project - 364
Committees - 63-98, 101-105
Congressional voting studies - 3-C-42-C
Dairy program - 377
Debt limit increase - 239
Franking privilege - 579
House rule changes - 597
Legislative veto - 572
Nicaragua covert aid - 129-130
Roll call votes - 2-H-145-H
Louisiana
Abortion laws - 308
Election results, 1983 - 3-B
Employment funds - 455
Public employees - 5-A
Low-income assistance. See Welfare and social services.
Lowery, Bill, R-Calif. (41)
Committees - 63-98, 101-105
Congressional voting studies - 3-C-42-C
Equal Rights Amendment - 297
Roll call votes - 2-H-145-H
Lowry, Mike, D-Wash. (7)
Committees - 63-98, 101-105
Congressional voting studies - 3-C-42-C
Election results, 1983 -4-B-5-B
Housing authorization - 282
Roll call votes - 2-H-145-H
LSC. See Legal Services Corporation.
Lugar, Richard G., R-Ind.
Adelman nomination - 214
Appropriations - 467
Coal leasing ban - 354
Committees - 44-62, 99-100
Congressional voting studies - 3-C-42-C
El Salvador aid - 161, 169
Presidential support - 20-C
Roll call votes - 2-S-60-S
United Nations authorization - 150
U.S.-Soviet relations - 150
U.S.-Vatican relations - 152, 168
Lujan, Manuel Jr., R-N.M. (1)
Committees - 63-98, 101-105
Congressional voting studies - 3-C-42-C
Public lands transfer - 345
Roll call votes - 2-H-145-H
Watt resignation - 327
Luken, Thomas A., D-Ohio (1)
Committees - 63-98, 101-105
Congressional voting studies - 3-C-42-C
Equal Rights Amendment - 297
Roll call votes - 2-H-145-H
Lunches, school. See School lunch and milk programs.
Lundine, Stan, D-N.Y. (34)
Committees - 63-98, 101-105
Congressional voting studies - 3-C-42-C
Roll call votes - 2-H-145-H
Lungren, Dan, R-Calif. (42)
Committees - 63-98, 101-105
Congressional voting studies - 3-C-42-C
Equal Rights Amendment - 297
Immigration reform bill - 287, 288, 290
Nuclear freeze resolution - 212
Refugee resettlement programs - 305
Roll call votes - 2-H-145-H

M

Mack, Connie, R-Fla. (13)
Committees - 63-98, 101-105
Congressional voting studies - 3-C-42-C
Roll call votes - 2-H-145-H
MacKay, Buddy, D-Fla. (6)
Committees - 63-98, 101-105
Congressional voting studies - 3-C-42-C
Roll call votes - 2-H-145-H
Madigan, Edward R., R-Ill. (15)
Acid rain - 340
Committees - 63-98, 101-105
Congressional voting studies - 3-C-42-C
Dairy, tobacco program - 380
FmHA programs - 385
NIH authorization - 410
Roll call votes - 2-H-145-H
Maganal, Alvaro - 158, 159
Mail. See Postal service.
Maine v. Thornton - 289
Maine - 308
Mansfield, Mike - 508
MAP. See Military Assistance Program.
Marbury v. Madison - 4-A
March for Life - 308
Marine Corps
Appropriations - 479-494
Authorization - 177, 185, 191, 192
Grenada invasion - 135
Headquaters bombing (Lebanon) - 121-123
Peace-keeping forces in Lebanon - 113-123, 484, 569, 5-C, 9-C, 36-E-38-E
Marine Mammal Commission - 473
Marine Protection Research and Sanctuaries Act of 1982 - 359-360
Maritime Administration
Appropriations - 473 (chart), 474, 478
Authorization - 544
Maritime affairs. See Ships and shipping.
Mark Twain National Forest - 343
Markey, Edward J., D-Mass. (7)
Committees - 63-98, 101-105
Congressional voting studies - 3-C-42-C
MX debate - 200
NRC authorization - 370
Nuclear freeze resolution - 209-210
Radio Marti - 140
Roll call votes - 2-H-145-H
Telephone rates - 547
Marlenee, Ron, R-Mont. (2)
Committees - 63-98, 101-105
Congressional voting studies - 3-C-42-C
Roll call votes - 2-H-145-H
Marriott, Dan, R-Utah (2)
Committees - 63-98, 101-105
Congressional voting studies - 3-C-42-C
Roll call votes - 2-H-145-H
Marsh v. Chambers - 12-A
Marshall, Thurgood
Abortions - 307
Legislative veto - 567
Supreme Court term, 1982-83 - 3-A-22-A
Marshall v. Lonberger - 7-A
Martin, David O'B., R-N.Y. (26)
Clean Air Act - 339
Committees - 63-98, 101-105
Congressional voting studies - 3-C-42-C
Roll call votes - 2-H-145-H
Martin, James G., R-N.C. (9)
Committees - 63-98, 101-105
Congressional voting studies - 3-C-42-C
Nuclear freeze resolution - 209
Roll call votes - 2-H-145-H
Martin, Lynn, R-Ill. (16)
Budget - 447
Committees - 63-98, 101-105
Congressional voting studies - 3-C-42-C
Roll call votes - 2-H-145-H

Martinez, Matthew G., D-Calif. (30)
  Committees - 63-96, 101-105
  Congressional voting studies - 3-C-42-C
  Roll call votes - 2-H-145-H
Martinez v. Bynum - 17-A
Maryland
  National trails - 346
  Abortion funding - 306
  Abortion laws - 308
  Abortion laws - 308
Mass transit. *(See also Urban Mass Transportation Administration.)*
  Appropriations - 448, 451, 453, 456, 457-462
Massachusetts
  Unemployment benefits - 275
  Abortion funding - 306
  Abortion laws - 308
Master list - 10-11
Maternal health programs. *See Child and maternal health programs.*
Mathematics education - 18, 396
Mathias, Charles McC. Jr., R-Md.
  Abscam investigation - 586
  Adelman nomination - 214
  Anti-crime proposal - 315, 316, 317
  Appropriations - 457, 489
  Arms control - 174
  Budget - 442
  Committees - 63-98, 101-105
  Congressional voting studies - 3-C-42-C
  Defense authorization - 188
  El Salvador aid - 169, 170
  Federal personnel rules - 603
  Foreign aid - 144, 523-524
  Franking privilege - 580
  International trade department proposal - 251
  National Security directive - 148
  Nuclear freeze resolution - 212
  Peacekeeping forces in Lebanon - 118, 123
  Record rentals - 313
  Roll call votes - 2-S-60-S
  Senate day-care facilities - 594
  Senate television broadcasting - 596
Matsui, Robert T., D-Calif. (3)
  Committees - 63-98, 101-105
  Congressional voting studies - 3-C-42-C
  Roll call votes - 2-H-145-H
Matsunaga, Spark M., D-Hawaii
  Committees - 44-62, 99-100
  Congressional voting studies - 3-C-42-C
  Natural gas pricing - 367
  Peace Academy proposal - 399
  Roll call votes - 2-S-60-S
Mattingly, Mack, R-Ga.
  Appropriations - 455, 467, 471, 491, 534
  Clinch River project - 365
  Coal leasing ban - 354
  Committees - 44-62, 99-100
  Congressional voting studies - 3-C-42-C
  Export controls - 255
  IMF funding - 244
  MX debate - 198
  Roll call votes - 2-S-60-S
  Senate day care facilities - 595
Mavroules, Nicholas, D-Mass. (6)
  Committees - 63-98, 101-105
  Congressional voting studies - 3-C-42-C
  Defense authorization - 180
  Roll call votes - 2-H-145-H
Mazzoli, Romano L., D-Ky. (3)
  Committees - 63-98, 101-105
  Congressional voting studies - 3-C-42-C
  Immigration reform bill - 285, 287, 288, 290
  Legal Services Corporation - 323
  Refugee resettlement programs - 304-305
  Roll call votes - 2-H-145-H
McCain, John, R-Ariz. (1)

  Committees - 63-98, 101-105
  Congressional voting studies - 3-C-42-C
  Roll call votes - 2-H-145-H
McCandless, Al, R-Calif. (37)
  Committees - 63-98, 101-105
  Congressional voting studies - 3-C-42-C
  Presidential support - 21-C
  Revenue sharing - 227-228
  Roll call votes - 2-H-145-H
McCloskey, Frank, D-Ind. (8)
  Committees - 63-98, 101-105
  Congressional voting studies - 3-C-42-C
  Defense authorization - 179
  Roll call votes - 2-H-145-H
McCloy-Zorin Agreement - 210
McClure, James A., R-Idaho
  Appropriations - 465, 466, 490, 538
  Clinch River breeder reactor - 365, 6-C
  Coal slurry pipelines - 551
  Committees - 44-62, 99-100
  Congressional voting studies - 3-C-42-C
  Energy preparedness - 371
  Immigration reform bill - 289
  MX debate - 198
  Natural gas pricing - 367-369
  Roll call votes - 2-S-60-S
  U.S.-Soviet relations - 150
  Water project - 355
  Watt resignation - 328
McCollum, Bill, R-Fla. (5)
  Bankruptcy laws - 320
  Committees - 63-98, 101-105
  Congressional voting studies - 3-C-42-C
  Equal Rights Amendment - 297
  Immigration reform bill - 288, 290
  Insanity defense - 315
  Refugee resettlement programs - 306
  Roll call votes - 2-H-145-H
McCurdy, Dave, D-Okla. (4)
  Appropriations - 469
  Committees - 63-98, 101-105
  Congressional voting studies - 3-C-42-C
  Roll call votes - 2-H-145-H
  Tax cap bill - 249
McDade, Joseph M., R-Pa. (10)
  Appropriations - 463, 465, 512
  Committees - 63-98, 101-105
  Congressional voting studies - 3-C-42-C
  Roll call votes - 2-H-145-H
McDonald, Larry P., D-Ga. (7)
  Committees - 63-98, 101-105
  Congressional voting studies - 3-C-42-C
  Death - 13, 136
  House rule changes - 596
  Most-favored-nation trade status - 265
  Party unity votes - 26-C
  Roll call votes - 2-H-145-H
  Window payments - 537
McDonnell Douglas Corp. - 493
McEwen, Bob, R-Ohio (6)
  Committees - 63-98, 101-105
  Congressional voting studies - 3-C-42-C
  Roll call votes - 2-H-145-H
McFarlane, Robert C. - 330
McGrath, Raymond J., R-N.Y.(5)
  Committees - 63-98, 101-105
  Congressional voting studies - 3-C-42-C
  Roll call votes - 2-H-145-H
McHugh, Matthew F., D-N.Y. (28)
  Appropriations - 480
  Committees - 63-98, 101-105
  Congressional voting studies - 3-C-42-C
  El Salvador aid - 157
  Foreign aid - 153
  Roll call votes - 2-H-145-H
McKernan, John R. Jr., R-Maine (1)
  Committees - 63-98, 101-105
  Congressional voting studies - 3-C-42-C
  Roll call votes - 2-H-145-H
McKinney, Stewart B., R-Conn. (4)
  Committees - 63-98, 101-105
  Congressional voting studies - 3-C-42-C

  Housing authorization - 282
  IMF funding - 244
  Roll call votes - 2-H-145-H
McNulty, James F. Jr., D-Ariz. (5)
  Committees - 63-98, 101-105
  Congressional voting studies - 3-C-42-C
  Roll call votes - 2-H-145-H
Measurement standards. *See Weights and measures.*
Media, communications. *See Communications and telecommunications.*
Medicaid, Medicare. *(See also Health Care Financing Administration.)*
  Abortion funding - 306, 507
  Appropriations - 506, 507
  Budget - 425, 433, 442
  Child health care plan - 419-420
  Handicapped infant care - 390
  Hospital Insurance Trust Fund - 219, 220
  Hospice payments - 398-399
  Hospital reimbursement - 219, 221
  Program revisions - 391-394
    Background - 392-393
    Congressional action - 393-394
    Provision - 391-392
  Refugee aid - 304-306
Medical care. *See Health.*
Medical research. *See Health; research and development.*
Meese, Edwin III
  Budget - 438
  Civil Rights Commission - 295
  Hunger in America - 416
  School prayer - 302
  Television syndication rights - 560
Melcher, John, D-Mont.
  Appropriations - 455, 462, 491
  Coal leasing ban - 354
  Committees - 44-62, 99-100
  Congressional voting studies - 3-C-42-C
  Defense authorization - 189
  IMF funding - 244
  Natural gas pricing - 367-368
  Roll call votes - 2-S-60-S
  Social Security rescue bill - 225
  Target price freeze - 384
Memphis Bank & Trust Co. v. Garner - 18-A
Mennonite Board of Missions v. Adams - 11-A
Mental health and illness. *(See also Alcoholism; Drug abuse.)*
  Appropriations - 449, 505
  Block grants - 506
  Insanity defense - 5-A, 19-E
  Insanity defense revision - 314, 315
  Veterans' counseling centers - 410-412
Mentally retarded persons. *See Handicapped persons.*
Merchant marine. *See Ships and shipping.*
Merit Systems Protection Board (MSPB)
  Appropriations - 510, 532 (chart)
  Nominations and confirmations - 30-A
Metcalf, Lee - 343
Methane gas. *See Natural gas.*
Metropolitan Edison Co. v. National Labor Relations Board (NLRB) - 15-A
Metropolitan Edison Co. v. People Against Nuclear Energy (PANE), United States Regulatory Commission (NRC) v. PANE - 16-A
Metzenbaum, Howard M., D-Ohio
  Aid to dislocated workers - 271
  Appropriations - 466, 491, 515, 539
  Bankruptcy laws - 321
  Budget - 439, 443
  Clark confirmation - 331
  Committees - 44-62, 99-100
  Congressional voting studies - 3-C-42-C
  Dam safety repairs - 349
  Defense authorization - 172, 187

  Energy preparedness - 371
  Legal Services Corporation - 324
  Maritime antitrust bill - 554-555
  Natural gas pricing - 368
  Roll call votes - 2-S-60-S
  Tobacco program - 378
  Watt resignation - 329
  Withholding tax revisions - 262-263
Mexico - 241
Meyer, Edward D. - 180
Mica, Daniel A., D-Fla. (14)
  Committees - 63-98, 101-105
  Congressional voting studies - 3-C-42-C
  El Salvador aid - 154, 163
  Nicaragua covert aid - 128, 129-130
  Roll call votes - 2-H-145-H
Michel, Robert H., R-Ill. (18)
  Appropriations - 539
  Budget - 437
  Censure proceedings - 580
  Civil Rights Commission - 295
  Clean Air Act - 340
  Committees - 63-98, 101-105
  Congressional voting studies - 3-C-42-C
  Dairy program - 377
  Equal Rights Amendment - 297
  Export controls - 256
  Grenada invasion - 135
  House rule changes - 597
  IMF funding - 248
  Nuclear freeze resolution - 207
  Roll call votes - 2-H-145-H
  Watt resignation - 329
Michigan
  Employment funds - 455
  Abortion funding - 306
Michigan v. Long - 6-A
Middle East. *(See also names of individual countries.)*
  Foreign aid - 144
  Foreign policy overview - 109-110
  Military construction funds - 470, 471
  Presidential messages (text) - 36-E-37-E
Middle-income housing assistance
  Appropriations - 496, 500
  Authorization - 278-279
  Mortgage revenue bonds - 276-277
  Mortgage subsidy bonds - 235
Midgetman missiles - 196, 199
Migrant farmworkers
  Health centers - 449 (chart), 457
  Immigration reform bill - 287-292
Mikulski, Barbara A., D-Md. (3)
  Abortion amendment - 310
  Committees - 63-98, 101-105
  Congressional voting studies - 3-C-42-C
  Roll call votes - 2-H-145-H
  Telephone rates - 547
Military affairs. *See Defense.*
Military aid. *See Foreign aid.*
Military construction - 469-472, 526
Military Appeals Court, U.S. *See Court of Military Appeals, U.S.*
Military Assistance Program (MAP)
  Appropriations - 524
  Authorizations - 141
  El Salvador - 154, 157, 162
  Foreign aid - 144
Military bases
  Civilian contractors - 189
  Military construction funds - 469-472
Military construction. *(See also Army Corps of Engineers.)*
  Appropriations - 469-472, 470 (chart)
  Authorization - 193-195
  Housing - 195
Military dependents
  Family housing
    FY 1983 appropriations - 454, 457
    Military construction funds - 195
  Schools - 189, 195
Military pay and benefits. *(See also Military retirement benefits.)*

Appropriations - 449
Authorization - 185-186, 192
Budget - 438
Military pensions. *See Military retirement benefits.*
Military personnel issues. *(See also Military health care; Military pay and benefits; Selective Service System; Veterans affairs.)*
Appropriations - 481
Authorization - 185-186
Justice code revisions - 311
Recruitment
Advertising - 481
GI bill proposals - 418
Student information - 189
Military procurement - 181-182, 193, 481, 490
Military retirement benefits *(See also Veterans affairs.)*
Appropriations - 481
Milk. *(See also School meal and milk programs.)*
Dairy assessment delay veto - 35-E-36-E
Dairy price supports - 375-380, 10-C
Dairy surplus - 13
Food assistance programs - 415, 516 (chart)
Miller, Clarence E., R-Ohio (10)
Appropriations - 534
Committees - 63-98, 101-105
Congressional voting studies - 3-C-42-C
Korean airline downing - 137
Roll call votes - 2-H-145-H
Miller, George, D-Calif. (7)
Child health care plan - 419
Committees - 63-98, 101-105
Congressional voting studies - 3-C-42-C
Deficit reduction proposals - 233
Immigration reform bill - 291
Roll call votes - 2-H-145-H
Miller, James C. III - 565
Mine Safety and Health Administration - 504, 506
Mineral leasing
Leasing ban - 350-354
Phosphate mining - 343
Wilderness areas - 328-329, 343, 344
Mineral Leasing Act of 1920 - 350
Minerals Management Service - 463
Mines and mining. *(See also Black lung benefits; Bureau of Mines.)*
Phosphate mining - 343
Research - 433
Safety - 504, 506
Mineta, Norman Y., D-Calif. (13)
Committees - 63-98, 101-105
Congressional voting studies - 3-C-42-C
Natural gas pricing - 367
Roll call votes - 2-H-145-H
Minish, Joseph G., D-N.J. (11)
Committees - 63-98, 101-105
Congressional voting studies - 3-C-42-C
Page sex charges - 583
Roll call votes - 2-H-145-H
Minneapolis Star & Tribune Co. v. Minnesota Commissioner of Revenue - 12-A
Minnesota
Abortion laws - 308
Draft registration requirement - 399
Education tax deductions - 395, 3-A, 4-A
Taxes - 5-A
Minority Business Development Agency - 472, 474
Minority business
Appropriations - 472, 474
Enterprise Zone program - 14-E-15-E
Minority assistance - 588
Minority groups. *See Aliens; Bilingual education; Blacks; Civil rights; Hispanics; Indians and Alaskan natives; Refugees; Women.*

Minuteman missiles - 198
Missile bases
Basing proposals - 195-205
Military construction - 193-195
Missiles. *(See also MX missile; Weapons.)*
Air-to-air - 482, 486
Anti-aircraft - 177, 178, 481
Anti-radar - 482, 486, 493
Antiballistic missile systems (ABM) - 176
Appropriations - 479-494, 488 (chart)
Arms control - 479, 484
Authorization - 175-193
Cruise missiles - 175, 183, 188, 192, 193, 195, 470, 471, 482, 486
Air-launched cruise (ALCM) - 175, 182
Ground-launched cruise (GLCM) - 175, 181, 183, 190-191, 195, 206-207, 470, 488 (chart)
Sea-launched cruise - 188
Dense pack - 199, 203
Deployment - 183, 195
HARM - 482, 486, 493
ICBMs - 182, 196, 200, 203, 489, 494, 7-C, 26-E-28-E
Key votes - 10-C
JTACMS - 177, 183, 191, 481, 487, 488
Midgetman - 196, 199
Minuteman - 198
MIRV - 196, 202-203
Pershing II - 175, 180, 181, 183, 191, 479, 486, 488 (chart), 510
Scowcroft Commission report - 195-197
Trident I - 175, 483, 488
Trident II - 175, 183, 190, 479, 486, 488, 494
Mississippi
Election results, 1983 - 4-B
Employment funds - 455
Highway construction bill - 536
National trails - 346
Water projects - 358
Missouri
Abortion laws - 307, 308
Harry S Truman historic site - 348
Wilderness areas - 343
Missouri. (ship) - 178, 185, 482
Missouri v. Hunter - 7-A
Mitchell, George J., D-Maine
Acid rain proposal - 341
Committees - 44-62, 99-100
Congressional voting studies - 3-C-42-C
Defense authorization - 189
EPA investigation - 335
NRC authorization - 371
Peacekeeping forces in Lebanon - 118
Roll call votes - 2-S-60-S
Mitchell, Parren J., D-Md. (7)
Committees - 63-98, 101-105
Congressional voting studies - 3-C-42-C
Federal contracts - 587
Martin Luther King holiday - 600
Roll call votes - 2-H-145-H
Moakley, Joe, D-Mass. (9)
Appropriations - 465
Committees - 63-98, 101-105
Congressional voting studies - 3-C-42-C
Defense authorization - 179
Roll call votes - 2-H-145-H
Mobilization planning. *See Emergency preparedness.*
Moffett, Toby - 583
Molinari, Guy V., R-N.Y. (14)
Committees - 63-98, 101-105
Congressional voting studies - 3-C-42-C
Roll call votes - 2-H-145-H
Mollohan, Alan B., D-W.Va. (1)
Committees - 63-98, 101-105
Congressional voting studies - 3-C-42-C
Roll call votes - 2-H-145-H
Mondale, Walter F. - 389
Monetary policy. *(See also Federal Reserve Board.)*

Budget - 446
Overview, 1983 - 217-218
Presidential messages - 7-E-12-E, 13-E-14-E
Volcker confirmation - 266-267
Money. *See Coins and currency.*
Money Lenders, The. (A. Sampson) - 242
Monsanto Co. v. Spray-Rite Service Corp. - 478
Montana
Abortion laws - 308
Coal and oil leasing - 328, 330, 353, 467
Coal leasing ban - 351
Wilderness areas - 328, 329, 342, 343
Montgomery, G. V. 'Sonny', D-Miss. (3)
Appropriations - 484
Committees - 63-98, 101-105
Congressional voting studies - 3-C-42-C
GI bill - 418
Peacekeeping forces in Lebanon - 115
Roll call votes - 2-H-145-H
Montreal Protocols - 300
Moody, Jim, D-Wis. (5)
Committees - 63-98, 101-105
Congressional voting studies - 3-C-42-C
IMF funding - 248
Roll call votes - 2-H-145-H
Moore, Henson, R-La. (6)
Committees - 63-98, 101-105
Congressional voting studies - 3-C-42-C
Deficit reduction proposals - 236
Roll call votes - 2-H-145-H
Moore, Powell A. - 117 (box)
Moorhead, Carlos J., R-Calif. (22)
Committees - 63-98, 101-105
Congressional voting studies - 3-C-42-C
Equal Rights Amendment - 296, 297
Handicapped education - 403
Immigration reform bill - 291
Legal Services Corporation - 322
Roll call votes - 2-H-145-H
Moral Majority - 301-302
Morocco
Foreign aid - 143, 144
Military construction funds - 194
Morris v. Slappy - 7-A
Morrison, Bruce A., D-Conn. (3)
Committees - 63-98, 101-105
Congressional voting studies - 3-C-42-C
Housing authorization - 283
Roll call votes - 2-H-145-H
Morrison, Sid, R-Wash. (4)
Committees - 63-98, 101-105
Congressional voting studies - 3-C-42-C
Immigration reform bill - 291
Roll call votes - 2-H-145-H
Morrison-Knudsen Construction Co. v. Director, Office of Workers' Compensation Programs, U.S. Department of Labor - 16-A
Morse, Bradford - 144
Mortgages and home loans. *(See also Farmers Home Administration; Federal Home Loan Bank Board; Federal Housing Administration; Government National Mortgage Association.)*
Appropriations - 457, 495-500, 511
Elderly housing projects - 495
Emergency Mortgage Aid - 8-C
FHA rates - 278
Legislative summary - 23
Mortgage assistance for unemployed - 267-268, 497
Mortgage revenue bonds - 276-277
Subsidy bonds - 235
Veteran assistance - 27, 495
Tax sales - 11-A
Moses H. Cone Memorial Hospital v. Mercury Construction Corp. - 19-A
Motor Carrier Act - 543
Motor Vehicle Manufacturers Association of the United States v. State Farm Mutual Automobile Insurance Co., Consumer Alert v. State Farm, Department of Transportation v. State Farm - 14-A

Motley, A. Tony - 25-A
Mountain States Legal Foundation - 328
Moynihan, Daniel Patrick, D-N.Y.
Appropriations - 455, 471, 508, 515
Budget - 439, 440
Committees - 44-62, 99-100
Congressional voting studies - 3-C-42-C
Dairy program - 377
Defense authorization - 186
EPA investigation - 335
Immigration reform bill - 290
Jordan military aid - 241
Korean airline downing - 137
Legislative veto - 572
Martin Luther King holiday - 601
Nicaragua covert aid - 124, 132
Revenue sharing - 229
Roll call votes - 2-S-60-S
Social Security rescue bill - 224
Mrazek, Robert J., D-N.Y. (3)
Committees - 63-98, 101-105
Congressional voting studies - 3-C-42-C
Roll call votes - 2-H-145-H
Mueller v. Allen - 395, 12-A
Mulberry, Richard - 351
Murkowski, Frank H., R-Alaska
Alaska sport hunting bill - 348
Committees - 44-62, 99-100
Congressional voting studies - 3-C-42-C
El Salvador aid - 161
Roll call votes - 2-S-60-S
Water projects - 355
Murphy, Austin J., D-Pa. (22)
Appropriations - 465
Coal slurry pipelines - 550
Committees - 63-98, 101-105
Congressional voting studies - 3-C-42-C
Korean airline downing - 137
Jobs bill, phase II program - 269
Roll call votes - 2-H-145-H
Murphy, John M. - 585
Murtha, John P., D-Pa. (12)
Abscam conviction - 585
Committees - 63-98, 101-105
Congressional voting studies - 3-C-42-C
Roll call votes - 2-H-145-H
MX missile
Appropriations - 204-205, 479-494, 488 (chart), 502, 503
Authorization - 175-176, 180-181, 186, 193, 201
Budget - 432
Basing
"Dense pack" - 176, 193, 195, 199, 203
Resolution terms - 195, 197, 198
Congressional overview, 1983 - 173-174
Deployment - 175
Key votes - 7-C, 9-C-10-C
Legislative summary - 16
Military construction funds - 193, 469-472
Nuclear freeze resolution - 7-C
President's Commission report - 26-E-28-E
Scowcroft Commission - 195-197
Myers, Michael 'Ozzie'
Abscam convictions - 585
Censure - 582
Myers, John T., R-Ind. (7)
Appropriations - 502
Committees - 63-98, 101-105
Congressional voting studies - 3-C-42-C
Roll call votes - 2-H-145-H

N

Nantahala National Forest - 346
Narcotics. *See Drug abuse.*

Natcher, William H., D-Ky. (2)
  Committees - 63-98, 101-105
  Congressional voting studies - 3-C-42-C
  Roll call votes - 2-H-145-H
Nation At Risk - 389
National Academy of Sciences (NAS)
  Acid rain report - 341
  Wild horses and burros study - 347
National Acid Precipitation Task Force
  - 341
National Aeronautics and Space Administration (NASA)
  Appropriations - 496-497, 499
  Authorization - 477, 589
  Construction funds - 536
  Weather satellites - 588-589
National Airport - 458, 461-462
National Archives - 595
National Association of Counties - 416
National Association of Greeting Card Publishers v. U.S. Postal Service, United Parcel Service of America v. U.S. Postal Service - 20-A
National Audubon Society - 329, 347
National Bureau of Standards
  Appropriation - 473 (chart)
  Authorization - 587
  Earthquake reduction - 591
National Cancer Institute - 409-410, 504
National Conference of Catholic Bishops - 308
National Commission on Excellence in Education - 18, 389, 400
National Commission on Libraries and Information Science - 505
National Commission on Social Security Reform - 219-226, 425, 7-C
National Consumer Telephone Resource Center - 546
National Council of Churches - 168
National Council of Senior Citizens - 222
National Credit Union Administration (NCUA) - 499
National debt. *See Budget, U.S.*
National defense. *See National security.*
National Education Association (NEA) - 389
National emergencies, preparedness. *See Emergency preparedness.*
National Endowment for Democracy - 148-149 (box)
National Endowment for the Arts - 463 (chart), 465, 466
National Endowment for the Humanities - 463 (chart), 465, 466
National Farmers Organization - 382
National Federation of Business and Professional Women's Clubs Inc. - 299
National Federation of Independent Business - 222
National forests
  Appropriations - 456
  Oil and gas leasing ban - 464
  RARE II wilderness bills - 342-344
  Timber sales - 466
National Governors' Association - 416
National Guard. *(See also Reserves, military.)*
  Air National Guard - 183, 189
  Appropriations - 479-494
  Authorization - 183, 189
  Educational benefits - 418-419
  Military construction funds - 193-195
National Health Service Corps - 506
National Heart, Lung and Blood Institute - 409-410, 504
National Highway Traffic Safety Administration (NHTSA)
  Appropriations - 458, 459 (chart), 460
  Nominations and confirmations - 28-A
National Historical Publications and Records Commission - 595

National Industrial Development Bank - 437, 444
National Institute of Allergy and Infectious Disease - 504
National Institute of Arthritis and Musculoskeletal Disease - 409, 504
National Institute on Alcohol Abuse and Alcoholism - 505
National Institute on Drug Abuse - 505
National Institutes of Health (NIH)
  Appropriations - 504-505
  Authorization proposals - 409-410
  Emergency fund - 417
National Institute on Occupational Safety and Health (NIOSH)- 409
National Labor Relations Board (NLRB) - 505
National Labor Relations Board v. Transportation Management Corp. - 15-A
National Library of Medicine - 504
National Mediation Board
  Appropriations - 505
  Nominations and confirmations - 30-A
National Milk Producers Federation - 376
National monuments. *See National parks and monuments.*
National Oceanic and Atmospheric Administration (NOAA)
  Appropriations
    FY 1983 supplemental - 510
    FY 1984 - 473 (chart), 474
  Authorization - 589
  Weather satellites - 589
National Organization for Women (NOW)
  Equal Rights Amendment - 297
  Women's equity issues - 299
National Park Service
  Appropriations
    FY 1983 supplemental - 448 (chart), 452, 453, 456
    FY 1984 - 463 (chart), 464, 466
National Parks and Conservation Association - 347
National parks and monuments. *(See also National forests.)*
  Alaska conservation act - 347
  Miscellaneous parks bill - 348-349
  Park protection bill - 348
National Public Radio - 558
National Railroad Passenger Corporation. *See Amtrak.*
National Research Council - 341
National Rifle Association - 347
NSC. *See National Security Council (NSC).*
National Science Board - 389
National Science Foundation (NSF)
  Appropriations - 496, 497, 499-500
  Authorization - 604
  Budget - 434
  Earthquake reduction - 591
  Educational summit proposal - 400
  Nominations and confirmations - 30-A
  Science education - 390
National sea grant program. *See Sea grant program.*
National security. *See Defense.*
National Security Council (NSC)
  Appropriations - 532 (chart)
  History - 330
  Joint Chiefs of Staff reorganization - 215
  Korean airline downing - 136
National Taxpayers Union - 222, 364
National Telecommunications and Information Administration - 473
National Trails System - 346
National Transportation Safety Board
  Appropriations - 458, 459 (chart), 461
  Authorization - 558

National Treasury Employees Union - 602
National Weather Service - 589
National wilderness preserves. *See Wilderness preservation areas.*
National Wildlife Federation - 329, 347, 353
National wildlife refuges. *See Wildlife and wildlife refuges.*
NATO. *See North Atlantic Treaty Organization.*
Natural disasters. *See Disaster relief; Emergency preparedness.*
Natural gas
  Leasing
    Administration policies - 327-332
    Leasing ban - 328-329, 344, 462-469
  Pricing
    Background - 366-367
    Congressional proposals - 367-369
    Controls - 369-370
  Soviet pipeline - 254, 255
Natural Gas Policy Act of 1978 - 325, 366, 369, 567
Natural resources. *See Environment.*
Natural resources conservation. *See Conservation.*
Naval Reserve
  Appropriations - 479-494
  Authorization - 186, 193-195
Naval ships. *(See also Submarines.)*
  Aegis anti-aircraft cruisers - 185, 192, 487, 491, 493
  Aircraft carriers - 178, 482
  Appropriations - 479-494
  Authorization - 178, 183, 184-185, 192
  Battleships - 183, 185, 192, 482
Navy. *(See also Naval ships.)*
  Appropriations - 479-494
  Authorization - 177, 178, 183, 186, 192
  Military construction funds - 469-472
Neal, Stephen L., D-N.C. (5)
  Committees - 63-98, 101-105
  Congressional voting studies - 3-C-42-C
  IMF funding - 244-246
  Roll call votes - 2-H-145-H
Near East. *See Middle East.*
Neas, Ralph G. - 294, 299
Nebraska
  Abortion laws - 308
  Power construction project - 510
  Prayer in state legislature - 4-A
Neighborhood development. *See Community development.*
Neighborhood Investment Corporation
  Appropriations - 496, 499
  Authorization - 278
Nelson, Bill, D-Fla. (11)
  Committees - 63-98, 101-105
  Congressional voting studies - 3-C-42-C
  Roll call votes - 2-H-145-H
Nelson, Gaylord - 329, 347
Nerve gas. *See Chemical and biological weapons.*
Netherlands - 195
Nevada
  Coal slurry pipelines - 550
  Employment funds - 455
Nevada v. United States, Truckee-Carson Irrigation District v. United States, Pyramid Lake Paiute Tribe of Indians v. Truckee-Carson Irrigation District - 17-A
New Deal - 4-A
New Hampshire - 343
New Jersey
  Medical plan - 393
  Redistricting - 4-A, 5-A, 5-B (box)
  Abortion funding - 306
New Jersey (ship) - 482

New Mexico
  Employment funds - 455
  Nuclear waste burial facility - 537
  Water projects - 358, 520-521
New Mexico v. Mescalero Apache Tribe - 17-A
New York.
  Election results, 1983 - 6-B
  Abortion funding - 306
Newport News Shipbuilding & Dry Dock Co. v. Equal Employment Opportunity Commission - 10-A
News media. *See Broadcasting; Freedom of the press; Print media and publishing.*
Nicaragua
  Congressional Democrats' policy - 31-E-32-E
  El Salvador aid - 157, 160
  Foreign aid
    Appropriations - 480, 491, 8-C
  Foreign policy overview - 111
  Human rights - 128
  Military aid
    Background - 124-126
    Congressional action - 126-132
    Provisions - 124
  Presidential message (text) - 28-E-31-E
Nicaraguan Democratic Force - 128
Nichols, Bill, D-Ala. (3)
  Appropriations - 485
  Committees - 63-98, 101-105
  Congressional voting studies - 3-C-42-C
  Defense authorization - 182
  Roll call votes - 2-H-145-H
Nickles, Don, R-Okla.
  Appropriations - 468
  Committees - 44-62, 99-100
  Congressional voting studies - 3-C-42-C
  Natural gas pricing - 368
  Roll call votes - 2-S-60-S
  Senate honoraria - 577
  Social Security rescue bill - 225
Nicolet National Forest - 344
Nielson, Howard C., R-Utah (3)
  Committees - 63-98, 101-105
  Congressional voting studies - 3-C-42-C
  Roll call votes - 2-H-145-H
NIOSH. *See National Institute of Occupational Safety and Health.*
Nixon, Richard
  Budget contol proposal - 238
  Clinch River project - 362
  Judicial appointments - 303
  Legislative veto - 566, 569
  Presidential support (box) - 19-C
  Revenue sharing - 226
  "Saturday night massacre" - 334
  Staff funding - 534
  U.S.-Vatican ties - 169
NOAA. *See National Oceanic and Atmospheric Administration.*
Nominations and confirmations
  Ambassadors - 27-A-28-A
  Cabinet - 25-A-27-A
  Independent agencies - 28-A-30-A
  Judiciary - 30-A-31-A
  Legal Services Corporation - 322, 324
  Major confirmations, 1983 - 23-A-31-A
  Regulatory agencies - 24-A
North Africa. *See Middle East.*
North Atlantic Treaty Organization (NATO)
  Appropriations - 469-472
  Authorization - 193-195
  Arms control - 206, 21-E
  Greece's commitment - 142
  Military construction funds - 193-195, 469-472
  Missile deployment - 175, 484
  Nuclear weapon deployment - 206
  Turkey's commitment - 142
North Carolina
  Abortion funding - 306

National trails - 346
Tax leasing plan - 603-604
Unemployment benefits - 275
Wilderness areas - 343
North Dakota
Abortion laws - 308
Coal leasing - 329, 467
Coal leasing ban - 353
FmHA loans - 385
Garrison Diversion project - 356-357, 500, 502, 503
Wilderness leasing - 329, 467
North Dakota v. United States - 17-A
North Yemen - 144
Norway - 472
NOW. *See National Organization for Women (NOW).*
Nowak, Henry J., D-N.Y. (33)
Committees - 63-98, 101-105
Congressional voting studies - 3-C-42-C
Equal Rights Amendment - 297
Roll call votes - 2-H-145-H
NRC. *See Nuclear Regulatory Commission.*
Nuclear energy. *(See also Breeder reactors; Nuclear non-proliferation; Nuclear power plants; Nuclear waste and spent fuel management; Uranium.)*
Appropriations - 501
Breeder technology - 362
Budget - 433
Export controls - 256
Fission energy research - 362
Key votes - 6-C
Nuclear non-proliferation
Arms control - 202
Freeze resolution
House action - 205-212
Key votes - 6-C, 8-C
Legislative summary - 16
Senate action - 212
Text - 210-211
Intermediate-range Nuclear Forces (INF) Talks - 479
Nuclear deterrence debate (box) - 202-203
Overview, 1983 - 173-174
Strategic Arms Limitation Treaty II (SALT II) - 490
Strategic Arms Reductions Talks (START)
ICMB ceiling - 174
Presidential messages (text) - 27-E-28-E, 33-E-34-E
Revised proposals - 200-201
Scowcroft Commission - 197
Technology transfers - 150, 152
Nuclear power plants
Clinch River project - 362-365
Construction - 3-A, 4-A
Licensing - 19, 370, 4-A
Supreme Court decision - 3-A, 4-A
Nuclear Regulatory Commission
Appropriations - 500-503
Authorization - 370-371
Licensing - 19, 370, 4-A
Nominations and confirmations - 24-A, 30-A
Nuclear safety. *See Nuclear power plants; Nuclear waste and spent fuel management.*
Nuclear waste and spent fuel management
Appropriations - 501, 537
Disposal facilities - 537
Ocean dumping - 360
Nuclear Waste Disposal Fund - 501
Nuclear weapons (general). *(See also Nuclear non-proliferation; Weapons.)*
Appropriations - 479-494
Authorization - 175-193
Budget - 432
Deployment - 195, 207, 484

Freeze resolution - 205-213
Nuclear deterrence debate (box) - 202-203
Nunn, Sam, D-Ga.
Committees - 44-62, 99-100
Congressional voting studies - 3-C-42-C
Defense authorization - 182, 187, 188, 191
Legislative veto - 571
Martin Luther King holiday - 602
MX debate - 197-198, 203-204
Nuclear freeze resolution - 212
Peacekeeping forces in Lebanon - 120
Presidential support - 21-C
Roll call votes - 2-S-60-S
Nurses and nursing - 409
Nutrition. *See Food and nutrition.*

O

Oakar, Mary Rose, D-Ohio (20)
Committees - 63-98, 101-105
Congressional voting studies - 3-C-42-C
Equal Rights Amendment - 297
Federal employee social security coverage - 574
Franking privilege - 579
IMF Funding - 244
Korean airline downing - 137
Peacekeeping forces in Lebanon - 120
Roll call votes - 2-H-145-H
Oberdorfer, Louis F. - 467
Oberstar, James L., D-Minn. (8)
Caribbean trade plan - 253
Committees - 63-98, 101-105
Congressional voting studies - 3-C-42-C
Natural gas pricing - 367
Public works jobs plan - 270
Roll call votes - 2-H-145-H
Obey, David R., D-Wis. (7)
Appropriations - 452, 480, 529, 536
Committees - 63-98, 101-105
Congressional voting studies - 3-C-42-C
Peacekeeping forces in Lebanon - 118-119
Pershing II deployment - 207
Roll call votes - 2-H-145-H
O'Brien, George M., R-Ill. (4)
Committees - 63-98, 101-105
Congressional voting studies - 3-C-42-C
MX debate - 199
Roll call votes - 2-H-145-H
Obscenity and pornography - 318
Occupational safety and health
Appropriations - 504-506
Black lung compensation - 505, 506, 510, 511, 513
Budget - 431
Mine safety - 50C
Occupational Safety and Health Administration (OSHA) - 504
Occupational Safety and Health Review Commission - 505
Oceans. *(See also Coastal zones; Fish and fishing; Harbors and ports; Maritime treaties and agreements; Outer continental shelf; Ships and shipping; Water pollution.)*
Ocean dumping - 360
Offshore drilling - 466-469
O'Connor, Sandra Day
Abortions - 307
Appointment - 302
Legislative veto - 567
Supreme Court term, 1982-83 - 3-A-22-A
Office of Consumer Affairs - 496, 499
Office of Federal Procurement Policy
Appropriations - 490, 532 (chart)
Authorization - 589
Legislative summary - 22

Office of International Cooperation and Development - 517
Office of Justice Assistance, Research and Statistics - 473
Office of Management and Budget (OMB)
Appropriations - 532
Budget - 435
Dairy program - 378
Federal program catalog - 591
Procurement authority - 589
Office of Personnel Management (OPM)
Appropriations - 510, 512, 513, 532 (chart)
Ethics office - 584
Pay-raise regulations - 512, 513, 531, 535
Personnel rules - 602-603
Office of Refugee Resettlement - 304
Office of Science and Technology Policy - 496, 499, 510
Office of Special Trade Representative. *See Office of the U.S. Trade Representative.*
Office of Surface Mining Reclamation and Enforcement - 466
Office of Technology Assessment (OTA) - 540
Office of the U.S. Trade Representative
Appropriations
FY 1983 supplemental - 509
FY 1984 - 473, 477 (charts)
International trade department proposal - 250
Nominations and confirmations - 25-A
Offshore drilling bans - 462-469
Ohio
Abortion ruling - 306
Election laws - 5-A
Employment funds - 455
Park funds - 349
Sulphuric emissions - 341
Water projects - 358
Oil imports
Energy preparedness bill - 371
Oil glut - 326
Oil industry. *(See also Windfall profits tax.)*
Antitrust exemption - 371
Energy preparedness bill - 371
Export controls - 254
Leasing bans - 328, 344, 462-469
Natural gas pricing
Background - 366-367
Congressional proposals - 367-369
Controls - 369-370
Offshore drilling - 466-469
Oil and gas leases - 328, 344, 462-469
Oil glut - 326
Oil reserves
Clark confirmation - 329-330
Emergency preparedness legislation - 371
Strategic petroleum reserve - 372, 462, 463, 466-469, 515
Oklahoma - 469
Old Age and Survivors program. *See Social security programs.*
Older Americans. *See Aged persons.*
Olim v. Wakinekona - 11-A
Olin, James R., D-Va. (6)
Committees - 63-98, 101-105
Congressional voting studies - 3-C-42-C
Roll call votes - 2-H-145-H
Oliver v. United States - 289
Oman - 470
Omnibus Judgeship Act - 303
O'Neill, Thomas P. Jr., D-Mass. (8)
Appropriations - 465, 527, 529
Budget - 437
Censure proceedings - 580

Committees - 63-98, 101-105
Congressional Budget Office - 443
Congressional voting studies - 3-C-42-C
Debt limit increase - 239
Deficit reduction proposals - 231, 236
El Salvador certification - 156
Equal Rights Amendment - 296-298, 11-C
Grenada invasion - 112, 135
Immigration reform bill - 285, 287, 292
Lebanon resolution - 113, 3-C, 5-C
Martin Luther King holiday - 601
MX debate - 201
Nicaragua covert aid - 129, 131
Nuclear freeze resolution - 207
Page sex charges - 583
Peacekeeping forces in Lebanon - 115, 117-119, 121, 9-C
Politics - 12, 13
Roll call votes - 2-H-145-H
Social Security rescue bill - 221, 223
Tax cap bill - 249
Withholding tax revisions- 261, 263
Oregon
Abortion funding - 306
Employment funds - 455
Lands bill veto - 38-E
Public lands transfer - 344-345
Wilderness areas - 343
Oregon v. Bradshaw - 7-A
Organization of American States (OAS) - 124, 130, 159, 163, 169
Organization for Economic Cooperation and Development - 555
Organization of Eastern Caribbean States (OECS) - 135
Organized labor. *See Labor, labor unions.*
Oritz, Solomon P., D-Texas (27)
Committees - 63-98, 101-105
Congressional voting studies - 3-C-42-C
Roll call votes - 2-H-145-H
Orphan Drug Act - 455
Osceola National Forest - 343
OSHA. *See Occupational Safety and Health Administration.*
Ottinger, Richard L., D-N.Y. (20)
Auto domestic content bill - 258-259
Committees - 63-98, 101-105
Clinch River project - 365
Congressional voting studies - 3-C-42-C
Electric utility charges - 372
NRC authorization - 370
Roll call votes - 2-H-145-H
Overseas Private Investment Corporation - 522 (chart)
Owens, Major R., D-N.Y. (12)
Committees - 63-98, 101-105
Congressional voting studies - 3-C-42-C
Roll call votes - 2-H-145-H
Oxley, Mike, R-Ohio (4)
Committee assignments - 63-98, 101-105
Congressional voting studies - 3-C-42-C
Public broadcasting authorization - 558
Roll call votes - 2-H-145-H

P

Pacific Gas & Electric Co. v. State Energy Resources Conservation and Development Commission - 16-A
Pacific Legal Foundation v. Watt - 353
Packard, Ron, R-Calif. (43)
Committees - 63-98, 101-105
Congressional voting studies - 3-C-42-C
Roll call votes - 2-H-145-H
Packwood, Bob, R-Ore.
Abortion amendment - 309, 310
Appropriations - 530, 536, 538
Cable television deregulation - 553

Clark confirmation - 331
Committees - 44-62, 99-100
Congressional voting studies - 3-C-42-C
Defense authorization - 186
Heckler nomination - 23-A
Roll call votes - 2-S-60-S
Sex-based insurance plans - 558
Telephone rates - 545
Trucking deregulation proposals - 543, 560
Page system -15, 580-583
Pakistan
Foreign aid - 143, 144, 513, 514 (box)
Military aid - 144
Narcotics control - 151
Palestine Liberation Organization (PLO)
Jordan - 135
Lebanese evacuation - 119
United Nations funding - 150
Pallas Shipping Agency Ltd. v. Duris - 16-A
Panama - 144, 157
Panama Canal Commission - 459, 510
Panetta, Leon E., D-Calif. (16)
Appropriations - 535
Budget - 447
Committees - 63-98, 101-105
Congressional voting studies - 3-C-42-C
Deficit reduction proposals - 233
Food assistance programs - 412
Immigration reform bill - 291
Roll call votes - 2-H-145-H
Target price freeze - 383-384
Paperwork Reduction Act - 591
Paraguay - 143
Paralyzed Veterans of America - 599
Parents and children. See *Family and marital issues.*
Parker, Barrington D. - 602
Parks and recreation areas. (See also *Public lands; Sports and recreation.*)
Appropriations - 448, 451, 453, 456, 463
Budget - 430
Land acquisition - 463
National parks and monuments - 348-349
Parochial schools. See *Private and parochial schools.*
Parole - 314
Parole Commission, U.S. - 473 (chart)
Parris, Stan, R-Va. (8)
Committees - 63-98, 101-105
Congressional voting studies - 3-C-42-C
Defense authorization - 181
Roll call votes - 2-H-145-H
Parties, political. See *Political parties.*
Pashayan, Charles Jr., R-Calif. (17)
Committees - 63-98, 101-105
Congressional voting studies - 3-C-42-C
Legislative veto - 571
Roll call votes - 2-H-145-H
Patent and Trademark Administration - 473 (chart)
Patents and trademarks. (See also *Copyrights*)
Protection of U.S. rights - 260
Supreme Court decision - 14-A
Patients' rights - 390
Patman, Bill, D-Texas (14)
Committees - 63-98, 101-105
Congressional voting studies - 3-C-42-C
Roll call votes - 2-H-145-H
Patterson, Jerry M., D-Calif. (38)
Committees - 63-98, 101-105
Congressional voting studies - 3-C-42-C
IMF funding - 247-248
Roll call votes - 2-H-145-H
Paul, Ron, R-Texas (22)
Committees - 63-98, 101-105
Congressional voting studies - 3-C-42-C
IMF funding - 244-245

Roll call votes - 2-H-145-H
Pay. See *Wages and salaries.*
Payment-in-kind (PIK) program
Appropriations - 509, 510, 517, 519
Background - 373-374, 380-381
Budget - 433
Cotton program (box) - 382
Farm recession relief - 385-386
Overview, 1983 - 373-374
Provisions - 381
Tax changes - 13, 380-383
Peace Corps
Appropriations - 522 (chart)
Authorization - 145
Peach, J. Dexter - 351
Pearson, James B.
Budget control proposal - 238
Senate rule changes - 598
Senate television broadcasting - 596
Pease, Don J., D-Ohio (13)
Auto domestic content bill - 259
Committees - 63-98, 101-105
Roll call votes - 2-H-145-H
Trade adjustment assistance - 252
Pell, Claiborne, D-R.I.
Committees - 44-62, 99-100
Congressional voting studies - 3-C-42-C
El Salvador aid - 155
Lebanon foreign aid - 117 (box)
Nuclear freeze resolution - 212
Peacekeeping forces in Lebanon - 118
Roll call votes - 2-S-60-S
Pell grants
Budget - 434, 507
Eligibility rules - 400-401
Pemigewasset Wilderness Area - 343
Pendleton, Clarence M. Jr. - 293
Penner, Rudolph G. - 443
Pennsylvania
Abortion laws - 306, 308
Employment funds - 455
Pennsylvania Avenue Development Commission - 349
Penny, Timothy J., D-Minn. (1)
Committees - 63-98, 101-105
Congressional voting studies - 3-C-42-C
Roll call votes - 2-H-145-H
Pensions. See *Retirement and pensions.*
Pentagon. See *Defense Department (DOD).*
People's Republic of China
Foreign aid - 145
Trade status - 264-265
U.S. exports - 255, 257
Pepper, Claude, D-Fla. (18)
Committees - 63-98, 101-105
Congressional voting studies - 3-C-42-C
Deficit reduction proposals - 236
Roll call votes - 2-H-145-H
Social Security rescue bill - 221-223
Percy, Charles H., R-Ill.
Adelman nomination - 213
Appropriations - 521
Committees - 44-62, 99-100
Congressional voting studies - 3-C-42-C
El Salvador aid - 156, 159, 161
Foreign aid authorization - 149-150, 521
Foreign policy role - 112, 142 (box)
Immigration reform bill - 292
International trade department proposal - 251
Korean airline downing - 137
MX debate - 197, 203-204
Nuclear freeze resolution - 212-213
Peacekeeping forces in Lebanon - 114, 118, 122
Roll call votes - 2-S-60-S
U.S. technology transfer - 150
Perkins, Carl D., D-Ky. (7)
Child nutrition programs - 417
Committees - 63-98, 101-105
Congressional voting studies - 3-C-42-C

Defense production - 266
Handicapped education - 403
Math-science education proposals - 396
Roll call votes - 2-H-145-H
Perle, Richard N. - 207
Perry, Robert M. - 333
Perry Education Association v. Perry Local Educators' Association - 12-A
Pershing II missiles
Appropriations - 479, 486, 510
Authorization - 175, 180, 181, 183, 191
Persian Gulf. See *Middle East.*
Personal rights. See *Civil rights.*
Peru - 144
Pesticides, pest control
Legislative summary - 14
Regulation program - 386
Peterson, R. Max - 343
Petri, Thomas E., R-Wis. (6)
Committees - 63-98, 101-105
Congressional voting studies - 3-C-42-C
Roll call votes - 2-H-145-H
Petroleum industry. See *Oil industry.*
Petroleum reserves. See *Oil reserves.*
Pharmaceutical industry. See *Drug industry.*
Philippines •
Foreign aid - 514 (box)
Military bases - 193
Philko Aviation Inc. v. Shacket - 17-A
Phosphate mining - 343
PHS. See *Public Health Service.*
Physicians
Federal contracts - 574
Medicare proposals - 394
Regulation - 473, 561
Pickett v. Brown - 11-A
Pickle, J.J., D-Texas (10)
Committees - 63-98, 101-105
Congressional voting studies - 3-C-42-C
Deficit reduction proposals - 234
Export controls - 256-257
Railroad retirement bill - 272
Roll call votes - 2-H-145-H
Social Security rescue bill - 222-223
Pierce, Lawrence W. - 302
PIK. See *Payment-in-kind (PIK) program.*
Pillsbury Co. v. Conboy - 7-A
Pipelines
Coal slurry pipelines - 544, 549-551, 9-C
Natural gas pricing - 366-370
Soviet gas and oil pipeline - 254, 255
Planned Parenthood Association of Kansas City, Mo. v. Ashcroft, Ashcroft v. Planned Parenthood Association of Kansas City, Mo. - 307, 10-A
Poisons. See *Hazardous substances.*
Poland
IMF funding - 243
U.S.-Soviet grain embargo (box) - 387
Police and law enforcement officers. See *Federal Bureau of Investigation; Searches and seizures; Secret Service.*
Political parties. See *Democratic Party; Republican Party.*
Politics and elections. See *Elections and politics.*
Pollution. (See also *Air pollution; Environmental health; Environmental Protection Agency; Hazardous substances; Waste disposal and treatment; Water pollution.*)
Acid rain - 151, 340-341
Budget - 430
Clean Air Act proposals - 339-340
POMCUS sites - 510
Poor, assistance to. See *Welfare and social services.*
Population. See *Birth control; Census, U.S.*
Pornography. See *Obscenity.*

Porter, John Edward, R-Ill. (10)
Appropriations - 480, 491
Committees - 63-98, 101-105
Congressional voting studies - 3-C-42-C
MX debate - 199, 200
Roll call votes - 2-H-145-H
rts. See *Harbors and ports.*
rtugal - 144
Post Office. See *Postal Service, U.S.*
Postal service
Appropriations - 529, 531-536, 532 (chart)
Budget - 540, 541
Franking privileges, congressional - 540, 541, 578-580
Mail fraud - 22
Subsidies - 534
Postal Service, U.S. - 529, 531-536, 532 (chart)
Postal Service Board of Governors, U.S. v. Aikens. - 9-A
Postsecondary education. (See also *Education Department; Student aid; Vocational education.*)
Appropriations - 505, 507
Budget - 431, 434
College housing programs - 496
Endowment aid - 397-398
Indian colleges - 395-396
Math-science education proposals - 396
Poverty assistance. See *Welfare and social services.*
Powell, Lewis F. Jr.
Abortion - 307
Legislative veto - 567, 570
Redistricting - 5-B
Supreme Court background - 3-A-5-A
Supreme Court term, 1982-83 - 3-A-22-A
Prescription drug industry. See *Drug industry.*
Presidency. See *Executive branch.*
President, U.S. See *Reagan, President Ronald; Executive branch.*
Presidential Dry River Wilderness - 343
Presidential messages (texts)
Arms control - 21-E, 22-E-26-E, 32-E-33-E
Budget messages - 7-E-12-E
Central America - 28-E-31-E
Civil Rights Commission - 38-E-39-E
Crime control - 19-E
Dairy assessment delay veto - 35-E-36-E
Desegregation funds veto - 35-E
Economic report - 12-E-14-E
Education legislation proposal - 20-E-21-E
Enterprise zones - 14-E-15-E
EPA Document Agreement - 16-E
Farm announcements veto - 34-E-35-E
Lebanon Resolution - 36-E-37-E
MX Commission - 26-E-28-E
Nuclear arms talks - 33-E-34-E
Oregon lands bill veto - 38-E
State of the Union - 3-E-7-E
Structural unemployment - 16-E-19-E
Tax leasing plan veto - 34-E
President's Council on Environmental Quality. See *Council on Environmental Quality.*
President's Council on Integrity and Efficiency - 11-E
Press freedom. See *Freedom of the press.*
Presser, Jackie - 271
Pressler, Larry, R-S.D.
Adelman nomination - 214
Appropriations - 477, 489
Clinch River project - 365
Committees - 44-62, 99-100
Defense authorization - 188
Foreign aid authorization - 141, 144
Franking privilege - 580

Roll call votes - 2-S-60-S
Trade reciprocity bill - 260
Water projects - 355
Weather satellites - 589
Preventive medicine
Child health care plan - 419-420
Disease control - 505, 506
Research - 409
Pribilof Islands - 345
Price-fixing. *See Antitrust and competition.*
Price, Melvin, D-Ill. (21)
Appropriations - 485
Committees - 63-98, 101-105
Congressional voting studies - 3-C-42-C
Defense authorization - 180, 181
MX debate - 202
Roll call votes - 2-H-145-H
Price supports, agricultural. *See Agricultural price supports.*
Print media and publishing. *(See also Government Printing Office.)*
Federal program catalog - 591
Freedom of the press - 5-A, 12-A
Historical publications - 595
Pre-publication review - 148, 152
Prisons and prisoners. *(See also Capital punishment; Parole.)*
District of Columbia overcrowding - 495
Drug treatment program - 314
Federal Prison System
FY 1983 supplemental - 449, 453, 510
FY 1984 appropriations - 473 (chart)
Supreme Court decisions - 11-A
Pritchard, Joel, R-Wash. (1)
Committees - 63-98, 101-105
Congressional voting studies - 3-C-42-C
MX debate - 199
Roll call votes - 2-H-145-H
Privacy protection. *See Freedom of information; Searches and seizures.)*
Private and parochial schools
Tax-exempt status - 3-A, 10-A
Tuition tax credits - 3-A, 4-A
Project Democracy - 148 (box)
Proxmire, William, D-Wis.
Appropriations - 466
Committees - 44-62, 99-100
Congressional voting studies - 3-C-42-C
Garrison Diversion project - 356
MX debate - 198
Project Democracy - 149
Roll call votes - 2-S-60-S
Pryor, David, D-Ark.
Appropriations - 489
Committees - 44-62, 99-100
Congressional voting studies - 3-C-42-C
Defense authorization - 186, 188, 190
Roll call votes - 2-S-60-S
Withholding tax revisions - 264
Psychological counseling. *See Mental health and illness.*
Public assistance. *See Welfare and social services.*
Public broadcasting - 558
Public debt. *See Budget, U.S.*
Public financing of elections. *See Campaign financing.*
Public health. *See Health.*
Public hospitals - 449 (chart)
Public housing and housing assistance. *(See also Middle-income housing assistance.)*
Appropriations
FY 1983 supplemental - 448 (chart), 511
FY 1984 - 495-500
Authorization - 277-283, 536, 537
Elderly and handicapped - 495, 496
Indian housing programs - 495
Public lands. *(See also Bureau of Land Management; Indian lands; National forests; Parks and recreation areas; Wilderness areas; Wildlife and wildlife refuges.)*

Coal leasing ban - 350-354
Conservation programs - 230
Federal seedling donations - 388
Lease sales - 350-351
Military and federal use - 345-346
Oil and gas leases - 328, 344, 462-469, 515
Oregon lands transfer - 344-345
Wetlands bill - 349
Wild horses and burros management - 346-347
Wilderness protection - 341
Public laws
List - 3-F-10-F
Totals (box) - 4
Public schools. *See Elementary and secondary education.*
Public Service Commission of New York v. Mid-Louisiana Gas Co., Arizona Electric Power Cooperative v. Mid-Louisiana Gas Co., Michigan v. Mid-Louisiana Gas Co., Federal Energy Regulatory Commission v. Mid-Louisiana Gas Co. - 17-A
Public service employment programs. *See Employment and training programs.*
Public utilities. *See Utilities.*
Publishing industry. *See Print media and publishing.*
Puerto Rico
Caribbean trade plan - 252-253
Judicial appointments - 302
Nutrition assistance - 516 (chart), 519
Pursell, Carl D. R-Mich. (2)
Committees - 63-98, 101-105
Congressional voting studies - 3-C-42-C
Roll call votes - 2-H-145-H

Q

Quayle, Dan, R-Ind.
Aid for dislocated workers - 270
Appropriations- 455, 467, 508
Budget - 438, 439
Committees - 44-62, 99-100
Congressional voting studies - 3-C-42-C
Defense authorization - 189
Coal leasing ban - 354
Roll call votes - 2-S-60-S
Quillen, James H., R-Tenn. (1)
Committees - 63-98, 101-105
Congressional voting studies - 3-C-42-C
Roll call votes - 2-H-145-H

R

Radio
Broadcast deregulation - 551-552
Cuban interference - 138-140
Public broadcasting authorization - 559
Radio Marti - 138-140, 473 (chart), 476, 477 (chart)
Senate broadcasting - 596
Radio Free Europe - 152
Radio Liberty
Baltic States - 153
Salaries and benefits - 152
Radio Marti
Appropriations - 476
Background - 21
Rahall, Nick J. II, D-W.Va. (4)
Coal surry pipelines - 550
Committees - 63-98, 101-105
Congressional voting studies - 3-C-42-C
Roll call votes - 2-H-145-H
Railroad Retirement Board
Appropriations - 505
Program revisions - 272-273
Nominations and confirmations - 30-A

Railroads. *(See also Amtrak; Conrail; Mass transit.)*
Appropriations - 449 (chart)
Rail-freight rates - 14-A
Railroad retirement bill - 24, 272-273
Unemployment benefits - 449 (chart)
Railway Association, U.S. - 459, 461
Ramirex, Blandina Cardenas - 292-295
Randolph, Jennings, D-W.Va.
Appropriations - 489
Clinch River project - 365
Committees - 44-62, 99-100
Congressional voting studies - 3-C-42-C
Martin Luther King holiday - 602
Peace Academy proposal - 399
Roll call votes - 2-S-60-S
Youth job programs - 230
Rangel, Charles B, D-N.Y. (16)
Committees - 63-98, 101-105
Congressional voting studies - 3-C-42-C
Roll call votes - 2-H-145-H
Rapid Deployment Force (RDF) - 194
Ras Banas - 194, 470-472
RARE II
Leasing ban - 344
Wilderness bills - 342-344
Ratchford, William R., D-Conn. (5)
Committees - 63-98, 101-105
Congressional voting studies - 3-C-42-C
Party unity votes - 27-C
Roll call votes - 2-H-145-H
Ray, Richard, D-Ga. (3)
Committees - 63-98, 101-105
Congressional voting studies - 3-C-42-C
Roll call votes - 2-H-145-H
Reagan, President Ronald. *(See also Executive branch; Nominations and confirmations; Presidential messages.)*
Agriculture
Dairy assessment delay veto - 35-E-36-E
Farm announcements veto - 34-E-35-E
Payment-in-kind (PIK) program - 381, 5-E
Arms control
Arms control agreement - 21-E
Address - 22-E-25-E
Budget
Administration plans - 425-434
Message (text) - 3-E-4-E
Resolution - 435-437
Civil rights - 292-295
Commerce and consumer affairs
Enterprise Zone program - 14-E-15-E, 17-E
Price fixing - 472
Congress
Presidential support - 18-C-25-C
Debt limit increase - 239-240
Defense
Anti-ballistic missiles - 176
Budget request - 479-494
Chemical weapons - 19-C
MX missile - 186, 195-205, 7-C, 26-E-28-E
Nuclear freeze resolution - 6-C, 207
Presidential messages (texts) - 21-C, 22-E-25-C, 32-E-33-E, 33-E-34-E
"Star Wars" speech - 173
Economic affairs
Budget message - 7-E-12-E
Economic report - 12-E-14-E
Enterprise Zone program - 14-E-15-E, 17-E
Jobs bill, phase II program - 268
Policy - 217-218
Presidential messages (text) - 3-E-4-E, 7-E-12-E, 12-E-14-E
Volcker confirmation - 266
Education
Desegregation funds veto - 35-E
Merit pay proposals - 389

Presidential messages - 5-E, 10-E, 20-E-21-E
Proposals - 20-E-21-E
School prayer - 302, 5-E
Tuition tax credits - 395
Energy
Emergency oil supplies - 371
Natural gas pricing - 366
Presidential messages - 10-E
Environment
Acid rain - 340
Burford contempt citation - 333
EPA investigation - 333
Water resources policy - 328
Watt resignation - 327-329
Wilderness leases - 328
Foreign affairs - 154
Central American policies - 28-E-31-E
East-West relations - 21-E, 22-E-25-E, 32-E-33-E, 33-E-34-E
El Salvador military aid - 523
Foreign aid authorization - 141
International Monetary Fund funding - 243
Korean airline downing - 136
Lebanese military aid - 113-118, 36-E-37-E
Most-favored nation trade status - 265
Nicaragua covert aid - 123-132
Overview, 1983 - 109-112
Peacekeeping forces in Lebanon - 115
Policy - 6-E
"Project Democracy" - 145
Soviet pipeline sanctions - 254, 255
U.S.-Soviet relations - 6-E
Vatican diplomatic ties - 152
Foreign aid
Caribbean Basin Initiative - 36-E-37-E
El Salvador - 523
Government operations
Federal employee pay raise - 577
Merit pay - 602-603
Presidential messages (text) - 11-E-12-E
Reorganization authority - 588
Health - 10-E
Housing - 280
IMF funding - 243
Law and justice
Crime control proposal - 312, 19-E
Judicial appointments - 302-304
Lebanon resolution - 5-C
Legal aid nominees - 324
Legislative summary - 12-28
Legislative veto - 565
Politics
Carter briefing papers - 594
Gender gap issues - 299
Refugees admissions - 304
Revenue sharing - 227-228
Social Security
Reform proposal - 3-E
Rescue bill - 221, 225
Space programs - 589
State of the Union address (text) - 3-E-7-E
Supreme Court decisions - 3-A, 4-A
Taxes
Budget resolution - 435
Caribbean Basin Initiative - 36-E-37-E
Enterprise Zone proposal - 14-E-15-E
Increase proposal - 11-C
Presidential message (text) - 15-E
Tax cap bill - 249-250
Tax leasing veto - 603-604, 34-E
Television syndication rights - 560
Vetoes
Anti-crime bill - 315
Dairy assessment - 35-E-36-E
Desegregation funds - 35-E
El Salvador certification - 156

Farm announcements - 34-E-35-E
Indian claims bill - 25-E-26-E
Indian land claim veto - 586-587
List (box) - 6
Oregon Lands bill - 38-E
Public lands transfer - 344-345
Tax leasing plan - 34-E
Transportation appropriation - 457
Water projects - 354
Welfare
  Food assistance programs - 412,
  415-416, 417
  Presidential messages - 3-E-39-E
  Social programs - 10-C
Regan v. Taxation with Representation of Washington, Taxation with Representation of Washington v. Regan - 12-A
Real estate business. *See Housing.*
Reclamation, land. *See Irrigation projects.*
Reclamation Safety of Dams Act - 349
Records
  Martin Luther King holiday - 600-602
  Rentals - 313
Recreation. *See Sports and recreation.*
Recreation areas. *See Parks and recreation areas.*
Reforestation - 456
Refugees. *(See also Aliens.)*
  Admissions (chart) - 305
  Appropriations - 505, 522 (chart)
  Authorization - 146 (box), 150, 152
  Bilingual education - 505, 507
  El Salvador - 148, 152
  Foreign aid - 522 (chart)
  Lebanese emergency aid - 148
  Resettlement programs - 304-306, 505
  Welfare and social services aid - 304, 305
Regan, Donald T.
  Appropriations - 536
  Budget control proposal - 238
  Deficit reduction proposals - 231
  Housing authorization - 283
  IMF funding - 248
  Revenue sharing - 227
Regional development. *See Community development.*
Regula, Ralph, R-Ohio (16)
  Appropriations - 480
  Committees - 63-98, 101-105
  Congressional voting studies - 3-C-42-C
  Roll call votes - 2-H-145-H
  Withholding tax revisions - 264
Regulatory process, agencies. *(See also Deregulation; Legislative veto.)*
  Membership - 24-A-30-A
  Regulatory process - 12-E
  Reorganization Act renewal - 588
  Supreme Court decisions - 14-A
Rehabilitation programs. *(See also Employment and training programs.)*
  Alcoholism rehabilitation programs - 505, 506
  Drug abuse rehabilitation programs - 314
  Handicapped persons - 18, 402-404
  Veterans' counseling centers - 410-412
  Vocational rehabilitation - 18
Rehnquist, William H.
  Abortions - 307
  Redistricting - 5-B
  Supreme Court term, 1982-83 - 3-A-22-A
Reid, Harry, D-Nev. (1)
  Committees - 63-98, 101-105
  Congressional voting studies - 3-C-42-C
  Roll call votes - 2-H-145-H
Religion and religious organizations. *(See also Freedom of religion; Private and parochial schools.)*
  School prayer - 301-302

U.S.-Vatican relations - 168-169
Rent subsidies, low-income housing. *See Public housing and housing assistance.*
Reorganization Act - 588
Republican Party. *(See also Elections and politics.)*
  Political report - 3-B-7-B
  Presidential support - 21-C-22-C
  Voting unity - 26-C-31-C
Research and development
  Agricultural programs - 518
  Animal subjects - 409
  Budget - 430, 431
  Defense - 481
  Dental - 504
  Earthquake hazard reduction - 591
  Energy
    Civilian - 365
    Conservation - 463
    Fossil - 465
    Geothermal - 501
    Research laboratories - 502
    Solar - 502-503
  Environmental Protection Agency (EPA) - 497-500
  Fetal research - 409
  Health - 23, 409-410
  Industrial policy proposals - 250-251
  Presidential message (text) - 10-E
  Water resources - 349
Research and Special Programs Administration - 459
Reserve fund - 444
Reserves, military. *(See also National Guard.)*
  Appropriations - 479-494
  Authorization - 185-186
  Buildup - 481
  Educational benefits - 418-419
  Military construction funds - 193-195
  Naval Reserve - 186
Reserves, petroleum. *See Oil reserves.*
Resource Conservation and Recovery Act of 1976
  EPA enforcement - 332-335
  Legislative summary - 19
  Reauthorization bill - 335-339
Retarded persons. *See Handicapped persons.*
Retirement and disability insurance - 431
Retirement and pensions. *(See also Federal retirement benefits; Military retirement benefits; Social security programs; Unemployment compensation.)*
  Age discrimination - 4-A
  Age discrimination - 4-A
  Pension equity bill - 276
  Railroad retirement - 272-273
  Retirement and disability insurance - 431
  Sex-based discrimination - 3-A, 9-A
  Social Security retirement age - 220, 223
  Supreme Court decisions - 3-A, 9-A
Revenue sharing. *(See also Countercyclical aid and targeted fiscal assistance.)*
  Appropriations - 496, 497
  Budget - 431
  Extension - 226-229
  Oil and gas drilling - 359
  Legislative summary - 17
Rhode Island - 455
Ribicoff, Abraham A.
  Budget control proposal - 238
  Senate rule change proposal - 598
  Senate television broadcasting - 596
Rice v. Rehner - 18-A
Richardson, Bill, D-N.M. (3)
  Committees - 63-98, 101-105
  Congressional voting studies - 3-C-42-C

Energy Committee appointment - 340
Revenue sharing - 228
Roll call votes - 2-H-145-H
Telephone rates - 548
Richardson, Elliot L. - 334
Richmond, Fred - 15
Ridge, Tom, R-Pa. (21)
  Committees - 63-98, 101-105
  Congressional voting studies - 3-C-42-C
  Defense production - 266
  Roll call votes - 2-H-145-H
Riegle, Donald W. Jr., D-Mich.
  Appropriations - 500
  Budget - 439
  Committees - 44-62, 99-100
  Congressional voting studies - 3-C-42-C
  Grenada press coverage - 241
  Housing authorization - 281
  Mortgage assistance - 267
  Party unity votes - 26-C
  Roll call votes - 2-S-60-S
  VISTA authorization - 398
Rights, civil. *See Civil rights.*
Rinaldo, Matthew J., R-N.J. (7)
  Budget - 437
  Committees - 63-98, 101-105
  Congressional voting studies - 3-C-42-C
  Radio Marti - 140
  Roll call votes - 2-H-145-H
  Telephone rates - 547-548
Ritter, Don, R-Pa. (15)
  Auto domestic content bill - 258
  Committees - 63-98, 101-105
  Congressional voting studies - 3-C-42-C
  Grenada invasion - 135
  Roll call votes - 2-H-145-H
Rivlin, Alice M.
  CBO directorship - 443
  Health insurance proposal - 406
Roadless area review and evaluation program. *See RARE II.*
Roads. *See Highways and roads.*
Roberts, Pat, R-Kan. (1)
  Committees - 63-98, 101-105
  Congressional voting studies - 3-C-42-C
  Roll call votes - 2-H-145-H
Robinson, J. Kenneth, R-Va. (7)
  Committees - 63-98, 101-105
  Congressional voting studies - 3-C-42-C
  Nicaragua covert aid - 131
  Roll call votes - 2-H-145-H
Rock Island Railroad - 460
Rodino, Peter W. Jr., D-N.J. (10)
  Bankruptcy court - 286
  Bankruptcy laws - 321
  Committees - 63-98, 101-105
  Congressional voting studies - 3-C-42-C
  Equal Rights Amendment - 298
  Immigration reform bill - 290, 292
  Insanity defense - 315
  Justice authorization - 312
  Legal Services Corporation - 323
  Legislative veto - 570
  Maritime antitrust bill - 556
  Roll call votes - 2-H-145-H
Roe, Robert A., D-N.J. (8)
  Appropriations - 498
  Committees - 63-98, 101-105
  Congressional voting studies - 3-C-42-C
  Roll call votes - 2-H-145-H
  Water projects - 357
Roe v. Wade - 307, 4-C
Roemer, Buddy, D-La. (4)
  Committees - 63-98, 101-105
  Congressional voting studies - 3-C-42-C
  Mortgage assistance - 268
  Mortgages and home loans - 8-C
  Roll call votes - 2-H-145-H
Rogers, Bernard - 122
Rogers, Harold, R-Ky. (5)
  Appropriations - 534
  Committees - 63-98, 101-105
  Congressional voting studies - 3-C-42-C

Roll call votes - 2-H-145-H
Roll call votes
  House roll call votes - 2-H-145-H
  Senate roll call votes - 2-S-60-S
Roman Catholic Church - 168-169
Romania - 264-265
Roosevelt, Franklin Delano
  El Salvador aid - 168, 169
  Supreme Court - 4-A
Rose, Charlie, D-N.C. (7)
  Committees - 63-98, 101-105
  Congressional voting studies - 3-C-42-C
  Dairy, tobacco program - 378, 380
  Roll call votes - 2-H-145-H
Rostenkowski, Dan, D-Ill. (8)
  Appropriations - 456, 530, 536
  Budget - 436
  Caribbean trade plan - 253
  Committees - 63-98, 101-105
  Congressional voting studies - 3-C-42-C
  Debt limit increase - 239
  Deficit reduction proposals - 231, 233, 236
  Medicare revisions - 392
  Roll call votes - 2-H-145-H
  Social Security rescue bill - 222-223
  Tax cap bill - 249
  Tuition tax credits - 395
  Unemployment benefits - 275
  Withholding tax revisions - 263
Rostow, Eugene V. - 213
Roth, Toby, R-Wis. (8)
  Committees - 63-98, 101-105
  Congressional voting studies - 3-C-42-C
  Export controls - 255-256
  International trade department proposal - 250-251
  Nicaragua covert aid - 128
  Peacekeeping forces in Lebanon - 119
  Roll call votes - 2-H-145-H
Roth, William V. Jr., R-Del.
  Committees - 44-62, 99-100
  Congressional voting studies - 3-C-42-C
  Mortgage revenue bonds - 277
  Peacekeeping forces in Lebanon - 118-119
  Roll call votes - 2-S-60-S
Roukema, Marge, R-N.J. (5)
  Committees - 63-96, 101-105
  Congressional voting studies - 3-C-42-C
  MX debate - 199
  Roll call votes - 2-H-145-H
Rowland, J. Roy, D-Ga. (8)
  Committees - 63-98, 101-105
  Congressional voting studies - 3-C-42-C
  Roll call votes - 2-H-145-H
Rowny, Edward L. - 180, 201
Roybal, Edward R., D-Calif. (25)
  Appropriations - 535
  Committees - 63-98, 101-105
  Congressional voting studies - 3-C-42-C
  Roll call votes - 2-H-145-H
Ruckelshaus, Jill - 292-295
Ruckelshaus, William D.
  Acid rain policy - 340
  Clean Water Act - 361
  Confirmation - 332, 334 (box), 23-A, 25-A, 29-A
  Congressional voting studies - 3-C-42-C
  EPA appropriations - 496, 498, 499
Ruckelshaus v. Sierra Club - 17-A
Rudd, Eldon, R-Ariz. (4)
  Appropriations - 533
  Committees - 63-98, 101-105
  Congressional voting studies - 3-C-42-C
  Korean airline downing - 137
  Roll call votes - 2-H-145-H
Rudman, Warren B., R-N.H.
  Appropriations - 455, 466, 467, 477, 478, 490
  Clinch River project - 365
  Committees - 44-62, 99-100
  Coal leasing ban - 354

Congressional voting studies - 3-C-42-C
Dairy program - 377-378
El Salvador aid - 159
Martin Luther King holiday - 602
MX debate - 198, 200
Roll call votes - 2-S-60-S
Rum - 252, 253
Rural affairs. (See also Agriculture and farming; Farm income stabilization and aid programs; Farmers Home Administration; Migrant farmworkers.)
Appropriations - 448 (chart), 452, 453, 457
Electrification bill - 388
Rural development funds - 386
Telephone rates - 14
Water grants - 452, 453, 457
Rural Electrification Administration (REA)
Appropriations - 516 (chart), 518-519
Interest rates - 388
Russia. See Soviet Union.
Russo, Marty, D-Ill. (3)
Committees - 63-98, 101-105
Congressional voting studies - 3-C-42-C
Equal Rights Amendment - 297
Roll call votes - 2-H-145-H
Tax cap bill - 249

S

Sabo, Martin Olav, D-Minn. (5)
Appropriations - 462, 480
Committees - 63-98, 101-105
Congressional voting studies - 3-C-42-C
Pershing II deployment - 207
Roll call votes - 2-H-145-H
Saccharin - 401-402
Safety. (See also Consumer product safety; Environmental health; Hazardous substances; National Highway Traffic Safety Administration; Nuclear power plants; Occupational safety and health.)
Boating - 511, 562
Drunk driving bill - 321
Safety board funding - 557-558
SALT II. See Strategic Arms Limitation Treaty.
Sampson, Anthony - 242
Sanderson, James - 333
Sandwich Range Wilderness - 343
Sarbanes, Paul S., D-Md.
Committees - 44-62, 99-100
Congressional voting studies - 3-C-42-C
Foreign aid - 141, 144
Lebanon foreign aid - 117
Peacekeeping forces in Lebanon - 118
Roll call votes - 2-S-60-S
Sasser, Jim, D-Tenn.
Budget - 439
Committees - 44-62, 99-100
Congressional voting studies - 3-C-42-C
MX debate - 198
Roll call votes - 2-S-60-S
Senate day care facilities - 595
Satellites
Anti-satellite missiles (ASAT)
Appropriations - 479, 480, 483, 494
Authorization - 181, 188, 191
Anti-missile - 173
Weather - 22, 477, 588-589
Savage, Gus, D-Ill. (2)
Committees - 63-98, 101-105
Congressional voting studies - 3-C-42-C
Roll call votes - 2-H-145-H
Savannah River L-Reactor - 503, 510
Savings and loan associations. See Banks and banking.
Sawyer, Harold S., R-Mich. (5)
Committees - 63-98, 101-105
Congressional voting studies - 3-C-42-C

Equal Rights Amendment - 296
Insanity defense - 315
Roll call votes - 2-H-145-H
Schaefer, Daniel L. R-Colo. (6)
Committees - 63-98
Congressional voting studies - 3-C-42-C
Election results - 6-B
Roll call votes - 2-H-145-H
Scheuer, James H., D-N.Y. (8)
Committees - 63-98, 101-105
Congressional voting studies - 3-C-42-C
EPA investigation - 335
Roll call votes - 2-H-145-H
Schmults, Edward C. - 478, 571
Schneider, Claudine, R-R.I. (2)
Budget - 437
Clinch River project - 365
Committees - 63-98, 101-105
Congressional voting studies - 3-C-42-C
Gender gap politics - 299
Party unity votes - 27-C
Presidential support - 21-C
Roll call votes - 2-H-145-H
Women's economic equity bills - 298
Scholarships. See Student aid.
School busing
Congressional action - 478, 508
Supreme Court decisions - 3-A
School desegregation. (See also School busing.)
Desegregation funds veto - 35-E
Supreme Court decisions - 3-A-5-A, 10-A
Tax-exempt private schools - 3-A, 10-A
Tuition tax credits - 18, 395, 3-A, 10-E, 20-E
School meal and milk programs
Appropriations - 518
Food assistance programs - 415
School prayer
Amendment proposals - 301-302
Presidential message - 5-E
Schools. See Elementary and secondary education.
Schroeder, Patricia, D-Colo. (1)
Abortion amendment - 310
Abortion funding - 533
Committees - 63-98, 101-105
Congressional pay raises - 578
Congressional voting studies - 3-C-42-C
Defense authorization - 182
Equal Rights Amendment - 286, 296
Federal personnel rules - 603
Railroad retirement bill - 272
Roll call votes - 2-H-145-H
Women's economic equity bills - 298
Schulze, Richard T., R-Pa. (5)
Committees - 63-98, 101-105
Congressional voting studies - 3-C-42-C
Roll call votes - 2-H-145-H
Social Security rescue bill - 222
Schumer, Charles E., D-N.Y. (10)
Committees - 63-98, 101-105
Congressional voting studies - 3-C-42-C
Housing authorization - 282
IMF funding - 244, 246
Most-favored-nation trade status - 265
Roll call votes - 2-H-145-H
Schweiker, Richard S. - 417
Science and technology. (See also National Science Foundation; Office of Science and Technology Policy; Office of Technology Assessment; Research and development.)
Appropriations - 473
Bilateral agreements - 146
Breeder technology - 362, 363
Budget - 430, 445 (chart)
Education proposals - 18, 390, 396-397
Foreign aid - 522 (chart)
Geothermal energy - 501
Trade reciprocity bill - 259-260

Scowcroft, Brent - 175, 180, 195
Scowcroft Commission
Basing recommendations - 195-196
Congressional reaction - 196-205
Defense authorization - 175, 180
Midgetman missile proposal - 196
Sea grant program - 360, 473 (chart), 476, 477 (chart)
Searches and seizures - 5-A, 6-A
Seas. See Oceans.
Second Roadless Area Review and Evaluation. See RARE II.
Secondary education. See Elementary and secondary education.
Securities. See Stocks, bonds, and securities.
Securities and Exchange Commission (SEC)
Insider trading curbs - 265
Nominations and confirmations - 24-A, 30-A
Seiberling, John F., D-Ohio (14)
Alaska hunting bill - 347
Committees - 63-98, 101-105
Congressional voting studies - 3-C-42-C
Defense authorization - 181
Park protection bill - 348
Roll call votes - 2-H-145-H
Watt resignation - 328
Wilderness areas - 343
Seko, Mobutu Sese - 143
Selective Service System
Appropriations - 496, 497, 499
Federal educational aid - 189, 418-419
Female personnel - 296
Senate. (See also Congressional elections; Nominations and confirmations.)
Day care center - 594-595
Ethics
Abscam investigation - 585-586
Franking privileges - 540, 541, 578-580
Leadership - 3-4
Legislative branch appropriations - 510, 539-542
Membership
Changes, 98th Congress - 5
Characteristics of 98th Congress - 29-31
Leadership - 3-4
Master list - 10-11
Seniority - 38-39
Pay and expenses - 577
Honoraria - 511, 512, 514, 515, 541, 577, 4-C
Pay increase - 15, 511, 512, 514, 515, 577-578, 4-C
Travel funds - 540, 541
Political report - 3-B-7-B
Rule changes - 598-599
Social Security coverage - 577
Television broadcasting - 15, 595-596
Votes
Conservative coalition - 37-C-42-C
Key votes - 4-C-7-C
Party unity - 26-C-31-C
Presidential support - 18-C-25-C
Roll call votes - 2-S-60-S
Voting participation - 32-C-36-C
Voting studies - 3-C-17-C
Senate committees (general). For committee action on a specific bill, see the topic of the legislation.
Assignments - 44-63, 99-100
Background - 42-43
Joint - 97-98
Sensenbrenner, F. James Jr., R-Wis. (9)
Appropriations - 502
Bankruptcy laws - 320
Civil Rights Commission - 293, 294
Committees - 63-98, 101-105
Congressional voting studies - 3-C-42-C
Equal Rights Amendment - 297
Immigration reform bill - 291

Justice authorization - 312
Math-science education proposals - 397
Roll call votes - 2-H-145-H
Sentencing of criminals. See Prisons and prisoners.
Sewers, sewage treatment plants - 448, 452, 457
Sex discrimination
Education - 300
Equal Rights Amendment - 296-298
Federally funded education programs - 397 (box)
Health benefits - 10-A
Insurance - 15, 300, 558
Presidential message - 5-E
Retirement plans - 10-A
Supreme Court decisions - 3-A, 10-A
Taxes - 300
Shamir, Yitzhak - 133
Shannon, James M., D-Mass. (5)
Committees - 63-98, 101-105
Congressional voting studies - 3-C-42-C
Roll call votes - 2-H-145-H
Sharp, Philip R., D-Ind. (2)
Committees - 63-98, 101-105
Congressional voting studies - 3-C-42-C
Natural gas pricing - 369
Roll call votes - 2-H-145-H
Shaw, E. Clay Jr., R-Fla. (15)
Committees - 63-98, 101-105
Congressional voting studies - 3-C-42-C
Equal Rights Amendment - 296
Immigration reform bill - 290
Insanity defense - 315
Roll call votes - 2-H-145-H
Shaw v. Delta Air Lines Inc. - 18-A
Shelby, Richard C., D-Ala. (7)
Committees - 63-98, 101-105
Congressional voting studies - 3-C-42-C
CPSC authorization - 557
Natural gas pricing - 369
Roll call votes - 2-H-145-H
Shepard v. National Labor Relations Board (NLRB) - 15-A
Ships and shipping. (See also Boats, boating; Coast Guard; Federal Maritime Commission; Harbors and ports; Maritime Administration; Naval ships; Oceans.)
Antitrust bill - 27, 544, 554-557
Authorization - 549
Longshoremen's compensation program - 271-272
Ocean-liner industry - 554-557
Shoshone National Forest - 344
Shultz, George P.
Acid rain - 340
Arms control policy - 214
Clark confirmation - 330
El Salvador aid - 155, 160, 166
El Salvador certification - 156
El Salvador human rights - 111
Foreign aid - 153
Nicaragua covert aid - 129, 131
Peacekeeping forces in Lebanon - 114-115
Project Democracy - 148 (box)
Shumway, Norman D., R-Calif. (14)
Committees - 63-98, 101-105
Congressional voting studies - 3-C-42-C
Roll call votes - 2-H-145-H
Wilderness areas - 343
Shuster, Bud, R-Pa. (9)
Coal slurry pipelines - 550
Committee assignments - 63-98, 101-105
Congressional voting studies - 3-C-42-C
Roll call votes - 2-H-145-H
Sikorski, Gerry, D-Minn. (6)
Committees - 63-98, 101-105
Congressional voting studies - 3-C-42-C
Energy Committee appointment - 340
Roll call votes - 2-H-145-H

Siljander, Mark D., R-Mich. (4)
Committees - 63-98, 101-105
Congressional voting studies - 3-C-42-C
Grenada invasion - 135
Nuclear freeze resolution - 208-209
Roll call votes - 2-H-145-H
Simon, Paul, D-Ill. (22)
Committees - 63-98, 101-105
Congressional voting studies - 3-C-42-C
Draft registration requirement - 399
Roll call votes - 2-H-145-H
Simopoulos v. Virginia - 10-A, 11-A
Simpson, Alan K., R-Wyo.
Anti-abortion amendment - 309
Clinch River project - 365
Committees - 44-62, 99-100
Congressional voting studies - 3-C-42-C
Economic development - 230
Immigration reform bill - 285, 287, 289
NRC authorization - 371
Roll call votes - 2-S-60-S
Sisisky, Norman, D-Va. (4)
Committees - 63-98, 101-105
Congressional voting studies - 3-C-42-C
Roll call votes - 2-H-145-H
Skeen, Joe, R-N.M. (2)
Committees - 63-98, 101-105
Congressional voting studies - 3-C-42-C
Roll call votes - 2-H-145-H
Skelton, Ike, D-Mo. (4)
Committees - 63-98, 101-105
Congressional voting studies - 3-C-42-C
Defense authorization - 179
Natural gas pricing - 367
Peacekeeping forces in Lebanon - 115
Roll call votes - 2-H-145-H
Slattery, Jim, D-Kan. (2)
Committees - 63-98, 101-105
Congressional voting studies - 3-C-42-C
Energy Committee appointment - 340
Roll call votes - 2-H-145-H
Small business. *(See also Federal contractors and consultants; Minority business; Small Business Administration.)*
Appropriations - 451, 453, 456, 509
Disaster loans - 233
Enterprise Zone proposal - 14-E-15-E
Export-Import Bank loans - 246
Federal contracts - 587-588
Minority assistance - 588
Small Business Administration (SBA)
Appropriations
FY 1983 supplemental - 448 (chart), 451, 453, 456, 509, 510
FY 1984 - 473 (chart), 474, 477 (chart)
Federal programs - 588
International trade department proposal - 250
Minority assistance - 588
Smith, Christopher H., R-N.J. (4)
Abortion funding - 533
Appropriations - 460, 535
Committees - 63-98, 101-105
Congressional voting studies - 3-C-42-C
Roll call votes - 2-H-145-H
Smith, Denny, R-Ore. (5)
Committees - 63-98, 101-105
Congressional voting studies - 3-C-42-C
Public lands transfer - 345
Roll call votes - 2-H-145-H
Wilderness areas - 343, 344
Smith, Larry, D-Fla. (16)
Committees - 63-98, 101-105
Congressional voting studies - 3-C-42-C
Defense authorization - 180
Equal Rights Amendment - 296
Foreign policy role - 142 (box)
Immigration reform bill - 288, 291, 292
Roll call votes - 2-H-145-H
Smith, John Lewis - 333
Smith, Mary Louise - 292-295
Smith, Neal, D-Iowa (4)

Appropriations - 456, 475
Committees - 63-98, 101-105
Congressional voting studies - 3-C-42-C
Export controls - 257
Roll call votes - 2-H-145-H
Smith, Robert F., R-Ore. (2)
Committees - 63-98, 101-105
Congressional voting studies - 3-C-42-C
Roll call votes - 2-H-145-H
Wilderness areas - 343, 344
Smith, Virginia, R-Neb. (3)
Committees - 63-98, 101-105
Congressional voting studies - 3-C-42-C
MX debate - 199
Roll call votes - 2-H-145-H
Smith, William French
EPA investigation - 312, 333
Legislative veto - 565
Wilderness leasing - 329
Smith v. Wade - 9-A
Smithsonian Institution - 463, 465
Snowe, Olympia J., R-Maine (2)
Abortion amendment - 310
Committees - 63-98, 101-105
Congressional voting studies - 3-C-42-C
Export controls - 255, 257
Gender gap politics - 299
MX debate - 199
Nicaragua covert aid - 129
Roll call votes - 2-H-145-H
Women's economic equity bills - 298
Snyder, Gene, R-Ky. (4)
Committees - 63-98, 101-105
Congressional voting studies - 3-C-42-C
Roll call votes - 2-H-145-H
Social Security Act Amendments of 1983
Background - 221-222
Congressional action - 222-226
Provisions - 219-221
Social Security Administration. *(See also Social security programs.)*
Appropriations - 510
Federal employee contributions - 573-576
Background - 576-577
Congressional action - 575-576
Provisions - 573-574
Rescue bill - 219-226
Background - 221-222
Congressional action - 222-226
Provisions - 219-221
Social Security Disability Insurance (SSDI) - 273
Social security programs
Appropriations - 504-509, 510, 511
Budget - 425, 432, 445 (chart)
Disability insurance program - 273-274
Key votes - 7-C
Legislative summary - 24
Old-Age and Survivors Insurance - 219
Presidential message - 4-E
Rescue bill - 219-226
Background - 221-222
Congressional action - 222-226
Provisions - 219-221
Retirement increase - 220, 223
Tax increase - 432
Social Service Block Grants - 452
Social welfare. *See Welfare and social services.*
Soil conservation - 452, 453, 456
Soil Conservation Service (SCS)
Appropriations - 453, 516 (chart), 518
Authorization bill - 354-359
Solar and renewable energies. *(See also Geothermal energy; Nuclear energy.)*
Appropriations - 496-500, 502
Budget - 433
Solar Energy and Energy Conservation Bank - 496-500
Solarz, Stephen J., D-N.Y. (13)

Committees - 63-98, 101-105
Congressional voting studies - 3-C-42-C
El Salvador aid - 162
Nicaragua covert aid - 130
Nuclear freeze resolution - 206, 208-209
Peacekeeping forces in Lebanon - 118
Roll call votes - 2-H-145-H
Solem v. Helm - 8-A
Solid wastes management. *See Wastes management.*
Solomon, Gerald B. H., R-N.Y. (24)
Committees - 63-98, 101-105
Congressional voting studies - 3-C-42-C
Draft registration requirement - 399
Export controls - 256
Jobs bill, phase II program - 269
Roll call votes - 2-H-145-H
Somoza, Anastasio - 125
South Africa
Foreign aid - 152
U.S. investments, export controls - 256, 257
U.S. technology transfer - 150
South Carolina - 503, 510
South Dakota - 5-A
South Dakota v. Neville - 7-A
South Korea
Korean airline downing - 20, 136-137, 175, 190, 257
Foreign aid - 514 (box)
Southeast Asia. *See Asia.*
Southeastern Power Administration - 501
Southwestern Power Administration - 501
Soviet Union. *(See also Strategic Arms Limitation Treaty.)*
Arms control
Deployment in Europe - 206-207
Joint Statement of Agreed Principles for Disarmament Negotiations - 210
Presidential messages (text) - 21-E, 22-E-25-E
Strategic Arms Reduction Talks (START) - 197-198, 200-201, 210
Chemical weapons - 11-C
El Salvador aid - 157, 160
Foreign trade - 387
Grenada presence - 135
ICBM - 196, 201-33
Immigration policies - 265
Korean airline downing - 136-137, 175, 190, 257
Nuclear weapons - 196, 198, 200
Oil and gas pipeline - 254, 255
Presidential messages (text) - 21-E, 22-E-25-E
Soviet studies program - 152
Syria support - 133
U.S. diplomats - 153
U.S. export controls - 253-257
U.S. grain pact (box) - 387
U.S. missile deployment - 480, 484
Washington D.C. embassy - 198
Space and space programs. *(See also National Aeronautics and Space Administration; Satellites.)*
Budget - 430, 445 (chart)
Space shuttle - 589
Spain - 514 (box)
Speakes, Larry - 156
Spanish-speaking Americans. *See Hispanics.*
Special Drawing Rights (SDRs) - 241, 245
Special interest groups. *See Lobbies, lobbying.*
Special Trade Representative, Office of. *See Office of the U.S. Trade Representative.*
Specter, Arlen, R-Pa.

Anti-crime proposal - 316, 317
Appropriations - 450, 467, 489, 508
Civil Rights Commission - 294, 295
Coal leasing ban - 354
Committees - 44-62, 99-100
Congressional voting studies - 3-C-42-C
El Salvador aid - 159
El Salvador human rights - 164
MX debate - 198
Party unity votes - 27-C
Peacekeeping forces in Lebanon - 120
Roll call votes - 2-S-60-S
Tax cap bill - 250
Trade reciprocity bill - 259
Speech freedom. *See Freedom of speech.*
Spence, Floyd, R-S.C. (2)
Censure proceedings - 580
Committees - 63-98, 101-105
Congressional voting studies - 3-C-42-C
Roll call votes - 2-H-145-H
Spent fuel management. *See Nuclear waste and radioactive materials management.*
Sports and recreation. *(See also Parks and recreation areas.)*
Alaska hunting bill - 347-348
Boating safety - 511, 562
Boxing commission - 586
SPR. *See Strategic Petroleum Reserve (SPR).*
Spratt, John M., D-S.C. (5)
Committees - 63-98, 101-105
Congressional voting studies - 3-C-42-C
Dairy program - 377
Roll call votes - 2-H-145-H
St. Elizabeths Hospital - 495, 505
St Germain, Fernand J., D-R.I. (1)
Appropriations - 536
Committees - 63-98, 101-105
Congressional voting studies - 3-C-42-C
Housing authorization - 248, 283
IMF funding - 244, 246
Roll call votes - 2-H-145-H
St. Lawrence Seaway Development Corporation - 28-A
St. Lucia - 135
St. Vincent - 135
Stafford, Robert T., R-Vt.
Acid rain - 341
Appropriations - 489
Budget - 442
Clark confirmation - 331
Clean Air Act - 340
Committees - 44-62, 99-101
Congressional voting studies - 3-C-42-C
Defense authorization - 187
Education spending - 6-C
Roll call votes - 2-S-60-S
Ruckelshaus confirmation - 332
Trucking deregulation proposals - 560
Tuition tax credits - 395
Youth job programs - 230
Staggers, Harley O. Jr., D-W.Va. (2)
Committees - 63-98, 101-105
Congressional voting studies - 3-C-42-C
Roll call votes - 2-H-145-H
Stangeland, Arlan, R-Minn. (7)
Committees - 63-98, 101-105
Congressional voting studies - 3-C-42-C
Roll call votes - 2-H-145-H
Stark, Fortney H. 'Pete', D-Calif. (9)
Committees - 63-98, 101-105
Congressional voting studies - 3-C-42-C
PIK program - 13, 381-383
Roll call votes - 2-H-145-H
START. *See Strategic Arms Reduction Talks.*
State and local government. *(See also Community development; Counter-cyclical aid and targeted fiscal assistance; District of Columbia; Impact aid; Revenue sharing; Urban affairs; names of individual states.)*

Courts, Supreme Court rulings - 5-A, 17-A-18-A
Enterprise Zone proposal - 14-E-15-E
Governors
Master list - 11
Political report - 3-B-4-B
Industrial Development Bonds - 235-236
Job training program - 450, 454
Justice assistance - 316
Legislative prayer - 4-A
Lobby registrations - 3-D-55-D
Redistricting - 5-A
Revenue sharing - 226-229
State powers - 5-A, 17-A-18-A
Supreme Court decisions - 5-A, 17-A-18-A
Taxation - 5-A
Unemployment insurance grants - 449, 504
State Department. *(See also Foreign Service, U.S.)*
Appropriations
FY 1983 supplemental - 509, 510
FY 1984 continuing resolution - 472-479, 527, 529
Authorization - 21, 145-153
Budget - 434
El Salvador human rights - 164
Nominations and confirmations - 27-A
State of the Union Address - 3-E-7-E
Stenholm, Charles W., D-Texas (17)
Auto domestic content bill - 259
Committees - 63-98, 101-105
Congressional voting studies - 3-C-42-C
Party unity votes - 27-C
Roll call votes - 2-H-145-H
Stennis, John C., D-Miss.
Committees - 44-62, 99-100
Congressional voting studies - 3-C-42-C
MX debate - 198
Roll call votes - 2-S-60-S
Stevens, John Paul
Abortions - 307
Congressional voting studies - 3-C-42-C
Legislative veto - 567
Supreme Court term, 1982-83 - 3-A-22-A
Stevens, Ted, R-Alaska
Alaska sport hunting bill - 348
Appropriations - 455, 457, 462, 485-490, 513, 515, 527, 538
Bankruptcy proposals - 321
Capitol bombing - 593
Committees - 44-62, 99-100
Congressional voting studies - 3-C-42-C
Defense authorization - 172
Federal employee social security coverage - 574-575
Federal personnel rules - 603
Franking privilege - 579
Maritime antitrust bill - 555
MX debate - 198
Presidential support - 20-C
Roll call votes - 2-S-60-S
Social Security rescue bill - 225
Television syndication rights - 560
Water projects - 355
Withholding tax revisions - 262
Stewart, Potter
Supreme Court term, 1982-1983 - 3-A-22-A
Stockman, David A.
Acid rain proposals - 340, 341
Agricultural marketing orders - 535
Appropriations
FY 1983 supplemental - 512, 514
FY 1984 continuing resolution- 461, 465, 495, 500, 516-518, 536, 537
Budget resolution - 435, 438
Carter briefing papers - 594
Child nutrition programs - 417
Clinch River project - 364

Coal leasing ban - 353
Defense authorization - 187
Farm programs - 373
Food assistance programs - 412, 415
Health insurance proposal - 390, 406
Housing authorization - 283
IMF funding - 248
Railroad retirement bill - 273
Student aid eligibility - 401
Water projects - 520
Stocks, bonds and securities. *(See also Securities and Exchange Commission.)*
Industrial Development Bonds - 235-236
Insider trading curbs - 265
Mortgage revenue bonds - 276-277
Supreme Court decisions - 14-A
Withholding tax revisions - 264
Stokes, Louis, D-Ohio (21)
Censure proceedings - 580
Committees - 63-98, 101-105
Congressional voting studies - 3-C-42-C
Grenada invasion - 136
Roll call votes - 2-H-145-H
Stone, Richard "Dick" - 126, 159, 160
Stonewall Jackson Dam - 500, 502, 503
Strategic Arms Limitation Treaty (SALT II)
Nuclear freeze resolution - 214
Presidential message (text) - 27-E
Strategic Arms Reduction Talks (START)
ICBM ceiling - 174
MX debate - 197, 200-204
Nuclear freeze resolution - 173-174, 210, 212
Presidential messages (text) - 27-E-28-E, 33-E-34-E
Revised proposals - 200-201
Scowcroft Commission - 197
Strategic Petroleum Reserve (SPR)
Appropriations - 462, 463, 466-469, 515
Legislative summary - 18-19
Stratton, Samuel S., D-N.Y. (23)
Appropriations - 484
Committees - 63-98, 101-105
Congressional voting studies - 3-C-42-C
Peacekeeping forces in Lebanon - 122
Roll call votes - 2-H-145-H
Studds, Gerry E., D-Mass. (10)
Appropriations - 460
Censure - 580-583
Committees - 63-98, 101-105
Congressional voting studies - 3-C-42-C
El Salvador aid - 155
Guatemalan foreign aid - 138
Nicaragua covert aid - 127
Page sex scandal - 15, 595
Peacekeeping forces in Lebanon - 118
Profile (box) - 582
Roll call votes - 2-H-145-H
Student aid
Appropriations - 449, 505
Budget plans - 434
Draft registration requirement - 399
Eligibility rules - 400-401
Guaranteed Student Loans - 400-401
Pell grants - 434, 507, 406
Presidential message - 20-E
Tuition tax credits - 18, 395, 432, 3-A, 10-E, 20-E
Veterans' education benefits
GI bill - 418-419
Vocational education - 599-600
Work study programs - 454, 457
Student Loan Marketing Association (Sallie Mae) - 400
Stump, Bob, D-Ariz. (3)
Committees - 63-98, 101-105
Congressional voting studies - 3-C-42-C
Roll call votes - 2-H-145-H
Submarines

Appropriations - 479, 482, 483, 488 (chart), 493
Authorization - 175, 185, 192
Trident submarines - 175, 488 (chart)
Subways. *See Mass transit.*
Sudan
Foreign aid - 513, 514 (box)
Military aid - 144
Sundquist, Don, R-Tenn. (7)
Committees - 63-98, 101-105
Congressional voting studies - 3-C-42-C
Roll call votes - 2-H-145-H
Superfund law - 332-335
Supplemental Security Income (SSI)
Appropriations - 505, 506
Refugee assistance - 305
Supreme Court. *(See also Supreme Court cases.)*
Abortion cases - 306-308, 10-A-11-A
Abscam appeals - 585
Antitrust law - 13-A-14-A
Appropriations - 473
Bankruptcy courts - 318
Business law - 13-A-15-A
Civil and individual rights - 4-A, 8-A-11-A
Child pornography bill - 318
Coal leasing ban - 353
Criminal law - 5-A, 6-A-8-A
Draft registration - 399
Education - 300, 395
Election law - 12-A-13-A
Energy law - 16-A-17-A
Environment - 17-A
Federal court powers - 19-A
First amendment rights - 4-A, 12-A
Franking privilege - 579-580
Freedom of religion - 302
Freedom of speech - 12-A
Freedom of the press - 12-A
Justices
Aging court - 4-A
List - 11
Labor law - 15-A-16-A
Legislative veto
Background - 565-566
Decision - 566-568, 570, 4-A, 19-A, 20-A-22-A (text)
Foreign policy implications - 569
Military court review - 311
Search and seizure - 6-A-7-A
State courts - 18-A
States - 5-A, 17-A-18-A
Taxation - 395, 3-A, 14-A-15-A
Term review, 1982-1983 - 3-A-22-A
Supreme Court cases
American Bank & Trust Co. v. Dallas County - 18-A
American Paper Institute Inc. v. American Electric Power Service Corp., Federal Energy Regulatory Commission (FERC) v. American Electric Power Service Corp. - 16-A
Anderson v. Celebrezze - 13-A
Arizona Governing Committee for Tax Deferred Annuity and Deferred Compensation Plans v. Norris - 10-A
Arizona v. California - 19-A
Arizona v. San Carlos Apache Tribe of Arizona, Montana v. Northern Cheyenne Tribe of the Northern Cheyenne Indian Reservation - 18-A
Arkansas Electric Cooperative Corp. v. Arkansas Public Commission - 16-A
Associated General Contractors of California Inc. v. California State Council of Carpenters - 13-A
Baker v. Carr - 5-B
Baltimore Gas & Electric Co. v. Natural Resources Defense Council Inc. - 16-A
BankAmerica Corp. v. United States - 14-A
Barclay v. Florida - 8-A

Barefoot v. Estelle - 5-A, 8-A
Beardon v. Georgia - 8-A
Belknap Inc. v. Hale - 16-A
Bell v. New Jersey - 17-A
Bell v. United States - 8-A
Bill Johnson's Restaurants Inc. v. National Labor Relations Board - 15-A
Block v. Neal - 20-A
Block v. North Dakota - 17-A
Bob Jones University v. United States, Goldsboro Christian Schools v. United States - 10-A
Bolger v. Youngs Drug Products Corp. - 12-A
Boston Firefighters Union, Local 718 v. Boston Chapter, NAACP, Boston Police Patrolmen's Association v. Castro, Beecher v. Boston Chapter, NAACP - 9-A
Bowen v. United States Postal Service - 15-A
Bowsher v. Merck & Co., Merck & Co. v. Bowsher - 20-A
Briscoe v. LaHue - 8-A
Brown v. Socialist Workers '74 Campaign Committee (Ohio) - 13-A
Brown v. Thomson - 13-A
Burlington Northern Inc. v. United States - 14-A
Bush v. Lucas - 12-A
California v. Ramos - 8-A
Chappell v. Wallace - 9-A
Chardon v. Soto - 9-A
City of Akron v. Akron Center for Reproductive Health Inc., Akron Center for Reproductive Health Inc. v. City of Akron - 306, 10-A
City of Lockhart, Texas v. United States - 13-A
City of Los Angeles v. Lyons - 19-A
City of Port Arthur, Texas v. United States - 13-A
City of Revere v. Massachusetts General Hospital - 17-A
Colorado v. New Mexico - 18-A
Commissioner of Internal Revenue v. Tufts - 15-A
Community Television of Southern California v. Gottfried, Federal Communications Commission (FCC) v. Gottfried - 11-A
Connecticut v. Johnson - 7-A
Connick v. Myers - 5-A, 12-A
Container Corporation of America v. Franchise Tax Board - 18-A
Crown, Cork & Seal Co. v. Parker - 9-A
DelCostello v. International Brotherhood of Teamsters, United Steelworkers of America v. Flowers - 15-A
Dickerson v. New Banner Institute Inc. - 8-A
Director, Office of Workers' Compensation Programs v. Perini North River Associates - 16-A
Dirks v. Securities and Exchange Commission - 14-A
District of Columbia Court of Appeals v. Feldman - 19-A
Edward J. DeBartolo Corp. v. National Labor Relations Board - 15-A-16-A
Energy Reserves Group Inc. v. Kansas Power & Light Co., Inc. - 16-A
Equal Employment Opportunity Commission v. Wyoming - 5-A, 17-A
Exxon Corp. v. Eagerton, Exchange Oil and Gas Corp. v. Eagerton - 18-A
Falls City Industries Inc. v. Vanco Beverage, Inc. - 13-A
Federal Election Commission v. National Right to Work Committee - 13-A
Federal Trade Commission v. Grolier Inc. - 20-A

First National City Bank v. Banco Para El Comercio Exterior de Cuba - 14-A
Florida v. Casal - 6-A
Florida v. Royer - 6-A
Franchise Tax Board of California v. Construction Laborers Vacation Trust for Southern California - 19-A
General Motors Corp. v. Devex Corp. - 14-A
Gillette Company v. Miner - 18-A
Grove City College v. Bell - 300, 397 (box)
Guardians Association v. Civil Service Commission of City of New York - 9-A
Haring v. Prosise - 9-A
Heckler v. Campbell - 20-A
Hensley v. Eckerhart - 9-A
Herman & MacLean v. Huddleston, Huddleston v. Herman & MacLean - 14-A
Hewitt v. Helms - 11-A
Hillsboro National Bank v. Commissioner of Internal Revenue, United States v. Bliss Dairy - 14-A
Idaho v. Oregon and Washington - 19-A
Illinois v. Abbott & Associates - 13-A
Illinois v. Andreas - 6-A
Illinois v. Gates - 5-A, 6-A
Illinois v. Lafayette - 6-A
Immigration and Naturalization Service v. Chadha, United States House of Representatives v. Chadha, United States Senate v. Chadha - 566-568, 570, 4-A, 19-A, 20-A-22-A
Jefferson County Pharmaceutical Association Inc. v. Abbott Laboratories - 13-A
Jim McNeff Inc. v. Todd - 15-A
Jones & Laughlin Steel Corp. v. Pfeifer - 16-A
Jones v. Barnes - 8-A
Jones v. United States - 7-A
Karcher v. Daggett - 12-A, 5-B
Kolender v. Lawson - 11-A
Kush v. Rutledge - 9-A
Landon v. Plasencia - 11-A
Larkin v. Grendel's Den - 12-A
Lehr v. Robertson - 11-A
Local 926, International Union of Operating Engineers, AFL-CIO v. Jones - 18-A
Lockheed Aircraft Corp. v. United States - 20-A
Maine v. Thornton - 289
Marbury v. Madison - 4-A
Marsh v. Chambers - 12-A
Marshall v. Lonberger - 7-A
Martinez v. Bynum - 17-A
Memphis Bank & Trust Co. v. Garner - 18-A
Mennonite Board of Missions v. Adams - 11-A
Metropolitan Edison Co. v. National Labor Relations Board (NLRB) - 15-A
Metropolitan Edison Co. v. People Against Nuclear Energy (PANE), United States Regulatory Commission (NRC) v. PANE - 16-A
Michigan v. Long - 6-A
Minneapolis Star & Tribune Co. v. Minnesota Commissioner of Revenue - 12-A
Missouri v. Hunter - 7-A
Monsanto Co. v. Spray-Rite Service Corp. - 478
Morris v. Slappy - 7-A
Morrison-Knudsen Construction Co. v. Director, Office of Workers' Compensation Programs, U.S. Department of Labor - 16-A
Moses H. Cone Memorial Hospital v. Mercury Construction Corp. - 19-A

Motor Vehicle Manufacturers Association of the United States v. State Farm Mutual Automobile Insurance Co., Consumer Alert v. State Farm, Department of Transportation v. State Farm - 14-A
Mueller v. Allen - 395, 12-A
National Association of Greeting Card Publishers v. U. S. Postal Service, United Parcel Service of America v. U. S. Postal Service - 20-A
National Labor Relations Board v. Transportation Management Corp. - 15-A
Nevada v. United States, Truckee-Carson Irrigation District v. United States, Pyramid Lake Paiute Tribe of Indians v. Truckee-Carson Irrigation District - 17-A
New Mexico v. Mescalero Apache Tribe - 17-A
Newport News Shipbuilding & Dry Dock Co. v. Equal Employment Opportunity Commission - 10-A
North Dakota v. United States - 17-A
Olim v. Wakinekona - 11-A
Oliver v. United States - 289
Oregon v. Bradshaw - 7-A
Pacific Gas & Electric Co. v. State Energy Resources Conservation and Development Commission - 16-A
Pallas Shipping Agency Ltd. v. Duris - 16-A
Perry Education Association v. Perry Local Educators' Association - 12-A
Philko Aviation Inc. v. Shacket - 17-A
Pickett v. Brown - 11-A
Pillsbury Co. v. Conboy - 7-A
Planned Parenthood Association of Kansas City, Mo. v. Ashcroft, Ashcroft v. Planned Parenthood Association of Kansas City, Mo. - 307, 10-A
Public Service Commission of New York v. Mid-Louisiana Gas Co., Arizona Electric Power Cooperative v. Mid-Louisiana Gas Co., Michigan v. Mid-Louisiana Gas Co., Federal Energy Regulatory Commission v. Mid-Louisiana Gas Co. - 17-A
Regan v. Taxation with Representation of Washington, Taxation with Representation of Washington v. Regan - 12-A
Rice v. Rehner - 18-A
Roe v. Wade - 307, 4-C
Ruckelshaus v. Sierra Club - 17-A
Shaw v. Delta Air Lines Inc. - 18-A
Shepard v. National Labor Relations Board (NLRB) - 15-A
Simopoulos v. Virginia - 307, 10-A-11-A
Smith v. Wade - 9-A
Solem v. Helm - 8-A
South Dakota v. Neville - 7-A
Texas v. Brown - 6-A
Texas v. New Mexico - 19-A
Tuten v. United States - 8-A
U.S. Postal Service Board of Governors v. Aikens - 9-A
United Brotherhood of Carpenters & Joiners of America, Local #610 v. Scott - 9-A
United States v. Baggot - 19-A
United States v. $8,850 in U.S. Currency - 11-A
United States v. Generix Drug Corp. - 14-A
United States v. Grace - 12-A
United States v. Hasting - 7-A
United States v. Knotts - 6-A
United States v. Mitchell - 20-A
United States v. Place - 6-A
United States v. Ptasynski - 15-A

United States v. Rodgers - 11-A
United States v. Rylander - 14-A
United States v. Security Industrial Bank - 14-A
United States v. Sells Engineering Inc. - 19-A
United States v. Villamonte-Marquez - 6-A
United States v. Whiting Pools Inc. - 14-A
Verlinden B. V. v. Central Bank of Nigeria - 19-A
W. R. Grace & Co. v. Local #759, International Union of the United Rubber, Cork, Linoleum and Plastic Workers of America - 15-A
Washington v. United States - 18-A
Watt v. Western Nuclear Inc. - 17-A
Wesberry v. Sanders - 5-B
White v. Massachusetts Council of Construction Employers - 17-A
Widmar v. Vincent - 302
Xerox Corp. v. County of Harris, Texas - 18-A
Zant v. Stephens - 8-A
Surface Transportation Assistance Act of 1982 - 543, 559
Susquehanna River Basin Commission - 501
Swift, Al, D-Wash. (2)
    Committee assignments - 63-98, 101-105
    Congressional voting studies - 3-C-42-C
    NRC authorization - 370
    Radio Marti - 140
    Roll call votes - 2-H-145-H
    Telephone rates - 547
Symms, Steven D., R-Idaho
    Appropriations - 490
    Budget - 440
    Civil Rights Commission - 295
    Committees - 44-62, 99-100
    Congressional voting studies - 3-C-42-C
    Korean airline downing - 137
    Roll call votes - 2-S-60-S
    Social Security rescue bill - 224, 226
    United Nations authorization - 147
    Water projects - 355
Synar, Mike, D-Okla. (2)
    Bankruptcy laws - 320
    Committees - 63-98, 101-105
    Congressional voting studies - 3-C-42-C
    NRC authorization - 370
    Roll call votes - 2-H-145-H
Synthetic fuels. (See also Solar and renewable energies.)
    Research - 465
Syria
    Economic aid - 525
    Foreign aid - 150, 152
    Lebanon conflict - 121
    Soviet support - 133

T

Taft-Hartley Act - 271
Tallon, Robin, D-S.C. (6)
    Committees - 63-98, 101-105
    Congressional voting studies - 3-C-42-C
    Roll call votes - 2-H-145-H
Tanks, military
    Appropriations - 487, 490, 492
    Authorization - 176-177, 183, 191
Tapes - 313, 601
Target prices. See Agricultural price supports.
Targeted fiscal assistance. See Countercyclical aid and targeted fiscal assistance.
Tariffs and duties.
    Caribbean Basin Initiative - 252-253

Trade reciprocity proposal - 259-260
Tauke, Tom, R-Iowa (2)
    Committees - 63-98, 101-105
    Congressional voting studies - 3-C-42-C
    Equal Rights Amendment - 297
    Health insurance proposal - 406
    Radio Marti - 140
    Roll call votes - 2-H-145-H
    Telephone rates - 547-548, 11-C
Tauzin, W. J. 'Billy', D-La. (3)
    Committees - 63-98, 101-105
    Congressional voting studies - 3-C-42-C
    Roll call votes - 2-H-145-H
Tax Court, U.S.
    Appropriations - 532
    Nominations and confirmations - 31-A
Tax reconciliation bill
    Medicare provisions - 391
    Withholding taxes - 261
Taxes and taxation. (See also Business taxes; Income taxes; Internal Revenue Service; Tariffs and duties; Windfall profits tax.)
    Budget
        Administration plans - 426, 432
        Federal deficit - 427
        Overview, 1983 - 217
        Reconciliation proposals - 231-239
        Resolution proposals - 439, 442, 444
    Caribbean trade incentives - 252-253
    Employer tax credits - 17-E
    Enterprise Zone proposal - 14-E-15-E
    Excise taxes
        Coal - 511
        Boating - 562
        Fishing - 562
        Oil windfall - 4-A
    Federal employees - 219
    House committee changes - 597
    Increase proposal - 11-C
    Jobless health insurance proposal - 405-408
    Key votes - 5-C
    Leasing plans - 234, 603-604
    Legislative summary - 17
    Payment-in-Kind program - 13, 381-383
    Presidential messages (texts) - 10-E, 15-E
    Railroad retirement program - 273
    Social Security
        Federal employee contributions - 573-576
        Increases - 219-226
    Supreme Court decisions - 3-A, 4-A, 11-A, 14-A, 18-A
    Tax cap bill - 249-250
    Tax-exempt status
        Leasing plans - 234
        Private and parochial schools - 3-A, 4-A, 10-A
        Veterans groups - 5-A
    Tax leasing veto - 34-E
    Tuition tax credits - 18, 395, 3-A, 10-E
    Withholding of interest and dividend income - 261-264
        Appropriations bill - 454
        Congressional action - 262-264
        Provisions of repeal - 261-262
    Women's equity proposal - 300
Tax-exempt organizations
    Divestiture of business holdings - 235
    Leasing plans - 234
Taylor, Gene, R-Mo. (7)
    Committees - 63-98, 101-105
    Congressional voting studies - 3-C-42-C
    Roll call votes - 2-H-145-H
Teamsters Union. See International Brotherhood of Teamsters.
Technology. See Science and technology.
Telecommunications. See Communications and telecommunications.
Television. (See also Cable television.)

Deregulation
  Broadcast - 15, 551-552
  Cable - 15, 552-554
  Senate broadcasting - 595-596
  Syndication rights - 14, 538, 544, 560-561
Tennessee
  Clinch River nuclear breeder reactor - 362, 500, 502
  Employment funds - 455
  National trails - 346
Tennessee-Tombigbee Waterway - 500, 502
Tennessee Valley Authority (TVA)
  Appropriations - 448 (chart), 452, 453, 500, 501
  Nuclear power - 363
Tenth Amendment - 5-A, 17-A-18-A
Terrorism
  Anti-terrorism aid - 143-144, 522 (chart)
  Capitol bombing - 592
Texas
  Election results, 1983 - 6-B
  Judicial appointments - 302
  Non-resident student education - 5-A
  Wildlife area - 345
Texas v. Brown - 6-A
Texas v. New Mexico - 19-A
Thailand - 151
Third World countries, aid to. See Foreign aid.
Thomas, Lindsay, D-Ga. (1)
  Committees - 63-98, 101-105
  Congressional voting studies - 3-C-42-C
  Roll call votes - 2-H-145-H
Thomas, William M., R-Calif. (20)
  Committees - 63-98, 101-105
  Congressional voting studies - 3-C-42-C
  Roll call votes - 2-H-145-H
Three Mile Island - 370
Thurmond, Strom, R-S.C.
  Anti-crime proposal - 318
  Anti-tampering bill - 314
  Appropriations - 476, 538
  Bankruptcy laws - 320, 321
  Civil Rights Commission - 294
  Committees - 44-62, 99-100
  Congressional Budget Office - 443
  Congressional voting studies - 3-C-42-C
  Immigration reform bill - 288
  Roll call votes - 2-S-60-S
  Senate rule change proposal - 598
  School prayer - 301-302
Timber industry - 343, 464, 466
Tobacco
  Federal tobacco program
    Legislative summary - 13
    Licensing system (box) - 369
    Price-support freeze - 375, 377, 378 (box)
    Provisions - 375-376
  Cigarette labeling - 22, 408-409
Todhunter, John A. - 333
Tombigbee Waterway. See Tennessee-Tombigbee Waterway.
Torres, Esteban Edward, D-Calif. (34)
  Committees - 63-98, 101-105
  Congressional voting studies - 3-C-42-C
  Roll call votes - 2-H-145-H
Torricelli, Robert G., D-N.J. (9)
  Committees - 63-98, 101-105
  Congressional voting studies - 3-C-42-C
  Nuclear freeze resolution - 206
  Roll call votes - 2-H-145-H
Tourism industry. See Travel and tourism industry.
Tower, John, R-Texas
  Appropriations - 489
  Budget - 439, 440
  Committees - 44-98, 99-101
  Congressional voting studies - 3-C-42-C
  Defense authorization - 187, 189

Grenada invasion - 135
Mortgage assistance - 267
MX debate - 202
Peacekeeping forces in Lebanon - 120, 121
Roll call votes - 2-S-60-S
Towns, Edolphus, D-N.Y. (11)
  Committees - 63-98, 101-105
  Congressional voting studies - 3-C-42-C
  Roll call votes - 2-H-145-H
Toxic substances. See Hazardous substances.
Tracked combat vehicles. See Tanks (military).
Trade Act of 1974
  Most-favored nation status - 265
  Trade adjustment aid - 251
  Trade reciprocity bill - 259-260
  Unemployment provisions - 505
Trade adjustment assistance
  Authorization - 251-252
  Reagan policy - 251
Trade, foreign. See Foreign trade.
Trade Representative, Office of. See Office of the U.S. Trade Representative.
Trademarks. See Patents and trademarks.
Traffic safety
  Air bags - 544
  Drunk driving legislation - 321
Trails, scenic and historic - 346
Trains. See Railroads.
Transportation. (See also Air transportation; Automobiles and automobile industry; Highways and roads; Mass transit; Railroads; Ships and shipping; Trucks and trucking.)
  Appropriations
    FY 1983 supplemental - 510
    FY 1984 - 457-462
  Budget - 430, 434, 445 (chart)
  Deregulation - 543
  Legislative summary - 26-27
  Overview, 1983 - 543-544
Transportation Department (DOT)
  Amtrak funding - 561
  Appropriations
    FY 1983 supplemental - 510
    FY 1984 - 457-462
  Budget - 434
  Nominations and confirmations - 28-A
Travel and Tourism Administration, U.S. - 472, 474
Travel and tourism industry - 554-557
Traxler, Bob, D-Mich. (8)
  Committees - 63-98, 101-105
  Congressional voting studies - 3-C-42-C
  Roll call votes - 2-H-145-H
Treasury bills - 426
Treasury Department. (See also Bureau of Alcohol, Tobacco and Firearms; Customs Service, U.S.; Internal Revenue Service.)
  Appropriations - 496, 499, 529, 532 (chart)
  Budget - 434
  Nominations and confirmations - 28-A
  Revenue sharing - 496, 499
Treaties and international agreements. (See also Strategic Arms Limitation Treaty; Strategic Arms Reduction Talks.)
  Limited Test Ban Treaty - 214
  Montreal Protocols 3 and 4 - 300-301
Trial procedures
  Cruel and unusual punishment - 8-A
  Double jeopardy - 7-A
  Due process - 7-A
  Equal protection - 8-A
  Fair trials - 7-A
  Right to counsel - 7-A
  Self-incrimination - 7-A
  Supreme Court rulings - 7-A-8-A

Trible, Paul S. Jr., R-Va. (1)
  Committees - 44-62, 99-100
  Congressional voting studies - 3-C-42-C
  Roll call votes - 2-S-60-S
Trident missiles
  Trident I - 175, 483, 488 (chart)
  Trident II - 175, 183, 190, 479, 486, 488 (chart), 494
Trident submarines
  Appropriations - 479, 483
  Authorization - 175
Trucking industry
  Antitrust immunity - 543
  Deregulation proposals - 559-560
  Truck user fees - 543
Truman, Harry S
  Historic site - 348
  U. S. Vatican relations - 169
Tsongas, Paul E., D-Mass.
  Adelman nomination - 214
  Alaska sport hunting bill - 348
  Appropriations - 468, 490
  Clark confirmation - 331
  Committees - 44-62, 99-100
  Congressional voting studies - 3-C-42-C
  Defense authorization - 188
  Equal Rights Amendment - 298
  Peacekeeping forces in Lebanon - 120
  Roll call votes - 2-S-60-S
Tuition tax credits - 432, 20-E
  Budget proposal - 432
  Legislative proposal - 395
  Presidential messages - 10-E, 20-E
  Supreme Court decision - 3-A
Tunisia
  Foreign aid - 143, 144
  Military aid - 144
Turkey
  Foreign aid - 141-143, 432, 513, 514 (box)
  Human rights - 142
  Military aid - 525
  Military construction - 195
Tuten v. United States - 8-A
Twentieth Century Fund - 389

U

U.N. See United Nations.
U.S. See other part of agency or organization name, e.g. Chamber of Commerce, U.S.; Railway Association, U.S.
U.S.S.R. See Soviet Union.
Udall, Morris K., D-Ariz. (2)
  Appropriations - 498
  Committees - 63-98, 101-105
  Coal leasing ban - 352-353
  Congressional voting studies - 3-C-42-C
  Korean airline downing - 137
  Public lands transfer - 345
  Roll call votes - 2-H-145-H
  Watt resignation - 328
Unemployment. See Employment and unemployment.
Unemployment compensation
  Appropriations - 447-457, 510
  Budget - 431, 444
  Extensions - 220-221, 224-225, 274-276
  Voucher program - 274, 17-E
Uniform Code of Military Justice - 311
Uniform Relocation Act - 587
Unions, labor. See Labor, labor unions.
United Auto Workers (UAW)
  Auto domestic content bill - 258
  Legislative summary - 26
United Brotherhood of Carpenters & Joiners of America, Local #610 v. Scott - 9-A
United Nations
  Authorization - 147, 150-151

Development Program - 144
United States Information Agency (USIA)
  Authorization - 145
  Radio Marti - 139
United States v. Baggot - 19-A
United States v. $8,850 in U.S. Currency - 11-A
United States v. Generix Drug Corp. - 14-A
United States v. Grace - 12-A
United States v. Hasting - 7-A
United States v. Knotts - 6-A
United States v. Mitchell - 20-A
United States v. Place - 6-A
United States v. Ptasynski - 15-A
United States v. Rodgers - 11-A
United States v. Rylander - 14-A
United States v. Security Industrial Bank - 14-A
United States v. Sells Engineering Inc. - 19-A
United States v. Villamonte-Marquez - 6-A
United States v. Whiting Pools Inc. - 14-A
United Technology - 482
Universities. See Postsecondary education.
Uranium - 362, 363
Urban affairs. See Community development; Mass transit; State and local government.
Urban development. See Community development.
Urban Development Action Grants (UDAGs)
  Appropriations
    FY 1983 supplemental - 448 (chart), 456
    FY 1984 - 495, 497, 499
  Authorization - 278
  Deficit reduction proposal - 235
Urban Park and Recreation Recovery Program - 452
Urban mass transit. See Mass transit.
Urban Mass Transportation Administration - 458, 459 (chart), 460
Utah
  Abortion laws - 308
  Wilderness study-area leasing - 464
Utilities. (See also Communications and telecommunications; Natural gas; Nuclear power plants; Rural Electrification Administration; Telephone and telegraph communications; Tennessee Valley Authority.)
  Acid rain - 151
  Construction charges - 372
  Natural gas pricing - 366
  Relocation assistance - 587
  Rural electrification bill - 388
Uruguay - 143

V

VA. See Veterans Administration.
Valentine, Tim, D-N.C. (2)
  Committees - 63-98, 101-105
  Congressional voting studies - 3-C-42-C
  Roll call votes - 2-H-145-H
Vandergriff, Tom, D-Texas (26)
  Committees - 63-98, 101-105
  Congressional voting studies - 3-C-42-C
  Equal Rights Amendment - 297
  Roll call votes - 2-H-145-H
Vander Jagt, Guy, R-Mich. (9)
  Committees - 63-98, 101-105
  Congressional voting studies - 3-C-42-C
  Equal Rights Amendment - 297
  IMF funding - 248

Roll call votes - 2-H-145-H
Tax cap bill - 250
Vatican - 152, 168-169
Vento, Bruce F., D-Minn. (4)
 Coal slurry pipelines - 550
 Committees - 63-98, 101-105
 Congressional voting studies - 3-C-42-C
 Roll call votes - 2-H-145-H
Verlinden B. V. v. Central Bank of Nigeria - 19-A
Vermont - 344
Veterans Administration (VA). *(See also Veterans affairs.)*
 Appropriations
  FY 1983 supplemental - 448 (chart), 451, 453, 509, 511
  FY 1984 - 496-500
 Budget - 429, 434
 Education programs - 418-419
 Health programs - 411-412
 Hospitals - 451, 453
 Housing programs - 429
 Job training program - 599-600
 Pension cost-of-living increases - 497
Veterans affairs
 Appropriations
  FY 1983 supplemental - 448 (chart), 451
  FY 1984 - 495-500
 Budget - 431, 448 (chart)
 Compensation COLAs - 233
 Cost-of-living raise - 495
 Disabled veterans - 495
 Education benefits and programs
  GI bill - 418-419
  Vocational education - 599-600
 Employment, job training programs
  Appropriations - 495-500, 536, 537
  Budget - 444
  Emergency bill - 599-600
 Health
  Agent Orange research - 536, 537
  Counseling centers - 410-412
  Veterans hospitals - 451, 453
 Legislative summary - 27
 Lobbying - 599
 Mortgage assistance - 267-268, 429, 495
Veterans of Foreign Wars - 599
Vetoes. *(See also Legislative veto.)*
 Anti-crime bill - 315
 Dairy assessments - 35-E-36-E
 Desegregation funds - 35-E
 El Salvador certification - 156
 Farm announcements - 34-E-35-E
 Indian claims bill - 25-E-26-E
 Indian land claim veto - 586-587
 List (box) - 6
 Oregon Lands bill - 38-E
 Public lands transfer - 344
 Tax leasing - 34-E, 603-604
Vietnam. *(See also Indochinese refugees.)*
 Agent Orange research - 536, 537
 Veterans' counseling centers - 410-412
 Veterans' employment programs - 599-600
Vietnam Veterans of America - 599
Virgin Islands - 252-253
Virginia
 Abortions - 307
 National trails - 346
 Water projects - 358
 Williamsburg Economic Summit - 217
VISTA. *See Volunteers in Service to America.*
Vocational education. *(See also Adult and continuing education; Employment and training programs.)*
 Appropriations - 505, 507
 Budget - 431
 Defense production bill - 266
 Veterans - 599-600

Vocational rehabilitation. *See Rehabilitation programs.*
Voice of America (VOA) - 139
Volcker, Paul A.
 Economic projections - 266-267
 Legislative summary - 17
 Monetary policy - 218
 Nominations and confirmations - 23-A
Volkmer, Harold L., D-Mo. (9)
 Committees - 63-98, 101-105
 Congressional voting studies - 3-C-42-C
 Immigration reform bill - 291
 Jobs bill, phase II program - 269
 Roll call votes - 2-H-145-H
Volunteers in Service to America - 398
Votes, congressional. *See Congressional votes.*
Voting (elections). *See Politics and elections.*
Vucanovich, Barbara F., R-Nev. (2)
 Committees - 63-98, 101-105
 Congressional voting studies - 3-C-42-C
 Equal Rights Amendment - 297
 Roll call votes - 2-H-145-H

W

W.R. Grace & Co. v. Local #759, International Union of the United Rubber, Cork, Linoleum and Plastic Workers of America - 15-A
Wages and salaries. *(See also Congress, Pay and expenses; Federal employees, Pay and benefits; Military pay and benefits.)*
 Job voucher proposal - 17-E
 Youth subminimum wage - 432, 11-E, 18-E
Waggonner, Joe D. - 221
Walgren, Doug, D-Pa. (18)
 Committees - 63-98, 101-105
 Congressional pay raises - 578
 Congressional voting studies - 3-C-42-C
 Roll call votes -2-H-145-H
Walker, Robert S., R-Pa. (16)
 Anti-crime grant program - 313
 Appropriations - 452, 475, 498, 541
 Committees - 63-98, 101-105
 Committee transcript alterations - 583
 Congressional voting studies - 3-C-42-C
 Jobs bill, phase II program - 269, 270
 Mortgage assistance - 268
 Revenue sharing - 227-228, 230
 Roll call votes -2-H-145-H
 Wilderness areas - 343, 344
Wallop, Malcolm, R-Wyo.
 Appropriations - 461, 467
 Central American intelligence activities - 131
 Coal slurry pipelines - 551
 Committees - 44-62, 99-100
 Congressional voting studies - 3-C-42-C
 Defense authorization - 188
 Roll call votes - 2-S-60-S
 Soviet embassy - 150
 Water projects - 355
War Powers Resolution
 Grenada invasion - 121, 135-136, 240
 Legislative veto - 147, 563, 565-566, 569, 573
 Peacekeeping forces in Lebanon - 113-123, 5-C, 9-C
Warner, John W., R-Va.
 Appropriations - 466
 Clinch River project - 365
 Committees - 44-62, 99-100
 Congressional voting studies - 3-C-42-C
 Defense authorization - 188
 IMF funding - 244
 Roll call votes - 2-S-60-S

Washington
 Election results, 1983 - 4-B
 Employment funds - 455
 Abortion funding - 306
Washington, D.C. *See District of Columbia.*
Washington, Harold, D-Ill. (1)
 Committees - 63-98, 101-105
 Congressional voting studies - 3-C-42-C
 Resignation - 5, 7-B
 Roll call votes - 2-H-145-H
Washington Metropolitan Area Transit Authority - 459
Washington Public Power Supply System (WPPSS) - 466
Washington v. United States - 18-A
Waste disposal and treatment. *(See also Hazardous wastes management; Nuclear waste and radioactive materials management.)*
 Clean water bill - 360-361
 Ocean dumping - 360
 Waste water treatment - 360
Water conservation
 Appropriations - 448 (chart)
 Water and erosion management - 388
Water pollution
 Acid rain - 151, 340-341
 Clean water bill - 360
 Nuclear reactor safety - 510
 Ocean dumping - 360
 Water Pollution Control Act - 360-361
Water projects
 Administration policies - 328
 Appropriations
  FY 1983 supplemental - 448 (chart), 452, 453, 455, 456, 510
  FY 1984 - 500-503, 501 (chart), 518-519, 520-521
 Authorization bill - 354-359
 Budget - 433
 Coastal Zone Management Program - 360
 Cost sharing - 355, 358
 Dam safety repair bill - 349
 Environmental impact statements - 358
 Flood control - 448 (chart), 452, 453, 456, 510
 Garrison Diversion project - 356-357, 500, 502, 503
 Inland Waterways Trust Fund - 358
 Legislative summary - 20
 Stonewall Jackson Dam - 500, 502, 503
 Tennessee-Tombigbee waterway - 500, 502
Water resources. *(See also Oceans; Water conservation; Water pollution; Water projects;)*
 Administration policy - 328
 Budget - 430, 448 (chart)
 Coal slurry pipelines - 26, 549-551, 9-C
 Drought relief - 375, 378, 387-388
 Indian water rights - 478, 587
 Research bill - 349
 Water and erosion management - 388
Water Resources Council
 Administration policy - 328
 Appropriations - 501
Water transportation. *See Ships and shipping.*
Watkins, Wes, D-Okla. (3)
 Committees - 63-98, 101-105
 Congressional voting studies - 3-C-42-C
 Roll call votes - 2-H-145-H
Watt, James G.
 Acid rain - 340
 Coal leasing ban - 350-354, 462, 467, 468, 5-C
 Resignation - 150, 325, 327-329, 332, 354
 Resource development policy - 327
 Water resources - 328

 Wilderness leasing - 328, 464
Watt v. Western Nuclear Inc. - 17-A
Waxman, Henry A., D-Calif. (24)
 Acid rain proposal - 341
 Child health care plan - 419-42
 Cigarette labeling - 408
 Clean Air Act - 339, 340
 Committees - 63-98, 10
 Congressional voting s
 CPSC authorization -
 Deficit reduction pro
 Health emergency fu
 Health insurance pro
 Immigration reform
 Legislative veto - 57
 NIH authorization -
 Roll call votes - 2-H
Weapons. *(See also A trol; Arms sales; Chem weapons; Missiles; N military.)*
 Appropriations - 479
 Authorization
 ...
 Procurement -
 Space lasers - 1,
 Spare parts - 182,
 Tanks - 488 (chart)
 Testing - 188, 193
Weather
 Drought impact - 374
 Satellites - 22, 477, 588-589
Weatherization, housing. *See Ho weatherization.*
Weaver, James, D-Ore. (4)
 Committees - 63-98, 101-105
 Congressional voting studies - 3-C-
 Public lands transfer - 345
 Roll call votes - 2-H-145-H
 Wilderness areas - 343
Weber, Vin, R-Minn. (2)
 Clinch River project - 364
 Committees - 63-98, 101-105
 Congressional voting studies - 3-
 Roll call votes - 2-H-145-H
Weicker, Lowell P. Jr., R-Conn.
 Appropriations - 450, 486, 4
 515
 Budget - 442, 443
 Clark confirmation - 331
 Committees - 44-62, 99-100
 Congressional voting studies
 Grenada invasion - 122
 MX debate - 198
 Natural gas pricing - 368
 Peacekeeping forces in Leb
 Radio Marti - 140
 Roll call votes - 2-S-60-S
Weights and measures
Weinberger, Caspar W.
 Budget - 435
 El Salvador aid - 155
 Family employment -
 Military sales to Jord
 MX debate - 197
 Nicaragua covert a
 Peacekeeping forc
Weiss, Ted, D-N.Y
 Child porr
 Committe
 Congr
 Grena
 Peac
 Revi
 Rol

Welfare and social services. (See also
ACTION; Aid to Families with Dependent Children; Child nutrition programs;
...munity Services Administration; Di-
...lief; Food stamps; Legal Services
...aid, Medicare; Public hous-
...istance; Social secu-
...mental Security In-
...compensation.)
...-457, 448 (chart),

...438, 441, 442, 445

... catalog - 591
...rograms
...ion proposals - 415-416
...I - 413-414
...nal action - 416
...s - 412-413
...- 10-C
... summary - 27-28
...proposals - 17-E
...e programs - 304-306
...y v. Sanders - 5-B
...ermany - 195, 479, 484
...Virginia
...ortion funding - 306
...nployment funds - 455
...onewall Jackson Dam - 500, 502,
503
...Sulphuric emissions - 341
...heat. See Grains.
...heat, Alan, D-Mo. (5)
Coal slurry pipelines - 550
Committees - 63-98, 101-105
Congressional voting studies - 3-C-42-C
Party unity votes - 27-C
Roll call votes - 2-H-145-H
...ite, Byron R.
...bortions - 307
...egislative veto - 567-568, 21-A-22-A
...edistricting - 5-B
...me Court term, 1982-83 - 3-A-22-

...se. See Executive branch.
...se Office - 532, 533
...ntain National Forest - 343
...Massachusetts Council of
...ion Employers - 17-A
...t, G. William, R-Va. (2)
...es - 63-98, 101-105
...al voting studies - 3-C-42-C
...orization - 181
...votes - 2-H-145-H
...arles, D-N.C. (3)
...ees - 63-98, 101-105
...onal voting studies - 3-C-42-C
...l votes - 2-H-145-H
...Bob, R-Kan. (5)
...-aid, 63-98, 101-105
...al voting studies - 3-C-42-C
...tes - 2-H-145-H
...rates - 548
...mie L., D-Miss. (1)
...ions - 447, 456, 478, 502,
..., 529, 536-537
...7, 194-195
...ing ban - 353
...es - 63-98, 101-105
...onal voting studies - 3-C-42-C
...ping forces in Lebanon - 118
...otes - 2-H-145-H
...m. See Women, infants and
...(C) program.
...s Z. - 146-147
...Vincent - 302
...oaming Horse and Burro
...- 346
...t of 1964 - 342
...reservation areas. (See
...forests.)
...n policies - 328
...rvation act - 347-348

Arizona wilderness bill - 341
Marine sanctuaries - 359
Oil, gas and mineral leasing ban - 328-
329, 343-344, 464
RARE II wilderness bills - 342-344
Wilderness Society - 353
Wildlife and wildlife refuges. (See also
Fish and Wildlife Service, U.S.)
Appropriations - 452, 453, 456
Alaska conservation act - 347-348
Endangered species protection - 152
Matagorda Island accord - 345
Pribilof Islands - 345
Wetlands bill - 349-350
Wild horses and burros management -
346-347
Williams, Harrison A. Jr. - 585-586
Williams, Lyle, R-Ohio (17)
Committees - 63-98, 101-105
Congressional voting studies - 3-C-42-C
Revenue sharing - 227-228
Roll call votes - 2-H-145-H
Williams, Pat, D-Mont. (1)
Committees - 63-98, 101-105
Congressional voting studies - 3-C-42-C
Handicapped education - 403
Roll call votes - 2-H-145-H
Williams, Roy Lee - 271
Wilson, Charles, D-Texas (2)
Committees - 63-98, 101-105
Censure - 582
El Salvador aid - 159, 168
Foreign aid - 134
Roll call votes - 2-H-145-H
Wilson, Pete, R-Calif.
Appropriations - 455, 469
Clark confirmation - 329
Committees - 44-62, 99-100
Congressional voting studies - 3-C-42-C
El Salvador aid - 160
Foreign aid - 525
Immigration reform bill - 289
Martin Luther King holiday - 602
Roll call votes - 2-S-60-S
Water projects - 355
Wilson, William A. - 152
Windfall profits tax - 4-A
Winn, Larry Jr., R-Kan. (3)
Committees - 63-98, 101-105
Congressional voting studies - 3-C-42-C
NSF authorization - 604
Roll call votes - 2-H-145-H
Wirth, Timothy E., D-Colo. (2)
Appropriations - 498
Broadcast deregulation - 551-552
Committees - 63-98, 101-105
Congressional voting studies - 3-C-42-C
Public broadcasting authorization - 558
Roll call votes - 2-H-145-H
Telephone rates - 545, 548, 11-C
Wisconsin
Employment funds - 455
Wilderness areas - 344
Wisconsin. (ship) - 482
Wise, Bob, D- W. Va. (3)
Appropriations - 502
Committees - 63-98, 101-105
Congressional voting studies - 3-C-42-C
Roll call votes - 2-H-145-H
Wolf, Frank R., R-Va. (10)
Appropriations - 465
Committees - 63-98, 101-105
Congressional voting studies - 3-C-42-C
Roll call votes - 2-H-145-H
Wolpe, Howard, D-Mich. (3)
Committees - 63-98, 101-105
Congressional voting studies - 3-C-42-C
Export control - 255
IMF funding - 248
Nuclear technology controls - 256
Roll call votes - 2-H-145-H
Women. (See also Abortion; Civil rights;
Family and marital issues; Sex discrimi-
nation.)

Appointments
Federal - 23-A
Judicial - 286, 302-304
Economic equity bill - 298-300
Equal Rights Amendment - 296-298
Gender gap - 299
Jobs legislation - 298-299
Pension reform - 299-300
Veteran health care - 411
**Women, Infants and Children (WIC)
Program**
Appropriations - 449 (chart), 452, 454,
457, 516 (chart), 518-519
Budget - 433, 415
Woods (forests). See Forests, forestry.
Work. See Employment and unemploy-
ment.
Workers' compensation. See Social Se-
curity Disability Insurance; Unemploy-
ment compensation.
World Bank. (See also International
Development Association.)
Appropriations - 513, 522 (chart), 525
Wortley, George C., R-N.Y. (27)
Committees - 63-98, 101-105
Congressional voting studies - 3-C-42-C
Housing authorization - 283
Mortgage assistance - 283
Roll call votes - 2-H-145-H
WPPSS. See Washington Public Power
Supply System (WPPSS).
Wright, Jim, D-Texas (12)
Appropriations - 450, 507, 528
Budget - 437-438
Capitol bombing - 593
Civil Rights Commission - 295
Clean Air Act - 340
Committees - 63-98, 101-105
Congressional voting studies - 3-C-42-C
Defense authorization - 180
El Salvador aid - 158, 170
Garrison Diversion project - 357
Handicapped education - 403
Health insurance proposal - 407
House rule changes - 597
Jobs bill, phase II program - 269
Legislative veto - 570
Nicaragua covert aid - 124, 128, 130-
131
Roll call votes - 2-H-145-H
Social programs - 10-C
Wyden, Ron, D-Ore. (3)
Committees - 63-98, 101-105
Congressional voting studies - 3-C-42-C
Roll call votes - 2-H-145-H
Wilderness areas - 343, 344
Wylie, Chalmers P., R-Ohio (15)
Censure proceedings - 582
Committees - 63-98, 101-105
Congressional voting studies - 3-C-42-C
Housing authorization - 283
IMF funding - 246, 248
Roll call votes - 2-H-145-H
Wyoming
Amtrak rerouting - 461
Coal leasing ban - 351
MX deployment - 182
Redistricting - 5-A
Water projects - 520-521
Wilderness areas - 344

X, Y, Z

Xerox Corp. v. County of Harris, Texas
- 18-A
Yates, Sidney R., D-Ill. (9)
Appropriations - 463-466
Coal leasing ban - 352
Committees - 63-98, 101-105
Congressional voting studies - 3-C-42-C

Roll call votes - 2-H-145-H
Watt resignation - 328
Yatron, Gus, D-Pa. (6)
Appropriations - 465
Committees - 63-98, 101-105
Congressional voting studies - 3-C-42-C
Equal Rights Amendment - 297
Foreign aid - 141-142
Roll call votes - 2-H-145-H
Young, C. W. Bill, R-Fla. (8)
Appropriations - 491
Committees - 63-98, 101-105
Congressional voting studies - 3-C-42-C
Nicaragua covert aid - 123, 129, 132
Roll call votes - 2-H-145-H
Young, Don, R-Alaska (AL)
Committees - 63-98, 101-105
Congressional voting studies - 3-C-42-C
Roll call votes - 2-H-145-H
Wilderness areas - 344
Young, Robert A., D-Mo. (2)
Committees - 63-98, 101-105
Congressional voting studies - 3-C-42-C
IMF funding - 248
Roll call votes - 2-H-145-H
Youth. (See also Children; Elementary
and secondary education; Job Corps;
Postsecondary education.)
Conservation jobs - 230 (box)
Employment and training programs
Presidential messages (text) - 18-E
Proposals - 229-231
Subminimum wage - 432, 11-E, 18-E
Youth Conservation Corps - 231
Zablocki, Clement J., D-Wis. (4)
Appropriations - 521, 529
Committees - 63-98, 101-105
Congressional voting studies - 3-C-42-C
Defense authorization - 179, 189, 190
El Salvador aid - 160, 169
Foreign aid - 109, 112, 140, 521
Legislative veto - 569, 571
MX debate - 199
Nicaragua covert aid - 126-127, 131
Nuclear freeze resolution - 205-206,
209-212
Peacekeeping forces in Lebanon - 114,
117, 119-120
Roll call votes - 2-H-145-H
State Department authorization - 147
War powers - 151
Zaire
Foreign aid - 143, 514 (box), 524
IMF funding - 243
Military aid - 144
Zant v. Stephens - 8-A
Zimbabwe - 144
Zorinsky, Edward, D-Neb.
Adelman nomination - 214
Appropriations - 467, 520
Coal leasing ban - 354
Committees - 44-62, 99-100
Congressional voting studies - 3-C-42-C
El Salvador - 161
Foreign aid - 141
Nuclear freeze resolution - 212
Party unity votes - 27-C
Peacekeeping forces in Lebanon - 118
Project Democracy - 149
Radio Marti - 139-140
Roll call votes - 2-S-60-S
Tax cap bill - 250
Zschau, Ed, R-Calif. (12)
Committees - 63-98, 101-105
Congressional voting studies - 3-C-42-C
Export control - 256
Nicaragua covert aid - 128
Roll call votes - 2-H-145-H

0

)
1-105
udies - 3-C-42-C
557
als - 236
- 417
al - 406
- 292

con-
ogical
nks

42-C

08,

2-C

119

21